2024
Harris
Indiana
Industrial Directory

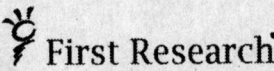

Published November 2024 next update November 2025

WARNING: Purchasers and users of this directory may not use this directory to compile mailing lists, other marketing aids and other types of data, which are sold or otherwise provided to third parties. Such use is wrongful, illegal and a violation of the federal copyright laws.

CAUTION: Because of the many thousands of establishment listings contained in this directory and the possibilities of both human and mechanical error in processing this information, Mergent Inc. cannot assume liability for the correctness of the listings or information on which they are based. Hence, no information contained in this work should be relied upon in any instance where there is a possibility of any loss or damage as a consequence of any error or omission in this volume.

Publisher

Mergent Inc.
444 Madison Ave
New York, NY 10022

©Mergent Inc All Rights Reserved
2024 Mergent Business Press
ISSN 1080-2614
ISBN 979-8-89251-083-7

TABLE OF CONTENTS

Summary of Contents & Explanatory Notes 4
User's Guide to Listings 6

Geographic Section
County/City Cross-Reference Index 9
Firms Listed by Location City 13

Standard Industrial Classification (SIC) Section
SIC Alphabetical Index 685
SIC Numerical Index 689
Firms Listed by SIC 695

Alphabetic Section
Firms Listed by Firm Name 951

Product Section
Industrial Product Index 1225
Firms Listed by Product Category 1239

SUMMARY OF CONTENTS

Number of Companies 17,065
Number of Decision Makers 21,684
Minimum Number of Employees 1

EXPLANATORY NOTES

How to Cross-Reference in This Directory

Sequential Entry Numbers. Each establishment in the Geographic Section is numbered sequentially (G-0000). The number assigned to each establishment is referred to as its "entry number." To make cross-referencing easier, each listing in the Geographic, SIC, Alphabetic and Product Sections includes the establishment's entry number. To facilitate locating an entry in the Geographic Section, the entry numbers for the first listing on the left page and the last listing on the right page are printed at the top of the page next to the city name.

Source Suggestions Welcome

Although all known sources were used to compile this directory, it is possible that companies were inadvertently omitted. Your assistance in calling attention to such omissions would be greatly appreciated. A special form on the facing page will help you in the reporting process.

Analysis

Every effort has been made to contact all firms to verify their information. The one exception to this rule is the annual sales figure, which is considered by many companies to be confidential information. Therefore, estimated sales have been calculated by multiplying the nationwide average sales per employee for the firm's major SIC/NAICS code by the firm's number of employees. Nationwide averages for sales per employee by SIC/NAICS codes are provided by the U.S. Department of Commerce and are updated annually. All sales—sales (est)—have been estimated by this method. The exceptions are parent companies (PA), division headquarters (DH) and headquarter locations (HQ) which may include an actual corporate sales figure—sales (corporate-wide) if available.

Types of Companies

Descriptive and statistical data are included for companies in the entire state. These comprise manufacturers, machine shops, fabricators, assemblers and printers. Also identified are corporate offices in the state.

Employment Data

This directory contains companies with 1 or more employees. The employment figure shown in the Geographic Section includes male and female employees and embraces all levels of the company: administrative, clerical, sales and maintenance. This figure is for the facility listed and does not include other plants or offices. It should be recognized that these figures represent an approximate year-round average. These employment figures are broken into codes A through G and used in the Product and SIC Sections to further help you in qualifying a company. Be sure to check the footnotes on the bottom of pages for the code breakdowns.

Standard Industrial Classification (SIC)

The Standard Industrial Classification (SIC) system used in this directory was developed by the federal government for use in classifying establishments by the type of activity they are engaged in. The SIC classifications used in this directory are from the 1987 edition published by the U.S. Government's Office of Management and Budget. The SIC system separates all activities into broad industrial divisions (e.g., manufacturing, mining, retail trade). It further subdivides each division. The range of manufacturing industry classes extends from two-digit codes (major industry group) to four-digit codes (product).

For example:

Industry Breakdown	Code	Industry, Product, etc.
*Major industry group	20	Food and kindred products
Industry group	203	Canned and frozen foods
*Industry	2033	Fruits and vegetables, etc.

*Classifications used in this directory

Only two-digit and four-digit codes are used in this directory.

Arrangement

1. The **Geographic Section** contains complete in-depth corporate data. This section is sorted by cities listed in alphabetical order and companies listed alphabetically within each city. A County/City Index for referencing cities within counties precedes this section.

> IMPORTANT NOTICE: It is a violation of both federal and state law to transmit an unsolicited advertisement to a facsimile machine. Any user of this product that violates such laws may be subject to civil and criminal penalties, which may exceed $500 for each transmission of an unsolicited facsimile. Mergent Inc. provides fax numbers for lawful purposes only and expressly forbids the use of these numbers in any unlawful manner.

2. The **Standard Industrial Classification (SIC) Section** lists companies under approximately 500 four-digit SIC codes. An alphabetical and a numerical index precedes this section. A company can be listed under several codes. The codes are in numerical order with companies listed alphabetically under each code.

3. The **Alphabetic Section** lists all companies with their full physical or mailing addresses and telephone number.

4. The **Product Section** lists companies under unique Harris categories. An index preceding this section lists all product categories in alphabetical order. Companies can be listed under several categories.

USER'S GUIDE TO LISTINGS

GEOGRAPHIC SECTION

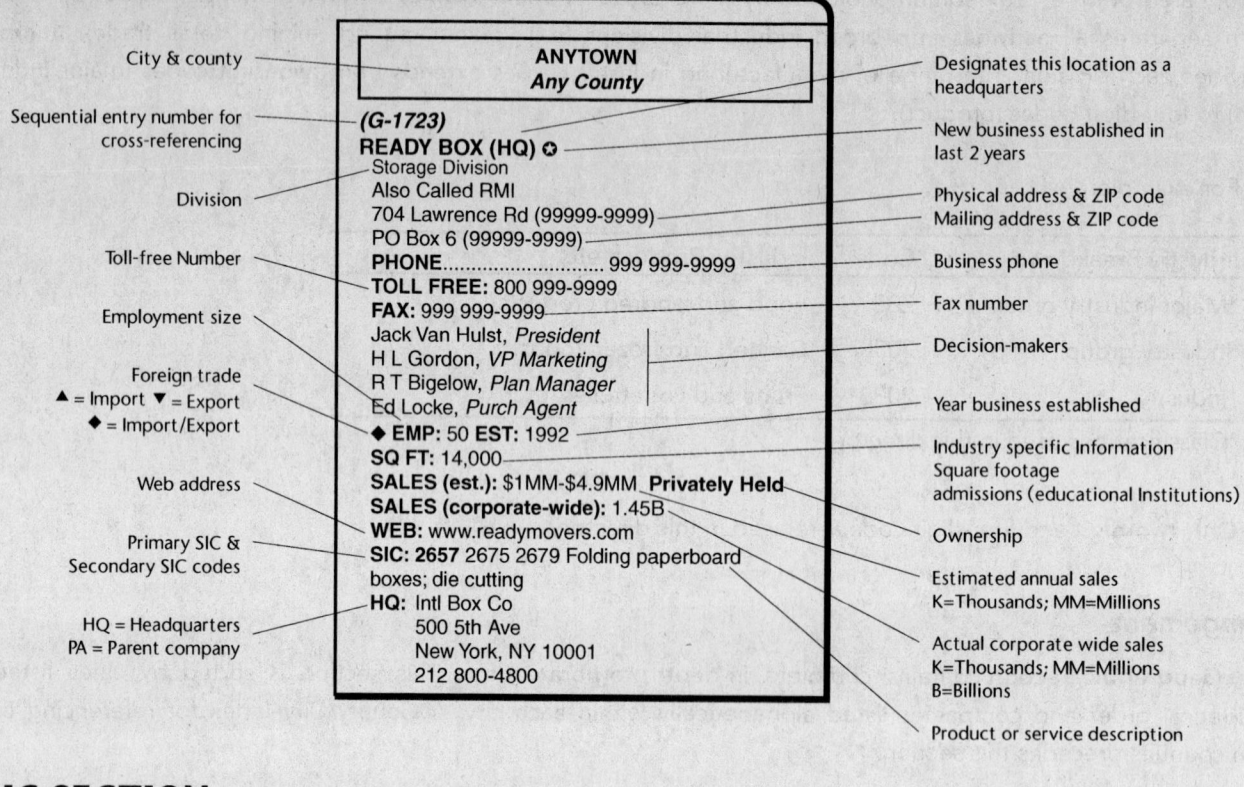

SIC SECTION

ALPHABETIC SECTION

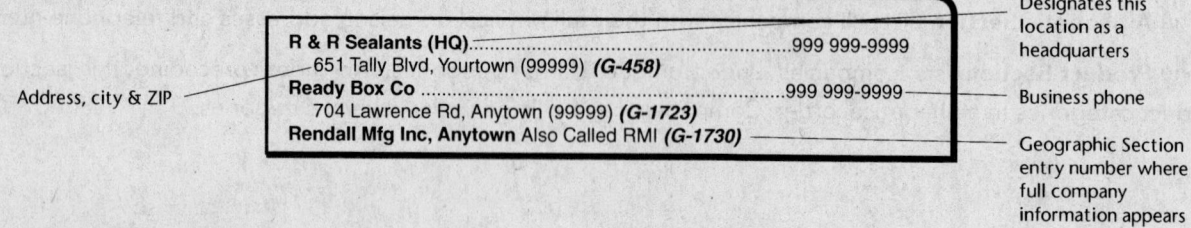

PRODUCT SECTION

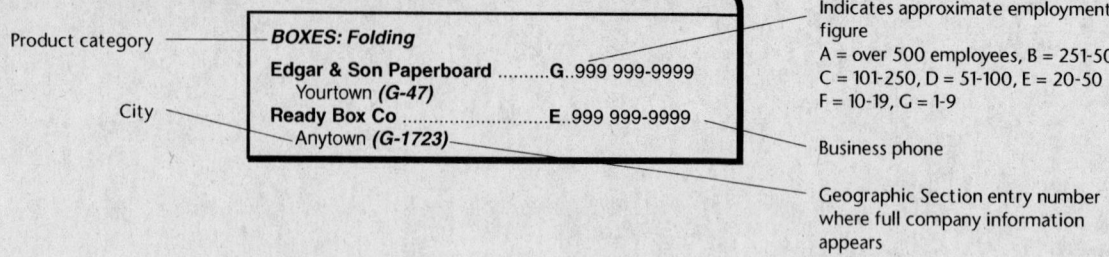

GEOGRAPHIC SECTION

Companies sorted by city in alphabetical order
In-depth company data listed

STANDARD INDUSTRIAL CLASSIFICATIONS

Alphabetical index of classification descriptions
Numerical index of classification descriptions
Companies sorted by SIC product groupings

ALPHABETIC SECTION

Company listings in alphabetical order

PRODUCT INDEX

Product categories listed in alphabetical order

PRODUCT SECTION

Companies sorted by product and manufacturing service classifications

GEOGRAPHIC SECTION

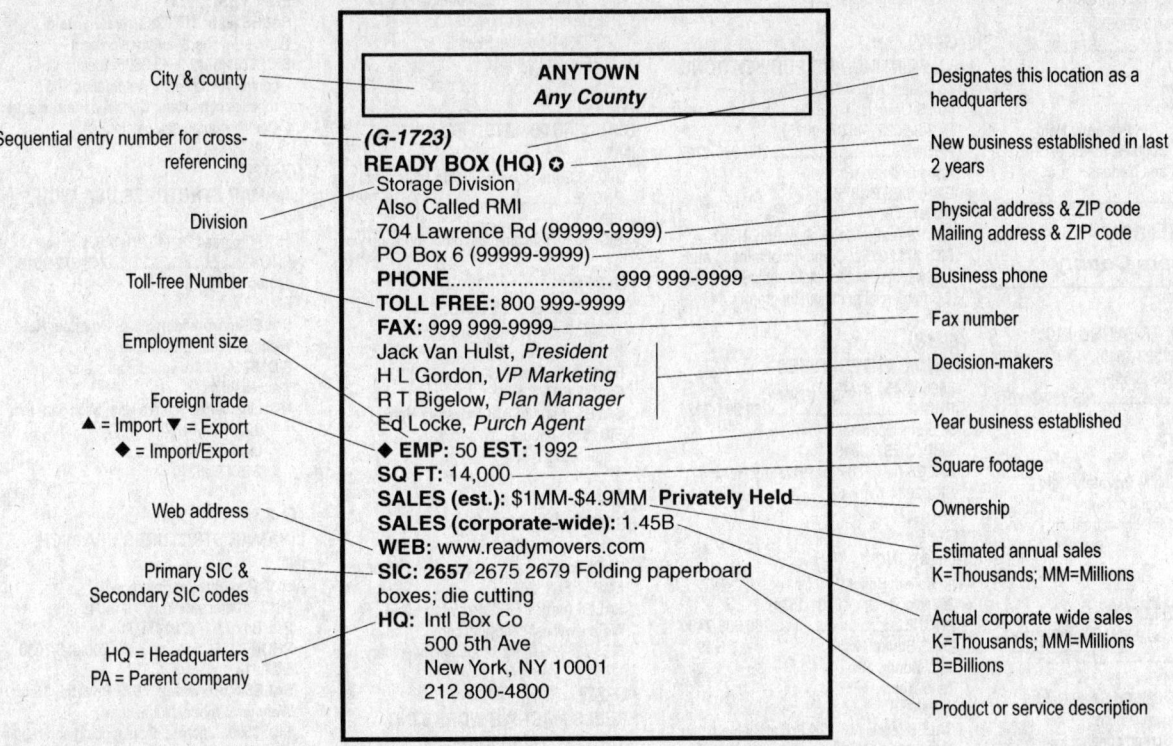

See footnotes for symbols and codes identification.
- This section is in alphabetical order by city.
- Companies are sorted alphabetically under their respective cities.
- To locate cities within a county refer to the County/City Cross Reference Index.

IMPORTANT NOTICE: It is a violation of both federal and state law to transmit an unsolicited advertisement to a facsimile machine. Any user of this product that violates such laws may be subject to civil and criminal penalties which may exceed $500 for each transmission of an unsolicited facsimile. Harris InfoSource provides fax numbers for lawful purposes only and expressly forbids the use of these numbers in any unlawful manner.

Akron
Fulton County

(G-1)
AKRON CONCRETE PRODUCTS INC (PA)
321 N Maple St (46910-9265)
P.O. Box 215 (46910-0215)
PHONE..................................574 893-4841
Pat Walgamuth, *Pr*
EMP: 8 **EST:** 1928
SQ FT: 16,234
SALES (est): 984.59K
SALES (corp-wide): 984.59K **Privately Held**
Web: www.akronconcreteproducts.com
SIC: 3272 Burial vaults, concrete or precast terrazzo

(G-2)
BUDDY EUGENE PUBLISHING LLC
2031 S 650 E (46910-9757)
PHONE..................................574 223-6048
Roger Bailey, *Prin*
EMP: 2 **EST:** 2010
SALES (est): 69.25K **Privately Held**
SIC: 2741 Miscellaneous publishing

(G-3)
CINDYS EMBROIDERY
202 W Walnut St (46910-9495)
PHONE..................................574 551-4521
Cindy Bucher, *Prin*
EMP: 1 **EST:** 2010
SALES (est): 46.8K **Privately Held**
SIC: 2395 Embroidery and art needlework

(G-4)
DRAGON ESP LTD
Also Called: Enviromental Services Pdts Mfg
8857 E State Road 14 (46910-9749)
PHONE..................................574 893-1569
Bobby Satterfield, *Pr*
▲ **EMP:** 20 **EST:** 1999
SQ FT: 60,000
SALES (est): 229.16K **Privately Held**
SIC: 3443 Dumpsters, garbage

(G-5)
FRENCH INTERNATIONAL COATINGS
15205 E 200 S (46910-9716)
PHONE..................................574 505-0774
Tyler French, *Prin*
EMP: 6 **EST:** 2017
SALES (est): 128.24K **Privately Held**
Web: www.apvcoatings.com
SIC: 3479 Metal coating and allied services

(G-6)
NORTHERN IND INDUS CATINGS LLC
619 E Main St (46910-9509)
PHONE..................................574 893-4621
EMP: 5 **EST:** 2009
SALES (est): 365.79K **Privately Held**
Web: www.niicoatings.com
SIC: 3479 1721 7532 Etching and engraving ; Industrial painting; Top and body repair and paint shops

(G-7)
PIKE LUMBER COMPANY INC (PA)
719 Front St (46910-9245)
P.O. Box 247 (46910-0247)
PHONE..................................574 893-4511
◆ **EMP:** 131 **EST:** 1904
SALES (est): 18.17MM
SALES (corp-wide): 18.17MM **Privately Held**
Web: www.pikelumber.com
SIC: 2421 Kiln drying of lumber

(G-8)
RUSSELL E MARTIN
Also Called: R & T Farm Supply
7585 E 350 S (46910-9768)
PHONE..................................574 354-2563
Russell E Martin, *Owner*
EMP: 1 **EST:** 2015
SALES (est): 38.28K **Privately Held**
SIC: 2519 5191 Lawn and garden furniture, except wood and metal; Farm supplies

(G-9)
SONOCO PRODUCTS COMPANY
Also Called: Industrial Products Div
1535 S State Road 19 (46910)
P.O. Box 338 (46910-0338)
PHONE..................................574 598-2731
Dedra Bockelman, *Brnch Mgr*
EMP: 51
SALES (corp-wide): 6.78B **Publicly Held**
Web: www.sonoco.com
SIC: 2631 Paperboard mills
PA: Sonoco Products Company
1 N 2nd St
Hartsville SC 29550
843 383-7000

(G-10)
TIC TOC TROPHY SHOP INC
930 E Rochester St (46910-9485)
P.O. Box 308 (46910-0308)
PHONE..................574 893-4234
TOLL FREE: 800
Chad Hartzler, Pr
EMP: 2 EST: 1956
SALES (est): 216.79K Privately Held
SIC: 3499 5999 Trophies, metal, except silver; Trophies and plaques

Albany
Delaware County

(G-11)
ALBANY METAL TREATING INC
400 S Gray St (47320-1549)
P.O. Box 65 (47320-0065)
PHONE..................765 789-6470
Marion Auker, Pr
EMP: 19 EST: 1978
SQ FT: 55,000
SALES (est): 2.65MM Privately Held
Web: www.albanymetal.com
SIC: 3398 3471 Metal heat treating; Plating and polishing

(G-12)
COOL CAYENNE LLC
7020 E County Road 900 N (47320-9010)
PHONE..................765 282-0977
EMP: 2 EST: 2004
SALES (est): 159.08K Privately Held
Web: www.coolcayenne.com
SIC: 2759 5651 Screen printing; Family clothing stores

(G-13)
MAKERS HAND WOODWORKING
6100 E Pottery Rd (47320-9715)
PHONE..................317 797-8776
EMP: 4 EST: 2015
SALES (est): 68.02K Privately Held
SIC: 2431 Millwork

(G-14)
PINSON MANUFACTURING CO LLC
500 W Walnut St (47320-1028)
PHONE..................217 273-8819
Leon M Pinson, Pr
EMP: 6 EST: 2021
SALES (est): 492.12K Privately Held
Web: www.pinsonmfg.com
SIC: 3599 Custom machinery

(G-15)
PRECISION PRINT LLC
10910 E County Road 500 N (47320-9554)
PHONE..................765 789-8799
Jon M Kern, Prin
EMP: 5 EST: 2016
SALES (est): 238.91K Privately Held
SIC: 2752 Commercial printing, lithographic

Albion
Noble County

(G-16)
ABC EMBROIDERY INC
Also Called: ABC Embroidery
3008 S 50 W (46701-9660)
PHONE..................260 636-7311
Vickie L Gaerte, Pr
Steven G Gaerte, VP
EMP: 5 EST: 1995
SALES (est): 497.2K Privately Held
Web: www.abcembroideryink.com
SIC: 2395 Embroidery products, except Schiffli machine

(G-17)
ALL PRINTING AND PUBLICATIONS
Also Called: Albion New ERA
407 S Orange St (46701-1132)
P.O. Box 25 (46701-0025)
PHONE..................260 636-2727
Robert Allman, Pr
EMP: 8 EST: 1872
SQ FT: 4,000
SALES (est): 431.1K Privately Held
SIC: 2711 2752 Commercial printing and newspaper publishing combined; Commercial printing, lithographic

(G-18)
B AND C ENTERPRISES
5095 W 450 S (46701-9483)
PHONE..................260 691-2171
Robert Hippensteel, Prin
EMP: 2 EST: 2008
SALES (est): 80.41K Privately Held
SIC: 2084 Wines

(G-19)
BONAR INC
Also Called: Bonar Well Drilling
307 Woods Dr (46701-1531)
PHONE..................260 636-7430
Eric L Bonar, Pr
Judy Bonar, Sec
Tenel Bonar, VP
▲ EMP: 5
SALES (est): 756.79K Privately Held
SIC: 1781 3053 Water well drilling; Gaskets, all materials

(G-20)
BURGESS ENTERPRISES LLC
Also Called: Burgess Auction Resale
441 S 400 E (46701-9517)
PHONE..................260 615-5194
◆ EMP: 4 EST: 2003
SQ FT: 3,340
SALES (est): 226.6K Privately Held
SIC: 3569 Filters

(G-21)
D & J TOOL CO INC
300 S 7th St (46701-1415)
PHONE..................260 636-2682
Delbert Smith, Pr
Janet Smith, Sec
EMP: 8 EST: 1978
SQ FT: 2,800
SALES (est): 894.46K Privately Held
SIC: 3544 Special dies and tools

(G-22)
D A MERRIMAN INC
2259 E State Road 8 (46701-9703)
PHONE..................260 636-3464
Don Merriman, Pr
Sally Merriman, VP
EMP: 2 EST: 2000
SALES (est): 127.31K Privately Held
SIC: 3999 0782 Lawn ornaments; Lawn and garden services

(G-23)
DEXTER AXLE COMPANY LLC
Also Called: Dexter Axle Division
500 S 7th St (46701-1419)
P.O. Box 108 (46701-0108)
PHONE..................260 636-2195
Dwight Busche, Brnch Mgr
EMP: 150
SALES (corp-wide): 1.41B Privately Held
Web: www.dexteraxle.com
SIC: 3714 Axles, motor vehicle
HQ: Dexter Axle Company Llc
2900 Industrial Pkwy E
Elkhart IN 46516

(G-24)
DIAL-X AUTOMATED EQUIPMENT INC
3903 S State Road 9 (46701-9634)
PHONE..................260 636-7588
EMP: 40
SIC: 3599 Machine and other job shop work

(G-25)
EBEY SALES & SERVICE
1037 E Baseline Rd (46701-9509)
PHONE..................260 636-3286
Brad Ebey, Owner
EMP: 2 EST: 2008
SALES (est): 86.87K Privately Held
SIC: 3651 Household audio and video equipment

(G-26)
ESTATES BY JUDI
441 S 400 E (46701-9517)
PHONE..................260 615-5195
EMP: 4 EST: 2017
SALES (est): 72.62K Privately Held
Web: www.estatesbyjudi.com
SIC: 3569 General industrial machinery, nec

(G-27)
FREELS MACHINE WORKS INC
489 S 75 E (46701-9563)
PHONE..................260 636-7948
Allen Freels, Pr
Shirley Freels, Contrlr
EMP: 1 EST: 1969
SQ FT: 2,500
SALES (est): 128.44K Privately Held
SIC: 3599 Machine shop, jobbing and repair

(G-28)
HAYES ENTERPRISES LLC
2174 N River Rd W (46701-9543)
PHONE..................260 636-3262
John P Hayes, Prin
EMP: 2 EST: 2008
SALES (est): 152.83K Privately Held
SIC: 3843 Dental hand instruments, nec

(G-29)
INTERNATIONAL WOOD INC
2425 E Us Highway 6 (46701-9794)
PHONE..................260 248-1491
Gavin Freel, Prin
EMP: 10 EST: 2014
SALES (est): 532.2K Privately Held
Web: www.woodworkingnetwork.com
SIC: 2431 Millwork

(G-30)
KNEPPERS INC
575 Weber Rd (46701-1472)
PHONE..................260 636-2180
Mike Knepper, Brnch Mgr
EMP: 9
Web: www.concretechute.com
SIC: 3713 Truck bodies and parts
PA: Knepper's, Inc.
1390 N 750 E
Avilla IN 46710

(G-31)
LIBERTY AUTOMATION LLC
4890 N 150 E (46701-9733)
PHONE..................574 524-0436
Steven Martz, Owner
Steven Michael Martz, Prin
EMP: 1 EST: 2014
SALES (est): 117.82K Privately Held
Web: www.liberty-automation.com
SIC: 1731 8742 3613 3625 Electronic controls installation; Automation and robotics consultant; Control panels, electric; Control equipment, electric

(G-32)
LINAMAR STRCTURES USA MICH INC
1510 Progress Dr (46701-1492)
PHONE..................248 372-9018
James Jarrell, Pr
EMP: 7
SALES (corp-wide): 5.89B Privately Held
Web: www.durashiloh.com
SIC: 3714 Motor vehicle parts and accessories
HQ: Linamar Structures Usa (Michigan) Inc.
32233 8 Mile Rd
Livonia MI 48152
248 477-6240

(G-33)
LINAMAR STRCTURES USA MICH INC
Also Called: Busche Enterprise
1612 Progress Dr (46701-1494)
P.O. Box 77 (46701-0077)
PHONE..................260 636-7030
EMP: 13
SALES (corp-wide): 5.89B Privately Held
Web: www.mobexglobal.com
SIC: 3599 Machine shop, jobbing and repair
HQ: Linamar Structures Usa (Michigan) Inc.
32233 8 Mile Rd
Livonia MI 48152
248 477-6240

(G-34)
LINAMAR STRCTURES USA MICH INC
Busche Workholding
600 S 7th St (46701-1421)
PHONE..................260 636-1069
Austin Pender, Genl Mgr
EMP: 38
SALES (corp-wide): 5.89B Privately Held
Web: www.mobexglobal.com
SIC: 3599 Machine shop, jobbing and repair
HQ: Linamar Structures Usa (Michigan) Inc.
32233 8 Mile Rd
Livonia MI 48152
248 477-6240

(G-35)
MOBEX GLOBAL US INC
Also Called: Mobex Global
1563 State Route #8 (46701)
PHONE..................319 269-3848
EMP: 1
SALES (corp-wide): 332.24MM Privately Held
Web: www.mobexglobal.com
SIC: 2819 Aluminum compounds
PA: Mobex Global U.S., Inc.
22122 Telegraph Rd
Southfield MI

(G-36)
NEWELL INDUSTRIAL LLC
200 E Park Dr (46701-1439)
PHONE..................260 636-3336
▲ EMP: 25
Web: www.newellindustrial.com
SIC: 3089 Extruded finished plastics products, nec

GEOGRAPHIC SECTION

Alexandria - Madison County (G-62)

(G-37)
NORTH AMERICAN EXTRUSN & ASSEM
200 E Park Dr (46701-1439)
PHONE.................................260 636-3336
Jack Caudill, *Prin*
▲ **EMP:** 9 **EST:** 2013
SALES (est): 226.15K **Privately Held**
SIC: 3089 Extruded finished plastics products, nec

(G-38)
OPI INC
Also Called: Orthopedic Precision Instrs
71 E 400 S Ste A (46701-9230)
P.O. Box 655 (46725-0655)
EMP: 4 **EST:** 2003
SALES (est): 759.81K **Privately Held**
Web: www.opimedical.com
SIC: 3599 Machine shop, jobbing and repair

(G-39)
ORR CABINET CO
Also Called: Orr Cabinetry
300 E Washington St (46701-1262)
PHONE.................................260 636-7757
Dale Orr, *Owner*
EMP: 5 **EST:** 1978
SQ FT: 2,000
SALES (est): 421.77K **Privately Held**
Web: www.orrcabinetry.com
SIC: 2434 Wood kitchen cabinets

(G-40)
PARKER-HANNIFIN CORPORATION
Also Called: Brass Products Division
903 N Orange St (46701-1523)
PHONE.................................260 636-2104
Russ Kalis, *Brnch Mgr*
EMP: 54
SALES (corp-wide): 19.93B **Publicly Held**
Web: www.parker.com
SIC: 3561 3491 3463 3432 Pumps and pumping equipment; Industrial valves; Nonferrous forgings; Plumbing fixture fittings and trim
PA: Parker-Hannifin Corporation
6035 Parkland Blvd
Cleveland OH 44124
216 896-3000

(G-41)
PRECISION MEDICAL INDS INC
907 Weber Rd (46701-1548)
PHONE.................................260 234-3112
Jeffrey Thornburgh, *Pr*
EMP: 5 **EST:** 2013
SALES (est): 597.42K **Privately Held**
Web: www.premedind.com
SIC: 2869 Silicones

(G-42)
QSI CUSTOM MACHINING
1512 Progress Dr (46701-1492)
PHONE.................................260 636-2341
EMP: 4 **EST:** 2016
SALES (est): 146.98K **Privately Held**
Web: www.qsiautomation.us
SIC: 3599 Machine shop, jobbing and repair

(G-43)
RICHARD K WILLIAMS
201 S Orange St (46701-1173)
PHONE.................................616 745-9319
EMP: 5 **EST:** 2019
SALES (est): 123.34K **Privately Held**
Web: www.kpcnews.com
SIC: 2711 Newspapers, publishing and printing

(G-44)
ROBERT BOSCH LLC
Also Called: Bosch Automotive
1613 Progress Dr (46701-1495)
PHONE.................................260 636-1005
Kurt Bendixen, *Pr*
EMP: 7
SALES (corp-wide): 230.19MM **Privately Held**
Web: www.bosch.us
SIC: 3714 Motor vehicle engines and parts
HQ: Robert Bosch Llc
38000 Hills Tech Dr
Farmington Hills MI 48331
248 876-1000

(G-45)
SHERMAN ENTERPRISES INC
4426 S 100 W (46701-9621)
PHONE.................................260 636-6225
Todd Sherman, *Owner*
EMP: 3 **EST:** 2000
SALES (est): 246.19K **Privately Held**
Web: www.teamse.com
SIC: 3449 Bars, concrete reinforcing: fabricated steel

(G-46)
TODD L WISE
5440 W 450 S (46701-9800)
PHONE.................................260 799-4828
Todd Wise, *Prin*
EMP: 2 **EST:** 2007
SALES (est): 131.25K **Privately Held**
SIC: 1442 Construction sand and gravel

Alexandria
Madison County

(G-47)
CABINET CRAFTERS CORP
120 S Sheridan St (46001-1944)
PHONE.................................765 724-7074
Tony Collins, *Pr*
EMP: 7 **EST:** 1998
SALES (est): 808.96K **Privately Held**
Web: www.cabinetcrafters.net
SIC: 2434 Wood kitchen cabinets

(G-48)
D1 MOLD & TOOL LLC
8201 N State Road 9 (46001-8649)
PHONE.................................765 378-0693
▲ **EMP:** 17 **EST:** 2002
SQ FT: 9,600
SALES (est): 2.21MM **Privately Held**
Web: www.d1moldandtool.com
SIC: 3544 Special dies and tools

(G-49)
DAN BARNETT WOODWORKING LLC
1570 E 1100 N (46001-9040)
PHONE.................................765 724-7828
Daniel Barnett, *Owner*
EMP: 1 **EST:** 2013
SALES (est): 76.89K **Privately Held**
SIC: 2431 Millwork

(G-50)
ELWOOD PUBLISHING COMPANY INC
Also Called: Alexandria Times-Tribune
1 Harrison Sq (46001-2054)
P.O. Box 85 (46036-0085)
PHONE.................................765 724-4469
Jack Barnes, *CEO*
EMP: 6
SALES (corp-wide): 8.23MM **Privately Held**
Web: www.elwoodpublishing.com
SIC: 2711 Newspapers, publishing and printing
HQ: Elwood Publishing Company Incorporated
317 S Anderson St
Elwood IN 46036
765 552-3355

(G-51)
ENERGY INC
Also Called: Airlift Services International
8201 N State Road 9 (46001-8649)
PHONE.................................765 948-3504
EMP: 6 **EST:** 1994
SALES (est): 590K **Privately Held**
Web: www.energy.gov
SIC: 1381 Drilling oil and gas wells

(G-52)
GLS MACHINING & DESIGN LLC
Also Called: GLS
12516 N 300 W (46001-8694)
PHONE.................................765 754-8248
Gary Glass, *Managing Member*
EMP: 5 **EST:** 2009
SQ FT: 6,000
SALES (est): 466.26K **Privately Held**
Web: www.glsmachining.com
SIC: 3569 Filters

(G-53)
J & H TOOL INC
109 S Clinton St (46001-2001)
PHONE.................................765 724-9691
Matthew Musgrave, *Pr*
Tommie Jones, *Pr*
Chris Wyatt, *Sec*
EMP: 5 **EST:** 1991
SQ FT: 5,000
SALES (est): 462.56K **Privately Held**
Web: j-h-tool.business.site
SIC: 3599 Machine shop, jobbing and repair

(G-54)
JAMES W HAGER
5731 N 100 E (46001-8795)
PHONE.................................765 643-0188
James W Hager, *Prin*
EMP: 6 **EST:** 2012
SALES (est): 62.63K **Privately Held**
SIC: 3423 3546 Hand and edge tools, nec; Power-driven handtools

(G-55)
MTS SYSTEMS CORPORATION
1611 S Harrison St (46001-2815)
PHONE.................................952 937-4000
Bill Allen, *Mgr*
EMP: 1
SALES (corp-wide): 16.11B **Publicly Held**
Web: www.mts.com
SIC: 3829 Measuring and controlling devices, nec
HQ: Mts Systems Corporation
14000 Technology Dr
Eden Prairie MN 55344
952 937-4000

(G-56)
NANNA S EMBROIDERY
169 E State Road 28 (46001-8920)
PHONE.................................765 724-3667
Nancy Cook, *Owner*
EMP: 1 **EST:** 1997
SALES (est): 65.71K **Privately Held**
Web: www.nanasembroidery.net
SIC: 3944 Games, toys, and children's vehicles

(G-57)
POET BRFINING - ALEXANDRIA LLC
Also Called: Poet Brfnng- Alexandria 21200
13179 N 100 E (46001-7703)
P.O. Box 717 (46001-0717)
PHONE.................................765 724-4384
Jeff Broin, *CEO*
Blake Hoffman, *Dir*
Doug Berven, *Dir*
Duane Sather, *Dir*
EMP: 2 **EST:** 2006
SALES (est): 2.3MM **Privately Held**
Web: www.poet.com
SIC: 2869 Ethyl alcohol, ethanol
PA: Poet, Llc
4615 N Lewis Ave
Sioux Falls SD 57104

(G-58)
RAM GRAPHICS INC
Also Called: Ram Apparel
1509 S Longwood Dr (46001-2819)
PHONE.................................765 724-7783
Ronald Ruby, *Pr*
Larry Mercer, *
Paulette Ruby, *
Patricia Mercer, *
EMP: 10 **EST:** 1976
SQ FT: 22,000
SALES (est): 533.43K **Privately Held**
SIC: 5136 5137 5094 5699 Men's and boy's clothing; Women's and children's clothing; Trophies; Customized clothing and apparel

(G-59)
RED GOLD LP
2595 W State Road 28 (46001-8673)
P.O. Box 83 (46036-0083)
PHONE.................................765 754-8750
EMP: 47 **EST:** 2001
SALES (est): 1.29MM **Privately Held**
Web: www.redgoldfoods.com
SIC: 3411 Food and beverage containers

(G-60)
REMINGTON MACHINE INC
6 Twin Oaks St (46001-1244)
PHONE.................................765 724-3389
David Remington, *Prin*
EMP: 11 **EST:** 2006
SALES (est): 198.91K **Privately Held**
Web: www.remingtonmachine.com
SIC: 3599 Machine shop, jobbing and repair

(G-61)
RESIN PARTNERS INC
Also Called: Home Design Products
602 S Fairview St (46001-2249)
P.O. Box 270 (46001-0270)
PHONE.................................765 724-7761
Mary Baber, *Brnch Mgr*
EMP: 79
SALES (corp-wide): 3.26MM **Privately Held**
Web: www.keter.com
SIC: 2519 Fiberglass and plastic furniture
HQ: Resin Partners, Inc.
6435 S Scatterfield Rd
Anderson IN 46013

(G-62)
ROBERT BURKHART
Also Called: Graphics 55
434 W State Road 28 (46001-8466)
PHONE.................................219 448-0365
EMP: 2 **EST:** 2011
SALES (est): 125.87K **Privately Held**
SIC: 2396 2395 Screen printing on fabric articles; Embroidery and art needlework

Alexandria - Madison County (G-63)   **GEOGRAPHIC SECTION**

(G-63)
TALON SYSTEMS INC
6548 N 100 W (46001-9302)
PHONE.................................765 393-1711
EMP: 1 EST: 1996
SQ FT: 5,000
SALES (est): 282.17K **Privately Held**
Web: www.talonsystems.net
SIC: 3559 Vibratory parts handling equipment

(G-64)
VINTAGE ROAD CANDLES
413 W 11th St Apt A8 (46001-2827)
PHONE.................................765 621-3561
Sarah Mullanix, *Prin*
EMP: 5 EST: 2017
SALES (est): 39.69K **Privately Held**
Web: www.vintageroadcandles.com
SIC: 3999 Candles

Alton
Crawford County

(G-65)
INDUSTRIAL CONTAINER SVCS LLC
Also Called: Ics-Cargo Clean
6213 Gheens Mill Road (47137)
PHONE.................................812 283-7659
Al Bauer, *Brnch Mgr*
EMP: 18
Web: www.mauserpackaging.com
SIC: 3443 3412 3411 Fabricated plate work (boiler shop); Metal barrels, drums, and pails; Metal cans
HQ: Industrial Container Services Llc
375 Northridge Rd Ste 600
Atlanta GA 30350
407 930-4182

Ambia
Benton County

(G-66)
HELENA AGRI-ENTERPRISES LLC
210 N 1st St (47917-8555)
PHONE.................................765 869-5518
EMP: 1
Web: www.helenaagri.com
SIC: 5191 2819 Chemicals, agricultural; Industrial inorganic chemicals, nec
HQ: Helena Agri-Enterprises, Llc
225 Schilling Blvd
Collierville TN 38017
901 761-0050

Amboy
Miami County

(G-67)
GRA-ROCK REDI MIX PRECAST LLC
5925 E 1050 S (46911)
P.O. Box 127 (46911)
PHONE.................................765 395-7275
EMP: 12 EST: 2016
SALES (est): 1.19MM **Privately Held**
Web: www.gra-rock.com
SIC: 3273 Ready-mixed concrete

Anderson
Madison County

(G-68)
3D PARTS MFG LLC
3248 Dr Martin Luther King Jr Blvd (46013-2004)
PHONE.................................317 860-6941
Josh Barber, *Managing Member*
▲ EMP: 5 EST: 2013
SQ FT: 3,000
SALES (est): 465.4K **Privately Held**
Web: www.3dpartsmfg.com
SIC: 3082 3312 Unsupported plastics profile shapes; Stainless steel

(G-69)
5 KNIGHT LLC ◆
2223 Sheridan St (46016-4180)
PHONE.................................219 680-6661
EMP: 2 EST: 2022
SALES (est): 62.38K **Privately Held**
SIC: 2099 7389 Food preparations, nec; Business services, nec

(G-70)
A1 PALLET LIQUIDATORS
2700 Indiana Ave (46012-1342)
PHONE.................................765 356-4020
EMP: 5 EST: 2016
SALES (est): 115.29K **Privately Held**
SIC: 2448 Pallets, wood and wood with metal

(G-71)
AAA SATELLITE LINK
1529 W 2nd St (46016-2405)
PHONE.................................765 642-7000
Lonnie Short, *Owner*
EMP: 6 EST: 2006
SALES (est): 120K **Privately Held**
SIC: 3663 Space satellite communications equipment

(G-72)
ADVANCE FILTER LLC
4515 Dr Martin Luther King Jr Blvd (46013)
PHONE.................................317 565-7009
EMP: 1 EST: 2010
SALES (est): 170.16K **Privately Held**
Web: www.advancefilterllc.com
SIC: 3569 Filters

(G-73)
AIR SIDE SYSTEMS LLC
3620 W 73rd St (46011)
PHONE.................................765 778-7895
John Reynolds, *Managing Member*
EMP: 1 EST: 2000
SALES (est): 267.43K **Privately Held**
Web: www.airsidesystems.com
SIC: 3564 Blowers and fans

(G-74)
AIRBUOYANT LLC
1508 E 7th St (46012-3423)
PHONE.................................765 623-9815
Pete V Bitar, *CEO*
EMP: 1 EST: 2010
SALES (est): 88.83K **Privately Held**
Web: www.airbuoyant.com
SIC: 3721 Aircraft

(G-75)
ALTAIR NANOTECHNOLOGIES INC
3019 Enterprise Dr (46013-8800)
PHONE.................................317 333-7617
Richard Lee, *Brnch Mgr*
EMP: 729
Web: www.altairnano.com
SIC: 2816 Inorganic pigments
PA: Altair Nanotechnologies Inc.
5190 Neil Rd
Reno NV 89502

(G-76)
AMERICAN PRINTING INDIANA LLC
1047 Broadway St (46012-2526)
PHONE.................................765 825-7600
Ron Smith, *Managing Member*
EMP: 7 EST: 2002
SALES (est): 942.32K **Privately Held**
SALES (corp-wide): 1.67MM **Privately Held**
SIC: 2759 Commercial printing, nec
PA: American Printing & Lithographing Co Inc
528 S 7th St
Hamilton OH 45011
513 867-0602

(G-77)
AMERICAN RUBBER CORP
1136 Dilts St (46017-1048)
PHONE.................................317 548-8455
Amit Patel, *Managing Member*
EMP: 3 EST: 2018
SALES (est): 72.87K **Privately Held**
Web: www.americanrubbercorp.com
SIC: 3069 3052 5085 3053 Rubber automotive products; Rubber hose; Gaskets and seals; Gasket materials

(G-78)
ANDERSON MEMORIAL PARK INC
Also Called: PARK DEVELOPEMENT
6805 Dr Martin Luther King Jr Blvd (46013-9706)
PHONE.................................765 643-3211
Diane Wiley, *Pr*
EMP: 10 EST: 1929
SALES (est): 380.48K **Privately Held**
Web: www.andersonmemorialpark.com
SIC: 6531 3272 6553 Cemetery management service; Burial vaults, concrete or precast terrazzo; Cemetery subdividers and developers

(G-79)
APOLOGIA EDUCTL MINISTRIES INC
1106 Meridian St Ste 340 (46016-1776)
P.O. Box 896844 (28289-6844)
PHONE.................................765 608-3280
Davis Carman, *Pr*
EMP: 21 EST: 1999
SQ FT: 550
SALES (est): 2.38MM **Privately Held**
Web: www.apologia.com
SIC: 2731 8299 Books, publishing and printing; Educational service, nondegree granting: continuing educ.

(G-80)
AVARI REEF LABS LLC
Also Called: Avari Labs
5217 S 100 E (46013-9540)
PHONE.................................317 201-9615
EMP: 2 EST: 2017
SALES (est): 58.43K **Privately Held**
SIC: 2048 7389 Fish food; Business Activities at Non-Commercial Site

(G-81)
BARBER MANUFACTURING CO INC (PA)
1824 Brown St (46016-1661)
P.O. Box 2454 (46018-2454)
PHONE.................................765 643-6905
John W Barber Junior, *Ch Bd*
Jeffery W Barber, *
James R Barber, *
Ron Feltner, *
Jack R Barber, *
▲ EMP: 93 EST: 1894
SQ FT: 80,000
SALES (est): 8.21MM
SALES (corp-wide): 8.21MM **Privately Held**
Web: www.barbermfg.com
SIC: 3495 Upholstery springs, unassembled

(G-82)
BARNETT-BATES CORPORATION
1415 Fairview St (46016-3523)
PHONE.................................815 726-5223
Robert H Barnett, *Pr*
Thomas C Barnett, *VP*
▲ EMP: 18 EST: 1926
SALES (est): 2.32MM **Privately Held**
Web: www.barnettbates.com
SIC: 3446 5085 Gratings, tread: fabricated metal; Valves and fittings

(G-83)
BEST WELD INC
1315 W 18th St (46016-3800)
PHONE.................................765 641-7720
Terry E Carl, *Pr*
EMP: 9 EST: 1992
SQ FT: 39,000
SALES (est): 270.11K **Privately Held**
Web: www.bestweld.net
SIC: 7539 3315 1799 Automotive repair shops, nec; Steel wire and related products ; Welding on site

(G-84)
BRISTOL VENTURES LLC
2698 N 400 W (46011-8758)
PHONE.................................765 649-8452
Charles Kile, *Prin*
EMP: 1 EST: 2008
SALES (est): 132.23K **Privately Held**
SIC: 2621 Paper mills

(G-85)
BROADWAY PRESS LLC
2112 Broadway St (46012-1605)
PHONE.................................765 644-8813
Richard L Zarse Ii, *Owner*
EMP: 5 EST: 1977
SQ FT: 3,500
SALES (est): 498.59K **Privately Held**
Web: www.gobroadwaypress.com
SIC: 2752 Offset printing

(G-86)
C & H SIGN INC CORPORATION
Also Called: C&H Plastic Letters & Signs
805 Morton St (46016-1355)
PHONE.................................765 642-7777
Linda L Laird, *Pr*
EMP: 2 EST: 1974
SQ FT: 800
SALES (est): 50K **Privately Held**
Web: www.candhsigns.com
SIC: 3993 Signs and advertising specialties

(G-87)
CABINETS PLUS BY PTRICK GEER I
6406 Production Dr (46013-9408)
PHONE.................................765 642-0329
Patrick Geer, *Pr*
Mary L Geer, *Sec*
EMP: 10 EST: 2001
SALES (est): 980.19K **Privately Held**
Web: www.cabinetsplus.us
SIC: 2434 Wood kitchen cabinets

(G-88)
CAPSTONE RAIL LLC
2302 Columbus Ave (46016-4538)
PHONE.................................877 242-4252
Brad Holtz, *VP*
EMP: 8 EST: 2016
SALES (est): 228.3K **Privately Held**

GEOGRAPHIC SECTION

Anderson - Madison County (G-112)

Web: www.capstonerail.com
SIC: 3446 Railings, banisters, guards, etc: made from metal pipe

(G-89)
CARRARA INDUSTRIES INC
1619 W 5th St (46016-1071)
PHONE.................................765 643-3430
EMP: 6 EST: 1993
SQ FT: 6,000
SALES (est): 501.72K Privately Held
Web: www.carraracoaters.com
SIC: 3479 Painting of metal products

(G-90)
CB FABRICATION
425 Sycamore St (46016-1044)
PHONE.................................765 649-1336
Chris Barkdull, Owner
EMP: 8 EST: 2007
SALES (est): 971.12K Privately Held
Web: www.cbfabricating.com
SIC: 3444 Sheet metalwork

(G-91)
CENTRAL COCA-COLA BTLG CO INC
Also Called: Coca-Cola
3200 E 38th St (46013-2657)
PHONE.................................765 642-9951
Scott Devall, Mgr
EMP: 60
SQ FT: 10,000
SALES (corp-wide): 45.75B Publicly Held
Web: www.coca-cola.com
SIC: 2086 Bottled and canned soft drinks
HQ: Central Coca-Cola Bottling Company, Inc.
    555 Taxter Rd Ste 550
    Elmsford NY 10523
    914 789-1100

(G-92)
CERLINE CERAMIC CORP
1415 Fairview St (46016-3523)
PHONE.................................765 649-7222
L William Hains, Pr
Margaret Hains, Sec
Robert A Hains, General Vice President
EMP: 1 EST: 1981
SQ FT: 10,000
SALES (est): 219.49K Privately Held
Web: www.mofabinc.com
SIC: 1799 5032 5169 3599 Coating of metal structures at construction site; Ceramic construction materials, excluding refractory; Adhesives, chemical; Machine and other job shop work

(G-93)
CITY OF ANDERSON
Also Called: Anderson Parking Authority
1035 Main St (46016-1745)
PHONE.................................765 648-6715
Wayne Wright, Brnch Mgr
EMP: 4
Web: www.cityofanderson.com
SIC: 9121 3559 Legislative bodies, Local government; Parking facility equipment and supplies
PA: City Of Anderson
    120 E 8th St
    Anderson IN 46016
    765 648-6034

(G-94)
CITY OF ANDERSON
Water Pollution Control
2801 Gene Gustin Way (46011-1900)
PHONE.................................765 648-6560
Nara Manor, Superintnt
EMP: 62

Web: www.cityofanderson.com
SIC: 3589 Water treatment equipment, industrial
PA: City Of Anderson
    120 E 8th St
    Anderson IN 46016
    765 648-6034

(G-95)
CNHI LLC
Also Called: Indiana Media Group
1133 Jackson St (46016-1433)
P.O. Box 1090 (46015-1090)
PHONE.................................765 640-4893
Mark Cohen, Brnch Mgr
EMP: 1
SALES (corp-wide): 34.97B Privately Held
Web: www.cnhi.com
SIC: 2711 Newspapers, publishing and printing
HQ: Cnhi, Llc
    445 Dexter Ave
    Montgomery AL 36104

(G-96)
COEUS TECHNOLOGY INC
2701 Entp Dr Ste 230 (46013)
PHONE.................................765 203-2304
Nathan J Richardson, Pr
David E Parker, VP
EMP: 6 EST: 2009
SQ FT: 700
SALES (est): 818.49K Privately Held
SIC: 2869 Accelerators, rubber processing: cyclic or acyclic

(G-97)
COMMUNITY HOLDINGS INDIANA INC
Also Called: Herald Bulletin, The
1133 Jackson St (46016-1433)
P.O. Box 1090 (46015-1090)
PHONE.................................765 622-1212
Joann Reed, Brnch Mgr
EMP: 10
SALES (corp-wide): 34.97B Privately Held
Web: www.heraldbulletin.com
SIC: 2711 Newspapers, publishing and printing
HQ: Community Holdings Of Indiana, Inc.
    3500 Colonnade Pkwy # 600
    Birmingham AL 35243

(G-98)
CONTINENTAL MANUFACTURING LLC
Also Called: Solas Ray Lighting
1524 Jackson St (46016-1621)
PHONE.................................765 778-9999
Bill Nagengast, *
▲ EMP: 50 EST: 2007
SALES (est): 9.06MM Privately Held
Web: www.solasray.com
SIC: 3714 Motor vehicle parts and accessories

(G-99)
COWPOKES INC
Also Called: Cowpokes Western Outfitters
1812 E 53rd St (46013-2830)
PHONE.................................765 642-3911
Jeff Boone, Pr
Lynnette Boone, Treas
EMP: 21 EST: 1993
SQ FT: 20,000
SALES (est): 2.4MM Privately Held
Web: www.cowpokesonline.com
SIC: 5699 5932 5947 5941 Western apparel; Antiques; Gift shop; Saddlery and equestrian equipment

(G-100)
DEBAMC INC
6501 Production Dr (46013-9407)
PHONE.................................765 608-2100
Rob Wineland, Pr
EMP: 18 EST: 1999
SQ FT: 28,500
SALES (est): 1.01MM Privately Held
Web: www.americanmetalcoatings.com
SIC: 3479 Coating of metals and formed products

(G-101)
DEER TRACK ARCHERY INC
648 W 500 S (46013-5412)
PHONE.................................765 643-6847
James Hasty, Pr
James Hasty, Owner
EMP: 2 EST: 1983
SALES (est): 115.1K Privately Held
Web: www.deertrackarchery.com
SIC: 5941 3949 Archery supplies; Targets, archery and rifle shooting

(G-102)
DERBY INDUSTRIES LLC
4301 W 73rd St (46011-8809)
PHONE.................................765 778-6104
▲ EMP: 7 EST: 2011
SALES (est): 201.61K Privately Held
Web: www.derbyindustries.com
SIC: 3999 Atomizers, toiletry

(G-103)
DILLON PATTERN WORKS INC
1010 W 21st St (46016-3907)
P.O. Box 41 (46015-0041)
PHONE.................................765 642-3549
Ronnie E Dillon, Pr
Prudy Dillon, Sec
EMP: 16 EST: 1970
SALES (est): 375.64K Privately Held
Web: www.andersonin.com
SIC: 3365 3543 Aluminum and aluminum-based alloy castings; Industrial patterns

(G-104)
DISCOUNT POWER EQUIPMENT
2650 E State Road 236 (46017-9757)
PHONE.................................765 642-0040
EMP: 4 EST: 2016
SALES (est): 108.79K Privately Held
Web: www.discountpowerequipment.com
SIC: 3524 1796 3714 3711 Lawn and garden equipment; Power generating equipment installation; Power transmission equipment, motor vehicle; Snow plows (motor vehicles), assembly of

(G-105)
DIVERSIFIED QULTY SVCS IND LLC
1315 W 18th St (46016-3800)
PHONE.................................765 644-7712
Sharon Montgomery, Pt
Will Nichols, Pr
Stacee Nichols, Sec
Kelli Perry, VP
Frank Shekell, Pt
EMP: 6 EST: 2004
SQ FT: 35,000
SALES (est): 498.72K Privately Held
Web: www.dqsicorp.com
SIC: 3537 Containers (metal), air cargo

(G-106)
DON HARTMAN OIL CO INC
Also Called: His
4193 Alexandria Pike (46012-9792)
PHONE.................................765 643-5026

William Inholt, Pr
Shirley Fox, Sec
EMP: 3 EST: 1950
SQ FT: 1,500
SALES (est): 346.59K Privately Held
SIC: 2911 5191 Petroleum refining; Fertilizer and fertilizer materials

(G-107)
DONALDSON COMPANY INC
Also Called: Donaldson Hydraulic Filters
6810 Layton Rd (46011)
PHONE.................................765 635-2285
Tod E Carpenter, Ch Bd
EMP: 3
SALES (corp-wide): 3.43B Publicly Held
Web: www.donaldson.com
SIC: 3599 Air intake filters, internal combustion engine, except auto
PA: Donaldson Company, Inc.
    1400 W 94th St
    Minneapolis MN 55431
    952 887-3131

(G-108)
DOUBLE T LEATHER INC
3320 Columbus Ave (46013-5354)
PHONE.................................765 393-3676
William Thompkins, Prin
EMP: 1 EST: 2009
SALES (est): 65.56K Privately Held
Web: wtomp58736.wixsite.com
SIC: 3199 Leather goods, nec

(G-109)
DOVEY CORPORATION
3220 W 25th St (46011-4617)
P.O. Box 2249 (46018-2249)
PHONE.................................765 649-2576
Kay Reed, Pr
Craig Smith, VP
▲ EMP: 23 EST: 1946
SQ FT: 18,000
SALES (est): 1.17MM Privately Held
Web: www.dovey.us
SIC: 3554 Corrugating machines, paper

(G-110)
DREWS PARTS LLC
705 E School St (46012)
PHONE.................................317 800-8713
Kelly Drew, Managing Member
EMP: 11 EST: 2013
SALES (est): 2.43MM Privately Held
Web: www.drewsparts.com
SIC: 3469 Metal stampings, nec

(G-111)
DUGOUT
2203 Broadway St (46012-1606)
PHONE.................................765 642-8528
Robert Stecher, Owner
EMP: 6 EST: 1985
SQ FT: 1,100
SALES (est): 491.26K Privately Held
SIC: 5699 2395 Sports apparel; Embroidery products, except Schiffli machine

(G-112)
E & B PAVING INC (HQ)
286 W 300 N (46012-1200)
PHONE.................................765 643-5358
Gary Stebbins, Pr
Larry Canterbury, *
John Eller, *
Ron Zink, *
Richard Knief, *
EMP: 25 EST: 1967
SQ FT: 6,000
SALES (est): 245.1MM
SALES (corp-wide): 814.09MM Privately Held

Anderson - Madison County (G-113)   **GEOGRAPHIC SECTION**

Web: www.irvmat.com
SIC: 1611 2951 1794 Highway and street paving contractor; Asphalt and asphaltic paving mixtures (not from refineries); Excavation work
PA: Irving Materials, Inc.
    8032 N State Road 9
    Greenfield IN 46140
    317 326-3101

(G-113)
EH BAARE CORPORATION (PA)
3620 W 73rd St (46011)
PHONE..................................765 778-7895
John R Reynolds, *Pr*
Richard Parsons, *Treas*
Johaannes P Jansen, *Sec*
EMP: 2 EST: 1920
SQ FT: 2,000
SALES (est): 23.8MM
SALES (corp-wide): 23.8MM **Privately Held**
Web: www.ehbaare.com
SIC: 3315 3444 Wire products, ferrous/iron: made in wiredrawing plants; Sheet metal specialties, not stamped

(G-114)
EMMANTONY PRODUCTIONS
1730 Lora St (46013-2742)
PHONE..................................765 649-5967
Roger Delillo, *Prin*
EMP: 1 EST: 2009
SALES (est): 38.61K **Privately Held**
SIC: 2731 Book publishing

(G-115)
ERTL ENTERPRISES INC
2316 Jefferson St (46016-4507)
PHONE..................................765 622-9900
Daniel A Ertl, *Pr*
EMP: 10 EST: 1996
SQ FT: 12,000
SALES (est): 2.43MM **Privately Held**
Web: www.ertlenterprises.com
SIC: 3519 Parts and accessories, internal combustion engines

(G-116)
ERTL FABRICATING INC
2316 Jefferson St (46016-4507)
PHONE..................................765 393-1376
EMP: 10 EST: 2011
SALES (est): 712.65K **Privately Held**
Web: www.ertlfabricating.com
SIC: 3449 Curtain wall, metal

(G-117)
FANCY CANDLE SOY LLC
1078 E 500 S (46013-9639)
PHONE..................................765 769-4042
Leidy Richardson, *Owner*
EMP: 5 EST: 2018
SALES (est): 110.45K **Privately Held**
Web: www.fancycandlesoy.com
SIC: 3999 Candles

(G-118)
FORGED ALLIANCE INC
Also Called: Barnett Bates
1415 Fairview St (46016-3523)
PHONE..................................815 726-3123
Bruce S Hains, *Prin*
EMP: 11 EST: 2017
SALES (est): 374K **Privately Held**
SIC: 3446 Architectural metalwork

(G-119)
GENERAL CAGE LLC
1106 Meridian St Ste 325 (46016-1776)
P.O. Box 104 (46036-0104)
PHONE..................................765 552-5039
◆ EMP: 10 EST: 1996
SQ FT: 108,000
SALES (est): 688.47K **Privately Held**
Web: www.westernpropertyadvisors.com
SIC: 3496 Cages, wire

(G-120)
GENTRYS CABINET INC
415 Main St (46016-1529)
PHONE..................................765 643-6611
Tim Miller, *Prin*
EMP: 5 EST: 2013
SALES (est): 95.31K **Privately Held**
Web: www.gentryscabinet.com
SIC: 2434 Wood kitchen cabinets

(G-121)
GET NOTICED PORTABLE SIGNS
1842 Lowell Ave (46011-2126)
PHONE..................................765 649-6645
Alvin Renschler, *Owner*
EMP: 2 EST: 2008
SALES (est): 143.68K **Privately Held**
SIC: 3993 Signs and advertising specialties

(G-122)
GO ELECTRIC INC
1920 Purdue Pkwy Ste 400 (46016-5579)
PHONE..................................765 400-1347
Lisa M Laughner, *Pr*
EMP: 1 EST: 2011
SQ FT: 30,000
SALES (est): 10MM
SALES (corp-wide): 7.96B **Privately Held**
Web: www.saft.com
SIC: 3621 3629 Generators for gas-electric or oil-electric vehicles; Battery chargers, rectifying or nonrotating
HQ: Saft America Inc
    13575 Waterworks St
    Jacksonville FL 32221
    904 861-1501

(G-123)
GREAT DEALS MAGAZINE
1232 Broadway St Ste 300 (46012-2564)
PHONE..................................765 649-3302
Jim Mougeotte, *Owner*
EMP: 10 EST: 2012
SALES (est): 820.85K **Privately Held**
Web: www.greatdealsmagazine.net
SIC: 3661 5192 Modems; Magazines

(G-124)
H&H MEDIA LLC
Also Called: N2 Publishing
1805 Sheffield Ct (46011-1367)
PHONE..................................317 213-0480
Jared Price, *Prin*
EMP: 5 EST: 2018
SALES (est): 227.31K **Privately Held**
Web: www.strollmag.com
SIC: 2741 Miscellaneous publishing

(G-125)
HELIX SIGNWORX LLC
530 W 6th St (46016-1151)
PHONE..................................765 203-1381
EMP: 5 EST: 2016
SALES (est): 76.2K **Privately Held**
SIC: 3993 Signs and advertising specialties

(G-126)
HELLO NATURE USA INC (PA)
1800 Purdue Pkwy (46016-5580)
PHONE..................................765 615-1900
Luca Bonini, *CEO*
Jonathan D Leman, *VP Sls*
Matteo Pra, *CFO*
▲ EMP: 2 EST: 2013
SALES (est): 3.87MM
SALES (corp-wide): 3.87MM **Privately Held**
SIC: 2873 Fertilizers: natural (organic), except compost

(G-127)
HOBBS AUTO DIAGNOSTICS & REPR
3594 N State Road 9 (46012-1242)
PHONE..................................765 606-1490
Christopher Hobbs, *Owner*
EMP: 1 EST: 2020
SALES (est): 60K **Privately Held**
Web: hobbsautomotiverepair.business.site
SIC: 7538 7537 7699 3519 General automotive repair shops; Automotive transmission repair shops; Miscellaneous automotive repair services; Diesel engine rebuilding

(G-128)
HOLDER BEDDING INC
1923 W 8th St (46016-2513)
PHONE..................................765 642-1256
Mark Beaman, *Mgr*
EMP: 3
SALES (corp-wide): 1MM **Privately Held**
Web: www.holderbedding.net
SIC: 2515 5712 Mattresses, containing felt, foam rubber, urethane, etc.; Mattresses
PA: Holder Bedding Inc
    230 Farabee Dr N
    Lafayette IN 47905
    765 447-7907

(G-129)
HOOSIER PRESS INC
1027 Meridian St (46016-1749)
PHONE..................................765 649-3716
Woody Farmer, *Pr*
Dan Shaw, *VP*
EMP: 3 EST: 1981
SQ FT: 3,100
SALES (est): 248.76K **Privately Held**
SIC: 2752 Offset printing

(G-130)
HY-PRO CORPORATION
Also Called: Hy-Pro Filtration
6810 Layton Rd (46011-9494)
PHONE..................................317 849-3535
Larry Hoeg, *Pr*
Aaron Hoeg, *Treas*
▲ EMP: 100 EST: 1986
SQ FT: 90,000
SALES (est): 22.06MM
SALES (corp-wide): 3.43B **Publicly Held**
Web: www.hyprofiltration.com
SIC: 3569 Filter elements, fluid, hydraulic line
PA: Donaldson Company, Inc.
    1400 W 94th St
    Minneapolis MN 55431
    952 887-3131

(G-131)
HY-TECH MACHINING SYSTEMS LLC
2900 S Scatterfield Rd (46013-1817)
P.O. Box 3223 (46018-3223)
PHONE..................................765 649-6852
Stan Lay, *Pr*
Joseph Lay, *Managing Member*
EMP: 28 EST: 1999
SQ FT: 30,000
SALES (est): 2.34MM **Privately Held**
Web: www.htmachines.com

(G-132)
I POWER ENERGY SYSTEMS LLC
4640 Dr Martin Luther King Jr Blvd (46013-2317)
PHONE..................................765 621-9980
EMP: 8 EST: 2005
SQ FT: 66,000
SALES (est): 725.11K **Privately Held**
Web: www.ipoweres.com
SIC: 3621 Generator sets: gasoline, diesel, or dual-fuel

(G-133)
ID GRAPHICS INCORPORATED
416 W 11th St (46016)
PHONE..................................765 649-9988
Dan Wehner, *Pr*
EMP: 5 EST: 2007
SALES (est): 306.68K **Privately Held**
Web: www.idgraphics.net
SIC: 2261 2395 Screen printing of cotton broadwoven fabrics; Embroidery and art needlework

(G-134)
IPOWER TECHNOLOGIES INC
Also Called: I Power
4640 Dr Martin Luther King Jr Blvd (46013-2317)
PHONE..................................317 574-0103
James E Luckman, *Pr*
John H Combes, *V Ch Bd*
EMP: 9 EST: 2002
SALES (est): 391.71K **Privately Held**
SIC: 3621 Power generators

(G-135)
IRVING MATERIALS INC
Also Called: I M I
1601 N Scatterfield Rd (46012-1584)
PHONE..................................765 644-8819
Doug Layman, *Brnch Mgr*
EMP: 8
SALES (corp-wide): 814.09MM **Privately Held**
Web: www.irvmat.com
SIC: 3273 Ready-mixed concrete
PA: Irving Materials, Inc.
    8032 N State Road 9
    Greenfield IN 46140
    317 326-3101

(G-136)
IRVING MATERIALS INC
5002 S State Road 67 (46013-9784)
PHONE..................................765 778-4760
EMP: 10
SALES (corp-wide): 814.09MM **Privately Held**
Web: www.irvmat.com
SIC: 3273 5032 1442 Ready-mixed concrete; Stone, crushed or broken; Construction sand and gravel
PA: Irving Materials, Inc.
    8032 N State Road 9
    Greenfield IN 46140
    317 326-3101

(G-137)
J & J PRINTING CO
2107 State St (46012)
PHONE..................................765 642-6642
John D Bagley, *Owner*
EMP: 3 EST: 1975
SALES (est): 239.56K **Privately Held**
Web: www.jandjprinting.com
SIC: 2752 Offset printing

GEOGRAPHIC SECTION
Anderson - Madison County (G-162)

(G-138)
JAM PRINTING INC
Also Called: PIP Printing & Marketting Svcs
1200 Meridian St (46016-1715)
PHONE..................765 649-9292
John Specht, *Pr*
EMP: 10 **EST:** 2009
SALES (est): 501.53K **Privately Held**
Web: www.jamprinting.biz
SIC: 2752 8742 Offset printing; Marketing consulting services

(G-139)
JANELLE DAVIS
Also Called: Amor Couture
1604 S Madison Ave (46016-3458)
PHONE..................765 635-6233
Janelle Davis, *CEO*
EMP: 1
SALES (est): 39.69K **Privately Held**
SIC: 3999 5621 Hair and hair-based products; Women's clothing stores

(G-140)
JCJ FABRICATION LLC
1653 W 500 S (46013-9732)
PHONE..................765 621-9556
Chad Sturgeon, *Pr*
EMP: 4 **EST:** 2017
SALES (est): 103.91K **Privately Held**
Web: jcj-fabrication-llc.business.site
SIC: 3999 Manufacturing industries, nec

(G-141)
KETER NORTH AMERICA INC
Also Called: Keter North America, Inc.
6435 S Scatterfield Rd (46013-9619)
PHONE..................765 298-6800
EMP: 84
Web: www.keter.com
SIC: 2392 2519 Household furnishings, nec; Lawn and garden furniture, except wood and metal
HQ: Keter North America Llc
901 W Yamato Rd Ste 180
Boca Raton FL 33431

(G-142)
KETER US INC (DH)
Also Called: US Leisure
6435 S Scatterfield Rd (46013)
PHONE..................317 575-4700
Thom Lombardo, *Pr*
Stacey Byers, *
◆ **EMP:** 200 **EST:** 1996
SQ FT: 100,000
SALES (est): 99.17MM
SALES (corp-wide): 3.26MM **Privately Held**
Web: www.keter.com
SIC: 2519 Fiberglass and plastic furniture
HQ: Jardin Netherlands B.V.
Ericssonstraat 17
Rijen NB 5121
161228300

(G-143)
KIRBY RISK CORPORATION
Also Called: Kirby Risk Electrical Supply
633 Broadway St (46012-2921)
PHONE..................765 643-3384
Bryan Jones, *Prin*
EMP: 3
SALES (corp-wide): 501.02MM **Privately Held**
Web: www.kirbyrisk.com
SIC: 5063 7694 Electrical supplies, nec; Rewinding stators
PA: Kirby Risk Corporation
1815 Sagamore Pkwy N
Lafayette IN 47904

765 448-4567

(G-144)
KLEENFLOW LLC
4515 Dr Martin Luther King Jr Blvd (46013)
PHONE..................317 912-0027
Jason Short, *Owner*
EMP: 5 **EST:** 2014
SALES (est): 165.73K **Privately Held**
Web: www.kleenflow.com
SIC: 3559 Special industry machinery, nec

(G-145)
L M PRODUCTS INC
1325 Meridian St (46016-1828)
PHONE..................765 643-3802
Larry Mechem Junior, *Pr*
Larry Mechem Senior, *Stockholder*
EMP: 30 **EST:** 1979
SQ FT: 7,000
SALES (est): 481.06K **Privately Held**
Web: lm-products.myshopify.com
SIC: 3199 3161 Straps, leather; Musical instrument cases

(G-146)
LAMINAR FITTINGS INC
1136 Dilts St Bldg 3 (46017-1048)
PHONE..................833 855-1020
Hiren Jetani, *CEO*
EMP: 5 **EST:** 2020
SALES (est): 59.19K **Privately Held**
Web: www.laminarfittings.com
SIC: 3599 Machine shop, jobbing and repair

(G-147)
LOST LEGENDS PUBLISHING LLC
158 Chariot Dr (46013-1081)
PHONE..................765 606-5342
EMP: 4 **EST:** 2019
SALES (est): 40.16K **Privately Held**
Web: www.lostlegendspublishing.us
SIC: 2741 Miscellaneous publishing

(G-148)
LOST REALMS PUBLISHING LLC
1231 Redwood Dr (46011-2815)
PHONE..................319 230-3666
Michelle M Hannan Poyner, *Pr*
EMP: 5 **EST:** 2017
SALES (est): 76.26K **Privately Held**
SIC: 2741 Miscellaneous publishing

(G-149)
LOVE-TOI LLC
1251 Flint Ct (46013)
PHONE..................317 537-7635
Annetoinette M Foreman, *CEO*
EMP: 1 **EST:** 2020
SALES (est): 85.31K **Privately Held**
SIC: 5999 2844 Cosmetics; Cosmetic preparations

(G-150)
MADISON MILLWORK INC
707 Jackson St (46016-1416)
PHONE..................765 649-7883
Gregory Hecht, *Pr*
Rhonda Hecht, *Sec*
EMP: 8 **EST:** 1991
SQ FT: 7,500
SALES (est): 957.86K **Privately Held**
Web: www.madisonmillwork.com
SIC: 2431 Millwork

(G-151)
MANCOR INDIANA INC
7825 American Way (46013-9669)
PHONE..................765 779-4800
Art Church, *CEO*
Craig Sloan, *
Jeffrey A Abrams, *
▲ **EMP:** 49 **EST:** 2006
SALES (est): 10.5MM
SALES (corp-wide): 156.64MM **Privately Held**
Web: www.mancor.com
SIC: 3714 Motor vehicle parts and accessories
PA: Mancor Canada Inc
2485 Speers Rd
Oakville ON L6L 2
905 827-3737

(G-152)
MEXABILLY BROTHERS LLC
1410 Chesterfield Dr (46012-4436)
PHONE..................765 621-6334
Owen Tungate, *Prin*
EMP: 5 **EST:** 2018
SALES (est): 103.91K **Privately Held**
SIC: 2759 Screen printing

(G-153)
MID AMERICA PROTOTYPING INC
428 E 21st St (46016-4412)
PHONE..................765 643-3200
Todd Wetz, *Pr*
Kimberly Wetz, *VP*
EMP: 3 **EST:** 2006
SQ FT: 6,000
SALES (est): 330.91K **Privately Held**
Web: www.mapi.biz
SIC: 3999 Miniatures

(G-154)
MILL STEEL CO
444 E 29th St (46016-5319)
PHONE..................765 622-4545
EMP: 10
SALES (corp-wide): 175.49MM **Privately Held**
Web: www.millsteel.com
SIC: 5051 3316 Steel; Cold-rolled strip or wire
PA: The Mill Steel Co
2905 Lucerne Dr Se
Grand Rapids MI 49546
800 247-6455

(G-155)
MITCHELL SMITH RACING
Also Called: Mitchell Smith Auto Service
4570 W State Road 32 (46011-1542)
PHONE..................765 640-0237
Mitchell Smith, *Owner*
EMP: 9 **EST:** 1984
SALES (est): 866.73K **Privately Held**
Web: www.mitchsmithauto.com
SIC: 3519 7549 7538 Internal combustion engines, nec; High performance auto repair and service; General automotive repair shops

(G-156)
MJ AIRCRAFT INC
262 Airport Rd (46017-9550)
PHONE..................765 378-7700
Susie Newman, *Pr*
Alex Buse, *VP*
EMP: 15 **EST:** 1967
SQ FT: 10,000
SALES (est): 1.58MM **Privately Held**
Web: www.mjaircraft.com
SIC: 4581 2531 Aircraft servicing and repairing; Seats, aircraft

(G-157)
MOFAB INC
Also Called: Ornamental Division
619 W 14th St (46016-3502)
PHONE..................765 649-5577
Bruce Hains, *Mgr*
EMP: 8
SQ FT: 6,000
SALES (corp-wide): 9.8MM **Privately Held**
Web: www.mofabinc.com
SIC: 3446 5999 1799 Architectural metalwork; Awnings; Fence construction
PA: Mofab Inc
1415 Fairview St
Anderson IN 46016
765 649-5577

(G-158)
MOFAB INC
Also Called: Ornamental Division
1424 Fairview St (46016-3552)
PHONE..................765 649-1288
Bruce Hains, *Mgr*
EMP: 2
SALES (corp-wide): 9.8MM **Privately Held**
Web: www.mofabinc.com
SIC: 3441 5051 Fabricated structural metal; Steel
PA: Mofab Inc
1415 Fairview St
Anderson IN 46016
765 649-5577

(G-159)
MOFAB INC (PA)
1415 Fairview St (46016-3524)
PHONE..................765 649-5577
L William Hains, *Ch Bd*
Max W Hains, *
Bruce S Hains, *
Robert Moffatt, *
EMP: 50 **EST:** 1958
SQ FT: 60,000
SALES (est): 9.8MM
SALES (corp-wide): 9.8MM **Privately Held**
Web: www.mofabinc.com
SIC: 3441 5051 3446 Fabricated structural metal; Steel; Ornamental metalwork

(G-160)
MONDAY VOIGT PRODUCTS INC
804 Hazlett St (46016-2324)
PHONE..................317 224-7920
Lacinda Monday, *CEO*
Kurt Voigt, *Pr*
EMP: 12 **EST:** 2005
SQ FT: 50,000
SALES (est): 12MM **Privately Held**
Web: www.mondayvoigtproducts.com
SIC: 5063 3568 Transformers and transmission equipment; Power transmission equipment, nec

(G-161)
MORIROKU TECHNOLOGY N AMER INC
3511 W 73rd St (46011-9606)
PHONE..................765 221-7576
EMP: 1
SIC: 3089 Injection molded finished plastics products, nec
HQ: Moriroku Technology North America Inc.
15000 Industrial Pkwy
Marysville OH 43040
937 548-3217

(G-162)
MOUGEOTTE PUBLISHING INC
1232 Broadway St Ste 300 (46012-2564)
PHONE..................765 649-3302
Kathy L Mougeotte, *Pr*
EMP: 5 **EST:** 2016
SALES (est): 50.03K **Privately Held**

Anderson - Madison County (G-163)

GEOGRAPHIC SECTION

SIC: 2741 Miscellaneous publishing

(G-163)
MUHLEN SOHN INC
Also Called: Muhlen Sohn Industries, L.P.
3019 Enterprise Dr (46013-8800)
PHONE..................765 640-9674
Petra Muhlen, *Pr*
▲ EMP: 18 EST: 2005
SQ FT: 60,000
SALES (est): 4.5MM
SALES (corp-wide): 2.59MM **Privately Held**
Web: www.muehlen-sohn.de
SIC: 2296 Cord and fabric for reinforcing industrial belting
PA: Muhlen Sohn Gmbh & Co.Kg
Lindenstr. 16/1
Blaustein BW 89134
73048010

(G-164)
MY GOODIES SNACK VENDING LLC
1905 E Balsam Ct (46011-2708)
PHONE..................317 653-7395
EMP: 1
SALES (est): 60.62K **Privately Held**
SIC: 7389 3581 Business Activities at Non-Commercial Site; Automatic vending machines

(G-165)
N-COMPLETE INC
804 Lincoln St (46016-1320)
P.O. Box 2309 (46018-2309)
PHONE..................765 649-2244
EMP: 10 EST: 2012
SALES (est): 449.39K **Privately Held**
SIC: 3537 Trucks, tractors, loaders, carriers, and similar equipment

(G-166)
NATES LLC
2224 Meridian St (46016)
PHONE..................765 400-4613
Nathan Paul Isadore Mcgill, *Pr*
EMP: 3 EST: 2020
SALES (est): 137.15K **Privately Held**
Web: www.naturenatesllc.com
SIC: 2099 Food preparations, nec

(G-167)
NATURAL COATING SYSTEMS
3220 W 25th St (46011-4617)
PHONE..................765 642-2464
Chuck Thomas, *Prin*
EMP: 2 EST: 2005
SALES (est): 91.06K **Privately Held**
SIC: 3479 Coating of metals and formed products

(G-168)
NEWCO METALS INC
1515 E 22nd St (46016-4613)
PHONE..................765 644-6649
Chris Rasmussen, *Brnch Mgr*
EMP: 1
SALES (corp-wide): 9.93MM **Privately Held**
Web: www.newcometals.com
SIC: 5093 5051 3341 Nonferrous metals scrap; Metals service centers and offices; Secondary nonferrous metals
PA: Newco Metals, Inc.
7268 S State Road 13
Pendleton IN 46064
317 485-7721

(G-169)
NINAS SCRUB BOUTIQUE LLC
1735 Lockerbie Ct (46011-3173)
PHONE..................833 445-1955
EMP: 4 EST: 2021
SALES (est): 75K **Privately Held**
SIC: 2211 Scrub cloths

(G-170)
NTK PRCSION AXLE CORP - ANDRSO
7635 S Layton Rd (46011-9496)
PHONE..................765 221-7800
EMP: 10 EST: 2019
SALES (est): 772.68K **Privately Held**
SIC: 3312 Blast furnaces and steel mills

(G-171)
OAKLEY BROTHERS DISTILLERY
34 W 8th St (46016-1406)
PHONE..................765 274-5590
EMP: 8 EST: 2018
SALES (est): 489.32K **Privately Held**
Web: www.oakleybrothersdistillery.online
SIC: 2085 Distilled and blended liquors

(G-172)
OAKLIEF LLC
3211 Jay Dr (46012-1217)
PHONE..................765 642-9010
Losie W Wools, *Pr*
Jerry Wools, *Pt*
EMP: 2 EST: 1982
SALES (est): 155K **Privately Held**
SIC: 2511 Whatnot shelves: wood

(G-173)
ON THE GO LOGISTICS LLC
1426 Dewey St (46016-3121)
PHONE..................765 810-7454
EMP: 1
SALES (est): 60.08K **Privately Held**
SIC: 3537 Trucks: freight, baggage, etc.: industrial, except mining

(G-174)
OPEN GATE LLC
Also Called: Open Gate Design & Decor
2834 N 900 W (46011-9128)
PHONE..................765 734-1314
EMP: 17 EST: 2015
SALES (est): 1.99MM **Privately Held**
Web: www.opengatedesign.com
SIC: 3446 Fences, gates, posts, and flagpoles

(G-175)
PARALLAX GROUP INC
600 Broadway St (46012-2922)
P.O. Box 2698 (46018-2698)
PHONE..................800 443-4859
Joseph Brandon, *Pr*
EMP: 7 EST: 2016
SALES (est): 826.62K **Privately Held**
Web: www.parallaxpower.com
SIC: 3799 Recreational vehicles

(G-176)
PERFECTO TOOL & ENGINEERING CO
1124 W 53rd St (46013-1305)
P.O. Box 2039 (46018-2039)
PHONE..................765 644-2821
Stephen D Skaggs, *Pr*
Andrew Skaggs, *
Chris Sharp, *
▼ EMP: 40 EST: 1955
SQ FT: 37,000
SALES (est): 7.45MM **Privately Held**
Web: www.perfecto.com
SIC: 3599 3544 3469 Custom machinery; Dies and die holders for metal cutting, forming, die casting; Machine parts, stamped or pressed metal

(G-177)
PHINIA USA LLC (DH)
6512 Production Dr (46013-9407)
PHONE..................765 778-6879
◆ EMP: 340 EST: 1994
SALES (est): 343.11MM
SALES (corp-wide): 3.5B **Publicly Held**
Web: www.phinia.com
SIC: 3714 Motor vehicle parts and accessories
HQ: Phinia Jersey Holdings Llc
3850 Hamlin Rd
Auburn Hills MI 48326
248 754-9200

(G-178)
PHOENIX PRESS INC
Also Called: Quality Printing
1047 Broadway St (46012-2526)
PHONE..................765 644-3959
Steve Harney, *Pr*
John Oblazney, *
EMP: 70 EST: 1963
SQ FT: 40,000
SALES (est): 9.71MM **Privately Held**
Web: www.quality-printing.com
SIC: 2752 2789 2053 Offset printing; Bookbinding and related work; Frozen bakery products, except bread

(G-179)
PIERCE TRACY
4663 State Road 32 E (46017-9511)
PHONE..................765 748-2361
Tracy Pierce, *Owner*
EMP: 6 EST: 1993
SALES (est): 110.71K **Privately Held**
SIC: 3537 Industrial trucks and tractors

(G-180)
PLASTICRAFT-COMPLETE ACRYLICS
4441 S Scatterfield Rd (46013-2944)
PHONE..................765 610-9502
Stan Boyd, *Prin*
EMP: 6 EST: 2011
SALES (est): 231.63K **Privately Held**
SIC: 3083 Plastics finished products, laminated

(G-181)
PROTRON LLC
1812 Mounds Rd Ste X (46016-5753)
PHONE..................765 313-1595
Todd Utley, *Prin*
EMP: 1 EST: 2014
SQ FT: 8,000
SALES (est): 67.86K **Privately Held**
SIC: 3613 3612 3621 7699 Knife switches, electric; Voltage regulating transformers, electric power; Control equipment for electric buses and locomotives; Medical equipment repair, non-electric

(G-182)
RAINE INC
6401 S Madison Ave (46013-3336)
P.O. Box 2219 (46018-2219)
PHONE..................765 622-7687
Raine Ii John, *Pr*
EMP: 12 EST: 1986
SQ FT: 13,000
SALES (est): 1.06MM **Privately Held**
Web: www.raineinc.com

SIC: 2311 5131 2393 3161 Military uniforms, men's and youths': purchased materials; Nylon piece goods, woven; Textile bags; Luggage

(G-183)
REBOUND PROJECT LLP
1125 N Madison Ave (46011-1211)
PHONE..................765 621-5604
Eric Foley, *Pt*
Rob Spaulding, *Pt*
EMP: 2 EST: 2018
SALES (est): 72.43K **Privately Held**
SIC: 8748 6794 7372 Business consulting, nec; Music licensing to radio stations; Application computer software

(G-184)
RECYCLE DESIGN INC
804 Hazlett St (46016-2324)
PHONE..................765 374-0316
Edward Boutwell, *Pr*
EMP: 4 EST: 2009
SQ FT: 1,600
SALES (est): 498.34K **Privately Held**
Web: www.recycledesign.com
SIC: 2531 Benches for public buildings

(G-185)
RESIN PARTNERS INC (DH)
Also Called: Home Design Products
6435 S Scatterfield Rd (46013-9619)
PHONE..................765 298-6800
Sami Sagol, *Ch Bd*
Yossi Sagol, *
Jeff Flagg, *
◆ EMP: 130 EST: 1992
SQ FT: 500,000
SALES (est): 38.43MM
SALES (corp-wide): 3.26MM **Privately Held**
Web: www.keter.com
SIC: 3089 Boxes, plastics
HQ: Keter Us, Inc.
6435 S Scatterfield Rd
Anderson IN 46013
317 575-4700

(G-186)
RUBY ENTERPRISES INC
Also Called: Soft Stop
1150 W 29th St (46016-6001)
PHONE..................765 649-2060
John Ruby, *Owner*
Jill Ruby, *Owner*
EMP: 7 EST: 1941
SQ FT: 8,000
SALES (est): 473.81K **Privately Held**
Web: www.sofstop.com
SIC: 2299 5999 Padding and wadding, textile ; Awnings

(G-187)
RUGGED COMPANY
3404 Clark St (46013-5339)
PHONE..................317 441-0927
EMP: 4 EST: 2015
SALES (est): 239.22K **Privately Held**
Web: www.ruggedcompany.com
SIC: 2844 5999 5122 Perfumes, cosmetics and other toilet preparations; Toiletries, cosmetics, and perfumes; Toiletries

(G-188)
RUSSELL BEEMAN LOGGING INC
4935 E County Road 67 (46017-9548)
PHONE..................765 387-0064
EMP: 4 EST: 2018
SALES (est): 81.72K **Privately Held**
SIC: 2411 Logging

GEOGRAPHIC SECTION

Anderson - Madison County (G-216)

(G-189)
S&S STEEL SERVICES INC
444 E 29th St (46016-5319)
P.O. Box 129 (46017-0129)
PHONE.................................765 622-4545
EMP: 120
Web: www.sssteelservices.com
SIC: 5051 3316 Metals service centers and offices; Cold-rolled strip or wire

(G-190)
SER NORTH AMERICA LLC
3025 Dr Martin Luther King Jr Blvd (46016-4851)
PHONE.................................765 639-0300
Lorenzo Ferro, *Managing Member*
Massimo Pavin, *Managing Member*
Roberto Panzarasa, *Managing Member*
EMP: 11 EST: 2019
SALES (est): 1.28MM **Privately Held**
Web: www.sirmax.com
SIC: 3089 Plastics containers, except foam

(G-191)
SHORTS MACHINE SHOP
509 E 29th St (46016-5322)
PHONE.................................765 622-6259
David Short, *Owner*
Dave Short, *Owner*
EMP: 7 EST: 1998
SALES (est): 489.69K **Privately Held**
SIC: 3599 Machine shop, jobbing and repair

(G-192)
SIGN PROS INC
633 Jackson St (46016-1156)
P.O. Box 233 (46017-0233)
PHONE.................................765 642-1175
Ronald Kinder, *Pr*
EMP: 3 EST: 1991
SALES (est): 251.03K **Privately Held**
Web: www.signprosga.com
SIC: 3993 Signs and advertising specialties

(G-193)
SIGNART & VINYL LLC
5132 W State Road 32 (46011-1582)
PHONE.................................765 644-5290
EMP: 4 EST: 2019
SALES (est): 55.01K **Privately Held**
Web: www.signartandvinyl.com
SIC: 3993 Signs and advertising specialties

(G-194)
SIRMAX NORTH AMERICA INC
2915 Dr Martin Luther King Jr Blvd (46016)
PHONE.................................765 639-0300
Massimo Pavin, *CEO*
Massimo Pavin, *Pr*
Lorenzo Ferro, *
Roberto Pavin, *
▲ EMP: 92 EST: 2015
SALES (est): 67.51MM
SALES (corp-wide): 432.97MM **Privately Held**
Web: www.sirmax.com
SIC: 2295 Resin or plastic coated fabrics
HQ: Sirmax Spa
  Viale Dell'artigianato 42
  Cittadella PD 35013
  049 944-1118

(G-195)
SOUDER DERYL CO
Also Called: Souder Walling
2918 Harbur Blvd (46011-9215)
PHONE.................................765 565-6719
Deryl Souder, *Owner*
EMP: 1 EST: 1972
SALES (est): 60.73K **Privately Held**

SIC: 3548 Welding and cutting apparatus and accessories, nec

(G-196)
SPEARS HOLDINGS INC
3574 E State Road 236 (46017-9713)
PHONE.................................765 378-4908
John Spears, *Pr*
EMP: 5 EST: 1997
SALES (est): 440.34K **Privately Held**
Web: www.speartech.com
SIC: 3714 Motor vehicle parts and accessories

(G-197)
SPECTRUM MARKETING
1629 Pearl St (46016-2022)
PHONE.................................765 643-5566
Donna Trueblood, *Mgr*
EMP: 2 EST: 1984
SQ FT: 2,500
SALES (est): 149.65K **Privately Held**
SIC: 7389 2396 7641 2262 Embroidery advertising; Screen printing on fabric articles; Reupholstery and furniture repair; Finishing plants, manmade

(G-198)
SPEEDCRAFT PROTOTYPES
141 W 14th St (46016-1635)
PHONE.................................765 644-6449
Scott Campbell, *Owner*
EMP: 1 EST: 1980
SALES (est): 71K **Privately Held**
Web: www.simulationfx.com
SIC: 3544 7692 1799 Special dies and tools; Welding repair; Special trade contractors, nec

(G-199)
SPOTLIGHT ON DRAMA LLC
3551 W 8th Street Rd (46011-9170)
PHONE.................................765 643-7170
EMP: 5 EST: 2018
SALES (est): 88.81K **Privately Held**
SIC: 3648 Lighting equipment, nec

(G-200)
STANDOUT CREATIONS LLC
1078 E 500 S (46013-9639)
P.O. Box 1412 (46015-1412)
PHONE.................................765 203-9110
William Richardson, *Pr*
EMP: 4 EST: 2014
SALES (est): 166.34K **Privately Held**
Web: www.standoutcreations.com
SIC: 2759 Screen printing

(G-201)
STITCH GLITCH
2210 Crestwood Dr (46016-2750)
PHONE.................................765 274-1435
Michael Dewalt, *Prin*
EMP: 5 EST: 2016
SALES (est): 51.15K **Privately Held**
SIC: 2395 Embroidery and art needlework

(G-202)
SUPERIOR KREATIONS INC
1926 E 53rd St (46013-2832)
PHONE.................................765 635-3729
Shelley Broshar, *Prin*
EMP: 5 EST: 2015
SALES (est): 264.43K **Privately Held**
Web: www.superiorkreationsinc.com
SIC: 3993 Signs and advertising specialties

(G-203)
SURFACE GENERATION TECH LLC
56 Beauvoir Cir (46011-1907)

PHONE.................................765 425-2741
David Chobany, *Prin*
EMP: 1 EST: 2020
SALES (est): 53.15K **Privately Held**
Web: www.surface-generation.com
SIC: 3291 3714 3795 Abrasive products; Motor vehicle parts and accessories; Tanks and tank components

(G-204)
TECNOPLAST USA LLC
3619 W 73rd St Ste 1 (46011-9608)
PHONE.................................317 769-4929
Gloria Da Ros, *CEO*
Ronnie Da Ros, *VP*
▲ EMP: 7 EST: 2011
SQ FT: 40,000
SALES (est): 1.17MM
SALES (corp-wide): 303.71K **Privately Held**
Web: www.tecnoplastonline.it
SIC: 3089 Hardware, plastics
PA: Tecnoplast Srl
  Via Del Fangario 22
  Cagliari CA
  070 208-0026

(G-205)
TERRANCE A SMITH DISTRIBUTING
2215 N Madison Ave (46011-9583)
PHONE.................................765 644-3396
Terrance A Smith, *Pr*
Terrance A Smith Prestreas, *Prin*
▲ EMP: 48 EST: 1945
SQ FT: 800,000
SALES (est): 4.15MM **Privately Held**
Web: www.tasmithdist.com
SIC: 5181 2082 Beer and other fermented malt liquors; Malt beverages

(G-206)
TETRASOLV INC
Also Called: Tetrasolv Filtration
444 E 29th St (46016-5319)
PHONE.................................765 643-3941
◆ EMP: 10 EST: 1995
SALES (est): 2.26MM **Privately Held**
Web: www.tetrasolv.com
SIC: 3677 Filtration devices, electronic

(G-207)
TOP IN SOUND INC
3273 N State Road 9 (46012-1235)
PHONE.................................765 649-8111
Patrick E Topolsky, *Pr*
EMP: 8 EST: 1974
SALES (est): 820.51K **Privately Held**
Web: www.pinnaclesystemsllc.com
SIC: 3699 5731 7812 Electric sound equipment; Radio, television, and electronic stores; Audio-visual program production

(G-208)
TRE PAPER COMPANY
5395 S 50 W (46013-9500)
PHONE.................................765 649-2536
Robert T Mier, *Pr*
EMP: 9 EST: 1994
SQ FT: 25,000
SALES (est): 560.84K **Privately Held**
Web: www.treepackaging.com
SIC: 2653 2675 2657 Corrugated and solid fiber boxes; Die-cut paper and board; Folding paperboard boxes

(G-209)
TRU-CUT INC
3111 S Madison Ave (46016-6011)
PHONE.................................765 683-9920
Kevin Elpers, *Pr*
Brian Elpers, *

Tony Anderson, *OF SLS Marketing**
▲ EMP: 23 EST: 1998
SQ FT: 90,000
SALES (est): 1.83MM **Privately Held**
Web: www.trucutinc.com
SIC: 2431 Millwork

(G-210)
TSPDESIGN LLC ✪
1029 Redrock Dr (46013-3768)
PHONE.................................317 785-8663
EMP: 1 EST: 2022
SALES (est): 69.27K **Privately Held**
SIC: 3999 7389 Barber and beauty shop equipment; Business Activities at Non-Commercial Site

(G-211)
ULLOM WOODWORKS
4740 E 200 N (46012-9439)
PHONE.................................765 610-3188
EMP: 4 EST: 2017
SALES (est): 73.71K **Privately Held**
SIC: 2431 Millwork

(G-212)
UNIQUE GLOBAL SOLUTIONS LLC
5729 S 200 E (46017-9536)
PHONE.................................765 779-5030
EMP: 2 EST: 2009
SALES (est): 225.39K **Privately Held**
SIC: 2522 7389 Office furniture, except wood; Business services, nec

(G-213)
VEE ENGINEERING INC (PA)
3620 W 73rd St (46011-9608)
PHONE.................................765 778-7895
John Reynolds, *Pr*
David Lawson Senior, *VP*
EMP: 2 EST: 1967
SQ FT: 2,000
SALES (est): 9.88MM
SALES (corp-wide): 9.88MM **Privately Held**
Web: www.veeengineering.com
SIC: 3089 Injection molded finished plastics products, nec

(G-214)
VMS PRODUCTS INC
6055 S White Oaks Dr (46013-9761)
P.O. Box 471 (46064-0471)
PHONE.................................888 321-4698
Colleen Baird, *Pr*
EMP: 1 EST: 2013
SALES (est): 130.74K **Privately Held**
Web: www.vmsproducts.net
SIC: 4491 5085 3429 4783 Marine cargo handling; Industrial supplies; Security cable locking systems; Packing and crating

(G-215)
WANDA HARRINGTON
Also Called: Bush Trophy Case & Embroidery
5215 S 100 W (46013-9404)
PHONE.................................765 642-1628
Wanda Harrington, *Owner*
EMP: 3 EST: 1981
SQ FT: 1,200
SALES (est): 218.26K **Privately Held**
SIC: 5999 2395 Trophies and plaques; Embroidery products, except Schiffli machine

(G-216)
WARNER PRESS INC
2902 Enterprise Dr (46013-9667)
PHONE.................................800 741-7721
EMP: 12 EST: 2017

Anderson - Madison County (G-217)

SALES (est): 492.93K **Privately Held**
Web: www.warnerpress.com
SIC: 2741 Miscellaneous publishing

(G-217)
WHITE RIVER PRESS INC
914 Park Ave (46012-4011)
PHONE..........................317 507-4684
EMP: 2
SALES (est): 115K **Privately Held**
SIC: 2759 Commercial printing, nec

(G-218)
XTREME ADS LIMITED
Also Called: Xtreme Alternative Def Systems
1735 W 53rd St (46013-1105)
PHONE..........................765 644-7323
Peter V Bitar, *Pr*
EMP: 23 EST: 1997
SQ FT: 80,000
SALES (est): 2.96MM **Privately Held**
SIC: 3812 8711 Defense systems and equipment; Engineering services

(G-219)
YOUNGS FREIGHT & LOGISTICS LLC ◆

4511 Columbus Ave Apt B-12 (46013-5102)
PHONE..........................765 639-7888
EMP: 1 EST: 2022
SALES (est): 60.08K **Privately Held**
SIC: 3537 7389 Trucks: freight, baggage, etc.: industrial, except mining; Business Activities at Non-Commercial Site

(G-220)
YOUTH JAM LLC
2017 Heather Rd (46012-9476)
PHONE..........................765 644-6375
Vera Magnum, *Prin*
EMP: 2 EST: 2008
SALES (est): 83.5K **Privately Held**
SIC: 2033 Canned fruits and specialties

Andrews
Huntington County

(G-221)
DAVIS EXTERIORS INC
2272 E N 800 (46702)
PHONE..........................260 786-1600
EMP: 4
SALES (est): 130.79K **Privately Held**
SIC: 3442 Window and door frames

(G-222)
W & W LOCKER
8896 W 600 N (46702-9507)
PHONE..........................260 344-3400
Gary Lopshire, *Owner*
EMP: 3 EST: 2007
SALES (est): 204.85K **Privately Held**
SIC: 2011 Meat packing plants

Angola
Steuben County

(G-223)
A GREAT STITCH
800 Lane 440 Lake James (46703-9092)
PHONE..........................317 698-3743
Andrew Stefanek, *Prin*
EMP: 4 EST: 2015
SALES (est): 60.77K **Privately Held**
SIC: 2395 Embroidery and art needlework

(G-224)
AARDVARK VINYL SIGNS
1875 W 275 N (46703-9540)
PHONE..........................260 833-0800
Josh Kugler, *Owner*
EMP: 3 EST: 2005
SALES (est): 228.76K **Privately Held**
SIC: 3993 Signs and advertising specialties

(G-225)
ALICON LLC
4720 W 200 N (46703-8777)
PHONE..........................260 687-1259
EMP: 1
SALES (est): 69.27K **Privately Held**
SIC: 3569 7389 General industrial machinery, nec; Business services, nec

(G-226)
AMI INDUSTRIES INC
1501 Wohlert St (46703-1064)
PHONE..........................989 786-3755
EMP: 3
SALES (corp-wide): 23.8MM **Privately Held**
Web: www.ami-lewiston.com
SIC: 3559 Automotive related machinery
PA: Ami Industries, Inc.
5093 N Red Oak Rd
Lewiston MI 49756
989 786-3755

(G-227)
ANGOLA CANVAS CO
2301 N Wayne St (46703-9110)
PHONE..........................260 665-9913
Richard A Hocker, *Pr*
Barbara Hocker, *Sec*
EMP: 10
SQ FT: 6,700
SALES (est): 822.49K **Privately Held**
Web: www.angolacanvascompany.com
SIC: 2394 3732 Convertible tops, canvas or boat: from purchased materials; Boatbuilding and repairing

(G-228)
ANGOLA WIRE PRODUCTS INC
Also Called: A W Manufacturing
1300 Wohlert St (46703-1059)
PHONE..........................260 665-3061
Todd Boots, *Mgr*
EMP: 1
SALES (corp-wide): 20.63MM **Privately Held**
Web: www.angolawire.com
SIC: 3496 5051 3599 Miscellaneous fabricated wire products; Metals service centers and offices; Machine shop, jobbing and repair
PA: Angola Wire Products, Inc.
803 Wohlert St
Angola IN 46703
260 665-9447

(G-229)
ANGOLA WIRE PRODUCTS INC (PA)
803 Wohlert St (46703-1079)
PHONE..........................260 665-9447
Michael G Heroy, *CEO*
Mark F Mangan, *
John Brockett, *
David F Heroy, *Stockholder*
Dennis H Heiney, *Stockholder*
▲ EMP: 170 EST: 1960
SALES (est): 20.63MM
SALES (corp-wide): 20.63MM **Privately Held**
Web: www.angolawire.com

SIC: 3479 3496 Coating of metals and formed products; Shelving, made from purchased wire

(G-230)
APEX INDUSTRIES LLC
309 W Stocker St (46703-1023)
PHONE..........................260 624-5003
Cody E Sholl, *CEO*
EMP: 5 EST: 2017
SALES (est): 39.69K **Privately Held**
Web: www.apexindpro.com
SIC: 3999 Manufacturing industries, nec

(G-231)
ASTBURY WATER TECHNOLOGY INC
601 W 400 N (46703-9516)
PHONE..........................260 668-8900
Daniel Astbury, *Owner*
EMP: 4
SALES (corp-wide): 10.12MM **Privately Held**
Web: www.astburygroup.com
SIC: 2899 3826 Water treating compounds; Water testing apparatus
PA: Astbury Water Technology, Incorporated
5940 W Raymond St
Indianapolis IN 46241
317 328-7153

(G-232)
AUTOFORM TOOL & MFG LLC
Also Called: Atm
1501 Wohlert St (46703-1064)
PHONE..........................260 624-2014
EMP: 240 EST: 1996
SQ FT: 135,000
SALES (est): 49.51MM
SALES (corp-wide): 1.66B **Publicly Held**
SIC: 3714 5084 3463 3462 Motor vehicle parts and accessories; Industrial machinery and equipment; Pump, compressor, turbine, and engine forgings, except auto; Pump, compressor, and turbine forgings
PA: Park-Ohio Holdings Corp.
6065 Parkland Blvd
Cleveland OH 44124
440 947-2000

(G-233)
BARIL COATINGS USA LLC
401 Growth Pkwy (46703-9323)
PHONE..........................260 665-8431
David P Harmon Junior, *CEO*
Joseph Rabensteine, *
EMP: 45 EST: 2006
SQ FT: 24,000
SALES (est): 9.46MM **Privately Held**
Web: www.barilcoatings.us
SIC: 2851 Lacquers, varnishes, enamels, and other coatings

(G-234)
BEST-ONE TIRE & AUTO CARE OF A
1101 N Wayne St (46703-2342)
PHONE..........................260 665-7330
Paul Zurcher, *Pr*
EMP: 9 EST: 1982
SQ FT: 11,000
SALES (est): 2.07MM **Privately Held**
Web: www.bestonetire.com
SIC: 5531 7534 Automotive tires; Tire repair shop

(G-235)
BOAT LIFT GUYS INC
207 Hoosier Dr Ste 1 (46703-9315)
PHONE..........................260 667-3057
Troy Helwig, *Prin*
EMP: 6 EST: 2014

SALES (est): 553.45K **Privately Held**
Web: www.boatliftguys.com
SIC: 3536 Boat lifts

(G-236)
BOYD SIGN COMPANY
495 Lane 298 Crooked Lk (46703-8144)
PHONE..........................260 833-2257
Randy Boyd, *Owner*
EMP: 1 EST: 1976
SALES (est): 90.55K **Privately Held**
SIC: 3993 Signs and advertising specialties

(G-237)
BSC VNTRES ACQUISITION SUB LLC
Also Called: Triton Plant
100 Woodhull Dr (46703-9339)
PHONE..........................260 665-7521
Victor Clark, *Brnch Mgr*
EMP: 65
SQ FT: 90,000
SALES (corp-wide): 126.11MM **Privately Held**
Web: www.bscventures.com
SIC: 2677 2791 Envelopes; Typesetting
HQ: Bsc Ventures Llc
7702 Plantation Rd
Roanoke VA 24019
540 362-3311

(G-238)
BUDGET INKS LLC
45 S Public Sq (46703-1926)
PHONE..........................877 636-4657
James Schall, *Managing Member*
EMP: 5 EST: 2015
SALES (est): 496.4K **Privately Held**
Web: www.budget-inks.com
SIC: 2893 Printing ink

(G-239)
CHAPMANS CIDER COMPANY LLC
300 Industrial Dr (46703-1053)
PHONE..........................260 444-1194
EMP: 7 EST: 2012
SALES (est): 701.15K **Privately Held**
Web: www.chapmansbrewing.com
SIC: 2082 Malt beverages

(G-240)
CLARK MILLWORKS
1587 S Old Us Highway 27 (46703-8956)
PHONE..........................260 665-1270
Stephen Clark, *Pt*
Tim Fournier, *Pt*
EMP: 2 EST: 1988
SALES (est): 179.93K **Privately Held**
Web: www.clarkmillworks.com
SIC: 2431 Moldings and baseboards, ornamental and trim

(G-241)
CLASSIC SIGN & AWNING
P.O. Box 335 (46703-0335)
PHONE..........................260 665-6663
EMP: 6 EST: 1996
SALES (est): 231.5K **Privately Held**
SIC: 5999 3993 Awnings; Signs and advertising specialties

(G-242)
CONCEPT CARS INC
1280 N 290 W (46703-9004)
PHONE..........................260 668-7553
Steve Asztalos, *Pr*
EMP: 7 EST: 1976
SQ FT: 10,000
SALES (est): 562.43K **Privately Held**
SIC: 3711 Automobile assembly, including specialty automobiles

GEOGRAPHIC SECTION

Angola - Steuben County (G-267)

(G-243)
COUNTY OF STEUBEN
Also Called: Steuben County Parks
100 Lane 101 Crooked Lk (46703-9162)
PHONE..................260 833-2401
Eric Ditmars, *Dir*
EMP: 3
Web: co.steuben.in.us
SIC: 2531 Picnic tables or benches, park
PA: County Of Steuben
317 S Wayne St Ste 2 J
Angola IN 46703

(G-244)
CUSTOM POLISH & CHROME
114 Lange Ln (46703-2164)
PHONE..................260 665-7448
EMP: 3
SALES (est): 307.15K **Privately Held**
SIC: 3471 Polishing, metals or formed products

(G-245)
CUT-PRO INDEXABLE TOOLING LLC
212 Growth Pkwy (46703-9331)
P.O. Box 657 (46703-0657)
PHONE..................260 668-2400
EMP: 2 **EST:** 2002
SQ FT: 2,500
SALES (est): 180.11K **Privately Held**
Web: www.cutproindexabletooling.com
SIC: 3541 Machine tools, metal cutting type

(G-246)
E M F CORP (PA)
Also Called: E M F
505 Pokagon Trl (46703-9320)
P.O. Box 389 (46703-0389)
PHONE..................260 665-9541
Steve Daugherty, *CEO*
Howards Sanders, *
Jacqueline Poe, *
▲ **EMP:** 40 **EST:** 1970
SQ FT: 175,000
SALES (est): 24.52MM
SALES (corp-wide): 24.52MM **Privately Held**
Web: www.emfusa.com
SIC: 3643 3699 3694 Cord connectors, electric; Electrical equipment and supplies, nec; Engine electrical equipment

(G-247)
EJ BROOKS COMPANY (HQ)
Also Called: Tydenbrooks
409 Hoosier Dr (46703)
PHONE..................800 348-4777
TOLL FREE: 800
Robert Logeman, *CEO*
Phil Whitley, *
◆ **EMP:** 75 **EST:** 1983
SALES (est): 73.4MM
SALES (corp-wide): 3.08B **Privately Held**
Web: www.tydenbrooks.com
SIC: 3053 Gaskets and sealing devices
PA: Madison Industries Holdings Llc
444 W Lake St Ste 4400
Chicago IL 60606
312 277-0156

(G-248)
ELECTRIC-TEC LLC
Also Called: Electri-Tec
509 Growth Pkwy (46703-9324)
PHONE..................260 665-1252
Bill Khorshid, *
Greg Baker, *
EMP: 45 **EST:** 2012
SQ FT: 30,000
SALES (est): 11.59MM
SALES (corp-wide): 52.79MM **Privately Held**
Web: www.electritec.com
SIC: 3679 Harness assemblies, for electronic use: wire or cable
PA: Khorporate Holdings, Inc.
6492 State Road 205
Laotto IN 46763
260 357-3365

(G-249)
ERIE HAVEN INC
1310 W Maumee St (46703-1359)
PHONE..................260 665-2052
EMP: 5 **EST:** 2013
SALES (est): 85.02K **Privately Held**
SIC: 3273 Ready-mixed concrete

(G-250)
FEDDEMA INDUSTRIES INC
Also Called: Special Cutting Tools
1305 Wohlert St (46703-1060)
P.O. Box 246 (46703-0246)
PHONE..................260 665-6463
Leonard Feddema, *Pr*
EMP: 31 **EST:** 1968
SQ FT: 9,800
SALES (est): 1.15MM **Privately Held**
Web: www.specialcuttingtools.net
SIC: 3599 3545 Machine shop, jobbing and repair; Machine tool accessories

(G-251)
FLEX-N-GATE LLC
3000 Woodhull Dr (46703-9318)
PHONE..................260 665-8288
Matt Tacia, *Brnch Mgr*
EMP: 6
SALES (corp-wide): 1.57B **Privately Held**
Web: www.flex-n-gate.com
SIC: 3465 3714 Automotive stampings; Motor vehicle parts and accessories
PA: Flex-N-Gate Llc
1306 E University Ave
Urbana IL 61802
217 384-6600

(G-252)
FOODS ALIVE INC
1600 Wohlert St (46703-1065)
P.O. Box 210 (46703-0210)
PHONE..................260 488-4497
Ellen Moor, *Pr*
Michael Moor, *CEO*
Matt Alvord, *VP*
EMP: 14 **EST:** 2003
SALES (est): 2.25MM **Privately Held**
Web: www.foodsalive.com
SIC: 2099 Food preparations, nec

(G-253)
FREDA INC
401 Growth Pkwy (46703-9323)
PHONE..................260 665-8431
David Harman Senior, *Pr*
EMP: 10 **EST:** 1964
SQ FT: 12,000
SALES (est): 1.55MM **Privately Held**
SIC: 1799 2891 Epoxy application; Epoxy adhesives

(G-254)
G & S SUPER ABRASIVES INC
1601 Wohlert St (46703-1066)
P.O. Box 461 (46703-0461)
PHONE..................260 665-5562
Paul M Jordan, *Pr*
Lisa Jordan, *Treas*
Christy Vangompel, *Contrlr*
EMP: 22 **EST:** 1981
SQ FT: 8,400
SALES (est): 448.64K **Privately Held**
Web: www.gssuperabrasives.com
SIC: 3291 3541 3545 Hones; Grinding, polishing, buffing, lapping, and honing machines; Machine tool accessories

(G-255)
GENERAL PRODUCTS DELAWARE CORPORATION
Also Called: General Products
1411 Wohlert St (46703-1062)
PHONE..................260 668-1440
▲ **EMP:** 335
SIC: 3599 3462 3369 Machine shop, jobbing and repair; Iron and steel forgings; Nonferrous foundries, nec

(G-256)
GRAPHICS UNLMTED MCRPUBLISHING
740 E 50 N (46703-9557)
PHONE..................260 665-3443
Jeanie Miller, *Owner*
EMP: 4 **EST:** 1996
SALES (est): 222.15K **Privately Held**
Web: www.thegraphicsunlimited.com
SIC: 2759 Screen printing

(G-257)
HEIDELBERG MTLS STHWEST AGG LL
HEIDELBERG MATERIALS SOUTHWEST AGG LLC
260 E 300 N (46703-7503)
PHONE..................260 665-2626
EMP: 5
SALES (corp-wide): 23.02B **Privately Held**
Web: www.heidelbergmaterials.com
SIC: 3273 Ready-mixed concrete
HQ: Hanson Aggregates Llc
8505 Freport Pkwy Ste 500
Irving TX 75063
469 417-1200

(G-258)
HI-PRO INC
Also Called: Hpi Wire Assemblies
1410 Wohlert St Ste C (46703-1061)
P.O. Box 480 (46703-0480)
PHONE..................260 665-5038
Wally Stevens, *Pr*
Stephanie Gaff, *Stockholder*
Robert Hiatt, *Stockholder*
▲ **EMP:** 10 **EST:** 2006
SQ FT: 22,000
SALES (est): 2.13MM **Privately Held**
Web: www.hiproinc.com
SIC: 3679 Harness assemblies, for electronic use: wire or cable

(G-259)
HIGHLAND COMPUTER FORMS INC
1510 Wohlert St (46703-1063)
PHONE..................260 665-6268
Robert Jones, *Mgr*
EMP: 19
SALES (corp-wide): 22.01MM **Privately Held**
Web: www.hcf.com
SIC: 2761 Computer forms, manifold or continuous
PA: Highland Computer Forms, Inc.
1025 W Main St
Hillsboro OH 45133
937 393-4215

(G-260)
HOLCIM - MWR INC
1310 W Maumee St (46703-1359)
PHONE..................260 665-2052
Gary Manley, *Brnch Mgr*
EMP: 2

Web: www.aggregatemn.com
SIC: 3273 Ready-mixed concrete
HQ: Holcim - Mwr, Inc.
2815 Dodd Rd
Eagan MN 55121

(G-261)
HOOSIER PLASTICS INC
2535 N 200 W (46703-9350)
PHONE..................812 232-5027
EMP: 6 **EST:** 2017
SALES (est): 698.88K **Privately Held**
Web: www.hoosierp.com
SIC: 3089 Injection molding of plastics

(G-262)
HUDSON AQUATIC SYSTEMS LLC
1100 Wohlert St (46703-1034)
PHONE..................260 665-1635
George Hunter, *Pr*
Tom Ellis, *Prin*
▼ **EMP:** 14 **EST:** 2010
SQ FT: 42,000
SALES (est): 2.66MM **Privately Held**
Web: www.hudsonaquatic.com
SIC: 3949 Water sports equipment

(G-263)
IMP HOLDINGS LLC
Also Called: Indiana Marine Products
409 Growth Pkwy (46703-9323)
PHONE..................260 665-6112
EMP: 80
Web: www.indianamarine.com
SIC: 3694 3089 Engine electrical equipment; Thermoformed finished plastics products, nec

(G-264)
JOHNNY LEMAS
2314 N 200 W (46703-9125)
P.O. Box 61 (46703-0061)
PHONE..................260 833-8850
Johnny Lemas, *Prin*
▲ **EMP:** 3 **EST:** 2001
SALES (est): 422.52K **Privately Held**
Web: www.johnnylemasfireworks.com
SIC: 2899 5961 Fireworks; Catalog and mail-order houses

(G-265)
JOMARK INC
Also Called: Greenman's Printing & Imaging
40 Lane 274 Crooked Lk (46703-8121)
PHONE..................248 478-2600
William Greenman, *Pr*
EMP: 15 **EST:** 1978
SALES (est): 397.94K **Privately Held**
SIC: 2752 7338 2791 2759 Offset printing; Secretarial and court reporting; Typesetting; Commercial printing, nec

(G-266)
JROWE SIGNS
311 S Superior St (46703-1816)
PHONE..................260 668-7100
Judy Rowe, *Owner*
EMP: 2 **EST:** 2007
SQ FT: 2,000
SALES (est): 68.23K **Privately Held**
Web: www.jrowesigns.com
SIC: 3993 Electric signs

(G-267)
KAS SATELLITE & CABLE INC (PA)
Also Called: King's Antenna Service
60 Lane 165 Jimmerson Lk (46703-9179)
P.O. Box 1027 (46703-5027)
PHONE..................260 833-3941
King D Oberlin, *Pr*

Angola - Steuben County (G-268)

Lori Oberlin, *VP*
EMP: 3 **EST:** 1969
SQ FT: 2,000
SALES (est): 458.64K
SALES (corp-wide): 458.64K **Privately Held**
Web: www.kassatellite.net
SIC: 3651 Home entertainment equipment, electronic, nec

(G-268)
KIRK ENTERPRISE SOLUTIONS INC
333 Hoosier Dr (46703-9336)
PHONE..................260 665-3670
Jeff Kirk, *Pt*
Mike Kirk, *Pt*
EMP: 5 **EST:** 1977
SQ FT: 5,000
SALES (est): 502.98K **Privately Held**
Web: www.kirkphoto.com
SIC: 3599 Machine shop, jobbing and repair

(G-269)
KNOX INC
Also Called: Dodge Heating and Coolg Contrs
101 Fox Lake Rd (46703-2162)
PHONE..................260 665-6617
Roger Knox, *Pr*
Deborah Knox, *Sec*
EMP: 12 **EST:** 1926
SQ FT: 4,800
SALES (est): 288.8K **Privately Held**
Web: www.mastersheatcool.com
SIC: 1711 3444 Warm air heating and air conditioning contractor; Sheet metalwork

(G-270)
KPC MEDIA GROUP INC
Also Called: Kpc Media Group
45 S Public Sq (46703-1926)
PHONE..................678 645-0000
Lindsay Brown, *Brnch-Mgr*
EMP: 16
SALES (corp-wide): 23.55MM **Privately Held**
Web: www.fwbusiness.com
SIC: 2711 Newspapers, publishing and printing
PA: Kpc Media Group Inc.
102 N Main St
Kendallville IN 46755
260 347-0400

(G-271)
LEATHER YODER COMPANY LLC
2064 N 130 W (46703)
P.O. Box 71 (46703)
PHONE..................260 833-4030
EMP: 5 **EST:** 2019
SALES (est): 101.23K **Privately Held**
SIC: 3199 Leather goods, nec

(G-272)
LEDINGEDGE LIGHTING INC
505 Pokagon Trl (46703-9320)
PHONE..................805 383-8493
Jo Fletcher, *Brnch Mgr*
EMP: 7
Web: www.ledingedge.com
SIC: 3648 Lighting equipment, nec
PA: Ledingedge Lighting, Inc.
600 N Bullard Ave Ste 4
Goodyear AZ 85338

(G-273)
LOMONT HOLDINGS CO INC
Also Called: Illuminated Image
1825 W Maumee St (46703-7066)
P.O. Box 537 (46703-0537)
PHONE..................800 545-9023
Barbara Lomont, *Pr*
EMP: 35 **EST:** 1989
SQ FT: 37,000
SALES (est): 4.03MM **Privately Held**
Web: www.illuminatedimage.com
SIC: 2394 3646 3829 2396 Awnings, fabric; made from purchased materials; Fluorescent lighting fixtures, commercial; Measuring and controlling devices, nec; Fabric printing and stamping

(G-274)
MAT MATRS OF INDIANA INC
205 Industrial Dr (46703-1052)
P.O. Box 193 (46703-0193)
PHONE..................260 624-2882
Brad Walker, *Pr*
EMP: 1 **EST:** 2004
SALES (est): 115.08K **Privately Held**
SIC: 2273 Mats and matting

(G-275)
METAL SPINNERS INC (PA)
914 Wohlert St (46703)
P.O. Box 269 (46703)
PHONE..................260 665-2158
Olin M Wiland, *Pr*
EMP: 15 **EST:** 1941
SALES (est): 45.97MM
SALES (corp-wide): 45.97MM **Privately Held**
Web: www.samuel.com
SIC: 3469 3449 3341 Spinning metal for the trade; Miscellaneous metalwork; Secondary nonferrous metals

(G-276)
MIRAGE COMPUTERS INC
1220 S Wayne St (46703-6970)
P.O. Box 1100 (46703-5100)
PHONE..................260 665-5072
Michael Davis, *Pr*
Michelle Davis, *Sec*
EMP: 9 **EST:** 1984
SALES (est): 488.92K **Privately Held**
SIC: 7373 7371 5045 7379 Computer systems analysis and design; Computer software development; Computers, nec; Computer related consulting services

(G-277)
MORGAN OLSON LLC
300 Growth Pkwy (46703-9326)
PHONE..................269 659-0243
Kathy Schumacher, *Brnch Mgr*
EMP: 133
SALES (corp-wide): 1.62B **Privately Held**
Web: www.morganolson.com
SIC: 3713 Truck bodies (motor vehicles)
HQ: Morgan Olson, Llc
1801 S Nottawa St
Sturgis MI 49091
269 659-0200

(G-278)
NORTHEAST WOODWORKING
1450 N 140 W (46703-9498)
PHONE..................260 665-1986
EMP: 4 **EST:** 2016
SALES (est): 65.86K **Privately Held**
SIC: 2431 Millwork

(G-279)
OWENS CORNING SALES LLC
Also Called: Owens Corning
1211 Wohlert St (46703-1058)
PHONE..................260 665-7318
Mike Aiello, *Mgr*
EMP: 2
SQ FT: 6,000
SIC: 3296 Fiberglass insulation
HQ: Owens Corning Sales, Llc
1 Owens Corning Pkwy
Toledo OH 43659
419 248-8000

(G-280)
PARAGON MANUFACTURING INC
700 Wohlert St (46703-1029)
P.O. Box 814 (46703-0814)
PHONE..................260 665-1492
EMP: 15 **EST:** 1994
SQ FT: 5,000
SALES (est): 883.76K **Privately Held**
Web: www.noisedamp.com
SIC: 3446 Partitions and supports/studs, including acoustical systems

(G-281)
PARKWAY INVESTOR GROUP INC
Also Called: Electri-Tec
509 Growth Pkwy (46703-9324)
PHONE..................260 665-1252
▲ **EMP:** 25
SIC: 3679 Harness assemblies, for electronic use: wire or cable

(G-282)
PATRICK INDUSTRIES INC
Also Called: Indiana Marine Products
409 Growth Pkwy (46703-9323)
PHONE..................260 665-6112
Todd M Cleveland, *CEO*
EMP: 80
SALES (corp-wide): 3.47B **Publicly Held**
Web: www.patrickind.com
SIC: 3089 3694 Thermoformed finished plastics products, nec; Harness wiring sets, internal combustion engines
PA: Patrick Industries, Inc.
107 W Franklin St
Elkhart IN 46516
574 294-7511

(G-283)
PERRY PRODUCTS INC
959 Growth Pkwy (46703-9338)
PHONE..................260 316-8816
Matthew Perry, *Pr*
EMP: 4 **EST:** 2004
SQ FT: 3,000
SALES (est): 392.23K **Privately Held**
SIC: 3423 7699 Hand and edge tools, nec; Tool repair services

(G-284)
POLYFUSION LLC
395 Lane 101 (46703)
PHONE..................260 624-7659
Dennis Springer, *CEO*
EMP: 5 **EST:** 2013
SALES (est): 239.33K **Privately Held**
Web: www.polyfusionllc.com
SIC: 2821 Plastics materials and resins

(G-285)
POLYFUSION LLC
959 Growth Pkwy Ste D (46703-9338)
P.O. Box 629 (46703-0629)
PHONE..................260 624-7659
EMP: 4 **EST:** 2015
SALES (est): 156.77K **Privately Held**
Web: www.polyfusionllc.com
SIC: 2899 Chemical preparations, nec

(G-286)
POWERS HARDWOODS
Also Called: Powers Farms
8090 E 40 S (46703-8249)
PHONE..................260 665-5498
Dewey Powers, *Owner*
EMP: 1 **EST:** 1978
SALES (est): 92.37K **Privately Held**
Web: www.powershardwoods.com
SIC: 2435 0211 0139 Panels, hardwood plywood; Beef cattle feedlots; Hay farm

(G-287)
PRECISION EDGE SRGCAL PDTS LLC
1910 N Wayne St (46703-9100)
PHONE..................260 624-3123
John Truckey, *Pr*
EMP: 53
Web: www.eva-lution.net
SIC: 3841 Surgical and medical instruments
PA: Precision Edge Surgical Products Company Llc
415 W 12th Ave
Sault Sainte Marie MI 49783

(G-288)
PRECISION TECHNOLOGIES I LLC
200 Industrial Dr (46703-1051)
PHONE..................260 668-7500
Joe Honer, *Pr*
EMP: 10 **EST:** 2007
SQ FT: 14,000
SALES (est): 1.5MM **Privately Held**
SIC: 3441 Fabricated structural metal

(G-289)
PRINTING PLACE INC
1500 N Wayne St Ste B (46703-2305)
P.O. Box 688 (46703-0688)
PHONE..................260 665-8444
Robert Osterholt, *Pr*
Jane Osterholt, *Treas*
EMP: 10 **EST:** 1985
SQ FT: 5,500
SALES (est): 666.84K **Privately Held**
Web: www.printingplace.com
SIC: 2752 2791 2789 2759 Offset printing; Typesetting; Bookbinding and related work; Commercial printing, nec

(G-290)
PULLMAN COMPANY
Also Called: Tenneco
503 Weatherhead St (46703-1057)
PHONE..................260 667-2200
Steven Hoeper, *Mgr*
EMP: 257
SQ FT: 90,000
SALES (corp-wide): 18.04B **Privately Held**
Web: www.tenneco.com
SIC: 3714 Motor vehicle transmissions, drive assemblies, and parts
HQ: The Pullman Company
1 International Dr
Monroe MI 48161
734 243-8000

(G-291)
R R DONNELLEY & SONS COMPANY
611 W Mill St (46703-1021)
PHONE..................260 624-2350
Jack N Curtis, *Brnch Mgr*
EMP: 400
SQ FT: 180,000
SALES (corp-wide): 15B **Privately Held**
Web: www.rrd.com
SIC: 2761 2672 Manifold business forms; Paper; coated and laminated, nec
HQ: R. R. Donnelley & Sons Company
35 W Wacker Dr
Chicago IL 60601
312 326-8000

(G-292)
RISE INC
907 S Wayne St (46703-2124)
PHONE..................260 665-9408

GEOGRAPHIC SECTION
Arcadia - Hamilton County (G-317)

Denise Payton, *Dir*
Doctor Donald Mason, *Pr*
David D Wilson, *
Joyce A Hevel, *
EMP: 68 **EST:** 1964
SALES (est): 541.04K **Privately Held**
Web: www.easterseals nei.org
SIC: 8331 2789 Sheltered workshop; Bookbinding and related work

(G-293)
SPEEDWAY REDI MIX INC
Also Called: SPEEDWAY REDI MIX INC
260 E 300 N (46703-7503)
PHONE 260 665-5999
EMP: 8
Web: www.speedwayredimix.com
SIC: 3273 Ready-mixed concrete
PA: Speedway Redi-Mix Inc
   4820 Industrial Rd
   Fort Wayne IN 46825

(G-294)
STEFFY WOOD PRODUCTS INC
Also Called: Steffy Wood Products
701 W Mill St (46703-1046)
PHONE 260 665-8016
John Steffy, *Pr*
Donna Steffy, *
Eva Speaker, *
EMP: 19 **EST:** 1998
SQ FT: 18,000
SALES (est): 2.22MM **Privately Held**
Web: www.childrensfactory.com
SIC: 2521 Cabinets, office: wood

(G-295)
STEUBEN COUNTY WELDING & FABG
2797 Woodhull Dr (46703-9348)
PHONE 260 665-3001
Jeff Counterman, *Pr*
Derek Craig, *VP*
EMP: 4 **EST:** 1976
SQ FT: 7,200
SALES (est): 481.56K **Privately Held**
Web: www.steubenfabandeng.com
SIC: 3498 3317 Fabricated pipe and fittings; Welded pipe and tubes

(G-296)
STOFFEL SEALS CORPORATION (DH)
409 Hoosier Dr (46703-9335)
PHONE 845 353-3800
Ian Morton, *CEO*
Jerome Anderson, *
Andrew Rattray, *
Miguel Companioni, *
◆ **EMP:** 50 **EST:** 1941
SQ FT: 40,000
SALES (est): 43.82MM
SALES (corp-wide): 418.09MM **Privately Held**
Web: www.tydenbrooks.com
SIC: 3089 3993 2759 2671 Identification cards, plastics; Signs and advertising specialties; Commercial printing, nec; Paper; coated and laminated packaging
HQ: Tyden Group Holdings Corp.
   1209 N Orange St
   Wilmington DE 19801
   740 420-6777

(G-297)
T & S EQUIPMENT COMPANY
2999 N Wayne St (46703-9122)
P.O. Box 496 (46703-0496)
PHONE 260 665-9521
Ralph D Trine, *Pr*
▲ **EMP:** 56 **EST:** 1952

SQ FT: 83,000
SALES (est): 2.96MM **Privately Held**
Web: www.vestil.com
SIC: 3448 3999 Ramps, prefabricated metal; Dock equipment and supplies, industrial

(G-298)
THRASHER WELDING AND MCH SP
2085 S 600 W (46703-9670)
PHONE 260 475-5550
EMP: 6 **EST:** 1993
SALES (est): 263.04K **Privately Held**
Web: www.thrasherproducts.com
SIC: 7692 Welding repair

(G-299)
TITAN METAL SPINNING INC
1000 Crestview Dr (46703-2210)
PHONE 260 665-1067
Roy A Meyer, *Pr*
Cindy Meyer, *Sec*
EMP: 9 **EST:** 2002
SALES (est): 1.02MM **Privately Held**
Web: www.wenzelmetalspinning.com
SIC: 3469 Stamping metal for the trade

(G-300)
TLA SIGNS INC
2175 W 175 N (46703-9168)
PHONE 260 833-2402
Terry Archbold, *Pr*
EMP: 2 **EST:** 1996
SALES (est): 140.54K **Privately Held**
Web: www.tlasigns.net
SIC: 3993 Signs and advertising specialties

(G-301)
TOMAHAWK LOG & COUNTY HOMES
280 Lane 100 Pine Canyon Lk (46703-8721)
PHONE 260 833-6429
Steve Foor, *Pr*
EMP: 1 **EST:** 2000
SALES (est): 108.75K **Privately Held**
SIC: 2452 Log cabins, prefabricated, wood

(G-302)
TRAFFIC TECHNICAL SUPPORT INC
840 S 650 W (46703-9666)
PHONE 260 665-1575
Michael Mc Allister, *Pr*
EMP: 1 **EST:** 1999
SALES (est): 118.27K **Privately Held**
SIC: 3669 Traffic signals, electric

(G-303)
UNIVERTICAL HOLDINGS INC (HQ)
203 Weatherhead St (46703-1024)
PHONE 260 665-1500
Eiitsu Masaki, *CEO*
Junichi Kitagaki, *CFO*
EMP: 9 **EST:** 2012
SALES (est): 27.49MM **Privately Held**
Web: www.univertical.com
SIC: 5051 3339 Ferrous metals; Primary nonferrous metals, nec
PA: Alconix Corporation
   2-11-1, Nagatacho
   Chiyoda-Ku TKY 100-0

(G-304)
UNIVERTICAL LLC
203 Weatherhead St (46703-1024)
PHONE 260 665-1500
◆ **EMP:** 15 **EST:** 1955
SALES (est): 9.32MM **Privately Held**
Web: www.univertical.com
SIC: 3331 2899 Refined primary copper products; Chemical preparations, nec
HQ: Univertical Holdings, Inc.

203 Weatherhead St
Angola IN 46703
260 665-1500

(G-305)
VESTIL MANUFACTURING CORP
749 Growth Pkwy (46703-9365)
PHONE 260 665-7586
EMP: 4
SALES (corp-wide): 90.4MM **Privately Held**
Web: www.vestil.com
SIC: 3999 Dock equipment and supplies, industrial
PA: Vestil Manufacturing Corp.
   2999 N Wayne St
   Angola IN 46703
   260 665-7586

(G-306)
VESTIL MANUFACTURING CORP (PA)
2999 N Wayne St (46703-9122)
P.O. Box 507 (46703-0507)
PHONE 260 665-7586
Ralph Trine, *Pr*
Sheri Trine, *
◆ **EMP:** 228 **EST:** 1967
SQ FT: 140,000
SALES (est): 90.4MM
SALES (corp-wide): 90.4MM **Privately Held**
Web: www.vestil.com
SIC: 3999 3535 3069 Dock equipment and supplies, industrial; Conveyors and conveying equipment; Molded rubber products

(G-307)
VESTIL MANUFACTURING CORP
705 W Maumee St (46703-1434)
P.O. Box 496 (46703-0496)
PHONE 800 348-0860
EMP: 9 **EST:** 2019
SALES (est): 68.52K **Privately Held**
Web: www.vestil.com
SIC: 3999 Manufacturing industries, nec

(G-308)
WEISSAIR
905 Bluffview Dr (46703-2238)
PHONE 260 466-7693
Brent Weisenhower, *Managing Member*
EMP: 1 **EST:** 2011
SALES (est): 60.98K **Privately Held**
SIC: 3559 Foundry, smelting, refining, and similar machinery

Arcadia
Hamilton County

(G-309)
CARTER ENTERPRISES INC
119 W Main St (46030)
P.O. Box 583 (46030-0583)
PHONE 317 984-1497
John A Carter, *Pr*
John Carter, *Prin*
EMP: 8 **EST:** 2004
SALES (est): 553.93K **Privately Held**
Web: www.carterent.com
SIC: 3999 Manufacturing industries, nec

(G-310)
CASES MARINE SERVICE INC
6281 E 261st St (46030-9754)
PHONE 317 379-0020
Rodney A Case, *Owner*
EMP: 5 **EST:** 2015

SALES (est): 230.44K **Privately Held**
Web: www.casesmarine.com
SIC: 3523 Farm machinery and equipment

(G-311)
CONFLUENCE PHARMACEUTICALS LLC
27628 Will Parker Rd (46030-9455)
PHONE 317 379-7498
Boyd W Sturdevant Junior, *Ch*
Steven Johns, *Pr*
EMP: 2 **EST:** 2010
SALES (est): 225.97K **Privately Held**
Web: www.confluencepharma.com
SIC: 2834 Pharmaceutical preparations

(G-312)
DEBRA SCHNEIDER
Also Called: A Lit'le Bit of Heaven Farm
25610 Salem Church Rd (46030-9494)
PHONE 317 420-9360
Debra Schneider, *Owner*
EMP: 2 **EST:** 2002
SALES (est): 92.9K **Privately Held**
SIC: 2824 Organic fibers, noncellulosic

(G-313)
DURA PRODUCTS INC
504 Demoss Ave (46030)
PHONE 855 502-3872
▲ **EMP:** 16 **EST:** 1971
SALES (est): 2.64MM **Privately Held**
Web: www.duraproducts.com
SIC: 3561 Pumps and pumping equipment

(G-314)
LINEAR TECHNOLOGY LLC
18 Point Ln (46030-9634)
PHONE 317 443-1169
Tom Luthman, *Mgr*
EMP: 1
SALES (corp-wide): 12.31B **Publicly Held**
Web: www.analog.com
SIC: 3674 Integrated circuits, semiconductor networks, etc.
HQ: Linear Technology Llc
   1630 Mccarthy Blvd
   Milpitas CA 95035
   408 432-1900

(G-315)
MOORES COUNTRY WOOD CRAFTING
507 Demoss Ave (46030)
P.O. Box 389 (46030-0389)
PHONE 317 984-3326
Robert David Moore, *Pr*
Thomas Henson, *Sec*
EMP: 12 **EST:** 1981
SQ FT: 35,000
SALES (est): 443.25K **Privately Held**
SIC: 2511 3231 2499 Wood household furniture; Products of purchased glass; Decorative wood and woodwork

(G-316)
RAM NORTH AMERICA INC
25415 State Road 19 (46030-9522)
PHONE 317 984-1971
Leanne Yeary, *Pr*
EMP: 10 **EST:** 2010
SALES (est): 655.6K **Privately Held**
Web: www.ramnorthamerica.com
SIC: 3089 3272 Panels, building: plastics, nec; Panels and sections, prefabricated concrete

(G-317)
REHCO PRODUCTS INC
700 S East St (46030)

Arcadia - Hamilton County (G-318)

P.O. Box 430 (46030-0430)
PHONE.................317 984-3319
John Hawkins, Pr
Robert L Hawkins, VP
Wanda Hawkins, Sec
EMP: 10 EST: 1945
SQ FT: 40,000
SALES (est): 784.92K Privately Held
Web: www.rehcoproducts.com
SIC: 3599 Machine shop, jobbing and repair

(G-318)
SYLVIA KAY HARTLEY (PA)
Also Called: Hartley Interiors
103 E Main St (46030)
P.O. Box 476 (46030-0476)
PHONE.................317 984-3424
Sylvia Kay Hartley, Owner
EMP: 2
SQ FT: 20,000
SALES (est): 491.07K
SALES (corp-wide): 491.07K Privately Held
Web: www.hartleyfuneralhomes.com
SIC: 2512 5712 Upholstered household furniture; Furniture stores

(G-319)
VIBCON CORPORATION
6660 E 266th St Ste 200 (46030-9751)
P.O. Box 1778 (46061-1778)
PHONE.................317 984-3543
Jeffrey Anderson, Pr
EMP: 12 EST: 1982
SQ FT: 20,000
SALES (est): 1.2MM Privately Held
Web: www.vibcon.com
SIC: 3559 3535 Vibratory parts handling equipment; Conveyors and conveying equipment

(G-320)
WITHAM ANTHONY J SIGN PROD
Also Called: A J Witham Sign Production
26266 Devaney Rd (46030-9756)
PHONE.................317 984-3765
Anthony J Witham, Owner
EMP: 1 EST: 1985
SALES (est): 105.92K Privately Held
Web: www.putmeinsports.com
SIC: 7389 3993 Lettering and sign painting services; Signs and advertising specialties

Argos
Marshall County

(G-321)
E Z WELDING
20954 Michigan Rd (46501-9796)
PHONE.................574 892-6417
Earl Zimmerman, Owner
EMP: 1 EST: 2003
SALES (est): 40K Privately Held
SIC: 7692 Welding repair

(G-322)
FARMWAY WELDING
20097 Gumwood Rd (46501-9788)
PHONE.................574 498-6147
David Oberholtzer, Prin
EMP: 1 EST: 2009
SALES (est): 95.12K Privately Held
SIC: 7692 Welding repair

(G-323)
IN STITCHZ & SIGNZ LLC
11189 State Road 10 (46501-9515)
PHONE.................574 892-5956
EMP: 3 EST: 2019
SALES (est): 106.04K Privately Held
Web: www.institchz.com
SIC: 2395 Embroidery and art needlework

(G-324)
JLE FABRICATING LLC
402 West St (46501-1281)
PHONE.................574 341-4034
EMP: 5 EST: 2021
SALES (est): 280.93K Privately Held
Web: www.jlefabricating.com
SIC: 3549 7389 Wiredrawing and fabricating machinery and equipment, ex. die; Business Activities at Non-Commercial Site

(G-325)
NORTH CENTRAL PALLETS INC
13990 State Road 10 (46501-9572)
P.O. Box 840 (46563-0840)
PHONE.................574 892-6142
Patrick Hanley, Pr
J Shawn Hanley, *
Caroline W Hanley, *
EMP: 35 EST: 1974
SQ FT: 10,000
SALES (est): 2.2MM Privately Held
Web: www.ncpallets.com
SIC: 2448 Pallets, wood

(G-326)
STAMPCRAFTER
324 Weidner Ave (46501-1030)
PHONE.................574 892-5206
Paul J Phillips, Owner
EMP: 4 EST: 2010
SALES (est): 79.41K Privately Held
Web: www.thestampcrafter.com
SIC: 3953 Postmark stamps, hand: rubber or metal

(G-327)
T I B INC
Also Called: Ameri-Can Engineering
775 N Michigan St (46501-1171)
PHONE.................574 892-5151
David Harling, Pr
Ron Bird, Stockholder
Gladys Bird, Stockholder
Keegan Campbell, VP
Elizabeth Campbell, CFO
▼ EMP: 22 EST: 1988
SQ FT: 25,000
SALES (est): 5MM Privately Held
Web: www.ameri-can.com
SIC: 3799 Boat trailers

(G-328)
VAN DER WEELE JON D
Also Called: Mr Trophy
200 W Walnut St (46501-1026)
PHONE.................574 892-5005
Jon D Van Der Weele, Owner
EMP: 3 EST: 1975
SQ FT: 4,096
SALES (est): 307.87K Privately Held
Web: www.radioshack.com
SIC: 5999 3993 5731 Trophies and plaques; Signs and advertising specialties; Radio, television, and electronic stores

Arlington
Rush County

(G-329)
ORIGINAL TRACTOR CAB CO INC
6849 West Front St (46104)
P.O. Box 97 (46104)
PHONE.................765 663-2214
Wayne D Williams, CEO
Robert S Williams, VP
Phil Vogelgesang, Sec
EMP: 15 EST: 1939
SQ FT: 60,000
SALES (est): 2.05MM Privately Held
Web: www.originalcab.com
SIC: 3524 3446 3523 3713 Snowblowers and throwers, residential; Flagpoles, metal; Cabs, tractors, and agricultural machinery; Truck and bus bodies

Ashley
Dekalb County

(G-330)
ASHLEY INDUSTRIAL MOLDING INC (PA)
310 S Wabash St (46705-5266)
P.O. Box 398 (46705-0398)
PHONE.................260 587-9155
Rod Schoon, Ch Bd
Rod Schoon, Pr
Mike Morgan, CFO
Scott Pflughoeft, CEO
♦ EMP: 91 EST: 2001
SALES (est): 41.43MM
SALES (corp-wide): 41.43MM Privately Held
Web: www.ashinmold.com
SIC: 3089 Molding primary plastics

(G-331)
COMPLETE FINISH INC
200 S Parker Dr (46705-5250)
P.O. Box 400 (46705-0400)
PHONE.................260 587-3588
James Clifford, Pr
EMP: 17 EST: 1996
SQ FT: 15,000
SALES (est): 1.04MM Privately Held
Web: www.complete-finish-inc.com
SIC: 3471 Sand blasting of metal parts

(G-332)
CUSTOM BOTTLING & PACKG INC
101 S Parker Dr (46705-9649)
P.O. Box 9 (46705-0009)
PHONE.................877 401-7195
Kriss Stackhouse, Pr
EMP: 25 EST: 2010
SALES (est): 4.15MM Privately Held
Web: www.cbpin.com
SIC: 2842 7389 Specialty cleaning; Packaging and labeling services

(G-333)
K TECH SPECIALTY COATINGS INC
111 W Garfield St (46705-5232)
P.O. Box 428 (46705-0428)
PHONE.................260 587-3888
Wayne Klink, Pr
Tony Winters, Sec
Carol Klink, Sec
EMP: 10 EST: 2008
SALES (est): 2.43MM Privately Held
Web: www.ktechcoatings.com
SIC: 2952 Asphalt felts and coatings

(G-334)
MTR MACHINING CONCEPT INC
2878 W 800 S (46705-9625)
P.O. Box 383 (46705-0383)
PHONE.................260 587-3381
Mervin Topp, Pr
Richard Bowers, VP
EMP: 9 EST: 1963
SQ FT: 4,000
SALES (est): 1.01MM Privately Held
Web: www.mtrmachine.com
SIC: 3462 7699 Gears, forged steel; Industrial equipment services

(G-335)
PARKER-HANNIFIN CORPORATION
201 S Parker Dr (46705-5250)
P.O. Box 368 (46705-0368)
PHONE.................260 587-9102
Kurt Peter, Mgr
EMP: 46
SALES (corp-wide): 19.93B Publicly Held
Web: www.parker.com
SIC: 3599 3592 3498 3312 Tubing, flexible metallic; Carburetors, pistons, piston rings and valves; Fabricated pipe and fittings; Blast furnaces and steel mills
PA: Parker-Hannifin Corporation
6035 Parkland Blvd
Cleveland OH 44124
216 896-3000

(G-336)
ROYAL ARC WELDING COMPANY
640 County Road 27 (46705-9709)
PHONE.................260 587-3711
Joe Rosen, Brnch Mgr
EMP: 1
SALES (corp-wide): 12.74MM Privately Held
Web: www.royalarc.com
SIC: 3536 Cranes, industrial plant
PA: Royal Arc Welding Company
23851 Vreeland Rd
Flat Rock MI 48134
734 789-9099

(G-337)
TI AUTOMOTIVE INC
507 H L Thompson Jr Dr (46705-0050)
P.O. Box 397 (46705-0397)
PHONE.................260 587-6100
Lorie Casiano, Mgr
▲ EMP: 7 EST: 2001
SALES (est): 989.43K Privately Held
Web: aftermarket.tiautomotive.com
SIC: 3714 Motor vehicle parts and accessories

(G-338)
TI GROUP AUTO SYSTEMS LLC
507 H L Thompson Jr Dr (46705-0050)
P.O. Box 397 (46705-0397)
PHONE.................260 587-6100
Lori Casiano, Mgr
EMP: 53
SALES (corp-wide): 3.82B Privately Held
Web: www.tifluidsystems.com
SIC: 3356 3714 Nonferrous rolling and drawing, nec; Motor vehicle parts and accessories
HQ: Ti Group Automotive Systems, Llc
2020 Taylor Rd
Auburn Hills MI 48326
248 296-8000

(G-339)
TRIBUTE PRECAST SYSTEMS LLC
110 Canopy Dr (46705-3500)
P.O. Box 413 (46705-0413)
PHONE.................260 587-9555
Christine Hentges, Pr
Bill Toson, Prin
Timothy Hentges, Prin
EMP: 5 EST: 2006
SALES (est): 461.36K Privately Held
Web: www.tributeinc.com
SIC: 3272 Precast terrazzo or concrete products

GEOGRAPHIC SECTION Auburn - Dekalb County (G-363)

(G-340)
WELDER ON WAY LLC
Also Called: Ibr
351 County Road 35 (46705-9758)
PHONE..............................260 920-4705
Adam Smith, *Managing Member*
Logan Zuber, *Prin*
EMP: 9 **EST:** 2017
SALES (est): 1.2MM **Privately Held**
SIC: 2611 Pulp mills, mechanical and recycling processing

Atlanta
Hamilton County

(G-341)
CUSTOM BLACKSMITH SHOP
Also Called: Custom Blacksmithing
29579 N State Road 19 (46031-9623)
PHONE..............................765 292-2745
Kurt Fehrenbach, *Owner*
Rick Bagby, *Mgr*
EMP: 2 **EST:** 1985
SQ FT: 5,400
SALES (est): 120K **Privately Held**
Web: www.custom-blacksmithing.com
SIC: 3462 1799 Iron and steel forgings; Welding on site

(G-342)
SHUCKS WLDG & FABRICATION LLC
4588 S 200 E (46031-9582)
PHONE..............................317 409-8526
EMP: 5 **EST:** 2020
SALES (est): 27.6K **Privately Held**
SIC: 7692 Welding repair

Attica
Fountain County

(G-343)
ATTICA READY MIXED CONCRETE (PA)
104 W Sycamore St (47918-1833)
PHONE..............................765 762-2424
Steve Wagner, *Pr*
EMP: 18 **EST:** 1952
SQ FT: 1,400
SALES (est): 2.3MM
SALES (corp-wide): 2.3MM **Privately Held**
SIC: 3273 5251 Ready-mixed concrete; Hardware stores

(G-344)
BRUCE A HODSON
4309 N Ruppert Rd (47918-8050)
PHONE..............................765 212-7757
Bruce A Hodson, *Prin*
EMP: 1 **EST:** 2001
SALES (est): 65.3K **Privately Held**
SIC: 2834 Druggists' preparations (pharmaceuticals)

(G-345)
C&D TECHNOLOGIES INC
200 W Main St (47918-1344)
P.O. Box 279 (47918-0279)
PHONE..............................765 762-2461
Dale Brown, *Mgr*
EMP: 240
SALES (corp-wide): 3.44B **Privately Held**
Web: www.cdtechno.com
SIC: 3691 3692 3661 Storage batteries; Primary batteries, dry and wet; Telephone and telegraph apparatus
HQ: C&D Technologies, Inc.
  200 Precision Rd
  Horsham PA 19044
  215 619-2700

(G-346)
COREY KERST
Also Called: Kerst Pallet
945 N Milligan Hill Rd (47918-7860)
PHONE..............................765 585-3026
Corey Kerst, *Owner*
EMP: 2 **EST:** 1985
SALES (est): 174.55K **Privately Held**
SIC: 2448 Pallets, wood

(G-347)
COUNTRY CHARM
Also Called: Real Log Homes
2721 E Flint Rd (47918-8235)
PHONE..............................765 572-2588
David L Hatke, *Owner*
EMP: 4 **EST:** 1985
SALES (est): 247.74K **Privately Held**
Web: www.kc1.com
SIC: 2452 Log cabins, prefabricated, wood

(G-348)
FOUNTAIN COUNTY NEIGHBOR
Also Called: Messenger, The
113 S Perry St (47918-1349)
PHONE..............................765 762-2411
Greg Willhite, *Prin*
EMP: 3 **EST:** 1856
SALES (est): 280.31K **Privately Held**
Web: www.newsbug.info
SIC: 2711 Newspapers, publishing and printing
HQ: The Times Republic
  1492 E Walnut St
  Watseka IL 60970
  815 432-5227

(G-349)
GECKOS
111 S Perry St (47918-1349)
PHONE..............................765 762-0822
Mark Palmer, *Owner*
EMP: 3 **EST:** 1994
SALES (est): 159.61K **Privately Held**
Web: www.geckosgraffiti.com
SIC: 5699 3993 2396 Uniforms and work clothing; Signs and advertising specialties; Automotive and apparel trimmings

(G-350)
GLORIA J BURNWORTH
Also Called: B & G Woodworking
2875 N 70 W (47918-8082)
PHONE..............................765 366-3950
Gloria J Burnworth, *Owner*
EMP: 2 **EST:** 2006
SALES (est): 98.2K **Privately Held**
SIC: 2511 Wood household furniture

(G-351)
HILL TOP WELDING LLC
217 N State Road 55 (47918-7769)
PHONE..............................765 585-2549
Chris Reifel, *Owner*
EMP: 2 **EST:** 2007
SALES (est): 159.98K **Privately Held**
Web: stores.hilltopwelding.com
SIC: 7692 Welding repair

(G-352)
HOME CITY ICE COMPANY
Also Called: Home City Ice
200 S Market St (47918-1371)
PHONE..............................765 762-6096
Chris Van Dywater, *Mgr*
EMP: 10
SALES (corp-wide): 100.42MM **Privately Held**
Web: www.homecityice.com
SIC: 2097 Manufactured ice
PA: The Home City Ice Company
  6045 Bridgetown Rd Ste 1
  Cincinnati OH 45248
  513 574-1800

(G-353)
NEUMAYR LUMBER CO INC
Also Called: Do It Best
401 S Union St (47918-1496)
P.O. Box 399 (47918-0399)
PHONE..............................765 764-4148
Martha L Neumayr, *Pr*
Rick Turpin, *VP*
Kathy Turpin, *Treas*
Marti Martigus, *Sec*
EMP: 10 **EST:** 1939
SQ FT: 3,000
SALES (est): 996.66K **Privately Held**
Web: www.neumayrlumber.com
SIC: 5251 2448 Hardware stores; Pallets, wood

(G-354)
SWANSON WOODWORKING
2949 E 950 N (47918-8039)
PHONE..............................765 585-0328
Randy Swanson, *Owner*
EMP: 1 **EST:** 2004
SALES (est): 49.09K **Privately Held**
SIC: 2431 Millwork

(G-355)
T W BRACKETT & ASSOC LLC
Also Called: Shore Measuring Systems
103 N Perry St (47918-1347)
PHONE..............................765 769-3000
James Brackett, *Senior Member*
EMP: 6 **EST:** 2019
SALES (est): 804.55K **Privately Held**
Web: www.shopmoisturetesters.com
SIC: 3823 5083 Moisture meters, industrial process type; Agricultural machinery and equipment

(G-356)
THE HARRISON STEEL CASTINGS CO (PA)
900 S Mound St (47918-1632)
P.O. Box 60 (47918-0060)
PHONE..............................765 762-2481
Ann S Harrison, *Ch*
G Edward Curtis, *
Geoffrey H Curtis, *
Trevor H Curtis, *
Wade C Harrison Iii, *Sec*
▲ **EMP:** 800 **EST:** 1906
SALES (est): 93.53MM
SALES (corp-wide): 93.53MM **Privately Held**
Web: www.hscast.com
SIC: 3325 Alloy steel castings, except investment

Atwood
Kosciusko County

(G-357)
PRIMIX CORPORATION
510 East Main Street (46502)
PHONE..............................574 858-0069
Carl J Fischer, *CEO*
Sonja Gilman, *CFO*
▲ **EMP:** 3 **EST:** 1998
SQ FT: 30,000
SALES (est): 252.06K **Privately Held**
Web: www.primix.com
SIC: 2491 Railroad cross-ties, treated wood

(G-358)
SWANSONS SERVICE CENTER
U S 30 & County Road 650 W (46502)
PHONE..............................574 858-9406
Tony Swanson, *Prin*
EMP: 3 **EST:** 2002
SALES (est): 153.8K **Privately Held**
SIC: 3599 Machine shop, jobbing and repair

Auburn
Dekalb County

(G-359)
1ST ATTACK ENGINEERING INC
5709 County Road 35 (46706-9719)
PHONE..............................260 837-2435
Jeffrey Cook, *Pr*
EMP: 4 **EST:** 2013
SALES (est): 483.53K **Privately Held**
Web: www.1stattack.com
SIC: 3711 Fire department vehicles (motor vehicles), assembly of

(G-360)
AFSOL INC
6869 County Road 11a (46706-9525)
PHONE..............................260 357-0788
EMP: 4 **EST:** 2016
SALES (est): 65.44K **Privately Held**
SIC: 3489 Ordnance and accessories, nec

(G-361)
ALUDYNE NORTH AMERICA LLC
1200 Power Dr (46706-2671)
PHONE..............................260 925-4711
Andreas Weller, *CEO*
EMP: 374
SQ FT: 68,000
SALES (corp-wide): 631.06MM **Privately Held**
Web: www.aludyne.com
SIC: 3465 Automotive stampings
HQ: Aludyne North America Llc
  300 Galleria Ofcntr Ste 5
  Southfield MI 48034
  248 728-8700

(G-362)
AUBURN GEAR LLC (PA)
Also Called: Auburn Gear
400 E Auburn Dr (46706-3400)
PHONE..............................260 925-3200
Shane Terblanche, *Pr*
George E Callas, *
Elizabeth Callas, *
▲ **EMP:** 149 **EST:** 1982
SQ FT: 250,000
SALES (est): 24.28MM
SALES (corp-wide): 24.28MM **Privately Held**
Web: www.auburngear.com
SIC: 3714 3566 3568 Differentials and parts, motor vehicle; Speed changers, drives, and gears; Power transmission equipment, nec

(G-363)
AUBURN HARDWOOD MOLDING
1109 W Auburn Dr (46706-3459)
PHONE..............................260 925-5959
Brian Rugsegger, *Pr*
EMP: 6 **EST:** 2008
SALES (est): 94.3K **Privately Held**
Web: www.auburnhardwood.com
SIC: 3089 Molding primary plastics

(G-364)
AUBURN MANUFACTURING INC
1000 W Auburn Dr (46706-3447)
P.O. Box 6078 (46706-6078)
PHONE..................260 925-8651
Cris Horton, CEO
Cris Horton, Pr
Angela Horton, VP
EMP: 20 **EST:** 1998
SQ FT: 12,000
SALES (est): 6.39MM **Privately Held**
Web: www.auburnmanufacturing.com
SIC: 3714 3451 Motor vehicle parts and accessories; Screw machine products

(G-365)
AUBURN SMOKE N VAPE LLC ◆
1029 W 7th St (46706)
PHONE..................260 572-6021
EMP: 3 **EST:** 2022
SALES (est): 136.08K **Privately Held**
SIC: 3999 Tobacco pipes, pipestems, and bits

(G-366)
AWARDMAKERSNET INC
1916 Wayne St (46706-3515)
PHONE..................260 925-4672
Jordan Bavis, Pr
Carol Bavis, Pr
Sandy Griffin, Mgr
EMP: 6 **EST:** 1971
SQ FT: 600
SALES (est): 515.15K **Privately Held**
Web: www.awardmakers.net
SIC: 3499 5999 Trophies, metal, except silver; Trophies and plaques

(G-367)
BALL BRASS AND ALUMINUM FOUNDRY INC
525 Hazel St (46706-2700)
P.O. Box 110 (46706-0110)
PHONE..................260 925-3515
▲ **EMP:** 28 **EST:** 1940
SALES (est): 5.32MM
SALES (corp-wide): 39.4MM **Privately Held**
Web: www.ballbrass.com
SIC: 3365 3366 3325 Aluminum and aluminum-based alloy castings; Castings (except die), nec, brass; Steel foundries, nec
HQ: Evans Industries, Inc.
3150 Livernois Rd Ste 170
Troy MI 48083
313 259-2266

(G-368)
BARON EMBROIDERY CORP
Also Called: Vigred Sports
103 S Main St (46706-2355)
PHONE..................260 484-8700
Brian Thomas, Pr
EMP: 9 **EST:** 2007
SALES (est): 408.66K **Privately Held**
Web: www.bigred-auburn.com
SIC: 2395 Embroidery products, except Schiffli machine

(G-369)
BEST-ONE TIRE & SVC AUBURN INC
1712 Wayne St (46706-3511)
PHONE..................260 925-2782
EMP: 2 **EST:** 2010
SALES (est): 259.13K **Privately Held**
Web: www.bestoneofauburn.com
SIC: 5531 7534 Automotive tires; Tire repair shop

(G-370)
BRALIN LASER SERVICES INC
2233 County Road 72 (46706)
P.O. Box 88 (46738)
PHONE..................260 357-6511
Bill Hohler, Pr
EMP: 24 **EST:** 1998
SQ FT: 12,000
SALES (est): 4.28MM **Privately Held**
Web: www.bralinlaser.com
SIC: 3441 Fabricated structural metal

(G-371)
BYE BUY CCI INC
1937 Jacob St (46706-3516)
P.O. Box 143 (46706-0143)
PHONE..................260 925-0623
Terry Hines, CEO
Vincent Hines, VP
EMP: 18 **EST:** 1986
SQ FT: 64,345
SALES (est): 3.36MM **Privately Held**
Web: www.customcoatinginc.com
SIC: 3471 Electroplating of metals or formed products
PA: Marksans Pharma Limited
11th Floor Grandeur, Off Veera Desai Extension Road,
Mumbai MH 40005

(G-372)
C & A TOOL ENGINEERING INC
Also Called: C & A TOOL ENGINEERING INC.
1015 W 15th St (46706-2047)
PHONE..................260 693-2167
Ward Krause, Brnch Mgr
EMP: 105
Web: www.catool.com
SIC: 3544 3545 Diamond dies, metalworking ; Machine tool accessories
HQ: C & A Tool Engineering Inc
4100 N Us 33
Churubusco IN 46723
260 693-2167

(G-373)
C & P WOODWORKING INC
7108 County Road 17 (46706)
PHONE..................260 637-3088
Carter Porter, Pr
EMP: 1 **EST:** 1987
SALES (est): 12.66K **Privately Held**
SIC: 2511 Wood household furniture

(G-374)
CARLEX GLASS AMERICA LLC
Also Called: Carlex Glass Ind Inc-Auburn
1900 Center St (46706-9685)
PHONE..................260 925-5656
Jeff Fraelich, Mgr
EMP: 400
Web: www.carlex.com
SIC: 3231 3211 Windshields, glass: made from purchased glass; Flat glass
PA: Carlex Glass America, Llc
7200 Centennial Blvd
Nashville TN 37209

(G-375)
CCT ENTERPRISES LLC
530 North St (46706-1622)
PHONE..................260 925-1420
Kurt Herman, Prin
Dan Nagel, *
EMP: 35 **EST:** 2010
SALES (est): 5.19MM **Privately Held**
Web: www.cct-ent.com

SIC: 3469 7539 3599 3714 Metal stampings, nec; Machine shop, automotive; Machine shop, jobbing and repair; Motor vehicle parts and accessories

(G-376)
CLASSIC CITY TOOL & ENGINEERING INC
1101 W Auburn Dr (46706-3459)
PHONE..................260 925-1420
EMP: 10 **EST:** 1987
SALES (est): 560.78K **Privately Held**
SIC: 3544 3599 Industrial molds; Machine and other job shop work

(G-377)
CNA TOOL ENGINEERING INC
1015 W 15th St (46706-2047)
P.O. Box 471 (46706-0471)
PHONE..................260 927-2298
Jeremy Kilgore, Prin
EMP: 7 **EST:** 2008
SALES (est): 130.79K **Privately Held**
SIC: 3841 Surgical and medical instruments

(G-378)
CONTITECH USA INC
725 W 15th St (46706-2136)
PHONE..................260 925-0700
Richard Meeks, Brnch Mgr
EMP: 301
SALES (corp-wide): 45.02B **Privately Held**
Web: www.continental-industry.com
SIC: 3061 Mechanical rubber goods
HQ: Contitech Usa, Inc.
325 E 10th St
Halstead KS 67056

(G-379)
CONTITECH USA INC
207 S West St (46706)
PHONE..................260 925-0700
Jeff Walker, Brnch Mgr
EMP: 500
SALES (corp-wide): 45.02B **Privately Held**
Web: www.continental-industry.com
SIC: 3061 Mechanical rubber goods
HQ: Contitech Usa, Inc.
325 E 10th St
Halstead KS 67056

(G-380)
COOPER-STANDARD AUTOMOTIVE INC
Also Called: Cooper
725 W 11th St (46706-2022)
PHONE..................260 637-5824
Connie Lepley, Mgr
EMP: 40
SALES (corp-wide): 2.82B **Publicly Held**
Web: www.cooperstandard.com
SIC: 3714 Motor vehicle parts and accessories
HQ: Cooper-Standard Automotive Inc.
40300 Traditions Dr
Northville MI 48168
248 596-5900

(G-381)
CUPKAS BEE GOOD MEADERY LLC
112 N Main St (46706-1857)
PHONE..................260 927-3837
EMP: 1
SALES (corp-wide): 65.93K **Privately Held**
Web: www.beegoodmeadery.com
SIC: 2084 Wines
PA: Cupka's Bee Good Meadery, Llc
819 N Indiana Ave
Auburn IN 46706
260 927-3837

(G-382)
CUPKAS BEE GOOD MEADERY LLC (PA)
819 N Indiana Ave (46706-1105)
PHONE..................260 927-3837
Thomas Cupka, Managing Member
EMP: 4 **EST:** 2021
SALES (est): 65.93K
SALES (corp-wide): 65.93K **Privately Held**
Web: www.beegoodmeadery.com
SIC: 2084 Wines

(G-383)
CUSTOM MFG & FABRICATION LLC
5536 County Road 31 (46706-9656)
PHONE..................260 908-1088
EMP: 7 **EST:** 2017
SALES (est): 237.78K **Privately Held**
Web: www.cmf-auburn.com
SIC: 3999 Manufacturing industries, nec

(G-384)
D & J FABRICATION AND WELDING
2471 County Road 64 (46706-9620)
PHONE..................260 414-0300
Vern Kelly, Prin
EMP: 1 **EST:** 2012
SALES (est): 37.19K **Privately Held**
SIC: 7692 Welding repair

(G-385)
DAYSPRING COMMUNITY CHURCH INC
2305 N Indiana Ave (46706-1085)
PHONE..................260 925-4599
Stephen Buckner, Pr
EMP: 10 **EST:** 1983
SALES (est): 274.02K **Privately Held**
Web: www.dayspringchurch.com
SIC: 8661 7372 Christian and Reformed Church; Application computer software

(G-386)
DEKALB METAL FINISHING INC
625 W 15th St (46706)
P.O. Box 70 (46706)
PHONE..................260 925-1820
Dennis Fry, Pr
EMP: 60 **EST:** 1946
SQ FT: 30,000
SALES (est): 4.49MM **Privately Held**
Web: www.dekalbmetal.com
SIC: 3471 Electroplating of metals or formed products

(G-387)
EATON CORPORATION
201 Brandon St (46706-1643)
PHONE..................260 925-3800
Ken Davis, Brnch Mgr
EMP: 135
SQ FT: 350,000
Web: www.dix-eaton.com
SIC: 3714 3713 3568 3537 Clutches, motor vehicle; Truck and bus bodies; Power transmission equipment, nec; Industrial trucks and tractors
HQ: Eaton Corporation
1000 Eaton Blvd
Cleveland OH 44122
440 523-5000

(G-388)
ENVISION GRAPHICS INC
118 W 9th St (46706-2225)
PHONE..................260 925-2266
Fritz Busch, Pr
Byron Wentworth, Prin
EMP: 5 **EST:** 1988
SALES (est): 437.67K **Privately Held**

GEOGRAPHIC SECTION

Auburn - Dekalb County (G-412)

SIC: 2752 Offset printing

(G-389)
ERIE-HAVEN INC
1204 S Union St (46706-2934)
PHONE.............................260 478-1674
Duane Ellert, *Mgr*
EMP: 2
SALES (corp-wide): 6.22MM **Privately Held**
Web: www.eriehaven.com
SIC: 3273 Ready-mixed concrete
PA: Erie-Haven Inc
  3909 Limestone Dr
  Fort Wayne IN 46809
  260 478-1674

(G-390)
FABTRON CORPORATION
1820 Sprott St (46706-3429)
PHONE.............................260 925-5770
Kevin Marquardt, *Pr*
Cina Marquardt, *Sec*
Wyatt Decker, *Mgr*
EMP: 3 **EST:** 1986
SQ FT: 17,000
SALES (est): 416.64K **Privately Held**
Web: www.fabtroncorp.com
SIC: 3441 Fabricated structural metal

(G-391)
FOLEY PATTERN COMPANY INC
500 W 11th St (46706-2142)
P.O. Box 150 (46706-0150)
PHONE.............................260 925-4113
Ellen E Stahly, *Pr*
Stephen Foley, *VP*
EMP: 25 **EST:** 1920
SQ FT: 35,000
SALES (est): 2.23MM **Privately Held**
SIC: 3365 3543 Aluminum and aluminum-based alloy castings; Industrial patterns

(G-392)
FXI INC
Also Called: Foamex
2211 Wayne St (46706-3518)
P.O. Box 606 (46706-0606)
PHONE.............................260 925-1073
Steve Setzer, *Brnch Mgr*
EMP: 1
SQ FT: 136,000
Web: www.fxi.com
SIC: 3086 Plastics foam products
HQ: Fxi, Inc.
  100 W Matsonford Rd
  Radnor PA 19087

(G-393)
FXI AUBURN
2211 Wayne St (46706-3518)
PHONE.............................260 925-1073
John Cowles, *Pr*
Harold J Earley, *VP*
EMP: 23 **EST:** 2010
SALES (est): 4.29MM **Privately Held**
Web: www.fxi.com
SIC: 3086 Plastics foam products

(G-394)
GFW FABRICATION
1905 Jacob St (46706-3527)
PHONE.............................260 333-7252
EMP: 4 **EST:** 2019
SALES (est): 76.14K **Privately Held**
SIC: 3599 Machine shop, jobbing and repair

(G-395)
HECK OF A LOPE ✪
4809 County Road 51 (46706-9753)
PHONE.............................260 570-3192
Christopher Chapman, *CEO*
EMP: 5 **EST:** 2022
SALES (est): 101.49K **Privately Held**
SIC: 3949 Sporting and athletic goods, nec

(G-396)
HERMAC INCORPORATED
540 North St (46706-1622)
P.O. Box 129 (46706-0129)
PHONE.............................260 925-0312
Kathy Mc Aninch, *Pr*
EMP: 36 **EST:** 1973
SQ FT: 11,000
SALES (est): 2.47MM **Privately Held**
SIC: 3679 Harness assemblies, for electronic use: wire or cable

(G-397)
HK MANUFACTURING INC
203 Hunters Rdg (46706-9116)
PHONE.............................260 925-1680
Elisa Kruse, *Owner*
EMP: 5 **EST:** 2018
SALES (est): 68.27K **Privately Held**
Web: www.hkmanufacturing.com
SIC: 3999 Manufacturing industries, nec

(G-398)
KDZ KUSTOMS LLC
Also Called: Kdz Motorcycle Sales and Svc
521 Ley Dr (46706-2073)
PHONE.............................260 927-0533
Jeff Lindbloom, *Managing Member*
EMP: 1 **EST:** 2003
SALES (est): 128.25K **Privately Held**
Web: www.kdzkustoms.com
SIC: 3751 Motorcycles and related parts

(G-399)
KINEDYNE
3486 County Road 36 (46706-9431)
PHONE.............................260 403-5149
EMP: 4 **EST:** 2017
SALES (est): 48.36K **Privately Held**
Web: www.kinedyne.com
SIC: 3714 Motor vehicle parts and accessories

(G-400)
KPC MEDIA GROUP INC
Evening Star, The
118 W 9th St (46706-2225)
PHONE.............................260 925-2611
Terry Housholder, *Pr*
EMP: 15
SQ FT: 2,000
SALES (corp-wide): 23.55MM **Privately Held**
Web: www.fwbusiness.com
SIC: 2711 Newspapers: publishing only, not printed on site
PA: Kpc Media Group Inc.
  102 N Main St
  Kendallville IN 46755
  260 347-0400

(G-401)
KPC MEDIA GROUP INC
Also Called: Butler Bulletin
118 W 9th St (46706-2225)
P.O. Box 39 (46721-0039)
PHONE.............................260 868-5501
EMP: 1
SALES (corp-wide): 23.55MM **Privately Held**
Web: www.fwbusiness.com
SIC: 2711 Newspapers, publishing and printing
PA: Kpc Media Group Inc.
  102 N Main St
  Kendallville IN 46755
  260 347-0400

(G-402)
LANE BYLER INC
5858 County Road 35 (46706-9652)
PHONE.............................260 920-4377
Alvin J R Byler Junior, *Pr*
EMP: 9 **EST:** 2017
SALES (est): 512.5K **Privately Held**
Web: www.bylerlanewinery.com
SIC: 2084 Wines

(G-403)
LOUD CLEAR COMMUNICATIONS LLC
6439 County Road 29 (46706-9697)
P.O. Box 260 (46765-0260)
PHONE.............................260 433-9479
Andrew Hollins, *Prin*
EMP: 2 **EST:** 2018
SALES (est): 245.42K **Privately Held**
Web: www.loudnclearllc.com
SIC: 4899 3699 3575 7382 Data communication services; Security devices; Computer terminals, monitors and components; Security systems services

(G-404)
MARSHALL SIGNS
1270 Rohm Dr (46706-2056)
PHONE.............................260 350-1492
EMP: 2 **EST:** 1995
SALES (est): 64.85K **Privately Held**
SIC: 3993 Signs, not made in custom sign painting shops

(G-405)
MESSENGER LLC
Also Called: Messenger
318 E 7th St (46706-1804)
PHONE.............................260 925-1700
Kevin Keane, *Managing Member*
▲ **EMP:** 183 **EST:** 2009
SALES (est): 45.55MM **Privately Held**
Web: www.messengerstationery.com
SIC: 2752 Commercial printing, lithographic
PA: Prairie Capital, L.P.
  191 N Wacker Dr Ste 800
  Chicago IL 60606

(G-406)
METAL TECHNOLOGIES INC (PA)
1537 W Auburn Dr (46706)
PHONE.............................812 384-9800
Doug Conrad, *Pr*
Larry Parsons, *
▲ **EMP:** 65 **EST:** 1997
SQ FT: 219,000
SALES (est): 24.09MM **Privately Held**
Web: www.metaltechnologiesinc.com
SIC: 3441 3559 Fabricated structural metal; Automotive related machinery

(G-407)
METAL TECHNOLOGIES AUBURN LLC
1537 W Auburn Dr (46706-3329)
PHONE.............................260 527-1410
Matthew Setter, *CEO*
▼ **EMP:** 280 **EST:** 2005
SALES (est): 89.93MM
SALES (corp-wide): 261.85MM **Privately Held**
Web: www.metal-technologies.com
SIC: 3315 Steel wire and related products
PA: Metal Technologies Of Indiana Llc
  1401 S Grandstaff Dr
  Auburn IN 46706
  260 925-4717

(G-408)
METAL TECHNOLOGIES INC ALABAMA (PA)
1401 S Grandstaff Dr (46706-2664)
PHONE.............................260 925-4717
Matthew J Fetter, *Pr*
Rick James, *
EMP: 60 **EST:** 1997
SALES (est): 23.45MM
SALES (corp-wide): 23.45MM **Privately Held**
Web: www.metal-technologies.com
SIC: 8711 3321 Acoustical engineering; Gray iron castings, nec

(G-409)
METAL TECHNOLOGIES INDIANA LLC (PA)
Also Called: Metal Technologies
1401 S Grandstaff Dr (46706-2664)
PHONE.............................260 925-4717
Rick James, *CEO*
Jeffrey L Turner, *
◆ **EMP:** 170 **EST:** 1997
SALES (est): 261.85MM
SALES (corp-wide): 261.85MM **Privately Held**
Web: www.metal-technologies.com
SIC: 3321 3443 Gray and ductile iron foundries; Metal parts

(G-410)
MILWAUKEE DUCTILE IRON INC
Also Called: West Allis Ductile Iron
1401 S Grandstaff Dr (46706-2664)
PHONE.............................260 925-4717
Rick James, *Ch*
Keith Turner, *Pr*
EMP: 1 **EST:** 1999
SQ FT: 400,000
SALES (est): 2.5MM
SALES (corp-wide): 261.85MM **Privately Held**
Web: www.ductile.org
SIC: 3321 Ductile iron castings
PA: Metal Technologies Of Indiana Llc
  1401 S Grandstaff Dr
  Auburn IN 46706
  260 925-4717

(G-411)
MINNEAPOLIS DIE CASTING LLC
Also Called: Metal Tech - Mnnpolis Die Cast
1401 S Grandstaff Dr (46706-2664)
PHONE.............................763 536-5500
EMP: 116 **EST:** 2009
SALES (est): 38.41MM
SALES (corp-wide): 261.85MM **Privately Held**
SIC: 3365 3321 Aluminum and aluminum-based alloy castings; Gray iron castings, nec
HQ: Key 3 Casting, Llc
  301 Commerce St Ste 3200
  Fort Worth TX 76102

(G-412)
MTI MEXICO MACHINING LLC
1401 S Grandstaff Dr (46706-2664)
PHONE.............................260 925-4717
Matthew Fetter, *Managing Member*
EMP: 1 **EST:** 2021
SALES (est): 540.21K
SALES (corp-wide): 23.45MM **Privately Held**
SIC: 3366 Machinery castings, copper or copper-base alloy
PA: Metal Technologies, Inc. Of Alabama
  1401 S Grandstaff Dr
  Auburn IN 46706
  260 925-4717

Auburn - Dekalb County (G-413)

(G-413)
NORTHERN FOUNDRY LLC
1401 S Grandstaff Dr (46706-2664)
PHONE.....................218 263-8871
EMP: 6 EST: 2016
SALES (est): 139.84K Privately Held
Web: www.metal-technologies.com
SIC: 3599 Machine shop, jobbing and repair

(G-414)
NUCOR REBAR FABRICATION S LLC (PA)
1342 S Grandstaff Dr (46706)
P.O. Box 627 (46706)
PHONE.....................260 925-5440
EMP: 56 EST: 2004
SALES (est): 110.7MM
SALES (corp-wide): 110.7MM Privately Held
Web: www.harrisrebar.com
SIC: 3441 Fabricated structural metal

(G-415)
PERPETUAL INDUSTRIES INC
Also Called: Professional Services Sector
2193 Rotunda Dr (46706-0039)
PHONE.....................702 707-9811
Brent W Bedford, CEO
EMP: 25 EST: 2005
SALES (est): 2.4MM Privately Held
Web: www.perpetualindustries.com
SIC: 3823 Process control instruments

(G-416)
PETROGAS INTERNATIONAL CORP
2444 Woodland Trl (46706-9688)
PHONE.....................260 484-0859
Pablo Migros, CEO
EMP: 5 EST: 2005
SALES (est): 497.81K Privately Held
SIC: 2813 Industrial gases

(G-417)
PRECISION GAGE LLC
1401 S Grandstaff Dr (46706-2664)
PHONE.....................260 925-4717
EMP: 8 EST: 2017
SALES (est): 947.95K Privately Held
Web: www.precisiongageco.com
SIC: 3321 Cooking utensils, cast iron

(G-418)
RAAC LLC ◊
Also Called: Custom Coating Inc
1937 Jacob St (46706-3516)
PHONE.....................260 925-0623
Richard Allen, Managing Member
EMP: 25 EST: 2023
SALES (est): 3.7MM Privately Held
SIC: 3479 Coating of metals and formed products

(G-419)
RIEKE LLC (HQ)
Also Called: Rieke Packaging Systems
500 W 7th St (46706-2006)
PHONE.....................260 925-3700
Fabio Salik, Pr
◆ EMP: 310 EST: 1978
SQ FT: 195,000
SALES (est): 81.12MM
SALES (corp-wide): 893.55MM Publicly Held
Web: www.riekepackaging.com
SIC: 3466 3089 Closures, stamped metal; Fittings for pipe, plastics
PA: Trimas Corporation
38505 Wodward Ave Ste 200
Bloomfield Hills MI 48304
248 631-5450

(G-420)
SCOT INDUSTRIES INC
1729 W Auburn Dr (46706-3343)
PHONE.....................260 927-0262
Tony Nondorf, Brnch Mgr
EMP: 101
SALES (corp-wide): 84.51MM Privately Held
Web: www.scotindustries.com
SIC: 3498 Fabricated pipe and fittings
PA: Scot Industries, Inc.
3756 F M 250 N
Lone Star TX 75668
903 639-2551

(G-421)
SCP HOLDINGS INC
1700 S Indiana Ave (46706-3414)
PHONE.....................260 925-2588
James A Buchanan, CEO
Paul Schlueter, VP Sls
Ryan Criswell, Dir Fin
EMP: 8 EST: 2016
SALES (est): 1.29MM Privately Held
Web: www.scplimited.com
SIC: 2899 Igniter grains, boron potassium nitrate

(G-422)
SEILER EXCAVATING INC
6310 County Road 31 (46706-9682)
PHONE.....................260 925-0507
Larry Seiler, Pr
Donna Seiler, VP
EMP: 7 EST: 1988
SALES (est): 880K Privately Held
SIC: 1794 7692 Excavation work; Welding repair

(G-423)
SIMPLEX COMPUTER SERVICES
1405 Willow Dr (46706-3215)
PHONE.....................260 570-7062
Tina Reighter, Prin
EMP: 1 EST: 2003
SALES (est): 43.04K Privately Held
SIC: 7374 7371 7372 7378 Data processing and preparation; Computer software systems analysis and design, custom; Prepackaged software; Computer maintenance and repair

(G-424)
SOFTEXPERT USA LLC
625 W 15th St (46706-2133)
P.O. Box 70 (46706-0070)
PHONE.....................260 925-7674
EMP: 9 EST: 2008
SALES (est): 194.41K Privately Held
Web: www.softexpert.com
SIC: 2451 Mobile homes

(G-425)
SPECILZED CMPNENT PRTS LTD LLC
Also Called: Scp Limited
1700 S Indiana Ave (46706-3414)
P.O. Box 560 (46706-0560)
PHONE.....................260 925-2588
James A Buchanan, CEO
▲ EMP: 150 EST: 1988
SQ FT: 27,000
SALES (est): 23.44MM Privately Held
Web: www.scplimited.com
SIC: 3491 Gas valves and parts, industrial

(G-426)
STE ACQUISITION LLC
Also Called: Revelation Medical Devices
1105 W Auburn Dr (46706-3459)
PHONE.....................260 925-1382
Jeff Ondrla, Managing Member
EMP: 23 EST: 2015
SALES (est): 1.41MM Privately Held
SIC: 3841 Surgical and medical instruments

(G-427)
SUPERIOR EQUIPMENT & MFG
717 Lakeshore Dr (46706-2615)
P.O. Box 97 (46793-0097)
PHONE.....................260 925-0152
Brian Ruegsegger, Pr
Sandra Rhaos, Sec
EMP: 2 EST: 1979
SQ FT: 2,600
SALES (est): 156.9K Privately Held
Web: www.superiorequipmfg.com
SIC: 3441 Fabricated structural metal

(G-428)
SURFIS INC
P.O. Box 414 (46706-0414)
PHONE.....................260 357-3475
William D Shetterly, Pr
Douglas Shetterly, VP
EMP: 7 EST: 1996
SALES (est): 219.66K Privately Held
SIC: 3644 Insulators and insulation materials, electrical

(G-429)
THE DEATON FAMILY COMPANY
318 E 7th St (46706-1804)
PHONE.....................815 726-6234
EMP: 80
Web: www.cigfh.ca
SIC: 2759 2789 2791 2752 Engraving, nec; Binding only: books, pamphlets, magazines, etc.; Typesetting; Commercial printing, lithographic

(G-430)
THREE DAUGHTERS CORP
Also Called: Rathburn Tool & Manufacturing
5005 County Road 29 (46706-9601)
PHONE.....................260 925-2128
Angela Holt, Pr
EMP: 30 EST: 1983
SALES (est): 4.18MM Privately Held
Web: www.rathburntool.com
SIC: 7539 3599 Machine shop, automotive; Machine shop, jobbing and repair

(G-431)
TOWER ATMTIVE OPRTONS USA II L
Also Called: Tower Automotive
801 W 15th St (46706-2030)
PHONE.....................260 920-1500
Don Stroud, Mgr
EMP: 155
SALES (corp-wide): 3.1B Privately Held
Web: www.autokiniton.com
SIC: 3465 Automotive stampings
HQ: Tower Automotive Operations Usa Ii, Llc
17672 N Laurel Park Dr 400e
Livonia MI 48152

(G-432)
TRIMAS CORPORATION
500 W 7th St (46706-2006)
PHONE.....................260 925-3700
EMP: 10
SALES (corp-wide): 893.55MM Publicly Held
Web: www.trimas.com
SIC: 3799 Trailer hitches
PA: Trimas Corporation
38505 Wodward Ave Ste 200
Bloomfield Hills MI 48304
248 631-5450

(G-433)
VANS TV & APPLIANCE INC
Also Called: Van's Home Center
106 Peckhart Ct (46706-9589)
PHONE.....................260 927-8267
EMP: 10 EST: 1994
SQ FT: 40,000
SALES (est): 1.87MM Privately Held
Web: www.vanshomecenter.com
SIC: 5722 5731 2515 2512 Electric household appliances, major; Television sets; Mattresses and foundations; Upholstered household furniture

(G-434)
WEST ALLIS GRAY IRON
Also Called: Metal Technologies
1401 S Grandstaff Dr (46706-2664)
PHONE.....................260 925-4717
Keith Turner, Prin
EMP: 25 EST: 1997
SQ FT: 5,000
SALES (est): 313.93K Privately Held
SIC: 3325 3321 Steel foundries, nec; Gray and ductile iron foundries

(G-435)
ZIM CORP
5715 Garman Rd (46706-9337)
PHONE.....................260 438-2110
Joseph Zimmerman, Pr
EMP: 8 EST: 2008
SALES (est): 148.03K Privately Held
SIC: 3549 Assembly machines, including robotic

Aurora
Dearborn County

(G-436)
AFTER HOURS EMBROIDERY
406 2nd St (47001-1326)
PHONE.....................812 926-9355
Donna Ashley, Pt
Charles Ashley, Pt
EMP: 2 EST: 1999
SALES (est): 106.67K Privately Held
SIC: 2395 2759 Embroidery and art needlework; Screen printing

(G-437)
ALL-RITE READY MIX INC
10513 Morgan Branch Rd (47001-8248)
PHONE.....................812 926-0920
EMP: 10
SALES (corp-wide): 7.02MM Privately Held
SIC: 3273 5251 Ready-mixed concrete; Tools
PA: All-Rite Ready Mix, Inc
139 Aristocrat Dr
Florence KY 41042
859 371-3314

(G-438)
AURORA CASKET COMPANY LLC
50 Factory (47001)
PHONE.....................812 926-1110
Linda Bushman, Mgr
EMP: 2
SALES (corp-wide): 1.88B Publicly Held
Web: www.auroracasket.com
SIC: 3995 Burial caskets
HQ: Aurora Casket Company, Llc
10944 Marsh Rd
Aurora IN 47001
800 457-1111

GEOGRAPHIC SECTION

Austin - Scott County (G-464)

(G-439)
AURORA CASKET COMPANY LLC (HQ)
Also Called: Matthews Aurora Fnrl Solutions
10944 Marsh Rd (47001-2328)
P.O. Box 29 (47001-0029)
PHONE..................800 457-1111
Michael Quinn, *Pr*
◆ **EMP**: 450 **EST**: 1937
SQ FT: 309,000
SALES (est): 41.73MM
SALES (corp-wide): 1.88B **Publicly Held**
Web: www.auroracasket.com
SIC: 7261 3995 3281 Funeral service and crematories; Burial caskets; Urns, cut stone
PA: Matthews International Corporation
2 N Shore Ctr
Pittsburgh PA 15212
412 442-8200

(G-440)
BATESVILLE PRODUCTS INC
Also Called: Huber Industries
10367 Randall Ave (47001-9390)
PHONE..................812 926-4230
EMP: 17
SALES (corp-wide): 9.1MM **Privately Held**
Web: www.batesvilleproducts.com
SIC: 3369 3365 Nonferrous foundries, nec; Aluminum foundries
PA: Batesville Products, Inc.
434 Margaret St
Lawrenceburg IN 47025
513 381-2057

(G-441)
COLOR GLO
5083 Country Hills Dr (47001-1777)
PHONE..................812 926-2639
Steve Gray, *Pr*
Laurie Gray, *CFO*
EMP: 2 **EST**: 2005
SALES (est): 93.62K **Privately Held**
Web: www.colorglo.com
SIC: 7699 3111 Leather goods, cleaning and repair; Leather tanning and finishing

(G-442)
D & S MACHINE PRODUCTS INC
6965 Us Highway 50 (47001-2286)
PHONE..................812 926-6250
EMP: 35
Web: www.dandsmachine.com
SIC: 3451 Screw machine products

(G-443)
DIAMOND CONSTRUCTION SVCS LLC
6534 Hartford Pike (47001-9204)
PHONE..................513 314-3609
EMP: 2 **EST**: 2013
SALES (est): 209.33K **Privately Held**
SIC: 3536 Hoists, cranes, and monorails

(G-444)
FRED BRANDT CO
Also Called: Brandt's
N Hogan Rd (47001)
P.O. Box 44 (47001-0044)
PHONE..................812 926-0009
Fred Brandt, *Owner*
EMP: 1 **EST**: 1970
SQ FT: 2,000
SALES (est): 93.7K **Privately Held**
SIC: 3599 Machine shop, jobbing and repair

(G-445)
HOTMIX INC (PA)
110 Forest Ave (47001-1065)
P.O. Box 67 (47001-0067)
PHONE..................812 926-1471
Randy Wanstrath, *Pr*
Keith Mosier, *VP*
EMP: 4 **EST**: 1965
SQ FT: 5,000
SALES (est): 592.25K
SALES (corp-wide): 592.25K **Privately Held**
Web: www.hotmixparts.com
SIC: 2951 Asphalt and asphaltic paving mixtures (not from refineries)

(G-446)
KAISER PICKLES LLC
6965 Us Highway 50 (47001-2286)
PHONE..................812 954-5115
David Kaiser, *CEO*
EMP: 1
SALES (corp-wide): 25.8MM **Privately Held**
Web: www.kaiserpickles.com
SIC: 2035 Pickles, sauces, and salad dressings
HQ: Kaiser Pickles, Llc
500 York St
Cincinnati OH 45214
513 621-2053

(G-447)
KLEEMAN CABINETRY
9814 Hueseman Rd (47001-9175)
PHONE..................812 926-0428
Thomas E Kleeman, *Owner*
Thomas Kleeman, *Owner*
EMP: 2 **EST**: 1998
SALES (est): 122.54K **Privately Held**
SIC: 2431 Woodwork, interior and ornamental, nec

(G-448)
KOMA INTEGRATION
10778 Randall Ave (47001-8340)
PHONE..................812 557-6009
EMP: 6 **EST**: 2017
SALES (est): 98.04K **Privately Held**
Web: www.komaprecision.com
SIC: 3599 Machine shop, jobbing and repair

(G-449)
MCFEELYS INC
340 2nd St (47001-1304)
PHONE..................800 443-7937
Peter Putterman, *Pr*
EMP: 15 **EST**: 2013
SALES (est): 2.3MM **Privately Held**
Web: www.mcfeelys.com
SIC: 5085 3553 Fasteners and fastening equipment; Woodworking machinery

(G-450)
MULTIPLE MACHINING
312 3rd St (47001-1310)
PHONE..................812 926-0798
EMP: 7 **EST**: 2017
SALES (est): 60.74K **Privately Held**
Web: www.multiplemachining.com
SIC: 3599 Machine shop, jobbing and repair

(G-451)
PAUL H ROHE COMPANY INC
110 Forest Ave (47001-1065)
P.O. Box 67 (47001-0067)
PHONE..................812 926-1471
James P Jurgenson, *Pr*
Mark Richardson, *
H Blake Michaels, *
EMP: 43 **EST**: 1930
SQ FT: 10,000
SALES (est): 4.4MM
SALES (corp-wide): 25.39MM **Privately Held**
Web: www.jrjnet.com
SIC: 2951 1442 1422 Asphalt and asphaltic paving mixtures (not from refineries); Construction sand and gravel; Crushed and broken limestone
PA: Morrow Gravel Company Inc
11641 Mosteller Rd
Cincinnati OH 45241
513 771-0820

(G-452)
PINPOINT PRINTER
541 Green Blvd (47001-1501)
PHONE..................812 577-0630
EMP: 4 **EST**: 2014
SALES (est): 127.01K **Privately Held**
SIC: 2752 Commercial printing, lithographic

(G-453)
POND DOCTORS INC
Also Called: Pond Doctor
11343 Coyote Run Rd (47001-8062)
PHONE..................812 744-5258
Robert Atkins, *Pr*
EMP: 1 **EST**: 1924
SQ FT: 3,500
SALES (est): 167.71K **Privately Held**
SIC: 1629 3564 Pond construction; Air purification equipment

(G-454)
QUILT BUG
11860 Creekside (47001-7719)
PHONE..................812 926-3092
Bev Desalvo, *Owner*
EMP: 1 **EST**: 2002
SALES (est): 53K **Privately Held**
Web: www.quiltbug.net
SIC: 2395 Quilting and quilting supplies

(G-455)
SPECIALTY ADHESIVE FILM CO (PA)
Also Called: USA Flap
10510 Randall Ave (47001-9496)
P.O. Box 150 (47001-0150)
PHONE..................812 926-0156
John Mahn Junior, *Pr*
EMP: 35 **EST**: 1965
SQ FT: 25,000
SALES (est): 5.55MM
SALES (corp-wide): 5.55MM **Privately Held**
Web: www.usaflap.com
SIC: 2672 3081 2891 Adhesive backed films, foams and foils; Unsupported plastics film and sheet; Laminating compounds

(G-456)
SPORTS SCREEN IMPACT
718 Green Blvd (47001-1506)
PHONE..................812 926-9355
Casey Roberts, *Owner*
EMP: 9 **EST**: 2011
SALES (est): 471.75K **Privately Held**
Web: www.impactsportsink.com
SIC: 2759 Screen printing

(G-457)
STEDMAN MACHINE COMPANY INC
Also Called: Eagle Crusher Co
129 Franklin St (47001-1064)
PHONE..................812 926-0038
Chris Nawalaniec, *Pr*
Mike Tinkey, *
EMP: 71 **EST**: 2016
SALES (est): 16.53MM **Privately Held**
Web: www.stedman-machine.com
SIC: 3532 8711 3541 3531 Rock crushing machinery, stationary; Engineering services ; Machine tools, metal cutting type; Construction machinery

(G-458)
VALLEY ASPHALT CORPORATION
Also Called: Rohe, Paul H
110 Forest Ave (47001-1065)
PHONE..................812 926-1471
EMP: 1
SALES (corp-wide): 225.16MM **Privately Held**
Web: www.jrjnet.com
SIC: 2951 Asphalt paving mixtures and blocks
HQ: Valley Asphalt Corporation
11641 Mosteller Rd
Cincinnati OH 45241
513 771-0820

(G-459)
WEAVERS WELDING
4572 Salem Rdg (47001-9222)
PHONE..................812 438-3425
Troy Weaver, *Prin*
EMP: 1 **EST**: 2010
SALES (est): 61.76K **Privately Held**
SIC: 7692 Welding repair

(G-460)
WILD HAIR CANVAS SHOP
605 Green Blvd (47001-1503)
PHONE..................812 290-1086
Gill Apmadoc, *Owner*
EMP: 2 **EST**: 1998
SALES (est): 94.57K **Privately Held**
Web: www.custom-boat-covers.com
SIC: 2394 Canvas and related products

(G-461)
WILLIS MACHINING INC
18395 Hogan Hill Rd (47001-7520)
PHONE..................812 744-1100
Dave Willis, *Owner*
EMP: 1 **EST**: 2008
SALES (est): 98.12K **Privately Held**
SIC: 3599 Machine shop, jobbing and repair

Austin
Scott County

(G-462)
AJEM WELDING
261 E State Road 256 (47102-8770)
PHONE..................812 595-3541
Amy K Youngblood, *Owner*
EMP: 2 **EST**: 2006
SALES (est): 91.26K **Privately Held**
SIC: 3441 Fabricated structural metal

(G-463)
AUSTIN TRI-HAWK AUTOMOTIVE INC
2001 West Just Industrial Parkway (47102)
P.O. Box 40 (47102-0040)
PHONE..................812 794-0062
Tri Hawk, *CEO*
Tetsuo Kikuchi, *
Manabu Yoshiike, *
Ryuichi Takayama, *
Michael Murry, *
▲ **EMP**: 170 **EST**: 1997
SQ FT: 184,000
SALES (est): 43.51MM **Privately Held**
Web: www.tri-hawk.com
SIC: 3469 Stamping metal for the trade
PA: G-Tekt Corporation
1-11-20, Sakuragicho, Omiya-Ku
Saitama STM 330-0

(G-464)
DEHART PALLET & LUMBER CO
Also Called: De Harts Pallet & Lbr Mfg Co
2737 E State Road 256 (47102-8424)

PHONE..................812 794-2974
Charles W Tutterow, Pr
Joanna Tutterow, Sec
EMP: 13 **EST:** 1968
SALES (est): 336.52K **Privately Held**
SIC: 2421 2448 2426 Sawmills and planing mills, general; Pallets, wood; Hardwood dimension and flooring mills

(G-465)
GARTECH ENTERPRISES INC
3037 W State Road 256 (47102-8905)
PHONE..................812 794-4796
Don Hounshell, Pr
EMP: 17 **EST:** 1990
SQ FT: 7,000
SALES (est): 3.28MM **Privately Held**
Web: www.gartechenterprises.com
SIC: 3679 3714 Harness assemblies, for electronic use: wire or cable; Automotive wiring harness sets

(G-466)
JASON BABBS
3869 N Whitsett Rd (47102-8446)
PHONE..................812 595-9073
Jason Babbs, Prin
EMP: 5 **EST:** 2017
SALES (est): 46.08K **Privately Held**
SIC: 3993 Signs and advertising specialties

(G-467)
MORGAN FOODS INC
90 W Morgan St (47102-1741)
PHONE..................812 794-1170
John S Morgan, Ch Bd
Kelly Morgan Maciejak, *
Lawrence M Higdon, VP
▲ **EMP:** 550 **EST:** 1901
SQ FT: 1,000,000
SALES (est): 207.98MM **Privately Held**
Web: www.morganfoods.com
SIC: 2032 Soups, except seafood: packaged in cans, jars, etc.

(G-468)
P-AMERICAS LLC
Also Called: Pepsico
1402 W State Road 256 (47102-8904)
P.O. Box 69 (47102-0069)
PHONE..................812 794-4455
Rodney Coleman, Dir
EMP: 1
SALES (corp-wide): 86.39B **Publicly Held**
Web: www.pepsico.com
SIC: 2086 Carbonated soft drinks, bottled and canned
HQ: P-Americas Llc
  1 Pepsi Way
  Somers NY 10589
  336 896-5740

(G-469)
PEACOCK LOGGING INC
2376 E Harrod Rd (47102-8331)
PHONE..................812 794-3579
Clinton Peacock, Pr
EMP: 1 **EST:** 1998
SALES (est): 79.72K **Privately Held**
SIC: 2411 Logging camps and contractors

(G-470)
RAKK LLC
491 W Main St (47102-1553)
PHONE..................812 271-4300
EMP: 5 **EST:** 2021
SALES (est): 104.73K **Privately Held**

SIC: 7389 1389 1541 Business Activities at Non-Commercial Site; Construction, repair, and dismantling services; Renovation, remodeling and repairs: industrial buildings

Avilla
Noble County

(G-471)
ACCEL INTERNATIONAL
302 Progress Way (46710-9668)
PHONE..................260 897-9990
Dan Cole, Ofcr
▲ **EMP:** 13 **EST:** 2009
SALES (est): 4.93MM **Privately Held**
Web: www.accelinternational.com
SIC: 3496 3357 3315 Miscellaneous fabricated wire products; Nonferrous wiredrawing and insulating; Steel wire and related products

(G-472)
AMERICAN BINDERS LLC
134 Green Dr Ste D (46710-9520)
P.O. Box 713 (46710-0713)
PHONE..................260 827-7799
Rick A Ross, Prin
EMP: 1 **EST:** 2019
SALES (est): 61.24K **Privately Held**
SIC: 2211 Canvas

(G-473)
BURNS CABINETS AND DISP INC
140 Green Dr (46710)
PHONE..................260 897-2219
Patrick Burns, Pr
EMP: 2 **EST:** 1987
SQ FT: 9,000
SALES (est): 248.51K **Privately Held**
Web: www.burnsdistributing.com
SIC: 2542 2434 Partitions and fixtures, except wood; Wood kitchen cabinets

(G-474)
DANA INCORPORATED
301 Progress Way (46710-9668)
PHONE..................260 897-2827
EMP: 5
Web: www.dana.com
SIC: 3714 Motor vehicle parts and accessories
PA: Dana Incorporated
  3939 Technology Dr
  Maumee OH 43537

(G-475)
DIVERSIFIED PATTERN ENGRG INC
100 Progress Way (46710-9609)
P.O. Box 230 (46710-0230)
PHONE..................260 897-3771
James Parker, Pr
EMP: 25 **EST:** 1975
SQ FT: 21,000
SALES (est): 2.14MM **Privately Held**
Web: www.diversifiedpatternco.com
SIC: 3543 Foundry patternmaking

(G-476)
ETA FABRICATION INC
Also Called: Eta Engineering
10605 E Baseline Rd (46710-9646)
PHONE..................260 897-3711
Samuel Adams, Pr
EMP: 14 **EST:** 1991
SALES (est): 1.4MM **Privately Held**
Web: www.etafab.com
SIC: 3444 3564 3441 Sheet metalwork; Blowers and fans; Fabricated structural metal

(G-477)
HOLLINGSHEAD MIXER COMPANY LLC
200 Dekko Dr (46710)
PHONE..................260 897-4397
Jeff Hollingshead, CEO
EMP: 90 **EST:** 2021
SALES (est): 20.54MM
SALES (corp-wide): 1.05B **Privately Held**
Web: www.smyrnareadymix.com
SIC: 3273 Ready-mixed concrete
PA: Smyrna Ready Mix Concrete, Llc
  1000 Hollingshead Cir
  Murfreesboro TN 37129
  615 355-1028

(G-478)
ILLINOIS NI CAST LLC
Also Called: Alloy Engineering & Casting Co
105 Progress Way (46710-9609)
P.O. Box 609 (46710-0609)
PHONE..................260 897-3768
EMP: 12 **EST:** 2005
SALES (est): 348.82K **Privately Held**
SIC: 3317 Steel pipe and tubes

(G-479)
JO MORY INC
Also Called: J O Mory Sheet Metal Division
201 Progress Way (46710-9684)
PHONE..................260 897-3541
Thomas Nott, Mgr
EMP: 11
SALES (corp-wide): 16.4MM **Privately Held**
Web: www.jomory.com
SIC: 3444 1761 1711 Sheet metalwork; Roofing, siding, and sheetmetal work; Plumbing, heating, air-conditioning
PA: J.O. Mory, Inc.
  7470 S State Road 3
  South Milford IN 46786
  260 351-2221

(G-480)
JOHN LEY MONUMENT SALES INC
101 Progress Way (46710-9609)
P.O. Box 5 (46710-0005)
PHONE..................260 347-7346
Anthony J Ley, Pr
Anthony J Ley, VP
Margaret E Ley, Sec
Regina Ley, VP
EMP: 5 **EST:** 1957
SQ FT: 3,200
SALES (est): 494.24K **Privately Held**
Web: www.johnleymonument.com
SIC: 5999 3281 Monuments, finished to custom order; Cut stone and stone products

(G-481)
KAUTEX INC
210 Green Dr (46710-9517)
P.O. Box 795 (46710-0795)
PHONE..................260 897-3250
Greg Fuller, Brnch Mgr
EMP: 1
SALES (corp-wide): 12.87B **Publicly Held**
Web: www.kautex.com
SIC: 3714 Gas tanks, motor vehicle
HQ: Kautex Inc.
  800 Tower Dr Ste 200
  Troy MI 48098
  248 616-5100

(G-482)
KENDALVILLE MALL
109 N Baum St (46710-5231)
PHONE..................260 897-2697
EMP: 4 **EST:** 2017
SALES (est): 87.43K **Privately Held**

SIC: 6512 2711 Theater building, ownership and operation; Newspapers

(G-483)
KNEPPERS INC (PA)
1390 N 750 E (46710-9624)
PHONE..................260 636-2180
Greg Knepper, Pr
Kelly Knepper, Sec
EMP: 3 **EST:** 1993
SALES (est): 969.75K **Privately Held**
Web: www.concretechute.com
SIC: 3713 Truck bodies and parts

(G-484)
KRETLER TOOL & ENGINEERING INC
104 Well St (46710-1002)
P.O. Box 610 (46710-0610)
PHONE..................260 897-2662
John Kretler, Pr
Cynthia Kretler, VP
EMP: 7 **EST:** 1992
SQ FT: 10,000
SALES (est): 747.74K **Privately Held**
SIC: 3312 Tool and die steel

(G-485)
LAKE LITE INC
100 Industrial Dr (46710-0020)
P.O. Box 414 (46763-0414)
PHONE..................260 918-2758
Jeffrey Martzall, Pr
Keith L Henley Junior, VP
EMP: 3 **EST:** 2004
SALES (est): 470.85K **Privately Held**
Web: www.lakelite.com
SIC: 3731 5551 Lighters, marine: building and repairing; Marine supplies and equipment

(G-486)
LAOTTO BREWING LLC
7530 E Swan Rd (46710-9726)
PHONE..................260 897-3152
David Koepper, Prin
EMP: 5 **EST:** 2015
SALES (est): 138.23K **Privately Held**
Web: www.laottobrewing.com
SIC: 2082 Malt beverages

(G-487)
LINAMAR STRCTURES USA MICH INC
100 Progress Way (46710-9669)
PHONE..................260 636-7030
Joseph Perkins, CEO
EMP: 6
SALES (corp-wide): 5.89B **Privately Held**
Web: www.mobexglobal.com
SIC: 3365 Machinery castings, aluminum
HQ: Linamar Structures Usa (Michigan) Inc.
  32233 8 Mile Rd
  Livonia MI 48152
  248 477-6240

(G-488)
MARK DEKONINDK
Also Called: Mark's Woodshop
176 County Road 52 (46710-9512)
PHONE..................260 357-5443
Mark Dekonindk, Owner
EMP: 1 **EST:** 1992
SALES (est): 100.32K **Privately Held**
Web: www.markswoodshopinc.com
SIC: 2499 Decorative wood and woodwork

(G-489)
MCLAUGHLIN SERVICES LLC (PA)
Also Called: McLaughlin Furnace Group

GEOGRAPHIC SECTION   Avon - Hendricks County (G-515)

150 Eagle Dr (46710-0017)
P.O. Box 639 (46710-0639)
PHONE.................................260 897-4328
EMP: 2 EST: 2007
SALES (est): 3.51MM Privately Held
Web: www.mclaughlinsvc.com
SIC: 3398 Metal heat treating

(G-490)
NOBLE COUNTY WELDING INC
Also Called: Noble Industrial Fabrications
635 S Van Scoyoc St (46710-9516)
PHONE.................................260 897-4082
Wayne Diehm, Pr
EMP: 11 EST: 1990
SQ FT: 16,500
SALES (est): 991.24K Privately Held
SIC: 7692 3441 Welding repair; Fabricated structural metal

(G-491)
ONXX TOOL INC
135 Nicholas Pl (46710-0069)
P.O. Box 375 (46763-0375)
PHONE.................................260 897-3530
EMP: 8 EST: 1990
SQ FT: 7,500
SALES (est): 990.2K Privately Held
Web: www.onxxtool.com
SIC: 3544 Special dies and tools

(G-492)
PEERLESS MANUFACTURING LLC (PA)
2084 N 800 E (46710-9696)
P.O. Box 206 (46710-0206)
PHONE.................................260 760-0880
EMP: 5 EST: 2012
SALES (est): 495.24K
SALES (corp-wide): 495.24K Privately Held
Web: www.peerlessmfg.cc
SIC: 3999 Manufacturing industries, nec

(G-493)
RON NAWROCKI
Also Called: Graphics Plus
1415 S 650 E (46710-9710)
PHONE.................................260 437-5323
Ron Nawrocki, Owner
EMP: 1 EST: 2000
SALES (est): 60K Privately Held
SIC: 3993 Signs and advertising specialties

(G-494)
SCHER MAIHEM PUBLISHING LTD
Also Called: Midwest Film Factory
109 N Baum St (46710-5231)
P.O. Box 313 (46710-0313)
PHONE.................................260 897-2697
Julia Scher, Pr
Claire Tindall, VP
EMP: 3 EST: 2016
SALES (est): 196.96K Privately Held
Web: www.midwestfilmfactory.com
SIC: 2741 7335 Miscellaneous publishing; Commercial photography

(G-495)
SHANK WELDING INC
7056 E 100 N (46710-9623)
PHONE.................................260 897-2068
Michael Shank, Pr
Jacob Patrick, Prin
EMP: 2 EST: 1983
SALES (est): 149.72K Privately Held
Web: www.shankweldinginc.com
SIC: 7692 3441 Automotive welding; Fabricated structural metal

(G-496)
TERNET METAL FINISHING INC
150 Green Dr (46710-9518)
P.O. Box 725 (46710-0725)
PHONE.................................260 897-3903
EMP: 6 EST: 1995
SQ FT: 20,000
SALES (est): 512.01K Privately Held
SIC: 3471 Electroplating of metals or formed products

(G-497)
UNLIMITED MANUFACTURING LLC
702 N Main St (46710-9658)
PHONE.................................260 515-3332
EMP: 5 EST: 2017
SALES (est): 199.69K Privately Held
Web: www.unlimitedmanufacturing.com
SIC: 3999 Manufacturing industries, nec

(G-498)
VICTOR REINZ VALVE SEALS LLC
Also Called: Dana Sealing Products
301 Progress Way (46710-9668)
P.O. Box 559 (46710-0559)
PHONE.................................260 897-2827
▲ EMP: 100 EST: 1985
SQ FT: 80,000
SALES (est): 28.31MM Publicly Held
Web: www.dana.com
SIC: 3592 Valves, aircraft
HQ: Dana Sealing Products, Llc
    3939 Technology Dr
    Maumee OH 43537

(G-499)
WICK - FAB INC
Also Called: Wickfab Steel Fabrication
307 E Fourth St (46710-9521)
PHONE.................................260 897-3303
Joe Cochran, Pr
EMP: 45 EST: 1993
SALES (est): 4.97MM Privately Held
Web: www.wickfabinc.com
SIC: 3441 Fabricated structural metal

(G-500)
WIRCO INC (PA)
105 Progress Way (46710-9609)
P.O. Box 609 (46710-0609)
PHONE.................................260 897-3768
Dennis L Wright, CEO
Chad Wright, *
Christopher M Dankert, *
Wendy Evans, *
EMP: 120 EST: 1984
SQ FT: 50,000
SALES (est): 42.54MM
SALES (corp-wide): 42.54MM Privately Held
Web: www.wirco.com
SIC: 3544 3322 3496 3599 Industrial molds; Malleable iron foundries; Woven wire products, nec; Machine shop, jobbing and repair

Avon
Hendricks County

(G-501)
3JM HAULING LLC ✪
10143 Morning Light Dr (46123-9838)
PHONE.................................317 518-0750
EMP: 1 EST: 2022
SALES (est): 60.08K Privately Held
SIC: 3537 7389 Trucks, tractors, loaders, carriers, and similar equipment; Business Activities at Non-Commercial Site

(G-502)
A & A MACHINE SERVICE INC
4830 E Main St (46123-9194)
P.O. Box 388 (46122-0388)
PHONE.................................317 745-7367
Jerry Morgan, Pr
Bryan Morgan, VP
EMP: 9 EST: 1971
SQ FT: 8,000
SALES (est): 967.36K Privately Held
SIC: 3545 7389 Gauges (machine tool accessories); Grinding, precision: commercial or industrial

(G-503)
ACME MASKING COMPANY INC
240 Production Dr (46123-7030)
PHONE.................................317 272-6202
William H Bailey Junior, Pr
EMP: 30 EST: 1951
SQ FT: 25,000
SALES (est): 2.82MM Privately Held
Web: www.acmemasking.com
SIC: 3069 3544 Molded rubber products; Industrial molds

(G-504)
AO INC
Also Called: Newspaper Solutions
9227 E Us Highway 36 (46123-7929)
PHONE.................................317 280-3000
Ronald Musgrave, Pr
Steven Peterka, VP
EMP: 4 EST: 2005
SQ FT: 2,500
SALES (est): 299.67K Privately Held
Web: www.lightsalive.com
SIC: 3648 7389 Stage lighting equipment; Printers' services: folding, collating, etc.

(G-505)
ASCL PRINTWEAR LLC
1238 Eton Way (46123-5593)
PHONE.................................317 507-0548
Carolyn Mcclain, Prin
EMP: 5 EST: 2016
SALES (est): 67.65K Privately Held
Web: www.asclprintwear.com
SIC: 2759 Screen printing

(G-506)
BATH & BODY WORKS LLC
10343 E Us Highway 36 (46123-7988)
PHONE.................................317 209-1517
Denise Newkirk, Brnch Mgr
EMP: 11
SALES (corp-wide): 7.43B Publicly Held
Web: www.bathandbodyworks.com
SIC: 5999 2844 Perfumes and colognes; Perfumes, cosmetics and other toilet preparations
HQ: Bath & Body Works, Llc
    7 Limited Pkwy E
    Reynoldsburg OH 43068

(G-507)
BEACON SIGN COMPANY LLC
9305 E Us Highway 36 (46123-7977)
PHONE.................................317 272-2388
Robert Alltop, Pt
Linda Alltop, Pt
EMP: 2 EST: 2001
SALES (est): 249.55K Privately Held
Web: www.beaconsign.biz
SIC: 3993 Signs and advertising specialties

(G-508)
BIG DIPPER INC
Also Called: Acme Coatings
240 Production Dr (46123-7030)

PHONE.................................317 272-6202
Michael Kays, Mgr
EMP: 13 EST: 2021
SALES (est): 589.67K Privately Held
SIC: 3479 Coating of metals and formed products

(G-509)
BREINER COMPANY INC
259 Production Dr (46123-7030)
PHONE.................................317 272-2521
William T Lucas Junior, Pr
William T Lucas Senior, Ch Bd
Frances Lucas, Sec
EMP: 15 EST: 1940
SQ FT: 20,000
SALES (est): 2.35MM Privately Held
Web: www.breinerco.com
SIC: 3053 Gaskets, all materials

(G-510)
CDP LOGISTICS INC
1943 Collingwood Dr (46123-7200)
PHONE.................................773 968-1455
Carlos Prunty, Dir
Morrissa Prunty, Dir
EMP: 2
SALES (est): 249.76K Privately Held
SIC: 3715 4213 Truck trailers; Trucking, except local

(G-511)
CONCEPTS CABINET SHOP INC (PA)
7599 E Us Highway 36 (46123-7171)
PHONE.................................317 272-7430
Aaron Albers, CEO
EMP: 5 EST: 2005
SALES (est): 985.05K
SALES (corp-wide): 985.05K Privately Held
Web: www.conceptsthecabinetshop.com
SIC: 2434 Wood kitchen cabinets

(G-512)
DEVIL DOC COFFEE
6576 Kings Ct (46123-9075)
PHONE.................................317 417-8486
Neil Chapman, Owner
EMP: 1 EST: 2021
SALES (est): 60.25K Privately Held
SIC: 2095 Coffee roasting (except by wholesale grocers)

(G-513)
DIMO MULTISERVICES LLC ✪
7998 Cobblesprings Dr (46123-8786)
PHONE.................................463 256-0561
Omar R Diaz C, CEO
Omar R Diaz Cespede, Managing Member
EMP: 15 EST: 2022
SALES (est): 735.42K Privately Held
SIC: 5199 2211 7389 8742 Advertising specialties; Print cloths, cotton; Advertising, promotional, and trade show services; Marketing consulting services

(G-514)
DWG GLOBAL SERVICES LLC
1986 Devonshire Ave (46123)
PHONE.................................469 605-0567
EMP: 2 EST: 2021
SALES (est): 62.38K Privately Held
SIC: 2087 Beverage bases, concentrates, syrups, powders and mixes

(G-515)
E SQUARED MOTORSPORTS LLC
1511 N County Road 600 E (46123-9582)
PHONE.................................317 626-2937
EMP: 4 EST: 2012

Avon - Hendricks County (G-516) GEOGRAPHIC SECTION

SALES (est): 162.07K **Privately Held**
SIC: 3644 Raceways

(G-516)
ELECTRIC PLUS INC
173 S County Road 525 E (46123-9058)
PHONE.....................317 718-0100
Timothy Whicker, *Pr*
Timothy A Whicker, *
EMP: 100 EST: 2006
SQ FT: 1,000
SALES (est): 24.37MM **Privately Held**
Web: www.electricplus.com
SIC: 1731 3634 General electrical contractor; Electric housewares and fans

(G-517)
ELITE HAND CAR WASH & MORE LLC
8403 E Us Highway 36 Ste C (46123-7961)
PHONE.....................317 500-8308
Antoine Hawkins, *Managing Member*
EMP: 1 EST: 2021
SALES (est): 50.76K **Privately Held**
SIC: 3589 Car washing machinery

(G-518)
EMBROIDERY N BEYOND
2048 Whitetail Ct (46123-7389)
PHONE.....................540 903-4861
Manuela Bretherick, *Prin*
EMP: 1 EST: 2012
SALES (est): 59.97K **Privately Held**
Web: www.embroiderynbeyond.com
SIC: 2395 Embroidery products, except Schiffli machine

(G-519)
FENCESCAPES LLC
Also Called: Construction
1385 Balsam Fir Pass (46123-6848)
PHONE.....................317 210-3912
Jeremy Miller, *Owner*
EMP: 12 EST: 1991
SALES (est): 589.89K **Privately Held**
SIC: 1799 3089 5039 Fence construction; Fences, gates, and accessories: plastics; Wire fence, gates, and accessories

(G-520)
FIGG PUBLISHING INC
8103 E Us Highway 36 Ste W (46123-7964)
PHONE.....................317 797-2022
Tonya Figg, *Prin*
EMP: 6 EST: 2008
SALES (est): 104.52K **Privately Held**
SIC: 2741 Miscellaneous publishing

(G-521)
GINAS CREATIVE JEWELRY INC
8100 E Us Highway 36 Ste 7 (46123-8284)
PHONE.....................317 272-0032
Gina Fisher, *Pr*
Bill Fisher, *VP*
EMP: 6 EST: 1991
SQ FT: 1,875
SALES (est): 568.95K **Privately Held**
Web: www.ginascreativejewelryin.com
SIC: 5944 3911 7631 Jewelry, precious stones and precious metals; Jewelry, precious metal; Jewelry repair services

(G-522)
HAMMERTECHRACECARS LLC
6396 Granny Smith Ln (46123-7726)
PHONE.....................765 412-8824
Tony Derhammer, *Owner*
EMP: 5 EST: 2018
SALES (est): 183.94K **Privately Held**
Web: www.hammertechracecars.com
SIC: 3999 Manufacturing industries, nec

(G-523)
HARLAN BAKERIES LLC (PA)
Also Called: Harlan Bakeries
7597 E Us Highway 36 (46123)
PHONE.....................317 272-3600
Hugh Harlan, *Pr*
Hal Harlan, *Ex VP*
Doug Harlan, *Ex VP*
▲ EMP: 3 EST: 2007
SALES (est): 1.18B **Privately Held**
Web: www.harlanfoods.com
SIC: 5149 2051 2045 Bakery products; Bread, cake, and related products; Prepared flour mixes and doughs

(G-524)
HARLAN BAKERIES-AVON LLC
7597 E Us Highway 36 (46123-7171)
PHONE.....................317 272-3600
Hugh Harlan, *Prin*
Hal Harlan, *
Paul G Hayden, *
John P Menne, *Prin*
Doug H Harian, *
▲ EMP: 375 EST: 1985
SQ FT: 225,000
SALES (est): 100.92MM **Privately Held**
Web: www.harlanfoods.com
SIC: 5149 2051 2045 Bakery products; Bread, cake, and related products; Prepared flour mixes and doughs
PA: Harlan Bakeries, Llc
    7597 E Us Hwy 36
    Avon IN 46123

(G-525)
HELP HELP LLC
Also Called: Say Help
1935 Acorn Ct (46123-9438)
PHONE.....................317 910-6631
EMP: 4 EST: 2017
SALES (est): 178.93K **Privately Held**
SIC: 7372 7389 Application computer software; Business Activities at Non-Commercial Site

(G-526)
IN THE AM LLC
319 Angelina Way (46123-5533)
PHONE.....................408 836-8200
Marquita Adagbada, *CEO*
EMP: 4 EST: 2021
SALES (est): 73.72K **Privately Held**
SIC: 2741 Miscellaneous publishing

(G-527)
INCENSE INCENSE
5599 Springhollow Ct (46123-7341)
PHONE.....................317 544-9444
Amanda Lebrun, *Prin*
EMP: 4 EST: 2017
SALES (est): 124.71K **Privately Held**
Web: www.incense-incense.com
SIC: 2899 Incense

(G-528)
JANI INDUSTRIES INC
2256 N County Road 800 E (46123-8571)
PHONE.....................317 985-3916
Devendra Jani Junior, *Prin*
EMP: 5 EST: 2005
SALES (est): 193.85K **Privately Held**
SIC: 3999 Manufacturing industries, nec

(G-529)
JT PRINTING LLC
Also Called: Full Circle Printing & Mktg
77 Park Place Blvd (46123-6536)
PHONE.....................317 271-7700
James Tolley, *Pr*
Charles Dorton, *Genl Mgr*
EMP: 5 EST: 2013
SQ FT: 2,800
SALES (est): 401.83K **Privately Held**
SIC: 2759 Commercial printing, nec

(G-530)
KAMREX INC
7367 Business Center Dr (46123-8662)
PHONE.....................317 204-3779
Rex Doom, *Pr*
Pam Elsey, *Sec*
EMP: 24 EST: 1978
SQ FT: 8,000
SALES (est): 482.93K **Privately Held**
Web: www.kamrex.com
SIC: 2721 8743 2731 Trade journals: publishing only, not printed on site; Public relations and publicity; Book publishing

(G-531)
KEYSTONE ENGINEERING & MFG LLC ◊
9786 E County Road 200 N (46123)
PHONE.....................317 319-7639
Andrea Latham, *Managing Member*
EMP: 8 EST: 2023
SALES (est): 285.68K **Privately Held**
SIC: 3999 Manufacturing industries, nec

(G-532)
KEYSTONE ENGRG & MFG CORP (PA)
9786 E County Road 200 N (46123-9044)
PHONE.....................317 271-6192
Chester Latham, *Pr*
▲ EMP: 19 EST: 1982
SQ FT: 20,000
SALES (est): 2.27MM
SALES (corp-wide): 2.27MM **Privately Held**
Web: www.keystonecutter.com
SIC: 3531 3532 Construction machinery; Mining machinery

(G-533)
KEYSTONE INDUSTRIAL FLRG LLC
7029 E County Road 200 N (46123-8549)
PHONE.....................317 403-8747
Robbie Sarkine, *Owner*
EMP: 4 EST: 2011
SALES (est): 258.78K **Privately Held**
SIC: 2851 Lacquers, varnishes, enamels, and other coatings

(G-534)
KING MACHINING INC
5574 Station Hill Dr (46123-7701)
PHONE.....................317 271-3132
Barry King, *Pr*
Jeanna King, *CFO*
EMP: 6 EST: 1995
SALES (est): 452K **Privately Held**
Web: www.kingmachining.com
SIC: 3599 Machine shop, jobbing and repair

(G-535)
KUMAR BROTHERS INC
432 Huron Ter Apt B (46123-7892)
PHONE.....................317 410-2450
Fnu Kumar, *Prin*
EMP: 6 EST: 2018
SALES (est): 201.22K **Privately Held**
SIC: 3714 Motor vehicle parts and accessories

(G-536)
LIMANIS POP UP CONCESSIONS LLC
137 Production Dr (46123-7082)
PHONE.....................317 966-1507
Limani Smith, *Mgr*
EMP: 3 EST: 2021
SALES (est): 312.56K **Privately Held**
SIC: 2599 Food wagons, restaurant

(G-537)
MEARS MACHINE CORP (PA)
9973 E Us Highway 36 (46123-7987)
PHONE.....................317 271-6041
EMP: 65 EST: 1966
SALES (est): 18.66MM
SALES (corp-wide): 18.66MM **Privately Held**
Web: www.mearsmachine.com
SIC: 3728 Aircraft assemblies, subassemblies, and parts, nec

(G-538)
MOODY MEATS
235 N Avon Ave (46123-8476)
PHONE.....................317 272-4533
Adam Moody, *Pr*
EMP: 2 EST: 2005
SALES (est): 95.19K **Privately Held**
Web: www.moodysbutchershop.com
SIC: 2011 5421 Meat packing plants; Meat and fish markets

(G-539)
NELMAR PRINTING CO
Also Called: Nelmar Engraving Company
573 Othello Way (46123-8464)
PHONE.....................317 504-7840
Nelson C Martin, *Owner*
EMP: 1 EST: 2010
SALES (est): 67.81K **Privately Held**
SIC: 2752 Commercial printing, lithographic

(G-540)
NEW AQUA LLC (HQ)
Also Called: Aqua Systems
7785 E Us Highway 36 (46123)
PHONE.....................317 272-3000
Donald Line, *Managing Member*
Bret Petty, *
EMP: 70 EST: 1980
SQ FT: 60,000
SALES (est): 26.18MM
SALES (corp-wide): 35.47MM **Privately Held**
Web: www.aquasystems.com
SIC: 3589 7389 5074 5149 Water filters and softeners, household type; Water softener service; Water purification equipment; Water, distilled
PA: Franklin Electric Company
    5 2nd St
    Trenton NJ 08611
    856 963-0541

(G-541)
NEW READERS PRESS
6414 Woodhaven Ct (46123-7220)
PHONE.....................317 514-6515
EMP: 2 EST: 2002
SALES (est): 75.14K **Privately Held**
Web: www.proliteracy.org
SIC: 2741 Miscellaneous publishing

(G-542)
NOVA MANUFACTURING
1153 S Avon Ave (46123-7662)
PHONE.....................512 750-5165
Steve Poalson, *Prin*
EMP: 5 EST: 2017

GEOGRAPHIC SECTION

Bargersville - Johnson County (G-567)

SALES (est): 67.03K **Privately Held**
SIC: 3999 Manufacturing industries, nec

(G-543)
NUMARK INDUSTRIES COMPANY LTD
7124 E County Road 150 S Ste B (46123-2000)
PHONE......................317 718-2502
Clifton Lee, *Prin*
Tracy Moore, *Ex VP*
▲ EMP: 10 EST: 2001
SQ FT: 3,000
SALES (est): 822.33K **Privately Held**
Web: www.numark.com
SIC: 2511 Wood lawn and garden furniture

(G-544)
PHOENIX FBRCATORS ERECTORS LLC (PA)
182 S County Road 900 E (46123-8973)
PHONE......................317 271-7002
Jeffery A Short, *Pr*
Charles Lakin, *
Eugene M Rothgerber Junior, *VP*
Timothy F Yohler, *
EMP: 110 EST: 1986
SQ FT: 70,000
SALES (est): 95.03MM
SALES (corp-wide): 95.03MM **Privately Held**
Web: www.phoenixtank.com
SIC: 3443 Water tanks, metal plate

(G-545)
PPG ARCHITECTURAL FINISHES INC
Also Called: Porter Paints
5201 E Us Highway 36 Ste 209 (46123-7837)
PHONE......................317 745-0427
Lisa Dyer, *Mgr*
EMP: 3
SALES (corp-wide): 17.65B **Publicly Held**
Web: www.ppgpaints.com
SIC: 2851 Paints and allied products
HQ: Ppg Architectural Finishes, Inc.
 1 Ppg Pl
 Pittsburgh PA 15272
 412 434-3131

(G-546)
PPG INDUSTRIES INC
Also Called: PPG 4366
5201 E Us Highway 36 Ste 209 (46123-7837)
PHONE......................317 745-0427
Jason Ingram, *Mgr*
EMP: 4
SALES (corp-wide): 17.65B **Publicly Held**
Web: www.ppg.com
SIC: 2851 Paints and allied products
PA: Ppg Industries, Inc.
 1 Ppg Pl
 Pittsburgh PA 15272
 412 434-3131

(G-547)
REXNORD INDUSTRIES LLC
1304 Turfway Dr (46123-8385)
PHONE......................317 273-5500
Dean Vlasak, *Prin*
EMP: 52
SQ FT: 470,000
SALES (corp-wide): 6.25B **Publicly Held**
SIC: 3568 Couplings, shaft: rigid, flexible, universal joint, etc.
HQ: Rexnord Industries, Llc
 111 W Michigan St
 Milwaukee WI 53203
 414 643-3000

(G-548)
RLAY EXPRESS INC
230 Oxmoor Way Apt I (46123-1163)
PHONE......................754 265-8555
Romeo Saint Hilaire, *CEO*
EMP: 4 EST: 2019
SALES (est): 230.57K **Privately Held**
SIC: 3537 7389 Trucks, tractors, loaders, carriers, and similar equipment; Business Activities at Non-Commercial Site

(G-549)
ROGERS MARKETING & PRTG INC
Also Called: Sav-or Pack
7588 E County Road 100 S (46123-7536)
P.O. Box 42212 (46242-0212)
PHONE......................317 838-7203
Jeff Rogers, *Pr*
EMP: 4 EST: 1980
SQ FT: 9,000
SALES (est): 498.14K **Privately Held**
Web: www.rogersmp.com
SIC: 8742 2759 Marketing consulting services; Commercial printing, nec

(G-550)
SHALOM TRANS LLC
297 Shiloh Crossing Dr (46123-7162)
PHONE......................317 712-6765
Birikti Habtemikael, *Managing Member*
EMP: 41 EST: 2016
SALES (est): 5.06MM **Privately Held**
SIC: 3537 7389 Trucks: freight, baggage, etc.: industrial, except mining; Business services, nec

(G-551)
SPECTRUM PRINT AND MKTG LLC
7575 E County Road 150 S (46123-8193)
PHONE......................317 908-7471
Rhonda Dorton, *Owner*
EMP: 2 EST: 2015
SALES (est): 45.98K **Privately Held**
Web: www.spectrumprintandmarketing.com
SIC: 2752 Offset printing

(G-552)
TIMES LEADER PUBLICATIONS LLC
Also Called: Southside Times The
5252 E Main St (46123-9719)
PHONE......................317 300-8782
Brian Kelly, *CEO*
EMP: 10 EST: 2006
SALES (est): 810.47K **Privately Held**
Web: www.myiconmedia.com
SIC: 2711 Newspapers, publishing and printing

(G-553)
TMA ENTERPRISES INC
Also Called: Embroidme
7900 E Us Highway 36 Ste C (46123-7871)
PHONE......................317 272-0694
Thomas M Albert, *Pr*
EMP: 4 EST: 2006
SQ FT: 1,800
SALES (est): 435.83K **Privately Held**
Web: www.fullypromoted.com
SIC: 5949 2759 Sewing, needlework, and piece goods; Screen printing

(G-554)
TRACARON DESIGNS INC
6498 Crystal Springs Dr (46123-8731)
PHONE......................317 839-9006
Carol Clayton, *CEO*
Tracy Clayton, *Sec*
EMP: 2 EST: 1998
SALES (est): 158.32K **Privately Held**
SIC: 2434 Wood kitchen cabinets

(G-555)
TRANSMED ASSOCIATES INC (PA)
Also Called: Maxcare Bionics
8131 Kingston St Ste 700 (46123-9120)
P.O. Box 225 (46122-0225)
PHONE......................317 293-9993
Wilber Haynes, *Pr*
EMP: 1 EST: 2005
SQ FT: 2,000
SALES (est): 203.64K
SALES (corp-wide): 203.64K **Privately Held**
SIC: 3842 Limbs, artificial

(G-556)
US ENZYME LLC
137 Production Dr Ste A (46123-7083)
PHONE......................317 268-4975
EMP: 9 EST: 2009
SALES (est): 230.82K **Privately Held**
Web: www.usenzyme.com
SIC: 2869 Enzymes

(G-557)
WOODLAND MANUFACTURING & SUP
Also Called: Old Bob's
10896 E Us Highway 36 (46123-7916)
PHONE......................317 271-2266
Jonathan Williams, *Pr*
Shirley Williams, *Sec*
EMP: 16 EST: 1975
SQ FT: 10,000
SALES (est): 480.6K **Privately Held**
Web: www.oldbobs.com
SIC: 2452 5719 5211 5231 Prefabricated buildings, wood; Kitchenware; Lumber and other building materials; Paint, glass, and wallpaper stores

Bainbridge
Putnam County

(G-558)
AIRPLANE ANNUALS
517 E County Road 825 N (46105-9521)
PHONE......................817 528-6545
Mark Currie, *Owner*
EMP: 2 EST: 2008
SALES (est): 143.49K **Privately Held**
Web: www.airplane-annuals.com
SIC: 3721 Aircraft

(G-559)
BROCKS INCORPORATED
6541 N Us Highway 231 (46105-9681)
PHONE......................765 721-3068
Fount Brock, *Owner*
EMP: 6 EST: 2010
SALES (est): 316.21K **Privately Held**
SIC: 2411 Logging

(G-560)
CENTURY CONCRETE INC
Also Called: Century Memorial
3725 W Us Highway 36 (46105-9650)
PHONE......................765 739-6210
Martin Evens, *Pr*
Mary Jane Evens, *Sec*
EMP: 4 EST: 1961
SQ FT: 500
SALES (est): 53.26K **Privately Held**
Web: www.centuryconcreteinc.com
SIC: 3273 Ready-mixed concrete

(G-561)
CERTIFIED WELDING COMPANY INC
5355 E County Road 500 N (46105-9590)
PHONE......................765 522-3238
Phillip Stjohn, *Pr*
EMP: 3 EST: 1964
SQ FT: 800
SALES (est): 93.08K **Privately Held**
SIC: 7692 Welding repair

(G-562)
FENWICK MOTOR SPORTS
112 S Washington St (46105-9725)
PHONE......................765 522-1354
Rooney Fenwick, *Owner*
EMP: 4 EST: 2009
SALES (est): 180K **Privately Held**
SIC: 5012 3714 Automobiles and other motor vehicles; Motor vehicle parts and accessories

(G-563)
HARRIS STONE SERVICE INC
5581 N County Road 25 W (46105-9698)
PHONE......................765 522-6241
Gilbert Harris, *Pr*
William Davis Junior, *Pr*
Shirley F Harris, *VP*
Kenneth R Davies, *Sec*
EMP: 10 EST: 1954
SALES (est): 455.7K **Privately Held**
SIC: 1422 3274 Crushed and broken limestone; Lime

(G-564)
TIMBER ARTS LLC
3057 E County Road 800 N (46105-9545)
PHONE......................765 522-4121
Jim Crosbie, *Owner*
EMP: 1 EST: 1982
SQ FT: 5,000
SALES (est): 176.02K **Privately Held**
Web: www.timberarts.co.nz
SIC: 2431 Millwork

Bargersville
Johnson County

(G-565)
ELEMENT ARMAMENT LLC
5120 N 400 W (46106-9375)
PHONE......................317 442-7924
Daniel Hill, *Prin*
EMP: 4 EST: 2018
SALES (est): 249.96K **Privately Held**
Web: www.elementarmament.com
SIC: 2819 Industrial inorganic chemicals, nec

(G-566)
FIRED UP TEES LLC
6740 W 150 N (46106-9450)
PHONE......................317 412-4113
Meagan Modlin, *Prin*
EMP: 5 EST: 2018
SALES (est): 144.28K **Privately Held**
Web: www.fireduptees.net
SIC: 2759 Screen printing

(G-567)
HEARTLAND EXPRESS LLC
465 S Baldwin St (46106-8404)
PHONE......................317 422-1438
Dustin Martin, *Prin*
EMP: 1 EST: 2006
SALES (est): 55.77K **Privately Held**
Web: www.heartlandexpress.com
SIC: 2741 Miscellaneous publishing

Bargersville - Johnson County (G-568) GEOGRAPHIC SECTION

(G-568)
HUCKLEBERRY WINERY
3057 Amber Way (46106-8363)
PHONE...................317 850-4445
Cheryl Riddle, *Prin*
EMP: 5 EST: 2016
SALES (est): 110.26K **Privately Held**
SIC: 2084 Wines

(G-569)
KINNEY DEFENSE SOLUTIONS
933 Quarterhorse Run (46106-8752)
PHONE...................812 360-6189
EMP: 4 EST: 2013
SALES (est): 64.25K **Privately Held**
SIC: 3812 Defense systems and equipment

(G-570)
MOODY CANDLES LLC
4162 W Whiteland Rd (46106-9074)
PHONE...................317 535-2969
Laura Gieseking, *Prin*
EMP: 4 EST: 2018
SALES (est): 88.94K **Privately Held**
SIC: 3999 Candles

(G-571)
P & A MACHINE COMPANY INC
4985 Kerrington Blvd (46106-8311)
P.O. Box 3305 (46206-3305)
PHONE...................317 634-3673
Paul A Coffey, *Pr*
Lisa Coffey, *Sec*
EMP: 7 EST: 1980
SALES (est): 575.58K **Privately Held**
SIC: 3599 3469 Machine shop, jobbing and repair; Machine parts, stamped or pressed metal

(G-572)
PRECISION FIBER SOLUTIONS LLC
3950 W Smokey Row Rd (46106-9716)
PHONE...................317 421-9642
Andrew Aiello, *Prin*
EMP: 8 EST: 2016
SALES (est): 451.73K **Privately Held**
SIC: 3599 Industrial machinery, nec

(G-573)
SOJOURN TECHNOLOGIES INC
3485 W 100 N (46106-9583)
PHONE...................317 422-1254
Joseph Perrin, *Pr*
EMP: 3 EST: 1999
SALES (est): 140K **Privately Held**
SIC: 3579 Dictating machines

(G-574)
SORLEY HORNS LLC
7295 W 350 N (46106-9335)
PHONE...................317 258-2718
Darin Sorley, *Managing Member*
EMP: 1 EST: 2000
SALES (est): 126.05K **Privately Held**
Web: www.sorleyhorns.com
SIC: 3931 Musical instruments

Batesville
Ripley County

(G-575)
A & M TOOL INC
23102 Vote Rd (47006-9539)
PHONE...................812 934-6533
Albert A Rogier, *Pr*
Mary Rogier, *VP*
EMP: 8 EST: 1991
SALES (est): 795.86K **Privately Held**
Web: www.amtoolinc.com
SIC: 3599 3542 Machine shop, jobbing and repair; Presses: forming, stamping, punching, sizing (machine tools)

(G-576)
ALLEN MEDICAL SYSTEMS INC
1069 State Road 46 E (47006)
PHONE...................978 266-4286
EMP: 5
SALES (corp-wide): 14.81B **Publicly Held**
SIC: 3841 Surgical and medical instruments
HQ: Allen Medical Systems, Inc.
100 Discovery Way Ste 100 # 100
Acton MA 01720
978 263-7727

(G-577)
ALLEN MEDICAL SYSTEMS INC
Also Called: Baxter
93 N Coonhunters Rd (47006)
PHONE...................812 931-2512
EMP: 6
SALES (corp-wide): 14.81B **Publicly Held**
SIC: 3841 Surgical and medical instruments
HQ: Allen Medical Systems, Inc.
100 Discovery Way Ste 100 # 100
Acton MA 01720
978 263-7727

(G-578)
ANODYNE MEDICAL DEVICE INC (DH)
Also Called: Tridien Medical
1069 State Road 46 E (47006-7520)
PHONE...................954 340-0500
Bernie Laurel, *Pr*
Eric Bello, *
▲ EMP: 81 EST: 2006
SALES (est): 105.75MM
SALES (corp-wide): 14.81B **Publicly Held**
SIC: 2599 Hospital beds
HQ: Hill-Rom Holdings, Inc.
130 E Randolph St # 1000
Chicago IL 60601
312 819-7200

(G-579)
ANTIQUES AT 200 EAST LLC
1211 Lammers Pike (47006-7772)
PHONE...................812 933-0863
Larry Beard, *Mgr*
EMP: 2
Web: www.cornercurio.com
SIC: 3444 Sheet metalwork
PA: Antiques At 200 East, Llc
200 E Broad St
Quakertown PA 18951

(G-580)
BATESVILLE CASKET COMPANY LLC (HQ)
Also Called: Batesville Management Services
1 Batesville Blvd (47006-9229)
PHONE...................800 622-8373
Christopher H Trainor, *CEO*
Douglas Kunkel, *
John Zerkel, *
Mark Evans, *
Thomas J Miller, *
◆ EMP: 1300 EST: 1884
SQ FT: 700,000
SALES (est): 722.09MM
SALES (corp-wide): 940.38MM **Privately Held**
Web: www.batesville.com
SIC: 3995 Burial caskets
PA: BI Memorial Partners Llc
100 Frst Stmford Pl Ste 3
Stamford CT 06902
203 423-3935

(G-581)
BATESVILLE CASKET COMPANY INC
Also Called: Stamping Plant
100 Eastern Ave (47006)
PHONE...................812 934-7010
Dennis Knigga, *Genl Mgr*
EMP: 12
SALES (corp-wide): 940.38MM **Privately Held**
Web: www.batesville.com
SIC: 3995 Burial caskets
HQ: Batesville Casket Company, Llc
1 Batesville Blvd
Batesville IN 47006
800 622-8373

(G-582)
BATESVILLE INTERACTIVE LLC
Also Called: Batesville Interactive, Inc.
1 Batesville Blvd (47006-7756)
PHONE...................812 932-0164
Christopher H Trainor, *Ex Dir*
EMP: 4 EST: 2014
SALES (est): 889.14K **Publicly Held**
Web: www.batesville.com
SIC: 3995 Burial caskets
PA: Hillenbrand, Inc.
1 Batesville Blvd
Batesville IN 47006

(G-583)
BATESVILLE SERVICES LLC (HQ)
1 Batesville Blvd (47006-7756)
PHONE...................800 622-8373
Christopher H Trainor, *CEO*
Douglas Kunkel, *
EMP: 250 EST: 1998
SALES (est): 165.27MM
SALES (corp-wide): 940.38MM **Privately Held**
Web: www.batesville.com
SIC: 3995 Burial caskets
PA: BI Memorial Partners Llc
100 Frst Stmford Pl Ste 3
Stamford CT 06902
203 423-3935

(G-584)
BATESVILLE TOOL & DIE INC
177 Six Pine Ranch Rd (47006-9540)
PHONE...................812 934-5616
Jody Fledderman, *Pr*
Jody Fledderman, *Ch Bd*
Robert Holtel, *TLNG*
Gene Lambert, *VP Sls*
Jay Fledderman, *VP Mfg*
▲ EMP: 450 EST: 1978
SQ FT: 217,400
SALES (est): 82.44MM
SALES (corp-wide): 97.86MM **Privately Held**
Web: www.btdinc.com
SIC: 3469 3544 Stamping metal for the trade; Special dies and tools
PA: Btd Manufacturing, Inc.
177 Six Pine Ranch Rd
Batesville IN 47006
812 934-5616

(G-585)
BTD MANUFACTURING INC (PA)
177 Six Pine Ranch Rd (47006-9248)
PHONE...................812 934-5616
Jody Fledderman, *Pr*
Ron Fledderman, *Ch Bd*
Ronda Green, *Materials Vice President*
Gene Lambert, *VP Sls*
Jay Fledderman, *VP Mfg*
EMP: 8 EST: 2000
SALES (est): 97.86MM
SALES (corp-wide): 97.86MM **Privately Held**
Web: www.btdinc.com
SIC: 3469 3544 Stamping metal for the trade; Special dies and tools

(G-586)
ECKSTEIN WELDING & FABRICATION
11385 N Delaware Rd (47006-7995)
PHONE...................812 934-2059
Maurice Eckstein, *Pt*
Helen Eckstein, *Pt*
EMP: 2 EST: 1971
SALES (est): 86.55K **Privately Held**
SIC: 7692 0111 0212 0213 Welding repair; Wheat; Beef cattle, except feedlots; Hogs

(G-587)
ENHANCED MFG SOLUTIONS INC
23 Hillcrest Estates Dr (47006-9590)
PHONE...................812 932-1101
Mike Femeyer, *Prin*
EMP: 2 EST: 2009
SALES (est): 150.71K **Privately Held**
Web: www.enhancedmfg.com
SIC: 3999 Manufacturing industries, nec

(G-588)
ERTEL CELLARS WINERY INC
3794 E County Road 1100 N (47006-8562)
PHONE...................812 933-1500
Thomas Ertel, *Prin*
EMP: 6 EST: 2006
SALES (est): 469.37K **Privately Held**
Web: www.ertelcellarswinery.com
SIC: 2084 Wines

(G-589)
HILL-ROM INC (DH)
Also Called: Hill-Rom
1069 State Road 46 E (47006)
PHONE...................812 934-7777
◆ EMP: 2000 EST: 1929
SALES (est): 1.62B
SALES (corp-wide): 14.81B **Publicly Held**
Web: www.hillrom.com
SIC: 2599 7352 3842 Hospital beds; Medical equipment rental; Surgical appliances and supplies
HQ: Hill-Rom Holdings, Inc.
130 E Randolph St # 1000
Chicago IL 60601
312 819-7200

(G-590)
HILLENBRAND INC (PA)
Also Called: Hillenbrand
1 Batesville Blvd (47006)
PHONE...................812 931-5000
Kimberly K Ryan, *Pr*
Helen W Cornell, *
Robert M Vanhimbergen, *Sr VP*
Nicholas R Farrell, *Sr VP*
Aneesha Arora, *Chief Human Resources Officer*
EMP: 3800 EST: 1906
SALES (est): 2.83B **Publicly Held**
Web: hillenbrand.com
SIC: 3559 3556 3532 3089 Recycling machinery; Food products machinery; Separating machinery, mineral; Injection molding of plastics

(G-591)
HILLENBRAND LUXEMBOURG INC (DH)
1 Batesville Blvd (47006-7756)
PHONE...................812 934-7500
EMP: 33 EST: 2020
SALES (est): 23.66MM **Publicly Held**
Web: www.hillenbrand.com

GEOGRAPHIC SECTION
Bedford - Lawrence County (G-616)

SIC: 3995 Burial caskets
HQ: Milacron Llc
   10200 Alliance Rd Ste 200
   Cincinnati OH 45242

(G-592)
ITS PERSONAL LASER ENGRAVING
3243 County Rd 1150 E (47006)
PHONE..................812 934-6657
Debbie Rippetoe, *Owner*
EMP: 2 EST: 2003
SALES (est): 75.56K **Privately Held**
Web: www.itspersonal-online.com
SIC: 2796 Engraving platemaking services

(G-593)
JOANS TSHIRT PRINTING LLC
103 N Main St (47006-1245)
PHONE..................812 934-2616
EMP: 3 EST: 2020
SALES (est): 92.3K **Privately Held**
SIC: 2752 Commercial printing, lithographic

(G-594)
K-TRON AMERICA INC
1 Batesville Blvd (47006-7756)
PHONE..................812 934-7000
EMP: 95 EST: 2015
SALES (est): 802.82K
SALES (corp-wide): 488.94MM **Publicly Held**
SIC: 3532 Mining machinery
PA: Shoals Technologies Group, Inc.
   1400 Shoals Way
   Portland TN 37148
   615 451-1400

(G-595)
LE KEM OF INDIANA INC
1863 Lammers Pike (47006-7774)
PHONE..................812 932-5536
Esther Feagins, *CEO*
Esther Feagin, *CEO*
Paul Feagin, *Pr*
Alicia Powers, *Sec*
Michael Faegins, *Prin*
EMP: 4 EST: 1985
SQ FT: 25,000
SALES (est): 488.32K **Privately Held**
Web: www.lekem.com
SIC: 2899 Chemical preparations, nec

(G-596)
LINKEL COMPANY (PA)
1081 Morris Rd (47006-8490)
PHONE..................812 934-5190
EMP: 5 EST: 1983
SQ FT: 25,000
SALES (est): 1.98MM
SALES (corp-wide): 1.98MM **Privately Held**
Web: www.linkelco.com
SIC: 3531 Drags, road (construction and road maintenance equipment)

(G-597)
METALFOR LLC
1358 Tekulve Rd (47006-9187)
PHONE..................812 212-2248
EMP: 1 EST: 2007
SALES (est): 81.63K **Privately Held**
SIC: 3446 Architectural metalwork

(G-598)
NEW POINT STONE CO INC
Also Called: Napolean Quarry
8792 N County Road 300 W (47006-8750)
PHONE..................812 852-4325
Steve Wanstrath, *Mgr*
EMP: 8

SALES (corp-wide): 8.86MM **Privately Held**
Web: www.newpointstone.com
SIC: 1422 Crushed and broken limestone
PA: New Point Stone Co Inc
   992 S County Road 800 E
   Greensburg IN 47240
   812 663-2021

(G-599)
OLDENBURG PALLET INC
19349 Tony Rd (47006-9350)
PHONE..................812 933-0568
Douglas Davidson, *VP*
Billie Davidson, *Sec*
Delma Davidson, *Pr*
EMP: 7 EST: 1986
SQ FT: 4,580
SALES (est): 985.4K **Privately Held**
Web: www.fengshuigiftsandarts.com
SIC: 2448 2421 Pallets, wood; Lumber: rough, sawed, or planed

(G-600)
PRO PRINTS
394 Northside Dr (47006-7007)
PHONE..................812 932-3800
John Webber, *CEO*
EMP: 8 EST: 2012
SALES (est): 896.05K **Privately Held**
Web: www.pro-prints.com
SIC: 2752 Commercial printing, lithographic

(G-601)
RAVER READY MIX CONCRETE LLC
3013 N Huntersville Rd (47006-9542)
PHONE..................812 662-7900
EMP: 8 EST: 2004
SALES (est): 906.05K **Privately Held**
Web: www.raverconcrete.com
SIC: 3273 Ready-mixed concrete

(G-602)
RED FORGE INC
Also Called: Weld & Fabrication Shop
4552 State Road 46 E (47006-7533)
PHONE..................812 934-9641
Robert Maple, *CEO*
EMP: 3 EST: 2000
SQ FT: 4,500
SALES (est): 163.24K **Privately Held**
Web: www.redforgeweld.com
SIC: 7692 Welding repair

(G-603)
RICCA CHEMICAL COMPANY LLC
1490 Lammers Pike (47006-8631)
PHONE..................812 932-1161
Paul Brandon, *Mgr*
EMP: 27
SALES (corp-wide): 48.53MM **Privately Held**
Web: www.riccachemical.com
SIC: 2899 Chemical preparations, nec
PA: Ricca Chemical Company, Llc
   448 W Fork Dr
   Arlington TX 76012
   817 274-2912

(G-604)
ROCK CREEK 2019 INC
1646 Lammers Pike (47006-7752)
PHONE..................812 933-0388
Dale Meyer, *Pr*
Bernadette Meyer, *
▲ EMP: 45 EST: 1992
SQ FT: 55,000
SALES (est): 4.82MM **Privately Held**
SIC: 2511 Wood household furniture

(G-605)
RODNEY SLOAN LOGGING INC
Also Called: Sloan, Rodney Logging
1324 E Salem Rd (47006-8576)
PHONE..................812 934-5321
Rodney Sloan, *Owner*
EMP: 6 EST: 1976
SALES (est): 443.5K **Privately Held**
SIC: 2411 2421 Logging camps and contractors; Sawmills and planing mills, general

(G-606)
THE FINDLAY PUBLISHING CO
Also Called: Radio Station Wrbi
133 S Main St (47006-1344)
P.O. Box 201 (47006-0201)
PHONE..................812 222-8000
Ron Green, *Mgr*
EMP: 8
SALES (corp-wide): 20.16MM **Privately Held**
Web: www.wrbiradio.com
SIC: 4832 2711 Radio broadcasting stations; Newspapers
PA: Findlay Publishing Company, The (Inc)
   701 W Sandusky St
   Findlay OH
   419 422-4545

(G-607)
THE OFFICE SHOP INC (PA)
131 Batesville Shopping Vlg (47006-1299)
PHONE..................812 934-5611
TOLL FREE: 800
EMP: 20 EST: 1978
SALES (est): 2.23MM
SALES (corp-wide): 2.23MM **Privately Held**
Web: www.officeshop.net
SIC: 5999 5943 5712 5734 Business machines and equipment; Office forms and supplies; Office furniture; Computer and software stores

(G-608)
TIM WEBERDING WOODWORKING LLC
117 N Main St (47006-1245)
PHONE..................865 430-8811
Tim Weberding, *Owner*
EMP: 8 EST: 2016
SALES (est): 213.04K **Privately Held**
Web: www.timweberding.com
SIC: 2431 Millwork

(G-609)
TRADE & INDUSTRIAL SUPPLY INC
1101 N Pocket Rd (47006-8448)
PHONE..................812 537-1300
Randy Sizemore, *Brnch Mgr*
EMP: 1
SALES (corp-wide): 8.5MM **Privately Held**
Web: www.tisupply.com
SIC: 1321 Propane (natural) production
PA: Trade & Industrial Supply Inc
   40 Doughty Rd
   Lawrenceburg IN 47025
   812 537-1300

(G-610)
WEBERDINGS CARVING SHOP INC
1230 State Road 46 E (47006-9185)
PHONE..................812 934-3710
W G Weberding Junior, *Pr*
Terry Weberding, *Pr*
Timothy Weberding, *VP*
William G Weberding Junior, *Pr*
EMP: 10 EST: 1943
SQ FT: 28,000
SALES (est): 475.98K **Privately Held**

Web: www.weberding.com
SIC: 2499 2426 3543 2531 Carved and turned wood; Carvings, furniture: wood; Industrial patterns; Public building and related furniture

(G-611)
WERNER CUSTOM WOODWORKING
3589 W Napoleon Main St (47006-9631)
PHONE..................812 852-0029
Jacob Werner, *Prin*
EMP: 4 EST: 2019
SALES (est): 97.59K **Privately Held**
SIC: 2431 Millwork

Bath
Franklin County

(G-612)
YANKEE MADE WOODWORKS LLC
13141 Springfield Rd (47010-9710)
PHONE..................513 607-3152
James Dwight Johnson, *Admn*
EMP: 5 EST: 2016
SALES (est): 69.56K **Privately Held**
SIC: 2431 Millwork

Battle Ground
Tippecanoe County

(G-613)
OKOS FAMILY FARMS LLC
4505 Pretty Prairie Rd (47920-9701)
PHONE..................765 567-2750
EMP: 1 EST: 2006
SALES (est): 91.06K **Privately Held**
SIC: 3448 Farm and utility buildings

(G-614)
SPECIALTY MACHINE AND CNC INC
Also Called: Machine Shop
100 W 1250 S (47920-8023)
P.O. Box 192 (46923-0192)
PHONE..................765 346-0774
Zachary T Owen, *Owner*
EMP: 10 EST: 2017
SALES (est): 434.53K **Privately Held**
Web: www.specialtymachinecnc.com
SIC: 3599 Machine shop, jobbing and repair

Bedford
Lawrence County

(G-615)
37 PIPE & SUPPLY LLC
8987 S.R. 37 (47421)
PHONE..................812 275-5676
Joyce Mounce, *Managing Member*
EMP: 6 EST: 2015
SALES (est): 678.92K **Privately Held**
Web: www.37pipeandsupply.net
SIC: 3444 3317 3321 Pipe, sheet metal; Seamless pipes and tubes; Water pipe, cast iron

(G-616)
ACCURACY LASER FABRICATION LLC
2120 Dixie Hwy (47421)
PHONE..................812 322-6431
John Stith, *CEO*
EMP: 1 EST: 2018
SALES (est): 57.45K **Privately Held**
Web: www.accuracylaser.com

Bedford - Lawrence County (G-617)

GEOGRAPHIC SECTION

SIC: 3444 7389 3699 Sheet metalwork; Metal cutting services; Laser systems and equipment

(G-617)
ACE PRINTING
68 Miami Dr (47421-7639)
PHONE..............................812 275-3412
Paul V Sanders, *Prin*
EMP: 1 EST: 2002
SALES (est): 73.19K **Privately Held**
Web: www.aceprinting.net
SIC: 2752 Offset printing

(G-618)
ADEPT LLC
677 Guthrie Rd (47421-7900)
P.O. Box 335 (47420-0335)
PHONE..............................812 275-8899
EMP: 1 EST: 2004
SALES (est): 94.4K **Privately Held**
SIC: 3999 Manufacturing industries, nec

(G-619)
ARCHITECTURAL STONE SALES INC
Also Called: Bedford Cut Stone Co
1728 30th St (47421-5450)
PHONE..............................812 279-2421
Gary Evans, *Pr*
Mary C Evans, *
EMP: 13 EST: 1965
SALES (est): 920.19K **Privately Held**
Web: www.architecturalstonesales.com
SIC: 3281 Cut stone and stone products

(G-620)
ARCTIC GLACIER USA INC
2404 U St Bedford (47421)
PHONE..............................800 562-1990
EMP: 17
SALES (corp-wide): 576.1MM **Privately Held**
Web: www.arcticglacier.com
SIC: 2097 Manufactured ice
HQ: Arctic Glacier U.S.A., Inc.
307 23rd Street Ext
Pittsburgh PA 15215
800 562-1990

(G-621)
B & B SAWMILL INC
7142 Leatherwood Rd (47421-8784)
PHONE..............................812 834-5072
Lloyd J Beyers Ii, *Prin*
EMP: 9 EST: 2008
SALES (est): 463.23K **Privately Held**
SIC: 2421 Sawmills and planing mills, general

(G-622)
BEDFORD CRANE SERVICE LLC
957 J St (47421-2630)
P.O. Box 668 (47421-0668)
PHONE..............................812 275-4411
Jospeh W Elliott, *Pr*
Sherry Elliott, *
Joseph S Elliott, *
Thomas Elliott, *
EMP: 12 EST: 1902
SALES (est): 234.38K **Privately Held**
Web: www.iseco-bcs.com
SIC: 3441 Bridge sections, prefabricated, highway

(G-623)
BEDFORD LIMESTONE SUPPLIERS
1319 Breckenridge Rd (47421-1507)
P.O. Box 654 (47421-0654)
PHONE..............................812 279-9120
Robert E Robbins, *Pr*
Betty Robbins, *Sec*
EMP: 16 EST: 1969
SQ FT: 16,900
SALES (est): 969.37K **Privately Held**
Web: www.bedfordlimestone.com
SIC: 1422 Crushed and broken limestone

(G-624)
BEDFORD MACHINE & TOOL INC
2103 John Williams Blvd (47421-9800)
PHONE..............................812 275-1948
Paul Douglas Conrad, *Pr*
Lawrence Parsons, *
EMP: 46 EST: 1987
SQ FT: 94,000
SALES (est): 6.48MM **Privately Held**
Web: www.bedfordmachine.com
SIC: 3599 Machine shop, jobbing and repair

(G-625)
BEDFORD STONECRAFTERS INC
3160 Mitchell Rd (47421-5432)
PHONE..............................812 275-2646
Kenny Simpson, *Pr*
Missy Simpson, *VP*
EMP: 7 EST: 1999
SALES (est): 470.13K **Privately Held**
Web: www.bedfordchamber.com
SIC: 3281 Limestone, cut and shaped

(G-626)
CHASE BEFORD
1602 I St (47421-3859)
PHONE..............................812 277-7028
Jody Cobb, *Prin*
EMP: 1 EST: 2010
SALES (est): 82.36K **Privately Held**
SIC: 3578 Automatic teller machines (ATM)

(G-627)
CORAL DOG CANDLES
2412 M St (47421-5036)
PHONE..............................812 797-4050
Andrea Talbot, *Prin*
EMP: 4 EST: 2016
SALES (est): 55.12K **Privately Held**
SIC: 3999 Candles

(G-628)
CUMMINGS MACHINE SHOP
1200 K St (47421-2901)
PHONE..............................812 275-5542
EMP: 4 EST: 2019
SALES (est): 115K **Privately Held**
SIC: 3599 Machine shop, jobbing and repair

(G-629)
DARNER GOLDEN PUBLISHING LLC
202 Heltonville Rd W (47421-9385)
PHONE..............................812 675-0897
Donna Washburne, *Admn*
EMP: 5 EST: 2014
SALES (est): 69.54K **Privately Held**
SIC: 2741 Miscellaneous publishing

(G-630)
DIAMOND STONE TECHNOLOGIES INC
2237 Industrial Dr (47421-5652)
PHONE..............................812 276-6043
EMP: 15 EST: 2007
SQ FT: 10,000
SALES (est): 2.39MM **Privately Held**
Web: www.diamondstonetechnologies.com
SIC: 3545 Cutting tools for machine tools

(G-631)
DNA DESIGNS LLC
121 Robin Hood Ln (47421-6416)
PHONE..............................812 329-1310
Rebecca Delphia, *Prin*
EMP: 3 EST: 2020
SALES (est): 30.77K **Privately Held**
Web: www.dnastore.biz
SIC: 2759 Screen printing

(G-632)
E & H BRIDGE AND GRATING INC
1 Lavender Ln (47421-7464)
PHONE..............................812 277-8343
EMP: 9 EST: 1992
SALES (est): 691.89K **Privately Held**
SIC: 3499 3446 Fire- or burglary-resistive products; Gratings, tread: fabricated metal

(G-633)
E & H BRIDGE INC
8136 State Road 158 (47421-8595)
PHONE..............................812 279-2308
EMP: 3 EST: 1993
SALES (est): 335.8K **Privately Held**
Web: www.ehbridge.com
SIC: 3441 Fabricated structural metal

(G-634)
E & R FABRICATING INC
8854 State Road 37 (47421-8300)
PHONE..............................812 275-0388
Ernie Mccullough, *Pr*
Ernie Mc Cullough, *Pr*
Sam Bair, *Corporate Secretary*
EMP: 5 EST: 1987
SQ FT: 6,400
SALES (est): 455.62K **Privately Held**
SIC: 3444 1799 Sheet metalwork; Welding on site

(G-635)
EVANS LIMESTONE CO
1201 Limestone Dr (47421-9155)
P.O. Box 714 (47421-0714)
PHONE..............................812 279-9744
Steve Evans, *Pr*
Larry Evans, *
EMP: 18 EST: 1973
SQ FT: 18,000
SALES (est): 962.92K **Privately Held**
Web: www.evanslimestone.com
SIC: 3281 Cut stone and stone products

(G-636)
FLINN FRMS BDFORD FEED SEED IN
917 17th St (47421-4205)
PHONE..............................812 279-4136
David Flinn, *Pr*
Brad Flinn, *VP*
Linda Flinn, *Sec*
EMP: 6 EST: 1968
SALES (est): 660K **Privately Held**
Web: www.flinnfarms.com
SIC: 0115 0116 2048 5191 Corn; Soybeans; Livestock feeds; Animal feeds

(G-637)
GARYS WELDING & MACHINING LLC
Also Called: Gary's Welding and Machining
411 County Complex Rd (47421-7493)
PHONE..............................812 279-6780
Gary Earl, *Owner*
EMP: 3 EST: 1985
SQ FT: 2,600
SALES (est): 240.4K **Privately Held**
Web: www.lsasbestoslaw.com
SIC: 7692 3441 Welding repair; Fabricated structural metal

(G-638)
GENERAL MOTORS LLC
Also Called: General Motors
105 Gm Dr (47421-1558)
PHONE..............................812 279-7321
EMP: 365
Web: www.gm.com
SIC: 3363 Aluminum die-castings
HQ: General Motors Llc
300 Rnaissance Ctr Ste L1
Detroit MI 48243

(G-639)
GEO-FLO CORPORATION
905 Williams Park Dr (47421-6713)
PHONE..............................812 275-8513
Thomas E Miller, *Pr*
▲ EMP: 12 EST: 1988
SQ FT: 10,000
SALES (est): 2.33MM **Privately Held**
Web: www.geo-flo.com
SIC: 3585 1711 Refrigeration and heating equipment; Heating and air conditioning contractors

(G-640)
HARRISON CONCRETE
1218 7th St (47421-2328)
PHONE..............................812 275-6682
Travis Harrison, *Prin*
EMP: 2 EST: 2004
SALES (est): 118.38K **Privately Held**
Web: www.harrisonconcreteinc.com
SIC: 3273 Ready-mixed concrete

(G-641)
HOOSIER TIMES INC
Rainbow Printing
2139 16th St (47421-3003)
P.O. Box 97 (47421-0097)
PHONE..............................812 275-3372
Tony Strahl, *Genl Mgr*
EMP: 119
SALES (corp-wide): 3.28B **Publicly Held**
Web: www.heraldtimesonline.com
SIC: 2711 2752 Newspapers: publishing only, not printed on site; Commercial printing, lithographic
HQ: Hoosier Times, Inc.
1840 S Walnut St
Bloomington IN 47401
812 331-4270

(G-642)
IN-FAB INC
2030 John Williams Blvd (47421-9649)
PHONE..............................812 279-8144
Jay Mccolough, *Pr*
Ay Mccollough, *Pr*
EMP: 6 EST: 2012
SALES (est): 2.36MM **Privately Held**
Web: www.in-fabinc.com
SIC: 3441 Fabricated structural metal

(G-643)
INDIANA CUT STONE INC
616 Guthrie Rd (47421-7900)
P.O. Box 13 (47434-0013)
PHONE..............................812 275-0264
Kathy Baker Heckard, *Pr*
Don Baker, *Pr*
Ernie Baker, *VP*
Linda Baker, *Sec*
EMP: 18 EST: 1997
SALES (est): 2.44MM **Privately Held**
Web: www.indystone.com
SIC: 3281 Limestone, cut and shaped

(G-644)
INDIANA FABRIC SOLUTIONS INC
2030 John Williams Blvd (47421-9649)
PHONE..............................812 279-0255
Patricia Mccullough, *Pr*
Angela Mccullough, *VP*

GEOGRAPHIC SECTION Bedford - Lawrence County (G-671)

EMP: 29 EST: 2015
SALES (est): 2MM **Privately Held**
SIC: 2399 Automotive covers, except seat and tire covers

(G-645)
INDIANA LMSTONE ACQISITION LLC
Also Called: Indiana Lime Stone Co
7056 State Road 158 (47421-8584)
PHONE..................................812 275-5556
Matt Howard, *CEO*
EMP: 55
SALES (corp-wide): 2.1MM **Privately Held**
Web: www.indianalimestonecompany.com
SIC: 3281 1411 Limestone, cut and shaped; Limestone, dimension-quarrying
HQ: Indiana Limestone Acquisition, Llc
120 W 7th St Ste 210
Bloomington IN 47404
812 275-3341

(G-646)
INDIANA QUARRIERS & CARVERS
562 Kentucky Hollow Rd (47421-8013)
P.O. Box 389 (47464-0389)
PHONE..................................812 935-8383
John Steckling, *Pr*
EMP: 12 EST: 2011
SALES (est): 2.07MM **Privately Held**
Web: www.iqcstone.com
SIC: 1411 Dimension stone

(G-647)
INDIANA STEEL & ENGRG INC (PA)
957 J St (47421-2630)
P.O. Box 668 (47421-0668)
PHONE..................................812 275-3363
Joseph W Elliott, *Pr*
Joseph S Elliott, *
Thomas S Elliott, *
Laura Elliott, *
EMP: 29 EST: 1962
SQ FT: 50,000
SALES (est): 2.38MM
SALES (corp-wide): 2.38MM **Privately Held**
Web: www.iseco-bcs.com
SIC: 3441 3536 3444 Bridge sections, prefabricated, highway; Cranes, overhead traveling; Sheet metalwork

(G-648)
INDIANA STONE WORKS
11438 Us Highway 50 W (47421-8336)
PHONE..................................812 279-0448
Donovan D Short, *Pr*
Theresa Short, *Sec*
▼ EMP: 9 EST: 1990
SQ FT: 10,000
SALES (est): 862.88K **Privately Held**
SIC: 1411 3281 Limestone, dimension-quarrying; Cut stone and stone products

(G-649)
IRVING MATERIALS INC
Also Called: I M I
1307 Bundy Ln (47421-9382)
PHONE..................................812 275-7450
Eric Belth, *Brnch Mgr*
EMP: 8
SALES (corp-wide): 814.09MM **Privately Held**
Web: www.irvmat.com
SIC: 3273 Ready-mixed concrete
PA: Irving Materials, Inc.
8032 N State Road 9
Greenfield IN 46140
317 326-3101

(G-650)
J&K GENERATIONS
1233 Brown Station Rd (47421-8928)
PHONE..................................812 508-1094
Kallie Lively, *Pt*
Josh Lively, *Pt*
EMP: 3 EST: 2021
SALES (est): 99.01K **Privately Held**
SIC: 5169 3999 3411 Detergents and soaps, except specialty cleaning; Candles; Food and beverage containers

(G-651)
KELSIE PIERCE
234 Rawlins Mill Rd (47421-7648)
PHONE..................................812 279-1335
Kelsie Pierce, *Owner*
EMP: 1 EST: 1966
SALES (est): 70K **Privately Held**
SIC: 2411 Logging

(G-652)
KERNS SPEED SHOP
Also Called: Kern's Speed & Racing Products
203 Newton St (47421-1745)
PHONE..................................812 275-4289
Claude Kern, *Owner*
EMP: 2 EST: 1962
SALES (est): 118.11K **Privately Held**
SIC: 7538 3599 General automotive repair shops; Machine shop, jobbing and repair

(G-653)
KOPELOV CUT STONE INC
2321 39th St (47421-5605)
P.O. Box 983 (47421-0983)
PHONE..................................812 675-0099
Labe Kopelov, *Pr*
EMP: 5 EST: 2015
SALES (est): 99.22K **Privately Held**
Web: www.kopelovcutstone.com
SIC: 3281 Cut stone and stone products

(G-654)
LAND OF INDIANA INC
10 Pinewood Dr (47421-6684)
P.O. Box 157 (47421-0157)
PHONE..................................812 788-1560
Larry Morin, *Pr*
Melody Morin, *Sec*
EMP: 11 EST: 1993
SALES (est): 443.63K **Privately Held**
Web: www.land-of-indiana.com
SIC: 2435 6531 Hardwood veneer and plywood; Real estate brokers and agents

(G-655)
LARRYS MARINE CANVAS
2107 Park Ave (47421-4044)
PHONE..................................252 725-2902
EMP: 4 EST: 2013
SALES (est): 67.09K **Privately Held**
SIC: 2211 Canvas

(G-656)
LASERTECH INC
4684 Dixie Hwy (47421-8247)
PHONE..................................812 277-1321
EMP: 2 EST: 1994
SQ FT: 1,500
SALES (est): 165.05K **Privately Held**
Web: www.lasertech.com
SIC: 3955 7378 Print cartridges for laser and other computer printers; Computer maintenance and repair

(G-657)
MERRIMAN STEEL AND EQUIPMENT
Also Called: Merriman Kiln & Mill Service
10430 Tunnelton Rd (47421-7887)
PHONE..................................812 849-2784
Kenneth H Merriman, *Pr*
EMP: 5 EST: 1975
SQ FT: 20,000
SALES (est): 490.81K **Privately Held**
Web: www.merrimansteel.com
SIC: 3559 Kilns, cement

(G-658)
MICHAEL J MEYER D M D P C
1504 Dental Dr (47421-3574)
PHONE..................................812 275-7112
Michael Meyer, *Pr*
EMP: 8 EST: 2001
SALES (est): 525.7K **Privately Held**
SIC: 3843 Enamels, dentists'

(G-659)
NORLIGHTSPRESSCOM
762 State Road 458 (47421-7545)
PHONE..................................812 675-8054
Vorris D Justesen, *CEO*
Sammie L Justesen, *VP*
EMP: 5 EST: 2009
SALES (est): 248.86K **Privately Held**
Web: www.norlightspress.com
SIC: 2741 Miscellaneous publishing

(G-660)
POWELL WOODWORKING LLC
196 Bartlettsville Rd (47421-7946)
PHONE..................................812 279-5029
Darin Powell, *Prin*
EMP: 5 EST: 2018
SALES (est): 94.13K **Privately Held**
Web: www.powellwoodworking.net
SIC: 2431 Millwork

(G-661)
PYNCO INC
2605 35th St (47421-5525)
PHONE..................................812 275-0900
Bill Ansley, *COO*
EMP: 24 EST: 1987
SQ FT: 1,800
SALES (est): 2.2MM **Privately Held**
Web: www.pynco.com
SIC: 3728 8731 Aircraft parts and equipment, nec; Electronic research

(G-662)
QUICK TO FIX LLC
Also Called: Handyman and Tree Service
518 16th St (47421-3817)
PHONE..................................812 660-2044
Brian Barker, *Pr*
EMP: 1 EST: 2017
SALES (est): 95.17K **Privately Held**
SIC: 1389 Construction, repair, and dismantling services

(G-663)
RAINBOW PRINTING LLC
2139 16th St (47421-3003)
P.O. Box 97 (47421-0097)
PHONE..................................812 275-3372
EMP: 10 EST: 1994
SQ FT: 10,000
SALES (est): 2.01MM **Privately Held**
Web: www.indianaprinting.com
SIC: 2752 Offset printing

(G-664)
RC ENTERPRISES
2611 16th St 301 (47421-3503)
PHONE..................................812 279-2755
Randall Corwin, *Owner*
EMP: 2 EST: 1974
SALES (est): 70.47K **Privately Held**

SIC: 3915 Jewelers' materials and lapidary work

(G-665)
REAL WOOD WORKS
2802 North South Poor Farm Rd (47421-9272)
PHONE..................................812 277-1462
David Stoops, *Owner*
EMP: 2 EST: 1998
SALES (est): 130.94K **Privately Held**
SIC: 2431 5712 Interior and ornamental woodwork and trim; Cabinet work, custom

(G-666)
RECYCLING SERVICES INDIANA INC
Also Called: Newco Metals Processing
1202 Breckenridge Rd (47421-1506)
PHONE..................................812 279-8114
Gary Wade, *Pr*
Paul Boening, *
EMP: 37 EST: 1998
SALES (est): 8.43MM **Privately Held**
SIC: 3341 Aluminum smelting and refining (secondary)

(G-667)
RED GATE FARMS INC
Also Called: Carousel Winery
8987 State Road 37 (47421-8301)
PHONE..................................812 277-9750
Sue Wilson, *Pr*
EMP: 8 EST: 2005
SALES (est): 418.05K **Privately Held**
Web: www.redgatefarms.com
SIC: 2084 5921 Wines; Wine

(G-668)
RIGHTCOLORS LLC
2190 Coveyville Rd (47421-7265)
PHONE..................................812 675-8775
EMP: 4 EST: 2017
SALES (est): 148.19K **Privately Held**
Web: www.rightcolors.com
SIC: 2752 Commercial printing, lithographic

(G-669)
RIVERSIDE PRINTING CO
1407 I St (47421)
PHONE..................................812 275-1950
Michael L Chapman, *Owner*
EMP: 3 EST: 1972
SALES (est): 235.61K **Privately Held**
Web: www.riversideprinting.com
SIC: 2752 3953 2759 Offset printing; Marking devices; Engraving, nec

(G-670)
ROBERT D MEADOWS
3568 Peerless Rd (47421-8109)
PHONE..................................812 797-8294
Robert Meadows, *Owner*
EMP: 4 EST: 2014
SALES (est): 156.28K **Privately Held**
SIC: 3441 Fabricated structural metal

(G-671)
SAMCO INC
1000 U St (47421-2704)
P.O. Box 721 (47421-0721)
PHONE..................................812 279-8131
Marvin Stahl, *Pr*
EMP: 20 EST: 1974
SQ FT: 20,000
SALES (est): 1.79MM **Privately Held**
Web: www.samcoinc.net
SIC: 3469 Stamping metal for the trade

Bedford - Lawrence County (G-672)

(G-672)
SIGMA STEEL INC (PA)
Also Called: Fab Con
1218 5th St (47421-2304)
P.O. Box 305 (47421-0305)
PHONE....................812 275-4489
Dean Tackett, *Pr*
Richard Derrington, *VP*
Jerry Covey, *Sec*
EMP: 25 **EST:** 1978
SQ FT: 7,800
SALES (est): 2.39MM
SALES (corp-wide): 2.39MM **Privately Held**
Web: www.sigmasteel.com
SIC: 3449 3441 3448 3446 Curtain walls for buildings, steel; Building components, structural steel; Prefabricated metal buildings and components; Architectural metalwork

(G-673)
SMITH GROUP PRECISION LLC
Also Called: Panther Werks
2124 Dixie Hwy (47421-8226)
PHONE....................855 927-6224
EMP: 7 **EST:** 2020
SALES (est): 270.4K **Privately Held**
SIC: 3484 Small arms

(G-674)
STANDISH STEEL INC
280 Standish Steel Dr (47421-6866)
PHONE....................812 834-5255
James K Standish, *Pr*
Michael Waggoner, *Assistant Finance*
Laura Waggoner, *Sec*
EMP: 12 **EST:** 1978
SQ FT: 15,560
SALES (est): 975.83K **Privately Held**
Web: www.standishsteelinc.com
SIC: 3599 Machine shop, jobbing and repair

(G-675)
STONE CITY IRONWORKS INC
1519 G St (47421-3827)
PHONE....................812 279-3023
EMP: 30 **EST:** 1995
SALES (est): 4.89MM **Privately Held**
Web: www.stonecityironworks.com
SIC: 3441 Fabricated structural metal

(G-676)
STONE CITY PRODUCTS INC
1206 7th St (47421-2328)
PHONE....................812 275-3373
Stewart D Rariden, *Pr*
Robert Burgess, *
Andrew Rariden, *
Denise Maple, *
▼ **EMP:** 87 **EST:** 1946
SQ FT: 80,000
SALES (est): 24.15MM **Privately Held**
Web: www.stonecityproducts.com
SIC: 3469 Stamping metal for the trade

(G-677)
TEK PRINT LLC
812 14th St (47421-3326)
PHONE....................812 336-2525
Elena Hartzell, *Prin*
EMP: 2 **EST:** 2013
SALES (est): 149.92K **Privately Held**
SIC: 2752 Offset printing

(G-678)
THORNES HOMES INC
3211 State Road 37 S (47421-9105)
PHONE....................812 275-4656
John David Thorne, *Pr*
Kathy Thorne, *Sec*
EMP: 7 **EST:** 1982
SQ FT: 2,700
SALES (est): 668.98K **Privately Held**
Web: www.thorneshomes.com
SIC: 5271 7699 2451 6531 Mobile home dealers; Mobile home repair; Mobile homes ; Broker of manufactured homes, on site

(G-679)
UNION OPTICAL EYECARE CTR INC
3343 Michael Ave (47421-3535)
PHONE....................812 279-3466
EMP: 5 **EST:** 2010
SALES (est): 216.58K **Privately Held**
Web: www.unionoptical.net
SIC: 8042 3827 Offices and clinics of optometrists; Glasses, field or opera

(G-680)
USA BASSIN LLC
P.O. Box 1126 (47421-1126)
PHONE....................812 276-8043
Kevin Yearly, *Prin*
EMP: 10 **EST:** 2010
SALES (est): 198.06K **Privately Held**
Web: www.usabassin.com
SIC: 2077 Fish oil

(G-681)
W F MEYERS COMPANY INC
1008 13th St (47421-3202)
P.O. Box 426 (47421-0426)
PHONE....................812 275-4485
Kenneth G Barnes, *Pr*
Mary Albright Barnes, *
Patricia J Hedrick, *
John L Keltner Junior, *Contrlr*
▲ **EMP:** 50 **EST:** 1888
SQ FT: 10,800
SALES (est): 4.31MM **Privately Held**
Web: www.wfmeyers.com
SIC: 3545 Diamond cutting tools for turning, boring, burnishing, etc.

(G-682)
WHITNEY TOOL COMPANY INC
906 R St (47421-2497)
PHONE....................812 275-4491
Linda Flynn, *Pr*
Geri Espy, *
Bob O'callaghan, *Secretary General*
Euretta Griggs, *
Sandi Hudson, *
EMP: 30 **EST:** 1970
SQ FT: 17,200
SALES (est): 4.65MM **Privately Held**
Web: www.whitneytool.com
SIC: 3545 Cutting tools for machine tools

(G-683)
WILSONS LOCKER & PROC PLANT
Also Called: Wilsons Slaughtering & Proc
2018 Blue Spring Caverns Rd (47421-8213)
PHONE....................812 358-2632
Ed Branum, *Mgr*
EMP: 2 **EST:** 1892
SALES (est): 85.48K **Privately Held**
SIC: 0751 2013 2011 Slaughtering: custom livestock services; Sausages and other prepared meats; Meat packing plants

(G-684)
WOODS CABINETS
2615 Broadview Dr (47421-5266)
PHONE....................812 279-6494
Jack Woods, *Prin*
EMP: 1 **EST:** 2006
SALES (est): 112.55K **Privately Held**
SIC: 2434 Wood kitchen cabinets

Beech Grove
Marion County

(G-685)
ADM MILLING CO
Also Called: ADM
854 Bethel Ave (46107-1142)
P.O. Box 610 (46107-0610)
PHONE....................317 783-3321
EMP: 8
SALES (corp-wide): 93.94B **Publicly Held**
Web: www.adm.com
SIC: 2041 Flour mills, cereal (except rice)
HQ: Adm Milling Co.
4666 E Faries Pkwy
Decatur IL 62526
913 491-9400

(G-686)
ARCHER-DANIELS-MIDLAND COMPANY
Also Called: ADM
854 Bethel Ave (46107-1142)
P.O. Box 610 (46107-0610)
PHONE....................317 783-3321
Kandi Kaiser, *Brnch Mgr*
EMP: 4
SALES (corp-wide): 93.94B **Publicly Held**
Web: www.adm.com
SIC: 2041 Flour and other grain mill products
PA: Archer-Daniels-Midland Company
77 W Wacker Dr Ste 4600
Chicago IL 60601
312 634-8100

(G-687)
BUNDOO LABORATORIES LLC ◆
17 N 5th Ave (46107-1325)
PHONE....................317 978-5574
Sharita Bundoo, *CEO*
EMP: 1 **EST:** 2023
SALES (est): 72.15K **Privately Held**
SIC: 8734 2899 Testing laboratories; Drug testing kits, blood and urine

(G-688)
BUSINESS ART & DESIGNS INC
402 Main St (46107-1838)
PHONE....................317 782-9108
Bart Heldman, *Pr*
EMP: 4 **EST:** 1992
SQ FT: 1,700
SALES (est): 431.04K **Privately Held**
Web: www.businessart.com
SIC: 7336 3993 2752 Graphic arts and related design; Signs and advertising specialties; Transfers, decalcomania or dry: lithographed

(G-689)
FISCHER WOODCRAFT INCORPORATED
1024 Timber Grove Pl (46107-3002)
PHONE....................317 627-6035
Glenn D Fischer, *CEO*
EMP: 4 **EST:** 1991
SALES (est): 420K **Privately Held**
SIC: 2431 Woodwork, interior and ornamental, nec

(G-690)
GOOD MORNING PUBLISHING CO
415 Main St (46107-1837)
PHONE....................317 782-8381
Marcia Wolfla, *Pr*
EMP: 1 **EST:** 1997
SALES (est): 73K **Privately Held**
SIC: 2731 Book publishing

(G-691)
HOOSIER TIMES INC
Also Called: Southside Times
301 Main St (46107-1835)
PHONE....................812 332-4401
Roger Huntzinger, *Mgr*
EMP: 10
SALES (corp-wide): 3.28B **Publicly Held**
Web: www.heraldtimesonline.com
SIC: 2711 Newspapers, publishing and printing
HQ: Hoosier Times, Inc.
1840 S Walnut St
Bloomington IN 47401
812 331-4270

(G-692)
INDY CONTROL CORPORATION
308 Main St (46107-1836)
PHONE....................317 787-4639
Anthony White, *Pr*
EMP: 7 **EST:** 2006
SALES (est): 816.75K **Privately Held**
Web: www.indycontrol.com
SIC: 3699 Electrical equipment and supplies, nec

(G-693)
J P CORPORATION
227 Main St (46107-1883)
PHONE....................317 783-1000
Wanda J Petty, *Pr*
James F Petty, *Ch Bd*
Charles K Petty, *VP*
Mark Petty, *VP*
Tina Matthis, *Sec*
EMP: 9 **EST:** 1964
SQ FT: 3,200
SALES (est): 1.48MM **Privately Held**
Web: www.jp-corp.net
SIC: 3599 3544 7389 Machine shop, jobbing and repair; Special dies and tools; Engraving service

(G-694)
JCI JONES CHEMICALS INC
600 Bethel Ave (46107-1356)
PHONE....................317 787-8382
Tim Beusey, *Mgr*
EMP: 21
SALES (corp-wide): 196.9MM **Privately Held**
Web: www.jcichem.com
SIC: 2812 2819 Chlorine, compressed or liquefied; Industrial inorganic chemicals, nec
PA: Jci Jones Chemicals, Inc.
1765 Ringling Blvd
Sarasota FL 34236
941 330-1537

(G-695)
JWCANDLE CO LLC
4344 Malden Ct Apt C (46107-2930)
PHONE....................317 661-1066
Latiya Webb, *Managing Member*
EMP: 1 **EST:** 2020
SALES (est): 52.3K **Privately Held**
SIC: 3999 Candles

(G-696)
KATALYST CORPORATION
Also Called: Katalyst Industrial Coatings
176 Schaff St (46107-1923)
PHONE....................317 783-6500
Kenny Westell, *Owner*
EMP: 3 **EST:** 2008
SQ FT: 8,000
SALES (est): 733.1K **Privately Held**
Web: www.katalystcorporation.com

GEOGRAPHIC SECTION

Berne - Adams County (G-721)

SIC: 2851 Paints and allied products

(G-697)
KRUKEMEIER MACHINE & TOOL CO
4949 Subway St (46107-1358)
PHONE..............................317 784-7042
Jeff J Krukemieier, *VP*
EMP: 27 EST: 1946
SQ FT: 13,500
SALES (est): 2.64MM **Privately Held**
Web: www.krukemeier.com
SIC: 3544 3545 3469 Special dies and tools; Gauge blocks; Metal stampings, nec

(G-698)
L & L ENGINEERING CO INC
4925 Subway St (46107-1358)
PHONE..............................317 786-6886
Jerry Kuner, *Pr*
EMP: 8 EST: 1952
SQ FT: 6,000
SALES (est): 840.41K **Privately Held**
Web: l-l-engineering-co-inc.business.site
SIC: 3599 7692 3544 Machine shop, jobbing and repair; Welding repair; Special dies, tools, jigs, and fixtures

(G-699)
L & R MACHINE CO INC
3136 S Emerson Ave (46107-3337)
P.O. Box 160 (46107-0160)
PHONE..............................317 787-7251
Robert D Litson, *Pr*
Barbara Litson-fugate, *VP*
EMP: 5 EST: 1960
SQ FT: 7,000
SALES (est): 374.15K **Privately Held**
SIC: 3599 7692 Machine shop, jobbing and repair; Welding repair

(G-700)
NATURALEE TWISTED LLC
5 Kiefer Ct (46107-2513)
PHONE..............................317 523-1012
EMP: 1 EST: 2021
SALES (est): 39.69K **Privately Held**
Web: www.naturaleetwisted.com
SIC: 3999 Hair and hair-based products

(G-701)
RAY MARKETING LLC
Also Called: PCI By Ray Marketing
619 Memorial Dr (46107-2230)
PHONE..............................317 782-0940
EMP: 5 EST: 2012
SALES (est): 122.91K **Privately Held**
SIC: 3993 Signs and advertising specialties

Bennington
Switzerland County

(G-702)
BYLER SAWMILL
9435 State Road 250 (47011-1515)
PHONE..............................812 577-5761
Daniel Byler, *Owner*
EMP: 8 EST: 2005
SALES (est): 475.14K **Privately Held**
SIC: 2421 7389 Sawmills and planing mills, general; Business Activities at Non-Commercial Site

Berne
Adams County

(G-703)
AMISH COUNTRY POPCORN INC
5433 S 150 E (46711-9157)
PHONE..............................260 589-8513
Brian Lehman, *CEO*
EMP: 20 EST: 1980
SALES (est): 1.89MM **Privately Held**
Web: www.amishcountrypopcorn.com
SIC: 2099 5145 Popcorn, packaged: except already popped; Popcorn and supplies

(G-704)
ANNIES PUBLISHING LLC
Also Called: True Colors Pubg & Design
306 E Parr Rd (46711-1138)
P.O. Box 5000 (75755-5000)
PHONE..............................260 589-4000
▲ EMP: 211 EST: 1995
SALES (est): 44.86MM
SALES (corp-wide): 47.93MM **Privately Held**
Web: www.drgnetwork.com
SIC: 5961 2732 Catalog sales; Book printing
PA: Drg Management Corporation
    269 S Jefferson St
    Berne IN 46711
    260 589-4000

(G-705)
BERNE LOCKER STORAGE
206 High St (46711-1538)
PHONE..............................260 589-2806
Donald Neuenschwand, *Owner*
EMP: 5 EST: 1953
SALES (est): 302.9K **Privately Held**
SIC: 2011 Meat packing plants

(G-706)
CITY OF BERNE
428 Wind Ridge Trl (46711-2375)
PHONE..............................260 849-4038
Gwen Muller, *Brnch Mgr*
EMP: 2
Web: www.cityofberne.com
SIC: 3911 Cigar and cigarette accessories
PA: City Of Berne
    158 W Franklin St
    Berne IN 46711
    260 589-8526

(G-707)
CTS CORPORATION
CTS Resistor/Electrocomponents
406 E Parr Rd (46711-1271)
PHONE..............................574 293-7511
Dave Poole, *Brnch Mgr*
EMP: 3
SALES (corp-wide): 550.42MM **Publicly Held**
Web: www.ctscorp.com
SIC: 3613 Switchgear and switchboard apparatus
PA: Cts Corporation
    4925 Indiana Ave
    Lisle IL 60532
    630 577-8800

(G-708)
D R G PUBLISHING
306 E Parr Rd (46711-1138)
PHONE..............................260 589-4000
EMP: 14 EST: 2019
SALES (est): 207.89K **Privately Held**
Web: www.drgnetwork.com
SIC: 2741 Miscellaneous publishing

(G-709)
DYNAMIC RESOURCE GROUP INC
Also Called: DRG
269 S Jefferson St (46711-2159)
PHONE..............................260 589-4000
Roger Muselman, *Ch Bd*
Chuck Croft, *CEO*
Thomas C Muselman, *Pr*
Karen E Thomas, *Sec*
Tyler Kitt, *Prin*
EMP: 26 EST: 1998
SALES (est): 1.48MM **Privately Held**
SIC: 2721 Magazines: publishing and printing

(G-710)
EP GRAPHICS INC (HQ)
Also Called: Mignone Communications
169 S Jefferson St (46711-2157)
PHONE..............................877 589-2145
Tyler N Kitt, *Pr*
Thomas C Muselman, *
Roger C Muselman, *
▲ EMP: 155 EST: 1926
SQ FT: 200,000
SALES (est): 47.5MM **Privately Held**
Web: www.epgraphics.com
SIC: 2752 Offset printing
PA: Drg Holdings, Llc
    169 S Jefferson St
    Berne IN 46711

(G-711)
FCC (ADAMS) LLC (HQ)
Also Called: FCC North America
936 E Parr Rd (46711-1267)
PHONE..............................260 589-8555
Shinsuke Kambara, *Pr*
▲ EMP: 356 EST: 2003
SALES (est): 109.6MM **Privately Held**
Web: www.fcc-na.com
SIC: 3714 Clutches, motor vehicle
PA: F.C.C.Co., Ltd.
    7000-36, Hosoechonakagawa,
    Hamana-Ku
    Hamamatsu SZO 431-1

(G-712)
GYPSY MOON RAGDOLLS INC
423 Wabash St (46711-2021)
PHONE..............................260 589-2852
Tamela Christian, *Pr*
EMP: 2 EST: 2002
SALES (est): 120.06K **Privately Held**
SIC: 2621 Stationary, envelope and tablet papers

(G-713)
HAINES ENGINEERING INC
6262 S 550 E (46711-9227)
PHONE..............................260 589-3388
Norman Haines, *Owner*
EMP: 7 EST: 1956
SALES (est): 756.09K **Privately Held**
Web: www.hainesengineering.com
SIC: 3523 3534 Elevators, farm; Elevators and moving stairways

(G-714)
HITZER INC
269 E Main St (46711-1209)
PHONE..............................260 589-8536
Dean Lehman, *Pr*
Claren Lehman, *Treas*
Cindy Lehman, *Sec*
EMP: 16 EST: 1975
SQ FT: 10,200
SALES (est): 798.85K **Privately Held**
Web: www.hitzer.com
SIC: 3433 2542 Stoves, wood and coal burning; Racks, merchandise display or storage: except wood

(G-715)
J D DIGGING
2636 E State Road 218 (46711-9121)
PHONE..............................260 589-2984
Jerry Double, *Owner*
EMP: 1 EST: 2000
SALES (est): 98.2K **Privately Held**
SIC: 3531 Bulldozers (construction machinery)

(G-716)
JL MANFCTURING FABRICATION INC
Also Called: J L Mfg & Fab
3633 E 800 S (46711-9201)
PHONE..............................260 589-3723
Shirley Lehman, *Pr*
EMP: 2 EST: 1991
SALES (est): 205.76K **Privately Held**
SIC: 3549 3523 Wiredrawing and fabricating machinery and equipment, ex. die; Farm machinery and equipment

(G-717)
K&M FASTENERS LLC
365 W Compromise St (46711-1419)
PHONE..............................260 525-8989
Mark Morgan, *Prin*
EMP: 5 EST: 2017
SALES (est): 101.47K **Privately Held**
SIC: 3965 Fasteners

(G-718)
MAFCO & POSEIDON BARGE
750 E Parr Rd (46711-1269)
PHONE..............................260 589-9000
EMP: 6 EST: 2014
SALES (est): 163.34K **Privately Held**
Web: www.poseidonbarge.com
SIC: 3462 Iron and steel forgings

(G-719)
MICRO-PRECISION OPERATIONS
525 Berne St (46711-1246)
PHONE..............................260 589-2136
William Bertke, *General Vice President*
EMP: 17 EST: 1960
SQ FT: 120,000
SALES (est): 754.41K **Privately Held**
Web: www.micromaticllc.com
SIC: 3625 3829 3549 3593 Actuators, industrial; Measuring and controlling devices, nec; Assembly machines, including robotic; Fluid power cylinders and actuators

(G-720)
MICROMATIC LLC (PA)
525 Berne St (46711-1298)
PHONE..............................260 589-2136
Rick Bush, *CEO*
Richard A Bush, *
Gregory Myer, *
▼ EMP: 83 EST: 2005
SQ FT: 100,000
SALES (est): 18.29MM
SALES (corp-wide): 18.29MM **Privately Held**
Web: www.micromaticllc.com
SIC: 3599 3593 Custom machinery; Fluid power cylinders and actuators

(G-721)
O & R PRECISION GRINDING INC
225 Heritage Trl (46711)
PHONE..............................260 368-9394
Joshua Oswalt, *Prin*
Joshua Oswalt, *Pr*
EMP: 38 EST: 1978
SALES (est): 4.69MM **Privately Held**
Web: www.orprecision.com

SIC: 3544 7692 Special dies and tools; Welding repair

(G-722)
POSEIDON LLC
Also Called: Poseidon Barge
725 E Parr Rd (46711-1270)
PHONE..................................260 422-8767
Mary Habegger-fox, *CEO*
Donnie Fain, *CEO*
Mary Habegger-fox, *Pr*
▲ **EMP:** 117 **EST:** 1986
SQ FT: 7,200
SALES (est): 13.91MM **Privately Held**
Web: www.poseidonbarge.com
SIC: 7353 3731 3441 3471 Heavy construction equipment rental; Shipbuilding and repairing; Fabricated structural metal; Finishing, metals or formed products

(G-723)
RTX CORPORATION
917 Liechty Rd (46711-1262)
PHONE..................................260 589-7207
EMP: 360
SALES (corp-wide): 68.92B **Publicly Held**
Web: www.rtx.com
SIC: 3724 Aircraft engines and engine parts
PA: Rtx Corporation
1000 Wilson Blvd
Arlington VA 22209
781 522-3000

(G-724)
SANTOS HERRERA
Also Called: Herrera Seamless Gutters
654 Fulton St (46711-2320)
PHONE..................................260 849-3454
Santos Herrera, *Owner*
EMP: 10 **EST:** 2020
SALES (est): 111K **Privately Held**
SIC: 1389 Construction, repair, and dismantling services

(G-725)
SCHWARTZ MANUFACTURING INC
Also Called: Schwartz Elmer D Mfg Co
1261 W 200 S (46711-9779)
P.O. Box 124 (46711-0124)
PHONE..................................260 589-3865
Elmer D Schwartz, *Pr*
Emma Schwartz, *Sec*
▲ **EMP:** 4 **EST:** 1968
SALES (est): 317.73K **Privately Held**
SIC: 0191 3999 5941 General farms, primarily crop; Candles; Bait and tackle

(G-726)
SMITH BROTHERS BERNE INC (PA)
356 Monroe St (46711-1266)
P.O. Box 270 (46711-0270)
PHONE..................................260 589-2131
S W Lehman, *Pr*
Frederick A Lehman, *
R Muselman, *
Thomas Muselman, *
▲ **EMP:** 505 **EST:** 1926
SQ FT: 380,000
SALES (est): 48.77MM
SALES (corp-wide): 48.77MM **Privately Held**
Web: www.smithbrothersfurniture.com
SIC: 2512 Upholstered household furniture

(G-727)
SPORT FORM INC
151 W Main St (46711-1548)
PHONE..................................260 589-2200
Haidi Fear, *Pr*
Ladonna Habegger, *Pr*
EMP: 3 **EST:** 1989

SQ FT: 2,000
SALES (est): 240.07K **Privately Held**
Web: www.gotosportform.com
SIC: 2396 5136 5137 Screen printing on fabric articles; Sportswear, men's and boys'; Sportswear, women's and children's

(G-728)
ST HENRY TILE CO INC
Also Called: Berne Ready Mix
155 E Buckeye St (46711)
P.O. Box 29 (46711)
PHONE..................................260 589-2880
Gene Subler, *Brnch Mgr*
EMP: 27
SQ FT: 15,000
SALES (corp-wide): 24.3MM **Privately Held**
Web: www.sthenrytileco.com
SIC: 3271 5211 3273 Blocks, concrete or cinder: standard; Cement; Ready-mixed concrete
PA: The St Henry Tile Co Inc
281 W Washington St
Saint Henry OH 45883
419 678-4841

(G-729)
SWISS WOODWORKING LLC
371 W 500 S (46711-9709)
PHONE..................................260 849-9669
Melvin Schwartz, *Prin*
EMP: 6 **EST:** 2008
SALES (est): 128.31K **Privately Held**
SIC: 2431 Millwork

(G-730)
WEAVER LOGGING INCORPORATED
2896 West St (46711)
PHONE..................................260 589-9985
Tex Weaver, *Owner*
EMP: 2 **EST:** 2005
SALES (est): 237.22K **Privately Held**
SIC: 2411 Logging camps and contractors

(G-731)
WICKEY CANVAS OUTDOOR COOKING
747 E 350 S (46711)
PHONE..................................260 223-8890
Stephen H Wickey, *Owner*
EMP: 1 **EST:** 2009
SALES (est): 56.68K **Privately Held**
SIC: 2394 Canvas and related products

Beverly Shores
Porter County

(G-732)
SPEEDHOOK SPECIALISTS INC
845 E Lake Front Dr (46301-0108)
P.O. Box 617 (46301-0617)
PHONE..................................219 378-6369
Michael Grynecki, *CEO*
Michael Grynecki, *Pr*
Melanie Germek, *Admn*
EMP: 4 **EST:** 1989
SALES (est): 424.52K **Privately Held**
Web: www.speedhook.com
SIC: 5099 3999 Lifesaving and survival equipment (non-medical); Feathers and feather products

Bicknell
Knox County

(G-733)
CUSTOM INSPIRATIONAL SIGNS
12008 E Ragsdale Rd (47512-8017)
PHONE..................................315 715-1893
Paul Askew, *Prin*
EMP: 4 **EST:** 2019
SALES (est): 46.08K **Privately Held**
SIC: 3993 Signs and advertising specialties

(G-734)
HERMETIC COIL CO INC
Also Called: Herco
12005 E Davis Ln (47512-9681)
P.O. Box 219 (47512-0219)
PHONE..................................812 735-2400
David Barton, *CEO*
Debra J Barton, *
EMP: 27 **EST:** 1955
SQ FT: 15,000
SALES (est): 2.65MM **Privately Held**
Web: www.illprec.com
SIC: 3544 3559 3677 Special dies and tools; Plastics working machinery; Electronic coils and transformers

(G-735)
M&M FABRICATION LLC
Also Called: Basiloid Products
7382 Russell Dr (47512-9666)
PHONE..................................812 692-5511
Rob French, *Admn*
EMP: 20 **EST:** 2011
SALES (est): 1.99MM **Privately Held**
SIC: 3441 Fabricated structural metal

(G-736)
ON THE BALL RMDLG & REPR LLP
212 W 9th St (47512-1222)
PHONE..................................812 910-9408
Hali Greenlee, *Pt*
EMP: 2
SALES (est): 72.16K **Privately Held**
SIC: 1389 Construction, repair, and dismantling services

(G-737)
SCEPTER INC
6467 N Scepter Rd (47512-8228)
PHONE..................................812 735-2600
John Vulvac, *Brnch Mgr*
EMP: 13
Web: www.scepterinc.com
SIC: 3334 3341 Primary aluminum; Secondary nonferrous metals
PA: Scepter, Inc
1485 Scepter Ln
Waverly TN 37185

Birdseye
Dubois County

(G-738)
CAMPBELL LOGGING LLC
9100 W State Road 64 (47513-0017)
PHONE..................................812 972-6280
Jerrud Campbell, *Prin*
EMP: 6 **EST:** 2017
SALES (est): 180.95K **Privately Held**
SIC: 2411 Logging camps and contractors

Bloomfield
Greene County

(G-739)
A J BROWN ARMS COMPANY
709 N Washington St (47424-1043)
PHONE..................................812 384-1056
Alan J Brown, *Owner*
EMP: 1 **EST:** 1983
SALES (est): 65.51K **Privately Held**
Web: www.ajbrownarms.com
SIC: 3999 Badges, metal: policemen, firemen, etc.

(G-740)
BLOOMFIELD MFG CO INC
Also Called: Kant Slam Door Check Company
46 W Spring St (47424-1473)
P.O. Box 228 (47424-0228)
PHONE..................................812 384-4441
E Austin Harrah, *CEO*
Steve Workman, *
Steve Dowden, *
Lyndal Schantz, *
Vanessa Harrah, *Stockholder*
◆ **EMP:** 40 **EST:** 1895
SQ FT: 55,000
SALES (est): 4.84MM **Privately Held**
Web: www.hi-lift.com
SIC: 3423 3429 Jacks: lifting, screw, or ratchet (hand tools); Door opening and closing devices, except electrical

(G-741)
C & C WELDING & FABG INC
32 W Judson St (47424-1658)
PHONE..................................812 384-8089
Troy Carmichael, *Pr*
John Combs, *VP*
EMP: 4 **EST:** 1999
SALES (est): 223.47K **Privately Held**
SIC: 7692 Welding repair

(G-742)
CARMICHAEL WELDING INC
9136 E State Road 54 (47424-5900)
PHONE..................................812 825-5156
Ira E Carmichael, *Pr*
Sheri L Carmichael, *Sec*
EMP: 5 **EST:** 1998
SQ FT: 1,200
SALES (est): 483.25K **Privately Held**
SIC: 7692 1799 4212 Welding repair; Welding on site; Local trucking, without storage

(G-743)
CAVE COMPANY PRINTING INC
5282 S Black Ankle Rd (47424-5519)
PHONE..................................812 863-4333
Don Cave, *Prin*
EMP: 5 **EST:** 2008
SALES (est): 59.52K **Privately Held**
SIC: 2752 Commercial printing, lithographic

(G-744)
CIMENTOS N VOTORANTIM AMER INC
Also Called: Praire Material
993 In 54 (47424)
PHONE..................................812 384-9463
EMP: 47
Web: www.prairie.com
SIC: 1442 Construction sand and gravel
PA: Votorantim Cimentos North America, Inc.
7601 W 79th St
Bridgeview IL 60455

GEOGRAPHIC SECTION   Bloomington - Monroe County (G-771)

(G-745)
DIANAS BEAUTY SALON
595 Forest Dr (47424-1063)
PHONE.....................812 699-7904
Diana Harris, *Owner*
EMP: 1 **EST:** 2001
SALES (est): 58.4K **Privately Held**
SIC: 2844 Shampoos, rinses, conditioners: hair

(G-746)
GREENE COUNTY PALLETS INC
1338 N Harv-Wright Rd (47424)
P.O. Box 344 (47424)
PHONE.....................812 384-8362
Blake Hutchison, *Pr*
Hanna Hutchinson, *VP*
EMP: 18 **EST:** 1994
SALES (est): 1.56MM **Privately Held**
SIC: 2448 7389 Pallets, wood; Business Activities at Non-Commercial Site

(G-747)
HAYWOOD PRINTING CO
2015 W State Road 54 (47424-5197)
P.O. Box 349 (47424-0349)
PHONE.....................812 384-8639
Paul Haywood, *Owner*
EMP: 1 **EST:** 1946
SQ FT: 6,000
SALES (est): 133.43K **Privately Held**
SIC: 2759 2752 Letterpress printing; Commercial printing, lithographic

(G-748)
HERBS REBEL INC
247 S Franklin St (47424-1408)
PHONE.....................812 762-4400
Jason Edwards, *CEO*
EMP: 10 **EST:** 2020
SALES (est): 666.22K **Privately Held**
Web: www.rebelherbs.com
SIC: 2023 Dietary supplements, dairy and non-dairy based

(G-749)
IMI BLOOMFIELD
9 E Judson St (47424-1651)
PHONE.....................812 384-0045
Norma Bell, *Prin*
EMP: 6 **EST:** 2012
SALES (est): 85.37K **Privately Held**
SIC: 3273 Ready-mixed concrete

(G-750)
JER-MAUR CORPORATION
Also Called: Main Street Sports
119 E Main St (47424-1419)
PHONE.....................812 384-8290
TOLL FREE: 800
EMP: 3 **EST:** 1995
SQ FT: 1,100
SALES (est): 224.17K **Privately Held**
SIC: 2396 2395 5941 5999 Screen printing on fabric articles; Embroidery products, except Schiffli machine; Sporting goods and bicycle shops; Trophies and plaques

(G-751)
METAL TECHNOLOGIES INC
Rr #1, Sr 54 E (47424)
PHONE.....................812 384-9800
Craig Duncan, *Brnch Mgr*
EMP: 237
Web: www.metaltechnologiesinc.com
SIC: 3441 Fabricated structural metal
PA: Metal Technologies, Inc.
1537 West Auburn Dr
Auburn IN 46706

(G-752)
MICHAEL AND SONS INCORPORATED (PA)
2606 E Calvertville Rd (47424)
PHONE.....................812 876-4736
Edward Michael, *Pr*
Larry Michael, *VP*
Jackie Michael, *Sec*
EMP: 16 **EST:** 1967
SQ FT: 7,050
SALES (est): 1.77MM
SALES (corp-wide): 1.77MM **Privately Held**
Web: www.michaelandsons.net
SIC: 3281 Granite, cut and shaped

(G-753)
MILLER WELDING LLC
2139 S Iron Mountain Rd (47424-7467)
PHONE.....................812 381-0800
Josiah W Miller, *Admn*
EMP: 5 **EST:** 2012
SALES (est): 74.65K **Privately Held**
SIC: 7692 Welding repair

(G-754)
MILLROSE CUSTOM WOODWORKING
12 S Harrison St (47424-1147)
PHONE.....................812 699-5101
David Miller, *Prin*
EMP: 4 **EST:** 2019
SALES (est): 70.83K **Privately Held**
SIC: 2431 Millwork

(G-755)
PARAGON FORCE INC
280 Northgate Blvd Ste A (47424-7141)
PHONE.....................812 384-3040
Sherri A Davis, *Pr*
Sherri Davis, *
EMP: 73 **EST:** 2009
SQ FT: 10,000
SALES (est): 4.65MM **Privately Held**
Web: www.paragonforce.com
SIC: 8741 3599 Business management; Machine and other job shop work

(G-756)
ROLLISON AIRPLANE COMPANY INC
County Road 300 S (47424)
PHONE.....................812 384-4972
Rob Rollison, *Pr*
EMP: 3 **EST:** 1993
SQ FT: 5,000
SALES (est): 298.08K **Privately Held**
Web: www.airplanegear.com
SIC: 3721 Aircraft

(G-757)
SHAPE SHIFTERS INC
420 N State Road 45 (47424-5919)
PHONE.....................812 400-0580
Michelle Hardy, *Prin*
Justin Hardy, *Prin*
EMP: 2 **EST:** 2018
SALES (est): 133.02K **Privately Held**
Web: www.shapeshiftersin.com
SIC: 3441 Fabricated structural metal

(G-758)
UNIQUE SIGNS
1650 N Warren Rd (47424-4769)
PHONE.....................812 384-4967
EMP: 2 **EST:** 1993
SALES (est): 101.53K **Privately Held**
SIC: 3993 Signs and advertising specialties

Bloomingdale
Parke County

(G-759)
FUTUREX INDUSTRIES INC
Formflex
80 E Smith St (47832)
PHONE.....................765 498-8900
Brent Thompson, *Mgr*
EMP: 35
SALES (corp-wide): 48.34MM **Privately Held**
Web: www.futurexind.com
SIC: 3089 3081 2782 Molding primary plastics; Unsupported plastics film and sheet; Blankbooks and looseleaf binders
PA: Futurex Industries, Inc.
70 N Main St
Bloomingdale IN 47832
765 498-3900

(G-760)
FUTUREX INDUSTRIES INC (PA)
Also Called: Formflex
70 N Main St (47832-8001)
P.O. Box 158 (47832-0158)
PHONE.....................765 498-3900
Richard J Kremer, *Pr*
Brent Thompson, *
George C Moravcik, *
▲ **EMP:** 145 **EST:** 1970
SQ FT: 100,000
SALES (est): 48.34MM
SALES (corp-wide): 48.34MM **Privately Held**
Web: www.formflexproducts.com
SIC: 2865 3081 Styrene; Plastics film and sheet

(G-761)
MYERS WOOD PRODUCTS
1287 E 1200 N (47832-8050)
PHONE.....................765 597-2147
EMP: 5 **EST:** 1998
SQ FT: 10,000
SALES (est): 450K **Privately Held**
SIC: 2448 Pallets, wood

(G-762)
TURKEY RUN DISTILLERY LLC
992 E State Road 47 (47832-8061)
PHONE.....................765 505-2044
Colten Lambermont, *Prin*
EMP: 6 **EST:** 2016
SALES (est): 187.82K **Privately Held**
SIC: 2085 Distilled and blended liquors

(G-763)
WOODY ENTERPRISES LLC
7880 N Roaring Creek Rd (47832-8113)
PHONE.....................765 498-7300
EMP: 1 **EST:** 2011
SALES (est): 81.25K **Privately Held**
Web: www.woody-enterprises.com
SIC: 8711 4841 3663 Consulting engineer; Direct broadcast satellite services (DBS); Satellites, communications

Bloomington
Monroe County

(G-764)
1Z2Z IMPRINTS
3815 E Tamarron Dr (47408-2820)
PHONE.....................303 918-8979
Lynnn Mccutchen, *Managing Member*
EMP: 2 **EST:** 2011
SALES (est): 94.66K **Privately Held**
SIC: 2759 Imprinting

(G-765)
39 DEGREES NORTH LLC
Also Called: 39 Degrees
908 N Walnut St (47404-3525)
P.O. Box 1937 (47402-1937)
PHONE.....................855 447-3939
EMP: 19 **EST:** 2004
SQ FT: 1,600
SALES (est): 940.14K **Privately Held**
Web: www.geoconvergence.com
SIC: 7371 2741 Computer software development; Atlas, map, and guide publishing

(G-766)
3D STONE INC
6700 S Victor Pike (47403-9758)
PHONE.....................812 824-5805
David Whaley, *Pr*
Carol Whaley, *
EMP: 48 **EST:** 1992
SALES (est): 8.72MM **Privately Held**
Web: www.3dstoneinc.com
SIC: 1422 Limestones, ground

(G-767)
3D STONE PURCHASER INC
6700 S Victor Pike (47403-9758)
PHONE.....................812 824-5805
Kurt Michael Sendek, *Pr*
Lily Serena Sendek, *
Chris Puderbaugh, *
EMP: 14 **EST:** 2015
SQ FT: 3,000
SALES (est): 1.75MM **Privately Held**
Web: www.3dstoneinc.com
SIC: 3281 Limestone, cut and shaped

(G-768)
A S P PARROTT SIGNS
1820 S Walnut St (47401-7719)
PHONE.....................812 325-9102
EMP: 5 **EST:** 2009
SALES (est): 130.51K **Privately Held**
SIC: 3993 Signs and advertising specialties

(G-769)
A-1 SCREENPRINTING LLC
Also Called: Underground Printing
512 E Kirkwood Ave (47408-4059)
PHONE.....................812 558-0286
EMP: 2
Web: www.undergroundshirts.com
SIC: 2759 Screen printing
PA: A-1 Screenprinting, Llc
1476 Seaver Way
Ypsilanti MI 48197

(G-770)
ABR IMAGES INC
Also Called: A B R Imagery
3808 W Vernal Pike (47404-2534)
PHONE.....................866 342-4764
Ross L Thackery, *Pr*
▲ **EMP:** 13 **EST:** 2001
SALES (est): 754.38K **Privately Held**
Web: www.abrprint.com
SIC: 2759 Screen printing

(G-771)
ABRACADABRA GRAPHICS
5144 E State Road 45 (47408-9672)
PHONE.....................812 336-1971
Sally Watkins, *Pt*
James R Watkins, *Pt*
EMP: 4 **EST:** 1982
SQ FT: 2,500
SALES (est): 192.55K **Privately Held**

Bloomington - Monroe County (G-772)   GEOGRAPHIC SECTION

Web: www.abragraphics.com
SIC: 2759 5199 2395 Screen printing; Advertising specialties; Embroidery products, except Schiffli machine

(G-772)
ACCENT LIMESTONE & CARVING INC
5900 N Maple Grove Rd (47404-9012)
PHONE..................812 876-7040
Michael Donham, *Pr*
Julie Donham, *Treas*
EMP: 3 EST: 2000
SALES (est): 237.98K Privately Held
Web: www.accentlimestone.com
SIC: 3281 1741 Limestone, cut and shaped; Stone masonry

(G-773)
ADVANCED DESIGNS CORP (PA)
1169 W 2nd St (47403-2160)
P.O. Box 1907 (47402-1907)
PHONE..................812 333-1922
Martin Riess, *CEO*
Matthew Mcgrath, *Pr*
Teri A Riess, *VP*
EMP: 14 EST: 1981
SQ FT: 2,700
SALES (est): 2.45MM
SALES (corp-wide): 2.45MM Privately Held
Web: www.doprad.com
SIC: 3829 7371 Weather tracking equipment; Computer software development

(G-774)
ADVANTEX INC
5981 E State Road 45 (47408-9680)
PHONE..................812 339-6479
Joe Galoupo, *Pr*
EMP: 3 EST: 1982
SALES (est): 192.38K Privately Held
Web: www.advantexinc.com
SIC: 2759 Screen printing

(G-775)
AGATE WORKSHOP
103 N College Ave (47404-3977)
PHONE..................812 333-0900
Steve Volan, *Owner*
EMP: 3 EST: 1996
SALES (est): 22.33K Privately Held
SIC: 2741 Telephone and other directory publishing

(G-776)
AIBMR LIFE SCIENCES INC
205 N College Ave Ste 513 (47404-3952)
PHONE..................812 822-1400
Alex Schauss, *Brnch Mgr*
EMP: 4
SALES (corp-wide): 812.37K Privately Held
Web: www.aibmr.com
SIC: 2023 Dietary supplements, dairy and non-dairy based
PA: Aibmr Life Sciences Inc
    2800 E Madison St Ste 202
    Seattle WA 98112
    253 286-2888

(G-777)
ALLONS-Y FOR INV & TECH LLC
1161 S Adams St Apt 11 (47403-2183)
PHONE..................260 206-4445
EMP: 2
SALES (est): 56.54K Privately Held
SIC: 7372 7389 Application computer software; Business Activities at Non-Commercial Site

(G-778)
AMERICAN COLORS CLOTHING
314 E Kirkwood Ave (47408-3552)
PHONE..................812 822-0476
EMP: 7 EST: 2016
SALES (est): 45.04K Privately Held
Web: www.americancolorsclothing.com
SIC: 2394 Cloth, drop (fabric): made from purchased materials

(G-779)
AMERICAN SCHOOL HEALTH ASSN
Also Called: ASHA
3011 S Xavier Ct (47401-6883)
PHONE..................703 506-7675
Linda Morse, *Pr*
EMP: 8 EST: 1926
SALES (est): 433.36K Privately Held
Web: www.ashaweb.org
SIC: 2721 8621 Trade journals: publishing only, not printed on site; Health association

(G-780)
AMERIFORCE MEDIA LLC
304 W Kirkwood Ave Apt 100 (47404-5233)
PHONE..................812 961-9478
Peter Rumley, *Acctnt*
Ted Wadsworth, *Managing Member*
EMP: 4 EST: 2015
SALES (est): 291.4K Privately Held
Web: www.usmilitarypublishing.com
SIC: 2721 Magazines: publishing only, not printed on site

(G-781)
APPAREL DESIGN GROUP
671 S Landmark Ave (47403-2087)
P.O. Box 3321 (47402-3321)
PHONE..................812 339-3355
Dick Huffman, *Pr*
EMP: 5 EST: 2000
SALES (est): 392.93K Privately Held
SIC: 2759 2752 Screen printing; Commercial printing, lithographic

(G-782)
AQUABEE COOLERS LLC
5293 N Targhee Ct (47404-8001)
PHONE..................615 947-7962
Thomas Kpabar, *Managing Member*
EMP: 1 EST: 2021
SALES (est): 61.6K Privately Held
Web: www.aquabeecooler.com
SIC: 3429 Ice chests or coolers, portable, except foam plastic

(G-783)
ARCTIC ICE EXPRESS INC
2423 W Industrial Park Dr (47404-2601)
PHONE..................812 333-0423
Garnet Don Kinser, *Pr*
Pamela A Kinser, *Treas*
EMP: 12 EST: 1988
SQ FT: 10,000
SALES (est): 187.2K Privately Held
SIC: 2097 Manufactured ice

(G-784)
ARGENTUM JEWELRY INC
205 N College Ave Ste 100 (47404-3954)
P.O. Box 1221 (47402-1221)
PHONE..................812 336-3100
Eugene Foltzer, *Pr*
Sally Walker, *Pr*
EMP: 5 EST: 1973
SALES (est): 658.38K Privately Held
Web: www.argentum-jewelry.com
SIC: 5944 3911 Jewelry, precious stones and precious metals; Jewelry, precious metal

(G-785)
ATRIUM WEB SERVICES LLC
3709 E Devonshire Ln (47408-9669)
PHONE..................812 322-6904
Ravi Zacharias, *Prin*
EMP: 6 EST: 2010
SALES (est): 122.9K Privately Held
Web: www.mycareercrna.biz
SIC: 3993 Signs and advertising specialties

(G-786)
AUTHOR SOLUTIONS LLC (PA)
Also Called: A S I
1663 S Liberty Dr (47403-5161)
PHONE..................812 339-6000
William Elliott, *Pr*
Gregory Wallis, *
William Becher, *
Jack Bowen, *
Keith Ogorek, *
▼ EMP: 250 EST: 2001
SQ FT: 25,000
SALES (est): 215.46MM
SALES (corp-wide): 215.46MM Privately Held
Web: www.authorsolutions.com
SIC: 2731 Books, publishing only

(G-787)
AUTO TEMP CTRL SPECIALISTS INC
Also Called: A T C Specialists
1001 S Walnut St (47401-5821)
PHONE..................812 333-2963
EMP: 5 EST: 1995
SQ FT: 10,000
SALES (est): 498.81K Privately Held
Web: www.recoverall.com
SIC: 3585 Air conditioning, motor vehicle

(G-788)
AXECALIBUR LLC ◆
3604 W 3rd St (47404-4860)
PHONE..................812 822-1157
Tammy Carson, *CEO*
EMP: 1 EST: 2022
SALES (est): 52.02K Privately Held
Web: www.axecaliburs.com
SIC: 7929 3949 5812 Entertainers; Targets, archery and rifle shooting; Restaurant, family: independent

(G-789)
B & L SHTMTL ROFG A TCTA AMER
Also Called: B L
1301 N Monroe St (47404-3377)
PHONE..................812 332-4309
David J Lee, *Pr*
Dan Mirer, *
Michael Kilber, *
EMP: 40 EST: 1968
SQ FT: 16,000
SALES (est): 3.7MM
SALES (corp-wide): 823.93MM Privately Held
Web: www.blsheetmetalroofing.com
SIC: 1761 3446 Roofing contractor; Architectural metalwork
PA: Tecta America Corp.
    9450 W Bryn Mawr Ave Ste
    Rosemont IL 60018
    847 581-3888

(G-790)
B G HOADLEY QUARRIES INC (PA)
3211 W Arlington Rd (47404-1563)
P.O. Box 1224 (47402-1224)
PHONE..................812 332-1447
Patsy H Fell, *Pr*
Bert H Fell Junior, *VP*
David R Fell, *
James Johnson, *

EMP: 40 EST: 1927
SALES (est): 4.63MM
SALES (corp-wide): 4.63MM Privately Held
Web: www.bghoadleyquarries.com
SIC: 1411 Limestone, dimension-quarrying

(G-791)
B2C2 LLC
Also Called: Fastsigns
2664 S Sunflower Dr (47403)
PHONE..................808 533-4128
▲ EMP: 6 EST: 2012
SALES (est): 458.45K Privately Held
Web: www.b2c2.com
SIC: 3993 Signs and advertising specialties

(G-792)
BALBOA PRESS
1663 S Liberty Dr (47403-5161)
PHONE..................812 671-9756
Louise Hay, *Prin*
EMP: 1 EST: 2010
SALES (est): 420.87K Privately Held
Web: www.balboapress.com
SIC: 2741 Miscellaneous publishing

(G-793)
BAMBOO US BIDCO LLC
Also Called: Baxter Biosciences
1801 N Curry Pike (47404)
PHONE..................812 355-5289
▲ EMP: 6
SALES (corp-wide): 482.9MM Privately Held
Web: www.baxter.com
SIC: 2834 Pharmaceutical preparations
PA: Bamboo Us Bidco Llc
    400 Interpace Pkwy
    Parsippany NJ 07054
    336 259-8000

(G-794)
BAMBOO US BIDCO LLC
2000 N Curry Pike (47402)
PHONE..................812 333-0887
Patrick Adams, *Brnch Mgr*
EMP: 624
SALES (corp-wide): 482.9MM Privately Held
Web: www.baxter.com
SIC: 3841 Surgical and medical instruments
PA: Bamboo Us Bidco Llc
    400 Interpace Pkwy
    Parsippany NJ 07054
    336 259-8000

(G-795)
BARRY COMPANY INC
2037 S Yost Ave (47403-3189)
PHONE..................812 333-1850
Tim Wagner, *Brnch Mgr*
EMP: 6
SALES (corp-wide): 19.11MM Privately Held
Web: www.barrycompany.net
SIC: 3432 5074 5251 5999 Plumbing fixture fittings and trim; Plumbing and hydronic heating supplies; Hardware stores; Plumbing and heating supplies
PA: Barry Company Inc
    1145 E Maryland St
    Indianapolis IN 46202
    317 637-5327

(G-796)
BAUGH ENTERPRISES INC
125 S Westplex Ave (47404-5080)
PHONE..................812 334-8189
Loyce B Keough, *Pr*
Larry Biggerstaff, *Sec*

GEOGRAPHIC SECTION   Bloomington - Monroe County (G-822)

EMP: 18 **EST:** 1982
SQ FT: 12,000
SALES (est): 481.43K **Privately Held**
Web: www.baughfineprint.com
SIC: 2752 7331 5199 7371 Offset printing; Mailing service; Advertising specialties; Computer software systems analysis and design, custom

(G-797)
BAXTER INTL
3249 S Southern Oaks Dr (47401-8000)
PHONE................812 355-4283
EMP: 4 **EST:** 2019
SALES (est): 66.62K **Privately Held**
Web: www.baxter.com
SIC: 2834 Pharmaceutical preparations

(G-798)
BAXTER PHRM SOLUTIONS LLC (HQ)
Also Called: Simtra Biopharma Solutions
927 S Curry Pike (47403)
PHONE................812 333-0887
Franco Negron, *CEO*
Tim Donovan, *
Ray Guidotti, *
Mike Macrie, *CIO*
▲ **EMP:** 235 **EST:** 2001
SALES (est): 482.9MM
SALES (corp-wide): 482.9MM **Privately Held**
Web: biopharmasolutions.baxter.com
SIC: 2834 Pharmaceutical preparations
PA: Bamboo Us Bidco Llc
400 Interpace Pkwy
Parsippany NJ 07054
336 259-8000

(G-799)
BAXTER PHRM SOLUTIONS LLC
Also Called: Simtra Biopharma Solutions
927 S Curry Pike (47403-2624)
PHONE................812 355-7167
Patrick Adams, *Brnch Mgr*
EMP: 997
SALES (corp-wide): 482.9MM **Privately Held**
Web: www.baxter.com
SIC: 3841 Surgical and medical instruments
HQ: Baxter Pharmaceutical Solutions Llc
927 S Curry Pike
Bloomington IN 47403

(G-800)
BE LOVED TRANSPORTATION INC
2514 S Rogers St (47403-3691)
PHONE................812 207-2610
EMP: 1 **EST:** 2010
SALES (est): 147.37K **Privately Held**
Web: www.belovedtransportation.com
SIC: 3799 Transportation equipment, nec

(G-801)
BELLS AND WHISTLES LLC
3747 E Stipp Rd (47401-9451)
PHONE................317 315-3129
Gregory English, *Owner*
EMP: 5 **EST:** 2016
SALES (est): 48.02K **Privately Held**
Web: www.goacegroup.com
SIC: 3999 Manufacturing industries, nec

(G-802)
BERRY GLOBAL INC
4100 W Profile Pkwy (47404-2546)
PHONE................812 334-7090
EMP: 58
Web: www.berryglobal.com

SIC: 3089 3081 Bottle caps, molded plastics; Unsupported plastics film and sheet
HQ: Berry Global, Inc.
101 Oakley St
Evansville IN 47710

(G-803)
BEST BEERS LLC
1100 S Strong Dr (47403-8742)
PHONE................812 332-1234
Jamie Per, *Prin*
John Miller, *
EMP: 36 **EST:** 2003
SALES (est): 2.13MM **Privately Held**
Web: www.bestbeersinc.com
SIC: 2082 Beer (alcoholic beverage)

(G-804)
BEST BICYCLE INC
Also Called: Bike Jerseys .com
4012 E 10th St (47408)
PHONE................812 336-2724
Hank West, *Pr*
Margie West, *Sec*
EMP: 3 **EST:** 1986
SQ FT: 2,500
SALES (est): 400K **Privately Held**
Web: www.bikejerseys.com
SIC: 5941 3751 Bicycle and bicycle parts; Bicycles and related parts

(G-805)
BIBLICAL ENTERPRISES LLC
3428 S Burks Ct (47401-8462)
PHONE................812 391-0071
EMP: 2 **EST:** 2012
SALES (est): 167.94K **Privately Held**
SIC: 2732 Books, printing and binding

(G-806)
BIG RED LIQUORS INC
Also Called: Karton King
435 S Walnut St (47401-4613)
PHONE................812 339-9552
Mark Mc Allister, *Owner*
EMP: 4
SALES (corp-wide): 24.98MM **Privately Held**
Web: www.bigredliquors.com
SIC: 5993 2111 5963 5921 Tobacco stores and stands; Cigarettes; Direct selling establishments; Liquor stores
PA: Big Red Liquors Inc
5445 S East St
Indianapolis IN 46227
812 339-7345

(G-807)
BILLS FURNITURE
1509 E Elliston Dr (47401-8611)
PHONE................317 695-8347
William Vaughn, *Owner*
EMP: 1 **EST:** 2001
SALES (est): 55K **Privately Held**
SIC: 2511 Wood household furniture

(G-808)
BIOMEDIX-INC
3895 W Vernal Pike (47404-2533)
PHONE................812 355-7000
FAX: 812 355-7001
▲ **EMP:** 17
SQ FT: 22,500
SALES (est): 4.7MM **Privately Held**
Web: www.biomedix-inc.com
SIC: 3841 Surgical and medical instruments

(G-809)
BLACKWOOD SOLUTIONS LLC
1901 S Liberty Dr (47403-5146)

P.O. Box 486 (47402-0486)
PHONE................812 676-8770
Jason M Feagans, *Pr*
Nathan Broadfoot, *
Jamie Feagans, *
Ryan Conrad, *
EMP: 85 **EST:** 2015
SALES (est): 10.27MM **Privately Held**
Web: www.bwoodsolutions.com
SIC: 4214 2411 5989 4953 Local trucking with storage; Fuel wood harvesting; Wood (fuel); Recycling, waste materials

(G-810)
BLOOMINGTON CON SURFACES CORP
3650 S Kingsbury Ave (47401-8750)
PHONE................812 345-0011
EMP: 2 **EST:** 2011
SALES (est): 139.98K **Privately Held**
SIC: 2851 Paints and allied products

(G-811)
BLOOMINGTON COOKIES LLC
Also Called: Crumbl- Bloomington
1155 S College Mall Rd Ste B (47401-6168)
PHONE................812 668-7779
EMP: 80 **EST:** 2021
SALES (est): 3.82MM **Privately Held**
Web: www.crumblcookies.com
SIC: 2052 Cookies and crackers

(G-812)
BLOOMINGTON LETTER SHOP
5717 S Rogers St (47403-4637)
PHONE................812 824-6363
Larry Stidd, *Owner*
EMP: 1 **EST:** 1946
SQ FT: 1,200
SALES (est): 96.67K **Privately Held**
Web: www.security-specialists.net
SIC: 2759 2752 Letterpress printing; Offset printing

(G-813)
BLOOMINGTON STITCHERY LLC
325 W Persimmon Ct (47403-4624)
PHONE................208 371-9598
Olivia Wendell, *Owner*
EMP: 5 **EST:** 2017
SALES (est): 47.21K **Privately Held**
Web: www.bloomingtonstitchery.com
SIC: 2395 Embroidery and art needlework

(G-814)
BOOMERANG SOLUTIONS
416 S Washington St (47401-4636)
PHONE................812 822-2125
EMP: 1 **EST:** 2012
SALES (est): 80.38K **Privately Held**
Web: www.bsg-corp.com
SIC: 3949 Boomerangs

(G-815)
BRIDGESTONE RET OPERATIONS LLC
Also Called: Firestone
219 S Walnut St (47404-6116)
PHONE................812 332-2119
Kelly Anderson, *Mgr*
EMP: 10
Web: www.bridgestoneamericas.com
SIC: 5531 7534 Automotive tires; Rebuilding and retreading tires
HQ: Bridgestone Retail Operations, Llc
200 4th Ave S Ste 100
Nashville TN 37201
630 259-9000

(G-816)
BROWN RIDGE STUDIO
625 N Lwer Brdie Glyan Rd (47408)
PHONE................812 335-0643
David Beery, *Owner*
EMP: 2 **EST:** 1995
SALES (est): 127.61K **Privately Held**
SIC: 2426 Turnings, furniture: wood

(G-817)
BRUMMETT ENTERPRISES LLC
3101 W Arlington Rd (47404-1561)
PHONE................812 325-6993
EMP: 5 **EST:** 2007
SALES (est): 82.08K **Privately Held**
Web: www.brummettenterprise.com
SIC: 1422 Crushed and broken limestone

(G-818)
BULENT GUMUSEL ✪
3366 S Oaklawn Cir (47401-8546)
P.O. Box 811 (47402-0811)
PHONE................812 803-5912
Bulent Gumusel, *Pr*
EMP: 1 **EST:** 2022
SALES (est): 54.05K **Privately Held**
SIC: 2834 7389 Pharmaceutical preparations; Business Activities at Non-Commercial Site

(G-819)
BUTLER VINEYARDS (PA)
Also Called: Butler Winery
6200 E Robinson Rd (47408-9380)
PHONE................812 332-6660
James Butler, *Pr*
EMP: 2 **EST:** 1982
SALES (est): 215.24K
SALES (corp-wide): 215.24K **Privately Held**
Web: www.butlerwinery.com
SIC: 2084 Wines

(G-820)
CARDINAL SPIRITS LLC
922 S Morton St (47403-2566)
P.O. Box 2282 (47402-2282)
PHONE................812 202-6789
Adam Christopher Quirk, *Managing Member*
Jeff Wuslich, *
▲ **EMP:** 30 **EST:** 2013
SQ FT: 4,500
SALES (est): 3.44MM **Privately Held**
Web: www.cardinalspirits.com
SIC: 2085 Distilled and blended liquors

(G-821)
CARLISLE COMPANIES INC
Carlisle Motion Control Inds
1031 E Hillside Dr (47401-6586)
PHONE................812 334-8793
EMP: 4
SALES (corp-wide): 4.59B **Publicly Held**
Web: www.carlisle.com
SIC: 2952 Roofing materials
PA: Carlisle Companies Incorporated
16430 N Scttsdale Rd Ste
Scottsdale AZ 85254
480 781-5000

(G-822)
CARLISLE INDUS BRAKE FRCTION I
1031 E Hillside Dr (47401-6586)
PHONE................812 336-3811
D Christian Koch, *Pr*
Steven J Ford, *
Kevin Zdimal, *
◆ **EMP:** 283 **EST:** 1989
SALES (est): 97.33MM
SALES (corp-wide): 4.59B **Publicly Held**

Bloomington - Monroe County (G-823) — GEOGRAPHIC SECTION

Web: www.carlislecbf.com
SIC: 3714 Motor vehicle brake systems and parts
PA: Carlisle Companies Incorporated
16430 N Scttsdale Rd Ste
Scottsdale AZ 85254
480 781-5000

(G-823)
CATALENT INDIANA LLC
3770 W Jonathan Dr (47404-4843)
PHONE..................812 355-6746
Matt Van Hoosier, Brnch Mgr
EMP: 1
Web: www.catalent.com
SIC: 2834 Pharmaceutical preparations
HQ: Catalent Indiana, Llc
1300 S Patterson Dr
Bloomington IN 47403
812 355-6746

(G-824)
CATALENT INDIANA LLC (DH)
1300 S Patterson Dr (47403)
P.O. Box 970 (47402)
PHONE..................812 355-6746
John Chiminski, CEO
EMP: 500 EST: 2004
SALES (est): 98.44MM Publicly Held
Web: biologics.catalent.com
SIC: 8731 2834 Biotechnical research, commercial; Pharmaceutical preparations
HQ: Indiana Catalent Holdings Llc
14 Schoolhouse Rd
Somerset NJ 08873
732 537-6200

(G-825)
CATALENT PHARMA SOLUTIONS INC
Also Called: Catalent Pharma Services
1300 S Patterson Dr (47403-4828)
PHONE..................812 355-4498
EMP: 66
Web: www.catalent.com
SIC: 2834 3841 Pharmaceutical preparations; Medical instruments and equipment, blood and bone work
HQ: Catalent Pharma Solutions, Inc.
14 Schoolhouse Rd
Somerset NJ 08873

(G-826)
CENTER FOR DAGNSTC IMAGING CDI
3802 W Industrial Blvd Ste 4 (47403-5141)
PHONE..................812 331-7727
EMP: 7 EST: 2018
SALES (est): 86.67K Privately Held
Web: www.rayusradiology.com
SIC: 3841 Surgical and medical instruments

(G-827)
CENTER FOR THE STUDY KNWLDGE D
Also Called: Not For Profit 501c3 RES Inst
1441 S Fenbrook Ln Ste 300 (47401)
PHONE..................812 361-4424
Margaret M Clements, Dir
EMP: 1 EST: 2011
SALES (est): 118.13K Privately Held
Web: www.knowledgediffusion.org
SIC: 8733 7371 7372 8231 Noncommercial research organizations; Computer software systems analysis and design, custom; Business oriented computer software; Specialized libraries

(G-828)
CENTRAL COCA-COLA BTLG CO INC
Also Called: Coca-Cola
1701 S Liberty Dr (47403-5119)
PHONE..................800 241-2653
EMP: 23
SALES (corp-wide): 45.75B Publicly Held
Web: www.coca-cola.com
SIC: 2086 8741 Bottled and canned soft drinks; Management services
HQ: Central Coca-Cola Bottling Company, Inc.
555 Taxter Rd Ste 550
Elmsford NY 10523
914 789-1100

(G-829)
CIRCLE - PROSCO INC (PA)
Also Called: C.P.i
401 N Gates Dr (47404-4824)
PHONE..................812 339-3653
Douglas K Parker, Pr
Patricia K Parker, *
▲ EMP: 25 EST: 1971
SQ FT: 38,000
SALES (est): 19.24MM
SALES (corp-wide): 19.24MM Privately Held
Web: www.circleprosco.com
SIC: 2841 Detergents, synthetic organic or inorganic alkaline

(G-830)
CMBF LLC
1031 E Hillside Dr (47401-6586)
PHONE..................812 336-3811
EMP: 9 EST: 2021
SALES (est): 1.16MM Privately Held
SIC: 3499 Friction material, made from powdered metal

(G-831)
COCA-COLA BOTTLING CO
Also Called: Coca-Cola
1701 S Liberty Dr Box 2 (47403-5119)
PHONE..................812 332-4434
Marvin J Herb, Pr
EMP: 31
SALES (est): 3.16MM Privately Held
Web: www.coca-cola.com
SIC: 2086 4226 Bottled and canned soft drinks; Special warehousing and storage, nec

(G-832)
COIS COILLTE WOODWORKING LLC
2116 S Smith Rd (47401-8916)
PHONE..................812 340-3718
EMP: 4 EST: 2017
SALES (est): 89.55K Privately Held
SIC: 2431 Millwork

(G-833)
COLLECTIVE PRESS INC
401 W 6th St Ste J (47404-4016)
P.O. Box 3494 (47402-3494)
PHONE..................812 325-1385
EMP: 2 EST: 2011
SALES (est): 124.43K Privately Held
Web: www.thecollectivepress.com
SIC: 2741 Miscellaneous publishing

(G-834)
COLOPHON BOOK ARTS SUPPLY LLC
5400 N Brummetts Creek Rd (47408-9417)
PHONE..................812 671-0577
Mary G Uthuppuru, Pr
EMP: 1 EST: 1974
SALES (est): 104.79K Privately Held
Web: www.colophonbookarts.com
SIC: 5999 2789 Artists' supplies and materials; Bookbinding and related work

(G-835)
CONDER WATER SERVICES
7691 W Kirksville Rd (47403-9534)
PHONE..................812 825-9883
Gary Conder, Owner
EMP: 1 EST: 2000
SALES (est): 103.77K Privately Held
SIC: 0191 3713 General farms, primarily crop; Farm truck bodies

(G-836)
COOK AIRCRAFT LEASING INC
750 N Daniels Way (47404-9120)
PHONE..................812 339-2044
Carol Seaman, Pr
EMP: 9 EST: 2015
SALES (est): 154.13K Privately Held
SIC: 3728 Aircraft parts and equipment, nec

(G-837)
COOK BIODEVICE LLC
750 N Daniels Way (47404-9120)
PHONE..................800 265-0945
Rob Lyles, Pr
Michael Cole, Finance
EMP: 7 EST: 2016
SALES (est): 115.05K Privately Held
Web: www.cookmedical.com
SIC: 3841 Surgical and medical instruments

(G-838)
COOK GROUP INCORPORATED (PA)
750 N Daniels Way (47404)
P.O. Box 489 (47402)
PHONE..................812 339-2235
William A Cook, Ch Bd
Kem Hawkins, Pr
Stephen L Ferguson, Ex VP
Robert K Irie, VP
John Kamstra, VP
EMP: 10 EST: 1963
SQ FT: 1,500
SALES (est): 1.61B
SALES (corp-wide): 1.61B Privately Held
Web: www.cookgroup.com
SIC: 3841 3821 3845 6411 Surgical instruments and apparatus; Pipettes, hemocytometer; Pacemaker, cardiac; Insurance agents, nec

(G-839)
COOK INCORPORATED
1025 W Acuff Rd (47404-9295)
PHONE..................812 339-2235
David Reed, Mgr
EMP: 1
SALES (corp-wide): 1.61B Privately Held
Web: www.cookmedical.com
SIC: 3841 Surgical and medical instruments
HQ: Cook Incorporated
750 Daniels Way
Bloomington IN 47404
812 339-2235

(G-840)
COOK INCORPORATED (HQ)
Also Called: Cook Endoscopy
750 N Daniels Way (47404)
P.O. Box 489 (47402)
PHONE..................812 339-2235
M Kem Hawkins, Pr
Phyllis Mccullough, Pr
Thomas Osborne, *
Brian Bates, *
Steve Ferguson, *
▲ EMP: 1750 EST: 1963
SQ FT: 40,000
SALES (est): 422.14MM
SALES (corp-wide): 1.61B Privately Held
Web: www.cookmedical.com
SIC: 3841 Catheters
PA: Cook Group Incorporated
750 Daniels Way
Bloomington IN 47404
812 339-2235

(G-841)
COOK INCORPORATED
Also Called: Cook Medical
1700 N Curry Pike (47404-1485)
PHONE..................812 339-2235
Derek Voskuil, Pr
EMP: 955 EST: 1977
SALES (est): 625MM Privately Held
Web: www.cookmedical.com
SIC: 3841 Medical instruments and equipment, blood and bone work

(G-842)
COOK MEDICAL HOLDINGS LLC (HQ)
750 N Daniels Way (47404-9120)
PHONE..................812 339-2235
Pete Yonkman, Pr
EMP: 1 EST: 2016
SALES (est): 5.56MM
SALES (corp-wide): 1.61B Privately Held
Web: www.cookgroup.com
SIC: 3841 3842 8731 Surgical instruments and apparatus; Surgical appliances and supplies; Medical research, commercial
PA: Cook Group Incorporated
750 Daniels Way
Bloomington IN 47404
812 339-2235

(G-843)
COOK MEDICAL INC
301 N Curry Pike (47404)
PHONE..................812 822-1402
EMP: 73 EST: 2018
SALES (est): 240.51K Privately Held
Web: www.cookmedical.com
SIC: 3841 Surgical and medical instruments

(G-844)
COOK MEDICAL LLC
400 N Daniels Way (47404-9155)
PHONE..................812 339-2235
Phyllis Mccullough, Pr
EMP: 628
SALES (corp-wide): 1.61B Privately Held
Web: www.cookmedical.com
SIC: 3841 3842 Surgical and medical instruments; Surgical appliances and supplies
HQ: Cook Medical Llc
750 Daniels Way
Bloomington IN 47404
812 339-2235

(G-845)
COOK MEDICAL LLC (HQ)
Also Called: Cook Medical
750 N Daniels Way (47404)
P.O. Box 4195 (47402)
PHONE..................812 339-2235
M Kem Hawkins, Pr
Robert L Santa, Sec
John Kamstra, CFO
Cynthia Kretz, VP
▼ EMP: 393 EST: 2003
SALES (est): 76.93MM
SALES (corp-wide): 1.61B Privately Held
Web: www.cookmedical.com
SIC: 3842 3841 Surgical appliances and supplies; Catheters
PA: Cook Group Incorporated
750 Daniels Way
Bloomington IN 47404
812 339-2235

GEOGRAPHIC SECTION
Bloomington - Monroe County (G-873)

(G-846)
COOK MEDICAL LLC
Also Called: Cook Polymer Technology
1800 N Curry Pike (47404)
PHONE.................812 323-4500
EMP: 628
SALES (corp-wide): 1.61B **Privately Held**
SIC: 3842 3841 Surgical appliances and supplies; Catheters
HQ: Cook Medical Llc
750 Daniels Way
Bloomington IN 47404
812 339-2235

(G-847)
COOK MEDICAL TECHNOLOGIES LLC
750 N Daniels Way (47404-9120)
PHONE.................812 339-2235
Pete Yonkman, *Pr*
EMP: 10 **EST:** 2010
SALES (est): 4.79MM
SALES (corp-wide): 1.61B **Privately Held**
Web: www.cookmedical.com
SIC: 3841 Surgical and medical instruments
HQ: Cook Medical Holdings Llc
750 N Daniels Way
Bloomington IN 47404
812 339-2235

(G-848)
COOK REGENTEC LLC
Also Called: Cook Regentec
500 W Simpson Chapel Rd (47404-9426)
PHONE.................800 265-0945
Jill Warfield, *Brnch Mgr*
EMP: 75
SALES (corp-wide): 1.61B **Privately Held**
Web: www.cookregentec.com
SIC: 3841 Surgical and medical instruments
HQ: Cook Regentec Llc
1102 Indiana Ave
Indianapolis IN 46202
800 265-0945

(G-849)
COSTUMES BY DESIGN
1912 S Montclair Ave (47401-6810)
PHONE.................812 334-2029
Jan Lamm, *Owner*
EMP: 1 **EST:** 2009
SALES (est): 68.05K **Privately Held**
Web: www.mycostumesbydesign.com
SIC: 7389 2389 Design services; Costumes

(G-850)
CRUSHER PARTS DIRECT LLC
3905 W Farmer Ave (47403-5152)
P.O. Box 133 (47458-0133)
PHONE.................812 822-1463
Edd Perdue, *Owner*
EMP: 4 **EST:** 2014
SQ FT: 7,900
SALES (est): 492.7K **Privately Held**
Web: www.crusherpartsdirect.com
SIC: 3531 Crushers, grinders, and similar equipment

(G-851)
CUSTOM WOODWORKING
732 S Village Dr (47403-1954)
PHONE.................812 339-6601
Vincent Payne, *Prin*
EMP: 5 **EST:** 2009
SALES (est): 231.72K **Privately Held**
SIC: 2431 Millwork

(G-852)
DAVID L PHILLIPS
Also Called: David L Phillips Services
3603 W Woodcliff Ct (47403-4130)
PHONE.................312 937-0299
David Phillips, *Owner*
EMP: 1 **EST:** 2003
SALES (est): 74.61K **Privately Held**
SIC: 2741 Miscellaneous publishing

(G-853)
DECKER SALES INC
5100 E Four Boys Trl (47408-9299)
PHONE.................812 330-1580
Chuck Decker, *Pr*
EMP: 3 **EST:** 1999
SALES (est): 229.41K **Privately Held**
SIC: 3714 Motor vehicle body components and frame

(G-854)
DIALECTICAL PUBLISHING LLC
3008 E Daniel St (47401-4391)
PHONE.................812 650-1094
John Hitchcock, *Prin*
EMP: 4 **EST:** 2019
SALES (est): 88.71K **Privately Held**
SIC: 2741 Miscellaneous publishing

(G-855)
DIESEL PUNK CORE
3520 S Mcdougal St (47403-4638)
PHONE.................812 631-0606
Judder Leinenbach, *Pr*
EMP: 4 **EST:** 2018
SALES (est): 87.26K **Privately Held**
Web: www.dieselpunkcore.com
SIC: 3714 Motor vehicle parts and accessories

(G-856)
DIGITAL IMAGE EDITIONS
117 E Wylie Rd (47408-9764)
PHONE.................812 876-4770
EMP: 5 **EST:** 2013
SALES (est): 81.51K **Privately Held**
Web: www.digitalimageeditions.com
SIC: 2752 Commercial printing, lithographic

(G-857)
DILLMAN FARM INCORPORATED
4955 W State Road 45 (47403-9362)
PHONE.................812 825-5525
Cary Dillman, *Pr*
EMP: 8 **EST:** 1970
SQ FT: 2,160
SALES (est): 2.32MM **Privately Held**
Web: www.dillmanfarm.com
SIC: 2033 2041 2021 Fruit butters: packaged in cans, jars, etc.; Flour and other grain mill products; Creamery butter

(G-858)
DOUBLE E DISTRIBUTING CO INC
Also Called: Double E Dstrbtng Co
2214 E Rock Creek Dr (47401-6852)
PHONE.................812 334-2220
Natalie Epstein, *Pr*
EMP: 1 **EST:** 1976
SQ FT: 900
SALES (est): 252.3K **Privately Held**
Web: www.doubleedistributing.com
SIC: 3299 5199 Built-up mica; Artists' materials

(G-859)
DRC MACHINING LLC
13968 Thacker Rd (47403-8923)
PHONE.................812 825-5783
EMP: 1 **EST:** 2015
SALES (est): 118.06K **Privately Held**
SIC: 3495 Mechanical springs, precision

(G-860)
ELECTRIC PLUS
1030 W 17th St (47404-3390)
PHONE.................812 336-4992
EMP: 10 **EST:** 2017
SALES (est): 1.11MM **Privately Held**
Web: www.electricplus.com
SIC: 3699 1731 Electrical equipment and supplies, nec; Electrical work

(G-861)
ENGRAVING AND STAMP CENTER INC
218 N Madison St (47404-3961)
PHONE.................812 336-0606
Jan Snoddy, *Pr*
Ron Snoddy, *Sec*
EMP: 3 **EST:** 1971
SQ FT: 5,000
SALES (est): 287.51K **Privately Held**
Web: www.bloomingtonmerchants.com
SIC: 3069 2759 Stationer's rubber sundries; Engraving, nec

(G-862)
ERIC ISAACSON
Also Called: Eric Isaacson Software
416 E University St (47403-4739)
PHONE.................812 339-1811
Eric Isaacson, *Owner*
EMP: 1 **EST:** 1986
SALES (est): 250K **Privately Held**
Web: www.eji.com
SIC: 7371 7372 Computer software development; Prepackaged software

(G-863)
EVERYWHERE SIGNS LLC
2630 N Walnut St (47404-2008)
PHONE.................812 323-1471
EMP: 5 **EST:** 1993
SQ FT: 1,800
SALES (est): 457.67K **Privately Held**
Web: www.everywheresigns.com
SIC: 3993 Signs and advertising specialties

(G-864)
FAZTECH LLC
7069 S Leisure Ln (47401-9082)
PHONE.................812 327-0926
EMP: 5 **EST:** 2005
SALES (est): 433.08K **Privately Held**
Web: www.faztechusa.com
SIC: 3569 8731 3845 Liquid automation machinery and equipment; Commercial physical research; Respiratory analysis equipment, electromedical

(G-865)
FERRILL-FISHER INCORPORATED
8768 N Wayport Rd (47404)
PHONE.................812 935-9000
John L Fisher, *Prin*
EMP: 5 **EST:** 2015
SALES (est): 300.6K **Privately Held**
Web: www.ferrillfisher.com
SIC: 2295 Metallizing of fabrics

(G-866)
FIBER TECHNOLOGIES LLC
2517 E Caray Ct (47401-8571)
PHONE.................812 569-4641
EMP: 2 **EST:** 2004
SQ FT: 200
SALES (est): 152.41K **Privately Held**
Web: www.fibertechnologiesllc.com
SIC: 2821 Plastics materials and resins

(G-867)
GET PUBLISHED INC
Also Called: Iuniverse
1663 S Liberty Dr Ste 200 (47403-5161)
PHONE.................812 334-5279
Bill Elliot, *Pr*
EMP: 500 **EST:** 2009
SALES (est): 21.94MM **Privately Held**
Web: www.authorlearningcenter.com
SIC: 2731 Book publishing

(G-868)
GOOD EARTH COMPOST LLC
650 E Empire Mill Rd (47401-9273)
PHONE.................812 824-7928
EMP: 2 **EST:** 1977
SQ FT: 2,500
SALES (est): 300K **Privately Held**
Web: www.gogoodearth.com
SIC: 2493 Reconstituted wood products

(G-869)
GRAPHIC VISIONS
Also Called: Graphic Vsons Screen Prtg Sgns
1314 W Kirkwood Ave (47404-5062)
P.O. Box 1336 (47402-1336)
PHONE.................812 331-7446
Rob Hudson, *Owner*
EMP: 3 **EST:** 1983
SQ FT: 2,500
SALES (est): 215.64K **Privately Held**
Web: www.graphicvisionsbloomington.com
SIC: 7336 2759 3993 Graphic arts and related design; Screen printing; Signs and advertising specialties

(G-870)
GREEN NURSERY INC
Also Called: Green Nursery, The
101 W Kirkwood Ave Ste 107 (47404-6129)
PHONE.................812 269-2220
Scott Noroozi, *CEO*
▲ **EMP:** 5 **EST:** 2006
SQ FT: 2,200
SALES (est): 493.11K **Privately Held**
Web: www.thegreennursery.com
SIC: 5993 2833 Cannabis store; Drugs and herbs: grading, grinding, and milling

(G-871)
GRIFFIN CLARK LLC
2738 S Pinehurst Dr (47403-3413)
PHONE.................765 491-9059
Griffin Clark, *Owner*
EMP: 1 **EST:** 2013
SALES (est): 41.31K **Privately Held**
SIC: 7699 1711 3731 Boiler and heating repair services; Plumbing, heating, air-conditioning; Shipbuilding and repairing

(G-872)
GRINER ENGINEERING INC
2500 N Curry Pike (47404-1431)
PHONE.................812 332-2220
John Griner, *Pr*
EMP: 75 **EST:** 1976
SQ FT: 24,000
SALES (est): 9.21MM **Privately Held**
Web: www.griner.com
SIC: 3599 Machine shop, jobbing and repair

(G-873)
HALL SIGNS INC
4495 W Vernal Pike (47404-9333)
P.O. Box 515 (47402-0515)
PHONE.................812 332-9355
Larry Hall, *Pr*
Patsy Hall, *Sec*
◆ **EMP:** 75 **EST:** 1949

Bloomington - Monroe County (G-874)

SQ FT: 75,000
SALES (est): 4.94MM **Privately Held**
Web: www.hallsigns.com
SIC: 3993 Signs, not made in custom sign painting shops

(G-874)
HAMBLEN MACHINE INC
1830 S Walnut St (47401-7719)
PHONE..................................812 330-6685
Benjamin Hamblen, *Pr*
EMP: 15 EST: 2009
SQ FT: 4,800
SALES (est): 505.95K **Privately Held**
Web: www.hamblenmachine.com
SIC: 3599 Machine shop, jobbing and repair

(G-875)
HARTZELLS HOMEMADE ICE CREAM
107 N Dunn St (47408-4047)
PHONE..................................812 332-3502
Hartzell Martel, *Owner*
EMP: 7 EST: 2009
SALES (est): 137.77K **Privately Held**
Web: www.hartzellsicecream.com
SIC: 2052 Cones, ice cream

(G-876)
HEITINK VENEERS INCORPORATED
1141 N Sunrise Greetings Ct (47404-2547)
P.O. Box 5176 (47407-5176)
PHONE..................................812 336-6436
Gerrit Heitink, *Pr*
Jan Berend Heitink, *
Vera Heitink, *
▲ EMP: 42 EST: 1983
SQ FT: 50,000
SALES (est): 4.87MM **Privately Held**
Web: www.heitink.us
SIC: 2435 5031 Veneer stock, hardwood; Veneer

(G-877)
HI-RISE SIGN & LIGHTING LLC
Also Called: Hi-Rise & Sign Services
6524 W Ison Rd (47403-8003)
PHONE..................................812 825-4448
Jeffery A Arbuckle, *Prin*
EMP: 7 EST: 2012
SALES (est): 442.76K **Privately Held**
Web: www.hirisesign.com
SIC: 3993 Signs and advertising specialties

(G-878)
HOLLERS WELDING LLC
13983 E Gardner Rd (47403-9000)
PHONE..................................812 825-9834
Jason Hollers, *Prin*
EMP: 1 EST: 2007
SALES (est): 47.72K **Privately Held**
Web: www.hollerswelding.com
SIC: 7692 Welding repair

(G-879)
HOOSIER CAB COMPANY LLC
500 S Morton St Ste 20 (47403-2420)
PHONE..................................812 822-2508
Julie Wonder, *Prin*
EMP: 5 EST: 2016
SALES (est): 102.8K **Privately Held**
SIC: 3674 Semiconductors and related devices

(G-880)
HOOSIER HELICOPTER SVCS INC
7900 N Thames Dr (47408-9337)
PHONE..................................812 935-5296
Wallace Kinder, *Pr*
EMP: 1 EST: 2001

SALES (est): 95K **Privately Held**
SIC: 3721 Helicopters

(G-881)
HOOSIER RECLAIMED TIMBER
5660 N Murat Rd (47408-9531)
PHONE..................................812 322-3912
EMP: 6 EST: 2012
SALES (est): 293.96K **Privately Held**
Web: www.hoosierreclaimedtimber.net
SIC: 2431 Millwork

(G-882)
HOOSIER TIMES INC (DH)
Also Called: Herald Times
1840 S Walnut St (47401-7733)
P.O. Box 909 (47402-0909)
PHONE..................................812 331-4270
Scott C Schurz, *Pr*
Mayer Malloney, *
Linda Breeden, *
Eric Mcintosh, *Treas*
EMP: 230 EST: 1966
SALES (est): 40.17MM
SALES (corp-wide): 3.28B **Publicly Held**
Web: www.heraldtimesonline.com
SIC: 2711 4813 2791 2752 Newspapers: publishing only, not printed on site; Online service providers; Typesetting; Commercial printing, lithographic
HQ: Schurz Communications, Inc.
1301 E Douglas Rd Ste 200
Mishawaka IN 46545
574 247-7237

(G-883)
HOOSIER TIRE & RETREADING INC
5200 W State Road 46 (47404-9695)
PHONE..................................812 876-8286
Gary Burton, *Pr*
EMP: 10 EST: 1990
SQ FT: 10,000
SALES (est): 844.49K **Privately Held**
SIC: 7534 5531 Tire retreading and repair shops; Automotive tires

(G-884)
HOOSIER WOOD WORKS
118 E Ridgeview Dr (47401-7316)
PHONE..................................812 325-9823
Roger Kugler, *Owner*
EMP: 5 EST: 2008
SALES (est): 107.78K **Privately Held**
Web: www.hoosierwoodworks.com
SIC: 2431 Millwork

(G-885)
HUNTSMAN INTL TRDG CORP
4100 W Profile Pkwy (47404-2546)
PHONE..................................812 334-7090
EMP: 70
SALES (corp-wide): 6.11B **Publicly Held**
Web: www.huntsman.com
SIC: 2821 Plastics materials and resins
HQ: Huntsman International Trading Corporation
10003 Woodloch Forest Dr # 260
The Woodlands TX 77380

(G-886)
IN CASE OF EMERGENCY PRESS
1112 S Morton St (47403-4744)
P.O. Box 26 (47402-0026)
PHONE..................................812 650-3352
EMP: 6 EST: 2016
SALES (est): 160.51K **Privately Held**
Web: www.incaseofemergencypress.com
SIC: 2396 Screen printing on fabric articles

(G-887)
INDEPENDENT LIMESTONE CO LLC
6001 S Rockport Rd (47423-9152)
P.O. Box 26 (47426-0026)
PHONE..................................812 824-4951
EMP: 25 EST: 1927
SQ FT: 1,400
SALES (est): 2.38MM **Privately Held**
Web: www.independentlimestone.com
SIC: 1411 Limestone, dimension-quarrying

(G-888)
INDIANA LMSTONE ACQISITION LLC (DH)
Also Called: Indiana Limestone Company
120 W 7th St Ste 210 (47404-3839)
PHONE..................................812 275-3341
Matthew Howard, *CEO*
Duffe Elkins, *COO*
▲ EMP: 28 EST: 1926
SALES (est): 14.1MM
SALES (corp-wide): 2.1MM **Privately Held**
Web: www.indianalimestonecompany.com
SIC: 3281 1411 Cut stone and stone products; Limestone, dimension-quarrying
HQ: Polycor Inc
100-76 Rue Saint-Paul
Quebec QC G1K 3
418 692-4695

(G-889)
INDIANA LUMBER INC
8215 S State Road 446 (47401-9742)
PHONE..................................812 837-9493
Dennis Blackwell, *Pr*
May Blackwell, *Sec*
EMP: 8 EST: 1986
SQ FT: 7,000
SALES (est): 736.15K **Privately Held**
Web: www.myblacklumber.com
SIC: 2431 5713 Moldings, wood: unfinished and prefinished; Carpets

(G-890)
INDIANA METAL CRAFT INC
4602 W Innovation Dr (47404-8713)
P.O. Box 546 (47402-0546)
PHONE..................................812 336-2362
Ronald D Davis, *Pr*
▲ EMP: 80 EST: 1988
SQ FT: 27,000
SALES (est): 6.38MM **Privately Held**
Web: www.indianaimc.com
SIC: 3993 Advertising novelties

(G-891)
INTERNATIONAL A I INC
7909 S Fairfax Rd (47401-8955)
PHONE..................................812 824-2473
Bradley S Blume, *Pr*
Clem Blume, *VP*
EMP: 3 EST: 1978
SQ FT: 8,600
SALES (est): 564.25K **Privately Held**
Web: www.internationalai.com
SIC: 5191 3523 Farm supplies; Poultry brooders, feeders and waterers

(G-892)
IRVING MATERIALS INC
Also Called: I M I
1800 N Kinser Pike (47404-1900)
PHONE..................................812 333-8530
EMP: 11
SALES (corp-wide): 814.09MM **Privately Held**
Web: www.irvmat.com
SIC: 3273 Ready-mixed concrete
PA: Irving Materials, Inc.
8032 N State Road 9

Greenfield IN 46140
317 326-3101

(G-893)
IU INTERNATIONAL SVC CTR
601 E Kirkwood Ave (47405-1223)
PHONE..................................812 855-9086
EMP: 12 EST: 2017
SALES (est): 110.88K **Privately Held**
Web: www.idsnews.com
SIC: 2711 Newspapers, publishing and printing

(G-894)
IUNIVERSE INC
1663 S Liberty Dr (47403-5161)
PHONE..................................812 330-2909
Kevin Weiss, *Pr*
Tony Arndt, *
▼ EMP: 342 EST: 1996
SALES (est): 1.55MM
SALES (corp-wide): 215.46MM **Privately Held**
Web: www.iuniverse.com
SIC: 2731 Book publishing
PA: Author Solutions Llc
1663 S Liberty Dr
Bloomington IN 47403
812 339-6000

(G-895)
JACK FORNEY
512 W 15th St (47404-3416)
P.O. Box 943 (47402-0943)
PHONE..................................812 334-1259
Jack Forney, *Owner*
▲ EMP: 1 EST: 1974
SALES (est): 64.93K **Privately Held**
SIC: 3911 Jewelry, precious metal

(G-896)
JERDEN INDUSTRIES INC
1104 S Morton St (47403-4798)
PHONE..................................812 332-1762
William D Jerden, *Pr*
EMP: 21 EST: 1969
SQ FT: 19,000
SALES (est): 550.31K **Privately Held**
Web: www.jerdenindustries.com
SIC: 3451 Screw machine products

(G-897)
JERICO METAL SPECIALTIES INC
1111 W 17th St Ste 1 (47404-3003)
P.O. Box 7016 (47407-7016)
PHONE..................................812 339-3182
EMP: 11 EST: 1996
SQ FT: 10,000
SALES (est): 2.28MM **Privately Held**
Web: www.jericometals.com
SIC: 3441 Fabricated structural metal

(G-898)
K W DEER PROCESSING
1715 E Rayletown Rd (47401-9353)
PHONE..................................812 824-2492
EMP: 6 EST: 1996
SALES (est): 335.69K **Privately Held**
Web: www.kwdeerprocessing.com
SIC: 2011 Meat packing plants

(G-899)
KC DESIGNS
Also Called: K C Designs Printing
2801 W Bristol Rd (47404-1207)
PHONE..................................812 876-4020
Karl Clark, *Owner*
EMP: 2 EST: 1992
SALES (est): 132.28K **Privately Held**
Web: www.kcdesignsprinting.com

GEOGRAPHIC SECTION　　　　　　　　　　　　　　　　　　　　　　　Bloomington - Monroe County (G-924)

SIC: 2752 Offset printing

(G-900)
KENNEY ORTHPDICS BLMINGTON LLC
Also Called: Kenney Orthopedics
474 S Landmark Ave (47403-5000)
PHONE..............................812 727-3651
EMP: 4 EST: 2018
SALES (est): 454.57K
SALES (corp-wide): 23.4MM Privately Held
Web: www.kenneyorthopedics.com
SIC: 3842 Surgical appliances and supplies
PA: Kenney Ortho Group, Inc.
　　208 Normandy Ct
　　Nicholasville KY 40356
　　859 241-1015

(G-901)
KETCH PUBLISHING
4675 N Benton Dr (47408-9503)
PHONE..............................812 327-0072
Allen Ketchersid, Prin
EMP: 2 EST: 2010
SALES (est): 113.81K Privately Held
Web: www.numaproject.com
SIC: 2741 Miscellaneous publishing

(G-902)
KNOWLEDGE DIFFUSION GAMES LLC
Also Called: Knowledge Diffusion Games
1441 S Fenbrook Ln Ste 100 (47401)
PHONE..............................812 361-4424
Margaret Clements, Pr
EMP: 2 EST: 2015
SQ FT: 500
SALES (est): 90.72K Privately Held
Web: www.knowledgediffusion.org
SIC: 7373 7379 7372 Value-added resellers, computer systems; Online services technology consultants; Application computer software

(G-903)
KP PHARMACEUTICAL TECH INC
1212 W Rappel Ave (47404-1702)
PHONE..............................812 330-8121
Rajinder Matharu, Pr
Joythi Matharu, *
EMP: 25 EST: 1997
SQ FT: 7,000
SALES (est): 4.99MM Privately Held
Web: www.kppt.com
SIC: 2834 8731 Pharmaceutical preparations; Commercial physical research

(G-904)
KURVY KURVES KOUTURE LLC
1100 N Crescent Rd Apt A208 (47404-2919)
PHONE..............................812 340-6090
Ebony Holmes, Managing Member
EMP: 12 EST: 2019
SALES (est): 997.25K Privately Held
Web: www.kurvykurveskouture.com
SIC: 2335 Women's, junior's, and misses' dresses

(G-905)
LAKOTA LANGUAGE CONSORTIUM
Also Called: LAKOTA LANGUAGE CONSORTIUM
1720 N Kinser Pike (47404-2210)
PHONE..............................888 525-6828
Wilhelm Meya, Ex Dir
▲ EMP: 10 EST: 2004
SALES (est): 897.68K Privately Held
Web: www.lakhota.org

SIC: 8299 2731 Language school; Book publishing

(G-906)
LAMINATED TOPS CENTRAL IND INC
711 E Dillman Rd (47401-9288)
PHONE..............................812 824-6299
Richard Raake, Pr
Robert Raake, *
Richard Raake, VP
Margaret Raake, *
EMP: 25 EST: 1969
SQ FT: 20,000
SALES (est): 2.89MM Privately Held
Web: www.laminatedtops.com
SIC: 5211 2541 Counter tops; Wood partitions and fixtures

(G-907)
LAS ARRIBES LLC
Also Called: Manolos Wines
8768 N Wayport Rd (47404-9463)
PHONE..............................317 892-9463
Manuel Hernandez Martin, Brnch Mgr
EMP: 20
SIC: 2084 Wines, brandy, and brandy spirits
PA: Las Arribes Llc
　　6700 S Church Rd
　　Bloomington IN 47401

(G-908)
LEARFIELD SPORTS
1710 N Kinser Pike (47404-2210)
PHONE..............................812 339-7201
EMP: 1 EST: 2009
SALES (est): 72.46K Privately Held
Web: www.learfield.com
SIC: 3949 Sporting and athletic goods, nec

(G-909)
LEE SUPPLY CORP
Also Called: LEE SUPPLY CORP.
1821 W 3rd St (47404-5206)
P.O. Box 757 (47402-0757)
PHONE..............................812 333-4343
David Barnes, Brnch Mgr
EMP: 12
SALES (corp-wide): 70.28MM Privately Held
Web: www.gotolee.com
SIC: 5712 5074 3432 Cabinet work, custom; Plumbing and hydronic heating supplies; Plumbing fixture fittings and trim
PA: Lee Supply Corp
　　6610 Guion Rd
　　Indianapolis IN 46268
　　317 290-2500

(G-910)
LENNIES INC
Also Called: Bloomington Brewing Co
514 E Kirkwood Ave (47408-4059)
P.O. Box 6955 (47407-6955)
PHONE..............................812 323-2112
Jeffrey Mease, Pr
Lennie Dare, *
EMP: 40 EST: 1989
SALES (est): 872.12K Privately Held
Web: www.bloomingtonbrew.com
SIC: 5812 2082 Chicken restaurant; Beer (alcoholic beverage)

(G-911)
LG METALWORKS LLC
4200 N Mount Gilead Rd (47408-9631)
PHONE..............................812 333-4344
EMP: 1 EST: 2013
SALES (est): 160.95K Privately Held
Web: www.lgmetalworks.org
SIC: 3599 7389 Machine shop, jobbing and repair; Business services, nec

(G-912)
LK TECHNOLOGIES INC
1590 S Liberty Dr Ste A (47403-5167)
PHONE..............................812 332-4449
Larry Kesmodel, Pr
Greg Hepfer, Dir
EMP: 5 EST: 1985
SQ FT: 14,000
SALES (est): 687.34K Privately Held
Web: www.lktech.com
SIC: 3826 5049 Spectroscopic and other optical properties measuring equip.; Scientific instruments

(G-913)
LONG LEATHER WORKS LLC
518 W 4th St (47404-5128)
PHONE..............................812 336-5309
Michael O Long, Owner
EMP: 3 EST: 1982
SALES (est): 166.34K Privately Held
Web: www.longleatherworks.com
SIC: 3172 Personal leather goods, nec

(G-914)
MADDOCK CONSTRUCTION EQP LLC
239 W Grimes Ln (47403-3015)
PHONE..............................812 349-3000
David Maddock, *
EMP: 25 EST: 2013
SQ FT: 90,000
SALES (est): 2.06MM Privately Held
Web: www.maddockcorp.com
SIC: 3531 Construction machinery attachments

(G-915)
MARCO PLASTICS INC
1616 S Huntington Dr (47401-6619)
P.O. Box 2133 (47402-2133)
PHONE..............................812 333-0062
Martin P Witkiewicz, Pr
Donna Witkiewicz, Sec
Joseph Witkiewicz, Genl Mgr
EMP: 12 EST: 1980
SQ FT: 12,000
SALES (est): 2.07MM Privately Held
Web: www.marcoplasticsinc.com
SIC: 3089 Injection molding of plastics

(G-916)
MCD MACHINE INCORPORATED
2345 W Industrial Park Dr (47404-2602)
PHONE..............................812 339-1240
Melinda Davis, Pr
Cj Davis, VP
EMP: 9 EST: 2003
SALES (est): 1.02MM Privately Held
Web: www.mcdmachineinc.com
SIC: 3599 3449 3444 Machine shop, jobbing and repair; Miscellaneous metalwork; Sheet metalwork

(G-917)
METROPOLITAN PRINTING SVCS LLC
Also Called: Metropolitan Printing, Rrd
720 S Morton St (47403-2498)
PHONE..............................812 332-7279
Mark Leggio, Pr
Wes Menefee, *
EMP: 175 EST: 1967
SQ FT: 23,000
SALES (est): 3.35MM
SALES (corp-wide): 15B Privately Held
SIC: 2752 Offset printing
HQ: Consolidated Graphics, Inc.
　　5858 Westheimer Rd # 200
　　Houston TX 77057

(G-918)
MICHAEL DUFF
Also Called: Berg Bows
4615 E State Road 45 (47408-9668)
PHONE..............................812 336-8994
EMP: 1 EST: 1957
SALES (est): 85.37K Privately Held
Web: www.bergbows.com
SIC: 3931 7929 String instruments and parts; Entertainers and entertainment groups

(G-919)
MIDWEST COLOR PRINTING LLC
2458 S Walnut St (47401-7730)
PHONE..............................812 822-2947
Michael Richardson, Managing Member
EMP: 5 EST: 2007
SQ FT: 1,200
SALES (est): 976.71K Privately Held
Web: www.midwestcolorprinting.com
SIC: 2752 Offset printing

(G-920)
MIRWEC FILM INCORPORATED
Also Called: Mirwec Coating
601 S Liberty Dr (47403-1925)
P.O. Box 2263 (47402-2263)
PHONE..............................812 331-7194
Yoshinari Yasui, Pr
Albert J Velasquez, Sec
▲ EMP: 19 EST: 1988
SQ FT: 13,000
SALES (est): 4.62MM Privately Held
Web: www.mirwec-coating.com
SIC: 3081 Polypropylene film and sheet
PA: Yasui Seiki Co., Ltd.
　　1-5-1, Kadosawabashi
　　Ebina KNG 243-0

(G-921)
MISTER HICBACHI
4400 E 3rd St (47401-5548)
PHONE..............................812 339-6288
EMP: 6 EST: 2011
SALES (est): 69.72K Privately Held
SIC: 3421 Table and food cutlery, including butchers'

(G-922)
MOBILE POWER WASHING LLC
Also Called: We Do Everything
4693 N Brookbank Dr (47404-8900)
PHONE..............................219 863-0066
EMP: 10 EST: 2019
SALES (est): 485.55K Privately Held
SIC: 1799 3569 Exterior cleaning, including sandblasting; Blast cleaning equipment, dustless

(G-923)
MOLD STOPPERS OF INDIANA
1135 N Logan Rd (47404-2580)
PHONE..............................812 325-1609
Michelle Galloway, Prin
EMP: 2 EST: 2013
SALES (est): 85.4K Privately Held
Web: www.moldstoppersofindiana.com
SIC: 3544 Industrial molds

(G-924)
MONROE COUNTY REGIONAL SEWER
P.O. Box 362 (47402-0362)
PHONE..............................812 824-9005
Gary Lentz, Pr
EMP: 3 EST: 2003
SALES (est): 201.71K Privately Held
SIC: 3589 Sewage and water treatment equipment

Bloomington - Monroe County (G-925) — GEOGRAPHIC SECTION

(G-925)
MR COPY INC
501 E 10th St (47408-3699)
PHONE..................812 334-2679
Mary Seeber, *Pr*
EMP: 4 EST: 1958
SALES (est): 368.46K **Privately Held**
Web: www.copysales.com
SIC: **2752** 7334 Offset printing; Photocopying and duplicating services

(G-926)
MSP AVIATION INC
Also Called: MSP
239 W Grimes Ln (47403-3015)
PHONE..................812 333-6100
John Goode, *Pr*
Jennifer Cowden, *
EMP: 30 EST: 2002
SQ FT: 20,000
SALES (est): 7.47MM **Privately Held**
Web: www.msp-aviation.com
SIC: **3728** Aircraft parts and equipment, nec

(G-927)
MWF LLC
3000 S Walnut Street Pike Apt F6 (47401)
PHONE..................812 936-5303
EMP: 6 EST: 2007
SALES (est): 243.56K **Privately Held**
SIC: **3087** Custom compound purchased resins

(G-928)
MYFIN INC
Also Called: Tap, The
101 N College Ave (47404-3947)
PHONE..................812 287-8579
Mallory Korpalski, *Acctg Mgr*
EMP: 12 EST: 2013
SALES (est): 915.72K **Privately Held**
Web: www.thetapbeerbar.com
SIC: **2082** 2599 Beer (alcoholic beverage); Bar, restaurant and cafeteria furniture

(G-929)
NEW PHILOSOPHER PRSS
5156 N Brummetts Creek Rd (47408-9616)
PHONE..................812 964-0786
Fran Weisman, *Owner*
EMP: 2 EST: 1999
SALES (est): 90.76K **Privately Held**
SIC: **2741** Miscellaneous publishing

(G-930)
NEWTONS LEGACY WDWKG ENGRV LLC
2920 N Hartstrait Rd (47404-9529)
PHONE..................812 322-3360
Regina Newton, *Prin*
EMP: 5 EST: 2016
SALES (est): 54.13K **Privately Held**
Web: www.newtonslegacy.com
SIC: **2431** Millwork

(G-931)
NUAXON BIOSCIENCE INC
899 S College Mall Rd Unit 161 (47401-6301)
P.O. Box 353 (47424-0353)
PHONE..................812 762-4400
Girish Soman, *Ch Bd*
Jason Edwards, *CEO*
Tena Edwards, *COO*
EMP: 3 EST: 2013
SALES (est): 282.32K **Privately Held**
Web: www.nuaxon.com
SIC: **2833** Medicinals and botanicals

(G-932)
OAK & STONE EXCAVATING & CNSTR
7811 W Eller Rd (47403-9112)
PHONE..................812 361-6901
Amy Deckard, *Prin*
EMP: 6 EST: 2020
SALES (est): 268.59K **Privately Held**
Web: www.oakandstoneexcavating.com
SIC: **3531** Plows: construction, excavating, and grading

(G-933)
OHIO RIVER VENEER LLC
650 E Empire Mill Rd (47401-9273)
P.O. Box 169 (47426-0169)
PHONE..................812 824-7928
EMP: 10 EST: 2002
SQ FT: 1,200
SALES (est): 422.54K **Privately Held**
Web: www.orveneer.com
SIC: **2411** Logging camps and contractors

(G-934)
OHM AUTOMOTIVE LLC
Also Called: Custom Manufacturing Solutions
3748 S Claybridge Dr (47401-8565)
PHONE..................812 879-5455
EMP: 8 EST: 2012
SALES (est): 516.89K **Privately Held**
SIC: **7538** 7692 General automotive repair shops; Welding repair

(G-935)
OLIVER WINE COMPANY INC (HQ)
Also Called: Oliver Winery
200 E Winery Rd (47404)
PHONE..................812 876-5800
Julie Adams, *CEO*
Bill Oliver, *
Pete Batule, *
▲ EMP: 53 EST: 1972
SQ FT: 30,000
SALES (est): 28.65MM
SALES (corp-wide): 55.33MM **Privately Held**
Web: www.oliverwinery.com
SIC: **5921** 2084 Wine; Wines
PA: Nexphase Capital, Lp
600 Lexington Ave
New York NY 10022
212 878-6000

(G-936)
ON THE GO PORTABLE WATER SOFTE
3905 W Roll Ave (47403-3181)
PHONE..................260 482-9614
Benjamin Scherschel, *Pr*
EMP: 10 EST: 2004
SALES (est): 992.56K **Privately Held**
Web: www.portablewatersoftener.com
SIC: **3589** 7389 Water filters and softeners, household type; Water softener service

(G-937)
ONE-STOP TRAVEL SHOP INC
317 E Dodds St (47401-4787)
PHONE..................812 339-9496
EMP: 2 EST: 1994
SQ FT: 600
SALES (est): 189.48K **Privately Held**
Web: www.1ststoptravelstore.com
SIC: **3161** Traveling bags

(G-938)
ORGANIZED LIVING INC
1500 S Strong Dr (47403-8741)
PHONE..................812 334-8839
Roy Hammon, *Brnch Mgr*
EMP: 170
SALES (corp-wide): 44.13MM **Privately Held**
Web: www.organizedliving.com
SIC: **2542** 5211 1799 Partitions and fixtures, except wood; Closets, interiors and accessories; Home/office interiors finishing, furnishing and remodeling
PA: Organized Living Inc.
3100 E Kemper Rd
Cincinnati OH 45241
513 489-9300

(G-939)
ORION GLOBAL SOURCING INC
1516 S Walnut St (47401-7711)
PHONE..................812 332-3338
Ian Munnoch, *Pr*
Alan Carlson, *VP*
▲ EMP: 4 EST: 2003
SQ FT: 1,500
SALES (est): 625.49K **Privately Held**
SIC: **3679** 7373 7389 Electronic circuits; Computer integrated systems design; Printed circuitry graphic layout

(G-940)
P-AMERICAS LLC
Also Called: Pepsico
214 W 17th St (47404-3536)
PHONE..................812 332-1200
Rick Nicolas, *Brnch Mgr*
EMP: 1
SALES (corp-wide): 86.39B **Publicly Held**
Web: www.pepsico.com
SIC: **2086** Carbonated soft drinks, bottled and canned
HQ: P-Americas Llc
1 Pepsi Way
Somers NY 10589
336 896-5740

(G-941)
PALIBRIO
1663 S Liberty Dr (47403-5161)
PHONE..................812 671-9757
Andrew Phillips, *CEO*
EMP: 2 EST: 2010
SALES (est): 156.65K **Privately Held**
Web: www.xlibris.com
SIC: **2731** Book publishing

(G-942)
PATRICK J FSCHER PIPE ORGAN SV
510 E University St (47401-4829)
PHONE..................978 314-7312
Patrick Fischer, *Prin*
EMP: 4 EST: 2019
SALES (est): 45.13K **Privately Held**
SIC: **3931** Pipes, organ

(G-943)
PATRIOT INDUSTRIES LLC ◆
Also Called: Patriot Industries
8917 N Old State Road 37 (47408-9727)
PHONE..................574 370-7899
Matthew Reiman, *Prin*
EMP: 1 EST: 2022
SALES (est): 27.98K **Privately Held**
Web: www.patriotsas.com
SIC: **3484** 5091 5099 Small arms; Sporting and recreation goods; Durable goods, nec

(G-944)
PENGUIN ENTERPRISES LLC
Also Called: Chocolate Moose, The
401 S Walnut St (47401-4613)
P.O. Box 1685 (47402-1685)
PHONE..................812 333-0475
Justin Loveless, *Managing Member*
EMP: 45 EST: 2012
SQ FT: 1,800
SALES (est): 3.26MM **Privately Held**
Web: www.moosebtown.com
SIC: **2024** Ice cream and frozen deserts

(G-945)
PEPSI-COLA METRO BTLG CO INC
Also Called: Pepsi-Cola
214 W 17th St (47404-3536)
PHONE..................812 332-1200
Ted Ness, *Mgr*
EMP: 18
SALES (corp-wide): 86.39B **Publicly Held**
Web: www.pepsico.com
SIC: **2086** 5149 Carbonated soft drinks, bottled and canned; Beverages, except coffee and tea
HQ: Pepsi-Cola Metropolitan Bottling Company, Inc.
700 Anderson Hill Rd
Purchase NY 10577
914 767-6000

(G-946)
PERSPICACITY LLC
4718 E Donington Dr (47401-8598)
P.O. Box 5904 (47407-5904)
PHONE..................812 650-2080
Justin Stimson, *Dir*
EMP: 1 EST: 2009
SALES (est): 56.16K **Privately Held**
SIC: **7371** 7372 Computer software systems analysis and design, custom; Application computer software

(G-947)
PHONOZOIC
1208 W 8th St (47404-3611)
PHONE..................812 331-0047
Patrick Feaster, *Prin*
EMP: 4 EST: 2011
SALES (est): 72.25K **Privately Held**
Web: www.phonozoic.net
SIC: **2741** Miscellaneous publishing

(G-948)
PRAIRIE GROUP INC
7100 S Old State Road 37 (47403)
PHONE..................812 824-1355
EMP: 6 EST: 2019
SALES (est): 165.09K **Privately Held**
Web: www.prairie.com
SIC: **3273** Ready-mixed concrete

(G-949)
QUALITY VAULT COMPANY
Also Called: Sexton
1908 W Allen St (47403-2840)
PHONE..................812 336-8127
Mark Sexton, *Pr*
Michael Sexton, *VP*
Tina Sexton, *Sec*
EMP: 5 EST: 1978
SALES (est): 239.52K **Privately Held**
SIC: **3272** 5087 Burial vaults, concrete or precast terrazzo; Concrete burial vaults and boxes

(G-950)
QUANTUM 7 GROUP LLC
3523 E Harbor Dr (47401-8884)
PHONE..................812 824-9378
William V West, *Owner*
EMP: 7 EST: 2013
SALES (est): 184.16K **Privately Held**
SIC: **3572** Computer storage devices

(G-951)
RAKE CABINET & SURFC SOLUTIONS

705 E Dillman Rd (47401-9288)
PHONE..................812 824-8338
EMP: 1 **EST:** 2008
SALES (est): 101.98K **Privately Held**
Web: www.rakesolutions.com
SIC: 3553 Cabinet makers' machinery

(G-952)
RB CONCEPTS
Also Called: RB Apparel
8451 S Marcy Ct (47401-7208)
PHONE..................317 735-2172
Rick Bomberger, *CEO*
EMP: 7 **EST:** 1985
SALES (est): 270K **Privately Held**
Web: www.rbconcepts.net
SIC: 2231 Apparel and outerwear broadwoven fabrics

(G-953)
REEARTH TECHNOLOGIES
706 W Allen St (47403-4706)
PHONE..................812 219-6517
Colin Roy-ehri, *Owner*
EMP: 1 **EST:** 2013
SALES (est): 50.76K **Privately Held**
Web: www.reearthtechnologies.com
SIC: 3585 3674 Air conditioning equipment, complete; Solar cells

(G-954)
REED QUARRIES INC
2950 N Prow Rd (47404-1602)
P.O. Box 64 (47402-0064)
PHONE..................812 332-2771
Edward M Reed, *Pr*
Stephen M Reed, *VP*
EMP: 10 **EST:** 1941
SQ FT: 1,200
SALES (est): 510.78K **Privately Held**
Web: www.reedquarries.com
SIC: 1411 Limestone, dimension-quarrying

(G-955)
RICHARD M JUDD
Also Called: Judd Associates
508 W 3rd St (47404-5112)
P.O. Box 205 (95628-0205)
PHONE..................916 704-3364
Richard Judd, *Owner*
EMP: 1 **EST:** 2004
SALES (est): 124.01K **Privately Held**
SIC: 1081 1382 Metal mining services; Oil and gas exploration services

(G-956)
RICHARDSON ENTPS BLMINGTON LLC
Also Called: Fastsigns
2454 S Walnut St (47401-7730)
PHONE..................812 287-8179
EMP: 4 **EST:** 2013
SQ FT: 2,000
SALES (est): 416.25K **Privately Held**
Web: www.fastsigns.com
SIC: 3993 Signs and advertising specialties

(G-957)
RICHCRAFT WOOD PRODUCTS LLC
Also Called: Richcraft Wood Product
4655 W Richland Plaza Dr (47404-9777)
PHONE..................812 320-7884
Jay Richardson, *Managing Member*
EMP: 3 **EST:** 1980
SQ FT: 1,800
SALES (est): 248.74K **Privately Held**
Web: www.richcraftwoodproducts.com
SIC: 2511 Wood household furniture

(G-958)
RIGHTREZ INC
3010 E David Dr (47401-4470)
PHONE..................812 219-1893
Michael C Vonforester, *CEO*
Jim Quinn, *Pr*
Huff Templeton, *COO*
EMP: 3 **EST:** 2003
SALES (est): 230.26K **Privately Held**
Web: www.rightrez.com
SIC: 7372 Prepackaged software

(G-959)
ROGERS GROUP INC
550 S Adams St (47403-2165)
PHONE..................812 333-6324
Mike Agee, *VP*
EMP: 105
SALES (corp-wide): 1.05B **Privately Held**
Web: www.rogersgroupincint.com
SIC: 5032 1794 2431 2426 Stone, crushed or broken; Excavation work; Millwork; Hardwood dimension and flooring mills
PA: Rogers Group, Inc.
421 Great Cir Rd
Nashville TN 37228
615 242-0585

(G-960)
ROGERS GROUP INC
2944 E Covenanter Dr (47401-5494)
PHONE..................812 332-6341
Neil Woldridge, *Mgr*
EMP: 86
SALES (corp-wide): 1.05B **Privately Held**
Web: www.rogersgroupincint.com
SIC: 1221 5032 Bituminous coal and lignite-surface mining; Stone, crushed or broken
PA: Rogers Group, Inc.
421 Great Cir Rd
Nashville TN 37228
615 242-0585

(G-961)
ROGERS GROUP INC
Also Called: Bloomington Crushed Stone
1100 N Oard Rd (47404-9365)
PHONE..................812 333-8560
Dana Boyd, *Mgr*
EMP: 81
SALES (corp-wide): 1.05B **Privately Held**
Web: www.rogersgroupincint.com
SIC: 1422 5032 Crushed and broken limestone; Stone, crushed or broken
PA: Rogers Group, Inc.
421 Great Cir Rd
Nashville TN 37228
615 242-0585

(G-962)
ROGERS GROUP INC
Also Called: Bloomington Asphalt & Cnstr
1110 N Oard Rd (47404-9365)
PHONE..................812 333-8550
Gary Barrow, *Mgr*
EMP: 19
SALES (corp-wide): 1.05B **Privately Held**
Web: www.rogersgroupincint.com
SIC: 1611 2951 General contractor, highway and street construction; Asphalt paving mixtures and blocks
PA: Rogers Group, Inc.
421 Great Cir Rd
Nashville TN 37228
615 242-0585

(G-963)
ROSMARINO CANDLES LLC
310 S High St (47401-7810)
PHONE..................970 218-2835
Rachel Whitcomb, *Prin*
EMP: 5 **EST:** 2018
SALES (est): 195.86K **Privately Held**
Web: www.rosmarinocandles.com
SIC: 3999 Candles

(G-964)
RUSH HOUR STATION
421 E 3rd St (47401-3630)
PHONE..................812 323-7874
EMP: 4 **EST:** 2011
SALES (est): 192.35K **Privately Held**
Web: www.rushhourstation.com
SIC: 3421 Table and food cutlery, including butchers'

(G-965)
SABIN CORPORATION
Also Called: Cook Polymer Technology
3800 W Constitution Ave (47403-3176)
P.O. Box 788 (47402-0788)
PHONE..................812 323-4500
William A Cook, *Pr*
Dave Lessard, *General Vice President**
John R Kamstra, *
Stpehen L Ferguson, *
▲ **EMP:** 235 **EST:** 1969
SQ FT: 70,000
SALES (est): 45.96MM
SALES (corp-wide): 1.61B **Privately Held**
Web: www.cookmedical.com
SIC: 3082 3089 3083 Tubes, unsupported plastics; Molding primary plastics; Laminated plastics plate and sheet
PA: Cook Group Incorporated
750 Daniels Way
Bloomington IN 47404
812 339-2235

(G-966)
SANDY ISLAND PRESS
1215 E Fairwood Dr (47408-9710)
PHONE..................812 360-7288
Jennifer Mackinday, *Prin*
EMP: 1 **EST:** 2010
SALES (est): 67.32K **Privately Held**
Web: www.sandyislandpress.com
SIC: 2741 Miscellaneous publishing

(G-967)
SCOTT NAYLOR
7170 N Old State Road 37 (47408-9445)
PHONE..................812 336-5361
Jay Naylor, *Owner*
EMP: 1 **EST:** 2003
SALES (est): 16.35K **Privately Held**
SIC: 3523 Driers (farm): grain, hay, and seed

(G-968)
SELECT EMBROIDERY/TOP IT OFF
Also Called: Select Embroidery
1713 N College Ave Ste 3 (47408-2479)
PHONE..................812 337-8049
EMP: 10 **EST:** 1992
SALES (est): 339.01K **Privately Held**
SIC: 5699 2395 2396 Customized clothing and apparel; Embroidery products, except Schiffli machine; Automotive and apparel trimmings

(G-969)
SIB INC
Also Called: Scholars Inn Bakehouse
573 W Simpson Chapel Rd (47404-9426)
PHONE..................812 331-6029
EMP: 15 **EST:** 1995
SQ FT: 30,000
SALES (est): 1.13MM **Privately Held**
Web: www.scholarsinn.com
SIC: 2051 Bakery: wholesale or wholesale/retail combined

(G-970)
SIGN GUY
4079 N Brookwood Dr (47404-9602)
PHONE..................812 345-2515
John Huber, *Prin*
EMP: 5 **EST:** 2010
SALES (est): 94.57K **Privately Held**
Web: www.thewholesalesignguy.com
SIC: 3993 Signs and advertising specialties

(G-971)
SIGN TOGETHER
2103 S Georgetown Rd (47401-6774)
PHONE..................812 219-2338
Cynthia Johnson, *Prin*
EMP: 1 **EST:** 2011
SALES (est): 81.08K **Privately Held**
SIC: 3993 Signs and advertising specialties

(G-972)
SIGNRITE
2351 W Thrasher Rd (47403-9420)
PHONE..................812 320-5245
Jeff Nelson, *Prin*
EMP: 1 **EST:** 2011
SALES (est): 95.52K **Privately Held**
Web: www.signritesolutions.com
SIC: 3993 5046 1799 Signs and advertising specialties; Signs, electrical; Sign installation and maintenance

(G-973)
SIGNS NOW
2500 W Industrial Park Dr (47404)
PHONE..................812 323-2776
Roger Watkins, *Owner*
EMP: 1 **EST:** 2010
SALES (est): 87.88K **Privately Held**
Web: www.signsnow.com
SIC: 3993 Signs and advertising specialties

(G-974)
SLAVICA PUBLISHERS
1430 N Willis Dr (47404-2146)
PHONE..................812 856-4186
George Fowler, *Dir*
EMP: 6 **EST:** 2015
SALES (est): 48.16K **Privately Held**
Web: slavica.indiana.edu
SIC: 2741 Miscellaneous publishing

(G-975)
SMART DISPLAYS LLC
5660 N Murat Rd (47408-9531)
PHONE..................812 322-3912
EMP: 7 **EST:** 2010
SALES (est): 182.37K **Privately Held**
Web: www.recognitionphotodisplays.com
SIC: 3993 Signs and advertising specialties

(G-976)
SMILING CROSS INC
Also Called: Smile Promotions
700 S College Ave Ste A (47403)
P.O. Box 8122 (47407)
PHONE..................812 323-9290
Rula Hanania, *Pr*
Alejandra Haddad, *Pr*
Michelle Heitink, *Treas*
EMP: 7 **EST:** 2003
SALES (est): 2.44MM **Privately Held**
Web: www.smilingcross.com
SIC: 5136 5199 2752 7336 Men's and boys' sportswear and work clothing; Advertising specialties; Promotional printing, lithographic; Silk screen design

Bloomington - Monroe County (G-977)

(G-977)
SOCIETY FOR ETHNMUSICOLOGY INC
800 E 3rd St (47405-3657)
PHONE.....................812 855-6672
Anne Rasmussen, *Pr*
Stephen Stuempfle, *Dir*
EMP: 2 **EST:** 1956
SALES (est): 646.67K **Privately Held**
SIC: 2721 Periodicals, publishing only

(G-978)
SOUTHFIELD CORPORATION
7100 S Old State Road 37 (47403-9427)
PHONE.....................812 824-1355
Greg Petro, *Mgr*
EMP: 23
SALES (corp-wide): 99.17MM **Privately Held**
Web: www.brickworkssupply.com
SIC: 3273 3271 1442 Ready-mixed concrete; Concrete block and brick; Construction sand and gravel
PA: Southfield Corporation
  8995 W 95th St
  Palos Hills IL 60465
  708 344-1000

(G-979)
STILLIONS SAW MILL
Also Called: Stillions Sawmill
7208 S Rockport Rd (47403-9157)
PHONE.....................812 824-6542
Dan Stillion, *Owner*
EMP: 4 **EST:** 1977
SALES (est): 230.83K **Privately Held**
SIC: 2421 Lumber: rough, sawed, or planed

(G-980)
STONEFLY PRESS LLC
3001 S Forrester St (47401-4494)
PHONE.....................812 369-4147
Robert D Clouse, *Owner*
EMP: 1 **EST:** 2011
SALES (est): 72K **Privately Held**
Web: www.stonefly.com
SIC: 2741 Miscellaneous publishing

(G-981)
STUDIO INDIANA
430 N Sewell Rd (47408-9408)
PHONE.....................812 332-5073
John Bower, *Owner*
EMP: 2 **EST:** 2005
SALES (est): 90.48K **Privately Held**
Web: www.studioindiana.com
SIC: 2731 Book publishing

(G-982)
SUGAR DADDYS SWEET SHOP
5340 S Old State Road 37 (47401-7517)
PHONE.....................812 824-2253
Deanna Hawkins, *Owner*
EMP: 1 **EST:** 2005
SALES (est): 97.05K **Privately Held**
Web: www.sugardaddyscakesandcatering.com
SIC: 2052 Bakery products, dry

(G-983)
TANGUERO INC
Also Called: CUARTETO TANGUERO
3315 S Daniel Ct (47401-7114)
PHONE.....................415 236-2642
Benjamin Bogart, *Prin*
Benjamin Bogart, *Pr*
Daniel Stein, *Treas*
EMP: 2 **EST:** 2016
SALES (est): 70.82K **Privately Held**
Web: www.moretango.org

SIC: 7929 2731 8299 7911 Entertainment group; Book music: publishing only, not printed on site; Musical instrument lessons; Dance instructor and school services

(G-984)
TASUS CORPORATION (HQ)
300 N Daniels Way (47404)
PHONE.....................812 333-6500
Yasuyuki O'hara, *Ch*
Melanie Walker, *
Craig Slater, *
▲ **EMP:** 206 **EST:** 1986
SALES (est): 370.29MM **Privately Held**
Web: www.tasus.com
SIC: 3089 7389 Injection molding of plastics; Trading stamp promotion and redemption
PA: Tsuchiya Hc.Ltd.
  2-9-29, Kamimaezu, Naka-Ku
  Nagoya AIC 460-0

(G-985)
TEC PHOTOGRAPHY
Also Called: Beautiful Brides By TEC
1011 W Gourley Pike (47404-2132)
PHONE.....................812 332-9847
Terence E Comstock, *Owner*
EMP: 2 **EST:** 1972
SALES (est): 101.28K **Privately Held**
Web: www.tecphotography.com
SIC: 7221 2759 Photographer, still or video; Letterpress printing

(G-986)
TENDRE PRESS LLC
134 N Overhill Dr (47408-4243)
PHONE.....................812 606-9563
Ann Kreilkamp, *Prin*
EMP: 2 **EST:** 2009
SALES (est): 83.46K **Privately Held**
Web: www.tendrepress.com
SIC: 2741 Miscellaneous publishing

(G-987)
TEXACON CUT STONE LLC
4790 Fluck Mill Rd (47403-8900)
PHONE.....................812 824-3211
James Pittman, *Stockholder*
EMP: 6 **EST:** 2013
SALES (est): 921.27K **Privately Held**
Web: www.texaconcutstone.com
SIC: 3281 Cut stone and stone products

(G-988)
TIMBER HAWK BOWS INC
7895 S State Road 446 (47401-9741)
PHONE.....................812 837-9340
Scott Mitchell, *Pr*
EMP: 1 **EST:** 1999
SALES (est): 117.18K **Privately Held**
Web: www.timberhawkbows.com
SIC: 3949 Bows, archery

(G-989)
TIMOTHY REED CARRY ME MUS PUBG
610 S Washington St Apt D (47401-3626)
PHONE.....................812 322-7187
EMP: 4 **EST:** 2016
SALES (est): 61.14K **Privately Held**
SIC: 2741 Miscellaneous publishing

(G-990)
TODDS WLDG & STL FABRICATION
Also Called: Todd's Wldg & Stl Fabricator
4810 S Old State Road 37 (47401-7420)
PHONE.....................812 824-2407
Robert Todd, *Owner*
EMP: 1 **EST:** 1980
SALES (est): 73.99K **Privately Held**

SIC: 7692 3441 Welding repair; Fabricated structural metal

(G-991)
TRAFFORD HOLDINGS LTD
Also Called: Trafford Publishing
1663 S Liberty Dr (47403-5161)
PHONE.....................888 232-4444
EMP: 221 **EST:** 2010
SALES (est): 966.81K
SALES (corp-wide): 215.46MM **Privately Held**
Web: www.trafford.com
SIC: 2731 Books, publishing only
PA: Author Solutions Llc
  1663 S Liberty Dr
  Bloomington IN 47403
  812 339-6000

(G-992)
TRANE US INC
Also Called: Trane
1458 S Liberty Dr (47403-5118)
PHONE.....................800 285-2487
EMP: 6
Web: www.trane.com
SIC: 3585 Refrigeration and heating equipment
HQ: Trane U.S. Inc.
  800-E Beaty St
  Davidson NC 28036
  704 655-4000

(G-993)
TRI STATE TIMBER LLC
3490 E Saddlebrook Ct (47401-8554)
PHONE.....................812 327-8161
EMP: 6 **EST:** 2018
SALES (est): 248.09K **Privately Held**
SIC: 2421 Sawmills and planing mills, general

(G-994)
TRUFAB STAINLESS INC
2126 W Industrial Park Dr (47404-2687)
PHONE.....................812 287-8278
Drew Hoffman, *Prin*
EMP: 13 **EST:** 2013
SALES (est): 1.16MM **Privately Held**
Web: www.trufabstainless.com
SIC: 3441 Fabricated structural metal

(G-995)
TRUSTEES INDIANA UNIVERSITY
Also Called: Indiana Law Journal
211 S Indiana Ave Rm 9 (47405-7001)
PHONE.....................812 855-7995
Shirley Wright, *Mgr*
EMP: 1
SALES (corp-wide): 1.64B **Privately Held**
Web: bloomington.iu.edu
SIC: 2711 8221 Newspapers, publishing and printing; University
PA: Trustees Indiana University
  107 S Indiana Ave
  Bloomington IN 47405
  812 855-4848

(G-996)
TRUSTEES INDIANA UNIVERSITY
Also Called: Indiana Daily Student
120 Ernie Pyle Hall Ind University (47405)
PHONE.....................812 855-0763
Dave Adams, *Prin*
EMP: 29
SALES (corp-wide): 1.64B **Privately Held**
Web: www.idsnews.com
SIC: 2711 2731 Newspapers: publishing only, not printed on site; Book publishing
PA: Trustees Indiana University
  107 S Indiana Ave

Bloomington IN 47405
812 855-4848

(G-997)
TRUSTEES INDIANA UNIVERSITY
Also Called: Indiana Review
465 Ballantine Hall 1020 E Kirkwood Ave (47405)
PHONE.....................812 855-3439
Abdel Shakur, *Prin*
EMP: 8
SALES (corp-wide): 1.64B **Privately Held**
Web: bloomington.iu.edu
SIC: 2721 8221 Magazines: publishing only, not printed on site; University
PA: Trustees Indiana University
  107 S Indiana Ave
  Bloomington IN 47405
  812 855-4848

(G-998)
TRUSTEES INDIANA UNIVERSITY
Also Called: Slavica Publishers
2611 E 10th St Rm 160 (47408-2603)
PHONE.....................812 856-4186
EMP: 4
SALES (corp-wide): 1.64B **Privately Held**
Web: bloomington.iu.edu
SIC: 2721 8221 Trade journals: publishing and printing; University
PA: Trustees Indiana University
  107 S Indiana Ave
  Bloomington IN 47405
  812 855-4848

(G-999)
TRUSTEES INDIANA UNIVERSITY
Also Called: Linguistics Club
900 E 7th St (47405-3905)
PHONE.....................812 855-4848
Robin Gress, *Mgr*
EMP: 17
SALES (corp-wide): 1.64B **Privately Held**
Web: bloomington.iu.edu
SIC: 2741 8221 Miscellaneous publishing; University
PA: Trustees Indiana University
  107 S Indiana Ave
  Bloomington IN 47405
  812 855-4848

(G-1000)
TU JINGHUA
3405 E Longview Ave # 10 (47408-4323)
PHONE.....................812 327-3819
Jinghua Tu, *Owner*
EMP: 1 **EST:** 2014
SALES (est): 49.36K **Privately Held**
SIC: 3663 Radio and t.v. communications equipment

(G-1001)
TURNER MINING GROUP LLC
304 W Kirkwood Ave Apt 100 (47404)
PHONE.....................812 277-9077
Keaton Turner, *Pr*
Jeff Turner, *
Paul Moran, *CCO**
EMP: 200 **EST:** 2017
SALES (est): 29.75MM **Privately Held**
Web: www.turnermining.com
SIC: 1081 Metal mining services

(G-1002)
TUSCA 2
3815 N Collins Dr (47404-9344)
PHONE.....................812 876-2857
Joel Milam, *Pt*
EMP: 5 **EST:** 2016
SALES (est): 178.77K **Privately Held**

GEOGRAPHIC SECTION

SIC: 3499 Fabricated metal products, nec

(G-1003)
UGO BARS LLC
1019 W Howe St (47403-2238)
PHONE.............................812 322-3499
Tracy Gates, *Prin*
EMP: 5 **EST:** 2013
SALES (est): 91.1K **Privately Held**
SIC: 2064 Candy and other confectionery products

(G-1004)
UNIVERSITY PUBLISHING CORP
310 S Washington St (47401-3529)
P.O. Box 1311 (47402-1311)
PHONE.............................812 339-9033
Dennis Campbell, *Prin*
EMP: 20 **EST:** 1967
SQ FT: 10,000
SALES (est): 1.17MM **Privately Held**
SIC: 2741 2791 2789 2752 Directories, nec: publishing only, not printed on site; Typesetting; Bookbinding and related work; Commercial printing, lithographic

(G-1005)
UPLAND BREWING COMPANY INC (PA)
Also Called: Upland Brewing Co.
350 W 11th St (47404-3720)
PHONE.............................812 330-7421
Douglas G Dayhoff, *Pr*
Mark Sattinger, *
EMP: 16 **EST:** 1996
SALES (est): 4.5MM
SALES (corp-wide): 4.5MM **Privately Held**
Web: www.uplandbeer.com
SIC: 2082 5813 5812 Beer (alcoholic beverage); Drinking places; Eating places

(G-1006)
VERY VOCAL VIKING
948 E Chambers Pike (47408-9232)
P.O. Box 903 (47402-0903)
PHONE.............................317 919-8903
Troy Maynard, *Prin*
EMP: 4 **EST:** 2018
SALES (est): 49.66K **Privately Held**
Web: www.veryvocalviking.com
SIC: 2741 Miscellaneous publishing

(G-1007)
VINCENT ALIANO ELC & HVAC INC
5128 W Vernal Pike (47404-8712)
PHONE.............................812 332-3332
EMP: 2 **EST:** 2008
SALES (est): 150.88K **Privately Held**
SIC: 3699 1711 Electrical equipment and supplies, nec; Heating systems repair and maintenance

(G-1008)
WEIGHTS & MEASURES
119 W 7th St (47404-3926)
PHONE.............................812 349-2566
Scott Sowder, *Dir*
EMP: 1 **EST:** 1993
SALES (est): 210.08K **Privately Held**
SIC: 3596 Scales and balances, except laboratory

(G-1009)
WESTBOW PRESS
1663 S Liberty Dr (47403-5161)
PHONE.............................866 928-1240
EMP: 46 **EST:** 2019
SALES (est): 2.4MM
SALES (corp-wide): 10.09B **Publicly Held**
Web: www.westbowpress.com

SIC: 2741 Miscellaneous publishing
HQ: The Zondervan Corporation L L C
3900 Sparks Dr Se
Grand Rapids MI 49546
616 698-6900

(G-1010)
WILBERT SEXTON CORPORATION
2332 W 3rd St (47404-5219)
PHONE.............................812 334-0883
Mark Sexton, *Brnch Mgr*
EMP: 1
SALES (corp-wide): 2.46MM **Privately Held**
Web: www.sextonwilbertconcrete.com
SIC: 3281 Burial vaults, stone
PA: Wilbert Sexton Corporation
1908 W Allen St
Bloomington IN 47403
812 336-6469

(G-1011)
WILBERT SEXTON CORPORATION (PA)
Also Called: Sexton Vault Company
1908 W Allen St (47403-2840)
PHONE.............................812 336-6469
Mark Sexton, *Pr*
Tina Sexton, *Sec*
Everett J Sexton, *Ch Bd*
EMP: 8 **EST:** 1946
SQ FT: 5,500
SALES (est): 2.46MM
SALES (corp-wide): 2.46MM **Privately Held**
Web: www.sextonwilbertconcrete.com
SIC: 3272 Burial vaults, concrete or precast terrazzo

(G-1012)
WILLIAMS BROS HLTH CARE PHRM I
Also Called: United Drugs
574 S Landmark Ave (47403-3239)
PHONE.............................812 335-0000
Nathan Jabhart, *Mgr*
EMP: 40
SALES (corp-wide): 88.5MM **Privately Held**
Web: www.williamsbrospharmacy.com
SIC: 5912 7352 5999 5169 Drug stores; Medical equipment rental; Telephone and communication equipment; Oxygen
PA: Williams Bros. Health Care Pharmacy, Inc.
10 Williams Brothers Dr
Washington IN 47501
812 254-2497

(G-1013)
WINE AND CANVAS DEV LLC
135 N Gates Dr Ste 3 (47404-4894)
PHONE.............................812 345-1019
EMP: 1
SALES (corp-wide): 805.52K **Privately Held**
Web: www.wineandcanvas.com
SIC: 2211 Canvas
PA: Wine And Canvas Development Llc
1760 Cholla Ter
Indianapolis IN 46240
317 345-1567

(G-1014)
WINSPEAR PUBLISHING LLC
209 E Grimes Ln (47401-5837)
PHONE.............................812 204-7973
EMP: 4 **EST:** 2016
SALES (est): 48.98K **Privately Held**
SIC: 2741 Miscellaneous publishing

(G-1015)
WINTERS ASSOC PRMTNAL PDTS INC (PA)
Also Called: Thadco
1048 W 17th St (47404-3338)
P.O. Box 2579 (47402-2579)
PHONE.............................812 330-7000
Kathy Slankard, *Pr*
Kathy A Slinkard, *Sec*
Kelly Slinkard, *Sec*
EMP: 13 **EST:** 1975
SQ FT: 10,000
SALES (est): 2.06MM
SALES (corp-wide): 2.06MM **Privately Held**
Web: www.wintersassociates.com
SIC: 5199 3993 2396 2395 Advertising specialties; Signs and advertising specialties; Automotive and apparel trimmings; Pleating and stitching

(G-1016)
WRACO ENTERPRISES INC
Also Called: Fine Print
125 S Westplex Ave (47404)
P.O. Box 1401 (47402)
PHONE.............................812 339-3987
Joe Wray, *Pr*
EMP: 8 **EST:** 1977
SQ FT: 8,500
SALES (est): 461.73K **Privately Held**
Web: www.fineprint125.com
SIC: 2752 Offset printing

(G-1017)
XLIBRIS CORPORATION
1663 S Liberty Dr Ste 200 (47403-5161)
PHONE.............................812 671-9162
Joe Steinbach, *Pr*
▲ **EMP:** 436 **EST:** 1999
SQ FT: 21,000
SALES (est): 2.4MM
SALES (corp-wide): 215.46MM **Privately Held**
Web: www.xlibris.com
SIC: 2731 7375 Book publishing; Information retrieval services
PA: Author Solutions Llc
1663 S Liberty Dr
Bloomington IN 47403
812 339-6000

(G-1018)
YELLOW CAT LLC
1419 S Winfield Rd (47401-6151)
PHONE.............................913 213-4570
EMP: 5 **EST:** 2018
SALES (est): 248.01K **Privately Held**
SIC: 3647 Vehicular lighting equipment

(G-1019)
ZEPTO SYSTEMS INCORPORATED
3110 S Mulberry Ln (47401-2424)
PHONE.............................812 323-0642
Kelly Souza, *Prin*
EMP: 2 **EST:** 2006
SALES (est): 194.8K **Privately Held**
Web: www.zeptosystems.com
SIC: 3675 Electronic capacitors

Bluffton
Wells County

(G-1020)
20/20 CUSTOM MOLDED PLAS LLC
785 Decker Dr (46714-9787)
PHONE.............................260 565-2020
David E Rupp, *Brnch Mgr*
EMP: 499

SALES (corp-wide): 26.24MM **Privately Held**
Web: www.2020cmp.com
SIC: 3089 Injection molding of plastics
PA: 20/20 Custom Molded Plastics, Llc
14620 Selwyn Dr
Holiday City OH 43543
419 485-2020

(G-1021)
ABC TRUCK & EQUIPMENT LLC
941 N Main St # B (46714-1317)
PHONE.............................260 565-3307
Jason Troxel, *Mng Pt*
EMP: 2 **EST:** 2005
SALES (est): 260.39K **Privately Held**
Web: www.abctruckequipment.com
SIC: 3711 Motor vehicles and car bodies

(G-1022)
ADAMSWELLS PHONEBOOKS LLC
125 N Johnson St (46714-1907)
PHONE.............................260 622-6046
Mark F Miller, *Admn*
EMP: 5 **EST:** 2017
SALES (est): 46.79K **Privately Held**
Web: phonebook.adamswells.com
SIC: 2741 Globe covers (maps): publishing only, not printed on site

(G-1023)
ALMCO STEEL PRODUCTS CORP
59 N Oak Street Ext (46714-1499)
PHONE.............................260 824-1118
EMP: 120 **EST:** 1946
SALES (est): 13.75MM **Privately Held**
Web: www.almcosteel.com
SIC: 3469 3465 Metal stampings, nec; Automotive stampings

(G-1024)
AMERICAN AXLE & MFG INC
Also Called: AAM Bluffton
131 W Harvest Rd (46714-9007)
PHONE.............................260 824-6800
EMP: 50
SALES (corp-wide): 6.08B **Publicly Held**
Web: www.aam.com
SIC: 3714 Motor vehicle parts and accessories
HQ: American Axle & Manufacturing, Inc.
One Dauch Dr
Detroit MI 48211

(G-1025)
ARCHER-DANIELS-MIDLAND COMPANY
Also Called: ADM
1800 W Western Ave (46714-9788)
PHONE.............................260 824-0079
Russ Johnson, *Brnch Mgr*
EMP: 23
SALES (corp-wide): 93.94B **Publicly Held**
Web: www.adm.com
SIC: 2041 5191 Flour and other grain mill products; Farm supplies
PA: Archer-Daniels-Midland Company
77 W Wacker Dr Ste 4600
Chicago IL 60601
312 634-8100

(G-1026)
AT FERRELL COMPANY INC (PA)
1440 S Adams St (46714-9793)
PHONE.............................260 824-3400
Tom Haines, *Ch*
B Steven Stuller, *
Dale Zeigler, *
◆ **EMP:** 42 **EST:** 1980
SQ FT: 58,000
SALES (est): 9.78MM

Bluffton - Wells County (G-1027)

SALES (corp-wide): 9.78MM **Privately Held**
Web: www.atferrell.com
SIC: 3523 Farm machinery and equipment

(G-1027)
AUTO & SIGN SPECIALTIES INC
Also Called: Baller Signs
3124 E State Road 124 (46714-9301)
P.O. Box 51 (46714-0051)
PHONE..................260 824-1987
Steve B Baller, *Owner*
EMP: 3 EST: 1984
SALES (est): 223.1K **Privately Held**
Web: www.ballersigns.com
SIC: 3993 Signs and advertising specialties

(G-1028)
BALLER SIGNS INC
3124 E State Road 124 (46714-9301)
PHONE..................260 824-1987
Clint Gerber, *Pr*
EMP: 1 EST: 2005
SALES (est): 46.08K **Privately Held**
Web: www.ballersigns.com
SIC: 3993 Signs and advertising specialties

(G-1029)
BLACK GOLD VENTURES IND LLC
2829 E State Road 124 (46714-9375)
P.O. Box 331 (46714-0331)
PHONE..................260 820-0771
Timothy L Drayer, *Mgr*
EMP: 7 EST: 2015
SALES (est): 199.9K **Privately Held**
SIC: 1382 Oil and gas exploration services

(G-1030)
BLUFFTON MOTOR WORKS LLC
(HQ)
410 E Spring St (46714-3737)
PHONE..................260 827-2200
Silvio Billo, *Pr*
Michael Brower, *
▲ EMP: 1 EST: 2006
SALES (est): 91.58MM **Privately Held**
Web: www.weg-cm.com
SIC: 3621 Motors, electric
PA: Weg Sa
   Av. Prefeito Waldemar Grubba 3300
   Jaragua Do Sul SC 89257

(G-1031)
BLUFFTON RUBBER
810 Lancaster St (46714-1700)
P.O. Box 255 (46714-0255)
PHONE..................260 824-4501
EMP: 2 EST: 2010
SALES (est): 137.91K **Privately Held**
Web: www.brcrubbergroup.com
SIC: 3061 Mechanical rubber goods

(G-1032)
BRC RUBBER & PLASTICS INC
810 Lancaster St (46714-1716)
P.O. Box 255 (46714-0255)
PHONE..................260 827-0871
Guy Broderick, *Mgr*
EMP: 21
SALES (corp-wide): 95.9MM **Privately Held**
Web: www.brcrp.com
SIC: 3061 3053 3069 Automotive rubber goods (mechanical); Gaskets; packing and sealing devices; Molded rubber products
PA: Brc Rubber & Plastics, Inc.
   1029a W State Blvd
   Fort Wayne IN 46808
   260 693-2171

(G-1033)
CARRERA MANUFACTURING INC
Also Called: W & M Manufacturing
2085 Commerce Dr (46714-9288)
PHONE..................260 726-9800
James D Hiester, *Pr*
EMP: 75 EST: 2007
SALES (est): 9.95MM **Privately Held**
Web: www.carreramfg.com
SIC: 3089 Injection molding of plastics

(G-1034)
DEDRICK TOOL & DIE INC
2929 E State Road 124 (46714-9366)
PHONE..................260 824-3334
Deborah Dedrick, *Pr*
EMP: 7 EST: 1979
SQ FT: 7,000
SALES (est): 864.4K **Privately Held**
Web: www.dedricktool.com
SIC: 3544 Special dies and tools

(G-1035)
EDGE MANUFACTURING INC
1274 S Adams St (46714-9384)
PHONE..................260 827-0482
Eric Gerber, *Pr*
Doug Gerber, *
Lori Gerber, *
EMP: 30 EST: 1997
SQ FT: 20,000
SALES (est): 4.99MM **Privately Held**
Web: www.edgemanufacturing.com
SIC: 3441 Fabricated structural metal

(G-1036)
ERIE-HAVEN INC
235 S Adams St (46714-9034)
PHONE..................260 353-1133
Cherie Moser, *Brnch Mgr*
EMP: 10
SALES (corp-wide): 6.22MM **Privately Held**
Web: www.eriehaven.com
SIC: 3273 Ready-mixed concrete
PA: Erie-Haven Inc
   3909 Limestone Dr
   Fort Wayne IN 46809
   260 478-1674

(G-1037)
HMS ZOO DIETS INC
43 Sunrise Way (46714-1225)
PHONE..................260 824-5157
EMP: 2 EST: 1983
SALES (est): 197.54K **Privately Held**
SIC: 2048 Prepared feeds, nec

(G-1038)
INVENTURE FOODS INC
705 W Dustman Rd (46714-1178)
PHONE..................260 824-2800
Teri Huffman, *CFO*
EMP: 37
SALES (corp-wide): 732.3MM **Privately Held**
SIC: 2096 Potato chips and similar snacks
HQ: Inventure Foods, Inc.
   900 High St
   Hanover PA 17331

(G-1039)
IRVING MATERIALS INC
Also Called: I M I
2321 E 150 N (46714-9237)
PHONE..................260 824-3428
Joe Langel, *Brnch Mgr*
EMP: 10
SALES (corp-wide): 814.09MM **Privately Held**
Web: www.irvmat.com
SIC: 3273 Ready-mixed concrete
PA: Irving Materials, Inc.
   8032 N State Road 9
   Greenfield IN 46140
   317 326-3101

(G-1040)
MATALCO BLUFFTON LLC
1390 S Adams St (46714-9030)
PHONE..................260 353-3100
Tom Horter, *Pr*
▲ EMP: 68 EST: 2008
SQ FT: 100
SALES (est): 22.65MM
SALES (corp-wide): 6.29MM **Privately Held**
Web: www.alexinllc.com
SIC: 3354 Aluminum extruded products
HQ: Matalco Inc
   850 Intermodal Dr
   Brampton ON L6T 0
   905 790-2511

(G-1041)
MESHBERGER BROTHERS STONE CORPORATION
6311 W State Road 218-1 (46714-9509)
P.O. Box 345 (46711-0345)
PHONE..................260 334-5311
EMP: 70
SIC: 1422 2951 Crushed and broken limestone; Paving mixtures

(G-1042)
METALDYNE M&A BLUFFTON LLC
Also Called: Bluffton Plant
131 W Harvest Rd (46714-9007)
PHONE..................260 824-6800
Thomas A Amato, *CEO*
Mark Blaufuss, *CFO*
Ben Schmidt, *VP*
Christoph Guhe, *VP*
Robert Defauw, *VP*
◆ EMP: 90 EST: 2009
SQ FT: 190
SALES (est): 4.36MM
SALES (corp-wide): 6.08B **Publicly Held**
Web: www.aam.com
SIC: 7537 3714 Automotive transmission repair shops; Motor vehicle engines and parts
HQ: Metaldyne Sinterforged Products, Llc
   3100 N State Highway 3
   North Vernon IN 47265

(G-1043)
MPS INTERNATIONAL LLC
Also Called: Crown Unlimited Machine
941 N Main St (46714-1317)
PHONE..................260 824-2630
▲ EMP: 50 EST: 2007
SALES (est): 2.3MM **Privately Held**
Web: www.crownunlimited.com
SIC: 3498 Tube fabricating (contract bending and shaping)

(G-1044)
MULTI FIBER LLC
1000 W Wiley Ave (46714)
PHONE..................260 353-1510
EMP: 19 EST: 2018
SALES (est): 3.2MM **Privately Held**
SIC: 2823 Cellulosic manmade fibers

(G-1045)
NEOTI LLC
Also Called: Neoti
910 Lancaster St (46714-1744)
P.O. Box 444 (46714-0444)
PHONE..................260 494-1499
Derek W Myers, *Managing Member*
▲ EMP: 18 EST: 2006
SALES (est): 1.65MM **Privately Held**
Web: www.neoti.com
SIC: 3993 3674 Electric signs; Light emitting diodes

(G-1046)
NEWS-BANNER PUBLICATIONS INC
Also Called: Echo, The
125 N Johnson St (46714-1926)
P.O. Box 436 (46714-0436)
PHONE..................260 824-0224
Mark Miller, *Pr*
Diane Witwer, *
George B Witwer, *
EMP: 38 EST: 1892
SQ FT: 6,250
SALES (est): 2.13MM **Privately Held**
Web: www.news-banner.com
SIC: 2711 8611 2752 2741 Newspapers: publishing only, not printed on site; Business associations; Commercial printing, lithographic; Miscellaneous publishing

(G-1047)
PARLOR CITY TROPHY & AP INC
125 N Main St (46714-2045)
PHONE..................260 824-0216
Tracy Pace, *Pt*
Elanie Line, *Pt*
EMP: 2 EST: 1992
SALES (est): 186.5K **Privately Held**
Web: pcta.imprintableapparel.com
SIC: 5999 2759 Trophies and plaques; Screen printing

(G-1048)
POORE BROTHERS - BLUFFTON LLC
Also Called: Wabash Snacks
705 W Dustman Rd (46714-1178)
PHONE..................260 824-2800
EMP: 102 EST: 1998
SALES (est): 2.17MM
SALES (corp-wide): 732.3MM **Privately Held**
SIC: 2096 5145 2099 Potato chips and similar snacks; Confectionery; Food preparations, nec
HQ: Inventure Foods, Inc.
   900 High St
   Hanover PA 17331

(G-1049)
PRETZELS LLC (PA)
123 W Harvest Rd (46714)
P.O. Box 503 (46714)
PHONE..................800 456-4838
Greg Pearson, *CEO*
Craig Anderson, *
Mike Kaczynski, *
▼ EMP: 163 EST: 1978
SQ FT: 200,000
SALES (est): 121.47MM
SALES (corp-wide): 121.47MM **Privately Held**
Web: www.pretzels-inc.com
SIC: 2099 2052 Food preparations, nec; Pretzels

(G-1050)
PRINT SOURCE CORPORATION
213 E Perry St (46714-2156)
P.O. Box 23 (46711-0023)
PHONE..................260 824-3911
Terry W Steffen, *Pr*
Gloria J Steffen, *Sec*
EMP: 3 EST: 1970
SQ FT: 2,200

SALES (est): 450K **Privately Held**
Web: www.eprintery.com
SIC: 2752 Offset printing

(G-1051)
RITTENHOUSE SQUARE
312 S Main St (46714-2519)
PHONE..................260 824-4200
George Rittenhouse, *Pt*
EMP: 6 **EST:** 1983
SQ FT: 3,000
SALES (est): 399.6K **Privately Held**
Web: www.rittenhousehotel.com
SIC: 2389 7011 Theatrical costumes; Hotels

(G-1052)
ROCK CREEK STONE LLC
781 N 500 W (46714-9752)
P.O. Box 6 (46714-0006)
PHONE..................260 694-6880
Darin Johnson, *Brnch Mgr*
EMP: 65
SALES (corp-wide): 797.87K **Privately Held**
SIC: 1422 Cement rock, crushed and broken-quarrying
PA: Rock Creek Stone, Llc
  717 Riverview Dr
  Bluffton IN 46714
  260 249-4446

(G-1053)
SIMPLY SILVER
1165 Fawncrest Ct (46714-3868)
PHONE..................260 824-4667
Wayne Barker, *Prin*
EMP: 2 **EST:** 2004
SALES (est): 119.71K **Privately Held**
SIC: 3914 Silverware

(G-1054)
SNIDER TIRE INC
Also Called: Snider Tire
1400 W Wiley Ave (46714-2245)
PHONE..................260 824-4520
Dave Double, *Mgr*
EMP: 51
SALES (corp-wide): 436.36MM **Privately Held**
Web: www.sniderfleet.com
SIC: 5531 7534 Automotive tires; Tire retreading and repair shops
PA: Snider Tire, Inc.
  1081 Red Ventures Dr
  Fort Mill SC 29707
  336 691-5480

(G-1055)
SPD PERFORMANCE PLUS LLC
476 N 500 W (46714-9752)
PHONE..................260 433-6192
Shaun Donaghy, *Prin*
EMP: 4 **EST:** 2019
SALES (est): 135.68K **Privately Held**
SIC: 3714 Motor vehicle parts and accessories

(G-1056)
STANDARD PLASTIC CORPORATION
850 Decker Dr (46714-9769)
P.O. Box 355 (46714-0355)
PHONE..................260 824-0214
Philip E Leonard, *Pr*
EMP: 13 **EST:** 1955
SQ FT: 36,000
SALES (est): 1.47MM **Privately Held**
SIC: 3089 Injection molded finished plastics products, nec

(G-1057)
STAR ENGINEERING & MCH CO INC
1717 Lancaster St (46714-1512)
PHONE..................260 824-4825
Keith Steffen, *Pr*
Eric Steffen, *
Paul Simon, *
◆ **EMP:** 38 **EST:** 1965
SQ FT: 39,000
SALES (est): 6.82MM
SALES (corp-wide): 9.29MM **Privately Held**
Web: www.star-eng.com
SIC: 3599 3568 7692 Machine shop, jobbing and repair; Power transmission equipment, nec; Welding repair
PA: U. S. Group, Inc.
  3667 Merriweather Ln
  Rochester Hills MI 48306
  313 372-7900

(G-1058)
STUDABKER SPCLTY WOODWORKS LLC
4755 E 300 S (46714-9481)
PHONE..................260 273-1326
EMP: 5 **EST:** 2013
SALES (est): 170.21K **Privately Held**
Web: www.studabakerwoodworks.com
SIC: 2431 Millwork

(G-1059)
SUPER-PUFFT SNACKS USA INC
705 W Dustman Rd (46714-1178)
PHONE..................850 295-9891
EMP: 1
SALES (corp-wide): 14.54B **Privately Held**
Web: www.superpufft.com
SIC: 2096 Cheese curls and puffs
HQ: Super-Pufft Snacks Usa, Inc.
  700 W Lance Dr
  Perry FL 32348
  850 371-5364

(G-1060)
SWEET OBSSSONS BAKE SHOPPE LLC
111 E Market St (46714-2016)
PHONE..................260 273-2145
Rachel Rinehart, *Managing Member*
EMP: 5 **EST:** 2017
SALES (est): 166.04K **Privately Held**
SIC: 2051 Bakery: wholesale or wholesale/retail combined

(G-1061)
TEAM MANTRA WEAR LLC
979 N Main St (46714-1317)
PHONE..................260 273-0421
EMP: 6 **EST:** 2016
SALES (est): 327.61K **Privately Held**
Web: www.teammantrawear.com
SIC: 2759 Screen printing

(G-1062)
TEAM MANTRA WEAR LLC
4126 N 100 E (46714-9218)
PHONE..................260 827-0061
John Johnson, *Owner*
EMP: 8 **EST:** 2014
SALES (est): 328.56K **Privately Held**
Web: www.teammantrawear.com
SIC: 2759 Screen printing

(G-1063)
TERHUNE WELDING SHOP
3390 N State Road 1 (46714-9209)
PHONE..................260 565-3446
Rex Terhune, *Prin*
EMP: 1 **EST:** 2008

SALES (est): 28.27K **Privately Held**
SIC: 7692 Welding repair

(G-1064)
TROYER BROTHERS INC
6691 W State Rd 124 (46714)
PHONE..................260 565-2244
Mark Troyer, *Pr*
Zach Geisel, *Engg Mgr*
Paul Troyer, *Prin*
Dan Jones, *Prin*
Dale Cole, *Prin*
EMP: 26 **EST:** 2005
SALES (est): 6.43MM **Privately Held**
Web: www.troyerbrothers.net
SIC: 3699 5084 Laser welding, drilling, and cutting equipment; Hydraulic systems equipment and supplies

(G-1065)
UPTGRAFT WELDING
3295 E 450 S (46714-9465)
PHONE..................260 824-4624
Charlie Uptgraft, *Owner*
EMP: 1 **EST:** 1976
SALES (est): 37.2K **Privately Held**
SIC: 7692 Welding repair

(G-1066)
UTZ QUALITY FOODS LLC
1955 Lancaster St Ste 1 (46714)
PHONE..................717 443-7230
Howard Friedman, *CEO*
EMP: 1
SALES (corp-wide): 732.3MM **Privately Held**
Web: www.utzsnacks.com
SIC: 2096 Potato chips and similar snacks
PA: Utz Quality Foods, Llc
  900 High St
  Hanover PA 17331
  800 367-7629

(G-1067)
V-TECH ENGINEERING INC
118 E Wabash St (46714-2025)
PHONE..................260 824-4322
EMP: 15
Web: www.vtei.com
SIC: 1796 3679 Machinery installation; Electronic switches

(G-1068)
VALERO RENEWABLE FUELS CO LLC
Also Called: Valero Bluffton Ethanol Plant
1441 S Adams St (46714-9793)
P.O. Box 297 (46714-0297)
PHONE..................260 846-0011
EMP: 61
SALES (corp-wide): 144.77B **Publicly Held**
Web: www.valero.com
SIC: 2869 Ethyl alcohol, ethanol
HQ: Valero Renewable Fuels Company, Llc
  1 Valero Way
  San Antonio TX 78249

(G-1069)
WEAVER WOODWORKING
7795 E 300 S (46714-9321)
PHONE..................260 565-3647
Eli Weaver, *Prin*
EMP: 6 **EST:** 2010
SALES (est): 170.68K **Privately Held**
SIC: 2431 Millwork

(G-1070)
WEG ELECTRIC CORP
Also Called: Weg Commercial Motors

410 E Spring St (46714-3737)
PHONE..................260 827-2200
EMP: 93
Web: www.weg-cm.com
SIC: 3612 Power and distribution transformers
HQ: Weg Electric Corp.
  6655 Sugarloaf Pkwy
  Duluth GA 30097

(G-1071)
YODERS QUALITY BARNS LLC
7207 E State Road 124 (46714-9334)
PHONE..................260 565-4122
John Yoder, *Owner*
EMP: 2 **EST:** 2000
SALES (est): 237.74K **Privately Held**
Web: www.yodersqualitybarns.com
SIC: 3448 Prefabricated metal buildings and components

Boggstown
Shelby County

(G-1072)
BIKES-N-TRIKES INCORPORATED
6597 W 300 N (46110-9708)
PHONE..................317 835-4544
Art Bensheimer, *CEO*
EMP: 3 **EST:** 2000
SQ FT: 3,000
SALES (est): 231.5K **Privately Held**
SIC: 3751 7699 Motorcycles, bicycles and parts; Motorcycle repair service

(G-1073)
GREENWOOD LIGHT & SIGN SERVICE
7955 W 400 N (46110-9730)
PHONE..................317 840-5729
EMP: 4 **EST:** 2010
SALES (est): 64.09K **Privately Held**
SIC: 3993 Signs and advertising specialties

(G-1074)
JOHNSONS WELDING INC
7908 W 525 N (46110-9728)
PHONE..................317 835-2438
Danny Johnson, *Prin*
EMP: 2 **EST:** 2000
SALES (est): 97.28K **Privately Held**
SIC: 7692 Welding repair

(G-1075)
OCCOUTDOORS INC
6597 W 300 N (46110-9708)
PHONE..................317 862-2584
David Fagel, *Pr*
▼ **EMP:** 1 **EST:** 2009
SALES (est): 236.6K **Privately Held**
Web: www.occoutdoors.com
SIC: 2531 Public building and related furniture

(G-1076)
RPF INC
6643 W Boggstown Rd (46110-9703)
PHONE..................317 727-6386
James Townsend, *Pr*
EMP: 5 **EST:** 2009
SALES (est): 326.63K **Privately Held**
SIC: 2499 Food handling and processing products, wood

(G-1077)
WITHAM MACHINE LLC
8429 W 525 N (46110-9726)
PHONE..................317 835-2076
David Witham, *Owner*

Boonville
Warrick County

(G-1078)
A-FAB LLC
977 Hyrock Blvd (47601-9571)
P.O. Box 548 (47601-0548)
PHONE.................................812 897-0900
▲ **EMP:** 13 **EST:** 2008
SALES (est): 2.29MM **Privately Held**
Web: www.afcoracing.com
SIC: 3714 5015 Motor vehicle parts and accessories; Motor vehicle parts, used

(G-1079)
AFCO PERFORMANCE GROUP LLC (PA)
Also Called: Afco Racing Products
977 Hyrock Blvd (47601-9571)
P.O. Box 548 (47601-0548)
PHONE.................................812 897-0900
Jeff Scales, *Pr*
EMP: 15 **EST:** 2008
SALES (est): 4.87MM
SALES (corp-wide): 4.87MM **Privately Held**
Web: www.dynatechheaders.com
SIC: 3465 5013 Body parts, automobile: stamped metal; Automotive supplies and parts

(G-1080)
AMERICAN FABRICATING
1302 N Rockport Rd (47601-2346)
P.O. Box 548 (47601-0548)
PHONE.................................812 897-0900
EMP: 6 **EST:** 2010
SALES (est): 247.66K **Privately Held**
SIC: 3441 Fabricated structural metal

(G-1081)
B-HIVE PRINTING
Also Called: Shipping Plus
804 W Main St (47601-3004)
PHONE.................................812 897-3905
Gail Bailey, *Owner*
EMP: 4 **EST:** 1981
SQ FT: 4,000
SALES (est): 238.71K **Privately Held**
Web: www.b-hiveprinting.com
SIC: 2752 2759 Offset and photolithographic printing; Promotional printing

(G-1082)
BILLY R RANSOM
Also Called: Billy R Ransom Logging
665 Heritage Ln (47601-9715)
PHONE.................................812 897-5921
Billy R Ransom, *Owner*
EMP: 1 **EST:** 1981
SALES (est): 78.15K **Privately Held**
SIC: 2411 Logging camps and contractors

(G-1083)
BST CORP
1066 Hunter Blvd (47601-8710)
PHONE.................................812 925-7911
Lawrence Steenberg, *Pr*
EMP: 2 **EST:** 2001
SALES (est): 174.05K **Privately Held**
SIC: 1389 Oil field services, nec

EMP: 2 **EST:** 1988
SALES (est): 177.55K **Privately Held**
Web: www.withammachine.com
SIC: 2673 Bags: plastic, laminated, and coated

(G-1084)
BUXTON ENGINEERING INC
1322 S Rockport Rd (47601-7923)
PHONE.................................812 897-3609
Brad Buxton, *Pr*
EMP: 2 **EST:** 1988
SALES (est): 187.98K **Privately Held**
Web: www.buxtonengineering.com
SIC: 3599 Machine shop, jobbing and repair

(G-1085)
CLIENTS CHOICE LTD
2144 Wildwood Dr (47601-9340)
PHONE.................................812 853-2911
Rosanna Clayton, *Pr*
EMP: 2 **EST:** 1990
SALES (est): 110.99K **Privately Held**
SIC: 3993 Advertising artwork

(G-1086)
COVEY RISE MINERALS LLC
1617 S 1st St (47601-2123)
PHONE.................................812 897-2356
Vito Amiano, *Managing Member*
EMP: 1 **EST:** 2013
SALES (est): 74.62K **Privately Held**
SIC: 1382 5052 1389 Oil and gas exploration services; Coal and other minerals and ores; Oil consultants

(G-1087)
INDUSTRIAL WOODKRAFT INC (PA)
811 Hyrock Blvd (47601)
P.O. Box 591 (47601-0591)
PHONE.................................812 897-4893
Stewart Phillips, *Pr*
Thad Leinenbach, *
Shirley Phillips, *
David Lockhart, *
▼ **EMP:** 50 **EST:** 1979
SQ FT: 64,000
SALES (est): 4.45MM
SALES (corp-wide): 4.45MM **Privately Held**
Web: www.industrialwoodkraft.com
SIC: 2448 2449 2441 Pallets, wood; Wood containers, nec; Nailed wood boxes and shook

(G-1088)
LINCOLN INDUSTRIES INC
110 W Division St (47601-1919)
P.O. Box 621 (47601-0621)
PHONE.................................812 897-0715
Seyed K Saboohi, *Pr*
John Zoeller, *Sec*
Gregory A Dueffert, *Sec*
▲ **EMP:** 50 **EST:** 1981
SQ FT: 19,500
SALES (est): 7.93MM
SALES (corp-wide): 197.28MM **Privately Held**
Web: www.lincolnind.com
SIC: 3089 Injection molding of plastics
PA: Zoeller Company
3649 Cane Run Rd
Louisville KY 40211
502 778-2731

(G-1089)
LITTLE MFG LLC
2122 N State Route 61 (47601-8341)
PHONE.................................812 453-8137
Alan Elzer, *Prin*
EMP: 6 **EST:** 2013
SALES (est): 152.39K **Privately Held**
SIC: 3999 Manufacturing industries, nec

(G-1090)
MILES FARM SUPPLY LLC
Also Called: Miles Farm Service
7187 State Hwy 66 E (47601)
PHONE.................................812 359-4463
Mike Rose, *Mgr*
EMP: 98
SALES (corp-wide): 29.21MM **Privately Held**
Web: www.milesfarmsupply.com
SIC: 5191 5083 1541 2875 Chemicals, agricultural; Agricultural machinery and equipment; Grain elevator construction; Fertilizers, mixing only
PA: Miles Farm Supply, Llc
2760 Keller Rd
Owensboro KY 42301
270 926-2420

(G-1091)
MINE SYSTEM SOLUTIONS LLC ◆
Also Called: Mss
2355 Eby Rd (47601-8306)
P.O. Box 356 (42461-0356)
PHONE.................................270 952-5422
EMP: 5 **EST:** 2022
SALES (est): 551.1K **Privately Held**
Web: www.minesystemsolutions.com
SIC: 3532 Mining machinery

(G-1092)
MINING MACHINE PARTS INC
420 S 3rd St (47601-1726)
P.O. Box 529 (47601-0529)
PHONE.................................812 897-1256
Wayne Anderson, *Pr*
Mary Kay Anderson, *Sec*
EMP: 8 **EST:** 1976
SQ FT: 3,600
SALES (est): 2.18MM **Privately Held**
SIC: 5082 3599 Mining machinery and equipment, except petroleum; Machine shop, jobbing and repair

(G-1093)
MOHLER TECHNOLOGY INC ◆
2355 Eby Rd (47601-8306)
PHONE.................................812 897-2900
Stephen S Mohler, *Pr*
EMP: 39 **EST:** 2022
SALES (est): 5.07MM **Privately Held**
Web: www.mohler.com
SIC: 3621 5063 7694 Motors, electric; Electrical supplies, nec; Rewinding services

(G-1094)
NIX SANITARY SERVICE
703 S 2nd St (47601-1961)
PHONE.................................812 785-1158
TOLL FREE: 888
EMP: 6 **EST:** 1957
SALES (est): 521.13K **Privately Held**
Web: www.nixsanitaryservices.com
SIC: 3795 7359 Tanks and tank components ; Portable toilet rental

(G-1095)
PERFORMANCE ROD & CUSTOM INC
6200 N State Route 61 (47601-9428)
P.O. Box 207 (47601-0207)
PHONE.................................812 897-5805
Duane Davis, *Pr*
EMP: 8 **EST:** 2000
SQ FT: 2,200
SALES (est): 947.09K **Privately Held**
Web: www.prchotrod.com
SIC: 3714 Connecting rods, motor vehicle engine

(G-1096)
S & S MACHINE SHOP INC (PA)
Also Called: Ralph West
298 Essex Dr (47601-9647)
P.O. Box 779 (47601-0779)
PHONE.................................812 897-5343
EMP: 31 **EST:** 1983
SALES (est): 3.75MM
SALES (corp-wide): 3.75MM **Privately Held**
Web: www.ssmachineshop.com
SIC: 3532 Mining machinery

(G-1097)
SHIRTS AND STUFFS HAPPENS
956 W Main St (47601-1598)
PHONE.................................812 217-8390
Teresa Shanks, *Owner*
EMP: 3 **EST:** 2018
SALES (est): 50.69K **Privately Held**
SIC: 3993 Signs and advertising specialties

(G-1098)
SONS OF THUNDER
Also Called: Alliance Machine
1233 Mount Gilead Rd (47601-9302)
PHONE.................................812 897-4908
Mike Winge, *Owner*
EMP: 2 **EST:** 2004
SALES (est): 194K **Privately Held**
Web: www.alliancearmament.com
SIC: 3482 Small arms ammunition

(G-1099)
TANGLEWOOD LLC
4742 W County Road 1060 N (47601-7528)
PHONE.................................607 621-1189
Jessica Mcdaniel, *Prin*
EMP: 6 **EST:** 2016
SALES (est): 41.52K **Privately Held**
Web: www.tanglewoodeventsbarn.com
SIC: 2499 Wood products, nec

(G-1100)
TRUSS SYSTEMS INC
3555 Hwy 62 W (47601)
P.O. Box 191 (47601-0191)
PHONE.................................812 897-3064
Stewart Phillips, *Pr*
Shirley Phillips, *Sec*
EMP: 14 **EST:** 1997
SALES (est): 799.29K **Privately Held**
Web: www.trusssystemsinc.net
SIC: 2439 Trusses, wooden roof

(G-1101)
WILHITE INDUSTRIES INC
5833 S Yankeetown Rd (47601-8282)
PHONE.................................812 853-8771
Charles F Wilhite, *Pr*
Jeanne Wilhite, *Sec*
EMP: 7 **EST:** 1980
SQ FT: 6,500
SALES (est): 513.41K **Privately Held**
SIC: 3544 Special dies, tools, jigs, and fixtures

Borden
Clark County

(G-1102)
ABSOLUTE CUSTOM COINS INC
Also Called: Absolute Coins
130 East St (47106-8947)
PHONE.................................812 733-4043
EMP: 3 **EST:** 2011
SALES (est): 316.04K **Privately Held**
Web: www.absolutecustomcoins.com

SIC: 3469 Metal stampings, nec

(G-1103)
ABSOLUTE WELDING INC
130 East St (47106)
P.O. Box 483 (47124)
PHONE.....................812 923-8001
EMP: 14 EST: 1994
SQ FT: 2,000
SALES (est): 961.78K Privately Held
Web: www.absolutewelding.com
SIC: 7692 Welding repair

(G-1104)
AGORA BRANDS GROUP INC
116 West St (47106-8919)
PHONE.....................615 802-0086
John Osland, *
Erik Del Villar, Board Director*
Angel Hughes, Board Director*
Leshia Mitic, Board Director*
EMP: 25 EST: 2017
SALES (est): 525.69K Privately Held
SIC: 7371 7372 7379 7373 Computer software systems analysis and design, custom; Application computer software; Computer related consulting services; Systems software development services

(G-1105)
ALS WOODCRAFT INC
435 E Main St (47106-8907)
P.O. Box 117 (47106-0117)
PHONE.....................812 967-4458
Jeff Hunt, Pr
Mildred Hunt, VP
Susan Hunt, Sec
EMP: 10 EST: 1982
SQ FT: 9,600
SALES (est): 678.84K Privately Held
Web: www.scenicvalleywoodproducts.com
SIC: 2426 2511 Dimension, hardwood; Wood household furniture

(G-1106)
CHAPPELLES SHEET METAL SHOP
14504 State Road 60 (47106-8587)
PHONE.....................812 246-2121
EMP: 1 EST: 1973
SALES (est): 119.61K Privately Held
SIC: 3444 Ducts, sheet metal

(G-1107)
CUSTOMER 1ST LLC
21005 Souders Rd (47106-9703)
PHONE.....................812 733-4638
Jack Hurst, Brnch Mgr
EMP: 1
SALES (corp-wide): 449.61K Privately Held
Web: www.customer1st.com
SIC: 3499 Safes and vaults, metal
PA: Customer 1st Llc
    8899 E Daily Rd Lot 51
    Pekin IN 47165
    877 768-9970

(G-1108)
FASKE WOOD MOULDING INC
10215 Saint Johns Rd (47106-8303)
PHONE.....................812 923-5061
Connie Senn, Pr
Francis C Senn, VP
D Wayne Stephens, VP
Carol J Stephens, Sec
EMP: 14 EST: 1963
SQ FT: 22,000
SALES (est): 420.33K Privately Held
SIC: 2431 Moldings, wood: unfinished and prefinished

(G-1109)
GREEN BANNER PUBLICATIONS INC (PA)
Also Called: Banner Publications
215 Money Hollow Rd (47106-8597)
P.O. Box 38 (47165-0038)
PHONE.....................812 967-3176
Joseph V Green, Pr
Jill B Green, *
Wanda A Green, *
EMP: 25 EST: 1933
SALES (est): 2.18MM
SALES (corp-wide): 2.18MM Privately Held
Web: www.gbpnews.com
SIC: 2711 2752 2791 2789 Newspapers, publishing and printing; Offset printing; Typesetting; Bookbinding and related work

(G-1110)
HUBER ORCHARDS INC
Also Called: Huber's Orchard & Winery
19816 Huber Rd (47106-8309)
PHONE.....................812 923-9463
Greg Huber, CEO
Ted Huber, *
▲ EMP: 90 EST: 1961
SQ FT: 15,000
SALES (est): 9.89MM Privately Held
Web: www.huberwinery.com
SIC: 0175 2022 0161 2084 Deciduous tree fruits; Natural cheese; Vegetables and melons; Wines, brandy, and brandy spirits

(G-1111)
KENTUCKY WOOD FLOORS LLC
533 Louis Smith Rd (47106-8100)
PHONE.....................812 256-2164
EMP: 1 EST: 2004
SALES (est): 492.57K
SALES (corp-wide): 48.06MM Privately Held
Web: www.koetterwoodworking.com
SIC: 2431 Millwork
PA: Koetter Woodworking Inc
    533 Louis Smith Rd
    Borden IN 47106
    812 923-8875

(G-1112)
KOETTER WOODWORKING
Also Called: Koetter Sawmill
533 Louis Smith Rd (47106-8107)
PHONE.....................812 923-8875
Tom Koetter, Owner
EMP: 10 EST: 2002
SALES (est): 594K Privately Held
Web: www.koetterwoodworking.com
SIC: 2499 2421 Decorative wood and woodwork; Sawmills and planing mills, general

(G-1113)
KOETTER WOODWORKING INC (PA)
533 Louis Smith Rd (47106-8107)
PHONE.....................812 923-8875
Randall F Koetter, Pr
Gerald Koetter, *
Richard A Koetter, *
Brian Koetter, *
Thomas C Koetter Junior, Treas
◆ EMP: 270 EST: 1959
SQ FT: 650,000
SALES (est): 48.06MM
SALES (corp-wide): 48.06MM Privately Held
Web: www.koetterwoodworking.com
SIC: 2431 Doors and door parts and trim, wood

(G-1114)
LIFE GARDEN PUBLISHING INC
908 Sunset Cir (47106-8501)
PHONE.....................812 246-2113
EMP: 2
SALES (est): 59.23K Privately Held
SIC: 2741 Miscellaneous publishing

(G-1115)
LM SUGARBUSH LLC
29618 Green Rd (47106-8013)
PHONE.....................812 967-4491
Nicholas Reisenbichler, Owner
Michael Georing, Owner
Leane Georing, Mgr
EMP: 2 EST: 1983
SALES (est): 93.97K Privately Held
Web: www.lmsugarbush.com
SIC: 2099 Maple syrup

(G-1116)
NORTHTECH MACHINE LLC
102 Walnut St (47106-8318)
P.O. Box 278 (47106-0278)
PHONE.....................812 967-7400
Brandon Koetter, Managing Member
EMP: 18 EST: 2016
SALES (est): 1.4MM Privately Held
Web: www.northtechmachine.com
SIC: 3553 Woodworking machinery

(G-1117)
PAM C JONES ENTERPRISES INC
Also Called: Pam C Jnes Typography Graphics
3007 Crone Rd (47106-9320)
P.O. Box 1623 (47151-1623)
PHONE.....................812 294-1862
EMP: 1 EST: 1989
SALES (est): 118.33K Privately Held
SIC: 2752 7336 Offset printing; Graphic arts and related design

Boswell
Benton County

(G-1118)
MANTA RUGS
305 N Harrison St (47921-8526)
PHONE.....................765 869-5940
EMP: 2
SQ FT: 2,200
SALES (est): 90K Privately Held
SIC: 2273 Carpets and rugs

Bourbon
Marshall County

(G-1119)
1 COMPOSITES LLC
606 W Center St (46504-1170)
PHONE.....................260 665-6112
EMP: 8 EST: 2018
SALES (est): 1.31MM Privately Held
SIC: 3714 Motor vehicle parts and accessories

(G-1120)
CT POLYMERS LLC
12340 Elm Rd (46504-9608)
PHONE.....................574 598-6132
Chris Roseri, Managing Member
EMP: 12 EST: 2018
SQ FT: 50,000
SALES (est): 2.82MM Privately Held
Web: www.ctpolymers.com

SIC: 2822 Ethylene-propylene rubbers, EPDM polymers

(G-1121)
FAULKNER FABRICATING INC
4050 Lincoln Hwy (46504-9610)
P.O. Box 61 (46504-0061)
PHONE.....................574 342-0022
Jerry Faulkner, Pr
EMP: 17 EST: 1990
SQ FT: 7,500
SALES (est): 4.99MM Privately Held
Web: www.faulknerfabricating.com
SIC: 3441 Fabricated structural metal

(G-1122)
HARMONY PRESS INC (PA)
Also Called: Harmony Marketing Group
115 N Main St (46504-1645)
PHONE.....................800 525-3742
Joel Harman, CEO
Timothy J Harman, *
Gary Price, *
Jim Pattison, *
Rita C Harman, *
EMP: 38 EST: 1941
SQ FT: 30,000
SALES (est): 9.88MM
SALES (corp-wide): 9.88MM Privately Held
Web: www.hmktgroup.com
SIC: 2759 2752 7331 Letterpress printing; Offset printing; Direct mail advertising services

(G-1123)
KLINGERMAN WELDING
409 W Jackson St (46504-1233)
PHONE.....................574 342-7375
Mark Klingerman, Owner
EMP: 1 EST: 1969
SQ FT: 5,000
SALES (est): 67.05K Privately Held
SIC: 7692 Welding repair

(G-1124)
NICORR LLC
4050 Lincoln Hwy (46504-9610)
P.O. Box 165 (46504-0165)
PHONE.....................574 342-0700
EMP: 9 EST: 2006
SQ FT: 5,000
SALES (est): 961.84K Privately Held
Web: www.nicorr.com
SIC: 3291 Abrasive metal and steel products

(G-1125)
NORTHERN INDIANA MANUFACTURING (PA)
202 S Ecker Ave (46504-1220)
P.O. Box 46 (46504-0046)
PHONE.....................574 342-2105
Robert Dragani Senior, Pr
▲ EMP: 44 EST: 1945
SQ FT: 140,000
SALES (est): 8.98MM
SALES (corp-wide): 8.98MM Privately Held
Web: northernindiana.weebly.com
SIC: 3451 3599 3398 3229 Screw machine products; Machine and other job shop work; Metal heat treating; Pressed and blown glass, nec

(G-1126)
PERFORMANCE CNC LLC
1338 12th Rd (46504-9682)
PHONE.....................574 780-4864
George Marks, Pr
EMP: 3 EST: 2010
SALES (est): 250.3K Privately Held

Bourbon - Marshall County (G-1127)

Web: www.performancecncllc.com
SIC: 3451 3841 Screw machine products; Surgical and medical instruments

(G-1127)
SHELLS INC
502 Old Us Highway 30 E (46504-1644)
PHONE................................574 342-2673
John Administer, *Mgr*
EMP: 75
SALES (corp-wide): 23MM **Privately Held**
Web: www.shellsinc.com
SIC: 3543 Foundry cores
PA: Shells, Inc.
  1245 S Cleveland Massillo
  Copley OH 44321
  330 808-5558

(G-1128)
SLABAUGH METAL FAB LLC
1860 12th Rd (46504-9595)
PHONE................................574 342-0554
James Slabaugh, *Pr*
EMP: 45 EST: 1990
SALES (est): 4.69MM **Privately Held**
SIC: 3444 Sheet metalwork

(G-1129)
TEREX CORPORATION
Also Called: Terex
4470 Lincoln Hwy (46504-9610)
PHONE................................574 342-0086
Michael Charles, *Mgr*
EMP: 7
SQ FT: 10,000
SALES (corp-wide): 5.15B **Publicly Held**
Web: www.terex.com
SIC: 3531 Construction machinery
PA: Terex Corporation
  45 Glover Ave Fl 4
  Norwalk CT 06850
  203 222-7170

(G-1130)
WHITEMAN EMBROIDERY
8091 Elm Rd (46504-9626)
PHONE................................574 342-3697
EMP: 3 EST: 2018
SALES (est): 38.61K **Privately Held**
SIC: 2395 Embroidery and art needlework

Brazil
Clay County

(G-1131)
ADVANCED DRAINAGE SYSTEMS INC
2340 E Us Highway 40 (47834-7638)
P.O. Box 367 (47834-0367)
PHONE................................812 443-2080
EMP: 6
SALES (corp-wide): 2.87B **Publicly Held**
Web: www.adspipe.com
SIC: 3084 Plastics pipe
PA: Advanced Drainage Systems, Inc.
  4640 Trueman Blvd
  Hilliard OH 43026
  614 658-0050

(G-1132)
AIRFX USA LLC (PA)
1484 E County Road 600 N (47834)
PHONE................................812 878-8135
Jeff Stark, *Pr*
EMP: 6 EST: 2019
SALES (est): 1.01MM
SALES (corp-wide): 1.01MM **Privately Held**
Web: www.airfxusa.com

SIC: 3714 Motor vehicle parts and accessories

(G-1133)
ATV PARTS BARN LLC
10997 N Meridian Street Rd (47834-6910)
PHONE................................812 251-6113
EMP: 1 EST: 2014
SALES (est): 61.48K **Privately Held**
SIC: 5571 7694 All-terrain vehicles; Motor repair services

(G-1134)
BLACKFOOT POWDER COATING
5729 N State Road 59 (47834-7485)
PHONE................................812 531-9315
Rebecca M Bower, *Owner*
EMP: 7 EST: 2017
SALES (est): 62.42K **Privately Held**
SIC: 3479 Coating of metals and formed products

(G-1135)
BRAZIL AUTO & ELECTRIC
1106 N Harrison St (47834-1331)
PHONE................................812 442-0060
Dennis Stultz, *Owner*
EMP: 1 EST: 1990
SALES (est): 96.87K **Privately Held**
SIC: 3519 Gasoline engines

(G-1136)
BRITT TOOL INC
949 E National Ave (47834-2705)
P.O. Box 554 (47834-0554)
PHONE................................812 446-0503
EMP: 80 EST: 1986
SALES (est): 10.24MM **Privately Held**
Web: www.brittaero.com
SIC: 3544 Special dies and tools

(G-1137)
BURKES GARDEN WOOD PDTS LLC
Also Called: Classic Baluster
4774 S 1000 E (47834-8469)
PHONE................................765 344-1724
Joe Glick, *Mgr*
EMP: 20
SALES (corp-wide): 2.79MM **Privately Held**
SIC: 2431 Porch work, wood
PA: Burkes' Garden Wood Products Llc
  1400 E Polymer Dr
  Terre Haute IN

(G-1138)
CLASSIC MANUFACTURING CO LLC
4774 S 1000 E (47834-8469)
PHONE................................765 344-1619
Samuel Fisher, *Managing Member*
John Fisher, *
Samuel Cook, *
John Beiler, *
EMP: 23 EST: 2009
SALES (est): 2.68MM **Privately Held**
SIC: 2421 Outdoor wood structural products

(G-1139)
CLOVER SIGNS CO
100 N Meridian St (47834-2172)
PHONE................................812 442-7446
Melisa Allender, *Pr*
EMP: 10 EST: 1997
SALES (est): 995.3K **Privately Held**
Web: www.cloversign.com
SIC: 3993 Electric signs

(G-1140)
EASTERN BANNER SUPPLY CORP
932 W National Ave (47834-2440)

PHONE................................812 448-2222
Melissa Allender, *Pr*
Jacquelyn E Hunt, *Pr*
Steve Hunt, *VP*
EMP: 3 EST: 1985
SQ FT: 7,200
SALES (est): 161.61K **Privately Held**
Web: www.easternbannersupply.com
SIC: 2399 Banners, made from fabric

(G-1141)
ENHANCED EMBROIDERY
3318 W County Road 900 N (47834-7939)
PHONE................................812 448-8452
EMP: 3 EST: 2019
SALES (est): 37.35K **Privately Held**
SIC: 2395 Embroidery and art needlework

(G-1142)
EXACTIFAB
10309 N Industrial Park Dr (47834-7322)
P.O. Box 315 (47834-0315)
PHONE................................812 420-2723
Noel Short, *Ch Bd*
Stephen Short, *Pr*
Scott Short, *VP*
Robert Drake, *VP*
Laura Clark, *Off Mgr*
EMP: 7 EST: 2014
SQ FT: 4,560
SALES (est): 481.55K **Privately Held**
Web: www.exactifab.com
SIC: 3451 Screw machine products

(G-1143)
GREAT DANE LLC
Also Called: Great Dane Trailers
2664 E Us Highway 40 (47834-7127)
PHONE................................812 443-4711
Gary Parker, *Mgr*
EMP: 900
SALES (corp-wide): 1.98B **Publicly Held**
Web: www.greatdane.com
SIC: 3715 3537 Truck trailers; Industrial trucks and tractors
HQ: Great Dane Llc
  222 N La Salle St Ste 920
  Chicago IL 60601

(G-1144)
HANCOR INC
2340 E Us Highway 40 (47834-7638)
P.O. Box 367 (47834-0367)
PHONE................................812 443-2080
Frank Mitchell, *Brnch Mgr*
EMP: 40
SQ FT: 16,000
SALES (corp-wide): 2.87B **Publicly Held**
Web: www.adspipe.com
SIC: 3089 3494 3084 3083 Plastics hardware and building products; Valves and pipe fittings, nec; Plastics pipe; Laminated plastics plate and sheet
HQ: Hancor, Inc.
  4640 Trueman Blvd
  Hilliard OH 43026
  614 658-0050

(G-1145)
INDIANA OXIDE CORPORATION
Also Called: Corporate Office
10665 N State Road 59 (47834-6961)
P.O. Box 423 (47834-0423)
PHONE................................812 446-2525
Greg Stevens, *Pr*
EMP: 15 EST: 1990
SALES (est): 2.69MM **Privately Held**
SIC: 2819 Lead compounds or salts, inorganic, not used in pigments

(G-1146)
INDIANA POWDER COATINGS INC
9413 N Tower Rd (47834)
PHONE................................615 347-2787
Mike Mccracken, *Pr*
EMP: 28 EST: 2021
SALES (est): 1.12MM **Privately Held**
Web: www.indianapowdercoatings.com
SIC: 3479 Coating of metals and formed products

(G-1147)
INNOVATIVE PRINTING SVCS INC
Also Called: A Plus Printing
219 W Church St (47834-2163)
PHONE................................812 443-1007
EMP: 4 EST: 1995
SQ FT: 2,500
SALES (est): 427.25K **Privately Held**
Web: www.aplusprinting.org
SIC: 2752 Offset printing

(G-1148)
IRVING MATERIALS INC
305 N Murphy Ave (47834-1552)
PHONE................................812 443-4661
Cliff Romas, *Prin*
EMP: 6
SALES (corp-wide): 814.09MM **Privately Held**
Web: www.irvmat.com
SIC: 3273 Ready-mixed concrete
PA: Irving Materials, Inc.
  8032 N State Road 9
  Greenfield IN 46140
  317 326-3101

(G-1149)
IVC INDUSTRIAL COATINGS INC
2831 E Industrial Park Dr (47834-7338)
PHONE................................812 442-5080
Michael Mccracken, *Pr*
Kevin S Mccracken, *VP*
Mark Mccracken, *Stockholder*
Allyn L Mccracken, *Stockholder*
Michael Mccracken Junior, *Stockholder*
♦ EMP: 108 EST: 1978
SQ FT: 3,000
SALES (est): 25.55MM
SALES (corp-wide): 17.65B **Publicly Held**
Web: www.ppgindustrialcoatings.com
SIC: 2851 Enamels, nec
PA: Ppg Industries, Inc.
  1 Ppg Pl
  Pittsburgh PA 15272
  412 434-3131

(G-1150)
J & N METAL PRODUCTS LLC
33 N County Road 250 W (47834-7496)
PHONE................................812 864-2600
EMP: 56 EST: 2006
SALES (est): 5.37MM **Privately Held**
Web: www.jnmetalproducts.com
SIC: 3599 Machine shop, jobbing and repair

(G-1151)
KINETICS XCAVATING LLC ⊙
8391 N County Road 100 E (47834-8505)
PHONE................................812 208-9892
EMP: 1 EST: 2022
SALES (est): 60.08K **Privately Held**
Web: www.kineticsxcavating.com
SIC: 3531 7389 Plows: construction, excavating, and grading; Business services, nec

(G-1152)
MAURER CONSTRUCTORS INC
10109 N Harmony Border St (47834-7714)

GEOGRAPHIC SECTION

Bremen - Marshall County (G-1175)

PHONE.............................812 236-5950
Mitch Maurer, *Pr*
EMP: 4 **EST:** 2008
SALES (est): 468.89K **Privately Held**
Web: www.maurerconstructors.com
SIC: 3448 Prefabricated metal buildings and components

(G-1153)
METALS AND ADDITIVES LLC
Indiana Oxide
10665 N State Road 59 (47834-6961)
P.O. Box 423 (47834-0423)
PHONE.............................812 446-2525
Jeff Smith, *Brnch Mgr*
EMP: 6
SALES (corp-wide): 24.81MM **Privately Held**
Web: www.pagholdings.com
SIC: 2819 3356 2899 Lead compounds or salts, inorganic, not used in pigments; Nonferrous rolling and drawing, nec; Chemical preparations, nec
PA: Metals And Additives, Llc
 5929 Lakeside Blvd
 Indianapolis IN 46278
 317 290-5007

(G-1154)
MORRIS HOLDING COMPANY LLC (PA)
1015 E Mechanic St (47834-3321)
PHONE.............................812 446-6141
EMP: 125 **EST:** 1995
SQ FT: 42,500
SALES (est): 23.71MM **Privately Held**
SIC: 3714 3599 Motor vehicle transmissions, drive assemblies, and parts; Machine shop, jobbing and repair

(G-1155)
MORRIS MFG & SLS CORP
1015 E Mechanic St (47834-3321)
PHONE.............................812 446-6141
Michael L Morris, *Pr*
EMP: 200 **EST:** 1962
SQ FT: 42,500
SALES (est): 23.71MM **Privately Held**
Web: www.morrismfg.com
SIC: 3714 3599 Motor vehicle transmissions, drive assemblies, and parts; Machine shop, jobbing and repair
PA: Morris Holding Company, Llc
 1015 E Mechanic St
 Brazil IN 47834

(G-1156)
MS MANUFACTURING LLC
Also Called: Kihm Metal Technologies
301 N Murphy Ave (47834-1552)
PHONE.............................812 442-7468
Bryan Davis, *Pr*
EMP: 45 **EST:** 2006
SQ FT: 20,000
SALES (est): 4.78MM **Privately Held**
Web: www.kihmmetaltech.com
SIC: 3499 Machine bases, metal

(G-1157)
NICOSIN EXTURSION INC
2058 W County Road 1200 N (47834)
PHONE.............................812 442-6751
EMP: 5 **EST:** 2020
SALES (est): 154.88K **Privately Held**
Web: www.nicosinextrusion.com
SIC: 3089 Injection molding of plastics

(G-1158)
NP CONVERTERS INC
Also Called: National Printing Converters
18 S Murphy Ave (47834-8297)
PHONE.............................812 448-2555
Brian Buckely, *Pr*
EMP: 51
SALES (corp-wide): 6.95MM **Privately Held**
Web: www.nationalcustomlabels.com
SIC: 7374 2761 2672 2671 Data processing and preparation; Manifold business forms; Paper; coated and laminated, nec; Paper; coated and laminated packaging
PA: Np Converters, Inc.
 16133 Ventura Blvd 741
 Encino CA 91436
 818 906-7936

(G-1159)
OTTER CREEK CHRISTIAN CHURCH
6299 N Crow St (47834-9300)
PHONE.............................812 446-5300
EMP: 1 **EST:** 1996
SALES (est): 58K **Privately Held**
SIC: 8661 7241 5719 3546 Catholic Church; Barber shops; Venetian blinds; Saws and sawing equipment

(G-1160)
P P G INDUSTRIES INC
Also Called: Brazil Industrial Coatings
2831 E Industrial Park Dr (47834-7338)
PHONE.............................812 442-5080
EMP: 10 **EST:** 1901
SALES (est): 521.42K **Privately Held**
SIC: 3999 Manufacturing industries, nec

(G-1161)
PAG HOLDINGS INC
Also Called: PAG HOLDINGS, INC.
10665 N State Road 59 (47834-6961)
PHONE.............................814 446-2525
EMP: 1
SALES (corp-wide): 24.81MM **Privately Held**
Web: www.pagholdings.com
SIC: 2861 Gum and wood chemicals
HQ: Pag Holdings, Llc
 5929 Lakeside Blvd
 Indianapolis IN 46278

(G-1162)
POOL SHOP
Also Called: Wiburn Jones Construction
1202 W Hendrix St (47834-6812)
PHONE.............................812 446-0026
Wilburn Jones, *Owner*
EMP: 1 **EST:** 1988
SALES (est): 66.39K **Privately Held**
SIC: 5999 5719 3546 5231 Spas and hot tubs; Venetian blinds; Saws and sawing equipment; Glass

(G-1163)
PROCESS DEVELOPMENT & FABRICATION INC
Also Called: P D F
10102 N Murphy Rd (47834-7065)
P.O. Box 493 (47834-0493)
PHONE.............................812 443-6000
◆ **EMP:** 105 **EST:** 1993
SALES (est): 15MM **Privately Held**
Web: www.pdf-inc.com
SIC: 3441 Fabricated structural metal

(G-1164)
PROTEQ CUSTOM GEAR LLC
3057 W County Road 1200 N (47834-6903)
PHONE.............................812 201-6002
Stephen Brannan, *Prin*
EMP: 6 **EST:** 2014
SALES (est): 149.44K **Privately Held**
Web: www.proteqcustomgear.com

SIC: 3949 Sporting and athletic goods, nec

(G-1165)
SMITHFIELD FOODS INC
195 N Sherman St (47834-2060)
PHONE.............................812 446-2328
EMP: 10
Web: www.smithfieldfoods.com
SIC: 2011 Meat packing plants
HQ: Smithfield Foods, Inc.
 200 Commerce St
 Smithfield VA 23430
 757 365-3000

(G-1166)
TECHNIFAB PRODUCTS INC (PA)
Also Called: Technifab
10339 N Industrial Park Dr (47834-7322)
P.O. Box 315 (47834-0315)
PHONE.............................812 442-0520
Noel Short, *CEO*
Noel Short, *CEO*
Steve Short, *Pr*
Rob Drake, *VP*
Scott D Short, *Sec*
▲ **EMP:** 46 **EST:** 1992
SQ FT: 43,000
SALES (est): 12.83MM **Privately Held**
Web: www.technifab.com
SIC: 3559 3498 Cryogenic machinery, industrial; Fabricated pipe and fittings

(G-1167)
TIMBERLINE INDUSTRIES LLC
Also Called: Timberline Industries
1892 E Us Highway 40 (47834-7637)
P.O. Box 334 (47834-0334)
PHONE.............................812 442-0949
Christopher Miller, *Owner*
EMP: 6 **EST:** 1985
SQ FT: 6,000
SALES (est): 856.77K **Privately Held**
Web: www.timberlineindustries.com
SIC: 5087 3429 Caskets; Casket hardware

(G-1168)
UNITED CCP INC
301 N Murphy Ave (47834-1552)
P.O. Box 404 (47834-0404)
PHONE.............................812 442-7468
Timothy C Callahan, *Pr*
Grady Paddock, *VP*
David Callahan, *Sec*
Grady Don Paddock, *VP*
David C Callahan, *Sec*
EMP: 24 **EST:** 2000
SQ FT: 35,000
SALES (est): 781.2K **Privately Held**
Web: www.umdi-usa.com
SIC: 3312 Tool and die steel

(G-1169)
VANEX INC
Also Called: Vanex Color
1825 E National Ave (47834-2825)
PHONE.............................618 244-1413
Jim W Montgomery, *Pr*
Christina Campbell, *
W Ray Grubb, *
Kenneth Brandt, *
EMP: 25 **EST:** 1962
SALES (est): 8.12MM
SALES (corp-wide): 17.65B **Publicly Held**
SIC: 2851 Paints: oil or alkyd vehicle or water thinned
PA: Ppg Industries, Inc.
 1 Ppg Pl
 Pittsburgh PA 15272
 412 434-3131

Bremen
Marshall County

(G-1170)
ACCRALINE INC
Also Called: Accraline Inc-Metal Surgeons
1420 W Bike St (46506-2199)
PHONE.............................574 546-3484
Richard D Cormican, *Pr*
Mark Cormican, *
Cris Cormican, *
▲ **EMP:** 35 **EST:** 1968
SQ FT: 36,000
SALES (est): 2.45MM **Privately Held**
Web: www.accraline.com
SIC: 3599 Machine shop, jobbing and repair

(G-1171)
AJ SCREEN PRINTING LLC
9545 Tyler Rd (46506-9642)
PHONE.............................574 274-4333
EMP: 4 **EST:** 2018
SALES (est): 243.7K **Privately Held**
Web: www.ajscreenprinting.com
SIC: 2752 Commercial printing, lithographic

(G-1172)
ALMEGA/TRU-FLEX INC
Also Called: Almega Wire Products
3917 State Road 106 (46506-9066)
P.O. Box 67 (46506-0067)
PHONE.............................574 546-2113
Elmo Hurst, *CEO*
Douglas Pomeroy, *
Joe E Miller, *
John Maurer, *
Arthur Stamas, *
◆ **EMP:** 50 **EST:** 1982
SQ FT: 42,000
SALES (est): 9.55MM **Privately Held**
Web: www.almegatf.com
SIC: 3679 3643 3694 3357 Harness assemblies, for electronic use: wire or cable ; Power line cable; Engine electrical equipment; Nonferrous wiredrawing and insulating

(G-1173)
ARTISTIC STONE MFG LLC
5958 4th Rd (46506-9322)
PHONE.............................574 546-3771
Marlin M Miller, *Owner*
EMP: 6 **EST:** 2017
SALES (est): 46.23K **Privately Held**
SIC: 3999 Manufacturing industries, nec

(G-1174)
BCI SOLUTIONS INC
Also Called: Bremen Castings, Inc.
500 N Baltimore St (46506-1177)
P.O. Box 129 (46506-0129)
PHONE.............................574 546-2411
Jb Brown, *CEO*
Charles Kalupa, *Pr*
Geoffrey Meester, *VP*
Frederick Bachman, *CFO*
EMP: 220 **EST:** 1939
SQ FT: 129,000
SALES (est): 38.23MM **Privately Held**
Web: www.bcisolutions.com
SIC: 3321 7539 3599 Ductile iron castings; Machine shop, automotive; Machine shop, jobbing and repair

(G-1175)
BETTER WAY PRODUCTS
3659 Destiny Dr (46506-9076)
PHONE.............................574 546-2868
Cletis Miller, *Pr*

Bremen - Marshall County (G-1176)

EMP: 9 EST: 2018
SALES (est): 241.23K **Privately Held**
Web: www.betterwayproducts.com
SIC: 2821 Plastics materials and resins

(G-1176)
BORKHOLDER WOOD PRODUCTS INC
2060 5th Rd (46506-9327)
PHONE..................574 546-2613
Marvin Borkholder, *Pr*
EMP: 6 EST: 1986
SALES (est): 492.22K **Privately Held**
Web: www.borkholderbuildings.com
SIC: 2431 Moldings, wood: unfinished and prefinished

(G-1177)
BREMEN COMPOSITES LLC
Also Called: Switzer Buildings
425 Industrial Dr (46506-2111)
PHONE..................574 546-3791
Alvin Hildenbrand, *
EMP: 70 EST: 2003
SALES (est): 9.71MM **Privately Held**
Web: www.bremencomposites.com
SIC: 3089 Automotive parts, plastic

(G-1178)
BREMEN CORPORATION (HQ)
405 Industrial Dr (46506-2100)
PHONE..................574 546-4238
Wayne Blessing, *Pr*
James Smith, *
Conrad D Chapman, *
▲ EMP: 300 EST: 1969
SQ FT: 46,000
SALES (est): 60.11MM
SALES (corp-wide): 198.24MM **Privately Held**
SIC: 3086 Packaging and shipping materials, foamed plastics
PA: Creative Foam Corporation
    300 N Alloy Dr
    Fenton MI 48430
    810 629-4149

(G-1179)
BREMTOWN FINE CSTM CBNETRY INC
1456 State Rd 331 (46506)
P.O. Box 409 (46506)
PHONE..................574 546-2781
Timothy Johnson, *Pr*
Nita R Gerig, *Stockholder*
EMP: 55 EST: 1979
SQ FT: 50,000
SALES (est): 5.15MM **Privately Held**
Web: www.bremtown.com
SIC: 2434 Vanities, bathroom: wood

(G-1180)
COLEMAN CABLE LLC
Also Called: South Wire
515 Enterprise Dr (46506)
PHONE..................574 546-5115
EMP: 47
SALES (corp-wide): 1.7B **Privately Held**
Web: www.colemancable.com
SIC: 3643 Power line cable
HQ: Coleman Cable, Llc
    1 Overlook Pt
    Lincolnshire IL 60069
    847 672-2300

(G-1181)
COOPER-STANDARD AUTOMOTIVE INC
Also Called: Cooper
501 High Rd (46506-1040)
PHONE..................574 546-5938
Keiji Kyomoto, *Brnch Mgr*
EMP: 20
SALES (corp-wide): 2.82B **Publicly Held**
Web: www.cooperstandard.com
SIC: 3443 Heat exchangers, condensers, and components
HQ: Cooper-Standard Automotive Inc.
    40300 Traditions Dr
    Northville MI 48168
    248 596-5900

(G-1182)
CORNERSTONE MOULDING INC
1586 3rd Rd (46506-9608)
PHONE..................574 546-4249
Eddie Berkholder, *Pr*
Darryl Yoder, *VP*
Fred Miller, *Off Mgr*
Darrell Yoder, *VP*
EMP: 23 EST: 2004
SALES (est): 1.82MM **Privately Held**
SIC: 2431 Moldings, wood: unfinished and prefinished

(G-1183)
COUNTY LINE WOODWORKING
11594 N 1100 W (46506-9501)
PHONE..................574 935-7107
EMP: 5 EST: 2005
SALES (est): 257.6K **Privately Held**
SIC: 2499 Decorative wood and woodwork

(G-1184)
CREATIVE FOAM CORPORATION
405 Industrial Dr (46506-2111)
PHONE..................574 546-4238
Kent Lutian, *Brnch Mgr*
EMP: 64
SALES (corp-wide): 198.24MM **Privately Held**
Web: www.creativefoam.com
SIC: 3086 Packaging and shipping materials, foamed plastics
PA: Creative Foam Corporation
    300 N Alloy Dr
    Fenton MI 48430
    810 629-4149

(G-1185)
DAILY CO
4502 W Shore Dr (46506-9359)
PHONE..................574 546-5126
EMP: 1 EST: 1983
SALES (est): 126.95K **Privately Held**
SIC: 3448 Prefabricated metal buildings and components

(G-1186)
DIGGER SPECIALTIES INC
3639 Destiny Dr (46506-9076)
PHONE..................574 546-2811
Ray A Helmuth, *Brnch Mgr*
EMP: 4
SALES (corp-wide): 22.78MM **Privately Held**
Web: www.diggerspecialties.com
SIC: 3089 Plastics hardware and building products
PA: Digger Specialties, Inc.
    3446 Us Hwy 6
    Bremen IN 46506
    574 546-5999

(G-1187)
DIGGER SPECIALTIES INC (PA)
3446 Us Highway 6 (46506)
P.O. Box 241 (46506)
PHONE..................574 546-5999
Loren Graber, *Pr*
Everett Hochstetler, *
Esther Graber, *
Margaret Borkholder, *
▲ EMP: 65 EST: 1990
SQ FT: 8,800
SALES (est): 22.78MM
SALES (corp-wide): 22.78MM **Privately Held**
Web: www.diggerspecialties.com
SIC: 3089 Plastics hardware and building products

(G-1188)
DUTCH KETTLE LLC
6375 Fir Rd (46506-9718)
PHONE..................574 546-4033
EMP: 10 EST: 2008
SALES (est): 940.89K **Privately Held**
Web: www.thedutchkettle.com
SIC: 2033 Jams, including imitation: packaged in cans, jars, etc.

(G-1189)
DYNAMIC FINISH SOLUTIONS LLC
1319 W North St (46506-2049)
PHONE..................574 529-0121
Ed Yutzy, *Prin*
EMP: 7 EST: 2017
SALES (est): 775.76K **Privately Held**
Web: www.dynamicfinishsolutions.com
SIC: 2851 Wood stains

(G-1190)
EDGEWOOD METAL FAB LLC
1265 B Rd (46506-9795)
PHONE..................574 546-5947
Raymond Helmuth, *Prin*
EMP: 2 EST: 2009
SALES (est): 225.04K **Privately Held**
SIC: 3441 Fabricated structural metal

(G-1191)
FIRST IMPRESSIONS EMBROIDARY
4763 Fir Rd (46506-9706)
PHONE..................574 276-0750
Betty Ahlenius, *Owner*
EMP: 1 EST: 1999
SALES (est): 47.71K **Privately Held**
SIC: 2395 Embroidery products, except Schiffli machine

(G-1192)
GEN Y HITCH
621 E Plymouth St (46506-1269)
PHONE..................574 218-6363
Donna Drepin, *Mktg Mgr*
EMP: 5 EST: 2020
SALES (est): 42.55K **Privately Held**
Web: www.genyhitch.com
SIC: 3999 Manufacturing industries, nec

(G-1193)
GRAPHIX UNLIMITED INC
3947 State Road 106 (46506-9066)
PHONE..................574 546-3770
Bernie Erickson, *Pr*
EMP: 40 EST: 1990
SQ FT: 14,000
SALES (est): 4.59MM **Privately Held**
Web: www.graphixunlimited.com
SIC: 2759 2675 2396 Decals: printing, nsk; Die-cut paper and board; Automotive and apparel trimmings

(G-1194)
GRIZZLY RIDGE HARDWOODS LLC
1820 Dogwood Rd (46506-9075)
PHONE..................574 546-3600
EMP: 1 EST: 2007
SALES (est): 112.41K **Privately Held**
SIC: 2435 Plywood, hardwood or hardwood faced

(G-1195)
HANWHA MACHINERY AMERICA CORP
Also Called: Universal Bearing
431 N Birkey St (46506-2016)
P.O. Box 38 (46506-0038)
PHONE..................574 546-2261
Young Tae Kim, *Pr*
Dave Ketcham, *VP Fin*
EMP: 93 EST: 1959
SQ FT: 300,000
SALES (est): 696.67K **Privately Held**
SIC: 3714 5085 Bearings, motor vehicle; Bearings
PA: Hanwha Corporation
    86 Cheonggyecheon-Ro, Jung-Gu
    Seoul 04541

(G-1196)
HEADSIGHT INC
4845 3b Rd (46506-9762)
PHONE..................574 546-5022
Richard Gramm, *Pr*
▲ EMP: 8 EST: 2000
SALES (est): 1.24MM **Privately Held**
Web: www.headsight.com
SIC: 3523 Farm machinery and equipment

(G-1197)
INDIANA CARTON COMPANY INC
1721 W Bike St (46506-2123)
PHONE..................574 546-3848
David L Petty, *CEO*
James C Petty, *
Kenneth Petty, *
John Hummer, *
Matthew Petty, *
▲ EMP: 95 EST: 1933
SQ FT: 162,000
SALES (est): 19.23MM **Privately Held**
Web: www.indianacarton.com
SIC: 2653 Boxes, corrugated: made from purchased materials

(G-1198)
INTERNATIONAL WIRE GROUP INC
833 Legner St (46506-1060)
PHONE..................574 546-4680
Joe Choquette, *Brnch Mgr*
EMP: 30
SALES (corp-wide): 558.95MM **Privately Held**
Web: www.internationalwire.com
SIC: 3357 3351 Nonferrous wiredrawing and insulating; Wire, copper and copper alloy
HQ: International Wire Group, Inc.
    12 Masonic Ave
    Camden NY 13316

(G-1199)
JC CREATIONS LLC
219 W Dewey St (46506-1117)
PHONE..................574 248-0126
EMP: 1 EST: 2009
SALES (est): 111.2K **Privately Held**
SIC: 3799 Trailers and trailer equipment

(G-1200)
JOHNS MANVILLE CORPORATION
1215 W Dewey St (46506-2063)
PHONE..................574 546-4666
Ray Darmer, *Mgr*
EMP: 101
SALES (corp-wide): 364.48B **Publicly Held**
Web: www.jm.com

SIC: 3086 Plastics foam products
HQ: Johns Manville Corporation
    717 17th St
    Denver CO 80202
    303 978-2000

(G-1201)
KAUFFMAN ENGINEERING LLC
Also Called: Bremen Wire Products
510 E 2nd St (46506-1050)
P.O. Box 658 (46947-0658)
PHONE..................574 732-2154
Tom Gay, *Brnch Mgr*
EMP: 59
SQ FT: 20,500
SALES (corp-wide): 140.92MM **Privately Held**
Web: www.kewire.com
SIC: 3679 Harness assemblies, for electronic use: wire or cable
PA: Kauffman Engineering, Llc
    595 Bond St
    Lincolnshire IL 60069
    765 482-5640

(G-1202)
KEMCO MANUFACTURING LLC
617 E Plymouth St (46506-1269)
PHONE..................574 546-2025
Ervin Miller, *Prin*
EMP: 6 EST: 2013
SALES (est): 245.1K **Privately Held**
Web: www.kemco-usa.com
SIC: 3999 Manufacturing industries, nec

(G-1203)
LAUDEMAN PLACE INC
1851 Dogwood Rd (46506-9074)
P.O. Box 250 (46506-0250)
PHONE..................574 546-4404
Connie Laudeman, *Pr*
EMP: 19 EST: 1968
SALES (est): 493.11K **Privately Held**
Web: www.tjsnuggles.com
SIC: 2394 Awnings, fabric: made from purchased materials

(G-1204)
MADISON MANUFACTURING INC
66990 State Road 331 (46506-9478)
PHONE..................574 633-4333
EMP: 40 EST: 1995
SQ FT: 20,000
SALES (est): 4.06MM **Privately Held**
Web: www.madisonmfg.com
SIC: 3714 3523 Motor vehicle body components and frame; Farm machinery and equipment

(G-1205)
MEL-RHON INC
Also Called: Mrs T'S Bakery
124 E Plymouth St (46506-1236)
PHONE..................574 546-4559
Rhonda Triplet, *Pt*
EMP: 4 EST: 1993
SALES (est): 244.87K **Privately Held**
Web: www.mrs-t.com
SIC: 2051 Bakery: wholesale or wholesale/retail combined

(G-1206)
MINT CITY SEWING & TACK LLC
2320 4c Rd (46506)
PHONE..................574 546-2230
EMP: 4 EST: 2016
SALES (est): 73.73K **Privately Held**
SIC: 2399 Fabricated textile products, nec

(G-1207)
MJ FINISHING LLC
5311 E County Line Rd (46506-9745)
PHONE..................574 646-2080
Mathew Schmucker, *Owner*
EMP: 4 EST: 2006
SALES (est): 391.42K **Privately Held**
Web: www.mjfinishingllc.com
SIC: 2499 Decorative wood and woodwork

(G-1208)
NISHIKAWA COOPER LLC
501 High Rd (46506-1040)
PHONE..................260 593-2156
EMP: 89
Web: www.niscoseals.com
SIC: 3053 Gaskets; packing and sealing devices
HQ: Nishikawa Cooper Llc
    324 Morrow St
    Topeka IN 46571
    260 593-2156

(G-1209)
OMEGA PROCESS SOLUTIONS LLC
860 Legner St # 870 (46506-1062)
P.O. Box 5240 (37841-5240)
PHONE..................574 546-5606
EMP: 36 EST: 2017
SALES (est): 4.86MM **Privately Held**
Web: www.omegapro-us.com
SIC: 3052 Rubber and plastics hose and beltings

(G-1210)
OMEGA PRODUCTS INC
870 Legner St (46506-1062)
P.O. Box 86 (46506-0086)
PHONE..................574 546-5606
William B Lentz, *Pr*
Ronald C Miller, *
Suzette Lentz, *
▼ EMP: 42 EST: 1999
SQ FT: 15,000
SALES (est): 3.59MM **Privately Held**
SIC: 3052 Rubber hose

(G-1211)
OZINGA BROS INC
524 N Bowen Ave (46506-2006)
PHONE..................574 546-2550
EMP: 23
SALES (corp-wide): 552.21MM **Privately Held**
Web: www.ozinga.com
SIC: 3273 Ready-mixed concrete
PA: Ozinga Bros., Inc.
    19001 Old Lagrange Rd # 3
    Mokena IL 60448
    708 326-4200

(G-1212)
PATRICK INDUSTRIES INC
Also Called: Charleston
1849 Dogwood Rd (46506-9074)
PHONE..................574 546-5222
Toni Swiheart, *Brnch Mgr*
EMP: 16
SALES (corp-wide): 3.47B **Publicly Held**
Web: www.patrickind.com
SIC: 3089 Gutters (glass fiber reinforced), fiberglass or plastics
PA: Patrick Industries, Inc.
    107 W Franklin St
    Elkhart IN 46516
    574 294-7511

(G-1213)
PERMALATT PRODUCTS INC (PA)
3462 Us Highway 6 (46506-9062)
P.O. Box 405 (46506-0405)
PHONE..................574 546-6311
EMP: 4 EST: 1997
SALES (est): 932.63K **Privately Held**
Web: www.permalatt.com
SIC: 3089 Plastics hardware and building products

(G-1214)
PETROLEUM SOLUTIONS INC
809 Douglas Rd (46506-9602)
P.O. Box 389 (46506-0389)
PHONE..................574 546-2133
John Kuhns, *CEO*
EMP: 4 EST: 2012
SALES (est): 933.64K **Privately Held**
Web: www.pslubricants.com
SIC: 2992 5172 2911 Lubricating oils and greases; Lubricating oils and greases; Fuel additives

(G-1215)
PROTEC PANEL & TRUSS MFG LLC
323 High Rd (46506)
PHONE..................574 281-9080
EMP: 75 EST: 2018
SALES (est): 6.02MM **Privately Held**
Web: www.protecmfg.com
SIC: 2439 Trusses, wooden roof

(G-1216)
RADIATOR SPECIALTY COMPANY
Omega Products
860 Legner St 870 (46506)
PHONE..................574 546-5606
Scott Sickmiller, *Mgr*
EMP: 65
SALES (corp-wide): 45.45MM **Privately Held**
Web: www.rscbrands.com
SIC: 3052 Rubber hose
PA: Radiator Specialty Company Inc
    600 Radiator Rd
    Indian Trail NC 28079
    704 688-2302

(G-1217)
RARE EARTH INC
68114 Lake Trl (46506-7805)
PHONE..................574 850-1924
EMP: 5 EST: 2014
SALES (est): 55.17K **Privately Held**
Web: www.polarisrem.com
SIC: 3499 Fabricated metal products, nec

(G-1218)
RENTOWN CABINETS LLC
2735 Birch Rd (46506-9042)
PHONE..................574 546-2569
Dennis Hochstetler, *Pr*
EMP: 3 EST: 1986
SALES (est): 191.57K **Privately Held**
Web: www.rentowncabinets.com
SIC: 2434 Wood kitchen cabinets

(G-1219)
SCHWARTZ WHEEL CO
2750 3b Rd (46506-8717)
PHONE..................574 546-0101
Jerry Schwartz, *Prin*
EMP: 9 EST: 2009
SALES (est): 129.79K **Privately Held**
SIC: 3312 Blast furnaces and steel mills

(G-1220)
SCHWARTZS WHEEL & CLIP C
Also Called: Schwartz's Wheel Repair
4199 Cedar Rd (46506-9755)
PHONE..................574 546-1302
John Schwartz, *Prin*

John Schwartz, *Owner*
EMP: 2 EST: 1998
SALES (est): 202.53K **Privately Held**
SIC: 3799 Carriages, horse drawn

(G-1221)
SIGN DEALS DELIVERED
2949 2b Rd (46506-9049)
PHONE..................574 276-7404
Anjie Brenda, *Ofcr*
EMP: 4 EST: 2007
SALES (est): 49.4K **Privately Held**
Web: www.signdealsdelivered.com
SIC: 3993 Signs and advertising specialties

(G-1222)
SOUTHWIRE COMPANY LLC
Also Called: Southwire East Insulating
515 Copperfield Way (46506-8842)
PHONE..................574 546-5115
EMP: 64
SALES (corp-wide): 1.7B **Privately Held**
Web: www.southwire.com
SIC: 3351 3355 3357 3559 Copper rolling and drawing; Aluminum rolling and drawing, nec; Nonferrous wiredrawing and insulating; Frame straighteners, automobile (garage equipment)
PA: Southwire Company, Llc
    One Southwire Dr
    Carrollton GA 30119
    770 832-4529

(G-1223)
SPEEDSTERS
119 N Liberty Dr (46506-2041)
PHONE..................574 546-4656
EMP: 6 EST: 2019
SALES (est): 87.26K **Privately Held**
Web: www.speedsterowners.com
SIC: 3711 Motor vehicles and car bodies

(G-1224)
STEVE WEAVER ART
113 N Center St (46506-1505)
PHONE..................574 546-3530
Steve Weaver, *Pt*
EMP: 1 EST: 1980
SQ FT: 1,800
SALES (est): 145.52K **Privately Held**
Web: www.steveweaverarts.com
SIC: 2752 2759 Offset printing; Screen printing

(G-1225)
SUMMIT MFG & MACHINING INC
723 High Rd (46506-1067)
P.O. Box 9 (46506-0009)
PHONE..................574 546-4571
EMP: 18 EST: 1993
SQ FT: 12,000
SALES (est): 2.16MM **Privately Held**
Web: www.summitmmi.com
SIC: 3599 Machine shop, jobbing and repair

(G-1226)
SUPERIOR COATINGS INC
1730 W Dewey St (46506-2133)
PHONE..................574 546-0591
Toby Lakins, *Pr*
EMP: 9 EST: 2005
SQ FT: 10,000
SALES (est): 992.32K **Privately Held**
Web: www.superiorcoatingsin.com
SIC: 3449 Plastering accessories, metal

(G-1227)
SURFACE ELEMENTS INC
506 E North St (46506-1271)
PHONE..................574 546-5455

Bremen - Marshall County (G-1228) — GEOGRAPHIC SECTION

EMP: 10 EST: 2009
SALES (est): 211.84K Privately Held
SIC: 2819 Elements

(G-1228)
VERNS WOODWORKING
491 4th Rd (46506-9082)
PHONE..................574 773-7930
EMP: 4 EST: 2017
SALES (est): 76.82K Privately Held
SIC: 2431 Millwork

(G-1229)
WALNUT LANE WOODWORKING
12530 Shively Rd (46506-9412)
PHONE..................574 633-2114
EMP: 5 EST: 2013
SALES (est): 201.07K Privately Held
SIC: 2431 Millwork

(G-1230)
WILLIAM LEMAN CO (PA)
114 N Center St (46506-1563)
PHONE..................574 546-2371
Eugene Zimmer, Pr
Tom Stiles, VP
Brian Shappell, Ex VP
Verdon Feldman, Sec
EMP: 20 EST: 1911
SQ FT: 100,000
SALES (est): 1.63MM
SALES (corp-wide): 1.63MM Privately Held
SIC: 2087 Extracts, flavoring

(G-1231)
WOODYS PAINT SPOT LTD
3860 W Shore Dr (46506-9366)
PHONE..................574 255-0348
Michael E Wood, Pr
EMP: 8 EST: 1983
SQ FT: 4,800
SALES (est): 817.53K Privately Held
SIC: 2851 Paints and allied products

(G-1232)
YODER WOODWORKING INC
2534 State Road 331 (46506-9051)
PHONE..................574 546-5100
EMP: 3 EST: 1994
SALES (est): 232.57K Privately Held
Web: www.yoderwoodworking.com
SIC: 3429 Cabinet hardware

Brimfield
Noble County

(G-1233)
PLAS-TECH MOLDING & DESIGN INC
7037 N Triplett St B (46794-9799)
PHONE..................260 761-3006
Dennis Berkey, Pr
Elaine Berkey, VP
EMP: 23 EST: 1986
SQ FT: 30,000
SALES (est): 987.8K Privately Held
SIC: 3089 Injection molding of plastics

Bringhurst
Carroll County

(G-1234)
ADVANTAGE EMBROIDERY INC
1059 E 400 S (46913-9561)
PHONE..................765 471-0188
Susan Moore, Pr
Renee Dexter, Sec
EMP: 2 EST: 1996
SQ FT: 1,800
SALES (est): 365.32K Privately Held
Web: www.embroiderypatches.com
SIC: 2395 Embroidery products, except Schiffli machine

(G-1235)
B & B ENGINEERING INC
7102 E 300 S (46913-9684)
PHONE..................765 566-3460
EMP: 4 EST: 1985
SQ FT: 6,000
SALES (est): 390.55K Privately Held
Web: www.bbengineering1.com
SIC: 3544 Special dies and tools

(G-1236)
GRAPHICS EMPORIUM
2540 E 200 S (46913-9545)
PHONE..................574 967-4627
Terry Langston, Owner
EMP: 1 EST: 1998
SALES (est): 66.71K Privately Held
Web: www.graphicsemporium.com
SIC: 3993 Signs and advertising specialties

(G-1237)
JIMS WELDING & REPAIR LLC
2359 E 400 S (46913-9565)
PHONE..................765 564-1797
Jim Brewer, Prin
EMP: 5 EST: 2010
SALES (est): 252.76K Privately Held
SIC: 7692 5051 Welding repair; Metal wires, ties, cables, and screening

(G-1238)
WORK ROOM
1415 E 400 S (46913-9562)
PHONE..................765 268-2634
EMP: 1 EST: 1994
SALES (est): 60.98K Privately Held
SIC: 2391 Curtains and draperies

(G-1239)
ZINN KITCHENS INC
Also Called: Zinn Cabinets Plus
1211 S Center St (46913-9621)
P.O. Box 7 (46929-0007)
PHONE..................574 967-4179
TOLL FREE: 800
Gregg Zinn, Pr
Dale Zinn, *
Mary Zinn, *
Tony Fife, *
EMP: 22 EST: 1955
SQ FT: 27,000
SALES (est): 511.49K Privately Held
Web: www.zinnkitchens.com
SIC: 2434 5722 Wood kitchen cabinets; Household appliance stores

Bristol
Elkhart County

(G-1240)
ABERCROMBIE TEXTILES I LLC
103 Hinsdale Farm Rd (46507-9167)
PHONE..................574 848-5100
John Regan, Brnch Mgr
EMP: 5
SALES (corp-wide): 4.79MM Privately Held
Web: www.cryptonmills.com
SIC: 2295 5131 2262 Laminating of fabrics; Upholstery fabrics, woven; Finishing plants, manmade
PA: Abercrombie Textiles I, Llc
1322 Mount Sinai Ch Rd
Shelby NC 28152
704 487-1245

(G-1241)
ABSOLUTE CALIBER LLC
50839 Oak Tree Ln (46507-9063)
PHONE..................574 303-4365
Amedee Mosier, Prin
EMP: 4 EST: 2017
SALES (est): 48.59K Privately Held
Web: www.absolutecaliber.com
SIC: 3599 Machine shop, jobbing and repair

(G-1242)
ALLIANCE ALUMINUM PRODUCTS INC
1649 Commerce Dr (46507-9348)
PHONE..................574 848-4300
Ramon D Barnes Junior, Pr
Christopher W Rody, *
EMP: 70 EST: 2008
SALES (est): 4.57MM
SALES (corp-wide): 162.61MM Privately Held
Web: www.alliancealum.com
SIC: 3354 Aluminum extruded products
PA: Eastern Metal Supply, Inc.
3600 23rd Ave S
Lake Worth FL 33461
561 533-6061

(G-1243)
AMERI-KART CORP
Also Called: Sherwood Plastics
1667 Commerce Dr (46507)
PHONE..................225 642-7874
Eric Gottuso, Pr
EMP: 88
SALES (corp-wide): 813.07MM Publicly Held
Web: www.myersengineeredsolutions.com
SIC: 2821 3444 3083 Plastics materials and resins; Sheet metalwork; Laminated plastics plate and sheet
HQ: Ameri-Kart Corp.
1667 Commerce Dr
Bristol IN 46507

(G-1244)
AMERI-KART CORP (HQ)
1667 Commerce Dr (46507)
P.O. Box P.O. Box 368 (46507)
PHONE..................574 848-7462
Bob Wagner, Mgr
▲ EMP: 120 EST: 1992
SALES (est): 46.13MM
SALES (corp-wide): 813.07MM Publicly Held
Web: www.myersengineeredsolutions.com
SIC: 3089 3537 2821 5162 Garbage containers, plastics; Tables, lift: hydraulic; Plastics materials and resins; Plastics products, nec
PA: Myers Industries, Inc.
1293 S Main St
Akron OH 44301
330 253-5592

(G-1245)
AMERI-KART(MI) CORP
1667 Commerce Dr (46507-9348)
PHONE..................269 641-5811
Mike O'brien, Genl Mgr
▲ EMP: 65 EST: 1969
SALES (est): 1.7MM
SALES (corp-wide): 813.07MM Publicly Held
SIC: 3089 Injection molding of plastics
PA: Myers Industries, Inc.
1293 S Main St
Akron OH 44301
330 253-5592

(G-1246)
AR-TEE ENTERPRISES INC
19874 County Road 6 (46507-9759)
P.O. Box 562 (46507-0562)
PHONE..................574 848-5543
Bruce Miller, Pr
EMP: 6 EST: 1983
SQ FT: 8,000
SALES (est): 760.3K Privately Held
SIC: 3089 3544 Injection molded finished plastics products, nec; Industrial molds

(G-1247)
AVR PRODUCTS INC
Also Called: Vista Plastic
53689 Pheasant Ridge Dr (46507-9006)
PHONE..................574 294-6101
Bernie Fassler, Pr
EMP: 5 EST: 2001
SALES (est): 819.49K Privately Held
SIC: 5085 3089 Gaskets; Plastics hardware and building products

(G-1248)
B D CUSTOM MANUFACTURING INC
1100 Bloomingdale Dr (46507-8403)
PHONE..................574 848-0925
EMP: 14 EST: 1993
SQ FT: 18,000
SALES (est): 2.42MM Privately Held
Web: www.bdcustommfg.com
SIC: 3089 Injection molding of plastics

(G-1249)
BAY BRIDGE MFG INC
Also Called: Bay Bridge Manufacturing
1301 Commerce Dr (46507-9349)
P.O. Box 215 (46507-0215)
PHONE..................574 848-7477
Dennis F Mccarthy, Pr
Merril M Mccarthy, Sec
EMP: 49 EST: 1983
SALES (est): 5.07MM Privately Held
Web: www.baybridgemfg.com
SIC: 3713 Truck bodies (motor vehicles)

(G-1250)
BRINCO MANUFACTURING INC
51650 County Road 133 (46507-9800)
PHONE..................574 213-1008
Jason Schmidt, Pr
EMP: 1 EST: 2019
SALES (est): 531.9K Privately Held
Web: brincomanufacturing.isolvedhire.com
SIC: 3312 Blast furnaces and steel mills

(G-1251)
BRISTOL INTGRTED TLING ATMTN L
Also Called: Bristol Tool and Die
689 Commerce Dr (46507-9355)
PHONE..................574 848-5354
Charles S Reitsma, Managing Member
EMP: 15 EST: 2019
SALES (est): 1.06MM Privately Held
Web: www.bristoltoolanddie.com
SIC: 3599 Machine shop, jobbing and repair

(G-1252)
BRISTOL TOOL AND DIE INC
710 Commerce Dr (46507-9354)
PHONE..................574 848-5354
Brian Price, Pr
EMP: 18 EST: 1999

GEOGRAPHIC SECTION Bristol - Elkhart County (G-1277)

SQ FT: 13,000
SALES (est): 1.81MM Privately Held
Web: www.rsetool.com
SIC: 3599 3545 3544 Machine shop, jobbing and repair; Machine tool accessories; Special dies, tools, jigs, and fixtures

(G-1253)
CHEM TECH INC
501 Bloomingdale Dr (46507-9610)
PHONE.............................574 848-1001
Dennis J Brosh, Pr
EMP: 12 EST: 1991
SQ FT: 20,000
SALES (est): 2.44MM Privately Held
SIC: 2891 Adhesives

(G-1254)
COMBINED TECHNOLOGIES INC (PA)
Also Called: CTI
503 Bloomingdale Dr (46507-9610)
PHONE.............................847 968-4855
Jerry Thompson, Pr
EMP: 9 EST: 2000
SQ FT: 160,000
SALES (est): 4.93MM
SALES (corp-wide): 4.93MM Privately Held
Web: www.ctipack.com
SIC: 2631 2657 2653 3565 Container, packaging, and boxboard; Folding paperboard boxes; Corrugated and solid fiber boxes; Bottling machinery: filling, capping, labeling

(G-1255)
COUNTRY CRAFT CABINETS LLC
17090 State Road 120 (46507-9593)
PHONE.............................574 596-8624
EMP: 4 EST: 2012
SALES (est): 127.79K Privately Held
SIC: 2434 Wood kitchen cabinets

(G-1256)
DOYLE MANUFACTURING INC
2108 Blakesley Pkwy (46507-7000)
P.O. Box 1474 (46507-1474)
PHONE.............................574 848-5624
Myron Miller, Pr
Mark E Miller, VP
EMP: 4 EST: 1989
SALES (est): 400.53K Privately Held
Web: www.doyleblocks.com
SIC: 3825 Test equipment for electronic and electrical circuits

(G-1257)
DYNAMIC PACKG SOLUTIONS INC
406 Kesco Dr (46507-8991)
PHONE.............................574 848-1410
Frank D Massa, CEO
Tracy Lute, *
EMP: 175 EST: 2007
SQ FT: 40,000
SALES (est): 11.31MM Privately Held
Web: www.dynamicclearsolutions.com
SIC: 2671 Paper; coated and laminated packaging

(G-1258)
EARTHWAY PRODUCTS LLC
1009 Maple St (46507-8328)
P.O. Box 547 (46507-0547)
PHONE.............................574 848-7491
Cinda Mckinney, Ch Bd
Cinda Mckinney, Ch
H Douglas Schrock, *
Sara Barrett, *
Kenneth Pickett, *
◆ EMP: 100 EST: 1965

SQ FT: 180,000
SALES (est): 18.32MM Privately Held
Web: www.earthway.com
SIC: 3523 Farm machinery and equipment

(G-1259)
EMBER RECRTL VEHICLES INC
710 Commerce Dr (46507-9354)
PHONE.............................844 732-4204
Ashley Lehman, CEO
EMP: 75
SALES (est): 4.34MM Privately Held
Web: www.emberrv.com
SIC: 3799 Recreational vehicles

(G-1260)
F B C INC (PA)
Also Called: Custom Formulating & Blending
1123 Commerce Dr (46507-9351)
PHONE.............................574 848-5288
John E Ray, Pr
Raj Bedi, Stockholder*
▼ EMP: 24 EST: 1990
SALES (est): 9.72MM Privately Held
Web: www.customformulating.com
SIC: 2842 2992 Cleaning or polishing preparations, nec; Lubricating oils and greases

(G-1261)
FOREST RIVER INC
U S Cargo
17645 Commerce Dr (46507-9350)
PHONE.............................574 848-1335
Joseph Greenlee, Brnch Mgr
EMP: 271
SALES (corp-wide): 364.48B Publicly Held
Web: www.forestriverinc.com
SIC: 3715 3792 Demountable cargo containers; Tent-type camping trailers
HQ: Forest River, Inc.
900 County Rd 1 N
Elkhart IN 46514

(G-1262)
FRUIT HILLS WINERY ORCHRD LLC
55503 State Road 15 (46507-9505)
PHONE.............................574 848-9463
EMP: 2 EST: 2010
SALES (est): 159.24K Privately Held
Web: www.fruithillswinery.com
SIC: 2084 Wines

(G-1263)
FT GROUP LLC
Also Called: Impact Trailers
19224 County Road 8 (46507-9706)
PHONE.............................574 322-4369
EMP: 8 EST: 2018
SQ FT: 110,000
SALES (est): 1.39MM
SALES (corp-wide): 4.57MM Privately Held
Web: www.formulatrailers.com
SIC: 3715 Truck trailers
PA: Ft Indiana, Llc
19224 County Road 8
Bristol IN 46507
574 622-0827

(G-1264)
GRACE STEEL CORPORATION (PA)
21601 Durham Way (46507-9010)
PHONE.............................574 218-6600
David Andre, CEO
EMP: 5 EST: 2015
SALES (est): 2.46MM
SALES (corp-wide): 2.46MM Privately Held
Web: www.steelgrace.com

SIC: 3291 Abrasive metal and steel products

(G-1265)
GREAT LAKES LAMINATION INC (PA)
1103 Maple St (46507-8330)
PHONE.............................574 389-9663
Mark E Smith, Pr
EMP: 1 EST: 2018
SALES (est): 1.02MM
SALES (corp-wide): 1.02MM Privately Held
SIC: 2655 Containers, laminated phenolic and vulcanized fiber

(G-1266)
HINSDALE FARMS LTD
605 Kesco Dr (46507-8980)
P.O. Box 1399 (46507-1399)
PHONE.............................574 848-0344
Milton C Smith, Pr
Philip M Smith, VP
EMP: 2 EST: 1997
SALES (est): 247.37K Privately Held
SIC: 2013 Sausages and other prepared meats

(G-1267)
HYMER GROUP USA LLC
1220 Maple St (46507-8335)
PHONE.............................574 970-7460
EMP: 1 EST: 2020
SALES (est): 249.99K
SALES (corp-wide): 11.12B Publicly Held
SIC: 3799 Recreational vehicles
PA: Thor Industries, Inc.
601 E Beardsley Ave
Elkhart IN 46514
574 970-7460

(G-1268)
JEC STEEL COMPANY (PA)
1151 Bloomingdale Dr (46507-8403)
PHONE.............................574 326-3829
Jeremy Seniff, Pr
EMP: 5 EST: 2014
SALES (est): 1.14MM
SALES (corp-wide): 1.14MM Privately Held
Web: www.jecsteelcompany.com
SIC: 3325 5051 Steel foundries, nec; Iron and steel (ferrous) products

(G-1269)
LASALLE BRISTOL CORPORATION
Lasalle Lighting
1203 N Division St (46507-8931)
P.O. Box 98 (46515-0098)
PHONE.............................574 295-4400
Dwayne Rosenberry, VP
EMP: 10
SQ FT: 88,816
SALES (corp-wide): 3.47B Publicly Held
Web: www.lasallebristol.com
SIC: 5023 3645 Floor coverings; Residential lighting fixtures
HQ: Lasalle Bristol Corporation
601 County Road 17
Elkhart IN 46516
574 295-8400

(G-1270)
LAVENDER PATCH FABR QUILTS LLC
20615 Baltimore Oriole Dr (46507-8531)
P.O. Box 114 (46507-0114)
PHONE.............................574 848-0011
Patricia Harris, Prin
EMP: 4 EST: 2011
SALES (est): 188.87K Privately Held

Web: www.lavenderpatchquilts.com
SIC: 2395 Quilted fabrics or cloth

(G-1271)
LEWIS PROPERTY SOLUTIONS LLC
1403 Pike Dr (46507-8847)
PHONE.............................574 361-0168
EMP: 2 EST: 2011
SALES (est): 227.13K Privately Held
Web: www.thewaterfallgroup.com
SIC: 1389 Construction, repair, and dismantling services

(G-1272)
MARINE GROUP LLC
Also Called: Misty Harbor
11 Lakota Ln (46507)
P.O. Box 579 (46507-0579)
PHONE.............................574 622-0490
George Thomas, CEO
Jeff Miller, *
EMP: 125 EST: 2007
SALES (est): 9.15MM Privately Held
Web: www.viaggiopontoonboats.com
SIC: 3732 Boatbuilding and repairing

(G-1273)
MARK-LINE INDUSTRIES LLC
51687 County Road 133 (46507-9800)
P.O. Box 277 (46507-0277)
PHONE.............................574 825-5851
EMP: 125
Web: www.marklinepa.com
SIC: 2451 Mobile buildings: for commercial use

(G-1274)
MISSION WOODWORKING INC
502 Kesco Dr (46507-9466)
PHONE.............................574 848-5697
Kevin Beck, Pr
Patty Beck, *
Gary Horst, Stockholder*
EMP: 26 EST: 1998
SALES (est): 2.44MM Privately Held
Web: www.missionwoodworking.com
SIC: 2511 2541 Storage chests, household: wood; Table or counter tops, plastic laminated

(G-1275)
MOLDED FOAM LLC
Also Called: Molded Foam Products
1203 S Division St (46507-9160)
PHONE.............................574 848-1500
▼ EMP: 40 EST: 2009
SALES (est): 4.85MM Privately Held
Web: www.moldedfoamproducts.com
SIC: 3086 Plastics foam products

(G-1276)
MOLDED FOAM PRODUCTS INC
1203 S Division St (46507-9160)
PHONE.............................574 848-1500
EMP: 15
SIC: 2821 Polyurethane resins

(G-1277)
MONOGRAM COMFORT FOODS LLC
605 Kesco Dr (46507-8980)
PHONE.............................574 848-0344
Wes Jackson, Managing Member
EMP: 100 EST: 2007
SQ FT: 35,000
SALES (est): 12.96MM Privately Held
Web: www.monogramfoods.com
SIC: 2013 Sausages and other prepared meats
PA: Monogram Food Solutions, Llc
530 Oak Court Dr Ste 400

Bristol - Elkhart County (G-1278)

(G-1278)
MONOGRAM FOOD SOLUTIONS LLC
605 Kesco Dr (46507)
PHONE.....................574 848-0344
Karl Schledwitz, *Brnch Mgr*
EMP: 1
Web: www.monogramfoods.com
SIC: 2013 Sausages and other prepared meats
PA: Monogram Food Solutions, Llc
530 Oak Court Dr Ste 400
Memphis TN 38117

(G-1279)
MONOGRAM FROZEN FOODS LLC
605 Kesco Dr (46507)
P.O. Box 1399 (46507)
PHONE.....................574 848-0344
Rob Shuster, *Managing Member*
Jocelyn Brown, *
Phillip Smith, *
▲ EMP: 250 EST: 1949
SQ FT: 113,000
SALES (est): 15.31MM **Privately Held**
Web: www.monogramfoods.com
SIC: 2013 Sausages and other prepared meats

(G-1280)
MPR CORPORATION
Also Called: Fabric Services
103 Hinsdale Farm Rd (46507-9167)
PHONE.....................574 848-5100
John Wuori, *Pr*
Steve Kercher, *
▲ EMP: 48 EST: 1988
SQ FT: 80,000
SALES (est): 8.5MM **Privately Held**
SIC: 5131 2211 2295 Upholstery fabrics, woven; Broadwoven fabric mills, cotton; Laminating of fabrics

(G-1281)
NIBLOCK EXCAVATING INC (PA)
Also Called: Michiana Directional Drilling
906 Maple St (46507)
P.O. Box 211 (46507)
PHONE.....................574 848-4437
Gary Niblock, *Pr*
Richard Niblock, *
EMP: 100 EST: 1971
SQ FT: 2,500
SALES (est): 14.26MM
SALES (corp-wide): 14.26MM **Privately Held**
Web: www.niblockexc.com
SIC: 2951 1771 1611 1794 Asphalt and asphaltic paving mixtures (not from refineries); Foundation and footing contractor; Highway and street paving contractor; Excavation work

(G-1282)
PANDA PRINTS
19647 County Road 8 (46507-9709)
PHONE.....................574 322-1050
Amanda Hatton, *Prin*
EMP: 5 EST: 2016
SALES (est): 83.91K **Privately Held**
SIC: 2752 Commercial printing, lithographic

(G-1283)
QUALITY GALVANIZED PDTS INC
Also Called: Galvanized Division
19473 County Road 8 (46507-9708)
P.O. Box 369 (46507-0369)
PHONE.....................574 848-5151
Chris Sutterby, *Genl Mgr*
Louis Chadwick, *Pr*
EMP: 8 EST: 2000
SQ FT: 15,000
SALES (est): 1.09MM **Privately Held**
Web: www.tcourse.com
SIC: 3444 Sheet metalwork

(G-1284)
RECORD / PLAY TEK INC
Also Called: Rpt
110 E Vistula St (46507)
P.O. Box 790 (46507-0790)
PHONE.....................574 848-5233
Michael H Stoll, *Pr*
John Haines, *VP*
EMP: 6 EST: 1997
SQ FT: 9,500
SALES (est): 485.3K **Privately Held**
SIC: 3651 Household audio and video equipment

(G-1285)
RESCHCOR INC (PA)
Also Called: Omega
2123 Blakesley Pkwy (46507-7000)
PHONE.....................574 295-2413
Tom Reschly, *Pr*
Jim Reschly, *
James Reschly, *
Dave Kieper, *
EMP: 91 EST: 1983
SQ FT: 42,700
SALES (est): 20.25MM
SALES (corp-wide): 20.25MM **Privately Held**
Web: www.reschcor.com
SIC: 3089 Extruded finished plastics products, nec

(G-1286)
REV RENEGADE LLC
Also Called: Renegade Rv
52216 State Road 15 (46507-9524)
PHONE.....................574 966-0166
EMP: 48 EST: 2004
SALES (est): 11.7MM **Publicly Held**
Web: www.renegaderv.com
SIC: 3711 Ambulances (motor vehicles), assembly of
PA: Rev Group, Inc.
245 S Exec Dr Ste 100
Brookfield WI 53005

(G-1287)
RICHARD SHEETS
15569 State Road 120 (46507-9241)
PHONE.....................574 536-8247
Richard Sheets, *Owner*
EMP: 2 EST: 2003
SQ FT: 1,092
SALES (est): 140K **Privately Held**
SIC: 3711 Truck tractors for highway use, assembly of

(G-1288)
ROBERT WEED PLYWOOD CORP
705 Maple St (46507-9103)
P.O. Box 487 (46507-0487)
PHONE.....................574 848-7631
David Weed, *Pr*
Thomas Longworth, *VP*
Michael Cosentino, *Sec*
Gary D Boyn, *Sec*
▲ EMP: 350 EST: 1966
SQ FT: 616,000
SALES (est): 79.62MM **Privately Held**
Web: www.robertweedcorp.com
SIC: 5031 2435 2431 Plywood; Panels, hardwood plywood; Moldings and baseboards, ornamental and trim

(G-1289)
RS PALLET INC
19816 County Road 6 (46507-9759)
PHONE.....................574 596-8777
Sie W Sharp Junior, *Owner*
EMP: 6 EST: 2016
SALES (est): 106.96K **Privately Held**
SIC: 2448 Pallets, wood

(G-1290)
SHA-DO CORP
1501 Bloomingdale Dr (46507-9184)
PHONE.....................574 848-9296
Donald Gingerich, *Pr*
EMP: 9 EST: 1993
SQ FT: 20,000
SALES (est): 1.04MM **Privately Held**
Web: www.shadocorp.com
SIC: 3469 Stamping metal for the trade

(G-1291)
SHYFT GROUP USA INC
603 Earthway Blvd (46507-9182)
PHONE.....................574 848-2000
EMP: 8
SALES (corp-wide): 872.2MM **Publicly Held**
Web: www.spartanrvchassis.com
SIC: 3713 Truck and bus bodies
HQ: The Shyft Group Usa Inc
1000 Reynolds Rd
Charlotte MI 48813
517 543-6400

(G-1292)
SIERRA MOTOR CORP
Also Called: Sierra Interiors
19224 County Road 8 (46507-9706)
PHONE.....................574 848-1300
Michael W Greene, *Pr*
Kathie Greene, *
Bryan Greene, *Stockholder*
EMP: 60 EST: 1987
SQ FT: 102,000
SALES (est): 8.72MM **Privately Held**
Web: www.sierrainteriors.com
SIC: 3799 Horse trailers, except fifth-wheel type

(G-1293)
STOUTCO INC (PA)
1 Stoutco Dr (46507)
P.O. Box 309 (46507-0309)
PHONE.....................574 848-4411
EMP: 100 EST: 1959
SALES (est): 10MM
SALES (corp-wide): 10MM **Privately Held**
Web: www.stoutcoinc.com
SIC: 3449 Bars, concrete reinforcing: fabricated steel

(G-1294)
TALON PRODUCTS LLC
1690 Commerce Dr (46507)
P.O. Box 508 (46507)
PHONE.....................574 218-0100
EMP: 14 EST: 2015
SALES (est): 4.54MM **Privately Held**
Web: www.talonproducts.com
SIC: 3229 Glass fiber products

(G-1295)
UTILIMASTER HOLDINGS INC
603 Earthway Blvd (46507-9182)
P.O. Box 585 (46573-0585)
PHONE.....................800 237-7806
◆ EMP: 750
Web: www.utilimaster.com
SIC: 3713 3711 Truck and bus bodies; Motor vehicles and car bodies

(G-1296)
UTILIMASTER SERVICES LLC
603 Earthway Blvd (46507-9182)
PHONE.....................800 582-3454
◆ EMP: 404 EST: 2005
SQ FT: 40,000
SALES (est): 46.34MM
SALES (corp-wide): 872.2MM **Publicly Held**
Web: www.utilimaster.com
SIC: 3537 Industrial trucks and tractors
HQ: The Shyft Group Usa Inc
1000 Reynolds Rd
Charlotte MI 48813
517 543-6400

(G-1297)
VANDELAY INDUSTRIES IND INC
802 W Vistula St (46507-9145)
PHONE.....................574 202-2367
Jeffrey Beachy, *Prin*
EMP: 4 EST: 2019
SALES (est): 78.93K **Privately Held**
SIC: 3999 Manufacturing industries, nec

(G-1298)
WATCHDOG MANUFACTURING LLC
21601 Durham Way (46507-9010)
PHONE.....................574 218-6604
Pam P Andre, *Prin*
EMP: 7 EST: 2018
SALES (est): 314.5K **Privately Held**
SIC: 3999 Manufacturing industries, nec

Bristow
Perry County

(G-1299)
BRISTOW MILLING CO LLC
4721 Water St (47515-8883)
P.O. Box 51 (47515-0051)
PHONE.....................812 843-5176
Matt Esarey, *Managing Member*
EMP: 3 EST: 1941
SQ FT: 10,000
SALES (est): 278.46K **Privately Held**
SIC: 2048 5191 5261 Prepared feeds, nec; Farm supplies; Fertilizer

(G-1300)
MATTHEW SCHLACHTER
24170 Cattail Rd (47515-9736)
PHONE.....................812 686-5486
Matthew Schlachter, *Owner*
EMP: 1 EST: 2019
SALES (est): 39.59K **Privately Held**
SIC: 2076 Vegetable oil mills, nec

(G-1301)
UBELHOR CONSTRUCTION INC
Also Called: Ubelhor Woodworking
26018 State Road 145 (47515-8865)
PHONE.....................812 357-2220
EMP: 13 EST: 1986
SQ FT: 33,000
SALES (est): 495.71K **Privately Held**
SIC: 2431 Moldings, wood: unfinished and prefinished

(G-1302)
WINZERWALD WINERY LLC
26300 N Indian Lake Rd (47515-9117)
PHONE.....................812 357-7000
EMP: 2 EST: 2003
SALES (est): 222.49K **Privately Held**
Web: www.winzerwaldwinery.com
SIC: 2084 Wines

Brook
Newton County

(G-1303)
BROOK LOCKER PLANT
243 W Main St (47922-8723)
P.O. Box 451 (47922-0451)
PHONE...............................219 275-2611
Jeff Lafflon, *Pr*
EMP: 4 **EST:** 1945
SQ FT: 2,300
SALES (est): 388.79K **Privately Held**
SIC: 2011 5421 Meat packing plants; Meat markets, including freezer provisioniers

(G-1304)
CASCADES HOLDING US INC
Also Called: Cascades Moulded Pulp-Indiana
3126 E 500 S (47922-8738)
PHONE...............................219 697-2900
EMP: 320
SALES (corp-wide): 3.32B **Privately Held**
Web: recovery.cascades.com
SIC: 2621 Wrapping and packaging papers
HQ: Cascades Holding Us Inc.
   4001 Packard Rd
   Niagara Falls NY 14303
   716 285-3681

(G-1305)
LIGHT PRINTING CO
9054 S 335 E (47922-8871)
PHONE...............................815 429-3724
James Light, *Owner*
EMP: 1 **EST:** 1980
SALES (est): 82.63K **Privately Held**
SIC: 2752 2791 Offset printing; Typesetting

(G-1306)
PT TOOL MACHINE
5183 E 894 S (47922-8663)
PHONE...............................219 275-3633
Mike W Wentzel, *Pt*
Wayne Wentzel, *Pt*
EMP: 4 **EST:** 1998
SALES (est): 378.3K **Privately Held**
SIC: 3544 Special dies, tools, jigs, and fixtures

(G-1307)
UFP LLC
3126 E 500 S (47922-8738)
PHONE...............................219 697-2900
▲ **EMP:** 2
SIC: 2679 Pressed fiber and molded pulp products, except food products

Brookston
White County

(G-1308)
BLUME METAL SALES LLC
695 W State Road 18 (47923-8200)
PHONE...............................765 490-0600
EMP: 4 **EST:** 2010
SALES (est): 255.05K **Privately Held**
SIC: 3444 Sheet metalwork

(G-1309)
CARTER MANUFACTURING COMPANY
896 E Carter Ct (47923-8297)
PHONE...............................765 563-3666
A J Batt, *Pr*
EMP: 3 **EST:** 1965
SQ FT: 6,000
SALES (est): 252.68K **Privately Held**
Web: www.cartermfgco.com
SIC: 3523 Planting machines, agricultural

(G-1310)
CONAGRA BRANDS INC
Also Called: Orville Redenbacher Popcorn
162 E 900 S (47923-8234)
PHONE...............................765 563-3182
Kent Korniak, *Brnch Mgr*
EMP: 61
SALES (corp-wide): 12.05B **Publicly Held**
Web: www.conagrabrands.com
SIC: 2099 Food preparations, nec
PA: Conagra Brands, Inc.
   222 W Mdse Mart Plz Ste 1
   Chicago IL 60654
   312 549-5000

(G-1311)
HUNTER NUTRITION INC
Also Called: Hunter Sheep Nutrition
200 Ns St (47923)
PHONE...............................765 563-1003
Jeffrey A Hunter, *Pr*
EMP: 10 **EST:** 1982
SALES (est): 2.16MM **Privately Held**
Web: www.hunternutrition.com
SIC: 2048 5191 5999 5211 Feed concentrates; Feed; Feed and farm supply; Fencing

(G-1312)
LEMAN ENGRG & CONSULTING INC
520 E 1050 S (47923-8362)
PHONE...............................574 870-7732
Randy Leman, *CEO*
EMP: 6 **EST:** 2013
SALES (est): 1MM **Privately Held**
Web: www.lemanengineering.com
SIC: 3613 8711 Panelboards and distribution boards, electric; Consulting engineer

(G-1313)
TERRA DRIVE SYSTEMS INC
Also Called: TDS
9098 W 800 S (47923-8048)
PHONE...............................219 279-2801
Daniel Dickinson, *Pr*
C Phillip Joy, *
Mark Hampshire, *
Jeffrey A Kropfl, *
◆ **EMP:** 110 **EST:** 1974
SQ FT: 80,000
SALES (est): 24.51MM
SALES (corp-wide): 25.51MM **Privately Held**
Web: www.tdsdrive.com
SIC: 3594 5084 Hydrostatic drives (transmissions); Hydraulic systems equipment and supplies
PA: Equity Hci Partners L P
   1730 Pennsylvania Ave Nw
   Washington DC 20006
   847 291-9259

(G-1314)
TWINROCKER HAND MADE PAPER INC
100 E 3rd St (47923)
P.O. Box 413 (47923-0413)
PHONE...............................765 563-3119
Kathryn Clark, *Pr*
Howard Clark, *VP*
Travis Becker, *Sec*
EMP: 6 **EST:** 1971
SQ FT: 5,000
SALES (est): 919.22K **Privately Held**
Web: www.twinrocker.com
SIC: 2621 5999 Art paper; Artists' supplies and materials

Brookville
Franklin County

(G-1315)
ABBOTT INC
1049 Main St (47012-1431)
PHONE...............................765 647-2523
Taya Abbott, *Brnch Mgr*
EMP: 58
Web: www.abbott.com
SIC: 2834 Pharmaceutical preparations
PA: Abbott, Inc.
   5396 N Fortville Pike
   Greenfield IN

(G-1316)
AMS EMBROIDERY & SIGNS LLC
110 S Main St Unit A (47012-6302)
PHONE...............................513 313-1613
Mark Reese, *Admn*
EMP: 6 **EST:** 2015
SALES (est): 120.76K **Privately Held**
SIC: 3993 Signs and advertising specialties

(G-1317)
CHARLES KOLB SONS LOGGING
1135 John St (47012-1041)
PHONE...............................765 647-4309
James Kolb, *Owner*
EMP: 5 **EST:** 2015
SALES (est): 84.34K **Privately Held**
SIC: 2411 Logging camps and contractors

(G-1318)
COMPLETE PACKAGING GROUP INC
9021 State Road 101 (47012-8813)
PHONE...............................765 547-1300
Jeff Roper, *Pr*
EMP: 3 **EST:** 2020
SALES (est): 100K **Privately Held**
Web: www.completepackaginggroup.com
SIC: 2821 Plastics materials and resins

(G-1319)
DR PEPPER BOTTLING CO
261 Webers Ln (47012-9642)
PHONE...............................765 647-3576
Kelly Joerger, *Mgr*
EMP: 8 **EST:** 2010
SALES (est): 87.58K **Privately Held**
Web: www.drpepper.com
SIC: 2086 Soft drinks: packaged in cans, bottles, etc.

(G-1320)
FRED SCHOCK COMPANY INC
P.O. Box 212 (47353-0212)
PHONE...............................765 647-4648
Joann Sottong, *Pr*
Clark Sperry, *VP*
James Sottong, *Sec*
EMP: 10 **EST:** 1953
SALES (est): 913.76K **Privately Held**
SIC: 3069 3089 Washers, rubber; Washers, plastics

(G-1321)
G & J PUBLISHING LLC
11146 Liberty Pike (47012-9709)
PHONE...............................765 914-3378
EMP: 5 **EST:** 2019
SALES (est): 81.3K **Privately Held**
SIC: 2741 Miscellaneous publishing

(G-1322)
GREG MINER
Also Called: Brookville Tool Co
10068 Oxford Pike (47012-9285)
PHONE...............................765 647-1012
Greg Miner, *Owner*
EMP: 3 **EST:** 1988
SQ FT: 2,428
SALES (est): 201.45K **Privately Held**
SIC: 3599 Machine shop, jobbing and repair

(G-1323)
HAUTAU TUBE CUTOFF SYSTEMS LLC
11199 State Road 101 (47012-8817)
PHONE...............................765 647-1600
EMP: 10 **EST:** 2003
SQ FT: 13,000
SALES (est): 2.06MM **Privately Held**
Web: www.hautau.com
SIC: 3541 8711 3354 Deburring machines; Designing: ship, boat, machine, and product ; Aluminum extruded products

(G-1324)
HUELSEMAN PRINTING CO
Also Called: Graphic Enterprises
9085 Bath Rd (47012-9769)
PHONE...............................765 647-3947
James C Huelseman, *Pt*
Mary Huelseman, *Pt*
EMP: 2 **EST:** 1982
SQ FT: 3,000
SALES (est): 164.1K **Privately Held**
SIC: 2752 Offset printing

(G-1325)
HUFFMAN METALWORKS LLC
16098 Messerschmidt Rd (47012-9296)
PHONE...............................574 835-0783
EMP: 1 **EST:** 2021
SALES (est): 50K **Privately Held**
Web: www.huffmanmetalworks.com
SIC: 7692 Welding repair

(G-1326)
INLINE SHIRT PRINTING LLC
5062 State Road 252 (47012-9456)
PHONE...............................765 647-6356
Dustin Grimmeissen, *Prin*
EMP: 6 **EST:** 2008
SALES (est): 82.5K **Privately Held**
SIC: 2752 Commercial printing, lithographic

(G-1327)
IRVING MATERIALS INC
Also Called: I M I
1352 Fairfield Ave (47012-1030)
PHONE...............................765 647-6533
EMP: 6
SALES (corp-wide): 814.09MM **Privately Held**
Web: www.irvmat.com
SIC: 3273 Ready-mixed concrete
PA: Irving Materials, Inc.
   8032 N State Road 9
   Greenfield IN 46140
   317 326-3101

(G-1328)
LANE LEGACY VINEYARD
12330 Whitcomb Rd (47012-9779)
PHONE...............................937 902-7738
Richard D Bodnar, *Owner*
EMP: 3 **EST:** 2015
SALES (est): 45.99K **Privately Held**
SIC: 2084 Wines

Brookville - Franklin County (G-1329) — GEOGRAPHIC SECTION

(G-1329)
NOBBE CONCRETE PRODUCTS INC
11177 Us Highway 52 (47012-9674)
PHONE.................................765 647-4017
Paul Nobbe, *Pr*
Phil Nobbe, *Sec*
Craig Nobbe, *VP*
EMP: 4 **EST:** 1967
SQ FT: 860
SALES (est): 352.2K **Privately Held**
SIC: 3553 3531 Woodworking machinery; Bituminous, cement and concrete related products and equip.

(G-1330)
OWENS CORNING SALES LLC
Also Called: Owens Corning
6102 Holland Rd (47012-9204)
PHONE.................................765 647-2857
Dave White, *Brnch Mgr*
EMP: 2
SIC: 3296 Mineral wool
HQ: Owens Corning Sales, Llc
    1 Owens Corning Pkwy
    Toledo OH 43659
    419 248-8000

(G-1331)
OWENS CORNING SALES LLC
Also Called: Owens Corning
128 W 8th St (47012-1458)
PHONE.................................765 647-4131
Martin Bever, *Mgr*
EMP: 250
SQ FT: 50,000
Web: www.owenscorning.com
SIC: 3296 Fiberglass insulation
HQ: Owens Corning Sales, Llc
    1 Owens Corning Pkwy
    Toledo OH 43659
    419 248-8000

(G-1332)
P-AMERICAS LLC
Also Called: Pepsico
261 Webers Ln (47012-9642)
PHONE.................................765 647-3576
Erick Lilley, *Mgr*
EMP: 1
SALES (corp-wide): 86.39B **Publicly Held**
Web: www.pepsico.com
SIC: 2086 Carbonated soft drinks, bottled and canned
HQ: P-Americas Llc
    1 Pepsi Way
    Somers NY 10589
    336 896-5740

(G-1333)
ROCCA INDUSTRIES LLC
28847 Central Dr (47012-8314)
PHONE.................................812 576-1011
Joseph Bamonte, *Owner*
EMP: 1 **EST:** 2014
SALES (est): 48.71K **Privately Held**
Web: www.roccaindustries.com
SIC: 3999 Manufacturing industries, nec

(G-1334)
ROCK GARDEN ENGRAVING
268 Main St (47012-1349)
PHONE.................................765 647-3357
Sam Schuck, *Owner*
EMP: 2 **EST:** 1996
SALES (est): 77.19K **Privately Held**
Web: www.rockgardenengraving.com
SIC: 2759 Engraving, nec

(G-1335)
SPERRY & RICE MANUFACTURING COMPANY LLC
9146 Us Highway 52 (47012-9657)
PHONE.................................765 647-4141
EMP: 158
SIC: 3052 Rubber and plastics hose and beltings

(G-1336)
TARVER WOLFF LLC
1149 Brookhaven Rd (47012)
P.O. Box 112 (47012-0112)
PHONE.................................765 265-7416
▲ **EMP:** 5 **EST:** 2008
SQ FT: 2,000
SALES (est): 255.37K **Privately Held**
Web: www.warfytr.com
SIC: 3949 Team sports equipment

(G-1337)
THOMPSON MACHINING SVCS INC
11040 State Road 101 (47012-9527)
PHONE.................................765 647-3451
EMP: 12 **EST:** 1997
SQ FT: 6,000
SALES (est): 1.79MM **Privately Held**
Web: www.thompsonmachiningservices.com
SIC: 3544 Special dies and tools

(G-1338)
TW ENTERPRISES LLC
9021 Meyer Rd (47012-8934)
PHONE.................................513 520-8453
Alex Tebbe, *Pr*
EMP: 2 **EST:** 2017
SALES (est): 96.59K **Privately Held**
SIC: 3842 5047 7389 Personal safety equipment; Industrial safety devices: first aid kits and masks; Business Activities at Non-Commercial Site

(G-1339)
VOEGELE AUTO SUPPLY LLC
12 Murphy St (47012-1338)
PHONE.................................765 647-3541
EMP: 4 **EST:** 2006
SALES (est): 258.67K **Privately Held**
SIC: 3714 Motor vehicle parts and accessories

(G-1340)
WHITEWATER PRINT SOLUTIONS LLC
10108 State Road 101 (47012-8620)
PHONE.................................513 405-3452
Tim Cunningham, *CEO*
EMP: 2 **EST:** 2011
SALES (est): 131.9K **Privately Held**
SIC: 2752 Advertising posters, lithographed

(G-1341)
WHITEWATER PUBLICATIONS INC
Also Called: Brookville Democrat
531 Main St (47012-1407)
P.O. Box 38 (47012-0038)
PHONE.................................765 647-4221
Gary Wolf, *Treas*
Donald G Sintz, *
Arthur C Feller, *
EMP: 12 **EST:** 1943
SQ FT: 2,800
SALES (est): 427.96K **Privately Held**
Web: www.whitewaterpub.com
SIC: 2711 2789 2759 2752 Job printing and newspaper publishing combined; Bookbinding and related work; Commercial printing, nec; Commercial printing, lithographic

(G-1342)
WILLIAM BROWNING
Also Called: Browning, William Logging
7015 Jefferson St (47012-9488)
PHONE.................................765 647-6397
William Browning, *Owner*
Viola Browning, *Sec*
EMP: 2 **EST:** 1972
SALES (est): 121.36K **Privately Held**
SIC: 2411 Logging camps and contractors

Brownsburg
Hendricks County

(G-1343)
ACHATES LLC
481 Southpoint Cir (46112-2205)
PHONE.................................317 852-6978
Brian Richardson, *CEO*
EMP: 17 **EST:** 2018
SALES (est): 699.65K **Privately Held**
SIC: 3599 3999 Machine shop, jobbing and repair; Manufacturing industries, nec

(G-1344)
ADVANTAGE COMPONENTS CORP
6320 Wings Ct (46112-8610)
PHONE.................................317 784-0299
Steve Vogel, *Pr*
George Hilgemeier, *CEO*
Roger Beal, *VP*
EMP: 5 **EST:** 1999
SALES (est): 497.24K **Privately Held**
SIC: 3599 Machine shop, jobbing and repair

(G-1345)
AMERICAN BUSINESS FORMS I
328 Acre Ave (46112-1318)
PHONE.................................317 852-8956
Randy Keen, *Owner*
EMP: 5 **EST:** 2005
SALES (est): 245.44K **Privately Held**
Web: www.abfgroup.net
SIC: 2752 Offset printing

(G-1346)
ANDRESEN GRAPHIC PROCESSORS
10843 E County Road 950 N (46112-9632)
PHONE.................................317 291-7071
Jon Andresen, *VP*
Ann Andresen, *Pr*
EMP: 10 **EST:** 1983
SQ FT: 5,000
SALES (est): 480.94K **Privately Held**
SIC: 2759 Screen printing

(G-1347)
ANIMALSINKCOM LLC
7489 Windridge Way (46112-8984)
PHONE.................................317 496-8467
Sean M Clapp, *Prin*
EMP: 4 **EST:** 2010
SALES (est): 467.35K **Privately Held**
Web: www.animalsink.com
SIC: 2833 Animal based products

(G-1348)
ART OVATION
7615 S State Road 267 (46112-9101)
PHONE.................................317 769-4301
EMP: 3 **EST:** 1994
SQ FT: 1,600
SALES (est): 162.98K **Privately Held**
Web: www.artovationhotel.com
SIC: 2399 5999 Banners, pennants, and flags; Banners, flags, decals, and posters

(G-1349)
AVT COMPOSITES
1652 E Northfield Dr Ste 2400 (46112-2465)
PHONE.................................317 286-7575
EMP: 3 **EST:** 2017
SALES (est): 233.32K **Privately Held**
SIC: 3728 Aircraft parts and equipment, nec

(G-1350)
BIOLOGICS MODULAR LLC
Also Called: Cleanroomsusa
1533 E Northfield Dr Ste 600 (46112)
PHONE.................................317 626-4093
Clark Byrum Junior, *CEO*
EMP: 6 **EST:** 2009
SALES (est): 1.03MM **Privately Held**
Web: www.cleanroomsusa.com
SIC: 3448 5039 Prefabricated metal buildings and components; Prefabricated structures

(G-1351)
BLUE MOON OIL COMPANY LLC
10359 N County Road 650 E (46112-9510)
PHONE.................................317 892-2499
Bruce Steinman, *Prin*
EMP: 1 **EST:** 2005
SALES (est): 100.13K **Privately Held**
SIC: 1381 Drilling oil and gas wells

(G-1352)
BOMBTRACK FABRICATION
45 Mardale Dr Ste G (46112-9441)
P.O. Box 1227 (46112-5227)
PHONE.................................317 286-7711
Joseph Barszcz, *Prin*
EMP: 8 **EST:** 2016
SALES (est): 455.6K **Privately Held**
Web: www.bombtrackfabrication.com
SIC: 3441 Fabricated structural metal

(G-1353)
BRUNSWICK CORPORATION
Also Called: Mercury Marine
4857 N Ronald Reagan Pkwy (46112-9567)
PHONE.................................866 278-6942
David M Foulkes, *CEO*
EMP: 1
SALES (corp-wide): 6.4B **Publicly Held**
Web: www.brunswick.com
SIC: 3732 Boatbuilding and repairing
PA: Brunswick Corporation
    26125 N Rvrwods Blvd Ste
    Mettawa IL 60045
    847 735-4700

(G-1354)
BUTTONS GALORE INC
110 E College Ave (46112-1207)
PHONE.................................800 626-8168
Joseph V Batic, *Pr*
EMP: 10 **EST:** 2007
SALES (est): 840K **Privately Held**
Web: www.coasterstonepromo.com
SIC: 3993 Signs and advertising specialties

(G-1355)
BUZTRONICS INC
464 Southpoint Cir Ste 100 (46112)
P.O. Box 415 (46112-0415)
PHONE.................................317 876-3413
Edward D Lewis, *Pr*
Terry Sanderson, *
▲ **EMP:** 43 **EST:** 1989
SQ FT: 70,000
SALES (est): 2.9MM **Privately Held**
Web: www.buztronics.com
SIC: 3999 Novelties, bric-a-brac, and hobby kits

Brownsburg - Hendricks County (G-1384)

(G-1356)
C F ROARK WLDG ENGRG CO INC
136 N Green St (46112-1238)
P.O. Box 67 (46112-0067)
PHONE..................317 852-3163
Charles T Roark, *Pr*
William Golay, *
Charles F Roark, *
Constance Kemp, *
Chris Roark Jones, *
EMP: 105 **EST:** 1949
SQ FT: 60,000
SALES (est): 15.73MM **Privately Held**
Web: www.roarkfab.com
SIC: 3728 3769 Aircraft parts and equipment, nec; Casings, missiles and missile components: storage

(G-1357)
CANDY COM
1207 E Northfield Dr (46112-2426)
PHONE..................317 939-0102
EMP: 5 **EST:** 2020
SALES (est): 68.62K **Privately Held**
SIC: 2064 Candy and other confectionery products

(G-1358)
CAPTIVE-AIRE SYSTEMS INC
20 Airport Rd Ste 500 (46112-2045)
PHONE..................317 852-3770
Dave Miller, *Mgr*
EMP: 1
SALES (corp-wide): 485.13MM **Privately Held**
Web: www.captiveaire.com
SIC: 3444 Sheet metalwork
PA: Captive-Aire Systems, Inc.
    4641 Pragon Pk Rd Ste 104
    Raleigh NC 27616
    919 882-2410

(G-1359)
CHECKERED PAST RACING PDTS LLC
481 Southpoint Cir Ste 8 (46112-2206)
PHONE..................317 852-6978
Gregg O Goff, *Managing Member*
EMP: 4 **EST:** 2001
SALES (est): 496.56K **Privately Held**
Web: www.checkeredpastmachine.com
SIC: 3599 Machine shop, jobbing and repair

(G-1360)
COMPOSITE SPECIALTIES
464 Johnson Ln Ste D (46112-7811)
PHONE..................317 852-1408
Jeff E Burnette, *Owner*
EMP: 2 **EST:** 2003
SALES (est): 240K **Privately Held**
Web: www.compositespecialties.com
SIC: 3624 Fibers, carbon and graphite

(G-1361)
CRANKSHAFT BREWING CO
1630 E Northfield Dr (46112-2498)
PHONE..................317 939-0138
EMP: 5 **EST:** 2015
SALES (est): 125.83K **Privately Held**
SIC: 5921 2082 Liquor stores; Malt beverages

(G-1362)
D & E PRINTING COMPANY INC
2 E Main St (46112-1214)
PHONE..................317 852-9048
Eric Mizell, *Pr*
Sarah Mizell, *Sec*
EMP: 8 **EST:** 1990
SQ FT: 3,000
SALES (est): 1.06MM **Privately Held**
Web: www.dandeprinting.com
SIC: 2752 Offset printing

(G-1363)
DAPPERED MAN LLC
1060 E Main St Ste 417 (46112-1408)
PHONE..................317 520-1194
EMP: 4 **EST:** 2019
SALES (est): 127.94K **Privately Held**
Web: www.dapperedmanbbg.com
SIC: 2381 Fabric dress and work gloves

(G-1364)
DON SCHUMACHER MOTOR SPT INC
Also Called: DSM Precision Manufacturing
1681 E Northfield Dr Ste B (46112-2486)
PHONE..................317 286-4380
Don Schumacher, *Prin*
Chad Osier, *
EMP: 27 **EST:** 1999
SALES (est): 2.82MM **Privately Held**
SIC: 3599 Machine shop, jobbing and repair

(G-1365)
DON SCHUMACHER RACING CORP
1681 E Northfield Dr Ste A (46112-2486)
PHONE..................317 858-0356
Donald A Schumacher, *Pr*
Mike Lewis, *
▲ **EMP:** 35 **EST:** 1963
SQ FT: 33,000
SALES (est): 5.24MM **Privately Held**
Web: www.dsrperformance.com
SIC: 3711 Automobile assembly, including specialty automobiles

(G-1366)
FAYETTE WELDING SERVICE INC
7555 S State Road 267 (46112-8992)
PHONE..................317 852-2929
Don Schooler, *Pr*
Mary Schooler, *Sec*
EMP: 2 **EST:** 1952
SQ FT: 3,000
SALES (est): 136.76K **Privately Held**
SIC: 7692 7699 Welding repair; Farm machinery repair

(G-1367)
FIGID PRESS LLC
1299 Spring Lake Dr (46112-8173)
PHONE..................717 809-0092
John Alling Graham Junior, *Owner*
EMP: 4 **EST:** 2017
SALES (est): 62.16K **Privately Held**
SIC: 2741 Miscellaneous publishing

(G-1368)
FOX UNIFORM INC
468 Southpoint Cir Ste 100 (46112)
PHONE..................317 350-2684
Peter Fox, *Pr*
EMP: 2 **EST:** 2020
SALES (est): 161.25K **Privately Held**
Web: www.renenusa.com
SIC: 2386 Leather and sheep-lined clothing

(G-1369)
FRANCINE BOND INSUR AGCY INC
316 Prebster Dr (46112-7743)
PHONE..................317 262-2250
EMP: 3 **EST:** 2018
SALES (est): 80.8K **Privately Held**
SIC: 3465 Automotive stampings

(G-1370)
FRESH HAMPER LLC
3135 N State Road 267 Ste B (46112-8862)
PHONE..................317 452-6023
EMP: 1 **EST:** 2020
SALES (est): 80K **Privately Held**
SIC: 3582 Washing machines, laundry: commercial, incl. coin-operated

(G-1371)
FUEL BLADDER DISTRIBUTORS INC
Also Called: S.B.I.
3800 N State Road 267 Ste B (46112-8166)
PHONE..................317 852-9156
Keith A Wagoner, *Pr*
Louis Billanueba, *VP*
Debra F Wagoner, *Stockholder*
Alejandra Billanueva, *Stockholder*
EMP: 3 **EST:** 2007
SQ FT: 600
SALES (est): 286.05K **Privately Held**
SIC: 3069 Fuel tanks, collapsible: rubberized fabric

(G-1372)
INDY METAL FINISHING CO
468 Southpoint Cir Ste 500 (46112)
PHONE..................317 858-5353
Carly Lawrence, *Pr*
EMP: 5 **EST:** 2008
SALES (est): 487.24K **Privately Held**
Web: www.indymetalfinishing.com
SIC: 3471 Electroplating of metals or formed products

(G-1373)
INDY PRFMCE COMPOSITES INC
1185 E Northfield Dr Ste A (46112-2508)
PHONE..................317 858-7793
Jeffery L West, *Pr*
Linas A Paskus, *VP*
EMP: 7 **EST:** 2003
SQ FT: 10,000
SALES (est): 1.09MM **Privately Held**
Web: www.indyperformancecompositesinc.com
SIC: 3624 Fibers, carbon and graphite

(G-1374)
INDY WIRING SERVICES LLC
150 Gasoline Aly (46112)
PHONE..................317 371-7044
EMP: 2 **EST:** 2010
SALES (est): 202.36K **Privately Held**
Web: www.indywiring.net
SIC: 3357 Appliance fixture wire, nonferrous

(G-1375)
INTEGRATED ORTHOTIC LAB INC
1630 E Northfield Dr Ste 400 (46112-2498)
PHONE..................317 852-4640
Gary Oswald, *Pr*
EMP: 7 **EST:** 2007
SALES (est): 967.45K **Privately Held**
Web: www.io-lab.com
SIC: 5661 3149 Custom and orthopedic shoes; Children's footwear, except athletic

(G-1376)
INTER PRINT AT IONS
10630 E County Road 750 N (46112-9682)
PHONE..................765 404-0887
Cari Bowersock, *Prin*
EMP: 5 **EST:** 2016
SALES (est): 121.17K **Privately Held**
SIC: 2752 Offset printing

(G-1377)
JLM LUBRICANTS USA LLC
1110 Windhaven Cir Apt B (46112-7919)
PHONE..................317 500-1012
Lex Joon, *Prin*
EMP: 5 **EST:** 2017
SALES (est): 100.45K **Privately Held**
SIC: 3714 Motor vehicle parts and accessories

(G-1378)
JRS CUSTOM FABRICATION
602 E Main St (46112-1423)
PHONE..................317 852-4964
John Stanbrough, *Owner*
EMP: 1 **EST:** 1993
SALES (est): 135.29K **Privately Held**
Web: www.jrscustomfabrications.com
SIC: 7692 Welding repair

(G-1379)
K & K CABINETS & SUPPLY
1640 S Green St Ste A (46112-8168)
PHONE..................317 852-4808
Francis Konovsek, *Owner*
EMP: 1 **EST:** 1998
SALES (est): 96.34K **Privately Held**
Web: www.the-birds.net
SIC: 2434 Wood kitchen cabinets

(G-1380)
KAMPLAIN MACHINE COMPANY INC
7785 Maloney Rd (46112-8406)
PHONE..................317 388-9111
Greg Kamplain, *Pr*
Judy Kamplain, *Sec*
EMP: 5 **EST:** 1986
SALES (est): 449.73K **Privately Held**
Web: www.kamplainmachine.com
SIC: 3599 Machine shop, jobbing and repair

(G-1381)
KASNAK RESTORATIONS INC
Also Called: Kasnak Designs
5505 N County Road 1000 E (46112-8707)
PHONE..................317 852-9770
Robert Kasnak, *Pr*
Leslie Kasnak, *Sec*
EMP: 3 **EST:** 1976
SQ FT: 2,700
SALES (est): 248.54K **Privately Held**
Web: www.kasnakrestorations.com
SIC: 7641 2511 Antique furniture repair and restoration; Wood household furniture

(G-1382)
KERRIA INDUSTRIES INC
668 Albatross Ln (46112-7483)
PHONE..................317 852-4542
Ronan Miot, *Prin*
EMP: 5 **EST:** 2018
SALES (est): 39.69K **Privately Held**
SIC: 3999 Manufacturing industries, nec

(G-1383)
KILLER MACHINING SOLUTIONS LLC
1650 E Northfield Dr Ste 1400 (46112-2466)
PHONE..................813 786-2309
EMP: 1 **EST:** 2009
SQ FT: 5,000
SALES (est): 130K **Privately Held**
Web: www.killermachiningsolutions.com
SIC: 3541 Numerically controlled metal cutting machine tools

(G-1384)
LAPP USA INC
1665 W Northfield Dr (46112-9588)
PHONE..................973 660-9700
EMP: 148
SALES (corp-wide): 355.83K **Privately Held**
Web: www.lapp.com
SIC: 3643 Power line cable
HQ: Lapp Usa, Inc.

Brownsburg - Hendricks County (G-1385)

29 Hanover Rd
Florham Park NJ 07932
973 660-9700

(G-1385)
MARK PEISER MANUFACTURING INC
3800 A Hway 267 N (46112)
PHONE.................................317 698-5376
Mark Peiser, *Pr*
EMP: 1 **EST:** 2005
SALES (est): 242.9K **Privately Held**
SIC: 3999 Barber and beauty shop equipment

(G-1386)
MAVRICK ENTRMT NETWRK INC
Also Called: Mavtv Motorsports
480 Southpoint Cir (46112)
PHONE.................................317 779-1237
Morgan Lucas, *Pr*
Charlotte Lucas, *VP*
Matt Kimmick, *CFO*
Jason Bonikowske, *Sec*
EMP: 4 **EST:** 2003
SALES (est): 301.58K **Privately Held**
SIC: 2741 Internet publishing and broadcasting
PA: Lucas Oil Products, Inc.
  1310 E 96th St
  Indianapolis IN 46240

(G-1387)
MELTING POINT METALWORKS LLC
70 Mardale Dr Ste D (46112-7871)
PHONE.................................317 984-0037
James Schmiedicke, *Prin*
EMP: 5 **EST:** 2019
SALES (est): 148.63K **Privately Held**
Web: www.mpmworks.com
SIC: 3398 Metal heat treating

(G-1388)
MIATA HUBS LLC
9572 Edgewater Ct (46112-8671)
PHONE.................................240 298-7368
Justin Lee, *Owner*
EMP: 5 **EST:** 2018
SALES (est): 97.07K **Privately Held**
Web: www.miatahubs.com
SIC: 3714 Motor vehicle parts and accessories

(G-1389)
MINDYS BROWNSBURG SIGNS INC
237 Harts Ford Way (46112-8136)
PHONE.................................317 939-0921
Melinda Bennett, *Prin*
EMP: 3 **EST:** 2018
SALES (est): 103.07K **Privately Held**
Web: www.mindysbrownsburgsigns.com
SIC: 3993 Signs and advertising specialties

(G-1390)
NITRO ALLEY GRAPHIX LLC
1185 E Northfield Dr Ste A (46112-2508)
PHONE.................................317 286-3294
Randy Garnett, *Prin*
EMP: 3 **EST:** 2010
SALES (est): 238.6K **Privately Held**
Web: www.nitroalleygraphix.com
SIC: 3993 Signs and advertising specialties

(G-1391)
NORTHSIDE PATTERN WORKS INC
10222 Terri Ln (46112-8981)
PHONE.................................317 290-0501
Don Holbrook, *Pr*
Diane Holbrook, *Sec*
EMP: 4 **EST:** 1938
SALES (est): 308.32K **Privately Held**
Web: www.amandahairbraiding.com
SIC: 3543 Industrial patterns

(G-1392)
NOVARTIS CORPORATION
30 Lakeshore Pl (46112-1741)
PHONE.................................317 852-3839
Stan Jerrodo, *Mgr*
EMP: 4
Web: www.novartis.com
SIC: 2834 Pharmaceutical preparations
HQ: Novartis Corporation
  1 Health Plz
  East Hanover NJ 07936
  212 307-1122

(G-1393)
ORANO MED LLC
1145 E Northfield Dr (46112-2425)
PHONE.................................469 638-0632
EMP: 9 **EST:** 2012
SALES (est): 74.44K **Privately Held**
SIC: 2834 Pharmaceutical preparations

(G-1394)
OVER GLOBE LLC (PA)
3105 Nw 107th Ave Ste 506 (46112)
PHONE.................................305 607-6472
Edgar Diaz, *Managing Member*
EMP: 2 **EST:** 2016
SALES (est): 149.04K
SALES (corp-wide): 149.04K **Privately Held**
Web: www.otgws.com
SIC: 3589 7389 Water treatment equipment, industrial; Business services, nec

(G-1395)
POPPY CO
10915 N State Road 267 (46112-9297)
PHONE.................................317 442-2491
EMP: 5 **EST:** 2010
SALES (est): 172.71K **Privately Held**
Web: www.poppycompany.com
SIC: 3089 Plastics boats and other marine equipment

(G-1396)
PTG INC
5838 E County Road 800 N (46112-8818)
PHONE.................................317 892-4625
Peter Bloyd, *Pr*
EMP: 3 **EST:** 1999
SALES (est): 246.04K **Privately Held**
SIC: 2431 Millwork

(G-1397)
RED CHAIR DESIGNS
10185 Terri Ln (46112-8723)
PHONE.................................317 852-9880
Karen Midkiff, *Owner*
EMP: 1 **EST:** 2003
SALES (est): 71.57K **Privately Held**
Web: www.redchairdesigns.com
SIC: 2512 Upholstered household furniture

(G-1398)
ROADHOG INC
464 Southpoint Cir Ste A (46112-2269)
PHONE.................................317 858-7050
Christopher Zanetis, *Pr*
EMP: 22 **EST:** 2004
SALES (est): 3.95MM **Privately Held**
Web: www.roadhoginc.com
SIC: 3542 Mechanical (pneumatic or hydraulic) metal forming machines

(G-1399)
ROW PRINTING INC
7177 Golden Oak (46112-9168)
PHONE.................................317 796-3289
EMP: 7 **EST:** 2018
SALES (est): 249.48K **Privately Held**
Web: www.rowprinting.com
SIC: 2752 Offset printing

(G-1400)
ROW PRINTING INC
5860 Walkabout Way (46112-2914)
PHONE.................................317 441-4301
Sandra Laycock, *Owner*
EMP: 5 **EST:** 2018
SALES (est): 162.14K **Privately Held**
Web: www.rowprinting.com
SIC: 2752 Offset printing

(G-1401)
SCUTT TOOL & DIE INC
3245 N State Road 267 (46112-8894)
PHONE.................................317 858-8725
Rusty Scutt, *Pr*
EMP: 2 **EST:** 1970
SALES (est): 242.06K **Privately Held**
Web: www.scutttoolanddie.com
SIC: 3599 Machine shop, jobbing and repair

(G-1402)
SEVIER MANUFACTURING
103 Oak Hill Dr (46112-8361)
PHONE.................................317 892-2784
Larry Lukins, *Owner*
EMP: 2 **EST:** 1997
SALES (est): 68.99K **Privately Held**
SIC: 3949 Buckets, fish and bait

(G-1403)
SIX SIX SUBLIMATION LLC
Also Called: Six Six Graphics
1531 E Northfield Dr Ste 300 (46112)
PHONE.................................317 858-5211
Aaron Swearingen, *Prin*
EMP: 3 **EST:** 2008
SALES (est): 232.44K **Privately Held**
Web: www.sixsixapparel.com
SIC: 2759 Screen printing

(G-1404)
SOUTHERN MECHATRONICS CO INC
708 S Locust Ln (46112-1530)
EMP: 7 **EST:** 1999
SQ FT: 15,000
SALES (est): 671.05K **Privately Held**
SIC: 3552 3542 Textile machinery; Mechanical (pneumatic or hydraulic) metal forming machines

(G-1405)
SURCLEAN INC
463 Southpoint Cir Ste 300 (46112)
PHONE.................................248 791-2226
Susan Sprentall, *Pr*
Donald Sprentall, *Dir*
Michael Malloure, *Dir*
Beverly Wall, *Treas*
Michael Nardozzi, *COO*
EMP: 11 **EST:** 2015
SALES (est): 415.46K **Privately Held**
Web: www.surclean.com
SIC: 7699 3569 3823 3545 Industrial machinery and equipment repair; Assembly machines, non-metalworking; Process control instruments; Machine tool accessories

(G-1406)
TEACH ME STUFF
355 Andscott Dr (46112-2030)
PHONE.................................317 550-6319
Joan Kopacz, *Owner*
EMP: 4 **EST:** 2018
SALES (est): 71.67K **Privately Held**
SIC: 3999 Manufacturing industries, nec

(G-1407)
TECHNA FIT OF INDIANA
493 Southpoint Cir # B (46112-2203)
PHONE.................................317 350-2153
Stuart Trotter, *Pr*
EMP: 5 **EST:** 2012
SALES (est): 143.16K **Privately Held**
Web: www.techna-fit.com
SIC: 3465 Body parts, automobile: stamped metal

(G-1408)
TECHNA-FIT INC
493 Southpoint Cir # B (46112-2203)
PHONE.................................317 350-2153
▲ **EMP:** 5 **EST:** 1996
SALES (est): 961.09K **Privately Held**
Web: www.technafitstore.com
SIC: 3714 3492 Motor vehicle brake systems and parts; Hose and tube fittings and assemblies, hydraulic/pneumatic

(G-1409)
TONY STEWART RACING ENTPS LLC
438 Southpoint Cir (46112-2203)
PHONE.................................317 858-8620
Anthony Stewart, *Managing Member*
EMP: 7 **EST:** 2003
SALES (est): 601.03K **Privately Held**
Web: www.tonystewartracing.com
SIC: 3711 Automobile assembly, including specialty automobiles

(G-1410)
TRU BORE COMPANY
Also Called: American Translifts Company
213 E Main St (46112-1217)
PHONE.................................317 442-6766
John Suiter, *Owner*
EMP: 1 **EST:** 2001
SALES (est): 150K **Privately Held**
SIC: 1381 Directional drilling oil and gas wells

(G-1411)
TWW FABRICATON & MACHINE LLC
55 Mardale Dr (46112-9444)
PHONE.................................985 637-8234
Justin Doucet, *Pr*
EMP: 1 **EST:** 2016
SALES (est): 70.47K **Privately Held**
SIC: 3599 Machine shop, jobbing and repair

(G-1412)
VIVID INTERNET PUBLISHING
4105 N County Road 900 E (46112-9496)
PHONE.................................317 858-3882
Jamie Schmiedicke, *Prin*
EMP: 1 **EST:** 2003
SALES (est): 55.12K **Privately Held**
Web: www.vividserver.com
SIC: 2741 Miscellaneous publishing

(G-1413)
WESTON FOODS US HOLDINGS LLC (HQ)
Also Called: Maplehurst Bakeries
50 Maplehurst Dr (46112-9085)
PHONE.................................317 858-9000
Benin Roy, *CEO*
Robert Balcom, *
EMP: 621 **EST:** 1986
SALES (est): 770.08MM
SALES (corp-wide): 1.22B **Privately Held**

SIC: **2051 2052** Bread, all types (white, wheat, rye, etc); fresh or frozen; Cookies and crackers
PA: Fgf Brands Inc
1295 Ormont Dr
Toronto ON M9L 2
905 761-3333

(G-1414)
XWIND LLC
1185 E Northfield Dr Ste C (46112-2507)
PHONE.................................317 350-2080
EMP: 7 EST: 2011
SALES (est): 485.53K **Privately Held**
Web: www.xwindflight.com
SIC: 3699 Flight simulators (training aids), electronic

(G-1415)
YOUNG & KENADY INCORPORATED
Also Called: Descon
463 Southpoint Cir Ste 600 (46112)
PHONE.................................317 852-6300
Michael Young, *Pr*
Jerry Young, *VP*
EMP: 9 EST: 1997
SQ FT: 7,000
SALES (est): 850.6K **Privately Held**
Web: www.desconinc.com
SIC: 7336 3999 3993 Commercial art and graphic design; Education aids, devices and supplies; Signs and advertising specialties

Brownstown
Jackson County

(G-1416)
AIM MEDIA INDIANA OPER LLC
Jackson Co Banner
116 E Cross St (47220-2011)
PHONE.................................812 358-2111
Melissa Bane, *Brnch Mgr*
EMP: 3
SALES (corp-wide): 26.88MM **Privately Held**
Web: www.aimmediaindiana.com
SIC: 2711 Commercial printing and newspaper publishing combined
PA: Aim Media Indiana Operating, Llc
2980 N National Rd # A
Columbus IN 47201
812 372-7811

(G-1417)
BROWNSTOWN QLTY TL AUTOMTN LLC
593 S State Road 135 (47220-9778)
PHONE.................................812 358-9059
Jared Cummings, *Managing Member*
EMP: 9 EST: 2015
SALES (est): 676.72K **Privately Held**
Web: www.bqtd.com
SIC: 3599 Machine shop, jobbing and repair

(G-1418)
BROWNSTOWN QULTY TL DESIGN INC
1408 E State Road 250 (47220-9666)
PHONE.................................812 358-4593
Anthony Nehrt, *Pr*
Sue Nehrt, *Ex VP*
EMP: 10 EST: 1994
SQ FT: 7,520
SALES (est): 1.38MM **Privately Held**
Web: www.bqtd.com
SIC: 3544 Dies and die holders for metal cutting, forming, die casting

(G-1419)
COCKERHAMS SIGNS & GRAPHICS
1130 S County Road 150 W (47220-9611)
PHONE.................................812 358-3737
Steve Cockerham, *Owner*
EMP: 2 EST: 1999
SALES (est): 135.39K **Privately Held**
Web: www.docmikedds.com
SIC: 3993 Signs, not made in custom sign painting shops

(G-1420)
CPC
Also Called: Custom Printing Co
811 Bloomington Rd (47220-1246)
P.O. Box 142 (47220-0142)
PHONE.................................812 358-5010
Tammy Weaver, *Prin*
Steve Weaver, *Prin*
EMP: 3 EST: 2008
SALES (est): 248.18K **Privately Held**
Web: www.cpc-tees.com
SIC: 2752 Offset printing

(G-1421)
CRAIGS PRINTING CO
811 Bloomington Rd (47220-1246)
P.O. Box 142 (47220-0142)
PHONE.................................812 358-5010
Dennis Craig, *Owner*
EMP: 4 EST: 1979
SQ FT: 3,500
SALES (est): 211.76K **Privately Held**
SIC: 2752 2759 Offset printing; Screen printing

(G-1422)
DARLAGE SAWMILL
1564 S County Road 100 E (47220-9620)
PHONE.................................812 358-3574
Randy Darlage, *Owner*
EMP: 1 EST: 1976
SALES (est): 81.31K **Privately Held**
SIC: 2421 Sawmills and planing mills, general

(G-1423)
GOLDEN AGE AEROPLANE WORKS LLC
2375 E State Road 250 (47220-9694)
PHONE.................................812 358-5778
Timothy O'conner, *Owner*
Gayla O'connor, *Managing Member*
EMP: 2 EST: 2006
SALES (est): 163.38K **Privately Held**
Web: www.peashooter.net
SIC: 3721 Airplanes, fixed or rotary wing

(G-1424)
IST LIQUIDATING INC
848 W Sweet St (47220-9557)
P.O. Box 316 (47220-0316)
PHONE.................................812 358-3894
EMP: 45
SIC: 3317 Steel pipe and tubes

(G-1425)
MARK HACKMAN
Also Called: Hackman Borthers Show Feed
3640 S County Road 400 E (47220-9691)
PHONE.................................812 522-8257
Mark Hackman, *Prin*
EMP: 3 EST: 1999
SALES (est): 239.98K **Privately Held**
Web: www.hackmanshowfeeds.com
SIC: 2048 Prepared feeds, nec

(G-1426)
REIDCO INC
Also Called: Marion-Kay Spices
1351 W Us Highway 50 (47220-9530)
PHONE.................................812 358-3000
Kordell Reid, *Pr*
Pam Warren, *Sec*
Kordell Reid, *Prin*
Tam Warren, *CFO*
EMP: 22 EST: 1986
SQ FT: 50,000
SALES (est): 2.42MM **Privately Held**
Web: www.marionkay.com
SIC: 2099 5149 5499 Seasonings and spices ; Spices and seasonings; Spices and herbs

(G-1427)
SCHROER DRAPERY
5542 E State Road 250 (47220-9651)
PHONE.................................812 523-3633
EMP: 4
SALES (est): 292.91K **Privately Held**
SIC: 2391 Draperies, plastic and textile: from purchased materials

(G-1428)
WERRCO INC
Also Called: Werrco Tools & Machines
5994 W State Road 58 (47220-9750)
PHONE.................................812 497-3500
James Mann, *Pr*
April Mann, *Mgr*
EMP: 5 EST: 1955
SQ FT: 4,000
SALES (est): 517.88K **Privately Held**
Web: www.werrco.com
SIC: 3544 Dies and die holders for metal cutting, forming, die casting

Brownsville
Union County

(G-1429)
BRAD GOODMAN
3855 N County Road 550 E (47325-9245)
PHONE.................................765 993-2007
Brad Goodman, *Prin*
EMP: 5 EST: 2010
SALES (est): 60.08K **Privately Held**
Web: www.iops360.com
SIC: 7372 Prepackaged software

(G-1430)
BUCK HOLLOW CNC LLC
Also Called: Machining
579 N County Road 500 E (47325-9213)
PHONE.................................717 269-9322
James Rhoads, *Pr*
EMP: 1 EST: 2019
SALES (est): 76.47K **Privately Held**
SIC: 3999 Manufacturing industries, nec

(G-1431)
EAST FORK STUDIO & PRESS INC
104 Ne First St (47325-9731)
PHONE.................................765 458-6103
James Kaufman, *Prin*
EMP: 5 EST: 2010
SALES (est): 98K **Privately Held**
SIC: 2741 Miscellaneous publishing

(G-1432)
TJ PERFORMANCE LLC
4331 N Jobe Rd (47325-9405)
PHONE.................................765 580-0481
Mike Jobe, *Owner*
EMP: 7 EST: 2011
SALES (est): 223.38K **Privately Held**

SIC: 2992 Lubricating oils and greases

Bruceville
Knox County

(G-1433)
TRIMAX MACHINE LLC
5852 N Rod And Gun Clb (47516-6005)
PHONE.................................812 887-9281
EMP: 3 EST: 2011
SALES (est): 172.97K **Privately Held**
Web: www.trimaxmachine.com
SIC: 3559 Automotive related machinery

Bryant
Jay County

(G-1434)
BRYANT MACHINING & WELDING LLC
1015 E State Road 67 (47326-9105)
P.O. Box 186 (47326-0186)
PHONE.................................260 997-6059
Diane Stults, *Prin*
EMP: 4 EST: 1979
SALES (est): 240.61K **Privately Held**
SIC: 3599 3548 Machine shop, jobbing and repair; Welding apparatus

(G-1435)
HI-TECH TURNING
303 N Hendricks St (47326-9068)
P.O. Box 74 (47326-0074)
PHONE.................................260 997-6668
EMP: 2 EST: 1997
SALES (est): 200K **Privately Held**
SIC: 3599 Machine shop, jobbing and repair

(G-1436)
RICHARDS RESTAURANT INC
Also Called: Bear Creek Farms
8341 N 400 E (47326-9003)
PHONE.................................260 997-6823
Carla Greens, *Mgr*
EMP: 10
SALES (corp-wide): 12MM **Privately Held**
Web: www.richardsrestaurants.com
SIC: 5812 2035 Restaurant, family: chain; Dressings, salad: raw and cooked (except dry mixes)
PA: Richards Restaurant, Inc.
8339 N 400 E
Bryant IN
260 997-6823

(G-1437)
T-FLYERZ PRINTING AND PROM LLC
6073 N Us Highway 27 (47326-8832)
PHONE.................................260 729-7392
EMP: 2 EST: 2012
SALES (est): 123.49K **Privately Held**
Web: www.tflyerz.com
SIC: 2752 Commercial printing, lithographic

Buffalo
White County

(G-1438)
HITES HARDWOOD LUMBER CORP
309 S East St (47925)
P.O. Box 162 (47925-0162)
PHONE.................................574 278-7783
Lewis Hites, *Pr*
EMP: 10 EST: 1972
SALES (est): 163.88K **Privately Held**

Buffalo - White County (G-1439)

SIC: 2421 Sawmills and planing mills, general

(G-1439)
LEIS MACHINE SHOP INC
6033 E Hwy 16 (47925)
P.O. Box 227 (47925-0227)
PHONE...................574 278-6000
Otto Richard Leis, *Pr*
Patsy Leis, *Sec*
EMP: 5 EST: 1989
SALES (est): 363.98K Privately Held
SIC: 3599 Machine shop, jobbing and repair

Bunker Hill
Miami County

(G-1440)
ARIZONA ISOTOPE SCIENCE RES
7796 S Innovation Way (46914-9609)
PHONE...................702 219-1243
Wade Brooksby, *Pr*
Sheldon Trubatch, *Sec*
EMP: 3 EST: 2018
SALES (est): 519.35K Privately Held
SIC: 2819 Isotopes, radioactive

(G-1441)
GVM INC
8497 S Us Highway 31 (46914-9485)
PHONE...................765 689-5010
EMP: 2
SALES (corp-wide): 24MM Privately Held
Web: www.gvminc.com
SIC: 3523 Fertilizing, spraying, dusting, and irrigation machinery
PA: Gvm, Inc.
   374 Heidlersburg Rd
   Biglerville PA 17307
   717 677-6197

(G-1442)
NUKEMED INC ✪
Also Called: Spectronrx
3358 W 800 S (46914-9614)
PHONE...................765 437-1631
Kelli Lightfoot, *CEO*
EMP: 6 EST: 2024
SALES (est): 78.58K Privately Held
SIC: 2834 Pharmaceutical preparations

(G-1443)
PEN PRODUCTS MIAMI COR FCILTY
3063w 800 S (46914-9473)
PHONE...................765 689-8920
Sandra Roark, *Mgr*
EMP: 8 EST: 2009
SALES (est): 244.46K Privately Held
SIC: 3716 Motor homes

(G-1444)
TIMOTHY WHITE
Also Called: Gold Medal Awards
191 S Elm St (46914-1517)
P.O. Box 214 (46914-0214)
PHONE...................765 689-8270
Timothy White, *Owner*
EMP: 4 EST: 2017
SALES (est): 155.59K Privately Held
Web: www.gold-medal-awards.com
SIC: 3499 Novelties and giftware, including trophies

Burket
Kosciusko County

(G-1445)
WARSAW BLACK OXIDE INC
310 S Walnut St (46508)
P.O. Box 38 (46508-0038)
PHONE...................574 491-2975
Craig Doran, *Pr*
◆ EMP: 22 EST: 1952
SQ FT: 40,000
SALES (est): 2.49MM Privately Held
SIC: 2899 Plating compounds

Burlington
Carroll County

(G-1446)
SUGAR CODED SOFTWARE LLC
604 E 7th St (46915-9441)
PHONE...................858 652-0797
Tyler Sugar, *Owner*
EMP: 4 EST: 2015
SALES (est): 70.63K Privately Held
SIC: 7372 Prepackaged software

(G-1447)
WILDCAT JAVA LLC (PA)
716 Michigan Rd (46915-1507)
PHONE...................765 438-3682
Steven Larson, *Managing Member*
EMP: 1 EST: 2019
SALES (est): 129.42K
SALES (corp-wide): 129.42K Privately Held
SIC: 2095 Coffee roasting (except by wholesale grocers)

Burney
Decatur County

(G-1448)
RIVERA SCREENPRINTING
1010 E State Road 46 (47240-7723)
PHONE...................812 663-0816
Jamie Rivera, *Owner*
EMP: 3 EST: 2004
SALES (est): 190.9K Privately Held
SIC: 2759 Screen printing

Burns Harbor
Porter County

(G-1449)
CLEVELAND-CLIFFS BURNS HARBOR (DH)
250 W Us Highway 12 (46304-9727)
PHONE...................219 787-2120
Lourenco Goncalves, *Ch*
John Brett, *
Wendell Carter, *
John Battisti, *
Gregory Ludkovsky, *
◆ EMP: 707 EST: 2003
SALES (est): 463.44MM
SALES (corp-wide): 22B Publicly Held
Web: www.clevelandcliffs.com
SIC: 3312 Blast furnaces and steel mills
HQ: Cleveland-Cliffs Steel Llc
   1 S Dearborn St Fl 19
   Chicago IL 60603
   312 346-0300

(G-1450)
CLEVELAND-CLIFFS BURNS HBR LLC
250 W Us Highway 12 (46304-9727)
PHONE...................219 787-2120
EMP: 1184
SALES (corp-wide): 22B Publicly Held
Web: www.clevelandcliffs.com
SIC: 3312 Blast furnaces and steel mills
HQ: Cleveland-Cliffs Burns Harbor Llc
   250 W Us Highway 12
   Burns Harbor IN 46304
   219 787-2120

(G-1451)
CLEVELAND-CLIFFS INC
250 W Us Highway 12 (46304-9727)
PHONE...................219 787-2120
John Miller, *Brnch Mgr*
EMP: 500
SALES (corp-wide): 22B Publicly Held
Web: www.clevelandcliffs.com
SIC: 3312 Blast furnaces and steel mills
PA: Cleveland-Cliffs Inc.
   200 Public Sq Ste 3300
   Cleveland OH 44114
   216 694-5700

(G-1452)
ISG BURNS HARBOR SERVICES LLC
250 W Us Highway 12 (46304-9727)
PHONE...................219 787-2120
EMP: 15 EST: 2010
SALES (est): 945.29K Privately Held
Web: www.burnsharbor-in.gov
SIC: 3312 Blast furnaces and steel mills

(G-1453)
J & F STEEL CORPORATION
310 Tech Dr (46304-8843)
PHONE...................219 764-3500
J Schoettert, *Pr*
M Pisacane, *Sec*
EMP: 8 EST: 1996
SALES (est): 120.12K Privately Held
SIC: 3449 Bars, concrete reinforcing: fabricated steel

(G-1454)
METAL SERVICES LLC
250 W Us Highway 12 (46304-9727)
P.O. Box 619 (46304-0619)
PHONE...................219 787-1514
EMP: 1
SALES (corp-wide): 405.6MM Privately Held
Web: www.phoenixglobal.com
SIC: 3295 Perlite, aggregate or expanded
HQ: Metal Services Llc
   4 Radnor Corp Ctr Ste 520
   Radnor PA 19087

(G-1455)
RYERSON TULL INC (DH)
310 Tech Dr (46304-8843)
PHONE...................219 764-3500
Edward J Lehner, *CEO*
Erich Schnaufer, *
▲ EMP: 75 EST: 1979
SALES (est): 51.88MM Publicly Held
Web: www.ryerson.com
SIC: 5051 3316 3312 Steel; Cold finishing of steel shapes; Blast furnaces and steel mills
HQ: Joseph T. Ryerson & Son, Inc.
   227 W Monroe St Fl 27
   Chicago IL 60606
   312 292-5000

(G-1456)
TMS INTERNATIONAL LLC
251 E Us Rt 12 (46304)
PHONE...................219 787-5220
EMP: 10
Web: www.tmsinternational.com
SIC: 3312 Blast furnaces and steel mills
HQ: Tms International, Llc
   Southside Wrks Bldg 1 3f
   Pittsburgh PA 15203
   412 678-6141

(G-1457)
VITAL INDUS SOLUTIONS CORP ✪
225 W Dunes Hwy (46304-1274)
PHONE...................219 916-7648
EMP: 1 EST: 2023
SALES (est): 78.58K Privately Held
SIC: 3569 General industrial machinery, nec

Burrows
Carroll County

(G-1458)
HEISE WELDING SERVICE
1 Bk South Of Main (46916)
P.O. Box 70 (46916-0070)
PHONE...................574 652-4631
Raymond Heise, *Owner*
EMP: 1 EST: 1966
SALES (est): 29K Privately Held
SIC: 7692 Welding repair

Butler
Dekalb County

(G-1459)
AVF MACHINING
5850 County Road 24 (46721-9633)
PHONE...................260 760-1531
EMP: 7 EST: 2008
SALES (est): 168.7K Privately Held
SIC: 3599 Machine shop, jobbing and repair

(G-1460)
CENTER CONCRETE INC
Also Called: CENTER CONCRETE INC
4225 County Road 79 (46721-9774)
PHONE...................800 453-4224
Don Pahl, *Brnch Mgr*
EMP: 9
Web: www.centerconcreteinc.com
SIC: 3273 Ready-mixed concrete
PA: Center Concrete, Inc.
   8790 Us Rt 6
   Edgerton OH 43517

(G-1461)
COLOR MASTER INC (PA)
810 S Broadway St (46721-9514)
P.O. Box 338 (46721-0338)
PHONE...................260 868-2320
Philip Schlink, *CEO*
Kyle Skaggs, *
EMP: 71 EST: 1991
SQ FT: 48,000
SALES (est): 24.36MM Privately Held
Web: www.color-master.com
SIC: 3089 3087 Coloring and finishing of plastics products; Custom compound purchased resins

(G-1462)
DEKALB MOLDED PLASTICS COMPANY (PA)
550 W Main St (46721)
P.O. Box 129 (46721)

PHONE.....................260 868-2105
Rick Walters, *Pr*
Jeff Rodgers, *CEO*
Lisa Cashel Ctrl, *Prin*
▲ **EMP: 99 EST:** 1997
SQ FT: 80,000
SALES (est): 23.93MM
SALES (corp-wide): 23.93MM **Privately Held**
Web: www.dekalbplastics.com
SIC: 3089 Injection molding of plastics

(G-1463)
EMPIRE INDUSTRIES INC
5631 County Road 16 (46721-9649)
PHONE.....................260 908-0996
Dexter Thain, *Prin*
EMP: 12 **EST:** 2014
SALES (est): 221.3K **Privately Held**
Web: www.empireindustries.com
SIC: 3999 Manufacturing industries, nec

(G-1464)
G W ENTERPRISES
7063 County Road 24 (46721-9662)
PHONE.....................260 868-2555
Gloria Wood, *Owner*
EMP: 3 **EST:** 1997
SALES (est): 248.44K **Privately Held**
SIC: 3625 Truck controls, industrial battery

(G-1465)
HEIDTMAN STEEL PRODUCTS INC
Also Called: Hs Processing
4400 County Road 59 (46721-9746)
PHONE.....................419 691-4646
Sarah Brown, *Brnch Mgr*
EMP: 56
SALES (corp-wide): 230.06MM **Privately Held**
Web: www.heidtman.com
SIC: 3312 3316 3471 3444 Blast furnaces and steel mills; Cold finishing of steel shapes; Plating and polishing; Sheet metalwork
HQ: Heidtman Steel Products, Inc.
2401 Front St
Toledo OH 43605
419 691-4646

(G-1466)
HENDRICKSON INTERNATIONAL CORP
Also Called: Hendrickson Suspension
201 W Cherry St (46721-1441)
PHONE.....................260 868-2131
EMP: 4
SQ FT: 44,000
SALES (corp-wide): 758.84MM **Privately Held**
Web: www.hendrickson-intl.com
SIC: 3714 Motor vehicle parts and accessories
HQ: Hendrickson International Corporation
840 S Frontage Rd
Woodridge IL 60517

(G-1467)
INTERNATIONAL ENGLISH INC
Also Called: National Stock Dog Registry
3597 County Road 75 (46721-9708)
P.O. Box 402 (46721-0402)
PHONE.....................260 868-2670
Rebecca Gorney, *Pr*
David J Gorney, *VP*
Juanita Russell, *Sec*
EMP: 3 **EST:** 1954
SALES (est): 165.74K **Privately Held**
SIC: 0752 2721 Animal breeding services; Periodicals

(G-1468)
INTERNATIONAL PAPER COMPANY
Also Called: International Paper
2626 County Road 71 (46721-9406)
PHONE.....................260 868-2151
John Chambers, *Genl Mgr*
EMP: 85
SQ FT: 132,000
SALES (corp-wide): 18.92B **Publicly Held**
Web: www.internationalpaper.com
SIC: 2621 Paper mills
PA: International Paper Company
6400 Poplar Ave
Memphis TN 38197
901 419-7000

(G-1469)
IRON DYNAMICS INC
4500 County Road 59 (46721-9747)
PHONE.....................260 868-8800
Keith E Busse, *Pr*
Tracy L Shellabarger, *
▲ **EMP:** 243 **EST:** 1995
SQ FT: 50,000
SALES (est): 4.38MM **Publicly Held**
Web: www.steeldynamics.com
SIC: 3312 Primary finished or semifinished shapes
PA: Steel Dynamics, Inc.
7575 W Jefferson Blvd
Fort Wayne IN 46804

(G-1470)
LEVY ENVIRONMENTAL SERVICES CO
Also Called: Butler Mill Service Company
4506 County Road 59 (46721-9747)
PHONE.....................260 868-5123
EMP: 50
SALES (corp-wide): 513.22MM **Privately Held**
Web: www.edwclevy.com
SIC: 3295 Slag, crushed or ground
HQ: Levy Environmental Services Company
9300 Dix
Dearborn MI 48120

(G-1471)
MOLD SERVICE INC
2911 County Road 59 (46721-9624)
PHONE.....................260 868-2920
Beverly Martin, *Pr*
Delbert E Martin, *Sec*
EMP: 7 **EST:** 1960
SQ FT: 6,000
SALES (est): 533.99K **Privately Held**
Web: www.moldserviceinc.com
SIC: 3544 Special dies and tools

(G-1472)
MULTIMATIC INDIANA INC (DH)
201 Re Jones Rd (46721-9570)
PHONE.....................260 868-1000
Peter Czapka, *Pr*
Martin Bressel, *
◆ **EMP:** 35 **EST:** 1999
SQ FT: 25,000
SALES (est): 99.19MM
SALES (corp-wide): 9.14B **Privately Held**
SIC: 3465 Body parts, automobile: stamped metal
HQ: Multimatic Inc.
8688 Woodbine Ave Suite 200
Markham ON L3R 8
905 474-7399

(G-1473)
NEW MLLENNIUM BLDG SYSTEMS LLC
6115 County Road 42 (46721-9743)
PHONE.....................260 868-6000
EMP: 101
Web: www.newmill.com
SIC: 3441 Joists, open web steel: long-span series
HQ: New Millennium Building Systems Llc
1690 Brdway Bldg 19 Ste 1
Fort Wayne IN 46802
260 969-3500

(G-1474)
NEW PROCESS STEEL LP
N P S
4258 County Road 61 (46721-9557)
PHONE.....................260 868-1445
Todd Hoover, *Manager*
EMP: 38
SALES (corp-wide): 331.14MM **Privately Held**
Web: www.nps.cc
SIC: 3479 3316 3353 5051 Galvanizing of iron, steel, or end-formed products; Sheet, steel, cold-rolled, nec: from purchased hot-rolled; Coils, sheet aluminum; Metals service centers and offices
PA: New Process Steel, L.P.
1322 N Post Oak Rd
Houston TX 77055
713 686-9631

(G-1475)
PETTIGREW
7725 County Road 32 (46721-9704)
PHONE.....................260 868-2032
Dennis Pettigrew, *Owner*
EMP: 2 **EST:** 2003
SALES (est): 74.21K **Privately Held**
SIC: 3421 Knife blades and blanks

(G-1476)
SERVICE STEEL FRAMING INC
206 Depot St (46721-1312)
P.O. Box 339 (46721-0339)
PHONE.....................260 868-5853
Andy Hollman, *Pr*
Pat Hollman, *Stockholder*
Earl Mullett, *Stockholder*
EMP: 13 **EST:** 1989
SQ FT: 12,000
SALES (est): 2.22MM **Privately Held**
Web: www.servicesteelframing.com
SIC: 3441 Fabricated structural metal

(G-1477)
SHULL MCH & FIREARMS SVC INC
3877 County Road 49 (46721-9620)
PHONE.....................260 925-4198
Edwin M Shull, *Pr*
EMP: 2 **EST:** 1978
SALES (est): 245.77K **Privately Held**
SIC: 3599 Machine shop, jobbing and repair

(G-1478)
SHULL TACTICAL CONCEPTS INC
3877 County Road 49 (46721-9620)
PHONE.....................260 316-9224
EMP: 1 **EST:** 2013
SALES (est): 106.66K **Privately Held**
Web: www.shulltacticalconcepts.com
SIC: 3949 Targets, archery and rifle shooting

(G-1479)
STAFFORD GRAVEL INC
4225 County Road 79 (46721-9774)
PHONE.....................260 868-2503
EMP: 10 **EST:** 1991
SALES (est): 514.61K **Privately Held**
Web: www.staffordgravel.com
SIC: 1442 Gravel and pebble mining

(G-1480)
STEEL DYNAMICS INC
Flat Roll Division
4500 County Road 59 (46721-9747)
PHONE.....................260 868-8000
Charlie Trowbridge, *Brnch Mgr*
EMP: 650
Web: www.steeldynamics.com
SIC: 3312 Plate, sheet and strip, except coated products
PA: Steel Dynamics, Inc.
7575 W Jefferson Blvd
Fort Wayne IN 46804

(G-1481)
STEEL DYNAMICS SLS N AMER INC
4500 County Road 59 (46721-9747)
PHONE.....................260 868-8000
Jordan Breiner, *Brnch Mgr*
EMP: 800
Web: www.steeldynamics.com
SIC: 3312 Blast furnaces and steel mills
HQ: Steel Dynamics Sales North America, Inc.
7575 W Jefferson Blvd
Fort Wayne IN 46804
260 969-3500

Butlerville
Jennings County

(G-1482)
CARGO SKIFF CORPORATION
1280 N County Road 500 E (47223-9685)
PHONE.....................812 873-6349
Daniel L Pohle, *Pr*
EMP: 5 **EST:** 2009
SALES (est): 266.7K **Privately Held**
Web: www.cargoskiff.com
SIC: 3731 Commercial cargo ships, building and repairing

(G-1483)
GREG ABPLANALP LOGGING LLC
1395 N County Road 615 E (47223-9698)
PHONE.....................812 873-8463
Greg Abplanalp, *Prin*
EMP: 5 **EST:** 2019
SALES (est): 242.95K **Privately Held**
SIC: 2411 Logging camps and contractors

(G-1484)
JENNINGS COUNTY PALLETS INC
5195 E Us Highway 50 (47223-9662)
P.O. Box 307 (47265-0307)
PHONE.....................812 458-6288
EMP: 45 **EST:** 1994
SALES (est): 4.8MM **Privately Held**
SIC: 2448 5031 4213 Pallets, wood; Lumber, plywood, and millwork; Trucking, except local

(G-1485)
JENNINGS COUNTY PALLETS INC
5195 E Us Highway 50 (47223-9662)
P.O. Box 307 (47265-0307)
PHONE.....................812 458-6288
EMP: 25
SIC: 2448 Pallets, wood
PA: Jennings County Pallets Inc
5195 E Us Highway 50
Butlerville IN 47223

(G-1486)
KELLER TOOL
Also Called: Keller Tools
1085 N County Road 500 E (47223-9689)
PHONE.....................812 873-7344
Kenneth Keller, *Owner*

Butlerville - Jennings County (G-1487)

Natalie Keller, *Mgr*
EMP: 2 **EST:** 1998
SALES (est): 125.98K **Privately Held**
SIC: 3544 Special dies and tools

(G-1487)
P&Y FARM FRESH MARKET LLC
800 S County Road 600 E (47223-9511)
PHONE.................................812 767-1902
EMP: 1 **EST:** 2019
SALES (est): 67.67K **Privately Held**
SIC: 2011 Variety meats, fresh edible organs

(G-1488)
STAPLES PIPE & MUFFLER (PA)
1365 S County Road 650 E (47223-9529)
PHONE.................................812 522-3569
Angela Staples, *Pr*
EMP: 2 **EST:** 2012
SALES (est): 248.37K
SALES (corp-wide): 248.37K **Privately Held**
Web: www.staplespipeandmuffler.com
SIC: 5013 3498 Automotive supplies and parts; Fabricated pipe and fittings

Cambridge City
Wayne County

(G-1489)
ABF WELDING & PIPE LLC
308 N 3rd St (47327-1331)
PHONE.................................765 977-7349
Thomas Alan Bertsch, *Admn*
EMP: 6 **EST:** 2013
SALES (est): 185.45K **Privately Held**
SIC: 7692 Welding repair

(G-1490)
ANTHONY SMITH
Also Called: Smith's Radiator Service
9 E Front St (47327-1214)
PHONE.................................765 478-5325
Anthony Smith, *Owner*
EMP: 1 **EST:** 1987
SQ FT: 1,240
SALES (est): 101.68K **Privately Held**
Web: www.smithsradiator.com
SIC: 3714 7539 Radiators and radiator shells and cores, motor vehicle; Automotive repair shops, nec

(G-1491)
BIOTA BIOSCIENCES INC
16239 Wagner Rd (47327-9725)
PHONE.................................765 702-3744
Thomas E Spike, *Pr*
EMP: 1 **EST:** 2009
SALES (est): 117.88K **Privately Held**
SIC: 2834 Pharmaceutical preparations

(G-1492)
CONVERTO MFG CO INC
220 S Green St (47327)
P.O. Box 287 (47327-0287)
PHONE.................................765 478-3205
Clarence France, *Pr*
Brenda Chandler, *Sec*
EMP: 7 **EST:** 1939
SQ FT: 40,000
SALES (est): 838.39K **Privately Held**
Web: www.convertomfg.com
SIC: 3537 Truck trailers, used in plants, docks, terminals, etc.

(G-1493)
DESIGN & MFG SOLUTIONS LLC
15421 W Hunnicut Rd (47327-9729)
P.O. Box 336 (47327-0336)
PHONE.................................765 478-9393
Travis Wadle, *Managing Member*
EMP: 10 **EST:** 2007
SALES (est): 849.59K **Privately Held**
Web: www.design-manufacturing.com
SIC: 3599 Machine shop, jobbing and repair

(G-1494)
FAB-TECH INDUSTRIES INC
14271 W Us Highway 40 (47327-9403)
PHONE.................................765 478-4191
Ken Banning, *Pr*
Jill Banning, *Sec*
EMP: 5 **EST:** 1989
SQ FT: 10,000
SALES (est): 475.81K **Privately Held**
Web: fab-tech-industries-inc.business.site
SIC: 3547 3441 Pipe and tube mills; Fabricated structural metal

(G-1495)
HM LOWRY ENTERPRISES LLC ⊙
13072 W Us Highway 40 (47327-9314)
PHONE.................................765 524-8435
EMP: 2 **EST:** 2022
SALES (est): 92.67K **Privately Held**
SIC: 2026 7389 Cream, sour; Business Activities at Non-Commercial Site

(G-1496)
IRVING MATERIALS INC
Also Called: I M I
14413 W Us Highway 40 (47327-9403)
PHONE.................................765 478-4914
Steve Lewis, *Brnch Mgr*
EMP: 8
SALES (corp-wide): 814.09MM **Privately Held**
Web: www.irvmat.com
SIC: 3273 5032 Ready-mixed concrete; Concrete and cinder building products
PA: Irving Materials, Inc.
8032 N State Road 9
Greenfield IN 46140
317 326-3101

(G-1497)
JANIS BUHL
Also Called: Wayne Newspapers
26 W Church St (47327-1615)
PHONE.................................765 478-5448
Janis Buhl, *Owner*
EMP: 8 **EST:** 2001
SALES (est): 335.28K **Privately Held**
SIC: 2711 Newspapers

(G-1498)
KIDS AT HEART PUBLISHING LLC
219 W Main St (47327-1122)
PHONE.................................765 478-5773
Shelley Davis, *Owner*
EMP: 10 **EST:** 2016
SALES (est): 50.03K **Privately Held**
Web: www.kidsatheartpublishing.com
SIC: 2741 Miscellaneous publishing

(G-1499)
MILLERS WOOD SPECIALTIES INC
850 E Church St (47327-1481)
P.O. Box 31 (47327-0031)
PHONE.................................765 478-3248
EMP: 50 **EST:** 1979
SALES (est): 1.38MM **Privately Held**
SIC: 7699 2441 Pallet repair; Boxes, wood

(G-1500)
POWCO INC
Also Called: Powell Paving Company
2583 S State Road 1 (47327-9333)
PHONE.................................765 334-4210
Randall Powell, *Pr*
Kimberly Powell, *Sec*
EMP: 10 **EST:** 1952
SQ FT: 13,000
SALES (est): 991.45K **Privately Held**
SIC: 2951 Asphalt paving mixtures and blocks

(G-1501)
REGAL MANUFACTURING COMPANY
502 S Green St (47327-1645)
P.O. Box 31 (47327-0031)
PHONE.................................765 334-8118
Robert Miller, *Pr*
EMP: 1 **EST:** 2016
SALES (est): 230.92K **Privately Held**
Web: www.regalmc.com
SIC: 2281 Yarn spinning mills

(G-1502)
RIHM INC (PA)
Also Called: Rihm Foods
8360 E County Road 950 S (47327-9608)
P.O. Box 148 (47327-0148)
PHONE.................................765 478-3426
James Rihm, *Pr*
Gerald Rihm, *Sec*
Donald Rihm, *Treas*
EMP: 5 **EST:** 1926
SQ FT: 2,000
SALES (est): 1.26MM
SALES (corp-wide): 1.26MM **Privately Held**
Web: www.rihmfoods.com
SIC: 5411 5921 2013 2011 Grocery stores, independent; Liquor stores; Sausages and other prepared meats; Beef products, from beef slaughtered on site

(G-1503)
ROGERS ENGINEERING AND MFG CO
112 S Center St (47327-1243)
PHONE.................................765 478-5444
William A Rogers, *Pr*
Steve Rogers, *
William Rogersjr, *
Denise Rogers, *
◆ **EMP:** 45 **EST:** 1972
SQ FT: 100,000
SALES (est): 8.69MM **Privately Held**
Web: www.rogersengineering.net
SIC: 3567 3444 7692 3398 Industrial furnaces and ovens; Sheet metalwork; Welding repair; Metal heat treating

(G-1504)
WESTERN WAYNE NEWS
Also Called: Mettle Creek
26 W Church St (47327-1615)
P.O. Box 337 (47327-0337)
PHONE.................................765 478-5448
Janis Buhl, *Owner*
EMP: 3 **EST:** 1991
SALES (est): 198.72K **Privately Held**
Web: www.westernwaynenews.com
SIC: 2711 Newspapers, publishing and printing

(G-1505)
WESTERN WYNE RGONAL SEWAGE DST
200 S Plum St (47327)
PHONE.................................765 478-3788
Darleene Druley, *Superintnt*
EMP: 3 **EST:** 1974
SALES (est): 200.59K **Privately Held**
SIC: 3589 Water treatment equipment, industrial

Camby
Morgan County

(G-1506)
AARON MCWHIRTER
Also Called: Pro Stop Mechanical Shop
6272 E Pemboke Ct (46113-9649)
PHONE.................................307 256-0070
Aaron Mcwhirter, *Owner*
Brett Mc Whirter, *Owner*
EMP: 1
SQ FT: 41,000
SALES (est): 50K **Privately Held**
SIC: 3549 Metalworking machinery, nec

(G-1507)
BACK TO EDEN HERBS CORP
Also Called: Back To Eden Herbs Shop
8411 Windfall Ln Ste 60 (46113-8027)
PHONE.................................317 455-1033
Candice Long, *CEO*
EMP: 1 **EST:** 2020
SALES (est): 31.39K **Privately Held**
SIC: 5499 2048 Spices and herbs; Mineral feed supplements

(G-1508)
CENTURY STEEL FABRICATING INC
4421 E County Line Rd (46113)
PHONE.................................317 834-1295
Greg Sheets, *Pr*
Connie R Sheets, *Sec*
EMP: 14 **EST:** 1997
SQ FT: 7,200
SALES (est): 2.31MM **Privately Held**
Web: www.centurysteel.net
SIC: 3441 Fabricated structural metal

(G-1509)
DIGITAL DESIGN GENIUS ⊙
9174 Bainbridge Dr (46113-8004)
PHONE.................................317 515-3680
Hephzibah Igwe, *Managing Member*
EMP: 4 **EST:** 2023
SALES (est): 68.7K **Privately Held**
SIC: 7389 7311 7336 7372 Design services; Advertising consultant; Commercial art and graphic design; Application computer software

(G-1510)
GARDEN OF REMEDIES INC ⊙
8411 Windfall Ln (46113-8027)
P.O. Box 95 (46113-0095)
PHONE.................................463 241-5991
Candice Long, *CEO*
EMP: 2 **EST:** 2022
SALES (est): 92.67K **Privately Held**
SIC: 2023 Dietary supplements, dairy and non-dairy based

(G-1511)
JIM LEMONS MODELS
Also Called: Jim Lemons Cnstr & Models
13575 N Western Rd (46113-8494)
PHONE.................................317 831-5133
James Lemons, *Owner*
EMP: 1 **EST:** 2009
SALES (est): 65.33K **Privately Held**
SIC: 3562 Casters

(G-1512)
MERCER MACHINE COMPANY INC
10356 Leases Corner Ct (46113-9010)
PHONE.................................317 241-9903
Tracy Robinson, *Pr*
Brian Robinson, *VP*
EMP: 15 **EST:** 1954
SALES (est): 1.92MM **Privately Held**

Web: www.mercermachine.net
SIC: 3599 Machine shop, jobbing and repair

(G-1513)
RENK SYSTEMS CORPORATION
8880 Union Mills Dr (46113-9705)
PHONE.....................317 455-1367
Tadeusz Trzesniowski, *CEO*
Joerg Cordes, *Pr*
David Williams Russell, *VP*
Kerstin Buchheister, *Treas*
EMP: 20 **EST:** 2004
SQ FT: 10,000
SALES (est): 5.13MM
SALES (corp-wide): 500.31K Privately Held
Web: www.renk.com
SIC: 3825 Engine electrical test equipment
HQ: Renk Gmbh
Gogginger Str. 73
Augsburg BY 86159
82157000

(G-1514)
STEVEN SMITH
13965 N State Road 67 (46113-8354)
PHONE.....................317 455-1086
Steven Smith, *Prin*
EMP: 1 **EST:** 2010
SALES (est): 93.12K Privately Held
Web: www.smithtea.com
SIC: 3578 Coin counters

(G-1515)
SUNRISE PIGMENT USA LLC ✪
13173 N Brick Chapel Dr (46113-8814)
PHONE.....................773 449-8265
James E Bailey Junior, *Mgr*
EMP: 1 **EST:** 2022
SALES (est): 47.23K Privately Held
SIC: 2816 Inorganic pigments

(G-1516)
WHATEVER IT TKES HM IMPRVS LLC
10625 Tilford Dr Apt 2e (46113-8996)
PHONE.....................317 494-9568
EMP: 5 **EST:** 2020
SALES (est): 131.61K Privately Held
SIC: 1389 Construction, repair, and dismantling services

(G-1517)
XFMRS INC
7570 E Landersdale Rd (46113-8512)
PHONE.....................317 834-1066
Anthony E Imburia, *Pr*
Cheri Imburgia, *Prin*
Tony Imburgia, *VP Opers*
Valarie Wareham, *Treas*
Randell Barnhorst, *Treas*
▲ **EMP:** 1100 **EST:** 1992
SQ FT: 7,500
SALES (est): 46.68MM Privately Held
Web: www.xfmrs.com
SIC: 3677 5065 3612 Electronic transformers ; Electronic parts and equipment, nec; Transformers, except electric

(G-1518)
XFMRS HOLDINGS INC (PA)
7570 E Landersdale Rd (46113-8512)
PHONE.....................317 834-1066
Anthony Imburgia, *Pr*
Joe Huff, *VP*
EMP: 18 **EST:** 1998
SALES (est): 60.14MM
SALES (corp-wide): 60.14MM Privately Held
Web: www.xfmrs.com
SIC: 3699 Electrical equipment and supplies, nec

Camden
Carroll County

(G-1519)
DELAPLANE & SON NEON & SIGN
Also Called: Delaplane Son Neon & Sign Svc
7768 E 550 N (46917-9594)
PHONE.....................574 859-3431
TOLL FREE: 800
Robert K Delaplane, *Pr*
Deborah Delaplane, *Sec*
EMP: 5 **EST:** 1983
SALES (est): 400K Privately Held
SIC: 3993 5046 Neon signs; Neon signs

(G-1520)
HOG SLAT INCORPORATED
200 N Meridian Line Rd (46917)
P.O. Box 26 (46917-0026)
PHONE.....................574 967-4145
Richard Hicks, *Brnch Mgr*
EMP: 51
SALES (corp-wide): 538.94MM Privately Held
Web: www.hogslat.com
SIC: 3523 2048 Hog feeding, handling, and watering equipment; Prepared feeds, nec
PA: Hog Slat, Incorporated
206 Fayetteville St
Newton Grove NC 28366
800 949-4647

(G-1521)
LESH ADVERTISING INC
6938 E State Road 218 (46917-9416)
PHONE.....................574 859-2141
TOLL FREE: 800
Jeffery Lesh, *Pr*
Cindy Lesh, *VP*
EMP: 3 **EST:** 1949
SALES (est): 160.72K Privately Held
SIC: 3993 1799 Signs, not made in custom sign painting shops; Sign installation and maintenance

(G-1522)
WILLIAMS WOODSHOP
2171 E 300 N (46917-9342)
PHONE.....................574 686-2324
William Brubaker, *Owner*
EMP: 1 **EST:** 2008
SALES (est): 86.36K Privately Held
SIC: 2499 7389 Wood products, nec; Business Activities at Non-Commercial Site

Campbellsburg
Washington County

(G-1523)
GREENE WOODWORKING & GLASS LLC
Also Called: Vase Candle
10136 W Suder Ln (47108-6527)
PHONE.....................812 755-4331
Rhonda Greene, *Owner*
EMP: 1 **EST:** 1990
SALES (est): 96.48K Privately Held
Web: www.vasecandle.com
SIC: 3231 5231 Mosaics, glass: made from purchased glass; Glass, leaded or stained

(G-1524)
HAWK PRECISION COMPONENTS INC
596 W Oak St (47108-9105)
P.O. Box 68 (47108-0068)
PHONE.....................812 755-4501
Paul Moser, *Prin*
EMP: 4 **EST:** 2013
SALES (est): 113.23K Privately Held
SIC: 3399 Powder, metal

(G-1525)
NETSHAPE TECHNOLOGIES LLC
Also Called: Mpp
596 W Oak St (47108-9105)
PHONE.....................317 805-3764
EMP: 49 **EST:** 2018
SALES (est): 3.09MM Privately Held
Web: www.mppinnovation.com
SIC: 3999 Manufacturing industries, nec

(G-1526)
NST TECHNOLOGIES MIM LLC
Also Called: Helsel
596 W Oak St (47108-9105)
PHONE.....................812 755-4501
Rhett Luecke, *Brnch Mgr*
EMP: 150
SALES (corp-wide): 154.49MM Privately Held
Web: www.mppinnovation.com
SIC: 3399 3566 3561 3545 Powder, metal; Speed changers, drives, and gears; Pumps and pumping equipment; Machine tool accessories
HQ: Nst Technologies Mim Llc
14670 Cumberland Rd
Noblesville IN 46060
812 248-9273

(G-1527)
ON SITE WELDING & MAINTENANCE
7632 E County Road 240 N (47108-7922)
PHONE.....................812 755-4184
Josh Wallace, *Prin*
EMP: 2 **EST:** 2004
SALES (est): 145.07K Privately Held
SIC: 7692 Welding repair

Canaan
Jefferson County

(G-1528)
THUNDER ROLLS EXPRESS
13449 State Road 129 (47224-9544)
PHONE.....................812 667-5111
Joseph Womack, *Owner*
EMP: 7 **EST:** 2006
SALES (est): 131.99K Privately Held
SIC: 2741 Miscellaneous publishing

Cannelburg
Daviess County

(G-1529)
CANNELBURG PROC PLANT LLC
204 S Main St (47519-5109)
PHONE.....................812 486-3223
Daniel Genrich, *Owner*
EMP: 9 **EST:** 1999
SALES (est): 498.78K Privately Held
SIC: 2011 Meat packing plants

(G-1530)
DAVIESS COUNTY METAL SALES
9929 E Us Highway 50 (47519-5021)
PHONE.....................812 486-4299
John Lengacher, *Pr*
Kenny Swartzentruber Junior, *Sec*
EMP: 97 **EST:** 1983
SQ FT: 150,000
SALES (est): 45.3MM Privately Held
Web: www.dcmetal.com
SIC: 3444 2439 Roof deck, sheet metal; Trusses, wooden roof

Cannelton
Perry County

(G-1531)
AUSTINS METAL MAFIA INC
8175 Boyd Rd (47520-6841)
PHONE.....................812 619-6115
Eddie Austin, *Pr*
EMP: 6 **EST:** 2017
SALES (est): 322.14K Privately Held
Web: austins-metal-mafiainc.business.site
SIC: 3999 Manufacturing industries, nec

(G-1532)
BEST CHAIRS INCORPORATED
Highway 66 E (47520)
P.O. Box 158 (47532-0158)
PHONE.....................812 367-1761
Don Gill, *Mgr*
EMP: 131
SALES (corp-wide): 225MM Privately Held
Web: www.besthf.com
SIC: 2512 2514 2511 Chairs: upholstered on wood frames; Metal household furniture; Wood household furniture
PA: Best Chairs Incorporated
1 Best Dr
Ferdinand IN 47532
812 367-1761

(G-1533)
BLUE HERON VINEYARDS LLC
5330 Blue Heron Ln (47520-5817)
PHONE.....................812 619-6045
Gary Dauby, *Owner*
▲ **EMP:** 3 **EST:** 2005
SALES (est): 182.42K Privately Held
Web: www.blueheronvines.com
SIC: 2084 Wines

(G-1534)
CAN-CLAY CORP
402 Washington St (47520-1240)
EMP: 24 **EST:** 1982
SQ FT: 7,000
SALES (est): 1.87MM Privately Held
Web: www.canclay.com
SIC: 3255 3259 Clay refractories; Sewer pipe or fittings, clay

(G-1535)
DENNIS ETIENNES LOGGING INC
14370 Ureka Rd (47520-5065)
PHONE.....................812 843-4518
Dennis Etienne, *Owner*
EMP: 5 **EST:** 2017
SALES (est): 77.19K Privately Held
SIC: 2411 Logging camps and contractors

(G-1536)
EXPRESS MACHINE
6115 Sugar Maple Rd (47520-6768)
PHONE.....................812 719-5979
EMP: 2 **EST:** 2010
SALES (est): 60.24K Privately Held
SIC: 3541 Machine tools, metal cutting type

Carbon
Clay County

(G-1537)
CLUTCH GRAPHICS
14650 N Oak St (47837)
PHONE..................812 244-9673
Christopher Mcvay, *Prin*
EMP: 1 EST: 2017
SALES (est): 48.55K **Privately Held**
SIC: 2741 Business service newsletters: publishing and printing

(G-1538)
PIKE LUMBER COMPANY INC
440 W County Rd1450 N (47837)
P.O. Box 255 (47837-0255)
PHONE..................574 893-4511
Jim Steen, *Mgr*
EMP: 37
SALES (corp-wide): 18.17MM **Privately Held**
Web: www.pikelumber.com
SIC: 5211 2426 2421 Planing mill products and lumber; Hardwood dimension and flooring mills; Sawmills and planing mills, general
PA: Pike Lumber Company, Inc.
719 Front St
Akron IN 46910
574 893-4511

Carlisle
Sullivan County

(G-1539)
5M POULTRY LLC
10977 S County Road 500 E (47838-8084)
PHONE..................812 890-5558
Joseph D Mccormick, *Owner*
EMP: 5 EST: 2016
SALES (est): 214.3K **Privately Held**
SIC: 3151 Mittens, leather

(G-1540)
CARLISLE MINE
1466 E State Road 58 (47838-8181)
PHONE..................812 398-2200
EMP: 5 EST: 2019
SALES (est): 158.7K **Privately Held**
Web: www.halladorenergy.com
SIC: 1382 Oil and gas exploration services

(G-1541)
GLASS MOLDERS POTTERY PLA
2126 E County Road 7 Se (47838-8089)
PHONE..................812 398-6222
Roy Terrell, *Pr*
EMP: 1 EST: 1999
SALES (est): 81.12K **Privately Held**
SIC: 3089 Molding primary plastics

(G-1542)
PEABODY BEAR RUN MINING LLC
7255 E County Road 600 S (47838-8042)
PHONE..................314 342-7676
EMP: 118
SALES (corp-wide): 4.95B **Publicly Held**
Web: www.peabodyenergy.com
SIC: 1221 Bituminous coal and lignite-surface mining
HQ: Peabody Bear Run Mining Llc
701 Market St
Saint Louis MO 63101
314 342-3400

(G-1543)
RUSSELL L ROOKSBERRY
Also Called: Bucktown Metal Works
6142 S State Road 159 (47838-8110)
PHONE..................812 659-1683
Russell L Rooksberry, *Owner*
EMP: 1 EST: 2004
SALES (est): 72.73K **Privately Held**
SIC: 3599 Amusement park equipment

(G-1544)
TRAVIS C AND JAN B PAGE
9606 S County Road 18 Sw (47838-8373)
PHONE..................812 398-5507
Travis Page, *Owner*
EMP: 2 EST: 2005
SALES (est): 202.17K **Privately Held**
SIC: 2452 Farm and agricultural buildings, prefabricated wood

Carmel
Hamilton County

(G-1545)
3OE SCIENTIFIC LLC
424 W Main St (46032-1622)
PHONE..................317 869-7602
EMP: 10 EST: 2018
SALES (est): 747.76K **Privately Held**
Web: www.3oescientific.com
SIC: 7389 3842 Business Activities at Non-Commercial Site; Surgical appliances and supplies

(G-1546)
A YARD ART
305 3rd Ave Ne (46032-1945)
PHONE..................317 862-1486
Darcy Adler, *Prin*
EMP: 5 EST: 2002
SALES (est): 184.32K **Privately Held**
Web: www.ayardart.com
SIC: 3993 Signs and advertising specialties

(G-1547)
AB&B SERVICES LLC
550 Congressional Blvd (46032-5609)
PHONE..................317 405-7219
EMP: 4
SALES (est): 101.26K **Privately Held**
SIC: 1389 Construction, repair, and dismantling services

(G-1548)
ABS MFG REP INC
1950 E Greyhound Pass Ste 18 (46033-7787)
PHONE..................317 407-0406
W Klingensmithmark, *Pr*
EMP: 6 EST: 2013
SALES (est): 67.76K **Privately Held**
SIC: 3999 Manufacturing industries, nec

(G-1549)
ADAPTIVE TECH SOLUTIONS LLC
14915 Silver Thorne Way (46033-8977)
PHONE..................317 762-4363
EMP: 2 EST: 2018
SALES (est): 65.53K **Privately Held**
Web: www.adaptivetechsolutionsindy.com
SIC: 7373 3651 Systems integration services; Household audio and video equipment

(G-1550)
ADELL GROUP LLC
1385 Sierra Spgs 5 (46280-2706)
PHONE..................317 507-6158
Jeffrey L Adell, *Ch*
EMP: 6 EST: 2013
SALES (est): 55.22K **Privately Held**
SIC: 3714 Motor vehicle parts and accessories

(G-1551)
ADEPT TOOL AND ENGINEERING
11307 Green St (46033-3738)
PHONE..................317 896-9250
EMP: 8 EST: 2017
SALES (est): 115.78K **Privately Held**
SIC: 3599 5084 Machine shop, jobbing and repair; Tool and die makers equipment

(G-1552)
ADVANCED MTLWRKING PRCTCES LLC
Also Called: AMP
4511 W 99th St (46032-7718)
PHONE..................317 337-0441
EMP: 6 EST: 2021
SALES (est): 250.52K **Privately Held**
SIC: 3444 Sheet metalwork

(G-1553)
ALLEGION LLC
11819 Pennsylvania St (46032-4555)
PHONE..................317 810-3700
EMP: 26 EST: 2013
SALES (est): 1.38MM **Privately Held**
SIC: 3699 Security devices
PA: Allegion Public Limited Company
D Block D
Dublin D02 V

(G-1554)
ALLEGION PUBLIC LTD COMPANY
11819 Pennsylvania St (46032-4555)
PHONE..................317 810-3700
EMP: 72
Web: www.allegion.com
SIC: 6722 5065 3429 5251
; Security control equipment and systems; Motor vehicle hardware; Door locks and lock sets
PA: Allegion Public Limited Company
D Block D
Dublin D02 V

(G-1555)
ALLEGION S&S HOLDING CO INC (HQ)
11819 Pennsylvania St (46032-4555)
PHONE..................317 810-3700
David D Petratis, *CEO*
EMP: 500 EST: 2013
SALES (est): 883.61MM **Privately Held**
Web: www.allegion.com
SIC: 3429 Locks or lock sets
PA: Allegion Public Limited Company
D Block D
Dublin D02 V

(G-1556)
ALLEGION US HOLDING CO INC (HQ)
11819 Pennsylvania St (46032-4555)
P.O. Box 4265 (46082-4265)
PHONE..................317 810-3700
David D Petratis, *Pr*
EMP: 20 EST: 2013
SALES (est): 526.2MM **Privately Held**
Web: www.allegion.com
SIC: 3429 Locks or lock sets
PA: Allegion Public Limited Company
D Block D
Dublin D02 V

(G-1557)
ALLEGRO MICROSYSTEMS LLC
11711 Pennsylvania St Ste 240 (46032-4559)
PHONE..................765 854-2263
Deb Mund, *Brnch Mgr*
EMP: 2
Web: www.allegromicro.com
SIC: 3674 Semiconductors and related devices
HQ: Allegro Microsystems, Llc
955 Perimeter Rd
Manchester NH 03103

(G-1558)
ALSONS CORPORATION
55 E 111th St (46280-1071)
PHONE..................800 421-0001
▲ EMP: 92
SIC: 3431 Plumbing fixtures: enameled iron, cast iron,or pressed metal

(G-1559)
ALWAYS FULL LLC ◆
1105 W 136th St (46032-8835)
PHONE..................317 727-9639
Steve R Booher, *CEO*
EMP: 5 EST: 2023
SALES (est): 62.01K **Privately Held**
SIC: 3999 Pet supplies

(G-1560)
ANDERSON AMISH CABINETS LLC
14545 John Paul Way (46032-1211)
PHONE..................317 575-9277
EMP: 1 EST: 2006
SALES (est): 83.65K **Privately Held**
Web: www.amishkitchencabinets.net
SIC: 2434 Wood kitchen cabinets

(G-1561)
APPLE III LLC
3928 Kitty Hawk Ct (46033-4801)
PHONE..................317 691-2869
Tamara A Haubry, *Pr*
EMP: 5 EST: 2018
SALES (est): 94.83K **Privately Held**
SIC: 3571 Electronic computers

(G-1562)
APTIV SERVICES US LLC
Also Called: Delphi
13085 Hamilton Crossing Blvd Ste X (46032-1412)
PHONE..................765 451-0732
Daniel Frazier, *Brnch Mgr*
EMP: 209
SALES (corp-wide): 20.05B **Privately Held**
Web: www.aptiv.com
SIC: 3714 Motor vehicle parts and accessories
HQ: Aptiv Services Us, Llc
5725 Innovation Dr
Troy MI 48098

(G-1563)
ARC INDUSTRIES LLC
6561 Iroquois Ln (46033-5000)
PHONE..................317 753-1607
Renay Pegg, *Owner*
EMP: 5 EST: 2015
SALES (est): 99.64K **Privately Held**
Web: www.arcindustriesllc.com
SIC: 3999 Manufacturing industries, nec

(G-1564)
ARTFUL LIVING
645 Mcnamara Ct (46032-5058)
PHONE..................317 764-7232
EMP: 3 EST: 2018
SALES (est): 50.14K **Privately Held**
Web: www.artfulliving.com
SIC: 2741 Miscellaneous publishing

GEOGRAPHIC SECTION
Carmel - Hamilton County (G-1591)

(G-1565)
ARTISTIC COMPOSITE PALLETS LLC
Also Called: Worlds Best Pallets, The
4518 W 99th St (46032-7715)
PHONE.............................317 960-5813
Sean Regan, *Managing Member*
Garrett Clark, *
Ashley Warren, *
William Bastian Ii, *Managing Member*
EMP: 30 EST: 2020
SALES (est): 4.18MM **Privately Held**
Web: www.artisticpallets.com
SIC: 2448 3089 Pallets, wood and wood with metal; Thermoformed finished plastics products, nec

(G-1566)
BELDEN INC
401 Pennsylvania Pkwy (46280-1385)
PHONE.............................317 818-6300
Denis Suggs, *Pr*
EMP: 239
SALES (corp-wide): 2.51B **Publicly Held**
Web: www.belden.com
SIC: 3357 Nonferrous wiredrawing and insulating
PA: Belden Inc.
 1 N Brentwood Blvd Fl 15
 Saint Louis MO 63105
 314 854-8000

(G-1567)
BETTA CALL PAUL 4 CBD LLC
1015 Oswego Rd (46032-2646)
PHONE.............................317 675-6060
Paul Shea, *Prin*
EMP: 5 EST: 2018
SALES (est): 126.4K **Privately Held**
Web: www.bettacallpaul4cbd.com
SIC: 3999

(G-1568)
BLUSH AND BOBBY PINS LLC
600 E Carmel Dr Ste 249 (46032-3064)
PHONE.............................317 789-5166
Stephanie Baker, *Prin*
▲ EMP: 4 EST: 2011
SALES (est): 70.38K **Privately Held**
Web: www.blushandbobbypins.com
SIC: 3452 Pins

(G-1569)
BOLSTRA LLC
12400 N Meridian St Ste 120 (46032-4600)
PHONE.............................317 660-9131
Haresh Gangwani, *CEO*
David Cochran, *COO*
Steve Ehrlich, *COO*
EMP: 2 EST: 2014
SALES (est): 235.6K **Privately Held**
Web: www.bolstra.com
SIC: 7372 Business oriented computer software

(G-1570)
BONACCORSI WINE COMPANY LLC
12586 Pembrooke Cir (46032-8339)
PHONE.............................310 777-3704
Michael Bonaccorsi, *Prin*
EMP: 1 EST: 2001
SALES (est): 53.4K **Privately Held**
SIC: 2084 Wines

(G-1571)
BONNER & ASSOCIATES
12310 Windsor Dr (46033-3144)
PHONE.............................317 571-3911
EMP: 5
SQ FT: 3,000
SALES (est): 500K **Privately Held**

SIC: 3613 5063 Control panels, electric; Light bulbs and related supplies

(G-1572)
BRAHM CORPORATION
3555 Sedgemoor Cir (46032-9095)
P.O. Box 994 (63006-0994)
PHONE.............................317 502-3133
Bhavook Tripathi, *Pr*
Mariah Carlisle, *VP*
EMP: 1 EST: 2016
SALES (est): 186.4K **Privately Held**
SIC: 3441 Fabricated structural metal

(G-1573)
BRICKWORKS SUPPLY CENTER LLC
Also Called: Edgewood Building Supply
430 W Carmel Dr (46032-2530)
PHONE.............................317 786-9208
Andy Whiller, *Mgr*
EMP: 24
SALES (corp-wide): 8.9MM **Privately Held**
Web: www.brickworkssupply.com
SIC: 5211 5032 3272 Brick; Drywall materials; Concrete products, precast, nec
PA: Brickworks Supply Center Llc
 1580 E Epler Ave
 Indianapolis IN 46227
 317 846-6060

(G-1574)
BUCKINGHAM PALLETS INC
12325 Camberly Ln (46033-3109)
PHONE.............................317 846-8601
Kenneth H Karsh, *Pr*
Denise Karsh, *VP*
Kerry Cronin, *Frmn Supr*
EMP: 8 EST: 1982
SQ FT: 14,000
SALES (est): 186.52K **Privately Held**
SIC: 2448 5031 Pallets, wood; Pallets, wood

(G-1575)
BUDDY COVERS INC
201 W Greyhound Pass (46032-7006)
PHONE.............................317 846-5766
EMP: 1 EST: 1999
SALES (est): 100K **Privately Held**
Web: www.buddycovers.com
SIC: 3949 5661 5091 Snow skiing equipment and supplies, except skis; Footwear, athletic; Athletic goods

(G-1576)
BURKS DOOR & SASH INC
Also Called: Shannon Door
599 3rd Ave Sw (46032-2084)
PHONE.............................317 844-2484
Kent Shively, *Pr*
Peter B Burks, *Stockholder*
EMP: 32 EST: 1977
SQ FT: 17,000
SALES (est): 798.83K **Privately Held**
Web: www.shannondoorco.com
SIC: 2431 Woodwork, interior and ornamental, nec

(G-1577)
BUZZI UNICEM USA INC
10333 N Meridian St Ste 235 (46290-1081)
PHONE.............................317 706-3352
EMP: 25
SALES (corp-wide): 4.69B **Privately Held**
Web: www.buzziunicemusa.com
SIC: 3241 Portland cement
HQ: Buzzi Unicem Usa Inc
 100 Brodhead Rd Ste 230
 Bethlehem PA 18017
 610 882-5000

(G-1578)
CANATURE USA INC (PA)
Also Called: Canature
9760 Mayflower Park Dr Ste 110 (46032)
PHONE.............................877 771-6789
Jeffrey L Warner, *Pr*
Michale Fiorante, *Sec*
▲ EMP: 7 EST: 1986
SALES (est): 2.23MM
SALES (corp-wide): 2.23MM **Privately Held**
Web: www.canaturewg.com
SIC: 3589 Swimming pool filter and water conditioning systems

(G-1579)
CAPTIVATED LLC
5483 Kenwood Pl (46033-8848)
PHONE.............................317 554-7400
Bryan Anderson, *Pr*
EMP: 2 EST: 2015
SALES (est): 107.74K **Privately Held**
Web: www.captivated.works
SIC: 7372 7389 Business oriented computer software; Business Activities at Non-Commercial Site

(G-1580)
CARMEL INDIANA
881 3rd Ave Sw Ste 101 (46032-3158)
PHONE.............................317 575-9942
EMP: 7 EST: 2017
SALES (est): 150.9K **Privately Held**
Web: carmel.in.gov
SIC: 2844 Perfumes, cosmetics and other toilet preparations

(G-1581)
CARMEL TROPHIES PLUS LLC
Also Called: Carmel Trophies Plus
411 N Rangeline Rd (46032-1748)
PHONE.............................317 844-3770
Ford Wilson, *Owner*
EMP: 4 EST: 1984
SALES (est): 307.73K **Privately Held**
Web: www.carmelawards.com
SIC: 5999 3479 Trophies and plaques; Etching and engraving

(G-1582)
CARMEL WELDING AND SUP CO INC
550 S Rangeline Rd (46032)
PHONE.............................317 846-3493
William K Wiggam Senior, *Owner*
William K Wiggam Junior, *Sec*
EMP: 24 EST: 1948
SQ FT: 15,000
SALES (est): 854.88K **Privately Held**
Web: www.carmelwelding.com
SIC: 5261 7692 7513 Lawn and garden equipment; Welding repair; Truck rental and leasing, no drivers

(G-1583)
CATHOLIC WOODWORKER
14844 Admiral Way N (46032-5155)
PHONE.............................317 413-4276
Jonathan Conrad, *Prin*
EMP: 4 EST: 2019
SALES (est): 93.79K **Privately Held**
Web: www.catholicwoodworker.com
SIC: 2431 Millwork

(G-1584)
CENTRAL INDIANA ETHANOL LLC
12911 N Meridian St Ste 101 (46032-1462)
PHONE.............................765 384-4001
Ryan Drook, *Pr*
EMP: 1
SALES (corp-wide): 65.49MM **Privately Held**

Web: www.cie.us
SIC: 2819 Industrial inorganic chemicals, nec
PA: Central Indiana Ethanol, Llc
 2955 W Delphi Pike
 Marion IN 46952
 765 384-4001

(G-1585)
CHEERCUSSION LLC
1091 3rd Ave Sw (46032-2523)
PHONE.............................317 762-4009
Patrick Cowherd, *COO*
EMP: 10 EST: 2011
SQ FT: 3,500
SALES (est): 1.05MM **Privately Held**
Web: www.cheercussion.com
SIC: 3949 Helmets, athletic

(G-1586)
CHERRY HILL VINEYARD LLC
10236 Ditch Rd (46032-9613)
PHONE.............................317 846-5170
Michael P Sweeney, *Prin*
EMP: 5 EST: 2005
SALES (est): 427.29K **Privately Held**
Web: www.cherryhillwinery.com
SIC: 2084 Wines

(G-1587)
CIRCLE CITY MEDICAL INC
Also Called: Bell-Horn
10850 Ruby Ct (46032-9303)
PHONE.............................317 228-1144
Todd Katz, *Pr*
▲ EMP: 7 EST: 1993
SQ FT: 6,000
SALES (est): 195.43K **Privately Held**
SIC: 3842 Braces, orthopedic

(G-1588)
CISCO SYSTEMS INC
Also Called: Cisco Systems
11711 N Meridian St Ste 250 (46032-6977)
PHONE.............................317 816-5200
EMP: 5
SALES (corp-wide): 53.8B **Publicly Held**
Web: www.cisco.com
SIC: 3577 Data conversion equipment, media-to-media: computer
PA: Cisco Systems, Inc.
 170 W Tasman Dr
 San Jose CA 95134
 408 526-4000

(G-1589)
CLASSIC CABINETS LLC
723 S Rangeline Rd (46032-2537)
PHONE.............................317 507-3775
EMP: 4 EST: 2018
SALES (est): 92.43K **Privately Held**
SIC: 2434 Wood kitchen cabinets

(G-1590)
CLINICAL ARCHITECTURE LLC (PA)
11611 N Meridian St Ste 500 (46032-4542)
PHONE.............................317 580-8400
Bob Taylor, *Chief Medical Information Officer*
EMP: 40 EST: 2007
SALES (est): 9.48MM **Privately Held**
Web: www.clinicalarchitecture.com
SIC: 8742 7372 Hospital and health services consultant; Application computer software

(G-1591)
COATS WRIGHT DE SIGN
200 S Rangeline Rd Ste 122 (46032-1941)
PHONE.............................317 569-5980
EMP: 4 EST: 2019
SALES (est): 46.08K **Privately Held**

Carmel - Hamilton County (G-1592) — GEOGRAPHIC SECTION

Web: www.coatswrightdesign.com
SIC: 3993 Signs and advertising specialties

(G-1592)
COMBI INSTIITUTE INC
12570 Lynnwood Blvd (46033-8816)
PHONE..................602 269-2288
EMP: 6 EST: 2019
SALES (est): 128.79K Privately Held
SIC: 3272 Concrete products, nec

(G-1593)
CONSTRUCTION BUS MEDIA LLC (HQ)
350 Monon Blvd (46032-2385)
PHONE..................847 359-6493
EMP: 1 EST: 2002
SALES (est): 497.73K
SALES (corp-wide): 17.11MM Privately Held
Web: www.arch-products.com
SIC: 2721 Magazines: publishing only, not printed on site
PA: Endeavor Business Media, Llc
30 Burton Hills Blvd # 185
Nashville TN 37215
800 547-7377

(G-1594)
CONTEGO INTERNATIONAL INC
334 W Greyhound Pass (46032-7007)
PHONE..................317 580-0665
EMP: 1
SALES (corp-wide): 7.5MM Privately Held
Web: www.contegointernational.com
SIC: 2851 Paints and allied products
PA: Contego International, Inc.
1013 Arthur St
Rochester IN 46975
574 223-5989

(G-1595)
CONZER SECURITY INC
1089 3rd Ave Sw Ste 200 (46032-7583)
PHONE..................317 580-9460
Dave Conley, Pr
Jeremiah Conley, COO
EMP: 4 EST: 1999
SALES (est): 542.88K Privately Held
Web: www.conzer.com
SIC: 3699 Security devices

(G-1596)
COOPERATIVE VENTURES IND CORP
Also Called: Mobius Learning
11550 N Meridian St Ste 180 (46032-6957)
PHONE..................317 564-4695
Edward J Cross, CEO
EMP: 7 EST: 2010
SQ FT: 1,200
SALES (est): 226.1K Privately Held
Web: www.mobiuslearning.com
SIC: 8331 7374 7372 Manpower training; Computer graphics service; Educational computer software

(G-1597)
CORSICA SCENTS LLC
12574 Meeting House Rd (46032-7250)
PHONE..................603 219-1287
EMP: 5 EST: 2020
SALES (est): 147.15K Privately Held
Web: www.corsicascents.com
SIC: 2844 Perfumes, cosmetics and other toilet preparations

(G-1598)
CORTEX SAFETY TECHNOLOGIES LLC
Also Called: Millercarlson
421 S Rangeline Rd (46032-2138)
PHONE..................317 414-5607
S Carlson Curtis, Managing Member
Michael Miller, Managing Member
Stephanie Carlson Curtis, Managing Member
EMP: 2 EST: 2015
SQ FT: 1,200
SALES (est): 93.2K Privately Held
SIC: 7389 8734 3586 5015 Personal service agents, brokers, and bureaus; Product testing laboratory, safety or performance; Measuring and dispensing pumps; Automotive supplies, used: wholesale and retail

(G-1599)
COTTOM AUTOMATED BUS SOLUTI
13295 Illinois St Ste 313 (46032-3022)
PHONE..................317 853-6531
John Cottom, Mng Pt
EMP: 5 EST: 2011
SALES (est): 434.93K Privately Held
SIC: 2542 5046 Shelving, office and store, except wood; Shelving, commercial and industrial

(G-1600)
CROSSROADS SOURCING GROUP LTD
737 Edison Way (46032-8223)
PHONE..................847 940-4123
Michael Kirby, Pr
Marie C Kirby, Sec
▲ EMP: 8 EST: 1998
SALES (est): 237.11K Privately Held
SIC: 2821 Plastics materials and resins

(G-1601)
CROWN PRODUCTS & SERVICES INC (PA)
12821 E New Market St Ste 310 (46032-7258)
PHONE..................317 564-4799
Doug Simmons, Pr
EMP: 4 EST: 2012
SALES (est): 470.25K
SALES (corp-wide): 470.25K Privately Held
Web: www.crownps.us
SIC: 3585 Air conditioning units, complete: domestic or industrial

(G-1602)
CURRENT PUBLISHING LLC
30 S Rangeline Rd (46032-2131)
PHONE..................317 489-4444
Brian Kelly, Prin
EMP: 39 EST: 2008
SALES (est): 1.27MM Privately Held
Web: www.youarecurrent.com
SIC: 2741 Miscellaneous publishing

(G-1603)
CUSTOMBANNERLAB
614 S Rangeline Rd (46032-2143)
PHONE..................317 956-3898
EMP: 5 EST: 2017
SALES (est): 81.58K Privately Held
Web: www.custombannerlab.com
SIC: 3993 Signs and advertising specialties

(G-1604)
DAILY MONEY MANAGERS IND LLC
P.O. Box 1086 (46082-1086)
PHONE..................317 797-0012
EMP: 1 EST: 2012
SALES (est): 201.1K Privately Held

SIC: 2711 Newspapers, publishing and printing

(G-1605)
DAVID TORTORA
Also Called: Accent Bicycles
11700 Oak Tree Way (46032-8269)
PHONE..................317 506-6902
David Tortora, Owner
EMP: 4 EST: 2015
SALES (est): 232.19K Privately Held
Web: www.accentbicycles.com
SIC: 3751 7389 Bicycles and related parts; Business services, nec

(G-1606)
DESIGN MSA INC
Also Called: M S Aronstam Jewelers
200 S Rangeline Rd Ste 217 (46032-1940)
PHONE..................317 817-9000
Marc Aronstam, Pr
EMP: 6 EST: 1979
SQ FT: 4,000
SALES (est): 829.65K Privately Held
Web: www.aronstam.com
SIC: 5944 3911 Jewelry, precious stones and precious metals; Jewelry apparel

(G-1607)
DESTRO MACHINES LLC
15015 Silver Thorne Way (46033-8979)
PHONE..................412 999-1619
Charles Destro, Managing Member
EMP: 2 EST: 2015
SALES (est): 86.27K Privately Held
Web: www.destromachines.com
SIC: 3949 Water sports equipment

(G-1608)
DIAGNOTION LLC
11611 N Meridian St Ste 455 (46032-6953)
PHONE..................317 853-1180
Richard Vanrooyen, Pr
EMP: 6 EST: 2017
SALES (est): 93.13K Privately Held
Web: www.diagnotion.com
SIC: 7372 Prepackaged software

(G-1609)
DOMCO LLC
10741 Downing St (46033-3853)
PHONE..................317 902-4404
EMP: 1 EST: 2005
SALES (est): 53.5K Privately Held
SIC: 1382 Geological exploration, oil and gas field

(G-1610)
DORON DISTRIBUTION INC
Also Called: Traffic Signal Company
1277 Helford Ln (46032-8330)
PHONE..................317 594-9259
Christine Doron, Pr
William Doron, VP
EMP: 6 EST: 1982
SALES (est): 845.96K Privately Held
Web: www.trafficsignalcompany.com
SIC: 3625 5063 Control equipment, electric; Signaling equipment, electrical

(G-1611)
DOUGLAS DYE AND ASSOCIATES INC
Also Called: Dye Woodworks
501 Industrial Dr (46032-4207)
PHONE..................317 844-1709
Douglas Dye, Pr
Lisa K Dye, VP
EMP: 5 EST: 1977
SQ FT: 13,500

SALES (est): 479.18K Privately Held
Web: www.dyewoodworks.net
SIC: 2434 2511 2436 7641 Wood kitchen cabinets; Wood household furniture; Veneer stock, softwood; Furniture repair and maintenance

(G-1612)
DOW AGROSCIENCES LLC
Also Called: Cargill Hybrid Seeds
457 3rd Ave Sw (46032-2062)
PHONE..................317 846-7873
Jerry Ravencraft, Brnch Mgr
EMP: 5
SQ FT: 20,000
SALES (corp-wide): 17.23B Publicly Held
Web: www.corteva.com
SIC: 2879 Agricultural chemicals, nec
HQ: Corteva Agriscience Llc
9330 Zionsville Rd
Indianapolis IN 46268

(G-1613)
DSH INDIANA INC
Also Called: Coasterstone
4250 W 99th St (46032-7797)
PHONE..................317 704-8130
David Glenn, Pr
▲ EMP: 1 EST: 2011
SALES (est): 763.18K Privately Held
Web: www.coasterstone.com
SIC: 3229 Art, decorative and novelty glassware

(G-1614)
DWYER ENTERPRISES
12075 Waterford Ln (46033-5501)
PHONE..................317 573-9628
William M Dwyer, Pr
EMP: 2 EST: 1977
SALES (est): 150K Privately Held
SIC: 3714 Motor vehicle body components and frame

(G-1615)
E & E GARAGE DOORS LLC
10155 N College Ave (46280-1633)
PHONE..................317 575-9677
Ed Kikendall, Owner
EMP: 1 EST: 1989
SALES (est): 93.23K Privately Held
Web: www.eedoors.com
SIC: 1751 3699 Garage door, installation or erection; Door opening and closing devices, electrical

(G-1616)
E & H INDUSTRIAL SERVICES LLC
963 Orlando St (46032-1044)
PHONE..................317 569-8819
EMP: 19 EST: 2013
SALES (est): 459.51K Privately Held
Web: www.eh-industrialservices.com
SIC: 7692 Welding repair

(G-1617)
E-MOTION LLC
493 Ironwood Dr (46033-1928)
PHONE..................317 379-5761
James Kulaga, Prin
EMP: 5 EST: 2018
SALES (est): 100.54K Privately Held
Web: www.emotion-technologies.de
SIC: 3714 Motor vehicle parts and accessories

(G-1618)
EAST COAST TREASURE FINDS LLC ✪
4000 W 106th St Ste 125-154 (46032-7720)

GEOGRAPHIC SECTION

Carmel - Hamilton County (G-1645)

PHONE.....................845 879-8744
Franjoli Rivera, *Managing Member*
EMP: 1 **EST:** 2023
SALES (est): 73.54K **Privately Held**
SIC: 3161 Clothing and apparel carrying cases

(G-1619)
ECO PARTNERS INC
515 Twin Oaks Dr (46032-9722)
P.O. Box 496 (46082-0496)
PHONE.....................317 450-3346
Elizabeth Roe, *Pr*
Gary Roe, *VP*
EMP: 4 **EST:** 1990
SALES (est): 454.61K **Privately Held**
Web: www.ecopartnersinc.com
SIC: 2721 Periodicals, publishing only

(G-1620)
EMERSON ELECTRIC CO
Also Called: Emerson
1517 Springmill Ponds Blvd (46032-8539)
PHONE.....................317 574-3170
Greg Showwalter, *Brnch Mgr*
EMP: 1
SALES (corp-wide): 15.16B **Publicly Held**
Web: www.emerson.com
SIC: 3823 Process control instruments
PA: Emerson Electric Co.
  8000 W Florissant Ave
  Saint Louis MO 63136
  314 553-2000

(G-1621)
ENDEAVOR PRECISION INC
5304 Woodfield Dr (46033-9450)
PHONE.....................317 903-0532
David Eugene Langenkamp, *Owner*
EMP: 6 **EST:** 2018
SALES (est): 141.38K **Privately Held**
Web: www.endeavorprecision.com
SIC: 3599 Machine shop, jobbing and repair

(G-1622)
ENERGY HARNESS CORPORATION
13335 Mercer St (46032-4423)
PHONE.....................239 246-1958
EMP: 4
SALES (corp-wide): 2.7MM **Privately Held**
Web: www.energyharness.com
SIC: 3646 Commercial lighting fixtures
PA: Energy Harness Corporation
  71 Mid Cape Ter Ste 8
  Cape Coral FL 33991
  239 790-3300

(G-1623)
ENERGYPOINT LLC
12400 N Meridian St Ste 180 (46032-4685)
PHONE.....................317 275-7979
EMP: 7 **EST:** 2013
SALES (est): 158.28K **Privately Held**
SIC: 3643 Power outlets and sockets

(G-1624)
ENTEGRATA INC
1950 E Greyhound Pass Ste 18 (46033-7787)
PHONE.....................949 244-1646
Thomas Baldwin, *CEO*
EMP: 3
SALES (est): 128.77K **Privately Held**
SIC: 7372 Prepackaged software

(G-1625)
ENVIRON CORPORATION
550 Congressional Blvd Ste 115 (46032)
PHONE.....................317 774-0541
Alonzo Young, *Ch*

Al Young, *Ch*
Aaron Carson, *CEO*
Jacque Brooks, *Sec*
EMP: 1 **EST:** 2006
SALES (est): 178.57K **Privately Held**
SIC: 3273 7389 Ready-mixed concrete; Business Activities at Non-Commercial Site

(G-1626)
ENVISTA LLC (PA)
11555 N Meridian St Ste 300 (46032-1677)
PHONE.....................317 208-9100
John Stitz, *CEO*
EMP: 100 **EST:** 2002
SALES (est): 81.42MM **Privately Held**
Web: www.envistacorp.com
SIC: 8742 7372 Banking and finance consultant; Application computer software

(G-1627)
ENVISTA CONCEPTS LLC
11711 N Meridian St Ste 415 (46032-4534)
PHONE.....................317 208-9100
EMP: 208 **EST:** 2003
SALES (est): 2.38MM **Privately Held**
Web: www.envistacorp.com
SIC: 7372 4731 Application computer software; Freight transportation arrangement
PA: Envista, Llc
  11555 N Meridian St # 300
  Carmel IN 46032

(G-1628)
ENVISTA ENTP SOLUTIONS LLC
11711 N Meridian St Ste 415 (46032-4534)
PHONE.....................317 208-9100
Jim Barnes, *Managing Member*
John Stitz, *Managing Member*
Davison Schopmeyer, *Managing Member*
Mike Kasperski, *Managing Member*
Ken Mullen, *Managing Member*
EMP: 105 **EST:** 2008
SALES (est): 1.14MM **Privately Held**
Web: www.envistacorp.com
SIC: 7372 8742 Application computer software; Banking and finance consultant
PA: Envista, Llc
  11555 N Meridian St # 300
  Carmel IN 46032

(G-1629)
ENVISTA FREIGHT MANAGMENT LLC
11711 N Meridian St Ste 415 (46032-4534)
PHONE.....................317 208-9100
Jim Barnes, *Managing Member*
John Stitz, *Managing Member*
Davison Schopmeyer, *Managing Member*
Mike Kasperski, *Managing Member*
Ken Mullen, *Managing Member*
EMP: 132 **EST:** 2008
SALES (est): 4.6MM **Privately Held**
Web: www.envistacorp.com
SIC: 7372 4731 Application computer software; Freight transportation arrangement
PA: Envista, Llc
  11555 N Meridian St # 300
  Carmel IN 46032

(G-1630)
EVIA CUSTOM CABINETS LLC
14221 Avian Way (46033-8304)
PHONE.....................317 987-5504
EMP: 4 **EST:** 2012
SALES (est): 122.96K **Privately Held**
SIC: 2434 Wood kitchen cabinets

(G-1631)
EXPRESS BINDING INC
1769 E 106th St (46032-4000)
PHONE.....................317 269-8114
EMP: 5 **EST:** 1997
SALES (est): 311.35K **Privately Held**
Web: www.expressbind.com
SIC: 2789 Binding only: books, pamphlets, magazines, etc.

(G-1632)
FANATICS
12011 Hoover Rd (46032-7905)
PHONE.....................317 844-5478
Dane Love, *Owner*
EMP: 1 **EST:** 1997
SALES (est): 86.47K **Privately Held**
Web: www.fanatics.com
SIC: 2521 Benches, office: wood

(G-1633)
FAST HOLSTER LLC
10376 Harrow Pl (46280-1449)
PHONE.....................317 727-5243
Jerry Clark, *Pr*
EMP: 5 **EST:** 2010
SALES (est): 223.46K **Privately Held**
SIC: 3199 Holsters, leather

(G-1634)
FAVOR IT PROMOTIONS INC
Also Called: Aef Emblem
4250 W 99th St (46032-7797)
PHONE.....................317 733-1112
Andrew Falender, *Pr*
EMP: 10 **EST:** 1991
SQ FT: 2,000
SALES (est): 954.1K **Privately Held**
Web: www.favor-it.com
SIC: 5961 5199 2395 Clothing, mail order (except women's); Advertising specialties; Embroidery and art needlework

(G-1635)
FINVANTAGE LLC
Also Called: Finvantage Solutions
275 Medical Dr Unit 633 (46082-0155)
P.O. Box 633 (46082-0633)
PHONE.....................317 500-4949
Daniel Traub, *CEO*
EMP: 10 **EST:** 2011
SALES (est): 471.51K **Privately Held**
Web: www.finvantage.com
SIC: 7372 7389 8742 Prepackaged software; Purchasing service; Materials mgmt. (purchasing, handling, inventory) consultant

(G-1636)
FIRST DATABANK INC
10 E Main St (46032)
P.O. Box 40930 (46240)
PHONE.....................317 571-7200
Mary Dial, *Brnch Mgr*
EMP: 1
SALES (corp-wide): 4.29B **Privately Held**
Web: www.fdbhealth.com
SIC: 2741 7375 Technical manuals: publishing only, not printed on site; Information retrieval services
HQ: First Databank, Inc.
  2 Tower Pl Ste 2100
  South San Francisco CA 94080
  650 588-5454

(G-1637)
G&S RESEARCH INC
3511 E Carmel Dr (46033-4314)
PHONE.....................317 815-1443
George E Grubb, *Prin*
EMP: 1 **EST:** 2001

SALES (est): 63.82K **Privately Held**
SIC: 2819 Industrial inorganic chemicals, nec

(G-1638)
GALBE MAGAZINE LLC
10540 Combs Ave (46280-1440)
PHONE.....................248 742-5231
EMP: 2 **EST:** 2015
SALES (est): 110.69K **Privately Held**
SIC: 2721 7389 Magazines: publishing and printing; Business Activities at Non-Commercial Site

(G-1639)
GAMER ENERGY LLC
13644 N Meridian St (46032-1358)
PHONE.....................317 660-9262
EMP: 5 **EST:** 2020
SALES (est): 62.38K **Privately Held**
SIC: 2086 Carbonated beverages, nonalcoholic: pkged. in cans, bottles

(G-1640)
GCI LLC
484 E Carmel Dr Ste 142 (46032)
PHONE.....................317 574-4970
EMP: 6 **EST:** 2008
SQ FT: 1,400
SALES (est): 555.04K **Privately Held**
Web: www.genchemintrnational.com
SIC: 2899 Water treating compounds

(G-1641)
GLOBALTECH MANUFACTURING LLC
14465 Welford Way (46032-7738)
PHONE.....................317 571-1910
Lixin Fan, *Admn*
EMP: 8 **EST:** 2008
SALES (est): 223.33K **Privately Held**
SIC: 3559 Sewing machines and attachments, industrial, nec

(G-1642)
GMV LLC
9621 Bramblewood Way (46032-9100)
PHONE.....................765 635-4842
EMP: 1 **EST:** 2020
SALES (est): 56.46K **Privately Held**
Web: www.gmv.com
SIC: 3089 Automotive parts, plastic

(G-1643)
GRAPE ARBOR PUBLISHING LLC
66 Rosewalk Cir Apt 1b (46032-2982)
PHONE.....................317 219-9337
Susan H Miller, *Owner*
EMP: 4 **EST:** 2017
SALES (est): 30.48K **Privately Held**
SIC: 2741 Miscellaneous publishing

(G-1644)
GREEN TEK LLC
4925 Jennings Dr (46033-9786)
PHONE.....................317 294-1614
Kimberly Suder, *Brnch Mgr*
EMP: 10
SALES (corp-wide): 115.24K **Privately Held**
Web: www.green-tek.com
SIC: 5169 2952 Organic chemicals, synthetic; Roofing felts, cements, or coatings, nec
PA: Green Tek Llc
  26283 Hummingbird Rd
  South Bend IN

(G-1645)
GRUMBLE GAMES LLC
12975 Limberlost Dr (46033-8705)
PHONE.....................317 941-6433

EMP: 1
SALES (est): 60.62K Privately Held
SIC: 7389 7372 Business Activities at Non-Commercial Site; Prepackaged software

(G-1646)
H 2 GOLF LLC
3435 Briar Creek Ln (46033-4105)
PHONE....................317 605-4720
EMP: 5 EST: 2017
SALES (est): 52.2K Privately Held
SIC: 3949 Sporting and athletic goods, nec

(G-1647)
HALO LLC (PA)
10585 N Meridian St Fl 3 (46290-1069)
PHONE....................317 575-5992
William A Bastian Ii, CEO
▼ EMP: 90 EST: 2000
SQ FT: 69,000
SALES (est): 10.2MM Privately Held
SIC: 8711 3535 Engineering services; Conveyors and conveying equipment

(G-1648)
HANCO INC
Also Called: Classico Seating
1374 Clay Spring Dr (46032-9754)
P.O. Box 48 (46970-0048)
▲ EMP: 45 EST: 1963
SQ FT: 100,000
SALES (est): 3.83MM
SALES (corp-wide): 21.68MM Privately Held
Web: www.classicoseating.com
SIC: 2599 Restaurant furniture, wood or metal
PA: Facility Concepts, Inc.
 4881 S Perry Worth Rd
 Whitestown IN 46075
 800 915-8890

(G-1649)
HANSA MEDICAL PRODUCTS INC
2000 W 106th St (46032-7918)
PHONE....................317 815-0708
Eric Blom, Pr
EMP: 2 EST: 1980
SALES (est): 125.22K Privately Held
SIC: 3841 Surgical and medical instruments

(G-1650)
HARTWARE TECHNOLOGIES
13099 Tarkington Cmn (46033-9352)
PHONE....................317 439-5816
Timothy Heston, Prin
EMP: 4 EST: 2017
SALES (est): 47.86K Privately Held
SIC: 7692 Welding repair

(G-1651)
HAVEN TECHNOLOGIES INC (PA)
873 W Carmel Dr (46032-5804)
PHONE....................317 740-0419
EMP: 30 EST: 2015
SALES (est): 4.73MM Privately Held
Web: www.isotunes.com
SIC: 3679 3663 3651 Headphones, radio; Mobile communication equipment; Music distribution apparatus

(G-1652)
HEAGY VINEYARDS LLC
10330 Holaday Dr (46032-4049)
PHONE....................317 752-4484
Raye Heagy, Prin
EMP: 5 EST: 2014
SALES (est): 205.33K Privately Held
Web: www.heagyvineyards.com
SIC: 2084 Wines

(G-1653)
HEARTLAND INDUSTRIES INC
861 N Rangeline Rd (46032-1349)
PHONE....................317 569-1718
EMP: 1 EST: 2009
SALES (est): 85.21K Privately Held
SIC: 3448 Prefabricated metal buildings and components

(G-1654)
HENNESSEY MONTAGE PRINTS
6471 Brauer Ln (46033-8839)
PHONE....................317 841-7562
John M Hennessey, Prin
EMP: 3 EST: 2016
SALES (est): 111.17K Privately Held
Web: www.hennesseymontageprints.com
SIC: 2752 Commercial printing, lithographic

(G-1655)
HERON BLUE PUBLICATIONS LLC
11157 Valeside Cres (46032-9159)
PHONE....................317 696-0674
Mark Guidone, VP
EMP: 7 EST: 2010
SALES (est): 100.48K Privately Held
SIC: 2741 Miscellaneous publishing

(G-1656)
HOFFMAN SLS & SPECIALTY CO INC
3222 Birch Canyon Dr (46033-3968)
P.O. Box 20398 (46220-0398)
PHONE....................317 846-6428
Jack Hoffman, Pr
Elinor Hoffman, Sec
EMP: 3 EST: 1985
SALES (est): 519.24K Privately Held
SIC: 5074 5084 3491 Steam fittings; Industrial machinery and equipment; Steam traps

(G-1657)
HOME MAG PUB INDIANAPOLIS
301 E Carmel Dr Ste C100 (46032-2890)
PHONE....................317 810-1341
Edward Enslin, CEO
EMP: 6 EST: 2017
SALES (est): 105.95K Privately Held
SIC: 2741 Miscellaneous publishing

(G-1658)
HOOSIER TRIBUNE CORP
Also Called: Hoosier Tribune, The
12659 Enclave Ct (46032-2332)
PHONE....................907 570-8888
Kevin Robert Patterson, CEO
Jan Need, Treas
Jill Vandegriff, Sec
Kevin Patterson, CEO
EMP: 1 EST: 2016
SALES (est): 52.61K Privately Held
SIC: 2711 8641 Newspapers: publishing only, not printed on site; Civic associations

(G-1659)
HORTON FAN SYSTEMS INC
Also Called: Horton
201 W Carmel Dr (46032-2527)
P.O. Box 9455 (55440-9455)
PHONE....................317 249-9100
▲ EMP: 131
SIC: 3564 Blowers and fans

(G-1660)
HOT HEART PRESS LLC
10617 Jordan Rd (46032-4065)
PHONE....................317 846-6057
Cheryl Reynon, Owner
EMP: 5 EST: 2017

SALES (est): 74.14K Privately Held
SIC: 2741 Miscellaneous publishing

(G-1661)
HOWMEDICA OSTEONICS CORP
Stryker Orthopaedics Division
12348 Hancock St (46032-5807)
PHONE....................317 587-2008
Michael P Mogul, Brnch Mgr
EMP: 9
SALES (corp-wide): 20.5B Publicly Held
Web: www.patientwebsitecontent.com
SIC: 3842 Surgical appliances and supplies
HQ: Howmedica Osteonics Corp.
 325 Corporate Dr
 Mahwah NJ 07430
 201 831-5000

(G-1662)
HP INC
Also Called: HP
201 W 103rd St Ste 240 (46290-1114)
PHONE....................317 566-6200
Charla Ireland, Mgr
EMP: 5
SQ FT: 40,000
SALES (corp-wide): 53.72B Publicly Held
Web: www.hp.com
SIC: 3571 Personal computers (microcomputers)
PA: Hp Inc.
 1501 Page Mill Rd
 Palo Alto CA 94304
 650 857-1501

(G-1663)
IMMINENT SOFTWARE INC
6575 Brauer Ln (46033-8841)
PHONE....................317 340-4562
Qing Ye, Prin
EMP: 2 EST: 2008
SALES (est): 159.57K Privately Held
SIC: 7372 Prepackaged software

(G-1664)
IN BUSINESS FOR LIFE INC
12400 N Meridian St Ste 150 (46032-4600)
PHONE....................317 691-6169
Christopher Mellard Mann, Dir
EMP: 7 EST: 2016
SALES (est): 123.45K Privately Held
SIC: 2759 Business forms: printing, nsk

(G-1665)
INDIANA ARTISAN INC
22 N Rangeline Rd (46032-1741)
PHONE....................317 607-8715
Eric Freeman, Prin
EMP: 1 EST: 2010
SALES (est): 181.3K Privately Held
Web: www.indianaartisan.org
SIC: 2084 Wines

(G-1666)
INDIANA CITY BREWING LLC
1036 W 136th St (46032-1314)
PHONE....................317 643-1103
EMP: 10 EST: 2012
SALES (est): 333.25K Privately Held
Web: www.frankiebunz.com
SIC: 5813 2082 5181 Tavern (drinking places); Beer (alcoholic beverage); Beer and ale

(G-1667)
INDIGO BIOAUTOMATION INC
385 City Center Dr Ste 200 (46032-3806)
PHONE....................317 493-2400
Randall K Julian, CEO
John Stewart, *

EMP: 35 EST: 2004
SALES (est): 4.64MM Privately Held
Web: www.indigobio.com
SIC: 7372 Prepackaged software

(G-1668)
INDYCOAST PARTNERS LLC
2258 Finchley Rd (46032-7347)
PHONE....................317 454-1050
David W Carfolite, Prin
EMP: 4 EST: 2009
SALES (est): 105.44K Privately Held
Web: www.indycoast.com
SIC: 2836 Culture media

(G-1669)
INFINITE AI INC
1950 E Greyhound Pass Ste 18-169 (46033-7787)
PHONE....................317 965-4850
Nathan Clark, CEO
Derek Knutsen, Dir
EMP: 4 EST: 2013
SQ FT: 300
SALES (est): 254.63K Privately Held
Web: www.infiniteai.com
SIC: 7371 7372 Computer software systems analysis and design, custom; Application computer software

(G-1670)
INNOVTIVE NUROLOGICAL DVCS LLC
Also Called: Cervella
13295 Illinois St Ste 312 (46032-3022)
PHONE....................317 674-2999
EMP: 1 EST: 2018
SALES (est): 79.45K Privately Held
Web: www.cervella.us
SIC: 3841 Surgical and medical instruments

(G-1671)
INSIGHT LPR LLC
11350 N Meridian St Ste 200 (46032)
PHONE....................855 862-5468
EMP: 15 EST: 2018
SALES (est): 4.25MM Privately Held
Web: www.insightlpr.com
SIC: 5043 3861 Photographic equipment and supplies; Photographic equipment and supplies

(G-1672)
INTEGRITY FIBER SUPPLY LLC (HQ)
10 W Carmel Dr Ste 300 (46032)
PHONE....................317 290-1140
Rick Torbeck, Managing Member
EMP: 44 EST: 2014
SALES (est): 71.7MM
SALES (corp-wide): 573.33MM Privately Held
Web: www.intfiber.com
SIC: 2611 Pulp mills, mechanical and recycling processing
PA: Schwarz Partners, L.P.
 10 W Carmel Dr Ste 300
 Carmel IN 46032
 317 290-1140

(G-1673)
IP SOFTWARE INC
10333 N Meridian St (46290-1150)
PHONE....................317 569-1313
Thomas Millay, CEO
EMP: 2 EST: 2013
SALES (est): 150.43K Privately Held
Web: www.ipanalytx.com
SIC: 7372 Prepackaged software

GEOGRAPHIC SECTION
Carmel - Hamilton County (G-1700)

(G-1674)
ITAPMENU LLC
14300 Clay Terrace Blvd Ste 200
(46032-3629)
PHONE..........................855 687-4827
Shawn Mccool, *Pr*
Michael Wilson, *Pr*
Ozan Selcuk, *VP*
EMP: 7 **EST:** 2011
SQ FT: 5,000
SALES (est): 627.26K Privately Held
Web: www.itapmenu.com
SIC: 7372 Business oriented computer software

(G-1675)
J PLUS PRODUCTS INC
4000 W 106th St Ste 125-217
(46032-7720)
PHONE..........................317 660-1003
Joseph Acklin, *Pr*
Joseph T Acklin, *Prin*
EMP: 1 **EST:** 2006
SALES (est): 129.84K Privately Held
SIC: 3089 Plastics hardware and building products

(G-1676)
JACOBS COMPANY LLC
10661 Winterwood (46032-8258)
PHONE..........................317 818-8500
EMP: 16 **EST:** 2011
SALES (est): 55.22K Privately Held
Web: www.jacobs.com
SIC: 2752 Commercial printing, lithographic

(G-1677)
JERRELS & COMPANY LLC
135 Parkview Rd (46032-5125)
PHONE..........................317 691-6045
Beth Jerrels, *Prin*
EMP: 4 **EST:** 2010
SALES (est): 75.47K Privately Held
Web: www.champagneandlipstick.com
SIC: 2844 Lipsticks

(G-1678)
JI WOODWORKING LLC
5770 Osprey Way (46033-8935)
PHONE..........................317 910-2976
Jeremy Iacocca, *Owner*
EMP: 5 **EST:** 2017
SALES (est): 43.89K Privately Held
SIC: 2431 Millwork

(G-1679)
JMR FABRICATION LLC
10636 Winterwood (46032-9688)
PHONE..........................317 682-7841
John M Roach Iii, *CEO*
EMP: 6 **EST:** 2020
SALES (est): 77.23K Privately Held
Web: www.jmrmfg.com
SIC: 3599 Machine shop, jobbing and repair

(G-1680)
KENNEY ORTHOPEDICS CARMEL LLC (HQ)
10435 N Pennsylvania St (46280-1097)
PHONE..........................317 993-3664
John M Kenney, *Managing Member*
EMP: 2 **EST:** 2015
SALES (est): 1.04MM
SALES (corp-wide): 23.4MM Privately Held
Web: www.kenneyorthopedics.com
SIC: 3842 Surgical appliances and supplies
PA: Kenney Ortho Group, Inc.
208 Normandy Ct
Nicholasville KY 40356

859 241-1015

(G-1681)
KILE ENTERPRISES INC
Also Called: AlphaGraphics
1051 3rd Ave Sw (46032-7568)
PHONE..........................317 844-6629
Michael Kile, *Pr*
Rhonda Kile, *Prin*
EMP: 15 **EST:** 2006
SALES (est): 893.75K Privately Held
Web: www.alphagraphics.com
SIC: 2752 Commercial printing, lithographic

(G-1682)
LAPTOP PUBLISHING LLC
3531 Rolling Springs Dr (46033-4452)
P.O. Box 3501 (46082-3501)
PHONE..........................317 379-5716
EMP: 4 **EST:** 2013
SALES (est): 74.21K Privately Held
Web: www.laptoppublishing.com
SIC: 2741 Miscellaneous publishing

(G-1683)
LEXINGTON PHRMCTICALS LABS LLC
14300 Clay Terrace Blvd Ste 249
(46032-3629)
PHONE..........................317 566-9750
EMP: 6 **EST:** 2013
SALES (est): 175.26K Privately Held
SIC: 2834 Pharmaceutical preparations

(G-1684)
LINNEAS LIGHTS LLC
839 W Carmel Dr (46032-5804)
P.O. Box 238 (46082-0238)
PHONE..........................317 324-4002
Laura L Cler, *Managing Member*
EMP: 3 **EST:** 2009
SALES (est): 418.68K Privately Held
Web: www.linneaandco.com
SIC: 3999 Candles

(G-1685)
LONE STAR INDUSTRIES INC (DH)
Also Called: Buzzi Unicem
10401 N Meridian St Ste 120 (46290-1090)
PHONE..........................317 706-3314
Massimo Toso, *Pr*
Nancy Krial, *
Patrick Lydon, *
▲ **EMP:** 100 **EST:** 1919
SALES (est): 358.89MM
SALES (corp-wide): 4.69B Privately Held
Web: www.lonestarind.com
SIC: 3241 3273 Portland cement; Ready-mixed concrete
HQ: Rc Lonestar Inc.
100 Brodhead Rd Ste 230
Bethlehem PA 18017

(G-1686)
LUXLY LLC
Also Called: Barnes Executive Trnsp
14549 Brackney Ln (46032-7743)
PHONE..........................617 415-8031
Sheldon Barnes, *Managing Member*
EMP: 3 **EST:** 2017
SALES (est): 135.97K Privately Held
SIC: 7363 7372 Chauffeur service; Application computer software

(G-1687)
LUXXEEN AMERICA CORPORATION ✪
3850 Birkdale Dr (46033-6610)
PHONE..........................888 589-9336
Hamid Dalir, *Pr*

EMP: 10 **EST:** 2022
SALES (est): 356.63K Privately Held
Web: www.luxxeen.com
SIC: 2676 Towels, napkins, and tissue paper products

(G-1688)
M&M INTERACTIVE INC
1661 Gotland Dr (46032-8844)
PHONE..........................317 708-1250
EMP: 5 **EST:** 2016
SALES (est): 50.49K Privately Held
Web: www.mandminteractive.com
SIC: 3652 Prerecorded records and tapes

(G-1689)
MACDESIGN INC
1009 3rd Ave Sw (46032-7568)
PHONE..........................317 580-9390
Cathey Brosseau, *Pr*
EMP: 2 **EST:** 2002
SALES (est): 201.43K Privately Held
Web: www.macdesignsinc.com
SIC: 2759 Screen printing

(G-1690)
MACO PRESS INC
560 3rd Ave Sw (46032)
P.O. Box 329 (46082)
PHONE..........................317 846-5754
Eric Seidensticker, *Pr*
George Seidensticker, *Treas*
Tomeen Seidensticker, *Sec*
EMP: 3 **EST:** 1913
SQ FT: 4,000
SALES (est): 257.07K Privately Held
Web: www.macopress.com
SIC: 2752 2759 Offset printing; Letterpress printing

(G-1691)
MAPLE LEAF GRAPHICS INC
Also Called: Skjodt Ink
13540 Kensington Pl (46032-5360)
PHONE..........................317 410-0321
Charles Skjodt, *Pr*
EMP: 3 **EST:** 1997
SALES (est): 222.73K Privately Held
SIC: 2752 Offset printing

(G-1692)
MARTIN MARIETTA MATERIALS INC
Also Called: Carmel Sand & Gravel
11010 Hazel Dell Pkwy (46280-2923)
PHONE..........................317 846-8540
EMP: 6
Web: www.martinmarietta.com
SIC: 1422 Crushed and broken limestone
PA: Martin Marietta Materials Inc
4123 Parklake Ave
Raleigh NC 27612

(G-1693)
MARTIN MARIETTA MATERIALS INC
Also Called: Martin Marietta Aggregates
12220 N Meridian Ste 100 (46032-6987)
PHONE..........................317 573-4460
John Tiberi, *VP*
EMP: 12
Web: www.martinmarietta.com
SIC: 1422 Crushed and broken limestone
PA: Martin Marietta Materials Inc
4123 Parklake Ave
Raleigh NC 27612

(G-1694)
MARTIN MARIETTA MATERIALS INC
Also Called: North Indianapolis Quarry
9825 Gray Rd (46280-1965)
PHONE..........................317 846-5942

Bob Rysinski, *Mgr*
EMP: 15
Web: www.martinmarietta.com
SIC: 1422 Crushed and broken limestone
PA: Martin Marietta Materials Inc
4123 Parklake Ave
Raleigh NC 27612

(G-1695)
MBX BIOSCIENCES INC
Also Called: Mbx
11711 N Meridian St Ste 300 (46032)
PHONE..........................317 659-0200
P Kent Hawryluk, *Pr*
Richard Bartram, *CFO*
Salomon Azoulay, *Chief Medical Officer*
EMP: 36 **EST:** 2018
SALES (est): 3.47MM Privately Held
Web: www.mbxbio.com
SIC: 8731 2834 Biotechnical research, commercial; Pharmaceutical preparations

(G-1696)
MCBETH DESIGNS INC
820 W Main St (46032-1430)
PHONE..........................317 848-7313
Beth Porter, *Pr*
Wade Porter, *Sec*
EMP: 2 **EST:** 2002
SALES (est): 147.63K Privately Held
Web: www.macdesignsinc.com
SIC: 2395 Embroidery and art needlework

(G-1697)
MERIDIAN RESOURCES LLC
13329 Dumbarton St (46032-7322)
PHONE..........................812 463-2281
Mark J Henning, *CEO*
Ericson D Briggs, *COO*
David L Briggs, *Prin*
EMP: 3 **EST:** 2017
SALES (est): 239.68K Privately Held
Web: www.meridianresourcesllc.com
SIC: 8999 8711 1311 Geological consultant; Consulting engineer; Crude petroleum and natural gas production

(G-1698)
MESH SYSTEMS LLC (PA)
801 Congressional Blvd Ste 300
(46032-5900)
PHONE..........................317 661-4800
Richard V Baxter Junior, *CEO*
Robert Wynne, *
Douglas Brune, *
EMP: 31 **EST:** 2005
SALES (est): 5.03MM
SALES (corp-wide): 5.03MM Privately Held
Web: www.meshsystems.com
SIC: 8711 7372 Electrical or electronic engineering; Application computer software

(G-1699)
MESSAGENET SYSTEMS INC
Also Called: Orchid Systems
1905 S New Market St Ste 269
(46032-7424)
PHONE..........................317 566-1677
Kevin L Brown, *Pr*
Jerome P Geis, *Sec*
EMP: 6 **EST:** 1996
SALES (est): 952.38K Privately Held
Web: www.messagenetsystems.com
SIC: 3669 Intercommunication systems, electric

(G-1700)
MITCHELL MARKETING GROUP INC
Also Called: Mr. Canary Company
2621 Towne Dr (46032-9748)

PHONE...................................317 816-7010
EMP: 1 EST: 1995
SALES (est): 243.63K Privately Held
Web: www.mrcanary.com
SIC: 2048 Bird food, prepared

(G-1701)
MOLTI GUSTI LLC
3812 Vanguard Cir (46032-9330)
PHONE...................................317 660-5692
Joseph F Albano, *Prin*
EMP: 1 EST: 2010
SALES (est): 97.98K Privately Held
SIC: 3421 Table and food cutlery, including butchers'

(G-1702)
MOORE SERVICES INCORPORATED
403 Industrial Dr (46032-4205)
PHONE...................................317 571-9800
John A Moore, *Pr*
Lisa Rork, *Mgr*
EMP: 5 EST: 1985
SALES (est): 480K Privately Held
SIC: 2752 Offset printing

(G-1703)
NEBO RIDGE ENTERPRISES LLC
Also Called: Nebo Ridge Bicycles
4335 W 106th St Ste 900 (46032-7754)
PHONE...................................317 471-1089
EMP: 4 EST: 2004
SALES (est): 215.92K Privately Held
Web: www.neboridge.com
SIC: 8748 5941 2389 Business consulting, nec; Sporting goods and bicycle shops; Apparel for handicapped

(G-1704)
NEPTUNE FLOTATION LLC
11405 Pennsylvania St Ste 106 (46032-6905)
PHONE...................................317 588-3600
Andrew W Elder, *Pr*
EMP: 10 EST: 2012
SALES (est): 1.1MM Privately Held
Web: www.pipefloat.com
SIC: 3089 Molding primary plastics

(G-1705)
NICKPRINT INC (PA)
484 E Carmel Dr (46032-2812)
PHONE...................................317 489-3033
Nick Bryant, *Prin*
EMP: 1 EST: 2010
SALES (est): 285.68K
SALES (corp-wide): 285.68K Privately Held
Web: www.nickprint.com
SIC: 2759 Screen printing

(G-1706)
NINEPLUS TABLES LLC
Also Called: Hyderabad House
14238 Chariots Whisper Dr (46074-8196)
PHONE...................................317 471-7606
EMP: 6 EST: 2019
SALES (est): 296.57K Privately Held
Web: usa.nineplus.com
SIC: 3949 Sporting and athletic goods, nec

(G-1707)
NO-LOAD FUND INVESTOR INC
10534 Coppergate (46032-9203)
PHONE...................................317 571-1471
Mark Salzingeo, *Pr*
EMP: 2 EST: 1979
SQ FT: 1,400
SALES (est): 123.23K Privately Held

SIC: 2731 Books, publishing and printing

(G-1708)
NORTHSIDE WLDG FABRICATION LLC
375 E 106th St (46280-1323)
PHONE...................................317 844-2240
Stephen A Perry, *Owner*
EMP: 1 EST: 2011
SALES (est): 46.49K Privately Held
SIC: 7692 Welding repair

(G-1709)
NSCI
301 American Way N (46032-7697)
PHONE...................................317 820-6526
EMP: 5 EST: 2017
SALES (est): 227.08K Privately Held
SIC: 3315 Steel wire and related products

(G-1710)
OEHLERS WOODS
1481 W 136th St (46032-8838)
PHONE...................................317 848-2698
Eric Oehler, *Owner*
EMP: 1 EST: 1975
SALES (est): 96.24K Privately Held
SIC: 2511 2541 2434 Wood household furniture; Wood partitions and fixtures; Wood kitchen cabinets

(G-1711)
ON-SITE WLDG MLLRIGHT SVCS LLC
9844 Chambray Dr (46280-1844)
PHONE...................................317 843-9773
Joy Sullivan, *Prin*
EMP: 1 EST: 2009
SALES (est): 96.92K Privately Held
Web: www.onsiteweldingandmillwright.com
SIC: 7692 Welding repair

(G-1712)
OPRATO SOFTWARE LLC
14155 Wicksworth Way (46032-9171)
PHONE...................................317 573-0168
Vijay Akella, *Owner*
EMP: 5 EST: 2014
SALES (est): 93.19K Privately Held
SIC: 7372 Prepackaged software

(G-1713)
OUT THE BOX TRANSIT INC
13295 Illinois St (46032-3019)
PHONE...................................317 523-0061
Comiesee Sampson, *Prin*
EMP: 5 EST: 2021
SALES (est): 352.28K Privately Held
SIC: 3537 7389 Trucks, tractors, loaders, carriers, and similar equipment; Business Activities at Non-Commercial Site

(G-1714)
PARADIGM INDUSTRIES INC
Also Called: Chemstation
12236 Hancock St (46032-5805)
PHONE...................................317 574-8590
Mark O'connell, *Pr*
EMP: 9 EST: 1985
SQ FT: 3,500
SALES (est): 2.41MM Privately Held
Web: www.paradigmindustries.net
SIC: 5169 2841 7349 Chemical additives; Soap and other detergents; Chemical cleaning services

(G-1715)
PARKE COUNTY WOOD YOU LIKE
12224 Castle Ct (46033-3114)
P.O. Box 1051 (46082-1051)
PHONE...................................317 575-9530
Jayne Sanftleben, *Prin*
EMP: 5 EST: 2016
SALES (est): 69.66K Privately Held
SIC: 2499 Wood products, nec

(G-1716)
PERFECT SEATING
1016 3rd Ave Sw (46032-2550)
PHONE...................................317 564-8173
EMP: 4 EST: 2019
SALES (est): 204.94K Privately Held
Web: www.perfectseating.net
SIC: 2211 Broadwoven fabric mills, cotton

(G-1717)
PHOENIX WOODWORKING CO LLC
3865 Penzance Pl (46032-8325)
PHONE...................................317 340-0726
EMP: 5 EST: 2017
SALES (est): 69.56K Privately Held
SIC: 2431 Millwork

(G-1718)
PINE CONE II LLC
11555 N Meridian St Ste 560 (46032-6934)
PHONE...................................463 232-3138
EMP: 5 EST: 2020
SALES (est): 78.43K Privately Held
Web: www.carmelpinecone.com
SIC: 7372 Business oriented computer software

(G-1719)
PIP MARKETING SIGNS PRINT
Also Called: PIP Printing
11711 Pennsylvania St Ste 107 (46032-4559)
PHONE...................................317 843-5755
Tony Kisstner, *Prin*
EMP: 2 EST: 2000
SALES (est): 385.66K Privately Held
Web: www.pip.com
SIC: 2752 2791 2789 Offset printing; Typesetting; Bookbinding and related work

(G-1720)
POLICYSTAT LLC
550 Congressional Blvd Ste 100 (46032-5609)
PHONE...................................317 644-1296
Steven Ehrlich, *Pr*
EMP: 73 EST: 2008
SALES (est): 9.71MM Privately Held
Web: www.rldatix.com
SIC: 7371 7372 Computer software development; Prepackaged software
PA: Icontracts, Inc.
100 Southgate Pkwy
Morristown NJ 07960

(G-1721)
POWDER LLC
1791 Hourglass Dr (46032-7203)
PHONE...................................317 581-9271
Mihir M Patel, *Owner*
EMP: 7 EST: 2018
SALES (est): 77.38K Privately Held
Web: www.schaferpowdercoating.com
SIC: 3479 Coating of metals and formed products

(G-1722)
PPG ARCHITECTURAL FINISHES INC
Also Called: Glidden Professional Paint Ctr
148 W Carmel Dr (46032-2526)

PHONE...................................317 575-8011
Brad Tnksley, *Mgr*
EMP: 2
SALES (corp-wide): 17.65B Publicly Held
Web: www.ppgpaints.com
SIC: 2851 Paints and allied products
HQ: Ppg Architectural Finishes, Inc.
1 Ppg Pl
Pittsburgh PA 15272
412 434-3131

(G-1723)
PPG ARCHITECTURAL FINISHES INC
Also Called: Porter Paints
148 W Carmel Dr (46032-2526)
PHONE...................................317 575-8011
Asa Crandall, *Mgr*
EMP: 3
SALES (corp-wide): 17.65B Publicly Held
Web: www.ppgpaints.com
SIC: 2851 Paints and allied products
HQ: Ppg Architectural Finishes, Inc.
1 Ppg Pl
Pittsburgh PA 15272
412 434-3131

(G-1724)
PPG ARCHITECTURAL FINISHES INC
Also Called: Porter Paints
10111 N Michigan Rd (46032-7945)
PHONE...................................317 471-8250
Doug Maves, *Mgr*
EMP: 7
SALES (corp-wide): 17.65B Publicly Held
Web: www.ppg.com
SIC: 2851 Paints and allied products
HQ: Ppg Architectural Finishes, Inc.
1 Ppg Pl
Pittsburgh PA 15272
412 434-3131

(G-1725)
PPG INDUSTRIES INC
Also Called: PPG 4369
10111 N Michigan Rd (46032-7945)
PHONE...................................317 870-0345
Doug Nave, *Brnch Mgr*
EMP: 4
SALES (corp-wide): 17.65B Publicly Held
Web: www.ppgpaints.com
SIC: 2851 Paints and allied products
PA: Ppg Industries, Inc.
1 Ppg Pl
Pittsburgh PA 15272
412 434-3131

(G-1726)
PRATT-KULSRUD LLC
13021 Abraham Run (46033)
PHONE...................................317 844-9122
EMP: 1 EST: 2013
SALES (est): 55.27K Privately Held
Web: www.van-griner.com
SIC: 2741 Miscellaneous publishing

(G-1727)
PRECISION ADDITIVE SOLUTIONS ◐
12950 Old Meridian St Apt 2005 (46032)
PHONE...................................419 320-6978
Thomas Stone, *CEO*
EMP: 2 EST: 2023
SALES (est): 83.76K Privately Held
SIC: 3552 Textile machinery

(G-1728)
PRESTONCBD LLC (PA)
13391 Mercer St (46032-4423)
PHONE...................................317 407-7068
Edward Preston Aguilar, *Owner*
EMP: 5 EST: 2018
SALES (est): 523.13K

GEOGRAPHIC SECTION   Carmel - Hamilton County (G-1755)

SALES (corp-wide): 523.13K Privately Held
SIC: 3999

(G-1729)
PREVINEX LLC
Also Called: Previnex
38 W Main St (46032-1764)
PHONE....................877 212-0310
David Block, CEO
EMP: 9 EST: 2013
SALES (est): 770.02K Privately Held
Web: www.previnex.com
SIC: 7371 2023 Computer software development and applications; Dietary supplements, dairy and non-dairy based

(G-1730)
PRIORITY PRESS INC
Also Called: Press 96
9609 N College Ave (46280-1627)
PHONE....................317 848-9695
Norm Melzer, Owner
EMP: 2
SALES (corp-wide): 9.15MM Privately Held
Web: www.priority-press.com
SIC: 2759 5112 5049 Commercial printing, nec; Computer paper; Engineers' equipment and supplies, nec
PA: Priority Press, Inc.
    4026 W 10th St
    Indianapolis IN 46222
    317 241-4234

(G-1731)
PROUD SPIRITS INC
Also Called: Live Proud Spirits
111 W Main St Ste 100 (46032-2064)
PHONE....................301 775-0386
Susan Kloss, COO
EMP: 7 EST: 2016
SALES (est): 62.38K Privately Held
Web: www.liveproud.com
SIC: 2084 Brandy spirits

(G-1732)
PZM INDIANA LLC
4511 W 99th St (46032-7718)
PHONE....................317 337-0441
Ken Edwards, Managing Member
◆ EMP: 5 EST: 2007
SALES (est): 458.45K Privately Held
Web: www.advancedmetalworking.com
SIC: 3444 Sheet metalwork

(G-1733)
R2 PHARMA LLC
11550 N Meridian St Ste 290 (46032-6956)
PHONE....................317 810-6205
William Culpepper, CEO
Mike Puckett, CFO
EMP: 7 EST: 2016
SALES (est): 84K Privately Held
SIC: 2834 Pharmaceutical preparations

(G-1734)
RACE CARS USA LLC
1530 Woodlake Ct (46032-9596)
PHONE....................317 508-3500
Tom Mccullough, Mng Pt
EMP: 8 EST: 2016
SALES (est): 232.84K Privately Held
SIC: 3711 Automobile assembly, including specialty automobiles

(G-1735)
RC ENTERPRISE LLC
581 S Rangeline Rd (46032-2100)
PHONE....................317 935-5628
Mark Cabbell, CEO
EMP: 2 EST: 2018
SALES (est): 320K Privately Held
Web: www.rcenterprise1.com
SIC: 1389 7389 Construction, repair, and dismantling services; Business Activities at Non-Commercial Site

(G-1736)
RED STITCH CREATIVE LLC
3547 Tahoe Rd (46033-4143)
PHONE....................202 255-8940
Bryan Avery, Owner
EMP: 6 EST: 2015
SALES (est): 77.47K Privately Held
SIC: 2395 Embroidery and art needlework

(G-1737)
REEDER & KLINE MACHINE CO INC
14042 Plantation Wood Ln (46033-9570)
PHONE....................317 846-6591
Lawrence C Sparks Iii, Pr
David Cole, *
EMP: 10 EST: 1947
SALES (est): 243.95K Privately Held
SIC: 3599 3541 Machine shop, jobbing and repair; Machine tools, metal cutting type

(G-1738)
RELEVO INC
Also Called: Relevo
5883 William Conner Way (46033-8825)
PHONE....................317 644-0099
Brian Southard, Pr
Jeffrey Southard, Prin
EMP: 3 EST: 2015
SALES (est): 318.15K Privately Held
SIC: 2834 2844 Pharmaceutical preparations ; Cosmetic preparations

(G-1739)
RELEVO LABS LLC
5883 William Conner Way (46033-8825)
PHONE....................317 900-6949
Brian Southard, Pr
Jeff Southard, Research & Development
EMP: 5 EST: 2015
SQ FT: 1,200
SALES (est): 614.49K Privately Held
SIC: 5999 2842 2844 Toiletries, cosmetics, and perfumes; Sanitation preparations, disinfectants and deodorants; Deodorants, personal

(G-1740)
RELIV
12738 Kiawah Dr (46033-8374)
PHONE....................317 507-1548
Gail Harpold, Prin
EMP: 5 EST: 2011
SALES (est): 82.64K Privately Held
Web: www.reliv.com
SIC: 2834 Vitamin, nutrient, and hematinic preparations for human use

(G-1741)
REMEDIUM SERVICES GROUP LLC
Also Called: Southside Solidification Svcs
11711 N College Ave Ste 170 (46032-5634)
PHONE....................317 660-6868
Tom Mccullough, Mng Pt
Gary Meyer, CFO
EMP: 10 EST: 2008
SALES (est): 2.49MM Privately Held
SIC: 2819 5093 Inorganic metal compounds or salts, nec; Metal scrap and waste materials

(G-1742)
ROAJER LLC
13865 Barberry Ct (46033-9581)
PHONE....................317 348-4640
Antonet Kanickainathan, Prin
Antonet Nirmala Kanickainathan, Prin
EMP: 1 EST: 2015
SALES (est): 22.9K Privately Held
SIC: 7929 7372 Entertainers and entertainment groups; Home entertainment computer software

(G-1743)
ROB PASSARELLI
219 E Admiral Way S (46032-5122)
PHONE....................317 340-8597
Rob Passarelli, Owner
EMP: 4 EST: 2019
SALES (est): 81.49K Privately Held
SIC: 3599 8711 7389 Machine and other job shop work; Engineering services; Drafting service, except temporary help

(G-1744)
ROBERT J STANKOVICH
12412 Windbush Way (46033-9151)
PHONE....................317 844-0886
Robert Stankovich, Prin
EMP: 6 EST: 2010
SALES (est): 81.76K Privately Held
SIC: 2834 Pharmaceutical preparations

(G-1745)
ROOMWORKS LLC ✪
200 S Rangeline Rd Ste 116 (46032-1940)
PHONE....................317 846-2090
Amy Kreutz, Managing Member
EMP: 1 EST: 2022
SALES (est): 69.27K Privately Held
SIC: 2434 Wood kitchen cabinets

(G-1746)
ROUGH NOTES COMPANY INC (PA)
Also Called: Insurance Publishing Plus
11690 Technology Dr (46032-5628)
P.O. Box 1990 (46082-1990)
PHONE....................317 582-1600
EMP: 25 EST: 1931
SQ FT: 15,000
SALES (est): 5.54MM Privately Held
Web: www.roughnotes.com
SIC: 2721 2741 Trade journals: publishing and printing; Art copy: publishing and printing

(G-1747)
ROUND WORLD PRODUCTS INC
75 Executive Dr Ste B (46032-2993)
P.O. Box 1792 (46082-1792)
PHONE....................317 257-7352
Christian M Knoebel, Pr
▲ EMP: 7 EST: 2010
SALES (est): 230.1K Privately Held
Web: www.waypointgeographic.com
SIC: 2741 Globe covers (maps): publishing only, not printed on site

(G-1748)
RS USED OIL SERVICES INC
4501 W 99th St Ste 1000 (46032-7768)
PHONE....................866 778-7336
Ron Winkle, Pr
EMP: 10 EST: 2002
SALES (est): 490.45K Privately Held
SIC: 1389 Oil and gas field services, nec

(G-1749)
RUMOHR
3930 Madeline Ln (46033-8427)
PHONE....................317 750-5911
Tom Rumohr, Prin
EMP: 6 EST: 2010
SALES (est): 189.01K Privately Held

SIC: 3599 Machine shop, jobbing and repair

(G-1750)
RYOBI PRESS PARTS
478 Gradle Dr Ste C (46032-2536)
PHONE....................800 901-3304
Paul Lippincott, Prin
EMP: 4 EST: 2018
SALES (est): 82.41K Privately Held
Web: www.ryobipressparts.com
SIC: 2741 Miscellaneous publishing

(G-1751)
SAHASRA TECHNOLOGIES CORP (PA)
Also Called: Stlogics
1119 Keystone Way Ste 301 (46032-3356)
PHONE....................317 845-5326
Priya Prasad, CEO
Sandeep Allam, *
Harikrishna Allam, *
EMP: 50 EST: 2004
SALES (est): 9.76MM
SALES (corp-wide): 9.76MM Privately Held
Web: www.stlogics.com
SIC: 7371 7372 Computer software development; Publisher's computer software

(G-1752)
SCHLAGE LOCK COMPANY LLC (HQ)
Also Called: Allegion
11819 Pennsylvania St (46032)
PHONE....................317 810-3700
◆ EMP: 500 EST: 1920
SALES (est): 609.63MM Privately Held
Web: www.schlage.com
SIC: 3429 Locks or lock sets
PA: Allegion Public Limited Company
    D Block D
    Dublin D02 V

(G-1753)
SCHWARZ PARTNERS LP (PA)
10 W Carmel Dr Ste 300 (46032-3365)
PHONE....................317 290-1140
Jack Schwarz, Mng Pt
John Schwarz, *
Jeff Schwarz, *
Betty Uebelhor, *
EMP: 35 EST: 1995
SQ FT: 6,000
SALES (est): 573.33MM
SALES (corp-wide): 573.33MM Privately Held
Web: www.schwarzpartners.com
SIC: 2679 Paper products, converted, nec

(G-1754)
SCOTT G KIRK
14165 Warbler Way N (46033-9651)
PHONE....................317 843-1703
Scott Kirk, Prin
EMP: 5 EST: 2014
SALES (est): 64.91K Privately Held
SIC: 3841 Surgical and medical instruments

(G-1755)
SDF ENGINEERING LLC
Also Called: Maritime Design Services
13786 Langley Dr (46032-5239)
PHONE....................317 674-2643
EMP: 1 EST: 2014
SALES (est): 74.94K Privately Held
Web: www.sdfmarine.net
SIC: 3731 4931 5169 5084 Submarines, building and repairing; Cogeneration of electric power; Industrial chemicals; Oil refining machinery, equipment, and supplies

Carmel - Hamilton County (G-1756) GEOGRAPHIC SECTION

(G-1756)
SECURITY PAKS INTL LLC
11405 Pennsylvania St Ste 106
(46032-6905)
PHONE..........................317 536-2662
Andrew Elder, *Managing Member*
EMP: 10 **EST:** 2006
SALES (est): 935.37K **Privately Held**
Web: www.securitypaks.com
SIC: 3086 Plastics foam products

(G-1757)
SEIBERTSPACE INDUSTRIES LLC
13476 Spotswood St (46032-7339)
PHONE..........................317 566-0014
Andrew Miroff, *Prin*
EMP: 1 **EST:** 2014
SALES (est): 73.32K **Privately Held**
SIC: 3999 Manufacturing industries, nec

(G-1758)
SEPRO CORPORATION (PA)
11550 N Meridian St Ste 600 (46032-4565)
PHONE..........................317 580-8282
William H Culpepper Junior, *Pr*
David Kessenich, *
Michael Puckett, *
Patrick O'keefe, *Treas*
Matthew Halverson, *
▲ **EMP:** 35 **EST:** 1993
SQ FT: 15,000
SALES (est): 69.23MM **Privately Held**
Web: www.sepro.com
SIC: 2879 7389 Agricultural disinfectants;
    Mapmaking services

(G-1759)
SHEETS LLC
10 W Carmel Dr Ste 300 (46032-3365)
PHONE..........................317 290-1140
EMP: 5 **EST:** 2001
SQ FT: 12,000
SALES (est): 3.89MM
SALES (corp-wide): 573.33MM **Privately Held**
Web: www.schwarzpartners.com
SIC: 2679 Corrugated paper: made from purchased material
PA: Schwarz Partners, L.P.
    10 W Carmel Dr Ste 300
    Carmel IN 46032
    317 290-1140

(G-1760)
SIGNS OF PROGRESS LLC
5363 Randolph Crescent Dr (46033-0006)
PHONE..........................317 340-7225
EMP: 5 **EST:** 2017
SALES (est): 71.85K **Privately Held**
SIC: 3993 Signs and advertising specialties

(G-1761)
SILK MOUNTAIN CREATIONS INC
1117 S Rangeline Rd (46032-2545)
PHONE..........................317 815-1660
David J Malone, *Prin*
EMP: 7 **EST:** 2007
SALES (est): 253.72K **Privately Held**
Web: www.silkmountaincreations.com
SIC: 2391 Draperies, plastic and textile: from purchased materials

(G-1762)
SIMPLY SAIDAHS LLC
Also Called: Simply Sdahs Natural Skin Care
4000 W 106th St Ste 125-130
(46032-7720)
PHONE..........................317 650-4256
EMP: 1 **EST:** 2014
SALES (est): 51.95K **Privately Held**

SIC: 2844 7389 Face creams or lotions;
    Business services, nec

(G-1763)
SKY CRYPTOASSETS LLC
Also Called: Noahvpn
14530 Baldwin Ln (46032-7734)
PHONE..........................949 903-6896
EMP: 1 **EST:** 2018
SALES (est): 46.23K **Privately Held**
SIC: 4813 7372 7389 Internet host services;
    Application computer software; Business Activities at Non-Commercial Site

(G-1764)
SMART PERGOLA
12958 Brighton Ave (46032-9282)
PHONE..........................317 987-7750
Claudio Bertolini, *Owner*
EMP: 5 **EST:** 2016
SALES (est): 193.75K **Privately Held**
Web: www.thesmartpergola.com
SIC: 3999 Manufacturing industries, nec

(G-1765)
SNAKE SANDBAGS LLC
1300 E 86th St Unit 90165 (46290-4606)
PHONE..........................317 721-1006
EMP: 4 **EST:** 2012
SALES (est): 57.19K **Privately Held**
Web: www.snakesandbags.com
SIC: 3999 Manufacturing industries, nec

(G-1766)
SOPHISTCTED LVING INDIANAPOLIS
200 S Rangeline Rd Ste 212 (46032-1940)
PHONE..........................317 565-4555
EMP: 16 **EST:** 2019
SALES (est): 71.13K **Privately Held**
Web: www.sophisticatedlivingmag.com
SIC: 2721 Periodicals

(G-1767)
SOUTHFIELD CORPORATION
Also Called: Indiana Brick Co.
430 W Carmel Dr (46032-2530)
PHONE..........................317 846-6060
EMP: 32
SALES (corp-wide): 99.17MM **Privately Held**
Web: www.brickworkssupply.com
SIC: 3273 1442 3241 Ready-mixed concrete
    ; Common sand mining; Natural cement
PA: Southfield Corporation
    8995 W 95th St
    Palos Hills IL 60465
    708 344-1000

(G-1768)
SPECIALTY MANUFACTURERS INC
11595 N Meridian St Ste 705 (46032-6947)
PHONE..........................317 241-1111
John W Lucas Junior, *Brnch Mgr*
EMP: 5
SALES (corp-wide): 22.09MM **Privately Held**
Web: www.spcmfg.com
SIC: 3089 Injection molding of plastics
PA: Specialty Manufacturers, Inc.
    2410 Executive Dr Ste 201
    Indianapolis IN
    317 241-1111

(G-1769)
SPECIALTY MANUFACTURING
11595 N Meridian St # 705 (46032-6947)
PHONE..........................317 587-4999
EMP: 7
SALES (est): 348.16K **Privately Held**
Web: www.gosm.com

SIC: 3999 Manufacturing industries, nec

(G-1770)
SPECTACLES OF CARMEL INC
30 1st St Sw (46032-2102)
PHONE..........................317 848-9081
EMP: 6 **EST:** 2017
SALES (est): 422.75K **Privately Held**
SIC: 3851 Spectacles

(G-1771)
STRAHMAN HOLDINGS INC (HQ)
10201 N Illinois St Ste 200 (46290-1114)
PHONE..........................317 818-5030
Jeff Graby, *CEO*
Brent Showalter, *Prin*
Eric Derheimer, *Asst Dir*
EMP: 1 **EST:** 2013
SALES (est): 9.79MM
SALES (corp-wide): 38.27MM **Privately Held**
SIC: 3494 Valves and pipe fittings, nec
PA: Flow Control Holdings, Llc
    900 N Michigan Ave # 1800
    Chicago IL 60611
    312 649-5666

(G-1772)
SUGAR CREEK HOPS LLC
1128 Laurelwood (46032-8747)
PHONE..........................317 319-1164
Spencer Gray, *Prin*
EMP: 5 **EST:** 2014
SALES (est): 64.05K **Privately Held**
Web: www.2track.info
SIC: 2082 Malt beverages

(G-1773)
SUGAR CREEK VINYRD WINERY INC
1324 Helford Ln (46032-8334)
PHONE..........................317 844-3785
David Phillips, *Prin*
EMP: 3 **EST:** 2011
SALES (est): 241.78K **Privately Held**
Web: www.sugarcreekwinery.com
SIC: 2084 Wines

(G-1774)
SWEET THINGS INC (PA)
Also Called: Sweet Things Candy & Gifts
1481 Sunray Dr Apt 105 (46280-2961)
PHONE..........................317 872-8720
Penni Brodey, *Pr*
Ronald Brodey, *Sec*
EMP: 10 **EST:** 1981
SALES (est): 1.26MM
SALES (corp-wide): 1.26MM **Privately Held**
Web: www.sweetthingsinc.com
SIC: 5441 5145 2066 Candy; Confectionery;
    Chocolate and cocoa products

(G-1775)
TALENT CABINET LLC
10903 Yorktown Xing (46032-8669)
PHONE..........................317 733-2149
Louise Jackson, *Prin*
EMP: 5 **EST:** 2016
SALES (est): 67.02K **Privately Held**
Web: www.talentcabinet.com
SIC: 2434 Wood kitchen cabinets

(G-1776)
TC HEARTLAND LLC (PA)
Also Called: Heartland Food Products Group
14390 Clay Terrace Blvd Ste 205 (46032)
PHONE..........................317 566-9750
▼ **EMP:** 967 **EST:** 2004
SALES (est): 288.9MM **Privately Held**
Web: www.heartlandfpg.com

SIC: 2087 Beverage bases, concentrates,
    syrups, powders and mixes

(G-1777)
TELAMON CORPORATION (PA)
1000 E 116th St (46032-3416)
PHONE..........................317 818-6888
Stanley Chen, *CEO*
Albert M Chen, *Ch*
▲ **EMP:** 200 **EST:** 1980
SQ FT: 130,000
SALES (est): 674.34MM
SALES (corp-wide): 674.34MM **Privately Held**
Web: www.telamon.com
SIC: 4813 8711 3357 Proprietary online
    service networks; Engineering services;
    Communication wire

(G-1778)
TELAMON ENTP VENTURES LLC
1000 E 116th St (46032-3416)
PHONE..........................317 818-6888
Jessie Wang, *Admn*
EMP: 11 **EST:** 2016
SALES (est): 486.31K **Privately Held**
Web: www.telamon.com
SIC: 8999 3845 7374 Scientific consulting;
    Electromedical equipment; Data processing and preparation

(G-1779)
TELAMON INTERNATIONAL CORP (HQ)
Also Called: Venture & Alliance Group
1000 E 116th St (46032)
PHONE..........................317 818-6888
Stan Chen, *CEO*
Stan Cheng, *CEO*
Albert Chen, *Ch Bd*
◆ **EMP:** 51 **EST:** 1985
SQ FT: 10,000
SALES (est): 89.19MM
SALES (corp-wide): 674.34MM **Privately Held**
Web: www.telamon.com
SIC: 5065 3661 Connectors, electronic;
    Fiber optics communications equipment
PA: Telamon Corporation
    1000 E 116th St
    Carmel IN 46032
    317 818-6888

(G-1780)
TELAMON SPV LLC
1000 E 116th St (46032-3416)
PHONE..........................800 788-6680
Stephanie Kim, *Pr*
Kevin P Burns, *Mgr*
Jessie Wang, *Mgr*
EMP: 6 **EST:** 2010
SALES (est): 70.5K **Privately Held**
SIC: 4813 3357 Proprietary online service
    networks; Communication wire

(G-1781)
TELAMON TECHNOLOGIES CORP
Also Called: Telamon International
1000 E 116th St (46032)
PHONE..........................317 818-6888
Stanley Chen, *CEO*
Alex Paskoff, *
Sarah Reisman, *
Kathleen Mcjohn, *Sec*
◆ **EMP:** 585 **EST:** 1982
SQ FT: 100,000
SALES (est): 492.07MM
SALES (corp-wide): 674.34MM **Privately Held**
Web: www.telamon.com

SIC: 3661 Telephones and telephone apparatus
PA: Telamon Corporation
1000 E 116th St
Carmel IN 46032
317 818-6888

(G-1782)
TELEIOS INC
191 Aspen Way (46032-2120)
PHONE..................317 509-1596
David B Robertson, Acctg Mgr
EMP: 6 EST: 2016
SALES (est): 92.36K Privately Held
Web: www.teleiosresearch.com
SIC: 3599 Machine shop, jobbing and repair

(G-1783)
TEMPEST TECHNICAL SALES INC (PA)
13295 Illinois St Ste 329 (46032-3042)
PHONE..................317 844-9236
Kevin Chatterton, Pr
Lynn Wuertemberger, Pr
Kevin Chatterton, Prin
EMP: 5 EST: 2003
SQ FT: 1,900
SALES (est): 1.01MM
SALES (corp-wide): 1.01MM Privately Held
Web: www.tempesttechsales.com
SIC: 3679 3675 3677 3625 Microwave components; Electronic capacitors; Electronic coils and transformers; Switches, electronic applications

(G-1784)
TEXAS INSTRUMENTS INCORPORATED
Also Called: Texas Instruments
12900 N Meridian St Ste 175 (46032-5402)
PHONE..................317 574-2611
Ken Smith, Brnch Mgr
EMP: 3
SALES (corp-wide): 17.52B Publicly Held
Web: www.ti.com
SIC: 3674 Semiconductors and related devices
PA: Texas Instruments Incorporated
12500 Ti Blvd
Dallas TX 75243
214 479-3773

(G-1785)
TGX MEDICAL SYSTEMS LLC
1016 Pine Hill Way (46032-7701)
PHONE..................317 575-0300
EMP: 10 EST: 2005
SALES (est): 915.39K Privately Held
Web: www.tgxmedical.com
SIC: 7372 Business oriented computer software

(G-1786)
TIMELESSMUSICGROUP LLC
9758 Innisbrook Blvd (46032-9386)
PHONE..................317 721-6671
EMP: 1
SALES (est): 46.43K Privately Held
SIC: 2782 7389 Record albums; Business Activities at Non-Commercial Site

(G-1787)
TITAN BATS LLC
14045 Pecos Ct (46033-8398)
PHONE..................317 670-8370
Todd E Stephens, Owner
EMP: 6 EST: 2014
SALES (est): 123.87K Privately Held
Web: www.titanbats.com

SIC: 3949 Sporting and athletic goods, nec

(G-1788)
TK SOFTWARE INC (PA)
11495 Pennsylvania St Ste 220 (46032-6935)
PHONE..................317 569-8887
Arthur Eaton, Prin
EMP: 3 EST: 2008
SALES (est): 992.18K
SALES (corp-wide): 992.18K Privately Held
Web: www.tksoftwareinc.com
SIC: 7372 Application computer software

(G-1789)
TPC SOFTWARE INC
490 Tulip Poplar Crst (46033-1983)
PHONE..................317 844-1480
Dale Mansberger, Pr
EMP: 5 EST: 1999
SALES (est): 286.64K Privately Held
SIC: 7372 Prepackaged software

(G-1790)
TRAVELHOST MAG INDIANAPOLIS
10254 Tammer Dr (46032-9737)
PHONE..................317 416-7780
Randy Claybrook, Pr
EMP: 1 EST: 2013
SALES (est): 85.39K Privately Held
Web: www.travelhostindy.com
SIC: 2721 Periodicals

(G-1791)
TWE WHOLESALE INC
9777 Colonial Dr (46032-9264)
PHONE..................317 450-5409
Thomas Emerson, Pr
EMP: 1 EST: 2007
SALES (est): 67.95K Privately Held
SIC: 2084 Wines

(G-1792)
U-NITT LLC
13640 Akers Dr (46074-2316)
PHONE..................812 251-9980
Julie Feng, CEO
▲ EMP: 2 EST: 2007
SALES (est): 194.61K Privately Held
Web: www.u-nitt.com
SIC: 5261 5072 3651 5051 Lawn ornaments; Garden tools, hand; Video camera-audio recorders, household use; Copper products

(G-1793)
ULTRA ATHLETE LLC
2800 N Meridian St Ste 125 (46032)
PHONE..................317 520-9898
EMP: 2 EST: 1998
SALES (est): 235.7K Privately Held
Web: www.ultraankle.com
SIC: 3842 Braces, orthopedic

(G-1794)
UNITED FEEDS
1513 Brook Mill Ct (46032-9104)
PHONE..................317 627-5637
EMP: 7 EST: 1946
SALES (est): 534.28K Privately Held
SIC: 2048 Prepared feeds, nec

(G-1795)
UNITED LEAK DETECTION INC
P.O. Box 4447 (46082-4447)
PHONE..................317 848-4447
John Jenson, Prin
EMP: 5 EST: 2008
SALES (est): 186.72K Privately Held
Web: www.unitedleak.com

SIC: 3829 Liquid leak detection equipment

(G-1796)
US OILFIELD COMPANY LLC
Also Called: US Solids Control
8925 N Meridian Ste Ste 120 (46032)
PHONE..................888 584-7565
John Bales, Pr
Martin Shraeder, CFO
EMP: 10 EST: 2013
SALES (est): 475.87K Privately Held
SIC: 1389 1381 Oil field services, nec; Directional drilling oil and gas wells

(G-1797)
VISUAL COMPONENTS N AMER CORP
Also Called: Visual Components
550 Congressional Blvd Ste 350 (46032)
PHONE..................855 823-3746
Rober Axtman, Pr
EMP: 4 EST: 2013
SALES (est): 578.31K Privately Held
Web: www.visualcomponents.com
SIC: 7372 Prepackaged software
HQ: Visual Components Oy
Vanrikinkuja 2
Espoo 02600

(G-1798)
W MICHAEL SSAN WLLS FNDTION I
4929 Deer Ridge Dr S (46033)
PHONE..................317 844-6006
Michael Wells, Owner
W Michel, Owner
EMP: 1 EST: 1996
SALES (est): 8.07K Privately Held
SIC: 3357 Nonferrous wiredrawing and insulating

(G-1799)
WASEVE LLC
12750 Horseferry Rd Ste 100 (46032-7265)
PHONE..................443 204-7976
Diana Eleojo Agada, Managing Member
EMP: 1 EST: 2018
SALES (est): 156.63K Privately Held
SIC: 8732 7372 8742 7379 Business analysis ; Business oriented computer software; Management information systems consultant; Computer related services, nec

(G-1800)
WEAVER AIR PRODUCTS LLC
1033 3rd Ave Sw Ste 212 (46032-7593)
PHONE..................317 848-4420
Jon Weaver, Owner
EMP: 3 EST: 2009
SALES (est): 382.67K Privately Held
Web: www.weaverairproducts.com
SIC: 2813 Industrial gases

(G-1801)
WEAVER POPCORN BULK LLC (PA)
303 Congressional Blvd Pmb 200 (46032-5631)
PHONE..................765 357-8413
EMP: 28 EST: 2018
SALES (est): 8.24MM
SALES (corp-wide): 8.24MM Privately Held
SIC: 3589 Popcorn machines, commercial

(G-1802)
WELL SPRING AUTOMATION LLC (PA)
366 Ridgepoint Dr (46032-2595)
PHONE..................317 324-1119
Berin Mckeown, Managing Member
EMP: 6 EST: 2016

SALES (est): 3.12MM
SALES (corp-wide): 3.12MM Privately Held
Web: www.wellspring.biz
SIC: 1389 Detection and analysis service, gas

(G-1803)
WELLSPRING WATER SERVICES LLC
366 Ridgepoint Dr (46032-2595)
PHONE..................337 962-5767
EMP: 5 EST: 2011
SALES (est): 3.12MM
SALES (corp-wide): 3.12MM Privately Held
SIC: 1382 Oil and gas exploration services
PA: Well Spring Automation Llc
366 Ridgepoint Dr
Carmel IN 46032
317 324-1119

(G-1804)
WESTWOOD PAPER COMPANY
4489 Camborne Dr (46033-2461)
PHONE..................317 843-1212
Jill W Sowder, Owner
EMP: 5 EST: 2006
SALES (est): 217.3K Privately Held
Web: www.westwoodpaper.com
SIC: 2754 Stationery and invitation printing, gravure

(G-1805)
WILEY INDUSTRIES INCORPORATED
1311 Woodgate Dr (46033-8504)
PHONE..................317 574-1477
Shannon Wiley, Prin
EMP: 2 EST: 2006
SALES (est): 133.77K Privately Held
SIC: 3999 Manufacturing industries, nec

(G-1806)
WILLIAM E STEINER
5254 Faye Ct (46033-7218)
PHONE..................317 575-9018
William E Steiner, Prin
EMP: 4 EST: 2017
SALES (est): 67.56K Privately Held
Web: www.stampalbums.com
SIC: 2752 Commercial printing, lithographic

(G-1807)
WOOD TRUSS SYSTEMS INC
784 Eden Woods Pl (46033-3015)
PHONE..................765 751-9990
EMP: 4 EST: 1987
SALES (est): 430.31K Privately Held
Web: www.woodtechsystems.com
SIC: 3541 Die sinking machines

(G-1808)
WOODFIELD PRINTING INC
9700 Lake Shore Dr E Ste E (46280-1997)
P.O. Box 1018 (46074-1018)
PHONE..................317 848-2000
Greg Pinkman, Pr
Bonnie Pinkman, Sec
EMP: 4 EST: 1988
SQ FT: 2,100
SALES (est): 307.79K Privately Held
Web: www.woodfieldprinting.com
SIC: 2752 2759 Offset printing; Commercial printing, nec

(G-1809)
WOUNDVISION LLC
10585 N Meridian St Ste 110 (46290-4513)
PHONE..................317 775-6054
EMP: 5 EST: 2012

Carmel - Hamilton County (G-1810)

GEOGRAPHIC SECTION

SALES (est): 999.55K **Privately Held**
Web: www.woundvision.com
SIC: 3578 Billing machines

(G-1810)
XPEDITED TRUCKING INC ◆
880 Monon Green Blvd (46032)
PHONE.....................463 223-7366
Nijhel Mccown, *Pr*
EMP: 10 EST: 2022
SALES (est): 548.55K **Privately Held**
SIC: 3537 7389 Trucks, tractors, loaders, carriers, and similar equipment; Business services, nec

(G-1811)
YOGURTZ
12561 N Meridian St (46032-9150)
PHONE.....................317 853-6600
Amy P Biggs, *Genl Mgr*
EMP: 6 EST: 2012
SALES (est): 158.89K **Privately Held**
Web: www.yogurtz.net
SIC: 2026 Yogurt

(G-1812)
ZANA PEABODY PUBLISHING LLC
550 Congressional Blvd Ste 115 (46032-5609)
PHONE.....................463 210-5111
EMP: 1 EST: 2021
SALES (est): 69.27K **Privately Held**
SIC: 2741 Miscellaneous publishing

Cartersburg
Hendricks County

(G-1813)
DININGER MACHINE SERVICE
6398 Amber Pass (46168-9381)
PHONE.....................317 839-6090
Douglas Meyer, *Owner*
EMP: 2 EST: 2000
SALES (est): 76.36K **Privately Held**
SIC: 3599 Machine shop, jobbing and repair

Carthage
Rush County

(G-1814)
GOOSECREEK WOODWORKING LLC
6140 W 1100 N (46115-9593)
PHONE.....................317 557-9189
EMP: 4 EST: 2019
SALES (est): 75.6K **Privately Held**
SIC: 2431 Millwork

(G-1815)
INTEGRATED SYSTEMS MGT INC
7002 W 1000 N # B (46115-9584)
P.O. Box 204 (46115-0204)
PHONE.....................765 565-6108
Mark Cosat, *Owner*
EMP: 3 EST: 1996
SALES (est): 257.45K **Privately Held**
Web: www.ismi-gunsprings.com
SIC: 3495 Gun springs, precision

(G-1816)
ONU ACRES LLC
9350 W 800 N (46115-9732)
PHONE.....................765 565-1355
James Owen, *Managing Member*
EMP: 2 EST: 2010
SALES (est): 79.22K **Privately Held**

SIC: 2211 2011 Alpacas, cotton; Lamb products, from lamb slaughtered on site

(G-1817)
RESET FAMILY SOLUTIONS LLC
501 N East St (46115-0020)
PHONE.....................317 699-2990
Latia Searcy, *CEO*
EMP: 3 EST: 2021
SALES (est): 179.77K **Privately Held**
SIC: 7299 3799 Banquet hall facilities; Transportation equipment, nec

(G-1818)
SIGNS BY SULANE INC
5920 W 850 N (46115-9456)
PHONE.....................765 565-6773
Tom Dennis, *Owner*
Barbara Dennis, *Owner*
EMP: 2 EST: 2001
SALES (est): 96.67K **Privately Held**
SIC: 3993 Signs and advertising specialties

(G-1819)
TRIPLE J IRONWORKS INC
211 S Main St (46115-9629)
P.O. Box 467 (46115-0467)
PHONE.....................765 544-9152
Joseph Collingwood Iii, *Pr*
Joseph Collingwood Iv, *VP*
EMP: 5 EST: 1996
SALES (est): 440K **Privately Held**
SIC: 3444 1791 1796 Sheet metalwork; Structural steel erection; Installing building equipment

(G-1820)
WWW WRITING CO
10700 N Carthage Pike (46115-9577)
PHONE.....................317 498-4041
Katherine Ann Smith, *Owner*
EMP: 1 EST: 2013
SALES (est): 26.63K **Privately Held**
Web: www.writing.com
SIC: 2741 Miscellaneous publishing

Cayuga
Vermillion County

(G-1821)
FABSTAR INC
200 E Maple St (47928-8243)
PHONE.....................765 230-0261
Steve York, *Pr*
Mark York, *VP*
Randal York, *VP*
EMP: 18 EST: 1994
SQ FT: 22,000
SALES (est): 639.17K **Privately Held**
Web: www.fabstar.com
SIC: 3443 Industrial vessels, tanks, and containers

(G-1822)
INTERNATIONAL PAPER COMPANY
Also Called: International Paper
2585 E 200 N (47928-8153)
PHONE.....................765 492-3341
EMP: 5
SALES (corp-wide): 18.92B **Publicly Held**
Web: www.internationalpaper.com
SIC: 2653 Boxes, corrugated: made from purchased materials
PA: International Paper Company
6400 Poplar Ave
Memphis TN 38197
901 419-7000

(G-1823)
JOHN GEBHART WOODWORKINGS
Also Called: Gebhart's Woodworking & Lumber
5352 N Fable St (47928-8057)
PHONE.....................765 492-3898
John Gebhart, *Owner*
EMP: 2 EST: 1982
SALES (est): 109.94K **Privately Held**
SIC: 2431 5211 Woodwork, interior and ornamental, nec; Millwork and lumber

Cedar Grove
Franklin County

(G-1824)
SCHINDLER WOODWORK
6006 English Hill Rd (47016-9625)
PHONE.....................513 314-5943
Cody Schindler, *Prin*
EMP: 5 EST: 2017
SALES (est): 68.1K **Privately Held**
SIC: 2431 Millwork

(G-1825)
SRK FILTERS LLC
5010 Beesley Rd (47016-9618)
PHONE.....................765 647-9962
Steve Kahles, *Prin*
EMP: 2 EST: 2010
SALES (est): 233.87K **Privately Held**
SIC: 3569 Filters

Cedar Lake
Lake County

(G-1826)
A & T CNSTR & EXCVTG INC
10212 W 128th Ave (46303-8348)
PHONE.....................219 314-2439
Christine Suttinger, *Pr*
EMP: 3 EST: 2016
SALES (est): 159.51K **Privately Held**
Web: www.aandtconstructioninc.com
SIC: 3531 1795 Buckets, excavating: clamshell, concrete, dragline, etc.; Wrecking and demolition work

(G-1827)
ARMOUR PATTERN INC
9121 W 133rd Ave (46303-8566)
PHONE.....................219 374-9325
Bert Lawrence, *Pr*
EMP: 1 EST: 1986
SALES (est): 102.31K **Privately Held**
SIC: 3543 Industrial patterns

(G-1828)
CAMILLES STUDIO
11650 Wicker Ave (46303-9793)
PHONE.....................219 365-5902
Edward Mitchell, *Owner*
EMP: 3 EST: 1965
SALES (est): 202.63K **Privately Held**
Web: www.camillestudios.com
SIC: 3271 5032 Concrete block and brick; Brick, stone, and related material

(G-1829)
CEDAR SHACK
11300 W 131st Pl (46303-9347)
PHONE.....................219 682-5531
Ralph Ells, *Owner*
EMP: 2 EST: 2003
SALES (est): 60.98K **Privately Held**
SIC: 3229 Candlesticks, glass

(G-1830)
DOWN RANGE INDUSTRIES LLC
11214 Daisy Ln (46303-7184)
PHONE.....................219 895-0834
EMP: 6 EST: 2020
SALES (est): 50K **Privately Held**
Web: www.downrangeind.com
SIC: 3317 Steel pipe and tubes

(G-1831)
GLASS SURGEONS INC
12604 Havenwood Pass (46303-8692)
PHONE.....................219 374-2500
Jack Olthoff, *Owner*
EMP: 2 EST: 1990
SALES (est): 105.19K **Privately Held**
Web: www.glasssurgeonsin.com
SIC: 3231 Windshields, glass: made from purchased glass

(G-1832)
GUND COMPANY INC
Also Called: MM&m Electrical Supply
10501 W 133rd Ave (46303-8577)
P.O. Box 376 (46303-0376)
PHONE.....................219 374-9944
Jeff Taylor, *Mgr*
EMP: 23
SALES (corp-wide): 89.99MM **Privately Held**
Web: www.thegundcompany.com
SIC: 3644 Insulators and insulation materials, electrical
PA: The Gund Company Inc
9333 Dielman Indus Dr
Saint Louis MO 63132
314 423-5200

(G-1833)
KOUDER INSTRUMENT SERVICE CO
Also Called: Kisco
9003 W 142nd Pl (46303-9097)
P.O. Box 572 (46303-0572)
PHONE.....................219 374-5935
Dan Kouder, *Pr*
Judy Kouder, *Sec*
EMP: 1 EST: 1985
SALES (est): 81K **Privately Held**
SIC: 7629 3613 Electronic equipment repair; Control panels, electric

(G-1834)
NWI SIGNS
10726 W 151st Ave (46303-9059)
PHONE.....................219 796-0948
EMP: 4 EST: 2012
SALES (est): 78.36K **Privately Held**
Web: www.simkosigns.com
SIC: 3993 Signs and advertising specialties

(G-1835)
OTTOSONS INDUSTRIES INC
12742 Wicker Ave Ste B (46303-9251)
PHONE.....................219 365-8330
Mark Speichert, *Pr*
Fred Spiechert, *VP*
EMP: 7 EST: 1971
SQ FT: 5,600
SALES (est): 374.88K **Privately Held**
Web: www.ottosonsindustries.com
SIC: 7699 3599 Hydraulic equipment repair; Machine shop, jobbing and repair

(G-1836)
SHOCKTECH USA COMPANY
8603 W 132nd Pl (46303-9508)
PHONE.....................708 557-6952
Dan Love, *Prin*
EMP: 4 EST: 2017
SALES (est): 60.8K **Privately Held**

Web: www.shocktechusa.com
SIC: 3949 Sporting and athletic goods, nec

(G-1837)
SIGNS BY DON
12998 Oakdale Pl (46303-8984)
PHONE.................................219 374-6754
Donald J Fair, *Owner*
EMP: 1 **EST:** 1987
SALES (est): 62.68K **Privately Held**
SIC: 3993 Signs and advertising specialties

(G-1838)
STERLING MACHINE CO INC
10501 W 133rd Ave Lot 6 (46303-8578)
P.O. Box 2026 (46303-2026)
PHONE.................................219 374-9360
Anthony Gatto, *Pr*
Dave Peterson, *VP*
John Allen, *Treas*
EMP: 5 **EST:** 1994
SQ FT: 6,400
SALES (est): 466.05K **Privately Held**
Web: www.horstengineering.com
SIC: 3599 Machine shop, jobbing and repair

(G-1839)
TALL OAKS WOODWORKING
12608 Tall Oaks Dr (46303-8787)
PHONE.................................708 275-5723
Alan Wojcik, *Prin*
EMP: 5 **EST:** 2018
SALES (est): 54.13K **Privately Held**
SIC: 2431 Millwork

(G-1840)
WEDGE GUYS LLC
11121 Hickory Grove Rd (46303-1301)
PHONE.................................708 362-0731
Matthew Isaacson, *Prin*
EMP: 4 **EST:** 2015
SALES (est): 207.65K **Privately Held**
Web: www.wedgeguys.com
SIC: 3949 Sporting and athletic goods, nec

Celestine
Dubois County

(G-1841)
GESSNER WOODWORKING
106 N 1000 E (47521-9648)
PHONE.................................812 389-2594
Mark Gessner, *Owner*
EMP: 2 **EST:** 1984
SALES (est): 93.29K **Privately Held**
SIC: 2499 Decorative wood and woodwork

(G-1842)
MASTERBRAND CABINETS LLC
6385 East State Road 164 (47521)
P.O. Box 420 (47547-0420)
PHONE.................................812 482-2527
Gene Buechlein, *Brnch Mgr*
EMP: 14
SALES (corp-wide): 2.73B **Publicly Held**
Web: www.woodcrestcabinets.ca
SIC: 2434 Wood kitchen cabinets
HQ: Masterbrand Cabinets Llc
   3300 Entp Pkwy Ste 300
   Beachwood OH 44122
   812 482-2527

(G-1843)
SANDER PROCESSING INCORPORATED (PA)
6614 E State Road 164 (47521-5401)
P.O. Box 68 (47521-0068)
PHONE.................................812 481-0044
Chris Sander, *Pr*

Kent Sander, *Sec*
Randy Sander, *Treas*
EMP: 10 **EST:** 1988
SALES (est): 1.9MM **Privately Held**
Web: www.sanderprocessing.com
SIC: 2013 2011 Sausages and other prepared meats; Meat packing plants

Centerpoint
Clay County

(G-1844)
GREEN MOUNTAIN INDUSTRIES LLC
603 W State Road 46 (47840-8274)
PHONE.................................812 585-1531
Hansford Mann, *Prin*
EMP: 5 **EST:** 2017
SALES (est): 127.13K **Privately Held**
SIC: 3999 Manufacturing industries, nec

(G-1845)
HEB DEVELOPMENT LLC
200 N State Road 59 (47840-8270)
PHONE.................................616 363-3825
Bill Mast, *Mng Pt*
EMP: 36
SALES (corp-wide): 2.31MM **Privately Held**
SIC: 3251 Structural brick and blocks
PA: Heb Development, Llc
   1946 Turner Ave Nw
   Grand Rapids MI 49504
   616 363-3825

(G-1846)
POLAND CHAPEL HISTORICAL SOC
5251 N Candlestick Corner Rd (47840-8131)
PHONE.................................213 977-2280
EMP: 4 **EST:** 2016
SALES (est): 39.59K **Privately Held**
SIC: 2023 Dry, condensed and evaporated dairy products

(G-1847)
R BOOE & SON HARDWOODS INC
481 N Meridian Rd (47840-8378)
PHONE.................................812 835-2663
Richard Booe, *Pr*
EMP: 35 **EST:** 1978
SQ FT: 3,000
SALES (est): 1.09MM **Privately Held**
SIC: 2421 Sawmills and planing mills, general

Centerville
Wayne County

(G-1848)
CHARLES BANE
Also Called: Pmp Enterprise
2009 Willow Grove Rd (47330-9667)
P.O. Box 116 (47330-0116)
PHONE.................................765 855-5100
Charles Bane, *Owner*
EMP: 3 **EST:** 1988
SQ FT: 1,300
SALES (est): 212.91K **Privately Held**
SIC: 3543 Foundry patternmaking

(G-1849)
GOLDEN ENGINEERING INC
6364 Means Rd (47330)
P.O. Box 185 (47330)
PHONE.................................765 855-3493
◆ **EMP:** 24 **EST:** 1972
SALES (est): 4MM **Privately Held**
Web: www.goldenengineering.com

SIC: 3844 X-ray apparatus and tubes

(G-1850)
JE MNNIX WELL SRVCING MINI E
5997 Smoker Rd (47330-9746)
PHONE.................................765 855-5464
EMP: 5 **EST:** 2021
SALES (est): 83.29K **Privately Held**
SIC: 1389 Oil field services, nec

(G-1851)
LOADED DOUGH COOKIE CO LLC
306 Deerfield Way (47330-9548)
PHONE.................................765 969-6513
EMP: 1 **EST:** 2015
SALES (est): 39.59K **Privately Held**
Web: www.loadeddough.com
SIC: 2045 5461 Doughs, frozen or refrigerated: from purchased flour; Cookies

(G-1852)
MINNIX J E WELL SERVICING
5997 Smoker Rd (47330-9746)
PHONE.................................765 855-5464
Joshua Minnix, *Owner*
EMP: 1 **EST:** 2004
SALES (est): 141.6K **Privately Held**
SIC: 1389 Oil field services, nec

(G-1853)
SCHEFFLER HARTMUT ROMANUS
Also Called: Hs Custom Manufacturing
7798 George Doherty Rd (47330-9615)
PHONE.................................765 855-2917
EMP: 1 **EST:** 2011
SALES (est): 96.06K **Privately Held**
SIC: 3449 Miscellaneous metalwork

(G-1854)
SHAFER STONEWARE
610 N Morton Ave (47330-1002)
PHONE.................................765 855-2409
Scott Shafer, *Owner*
EMP: 1 **EST:** 2001
SALES (est): 73.59K **Privately Held**
Web: www.shaferstonewarepottery.com
SIC: 3269 Stoneware pottery products

(G-1855)
WARM GLOW CANDLE COMPANY
519 W Water St (47330-1055)
P.O. Box 127 (47330-0127)
PHONE.................................765 855-5483
Jacquelyn Carberry, *Pr*
EMP: 23 **EST:** 1997
SALES (est): 2.34MM **Privately Held**
Web: www.warmglow.com
SIC: 3999 Candles

(G-1856)
WARM GLOW CANDLE OUTLET
2131 N Centerville Rd (47330-9608)
PHONE.................................765 855-2000
Jackie Carveri, *Owner*
EMP: 2 **EST:** 2002
SALES (est): 248.02K **Privately Held**
Web: www.warmglow.com
SIC: 3999 Candles

Chalmers
White County

(G-1857)
BROWN & BROWN FUEL
5774 S State Road 43 (47929-8000)
PHONE.................................219 984-5173
EMP: 4 **EST:** 2015
SALES (est): 158.98K **Privately Held**

SIC: 2869 Fuels

(G-1858)
KEN ANLIKER
Also Called: Anliker Machine
2785 S 75 W (47929-8065)
PHONE.................................219 984-5676
Ken Anliker, *Owner*
EMP: 3 **EST:** 1998
SQ FT: 30,000
SALES (est): 245.32K **Privately Held**
SIC: 3599 3548 Machine and other job shop work; Welding apparatus

Chandler
Warrick County

(G-1859)
CLOUD DEFENSIVE LLC
Also Called: Cloud Defensive
612 Grace Way (47610-9029)
PHONE.................................813 492-5683
EMP: 6 **EST:** 2018
SALES (est): 1.08MM **Privately Held**
Web: www.clouddefensive.com
SIC: 3949 3648 3643 5091 Shooting equipment and supplies, general; Flashlights; Electric switches; Hunting equipment and supplies

(G-1860)
DWD MILLER INC
10399 Telephone Rd (47610-9669)
PHONE.................................812 853-8497
EMP: 4 **EST:** 1993
SALES (est): 650.4K **Privately Held**
SIC: 3523 Driers (farm): grain, hay, and seed

(G-1861)
ELECTRONICS RESEARCH INC (PA)
7777 Gardner Rd (47610-9219)
PHONE.................................812 925-6000
◆ **EMP:** 150 **EST:** 1944
SALES (est): 33.44MM
SALES (corp-wide): 33.44MM **Privately Held**
Web: www.eriinc.com
SIC: 3663 3651 3441 Antennas, transmitting and communications; Household audio and video equipment; Fabricated structural metal

(G-1862)
HOOSIER STAMPING LLC
7988 Gardner Rd (47610-9023)
PHONE.................................812 426-2778
▲ **EMP:** 2 **EST:** 2010
SALES (est): 319.15K **Privately Held**
SIC: 3469 Stamping metal for the trade

(G-1863)
K M SPECIALTY PUMPS INC
8055 State Route 62 W (47610)
P.O. Box P.O. Box 99 (47610)
PHONE.................................812 925-3000
C Russell Welder, *Pr*
Devin Allen, *Prin*
▲ **EMP:** 10 **EST:** 1982
SQ FT: 20,000
SALES (est): 2.12MM **Privately Held**
Web: www.kmspecialty.com
SIC: 7699 3593 Hydraulic equipment repair; Fluid power cylinders, hydraulic or pneumatic

(G-1864)
MID AMERICA POWERED VEHICLES
Also Called: Mid-America Golf Car
1699 S Stevenson Station Rd (47610)

Chandler - Warrick County (G-1865)

P.O. Box 5749 (47716)
PHONE..................................812 925-7745
TOLL FREE: 888
EMP: 7 EST: 1995
SQ FT: 9,600
SALES (est): 2.09MM **Privately Held**
Web: www.golfcartonline.com
SIC: 5599 5088 7999 7699 Golf cart, powered; Golf carts; Golf cart, power, rental ; Golf club and equipment repair

(G-1865)
QUALITY COATINGS INC
1700 N State St (47610-9738)
PHONE..................................812 925-3314
Gerald R Lewis, *Pr*
Donald R Lewis, *VP*
Troy Ellis Lewis, *Ex VP*
EMP: 15 EST: 1976
SQ FT: 50,000
SALES (est): 2.44MM **Privately Held**
Web: www.qcipaint.com
SIC: 2851 Paints: oil or alkyd vehicle or water thinned

(G-1866)
SMARTER HOME TECHNOLOGY INC
355 Fuquay Rd (47610-9401)
PHONE..................................815 677-6885
Travis Carter, *Pr*
EMP: 4 EST: 2020
SALES (est): 69.85K **Privately Held**
SIC: 3651 Home entertainment equipment, electronic, nec

(G-1867)
STEPHENS WELDING LLC
1000 S State St (47610-8600)
PHONE..................................812 925-6033
Timothy D Stephens, *Prin*
EMP: 1 EST: 2010
SALES (est): 42.23K **Privately Held**
SIC: 7692 Welding repair

(G-1868)
WATERWAYS EQUIPMENT EXCH INC (PA)
1699 S Stevenson Station Rd (47610-9233)
P.O. Box 5004 (47716-5004)
PHONE..................................812 925-8104
Paul Legeay Iii, *Pr*
EMP: 2 EST: 1998
SALES (est): 474.61K
SALES (corp-wide): 474.61K **Privately Held**
Web: www.waterwaysequipment.com
SIC: 3731 Shipbuilding and repairing

Charlestown
Clark County

(G-1869)
ACTION EMBROIDERY INC
300 Pike St (47111-8608)
PHONE..................................850 626-1796
Denise Harper-higgs, *Pr*
Melony Worall, *VP*
EMP: 2 EST: 1976
SALES (est): 85.5K **Privately Held**
Web: www.actionembroideryinc.com
SIC: 7299 2261 Stitching services; Screen printing of cotton broadwoven fabrics

(G-1870)
AGGROCK QUARRIES INC
Also Called: Hanson Aggregates
5421 County Road 403 (47111-9646)
P.O. Box 275 (47172-0275)
PHONE..................................812 246-2582
Clay Vibbert, *Mgr*
John Lorsen, *Prin*
EMP: 9 EST: 2002
SALES (est): 593.96K **Privately Held**
SIC: 5032 1422 Stone, crushed or broken; Crushed and broken limestone

(G-1871)
ALLERGAN SALES LLC
1250 Patrol Rd (47111-8670)
PHONE..................................888 786-6471
EMP: 11 EST: 2002
SALES (est): 139.34K **Privately Held**
Web: www.abbvie.com
SIC: 2834 Pharmaceutical preparations

(G-1872)
C-WAY TOOL AND DIE INC
103 Industrial Way (47111-1246)
PHONE..................................812 256-6341
Bobby W Caudill, *Pr*
Bob Caudill, *Pr*
EMP: 9 EST: 1973
SQ FT: 9,600
SALES (est): 610.91K **Privately Held**
SIC: 3545 7692 3544 Machine tool accessories; Welding repair; Special dies, tools, jigs, and fixtures

(G-1873)
CHRYSO INC
10600 Highway 62 Unit 7 (47111-1250)
P.O. Box 129 (47111-0129)
PHONE..................................812 256-4220
◆ EMP: 20 EST: 1993
SALES (est): 5.29MM
SALES (corp-wide): 402.18MM **Privately Held**
Web: www.chryso.com
SIC: 3821 Crushing and grinding apparatus, laboratory
HQ: Chryso
   Tour Saint Gobain
   Courbevoie 92400

(G-1874)
DA INC (DH)
1800 Patrol Rd (47111-8509)
PHONE..................................812 730-2130
Katsuhiko Banno, *CEO*
Jeff Smith, *Pr*
Kenji Kanii, *Treas*
Yuji Matsuura, *Sec*
▲ EMP: 20 EST: 1988
SQ FT: 90,000
SALES (est): 53.67MM **Privately Held**
Web: www.daiwa-da.com
SIC: 3089 Injection molding of plastics
HQ: Kojima Industries Corporation
   3-30, Shimoichibacho
   Toyota AIC 471-0

(G-1875)
EARTH FIRST KENTUCKIANA INC (PA)
Also Called: Earth First
5511 County Road 403 (47111-9680)
P.O. Box 123 (47172-0123)
PHONE..................................812 923-1227
EMP: 10 EST: 1993
SQ FT: 6,400
SALES (est): 4.12MM **Privately Held**
Web: www.earth-first.com
SIC: 5261 2499 5251 5191 Lawn and garden supplies; Mulch or sawdust products, wood; Tools; Garden supplies

(G-1876)
EXTREME TRAILER SERVICE LLC
117 Industrial Way (47111-1246)
PHONE..................................812 406-1984
Jeffrey K Wenning, *Prin*
EMP: 25 EST: 2010
SALES (est): 2.45MM **Privately Held**
Web: www.extremetrailerservice.com
SIC: 3537 Trucks: freight, baggage, etc.: industrial, except mining

(G-1877)
H & H METAL PRODUCTS INC
104 Industrial Way (47111-1247)
PHONE..................................812 256-0444
EMP: 10 EST: 1996
SQ FT: 18,000
SALES (est): 2.46MM **Privately Held**
Web: www.hhmetalproducts.com
SIC: 3444 Metal roofing and roof drainage equipment

(G-1878)
HARPRING STEEL INC
109 Industrial Way (47111-1246)
P.O. Box 306 (47111-0306)
PHONE..................................812 256-6326
Jerry Cooper, *Pr*
Julia Cooper, *Sec*
EMP: 5 EST: 1983
SQ FT: 18,000
SALES (est): 521.86K **Privately Held**
Web: www.harpringsteel.com
SIC: 3441 1791 Building components, structural steel; Structural steel erection

(G-1879)
LOTUS DESIGNS LLC
113 Industrial Way (47111-1246)
PHONE..................................812 206-7281
David Lemay, *Owner*
EMP: 3 EST: 2004
SALES (est): 203.87K **Privately Held**
Web: www.lotusdesignlab.com
SIC: 3993 Signs and advertising specialties

(G-1880)
LSC COMMUNICATIONS US LLC
100 Quality Ct (47111-1150)
P.O. Box 157 (47111-0157)
PHONE..................................812 256-3396
Kyra Stevens, *Mgr*
EMP: 1
SALES (corp-wide): 8.23B **Privately Held**
Web: www.lsccom.com
SIC: 2759 Commercial printing, nec
HQ: Lsc Communications Us, Llc
   4101 Winfield Rd
   Warrenville IL 60555
   844 572-5720

(G-1881)
LUCAS OIL PRO PLLING PRMOTIONS
5511 County Road 403 (47111-9680)
PHONE..................................812 246-3350
Kristi Chastain, *Mgr*
EMP: 2 EST: 2006
SALES (est): 157.28K **Privately Held**
Web: www.propulling.com
SIC: 1389 Construction, repair, and dismantling services

(G-1882)
MEDLINE INDUSTRIES LP
251 Hilton Dr (47111)
PHONE..................................800 633-5463
EMP: 5
SALES (corp-wide): 7.75B **Privately Held**
Web: www.medline.com
SIC: 3841 Surgical and medical instruments
PA: Medline Industries, Lp
   3 Lakes Dr
   Northfield IL 60093
   800 633-5463

(G-1883)
MEDTECH LLC
3322 Nine Penny Ln (47111-8897)
P.O. Box 370 (47111-0370)
PHONE..................................330 715-6864
Timothy Zeis, *Prin*
EMP: 5 EST: 2019
SALES (est): 143.61K **Privately Held**
SIC: 3599 Machine shop, jobbing and repair

(G-1884)
MIKES CREATIVE WOODWORKS LLC
2405 Arrowhead Dr (47111-9312)
PHONE..................................502 649-3665
EMP: 4 EST: 2016
SALES (est): 131.3K **Privately Held**
SIC: 2431 Millwork

(G-1885)
MITTERA GROUP INC
Also Called: Mittera Charlestown
100 Quality Ct (47111-1150)
PHONE..................................812 256-3396
EMP: 1
SALES (corp-wide): 487.58MM **Privately Held**
Web: www.mittera.com
SIC: 2711 Newspapers, publishing and printing
PA: Mittera Group, Inc.
   1312 Locust St Ste 202
   Des Moines IA 50309
   515 343-5353

(G-1886)
MULZER CRUSHED STONE INC
Also Called: Mulzer Security
15602 Charlestown Bethlehem Rd (47111-9423)
PHONE..................................812 256-3346
EMP: 27
SALES (corp-wide): 34.95B **Privately Held**
Web: www.mulzer.com
SIC: 5032 1422 Brick, stone, and related material; Crushed and broken limestone
HQ: Mulzer Crushed Stone Inc
   534 Mozart St
   Tell City IN 47586
   812 547-7921

(G-1887)
NEWTON BUSINESS FORMS
104 Bates Dr (47111-8913)
PHONE..................................812 256-5399
EMP: 2 EST: 1995
SALES (est): 119.07K **Privately Held**
SIC: 2759 Invitation and stationery printing and engraving

(G-1888)
NIBCO INC
204 Pike St (47111-9612)
PHONE..................................812 256-8500
Mark Lecker, *Mgr*
EMP: 10
SALES (corp-wide): 509.67MM **Privately Held**
Web: www.nibco.com
SIC: 3089 Fittings for pipe, plastics
PA: Nibco Inc.
   1516 Middlebury St
   Elkhart IN 46516
   574 295-3000

(G-1889)
OHIO VLY FUEL INJCTION SVC INC
5905 Stacy Rd (47111-9691)
PHONE..................................812 987-5857
Mark Ward, *Owner*

EMP: 6 EST: 2010
SALES (est): 151.89K Privately Held
SIC: 2869 Fuels

(G-1890)
PATRICIA J NICKELS INC
8324 Cypress Dr (47111-9660)
PHONE.................502 489-4358
Patricia Mtiberi, Prin
EMP: 6 EST: 2012
SALES (est): 134.8K Privately Held
SIC: 3356 Nickel

(G-1891)
PRINT 2 FINISH LLC
231 Butler Ave (47111-2007)
PHONE.................812 256-5515
EMP: 5 EST: 2019
SALES (est): 83.91K Privately Held
Web: www.print2finish.com
SIC: 2752 Commercial printing, lithographic

(G-1892)
PROVISA INTERNATIONAL INC
6303 21st Century Dr (47111-7716)
PHONE.................812 207-9137
Fridsteinn Stefansson, Owner
EMP: 1 EST: 2013
SALES (est): 61.36K Privately Held
Web: www.workweartradingpost.com
SIC: 2323 Men's and boy's neckwear

(G-1893)
SOUTHERN IND LNNGS CATINGS INC
113 Industrial Way (47111-1246)
PHONE.................812 206-7250
Dave Lamy, Prin
EMP: 2 EST: 2008
SALES (est): 212.12K Privately Held
SIC: 3799 Trailer hitches

(G-1894)
SPECIALTY MFG IND INC
Also Called: Speciality Manufacturing
15412 Highway 62 Ste 2 (47111-7723)
PHONE.................812 256-4633
John M Callis, Pr
Rex Callis, Sec
James Clapp, Stockholder
▲ EMP: 22 EST: 1988
SQ FT: 22,000
SALES (est): 3MM Privately Held
Web: www.gosm.com
SIC: 3082 3085 3561 Unsupported plastics profile shapes; Plastics bottles; Pumps and pumping equipment

(G-1895)
VIKING GROUP INC
Chemtrol Division
105 Quality Ct (47111-1149)
PHONE.................812 256-8500
Franco Negron, Mgr
EMP: 255
SQ FT: 27,000
SALES (corp-wide): 2.67MM Privately Held
Web: www.vikinggroupinc.com
SIC: 3089 3084 Fittings for pipe, plastics; Plastics pipe
HQ: Viking Group, Inc.
   5150 Beltway Dr. Se
   Caledonia MI 49316

(G-1896)
WEATHERALL INDIANA INC
Also Called: Weatherall Company
106 Industrial Way (47111-1247)
PHONE.................812 256-3378
James Mccain, Pr
Chris Miloe, Sec
▼ EMP: 17 EST: 1982
SQ FT: 14,000
SALES (est): 2.42MM Privately Held
Web: www.weatherall.com
SIC: 2851 2891 Wood stains; Caulking compounds

Chesterfield
Madison County

(G-1897)
MORGAN AUTOMOTIVE
4443 State Road 32 E (46017-9525)
PHONE.................765 378-0593
Mike Morgan, Owner
EMP: 7 EST: 2007
SALES (est): 244.24K Privately Held
Web: www.morganautomotiveservice.com
SIC: 7538 7539 7694 7699 Engine repair; Automotive repair shops, nec; Rebuilding motors, except automotive; Engine repair and replacement, non-automotive

(G-1898)
SMITHS ENTERPRISES INC
Also Called: Reversible Rollers
1124 Dilts St (46017-1048)
P.O. Box 610 (46015-0610)
PHONE.................765 378-6267
Kevin Smith, Pr
Amy Smith, VP
Karen Smith, VP
EMP: 8 EST: 1982
SQ FT: 6,000
SALES (est): 961.45K Privately Held
SIC: 3089 Molding primary plastics

(G-1899)
THOMAS CUSTOM LIGHTING
207 South St (46017-1741)
PHONE.................765 378-5472
Thomas Watson, Owner
EMP: 1 EST: 1994
SALES (est): 71K Privately Held
SIC: 3646 Commercial lighting fixtures

Chesterton
Porter County

(G-1900)
ACCUCAST INDUSTRIES
1631 Pioneer Trl (46304-9383)
PHONE.................219 929-1137
EMP: 5 EST: 2000
SQ FT: 2,184
SALES (est): 242.11K Privately Held
Web: www.brickworkssupply.com
SIC: 3272 Stone, cast concrete

(G-1901)
ALUMINUM WLDG & MCH WORKS INC
225 W Dunes Hwy (46304-1274)
PHONE.................219 787-8066
Daryl T Boothe Junior, CEO
EMP: 6 EST: 1959
SALES (est): 471.14K Privately Held
Web: www.al2weld.com
SIC: 7699 3449 5084 5051 Industrial machinery and equipment repair; Miscellaneous metalwork; Welding machinery and equipment; Tubing, metal

(G-1902)
ANDRITZ HERR-VOSS STAMCO INC
1079 Lot #1, Industry Drive (46304-8853)
PHONE.................219 764-8586
EMP: 1
SALES (corp-wide): 7.83B Privately Held
Web: www.andritz.com
SIC: 3559 Metal finishing equipment for plating, etc.
HQ: Andritz Herr-Voss Stamco, Inc.
   130 Main St
   Callery PA 16024
   724 538-3180

(G-1903)
ARDENA COMPANY
1423 Parmaker (46304-8829)
PHONE.................219 926-1018
EMP: 4 EST: 2017
SALES (est): 57.11K Privately Held
Web: www.ardena.com
SIC: 2834 Pharmaceutical preparations

(G-1904)
ASHLEYS JEWELRY BY DESIGN LTD
2450 Idaho St (46304-3020)
PHONE.................219 926-9039
EMP: 5 EST: 1994
SALES (est): 500.02K Privately Held
Web: www.ashleysjewelrybydesign.com
SIC: 5944 3911 Jewelry, precious stones and precious metals; Jewelry, precious metal

(G-1905)
ASPIRE LIFESTYLE INC
709 Plaza Dr Ste 2-154 (46304-1572)
PHONE.................219 814-2591
Jerry Stallings, CEO
EMP: 4 EST: 2016
SALES (est): 87K Privately Held
SIC: 7372 8742 Business oriented computer software; Marketing consulting services

(G-1906)
B & N RENTALS LLC
1506 Washington Ave (46304-2870)
PHONE.................219 850-3304
EMP: 2
SALES (est): 74.03K Privately Held
SIC: 1389 7389 Construction, repair, and dismantling services; Business Activities at Non-Commercial Site

(G-1907)
BUTLER VINEYARDS
401 Broadway (46304-2347)
PHONE.................219 929-1400
EMP: 1
SALES (corp-wide): 215.24K Privately Held
Web: www.butlerwinery.com
SIC: 2084 Wines
PA: Butler Vineyards
   6200 E Robinson Rd
   Bloomington IN 47408
   812 332-6660

(G-1908)
CEC CONTROLS COMPANY INC
100 Brown Ave (46304-2387)
PHONE.................219 728-6007
EMP: 9 EST: 2019
SALES (est): 230.24K Privately Held
Web: www.ceccontrols.com
SIC: 3823 Process control instruments

(G-1909)
CHAD SIMONS
803 Shannon Dr (46304-3162)
PHONE.................219 405-1620
Chad Simons, Prin
EMP: 8 EST: 2009
SALES (est): 205.59K Privately Held
SIC: 2851 Removers and cleaners

(G-1910)
CHESTERTON PRINTING CO
102 Brown Ave (46304-2424)
PHONE.................219 250-2896
EMP: 6 EST: 2019
SALES (est): 143.55K Privately Held
Web: www.chestertonprinting.com
SIC: 2752 Offset printing

(G-1911)
CHICAGO COLD ROLLING LLC
250 W Us Highway 12 (46304-9727)
PHONE.................219 787-2021
R Kevin Stevick, CEO
John Van Proyen, CFO
Klaus Guip, VP Mfg
EMP: 27 EST: 1995
SALES (est): 258.48K Privately Held
SIC: 3316 Cold finishing of steel shapes

(G-1912)
CLC EMBROIDERY LLC (PA)
332 Wake Robin Dr (46304)
PHONE.................219 395-9600
Joyce M Thomas, Owner
EMP: 2 EST: 2007
SALES (est): 140.01K
SALES (corp-wide): 140.01K Privately Held
SIC: 2395 Embroidery products, except Schiffli machine

(G-1913)
CLEANINTERNET INC
1070 S Calumet Rd Unit 892 (46304-7782)
PHONE.................866 752-5326
Daniel Granquist, Pr
Robert Grant, VP
Joe Labate, VP
Bobby Fowler, VP
EMP: 5 EST: 1998
SALES (est): 888.63K Privately Held
Web: www.cleaninter.net
SIC: 7372 Application computer software

(G-1914)
CLEVELAND-CLIFFS STEEL LLC
250 W Us Highway 12 (46304-9727)
P.O. Box 2928 (46304-5428)
PHONE.................219 787-2120
Jackie Wilson, Mgr
EMP: 79
SALES (corp-wide): 22B Publicly Held
Web: www.clevelandcliffs.com
SIC: 3312 3325 3356 3316 Blast furnaces and steel mills; Rolling mill rolls, cast steel; Tin; Cold finishing of steel shapes
HQ: Cleveland-Cliffs Steel Llc
   1 S Dearborn St Fl 19
   Chicago IL 60603
   312 346-0300

(G-1915)
CLEVELND-CLFFS MNORCA MINE INC
P.O. Box 2928 (46304-5428)
PHONE.................219 787-2002
EMP: 311
SALES (corp-wide): 22B Publicly Held
SIC: 1011 Iron ore pelletizing
HQ: Cleveland-Cliffs Minorca Mine Inc.
   3210 Watling St
   East Chicago IN 46312
   219 399-1200

Chesterton - Porter County (G-1916) GEOGRAPHIC SECTION

(G-1916)
CMS TECHNOLOGIES INC
147 N Jackson Blvd Ste 1x (46304-2079)
PHONE..................................219 395-8272
Phil Glaeser, *Prin*
Mark Schlichting, *Prin*
Gary Craig, *Prin*
EMP: 5 EST: 1998
SALES (est): 476.33K **Privately Held**
SIC: 3089 Injection molding of plastics

(G-1917)
DELUX ILLUMINATION
217 S 13th St (46304-2103)
PHONE..................................219 331-9525
Alvin F Udvare Junior, *Owner*
EMP: 5 EST: 2016
SALES (est): 71.42K **Privately Held**
SIC: 2782 Blankbooks and looseleaf binders

(G-1918)
DELUXE WHEEL COMPANY
1457 N Veden Rd (46304-9551)
PHONE..................................219 395-8003
Barry Perlin, *Pr*
EMP: 1 EST: 2014
SALES (est): 113.93K **Privately Held**
Web: www.deluxewheels.com
SIC: 2782 Checkbooks

(G-1919)
DESIGN ENGINEERING
Also Called: Design Engineering Company
600 River Dr (46304-1421)
PHONE..................................219 926-2170
Al Rioli, *Owner*
EMP: 5 EST: 1997
SQ FT: 1,096
SALES (est): 85.21K **Privately Held**
Web: www.designandengineering.com
SIC: 3694 8711 3511 Engine electrical equipment; Engineering services; Turbines and turbine generator sets

(G-1920)
DLM FABRICATION
122 Washington Ave (46304-3252)
PHONE..................................219 393-8820
Michael Rollins, *Prin*
EMP: 4 EST: 2017
SALES (est): 52.96K **Privately Held**
Web: www.dlmfabrication.com
SIC: 7692 Welding repair

(G-1921)
DUNE RIDGE WINERY LLC
1240 W Beam St (46304-8910)
PHONE..................................219 548-4605
EMP: 2 EST: 1998
SALES (est): 96.06K **Privately Held**
SIC: 2084 Wines

(G-1922)
ELECTRO SEAL CORPORATION
Also Called: Northern Indiana Mfg
914 Broadway (46304-2233)
P.O. Box 46 (46304)
PHONE..................................219 926-8606
Robert B Dragani, *Pr*
EMP: 9 EST: 1974
SQ FT: 10,000
SALES (est): 3.5MM **Privately Held**
Web: www.electroseal.net
SIC: 3398 Brazing (hardening) of metal

(G-1923)
ESPI ENTERPRISES INC
Custom Packing and Seals
307 Melton Rd Ste B (46304-9777)
PHONE..................................219 787-8711
Dennis D Errichiello, *VP*
EMP: 3
SALES (corp-wide): 1.7MM **Privately Held**
Web: www.espsealing.com
SIC: 5085 3053 Packing, industrial; Gaskets; packing and sealing devices
PA: Espi Enterprises, Inc.
    10145 Queensway
    Chagrin Falls OH 44023
    440 543-8108

(G-1924)
F B MFG
864 N Calumet Ave (46304-9361)
P.O. Box 2323 (46304-0423)
PHONE..................................219 406-1318
EMP: 19 EST: 2019
SALES (est): 377.1K **Privately Held**
Web: www.fbmfg.com
SIC: 3599 Machine shop, jobbing and repair

(G-1925)
FABRICATED METALS CORP
2180 N State Road 149 (46304-8819)
PHONE..................................219 734-6896
William Moore, *Brnch Mgr*
EMP: 5
Web: www.fabricatedmetals.com
SIC: 3441 Fabricated structural metal
PA: Fabricated Metals Corp.
    4991a W Us Highway 20
    Michigan City IN 46360

(G-1926)
FIREFLIES LTD
1505 S Calumet Rd (46304-3390)
PHONE..................................219 728-6245
EMP: 7 EST: 2016
SALES (est): 246.4K **Privately Held**
Web: www.firefliesfamilyfun.com
SIC: 3674 Semiconductors and related devices

(G-1927)
FISH FACTORY
676 Mississinewa Rd (46304-1409)
PHONE..................................219 929-9375
EMP: 4 EST: 2009
SALES (est): 94.18K **Privately Held**
SIC: 2741 Miscellaneous publishing

(G-1928)
FOUR PART INC
Also Called: Datagraphic Printing
132 S Calumet Rd (46304-2447)
PHONE..................................219 926-7777
Catherine Dudak, *Pr*
Ernest Darr, *Stockholder*
Richard Halstead, *Stockholder*
Kathrin Dudak, *Pr*
EMP: 5 EST: 1989
SALES (est): 372.38K **Privately Held**
Web: www.datagraphicchesterton.com
SIC: 2752 Offset printing

(G-1929)
FRESH NEWS LLC
509 S Park Dr (46304-2937)
PHONE..................................219 929-5558
Dana Gilbertson, *Owner*
EMP: 4 EST: 2017
SALES (est): 116.26K **Privately Held**
Web: www.my-fresh-news.com
SIC: 2711 Newspapers, publishing and printing

(G-1930)
GRAPHIC22 INC
Also Called: Graphic 22
1505 N State Road 149 Ste 2 (46304-3454)
PHONE..................................219 921-5409
Marilyn Busch, *Pr*
EMP: 2 EST: 1999
SALES (est): 240.8K **Privately Held**
SIC: 2261 2262 2759 5099 Printing of cotton broadwoven fabrics; Printing, manmade fiber and silk broadwoven fabrics; Letterpress and screen printing; Signs, except electric

(G-1931)
GRAPHICALLY SPEAKING
349 Sand Creek Dr (46304-1554)
PHONE..................................219 921-1572
Lori Clair, *Prin*
EMP: 2 EST: 2007
SALES (est): 65.32K **Privately Held**
Web: www.graphicallyspeakingsigns.com
SIC: 3993 Signs and advertising specialties

(G-1932)
GRINDCO INC
Also Called: Heco
288 W 1050 N (46304-8806)
P.O. Box 819 (46304-0819)
PHONE..................................219 763-6130
Adam Bellar, *Pr*
EMP: 44 EST: 1965
SQ FT: 20,000
SALES (est): 7.36MM **Privately Held**
Web: www.hecomach.com
SIC: 3599 Custom machinery

(G-1933)
GRNWMAN LLC
1212 Jefferson Ave (46304-2924)
PHONE..................................219 359-9237
EMP: 1
SALES (est): 42.55K **Privately Held**
SIC: 2339 7389 Women's and misses' accessories; Business Activities at Non-Commercial Site

(G-1934)
HAMPTON IRONWORKS INC
542 Dunewood Dr (46304-3131)
PHONE..................................219 929-6448
Bob Hampton, *Prin*
EMP: 2 EST: 2005
SALES (est): 311.99K **Privately Held**
SIC: 3446 Architectural metalwork

(G-1935)
HEFTER INDUSTRIES
133 S Calumet Rd (46304-2433)
PHONE..................................219 728-1159
EMP: 5 EST: 2015
SALES (est): 64.76K **Privately Held**
SIC: 3999 Manufacturing industries, nec

(G-1936)
HELP4U PUBLICATIONS LLC
86 E Oak Hill Rd (46304-1363)
PHONE..................................219 771-0189
David J Olson, *Admn*
EMP: 5 EST: 2016
SALES (est): 40.51K **Privately Held**
Web: www.help4uministries.com
SIC: 2741 Miscellaneous publishing

(G-1937)
INDIANA FLAME SERVICE
250 W Us Highway 12 (46304-9727)
P.O. Box 771 (46368-0771)
PHONE..................................219 787-7129
Howard Paterson, *Pr*
EMP: 26 EST: 2003
SALES (est): 2.4MM **Privately Held**
Web: www.indianaflame.net
SIC: 3553 Scarfing machines, woodworking

(G-1938)
INDUSTRIAL ORGANIC INKS INC
1608 Fox Point Dr (46304-3147)
PHONE..................................219 878-0613
Catherine Swigon, *Pr*
EMP: 3 EST: 1999
SALES (est): 247.35K **Privately Held**
SIC: 2893 Printing ink

(G-1939)
JB BOND CONSTRUCTION LLC
252 E Burdick Rd (46304-9303)
PHONE..................................219 628-4606
Joy Bond, *Prin*
EMP: 8 EST: 2013
SALES (est): 470.2K **Privately Held**
SIC: 1521 3531 General remodeling, single-family houses; Buckets, excavating: clamshell, concrete, dragline, etc.

(G-1940)
JPS CANDLES LLC
1735 Indian Boundary Rd (46304-2627)
PHONE..................................219 728-8210
Jordan Pendleton, *Prin*
EMP: 1 EST: 2013
SALES (est): 57.13K **Privately Held**
SIC: 3999 Candles

(G-1941)
KNOWLEDGE TRADING NETWORK LLC
346 E 1200 N (46304-9525)
P.O. Box 2205 (46304-0305)
PHONE..................................219 309-5360
Peter F Brown, *Prin*
EMP: 1 EST: 2001
SALES (est): 81K **Privately Held**
Web: www.knotranet.com
SIC: 7372 Business oriented computer software

(G-1942)
KSN TECHNOLOGIES INC
364 Indian Boundary Rd Ste A (46304)
P.O. Box 624 (46304)
PHONE..................................219 877-4770
Kareem Khan, *CEO*
Rukhsana Khan, *
EMP: 26 EST: 2005
SALES (est): 2.05MM **Privately Held**
Web: www.ksntech.com
SIC: 7379 7371 7372 8748 Computer related consulting services; Software programming applications; Business oriented computer software; Business consulting, nec

(G-1943)
LANDMARK SIGNS INC
Also Called: Landmark Signs Group
7424 Industrial Ave (46304-8804)
PHONE..................................219 762-9577
Allen C O'brien, *Pr*
Mary O'brien, *VP*
EMP: 68 EST: 1999
SALES (est): 9.85MM **Privately Held**
Web: www.landmarksign.com
SIC: 3993 Electric signs

(G-1944)
LEGACY SCREEN PRINTING PROMOTI
1086 N State Road 149 (46304-8981)
PHONE..................................219 262-4000
EMP: 7 EST: 2016
SALES (est): 496.88K **Privately Held**
Web: www.legacyscreenprinting.net

GEOGRAPHIC SECTION
Churubusco - Whitley County (G-1974)

SIC: 2759 Screen printing

(G-1945)
LINDA CONTROLS LLC
402 E 1500 N (46304-9553)
PHONE.................................219 926-6979
EMP: 1 EST: 2010
SALES (est): 58.34K Privately Held
SIC: 3823 Process control instruments

(G-1946)
MANUFACTURING SOLUTION INTL
1145 Max Mochal Hwy (46304-9429)
PHONE.................................219 841-9434
EMP: 5 EST: 2017
SALES (est): 106.92K Privately Held
SIC: 3999 Manufacturing industries, nec

(G-1947)
MARTINSON CABINET SHOP
Also Called: Martinson Custom Kitchens
1245 W Us Highway 20 (46304-9409)
P.O. Box 867 (46304-0867)
PHONE.................................219 926-1566
Ronald Martinson, Owner
EMP: 4 EST: 1956
SQ FT: 6,000
SALES (est): 167.79K Privately Held
SIC: 2434 Wood kitchen cabinets

(G-1948)
MGM ENTERPRISES
1493 Hogan Ave (46304-9396)
PHONE.................................219 395-1888
George S Mcnally, Owner
EMP: 1 EST: 2010
SALES (est): 64K Privately Held
SIC: 3743 Freight cars and equipment

(G-1949)
MULLIN SIGN STUDIO
48 E 1050 N (46304-9345)
PHONE.................................219 926-8937
John Mullin, Owner
EMP: 5 EST: 2011
SALES (est): 68.85K Privately Held
SIC: 3993 Signs and advertising specialties

(G-1950)
NOTARY HAYES LLC
1050 Broadway Ste 19 (46304-2170)
PHONE.................................219 292-4531
EMP: 1
SALES (est): 69.27K Privately Held
SIC: 3953 Seal presses, notary and hand

(G-1951)
ONSITE CONSTRUCTION SERVICES
416 Jefferson Ave (46304-3237)
PHONE.................................312 723-8060
Kevin Ohare, CEO
Brianne Ohare, *
Arturo Perkitny, *
Zachary Perkitny, *
EMP: 25 EST: 2017
SALES (est): 1.11MM Privately Held
Web: www.onsiteconstructionservicesinc.com
SIC: 1795 1799 1389 7349 Demolition, buildings and other structures; Construction site cleanup; Construction, repair, and dismantling services; Building maintenance services, nec

(G-1952)
OSTERFELD INDUSTRIES
1050 Broadway # Stsuite8 (46304-2170)
PHONE.................................219 926-4646
Heather Harwood, Prin
EMP: 2 EST: 2004

SALES (est): 60.77K Privately Held
SIC: 3999 Manufacturing industries, nec

(G-1953)
P JS CUSTOM EMBROIDERING LLC
252 Haglund Rd (46304-9757)
PHONE.................................219 787-9161
James Constantine, Prin
EMP: 2 EST: 2010
SALES (est): 53.34K Privately Held
SIC: 2395 Embroidery and art needlework

(G-1954)
PREMIER LUMBER COMPANY INC
6717 Atcheson Dr (46304)
PHONE.................................219 801-6018
Sergio Magana, Pr
Esperanza Magana, VP
EMP: 7 EST: 2009
SALES (est): 80.45K Privately Held
Web: www.expiredwixdomain.com
SIC: 2448 Pallets, wood

(G-1955)
PURRFECTPLAY LLC
790 Graham Dr (46304-1660)
PHONE.................................219 926-7604
Pamela Wheelock, Owner
EMP: 3 EST: 2010
SALES (est): 175.13K Privately Held
Web: www.purrfectplay.com
SIC: 3944 Games, toys, and children's vehicles

(G-1956)
RCI HV INC
Also Called: Herr-Voss Stamco Roll Center
1079 Industry Dr (46304-8853)
PHONE.................................724 538-3180
▲ EMP: 60
SIC: 3549 3471 Coilers (metalworking machines); Plating and polishing

(G-1957)
RIMSMITH TOOL LLC
830 Sidewalk Rd (46304-9662)
PHONE.................................219 926-8665
Herbert S Lasser, Managing Member
EMP: 8 EST: 2009
SALES (est): 120.52K Privately Held
SIC: 3545 Machine tool accessories

(G-1958)
SSP TECHNOLOGIES INC
709 Plaza Dr Ste 2 (46304)
PHONE.................................888 548-4668
Gert F Semler, Pr
Gert F Semler, Admn
EMP: 4 EST: 2016
SALES (est): 512.75K Privately Held
Web: www.ssptechnologies.com
SIC: 3589 Shredders, industrial and commercial

(G-1959)
STOUT PLASTIC WELD
Also Called: U-Haul
425 S 15th St (46304-2027)
PHONE.................................219 926-7622
Terry Tharp, Pt
Scott Tharp, Pt
EMP: 10 EST: 1986
SQ FT: 1,400
SALES (est): 255.65K Privately Held
Web: offline.uhaul.com
SIC: 7513 3829 7692 Truck rental and leasing, no drivers; Testing equipment: abrasion, shearing strength, etc.; Welding repair

(G-1960)
THREE MOONS FIBERWORKS LLC
402 Broadway (46304-2318)
PHONE.................................219 841-5387
Rebecca Riley-vargas, Admn
EMP: 8 EST: 2018
SALES (est): 53.34K Privately Held
Web: www.threemoonsfiberworks.com
SIC: 2284 Thread mills

(G-1961)
TRINITY DISPLAYS LLC
Also Called: Trinity Displays
1579 S Calumet Rd (46304-3301)
PHONE.................................219 201-8733
EMP: 5 EST: 2009
SALES (est): 502.63K Privately Held
Web: www.trinitydisplays.com
SIC: 3999 7389 Advertising display products; Business Activities at Non-Commercial Site

(G-1962)
TWO STICKS INC
147 E Us Highway 20 (46304-9216)
PHONE.................................219 926-7910
EMP: 2 EST: 2011
SALES (est): 184.25K Privately Held
SIC: 3537 Trucks: freight, baggage, etc.: industrial, except mining

(G-1963)
UNIQUE SPECIALTY SERVICES LLC
307 S 18th St (46304-2041)
PHONE.................................219 395-8898
Deborah Wilson, Prin
EMP: 2 EST: 1999
SALES (est): 70K Privately Held
SIC: 3479 Coating of metals and formed products

(G-1964)
URSCHEL LABORATORIES INC (PA)
1200 Cutting Edge Dr (46304-3554)
PHONE.................................219 464-4811
Robert R Urschel, Ch Bd
Patrick C Urschel, *
Daniel R Urschel, *
Daniel Marchetti, *
◆ EMP: 415 EST: 1910
SQ FT: 250,000
SALES (est): 134.23MM
SALES (corp-wide): 134.23MM Privately Held
Web: nl.urschel.com
SIC: 3556 Cutting, chopping, grinding, mixing, and similar machinery

(G-1965)
URSCHELAIR LEASING LLC
1200 Cutting Edge Dr (46304-3554)
PHONE.................................219 464-4811
EMP: 2 EST: 2010
SALES (est): 241.14K Privately Held
SIC: 3556 7374 Food products machinery; Data processing and preparation

(G-1966)
VARIED PRODUCTS INDIANA INC
2180 N State Road 149 (46304-8819)
PHONE.................................219 763-2526
Dennis L Willard, Pr
EMP: 25 EST: 1975
SQ FT: 43,500
SALES (est): 727.41K Privately Held
Web: www.variedproducts.com
SIC: 3443 3441 Fabricated plate work (boiler shop); Fabricated structural metal

(G-1967)
WEBSTERS PROTECTIVE CASES INC
Also Called: Webster's Billing Services
709 Plaza Dr Ste 2-224 (46304-1572)
PHONE.................................219 263-3039
Connie Webster, Pr
EMP: 1 EST: 2008
SALES (est): 53.94K Privately Held
Web: www.webstersbags.com
SIC: 2393 Canvas bags

(G-1968)
WELDING CENTER
1951 Jacob Ln (46304-5305)
PHONE.................................219 921-1509
Rob Sufana, Prin
EMP: 1 EST: 2010
SALES (est): 53K Privately Held
SIC: 7692 Welding repair

(G-1969)
ZENO COMPANIES INC
505 Grant Ave (46304-2361)
PHONE.................................219 728-5126
Amy Rossetti, Prin
EMP: 6 EST: 2013
SALES (est): 483.58K Privately Held
SIC: 3993 Signs and advertising specialties

(G-1970)
ZENO SIGNS LLC
119 Broadway (46304-2476)
PHONE.................................219 250-2896
Zeno Rossetti, Owner
EMP: 5 EST: 2018
SALES (est): 150.43K Privately Held
SIC: 3993 Signs and advertising specialties

Churubusco
Whitley County

(G-1971)
143 BERKLEY LLC
6455 E Mcguire Rd (46723-9341)
PHONE.................................260 414-0369
Angela Knezevich, Prin
EMP: 4 EST: 2018
SALES (est): 93.47K Privately Held
Web: www.143berkley.com
SIC: 7372 Prepackaged software

(G-1972)
BENT TREE CUSTOM SAWING LLC
9309 Bryie Rd (46723-9207)
PHONE.................................260 693-9781
Dave Scheiber, Managing Member
EMP: 1 EST: 2005
SALES (est): 100.49K Privately Held
SIC: 2421 Custom sawmill

(G-1973)
BMC MARKETING CORP
300 E Pleasant St (46723-1809)
PHONE.................................260 693-2193
Steven Barcus, Pr
EMP: 2 EST: 1984
SQ FT: 7,500
SALES (est): 227.92K Privately Held
SIC: 3544 Special dies, tools, jigs, and fixtures

(G-1974)
BRC RUBBER & PLASTICS INC
589 S Main St (46723-2219)
PHONE.................................260 203-5300
Chuck Chaffee, Mgr
EMP: 17

Churubusco - Whitley County (G-1975)

SALES (corp-wide): 95.9MM **Privately Held**
Web: www.brcrp.com
SIC: 3061 3714 3053 Automotive rubber goods (mechanical); Motor vehicle parts and accessories; Gaskets; packing and sealing devices
PA: Brc Rubber & Plastics, Inc.
1029a W State Blvd
Fort Wayne IN 46808
260 693-2171

(G-1975)
BROWNS WOODWORKING LIMITED
4966 N 550 E (46723-9726)
PHONE..................260 693-2868
Maribeth Brown, *Prin*
EMP: 1 EST: 2006
SALES (est): 120.75K **Privately Held**
SIC: 2431 Millwork

(G-1976)
C & A TOOL ENGINEERING INC
Also Called: C & A TOOL ENGINEERING INC.
105 S Main St (46723-1712)
P.O. Box 194 (46723-0194)
PHONE..................260 693-2167
EMP: 2
Web: www.catool.com
SIC: 3544 Special dies, tools, jigs, and fixtures
HQ: C & A Tool Engineering Inc
4100 N Us 33
Churubusco IN 46723
260 693-2167

(G-1977)
C & A TOOL ENGINEERING INC
Also Called: C & A TOOL ENGINEERING INC.
118 N Main St (46723-1798)
P.O. Box 94 (46723-0094)
PHONE..................260 693-2167
EMP: 105
Web: www.catool.com
SIC: 3544 Special dies, tools, jigs, and fixtures
HQ: C & A Tool Engineering Inc
4100 N Us 33
Churubusco IN 46723
260 693-2167

(G-1978)
C & A TOOL ENGINEERING INC
Also Called: C & A TOOL ENGINEERING INC.
100 Cole St (46723)
PHONE..................260 693-2167
Richard Conrow, *Brnch Mgr*
EMP: 2
Web: www.catool.com
SIC: 3544 Diamond dies, metalworking
HQ: C & A Tool Engineering Inc
4100 N Us 33
Churubusco IN 46723
260 693-2167

(G-1979)
C & A TOOL ENGINEERING INC
Also Called: C & A TOOL ENGINEERING INC.
411 S Mulberry St (46723-2208)
PHONE..................260 693-2167
Richard Conrow, *Prin*
EMP: 2
Web: www.catool.com
SIC: 3544 Diamond dies, metalworking
HQ: C & A Tool Engineering Inc
4100 N Us 33
Churubusco IN 46723
260 693-2167

(G-1980)
C & A TOOL ENGINEERING INC
Also Called: C & A TOOL ENGINEERING INC.
119 S Mulberry St (46723)
PHONE..................260 693-2167
Richard Conrow, *Brnch Mgr*
EMP: 2
Web: www.catool.com
SIC: 3544 Diamond dies, metalworking
HQ: C & A Tool Engineering Inc
4100 N Us 33
Churubusco IN 46723
260 693-2167

(G-1981)
C & A TOOL ENGINEERING INC
Also Called: C & A TOOL ENGINEERING INC.
101 N Main St (46723-1708)
P.O. Box 94 (46723-0094)
PHONE..................260 693-2167
Richard Conrow, *Brnch Mgr*
EMP: 105
Web: www.catool.com
SIC: 3544 Diamond dies, metalworking
HQ: C & A Tool Engineering Inc
4100 N Us 33
Churubusco IN 46723
260 693-2167

(G-1982)
C & A TOOL ENGINEERING INC (HQ)
4100 N Us 33 (46723)
P.O. Box 94 (46723-0094)
PHONE..................260 693-2167
John Halverson, *Pr*
Sara Conrow, *
Robert Marr, *
EMP: 360 EST: 1977
SQ FT: 230,000
SALES (est): 90.33MM **Privately Held**
Web: www.catool.com
SIC: 3544 3545 Diamond dies, metalworking; Machine tool accessories
PA: Minebea Mitsumi Inc.
1-9-3, Higashishimbashi
Minato-Ku TKY 105-0

(G-1983)
CENTERLINE MANUFACTURING
18628 Wappes Rd (46723-9273)
PHONE..................260 348-7400
Roger Bruck, *Prin*
EMP: 5 EST: 2016
SALES (est): 79.77K **Privately Held**
Web: www.clmanufacturing.com
SIC: 3599 Machine shop, jobbing and repair

(G-1984)
EDWIN COE LLC
Also Called: Edwin Coe Spirits
6675 E Us Highway 33 (46723-9559)
PHONE..................260 438-7678
Joe Collins, *Managing Member*
EMP: 6 EST: 2016
SALES (est): 246.29K **Privately Held**
Web: www.edwincoespirits.com
SIC: 2085 Distilled and blended liquors

(G-1985)
IDEAL PRO CNC INC
6231 N 650 E (46723-9799)
P.O. Box 217 (46763-0217)
PHONE..................260 693-1954
EMP: 8 EST: 2007
SALES (est): 167.94K **Privately Held**
SIC: 3423 Hand and edge tools, nec

(G-1986)
KEYSTONE CONCRETE INC (PA)
12628 Us Highway 33 N (46723-9468)
P.O. Box 121 (46723-0121)
PHONE..................260 693-6437
Mike Hatfield, *Pr*
William Hatfield, *
Dan Hatfield, *
EMP: 26 EST: 1962
SQ FT: 8,000
SALES (est): 4.2MM
SALES (corp-wide): 4.2MM **Privately Held**
Web: www.keystoneconcreteinc.com
SIC: 3273 Ready-mixed concrete

(G-1987)
SUMMIT BUSINESS PRODUCTS INC
4506 S State Road 9 57 (46723-9606)
PHONE..................260 244-1820
James Gingerich, *Pr*
EMP: 7 EST: 1979
SALES (est): 473.44K **Privately Held**
Web: www.summitbp.com
SIC: 2752 Offset printing

(G-1988)
SURE TOOL & ENGINEERING INC
302 W Pleasant St (46723-2102)
PHONE..................260 693-2193
Steve E Barcus, *Pr*
EMP: 6 EST: 1979
SQ FT: 7,500
SALES (est): 500K **Privately Held**
SIC: 3544 3545 Special dies and tools; Machine tool accessories

(G-1989)
SWAGS WELDING SERVICES LLC
6650 E Mcguire Rd (46723-9333)
PHONE..................260 417-7510
EMP: 4 EST: 2011
SALES (est): 155.34K **Privately Held**
SIC: 7692 Welding repair

(G-1990)
TACAIR PUBLICATIONS LLC
15922 Wappes Rd (46723-9438)
PHONE..................260 429-7975
Michael Benolkin, *Owner*
EMP: 2 EST: 1997
SALES (est): 96.75K **Privately Held**
Web: www.tacair-press.com
SIC: 2741 Miscellaneous publishing

(G-1991)
TECHNCAL CNTROLS/SOLUTIONS INC
2640 N 825 E (46723-9529)
PHONE..................260 416-0329
Nancy Guisinger, *Pr*
EMP: 7 EST: 1999
SALES (est): 852.92K **Privately Held**
Web: www.tcsforcomfort.com
SIC: 3829 Measuring and controlling devices, nec

(G-1992)
U S S INC
Also Called: Utility Systems Specialists
9745 E State Road 205-57 (46723-9102)
PHONE..................260 693-1172
Diane Monroe, *Pr*
Carl Monroe, *VP*
EMP: 6 EST: 2000
SQ FT: 5,000
SALES (est): 992.82K **Privately Held**
Web: www.usspecialists.com
SIC: 3812 3728 Aircraft control systems, electronic; R and D by manuf., aircraft parts and auxiliary equipment

(G-1993)
WHITE HOUSE VENTURES LLC
4960 S 600 E-57 (46723-9120)
PHONE..................260 693-3032
EMP: 1 EST: 2004
SALES (est): 14.11K **Privately Held**
SIC: 3581 Automatic vending machines

Cicero
Hamilton County

(G-1994)
BEEFREE INC
20935 State Road 19 (46034-9369)
PHONE..................317 402-1019
Jennifer Wiese, *Prin*
EMP: 7 EST: 2010
SALES (est): 1.16MM **Privately Held**
Web: www.beefreegf.com
SIC: 5411 2043 Grocery stores; Cereal breakfast foods

(G-1995)
CREATIONS IN CANVAS VINYL
1669 Cape Charles Ct (46034-9626)
PHONE..................317 984-5712
EMP: 4 EST: 2017
SALES (est): 46.58K **Privately Held**
SIC: 2211 Canvas

(G-1996)
FRIDGE MAG
1025 Freshwater Ln (46034-9208)
PHONE..................317 442-2872
Scott Wahl, *Owner*
EMP: 5 EST: 2014
SALES (est): 94.55K **Privately Held**
SIC: 3499 Fabricated metal products, nec

(G-1997)
IRIS RUBBER CO INC
10 E Jackson St (46034-5040)
P.O. Box 737 (46034-0737)
PHONE..................317 984-3561
Steve Stewart, *Pr*
David Evans, *VP*
EMP: 17 EST: 1956
SQ FT: 7,700
SALES (est): 492.19K **Privately Held**
Web: www.irisrubber.com
SIC: 3069 3599 3061 3053 Molded rubber products; Machine shop, jobbing and repair; Mechanical rubber goods; Gaskets; packing and sealing devices

(G-1998)
LINDE INC
Also Called: Praxair
1420 Bayswater Ln (46034-9404)
PHONE..................317 984-7002
EMP: 1
Web: www.lindeus.com
SIC: 2813 Industrial gases
HQ: Linde Inc.
10 Riverview Dr
Danbury CT 06810
203 837-2000

(G-1999)
PING CUSTOM DRAPERY WORKROOM
Also Called: Ping's Custom Drapery
11313 E 234th St (46034-9462)
PHONE..................317 984-3251
Mary Beth Ping, *Owner*
EMP: 2 EST: 1967
SQ FT: 2,000
SALES (est): 77K **Privately Held**
Web: www.pingdrapery.com

SIC: 2391 Curtains and draperies

(G-2000)
RANDOLPH CARPET-TILE CLEANING
59 W Armitage Dr (46034-9321)
PHONE.....................317 401-2300
Jeff Randolph, Mgr
EMP: 4 EST: 2017
SALES (est): 79.98K Privately Held
SIC: 3582 Commercial laundry equipment

(G-2001)
SYSTEM SOLUTIONS INC
4 Forest Bay Ln (46034-9744)
PHONE.....................317 877-7572
Michael O'cull, Pr
EMP: 2 EST: 1996
SALES (est): 224.66K Privately Held
Web: www.systemsolutionsinc.com
SIC: 3825 Test equipment for electronic and electrical circuits

(G-2002)
UNRIVALED INTERIORS LLC (PA)
24000 Twilight Hills Dr (46034)
PHONE.....................317 509-0496
Jason Cosand, Prin
EMP: 1 EST: 2017
SALES (est): 27.98K
SALES (corp-wide): 27.98K Privately Held
Web: www.unrivaledinteriors.com
SIC: 3531 Construction machinery

(G-2003)
UNRIVALED INTERIORS LLC
24000 Twilight Hills Dr (46034-9544)
PHONE.....................317 509-0496
Jason Cosand, Brnch Mgr
EMP: 1
SALES (corp-wide): 27.98K Privately Held
Web: www.unrivaledinteriors.com
SIC: 3531 7389 Blades for graders, scrapers, dozers, and snow plows; Interior design services
PA: Unrivaled Interiors Llc
24000 Twighlight Hills Dr
Cicero IN 46034
317 509-0496

Clarks Hill
Tippecanoe County

(G-2004)
LYNN BECK
9950 S 1000 E (47930-9268)
PHONE.....................765 523-2260
Lynn Beck, Prin
EMP: 5 EST: 2010
SALES (est): 110.84K Privately Held
SIC: 2741 Miscellaneous publishing

Clarksville
Clark County

(G-2005)
A-1 PALLET CO INC CLARKSVILLE
Also Called: A-1 Pallet
1507 Progress Way (47129-9231)
PHONE.....................812 288-6339
Billy Waters, Owner
EMP: 30
Web: www.a1palletco.com
SIC: 2448 Pallets, wood
PA: A-1 Pallet Co. Of Clarksville, Inc
940 Cottonwood Dr
Clarksville IN 47129

(G-2006)
A-1 PALLET CO OF CLARKSVILLE (PA)
940 Cottonwood Dr (47129-1042)
P.O. Box 2366 (47131-2366)
PHONE.....................812 288-6339
EMP: 1 EST: 1990
SQ FT: 27,000
SALES (est): 3.78MM Privately Held
SIC: 2448 2449 Wood pallets and skids; Wood containers, nec

(G-2007)
BAERDEN PRIMITIVES LLC
2316 Gutford Rd (47129-9048)
PHONE.....................502 909-7045
EMP: 3 EST: 2017
SALES (est): 96.03K Privately Held
Web: www.baerdenprimitives.com
SIC: 3999 Candles

(G-2008)
BAIRD ICE CREAM CO
110 N Randolph Ave (47129-2714)
PHONE.....................812 283-3345
Randall C Baird, Owner
EMP: 4 EST: 1918
SQ FT: 2,500
SALES (est): 429.89K Privately Held
SIC: 2023 Ice cream mix, unfrozen: liquid or dry

(G-2009)
BIG BRUHS SEASONING LLP
209 Altra Dr (47129-2221)
P.O. Box 2503 (47131-2503)
PHONE.....................502 751-5516
Virgil Cash, Mng Pt
EMP: 7
SALES (est): 286.99K Privately Held
SIC: 2099 7389 Seasonings: dry mixes; Business Activities at Non-Commercial Site

(G-2010)
BOTTOM LINE MANAGEMENT INC
Also Called: Hearthcraft
1410 Johnson Ln (47129-1402)
PHONE.....................812 944-7388
Shahla Javid, Pr
Doug Longest, Treas
Shahriar Javid, VP
Kamran Javid, VP
▲ EMP: 15 EST: 1988
SQ FT: 30,000
SALES (est): 2.24MM Privately Held
SIC: 3429 5199 3589 Fireplace equipment, hardware: andirons, grates, screens; Art goods and supplies; Commercial cooking and foodwarming equipment

(G-2011)
CD GRAFIX LLC
632 Providence Way Ste 3 (47129-1530)
P.O. Box 3354 (47131-3354)
PHONE.....................812 945-4443
EMP: 4 EST: 1999
SALES (est): 226.53K Privately Held
Web: www.cdgrafix.com
SIC: 2759 Screen printing

(G-2012)
CENTENNIAL GROUP INC
Also Called: Centennial Graphics Group
1330 Woerner Ave (47129-3105)
PHONE.....................812 948-2886
Gerald Durnell, Pr
Kaye Durnell, VP
EMP: 10 EST: 1986
SALES (est): 905.25K Privately Held
Web: www.centennial-group.com

SIC: 2789 Binding and repair of books, magazines, and pamphlets

(G-2013)
CLASSIC BUILDINGS INC
Also Called: Premier Homes
2709 Blackiston Mill Rd (47129-9020)
PHONE.....................812 944-5821
Jeff Corbett, Pr
EMP: 30 EST: 1983
SQ FT: 1,800
SALES (est): 4.5MM Privately Held
Web: www.classicbuildings.com
SIC: 2452 1542 3448 Prefabricated wood buildings; Commercial and office buildings, prefabricated erection; Prefabricated metal buildings and components

(G-2014)
CLASSIC TRUSS WD CMPONENTS INC
2709 Blackiston Mill Rd (47129-9020)
PHONE.....................812 944-5821
TOLL FREE: 800
Jeff Corbett, Pr
EMP: 43 EST: 1993
SALES (est): 11.96MM Privately Held
Web: www.classictruss.com
SIC: 2439 Trusses, wooden roof

(G-2015)
DNM CONVERTERS & CORES
107 E Lynnwood Dr (47129-1733)
PHONE.....................502 599-5225
Debbie Popplewell, Pt
Mike Popplewell, Pt
EMP: 2 EST: 2002
SALES (est): 158.1K Privately Held
SIC: 3356 Precious metals

(G-2016)
GHK TRUSS LLC (PA)
521 N Clark Blvd (47129-2449)
P.O. Box 2696 (47131-2696)
PHONE.....................812 282-6600
Michael G Gilley, Pr
Michael L Harlowe, VP
James M Kulaga, VP
EMP: 20 EST: 2007
SALES (est): 4.89MM
SALES (corp-wide): 4.89MM Privately Held
Web: www.ghktruss.com
SIC: 2439 Trusses, wooden roof

(G-2017)
H & H HOME IMPROVEMENT INC
1120 N Taggart Ave (47129-1848)
PHONE.....................812 288-8700
Rick Hauber, Pr
Tim Hauber, VP
EMP: 4 EST: 1971
SQ FT: 3,500
SALES (est): 438.53K Privately Held
SIC: 1761 1521 1751 3444 Siding contractor ; Single-family housing construction; Window and door (prefabricated) installation ; Awnings, sheet metal

(G-2018)
HAIR NECESSITIES
711 E Lewis And Clark Pkwy Ste 105 (47129-2284)
PHONE.....................812 288-5887
Joyce Douglas, Owner
EMP: 2 EST: 2005
SALES (est): 179.79K Privately Held
Web: www.hair-necessities.com
SIC: 3999 Hair and hair-based products

(G-2019)
IMI SOUTH LLC
1221 Highway 31 E (47129-9601)
PHONE.....................812 284-9732
EMP: 8
SALES (corp-wide): 814.09MM Privately Held
Web: www.irvmat.com
SIC: 3273 Ready-mixed concrete
HQ: Imi South, Llc
1440 Selinda Ave
Louisville KY 40213
502 456-6930

(G-2020)
J & J PALLET CORP
640 Miller Ave (47129-2457)
PHONE.....................812 288-4487
EMP: 90
SALES (corp-wide): 8.49MM Privately Held
Web: www.jjpallet.com
SIC: 2448 Pallets, wood
PA: J & J Pallet Corp
2234 E Market St
New Albany IN 47150
812 944-8670

(G-2021)
JLR MECHANICAL INC
Also Called: Jlr Welding & Fabrication
2020 Hospitality Way (47129)
PHONE.....................502 551-6879
Jill Tuell, Pr
Kevin Brumley, VP
Kyle Tuell, VP
EMP: 3 EST: 2020
SALES (est): 96.94K Privately Held
SIC: 7692 Welding repair

(G-2022)
JUDKINS SR RENALDO G
Also Called: Troop Enterprises
2315 Birch Dr (47129-1256)
PHONE.....................812 944-4251
Renaldo G Judkins Senior, Owner
EMP: 1 EST: 2005
SALES (est): 82K Privately Held
SIC: 2678 Stationery products

(G-2023)
MIKE MUGLER
Also Called: M & M Printing
1907 Majestic Meadows Dr (47129-9076)
PHONE.....................812 945-4266
Mike Mugler, Owner
EMP: 2 EST: 1984
SALES (est): 50K Privately Held
SIC: 2752 Offset printing

(G-2024)
MUSIC STORE
307 W Lewis And Clark Pkwy (47129-1647)
PHONE.....................812 949-3004
Paul Starks, Owner
EMP: 2 EST: 2005
SALES (est): 155.13K Privately Held
Web: www.drummersuperstore.com
SIC: 3679 5736 Recording heads, speech and musical equipment; Musical instrument stores

(G-2025)
PINEAPPLE SOFTWARE INC
1801 Creekside Dr (47129-9029)
PHONE.....................812 987-8277
Chad Hinton, Admn
EMP: 6 EST: 2015
SALES (est): 135.56K Privately Held

Clarksville - Clark County (G-2026)

SIC: 7372 Prepackaged software

(G-2026)
PPG INDUSTRIES INC
Also Called: PPG 4312
319 E Lewis And Clark Pkwy (47129-1725)
PHONE.................................812 948-9253
Aaron Ingle, Mgr
EMP: 1
SALES (corp-wide): 17.65B **Publicly Held**
Web: www.ppgpaints.com
SIC: 2851 Paints and allied products
PA: Ppg Industries, Inc.
1 Ppg Pl
Pittsburgh PA 15272
412 434-3131

(G-2027)
PQ LLC
1101 Quartz Rd (47129-3260)
P.O. Box 669 (47131-0669)
PHONE.................................812 288-7186
Jeff Sayffer, Mgr
EMP: 74
SALES (corp-wide): 575.98MM **Privately Held**
Web: www.pqcorp.com
SIC: 2819 Industrial inorganic chemicals, nec
PA: Pq Llc
300 Lindenwood Dr
Malvern PA 19355
610 651-4200

(G-2028)
PRECISION AUTOMATION COMPANY
Also Called: Altek Mfg. Co.
2120 Addmore Ln (47129)
P.O. Box Po Box2188 (47131)
PHONE.................................812 283-7963
G Frederick Rexon Senior, Ch
Glen A Morris, *
J William Huffmon Junior, VP
Robert J Daily, *
Steven Fischer, *
EMP: 34 EST: 1953
SQ FT: 35,000
SALES (est): 5.93MM **Privately Held**
Web: www.pacomanufacturing.com
SIC: 3549 3565 Metalworking machinery, nec ; Packaging machinery

(G-2029)
PRECISION SYSTEMS
478 Accrusia Ave (47129-2832)
PHONE.................................812 283-4904
Ron Eicher, Owner
EMP: 1 EST: 1994
SALES (est): 91.82K **Privately Held**
Web: www.precisionsystemsinc.com
SIC: 3825 Engine electrical test equipment

(G-2030)
REEDERS CLEANERS INC
1205 Eastern Blvd (47129-1701)
PHONE.................................812 945-4833
Douglas Nalley, Pr
EMP: 7 EST: 1923
SALES (est): 405.68K **Privately Held**
SIC: 2842 Drycleaning preparations

(G-2031)
ROSSWYVERN PRESS LLC
2224 Birch Dr (47129-1214)
PHONE.................................859 421-0864
Neviana Dimova, Admn
EMP: 2 EST: 2012
SALES (est): 100.58K **Privately Held**
SIC: 2741 Miscellaneous publishing

(G-2032)
S R WOOD INC
Also Called: Sr Wood
1801 Progress Way (47129-9205)
PHONE.................................812 288-9201
EMP: 35 EST: 1970
SALES (est): 3.14MM **Privately Held**
Web: www.srwoodinc.com
SIC: 2679 Wallboard, decorated: made from purchased material

(G-2033)
SAYBOLT
1223 Providence Way (47129-1546)
PHONE.................................812 944-5001
EMP: 5 EST: 2019
SALES (est): 168.79K **Privately Held**
SIC: 1389 Oil field services, nec

(G-2034)
SAYBOLT LP
905 Eastern Blvd Ste C (47129-1961)
PHONE.................................812 282-7242
Jim Rasdom, Mgr
EMP: 3
Web: www.corelab.com
SIC: 1389 Oil field services, nec
HQ: Saybolt Lp
6316 Windfern Rd
Houston TX 77040
713 328-2673

(G-2035)
SEATON SPRINGS INC
Also Called: Signs Now
632 Eastern Blvd Ste B (47129-2463)
PHONE.................................812 282-2440
EMP: 3
Web: www.signsnow.com
SIC: 3993 Signs and advertising specialties
PA: Seaton Springs, Inc.
1700 Research Dr
Louisville KY 40299

(G-2036)
SIDDHI INTEGRATED MFG SVCS INC
Also Called: Sims
1513 Lynch Ln (47129)
PHONE.................................502 298-8640
Neelam Puneet Neotia, Pr
Tanay Neotia, Dir
EMP: 4 EST: 2021
SALES (est): 290.68K **Privately Held**
Web: www.simfgservices.com
SIC: 3559 3498 Semiconductor manufacturing machinery; Fabricated pipe and fittings

(G-2037)
SORBTECH INC
1305 Veterans Pkwy Ste 1000 (47129-7792)
PHONE.................................812 944-9108
Deborah Payne, Owner
Deborah S Payne, Pr
James O Payne, VP
Joanna Kilburn, Sec
EMP: 3 EST: 1991
SALES (est): 279.17K **Privately Held**
Web: www.sorbtechinc.com
SIC: 5169 8748 8742 2842 Specialty cleaning and sanitation preparations; Environmental consultant; Transportation consultant; Sweeping compounds, oil or water absorbent, clay or sawdust

(G-2038)
STEAMIN DEMON INC
1041 S Clark Blvd (47129-3019)
PHONE.................................812 288-6754
Mike Downey, Pr
EMP: 2 EST: 1993
SQ FT: 3,000
SALES (est): 223.1K **Privately Held**
Web: www.steamindemon.com
SIC: 3635 Carpet shampooer

(G-2039)
TIDY JANITORIAL SERVICES LLC
Also Called: Insurance
1450 Blackiston View Dr (47129-2060)
PHONE.................................502 807-9847
Bruce Willis, CEO
EMP: 1 EST: 2014
SALES (est): 46.79K **Privately Held**
SIC: 3711 3537 Trucks, pickup, assembly of; Trucks: freight, baggage, etc.: industrial, except mining

(G-2040)
UNITED SERVICES INC (PA)
Also Called: U.S.I. Custom Blinds
118 W Lewis And Clark Pkwy (47129-1732)
PHONE.................................812 989-3320
EMP: 8 EST: 1993
SQ FT: 4,000
SALES (est): 1.02MM **Privately Held**
SIC: 2591 Window blinds

(G-2041)
VALLEY SCALE COMPANY LLC
Also Called: VSC
751 W Kenwood Ave (47129-2569)
PHONE.................................812 282-5269
Arlis Guffey, Ch
Matthew S Guffey, CEO
EMP: 15 EST: 1968
SQ FT: 4,500
SALES (est): 2.4MM **Privately Held**
Web: www.thinkvsc.com
SIC: 7699 3596 1389 Scale repair service; Railroad track scales; Testing, measuring, surveying, and analysis services

Clay City
Clay County

(G-2042)
CORY WILLIAMSON
6745 S County Road 200 E (47841-8061)
PHONE.................................812 242-0400
Cory Williamson, Prin
EMP: 6 EST: 2010
SALES (est): 175.63K **Privately Held**
SIC: 2411 Logging

(G-2043)
HARRIS BURIAL SERVICE INC
1440 W County Road 800 S (47841-8229)
PHONE.................................812 939-3605
Eric Harris, Prin
EMP: 5 EST: 2000
SALES (est): 374.2K **Privately Held**
SIC: 3272 Burial vaults, concrete or precast terrazzo

(G-2044)
IRONHORSE DETAILING INC
8445 S State Road 59 (47841-8206)
P.O. Box 132 (47841-0132)
PHONE.................................812 939-3300
James Zimmerman, Pr
EMP: 2 EST: 2009
SALES (est): 138.32K **Privately Held**
SIC: 3449 Bars, concrete reinforcing: fabricated steel

(G-2045)
LOGGERS INCORPORATED
7755 S County Rd 50 (47841)
P.O. Box 122 (47841-0122)
PHONE.................................812 939-2797
Marvin Booe Junior, Pr
Marvin Booe Junior, Pr
James Booe, *
EMP: 21 EST: 1965
SQ FT: 1,800
SALES (est): 1.19MM **Privately Held**
Web: www.digital-loggers.com
SIC: 2421 2431 2411 Sawmills and planing mills, general; Millwork; Logging

(G-2046)
PIONEER CANE & HANDLE CO
3016 E River Rd (47841-8056)
PHONE.................................812 859-4415
Dale Killion, Owner
EMP: 2 EST: 1970
SALES (est): 108.54K **Privately Held**
SIC: 2499 Handles, wood

(G-2047)
TILTED COMPASS WINERY LLC
1461 W State Road 246 (47841-8215)
PHONE.................................812 691-1766
Thad D Shidler, Prin
EMP: 6 EST: 2018
SALES (est): 107.53K **Privately Held**
Web: www.tiltedcompasswinery.com
SIC: 2084 Wines

(G-2048)
WAITE ADEL (MARLANE)
Also Called: The Education Connection
4810 S Whippoorwill Lk Dr (47841-8028)
PHONE.................................812 939-2252
EMP: 1
SALES (est): 54.42K **Privately Held**
SIC: 2741 Miscellaneous publishing

(G-2049)
WREATH INC
500 E 10th St (47841-1534)
P.O. Box 21 (47841-0021)
PHONE.................................812 939-3439
Laura Wells, Prin
EMP: 5 EST: 2010
SALES (est): 54.61K **Privately Held**
SIC: 3999 Wreaths, artificial

Claypool
Kosciusko County

(G-2050)
APEX PROCUREMENT LLC
4802 E State Road 14 (46510-9195)
PHONE.................................574 304-2679
EMP: 3
SALES (est): 242.65K **Privately Held**
SIC: 3069 Fabricated rubber products, nec

(G-2051)
CALHOUN LOGGING CORPORATION
9543 S State Road 13 (46510-8848)
PHONE.................................260 839-0268
EMP: 4 EST: 2018
SALES (est): 84.34K **Privately Held**
SIC: 2411 Logging

(G-2052)
DOUGLAS DRUDGE
1384 W 600 S (46510-8926)
PHONE.................................574 566-2210
Douglas Drudge, Owner
EMP: 1 EST: 1992

SALES (est): 60.85K **Privately Held**
SIC: 7692 Welding repair

(G-2053)
HEARTHGLOW INC
3902 E State Road 14 (46510)
PHONE.................................260 839-3205
Roger Presl, *Pr*
Kathryn Presl, *Sec*
EMP: 9 EST: 1989
SALES (est): 922.66K **Privately Held**
Web: www.qualityhardwood.net
SIC: 2411 Fuel wood harvesting

(G-2054)
JP MACHINE SHOP LLC
2661 E 1000 S (46510-9173)
PHONE.................................574 453-7617
EMP: 5 EST: 2012
SALES (est): 81.49K **Privately Held**
Web: www.jpmachineshop.com
SIC: 3599 Machine shop, jobbing and repair

(G-2055)
LOUIS DREYFUS CO AG INDS LLC
7344 S State Road 15 (46510-9289)
EMP: 5119
SIC: 6221 2869 Commodity contracts brokers, dealers; Glycerin
HQ: Louis Dreyfus Company Agricultural Industries Llc
40 Danbury Rd
Wilton CT 06897

(G-2056)
QUALITY HARDWOOD PRODUCTS INC
3902 E State Road 14 (46510)
PHONE.................................260 982-2043
Roger Presl, *Pr*
Kathryn Presl, *Sec*
EMP: 11 EST: 1973
SALES (est): 978.19K **Privately Held**
Web: www.qualityhardwood.net
SIC: 2421 2426 Custom sawmill; Hardwood dimension and flooring mills

(G-2057)
SILAS BEACHLER
Also Called: Beachlers Sugar Bush
9569 S 600 E (46510-9019)
PHONE.................................260 578-1625
Silas Beachler, *Owner*
EMP: 1 EST: 2020
SALES (est): 100K **Privately Held**
SIC: 2099 Sugar, industrial maple

(G-2058)
STEVEN RAY HUGHES
Also Called: Hughes Custom Smokers
5972 S 450 W (46510-9713)
PHONE.................................574 491-2128
Steven R Hughes, *Owner*
EMP: 5 EST: 2016
SALES (est): 145.51K **Privately Held**
SIC: 3631 0291 Barbecues, grills, and braziers (outdoor cooking); General farms, primarily animals

Clayton
Hendricks County

(G-2059)
HUBBARD WELDING
10114 S County Road 100 W (46118-9248)
PHONE.................................317 539-2758
Ray Hubbard, *Owner*
EMP: 2 EST: 1969
SALES (est): 113.71K **Privately Held**

SIC: 7692 Welding repair

(G-2060)
JONESYS FABRICATION LLC ✪
9913 S County Road 25 W (46118)
PHONE.................................317 504-6511
EMP: 4 EST: 2022
SALES (est): 62.01K **Privately Held**
SIC: 3599 Machine shop, jobbing and repair

(G-2061)
KK HALL INC
6774 S County Road 400 E (46118-9442)
PHONE.................................317 839-8329
EMP: 1 EST: 1979
SALES (est): 110K **Privately Held**
SIC: 3679 Electronic circuits

(G-2062)
TRIVETT CONTRACTING INC
5981 Liberty Pkwy (46118-8838)
PHONE.................................317 539-5150
Daniel V Trivett, *Pr*
EMP: 28 EST: 1997
SALES (est): 4.9MM **Privately Held**
Web: www.trivettcontracting.com
SIC: 1541 1799 3449 1796 Renovation, remodeling and repairs: industrial buildings; Dock equipment installation, industrial; Bars, concrete reinforcing: fabricated steel; Machine moving and rigging

Clermont
Marion County

(G-2063)
DR RESTORATIONS INC
Also Called: Exclusive Reality
4252 N Raceway Rd (46234-9248)
PHONE.................................317 646-7150
Joe Robey, *Asst Sec*
Bianca Broyles, *CFO*
Ray Hubbard, *VP*
EMP: 9 EST: 2017
SALES (est): 493.01K **Privately Held**
Web: www.drrestoration.com
SIC: 1799 1742 1721 2431 Construction site cleanup; Drywall; Painting and paper hanging; Window frames, wood

Clinton
Vermillion County

(G-2064)
BI-STATE ASPHALT
14516 S 200 E (47842-7554)
PHONE.................................765 832-5000
TOLL FREE: 866
Dave Cotton, *Owner*
EMP: 3 EST: 1997
SALES (est): 390.22K **Privately Held**
Web: www.paverservingclintonindiana.com
SIC: 1611 3479 Surfacing and paving; Coating or wrapping steel pipe

(G-2065)
D ROBERTSON GRAVEL CO INC
3499 E 1850 S (47842-7207)
P.O. Box 176 (47842-0176)
PHONE.................................765 832-2768
Donnetta Domeika, *Pr*
Donald R Robertson, *Pr*
Karen Robertson, *Sec*
EMP: 10 EST: 1947
SALES (est): 964.82K **Privately Held**
SIC: 1442 5211 Gravel mining; Sand and gravel

(G-2066)
ELANCO US INC
Elanco Clinton Laboratory
10500 S State Road 63 (47842-7696)
P.O. Box 99 (47842-0099)
PHONE.................................765 832-4400
George Rogers, *Brnch Mgr*
EMP: 1
SALES (corp-wide): 4.42B **Publicly Held**
Web: www.elanco.com
SIC: 2834 Pharmaceutical preparations
HQ: Elanco Us Inc.
2500 Innovation Way N
Greenfield IN 46140

(G-2067)
FEATHER CREEK CALLS
860 E 1375 S (47842-7548)
PHONE.................................812 229-1124
Richard Buker, *Owner*
EMP: 2 EST: 2018
SALES (est): 78.06K **Privately Held**
SIC: 3949 Sporting and athletic goods, nec

(G-2068)
IEA CONSTRUCTORS INC
Also Called: IEA CONSTRUCTORS, INC.
3900 White Ave (47842-1160)
PHONE.................................765 832-8526
EMP: 66
SALES (corp-wide): 12B **Publicly Held**
Web: www.iea.net
SIC: 3799 Carriages, horse drawn
HQ: Iea Constructors, Llc
6325 Digital Way Ste 460
Indianapolis IN 46278
765 832-8526

(G-2069)
IEA EQUIPMENT MANAGEMENT LLC
3900 White Ave (47842-1160)
P.O. Box 249 (47842-0249)
PHONE.................................765 832-2800
Paul M Daily, *CEO*
Creighton K Kim Early, *CFO*
EMP: 251 EST: 2012
SALES (est): 21.32MM
SALES (corp-wide): 12B **Publicly Held**
SIC: 3799 Trailers and trailer equipment
HQ: Infrastructure And Energy Alternatives, Inc.
6625 Network Way
Indianapolis IN 46278
765 828-2580

(G-2070)
IEA MANAGEMENT SERVICES INC
3900 White Ave (47842-1160)
P.O. Box 249 (47842-0249)
PHONE.................................765 832-8526
David R Helwig, *CEO*
David Bostwick, *Sec*
EMP: 2 EST: 2012
SALES (est): 1.31MM
SALES (corp-wide): 12B **Publicly Held**
SIC: 3799 Trailers and trailer equipment
HQ: Infrastructure And Energy Alternatives, Inc.
6625 Network Way
Indianapolis IN 46278
765 828-2580

(G-2071)
LUND CUSTOM CALLS LLC
801 S 4th St (47842-2221)
PHONE.................................812 242-0566
Robert D Lund, *Prin*
EMP: 3 EST: 2019
SALES (est): 109.44K **Privately Held**
Web: www.lundcustomcalls.com

SIC: 3949 Sporting and athletic goods, nec

(G-2072)
MRRX MOBILE RAILCAR REPAIR LLC
Also Called: Small Repairs/Mobile For Ind
1020 W Trinity Ave (47842-9215)
PHONE.................................812 251-0055
Anna Kelsheimer, *Owner*
EMP: 4 EST: 2018
SALES (est): 26.07K **Privately Held**
SIC: 7699 7692 Repair services, nec; Welding repair

(G-2073)
NG OPERATIONS LLC
Also Called: National Gypsum Company
75 Ivy Ln (47842-7188)
P.O. Box 367 (47842-0367)
PHONE.................................765 828-0898
George Schmalz, *Manager*
EMP: 30
SALES (corp-wide): 795.88MM **Privately Held**
Web: www.nationalgypsum.com
SIC: 3275 Gypsum products
HQ: Proform Finishing Products, Llc
2001 Rexford Rd
Charlotte NC 28211

(G-2074)
NG OPERATIONS LLC
Also Called: NG OPERATIONS, LLC
2230 N Main St (47842-7160)
PHONE.................................765 828-0371
Charlie Cowman, *Brnch Mgr*
EMP: 92
SALES (corp-wide): 795.88MM **Privately Held**
Web: www.nationalgypsum.com
SIC: 3275 Gypsum products
HQ: Proform Finishing Products, Llc
2001 Rexford Rd
Charlotte NC 28211

(G-2075)
PERMABASE BUILDING PDTS LLC
75 Ivy Ln (47842-7188)
PHONE.................................765 828-0898
EMP: 6
SALES (est): 86.73K **Privately Held**
Web: www.permabase.com
SIC: 2452 Prefabricated wood buildings

(G-2076)
ROSKOVENSKI SAND & GRAVEL INC
3200 E 1850 S (47842-7207)
PHONE.................................765 832-6748
Thomas Robert Roskovensky, *Pr*
EMP: 6 EST: 2001
SALES (est): 349.29K **Privately Held**
Web: www.thechurchstop.org
SIC: 1442 Gravel mining

(G-2077)
ROSSKOVENSKI CONCRETE & RDYMX
12927 S State Road 63 (47842-7161)
PHONE.................................765 832-6103
John Rosskovenski, *Owner*
EMP: 5 EST: 1968
SQ FT: 5,000
SALES (est): 450K **Privately Held**
SIC: 3272 3273 Burial vaults, concrete or precast terrazzo; Ready-mixed concrete

(G-2078)
SUSTAINABLE SOURCING LLC
10500 S State Road 63 (47842-7696)
PHONE.................................765 505-2338

Scott Lewis, Mgr
EMP: 38
Web: www.sustainablesourcingllc.com
SIC: 2077 Animal and marine fats and oils
PA: Sustainable Sourcing Llc
19633 S La Grange Rd
Mokena IL 60448

(G-2079)
THOMAS PRODUCTS & SERVICES INC
109 W Harrison St (47842-7254)
PHONE.................................217 463-3999
Dennis Thomas, Prin
EMP: 9 EST: 2016
SALES (est): 147.49K Privately Held
SIC: 3999 Manufacturing industries, nec

(G-2080)
USELMAN PACKING CO
75 E 4th St (47842-7040)
PHONE.................................765 832-2112
Garry Uselman, Owner
EMP: 5 EST: 1975
SALES (est): 505.86K Privately Held
SIC: 2011 5147 Meat packing plants; Meats and meat products

Cloverdale
Putnam County

(G-2081)
243 QUARRY
8090 S State Road 243 (46120-9692)
PHONE.................................765 653-4100
Tom Thingst, Prin
EMP: 7 EST: 2010
SALES (est): 167.38K Privately Held
SIC: 1481 Mine and quarry services, nonmetallic minerals

(G-2082)
ASSURANCE WASTE MANAGEMENT LLC ◆
11048 W Awbrey Rd (46120)
PHONE.................................765 341-4431
David A Rogers, CEO
EMP: 6 EST: 2024
SALES (est): 68.7K Privately Held
SIC: 8748 3443 Environmental consultant; Dumpsters, garbage

(G-2083)
BILLY D SNIDER
Also Called: Bills Pallets
294 Bubble Loo Rd (46120-8882)
PHONE.................................765 795-6426
Billy D Snider, Prin
EMP: 4 EST: 2012
SALES (est): 243.46K Privately Held
SIC: 2448 Pallets, wood and wood with metal

(G-2084)
COMPTONS WOODWORKING LLC ◆
11275 S Meridian Line Rd (46120-9185)
PHONE.................................765 712-0568
EMP: 1 EST: 2022
SALES (est): 54.13K Privately Held
Web: www.comptonswoodworking.com
SIC: 2431 7389 Woodwork, interior and ornamental, nec; Business services, nec

(G-2085)
HANSON AGRIGOODS MIDWEST INC
8950 S State Road 243 (46120-9698)
P.O. Box 328 (46120-0328)
PHONE.................................317 635-9048
Jack Thompson, Superintnt
EMP: 8 EST: 1999
SALES (est): 1.14MM Privately Held
SIC: 5032 1499 Aggregate; Asphalt mining and bituminous stone quarrying

(G-2086)
HEIDELBERG MTLS MDWEST AGG INC
State Road 243 Cty Rd 900 S (46120)
P.O. Box 328 (46120-0328)
PHONE.................................765 653-7205
EMP: 1
SALES (corp-wide): 23.02B Privately Held
SIC: 1422 5032 Limestones, ground; Stone, crushed or broken
HQ: Heidelberg Materials Midwest Agg, Inc.
300 E John Carpenter Fwy
Irving TX

(G-2087)
IOWA LIMESTONE COMPANY
Also Called: Ilc Resources
8114 S State Road 243 (46120-9693)
PHONE.................................317 981-7919
EMP: 12
SALES (corp-wide): 56.31MM Privately Held
Web: www.ilcresources.com
SIC: 1422 Crushed and broken limestone
PA: Iowa Limestone Company
3301 106th Cir
Urbandale IA 50322
515 243-3160

(G-2088)
MAPCO
7230 E County Road 1000 S (46120-9039)
PHONE.................................765 795-3179
Mark Pitt, Owner
EMP: 1 EST: 1999
SALES (est): 36.58K Privately Held
SIC: 7692 Welding repair

(G-2089)
MID-STATE AUTOMATION INC
12389 Camp Otto Rd (46120-8098)
PHONE.................................765 795-5500
John Dougherty, Pr
Jacqueline Dougherty, Contrlr
EMP: 5 EST: 1985
SQ FT: 4,500
SALES (est): 462.05K Privately Held
Web: www.mid-stateautomation.com
SIC: 3559 1796 Vibratory parts handling equipment; Machinery installation

(G-2090)
MORTON BUILDINGS INC
6215 S Us Highway 231 (46120-9635)
PHONE.................................765 653-9781
Cliff Baumgatner, Brnch Mgr
EMP: 16
SALES (corp-wide): 213.04MM Privately Held
Web: www.mortonbuildings.com
SIC: 3448 Prefabricated metal buildings and components
PA: Morton Buildings, Inc.
252 W Adams St
Morton IL 61550
800 447-7436

(G-2091)
NALC LLC
8090 S State Road 243 (46120-9692)
PHONE.................................502 548-9590
Greg Gould, Prin
Greg Gould, CEO
Richard Boyd, *
Thomas Hingst, *
Cari Hylton, *
EMP: 9 EST: 2014
SQ FT: 10,000
SALES (est): 775.36K Privately Held
Web: www.nalcllc.com
SIC: 1422 Crushed and broken limestone

(G-2092)
OHIO RIVER TRADING CO
8090 S State Road 243 (46120-9692)
PHONE.................................765 653-4100
Tom Thingst, Owner
EMP: 4 EST: 2008
SALES (est): 192K Privately Held
SIC: 3281 Cut stone and stone products

(G-2093)
POET BRFINING - CLOVERDALE LLC
Also Called: Poet Boprocessing - Cloverdale
2265 E County Road 800 S (46120-8431)
PHONE.................................765 795-3235
Jeff Lautt, CFO
Luke Logan, Genl Mgr
EMP: 56 EST: 2009
SQ FT: 4,000
SALES (est): 25.68MM Privately Held
Web: www.poet.com
SIC: 2869 Ethyl alcohol, ethanol
PA: Poet, Llc
4615 N Lewis Ave
Sioux Falls SD 57104

(G-2094)
PUTNAM PLASTICS INC (PA)
30 W Stardust Rd (46120)
P.O. Box 258 (46120)
PHONE.................................765 795-6102
Brad Query, Pr
Chris Query, *
Marla Corbin, *
EMP: 35 EST: 1975
SQ FT: 35,000
SALES (est): 5.45MM
SALES (corp-wide): 5.45MM Privately Held
Web: www.putnamplasticsinc.com
SIC: 2673 Plastic bags: made from purchased materials

(G-2095)
RONNIE ELMORE JR
1193 E State Road 42 (46120-8759)
PHONE.................................765 719-1681
Ronnie Elmore Junior, Prin
EMP: 5 EST: 2013
SALES (est): 119.75K Privately Held
SIC: 2752 Commercial printing, lithographic

(G-2096)
RUSSS CUSTOM WELDING CORP
673 W County Road 1000 S (46120-9494)
PHONE.................................765 795-5795
Russell Plamondon, Pr
EMP: 1 EST: 2005
SALES (est): 90.43K Privately Held
SIC: 7692 Welding repair

(G-2097)
SCORPION PRTCTIVE COATINGS INC
6184 S Us Highway 231 (46120-9636)
PHONE.................................800 483-9087
Clayton Tomasino, Pr
Randolph Tomasino, VP
Greg Tomasino, VP
Nancy Brush, Sec
Gregory R Romasino, Sec
▲ EMP: 15 EST: 1996
SALES (est): 4.79MM Privately Held
Web: www.scorpioncoatings.com
SIC: 3479 Coating of metals and formed products

(G-2098)
SIGNPLEX LLC
4 W Market St (46120-8424)
P.O. Box 775 (46120-0775)
PHONE.................................765 795-7446
Wayne Meyer, Owner
EMP: 3 EST: 2004
SALES (est): 202.32K Privately Held
Web: www.signplex.com
SIC: 3993 Signs and advertising specialties

(G-2099)
STANDARD FOR SUCCESS LLC
10741 S County Road 850 E (46120)
PHONE.................................844 737-3825
Todd Whitlock, CEO
EMP: 10 EST: 2012
SALES (est): 2.54MM
SALES (corp-wide): 3.13MM Privately Held
Web: www.educationadvanced.com
SIC: 7372 8748 Educational computer software; Educational consultant
PA: Education Advanced, Inc.
2702 E 5th St Ste 372
Tyler TX 75701
903 858-4497

Coal City
Owen County

(G-2100)
LEDGERWOOD & SONS SAWMILL LLC
246 Pleasant View Rd (47427-7948)
PHONE.................................812 939-8212
Larry Ledgerwoodm, Owner
EMP: 3 EST: 2001
SALES (est): 232.37K Privately Held
SIC: 2421 Lumber: rough, sawed, or planed

(G-2101)
RODS WELDING SHOP
Also Called: Rod Welding and Auto
2135 Beech Church Rd (47427-7811)
PHONE.................................812 859-4250
Rod Schmaltz, Owner
EMP: 2 EST: 1987
SQ FT: 3,000
SALES (est): 40K Privately Held
SIC: 7692 Welding repair

Coatesville
Putnam County

(G-2102)
ADVANCED PRTCTIVE SLUTIONS LLC
639 Gettysburg (46121-8960)
P.O. Box 131 (46121-0131)
PHONE.................................765 720-9574
EMP: 3 EST: 2016
SALES (est): 145.68K Privately Held
Web: www.advancedprotectivesolutions.com
SIC: 7389 3545 7381 8742 Personal service agents, brokers, and bureaus; Machine knives, metalworking; Protective services, guard; Management consulting services

(G-2103)
ARNOLD BROTHERS CONSTRUCTION
7483 W County Road 350 S (46121-9151)
PHONE.................................317 775-5523
Mark Arnold, Pt
EMP: 8

SALES (est): 78.52K **Privately Held**
SIC: 3715 Truck trailers

(G-2104)
CARRIAGE HOUSE WOODWORKING INC
8043 S Putnam County Rd (46121-9100)
PHONE..................................317 406-3042
James A Barker, *Pr*
Rita Barker, *Sec*
EMP: 2 **EST:** 1993
SALES (est): 245.9K **Privately Held**
Web: www.chweinc.com
SIC: 2434 5712 Wood kitchen cabinets; Customized furniture and cabinets

(G-2105)
EXHIBIT A PLASTICS LLC
4170 S State Road 75 (46121-9114)
P.O. Box 230 (46121-0230)
PHONE..................................765 386-6702
EMP: 16 **EST:** 2002
SQ FT: 12,000
SALES (est): 741.57K **Privately Held**
Web: www.exhibitaplastics.com
SIC: 3089 Injection molding of plastics

(G-2106)
HERITAGE LAKE COMMUNITY SVCS
26 Gettysburg (46121-8955)
PHONE..................................317 766-4118
EMP: 2 **EST:** 2010
SALES (est): 18.85K **Privately Held**
Web: www.hlpoa.us
SIC: 2711 Newspapers

(G-2107)
MCPUBS INC
2785 S County Road 1000 E (46121-9385)
PHONE..................................317 539-6461
Michael B Mccammack, *Prin*
EMP: 7 **EST:** 2012
SALES (est): 72.47K **Privately Held**
SIC: 2721 Magazines: publishing only, not printed on site

(G-2108)
MULLIS CUSTOM FRAMING LLC
246 Victory HI (46121-8963)
PHONE..................................317 627-4024
Joyce Mullis, *Prin*
EMP: 1 **EST:** 2010
SALES (est): 49.56K **Privately Held**
SIC: 2499 Picture frame molding, finished

(G-2109)
SAWMILL PRIDE LLC
5056 Milton St (46121-9706)
P.O. Box 216 (46121-0216)
PHONE..................................317 442-2958
Joe Vieira, *Pr*
EMP: 1 **EST:** 2001
SALES (est): 160K **Privately Held**
SIC: 2421 Sawmills and planing mills, general

(G-2110)
TEXTRON OUTDOOR POWER EQP INC (HQ)
6302 E County Road 100 N (46121-9689)
PHONE..................................704 504-6600
Scott A Ernest, *Pr*
Dana L Goldberg, *VP*
James Pennoyer, *CFO*
Eric Salander, *Treas*
▲ **EMP:** 3 **EST:** 2014
SALES (est): 4.43MM
SALES (corp-wide): 12.87B **Publicly Held**
SIC: 3524 Lawn and garden equipment
PA: Textron Inc.

40 Westminster St
Providence RI 02903
401 421-2800

Colburn
Tippecanoe County

(G-2111)
TOYOTA TSUSHO AMERICA INC
5440 Haggerty Ln (47905-9402)
PHONE..................................765 449-3500
Jack Porman, *Mgr*
EMP: 90
Web: www.taiamerica.com
SIC: 4225 4226 3674 3679 Warehousing, self storage; Automobile dead storage; Fuel cells, solid state; Antennas, receiving
HQ: Toyota Tsusho America, Inc.
825 3rd Ave Fl 10
New York NY 10022
212 355-3600

(G-2112)
TRI-ESCO INC
101 N 36th St (47905-4784)
P.O. Box 6386 (47903-6386)
PHONE..................................765 446-7937
EMP: 14
SALES (corp-wide): 2.84MM **Privately Held**
Web: www.triesco.com
SIC: 1542 1771 1794 7692 Commercial and office building, new construction; Concrete work; Excavation work; Welding repair
PA: Tri-Esco Inc.
3221 Imperial Pkwy
Lafayette IN 47909
765 446-7937

Colfax
Clinton County

(G-2113)
THIS OLD FARM INC
Also Called: This Old Farm
9572 W County Road 650 S (46035-9424)
PHONE..................................765 324-2161
EMP: 20 **EST:** 2009
SALES (est): 996.11K **Privately Held**
Web: www.thisoldfarm.com
SIC: 0191 2013 General farms, primarily crop ; Prepared beef products, from purchased beef

Columbia City
Whitley County

(G-2114)
80/20 LLC
1701 S 400 E (46725)
PHONE..................................260 248-8030
Don Wood, *Pr*
David Wood, *
Scott Brown, *
◆ **EMP:** 300 **EST:** 1990
SALES (est): 82.2MM **Privately Held**
Web: www.8020.net
SIC: 3354 Shapes, extruded aluminum, nec

(G-2115)
ACCU-TOOL INC
831 E Short St (46725-8743)
PHONE..................................260 248-4529
EMP: 7 **EST:** 1994
SQ FT: 9,000
SALES (est): 651.96K **Privately Held**
Web: www.accutoolinc.com
SIC: 3599 Machine shop, jobbing and repair

(G-2116)
ACME INDUSTRIAL INC
2380 E Cardinal Dr (46725-8789)
PHONE..................................260 422-6518
EMP: 30 **EST:** 1995
SQ FT: 25,000
SALES (est): 832.29K **Privately Held**
SIC: 3599 Machine shop, jobbing and repair

(G-2117)
ADHESIVE SOLUTIONS COMPANY LLC (PA)
4201 N 450 E (46725-9352)
PHONE..................................260 691-0304
EMP: 2 **EST:** 1997
SQ FT: 2,000
SALES (est): 280.36K
SALES (corp-wide): 280.36K **Privately Held**
Web: www.adhesivesolutions.com
SIC: 2891 5169 5085 Adhesives; Adhesives and sealants; Adhesives, tape and plasters

(G-2118)
AJ MACHINE INC
2441 E Business 30 (46725-8768)
PHONE..................................260 248-4900
Ronda Mcclure, *Pr*
EMP: 25 **EST:** 2002
SALES (est): 2.39MM **Privately Held**
Web: www.ajmachineinc.com
SIC: 3599 Machine shop, jobbing and repair

(G-2119)
ALLIANCE FEED LLC
2560 S 600 E (46725)
PHONE..................................260 244-6100
Dewey A Bucher, *Pr*
EMP: 1 **EST:** 2018
SALES (est): 844.43K **Privately Held**
Web: www.keystonecoop.com
SIC: 2048 Livestock feeds

(G-2120)
ASW LLC
Also Called: American Sportworks
2499 S 600 E Ste 102 (46725-9029)
PHONE..................................260 432-1596
Jeff Banister, *Pr*
Josh Graham Ctrl, *Prin*
EMP: 140 **EST:** 1959
SALES (est): 17.74MM **Privately Held**
Web: www.landmaster.com
SIC: 3799 Recreational vehicles

(G-2121)
AUTOLIV ASP INC
Also Called: Autoliv Steering Whl Facility
5627 E Rail Connect Dr (46725-0077)
PHONE..................................801 620-8018
Jason Vincent, *Brnch Mgr*
EMP: 407
SALES (corp-wide): 10.47B **Publicly Held**
Web: www.autoliv.com
SIC: 3714 Motor vehicle parts and accessories
HQ: Autoliv Asp, Inc.
1320 Pacific Dr
Auburn Hills MI 48326

(G-2122)
BAINS PACKING AND RFRGN
Also Called: Bains' Packing & Refrigeration
3922 E Old Trail Rd (46725-9013)
PHONE..................................260 244-5209
Ralph D Bain, *Pt*
George A Bain, *Pt*

EMP: 10 **EST:** 1945
SQ FT: 7,000
SALES (est): 613.32K **Privately Held**
SIC: 2011 Meat packing plants

(G-2123)
BEST CUSTOM CABINET REFACING
6821 S 275 W (46725-8078)
PHONE..................................260 459-1448
Caroline Dennis-rogers, *Owner*
EMP: 2 **EST:** 2001
SALES (est): 177.86K **Privately Held**
Web: www.bestcabinetfw.com
SIC: 2434 Wood kitchen cabinets

(G-2124)
BETTER VISIONS PC
Also Called: City Vision Center
513 N Line St (46725-1229)
PHONE..................................260 244-7542
Andrew B Hogue, *Pr*
Dennis D Sutton, *Prin*
EMP: 10 **EST:** 1999
SALES (est): 272.33K **Privately Held**
Web: www.visionsource-cityvisioncenter.com
SIC: 5995 3827 Contact lenses, prescription; Aiming circles (fire control equipment)

(G-2125)
BOWSMAN TANK CO
115 W Spencer St (46725-2413)
PHONE..................................260 244-7129
Robert Bowsman, *Owner*
EMP: 1 **EST:** 1952
SALES (est): 94.94K **Privately Held**
SIC: 3272 Septic tanks, concrete

(G-2126)
BRAID DEN INC
4532 E Park 30 Dr (46725-8869)
PHONE..................................260 244-2995
Chad Heathco, *Pr*
◆ **EMP:** 39 **EST:** 1990
SQ FT: 50,000
SALES (est): 10.01MM **Privately Held**
Web: www.breydenproducts.com
SIC: 3496 Miscellaneous fabricated wire products
PA: Precision Products Group, Inc.
8770 Guion Rd Ste A
Indianapolis IN 46268

(G-2127)
BRIDGESTONE RET OPERATIONS LLC
Also Called: Firestone
651 Country Side Dr (46725-1101)
PHONE..................................260 447-2596
Tom Spencer, *Mgr*
EMP: 6
Web: www.bridgestoneamericas.com
SIC: 5531 7534 Automotive tires; Rebuilding and retreading tires
HQ: Bridgestone Retail Operations, Llc
200 4th Ave S Ste 100
Nashville TN 37201
630 259-9000

(G-2128)
C & R PLATING CORP
302 Factory St (46725-2761)
P.O. Box 247 (46725-0247)
PHONE..................................586 755-4900
Bob Burger, *CEO*
Dennis Blaugh, *
EMP: 36 **EST:** 1965
SQ FT: 13,772
SALES (est): 4.54MM
SALES (corp-wide): 21.41MM **Privately Held**

Web: www.kcjplating.com
SIC: 3471 Electroplating of metals or formed products
PA: K.C. Jones Plating Co.
2845 E 10 Mile Rd
Warren MI 48091
586 755-4900

(G-2129)
CAPITOL SOURCE NETWORK
366 E 600 N (46725-8915)
PHONE..........................260 248-9747
Thomas Lehman, VP
▼ EMP: 5 EST: 2011
SQ FT: 5,000
SALES (est): 202.28K Privately Held
SIC: 2086 Carbonated soft drinks, bottled and canned

(G-2130)
CHROMASOURCE INC
Also Called: Chromasource
2433 S Cr 600 E (46725)
P.O. Box P.O. Box 8300 (46898)
PHONE..........................260 420-3000
▲ EMP: 140 EST: 1995
SQ FT: 130,000
SALES (est): 24.29MM Privately Held
Web: www.chromasource.com
SIC: 2752 7336 Offset printing; Commercial art and graphic design

(G-2131)
CHS LEGACY COMPANY
2921 E Crescent Ave (46725-9315)
P.O. Box 13343 (46868-3343)
PHONE..........................260 456-3596
Terri Parker, CFO
Scott Sanderson, Pr
Chuck Sanderson, VP
EMP: 9 EST: 1964
SALES (est): 1MM Privately Held
Web: www.superiorwaterconditioners.com
SIC: 3589 Water treatment equipment, industrial

(G-2132)
CITY OF COLUMBIA CITY
925 E Van Buren St (46725-1916)
PHONE..........................260 248-5118
Mike Dear, Brnch Mgr
EMP: 7
Web: www.columbiacity.net
SIC: 3589 Water treatment equipment, industrial
PA: City Of Columbia City
112 S Chauncey St Rm C
Columbia City IN 46725
260 248-5100

(G-2133)
CLAYWOOD CREATION
111 S Briarwood Ln (46725-8709)
PHONE..........................260 244-7719
Jerry Krider, Owner
EMP: 4 EST: 1991
SALES (est): 158.76K Privately Held
SIC: 3944 Puzzles

(G-2134)
COLUMBIA CITY PLASTICS INC
831 E Short St (46725-8743)
P.O. Box 86 (46725-0086)
PHONE..........................260 244-0065
EMP: 15 EST: 2016
SALES (est): 872.08K Privately Held
Web: www.columbiacityplastics.com
SIC: 3089 Injection molding of plastics

(G-2135)
COUNTRY WOODCRAFTS INC
2283 E State Road 205 (46725-9010)
PHONE..........................260 244-7578
EMP: 2 EST: 1983
SALES (est): 172.34K Privately Held
SIC: 3944 Craft and hobby kits and sets

(G-2136)
DANFOSS POWER SOLUTIONS II LLC
1380 S Williams Dr (46725-8750)
PHONE..........................260 248-5800
Tom Schlemmer, Brnch Mgr
EMP: 1
SALES (corp-wide): 11.6B Privately Held
SIC: 3625 Motor controls and accessories
HQ: Danfoss Power Solutions Ii, Llc
2800 E 13th St
Ames IA 50010
515 239-6000

(G-2137)
DEL PALMA ORTHOPEDICS LLC
5865 E State Road 14 (46725-9237)
PHONE..........................260 625-3169
Andrew Palmer, Managing Member
EMP: 3 EST: 2008
SALES (est): 285.95K Privately Held
Web: www.delpalmaortho.com
SIC: 3842 Orthopedic appliances

(G-2138)
DOT AMERICA INC
335 Towerview Dr (46725-8799)
PHONE..........................260 244-5700
Michael Venturini, Pr
EMP: 17 EST: 2013
SQ FT: 17,000
SALES (est): 4.81MM Privately Held
Web: www.dot-coatingusa.com
SIC: 3471 Finishing, metals or formed products
HQ: Dot Gmbh
Charles-Darwin-Ring 1a
Rostock MV 18059
38140335

(G-2139)
DPS PRINTING LLC
950 Liberty Dr (46725-1123)
PHONE..........................260 503-9681
Ryan Carper, Prin
EMP: 2 EST: 2011
SALES (est): 212.74K Privately Held
SIC: 2752 Offset printing

(G-2140)
DULCIUS VINEYARDS LLC
2573 W 500 S-57 (46725-9444)
PHONE..........................260 602-9259
Scott O Fergusson, Pt
EMP: 4 EST: 2014
SALES (est): 93.66K Privately Held
Web: www.dulciusvineyards.com
SIC: 2084 Wines

(G-2141)
DYNAMIC COMPOSITES LLC
2670 S 700 E (46725-9044)
PHONE..........................260 625-8686
EMP: 4 EST: 2005
SALES (est): 468.8K Privately Held
SIC: 3272 5051 Ties, railroad: concrete; Rails and accessories

(G-2142)
ERAPSCO
Also Called: Sonobuoy Tech Systems
4868 E Park 30 Dr (46725-8861)
PHONE..........................386 740-5361
Roland Fritts, Mng Pt
Eric Webster, Pr
EMP: 1 EST: 1989
SALES (est): 191.62K Privately Held
Web: www.erapsco.com
SIC: 3443 Fabricated plate work (boiler shop)

(G-2143)
ERS AUTOMATION INC
1420 S 500 E (46725-9049)
PHONE..........................260 341-8114
EMP: 5 EST: 1995
SQ FT: 1,000
SALES (est): 393.38K Privately Held
Web: www.ersautomation.com
SIC: 7373 3625 Systems integration services; Relays and industrial controls

(G-2144)
ESSEX FRKAWA MGNT WIRE USA LLC
Also Called: Essex Wire & Cable Division
2499 S 600 E (46725-9029)
PHONE..........................260 424-1708
Ron Stiltner, Brnch Mgr
EMP: 7
Web: www.essexfurukawa.com
SIC: 4841 3315 Cable television services; Steel wire and related products
HQ: Essex Furukawa Magnet Wire Usa Llc
5770 Pwr Frry Rd Nw Ste 3
Atlanta GA 30327
770 657-6000

(G-2145)
ESSEX FRKAWA MGNT WIRE USA LLC
Superior Essex
2601 S 600 E (46725-9097)
PHONE..........................260 248-5500
William Nicolson, Mgr
EMP: 24
Web: www.essexfurukawa.com
SIC: 3357 Nonferrous wiredrawing and insulating
HQ: Essex Furukawa Magnet Wire Usa Llc
5770 Pwr Frry Rd Nw Ste 3
Atlanta GA 30327
770 657-6000

(G-2146)
ESSEX FRKAWA MGNT WIRE USA LLC
2580 S 600 St E (46725-9097)
PHONE..........................260 248-5500
David Hockerman, Mgr
EMP: 12
Web: www.essexfurukawa.com
SIC: 3357 3496 3315 Building wire and cable, nonferrous; Miscellaneous fabricated wire products; Steel wire and related products
HQ: Essex Furukawa Magnet Wire Usa Llc
5770 Pwr Frry Rd Nw Ste 3
Atlanta GA 30327
770 657-6000

(G-2147)
FORT WAYNE METALS RES PDTS LLC
Also Called: Fort Wayne Metals
2300 E Cardinal Dr (46725-8789)
PHONE..........................260 747-4154
EMP: 1
SALES (corp-wide): 112.25MM Privately Held
Web: www.fwmetals.com
SIC: 3315 Wire, steel: insulated or armored

PA: Fort Wayne Metals Research Products, Llc
9609 Ardmore Ave
Fort Wayne IN 46809
260 747-4154

(G-2148)
GATOR CASES INC
Also Called: Gator Cases
2499 S 600 E (46725-9029)
PHONE..........................260 627-8070
Crystal Morris, Pr
▲ EMP: 10 EST: 2011
SALES (est): 2.3MM Privately Held
Web: www.gatorco.com
SIC: 3523 Farm machinery and equipment

(G-2149)
GENERAL MACHINE BROKERS INC
1295 E 600 N (46725-8944)
PHONE..........................260 691-3800
Michael D Worthman, Pr
EMP: 7 EST: 2001
SALES (est): 232.41K Privately Held
SIC: 3599 Machine shop, jobbing and repair

(G-2150)
HINEN PRINTING CO
117 W Market St (46725-2311)
PHONE..........................260 248-8984
Jeff Hinen, Owner
EMP: 8 EST: 1988
SQ FT: 6,000
SALES (est): 864.79K Privately Held
Web: www.hinenprinting.com
SIC: 2759 2791 2789 2752 Screen printing; Typesetting; Bookbinding and related work; Commercial printing, lithographic

(G-2151)
HOLMES & COMPANY LLC
807 E Ellsworth St (46725-2508)
P.O. Box 370 (46725-0370)
PHONE..........................260 244-6149
Daniel E Almendinger, Pr
Stephanie J Greer, *
Larry Almendinger, *
◆ EMP: 50 EST: 1983
SQ FT: 100,000
SALES (est): 4.42MM Privately Held
Web: holmescompanyinc.yolasite.com
SIC: 2421 Sawmills and planing mills, general

(G-2152)
HORIZON PUBLICATIONS INC
Also Called: Post and Mail
927 W Connexion Way (46725-1031)
P.O. Box 39 (46755-0039)
PHONE..........................260 244-5153
Doug Brown, Brnch Mgr
EMP: 6
SALES (corp-wide): 47.1MM Privately Held
Web: www.horizonpublicationsinc.com
SIC: 2711 Newspapers, publishing and printing
PA: Horizon Publications, Inc.
1120 N Carbon St Ste 100
Marion IL 62959
618 993-1711

(G-2153)
HUTHONE LLC
707 Burke St (46725-7751)
PHONE..........................260 248-2384
Charles Grabach, Prin
EMP: 7 EST: 2015
SALES (est): 154.28K Privately Held
SIC: 3471 Plating of metals or formed products

Columbia City - Whitley County (G-2179)

(G-2154)
IMPACT CNC LLC (PA)
2651 S 600 E (46725-9097)
P.O. Box 669 (46725-0669)
PHONE.....................260 244-5511
Jerry Busche, *Pr*
Bret Sherwin, *
Karen Harpel, *
EMP: 75 **EST:** 2011
SQ FT: 29,400
SALES (est): 17MM
SALES (corp-wide): 17MM **Privately Held**
Web: www.impactcnc.net
SIC: 3577 Computer peripheral equipment, nec

(G-2155)
INDIANA MATERIALS PROC LLC
5750 E Rail Connect Dr (46725-9498)
PHONE.....................260 244-6026
Abid Bengali, *Owner*
EMP: 15 **EST:** 2012
SALES (est): 1.03MM **Privately Held**
SIC: 3999 Barber and beauty shop equipment

(G-2156)
INK SPOT TATTOO
302 S Main St (46725-2142)
PHONE.....................260 244-0025
Sean Blaine, *Owner*
EMP: 6 **EST:** 2004
SALES (est): 158.35K **Privately Held**
SIC: 2752 Offset printing

(G-2157)
IOTRON INDUSTRIES USA INC
Also Called: Sterigenics
4394 E Park 30 Dr (46725-8517)
PHONE.....................260 212-1722
EMP: 20 **EST:** 2010
SALES (est): 4.61MM
SALES (corp-wide): 1.05B **Publicly Held**
Web: www.sterigenics.com
SIC: 3671 Electron beam (beta ray) generator tubes
HQ: Sterigenics Radiation Technologies Canada, Inc
1425 Kebet Way
Port Coquitlam BC
604 945-8838

(G-2158)
J MILLER CABINET COMPANY INC
Also Called: J Miller Cabinet Company
5874 N 350 E (46725-9373)
PHONE.....................260 691-2032
Steven Marschand, *Pr*
Cheryl Marschand, *Sec*
EMP: 8 **EST:** 1949
SQ FT: 10,000
SALES (est): 851.93K **Privately Held**
Web: www.patrioteer.org
SIC: 2511 2434 Wood household furniture; Vanities, bathroom: wood

(G-2159)
JEANNIE AND RACHEL HEIDENREICH
1240 N Airport Rd (46725-8619)
PHONE.....................260 244-4583
Jeannie Heidenreich, *Prin*
EMP: 2 **EST:** 2005
SALES (est): 60.18K **Privately Held**
SIC: 7539 3621 Alternators and generators, rebuilding and repair; Starters, for motors

(G-2160)
JIGSAW CREATIONS LLC
5867 N 350 E (46725-9341)
PHONE.....................260 691-2196
Lory Norden, *Owner*
EMP: 2 **EST:** 2010
SALES (est): 129.51K **Privately Held**
Web: www.jigsawcreations.com
SIC: 3944 Puzzles

(G-2161)
JMS MACHINE INC
307 Diamond Ave (46725-2448)
P.O. Box 422 (46725-0422)
PHONE.....................260 244-0077
Jonathan Smith, *Pr*
Michelle Smith, *VP*
EMP: 2 **EST:** 2004
SALES (est): 266.5K **Privately Held**
Web: jmsmachine.tripod.com
SIC: 3599 Custom machinery

(G-2162)
KILGORE MANUFACTURING CO INC
Also Called: Kilgore Mfg Plant No 1
445 S Line St (46725-2443)
PHONE.....................260 248-2002
John E Hicks, *Pr*
◆ **EMP:** 63 **EST:** 1984
SQ FT: 25,000
SALES (est): 9.86MM **Privately Held**
Web: www.kilgoremfg.com
SIC: 3841 3492 5047 3052 Surgical and medical instruments; Hose and tube fittings and assemblies, hydraulic/pneumatic; Medical and hospital equipment; Rubber and plastics hose and beltings

(G-2163)
KYOCERA SGS PRECISION TLS INC
Also Called: SGS Tool
201 Towerview Dr (46725-8799)
PHONE.....................260 244-7677
Drew Johnson, *Prin*
EMP: 14 **EST:** 2009
SALES (est): 2.57MM **Privately Held**
Web: www.ksptmedical.com
SIC: 3545 Cutting tools for machine tools

(G-2164)
L B FOSTER COMPANY
2658 S 700 E (46725-9044)
PHONE.....................260 244-2887
Joe Flores, *Prin*
EMP: 5
SALES (corp-wide): 543.74MM **Publicly Held**
Web: www.lbfoster.com
SIC: 3312 Railroad crossings, steel or iron
PA: L. B. Foster Company
415 Holiday Dr Ste 100
Pittsburgh PA 15220
412 928-3400

(G-2165)
LAKESIDE EMBROIDERY
735 E Spear Rd (46725-8963)
PHONE.....................260 691-3289
Lisa Wilson, *Prin*
EMP: 1 **EST:** 2004
SALES (est): 42K **Privately Held**
SIC: 2395 Embroidery and art needlework

(G-2166)
LATHE SPECIALTIES CO INC
2299 E Business 30 (46725-8426)
PHONE.....................260 244-3629
Dewey Lackey, *Pr*
EMP: 9 **EST:** 1976
SQ FT: 5,600
SALES (est): 737.73K **Privately Held**
SIC: 3599 Machine shop, jobbing and repair

(G-2167)
LEAR CORPORATION
Also Called: Advanced Assembly
2101 S 600 E (46725-9029)
PHONE.....................260 244-1700
Jerry Leamere, *Mgr*
EMP: 99
SALES (corp-wide): 23.47B **Publicly Held**
Web: www.lear.com
SIC: 3714 Motor vehicle parts and accessories
PA: Lear Corporation
21557 Telegraph Rd
Southfield MI 48033
248 447-1500

(G-2168)
LEVY ENVIRONMENTAL SERVICES CO
Also Called: Columbia City Mill Service
2734 S 800 E (46725-8892)
PHONE.....................260 625-4930
Tammie Lowrance, *Brnch Mgr*
EMP: 50
SALES (corp-wide): 513.22MM **Privately Held**
Web: www.edwclevy.com
SIC: 3295 Slag, crushed or ground
HQ: Levy Environmental Services Company
9300 Dix
Dearborn MI 48120

(G-2169)
MACH MEDICAL LLC
4707 E Park 30 Dr (46725-8871)
PHONE.....................260 229-1514
Stephen Rozow, *Pr*
Chad Blair, *Finance Leader**
EMP: 30 **EST:** 2019
SALES (est): 3.56MM **Privately Held**
Web: www.machmedicalcmo.com
SIC: 3841 Surgical and medical instruments

(G-2170)
MICHFAB MACHINERY
201 Towerview Dr (46725-8799)
PHONE.....................260 244-6117
Scott Richmond, *Prin*
EMP: 7 **EST:** 2016
SALES (est): 81.49K **Privately Held**
Web: www.michfab.com
SIC: 3599 Industrial machinery, nec

(G-2171)
MICROPULSE INC (PA)
5865 E State Road 14 (46725-9237)
PHONE.....................260 625-3304
Brian G Emerick, *
Brian G Emerick, *
Sonya Emerick, *
Brian More, *
EMP: 239 **EST:** 1988
SQ FT: 105,000
SALES (est): 42.37MM
SALES (corp-wide): 42.37MM **Privately Held**
Web: www.micropulseinc.com
SIC: 3841 Surgical and medical instruments

(G-2172)
MOO-OVER LLC
207 W Van Buren St (46725-2037)
PHONE.....................260 224-2108
Julie Hurd, *CEO*
EMP: 9 **EST:** 2018
SALES (est): 723.98K **Privately Held**
Web: www.moo-over.com
SIC: 2024 Nondairy based frozen desserts

(G-2173)
NANOVIS LLC (PA)
5865 E State Road 14 (46725-9237)
PHONE.....................260 625-1502
Matt Hedrick, *Bd of Dir*
Brian Emerick, *Bd of Dir*
Steve Gerrish, *Bd of Dir*
Brian More, *Bd of Dir*
EMP: 5 **EST:** 2008
SQ FT: 3,000
SALES (est): 1.85MM **Privately Held**
Web: www.nanovistechnology.com
SIC: 3841 Surgical and medical instruments

(G-2174)
NIBLOCK EXCAVATING INC
1080 Spartan Dr Ste C (46725-1043)
PHONE.....................260 248-2100
EMP: 4
SALES (corp-wide): 14.26MM **Privately Held**
Web: www.niblockexc.com
SIC: 2951 1794 1771 1611 Asphalt paving mixtures and blocks; Excavation work; Concrete work; Highway and street construction
PA: Niblock Excavating Inc
906 Maple St
Bristol IN 46507
574 848-4437

(G-2175)
NUMERIX INC
406 Diamond Ave Ste B (46725-2451)
PHONE.....................260 248-2942
Jeffrey Johnson, *Pr*
EMP: 7 **EST:** 2002
SQ FT: 7,000
SALES (est): 970.92K **Privately Held**
Web: www.numerixinc.com
SIC: 3599 Machine shop, jobbing and repair

(G-2176)
OAK VIEW TOOLING INC
724 E Swihart St (46725-2767)
PHONE.....................260 244-7677
Matthew T Dahms, *Pr*
Tonnette Dahms, *VP*
EMP: 14 **EST:** 2002
SQ FT: 5,000
SALES (est): 347.95K **Privately Held**
Web: www.oakviewtooling.com
SIC: 3599 Machine shop, jobbing and repair

(G-2177)
OLD WORLD FUDGE & CDS DOGS LLC
206 Raleigh Ct (46725-7424)
PHONE.....................260 610-2249
Cris Lamb, *Pr*
EMP: 6 **EST:** 2014
SALES (est): 93.9K **Privately Held**
SIC: 2064 Fudge (candy)

(G-2178)
ORR MOTOR SPORTS
3151 S State Road 9 (46725-9665)
PHONE.....................260 244-2681
Jason Orr, *Owner*
EMP: 1 **EST:** 2000
SALES (est): 243.48K **Privately Held**
Web: www.weserveullc.com
SIC: 5571 3751 Motorcycles; Motorcycle accessories

(G-2179)
PDQ WORKHOLDING LLC
Also Called: P D Q
1100 S Williams Dr # 1 (46725)
P.O. Box 371 (46725)

Columbia City - Whitley County (G-2180)

PHONE............................260 244-2919
Jerry Busche, *Managing Member*
▲ **EMP:** 25 **EST:** 2010
SALES (est): 5.83MM **Privately Held**
Web: www.pdqwh.com
SIC: 3553 Woodworking machinery

(G-2180)
PHILLIPS DIVERSIFIED SERVICES
309 N Washington St (46725-1718)
P.O. Box 161 (46725-0161)
PHONE............................260 248-2975
John Phillips, *Owner*
EMP: 6 **EST:** 1979
SALES (est): 235.58K **Privately Held**
SIC: 2759 Invitations: printing, nsk

(G-2181)
PINE VALLEY MUNITIONS INC
Also Called: Pvm
555 N Line St (46725)
PHONE............................260 818-6113
Quinlan Wall, *Pr*
EMP: 6 **EST:** 2019
SALES (est): 415.91K **Privately Held**
SIC: 3483 5941 5099 Ammunition components; Ammunition; Firearms and ammunition, except sporting

(G-2182)
POPTIQUE POPCORN LLC
120 W Walker Way Ste C (46725-1339)
PHONE............................260 244-3745
EMP: 4 **EST:** 2008
SALES (est): 312.94K **Privately Held**
Web: www.poptiquepopcorn.com
SIC: 2064 Popcorn balls or other treated popcorn products

(G-2183)
PRECISION PLASTICS INDIANA INC
Also Called: Precision Plastics
900 W Connexion Way (46725-1028)
PHONE............................260 244-6114
Ronald R Richey, *Pr*
Ryan B Richey, *
Terry Farber, *
EMP: 150 **EST:** 1955
SQ FT: 75,000
SALES (est): 21.86MM **Privately Held**
Web: www.titusplus.com
SIC: 3089 3544 Injection molded finished plastics products, nec; Industrial molds

(G-2184)
PYROTEK INCORPORATED
4447 E Park 30 Dr (46725-8872)
PHONE............................260 248-4141
Scott Denning, *Brnch Mgr*
EMP: 96
SALES (corp-wide): 462.43MM **Privately Held**
Web: www.pyrotek.com
SIC: 3229 8748 Glass fiber products; Business consulting, nec
PA: Pyrotek Incorporated
705 W 1st Ave
Spokane WA 99201
509 926-6212

(G-2185)
QIG LLC
Also Called: Quality Inspection and Gage
225 Towerview Dr (46725-8799)
PHONE............................260 244-3591
EMP: 20 **EST:** 1982
SQ FT: 20,000
SALES (est): 2.24MM **Privately Held**
Web: www.qigage.com

SIC: 3599 3541 8734 Custom machinery; Machine tools, metal cutting type; Calibration and certification

(G-2186)
QUALITEX INC
4185 E Park 30 Dr (46725-7587)
PHONE............................260 244-7839
◆ **EMP:** 10 **EST:** 1993
SQ FT: 10,000
SALES (est): 3.17MM **Privately Held**
Web: www.qualitexinc.net
SIC: 7549 3674 Inspection and diagnostic service, automotive; Strain gages, solid state

(G-2187)
R & R MANUFACTURING
Also Called: R & R
1150 W 150 N (46725-9586)
P.O. Box 84 (46725-0084)
PHONE............................260 244-5621
Randy L Plew, *Owner*
EMP: 3 **EST:** 1972
SQ FT: 5,100
SALES (est): 236.15K **Privately Held**
Web: www.postboxx.com
SIC: 3444 Mail (post office) collection or storage boxes, sheet metal

(G-2188)
REELCRAFT INDUSTRIES INC
2842 E Business 30 (46725-8451)
P.O. Box 248 (46725-0248)
PHONE............................855 634-9109
Robert Law, *Pr*
Jeffrey Delisi, *
Drew Cross, *
◆ **EMP:** 177 **EST:** 1971
SQ FT: 80,000
SALES (est): 45.07MM
SALES (corp-wide): 3.08B **Privately Held**
Web: www.reelcraft.com
SIC: 3496 3499 3429 Miscellaneous fabricated wire products; Reels, cable: metal ; Hardware, nec
PA: Madison Industries Holdings Llc
444 W Lake St Ste 4400
Chicago IL 60606
312 277-0156

(G-2189)
RESTORATION MED POLYMERS LLC
4474 E Park 30 Dr (46725-8872)
PHONE............................260 625-1573
EMP: 48 **EST:** 2015
SALES (est): 15.33MM **Privately Held**
Web: www.rmpoly.com
SIC: 3841 Diagnostic apparatus, medical

(G-2190)
RICHARD J BAGAN INC
Also Called: Montech USA
1280 S Williams Dr (46725-7528)
P.O. Box 169 (46725-0169)
PHONE............................260 244-5115
Richard J Bagan, *Pr*
EMP: 50 **EST:** 1974
SQ FT: 32,000
SALES (est): 8.42MM **Privately Held**
Web: www.rjbagan.com
SIC: 7629 5084 3613 Electronic equipment repair; Instruments and control equipment; Panel and distribution boards and other related apparatus

(G-2191)
RICKIE ALLAN PEASE
Also Called: Rick's Tool Company
406 Diamond Ave (46725-2450)
P.O. Box 151 (46725-0151)

PHONE............................260 244-7579
Rickie Allan Pease, *Owner*
Rick Pease, *Owner*
EMP: 6 **EST:** 2003
SALES (est): 220K **Privately Held**
SIC: 3542 Thread rolling machines

(G-2192)
ROBCO ENGINEERED RBR PDTS INC
707 E Short St (46725-7400)
PHONE............................260 248-2888
Mark Roberts, *Pr*
Robert Holler, *VP*
Gwenn Roberts, *Sec*
EMP: 10 **EST:** 1996
SQ FT: 6,500
SALES (est): 973.8K **Privately Held**
Web: www.endvibes.com
SIC: 3069 3829 Rubber floorcoverings/mats and wallcoverings; Measuring and controlling devices, nec

(G-2193)
RTC
Also Called: RTC Threaders
1901 N Airport Rd (46725-8677)
PHONE............................260 503-9770
Rick A Pease, *Owner*
EMP: 6 **EST:** 2005
SALES (est): 402.31K **Privately Held**
Web: www.rtc.com
SIC: 3451 7389 Screw machine products; Business Activities at Non-Commercial Site

(G-2194)
RUNNING AROUND SCREEN PRTG LLC
227 W Van Buren St (46725-2037)
PHONE............................260 248-1216
Joann Bird, *Owner*
EMP: 9 **EST:** 2009
SALES (est): 479.81K **Privately Held**
Web: www.runningaroundscreenprinting.com
SIC: 2759 Screen printing

(G-2195)
SAILRITE ENTERPRISES INC
2390 E 100 S (46725-9800)
PHONE............................260 244-4647
Hallie R Grant, *Pr*
Matthew M Grant, *VP*
◆ **EMP:** 19 **EST:** 1969
SALES (est): 4.86MM **Privately Held**
Web: www.sailrite.com
SIC: 5961 3639 Catalog and mail-order houses; Sewing machines and attachments, domestic

(G-2196)
SCHWARTZVILLE PALLET
4861 W 300 S (46725-9722)
PHONE............................260 244-4144
EMP: 4 **EST:** 2015
SALES (est): 108.33K **Privately Held**
SIC: 2448 Pallets, wood and wood with metal

(G-2197)
SIMMONS EQUIPMENT SALES INC
6025 S State Road 9 (46725-9662)
PHONE............................260 625-3308
Wallace E Simmons, *Pr*
Martha Simmons, *Sec*
EMP: 10 **EST:** 1971
SQ FT: 5,000
SALES (est): 768.42K **Privately Held**

SIC: 4214 5082 1389 Local trucking with storage; Road construction equipment; Construction, repair, and dismantling services

(G-2198)
SMED - TA/TD LLC
4707 E Park 30 Dr (46725-8871)
P.O. Box 330 (46725-0330)
PHONE............................260 625-3347
EMP: 2 **EST:** 2010
SALES (est): 100K **Privately Held**
SIC: 3841 Surgical and medical instruments

(G-2199)
SORDELET TOOL & DIE INC
2765 E Crescent Ave (46725-9316)
PHONE............................260 483-7258
Daniel Sordelet, *Pr*
Teresa Sordelet, *Sec*
EMP: 5 **EST:** 1969
SALES (est): 372.93K **Privately Held**
SIC: 3599 Machine shop, jobbing and repair

(G-2200)
SOURCE PRODUCTS INC
9875 S Washington Rd (46725-9623)
PHONE............................260 424-0864
John Wainwright, *Pr*
EMP: 3 **EST:** 1998
SQ FT: 2,700
SALES (est): 360.82K **Privately Held**
Web: www.sourceproducts.com
SIC: 5063 3646 Lighting fixtures, commercial and industrial; Commercial lighting fixtures

(G-2201)
SPEEDWAY REDI MIX INC
Also Called: Columbia City Ready Mix
400 S Whitley St (46725-2629)
P.O. Box 447 (46725-0447)
PHONE............................260 244-7205
Robert E Hursey, *Mgr*
EMP: 6
Web: www.speedwayredimix.com
SIC: 3273 Ready-mixed concrete
PA: Speedway Redi-Mix Inc
4820 Industrial Rd
Fort Wayne IN 46825

(G-2202)
STEEL DYNAMICS INC
Structural & Rail Division
2601 S County Rd 700 E (46725)
PHONE............................866 740-8700
John Nolan, *Mgr*
EMP: 574
Web: www.steeldynamics.com
SIC: 3312 Plate, sheet and strip, except coated products
PA: Steel Dynamics, Inc.
7575 W Jefferson Blvd
Fort Wayne IN 46804

(G-2203)
STEEL TANK & FABRICATING CORP
Also Called: Stafco
365 S James St (46725-8721)
P.O. Box 210 (46725-0210)
PHONE............................260 248-8971
TOLL FREE: 800
Patrick W Kennedy, *Pr*
Patrick W Kennedy, *Pr*
Carl T Norris, *General Vice President*
Gerald A Hemmelgarn, *VP Fin*
Gene Dietz, *Sec*
EMP: 20 **EST:** 1952
SQ FT: 15,000
SALES (est): 2.06MM **Privately Held**
Web: www.steeltankandfabricating.com

SIC: 3443 3714 3444 3441 Fabricated plate work (boiler shop); Motor vehicle parts and accessories; Sheet metalwork; Fabricated structural metal

(G-2204)
SUMMIT INDUSTRIAL TECH INC
501 W Van Buren St Ste C (46725-2077)
P.O. Box 507 (46725-0507)
PHONE..........................260 494-3461
Kevin Milliman, Pr
EMP: 3 **EST:** 2015
SALES (est): 247.71K Privately Held
SIC: 3559 Plastics working machinery

(G-2205)
T W MACHINE & GRINDING
7150 N 350 W (46725-9167)
PHONE..........................260 799-4236
Tom Wise, Prin
EMP: 6 **EST:** 2008
SALES (est): 163.91K Privately Held
SIC: 3599 Grinding castings for the trade

(G-2206)
TITUS PRECISION COMPANY
900 W Connexion Way (46725)
PHONE..........................260 244-6114
Matthew T Hurley, Pr
Ronald P Salkie, Treas
EMP: 6 **EST:** 2021
SALES (est): 674.48K Privately Held
Web: www.titusplus.com
SIC: 3495 3089 Precision springs; Injection molding of plastics

(G-2207)
TITUS TOOL COMPANY INC
Also Called: Titus Plus
900 W Connexion Way (46725-1028)
PHONE..........................206 447-1489
Matthew Hurley, Pr
Walter Zabriskie, Ch Bd
Sidney N Mendelsohn Junior, Sec
Ben Lee, Treas
▲ **EMP:** 12 **EST:** 1980
SALES (est): 7.23MM
SALES (corp-wide): 3.69MM Privately Held
Web: www.titusplus.com
SIC: 5085 3429 Fasteners and fastening equipment; Hardware, nec
PA: Titus International Ltd
  Brook Business
  Uxbridge MIDDX UB8 2
  189 520-3730

(G-2208)
TURNBOW PROSTHETICS LLC
522 W 1000 S (46725-9627)
PHONE..........................260 396-2234
Kent Turnbow, Brnch Mgr
EMP: 1
SALES (corp-wide): 207.56K Privately Held
Web: www.turnbowprosthetics.com
SIC: 3842 Prosthetic appliances
PA: Turnbow Prosthetics, Llc
  561 W Connexion Way
  Columbia City IN 46725
  260 244-0099

(G-2209)
UNDERSEA SENSOR SYSTEMS INC (DH)
Also Called: Ultra Electronics
4868 E Park 30 Dr (46725-8861)
PHONE..........................260 248-3500
David C Jost, CEO
◆ **EMP:** 43 **EST:** 1998
SQ FT: 150,000
SALES (est): 99.69MM
SALES (corp-wide): 2.67MM Privately Held
Web: www.umaritime.com
SIC: 3812 Nautical instruments
HQ: Ultra Electronics Holdings Limited
  Unit C1 Knaves Beech Business Centre
  High Wycombe BUCKS HP10
  208 813-4321

(G-2210)
VANGUARD MACHINE INC
965 W Ryan Rd (46725-8402)
PHONE..........................260 508-6044
Sean Oldfather, Prin
EMP: 11
SALES (est): 531.19K Privately Held
SIC: 3599 Machine and other job shop work

(G-2211)
VIKING INC
2740 E Business 30 (46725-8890)
P.O. Box 130 (46725-0130)
PHONE..........................260 244-6141
Mary L Schwenn, Pr
Donald A Schwenn, *
Steven Schwenn, *
EMP: 22 **EST:** 1949
SQ FT: 70,000
SALES (est): 2.19MM Privately Held
Web: www.vikinginc.com
SIC: 3714 3429 3061 Exhaust systems and parts, motor vehicle; Hardware, nec; Mechanical rubber goods

Columbus
Bartholomew County

(G-2212)
ACCURATE TURNING SOLUTIONS ✪
4141 W Carr Hill Rd (47201-8949)
PHONE..........................812 603-6612
Brian Rose, Genl Pt
Joshua Jeffries, Genl Pt
EMP: 2 **EST:** 2022
SALES (est): 106.53K Privately Held
SIC: 3599 7389 Machine and other job shop work; Business services, nec

(G-2213)
ACE WELDING AND MACHINE INC
2461 N Indianapolis Rd (47201-3521)
PHONE..........................812 379-9625
Dale L Goddard, Pr
EMP: 6 **EST:** 1969
SQ FT: 10,000
SALES (est): 481.75K Privately Held
Web: www.ace-welding.com
SIC: 7692 3444 3443 Welding repair; Sheet metalwork; Fabricated plate work (boiler shop)

(G-2214)
ADVANCED MOLD & ENGINEERING
7980 S International Dr (47201-3033)
PHONE..........................812 342-9000
Myron Moorman, CEO
EMP: 12 **EST:** 1994
SQ FT: 7,000
SALES (est): 1.85MM Privately Held
Web: www.advancedmoldandeng.com
SIC: 3544 Industrial molds

(G-2215)
AIM MEDIA INDIANA OPER LLC
Republic, The
2980 N National Rd Ste A (47201-3234)
PHONE..........................812 372-7811
Chuck Wells, Brnch Mgr
EMP: 84
SALES (corp-wide): 26.88MM Privately Held
Web: www.aimmediaindiana.com
SIC: 2711 Commercial printing and newspaper publishing combined
PA: Aim Media Indiana Operating, Llc
  2980 N National Rd # A
  Columbus IN 47201
  812 372-7811

(G-2216)
AIM MEDIA INDIANA OPER LLC (PA)
2980 N National Rd # A (47201)
P.O. Box 3011 (47202)
PHONE..........................812 372-7811
Jeremy Halbreich, CEO
Rick Starks, *
Jeff Rogers, *
EMP: 80 **EST:** 2015
SQ FT: 23,000
SALES (est): 26.88MM
SALES (corp-wide): 26.88MM Privately Held
Web: www.aimmediaindiana.com
SIC: 2741 2711 Miscellaneous publishing; Commercial printing and newspaper publishing combined

(G-2217)
AMERICAN AXLE MANUFACTURI
2805 Norcross Dr (47201-4911)
PHONE..........................812 418-7726
EMP: 12 **EST:** 2019
SALES (est): 3.68MM Privately Held
SIC: 3999 Manufacturing industries, nec

(G-2218)
AMERICAN URN INC
Also Called: A U I
2315 N Cherry St (47201-4321)
PHONE..........................812 379-5555
John J Head, Pr
Carter Jerman, VP
Joe Jerman, Treas
EMP: 1 **EST:** 1992
SQ FT: 6,000
SALES (est): 88.69K Privately Held
Web: www.auinc.com
SIC: 3281 5099 Urns, cut stone; Monuments and grave markers

(G-2219)
AMERICAS COML TRNSP RES CO LLC
Also Called: Act Research
4440 Middle Rd (47203-1831)
PHONE..........................812 379-2085
Kenneth Vieth Senior, Pr
Kenneth Vieth Junior, Managing Member
EMP: 14 **EST:** 1986
SQ FT: 3,000
SALES (est): 2.49MM Privately Held
Web: www.actresearch.net
SIC: 8732 2721 Economic research; Statistical reports (periodicals): publishing and printing

(G-2220)
ANGEL ARC WELDING
7551 Hartshaven Ln (47201-3405)
PHONE..........................812 322-9027
EMP: 4 **EST:** 2019
SALES (est): 25.09K Privately Held
SIC: 7692 Welding repair

(G-2221)
APPLIED LABORATORIES INC (HQ)
1600 W Brian Dr (47201)
P.O. Box 2127 (47202)
PHONE..........................812 372-2607
Anthony Moravec, CEO
▲ **EMP:** 38 **EST:** 1984
SQ FT: 80,000
SALES (est): 28.2MM
SALES (corp-wide): 48.72MM Privately Held
Web: www.appliedlabs.com
SIC: 2834 Pharmaceutical preparations
PA: Blairex Laboratories, Inc.
  1600 W Brian Dr
  Columbus IN 47201
  812 378-1864

(G-2222)
AUSTIN POWDER COMPANY
13468 W Old Nashville Rd (47201-8723)
PHONE..........................812 342-1237
EMP: 8
SALES (corp-wide): 749.73MM Privately Held
Web: www.austinpowder.com
SIC: 2892 Black powder (explosive)
HQ: Austin Powder Company
  25800 Science Park Dr # 300
  Cleveland OH 44122
  216 464-2400

(G-2223)
AUTOMATED DRIVE & DESIGN LLC
6350 Inwood Dr (47201-8449)
PHONE..........................812 342-0809
EMP: 5 **EST:** 1996
SALES (est): 419.01K Privately Held
Web: www.adandd.com
SIC: 3823 Differential pressure instruments, industrial process type

(G-2224)
B B & H TOOL OF COLUMBUS INC
2775 Roadway Dr (47201-7441)
PHONE..........................812 372-3707
Jerrett Deckard, Pr
Dale G Behrman, Treas
EMP: 14 **EST:** 1979
SQ FT: 7,500
SALES (est): 443.85K Privately Held
Web: b-b-h-tool-of-columbus-inc.business.site
SIC: 3544 Special dies and tools

(G-2225)
B&H CAPITAL INC
3460 Commerce Dr (47201-2204)
PHONE..........................812 376-9301
EMP: 300
SIC: 2653 2679 Boxes, corrugated: made from purchased materials; Excelsior, paper: made from purchased paper

(G-2226)
BETTNER WIRE COATING DIES INC
1230 Jackson St (47201-5774)
P.O. Box 872 (47202-0872)
PHONE..........................812 372-2732
Howard Bettner, Pr
Max Bettner, VP Mfg
Gerald Bettner, VP
Nelson Bettner, VP
Edith Bettner, Sec
EMP: 15 **EST:** 1987
SQ FT: 4,000
SALES (est): 517.03K Privately Held
Web: www.bettner.com
SIC: 3496 Miscellaneous fabricated wire products

(G-2227)
BOOTH SIGNS INC
Also Called: Fastsigns
1307 12th St (47201-5604)

Columbus - Bartholomew County (G-2228)

PHONE.............................812 376-7446
Donna Booth, *Pr*
EMP: 8 **EST:** 2013
SALES (est): 261.58K **Privately Held**
Web: www.fastsigns.com
SIC: 3993 Signs and advertising specialties

(G-2228)
BOYER MACHINE & TOOL CO INC
1080 S Gladstone Ave (47201-9520)
P.O. Box 422 (47202-0422)
PHONE.............................812 379-9581
William Boyer, *CEO*
David Boyer, *
Jennifer Wilson, *
▲ **EMP:** 45 **EST:** 1964
SQ FT: 33,998
SALES (est): 8.49MM **Privately Held**
Web: www.boyermachine.com
SIC: 3599 3569 5013 Machine shop, jobbing and repair; Assembly machines, non-metalworking; Automotive supplies and parts

(G-2229)
BRENT DEVERS
Also Called: Town Planner
1207 Washington St (47201-5721)
PHONE.............................812 657-3786
Brent Devers, *Prin*
EMP: 4 **EST:** 2019
SALES (est): 93.47K **Privately Held**
Web: www.townplanner.com
SIC: 2741 Miscellaneous publishing

(G-2230)
BRIAN T KLEM
Also Called: Laundry Room, The
4270 W Jonathan Moore Pike (47201-9585)
PHONE.............................812 342-4080
Brian Klem, *Owner*
EMP: 5 **EST:** 2000
SALES (est): 303.34K **Privately Held**
SIC: 3582 Washing machines, laundry: commercial, incl. coin-operated

(G-2231)
BUSINESS & INDUSTRIAL PDTS CO
Also Called: B I P C O
3552 Mockingbird Dr (47203-1333)
PHONE.............................812 376-6149
John Dougherty, *Pr*
EMP: 4 **EST:** 1990
SALES (est): 227.09K **Privately Held**
SIC: 3993 Advertising novelties

(G-2232)
C & S PROTOTYPING LLC
3345 Commerce Dr (47201-2201)
PHONE.............................812 343-8618
Steve Vawter, *Managing Member*
EMP: 1 **EST:** 2010
SALES (est): 223.01K **Privately Held**
Web: www.csprototyping.com
SIC: 3599 Machine shop, jobbing and repair

(G-2233)
CAPCO LLC
1349 Arcadia Dr (47201-8445)
PHONE.............................812 375-1700
Jun Hashizume, *VP*
▲ **EMP:** 84 **EST:** 1997
SQ FT: 24,000
SALES (est): 11.27MM **Privately Held**
Web: www.capco-llc.com
SIC: 3469 Stamping metal for the trade

(G-2234)
CARLTON WEST OIL COMPANY LLC
3237 Nugent Blvd (47203-1609)
PHONE.............................812 375-9689
William Haeberle, *Prin*
EMP: 6 **EST:** 2015
SALES (est): 366.76K **Privately Held**
SIC: 1311 Crude petroleum production

(G-2235)
CE SYSTEMS INC
Also Called: Cunningham Precision
1045 S Gladstone Ave (47201)
P.O. Box 348 (47202)
PHONE.............................812 372-8234
Mike Miller, *Pr*
Joseph Cunningham, *
▼ **EMP:** 34 **EST:** 1971
SQ FT: 32,000
SALES (est): 3.82MM **Privately Held**
Web: www.ce-systems.com
SIC: 3321 3365 3322 Gray and ductile iron foundries; Aluminum foundries; Malleable iron foundries

(G-2236)
CIDERLEAF TEA COMPANY INC
4525 Progress Dr (47201-8819)
PHONE.............................812 375-1937
Lalith Paranavitana, *Pr*
Doctor Randall Pflueger, *VP*
EMP: 2 **EST:** 2017
SALES (est): 64.39K **Privately Held**
SIC: 2099 Food preparations, nec

(G-2237)
CLEVELND-CLFFS TBLAR CMPNNTS L
150 W 450 S (47201-8872)
PHONE.............................812 341-3200
EMP: 148
SALES (corp-wide): 22B **Publicly Held**
Web: www.clevelandcliffs.com
SIC: 3317 Steel pipe and tubes
HQ: Cleveland-Cliffs Tubular Components Llc
30400 E Broadway St
Walbridge OH 43465
419 661-4150

(G-2238)
CMI PGI HOLDINGS LLC (HQ)
500 Jackson St (47201)
P.O. Box 3005 (47202)
PHONE.............................812 377-5000
Donald G Jackson, *Mgr*
Kevin Caudill, *Mgr*
EMP: 16 **EST:** 2011
SALES (est): 7.19MM
SALES (corp-wide): 34.06B **Publicly Held**
SIC: 3463 Engine or turbine forgings, nonferrous
PA: Cummins Inc.
500 Jackson St
Columbus IN 47201
812 377-5000

(G-2239)
CNS CUSTOM WOODWORKS INC
1053 Hummingbird Ln (47203-1310)
PHONE.............................812 350-2431
Scott Daugherty, *Pr*
EMP: 2 **EST:** 2012
SALES (est): 184.68K **Privately Held**
SIC: 2431 Millwork

(G-2240)
COCA COLA BOTTLING COMPANY I
Also Called: Coca-Cola
1334 Washington St (47201-5724)
PHONE.............................812 376-3381
Albert H Schumaker Ii, *Pr*
William Russell, *
EMP: 30 **EST:** 1886
SQ FT: 25,000
SALES (est): 3.1MM **Privately Held**
Web: www.columbuscoke.com
SIC: 2086 Bottled and canned soft drinks

(G-2241)
COLUMBUS CABINETRY LLC
1117 16th St (47201-5651)
PHONE.............................812 447-1005
Melissa Butiste, *Prin*
EMP: 5 **EST:** 2017
SALES (est): 81.17K **Privately Held**
Web: www.columbuscarpetinc.com
SIC: 2434 Wood kitchen cabinets

(G-2242)
COLUMBUS CSTM CBINETS FURN LLC
4475 Middle Rd (47203-1832)
PHONE.............................812 379-9411
EMP: 7 **EST:** 1980
SALES (est): 489.71K **Privately Held**
SIC: 7641 2519 2434 Antique furniture repair and restoration; Household furniture, except wood or metal: upholstered; Wood kitchen cabinets

(G-2243)
COLUMBUS ENGINEERING INC
Also Called: Cei
6600 S 50 W (47201-3964)
PHONE.............................812 342-1231
Burdett Noblitt, *Pr*
Ann Noblitt, *
Mike Noblitt, *
EMP: 35 **EST:** 1954
SQ FT: 45,000
SALES (est): 4.23MM **Privately Held**
Web: www.colengi.com
SIC: 3444 Sheet metalwork

(G-2244)
COLUMBUS INDUSTRIAL ELECTRIC
1625 N Indianapolis Rd (47201-3521)
PHONE.............................812 372-8414
Steven M Deppe, *Pr*
Mary Deppe, *CEO*
Francis Deppe, *VP*
Susan Chandler, *Sec*
Helen A Deppe, *Treas*
EMP: 13 **EST:** 1974
SQ FT: 31,000
SALES (est): 2.26MM **Privately Held**
Web: www.ciemotors.com
SIC: 7694 Electric motor repair

(G-2245)
COLUMBUS OPTICAL SERVICE INC
Also Called: Columbus Wholesale Optical
2475 Cottage Ave (47201-4476)
P.O. Box 259 (47202-0259)
PHONE.............................812 372-4117
Charles Oliver, *Pr*
Robert De Ment, *VP*
John Oliver, *VP*
EMP: 6 **EST:** 1964
SQ FT: 2,200
SALES (est): 492.89K **Privately Held**
Web: www.columbusoptical.com
SIC: 3851 5995 Eyeglasses, lenses and frames; Eyeglasses, prescription

(G-2246)
COLUMBUS PALLET CORP
1520 14th St (47201-5613)
P.O. Box 1189 (47202-1189)
PHONE.............................812 372-7272
Matt A Sebahar, *Pr*
EMP: 6 **EST:** 1984
SQ FT: 10,000
SALES (est): 564.31K **Privately Held**
SIC: 2448 Pallets, wood

(G-2247)
COLUMBUS VAULT CO
3100 S Us Highway 31 (47201-9099)
PHONE.............................812 372-3210
Ted Shanks, *Prin*
EMP: 7 **EST:** 2006
SALES (est): 81.8K **Privately Held**
SIC: 3272 Burial vaults, concrete or precast terrazzo

(G-2248)
CREATIVE TOOL AND MACHINING
4010 Middle Rd (47203-1835)
PHONE.............................812 378-3562
Angela Bailey, *Pr*
Gregory Exner, *Pr*
Angela Bailey, *Sec*
EMP: 20 **EST:** 1984
SQ FT: 17,500
SALES (est): 2.04MM **Privately Held**
Web: www.creativetool.net
SIC: 3599 3544 Machine shop, jobbing and repair; Special dies, tools, jigs, and fixtures

(G-2249)
CREGG CUSTOM CABINETS
12230 W 525 S (47201-3918)
PHONE.............................812 342-3605
Andy Cregg, *Owner*
EMP: 1 **EST:** 1997
SALES (est): 101.58K **Privately Held**
SIC: 2434 Wood kitchen cabinets

(G-2250)
CUMMINS AMERICAS INC (HQ)
Also Called: Cummins Engine
500 Jackson St (47201-6258)
PHONE.............................812 377-5000
Thomas Linebarger, *Ch*
Theodore M Solso, *Pr*
Mark Gestle, *VP*
Mario Rose, *Sec*
◆ **EMP:** 1 **EST:** 1965
SQ FT: 1,000
SALES (est): 33.74MM
SALES (corp-wide): 34.06B **Publicly Held**
SIC: 5084 3519 Engines and parts, diesel; Internal combustion engines, nec
PA: Cummins Inc.
500 Jackson St
Columbus IN 47201
812 377-5000

(G-2251)
CUMMINS CDC HOLDING INC
Also Called: Cummins
500 Jackson St (47201-6258)
PHONE.............................812 312-3162
Jennifer Rumsey, *CEO*
EMP: 50000 **EST:** 2002
SALES (est): 400.07MM
SALES (corp-wide): 34.06B **Publicly Held**
SIC: 3714 Motor vehicle parts and accessories
PA: Cummins Inc.
500 Jackson St
Columbus IN 47201
812 377-5000

(G-2252)
CUMMINS DIST HOLDCO INC (HQ)
Also Called: Cummins
500 Jackson St (47201-6258)
PHONE.............................812 377-5000
David Geraghty, *Ex Dir*

EMP: 24 **EST:** 2014
SALES (est): 7.77MM
SALES (corp-wide): 34.06B **Publicly Held**
Web: greatplains.cummins.com
SIC: 5091 3519 Sporting and recreation goods; Internal combustion engines, nec
PA: Cummins Inc.
500 Jackson St
Columbus IN 47201
812 377-5000

(G-2253)
CUMMINS EMISSION SOLUTIONS INC (HQ)
Also Called: Cummins
500 Jackson St (47201-6258)
PHONE...............615 986-2596
EMP: 57 **EST:** 2007
SALES (est): 58.99MM
SALES (corp-wide): 34.06B **Publicly Held**
SIC: 3714 3519 Exhaust systems and parts, motor vehicle; Internal combustion engines, nec
PA: Cummins Inc.
500 Jackson St
Columbus IN 47201
812 377-5000

(G-2254)
CUMMINS EMSSION SLTONS CLMBUS ✪
500 Jackson St (47201-6258)
PHONE...............800 286-6467
EMP: 29 **EST:** 2023
SALES (est): 7.61MM
SALES (corp-wide): 34.06B **Publicly Held**
SIC: 3519 3694 3621 Internal combustion engines, nec; Engine electrical equipment; Generator sets: gasoline, diesel, or dual-fuel
PA: Cummins Inc.
500 Jackson St
Columbus IN 47201
812 377-5000

(G-2255)
CUMMINS ENGINE HOLDING COMPANY
Also Called: Cummins
500 Jackson St (47201-6258)
PHONE...............812 377-5000
F Joseph Loughrey, *Pr*
Mark R Gerstle, *Sec*
James A Henderson, *VP*
Richard Joseph Freeland, *Pr*
James Lyons, *VP*
◆ **EMP:** 452 **EST:** 1980
SALES (est): 32.99MM
SALES (corp-wide): 34.06B **Publicly Held**
SIC: 3714 Motor vehicle parts and accessories
PA: Cummins Inc.
500 Jackson St
Columbus IN 47201
812 377-5000

(G-2256)
CUMMINS FILTRATION IP INC
500 Jackson St (47201)
PHONE...............615 514-7339
Greg Hoverson, *Pr*
Rakesh Gangwani, *Sec*
Toni Hickey, *Treas*
EMP: 6 **EST:** 2000
SALES (est): 8.88MM
SALES (corp-wide): 1.63B **Publicly Held**
SIC: 3564 Blowers and fans
HQ: Cummins Filtration Inc
26 Century Blvd Ste 500
Nashville TN 37214
812 312-3162

(G-2257)
CUMMINS FRANCHISE HOLDCO LLC
Also Called: Cummins
500 Jackson St (47201-6258)
PHONE...............812 377-5000
Zach Gillen, *Mgr*
EMP: 53 **EST:** 2015
SALES (est): 6.45MM
SALES (corp-wide): 34.06B **Publicly Held**
SIC: 3714 Motor vehicle parts and accessories
PA: Cummins Inc.
500 Jackson St
Columbus IN 47201
812 377-5000

(G-2258)
CUMMINS INC
7660 S International Dr (47201-3003)
P.O. Box 1789 (47202-1789)
PHONE...............812 377-5298
EMP: 51
SALES (corp-wide): 34.06B **Publicly Held**
Web: www.cummins.com
SIC: 3714 Motor vehicle parts and accessories
PA: Cummins Inc.
500 Jackson St
Columbus IN 47201
812 377-5000

(G-2259)
CUMMINS INC
910 S Marr Rd (47201-7440)
PHONE...............812 377-2932
Chad Rolfe, *Brnch Mgr*
EMP: 3
SALES (corp-wide): 34.06B **Publicly Held**
Web: www.cummins.com
SIC: 3714 3694 3621 3519 Motor vehicle parts and accessories; Engine electrical equipment; Generator sets: gasoline, diesel, or dual-fuel; Engines, diesel and semi-diesel or dual-fuel
PA: Cummins Inc.
500 Jackson St
Columbus IN 47201
812 377-5000

(G-2260)
CUMMINS INC
5175 N Warren Dr Ste 100 (47203-1702)
PHONE...............812 377-9914
EMP: 2
SALES (corp-wide): 34.06B **Publicly Held**
Web: www.cummins.com
SIC: 3714 Motor vehicle parts and accessories
PA: Cummins Inc.
500 Jackson St
Columbus IN 47201
812 377-5000

(G-2261)
CUMMINS INC
2879 Prairie Stream Way (47203-9046)
PHONE...............812 377-0150
EMP: 3
SALES (corp-wide): 34.06B **Publicly Held**
Web: www.cummins.com
SIC: 3714 Motor vehicle parts and accessories
PA: Cummins Inc.
500 Jackson St
Columbus IN 47201
812 377-5000

(G-2262)
CUMMINS INC
525 Jackson St (47201)
PHONE...............765 430-0093
James Kim, *Mgr*
EMP: 4
SALES (corp-wide): 34.06B **Publicly Held**
Web: www.cummins.com
SIC: 3714 Motor vehicle parts and accessories
PA: Cummins Inc.
500 Jackson St
Columbus IN 47201
812 377-5000

(G-2263)
CUMMINS INC
1350 Arcadia Dr (47201)
PHONE...............812 376-0742
Floyd Rutan, *Dir*
EMP: 11
SALES (corp-wide): 34.06B **Publicly Held**
Web: www.cummins.com
SIC: 3714 Motor vehicle parts and accessories
PA: Cummins Inc.
500 Jackson St
Columbus IN 47201
812 377-5000

(G-2264)
CUMMINS INC
1825 W 450 S (47201-3044)
PHONE...............812 524-6455
EMP: 6
SALES (corp-wide): 34.06B **Publicly Held**
Web: www.cummins.com
SIC: 5013 3519 Motor vehicle supplies and new parts; Internal combustion engines, nec
PA: Cummins Inc.
500 Jackson St
Columbus IN 47201
812 377-5000

(G-2265)
CUMMINS INC
4303 Washington St (47203-1140)
PHONE...............317 460-9843
EMP: 4
SALES (corp-wide): 34.06B **Publicly Held**
Web: www.cummins.com
SIC: 3519 Internal combustion engines, nec
PA: Cummins Inc.
500 Jackson St
Columbus IN 47201
812 377-5000

(G-2266)
CUMMINS INC
Also Called: Cummins Clmbus Mdrnge Eng Plan
2725 W County Road 450 (47201)
PHONE...............812 377-7739
EMP: 6
SALES (corp-wide): 34.06B **Publicly Held**
Web: www.cummins.com
SIC: 3519 Internal combustion engines, nec
PA: Cummins Inc.
500 Jackson St
Columbus IN 47201
812 377-5000

(G-2267)
CUMMINS INC
3540 W 450 S (47201-8870)
PHONE...............812 374-4774
EMP: 33
SALES (corp-wide): 34.06B **Publicly Held**
Web: www.cummins.com
SIC: 3519 Internal combustion engines, nec
PA: Cummins Inc.
500 Jackson St
Columbus IN 47201
812 377-5000

(G-2268)
CUMMINS INC
Also Called: Cummins Fuel Systems
1460 N National Rd (47201-5577)
PHONE...............812 377-6072
Per Lange, *Genl Mgr*
EMP: 36
SALES (corp-wide): 34.06B **Publicly Held**
Web: www.cummins.com
SIC: 3519 Internal combustion engines, nec
PA: Cummins Inc.
500 Jackson St
Columbus IN 47201
812 377-5000

(G-2269)
CUMMINS INC
Also Called: Cummins Technical Center
1900 Mckinley Ave (47201-6414)
P.O. Box 3005 (47202-3005)
PHONE...............812 377-7000
Sean Milloy, *Mgr*
EMP: 350
SALES (corp-wide): 34.06B **Publicly Held**
Web: www.cummins.com
SIC: 3519 Internal combustion engines, nec
PA: Cummins Inc.
500 Jackson St
Columbus IN 47201
812 377-5000

(G-2270)
CUMMINS INC
Also Called: Cummins Sales and Service
500 Jackson St (47201-6258)
PHONE...............812 312-3162
EMP: 4
SALES (corp-wide): 34.06B **Publicly Held**
Web: www.cummins.com
SIC: 3519 3694 Internal combustion engines, nec; Engine electrical equipment
PA: Cummins Inc.
500 Jackson St
Columbus IN 47201
812 377-5000

(G-2271)
CUMMINS INC (PA)
Also Called: Cummins
500 Jackson St (47201)
P.O. Box 3005 (47202)
PHONE...............812 377-5000
Jennifer Rumsey, *Ch Bd*
Mark A Smith, *VP*
Nicole Y Lamb-hale, *CLO*
Marvin Boakye, *Chief Human Resource Officer*
Sharon R Barner, *VP*
EMP: 2565 **EST:** 1919
SALES (est): 34.06B
SALES (corp-wide): 34.06B **Publicly Held**
Web: www.cummins.com
SIC: 3519 3694 3621 Internal combustion engines, nec; Engine electrical equipment; Generator sets: gasoline, diesel, or dual-fuel

(G-2272)
CUMMINS INC
2851 State St (47201-7449)
PHONE...............812 377-8601
EMP: 6
SALES (corp-wide): 34.06B **Publicly Held**
Web: www.cummins.com
SIC: 3519 3714 3694 3621 Internal combustion engines, nec; Motor vehicle parts and accessories; Engine electrical equipment; Generator sets: gasoline, diesel, or dual-fuel
PA: Cummins Inc.
500 Jackson St
Columbus IN 47201

Columbus - Bartholomew County (G-2273)

812 377-5000

(G-2273)
CUMMINS INC
301 Jackson St (47201)
PHONE..................812 378-2874
EMP: 13
SALES (corp-wide): 34.06B **Publicly Held**
Web: www.cummins.com
SIC: 3519 3714 3694 3621 Internal combustion engines, nec; Motor vehicle parts and accessories; Engine electrical equipment; Generator sets: gasoline, diesel, or dual-fuel
PA: Cummins Inc.
500 Jackson St
Columbus IN 47201
812 377-5000

(G-2274)
CUMMINS POWER SYSTEMS LLC
Also Called: CMI
500 Jackson St (47201-6258)
PHONE..................410 590-8700
Mark Zannino, *Prin*
EMP: 8000 **EST:** 2018
SALES (est): 99.45MM
SALES (corp-wide): 34.06B **Publicly Held**
SIC: 3714 Motor vehicle parts and accessories
PA: Cummins Inc.
500 Jackson St
Columbus IN 47201
812 377-5000

(G-2275)
CUMMINS-SCANIA XPI MFG LLC (PA)
Also Called: Cummins
1460 N National Rd (47201-5577)
PHONE..................812 377-5000
EMP: 7 **EST:** 2005
SALES (est): 13.73MM **Privately Held**
SIC: 3714 3519 Motor vehicle parts and accessories; Internal combustion engines, nec

(G-2276)
CUNNINGHAM PATTERN & ENGRG INC
4399 N Us Hwy 31 (47201-8558)
P.O. Box 854 (47202-0854)
PHONE..................812 379-9571
Mike Miller, *Pr*
EMP: 16 **EST:** 1965
SQ FT: 10,500
SALES (est): 2.47MM **Privately Held**
Web: www.cunninghamprecision.com
SIC: 3366 3599 3543 7374 Castings (except die), nsk; Machine shop, jobbing and repair; Industrial patterns; Optical scanning data service

(G-2277)
CUSTOMIZED MACHINING INC
8101 Sunset Ct (47201-2542)
PHONE..................765 490-7894
Troy Boggs, *Pr*
EMP: 4 **EST:** 2020
SALES (est): 90.8K **Privately Held**
SIC: 3599 Machine shop, jobbing and repair

(G-2278)
DARLAGE METALWORX LLC
1647 Washington St (47201-5124)
PHONE..................812 341-5530
Amanda Darlage, *Owner*
EMP: 4 **EST:** 2018
SALES (est): 85.5K **Privately Held**
Web: www.darlagemetalworx.com
SIC: 7692 Welding repair

(G-2279)
DARLING INGREDIENTS INC
Also Called: Columbus Transfer Station
345 Water St (47201-6771)
P.O. Box 301 (47202-0301)
PHONE..................317 708-3070
James Hollenbaugh, *Bmch Mgr*
EMP: 1
SALES (corp-wide): 6.79B **Publicly Held**
Web: www.darlingii.com
SIC: 2077 Animal and marine fats and oils
PA: Darling Ingredients Inc.
5601 N Macarthur Blvd
Irving TX 75038
972 717-0300

(G-2280)
DAVIDS INC
905 S Gladstone Ave (47201-9520)
P.O. Box 1031 (47202-1031)
PHONE..................812 376-6870
Michelle David, *Pr*
Jeffery David, *Sec*
EMP: 19 **EST:** 1976
SQ FT: 4,200
SALES (est): 916.67K **Privately Held**
Web: www.davidsinc.com
SIC: 3446 7692 3444 Fences, gates, posts, and flagpoles; Welding repair; Sheet metalwork

(G-2281)
DEBRA RICHARD
Also Called: Blackthorn Design Studio
4927 Denny (47201-8593)
PHONE..................812 379-4927
Debra Richard, *Owner*
EMP: 1 **EST:** 1988
SALES (est): 38.18K **Privately Held**
SIC: 7336 3993 Commercial art and graphic design; Signs and advertising specialties

(G-2282)
DEVENING BLOCK INC (PA)
895 Jonesville Rd (47201-7548)
P.O. Box 566 (47202-0566)
PHONE..................812 372-4458
Harry E Horn, *Pr*
Harry Horn, *
Steve Horn, *
EMP: 30 **EST:** 1952
SQ FT: 10,000
SALES (est): 5.29MM
SALES (corp-wide): 5.29MM **Privately Held**
SIC: 3271 5032 Concrete block and brick; Brick, stone, and related material

(G-2283)
DIAMET
8841 W 450 S (47201-5026)
PHONE..................812 379-4606
EMP: 4 **EST:** 2014
SALES (est): 214.85K **Privately Held**
SIC: 3714 Motor vehicle parts and accessories

(G-2284)
DIRECT INNOVATIONS LLC
4251 Fairlawn Dr (47203-2720)
PHONE..................812 343-6085
EMP: 1 **EST:** 2016
SALES (est): 58.16K **Privately Held**
SIC: 3441 Fabricated structural metal

(G-2285)
DOREL HOME FURNISHINGS INC
2525 State St (47201-7443)
PHONE..................812 372-0141
Troy Franks, *Bmch Mgr*

EMP: 67
SALES (corp-wide): 1.39B **Privately Held**
Web: www.ameriwoodhome.com
SIC: 2511 Console tables: wood
HQ: Dorel Home Furnishings, Inc.
410 E 1st St S
Wright City MO 63390
636 745-3351

(G-2286)
DOREL JUVENILE GROUP INC
505 S Cherry St (47201)
PHONE..................812 372-0141
Chuck Caldwell, *Mgr*
EMP: 3
SALES (corp-wide): 1.39B **Privately Held**
Web: na.doreljuvenile.com
SIC: 3089 Plastics kitchenware, tableware, and houseware
HQ: Dorel Juvenile Group, Inc.
2525 State St
Columbus IN 47201
800 457-5276

(G-2287)
DOREL JUVENILE GROUP INC
Also Called: Safety First
2525 State St (47201-7494)
PHONE..................812 372-0141
David Taylor, *CEO*
EMP: 114
SALES (corp-wide): 1.39B **Privately Held**
Web: na.doreljuvenile.com
SIC: 3944 Games, toys, and children's vehicles
HQ: Dorel Juvenile Group, Inc.
2525 State St
Columbus IN 47201
800 457-5276

(G-2288)
DOREL JUVENILE GROUP INC
500 S Gladstone Ave (47201-9520)
PHONE..................812 314-6629
Dale Fear, *Mgr*
EMP: 10
SALES (corp-wide): 1.39B **Privately Held**
Web: www.dorel.com
SIC: 3944 Baby carriages and restraint seats
HQ: Dorel Juvenile Group, Inc.
2525 State St
Columbus IN 47201
800 457-5276

(G-2289)
DOREL JUVENILE GROUP INC (DH)
Also Called: Cosco Home & Office Pdts Div
2525 State St (47201-7494)
P.O. Box 2609 (47202-2609)
PHONE..................800 457-5276
Nicolas Duran, *Pr*
Steven E Willeke, *
◆ **EMP:** 125 **EST:** 1984
SQ FT: 897,000
SALES (est): 112.23MM
SALES (corp-wide): 1.39B **Privately Held**
Web: na.doreljuvenile.com
SIC: 3944 Baby carriages and restraint seats
HQ: Dorel U.S.A., Inc.
2525 State St
Columbus IN 47201

(G-2290)
DOREL USA INC (HQ)
Also Called: Safety 1st Cosco
2525 State St (47201-7443)
PHONE..................812 372-0141
Nick Costides, *Pr*
Steve Willeke, *
Tim Ferguson, *
◆ **EMP:** 75 **EST:** 1991

SQ FT: 897,000
SALES (est): 204.79MM
SALES (corp-wide): 1.39B **Privately Held**
Web: www.dorel.com
SIC: 3944 2511 2514 Strollers, baby (vehicle); High chairs, children's: wood; Cribs: metal
PA: Les Industries Dorel Inc
1255 Av Greene Bureau 300
Westmount QC H3Z 2
514 934-3034

(G-2291)
DSE INC
Also Called: Screen Tech Designs
2651 Cessna Dr (47203-1877)
P.O. Box 686 (47202-0686)
PHONE..................812 376-0310
Paul Saddler, *Pr*
Scott Saddler, *
Jesse Saddler, *
EMP: 30 **EST:** 1982
SQ FT: 18,000
SALES (est): 2.57MM **Privately Held**
Web: www.stdesigns.com
SIC: 2759 3479 2396 2851 Screen printing; Painting, coating, and hot dipping; Automotive and apparel trimmings; Paints and allied products

(G-2292)
DWG DESIGN SERVICES CORP
Also Called: .dwg Tooling Technologies
1220 Washington St (47201-5746)
PHONE..................812 372-0864
William Dirk Rader, *Pr*
Gary Akin, *Sec*
Phil Miles, *Treas*
EMP: 4 **EST:** 2001
SQ FT: 1,800
SALES (est): 437.51K **Privately Held**
Web: www.dwgservices.com
SIC: 3544 Special dies and tools

(G-2293)
E F M CORPORATION
Also Called: Product Engineering Company
1480 14th St (47201-5611)
PHONE..................812 372-4421
James Eversole, *Pr*
James Eversole, *Pr*
Lloyd D Meyer, *
EMP: 100 **EST:** 1945
SQ FT: 44,600
SALES (est): 6.78MM **Privately Held**
SIC: 3544 Special dies and tools

(G-2294)
ED LLOYD CO
13240 S 100 W (47201-4711)
PHONE..................812 342-2505
Ed Lloyd, *Owner*
EMP: 2 **EST:** 1996
SALES (est): 100K **Privately Held**
SIC: 2511 2431 Wood household furniture; Interior and ornamental woodwork and trim

(G-2295)
EJL TECH
461 S Mapleton St Ste B (47201-7362)
PHONE..................812 374-8808
EMP: 6 **EST:** 2011
SALES (est): 85.96K **Privately Held**
SIC: 3663 Radio and t.v. communications equipment

(G-2296)
ELEMENT CLUMBUS
8800 N Us Highway 31 (47201-4863)
PHONE..................812 526-2329
EMP: 4 **EST:** 2018
SALES (est): 142.61K **Privately Held**

SIC: 2819 Elements

(G-2297)
EM PRINTING & EMBROIDERY LLC
2221 Pear Tree Ct (47201-2740)
PHONE..................................812 373-0082
Michael R Bodart, *Owner*
EMP: 6 **EST:** 2014
SALES (est): 185.7K **Privately Held**
SIC: 2752 Commercial printing, lithographic

(G-2298)
ENKEI AMERICA INC (PA)
2900 Inwood Dr (47201-9758)
PHONE..................................812 373-7000
Makoto Miura, *CEO*
◆ **EMP:** 645 **EST:** 1985
SQ FT: 246,000
SALES (est): 84.1MM
SALES (corp-wide): 84.1MM **Privately Held**
Web: www.enkei.com
SIC: 3714 3365 Wheels, motor vehicle; Aluminum foundries

(G-2299)
ENKEI AMERICA MOLDINGS INC
2680 Norcross Dr (47201-8844)
PHONE..................................812 373-7000
Junichi Suzuki, *Pr*
▲ **EMP:** 1 **EST:** 2005
SALES (est): 3.13MM
SALES (corp-wide): 84.1MM **Privately Held**
Web: www.enkei.com
SIC: 3363 Aluminum die-castings
PA: Enkei America, Inc.
    2900 Inwood Dr
    Columbus IN 47201
    812 373-7000

(G-2300)
EYB PROMOTIONS
3490 Commerce Dr (47201-2204)
PHONE..................................812 376-3212
Sally Johnson, *Managing Member*
EMP: 4 **EST:** 2007
SALES (est): 229.18K **Privately Held**
Web: www.eybpromotions.com
SIC: 2395 Embroidery products, except Schiffli machine

(G-2301)
FALCON MANUFACTURING LLC
6200 S International Dr (47201-3034)
PHONE..................................317 884-3600
EMP: 15 **EST:** 2012
SQ FT: 468,000
SALES (est): 4.26MM **Privately Held**
Web: www.falcon-manufacturing.com
SIC: 3511 Turbines and turbine generator sets
PA: The Phoenix Group Inc
    164 S Park Blvd
    Greenwood IN 46143

(G-2302)
FAURECIA EMSSONS CTRL TECH USA
830 W 450 S (47201-5699)
PHONE..................................812 341-2000
Michael R Manson, *of*
EMP: 350
SALES (corp-wide): 100.93MM **Privately Held**
Web: www.faurecia.com
SIC: 3714 Air conditioner parts, motor vehicle
HQ: Faurecia Emissions Control
    Technologies Usa, Llc
    2800 High Meadow Cir
    Auburn Hills MI 48326

(G-2303)
FAURECIA EMSSONS CTRL TECH USA
Gladstone Div
601 S Gladstone Ave (47201-9520)
PHONE..................................812 348-4305
Mark Fraser, *Mgr*
EMP: 900
SALES (corp-wide): 100.93MM **Privately Held**
Web: www.faurecia.com
SIC: 3714 Motor vehicle parts and accessories
HQ: Faurecia Emissions Control
    Technologies Usa, Llc
    2800 High Meadow Cir
    Auburn Hills MI 48326

(G-2304)
FAURECIA EMSSONS CTRL TECH USA
17th Street Warehouse (47201)
PHONE..................................812 565-5214
EMP: 370
SALES (corp-wide): 100.93MM **Privately Held**
Web: www.faurecia.com
SIC: 3714 Exhaust systems and parts, motor vehicle
HQ: Faurecia Emissions Control
    Technologies Usa, Llc
    2800 High Meadow Cir
    Auburn Hills MI 48326

(G-2305)
FAURECIA EMSSONS CTRL TECH USA
Also Called: Faurecia Emissions Ctrl Tech
950 W 450 S Bldg 1 (47201-1520)
P.O. Box 3070 (47202-3070)
PHONE..................................812 341-2000
Buddy Wacaser, *Mgr*
EMP: 400
SALES (corp-wide): 100.93MM **Privately Held**
Web: www.faurecia.com
SIC: 3714 Exhaust systems and parts, motor vehicle
HQ: Faurecia Emissions Control
    Technologies Usa, Llc
    2800 High Meadow Cir
    Auburn Hills MI 48326

(G-2306)
FAURECIA EXHAUST SYSTEMS LLC
Also Called: Faurecia Emissions Control TEC
950 W 450 S (47201-1520)
PHONE..................................812 341-2079
EMP: 182
SALES (corp-wide): 100.93MM **Privately Held**
SIC: 3714 Exhaust systems and parts, motor vehicle
HQ: Faurecia Emissions Control Systems Na, Llc
    543 Matzinger Rd
    Toledo OH 43612
    812 341-2000

(G-2307)
FIRST METALS & PLASTICS INC
3805 Jonesville Rd (47201-7703)
P.O. Box 943 (47202-0943)
PHONE..................................812 379-4400
John Counceller, *Pr*
John D Counceller, *
Andrew Counceller, *
EMP: 32 **EST:** 2003
SQ FT: 50,000
SALES (est): 4.25MM **Privately Held**
Web: www.firstmetals.us

SIC: 3441 3089 Fabricated structural metal; Plastics processing

(G-2308)
FIRST METALS & PLASTICS TECHNOLOGIES INC
3805 Jonesville Rd (47201-7703)
P.O. Box 943 (47202-0943)
PHONE..................................812 379-4400
EMP: 50
Web: www.firstmetals.us
SIC: 3469 3089 Stamping metal for the trade ; Injection molding of plastics

(G-2309)
FLAMBEAU INC
4325 Middle Rd (47203-1882)
PHONE..................................812 372-4899
EMP: 5
Web: www.flambeau.com
SIC: 3089 Injection molding of plastics
HQ: Flambeau, Inc.
    801 Lynn Ave
    Baraboo WI 53913
    800 352-6266

(G-2310)
FLAMBEAU INC
4325 Middle Rd (47203-1882)
PHONE..................................812 372-4899
Rick Coffing, *Mgr*
EMP: 6
Web: www.flambeau.com
SIC: 3089 3949 3944 3469 Pallets, plastics; Decoys, duck and other game birds; Games, toys, and children's vehicles; Metal stampings, nec
HQ: Flambeau, Inc.
    801 Lynn Ave
    Baraboo WI 53913
    800 352-6266

(G-2311)
FUTURE TOOL & ENGRG CO INC
3400 Scott Dr (47201-4025)
PHONE..................................812 376-8699
Phil Westerfield, *Pr*
Phyllis Westerfield, *Sec*
EMP: 12 **EST:** 1992
SQ FT: 6,500
SALES (est): 1.9MM **Privately Held**
Web: www.futuretool.net
SIC: 3544 Special dies and tools

(G-2312)
G N HOLDINGS INC
4735 N Indianapolis Rd (47203-9440)
P.O. Box 908 (47202-0908)
PHONE..................................812 372-9969
EMP: 25
SIC: 3599 Machine and other job shop work

(G-2313)
GILLEYS REPAIR AND WELDING
1501 Wrenwood Dr (47201-8457)
PHONE..................................812 374-6009
Brandon Gilley, *Prin*
EMP: 4 **EST:** 2018
SALES (est): 47.61K **Privately Held**
SIC: 7692 Welding repair

(G-2314)
GRANITE ENGRG & TL CO INC (PA)
51 S Us Highway 31 (47201)
PHONE..................................812 375-9077
Joseph Harvey, *Pr*
Michael Coons, *VP*
Gregg Fields, *Genl Mgr*
EMP: 10 **EST:** 1993
SQ FT: 10,000

SALES (est): 1.2MM **Privately Held**
Web: www.graniteengineering.com
SIC: 3544 Special dies and tools

(G-2315)
GRIFFIN INDUSTRIES LLC
345 Water St (47201-6771)
P.O. Box 301 (47202-0301)
PHONE..................................812 379-9528
Tim Shuffet, *Mgr*
EMP: 62
SALES (corp-wide): 6.79B **Publicly Held**
Web: www.griffinind.com
SIC: 2077 2048 2011 Grease rendering, inedible; Prepared feeds, nec; Meat packing plants
HQ: Griffin Industries Llc
    4221 Alexandria Pike
    Cold Spring KY 41076
    859 781-2010

(G-2316)
HERITAGE DISTRIBUTING COMPANY
Also Called: Ninth Avenue Foods
6350 S 175 W (47201-9366)
PHONE..................................317 413-6514
Zach Pavlik, *Mgr*
EMP: 1
SIC: 2026 Milk processing (pasteurizing, homogenizing, bottling)
PA: Heritage Distributing Company
    5743 Smithway St Ste 105
    Commerce CA 90040

(G-2317)
HITARTH LLC
1609 Cottage Ave Ste G (47201-1200)
PHONE..................................812 372-1744
Vijender Kumar, *Prin*
EMP: 6 **EST:** 2016
SALES (est): 114.66K **Privately Held**
SIC: 3599 Industrial machinery, nec

(G-2318)
HOME NEWS ENTERPRISES LLC
333 2nd St (47201-6709)
P.O. Box 3011 (47202-3011)
PHONE..................................800 876-7811
EMP: 425
SIC: 2752 2711 Offset printing; Newspapers, publishing and printing

(G-2319)
HOOSIER MACHINE COMPANY LLC
2875 N State Road 9 (47203-9648)
PHONE..................................317 965-5901
EMP: 4 **EST:** 2019
SALES (est): 89.99K **Privately Held**
Web: www.hoosiermachinecompany.com
SIC: 3599 Machine shop, jobbing and repair

(G-2320)
HORN PRE-CAST INC
895 Jonesville Rd (47201-7548)
P.O. Box 566 (47202-0566)
PHONE..................................812 372-4458
Harry E Horn, *Pr*
Harry Horn, *Pr*
Steve Horn, *VP*
EMP: 10 **EST:** 1968
SQ FT: 10,000
SALES (est): 1.41MM
SALES (corp-wide): 5.29MM **Privately Held**
SIC: 3272 Concrete products, precast, nec
PA: Devening Block Inc
    895 Jonesville Rd
    Columbus IN 47201
    812 372-4458

Columbus - Bartholomew County (G-2321)

(G-2321)
IMPACT FORGE GROUP INC
2705 Norcross Dr (47201-4910)
PHONE..................812 342-5527
Andrew Bannoy, *Contrlr*
EMP: 174
SALES (corp-wide): 6.08B **Publicly Held**
Web: www.impactforge.com
SIC: 3462 Iron and steel forgings
HQ: Impact Forge Group, Inc
   2805 Norcross Dr
   Columbus IN 47201

(G-2322)
IMPACT FORGE GROUP INC (DH)
2805 Norcross Dr (47201)
P.O. Box 1847 (47202)
PHONE..................812 342-4437
George Thanopolous, *CEO*
Dennis Potter, *VP*
Michael Keslar, *Sec*
EMP: 1 EST: 2006
SALES (est): 86.47MM
SALES (corp-wide): 6.08B **Publicly Held**
Web: www.impactforge.com
SIC: 3462 3463 Iron and steel forgings; Nonferrous forgings
HQ: American Axle & Manufacturing, Inc.
   One Dauch Dr
   Detroit MI 48211

(G-2323)
INDIANA NEWS MEDIA LLC
10132 N Hickory Ln (47203-9264)
PHONE..................812 703-2025
Larry D Simpson, *Brnch Mgr*
EMP: 2
Web: www.alabamapersonalinjurylawyers.org
SIC: 2711 Job printing and newspaper publishing combined
PA: Indiana News Media Llc
   645 Harrison St
   Hope IN 47246

(G-2324)
INDIANA PRECAST INC
895 Jonesville Rd (47201)
PHONE..................812 372-7771
Keith Bauer, *Pr*
EMP: 20 EST: 2016
SQ FT: 1,000
SALES (est): 2.47MM **Privately Held**
SIC: 3272 Precast terrazzo or concrete products

(G-2325)
INDIANA RESEARCH INSTITUTE
Also Called: AEC America
1402 Hutchins Ave (47201-5630)
P.O. Box 1815 (47202-1815)
PHONE..................812 378-5363
Sue Jane Chang, *Pr*
EMP: 1
Web: www.indianaresearch.us
SIC: 3825 4225 3694 3714 Engine electrical test equipment; General warehousing and storage; Engine electrical equipment; Rebuilding engines and transmissions, factory basis
PA: Indiana Research Institute
   4571 N Long Rd
   Columbus IN 47203

(G-2326)
INDIANA RESEARCH INSTITUTE (PA)
4571 N Long Rd (47203-9012)
PHONE..................812 378-4221
Sue Jane Chang, *Pr*
▲ EMP: 8 EST: 1991
SALES (est): 3.34MM **Privately Held**
Web: www.indianaresearch.us
SIC: 3825 8734 3599 Engine electrical test equipment; Testing laboratories; Machine and other job shop work

(G-2327)
ITSUWA AMERICA INC
1349 Arcadia Dr (47201-8445)
PHONE..................812 375-0323
Hisashi Ando, *Prin*
EMP: 16 EST: 2008
SALES (est): 57.2K **Privately Held**
Web: www.itsuwausa.com
SIC: 3479 Coating of metals and formed products

(G-2328)
ITSUWA USA LLC
1349 Arcadia Dr (47201-8445)
PHONE..................812 375-0323
Akira Hayashi, *Prin*
▲ EMP: 80 EST: 2008
SALES (est): 6.2MM **Privately Held**
Web: www.itsuwausa.com
SIC: 3479 Coating of metals and formed products

(G-2329)
JCMZ ENTERPRISES INC
725 S Mapleton St (47201-7354)
PHONE..................812 372-0288
Donald Smith, *CEO*
EMP: 40 EST: 1977
SQ FT: 40,000
SALES (est): 8.08MM **Privately Held**
Web: www.pyramidpaper.com
SIC: 2653 3086 Boxes, corrugated: made from purchased materials; Packaging and shipping materials, foamed plastics

(G-2330)
JEM PRINTING INC
Also Called: PIP Printing
808 3rd St Ste C (47201-2403)
PHONE..................812 376-9264
Jeanne G Lucas, *Pr*
Mark A Lucas, *Treas*
EMP: 3 EST: 2007
SALES (est): 469.7K **Privately Held**
Web: www.pip.com
SIC: 2752 Offset printing

(G-2331)
JOHNSONS ORTHTICS PRSTHTICS LL
941 25th St (47201)
PHONE..................812 372-2800
Greg Johnson, *Pr*
EMP: 2 EST: 2013
SQ FT: 1,140
SALES (est): 170K **Privately Held**
SIC: 3842 Orthopedic appliances

(G-2332)
JW MACHINING LLC
12775 W Becks Grove Rd (47201-9077)
PHONE..................812 344-6753
EMP: 8 EST: 2015
SALES (est): 623.02K **Privately Held**
Web: www.jwolfmachining.com
SIC: 3599 Air intake filters, internal combustion engine, except auto

(G-2333)
KEITH KUNZ MOTORSPORTS LLC
4575 Kelly St (47203-1752)
PHONE..................812 372-8494
Keith Kunz, *Pr*
EMP: 1 EST: 2000
SALES (est): 188.48K **Privately Held**
Web: www.keithkunzmotorsports.com
SIC: 3799 Go-carts, except children's

(G-2334)
KENNEY ORTHPEDICS COLUMBUS LLC
2525 California St Ste B (47201-3671)
PHONE..................812 214-4623
John M Kenney, *Managing Member*
EMP: 10 EST: 2015
SALES (est): 1.26MM
SALES (corp-wide): 23.4MM **Privately Held**
Web: www.kenneyorthopedics.com
SIC: 3842 Surgical appliances and supplies
PA: Kenney Ortho Group, Inc.
   208 Normandy Ct
   Nicholasville KY 40356
   859 241-1015

(G-2335)
KING OF MOUNTAIN KOM EMB LLC
1998 Creekstone Dr (47201-1462)
PHONE..................812 799-0611
Jeremiah Kratzer, *Prin*
EMP: 5 EST: 2015
SALES (est): 45.96K **Privately Held**
SIC: 2395 Embroidery and art needlework

(G-2336)
KOUSEI USA INC
2396 Norcross Dr Ste C (47201-8327)
PHONE..................812 373-7315
Atsuo Suga, *Pr*
EMP: 5 EST: 2014
SALES (est): 122.94K **Privately Held**
Web: www.kouseius.com
SIC: 3465 Body parts, automobile: stamped metal

(G-2337)
KUSTOM KILMS LLC
2410 Chestnut St (47201-4271)
P.O. Box 1944 (47202-1944)
PHONE..................317 512-5813
EMP: 5 EST: 2011
SALES (est): 279.31K **Privately Held**
SIC: 2491 Wood preserving

(G-2338)
LEAR MACHINING & WATERJET INC
Also Called: Lear Machining & Waterjet
4056 N Long Rd (47203-9057)
P.O. Box 403 (47202-0403)
PHONE..................812 418-8111
Andrew L Long, *Prin*
EMP: 6 EST: 2010
SALES (est): 717.83K **Privately Held**
Web: www.learmachining.com
SIC: 3599 Machine shop, jobbing and repair

(G-2339)
LEES READY-MIX & TRUCKING INC
Also Called: Lee's Ready-Mix
1460 Blessing Rd (47201)
PHONE..................812 372-1800
Mark Hensley, *Brnch Mgr*
EMP: 15
SALES (corp-wide): 7.41MM **Privately Held**
SIC: 4212 3273 1442 Light haulage and cartage, local; Ready-mixed concrete; Construction sand and gravel
PA: Lee's Ready-Mix & Trucking Inc
   701 Hodell St Ste 101
   Shelbyville IN 46176

(G-2340)
LER TECHFORCE LLC (PA)
305 Franklin St (47201-6731)
PHONE..................812 373-0870
David Glass, *Managing Member*
Ryan Hou,
EMP: 232 EST: 2001
SALES (est): 25.39MM
SALES (corp-wide): 25.39MM **Privately Held**
Web: www.lertechforce.com
SIC: 7371 3999 Computer software development; Stage hardware and equipment, except lighting

(G-2341)
LIBERTY ADVANCE MACHINE INC
3210 Scott Dr (47201-4046)
P.O. Box 2247 (47202-2247)
PHONE..................812 372-1010
EMP: 3 EST: 1981
SQ FT: 5,000
SALES (est): 319.8K **Privately Held**
Web: www.libertyadvance.com
SIC: 3599 Machine shop, jobbing and repair

(G-2342)
LINDAL NORTH AMERICA INC
6010 S International Dr (47201-3046)
PHONE..................812 657-7142
Phil Lever, *Pr*
Matthias Woelk, *VP*
▲ EMP: 75 EST: 2006
SQ FT: 100,000
SALES (est): 30.3MM
SALES (corp-wide): 391.59MM **Privately Held**
Web: www.lindalgroup.com
SIC: 3565 Packaging machinery
HQ: Lindal Group Holding Gmbh
   Brandstwiete 1
   Hamburg HH 20457
   40200075100

(G-2343)
LINDE GAS & EQUIPMENT INC
Also Called: Praxair
111 S National Rd (47201-7855)
PHONE..................812 376-3314
John Bryant, *Mgr*
EMP: 1
Web: www.lindeus.com
SIC: 5084 5169 3548 Welding machinery and equipment; Chemicals and allied products, nec; Welding apparatus
HQ: Linde Gas & Equipment Inc.
   10 Riverview Dr
   Danbury CT 06810
   844 445-4633

(G-2344)
LLC BLACK JEWELL
Also Called: Black Jewell Popcorn
417 Washington St (47201-6757)
P.O. Box 27 (47202-0027)
PHONE..................800 948-2302
EMP: 42 EST: 2013
SALES (est): 1MM **Privately Held**
Web: www.blackjewell.com
SIC: 2099 Popcorn, packaged: except already popped

(G-2345)
LLC TIPTON MILLS
835 S Mapleton St (47201-7359)
EMP: 2 EST: 2009
SALES (est): 1.14MM
SALES (corp-wide): 2.4MM **Privately Held**
Web: www.tiptonmills.com
SIC: 2066 Chocolate and cocoa products
PA: Buffalo Blends, Inc.
   108 Henning Dr
   Orchard Park NY 14127
   716 825-4422

Columbus - Bartholomew County (G-2370)

(G-2346)
LOVE TO STITCH LLC
1097 Westview Point Dr (47201-2507)
PHONE.................................812 342-8565
Donna M Turner, *Owner*
EMP: 3 **EST:** 2016
SALES (est): 58.64K **Privately Held**
SIC: 2395 Embroidery and art needlework

(G-2347)
LUCAS CUSTOM INSTRUMENTS LLC
13360 W Becks Grove Rd (47201-7598)
P.O. Box 1404 (47202-1404)
PHONE.................................812 342-3093
Randy Lucas, *Owner*
EMP: 2 **EST:** 1988
SALES (est): 91.6K **Privately Held**
Web: www.lucasguitars.com
SIC: 3931 Guitars and parts, electric and nonelectric

(G-2348)
MARIAH FOODS CORP
Also Called: Peer Foods
1333 Indiana Ave (47201-6986)
P.O. Box 548 (47202-0548)
PHONE.................................812 378-3366
▲ **EMP:** 150 **EST:** 1996
SALES (est): 47.08MM
SALES (corp-wide): 54.3MM **Privately Held**
Web: www.peerfoods.com
SIC: 2011 Meat packing plants
PA: Peer Foods Group, Inc.
    1200 W 35th St Fl 3
    Chicago IL 60609
    773 927-1440

(G-2349)
MARIAH RETAIL STORE
52 Stadler Dr (47201-6911)
P.O. Box 548 (47202-0548)
PHONE.................................812 372-8712
Sue Barringer, *Mgr*
EMP: 1 **EST:** 2001
SALES (est): 73.34K **Privately Held**
Web: www.peerfoods.com
SIC: 2011 Meat packing plants

(G-2350)
MASTER POWER TRANSMISSION INC
3300 10th St (47201-5503)
PHONE.................................812 378-2270
EMP: 33
Web: www.master-pt.com
SIC: 3728 Gears, aircraft power transmission
PA: Master Power Transmission, Inc.
    19 Airview Dr
    Greenville SC 29607

(G-2351)
MDL MOLD & DIE COMPONENTS INC
1130 Industrial Rd Ste B (47203-9467)
P.O. Box 439 (46124-0439)
PHONE.................................812 373-0021
Arthur Beck, *Pr*
Owen Gall, *Prin*
▲ **EMP:** 4 **EST:** 1998
SALES (est): 474.2K **Privately Held**
Web: www.mdlcomponents.com
SIC: 3544 Special dies and tools

(G-2352)
METAL FABRICATED PRODUCTS CO
925 S Marr Rd (47201-7439)
PHONE.................................812 372-7430
Tom Keith Johnson, *Pr*
EMP: 2 **EST:** 1977
SQ FT: 2,000
SALES (est): 229.36K **Privately Held**
Web: www.metal-fabricators.org
SIC: 3599 Machine shop, jobbing and repair

(G-2353)
MI TIERRA
1461 Central Ave (47201-5303)
PHONE.................................812 376-0668
Jorge Delgadillo, *Owner*
EMP: 3 **EST:** 2005
SALES (est): 199.37K **Privately Held**
SIC: 2099 5141 5411 5812   Tortillas, fresh or refrigerated; Groceries, general line; Grocery stores; Eating places

(G-2354)
MICHAEL D METZ
Also Called: Metzgas Exterior
6615 W Ohio Ridge Rd (47201-4664)
P.O. Box 2 (47280-0002)
PHONE.................................812 526-9606
Michael D Metz, *Owner*
EMP: 1 **EST:** 2000
SALES (est): 86.89K **Privately Held**
SIC: 3444 Metal flooring and siding

(G-2355)
MIK MOCHA PRINTS LLC
4637 Clairmont Dr (47203-4763)
PHONE.................................812 376-8891
Mikala Lomax, *Prin*
EMP: 5 **EST:** 2017
SALES (est): 82.51K **Privately Held**
SIC: 2752 Commercial printing, lithographic

(G-2356)
MILESTONE CONTRACTORS LP
3410 S 650 E (47203-9554)
P.O. Box 3004 (47202-3004)
PHONE.................................812 579-5248
TOLL FREE: 800
EMP: 70
SALES (corp-wide): 894.43MM **Privately Held**
Web: www.milestonelp.com
SIC: 1611 1623 1622 2951   Highway and street paving contractor; Water, sewer, and utility lines; Bridge construction; Asphalt paving mixtures and blocks
HQ: Milestone Contractors, L.P.
    5757 Decatur Blvd Ste 250
    Indianapolis IN 46241
    317 788-6885

(G-2357)
MORGAN ADHESIVES COMPANY LLC
Also Called: Mactac
2576 Norcross Dr (47201-3808)
PHONE.................................812 342-2004
Dennis Faltynski, *Mgr*
EMP: 327
Web: www.mactac.com
SIC: 2891 3565 2672   Adhesives and sealants; Packaging machinery; Paper; coated and laminated, nec
HQ: Morgan Adhesives Company, Llc
    4560 Darrow Rd
    Stow OH 44224
    330 688-1111

(G-2358)
MOVIE POSTER PRINT
4114 Washington St (47203-1135)
PHONE.................................812 679-7301
Ryan Walton, *Prin*
EMP: 5 **EST:** 2013
SALES (est): 101.49K **Privately Held**
SIC: 2752 Commercial printing, lithographic

(G-2359)
NAGAKURA ENGRG WORKS CO INC
Also Called: N.E.W. Indiana Co.,
630 S Mapleton St (47201-7360)
PHONE.................................812 375-1382
▲ **EMP:** 169 **EST:** 1994
SQ FT: 37,500
SALES (est): 21.29MM **Privately Held**
Web: www.nagakurausa.com
SIC: 3714 3462   Motor vehicle transmissions, drive assemblies, and parts; Iron and steel forgings
HQ: Nagakura Mfg.Co.,Ltd.
    606, Momozato
    Numazu SZO 410-0

(G-2360)
NOBLITT INTERNATIONAL CORP
Also Called: Noblitt Fabricating
4572 N Long Rd (47203-9055)
PHONE.................................812 372-9969
EMP: 10 **EST:** 2008
SALES (est): 309.67K **Privately Held**
SIC: 3599 Machine shop, jobbing and repair

(G-2361)
NOBLITT INTERNATIONAL CORP
Also Called: Noblitt Fabricating
4735 N Indianapolis Rd (47203-9440)
P.O. Box 646 (47202-0646)
PHONE.................................812 372-9969
Curt Aton, *Pr*
EMP: 30 **EST:** 2008
SALES (est): 4.33MM **Privately Held**
Web: www.noblittfab.com
SIC: 3363 Aluminum die-castings

(G-2362)
NTN DRIVESHAFT INC
8251 S International Dr (47201-9329)
PHONE.................................812 342-7000
Tohru Tomiyama, *Pr*
Nobuo Satoh, *
Tom Fowler, *
Takanobu Ozawa, *
Hidekazu Asaba, *
▲ **EMP:** 1000 **EST:** 1989
SQ FT: 1,200,000
SALES (est): 228.87MM **Privately Held**
Web: www.ntnamericas.com
SIC: 3714 Motor vehicle parts and accessories
HQ: Ntn Usa Corporation
    1600 E Bishop Ct
    Mount Prospect IL 60056

(G-2363)
NUGENT SAND COMPANY
5205 W State Road 46 (47201-8725)
P.O. Box 802 (47202-0802)
PHONE.................................812 372-7508
EMP: 8
SALES (corp-wide): 24.75MM **Privately Held**
Web: www.nugentsand.com
SIC: 1442 Gravel and pebble mining
PA: Nugent Sand Company
    1833 River Rd
    Louisville KY 40206
    502 584-0158

(G-2364)
OESTERLING CHIMNEY SWEEP INC
2360 N National Rd (47201-3732)
PHONE.................................812 372-3512
Daina Ross, *Mgr*
EMP: 4
SALES (corp-wide): 491.9K **Privately Held**
Web: www.oesterlingchimneysweep.com
SIC: 1741 3433   Chimney construction and maintenance; Stoves, wood and coal burning
PA: Oesterling Chimney Sweep Inc
    209 N Walnut St
    Batesville IN 47006
    812 934-3512

(G-2365)
OMNICELL CO
1015 Rocky Ford Rd (47201-1346)
PHONE.................................812 376-0747
Brian Heaton, *Prin*
EMP: 2 **EST:** 2001
SALES (est): 112.82K **Privately Held**
Web: www.omnicell.com
SIC: 3571 Electronic computers

(G-2366)
ORIGINAL BRDFORD SOAP WRKS INC
7667 S International Dr (47201-3004)
PHONE.................................812 342-6854
Tim Johns, *Brnch Mgr*
EMP: 100
SALES (corp-wide): 227.55MM **Privately Held**
Web: www.bradfordsoap.com
SIC: 2841 Soap: granulated, liquid, cake, flaked, or chip
HQ: The Original Bradford Soap Works Inc
    200 Providence St
    West Warwick RI 02893
    401 821-2141

(G-2367)
ORKA TECHNOLOGIES LLC
2182 W 500 N (47201-9167)
PHONE.................................812 378-9842
Karen Orisich, *Pr*
EMP: 2 **EST:** 2002
SALES (est): 134.76K **Privately Held**
SIC: 3648 Flashlights

(G-2368)
OSR INC
6893 S International Dr (47201-3039)
PHONE.................................812 342-7642
Shinichi Kimura, *Pr*
▲ **EMP:** 10 **EST:** 2002
SALES (est): 2.35MM **Privately Held**
Web: www.osrfasteners.com
SIC: 3429 Hardware, nec
PA: Owari Precise Products Co.,Ltd.
    2345-1, Haneuchi, Shimoicho
    Owariasahi AIC 488-0

(G-2369)
PACHECO WINERY LTD LBLTY CO
602 3rd St (47201-6811)
PHONE.................................812 799-0683
Doug Pacheco, *Owner*
EMP: 10 **EST:** 2013
SALES (est): 598.25K **Privately Held**
SIC: 2084 Wines

(G-2370)
PACKAGING CORPORATION AMERICA
Also Called: PCA
3460 Commerce Dr (47201-2204)
PHONE.................................812 376-9301
Rick Hartwick, *Brnch Mgr*
EMP: 300
SALES (corp-wide): 8.48B **Publicly Held**
Web: www.packagingcorp.com
SIC: 2653 Boxes, corrugated: made from purchased materials
PA: Packaging Corporation Of America
    1 N Field Ct

Columbus - Bartholomew County (G-2371)

Lake Forest IL 60045
847 482-3000

(G-2371)
PAF CONSTRUCTION LLC
4840 Progress Dr (47201)
PHONE..................812 496-4669
Jeremiah Percival, *Pr*
Jeremiah Percival, *Managing Member*
Nick Likens, *Sec*
EMP: 20 **EST:** 2018
SALES (est): 1.03MM **Privately Held**
Web: www.pafconstruction.com
SIC: 3731 0919 1629 1794 Dredges, building and repairing; Oyster shells, dredging; Dredging contractor; Excavation work

(G-2372)
PAMELA TAULMAN
Also Called: Indiana Custom Machining
982 S Marr Rd (47201-7440)
PHONE..................812 378-5008
Pamela Taulman, *Owner*
EMP: 12 **EST:** 2005
SQ FT: 18,000
SALES (est): 471.56K **Privately Held**
SIC: 3599 Machine shop, jobbing and repair

(G-2373)
PCA SUTHERN IND CORRUGATED LLC
3460 Commerce Dr (47201-2204)
PHONE..................812 376-9301
EMP: 34 **EST:** 2016
SALES (est): 2.28MM
SALES (corp-wide): 8.48B **Publicly Held**
Web: www.packagingcorp.com
SIC: 2653 Boxes, corrugated: made from purchased materials
PA: Packaging Corporation Of America
1 N Field Ct
Lake Forest IL 60045
847 482-3000

(G-2374)
PEER FOODS GROUP INC
P.O. Box 548 (47202-0548)
PHONE..................773 927-1440
Larry O'connell, *Pr*
EMP: 1
SALES (corp-wide): 54.3MM **Privately Held**
Web: www.peerfoods.com
SIC: 2013 Sausages and other prepared meats
PA: Peer Foods Group, Inc.
1200 W 35th St Fl 3
Chicago IL 60609
773 927-1440

(G-2375)
PENTZER PRINTING INC
4505 Kelly St (47203-1752)
PHONE..................812 372-2896
EMP: 14 **EST:** 1902
SALES (est): 1.48MM **Privately Held**
Web: www.pentzerprinting.com
SIC: 2752 2759 Offset printing; Commercial printing, nec

(G-2376)
PERMAWICK COMPANY INC
3110 Permawick Dr (47201-7468)
PHONE..................812 376-0703
Dennis Sabau, *Mgr*
EMP: 10
SALES (corp-wide): 4.87MM **Privately Held**
Web: www.permawick.com

SIC: 2992 2241 Lubricating oils and greases; Wicking
PA: Permawick Company, Inc.
255 E Brown St Ste 100
Birmingham MI 48009
248 433-3500

(G-2377)
PHILLIPS COMPANY INC (PA)
Also Called: Pdi
6330 E 100 S (47201-9786)
P.O. Box 611 (47202-0611)
PHONE..................812 378-3797
Valerie A Phillips, *CEO*
▲ **EMP:** 34 **EST:** 1986
SQ FT: 9,600
SALES (est): 9.39MM
SALES (corp-wide): 9.39MM **Privately Held**
Web: www.thephillipscompany.com
SIC: 3714 Motor vehicle parts and accessories

(G-2378)
PHOENIX ASSEMBLY INDIANA LLC
6200 S International Dr (47201-3034)
PHONE..................317 884-3600
Tom Beck, *Mgr*
▲ **EMP:** 1 **EST:** 2010
SALES (est): 1.78MM **Privately Held**
Web: www.falcon-manufacturing.com
SIC: 3569 4225 4731 8741 Assembly machines, non-metalworking; General warehousing; Freight transportation arrangement; Industrial management
HQ: Phoenix Assembly, Llc
164 S Park Blvd
Greenwood IN 46143
317 884-3600

(G-2379)
PMG INDIANA LLC (DH)
1751 Arcadia Dr (47201)
PHONE..................812 379-4606
Doctor Michael Krehl, *CEO*
John Von Arx, *Pr*
Juan Miguel Garca Vzquez, *
John Lewis, *
Toni Wendel, *
▲ **EMP:** 200 **EST:** 1988
SQ FT: 144,000
SALES (est): 44.95MM
SALES (corp-wide): 242.12K **Privately Held**
Web: www.pmgsinter.com
SIC: 3714 Motor vehicle engines and parts
HQ: Plansee Group Functions Austria Gmbh
Metallwerk Plansee-StraBe 71
Reutte 6600
56726000

(G-2380)
PRECISE TOOLING SOLUTIONS INC
Also Called: Precise Plate
3150 Scott Dr (47201-4045)
PHONE..................812 378-0247
Donald Dumoulin, *CEO*
▲ **EMP:** 29 **EST:** 1979
SQ FT: 30,000
SALES (est): 4.77MM **Privately Held**
Web: www.precisetooling.com
SIC: 3089 Injection molding of plastics

(G-2381)
PRESTIGE PRINTING INC
Also Called: You Can Do It Printer
1307 12th St (47201-5604)
PHONE..................812 372-2500
TOLL FREE: 800
Frank Miller, *Pr*

Jenny Miller, *Sec*
EMP: 23 **EST:** 1987
SQ FT: 7,000
SALES (est): 837.58K **Privately Held**
Web: www.prestigeteam.biz
SIC: 2752 Offset printing

(G-2382)
PRO-FORM PLASTICS INC
15200 S Jonesville Rd (47201-2717)
PHONE..................812 522-4433
EMP: 19 **EST:** 2020
SALES (est): 2.7MM **Privately Held**
SIC: 3089 Injection molding of plastics

(G-2383)
QUALITY MACHINE & TOOL WORKS
1201 Michigan Ave (47201-5635)
PHONE..................812 379-2660
Billy Mullins, *Pr*
Kippe Detty, *
▲ **EMP:** 75 **EST:** 1951
SQ FT: 90,000
SALES (est): 8.47MM **Privately Held**
Web: www.qmtw.net
SIC: 3599 Machine shop, jobbing and repair

(G-2384)
QUALTRONICS LLC
4775 Progress Dr (47201-2853)
PHONE..................812 375-8880
EMP: 25 **EST:** 1996
SALES (est): 4.68MM
SALES (corp-wide): 6.37MM **Privately Held**
Web: www.qualtronics.net
SIC: 3694 7389 Harness wiring sets, internal combustion engines; Business Activities at Non-Commercial Site
PA: Second Flight Capital, Llc
7450 Rossmore Ct
Dayton OH

(G-2385)
R & J EXCVTG & SEALCOATING LLC ◆
1240 11th St (47201-5601)
PHONE..................812 799-1849
EMP: 6 **EST:** 2022
SALES (est): 261.54K **Privately Held**
SIC: 2952 Asphalt felts and coatings

(G-2386)
REPUBLIC INC
333 2nd St (47201-6795)
PHONE..................812 342-8028
Isaac M Brown, *Owner*
Neil Thompson, *Prin*
EMP: 32 **EST:** 2004
SALES (est): 2.2MM **Privately Held**
Web: www.therepublic.com
SIC: 2711 Commercial printing and newspaper publishing combined

(G-2387)
RIGHTWAY FASTENERS INC
Also Called: RFI
7945 S International Dr (47201-9329)
PHONE..................812 342-2700
Yuta Takashima, *Pr*
Yasutaka Hasegawa, *
Satoshi Furuto, *
▲ **EMP:** 200 **EST:** 1991
SQ FT: 350,000
SALES (est): 46.98MM **Privately Held**
Web: www.rfiusa.com
SIC: 3965 3479 Fasteners; Painting, coating, and hot dipping
PA: Meido Tekko, K.K.
4-5, Sangencho
Toyota AIC 471-0

(G-2388)
SABIC INNOVATIVE PLAS US LLC
945 S Marr Rd (47201-7439)
PHONE..................812 372-0197
John Curvey, *Mgr*
EMP: 58
Web: www.sabic.com
SIC: 2821 3083 Molding compounds, plastics; Laminated plastics plate and sheet
HQ: Sabic Innovative Plastics Us Llc
2500 Ctywest Blvd Ste 100
Houston TX 77042

(G-2389)
SELECTRIC SIGNS
3055 State St (47201-7453)
PHONE..................812 378-6129
EMP: 5 **EST:** 2018
SALES (est): 80.87K **Privately Held**
Web: www.selectricsigns.com
SIC: 3993 Signs and advertising specialties

(G-2390)
SETSER FABRICATING LLC
15601 E 225 N (47203-9609)
PHONE..................812 546-2169
Jason A Setser, *Managing Member*
EMP: 7 **EST:** 2008
SALES (est): 418.71K **Privately Held**
SIC: 2381 7389 Fabric dress and work gloves; Business services, nec

(G-2391)
SGS CYBERMETRIX INC (HQ)
2860 N National Rd A (47201-3746)
PHONE..................800 713-1203
Christine Mullholand, *CEO*
Peter Palladino, *Pr*
David Bartels, *VP*
Judy Kopp, *Operations Finance*
Bruce Thomason, *Engr*
EMP: 3 **EST:** 1992
SALES (est): 9.22MM **Privately Held**
Web: www.sgs.com
SIC: 7371 3825 3625 8711 Computer software development; Analog-digital converters, electronic instrumentation type; Motor controls, electric; Consulting engineer
PA: Fenaco Genossenschaft
Erlachstrasse 5
Bern BE 3012

(G-2392)
SIGN ARAMA
3192 Washington St (47201-2942)
PHONE..................812 657-7449
Barry Davis, *CEO*
EMP: 2 **EST:** 2012
SALES (est): 159.44K **Privately Held**
Web: www.signarama.com
SIC: 3993 Signs and advertising specialties

(G-2393)
SIMMONS WINERY & FARM MKT INC
8111 E 450 N (47203-8106)
PHONE..................812 546-0091
David Simmons, *Pr*
Brenda Simmons, *Sec*
EMP: 2 **EST:** 2000
SALES (est): 246.54K **Privately Held**
Web: www.simmonswinery.com
SIC: 2084 Wines

(G-2394)
SMITH CUSTOM CABINETS
1196 N Nelson Ridge Rd (47201-3493)
PHONE..................812 342-4797
EMP: 1 **EST:** 1991
SALES (est): 57.55K **Privately Held**

SIC: 2434 Wood kitchen cabinets

(G-2395)
STAR TOOL INC
Also Called: Star Tools
4489 Middle Rd (47203-1832)
P.O. Box 68 (47202-0068)
PHONE..................812 372-6730
R Stephen Taylor, Pr
Roger Lee, VP
EMP: 22 **EST:** 1984
SQ FT: 13,600
SALES (est): 465.19K **Privately Held**
Web: www.startoolsupply.com
SIC: 3544 3549 Special dies and tools; Metalworking machinery, nec

(G-2396)
STERLING INDUSTRIES INC
4015 N Long Rd (47203-9057)
PHONE..................812 376-6560
EMP: 25 **EST:** 1996
SQ FT: 20,000
SALES (est): 4.86MM **Privately Held**
Web: www.sterlingindustriesusa.com
SIC: 3599 Machine shop, jobbing and repair

(G-2397)
STRYTEN ENERGY LLC
2405 Norcross Dr (47201-8844)
PHONE..................812 342-0139
EMP: 65
SALES (corp-wide): 8.23B **Privately Held**
Web: www.stryten.com
SIC: 3089 Injection molding of plastics
HQ: Stryten Energy Llc
  5925 Cabot Pkwy
  Alpharetta GA 30005
  678 566-9000

(G-2398)
SUNRIGHT AMERICA INC
6205 S International Dr (47201-3034)
PHONE..................812 342-3430
Yoshi Ota, Pr
Toshiaki Takeuchi, *
▲ **EMP:** 150 **EST:** 2002
SQ FT: 170,000
SALES (est): 23.19MM **Privately Held**
Web: www.sunrightamerica.com
SIC: 3452 Bolts, nuts, rivets, and washers
PA: Sugiura Seisakusho Co.,Ltd.
  33, Ninowari, Terazucho
  Nishio AIC 444-0

(G-2399)
SUPERIOR LAYOUT
1417 Chestnut St (47201-8023)
P.O. Box 4 (47246-0004)
PHONE..................812 371-1709
Jerry Wilson, Prin
EMP: 2 **EST:** 2010
SALES (est): 204.71K **Privately Held**
Web: www.superiorlayout.com
SIC: 3441 Fabricated structural metal

(G-2400)
SWI
3475 W International Ct (47201-3022)
PHONE..................812 342-2409
EMP: 4 **EST:** 2007
SALES (est): 446.51K **Privately Held**
SIC: 3312 Stainless steel

(G-2401)
TECHCOM INC
4630 Progress Dr (47201-7825)
PHONE..................812 372-0960
Bud Mantyla, Mgr
EMP: 10
SALES (corp-wide): 2.62MM **Privately Held**
Web: www.techcom.com
SIC: 7336 3999 Graphic arts and related design; Models, general, except toy
PA: Techcom, Inc.
  7515 Company Dr Ste A
  Indianapolis IN 46237
  317 865-2530

(G-2402)
TIPTON MILLS FOODS LLC
Also Called: Tipton Mills
835 S Mapleton St (47201-7359)
PHONE..................812 372-0900
David M Harding, CEO
EMP: 90 **EST:** 2015
SALES (est): 9.14MM **Privately Held**
Web: www.tiptonmills.com
SIC: 2099 Food preparations, nec

(G-2403)
TONY LONDON CO INC
4630 Progress Dr # A (47201-7825)
P.O. Box 1594 (47202-1594)
PHONE..................812 373-0748
Norman London, Pr
EMP: 1 **EST:** 1998
SALES (est): 216.96K **Privately Held**
Web: www.eventshirts.in
SIC: 2261 Screen printing of cotton broadwoven fabrics

(G-2404)
TOOL DYNAMICS LLC
835 S Marr Rd (47201-7437)
PHONE..................812 379-4243
John Wither, Managing Member
Dana Byrkett, Off Mgr
Shane Hankins, Sls Mgr
EMP: 35 **EST:** 2001
SQ FT: 2,500
SALES (est): 4.78MM **Privately Held**
Web: www.tool-dynamics.com
SIC: 3398 Metal heat treating

(G-2405)
TOUCHDOWN MACHINING INC
432 S Mapleton St (47201-7327)
PHONE..................812 378-0300
Michael T Moore, Pr
Kristine R Moore, Sec
EMP: 7 **EST:** 1994
SALES (est): 1.06MM **Privately Held**
Web: www.touchdownmachine.com
SIC: 3599 Machine shop, jobbing and repair

(G-2406)
TOYOTA MATERIAL HANDLING INC (DH)
Also Called: Toyota
5559 Inwood Dr (47201)
PHONE..................800 381-5879
Jeff Rufener, Pr
Hitoshi Matsuoka, *
Brett Wood, *
▲ **EMP:** 100 **EST:** 2001
SQ FT: 75,000
SALES (est): 123.54MM **Privately Held**
Web: www.toyotaforklift.com
SIC: 5084 3537 Materials handling machinery; Forklift trucks
HQ: Toyota Industries North America, Inc.
  3030 Barker Dr
  Columbus IN 47201
  812 341-3810

(G-2407)
TURNERS MACHINING SPECIALTIES INC
820 Repp Dr (47201-7474)
PHONE..................812 372-9472
EMP: 24 **EST:** 1992
SALES (est): 2.55MM **Privately Held**
Web: www.turnersmachining.com
SIC: 3599 7692 Machine shop, jobbing and repair; Welding repair

(G-2408)
TWB OF INDIANA
3030 Barker Dr (47201-9611)
PHONE..................812 342-6000
EMP: 6 **EST:** 2016
SALES (est): 87.26K **Privately Held**
Web: www.twbcompany.com
SIC: 3714 Motor vehicle parts and accessories

(G-2409)
UNIQUE PRODUCTS
3129 25th St (47203-2436)
PHONE..................812 376-8887
Jo Ann Swank, Pr
EMP: 2 **EST:** 1992
SQ FT: 2,000
SALES (est): 166.21K **Privately Held**
Web: www.uniqueinc.com
SIC: 3949 Billiard and pool equipment and supplies, general

(G-2410)
UNITED INDUSTRIAL & WLDG LLC
Also Called: Uiw Supply
8720 N Us Highway 31 (47201-9170)
PHONE..................812 526-4050
Charles Short, Managing Member
EMP: 7 **EST:** 2006
SQ FT: 4,000
SALES (est): 876.47K **Privately Held**
Web: www.uiwsupply.com
SIC: 7692 Welding repair

(G-2411)
VERNATHERM LLC
Also Called: Vernatherm By Vernet
910 S Gladstone Ave (47201-9520)
P.O. Box 3060 (06011-3060)
PHONE..................860 582-6776
Walter E Rose, Managing Member
Kevin Lamb, *
▲ **EMP:** 42 **EST:** 1988
SALES (est): 5.48MM **Privately Held**
Web: www.vernathermbyvernet.com
SIC: 3491 Industrial valves

(G-2412)
VERNET US CORPORATION
Also Called: Permo Wick
835 S Marr Rd (47201-7437)
PHONE..................812 372-0281
Dennis Sabau, Mgr
EMP: 77
SALES (corp-wide): 848.51K **Privately Held**
Web: www.vernet-group.com
SIC: 3714 3822 Thermostats, motor vehicle; Environmental controls
HQ: Vernet Us Corporation
  910 S Gladstone Ave
  Columbus IN 47201
  812 372-0281

(G-2413)
VERNET US CORPORATION (DH)
Also Called: Vernet Group
910 S Gladstone Ave (47201)
PHONE..................812 372-0281
Kurt Kushner, CEO
Benoit Halard, *
Dennis Sabau, *
▲ **EMP:** 110 **EST:** 1976
SQ FT: 57,000
SALES (est): 53.28MM
SALES (corp-wide): 848.51K **Privately Held**
Web: www.vernet.us
SIC: 3714 3822 Thermostats, motor vehicle; Environmental controls
HQ: Vernet
  21 A 27
  Ollainville 91340
  169268282

(G-2414)
VICKIE HILDRETH
2331 N Marr Rd (47203-3445)
PHONE..................812 350-3575
Vickie Hildreth, Prin
EMP: 4 **EST:** 2011
SALES (est): 126.04K **Privately Held**
Web: www.vickiessalon.com
SIC: 3999 Hair, dressing of, for the trade

(G-2415)
VOGEL BROTHERS CORPORATION
860 Repp Dr (47201-7474)
PHONE..................812 376-2775
Donald E Vogel, Pr
David S Vogel, *
Virginia B Vogel, *
EMP: 22 **EST:** 1951
SQ FT: 10,000
SALES (est): 463.2K **Privately Held**
SIC: 3421 Scissors, shears, clippers, snips, and similar tools

(G-2416)
WEAVER FINE FURN CABINETS INC
14400 W Georgetown Rd (47201-8716)
PHONE..................812 342-4833
Rob Weaver, Pr
Diane Weaver, VP
EMP: 3 **EST:** 1999
SALES (est): 240.14K **Privately Held**
Web: www.weaverfinefurniture.com
SIC: 5712 2519 Cabinet work, custom; Household furniture, except wood or metal: upholstered

(G-2417)
WESTROCK CP LLC
3101 State St (47201-7455)
PHONE..................812 372-8873
Tim Barry, Brnch Mgr
EMP: 1
SALES (corp-wide): 20.31B **Privately Held**
Web: www.westrock.com
SIC: 2653 Boxes, corrugated: made from purchased materials
HQ: Westrock Cp, Llc
  1000 Abernathy Rd Ste 125
  Atlanta GA 30328

(G-2418)
WESTROCK RKT LLC
Also Called: Rock-Tenn Paperboard Products
3101 State St (47201-7455)
PHONE..................812 372-8873
Rick Hollin, Mgr
EMP: 27
SALES (corp-wide): 20.31B **Privately Held**
Web: www.westrock.com
SIC: 2679 2675 2631 Paperboard products, converted, nec; Die-cut paper and board; Paperboard mills
HQ: Westrock Rkt, Llc
  1000 Abernathy Rd Ste 125
  Atlanta GA 30328
  770 448-2193

Columbus - Bartholomew County (G-2419)

(G-2419)
WILBERT SEXTON CORPORATION
3100 S Us Highway 31 (47201-9099)
PHONE..............................812 372-3210
EMP: 2
SALES (corp-wide): 2.46MM Privately Held
Web: www.sextonwilbertconcrete.com
SIC: 3272 Burial vaults, concrete or precast terrazzo
PA: Wilbert Sexton Corporation
1908 W Allen St
Bloomington IN 47403
812 336-6469

(G-2420)
WINE AND CANVAS DEV LLC
1005 Hawthorne Dr (47203-1621)
PHONE..............................317 914-2806
Mary Zwerneman, Mgr
EMP: 5
SALES (corp-wide): 805.52K Privately Held
Web: www.wineandcanvas.com
SIC: 2084 Wines, brandy, and brandy spirits
PA: Wine and Canvas Development Llc
1760 Cholla Ter
Indianapolis IN 46240
317 345-1567

Commiskey
Jennings County

(G-2421)
QUALITY PALLETS INC
8740 W County Road 700 S (47227-9437)
P.O. Box 725 (47274-0725)
PHONE..............................812 873-6818
Evelyn J Willhite, Pr
Robert D Willhite, VP
EMP: 9 EST: 2003
SALES (est): 805.61K Privately Held
SIC: 2448 Pallets, wood

(G-2422)
SPARKMAN PALLET & LUMBER INC
9197 N Jake Gayle Rd (47227-9322)
PHONE..............................812 873-6052
EMP: 9 EST: 1983
SQ FT: 14,000
SALES (est): 619.27K Privately Held
SIC: 2448 Pallets, wood

Connersville
Fayette County

(G-2423)
ADVANCED PRODUCTS TECH INC
5430 Western Ave (47331-9705)
P.O. Box 247 (47331-0247)
PHONE..............................765 827-1166
Tim Hinds, Pr
EMP: 7 EST: 1990
SQ FT: 10,000
SALES (est): 659.3K Privately Held
Web: www.advproducts.com
SIC: 3552 3544 Dyeing, drying, and finishing machinery and equipment; Special dies, tools, jigs, and fixtures

(G-2424)
ADVANTAGE WIRE & MACHINE INC
5480 Industrial Ave (47331-7708)
PHONE..............................765 698-4643
Steven Mitchell, Pr
Howard V Hopkins, Pr
Steven A Mithcell, VP
EMP: 8 EST: 2005
SALES (est): 694.82K Privately Held
SIC: 3496 Miscellaneous fabricated wire products

(G-2425)
ARMORITE AMMO LLC
901 W 21st St (47331-1703)
PHONE..............................765 825-7527
EMP: 2
SALES (est): 92.67K Privately Held
SIC: 3482 Small arms ammunition

(G-2426)
ARROW METALS INC
1527 Vermont Ave (47331-2239)
PHONE..............................765 825-4443
Raymond Logan, Pr
EMP: 20 EST: 1974
SQ FT: 60,000
SALES (est): 967.38K Privately Held
SIC: 1761 1791 3446 3444 Sheet metal work, nec; Structural steel erection; Architectural metalwork; Sheet metalwork

(G-2427)
B&B GOODIEZ
911 1/2 Western Ave (47331-1667)
PHONE..............................765 338-6833
EMP: 4
SALES (est): 83K Privately Held
SIC: 2051 Bread, cake, and related products

(G-2428)
BELL GRAPHICS AND DESIGN LLC
Also Called: Brunsman Graphic Design
3207 Iowa Ave (47331-2546)
PHONE..............................765 825-7441
Craig Bell, Pr
Chris Bell, VP
EMP: 3 EST: 1997
SQ FT: 3,500
SALES (est): 231.31K Privately Held
SIC: 2759 Commercial printing, nec

(G-2429)
BEST MACHINE COMPANY INC
1830 Virginia Ave (47331-2832)
P.O. Box 577 (47331-0577)
PHONE..............................765 827-0250
Lisa Brown, Pr
EMP: 4 EST: 1997
SALES (est): 328.45K Privately Held
SIC: 3599 Machine shop, jobbing and repair

(G-2430)
C & P ENGINEERING AND MFG INC
1605 Kentucky Ave (47331-1620)
P.O. Box 672 (47331-0672)
PHONE..............................765 825-4293
Tim Patterson, Pr
EMP: 17 EST: 1973
SQ FT: 15,600
SALES (est): 884.64K Privately Held
Web: www.candpengmfg.com
SIC: 3441 3535 3444 Fabricated structural metal; Conveyors and conveying equipment; Sheet metalwork

(G-2431)
COACH LINE MOTORS
Also Called: Cherry Hill Shopping Park
2516 Western Ave (47331-1802)
PHONE..............................765 825-7893
Robert Cavins, Owner
Sharon Cavins, Off Mgr
EMP: 2 EST: 1966
SALES (est): 440.66K Privately Held
SIC: 5521 3716 7993 6512 Automobiles, used cars only; Recreational van conversion (self-propelled), factory basis; Amusement arcade; Shopping center, property operation only

(G-2432)
CODYBRO LLC
Also Called: C5 Printing & Graphic Design
3207 Iowa Ave (47331-2546)
P.O. Box 385 (47331-0385)
PHONE..............................765 827-5441
EMP: 5 EST: 2012
SALES (est): 243.52K Privately Held
SIC: 2782 2396 2621 2732 Looseleaf forms and fillers, pen ruled or printed only; Screen printing on fabric articles; Book, bond and printing papers; Books, printing and binding

(G-2433)
CONNERSVILLE PAINT MFGCO
196 Water St (47331-1979)
PHONE..............................765 825-4111
Glen Findley, Pr
EMP: 5 EST: 2013
SALES (est): 87.95K Privately Held
SIC: 2851 Paints and allied products

(G-2434)
CP INC
27100 Hall Rd (47331)
P.O. Box 1049 (47331-8049)
PHONE..............................765 825-4111
Glen Findley, Pr
Scott Findley, *
Nancy Findley, *
Mark Keifer, *
Bill Corbett, *
EMP: 32 EST: 1946
SQ FT: 10,000
SALES (est): 2.4MM Privately Held
Web: www.cpincpaints.com
SIC: 2851 Paints and allied products

(G-2435)
DIECO OF INDIANA INC
5130 Western Ave (47331-9703)
P.O. Box 266 (47331-0266)
PHONE..............................765 825-4151
Carson Stevens, Pr
Richard Stevens, Sec
EMP: 16 EST: 1967
SQ FT: 4,000
SALES (est): 440.71K Privately Held
SIC: 3544 Special dies and tools

(G-2436)
DRESSER LLC
Also Called: Dresser Roots Blowers & Cmpsr
900 W Mount St (47331-1675)
PHONE..............................765 827-9200
EMP: 55
SALES (corp-wide): 25.51B Publicly Held
Web: www.dresserutility.com
SIC: 3491 3825 3594 3593 Industrial valves; Instruments to measure electricity; Fluid power pumps and motors; Fluid power cylinders and actuators
HQ: Dresser, Llc
4425 Westway Park Blvd
Houston TX 77041
262 549-2626

(G-2437)
DUNGAN AERIAL SERVICE INC
4290 N County Road 450 W (47331-9685)
P.O. Box 78 (46127-0078)
PHONE..............................765 827-1355
Jeff Dungan, Pr
EMP: 4 EST: 2009
SALES (est): 238.52K Privately Held
SIC: 2741 Internet publishing and broadcasting

(G-2438)
FAYETTE TOOL AND ENGINEERING
5432 Western Ave (47331-9705)
P.O. Box 716 (47331-0716)
PHONE..............................765 825-7518
Gary B Adams, Pr
Shelly Goodson, *
▲ EMP: 72 EST: 1976
SQ FT: 50,000
SALES (est): 8.93MM Privately Held
Web: www.fayettetool.com
SIC: 3544 3465 Special dies and tools; Automotive stampings

(G-2439)
H&E CUTTER GRINDING INC
6251 Industrial Ave N (47331-7729)
PHONE..............................765 825-0541
Jerry D Miller Ii, Pr
Michael Morgan, *
Gene Hood, *
EMP: 40 EST: 1985
SQ FT: 7,200
SALES (est): 3.25MM Privately Held
SIC: 3599 Machine shop, jobbing and repair

(G-2440)
HOMEMARK CABINETRY LLC ✪
4747 Western Ave (47331)
PHONE..............................678 234-4519
Rajan Shah, Managing Member
EMP: 27 EST: 2022
SALES (est): 2.47MM Privately Held
Web: www.homemarkcabinets.com
SIC: 2434 Wood kitchen cabinets

(G-2441)
HOWDEN COMPRESSORS INC
900 W Mount St (47331)
PHONE..............................610 313-9800
Jim Fairbairn, Pr
◆ EMP: 10 EST: 1998
SALES (est): 1.02MM Privately Held
Web: www.chartindustries.com
SIC: 3443 Fabricated plate work (boiler shop)

(G-2442)
HYDRO EXTRUSION USA LLC
5120 Western Ave (47331-9703)
PHONE..............................765 825-1141
Pat Wooley, Sls Dir
EMP: 133
SQ FT: 32,000
Web: www.hydro.com
SIC: 3354 Aluminum extruded products
HQ: Hydro Extrusion Usa, Llc
6250 N River Rd Ste 5000
Rosemont IL 60018

(G-2443)
I V S
7079 S County Road 200 E (47331-8906)
PHONE..............................765 914-5268
William J Bresnahan, Prin
EMP: 2 EST: 2010
SALES (est): 85.68K Privately Held
SIC: 3841 Surgical and medical instruments

(G-2444)
INDIANA TOOL INC
6260 Industrial Ave N (47331-7729)
P.O. Box 314 (47331-0314)
PHONE..............................765 825-7117
Brian D Fohl, Pr
Bryan Pflum, VP
EMP: 10 EST: 1997
SQ FT: 6,000

GEOGRAPHIC SECTION — Connersville - Fayette County (G-2469)

SALES (est): 912.28K **Privately Held**
SIC: 3312 Tool and die steel and alloys

(G-2445)
INDILEX ALUMINUM SOLUTIONS
5120 Western Ave (47331-9703)
P.O. Box 286 (47331-0286)
PHONE..................765 825-1141
Bob Jay, *Mgr*
EMP: 1 EST: 2010
SALES (est): 124.03K **Privately Held**
SIC: 3354 Aluminum extruded products

(G-2446)
IRVING MATERIALS INC
Also Called: I M I
1998 S State Road 121 (47331-8661)
PHONE..................765 825-2581
Don Steinard, *Mgr*
EMP: 8
SALES (corp-wide): 814.09MM **Privately Held**
Web: www.irvmat.com
SIC: 3273 Ready-mixed concrete
PA: Irving Materials, Inc.
  8032 N State Road 9
  Greenfield IN 46140
  317 326-3101

(G-2447)
JACOBS & BRICHFORD LLC
2957 S State Road 1 (47331-8942)
PHONE..................765 692-0056
Mathew Brichford, *Brnch Mgr*
EMP: 5
SALES (corp-wide): 241.43K **Privately Held**
Web: www.jandbcheese.com
SIC: 2026 Fermented and cultured milk products
PA: Jacobs & Brichford Llc
  3892 S Base Rd
  Connersville IN

(G-2448)
KATHERINE MACKEY
Also Called: Mackey's Drapes
409 Ridge Rd (47331-1262)
PHONE..................765 825-0634
Katherine Mackey, *Owner*
EMP: 1 EST: 1984
SALES (est): 99.58K **Privately Held**
SIC: 2391 2392 Curtains and draperies; Bedspreads and bed sets; made from purchased materials

(G-2449)
KEENER CORPORATION
950 Conwell St (47331-2060)
PHONE..................765 825-2100
Gary Keener Senior, *CEO*
Mark Keener, *
▲ EMP: 166 EST: 1977
SQ FT: 40,000
SALES (est): 6.59MM
SALES (corp-wide): 21.24MM **Privately Held**
Web: www.forge-racks.com
SIC: 3535 Conveyors and conveying equipment
PA: Keener Metal Fabricating, Llc
  950 Conwell St
  Connersville IN 47331
  765 825-2100

(G-2450)
KEENER METAL FABRICATING LLC (PA)
Also Called: Forge Racks and Dunnage
950 Conwell St (47331-2060)
PHONE..................765 825-2100

Jim Baich, *CEO*
Mark Keener, *CAO*
John Crotty, *CFO*
Brant Miller, *Pt*
Ryan Kelley, *Pt*
EMP: 28 EST: 2021
SALES (est): 21.24MM
SALES (corp-wide): 21.24MM **Privately Held**
SIC: 3291 Abrasive metal and steel products

(G-2451)
KELLER PERFORMANCE CENTER
300 E 30th St (47331-3155)
PHONE..................765 827-5225
Andy Keller, *Owner*
EMP: 1 EST: 1997
SALES (est): 191.23K **Privately Held**
Web: www.kellerperformance.com
SIC: 3714 Motor vehicle engines and parts

(G-2452)
KENLEY CORPORATION
5540 Western Ave (47331-7721)
PHONE..................765 825-7150
EMP: 2 EST: 1995
SQ FT: 30,000
SALES (est): 218.44K **Privately Held**
Web: www.kenleycorporation.com
SIC: 3441 Fabricated structural metal

(G-2453)
MAC MACHINE & METAL WORKS INC
100 N Grand Ave (47331-1937)
P.O. Box 609 (47331-0609)
PHONE..................765 825-4121
John Malone, *Pr*
David M Krepp, *
Steven E Krepp, *
Janet S Malone, *Stockholder**
▼ EMP: 36 EST: 1951
SQ FT: 25,100
SALES (est): 2.68MM **Privately Held**
Web: www.mmmw.com
SIC: 3544 3469 Special dies and tools; Metal stampings, nec

(G-2454)
MCCOMBS AND SON COMPANY
201 W 6th St (47331-1503)
PHONE..................765 825-4581
Robert Mccombs, *Pr*
Nancy Mccombs, *Treas*
Marcia S Mccombs, *CEO*
EMP: 6 EST: 1906
SQ FT: 4,784
SALES (est): 443.89K **Privately Held**
SIC: 3312 Plate, steel

(G-2455)
MCCOMBS FABRICATION LLC
1400 Madison St (47331-3342)
PHONE..................765 265-0594
Chase Mccombs, *Pr*
EMP: 1 EST: 2015
SALES (est): 211.48K **Privately Held**
Web: mccombs-fabrication.business.site
SIC: 3441 Fabricated structural metal

(G-2456)
MEADOWLARK WDWKG CABINETRY LLC
105 W 24th St (47331-2940)
PHONE..................765 541-3660
Robert Ferguson, *Managing Member*
EMP: 1 EST: 2009
SALES (est): 234.94K **Privately Held**
SIC: 2431 7389 Millwork; Business Activities at Non-Commercial Site

(G-2457)
MOORE PRECISION MACHINING LLC (PA)
1400 Madison St (47331-3342)
PHONE..................765 265-2386
David A Moore, *Managing Member*
David A Moore Mng Mbg, *Prin*
Jonathan B Moore, *Managing Member*
EMP: 2 EST: 2008
SQ FT: 1,000
SALES (est): 939.29K
SALES (corp-wide): 939.29K **Privately Held**
Web: www.mooreprecisionmachining.com
SIC: 3599 Machine shop, jobbing and repair

(G-2458)
NEWS EXAMINER CIRCULATION DEPT
406 N Central Ave (47331-1926)
PHONE..................765 825-2914
Tina West, *Prin*
EMP: 6 EST: 2007
SALES (est): 74.79K **Privately Held**
Web: www.newsexaminer.com
SIC: 2711 Newspapers, publishing and printing

(G-2459)
P & E PRODUCTS
637 W 17th St (47331-2214)
PHONE..................765 969-2644
Bruce Rea, *Owner*
Bruce Rea, *Pr*
EMP: 6 EST: 1988
SQ FT: 8,000
SALES (est): 484.96K **Privately Held**
Web: www.pandeproducts.com
SIC: 3441 Fabricated structural metal

(G-2460)
PARTS PRO AUTO PRFRORMANCE LLC
510 E 5th St (47331-2608)
PHONE..................765 825-5545
Robert Boll, *CEO*
EMP: 6 EST: 2018
SALES (est): 193.14K **Privately Held**
SIC: 3559 Automotive maintenance equipment

(G-2461)
PH CUSTOM LURES LLC
3984 S County Road 350 E (47331-9496)
PHONE..................765 541-0726
Phillip Hunt, *Admn*
EMP: 5 EST: 2014
SALES (est): 102.59K **Privately Held**
Web: phcustomlures.myshopify.com
SIC: 3949 Lures, fishing; artificial

(G-2462)
POULTRY PRESS
943 N My Ln (47331-8217)
P.O. Box 542 (47331-0542)
PHONE..................765 827-0932
Bill Wulff, *Owner*
EMP: 1 EST: 1914
SALES (est): 7.25K **Privately Held**
Web: www.poultrypress.com
SIC: 2711 Newspapers, publishing and printing

(G-2463)
POWERRAIL HOLDINGS INC
Also Called: Powerrail Mfg
1321 N Illinois Ave (47331-1606)
PHONE..................765 827-4660
Tom Casper Managing, *Brnch Mgr*

EMP: 1
SALES (corp-wide): 51.33MM **Privately Held**
Web: www.epowerrail.com
SIC: 3743 Locomotives and parts
PA: Powerrail Holdings, Inc.
  182 Susquehanna Ave
  Exeter PA 18643
  570 883-7005

(G-2464)
QUALITY TOOL DESIGN INC
1645 E County Road 175 N (47331-9135)
PHONE..................765 377-4055
EMP: 2
SALES (est): 110K **Privately Held**
SIC: 3544 Special dies, tools, jigs, and fixtures

(G-2465)
ROOTS BLOWERS LLC (HQ)
900 W Mount St (47331)
PHONE..................765 827-9200
◆ EMP: 100 EST: 2015
SALES (est): 98.13MM
SALES (corp-wide): 6.88B **Publicly Held**
Web: www.chartindustries.com
SIC: 3564 3563 Blowers and fans; Air and gas compressors
PA: Ingersoll Rand Inc.
  525 Harbor Pl Dr Ste 600
  Davidson NC 28036
  704 896-4000

(G-2466)
SMI SELLER INC
P.O. Box 102349 (30368-2349)
PHONE..................765 825-3121
▲ EMP: 650
SIC: 3714 Motor vehicle parts and accessories

(G-2467)
STANT CORPORATION
1620 Columbia Ave (47331)
PHONE..................765 825-3122
Marlon Bailey, *Pr*
EMP: 84 EST: 2018
SALES (est): 10.58MM
SALES (corp-wide): 54.92MM **Privately Held**
Web: www.stant.com
SIC: 3714 Motor vehicle parts and accessories
PA: H.I.G. Capital, Llc
  1450 Brickell Ave 31st Fl
  Miami FL 33131
  305 379-2322

(G-2468)
STANT MANUFACTURING INC
1620 Columbia Ave (47331-1672)
PHONE..................870 247-5480
▲ EMP: 1400
Web: www.stant.com
SIC: 3491 Automatic regulating and control valves

(G-2469)
STANT USA CORP
Cv Plant
1620 Columbia Ave (47331-1672)
PHONE..................765 825-3121
Rick Barnett, *Manager*
EMP: 350
SALES (corp-wide): 6.55B **Privately Held**
Web: www.stant.com
SIC: 3714 Motor vehicle parts and accessories
HQ: Stant Usa Corp.
  1620 Columbia Ave

Connersville - Fayette County (G-2470)

Connersville IN 47331

(G-2470)
STANT USA CORP (HQ)
1620 Columbia Ave (47331-1672)
P.O. Box 899 (47331-0899)
PHONE..................765 825-3121
Gary Masse, *CEO*
David Roys, *
Thomas Zambelli, *
◆ **EMP:** 229 **EST:** 2009
SQ FT: 190,000
SALES (est): 377.24MM
SALES (corp-wide): 6.55B **Privately Held**
Web: www.stant.com
SIC: 3714 5013 3519 Motor vehicle parts and accessories; Automotive supplies and parts; Diesel engine rebuilding
PA: Cerberus Capital Management, L.P.
875 3rd Ave
New York NY 10022
212 891-2100

(G-2471)
TAGGARTS CUSTOM SNDBLST LLC
1740 Georgia Ave (47331-1673)
PHONE..................765 825-4584
EMP: 3 **EST:** 2007
SALES (est): 209.09K **Privately Held**
SIC: 3589 Sandblasting equipment

(G-2472)
TATMAN INC
Also Called: Commercial Printing Service
815 N Central Ave (47331-2049)
P.O. Box 719 (47331-0719)
PHONE..................765 825-2164
TOLL FREE: 800
Jamison Tatman, *Ch Bd*
Marilyn Kinzler, *
Janet Rose, *
Melody Crawford, *
EMP: 25 **EST:** 1934
SQ FT: 13,500
SALES (est): 2.26MM **Privately Held**
Web: www.cpsprints.com
SIC: 2752 2759 2791 2789 Offset printing; Letterpress printing; Typesetting; Bookbinding and related work

(G-2473)
TERRA HEALTH NORTH AMERICA LLC
725 W 21st St (47331-1750)
PHONE..................317 675-9990
EMP: 4 **EST:** 2021
SALES (est): 154.77K **Privately Held**
SIC: 3069 Medical sundries, rubber

(G-2474)
VORZEIGEN MACHINING INC
5650 Industrial Ave S (47331-7715)
P.O. Box 608 (47331-0608)
PHONE..................765 827-1500
Austin B Cummings, *Pr*
John Godar, *VP*
EMP: 23 **EST:** 2002
SQ FT: 15,000
SALES (est): 1.31MM **Privately Held**
Web: www.vorzeigen.com
SIC: 3599 Machine shop, jobbing and repair

(G-2475)
WHITLOCKS PRESSURE WASH
5649 Industrial Ave S (47331-7715)
P.O. Box 391 (47331-0391)
PHONE..................765 825-5868
Bob Whitlock, *Owner*
Carol Whitlock, *Prin*
EMP: 10 **EST:** 1980
SALES (est): 527.55K **Privately Held**
Web: www.whitlockspressurewash.com
SIC: 7699 7542 5087 3471 Industrial equipment cleaning; Carwash, self-service; Carwash equipment and supplies; Plating and polishing

Converse
Miami County

(G-2476)
12 STONE VENTURES INC
9488 N W 100 (46919)
P.O. Box 253 (46919-0253)
PHONE..................765 573-4605
Ryan Frank, *Prin*
EMP: 5 **EST:** 2016
SALES (est): 130.76K **Privately Held**
SIC: 2721 Periodicals

(G-2477)
JW PACKAGING LLC ✪
Also Called: Uncle Als Breading
204 W Railroad St (46919-2101)
PHONE..................317 414-9038
Mary Beth Morrow, *Managing Member*
EMP: 1 **EST:** 2023
SALES (est): 69.27K **Privately Held**
SIC: 2045 Prepared flour mixes and doughs

(G-2478)
NORTH CENTRAL IND SHAVINGS LLC
307 E Dunn St (46919-2121)
PHONE..................765 395-3875
Toby Middlesworth, *Prin*
EMP: 8 **EST:** 2011
SALES (est): 272K **Privately Held**
Web: www.pellhot.com
SIC: 2421 Sawdust and shavings

(G-2479)
OAK HILL WINERY LLC
111 E Marion St (46919-2105)
P.O. Box 549 (46919-0549)
PHONE..................765 395-3632
Betty Moulton, *VP*
EMP: 2 **EST:** 2001
SALES (est): 181.96K **Privately Held**
Web: www.oakhillwines.com
SIC: 2084 Wines

(G-2480)
SMITHS WOODCRAFT
4804 N 1300 E 34 (46919-9625)
PHONE..................765 395-8044
Kent Smith, *Owner*
EMP: 1 **EST:** 1983
SALES (est): 83.83K **Privately Held**
Web: www.woodcraftspecialty.com
SIC: 2519 Furniture, household: glass, fiberglass, and plastic

Corunna
Dekalb County

(G-2481)
CHARLESTON METAL PRODUCTS INC
1746 Us Highway 6 (46730-9713)
PHONE..................260 281-9972
Rod Evans, *Brnch Mgr*
EMP: 19
SALES (corp-wide): 17.54MM **Privately Held**
Web: www.charlestonmetal.com
SIC: 3599 Machine shop, jobbing and repair
PA: Charleston Metal Products Inc
350 Grant St
Waterloo IN 46793
260 837-8211

(G-2482)
FRISKNEY GEAR & MACHINE CORP
Also Called: Friskney Gear Division
106 N Bridge St (46730-1000)
P.O. Box 122 (46730-0122)
PHONE..................260 281-2200
Randy Thomas, *Pr*
EMP: 4 **EST:** 1963
SALES (est): 295.22K **Privately Held**
SIC: 3599 3568 Machine shop, jobbing and repair; Power transmission equipment, nec

Corydon
Harrison County

(G-2483)
4INK FULLFILLMENT SERVICES
Also Called: 4ink
2070 Highway 337 Nw # 101 (47112-2080)
PHONE..................812 738-4465
Ronald Bays, *Pr*
EMP: 4 **EST:** 2016
SALES (est): 450K **Privately Held**
Web: www.4ink.com
SIC: 2759 5699 Screen printing; T-shirts, custom printed

(G-2484)
ALLIED APPLICATIONS LLC
723 Quarry Rd Nw (47112-6921)
PHONE..................502 817-6478
EMP: 15 **EST:** 2010
SQ FT: 30,000
SALES (est): 2.34MM **Privately Held**
Web: www.alliedapplicationsinc.com
SIC: 3479 Coating of metals and formed products

(G-2485)
AMERICAN MAINT & TRAINING INC
300 E Walnut St (47112-1230)
PHONE..................812 738-4230
Spencer Wendelin, *Pr*
Pete G Bell, *VP*
Kathryn M Kunz, *Sec*
EMP: 14 **EST:** 1997
SQ FT: 2,800
SALES (est): 993K **Privately Held**
SIC: 7349 3743 8611 Building maintenance services, nec; Industrial locomotives and parts; Trade associations

(G-2486)
AWNINGTEC USA INCORPORATED
3265 Highway 62 Nw (47112-6709)
P.O. Box 837 (47112-0837)
PHONE..................812 734-0423
Mansen Way, *Pr*
▲ **EMP:** 20 **EST:** 1997
SQ FT: 15,000
SALES (est): 2.32MM **Privately Held**
Web: www.awningtecusa.com
SIC: 3444 Awnings and canopies

(G-2487)
BARKS WLDG SUPS & FARMING INC
6125 Highway 135 Sw (47112-6068)
PHONE..................812 732-4366
Waunita Barks, *Owner*
EMP: 3 **EST:** 1957
SALES (est): 247.96K **Privately Held**
SIC: 7692 5051 Welding repair; Steel

(G-2488)
BLUE RIVER SERVICES INC
Also Called: General Mrgans Scrnprint Shppe
101 N Mulberry St (47112-1211)
P.O. Box 547 (47112-0547)
PHONE..................812 738-2437
Daniel Lowe, *Brnch Mgr*
EMP: 35
SALES (corp-wide): 20.93MM **Privately Held**
Web: www.brsinc.org
SIC: 2759 Screen printing
PA: Blue River Services, Inc.
1365 Old Hwy 135 Nw
Corydon IN 47112
812 738-3836

(G-2489)
C & R CNSTR & CONSULTING LLC
Also Called: C & R Construction
598 Schwartz Rd Nw (47112-6988)
PHONE..................812 738-4493
Lacy L Crosier, *Managing Member*
EMP: 4 **EST:** 2013
SQ FT: 1,000
SALES (est): 1.07MM **Privately Held**
Web: www.c-rconstruction.com
SIC: 1611 1794 1622 2951 Concrete construction: roads, highways, sidewalks, etc.; Excavation work; Bridge construction; Asphalt paving mixtures and blocks

(G-2490)
CHASE N CORYDON
1881 Old Highway 135 Nw (47112-2012)
PHONE..................812 738-3032
Jamie Diamon, *Pr*
Tony Myers, *Mgr*
EMP: 10 **EST:** 2010
SALES (est): 563.25K **Privately Held**
Web: www.chase.com
SIC: 3578 Automatic teller machines (ATM)

(G-2491)
CLINE BROTHERS WELDING INC
3490 Highway 62 Ne (47112-7714)
PHONE..................812 738-3537
Ron Cline, *Pt*
Don Cline, *Pt*
EMP: 2 **EST:** 1975
SALES (est): 146.18K **Privately Held**
SIC: 3444 7692 Sheet metalwork; Welding repair

(G-2492)
CLOAK GAMING LLC
2225 Heritage Way Nw Apt 75 (47112-2095)
PHONE..................502 563-8790
Matthew H Greenwald, *Managing Member*
EMP: 1 **EST:** 2019
SALES (est): 30.62K **Privately Held**
SIC: 3944 Board games, children's and adults'

(G-2493)
COFFMAN DALLAS LOG & EXCVTG
Also Called: Coffman Dallas Logging
2045 Dixie Rd Sw (47112-6395)
PHONE..................812 738-1528
Dallas Coffman, *Owner*
EMP: 1 **EST:** 1999
SALES (est): 105.63K **Privately Held**
SIC: 2411 Logging camps and contractors

(G-2494)
COFFMAN LOGGING
2190 Lickford Bridge Rd Sw (47112-6029)
PHONE..................812 732-4857
Allan Coffman, *Owner*

GEOGRAPHIC SECTION
Corydon - Harrison County (G-2521)

EMP: 4 EST: 2001
SALES (est): 387.53K **Privately Held**
SIC: 2411 Logging camps and contractors

(G-2495)
CORYDON MACHINE & TOOL CO INC
615 Quarry Rd Nw (47112-6920)
PHONE.................812 738-3107
Steven Yahraus, *Pr*
Kevin Rowe, *
Elsie Yahraus, *
EMP: 38 EST: 1979
SQ FT: 27,000
SALES (est): 4.58MM **Privately Held**
Web: www.corydonmachine.com
SIC: 3544 3599 Special dies and tools; Machine shop, jobbing and repair

(G-2496)
FERREE LOGGING LLC
2150 Leonard Rd Nw (47112-6867)
PHONE.................812 786-1676
Andrew Ferree, *Prin*
EMP: 7 EST: 2017
SALES (est): 220.18K **Privately Held**
SIC: 2411 Logging

(G-2497)
FRED SMITH STORE FIXTURES
3700 Commerce Way Nw (47112-6976)
PHONE.................812 347-2363
EMP: 11 EST: 2019
SALES (est): 400.85K **Privately Held**
Web: www.fssf.us
SIC: 3089 Plastics products, nec

(G-2498)
HOEHN HARDWOODS
2285 Fogel Rd Se (47112-7959)
PHONE.................812 968-3242
Walter Hoehn, *Owner*
EMP: 3 EST: 2000
SALES (est): 129.68K **Privately Held**
SIC: 2435 Plywood, hardwood or hardwood faced

(G-2499)
ICON METAL FORMING LLC
2190 Landmark Ave Ne (47112-2016)
PHONE.................812 738-5900
EMP: 380 EST: 2005
SALES (est): 49.31MM
SALES (corp-wide): 3.89B **Privately Held**
SIC: 3714 1761 Motor vehicle parts and accessories; Sheet metal work, nec
HQ: Martinrea Industries, Inc.
10501 Mi State Road 52
Manchester MI 48158
734 428-2400

(G-2500)
IMI SOUTH LLC
3060 Cline Rd Nw (47112-6904)
PHONE.................812 738-4173
EMP: 6
SALES (corp-wide): 814.09MM **Privately Held**
Web: www.irvmat.com
SIC: 3273 Ready-mixed concrete
HQ: Imi South, Llc
1440 Selinda Ave
Louisville KY 40213
502 456-6930

(G-2501)
INDIANA HOME PRO LLC
200 S Capitol Ave (47112-1010)
PHONE.................812 968-4822
Jason Lawyer, *Managing Member*
EMP: 6 EST: 2018
SALES (est): 276.17K **Privately Held**
SIC: 8742 1389 Retail trade consultant; Construction, repair, and dismantling services

(G-2502)
JJS ENTERPRISE LLC
2689 Breckenridge Rd Ne (47112-8320)
PHONE.................812 736-0062
EMP: 1
SALES (est): 64.69K **Privately Held**
SIC: 1389 Construction, repair, and dismantling services

(G-2503)
KASGRO RAIL CAR MANAGEMENT
209 N Capitol Ave (47112-1142)
PHONE.................812 347-3888
Harry Ketterman, *Pr*
EMP: 7 EST: 1993
SALES (est): 1.49MM **Privately Held**
Web: www.kasgro.com
SIC: 3743 Railroad equipment
PA: Kasgro Rail Corp.
121 Rundle Rd
New Castle PA 16102

(G-2504)
LUCAS OIL RACING INC
Also Called: Lucas Oil
3199 Harrison Way Nw (47112-6903)
PHONE.................812 738-1147
Charlotte Lucas, *Sec*
Robert E Patison, *Prin*
◆ EMP: 15 EST: 2003
SALES (est): 5.28MM **Privately Held**
Web: www.lucasoil.com
SIC: 3533 Well logging equipment
PA: Lucas Oil Products, Inc.
1310 E 96th St
Indianapolis IN 46240

(G-2505)
MORGAN NYE
Also Called: Morgan Nye Welding
442 Quarry Rd Nw (47112-6918)
PHONE.................812 738-4587
Morgan Nye, *Owner*
EMP: 1 EST: 1997
SALES (est): 127.06K **Privately Held**
SIC: 7692 Welding repair

(G-2506)
MOSIER PALLET & LUMBER CO
Also Called: Mosier Log Homes
3600 Tee Rd Ne (47112-7459)
PHONE.................812 366-4817
Russell Mosier, *Pr*
EMP: 5 EST: 1989
SALES (est): 499.48K **Privately Held**
SIC: 2452 Prefabricated wood buildings

(G-2507)
NACHURS ALPINE SOLUTIONS LLC
Also Called: Natures Alpine Solutions
3185 Cline Rd Nw (47112-6905)
PHONE.................812 738-1333
Doris Beuser, *Mgr*
EMP: 5
SALES (corp-wide): 3.23B **Privately Held**
Web: www.nachurs.com
SIC: 2875 5261 Fertilizers, mixing only; Fertilizer
HQ: Nachurs Alpine Solutions, Llc
421 Leader St
Marion OH 43302
740 382-5701

(G-2508)
OBANNON PUBLISHING COMPANY
Also Called: Corydon Democrat, The
117 W Walnut St (47112-1528)
PHONE.................812 738-4552
Jon L O'bannon, *Ch Bd*
Frank L O'bannon, *Ch Bd*
Dennis Huber, *
EMP: 26 EST: 1943
SALES (est): 840.12K **Privately Held**
Web: www.madisoncourier.com
SIC: 2711 2754 Job printing and newspaper publishing combined; Job printing: gravure

(G-2509)
OWENS MACHINERY INC
3194 Fogel Rd Se (47112-7968)
PHONE.................812 968-3285
Fredrick Owen, *Pr*
Kay Owen, *Sec*
J R Eckart, *Stockholder*
EMP: 7 EST: 1979
SALES (est): 483.29K **Privately Held**
Web: www.owensmachinery.com
SIC: 7389 3554 Relocation service; Corrugating machines, paper

(G-2510)
PEYTON TECHNICAL SERVICES LLC
1548 Highway 62 Nw (47112-5131)
PHONE.................812 738-2016
EMP: 10 EST: 2005
SALES (est): 966.57K **Privately Held**
Web: www.ptsarcflash.com
SIC: 3842 Personal safety equipment

(G-2511)
PFEIFFER WINERY & VINEYARD INC
Also Called: Trutle Run Winery
940 Saint Peters Church Rd Ne (47112-8351)
PHONE.................812 952-2650
EMP: 2 EST: 1998
SALES (est): 208.56K **Privately Held**
Web: www.turtlerunwinery.com
SIC: 2084 Wines

(G-2512)
POWDER BLUE
723 Quarry Rd Nw (47112-6921)
PHONE.................918 835-2629
Bud Slusher, *VP*
EMP: 18 EST: 2008
SALES (est): 997.5K **Privately Held**
SIC: 2851 Coating, air curing

(G-2513)
QUICKS MACHINE AND TOOL INC
5523 Corydon Ridge Rd Ne (47112-7039)
PHONE.................812 952-2135
Terry Quick, *Pr*
Virginia Quick, *Sec*
EMP: 2 EST: 1989
SQ FT: 4,000
SALES (est): 213.33K **Privately Held**
SIC: 3599 Machine shop, jobbing and repair

(G-2514)
S & S COMPONENTS INC
1050 Driftwood Dr Ne (47112-8217)
PHONE.................812 734-1104
Sandra Taylor, *Pr*
EMP: 1 EST: 2001
SALES (est): 122.42K **Privately Held**
SIC: 3599 Machine shop, jobbing and repair

(G-2515)
SCOUT MOUNTAIN FARM - HIDEAWAY
2145 Scout Mountain Rd Nw (47112-6678)
PHONE.................812 738-7196
Michael Schad, *Owner*
EMP: 5 EST: 2008
SALES (est): 164.83K **Privately Held**
Web: www.scoutmountainfarm.com
SIC: 2084 Wines

(G-2516)
SIMCO OF SOUTHERN INDIANA
2585 W Heidelberg Rd Sw (47112-6304)
P.O. Box 282 (47140-0282)
PHONE.................812 890-6225
Tom Wieckowski, *Prin*
EMP: 12 EST: 2018
SALES (est): 660.74K **Privately Held**
Web: www.simcosouthernindiana.com
SIC: 2621 Insulation siding, paper

(G-2517)
TAKEDA
1205 Todd Ln Nw (47112-6872)
PHONE.................812 972-0957
EMP: 15 EST: 2009
SALES (est): 372.74K **Privately Held**
Web: www.takeda.com
SIC: 2834 Pharmaceutical preparations

(G-2518)
TAKEDA PHARMACEUTICALS USA INC
1860 Andrew Ct Nw (47112-6974)
PHONE.................812 738-0452
Jarrod Bulleit, *Prin*
EMP: 1
Web: www.takeda.com
SIC: 2834 Pharmaceutical preparations
HQ: Takeda Pharmaceuticals U.S.A., Inc.
500 Kendall St
Cambridge MA 02142
877 825-3327

(G-2519)
TRUSTY TIRES INC
Also Called: Trusty Sons Tire Inc/Goodyear
1074 Old Forest Rd Nw (47112-1909)
PHONE.................812 738-4212
Steve Trusty, *Pr*
EMP: 8
SALES (corp-wide): 2.98MM **Privately Held**
Web: www.trustytireinc.com
SIC: 5531 7534 5014 Automotive tires; Tire repair shop; Tires, used
PA: Trusty Tires, Inc.
7223 S Mifflin W Fork Rd
English IN 47118
812 739-4395

(G-2520)
TYSON FOODS INC
Tyson
545 Valley Rd (47112-1747)
P.O. Box 545 (47112-0545)
PHONE.................812 738-3219
David Wahittington, *Brnch Mgr*
EMP: 27
SQ FT: 1,000
SALES (corp-wide): 52.88B **Publicly Held**
Web: www.tysonfoods.com
SIC: 2015 Chicken slaughtering and processing
PA: Tyson Foods, Inc.
2200 W Don Tyson Pkwy
Springdale AR 72762
479 290-4000

(G-2521)
WARREN PRINTING SERVICES LLC
217 E Chestnut St (47112-1107)
PHONE.................812 738-6508
Larry Warren, *Prin*

Corydon - Harrison County (G-2522)

EMP: 10 EST: 2008
SALES (est): 491.78K **Privately Held**
Web: www.warrenprinting.com
SIC: 2759 Screen printing

(G-2522)
WHITAKERR DALEMON
Also Called: Whitaker Skid and Crate
1240 Old North Bridge Rd Ne (47112-2259)
PHONE..................................812 738-2396
Dale Whitaker, *Owner*
EMP: 4 EST: 2007
SALES (est): 479.04K **Privately Held**
SIC: 2441 2448 Boxes, wood; Cargo containers, wood

(G-2523)
WHITE EAGLE INDUS GROUP LLC
205 W Poplar St (47112-1033)
PHONE..................................270 577-2415
EMP: 1 EST: 2017
SALES (est): 54.1K **Privately Held**
SIC: 3541 Grinding, polishing, buffing, lapping, and honing machines

(G-2524)
ZIMMERMAN ART GLASS LLC
300 E Chestnut St (47112-1202)
PHONE..................................812 738-2206
Kerry Zimmerman, *Pt*
EMP: 2 EST: 1960
SALES (est): 228.03K **Privately Held**
Web: www.artzglass.com
SIC: 3229 Glassware, art or decorative

Covington
Fountain County

(G-2525)
170 TACTICAL INC
406 Liberty St (47932-1244)
P.O. Box 144 (47932-0144)
PHONE..................................765 793-7932
Lance Dillon, *Owner*
EMP: 6 EST: 2015
SALES (est): 52.9K **Privately Held**
SIC: 3489 Ordnance and accessories, nec

(G-2526)
ABC FIX-N-FAB WELDING LLC
1106 N Portland Arch Rd (47932-8072)
PHONE..................................765 230-6492
Paula Kay Lyons, *Owner*
EMP: 5 EST: 2018
SALES (est): 63.22K **Privately Held**
SIC: 7692 Welding repair

(G-2527)
BIO-ALTERNATIVE LLC
11778 S 600 W (47932-7904)
P.O. Box 727 (61803-0727)
PHONE..................................765 793-5731
EMP: 28
Web: www.bio-alternative.com
SIC: 2869 Fuels

(G-2528)
DESIGNS 4 U INC
1350 W 100 N (47932-8107)
PHONE..................................765 793-3026
Brenda Hardy, *Pr*
Stan Hardy, *VP*
EMP: 2 EST: 2001
SALES (est): 44K **Privately Held**
SIC: 3993 2329 2339 2389 Signs and advertising specialties; Men's and boys' athletic uniforms; Uniforms, athletic: women's, misses', and juniors'; Uniforms and vestments

(G-2529)
ELDON FRANCE
Also Called: Just For Karts
1484 S Stringtown Rd (47932-8013)
PHONE..................................765 793-2743
Eldon France, *Owner*
EMP: 1 EST: 2010
SALES (est): 29K **Privately Held**
SIC: 3944 Go-carts, children's

(G-2530)
FLEX-N-GATE LLC
Also Called: Masterguard LLC
11778 S 600 W (47932-7904)
P.O. Box 228 (47932-0228)
PHONE..................................765 793-5732
Jeffrey Satyshur, *Mgr*
EMP: 1
SALES (corp-wide): 1.57B **Privately Held**
Web: www.flex-n-gate.com
SIC: 3714 Motor vehicle parts and accessories
PA: Flex-N-Gate Llc
  1306 E University Ave
  Urbana IL 61802
  217 384-6600

(G-2531)
MIDWEST BIO-PRODUCTS INC
618 Liberty St (47932-1531)
PHONE..................................765 793-3426
Masakazu Miyagi, *Pr*
Mary Patricia Miyagi, *Sec*
EMP: 5 EST: 1981
SALES (est): 723.63K **Privately Held**
SIC: 2869 Enzymes

(G-2532)
PARISH TIRE & BATTERY SHOP
416 3rd St (47932-1116)
PHONE..................................765 793-3191
Robert H Baldin, *Owner*
EMP: 4
SQ FT: 2,000
SALES (est): 262.86K **Privately Held**
SIC: 5531 7539 7534 7549 Automotive tires; Wheel alignment, automotive; Tire repair shop; Towing service, automotive

(G-2533)
RECKON WITH IT TEES STUFF LLC
1853 S Towpath Rd (47932-8046)
PHONE..................................765 585-3610
EMP: 4 EST: 2016
SALES (est): 57.61K **Privately Held**
SIC: 2759 Screen printing

(G-2534)
STEEL GRIP INC
1200 Pearl St (47932-1466)
P.O. Box 174 (47932-0174)
PHONE..................................765 793-3652
Dave Mason, *Mgr*
EMP: 2
SALES (corp-wide): 15.25MM **Privately Held**
Web: www.steelgripinc.com
SIC: 3842 Personal safety equipment
PA: Steel Grip, Inc.
  1501 E Voorhees St
  Danville IL 61832
  217 442-6240

Craigville
Wells County

(G-2535)
MODULAR GREEN SYSTEMS LLC
5889 N 700 W-1 (46731-9505)
PHONE..................................260 547-4121
EMP: 2
SALES (est): 86.73K **Privately Held**
SIC: 2421 7389 Outdoor wood structural products; Business Activities at Non-Commercial Site

Crandall
Harrison County

(G-2536)
CORRQUEST AUTOMATION INC
2060 Highway 335 Ne (47114-9407)
PHONE..................................812 596-0049
Brian Wellman Mech Lead, *Brnch Mgr*
EMP: 2
SALES (corp-wide): 4.93MM **Privately Held**
Web: www.corrquest.com
SIC: 1731 3554 Banking machine installation and service; Paper industries machinery
PA: Corrquest Automation, Inc.
  5253 Old Salem Rd Ne
  Albany OR 97321
  503 305-3810

Crane
Martin County

(G-2537)
DLA DOCUMENT SERVICES
300 Highway 361 Bldg 18 (47522-4000)
PHONE..................................812 854-1465
Bob Clark, *Mgr*
EMP: 2
Web: documentservices.dla.mil
SIC: 2752 9711 Commercial printing, lithographic; National security
HQ: Dla Document Services
  5450 Carlisle Pike Bldg 9
  Mechanicsburg PA 17050
  717 605-2362

(G-2538)
HONEYWELL INTERNATIONAL INC
Also Called: Honeywell
3330n 138b (47522)
PHONE..................................812 854-4450
EMP: 2
Web: www.honeywell.com
SIC: 3724 Aircraft engines and engine parts
PA: Honeywell International Inc.
  855 S Mint St
  Charlotte NC 28202

(G-2539)
L3HARRIS TECHNOLOGIES INC
Also Called: Exelis Inc., Electronic
27548 N 1400 E (47522)
PHONE..................................812 202-5171
EMP: 3
SALES (corp-wide): 19.42B **Publicly Held**
Web: www.l3harris.com
SIC: 3812 Defense systems and equipment
PA: L3harris Technologies, Inc.
  1025 W Nasa Blvd
  Melbourne FL 32919
  321 727-9100

(G-2540)
L3HARRIS TECHNOLOGIES INC
27548 N 1400 E (47522)
PHONE..................................812 202-5171
EMP: 5
SALES (corp-wide): 19.42B **Publicly Held**
Web: www.l3harris.com
SIC: 3823 3812 Process control instruments; Search and navigation equipment
PA: L3harris Technologies, Inc.
  1025 W Nasa Blvd
  Melbourne FL 32919
  321 727-9100

(G-2541)
UNITED STATES DEPT OF NAVY
Also Called: Military Facilitie
300 Highway 36 (47522)
PHONE..................................812 854-1762
Karl Mcclure, *Dir*
▲ EMP: 6
Web: www.navy.mil
SIC: 3483 Ammunition, except for small arms, nec
HQ: United States Department Of The Navy
  1200 Navy Pentagon
  Washington DC 20350

Crawfordsville
Montgomery County

(G-2542)
ACUITY BRANDS INC
1304 E Elmore St (47933-3170)
PHONE..................................765 362-1837
EMP: 5
SALES (corp-wide): 3.95B **Publicly Held**
Web: www.acuitybrands.com
SIC: 3646 Commercial lighting fixtures
PA: Acuity Brands, Inc.
  1170 Pchtree St Ne Ste 23
  Atlanta GA 30309
  404 853-1400

(G-2543)
ACUITY BRANDS LIGHTING INC
Lithonia Lighting
1615 E Elmore St (47933-3122)
PHONE..................................765 362-1837
Bert Kerr, *Brnch Mgr*
EMP: 500
SALES (corp-wide): 3.95B **Publicly Held**
Web: lithonia.acuitybrands.com
SIC: 3646 3641 Commercial lighting fixtures; Electric lamps
HQ: Acuity Brands Lighting, Inc.
  1170 Peachtree St Ne # 23
  Atlanta GA 30309

(G-2544)
ALLEN MONUMENT COMPANY (PA)
212 Hamilton St (47933-1915)
PHONE..................................765 362-8886
Randall Allen, *Pr*
Missy Allen, *Prin*
EMP: 3 EST: 1993
SALES (est): 878.9K
SALES (corp-wide): 878.9K **Privately Held**
Web: www.allenmonuments.com
SIC: 5999 3272 3281 Monuments, finished to custom order; Monuments and grave markers, except terrazzo; Monument or burial stone, cut and shaped

(G-2545)
ARCHER-DANIELS-MIDLAND COMPANY
Also Called: ADM
3696 E 510 S (47933-8290)
PHONE..................................765 362-2965
Ken Martin, *Mgr*
EMP: 4
SALES (corp-wide): 93.94B **Publicly Held**
Web: www.adm.com
SIC: 2041 Flour and other grain mill products
PA: Archer-Daniels-Midland Company

GEOGRAPHIC SECTION
Crawfordsville - Montgomery County (G-2569)

77 W Wacker Dr Ste 4600
Chicago IL 60601
312 634-8100

(G-2546)
BANJO CORPORATION
150 Banjo Dr (47933-9603)
PHONE...................765 362-7367
▲ **EMP:** 200 **EST:** 1959
SALES (est): 32.33MM
SALES (corp-wide): 3.27B **Publicly Held**
Web: www.banjocorp.com
SIC: 3561 3494 Pumps and pumping equipment; Valves and pipe fittings, nec
PA: Idex Corporation
3100 Sanders Rd Ste 301
Northbrook IL 60062
847 498-7070

(G-2547)
BERTELSMANN PUBG GROUP INC
1019 N State Road 47 (47933-7131)
PHONE...................410 386-7717
EMP: 2
SALES (corp-wide): 54.57MM **Privately Held**
Web: www.bertelsmann.com
SIC: 2731 Books, publishing only
HQ: Bertelsmann Publishing Group, Inc.
1540 Broadway Fl 24
New York NY 10036
212 782-1000

(G-2548)
BOGGS FABG SOLUTIONS INC
3902 W Offield Monument Rd (47933-6952)
PHONE...................317 852-5107
William Boggs, *Prin*
Janet Boggs, *Prin*
EMP: 2 **EST:** 1999
SALES (est): 210K **Privately Held**
Web: www.boggsfsi.com
SIC: 3599 Machine shop, jobbing and repair

(G-2549)
BOM CORPORATION
Also Called: Toner Tek
3370 E State Road 32 (47933-9620)
P.O. Box 871 (47933-0871)
PHONE...................765 361-0382
EMP: 39
SQ FT: 10,000
SALES (est): 5.2MM **Privately Held**
SIC: 3955 3861 Print cartridges for laser and other computer printers; Photographic equipment and supplies

(G-2550)
C&F FABRICATING LLC
1831 E Elmore St (47933-3126)
PHONE...................765 362-5922
EMP: 2 **EST:** 2010
SALES (est): 442.52K **Privately Held**
Web: www.cffabricating.com
SIC: 3444 Sheet metalwork

(G-2551)
CERAMIC FIBER ENTERPRISES INC
503 W 300 N (47933)
P.O. Box 72 (47933)
PHONE...................765 362-2179
David Kitko, *Pr*
EMP: 8 **EST:** 2015
SALES (est): 755.95K **Privately Held**
Web: www.cfeworld.com
SIC: 3299 Ceramic fiber

(G-2552)
CHARLES COONS
Also Called: Hillcrest Mobile Homes Court
2401 Indianapolis Rd (47933-3173)
PHONE...................765 362-6509
Charles Coons, *Owner*
EMP: 3 **EST:** 1954
SQ FT: 2,400
SALES (est): 177.43K **Privately Held**
SIC: 6515 1741 6514 2396 Mobile home site operators; Masonry and other stonework; Dwelling operators, except apartments; Automotive and apparel trimmings

(G-2553)
CLOSURE SYSTEMS INTL HLDNGS IN
Also Called: Alcoa Csi
1604 E Elmore St (47933-3121)
PHONE...................765 364-6300
EMP: 2
Web: www.csiclosures.com
SIC: 3334 Primary aluminum
PA: Closure Systems International Holdings Llc
7820 Innvtion Blvd Ste 10
Indianapolis IN 46278

(G-2554)
CLOSURE SYSTEMS INTL INC
Also Called: Csi
1205 E Elmore St (47933-3116)
PHONE...................765 364-6300
EMP: 367
Web: www.csiclosures.com
SIC: 3334 3089 Primary aluminum; Bottle caps, molded plastics
HQ: Closure Systems International, Inc.
7820 Innovation Blvd # 100
Indianapolis IN 46278
317 390-5000

(G-2555)
COOPERS WOOD HEAT SUPPLY LLC
Also Called: Cooper's Custom Hardwoods
3506 W Offield Monument Rd (47933-6930)
PHONE...................765 918-1039
Brian Cooper, *Pr*
EMP: 6 **EST:** 2013
SALES (est): 52.4K **Privately Held**
Web: www.cooperscustomhardwoods.com
SIC: 2426 Hardwood dimension and flooring mills

(G-2556)
CPM ACQUISITION CORP
Also Called: California Pellet Mill Company
1114 E Wabash Ave (47933-2635)
P.O. Box 647 (47933-0647)
PHONE...................765 362-2600
EMP: 12
SALES (corp-wide): 227.38MM **Privately Held**
Web: www.cpmroskamp.com
SIC: 3523 3559 3312 3544 Feed grinders, crushers, and mixers; Refinery, chemical processing, and similar machinery; Blast furnaces and steel mills; Special dies, tools, jigs, and fixtures
HQ: Cpm Acquisition Corp.
4050 Leversee Rd
Waterloo IA 50703
319 232-8444

(G-2557)
CRAWFORD INDUSTRIES LLC (HQ)
Also Called: Innovative Consumer Packaging
1414 Crawford Dr (47933-9740)
PHONE...................800 428-0840
George L Faulstich Junior, *CEO*
Kendall Faulstich,
▲ **EMP:** 30 **EST:** 1999
SQ FT: 85,000
SALES (est): 25.04MM
SALES (corp-wide): 344.31MM **Privately Held**
Web: www.spartech.com
SIC: 3089 Injection molding of plastics
PA: Spartech Llc
11650 Lkeside Crossing Ct
Saint Louis MO 63146
314 569-7400

(G-2558)
CROSSROADS FURNITURE CO LLC
121 N Washington St (47933-1734)
PHONE...................765 307-2095
Stacee Cornett, *Managing Member*
EMP: 10 **EST:** 2018
SALES (est): 1.03MM **Privately Held**
Web: www.crossroadsfurniturecompany.com
SIC: 5712 2515 Furniture stores; Mattresses and foundations

(G-2559)
CROSSROADS ORTHOTICS & CNSLTN
821 S Washington St (47933-3546)
PHONE...................765 359-0041
Jenifer L Furness, *Owner*
EMP: 3 **EST:** 2008
SALES (est): 537.94K **Privately Held**
Web: www.crossroadsorthotics.com
SIC: 3842 Orthopedic appliances

(G-2560)
CROWN CORK & SEAL USA INC
Also Called: Crown Cork & Seal
400 N Walnut St (47933-1300)
PHONE...................765 362-3200
Robert Bourque, *Brnch Mgr*
EMP: 141
SQ FT: 100,000
SALES (corp-wide): 12.01B **Publicly Held**
Web: www.crowncork.com
SIC: 3411 Metal cans
HQ: Crown Cork & Seal Usa, Inc.
770 Township Line Rd
Yardley PA 19067
215 698-5100

(G-2561)
CURRENT TECHNOLOGIES INC
Frontage Rd (47933)
P.O. Box 21 (47933-0021)
PHONE...................765 364-0490
Susan Hapak, *Pr*
EMP: 15 **EST:** 1968
SQ FT: 9,000
SALES (est): 911.45K **Privately Held**
Web: www.currtechinc.com
SIC: 3842 3821 Bandages and dressings; Laboratory apparatus and furniture

(G-2562)
D P WOODS UNLIMITED
2407 N Everett St (47933-1010)
PHONE...................765 362-3625
Daniel Harwood, *Prin*
EMP: 2 **EST:** 2008
SALES (est): 100.28K **Privately Held**
SIC: 2741 Miscellaneous publishing

(G-2563)
DND DUST CONTROL INC
Also Called: D N D Oil Company
2209 Indianapolis Rd (47933-3140)
P.O. Box 329 (47965-0329)
PHONE...................765 362-3774

Danny Fisher, *Pr*
EMP: 1 **EST:** 1999
SALES (est): 1.16MM
SALES (corp-wide): 676.37MM **Privately Held**
SIC: 2992 Lubricating oils and greases
HQ: Petrochoice Llc
933 1st Ave
King Of Prussia PA 19406
888 575-1226

(G-2564)
DUBOSE STRAPPING INC
4414 E 400 S (47933-7958)
PHONE...................765 361-0000
EMP: 29
Web: www.dubosestrapping.com
SIC: 3499 Strapping, metal
PA: Dubose Strapping, Inc.
906 Industrial Dr
Clinton NC 28328

(G-2565)
EDW C LEVY CO
Whitesville Mill Service
New Core Rd (47933)
PHONE...................765 364-9251
Mike Perkins, *Mgr*
EMP: 3
SALES (corp-wide): 513.22MM **Privately Held**
Web: www.edwclevy.com
SIC: 3295 3281 Slag, crushed or ground; Cut stone and stone products
PA: Edw. C. Levy Co.
9300 Dix
Dearborn MI 48120
313 429-2200

(G-2566)
FERRELLGAS LP
Also Called: Ferrellgas
2111b Indianapolis Rd (47933-3138)
PHONE...................574 936-2725
EMP: 8
Web: www.ferrellgas.com
SIC: 5984 2813 Liquefied petroleum gas, delivered to customers' premises; Industrial gases
HQ: Ferrellgas, L.P.
1 Liberty Plz
Liberty MO 64068

(G-2567)
FLOW CENTER PRODUCTS INC
2065 S Nucor Rd (47933-7970)
P.O. Box 509 (47933-0509)
PHONE...................765 364-9460
▲ **EMP:** 5 **EST:** 2002
SALES (est): 461.49K **Privately Held**
Web: www.flowcenterproducts.com
SIC: 3585 Refrigeration and heating equipment

(G-2568)
FRICTION PRODUCTS COMPANY LLC
1204 Darlington Ave (47933-1958)
PHONE...................765 362-3500
▲ **EMP:** 916
SIC: 3714 3624 Power transmission equipment, motor vehicle; Carbon and graphite products

(G-2569)
GEARBOX LM HOLDINGS INC (PA)
711 Tech Dr (47933-1400)
PHONE...................765 362-3500
Lorenzo Muhammad, *Managing Member*
EMP: 8 **EST:** 2020
SALES (est): 49.09MM

Crawfordsville - Montgomery County (G-2570)

SALES (corp-wide): 49.09MM **Privately Held**
Web: www.raybestospowertrain.com
SIC: 3714 Motor vehicle parts and accessories

(G-2570)
GHOST FORGE L T D (PA)
Also Called: Ghost Frge Rubenesque Fashions
1009 S Elm St (47933-3515)
PHONE..................................765 362-8654
Joann V Sykes, *Pr*
Robert Sykes Junior Factor, *Prin*
James R Shillings, *VP*
Joann Seibert, *CEO*
▼ EMP: 3 EST: 1998
SALES (est): 439.39K
SALES (corp-wide): 439.39K **Privately Held**
Web: www.ghostforge.com
SIC: 2389 Costumes

(G-2571)
GREFCO MINERALS INC
Dicaperl/Mineral Products Div
2510 N Concord Rd (47933-7807)
P.O. Box 48 (47933-0048)
PHONE..................................765 362-6000
William Staten, *Mgr*
EMP: 17
Web: www.dicalite.com
SIC: 3295 Minerals, ground or treated
HQ: Grefco Minerals Inc.
1 Bala Ave Ste 310
Bala Cynwyd PA 19004
610 660-8820

(G-2572)
GRUNDY WOODWORKS
600 W Main St (47933-1626)
PHONE..................................765 337-4596
Sean Grundy, *Prin*
EMP: 5 EST: 2017
SALES (est): 54.13K **Privately Held**
SIC: 2431 Millwork

(G-2573)
GUARANTEED LIGHTING & SIGNS
6490 S 200 W (47933-6326)
PHONE..................................765 866-1229
Marty Paris, *Owner*
EMP: 1 EST: 2000
SALES (est): 71.39K **Privately Held**
SIC: 3993 Signs and advertising specialties

(G-2574)
GUARDIAN TECH GROUP IND LLC
1100 E Elmore St (47933-3573)
PHONE..................................765 364-0863
Charles Hudson, *Pr*
Brian Hudson, *CEO*
EMP: 7 EST: 2004
SQ FT: 24,000
SALES (est): 779.35K **Privately Held**
Web: www.guardiancnc.com
SIC: 3599 Machine shop, jobbing and repair

(G-2575)
H H PALLET
1977 N 175 W (47933-6107)
PHONE..................................765 505-1682
EMP: 4 EST: 2018
SALES (est): 148.56K **Privately Held**
SIC: 2448 Wood pallets and skids

(G-2576)
H H PALLET
3450 E State Road 32 (47933)
PHONE..................................765 323-3117

EMP: 3 EST: 2020
SALES (est): 119.91K **Privately Held**
SIC: 2448 Pallets, wood

(G-2577)
HERITAGE PRODUCTS INC
2000 Smith Ave (47933-1055)
PHONE..................................765 364-9002
Takaharu Miyake, *Pr*
Tatsunori Shigeta, *
Bryan Y Funai, *
◆ EMP: 216 EST: 1988
SQ FT: 195,000
SALES (est): 47.79MM **Privately Held**
Web: www.heritageproductsinc.com
SIC: 3465 Body parts, automobile: stamped metal
PA: Hiruta Kogyo Co., Ltd.
1410, Mobira
Kasaoka OKA 714-0

(G-2578)
HT ENTERPRISES INC
Also Called: Hi-Temp Refractories
5070 N Old State Road 55 (47933-8138)
P.O. Box 414 (47940-0414)
PHONE..................................765 794-4174
Tim Foster, *Pr*
Tom Mccormick, *Sec*
EMP: 6 EST: 1998
SALES (est): 496.56K **Privately Held**
Web: www.htent.com
SIC: 3255 Tile and brick refractories, except plastic

(G-2579)
INTERNATIONAL PAPER COMPANY
Also Called: International Paper
1823 E Elmore St (47933-3126)
PHONE..................................765 359-0107
Cj Wilson, *Brnch Mgr*
EMP: 5
SALES (corp-wide): 18.92B **Publicly Held**
Web: www.internationalpaper.com
SIC: 2631 Paperboard mills
PA: International Paper Company
6400 Poplar Ave
Memphis TN 38197
901 419-7000

(G-2580)
INTERNATIONAL PAPER COMPANY
Also Called: International Paper
801 N Englewood Dr (47933-9741)
PHONE..................................765 364-5342
Gary Huxhold, *Brnch Mgr*
EMP: 70
SALES (corp-wide): 18.92B **Publicly Held**
Web: www.internationalpaper.com
SIC: 2653 Boxes, corrugated: made from purchased materials
PA: International Paper Company
6400 Poplar Ave
Memphis TN 38197
901 419-7000

(G-2581)
IRVING MATERIALS INC
Also Called: I M I
3350 E State Road 32 (47933-9620)
PHONE..................................765 362-6904
Don Russell, *Mgr*
EMP: 8
SALES (corp-wide): 814.09MM **Privately Held**
Web: www.irvmat.com
SIC: 3273 Ready-mixed concrete
PA: Irving Materials, Inc.
8032 N State Road 9
Greenfield IN 46140
317 326-3101

(G-2582)
JARROD ZACHARY WELD
3384 E State Road 32 (47933-9620)
PHONE..................................765 230-6424
Jarrod Zachery, *Prin*
EMP: 6 EST: 2007
SALES (est): 96.89K **Privately Held**
SIC: 7692 Welding repair

(G-2583)
KROGER LIMITED PARTNERSHIP II
Pace Dairy Foods
800 N Englewood Dr (47933-9741)
PHONE..................................765 364-5200
Pat Dilts, *Prin*
EMP: 1
SALES (corp-wide): 150.04B **Publicly Held**
Web: www.thekrogerco.com
SIC: 2022 Natural cheese
HQ: Kroger Limited Partnership Ii
1014 Vine St
Cincinnati OH 45202
513 762-4000

(G-2584)
LASERWASH
1529 S Washington St (47933-3814)
PHONE..................................765 359-0582
Mark Addler, *Mgr*
EMP: 2 EST: 2010
SALES (est): 148.49K **Privately Held**
Web: www.laserwashmycar.com
SIC: 3589 Car washing machinery

(G-2585)
LIGHTNING PRINTING
115 N Washington St (47933-1734)
PHONE..................................765 362-5999
EMP: 4 EST: 2012
SALES (est): 186.57K **Privately Held**
SIC: 2759 Screen printing

(G-2586)
LSC COMMUNICATIONS INC
Lakeside Books Company
600 W State Road 32 (47933-8967)
PHONE..................................765 364-2247
EMP: 130
SALES (corp-wide): 8.23B **Privately Held**
Web: www.lsccom.com
SIC: 2732 2721 Book printing; Magazines: publishing and printing
HQ: Lsc Communications, Inc.
4101 Winfield Rd
Warrenville IL 60555
844 572-5720

(G-2587)
LSC COMMUNICATIONS US LLC
600 W State Road 32 (47933-8967)
PHONE..................................765 362-1300
EMP: 1
SALES (corp-wide): 8.23B **Privately Held**
Web: www.lsccom.com
SIC: 2732 2721 2621 Book printing; Magazines: publishing and printing; Catalog, magazine, and newsprint papers
HQ: Lsc Communications Us, Llc
4101 Winfield Rd
Warrenville IL 60555
844 572-5720

(G-2588)
MCCLAMROCH AG LLC
Also Called: Perry Equipment
115 W 580 N (47933-7307)
PHONE..................................765 362-4495
Tom Mcclamroch, *Pr*
EMP: 7 EST: 1982

SALES (est): 1.26MM **Privately Held**
Web: www.perry-equip.com
SIC: 3535 Conveyors and conveying equipment

(G-2589)
MIDWEST BALE TIES INC
1200 E Wabash Ave (47933-2636)
P.O. Box 66 (47933-0066)
PHONE..................................765 364-0113
John Kendricks, *Pr*
Jason Ramsey, *VP*
EMP: 18 EST: 1998
SQ FT: 30,000
SALES (est): 9MM **Privately Held**
Web: www.midwestbaleties.com
SIC: 3315 Wire, steel: insulated or armored

(G-2590)
MIDWEST WILLYS LLC
3708 S 100 E (47933-8817)
PHONE..................................765 362-2247
EMP: 1 EST: 2004
SALES (est): 158.72K **Privately Held**
Web: www.midwestwillys.com
SIC: 3089 Automotive parts, plastic

(G-2591)
MILLERS LOCKER PLANT
1979 N Summer Dr (47933-8297)
PHONE..................................765 234-2381
James P Miller, *Pt*
Linda L Miller, *Pt*
EMP: 2 EST: 1945
SQ FT: 4,000
SALES (est): 103.62K **Privately Held**
SIC: 0751 2013 5421 Slaughtering: custom livestock services; Sausages and other prepared meats; Freezer provisioners, meat

(G-2592)
NATHANIEL BOWMAN
Also Called: Everybody
1107 Durham Dr (47933-3506)
Rural Route 1107 Durham Dr (47933)
PHONE..................................765 365-2358
N Emmett Bowman, *Owner*
EMP: 1 EST: 2021
SALES (est): 31.29K **Privately Held**
SIC: 2395 Embroidery and art needlework

(G-2593)
NEW MARKET PLASTICS INC (PA)
Also Called: Gator Buckets
3206 S Us Highway 231 (47933-9448)
PHONE..................................317 758-5494
Kerry Hopkins, *Pr*
EMP: 11 EST: 1991
SALES (est): 942.4K
SALES (corp-wide): 942.4K **Privately Held**
Web: www.gatorbuckets.com
SIC: 3089 Injection molded finished plastics products, nec

(G-2594)
NEWTON WLDG & FABRICATION LLC
1020 E College St (47933-2914)
PHONE..................................765 365-5129
EMP: 9 EST: 2014
SALES (est): 490.93K **Privately Held**
SIC: 7692 Welding repair

(G-2595)
NKAHOOTS BDY BATH BUTTERS LLC
1412 E Main St (47933-2003)
PHONE..................................317 559-2442
EMP: 2 EST: 2020
SALES (est): 74.42K **Privately Held**

GEOGRAPHIC SECTION
Crawfordsville - Montgomery County (G-2619)

Web: www.nkahootsbbb.com
SIC: 2841 Soap and other detergents

(G-2596)
NOR-COTE INTERNATIONAL INC
506 Lafayette Ave (47933-1336)
PHONE..................................800 488-9180
EMP: 1
SALES (corp-wide): 17.57MM Privately Held
Web: www.norcote.com
SIC: 2893 Printing ink
PA: Nor-Cote International, Inc.
605 Lafayette Ave
Crawfordsville IN 47933
800 488-9180

(G-2597)
NOR-COTE INTERNATIONAL INC (PA)
Also Called: Nor-Cote International
605 Lafayette Ave (47933-1339)
P.O. Box 668 (47933-0668)
PHONE..................................800 488-9180
Norman G Wolcott Junior, Ch Bd
Charles Mchargue, COO
▲ EMP: 42 EST: 1976
SQ FT: 20,000
SALES (est): 17.57MM
SALES (corp-wide): 17.57MM Privately Held
Web: www.norcote.com
SIC: 2893 Duplicating ink

(G-2598)
NUCOR CORPORATION
Nucor Steel - Indiana
4537 S Nucor Rd (47933-7969)
P.O. Box 907 (47933-0907)
PHONE..................................765 364-1323
Jeff Powers, Genl Mgr
EMP: 760
SALES (corp-wide): 34.71B Publicly Held
Web: www.nucor.com
SIC: 3312 3316 Blast furnaces and steel mills; Cold finishing of steel shapes
PA: Nucor Corporation
1915 Rexford Rd
Charlotte NC 28211
704 366-7000

(G-2599)
NUCOR STEEL CORP
4537 S Nucor Rd (47933-7969)
PHONE..................................765 364-1323
Jeff Powers, Prin
EMP: 41 EST: 2018
SALES (est): 48.4MM
SALES (corp-wide): 34.71B Publicly Held
Web: www.nucor.com
SIC: 3312 Blast furnaces and steel mills
PA: Nucor Corporation
1915 Rexford Rd
Charlotte NC 28211
704 366-7000

(G-2600)
PAPER OF MONTGOMERY COUNTY
201 E Jefferson St Ste 200 (47933-2804)
P.O. Box 272 (47933-0272)
PHONE..................................765 361-8888
Tim Timmons, Pt
Jeff Bannon, Pt
EMP: 2 EST: 2004
SALES (est): 180.24K Privately Held
Web: www.thepaper24-7.com
SIC: 2711 Commercial printing and newspaper publishing combined

(G-2601)
PENGUIN RANDOM HOUSE LLC
1019 N State Road 47 (47933-7131)
PHONE..................................800 733-3000
EMP: 11
SALES (corp-wide): 54.57MM Privately Held
Web: global.penguinrandomhouse.com
SIC: 2731 Books, publishing only
HQ: Penguin Random House Llc
1745 Broadway
New York NY 10019
212 782-9000

(G-2602)
PENGUIN RANDOM HOUSE LLC
1021 N State Road 47 (47933-7131)
PHONE..................................765 362-5125
EMP: 54
SALES (corp-wide): 54.57MM Privately Held
Web: www.prhspeakers.com
SIC: 2731 Books, publishing only
HQ: Penguin Random House Llc
1745 Broadway
New York NY 10019
212 782-9000

(G-2603)
PERFORMANCE MSTR COIL PROC INC
3752 E 350 S (47933-9464)
PHONE..................................765 364-1300
James Harrington, Pr
Richard Magnini, VP
James Jensen, Pr
Anthony Aiardo, Sec
Antoinette Magnini, Prin
EMP: 22 EST: 1997
SALES (est): 3.25MM Privately Held
SIC: 3677 Electronic coils and transformers

(G-2604)
PHANTOM NEON LLC
Also Called: Phantom Signs
100 E North St (47933-1738)
PHONE..................................765 362-2221
Yvonne Rincon, Managing Member
Yvonne Neal, Owner
Juan Rincon, Managing Member
EMP: 4 EST: 2008
SALES (est): 364.37K Privately Held
Web: www.phantomneon.com
SIC: 2759 3993 Posters, including billboards: printing, nsk; Neon signs

(G-2605)
PRO LINK
400 Fairlane Dr (47933-2132)
PHONE..................................765 225-1051
EMP: 1 EST: 1995
SALES (est): 85.7K Privately Held
Web: www.prolinkgs.com
SIC: 2759 Commercial printing, nec

(G-2606)
PURITAN WATER CONDITIONING
216 Lafayette Ave (47933-1609)
P.O. Box 778 (47933-0778)
PHONE..................................765 362-6340
TOLL FREE: 800
Jeff Hockersmith, Pr
Jan Cash, Sec
Gary Hockersmith, VP
EMP: 10 EST: 1905
SQ FT: 7,200
SALES (est): 932.61K Privately Held
Web: www.puritanwater.net

SIC: 3589 5999 7389 Water filters and softeners, household type; Water purification equipment; Water softener service

(G-2607)
R R DONNELLEY & SONS COMPANY
R R Donnelley
1009 Sloan St (47933-2743)
PHONE..................................765 362-1300
Gary Calleo, Dir
EMP: 113
SALES (corp-wide): 15B Privately Held
Web: www.rrd.com
SIC: 2732 2789 Books, printing only; Bookbinding and related work
HQ: R. R. Donnelley & Sons Company
35 W Wacker Dr
Chicago IL 60601
312 326-8000

(G-2608)
RAYBESTOS AFTERMARKET PDTS CO
204 Maple St (47933)
PHONE..................................765 359-1943
EMP: 4 EST: 2019
SALES (est): 147K Privately Held
Web: www.raybestospowertrain.com
SIC: 3714 Motor vehicle parts and accessories

(G-2609)
RAYBESTOS POWERTRAIN
1204 Darlington Ave (47933-1900)
PHONE..................................765 362-3500
John Butz, Pr
EMP: 99 EST: 2015
SALES (est): 5.7MM Privately Held
Web: www.raybestospowertrain.com
SIC: 3714 Motor vehicle parts and accessories

(G-2610)
RAYTECH CORP
711 Tech Dr (47933-1400)
PHONE..................................765 359-2882
John Butz, COO
EMP: 6 EST: 2019
SALES (est): 186.35K Privately Held
Web: www.raybestospowertrain.com
SIC: 3714 Motor vehicle parts and accessories

(G-2611)
RAYTECH POWERTRAIN LLC
Also Called: Raytech Powertrain
204 Maple St (47933-1922)
PHONE..................................812 268-0322
▲ EMP: 200
Web: www.raybestospowertrain.com
SIC: 3714 Anti-sway devices, motor vehicle

(G-2612)
RB MACHINE COMPANY
2907 S 550 E (47933-7954)
PHONE..................................765 364-6716
Ron Beach, Pr
EMP: 2 EST: 1987
SALES (est): 206.24K Privately Held
Web: www.rbmachineco.com
SIC: 3599 Machine shop, jobbing and repair

(G-2613)
RBM MANUFACTURING INC
566 S 200 E (47933-7932)
PHONE..................................765 364-6933
Ralph R Stevens, Pr
Todd A Stevens, Treas
EMP: 5 EST: 1992

SQ FT: 4,320
SALES (est): 504.71K Privately Held
Web: www.rbmmb.com
SIC: 3469 Stamping metal for the trade

(G-2614)
RED HAWK CHOPPERS INC
Also Called: Redhawk Choppers
419 Lafayette Ave (47933-1614)
PHONE..................................765 307-2269
Dan Joseph Wemer Junior, Pr
EMP: 5 EST: 2016
SALES (est): 202.93K Privately Held
Web: www.redhawkchoppers.com
SIC: 3751 Motorcycles and related parts

(G-2615)
SIZZLIN SOUND PRODUCTIONS LLC
2297 E Traction Rd (47933-8032)
PHONE..................................765 376-0129
Rich Bell, Pr
Rich Bell, Owner
Tammy Bell, Pt
EMP: 6 EST: 1993
SALES (est): 288.59K Privately Held
Web: www.sizzlinsoundsproductions.com
SIC: 7359 7812 3999 Audio-visual equipment and supply rental; Audio-visual program production; Stage hardware and equipment, except lighting

(G-2616)
SOLEMA USA INC
315 Glenn St (47933-2363)
P.O. Box 472 (47933-0472)
PHONE..................................765 361-0806
C Scott Ellis Prinicpal, Prin
C Scott Ellis, Pr
Michelle Ellis, VP
▲ EMP: 4 EST: 1999
SALES (est): 380K Privately Held
Web: www.solema.it
SIC: 2732 Books, printing and binding

(G-2617)
SOMMER METALCRAFT LLC
Also Called: Sommer
315 Poston Dr (47933-3050)
P.O. Box 688 (47933-0688)
PHONE..................................765 362-6200
▼ EMP: 90 EST: 1910
SALES (est): 8.25MM Privately Held
Web: www.sommercorp.com
SIC: 3496 Woven wire products, nec

(G-2618)
SQUEEGEEPIE MERCH CO LLC ✪
600 Mill St (47933-3439)
PHONE..................................765 376-6358
Zachary Benge, CEO
EMP: 1 EST: 2023
SALES (est): 62.43K Privately Held
SIC: 8611 2759 7336 7389 Merchants' association; Screen printing; Silk screen design; Design services

(G-2619)
STEEL TECHNOLOGIES LLC
3560 S Nucor Rd (47933-7968)
PHONE..................................765 362-3110
EMP: 102
Web: www.steeltechnologies.com
SIC: 3316 3312 Cold-rolled strip or wire; Sheet or strip, steel, hot-rolled
HQ: Steel Technologies Llc
700 N Hurstbourne Pkwy # 400
Louisville KY 40222
502 245-2110

Crawfordsville - Montgomery County (G-2620)

(G-2620)
SUGAR CREEK FABRICATORS INC
503 W 300 N (47933-9088)
P.O. Box 72 (47933-0072)
PHONE.................................765 361-0891
Greg Funk, *Owner*
EMP: 7 **EST:** 2008
SALES (est): 881.98K **Privately Held**
SIC: 3446 Ornamental metalwork

(G-2621)
SYSTEMS CONTRACTING CORP
4537 S Nucor Rd (47933-7969)
PHONE.................................765 361-2991
Phil Collins, *Mgr*
EMP: 21 **EST:** 1995
SALES (est): 271.79K **Privately Held**
Web: contracting.tsg.bz
SIC: 3547 Pipe and tube mills

(G-2622)
T K FABRICATING
6331 W 200 S (47933-6915)
PHONE.................................765 866-0755
Tom Klepfer, *Owner*
EMP: 1 **EST:** 1988
SQ FT: 10,000
SALES (est): 238.88K **Privately Held**
Web: www.tkfabricating.com
SIC: 3599 Custom machinery

(G-2623)
TEMPLE INLAND
801 N Englewood Dr (47933-9741)
P.O. Box 508 (47933-0508)
PHONE.................................765 362-1074
EMP: 5 **EST:** 2016
SALES (est): 246.08K **Privately Held**
SIC: 5113 2621 Patterns, paper; Paper mills

(G-2624)
TEMPUR PRODUCTION USA LLC
3200 Comfort Dr (47933)
PHONE.................................859 455-1000
EMP: 55
SALES (corp-wide): 4.93B **Publicly Held**
SIC: 5712 2515 Mattresses; Mattresses and bedsprings
HQ: Tempur Production Usa, Llc
203 Tempur Pedic Dr # 102
Duffield VA 24244
276 431-7150

(G-2625)
W & W FABRICATING INC
2597 S Us Highway 231 (47933-9488)
P.O. Box 602 (47933-0602)
PHONE.................................765 362-2182
Dan D Walden, *Pr*
Mary Walden, *Sec*
EMP: 2 **EST:** 1985
SQ FT: 261,000
SALES (est): 296.66K **Privately Held**
Web: www.waldentransportandrecycle.com
SIC: 3444 5051 Sheet metalwork; Steel

(G-2626)
WABASH CLUB RAYBESTOS PDTS CO
1204 Darlington Ave (47933-1958)
PHONE.................................765 359-2862
Harold Pope, *Prin*
EMP: 2 **EST:** 2008
SALES (est): 576.66K **Privately Held**
Web: www.raybestospowertrain.com
SIC: 3714 Motor vehicle parts and accessories

(G-2627)
WILSON ENTERPRISES INC
Also Called: Wilson Autotech
2008 Indianapolis Rd (47933-3136)
PHONE.................................765 362-1089
Diane Wilson, *Pr*
Mark Wilson, *Sec*
EMP: 8 **EST:** 1988
SQ FT: 6,400
SALES (est): 973.05K **Privately Held**
Web: www.wilsonsautotech.net
SIC: 7549 2759 Automotive maintenance services; Screen printing

(G-2628)
YES FEED & SUPPLY LLC
Also Called: Associated Mfg & Packg
2065 S Nucor Rd (47933-7970)
PHONE.................................765 361-9821
EMP: 3 **EST:** 2007
SALES (est): 244.29K **Privately Held**
SIC: 3999 Manufacturing industries, nec

Cromwell
Noble County

(G-2629)
ALUMINUM CONVERSION INC
204 Parkway (46732)
P.O. Box 137 (46732-0137)
PHONE.................................260 856-2180
Smith Michael A, *Pr*
Pamela Smith, *Sec*
▲ **EMP:** 4 **EST:** 1981
SQ FT: 3,500
SALES (est): 497.17K **Privately Held**
SIC: 3341 Secondary nonferrous metals

(G-2630)
FREEDOM ACRES INC
458 Olive St (46732-1122)
P.O. Box 278 (46732-0278)
PHONE.................................260 856-3059
Michael E Hatfield, *Pr*
EMP: 14 **EST:** 2003
SQ FT: 6,000
SALES (est): 973.52K **Privately Held**
Web: www.freedomwireinc.com
SIC: 3679 Harness assemblies, for electronic use: wire or cable

(G-2631)
LAKETRONICS INC
2 Moore St (46732-1117)
P.O. Box 338 (46732-0338)
PHONE.................................260 856-4588
EMP: 25 **EST:** 1974
SALES (est): 4.72MM **Privately Held**
Web: www.laketronicsinc.com
SIC: 3679 3694 3625 Harness assemblies, for electronic use: wire or cable; Engine electrical equipment; Relays and industrial controls

(G-2632)
OH HUNT LINES INC
591 N Jefferson St (46732-9547)
PHONE.................................260 856-2125
Dave Martin, *Pr*
EMP: 7 **EST:** 2002
SALES (est): 505.48K **Privately Held**
SIC: 3621 Motors, electric

(G-2633)
STEVES PALLETS
3868 N 1025 W (46732-9744)
PHONE.................................260 856-2047
Steve Sturgill, *Owner*
EMP: 8 **EST:** 2002
SALES (est): 528.47K **Privately Held**
SIC: 2448 Pallets, wood

Cross Plains
Ripley County

(G-2634)
FUR REAL TAXIDERMY LLC
4339 E County Road 900 S (47017-8961)
PHONE.................................812 667-6365
Cheryl Mathews, *Prin*
EMP: 2 **EST:** 2010
SALES (est): 62.35K **Privately Held**
SIC: 3999 Furs

Crothersville
Jackson County

(G-2635)
AISIN CHEMICAL INDIANA LLC
1004 Industrial Way (47229-9415)
PHONE.................................812 793-2888
Yoshiaki Yasui, *CEO*
Hiroshi Tanida, *
Masashi Nagino, *
Masayuki Isogami, *
▲ **EMP:** 50 **EST:** 2005
SALES (est): 12.49MM **Privately Held**
Web: www.aisinchemin.com
SIC: 3499 Friction material, made from powdered metal
HQ: Aisin Chemical Co.,Ltd.
1141-1, Okawagawara, Fujiokainocho
Toyota AIC 470-0

(G-2636)
AISIN DRIVETRAIN INC
1001 Industrial Way (47229-9415)
PHONE.................................812 793-2427
George S Turpin, *Pr*
Scott Turpin, *
Scott Shade, *
Junji Miyagawa, *
Hiroshi Tanida, *
▲ **EMP:** 130 **EST:** 1996
SQ FT: 350,000
SALES (est): 49.13MM **Privately Held**
Web: www.aisindrive.com
SIC: 3714 3566 3568 Transmissions, motor vehicle; Torque converters, except auto; Power transmission equipment, nec
HQ: Aisin Holdings Of America, Inc.
1665 E 4th St
Seymour IN 47274
812 524-8144

(G-2637)
BISHOP REPAIR
4514 S County Road 700 E (47229-9726)
PHONE.................................812 523-3246
Robert Bishop, *Pt*
EMP: 2 **EST:** 1993
SALES (est): 232.68K **Privately Held**
Web: www.terrorstudies.org
SIC: 3599 Machine shop, jobbing and repair

(G-2638)
CERRO WIRE LLC
1002 Industrial Way (47229-9415)
PHONE.................................812 793-2929
Rick Mcdold, *Brnch Mgr*
EMP: 70
SALES (corp-wide): 364.48B **Publicly Held**
Web: www.cerrowire.com
SIC: 3357 3351 Nonferrous wiredrawing and insulating; Wire, copper and copper alloy
HQ: Cerro Wire Llc
1099 Thompson Rd Se
Hartselle AL 35640
256 773-2522

(G-2639)
CROTHERSVILLE TIMES
510 Moore St Ste 100 (47229-1622)
P.O. Box 141 (47229-0141)
PHONE.................................812 793-2188
Curt Kovener, *Owner*
EMP: 1 **EST:** 1947
SALES (est): 81.06K **Privately Held**
Web: www.crothersvilletimes.com
SIC: 2711 Newspapers, publishing and printing

(G-2640)
FROSTBITE PRESS LLC
6679 S County Road 1025 E (47229-9733)
PHONE.................................812 216-1372
Vera Michelle Watts, *Prin*
EMP: 4 **EST:** 2019
SALES (est): 87.74K **Privately Held**
SIC: 2741 Miscellaneous publishing

(G-2641)
K TECH SUPPLY
12740 E County Road 400 S (47229-9689)
PHONE.................................812 793-3352
Scott Kovener, *Prin*
EMP: 1 **EST:** 2001
SALES (est): 101.63K **Privately Held**
SIC: 7534 5099 Rebuilding and retreading tires; Durable goods, nec

(G-2642)
MASTERSBILT CHASSIS INC
Also Called: Master Built Racing Accessory
6520 S Us Highway 31 (47229-9643)
P.O. Box 144 (47229-0144)
PHONE.................................812 793-3666
Keith Masters, *Pr*
Adrian Masters, *Sec*
EMP: 9 **EST:** 1982
SQ FT: 3,200
SALES (est): 442.49K **Privately Held**
Web: www.mastersbilt.com
SIC: 3711 5531 3714 Automobile assembly, including specialty automobiles; Automotive parts; Motor vehicle parts and accessories

(G-2643)
PRO SERIES PRODUCTS LLC
208 N Armstrong St (47229-1004)
PHONE.................................812 793-3506
EMP: 5 **EST:** 2008
SALES (est): 264.4K **Privately Held**
Web: www.proseriesproducts.com
SIC: 3999 Manufacturing industries, nec

(G-2644)
PRO-FORM PLASTICS INC
11624 E State Road 250 (47229-9621)
PHONE.................................812 522-4433
▼ **EMP:** 30 **EST:** 1996
SQ FT: 32,000
SALES (est): 4.97MM **Privately Held**
Web: www.proformcp.com
SIC: 2431 3423 3089 Trim, wood; Cutting dies, except metal cutting; Thermoformed finished plastics products, nec

(G-2645)
S-TECH INC
208 N Armstrong St (47229-1004)
PHONE.................................812 793-3506
Dale Schmelzle, *Pr*
EMP: 6 **EST:** 2005
SALES (est): 456.98K **Privately Held**
SIC: 7692 Welding repair

Crown Point — Lake County (G-2675)

(G-2646)
SEW BEAUTIFUL EMBROIDRY
5084 S County Road 1060 E (47229-9771)
PHONE.................812 793-2245
Gernetta Land, *Owner*
EMP: 4 EST: 2015
SALES (est): 46.14K **Privately Held**
SIC: 2395 Embroidery and art needlework

Crown Point
Lake County

(G-2647)
1109 169TH LLC
1109 Churchill Ln (46307-5068)
PHONE.................219 671-5052
Ryan M Stojkovich, *Managing Member*
EMP: 1 EST: 2018
SALES (est): 74.14K **Privately Held**
SIC: 3531 Construction machinery

(G-2648)
ADAMS SMITH (PA)
Also Called: Lakeshore Graphics
10431 Floyd St (46307-2999)
PHONE.................219 661-2812
Smith Adams, *Owner*
EMP: 5 EST: 1991
SALES (est): 366.39K **Privately Held**
SIC: 2759 Commercial printing, nec

(G-2649)
ADVANCED BOILER CTRL SVCS INC (PA)
7515 Cline Ave (46307-9607)
PHONE.................708 429-7066
Robert Burrink, *Pr*
EMP: 15 EST: 1986
SALES (est): 2.23MM
SALES (corp-wide): 2.23MM **Privately Held**
Web: www.boiler-controls.com
SIC: 3823 Boiler controls: industrial, power, and marine type

(G-2650)
ANDERSON & ANDERSON TRCKG INC
104 W Hack Ct (46307-3938)
PHONE.................219 661-7547
John Anderson, *CEO*
EMP: 1 EST: 2021
SALES (est): 60.08K **Privately Held**
SIC: 3537 Trucks: freight, baggage, etc.: industrial, except mining

(G-2651)
ASSOCIATED WORLD MUSIC LLC
2125 W 96th Pl (46307-2017)
PHONE.................219 512-4511
Aaron Olson, *Managing Member*
EMP: 2 EST: 2020
SALES (est): 88.38K **Privately Held**
SIC: 3651 Music distribution apparatus

(G-2652)
ASTRAL AURAS LLC
9800 Connecticut Dr (46307-7840)
PHONE.................219 628-5258
EMP: 4 EST: 2021
SALES (est): 39.69K **Privately Held**
Web: www.astralauras.com
SIC: 3999 Candles

(G-2653)
BD MEDICAL DEVELOPMENT INC
1140 Millennium Dr (46307-7533)
PHONE.................219 310-8551
Bill Depel, *Pr*
EMP: 5 EST: 2010
SALES (est): 355.91K **Privately Held**
SIC: 3841 2821 Medical instruments and equipment, blood and bone work; Molding compounds, plastics

(G-2654)
BEAR KOMPLEX
1001 E Summit St (46307-2727)
PHONE.................317 600-5833
EMP: 5 EST: 2019
SALES (est): 277.08K **Privately Held**
Web: www.bearkomplex.com
SIC: 3949 Sporting and athletic goods, nec

(G-2655)
BERG
393 Golden Oak Ct (46307-8275)
PHONE.................219 226-4350
Vincent Berg, *Prin*
EMP: 6 EST: 2010
SALES (est): 91.47K **Privately Held**
Web: www.borusanbergpipe.com
SIC: 3444 Sheet metalwork

(G-2656)
BIBLICAL PUBLISHING SVCS INC
307 E Clark St (46307-4044)
PHONE.................219 213-2078
EMP: 4 EST: 2016
SALES (est): 59.45K **Privately Held**
Web: www.liubakkastudio.com
SIC: 2741 Miscellaneous publishing

(G-2657)
BLUSH BATH BOMBS BY AMOR
6650 Rohrman Rd (46307-9184)
PHONE.................219 313-3993
Amor Monjes, *Prin*
EMP: 4 EST: 2018
SALES (est): 83.99K **Privately Held**
SIC: 2844 Bath salts

(G-2658)
BOBBY LITTLE CREATIONS
610 W Joliet St (46307-3813)
PHONE.................219 313-5102
Bob Wright, *Pr*
Bob Wright, *Owner*
EMP: 5 EST: 1996
SALES (est): 284.59K **Privately Held**
Web: www.littlebobbycreations.com
SIC: 2676 5947 Infant and baby paper products; Gift, novelty, and souvenir shop

(G-2659)
BOLTTECH MANNINGS INC
Also Called: Bolttech Mannings, Inc.
1170 Arrowhead Ct (46307-7536)
PHONE.................219 310-8389
EMP: 5
SALES (corp-wide): 60.23MM **Privately Held**
Web: www.bolttechmannings.com
SIC: 3546 Power-driven handtools
PA: Bolttech Mannings Llc
 103 Equity Dr
 Greensburg PA 15601
 724 872-4873

(G-2660)
BOOK OF US LLC
8041 Pine Island Ct Apt B38 (46307-4719)
PHONE.................331 256-5953
EMP: 2 EST: 2021
SALES (est): 30K **Privately Held**
SIC: 2731 Books, publishing and printing

(G-2661)
BORMAN DISTRIBUTING INC
650 E 119th Pl (46307-0164)
PHONE.................219 713-8523
Robert Borman, *Pr*
EMP: 2 EST: 2016
SALES (est): 207.16K **Privately Held**
SIC: 2051 Bakery, for home service delivery

(G-2662)
BROGAN PHARMACEUTICALS LLC
9800 Connecticut Dr (46307-7840)
PHONE.................219 644-3693
EMP: 15 EST: 2004
SQ FT: 10,500
SALES (est): 727.46K **Privately Held**
SIC: 2834 Pharmaceutical preparations

(G-2663)
BUILDING INDIANA
1255 Erie Ct Ste C (46307-2770)
PHONE.................219 226-0300
EMP: 7 EST: 2019
SALES (est): 128.75K **Privately Held**
Web: www.buildingindiana.com
SIC: 2399 Fabricated textile products, nec

(G-2664)
CARGO SKI TRANSPORT INC
Also Called: CST
9528 Cleveland St (46307-2020)
PHONE.................219 448-9888
Dejan Kitevski, *Pr*
EMP: 9 EST: 2013
SALES (est): 476.94K **Privately Held**
SIC: 3715 Trailers or vans for transporting horses

(G-2665)
CHIEF POWERBOATS INC
280 Wood St (46307-4100)
PHONE.................219 775-7024
Scott Grady, *Pr*
Rosemarie Grady, *Sec*
Daryl Grady, *Stockholder*
EMP: 5 EST: 2004
SALES (est): 476.04K **Privately Held**
Web: www.chiefpowerboats.com
SIC: 3732 Boatbuilding and repairing

(G-2666)
CLUSTER PACKAGING LLC
10769 Bdwy Ave Ste 146 (46307-7316)
PHONE.................612 803-1056
Bill Zimmerman, *Pr*
EMP: 5 EST: 2010
SALES (est): 110K **Privately Held**
Web: www.clusterpackaging.com
SIC: 5199 3089 Packaging materials; Blow molded finished plastics products, nec

(G-2667)
CONSULTECH5
3056 Sunrise Dr (46307-8431)
PHONE.................219 712-2801
Lisa Ghezzi, *Owner*
EMP: 1 EST: 2006
SALES (est): 96K **Privately Held**
SIC: 3579 Sorters, filing (office)

(G-2668)
CROWN BRICK & SUPPLY INC (PA)
820 Thomas St (46307-3497)
PHONE.................219 663-7880
EMP: 21 EST: 1995
SQ FT: 9,000
SALES (est): 4.06MM **Privately Held**
Web: www.crownbrick.com
SIC: 5032 3271 Brick, stone, and related material; Concrete block and brick

(G-2669)
CROWN MTAL FBRICATORS ERECTORS
1031 E Summit St (46307-2727)
P.O. Box 179 (46308-0179)
PHONE.................219 661-8277
Gerhard Kurt King, *Owner*
Christine King, *VP*
EMP: 5 EST: 1980
SQ FT: 10,000
SALES (est): 951.76K **Privately Held**
Web: www.crownmetalfab.com
SIC: 3441 Fabricated structural metal

(G-2670)
CROWN POINT PRINTING LLC
1082 Breuckman Dr (46307-7530)
PHONE.................219 226-0900
EMP: 4 EST: 2020
SALES (est): 109.25K **Privately Held**
Web: www.crownpointprinting.com
SIC: 2752 Offset printing

(G-2671)
CROWN POINT SHOPPING NEWS
Also Called: Star
112 W Clark St (46307-3918)
PHONE.................219 663-4212
Andrew Steel, *Prin*
Andrew Steel, *Owner*
EMP: 4 EST: 1966
SQ FT: 3,000
SALES (est): 256.97K **Privately Held**
Web: www.cps.k12.in.us
SIC: 2741 Shopping news: publishing and printing

(G-2672)
D TIMBER INC
14405 Clark St (46307-9497)
PHONE.................219 374-8085
Dennis A Ohhof, *Prin*
EMP: 6 EST: 2001
SALES (est): 457.21K **Privately Held**
SIC: 2411 Timber, cut at logging camp

(G-2673)
DANUBIUS MACHINE INC
11205 Delaware Pkwy (46307-7812)
PHONE.................219 662-7787
EMP: 7 EST: 2007
SALES (est): 868.26K **Privately Held**
Web: www.danubiusmachine.com
SIC: 3541 Vertical turning and boring machines (metalworking)

(G-2674)
DAWN FOOD PRODUCTS INC
Also Called: Dawn Food Products Frozen Div
9601 Georgia St (46307-9846)
PHONE.................800 333-3296
W Denson, *Brnch Mgr*
EMP: 104
SQ FT: 27,000
SALES (corp-wide): 1.73B **Privately Held**
Web: www.dawnfoods.com
SIC: 2051 Croissants, except frozen
HQ: Dawn Food Products, Inc.
 3333 Sargent Rd
 Jackson MI 49201

(G-2675)
DEG CORP
Also Called: Wilson Iron Works
1150 E Summit St (46307-2729)
PHONE.................219 663-7900
Darrin Grabek, *Prin*
EMP: 18 EST: 2007
SALES (est): 839.69K **Privately Held**
Web: www.wilsoniron.com

Crown Point - Lake County (G-2676)

SIC: 3441 Fabricated structural metal

(G-2676)
DELUXE AKIO 606 LTD LBLTY CO
525 W 93rd Pl Apt 213 (46307-6200)
PHONE.................................708 682-2780
EMP: 1 EST: 2020
SALES (est): 88K **Privately Held**
SIC: 3799 Transportation equipment, nec

(G-2677)
DLA CONSTRUCTION
3467 Highland Ct (46307-8925)
PHONE.................................404 992-0805
Debbie Agnew, *CEO*
EMP: 1 EST: 2020
SALES (est): 200K **Privately Held**
Web: www.dla.mil
SIC: 2421 Building and structural materials, wood

(G-2678)
DON TAYLOR
9524 Cleveland St (46307-2020)
PHONE.................................219 662-0597
Donald Taylor, *Owner*
EMP: 6 EST: 2015
SALES (est): 115.66K **Privately Held**
Web: www.scbi.org
SIC: 2711 Newspapers, publishing and printing

(G-2679)
DONALD L GARD
11629 Burr St (46307-8766)
PHONE.................................219 663-7945
Donald L Gard, *Pr*
EMP: 3 EST: 2005
SALES (est): 165.11K **Privately Held**
SIC: 3582 Washing machines, laundry: commercial, incl. coin-operated

(G-2680)
ENGINEERED PRODUCTS INC
1203 E Summit St (46307-2730)
PHONE.................................219 662-2080
Robert A Scott Senior, *Pr*
EMP: 2 EST: 1999
SALES (est): 280.19K **Privately Held**
Web: www.superiorwallembrace.com
SIC: 3271 Blocks, concrete: landscape or retaining wall

(G-2681)
ERNESTINE FOODS INC
9800 Connecticut Dr (46307-7840)
PHONE.................................219 274-0188
Chastidy S Dix, *CEO*
EMP: 7 EST: 2013
SALES (est): 365.97K **Privately Held**
Web: www.ernestinefoods.com
SIC: 5499 2051 Gourmet food stores; Bagels, fresh or frozen

(G-2682)
EXACT SHTMTL & SKYLIGHTS INC
763 Seminole Ct (46307-5200)
PHONE.................................219 670-3520
EMP: 7 EST: 2012
SALES (est): 93.14K **Privately Held**
SIC: 3444 Sheet metalwork

(G-2683)
EXPEDITION LOG HOMES
11091 Marion Pl (46307-9428)
PHONE.................................219 663-5555
EMP: 2 EST: 1991
SALES (est): 170K **Privately Held**
Web: www.expeditionloghomes.com

SIC: 2452 1521 Log cabins, prefabricated, wood; Single-family housing construction

(G-2684)
FINITE FILTATION COMPANY
120 Las Olas Ct (46307-8432)
PHONE.................................219 789-8084
Rick P Schultz, *CEO*
EMP: 2 EST: 2009
SALES (est): 147.1K **Privately Held**
SIC: 3549 Metalworking machinery, nec

(G-2685)
FIVES N AMERCN COMBUSTN INC
730 N Main St (46307-3236)
PHONE.................................219 662-9600
EMP: 4
SALES (corp-wide): 2.12MM **Privately Held**
Web: www.fivesgroup.com
SIC: 3433 Heating equipment, except electric
HQ: Fives North American Combustion, Inc.
4455 E 71st St
Cleveland OH 44105
216 271-6000

(G-2686)
FORENSIC SANE SOFTWARE LLC
5201 Fountain Dr Ste B (46307-1086)
PHONE.................................219 232-6576
Nancy Healy, *Managing Member*
EMP: 2 EST: 2011
SALES (est): 250K **Privately Held**
Web: www.forensicsoftwaresolutions.com
SIC: 7372 Prepackaged software

(G-2687)
FORESEE LLC
158 N Main St (46307-4063)
PHONE.................................219 226-9663
EMP: 11 EST: 2007
SALES (est): 12.21K **Privately Held**
Web: www.verint.com
SIC: 3423 Carpenters' hand tools, except saws: levels, chisels, etc.

(G-2688)
FUEL FABRICATION LLC
14727 Reeder Ct (46307-8514)
PHONE.................................219 390-7022
Joseph Ponziano, *Prin*
EMP: 5 EST: 2015
SALES (est): 50.64K **Privately Held**
SIC: 3999 Manufacturing industries, nec

(G-2689)
GLENS MOBILE WELDING
12207 Burr St (46307-8734)
PHONE.................................219 663-2668
Glen Whitmer, *Prin*
EMP: 1 EST: 1997
SALES (est): 70K **Privately Held**
SIC: 7692 Welding repair

(G-2690)
GOOD NEWS NETWORK LLC
1950 Pecan Ct (46307-1080)
PHONE.................................812 219-2376
Giavonni Nickson, *CEO*
EMP: 5 EST: 2019
SALES (est): 84.23K **Privately Held**
Web: www.goodnewsnetwork.org
SIC: 2741 Miscellaneous publishing

(G-2691)
HAIR OF FERRET
339 Maple Ln (46307-4544)
P.O. Box 599 (46308-0599)
PHONE.................................219 663-1599

EMP: 2 EST: 2000
SALES (est): 203.32K **Privately Held**
Web: www.hairoftheferret.com
SIC: 2035 Pickles, sauces, and salad dressings

(G-2692)
HEARTLAND ADHESIVES INC
7519 Boardwalk (46307-8254)
PHONE.................................219 310-8645
James Pohlman, *Pr*
Tracy Pohlman, *VP*
▲ EMP: 7 EST: 2007
SALES (est): 981.06K **Privately Held**
Web: www.gdiadhesives.com
SIC: 2891 Adhesives

(G-2693)
HOBART LOCKER & MEAT PKG CO
8602 Randolph St (46307-8818)
PHONE.................................219 942-5952
Peter Urenovich, *Pr*
EMP: 4 EST: 1946
SQ FT: 4,000
SALES (est): 414.05K **Privately Held**
SIC: 2011 5147 Meat packing plants; Meats, cured or smoked

(G-2694)
HPC INTERNATIONAL INC
5261 Fountain Dr Ste A (46307-1089)
PHONE.................................219 922-4868
Hilton Hudson Ii, *Pr*
EMP: 13 EST: 1996
SALES (est): 1.01MM **Privately Held**
Web: www.hpcinternationalinc.com
SIC: 2731 Book publishing

(G-2695)
IMCO INDUSTRIAL MACHINE CORP
Also Called: Imco
1201 S Main St (46307-8481)
P.O. Box 943 (46308-0943)
PHONE.................................219 663-6100
Steve Higgins, *Pr*
Mark Mcgurk, *VP*
Shirley Crapbis, *Sec*
EMP: 34 EST: 1967
SQ FT: 18,000
SALES (est): 865.54K **Privately Held**
SIC: 3599 Machine shop, jobbing and repair

(G-2696)
INDUSTRIAL MACHINING INC
1201 Merrillville Rd (46307-2725)
PHONE.................................219 663-6100
Shirley Krebes, *Prin*
EMP: 11 EST: 2003
SALES (est): 258.01K **Privately Held**
SIC: 3599 Machine shop, jobbing and repair

(G-2697)
INNOVATIVE ENERGY INC
Also Called: Ratech Industries
1204 Erie Ct (46307-2743)
PHONE.................................219 696-3639
Robert Wadsworth, *Pr*
Mary Wadsworth, ◆
▲ EMP: 35 EST: 1980
SALES (est): 5.99MM **Privately Held**
Web: www.innovativeenergy.com
SIC: 2671 5033 Paper; coated and laminated packaging; Insulation materials

(G-2698)
JAC JMR INC
Also Called: Quality Imprssons Print Design
1421 E Summit St (46307)
PHONE.................................219 663-6700
Judy Cruse, *Pr*

EMP: 3 EST: 2008
SALES (est): 917.06K **Privately Held**
Web: www.qualityimpressionsinc.com
SIC: 5085 5084 2759 Industrial supplies; Printing trades machinery, equipment, and supplies; Commercial printing, nec

(G-2699)
JADCO LTD
Also Called: Heritage Flower Company
401 N Jackson St (46307-3368)
P.O. Box 267 (46308-0267)
PHONE.................................219 661-2065
Richard J Amodeo, *Pr*
Cathleen A Amodeo, *Sec*
▲ EMP: 10 EST: 1960
SQ FT: 3,000
SALES (est): 2.07MM **Privately Held**
Web: www.heritageflower.com
SIC: 5193 3999 Artificial flowers; Wreaths, artificial

(G-2700)
JAY COSTAS COMPANIES INC
Also Called: Oil and Go
1492 N Main St (46307-2302)
PHONE.................................219 663-4364
EMP: 6
SALES (corp-wide): 3.64MM **Privately Held**
SIC: 1389 Oil field services, nec
PA: Jay Costas Companies, Inc.
121 Lincolnway
Valparaiso IN 46383
219 464-9819

(G-2701)
JD MATERIALS
11563 Baker St (46307-4262)
PHONE.................................219 662-1418
James D Miller, *Prin*
EMP: 9 EST: 2010
SALES (est): 212.6K **Privately Held**
SIC: 3537 Industrial trucks and tractors

(G-2702)
JEROME PAGELL
1752 Broadacre Rd (46307-9317)
PHONE.................................219 226-0591
Jerome Pagell, *Owner*
EMP: 1 EST: 2004
SALES (est): 92.05K **Privately Held**
SIC: 3651 Home entertainment equipment, electronic, nec

(G-2703)
JOHNS ARCHTCTRAL MET SOLUTIONS
800 E Porter St (46307)
PHONE.................................219 440-2116
Arron Johns, *Pr*
EMP: 10 EST: 2016
SALES (est): 242.17K **Privately Held**
SIC: 3444 5039 Siding, sheet metal; Architectural metalwork

(G-2704)
JOHNSON CONTROLS INC
Also Called: Johnson Controls
2293 N Main St (46307-1854)
PHONE.................................219 736-7105
George Kosides, *Owner*
EMP: 16
Web: www.johnsoncontrols.com
SIC: 2531 Seats, automobile
HQ: Johnson Controls, Inc.
5757 N Green Bay Ave
Milwaukee WI 53209
866 496-1999

Crown Point - Lake County (G-2732)

(G-2705)
JORH FRAME & MOULDING CO INC
Also Called: Jorh Frame
2909 Morningside Dr (46307-5190)
PHONE..............................708 747-3440
Gordon N Harrington Junior, *Pr*
Patricia Harrington, *Sec*
EMP: 5 **EST:** 1972
SALES (est): 340.84K **Privately Held**
SIC: 2499 Picture frame molding, finished

(G-2706)
JP TECHNOLOGY INC
10769 Broadway (46307-7316)
PHONE..............................219 947-2525
Jerry Pagell, *Pr*
EMP: 3 **EST:** 2004
SALES (est): 351.39K **Privately Held**
Web: www.jphometechnology.com
SIC: 3651 Home entertainment equipment, electronic, nec

(G-2707)
KA CROWN POINT INC
1650 Blue Heron Ct (46307-5076)
PHONE..............................219 595-5276
Rahul Patel, *Owner*
EMP: 10 **EST:** 2018
SALES (est): 184.11K **Privately Held**
Web: crownpoint.in.gov
SIC: 2434 Wood kitchen cabinets

(G-2708)
KENSINGTON WATCH SERVICES
146 N Main St (46307-4063)
PHONE..............................219 306-5499
EMP: 1
SALES (est): 53.29K **Privately Held**
SIC: 7631 3911 Watch repair; Jewelry, precious metal

(G-2709)
KIEMLE-HANKINS COMPANY
Also Called: Kh
1011 E Summit St (46307-2727)
PHONE..............................219 213-2643
EMP: 17
SALES (corp-wide): 14.06MM **Privately Held**
Web: www.kiemlehankins.com
SIC: 7694 Electric motor repair
PA: The Kiemle-Hankins Company
  94 H St
  Perrysburg OH 43551
  419 661-2430

(G-2710)
KIPPS PLUMBING INC
800 E North St Ste 1 (46307-3389)
PHONE..............................219 661-9320
Brian Tipp, *Pr*
EMP: 1 **EST:** 2005
SALES (est): 123.06K **Privately Held**
Web: www.yourpenguy.com
SIC: 3432 Plumbing fixture fittings and trim

(G-2711)
KONECRANES INC
Also Called: Crane Pro Services
1255 Erie Ct Ste B (46307-2770)
PHONE..............................219 661-9602
Heather Hughes, *Mgr*
EMP: 10
Web: www.konecranes.com
SIC: 3536 Hoists, cranes, and monorails
HQ: Konecranes, Inc.
  4401 Gateway Blvd
  Springfield OH 45502

(G-2712)
KONRADY GRAPHICS INC
4070 Bush Hill Ct (46307-8953)
P.O. Box 174 (46308-0174)
PHONE..............................219 662-0436
Thomas E Konrady, *Pr*
Kimberly Konrady, *Pr*
EMP: 4 **EST:** 1983
SALES (est): 270.44K **Privately Held**
Web: www.konradyplastics.com
SIC: 3993 Signs and advertising specialties

(G-2713)
KUMAS DUMPSTER RENTALS LLC
8145 Mount Ct Apt C (46307-1234)
PHONE..............................662 422-1508
EMP: 1 **EST:** 2021
SALES (est): 56.47K **Privately Held**
SIC: 3443 Dumpsters, garbage

(G-2714)
KWIK KOPY PRINTING
1180 N Main St (46307)
PHONE..............................219 663-7799
EMP: 5 **EST:** 2019
SALES (est): 241.94K **Privately Held**
Web: www.nwiprintpro.com
SIC: 2759 Thermography

(G-2715)
LEANING PALMS LLC
735 Quinlan Ct (46307-9825)
PHONE..............................630 886-8924
EMP: 1 **EST:** 2012
SALES (est): 63.33K **Privately Held**
SIC: 7371 7372 7389 Computer software development and applications; Business oriented computer software; Business services, nec

(G-2716)
LEASELINKS LLC
631 W South St (46307-4321)
PHONE..............................312 810-0788
Johnson Frederick, *Prin*
EMP: 5 **EST:** 2016
SALES (est): 132.99K **Privately Held**
Web: www.leasepipeline.com
SIC: 7372 Prepackaged software

(G-2717)
LEROY E DOTY CABINET SHOP
Also Called: Doty, Leroy E. Builder
4514 W 105th Ave (46307-2501)
PHONE..............................219 663-1139
Leroy E Doty, *Owner*
EMP: 3 **EST:** 1955
SALES (est): 245.82K **Privately Held**
SIC: 1521 2434 2521 General remodeling, single-family houses; Wood kitchen cabinets ; Cabinets, office: wood

(G-2718)
LGS PLUMBING INC
1110 E Summit St (46307-2729)
PHONE..............................219 663-2177
Daniel Smith, *Pr*
Adam J Smith, *
EMP: 25 **EST:** 1983
SALES (est): 4.88MM **Privately Held**
Web: www.lgsplumbing.com
SIC: 3432 1623 Plastic plumbing fixture fittings, assembly; Underground utilities contractor

(G-2719)
LIGHTCRAFTERS NANOTECH LLC
Also Called: Nano X Labs, LLC
9188 Vigo St (46307-8623)
PHONE..............................610 844-8341
EMP: 4 **EST:** 2019
SALES (est): 174.83K **Privately Held**
SIC: 2819 Chemicals, high purity: refined from technical grade

(G-2720)
LITTLE BROWN BEARS
317 S Main St (46307-7758)
PHONE..............................219 663-9037
Melisa F Brown, *Owner*
EMP: 1 **EST:** 1989
SALES (est): 40.89K **Privately Held**
SIC: 3942 Stuffed toys, including animals

(G-2721)
MAGNUM INTERNATIONAL INC
11494 Broadway (46307-7106)
P.O. Box 1727 (60409-7727)
PHONE..............................708 889-9999
David Creech, *Pr*
Thomas S Eisner, *
◆ **EMP:** 50 **EST:** 1982
SQ FT: 2,600
SALES (est): 5.93MM **Privately Held**
Web: www.magnuminternationalinc.com
SIC: 2851 5162 5169 Coating, air curing; Plastics materials, nec; Chemicals, industrial and heavy

(G-2722)
MANIC MEADERY
1003 E Summit St (46307-2771)
PHONE..............................219 614-1846
EMP: 6 **EST:** 2018
SALES (est): 102.16K **Privately Held**
Web: www.manicmeadery.com
SIC: 2084 Wines

(G-2723)
MH VALE PC
3805 W 107th Ln (46307-2951)
PHONE..............................219 661-0867
Marlene H Vale, *Prin*
EMP: 3 **EST:** 2001
SALES (est): 205.02K **Privately Held**
SIC: 3491 Industrial valves

(G-2724)
MICROWORKS INC
2200 W 97th Pl (46307-2344)
PHONE..............................219 661-8620
Dan Henderson, *Pr*
EMP: 6 **EST:** 1996
SALES (est): 2.09MM **Privately Held**
Web: www.mwiconsulting.com
SIC: 2835 Microbiology and virology diagnostic products
PA: Infinity Laboratories, Inc.
  230 3rd St Ste 200
  Castle Rock CO 80104

(G-2725)
MIDWEST AEROSPACE CASTING LLC ✪
899 E 99th Ct (46307)
PHONE..............................708 597-1300
Robert Littlefield, *Managing Member*
EMP: 6 **EST:** 2022
SALES (est): 537.18K **Privately Held**
SIC: 3365 Aerospace castings, aluminum

(G-2726)
NORTHWEST IND BACKFLOW TESTERS
5910 E 129th Ave (46307-9055)
PHONE..............................219 663-8390
Dennis Hamilton, *Owner*
EMP: 1 **EST:** 1997
SALES (est): 108.31K **Privately Held**
Web: www.aship.org
SIC: 1389 Testing, measuring, surveying, and analysis services

(G-2727)
OUTFIELD PRSNLZED SPT BLLS INC
12880 Jefferson Dr (46307-7955)
PHONE..............................219 661-8942
David K De Espinosa, *Prin*
EMP: 5 **EST:** 2007
SALES (est): 120.71K **Privately Held**
SIC: 2752 Offset printing

(G-2728)
OZINGA BROS INC
1211 E Summit St (46307-2730)
PHONE..............................219 662-0925
TOLL FREE: 800
Chad Biggs, *Mgr*
EMP: 34
SALES (corp-wide): 552.21MM **Privately Held**
Web: www.ozinga.com
SIC: 3273 Ready-mixed concrete
PA: Ozinga Bros., Inc.
  19001 Old Lagrange Rd # 3
  Mokena IL 60448
  708 326-4200

(G-2729)
P&E ENTERPRISES
3936 S Lakeshore Dr (46307-8943)
PHONE..............................219 226-9524
Eric Nelson, *Owner*
EMP: 1 **EST:** 2003
SALES (est): 90.81K **Privately Held**
SIC: 3911 Jewelry, precious metal

(G-2730)
PHIL & SON INC
871 N Madison St (46307-8212)
PHONE..............................219 663-5757
Allen Pante, *Pr*
Alfred Pante, *Pr*
Vicky Pante, *Sec*
EMP: 8 **EST:** 1972
SQ FT: 7,200
SALES (est): 857K **Privately Held**
Web: www.philandson.com
SIC: 7699 1731 5063 3699 Locksmith shop; Fire detection and burglar alarm systems specialization; Burglar alarm systems; Security control equipment and systems

(G-2731)
PLOOG ENGINEERING CO INC
814 N Indiana Ave (46307-3447)
P.O. Box 341 (46308-0341)
PHONE..............................219 663-2854
Max H Ploog, *Pr*
Ploog Gisela M, *Sec*
EMP: 8 **EST:** 1981
SQ FT: 6,400
SALES (est): 989.03K **Privately Held**
SIC: 2899 3599 3544 Soil testing kits; Machine shop, jobbing and repair; Special dies and tools

(G-2732)
POINT MEDICAL CORPORATION
871 E Summit St (46307-2700)
PHONE..............................219 663-1775
Timothy M Schweikert, *Pr*
John C Stevens, *Treas*
▲ **EMP:** 695 **EST:** 1990
SALES (est): 39.37MM **Privately Held**
Web: www.pointmedical.com
SIC: 3841 3842 Surgical and medical instruments; Surgical appliances and supplies

Crown Point - Lake County (G-2733) — GEOGRAPHIC SECTION

(G-2733)
PORTER COUNTY FABRICATORS LTD
13405 Montgomery St (46307-9258)
PHONE.....................219 663-4665
EMP: 8 EST: 1992
SALES (est): 559.87K Privately Held
SIC: 3498 Fabricated pipe and fittings

(G-2734)
POWDERCOIL TECHNOLOGIES LLC
9800 Connecticut Dr (46307)
PHONE.....................708 634-2343
Robert Mcshane, *Managing Member*
EMP: 2 EST: 2016
SQ FT: 1,000
SALES (est): 252.14K Privately Held
SIC: 3479 Coating of metals and formed products

(G-2735)
PREFERRED METAL SERVICE INC
1146 Sunnyslope Dr (46307-9312)
PHONE.....................219 988-2386
William M Glass, *Pr*
D Joyce Glass, *Sec*
EMP: 2 EST: 2001
SQ FT: 1,774
SALES (est): 175.54K Privately Held
SIC: 5051 3493 Sheets, metal; Steel springs, except wire

(G-2736)
PRINT SOLUTIONS OF INDIANA
1744 Beachview Ct (46307-9411)
PHONE.....................219 988-4186
Sherrie Matthews, *Prin*
EMP: 1 EST: 2005
SALES (est): 175.44K Privately Held
Web: www.printsolutions11.com
SIC: 2752 Offset printing

(G-2737)
PRO-FAB SHEET METAL IND INC
880 E 99th Ct Ste B (46307-7893)
EMP: 1 EST: 2008
SALES (est): 751.9K Privately Held
Web: www.profabsm.com
SIC: 3444 Sheet metal specialties, not stamped

(G-2738)
PROFESSIONALLY POLISHED LLC ✪
1716 Beachview Ct (46307-9315)
PHONE.....................219 779-7664
Rachel Slack, *Managing Member*
EMP: 5 EST: 2022
SALES (est): 62.01K Privately Held
SIC: 2842 Cleaning or polishing preparations, nec

(G-2739)
PYRO SHIELD INC
1171 Erie Ct (46307-2750)
PHONE.....................219 661-8600
Donald J Murphy, *Pr*
Andrew Passage, *Sec*
▲ EMP: 15 EST: 1997
SQ FT: 23,000
SALES (est): 2.09MM Privately Held
Web: www.pyroshield.com
SIC: 2211 Canvas and other heavy, coarse fabrics: cotton

(G-2740)
RACE ENGINEERING
725 E Goldsborough St Ste 2 (46307-3393)
PHONE.....................219 661-8904
Dennis Rys, *Pr*
Kevin Rys, *VP*
EMP: 2 EST: 1998
SALES (est): 227.7K Privately Held
Web: www.raceeng.com
SIC: 3714 Motor vehicle parts and accessories

(G-2741)
RAGING ROCKET WEB DESIGN LLC
9800 Connecticut Dr (46307-7840)
PHONE.....................219 381-5027
EMP: 4 EST: 2018
SALES (est): 198.07K Privately Held
Web: www.ragingrocket.com
SIC: 2741 7336 8742 Internet publishing and broadcasting; Graphic arts and related design; Marketing consulting services

(G-2742)
REDAB INDUSTRIES INC
10425 Maine Dr (46307-7069)
PHONE.....................219 484-8382
EMP: 2 EST: 2010
SALES (est): 170.38K Privately Held
SIC: 3999 Manufacturing industries, nec

(G-2743)
REGION COMMUNICATIONS INC
Also Called: Winfield American, The
7590 E 109th Ave (46307-8631)
P.O. Box 505 (46308-0505)
PHONE.....................219 662-8888
Mike Kucic, *Pr*
Mike Gooldy, *VP*
EMP: 2 EST: 2003
SALES (est): 141.97K Privately Held
Web: www.winfieldamerican.com
SIC: 2711 Newspapers: publishing only, not printed on site

(G-2744)
REGIONAL DATA SERVICES INC
1260 Arrowhead Ct (46307-8222)
PHONE.....................219 661-3200
Rosalind Henderson, *Pr*
Lori Schuffert, *Mgr*
EMP: 16 EST: 1985
SALES (est): 562.03K Privately Held
Web: www.rdsgym.com
SIC: 7371 7372 Computer software development; Prepackaged software

(G-2745)
RIDDELL TECHNOLOGIES LLC
Also Called: Riddell Technologies
1351 W 95th Ct (46307-2270)
PHONE.....................219 213-9602
EMP: 4 EST: 2014
SALES (est): 147.97K Privately Held
SIC: 7378 3571 5734 7371 Computer maintenance and repair; Computers, digital, analog or hybrid; Computer software and accessories; Computer software development

(G-2746)
ROAST HAUS COFFEE LLC
Also Called: Ffeine
1085 Millennium Dr (46307-7532)
PHONE.....................224 544-9550
EMP: 3 EST: 2020
SALES (est): 62.38K Privately Held
SIC: 2095 Roasted coffee

(G-2747)
ROHDER MACHINE & TOOL INC
1023 E Summit St (46307-2794)
PHONE.....................219 663-3697
Daniel J Rohder, *Pr*
Laurie G Rohder, *Sec*
EMP: 26 EST: 1968
SQ FT: 7,000
SALES (est): 960.41K Privately Held
Web: www.rohdermachineandbolt.com
SIC: 3452 3599 Bolts, metal; Machine shop, jobbing and repair

(G-2748)
SCHMIGBOB LLC
5366 E 111th Ave (46307-5600)
PHONE.....................219 781-7991
Matthew Bigelow, *Prin*
EMP: 4 EST: 2015
SALES (est): 102.01K Privately Held
SIC: 3999 Manufacturing industries, nec

(G-2749)
SCOTT STEEL SERVICES INC
1203 E Summit St (46307-2730)
PHONE.....................219 663-4740
Robert A Scott, *Pr*
EMP: 4 EST: 1999
SALES (est): 951.72K Privately Held
Web: www.scottsteelservicesinc.com
SIC: 3441 Fabricated structural metal

(G-2750)
SHAW POLYMERS HOLDINGS LLC (PA)
400 N Indiana Ave (46307-3410)
PHONE.....................219 779-9450
Jim Adams, *Pr*
Kelly Gillig, *Prin*
EMP: 7 EST: 1997
SQ FT: 1,500
SALES (est): 4.19MM
SALES (corp-wide): 4.19MM Privately Held
Web: www.shawpolymers.com
SIC: 2821 5162 Plastics materials and resins ; Plastics materials and basic shapes

(G-2751)
SIGNIFIED SIGNS INC
8356 E 137th Ave (46307-9024)
P.O. Box 300 (46308-0300)
PHONE.....................219 712-7385
EMP: 2 EST: 1993
SALES (est): 150K Privately Held
SIC: 3993 Signs and advertising specialties

(G-2752)
SIGNS AP & AWARDS ON TIME LLC
Also Called: Visual Communication Mfg
10740 Broadway (46307-7310)
PHONE.....................219 661-4488
Matthew Brauer, *Owner*
EMP: 2 EST: 2020
SALES (est): 80.34K Privately Held
SIC: 5621 1799 2759 7389 Ready-to-wear apparel, women's; Sign installation and maintenance; Screen printing; Sign painting and lettering shop

(G-2753)
SIGNS ON TIME INC
10740 Broadway (46307-7310)
PHONE.....................219 661-4488
EMP: 10 EST: 1991
SALES (est): 248.79K Privately Held
Web: www.signsontime.com
SIC: 3993 Signs, not made in custom sign painting shops

(G-2754)
SIGNS OVERNITE INC
8304 Cline Ave (46307-9612)
PHONE.....................219 365-4088
Jamie Quint, *Owner*
EMP: 2 EST: 2008
SALES (est): 167.13K Privately Held
Web: www.signsovernite.net
SIC: 3993 Signs and advertising specialties

(G-2755)
SIMKO SIGNS LLC
7570 E 109th Ave (46307-8631)
PHONE.....................219 308-6000
Rob Moreth, *Owner*
EMP: 2 EST: 2007
SALES (est): 213.61K Privately Held
Web: www.simkosigns.com
SIC: 3993 Signs and advertising specialties

(G-2756)
SIMPLIFIED IMAGING LLC
1126 Arrowhead Ct (46307-6801)
PHONE.....................219 663-5122
Gerald G Gross, *Prin*
EMP: 6 EST: 2009
SALES (est): 470.79K Privately Held
SIC: 2759 Laser printing

(G-2757)
SITTIN PRETTY LLC
9470 Randolph St (46307-8628)
PHONE.....................219 947-4121
EMP: 3
SALES (est): 195.52K Privately Held
SIC: 3999 Pet supplies

(G-2758)
SKIPPER ROTA CORPORATION
130 E 168th St (46307)
P.O. Box 219 (60473-0219)
PHONE.....................708 331-0660
EMP: 18
SIC: 3556 7692 Food products machinery; Welding repair

(G-2759)
SMALLTOWN COFFEE CO LLC
306 E Goldsborough St (46307-3230)
PHONE.....................816 288-0687
Annette Mckeown, *Managing Member*
EMP: 12 EST: 2016
SALES (est): 367.74K Privately Held
Web: www.smalltown.coffee
SIC: 5812 2095 Coffee shop; Coffee roasting (except by wholesale grocers)

(G-2760)
SONAM TECHNOLOGIES LLC
9800 Connecticut Dr (46307-7840)
PHONE.....................844 887-6626
Christopher Hanson, *Prin*
Michael Hanson, *Prin*
EMP: 2 EST: 2016
SALES (est): 126.17K Privately Held
SIC: 3829 Physical property testing equipment

(G-2761)
SOPHYSA USA INC
503 E Summit St Ste 5 (46307-3477)
PHONE.....................219 663-7711
Philippe Negre, *Pr*
Steve Egan, *VP*
EMP: 5 EST: 2006
SALES (est): 593.78K Privately Held
Web: www.sophysa.com
SIC: 3841 Surgical and medical instruments

(G-2762)
TDK GRAPHICS INC
Also Called: Tdk Graphics
1180 N Main St (46307-2715)
PHONE.....................219 663-7799
TOLL FREE: 800
Tim Koedyker, *Pr*

EMP: 13 EST: 1985
SQ FT: 3,200
SALES (est): 1.98MM **Privately Held**
Web: www.nwiprintpro.com
SIC: **2752** 7334 7389 Offset printing; Photocopying and duplicating services; Printers' services: folding, collating, etc.

(G-2763)
THERMAL TECH & TEMP INC
880 N Madison St (46307-8212)
P.O. Box 1304 (46308-1304)
PHONE.....................................219 213-2093
Tasha Gomez, *Pr*
EMP: 12 EST: 2017
SALES (est): 2.2MM **Privately Held**
Web: www.thermaltechtemp.com
SIC: **3567** Induction heating equipment

(G-2764)
TNT TOP NOTCH TEES
1552 Happy Valley Rd (46307-9300)
PHONE.....................................219 775-3812
EMP: 4 EST: 2015
SALES (est): 88K **Privately Held**
SIC: **2759** Screen printing

(G-2765)
TOP FUEL CROSSFIT INC
1674 E North St (46307-8568)
PHONE.....................................219 281-7001
Michael Young, *Mgr*
EMP: 8 EST: 2015
SALES (est): 97.19K **Privately Held**
Web: www.break90crossfit.com
SIC: **2869** Fuels

(G-2766)
TOWN & COUNTRY INDUSTRIES INC
Also Called: Town & Country Printing
10187 Florida Ln (46307-7577)
P.O. Box 1279 (46308-1279)
PHONE.....................................219 712-0893
EMP: 28
Web: www.avonlogowear.com
SIC: **3993** 2752 Signs and advertising specialties; Promotional printing, lithographic

(G-2767)
TOWN WELDER
9306 Grand Blvd (46307-8829)
PHONE.....................................219 945-1311
Matt Siegel, *Prin*
EMP: 1 EST: 2005
SALES (est): 49.06K **Privately Held**
SIC: **7692** Welding repair

(G-2768)
TURBONETICS HOLDINGS INC (HQ)
Also Called: Turbonetics
9401 Georgia St Ste 2 (46307-6528)
PHONE.....................................805 581-0333
Joe Krivickas, *Genl Mgr*
Greg Papp, *
▲ EMP: 27 EST: 2006
SALES (est): 8.65MM **Publicly Held**
Web: www.turboneticsinc.com
SIC: **3443** Heat exchangers, condensers, and components
PA: Westinghouse Air Brake Technologies Corporation
30 Isabella St
Pittsburgh PA 15212

(G-2769)
US PREMIER BUSINESS LLC
Also Called: Wholesale
8188 Durbin Ter Apt D (46307-1265)
PHONE.....................................540 822-0329

Musab Keelani, *Managing Member*
EMP: 1 EST: 2018
SALES (est): 80.13K **Privately Held**
SIC: **5199** 1389 General merchandise, non-durable; Construction, repair, and dismantling services

(G-2770)
UTILITIES AVI SPECIALISTS INC
401 W Summit St (46307-2601)
P.O. Box 810 (46308-0810)
PHONE.....................................219 662-8175
Robert Feerst, *Pr*
Patricia Feerst, *VP*
EMP: 2 EST: 1995
SALES (est): 285.58K **Privately Held**
Web: www.helicoptersafety.com
SIC: **3721** 8742 Helicopters; Planning consultant

(G-2771)
VKF RENZEL USA CORP
1311 Merrillville Rd (46307-2708)
PHONE.....................................219 661-6300
Heinz Renzel, *Pr*
▲ EMP: 10 EST: 2002
SQ FT: 4,000
SALES (est): 2.4MM
SALES (corp-wide): 126.55MM **Privately Held**
Web: www.renzelusa.com
SIC: **3993** Signs and advertising specialties
HQ: Vkf Renzel Gmbh
Im Geer 15
Isselburg NW 46419
28749100

(G-2772)
VOTER REGISTRATION
2293 N Main St (46307-1854)
PHONE.....................................219 755-3795
Sally Lasota, *Ex Dir*
EMP: 3 EST: 2010
SALES (est): 219.01K **Privately Held**
Web: lakecounty.in.gov
SIC: **3579** Office machines, nec

(G-2773)
WELLSOURCE NUTRACEUTICALS LLC
9800 Connecticut Dr (46307-7840)
PHONE.....................................219 213-6173
EMP: 6 EST: 2016
SALES (est): 397.32K **Privately Held**
Web: www.histamineshieldplus.com
SIC: **2023** 5499 5122 Dietary supplements, dairy and non-dairy based; Vitamin food stores; Vitamins and minerals

(G-2774)
WIW INC
424 Wessex Rd (46307)
P.O. Box 704 (46308-0704)
PHONE.....................................219 663-7900
Darren Grabek, *Pr*
Kay Grabek, *
Brian Sadewasser, *
EMP: 25 EST: 1945
SQ FT: 12,000
SALES (est): 2.74MM **Privately Held**
Web: www.wilsoniron.com
SIC: **3441** 3446 Fabricated structural metal; Architectural metalwork

(G-2775)
WORTH PUBLICATIONS LLC
13398 Hayes Ct (46307-7807)
P.O. Box 683 (46308-0583)
PHONE.....................................219 808-4001
EMP: 3 EST: 2013
SALES (est): 61.51K **Privately Held**

Web: www.worthpublications.com
SIC: **2741** Miscellaneous publishing

(G-2776)
XOXO INVITES
1958 Springvale Dr (46307-5317)
PHONE.....................................773 744-2504
EMP: 3 EST: 2016
SALES (est): 76.09K **Privately Held**
Web: www.xoxoinvites.com
SIC: **2759** Invitation and stationery printing and engraving

Culver
Marshall County

(G-2777)
ACPI WOOD PRODUCTS LLC
515 W Mill St (46511-1403)
PHONE.....................................574 842-2066
EMP: 67
SALES (corp-wide): 2.54B **Privately Held**
Web: www.medallioncabinetry.com
SIC: **5099** 2434 Wood and wood by-products; Wood kitchen cabinets
HQ: Acpi Wood Products, Llc
1 Medallion Way
Waconia MN 55387
952 442-5171

(G-2778)
ACURA PHARMACEUTICAL TECH
16235 State Road 17 (46511-9010)
PHONE.....................................574 842-3305
Peter A Clemens, *VP*
James Emigh, *VP*
Robert Seiser, *Treas*
EMP: 8 EST: 1976
SQ FT: 40,000
SALES (est): 1.42MM
SALES (corp-wide): 1.85MM **Publicly Held**
Web: www.acurapharm.com
SIC: **2834** Pharmaceutical preparations
HQ: Acura Pharmaceuticals, Inc.
616 N North Ct Ste 120
Palatine IL 60067
847 705-7709

(G-2779)
ALL STAR MANUFACTURING INC
18243 W Shore Cir (46511)
PHONE.....................................574 293-8141
Melissa Henderson, *Prin*
EMP: 6 EST: 2016
SALES (est): 39.69K **Privately Held**
SIC: **3448** Prefabricated metal buildings

(G-2780)
BEHNKE ENGINEERING
321 E Washington St (46511-1535)
PHONE.....................................574 842-2327
Ed Behnke, *Owner*
EMP: 1 EST: 1986
SALES (est): 100.26K **Privately Held**
SIC: **3695** 8711 Computer software tape and disks: blank, rigid, and floppy; Consulting engineer

(G-2781)
MEDALLION CABINETRY
515 W Mill St (46511-1403)
PHONE.....................................574 842-2066
EMP: 11 EST: 2019
SALES (est): 576.88K **Privately Held**
Web: www.medallioncabinetry.com
SIC: **2434** Wood kitchen cabinets

(G-2782)
THUNDRBIRD TRADITIONAL ARCHERY
306 N Ohio St (46511-1524)
PHONE.....................................812 699-1099
EMP: 3 EST: 1995
SALES (est): 96.01K **Privately Held**
SIC: **3949** Bows, archery

Cutler
Carroll County

(G-2783)
CD & WS BORDNER ENTPS INC
Also Called: Bordners Truck Repair & Algnmt
6559 S State Road 75 (46920-9361)
P.O. Box 355 (46920-0355)
PHONE.....................................765 268-2120
Dave Bordner, *Pr*
Wendy Bordner, *Sec*
EMP: 2 EST: 1999
SQ FT: 4,500
SALES (est): 253.35K **Privately Held**
SIC: **1799** 7538 3523 7231 Welding on site; General truck repair; Driers (farm): grain, hay, and seed; Hairdressers

(G-2784)
FRAZIER AVIATION LLC
Also Called: Team Rocket Aircraft
7237 S State Road 75 (46920-9617)
PHONE.....................................888 835-9269
Vincent A Frazier, *Managing Member*
EMP: 1 EST: 2007
SALES (est): 66.91K **Privately Held**
Web: www.f1aircraft.com
SIC: **3728** Aircraft parts and equipment, nec

Cynthiana
Posey County

(G-2785)
B B MINING INC (PA)
11700 Water Tank Rd (47612-9528)
PHONE.....................................812 845-2717
Steve Blankenberger, *Pr*
Donald Blankenberger, *VP*
Pat Blankenberger, *Sec*
David Blankenberger, *Treas*
Rick Blankenberger, *Asst Tr*
EMP: 3 EST: 1991
SALES (est): 4.16MM **Privately Held**
Web: www.blankenbergerbros.com
SIC: **1241** Coal mining services

(G-2786)
B STEVENS SERVICE LLC
10470 Evansville St (47612-9542)
PHONE.....................................812 622-2039
Bradley B Stevens, *Managing Member*
EMP: 3 EST: 2015
SALES (est): 255.65K **Privately Held**
SIC: **3499** 3441 Metal household articles; Fabricated structural metal

(G-2787)
DRILLMASTER CORP
8900 Highway 65 Ste 5 (47612-9571)
P.O. Box 83 (47612-0083)
PHONE.....................................732 919-3088
John K Marshall, *CEO*
EMP: 7 EST: 1972
SALES (est): 64.25K **Privately Held**
Web: www.drillmastersmarching.com
SIC: **3149** Athletic shoes, except rubber or plastic

(G-2788)
PEARISON INC
Also Called: Band Shoppe
8900 Highway 65 (47612-9571)
P.O. Box 428 (47612-0428)
PHONE..................................812 963-8890
EMP: 58 EST: 1966
SALES (est): 2.49MM Privately Held
Web: www.pearison.com
SIC: 2389 5131 Band uniforms; Flags and banners

Dale
Spencer County

(G-2789)
C&S MACHINERY INC
5440 E 2150 N (47523)
P.O. Box 313 (47579-0313)
PHONE..................................812 937-2160
William Sexton, Pr
EMP: 8 EST: 2008
SALES (est): 238.71K Privately Held
SIC: 3569 General industrial machinery, nec

(G-2790)
FRITHS CUSTOM WELD
9 E Elm St (47523-9359)
PHONE..................................812 937-2618
EMP: 1 EST: 1990
SALES (est): 43.19K Privately Held
SIC: 7692 Welding repair

(G-2791)
MULZER CRUSHED STONE INC
4590 E Aw Mulzer Dr (47523)
P.O. Box 28 (47523-0028)
PHONE..................................812 937-2442
Kenneth Mulzer, Pr
EMP: 2
SALES (corp-wide): 34.95B Privately Held
Web: www.mulzer.com
SIC: 1422 Crushed and broken limestone
HQ: Mulzer Crushed Stone Inc
    534 Mozart St
    Tell City IN 47586
    812 547-7921

(G-2792)
SPENCER INDUSTRIES INC (PA)
902 Buffaloville Rd (47523-9057)
PHONE..................................812 937-4561
TOLL FREE: 800
Tom Messmer, Pr
Jarid Hirt, *
Eric Olinger, *
◆ EMP: 190 EST: 1969
SQ FT: 400,000
SALES (est): 33.8MM
SALES (corp-wide): 33.8MM Privately Held
Web: www.spencerindustries.com
SIC: 3089 Thermoformed finished plastics products, nec

(G-2793)
STECKLER GRASSFED LLC
21477 N County Road 600 E (47523-9369)
PHONE..................................812 683-3098
EMP: 6 EST: 2019
SALES (est): 236.56K Privately Held
Web: www.stecklergrassfedfarms.com
SIC: 2022 Natural cheese

(G-2794)
THERMWOOD CORPORATION
904 Buffaloville Rd (47523)
P.O. Box 436 (47523)
PHONE..................................812 937-4476
Kenneth Susnjara, CEO
David Hildenbrand, *
Linda Susnjara, *
Michael Hardesty, *
Rebecca Fuller, *
◆ EMP: 96 EST: 1969
SQ FT: 170,000
SALES (est): 21.01MM Privately Held
Web: www.thermwood.com
SIC: 3599 Machine shop, jobbing and repair

Daleville
Delaware County

(G-2795)
AUTOFARM MOBILITY LLC
Also Called: McCrocklin Mobility
9004 S County Road 800 W (47334-9420)
PHONE..................................317 410-0070
Jim Autofarm, Pr
James Kissling, *
EMP: 8 EST: 2014
SALES (est): 2.56MM Privately Held
Web: www.autofarmmobility.com
SIC: 5511 5047 3711 5599 Automobiles, new and used; Medical equipment and supplies; Ambulances (motor vehicles), assembly of; Golf cart, powered

(G-2796)
C A LAKEY FAMILY SAW MILL INC
9491 S County Road 900 W (47334-9703)
PHONE..................................765 378-7528
Charles A Lakey, Owner
EMP: 1 EST: 1970
SALES (est): 64K Privately Held
SIC: 2421 Custom sawmill

(G-2797)
CASH & CARRY LUMBER CO INC
Also Called: Fuller Architectural Hardwoods
14113 W Main St (47334-9758)
P.O. Box 427 (47334-0427)
PHONE..................................765 378-7575
Fred W Fuller Ii, Pr
William Smith, CEO
Ed Orem, CFO
EMP: 26 EST: 1946
SQ FT: 40,000
SALES (est): 2.85MM Privately Held
Web: www.fahwoods.com
SIC: 2431 Millwork

(G-2798)
CHESTERFIELD TOOL & ENGRG INC
13710 W Commerce Rd (47334-9347)
P.O. Box 566 (47334-0566)
PHONE..................................765 378-5101
Rick A Ray, Pr
Gregory A Julian, *
Luannen Julian, *
EMP: 25 EST: 1960
SQ FT: 50,000
SALES (est): 2.84MM Privately Held
Web: www.chesterfieldtool.com
SIC: 3829 3544 3545 3599 Measuring and controlling devices, nec; Special dies, tools, jigs, and fixtures; Gauges (machine tool accessories); Machine shop, jobbing and repair

(G-2799)
FILLMANNS INDUSTRIES LLC
3921 S Highbanks Rd (47334-9609)
PHONE..................................765 744-4772
Peter Fillmann, Prin
EMP: 2 EST: 2009
SALES (est): 110.25K Privately Held
SIC: 3999 Manufacturing industries, nec

(G-2800)
JERRY LAMBERT
10010 S County Road 900 W (47334-9704)
PHONE..................................765 378-7599
Jerry Lambert, Owner
EMP: 2 EST: 2000
SALES (est): 130K Privately Held
SIC: 7692 Welding repair

(G-2801)
PRECISION ABRASIVE MACHINERY
14200 W Commerce Rd (47334-9345)
P.O. Box 543 (47334-0543)
PHONE..................................765 378-3315
Edward J Kerr, Pr
Darlene Kerr, VP
EMP: 5 EST: 1977
SQ FT: 10,000
SALES (est): 494.09K Privately Held
Web: www.precisionabrasive.com
SIC: 3599 Machine shop, jobbing and repair

(G-2802)
SAGAMORE READY-MIX LLC
8700 S County Road 600 W (47334-9491)
PHONE..................................765 759-8999
EMP: 4
SALES (corp-wide): 4.31MM Privately Held
Web: www.sagamorereadymix.com
SIC: 3273 Ready-mixed concrete
PA: Sagamore Ready-Mix, Llc
    9170 E 131st St
    Fishers IN 46038
    317 570-6201

Dana
Vermillion County

(G-2803)
CARGILL INCORPORATED
Also Called: Cargill
225 E Briarwood Ave (47847)
P.O. Box 363 (47847-0363)
PHONE..................................765 665-3326
Ericka Umbargar, Mgr
EMP: 8
SALES (corp-wide): 159.59B Privately Held
Web: www.cargill.com
SIC: 2048 Prepared feeds, nec
PA: Cargill, Incorporated
    15407 Mcginty Rd W
    Wayzata MN 55391
    800 227-4455

(G-2804)
DAVERN MACHINE SHOP
Also Called: John Davern
1248 E 500 S (47847-8026)
P.O. Box 601 (47847-0601)
PHONE..................................765 505-1051
John M Davern, Owner
Martha Davern, Sec
EMP: 2 EST: 1996
SALES (est): 201.13K Privately Held
SIC: 3523 1799 Farm machinery and equipment; Welding on site

Danville
Hendricks County

(G-2805)
4 PISTON RACING
200 Colin Ct (46122-7933)
PHONE..................................317 902-0200
Luke Wilson, Prin
EMP: 5 EST: 2015
SALES (est): 228.84K Privately Held
Web: www.4pistonracing.com
SIC: 3714 Motor vehicle parts and accessories

(G-2806)
AIR KIT LLC
2985 S County Road 300 E (46122-9447)
PHONE..................................317 745-0656
Jeff Mears, Managing Member
EMP: 1 EST: 2004
SALES (est): 102.66K Privately Held
Web: www.airkitllc.com
SIC: 3728 Aircraft parts and equipment, nec

(G-2807)
BIO-RESPONSE SOLUTIONS INC
200 Colin Ct (46122-7933)
PHONE..................................317 386-3500
Joseph H Wilson, CEO
Lucus J Wilson, Pr
▲ EMP: 10 EST: 2006
SQ FT: 9,000
SALES (est): 2.29MM Privately Held
Web: www.bioresponsesolutions.com
SIC: 3589 5169 Water treatment equipment, industrial; Alkalines

(G-2808)
BLENDED LLC
148 1/2 S Washington St (46122)
PHONE..................................317 268-8005
EMP: 5 EST: 2016
SALES (est): 73.02K Privately Held
SIC: 2086 Bottled and canned soft drinks

(G-2809)
CONVEYORS INC
3434 S State Road 39 (46122-7962)
PHONE..................................317 539-5472
George Phillips, Pr
Debra Phillips, Sec
EMP: 5 EST: 1987
SQ FT: 8,000
SALES (est): 806.22K Privately Held
Web: www.conveyorsinc.net
SIC: 3535 Conveyors and conveying equipment

(G-2810)
CYGNUS HOME SERVICE LLC
Also Called: Schwan's Home Service
2700 E Main St (46122-9085)
PHONE..................................317 882-6624
Bruce Cochrin, Pr
EMP: 56
SALES (corp-wide): 448.71MM Privately Held
Web: www.yelloh.com
SIC: 2038 4215 Pizza, frozen; Parcel delivery, vehicular
PA: Cygnus Home Service, Llc
    115 W College Dr
    Marshall MN 56258
    507 532-3274

(G-2811)
F & S SIGNAGE SOLUTIONS INC
2765 S County Road 250 W (46122-7987)
P.O. Box 841 (46122-0841)
PHONE..................................317 539-2086
Kyle Freeman, Prin
EMP: 5 EST: 2015
SALES (est): 142.45K Privately Held
Web: www.fandssignagesolutions.com
SIC: 3993 Signs and advertising specialties

GEOGRAPHIC SECTION

Darmstadt - Vanderburgh County (G-2836)

(G-2812)
FLAVOR BURST LLC
Also Called: Flavor Burst
499 Commerce Dr (46122-7848)
PHONE.................................317 745-2952
Timothy Gerber, Pr
Thomas Gerber, VP Opers
◆ EMP: 20 EST: 2002
SQ FT: 35,000
SALES (est): 4.66MM
SALES (corp-wide): 4.04B Publicly Held
Web: www.flavorburst.com
SIC: 3556 5149 Ice cream manufacturing machinery; Syrups, except for fountain use
PA: The Middleby Corporation
1400 Toastmaster Dr
Elgin IL 60120
847 741-3300

(G-2813)
FREEMAN SIGNS
2949 E Main St (46122-9445)
P.O. Box 841 (46122-0841)
PHONE.................................317 386-3453
Kyle Freeman, Pr
EMP: 4 EST: 2015
SALES (est): 182.57K Privately Held
Web: www.freemansigns.com
SIC: 3993 Signs and advertising specialties

(G-2814)
J GAME VENTURES LLC
3105 Garden View Ter Apt F (46122-8671)
PHONE.................................812 241-7096
Jeffrey Mcgowan, Pr
EMP: 5 EST: 2016
SALES (est): 229.52K Privately Held
SIC: 3429 Furniture, builders' and other household hardware

(G-2815)
JAMES BRUMMETT
Also Called: Battlefield Tech Unlimited
212 Woodberry Dr (46122-7860)
PHONE.................................317 724-4131
EMP: 1 EST: 2011
SALES (est): 7.12K Privately Held
SIC: 3489 Ordnance and accessories, nec

(G-2816)
KADEL ENGINEERING CORPORATION
1627 E Main St (46122-9468)
PHONE.................................317 745-2798
David Alexander, Pr
Keith Alexander, *
Sheri Lemon, *
Dolores Alexander, *
EMP: 35 EST: 1966
SQ FT: 22,000
SALES (est): 4.1MM Privately Held
Web: www.kadel.com
SIC: 3679 Cryogenic cooling devices for infrared detectors, masers

(G-2817)
L&N WELDING LLC
121 Commerce Dr Ste 306 (46122-7856)
PHONE.................................317 372-9554
Nick Albright, Owner
EMP: 8 EST: 2014
SALES (est): 225.81K Privately Held
Web: www.lnweldingllc.com
SIC: 7692 Welding repair

(G-2818)
LEACH & SONS WATERCARE (PA)
Also Called: Leach and Sons Water Systems
671 E Main St # E (46122-1939)
PHONE.................................317 248-8954
Paul Leach, Owner
EMP: 4 EST: 1982
SALES (est): 603.16K
SALES (corp-wide): 603.16K Privately Held
Web: www.leachsons.com
SIC: 7389 3589 Water softener service; Water filters and softeners, household type

(G-2819)
MAGWERKS CORPORATION
Also Called: Magwerks
501 Commerce Dr (46122-7976)
PHONE.................................317 241-8011
▲ EMP: 15 EST: 1985
SQ FT: 50,000
SALES (est): 2.31MM Privately Held
Web: www.magwerks.com
SIC: 3829 Physical property testing equipment

(G-2820)
MEARS MACHINE CORP
2983 S County Road 300 E (46122-9447)
PHONE.................................317 745-0656
Jeff Mears, Pr
EMP: 39
SALES (corp-wide): 18.66MM Privately Held
Web: www.mearsmachine.com
SIC: 3599 Machine shop, jobbing and repair
PA: Mears Machine Corp
9973 E Us Highway 36
Avon IN 46123
317 271-6041

(G-2821)
NU WAVE MANUFACTURING LLC
3173 E Main St (46122-9404)
P.O. Box 793 (46122-0793)
PHONE.................................317 989-4703
Mary E Peyton, Pr
EMP: 5 EST: 2014
SALES (est): 124.65K Privately Held
Web: www.nuwavescaffold.com
SIC: 3999 Manufacturing industries, nec

(G-2822)
OWEN WOODWORKING
3012 S State Road 39 (46122-7961)
PHONE.................................317 331-6936
Jason Owen, Owner
EMP: 2 EST: 2001
SALES (est): 145.93K Privately Held
SIC: 2431 Millwork

(G-2823)
PALLADIN SERVICES INC
1425 N County Road 200 W (46122-8839)
PHONE.................................317 745-6741
Richard Fried, Pr
EMP: 1 EST: 1995
SALES (est): 65K Privately Held
Web: www.palladinusa.com
SIC: 3441 Fabricated structural metal

(G-2824)
QUALITY HYDRAULIC MCH SVC INC
4905 E County Road 450 N (46122-9307)
PHONE.................................317 892-2596
Richard Russell, Pr
Linda Russell, VP
EMP: 3 EST: 1991
SALES (est): 274.91K Privately Held
SIC: 3498 3699 Tube fabricating (contract bending and shaping); Electrical equipment and supplies, nec

(G-2825)
REPUBLICAN
Also Called: Republican Newspaper
6 E Main St (46122-1818)
P.O. Box 149 (46122-0149)
PHONE.................................317 745-2777
Betty Weesner, Owner
EMP: 3 EST: 1847
SALES (est): 230.21K Privately Held
Web: www.therepublicannewspaper.com
SIC: 2711 Newspapers, publishing and printing

(G-2826)
SCHUHLER WOODWORKING LLC
414 Western Dr (46122-1547)
PHONE.................................317 626-0452
EMP: 1 EST: 2005
SALES (est): 109.09K Privately Held
Web: www.schuhlerwoodworking.com
SIC: 2431 2517 Woodwork, interior and ornamental, nec; Radio cabinets and cases, wood

(G-2827)
SCOTTS FASTENERS & SUPPLY LLC
1945 W County Road 300 S (46122-8135)
P.O. Box 671 (46122-0671)
PHONE.................................317 372-8743
Douglas Scott, Managing Member
EMP: 4 EST: 2010
SALES (est): 227.04K Privately Held
Web: www.scottsfasteners.com
SIC: 3965 Fasteners

(G-2828)
SIMS CABINET CO INC (PA)
778 Robertson Ct (46122)
P.O. Box 22385 (46222)
PHONE.................................317 634-1747
James D Sims, Pr
James Sims, *
Becky Sparks, *
Richard Sims, *
EMP: 35 EST: 1961
SQ FT: 16,000
SALES (est): 4.46MM
SALES (corp-wide): 4.46MM Privately Held
Web: www.simscabinetco.com
SIC: 3083 2541 2434 Plastics finished products, laminated; Wood partitions and fixtures; Wood kitchen cabinets

(G-2829)
TRI-K MACHINING INC
Also Called: Tri-K Machining
120 Commerce Dr (46122-7975)
PHONE.................................317 244-7724
EMP: 19 EST: 1997
SALES (est): 1.8MM Privately Held
Web: www.tri-k.net
SIC: 3599 Machine shop, jobbing and repair

(G-2830)
WILSON PRINTING
527 N County Road 50 E (46122-9502)
PHONE.................................317 745-5868
Rex Wilson, Pr
EMP: 2 EST: 1975
SALES (est): 129.98K Privately Held
Web: www.wilsonprint.com
SIC: 2752 Offset printing

Darlington
Montgomery County

(G-2831)
ANDERSON PRODUCTS
700 E Rd (47940)
PHONE.................................765 794-4242
Jack Anderson, Pt
Charles Anderson, Pt
EMP: 2 EST: 1989
SALES (est): 131.58K Privately Held
Web: www.andersonproducts.net
SIC: 3089 Injection molding of plastics

(G-2832)
B & H INDUSTRIES CORPORATION
6425 E South St (47940)
P.O. Box 460 (47940-0460)
PHONE.................................765 794-4428
Lance Hopper, CEO
Lance Hopper, Pr
Jaye Dee Hopper, VP
EMP: 3 EST: 1964
SQ FT: 6,300
SALES (est): 409.35K Privately Held
Web: www.bhindustriescorp.com
SIC: 3965 Fasteners

(G-2833)
JAMES CONNER WELDING LLC
5133 N 700 E (47940-7088)
PHONE.................................765 230-0455
James D Conner, Prin
EMP: 1 EST: 2008
SALES (est): 52.57K Privately Held
SIC: 7692 Welding repair

(G-2834)
SPI-BINDING COMPANY INC
610 South St (47940-7131)
P.O. Box 550 (47940-0550)
PHONE.................................765 794-4992
Linda Crispin, Pr
David Crispin, *
▲ EMP: 15 EST: 1972
SALES (est): 393.15K Privately Held
Web: www.spibinding.com
SIC: 2789 2782 2396 Bookbinding and related work; Blankbooks and looseleaf binders; Automotive and apparel trimmings

(G-2835)
VERTICAL VEGETATION MGT LLC
6655 E N 700 (47940)
P.O. Box 125 (47940-0125)
PHONE.................................765 366-4447
EMP: 10 EST: 2015
SALES (est): 370.48K Privately Held
SIC: 2591 Blinds vertical

Darmstadt
Vanderburgh County

(G-2836)
IMPERIAL PETROLEUM INC
11600 German Pines Dr (47725-9514)
PHONE.................................812 867-1433
EMP: 49
Web: www.imperialpetro.com
SIC: 1311 2911 1382 1389 Tar sands mining; Diesel fuels; Oil and gas exploration services; Servicing oil and gas wells

Dayton
Tippecanoe County

(G-2837)
BIRCH CANDLE COMPANY LLC
731 S St (47941-8017)
P.O. Box 400 (47941-0400)
PHONE..................................765 296-9425
Traci Bratton, *Managing Member*
EMP: 4 **EST:** 2021
SALES (est): 221.63K **Privately Held**
SIC: 3999 Candles

(G-2838)
WEE ENGINEER INC
Also Called: Williams Signs
282 Delaware St (47941-8025)
P.O. Box 39 (47941-0039)
PHONE..................................765 449-4280
Robert Parker, *Pr*
Charlotte E Parker, *Sec*
Seth Parker, *VP*
EMP: 16 **EST:** 1990
SQ FT: 8,800
SALES (est): 669.48K **Privately Held**
Web: www.wee-engineer.com
SIC: 3563 3561 5012 Tire inflators, hand or compressor operated; Industrial pumps and parts; Trucks, commercial

Decatur
Adams County

(G-2839)
A S M INC
Also Called: Precision Woodcrafters
125 W Grant St (46733-2316)
P.O. Box 149 (46733-0149)
PHONE..................................260 724-8220
Richard W Steury, *Pr*
Norm Steury, *Prin*
Patricia Steury, *Prin*
John Kowalczwk, *Prin*
Barbar Kowalczyk, *Prin*
EMP: 5 **EST:** 1998
SQ FT: 5,000
SALES (est): 492.84K **Privately Held**
SIC: 2499 2511 2449 2448 Decorative wood and woodwork; Silverware chests: wood; Wood containers, nec; Wood pallets and skids

(G-2840)
AIP/FW FUNDING INC (PA)
1031 E Us Highway 224 (46733-2737)
PHONE..................................212 627-2360
Dino Cusumano, *Pr*
Paul Bamatter, *VP*
EMP: 2 **EST:** 2009
SALES (est): 35.49MM **Privately Held**
SIC: 3716 Motor homes

(G-2841)
ALBERDING WOODWORKING INC
7050 N 200 W (46733-8849)
PHONE..................................260 728-9526
Stephen Alberding, *Pr*
Jeananne Alberding, *
EMP: 12 **EST:** 1980
SQ FT: 12,000
SALES (est): 454.04K **Privately Held**
SIC: 2431 3272 Doors and door parts and trim, wood; Housing components, prefabricated concrete

(G-2842)
ALL AMERICAN GROUP INC
309 S 13th St (46733-1852)
PHONE..................................260 724-7391
Machelle Bradbury, *Brnch Mgr*
EMP: 2
SIC: 3448 Prefabricated metal buildings and components
HQ: All American Group, Inc.
2831 Dexter Dr
Elkhart IN 46514
574 262-0123

(G-2843)
ALL AMERICAN HOMES INDIANA LLC
1418 S 13th St (46733-2170)
PHONE..................................260 724-9171
Chad Marchand, *VP*
EMP: 1 **EST:** 2000
SQ FT: 235,000
SALES (est): 3.82MM **Privately Held**
SIC: 2452 Modular homes, prefabricated, wood
HQ: All American Homes, Llc
2831 Dexter Dr
Elkhart IN 46514
574 266-3044

(G-2844)
AQUA BLAST CORP
1025 W Commerce Dr (46733)
P.O. Box 547 (46733)
PHONE..................................260 728-4433
David L Tumbleson, *CEO*
EMP: 11 **EST:** 1966
SQ FT: 12,000
SALES (est): 1.72MM **Privately Held**
Web: www.aquablast.com
SIC: 3589 5084 High pressure cleaning equipment; Industrial machine parts

(G-2845)
B & G ENTITY INC
125 W Grant St (46733-2316)
P.O. Box 965 (46733-0965)
PHONE..................................260 724-8874
Gary Sheets, *Pr*
Robert Mies, *VP*
EMP: 19 **EST:** 1988
SQ FT: 12,000
SALES (est): 830.49K **Privately Held**
Web: www.ttswireharness.com
SIC: 3496 Miscellaneous fabricated wire products

(G-2846)
BEARS DEN EMB & MORE LLC
530 E 900 N (46733-8454)
PHONE..................................260 724-4070
Pamela L Berdall, *Managing Member*
EMP: 5 **EST:** 2016
SALES (est): 275.2K **Privately Held**
Web: www.bearsdenembroidery.com
SIC: 2395 Embroidery products, except Schiffli machine

(G-2847)
BROKEN VESSEL SIGN CO LLC
3710 N Hickory Rd (46733-9317)
PHONE..................................260 273-2780
Mindy Yergler, *Prin*
EMP: 4 **EST:** 2018
SALES (est): 79.37K **Privately Held**
SIC: 3993 Signs and advertising specialties

(G-2848)
BUCHAN LOGGING INC
Also Called: Buchan Saw Mill
3333 E 600 N (46733-9114)
PHONE..................................260 749-4697
EMP: 10 **EST:** 1986
SALES (est): 610K **Privately Held**
Web: www.farmersgrainag.com
SIC: 2421 Sawmills and planing mills, general

(G-2849)
BUNGE NORTH AMERICA EAST LLC
1200 N 2nd St (46733-1175)
PHONE..................................260 724-2101
Doyle Smith, *Mgr*
EMP: 60
Web: www.bunge.com
SIC: 2075 2079 2077 Soybean oil mills; Edible fats and oils; Animal and marine fats and oils
HQ: Bunge North America (East), L.L.C.
1391 Tmbrlake Mnor Pkwy S
Chesterfield MO 63017
314 292-2000

(G-2850)
COMMERCIAL PRINT SHOP INC
Also Called: Complete Printing Service
210 S 2nd St (46733-1667)
P.O. Box 347 (46733-0347)
PHONE..................................260 724-3722
Charles A Brune, *Pr*
EMP: 5 **EST:** 1969
SQ FT: 2,000
SALES (est): 447.77K **Privately Held**
Web: www.completeprintingservice.com
SIC: 2752 7334 2759 Offset printing; Photocopying and duplicating services; Letterpress printing

(G-2851)
DECATUR PUBLISHING CO INC
Also Called: Decatur Daily Democrat
141 S 2nd St (46733-1664)
PHONE..................................260 724-2121
Ron Storey, *Mgr*
Ron Storey, *Prin*
Melanie Radler, *Pr*
EMP: 25 **EST:** 1857
SQ FT: 3,000
SALES (est): 452.62K **Privately Held**
Web: www.decaturdailydemocrat.com
SIC: 2711 Newspapers, publishing and printing

(G-2852)
DIETECH CORPORATION
1001 W Commerce Dr (46733-7541)
P.O. Box 237 (46733-0237)
PHONE..................................260 724-8946
Brent Saalfrank, *Pr*
Bryan Saalfrank, *Treas*
Brad Saalfrank, *Sec*
EMP: 8 **EST:** 1983
SALES (est): 804.06K **Privately Held**
Web: www.dietech-corp.com
SIC: 3544 3469 Special dies and tools; Metal stampings, nec

(G-2853)
DS WOODS CUSTOM CABINETS
2231 N Us Highway 27 (46733-9353)
PHONE..................................260 692-6565
EMP: 3 **EST:** 1994
SALES (est): 198.13K **Privately Held**
Web: www.dswoodscustomcabinets.com
SIC: 2434 Wood kitchen cabinets

(G-2854)
DWD INDUSTRIES LLC (DH)
1921 Patterson St (46733-1866)
PHONE..................................260 728-9272
▲ **EMP:** 50 **EST:** 1979
SQ FT: 27,000
SALES (est): 10.52MM **Privately Held**
Web: www.estevesgroup.com
SIC: 3544 Wire drawing and straightening dies
HQ: Diamond Tools Group B.V.
De Vest 1 C
Valkenswaard NB 5555
402082311

(G-2855)
ESTEVES-DWD LLC
Also Called: Esteves Group USA
1921 Patterson St (46733-1866)
PHONE..................................260 728-9272
EMP: 75 **EST:** 1998
SALES (est): 8.1MM **Privately Held**
Web: www.estevesgroup.com
SIC: 3544 Wire drawing and straightening dies
HQ: Diamond Tools Group B.V.
De Vest 1 C
Valkenswaard NB 5555
402082311

(G-2856)
FROM TREES TO THESE INC
6188 E 25 N (46733-8962)
PHONE..................................260 592-7397
EMP: 1
SQ FT: 5,600
SALES (est): 200K **Privately Held**
Web: www.fromtreestothese.com
SIC: 2511 Wood household furniture

(G-2857)
FUHRMAN PRECISION SERVICES INC
10484 N 200 W (46733-8759)
PHONE..................................260 728-9600
John Fuhrman, *Pr*
Jon Furhman, *Pr*
Danielle Furhman, *Sec*
EMP: 11 **EST:** 2000
SQ FT: 9,000
SALES (est): 951.13K **Privately Held**
Web: www.heritagewiredie.com
SIC: 3599 Machine shop, jobbing and repair

(G-2858)
GILPIN INC
1819 Patterson St (46733-1890)
PHONE..................................260 724-9155
Paul Gilpin, *Ch*
Todd Gilpin, *
▲ **EMP:** 30 **EST:** 1937
SQ FT: 70,000
SALES (est): 2.35MM **Privately Held**
Web: www.gilpininc.com
SIC: 3446 Stairs, fire escapes, balconies, railings, and ladders

(G-2859)
GOLDSHIELD FIBER GLASS INC
Also Called: Rev Group
2004 Patterson St (46733-1867)
P.O. Box 496 (46733-0496)
PHONE..................................260 728-2476
Dino Cusumano, *CEO*
Tim Sullivan, *
Larry L Mace, *
Dean Nolden, *
Forrest D Theobald, *
EMP: 250 **EST:** 1982
SQ FT: 150,000
SALES (est): 47.33MM **Privately Held**
Web: www.goldshield.com
SIC: 2221 Fiberglass fabrics
HQ: Fleetwood Enterprises, Inc.
1351 Pomona Rd Ste 230
Corona CA 92882
951 354-3000

GEOGRAPHIC SECTION

Decatur - Adams County (G-2885)

(G-2860)
H & S FABRICATION LLC
5342 N 400 W (46733-8593)
PHONE..................260 724-3656
EMP: 9 **EST:** 2013
SALES (est): 484.38K **Privately Held**
SIC: 7692 Welding repair

(G-2861)
H P SCHMITT PACKING CO INC
976 Waynesboro Rd (46733-2624)
PHONE..................260 724-3146
H P Schmitt Junior, *Pr*
EMP: 9 **EST:** 1940
SALES (est): 522.35K **Privately Held**
SIC: 2011 Meat packing plants

(G-2862)
HERITAGE WIRE DIE INC
10484 N 200 W (46733-8759)
PHONE..................260 728-9300
Jon M Fuhrman, *Pr*
EMP: 4 **EST:** 1987
SALES (est): 495.71K **Privately Held**
Web: www.heritagewiredie.com
SIC: 3544 Diamond dies, metalworking

(G-2863)
HOEHN ENGINEERED PRODUCTS LLC
5853 N Piqua Rd (46733-8903)
PHONE..................260 223-9158
EMP: 1 **EST:** 2013
SALES (est): 80.46K **Privately Held**
SIC: 3714 7389 Motor vehicle parts and accessories; Business Activities at Non-Commercial Site

(G-2864)
INTELLIRAY INC
10262 N 550 W (46733-7899)
PHONE..................260 547-4399
Timothy Blomenberg, *Pr*
Kristine Blomenberg, *CFO*
▼ **EMP:** 5 **EST:** 1997
SALES (est): 698.3K **Privately Held**
Web: www.idspd.com
SIC: 3679 Electronic switches

(G-2865)
JOSEPH M SCHMIDT
Also Called: Triple S Logging
7741 N 200 E (46733-9416)
PHONE..................260 223-3498
Joseph M Schmidt, *Prin*
EMP: 5 **EST:** 2010
SALES (est): 207.74K **Privately Held**
SIC: 2411 Logging camps and contractors

(G-2866)
KINGSFORD PRODUCTS INC (PA)
Also Called: Kingsford
1819 Patterson St (46733-1846)
PHONE..................740 862-4450
Roland Harrison, *Pr*
EMP: 18 **EST:** 1942
SALES (est): 3.48MM
SALES (corp-wide): 3.48MM **Privately Held**
SIC: 3315 3334 3496 Steel wire and related products; Primary aluminum; Miscellaneous fabricated wire products

(G-2867)
KYANN MANUFACTURING GROUP LLC
5232 N 375 E (46733-7957)
PHONE..................260 724-9721
Tyler Braun, *Owner*
EMP: 4 **EST:** 2017
SALES (est): 92.36K **Privately Held**
SIC: 3999 Manufacturing industries, nec

(G-2868)
LENNOXS LEGACY RESCUE INC
4777 N 375 E (46733)
PHONE..................260 223-3115
EMP: 6 **EST:** 2018
SALES (est): 263.81K **Privately Held**
Web: www.lennoxslegacyrescue.org
SIC: 3585 Refrigeration and heating equipment

(G-2869)
LINGENFELTER PRFMCE ENGRG INC
Also Called: Lingenfelter Racing
1557 Winchester Rd (46733-3109)
PHONE..................260 724-2552
Thomas Cress, *Pr*
▲ **EMP:** 23 **EST:** 1972
SQ FT: 24,000
SALES (est): 1.16MM **Privately Held**
Web: www.lingenfelter.com
SIC: 7549 5531 3519 3714 High performance auto repair and service; Automotive parts; Parts and accessories, internal combustion engines; Motor vehicle parts and accessories
PA: Lpe Assets, Llc
  7819 Lochlin Dr
  Brighton MI 48116

(G-2870)
LLAMA CORPORATION
2937 E 900 N (46733-9470)
P.O. Box 702 (46733-0702)
PHONE..................888 701-7432
Robert L Hakes, *Pr*
EMP: 3 **EST:** 2001
SALES (est): 244.96K **Privately Held**
Web: www.llamacorp.com
SIC: 8711 3533 3643 3663 Electrical or electronic engineering; Gas field machinery and equipment; Lightning protection equipment; Radio and t.v. communications equipment

(G-2871)
MANLEY MEATS INC
302 S 400 E (46733-9095)
PHONE..................260 592-7313
Roger Manley, *Pr*
Ronald Manley, *VP*
Steven Manley, *VP*
Marilyn Guyer, *Sec*
Alice Manley, *Treas*
▲ **EMP:** 14 **EST:** 1961
SQ FT: 7,500
SALES (est): 439.5K **Privately Held**
Web: www.manleymeats.com
SIC: 5421 2013 2011 Meat markets, including freezer provisioners; Canned meats (except baby food), from purchased meat; Meat packing plants

(G-2872)
MATCO PALLETS
2001 N St Rd 101 (46733-7000)
PHONE..................260 223-0585
EMP: 8 **EST:** 1977
SALES (est): 115.93K **Privately Held**
SIC: 2448 Pallets, wood and metal combination

(G-2873)
MID-STATES TOOL & MACHINE INC
2220 Patterson St (46733-1871)
PHONE..................260 728-9797
Jason Scheumann, *Prin*
Jason Scheumann, *CEO*
Sylvia Scheumann, *
EMP: 27 **EST:** 1977
SQ FT: 24,200
SALES (est): 3.02MM **Privately Held**
Web: www.midstatestool.com
SIC: 3599 Machine shop, jobbing and repair

(G-2874)
MINDS EYE GRAPHICS INC
958 Yorktown Rd (46733-2626)
P.O. Box 299 (46733-0299)
PHONE..................260 724-2050
Gregory F Kitson, *Pr*
Gregory F Kitson, *Pr*
Teresa Kitson, *Sec*
EMP: 13 **EST:** 1981
SALES (est): 386.87K **Privately Held**
Web: www.mindseyeg.com
SIC: 2759 Screen printing

(G-2875)
PANACEA PAINTING & COATING INC
1013 W Commerce Dr (46733-7541)
PHONE..................260 728-4222
EMP: 8 **EST:** 1993
SQ FT: 11,000
SALES (est): 734.62K **Privately Held**
Web: www.panaceapowder.com
SIC: 3479 Coating of metals and formed products

(G-2876)
PORTER INC
Also Called: Thunderbird Products
2200 W Monroe St (46733-3028)
P.O. Box 1003 (46733-5003)
PHONE..................800 736-7685
▲ **EMP:** 610 **EST:** 1976
SALES (est): 50.71MM **Privately Held**
Web: www.formulaboats.com
SIC: 3732 5088 5551 Motorboats, inboard or outboard: building and repairing; Marine supplies; Marine supplies, nec

(G-2877)
PRESTRESS SERVICES INC
Also Called: Marine Precast
7855 Nw Winchester Rd (46733-8825)
P.O. Box 111 (46733-0111)
PHONE..................260 724-7117
Bob Sawyer, *Pr*
EMP: 205
SALES (corp-wide): 21.52MM **Privately Held**
Web: www.prestressservices.com
SIC: 3272 3441 Prestressed concrete products; Fabricated structural metal
PA: Prestress Services, Inc.
  5501 Briar Hill Rd
  Lexington KY 40516
  859 299-0461

(G-2878)
R & K INCINERATOR INC
6125 W 100 S (46733-8355)
PHONE..................260 565-3214
Mark Kaehr, *Pr*
EMP: 3 **EST:** 1974
SALES (est): 429.96K **Privately Held**
Web: www.burnez.com
SIC: 3567 Incinerators, metal: domestic or commercial

(G-2879)
REV RECREATION GROUP INC
Also Called: Fleetwood Homes
1803 Winchester St (46733-2187)
PHONE..................260 724-4217
EMP: 58
Web: www.revrvgroup.com
SIC: 3716 2451 Motor homes; Mobile homes
HQ: Rev Recreation Group, Inc.
  1031 E Us Highway 224
  Decatur IN 46733

(G-2880)
REV RECREATION GROUP INC
Also Called: Fleetwood Homes
1420 Patterson St (46733-1839)
P.O. Box 1007 (46733-5007)
PHONE..................260 724-2418
Steve Heim, *Brnch Mgr*
EMP: 47
Web: www.revrvserviceandrepair.com
SIC: 3711 Motor vehicles and car bodies
HQ: Rev Recreation Group, Inc.
  1031 E Us Highway 224
  Decatur IN 46733

(G-2881)
REVENGE DESIGNS INC
Also Called: Revenge Designs
1040 S 11th St (46733)
PHONE..................260 724-4000
Peter Collorafi, *Pr*
EMP: 5 **EST:** 2005
SQ FT: 53,000
SALES (est): 381.67K **Privately Held**
Web: www.revengedesignsinc.com
SIC: 3711 Automobile bodies, passenger car, not including engine, etc.

(G-2882)
RING-R INC
Also Called: Ring-R Engineering
6691 W State Road 124 (46733-8330)
P.O. Box 462 (46714-0462)
PHONE..................260 565-3347
◆ **EMP:** 25
SIC: 3441 8711 Fabricated structural metal; Engineering services

(G-2883)
SILBERLINE MFG CO INC
Also Called: Silberline of Indiana
2010 Guy Brown Dr (46733-1882)
PHONE..................260 728-2111
Thomas E Anderson, *Mgr*
EMP: 39
SQ FT: 45,000
SALES (corp-wide): 46.08MM **Privately Held**
Web: www.silberline.com
SIC: 2819 Industrial inorganic chemicals, nec
PA: Silberline Manufacturing Co., Inc.
  130 Lincoln Dr
  Tamaqua PA 18252
  570 668-6050

(G-2884)
SOLAE
1200 N 2nd St (46733-1160)
PHONE..................260 724-2101
Ted Habegger, *Pr*
◆ **EMP:** 8 **EST:** 2005
SALES (est): 252.83K **Privately Held**
SIC: 2075 Soybean oil mills

(G-2885)
SP3
3531 W Us Highway 224 (46733-7504)
PHONE..................260 547-4150
Eric Koik, *Brnch Mgr*
EMP: 26
Web: www.sp3diamondtech.com
SIC: 3479 Aluminum coating of metal products
PA: Sp3
  1605 Wyatt Dr
  Santa Clara CA 95054

Decatur - Adams County (G-2886)

(G-2886)
TP/ELM ACQUISITION SBUSID INC (HQ)
Also Called: Elm Packaging
2110 Patterson St (46733-1869)
PHONE..................260 728-2161
Glen Davis, Contrlr
EMP: 100 **EST:** 1993
SQ FT: 100,000
SALES (est): 47.05MM
SALES (corp-wide): 996.3MM **Privately Held**
SIC: 3086 Cups and plates, foamed plastics
PA: Tekni-Plex, Inc.
460 E Swedesford Rd # 300
Wayne PA 19087
484 690-1520

(G-2887)
TROYER BROTHERS
6691 W State Road 124 (46733-8330)
PHONE..................260 589-2244
EMP: 23 **EST:** 2014
SALES (est): 817.49K **Privately Held**
Web: www.troyerbrothers.net
SIC: 3599 Machine shop, jobbing and repair

(G-2888)
UNIVERSAL METALCRAFT INC
4215 W 750 N (46733-7852)
PHONE..................260 547-4357
Donald Haines, Pr
Janelle Hartmann, *
EMP: 35 **EST:** 1969
SQ FT: 6,400
SALES (est): 4.96MM **Privately Held**
Web: www.universalmetalcraft.com
SIC: 3444 3599 Sheet metalwork; Machine shop, jobbing and repair

(G-2889)
XYZ MODEL WORKS
10334 N 500 W (46733-7838)
PHONE..................260 413-1873
Paul Ruble, Prin
EMP: 5 **EST:** 2010
SALES (est): 64.3K **Privately Held**
SIC: 3999 Novelties, bric-a-brac, and hobby kits

Delphi
Carroll County

(G-2890)
ANDERSONS AGRICULTURE GROUP LP
Grain Division
3902 N Anderson Dr (46923-8157)
PHONE..................765 564-6135
Joe Needham, Mgr
EMP: 10
SQ FT: 20,000
SALES (corp-wide): 14.75B **Publicly Held**
Web: www.andersonsinc.com
SIC: 5191 3523 3291 2842 Fertilizer and fertilizer materials; Farm machinery and equipment; Abrasive products; Polishes and sanitation goods
HQ: The Andersons Agriculture Group L P
1947 Briarfield Blvd
Maumee OH 43537
419 893-5050

(G-2891)
BRIM CONCRETE INC
2485 W Gravel Pit Rd (46923-8422)
PHONE..................765 564-4975
TOLL FREE: 800
EMP: 6
SALES (corp-wide): 2.22MM **Privately Held**
SIC: 3273 3272 Ready-mixed concrete; Floor slabs and tiles, precast concrete
PA: Brim Concrete Inc
614 W Fisher St
Monticello IN
574 583-7101

(G-2892)
CARROLL PAPERS INC
Also Called: Carroll County Comet
114 E Franklin St (46923-1210)
P.O. Box 26 (46929-0026)
PHONE..................765 564-2222
Joe Moss, Pr
EMP: 8
SALES (corp-wide): 727.07K **Privately Held**
Web: www.carrollcountycomet.com
SIC: 2711 Newspapers: publishing only, not printed on site
PA: Carroll Papers Inc
14 E Main St
Flora IN 46929
574 967-4135

(G-2893)
DELPHI BODY WORKS
313 S Washington St (46923-1542)
P.O. Box 30 (46923-0030)
PHONE..................765 564-2212
Richard C Bradshaw, Pr
James Huffer, Sec
EMP: 17 **EST:** 1848
SQ FT: 43,000
SALES (est): 1.94MM **Privately Held**
Web: www.delphibodyworks.com
SIC: 3713 5082 3715 3441 Truck bodies (motor vehicles); General construction machinery and equipment; Trailer bodies; Fabricated structural metal

(G-2894)
DELPHI PRODUCTS CO INC
2065 W Us Highway 421 (46923-8268)
P.O. Box 149 (46923-0149)
PHONE..................800 382-7903
Blair Underhill, Pr
Alan Girton, Sec
EMP: 10 **EST:** 1989
SQ FT: 20,000
SALES (est): 2.35MM **Privately Held**
Web: www.delphiproducts.com
SIC: 5083 3523 Agricultural machinery and equipment; Farm machinery and equipment

(G-2895)
DPC INC
Also Called: Delphi Products Company
2065 W Us Highway 421 (46923-8268)
P.O. Box 149 (46923-0149)
PHONE..................765 564-3752
Blair Underhill, Pr
Alan Girpon, VP
EMP: 24 **EST:** 1963
SQ FT: 20,000
SALES (est): 1.22MM **Privately Held**
SIC: 3523 5083 3446 3444 Barn, silo, poultry, dairy, and livestock machinery; Poultry equipment; Architectural metalwork; Sheet metalwork

(G-2896)
EFFICIENT PLAS SOLUTIONS INC
9745 N 850 W (46923-9224)
PHONE..................574 965-4690
Thomas Thompson, Prin
EMP: 7 **EST:** 2016
SALES (est): 99.06K **Privately Held**
SIC: 2821 Plastics materials and resins

(G-2897)
FRONTIER CARRIAGE
7872 W 1000 N (46923-8623)
PHONE..................574 965-4444
Shawn Bunnell, Owner
EMP: 2 **EST:** 2001
SALES (est): 76.63K **Privately Held**
Web: www.frontiercarriages.com
SIC: 3799 Carriages, horse drawn

(G-2898)
HOMETOWN SHIRTS & GRAPHIX LLC
101 S Washington St (46923-1538)
PHONE..................765 564-3066
EMP: 2 **EST:** 2013
SALES (est): 140K **Privately Held**
Web: www.hometownshirts.com
SIC: 2389 2396 2395 Apparel and accessories, nec; Screen printing on fabric articles; Embroidery products, except Schiffli machine

(G-2899)
INDIANA PACKERS CORPORATION (HQ)
6755 W 100 N (46923-9305)
P.O. Box 318 (46923-0318)
PHONE..................765 564-3680
Russ Yearwood, Pr
Masao Watanabe, Ch
Edward J Nelson, Pr
Randy Toleman, S&M/VP
James Hardison, Pers/VP
◆ **EMP:** 1350 **EST:** 1993
SQ FT: 312,000
SALES (est): 456.07MM **Privately Held**
Web: www.indianapackerscorp.com
SIC: 2011 2013 Pork products, from pork slaughtered on site; Sausages and other prepared meats
PA: Mitsubishi Corporation
2-3-1, Marunouchi
Chiyoda-Ku TKY 100-0

(G-2900)
JACOB ADAMS
108 E Main St (46923-1543)
PHONE..................765 564-2314
Jacob Adams, Owner
EMP: 1
SALES (est): 53.24K **Privately Held**
SIC: 2752 Commercial printing, lithographic

(G-2901)
KINZIE MILL WORK
852 S 800 W (46923-8990)
PHONE..................765 564-4355
Gerald Kinzie, Owner
EMP: 1 **EST:** 2001
SALES (est): 47.48K **Privately Held**
SIC: 2499 Decorative wood and woodwork

(G-2902)
MARK FOSTER
6954 N 980 W (46923-8672)
PHONE..................574 965-4558
Mark Foster, Owner
EMP: 1 **EST:** 2000
SALES (est): 83.07K **Privately Held**
SIC: 2431 Woodwork, interior and ornamental, nec

(G-2903)
MED GRIND INC
7848 N Us Highway 421 (46923-8691)
PHONE..................574 965-4040
Mike Cummings, Pr
EMP: 2 **EST:** 2006
SALES (est): 140.48K **Privately Held**
SIC: 3599 Grinding castings for the trade

(G-2904)
NICHOLAS MENDEL
Also Called: Ikonik Graphix
101 S Washington St (46923-1538)
PHONE..................574 870-8856
Nicholas Mendel, Owner
EMP: 2
SALES (est): 73.28K **Privately Held**
SIC: 2759 7389 Letterpress and screen printing; Business Activities at Non-Commercial Site

(G-2905)
P T I MACHINING INC
5395 W 200 N (46923-8265)
P.O. Box 587 (46923-0587)
PHONE..................765 564-9966
EMP: 6 **EST:** 1994
SQ FT: 15,000
SALES (est): 3.6MM **Privately Held**
Web: www.swissparts.com
SIC: 3599 Machine shop, jobbing and repair

(G-2906)
QGRAPHICS INC (PA)
108 E Main St (46923-1543)
P.O. Box 180 (46923-0180)
PHONE..................765 564-2314
Bret Hanaway, Pr
EMP: 5 **EST:** 1948
SQ FT: 3,000
SALES (est): 848.39K
SALES (corp-wide): 848.39K **Privately Held**
Web: www.qgraphicsinc.com
SIC: 2752 5943 Offset printing; Office forms and supplies

(G-2907)
READY SET GO INC
4280 W 700 N (46923-8309)
PHONE..................765 564-2847
Denise M Bender, Pr
EMP: 1 **EST:** 2000
SALES (est): 112.72K **Privately Held**
SIC: 3273 Ready-mixed concrete

(G-2908)
SKYLINE SIGNS INC
Also Called: Skyline Signs & Awnings
1989 W Mill St (46923-8582)
PHONE..................765 564-4422
Rob Johnson, Pr
Sue Johnson, VP
EMP: 2 **EST:** 2000
SALES (est): 121.54K **Privately Held**
Web: www.skylinesigns.net
SIC: 3993 Signs and advertising specialties

(G-2909)
TERRYS WELDING INC
9176 W 132 N (46923-9780)
P.O. Box 6384 (47903-6384)
PHONE..................765 564-3331
Greg Terry, Prin
EMP: 2 **EST:** 2005
SALES (est): 148.95K **Privately Held**
Web: www.oxygenchannel.com
SIC: 7692 Welding repair

(G-2910)
U S AGGREGATES INC
Us 421n (46923)
P.O. Box 315 (46923-0315)
PHONE..................765 564-2282
Bill Corbett, Brnch Mgr

EMP: 20
SALES (corp-wide): 894.43MM **Privately Held**
Web: www.usagg.com
SIC: **1442** 1422 5032 Gravel mining; Crushed and broken limestone; Limestone
HQ: U S Aggregates Inc
5400 W 86th St
Indianapolis IN 46268
317 872-6010

Demotte
Jasper County

(G-2911)
BELSTRA MILLING CO INC (PA)
424 15th St Se (46310-9367)
PHONE..............................219 987-4343
▲ EMP: 30 EST: 1954
SALES (est): 8.38MM
SALES (corp-wide): 8.38MM **Privately Held**
Web: www.belstramilling.com
SIC: **2048** 5191 Prepared feeds, nec; Farm supplies

(G-2912)
BOEZEMAN ENTERPRISES INC
Also Called: Boezeman Signs Graphic Design
9941 N 1200 W (46310-9071)
PHONE..............................219 345-2732
Lynn Boezeman, *Pr*
Marcia Boezeman, *VP*
EMP: 2 EST: 1995
SALES (est): 126.5K **Privately Held**
Web: www.boezemansigns.com
SIC: **3993** Signs and advertising specialties

(G-2913)
BROKEN MOLD CUSTOMS INC
1207 Daisy St Se (46310-8467)
P.O. Box 421 (47943-0421)
PHONE..............................219 863-1008
Becky A Trembly, *Prin*
EMP: 2 EST: 2010
SALES (est): 145.87K **Privately Held**
Web: www.brokenmoldcustoms.com
SIC: **3544** Industrial molds

(G-2914)
CUSTOM MFG INC
10020 N 1100 W (46310-9324)
PHONE..............................219 987-7716
Daniel Kingma, *Pr*
EMP: 1 EST: 2001
SALES (est): 150.5K **Privately Held**
SIC: **3599** Machine shop, jobbing and repair

(G-2915)
DEMOTTE DECORATIVE STONE INC
6611 W State Road 10 (46310-7800)
PHONE..............................219 987-5461
EMP: 3 EST: 2011
SALES (est): 195.93K **Privately Held**
Web: www.demottedecorativestone.com
SIC: **1411** Dimension stone

(G-2916)
FITZPATRICK SONS WOODWORKS LLC
9190 W 1100 N (46310-9457)
PHONE..............................219 987-2223
Bryan Fitzpatrick, *Owner*
EMP: 4 EST: 2018
SALES (est): 54.13K **Privately Held**
SIC: **2431** Millwork

(G-2917)
FLEX APPEALS FAMILY AND FRIEN
9985 Arrowhead Ln (46310-9776)
PHONE..............................219 863-3830
Rebecca R Singel, *Owner*
EMP: 1 EST: 2010
SALES (est): 44.19K **Privately Held**
SIC: **3357** Nonferrous wiredrawing and insulating

(G-2918)
GOLD STANDARD TRUSS LLC
817 15th St Se (46310-9371)
P.O. Box 517 (46310-0517)
PHONE..............................219 987-7781
Marv Veldt, *Manager*
EMP: 3 EST: 2008
SALES (est): 282.67K **Privately Held**
Web: www.goldstandardtruss.com
SIC: **3999** Manufacturing industries, nec

(G-2919)
K IRPCHEADSTART PROGRAM
10448 N 450 E (46310-8920)
PHONE..............................219 345-2011
Katherine Mendiola, *Brnch Mgr*
EMP: 2
Web: www.kirpc.net
SIC: **2752** Commercial printing, lithographic
PA: K Irpcheadstart Program
115 W Pearl St
Winamac IN 46996

(G-2920)
KANKAKEE VALLEY POST NEWS
Also Called: Action Plus Shopper & Shoppers
827 S Halleck St (46310-8342)
P.O. Box 110 (46310-0110)
PHONE..............................219 987-5111
Dan Hurd, *Pr*
EMP: 5 EST: 1932
SALES (est): 151.54K **Privately Held**
Web: www.newsbug.info
SIC: **2711** Newspapers, publishing and printing

(G-2921)
KNIP WELDING
8446 W 1000 N (46310-9444)
PHONE..............................219 987-5123
Kenny Knip, *Owner*
EMP: 2 EST: 2004
SALES (est): 87.83K **Privately Held**
Web: knippumps.wixsite.com
SIC: **7692** Welding repair

(G-2922)
LEGACY VULCAN LLC
Also Called: Demotte Yard
832 15th St Se - Sr231 (46310-9371)
P.O. Box 140 (46310-0140)
PHONE..............................219 987-3040
John Walstar, *Mgr*
EMP: 5
Web: www.vulcanmaterials.com
SIC: **3272** Concrete products, nec
HQ: Legacy Vulcan, Llc
1200 Urban Center Dr
Birmingham AL 35242
205 298-3000

(G-2923)
MENGEL WELDING COMPANY
12510 N 600 W (46310-8760)
PHONE..............................219 987-4079
Robert Mengel, *Prin*
EMP: 1 EST: 2009
SALES (est): 36.93K **Privately Held**
SIC: **7692** Welding repair

(G-2924)
MIDCOUNTY MACHINING INC
Also Called: Mid-County Machining
11694 Lilac Ct (46310)
PHONE..............................219 992-9380
Herbert Dresbaugh Junior, *Pr*
Herb Dresbaugh, *Pr*
Judy Dresbaugh, *VP*
EMP: 4 EST: 1998
SALES (est): 449.37K **Privately Held**
Web: www.studiom.org
SIC: **3599** Machine shop, jobbing and repair

(G-2925)
MR HEAT INC
11735 N State Road 55 (46310-9612)
PHONE..............................219 345-5629
TOLL FREE: 866
Raymond Thomas, *Pr*
Joe Thomas, *Pr*
EMP: 9 EST: 1998
SALES (est): 752.14K **Privately Held**
Web: www.mrheatinc.com
SIC: **3585** Heating and air conditioning combination units

(G-2926)
PRECISE TITLE INC
8917 24th St Sw (46310-9715)
PHONE..............................219 987-2286
Peter Georgopoulos, *Prin*
EMP: 6 EST: 2001
SALES (est): 80.88K **Privately Held**
SIC: **2389** Apparel and accessories, nec

(G-2927)
RACESTAR PUBLICATIONS
9054 Holmes Ter E (46310-9100)
PHONE..............................219 987-2096
Diva Rish, *Owner*
EMP: 1 EST: 1998
SALES (est): 78.9K **Privately Held**
Web: www.racestarpublications.com
SIC: **2721** Magazines: publishing only, not printed on site

(G-2928)
RE INDUSTRIES INC
1328 15th St Se Ste 4 (46310-9146)
PHONE..............................219 987-1764
David Repko, *Pr*
EMP: 4 EST: 2017
SALES (est): 159.2K **Privately Held**
SIC: **3999** Manufacturing industries, nec

(G-2929)
SHIELDS MECH & FABRICATION LLC
11474 Chateau Ln (46310-9350)
PHONE..............................219 863-3972
David Shields, *Prin*
EMP: 6 EST: 2015
SALES (est): 165.34K **Privately Held**
Web: www.shieldsmechanicalandfabrication.com
SIC: **3999** Manufacturing industries, nec

(G-2930)
TGE PUZZLE PIECES IN LIFE
2026 E 1130 N (46310-9660)
PHONE..............................219 345-2193
Samantha Poort, *Prin*
EMP: 4 EST: 2016
SALES (est): 41.02K **Privately Held**
Web: www.tgepuzzlepiecesinlifephotography.com
SIC: **3944** Puzzles

(G-2931)
VARSITY SPORTS INC
603 N Halleck St (46310-9545)
PHONE..............................219 987-7200
Scott Ericks, *Prin*
EMP: 7
SALES (corp-wide): 969.28K **Privately Held**
Web: www.varsitysportsin.com
SIC: **2759** 5941 5949 5999 Screen printing; Sporting goods and bicycle shops; Sewing, needlework, and piece goods; Trophies and plaques
PA: Varsity Sports Inc
134 N Broad St
Griffith IN 46319
219 924-5110

(G-2932)
WHEELS 4 TOTS INC
10700 W 1300 N (46310-8505)
P.O. Box 221 (46310-0221)
PHONE..............................219 987-6812
Jeff Martin, *Pr*
Donna Martin, *VP*
▲ EMP: 3 EST: 1999
SQ FT: 8,000
SALES (est): 373.16K **Privately Held**
Web: www.wheels4tots.com
SIC: **3714** Motor vehicle wheels and parts

(G-2933)
WRITE WORD
6834 Mercedes Ln (46310-9412)
PHONE..............................219 987-5254
Jacquelyn Getz, *Owner*
EMP: 1 EST: 1997
SALES (est): 61.32K **Privately Held**
SIC: **2741** Technical papers: publishing only, not printed on site

Denver
Miami County

(G-2934)
BEST FRIENDS INC
252 W Harrison St (46926-9318)
P.O. Box 26 (46926-0026)
PHONE..............................765 985-3872
Kevin Hostetler, *Pr*
Hayley Hostetler, *VP*
EMP: 2 EST: 2003
SALES (est): 253.16K **Privately Held**
Web: www.bestfriends.org
SIC: **2339** 7389 Women's and misses' athletic clothing and sportswear; Business services, nec

(G-2935)
IMPERIAL DESIGNS
6599 N State Road 19 (46926-9213)
PHONE..............................765 985-2712
Theresa Armstrong, *Owner*
EMP: 2 EST: 1997
SALES (est): 54.59K **Privately Held**
SIC: **2395** Embroidery and art needlework

(G-2936)
WOODCRAFTERS LLC
8472 N 100 E (46926-9120)
PHONE..............................765 469-5103
Chadd A Pattison, *Admn*
EMP: 6 EST: 2012
SALES (est): 120.94K **Privately Held**
SIC: **2511** Wood household furniture

Depauw
Harrison County

(G-2937)
CHURCHILL EQUIPMENT
4880 Adams Rd Nw (47115-8436)
PHONE.................................812 347-2592
Cameron Churchill, *Owner*
EMP: 1 **EST:** 1977
SALES (est): 107.35K **Privately Held**
Web: www.churchillequipment.com
SIC: 3523 Farm machinery and equipment

(G-2938)
FRED SMITH STORE FIXTURES INC
6405 Highway 337 Nw (47115)
P.O. Box P.O. Box 40 (47115)
PHONE.................................812 347-2363
Steven F Smith, *Sec*
EMP: 60 **EST:** 1962
SQ FT: 60,000
SALES (est): 9.79MM **Privately Held**
Web: www.fssf.us
SIC: 3089 Laminating of plastics

(G-2939)
JAMES HARPER ✪
Also Called: Harpers Headstone Care
426 E Main St Nw (47115)
PHONE.................................812 267-4251
James Harper, *Owner*
EMP: 2 **EST:** 2024
SALES (est): 70.89K **Privately Held**
SIC: 3272 7389 Monuments and grave markers, except terrazzo; Business Activities at Non-Commercial Site

Deputy
Jefferson County

(G-2940)
BAXTER LUMBER LLC
12876 W Deputy Pike Rd (47230-9309)
PHONE.................................812 873-6868
Donald Baxter, *Managing Member*
EMP: 17 **EST:** 1957
SQ FT: 4,000
SALES (est): 2.45MM **Privately Held**
Web: www.baxterlumberllc.com
SIC: 2421 Lumber: rough, sawed, or planed

(G-2941)
HOMESTEAD PROPERTIES INC
Also Called: Tiny Timbers
10214 W Deputy Pike Rd (47230-9090)
P.O. Box 126 (47230-0126)
PHONE.................................812 866-4415
EMP: 10 **EST:** 1986
SQ FT: 20,000
SALES (est): 1.31MM **Privately Held**
Web: www.tinytimbers.com
SIC: 2421 2426 Sawmills and planing mills, general; Hardwood dimension and flooring mills

(G-2942)
VIRES BACKHOE AND DUMPTRUC
2571 E Doty Mill Rd (47230-9603)
PHONE.................................812 595-1630
Billie Vires, *Prin*
EMP: 2 **EST:** 2008
SALES (est): 216.63K **Privately Held**
SIC: 3531 Backhoes

Dillsboro
Dearborn County

(G-2943)
BEVERLY INDUSTRIAL SERVICE INC
4233 S Farmers Retreat Rd (47018-9297)
PHONE.................................812 667-5047
Beverly Snyder, *Sec*
Cary Snyder, *Pr*
Teresa Meyer, *VP*
Howard Snyder, *Pr*
Glenda Lacey, *Contrlr*
EMP: 33 **EST:** 1980
SQ FT: 20,000
SALES (est): 897.45K **Privately Held**
Web: www.beverlyind.com
SIC: 7389 3545 Grinding, precision: commercial or industrial; Precision tools, machinists'

(G-2944)
CRAIG HYDRAULIC ENTERPRISES
Also Called: Global Odor Ctrl Tech Mid Amer
9790 Front St (47018-9342)
PHONE.................................812 432-5108
Tom Wafford, *Pr*
Berneta Wafford, *VP*
EMP: 2 **EST:** 1989
SALES (est): 249.21K **Privately Held**
SIC: 2899 Water treating compounds

(G-2945)
DOBBINS INTERIOR WOODWORKS
5916 E County Road 300 S (47018-7501)
PHONE.................................812 221-0058
Sheila Dobbins, *Prin*
EMP: 6 **EST:** 2010
SALES (est): 10.35K **Privately Held**
SIC: 2431 Millwork

(G-2946)
HELENA AGRI-ENTERPRISES LLC
5262 E Us Highway 50 (47018-8797)
PHONE.................................812 654-3177
Matthew Hirt, *Mgr*
EMP: 1
Web: www.helenaagri.com
SIC: 5191 2819 Chemicals, agricultural; Industrial inorganic chemicals, nec
HQ: Helena Agri-Enterprises, Llc
   225 Schilling Blvd
   Collierville TN 38017
   901 761-0050

(G-2947)
INDIANA PRECISION TOOLING INC
4233 S Farmers Retreat Rd (47018-9297)
PHONE.................................812 667-5141
Don Gooden, *Pr*
Judy Gooden, *VP*
EMP: 10 **EST:** 1987
SQ FT: 20,000
SALES (est): 696.88K **Privately Held**
SIC: 3423 3545 Hand and edge tools, nec; Machine knives, metalworking

(G-2948)
K&D CRAFTS
13020 Southfork Rd (47018-8837)
PHONE.................................812 667-2575
Kimberly Hess, *Owner*
EMP: 2 **EST:** 1997
SALES (est): 78.37K **Privately Held**
SIC: 3944 Craft and hobby kits and sets

(G-2949)
LAUGHERY SAWMILL
10678 W Laughery Creek Rd (47018-9381)
PHONE.................................812 432-5649
Steve Brown, *Owner*
EMP: 1 **EST:** 1979
SALES (est): 88.59K **Privately Held**
SIC: 2421 Sawmills and planing mills, general

(G-2950)
MULTIPLE MACHINING INC
10150 Lenover St (47018-9421)
P.O. Box 29 (47018-0029)
PHONE.................................812 432-5946
EMP: 23 **EST:** 1992
SQ FT: 20,000
SALES (est): 2.5MM **Privately Held**
Web: www.multiplemachining.com
SIC: 3599 Machine shop, jobbing and repair

(G-2951)
PERFORMANCE MACHINING INC
Also Called: Performance
13350 Us Highway 50 (47018-9603)
P.O. Box 457 (47018-0457)
PHONE.................................812 432-9180
Steve Ochs, *Pr*
Lavonne Ochs, *VP*
EMP: 6 **EST:** 1997
SALES (est): 466.73K **Privately Held**
SIC: 3599 Machine shop, jobbing and repair

(G-2952)
SAVOR FLAVOR LLC
13721 Prosperity Ridge Rd (47018-2500)
PHONE.................................812 667-1030
Linda Hurelbrink, *Mgr*
EMP: 5 **EST:** 2018
SALES (est): 121.19K **Privately Held**
SIC: 2087 Flavoring extracts and syrups, nec

(G-2953)
VISUAL IMPACT
8595 Hueseman Rd (47018-8937)
PHONE.................................812 432-3524
Renee Bedinghaus, *Owner*
EMP: 1 **EST:** 2001
SALES (est): 74.73K **Privately Held**
SIC: 3993 Signs and advertising specialties

Dubois
Dubois County

(G-2954)
MEYER CUSTOM WOODWORKING INC
2657 E State Road 56 (47527-9541)
PHONE.................................812 695-2021
Melvin Meyer, *Pr*
Dorothy Meyer, *Sec*
EMP: 9 **EST:** 1874
SQ FT: 12,000
SALES (est): 902.3K **Privately Held**
Web: www.meyercustomwoodworking.com
SIC: 2441 2434 8712 Cases, wood; Wood kitchen cabinets; Architectural services

(G-2955)
WISEMAN CUSTOM CABINETS INC
4501 E State Road 56 (47527-9505)
PHONE.................................812 678-3601
Doug Wiseman, *Prin*
Doug Wiseman, *Dir*
Hoyt Wiseman, *Pr*
EMP: 3 **EST:** 1997
SALES (est): 204.5K **Privately Held**
SIC: 2434 Wood kitchen cabinets

Dugger
Sullivan County

(G-2956)
C M ENGINEERING INC
8112 E Main St (47848-8087)
P.O. Box 215 (47848-0215)
PHONE.................................812 648-2038
James M Stringer, *Pr*
Dean Stringer, *VP*
EMP: 16 **EST:** 1991
SQ FT: 12,000
SALES (est): 2.17MM **Privately Held**
Web: www.cm-engineering.org
SIC: 3599 Machine shop, jobbing and repair

(G-2957)
INDUSTRIAL TRNING UNLMTED CORP
Also Called: Learnlab
8184 E Station (47848-4800)
P.O. Box 128 (47848-0128)
PHONE.................................812 961-8801
David Carpenter, *Pr*
Kambi Carpenter, *
▼ **EMP:** 39 **EST:** 2001
SQ FT: 15,800
SALES (est): 4.97MM **Privately Held**
Web: www.learnlab.biz
SIC: 3699 Electrical equipment and supplies, nec

(G-2958)
MISNER WELDING & CNSTR INC
6922 E County Road 425 S (47848)
P.O. Box 554 (47848-0554)
PHONE.................................812 648-2980
Walter R Misner, *Pr*
EMP: 8 **EST:** 1997
SALES (est): 112.77K **Privately Held**
SIC: 7692 Welding repair

(G-2959)
NMC INC
Also Called: Northside Machine
8068 E Main St (47848-5034)
PHONE.................................812 648-2636
Richard G Smith, *Pr*
Debra A Smith, *
Mike Smith, *
Denny Smith, *
EMP: 24 **EST:** 1965
SQ FT: 18,900
SALES (est): 4.94MM **Privately Held**
Web: www.northsidemachine.com
SIC: 3599 Machine shop, jobbing and repair

Dunkirk
Jay County

(G-2960)
ARDAGH GLASS INC
Also Called: ARDAGH GLASS INC.
524 E Center St (47336-1365)
P.O. Box 205 (47336-0205)
PHONE.................................765 768-7891
Mike Hart, *Manager*
EMP: 1
SALES (corp-wide): 2.67MM **Privately Held**
Web: www.ardaghgroup.com
SIC: 3221 Glass containers
HQ: Ardagh Glass Inc
   10194 Crsspint Blvd Ste 4
   Indianapolis IN 46256

GEOGRAPHIC SECTION

East Chicago - Lake County (G-2988)

(G-2961)
D RINKER TRANSPORT LLC
9975 W 200 S (47336-9034)
PHONE..................765 749-4120
James Rinker, *Managing Member*
EMP: 1 **EST:** 2007
SALES (est): 246.29K **Privately Held**
SIC: 5154 3537 Livestock; Trucks: freight, baggage, etc.: industrial, except mining

(G-2962)
HAWTHORNE PRODUCTS INC
16828 N State Road 167n (47336-9126)
P.O. Box 226 (47336-0226)
PHONE..................765 768-6585
Don Hobson, *Pr*
Edwin L Kinney, *VP*
▲ **EMP:** 6 **EST:** 1977
SALES (est): 981.12K **Privately Held**
Web: www.hawthorne-products.com
SIC: 2834 Veterinary pharmaceutical preparations

(G-2963)
SDP MANUFACTURING INC
400 Industrial Dr (47336-9607)
P.O. Box 44 (47320-0044)
PHONE..................765 768-5000
Stanely Douglas Pitman, *Pr*
Selena D Hall, *Sec*
EMP: 21 **EST:** 1974
SQ FT: 20,000
SALES (est): 2.2MM **Privately Held**
Web: www.sdpmfg.com
SIC: 3589 Sewer cleaning equipment, power

Dupont
Jefferson County

(G-2964)
J W P VINYL DESIGNS
Also Called: JP Signs
5210 E Private Road 415 S (47231-9665)
PHONE..................812 873-8744
Jeff Petro, *Owner*
EMP: 2 **EST:** 2000
SQ FT: 2,000
SALES (est): 63.77K **Privately Held**
SIC: 3993 Signs and advertising specialties

Dyer
Lake County

(G-2965)
A&J LOGISTIC LLC
905 Joliet St (46311-1922)
PHONE..................708 314-6817
EMP: 6 **EST:** 2021
SALES (est): 400K **Privately Held**
SIC: 3537 Trucks: freight, baggage, etc.: industrial, except mining

(G-2966)
AMERICAN PALLET & RECYCL INC (PA)
1203 Sheffield Ave (46311-1054)
PHONE..................219 322-4391
EMP: 2 **EST:** 1987
SALES (est): 1.08MM **Privately Held**
SIC: 2448 7699 Pallets, wood; Pallet repair

(G-2967)
AREA WELDING INC LLC
1503 215th St (46311-1621)
PHONE..................219 669-0981
EMP: 4 **EST:** 2018
SALES (est): 55.69K **Privately Held**

SIC: 7692 Welding repair

(G-2968)
BACK ALLEY CREATIONS LLC
927 Tyler Ave (46311-1036)
P.O. Box 1063 (46375-5563)
PHONE..................219 306-6590
Matt Riesterer, *Managing Member*
EMP: 1 **EST:** 2008
SALES (est): 71.94K **Privately Held**
Web: www.backalleycreations.com
SIC: 3255 Melting pots, glasshouse: clay

(G-2969)
CIRCLES LEGACY PUBLISHING LLC
3419 Violet Ln (46311-2796)
PHONE..................219 322-1278
John Joslin, *Prin*
EMP: 5 **EST:** 2011
SALES (est): 109.77K **Privately Held**
SIC: 2741 Miscellaneous publishing

(G-2970)
CLOUD 9 GRIPTAPE LLC
2710 Hillcrest Dr (46311-2160)
PHONE..................818 795-1082
EMP: 1 **EST:** 2014
SALES (est): 98.65K **Privately Held**
Web: www.cloud9griptape.com
SIC: 3949 Sporting and athletic goods, nec

(G-2971)
DYER SIGNWERKS INC
1000 Richard Rd (46311-1992)
P.O. Box 312 (46311-0312)
PHONE..................219 322-7722
Mike Bettenbender, *Prin*
EMP: 7 **EST:** 2007
SALES (est): 188.1K **Privately Held**
SIC: 2253 T-shirts and tops, knit

(G-2972)
DYER VAULT COMPANY INC
1750 Sheffield Ave (46311-1599)
PHONE..................219 865-2521
Gerald J Austgen, *Pr*
Susan Karvasale, *VP*
EMP: 20 **EST:** 1938
SQ FT: 4,000
SALES (est): 782.29K **Privately Held**
Web: www.dyervault.com
SIC: 3272 Concrete products, precast, nec

(G-2973)
EDDIE S GUITARS
2111 Northwinds Dr (46311-1882)
PHONE..................219 689-7007
Eddie Jones, *Owner*
EMP: 5 **EST:** 2008
SALES (est): 100K **Privately Held**
Web: www.eddiesguitars.com
SIC: 3931 Guitars and parts, electric and nonelectric

(G-2974)
F W A DECKS & FENCING
2401 Hickory Dr (46311-2217)
PHONE..................219 865-3275
Carolyn Ready, *Owner*
EMP: 6 **EST:** 1988
SALES (est): 381.02K **Privately Held**
Web: www.fwadecksandfencing.com
SIC: 3446 Fences, gates, posts, and flagpoles

(G-2975)
GUARDIAN MOLD PREVENT CORP
906 Jackson Pl (46311-1111)
PHONE..................708 878-5788
EMP: 8 **EST:** 2007

SALES (est): 261.13K **Privately Held**
Web: www.guardianmold.com
SIC: 3544 Industrial molds

(G-2976)
HADADY CORPORATION (PA)
1832 Lake St (46311-1547)
PHONE..................219 322-7417
Jane Sullivan, *Pr*
Roger Gordon, *
Peter Trybula, *
▲ **EMP:** 30 **EST:** 1973
SALES (est): 23.98MM
SALES (corp-wide): 23.98MM **Privately Held**
Web: www.hadadycorp.com
SIC: 3499 3743 3452 Machine bases, metal; Locomotives and parts; Pins

(G-2977)
LINKER MEDIA GROUP INC
905 Joliet St (46311-1922)
PHONE..................219 230-3777
Troy Linker, *CEO*
EMP: 1 **EST:** 2016
SALES (est): 222.04K **Privately Held**
Web: www.nwindianabusiness.com
SIC: 7319 2721 Advertising, nec; Magazines: publishing only, not printed on site

(G-2978)
MODERN MACHINE & GRINDING INC
2001 Clark Rd (46311-1704)
P.O. Box 247 (46311-0247)
PHONE..................219 322-1201
Bruce Givens, *Pr*
Tim Holzhauer, *VP Opers*
Dennis Reed, *VP Mktg*
EMP: 23 **EST:** 1970
SQ FT: 14,000
SALES (est): 2.23MM **Privately Held**
Web: www.modernshearblade.com
SIC: 3599 Machine shop, jobbing and repair

(G-2979)
NWI PRINT & MAIL LLC
1050 Flagstone Dr (46311-2184)
PHONE..................219 916-1358
Doug Pint, *Prin*
EMP: 2 **EST:** 2014
SALES (est): 118.26K **Privately Held**
Web: www.nwiprintandmail.com
SIC: 2752 Offset printing

(G-2980)
PDB II INC
2661 Tower Ct (46311-2363)
PHONE..................219 865-1888
Pat Ballwick, *CEO*
EMP: 2 **EST:** 2004
SALES (est): 106.58K **Privately Held**
SIC: 2389 Apparel and accessories, nec

(G-2981)
PRINTWERK GRAPHICS & DESIGN
1000 Richard Rd (46311-1992)
PHONE..................219 322-7722
Michael E Bettenbender, *Owner*
EMP: 3 **EST:** 1982
SQ FT: 2,800
SALES (est): 176.12K **Privately Held**
SIC: 2759 7331 Advertising literature: printing, nsk; Direct mail advertising services

(G-2982)
ROTECK ENTERPRISES INC
13801 77th Ave (46311-2573)
PHONE..................219 322-4132

Jason Roteck, *Pr*
EMP: 6 **EST:** 2001
SALES (est): 315K **Privately Held**
Web: www.roteck.com
SIC: 2752 Commercial printing, lithographic

(G-2983)
SPARK MARKETING LLC
2010 Georgia Ave (46311-7759)
P.O. Box 1113 (46375-5613)
PHONE..................219 301-0071
EMP: 3 **EST:** 2012
SALES (est): 226.94K **Privately Held**
Web: www.sparkmarketing.co
SIC: 8742 2759 7389 3993 Marketing consulting services; Letterpress and screen printing; Embroidery advertising; Signs and advertising specialties

(G-2984)
STAMP N SCRAP INK CORP
1043 Sheffield Ave (46311-1048)
PHONE..................219 440-7239
Pamela Nachel, *Prin*
EMP: 6 **EST:** 2016
SALES (est): 81.87K **Privately Held**
SIC: 2893 Printing ink

Earl Park
Benton County

(G-2985)
EARL PARK SIGN SHOP LLC
208 S Locust St (47942-8689)
PHONE..................219 474-6419
Frank Balensiefer, *Owner*
EMP: 1 **EST:** 1963
SALES (est): 80K **Privately Held**
Web: www.earlparksignshop.com
SIC: 3993 Electric signs

(G-2986)
FRANK BALENSIEFER
Also Called: Frank Balensiefer Painting
208 S Locust St (47942-8689)
PHONE..................219 474-6419
Frank Balensiefer, *Owner*
EMP: 1 **EST:** 1964
SALES (est): 100K **Privately Held**
SIC: 3993 Signs and advertising specialties

East Chicago
Lake County

(G-2987)
1632 INC
Also Called: Science Fiction Public
4202 Baring Ave (46312-2509)
PHONE..................219 398-4155
Eric Flint, *Pr*
EMP: 2 **EST:** 2015
SALES (est): 115.74K **Privately Held**
Web: www.1632.org
SIC: 2721 8999 7389 Magazines: publishing and printing; Author; Business services, nec

(G-2988)
ACDC CONTROL LLC ✪
5614 Homerlee Ave (46312-3917)
PHONE..................219 801-3900
Donald Brown, *Managing Member*
EMP: 1 **EST:** 2023
SALES (est): 69.27K **Privately Held**
SIC: 3571 7389 Electronic computers; Business Activities at Non-Commercial Site

East Chicago - Lake County (G-2989)

(G-2989)
AMERICAN SCRAP PROCESSING INC
3601 Canal St (46312-1605)
PHONE..................................219 398-1444
Frank Cozzi, *Pr*
Albert Cozzi, *
Gregory Cozzi, *
EMP: 223 **EST:** 1916
SQ FT: 5,000
SALES (est): 554.11K **Privately Held**
SIC: 5093 3341 Metal scrap and waste materials; Secondary nonferrous metals
HQ: Metal Management, Inc.
2425 S Wood St
Chicago IL 60608
773 890-4210

(G-2990)
ARCELORMITTAL HOLDINGS LLC (HQ)
3210 Watling St (46312-1716)
PHONE..................................219 399-1200
Lakshmi Mittal, *Ch Bd*
Michael G Rippey, *
◆ **EMP:** 95 **EST:** 1998
SALES (corp-wide): 2.74B **Privately Held**
Web: corporate.arcelormittal.com
SIC: 3312 1011 Blast furnaces and steel mills; Iron ores
PA: Arcelormittal
Boulevard D'avranches 24-26
Luxembourg 1160
47924405

(G-2991)
ASPHALT CUTBACKS INC
3000 Gary Rd (46312-3578)
PHONE..................................219 398-4230
Cleopatra Bizoukas, *Pr*
George Bizoukas, *VP*
EMP: 11 **EST:** 1984
SALES (est): 2.38MM **Privately Held**
Web: www.asphaltcutbacks.com
SIC: 2952 2951 Coating compounds, tar; Asphalt paving mixtures and blocks

(G-2992)
BEEMSTERBOER SLAG CORP
3210 Watling St (46312-1716)
PHONE..................................219 392-1930
William Mundel, *Owner*
EMP: 121
SALES (corp-wide): 20.99MM **Privately Held**
Web: www.beemcompanies.com
SIC: 3295 Slag, crushed or ground
PA: Beemsterboer Slag Corp.
3411 Sheffield Ave
Hammond IN 46327
773 785-6000

(G-2993)
BETOS BAR INC
1301 E Chicago Ave (46312-3518)
P.O. Box 94 (46312-0094)
PHONE..................................219 397-8247
Roberto Abille, *Pr*
EMP: 5 **EST:** 2004
SALES (est): 425.16K **Privately Held**
SIC: 3631 Barbecues, grills, and braziers (outdoor cooking)

(G-2994)
BUNNY BEAUTIFUL COSMETICS LLC
3416 Elm St (46312-2012)
PHONE..................................219 433-1698
Taquetta Wright, *Mgr*
EMP: 1 **EST:** 2021
SALES (est): 47.23K **Privately Held**
SIC: 2844 Cosmetic preparations

(G-2995)
CHICAGO FLAME HARDENING CO
5200 Railroad Ave Ste 1 (46312-3891)
PHONE..................................773 768-3608
Thomas J Farnsworth, *Ch Bd*
John Farnsworth, *
Gwen Farnsworth, *
EMP: 28 **EST:** 1956
SQ FT: 25,000
SALES (est): 3.19MM **Privately Held**
Web: www.cflame.com
SIC: 3398 3312 Metal burning; Blast furnaces and steel mills

(G-2996)
CLEVELAND-CLIFFS INDIANA HBR
Also Called: Cleveland-Cliffs Indiana Harbor
3210 Watling St (46312-1716)
PHONE..................................219 399-1200
EMP: 1
SALES (corp-wide): 22B **Publicly Held**
Web: www.clevelandcliffs.com
SIC: 3312 Blast furnaces and steel mills
1 S Dearborn St Fl 19
Chicago IL 60603
312 346-0300

(G-2997)
CLEVELAND-CLIFFS STEEL LLC
3001 E Columbus Dr (46312-2939)
PHONE..................................219 399-6500
Stephen Rogers, *Mgr*
EMP: 1
SALES (corp-wide): 22B **Publicly Held**
Web: www.clevelandcliffs.com
SIC: 3312 Blast furnaces and steel mills
HQ: Cleveland-Cliffs Steel Llc
1 S Dearborn St Fl 19
Chicago IL 60603
312 346-0300

(G-2998)
CLEVELAND-CLIFFS STEEL LLC
3300 Dickey Rd (46312-1644)
PHONE..................................312 346-0300
Richard Kalmas, *Pr*
EMP: 2
SALES (corp-wide): 22B **Publicly Held**
Web: www.clevelandcliffs.com
SIC: 3312 Blast furnaces and steel mills
HQ: Cleveland-Cliffs Steel Llc
1 S Dearborn St Fl 19
Chicago IL 60603
312 346-0300

(G-2999)
CLEVELAND-CLIFFS STEEL LLC
3001 Dickey Rd (46312-1610)
PHONE..................................219 399-1000
Wendel Carter, *Genl Mgr*
EMP: 1000
SALES (corp-wide): 22B **Publicly Held**
Web: www.clevelandcliffs.com
SIC: 3312 Blast furnaces and steel mills
HQ: Cleveland-Cliffs Steel Llc
1 S Dearborn St Fl 19
Chicago IL 60603
312 346-0300

(G-3000)
CLEVELAND-CLIFFS STEEL LLC
Also Called: Indiana Harbor
3210 Watling St (46312-1716)
PHONE..................................219 399-1200
Ladale Comb, *Manager*
EMP: 3435
SALES (corp-wide): 22B **Publicly Held**
Web: www.clevelandcliffs.com

SIC: 3312 Blast furnaces and steel mills
HQ: Cleveland-Cliffs Steel Llc
1 S Dearborn St Fl 19
Chicago IL 60603
312 346-0300

(G-3001)
CLEVELND-CLFFS MNORCA MINE INC (DH)
Also Called: Mittal Steel -Ihw- 3 Sp
3210 Watling St (46312-1716)
PHONE..................................219 399-1200
Peter D Southwich, *Ch Bd*
Madhu Ranade, *Pr*
Edward C Mccarthy, *Sec*
Gary Krall, *CEO*
◆ **EMP:** 5 **EST:** 1974
SALES (est): 236.36MM
SALES (corp-wide): 22B **Publicly Held**
SIC: 1011 Open pit iron ore mining, nec
HQ: Cleveland-Cliffs Steel Llc
1 S Dearborn St Fl 19
Chicago IL 60603
312 346-0300

(G-3002)
D & D TIRE SHOP LLC
Also Called: Dub City Tires
4707 Tod Ave (46312-3302)
PHONE..................................219 354-0402
Enrique Peralta, *Pr*
EMP: 9 **EST:** 2014
SALES (est): 132.77K **Privately Held**
SIC: 5531 7534 Automotive tires; Tire repair shop

(G-3003)
DIAMOND WATERJET
3468 Watling St (46312-1709)
PHONE..................................219 713-1727
EMP: 5 **EST:** 2017
SALES (est): 132.14K **Privately Held**
Web: www.diamondwaterjet.com
SIC: 3441 Fabricated structural metal

(G-3004)
EAST CHICAGO SHEARING
4303 Kennedy Ave (46312-2723)
PHONE..................................219 398-2933
EMP: 4 **EST:** 2016
SALES (est): 54.36K **Privately Held**
SIC: 3499 Fabricated metal products, nec

(G-3005)
EL POPULAR INC
910 E Chicago Ave (46312-3513)
P.O. Box 328 (46312-0328)
PHONE..................................219 397-3728
Edward Garza, *Pr*
EMP: 12 **EST:** 2002
SALES (est): 1.78MM **Privately Held**
Web: www.elpopular.com
SIC: 2011 2099 2035 2066 Meat packing plants; Seasonings and spices; Seasonings, meat sauces (except tomato and dry); Chocolate and cocoa products

(G-3006)
ELECTRIC COATING TECH LLC
Also Called: Material Sciences
4407 Railroad Ave (46312)
PHONE..................................219 378-1930
Steve Tatalovich, *
Charlie Keene, *
James L Todd, *
▼ **EMP:** 36 **EST:** 2003
SQ FT: 170,000
SALES (est): 9.44MM
SALES (corp-wide): 120.84MM **Privately Held**
Web: www.materialsciencescorp.com

SIC: 3479 Galvanizing of iron, steel, or end-formed products
PA: Material Sciences Corporation
6855 Commerce Blvd
Canton MI 48187
734 207-4444

(G-3007)
ENVIRI CORPORATION
5222 Indianapolis Blvd (46312-3838)
PHONE..................................219 397-0200
Henry W Knueppel, *Brnch Mgr*
EMP: 10
SALES (corp-wide): 2.07B **Publicly Held**
Web: www.enviri.com
SIC: 4953 2899 Refuse systems; Chemical preparations, nec
PA: Enviri Corporation
100-120 N 18th St # 17
Philadelphia PA 19103
267 857-8715

(G-3008)
FRIEDMAN INDUSTRIES INC
4303 Kennedy Ave (46312-2723)
PHONE..................................219 392-3400
Michael J Taylor, *Pr*
EMP: 35
SQ FT: 140,000
SALES (corp-wide): 516.25MM **Publicly Held**
Web: www.friedmanindustries.com
SIC: 5051 3316 Steel; Sheet, steel, cold-rolled, nec: from purchased hot-rolled
PA: Friedman Industries, Incorporated
1121 Judson Rd Ste 124
Longview TX 75601
903 758-3431

(G-3009)
GANNON MTAL FBRCATORS ERECTORS
418 E Chicago Ave (46312-3544)
P.O. Box 499 (46312-0499)
PHONE..................................219 398-0299
Nicholas M Paul, *Pr*
Joseph E Fraley, *Sec*
EMP: 9 **EST:** 1957
SQ FT: 25,000
SALES (est): 919.92K **Privately Held**
SIC: 3441 Fabricated structural metal

(G-3010)
GEMS QUALITY EXTENSIONS LLC
1211 W 149th St Apt 2f (46312-6420)
PHONE..................................219 501-6320
EMP: 1
SALES (est): 69.27K **Privately Held**
SIC: 2844 7389 Hair preparations, including shampoos; Business Activities at Non-Commercial Site

(G-3011)
GENERAL MACHINE SOLUTIONS INC
3550 Canal St (46312-1604)
PHONE..................................219 378-1700
Gail Moniuszko, *Prin*
EMP: 16 **EST:** 2013
SALES (est): 460.35K **Privately Held**
Web: www.generalmachinesolutions.com
SIC: 3599 Machine shop, jobbing and repair

(G-3012)
GRC ENTERPRISES INC
Also Called: Taylor Chain
3477 Watling St (46312-1708)
P.O. Box 481 (46312-0481)
PHONE..................................219 932-2220
Gerhard Volkmann, *Pr*
Henry Walma, *Contrlr*
EMP: 24 **EST:** 1983

GEOGRAPHIC SECTION

East Chicago - Lake County (G-3035)

SQ FT: 5,000
SALES (est): 1.56MM **Privately Held**
SIC: 3496 Chain, welded

(G-3013)
GREEN LAKE TUBE LLC (PA)
Also Called: Steel Manufacturing
4500 Euclid Ave (46312-3079)
PHONE..............................219 397-0495
EMP: 15 **EST:** 2010
SQ FT: 100,000
SALES (est): 2.82MM **Privately Held**
SIC: 3498 Tube fabricating (contract bending and shaping)

(G-3014)
HADADY MACHINING COMPANY INC (PA)
4809 Tod Ave (46312)
PHONE..............................708 474-8620
Peter Lanman, *Pr*
EMP: 12 **EST:** 1947
SALES (est): 4.95MM
SALES (corp-wide): 4.95MM **Privately Held**
Web: www.hadadyinc.com
SIC: 3599 3823 3593 Machine shop, jobbing and repair; Process control instruments; Fluid power cylinders and actuators

(G-3015)
HEIDTMAN STEEL PRODUCTS INC
4407 Railroad Ave (46312-4337)
PHONE..............................219 256-7426
EMP: 40
SALES (corp-wide): 230.06MM **Privately Held**
Web: www.heidtman.com
SIC: 5051 3316 Steel; Strip, steel, cold-rolled, nec: from purchased hot-rolled,
HQ: Heidtman Steel Products, Inc.
   2401 Front St
   Toledo OH 43605
   419 691-4646

(G-3016)
HEREXTENSIONS LLC ✪
4728 Baring Ave (46312-5302)
PHONE..............................219 466-4273
Lakisha Braboy, *CEO*
EMP: 1 **EST:** 2022
SALES (est): 69.27K **Privately Held**
SIC: 3999 7389 Hair and hair-based products ; Business Activities at Non-Commercial Site

(G-3017)
HOLCIM (US) INC
3210 Watling St (46312-1716)
P.O. Box 2974 (46312-7974)
PHONE..............................219 378-1193
Shawn Blacklock, *Proj Mgr*
EMP: 8
Web: www.holcim.us
SIC: 3273 3272 3271 1442 Ready-mixed concrete; Concrete products, nec; Blocks, concrete or cinder: standard; Construction sand and gravel
HQ: Holcim (Us) Inc.
   8700 W Bryn Mawr Ave Ste
   Chicago IL 60631

(G-3018)
HUMES & BERG MFG CO INC
4801 Railroad Ave (46312-3359)
PHONE..............................219 391-5880
Irwin Berg, *Pr*
Michael Berg, *Sec*
▲ **EMP:** 9 **EST:** 1935
SQ FT: 100,000
SALES (est): 964.97K **Privately Held**
Web: www.humesandberg.com
SIC: 3931 3161 Stands, music; Musical instrument cases

(G-3019)
ILLIANA GRINDING MACHINING INC
4450 Euclid Ave (46312-3045)
PHONE..............................219 306-0253
Ray Hunt, *Pr*
EMP: 7 **EST:** 1992
SALES (est): 487.61K **Privately Held**
SIC: 7389 3599 3423 Grinding, precision: commercial or industrial; Machine and other job shop work; Knives, agricultural or industrial

(G-3020)
INDIANA ARCELORMITTAL HARBOR LLC
Also Called: Arcelormittal Indiana Harbor W
3210 Watling St (46312-1716)
P.O. Box 2928 (46304-5428)
PHONE..............................219 399-1200
▲ **EMP:** 3435
SIC: 3312 Blast furnaces and steel mills

(G-3021)
INDIANA HARBOR COKE COMPANY LP
3210 Watling St (46312-1716)
P.O. Box 240 (46312-0240)
PHONE..............................219 397-5769
Frederick A Henderson, *CEO*
Kenneth J Schuett, *CEO*
▲ **EMP:** 122 **EST:** 1996
SALES (est): 24.99MM **Publicly Held**
SIC: 3312 Blast furnaces and steel mills
PA: Suncoke Energy, Inc.
   1011 Wrrnville Rd Ste 600
   Lisle IL 60532

(G-3022)
INDIANA PALLET COMPANY
724 E Chicago Ave (46312-6540)
P.O. Box 398 (46312-0398)
PHONE..............................219 398-4223
Sergio Magana, *Pr*
EMP: 26 **EST:** 1995
SQ FT: 250,000
SALES (est): 2.23MM **Privately Held**
Web: www.indianapallet.net
SIC: 2448 Pallets, wood

(G-3023)
INSIGHT EQUITY HOLDINGS LLC
4407 Railroad Ave (46312-4337)
PHONE..............................219 378-1930
Patrick J Murley, *CEO*
EMP: 405
Web: www.insightequity.com
SIC: 3312 Sheet or strip, steel, cold-rolled: own hot-rolled
PA: Insight Equity Holdings Llc
   1400 Civic Pl Ste 250
   Southlake TX 76092

(G-3024)
KEMIRA WATER SOLUTIONS INC
3761 Canal St (46312-1607)
PHONE..............................219 397-2646
Jerry Tenny, *CFO*
EMP: 52
SALES (corp-wide): 3.68B **Privately Held**
Web: www.kemira.com
SIC: 2819 Industrial inorganic chemicals, nec
HQ: Kemira Water Solutions, Inc.
   200 Gllria Pkwy Se Ste 15
   Atlanta GA 30339

(G-3025)
KOCSIS BROTHERS MACHINE CO
4321 Railroad Ave (46312-3455)
PHONE..............................219 397-8400
EMP: 1
SALES (corp-wide): 24.99MM **Privately Held**
Web: www.kocsisbros.com
SIC: 3599 7692 Machine shop, jobbing and repair; Welding repair
PA: Kocsis Brothers Machine Company
   11755 S Austin Ave
   Alsip IL 60803
   708 597-8110

(G-3026)
L&N SUPPLY LLC
4016 Deodar St (46312-2809)
P.O. Box 1850 (46384-1850)
PHONE..............................219 397-9500
EMP: 2 **EST:** 2011
SALES (est): 157.71K **Privately Held**
Web: www.nedealers.com
SIC: 3949 Shooting equipment and supplies, general

(G-3027)
LINDE INC
Praxair
4550 Kennedy Ave (46312-2736)
P.O. Box 501 (46312-0501)
PHONE..............................219 391-5100
Me Benefiel, *Mgr*
EMP: 25
Web: www.lindeus.com
SIC: 2813 Industrial gases
HQ: Linde Inc.
   10 Riverview Dr
   Danbury CT 06810
   203 837-2000

(G-3028)
LYONDLLBSELL ADVNCED PLYMERS I
4404 Euclid Ave (46312-3045)
PHONE..............................219 392-3375
EMP: 51
Web: www.lyondellbasell.com
SIC: 2869 Industrial organic chemicals, nec
HQ: Lyondellbasell Advanced Polymers Inc.
   1221 Mckinney St Ste 300
   Houston TX 77010
   713 309-7200

(G-3029)
METAL SERVICES LLC
3001 Dickey Rd (46312-1610)
P.O. Box 3070 (46312-8070)
PHONE..............................219 397-0650
Ed Front, *Brnch Mgr*
EMP: 1
SALES (corp-wide): 405.6MM **Privately Held**
Web: www.phoenixglobal.com
SIC: 3295 Perlite, aggregate or expanded
HQ: Metal Services Llc
   4 Radnor Corp Ctr Ste 520
   Radnor PA 19087

(G-3030)
NATIONAL MATERIAL COMPANY LLC
4506 Cline Ave (46312-3181)
PHONE..............................219 397-5088
EMP: 23
SALES (corp-wide): 582.04MM **Privately Held**
Web: www.nmlp.com
SIC: 3315 3341 3399 Wire, ferrous/iron; Aluminum smelting and refining (secondary) ; Aluminum atomized powder
HQ: National Material Company, L.L.C.
   1965 Pratt Blvd
   Elk Grove Village IL 60007

(G-3031)
NATIONAL MATERIAL LP
National Material Processing
4506 Cline Ave (46312-3181)
P.O. Box 29 (46312-0029)
PHONE..............................219 397-5088
Chris Sekella, *Mgr*
EMP: 119
SQ FT: 60,000
SALES (corp-wide): 582.04MM **Privately Held**
Web: www.interstatesteelco.com
SIC: 3471 5051 3312 Plating and polishing; Metals service centers and offices; Blast furnaces and steel mills
PA: National Material L.P.
   1965 Pratt Blvd
   Elk Grove Village IL 60007
   847 806-7200

(G-3032)
NEW STAR METALS INC
Also Called: Material Sciences
4407 Railroad Ave Ste 3a (46312)
PHONE..............................219 378-1930
▲ **EMP:** 20 **EST:** 1982
SQ FT: 205,000
SALES (est): 2.04MM **Privately Held**
Web: www.materialsciencescorp.com
SIC: 3479 Painting of metal products

(G-3033)
NORTHWEST INDUS SPECIALIST INC
4333 Indianapolis Blvd (46312-2627)
PHONE..............................219 397-7446
Joseph Wargo, *Pr*
Roger Wargo Junior, *VP*
Timothy King, *Treas*
EMP: 18 **EST:** 1981
SQ FT: 8,000
SALES (est): 2.27MM **Privately Held**
Web: www.nissigns.com
SIC: 5099 3993 Signs, except electric; Signs and advertising specialties

(G-3034)
PINDER POLYURETHANE & PLAS INC
481 E 151st St (46312-3844)
P.O. Box 433 (46312-0433)
PHONE..............................219 397-8248
Walter Tokarz, *Pr*
Janice Gaskill, *VP*
EMP: 6 **EST:** 1984
SQ FT: 15,000
SALES (est): 901.6K **Privately Held**
Web: www.pinderpolyurethane.com
SIC: 2851 5169 Polyurethane coatings; Polyurethane products

(G-3035)
PRECISION SURVEILLANCE CORP
Also Called: PSC
3468 Watling St (46312-1709)
PHONE..............................219 397-4295
Paul Smith, *Pr*
Christopher Cox, *
Pat Furlan, *
EMP: 50 **EST:** 1986
SQ FT: 40,000
SALES (est): 8.02MM **Privately Held**
Web: www.pscnuclear.com
SIC: 1796 1791 3441 8711 Machine moving and rigging; Iron work, structural; Fabricated structural metal; Structural engineering

---

(PA)=Parent Co (HQ)=Headquarters
✪ = New Business established in last 2 years

East Chicago - Lake County (G-3036)

(G-3036)
PROFESSNAL LOCOMOTIVE SVCS INC
4949 Huish Dr (46312-3768)
PHONE..................219 398-9123
EMP: 24 EST: 1996
SQ FT: 5,000
SALES (est): 2.15MM Privately Held
Web: www.plsworks.com
SIC: 4789 3743 Railroad maintenance and repair services; Locomotives and parts

(G-3037)
PROGRESS RAIL SERVICES CORP
Locomotive & Transit
175 W Chicago Ave (46312-3201)
PHONE..................219 397-5326
Mike Role, *Brnch Mgr*
EMP: 133
SALES (corp-wide): 67.06B Publicly Held
Web: www.progressrailstore.com
SIC: 4789 3312 7389 Railroad maintenance and repair services; Structural and rail mill products; Metal cutting services
HQ: Progress Rail Services Corporation
 1600 Progress Dr
 Albertville AL 35950
 800 476-8769

(G-3038)
REFRACTORY SERVICE CORPORATION (PA)
Also Called: R S C
4900 Cline Ave (46312-3559)
P.O. Box 2276 (46312-7276)
PHONE..................219 397-7108
Samuel F Bianchi, *Pr*
Laura Eikenmeyer, *
Cindy Bianchi, *
▲ EMP: 40 EST: 1980
SQ FT: 50,000
SALES (est): 5.91MM
SALES (corp-wide): 5.91MM Privately Held
Web: www.refractoryservice.net
SIC: 3297 7699 Castable refractories, nonclay; Industrial equipment services

(G-3039)
REGION AUTO DETAILING LLC
4317 Ivy St (46312-3026)
PHONE..................219 427-6318
EMP: 2 EST: 2020
SALES (est): 79.98K Privately Held
Web: www.regionautodetailing219.com
SIC: 3589 Car washing machinery

(G-3040)
ROBINSON STEEL CO INC
4303 Kennedy Ave (46312-2723)
P.O. Box 2854 (46312-7854)
PHONE..................219 398-4600
EMP: 250
SIC: 3312 5051 3444 3443 Sheet or strip, steel, hot-rolled; Metals service centers and offices; Sheet metalwork; Fabricated plate work (boiler shop)

(G-3041)
SAFETY-KLEEN SYSTEMS INC
Also Called: Safety-Kleen
601 Riley Rd (46312-1638)
PHONE..................219 397-1131
EMP: 18
SALES (corp-wide): 5.41B Publicly Held
Web: www.safety-kleen.com
SIC: 3559 Degreasing machines, automotive and industrial
HQ: Safety-Kleen Systems, Inc.
 6600 Chase Oaks Blvd
 Plano TX 75023
 972 265-2000

(G-3042)
SUNCOKE ENERGY INC
3210 Watling St (46312-1716)
PHONE..................219 397-0243
EMP: 1
Web: www.suncoke.com
SIC: 3312 Blast furnaces and steel mills
PA: Suncoke Energy, Inc.
 1011 Wrrnville Rd Ste 600
 Lisle IL 60532

(G-3043)
SUNCOKE LAKE TERMINAL LLC
3210 Watling St (46312-1716)
PHONE..................630 824-1963
EMP: 10 EST: 2013
SALES (est): 2.42MM Privately Held
Web: www.suncoke.com
SIC: 1389 Construction, repair, and dismantling services

(G-3044)
TMS INTERNATIONAL LLC
3001 Dickey Rd (46312-1610)
PHONE..................219 881-0155
EMP: 14
Web: www.tmsinternational.com
SIC: 3312 Blast furnaces and steel mills
HQ: Tms International, Llc
 Southside Wrks Bldg 1 3f
 Pittsburgh PA 15203
 412 678-6141

(G-3045)
TRADEBE GP
4343 Kennedy Ave (46312-2723)
PHONE..................800 388-7242
EMP: 742
SIC: 4953 7699 1389 Hazardous waste collection and disposal; Ship boiler and tank cleaning and repair, contractors; Lease tanks, oil field: erecting, cleaning, and repairing

(G-3046)
TRADEBE INDUSTRIAL SVCS LLC
Also Called: Tradebe
1433 E 83rd Ave Ste 200 (46312)
PHONE..................800 388-7242
Victor Creixell, *CEO*
Sergio Nusimovich Kolodny, *Prin*
EMP: 100 EST: 1981
SQ FT: 35,000
SALES (est): 9.78MM Privately Held
Web: www.tradebe.com
SIC: 7699 1389 Ship boiler and tank cleaning and repair, contractors; Lease tanks, oil field: erecting, cleaning, and repairing
HQ: Tradebe Environmental Services, Llc
 1433 E 83rd Ave Ste 200
 Merrillville IN 46410

(G-3047)
TRI-STATE METAL INC
220 W Chicago Ave (46312-3203)
PHONE..................219 397-0470
Salvadore Ortiz, *Pr*
Marrietta Peek, *
EMP: 25 EST: 1995
SALES (est): 943.7K Privately Held
Web: www.tri-statemetal.com
SIC: 3398 7389 Metal heat treating; Metal cutting services

(G-3048)
TRINITY PRODUCTS LLC
425 W 151st St (46312-3855)
PHONE..................636 639-5244
Chad Duffin, *Brnch Mgr*
EMP: 4 EST: 2020
SALES (est): 248.64K Privately Held
Web: www.trinityproducts.com
SIC: 3312 Blast furnaces and steel mills

(G-3049)
UNITED STATES GYPSUM COMPANY
301 Riley Rd (46312-1697)
PHONE..................219 392-4600
Neil Garceau, *Brnch Mgr*
EMP: 99
SALES (corp-wide): 16B Privately Held
Web: www.usg.com
SIC: 3275 Gypsum products
HQ: United States Gypsum Company
 550 W Adams St
 Chicago IL 60661
 312 606-4000

(G-3050)
UNITED STATES STEEL CORP
101 E 129th St (46312-1650)
PHONE..................219 391-2045
Dennis Henry, *Brnch Mgr*
EMP: 10
SALES (corp-wide): 18.05B Publicly Held
Web: www.ussteel.com
SIC: 3325 3312 Steel foundries, nec; Blast furnaces and steel mills
PA: United States Steel Corp
 600 Grant St
 Pittsburgh PA 15219
 412 433-1121

(G-3051)
UNIVERSAL SERVICES INC
Also Called: Patco Distribution
475 E 151st St (46312-3844)
P.O. Box 500 (46312-0500)
PHONE..................219 397-4373
Rich Haan, *Mgr*
EMP: 4 EST: 1988
SQ FT: 43,960
SALES (est): 485.42K Privately Held
SIC: 2911 2899 Greases, lubricating; Antifreeze compounds

(G-3052)
US METALS INC
425 W 151st St Ste 2 (46312-3856)
PHONE..................219 398-1350
Bob Qualey, *Brnch Mgr*
EMP: 5
SALES (corp-wide): 40.97MM Privately Held
Web: www.usmetals.com
SIC: 3449 5051 Bars, concrete reinforcing: fabricated steel; Metals service centers and offices
PA: U.S. Metals, Inc.
 19102 Gundle Rd
 Houston TX 77073
 281 443-7473

(G-3053)
VEOLIA WTS USA INC
Also Called: General Electric Betz
3210 Watling St (46312-1716)
PHONE..................219 397-0554
George Grote, *Mgr*
EMP: 2
Web: www.watertechnologies.com
SIC: 3295 Minerals, ground or treated
HQ: Veolia Wts Usa, Inc.
 3600 Horizon Blvd
 Trevose PA 19053
 866 439-2837

(G-3054)
VIDIMOS INC
3858 Indiana Harbor Dr (46312-2349)
P.O. Box 480 (46312-0480)
PHONE..................219 397-2728
Alfred Scott Vidimos, *Pr*
Christopher E Lawes, *
Adam Vidimos, *
Dan Vidimos, *
EMP: 80 EST: 1946
SQ FT: 54,000
SALES (est): 19.52MM Privately Held
Web: www.vidimos.com
SIC: 1761 3441 Sheet metal work, nec; Fabricated structural metal

(G-3055)
W R GRACE & CO-CONN
Also Called: W R Grace Davison Chemical Div
5215 Kennedy Ave (46312-3805)
PHONE..................219 398-2040
Patricia Winkley, *Mgr*
EMP: 27
SALES (corp-wide): 6.35B Privately Held
Web: www.grace.com
SIC: 2819 Industrial inorganic chemicals, nec
HQ: W. R. Grace & Co.-Conn.
 7500 Grace Dr
 Columbia MD 21044

(G-3056)
WARE INDUSTRIES INC
Also Called: WARE INDUSTRIES INC.
4245 Railroad Ave (46312-2549)
PHONE..................219 378-7100
Jim Watson, *Brnch Mgr*
EMP: 17
SALES (corp-wide): 120.44MM Privately Held
Web: www.marinoware.com
SIC: 3441 Fabricated structural metal
PA: Ware Industries, Inc.
 400 Metuchen Rd
 South Plainfield NJ 07080
 908 757-9000

(G-3057)
WINDY CITY COML TIRE & SVC LLC
444 E Chicago Ave (46312-3544)
PHONE..................773 530-1246
Jesus Velasquez, *Managing Member*
EMP: 2 EST: 2012
SALES (est): 201.72K Privately Held
SIC: 5531 7534 Automotive tires; Tire retreading and repair shops

(G-3058)
WORKING PITBULL KENNELL
4319 Indianapolis Blvd (46312-2627)
PHONE..................708 762-9725
Damon Holmes, *Owner*
EMP: 1 EST: 2019
SALES (est): 42.55K Privately Held
SIC: 2326 2331 Men's and boy's work clothing; Women's and misses' blouses and shirts

Eaton
Delaware County

(G-3059)
ARROWHEAD PLASTIC ENGRG INC
Also Called: Arrowhead Plastic Products
1155 N Hartford St (47338-8774)
P.O. Box 75 (47338-0075)
PHONE..................765 396-9113
EMP: 10
SALES (corp-wide): 10.53MM Privately Held

Web: www.arrowheadinc.com
SIC: 5162 3089 Plastics materials and basic shapes; Thermoformed finished plastics products, nec
PA: Arrowhead Plastic Engineering, Inc.
2909 S Hoyt Ave
Muncie IN 47302
765 286-0533

(G-3060)
EATON SEPTIC TANK COMPANY
14601 N State Road 3n (47338-8936)
PHONE.................................765 396-3275
Jack Ashcraft, Owner
EMP: 2 EST: 1978
SALES (est): 176.61K Privately Held
SIC: 3272 1711 Septic tanks, concrete; Septic system construction

(G-3061)
EDEN FOODS INC
Meridian Foods Division
201 E Babb Rd (47338-8807)
P.O. Box 155 (47338-0155)
PHONE.................................765 396-3344
Terry Evans, Genl Mgr
EMP: 33
SALES (corp-wide): 25.14MM Privately Held
Web: store.edenfoods.com
SIC: 2032 2033 Beans and bean sprouts, canned, jarred, etc.; Canned fruits and specialties
PA: Eden Foods, Inc.
701 Tecumseh Rd
Clinton MI 49236
517 456-7424

(G-3062)
GRAPHIC MENUS INC
Also Called: GMI
16555 N State Road 3n (47338-8944)
P.O. Box 247 (47338-0247)
PHONE.................................765 396-3003
Robert Schwindt, Pr
EMP: 16 EST: 1967
SQ FT: 5,000
SALES (est): 1.6MM Privately Held
Web: www.graphicmenus.com
SIC: 2752 2759 Menus, lithographed; Commercial printing, nec

(G-3063)
MERIT TOOL & MANUFACTURING INC
120 N Hartford St (47338)
P.O. Box 365 (47338-0365)
PHONE.................................765 396-9566
Phillip J Reber, Pr
Janet L Reber, Sec
EMP: 10 EST: 1987
SQ FT: 4,500
SALES (est): 896.89K Privately Held
Web: www.merittool.com
SIC: 3599 3544 3545 Machine shop, jobbing and repair; Jigs and fixtures; Gauges (machine tool accessories)

(G-3064)
OX INDUSTRIES INC
800 S Romy St Ste A (47338-8822)
PHONE.................................765 396-3317
Timothy Hagdnduch, Genl Mgr
EMP: 1
SALES (corp-wide): 117.54MM Privately Held
Web: www.oxindustries.com
SIC: 2631 Paperboard mills
PA: Ox Industries, Inc.
600 W Elm Ave
Hanover PA 17331

717 698-3329

(G-3065)
PALMETTO PLANTERS LLC
1153 N Hartford St (47338-8774)
P.O. Box 512 (47338-0512)
PHONE.................................765 396-4446
Anita Kishel, Pr
EMP: 6 EST: 2009
SALES (est): 124.2K Privately Held
Web: www.palmettoplanters.com
SIC: 3229 Glass fiber products

Economy
Wayne County

(G-3066)
H & H DESIGN & TOOL INC
222 2nd St (47339-9748)
P.O. Box 157 (47339-0157)
PHONE.................................765 886-6199
Jeff Himelick, Pr
Gene Himelick, VP
Leora Himelick, Treas
EMP: 8 EST: 1975
SQ FT: 3,000
SALES (est): 791.5K Privately Held
Web: www.hhdesignandtool.com
SIC: 3599 3535 3544 7692 Machine shop, jobbing and repair; Conveyors and conveying equipment; Special dies and tools; Welding repair

Edinburgh
Johnson County

(G-3067)
AMOS-HILL ASSOCIATES INC
112 Shelby Ave (46124-1042)
P.O. Box 7 (46124-0007)
PHONE.................................812 526-2671
William A Costoplos, Pr
Susanne Renner, *
◆ EMP: 150 EST: 1982
SALES (est): 23.23MM
SALES (corp-wide): 824.31K Privately Held
Web: www.koppensteiner.com
SIC: 2435 Veneer stock, hardwood
PA: Koppensteiner Furniere Gmbh & Co. Kg
Unterer Muhlweg 39
Wannweil BW 72827
712 151-0710

(G-3068)
BEACON INDUSTRIES INC
912 S Walnut St (46124-2001)
P.O. Box 355 (46124-0355)
PHONE.................................812 526-0100
Larry C Sparks, Pr
Michael Senteney, *
Christopher Senteney, *
EMP: 45 EST: 1989
SQ FT: 51,000
SALES (est): 5.25MM Privately Held
Web: www.beacon-industries.com
SIC: 3479 Coating of metals and formed products

(G-3069)
BO-WITT PRODUCTS INC
500 N Walnut St (46124-1099)
PHONE.................................812 526-5561
Jon Jacobson, Pr
William C Bobbs Junior, Prin
Julia Beaman, Prin
EMP: 35 EST: 1960

SQ FT: 15,000
SALES (est): 4.4MM Privately Held
Web: www.bowitt.com
SIC: 3644 Insulators and insulation materials, electrical

(G-3070)
CENTER LINE MOLD & TOOL INC
703 S Eisenhower Dr (46124-1809)
PHONE.................................812 526-0970
Scott Bringle, Pr
EMP: 15 EST: 1990
SQ FT: 13,000
SALES (est): 1.63MM Privately Held
Web: www.centerlinemold.com
SIC: 3544 Special dies and tools

(G-3071)
CHALLENGE PLASTIC PRODUCTS INC
110 W Industrial Dr (46124-1457)
P.O. Box 278 (46124-0278)
PHONE.................................812 526-0582
William Davis, Pr
William R Davis, VP
▲ EMP: 11 EST: 1990
SQ FT: 33,000
SALES (est): 1.75MM Privately Held
Web: www.fishingbuckets.com
SIC: 3089 Injection molding of plastics

(G-3072)
CL TECH INC
216 N Main St (46124-1027)
P.O. Box 277 (46124-0277)
PHONE.................................812 526-0995
Fred C Stadler, Pr
Roberta S Hehman, VP
Vaughan Hehman, Treas
EMP: 9 EST: 1988
SQ FT: 4,000
SALES (est): 1.34MM Privately Held
SIC: 3599 3544 Custom machinery; Jigs and fixtures

(G-3073)
COUNTRY COMPONENTS INC
8990 S Edinburgh Rd (46124-9451)
PHONE.................................812 345-9594
EMP: 3 EST: 2014
SALES (est): 222.06K Privately Held
Web: www.countrycomponents.com
SIC: 3599 Machine shop, jobbing and repair

(G-3074)
DANZER SERVICES INC (PA)
206 S Holland St (46124-1431)
P.O. Box 8 (46124-0008)
PHONE.................................812 526-2601
Hans-joachim Danzer, CEO
Dan Sullivan, Pr
Terry Simmonds, VP
Mike Bell, Treas
Dana Whitlock, Sec
◆ EMP: 2 EST: 1993
SALES (est): 72.35MM
SALES (corp-wide): 72.35MM Privately Held
Web: www.danzer.com
SIC: 2435 Hardwood veneer and plywood

(G-3075)
DANZER VENEER AMERICAS INC
206 S Holland St (46124-1431)
PHONE.................................812 526-6789
Greg Lottes, Pr
EMP: 12
Web: www.danzer.com
SIC: 2435 Hardwood veneer and plywood
HQ: Danzer Veneer Americas, Inc.
119 A I D Dr

Darlington PA 16115

(G-3076)
DAVIS MACHINE AND TOOL INC
920 S Walnut St (46124-2001)
P.O. Box 157 (46124-0157)
PHONE.................................812 526-2674
Elby Mcgaha, Pr
EMP: 10 EST: 1982
SQ FT: 15,000
SALES (est): 766.44K Privately Held
Web: www.indianagundrilling.com
SIC: 3544 3542 Industrial molds; Machine tools, metal forming type

(G-3077)
DITECH INC (PA)
1000 S Main St (46124-1377)
P.O. Box 125 (46124-0125)
PHONE.................................812 526-0850
Nathan J Dillingham, Pr
Wilma Dillingham, VP
Christopher A Dillingham, VP
Kimberly Bieker, VP
Timothy L Dillingham, VP
▲ EMP: 42 EST: 1992
SQ FT: 50,000
SALES (est): 10.05MM Privately Held
Web: www.ditech-hr.com
SIC: 7389 3444 8742 Packaging and labeling services; Sheet metalwork; Manufacturing management consultant

(G-3078)
DITECH INC
1151 S Walnut St (46124-9037)
PHONE.................................812 379-9756
EMP: 33
Web: www.ditech-hr.com
SIC: 7692 Welding repair
PA: Ditech Inc.
1000 S Main St
Edinburgh IN 46124

(G-3079)
DMB EMBROIDERY LLC
111 E Center Cross St (46124-1201)
PHONE.................................812 592-3301
Laura Burton, Owner
EMP: 1 EST: 2010
SALES (est): 61.92K Privately Held
Web: www.dmbembroidery.com
SIC: 2395 Embroidery products, except Schiffli machine

(G-3080)
DRUG PLASTICS CLOSURES INC
2875 W 800 N (46124-9572)
PHONE.................................812 526-0555
EMP: 24
SALES (corp-wide): 91.9MM Privately Held
Web: www.drugplastics.com
SIC: 3089 3466 Caps, plastics; Crowns and closures
HQ: Drug Plastics Closures, Inc.
850 Montgomery Ave
Boyertown PA 19512
610 367-5000

(G-3081)
DYNO ONE INC
14671 N 250 W (46124-9064)
PHONE.................................812 526-0500
Bill J Willis, Pr
Sandra K Willis, *
EMP: 24 EST: 1983
SQ FT: 76,000
SALES (est): 4.49MM Privately Held
Web: www.dyno-one.com

Edinburgh - Johnson County (G-3082) — GEOGRAPHIC SECTION

SIC: 3829 Measuring and controlling devices, nec

(G-3082)
EDINBURGH CONNECTOR CO LLC
Also Called: Connectronics
908 S Walnut St (46124-2001)
P.O. Box 246 (46124-0246)
PHONE..................812 526-8801
Enrique Morales, *CEO*
Megan Morales, *
EMP: 40 EST: 1985
SQ FT: 20,000
SALES (est): 5.49MM
SALES (corp-wide): 5.49MM **Privately Held**
Web: www.customrfconnectors.com
SIC: 3678 Electronic connectors
PA: Qnnect, Llc
　　 1382 W Jackson St
　　 Painesville OH 44077
　　 864 275-8970

(G-3083)
EDINBURGH SIGNS & GRAPICS
500 1/2 W Center Cross St (46124-9701)
PHONE..................812 526-6626
EMP: 1 EST: 2016
SALES (est): 46.08K **Privately Held**
SIC: 3993 Signs and advertising specialties

(G-3084)
G UNIT CORE INC
1015 S Walnut St (46124-9501)
PHONE..................812 526-2080
Anita Hancock, *Pr*
EMP: 7 EST: 2014
SALES (est): 213.51K **Privately Held**
Web: www.gunitcore.com
SIC: 3829 Measuring and controlling devices, nec

(G-3085)
GEORG UTZ INC
14000 N 250 W (46124-9070)
PHONE..................812 526-2240
Axel Ritzberger, *CEO*
Bruno Bucher, *
▲ EMP: 25 EST: 2003
SALES (est): 6.53MM **Privately Held**
Web: www.utzgroup.com
SIC: 7389 5131 2542 4225 Authors' agents and brokers; Textiles, woven, nec; Postal lock boxes, mail racks, and related products; Warehousing, self storage
HQ: Georg Utz Ag
　　 Augraben 4
　　 Bremgarten AG 5620

(G-3086)
HISADA AMERICA INC
1191 S Walnut St (46124-9015)
PHONE..................812 526-0756
Hiroyuki Tsutsui, *Pr*
Akio Saito, *
Makoto Fukui, *
Toro Mituhara, *
Hiro Tsutsui, *
▲ EMP: 250 EST: 1997
SQ FT: 72,000
SALES (est): 26.64MM **Privately Held**
Web: www.hisadaamerica.com
SIC: 3714 Motor vehicle parts and accessories
PA: Hisada Co.,Ltd.
　　 11, Saburo, Satocho
　　 Anjo AIC 446-0

(G-3087)
HOOSIER TOOL & DIE CO INC
Also Called: H T D
224 N Pleasant St (46124-1300)
PHONE..................812 376-8286
◆ EMP: 55
Web: www.htdteam.com
SIC: 3545 3544 Machine tool accessories; Special dies, tools, jigs, and fixtures

(G-3088)
K & L MACHINING INC
6973 S Us Highway 31 (46124-1068)
PHONE..................812 526-4840
Pete Knue, *Pr*
EMP: 4 EST: 2006
SQ FT: 2,500
SALES (est): 448K **Privately Held**
Web: www.klmachining.net
SIC: 3599 Machine shop, jobbing and repair

(G-3089)
KRAMER FURN & CAB MAKERS INC
12600 N Presidential Way (46124-9069)
PHONE..................812 526-2711
TOLL FREE: 800
Thomas H Kramer, *Pr*
EMP: 22 EST: 1972
SQ FT: 25,000
SALES (est): 784.5K **Privately Held**
Web: www.kramermakers.com
SIC: 2522 2511 2434 Office bookcases, wallcases and partitions, except wood; Wood household furniture; Wood kitchen cabinets

(G-3090)
LB MOLD INC
Also Called: Lb Mold
1031 S Main St (46124-1378)
PHONE..................812 526-2030
EMP: 22 EST: 1995
SQ FT: 15,000
SALES (est): 1.45MM **Privately Held**
SIC: 3544 Industrial molds

(G-3091)
MA METAL CO INC
216 N Main St (46124-1027)
PHONE..................812 526-2666
Peter Ariens, *CEO*
Robert Bosar, *
Ronnie Burton, *
Sumeet Dheer, *
EMP: 35 EST: 1946
SALES (est): 4.2MM **Privately Held**
Web: www.mametal.com
SIC: 3469 Stamping metal for the trade

(G-3092)
MANAR INC (PA)
Also Called: Tennplasco
905 S Walnut St (46124-2002)
PHONE..................812 526-2891
Eugene Nolen, *CEO*
Larry Johnson, *
◆ EMP: 100 EST: 1974
SQ FT: 50,000
SALES (est): 47.02MM
SALES (corp-wide): 47.02MM **Privately Held**
Web: www.manarinc.com
SIC: 3089 Molding primary plastics

(G-3093)
MANAR MEDICAL INC
906 S Walnut St (46124)
P.O. Box 313 (46124)
PHONE..................812 526-6734
Allan S Miller, *Pr*
Richard A Miller, *
Gene Nollan, *Stockholder*
Diane Barringer, *Stockholder*
▲ EMP: 40 EST: 1988
SQ FT: 16,000
SALES (est): 4.63MM **Privately Held**
Web: www.manarinc.com
SIC: 3089 Injection molding of plastics

(G-3094)
P M I LLC
12595 N Executive Dr (46124-9067)
PHONE..................812 374-3856
EMP: 7 EST: 2016
SALES (est): 215.01K **Privately Held**
SIC: 1081 Exploration, metal mining

(G-3095)
PACKAGING CORPORATION AMERICA
Also Called: PCA
12599 N Presidential Way (46124-9039)
PHONE..................812 526-5919
Robert Groob, *Mgr*
EMP: 5
SALES (corp-wide): 8.48B **Publicly Held**
Web: www.packagingcorp.com
SIC: 2653 Boxes, corrugated: made from purchased materials
PA: Packaging Corporation Of America
　　 1 N Field Ct
　　 Lake Forest IL 60045
　　 847 482-3000

(G-3096)
PEER FOODS GROUP INC
3013 W Presidential Way (46124)
PHONE..................812 703-2081
EMP: 8
SALES (corp-wide): 54.3MM **Privately Held**
Web: www.peerfoods.com
SIC: 2013 Sausages and other prepared meats
PA: Peer Foods Group, Inc.
　　 1200 W 35th St Fl 3
　　 Chicago IL 60609
　　 773 927-1440

(G-3097)
PENWAY INC
900 S Walnut St (46124)
P.O. Box 185 (46124)
PHONE..................812 526-2645
Alan Ryshavy, *Pr*
Anu Ryshavy, *
EMP: 30 EST: 1988
SALES (est): 3.75MM **Privately Held**
Web: www.penway-inc.com
SIC: 3443 Tanks, standard or custom fabricated: metal plate

(G-3098)
PHILLIPS COMPANY INC
1045 S Walnut St (46124-9501)
PHONE..................812 526-8250
EMP: 18
SALES (corp-wide): 9.39MM **Privately Held**
Web: www.thephillipscompany.com
SIC: 3714 Motor vehicle parts and accessories
PA: The Phillips Company Inc
　　 6330 E 100 S
　　 Columbus IN 47201
　　 812 378-3797

(G-3099)
QUICK TURN ANODIZING LLC
6973 S Us Highway 31 (46124-1068)
PHONE..................877 716-1150
Jann Powell, *Pr*
Trace Powell, *VP*
EMP: 16 EST: 2015
SQ FT: 11,000
SALES (est): 678.56K **Privately Held**
Web: www.quickturnanodizing.net
SIC: 3471 3479 Anodizing (plating) of metals or formed products; Rust proofing (hot dipping) of metals and formed products

(G-3100)
R & R TECHNOLOGIES LLC (PA)
7560 E County Line Rd (46124-1100)
PHONE..................812 526-2655
EMP: 30 EST: 1996
SQ FT: 55,000
SALES (est): 8.78MM **Privately Held**
Web: www.rrtech.com
SIC: 3089 Injection molding of plastics

(G-3101)
RJ FUEL SERVICES INC
6815 W State Road 252 (46124-9461)
P.O. Box 308 (47202-0308)
PHONE..................812 350-2897
Rita Gearhart, *Pr*
Robert Gearhart, *Mgr*
EMP: 2 EST: 2004
SALES (est): 253.62K **Privately Held**
Web: www.rjfuelservices.com
SIC: 3586 Oil pumps, measuring or dispensing

(G-3102)
SACOMA PROPERTIES LLC
955 S Walnut St (46124-2002)
PHONE..................812 526-5600
EMP: 10 EST: 2020
SALES (est): 2.42MM **Privately Held**
Web: www.sacoma.com
SIC: 3714 3499 Motor vehicle parts and accessories; Fire- or burglary-resistive products

(G-3103)
SAPP INC
Also Called: Sapp USA
600 S Kyle St (46124-1606)
PHONE..................317 512-8353
Diego Mancini, *Pr*
Claudio Apollonia, *Sec*
▲ EMP: 18 EST: 2013
SQ FT: 75,000
SALES (est): 495.58K **Privately Held**
SIC: 3542 3545 Die casting machines; Milling machine attachments (machine tool accessories)

(G-3104)
SHELBY GRAVEL INC
7520 E 650 S (46124-8904)
PHONE..................812 526-2731
Gregg Hebbe, *Brnch Mgr*
EMP: 10
SALES (corp-wide): 74.83MM **Privately Held**
Web: www.shelbymaterials.com
SIC: 5032 1442 Concrete mixtures; Gravel mining
PA: Shelby Gravel, Inc
　　 157 E Rampart St
　　 Shelbyville IN 46176
　　 317 398-4485

(G-3105)
SONOCO PRODUCTS COMPANY
Also Called: Sonoco Products
6502 S Us Highway 31 (46124-1070)
P.O. Box 188 (46124-0188)
PHONE..................812 526-5511
Vince Dimino, *Brnch Mgr*

EMP: 57
SALES (corp-wide): 6.78B **Publicly Held**
Web: www.sonoco.com
SIC: **2631** 3083 3081 2851 Paperboard mills; Laminated plastics plate and sheet; Unsupported plastics film and sheet; Paints and allied products
PA: Sonoco Products Company
 1 N 2nd St
 Hartsville SC 29550
 843 383-7000

(G-3106)
TRU-FLEX LLC
955 S Walnut St (46124-2002)
PHONE.................................812 526-5600
EMP: 1
Web: www.tru-flex.com
SIC: **3714** Motor vehicle parts and accessories
HQ: Tru-Flex, Llc
 2391 S State Road 263
 West Lebanon IN 47991

(G-3107)
TRUTEX EQUESTRIAN LLC
Also Called: Trutex Footing
7448 W Old State Road 252 (46124-9285)
PHONE.................................812 350-6368
EMP: 5 EST: 2018
SALES (est): 72K **Privately Held**
Web: www.trutexfooting.com
SIC: **3111** Equestrian leather products

(G-3108)
TSB LLC
12550 N Presidential Way (46124-9039)
PHONE.................................812 314-8331
Michael Riebl, *Managing Member*
Yoshitaka Tsune, *Dir*
EMP: 6 EST: 2011
SQ FT: 3,000
SALES (est): 343.91K **Privately Held**
SIC: **3425** Saw blades and handsaws

(G-3109)
TSUNE AMERICA LLC
12550 N Presidential Way (46124-9039)
PHONE.................................812 378-9875
▲ EMP: 17 EST: 1995
SQ FT: 3,500
SALES (est): 2.11MM **Privately Held**
Web: www.tsuneamerica.com
SIC: **3545** 5084 Machine tool accessories; Industrial machinery and equipment

(G-3110)
YANKEE CANDLE COMPANY INC
11740 Ne Executive Dr (46124-9180)
PHONE.................................812 526-5195
Sharon Canada, *Brnch Mgr*
EMP: 9
SALES (corp-wide): 8.13B **Publicly Held**
Web: www.yankeecandle.com
SIC: **5999** 5199 3999 Candle shops; Candles; Barber and beauty shop equipment
HQ: The Yankee Candle Company Inc
 16 Yankee Candle Way
 South Deerfield MA 01373
 413 665-8306

Elberfeld
Warrick County

(G-3111)
DAYLIGHT ENGINEERING INC
11022 Elberfeld Rd (47613-9449)
PHONE.................................812 983-2518
Thomas E Sawyer, *Pr*
Joanne Sawyer, *Sec*
EMP: 5 EST: 1969
SQ FT: 12,200
SALES (est): 897.99K **Privately Held**
Web: www.daylightengineering.com
SIC: **5085** 3533 1321 8711 Abrasives; Gas field machinery and equipment; Natural gas liquids production; Engineering services

(G-3112)
EURONIQUE INC
7633 Saint Johns Rd (47613)
P.O. Box 128 (47613)
PHONE.................................812 983-3337
Scott R Hasenour, *Pr*
David J Hasenour, *
EMP: 30 EST: 1999
SQ FT: 36,000
SALES (est): 4.65MM **Privately Held**
Web: www.euronique.us
SIC: **2541** Cabinets, lockers, and shelving

(G-3113)
FIBERTECH PLASTICS LLC
Also Called: Fibertech Plastics
11744 Blue Bell Rd (47613-9455)
PHONE.................................812 983-2642
Brent Rasche, *Pr*
Jp Engelbrecht, *Prin*
Randy Champion, *Prin*
Brent Rasche, *Prin*
Natalie Colvin, *Prin*
EMP: 80 EST: 2021
SALES (est): 7.69MM **Privately Held**
Web: www.fibertechplastics.com
SIC: **7699** 3089 2519 Plastics products repair; Plastics containers, except foam; Fiberglass and plastic furniture

(G-3114)
FTI INC
11744 Blue Bell Rd (47613-9455)
PHONE.................................812 983-2642
▼ EMP: 60 EST: 1991
SALES (est): 8.35MM **Privately Held**
Web: www.fibertechplastics.com
SIC: **3089** Plastics containers, except foam

(G-3115)
JAMES G HENAGER
Also Called: Henager
8837 S State Road 57 (47613-8445)
PHONE.................................812 795-2230
James G Henager, *Owner*
EMP: 3 EST: 1990
SALES (est): 177.07K **Privately Held**
Web: www.henagermuseum.com
SIC: **2431** 2434 2439 Millwork; Wood kitchen cabinets; Structural wood members, nec

(G-3116)
NORTH AMERICAN LIGHTING INC
Also Called: North American Lighting
11833 Industrial Park Dr (47613-9038)
PHONE.................................812 983-2663
EMP: 263
Web: www.nal.com
SIC: **3647** Vehicular lighting equipment
HQ: North American Lighting, Inc.
 2275 S Main St
 Paris IL 61944
 217 465-6600

(G-3117)
PEACOCK BAT CO
8466 Susott Rd (47613-9001)
PHONE.................................812 568-1006
Clay Peacock, *Ofcr*
EMP: 1 EST: 2013
SALES (est): 53.13K **Privately Held**
SIC: **3949** Sporting and athletic goods, nec

(G-3118)
STOLZ STRUCTURAL INC
7735 Saint Johns Rd (47613-9141)
P.O. Box 420 (47613-0420)
PHONE.................................812 983-4720
Linda Stolz, *Pr*
John Stolz, *Treas*
EMP: 7 EST: 1999
SALES (est): 936.22K **Privately Held**
SIC: **3449** Bars, concrete reinforcing: fabricated steel

(G-3119)
STONE COAL SERVICES LLC
5344 Gander Rd (47613-9188)
PHONE.................................812 455-8215
Dennis R Wilzbacher, *Pr*
EMP: 6 EST: 2010
SALES (est): 185.28K **Privately Held**
SIC: **1241** Coal mining services

(G-3120)
STUMP & GRIND
8827 S State Road 57 (47613-8445)
PHONE.................................812 453-2121
Terry Fowler, *Owner*
EMP: 5 EST: 2017
SALES (est): 80.93K **Privately Held**
SIC: **3599** Grinding castings for the trade

(G-3121)
SUPERIOR MFG INC
11333 Elberfeld Rd (47613-9452)
PHONE.................................812 983-9900
Lori A Bowman, *Pr*
Bradley S Lattner, *Sec*
EMP: 12 EST: 1995
SALES (est): 2.05MM **Privately Held**
SIC: **3715** Truck trailers

(G-3122)
SUPPRESS TEC LLC
7599 Saint Johns Rd (47613-9140)
PHONE.................................812 453-5813
Nicholas Stratman, *Prin*
EMP: 2 EST: 2017
SALES (est): 84.23K **Privately Held**
SIC: **3484** Guns (firearms) or gun parts, 30 mm. and below

Elizabeth
Harrison County

(G-3123)
ARTYS LOGGING INC
7800 E Highway 11 Se (47117-9130)
PHONE.................................812 969-3124
Jeff Lillpop, *Prin*
EMP: 3 EST: 2010
SALES (est): 240K **Privately Held**
SIC: **2411** Logging camps and contractors

(G-3124)
BEST VINEYARDS LLC
8373 Morgans Ln Se (47117-7408)
PHONE.................................812 969-9463
EMP: 3 EST: 2007
SALES (est): 241.19K **Privately Held**
Web: www.bestvineyardswinery.com
SIC: **2084** Wines

(G-3125)
GOLD CANYON CANDLES
3793 Doolittle Hill Rd Se (47117-8054)
PHONE.................................812 267-4477
Crissy Blackman, *Prin*
EMP: 4 EST: 2018
SALES (est): 93.36K **Privately Held**
Web: www.sunsetcanyoncandles.com
SIC: **3999** Candles

(G-3126)
GRANNYS LLC
7156 Black Creek Rd (47117-9632)
PHONE.................................812 969-3058
Mary Elisse Coulter, *Prin*
EMP: 1 EST: 2011
SALES (est): 82.7K **Privately Held**
SIC: **3421** Table and food cutlery, including butchers'

(G-3127)
GUY CARDBOARD
2860 N Highway 11 Se (47117-7747)
PHONE.................................812 989-4809
Jason Colligan, *Prin*
EMP: 6 EST: 2011
SALES (est): 82.08K **Privately Held**
SIC: **2631** Cardboard

(G-3128)
PRINTING IN TIME INC
8213 Lotticks Corner Rd Se (47117-7312)
PHONE.................................502 807-3545
Greg Hogle, *Pr*
EMP: 6 EST: 2015
SALES (est): 94.77K **Privately Held**
Web: printingintime.espwebsite.com
SIC: **2752** Offset printing

(G-3129)
SIMPSON ALLOY SERVICES INC
Also Called: Simpson Aerospace Services
7017 Old Highway 111 Se (47117-8447)
PHONE.................................812 969-2766
Dean Simpson, *Pr*
Kathy Simpson, *VP*
EMP: 8 EST: 1997
SQ FT: 7,500
SALES (est): 2.34MM **Privately Held**
Web: www.simpson-services.com
SIC: **3724** 3398 Aircraft engines and engine parts; Tempering of metal

(G-3130)
SMALL TOWN PRINTERS LLC
6265 Sand Hill Rd Se (47117-8232)
PHONE.................................812 596-1536
Kristy Hess, *Prin*
EMP: 6 EST: 2018
SALES (est): 149.65K **Privately Held**
Web: www.smalltownprinters.com
SIC: **2752** Commercial printing, lithographic

(G-3131)
WOOD LIGHTER CASES LLC
7705 Pine Hill Dr Se (47117-9139)
PHONE.................................812 969-3908
Jeff Ankrum, *Prin*
EMP: 4 EST: 2014
SALES (est): 88.68K **Privately Held**
Web: www.woodlightercases.com
SIC: **3523** Farm machinery and equipment

Elizabethtown
Bartholomew County

(G-3132)
QUANTUM TECHNOLOGIES LLC
7135 E 750 S (47232-9565)
P.O. Box 804 (46725-0804)
PHONE.................................765 426-0156
EMP: 2 EST: 2020
SALES (est): 85K **Privately Held**

Elizabethtown - Bartholomew County (G-3133)

SIC: 3589 8711 1731 3613 Servicing machines, except dry cleaning, laundry: coin-oper.; Engineering services; Electronic controls installation; Control panels, electric

(G-3133)
SMITHLAND BUTCHERING CO INC
11420 S Us Highway 31 (47232-9578)
PHONE.................317 729-5398
James Mc Curdy, *Pr*
Peggy Mc Curdy, *Sec*
EMP: 6 EST: 1965
SQ FT: 2,400
SALES (est): 432.57K **Privately Held**
SIC: 2011 5147 Meat packing plants; Meats, fresh

(G-3134)
WILSON MACHINE SHOP INC
7780 W County Road 800 N (47232-9425)
PHONE.................812 392-2774
Jeffrey Wilson, *Pr*
Joseph Wilson, *VP*
Brenda Reecer, *Sec*
EMP: 4 EST: 1978
SQ FT: 7,600
SALES (est): 306.63K **Privately Held**
SIC: 3599 7692 Machine shop, jobbing and repair; Welding repair

(G-3135)
WOEHR TOOL & DIE
110 Pennsylvania St (47232-5501)
PHONE.................408 313-1708
EMP: 5 EST: 2017
SALES (est): 226.22K **Privately Held**
Web: www.woehrtool.com
SIC: 3599 Machine shop, jobbing and repair

Elkhart
Elkhart County

(G-3136)
(EBS CMPSTES ENGNRED BNDED STR
Also Called: Ebsc
3506 Henke St (46514-7653)
PHONE.................574 266-3471
Ben Pearson, *Pr*
Dale Dewitt, *Sec*
EMP: 12 EST: 2006
SQ FT: 28,000
SALES (est): 2.25MM **Privately Held**
Web: www.ebscomposites.net
SIC: 3448 2452 Buildings, portable: prefabricated metal; Prefabricated wood buildings

(G-3137)
3W ENTERPRISES LLC
Also Called: 3w Enterprises
2727 Industrial Pkwy (46516-5402)
PHONE.................847 366-6555
EMP: 6 EST: 2004
SALES (est): 484.33K **Privately Held**
SIC: 2299 5084 3561 Burlap, jute; Water pumps (industrial); Pumps, domestic: water or sump

(G-3138)
A & M SYSTEMS INC
4121 Eastland Dr (46516-9031)
P.O. Box 89 (46515-0089)
PHONE.................574 522-5000
Jim Miller, *Pr*
Karey Aenis, *VP*
▲ EMP: 15 EST: 1999
SALES (est): 2.21MM **Privately Held**
Web: www.anmsystems.com

SIC: 3542 Headers

(G-3139)
A E TECHRON INC
Also Called: Ae Techron
2507 Warren St (46516-5759)
P.O. Box 2808 (46515-2808)
PHONE.................574 295-9495
▲ EMP: 13 EST: 1992
SQ FT: 15,000
SALES (est): 4.79MM **Privately Held**
Web: www.aetechron.com
SIC: 3651 Household audio equipment

(G-3140)
A ONE SIGNS & GRAPHICS
726 Middleton Run Rd (46516-5424)
PHONE.................574 293-7104
Marc Barfell, *Prin*
EMP: 6 EST: 2016
SALES (est): 152.61K **Privately Held**
SIC: 3993 Signs and advertising specialties

(G-3141)
A S V PLASTICS INC
419 Roske Dr (46516-9086)
PHONE.................574 264-9694
EMP: 11 EST: 1996
SALES (est): 1.11MM **Privately Held**
Web: www.asvplastics.com
SIC: 5162 3089 Plastics products, nec; Plastics processing

(G-3142)
A SHADE FASTER PRODUCTS LLC
23035 Lake Shore Dr (46514-9334)
PHONE.................574 584-5744
EMP: 1 EST: 2016
SALES (est): 72.07K **Privately Held**
SIC: 3444 Awnings and canopies

(G-3143)
A1 CAMPERS AND TRLRS MFG LLC
30063 Tower Rd (46516-1109)
PHONE.................574 227-2200
Robert Meredith, *Managing Member*
EMP: 1 EST: 2016
SALES (est): 52.44K **Privately Held**
SIC: 3715 5083 5261 Truck trailers; Lawn machinery and equipment; Lawn and garden equipment

(G-3144)
AAA WELDING INC
28338 County Road 24 (46517-9446)
PHONE.................574 293-5294
Bruce L Loucks, *Pr*
EMP: 1 EST: 2001
SALES (est): 63.87K **Privately Held**
SIC: 7692 Welding repair

(G-3145)
ABI PLASTICS LLC
2510 Middlebury St (46516-5512)
PHONE.................574 294-1700
Glen Unzicker, *Managing Member*
EMP: 2 EST: 2002
SALES (est): 240.41K **Privately Held**
SIC: 3089 Injection molding of plastics

(G-3146)
ABSOLUTE FABRICATION INC
1651 Toledo Rd (46516)
PHONE.................574 848-0300
Ryan Casey, *Pr*
EMP: 4 EST: 2018
SALES (est): 65.3K **Privately Held**
Web: www.absolutefabricating.com
SIC: 7692 Welding repair

(G-3147)
ACADEMY INC
21291 Buckingham Rd (46516-9703)
PHONE.................574 293-7113
Richard Eysol, *Pr*
Carolyn Eysol, *Sec*
EMP: 8 EST: 1987
SQ FT: 6,000
SALES (est): 937.54K **Privately Held**
SIC: 5211 1751 2434 Cabinets, kitchen; Cabinet and finish carpentry; Vanities, bathroom: wood

(G-3148)
ACCENT COMPLEX INC
Also Called: Accent Printing
515 East St (46516-3611)
PHONE.................574 522-2368
Joseph J Lidy, *Pr*
EMP: 2 EST: 1993
SALES (est): 245.09K **Privately Held**
Web: www.blackhoneyshats.com
SIC: 6512 2752 7389 2451 Commercial and industrial building operation; Commercial printing, lithographic; Telephone services; Mobile homes

(G-3149)
ACCRA-PAC INC
Also Called: Accra Pac
711 Middleton Run Rd (46516-5425)
PHONE.................574 295-0000
EMP: 1
SALES (corp-wide): 118.94MM **Privately Held**
Web: www.accrapacindia.net
SIC: 7389 5169 2844 4213 Packaging and labeling services; Chemicals and allied products, nec; Perfumes, cosmetics and other toilet preparations; Trucking, except local
HQ: Accra-Pac, Inc.
2730 Middlebury St
Elkhart IN 46516
574 295-0000

(G-3150)
ACCRA-PAC INC (DH)
Also Called: Kik Cusrtom Products
2730 Middlebury St (46516-5582)
P.O. Box 2988 (46515-2988)
PHONE.................574 295-0000
Jeffrey M Nodland, *CEO*
Ben W Kaak, *
Stratis Katsiris, *
William Smith, *
EMP: 67 EST: 1967
SQ FT: 170,000
SALES (est): 24.7MM
SALES (corp-wide): 118.94MM **Privately Held**
Web: www.accrapacindia.net
SIC: 3842 3633 2834 Surgical appliances and supplies; Household laundry equipment; Pharmaceutical preparations
HQ: Voyant Beauty Holdings, Inc.
6710 River Rd
Hodgkins IL 60525
708 482-8881

(G-3151)
ACCRA-PAC INC
Also Called: Voyant Beauty
1919 Superior St (46516-4707)
PHONE.................574 295-0000
Jeffrey M Nodland, *CEO*
▲ EMP: 70 EST: 1967
SQ FT: 424,000
SALES (est): 4.34MM **Privately Held**
Web: www.accrapacindia.net

SIC: 3842 3633 2834 Personal safety equipment; Household laundry equipment; Pharmaceutical preparations

(G-3152)
ACCUBUILT PLANT I
2811 Tuscany Dr (46514-7639)
PHONE.................574 389-9000
David Harvey, *Pr*
EMP: 7 EST: 2010
SALES (est): 138.61K **Privately Held**
Web: www.tuscanymotorco.com
SIC: 3713 Truck and bus bodies

(G-3153)
ACUTECH LLC
53905 County Road 9 Ste C (46514-5012)
P.O. Box 543 (46530-0543)
PHONE.................574 262-8228
Joe Bella, *Managing Member*
EMP: 10 EST: 2004
SQ FT: 7,000
SALES (est): 543K **Privately Held**
Web: www.acu-tech.net
SIC: 3555 Printing trades machinery

(G-3154)
ADAMS & WESTLAKE LTD
Also Called: Adlake
940 N Michigan St (46514-2216)
PHONE.................574 264-1141
Randy Schneider, *Pr*
Dg Elmore, *
EMP: 35 EST: 1857
SQ FT: 65,000
SALES (est): 2.52MM **Privately Held**
Web: www.adlake.com
SIC: 3743 Train cars and equipment, freight or passenger

(G-3155)
AIRJET INC
2101 Kinro Ct (46514-1697)
P.O. Box 1247 (46515-1247)
PHONE.................574 264-0123
David Leiter, *Pr*
EMP: 100 EST: 2004
SALES (est): 8.73MM
SALES (corp-wide): 22.85MM **Privately Held**
Web: www.continentalindustries.com
SIC: 3564 Ventilating fans: industrial or commercial
PA: Continental Industries Inc
100 W Windsor Ave
Elkhart IN 46514
574 262-4511

(G-3156)
AIRXCEL INC
1136 Verdant St (46516-9044)
PHONE.................574 294-5681
Michael A Higley, *Brnch Mgr*
EMP: 447
SQ FT: 27,000
SALES (corp-wide): 11.12B **Publicly Held**
Web: www.suburbanrv.com
SIC: 5012 4225 3822 Recreational vehicles, motor homes, and trailers; General warehousing; Water heater controls
HQ: Airxcel, Inc.
3050 N Saint Francis St
Wichita KS 67219

(G-3157)
AL-EX INC
3170 Windsor Ct (46514-5556)
PHONE.................574 206-0100
Rick L Newman, *Pr*
EMP: 2 EST: 2006
SALES (est): 245.41K **Privately Held**

Web: www.dein-alex.de
SIC: 3544 Extrusion dies

(G-3158)
AL-KO KOBER LLC
Also Called: Al-Ko Kober
21611 Protecta Dr (46516-9543)
P.O. Box 1367 (46515-1367)
PHONE..................................574 294-6651
▲ EMP: 203
SIC: 3714 5083 Gears, motor vehicle; Lawn and garden machinery and equipment

(G-3159)
ALL AMERICAN GROUP INC
Also Called: Coachmen Recreational Vehicle
1251 N Nappanee St (46514-1733)
PHONE..................................574 262-9889
Mel Williams, Mgr
EMP: 1
SIC: 3716 Motor homes
HQ: All American Group, Inc.
 2831 Dexter Dr
 Elkhart IN 46514
 574 262-0123

(G-3160)
ALL AMERICAN GROUP INC (HQ)
Also Called: Viking Formed Products
2831 Dexter Dr (46514-8225)
P.O. Box 1205 (17055-1205)
PHONE..................................574 262-0123
Richard M Lavers, Pr
Colleen A Zuhl, *
W Todd Woelfer, *
Martin L Miranda, *
◆ EMP: 45 EST: 1964
SQ FT: 138,680
SALES (est): 118.56MM Privately Held
SIC: 3716 3792 2452 3714 Motor homes; Travel trailers and campers; Modular homes, prefabricated, wood; Motor vehicle parts and accessories
PA: All American Group Holdings, Llc
 1450 Brickell Ave # 3100
 Miami FL 33131

(G-3161)
ALL AMERICAN GROUP INC
All American Homes
2831 Dexter Dr (46514-8225)
PHONE..................................574 262-0123
James P Skinner, Prin
EMP: 1
SIC: 2452 Modular homes, prefabricated, wood
HQ: All American Group, Inc.
 2831 Dexter Dr
 Elkhart IN 46514
 574 262-0123

(G-3162)
ALL AMERICAN HOMES LLC (DH)
2831 Dexter Dr (46514-8225)
PHONE..................................574 266-3044
Steve Sheinkman, CEO
EMP: 43 EST: 1970
SALES (est): 20.32MM Privately Held
Web: www.allamericanhomes.com
SIC: 2452 Modular homes, prefabricated, wood
HQ: All American Group, Inc.
 2831 Dexter Dr
 Elkhart IN 46514
 574 262-0123

(G-3163)
ALL PACKAGING EQUIPMENT CORP
1749 Fieldhouse Ave (46517-1410)
PHONE..................................574 294-3371
Michael Luke, VP
EMP: 4 EST: 2012
SQ FT: 3,200
SALES (est): 421.31K Privately Held
Web: www.allpackagingequipment.com
SIC: 3565 Packaging machinery

(G-3164)
ALL YOU NATURALLY LLC
1501 Cedar St (46514-1815)
PHONE..................................574 215-5425
Ann Johnson, Managing Member
EMP: 1 EST: 2013
SALES (est): 68K Privately Held
SIC: 2844 Perfumes, cosmetics and other toilet preparations

(G-3165)
ALL-STATE INDUSTRIES INC
409 Roske Dr Unit B (46516-9086)
PHONE..................................574 522-4245
EMP: 9
SALES (corp-wide): 99.48MM Privately Held
Web: www.all-stateind.com
SIC: 3999 Atomizers, toiletry
HQ: All-State Industries, Inc.
 500 S 18th St
 West Des Moines IA 50265
 515 223-5843

(G-3166)
ALLIANCE RV LLC
301 Benchmark Dr (46516-0001)
PHONE..................................574 312-5215
EMP: 48 EST: 2019
SALES (est): 9.13MM Privately Held
Web: www.alliancerv.com
SIC: 3799 Recreational vehicles

(G-3167)
ALTEC ENGINEERING INC (PA)
2401 W Mishawaka Rd (46517-4041)
PHONE..................................574 293-1965
Gary Robinson, Pr
Joane Robinson, *
Dennis J Jordan, *
EMP: 50 EST: 1988
SALES (est): 8.22MM Privately Held
Web: www.altecengineering.com
SIC: 3089 3088 2221 Molding primary plastics; Plastics plumbing fixtures; Fiberglass fabrics

(G-3168)
ALUMINUM EXTRUSIONS
3170 Windsor Ct (46514-5556)
PHONE..................................574 206-0100
Rick L Newman, Prin
EMP: 9 EST: 2008
SALES (est): 224.43K Privately Held
SIC: 3354 Aluminum extruded products

(G-3169)
AMC ACQUISITION CORPORATION
Also Called: American Millwork
4840 Beck Dr (46516-9569)
PHONE..................................215 572-0738
Tom Harper, Pr
Richard A Horwitz, *
Scott T Swick, *
EMP: 100 EST: 2003
SQ FT: 170,000
SALES: 13.71MM
SALES (corp-wide): 426.63MM Privately Held
Web: www.americanmillwork.com
SIC: 2431 Moldings and baseboards, ornamental and trim
PA: R.A.F. Industries, Inc.
 50 Monument Rd Ste 303
 Bala Cynwyd PA 19004
 215 572-0738

(G-3170)
AMERICAN ADVENTURES INC
2809 Ferndale Rd (46517-8783)
PHONE..................................574 875-6850
David Myers, Pr
EMP: 1 EST: 1992
SQ FT: 1,400
SALES (est): 20K Privately Held
SIC: 1521 2499 New construction, single-family houses; Ladders and stepladders, wood

(G-3171)
AMERICAN ELCTRNC CMPNENTS INC
Also Called: Durakool
913 10th St (46516)
PHONE..................................574 295-6330
Tom Henry, CEO
Mark Del Giudice, Pr
Thomas Thorelli, Sec
◆ EMP: 21 EST: 1995
SALES (est): 3.46MM Privately Held
Web: www.aecsensors.com
SIC: 3625 Relays, for electronic use

(G-3172)
AMERICAN ELKHART LLC
2304 Charlotte Ave (46517)
P.O. Box 272 (46561)
PHONE..................................574 293-0333
EMP: 18 EST: 2014
SQ FT: 30,000
SALES (est): 2.46MM Privately Held
Web: www.americanelkhart.com
SIC: 3053 Gaskets and sealing devices

(G-3173)
AMERICAN LIMB & ORTHOPEDIC CO
3614 S Nappanee St Ste 122 (46517-9291)
PHONE..................................574 522-3643
Norbert Fliess, Pr
EMP: 2
SALES (corp-wide): 1.57MM Privately Held
Web: www.americanlimbvalparaiso.com
SIC: 3842 5999 Limbs, artificial; Orthopedic and prosthesis applications
PA: American Limb & Orthopedic Co.
 2930 Mckinley Ave Ste A
 South Bend IN 46615
 574 287-3767

(G-3174)
AMERICAN MILLWORK LLC
4840 Beck Dr (46516-9569)
PHONE..................................574 295-4158
EMP: 7 EST: 2017
SALES (est): 205.72K Privately Held
Web: www.americanmillwork.com
SIC: 2431 Millwork

(G-3175)
AMERICAN STEEL RULE DIE INC
3401 Reedy Dr (46514-9413)
PHONE..................................574 262-3437
David Catanzarite, Pr
EMP: 8 EST: 1965
SQ FT: 5,000
SALES (est): 928.62K Privately Held
Web: www.asrd.com
SIC: 3544 2675 Dies, steel rule; Die-cut paper and board

(G-3176)
AMERICAN STONECAST PDTS INC
4315 Wyland Dr (46516-9501)
P.O. Box 2434 (46515-2434)
PHONE..................................574 206-0097
Kirk Veer, Pr
▼ EMP: 14 EST: 2001
SQ FT: 20,000
SALES (est): 474.89K Privately Held
Web: www.rv-sinks.com
SIC: 2541 Counter and sink tops

(G-3177)
AMERICAN TECHNOLOGY COMPONENTS INCORPORATED
Also Called: A T C
1147 N Michigan St (46514-2213)
PHONE..................................800 238-2687
▲ EMP: 160 EST: 1985
SALES (est): 32.41MM Privately Held
Web: www.atcomp.com
SIC: 3679 3613 Electronic switches; Panel and distribution boards and other related apparatus

(G-3178)
AMERICAN WAY MARKETING LLC
400 Pine Creek Ct (46516-9089)
P.O. Box 1681 (46515-1681)
PHONE..................................574 295-6633
Kathy Donahoe, Managing Member
▲ EMP: 17 EST: 1988
SQ FT: 8,200
SALES (est): 2.46MM Privately Held
Web: www.americanwaymktg.com
SIC: 5099 3991 Musical instruments parts and accessories; Brushes, except paint and varnish

(G-3179)
AMERICANA DEVELOPMENT INC
Also Called: Dexstar Wheel
400 Collins Rd (46516-5437)
PHONE..................................574 295-3535
Chi Yang, Brnch Mgr
EMP: 97
Web: www.dexstarwheel.com
SIC: 3714 Wheel rims, motor vehicle
PA: Americana Development, Inc.
 7095 Americana Pkwy
 Reynoldsburg OH 43068

(G-3180)
AMSAFE PARTNERS INC
Also Called: Am-Safe Commercial Products
3802 Gallatin Way (46514-7650)
PHONE..................................574 266-8330
EMP: 66
SALES (corp-wide): 39.49MM Privately Held
Web: www.amsafe.com
SIC: 3714 Motor vehicle parts and accessories
PA: Amsafe Partners, Inc.
 1043 N 47th Ave
 Phoenix AZ 85043
 602 850-2850

(G-3181)
ANABAPTIST MNNNITE BBLCAL SMNA
Also Called: Institute of Mennonite Studies
3003 Benham Ave (46517-1947)
PHONE..................................574 295-3726
Sara Wenger Shenk, Pr
Ron Ringenberg, *
EMP: 53 EST: 1958
SQ FT: 18,000
SALES (est): 4.56MM Privately Held
Web: www.ambs.edu
SIC: 8221 7372 Theological seminary; Application computer software

Elkhart - Elkhart County (G-3182) GEOGRAPHIC SECTION

(G-3182)
ANDERSON SILVER PLATING CO
541 Industrial Pkwy (46516-5482)
P.O. Box 961 (46515-0961)
PHONE..................574 294-6447
Michael Anderson, *Pr*
EMP: 18 **EST:** 1948
SQ FT: 30,000
SALES (est): 452.67K **Privately Held**
Web: www.andersonsilverplating.com
SIC: 3471 Electroplating of metals or formed products

(G-3183)
ANDRE CORP
3406 S Main St 8 (46517-3124)
PHONE..................574 293-0207
EMP: 5 **EST:** 2020
SALES (est): 158.1K **Privately Held**
Web: www.andrecorp.com
SIC: 3452 Bolts, nuts, rivets, and washers

(G-3184)
ANEW COMPANY INC
Also Called: Anewco
4811 Eastland Dr (46516-9634)
P.O. Box 2262 (46515-2262)
PHONE..................574 293-9088
Rick Hollar, *Pr*
Nona Hollar, *Sec*
EMP: 13 **EST:** 1981
SQ FT: 70,000
SALES (est): 435.1K **Privately Held**
SIC: 3231 2396 Ornamental glass: cut, engraved or otherwise decorated; Automotive and apparel trimmings

(G-3185)
APG INC
2825 Middlebury St (46516-5508)
P.O. Box 2988 (46515-2988)
PHONE..................574 295-0000
EMP: 70
SIC: 7389 5169 2844 Packaging and labeling services; Chemicals and allied products, nec; Perfumes, cosmetics and other toilet preparations

(G-3186)
API INDIANA INC
Also Called: Anco Products
2500 17th St (46517-1412)
PHONE..................574 293-5574
Lee R Anderson Senior, *Ch Bd*
William Beadie, *
Gregory Keup, *Treas*
◆ **EMP:** 75 **EST:** 1972
SQ FT: 154,000
SALES (est): 8.2MM
SALES (corp-wide): 6.93B **Publicly Held**
Web: www.ancoproducts.com
SIC: 3296 3089 Fiberglass insulation; Ducting, plastics
HQ: Api Group, Inc.
  1100 Old Highway 8 Nw
  New Brighton MN 55112
  651 636-4320

(G-3187)
AQUA LILY PRODUCTS LLC (PA)
1806 Conant St (46516-4755)
PHONE..................951 246-9610
Craig Cushman, *Prin*
EMP: 5 **EST:** 2010
SALES (est): 4.62MM
SALES (corp-wide): 4.62MM **Privately Held**
Web: www.aqualilypad.com
SIC: 3086 7389 Padding, foamed plastics; Business services, nec

(G-3188)
ARCH MED SLTIONS - ELKHART LLC
2921 Lavanture Pl (46514-8233)
PHONE..................574 264-3997
EMP: 10 **EST:** 2020
SALES (est): 1.07MM **Privately Held**
Web: www.archglobalprecision.com
SIC: 3826 Analytical instruments

(G-3189)
ARMOR CONTRACT MFG INC
300 Comet Ave (46514-5529)
PHONE..................574 327-2962
John Cullip, *Pr*
EMP: 14 **EST:** 2018
SALES (est): 549.68K **Privately Held**
Web: www.armorcontract.com
SIC: 3999 Manufacturing industries, nec

(G-3190)
ARMOR GROUP
300 Comet Ave (46514-5529)
PHONE..................574 293-1791
EMP: 8 **EST:** 2016
SALES (est): 200.25K **Privately Held**
Web: www.thearmorgroup.com
SIC: 3441 Fabricated structural metal

(G-3191)
ARRAN ISLE INC (HQ)
601 County Road 17 (46516-9505)
PHONE..................574 295-4400
Andrew Batson, *CEO*
EMP: 30 **EST:** 2016
SALES (est): 183.62MM
SALES (corp-wide): 3.47B **Publicly Held**
Web: www.lasallebristol.com
SIC: 5023 5021 5051 5033 Floor coverings; Household furniture; Aluminum bars, rods, ingots, sheets, pipes, plates, etc.; Siding, except wood
PA: Patrick Industries, Inc.
  107 W Franklin St
  Elkhart IN 46516
  574 294-7511

(G-3192)
ASA ELECTRONICS LLC (PA)
Also Called: Audiovox Spclized Applications
2602 Marina Dr (46514-8642)
PHONE..................574 264-3135
Tom Irions, *CEO*
◆ **EMP:** 110 **EST:** 1977
SALES (est): 24.19MM
SALES (corp-wide): 24.19MM **Privately Held**
Web: www.asaelectronics.com
SIC: 3651 5065 Amplifiers: radio, public address, or musical instrument; Electronic parts and equipment, nec

(G-3193)
ASANDERS GLOBAL LLC ◯
2125 Toledo Rd Apt 145 (46516-5564)
PHONE..................224 401-4050
Autro Sanders, *Managing Member*
EMP: 5 **EST:** 2022
SALES (est): 241.99K **Privately Held**
SIC: 3799 Transportation equipment, nec

(G-3194)
ASC INDUSTRIES INC
23325 County Road 6 (46514)
P.O. Box 1801 (46515)
PHONE..................574 264-1987
Greg Macri, *Pr*
Edward Ramsey, *
▲ **EMP:** 25 **EST:** 1984
SALES (est): 3.29MM **Privately Held**
Web: www.ascind.com

SIC: 3498 3444 Tube fabricating (contract bending and shaping); Sheet metalwork

(G-3195)
ASCOT ENTERPRISES INC
53706 County Road 9 (46514)
P.O. Box 697 (46515-0697)
PHONE..................877 773-7751
Howard Yoder, *Brnch Mgr*
EMP: 70
SALES (corp-wide): 41.85MM **Privately Held**
Web: www.ascotent.com
SIC: 2391 Draperies, plastic and textile: from purchased materials
PA: Ascot Enterprises Inc
  503 S Main St
  Nappanee IN 46550
  877 773-7751

(G-3196)
ASHLEY F WARD INC
Also Called: Ashley Ward
56883 Elk Ct (46516-1457)
PHONE..................574 294-1502
Richard Dudley, *Prin*
EMP: 1
SQ FT: 50,000
SALES (corp-wide): 3.38K **Privately Held**
Web: www.ashleyward.com
SIC: 3451 3494 3432 Screw machine products; Valves and pipe fittings, nec; Plumbing fixture fittings and trim
PA: Ashley F. Ward, Inc.
  7490 Easy St
  Mason OH 45040
  513 398-1414

(G-3197)
ASSA ABLOY DOOR GROUP LLC
Also Called: Dominion Building Products
53518 Cr 9n, Ste.B (46514-5577)
PHONE..................800 826-2617
Rick Weiss, *Mgr*
EMP: 1
SIC: 3499 3442 Doors, safe and vault: metal; Metal doors, sash, and trim
HQ: Assa Abloy Door Group, Llc
  9159 Telecom Dr
  Milan TN 38358
  731 686-8345

(G-3198)
ASSEMBLY MASTERS INC
56624 Elk Park Dr (46516)
P.O. Box 1091 (46546)
PHONE..................574 293-9026
Debra Walters, *Pr*
Debra Hanigosky, *Pr*
Larry J Gennicks, *VP*
EMP: 2 **EST:** 2000
SQ FT: 10,000
SALES (est): 442.72K **Privately Held**
Web: www.assemblymasters.com
SIC: 3679 Harness assemblies, for electronic use: wire or cable

(G-3199)
ATLAS COPCO COMPRESSORS
831 E Windsor Ave Unit 8 (46514-5568)
PHONE..................574 264-1033
EMP: 6 **EST:** 2005
SALES (est): 127.22K **Privately Held**
Web: www.atlascopco.com
SIC: 3563 Air and gas compressors

(G-3200)
ATLAS DIE LLC (HQ)
2000 Middlebury St (46516-5521)
PHONE..................574 295-0050
▲ **EMP:** 55 **EST:** 2002

SALES (est): 43.81MM
SALES (corp-wide): 165.78MM **Privately Held**
Web: www.atlasdie.com
SIC: 3423 3544 Cutting dies, except metal cutting; Dies, steel rule
PA: Auxo Investment Partners, Llc
  38 Commerce Ave Sw
  Grand Rapids MI 49503
  616 980-9810

(G-3201)
ATS MANUFACTURING INC
2026 Sterling Ave (46516-4220)
▼ **EMP:** 9 **EST:** 2011
SALES (est): 707.64K **Privately Held**
Web: ats-manufacturing-llc.hub.biz
SIC: 3841 Surgical and medical instruments

(G-3202)
ATWOOD MOBILE PRODUCTS INC
Also Called: Atwood Mobile Products
1120 N Main St (46514-3203)
P.O. Box 1627 (46515-1627)
PHONE..................574 264-2131
▲ **EMP:** 875
SIC: 3714 Motor vehicle parts and accessories

(G-3203)
ATWOOD MOBILE PRODUCTS LLC
5155 Verdant St (46516-9315)
PHONE..................574 266-4848
EMP: 81
SALES (corp-wide): 2.84B **Privately Held**
Web: www.dometic.com
SIC: 3714 Motor vehicle parts and accessories
HQ: Atwood Mobile Products Llc
  1120 N Main St
  Elkhart IN 46514

(G-3204)
ATWOOD MOBILE PRODUCTS LLC
2040 Toledo Rd (46516-5541)
PHONE..................574 264-2131
Timothy Stephens, *Pr*
EMP: 81
SALES (corp-wide): 2.84B **Privately Held**
Web: www.dometic.com
SIC: 3714 Motor vehicle parts and accessories
HQ: Atwood Mobile Products Llc
  1120 N Main St
  Elkhart IN 46514

(G-3205)
ATWOOD MOBILE PRODUCTS LLC
2701 Ada Dr (46514-8646)
PHONE..................574 264-2131
EMP: 81
SALES (corp-wide): 2.84B **Privately Held**
Web: www.dometic.com
SIC: 3714 Motor vehicle parts and accessories
HQ: Atwood Mobile Products Llc
  1120 N Main St
  Elkhart IN 46514

(G-3206)
ATWOOD MOBILE PRODUCTS LLC (DH)
Also Called: Atwood Solutions
1120 N Main St (46514-3203)
P.O. Box 1627 (46515-1627)
PHONE..................574 264-2131
▲ **EMP:** 100 **EST:** 2007
SALES (est): 97.88MM
SALES (corp-wide): 2.84B **Privately Held**
Web: www.dometic.com

GEOGRAPHIC SECTION
Elkhart - Elkhart County (G-3232)

SIC: 3714 Motor vehicle parts and accessories
HQ: Dometic Corporation
5600 N River Rd Ste 250
Rosemont IL 60018

(G-3207)
AXIS PRODUCTS INC
21611 Protecta Dr (46516-9543)
P.O. Box 1083 (46515-1083)
PHONE..................................574 266-8282
EMP: 150
Web: www.axisproducts.com
SIC: 3714 5013 Axles, motor vehicle; Trailer parts and accessories

(G-3208)
AXIS UNLIMITED LLC
Also Called: Midwest Industrial Tanks
3403 Reedy Dr (46514)
P.O. Box 2897 (46515)
PHONE..................................574 370-8923
Chelsi Bowers, Prin
EMP: 8 EST: 2015
SALES (est): 492.08K Privately Held
SIC: 3443 Tanks, lined: metal plate

(G-3209)
AXLE INC
53664 County Road 9 (46514-5028)
P.O. Box 2153 (46515-2153)
PHONE..................................574 264-9434
EMP: 4 EST: 1994
SQ FT: 17,500
SALES (est): 469.43K Privately Held
Web: www.axleinc.com
SIC: 3714 Motor vehicle parts and accessories

(G-3210)
B & B INDUSTRIES INC
1121 D I Dr (46514-8232)
PHONE..................................574 262-8551
Bill Bottoms, Pr
Judy Bottoms, *
Glenn Duncan, *
▲ EMP: 35 EST: 1989
SQ FT: 28,000
SALES (est): 2.52MM Privately Held
Web: www.billbottoms.com
SIC: 3711 Wreckers (tow truck), assembly of

(G-3211)
B INDUSTRIES INC
4000 E Bristol St Ste 3 (46514-6949)
PHONE..................................574 264-3290
EMP: 3 EST: 2020
SALES (est): 125.94K Privately Held
SIC: 3999 Manufacturing industries, nec

(G-3212)
B NICKELL WOODWORKING LLC
4848 Beck Dr (46516-9569)
PHONE..................................574 333-2863
EMP: 5 EST: 2016
SALES (est): 59.54K Privately Held
Web: www.bnickell.com
SIC: 2431 Millwork

(G-3213)
B&R MANUFACTURING INC
2503 Marina Dr (46514-8641)
PHONE..................................574 293-5669
◆ EMP: 6 EST: 2011
SALES (est): 229.15K Privately Held
Web: www.hadleyproducts.com
SIC: 3999 Manufacturing industries, nec

(G-3214)
B-D INDUSTRIES INC
1715 Fieldhouse Ave (46517-1410)
PHONE..................................574 295-1420
James P Denton, Pr
Michael Dills, VP
Carol A Denton, Sec
Robert K Denton Prestreas, Prin
Suzanne Marvel, Corporate Secretary
EMP: 15 EST: 1979
SQ FT: 13,000
SALES (est): 1.79MM Privately Held
Web: www.bdindustries.com
SIC: 3479 3728 3471 Coating of metals and formed products; Aircraft parts and equipment, nec; Anodizing (plating) of metals or formed products

(G-3215)
BAKER PROTOTYPE ENGRG INC
53050 Elkhart East Blvd (46514-9479)
PHONE..................................574 266-7223
James Baker, Pr
EMP: 3 EST: 2006
SALES (est): 249.57K Privately Held
SIC: 3541 Machine tools, metal cutting type

(G-3216)
BATES MACHINE INC
2921 Lavanture Pl (46514-8233)
PHONE..................................574 264-3997
EMP: 5 EST: 2019
SALES (est): 25.09K Privately Held
Web: www.archglobalprecision.com
SIC: 7692 Welding repair

(G-3217)
BATTLEWEAR COMPONENTS INC
1421 Lawndale Rd (46514-3714)
PHONE..................................574 262-4659
Jennifer Bennett, Pr
Aaron Bennett, VP
EMP: 2 EST: 2015
SALES (est): 188.63K Privately Held
Web: www.exfog.com
SIC: 3949 Sporting and athletic goods, nec

(G-3218)
BAYER HEALTHCARE LLC
3400 Middlebury St (46516-5586)
PHONE..................................574 262-6136
Mike Kofeldt, Mgr
EMP: 24
SALES (corp-wide): 51.78B Privately Held
Web: www.bayercare.com
SIC: 2834 Pharmaceutical preparations
HQ: Bayer Healthcare Llc
100 Bayer Blvd
Whippany NJ 07981
862 404-3000

(G-3219)
BEACHFRONT FURNITURE INC
60874 Ridgepoint Ct (46517-9100)
PHONE..................................574 875-0817
Brian Thompson, Sec
EMP: 6 EST: 2003
SQ FT: 35,000
SALES (est): 92.21K Privately Held
Web: 3459-us.all.biz
SIC: 2519 Garden furniture, except wood, metal, stone, or concrete

(G-3220)
BEAMS SEATBELTS INC
3802 Gallatin Way (46514-7650)
PHONE..................................574 970-2667
Dennis Pursel, Mgr
EMP: 2 EST: 2012
SALES (est): 375.91K
SALES (corp-wide): 6.58B Publicly Held
SIC: 3199 Seat belts, leather
HQ: Shield Restraint Systems, Inc.
3802 Gallatin Way
Elkhart IN 46514

(G-3221)
BECK INDUSTRIES LP
28707 La Rue St (46516-1673)
P.O. Box 8 (46515-0008)
PHONE..................................574 294-5621
EMP: 70 EST: 1993
SQ FT: 300,000
SALES (est): 5.01MM Privately Held
SIC: 2451 3317 3799 5051 Mobile home frames; Tubes, seamless steel; Trailers and trailer equipment; Iron and steel (ferrous) products

(G-3222)
BEEBE CABINET CO INC
22695 State Road 120 (46516-5369)
PHONE..................................574 293-3580
Richard Hunger, Pr
Judith Hunger, VP
EMP: 10 EST: 1935
SQ FT: 10,000
SALES (est): 422.2K Privately Held
SIC: 2541 2521 2511 2434 Cabinets, except refrigerated: show, display, etc.: wood; Wood office furniture; Wood household furniture; Wood kitchen cabinets

(G-3223)
BEST FORMED PLASTICS LLC
21209 Protecta Dr (46516-9539)
PHONE..................................574 293-6128
James V Stewart, Managing Member
Jane Stewart, Sec
EMP: 21 EST: 2006
SQ FT: 3,000
SALES (est): 3.63MM Privately Held
Web: www.bestformedplastics.com
SIC: 3089 Injection molding of plastics

(G-3224)
BIG DOG ADHESIVES LLC
435 Harrison St (46516-2771)
PHONE..................................574 350-2237
Louis Giovannini, Managing Member
EMP: 19 EST: 2017
SALES (est): 3.1MM Privately Held
Web: www.bigdogadhesives.com
SIC: 2891 Adhesives

(G-3225)
BIONIC PROSTHETICS AND ORTHO
3130a Windsor Ct (46514-5556)
PHONE..................................219 791-9200
Dheeraj Bhambini, Brnch Mgr
EMP: 1
Web: www.bionicpo.com
SIC: 3842 Surgical appliances and supplies
PA: Bionic Prosthetics And Orthotics Group Llc
8695 Connecticut St Ste E
Merrillville IN 46410

(G-3226)
BLESSING TOOL & DIE INC
24366 County Road 45 (46516-6056)
PHONE..................................574 875-1982
James Blessing, Pr
Leah Blessing, VP
EMP: 2 EST: 2012
SQ FT: 4,000
SALES (est): 250.2K Privately Held
SIC: 3544 Special dies and tools

(G-3227)
BLUE BYTE TECH SOLUTIONS LLC
28571 County Road 16 (46516-1531)
PHONE..................................574 903-5637
Edward Collins, Owner
EMP: 6 EST: 2008
SALES (est): 437.81K Privately Held
Web: www.bluebytetech.com
SIC: 5734 7374 7379 3661 Computer and software stores; Computer graphics service; Online services technology consultants; Communication headgear, telephone

(G-3228)
BLUE SKY LIFE STORIES LLC
53641 Michael Ct (46514-9027)
PHONE..................................574 298-1254
Dawn Szabo, Prin
EMP: 3 EST: 2016
SALES (est): 103.28K Privately Held
Web: www.blueskylifestories.com
SIC: 2741 Miscellaneous publishing

(G-3229)
BOCK ENGINEERING COMPANY INC
Also Called: Rug Works
4307 Wyland Dr (46516-9501)
PHONE..................................574 522-3191
James Bock, Pr
W E Mc Manimie, VP
Joann Bock, Sec
EMP: 5 EST: 1990
SQ FT: 80,000
SALES (est): 457.37K Privately Held
Web: www.bockrugworks.com
SIC: 2273 5023 Carpets and rugs; Floor coverings

(G-3230)
BOCK INDUSTRIES INC
Also Called: Bull Moose Tube
29851 County Road 20 (46517-8993)
P.O. Box 1037 (46515-1037)
PHONE..................................574 295-8070
John J Meyer, Pr
Stephen H Birk, *
◆ EMP: 22 EST: 1923
SQ FT: 550,000
SALES (est): 10.76MM
SALES (corp-wide): 197.93MM Privately Held
Web: www.bullmoosetube.com
SIC: 3317 Tubes, wrought: welded or lock joint
PA: Caparo Bull Moose, Inc.
1819 Clarkson Rd Ste 100
Chesterfield MO 63017
636 537-1249

(G-3231)
BODYCOTE THERMAL PROC INC
908 County Road 1 N (46514-8992)
PHONE..................................574 295-2491
Tom Williams, Brnch Mgr
EMP: 23
SQ FT: 2,700
SALES (corp-wide): 1B Privately Held
Web: www.bodycote.com
SIC: 3398 Metal heat treating
HQ: Bodycote Thermal Processing, Inc.
12750 Merit Dr Ste 1400
Dallas TX 75251
214 904-2420

(G-3232)
BONNELL ALUMINUM ELKHART INC
Also Called: Aacoa
2551 County Road 10 W (46514-8788)
PHONE..................................574 262-4685
W Brook Hamilton, Pr
John J Teeple, *

Elkhart - Elkhart County (G-3233) GEOGRAPHIC SECTION

Mark J North, *
EMP: 220 **EST:** 1972
SQ FT: 255,000
SALES (est): 25.51MM **Publicly Held**
Web: www.bonnellaluminum.com
SIC: 3471 Electroplating of metals or formed products
HQ: Bonnell Aluminum (Corporate), Inc.
25 Bonnell St
Newnan GA 30263
770 253-2020

(G-3233)
BOWMANS HOOF TRIMMING
28824 Country Ln (46514-1218)
PHONE..................574 522-2838
Harry Bowman, *Owner*
EMP: 1 **EST:** 2005
SALES (est): 115.56K **Privately Held**
SIC: 3462 Horseshoes

(G-3234)
BRASILIA PRESS INC
2911 Moose Trl (46514-8230)
P.O. Box 2023 (46515-2023)
PHONE..................574 262-9700
Paul Bender, *Pr*
Ilaine Bender, *Sec*
EMP: 6 **EST:** 1978
SALES (est): 839.06K **Privately Held**
Web: www.bendersweb.com
SIC: 5092 2741 Model kits; Miscellaneous publishing

(G-3235)
BRIANZA USA CORP
3503 Cooper Dr (46514-8639)
PHONE..................574 855-9520
Filippo Milani, *Prin*
▲ **EMP:** 9 **EST:** 2013
SALES (est): 518.66K **Privately Held**
SIC: 3089 Air mattresses, plastics

(G-3236)
BRIDGEVIEW MANUFACTURING LLC
5321 Beck Dr (46516-9251)
PHONE..................574 970-0116
EMP: 11 **EST:** 2010
SQ FT: 30,000
SALES (est): 528.1K **Privately Held**
SIC: 3799 Recreational vehicles

(G-3237)
BUDCO TOOL & DIE INC
56935 Elk Ct (46516-1460)
PHONE..................574 522-4004
James H Allen Junior, *Pr*
EMP: 20 **EST:** 1979
SQ FT: 9,800
SALES (est): 788.15K **Privately Held**
Web: www.budcotool.com
SIC: 3544 3545 Die sets for metal stamping (presses); Tools and accessories for machine tools

(G-3238)
BURSTON MARKETING INC
2802 Frederic Dr (46514)
P.O. Box 1726 (46515)
PHONE..................574 262-4005
Thomas Stout, *Pr*
▲ **EMP:** 18 **EST:** 1988
SQ FT: 20,000
SALES (est): 2.37MM **Privately Held**
Web: www.burston.com
SIC: 2396 2395 7336 5199 Screen printing on fabric articles; Embroidery and art needlework; Graphic arts and related design; Advertising specialties

(G-3239)
BUZZI UNICEM USA INC
55284 Corwin Rd (46514-8401)
PHONE..................574 674-8873
David A Pedzinski, *Prin*
EMP: 3
SALES (corp-wide): 4.69B **Privately Held**
Web: www.buzziunicemusa.com
SIC: 3241 Portland cement
HQ: Buzzi Unicem Usa Inc
100 Brodhead Rd Ste 230
Bethlehem PA 18017
610 882-5000

(G-3240)
BY-PASS PAINT SHOP INC (PA)
1132 N Nappanee St (46514-1792)
PHONE..................574 264-5334
Donato Del Prete, *Pr*
Florence Del Prete, *VP*
EMP: 15 **EST:** 1947
SQ FT: 40,000
SALES (est): 2.17MM
SALES (corp-wide): 2.17MM **Privately Held**
SIC: 2431 Moldings, wood: unfinished and prefinished

(G-3241)
C & G WIRING INC
1823 Leer Dr (46514-5447)
PHONE..................574 333-3433
Kenneth Brink, *Pr*
EMP: 15 **EST:** 1988
SALES (est): 2.52MM **Privately Held**
Web: www.cngwiring.com
SIC: 3679 Harness assemblies, for electronic use: wire or cable

(G-3242)
C & K MANUFACTURING INC
25943 Forest Hill Ave (46514-5002)
P.O. Box 3015 (46515-3015)
PHONE..................574 264-4063
Stephan K Clements, *Pr*
EMP: 16 **EST:** 2004
SQ FT: 20,000
SALES (est): 791.28K **Privately Held**
Web: www.ckmfginc.com
SIC: 3823 Computer interface equipment, for industrial process control

(G-3243)
C & L ELECTRIC MOTOR REPR INC
2910 Airport Pkwy (46514-9711)
PHONE..................574 533-2643
Charles Lewallen, *Pr*
Robert Kauffman, *VP*
EMP: 4 **EST:** 1967
SALES (est): 241.29K **Privately Held**
SIC: 7694 5063 Electric motor repair; Motors, electric

(G-3244)
C M I ENTERPRISES INC
Also Called: C M I Automotive of Indiana
2904 Leer Ct (46514-5448)
PHONE..................305 685-9651
Jorge Giraldo, *Prin*
EMP: 60
SALES (corp-wide): 28.77MM **Privately Held**
Web: www.cmi-enterprises.com
SIC: 5131 2295 7532 Knit fabrics; Coated fabrics, not rubberized; Van conversion
PA: C. M. I. Enterprises, Inc.
13145 Nw 45th Ave
Opa Locka FL 33054
305 622-6410

(G-3245)
CABINETRY SOLUTIONS LLC
2933 Thorne Dr (46514-8228)
PHONE..................574 326-3699
EMP: 4 **EST:** 2017
SALES (est): 151.02K **Privately Held**
Web: www.cabinetrysi.com
SIC: 2434 Wood kitchen cabinets

(G-3246)
CANA INC (PA)
Also Called: Cana Cabinetry
29194 Phillips St (46514-1050)
PHONE..................574 266-6566
David Geiger, *Pr*
George Forman, *CFO*
EMP: 5 **EST:** 1985
SALES (est): 9.66MM
SALES (corp-wide): 9.66MM **Privately Held**
Web: www.componentsbycana.com
SIC: 2431 Doors and door parts and trim, wood

(G-3247)
CARGO SYSTEMS INC
2603 Glenview Dr (46514-8709)
PHONE..................574 264-1600
John R Coble, *CEO*
Dallis Lindley, *Pr*
EMP: 5 **EST:** 1989
SQ FT: 9,200
SALES (est): 529.74K **Privately Held**
Web: www.cargosystems.com
SIC: 3493 Torsion bar springs

(G-3248)
CARVERS TRUCK AND TRAILER LLC
2946 Jami St (46514-9050)
PHONE..................574 343-2240
EMP: 7 **EST:** 2019
SALES (est): 517.84K **Privately Held**
SIC: 3715 Truck trailers

(G-3249)
CAST PRODUCTS LP (DH)
Also Called: Colorimetric
5400 Beck Dr (46516-9259)
P.O. Box 1368 (46515-1368)
PHONE..................574 294-2684
Dennis Schwartz, *Pt*
James Schwartz, *Pt*
Thomas Nagy, *Pt*
Brent Jagla, *Pt*
Chris White, *Pt*
▲ **EMP:** 35 **EST:** 1956
SALES (est): 8.88MM
SALES (corp-wide): 3.47B **Publicly Held**
Web: www.castproducts.com
SIC: 5074 5014 5084 5031 Plumbing fittings and supplies; Tires and tubes; Instruments and control equipment; Lumber, plywood, and millwork
HQ: Dehco, Inc.
5400 Beck Dr
Elkhart IN 46516
574 294-2684

(G-3250)
CENTURY FOAM INC (PA)
Also Called: Century Foam
2600 S Nappanee St (46517-1082)
P.O. Box 2207 (46515-2207)
PHONE..................574 293-5547
Thomas Teach, *Pr*
Sandra Teach, *
▲ **EMP:** 94 **EST:** 1981
SQ FT: 131,000
SALES (est): 24.93MM
SALES (corp-wide): 24.93MM **Privately Held**

Web: www.centuryfoam.com
SIC: 3086 Insulation or cushioning material, foamed plastics

(G-3251)
CHRISTIAN SOUND & SONG INC
56718 Coppergate Dr (46516-5678)
PHONE..................574 294-2893
Thomas Lefevre, *COO*
Charles Cooper, *CEO*
EMP: 3 **EST:** 1999
SALES (est): 163.43K **Privately Held**
SIC: 2721 8661 8742 Magazines: publishing and printing; Religious organizations; Training and development consultant

(G-3252)
CHUBBS STEEL SALES INC
Also Called: Griffin Trailers
57832 County Road 3 (46517-9366)
P.O. Box 64 (46561-0064)
PHONE..................574 295-3166
Roy Lee Griffin, *Pr*
Gwen Mae Griffin, *
EMP: 25 **EST:** 1994
SQ FT: 40,000
SALES (est): 2.57MM **Privately Held**
Web: www.griffintrailer.com
SIC: 5013 3799 Trailer parts and accessories; Trailers and trailer equipment

(G-3253)
CHURCHASSIST TECHNOLOGIES LLC
23879 Banyan Cir (46516-6042)
PHONE..................574 238-2307
Bruce Van Der, *Owner*
Bruce Vanderwolf, *Owner*
EMP: 1 **EST:** 2005
SALES (est): 67.95K **Privately Held**
Web: www.churchassist.com
SIC: 7372 Prepackaged software

(G-3254)
CLEER VISION WINDOWS INC
Also Called: Cleer Vision Tempered Glass
3401 County Road 6 E (46514-7662)
PHONE..................574 262-0449
Rick Collins, *Pr*
John Collins, *Ch Bd*
EMP: 46 **EST:** 1982
SQ FT: 180,000
SALES (est): 13.61MM
SALES (corp-wide): 11.12B **Publicly Held**
Web: www.cleervision.com
SIC: 3231 3442 Strengthened or reinforced glass; Metal doors, sash, and trim
HQ: Airxcel, Inc.
3050 N Saint Francis St
Wichita KS 67219

(G-3255)
CLOVER SHEET METAL COMPANY
28298 Clay St (46517-1072)
PHONE..................574 293-5912
David Collier, *CEO*
Stephen Collier, *Pr*
EMP: 10 **EST:** 1938
SQ FT: 14,000
SALES (est): 243.44K **Privately Held**
Web: www.cloversm.com
SIC: 1761 3444 Sheet metal work, nec; Sheet metalwork

(G-3256)
COLBERT PACKAGING CORPORATION
1511 W Lusher Ave (46517-1423)
PHONE..................574 295-6605
Tim Price, *Prin*

EMP: 90
SALES (corp-wide): 48.98MM **Privately Held**
Web: www.colbertpkg.com
SIC: 2657 2652 Folding paperboard boxes; Setup paperboard boxes
PA: Colbert Packaging Corporation
9949 58th Pl Ste 100
Kenosha WI 53144
847 367-5990

(G-3257)
COLLINS TRAILERS INC
Also Called: J B Enterprises
1053 Middleton Run Rd (46516-9253)
PHONE................574 294-2561
Joe Collins, *Pr*
Betty Collins, *VP*
EMP: 7 EST: 1988
SQ FT: 13,000
SALES (est): 622.43K **Privately Held**
SIC: 3799 5599 Trailers and trailer equipment; Utility trailers

(G-3258)
COMMODORE HOMES LLC
58096 County Road 7 (46517)
PHONE................574 533-7100
Bill Boor, *Pr*
EMP: 1200 EST: 2021
SALES (est): 115.92MM
SALES (corp-wide): 1.79B **Publicly Held**
Web: www.commodorehomes.com
SIC: 2452 Modular homes, prefabricated, wood
PA: Cavco Industries, Inc.
3636 N Centl Ave Ste 1200
Phoenix AZ 85012
602 256-6263

(G-3259)
COMPLEX PLASTICS LLC
23153 Circle Ln (46514-4579)
PHONE................574 389-9911
▲ EMP: 6 EST: 1967
SQ FT: 1,000
SALES (est): 462.92K **Privately Held**
Web: www.complexplastics.com
SIC: 3089 Injection molding of plastics

(G-3260)
COMPLEX PLASTICS LLC
2630 Sterling Ave (46516-4903)
PHONE................603 305-3043
EMP: 6 EST: 2018
SALES (est): 65.36K **Privately Held**
Web: www.complexplastics.com
SIC: 3089 Injection molding of plastics

(G-3261)
CONN-SELMER INC
Selmer Plant 2
2415 Industrial Pkwy (46516-5406)
P.O. Box 310 (46515-0310)
PHONE................574 522-1675
Heinz Mantel, *Mgr*
EMP: 87
SQ FT: 75,888
SALES (corp-wide): 528.25MM **Privately Held**
Web: www.connselmer.com
SIC: 3931 Musical instruments
HQ: Conn-Selmer, Inc.
600 Industrial Pkwy
Elkhart IN 46516
574 522-1675

(G-3262)
CONN-SELMER INC (DH)
Also Called: Selmer Paris
600 Industrial Pkwy (46516)
P.O. Box 310 (46515)
PHONE................574 522-1675
Stephen Zapf, *Pr*
Kimberly S Kirk, *
Judy Minik, *
◆ EMP: 75 EST: 1915
SQ FT: 25,000
SALES (est): 146.22MM
SALES (corp-wide): 528.25MM **Privately Held**
Web: www.connselmer.com
SIC: 3931 5736 Pianos, all types: vertical, grand, spinet, player, etc.; Pianos
HQ: Steinway Musical Instruments, Inc.
1133 Ave Of The Amrcas Fl
New York NY 10036

(G-3263)
CONN-SELMER INC
Vincent Bach Co
500 Industrial Pkwy (46516-5416)
P.O. Box 310 (46515-0310)
PHONE................574 295-6730
John Stoner, *Pr*
EMP: 45
SQ FT: 152,320
SALES (corp-wide): 528.25MM **Privately Held**
Web: www.connselmer.com
SIC: 3931 5099 Guitars and parts, electric and nonelectric; Musical instruments
HQ: Conn-Selmer, Inc.
600 Industrial Pkwy
Elkhart IN 46516
574 522-1675

(G-3264)
CONN-SELMER INC
1000 Industrial Pkwy (46516-5526)
PHONE................574 295-0079
Michael R Vickrey, *VP Fin*
EMP: 89
SALES (corp-wide): 528.25MM **Privately Held**
Web: www.connselmer.com
SIC: 3931 Woodwind instruments and parts
HQ: Conn-Selmer, Inc.
600 Industrial Pkwy
Elkhart IN 46516
574 522-1675

(G-3265)
CONTINENTAL INDUSTRIES INC (PA)
Also Called: Continental Register Co
100 W Windsor Ave (46514-5503)
P.O. Box 1248 (46515-1248)
PHONE................574 262-4511
David Leiter, *Pr*
Paul Leiter, *
Judith Leiter, *
EMP: 100 EST: 1952
SQ FT: 170,000
SALES (est): 22.85MM
SALES (corp-wide): 22.85MM **Privately Held**
Web: www.continentalindustries.com
SIC: 3444 3446 Sheet metalwork; Registers (air), metal

(G-3266)
CONVERSION COMPONENTS INC
51174 Creek Haven Dr (46514-6070)
P.O. Box 429 (46515-0429)
PHONE................574 264-4181
Jim Shreve, *Pr*
Beth Shreve, *Sec*
Max Reeder, *VP*
EMP: 4 EST: 1984
SALES (est): 450.52K **Privately Held**
Web: www.conversioncomponents.com
SIC: 3714 5013 Motor vehicle parts and accessories; Automotive hardware

(G-3267)
COOLSTREAM RV DUCTING INC
2019 W Lusher Ave (46517-1347)
PHONE................574 361-4271
Richard Moore, *Pr*
EMP: 19 EST: 2017
SALES (est): 1.19MM **Privately Held**
SIC: 3999 Barber and beauty shop equipment

(G-3268)
CORE WOOD COMPONENTS LLC
2995 Paul Dr Ste A (46514-8797)
PHONE................574 370-4457
Wendall Joe Campbell, *Pr*
Joe Campbell, *Prin*
EMP: 7 EST: 2014
SQ FT: 25,000
SALES (est): 893.5K **Privately Held**
SIC: 3553 5099 Woodworking machinery; Wood and wood by-products

(G-3269)
CRANE COMPOSITES INC
21067 Protecta Dr (46516-9704)
PHONE................574 295-9391
Julie Keith, *Brnch Mgr*
EMP: 1
SALES (corp-wide): 2.09B **Publicly Held**
Web: www.cranecomposites.com
SIC: 3089 Panels, building: plastics, nec
HQ: Crane Composites, Inc.
23525 W Eames St
Channahon IL 60410
815 467-8600

(G-3270)
CREATIVE CABINETS
30034 County Road 10 (46514-9776)
PHONE................574 264-9041
Tim Marshall, *Owner*
EMP: 5 EST: 1988
SALES (est): 186.44K **Privately Held**
Web: www.marshallscreativecabinets.com
SIC: 2434 Wood kitchen cabinets

(G-3271)
CREATIVE MANUFACTURING RV LLC
330 E Windsor Ave (46514-5565)
PHONE................574 333-3302
Rebecca L Belcher, *Pt*
Roger Reiff, *Pt*
EMP: 10 EST: 2010
SALES (est): 445.26K **Privately Held**
SIC: 3799 6399 Recreational vehicles; Warranty insurance, automobile

(G-3272)
CROSBIE FOUNDRY COMPANY INC
1600 Mishawaka St (46514-1898)
PHONE................574 262-1502
Daniel J Crosbie, *Pr*
Gregory A Crosbie, *
John F Crosbie, *
EMP: 19 EST: 1956
SQ FT: 18,500
SALES (est): 811.1K **Privately Held**
Web: www.crosbiefoundry.com
SIC: 3369 3366 Nonferrous foundries, nec; Copper foundries

(G-3273)
CROWN AUDIO INC
Also Called: Crown International
1718 W Mishawaka Rd (46517-9439)
PHONE................800 342-6939
◆ EMP: 450 EST: 1947
SALES (est): 92.11MM **Privately Held**
Web: www.crownaudio.com
SIC: 3651 3663 3823 Amplifiers: radio, public address, or musical instrument; Transmitting apparatus, radio or television; Analyzers, industrial process type
HQ: Harman International Industries Incorporated
400 Atlantic St Fl 15
Stamford CT 06901
203 328-3500

(G-3274)
CROWN EQUIPMENT CORPORATION
Also Called: Crown Lift Trucks
1125 Herman St (46516-9030)
PHONE................574 293-1264
Troy Boyer, *Mgr*
EMP: 4
SALES (corp-wide): 7.12B **Privately Held**
Web: www.crown.com
SIC: 3537 Lift trucks, industrial: fork, platform, straddle, etc.
PA: Crown Equipment Corporation
44 S Washington St
New Bremen OH 45869
419 629-2311

(G-3275)
CRUME INDUSTRIES LLC
1329 Freda Dr A (46514-5451)
PHONE................574 747-7683
Philip Crume, *Pr*
EMP: 1 EST: 2016
SALES (est): 56.15K **Privately Held**
SIC: 8711 5063 3569 7372 Engineering services; Electrical apparatus and equipment; Robots, assembly line: industrial and commercial; Prepackaged software

(G-3276)
CRYSTAL INDUSTRIES INC
28870 Phillips St (46514-1241)
PHONE................574 264-6166
Kevin Anthony, *Pr*
▲ EMP: 49 EST: 1999
SQ FT: 85,000
SALES (est): 4.72MM **Privately Held**
Web: www.crystalindustries.net
SIC: 3441 Fabricated structural metal

(G-3277)
CTS CORPORATION
905 N West Blvd (46514-1875)
PHONE................574 293-7511
EMP: 116
SALES (corp-wide): 550.42MM **Publicly Held**
Web: www.ctscorp.com
SIC: 3678 Electronic connectors
PA: Cts Corporation
4925 Indiana Ave
Lisle IL 60532
630 577-8800

(G-3278)
CTS ELCTRNIC CMPONENTS CAL INC
Also Called: Ierc
905 N West Blvd (46514-1875)
PHONE................574 523-3800
EMP: 6 EST: 1963
SQ FT: 6,140
SALES (est): 2.47MM
SALES (corp-wide): 550.42MM **Publicly Held**
Web: www.ctscorp.com
SIC: 3679 Electronic circuits
PA: Cts Corporation

Elkhart - Elkhart County (G-3279)

GEOGRAPHIC SECTION

4925 Indiana Ave
Lisle IL 60532
630 577-8800

(G-3279)
CULLIP INDUSTRIES INC
Also Called: Cullip Tool & Die
300 Comet Ave (46514-5529)
PHONE.....................574 293-8251
John Cullip, *Pr*
Marie Cullip, *Sec*
EMP: 23 **EST:** 1959
SQ FT: 10,400
SALES (est): 461.92K **Privately Held**
Web: www.cullipindustries.com
SIC: 3599 Machine shop, jobbing and repair

(G-3280)
CUMMINS AMERICAS INC
Also Called: Cummins
5125 Beck Dr (46516-9094)
PHONE.....................800 589-9027
David Boots, *Mgr*
EMP: 3
SQ FT: 2,000
SALES (corp-wide): 34.06B **Publicly Held**
SIC: 3621 Generators and sets, electric
HQ: Cummins Americas, Inc.
500 Jackson St
Columbus IN 47201
812 377-5000

(G-3281)
CUMMINS POWER GENERATION INC
Also Called: Cummins Onan
5125 Beck Dr Ste A (46516-9094)
PHONE.....................574 262-4611
EMP: 42
SALES (corp-wide): 34.06B **Publicly Held**
SIC: 3621 3519 Generators and sets, electric
; Internal combustion engines, nec
HQ: Cummins Power Generation Inc.
1400 73rd Ave Ne
Minneapolis MN 55432
763 574-5000

(G-3282)
CURTIS TOM TOOL AND DYE
622 Jay Dee St (46514-1353)
PHONE.....................574 293-3832
Ronald Curtis, *Owner*
EMP: 1 **EST:** 1947
SQ FT: 2,478
SALES (est): 66.27K **Privately Held**
SIC: 3469 Stamping metal for the trade

(G-3283)
CUSTOM WOOD PRODUCTS INC
1901 W Hively Ave (46517-4028)
P.O. Box 925 (46573-0925)
PHONE.....................574 522-3300
Kirti P Shah, *Pr*
Kirit P Shah, *
Raju K Shah, *
▲ **EMP:** 70 **EST:** 1988
SALES (est): 4.66MM **Privately Held**
Web: www.cwponline.com
SIC: 2511 2512 3714 2531 Dining room furniture: wood; Chairs: upholstered on wood frames; Motor vehicle parts and accessories; Public building and related furniture

(G-3284)
D & W INC
941 Oak St (46514-2287)
PHONE.....................574 264-9674
Anthony Warning, *Pr*
▲ **EMP:** 100 **EST:** 1967
SQ FT: 130,000
SALES (est): 14.35MM **Privately Held**

Web: www.dwmirrorglass.com
SIC: 3231 5075 Mirrored glass; Warm air heating equipment and supplies

(G-3285)
DAMON CORPORATION
Also Called: Breckenridge Recrtl Pk Trlrs
2958 Gateway Dr (46514-8600)
P.O. Box 1486 (46515-1486)
PHONE.....................574 262-2624
◆ **EMP:** 600
SIC: 3716 3792 Motor homes; Travel trailers and campers

(G-3286)
DAMON MOTOR COACH
604 Middleton Run Rd (46516-5447)
P.O. Box 2888 (46515-2888)
PHONE.....................574 536-3781
Bill Fenech, *Pr*
EMP: 25 **EST:** 2010
SALES (est): 2.03MM
SALES (corp-wide): 11.12B **Publicly Held**
Web: www.thormotorcoach.com
SIC: 3711 Motor vehicles and car bodies
PA: Thor Industries, Inc.
601 E Beardsley Ave
Elkhart IN 46514
574 970-7460

(G-3287)
DEC-O-ART INC
3914 Lexington Park Dr (46514-1194)
PHONE.....................574 294-6451
Anthony J Dosmann, *Pr*
Ronald Dosmann, *
Fredrick Dosmann, *
Carl Dosmann, *Quality*
EMP: 45 **EST:** 1971
SQ FT: 28,000
SALES (est): 9.71MM **Privately Held**
Web: www.dec-o-art.com
SIC: 2759 Screen printing

(G-3288)
DEHCO INC (HQ)
Also Called: Recreation Nation
5400 Beck Dr (46516-9259)
P.O. Box 1368 (46515-1368)
PHONE.....................574 294-2684
James T Schwartz, *CEO*
Thomas J Nagy, *
Pamela Austin, *
▲ **EMP:** 100 **EST:** 1999
SALES (est): 83.58MM
SALES (corp-wide): 3.47B **Publicly Held**
Web: www.dehco.com
SIC: 5031 5074 5014 5084 Lumber, plywood, and millwork; Plumbing fittings and supplies; Tires and tubes; Instruments and control equipment
PA: Patrick Industries, Inc.
107 W Franklin St
Elkhart IN 46516
574 294-7511

(G-3289)
DELIVERY CONCEPTS INC (PA)
29301 County Road 20 (46517-8990)
PHONE.....................574 522-3981
Anthony M Marchetti, *Pr*
Daniel Dulmentritt, *
Michael Oliva, *
Aaron A Marchetti, *
Rebecca Stanley, *
EMP: 25 **EST:** 1991
SQ FT: 12,000
SALES (est): 6.67MM
SALES (corp-wide): 6.67MM **Privately Held**
Web: www.deliveryconcepts.com

SIC: 3585 3713 Refrigeration and heating equipment; Specialty motor vehicle bodies

(G-3290)
DEXSTAR WHEEL COMPANY INC
400 Collins Rd (46516-5437)
PHONE.....................574 295-3535
▲ **EMP:** 60
SIC: 3714 Wheel rims, motor vehicle

(G-3291)
DEXTER AXLE COMPANY LLC
Also Called: Al-Ko Kober
21611 Protecta Dr (46516-9543)
PHONE.....................574 294-6651
Robert Murray, *Mgr*
EMP: 96
SALES (corp-wide): 1.41B **Privately Held**
Web: www.dexteraxle.com
SIC: 3714 Axles, motor vehicle
HQ: Dexter Axle Company Llc
2900 Industrial Pkwy E
Elkhart IN 46516

(G-3292)
DEXTER AXLE COMPANY LLC (HQ)
Also Called: Dexter Axle
2900 Industrial Pkwy (46516)
P.O. Box 250 (46515)
PHONE.....................574 295-7888
Adam W Dexter, *Pr*
Bryan S Thursby, *CCO**
◆ **EMP:** 70 **EST:** 1999
SQ FT: 43,000
SALES (est): 1.3B
SALES (corp-wide): 1.41B **Privately Held**
Web: www.dexteraxle.com
SIC: 3714 3442 Axles, motor vehicle; Metal doors, sash, and trim
PA: Dexko Global Inc.
39555 Orchrd Hl Pl Ste 52
Novi MI 48375
248 533-0029

(G-3293)
DEXTER AXLE COMPANY LLC
21608 Protecta Dr (46516-9532)
PHONE.....................574 294-6651
EMP: 203
SALES (corp-wide): 1.41B **Privately Held**
Web: www.dexteraxle.com
SIC: 3714 5083 Gears, motor vehicle; Lawn and garden machinery and equipment
HQ: Dexter Axle Company Llc
2900 Industrial Pkwy E
Elkhart IN 46516

(G-3294)
DEXTER CHASSIS GROUP INC
Also Called: Electrocoat Technologies
2501 Jeanwood Dr (46514-7615)
PHONE.....................574 266-7356
EMP: 99
SIC: 3799 1799 Trailers and trailer equipment; Welding on site

(G-3295)
DG MANUFACTURING INC
28564 Holiday Pl (46517-1155)
PHONE.....................574 294-7550
Tim Stankovich, *Pr*
Sherry Stankovich, *
EMP: 55 **EST:** 1986
SQ FT: 51,000
SALES (est): 5.16MM **Privately Held**
SIC: 3792 5561 Pickup covers, canopies or caps; Recreational vehicle parts and accessories

(G-3296)
DIANE VANDER VLIET
56045 Riverdale Dr (46514-1111)
PHONE.....................574 389-9360
EMP: 3 **EST:** 2016
SALES (est): 55.07K **Privately Held**
SIC: 1389 Oil field services, nec

(G-3297)
DIE-RITE MACHINE AND TOOL CORP
129 Rush Ct (46516-9644)
P.O. Box 2436 (46515-2436)
PHONE.....................574 522-2366
Monty K Craven, *Pr*
EMP: 8 **EST:** 1987
SQ FT: 12,000
SALES (est): 936.64K **Privately Held**
Web: www.die-ritemachine.com
SIC: 3544 3599 Special dies and tools; Machine shop, jobbing and repair

(G-3298)
DNA ENTERPRISES INC
Also Called: Canterbury R V
21710 County Road 10 (46514-4647)
P.O. Box 147 (46527-0147)
PHONE.....................574 534-0034
Kevin Wells, *Pr*
Tyler Steele, *
EMP: 34 **EST:** 1990
SALES (est): 2.93MM **Privately Held**
Web: www.canterburyrv.com
SIC: 3792 5012 Travel trailers and campers; Recreational vehicles, motor homes, and trailers

(G-3299)
DOMAR MACHINE & TOOL INC
56740 Elk Park Dr (46516-1448)
PHONE.....................574 295-8791
Doug Martin, *Pr*
Donna Martin, *VP*
▲ **EMP:** 6 **EST:** 1989
SQ FT: 10,000
SALES (est): 531.38K **Privately Held**
Web: www.classcustoms.com
SIC: 3469 Stamping metal for the trade

(G-3300)
DOMETIC
5155 Verdant St (46516-9315)
PHONE.....................574 266-4848
EMP: 114 **EST:** 2019
SALES (est): 16.49MM **Privately Held**
Web: www.dometic.com
SIC: 3714 Motor vehicle parts and accessories

(G-3301)
DOMETIC CORPORATION
Also Called: Dometic
5155 Verdant St (46516-9315)
PHONE.....................260 463-7657
John Waters, *Pr*
EMP: 375
SALES (corp-wide): 2.84B **Privately Held**
Web: www.dometic.com
SIC: 3585 3714 2394 Air conditioning units, complete: domestic or industrial; Motor vehicle parts and accessories; Canvas and related products
HQ: Dometic Corporation
5600 N River Rd Ste 250
Rosemont IL 60018

(G-3302)
DOUBLE T MANUFACTURING CORP
Also Called: S T Laminating
27139 County Road 6 (46514-5601)
P.O. Box 1371 (46515-1371)

PHONE..................574 262-1340
Gary Taska, Ch
Marlene Taska, Sec
EMP: 10 **EST:** 1974
SQ FT: 15,000
SALES (est): 933.01K **Privately Held**
Web: www.double-t-usa.com
SIC: 2541 2434 3714 2521 Counter and sink tops; Vanities, bathroom: wood; Motor vehicle parts and accessories; Wood office furniture

(G-3303)
DREAM LIGHTING INC
2111 Industrial Pkwy (46516-5410)
PHONE..................574 206-4888
Michael Cole Gilpin, Prin
▲ **EMP:** 18 **EST:** 2013
SALES (est): 2.83MM **Privately Held**
Web: www.dreamlightingled.com
SIC: 3646 Commercial lighting fixtures
PA: Power Panda Pty Ltd
58 Eastern Road
Browns Plains QLD 4118

(G-3304)
DUBOIS MANUFACTURING INC
30561 Old Us 20 (46514-9597)
PHONE..................574 674-6988
EMP: 3 **EST:** 2009
SALES (est): 227.31K **Privately Held**
SIC: 3999 Manufacturing industries, nec

(G-3305)
DURO INC
Also Called: Lee's Wood Products
24478 County Road 45 (46516-6043)
P.O. Box 2341 (46515-2341)
PHONE..................574 293-6860
Terry Rodino, Pr
EMP: 8 **EST:** 1985
SQ FT: 14,000
SALES (est): 1.32MM **Privately Held**
SIC: 2448 Pallets, wood

(G-3306)
DURO RECYCLING INC
Also Called: Recycled New
24478 County Road 45 (46516-6043)
P.O. Box 2341 (46515-2341)
PHONE..................574 522-2572
Terry Rodino, Pr
EMP: 18 **EST:** 1998
SALES (est): 954.15K **Privately Held**
Web: www.recyclednew.com
SIC: 2448 Pallets, wood

(G-3307)
DUROGREEN OUTDOOR LLC
4540 Pine Creek Rd (46516-9562)
PHONE..................574 327-6943
EMP: 10 **EST:** 2021
SALES (est): 89.23K **Privately Held**
SIC: 5021 2511 Outdoor and lawn furniture, nec; Wood lawn and garden furniture

(G-3308)
DYNAMIC AXLE LLC
25863 Northland Crossing Dr (46514)
P.O. Box 13 (49130-0013)
PHONE..................574 226-0242
EMP: 5 **EST:** 2012
SALES (est): 119.07K **Privately Held**
SIC: 3714 Motor vehicle parts and accessories

(G-3309)
DYNAMIC INDUSTRIAL GROUP LLC
54347 Highland Blvd (46514-2124)
PHONE..................574 295-5525

EMP: 48 **EST:** 2007
SALES (est): 421.04K **Privately Held**
Web: www.dynamicindustrial.com
SIC: 3441 Fabricated structural metal

(G-3310)
DYNAMIC METALS LLC (PA)
Also Called: Dynamic Aerospace and Defense
54347 Highland Blvd (46514-2124)
PHONE..................574 262-2497
Donald Nystrom, Pr
Dennis Nystrom, Sec
▼ **EMP:** 38 **EST:** 2003
SQ FT: 80,000
SALES (est): 27.27MM
SALES (corp-wide): 27.27MM **Privately Held**
Web: www.dynamicmetalsllc.com
SIC: 3441 Fabricated structural metal

(G-3311)
EASH LLC
Also Called: Eash Design
301 Benchmark Dr (46516-0001)
PHONE..................574 295-4450
Damon Marcott, Managing Member
EMP: 12 **EST:** 2015
SALES (est): 950.7K **Privately Held**
Web: www.eashdesign.com
SIC: 2541 5561 Table or counter tops, plastic laminated; Recreational vehicle parts and accessories

(G-3312)
EAST-T-WEST NORTH-TO-SOUTH INC
3000 County Road 6 W (46514-8681)
PHONE..................574 264-6664
Judith Reyes, Prin
EMP: 82 **EST:** 2017
SALES (est): 27.71K
SALES (corp-wide): 364.48B **Publicly Held**
Web: www.easttowestrv.com
SIC: 3799 Recreational vehicles
HQ: Forest River, Inc.
900 County Rd 1 N
Elkhart IN 46514

(G-3313)
EDWARDS PACE CO
28858 Ventura Dr (46517-8832)
PHONE..................574 522-5337
Mike Beckman, Prin
Lester Lee, *
EMP: 62 **EST:** 2010
SALES (est): 11.32MM
SALES (corp-wide): 1.62B **Privately Held**
SIC: 3715 Truck trailers
HQ: Truck Accessories Group, Llc
28858 Ventura Dr
Elkhart IN 46517
574 522-5337

(G-3314)
EFP LLC (HQ)
Also Called: EFP
223 Middleton Run Rd (46516-5488)
P.O. Box 2368 (46515-2368)
PHONE..................574 295-4690
Keith Arenz, Pr
Dennis Orban, *
▲ **EMP:** 64 **EST:** 1954
SQ FT: 230,000
SALES (est): 52.84MM
SALES (corp-wide): 1.62B **Privately Held**
Web: www.efppackaging.com
SIC: 3086 Insulation or cushioning material, foamed plastics
PA: J. B. Poindexter & Co., Inc.
600 Travis St Ste 400

Houston TX 77002
713 655-9800

(G-3315)
EJE INDUSTRIES LLC
2610 Sterling Ave (46516-4903)
PHONE..................574 326-3269
Eric Herrera, Pr
EMP: 6 **EST:** 2014
SALES (est): 317.65K **Privately Held**
Web: www.eje-ind.com
SIC: 3441 Fabricated structural metal

(G-3316)
ELECTRO-COAT TECHNOLOGIES
2501 Jeanwood Dr (46514-7615)
PHONE..................574 266-7356
Dennis Marcott, CEO
EMP: 19 **EST:** 1998
SALES (est): 194.29K **Privately Held**
Web: corporate.lippert.com
SIC: 3479 Coating of metals and formed products

(G-3317)
ELKCASES INC
Also Called: Sprunger Engineering
23143 Heaton Vis (46514-9340)
PHONE..................574 295-7700
Dale D Fahlbeck, CEO
Vicki Spicer, *
Kennard R Weaver, *
EMP: 8 **EST:** 1964
SQ FT: 33,000
SALES (est): 199.54K **Privately Held**
SIC: 3161 3089 Musical instrument cases; Plastics processing

(G-3318)
ELKHART BEDDING CO INC
2124 Sterling Ave (46516-4999)
PHONE..................574 293-6200
Chris Darr, Pr
Sandra Darr, Sec
EMP: 15 **EST:** 1942
SQ FT: 28,000
SALES (est): 2.23MM **Privately Held**
Web: www.elkhartbedding.com
SIC: 2515 Mattresses, innerspring or box spring

(G-3319)
ELKHART BINDING INC
51784 State Road 19 (46514-5801)
PHONE..................574 522-5455
Patrick C Berendt, Pr
EMP: 2 **EST:** 1989
SQ FT: 2,000
SALES (est): 193.47K **Privately Held**
SIC: 2789 Binding only: books, pamphlets, magazines, etc.

(G-3320)
ELKHART BRASS
1302 W Beardsley Ave (46514-1828)
PHONE..................574 266-3700
EMP: 20 **EST:** 2018
SALES (est): 3.14MM **Privately Held**
Web: www.elkhartbrass.com
SIC: 3999 Manufacturing industries, nec

(G-3321)
ELKHART BRASS MANUFACTURING CO
Also Called: Shreve Manufacturing
1302 W Beardsley Ave (46514-1828)
PHONE..................800 346-0250
EMP: 29
Web: www.elkhartbrass.com

SIC: 2542 5087 Partitions and fixtures, except wood; Firefighting equipment
HQ: Elkhart Brass Manufacturing Company Inc
1302 W Beardsley Ave
Elkhart IN 46514
574 295-8330

(G-3322)
ELKHART BRASS MANUFACTURING COMPANY INC (DH)
1302 W Beardsley Ave (46514-1828)
P.O. Box 1127 (46515-1127)
PHONE..................574 295-8330
◆ **EMP:** 151 **EST:** 1902
SALES (est): 29.78MM **Privately Held**
Web: www.elkhartbrass.com
SIC: 3569 3429 Firefighting apparatus; Nozzles, fire fighting
HQ: Safe Fleet Holdings Llc
6800 E 163rd St
Belton MO 64012
816 318-8000

(G-3323)
ELKHART BRISTOL CORP
1850 E Bristol St (46514-3918)
PHONE..................574 264-7600
EMP: 25 **EST:** 2010
SALES (est): 61K **Privately Held**
Web: www.epi-roto.com
SIC: 2621 Bristols

(G-3324)
ELKHART CASES INC
Also Called: Sprunger Engineering
23143 Heaton Vis (46514-9340)
PHONE..................574 295-7700
Dale Fehlbeck, Pr
▲ **EMP:** 10 **EST:** 1964
SALES (est): 231.33K **Privately Held**
Web: www.elkhartcatering.com
SIC: 3089 Injection molding of plastics

(G-3325)
ELKHART HINGE CO INC
1839 W Lusher Ave (46517-1394)
PHONE..................574 293-2841
Steve Holbert, Pr
Jayne Holbert, Sec
EMP: 10 **EST:** 1949
SQ FT: 12,000
SALES (est): 857.3K **Privately Held**
Web: www.elkharthinge.com
SIC: 3429 Furniture, builders' and other household hardware

(G-3326)
ELKHART LASER PRODUCTS LLC
116 Parker Ave (46516-4631)
PHONE..................574 304-7242
George W Varga, Pr
EMP: 5 **EST:** 2017
SALES (est): 185.93K **Privately Held**
Web: www.elkhartproducts.com
SIC: 3544 Special dies and tools

(G-3327)
ELKHART PLATING CORP
1913 14th St (46516-2278)
P.O. Box 74 (46515-0074)
PHONE..................574 294-1800
George Malcom, Pr
EMP: 18 **EST:** 1960
SQ FT: 15,000
SALES (est): 2.38MM **Privately Held**
Web: www.elkhartplating.com
SIC: 3471 Electroplating of metals or formed products

(G-3328)
ELKHART PRODUCTS CORPORATION (HQ)
1255 Oak St (46514)
P.O. Box 701 (28105)
PHONE....................................574 264-3181
Greg Heifler, *CEO*
Sean P O'connell, *VP*
Larry Johnson, *VP*
◆ **EMP:** 150 **EST:** 1969
SQ FT: 186,000
SALES (est): 86.24MM
SALES (corp-wide): 3.35B **Privately Held**
Web: www.elkhartproducts.com
SIC: 3498 Tube fabricating (contract bending and shaping)
PA: Aalberts N.V.
Stadsplateau 18
Utrecht UT
303079300

(G-3329)
ELKHART STEEL SERVICE INC (PA)
Also Called: Lape Steel
23321 C R 106 (46514)
PHONE....................................574 262-2552
Bradford J Miller, *Pr*
Michelle Miller, *
James M Hampel, *
EMP: 35 **EST:** 1979
SQ FT: 48,400
SALES (est): 4.61MM
SALES (corp-wide): 4.61MM **Privately Held**
Web: www.elkhartsteel.com
SIC: 3312 5051 Iron and steel products, hot-rolled; Steel

(G-3330)
ELKHART SUPPLY CORP
Also Called: E S C O
1126 Kent St (46514-1799)
PHONE....................................574 264-4156
Lewis Shaum, *Pr*
Gary L Shaum, *Sec*
▲ **EMP:** 23 **EST:** 1948
SQ FT: 15,000
SALES (est): 10.87MM **Privately Held**
Web: www.escousa.net
SIC: 5063 5074 3643 5065 Light bulbs and related supplies; Plumbing fittings and supplies; Electric switches; Electronic parts and equipment, nec

(G-3331)
ELKHART TOOL AND DIE INC
2400 15th St (46517-1416)
P.O. Box 1428 (46515-1428)
PHONE....................................574 295-8500
Brent H Brown, *Pr*
EMP: 25 **EST:** 1932
SQ FT: 40,000
SALES (est): 726.79K **Privately Held**
Web: www.postledistributors.com
SIC: 3544 Special dies and tools

(G-3332)
ENCORE RV LLC
2702 Ada Dr (46514-8646)
PHONE....................................574 327-6540
EMP: 20 **EST:** 2021
SALES (est): 1.09MM **Privately Held**
Web: www.encore-rv.com
SIC: 3799 Recreational vehicles

(G-3333)
EPW LLC
1500 W Hively Ave Ste A (46517-4033)
P.O. Box 1485 (46515-1485)
PHONE....................................574 293-5090
EMP: 15 **EST:** 2014
SALES (est): 2.14MM **Privately Held**
Web: www.epw.com
SIC: 3544 Industrial molds

(G-3334)
ESCO INDUSTRIES INC
1701 Conant St (46516-4716)
PHONE....................................574 522-4500
Kelly Rentfrow, *Genl Mgr*
EMP: 12
SALES (corp-wide): 22.41MM **Privately Held**
Web: www.escoindustries.com
SIC: 3275 Gypsum board
PA: Esco Industries, Inc.
185 Sink Hole Rd
Douglas GA 31533
912 384-1417

(G-3335)
EVANS METAL PRODUCTS CO INC
2400 Johnson St (46514-5578)
PHONE....................................574 264-2166
Evans Ii C David, *Pr*
Bruce W Reinks, *VP*
Lorraine S Evans, *Sec*
EMP: 14 **EST:** 1945
SQ FT: 12,000
SALES (est): 2.24MM **Privately Held**
Web: www.evansmetal.com
SIC: 3441 3446 Building components, structural steel; Ladders, for permanent installation: metal

(G-3336)
EVERYTHING ELSE LLC
1322 W Lexington Ave (46514-2048)
PHONE....................................574 350-7383
EMP: 1
SALES (est): 69.27K **Privately Held**
SIC: 3524 7389 Lawn and garden equipment; Business Activities at Non-Commercial Site

(G-3337)
EXACT-TECH MACHINING INC
1140 County Road 6 W (46514-8218)
PHONE....................................574 970-0197
EMP: 11 **EST:** 1984
SALES (est): 882.73K **Privately Held**
Web: www.exact-tech.com
SIC: 3599 Machine shop, jobbing and repair

(G-3338)
EXEMPLARY FOAM INC (PA)
Also Called: Exemplary Foam
1235 W Hively Ave (46517-1555)
PHONE....................................574 295-8888
John Petrofsky, *Pr*
Don Frandsen, *General Vice President*
◆ **EMP:** 12 **EST:** 2005
SQ FT: 18,000
SALES (est): 4.55MM
SALES (corp-wide): 4.55MM **Privately Held**
Web: www.exemplaryfoam.com
SIC: 3069 Foam rubber

(G-3339)
EXEMPLARY FOAM SOUTH LLC
Also Called: Foamfab
2600 S Nappanee St (46517-1082)
PHONE....................................423 302-0962
Steve Walker, *Mgr*
EMP: 10 **EST:** 2013
SALES (est): 618.37K **Privately Held**
SIC: 3086 Packaging and shipping materials, foamed plastics

(G-3340)
F & F SCREW MACHINE PRODUCTS
4302 Wyland Dr (46516-9519)
PHONE....................................574 293-0362
Roger Duffy, *Pr*
Blake Slack, *
Roger Duffy, *Sec*
EMP: 40 **EST:** 1959
SQ FT: 20,000
SALES (est): 4.83MM **Privately Held**
Web: www.ffmpinc.com
SIC: 3451 Screw machine products

(G-3341)
FAIRVIEW FITTINGS & MFG
23845 County Road 6 (46514-9691)
PHONE....................................574 206-8884
Ryan Yewchuck, *Mgr*
▲ **EMP:** 3 **EST:** 1969
SALES (est): 324.56K **Privately Held**
Web: www.fairviewfittings.com
SIC: 3089 Fittings for pipe, plastics

(G-3342)
FAN-TASTIC VENT
1120 N Main St (46514-3203)
PHONE....................................800 521-0298
Stephen Milks, *Owner*
EMP: 9 **EST:** 2013
SALES (est): 151.78K **Privately Held**
Web: www.dometic.com
SIC: 3564 Blowers and fans

(G-3343)
FARMER LEGACY INC
25575 Woodlawn Ave (46514-3826)
PHONE....................................574 264-4625
Harold Farmer, *Pr*
Evelyn Farmer, *VP*
EMP: 7 **EST:** 1965
SQ FT: 12,000
SALES (est): 844.84K **Privately Held**
SIC: 3272 Septic tanks, concrete

(G-3344)
FENDERS INC
5304 Beck Dr (46516-9251)
P.O. Box 2082 (46515-2082)
PHONE....................................574 293-3717
Herbert L Kirts, *Pr*
Diane Kirts, *Sec*
EMP: 7 **EST:** 2005
SQ FT: 16,500
SALES (est): 644.03K **Privately Held**
Web: www.fender.com
SIC: 3465 Fenders, automobile: stamped or pressed metal

(G-3345)
FIBER-TRON CORP
29877 Old Us 33 (46516-1428)
PHONE....................................574 294-8545
William Mccaslin, *Pr*
EMP: 16 **EST:** 1986
SQ FT: 30,000
SALES (est): 2.18MM **Privately Held**
SIC: 3716 3799 Motor homes; Recreational vehicles

(G-3346)
FIBROSAN INC
2926 Paul Dr (46514-8796)
PHONE....................................574 612-4736
Olga Soykan, *Pr*
Nese Ertenk, *Treas*
Florian A Stamm, *Sec*
EMP: 10 **EST:** 2018
SALES (est): 217.43K **Privately Held**
Web: www.fibrosan.com.tr
SIC: 2952 Roof cement: asphalt, fibrous, or plastic

(G-3347)
FIRST PLACE TROPHY INC
Also Called: 1st Place Trophy Shop
24888 County Road 20 (46517-3202)
PHONE....................................574 293-6147
Marvin Boht, *Pr*
EMP: 4 **EST:** 1988
SALES (est): 500.82K **Privately Held**
Web: www.bohttrophy.com
SIC: 5094 3089 5999 Trophies; Plastics hardware and building products; Trophies and plaques

(G-3348)
FLEXCO PRODUCTS INC
Also Called: Industrial Steel Co Division
2415 Bryant St (46516-5593)
P.O. Box 1582 (46515-1582)
PHONE....................................574 294-2502
Thomas Jellison, *CEO*
Susan Jellison, *
Brett Mitchell Jellison, *
EMP: 180 **EST:** 1977
SQ FT: 300,000
SALES (est): 47.59MM **Privately Held**
Web: www.flexcoproducts.com
SIC: 5051 3444 Sheets, metal; Sheet metal specialties, not stamped

(G-3349)
FLEXFORM TECHNOLOGIES LLC
4955 Beck Dr (46516-9092)
PHONE....................................574 295-3777
Gregg Baumbaugh, *Managing Member*
▲ **EMP:** 45 **EST:** 1999
SQ FT: 100,000
SALES (est): 8.76MM **Privately Held**
Web: www.flexformtech.com
SIC: 3711 Automobile assembly, including specialty automobiles

(G-3350)
FLEXIBLE CONCEPTS INC
1620 Middlebury St (46516-4713)
PHONE....................................574 296-0941
Beth Gerstbauer, *CEO*
Timothy Gerstbauer, *
Amy Brown, *
Fabian Gerstbauer, *
Tom Andrea, *
EMP: 52 **EST:** 1990
SQ FT: 60,000
SALES (est): 9.09MM **Privately Held**
Web: www.flexibleconcepts.com
SIC: 3599 3462 Machine shop, jobbing and repair; Iron and steel forgings

(G-3351)
FLEXSEALS MFG LLC
28255 Charlotte Ave Bldg 1 (46517-1196)
PHONE....................................574 293-0333
Clarence Miller, *Managing Member*
EMP: 2 **EST:** 2014
SALES (est): 272.52K **Privately Held**
Web: www.flexseals.com
SIC: 3089 Extruded finished plastics products, nec

(G-3352)
FOAMCRAFT INC
900 Industrial Pkwy (46516-5592)
P.O. Box 664076 (46266)
PHONE....................................574 293-8569
Jim Showalter, *Brnch Mgr*
EMP: 50
SALES (corp-wide): 92.24MM **Privately Held**
Web: www.foamcraftinc.com

GEOGRAPHIC SECTION
Elkhart - Elkhart County (G-3375)

SIC: **3086** 5199 Padding, foamed plastics; Foams and rubber
PA: Foamcraft Inc
9230 Harrison Park Ct
Indianapolis IN 46216
317 545-3626

(G-3353)
FOREST RIVER INC
3603 S Nappanee St (46517-1176)
PHONE.................................574 296-7700
EMP: 743
SALES (corp-wide): 364.48B **Publicly Held**
Web: www.forestriverinc.com
SIC: **3792** 3716 5012 Travel trailers and campers; Motor homes; Recreational vehicles, motor homes, and trailers
HQ: Forest River, Inc.
900 County Rd 1 N
Elkhart IN 46514

(G-3354)
FOREST RIVER INC
Also Called: Battisti Customs
3601 County Road 6 E (46514-7664)
PHONE.................................574 262-5466
EMP: 66
SALES (corp-wide): 364.48B **Publicly Held**
Web: www.forestriverinc.com
SIC: **3711** Buses, all types, assembly of
HQ: Forest River, Inc.
900 County Rd 1 N
Elkhart IN 46514

(G-3355)
FOREST RIVER INC
Dynamax
2745 Northland Dr (46514-7619)
P.O. Box 875 (46515-0875)
PHONE.................................574 262-3474
Peter J Liegl, Pr
EMP: 628
SALES (corp-wide): 364.48B **Publicly Held**
Web: www.dynamaxcorp.com
SIC: **3716** 3792 Motor homes; Travel trailers and campers
HQ: Forest River, Inc.
900 County Rd 1 N
Elkhart IN 46514

(G-3356)
FOREST RIVER INC (HQ)
Also Called: Forest River
900 County Road 1 N (46514)
P.O. Box 3030 (46515)
PHONE.................................574 389-4600
Peter J Liegl, Pr
Darrel O Ritchie, *
◆ EMP: 50 EST: 1995
SQ FT: 100,000
SALES (est): 2.03MM
SALES (corp-wide): 364.48B **Publicly Held**
Web: www.forestriverinc.com
SIC: **5561** 3799 Recreational vehicle dealers; Recreational vehicles
PA: Berkshire Hathaway Inc.
3555 Farnam St Ste 1440
Omaha NE 68131
402 346-1400

(G-3357)
FORMAL AFFAIRS TUXEDO SHOP
Also Called: Formal
23797 Us Highway 33 (46517-3517)
PHONE.................................574 875-6654
EMP: 3 EST: 1993
SALES (est): 196.45K **Privately Held**

Web: www.formalaffairs.net
SIC: **5621** 7299 2311 5699 Boutiques; Computer photography or portrait; Tuxedos: made from purchased materials; Formal wear

(G-3358)
FRED SIBLEY SR
Also Called: Fred Sibley Enterprises
25551 Homewood Ave (46514-5025)
PHONE.................................574 264-2237
Fred Sibley Senior, Owner
EMP: 2 EST: 1959
SQ FT: 5,500
SALES (est): 92.23K **Privately Held**
SIC: **3711** Automobile assembly, including specialty automobiles

(G-3359)
FTC LIQUIDATION INC
24615 County Road 45 Ste 4 (46516-5937)
PHONE.................................574 295-6700
Jack Wait Junior, Pr
▲ EMP: 10 EST: 1974
SQ FT: 80,000
SALES (est): 919.01K
SALES (corp-wide): 93.59MM **Privately Held**
Web: www.marshalltown.com
SIC: **3423** 5082 2491 Hand and edge tools, nec; Masonry equipment and supplies; Wood products, creosoted
PA: Marshalltown Company
104 S 8th Ave
Marshalltown IA 50158
641 753-5999

(G-3360)
FURRION LLC
2572 Links Dr Apt 3a (46514-5188)
PHONE.................................574 361-1325
EMP: 2
SALES (corp-wide): 3.78B **Publicly Held**
Web: www.furrion.com
SIC: **3663** Radio and t.v. communications equipment
HQ: Furrion, Llc
52567 Independence Ct
Elkhart IN 46514
574 327-6571

(G-3361)
FURRION LLC
1121 Herman St (46516-9030)
PHONE.................................574 327-6571
EMP: 3
SALES (corp-wide): 3.78B **Publicly Held**
Web: www.furrion.com
SIC: **3663** Radio and t.v. communications equipment
HQ: Furrion, Llc
52567 Independence Ct
Elkhart IN 46514
574 327-6571

(G-3362)
FURRION LLC (DH)
52567 Independence Ct (46514)
PHONE.................................574 327-6571
Aaron Fidler, Managing Member
EMP: 7 EST: 2007
SQ FT: 16,800
SALES (est): 17.29MM
SALES (corp-wide): 3.78B **Publicly Held**
Web: www.furrion.com
SIC: **3663** Radio and t.v. communications equipment
HQ: Lippert Components, Inc.
3501 County Rd 6 E
Elkhart IN 46514
574 535-1125

(G-3363)
FUTURE FOAM INC
1900 W Lusher Ave (46517-1310)
PHONE.................................574 294-7694
EMP: 41
SALES (corp-wide): 495.02MM **Privately Held**
Web: www.futurefoam.com
SIC: **2821** Polyurethane resins
PA: Future Foam, Inc.
1610 Ave N
Council Bluffs IA 51501
712 323-9122

(G-3364)
FUTURE FORM PLASTICS
612 Kollar St (46514-1358)
PHONE.................................574 293-4004
EMP: 13 EST: 2018
SALES (est): 1.81MM **Privately Held**
SIC: **3089** Injection molding of plastics

(G-3365)
G4 TOOL AND TECHNOLOGY INC
2907 Paul Dr (46514-8797)
P.O. Box 1711 (46515-1711)
PHONE.................................574 970-0844
Erin Mullet, Pr
EMP: 11 EST: 2014
SALES (est): 299.66K **Privately Held**
Web: www.g4tool.com
SIC: **3452** Bolts, nuts, rivets, and washers

(G-3366)
GASKA TAPE INC
1810 W Lusher Ave (46517-1395)
P.O. Box 1968 (46515-1968)
PHONE.................................574 294-5431
Jack Boyd Smith Junior, Pr
◆ EMP: 100 EST: 1965
SQ FT: 150,000
SALES (est): 24.92MM **Privately Held**
Web: www.gaska.com
SIC: **3086** 2821 3053 Insulation or cushioning material, foamed plastics; Thermoplastic materials; Gaskets, all materials

(G-3367)
GATEWAY BUILDERS & PROPERTIES
1001 Parkway Ave Ste 1 (46516-9347)
PHONE.................................574 295-9944
Dan Brekke, Owner
EMP: 5 EST: 2000
SALES (est): 273.91K **Privately Held**
Web: www.homesbygateway.com
SIC: **2789** Trade binding services

(G-3368)
GDC INC
22428 Elkhart East Blvd (46514-8150)
PHONE.................................574 533-3128
EMP: 48
SALES (corp-wide): 73.86MM **Privately Held**
Web: www.gdc-corp.com
SIC: **3089** Injection molding of plastics
PA: Gdc, Inc.
815 Logan St
Goshen IN 46528
574 533-3128

(G-3369)
GEM CITY TECHNOLOGIES
54347 Highland Blvd (46514-2124)
PHONE.................................937 252-8998
EMP: 11 EST: 2018
SALES (est): 485.97K **Privately Held**
Web: www.dynamicindustrial.com

SIC: **3599** Machine shop, jobbing and repair

(G-3370)
GEMEINHARDT MUSICAL INSTR LLC
Also Called: Gemstone Musical Instruments
3302 S Nappanee St (46517-1096)
PHONE.................................574 295-5280
▲ EMP: 40 EST: 1992
SQ FT: 33,000
SALES (est): 4.19MM
SALES (corp-wide): 4.19MM **Privately Held**
Web: www.gemeinhardt.com
SIC: **3931** 5736 Piccolos and parts; Musical instrument stores
PA: Bp Music Holdings Llc
317 Madison Ave
New York NY 10017
212 302-0066

(G-3371)
GEN T LLC
3008 Mobile Dr (46514-5524)
PHONE.................................574 266-0911
EMP: 1 EST: 2020
SALES (est): 500K **Privately Held**
SIC: **3713** Ambulance bodies

(G-3372)
GENERAL FASTENERS CO
2701 Decio Dr (46514)
PHONE.................................574 343-2413
EMP: 7 EST: 2020
SALES (est): 189.26K **Privately Held**
Web: www.genfast.com
SIC: **3965** Fasteners

(G-3373)
GENESIS PRODUCTS LLC
Also Called: Genesis Products, Plant 2
3130 Tuscany Dr (46514-7649)
PHONE.................................574 266-8293
Zack Nickell, Brnch Mgr
EMP: 131
SALES (corp-wide): 114.8MM **Privately Held**
Web: www.genesisproductsinc.com
SIC: **3479** 7389 2431 Aluminum coating of metal products; Laminating service; Doors, wood
PA: Genesis Products, Llc
1853 Eisenhower Dr S
Goshen IN 46526
877 266-8292

(G-3374)
GENESIS PRODUCTS LLC
Also Called: Welformed
2924 County Road 6 E (46514-7678)
PHONE.................................574 262-4054
EMP: 131
SALES (corp-wide): 114.8MM **Privately Held**
Web: www.genesisproductsinc.com
SIC: **2522** Panel systems and partitions, office: except wood
PA: Genesis Products, Llc
1853 Eisenhower Dr S
Goshen IN 46526
877 266-8292

(G-3375)
GENESIS PRODUCTS LLC
2608 Almac Ct (46514)
PHONE.................................877 266-8292
EMP: 41
SALES (corp-wide): 114.8MM **Privately Held**
Web: www.genesisproductsinc.com
SIC: **2431** Doors, wood
PA: Genesis Products, Llc

1853 Eisenhower Dr S
Goshen IN 46526
877 266-8292

(G-3376)
GEOCEL HOLDINGS CORPORATION
2504 Marina Dr (46514-8641)
P.O. Box 398 (46515-0398)
PHONE...................574 264-0645
▲ **EMP:** 65
Web: www.geocelholdings.com
SIC: 2891 Sealants

(G-3377)
GILLETTE GENERATORS INC
2921 Thorne Dr (46514-8228)
PHONE...................574 264-9639
◆ **EMP:** 25 **EST:** 1972
SALES (est): 4.71MM **Privately Held**
Web: www.gillettegenerators.com
SIC: 3621 Generator sets: gasoline, diesel, or dual-fuel

(G-3378)
GIRARD PRODUCTS LLC
Also Called: Girard Systems
4800 Beck Dr (46516-9569)
PHONE...................574 534-3328
Marcia Girard, *Brnch Mgr*
EMP: 2
SALES (corp-wide): 3.78B **Publicly Held**
Web: corporate.lippert.com
SIC: 3792 Trailer coaches, automobile
HQ: Girard Products, Llc
1361 Calle Avanzado
San Clemente CA 92673

(G-3379)
GLOBAL BUILDING PRODUCTS LLC
1121 Herman St (46516-9030)
PHONE...................574 296-6868
Andrew Carpenter, *Managing Member*
Clayton Bjurstrom, *
EMP: 32 **EST:** 2002
SQ FT: 43,000
SALES (est): 4.04MM **Privately Held**
Web: www.globalbuildingproducts.us
SIC: 3442 Window and door frames

(G-3380)
GLOBAL COMPOSITES INC
Also Called: Global Moulding
58190 County Road 3 (46517-9007)
PHONE...................574 522-9956
Gary L Beck, *Pr*
Stephen M Beck, *
EMP: 180 **EST:** 1981
SALES (est): 10.89MM **Privately Held**
Web: www.globalcompositesinc.com
SIC: 3229 Glass fibers, textile

(G-3381)
GLOBAL COMPOSITES INC
56807 Elk Park Dr (46516-1451)
PHONE...................574 294-7681
EMP: 7 **EST:** 2019
SALES (est): 101.32K **Privately Held**
SIC: 3296 Mineral wool

(G-3382)
GLOBAL GLASS INC
28967 Old Us 33 (46516-1600)
PHONE...................574 294-7681
Gary L Beck, *Pr*
Stephen M Beck, *
Ann M Beck, *
EMP: 18 **EST:** 1981
SQ FT: 36,000
SALES (est): 559.85K **Privately Held**
Web: www.globalmoldingtech.com

SIC: 3714 Motor vehicle body components and frame

(G-3383)
GLOBAL OZONE INNOVATIONS LLC
Also Called: Sanitation Equipment
425 Pine Creek Ct (46516-9089)
PHONE...................574 294-5797
EMP: 2 **EST:** 2003
SALES (est): 223.53K **Privately Held**
Web: www.sportsozone.com
SIC: 3949 5091 5941 7999 Sporting and athletic goods, nec; Sporting and recreation goods; Sporting goods and bicycle shops; Sporting goods rental, nec

(G-3384)
GOLDEN-HELVEY HOLDINGS INC
1020 County Road 6 W (46514-8299)
PHONE...................574 266-4500
Russell Golden, *Pr*
Steve Helvey, *
EMP: 70 **EST:** 1975
SQ FT: 55,000
SALES (est): 8.2MM **Privately Held**
Web: www.kessington.com
SIC: 3728 3842 Aircraft parts and equipment, nec; Implants, surgical

(G-3385)
GOWDY WOODWORKS
Also Called: Gowdy Woodworking
906 Plum St (46514-2203)
PHONE...................574 293-4399
EMP: 1 **EST:** 1974
SQ FT: 8,168
SALES (est): 50.87K **Privately Held**
SIC: 2499 Decorative wood and woodwork

(G-3386)
GRANITECH
3954 Lexington Park Dr (46514-1157)
PHONE...................574 674-6988
Mark Fessenden, *Pr*
Rick Farrell Junior, *VP*
Steve Jones, *Treas*
▲ **EMP:** 9 **EST:** 1998
SALES (est): 496.46K **Privately Held**
Web: www.granitech.net
SIC: 3281 2434 Marble, building: cut and shaped; Wood kitchen cabinets

(G-3387)
GRAPHICS FACTORY
400 W Crawford St (46514-2732)
PHONE...................574 264-0542
EMP: 4 **EST:** 2018
SALES (est): 82.64K **Privately Held**
Web: www.thegraphicsfactoryinc.com
SIC: 3993 Signs and advertising specialties

(G-3388)
GRAYSON GRAPHICS
3008 Mobile Dr (46514-5524)
PHONE...................574 264-6466
Lemar Mast, *Pr*
EMP: 2 **EST:** 2003
SALES (est): 174.77K **Privately Held**
SIC: 7336 3993 Commercial art and graphic design; Signs and advertising specialties

(G-3389)
GREAT LAKES FOREST PDTS INC (PA)
21861 Protecta Dr (46516)
PHONE...................574 389-9663
Mark E Smith, *Pr*
Jennifer L Smith, *
EMP: 102 **EST:** 1989
SALES (est): 66MM **Privately Held**

Web: www.glfp.net
SIC: 2421 5031 Resawing lumber into smaller dimensions; Lumber, plywood, and millwork

(G-3390)
GREAT LAKES LAMINATION INC
21861 Protecta Dr (46516-9544)
PHONE...................574 389-9663
EMP: 1
SALES (corp-wide): 1.02MM **Privately Held**
Web: www.glfp.net
SIC: 2655 Containers, laminated phenolic and vulcanized fiber
PA: Great Lakes Lamination, Inc.
1103 Maple St
Bristol IN 46507
574 389-9663

(G-3391)
GREEN STREAM COMPANY
29414 Phillips St (46514-1022)
P.O. Box 2341 (46515-2341)
PHONE...................574 293-1949
EMP: 168 **EST:** 2010
SQ FT: 66,000
SALES (est): 21.61MM **Privately Held**
Web: www.greenstreamcompany.com
SIC: 2448 4953 7699 Pallets, wood; Recycling, waste materials; Pallet repair

(G-3392)
GRIFFEN PLMBNG-HEATING-COOLING
Also Called: Griffen Plumbing & Heating
2310 Toledo Rd (46516-5537)
PHONE...................574 295-2440
Tood Mikel, *Pr*
Trisha Martin, *
Todd Mikel, *
Dawn Mikel, *
EMP: 39 **EST:** 1982
SQ FT: 10,000
SALES (est): 2.37MM **Privately Held**
Web: www.griffenph.com
SIC: 1711 3585 Plumbing contractors; Compressors for refrigeration and air conditioning equipment

(G-3393)
GVS TECHNOLOGIES LLC
5308 Beck Dr (46516-9251)
PHONE...................574 293-0974
Donald L Breiter, *Treas*
◆ **EMP:** 12 **EST:** 1983
SQ FT: 12,000
SALES (est): 186.86K **Privately Held**
Web: www.trpintl.com
SIC: 3599 3544 Machine shop, jobbing and repair; Special dies and tools

(G-3394)
H & A PRODUCTS INC
Also Called: Storm Trailers
28761 Holiday Pl (46517-1109)
PHONE...................574 226-0079
William D Aust, *Pr*
William Aust, *Pr*
EMP: 8 **EST:** 2009
SALES (est): 134.79K **Privately Held**
SIC: 2448 Cargo containers, wood and metal combination

(G-3395)
H L ENTERPRISE INC
Also Called: H L Enterprise
5321 Beck Dr (46516)
PHONE...................574 294-1112
EMP: 3 **EST:** 2010
SALES (est): 465.67K **Privately Held**

Web: www.hlenterpriseinc.com
SIC: 3799 Recreational vehicles

(G-3396)
HADLEY PRODUCTS LLC
Hadley Rv Trnst Spclty Vhcl Bu
319 Roske Dr (46516-9084)
PHONE...................574 266-3700
Michaele Dutton Cust, *Svc Mgr*
EMP: 1
SALES (corp-wide): 144.5MM **Privately Held**
Web: www.hadleyadvantage.com
SIC: 3799 Trailers and trailer equipment
HQ: Hadley Products Llc
4300 36th St Se
Grand Rapids MI 49512
616 530-1717

(G-3397)
HAMPELS WOODLAND PRODUCTS
61292 County Road 7 (46517-8945)
PHONE...................574 293-2124
EMP: 4 **EST:** 2011
SALES (est): 207.51K **Privately Held**
Web: www.hampelswoodlandproducts.com
SIC: 2491 Wood products, creosoted

(G-3398)
HARMAN PROFESSIONAL INC
Crown Audio
1718 W Mishawaka Rd (46517-9439)
PHONE...................574 294-8000
EMP: 450
SQ FT: 200,000
Web: www.jblpro.com
SIC: 3651 3663 3823 Amplifiers: radio, public address, or musical instrument; Transmitting apparatus, radio or television; Analyzers, industrial process type
HQ: Harman Professional, Inc.
8500 Balboa Blvd
Northridge CA 91325
818 893-8411

(G-3399)
HART INDUSTRIES INC
2907 Park Six Ct (46514-5445)
PHONE...................574 575-4657
Blake C Miller, *Pr*
EMP: 6 **EST:** 2017
SALES (est): 248.32K **Privately Held**
Web: www.hartengineeringgroup.com
SIC: 3999 Manufacturing industries, nec

(G-3400)
HART PLASTICS INC
Also Called: Harl Plastics
2907 Park Six Ct (46514-5445)
PHONE...................574 264-7060
Blake C Miller, *Pr*
EMP: 20 **EST:** 1984
SQ FT: 20,800
SALES (est): 2.44MM **Privately Held**
Web: www.hartplastics.com
SIC: 3089 3714 3429 Thermoformed finished plastics products, nec; Motor vehicle parts and accessories; Hardware, nec

(G-3401)
HAT PLUG US
1230 N Nappanee St (46514-1732)
PHONE...................574 575-2520
EMP: 5 **EST:** 2018
SALES (est): 137.6K **Privately Held**
SIC: 2759 Screen printing

GEOGRAPHIC SECTION — Elkhart - Elkhart County (G-3426)

(G-3402)
HAWK ENTERPRISES ELKHART INC (PA)
2902 Park Six Ct (46514-5445)
PHONE..................574 294-1910
Tom Kershner Junior, *Pr*
◆ **EMP:** 8 **EST:** 1995
SQ FT: 20,000
SALES (est): 3.23MM **Privately Held**
Web: www.hawkenterprises.com
SIC: 3589 Floor washing and polishing machines, commercial

(G-3403)
HELGESON STEEL INC
1130 Verdant St Ste 1 (46516-9330)
PHONE..................574 293-5576
Fred Helgeson, *Pr*
EMP: 14 **EST:** 1983
SQ FT: 25,000
SALES (est): 2.52MM **Privately Held**
Web: www.helgesonsteel.com
SIC: 3441 Building components, structural steel

(G-3404)
HERITAGE FINANCIAL GROUP INC (PA)
120 W Lexington Ave Ste 200 (46516-3117)
PHONE..................574 522-8000
L Craig Fulmer, *Ch Bd*
Dan A Morrison, *
Brian J Smith, *
Sharon Martin, *
EMP: 38 **EST:** 1980
SQ FT: 75,000
SALES (est): 17.95MM **Privately Held**
Web: www.hfgnet.com
SIC: 6531 6141 5521 2451 Real estate managers; Consumer finance companies; Used car dealers; Mobile homes

(G-3405)
HEYWOOD WILLIAMS INC
601 County Road 17 (46516-9505)
P.O. Box 98 (46515-0098)
PHONE..................574 295-8400
Larry Campbell, *Pr*
EMP: 9 **EST:** 2011
SALES (est): 165.78K **Privately Held**
Web: www.lasallebristol.com
SIC: 3083 Laminated plastics plate and sheet

(G-3406)
HIGHWATER MARINE LLC (PA)
Also Called: Godfrey Marine
4500 Middlebury St (46516-9068)
P.O. Box 1158 (46515-1158)
PHONE..................574 522-8381
▼ **EMP:** 69 **EST:** 2005
SALES (est): 26.2MM **Privately Held**
Web: www.rinkerboats.com
SIC: 3732 Boats, fiberglass: building and repairing

(G-3407)
HINGECRAFT CORPORATION
3601 Lexington Park Dr (46514-1165)
PHONE..................574 293-6543
Lanny Rogers, *Pr*
Carolyn Rogers, *Sec*
Scott Rogers, *VP*
Shelley Rogers, *Treas*
EMP: 25 **EST:** 1976
SQ FT: 50,000
SALES (est): 953.93K **Privately Held**
Web: www.hingecraft.com
SIC: 3429 Builders' hardware

(G-3408)
HOLIDAY HOUSE LLC
Also Called: Holiday House Trailers
25771 Miner Rd (46514-5019)
PHONE..................574 206-0016
EMP: 10 **EST:** 2018
SALES (est): 1.13MM **Privately Held**
Web: www.holidayhouserv.com
SIC: 5599 3711 3799 5012 Utility trailers; Motor homes, self contained, assembly of; Recreational vehicles; Recreational vehicles, motor homes, and trailers

(G-3409)
HOLLAND METAL FAB INC
1550 W Lusher Ave (46517-1422)
P.O. Box 1914 (46515-1914)
PHONE..................574 522-1434
Ted Holland, *Pr*
Lana Holland, *Sec*
EMP: 17 **EST:** 1995
SQ FT: 19,000
SALES (est): 461.28K **Privately Held**
SIC: 3429 Hardware, nec

(G-3410)
HOMETTE CORPORATION (HQ)
Also Called: Skyline Mainsfield
200 Nibco Pkwy Ste 200 (46516-3570)
P.O. Box 743 (46515-0743)
PHONE..................574 294-6521
Thomas Deranek, *CEO*
John Pilarski, *Sec*
EMP: 7 **EST:** 1956
SALES (est): 54.28K
SALES (corp-wide): 2.02B **Publicly Held**
Web: www.skylinehomes.com
SIC: 2452 3792 Modular homes, prefabricated, wood; Travel trailers and campers
PA: Skyline Champion Corporation
755 W Big Bevr Rd Ste 100
Troy MI 48084
248 614-8211

(G-3411)
HOOSIER CRANE SERVICE COMPANY
Also Called: Hoosier Crane
3500 Charlotte Ave (46517)
PHONE..................574 523-2945
Thomas Schmidt, *Pr*
Thomas R Schmidt Ii, *Pr*
▼ **EMP:** 100 **EST:** 2002
SQ FT: 29,000
SALES (est): 23.07MM **Privately Held**
Web: www.hoosiercrane.com
SIC: 3536 7389 Cranes, overhead traveling; Crane and aerial lift service

(G-3412)
HOWARD & SONS CEMENT PDTS INC
2912 Oakland Ave (46517-1507)
PHONE..................574 293-1906
James Howard, *Pr*
EMP: 6 **EST:** 1958
SQ FT: 3,360
SALES (est): 497.54K **Privately Held**
SIC: 3272 Concrete products, precast, nec

(G-3413)
HY-LINE ENTERPRISES INTL INC
25369 Vernon Xing (46514-6260)
PHONE..................574 294-1112
Mark Horita, *Pr*
Holly O'hara, *Ch*
Scott Dawson, *
▼ **EMP:** 20 **EST:** 1986
SQ FT: 36,100
SALES (est): 494.66K **Privately Held**
SIC: 3792 Travel trailer chassis

(G-3414)
HYCO MACHINE & MOLD INC
121 Rush Ct (46516-9644)
PHONE..................574 522-5847
Ron High, *Sec*
Barbara High, *Pr*
EMP: 3 **EST:** 1984
SQ FT: 6,000
SALES (est): 280.62K **Privately Held**
SIC: 3599 Machine shop, jobbing and repair

(G-3415)
HYDRO EXTRUSION USA LLC
3406 Reedy Dr (46514-7667)
PHONE..................574 262-2667
Pat Wooley, *Sls Dir*
EMP: 181
Web: www.hydro.com
SIC: 3354 Aluminum extruded products
HQ: Hydro Extrusion Usa, Llc
6250 N River Rd Ste 5000
Rosemont IL 60018

(G-3416)
IAM AW TL DIE MAKERS LL 229
2618 Lowell Ave (46516-5707)
PHONE..................574 333-5955
EMP: 6 **EST:** 2010
SALES (est): 71.82K **Privately Held**
SIC: 3544 Special dies and tools

(G-3417)
IKON GROUP
330 E Windsor Ave (46514-5565)
PHONE..................574 326-3661
Brandon Ambris, *Owner*
EMP: 7 **EST:** 2015
SALES (est): 459.9K **Privately Held**
SIC: 3799 Recreational vehicles

(G-3418)
IMAGINE LIKE GOD LLC
1020 E Beardsley Ave (46514-3507)
PHONE..................574 575-5023
EMP: 1 **EST:** 2019
SALES (est): 29K **Privately Held**
Web: www.imaginelikegod.com
SIC: 3161 Clothing and apparel carrying cases

(G-3419)
IMPERIAL STAMPING CORPORATION
Also Called: Imperial Stamping Company
4801 Middlebury St (46516-9054)
PHONE..................574 294-3780
Donald Mossey, *Ch*
John Conner, *
Allan J Ludwig, *
▲ **EMP:** 100 **EST:** 1973
SQ FT: 100,000
SALES (est): 6.73MM **Privately Held**
SIC: 3469 7692 3452 3446 Stamping metal for the trade; Welding repair; Bolts, nuts, rivets, and washers; Architectural metalwork

(G-3420)
IN STITCHES INC
Also Called: Insignia Promotions
135 Easy Shopping Pl (46516-3536)
PHONE..................574 294-2121
Sandra Singleton, *Pr*
EMP: 2 **EST:** 1990
SQ FT: 3,500
SALES (est): 242.54K **Privately Held**
Web: www.insigniapromos.com
SIC: 2395 Embroidery and art needlework

(G-3421)
INDIANA DISCOUNT TIRE COMPANY
Also Called: Discount Tire
3711 S Main St (46517-3547)
PHONE..................574 875-8547
Eric Emmons, *Mgr*
EMP: 7
SALES (corp-wide): 3.69B **Privately Held**
Web: www.discounttire.com
SIC: 5531 5015 7534 5013 Automotive tires; Tires, used: retail only; Tire repair shop; Wheels, motor vehicle
HQ: Indiana Discount Tire Company Inc
20225 N Scottsdale Rd
Scottsdale AZ 85255

(G-3422)
INDIANA PLASTICS LLC
Also Called: Impact Molding Elkhart
2221 Industrial Pkwy (46516-5409)
PHONE..................574 294-3253
EMP: 1 **EST:** 2018
SALES (est): 12.61MM
SALES (corp-wide): 130.92MM **Privately Held**
SIC: 3089 Injection molding of plastics
HQ: Thunderbird Plastics Llc
1501 Oakton St
Elk Grove Village IL

(G-3423)
INDUSTRIAL AXLE COMPANY LLC
21611 Protecta Dr (46516-9543)
PHONE..................574 294-6651
EMP: 42
SALES (corp-wide): 1.41B **Privately Held**
Web: www.dexteraxle.com
SIC: 3714 Axles, motor vehicle
HQ: Industrial Axle Company, Llc
21608 Protecta Dr
Elkhart IN 46516
574 295-6077

(G-3424)
INDUSTRIAL AXLE COMPANY LLC (DH)
21608 Protecta Dr (46516-9532)
PHONE..................574 295-6077
Adam Dexter, *Pr*
Bernie Bolka, *
EMP: 99 **EST:** 2014
SALES (est): 58.53MM
SALES (corp-wide): 1.41B **Privately Held**
Web: www.dexteraxle.com
SIC: 3714 Axles, motor vehicle
HQ: Dexter Axle Company Llc
2900 Industrial Pkwy E
Elkhart IN 46516

(G-3425)
INFINITY UV INC
4240 Pine Creek Rd (46516-9556)
PHONE..................269 625-3423
Andrew Carpenter, *Prin*
EMP: 6 **EST:** 2019
SALES (est): 316.07K **Privately Held**
Web: www.infinityuv.com
SIC: 3999 Manufacturing industries, nec

(G-3426)
INFOSOFT INC
2911 Moose Trl (46514-8230)
PHONE..................574 262-9800
Paul Bender, *Pr*
EMP: 10 **EST:** 1988
SALES (est): 527.11K **Privately Held**
Web: www.infosoft-inc.com
SIC: 7372 Prepackaged software

Elkhart - Elkhart County (G-3427)

(G-3427)
INNOCOR FOAM TECH - ACP INC
1900 W Lusher Ave (46517-1310)
P.O. Box 2057 (46515-2057)
PHONE.....................574 294-7694
Jerry Eagon, *Pr*
EMP: 1
Web: www.fxi.com
SIC: 3086 Plastics foam products
HQ: Innocor Foam Technologies - Acp, Inc.
  200 Schulz Dr Ste 2
  Red Bank NJ 07701
  732 945-6222

(G-3428)
INTEGRATED TECHNOLOGY LLC
221 W Lexington Ave (46516-3129)
PHONE.....................574 300-9412
EMP: 14 **EST:** 2018
SALES (est): 1.14MM **Privately Held**
Web: www.itghelp.com
SIC: 3559 Wheel balancing equipment, automotive

(G-3429)
INTERNATIONAL RDO & ELEC CORP
Also Called: Crown Broadcast Irec
2515 Toledo Rd (46516-5777)
PHONE.....................866 262-8910
Beryl J Loomis, *Pr*
Laurie Thompson, *Sec*
Sharon K Moore, *Treas*
EMP: 9 **EST:** 1959
SALES (est): 1.04MM **Privately Held**
Web: www.crownbroadcast.com
SIC: 3663 Transmitting apparatus, radio or television

(G-3430)
IRVINE SHADE & DOOR INC (PA)
Also Called: Irvine Window Coverings
1000 Verdant St (46516-9042)
PHONE.....................574 522-1446
Ben D Mausar Senior, *Pr*
Ron Green, *
Nick Donis, *
▲ **EMP:** 70 **EST:** 1988
SQ FT: 7,500
SALES (est): 8.87MM **Privately Held**
Web: www.irvineshadeanddoor.com
SIC: 2591 3089 2431 Window blinds; Doors, folding: plastics or plastics coated fabric; Millwork

(G-3431)
J J BABBITT CO
2201 Industrial Pkwy (46516-5486)
P.O. Box 1264 (46515-1264)
PHONE.....................574 315-1639
Eugene Reglein, *Ch*
William Reglein, *Pr*
▲ **EMP:** 2 **EST:** 1919
SQ FT: 20,000
SALES (est): 396.64K **Privately Held**
Web: www.jjbabbitt.com
SIC: 3931 Mouthpieces for musical instruments

(G-3432)
JESSEN MANUFACTURING CO INC
1409 W Beardsley Ave (46514-1827)
P.O. Box 549 (46515-0549)
PHONE.....................574 295-3836
Mark C Jessen, *Pr*
Mark C Jessen, *Pr*
John H Jessen Junior, *VP*
EMP: 70 **EST:** 1923
SQ FT: 90,000
SALES (est): 9.63MM **Privately Held**
Web: www.jessenmfg.com
SIC: 3451 Screw machine products

(G-3433)
JET TECHNOLOGIES INC
53893 N Park Ave (46514-5008)
P.O. Box 2848 (46515-2848)
PHONE.....................574 264-3613
EMP: 50 **EST:** 1996
SQ FT: 35,000
SALES (est): 9.59MM **Privately Held**
Web: www.jettechinc.com
SIC: 3089 Injection molding of plastics

(G-3434)
JMS ELECTRONICS CORPORATION
4400 Wyland Dr (46516-9520)
PHONE.....................574 522-0246
Alex Saharian, *Pr*
Michael Saharian, *
▲ **EMP:** 50 **EST:** 1973
SQ FT: 33,000
SALES (est): 5.82MM **Privately Held**
Web: www.polyelectronics.us
SIC: 3556 3625 3621 Smoking or roasting machinery, including ovens; Electric controls and control accessories, industrial; Motors and generators

(G-3435)
JOLAR ENTERPRISES
58052 Ox Bow Dr (46516-6340)
PHONE.....................574 875-8369
Joyce Parker, *Pt*
Raymond Parker, *Pt*
EMP: 2 **EST:** 1986
SALES (est): 131.74K **Privately Held**
SIC: 2499 5719 Decorative wood and woodwork; Housewares, nec

(G-3436)
JP INDUSTRIES INC
Also Called: Keline Manufacturing
726 Middleton Run Rd (46516-5424)
PHONE.....................574 293-8763
James E Pettit, *Pr*
EMP: 10 **EST:** 1991
SALES (est): 1MM **Privately Held**
SIC: 3743 7389 Railroad equipment; Engraving service

(G-3437)
JPC LLC
Also Called: Jpc Mat
2926 Paul Dr (46514-8796)
PHONE.....................574 293-8030
▲ **EMP:** 14 **EST:** 1993
SALES (est): 642.16K **Privately Held**
SIC: 3069 2273 5561 Mats or matting, rubber, nec; Carpets and rugs; Recreational vehicle parts and accessories

(G-3438)
JUS RITE ENGINEERING INC
56977 Elk Ct (46516-1460)
PHONE.....................574 522-9600
David A Bratton, *Pr*
John Binns, *
George P Kelsey, *
EMP: 28 **EST:** 1987
SQ FT: 26,000
SALES (est): 2.49MM **Privately Held**
Web: www.jrecorp.com
SIC: 3544 Jigs and fixtures

(G-3439)
JUSHI USA FIBERGLASS
3310 Middlebury St (46516)
PHONE.....................574 293-0061
EMP: 4 **EST:** 2019
SALES (est): 150.86K **Privately Held**

(G-3440)
K & K INC
2617 Glenview Dr (46514-8709)
PHONE.....................574 266-8040
Kirk Blank, *Pr*
EMP: 16 **EST:** 1997
SQ FT: 18,000
SALES (est): 2.48MM **Privately Held**
Web: www.intertoolgroup.com
SIC: 3544 3543 Special dies and tools; Industrial patterns

(G-3441)
K C FORM PLASTICS LLC
1009 Borg Rd (46514-5282)
PHONE.....................574 333-2523
EMP: 7 **EST:** 2012
SALES (est): 469.7K **Privately Held**
Web: kc-form-plastics.business.site
SIC: 3089 Injection molding of plastics

(G-3442)
K C MACHINE INC
56850 Elk Park Dr (46516-1450)
PHONE.....................574 293-1822
Gerald D Cline, *Pr*
Linda J Cline, *Sec*
EMP: 8 **EST:** 1978
SQ FT: 5,000
SALES (est): 955.31K **Privately Held**
SIC: 3544 3599 Jigs and fixtures; Machine and other job shop work

(G-3443)
K I B ENTERPRISES CORP
Also Called: K I B Electronics
1147 N Michigan St (46514-2213)
PHONE.....................574 262-0518
Michael A Hoover, *CEO*
▲ **EMP:** 130 **EST:** 1982
SALES (est): 24.32MM **Privately Held**
Web: www.kib.us
SIC: 3679 Electronic circuits

(G-3444)
K S MOLD INC
4650 Chester Dr (46516-9056)
PHONE.....................260 357-5141
EMP: 5 **EST:** 2019
SALES (est): 117.96K **Privately Held**
Web: www.ksmold.net
SIC: 3089 Injection molding of plastics

(G-3445)
K TOOL
700 W Beardsley Ave Ste 17 (46514-2232)
PHONE.....................574 296-9604
David Kehr, *Owner*
EMP: 1 **EST:** 1998
SALES (est): 46K **Privately Held**
Web: www.ktoolfirellc.com
SIC: 3599 Machine shop, jobbing and repair

(G-3446)
KAMDOER INC
4027 Timber Ct (46514-8656)
P.O. Box 1387 (46515-1387)
PHONE.....................574 293-2990
John Kamakian, *Ch*
Jacob Stoltyfus, *Vice Chairman**
Mike Doering, *
EMP: 21 **EST:** 1984
SQ FT: 37,000
SALES (est): 877.13K **Privately Held**
Web: www.wire-design.com
SIC: 3679 5063 Harness assemblies, for electronic use: wire or cable; Wire and cable

(G-3447)
KAMPCO STEEL PRODUCTS INC
57533 County Road 3 (46517-9502)
PHONE.....................574 294-5466
Francis E Freel, *Pr*
James Kamp, *
Susan Freel, *
EMP: 29 **EST:** 1972
SQ FT: 80,000
SALES (est): 5.24MM **Privately Held**
Web: www.kampco.com
SIC: 3714 Motor vehicle body components and frame

(G-3448)
KDS INDUSTRIES LLC
21790 Beck Dr (46516-9742)
PHONE.....................574 333-2720
EMP: 6 **EST:** 2012
SALES (est): 104.91K **Privately Held**
SIC: 2231 Upholstery fabrics, wool

(G-3449)
KELLMARK CORPORATION
2501 Ada Dr (46514-8644)
PHONE.....................574 264-9695
George Kelly, *Pr*
Vincent Kelly, *
James J Kelly, *
Luke A Latimer, *
David A Zuchegno, *
EMP: 13 **EST:** 1994
SQ FT: 40,000
SALES (est): 2.42MM **Privately Held**
Web: www.kellmark.com
SIC: 2752 2771 5199 3993 Calendars, lithographed; Greeting cards; Calendars; Signs and advertising specialties

(G-3450)
KEM KREST DEFENSE LLC
3221 Magnum Dr (46516-9021)
PHONE.....................574 389-2650
EMP: 10 **EST:** 2011
SALES (est): 2.75MM
SALES (corp-wide): 475.73MM **Privately Held**
Web: www.kemkrest.com
SIC: 3728 Aircraft parts and equipment, nec
PA: Kem Krest Llc
  3221 Magnum Dr
  Elkhart IN 46516
  574 389-2650

(G-3451)
KENNYLEEHOLMESCOM
25855 Kiser Ct (46514-5226)
PHONE.....................574 612-2526
EMP: 2 **EST:** 2010
SALES (est): 73.63K **Privately Held**
Web: www.kennyleeholmes.com
SIC: 7221 2396 5699 7336 Photographer, still or video; Screen printing on fabric articles; Customized clothing and apparel; Commercial art and graphic design

(G-3452)
KESSINGTON LLC
Also Called: Kessington Machine Products
1020 County Road 6 W (46514-8299)
PHONE.....................574 266-4500
Steve Helvey, *
EMP: 80 **EST:** 2011
SALES (est): 10.87MM **Privately Held**
Web: www.kessington.com
SIC: 3365 Aerospace castings, aluminum

(G-3453)
KEYLINE SALES INC
Also Called: Framed Art Division

2601 Marina Dr (46514)
P.O. Box 1861 (46515)
PHONE.................................574 294-5611
Taylor Futterknecht, *Pr*
Kenneth Lail, *Pr*
John M Wenzel, *VP*
Richard Torok, *VP*
Linda J Lail, *Sec*
EMP: 8 **EST:** 1981
SQ FT: 72,500
SALES (est): 955.14K **Privately Held**
Web: www.keylinesaleselkhart.com
SIC: 3799 5012 Recreational vehicles; Recreational vehicles, motor homes, and trailers

(G-3454)
KIBBECHEM INC
22243 Innovation Dr (46514-8684)
PHONE.................................574 266-1234
W Glen Kibbe, *Pr*
Laura M Rice, *
Shane Kibbe, *
Shannon Rice, *
Glenn E Killoren, *
▲ **EMP:** 28 **EST:** 1990
SALES (est): 9.13MM **Privately Held**
Web: www.kibbechem.com
SIC: 2899 2865 2816 3086 Foam charge mixtures; Color pigments, organic; Color pigments; Plastics foam products

(G-3455)
KINRO MANUFACTURING INC
P.O. Box 2888 (46515-2888)
PHONE.................................803 385-5171
Nick Heffner, *Brnch Mgr*
EMP: 104
SALES (corp-wide): 3.78B **Publicly Held**
Web: corporate.lippert.com
SIC: 3442 Metal doors, sash, and trim
HQ: Kinro Manufacturing, Inc.
    3501 County Road 6 E
    Elkhart IN 46514
    574 535-1125

(G-3456)
KINRO MANUFACTURING INC
Also Called: Kinro
3501 County Road 6 E (46514-7663)
PHONE.................................574 535-1125
Allan Hammond, *Mgr*
EMP: 44
SALES (corp-wide): 3.78B **Publicly Held**
Web: corporate.lippert.com
SIC: 3442 Shutters, door or window: metal
HQ: Kinro Manufacturing, Inc.
    200 Mmaroneck Ave Ste 301
    White Plains NY 10601
    817 483-7791

(G-3457)
KINRO MANUFACTURING INC (HQ)
Also Called: Starquest Products
3501 County Road 6 E (46514-7663)
PHONE.................................574 535-1125
Jason Lippert, *Ch*
Scott Mereness, *
Dominic Gattuso, *
▲ **EMP:** 35 **EST:** 1982
SQ FT: 9,500
SALES (est): 444.61MM
SALES (corp-wide): 3.78B **Publicly Held**
Web: corporate.lippert.com
SIC: 3442 Screen doors, metal
PA: Lci Industries
    3501 County Rd 6 E
    Elkhart IN 46514
    574 535-1125

(G-3458)
KITCHEN & BATH FIXTURES
3601 Charlotte Ave (46517-1192)
PHONE.................................574 296-7617
Jim Schwartz, *CEO*
EMP: 1 **EST:** 1996
SQ FT: 220,000
SALES (est): 137.59K **Privately Held**
SIC: 3469 Kitchen fixtures and equipment: metal, except cast aluminum

(G-3459)
KOBELCO CMPSR MFG IND INC
3000 Hammond Ave (46516-5919)
PHONE.................................574 295-3145
Kevin O Neill, *Pr*
Jay Killian, *
▲ **EMP:** 55 **EST:** 1965
SQ FT: 86,000
SALES (est): 13.39MM **Privately Held**
Web: www.kobelco-compressors.com
SIC: 3563 3599 Air and gas compressors including vacuum pumps; Machine shop, jobbing and repair
PA: Kobe Steel, Ltd.
    2-2-4, Wakinohamakaigandoori, Chuo-Ku
    Kobe HYO 651-0

(G-3460)
KROGER CO
Also Called: Kroger
130 W Hively Ave (46517-2113)
PHONE.................................574 294-6092
Brandon Wagner, *Mgr*
EMP: 1
SALES (corp-wide): 150.04B **Publicly Held**
Web: www.thekrogerco.com
SIC: 5411 2051 Supermarkets, chain; Bread, cake, and related products
PA: The Kroger Co
    1014 Vine St
    Cincinnati OH 45202
    513 762-4000

(G-3461)
L E JOHNSON PRODUCTS INC
1133 Lusher Ave (46516)
PHONE.................................574 293-5664
Larry Johnson, *Brnch Mgr*
EMP: 8
SALES (corp-wide): 28.16MM **Privately Held**
Web: www.johnsonhardware.com
SIC: 3429 Door opening and closing devices, except electrical
PA: L E Johnson Products Inc
    2100 Sterling Ave
    Elkhart IN 46516
    574 293-5664

(G-3462)
L E JOHNSON PRODUCTS INC (PA)
Also Called: Johnson Hardware
2100 Sterling Ave (46516-4909)
PHONE.................................574 293-5664
Larry A Johnson, *Pr*
Larry Johnson, *
Stephen Johnson, *
Scott Johnson, *
Drew Johnson, *
◆ **EMP:** 200 **EST:** 1959
SQ FT: 200,000
SALES (est): 28.16MM
SALES (corp-wide): 28.16MM **Privately Held**
Web: www.johnsonhardware.com
SIC: 3429 Door opening and closing devices, except electrical

(G-3463)
LA MICHOACANA
1854 Woodland Dr (46514-9284)
PHONE.................................574 293-9799
Adam Corona, *Prin*
EMP: 7 **EST:** 2010
SALES (est): 135.41K **Privately Held**
SIC: 2024 Ice cream, bulk

(G-3464)
LABEL LOGIC INC
Also Called: Label Logic
516 Pine Creek Ct (46516-9093)
P.O. Box 3002 (46515-3002)
PHONE.................................574 266-6007
Karen Cripe, *Pr*
Jeff Cripe, *
Doug Williams, *
EMP: 38 **EST:** 1996
SQ FT: 48,000
SALES (est): 9.29MM **Privately Held**
Web: www.label-logic.com
SIC: 2759 Labels and seals: printing, nsk

(G-3465)
LACAY FABRICATION AND MFG INC
2801 Glenview Dr (46514-8711)
PHONE.................................574 288-4678
Maryann Lacay, *CEO*
Ann M Filley, *
Joe Lacay, *Prin*
EMP: 24 **EST:** 1975
SQ FT: 54,000
SALES (est): 4.71MM **Privately Held**
Web: www.lacayfab.com
SIC: 3441 Fabricated structural metal

(G-3466)
LAKE COPPER CONDUCTORS LLC
4430 Eastland Dr (46516-9034)
PHONE.................................847 238-3000
Emile Tohme, *Pr*
Mary Oziemkowski, *CFO*
▲ **EMP:** 10 **EST:** 2008
SALES (est): 2.38MM **Privately Held**
Web: www.lakecable.com
SIC: 3351 Wire, copper and copper alloy

(G-3467)
LAKELAND PALLETS INC
Lafree Entps A Div Lkland Plle
2505 Middlebury St (46516-5513)
PHONE.................................574 674-5906
John Denhan, *Mgr*
EMP: 5
Web: www.lakelandpalletsinc.com
SIC: 2421 Lumber: rough, sawed, or planed
PA: Lakeland Pallets, Inc.
    3801 Kraft Ave Se
    Grand Rapids MI 49512

(G-3468)
LANDJET INTERNATIONAL
21240 Protecta Dr (46516-9535)
PHONE.................................574 970-7805
John Dingle, *Pr*
EMP: 9 **EST:** 2014
SALES (est): 189.9K **Privately Held**
Web: www.landjet.net
SIC: 3799 Recreational vehicles

(G-3469)
LASALLE BRISTOL CORPORATION (DH)
Also Called: Lasalle Bristol
601 County Road 17 (46516-9505)
P.O. Box 98 (46515-0098)
PHONE.................................574 295-8400
Andrew Batson, *Pr*
Robin L Robb, *
William J Schmuhl Junior, *Dir*
◆ **EMP:** 180 **EST:** 1961
SALES (est): 183.62MM
SALES (corp-wide): 3.47B **Publicly Held**
Web: www.lasallebristol.com
SIC: 5023 5021 5051 5033 Floor coverings; Household furniture; Aluminum bars, rods, ingots, sheets, pipes, plates, etc.; Siding, except wood
HQ: Arran Isle, Inc.
    601 County Road 17
    Elkhart IN 46516
    574 295-4400

(G-3470)
LASALLE BRISTOL CORPORATION
3933 E Jackson Blvd (46516-5228)
PHONE.................................574 293-5526
Crystal Jernigan, *Brnch Mgr*
EMP: 13
SALES (corp-wide): 3.47B **Publicly Held**
Web: www.lasallebristol.com
SIC: 5031 5075 3444 Molding, all materials; Warm air heating equipment and supplies; Sheet metalwork
HQ: Lasalle Bristol Corporation
    601 County Road 17
    Elkhart IN 46516
    574 295-8400

(G-3471)
LATCH GARD CO INC
1900 Fieldhouse Ave (46517-1315)
P.O. Box 425 (46573-0425)
PHONE.................................574 862-2373
Randall Moyer, *Pr*
David Geiger, *VP*
EMP: 7 **EST:** 1973
SALES (est): 678.22K **Privately Held**
Web: www.latchgard.com
SIC: 3429 3357 Door locks, bolts, and checks; Nonferrous wiredrawing and insulating

(G-3472)
LAYTON HOMES CORPORATION (HQ)
2520 Bypass Rd (46514-1518)
P.O. Box 743 (46515-0743)
PHONE.................................574 294-6521
Ronald Kloska, *Pr*
Joseph Fanchi, *VP*
Richard M Treckelo, *Sec*
EMP: 3 **EST:** 1962
SALES (est): 29.92MM
SALES (corp-wide): 2.02B **Publicly Held**
SIC: 3792 Travel trailers and campers
PA: Skyline Champion Corporation
    755 W Big Bevr Rd Ste 100
    Troy MI 48084
    248 614-8211

(G-3473)
LAYTON HOMES CORPORATION
Also Called: Layton Elkhart
411 County Road 15 (46516-9623)
PHONE.................................574 294-6521
Ralph Nichols, *Brnch Mgr*
EMP: 136
SALES (corp-wide): 2.02B **Publicly Held**
SIC: 3792 Travel trailers and campers
HQ: Layton Homes Corporation
    2520 Bypass Rd
    Elkhart IN 46514
    574 294-6521

(G-3474)
LAZZERINI CORPORATION
1011 Herman St (46516-9029)
PHONE.................................574 206-4769
Rocco Carbone, *Pr*

EMP: 11 EST: 2016
SALES (est): 242.32K Privately Held
Web: www.lazzerini.it
SIC: 2211 Upholstery fabrics, cotton

(G-3475)
LCI INDUSTRIES
1722 W Mishawaka Rd (46517-9404)
PHONE.................................574 535-1125
John Ries, Brnch Mgr
EMP: 2
SALES (corp-wide): 3.78B Publicly Held
Web: corporate.lippert.com
SIC: 3999 Atomizers, toiletry
PA: Lci Industries
   3501 County Rd 6 E
   Elkhart IN 46514
   574 535-1125

(G-3476)
LCI INDUSTRIES (PA)
3501 County Road 6 E (46514)
PHONE.................................574 535-1125
Jason D Lippert, Pr
James F Gero, Ch Bd
Lillian D Etzkorn, Ex VP
Andrew J Namenye, CLO
Eileen S Pruitt, Chief Human Resources Officer
EMP: 592 EST: 1962
SALES (est): 3.78B
SALES (corp-wide): 3.78B Publicly Held
Web: corporate.lippert.com
SIC: 3714 3715 3711 3442 Motor vehicle parts and accessories; Trailer bodies; Chassis, motor vehicle; Window and door frames

(G-3477)
LCI INDUSTRIES
3407 Cooper Dr (46514-8638)
PHONE.................................574 264-3521
EMP: 1
SALES (corp-wide): 3.78B Publicly Held
Web: corporate.lippert.com
SIC: 3714 Motor vehicle parts and accessories
PA: Lci Industries
   3501 County Rd 6 E
   Elkhart IN 46514
   574 535-1125

(G-3478)
LCI INDUSTRIES
3308 Charlotte Ave (46517-1189)
PHONE.................................574 312-6116
EMP: 2
SALES (corp-wide): 3.78B Publicly Held
Web: corporate.lippert.com
SIC: 3714 Motor vehicle parts and accessories
PA: Lci Industries
   3501 County Rd 6 E
   Elkhart IN 46514
   574 535-1125

(G-3479)
LCM REALTY LLC
3501 County Road 6 E (46514-7663)
PHONE.................................574 535-1125
EMP: 1 EST: 2018
SALES (est): 2.48MM
SALES (corp-wide): 3.78B Publicly Held
SIC: 3711 Chassis, motor vehicle
PA: Lci Industries
   3501 County Rd 6 E
   Elkhart IN 46514
   574 535-1125

(G-3480)
LEARMAN ELCTRNIC TL ASSCTESINC
58211 County Road 105 (46517)
PHONE.................................574 293-4641
EMP: 6 EST: 2019
SALES (est): 242.97K Privately Held
Web: www.inductionharden.com
SIC: 3398 Metal heat treating

(G-3481)
LEARMAN ELECTRONIC TOOL ASSOC
Also Called: Electronic Tool Associates
1513 S 6th St (46516-2546)
PHONE.................................574 226-0420
Tim Learman, Pr
Pat Learman, VP
EMP: 6 EST: 1955
SQ FT: 15,000
SALES (est): 461.57K Privately Held
Web: www.inductionharden.com
SIC: 3398 Metal heat treating

(G-3482)
LEARNING CEDAR WOODWORKING
28388 County Road 30 (46517-9517)
PHONE.................................574 862-1864
Dana Ramer, Owner
EMP: 1 EST: 2013
SALES (est): 75.18K Privately Held
SIC: 2431 Millwork

(G-3483)
LEGACY VULCAN LLC
Also Called: Elkhart Yard
2500 W Lusher Ave (46517-1067)
PHONE.................................574 293-1536
Chris Weinkauf, Brnch Mgr
EMP: 4
Web: www.vulcanmaterials.com
SIC: 3273 Ready-mixed concrete
HQ: Legacy Vulcan, Llc
   1200 Urban Center Dr
   Birmingham AL 35242
   205 298-3000

(G-3484)
LEONARD EATON TOOLING INC
435 Roske Dr (46516-9086)
PHONE.................................574 295-5041
Betty Hartman, Contrlr
EMP: 10 EST: 2015
SALES (est): 211.6K Privately Held
Web: www.bendtools.com
SIC: 3599 Machine shop, jobbing and repair

(G-3485)
LEPARK MOLD & TOOL
1147 N Michigan St (46516-2213)
PHONE.................................574 262-0518
Mike Hoover, Owner
EMP: 10 EST: 2009
SALES (est): 341.4K Privately Held
SIC: 3089 Injection molding of plastics

(G-3486)
LEXICON INCORPORATED
Also Called: Harman Specialty Group
1718 W Mishawaka Rd (46517-9439)
PHONE.................................203 328-3500
▲ EMP: 130
SIC: 3651 Audio electronic systems

(G-3487)
LEXINGTON LLC
Also Called: Domore Seating
2503 Banks Ct (46514-7675)
PHONE.................................574 295-8166
EMP: 25

Web: www.lexingtonproducts.com
SIC: 2531 Vehicle furniture

(G-3488)
LIFTCO INC
Also Called: Vb Air Suspension North Amer
3301 Reedy Dr (46514-7665)
PHONE.................................574 266-5551
Stanley Disher, CEO
John Disher, *
Patrick Disher, *
▲ EMP: 30 EST: 1992
SQ FT: 52,000
SALES (est): 2.5MM Privately Held
Web: www.liftcoinc.com
SIC: 3499 Stabilizing bars (cargo), metal

(G-3489)
LIPPERT CMPONENTS INTL SLS INC
3501 County Road 6 E (46514-7663)
PHONE.................................574 312-7480
EMP: 1 EST: 2018
SALES (est): 740.17K
SALES (corp-wide): 3.78B Publicly Held
Web: www.lippertcomponents.eu
SIC: 3711 Chassis, motor vehicle
PA: Lci Industries
   3501 County Rd 6 E
   Elkhart IN 46514
   574 535-1125

(G-3490)
LIPPERT COMPONENTS
625 Bower St (46514-2656)
PHONE.................................574 226-4088
EMP: 5 EST: 2018
SALES (est): 87.27K Privately Held
Web: www.lippertcomponents.eu
SIC: 3714 Motor vehicle parts and accessories

(G-3491)
LIPPERT COMPONENTS INC
3308 Charlotte Ave (46517-1189)
PHONE.................................574 295-1483
EMP: 9
SALES (corp-wide): 3.78B Publicly Held
Web: corporate.lippert.com
SIC: 3711 Chassis, motor vehicle
HQ: Lippert Components, Inc.
   3501 County Rd 6 E
   Elkhart IN 46514
   574 535-1125

(G-3492)
LIPPERT COMPONENTS INC
Also Called: Plant 83
57912 Charlotte Ave (46517-1189)
PHONE.................................574 535-1125
Jason Lippert, Brnch Mgr
EMP: 3
SALES (corp-wide): 3.78B Publicly Held
Web: corporate.lippert.com
SIC: 3711 3469 3444 3714 Chassis, motor vehicle; Stamping metal for the trade; Metal roofing and roof drainage equipment; Motor vehicle parts and accessories
HQ: Lippert Components, Inc.
   3501 County Rd 6 E
   Elkhart IN 46514
   574 535-1125

(G-3493)
LIPPERT COMPONENTS INC (HQ)
Also Called: Lippert
3501 County Road 6 E (46514)
P.O. Box 2888 (46514)
PHONE.................................574 535-1125
Jason D Lippert, Pr
L Douglas Lippert, *
Brian Hall, *

Rob Ford, *
Joe Thompson, CMO*
▲ EMP: 256 EST: 1956
SQ FT: 8,000
SALES (est): 1.45B
SALES (corp-wide): 3.78B Publicly Held
Web: www.lci1.com
SIC: 3711 3469 3444 3714 Chassis, motor vehicle; Stamping metal for the trade; Metal roofing and roof drainage equipment; Motor vehicle parts and accessories
PA: Lci Industries
   3501 County Rd 6 E
   Elkhart IN 46514
   574 535-1125

(G-3494)
LIPPERT COMPONENTS INC
2503 Banks Ct (46514-7675)
P.O. Box 2888 (46515-2888)
PHONE.................................574 295-8166
Jeff Wysong, Brnch Mgr
EMP: 25
SALES (corp-wide): 3.78B Publicly Held
Web: www.lci1.com
SIC: 2531 Vehicle furniture
HQ: Lippert Components, Inc.
   3501 County Rd 6 E
   Elkhart IN 46514
   574 535-1125

(G-3495)
LIPPERT COMPONENTS MFG INC (DH)
3501 County Road 6 E (46514)
P.O. Box 2888 (46515)
PHONE.................................574 535-1125
Jason Lippert, CEO
Lillian D Etzkorn, *
▲ EMP: 94 EST: 1998
SALES (est): 153.99MM
SALES (corp-wide): 3.78B Publicly Held
Web: corporate.lippert.com
SIC: 3711 Chassis, motor vehicle
HQ: Lippert Components, Inc.
   3501 County Rd 6 E
   Elkhart IN 46514
   574 535-1125

(G-3496)
LIPPERT EXTRUSIONS
1722 W Mishawaka Rd (46517-9404)
PHONE.................................574 312-6467
EMP: 10 EST: 2011
SALES (est): 196.61K Privately Held
SIC: 3999 Manufacturing industries, nec

(G-3497)
LITHOTONE INC (PA)
1313 W Hively Ave (46517-1594)
PHONE.................................574 294-5521
Robert Priebe, Pr
James Priebe, *
Timothy Coquillard, *
Kirk Lehman, *
EMP: 44 EST: 1962
SQ FT: 41,400
SALES (est): 5.86MM
SALES (corp-wide): 5.86MM Privately Held
Web: www.lithotone.com
SIC: 2752 Offset printing

(G-3498)
LIVINGS GRAPHICS INC
Also Called: Printers Plus
2111 Cassopolis St (46514-5115)
PHONE.................................574 264-4114
Kathy Livings, Pr
Joseph Livings, VP
EMP: 6 EST: 1982

GEOGRAPHIC SECTION

Elkhart - Elkhart County (G-3525)

SALES (est): 405.94K **Privately Held**
Web: www.printerspluselkhart.com
SIC: 2752 Offset printing

(G-3499)
LONE STAR INDUSTRIES INC
55284 Corwin Rd (46514-8401)
PHONE..................574 674-8873
David A Pedzinski, *Mgr*
EMP: 3
SQ FT: 2,000
SALES (corp-wide): 4.69B **Privately Held**
Web: www.lonestarind.com
SIC: 3241 Portland cement
HQ: Lone Star Industries Inc
10401 N Meridian St # 120
Carmel IN 46290
317 706-3314

(G-3500)
LOTEC INC
Also Called: Speedgrip Chuck
2000 Industrial Pkwy (46516-5411)
P.O. Box 596 (46515-0596)
PHONE..................574 294-1506
Nancy Renaud, *CEO*
David Copp, *
Michelle Endres, *
EMP: 30 EST: 1943
SQ FT: 47,200
SALES (est): 4.5MM **Privately Held**
Web: www.lotecinc.com
SIC: 3599 Machine shop, jobbing and repair

(G-3501)
LSR CONVERSIONS LLC
25771 Miner Rd (46514-5019)
PHONE..................574 206-9610
EMP: 10 EST: 2003
SQ FT: 18,000
SALES (est): 1.12MM **Privately Held**
Web: www.lsrconversions.net
SIC: 3792 Travel trailers and campers

(G-3502)
LTI HOLDINGS INC
53208 Columbia Dr (46514-8149)
PHONE..................574 389-1878
Bill Kuehne, *Brnch Mgr*
EMP: 1
Web: www.boydcorp.com
SIC: 3069 Bags, rubber or rubberized fabric
PA: Lti Holdings, Inc.
5960 Inglewood Dr Ste 115
Pleasanton CA 94588

(G-3503)
LUNARGLO LLC
22385 Via Pompeii (46516-9779)
PHONE..................574 294-2624
Judy A Barton, *Prin*
Rex Barton, *Prin*
EMP: 2 EST: 2016
SALES (est): 155.62K **Privately Held**
Web: www.lunarglo.com
SIC: 3648 Lighting equipment, nec

(G-3504)
LUXE TRUCKS LLC
Also Called: Utility Body Werks
3504 Henke St (46514-7653)
PHONE..................574 522-8372
George Thomas, *Managing Member*
Brian Shea, *Managing Member*
EMP: 15 EST: 2020
SALES (est): 1.15MM **Privately Held**
Web: www.luxefifthwheel.com
SIC: 3713 Truck and bus bodies

(G-3505)
M G PRODUCTS INC
4707 Chester Dr (46516-9641)
PHONE..................574 293-0752
EMP: 30 EST: 1995
SQ FT: 41,000
SALES (est): 2.34MM **Privately Held**
Web: www.mgproducts.com
SIC: 3599 Machine shop, jobbing and repair

(G-3506)
M-3 AND ASSOCIATES INC
2500 Ada Dr (46514-8644)
PHONE..................574 294-3988
Randy D Wilson, *Pr*
Linda Wilson, *Sec*
EMP: 21 EST: 1987
SALES (est): 963.97K **Privately Held**
Web: www.m3assoc.com
SIC: 3493 Torsion bar springs

(G-3507)
M-TEC CORPORATION
701 Collins Rd (46516-5420)
P.O. Box 1064 (46515-1064)
PHONE..................574 294-1060
William Banks Junior, *CEO*
John F Hughes, *
Dave Devon, *
EMP: 98 EST: 2002
SALES (est): 2.52MM
SALES (corp-wide): 3.78B **Publicly Held**
SIC: 3711 Cars, electric, assembly of
HQ: Lippert Components, Inc.
3501 County Rd 6 E
Elkhart IN 46514
574 535-1125

(G-3508)
MACH 1 PAPER AND POLY PDTS INC
1801 Minnie St (46516-5736)
PHONE..................574 522-4500
Thomas Reusser, *Pr*
EMP: 13 EST: 2011
SALES (est): 192.16K **Privately Held**
Web: www.mach1tube.com
SIC: 2679 2655 Paperboard products, converted, nec; Tubes, fiber or paper: made from purchased material

(G-3509)
MADDEN ENGINEERED PRODUCTS LLC
1317 Princeton St (46516-4106)
PHONE..................574 295-4292
EMP: 7 EST: 2019
SALES (est): 514.8K **Privately Held**
Web: www.maddenep.com
SIC: 3999 Atomizers, toiletry

(G-3510)
MAJESTIC DRAPERIES INC
59193 Green Valley Pkwy (46517-3427)
PHONE..................574 257-8465
Verna R Walker Huston, *Pr*
EMP: 2 EST: 1982
SQ FT: 1,000
SALES (est): 140K **Privately Held**
SIC: 2391 Curtains and draperies

(G-3511)
MANU SANGHA INC
3400 County Road 6 E (46514-7662)
PHONE..................219 262-5400
EMP: 4 EST: 2018
SALES (est): 95.22K **Privately Held**
SIC: 3999 Manufacturing industries, nec

(G-3512)
MARATHON HOMES CORPORATION
4420 Pine Creek Rd (46516-9560)
PHONE..................574 294-6441
Ron Berg, *Pr*
EMP: 45 EST: 1973
SQ FT: 20,000
SALES (est): 3.37MM **Privately Held**
SIC: 3792 Travel trailers and campers

(G-3513)
MARKLEY ENTERPRISE INC
2605 Whipple Ave (46516-5506)
PHONE..................574 295-4195
H Timothy Markley, *Pr*
Nancy Stanner, *
EMP: 75 EST: 1962
SQ FT: 16,000
SALES (est): 3.85MM **Privately Held**
Web: www.colwellcolour.com
SIC: 3161 5046 Sample cases; Store fixtures and display equipment

(G-3514)
MARSHALL & POE LLC (PA)
Also Called: Marshall & Poe Bus Cons & CP
818 Erwin St (46514-3370)
PHONE..................574 266-5244
Charles Marshall, *Owner*
Jeff Keccanowski, *
EMP: 24 EST: 1981
SALES (est): 1.15MM
SALES (corp-wide): 1.15MM **Privately Held**
Web: www.arrisconsulting.com
SIC: 7372 Prepackaged software

(G-3515)
MARSON INTERNATIONAL LLC
1001 Sako Ct (46516-9019)
PHONE..................574 295-4222
◆ EMP: 78 EST: 2001
SALES (est): 10MM **Privately Held**
Web: www.marsonintl.com
SIC: 3441 Fabricated structural metal

(G-3516)
MARTIN PROFESSIONAL INC
1718 W Mishawaka Rd (46517-9439)
PHONE..................574 294-8000
EMP: 9
Web: www.martin.com
SIC: 3646 Commercial lighting fixtures
HQ: Martin Professional, Inc.
3300 Corp Ave Ste 108
Weston FL 33331

(G-3517)
MARTIN TRUSS MFG LLC
62332 County Road 1 (46517-9724)
PHONE..................574 862-4457
Andrew Martin, *Owner*
EMP: 2 EST: 1993
SALES (est): 310.43K **Privately Held**
SIC: 2439 Trusses, wooden roof

(G-3518)
MARTYS DESKTOP PUBLISH
29200 County Road 20 # 69 (46517-9742)
PHONE..................715 520-7682
EMP: 2
SALES (est): 86.39K **Privately Held**
SIC: 2741 Miscellaneous publishing

(G-3519)
MAVERICK PACKAGING INC
3505 Reedy Dr (46514-7668)
PHONE..................574 264-2891
▲ EMP: 33 EST: 1998
SQ FT: 25,000

SALES (est): 4.49MM **Privately Held**
Web: www.maverickpackaging.com
SIC: 2844 5122 Hair preparations, including shampoos; Cosmetics, perfumes, and hair products

(G-3520)
MBSI HOLDINGS LLC
58120 County Road 3 (46517-9007)
PHONE..................574 295-1214
Rick Bedell, *Managing Member*
EMP: 3 EST: 2006
SALES (est): 293.01K **Privately Held**
SIC: 2452 Prefabricated wood buildings

(G-3521)
MCDOWELL ENTERPRISES INC
2010 Superior St (46516-4706)
P.O. Box 846 (46515-0846)
PHONE..................574 293-1042
Carol Mcdowell, *Pr*
James Loshbough, *
EMP: 25 EST: 1939
SQ FT: 25,000
SALES (est): 919.36K **Privately Held**
Web: www.mcdowellenterprisesinc.com
SIC: 3471 Plating of metals or formed products

(G-3522)
MECHANCAL ENGRG CNTRLS ATMTN C
Also Called: Meca
57236 Nagy Dr (46517-1019)
P.O. Box 519 (46515-0519)
PHONE..................574 294-7580
Jim Bour, *Pr*
Greg Dean, *VP*
EMP: 23 EST: 1993
SQ FT: 15,000
SALES (est): 1.32MM **Privately Held**
Web: www.mecacorp.net
SIC: 3613 3599 Panel and distribution boards and other related apparatus; Custom machinery

(G-3523)
MECK DIE INC
29029 Phillips St (46514-1024)
PHONE..................574 262-5441
Robert Wilkinson, *Pr*
Kathy Wilkinson, *VP*
EMP: 3 EST: 1976
SQ FT: 2,400
SALES (est): 385K **Privately Held**
Web: www.meckdie.com
SIC: 3544 Dies, steel rule

(G-3524)
MEDICAL STRUCTURES MFG CORP
1803 Minnie St (46516-5736)
PHONE..................574 612-0353
Thomas Cassity, *Prin*
EMP: 6 EST: 2005
SALES (est): 123.86K **Privately Held**
Web: www.medicalstructures.com
SIC: 3999 Manufacturing industries, nec

(G-3525)
MEDIX SPECIALTY VEHICLES LLC
3008 Mobile Dr (46514-5524)
PHONE..................574 266-0911
◆ EMP: 125 EST: 2001
SQ FT: 48,000
SALES (est): 19.81MM **Privately Held**
Web: www.medixambulance.com
SIC: 3711 Ambulances (motor vehicles), assembly of

Elkhart - Elkhart County (G-3526)

(G-3526)
MEER ENTERPRISES INC
21700 Protecta Dr (46516-9531)
PHONE..................574 522-7527
EMP: 65
SIC: 3089 Injection molded finished plastics products, nec

(G-3527)
METALCRAFT PRECISION MACHINING
Also Called: Metalcraft
56854 Elk Ct (46516-1456)
PHONE..................574 293-6700
Don Utz, Pr
Jeff Rhodes, VP
EMP: 25 EST: 1997
SQ FT: 20,000
SALES (est): 710.16K Privately Held
SIC: 3599 Machine shop, jobbing and repair

(G-3528)
METALCRAFTERS INC
2415 Bryant St (46516-5536)
PHONE..................574 294-2502
Thomas Jellison, Pr
EMP: 17 EST: 1993
SQ FT: 90,000
SALES (est): 650.49K Privately Held
SIC: 3799 Trailers and trailer equipment

(G-3529)
METZLER ENTERPRISE
2745 Homer Ave (46517-2627)
PHONE..................574 293-9267
Kenneth D Metzler, Prin
EMP: 1 EST: 2007
SALES (est): 109.94K Privately Held
Web: www.metzlerbrass.com
SIC: 3714 Motor vehicle parts and accessories

(G-3530)
MICHIANA BANDSAW & SUP CO LLC
2115 E Jackson Blvd (46516-4645)
P.O. Box 1864 (46515-1864)
PHONE..................574 293-5974
Scott Miller, Owner
EMP: 1 EST: 2001
SALES (est): 130.45K Privately Held
SIC: 3553 Bandsaws, woodworking

(G-3531)
MICHIANA ELKHART INC
51505 State Road 19 (46514-5814)
PHONE..................574 206-0620
EMP: 11 EST: 2009
SALES (est): 220.91K Privately Held
Web: www.michianametalfab.com
SIC: 2992 Lubricating oils

(G-3532)
MICHIANA FORKLIFT INC
Also Called: Michiana Compressor
2921 Moose Trl (46514-8230)
PHONE..................574 326-3702
Jennifer Kowalski, Pr
EMP: 13 EST: 2009
SALES (est): 1.32MM Privately Held
Web: www.michianaforklift.com
SIC: 3537 Forklift trucks

(G-3533)
MICHIANA METAL FABRICATION INC
1227 W Beardsley Ave (46514-2223)
PHONE..................574 256-9010
Shawn Winkelmann, Pr
EMP: 5 EST: 1989
SQ FT: 18,000
SALES (est): 499.91K Privately Held
Web: www.michianametalfab.com
SIC: 3544 Special dies and tools

(G-3534)
MICHIANA METAL FINISHING INC
2805 Frederic Dr (46514-7642)
PHONE..................574 206-0666
EMP: 3 EST: 2009
SALES (est): 169.28K Privately Held
Web: www.michianametalfab.com
SIC: 3471 Finishing, metals or formed products

(G-3535)
MICRO MACHINE WORKS INC
835 Lillian Ave (46516-5525)
P.O. Box 2082 (46515-2082)
PHONE..................574 293-1354
Herbert L Kirts, Pr
Diane Kirts, Sec
EMP: 8 EST: 1992
SQ FT: 1,350
SALES (est): 851.6K Privately Held
SIC: 3599 Machine shop, jobbing and repair

(G-3536)
MICROFORM INC
21053 Protecta Dr Ste A (46516-9335)
PHONE..................574 522-9851
EMP: 9 EST: 1989
SQ FT: 14,000
SALES (est): 977.76K Privately Held
Web: www.mform.com
SIC: 3444 3679 Sheet metalwork; Electronic circuits

(G-3537)
MID AMERICA SCREW PRODUCTS
Also Called: M.A.S. Products
21559 Protecta Dr (46516-9542)
PHONE..................574 294-6905
Steve Nauman, Pr
▲ EMP: 13 EST: 1983
SQ FT: 20,000
SALES (est): 629.51K Privately Held
Web: www.masinserts.com
SIC: 3451 Screw machine products

(G-3538)
MIDE PRODUCTS
53848 N Park Ave (46514-5000)
PHONE..................574 326-3060
Mike Riggle, Pr
EMP: 1 EST: 2013
SALES (est): 153.66K Privately Held
Web: www.mideproducts.com
SIC: 3524 Lawn and garden equipment

(G-3539)
MIDWAY SPECIALTY VEHICLES LLC
2940 Dexter Dr (46514-8226)
P.O. Box 1931 (46515-1931)
PHONE..................574 264-2530
Russ Gilpin, *
Gary Mathers, *
EMP: 48 EST: 2002
SQ FT: 78,000
SALES (est): 9.8MM Privately Held
Web: www.midwayspecialtyvehicles.com
SIC: 3711 Automobile assembly, including specialty automobiles

(G-3540)
MIDWEST PLASTICS COMPANY INC
1603 E Lake Dr W (46514-4210)
PHONE..................574 264-4994
Michael M Malloy, Brnch Mgr
EMP: 1
SALES (corp-wide): 461.57K Privately Held
SIC: 3089 Injection molding of plastics
PA: Midwest Plastics Company Inc
401 Lincolnway W
Osceola IN 46561
574 674-0161

(G-3541)
MIDWEST SANDBAGS LLC
2727 Industrial Pkwy (46516)
PHONE..................847 366-6555
Dave Wilman, Managing Member
EMP: 8 EST: 2017
SALES (est): 1.2MM Privately Held
Web: www.midwestsandbags.com
SIC: 2211 2299 2673 Bags and bagging, cotton; Bagging, jute; Bags: plastic, laminated, and coated

(G-3542)
MIDWEST WELDING FABRICATION
30182 Blue Spruce Dr (46514-9723)
PHONE..................574 226-8306
Ines Ambriz, Prin
EMP: 4 EST: 2019
SALES (est): 58.02K Privately Held
SIC: 7692 Welding repair

(G-3543)
MILFORD PROPERTY LLC
601 E Beardsley Ave (46514-3305)
PHONE..................574 970-7460
Todd Woelfer, Off Mgr
EMP: 13 EST: 2016
SALES (est): 1.52MM
SALES (corp-wide): 11.12B Publicly Held
SIC: 3716 Motor homes
PA: Thor Industries, Inc.
601 E Beardsley Ave
Elkhart IN 46514
574 970-7460

(G-3544)
MILLMARK ENTERPRISES INC
1935 Markle Ave (46517-1321)
P.O. Box 757 (46515-0757)
PHONE..................574 389-9904
Darin J Miller, Pr
Michelle Miller, Sec
EMP: 15 EST: 1998
SQ FT: 24,000
SALES (est): 2.44MM Privately Held
Web: www.millmarkenterprises.com
SIC: 3441 Fabricated structural metal

(G-3545)
MIN KO KYAW LLC
2730 Industrial Pkwy (46516-5401)
PHONE..................574 296-3500
Tina Leonard, Prin
EMP: 13 EST: 2012
SALES (est): 1.15MM Privately Held
SIC: 3714 Motor vehicle parts and accessories

(G-3546)
MISHAWAKA SHEET METAL LLC
28505 C R 20 W (46517)
PHONE..................574 294-5959
EMP: 60
Web: www.mishawakasheetmetal.com
SIC: 3444 Sheet metalwork

(G-3547)
MJB WOOD GROUP LLC
1600 Fieldhouse Ave Ste A (46517-1452)
PHONE..................574 295-5228
Sherry Ohman, Brnch Mgr
EMP: 6
SALES (corp-wide): 90.06MM Privately Held
Web: www.mjbwood.com
SIC: 5031 2499 Lumber: rough, dressed, and finished; Decorative wood and woodwork
PA: Mjb Wood Group, Llc
1585 High Meadows Way
Cedar Hill TX 75104
972 401-0005

(G-3548)
MOBILE/MODULAR EXPRESS II LLC
58120 County Road 3 (46517-9007)
PHONE..................574 295-1214
EMP: 8 EST: 2019
SALES (est): 198.83K Privately Held
Web: www.mobilemodular.com
SIC: 2452 Prefabricated wood buildings

(G-3549)
MODERN MUSCLE CAR FACTORY INC
30446 County Road 12 (46514-8937)
PHONE..................574 329-6390
EMP: 3 EST: 2014
SALES (est): 125.88K Privately Held
SIC: 2396 Automotive and apparel trimmings

(G-3550)
MOLDED ACSTCAL PDTS EASTON INC
3733 Lexington Park Dr (46514-1163)
PHONE..................610 253-7135
Sherry Mcshane, Mgr
EMP: 50
Web: www.mapeaston.com
SIC: 3296 Fiberglass insulation
PA: Molded Acoustical Products Of Easton, Inc.
3 Danforth Dr
Easton PA 18045

(G-3551)
MOR/RYDE INC
Also Called: Mor-Ryde Service Center
1966 Sterling Ave (46516-4221)
P.O. Box 579 (46515-0579)
PHONE..................574 293-1581
Robert Moore Senior, Ch Bd
Robert G Moore Junior, Pr
Rodney A Moore, Sec
EMP: 115 EST: 1966
SQ FT: 60,000
SALES (est): 24.08MM Privately Held
Web: www.morryde.com
SIC: 3714 Motor vehicle transmissions, drive assemblies, and parts

(G-3552)
MOREHEAD MACHINERY INC
30924 County Road 8 (46514-9710)
PHONE..................574 651-8671
Austin Morehead, Pr
EMP: 2 EST: 2017
SQ FT: 3,200
SALES (est): 208.57K Privately Held
Web: www.moreheadmachinery.com
SIC: 3599 Machine shop, jobbing and repair

(G-3553)
MORRYDE INTERNATIONAL INC
1536 Grant St (46514-3756)
PHONE..................574 293-1581
Robert Moore Senior, Prin
EMP: 15
Web: www.morryde.com
SIC: 3714 Motor vehicle parts and accessories
PA: Morryde International, Inc.
1966 Sterling Avenue
Elkhart IN 46516

GEOGRAPHIC SECTION

Elkhart - Elkhart County (G-3578)

(G-3554)
MORRYDE INTERNATIONAL INC
23208 Cooper Dr (46514-9741)
PHONE.................................574 293-1581
EMP: 15
Web: www.morryde.com
SIC: 3714 Motor vehicle parts and accessories
PA: Morryde International, Inc.
1966 Sterling Avenue
Elkhart IN 46516

(G-3555)
MORRYDE INTERNATIONAL INC (PA)
1966 Sterling Ave (46516)
P.O. Box 579 (46515)
PHONE.................................574 293-1581
Rodney Moore, CEO
Robert Moore Senior, Ch Bd
Robert Moore Junior, Pr
Rodney A Moore, *
EMP: 200 EST: 1982
SQ FT: 60,000
SALES (est): 48.57MM Privately Held
Web: www.morryde.com
SIC: 3449 3714 Bars, concrete reinforcing: fabricated steel; Motor vehicle transmissions, drive assemblies, and parts

(G-3556)
MOTOR ELECTRIC INC
4700 Eastland Dr (46516-9661)
P.O. Box 1571 (46515-1571)
PHONE.................................574 294-7123
Richard Karenke, Pr
Darren M Karenke, VP
Doris J Karenke, Sec
EMP: 7 EST: 1975
SQ FT: 10,000
SALES (est): 1.58MM Privately Held
SIC: 5063 7694 Motors, electric; Electric motor repair

(G-3557)
MOYERS INC
3502 Reedy Dr (46514-7668)
P.O. Box 157 (46515-0157)
PHONE.................................574 264-3119
Mark Moyer, Pr
Gunnar Erickson, *
EMP: 18 EST: 1980
SQ FT: 55,000
SALES (est): 396.46K Privately Held
Web: www.moyersinc.com
SIC: 3317 3499 3444 Seamless pipes and tubes; Chair frames, metal; Sheet metalwork

(G-3558)
MR PIN SHI PETER LEE
23329 Century Dr (46514-4291)
PHONE.................................574 264-9754
Peter Lee, Prin
EMP: 7 EST: 2010
SALES (est): 162.06K Privately Held
SIC: 3452 Pins

(G-3559)
MTS PRODUCTS CORP
28672 Holiday Pl (46517-1111)
PHONE.................................574 295-3142
David E Mount, Pr
Mary E Mount, *
Richard Farrough, *
◆ EMP: 45 EST: 1971
SQ FT: 50,000
SALES (est): 2.63MM Privately Held
Web: www.mtsproducts.com
SIC: 3161 3651 Cases, carrying, nec; Speaker systems

(G-3560)
MWSS INC ✪
2810 Bridger Ct (46514-7602)
PHONE.................................574 287-3365
EMP: 5 EST: 2022
SALES (est): 78.58K Privately Held
Web: www.geappliancesrecreationalliving.com
SIC: 3634 Electric household cooking appliances

(G-3561)
MX5 & ASSOCIATES INC
24615 County Road 45 Ste 2 (46516-5937)
PHONE.................................574 226-0733
Roger Merlin Mansfield, Pr
Travis Mansfield, COO
Renee Mansfield, Marketing
Spencer Mansfield, VP Prd
Robert Hesselgrave, Pur Mgr
EMP: 11 EST: 2018
SALES (est): 942.12K Privately Held
SIC: 3442 Window and door frames

(G-3562)
MYTURBOPC LLC
55348 Osborn Ave Ste C (46514-8487)
PHONE.................................574 350-9330
Shayne A Sherman, Prin
EMP: 3 EST: 2017
SALES (est): 77.52K Privately Held
Web: www.myturbopc.com
SIC: 7372 Prepackaged software

(G-3563)
NANOCHEM TECHNOLOGIES LLC
1203 Kent St (46514-1739)
PHONE.................................574 970-2436
▲ EMP: 50 EST: 2005
SALES (est): 7.97MM Privately Held
Web: www.nanochemtechnologies.com
SIC: 2851 Paints and paint additives

(G-3564)
NAP ASSET HOLDINGS LTD
900 Instamatic Dr (46516-5555)
PHONE.................................574 295-7651
EMP: 1
SALES (corp-wide): 43.28MM Privately Held
Web: www.peaktoolworks.com
SIC: 3545 Cutting tools for machine tools
PA: Nap Asset Holdings Ltd.
1180 Wernsing Rd
Jasper IN 47546
812 482-2000

(G-3565)
NEA LLC
Also Called: Allegra Print & Imaging
131 W Marion St (46516-3206)
PHONE.................................574 295-0024
EMP: 5 EST: 2003
SALES (est): 748.93K Privately Held
Web: www.nea.com
SIC: 2752 Offset printing

(G-3566)
NESTOR SALES LLC
205 County Road 17 (46516-5449)
PHONE.................................574 295-5535
EMP: 5
SALES (corp-wide): 1.47B Privately Held
Web: www.nestorsales.com
SIC: 3423 7699 Hand and edge tools, nec; Knife, saw and tool sharpening and repair
HQ: Nestor Sales Llc
7337 Bryan Dairy Rd
Largo FL 33777
727 544-6114

(G-3567)
NEWLETT INC
Also Called: Gemstone
435 Harrison St (46516-2771)
PHONE.................................574 294-8899
EMP: 52 EST: 2001
SALES (est): 4.68MM Privately Held
Web: www.gemstonesinks.com
SIC: 2541 Table or counter tops, plastic laminated

(G-3568)
NEXT GEN POWER HOLDINGS LLC
Also Called: Way Interglobal
3002 Coast Ct (46514)
PHONE.................................574 971-4490
▲ EMP: 5 EST: 2009
SQ FT: 13,000
SALES (est): 5.39MM
SALES (corp-wide): 3.78B Publicly Held
SIC: 3261 3792 Sinks, vitreous china; Travel trailers and campers
HQ: Furrion, Llc
52567 Independence Ct
Elkhart IN 46514
574 327-6571

(G-3569)
NHI-JRJ CORP ✪
316 Roske Dr (46516-9077)
PHONE.................................574 293-9690
EMP: 150 EST: 2023
SALES (est): 13.03MM Privately Held
Web: www.nativehardwoods.com
SIC: 2499 2431 2541 Decorative wood and woodwork; Doors, wood; Counter and sink tops
PA: Chase Manufacturing, Llc
506 S Oakland Ave
Nappanee IN 46550

(G-3570)
NIBCO INC (PA)
Also Called: Nibco
1516 Middlebury St (46516)
P.O. Box 1167 (46516)
PHONE.................................574 295-3000
Steven E Malm, CEO
Rex Martin, Ch
David Goodling, Senior Vice President Supply Chain
Chris Mason, Supply Chain Vice President
Cody Huffines, CIO
◆ EMP: 291 EST: 1909
SQ FT: 98,000
SALES (est): 509.67MM
SALES (corp-wide): 509.67MM Privately Held
Web: www.nibco.com
SIC: 3491 3089 3494 Industrial valves; Plastics hardware and building products; Pipe fittings

(G-3571)
NORCO INDUSTRIES INC
2600 Jeanwood Dr (46514-7657)
PHONE.................................574 262-3400
EMP: 1
SALES (corp-wide): 82.94MM Privately Held
Web: www.norcoind.com
SIC: 3569 Jacks, hydraulic
PA: Norco Industries, Inc
365 W Victoria St
Compton CA 90220
310 639-4000

(G-3572)
NORCO INDUSTRIES INC
2800 Northland Dr (46514-7670)
PHONE.................................800 347-2232

▲ EMP: 3
SALES (corp-wide): 82.94MM Privately Held
Web: www.norcoind.com
SIC: 3569 Jacks, hydraulic
PA: Norco Industries, Inc
365 W Victoria St
Compton CA 90220
310 639-4000

(G-3573)
NORCO INDUSTRIES INC
Adnik Manufacturing
2600 Jeanwood Dr (46514-7657)
PHONE.................................574 262-3400
Jeff Dick, Mgr
EMP: 210
SALES (corp-wide): 82.94MM Privately Held
Web: www.norcoind.com
SIC: 2531 3714 3452 Public building and related furniture; Motor vehicle parts and accessories; Bolts, nuts, rivets, and washers
PA: Norco Industries, Inc
365 W Victoria St
Compton CA 90220
310 639-4000

(G-3574)
NORTHERN BOX COMPANY INC
1328 Mishawaka St (46514-1809)
P.O. Box 985 (46515-0985)
PHONE.................................574 264-2161
Heidi Linder, Pr
Heidi A Linder, *
Christina J Linder, *
EMP: 25 EST: 1951
SQ FT: 70,000
SALES (est): 712.9K Privately Held
Web: www.welchpkg.com
SIC: 2653 Boxes, corrugated: made from purchased materials

(G-3575)
NORTHWEST INTERIORS INC
405 Pine Creek Ct (46516-9089)
PHONE.................................574 294-2326
James Mellott, Pr
Jan Mellott, Sec
EMP: 16 EST: 1983
SQ FT: 24,000
SALES (est): 3.99MM Privately Held
Web: www.northwestinteriors.com
SIC: 2391 Draperies, plastic and textile: from purchased materials

(G-3576)
NORTOOL PRECISION MACHINING TL
2600 Jeanwood Dr (46514-7657)
PHONE.................................574 262-3400
Jeff Dick, Asstg
EMP: 2 EST: 1998
SALES (est): 209.85K Privately Held
Web: www.norcoind.com
SIC: 3599 Machine shop, jobbing and repair

(G-3577)
NOTETECH INDUSTRIES LLC
21125 Protecta Dr (46516-9538)
PHONE.................................574 326-3188
EMP: 8 EST: 2018
SALES (est): 527.07K Privately Held
SIC: 3999 Manufacturing industries, nec

(G-3578)
OLD IP INC
2221 Industrial Pkwy (46516-5409)
PHONE.................................574 294-3253
▲ EMP: 30

Elkhart - Elkhart County (G-3579)   GEOGRAPHIC SECTION

SIC: 3089 Injection molding of plastics

(G-3579)
OMEGA NATIONAL PRODUCTS LLC
1010 Rowe St (46516-5507)
PHONE.................................574 295-5353
Michael Van Rooy, *VP*
EMP: 179
SALES (corp-wide): 313.35MM **Privately Held**
Web: www.omeganationalproducts.com
SIC: 2499 2452 3231 2431 Decorative wood and woodwork; Panels and sections, prefabricated, wood; Mirrored glass; Millwork
HQ: Omega National Products, Llc
    810 Baxter Ave
    Louisville KY 40204
    502 583-3038

(G-3580)
PANEL SOLUTIONS INC (PA)
Also Called: Panel Solutions/Tape Tech
5015 Verdant St (46516-9313)
PHONE.................................574 389-8494
Tom Zurek, *Pr*
Catherine Zurek, *VP*
Karen Ponciano, *CFO*
▲ EMP: 8 EST: 1998
SALES (est): 3.5MM
SALES (corp-wide): 3.5MM **Privately Held**
Web: www.panelsolutionsgroup.com
SIC: 2621 Wallpaper (hanging paper)

(G-3581)
PANEL SOLUTIONS INC
PS Designs
5015 Verdant St (46516)
PHONE.................................574 295-0222
Amanda Zurek, *Brnch Mgr*
EMP: 1
SALES (corp-wide): 3.5MM **Privately Held**
Web: www.panelsolutionsgroup.com
SIC: 2211 Draperies and drapery fabrics, cotton
PA: Panel Solutions, Inc.
    5015 Verdant St
    Elkhart IN 46516
    574 389-8494

(G-3582)
PANOLAM INDUSTRIES INC
25603 Borg Rd (46514-5273)
PHONE.................................574 264-0702
EMP: 92
Web: www.panolam.com
SIC: 3089 Panels, building: plastics, nec
HQ: Panolam Industries, Inc.
    2 Corporate Dr Ste 946
    Shelton CT 06484
    203 925-1556

(G-3583)
PARAMOUNT PLASTICS INC
2810 Jeanwood Dr (46514-7659)
PHONE.................................574 264-2143
Rex Lim, *Pr*
Jessie Prugh, *
EMP: 42 EST: 1982
SQ FT: 60,000
SALES (est): 5.46MM **Privately Held**
Web: www.paramountplastics.com
SIC: 3089 Injection molding of plastics

(G-3584)
PARR CORP
3200 County Road 6 E (46514-9695)
PHONE.................................574 264-9614
David Burger, *Pr*
Andrew Wiegand, *Sec*
▲ EMP: 11 EST: 2011

SALES (est): 173.96K **Privately Held**
SIC: 2891 Adhesives

(G-3585)
PARR HOLDINGS LLC
Also Called: Parr Technologies
3200 County Road 6 E (46514-9695)
PHONE.................................423 468-1855
▲ EMP: 20
SIC: 2891 Adhesives and sealants

(G-3586)
PARR TECHNOLOGIES LLC
3200 County Road 6 E (46514-9695)
PHONE.................................574 264-9614
Thomas Joyce, *Prin*
EMP: 8 EST: 2011
SALES (est): 208.73K **Privately Held**
Web: www.parrtechllc.com
SIC: 2891 Adhesives

(G-3587)
PATHFINDER COMMUNICATIONS CORP (PA)
Also Called: Federated Media
421 S 2nd St Ste 100 (46516-3230)
PHONE.................................574 295-2500
John F Dille Iii, *Pr*
Robert A Watson, *
EMP: 25 EST: 1970
SQ FT: 1,000
SALES (est): 24.04MM
SALES (corp-wide): 24.04MM **Privately Held**
Web: www.federatedmedia.com
SIC: 3993 2711 Signs and advertising specialties; Newspapers: publishing only, not printed on site

(G-3588)
PATRICK INDUSTRIES INC
Also Called: Alpha Systems
5120 Beck Dr (46516-9512)
PHONE.................................574 295-5206
David Smith Iii, *Brnch Mgr*
EMP: 16
SALES (corp-wide): 3.47B **Publicly Held**
Web: www.patrickind.com
SIC: 2891 3645 3442 Adhesives; Chandeliers, residential; Metal doors, sash, and trim
PA: Patrick Industries, Inc.
    107 W Franklin St
    Elkhart IN 46516
    574 294-7511

(G-3589)
PATRICK INDUSTRIES INC
Midwest Laminating Co
1926 W Lusher Ave (46517-1310)
PHONE.................................574 293-1521
Jeff Davis, *Genl Mgr*
EMP: 6
SALES (corp-wide): 3.47B **Publicly Held**
Web: www.patrickind.com
SIC: 3089 2542 2541 2511 Laminating of plastics; Partitions and fixtures, except wood; Wood partitions and fixtures; Wood household furniture
PA: Patrick Industries, Inc.
    107 W Franklin St
    Elkhart IN 46516
    574 294-7511

(G-3590)
PATRICK INDUSTRIES INC
2300 W Mishawaka Rd (46517-4040)
P.O. Box 638 (46515-0638)
PHONE.................................574 294-1975
EMP: 6
SALES (corp-wide): 3.47B **Publicly Held**

Web: www.patrickind.com
SIC: 3275 Gypsum products
PA: Patrick Industries, Inc.
    107 W Franklin St
    Elkhart IN 46516
    574 294-7511

(G-3591)
PATRICK INDUSTRIES INC
4906 Hoffman St Ste B (46516-9075)
PHONE.................................574 295-9660
David Daisy, *Mgr*
EMP: 18
SALES (corp-wide): 3.47B **Publicly Held**
Web: www.patrickind.com
SIC: 3275 Gypsum products
PA: Patrick Industries, Inc.
    107 W Franklin St
    Elkhart IN 46516
    574 294-7511

(G-3592)
PATRICK INDUSTRIES INC
1012 Borg Rd (46514-5282)
PHONE.................................574 294-8828
Brian Burke, *Brnch Mgr*
EMP: 60
SALES (corp-wide): 3.47B **Publicly Held**
Web: www.patrickind.com
SIC: 3275 2493 2435 5031 Gypsum products; Reconstituted wood products; Plywood, hardwood or hardwood faced; Building materials, exterior
PA: Patrick Industries, Inc.
    107 W Franklin St
    Elkhart IN 46516
    574 294-7511

(G-3593)
PATRICK INDUSTRIES INC (PA)
Also Called: Patrick
107 W Franklin St (46516)
P.O. Box 638 (46515)
PHONE.................................574 294-7511
Andy L Nemeth, *Ch Bd*
Jeffrey M Rodino, *Pr*
Kip B Ellis, *Ex VP*
Joel D Duthie, *CLO*
Stacey Amundson, *Chief Human Resource Officer*
▲ EMP: 306 EST: 1959
SQ FT: 35,000
SALES (est): 3.47B
SALES (corp-wide): 3.47B **Publicly Held**
Web: www.patrickind.com
SIC: 3275 2493 2435 5031 Gypsum products; Reconstituted wood products; Plywood, hardwood or hardwood faced; Building materials, exterior

(G-3594)
PATRICK INDUSTRIES INC
Also Called: L S Manufacturing
56741 Elk Park Dr (46516-1449)
PHONE.................................574 294-8828
EMP: 4
SALES (corp-wide): 3.47B **Publicly Held**
Web: www.patrickind.com
SIC: 3089 Plastics processing
PA: Patrick Industries, Inc.
    107 W Franklin St
    Elkhart IN 46516
    574 294-7511

(G-3595)
PATRICK INDUSTRIES INC
Praxis Group
1515 Leininger Ave (46517-1448)
PHONE.................................574 266-8400
EMP: 6
SALES (corp-wide): 3.47B **Publicly Held**

Web: www.patrickind.com
SIC: 2541 Table or counter tops, plastic laminated
PA: Patrick Industries, Inc.
    107 W Franklin St
    Elkhart IN 46516
    574 294-7511

(G-3596)
PATRICK INDUSTRIES INC
Also Called: Nickel Enterprises
3905 Lexington Park Dr (46514-1160)
P.O. Box 638 (46515-0638)
PHONE.................................574 294-5758
Jeff Davis, *Genl Mgr*
EMP: 5
SQ FT: 20,000
SALES (corp-wide): 3.47B **Publicly Held**
Web: www.patrickind.com
SIC: 2499 2541 2493 Decorative wood and woodwork; Wood partitions and fixtures; Reconstituted wood products
PA: Patrick Industries, Inc.
    107 W Franklin St
    Elkhart IN 46516
    574 294-7511

(G-3597)
PATRICK INDUSTRIES INC
Also Called: Mobilcraft Wood Products
1930 W Lusher Ave (46517-1310)
PHONE.................................574 293-1521
James Johnson, *Mgr*
EMP: 5
SQ FT: 20,000
SALES (corp-wide): 3.47B **Publicly Held**
Web: www.patrickind.com
SIC: 2431 8741 Doors, wood; Management services
PA: Patrick Industries, Inc.
    107 W Franklin St
    Elkhart IN 46516
    574 294-7511

(G-3598)
PATRICK INDUSTRIES INC
Adorn
1808 W Hively Ave (46517-4026)
PHONE.................................574 522-7710
Todd Cleveland, *Brnch Mgr*
EMP: 63
SALES (corp-wide): 3.47B **Publicly Held**
Web: www.patrickind.com
SIC: 2435 Hardwood veneer and plywood
PA: Patrick Industries, Inc.
    107 W Franklin St
    Elkhart IN 46516
    574 294-7511

(G-3599)
PATRICK INDUSTRIES INC
Also Called: Wire Design
2520 Industrial Pkwy (46516-5405)
P.O. Box 1387 (46515-1387)
PHONE.................................574 293-2990
Micheal Doering, *Brnch Mgr*
EMP: 85
SALES (corp-wide): 3.47B **Publicly Held**
Web: www.patrickind.com
SIC: 5063 3679 Wire and cable; Harness assemblies, for electronic use: wire or cable
PA: Patrick Industries, Inc.
    107 W Franklin St
    Elkhart IN 46516
    574 294-7511

(G-3600)
PATRICK INDUSTRIES INC
Also Called: Mishawaka Sheet Metal
28505 C R 20 W (46517)
PHONE.................................574 294-5959

GEOGRAPHIC SECTION

Elkhart - Elkhart County (G-3626)

Jeff Troyer, Mgr
EMP: 70
SALES (corp-wide): 3.47B **Publicly Held**
Web: www.patrickind.com
SIC: 3444 Sheet metalwork
PA: Patrick Industries, Inc.
107 W Franklin St
Elkhart IN 46516
574 294-7511

(G-3601)
PAULS SEATING INC
56912 Elk Ct (46516-1462)
PHONE..................574 522-0630
Paul Fizer, Pr
Brenda Fizer, VP
EMP: 8 **EST:** 1987
SQ FT: 5,000
SALES (est): 712.31K **Privately Held**
Web: www.paulsseating.net
SIC: 2531 Seats, automobile

(G-3602)
PHED MOBILITY LLC
55335 Corwin Rd (46514-8402)
PHONE..................574 226-4104
EMP: 5 **EST:** 2020
SALES (est): 800K **Privately Held**
Web: www.wheelchairgolfcarts.com
SIC: 3799 Transportation equipment, nec

(G-3603)
PHOENIX USA INC
3504 Cooper Dr (46514-8639)
PHONE..................574 266-2020
▲ **EMP:** 25 **EST:** 1996
SALES (est): 3.01MM **Privately Held**
Web: www.phoenixusa.com
SIC: 3716 Motor homes

(G-3604)
PIONEER PLASTICS CORPORATION
25603 Borg Rd (46514-5273)
PHONE..................574 264-0702
Rick Posthuma, Mgr
EMP: 189
Web: www.panolam.com
SIC: 3089 Injection molding of plastics
HQ: Pioneer Plastics Corporation
2 Corporate Dr Ste 946
Shelton CT 06484
203 925-1556

(G-3605)
PJW INC
56199 Parkway Ave (46516-9300)
PHONE..................574 295-1203
Pat Welch, Prin
EMP: 9 **EST:** 2011
SALES (est): 412.28K **Privately Held**
SIC: 3993 Signs and advertising specialties

(G-3606)
PLACON CORPORATION
2901 Oakland Ave (46517-1508)
PHONE..................608 278-4920
EMP: 17 **EST:** 2018
SALES (est): 2.77MM **Privately Held**
Web: www.placon.com
SIC: 3089 Plastics containers, except foam

(G-3607)
PLUMROSE USA INC
Also Called: Plumrose
24402 County Road 45 (46516-6043)
P.O. Box 160 (46515-0160)
PHONE..................574 295-8190
Mike Wilfert, Brnch Mgr
EMP: 250
SQ FT: 60,000
SALES (corp-wide): 19.78B **Publicly Held**
Web: www.jbsfoodsgroup.com
SIC: 2011 Meat packing plants
HQ: Plumrose Usa, Inc.
651 W Wash Blvd Ste 304
Chicago IL 60661

(G-3608)
PONTOON BOAT LLC
Also Called: Bennington
2805 Decio Dr (46514-7666)
PHONE..................574 264-6336
▼ **EMP:** 99 **EST:** 2009
SALES (est): 23.63MM
SALES (corp-wide): 8.93B **Publicly Held**
Web: www.benningtonmarine.com
SIC: 3732 Boatbuilding and repairing
PA: Polaris Inc.
2100 Highway 55
Medina MN 55340
763 542-0500

(G-3609)
PONTOONSTUFF INC
1165 Fremont Ct (46516-9320)
PHONE..................574 970-0003
Paul E Myers Junior, Dir
▲ **EMP:** 1 **EST:** 2005
SALES (est): 1.14MM **Privately Held**
Web: www.pontoonstuff.com
SIC: 2392 Boat cushions

(G-3610)
POSITRON CORPORATION (PA)
4614 Wyland Dr (46516-9787)
PHONE..................574 295-8777
Raymond J Sweers, Pr
EMP: 35 **EST:** 1992
SQ FT: 35,000
SALES (est): 8.61MM **Privately Held**
Web: www.positroncorp.com
SIC: 3083 Laminated plastics plate and sheet

(G-3611)
POSTLE ALUMINUM COMPANY LLC (HQ)
511 Pine Creek Ct (46516-9090)
PHONE..................574 389-0800
Dennis Marcott, CEO
EMP: 25 **EST:** 2006
SALES (est): 21.64MM
SALES (corp-wide): 11.12B **Publicly Held**
Web: www.postledistributors.com
SIC: 1081 Metal mining services
PA: Thor Industries, Inc.
601 E Beardsley Ave
Elkhart IN 46514
574 970-7460

(G-3612)
POSTLE OPERATING LLC
Also Called: Postle Aluminum
1503 Pierina Dr (46514-5286)
PHONE..................574 266-7720
EMP: 72
SALES (corp-wide): 11.12B **Publicly Held**
Web: www.postledistributors.com
SIC: 3355 5051 Extrusion ingot, aluminum: made in rolling mills; Aluminum bars, rods, ingots, sheets, pipes, plates, etc.
HQ: Postle Operating, Llc
511 Pine Creek Ct
Elkhart IN 46516
574 389-0800

(G-3613)
POSTLE OPERATING LLC (HQ)
Also Called: Temple
511 Pine Creek Ct (46516)
PHONE..................574 389-0800
Dennis Marcott, Managing Member
▲ **EMP:** 97 **EST:** 2006
SQ FT: 112,000
SALES (est): 97.86MM
SALES (corp-wide): 11.12B **Publicly Held**
Web: www.postledistributors.com
SIC: 3355 5051 Extrusion ingot, aluminum: made in rolling mills; Aluminum bars, rods, ingots, sheets, pipes, plates, etc.
PA: Thor Industries, Inc.
601 E Beardsley Ave
Elkhart IN 46514
574 970-7460

(G-3614)
PRECISION BUFFING & POLSG INC
Also Called: Precision Building
54194 Adams St (46514-3649)
P.O. Box 1423 (46515-1423)
PHONE..................574 262-3430
Lori Barry, Pr
EMP: 3 **EST:** 1985
SQ FT: 9,600
SALES (est): 314.6K **Privately Held**
SIC: 3471 Electroplating of metals or formed products

(G-3615)
PRECISION INDUSTRIES CORP
601 Wagner Ave (46516-2357)
P.O. Box 1923 (46515-1923)
PHONE..................574 522-2626
Sue Ellen Mc Kinnell, Pr
Jim Hays, SALES
EMP: 16 **EST:** 1990
SQ FT: 30,000
SALES (est): 482.23K **Privately Held**
Web: www.precisionindustriescorp.net
SIC: 3542 Pressing machines

(G-3616)
PRECISION STAMPING INC
720 Collins Rd (46516-5419)
P.O. Box 598 (46507-0598)
PHONE..................574 522-8987
EMP: 15 **EST:** 1997
SQ FT: 32,000
SALES (est): 2.92MM **Privately Held**
Web: www.precisionstampinginc.com
SIC: 3469 Stamping metal for the trade

(G-3617)
PREMIER FIBERGLASS CO INC
55080 Phillips St (46514-1202)
PHONE..................574 264-5457
EMP: 40 **EST:** 1992
SQ FT: 40,000
SALES (est): 4.69MM **Privately Held**
Web: www.premierfiberglassinc.com
SIC: 3089 Injection molding of plastics

(G-3618)
PRESERVING PAST
3764 E Jackson Blvd (46516-5205)
PHONE..................574 835-0833
Julie Cuppy, Prin
EMP: 5 **EST:** 2015
SALES (est): 79.16K **Privately Held**
Web: www.preservethepast.com
SIC: 2491 Wood preserving

(G-3619)
PRESTIGE TOOLING LLC
419 Harrison St (46516-2710)
PHONE..................269 470-4525
Nicholas Castelucci, Managing Member
EMP: 7 **EST:** 2019
SALES (est): 364.09K **Privately Held**
Web: www.prestigetooling.com
SIC: 3999 3544 Manufacturing industries, nec; Forms (molds), for foundry and plastics working machinery

(G-3620)
PRINT SHOP INC
51748 State Road 19 (46516-6772)
PHONE..................574 264-0023
Daniel Topolski, Pr
Diane Topolski, Sec
EMP: 5 **EST:** 1969
SALES (est): 376.32K **Privately Held**
Web: www.allegramarketingprint.com
SIC: 2752 Offset printing

(G-3621)
PRINTED BY ERIK INC
Also Called: AlphaGraphics
22158 Elkhart East Blvd (46514-8176)
PHONE..................574 295-1203
Erik Shultz, Pr
Pat Welch, Prin
EMP: 8 **EST:** 2017
SALES (est): 981.24K **Privately Held**
Web: www.alphagraphics.com
SIC: 2752 Commercial printing, lithographic

(G-3622)
PROAIR LLC
2900 County Road 6 W (46514-8297)
PHONE..................574 264-5494
EMP: 67
SALES (corp-wide): 129.36MM **Privately Held**
Web: www.proairllc.com
SIC: 3585 5075 Air conditioning, motor vehicle; Automotive air conditioners
HQ: Proair, Llc
6630 E State Highway 114
Haslet TX 46514
817 636-2308

(G-3623)
PROLON INC
1040 Sako Ct (46516-9019)
PHONE..................574 522-8900
Leroy Van Kirk, Prin
EMP: 45 **EST:** 1989
SQ FT: 20,000
SALES (est): 4.56MM **Privately Held**
Web: www.prolon.com
SIC: 3089 3082 Injection molding of plastics; Unsupported plastics profile shapes

(G-3624)
PROTO-FAB ACQUISITION INC
1615 Elreno St (46516-1937)
PHONE..................574 522-4245
EMP: 45
SIC: 3714 Instrument board assemblies, motor vehicle

(G-3625)
PUCK SUPPLY & MACHINE LLC
56644 Elk Park Dr (46516-1400)
PHONE..................574 293-3333
Joe Swald, Managing Member
EMP: 13 **EST:** 2009
SALES (est): 910.31K **Privately Held**
Web: www.pucksupply.com
SIC: 3089 5085 Injection molding of plastics; Industrial supplies

(G-3626)
Q P INC
530 E Lexington Ave Ste 155 (46516-3596)
PHONE..................574 295-6884
Randy Brewers, Pr
Benedict Brewers, Pr
Jack Miller, VP
Mike Brewers, Pr
EMP: 10 **EST:** 1991
SQ FT: 500
SALES (est): 695.24K **Privately Held**

Elkhart - Elkhart County (G-3627)

Web: www.qp-inc.com
SIC: 3677 3699 3621 7694 Coil windings, electronic; Electrical equipment and supplies, nec; Motors and generators; Coil winding service

(G-3627)
QMP INC
Also Called: Quality Metal Products
2925 Stephen Pl (46514-7701)
PHONE...................................574 262-1575
Shaylor King, Pr
Marjorie King, *
Tim King, *
▲ EMP: 40 EST: 1971
SALES (est): 4.36MM Privately Held
Web: www.qmp-elkhart.com
SIC: 3429 3544 3469 Motor vehicle hardware; Special dies, tools, jigs, and fixtures; Metal stampings, nec

(G-3628)
QPOLY LLC
56977 Elk Ct (46516)
P.O. Box 1305 (46530)
PHONE...................................574 386-4671
Michael Shaul, Pr
EMP: 6 EST: 2016
SALES (est): 285.38K Privately Held
Web: www.qpoly.com
SIC: 3069 Custom compounding of rubber materials

(G-3629)
QUAD 4 PLASTICS INC
Also Called: Quad 4
1840 Borneman Ave (46517-1334)
PHONE...................................574 293-8660
EMP: 34 EST: 1995
SQ FT: 17,500
SALES (est): 3.69MM Privately Held
Web: www.quad4plastics.com
SIC: 3089 Injection molding of plastics

(G-3630)
QUALITY ENGINEERED PDTS INC
56802 Elk Ct (46516-1456)
PHONE...................................574 294-6943
Dee Davis, Pr
▲ EMP: 15 EST: 1988
SQ FT: 8,000
SALES (est): 500.91K Privately Held
Web: www.qepdesign.com
SIC: 2672 Adhesive papers, labels, or tapes: from purchased material

(G-3631)
QUALITY FUEL SOLUTIONS
1001 Sako Ct (46516-9019)
PHONE...................................574 293-1423
Stan Wogoman, Prin
EMP: 1 EST: 2010
SALES (est): 86K Privately Held
SIC: 2869 Fuels

(G-3632)
QUALITY PLAS ENGRG ACQSTION CO
Also Called: D C C
2507 Decio Dr (46514-8647)
PHONE...................................574 262-2621
Rick Donati, Pr
▲ EMP: 30 EST: 1988
SQ FT: 33,000
SALES (est): 4.5MM Privately Held
Web: www.qualityplastics.net
SIC: 3089 3679 Injection molding of plastics; Harness assemblies, for electronic use: wire or cable

(G-3633)
QUALITY PNT PRSTNED FNSHES INC
28827 Old Us 33 (46516-1625)
PHONE...................................574 294-6944
Jesse Thrash Junior, Pr
Lorraine Thrash, Sec
EMP: 6 EST: 1987
SQ FT: 8,000
SALES (est): 473.67K Privately Held
Web: www.qualitypaintandprestained.com
SIC: 3479 1721 Painting, coating, and hot dipping; Commercial painting

(G-3634)
QUALITY STEEL & ALUM PDTS INC
Also Called: Dump & Go
28620 County Road 20 (46517-1131)
PHONE...................................574 295-8715
James R Reid, Pr
Carol R Reid, Sec
▲ EMP: 22 EST: 2000
SALES (est): 3.76MM Privately Held
Web: www.geterdumped.com
SIC: 5051 3715 Steel; Truck trailers

(G-3635)
QUALITY STEEL & ALUMINUM
56741 Elk Park Dr (46516-1449)
PHONE...................................574 294-7221
EMP: 2 EST: 2013
SALES (est): 164.91K Privately Held
SIC: 3544 Special dies and tools

(G-3636)
R & R REGULATORS INC
24545 County Road 45 (46516-5959)
PHONE...................................574 522-3500
Tom Reusser, Pr
Ruth Banner, Sec
EMP: 14 EST: 1981
SALES (est): 1.1MM Privately Held
SIC: 3694 5065 5088 3612 Automotive electrical equipment, nec; Rectifiers, electronic; Pulleys; Transformers, except electric

(G-3637)
RADON ENVIRONMENTAL INC
2320 Broadmoor Dr (46516-4067)
P.O. Box 4146 (46082-4146)
PHONE...................................317 843-0804
Michael Brennaman, Pr
EMP: 5 EST: 1988
SALES (est): 547.56K Privately Held
Web: www.radonenvironmental.com
SIC: 1799 8734 1389 Athletic and recreation facilities construction; Radiation laboratories; Construction, repair, and dismantling services

(G-3638)
RAMCO ENGINEERING INC
2805 Frederic Dr (46514)
PHONE...................................574 266-1455
Dee Anna Ryan, Pr
Deanna K Reed, *
▲ EMP: 38 EST: 1975
SQ FT: 60,000
SALES (est): 4.78MM Privately Held
Web: www.ramco-eng.com
SIC: 3231 3714 3713 Mirrors, truck and automobile: made from purchased glass; Motor vehicle parts and accessories; Truck and bus bodies

(G-3639)
RANCE ALUMINUM FABRICATION
3012 Mobile Dr (46514-5524)
PHONE...................................574 266-9028
Rod Rance, Pr
Cheryl Rance, *
EMP: 22 EST: 1974
SQ FT: 32,000
SALES (est): 1.17MM Privately Held
Web: www.rancealuminum.com
SIC: 3714 3537 3444 3792 Motor vehicle body components and frame; Industrial trucks and tractors; Sheet metalwork; Pickup covers, canopies or caps

(G-3640)
RAYCO MARKETING
29675 Old Us 20 (46514-9351)
PHONE...................................574 293-8416
Ray Petit, Owner
EMP: 4 EST: 2000
SALES (est): 229.43K Privately Held
Web: www.raycomarketing.com
SIC: 2759 Commercial printing, nec

(G-3641)
REBUILDING CNSLTING PCKG SLTON
636 Kollar St (46514-1358)
PHONE...................................574 389-1966
Ralph C Pennington, Managing Member
EMP: 6 EST: 2020
SALES (est): 1.5MM Privately Held
SIC: 3699 Household electrical equipment

(G-3642)
RECREATION BY DESIGN LLC
57420 County Road 3 (46517-9798)
PHONE...................................574 294-2117
▼ EMP: 75 EST: 1999
SALES (est): 9.34MM Privately Held
Web: www.recreationbydesign.us
SIC: 3792 Travel trailers and campers

(G-3643)
RECREATION VHCL TECHNICAL INST
3333 Middlebury St (46516-5587)
PHONE...................................574 549-9068
Craig Kirby, CEO
Kurt Hemmeler, Sr VP
EMP: 8 EST: 2018
SALES (est): 2.42MM Privately Held
Web: www.rvia.org
SIC: 3799 Recreational vehicles

(G-3644)
RECYCLING WORKS LLC
605 Mason St (46516-2760)
P.O. Box 1492 (46515-1492)
PHONE...................................574 293-3751
Charles Himes Junior, Pr
Stephen Himes, VP
EMP: 10 EST: 1968
SQ FT: 30,000
SALES (est): 2.42MM Privately Held
Web: www.wasteawaygroup.com
SIC: 5093 4953 3341 3231 Waste paper; Refuse systems; Secondary nonferrous metals; Products of purchased glass

(G-3645)
RED BEARD BEEF JERKY
1530 Cassopolis St Ste B (46514-3162)
PHONE...................................574 596-7054
Bernard Weyrick, Prin
EMP: 6 EST: 2018
SALES (est): 205.62K Privately Held
Web: www.redbeardjerky.com
SIC: 2013 Snack sticks, including jerky: from purchased meat

(G-3646)
REICH TOOL & DESIGN INC
Also Called: REICH TOOL & DESIGN, INC
1635 Woodfield Ct (46514-4708)
PHONE...................................574 849-6416
Frtiz Reich, Brnch Mgr
EMP: 12
SALES (corp-wide): 7.94MM Privately Held
Web: www.reichtool.com
SIC: 3544 Special dies and tools
PA: Reich Tool & Design, Inc.
W175n5750 Technology Dr
Menomonee Falls WI 53051
262 252-3440

(G-3647)
RESCHCOR INC
2711 Industrial Pkwy (46516-5402)
PHONE...................................574 295-2413
EMP: 9
SALES (corp-wide): 20.25MM Privately Held
Web: www.reschcor.com
SIC: 3089 Plastics processing
PA: Reschcor, Inc.
2123 Blakesley Pkwy
Bristol IN 46507
574 295-2413

(G-3648)
RITE-WAY STEEL INC
25687 Woodlawn Ave (46514-3825)
P.O. Box 28 (46515-0028)
PHONE...................................574 262-3465
Sam Igney, Pr
EMP: 10 EST: 1982
SQ FT: 22,000
SALES (est): 812.6K Privately Held
SIC: 3444 Studs and joists, sheet metal

(G-3649)
RIVER VALLEY PLASTICS INC
Also Called: Rvp
1090 D I Dr (46514-8294)
PHONE...................................574 262-5221
Harold J Mccracken Junior, Pr
Mitchell Mc Cracken, *
Paamela K Bidwell, *
EMP: 28 EST: 1974
SQ FT: 22,000
SALES (est): 4.98MM Privately Held
Web: www.rivervalleyplastics-injectionmolding.com
SIC: 3089 3544 Injection molding of plastics; Special dies and tools

(G-3650)
RIVERSIDE TOOL CORP (HQ)
3504 Henke St (46514)
PHONE...................................574 522-6798
Ronald Migedt, Pr
EMP: 26 EST: 1968
SQ FT: 14,000
SALES (est): 9.38MM Privately Held
Web: www.riversidetool.com
SIC: 7389 3545 Grinding, precision: commercial or industrial; Tools and accessories for machine tools
PA: Techniks, Llc
9930 E 56th St
Indianapolis IN 46236

(G-3651)
ROMAINE INCORPORATED
Also Called: Koldcare
2026 Sterling Ave (46516-4220)
PHONE...................................574 294-7101
John A Levy, Ch Bd
John Levy, Ch Bd
EMP: 11 EST: 1973

SQ FT: 10,000
SALES (est): 860.49K **Privately Held**
Web: www.koldcare.com
SIC: 3842 Bandages and dressings

(G-3652)
ROYALE PHOENIX INC
53972 N Park Ave (46514-5000)
P.O. Box 1664 (46515-1664)
PHONE.....................574 206-1216
Dan R Jourdan, *Pr*
Glenn J Berden, *VP*
EMP: 2 EST: 2006
SALES (est): 164.18K **Privately Held**
Web: www.royalephoenix.com
SIC: 3711 Motor homes, self contained, assembly of

(G-3653)
RPI COMPONENTS INC
2503 Whipple Ave (46516-5779)
PHONE.....................574 536-2283
Arthur Miller, *Pr*
Scott Tarnowski, *CEO*
EMP: 4 EST: 2019
SALES (est): 346.27K **Privately Held**
SIC: 2452 3448 Prefabricated wood buildings; Prefabricated metal components

(G-3654)
RTW ENTERPRISES INC
2924 County Road 6 E (46514-7678)
PHONE.....................574 294-3275
EMP: 40
SIC: 3679 2273 5063 Harness assemblies, for electronic use: wire or cable; Mats and matting; Wire and cable

(G-3655)
RUCO INC
Also Called: Regal Mold & Die
1817 Leer Dr (46514-5447)
PHONE.....................574 262-4110
Gary Rheude, *Pr*
Micheal Leamon, *
EMP: 28 EST: 1959
SQ FT: 25,000
SALES (est): 2.63MM **Privately Held**
Web: www.regalmold.com
SIC: 3544 Forms (molds), for foundry and plastics working machinery

(G-3656)
S H LEGGITT COMPANY
Also Called: Marshall Gas Controls
831 E Windsor Ave Unit 9 (46514-5568)
PHONE.....................574 264-0230
Trey Ywell, *Mgr*
EMP: 7
SALES (corp-wide): 22.27MM **Privately Held**
SIC: 3491 3451 3082 Gas valves and parts, industrial; Screw machine products; Tubes, unsupported plastics
PA: S. H. Leggitt Company
1000 Civic Ctr Loop
San Marcos TX 78666
956 504-6440

(G-3657)
SABINA LLC
127 S Main St (46516-3147)
PHONE.....................574 903-4688
Daniel Boecher, *Admn*
EMP: 7 EST: 2013
SALES (est): 88.01K **Privately Held**
SIC: 3599 Machine shop, jobbing and repair

(G-3658)
SAFE FLEET HOLDINGS LLC
3802 Gallatin Way (46514-7650)
PHONE.....................574 849-4619
EMP: 3
Web: www.elkhartbrass.com
SIC: 3569 Firefighting apparatus
HQ: Safe Fleet Holdings Llc
6800 E 163rd St
Belton MO 64012
816 318-8000

(G-3659)
SAFE FLEET MIRRORS
Also Called: Safe Fleet
319 Roske Dr (46516-9084)
PHONE.....................574 266-3700
Laurie Pepple, *Owner*
EMP: 23 EST: 2016
SALES (est): 4.21MM **Privately Held**
Web: www.safefleet.net
SIC: 3714 Motor vehicle parts and accessories

(G-3660)
SAILOR GROUP LLC
Also Called: Sailor Logistic
1400 W Bristol St (46514-1617)
P.O. Box 3003 (46515-3003)
PHONE.....................574 226-0362
Brent Sailor, *Pr*
EMP: 4 EST: 2013
SALES (est): 489.33K **Privately Held**
Web: www.sailorgroupllc.com
SIC: 8748 4789 3949 Business consulting, nec; Cargo loading and unloading services; Sporting and athletic goods, nec

(G-3661)
SAMARON CORP
Also Called: Troyer Products
3310 Magnum Dr (46516-9020)
PHONE.....................574 970-7070
Daniel Holtz, *CEO*
David Buck, *
EMP: 25 EST: 1976
SQ FT: 16,000
SALES (est): 4.57MM **Privately Held**
Web: www.troyerproducts.com
SIC: 5131 3429 8748 Piece goods and notions; Hardware, nec; Business consulting, nec

(G-3662)
SANDMAN PRODUCTS LLC
Also Called: Sandman Products
2604 Glenview Dr (46514-9243)
PHONE.....................574 264-7700
EMP: 7 EST: 1998
SQ FT: 6,000
SALES (est): 777.62K **Privately Held**
Web: www.sandmanproducts.com
SIC: 3553 Sanding machines, except portable floor sanders: woodworking

(G-3663)
SATELLITE INDUSTRIES
5313 Beck Dr (46516-9251)
PHONE.....................800 328-3332
EMP: 4 EST: 2019
SALES (est): 122.03K **Privately Held**
SIC: 3999 Manufacturing industries, nec

(G-3664)
SCG ACQUISITION COMPANY LLC
Also Called: Speedgrip Chuck Company
2000 Industrial Pkwy (46516-5411)
P.O. Box 596 (46515-0596)
PHONE.....................574 294-1506
EMP: 50 EST: 1962

SALES (est): 4.31MM **Privately Held**
Web: www.speedgrip.com
SIC: 3545 Machine tool attachments and accessories

(G-3665)
SCHUSTER SHEET METAL INC
418 Roske Dr (46516-9085)
PHONE.....................574 293-4802
Doug Livingston, *Pr*
EMP: 8 EST: 1946
SQ FT: 10,500
SALES (est): 978.82K **Privately Held**
Web: www.schustersheetmetal.com
SIC: 3444 Sheet metal specialties, not stamped

(G-3666)
SDG ELKHART LLC ✪
314 W High St (46516-2826)
P.O. Box 2913 (46515-2913)
PHONE.....................574 294-4646
EMP: 5 EST: 2022
SALES (est): 262.9K **Privately Held**
SIC: 3431 Metal sanitary ware

(G-3667)
SELECT TOOL AND ENG INC
59753 Park Side Dr (46517-4505)
PHONE.....................574 295-6197
Carl Esch, *CEO*
Mark Esch, *Pr*
EMP: 8 EST: 1988
SALES (est): 964.78K **Privately Held**
Web: www.selecttool.com
SIC: 3599 Machine shop, jobbing and repair

(G-3668)
SELKING INTERNATIONAL INC
Also Called: Selking International Inc
836 Verdant St (46516-9038)
PHONE.....................574 522-2001
Alan Jordan, *Brnch Mgr*
EMP: 9
SALES (corp-wide): 29.7MM **Privately Held**
Web: www.selkinginternational.com
SIC: 5012 7538 3537 Trucks, commercial; General automotive repair shops; Industrial trucks and tractors
HQ: Selking International, Llc
2807 Goshen Rd
Fort Wayne IN 46808

(G-3669)
SERVICE PRINTERS INC
28574 Phillips St (46514-1236)
PHONE.....................574 266-6710
▲ EMP: 28 EST: 1996
SQ FT: 36,000
SALES (est): 9.61MM **Privately Held**
Web: www.serviceprinterselkhart.com
SIC: 2752 2791 2789 Offset printing; Typesetting; Bookbinding and related work

(G-3670)
SERVOFLO CORPORATION
54503 Saddle Brook Xing (46514-4667)
PHONE.....................574 262-4171
Neal Thomas, *Prin*
EMP: 1 EST: 2010
SALES (est): 86.5K **Privately Held**
Web: www.servoflo.com
SIC: 3829 Measuring and controlling devices, nec

(G-3671)
SHARPS BATON MFG CORP
Also Called: Sharp's Creations
57330 Orchard Ridge Dr (46516-8904)

PHONE.....................574 214-9389
Jim Sharp, *Pr*
Mark Sharp, *Treas*
Linda Degetter, *Mgr*
Jim Sharp, *Mgr*
EMP: 8 EST: 1977
SQ FT: 1,600
SALES (est): 519.75K **Privately Held**
Web: www.starlinebaton.com
SIC: 3949 5949 3446 Batons; Notions, including trim; Architectural metalwork

(G-3672)
SHERWOOD INDUSTRIES INC
Also Called: Accessories By Sherwood
1805 Leer Dr (46514)
PHONE.....................574 262-2639
Steven Schemenauer, *Pr*
Elizabeth Sorg, *Stockholder*
Phyllis Schemenauer, *Sec*
◆ EMP: 25 EST: 1973
SQ FT: 120,000
SALES (est): 4.98MM **Privately Held**
Web: www.gosherwood.com
SIC: 5023 3231 Decorative home furnishings and supplies; Framed mirrors

(G-3673)
SHIELD RESTRAINT SYSTEMS INC
(HQ)
Also Called: Shield
3802 Gallatin Way (46514-7650)
PHONE.....................574 266-8330
◆ EMP: 120 EST: 1994
SQ FT: 50,000
SALES (est): 61.08MM
SALES (corp-wide): 6.58B **Publicly Held**
Web: www.seatbelts.net
SIC: 3714 Motor vehicle parts and accessories
PA: Transdigm Group Incorporated
1350 Euclid Ave Ste 1600
Cleveland OH 44115
216 706-2960

(G-3674)
SHROCK MANUFACTURING INC
2746 Jami St (46514-8792)
PHONE.....................574 264-4126
Fred Shrock, *Pr*
Scott Shrock, *
Janet Shrock, *
EMP: 35 EST: 1979
SQ FT: 68,000
SALES (est): 4.21MM **Privately Held**
Web: www.shrockmfg.com
SIC: 3499 Furniture parts, metal

(G-3675)
SIEMENS HLTHCARE DGNOSTICS INC
3400 Middlebury St (46516-5586)
P.O. Box 2297 (46515-2297)
PHONE.....................574 262-6139
EMP: 1
SALES (corp-wide): 84.48B **Privately Held**
Web: new.siemens.com
SIC: 2835 Diagnostic substances
HQ: Siemens Healthcare Diagnostics Inc.
511 Benedict Ave
Tarrytown NY 10591
914 631-8000

(G-3676)
SIGMA SWITCHES PLUS INC
Also Called: Sigma South Division
4703 Wyland Dr (46516-9681)
PHONE.....................574 294-5776
Daniel Rothbauer, *Ch Bd*
Brian Rothbauer, *Pr*
Debra May, *VP*

Elkhart - Elkhart County (G-3677)

▲ EMP: 11 EST: 1983
SQ FT: 12,000
SALES (est): 1.96MM Privately Held
Web: www.sigmaswitches.com
SIC: 3625 3613 Switches, electric power; Switchgear and switchboard apparatus

(G-3677)
SIGMA WIRE INTERNATIONAL LLC
4906 Hoffman St Ste B (46516-9075)
PHONE....................574 295-9660
EMP: 2
Web: www.sigma-wire.com
SIC: 3357 Automotive wire and cable, except ignition sets: nonferrous

(G-3678)
SIGNS OF TIMES
2201 S Nappanee St (46517-1354)
PHONE....................574 296-7464
Les Anderson, Prin
EMP: 3 EST: 2005
SALES (est): 210.08K Privately Held
Web: www.signsofthetimeselkhart.com
SIC: 3993 Signs, not made in custom sign painting shops

(G-3679)
SISSYS CERAMICS
30803 County Road 20 (46517-9758)
PHONE....................951 550-7728
EMP: 4 EST: 2009
SALES (est): 56.78K Privately Held
SIC: 3269 Pottery products, nec

(G-3680)
SJC INDUSTRIES CORP
Also Called: Marque
1110 D I Dr (46514-8231)
PHONE....................574 264-7511
Chris Graff, CEO
Charles Drake, *
James Evans, *
▼ EMP: 49 EST: 2005
SQ FT: 120,000
SALES (est): 5.3MM
SALES (corp-wide): 11.12B Publicly Held
Web: www.sjcind.com
SIC: 3713 Ambulance bodies
PA: Thor Industries, Inc.
    601 E Beardsley Ave
    Elkhart IN 46514
    574 970-7460

(G-3681)
SKYLINE CHAMPION CORPORATION
2520 Bypass Rd (46515)
P.O. Box 743 (46515-0743)
PHONE....................574 294-6521
EMP: 2
SALES (corp-wide): 2.02B Publicly Held
Web: www.skylinehomes.com
SIC: 2452 Prefabricated wood buildings
PA: Skyline Champion Corporation
    755 W Big Bevr Rd Ste 100
    Troy MI 48084
    248 614-8211

(G-3682)
SKYLINE CORPORATION
Nomad Travel Trailers
401 County Road 15 (46516-9623)
P.O. Box 1068 (46515-1068)
PHONE....................574 294-2463
Ken Mccain, Mgr
EMP: 135
SALES (corp-wide): 2.02B Publicly Held
Web: www.skylinehomes.com
SIC: 3792 2451 5012 Travel trailers and campers; Mobile homes; Recreational vehicles, motor homes, and trailers

PA: Skyline Champion Corporation
    755 W Big Bevr Rd Ste 100
    Troy MI 48084
    248 614-8211

(G-3683)
SKYLINE HOMES INC (HQ)
2520 Bypass Rd (46514-1518)
P.O. Box 743 (46515-0743)
PHONE....................574 294-6521
Jon Pilarski, CFO
EMP: 45 EST: 1960
SALES (est): 236.81MM
SALES (corp-wide): 2.02B Publicly Held
Web: www.skylinehomes.com
SIC: 2451 3792 Mobile homes; Travel trailers and campers
PA: Skyline Champion Corporation
    755 W Big Bevr Rd Ste 100
    Troy MI 48084
    248 614-8211

(G-3684)
SMART CHOICE MOBILE INC
4542 Elkhart Rd (46517-3571)
PHONE....................574 830-5727
Nabeel Aldeir, Prin
EMP: 22
SALES (corp-wide): 3.23MM Privately Held
Web: www.smartchoicemobile.com
SIC: 3661 Telephone sets, all types except cellular radio
PA: Smart Choice Mobile, Inc.
    7667 W 95th St Ste 300
    Hickory Hills IL 60457
    708 581-4904

(G-3685)
SMARTT INNOVATIONS INC
54160 Adams St (46514-3649)
PHONE....................574 266-5432
Cliffton R Smartt, Pr
Cassidy C Fritz, Prin
EMP: 10 EST: 2006
SQ FT: 3,200
SALES (est): 512.61K Privately Held
Web: www.coatingcompanyelkhart.com
SIC: 3479 3441 Coating of metals and formed products; Fabricated structural metal

(G-3686)
SMCO INC
Also Called: Ferret, Inc.
2505 Laura Ct (46517-1197)
P.O. Box 35 (46515-0035)
PHONE....................574 295-1482
Scott Mcmeekan, Pr
EMP: 30 EST: 1981
SQ FT: 28,000
SALES (est): 4.41MM Privately Held
Web: www.ferretrollforming.com
SIC: 3441 Fabricated structural metal

(G-3687)
SMOKERS IRON WORKS
Also Called: Plexiclass Awards Disc Tropies
30907 County Road 16 (46516-1037)
PHONE....................574 674-6683
John Smoker, Owner
EMP: 3 EST: 1991
SALES (est): 154.25K Privately Held
SIC: 3499 3873 Novelties and giftware, including trophies; Clocks, assembly of

(G-3688)
SOUTHSIDE MINI STORAGE
2031 W Mishawaka Rd (46517-4005)
PHONE....................574 293-3270
Carl Gilley, Pr
Jewelene Gilley, Sec

EMP: 5 EST: 1983
SQ FT: 6,400
SALES (est): 467.22K Privately Held
Web: www.southsideministoragerentals.com
SIC: 3716 Recreational van conversion (self-propelled), factory basis

(G-3689)
SOUTHSIDE PLATING WORKS INC
2010 Superior St (46516-4706)
PHONE....................219 293-5508
EMP: 2 EST: 2012
SALES (est): 76.71K Privately Held
SIC: 3471 Plating of metals or formed products

(G-3690)
SPECIAL METALS CORPORATION
2900 Higgins Blvd (46514-5449)
PHONE....................574 262-3451
William Belcher, Mgr
EMP: 259
SALES (corp-wide): 364.48B Publicly Held
Web: www.specialmetals.com
SIC: 5051 3341 Steel; Secondary nonferrous metals
HQ: Special Metals Corporation
    4832 Richmond Rd Ste 100
    Warrensville Heights OH 44128
    216 755-3030

(G-3691)
SPECIALIZED WOOD PRODUCTS INC
4221 Middlebury St (46516-9022)
PHONE....................574 522-6376
Leanna Miller, Pr
EMP: 24 EST: 1988
SQ FT: 32,000
SALES (est): 1.98MM Privately Held
Web: www.thewoodcompany.com
SIC: 2431 2499 Moldings, wood: unfinished and prefinished; Decorative wood and woodwork

(G-3692)
SPECIALTY WIRE TECHNOLOGIES
23651 Wilshire Blvd E (46516-6351)
PHONE....................260 750-1418
Mirza A Khoja, Pr
EMP: 10 EST: 2015
SALES (est): 151.81K Privately Held
SIC: 3493 Steel springs, except wire

(G-3693)
SPHEROS NORTH AMERICA INC
Also Called: Valeo Thrmal Coml Vhcles N Ame
22150 Challenger Dr (46514)
P.O. Box 1905 (46515)
PHONE....................734 218-7350
Mark Sondermann, Pr
Octavio Alejandro Rodriguez Garcia, Treas
▲ EMP: 8 EST: 2008
SALES (est): 5.08MM Privately Held
Web: www.valeo-thermalbus.com
SIC: 5074 5075 3465 Plumbing and hydronic heating supplies; Air conditioning and ventilation equipment and supplies; Body parts, automobile: stamped metal
HQ: Spheros Germany Gmbh
    Friedrichshafener Str. 7
    Gilching BY 82205
    810577210

(G-3694)
STALTARI ENTERPRISES INC
236 Marshall Blvd (46516-5016)
P.O. Box 1742 (46515-1742)

PHONE....................574 522-1988
Rosa Staltari, Owner
EMP: 1 EST: 1996
SALES (est): 152.99K Privately Held
SIC: 2621 Wallpaper (hanging paper)

(G-3695)
STANBIO LABORATORY LP
Efk Life Sciences
1814 Leer Dr (46514-5447)
PHONE....................830 249-0772
Cliff Yehle, Mgr
EMP: 1
SQ FT: 14,250
SALES (corp-wide): 65.58MM Privately Held
Web: www.ekfusa.com
SIC: 2835 Enzyme and isoenzyme diagnostic agents
HQ: Stanbio Laboratory, L.P.
    1261 N Main St
    Boerne TX 78006
    830 824-0772

(G-3696)
STANDARD LABEL CO INC
4200 Wyland Dr (46516-9509)
PHONE....................574 522-3548
Tom Wyncott, Pr
Kris Wyncott, VP
EMP: 12 EST: 1980
SQ FT: 20,000
SALES (est): 309.86K Privately Held
Web: www.standard-label.com
SIC: 2759 Labels and seals: printing, nsk

(G-3697)
STAR MANUFACTURING LLC
2772 Faith Ave (46514-7810)
PHONE....................574 329-6042
Allen Medford, Managing Member
EMP: 5 EST: 2010
SALES (est): 254.77K Privately Held
SIC: 3999 Manufacturing industries, nec

(G-3698)
STAR TOOL & DIE INC
53088 Faith Ave (46514-9373)
PHONE....................574 264-3815
EMP: 17 EST: 1994
SQ FT: 10,000
SALES (est): 544.31K Privately Held
Web: www.startooldie.com
SIC: 3544 3599 Special dies and tools; Machine shop, jobbing and repair

(G-3699)
STATE WIDE ALUMINUM INC
Also Called: State Wide Window
3518 County Road 6 E (46514)
P.O. Box 987 (46514)
PHONE....................574 262-2594
Jim Donohue, Pr
Larry Wolfe, *
Mike Beckman, *
◆ EMP: 175 EST: 1971
SQ FT: 75,000
SALES (est): 42.27MM
SALES (corp-wide): 1.62B Privately Held
Web: www.state-wide.com
SIC: 3714 3231 3444 Motor vehicle body components and frame; Strengthened or reinforced glass; Sheet metalwork
HQ: Truck Accessories Group, Llc
    28858 Ventura Dr
    Elkhart IN 46517
    574 522-5337

GEOGRAPHIC SECTION
Elkhart - Elkhart County (G-3726)

(G-3700)
STEINWAY PIANO COMPANY INC (DH)
600 Industrial Pkwy (46516-5414)
PHONE.....................574 522-1675
EMP: 100 EST: 1985
SQ FT: 25,000
SALES (est): 113.45MM
SALES (corp-wide): 528.25MM Privately Held
Web: www.connselmer.com
SIC: 3931 Pianos, all types: vertical, grand, spinet, player, etc.
HQ: Conn-Selmer, Inc.
  600 Industrial Pkwy
  Elkhart IN 46516
  574 522-1675

(G-3701)
STRUCTURAL COMPOSITES LLC
107 W Franklin St (46516-3214)
P.O. Box 638 (46515-0638)
PHONE.....................574 294-7511
EMP: 20 EST: 2018
SALES (est): 2.29MM
SALES (corp-wide): 3.47B Publicly Held
Web: www.patrickind.com
SIC: 3275 2493 Gypsum products; Reconstituted wood products
PA: Patrick Industries, Inc.
  107 W Franklin St
  Elkhart IN 46516
  574 294-7511

(G-3702)
STUDY STUDSTERS LLC ✪
616 Mcdonald St (46516-4111)
PHONE.....................574 635-1018
Howard L Thomas, *Managing Member*
EMP: 5 EST: 2022
SALES (est): 131.61K Privately Held
SIC: 1389 7389 Construction, repair, and dismantling services; Business Activities at Non-Commercial Site

(G-3703)
STYRENE SOLUTIONS LLC
115 E Windsor Ave (46514-5546)
PHONE.....................574 876-4610
EMP: 5 EST: 2018
SALES (est): 243.01K Privately Held
SIC: 2865 Styrene

(G-3704)
SUGGS CUSTOM DESIGN SOLUTIONS
336 W Garfield Ave (46516-2501)
PHONE.....................574 549-2174
Thadd Suggs, *CEO*
EMP: 3 EST: 2011
SALES (est): 234.06K Privately Held
SIC: 3315 Steel wire and related products

(G-3705)
SUMMIT LLC
Also Called: AlphaGraphics
660 County Road 15 (46516-9553)
PHONE.....................574 287-7468
Pat Welch, *Managing Member*
EMP: 8 EST: 2002
SALES (est): 961.68K Privately Held
Web: www.alphagraphics.com
SIC: 2752 Commercial printing, lithographic

(G-3706)
SUMMIT SEATING INC
2601 Northland Dr (46514-7614)
PHONE.....................574 264-9636
Ray Fink, *Prin*
EMP: 13 EST: 2001
SQ FT: 8,800
SALES (est): 318.18K Privately Held
Web: www.hsmtransportation.com
SIC: 2399 Seat covers, automobile

(G-3707)
SUPERIOR AXLE LLC
3001 Tuscany Dr (46514-7674)
PHONE.....................574 295-1905
James Roberts, *Managing Member*
EMP: 50
SALES (est): 526.56K Privately Held
Web: www.superiortireaxle.com
SIC: 7534 Vulcanizing tires and tubes

(G-3708)
SUPERIOR INDUS SOLUTIONS INC
Also Called: Superior Fiberglass & Resins
1030 All Pro Dr (46514-8815)
PHONE.....................574 264-0161
Wayne Dixon, *Mgr*
EMP: 18
SALES (corp-wide): 306.28MM Privately Held
Web: www.relyonsuperior.com
SIC: 2911 Petroleum refining
PA: Superior Industrial Solutions, Inc.
  1411 Roosevelt Ave # 250
  Indianapolis IN 46201
  317 781-4400

(G-3709)
SUPERIOR SEATING INC
21468 C St (46516-9670)
PHONE.....................574 389-9011
Cindy Battisti, *Pr*
John S Batisti, *Sec*
EMP: 15 EST: 2001
SQ FT: 8,000
SALES (est): 948.6K Privately Held
Web: www.superior-seats.com
SIC: 2531 Seats, automobile

(G-3710)
SUPERIOR TOOL & DIE CO INC (PA)
Also Called: Superior
2325 S Nappanee St (46517-1397)
PHONE.....................574 293-2591
Roy L Hershberger, *Pr*
Mary E Hershberger, *
Thomas Hershberger, *
EMP: 25 EST: 1952
SQ FT: 35,000
SALES (est): 4.76MM
SALES (corp-wide): 4.76MM Privately Held
Web: www.superiortd.com
SIC: 3599 3545 3544 Machine and other job shop work; Machine tool accessories; Special dies and tools

(G-3711)
SYNERGY INDUSTRIES INC
59264 Wilray Dr (46517-9490)
PHONE.....................574 320-2754
EMP: 5 EST: 2019
SALES (est): 103.68K Privately Held
Web: www.syn-ind.com
SIC: 3999 Manufacturing industries, nec

(G-3712)
T J B INC
2926 Paul Dr (46514-8796)
PHONE.....................219 293-8030
Terry Kraus, *Prin*
EMP: 6 EST: 2016
SALES (est): 102.53K Privately Held
SIC: 3443 Fabricated plate work (boiler shop)

(G-3713)
T SHORTER MANUFACTURING INC
2931 Dexter Dr (46514)
PHONE.....................574 264-4131
Terry Shorter, *Pr*
Jane Shorter, *Sec*
EMP: 3 EST: 1991
SQ FT: 10,000
SALES (est): 592.85K Privately Held
SIC: 3699 3931 3599 Fire control or bombing equipment, electronic; Musical instruments; Machine shop, jobbing and repair

(G-3714)
TAMCO MANUFACTURING CO
2717 Oakland Ave (46517-1558)
P.O. Box 1794 (46515-1794)
PHONE.....................574 294-1909
Tony Asoera, *Owner*
EMP: 4 EST: 1979
SQ FT: 25,000
SALES (est): 496.75K Privately Held
Web: www.tamcomfg.com
SIC: 5072 3559 Builders' hardware, nec; Plastics working machinery

(G-3715)
TATIANAS EMBROIDERY
59018 Jasmine Ct (46517-9566)
PHONE.....................574 875-1654
EMP: 4 EST: 2016
SALES (est): 140.46K Privately Held
SIC: 2395 Embroidery and art needlework

(G-3716)
TAYLOR MADE GROUP LLC
Also Called: Taylor Made Fabrics
3501 County Road 6 E (46514-7663)
PHONE.....................574 535-1125
Deanna Belcher, *Prin*
EMP: 64 EST: 2018
SALES (est): 9.62MM Privately Held
SIC: 3714 Motor vehicle parts and accessories

(G-3717)
TB PLASTIC EXTRUSIONS INC
54432 Adams St (46514-3647)
PHONE.....................574 266-7409
EMP: 50 EST: 2010
SALES (est): 4.92MM Privately Held
SIC: 3498 Fabricated pipe and fittings

(G-3718)
TCB INDUSTRIES INC
4519 Wyland Dr (46516-9642)
PHONE.....................574 522-3971
Tony Cunnane, *Prin*
Robert Loper, *Prin*
▲ EMP: 10 EST: 2004
SQ FT: 23,000
SALES (est): 219.17K Privately Held
SIC: 3743 Trackless trolley buses

(G-3719)
TEG HOLDINGS INC
1210 County Road 6 W (46514-8219)
PHONE.....................574 264-7514
Thomas E Graham, *Pr*
Tad Hayden, *
Kim Ottavi, *
EMP: 25 EST: 1973
SQ FT: 40,000
SALES (est): 24.9MM Privately Held
Web: www.plasticcomponentsinc.com
SIC: 3089 Injection molding of plastics

(G-3720)
TEKMODO LLC
1701 Conant St (46516-4716)
PHONE.....................574 970-5800
EMP: 10
SIC: 3089 Composition stone, plastics

(G-3721)
TEKMODO OZ HOLDINGS LLC
1701 Conant St (46516)
PHONE.....................574 970-5800
Marc Lacounte, *Pr*
Mark Hatley, *CFO*
EMP: 8 EST: 2018
SALES (est): 865.02K Privately Held
Web: www.tekmodo.net
SIC: 2273 Carpets, textile fiber

(G-3722)
TEKMODO STRUCTURES LLC
1701 Conant St (46516-4716)
PHONE.....................574 970-5800
EMP: 2 EST: 2012
SALES (est): 904.76K Privately Held
Web: www.tekmodo.com
SIC: 3089 Composition stone, plastics

(G-3723)
TENNECO AUTOMOTIVE OPER CO INC
Also Called: Tenneco
4825 Hoffman St (46516-9052)
PHONE.....................574 296-9400
EMP: 250
SALES (corp-wide): 18.04B Privately Held
Web: www.tenneco.com
SIC: 3714 Motor vehicle engines and parts
HQ: Tenneco Automotive Operating Company, Inc.
  500 N Field Dr
  Lake Forest IL 60045
  847 482-5000

(G-3724)
THE COMMODORE CORPORATION (PA)
Also Called: Manorwood Homes
58096 County Road 7 (46517)
P.O. Box 577 (46527-0577)
PHONE.....................574 533-7100
EMP: 45 EST: 1952
SALES (est): 85.9MM
SALES (corp-wide): 85.9MM Privately Held
Web: www.commodorehomes.com
SIC: 2452 Modular homes, prefabricated, wood

(G-3725)
THERMAL CERAMICS INC
Also Called: Morgan Thermal Ceramics
2730 Industrial Pkwy (46516-5401)
PHONE.....................574 296-3500
EMP: 38
SALES (corp-wide): 1.39B Privately Held
Web: www.morganthermalceramics.com
SIC: 3299 3255 3769 3714 Ceramic fiber; Brick, clay refractory; Space vehicle equipment, nec; Motor vehicle parts and accessories
HQ: Thermal Ceramics Inc.
  2102 Old Savannah Rd
  Augusta GA 30906
  706 796-4200

(G-3726)
THERMO BOND BUILDINGS LLC
58120 County Road 3 (46517-9007)
PHONE.....................574 295-1214
Shane Ryckeart, *Brnch Mgr*

Elkhart - Elkhart County (G-3727)

EMP: 85
Web: www.thermobond.com
SIC: 2451 Mobile buildings: for commercial use
PA: Thermo Bond Buildings Llc
109 E Pleasant St
Elk Point SD 57025

(G-3727)
THINK NORTH AMERICA INC
3221 Magnum Dr (46516-9021)
PHONE................................313 565-6781
EMP: 30
SIC: 3711 Motor vehicles and car bodies
PA: Think North America, Inc.
22226 Garrison St
Dearborn MI 48124

(G-3728)
THOR INDUSTRIES INC
Also Called: Thor Motor Coach
52570 Paul Dr (46514-8796)
PHONE................................574 264-2900
Arthur Konecny, Brnch Mgr
EMP: 31
SALES (corp-wide): 11.12B Publicly Held
Web: www.thorindustries.com
SIC: 3711 3716 Buses, all types, assembly of ; Motor homes
PA: Thor Industries, Inc.
601 E Beardsley Ave
Elkhart IN 46514
574 970-7460

(G-3729)
THOR INDUSTRIES INC
4221 Pine Creek Rd (46516-9557)
PHONE................................574 266-1111
Julie Delapaz, Brnch Mgr
EMP: 2
SALES (corp-wide): 11.12B Publicly Held
Web: www.thorindustries.com
SIC: 3716 Motor homes
PA: Thor Industries, Inc.
601 E Beardsley Ave
Elkhart IN 46514
574 970-7460

(G-3730)
THOR INDUSTRIES INC (PA)
Also Called: Thor
601 E Beardsley Ave (46514)
PHONE................................574 970-7460
Robert W Martin, Pr
Andy Graves, Ch Bd
Josef Hjelmaker, CIO
Colleen Zuhl, Sr VP
W Todd Woelfer, Sr VP
EMP: 310 EST: 1980
SQ FT: 1,465,000
SALES (est): 11.12B
SALES (corp-wide): 11.12B Publicly Held
Web: www.thorindustries.com
SIC: 3716 3799 3711 Motor homes; Recreational vehicles; Buses, all types, assembly of

(G-3731)
THOR INDUSTRIES INC
Also Called: Thor Motor Coach
28719 Jami St (46514-8794)
PHONE................................574 262-2624
Gary Groom, Brnch Mgr
EMP: 11
SALES (corp-wide): 11.12B Publicly Held
Web: www.thorindustries.com
SIC: 5012 3716 Recreational vehicles, motor homes, and trailers; Motor homes
PA: Thor Industries, Inc.
601 E Beardsley Ave
Elkhart IN 46514

574 970-7460

(G-3732)
THOR INDUSTRIES DATA CENTER
3080 Windsor Ct (46514-5555)
PHONE................................574 970-7460
EMP: 8 EST: 2020
SALES (est): 211.82K Privately Held
Web: www.thorindustries.com
SIC: 3799 Transportation equipment, nec

(G-3733)
THOR MOTOR COACH INC (HQ)
701 County Road 15 Ste 100 (46516)
P.O. Box 1486 (46515)
PHONE................................574 266-1111
Jeff Kime, Pr
▼ EMP: 246 EST: 1990
SALES (est): 80.47MM
SALES (corp-wide): 11.12B Publicly Held
Web: www.thormotorcoach.com
SIC: 3792 3716 Travel trailers and campers; Recreational van conversion (self-propelled), factory basis
PA: Thor Industries, Inc.
601 E Beardsley Ave
Elkhart IN 46514
574 970-7460

(G-3734)
TIME OUT TRAILERS INC
4636 Chester Dr (46516-9056)
PHONE................................574 294-7671
Blake Walters, Pr
Julie Walters, VP
EMP: 8 EST: 1978
SQ FT: 12,000
SALES (est): 959.1K Privately Held
Web: www.timeouttrailers.org
SIC: 3751 Motorcycle accessories

(G-3735)
TK METAL FORMING INC
57433 Nagy Dr (46517-1059)
P.O. Box 3037 (46515-3037)
PHONE................................574 293-2907
Timothy Utley, Pr
EMP: 12 EST: 2014
SALES (est): 2.23MM Privately Held
SIC: 3542 Machine tools, metal forming type

(G-3736)
TL INDUSTRIES INC
21746 Buckingham Rd (46516-9703)
PHONE................................419 666-8144
Randy Rush, Pr
Bonnie Rush, *
EMP: 25 EST: 1966
SQ FT: 25,000
SALES (est): 662.84K Privately Held
Web: www.tlindustries.com
SIC: 3792 Travel trailers and campers

(G-3737)
TL MOLD INC
24242 State Line Rd (46514-9451)
PHONE................................574 596-7875
Terri G Longacre, Prin
EMP: 6 EST: 2013
SALES (est): 73.22K Privately Held
SIC: 3544 Industrial molds

(G-3738)
TOGS POWDER COATING
1200 Oak St (46514-2200)
PHONE................................574 266-2850
EMP: 6 EST: 2020
SALES (est): 190.51K Privately Held
SIC: 3479 Coating of metals and formed products

(G-3739)
TOPSTITCH INC
921 Summa Dr (46516-9037)
EMP: 11 EST: 2011
SALES (est): 424.57K Privately Held
Web: www.topstitchusa.com
SIC: 2395 2759 Embroidery products, except Schiffli machine; Screen printing

(G-3740)
TORQUE ENGINEERING CORPORATION
2932 Thorne Dr (46514)
PHONE................................574 264-2628
Raymond Wedel, Pr
Rick Wedel, Dir
Michael Bennett, COO
I Paul Arcuri, VP
EMP: 18 EST: 1996
SQ FT: 34,000
SALES (est): 1.78MM Privately Held
Web: www.torque-eng.com
SIC: 3519 Marine engines

(G-3741)
TOUCHTRONICS INC
57315 Nagy Dr Ste A (46517-1081)
PHONE................................574 294-2570
Alice Poseley, Pr
Joan Young, Sec
Ron Mathia, Treas
Natalie Rose, Stockholder
EMP: 12 EST: 1983
SQ FT: 11,000
SALES (est): 2.93MM Privately Held
Web: www.touchtronics.com
SIC: 3625 Switches, electronic applications

(G-3742)
TRAMS DESIGN LLC
22834 Pine Arbor Dr Apt 1b (46516-9073)
PHONE................................574 206-3232
Tina Smart, Owner
EMP: 5 EST: 2021
SALES (est): 229.75K Privately Held
SIC: 2396 Automotive trimmings, fabric

(G-3743)
TRANS ATLANTIC PRODUCTS LLC
2778 Faith Ave (46514-7810)
PHONE................................574 262-0165
EMP: 10 EST: 2014
SALES (est): 980.14K Privately Held
Web: www.transatlanticprod.com
SIC: 3714 Motor vehicle parts and accessories

(G-3744)
TRANSHIELD INC (HQ)
2932 Thorne Dr (46514)
PHONE................................574 266-4118
James Glick, Pr
Matt Peat, *
Jeff Vold, *
Brian Mckenzie, VP Opers
◆ EMP: 40 EST: 1993
SQ FT: 31,050
SALES (est): 19.59MM
SALES (corp-wide): 3.47B Publicly Held
Web: www.transhield-usa.com
SIC: 2394 Liners and covers, fabric: made from purchased materials
PA: Patrick Industries, Inc.
107 W Franklin St
Elkhart IN 46516
574 294-7511

(G-3745)
TREDEGAR CORPORATION
2551 County Road 10 W (46514)

PHONE................................574 262-4685
EMP: 1
Web: www.tredegar.com
SIC: 3081 Plastics film and sheet
PA: Tredegar Corporation
1100 Boulders Pkwy
North Chesterfield VA 23225

(G-3746)
TRIANGLE RUBBER CO LLC
5333 E Beck Dr (46516-9251)
PHONE................................574 533-3118
Pat Liverman, Brnch Mgr
EMP: 32
SALES (corp-wide): 32MM Privately Held
Web: www.trianglerubberco.com
SIC: 2821 Plastics materials and resins
PA: Triangle Rubber Co., Llc
1924 Elkhart Rd
Goshen IN 46526
574 533-3118

(G-3747)
TRIM-LOK INC
1642 Gateway Ct (46514-8216)
PHONE................................574 227-1143
Darrly Torrey, Owner
EMP: 11 EST: 2015
SALES (est): 886.24K Privately Held
Web: www.trimlok.com
SIC: 3089 Molding primary plastics

(G-3748)
TROPHY HOMES INC
2730 Almac Ct (46514-7627)
PHONE................................574 264-4911
Olin Wenrick, Pr
EMP: 33 EST: 1971
SQ FT: 33,000
SALES (est): 2.28MM Privately Held
SIC: 3792 2451 House trailers, except as permanent dwellings; Mobile homes

(G-3749)
TRU-FORM METAL PRODUCTS INC
Also Called: Tru-Form
27200 D I Dr (46514-8294)
PHONE................................574 266-8020
Joseph Straughn, Pr
EMP: 19 EST: 1989
SQ FT: 15,000
SALES (est): 3.43MM Privately Held
Web: www.truformmetalproducts.com
SIC: 3465 Fenders, automobile: stamped or pressed metal

(G-3750)
TRUTH PUBLISHING COMPANY INC (PA)
Also Called: Elkhart Truth, The
421 S 2nd St Ste 100 (46516-3230)
P.O. Box 487 (46515-0487)
PHONE................................574 294-1661
John F Dille III, Pr
John F Dille Iii, Pr
Robert A Watson, *
▲ EMP: 185 EST: 1984
SQ FT: 30,000
SALES (est): 9.23MM
SALES (corp-wide): 9.23MM Privately Held
Web: www.elkharttruth.com
SIC: 2711 Newspapers, publishing and printing

(G-3751)
TUBE FORM SOLUTIONS LLC (PA)
435 Roske Dr (46516-9086)
PHONE................................574 295-5041
Michael Thomas, *
▲ EMP: 31 EST: 2010

GEOGRAPHIC SECTION
Elkhart - Elkhart County (G-3777)

SALES (est): 8.39MM
SALES (corp-wide): 8.39MM **Privately Held**
Web: www.tubeformsolutions.com
SIC: 3599 Machine shop, jobbing and repair

(G-3752)
TUBE FORM SOLUTIONS LLC
4221 Pine Creek Rd (46516-9557)
PHONE.................................574 266-5230
EMP: 1
SALES (corp-wide): 8.39MM **Privately Held**
Web: www.tubeformsolutions.com
SIC: 3599 Machine shop, jobbing and repair
PA: Tube Form Solutions, Llc
435 Roske Dr
Elkhart IN 46516
574 295-5041

(G-3753)
TUMACS LLC
Also Called: Tumacs Covers
3505 Cooper Dr (46514-8639)
PHONE.................................574 264-5000
▲ EMP: 20 EST: 2007
SALES (est): 233.85K **Privately Held**
Web: www.tumacscovers.com
SIC: 2394 Convertible tops, canvas or boat: from purchased materials

(G-3754)
TUSKIN EQUIPMENT CORPORATION
616 S 4th St (46516-2770)
PHONE.................................630 466-5590
Kristine O'dwyer, Pr
Jeffrey O'dwyer, Sec
EMP: 5 EST: 1991
SALES (est): 900K **Privately Held**
Web: www.tuskin.com
SIC: 3561 3559 Industrial pumps and parts; Plastics working machinery

(G-3755)
TWIN-AIR PRODUCTS INC
4602 Chester Dr (46516-9056)
PHONE.................................574 295-1129
Roger L Burks, Pr
Charlotte Burks, VP
▲ EMP: 6 EST: 1982
SQ FT: 15,000
SALES (est): 730K **Privately Held**
Web: www.twinairproducts.com
SIC: 3585 7532 Air conditioning, motor vehicle; Van conversion

(G-3756)
UINSPIRE LLC
1201 County Road 15 (46516-9648)
PHONE.................................574 575-6949
EMP: 1
SALES (est): 46.58K **Privately Held**
SIC: 2211 7389 Scrub cloths; Business services, nec

(G-3757)
ULTRA-FAB ACQUISITIONS INC
57985 State Road 19 (46517)
PHONE.................................574 294-7571
Searer Craig, Pr
Darryl Searer, Sec
◆ EMP: 15 EST: 1958
SQ FT: 24,000
SALES (est): 2.36MM **Privately Held**
Web: www.ultra-fab.com
SIC: 3429 Motor vehicle hardware

(G-3758)
UNITED PET FOODS INC
30809 Corwin Rd (46514-9394)
P.O. Box 250 (46561-0250)
PHONE.................................574 674-5981
Sally Davis, Pr
Diane Hershberger, Sec
Jeff Davis Plant, Prin
EMP: 10 EST: 1976
SQ FT: 33,000
SALES (est): 1.17MM **Privately Held**
SIC: 2048 Prepared feeds, nec

(G-3759)
UNITED PIES OF ELKHART INC
Also Called: United Pie
1016 Middlebury St (46516-4510)
PHONE.................................574 294-3419
Blanche Nichols, Pr
Frank Nichols, VP
EMP: 8 EST: 1970
SQ FT: 7,200
SALES (est): 975.21K **Privately Held**
SIC: 2051 2053 Pies, bakery: except frozen; Pies, bakery; frozen

(G-3760)
UNITED ROLL FORMING CORP
58288 County Road 3 (46517-9371)
PHONE.................................574 294-2800
Betty Glaum, Pr
James Glaum, *
◆ EMP: 35 EST: 1983
SQ FT: 65,000
SALES (est): 4.59MM **Privately Held**
Web: www.unitedrollforming.org
SIC: 3449 Custom roll formed products

(G-3761)
UNITED SHADE LLC
2780 County Road 6 W (46514-8295)
PHONE.................................574 262-0954
▲ EMP: 60 EST: 2002
SALES (est): 8.69MM
SALES (corp-wide): 11.12B **Publicly Held**
Web: www.unitedshade.com
SIC: 2591 Window shades
PA: Thor Industries, Inc.
601 E Beardsley Ave
Elkhart IN 46514
574 970-7460

(G-3762)
UNIVERSAL COATINGS LLC
1204 Pierina Dr (46514-5285)
PHONE.................................574 520-3403
Shawn Vertrees, Admn
EMP: 7 EST: 2016
SALES (est): 83.42K **Privately Held**
SIC: 3479 Metal coating and allied services

(G-3763)
UNIVERSAL PRECISION INSTRS INC
2921 Lavanture Pl (46514-8233)
PHONE.................................574 264-3997
Ron Drown, Pr
Robert Wozny, VP
Bill Harper, Sec
Larry Rembarger, Treas
EMP: 9 EST: 1978
SQ FT: 12,000
SALES (est): 1.48MM **Privately Held**
Web: www.archglobalprecision.com
SIC: 3599 3841 Machine shop, jobbing and repair; Surgical and medical instruments

(G-3764)
VAHALA FOAM INC
930 Herman St (46516-9311)
PHONE.................................574 293-1287
Dan Vahala, Ch Bd
Dave Vahala, *
EMP: 57 EST: 1991
SQ FT: 47,000
SALES (est): 9.89MM **Privately Held**
Web: www.vahalafoam.com
SIC: 5199 2821 3086 Foams and rubber; Plastics materials and resins; Insulation or cushioning material, foamed plastics

(G-3765)
VALENTINE WOODWORKING LLC
25810 Miner Rd (46514-5018)
PHONE.................................574 206-0697
Ron Valentine, Owner
EMP: 3 EST: 2003
SALES (est): 130K **Privately Held**
SIC: 2499 Decorative wood and woodwork

(G-3766)
VALLEY DISTRIBUTING INC
Also Called: Valley Manufacturing
2820 Lillian Ave (46514-9233)
P.O. Box 1684 (46515-1684)
PHONE.................................574 266-4455
Bill Harris Senior, Pr
EMP: 35 EST: 1986
SQ FT: 27,000
SALES (est): 3.7MM **Privately Held**
Web: www.valleymanufacturinginc.com
SIC: 3714 Motor vehicle body components and frame

(G-3767)
VALMONT INDUSTRIES INC
3403 Charlotte Ave (46517-1190)
PHONE.................................574 295-6942
Franco Garcay, Brnch Mgr
EMP: 78
SQ FT: 400,000
SALES (corp-wide): 4.17B **Publicly Held**
Web: www.valmont.com
SIC: 3441 Fabricated structural metal
PA: Valmont Industries, Inc.
15000 Valmont Plz
Omaha NE 68154
402 963-1000

(G-3768)
VANDELEIGH INDUSTRIES LLC
318 S Elkhart Ave Apt 409 (46516)
PHONE.................................574 326-3254
EMP: 4 EST: 2018
SALES (est): 88.51K **Privately Held**
SIC: 3999 Manufacturing industries, nec

(G-3769)
VERSATILE FABRICATION LLC
4431 Pine Creek Rd (46516-9561)
PHONE.................................574 293-8504
Will Gury, Pr
EMP: 9 EST: 2013
SALES (est): 1.73MM **Privately Held**
Web: www.versatilefabrication.com
SIC: 3469 3599 Ash trays, stamped metal; Machine and other job shop work

(G-3770)
VINCE ROGERS SIGNS INC
400 W Crawford St (46514-2732)
PHONE.................................574 264-0542
Michael Smoot, Pr
EMP: 2 EST: 1960
SQ FT: 3,200
SALES (est): 181.26K **Privately Held**
Web: www.thegraphicsfactoryinc.com
SIC: 3993 Signs and advertising specialties

(G-3771)
VISTA MANUFACTURING INC (PA)
53345 Columbia Dr (46514)
PHONE.................................574 264-0711
Tod E Tieszen, Pr
Allen Mazelin, *
Dwayne Tieszen, *
▲ EMP: 24 EST: 1979
SQ FT: 16,000
SALES (est): 8.69MM
SALES (corp-wide): 8.69MM **Privately Held**
Web: www.vistamfg.com
SIC: 3641 5063 Lamps, incandescent filament, electric; Lighting fixtures

(G-3772)
VISTA WORLDWIDE LLC
53345 Columbia Dr (46514-8153)
PHONE.................................574 264-0711
Joe Bonta, Pr
EMP: 6 EST: 2013
SALES (est): 174.59K **Privately Held**
Web: www.vistamfg.com
SIC: 3648 3677 3679 Lighting equipment, nec; Transformers power supply, electronic type; Electronic components, nec

(G-3773)
VITRACOAT AMERICA INC (PA)
2807 Marina Dr (46514-7669)
PHONE.................................574 262-2188
Eduardo Moussalli, Pr
Luis Moussali, VP
▼ EMP: 16 EST: 2000
SQ FT: 20,000
SALES (est): 6.23MM
SALES (corp-wide): 6.23MM **Privately Held**
Web: www.vitracoat.com
SIC: 3479 Coating of metals and formed products

(G-3774)
VIXEN COMPOSITES LLC
Also Called: Vixen
2965 Lavanture Pl (46514)
PHONE.................................574 970-1224
Gregg Fore, Managing Member
▲ EMP: 1 EST: 2009
SALES (est): 1.53MM
SALES (corp-wide): 11.12B **Publicly Held**
Web: www.vixencomposites.com
SIC: 3089 Air mattresses, plastics
PA: Thor Industries, Inc.
601 E Beardsley Ave
Elkhart IN 46514
574 970-7460

(G-3775)
VLB GROUP NORTH AMERICA LLC
435 Roske Dr (46516-9086)
PHONE.................................317 642-3425
Mike Thomas, Prin
Jeffrey Jacobs, Prin
Michael Thomas, Prin
Kile Snyder, Prin
EMP: 40 EST: 2021
SALES (est): 1.32MM **Privately Held**
Web: www.vlb-group.us
SIC: 3542 Machine tools, metal forming type

(G-3776)
WAIT INDUSTRIES LLC
Also Called: M-3 & Associates
2500 Ada Dr (46514)
PHONE.................................574 347-4320
EMP: 24 EST: 2017
SALES (est): 5.77MM **Privately Held**
Web: www.waitindustries.com
SIC: 3444 Sheet metalwork

(G-3777)
WALERKO TOOL AND ENGRG CORP
1935 W Lusher Ave (46517-1348)
PHONE.................................574 295-2233
Edward M Walerko Junior, Pr

Elkhart - Elkhart County (G-3778)

▲ **EMP:** 42 **EST:** 1952
SQ FT: 40,000
SALES (est): 4.81MM
SALES (corp-wide): 11.28MM **Privately Held**
Web: www.walerko.com
SIC: 3599 3724 Machine shop, jobbing and repair; Aircraft engines and engine parts
PA: Mno-Drek, Llc
  415 E Prairie Ronde St
  Dowagiac MI 49047
  269 783-4111

(G-3778)
WALLAR ADDITIONS INC (PA)
Also Called: American Sunspace
30012 County Road 10 (46514-9776)
PHONE..................574 262-1989
James Jeffrey Wallar, *Pr*
William Brad Wallar, *
EMP: 7 **EST:** 1976
SQ FT: 25,000
SALES (est): 4.93MM
SALES (corp-wide): 4.93MM **Privately Held**
Web: www.americansunspaceadditions.com
SIC: 6163 1799 3211 Loan brokers; Athletic and recreation facilities construction; Flat glass

(G-3779)
WALTER PIANO COMPANY INC
1705 County Road 6 E Ste 200 (46514-5594)
PHONE..................574 266-0615
TOLL FREE: 888
Charles R Walter, *Pr*
Barbara Walter, *VP*
▲ **EMP:** 15 **EST:** 1970
SQ FT: 70,000
SALES (est): 881.38K **Privately Held**
Web: www.walterpiano.com
SIC: 3931 5736 7699 Pianos, all types: vertical, grand, spinet, player, etc.; Pianos; Piano tuning and repair

(G-3780)
WATCHDOG MANUFACTURING LLC
57039 Rutledge Ct (46516-9011)
PHONE..................574 536-2445
EMP: 5 **EST:** 2016
SALES (est): 227.49K **Privately Held**
SIC: 3999 Manufacturing industries, nec

(G-3781)
WELCH PACKAGING KENTUCKY LLC (HQ)
1020 Herman St (46516-9028)
PHONE..................574 295-2460
Scott Welch, *CEO*
EMP: 25 **EST:** 2018
SALES (est): 10.55MM
SALES (corp-wide): 457.79MM **Privately Held**
SIC: 2679 Corrugated paper: made from purchased material
PA: Welch Packaging Group, Inc.
  1020 Herman St
  Elkhart IN 46516
  574 295-2460

(G-3782)
WELLCO HOLDINGS INC (DH)
1503 Mcnaughton Ave (46514-2243)
PHONE..................574 264-9661
Jeffrey M Wells, *Pr*
Victor Arko, *
Bill Peck, *
Phyllis M Wells, *
▼ **EMP:** 130 **EST:** 1958
SQ FT: 55,000
SALES (est): 49.04MM
SALES (corp-wide): 486.78MM **Privately Held**
Web: www.wellscargo.com
SIC: 3715 Demountable cargo containers
HQ: Universal Trailer Cargo Group
  12800 University Dr # 300
  Fort Myers FL 33907

(G-3783)
WHEELCHAIR HELP LLC
28423 Old Us 33 (46516-1719)
PHONE..................574 295-2220
Joe Lidy, *Owner*
EMP: 6 **EST:** 2014
SALES (est): 90.32K **Privately Held**
Web: www.wheelchairhelp.org
SIC: 3842 Wheelchairs

(G-3784)
WINDSOR STEEL INC
2210 Middlebury St (46516-5518)
P.O. Box 1064 (46515-1064)
PHONE..................574 294-1060
EMP: 12 **EST:** 2011
SALES (est): 1.89MM **Privately Held**
Web: www.windsorsteel.net
SIC: 3312 Blast furnaces and steel mills

(G-3785)
WINDSOR WARTCARE
3100 Windsor Ct (46514-5556)
PHONE..................574 266-6555
Dorwyn Collier, *Owner*
EMP: 4 **EST:** 2007
SALES (est): 464.16K **Privately Held**
Web: www.windsorworkcare.com
SIC: 2834 Medicines, capsuled or ampuled

(G-3786)
WINE & CANVAS SOUTH BEND LLC
51213 County Road 11 (46514-8557)
PHONE..................574 807-1562
EMP: 5 **EST:** 2012
SALES (est): 73.61K **Privately Held**
Web: www.wineandcanvas.com
SIC: 2211 Canvas

(G-3787)
WINE AND CANVAS
51197 Channel Ct (46514-9235)
PHONE..................574 514-9942
EMP: 4 **EST:** 2014
SALES (est): 68.44K **Privately Held**
Web: www.wineandcanvas.com
SIC: 2211 Canvas

(G-3788)
WISEGUYS SEATING & ACCESSRY CO
2701 Industrial Pkwy (46516-5441)
P.O. Box 211 (46515-0211)
PHONE..................574 294-6030
Jim Wise, *Pr*
Todd Lorang, *CEO*
EMP: 3 **EST:** 2002
SALES (est): 387.37K **Privately Held**
Web: www.wiseguys-seats.com
SIC: 2399 Seat covers, automobile

(G-3789)
WOOD CREATIONS INC
800 Industrial Pkwy (46516-5530)
PHONE..................574 522-7765
Carlos Gonzalez, *Prin*
EMP: 2 **EST:** 2010
SALES (est): 90.02K **Privately Held**
SIC: 2431 Millwork

(G-3790)
WOOD PARTS INC
4340 Pine Creek Rd (46516-9558)
PHONE..................574 326-3631
EMP: 10 **EST:** 2011
SALES (est): 499.64K **Privately Held**
SIC: 2499 Wood products, nec

(G-3791)
WOODPARTS INTERNATIONAL CORP
Also Called: Woodpart International
729 Mason St (46516-2700)
P.O. Box 1011 (46515-1011)
PHONE..................574 293-0566
Keith Butus, *Pr*
Carmen Butus, *Sec*
Peter Butus, *Stockholder*
▲ **EMP:** 15 **EST:** 1974
SQ FT: 38,000
SALES (est): 253.67K **Privately Held**
SIC: 2421 Specialty sawmill products

(G-3792)
WOODWRIGHT DOOR & TRIM INC
808 9th St (46516-2653)
P.O. Box 1943 (46515-1943)
PHONE..................574 522-1667
Bruce Shoup, *Pr*
EMP: 6 **EST:** 1989
SQ FT: 8,500
SALES (est): 430.25K **Privately Held**
SIC: 2431 5211 Moldings, wood: unfinished and prefinished; Door and window products

(G-3793)
WORLD RDO MSSNARY FLLWSHIP INC
Also Called: H C J B World Radio
2830 17th St (46517-4008)
PHONE..................574 970-4252
David Pasechnik, *Brnch Mgr*
EMP: 6
SALES (corp-wide): 6.91MM **Privately Held**
Web: www.reachbeyond.org
SIC: 3663 8711 4832 8661 Transmitter-receivers, radio; Engineering services; Radio broadcasting stations; Non-denominational church
PA: World Radio Missionary Fellowship, Inc.
  1065 Grdn Of The Gods Rd
  Colorado Springs CO 80907
  719 590-9800

(G-3794)
WORLDCELL EXTRUSIONS LLC
318 S Elkhart Ave (46516-0005)
PHONE..................574 333-2249
John Petrofsky, *Managing Member*
EMP: 1 **EST:** 2016
SALES (est): 247.27K **Privately Held**
SIC: 3061 Mechanical rubber goods

(G-3795)
WORLDWIDE BATTERY COMPANY LLC
2804 Jeanwood Dr Ste 5a (46514-7672)
PHONE..................248 830-8537
Dave Mast, *Ofcr*
EMP: 1
SALES (corp-wide): 22.57MM **Privately Held**
Web: www.worldwidebattery.com
SIC: 5063 3691 Batteries; Storage batteries
PA: Worldwide Battery Company, Llc
  9955 Westpoint Dr Ste 120
  Indianapolis IN 46256
  317 845-1330

(G-3796)
WORLDWIDE FOAM LTD (DH)
Also Called: Worldcell Extrusions
1806 Conant St (46516-4755)
PHONE..................574 968-8268
◆ **EMP:** 1 **EST:** 2008
SALES (est): 6.04MM
SALES (corp-wide): 17.79MM **Privately Held**
Web: www.worldwidefoam.com
SIC: 3086 Packaging and shipping materials, foamed plastics
HQ: Jacobs & Thompson Ltd.
  699 Port Rd
  Wurtland KY 41144
  800 387-7431

(G-3797)
XANTREX LLC (HQ)
541 Roske Dr Ste A (46516)
PHONE..................800 670-0707
Kevin Moschetti, *CEO*
John Kalbfleisch, *Genl Mgr*
EMP: 20 **EST:** 2018
SALES (est): 42.02MM
SALES (corp-wide): 100.76MM **Privately Held**
Web: www.xantrex.com
SIC: 3629 Inverters, nonrotating: electrical
PA: Mission Critical Electronics Llc
  1580 Sunflower Ave
  Costa Mesa CA 92626
  714 751-0488

(G-3798)
XANTREX LLC
541 Roske Dr Ste A (46516-9323)
PHONE..................800 670-0707
EMP: 180
SALES (corp-wide): 100.76MM **Privately Held**
Web: www.xantrex.com
SIC: 3629 Inverters, nonrotating: electrical
HQ: Xantrex Llc
  541 Roske Dr Ste A
  Elkhart IN 46516
  800 670-0707

(G-3799)
YELLOW DOG ANODIZING
2730 Almac Ct (46514-7627)
PHONE..................574 343-2247
EMP: 3 **EST:** 2012
SALES (est): 226.15K **Privately Held**
Web: www.yellowdogextrusion.com
SIC: 3471 Anodizing (plating) of metals or formed products

(G-3800)
YNWA INDUSTRIES INC
555 County Road 15 (46516)
PHONE..................574 295-6641
Chris Curtis, *Pr*
EMP: 100 **EST:** 1994
SQ FT: 115,000
SALES (est): 9.91MM **Privately Held**
Web: www.rctoolbox.com
SIC: 3469 3714 3444 3441 Boxes: tool, lunch, mail, etc.: stamped metal; Bumpers and bumperettes, motor vehicle; Sheet metalwork; Fabricated structural metal

Ellettsville
Monroe County

(G-3801)
BYBEE STONE COMPANY INC
6293 N Matthews Dr (47429-9424)
P.O. Box 308 (47429-0308)

PHONE...............................812 876-2215
William Bybee, *Pr*
George Bybee, *
Mary Beth Haas, *
Laura Bybee, *
Sharon Myers, *
EMP: 65 **EST:** 1862
SQ FT: 73,000
SALES (est): 4.49MM **Privately Held**
Web: www.bybeestone.com
SIC: 3281 Limestone, cut and shaped

(G-3802)
CHADS LLC
Also Called: Chad's Towing and Recovery
6679 W Mcneely St (47429-9444)
P.O. Box 593 (47429-0593)
PHONE...............................812 323-7377
Chad Stephens, *Prin*
EMP: 4 **EST:** 2009
SALES (est): 223.37K **Privately Held**
SIC: 7549 3713 3531 Towing service, automotive; Automobile wrecker truck bodies; Winches

(G-3803)
CHRISTOPHER ENGLE
Also Called: Hamster Press Klingel-Engle Pu
7251 W State Road 46 (47429-1029)
PHONE...............................812 876-3540
Terri Klinglehoefer, *Prin*
Christopher Engle, *Owner*
EMP: 2 **EST:** 1995
SALES (est): 73.33K **Privately Held**
SIC: 3944 Games, toys, and children's vehicles

(G-3804)
COMPUCOMICS
6079 N Holly Dr (47429-9462)
PHONE...............................812 876-1480
Roy Duncan, *Owner*
EMP: 3 **EST:** 1997
SALES (est): 104.25K **Privately Held**
SIC: 2721 Comic books: publishing only, not printed on site

(G-3805)
COOK GROUP INCORPORATED
Also Called: Cook Medical
6300 N Matthews Dr (47429-9495)
PHONE...............................812 331-1025
EMP: 11
SALES (corp-wide): 1.61B **Privately Held**
Web: www.cookgroup.com
SIC: 3841 Surgical and medical instruments
PA: Cook Group Incorporated
    750 Daniels Way
    Bloomington IN 47404
    812 339-2235

(G-3806)
COOK INCORPORATED
6600 W Mcneely St (47429-9444)
P.O. Box 489 (47429-0489)
PHONE...............................812 339-2235
Dan Brinson, *Mgr*
EMP: 1
SALES (corp-wide): 1.61B **Privately Held**
Web: www.cookmedical.com
SIC: 3841 Catheters
HQ: Cook Incorporated
    750 Daniels Way
    Bloomington IN 47404
    812 339-2235

(G-3807)
DIGITAL CARVINGS LLC
927 E Meadowlands Dr (47429-1086)
PHONE...............................812 269-6123
Bradley Edwards, *Owner*
EMP: 2 **EST:** 2011
SALES (est): 74.08K **Privately Held**
SIC: 2426 8742 Carvings, furniture: wood; General management consultant

(G-3808)
H L SIGNWORKS
616 N Robin Dr (47429-1635)
PHONE...............................812 325-5750
Robert Double, *Owner*
EMP: 2 **EST:** 1988
SALES (est): 75K **Privately Held**
SIC: 3993 Signs and advertising specialties

(G-3809)
HIGGINS DYAN
Also Called: Costume Delights
5680 W Mcneely St (47429-9411)
PHONE...............................812 876-0754
Dyan Higgins, *Owner*
EMP: 5 **EST:** 1980
SQ FT: 1,800
SALES (est): 422.01K **Privately Held**
Web: www.costumedelights.com
SIC: 2389 5699 7299 Costumes; Costumes and wigs; Costume rental

(G-3810)
NITE OWL PROMOTIONS INC
7011 N Red Hill Rd (47429-9748)
PHONE...............................812 876-3888
EMP: 1 **EST:** 1991
SALES (est): 247.47K **Privately Held**
Web: www.niteowlpromo.com
SIC: 2759 Screen printing

(G-3811)
PARSLEYS SEAL COATING INC
Also Called: Parsley Seal Coating Stripping
305 S Ridge Springs Ln (47429-1017)
PHONE...............................812 876-5450
Brent Parsley, *VP*
EMP: 2 **EST:** 2009
SALES (est): 146.24K **Privately Held**
SIC: 2951 Asphalt paving mixtures and blocks

(G-3812)
WOODLAND RIDGE WOODWORKING LLC
5182 W Woodland Rd (47429-9578)
PHONE...............................812 821-8032
Paul C Mizell, *Prin*
EMP: 5 **EST:** 2014
SALES (est): 138.57K **Privately Held**
SIC: 2431 Millwork

Elnora
Daviess County

(G-3813)
CAMPBELL PET COMPANY
Also Called: Paws Depot
120 N Odon St (47529-4720)
P.O. Box 128 (47529-0128)
PHONE...............................812 692-5208
Mary Henrichsen, *Pr*
EMP: 6
SALES (corp-wide): 2.5MM **Privately Held**
Web: www.campbellpet.com
SIC: 3199 5047 Dog furnishings: collars, leashes, muzzles, etc.: leather; Veterinarians' equipment and supplies
PA: Campbell Pet Company
    9606 Ne 126th Ave
    Vancouver WA 98682
    360 892-9786

(G-3814)
CORN PRO INC
5344 E 1250 N (47529-5060)
PHONE...............................812 636-4319
EMP: 8
SALES (est): 470.66K **Privately Held**
Web: www.cornpro.com
SIC: 3715 Truck trailers

(G-3815)
JOLLIFF DIESEL SERVICE LLC
7325 E 1500 N (47529-5031)
PHONE...............................812 692-5725
Phillip Jolliff, *Managing Member*
Sara Jolliff, *VP*
EMP: 2 **EST:** 1976
SQ FT: 2,208
SALES (est): 156.14K **Privately Held**
Web: jolliff-diesel-service.hub.biz
SIC: 3519 7538 0115 5172 Diesel engine rebuilding; Diesel engine repair: automotive ; Corn; Lubricating oils and greases

(G-3816)
SPECIAL FABRICATION SERVICES
418 East Hgwy 57 (47529-3019)
PHONE...............................812 384-5384
EMP: 5 **EST:** 2005
SALES (est): 74.09K **Privately Held**
SIC: 3441 Fabricated structural metal

Elwood
Madison County

(G-3817)
AEROMOTIVE MFG INC
8421 N 750 W (46036-8990)
PHONE...............................765 552-0668
Dorcia Stottlemyer, *Pr*
Charles Stottlemyer, *Sec*
EMP: 2 **EST:** 1989
SALES (est): 196.58K **Privately Held**
SIC: 3441 Fabricated structural metal

(G-3818)
AUNT NETTS COUNTRY CANDLES LLC
Also Called: Dream Mill
7374 West State Rd (46036)
PHONE...............................765 557-2770
EMP: 3 **EST:** 2007
SALES (est): 163.97K **Privately Held**
SIC: 3999 Manufacturing industries, nec

(G-3819)
CNM MACHINE TOOL REPAIR
9833 W Sunset Ln (46036-8829)
PHONE...............................765 552-3255
Chris Morgan, *Owner*
EMP: 1 **EST:** 2009
SALES (est): 72K **Privately Held**
SIC: 3541 Machine tool replacement & repair parts, metal cutting types

(G-3820)
DUNN-RITE PRODUCTS INC (PA)
2200 S J St (46036-2506)
PHONE...............................765 552-9433
Edward Dunn Junior, *Pr*
Douglas Dunn, *
Nancy Dunn, *Stockholder*
▲ **EMP:** 19 **EST:** 1981
SQ FT: 68,000
SALES (est): 4.3MM **Privately Held**
Web: www.dunnriteproducts.com
SIC: 3949 5091 Water sports equipment; Swimming pools, equipment and supplies

(G-3821)
ELSA LLC
Also Called: Elsa
1240 S State Road 37 (46036-3023)
PHONE...............................765 552-5200
Kiyokazu Sakamoto, *CEO*
Masataka Sakamoto, *
Takuya Yoshida, *
Yashihito Matsuoka, *
Hideo Nakamura, *
▲ **EMP:** 310 **EST:** 1987
SQ FT: 300,000
SALES (est): 47.14MM **Privately Held**
Web: www.elsallc.com
SIC: 3714 Exhaust systems and parts, motor vehicle
HQ: Elsa Corporation
    1240 S State Road 37
    Elwood IN 46036
    765 552-5200

(G-3822)
ELSA CORPORATION (DH)
Also Called: Elsa
1240 S State Road 37 (46036-3023)
PHONE...............................765 552-5200
Kiyokazu Sakamoto, *CEO*
Yasuhiko Matsuoka, *
Hideo Nakamura, *
Takuya Yoshida, *
▲ **EMP:** 350 **EST:** 1987
SQ FT: 400,000
SALES (est): 87.27MM **Privately Held**
Web: www.elsallc.com
SIC: 3714 Exhaust systems and parts, motor vehicle
HQ: Sakamoto Industry Co., Ltd.
    292, Besshocho
    Ota GNM 373-0

(G-3823)
ELWOOD PUBLISHING COMPANY INC (HQ)
Also Called: Call Leader
317 S Anderson St (46036-2018)
P.O. Box 85 (46036-0085)
PHONE...............................765 552-3355
Jack L Barnes, *Pr*
Charles Barnes, *
Judith Barnes, *
Brian Barnes, *
Robert Naash, *
EMP: 50 **EST:** 1894
SQ FT: 15,000
SALES (est): 3.76MM
SALES (corp-wide): 8.23MM **Privately Held**
Web: www.elwoodpublishing.com
SIC: 2711 Commercial printing and newspaper publishing combined
PA: Ray Barnes Newspaper Inc
    201 E Columbus St 207
    Kenton OH 43326
    419 674-4066

(G-3824)
ENDEAVOR PRECISION INC
2635 S F St (46036-2658)
PHONE...............................765 557-8694
EMP: 7 **EST:** 2018
SALES (est): 164.53K **Privately Held**
Web: www.endeavorprecision.com
SIC: 3599 Machine shop, jobbing and repair

(G-3825)
GOLDEN THREAD LLC
516 N Anderson St Ste C (46036-1295)
PHONE...............................765 557-7801
Penny Martin, *Owner*
EMP: 2 **EST:** 2006
SALES (est): 71.89K **Privately Held**

Elwood - Madison County

SIC: 2395 Embroidery products, except Schiffli machine

(G-3826)
IRVING MATERIALS INC
Also Called: I M I
2500 S D St (46036-2621)
PHONE..................................765 552-5041
Beutch Mey, Brnch Mgr
EMP: 3
SALES (corp-wide): 814.09MM **Privately Held**
Web: www.irvmat.com
SIC: 3273 Ready-mixed concrete
PA: Irving Materials, Inc.
 8032 N State Road 9
 Greenfield IN 46140
 317 326-3101

(G-3827)
JACKSONS WOODWORKS LLC
1609 N E St (46036-1330)
PHONE..................................765 623-0638
Cathy Swift, Admn
EMP: 6 EST: 2015
SALES (est): 216.56K **Privately Held**
Web: www.jacksonswoodworksllc.com
SIC: 2431 Millwork

(G-3828)
KADET PRODUCTS INC
2403 S J St (46036-2511)
PHONE..................................765 552-7341
Phillip Fettig, Ch
Page Fettig, Sec
Eric Fettig, Pr
EMP: 18 EST: 1984
SQ FT: 60,000
SALES (est): 895.38K **Privately Held**
Web: www.kadetproducts.com
SIC: 3471 Cleaning and descaling metal products

(G-3829)
LOYS SALES INC
Also Called: Loy's Music Center
715 S 22nd St (46036-2521)
PHONE..................................765 552-7250
Leslie J Richardson, Pr
Dan Richardson, VP
EMP: 5 EST: 1952
SQ FT: 4,000
SALES (est): 300K **Privately Held**
SIC: 3651 5731 8299 Household audio and video equipment; Radio, television, and electronic stores; Musical instrument lessons

(G-3830)
MANASEK ACQUISITION CO LLC
Also Called: Warner Bodies
11700 N State Road 37 (46036-9024)
PHONE..................................765 551-1600
EMP: 45 EST: 1939
SQ FT: 100,000
SALES (est): 4.78MM **Privately Held**
SIC: 3713 Truck bodies (motor vehicles)

(G-3831)
MANUFACTURED PRODUCTS INC
2700 S K St (46036-3109)
PHONE..................................765 552-2871
Eric Horn, Owner
EMP: 5 EST: 1990
SQ FT: 5,500
SALES (est): 393.53K **Privately Held**
Web: www.manufacturedproductsgroup.com
SIC: 3599 Machine shop, jobbing and repair

(G-3832)
MONOFOILUSA LLC
2635 S F St (46036-2658)
PHONE..................................317 340-9951
Nathan Richardson, CEO
EMP: 1 EST: 2015
SALES (est): 248.25K **Privately Held**
Web: www.monofoilusa.com
SIC: 2842 2879 2841 Sanitation preparations, disinfectants and deodorants; Insecticides and pesticides; Detergents, synthetic organic or inorganic alkaline

(G-3833)
PROGRESSIVE PLASTICS INC
2200 S J St (46036-2506)
PHONE..................................765 552-2004
Mike Leagre, Pr
Davis Herbert, VP
▲ EMP: 16 EST: 2004
SALES (est): 2.71MM **Privately Held**
Web: www.progressive-plastics.net
SIC: 3089 Injection molding of plastics
PA: Dunn-Rite Products, Inc.
 2200 S J St
 Elwood IN 46036

(G-3834)
RED GOLD INC
900 N D St (46036-1531)
PHONE..................................765 557-5500
EMP: 8 EST: 1934
SALES (est): 17.74K **Privately Held**
Web: www.redgoldfoods.com
SIC: 2033 Canned fruits and specialties

(G-3835)
RED GOLD INC
622 S 22nd St (46036-2518)
PHONE..................................765 557-5500
Brian Reichart, CEO
EMP: 5
SALES (corp-wide): 451.21MM **Privately Held**
Web: www.redgoldfoods.com
SIC: 2033 Tomato products, packaged in cans, jars, etc.
PA: Red Gold, Inc.
 1520 S 22nd St
 Elwood IN 46036
 765 557-5500

(G-3836)
RED GOLD INC
Also Called: Red Gold/Elwood
490 S 22nd St (46036-2514)
P.O. Box 83 (46036-0083)
PHONE..................................765 552-3386
EMP: 150
SALES (corp-wide): 431.68MM **Privately Held**
SIC: 2033 Tomato products, packaged in cans, jars, etc.
PA: Red Gold, Inc.
 1500 Tomato Country Way
 Elwood IN 46036
 765 557-5500

(G-3837)
RED GOLD INC (PA)
Also Called: Red Gold
1520 S 22nd St (46036)
P.O. Box 83 (46036)
PHONE..................................765 557-5500
◆ EMP: 200 EST: 1942
SALES (est): 451.21MM
SALES (corp-wide): 451.21MM **Privately Held**
Web: www.redgoldfoods.com

SIC: 2033 2035 Tomato products, packaged in cans, jars, etc.; Pickles, sauces, and salad dressings

(G-3838)
TERRONICS DEVELOPMENT CORP INC
7565 W 900 N (46036-8907)
PHONE..................................765 552-0808
Eduardo C Escallon, Pr
Johannes Almekinders, VP
Jennifer Swenson, Sec
EMP: 7 EST: 1984
SQ FT: 4,000
SALES (est): 1.1MM **Privately Held**
Web: www.terronics.com
SIC: 3564 Blowers and fans

(G-3839)
TRIM-A-DOOR CORPORATION
238 N 29th St (46036-1702)
PHONE..................................317 769-8746
EMP: 3
SALES (corp-wide): 4.35MM **Privately Held**
Web: www.trimadoor.com
SIC: 5031 2431 Door frames, all materials; Doors and door parts and trim, wood
PA: Trim-A-Door Corporation
 1824 N Home St
 Mishawaka IN 46545
 574 254-0300

English
Crawford County

(G-3840)
COLLUCI CONSTRUCTION-LOG HOMES
10591 Oriental Rd (47118-7515)
PHONE..................................812 843-5607
EMP: 2 EST: 1996
SALES (est): 105.69K **Privately Held**
SIC: 2452 7011 Log cabins, prefabricated, wood; Hotels and motels

(G-3841)
JIM RHODES LOGGING
2121 W State Road 62 (47118-6003)
PHONE..................................812 739-4221
Jim Rhodes, Owner
EMP: 2 EST: 2008
SALES (est): 140.36K **Privately Held**
SIC: 2411 Logging

(G-3842)
LANDMARK WOOD PRODUCTS INC
118 W Sawmill Rd (47118-6730)
P.O. Box 24 (47118-0024)
PHONE..................................812 338-2641
Terry Smith, Pr
Larry Smith, VP
Tim Smith, VP
EMP: 10 EST: 1983
SQ FT: 15,000
SALES (est): 478.89K **Privately Held**
Web: www.landmarkwood.com
SIC: 2421 Sawmills and planing mills, general

(G-3843)
MIDWEST CAVIAR LLC
439 E State Road 64 (47118-3609)
PHONE..................................812 338-3610
Vicki Cox, Owner
EMP: 4 EST: 2010
SALES (est): 241.48K **Privately Held**
Web: midwestcaviar.tripod.com

SIC: 2091 Caviar, preserved

(G-3844)
MULZER CRUSHED STONE INC
Also Called: Mulzer Crushed Stone
Old Hwy #64 E (47118)
PHONE..................................812 365-2145
Noel Kessens, Mgr
EMP: 34
SALES (corp-wide): 34.95B **Privately Held**
Web: www.mulzer.com
SIC: 1422 3274 Limestones, ground; Lime
HQ: Mulzer Crushed Stone Inc
 534 Mozart St
 Tell City IN 47586
 812 547-7921

(G-3845)
OHIO VALLEY CAVIAR
1927 E Shelton Rd (47118-6932)
PHONE..................................812 338-4367
Jessica Schigur, Owner
EMP: 2 EST: 2009
SALES (est): 245.21K **Privately Held**
SIC: 2092 Fresh or frozen packaged fish

(G-3846)
RIDDLE RIDGE WOODWORKS
1731 E Denton Rd (47118-6312)
PHONE..................................812 596-4503
EMP: 4 EST: 2012
SALES (est): 151.91K **Privately Held**
SIC: 2431 Millwork

(G-3847)
RONALD WRIGHT LOGGING LLC
61 S Pleasant Hill Rd (47118-6709)
P.O. Box 394 (47118-0394)
PHONE..................................812 338-2665
EMP: 5 EST: 1973
SALES (est): 449.8K **Privately Held**
Web: ronaldwrightlogging.wisebuyingmall.com
SIC: 2411 2421 Logging; Sawmills and planing mills, general

Etna Green
Kosciusko County

(G-3848)
FASTTIMES FABRICATION CUS
115 S Walnut St (46524-9419)
P.O. Box 210 (46524-0210)
PHONE..................................574 858-9222
Heath Roberts, Owner
EMP: 3 EST: 2007
SALES (est): 236.68K **Privately Held**
Web: www.fasttimesfabrication.com
SIC: 3441 Fabricated structural metal

(G-3849)
GULF STREAM PARTS & SERVICE
330 N Tower St (46524-9607)
PHONE..................................574 858-2850
EMP: 1 EST: 2010
SALES (est): 140.47K **Privately Held**
SIC: 3792 Travel trailers and campers

(G-3850)
STONEY RIDGS CANDLES
7630 W 640 N (46524-9534)
PHONE..................................574 453-6807
EMP: 4 EST: 2018
SALES (est): 189.1K **Privately Held**
SIC: 3999 Candles

GEOGRAPHIC SECTION

Evansville - Vanderburgh County (G-3876)

(G-3851)
WINONA POWDER COATING INC (PA)
9876 W Old Road 30 (46524-9562)
P.O. Box 170 (46524-0170)
PHONE..............................574 267-8311
Jamie Visker, *CEO*
Fred Fribley, *
▲ **EMP:** 40 **EST:** 1963
SQ FT: 25,000
SALES (est): 8.55MM
SALES (corp-wide): 8.55MM **Privately Held**
Web: www.winonapowder.com
SIC: 3479 Coating of metals and formed products

(G-3852)
WOODENWARE USA INC
9151 W 750 N (46524-9753)
PHONE..............................574 372-8400
Earl Chupp, *Prin*
EMP: 4 **EST:** 1991
SALES (est): 418.68K **Privately Held**
Web: www.woodenwareusainc.com
SIC: 2499 Woodenware, kitchen and household

Evanston
Spencer County

(G-3853)
MITCHELL L KLINE
13833 N County Road 1100 E (47531-8257)
PHONE..............................812 449-6518
Mitchell L Kline, *Prin*
EMP: 7 **EST:** 2008
SALES (est): 223.14K **Privately Held**
SIC: 2411 Logging

(G-3854)
SANDY LITTLE COAL COMPANY INC
12568 N State Road 245 (47531-8233)
P.O. Box 16 (47550-0016)
PHONE..............................812 529-8216
Don Foertsch, *Pr*
Mason Foertsch, *VP*
Linda Foertsch, *Sec*
EMP: 8 **EST:** 1974
SQ FT: 5,000
SALES (est): 928.24K **Privately Held**
SIC: 1221 Bituminous coal and lignite-surface mining

(G-3855)
STILL SAFETY PRODUCTS LLC
Also Called: Still Safety Sling
9285 N Cr600 East (47531-8197)
PHONE..............................855 249-0009
EMP: 1 **EST:** 2013
SALES (est): 55.46K **Privately Held**
SIC: 2339 7389 Aprons, except rubber or plastic: women's, misses', juniors'; Business Activities at Non-Commercial Site

Evansville
Vanderburgh County

(G-3856)
3-T CORP
Also Called: Clean Air of Evansville
2206 N Grand Ave (47711-3806)
PHONE..............................812 424-7878
Barbara Otto, *Pr*
Andrew Otto, *VP*
EMP: 12 **EST:** 1972

SQ FT: 12,000
SALES (est): 1.01MM **Privately Held**
SIC: 3564 5075 7699 Air cleaning systems; Air pollution control equipment and supplies; Industrial equipment services

(G-3857)
7R EXPRESS LLC
815 John St Ste 110 (47713-2746)
PHONE..............................833 611-3497
EMP: 1
SALES (est): 69.21K **Privately Held**
SIC: 3537 Trucks: freight, baggage, etc.: industrial, except mining

(G-3858)
A & A CUSTOM AUTOMATION INC (PA)
2125 Bergdolt Rd (47711-2845)
PHONE..............................812 464-3650
Kristie Chinn, *Pr*
EMP: 58 **EST:** 1989
SQ FT: 34,000
SALES (est): 9.45MM **Privately Held**
Web: www.aametal.com
SIC: 3544 Special dies and tools

(G-3859)
A & A PRCSION HTG COLG RFRGN L
1272 Maxwell Ave (47711-4153)
PHONE..............................812 401-1711
John Rice, *Prin*
EMP: 8 **EST:** 2013
SALES (est): 959.72K **Privately Held**
Web: www.youneedprecision.com
SIC: 3585 1711 3822 Refrigeration and heating equipment; Heating and air conditioning contractors; Air flow controllers, air conditioning and refrigeration

(G-3860)
A & AS BEAUTY BARN LLC
1127 Lincoln Ave Apt 629 (47714-1051)
PHONE..............................812 589-8559
Alina Keeney, *Managing Member*
EMP: 2 **EST:** 2020
SALES (est): 74.42K **Privately Held**
SIC: 2844 5999 Perfumes, cosmetics and other toilet preparations; Toiletries, cosmetics, and perfumes

(G-3861)
A TASTE OF COURT VALJEAN LLC
3011 Southeast Blvd (47714-4039)
PHONE..............................812 802-8584
Courtlandt Cannon Junior, *Mgr*
EMP: 1 **EST:** 2021
SALES (est): 41.75K **Privately Held**
SIC: 2099 Ready-to-eat meals, salads, and sandwiches

(G-3862)
A1 PALLETS INC
Also Called: A1 Pallet
1801 W Maryland St (47712-5337)
PHONE..............................812 425-0381
Larry Dunn, *Owner*
EMP: 5 **EST:** 1962
SQ FT: 4,000
SALES (est): 425.27K **Privately Held**
Web: www.a1palletsinc.com
SIC: 2448 Pallets, wood

(G-3863)
ABB INC
401 N Congress Ave (47715-2444)
PHONE..............................941 278-2200
EMP: 11 **EST:** 2018
SALES (est): 1.04MM **Privately Held**
Web: www.careers.abb

SIC: 3612 Transformers, except electric

(G-3864)
ABBP LLC
616 N Norman Ave (47711-5872)
PHONE..............................812 402-2000
EMP: 7 **EST:** 2007
SQ FT: 2,000
SALES (est): 949.42K **Privately Held**
SIC: 3086 Plastics foam products

(G-3865)
ABK TRACKING INC
1201 N Weinbach Ave (47711-4301)
P.O. Box 4715 (47724-0715)
PHONE..............................812 473-9554
Danny P Koester, *Pr*
Janet L Koester, *Sec*
EMP: 8 **EST:** 2010
SALES (est): 285.34K **Privately Held**
Web: www.abkkcc.com
SIC: 3663 Global positioning systems (GPS) equipment

(G-3866)
ACCLAIM GRAPHICS INC
Also Called: Print Tech
908 N Garvin St (47711-5168)
PHONE..............................812 424-5035
Joseph Birkhead, *Admn*
Joseph Birkhead, *Pr*
Kell Y Birkhead, *VP*
EMP: 5 **EST:** 1946
SQ FT: 7,600
SALES (est): 491.95K **Privately Held**
Web: www.acclaimgraphics.com
SIC: 2791 2789 2759 2752 Typesetting; Bookbinding and related work; Commercial printing, nec; Commercial printing, lithographic

(G-3867)
ACCURIDE CORPORATION
7140 Office Cir (47715-8235)
PHONE..............................812 962-5000
EMP: 152
Web: www.accuridecorp.com
SIC: 3714 Wheels, motor vehicle
HQ: Accuride Corporation
38777 6 Mile Rd Ste 410
Livonia MI 48152
812 962-5000

(G-3868)
ACCURIDE EMI LLC
7140 Office Cir (47715-8235)
PHONE..............................940 565-8505
EMP: 24 **EST:** 2009
SALES (est): 2.08MM **Privately Held**
Web: www.accuridecorp.com
SIC: 3714 3713 Motor vehicle parts and accessories; Truck and bus bodies

(G-3869)
ACE EXTRUSION LLC (PA)
14020 Highway 57 (47725-9638)
P.O. Box 6587 (47719-0587)
PHONE..............................812 868-8640
EMP: 17 **EST:** 2012
SQ FT: 20,000
SALES (est): 8.98MM
SALES (corp-wide): 8.98MM **Privately Held**
Web: www.aceextrusion.com
SIC: 3061 Mechanical rubber goods

(G-3870)
ACE EXTRUSION LLC
Also Called: Pipeconx
701 N 9th Ave (47712-5343)

PHONE..............................812 436-4840
EMP: 30
SALES (corp-wide): 8.98MM **Privately Held**
Web: www.aceextrusion.com
SIC: 3272 Pipe, concrete or lined with concrete
PA: Ace Extrusion Llc
14020 Highway 57
Evansville IN 47725
812 868-8640

(G-3871)
ACE EXTRUSION LLC
Extrusion Division
1800 W Maryland St (47712-5338)
P.O. Box 6288 (47719-0288)
PHONE..............................812 463-5230
Randolph Zahn, *Pr*
EMP: 30
SALES (corp-wide): 8.98MM **Privately Held**
Web: www.aceextrusion.com
SIC: 2891 3084 3086 Sealants; Plastics pipe; Packaging and shipping materials, foamed plastics
PA: Ace Extrusion Llc
14020 Highway 57
Evansville IN 47725
812 868-8640

(G-3872)
ACTION AMUSEMENT
1405 Allens Ln (47710-3365)
PHONE..............................812 422-9029
Jeff Monar, *Prin*
EMP: 1 **EST:** 1984
SALES (est): 69.56K **Privately Held**
SIC: 3999 Coin-operated amusement machines

(G-3873)
AD VISION GRAPHICS INC
Also Called: Zoo Zone
1820 N Hoosier Ave (47715-8542)
PHONE..............................812 476-4932
Greg Gray, *Pr*
Christina Nobles, *Mgr*
EMP: 6 **EST:** 1999
SALES (est): 473.28K **Privately Held**
Web: www.advision1.com
SIC: 3993 Signs and advertising specialties

(G-3874)
ADVANCE LEDS LLC
118 W Missouri St (47710-2150)
PHONE..............................844 815-8898
Jack Wishy, *Pr*
EMP: 1 **EST:** 2017
SALES (est): 67.86K **Privately Held**
SIC: 3646 Commercial lighting fixtures

(G-3875)
ADVANCED SIGN & LTG SVC INC
13350 N Green River Rd (47725-9768)
PHONE..............................812 430-2817
EMP: 2 **EST:** 2009
SALES (est): 113.39K **Privately Held**
SIC: 3993 Signs and advertising specialties

(G-3876)
ADVANTAGE PRINT SOLUTIONS
700 N Weinbach Ave (47711-5966)
PHONE..............................812 473-5945
EMP: 18 **EST:** 2019
SALES (est): 269.21K **Privately Held**
Web: www.advantageprintsolutionsinc.com
SIC: 2752 Commercial printing, lithographic

Evansville - Vanderburgh County (G-3877)

GEOGRAPHIC SECTION

(G-3877)
AGRISELECT EVANSVILLE LLC
11401 N Green River Rd (47725)
PHONE..................812 453-2235
Luke Snyder, *Managing Member*
David Papariella, *CFO*
EMP: 9 **EST:** 2021
SALES (est): 1.3MM **Privately Held**
SIC: 2879 Insecticides and pesticides

(G-3878)
AIRGAS USA LLC
Also Called: Airgas
2300 N Burkhardt Rd (47715-2156)
P.O. Box 5229 (47716-5229)
PHONE..................812 474-0440
Betty Slaughter, *Mgr*
EMP: 9
SALES (corp-wide): 114.13MM **Privately Held**
Web: www.airgas.com
SIC: 5169 5085 2813 Chemicals and allied products, nec; Industrial supplies; Industrial gases
HQ: Airgas Usa, Llc
  259 N Radnor Chester Rd
  Radnor PA 19087
  216 642-6600

(G-3879)
AL PERRY ENTERPRISES INC (PA)
9203 Petersburg Rd (47725-1479)
PHONE..................812 867-7727
EMP: 2 **EST:** 1993
SALES (est): 427.94K **Privately Held**
Web: www.alperry.com
SIC: 8748 5052 1241 Energy conservation consultant; Coal; Coal mining services

(G-3880)
ALL-WEATHER PRODUCTS INC
8346 Baumgart Rd (47725-1514)
PHONE..................812 867-6403
Roger Feightner, *Pr*
Juanita Feightner, *VP*
EMP: 9 **EST:** 1979
SQ FT: 13,000
SALES (est): 900.47K **Privately Held**
Web: www.allweatherproductsinc.com
SIC: 3442 5031 Storm doors or windows, metal; Doors, combination, screen-storm

(G-3881)
ALLISON QUALITY WDWKG LLC
9701 Saint Wendel Rd (47720-8563)
PHONE..................812 963-3359
Clay Allison, *Owner*
EMP: 1 **EST:** 2004
SALES (est): 171.28K **Privately Held**
SIC: 3553 Furniture makers machinery, woodworking

(G-3882)
ALTSTADT BUSINESS FORMS INC (PA)
Also Called: Allstade Business Forms
1550 Baker Ave (47710-2510)
P.O. Box 6422 (47719-0422)
PHONE..................812 425-3393
Mark Altstadt, *Pr*
Brenda Atlstadt, *VP*
EMP: 16 **EST:** 1964
SALES (est): 3.72MM
SALES (corp-wide): 3.72MM **Privately Held**
Web: www.altstadts.com
SIC: 5112 2752 5021 2761 Business forms; Forms, business: lithographed; Office furniture, nec; Manifold business forms

(G-3883)
ALVEYS SIGN CO INC
13100 Highway 57 (47725-7612)
PHONE..................812 867-2567
Kenneth Alvey, *Pr*
Helen Alvey, *
EMP: 45 **EST:** 1970
SQ FT: 51,635
SALES (est): 7.77MM **Privately Held**
Web: www.alveyssigns.com
SIC: 3993 1799 7532 7389 Electric signs; Sign installation and maintenance; Truck painting and lettering; Sign painting and lettering shop

(G-3884)
AMERICAN CO
2131 Covert Ave (47714-3709)
PHONE..................812 250-9575
EMP: 6 **EST:** 2011
SALES (est): 46.5K **Privately Held**
Web: www.nucorbuildingsystems.com
SIC: 3441 Fabricated structural metal

(G-3885)
AMERICAN CORRUGATED
3410 Claremont Ave (47712-4800)
PHONE..................812 425-4056
Robert Smock, *Mgr*
EMP: 1 **EST:** 2009
SALES (est): 77K **Privately Held**
Web: www.acm-corp.com
SIC: 2653 Boxes, corrugated: made from purchased materials

(G-3886)
AMERICAN WINDOW AND GLASS INC (PA)
2715 Lynch Rd (47711-2958)
PHONE..................812 464-9400
Jack Starks, *Pr*
Douglas Dockery, *
Ric Grant, *
Richard Grant, *
Patty Hertweck, *
EMP: 135 **EST:** 1988
SQ FT: 105,000
SALES (est): 22.94MM **Privately Held**
Web: www.americanwindowandglass.com
SIC: 3089 3442 3231 Awnings, fiberglass and plastics combination; Metal doors, sash, and trim; Products of purchased glass

(G-3887)
AMERIQUAL GROUP LLC
Also Called: Ameriqual Foods
18200 Highway 41 N (47725-9300)
PHONE..................812 867-1444
Neil Mcdonald, *CFO*
EMP: 12
SQ FT: 111,000
Web: www.ameriqual.com
SIC: 2099 Ready-to-eat meals, salads, and sandwiches
HQ: Ameriqual Group, Llc
  18200 Highway 41 N
  Evansville IN 47725
  812 867-1444

(G-3888)
AMERIQUAL GROUP LLC (DH)
Also Called: Ameriqual Packaging
18200 Highway 41 N (47725)
PHONE..................812 867-1444
Dennis Straub, *Pr*
Daniel Hermann, *Managing Member**
Eugene Aimone, *
Timothy Brauer, *
◆ **EMP:** 510 **EST:** 1987
SQ FT: 240,000
SALES (est): 253.89MM **Privately Held**
Web: www.ameriqual.com
SIC: 2099 Ready-to-eat meals, salads, and sandwiches
HQ: Ameriqual Group Holdings Llc
  18200 Highway 41 N
  Evansville IN 47725
  812 867-1300

(G-3889)
AMERLIGHT LLC (PA)
2800 Lynch Rd Ste B (47711-2928)
PHONE..................812 602-3452
James Vincent, *Managing Member*
▲ **EMP:** 17 **EST:** 2011
SQ FT: 110,000
SALES (est): 3.07MM
SALES (corp-wide): 3.07MM **Privately Held**
Web: www.amerlight.com
SIC: 3674 3646 5063 Light emitting diodes; Commercial lighting fixtures; Lighting fixtures

(G-3890)
AMROSIA METAL FABRICATION INC
1701 N Kentucky Ave (47711-3854)
PHONE..................812 425-5707
James D Burch, *Pr*
EMP: 9 **EST:** 2016
SALES (est): 150.48K **Privately Held**
SIC: 3441 Fabricated structural metal

(G-3891)
ANCHOR INDUSTRIES INC (PA)
1100 Burch Dr (47725-1702)
P.O. Box 3477 (47733-3477)
PHONE..................812 867-2421
◆ **EMP:** 88 **EST:** 1892
SALES (est): 45.75MM
SALES (corp-wide): 45.75MM **Privately Held**
Web: www.anchorinc.com
SIC: 2394 Canvas and related products

(G-3892)
ANCHOR INDUSTRIES INC
7701 Highway 41 N (47725-1700)
P.O. Box 7105 (46207-7105)
PHONE..................812 867-2421
Pete Mogavero, *CEO*
EMP: 152
SALES (corp-wide): 45.75MM **Privately Held**
Web: www.anchorinc.com
SIC: 3999 Barber and beauty shop equipment
PA: Anchor Industries Inc.
  1100 Burch Dr
  Evansville IN 47725
  812 867-2421

(G-3893)
APAR TECHNOLOGICAL INC
305 S Welworth Ave (47714-1425)
PHONE..................812 430-2025
Robert Becker, *Pr*
EMP: 1 **EST:** 2005
SALES (est): 115.28K **Privately Held**
SIC: 3441 3599 Fabricated structural metal; Machine and other job shop work

(G-3894)
APEX TOOL AND MANUFACTURING
2306 N New York Ave (47711-3934)
PHONE..................812 425-8121
Terry A Babb, *Pr*
B Jay Babb, *VP*
Susan B Babb, *Treas*
Nikki Turner, *Sec*
EMP: 28 **EST:** 1970
SQ FT: 18,000
SALES (est): 1.01MM **Privately Held**
Web: www.apextool.org
SIC: 3544 Special dies and tools

(G-3895)
APR PLASTICS INC ✪
3350 Claremont Ave (47712)
PHONE..................812 258-8888
Hyejin Bang, *Pr*
Bingchang Jia, *VP*
Jun Sheng, *CEO*
EMP: 11 **EST:** 2023
SALES (est): 255.56K **Privately Held**
SIC: 2821 Plastics materials and resins

(G-3896)
ARBEN CORPORATION
Also Called: Ameristamp Sign-A-Rama
1300 N Royal Ave (47715-7808)
PHONE..................812 477-7763
Walter A Valiant, *Pr*
Deborah A Valiant, *VP*
EMP: 20 **EST:** 1957
SQ FT: 8,400
SALES (est): 948.49K **Privately Held**
Web: www.signarama.com
SIC: 3953 3993 Marking devices; Signs, not made in custom sign painting shops

(G-3897)
ARC INDUSTRIES
615 W Virginia St (47710-1615)
PHONE..................812 471-1633
Margaret Boarman, *Pr*
◆ **EMP:** 3 **EST:** 2010
SALES (est): 248.24K **Privately Held**
Web: www.arcofevansville.org
SIC: 3999 Manufacturing industries, nec

(G-3898)
ARCPRO WELDING & PROP REPAIR
14121 Bickmeier Rd (47725-9359)
PHONE..................812 867-6383
Walter Schneider, *Pr*
EMP: 1 **EST:** 1997
SALES (est): 45.5K **Privately Held**
SIC: 7692 Welding repair

(G-3899)
ARMADA OPTICAL SERVICES INC
701 N Weinbach Ave Ste 410 (47711-5990)
PHONE..................812 476-6623
Lori L Miller, *Pr*
EMP: 12 **EST:** 1990
SQ FT: 2,800
SALES (est): 788.02K **Privately Held**
Web: www.armadaoptical.com
SIC: 3851 Eyeglasses, lenses and frames

(G-3900)
ARMOR PARENT CORP (HQ)
7140 Office Cir (47715)
PHONE..................812 962-5000
Alex Rose, *Pr*
EMP: 14 **EST:** 2016
SALES (est): 795.86MM **Privately Held**
SIC: 3714 3713 Wheel rims, motor vehicle; Truck bodies and parts
PA: Crestview Partners, L.P.
  590 Madison Ave Fl 36
  New York NY 10022

(G-3901)
ATLAS MACHINE AND SUPPLY INC
5001 Hitch Peters Rd (47711-2469)
PHONE..................812 423-7762
Todd Riley, *Mgr*
EMP: 10
SALES (corp-wide): 52.44MM **Privately Held**

GEOGRAPHIC SECTION
Evansville - Vanderburgh County (G-3926)

Web: www.atlasmachine.com
SIC: **5084** 3599 Compressors, except air conditioning; Machine shop, jobbing and repair
PA: Atlas Machine And Supply, Inc.
7000 Global Dr
Louisville KY 40258
502 584-7262

(G-3902)
AUDIENCE RESPONSE SYSTEMS INC
5611 E Morgan Ave Ste C (47715-3377)
PHONE..................................812 479-7507
EMP: 11 **EST:** 1988
SALES (est): 991.78K
SALES (corp-wide): 991.78K **Privately Held**
Web: www.audienceresponse.com
SIC: **3651** Audio electronic systems
PA: Campus Group Companies, Inc.
42 Oak Ave
Tuckahoe NY
914 961-1900

(G-3903)
AUTOMATED WELDING SERVICES INC
1401 Wimberg Rd (47710-4539)
PHONE..................................812 464-8784
Jeffrey W Wampler, *Prin*
EMP: 1 **EST:** 2002
SALES (est): 84.75K **Privately Held**
SIC: **7692** Welding repair

(G-3904)
AUTOMATION ENCLOSURES LLC
815 John St Ste 140 (47713-2746)
PHONE..................................812 453-8480
EMP: 7 **EST:** 2014
SALES (est): 879.51K **Privately Held**
Web: www.automationenclosures.com
SIC: **3496** Miscellaneous fabricated wire products

(G-3905)
AZTECA MILLING LP
Also Called: Azteca Milling Co
15700 Highway 41 N (47725-8525)
PHONE..................................812 867-3190
EMP: 1
Web: www.gruma.com
SIC: **2041** Flour and other grain mill products
HQ: Azteca Milling, L.P.
5601 Executive Dr Ste 650
Irving TX 75038
956 383-4911

(G-3906)
B&M PLASTICS INC
2300 Lynch Rd (47711-2951)
PHONE..................................812 422-0888
William Gillenwater Iii, *Prin*
EMP: 2 **EST:** 2008
SALES (est): 234.4K **Privately Held**
Web: www.bmplastics.com
SIC: **3089** Injection molding of plastics

(G-3907)
BABCOCKS COATINGS LLC
8410 Kneer Rd (47720-7410)
PHONE..................................812 624-2120
Tim Babcocks, *Owner*
EMP: 1 **EST:** 2004
SALES (est): 63.6K **Privately Held**
SIC: **3479** Coating of metals and formed products

(G-3908)
BAILEY TOOLS & SUPPLY INC
5716 E Morgan Ave Ste 9 (47715-2398)
PHONE..................................502 635-6348
Jims Keepes, *Mgr*
EMP: 4
SALES (corp-wide): 4.68MM **Privately Held**
Web: www.baileysafety.com
SIC: **3541** Electron-discharge metal cutting machine tools
PA: Bailey Tools & Supply, Inc.
1338 S Shelby St
Louisville KY 40217
502 635-6348

(G-3909)
BARGER ENGINEERING INC
2116 Lincoln Ave (47714-1600)
P.O. Box 2507 (47728-0507)
PHONE..................................812 476-3077
Gloria Barger, *Pr*
Hubert S Barger, *Pr*
EMP: 5 **EST:** 1960
SQ FT: 2,200
SALES (est): 867.49K **Privately Held**
Web: www.bargerengineering.com
SIC: **1311** 8711 1382 Crude petroleum production; Petroleum engineering; Oil and gas exploration services

(G-3910)
BARTONS SCREEN PRINTING
1938 N Green River Rd (47715-1908)
PHONE..................................812 422-4303
Larry Barton Junior, *Owner*
EMP: 1 **EST:** 2005
SALES (est): 123.4K **Privately Held**
SIC: **2759** Screen printing

(G-3911)
BARTONS TEEZ
1938 N Green River Rd (47715-1908)
PHONE..................................812 422-4303
EMP: 4 **EST:** 2019
SALES (est): 73.28K **Privately Held**
SIC: **2759** Commercial printing, nec

(G-3912)
BASIN ENERGY INC
514 Se 1st St (47713-1008)
PHONE..................................812 983-2519
Thomas Sawyer, *Pr*
EMP: 1 **EST:** 2005
SALES (est): 197.92K **Privately Held**
SIC: **1381** Service well drilling

(G-3913)
BELCHER PRINTING SERVICES
11437 Middle Mount Vernon Rd (47712-8402)
PHONE..................................812 305-1093
EMP: 1 **EST:** 2010
SALES (est): 61.87K **Privately Held**
SIC: **2752** Commercial printing, lithographic

(G-3914)
BENSON TOWER LLC
Also Called: Radio and Broadcasting Towers
10833 Sunset Dr (47712-9561)
PHONE..................................270 577-7598
Brandon Benson, *Admn*
EMP: 3 **EST:** 2019
SALES (est): 66.15K **Privately Held**
SIC: **1799** 1623 3663 Service and repair of broadcasting stations; Communication line and transmission tower construction; Radio and t.v. communications equipment

(G-3915)
BENTHALL BROS INC (PA)
15 Read St (47710-1399)
PHONE..................................800 488-5995
Dennis M Benthall, *Pr*
Richard L Zirkle, *Pr*
EMP: 20 **EST:** 1943
SQ FT: 23,000
SALES (est): 10.34MM
SALES (corp-wide): 10.34MM **Privately Held**
Web: www.benthallbros.com
SIC: **5031** 3496 3444 Doors, combination, screen-storm; Miscellaneous fabricated wire products; Sheet metalwork

(G-3916)
BERENDSEN INC
Also Called: Evansville Sales
460 E Sycamore St (47713-2776)
PHONE..................................812 423-6468
Carolyn Fischer, *Brnch Mgr*
EMP: 4
Web: www.bfpna.com
SIC: **5084** 3535 Hydraulic systems equipment and supplies; Pneumatic tube conveyor systems
HQ: Berendsen, Inc.
401 S Boston Ave Ste 1200
Tulsa OK 74103
918 592-3781

(G-3917)
BERRY FILM PRODUCTS CO INC
Also Called: Packerware
101 Oakley St (47710-1237)
PHONE..................................812 306-2690
EMP: 112 **EST:** 1986
SALES (est): 8.79MM **Publicly Held**
Web: www.berryglobal.com
SIC: **3089** Plastics containers, except foam
PA: Berry Global Group, Inc.
101 Oakley St
Evansville IN 47710

(G-3918)
BERRY GLOBAL INC (HQ)
Also Called: Berry Plastics
101 Oakley St (47710)
P.O. Box 959 (47706)
PHONE..................................812 424-2904
Stephen E Sterrett, *Ch Bd*
Kevin J Kwilinski, *
Mark Miles, *
Rodgers Greenawalt, *
Jason Greene, *
◆ **EMP:** 1200 **EST:** 1990
SALES (est): 3.43B **Publicly Held**
Web: www.berryglobal.com
SIC: **3089** 3081 Plastics containers, except foam; Unsupported plastics film and sheet
PA: Berry Global Group, Inc.
101 Oakley St
Evansville IN 47710

(G-3919)
BERRY GLOBAL INC
3245 Kansas Rd (47725-9757)
PHONE..................................812 867-6671
Bob Fella, *Mgr*
EMP: 48
Web: www.berryglobal.com
SIC: **3089** 3081 Bottle caps, molded plastics; Unsupported plastics film and sheet
HQ: Berry Global, Inc.
101 Oakley St
Evansville IN 47710

(G-3920)
BERRY GLOBAL ESCROW CORP
101 Oakley St (47710-1237)
P.O. Box 959 (47706-0959)
PHONE..................................812 424-2904
EMP: 9 **EST:** 2009
SALES (est): 88.97K **Privately Held**
SIC: **3089** Plastics containers, except foam

(G-3921)
BERRY GLOBAL GROUP INC (PA)
Also Called: BERRY
101 Oakley St (47710)
P.O. Box 959 (47706)
PHONE..................................812 424-2904
Kevin J Kwilinski, *CEO*
Mark W Miles, *CFO*
Jason K Greene, *CLO*
James M Till, *CAO*
▼ **EMP:** 2000 **EST:** 1967
SALES (est): 12.66B **Publicly Held**
Web: www.berryglobal.com
SIC: **3089** 3085 2673 3081 Plastics containers, except foam; Plastics bottles; Trash bags (plastic film): made from purchased materials; Plastics film and sheet

(G-3922)
BERRY PLAS TECHNICAL SVCS INC
101 Oakley St (47710-1237)
PHONE..................................812 424-2904
EMP: 10 **EST:** 1999
SALES (est): 279.82K **Privately Held**
SIC: **3089** Plastics products, nec

(G-3923)
BERRY PLASTICS ESCROW CORP
101 Oakley St (47710)
PHONE..................................812 424-2904
EMP: 13 **EST:** 2012
SALES (est): 4.81MM **Publicly Held**
Web: www.berryglobal.com
SIC: **3089** Bottle caps, molded plastics
HQ: Berry Global, Inc.
101 Oakley St
Evansville IN 47710

(G-3924)
BERRY PLASTICS GROUP INC
101 Oakley St (47710-1252)
PHONE..................................812 424-2904
EMP: 43 **EST:** 2006
SALES (est): 7.33MM **Privately Held**
Web: www.berryglobal.com
SIC: **3089** Plastics containers, except foam

(G-3925)
BERRY PLASTICS IK LLC
101 Oakley St (47710-1252)
PHONE..................................641 648-5047
Ira Boots, *Pr*
▲ **EMP:** 166 **EST:** 1992
SQ FT: 96,000
SALES (est): 22.22MM **Publicly Held**
Web: www.berryglobal.com
SIC: **3089** 2396 Injection molding of plastics; Automotive and apparel trimmings
HQ: Berry Global, Inc.
101 Oakley St
Evansville IN 47710

(G-3926)
BERRY PLASTICS OPCO INC
9845 Hedden Rd (47725-8905)
PHONE..................................812 402-2903
EMP: 2
Web: www.berryglobal.com
SIC: **3089** Bottle caps, molded plastics
HQ: Berry Plastics Opco, Inc.
101 Oakley St

Evansville - Vanderburgh County (G-3927)   GEOGRAPHIC SECTION

Evansville IN 47710

(G-3927)
BERRY PLASTICS OPCO INC (DH)
101 Oakley St (47710-1252)
PHONE..................................812 424-2904
EMP: 39 **EST:** 2002
SALES (est): 54.83MM **Publicly Held**
Web: www.berryglobal.com
SIC: 3089 Bottle caps, molded plastics
HQ: Berry Global, Inc.
  101 Oakley St
  Evansville IN 47710

(G-3928)
BEST-ONE LT LLC
6640 Toney Ln (47715-1774)
P.O. Box 187 (46772-0187)
PHONE..................................812 471-8473
Craig Morphett, *Managing Member*
EMP: 5 **EST:** 2002
SALES (est): 9.55MM **Privately Held**
Web: www.bestonetire.com
SIC: 5531 7534 Automotive tires; Tire repair shop
PA: Best One Tire & Service Of Evansville, Inc.
  1241 Tutor Ln
  Evansville IN 47715

(G-3929)
BETTER BUILT BARNS INC
4415 E Morgan Ave (47715-2253)
PHONE..................................812 477-2001
Terry Turpin, *Pr*
Frances Turpin, *VP*
EMP: 2 **EST:** 1997
SALES (est): 210K **Privately Held**
Web: www.betterbuiltbarns.org
SIC: 2421 Outdoor wood structural products

(G-3930)
BIG B DISTRIBUTORS INC
2727 N Kentucky Ave (47711-6203)
P.O. Box 996 (47706-0996)
PHONE..................................812 425-5235
David Alan Clark, *Pr*
David Alan Clark Presdient, *Prin*
Derek Clark, *VP*
▲ **EMP:** 10 **EST:** 1963
SQ FT: 2,000
SALES (est): 1.26MM
SALES (corp-wide): 41.27MM **Privately Held**
Web: www.bigbbarbecue.com
SIC: 2013 2035 Canned meats (except baby food), from purchased meat; Pickles, sauces, and salad dressings
PA: Clark Restaurant Service Inc.
  2803 Tamarack Dr
  Owensboro KY 42301
  270 684-1469

(G-3931)
BIG CONE INC
102 W Franklin St (47710-1312)
PHONE..................................812 424-1416
Kay A Mcatee, *Pr*
Mike Mcatee, *VP*
EMP: 3 **EST:** 2010
SALES (est): 257.34K **Privately Held**
Web: www.zestoonfranklin.com
SIC: 2024 Ice cream, bulk

(G-3932)
BIG STICK SOFTWARE
3415 E Boonville New Harmony Rd (47725)
PHONE..................................812 867-0694
Scott Titzer, *Prin*
EMP: 1 **EST:** 2003
SALES (est): 69.15K **Privately Held**

SIC: 7372 Prepackaged software

(G-3933)
BLACK AND GOLD ENERGY LLC
514 Se 1st St (47713-1008)
PHONE..................................812 618-6744
EMP: 2 **EST:** 2021
SALES (est): 75.37K **Privately Held**
Web: www.blackandgoldenergy.com
SIC: 1382 Oil and gas exploration services

(G-3934)
BLACK EQUIPMENT COMPANY S INC
1187 Burch Dr (47725-1701)
PHONE..................................812 477-6481
Jay D Bonnell, *Ex Dir*
EMP: 106 **EST:** 2016
SALES (est): 12.44MM **Privately Held**
Web: www.blackequipment.com
SIC: 5084 7694 7699 Lift trucks and parts; Motor repair services; Industrial truck repair

(G-3935)
BLUE RIVER TIMBER LLC
2997 Gethsemane Church Rd (47712)
PHONE..................................812 291-0411
Sandy Meyer, *Prin*
EMP: 7 **EST:** 2010
SALES (est): 151.65K **Privately Held**
SIC: 2411 Timber, cut at logging camp

(G-3936)
BMG INC
Also Called: Thrust Industries
10334 Hedden Rd (47725-8923)
PHONE..................................812 437-3643
EMP: 1
SALES (corp-wide): 1.03MM **Privately Held**
Web: www.thrustin.com
SIC: 3544 Special dies and tools
PA: Bmg, Inc.
  1601 N 1st Ave
  Evansville IN
  812 401-5660

(G-3937)
BODY PANELS CO
Also Called: BODY PANELS CO
1101 N Governor St (47711-5069)
PHONE..................................812 962-6262
Mrk Cowan, *Brnch Mgr*
EMP: 15
SALES (corp-wide): 4.37MM **Privately Held**
Web: www.bodypanelsco.com
SIC: 3465 Fenders, automobile: stamped or pressed metal
PA: Body Panels Company Llc
  2282 Whitten Rd
  Memphis TN
  901 372-6964

(G-3938)
BOEKE ROAD BAPTIST CHURCH INC
Also Called: Faith Music Missions
2601 S Boeke Rd (47714-4933)
P.O. Box 2463 (47728-0463)
PHONE..................................812 479-5342
Gayle Russ, *Religious Leader*
Gayle Russ, *Prin*
Pastor Ed Russ, *Prin*
EMP: 7 **EST:** 1972
SALES (est): 363.69K **Privately Held**
Web: www.boekeroadbaptist.org
SIC: 8661 3652 8211 Baptist Church; Magnetic tape (audio): prerecorded; Private combined elementary and secondary school

(G-3939)
BONDLINE ADHESIVES INC
500 N Woods Ave (47712-6448)
PHONE..................................812 423-4651
Diane D Fisher, *CEO*
Donald Berberich, *Stockholder*
EMP: 10 **EST:** 1966
SQ FT: 8,650
SALES (est): 1.22MM **Privately Held**
Web: www.bondline.net
SIC: 2891 2851 Adhesives; Paints and allied products

(G-3940)
BOOTZ MANUFACTURING CO LLC
Also Called: Bootz Industries
1600 N 1st Ave (47710-2708)
PHONE..................................812 423-5019
Peter J Desocio, *Pr*
EMP: 7
SALES (corp-wide): 582.45MM **Privately Held**
Web: www.bootz.com
SIC: 3431 Bathtubs: enameled iron, cast iron, or pressed metal
HQ: Bootz Manufacturing Company, Llc
  1400 Park St
  Evansville IN 47710
  812 423-5401

(G-3941)
BOOTZ MANUFACTURING CO LLC (HQ)
Also Called: Bootz Industries
1400 Park St (47710-2258)
P.O. Box 18010 (47719-1010)
PHONE..................................812 423-5401
Peter J Desocio, *Pr*
Thomas H Bootz, *VP*
Bill Weiman, *VP Fin*
◆ **EMP:** 20 **EST:** 1937
SQ FT: 125,000
SALES (est): 48.44MM
SALES (corp-wide): 582.45MM **Privately Held**
Web: www.bootz.com
SIC: 3431 Bathtubs: enameled iron, cast iron, or pressed metal
PA: American Bath Group, Llc
  500 E Border St
  Arlington TX 76010
  731 925-7656

(G-3942)
BOOTZ MANUFACTURING CO LLC
Also Called: Bootz Plumbing
2301 W Maryland St (47714-5301)
P.O. Box 18010 (47719-1010)
PHONE..................................812 425-4646
Jim Poor, *Mgr*
EMP: 103
SALES (corp-wide): 582.45MM **Privately Held**
Web: www.bootz.com
SIC: 4225 3432 3431 3261 General warehousing and storage; Plumbing fixture fittings and trim; Metal sanitary ware; Vitreous plumbing fixtures
HQ: Bootz Manufacturing Company, Llc
  1400 Park St
  Evansville IN 47710
  812 423-5401

(G-3943)
BOYER ENTERPRISES INC
Also Called: Soltek
12311 Edgewater Dr (47720-7911)
PHONE..................................812 773-3295
Steven D Boyer, *Pr*
EMP: 2 **EST:** 1996
SALES (est): 247.61K **Privately Held**

SIC: 3651 Audio electronic systems

(G-3944)
BPREX BRAZIL HOLDING INC
101 Oakley St (47710-1237)
PHONE..................................812 306-2764
EMP: 26 **EST:** 2001
SALES (est): 3.26MM **Publicly Held**
SIC: 3089 Plastics products, nec
PA: Berry Global Group, Inc.
  101 Oakley St
  Evansville IN 47710

(G-3945)
BPREX CLOSURE SYSTEMS LLC
101 Oakley St (47710-1237)
P.O. Box 959 (47706-0959)
PHONE..................................812 424-2904
▼ **EMP:** 19 **EST:** 2011
SALES (est): 7.22MM **Publicly Held**
SIC: 3089 Bottle caps, molded plastics
HQ: Berry Global, Inc.
  101 Oakley St
  Evansville IN 47710

(G-3946)
BPREX CLOSURES LLC (DH)
101 Oakley St (47710-1237)
P.O. Box 959 (47706-0959)
PHONE..................................812 424-2904
James M Kratochvil, *
EMP: 50 **EST:** 2011
SALES (est): 128.07MM **Publicly Held**
Web: www.berryglobal.com
SIC: 3089 Bottle caps, molded plastics
HQ: Berry Global, Inc.
  101 Oakley St
  Evansville IN 47710

(G-3947)
BPREX CLOSURES LLC
Also Called: Manufacturing Facility
3245 Kansas Rd (47725-9757)
PHONE..................................812 867-6671
Leslie De Walle, *Brnch Mgr*
EMP: 126
Web: www.berryglobal.com
SIC: 3089 Bottle caps, molded plastics
HQ: Bprex Closures, Llc
  101 Oakley St
  Evansville IN 47710
  812 424-2904

(G-3948)
BPREX HEALTHCARE PACKAGING INC
101 Oakley St (47710-1237)
PHONE..................................812 424-2904
EMP: 13 **EST:** 2020
SALES (est): 4.45MM **Publicly Held**
SIC: 3089 Plastics containers, except foam
PA: Berry Global Group, Inc.
  101 Oakley St
  Evansville IN 47710

(G-3949)
BRACKETT HEATING & AC INC
5233 Old Boonville Hwy (47715-2124)
PHONE..................................812 476-1138
Wayman E Brackett, *CEO*
David Brackett, *Pr*
Carla Boulware, *VP*
Darlene Brackett, *Sec*
EMP: 23 **EST:** 1943
SQ FT: 9,000
SALES (est): 2.15MM **Privately Held**
Web: www.brackettheatingandair.com
SIC: 1711 3444 Warm air heating and air conditioning contractor; Sheet metalwork

GEOGRAPHIC SECTION
Evansville - Vanderburgh County (G-3974)

(G-3950)
BRAKE SUPPLY COMPANY INC (HQ)
Also Called: Continental Advantage Eqp
5501 Foundation Blvd (47725)
PHONE.................812 467-1000
◆ **EMP:** 185 **EST:** 1946
SALES (est): 89.47MM
SALES (corp-wide): 915.49MM Privately Held
Web: www.brake.com
SIC: 5082 5084 5088 5013 Mining machinery and equipment, except petroleum; Industrial machinery and equipment; Marine propulsion machinery and equipment; Truck parts and accessories
PA: Koch Enterprises, Inc.
14 South Eleventh Avenue
Evansville IN 47712
812 465-9800

(G-3951)
BRIDGESTONE RET OPERATIONS LLC
Also Called: Firestone
4611 Washington Ave (47714-0896)
PHONE.................812 477-8818
James Decamps, *Mgr*
EMP: 9
Web: www.bridgestoneamericas.com
SIC: 5531 7534 Automotive tires; Rebuilding and retreading tires
HQ: Bridgestone Retail Operations, Llc
200 4th Ave S Ste 100
Nashville TN 37201
630 259-9000

(G-3952)
BRIDGESTONE RET OPERATIONS LLC
Also Called: Firestone
4401 N 1st Ave (47710-3621)
PHONE.................812 423-4451
Don Calloway, *Mgr*
EMP: 10
Web: www.bridgestoneamericas.com
SIC: 5531 7534 Automotive tires; Tire repair shop
HQ: Bridgestone Retail Operations, Llc
200 4th Ave S Ste 100
Nashville TN 37201
630 259-9000

(G-3953)
BRIGGS EXPLORATION PROD CO LLC
4424 Vogel Rd Ste 404 (47715-9003)
PHONE.................812 249-0564
Brandon Renner, *Admn*
EMP: 7 **EST:** 2015
SALES (est): 409.09K Privately Held
SIC: 1311 Crude petroleum production

(G-3954)
BRINKER MFG JEWELERS INC
111 S Green River Rd (47715-7338)
PHONE.................812 476-0651
Roland Brinker, *Pr*
Eula Jeanette Brinker, *Sec*
Dean Brinker, *VP*
EMP: 18 **EST:** 1972
SQ FT: 7,000
SALES (est): 2.53MM Privately Held
Web: www.brinkersjewelers.com
SIC: 5944 3911 Jewelry, precious stones and precious metals; Jewelry apparel

(G-3955)
BRISTOL MYERS
2400 W Lloyd Expy (47712-5095)
PHONE.................812 428-1927
EMP: 16 **EST:** 2016
SALES (est): 678.58K Privately Held
Web: www.bms.com
SIC: 2834 Pharmaceutical preparations

(G-3956)
BRISTOL-MYERS SQUIBB COMPANY
Also Called: Bristol-Myers Squibb
7503 Highway 57 (47725)
PHONE.................812 429-5505
Steven A Wolf, *Mgr*
EMP: 12
SALES (corp-wide): 45.01B Publicly Held
Web: www.bms.com
SIC: 2834 Pharmaceutical preparations
PA: Bristol-Myers Squibb Company
Route 206/Prvince Line Rd
Princeton NJ 08540
609 252-4621

(G-3957)
BURKERT-WALTON INC
1561 Allens Ln (47710-3370)
P.O. Box 4345 (47724-0345)
PHONE.................812 425-7157
William Heierman, *Pr*
Daniel E Heierman, *Sec*
EMP: 5 **EST:** 1906
SQ FT: 6,800
SALES (est): 486.4K Privately Held
Web: www.burkertwalton.net
SIC: 2752 2759 2732 Offset printing; Letterpress printing; Pamphlets: printing and binding, not published on site

(G-3958)
C & K UNITED SHTMTL & MECH
2805 Lincoln Ave Ste C (47714-1753)
P.O. Box 16095 (47716-1095)
PHONE.................812 423-5090
Maurice E Coates Junior, *Pr*
Maurice Coates, *
Pamela Rowe, *
Catherine Beckley, *
EMP: 30 **EST:** 1997
SQ FT: 4,500
SALES (est): 4.94MM Privately Held
Web: www.ckunited.com
SIC: 1711 1761 3444 5033 Mechanical contractor; Sheet metal work, nec; Sheet metalwork; Siding, except wood

(G-3959)
C & L SHEET METAL LLC
2263 E Tennessee St (47711-4837)
PHONE.................812 449-9126
Lyman Matherly, *Admn*
EMP: 8 **EST:** 2010
SALES (est): 697.97K Privately Held
SIC: 3444 Sheet metalwork

(G-3960)
CANVAS & CONVERSATION LLC
8515 Edinborough Rd (47725-6535)
PHONE.................812 425-5960
Willard Jones, *Prin*
EMP: 4 **EST:** 2010
SALES (est): 42K Privately Held
Web: www.canvasandconversation.com
SIC: 2211 Canvas

(G-3961)
CAPITAL TECH SOLUTIONS LLC
1112 S Villa Dr (47714-3248)
PHONE.................812 303-4357
Maverick Taylor, *Owner*
EMP: 11 **EST:** 2010
SALES (est): 1.51MM Privately Held
Web: www.capitaltechnologysolutions.com
SIC: 3823 Temperature measurement instruments, industrial

(G-3962)
CAPTIVE HOLDINGS LLC
101 Oakley St (47710-1237)
P.O. Box 959 (47706-0959)
PHONE.................812 424-2904
Irag Boots, *Prin*
EMP: 89 **EST:** 2004
SALES (est): 6.71MM Publicly Held
Web: www.berryglobal.com
SIC: 3089 Battery cases, plastics or plastics combination
HQ: Berry Global, Inc.
101 Oakley St
Evansville IN 47710

(G-3963)
CAPTIVE PLASTICS LLC (DH)
101 Oakley St (47710-1237)
PHONE.................812 424-2904
John Dezio, *COO*
Rick Carroll, *
Rolland Strasser, *
◆ **EMP:** 170 **EST:** 1969
SQ FT: 228,000
SALES (est): 183.92MM Publicly Held
Web: www.berryglobal.com
SIC: 3089 Plastics containers, except foam
HQ: Berry Global, Inc.
101 Oakley St
Evansville IN 47710

(G-3964)
CARLA CLARK
2507 Graham Ave (47714-3933)
PHONE.................812 598-4687
Carla Clark, *Owner*
EMP: 1
SALES (est): 65.99K Privately Held
SIC: 3999 Hair and hair-based products

(G-3965)
CASTERS IN MOTION USA LTD LLC
1513 N Cullen Ave (47715-2332)
PHONE.................812 437-4627
John W Smith, *Managing Member*
EMP: 4 **EST:** 2011
SALES (est): 253.56K Privately Held
Web: www.castersinmotion.com
SIC: 3562 Casters

(G-3966)
CATHOLIC PRESS OF EVANSVILLE
Also Called: Message The
4200 N Kentucky Ave (47711-2752)
P.O. Box 4169 (47724-0169)
PHONE.................812 424-5536
Tim Lillley, *Dir*
EMP: 5 **EST:** 1970
SALES (est): 447.77K Privately Held
Web: www.evdiomessage.org
SIC: 2711 8661 Newspapers: publishing only, not printed on site; Nonchurch religious organizations

(G-3967)
CELANESE CORPORATION
2300 Lynch Rd (47711-2951)
PHONE.................812 421-8900
EMP: 4
SALES (corp-wide): 10.94B Publicly Held
Web: www.celanese.com
SIC: 2819 Industrial inorganic chemicals, nec
PA: Celanese Corporation
222 Las Clnas Blvd W Ste
Irving TX 75039
877 295-0004

(G-3968)
CHAMP CONVERTERS INCORPORATED
1914 N Denby Ave (47711-3822)
PHONE.................812 424-2602
Kristene Miller, *CEO*
Steven Graves, *CFO*
EMP: 5 **EST:** 2011
SALES (est): 497.84K Privately Held
Web: www.champconverters.com
SIC: 3566 Speed changers, drives, and gears

(G-3969)
CHAMP TORQUE CONVERTERS INC
Also Called: Champ Converters
1914 N Denby Ave (47711-3822)
PHONE.................812 424-2602
Mike Mcgregor, *Pr*
Kirk Knight, *Pr*
Susan Knight, *VP*
EMP: 5 **EST:** 1960
SQ FT: 2,000
SALES (est): 489.84K Privately Held
Web: www.champconverters.com
SIC: 7539 3566 Torque converter repair, automotive; Torque converters, except auto

(G-3970)
CHAOS MACHINE DIVISION INC
424 N Willow Rd (47711-5761)
P.O. Box 4917 (47724-0917)
PHONE.................812 306-7380
Cameron Hadley, *CEO*
EMP: 1 **EST:** 2009
SALES (est): 140.21K Privately Held
Web: www.chaosmachinedivision.com
SIC: 3599 Machine shop, jobbing and repair

(G-3971)
CHICKEN AND SALSA INC
1513 S Green River Rd (47715-5659)
PHONE.................812 480-6580
Jose M Mosqueda Lopez, *Pr*
EMP: 7 **EST:** 2015
SALES (est): 150.9K Privately Held
SIC: 2099 Dips, except cheese and sour cream based

(G-3972)
CLASSIC INDUSTRIES INC
2308 Commercial Ct (47720-1328)
PHONE.................812 421-4006
Tom Buskavitz, *Pr*
Diane Buskavitz, *Sec*
EMP: 6 **EST:** 1992
SQ FT: 2,400
SALES (est): 944.93K Privately Held
Web: www.classicind.net
SIC: 3312 Tool and die steel

(G-3973)
CLOUD DEFENSIVE LLC
6045 Wedeking Ave (47715)
PHONE.................812 646-1762
Amy Tenbarge, *CEO*
Joel Epley, *
EMP: 30 **EST:** 2013
SALES (est): 1.17MM Privately Held
SIC: 3648 Flashlights

(G-3974)
COCA-COLA CONSOLIDATED INC
Also Called: Coca-Cola
3223 Interstate Dr (47715-1780)
PHONE.................812 228-3200
Johnnie Palmer, *Rgnl Mgr*
EMP: 137
SALES (corp-wide): 6.65B Publicly Held
Web: www.cokeconsolidated.com

Evansville - Vanderburgh County (G-3975) GEOGRAPHIC SECTION

SIC: 2086 Bottled and canned soft drinks
PA: Coca-Cola Consolidated, Inc.
4100 Coca-Cola Plz
Charlotte NC 28211
980 392-8298

(G-3975)
COLORMAX DIGITAL IMAGING INC (PA)
Also Called: Colormax Imaging
626 Court St (47708-1342)
PHONE..................812 477-3805
David Odell, Pr
Odell Virginia, Sec
EMP: 10 EST: 1978
SQ FT: 2,000
SALES (est): 2.27MM
SALES (corp-wide): 2.27MM Privately Held
Web: www.colormaxdigital.com
SIC: 2711 2752 Commercial printing and newspaper publishing combined; Commercial printing, lithographic

(G-3976)
COMMERCIAL COATINGS ASSOC LLC
800 E Oregon St (47711-5112)
P.O. Box 2493 (47728-0493)
PHONE..................812 773-3526
Kevin Casagrand, Prin
EMP: 9 EST: 2017
SALES (est): 953.65K Privately Held
Web: www.wecoatyourroof.com
SIC: 3479 Metal coating and allied services

(G-3977)
COMPOSITES UNLIMITED
1250 S Green River Rd (47715)
PHONE..................812 475-8621
EMP: 6 EST: 2019
SALES (est): 222.5K Privately Held
Web: www.compositesunlimitedllc.com
SIC: 3728 Aircraft parts and equipment, nec

(G-3978)
CONCRETE MONKEY STUDIOS LLC
236 Calle Del Prado (47712-2733)
P.O. Box 6021 (47719-0021)
PHONE..................812 630-2339
EMP: 1 EST: 2013
SALES (est): 42.75K Privately Held
SIC: 7371 3299 Computer software development; Architectural sculptures: gypsum, clay, papier mache, etc.

(G-3979)
CONCRETE SUPPLY LLC (PA)
4300 Vogel Rd (47715-2220)
PHONE..................812 474-6715
Murl Powell, *
EMP: 25 EST: 1935
SALES (est): 4.91MM
SALES (corp-wide): 4.91MM Privately Held
Web: www.jhrudolph.com
SIC: 3272 3273 Concrete products, nec; Ready-mixed concrete

(G-3980)
CONNECTONS SIGN LNGAGE INTRPRT
4500 Taylor Ave (47714-0879)
P.O. Box 14492 (47728-6492)
PHONE..................812 449-7140
EMP: 1 EST: 2007
SALES (est): 119.16K Privately Held
SIC: 3993 Signs and advertising specialties

(G-3981)
CONSOLIDATED RECYCLING CO INC
2406 Lynch Rd (47711-2953)
PHONE..................812 547-7951
EMP: 60
Web: www.chem-group.com
SIC: 2899 Oil treating compounds

(G-3982)
CONSTELLATION MOLD INC
4825 Hitch Peters Rd (47711-2481)
PHONE..................812 424-5338
Donald Kappert, Pr
Loretta Kappert, VP
◆ EMP: 18 EST: 1981
SQ FT: 26,500
SALES (est): 485.92K Privately Held
Web: www.constmold.com
SIC: 3544 Industrial molds

(G-3983)
CORE MINERALS OPERATING CO INC
25 Nw Riverside Dr Ste 310 (47708-1211)
P.O. Box 581 (62439-0581)
PHONE..................812 759-6950
James P Rode, Pr
John Gasser, CFO
Michael Mclear, Ex VP
EMP: 8 EST: 2006
SALES (est): 2.03MM Privately Held
Web: www.coreoperating.com
SIC: 1382 Oil and gas exploration services

(G-3984)
CORR-WOOD MANUFACTURING INC
10501 Hedden Rd (47725-8928)
PHONE..................812 867-0700
Dorothy Moors, Pr
EMP: 8 EST: 1973
SQ FT: 17,500
SALES (est): 364.24K Privately Held
Web: www.corrwoodmfg.com
SIC: 2499 2448 2449 Reels, plywood; Pallets, wood; Containers, plywood and veneer wood

(G-3985)
COUNTER DESIGN CO INC
2381 N Cullen Ave (47715-2185)
PHONE..................812 477-1243
Alvin C Tretter, Pr
EMP: 40 EST: 1976
SQ FT: 30,000
SALES (est): 3.03MM Privately Held
Web: www.counterdesignco.com
SIC: 2434 Wood kitchen cabinets

(G-3986)
COUNTRYSIDE PROPERTY LLC
1033 E Walnut St (47714-1039)
PHONE..................800 711-5926
George Madison, Managing Member
EMP: 1 EST: 2018
SALES (est): 240.88K Privately Held
SIC: 6531 1389 Real estate leasing and rentals; Construction, repair, and dismantling services

(G-3987)
COVALNCE SPCALTY ADHESIVES LLC (DH)
101 Oakley St (47710-1237)
PHONE..................812 424-2904
Thomas Salmon, Pr
▼ EMP: 500 EST: 2006
SALES (est): 478.97MM Publicly Held
Web: www.berryglobal.com
SIC: 2891 Adhesives
HQ: Berry Global, Inc.
101 Oakley St
Evansville IN 47710

(G-3988)
COVALNCE SPCIALTY COATINGS LLC (DH)
Also Called: Covalence Coated Products
101 Oakley St (47710-1237)
PHONE..................812 424-2904
Jeffrey D Thompson, Pr
◆ EMP: 50 EST: 2006
SALES (est): 135.45MM Publicly Held
Web: www.berryglobal.com
SIC: 2672 Coated paper, except photographic, carbon, or abrasive
HQ: Berry Global, Inc.
101 Oakley St
Evansville IN 47710

(G-3989)
CP POLYMER SOLUTIONS LLC
2301 Saint Joseph Ind Park Dr (47720-1250)
PHONE..................812 426-1350
Ben Schmidt, Managing Member
EMP: 8 EST: 2019
SALES (est): 477.45K Privately Held
SIC: 2295 Resin or plastic coated fabrics

(G-3990)
CPI HOLDING CORPORATION
101 Oakley St (47710-1237)
PHONE..................812 424-2904
EMP: 16 EST: 2020
SALES (est): 3.89MM Publicly Held
SIC: 3089 Plastics containers, except foam
PA: Berry Global Group, Inc.
101 Oakley St
Evansville IN 47710

(G-3991)
CRADDOCK FURNITURE CORPORATION
Also Called: Craddock Finishing
1400 W Illinois St (47710)
P.O. Box 269 (47702)
PHONE..................812 425-2691
John T Craddock, Pr
Terry W Husk, *
John Ryan Craddock, *
EMP: 40 EST: 1934
SQ FT: 60,000
SALES (est): 5.04MM Privately Held
Web: www.craddockfinishing.com
SIC: 3479 3089 Painting of metal products; Coloring and finishing of plastics products

(G-3992)
CRESCENT PLASTICS INC
600 N Cross Pointe Blvd (47715-9119)
PHONE..................812 428-9305
John C Schroeder, Pr
Belle A Fahrer, Sec
Ken Graves, VP
EMP: 125 EST: 1949
SALES (est): 19.83MM Privately Held
Web: www.crescentplastics.com
SIC: 3089 Thermoformed finished plastics products, nec

(G-3993)
CRESCNT-CRSLN-WBASH PLAS FNDTI
600 N Cross Pointe Blvd (47715-9119)
PHONE..................812 428-9300
EMP: 2 EST: 2010
SALES (est): 1.22MM Privately Held
Web: www.wabashplastics.com
SIC: 3089 Injection molding of plastics

(G-3994)
CRESLINE PLASTIC PIPE CO INC (PA)
600 N Cross Pointe Blvd (47715)
PHONE..................812 428-9300
John H Schroeder, Ch Bd
Richard A Schroeder, *
Tom Walker, *
Gary Richmond, *
Belle Fahrer, *
▲ EMP: 35 EST: 1966
SQ FT: 8,000
SALES (est): 105.38MM
SALES (corp-wide): 105.38MM Privately Held
Web: www.cresline.com
SIC: 3084 4213 Plastics pipe; Building materials transport

(G-3995)
CRESLINE-NORTHWEST LLC (PA)
600 N Cross Pointe Blvd (47715-9119)
PHONE..................812 428-9300
Richard Schroeder, Managing Member
Belle Fahrer, Sec
EMP: 10 EST: 2001
SQ FT: 15,000
SALES (est): 7.26MM
SALES (corp-wide): 7.26MM Privately Held
Web: www.cresline.com
SIC: 3084 Plastics pipe

(G-3996)
CRESLINE-WEST INC (PA)
600 N Cross Pointe Blvd (47715-9119)
PHONE..................812 428-9300
Richard A Schroeder, Pr
Belle Fahrer, Sec
John H Schroeder, Ch Bd
Tom Walker, VP Sls
Gary B Richmond, Asst VP
EMP: 5 EST: 1992
SQ FT: 15,000
SALES (est): 20.94MM Privately Held
Web: www.cresline.com
SIC: 3084 Plastics pipe

(G-3997)
CROSSPOINT POLYMER TECH LLC
2301 Saint Joseph Ind Park Dr (47720-1250)
PHONE..................812 426-1350
Ben Schmidt, Managing Member
Doug Wurmnest, *
Matt Minton, *
EMP: 47 EST: 2010
SALES (est): 25MM Privately Held
Web: www.cpptech.com
SIC: 3087 Custom compound purchased resins

(G-3998)
CROWN EQUIPMENT CORPORATION
Also Called: Crown Lift Trucks
2540 Diego Dr (47715-2906)
PHONE..................812 477-5511
David Smith, Mgr
EMP: 60
SALES (corp-wide): 7.12B Privately Held
Web: www.crown.com
SIC: 3537 Lift trucks, industrial: fork, platform, straddle, etc.
PA: Crown Equipment Corporation
44 S Washington St
New Bremen OH 45869
419 629-2311

GEOGRAPHIC SECTION
Evansville - Vanderburgh County (G-4026)

(G-3999)
CUMMINS CROSSPOINT LLC
Also Called: Cummins
7901 Highway 41 N (47725-1525)
PHONE..................812 867-4400
Ken Hurst, *Brnch Mgr*
EMP: 59
SQ FT: 21,000
SALES (corp-wide): 34.06B **Publicly Held**
Web: www.cummins.com
SIC: 5084 5063 3519 Engines and parts, diesel; Generators; Internal combustion engines, nec
HQ: Cummins Crosspoint Llc
   111 Monument Cir Ste 601
   Indianapolis IN 46204
   317 243-7979

(G-4000)
CURVO LABS INC (PA)
58 Adams Ave (47713-1310)
PHONE..................619 316-1202
Andrew S Perry, *CEO*
Kent Parker, *Ch Bd*
Steve Suhrheinrich, *COO*
Jenny Vance, *CRO*
EMP: 8 **EST:** 2012
SALES (est): 1.48MM
SALES (corp-wide): 1.48MM **Privately Held**
Web: www.curvolabs.com
SIC: 7372 Business oriented computer software

(G-4001)
CUSTOM BLIND AND SHADE COMPANY
21 W Sunrise Dr (47710-4659)
PHONE..................812 867-9280
EMP: 7 **EST:** 2021
SALES (est): 118.5K **Privately Held**
Web: www.customblindcompany.org
SIC: 2591 Window blinds

(G-4002)
CUSTOM BLIND CO
21 W Sunrise Dr (47710-4659)
PHONE..................812 867-9280
Jeff Goebel, *Pr*
EMP: 2 **EST:** 1999
SQ FT: 3,000
SALES (est): 223.66K **Privately Held**
SIC: 2591 Drapery hardware and window blinds and shades

(G-4003)
CUSTOM ENGINEERING INC
1900 Lynch Rd (47711-2896)
PHONE..................812 424-3879
Robert G Klassen, *Pr*
EMP: 10 **EST:** 1959
SQ FT: 11,000
SALES (est): 1.49MM **Privately Held**
Web: www.customengr.com
SIC: 3599 3544 Machine shop, jobbing and repair; Special dies and tools

(G-4004)
CUSTOM SEWING SERVICE
2644 N Heidelbach Ave (47711-3236)
PHONE..................812 428-7015
Jennifer Ziliak, *Owner*
EMP: 4 **EST:** 1993
SQ FT: 2,100
SALES (est): 351.37K **Privately Held**
Web: www.customsewingin.com
SIC: 2221 5131 5949 5714 Upholstery, tapestry, and wall covering fabrics; Piece goods and notions; Sewing, needlework, and piece goods; Draperies

(G-4005)
CUSTOM WOODWORKING
Also Called: Custom Wood Floor
3314 Kratzville Rd (47710-3358)
PHONE..................812 422-6786
Michael Alley, *Owner*
EMP: 4 **EST:** 2002
SALES (est): 192.61K **Privately Held**
Web: www.customwoodflooring.org
SIC: 2431 Millwork

(G-4006)
CWB SOFTWARE LLC
9811 Cove Ct (47711-6917)
PHONE..................812 760-3431
Robert Paul Humphrey, *Pr*
EMP: 5 **EST:** 2010
SALES (est): 86.82K **Privately Held**
Web: www.neysc.net
SIC: 7372 Prepackaged software

(G-4007)
DATA MAIL INCORPORATED
1014 Main St (47708-1837)
PHONE..................812 424-7835
Adam M Miller, *Pr*
Michael A Miller, *Pr*
EMP: 20 **EST:** 1979
SQ FT: 11,000
SALES (est): 3.17MM **Privately Held**
Web: www.datamailinc.com
SIC: 7331 7389 2752 Mailing service; Packaging and labeling services; Commercial printing, lithographic

(G-4008)
DAYSON GEOLOGICAL CONSULTING
501 Caranza Ct (47711-1627)
PHONE..................812 868-0957
Robert Dayson, *Owner*
EMP: 1 **EST:** 2002
SALES (est): 81.07K **Privately Held**
SIC: 1389 Oil consultants

(G-4009)
DCS CAR AUDIO
Also Called: Dc's Mobile Electronics
1732 W Franklin St Ste A (47712-5147)
PHONE..................812 437-8488
Dennis Chapman, *Owner*
EMP: 5 **EST:** 2002
SALES (est): 291.87K **Privately Held**
SIC: 3571 Electronic computers

(G-4010)
DELILAH CLUB COVERS LLC
4812 Tippecanoe Dr (47715-3234)
PHONE..................812 401-0012
Delilah Harvey, *Owner*
EMP: 2 **EST:** 2012
SALES (est): 75.78K **Privately Held**
Web: www.girlygolfer.com
SIC: 3949 Shafts, golf club

(G-4011)
DELUX INDUSTRIES INC
8230 Carrington Dr (47711-6380)
PHONE..................812 867-0655
EMP: 25 **EST:** 1972
SQ FT: 50,000
SALES (est): 2.39MM **Privately Held**
SIC: 3544 Dies, plastics forming

(G-4012)
DEXTEROUS MOLD AND TOOL INC
2535 Locust Creek Dr (47720-1558)
PHONE..................812 422-8046
Eugene Elpers, *Pr*
Earlene Elpers, *Sec*
EMP: 20 **EST:** 1979
SQ FT: 15,000
SALES (est): 2.44MM **Privately Held**
Web: www.dexterousmold.com
SIC: 3089 Injection molding of plastics

(G-4013)
DIRECTIONS PROMOTIONS
1363 E Chandler Ave (47714-1951)
PHONE..................812 746-2505
Janet Schultzius, *VP*
EMP: 5 **EST:** 2017
SALES (est): 47.56K **Privately Held**
Web: www.albrechtco.com
SIC: 3993 Signs and advertising specialties

(G-4014)
DIST COUNCIL 91
409 Millner Industrial Dr (47710-2545)
PHONE..................812 962-9191
Steven Stall, *Pr*
EMP: 4 **EST:** 2005
SALES (est): 374.32K **Privately Held**
Web: www.iupatdc91.com
SIC: 2851 8631 Paints, waterproof; Trade union

(G-4015)
DITTO SALES INC
1817 W Virginia St (47712-5206)
PHONE..................812 424-4098
John Evans, *Mgr*
EMP: 4
SALES (corp-wide): 31.67MM **Privately Held**
Web: www.dittosales.com
SIC: 2519 Household furniture, except wood or metal: upholstered
PA: Ditto Sales, Inc.
   2332 Cathy Ln
   Jasper IN 47546
   812 482-3043

(G-4016)
DLB CUSTOM EXTRUSIONS LLC
1618 Lynch Rd (47711)
PHONE..................812 423-6405
EMP: 16 **EST:** 2019
SALES (est): 2.73MM **Privately Held**
Web: www.dlbextrusions.com
SIC: 3089 Injection molding of plastics

(G-4017)
DOMAINDRESS LLC
331 Inwood Dr (47711-2223)
PHONE..................812 430-4856
EMP: 5 **EST:** 2020
SALES (est): 59.23K **Privately Held**
SIC: 2741 Internet publishing and broadcasting

(G-4018)
DONTSTOPTILLYOUGETENOUGH LLC
235 N Burkhardt Rd (47715-2729)
PHONE..................812 250-8262
EMP: 2
SALES (est): 93.54K **Privately Held**
SIC: 2254 Shirts and T-shirts (underwear), knit

(G-4019)
DONUT BANK INC (PA)
Also Called: Donut Bank Bakery
1031 E Diamond Ave (47711-3901)
PHONE..................812 426-0011
Harold A Kempf, *Pr*
Shirley A Kempf, *
EMP: 25 **EST:** 1967
SQ FT: 8,000
SALES (est): 9.31MM
SALES (corp-wide): 9.31MM **Privately Held**
Web: www.donutbank.com
SIC: 2051 5461 Doughnuts, except frozen; Retail bakeries

(G-4020)
DREAM CENTER EVANSVILLE INC
16 W Morgan Ave (47710-2532)
P.O. Box 4793 (47724-0793)
PHONE..................812 401-5558
Todd Morgan, *Prin*
EMP: 1 **EST:** 1998
SALES (est): 1.4MM **Privately Held**
Web: www.dreamcenterevansville.org
SIC: 2741 Catalogs: publishing and printing

(G-4021)
DUE NORTH INDUSTRIES CORP
5215 James Ave (47712-3984)
PHONE..................812 306-4043
Daniel Schweikhart, *CEO*
EMP: 1 **EST:** 2019
SALES (est): 39.69K **Privately Held**
SIC: 3999 Manufacturing industries, nec

(G-4022)
DYNAMIC FABRICATION LLC
2214 Saint Joseph Ind Park Dr (47720-1207)
PHONE..................812 305-5576
EMP: 5 **EST:** 2017
SALES (est): 194.78K **Privately Held**
Web: www.dynafabmetal.com
SIC: 3441 Fabricated structural metal

(G-4023)
DYNAMIC FABRICATION LLC
1331 Grove St (47710-2241)
PHONE..................812 305-5576
Kyle Gabbard, *Admn*
EMP: 7 **EST:** 2018
SALES (est): 524.83K **Privately Held**
Web: www.dynafabmetal.com
SIC: 3441 Fabricated structural metal

(G-4024)
EAGLE RIVER COAL LLC
Also Called: Eagle River Coal
250 N Cross Pointe Blvd (47715)
P.O. Box 7 (47567)
PHONE..................618 252-0490
EMP: 2 **EST:** 2009
SALES (est): 982.87K **Privately Held**
SIC: 1241 Coal mining services

(G-4025)
EARTHCARE LLC
3311 E Powell Ave (47714-0438)
PHONE..................812 455-9258
EMP: 4 **EST:** 2017
SALES (est): 72K **Privately Held**
Web: www.earthcarellc.com
SIC: 2875 Fertilizers, mixing only

(G-4026)
EAST CAST EROSION HOLDINGS LLC (HQ)
4609 E Boonville New Harmony Rd (47725)
PHONE..................812 867-4873
Zachary Snyder, *Managing Member*
EMP: 1 **EST:** 2021
SALES (est): 10.49MM
SALES (corp-wide): 49.41MM **Privately Held**
Web: www.westerngreen.com
SIC: 2211 Blankets and blanketings, cotton
PA: Western Excelsior Corporation
   4609 E Bnvlle New Hrmony
   Evansville IN 47725

Evansville - Vanderburgh County (G-4027)

GEOGRAPHIC SECTION

970 533-7412

(G-4027)
EDGETEK INC
10600 Highway 57 (47725-7650)
PHONE..............................812 868-1250
Sara E Seib, *Pr*
EMP: 6 **EST:** 1955
SQ FT: 3,800
SALES (est): 466.42K **Privately Held**
Web: www.edgetekinc.com
SIC: 3599 Machine shop, jobbing and repair

(G-4028)
EEMSCO INC
Also Called: Eemsco
600 W Eichel Ave (47710-2412)
P.O. Box 4717 (47724-0717)
PHONE..............................812 426-2224
John G Mathias Junior, *Pr*
EMP: 27 **EST:** 1920
SQ FT: 42,000
SALES (est): 4.74MM **Privately Held**
Web: www.eemsco.com
SIC: 3599 7694 Machine shop, jobbing and repair; Rewinding services

(G-4029)
EFP LLC
14636 Foundation Ave (47725-7717)
PHONE..............................812 602-0019
Chuck Harper, *Manager*
EMP: 35
SALES (corp-wide): 1.62B **Privately Held**
Web: www.efppackaging.com
SIC: 3086 Plastics foam products
HQ: Efp, Llc
223 Middleton Run Rd
Elkhart IN 46516
574 295-4690

(G-4030)
ELKO INC
Also Called: Elko Plastic Fabricators Div
940 N Boeke Rd (47711-4902)
PHONE..............................812 473-8400
Randall Kanter, *Pr*
EMP: 17 **EST:** 1954
SQ FT: 7,000
SALES (est): 895.78K **Privately Held**
Web: www.plasticfabinc.com
SIC: 3083 5211 5031 2541 Laminated plastics plate and sheet; Cabinets, kitchen; Kitchen cabinets; Wood partitions and fixtures

(G-4031)
ELPERS TRUCK EQUIPMENT LLC
8136 Baumgart Rd (47725-1510)
PHONE..............................812 423-5787
Greg Wilhite, *CFO*
EMP: 14 **EST:** 2003
SQ FT: 12,000
SALES (est): 4.66MM **Privately Held**
Web: www.elperstruck.com
SIC: 3537 Industrial trucks and tractors

(G-4032)
ELS INC
10435 Upper Mount Vernon Rd (47712-9604)
PHONE..............................812 985-2272
Elwanda Shrode, *Pr*
James W Shrode, *Sec*
EMP: 3 **EST:** 1971
SQ FT: 10,000
SALES (est): 261.31K **Privately Held**
SIC: 3599 Machine shop, jobbing and repair

(G-4033)
EMI LLC
Also Called: EMI Quality Plating
5701 Old Boonville Hwy (47715-2198)
PHONE..............................812 437-9100
Fran Gilchrist, *Pr*
Bill King, *VP*
Mark Dye, *VP*
EMP: 48 **EST:** 1999
SQ FT: 32,000
SALES (est): 6.3MM **Privately Held**
Web: www.emiplating.com
SIC: 3471 Electroplating of metals or formed products

(G-4034)
EMP OF EVANSVILLE
Also Called: News 4 U Magazine
4 Chestnut St (47713-1022)
PHONE..............................812 962-1309
Bashar Hamami, *Pr*
EMP: 10 **EST:** 2000
SALES (est): 177.86K **Privately Held**
SIC: 2721 Magazines: publishing and printing

(G-4035)
EMPIRE CONTRACTORS INC
Also Called: Construction
2200 Lexington Rd (47720)
P.O. Box 6327 (47719)
PHONE..............................812 424-3865
Jason M Martin, *Pr*
Thomas H Fleenor, *
Michael F Raber, *
Jason Martin, *
EMP: 100 **EST:** 1998
SQ FT: 8,000
SALES (est): 22.84MM **Privately Held**
Web: www.empire-contractors.com
SIC: 1541 1389 1771 1741 Industrial buildings, new construction, nec; Construction, repair, and dismantling services; Concrete work; Masonry and other stonework

(G-4036)
ENCOM POLYMERS LLC
Also Called: Encom Polymers
4825 N Spring St (47711)
PHONE..............................812 421-7700
Richard Kaskel Junior, *CEO*
Darrell Hughes, *
▲ **EMP:** 50 **EST:** 1999
SQ FT: 60,000
SALES (est): 23.37MM **Privately Held**
Web: www.encompolymers.com
SIC: 2821 Thermoplastic materials
HQ: Aurora Plastics, Llc
9280 Jefferson St
Streetsboro OH 44241

(G-4037)
ENGLEHARDT CUSTOM WDWKG LLC
4125 Kedzie Ave (47712-7894)
PHONE..............................812 425-9282
Barry Englehardt, *Owner*
EMP: 2 **EST:** 2011
SALES (est): 168.9K **Privately Held**
Web: www.plazadelamo.com
SIC: 2431 Millwork

(G-4038)
ENGLISH RESOURCES INC
816 Nw 2nd St (47708-1018)
P.O. Box 34 (47701-0034)
PHONE..............................812 423-6716
Ken English, *Pr*
Danny English, *VP*
Wanda English, *VP*
Judy Burkhart, *Sec*
▲ **EMP:** 4 **EST:** 1991
SQ FT: 4,600
SALES (est): 436.73K **Privately Held**
Web: www.englishresources.com
SIC: 1241 Coal mining services

(G-4039)
ENVALIOR ENGINEERING MATERIALS INC (DH)
Also Called: D S M
2267 W Mill Rd (47720)
PHONE..............................800 333-4237
◆ **EMP:** 230 **EST:** 1991
SALES (est): 96.46MM
SALES (corp-wide): 2.67MM **Privately Held**
Web: www.envalior.com
SIC: 2821 3087 3083 Acrylonitrile-butadiene-styrene resins, ABS resins; Custom compound purchased resins; Laminated plastics plate and sheet
HQ: Envalior B.V.
Urmonderbaan 22
Geleen LI 6167
467506500

(G-4040)
ENVALIOR ENGINEERING MTLS INC
2267 W Mill Rd (47720)
PHONE..............................812 435-7500
EMP: 7
SALES (corp-wide): 2.67MM **Privately Held**
Web: www.envalior.com
SIC: 2821 Plastics materials and resins
HQ: Envalior Engineering Materials Inc.
2267 W Mill Rd
Evansville IN 47720

(G-4041)
ENVALIOR ENGINEERING MTLS INC
1100 E Louisiana St (47711)
PHONE..............................812 435-7500
Steve Hartig, *Mgr*
EMP: 7
SALES (corp-wide): 2.67MM **Privately Held**
Web: www.envalior.com
SIC: 2821 3087 3083 Acrylonitrile-butadiene-styrene resins, ABS resins; Custom compound purchased resins; Laminated plastics plate and sheet
HQ: Envalior Engineering Materials Inc.
2267 W Mill Rd
Evansville IN 47720

(G-4042)
ENVIROGEN TECHNOLOGIES LLC ✪
1133 E Virginia St (47711-5724)
PHONE..............................812 319-4496
Steve Graves, *CEO*
Mark Miller, *VP*
EMP: 2 **EST:** 2022
SALES (est): 88.38K **Privately Held**
Web: www.envirogen.com
SIC: 3629 Electrical industrial apparatus, nec

(G-4043)
ENVIROPLAS LLC
15220 Foundation Ave (47725-9655)
PHONE..............................812 868-0808
▲ **EMP:** 60 **EST:** 1994
SALES (est): 41.63MM **Privately Held**
Web: www.auroraplastics.com
SIC: 3087 Custom compound purchased resins
HQ: Aurora Plastics, Llc
9280 Jefferson St
Streetsboro OH 44241

(G-4044)
ENVIROPLAS LLC
10100 Hedden Rd (47725-8919)
PHONE..............................812 868-0808
EMP: 90 **EST:** 1996
SALES (est): 120.18K **Privately Held**
SIC: 3087 Custom compound purchased resins

(G-4045)
ESCALADE INCORPORATED (PA)
Also Called: Escalade
817 Maxwell Ave (47711)
PHONE..............................812 467-1358
Walter P Glazer Junior, *Ch Bd*
Stephen R Wawrin, *VP Fin*
Patrick J Griffin, *Investor Relations*
EMP: 54 **EST:** 1922
SQ FT: 771,000
SALES (est): 263.57MM
SALES (corp-wide): 263.57MM **Publicly Held**
Web: www.escaladeinc.com
SIC: 3949 Ping-pong tables

(G-4046)
EVANSVILLE ARC INC
2515 Kotter Ave (47715-8512)
PHONE..............................812 471-1633
Andy Cosgrove, *Brnch Mgr*
EMP: 60
SALES (corp-wide): 5.62MM **Privately Held**
Web: www.arcofevansville.org
SIC: 8331 2653 Sheltered workshop; Corrugated and solid fiber boxes
PA: Evansville Arc, Inc.
615 W Virginia St
Evansville IN 47710
812 428-4500

(G-4047)
EVANSVILLE ASSN FOR THE BLIND
Also Called: EAB INDUSTRIES
500 N 2nd Ave (47710-1540)
P.O. Box 6445 (47719-0445)
PHONE..............................812 422-1181
Karla Horrell, *Dir*
EMP: 120 **EST:** 1919
SQ FT: 115,000
SALES (est): 1.28MM **Privately Held**
Web: www.evansvilleblind.org
SIC: 7699 2392 5087 Industrial equipment services; Mops, floor and dust; Janitors' supplies

(G-4048)
EVANSVILLE BINDERY INC
221 E Columbia St (47711-5047)
PHONE..............................812 423-2222
Gary Beshears, *Pr*
EMP: 4 **EST:** 1980
SQ FT: 6,000
SALES (est): 429.51K **Privately Held**
Web: www.evansvillebindery.com
SIC: 2759 2752 2789 2791 Business forms: printing, nsk; Offset printing; Bookbinding and related work; Typesetting

(G-4049)
EVANSVILLE BLOCK CO INC
Also Called: Miller Block Co
1700 W Franklin St Ste 14 (47712-5107)
P.O. Box 6325 (47719-0325)
PHONE..............................812 422-2864
Lawrence E Miller, *Pr*
Keith Milling, *VP*
EMP: 32 **EST:** 1946
SQ FT: 14,160
SALES (est): 1.19MM **Privately Held**

GEOGRAPHIC SECTION
Evansville - Vanderburgh County (G-4073)

SIC: 3271 5032 Architectural concrete: block, split, fluted, screen, etc.; Tile and clay products

(G-4050)
EVANSVILLE CORP DESIGN INC
Also Called: Office Furniture Liquidators
401 Nw 4th St (47708-1105)
PHONE..................812 426-0911
Michael Small, Pr
EMP: 6
SALES (corp-wide): 17.68MM **Privately Held**
Web: www.cdievv.com
SIC: 2522 Office furniture, except wood
PA: Evansville Corporate Design, Inc.
420 Nw 5th St Ste 300
Evansville IN 47708
812 422-3000

(G-4051)
EVANSVILLE COURIER CO (DH)
Also Called: Evansville Courier
300 E Walnut St (47713-1938)
P.O. Box 268 (47702-0268)
PHONE..................812 464-7500
Jack Pate, Edr
Daniel J Castellini, *
M Denise Kuprionis, *
E John Wolfzorn, *
EMP: 450 EST: 1845
SQ FT: 140,000
SALES (est): 22.97MM
SALES (corp-wide): 2.66B **Publicly Held**
Web: www.courierpress.com
SIC: 2711 2791 Newspapers, publishing and printing; Typesetting
HQ: Journal Media Group, Inc.
333 W State St
Milwaukee WI 53203
414 224-2000

(G-4052)
EVANSVILLE LITHOGRAPH CO INC
3112 E Walnut St (47714-1468)
PHONE..................812 477-0506
Joyce Freeman, Pr
EMP: 4 EST: 1955
SQ FT: 3,500
SALES (est): 301.77K **Privately Held**
Web: evansvillelithographco.samsbiz.com
SIC: 2752 Offset printing

(G-4053)
EVANSVILLE MARINE SERVICE INC (PA)
2300 Broadway Ave (47712-4916)
PHONE..................812 424-9278
EMP: 36 EST: 1994
SQ FT: 850
SALES (est): 8.76MM **Privately Held**
Web: www.ems-harbors.com
SIC: 4492 4491 3732 Towing and tugboat service; Waterfront terminal operation; Boatbuilding and repairing

(G-4054)
EVANSVILLE METAL PRODUCTS INC (PA)
Also Called: Refrigeration Sys of Evans
119 Ladonna Blvd (47711-1859)
PHONE..................812 423-5632
Rahmi Soyugenc, Pr
Marjorie Soyugenc, *
EMP: 65 EST: 1961
SQ FT: 156,000
SALES (est): 9.68MM
SALES (corp-wide): 9.68MM **Privately Held**

Web: www.internationalrevolvingdoor.com
SIC: 3442 3469 3479 3585 Metal doors; Stamping metal for the trade; Coating of metals with plastic or resins; Refrigeration and heating equipment

(G-4055)
EVANSVILLE METAL PRODUCTS INC
Refrigrtion Systems Evnsvlle D
2086 N 6th Ave (47710-2812)
PHONE..................812 421-6589
EMP: 1
SALES (corp-wide): 9.68MM **Privately Held**
Web: www.internationalrevolvingdoor.com
SIC: 3585 Refrigeration and heating equipment
PA: Evansville Metal Products Inc
119 Ladonna Blvd
Evansville IN 47711
812 423-5632

(G-4056)
EVANSVILLE PALLETS
2203 N Kentucky Ave (47711-3917)
PHONE..................812 550-0199
EMP: 5 EST: 2011
SALES (est): 76.11K **Privately Held**
SIC: 2448 Pallets, wood and wood with metal

(G-4057)
EVANSVILLE SHEET METAL WORKS INC
1901 W Maryland St (47712-5399)
PHONE..................812 423-7871
EMP: 65 EST: 1946
SALES (est): 8.36MM **Privately Held**
Web: www.cut2sizemetals.com
SIC: 3444 1711 5051 Sheet metalwork; Ventilation and duct work contractor; Steel

(G-4058)
EVANSVILLE THUNDERBOLTS
1 Se Martin Luther King Jr Blvd (47708-1801)
PHONE..................812 435-0872
Scott Schoenike, Prin
EMP: 16 EST: 2017
SALES (est): 67.51K **Privately Held**
Web: www.evansvillethunderbolts.com
SIC: 2711 Newspapers, publishing and printing

(G-4059)
EVANSVILLE TOOL & DIE INC
4900 N Saint Joseph Ave (47720-1222)
PHONE..................812 422-7101
Jack Dennis Droste, Pr
EMP: 15 EST: 1959
SQ FT: 27,000
SALES (est): 2.44MM **Privately Held**
Web: www.evansvilletoolanddie.com
SIC: 3544 Special dies and tools

(G-4060)
EVANSVLLE PRINT SPECIALIST INC
2217 W Franklin St (47712-5116)
PHONE..................812 423-5831
Butch Frank, Pr
Dorothy Wesley, VP
Glenda Floyd, VP
EMP: 2 EST: 1995
SQ FT: 2,500
SALES (est): 343.52K **Privately Held**
Web: www.evprint.com
SIC: 2759 2752 Screen printing; Commercial printing, lithographic

(G-4061)
EVANTEK MANUFACTURING INDS LLC
Also Called: EMI Quality Plating
5701 Old Boonville Hwy (47715-2198)
PHONE..................812 437-9100
William King, Managing Member
EMP: 8 EST: 2005
SQ FT: 32,000
SALES (est): 499.52K **Privately Held**
Web: www.emiplating.com
SIC: 2796 Platemaking services

(G-4062)
EVILLE IRON STREET RODS LTD
P.O. Box 3011 (47730-3011)
PHONE..................812 428-3764
EMP: 5 EST: 2001
SALES (est): 154.88K **Privately Held**
Web: www.frogfollies.org
SIC: 3312 Rods, iron and steel: made in steel mills

(G-4063)
EXPRESS MOTORS
1059 E Riverside Dr (47714-3454)
P.O. Box 14452 (47728-6452)
PHONE..................812 437-9495
Aadil Almoudaai, Owner
EMP: 4 EST: 2005
SALES (est): 244.22K **Privately Held**
SIC: 2741 Miscellaneous publishing

(G-4064)
FARM BOY MEATS OF EVANSVILLE
2761 N Kentucky Ave (47711)
P.O. Box 1984 (42302)
PHONE..................812 425-5231
Alan Clark, Pr
Richard W Bonenberger, *
EMP: 97 EST: 1952
SQ FT: 30,000
SALES (est): 21.3MM
SALES (corp-wide): 41.27MM **Privately Held**
Web: www.farmboyfoodservice.com
SIC: 2013 5113 5142 Beef, dried: from purchased meat; Industrial and personal service paper; Meat, frozen: packaged
PA: Clark Restaurant Service Inc.
2803 Tamarack Rd
Owensboro KY 42301
270 684-1469

(G-4065)
FARMERS MACHINE SHOP INC
1511 E Virginia St Ste C (47711-5702)
PHONE..................812 425-1238
Bill Farmer, Pr
Bill Farmer, Owner
EMP: 2 EST: 1987
SQ FT: 2,500
SALES (est): 184.69K **Privately Held**
SIC: 3599 Machine shop, jobbing and repair

(G-4066)
FEHRENBACHER CABINETS INC
8944 Big Cynthiana Rd (47720-7612)
PHONE..................812 963-3377
Peter Fehrenbacher, Pr
Zachary Fehrenbacher, *
Patrick Fehrenbacher, *
Jim Balbach, *
▲ EMP: 35 EST: 1961
SQ FT: 18,000
SALES (est): 2.36MM **Privately Held**
Web: www.fehrenbachercabinets.com

SIC: 5712 2541 2517 2511 Cabinet work, custom; Wood partitions and fixtures; Wood television and radio cabinets; Wood household furniture

(G-4067)
FELLWOCKS AUTOMOTIVE
10004 Darmstadt Rd (47710-5082)
PHONE..................812 867-3658
Ron Fellwock, Owner
EMP: 4 EST: 1918
SQ FT: 5,430
SALES (est): 232.2K **Privately Held**
SIC: 3053 3061 Gaskets; packing and sealing devices; Automotive rubber goods (mechanical)

(G-4068)
FIGTREE PRINT LLC
10101 Brook Meadow Dr (47711-7127)
PHONE..................978 503-1779
Michelle Marie Petie, Pr
EMP: 5 EST: 2016
SALES (est): 94.82K **Privately Held**
SIC: 2752 Offset printing

(G-4069)
FINEST GRADE PRODUCTS
2949 Arlington Ave (47712-4522)
P.O. Box 855 (47705-0855)
PHONE..................812 421-1976
Lee Horton, Owner
L E Horton, Owner
EMP: 2 EST: 1975
SALES (est): 118.78K **Privately Held**
SIC: 7372 5112 Application computer software; Business forms

(G-4070)
FISHER & COMPANY INCORPORATED
Also Called: Fisher Dynamics Evansville
2301 Saint George Rd (47711-2561)
PHONE..................586 746-2000
Alfred J Fisher Iii, Brnch Mgr
EMP: 69
SALES (corp-wide): 448.13MM **Privately Held**
Web: www.fisherco.com
SIC: 3714 Motor vehicle parts and accessories
PA: Fisher & Company, Incorporated
33300 Fisher Dr
Saint Clair Shores MI 48082
586 746-2000

(G-4071)
FISHER TOOL 2 INC
8231 Burch Park Dr (47725-1707)
PHONE..................812 867-8350
Logan Fisher, Pr
EMP: 8 EST: 2021
SALES (est): 657.69K **Privately Held**
SIC: 3544 Special dies and tools

(G-4072)
FIT TIGHT COVERS COMPANY INC
1200 N Willow Rd Ste 100 (47711-4784)
PHONE..................812 492-3370
James Gribbins, Pr
Calvin Brasel, *
EMP: 25 EST: 2009
SALES (est): 1.77MM **Privately Held**
Web: www.fittightcovers.com
SIC: 1742 3999 Insulation, buildings; Heating pads, nonelectric

(G-4073)
FL SMIDTH
1315 N Cullen Ave Ste 102 (47715-8248)

Evansville - Vanderburgh County (G-4074)

PHONE..................812 402-9210
T J Rhule, *Brnch Mgr*
EMP: 3 **EST:** 2012
SALES (est): 207.28K **Privately Held**
SIC: 3561 Pumps and pumping equipment

(G-4074)
FLAIR MOLDED PLASTICS INC
2521 Lynch Rd (47711-2954)
PHONE..................812 425-6155
Benedict A Brougham, *Ch*
Albert Brougham, *
Carolyn Wilkinson, *
Jackie Strange, *
EMP: 75 **EST:** 1965
SQ FT: 91,000
SALES (est): 9.13MM **Privately Held**
Web: www.flairplastics.com
SIC: 3089 Injection molding of plastics

(G-4075)
FLANDERS INC
8101 Baumgart Rd (47725)
PHONE..................812 867-7421
EMP: 11 **EST:** 2004
SALES (est): 63.84K **Privately Held**
Web: www.flandersinc.com
SIC: 7694 3621 Electric motor repair; Electric motor and generator parts

(G-4076)
FLANDERS ELECTRIC MOTOR SERVICE LLC (PA)
Also Called: Evansville-Baumgart - Flanders
8101 Baumgart Rd (47725)
P.O. Box 23130 (47725)
PHONE..................812 867-7421
◆ **EMP:** 182 **EST:** 1962
SALES (est): 98.14MM
SALES (corp-wide): 98.14MM **Privately Held**
Web: www.flanderselectric.com
SIC: 7694 3621 Electric motor repair; Electric motor and generator parts

(G-4077)
FLANDERS ELECTRIC MTR SVC LLC
500 E Buena Vista Rd (47711-2722)
PHONE..................812 867-4014
Allen Patterson, *Brnch Mgr*
EMP: 35
SALES (corp-wide): 98.14MM **Privately Held**
Web: www.flanderselectric.com
SIC: 7694 Electric motor repair
PA: Flanders Electric Motor Service, Llc
8101 Baumgart Rd
Evansville IN 47725
812 867-7421

(G-4078)
FLANDERS ELECTRIC MTR SVC LLC
1050 E Maryland St (47711-4756)
PHONE..................812 421-4300
Kyle Williams, *Brnch Mgr*
EMP: 69
SALES (corp-wide): 98.14MM **Privately Held**
Web: www.flanderselectric.com
SIC: 5999 7699 7694 5063 Motors, electric; Welding equipment repair; Armature rewinding shops; Electrical apparatus and equipment
PA: Flanders Electric Motor Service, Llc
8101 Baumgart Rd
Evansville IN 47725
812 867-7421

(G-4079)
FOCUS MOLD AND MACHINE INC
1145 Indy Ct (47725-6300)
PHONE..................812 422-9627
Stephen Gardner, *Pr*
Pam Gardner, *Sec*
Bryan Gardner, *VP*
EMP: 3 **EST:** 1998
SQ FT: 3,600
SALES (est): 362.54K **Privately Held**
Web: www.focusmold.com
SIC: 3089 3544 Injection molding of plastics; Special dies, tools, jigs, and fixtures

(G-4080)
FORTERRA CONCRETE INDS INC
1213 Stanley Ave (47711-3569)
PHONE..................812 426-5353
EMP: 33
SIC: 3999 Pipe cleaners
HQ: Forterra Concrete Industries, Inc.
4108 Dakota Ave
Nashville TN 37209
615 889-0700

(G-4081)
FRANK R KOMAR PC
4111 Washington Ave (47714-0886)
PHONE..................812 477-9110
Frank R Komar, *Pr*
EMP: 3 **EST:** 1975
SALES (est): 228.07K **Privately Held**
Web: www.komaraccounting.com
SIC: 8721 7372 Certified public accountant; Prepackaged software

(G-4082)
FUZION INDUSTRIES
2200 W Maryland St (47712-5308)
PHONE..................812 430-4037
Robert Taylor, *Prin*
EMP: 4 **EST:** 2018
SALES (est): 208.83K **Privately Held**
SIC: 3999 Manufacturing industries, nec

(G-4083)
GALLAGHER DRILLING INC (PA)
115 Se 3rd St Fl 2 (47708-1431)
P.O. Box 8275 (47716-8275)
PHONE..................812 477-6746
Victor R Gallagher Junior, *VP*
Michael D Gallagher, *
Shawn G Gallagher, *
Thomas R Bailey, *
Daniel G Gallager, *
EMP: 18 **EST:** 1957
SQ FT: 4,200
SALES (est): 1.54MM
SALES (corp-wide): 1.54MM **Privately Held**
Web: www.gallagherdrilling.com
SIC: 1311 1381 1389 Crude petroleum production; Drilling oil and gas wells; Gas compressing (natural gas) at the fields

(G-4084)
GARRETT PRTG & GRAPHICS INC
1405 N 1st Ave (47710-2407)
PHONE..................812 422-6005
Richard Wooley, *Pr*
Alicia Cave, *Sec*
EMP: 6 **EST:** 1981
SQ FT: 2,660
SALES (est): 495.36K **Privately Held**
Web: www.garrettprinting.us
SIC: 2752 Offset printing

(G-4085)
GAUGER WOODWORKING PLUS
2012 Koring Rd (47720-2346)

PHONE..................812 421-8223
Alan Gauger, *Prin*
EMP: 1 **EST:** 2003
SALES (est): 104.78K **Privately Held**
Web: www.gaugerwoodworking.com
SIC: 2431 Millwork

(G-4086)
GAUNT FAMILY LLC
7001 Red Wing Dr (47715-5251)
P.O. Box 779 (47705-0779)
PHONE..................812 473-3167
Nancy Gaunt, *Prin*
EMP: 2 **EST:** 2010
SALES (est): 74.06K **Privately Held**
SIC: 2741 Miscellaneous publishing

(G-4087)
GENERAL RBR PLAS OF EVANSVILLE (PA)
1902 N Kentucky Ave (47711-3879)
P.O. Box 4510 (47724-0510)
PHONE..................812 464-5153
W L Burnett, *Pr*
Dean Becher, *
Wanda De Witt, *
William R Ruez, *
▲ **EMP:** 25 **EST:** 1977
SQ FT: 20,000
SALES (est): 20.91MM
SALES (corp-wide): 20.91MM **Privately Held**
Web: www.generalrubberplastics.com
SIC: 5162 5085 3053 3052 Plastics resins; Rubber goods, mechanical; Gaskets; packing and sealing devices; Rubber and plastics hose and beltings

(G-4088)
GENERAL SIGNALS INC
5611 E Morgan Ave (47715-3377)
PHONE..................812 474-4256
Glenn Grant, *Pr*
Ronald L Mitchell, *Pr*
Michael S Ellenstein Junior, *VP*
Kirk Mitchell, *Sec*
EMP: 24 **EST:** 1954
SQ FT: 2,000
SALES (est): 7.45MM **Privately Held**
Web: www.generalsignals.com
SIC: 5088 3229 3743 Railroad equipment and supplies; Reflectors for lighting equipment, pressed or blown glass; Railroad equipment

(G-4089)
GEORGE KOCH SONS LLC (HQ)
10 S 11th Ave (47712-6800)
PHONE..................812 465-9600
EMP: 75 **EST:** 1998
SQ FT: 225,000
SALES (est): 46.06MM
SALES (corp-wide): 915.49MM **Privately Held**
Web: www.kochllc.com
SIC: 3549 3567 3535 Metalworking machinery, nec; Industrial furnaces and ovens; Conveyors and conveying equipment
PA: Koch Enterprises, Inc.
14 South Eleventh Avenue
Evansville IN 47712
812 465-9800

(G-4090)
GES SERVICES LLC
2705 N Red Bank Rd (47720-3446)
PHONE..................812 270-3090
Justin Kaercher, *Pr*
Jill Horstman, *Prin*
EMP: 4 **EST:** 2019
SALES (est): 207.52K **Privately Held**

Web: www.gesservicesinc.com
SIC: 1081 Metal mining exploration and development services

(G-4091)
GOAD CRANKSHAFT SERVICE INC
3514 E Morgan Ave (47715-2236)
PHONE..................812 477-1127
Larry Goad, *Pr*
EMP: 2 **EST:** 2005
SALES (est): 125.38K **Privately Held**
SIC: 3599 Crankshafts and camshafts, machining

(G-4092)
GOLF PLUS INC
5601 E Virginia St (47715-2640)
PHONE..................812 477-7529
EMP: 7 **EST:** 1995
SALES (est): 961.62K **Privately Held**
Web: www.golfplusstores.com
SIC: 5941 5611 3949 Golf goods and equipment; Clothing, sportswear, men's and boys'; Softball equipment and supplies

(G-4093)
GOOD POPPI LLC ✪
640 Kirkwood Dr (47715-7163)
PHONE..................812 319-1660
Sidney Kull, *Mgr*
EMP: 4 **EST:** 2022
SALES (est): 62.01K **Privately Held**
SIC: 2047 0752 Dog food; Training services, pet and animal specialties (not horses)

(G-4094)
GRAFAC INDUSTRIES INC
Also Called: Grafac Apparel
2315 E Morgan Ave (47711-4315)
PHONE..................812 474-0930
EMP: 3 **EST:** 1993
SALES (est): 471.7K **Privately Held**
Web: www.grafac.com
SIC: 2759 Screen printing

(G-4095)
GRAFCO INDUSTRIES LTD PARTNR (HQ)
101 Oakley St (47710-1237)
PHONE..................812 424-2904
Timothy Frank, *Pt*
Thomas Frank, *Pt*
EMP: 108 **EST:** 1978
SQ FT: 120,000
SALES (est): 17.3MM **Publicly Held**
Web: www.berryglobal.com
SIC: 3089 Plastics containers, except foam
PA: Berry Global Group, Inc.
101 Oakley St
Evansville IN 47710

(G-4096)
GREEN EARTH POLYMERS INC
4825 N Spring St (47711-2488)
PHONE..................812 602-4070
EMP: 3 **EST:** 2018
SALES (est): 334.5K **Privately Held**
Web: www.greenearthpolymers.com
SIC: 2822 Ethylene-propylene rubbers, EPDM polymers

(G-4097)
GREEN TREE PLASTICS LLC
1107 E Virginia St (47711-5724)
PHONE..................812 402-4127
▲ **EMP:** 8 **EST:** 2004
SALES (est): 1.38MM **Privately Held**
Web: www.greentreeplastics.com
SIC: 2821 Plastics materials and resins

Evansville - Vanderburgh County (G-4121)

(G-4098)
GREYSTONE LOGISTICS INC
9747 Morris Dr (47720-7541)
PHONE..............................812 459-9978
Warren Kruger, *CEO*
EMP: 1
Web: www.greystonepallets.com
SIC: 3089 Pallets, plastics
PA: Greystone Logistics, Inc.
1613 E 15th St
Tulsa OK 74120

(G-4099)
GRIBBINS SPECIALTY GROUP INC (PA)
1400 E Columbia St (47711-5222)
PHONE..............................812 422-3340
James Gribbins, *Pr*
Leslee Gribbins, *CEO*
Mark Gribbins, *VP*
Brian Willett, *VP*
EMP: 4 **EST:** 2009
SALES (est): 3.53MM
SALES (corp-wide): 3.53MM **Privately Held**
Web: www.gribbins.com
SIC: 1742 3999 Insulation, buildings; Heating pads, nonelectric

(G-4100)
H & S CUSTOM COUNTERTOPS INC
5705 E Morgan Ave (47715-2319)
P.O. Box 15743 (47716-0743)
PHONE..............................812 422-6314
Roert B Howard, *Pr*
Bruce W Spaulding, *Sec*
Robert B Howard, *Pr*
EMP: 2 **EST:** 2002
SALES (est): 245.17K **Privately Held**
SIC: 2541 Table or counter tops, plastic laminated

(G-4101)
H & W MOLDERS INC
1031 W Tennessee St (47710-2349)
PHONE..............................812 423-9340
EMP: 5 **EST:** 1995
SQ FT: 6,000
SALES (est): 705.55K **Privately Held**
SIC: 3089 Injection molding of plastics

(G-4102)
H W MOLDERS
1500 W Missouri St (47710-1844)
PHONE..............................812 423-3552
Robert Koons, *Mgr*
EMP: 6 **EST:** 2018
SALES (est): 97.87K **Privately Held**
SIC: 3089 Injection molding of plastics

(G-4103)
HARD HUSTLA MUZIK LLC
800 Sycamore St # 329 (47708-1820)
PHONE..............................812 214-1995
EMP: 1 **EST:** 2020
SALES (est): 16.2K **Privately Held**
Web: www.hardhustlamuzik.com
SIC: 7929 7922 7389 2782 Musician; Entertainment promotion; Recording studio, noncommercial records; Record albums

(G-4104)
HARTFORD BAKERY INC (HQ)
500 N Fulton Ave (47710-1571)
PHONE..............................812 425-4642
H Dean Short, *Pr*
R Jack Lewis Junior, *Sec*
Rodger L Lesh, *VP*
Peggy S Lewis, *Sec*
EMP: 59 **EST:** 1963
SQ FT: 115,000
SALES (est): 234.34K
SALES (corp-wide): 9.76MM **Privately Held**
Web: www.lewisbakeries.net
SIC: 2051 Bread, all types (white, wheat, rye, etc); fresh or frozen
PA: Lewis Brothers Bakeries Inc
500 N Fulton Ave
Evansville IN 47710
812 425-4642

(G-4105)
HERITAGE CUSTOM PRODUCTS
1915 W Illinois St (47712-5120)
P.O. Box 6465 (47719-0465)
PHONE..............................812 425-8639
Jerry Knight, *Pr*
EMP: 1 **EST:** 2002
SALES (est): 91.61K **Privately Held**
SIC: 2499 Wood products, nec

(G-4106)
HEY HEYS CANDLES LLC
2827 Egmont St (47712-4937)
PHONE..............................812 484-9956
Rita Williams, *Prin*
EMP: 4 **EST:** 2018
SALES (est): 65.99K **Privately Held**
SIC: 3999 Candles

(G-4107)
HOME - LITTLE CREEK WINERY
4116 Koressel Rd (47720-2236)
PHONE..............................812 319-3951
EMP: 4 **EST:** 2015
SALES (est): 70.4K **Privately Held**
Web: www.littlecreekwinery.com
SIC: 2084 Wines

(G-4108)
HONEYWELL INTERNATIONAL INC
Also Called: Honeywell
101 Plaza Dr Ste 103 (47715-3514)
PHONE..............................812 473-4163
Tom Giorgio, *Asst Sec*
EMP: 1
Web: www.honeywell.com
SIC: 3829 5045 Temperature sensors, except industrial process and aircraft; Computers, peripherals, and software
PA: Honeywell International Inc.
855 S Mint St
Charlotte NC 28202

(G-4109)
HOOSIER HOT RODS CLASSICS INC
5209 N Kerth Ave (47711-2348)
PHONE..............................812 768-5221
Kent Mann, *Pr*
EMP: 6 **EST:** 2007
SALES (est): 402.66K **Privately Held**
Web: www.hoosierhotrod.com
SIC: 3711 7532 Automobile assembly, including specialty automobiles; Antique and classic automobile restoration

(G-4110)
HOOSIER STAMPING & MFG CORP (DH)
Also Called: Hoosier Wheel
700 Schrader Dr (47712-4970)
P.O. Box 6447 (47719-0447)
PHONE..............................812 426-2778
Alex Webb, *Pr*
▲ **EMP:** 25 **EST:** 1967
SQ FT: 38,000
SALES (est): 23.16MM
SALES (corp-wide): 102.32MM **Privately Held**
Web: www.hoosierwheel.com
SIC: 3469 Stamping metal for the trade
HQ: Otr Engineered Solutions, Inc.
195 Chatillon Rd Ne Ste 4
Rome GA 30161

(G-4111)
HOUCHENS INDUSTRIES INC
Also Called: Buehler's Buy Low 4182
4635 N 1st Ave (47710-3625)
PHONE..............................812 467-7255
Eric Bedwell, *Mgr*
EMP: 12
Web: www.houchens.com
SIC: 5411 5912 2052 2051 Supermarkets, independent; Drug stores and proprietary stores; Cookies and crackers; Bread, cake, and related products
PA: Houchens Industries, Inc.
700 Church St
Bowling Green KY 42102

(G-4112)
HSM EAGLE LTD
Also Called: Eagle Bearing, Ltd.
6149 Wedeking Ave (47715-8532)
P.O. Box 327 (47629-0327)
PHONE..............................812 491-9667
Thomas J Johnson, *Pr*
▲ **EMP:** 5 **EST:** 1989
SALES (est): 453.01K **Privately Held**
Web: www.eaglebearing.com
SIC: 3562 Roller bearings and parts

(G-4113)
HUNTER VENETIAN BLIND CO
2419 Hialeah Dr (47715-1947)
PHONE..............................812 471-1100
Jerry Schaefer, *Owner*
EMP: 1 **EST:** 1949
SQ FT: 1,800
SALES (est): 43.55K **Privately Held**
Web: www.wwvenetianblindcompany.com
SIC: 7349 7699 1799 2591 Window blind cleaning; Venetian blind repair shop; Window treatment installation; Venetian blinds

(G-4114)
IET GLOBAL INC
225 W Morgan Ave Ste A (47710-2515)
PHONE..............................812 421-7810
Daniel Davis, *Pr*
Paul Speciale, *
EMP: 40 **EST:** 2018
SALES (est): 5.18MM **Privately Held**
Web: www.ietglobal.com
SIC: 3511 Turbines and turbine generator set units, complete

(G-4115)
IGOTKICKZ LLC
4913 Rolling Ridge Dr (47712-6560)
PHONE..............................812 893-7674
EMP: 1 **EST:** 2020
SALES (est): 77.14K **Privately Held**
SIC: 2329 Men's and boy's clothing, nec

(G-4116)
ILPEA INDUSTRIES INC
2500 Lynch Rd (47711-2955)
P.O. Box 779 (47705-0779)
PHONE..............................812 752-2526
Wayne Heverly, *Manager*
EMP: 106
Web: www.ilpeaindustries.com
SIC: 3999 Barber and beauty shop equipment
HQ: Ilpea Industries, Inc.
745 S Gardner St
Scottsburg IN 47170
812 752-2526

(G-4117)
IMAGINATION GRAPHICS
2323 W Franklin St (47712-5118)
PHONE..............................812 423-6503
Julie Williams, *Owner*
EMP: 2 **EST:** 1986
SQ FT: 2,500
SALES (est): 110K **Privately Held**
Web: www.imaginationts.com
SIC: 2759 Screen printing

(G-4118)
IMI SOUTHWEST INC (HQ)
1816 W Lloyd Expy (47712-5137)
PHONE..............................812 424-3554
Fred Irving, *CEO*
Mike Harmon, *VP*
Pete Irving, *Ch Bd*
Earl Brinker, *CEO*
EMP: 50 **EST:** 1948
SQ FT: 6,000
SALES (est): 21.26MM
SALES (corp-wide): 814.09MM **Privately Held**
SIC: 3273 Ready-mixed concrete
PA: Irving Materials, Inc.
8032 N State Road 9
Greenfield IN 46140
317 326-3101

(G-4119)
INDIANA DRILLING COMPANY INC (PA)
1410 N Cullen Ave (47715-2331)
P.O. Box 5269 (47716-5269)
PHONE..............................812 477-1575
Charles A Robinson, *Pr*
J Glenn Robinson, *VP*
EMP: 4 **EST:** 1979
SQ FT: 2,500
SALES (est): 752.92K
SALES (corp-wide): 752.92K **Privately Held**
SIC: 1381 Drilling oil and gas wells

(G-4120)
INDIANA PETROLEUM CONTRACTORS (PA)
1410 N Cullen Ave (47715-2331)
P.O. Box 5269 (47716-5269)
PHONE..............................812 477-1575
Charles A Robinson, *Pr*
EMP: 5 **EST:** 1978
SALES (est): 1.78MM
SALES (corp-wide): 1.78MM **Privately Held**
Web: www.indianaboringcontractors.com
SIC: 1389 Cementing oil and gas well casings

(G-4121)
INDIANA TUBE CORPORATION (DH)
2100 Lexington Rd (47720)
P.O. Box 3005 (47730)
PHONE..............................812 467-7155
John Whitenack, *Pr*
Joel Cunningham, *
Ron Hawkins, *
Ron Tenbarge, *
▼ **EMP:** 251 **EST:** 1973
SQ FT: 125,000
SALES (est): 64.31MM
SALES (corp-wide): 1.91B **Publicly Held**
Web: www.indianatube.com
SIC: 3317 Steel pipe and tubes
HQ: Handy & Harman
C/O Steel Partners
New York NY 10022
212 520-2300

Evansville - Vanderburgh County (G-4122)

(G-4122)
INDUCTION IRON INCORPORATED
403 N 7th Ave (47710-1417)
PHONE.................813 969-3300
Greg Nun, *Mgr*
EMP: 10
SALES (corp-wide): 2.67MM **Privately Held**
Web: www.inductioniron.com
SIC: 3449 3341 Miscellaneous metalwork; Secondary nonferrous metals
PA: Induction Iron Incorporated
  13909 N Dale Mbry Hwy # 203
  Tampa FL 33618
  813 969-3300

(G-4123)
INDUSTRIAL PLASTICS GROUP LLC
Also Called: Ipg
911 E Virginia St (47711-5657)
PHONE.................812 831-4053
Barry Cox, *Pr*
◆ **EMP:** 23 **EST:** 2001
SALES (est): 16.28MM
SALES (corp-wide): 102.03MM **Privately Held**
Web: www.iplasticsgroup.com
SIC: 2821 Plastics materials and resins
PA: Warehouse Services, Inc.
  58 S Burty Rd
  Piedmont SC 29673
  812 831-4053

(G-4124)
INDUSTRIAL SEWING MACHINE CO
Also Called: Tom Cooks
2750 N Burkhardt Rd Ste 107 (47715-1685)
P.O. Box 8243 (47716-8243)
PHONE.................812 425-2255
Edwina Cook, *Owner*
EMP: 3 **EST:** 1970
SQ FT: 5,000
SALES (est): 110K **Privately Held**
SIC: 7641 2391 5084 5984 Upholstery work; Curtains and draperies; Sewing machines, industrial; Liquefied petroleum gas dealers

(G-4125)
INDUSTRIAL TOOL & DIE CORP
2201 Lexington Rd (47720-1235)
PHONE.................812 424-9971
Charles Bryan Coughlin, *Pr*
Stacey L Coughlin, *Sec*
▲ **EMP:** 11 **EST:** 1961
SQ FT: 10,500
SALES (est): 989.61K **Privately Held**
Web: www.indtool.net
SIC: 3544 Special dies and tools

(G-4126)
INKWORKS STUDIO LLC
767 S Green River Rd (47715-4179)
PHONE.................812 401-6203
EMP: 6 **EST:** 2018
SALES (est): 93.33K **Privately Held**
Web: www.indianascreenprinting.com
SIC: 2759 Screen printing

(G-4127)
INTEGRAL TECHNOLOGIES INC
2605 Eastside Park Rd Ste 1 (47715-2177)
PHONE.................812 550-1770
Doug Bathauer, *Pr*
James Eagan, *Ch Bd*
Eli Dusenbury, *CFO*
Slobodan Pavlovic, *VP*
EMP: 4 **EST:** 1996
SQ FT: 800
SALES (est): 39.9K **Privately Held**
Web: www.itkg.net
SIC: 2821 Plastics materials and resins

(G-4128)
INTEGRATED ENERGY TECHNOLOGIES INC
225 W Morgan Ave Ste A (47710-2515)
P.O. Box 1146 (06340-1146)
PHONE.................812 421-7810
▲ **EMP:** 40
SIC: 3724 3714 3511 Exhaust systems, aircraft; Exhaust systems and parts, motor vehicle; Turbines and turbine generator sets and parts

(G-4129)
INTERMETCO PROCESSING INC
1901 W Louisiana St (47710-2268)
PHONE.................812 423-5914
Ron Morgan, *Pr*
EMP: 6 **EST:** 2008
SALES (est): 100.86K **Privately Held**
SIC: 3399 Brads: aluminum, brass, or other nonferrous metal or wire

(G-4130)
INTERNATIONAL STEEL COMPANY
Also Called: Interntonal Revolving Door Div
2138 N 6th Ave (47710-2814)
PHONE.................812 425-3311
Rahmi Soyugenc, *Pr*
Lewis Cheeney, *
Marjorie Soyugenc, *
▲ **EMP:** 70 **EST:** 1909
SQ FT: 156,000
SALES (est): 9.68MM
SALES (corp-wide): 9.68MM **Privately Held**
Web: www.internationalrevolvingdoor.com
SIC: 3442 3231 Metal doors; Products of purchased glass
PA: Evansville Metal Products Inc
  119 Ladonna Blvd
  Evansville IN 47711
  812 423-5632

(G-4131)
IRD GROUP INC
2138 N 6th Ave (47710-2814)
PHONE.................812 425-3311
James M Kratochvil, *Prin*
EMP: 20 **EST:** 2015
SQ FT: 135,000
SALES (est): 2.35MM **Privately Held**
Web: www.internationalrevolvingdoor.com
SIC: 3442 Metal doors

(G-4132)
IRVING MATERIALS INC
6000 Oak Grove Rd (47715-2359)
PHONE.................812 424-3551
EMP: 3
SALES (corp-wide): 814.09MM **Privately Held**
Web: www.irvmat.com
SIC: 3273 Ready-mixed concrete
PA: Irving Materials, Inc.
  8032 N State Road 9
  Greenfield IN 46140
  317 326-3101

(G-4133)
J A SMIT INC
Also Called: Powers Welding Shop
1500 N Fulton Ave (47710-2365)
P.O. Box 6975 (47719-0975)
PHONE.................812 424-8141
Larry R Smith, *Pr*
Sharon Smith, *Treas*
EMP: 6 **EST:** 1968
SALES (est): 1.01MM **Privately Held**
Web: www.powerswelding.com
SIC: 7692 3446 3443 3441 Welding repair; Architectural metalwork; Fabricated plate work (boiler shop); Fabricated structural metal

(G-4134)
J TROCKMAN & SONS INC
1017 Bayse St (47714-4180)
P.O. Box 682 (47704-0682)
PHONE.................812 425-5271
David Trockman, *Pr*
Jeffrey Trockman, *
▼ **EMP:** 36 **EST:** 1985
SQ FT: 28,000
SALES (est): 4.56MM **Privately Held**
Web: www.trockman.com
SIC: 5093 3341 Ferrous metal scrap and waste; Secondary nonferrous metals

(G-4135)
J&J SPRTS SCREEN PRTG SPRIT WR
3012 Covert Ave Ste B (47714-4094)
PHONE.................812 909-2686
Larry Hooper, *Prin*
EMP: 5 **EST:** 2018
SALES (est): 231.05K **Privately Held**
Web: www.jandjsportsevv.com
SIC: 2759 Screen printing

(G-4136)
JACK FROST LLC
Also Called: Honeywell Authorized Dealer
1401 N Fares Ave (47711-4729)
PHONE.................812 477-7244
H Scott Larsen, *
EMP: 40 **EST:** 1993
SALES (est): 4.52MM **Privately Held**
Web: www.jackfrostinc.com
SIC: 1711 3444 Warm air heating and air conditioning contractor; Sheet metalwork

(G-4137)
JACKSON SEED SERVICE LLC
14510 Old State Rd (47725-9407)
PHONE.................812 480-6555
Shawn Jackson, *Managing Member*
EMP: 5 **EST:** 2013
SALES (est): 196.91K **Privately Held**
Web: www.jacksonseedservice.com
SIC: 2824 Organic fibers, noncellulosic

(G-4138)
JAZ INDUSTRIAL LLC
13040 Reising Ln (47720-7919)
PHONE.................812 305-5692
Stephanie D Purcell, *Pr*
EMP: 11 **EST:** 2014
SALES (est): 508.5K **Privately Held**
Web: www.jazind.com
SIC: 3999 Manufacturing industries, nec

(G-4139)
JBM RACE CARS LLC
7901 Newburgh Rd (47715-4533)
PHONE.................812 305-3666
Mark Mcdonald, *Prin*
EMP: 2 **EST:** 2008
SALES (est): 132.07K **Privately Held**
Web: www.dragsters4sale.com
SIC: 3711 Automobile assembly, including specialty automobiles

(G-4140)
JEF ENTERPRISES INC (PA)
Also Called: Tri-State Trophies
1200 W Columbia St (47710-1400)
P.O. Box 6449 (47719-0449)
PHONE.................812 425-0628
Lisa Tanner, *Pr*
Harvey Tanner, *VP*
Beverley Frederking, *Stockholder*
EMP: 14 **EST:** 1967
SQ FT: 6,000
SALES (est): 2.29MM
SALES (corp-wide): 2.29MM **Privately Held**
Web: www.spamhaus.org
SIC: 5999 3993 Trophies and plaques; Signs and advertising specialties

(G-4141)
JEFF HURY HRDWOOD FLORS PNTG S
629 S Norman Ave (47714-2119)
PHONE.................812 204-8650
Jeff Haury, *Prin*
EMP: 3 **EST:** 2007
SALES (est): 185.99K **Privately Held**
Web: jeff-haury-hardwood-floor-service.hub.biz
SIC: 1752 1771 2426 Wood floor installation and refinishing; Flooring contractor; Flooring, hardwood

(G-4142)
JESHSOFT LLC
414 Mount Ashley Rd (47711-7167)
PHONE.................812 431-8603
Paul Hanson, *Managing Member*
EMP: 1 **EST:** 2008
SALES (est): 139.52K **Privately Held**
SIC: 7372 7389 Utility computer software; Business Activities at Non-Commercial Site

(G-4143)
JOE W MORGAN INC
Also Called: Henry Fligeltaub Co Div
1719 W Louisiana St (47710-2265)
P.O. Box 928 (47706-0928)
PHONE.................812 423-5914
Ronald Morgan, *Pr*
Alan N Shovers, *
John Mac Leod, *
EMP: 65 **EST:** 1971
SALES (est): 6.34MM **Privately Held**
Web: www.fligeltaub.com
SIC: 3341 5093 Aluminum smelting and refining (secondary); Ferrous metal scrap and waste

(G-4144)
JOHNSON CONTROLS INC
Also Called: Johnson Controls
8401 N Kentucky Ave Ste H (47725-6301)
PHONE.................812 868-1374
EMP: 12
Web: www.johnsoncontrols.com
SIC: 3822 2531 8744 Building services monitoring controls, automatic; Seats, automobile; Facilities support services
HQ: Johnson Controls, Inc.
  5757 N Green Bay Ave
  Milwaukee WI 53209
  866 496-1999

(G-4145)
JRI WOODWORKS
1601 Florence St (47710-2647)
PHONE.................812 401-1234
EMP: 5 **EST:** 2019
SALES (est): 126.44K **Privately Held**
Web: www.jriwoodworks.com
SIC: 2431 Millwork

(G-4146)
JT CUSTOM MACHINE SHOP LLC
3065 Cottage Dr (47711-4061)
PHONE.................812 827-1993

Jason Lueken, Prin
EMP: 5 **EST:** 2019
SALES (est): 89.79K **Privately Held**
SIC: 3599 Machine shop, jobbing and repair

(G-4147)
JZJ SERVICES LLC (PA)
Also Called: Pro-Tex-All
210 S Morton Ave (47713-2448)
PHONE..................812 424-8268
Richard Easterling, *Managing Member*
EMP: 24 **EST:** 2019
SALES (est): 2.12MM
SALES (corp-wide): 2.12MM **Privately Held**
Web: www.protexall.com
SIC: 2842 5087 5169 Polishes and sanitation goods; Janitors' supplies; Waxes, except petroleum

(G-4148)
KENDLE CUSTOM INC
Also Called: Aquathin A Wtr Prfction Evnsvl
11711 Boberg Rd (47712-8625)
PHONE..................812 985-5917
George Kendall, *Pr*
Troy Higgenson, *VP*
EMP: 2 **EST:** 1985
SALES (est): 162.32K **Privately Held**
SIC: 3589 Water purification equipment, household type

(G-4149)
KERR GROUP LLC
315 Se 2nd St (47713-1054)
PHONE..................812 424-2904
Ira Boots, *Pr*
EMP: 127
SIC: 3089 Closures, plastics
HQ: Kerr Group, Llc
    1846 Charter Ln Ste 209
    Lancaster PA 17601
    812 424-2904

(G-4150)
KERRY INC
1615 N Fulton Ave (47710-2755)
PHONE..................812 464-9151
EMP: 12
Web: www.kerry.com
SIC: 2099 Food preparations, nec
HQ: Kerry Inc.
    3400 Millington Rd
    Beloit WI 53511
    608 363-1200

(G-4151)
KERRY INC
DCA Modern Maid
1515 Park St (47710-2295)
PHONE..................812 464-9151
Joe Sstellern, *Brnch Mgr*
EMP: 115
SQ FT: 183,000
Web: www.kerry.com
SIC: 2041 2099 Doughs and batters; Food preparations, nec
HQ: Kerry Inc.
    3400 Millington Rd
    Beloit WI 53511
    608 363-1200

(G-4152)
KIC LLC
Also Called: Kic
7140 Office Cir (47715)
PHONE..................360 823-4440
Robin Kendrick, *CEO*
John Schneider, *Pr*
Stephen Martin, *Sec*
EMP: 30 **EST:** 2013
SALES (est): 9.93MM **Privately Held**
Web: www.kicintl.com
SIC: 4214 3715 Local trucking with storage; Bus trailers, tractor type
HQ: Accuride Corporation
    38777 6 Mile Rd Ste 410
    Livonia MI 48152
    812 962-5000

(G-4153)
KIMALCO INC
Also Called: Kimalco Mattress
213 W Division St Ste J (47710-1368)
PHONE..................812 463-3105
Kimberly Pike, *Pr*
Alice Pike, *Prin*
EMP: 5 **EST:** 2014
SALES (est): 478.97K **Privately Held**
Web: www.pikesmattress.com
SIC: 2515 Foundations and platforms

(G-4154)
KIRCHOFF CUSTOM SPORTS INC
311 Eissler Rd (47711-1551)
PHONE..................812 434-0355
Mike Kirchoff, *Prin*
EMP: 7 **EST:** 2009
SALES (est): 212.95K **Privately Held**
Web: www.sssservicessealcoating.com
SIC: 2759 Screen printing

(G-4155)
KITWANA KOUTURE LLC
705 Se 3rd St Apt B (47713-1140)
PHONE..................812 589-7135
EMP: 1 **EST:** 2020
SALES (est): 10K **Privately Held**
SIC: 2335 Women's, junior's, and misses' dresses

(G-4156)
KLEEN-RITE SUPPLY INC
Also Called: Krs
1101 E Diamond Ave (47711-3903)
PHONE..................812 422-7483
TOLL FREE: 800
Anthony D Richardt, *Pr*
EMP: 10 **EST:** 1981
SQ FT: 30,000
SALES (est): 2.39MM **Privately Held**
SIC: 5087 2842 Janitors' supplies; Cleaning or polishing preparations, nec

(G-4157)
KLEERBLUE SOLUTIONS
1601 Buchanan Rd (47720-5411)
PHONE..................800 320-2122
EMP: 6 **EST:** 2019
SALES (est): 138.61K **Privately Held**
Web: www.kleerbluesolutions.com
SIC: 3443 Fabricated plate work (boiler shop)

(G-4158)
KNIGHT DAVIS PUBLISHING LLC
1245 W Wortman Rd (47725-8861)
PHONE..................812 568-9646
Joelle Knight, *Prin*
EMP: 6 **EST:** 2017
SALES (est): 37.59K **Privately Held**
SIC: 2741 Miscellaneous publishing

(G-4159)
KOCH ENTERPRISES INC (PA)
Also Called: Koch Enterprises
14 S 11th Ave (47712)
PHONE..................812 465-9800
Robert Koch, *Ch*
James H Muehlbauer, *Vice Chairman*
Kevin R Koch, *Pr*
Susan E Parsons, *Sec*
◆ **EMP:** 7 **EST:** 1873
SALES (est): 915.49MM
SALES (corp-wide): 915.49MM **Privately Held**
Web: www.kochenterprises.com
SIC: 3363 5075 3559 5084 Aluminum die-castings; Air conditioning equipment, except room units, nec; Metal finishing equipment for plating, etc.; Industrial machinery and equipment

(G-4160)
KONECRANES INC
2400 Kotter Ave (47715-8509)
PHONE..................812 479-0488
Barb Watson, *Admn*
EMP: 9
Web: www.konecranes.com
SIC: 3536 Hoists, cranes, and monorails
HQ: Konecranes, Inc.
    4401 Gateway Blvd
    Springfield OH 45502

(G-4161)
LANIGAN HOLDINGS LLC
3400 Claremont Ave (47712-4800)
PHONE..................812 422-6912
Sara Hinsey, *Brnch Mgr*
EMP: 2
SALES (corp-wide): 48.44MM **Privately Held**
SIC: 3531 Crane carriers
PA: Lanigan Holdings Llc
    3111 167th St
    Hazel Crest IL 60429
    708 596-5200

(G-4162)
LASERTONE INC
Also Called: Ail
700 N Weinbach Ave Ste 101 (47711-5966)
PHONE..................812 473-5945
Mark Daily, *Pr*
EMP: 15 **EST:** 1988
SQ FT: 5,000
SALES (est): 1.43MM **Privately Held**
Web: www.advantageprintsolutionsinc.com
SIC: 3861 7629 5112 Toners, prepared photographic (not made in chemical plants); Business machine repair, electric; Computer and photocopying supplies

(G-4163)
LEED SAMPLES-FULFILLMENT
9700 Highway 57 (47725-9704)
PHONE..................812 867-4340
EMP: 11 **EST:** 2019
SALES (est): 556.25K **Privately Held**
Web: www.leedsamples.com
SIC: 2752 Offset printing

(G-4164)
LEED SELLING TOOLS CORP (PA)
9700 Highway 57 (47725-9704)
P.O. Box 68 (47545-0068)
PHONE..................812 867-4340
Douglas Edwards, *Pr*
Richard A Edwards, *
George K Grace, *
EMP: 42 **EST:** 1962
SQ FT: 19,000
SALES (est): 18.9MM
SALES (corp-wide): 18.9MM **Privately Held**
Web: www.leedsamples.com
SIC: 2789 2782 Swatches and samples; Sample books

(G-4165)
LETICA CORPORATION
101 Oakley St (47710-1237)
P.O. Box 5005 (48308-5005)
PHONE..................812 421-3136
Anton Letica, *CEO*
◆ **EMP:** 1800 **EST:** 1968
SALES (est): 47.76MM **Privately Held**
Web: www.letica.com
SIC: 2656 3089 Sanitary food containers; Plastics containers, except foam
HQ: Rpc Group Limited
    Suite 2
    Rushden NORTHANTS NN10

(G-4166)
LEWIS BROTHERS BAKERIES INC (PA)
Also Called: LEWIS BAKERIES
500 N Fulton Ave (47710)
PHONE..................812 425-4642
R Jack Lewis Junior, *Pr*
Peggy S Lewis, *Sec*
Jeffery J Sankovitch, *Treas*
▲ **EMP:** 200 **EST:** 1925
SQ FT: 100,000
SALES (est): 9.76MM
SALES (corp-wide): 9.76MM **Privately Held**
Web: www.lewisbakeries.net
SIC: 2051 5149 Bread, all types (white, wheat, rye, etc); fresh or frozen; Groceries and related products, nec

(G-4167)
LIGGETT GROUP LLC
1836 N Colony Rd (47715-2014)
PHONE..................812 479-7635
Von Fuchs, *Mgr*
EMP: 1
Web: www.liggettvectorbrands.com
SIC: 2111 Cigarettes
HQ: Liggett Group Llc
    100 Maple Ln
    Mebane NC 27302
    919 304-7700

(G-4168)
LIGHT & INK CORPORATION
Also Called: Link Graphics
1018 E Diamond Ave (47711-3902)
PHONE..................812 421-1400
Robert Fuchs, *Pr*
EMP: 8 **EST:** 1990
SQ FT: 9,000
SALES (est): 765.82K **Privately Held**
Web: www.linkgraphics.com
SIC: 2752 Offset printing

(G-4169)
LIGHT STIGMA LLC
10701 Greenleaf Dr (47712-8635)
PHONE..................812 550-7923
Joseph Priest, *Prin*
EMP: 1 **EST:** 2015
SALES (est): 57.54K **Privately Held**
SIC: 7372 Prepackaged software

(G-4170)
LINE-X
1804 Stringtown Rd (47711-4511)
PHONE..................812 491-9475
Matt Schapker, *Owner*
EMP: 2 **EST:** 2005
SALES (est): 150K **Privately Held**
Web: www.linex.com
SIC: 3479 7699 5531 Painting, coating, and hot dipping; Industrial equipment services; Truck equipment and parts

Evansville - Vanderburgh County (G-4171)

GEOGRAPHIC SECTION

(G-4171)
LIQUID NINJA ENERGY LLC
6050 Wedeking Ave Ste 14 (47715-2187)
PHONE..................812 746-2830
EMP: 12 **EST:** 2013
SQ FT: 4,000
SALES (est): 436.22K **Privately Held**
SIC: 2086 Carbonated beverages, nonalcoholic: pkged. in cans, bottles

(G-4172)
LITTLE BIRD PICTURE FRAMING
100 N Saint Joseph Ave (47712-5506)
PHONE..................812 437-0285
EMP: 5 **EST:** 2014
SALES (est): 123.61K **Privately Held**
SIC: 2499 Picture frame molding, finished

(G-4173)
LITTLE SUPER FINDINGS ✪
5115 Pollack Ave (47715)
PHONE..................812 430-3353
EMP: 1 **EST:** 2024
SALES (est): 65.62K **Privately Held**
SIC: 3911 7389 Jewelry, precious metal; Business Activities at Non-Commercial Site

(G-4174)
LIVELY MACHINE COMPANY INC
4404 Upper Mount Vernon Rd (47712-6418)
◆ **EMP:** 9 **EST:** 1952
SQ FT: 8,400
SALES (est): 1.34MM **Privately Held**
Web: www.livelymachine.com
SIC: 3599 Machine shop, jobbing and repair

(G-4175)
LOZANO WLDG & FABRICATION LLC
3816 E Morgan Ave (47715-2242)
PHONE..................812 550-1706
Cesar Lozano-capistran, *Pr*
EMP: 5 **EST:** 2016
SALES (est): 40.41K **Privately Held**
SIC: 7692 Welding repair

(G-4176)
LUBBER DUBBERS
6240 E Virginia St (47715-9126)
PHONE..................812 475-1725
EMP: 6 **EST:** 2017
SALES (est): 246.5K **Privately Held**
Web: www.lubberdubbers.com
SIC: 2369 Girl's and children's outerwear, nec

(G-4177)
LUCENT POLYMERS INC
Also Called: Lucent Polymers Acquisition
1700 Lynch Rd (47711-2848)
PHONE..................812 421-2216
▼ **EMP:** 100
Web: www.lucentpolymers.com
SIC: 2821 Plastics materials and resins

(G-4178)
LUXETREND LLC
1014 Mary St Apt 2 (47710-2049)
PHONE..................502 208-9344
EMP: 1
SALES (est): 68.7K **Privately Held**
SIC: 7389 3172 Business Activities at Non-Commercial Site; Cases, jewelry

(G-4179)
LYONDLLBSELL ADVNCED PLYMERS I
Also Called: Aschulman
820 E Columbia St (47711-5146)
PHONE..................812 202-1968
EMP: 50
Web: www.lyondellbasell.com
SIC: 2821 Molding compounds, plastics
HQ: Lyondellbasell Advanced Polymers Inc.
    1221 Mckinney St Ste 300
    Houston TX 77010
    713 309-7200

(G-4180)
LYONDLLBSELL ADVNCED PLYMERS I
5001 Ohara Dr (47711-2475)
PHONE..................713 309-7148
EMP: 51
Web: www.lyondellbasell.com
SIC: 2869 Industrial organic chemicals, nec
HQ: Lyondellbasell Advanced Polymers Inc.
    1221 Mckinney St Ste 300
    Houston TX 77010
    713 309-7200

(G-4181)
LYONDLLBSELL ADVNCED PLYMERS I
15000 Us Hwy 41 (47725-9360)
PHONE..................812 253-5203
EMP: 54
Web: www.lyondellbasell.com
SIC: 2869 Industrial organic chemicals, nec
HQ: Lyondellbasell Advanced Polymers Inc.
    1221 Mckinney St Ste 300
    Houston TX 77010
    713 309-7200

(G-4182)
MA PUBLISHING INC
2205 Bellemeade Ave Apt A (47714-2346)
PHONE..................812 217-0925
EMP: 4 **EST:** 2016
SALES (est): 56.87K **Privately Held**
SIC: 2741 Miscellaneous publishing

(G-4183)
MACO REPROGRAHICS LLC
600 Court St (47708-1342)
PHONE..................812 464-8108
EMP: 3 **EST:** 1966
SQ FT: 900
SALES (est): 467.61K **Privately Held**
Web: www.macoplanroom.com
SIC: 5049 7334 2752 Engineers' equipment and supplies, nec; Blueprinting service; Offset printing

(G-4184)
MADDENCO INC
4847 E Virginia St Ste G (47715-2611)
PHONE..................812 474-6245
Jay Adams, *Pr*
EMP: 16 **EST:** 1977
SQ FT: 4,500
SALES (est): 2.41MM **Privately Held**
Web: www.maddenco.com
SIC: 7372 5045 Business oriented computer software; Mainframe computers

(G-4185)
MAGELLAN INTEGRATION INC
318 Main St Ste 322 (47708-1484)
P.O. Box 110 (62363-0110)
PHONE..................812 492-4400
EMP: 38
SALES (est): 4.04MM **Privately Held**
SIC: 3674 Integrated circuits, semiconductor networks, etc.

(G-4186)
MALEY & WERTZ INC (PA)
Also Called: Maley & Wertz Lumber
900 E Columbia St (47711-5148)
P.O. Box 4537 (47724-0537)
PHONE..................812 425-3358
Mike Powers, *Pr*
Richard W Klipsch, *Dir*
Teresa Korff, *Sec*
▼ **EMP:** 21 **EST:** 1885
SQ FT: 1,500
SALES (est): 9.27MM
SALES (corp-wide): 9.27MM **Privately Held**
Web: www.maleyandwertz.com
SIC: 2421 Sawmills and planing mills, general

(G-4187)
MANNON L WALTERS INC
6015 Heckel Rd (47725-7338)
PHONE..................812 867-5946
Mannon L Walters, *Pr*
Betty Trabant, *Prin*
Sherry Roberts, *Sec*
Ronnie Rogers, *Sec*
Mike Newlin, *Sec*
EMP: 10 **EST:** 1989
SALES (est): 2.02MM **Privately Held**
Web: www.mannonoil.com
SIC: 1311 Crude petroleum production

(G-4188)
MANNON OIL LLC
6015 Heckel Rd (47725-7338)
PHONE..................812 867-5946
EMP: 12 **EST:** 2005
SALES (est): 637.94K **Privately Held**
Web: www.mannonoil.com
SIC: 1382 Oil and gas exploration services

(G-4189)
MARK EDWARD HAILS
Also Called: Hails' Jewelry Service
440 Tyler Ave (47715-3244)
PHONE..................812 437-1030
Mark E Hails, *Owner*
Mark Hails, *Owner*
EMP: 1 **EST:** 1985
SALES (est): 8.4K **Privately Held**
SIC: 3911 7631 Jewelry, precious metal; Jewelry repair services

(G-4190)
MARTIN HOLDING COMPANY LLC
Also Called: Indiana Cardinal
605 W Eichel Ave (47710-2411)
PHONE..................812 401-9988
Timothy R Martin, *Managing Member*
EMP: 47 **EST:** 2005
SQ FT: 200,000
SALES (est): 9.45MM **Privately Held**
Web: www.indianacardinal.com
SIC: 2821 Plastics materials and resins

(G-4191)
MASTER MANUFACTURING COMPANY
4703 Ohara Dr (47711-2495)
PHONE..................812 425-1561
John R Gannon Junior, *Pr*
Grace Donley, *
EMP: 41 **EST:** 1970
SQ FT: 74,000
SALES (est): 5.36MM **Privately Held**
Web: www.mastermfg.com
SIC: 3469 3423 Stamping metal for the trade; Ironworkers' hand tools

(G-4192)
MATRIXX-QTR INC
15000 Highway 41 N (47725-9360)
PHONE..................812 429-0901
▲ **EMP:** 55
SIC: 3087 Custom compound purchased resins

(G-4193)
MEAD JOHNSON & COMPANY LLC (DH)
Also Called: Mead Johnson Nutrition
2400 W Lloyd Expy (47721)
PHONE..................812 429-5000
Peter Kasper Jakobsen, *Pr*
Peter Kasper Jakobsen, *CEO*
Charles Urbain, *
◆ **EMP:** 121 **EST:** 1895
SQ FT: 875,000
SALES (est): 460.73MM
SALES (corp-wide): 18.21B **Privately Held**
Web: www.meadjohnson.com
SIC: 2099 2834 2032 Food preparations, nec; Pharmaceutical preparations; Canned specialties
HQ: Mead Johnson Nutrition Company
    225 N Canal St Fl 25
    Chicago IL 60606

(G-4194)
MEASURE PRESS INC
526 S Lincoln Park Dr (47714-1542)
PHONE..................812 473-0361
Robert Griffith, *Owner*
EMP: 5 **EST:** 2012
SALES (est): 9.06K **Privately Held**
Web: www.measurepress.com
SIC: 2741 Miscellaneous publishing

(G-4195)
MED PAD INCORPORATED
1411 Timberlake Rd (47710-4127)
PHONE..................812 422-6154
EMP: 1
SALES (est): 55.8K **Privately Held**
SIC: 2676 Napkins, sanitary: made from purchased paper

(G-4196)
MERIDIAN METALFORM INC
1025 W Tennessee St (47710-2349)
PHONE..................812 422-1524
David Walker, *Pr*
EMP: 7 **EST:** 1994
SALES (est): 675.39K **Privately Held**
Web: www.meridianmetalform.com
SIC: 3442 Casements, aluminum

(G-4197)
METAL FABRICATION LLC
1001 Mount Auburn Rd (47720-8226)
PHONE..................812 686-9430
EMP: 1
SALES (est): 70.48K **Privately Held**
SIC: 3499 Fabricated metal products, nec

(G-4198)
METAL MASTERS INC
4600 Broadway Ave (47712-4208)
P.O. Box 3501 (47734-3501)
PHONE..................812 421-9162
Tony May, *Pr*
Steve Vessel, *VP*
Lynda R Vessel, *Sec*
EMP: 3 **EST:** 1991
SALES (est): 327.04K **Privately Held**
SIC: 3441 Fabricated structural metal

(G-4199)
MEUTH CONSTRUCTION SUPPLY INC
Also Called: Meuth Construction Supply
2201 Bergdolt Rd (47711-2888)
PHONE..................812 424-8554
Delbert Meuth, *Brnch Mgr*

EMP: 1
SALES (corp-wide): 9.81MM **Privately Held**
Web: www.meuthconcrete.com
SIC: 3273 Ready-mixed concrete
PA: Meuth Construction Supply, Inc.
    703 8th St
    Henderson KY 42420
    270 827-8063

(G-4200)
MEYER OIL CO
19920 Ruffian Way (47725-7867)
PHONE.............................812 746-9525
EMP: 11
SALES (corp-wide): 24.71MM **Privately Held**
Web: www.mach1stores.com
SIC: 3599 Machine shop, jobbing and repair
PA: Meyer Oil Co.
    1505 W Main St
    Teutopolis IL
    217 857-3163

(G-4201)
MICHAEL R HARRIS
Also Called: Harris Oil Co
20 Nw 1st St Rear 208 (47708-1267)
PHONE.............................812 425-9411
R Michael Harris, *Owner*
Karen Baldman, *Sec*
EMP: 2 EST: 1966
SALES (est): 221.28K **Privately Held**
SIC: 1382 1381 Oil and gas exploration services; Drilling oil and gas wells

(G-4202)
MICO INDUSTRIES LLC
2301 Lexington Rd (47720-1237)
PHONE.............................812 480-3015
Brain Housman, *Owner*
EMP: 3 EST: 2004
SALES (est): 453.28K **Privately Held**
Web: www.mico-industries.com
SIC: 3552 Dyeing, drying, and finishing machinery and equipment

(G-4203)
MID MOUNTAIN MATERIALS INC
Also Called: Mid-Mountain Materials
1176 E Diamond Ave (47711-3904)
PHONE.............................812 550-5867
EMP: 17
SALES (corp-wide): 7.22MM **Privately Held**
Web: www.mid-mountain.com
SIC: 2295 Chemically coated and treated fabrics
PA: Mid Mountain Materials, Inc.
    5602 2nd Ave S
    Seattle WA 98108
    206 762-7600

(G-4204)
MID-AMERICA ENVIRONMENTAL LLC
Also Called: Alpha Laser and Imaging
5815 Metro Center Dr (47715-2651)
PHONE.............................812 475-1644
Aaron Althaus, *Managing Member*
EMP: 19 EST: 1999
SQ FT: 4,500
SALES (est): 4.08MM **Privately Held**
SIC: 3861 7629 Toners, prepared photographic (not made in chemical plants); Business machine repair, electric

(G-4205)
MIDWESTERN PET FOODS INC (PA)
9634 Hedden Rd (47725-9660)
PHONE.............................812 867-7466

◆ EMP: 17 EST: 1961
SALES (est): 25.37MM
SALES (corp-wide): 25.37MM **Privately Held**
Web: www.midwesternpetfoods.com
SIC: 2047 2048 Dog food; Prepared feeds, nec

(G-4206)
MILLMADE INCORPORATED
9 N Kentucky Ave (47711-5708)
P.O. Box 6565 (47719-0565)
PHONE.............................812 424-7778
Billy Grant, *Pr*
Dennis Grant, *VP*
EMP: 8 EST: 1987
SQ FT: 11,000
SALES (est): 926.15K **Privately Held**
Web: www.millmade.com
SIC: 2521 Wood office furniture

(G-4207)
MOBILE COMMUNICATIONS TECH
945 N Peerless Rd (47712-2933)
PHONE.............................812 423-7322
Steven Muensterman, *VP*
EMP: 2 EST: 2001
SALES (est): 175.09K **Privately Held**
SIC: 3651 4813 4899 FM and AM radio tuners; Telephone communication, except radio; Communication services, nec

(G-4208)
MOMINEE STUDIOS INC
5001 Lincoln Ave (47715-4113)
PHONE.............................812 473-1691
Jules Mominee, *Pr*
Terry Mominee, *Sec*
EMP: 4 EST: 1979
SALES (est): 346.52K **Privately Held**
Web: www.momineestudios.com
SIC: 3231 5231 Stained glass: made from purchased glass; Glass, leaded or stained

(G-4209)
MONSANTO COMPANY
Also Called: Monsanto
737 Rusher Ln (47725-7842)
PHONE.............................229 759-0034
Robert Clements, *Brnch Mgr*
EMP: 5
SALES (corp-wide): 51.78B **Privately Held**
Web: www.monsanto.com
SIC: 2879 Agricultural chemicals, nec
HQ: Monsanto Technology Llc.
    800 N Lindbergh Blvd
    Saint Louis MO 63167
    314 694-1000

(G-4210)
MOONEY COPY SERVICE INC
40 E Sycamore St (47713-1930)
PHONE.............................812 423-6626
Michael Dejean, *Pr*
Michael De Jean, *Pr*
EMP: 4 EST: 1945
SQ FT: 5,000
SALES (est): 390K **Privately Held**
Web: www.mooneyprinting.com
SIC: 2752 2759 Offset printing; Letterpress printing

(G-4211)
MOORE ENGINEERING & PROD CO (PA)
Also Called: Mepco
2104 Lincoln Ave (47714-1612)
P.O. Box 427 (62863-0427)
PHONE.............................812 479-1051
Lester D Moore, *Pr*
Joyce A Moore, *Sec*

EMP: 12 EST: 1967
SQ FT: 3,000
SALES (est): 1.2MM
SALES (corp-wide): 1.2MM **Privately Held**
SIC: 1311 8711 Crude petroleum production; Petroleum engineering

(G-4212)
MOORE MACHINE & GEAR INC
Also Called: Moore Machine & Gear
10920 N Saint Joseph Ave (47720-7195)
PHONE.............................812 963-3074
Alan Moore, *Pr*
Judy Lynch, *Sec*
EMP: 6 EST: 1962
SQ FT: 2,600
SALES (est): 472.74K **Privately Held**
Web: www.moorecustomgear.com
SIC: 3599 3566 Machine shop, jobbing and repair; Drives, high speed industrial, except hydrostatic

(G-4213)
MOORE METAL WORKS & A/C LLC
3712 Upper Mount Vernon Rd (47712-7868)
PHONE.............................812 422-9473
EMP: 25 EST: 1997
SALES (est): 2.42MM **Privately Held**
Web: www.mooremetalworks.com
SIC: 3444 Sheet metalwork

(G-4214)
MT PUBLISHING COMPANY INC
209 Nw 8th St (47708-1907)
P.O. Box 6802 (47719-0802)
PHONE.............................812 468-8022
Mark A Thompson, *Pr*
Cathy Thompson, *VP*
EMP: 8 EST: 1997
SALES (est): 492.85K **Privately Held**
Web: www.mtpublishing.com
SIC: 2741 Miscellaneous publishing

(G-4215)
MULTISEAL INC
Also Called: Multiseal
4320 Hitch Peters Rd (47711)
PHONE.............................812 428-3422
Gary M Rust, *Pr*
Robert C Rust, *
Larry Rust, *
EMP: 120 EST: 1991
SQ FT: 75,000
SALES (est): 22.07MM **Privately Held**
Web: www.multiseal-usa.com
SIC: 2891 Sealants

(G-4216)
MULZER CRUSHED STONE INC
Also Called: Evansville Materials
900 Nw Riverside Dr (47708-1058)
P.O. Box 3596 (47734-3596)
PHONE.............................844 480-6803
Russell Woosley, *Mgr*
EMP: 41
SALES (corp-wide): 34.95B **Privately Held**
Web: www.mulzer.com
SIC: 1422 1442 Limestones, ground; Construction sand and gravel
HQ: Mulzer Crushed Stone Inc
    534 Mozart St
    Tell City IN 47586
    812 547-7921

(G-4217)
N2 PUBLISHING
6709 E Oak St (47715-3535)
PHONE.............................812 449-0408
EMP: 5 EST: 2017
SALES (est): 65.01K **Privately Held**

Web: www.strollmag.com
SIC: 2741 Miscellaneous publishing

(G-4218)
NALIN MANUFACTURING LLC
2108 E Virginia St (47711-5954)
PHONE.............................812 401-9187
Andrew Nalin, *Prin*
EMP: 5 EST: 2011
SALES (est): 75K **Privately Held**
Web: www.nalinmfg.com
SIC: 3999 Manufacturing industries, nec

(G-4219)
NEEDLES CONTRACT EMB INC
2913 E Mulberry St (47714-2549)
PHONE.............................812 491-9636
Lynna M Townsend, *Prin*
EMP: 1 EST: 2006
SALES (est): 79K **Privately Held**
SIC: 2395 Embroidery and art needlework

(G-4220)
NELSON BROTHERS
7525 E Virginia St (47715)
PHONE.............................812 250-7520
EMP: 4 EST: 2019
SALES (est): 83.68K **Privately Held**
SIC: 2892 Explosives

(G-4221)
NORMAN TOOL INC
15415 Old State Rd (47725-8578)
PHONE.............................812 867-3496
Scott Norman, *Pr*
EMP: 4 EST: 1946
SQ FT: 7,350
SALES (est): 365.79K **Privately Held**
Web: www.normantool.com
SIC: 3544 Special dies and tools

(G-4222)
NOV OAK WOODWORKING
913 Washington Ave (47713-2259)
PHONE.............................812 422-1973
Donald Novack, *Prin*
EMP: 6 EST: 2000
SALES (est): 63.99K **Privately Held**
SIC: 2431 Millwork

(G-4223)
NOVA POLYMERS INCORPORATED
Also Called: Nova
2650 Eastside Park Rd (47715-2178)
P.O. Box 8278 (47716-8278)
PHONE.............................812 476-0339
Roger D Chapman, *Pr*
EMP: 40 EST: 1984
SQ FT: 78,000
SALES (est): 8.43MM **Privately Held**
Web: www.novapolymers.net
SIC: 2821 Thermoplastic materials

(G-4224)
NUSSMEIER ENGRAVING COMPANY
933 Main St (47708-1834)
PHONE.............................812 425-1339
Louis H Nussmeier, *Sec*
David Nussmeier, *Pr*
Steven D Nussmeier, *VP*
James L Nussmeier, *Dir*
EMP: 21 EST: 1916
SQ FT: 15,000
SALES (est): 927.6K **Privately Held**
Web: www.nussmeier.com
SIC: 2754 2791 2759 2752 Stationery and invitation printing, gravure; Typesetting; Commercial printing, nec; Commercial printing, lithographic

(G-4225)
OBRYAN BARREL COMPANY INC
5501 Old Boonville Hwy (47715-2130)
PHONE.................................812 479-6741
Arthur J O'bryan, *Pr*
Timothy O'bryan, *VP*
Daniel O'bryan, *VP*
Anna O'bryan, *Sec*
EMP: 30 **EST:** 1962
SQ FT: 10,000
SALES (est): 24.5MM **Privately Held**
Web: www.obryanbarrel.com
SIC: 5085 3412 Barrels, new or reconditioned; Barrels, shipping: metal

(G-4226)
OILFIELD RESEARCH INC
7825 Old Orchard Trl (47712-7324)
PHONE.................................812 424-2907
Marlin F Krieg, *Pr*
Carol Sue Roth, *Sec*
EMP: 2 **EST:** 1960
SALES (est): 174.41K **Privately Held**
SIC: 8711 1389 Petroleum engineering; Oil field services, nec

(G-4227)
OMNI PLASTICS LLC
Also Called: Omni Plastics
2300 Lynch Rd (47711-2951)
PHONE.................................812 422-0888
▲ **EMP:** 80
Web: www.omniplastics.com
SIC: 3083 2821 Laminated plastics plate and sheet; Plastics materials and resins

(G-4228)
ORG CHEM GROUP LLC (PA)
2406 Lynch Rd (47711-2953)
PHONE.................................812 464-4446
▲ **EMP:** 69 **EST:** 1996
SQ FT: 11,000
SALES (est): 69.12MM **Privately Held**
Web: www.chem-group.com
SIC: 2869 Industrial organic chemicals, nec

(G-4229)
ORTHOTIC & PROSTHETIC LAB
Also Called: O & P Lab
125 N Weinbach Ave Ste 310 (47711-6091)
PHONE.................................812 479-6298
Chad Allen, *Pr*
Elva Allen, *Sec*
EMP: 11 **EST:** 1990
SALES (est): 505.33K **Privately Held**
SIC: 3842 Limbs, artificial

(G-4230)
OVATION COMMUNICATIONS INC
Also Called: Kwik Kopy Business Center 130
1326 N Weinbach Ave (47711-4307)
PHONE.................................812 401-9100
EMP: 6 **EST:** 1986
SQ FT: 3,625
SALES (est): 709.99K **Privately Held**
Web: www.ovationgrafix.com
SIC: 2752 7334 7311 3993 Offset printing; Photocopying and duplicating services; Advertising agencies; Signs and advertising specialties

(G-4231)
OVER HILL & DALE SIGN STUDIO
12730 Highway 57 (47725-7646)
PHONE.................................812 867-1664
Dale Wright, *Owner*
EMP: 2 **EST:** 1963
SALES (est): 91.99K **Privately Held**
SIC: 3993 5099 Signs and advertising specialties; Signs, except electric

(G-4232)
PALLET RECYCLERS LLC
4200 Upper Mount Vernon Rd (47712-6429)
PHONE.................................812 402-0095
Art Green, *Pr*
EMP: 8 **EST:** 2002
SALES (est): 636.37K **Privately Held**
Web: www.palletrecyclers.com
SIC: 2448 Pallets, wood

(G-4233)
PARADISE INK INC
Also Called: Paradise Ink
619 N Burkhardt Rd Ste G (47715-7296)
P.O. Box 177 (47618-0177)
PHONE.................................812 402-4465
Julia Hudson, *CEO*
EMP: 2 **EST:** 2006
SALES (est): 244.92K **Privately Held**
Web: www.paradiseink.net
SIC: 5084 3577 Printing trades machinery, equipment, and supplies; Computer peripheral equipment, nec

(G-4234)
PARSON ADHESIVES INC
2545 Eastside Park Rd (47715-2175)
PHONE.................................812 401-7277
Pete Shaw, *Owner*
EMP: 116
SALES (corp-wide): 14.16MM **Privately Held**
Web: www.parsonadhesives.com
SIC: 2891 Adhesives
PA: Parson Adhesives Inc.
3345 W Auburn Rd Ste 107
Rochester Hills MI 48309
248 299-5585

(G-4235)
PEARL SCREEN PRINTING
428 Nw 3rd St (47708-1138)
PHONE.................................812 429-1686
EMP: 4 **EST:** 2019
SALES (est): 83.91K **Privately Held**
Web: www.pearlembroidery.net
SIC: 2759 Screen printing

(G-4236)
PGC MULCH LLC
Also Called: Pgc Landscaping & Mulch
1501 N 7th Ave (47710-2219)
PHONE.................................812 455-0700
Matt Dillon, *Managing Member*
EMP: 9 **EST:** 2013
SALES (est): 1.89MM **Privately Held**
Web: www.wwwpgcpros.com
SIC: 2499 7699 Mulch, wood and bark; Industrial tool grinding
PA: Pro Grass Cutters, Llc
1119 N Fulton Ave
Evansville IN 47710

(G-4237)
PGP INTERNATIONAL INC
5404 Foundation Blvd (47725-9652)
PHONE.................................812 867-5129
EMP: 38
SALES (corp-wide): 25.28B **Privately Held**
Web: www.pgpint.com
SIC: 2099 Food preparations, nec
HQ: Pgp International, Inc.
351 Hanson Way
Woodland CA 95776
530 662-5056

(G-4238)
PGP INTERNATIONAL INC
1901 N New York Ave (47711-3925)
PHONE.................................812 449-0650
Darimar Hernandez, *Mgr*
EMP: 38
SALES (corp-wide): 25.28B **Privately Held**
Web: www.pgpint.com
SIC: 2099 Almond pastes
HQ: Pgp International, Inc.
351 Hanson Way
Woodland CA 95776
530 662-5056

(G-4239)
PHASEFOUR LLP
715 S Burkhardt Rd (47715-4221)
PHONE.................................812 583-7247
Ryan Draper, *Prin*
EMP: 5 **EST:** 2017
SALES (est): 59.65K **Privately Held**
SIC: 2796 Engraving platemaking services

(G-4240)
PHIL JOHNSON
512 S Green River Rd (47715-7308)
PHONE.................................812 457-2433
Phil Johnson, *Pr*
EMP: 5 **EST:** 2017
SALES (est): 84.82K **Privately Held**
Web: www.homesinevansville.net
SIC: 7372 Prepackaged software

(G-4241)
PHILLIPS SIGNS & GRAPHICS
4800 Tecumseh Ln (47715-3220)
PHONE.................................812 499-3607
EMP: 7 **EST:** 2014
SALES (est): 227.35K **Privately Held**
Web: www.phillipssignsandgraphics.com
SIC: 3993 Signs and advertising specialties

(G-4242)
PIA AUTOMATION US INC (DH)
5825 Old Boonville Hwy (47715-2136)
PHONE.................................812 485-5500
Uwe Kruger, *Pr*
Nicole Garrison, *
EMP: 37 **EST:** 1963
SQ FT: 50,000
SALES (est): 22.4MM **Privately Held**
Web: www.piagroup.com
SIC: 3535 8711 3549 Robotic conveyors; Engineering services; Metalworking machinery, nec
HQ: Pia Automation Bad Neustadt Gmbh
Theodor-Jopp-Str. 6
Bad Neustadt A.D.Saale BY 97616
977163521000

(G-4243)
PICCOLO PRINTING
729 S Green River Rd (47715-4103)
PHONE.................................888 901-8648
EMP: 4 **EST:** 2018
SALES (est): 73.25K **Privately Held**
SIC: 2752 Commercial printing, lithographic

(G-4244)
PILLAR INNOVATIONS LLC
9844 Hedden Rd (47725-8904)
PHONE.................................812 474-9080
EMP: 6
SALES (corp-wide): 104.01MM **Privately Held**
Web: www.pillarinnovations.com
SIC: 3532 3569 7371 Mining machinery; Sprinkler systems, fire: automatic; Computer software development and applications
HQ: Pillar Innovations, Llc
92 Corporate Dr
Grantsville MD 21536

(G-4245)
PLASTIC EXTRUSIONS COMPANY
Also Called: Lattice Works
6500 Newburgh Rd (47715-4457)
PHONE.................................812 479-3232
John Michael Cohen, *Owner*
EMP: 3 **EST:** 1991
SQ FT: 3,500
SALES (est): 206.84K **Privately Held**
SIC: 3089 Extruded finished plastics products, nec

(G-4246)
PLIANT LLC
101 Oakley St (47710-1237)
PHONE.................................253 872-2253
Dwyane Nichols, *VP*
EMP: 48 **EST:** 2016
SALES (est): 4.84MM **Publicly Held**
Web: www.pliantcorp.com
SIC: 3081 Unsupported plastics film and sheet
PA: Berry Global Group, Inc.
101 Oakley St
Evansville IN 47710

(G-4247)
POLY-SEAL LLC (HQ)
101 Oakley St (47710-1237)
P.O. Box 959 (47706-0959)
PHONE.................................812 306-2573
▲ **EMP:** 87 **EST:** 1969
SQ FT: 240,000
SALES (est): 8.29MM **Publicly Held**
SIC: 3089 Closures, plastics
PA: Berry Global Group, Inc.
101 Oakley St
Evansville IN 47710

(G-4248)
POLYRAM COMPOUNDS LLC
15000 Foundation Ave (47725-7707)
PHONE.................................812 401-5830
Yuval Peleg, *CEO*
EMP: 13 **EST:** 2017
SALES (est): 3.05MM **Privately Held**
Web: www.polyram-group.com
SIC: 3087 Custom compound purchased resins
PA: Polyram Plastic Industries Ltd
Moshav
Ram-On 19205

(G-4249)
POLYWEAVE INDUSTRIES INC
11 S Kentucky Ave (47714-1004)
PHONE.................................812 467-0300
▲ **EMP:** 25 **EST:** 1995
SALES (est): 2.4MM **Privately Held**
SIC: 3081 Unsupported plastics film and sheet

(G-4250)
POWDER COATING BY EXPRESS LLC
1400 N Fares Ave (47711-4730)
PHONE.................................812 402-1010
Greg Schultheis, *Pr*
EMP: 12 **EST:** 2014
SALES (est): 937.23K **Privately Held**
Web: www.expresspowdercoatingandmediablast.com
SIC: 3479 Coating of metals and formed products

(G-4251)
PPG ARCHITECTURAL FINISHES INC
Also Called: Porter Paints
2211 N Burkhardt Rd Ste C (47715-2194)

GEOGRAPHIC SECTION Evansville - Vanderburgh County (G-4277)

PHONE.....................812 473-0339
EMP: 2
SALES (corp-wide): 17.65B Publicly Held
Web: www.ppgpaints.com
SIC: 2851 Paints and allied products
HQ: Ppg Architectural Finishes, Inc.
    1 Ppg Pl
    Pittsburgh PA 15272
    412 434-3131

(G-4252)
PPG INDUSTRIES INC
424 E Inglefield Rd (47725-9358)
PHONE.....................812 867-6601
Harry Nasab, Brnch Mgr
EMP: 3
SALES (corp-wide): 17.65B Publicly Held
Web: www.ppg.com
SIC: 2851 Paints and allied products
PA: Ppg Industries, Inc.
    1 Ppg Pl
    Pittsburgh PA 15272
    412 434-3131

(G-4253)
PPG INDUSTRIES INC
Also Called: PPG 4380
306 N 7th Ave (47710-1024)
PHONE.....................812 424-4774
Chris Shade, Brnch Mgr
EMP: 4
SALES (corp-wide): 17.65B Publicly Held
Web: www.ppg.com
SIC: 2851 Paints and allied products
PA: Ppg Industries, Inc.
    1 Ppg Pl
    Pittsburgh PA 15272
    412 434-3131

(G-4254)
PPG INDUSTRIES INC
Also Called: PPG 4382
2211 N Burkhardt Rd Ste D (47715-2194)
PHONE.....................812 473-0339
Chris Shade, Brnch Mgr
EMP: 4
SALES (corp-wide): 17.65B Publicly Held
Web: www.ppg.com
SIC: 2851 Paints and allied products
PA: Ppg Industries, Inc.
    1 Ppg Pl
    Pittsburgh PA 15272
    412 434-3131

(G-4255)
PRECISION SERVICES INC ✪
6601 W Mill Rd (47720-2037)
PHONE.....................812 602-8375
EMP: 6 EST: 2022
SALES (est): 117K Privately Held
Web: www.precision-services.com
SIC: 3599 Machine shop, jobbing and repair

(G-4256)
PREFERRED TANK & TOWER INC (PA)
5444 E Indiana St Pmb 374 (47715-2857)
P.O. Box 374 (47703-0374)
PHONE.....................270 826-7950
Karen Ferguson-johnston, Pr
Herman Johnston, Dir
EMP: 7 EST: 2007
SQ FT: 7,500
SALES (est): 1.85MM Privately Held
Web: www.preferredtankandtower.com
SIC: 3441 Building components, structural steel

(G-4257)
PRESIDENTIAL BATH & FIX LLC
215 Wedeking Ave (47711-3753)
PHONE.....................812 259-9817
EMP: 1
SALES (est): 41.07K Privately Held
SIC: 1389 7389 Construction, repair, and dismantling services; Business Activities at Non-Commercial Site

(G-4258)
PRIME SOURCE LLC
4609 E Boonville New Harmony Rd (47725)
PHONE.....................812 867-8921
EMP: 2
SALES (corp-wide): 152.46MM Privately Held
Web: www.albaughllc.com
SIC: 2879 Insecticides and pesticides
HQ: Prime Source Llc
    1525 Ne 36th St
    Ankeny IA 50021
    252 235-0043

(G-4259)
PRO FINISH
4825 Hitch Peters Rd (47711-2481)
PHONE.....................618 771-7207
EMP: 3 EST: 2018
SALES (est): 71.62K Privately Held
Web: www.profinishmoldpolishing.com
SIC: 3599 Machine shop, jobbing and repair

(G-4260)
PRO FINISH MOLD POLISHING
9918 Massey Dr (47725-7718)
PHONE.....................618 922-8161
John Mercer, Prin
EMP: 4 EST: 2017
SALES (est): 69.04K Privately Held
Web: www.profinishmoldpolishing.com
SIC: 3599 Machine shop, jobbing and repair

(G-4261)
PROKUMA INCORPORATED
110 N Main St (47711-5449)
PHONE.....................812 461-1681
Louis Meredith, Pr
EMP: 10 EST: 2017
SQ FT: 5,000
SALES (est): 1.23MM Privately Held
Web: www.prokuma.com
SIC: 3441 Fabricated structural metal

(G-4262)
PROTHERM SUPPLY INC
1409 E Maryland St (47711-5261)
PHONE.....................812 492-3386
James H Gribbins, Pr
EMP: 1 EST: 2009
SALES (est): 77.91K Privately Held
Web: www.prothermsupply.com
SIC: 3312 Pipes, iron and steel

(G-4263)
PSC INDUSTRIES INC
Also Called: P S C Fabricating
900 E Virginia St (47711-5645)
PHONE.....................812 425-9071
Susanna Durham, Dir
EMP: 12
SQ FT: 180,000
SALES (corp-wide): 1.71B Privately Held
Web: www.pscindustries.com
SIC: 5113 3086 2671 2631 Shipping supplies; Plastics foam products; Paper; coated and laminated packaging; Paperboard mills
HQ: Psc Industries, Inc.
    1100 W Market St
    Louisville KY 40203
    502 625-7700

(G-4264)
PULSE ENERGY SYSTEMS LLC
420 Nw 5th St Ste 2b (47708-1333)
P.O. Box 1253 (47706-1253)
PHONE.....................618 392-5502
EMP: 5 EST: 1995
SQ FT: 1,500
SALES (est): 579.06K Privately Held
SIC: 1311 Natural gas production

(G-4265)
PURINA ANIMAL NUTRITION LLC
2124 Lynch Rd (47711-2947)
PHONE.....................812 424-5501
Calvin Scott, Mgr
EMP: 1
SALES (corp-wide): 2.89B Privately Held
Web: www.purinamills.com
SIC: 2048 Prepared feeds, nec
HQ: Purina Animal Nutrition Llc
    100 Danforth Dr
    Gray Summit MO 63039

(G-4266)
PURINA MILLS LLC
Also Called: Purina Mills
2124 Lynch Rd (47711)
PHONE.....................812 424-5501
Calvin Scott, Mgr
EMP: 67
SQ FT: 20,000
SALES (corp-wide): 2.89B Privately Held
Web: www.purina.com
SIC: 2047 Dog and cat food
HQ: Purina Mills, Llc
    555 Mryvlle Univ Dr Ste 2
    Saint Louis MO 63141

(G-4267)
PYRO MICRO WELDING LLC
1901 Orchard Rd (47720-7638)
PHONE.....................812 431-3330
EMP: 3 EST: 2019
SALES (est): 71.01K Privately Held
SIC: 7692 Welding repair

(G-4268)
QUIREY QUALITY ENGINEERING
2251 Commercial Ct (47720-1325)
PHONE.....................812 963-6097
Larry Quirey, Owner
EMP: 5 EST: 2017
SALES (est): 76.65K Privately Held
SIC: 3944 Electronic game machines, except coin-operated

(G-4269)
R T W REFRACTORY INC
3141 Broadway Ave (47712-4611)
PHONE.....................812 468-4299
Jeffrey Redman, Pr
Angela Turner, *
Troy Tomlinson, *
EMP: 12 EST: 2001
SQ FT: 3,000
SALES (est): 747.91K Privately Held
Web: www.rtwrefractory.com
SIC: 3255 Clay refractories

(G-4270)
R2B2 INDUSTRIES LLC
Also Called: Pipeconx
701 N 9th Ave (47712-5343)
P.O. Box 18007 (47719-1007)
PHONE.....................812 436-4840
Gary K Price, Managing Member
EMP: 1 EST: 2011
SALES (est): 234.28K Privately Held
Web: www.pipeconx.com
SIC: 3494 Pipe fittings

(G-4271)
RABEN TIRE CO LLC
1108 N Fares Ave (47711-5238)
PHONE.....................812 465-5555
Larry Raben, Mgr
EMP: 10
SALES (corp-wide): 20.07B Publicly Held
Web: www.goodyearautoservice.com
SIC: 5531 7534 Automotive tires; Tire retreading and repair shops
HQ: Raben Tire Co., Llc
    2100 N New York Ave
    Evansville IN 47711
    812 465-5565

(G-4272)
RANDALL CORP
Also Called: Letter Shop, The
1105 E Virginia St (47711-5724)
P.O. Box 23264 (47724-1264)
PHONE.....................812 425-7122
Randy Chapman, Pr
EMP: 2 EST: 1953
SALES (est): 242.42K Privately Held
SIC: 2752 7699 7334 5999 Offset printing; Picture framing, custom; Photocopying and duplicating services; Art dealers

(G-4273)
RASURE PRINTS LLC
4001 Wood Castle Rd (47711-2777)
PHONE.....................812 454-6222
Adena Rasure, Prin
EMP: 5 EST: 2016
SALES (est): 78.7K Privately Held
SIC: 2752 Commercial printing, lithographic

(G-4274)
RC TRANSPORTATION LLC
1100 Independence Ave (47714-4549)
P.O. Box 2870 (47728-0870)
PHONE.....................812 424-7978
Leo King Junior, Prin
EMP: 55 EST: 1995
SALES (est): 2.06MM Publicly Held
Web: www.rctransportation.com
SIC: 2086 Soft drinks: packaged in cans, bottles, etc.
HQ: Royal Crown Bottling Corp.
    1100 Independence Ave
    Evansville IN 47714
    812 424-7978

(G-4275)
REALLY GOOD STUFF INC
9951 Hedden Rd (47725-8915)
PHONE.....................812 402-8275
EMP: 7 EST: 2018
SALES (est): 487.41K Privately Held
Web: www.reallygoodstuff.com
SIC: 2741 Miscellaneous publishing

(G-4276)
RECKITT BENCKISER LLC
2400 W Lloyd Expy (47712-5095)
PHONE.....................812 429-5000
Rakesh Kapoor, CEO
EMP: 28 EST: 2016
SALES (est): 2.38MM Privately Held
SIC: 2842 2035 Polishes and sanitation goods; Pickles, sauces, and salad dressings

(G-4277)
RED HEN SIGNS
306 Boehne Ave (47712-4710)
PHONE.....................812 430-0956
Jessica Wilson, Prin
EMP: 4 EST: 2017
SALES (est): 49.42K Privately Held

Evansville - Vanderburgh County (G-4278) — GEOGRAPHIC SECTION

SIC: 3993 Signs and advertising specialties

(G-4278)
RED SPOT PAINT & VARNISH CO
Also Called: Red Spot Uv/Vm Research
1001 E Louisiana St (47711-4745)
P.O. Box 418 (47703-0418)
PHONE..................................812 428-9100
Brenda Bosecker, Mgr
EMP: 3
Web: www.redspot.com
SIC: 2851 Paints and allied products
HQ: Red Spot Paint & Varnish Co Inc
1107 E Louisiana St
Evansville IN 47711
812 428-9100

(G-4279)
RED SPOT PAINT & VARNISH CO
1016 E Columbia St (47711-5100)
PHONE..................................812 428-9100
Reese Hamilton, Opers Mgr
EMP: 4
Web: www.redspot.com
SIC: 2851 3479 Paints and paint additives; Painting, coating, and hot dipping
HQ: Red Spot Paint & Varnish Co Inc
1107 E Louisiana St
Evansville IN 47711
812 428-9100

(G-4280)
RED SPOT PAINT & VARNISH CO
Also Called: A & D Building
1111 E Louisiana St (47711-4747)
PHONE..................................812 428-9100
John Phillips, Mgr
EMP: 4
Web: www.redspot.com
SIC: 2851 Plastics base paints and varnishes
HQ: Red Spot Paint & Varnish Co Inc
1107 E Louisiana St
Evansville IN 47711
812 428-9100

(G-4281)
RED SPOT PAINT & VARNISH CO (HQ)
1107 E Louisiana St (47711-4747)
P.O. Box 418 (47703-0418)
PHONE..................................812 428-9100
Akiro Takeda, Pr
David White, *
Jeffrey M Scheu, *
Jennifer L Smith, *
Timothy J Tanner, *
▲ EMP: 350 EST: 1903
SQ FT: 200,000
SALES (est): 189.23MM Privately Held
Web: www.redspot.com
SIC: 2851 Plastics base paints and varnishes
PA: Fujikura Kasei Co.,Ltd.
2-6-15, Shibakoen
Minato-Ku TKY 105-0

(G-4282)
REDSPOT PAINT AND VARNISH CO
1107 East La St (47711)
P.O. Box 418 (47703-0418)
PHONE..................................812 428-9100
EMP: 44 EST: 1903
SALES (est): 2.12MM Privately Held
Web: www.redspot.com
SIC: 2851 Paints and allied products

(G-4283)
REIS TIRE SALES INC
1512 W Columbia St (47710-1432)
P.O. Box 6354 (47719-0354)
PHONE..................................812 425-2229
Luke Reis, Pr

Joseph J Reis Junior, VP
EMP: 21 EST: 1918
SQ FT: 18,000
SALES (est): 1.47MM Privately Held
Web: www.reistire.com
SIC: 5531 5014 7534 Automotive tires; Automobile tires and tubes; Tire repair shop

(G-4284)
REPLAS OF TEXAS INC
15000 Highway 41 N (47725-9360)
PHONE..................................812 421-3600
Joe Dalley, Mgr
EMP: 4 EST: 2002
SALES (est): 332.01K Privately Held
SIC: 2821 Molding compounds, plastics

(G-4285)
RESIDUE WEST INC
Also Called: Residue Regency Pad
2625 Kotter Ave (47715-8508)
PHONE..................................731 587-9596
Dan Chadwick, Genl Mgr
EMP: 15
SALES (corp-wide): 4.81MM Privately Held
SIC: 3086 Padding, foamed plastics
PA: Residue West Inc.
4 Anchor Way
Port Washington NY 11050
516 883-8294

(G-4286)
RETRIEVING WITH EVIE
2515 Glenn Ave (47711-4039)
PHONE..................................812 455-5292
EMP: 4 EST: 2013
SALES (est): 39.69K Privately Held
Web: www.mtpublishing.com
SIC: 2741 Miscellaneous publishing

(G-4287)
REVSELLER LLC
5444 E Indiana St Pmb 215 (47715)
P.O. Box 792 (47629)
PHONE..................................800 619-6304
EMP: 2 EST: 2015
SALES (est): 68.41K Privately Held
Web: www.revseller.com
SIC: 7372 Application computer software

(G-4288)
RFBP INC
3245 Kansas Rd (47725-9757)
▼ EMP: 400
SIC: 3089 Caps, plastics

(G-4289)
RICKTOM PROMOTIONS LLC
4528 Moray Dr (47714-7517)
PHONE..................................812 430-0282
EMP: 1 EST: 2013
SALES (est): 77.19K Privately Held
SIC: 3993 7389 Advertising novelties; Business Activities at Non-Commercial Site

(G-4290)
RIX PRODUCTS INC
Also Called: Rix Products
3747 Hogue Rd (47712-6431)
PHONE..................................812 426-1749
Rick A Rideout, Pr
EMP: 6 EST: 1980
SQ FT: 5,400
SALES (est): 496.61K Privately Held
Web: www.rixproducts.com
SIC: 3089 3944 Injection molding of plastics; Railroad models: toy and hobby

(G-4291)
ROBINSON ENGINEERING & OIL CO (PA)
1410 N Cullen Ave (47715-2331)
P.O. Box 5269 (47716-5269)
PHONE..................................812 477-1575
Charles A Robinson, Pr
J Glenn Robinson, Pr
Charles H Robinson, VP
EMP: 10 EST: 1969
SQ FT: 2,500
SALES (est): 4.03MM Privately Held
SIC: 1311 8711 Crude petroleum production; Petroleum engineering

(G-4292)
ROLLS-ROYCE CORPORATION
225 W Morgan Ave Ste A (47710-2515)
PHONE..................................812 421-7810
Michael Lampert, Pr
EMP: 26
SALES (corp-wide): 20.55B Privately Held
Web: www.rolls-roycemotorcars.com
SIC: 3724 3728 Aircraft engines and engine parts; Aircraft parts and equipment, nec
HQ: Rolls-Royce Corporation
450 S Meridian St
Indianapolis IN 46225

(G-4293)
ROSIES HOLISTIC LIFESTYLE LLC
Also Called: Handmade Natural Products
5642 Ryan Ln (47712-9566)
PHONE..................................812 682-1212
EMP: 1 EST: 2021
SALES (est): 66.26K Privately Held
SIC: 2499 Beekeeping supplies, wood

(G-4294)
ROYAL CROWN BOTTLING CORP (HQ)
Also Called: RC Cola
1100 Independence Ave (47714-4549)
P.O. Box 2870 (47728-0870)
PHONE..................................812 424-7978
Nancy King Hodge, Pr
Chad Metten, *
David Palmer, CIO*
Gail L King, *
EMP: 125 EST: 1938
SQ FT: 115,000
SALES (est): 51.47MM Publicly Held
Web: www.keurigdrpepper.com
SIC: 2086 Soft drinks: packaged in cans, bottles, etc.
PA: Keurig Dr Pepper Inc.
53 South Ave
Burlington MA 01803

(G-4295)
ROYAL INC
Also Called: Royal Feeds
1210 N Fulton Ave (47710-2359)
PHONE..................................812 424-4925
EMP: 10
Web: websiteconnect.drb.com
SIC: 2085 7841 Distilled and blended liquors; Video tape rental
PA: Royal Inc.
1212 W Florida St
Evansville IN 47710

(G-4296)
SAIMAX PRODUCTS INC
2545 Eastside Park Rd (47715-2175)
PHONE..................................248 299-5585
▲ EMP: 1 EST: 2015
SALES (est): 54.72K Privately Held
SIC: 2891 Adhesives

(G-4297)
SATER ENTERPRISES
5401 Vogel Rd Ste 430 (47715-7837)
P.O. Box 1760 (90406-1760)
PHONE..................................812 477-1529
Ronald E Sater, Pr
Alvrone Sater, Pt
EMP: 6 EST: 1967
SQ FT: 6,250
SALES (est): 514.96K Privately Held
Web: www.fmfab.biz
SIC: 1311 6799 Crude petroleum production; Investors, nec

(G-4298)
SCHAFFSTEINS TRUCK CLEAN LLC
Also Called: Tc Graphics
601 N 9th Ave (47712-5342)
P.O. Box 6256 (47719-0256)
PHONE..................................812 464-2424
Alan Schaffstein, Pr
Thomas Schaffstein, Pr
Carol Schaffstein, Sec
EMP: 15 EST: 1972
SQ FT: 20,000
SALES (est): 2.28MM Privately Held
Web: www.schaffsteins.com
SIC: 7542 7532 3471 7336 Truck wash; Truck painting and lettering; Sand blasting of metal parts; Commercial art and graphic design

(G-4299)
SCHUCKERS ORNA IR WORKS CO
2211 Glenview Dr (47720-1255)
P.O. Box 6049 (47719-0049)
PHONE..................................812 422-7057
Robert Schecker, Pr
EMP: 1 EST: 1982
SALES (est): 232.13K Privately Held
Web: schucker.server308.com
SIC: 3446 3444 3441 Architectural metalwork; Sheet metalwork; Fabricated structural metal

(G-4300)
SCHUTTE LITHOGRAPHY INC
1207 Harrelton Ct (47714-0706)
PHONE..................................812 469-3500
EMP: 16 EST: 1977
SALES (est): 1.31MM Privately Held
Web: www.schuttelithography.com
SIC: 2752 2789 2759 Color lithography; Bookbinding and related work; Commercial printing, nec

(G-4301)
SCOTT PRINTING LLC
11545 Bohannon Dr (47725-9275)
PHONE..................................812 306-7477
Ryan Michael Scott, Pr
EMP: 5 EST: 2018
SALES (est): 92.3K Privately Held
Web: www.scottprintingevv.com
SIC: 2752 Commercial printing, lithographic

(G-4302)
SEAL CORP
1179 E Diamond Ave (47711-3903)
PHONE..................................812 868-0790
EMP: 8 EST: 2019
SALES (est): 387.67K Privately Held
Web: www.sealcorpusa.com
SIC: 2891 Adhesives and sealants

(G-4303)
SEALCORPUSA INC
1175 E Diamond Ave (47711-3903)
PHONE..................................866 868-0791
Ken Rust, Pr

Ken Rust, *Ch Bd*
Kenneth Rust, *
Barbara Rust, *
Tim Robards, *
▲ **EMP:** 80 **EST:** 1991
SQ FT: 35,000
SALES (est): 9.14MM Privately Held
Web: www.sealcorpusa.com
SIC: 2891 8732 Adhesives; Commercial nonphysical research

(G-4304)
SEIB MACHINE & TOOL CO INC
Also Called: Seibs Welding
14314 Bender Rd (47720-7213)
PHONE..............................812 453-6174
George Seib, *Pr*
EMP: 4 **EST:** 1979
SQ FT: 4,800
SALES (est): 339K Privately Held
SIC: 3699 7692 1761 Teaching machines and aids, electronic; Welding repair; Sheet metal work, nec

(G-4305)
SEPARATION BY DESIGN INC
1601 Buchanan Rd (47720-5411)
PHONE..............................812 424-1239
Roy W Jorgensen, *Pr*
Lee K Jorgensen, *
Amanda Jorgensen, *
EMP: 30 **EST:** 2005
SQ FT: 17,000
SALES (est): 4.82MM Privately Held
Web: www.separationbydesign.com
SIC: 3586 3569 Measuring and dispensing pumps; Gas separators (machinery)

(G-4306)
SEQUOIA NATIONAL LLC (PA)
Also Called: Tri-State Cylinder Head
1712 Read St (47710-2798)
PHONE..............................812 421-0095
Kyle Sharrer, *Pr*
Lucas Recker, *CFO*
EMP: 20 **EST:** 2017
SQ FT: 10,000
SALES (est): 2.31MM
SALES (corp-wide): 2.31MM Privately Held
Web: www.flotekheads.com
SIC: 3519 Parts and accessories, internal combustion engines

(G-4307)
SETCO LLC (DH)
Also Called: Berry
101 Oakley St (47710-1237)
PHONE..............................812 424-2904
Donald E Parodi, *
◆ **EMP:** 450 **EST:** 2003
SQ FT: 288,000
SALES (est): 117.52MM Publicly Held
Web: www.berryglobal.com
SIC: 3085 8711 3544 Plastics bottles; Engineering services; Special dies, tools, jigs, and fixtures
HQ: Berry Global, Inc.
  101 Oakley St
  Evansville IN 47710

(G-4308)
SEXTON PLYWOOD & VENEER CO
227 Rosemarie Ct (47715-7425)
PHONE..............................812 454-0488
EMP: 2
SALES (est): 69.44K Privately Held
SIC: 2435 Hardwood veneer and plywood

(G-4309)
SHELOVEXEMPRESS LLC ✪
235 N Burkhardt Rd (47715-2729)
PHONE..............................317 490-2097
Myiesha Stewart, *CEO*
EMP: 1 **EST:** 2022
SALES (est): 69.27K Privately Held
SIC: 3999 7389 Eyelashes, artificial; Business Activities at Non-Commercial Site

(G-4310)
SIGN A RAMA
Also Called: Sign-A-Rama
1300 N Royal Ave (47715-7808)
PHONE..............................812 477-7763
Walter Valiant, *Owner*
EMP: 2 **EST:** 2001
SALES (est): 253.52K Privately Held
Web: www.signarama.com
SIC: 3993 3953 Signs and advertising specialties; Marking devices

(G-4311)
SIGN GRAPHICS EVANSVILLE INC
6020 Feltman Dr (47711-1808)
PHONE..............................812 476-9151
Dana Dubuque, *Pr*
EMP: 6 **EST:** 1973
SQ FT: 4,000
SALES (est): 405.51K Privately Held
Web: www.signgraphicsinc.com
SIC: 3993 Signs, not made in custom sign painting shops

(G-4312)
SIGNCRAFTERS INC (PA)
1508 Stringtown Rd (47711-4593)
P.O. Box 4266 (47724-0266)
PHONE..............................812 424-9011
Bill G Dugan, *Pr*
EMP: 38 **EST:** 1974
SQ FT: 49,000
SALES (est): 5.08MM
SALES (corp-wide): 5.08MM Privately Held
Web: www.signcrafters-inc.com
SIC: 3993 Electric signs

(G-4313)
SIGNS MAGIC LLC
Also Called: Signs Now
716 N Weinbach Ave (47711-5966)
PHONE..............................812 473-5155
EMP: 7 **EST:** 2010
SQ FT: 5,000
SALES (est): 504.43K Privately Held
Web: www.signsnow.com
SIC: 3993 Signs and advertising specialties

(G-4314)
SILGAN WHITE CAP LLC
Also Called: Silgan Closures
2201 W Maryland St (47712-5394)
PHONE..............................812 425-6222
John Bugnitz, *Brnch Mgr*
EMP: 250
Web: www.silgancls.com
SIC: 3411 Metal cans
HQ: Silgan White Cap Llc
  1140 31st St
  Downers Grove IL 60515
  630 515-8383

(G-4315)
SINGER OPTICAL COMPANY INC
1401 N Royal Ave (47715-7827)
P.O. Box 3557 (47734-3557)
PHONE..............................812 423-1179
Martin Singer, *Pr*
Roger Singer, *Pr*
Martin E Singer, *VP*
EMP: 13 **EST:** 1948
SQ FT: 15,320
SALES (est): 893.33K Privately Held
Web: www.singeroptical.com
SIC: 3851 5048 Ophthalmic goods; Ophthalmic goods

(G-4316)
SISCO CORPORATION
Also Called: Sisco Box
1231 E Michigan St (47711-5720)
PHONE..............................812 422-2090
Larry Zeitler, *Genl Mgr*
EMP: 60
SALES (corp-wide): 7.68MM Privately Held
Web: www.siscobox.com
SIC: 2653 Boxes, corrugated: made from purchased materials
PA: Sisco Corporation
  1520 S Mill St
  Nashville IL 62263
  618 327-3066

(G-4317)
SK MARKTING STRTGIES LLC DBA A
10400 W Boonville New Harmony Rd (47720)
PHONE..............................812 962-0900
Stephanie Koch, *Pr*
EMP: 1 **EST:** 2016
SALES (est): 50.64K Privately Held
Web: www.theaxispointe.com
SIC: 7379 7372 7371 8742 Online services technology consultants; Application computer software; Computer software development; Management consulting services

(G-4318)
SLEEPMADECOM LLC
2625 Kotter Ave (47715-8508)
PHONE..............................662 350-0999
EMP: 43
SALES (corp-wide): 418.44K Privately Held
Web: www.eluxury.com
SIC: 2515 Mattresses and bedsprings
PA: Sleepmade.Com, Llc
  179 Tradewinds Dr N
  Columbus MS 39705
  662 386-2222

(G-4319)
SLM MRKTING COMMUNICATIONS INC
Also Called: Our Times Newspaper
605 S Evans Ave (47713-2332)
P.O. Box 2164 (47728-0164)
PHONE..............................812 426-7993
Sondra L Matthews, *Pr*
Demarco Hampton, *Prin*
EMP: 1 **EST:** 1983
SALES (est): 120.76K Privately Held
Web: www.ourtimesnewspaper.com
SIC: 2711 Newspapers: publishing only, not printed on site

(G-4320)
SMITH & BUTTERFIELD CO INC (DH)
Also Called: Smith & Butterfield
2800 Lynch Rd Ste D (47711-2913)
P.O. Box 3446 (47733-3446)
PHONE..............................812 422-3261
J Mac Aldridge, *Ch Bd*
James D Butterfield, *Pr*
EMP: 16 **EST:** 1866
SQ FT: 50,000
SALES (est): 4.27MM Privately Held
Web: www.smithbutterfield.com
SIC: 5021 5112 2752 5943 Office furniture, nec; Stationery and office supplies; Commercial printing, lithographic; Office forms and supplies
HQ: Stationers, Inc.
  100 Industrial Ln
  Huntington WV 25702
  304 528-2780

(G-4321)
SMITH & BUTTERFIELD CO INC
Also Called: Ips
2800 Lynch Rd Ste D (47711-2928)
P.O. Box 3446 (47733-3446)
PHONE..............................812 422-3261
Jim Butterfield, *Pr*
EMP: 1 **EST:** 1986
SQ FT: 1,760
SALES (est): 615.82K Privately Held
SIC: 5112 2752 Stationery and office supplies; Commercial printing, lithographic
HQ: Smith & Butterfield Co., Inc.
  2800 Lynch Rd Ste D
  Evansville IN 47711
  812 422-3261

(G-4322)
SMITHFIELD DIRECT LLC
8426 Baumgart Rd (47725-1516)
PHONE..............................812 867-6644
Andrew Kase, *Brnch Mgr*
EMP: 98
Web: carando.sfdbrands.com
SIC: 2011 Meat packing plants
HQ: Smithfield Direct, Llc
  4225 Naperville Rd # 600
  Lisle IL 60532

(G-4323)
SNAPPLE BEVERAGE CORP
1100 Independence Ave (47714-4549)
PHONE..............................812 424-7978
Rick Morse, *Prin*
EMP: 9 **EST:** 2015
SALES (est): 75.48K Privately Held
Web: www.snapple.com
SIC: 2086 Bottled and canned soft drinks

(G-4324)
SOUTHERN INDIANA WATERJET LLC
2286 Commercial Ct (47720-1326)
PHONE..............................812 457-3201
Mitch Happe, *Prin*
EMP: 7 **EST:** 2017
SALES (est): 72K Privately Held
Web: www.siwaterjet.com
SIC: 3599 Machine shop, jobbing and repair

(G-4325)
SOUTHWEST GRAFIX AND AP INC
2229 W Franklin St (47712-5116)
PHONE..............................812 425-5104
Mark Weidner, *Pr*
Roseann Weidner, *Sec*
EMP: 11 **EST:** 1985
SQ FT: 6,900
SALES (est): 403.73K Privately Held
Web: www.southwestgrafix.com
SIC: 2759 Screen printing

(G-4326)
SPARKLING CLEAN INC
Also Called: Dallas Towing Service
1018 Bayse St (47714-4129)
PHONE..............................812 422-4871
Jim Ray, *Mgr*
EMP: 4 **EST:** 1955
SALES (est): 204.18K Privately Held
Web: www.dallastowingservice.net

Evansville - Vanderburgh County (G-4327)   GEOGRAPHIC SECTION

SIC: 7549 5012 3711 Towing service, automotive; Commercial vehicles; Wreckers (tow truck), assembly of

(G-4327)
SPECIALTY COATINGS LLC
3301 N 1st Ave # B (47710-3205)
PHONE..................812 431-3375
Scot William Grossman, *Prin*
EMP: 7 EST: 2017
SALES (est): 198.49K **Privately Held**
Web: www.specialtycoatingsllc.com
SIC: 3479 Coating of metals and formed products

(G-4328)
SPECIALTY TOOLING INC
2391 Lexington Rd (47720-1237)
PHONE..................812 464-8521
Gregory Johann, *Pr*
Brenda Johann, *Sec*
Matthew Lovell, *Sls Mgr*
EMP: 10 EST: 1973
SQ FT: 6,400
SALES (est): 2.25MM **Privately Held**
Web: www.specialty-tooling.com
SIC: 3544 8711 Special dies and tools; Mechanical engineering

(G-4329)
SRG GLOBAL TRIM INC (DH)
Also Called: Srg Global Evansville
601 N Congress Ave (47715)
PHONE..................812 473-6200
Kevin Baird, *Pr*
David B Jaffe, *
Doug Girdler, *
Gregory J Mulawa, *
▲ EMP: 510 EST: 1964
SQ FT: 400,000
SALES (est): 129.26MM
SALES (corp-wide): 64.37B **Privately Held**
Web: www.srgglobal.com
SIC: 3089 Injection molded finished plastics products, nec
HQ: Srg Global, Llc
    800 Stephenson Hwy
    Troy MI 48083

(G-4330)
SS&C TECHNOLOGIES INC
110 N Fulton Ave (47710-1036)
PHONE..................812 266-2000
EMP: 11
SALES (corp-wide): 5.5B **Publicly Held**
Web: www.ssctech.com
SIC: 7372 Prepackaged software
HQ: Ss&C Technologies, Inc.
    80 Lamberton Rd
    Windsor CT 06095
    800 234-0556

(G-4331)
STEPHEN LIBS CANDY COMPANY INC
Also Called: Stephen Libs Finer Chocolate
6225 Vogel Rd (47715-4033)
PHONE..................812 473-0048
Stephen R Libs, *Pr*
Marjorie Libs, *Sec*
EMP: 10 EST: 1985
SALES (est): 907.32K **Privately Held**
Web: www.stephenlibschocolates.com
SIC: 2064 5441 2068 2066 Candy and other confectionery products; Candy; Salted and roasted nuts and seeds; Chocolate and cocoa products

(G-4332)
STERLING BERRY CORPORATION
101 Oakley St (47710-1237)
PHONE..................812 424-2904
Martin R Imbler, *Pr*
George Willbrandt, *VP*
Randy Becker, *OK Vice President*
▼ EMP: 99 EST: 1983
SALES (est): 4.75MM **Publicly Held**
Web: www.berryglobal.com
SIC: 3089 Cups, plastics, except foam
HQ: Berry Global, Inc.
    101 Oakley St
    Evansville IN 47710

(G-4333)
STERLING INDUSTRIAL LLC
Also Called: Industrial Contrs Shtmtl Div
1001 Mount Auburn Rd (47720-8226)
P.O. Box 208 (47702-0208)
PHONE..................812 423-7832
Brent Smith, *Brnch Mgr*
EMP: 238
SALES (corp-wide): 120.89MM **Privately Held**
Web: www.sterlingboiler.com
SIC: 1541 3471 3446 3444 Industrial buildings, new construction, nec; Plating and polishing; Architectural metalwork; Sheet metalwork
PA: Sterling Industrial, Llc
    401 Nw 1st St
    Evansville IN 47708
    812 479-5447

(G-4334)
STERLING INDUSTRIAL LLC (PA)
401 Nw 1st St (47708-1001)
P.O. Box 8004 (47716-8004)
PHONE..................812 479-5447
Daniel G Felker, *Pr*
Butch Bradley, *
Kenneth E Wahl, *
EMP: 231 EST: 1982
SALES (est): 120.89MM
SALES (corp-wide): 120.89MM **Privately Held**
Web: www.sterlingboiler.com
SIC: 1711 3443 Mechanical contractor; Fabricated plate work (boiler shop)

(G-4335)
STERNBERG INC
Also Called: Sternberg International Isuzu
8950 N Kentucky Ave (47725-1392)
P.O. Box 690 (47547-0690)
PHONE..................812 867-0077
TOLL FREE: 800
Derek Strumberg, *Genl Mgr*
EMP: 28
SALES (corp-wide): 66.82MM **Privately Held**
Web: www.sternbergs.com
SIC: 5511 3715 Automobiles, new and used; Truck trailers
PA: Sternberg, Inc.
    1781 S Us Highway 231
    Jasper IN 47546
    812 482-5125

(G-4336)
STRAIGHT TRIPPIN LLC ✪
2424 Antilles Dr (47725-7721)
PHONE..................812 484-6154
EMP: 2 EST: 2023
SALES (est): 87.69K **Privately Held**
SIC: 7372 Prepackaged software

(G-4337)
SUNBEAM PACKAGING SERVICES LLC
12518 Oak Gate Rd (47725-8390)
PHONE..................812 867-3551
Jeffrey Minnette, *Ofcr*
EMP: 1 EST: 2004
SALES (est): 156.26K **Privately Held**
SIC: 2631 Container, packaging, and boxboard

(G-4338)
SWEET SCENTS LLC
800 Sycamore St (47708-1820)
PHONE..................219 902-6853
Kalama Fox, *Mgr*
EMP: 1 EST: 2020
SALES (est): 60.62K **Privately Held**
Web: www.bakingsweetscents.com
SIC: 2844 Perfumes, cosmetics and other toilet preparations

(G-4339)
SYCAMORE ENTERPRISES INC
Also Called: Asbury Hall
2214 Saint Joseph Ind Park Dr (47720-1207)
P.O. Box 8062 (47716-8062)
PHONE..................812 477-2266
James R Egen, *Pr*
Deborah K Egen, *VP*
Don Bowen, *Treas*
EMP: 2 EST: 2014
SQ FT: 17,000
SALES (est): 449.67K **Privately Held**
Web: www.sycamoreworldwide.com
SIC: 5199 2323 2339 2396 General merchandise, non-durable; Men's and boys' neckties and bow ties; Neckwear and ties: women's, misses', and juniors'; Screen printing on fabric articles

(G-4340)
TEAM HANDY LLC
Also Called: Team Handy
14215 N Green River Rd (47725-9776)
P.O. Box 506 (47629-0506)
PHONE..................812 962-3630
Brad Huebner, *Pr*
EMP: 1 EST: 2009
SALES (est): 242.57K **Privately Held**
Web: www.teamhandy.com
SIC: 1389 Construction, repair, and dismantling services

(G-4341)
TESTIMONY PUBLICATIONS LLC
901 Jobes Ln (47712-4229)
PHONE..................812 602-3031
Ralph Michael Kough, *Owner*
EMP: 5 EST: 2015
SALES (est): 50.03K **Privately Held**
SIC: 2741 Miscellaneous publishing

(G-4342)
THERMO FISHER SCIENTIFIC INC
958 S Kenmore Dr Ste C (47714-7513)
PHONE..................812 477-2760
Georgetta Geuss, *Dir*
EMP: 10
SALES (corp-wide): 42.86B **Publicly Held**
Web: www.thermofisher.com
SIC: 3826 Analytical instruments
PA: Thermo Fisher Scientific Inc.
    168 3rd Ave
    Waltham MA 02451
    781 622-1000

(G-4343)
THOMAS E SLADE INC
Also Called: Slade Print
6220 Vogel Rd (47715-4014)
PHONE..................812 437-5233
Lisa Slade, *Pr*
Thomas E Slade, *VP*
EMP: 16 EST: 1993
SQ FT: 5,000
SALES (est): 2.49MM **Privately Held**
Web: www.slade.company
SIC: 2752 2759 7336 2791 Commercial printing, lithographic; Commercial printing, nec; Commercial art and graphic design; Typesetting

(G-4344)
THRUST INDUSTRIES INC
10334 Hedden Rd (47725-8923)
PHONE..................812 437-3643
Jim Stuteville, *Pr*
Tracy Stuteville, *Sec*
EMP: 10 EST: 1992
SQ FT: 12,000
SALES (est): 1.01MM **Privately Held**
Web: www.thrustin.com
SIC: 3089 3083 Casting of plastics; Laminated plastics plate and sheet

(G-4345)
THYME IN KITCHEN LLC
Also Called: Thyme In The Kitchen
2308 W Franklin St Ste A (47712-5161)
PHONE..................812 624-0344
Marcia C Jochem, *Prin*
EMP: 7 EST: 2013
SALES (est): 231.01K **Privately Held**
Web: www.thymeinthekitchen.com
SIC: 2099 Food preparations, nec

(G-4346)
TRANE US INC
Also Called: Trane
1024 E Sycamore St (47714-1011)
PHONE..................812 421-8725
Brett Palmer, *Mgr*
EMP: 19
Web: www.harshawtrane.com
SIC: 3585 Refrigeration and heating equipment
HQ: Trane U.S. Inc.
    800-E Beaty St
    Davidson NC 28036
    704 655-4000

(G-4347)
TRANSPORTATION TECH INDS (DH)
7140 Office Cir (47715-8235)
PHONE..................812 962-5000
Terrence Keating, *Pr*
Kenneth M Tallering, *VP*
Anthony A Donatelli, *Sr VP*
▲ EMP: 10 EST: 1901
SQ FT: 10,000
SALES (est): 350.02MM **Privately Held**
SIC: 2531 3714 3321 4741 Vehicle furniture; Motor vehicle wheels and parts; Ductile iron castings; Rental of railroad cars
HQ: Accuride Corporation
    38777 6 Mile Rd Ste 410
    Livonia MI 48152
    812 962-5000

(G-4348)
TRAYLOR INDUSTRIAL LLC (HQ)
835 N Congress Ave (47715)
PHONE..................812 428-3708
R Scott Thomas, *Pr*
Allen Harding, *
Steven Scott Owen, *
Kirk Alan Williams, *

GEOGRAPHIC SECTION
Evansville - Vanderburgh County (G-4371)

EMP: 175 EST: 1985
SALES (est): 60.68MM
SALES (corp-wide): 111.87MM **Privately Held**
Web: www.adconstructors.com
SIC: **3441** Fabricated structural metal
PA: Traylor Bros., Inc.
835 N Congress Ave
Evansville IN 47715
812 477-1542

(G-4349)
TRI-SKY LLC
13031 Balboa Dr (47725-6825)
PHONE..................................812 746-1678
EMP: 1 EST: 2021
SALES (est): 56.09K **Privately Held**
SIC: **3669** Communications equipment, nec

(G-4350)
TRI-STATE GUTTERTOPPER INC
Also Called: Construction
6901 Briar Ct (47711-1655)
PHONE..................................812 455-1460
John Buckingham, *Pr*
EMP: 3 EST: 2002
SALES (est): 229.28K **Privately Held**
SIC: **1761** 5211 1389 Gutter and downspout contractor; Lumber and other building materials; Construction, repair, and dismantling services

(G-4351)
TRI-STATE POWDER COATING LLC
800 Bayse St (47713-2902)
PHONE..................................812 425-7010
Billy G Tibbs, *Admn*
EMP: 10 EST: 2011
SALES (est): 743.88K **Privately Held**
Web: www.tristatepowdercoatings.com
SIC: **3479** Coating of metals and formed products

(G-4352)
TRI-STATE VETERINARY SUP INC
3300 Interstate Dr (47715-1781)
P.O. Box 4142 (47724-0142)
PHONE..................................812 477-4793
Lee Sorrell, *Pr*
Jean Sorrell, *Sec*
EMP: 5 EST: 1953
SQ FT: 3,000
SALES (est): 979.8K
SALES (corp-wide): 45.87MM **Privately Held**
Web: www.tristateequineandpet.com
SIC: **3999** Pet supplies
PA: Posey County Farm Bureau Cooperative Association, Inc.
817 W 4th St
Mount Vernon IN 47620
812 838-4468

(G-4353)
TRIVALENCE TECHNOLOGIES LLC
3001 Maxx Rd (47711)
PHONE..................................800 209-2517
David Richey, *CEO*
David Richey, *Managing Member*
Eric Stockton, *
Mark Larue, *
EMP: 41 EST: 2015
SALES (est): 5.91MM **Privately Held**
Web: www.trivalencetechnologies.com
SIC: **3089** Injection molding of plastics

(G-4354)
TSF CO INC
Also Called: Tri State Flasher Co
2930 Saint Philip Rd S (47712-9581)
PHONE..................................812 985-2630

TOLL FREE: 800
Eugene Barnhart, *Pr*
Bob Schenk, *
Patricia Schenk, *
Mathew Schenk, *
Jeanette H Barnhart, *
◆ EMP: 25 EST: 1959
SQ FT: 6,000
SALES (est): 2.77MM **Privately Held**
Web: www.tuff-jon.com
SIC: **3431** 7359 Portable chemical toilets, metal; Equipment rental and leasing, nec

(G-4355)
TUCKER PUBLISHING GROUP INC
Also Called: Evansville Living
25 Nw Riverside Dr Ste 200 (47708)
PHONE..................................812 426-2115
Todd Tucker, *Pr*
William Tucker Junior, *Sec*
Kristin Tucker, *Prin*
EMP: 17 EST: 1999
SALES (est): 1.68MM **Privately Held**
Web: www.webpublisherpro.com
SIC: **2741** Miscellaneous publishing

(G-4356)
TURONIS FORGET-ME-NOT INC
4 N Weinbach Ave (47711-6004)
PHONE..................................812 477-7500
Jerry Turner, *Pr*
EMP: 17 EST: 1964
SALES (est): 247.57K **Privately Held**
Web: www.turonis.com
SIC: **5812** 2082 Pizza restaurants; Malt beverages

(G-4357)
TWICE DAILY LLC
640 S Bennighof Ave (47714-2020)
PHONE..................................812 484-5417
EMP: 6 EST: 2014
SALES (est): 56.18K **Privately Held**
Web: www.twicedaily.com
SIC: **2711** Newspapers, publishing and printing

(G-4358)
ULTIMA PLASTICS LLC
5401 Highway 41 N Ste B (47711)
PHONE..................................812 459-1430
Gregory Riedford, *Managing Member*
EMP: 5 EST: 2018
SALES (est): 955.31K **Privately Held**
SIC: **3089** 7389 Novelties, plastics; Business services, nec

(G-4359)
UNDERDOG DINER LLP
2800 Lake Dr (47711-3614)
PHONE..................................812 598-2970
Amanda Green, *Pt*
EMP: 2 EST: 2021
SALES (est): 62.38K **Privately Held**
SIC: **2047** 7389 Dog food; Business Activities at Non-Commercial Site

(G-4360)
UNISEAL INC
1000 Grove St (47710-1824)
PHONE..................................812 425-1361
EMP: 43
Web: www.uniseal.com
SIC: **3084** 2891 3568 3498 Plastics pipe; Sealants; Power transmission equipment, nec; Fabricated pipe and fittings
HQ: Uniseal, Inc.
1014 Uhlhorn St
Evansville IN 47710
812 425-1361

(G-4361)
UNISEAL INC (HQ)
Also Called: Uniseal
1014 Uhlhorn St (47710)
P.O. Box 6288 (47719)
PHONE..................................812 425-1361
Changhyun Lee, *Pr*
Jang Woo Park, *CFO*
▲ EMP: 126 EST: 1984
SQ FT: 134,000
SALES (est): 42.26MM **Privately Held**
Web: www.uniseal.com
SIC: **2891** Sealants
PA: Lg Chem, Ltd.
128 Yeoui-Daero, Yeongdeungpo-Gu
Seoul 07336

(G-4362)
UNITED HERO APPAREL PRINTING
928 Beverly Ave (47710-3130)
PHONE..................................812 306-1998
EMP: 4 EST: 2017
SALES (est): 83.91K **Privately Held**
SIC: **2752** Commercial printing, lithographic

(G-4363)
UNIVERSAL OPERATING INC
1521 S Green River Rd (47715-5659)
PHONE..................................812 477-1584
William W Smith, *Pr*
William Gene Moser, *VP*
Nancy L Montgomery, *Sec*
EMP: 4 EST: 1953
SQ FT: 1,200
SALES (est): 469.04K **Privately Held**
Web: www.universalsalvage.net
SIC: **1381** 1311 Drilling oil and gas wells; Crude petroleum and natural gas production

(G-4364)
US LBM OPERATING CO 3009 LLC
Also Called: K & I Sash & Door
1700 N Kentucky Ave (47711-3824)
P.O. Box 4099 (47724-0099)
PHONE..................................812 464-2428
Mark C Hansen, *Brnch Mgr*
EMP: 1
SALES (corp-wide): 141.88MM **Privately Held**
Web: www.ki-lumber.com
SIC: **2439** 2431 2426 5031 Structural wood members, nec; Millwork; Hardwood dimension and flooring mills; Structural assemblies, prefabricated: wood
HQ: Us Lbm Operating Co. 3009, Llc
2150 E Lk Cook Rd Ste 101
Buffalo Grove IL 60089
706 266-8856

(G-4365)
US VALVES INC
640 S Hebron Ave (47714-4042)
PHONE..................................812 476-6662
Brian Ricci, *Pr*
Tanya Henson, *VP*
EMP: 2 EST: 1990
SQ FT: 1,200
SALES (est): 230K **Privately Held**
Web: www.officetraining.com
SIC: **3491** 3599 Valves, automatic control; Custom machinery

(G-4366)
VAN ZANDT ENTERPRISES INC
Also Called: Industrial Services Co
1701 N Kentucky Ave (47711-3854)
P.O. Box 6407 (47719-0407)
PHONE..................................812 423-3511
Edward L Vanzandt, *Pr*
Debra Van Zandt, *Sec*
EMP: 11 EST: 1979

SQ FT: 43,000
SALES (est): 491.11K **Privately Held**
SIC: **1721** 1799 2851 Commercial painting; Sandblasting of building exteriors; Paints and allied products

(G-4367)
VANDERGRIFF & ASSOCIATES INC
Also Called: Vander Parts Co
1930 Allens Ln (47720-1313)
P.O. Box 6306 (47719-0306)
PHONE..................................812 422-6033
Gary Van Dergriff, *Pr*
Gary D Vandergriff, *Pr*
Steve Vandergriff, *VP*
Janet Vandergriff, *Sec*
EMP: 5 EST: 1985
SQ FT: 30,000
SALES (est): 999.46K **Privately Held**
Web: www.vanderparts.com
SIC: **5082** 7629 3441 Mining machinery and equipment, except petroleum; Electrical repair shops; Fabricated structural metal

(G-4368)
VECTREN LLC (HQ)
Also Called: Vectren
1 Vectren Sq (47708)
PHONE..................................812 491-4000
Carl L Chapman, *CEO*
EMP: 1207 EST: 1999
SALES (est): 5.42B
SALES (corp-wide): 8.7B **Publicly Held**
Web: www.centerpointenergy.com
SIC: **4924** 4911 1241 1623 Natural gas distribution; Electric services; Coal mining services; Water, sewer, and utility lines
PA: Centerpoint Energy, Inc.
1111 Louisiana St
Houston TX 77002
713 207-1111

(G-4369)
VECTREN LLC
20 Nw 4th St (47708-1724)
PHONE..................................812 424-6411
Niel C Ellerbrook, *Brnch Mgr*
EMP: 3
SALES (corp-wide): 8.7B **Publicly Held**
Web: www.centerpointenergy.com
SIC: **4924** 4911 1241 4841 Natural gas distribution; Electric services; Coal mining services; Cable and other pay television services
HQ: Vectren, Llc
1 Vectren Sq
Evansville IN 47708
812 491-4000

(G-4370)
VECTREN POWER SUPPLY
P.O. Box 209 (47702-0209)
PHONE..................................812 491-4310
EMP: 7 EST: 2009
SALES (est): 4.53MM
SALES (corp-wide): 8.7B **Publicly Held**
SIC: **1389** Fire fighting, oil and gas field
HQ: Vectren, Llc
1 Vectren Sq
Evansville IN 47708
812 491-4000

(G-4371)
VERNON A STEVENS
3901 Bergdolt Rd (47711-2591)
PHONE..................................812 626-0010
Vernon A Stevens, *Owner*
EMP: 5 EST: 1989
SALES (est): 278.71K **Privately Held**
SIC: **3579** Postage meters

Evansville - Vanderburgh County (G-4372)

(G-4372)
VERNON L GOEDECKE COMPANY INC
1011 E Columbia St (47711-5213)
PHONE..................812 421-9633
Steve Schaar, *Mgr*
EMP: 1
SALES (corp-wide): 47.01MM **Privately Held**
Web: www.goedeckeonline.com
SIC: **3272** Concrete products, nec
PA: Vernon L. Goedecke Company, Inc.
   8000 Hall St Bldg 6
   Saint Louis MO 63147
   314 652-1810

(G-4373)
VICTOR R GALLAGHER
Also Called: Gallagher Drilling
P.O. Box 8275 (47716-8275)
PHONE..................812 425-8256
Victor Gallagher Junior, *Owner*
EMP: 4 EST: 1947
SALES (est): 124.24K **Privately Held**
SIC: **1311** Crude petroleum production

(G-4374)
VIGO COAL OPERATING CO INC (HQ)
Also Called: Vigo Coal Company
250 N Cross Pointe Blvd (47715-4073)
PHONE..................812 759-8446
John C Harman, *Pr*
Raymond T Purk, *
David J Beckman, *
EMP: 133 EST: 1977
SQ FT: 20,000
SALES (est): 127.84MM
SALES (corp-wide): 132.82MM **Privately Held**
SIC: **1221 8748** Surface mining, bituminous, nec; Business consulting, nec
PA: White Stallion Acquisition Llc
   250 N Cross Pointe Blvd
   Evansville IN

(G-4375)
VINTAGE PUBLISHING LLC
7643 Miranda Dr (47711-1501)
PHONE..................812 719-7200
Chad Schmidt, *Prin*
EMP: 4 EST: 2011
SALES (est): 51.2K **Privately Held**
Web: www.vintage-publishing.com
SIC: **2741** Miscellaneous publishing

(G-4376)
VISION IV INC
14110 Castle Brook Rd (47725-8320)
PHONE..................812 423-0119
Jackie Cozgrove, *Pr*
EMP: 20 EST: 1971
SALES (est): 2.39MM **Privately Held**
Web: www.visioniv.net
SIC: **2448** Pallets, wood

(G-4377)
WABASH PLASTICS INC (PA)
600 N Cross Pointe Blvd (47715-9119)
PHONE..................812 428-9300
John Schroeder, *Pr*
Belle Fahrer, *Sec*
◆ EMP: 4 EST: 1972
SALES (est): 39.46MM
SALES (corp-wide): 39.46MM **Privately Held**
Web: www.wabashplastics.com
SIC: **3089** Injection molded finished plastics products, nec

(G-4378)
WABASH PLASTICS INC
1300 Burch Dr (47725-1798)
PHONE..................812 867-2447
Ed Furniss, *Brnch Mgr*
EMP: 221
SALES (corp-wide): 39.46MM **Privately Held**
Web: www.wabashplastics.com
SIC: **3089** Injection molding of plastics
PA: Wabash Plastics, Inc.
   600 N Cross Pointe Blvd
   Evansville IN 47715
   812 428-9300

(G-4379)
WANNEMUEHLER DISTRIBUTION INC
516 N 7th Ave (47710-1420)
PHONE..................812 422-3251
Eugene Wannemuehler, *Pr*
EMP: 14 EST: 1991
SALES (est): 196.88K **Privately Held**
Web: www.heritageoil.com
SIC: **3713 5172** Tank truck bodies; Petroleum products, nec

(G-4380)
WCM TOOL & MACHINE INC
810 E Division St (47711-5664)
PHONE..................812 422-2315
EMP: 7 EST: 1995
SQ FT: 6,000
SALES (est): 644.58K **Privately Held**
SIC: **3544** Dies, plastics forming

(G-4381)
WESTERN EXCELSIOR CORPORATION (PA)
Also Called: Western Green
4609 E Boonville New Harmony Rd (47725)
PHONE..................970 533-7412
Norman Snyder, *Pr*
Exum Lewis, *Sec*
Zack Snyder, *CFO*
◆ EMP: 49 EST: 1989
SALES (est): 49.41MM
SALES (corp-wide): 49.41MM **Privately Held**
Web: www.westernexcelsior.com
SIC: **2429** Shavings and packaging, excelsior

(G-4382)
WESTERN KENTUCKY DRILLING
600 S Cullen Ave Apt 810 (47715-4166)
PHONE..................812 457-5639
William Endicott, *Owner*
EMP: 3 EST: 2010
SALES (est): 177.23K **Privately Held**
SIC: **1381** Drilling oil and gas wells

(G-4383)
WHIRLPOOL CORPORATION
Whirlpool
5401 Us Hwy 41n (47711-1962)
PHONE..................812 426-4000
Al Holaday, *Brnch Mgr*
EMP: 94
SALES (corp-wide): 19.45B **Publicly Held**
Web: www.whirlpoolcorp.com
SIC: **3585 3632** Refrigeration equipment, complete; Freezers, home and farm
PA: Whirlpool Corporation
   2000 N M-63
   Benton Harbor MI 49022
   269 923-5000

(G-4384)
WHITE CAP LLC
2201 W Maryland St (47712-5365)
PHONE..................812 425-6221
John Bugnitz, *Prin*
EMP: 8 EST: 2004
SALES (est): 95.24K **Privately Held**
SIC: **3999** Manufacturing industries, nec

(G-4385)
WILLIAM F SHIRLEY
Also Called: S & S Machine Co
2721 W Mill Rd (47720-1127)
PHONE..................812 426-2599
William F Shirley, *Owner*
EMP: 3 EST: 1978
SQ FT: 5,000
SALES (est): 180K **Privately Held**
SIC: **3599 7692** Machine shop, jobbing and repair; Welding repair

(G-4386)
WILLIAM L THEBY
650 Salem Ct (47715-7141)
PHONE..................812 477-6673
William L Theby, *Owner*
EMP: 5 EST: 2005
SALES (est): 135.12K **Privately Held**
Web: www.pchen.co
SIC: **2899** Chemical preparations, nec

(G-4387)
WILLIAMS JEWELERS INC
3101 Covert Ave (47714-4059)
PHONE..................812 475-1705
Daniel Williams, *Owner*
EMP: 3 EST: 1968
SQ FT: 1,500
SALES (est): 140K **Privately Held**
SIC: **3911 5944 7631** Jewelry, precious metal ; Jewelry, precious stones and precious metals; Jewelry repair services

(G-4388)
WINK ANTI TIP LLC
4936 Countrylane Dr (47715-7659)
PHONE..................812 305-3165
EMP: 4 EST: 2018
SALES (est): 186.69K **Privately Held**
Web: www.winkantitip.com
SIC: **3999** Manufacturing industries, nec

(G-4389)
WOOD SPC BY FEHRENBACHER INC
8920 Big Cynthiana Rd (47720-7606)
PHONE..................812 963-9414
Keith Fehrenbacher, *Pr*
Gary Fehrenbacher, *VP*
Chris Fehrenbacher, *Sec*
EMP: 22 EST: 1985
SQ FT: 14,000
SALES (est): 2.23MM **Privately Held**
Web: www.wsfinc.com
SIC: **2431** Doors and door parts and trim, wood

(G-4390)
WORLDWIDE BATTERY COMPANY LLC
6050 Wedeking Ave Ste 5 (47715-2187)
PHONE..................812 475-1326
EMP: 2
SALES (corp-wide): 22.57MM **Privately Held**
Web: www.worldwidebattery.com
SIC: **5063 3691** Batteries; Storage batteries
PA: Worldwide Battery Company, Llc
   9955 Westpoint Dr Ste 120
   Indianapolis IN 46256
   317 845-1330

(G-4391)
YESCO LLC
1300 N Royal Ave (47715-7808)
PHONE..................812 469-2292
EMP: 9 EST: 2015
SALES (est): 122.16K **Privately Held**
Web: www.yesco.com
SIC: **3993** Signs and advertising specialties

(G-4392)
ZEROCARB LLC
318 Main St Ste 101 (47708-1451)
PHONE..................812 214-1084
EMP: 3 EST: 2020
SALES (est): 280.96K **Privately Held**
Web: www.zerocarblyfe.com
SIC: **2038** Frozen specialties, nec

(G-4393)
ZIP ZONE GONE LLC
815 John St Ste 110 # 1017 (47713-2746)
PHONE..................812 604-0041
Sherry Walker, *Managing Member*
EMP: 2 EST: 2018
SALES (est): 244.38K **Privately Held**
Web: www.zipzonegone.com
SIC: **4789 4213 3537** Transportation services, nec; Trucking, except local; Trucks, tractors, loaders, carriers, and similar equipment

Fair Oaks
Jasper County

(G-4394)
AMP AMERICAS LLC
Also Called: AMP CNG
5431 E 600 N (47943-8034)
PHONE..................312 300-6700
EMP: 2
SALES (corp-wide): 6.03MM **Privately Held**
Web: www.ampamericas.com
SIC: **2869 5171** Fuels; Petroleum bulk stations
PA: Amp Americas, Llc
   2001 N Clybourn Ave # 400
   Chicago IL 60614
   312 300-6700

Fairbanks
Sullivan County

(G-4395)
FLOOR WORKS MFG & FAB
6224 W Walnut (47849)
PHONE..................812 394-2311
Mickey Fuson, *Owner*
EMP: 1 EST: 1986
SALES (est): 77.99K **Privately Held**
SIC: **3444** Sheet metal specialties, not stamped

Fairland
Shelby County

(G-4396)
ARBUCKLE INDUSTRIES INC
4990 N 550 W (46126-9807)
PHONE..................317 835-7489
David Arbuckle, *Pr*
Cinde Arbuckle, *VP*
EMP: 2 EST: 1990
SALES (est): 137.24K **Privately Held**
Web: www.arbuckleindustries.com

SIC: 3569 Robots, assembly line: industrial and commercial

(G-4397)
BEGLEY SIGN PAINTING INC
220 N Murnan Ln (46126-2009)
P.O. Box 212 (46126-0212)
PHONE.............................317 835-2027
John Begley, Pr
EMP: 2 EST: 1969
SALES (est): 132.75K Privately Held
SIC: 3993 Electric signs

(G-4398)
BROOKFIELD SAND & GRAVEL INC (PA)
8587 N 850 W (46126)
P.O. Box 60 (46126)
PHONE.............................317 835-2235
Charles Mc Curdy, Pr
EMP: 25 EST: 1976
SQ FT: 15,000
SALES (est): 7.96MM Privately Held
Web: www.brookfieldsandandgravel.com
SIC: 1442 Sand mining

(G-4399)
JUPITER ALUMINUM CORPORATION
Also Called: Jupiter Coil Coating
205 E Carey St (46126-9694)
PHONE.............................219 932-3322
Alex Gross, Mgr
EMP: 55
Web: www.jupiteraluminum.com
SIC: 3353 3479 Aluminum sheet, plate, and foil; Painting of metal products
PA: Jupiter Aluminum Corporation
1745 165th St Ste 6
Hammond IN 46320

(G-4400)
MARSTONE PRODUCTS LTD
Also Called: M P L
203 N Edgerton St (46126-2036)
P.O. Box 220 (46126-0220)
PHONE.............................800 466-7465
Thomas Crowley, Prin
Nancy Crawley, *
▲ EMP: 32 EST: 1962
SQ FT: 20,000
SALES (est): 4.72MM Privately Held
Web: www.mplcompany.net
SIC: 3281 Table tops, marble

(G-4401)
PRINTERS GROUP
4485 W 600 N (46126-9774)
PHONE.............................317 835-7720
Gene Taylor, Prin
EMP: 4 EST: 2016
SALES (est): 54.36K Privately Held
SIC: 2711 Newspapers

(G-4402)
R&H METALWORKS LLC
8142 N 700 W (46126-9665)
PHONE.............................317 513-8733
EMP: 1 EST: 2013
SALES (est): 64.01K Privately Held
SIC: 3499 7389 Metal household articles; Business Activities at Non-Commercial Site

(G-4403)
THOMAS L WEHR
Also Called: Wehr Engineering
8192 W 700 N (46126-9507)
PHONE.............................317 835-7824
Thomas Wehr, Owner
Kyle Wehr, VP
EMP: 4 EST: 1985

SQ FT: 2,560
SALES (est): 315.74K Privately Held
Web: www.glasmaster.com
SIC: 3569 3545 Firefighting and related equipment; Machine tool accessories

(G-4404)
TLK PRECISION INC
9609 N Pumpkinvine Rd (46126-9800)
PHONE.............................317 427-0123
EMP: 6 EST: 2008
SALES (est): 73.33K Privately Held
Web: www.tlk-precision.com
SIC: 3599 Machine shop, jobbing and repair

(G-4405)
TRUCK TRAILER REPAIR INDY LLC
11357 N Pheasant Run (46126-9578)
PHONE.............................317 755-2177
Michael Sprague, Pr
EMP: 1 EST: 2019
SALES (est): 55.37K Privately Held
SIC: 3715 Truck trailers

(G-4406)
WORLD CLASS FIBERGLASS
5694 N Private Road 660 W (46126-9460)
PHONE.............................317 512-3343
James Gatchett, Owner
EMP: 1 EST: 1988
SALES (est): 128.94K Privately Held
SIC: 3732 Boats, fiberglass: building and repairing

Fairmount
Grant County

(G-4407)
ALLEN C TERHUNE & ASSOCIATES
Also Called: News-Sun, The
122 S Main St (46928-1923)
PHONE.............................765 948-4164
Jim Terhune, Pr
Florence Terhune, Sec
EMP: 9 EST: 1872
SQ FT: 5,000
SALES (est): 486.58K Privately Held
SIC: 2752 2711 Offset printing; Newspapers

(G-4408)
BEAST CUSTOM ATHLETIC PRINTING
418 W Fifth St (46928-1320)
PHONE.............................765 610-6802
Philip Parker, Prin
EMP: 4 EST: 2016
SALES (est): 83.91K Privately Held
Web: www.beastprints.com
SIC: 2752 Commercial printing, lithographic

(G-4409)
FAIRMOUNT NEWS
122 S Main St (46928-1923)
P.O. Box 25 (46928-0025)
PHONE.............................765 948-4164
Jim Terhune, Pr
EMP: 4 EST: 2001
SALES (est): 163.32K Privately Held
SIC: 2711 Newspapers, publishing and printing

(G-4410)
GIBSON BROTHERS WELDING INC
1520 W 900 S (46928-9774)
PHONE.............................765 948-5775
Brian Gibson, Pr
Dale Gibson, Sec
EMP: 10 EST: 1989
SQ FT: 4,200

SALES (est): 953.43K Privately Held
Web: www.gibsonbrotherswelldinginc.com
SIC: 7692 3429 Welding repair; Fireplace equipment, hardware: andirons, grates, screens

(G-4411)
NORTH AMERICAN MFG INC
Also Called: American Mobile Power
619 E Jefferson St (46928-1817)
P.O. Box 65 (46928-0065)
PHONE.............................765 948-3337
EMP: 1 EST: 1994
SALES (est): 2.15MM Privately Held
Web: www.americanmobilepower.com
SIC: 3714 Motor vehicle parts and accessories

(G-4412)
PALLET BUILDER INC
1520 W 900 S (46928-9774)
P.O. Box 144 (46928-0144)
PHONE.............................765 948-3345
John Remmington, Mgr
EMP: 7
Web: www.thepalletbuilders.com
SIC: 2448 Pallets, wood
PA: The Pallet Builder Inc
112 Inks Dr
Winchester IN 47394

(G-4413)
SUE S SHEEP QUARTERS
11320 S Wheeling Pike (46928-9575)
PHONE.............................765 998-2067
Sue Parker, Prin
EMP: 1 EST: 2010
SALES (est): 43.68K Privately Held
SIC: 3199 Leather goods, nec

(G-4414)
WIMMER LIME SERVICE INC
7497 S 150 E (46928-9707)
P.O. Box 81 (46928-0081)
PHONE.............................765 948-4001
Kevin Wimmer, Pr
Tom Wimmer, Owner
Kevin Wimmer, Mgr
EMP: 17 EST: 1997
SALES (est): 1.39MM Privately Held
SIC: 3713 Dump truck bodies

Falmouth
Rush County

(G-4415)
BILL BANNER SIGNS
10697 N 600 E (46127-9793)
PHONE.............................765 209-2642
Bill Weaver, Owner
EMP: 4 EST: 2017
SALES (est): 88.96K Privately Held
SIC: 3993 Signs and advertising specialties

Farmersburg
Sullivan County

(G-4416)
BRAMPTON BRICK INC
1256 E County Road 950 N (47850-8111)
PHONE.............................812 397-2190
Jeffrey G Kerbel, Pr
Ken Mondor, *
Marilia Macias, *
David R Carter, *
Judy H Pryma, *
▲ EMP: 26 EST: 2006

SALES (est): 22.99MM Privately Held
SALES (corp-wide): 114.44MM Privately Held
Web: www.bramptonbrick.com
SIC: 5032 3271 Brick, stone, and related material; Architectural concrete: block, split, fluted, screen, etc.
PA: Brampton Brick Limited
225 Wanless Dr
Brampton ON L7A 1
905 840-1011

(G-4417)
BRYAN WARD
Also Called: B & G Box
247 W Hampton Dr (47850-9434)
PHONE.............................812 696-5126
Bryan Ward, Owner
EMP: 1 EST: 2001
SALES (est): 64.39K Privately Held
SIC: 2449 5999 Rectangular boxes and crates, wood; Packaging materials: boxes, padding, etc.

(G-4418)
DW INC
220 E Hampton St (47850-7014)
P.O. Box 230 (47850-0230)
PHONE.............................812 696-2149
EMP: 4 EST: 2018
SALES (est): 48.8K Privately Held
Web: www.dwincorp.com
SIC: 3999 Manufacturing industries, nec

(G-4419)
JEWETT PRINTING LLC
219 W Main St (47850-7095)
PHONE.............................812 232-0087
Larry Natailie, Managing Member
EMP: 4 EST: 2014
SALES (est): 249.17K Privately Held
Web: www.jewettprinting.com
SIC: 2752 Offset printing

(G-4420)
JEWETT PUBLICATIONS INC
Also Called: Jewett Printing
219 W Main St (47850-7095)
P.O. Box 390 (47850-0390)
PHONE.............................812 232-0087
EMP: 15
SIC: 2752 Post cards, picture: lithographed

(G-4421)
WRITERS OF VISION
4118 W County Road 975 N (47850-8268)
PHONE.............................812 239-6347
Darrell Case, Prin
EMP: 5 EST: 2015
SALES (est): 85.38K Privately Held
SIC: 3523 Farm machinery and equipment

Farmland
Randolph County

(G-4422)
BOBS WELDING & REPAIR LLC
6447 W 250 S (47340-9562)
PHONE.............................765 744-4192
EMP: 2 EST: 1996
SALES (est): 107.56K Privately Held
SIC: 7692 Welding repair

(G-4423)
BRANDING STITCH LLC
104 N Main St Ste 2 (47340-9403)
PHONE.............................765 468-8463
Denise Smith, Admn
EMP: 5 EST: 2018

Farmland - Randolph County (G-4424)   **GEOGRAPHIC SECTION**

SALES (est): 35.4K **Privately Held**
SIC: 2395 Embroidery and art needlework

(G-4424)
CONSOLIDATED PRINTING SVCS INC
201 E Henry St (47340-7006)
P.O. Box 446 (47340-0446)
PHONE..................................765 468-6033
Daniel Yuska, *Pr*
Jeffrey Brooks, *Sec*
EMP: 7 EST: 1959
SQ FT: 8,000
SALES (est): 129.77K **Privately Held**
SIC: 2752 2791 2789 2759 Offset printing; Typesetting; Bookbinding and related work; Commercial printing, nec

(G-4425)
FROM WOODS
1279 S 1000 W (47340-8909)
PHONE..................................765 468-7387
Wayne Gaydos, *Owner*
EMP: 1 EST: 1970
SALES (est): 106.73K **Privately Held**
SIC: 2431 Woodwork, interior and ornamental, nec

(G-4426)
MIDWEST RUBBER SALES INC
2135 N 900 W (47340-8942)
PHONE..................................765 468-7105
Rita R Buckner, *Pr*
James S Buckner, *VP*
EMP: 7 EST: 1976
SQ FT: 25,000
SALES (est): 574.45K **Privately Held**
Web: www.midwestrubbersales.com
SIC: 3069 Medical and laboratory rubber sundries and related products

(G-4427)
WILLIAMS PRINTING INC
201 E Henry St (47340-7006)
P.O. Box 268 (47340-0268)
PHONE..................................765 468-6033
Tammy Bousman, *Pr*
EMP: 3 EST: 2006
SALES (est): 242.22K **Privately Held**
SIC: 2752 Offset printing

Ferdinand
Dubois County

(G-4428)
AMERICAN WHITETAIL INC
8478 E State Road 62 (47532-7599)
P.O. Box 299 (47532-0299)
PHONE..................................812 937-7185
Ralph Harris, *Pr*
Robert Harris, *Stockholder*
Kenneth Harris, *Stockholder*
EMP: 10 EST: 1987
SQ FT: 18,000
SALES (est): 1.59MM **Privately Held**
Web: www.archerytargets.com
SIC: 3086 3949 Plastics foam products; Sporting and athletic goods, nec

(G-4429)
BEST CHAIRS INCORPORATED (PA)
Also Called: Best Chairs
1 Best Dr (47532-9537)
P.O. Box 158 (47532-0158)
PHONE..................................812 367-1761
Glenn A Lange, *CEO*
Clement M Lange Junior, *Ch*
Brian L Lange, *
Joseph L Lange, *
Gregory K Sicard, *Marketing*

◆ EMP: 700 EST: 1962
SALES (est): 225MM
SALES (corp-wide): 225MM **Privately Held**
Web: www.besthf.com
SIC: 2512 Chairs: upholstered on wood frames

(G-4430)
DUBOIS-SPNCER CUNTIES PUBG INC (PA)
Also Called: Spencer County Leader
113 W 6th St (47532-9517)
P.O. Box 38 (47532-0038)
PHONE..................................812 367-2041
Richard Tretter, *Pr*
Kathleen Tretter, *Sec*
EMP: 11 EST: 1906
SALES (est): 1.02MM
SALES (corp-wide): 1.02MM **Privately Held**
Web: www.ferdinandnews.com
SIC: 2711 Job printing and newspaper publishing combined

(G-4431)
FERDINAND MACHINE SHOP
825 Main St (47532-9792)
PHONE..................................812 367-2590
Leo Giesler Junior, *Pt*
Randy Oser, *Pt*
Jim Weyer, *Pt*
EMP: 4 EST: 1982
SQ FT: 5,000
SALES (est): 486.09K **Privately Held**
SIC: 3599 Machine shop, jobbing and repair

(G-4432)
FERDINAND PROCESSING INC
1182 E 5th St (47532-9780)
PHONE..................................812 367-2073
Paul Gogel, *Pr*
Paula Gogel, *VP*
EMP: 4 EST: 1988
SALES (est): 402.79K **Privately Held**
Web: www.ferdinandprocessing.net
SIC: 2011 Meat packing plants

(G-4433)
FIVE STARR INC
453 W 9th St (47532-9236)
P.O. Box 10 (47532-0010)
PHONE..................................812 367-1554
Kathy Weyer, *Pr*
EMP: 2 EST: 2008
SALES (est): 186.82K **Privately Held**
Web: www.weyerelectric.com
SIC: 3448 Buildings, portable: prefabricated metal

(G-4434)
HANKS SIGN SHOP LLC
330 Main St (47532-9710)
PHONE..................................812 367-2851
Hank Brahm, *Managing Member*
EMP: 3 EST: 1960
SALES (est): 198.58K **Privately Held**
SIC: 3993 Signs and advertising specialties

(G-4435)
HERB RAHMAN & SONS INC
9426 E County Road 2100 N (47532-7525)
PHONE..................................812 367-2513
Stan Rahman, *Pr*
Kenneth Rahman, *Sec*
EMP: 2 EST: 1978
SQ FT: 4,000
SALES (est): 154.07K **Privately Held**
SIC: 2434 Wood kitchen cabinets

(G-4436)
J & L UEBELHOR ENTERPRISES LLC
1440 Virginia St (47532-9192)
P.O. Box 125 (47532-0125)
PHONE..................................812 367-1591
Keith Uebelhor, *Managing Member*
EMP: 6 EST: 2002
SALES (est): 334.13K **Privately Held**
Web: www.uebelhor-tv.com
SIC: 3671 Television tubes

(G-4437)
JEFF HURST CUSTOM WDWKG INC
8134 S State Road 162 (47532-9437)
PHONE..................................812 367-1430
Jeff Hurst, *CEO*
EMP: 2 EST: 1995
SALES (est): 141.8K **Privately Held**
SIC: 2431 Woodwork, interior and ornamental, nec

(G-4438)
KNU LLC (PA)
Also Called: La-Z-Boy Contract Furniture
824 W 23rd St (47532)
P.O. Box 9 (47532)
PHONE..................................812 367-1761
Richard N Franey, *VP*
Steven M Wahl, *Treas*
▲ EMP: 33 EST: 2005
SALES (est): 22.67MM
SALES (corp-wide): 22.67MM **Privately Held**
Web: www.getknu.com
SIC: 2599 Hospital furniture, except beds

(G-4439)
LA-Z-BOY INC
1 Best Dr (47532-9537)
PHONE..................................812 367-0190
EMP: 6 EST: 2018
SALES (est): 181.89K **Privately Held**
Web: www.getknu.com
SIC: 2512 Upholstered household furniture

(G-4440)
LEIBERING DIMENSION INC
514 W 8th St (47532-9536)
P.O. Box 189 (47532-0189)
PHONE..................................812 367-2971
Shawn N Leibering, *Prin*
EMP: 9 EST: 2008
SALES (est): 242.02K **Privately Held**
Web: www.leiberingdimension.com
SIC: 2511 Wood household furniture

(G-4441)
LELAND MANUFACTURING
1 Best Dr (47532-9537)
PHONE..................................812 367-2068
Faron Lasher, *Prin*
EMP: 7 EST: 2014
SALES (est): 96.4K **Privately Held**
SIC: 3999 Manufacturing industries, nec

(G-4442)
MASTERBRAND CABINETS LLC
328 Main St (47532-9710)
PHONE..................................812 367-1104
EMP: 3
SALES (corp-wide): 2.73B **Publicly Held**
Web: www.masterbrand.com
SIC: 2434 Wood kitchen cabinets
HQ: Masterbrand Cabinets Llc
3300 Entp Pkwy Ste 300
Beachwood OH 44122
812 482-2527

(G-4443)
MASTERBRAND CABINETS LLC
614 W 3rd St (47532-9753)
PHONE..................................812 367-1104
Glen Maservy, *Mgr*
EMP: 42
SALES (corp-wide): 2.73B **Publicly Held**
Web: www.masterbrand.com
SIC: 2434 Vanities, bathroom: wood
HQ: Masterbrand Cabinets Llc
3300 Entp Pkwy Ste 300
Beachwood OH 44122
812 482-2527

(G-4444)
MIKE FISHER LOGGING
6480 E 850 S (47532-9460)
PHONE..................................812 357-2169
Mike Fisher, *Owner*
EMP: 1 EST: 1997
SALES (est): 77K **Privately Held**
SIC: 2411 Logging camps and contractors

(G-4445)
MOBEL INC (PA)
2130 Industrial Park Rd (47532-9470)
P.O. Box 130 (47532-0130)
PHONE..................................812 367-1214
Paul Ruhe, *CEO*
Kenneth Lampkin, *
EMP: 140 EST: 1971
SQ FT: 200,000
SALES (est): 4.9MM
SALES (corp-wide): 4.9MM **Privately Held**
Web: www.mobelinc.com
SIC: 2511 Wood bedroom furniture

(G-4446)
OEDING CORPORATION
443 W 16th St (47532-9173)
PHONE..................................812 367-1271
Gary Oeding, *Pr*
EMP: 3 EST: 1945
SALES (est): 226.48K **Privately Held**
SIC: 5984 2511 5712 Propane gas, bottled; Wood household furniture; Furniture stores

(G-4447)
PHILIPPS WOOD PROCESSING
8942 E County Road 1850 N (47532-7584)
PHONE..................................812 357-2824
Lee Philipps, *Owner*
EMP: 1 EST: 2000
SALES (est): 69.73K **Privately Held**
SIC: 2519 Household furniture, except wood or metal: upholstered

(G-4448)
PRINTING COMPANY LLC
8765 S Club Rd (47532-9331)
PHONE..................................812 367-2668
Karl Hinson, *Prin*
EMP: 5 EST: 2015
SALES (est): 111.68K **Privately Held**
SIC: 2752 Offset printing

(G-4449)
SUPERB TOOLING INC
250 Scenic Industrial Dr (47532-9736)
P.O. Box 227 (47532-0227)
PHONE..................................812 367-2102
Ron Buechler, *Pr*
EMP: 19 EST: 1985
SQ FT: 10,000
SALES (est): 2.28MM **Privately Held**
Web: www.superbtooling.com
SIC: 3599 Machine shop, jobbing and repair

▲ = Import ▼ = Export
◆ = Import/Export

GEOGRAPHIC SECTION

Fishers - Hamilton County (G-4474)

(G-4450)
UNIVERSAL PACKAGE LLC
Also Called: Universal Package Systems
435 Virginia St (47532)
P.O. Box 248 (47532-0248)
PHONE..................................812 937-3605
Mike Brandes, *Dir*
Jim Kulbeth, *Managing Member*
Jd Kulbeth, *Pr*
EMP: 18 **EST:** 2002
SQ FT: 24,000
SALES (est): 4.99MM Privately Held
Web: www.universalpackage.com
SIC: 2671 5085 Plastic film, coated or laminated for packaging; Bins and containers, storage

(G-4451)
WEBB WHEEL PRODUCTS INC
50 Scenic Industrial Dr (47532)
PHONE..................................812 548-0477
EMP: 1
SALES (corp-wide): 364.48B Publicly Held
Web: www.webbwheel.com
SIC: 3714 Motor vehicle brake systems and parts
HQ: Webb Wheel Products, Inc.
2310 Industrial Dr Sw
Cullman AL 35055
256 739-6660

Fillmore
Putnam County

(G-4452)
ARNOLD FAMILY WOODWORKS
3294 E County Road 50 S (46128-9642)
PHONE..................................765 246-6593
Greg Arnold, *Prin*
EMP: 5 **EST:** 2016
SALES (est): 65.5K Privately Held
SIC: 2431 Millwork

(G-4453)
GILLEYS WLDG & FABRICATION LLC
390 N County Road 475 E (46128-9398)
PHONE..................................765 720-0554
EMP: 4 **EST:** 2016
SALES (est): 27.6K Privately Held
SIC: 7692 Welding repair

(G-4454)
JOHN COLLIER LOGGING INC
9874 E Us Highway 40 (46128-9420)
PHONE..................................317 539-9663
John D Collier, *Pr*
EMP: 1 **EST:** 1993
SALES (est): 241.97K Privately Held
SIC: 2411 Logging camps and contractors

(G-4455)
LIBERTY INDS INVESTMENTS LLC
Also Called: Liberty Trailers
130 E Cemetery Rd (46128-9304)
PHONE..................................765 246-4031
Michael Gene Teso, *Pr*
Deanna Reeves, *
EMP: 62 **EST:** 2019
SALES (est): 4.76MM Privately Held
Web: www.libertytrailers.com
SIC: 3799 Trailers and trailer equipment

Fishers
Hamilton County

(G-4456)
3RD ROCK ENERGY SERVICES LLC
12658 Watford Way (46037-6270)
PHONE..................................314 750-2722
Mary Amos, *COO*
EMP: 1
SALES (corp-wide): 875.97K Privately Held
SIC: 1389 Hydraulic fracturing wells
PA: 3rd Rock Energy Services, Llc
748 S Highway 115
Kermit TX 79745
432 955-8784

(G-4457)
47TEE LLC
10526 Blue Springs Ln (46037-4052)
PHONE..................................317 373-8070
EMP: 4 **EST:** 2013
SALES (est): 66.19K Privately Held
Web: www.47tee.com
SIC: 2759 Screen printing

(G-4458)
AALBERTS HYDRNIC FLOW CTRL INC
Also Called: Flamco
9982 E 121st St (46037-9727)
PHONE..................................317 257-6050
▲ **EMP:** 40 **EST:** 1995
SQ FT: 10,000
SALES (est): 10.44MM
SALES (corp-wide): 3.35B Privately Held
Web: www.nexusvalve.com
SIC: 3491 Industrial valves
PA: Aalberts N.V.
Stadsplateau 18
Utrecht UT
303079300

(G-4459)
ACCUCAST INC
13352 Kimberlite Dr (46038-4819)
PHONE..................................317 849-5521
Steven A Robinson, *Pr*
EMP: 2 **EST:** 1990
SALES (est): 182.46K Privately Held
Web: www.accucastinc.com
SIC: 3321 8711 Gray iron castings, nec; Consulting engineer

(G-4460)
ACRO BIOMEDICAL CO LTD
12175 Visionary Way Ste 1160 (46038-3069)
PHONE..................................317 286-6788
Pao-chi Chu, *Pr*
EMP: 1 **EST:** 2014
SALES (est): 658.5K Privately Held
Web: www.acrobiomedicalco.com
SIC: 2836 Biological products, except diagnostic

(G-4461)
ALL-PHASE CONSTRUCTION CO LLC
10182 Orange Blossom Trl (46038-7465)
PHONE..................................317 345-7057
Elisha Madison, *
EMP: 3 **EST:** 2016
SALES (est): 98.5K Privately Held
SIC: 1389 1541 0782 1742 Construction, repair, and dismantling services; Industrial buildings and warehouses; Lawn care services; Drywall

(G-4462)
AM PUBLISHING INC
11650 Lantern Rd Ste 103 (46038-3095)
PHONE..................................317 806-0001
Steve Crell, *Admn*
EMP: 6 **EST:** 2009
SALES (est): 108.22K Privately Held
SIC: 2731 Books, publishing and printing

(G-4463)
AMERICAN RESOURCES CORPORATION (PA)
12115 Visionary Way (46038)
P.O. Box 606 (46038)
PHONE..................................317 855-9926
Mark C Jensen, *Ch Bd*
Thomas M Sauve, *
Kirk P Taylor, *CFO*
Tarlis R Thompson, *COO*
EMP: 231 **EST:** 2013
SALES (est): 39.47MM
SALES (corp-wide): 39.47MM Publicly Held
Web: www.americanresourcescorp.com
SIC: 1221 Coal preparation plant, bituminous or lignite

(G-4464)
ANDOVER COILS LLC
Also Called: Andover Coils
13865 Black Canyon Ct (46038-5358)
PHONE..................................765 447-1157
Michael Cole, *
Gregory Steward, *Managing Member**
Kurt Walterhouse, *Managing Member**
EMP: 65 **EST:** 2007
SALES (est): 7.85MM Privately Held
SIC: 3677 Electronic coils and transformers

(G-4465)
ANIPPE
11486 Enclave Blvd (46038-1590)
P.O. Box 41 (46038-0041)
PHONE..................................317 979-1110
EMP: 4 **EST:** 2011
SALES (est): 197.55K Privately Held
Web: www.anippe.com
SIC: 2211 Towels and toweling, cotton

(G-4466)
ATARAXIS MUSIC LLC
9128 Technology Ln (46038)
PHONE..................................626 945-6441
Rodney Gabriel, *Pr*
EMP: 2 **EST:** 2019
SALES (est): 96.26K Privately Held
SIC: 3931 Guitars and parts, electric and nonelectric

(G-4467)
ATTITUDE OF GRATITUDE ROCKS
11057 Allisonville Rd Ste 153 (46038-2698)
PHONE..................................317 331-0163
Tom Warmus, *Prin*
EMP: 1 **EST:** 2011
SALES (est): 62.05K Privately Held
Web: www.ascentofgratitude.com
SIC: 3961 Necklaces, except precious metal

(G-4468)
AUTOMATED BUS SOLUTIONS INC
8700 North St Ste 400 (46038-2865)
PHONE..................................317 257-9062
Roy Yates, *Pr*
Julie Yates, *Sec*
EMP: 12 **EST:** 1986
SALES (est): 1.85MM Privately Held
Web: www.abssd.com
SIC: 3579 Word processing equipment

(G-4469)
B6 TRANSPORTS LLC
11 Municipal Dr Ste 200 (46038-1634)
PHONE..................................317 975-0053
EMP: 1 **EST:** 2021
SALES (est): 250K Privately Held
Web: www.b6transports.com
SIC: 4789 3537 Transportation services, nec; Trucks, tractors, loaders, carriers, and similar equipment

(G-4470)
BANGS LABORATORIES INC
9025 Technology Dr (46038-4539)
PHONE..................................317 570-7020
Michael H Ott, *Ch Bd*
Chad Owen, *Pr*
EMP: 16 **EST:** 1988
SQ FT: 9,626
SALES (est): 4.56MM
SALES (corp-wide): 99.65MM Privately Held
Web: www.bangslabs.com
SIC: 2899 5169 8731 Chemical preparations, nec; Chemicals and allied products, nec; Commercial physical research
PA: Polysciences, Inc.
400 Valley Rd
Warrington PA 18976
215 343-6484

(G-4471)
BARRY COMPANY INC
13317 Britton Park Rd (46038-3500)
PHONE..................................317 578-2486
EMP: 3
SALES (corp-wide): 19.11MM Privately Held
Web: www.barrycompany.net
SIC: 5074 3498 Plumbing fittings and supplies; Pipe fittings, fabricated from purchased pipe
PA: Barry Company Inc
1145 E Maryland St
Indianapolis IN 46202
317 637-5327

(G-4472)
BAUER REY INC
11057 Allisonville Rd Ste 240 (46038-2698)
PHONE..................................317 731-2812
Cam Miller, *CEO*
EMP: 1 **EST:** 2013
SALES (est): 42.25K Privately Held
SIC: 7372 Application computer software

(G-4473)
BEE WINDOW INCORPORATED
Also Called: Faerber's Bee Window
115 Shadowlawn Dr (46038-2432)
PHONE..................................317 283-8522
George Faerber, *Pr*
Jeff Todd, *
Pamela J Faerber, *
EMP: 200 **EST:** 1983
SQ FT: 50,000
SALES (est): 20.13MM Privately Held
Web: www.beewindow.com
SIC: 3089 1521 5031 Windows, plastics; General remodeling, single-family houses; Metal doors, sash and trim

(G-4474)
BLEU ROOSTER DESIGNS
7444 River Highlands Dr (46038-1180)
PHONE..................................317 845-0889
Kim Sexson, *Pt*
EMP: 2 **EST:** 1999
SALES (est): 143.32K Privately Held

Fishers - Hamilton County (G-4475)

SIC: 2392 Cushions and pillows

(G-4475)
BLUSH SALON BOUTIQUE
11631 Maple St (46038-2803)
PHONE....................317 523-1635
EMP: 14 EST: 2015
SALES (est): 89.14K **Privately Held**
Web: www.blushsalonboutique.com
SIC: 2299 Jute and flax textile products

(G-4476)
BOGER CABINETRY & DESIGN INC
9721 Kincaid Dr (46037-9791)
PHONE....................317 588-6954
Steven Paul Ash, Pr
Steven Ash, Pr
Jacob Russell Boger, Genl Mgr
EMP: 6 EST: 2014
SQ FT: 4,500
SALES (est): 481.58K **Privately Held**
Web: www.bogercabinetry.com
SIC: 5251 5722 2434 Hardware stores; Kitchens, complete (sinks, cabinets, etc.); Wood kitchen cabinets

(G-4477)
BRYANT CONTROL INC
9925 E 126th St Ste 130 (46038-9477)
PHONE....................317 549-3355
Edward Henz, Pr
EMP: 10 EST: 1976
SALES (est): 1.05MM **Privately Held**
Web: www.bryantcontrol.com
SIC: 3613 5063 3625 Control panels, electric ; Electrical apparatus and equipment; Relays and industrial controls

(G-4478)
BUILDERS CONCRETE & SUPPLY CO INC
9170 E 131st St (46038-3545)
PHONE....................317 570-6201
EMP: 135
Web: www.bcconcrete.com
SIC: 3273 Ready-mixed concrete

(G-4479)
C&C TRANSPORTATION SERVICE LLC
Also Called: Trucking
10744 Springston Ct (46037-8979)
P.O. Box 502897 (46250-7897)
PHONE....................317 677-5060
EMP: 12 EST: 2011
SQ FT: 2,100
SALES (est): 2.18MM **Privately Held**
SIC: 3537 Truck trailers, used in plants, docks, terminals, etc.

(G-4480)
CABINETRY GREEN LLC
Also Called: Cabinetry Green
13818 Promise Rd (46038-3621)
PHONE....................317 842-1550
Hartman Jean-christophe, Admn
EMP: 5 EST: 2009
SALES (est): 212.81K **Privately Held**
Web: www.cabinetrygreen.com
SIC: 2434 Wood kitchen cabinets

(G-4481)
CAJ FOOD PRODUCTS INC
Also Called: Biotta Juices
11650 Olio Rd Ste 1000 (46037-7621)
PHONE....................888 524-6882
Matt Herzog, Pr
▲ EMP: 7 EST: 2008
SALES (est): 842.2K **Privately Held**
Web: www.biottajuices.com

SIC: 2037 2033 Fruit juices; Vegetable juices: fresh

(G-4482)
CALIFORNIA COLORS INC
508 Conner Creek Dr (46038-1819)
PHONE....................317 435-1351
EMP: 4 EST: 2010
SALES (est): 69.15K **Privately Held**
SIC: 2759 Screen printing

(G-4483)
CAROUSEL INDUSTRIES
10419 Corning Way (46038-3089)
PHONE....................317 674-8111
EMP: 7 EST: 2009
SALES (est): 119.2K **Privately Held**
Web: www.nwncarousel.com
SIC: 3999 Manufacturing industries, nec

(G-4484)
CASCADE METRIX LLC
12321 Hawks Nest Dr (46037-4215)
PHONE....................317 572-7094
Kislaya Kunjan, Managing Member
Frank Lloyd, Pr
Kislaya Kunjan Mng, Mgr
David Giddings, Chief Business Officer
EMP: 3 EST: 2016
SALES (est): 169.43K **Privately Held**
Web: www.cascademetrix.com
SIC: 3845 Patient monitoring apparatus, nec

(G-4485)
CEDRIC MORRIS
9783 E 116th St (46037-2822)
PHONE....................678 718-0012
Cedric Morris, Owner
EMP: 2 EST: 2021
SALES (est): 95.58K **Privately Held**
SIC: 3537 Trucks: freight, baggage, etc.: industrial, except mining

(G-4486)
CHAPDELLS TREE & PLANT DESIGN
11480 E 111th St (46037-3610)
PHONE....................317 845-9980
Nils Nordell, Pr
EMP: 2 EST: 1971
SQ FT: 1,500
SALES (est): 130K **Privately Held**
Web: www.usvapers.com
SIC: 3999 Plants, artificial and preserved

(G-4487)
CIGAR EXCLUSIVE LLC
12995 Star Dr (46037-5982)
PHONE....................317 778-2826
EMP: 5 EST: 2021
SALES (est): 125K **Privately Held**
SIC: 3634 Cigar lighters, electric

(G-4488)
CINDYS IN STITCHES INC
9836 N By Northeast Blvd (46037-9709)
PHONE....................317 841-1408
Cynthia Hannon, Pt
Cindy Johnson, Pt
EMP: 2 EST: 2002
SALES (est): 162.92K **Privately Held**
Web: www.cindysinstitches.com
SIC: 2395 Embroidery products, except Schiffli machine

(G-4489)
CKH TWO INC
Also Called: I W I
9160 Ford Cir (46038-3000)
PHONE....................317 841-7800
EMP: 29

SIC: 2431 2521 Millwork; Wood office furniture

(G-4490)
CLARK TIRE FISHERS INC
12371 Reynolds Dr (46038-9264)
P.O. Box 195 (46038-0195)
PHONE....................317 842-0544
Dave Smith, Pr
David W Smith, VP
EMP: 8 EST: 1975
SQ FT: 13,000
SALES (est): 911.41K **Privately Held**
Web: www.clarktirefishers.com
SIC: 5531 7534 5014 Automotive tires; Tire repair shop; Automobile tires and tubes

(G-4491)
CLARKE INDUSTRIAL SYSTEMS INC
Also Called: Ifp Automation
9084 Technology Dr Ste 150 (46038)
P.O. Box 80310 (46898-0310)
PHONE....................260 489-4575
EMP: 35 EST: 1976
SALES (est): 9.45MM **Privately Held**
Web: www.ifp1.com
SIC: 5084 3699 Industrial machinery and equipment; Electrical equipment and supplies, nec

(G-4492)
COLLECTIVE PUBLISHING LLC
12313 Ostara Ct (46037-8756)
PHONE....................317 418-0503
Neil Lucas, Prin
EMP: 6 EST: 2016
SALES (est): 237.51K **Privately Held**
Web: www.collectivepub.com
SIC: 2741 Miscellaneous publishing

(G-4493)
COMPOSITION LLC
14048 Woodlark Dr (46038-4524)
PHONE....................317 979-7214
EMP: 4 EST: 2014
SALES (est): 68.92K **Privately Held**
SIC: 2791 Typesetting

(G-4494)
CONTECH ENGNERED SOLUTIONS LLC
10130 Bahamas Cir (46037-9739)
PHONE....................317 407-4914
Christa Petzke, Prin
EMP: 4
Web: www.conteches.com
SIC: 3443 Fabricated plate work (boiler shop)
HQ: Contech Engineered Solutions Llc
9025 Centre Pointe Dr # 400
West Chester OH 45069
513 645-7000

(G-4495)
CORVANO LLC
11309 Guy St (46038-5452)
PHONE....................317 403-0471
Gerry Bailey, Pr
John Millspaugh, Ex VP
EMP: 2 EST: 2016
SALES (est): 103.16K **Privately Held**
Web: www.corvano.com
SIC: 7372 8748 Business oriented computer software; Systems engineering consultant, ex. computer or professional

(G-4496)
COUNTERPART
12115 Visionary Way (46038-3069)
PHONE....................317 587-1621
Teresa Tatum, Prin

EMP: 73 EST: 2018
SALES (est): 917.9K **Privately Held**
Web: www.counterpart.biz
SIC: 3652 Prerecorded records and tapes

(G-4497)
CROSSROADS FRT SOLUTIONS LLC
Also Called: Www.crssrdsfreightsolutionscom
11 Municipal Dr Ste 200 (46038-1634)
PHONE....................800 425-0282
Robert Williams, Pr
EMP: 1 EST: 2019
SALES (est): 437.97K **Privately Held**
Web: www.crossroadsfreightsolutions.com
SIC: 3537 Trucks, tractors, loaders, carriers, and similar equipment

(G-4498)
CROWDPIXIE LLC
7594 Timber Springs Dr N (46038-3203)
PHONE....................317 578-3137
Eugene Odonnell, Pr
Scott Jones, CEO
EMP: 2 EST: 2014
SALES (est): 126.08K **Privately Held**
Web: www.crowdpixie.com
SIC: 7372 7389 Application computer software; Business services, nec

(G-4499)
CUSTOM EMBROIDERY
11695 Sunnybrook Pl (46038-2732)
PHONE....................317 459-6603
EMP: 6 EST: 2013
SALES (est): 82.11K **Privately Held**
Web: www.custombroideryindiana.com
SIC: 2395 Embroidery products, except Schiffli machine

(G-4500)
DAILEY SIGNS LLC
10087 Allisonville Rd Ste G (46038-2122)
PHONE....................317 436-7550
David Dailey, Acctg Mgr
EMP: 1 EST: 2012
SALES (est): 79.41K **Privately Held**
Web: www.daileysigns.com
SIC: 3993 Signs and advertising specialties

(G-4501)
DAIRYCHEM LABORATORIES INC (PA)
9120 Technology Ln (46038-2839)
P.O. Box 6207 (46038-6207)
PHONE....................317 849-8400
Daniel Church, Pr
Diana Church, Sec
▲ EMP: 48 EST: 1993
SQ FT: 16,700
SALES (est): 36MM **Privately Held**
Web: www.dairychem.com
SIC: 2087 Extracts, flavoring

(G-4502)
DAVID INDUS PROCESS PDTS INC
Also Called: David Company
10142 Brooks School Rd Ste 102 (46038-3840)
PHONE....................317 577-0351
Martha Jane Watrous, Pr
David Watrous, Pr
M Jane Watrous, VP
EMP: 5 EST: 1993
SALES (est): 740.16K **Privately Held**
SIC: 5074 2759 Pipes and fittings, plastic; Visiting cards (including business): printing, nsk

GEOGRAPHIC SECTION
Fishers - Hamilton County (G-4530)

(G-4503)
DELANEY WINDOW FASHIONS LLC
14297 Delaney Dr (46038-5244)
PHONE.................................317 567-7672
EMP: 5 EST: 2014
SALES (est): 142.28K **Privately Held**
SIC: **2591** 5023 Drapery hardware and window blinds and shades; Homefurnishings

(G-4504)
DISASTER MASTERS INC
Also Called: 1970
12621 Walrond Rd (46037-6632)
PHONE.................................317 385-2216
David Parker, *CEO*
EMP: 1 EST: 2016
SALES (est): 57.15K **Privately Held**
Web: www.disastermasters.com
SIC: **2842** Disinfectants, household or industrial plant

(G-4505)
DREAM THEORY PUBLISHING LLC
11145 Harriston Dr (46037-9141)
PHONE.................................317 598-0320
Robyne Harris, *Prin*
EMP: 5 EST: 2016
SALES (est): 65.42K **Privately Held**
SIC: **2741** Miscellaneous publishing

(G-4506)
DYNOMAX
11797 Belle Plaine Blvd (46037-4125)
PHONE.................................317 835-3813
Michael Blanner, *Engr*
EMP: 4 EST: 2018
SALES (est): 43.26K **Privately Held**
Web: www.dynomax.com
SIC: **3714** Motor vehicle parts and accessories

(G-4507)
DYTEC-NCI LLC
8500 E 116th St Unit 6156 (46038-0564)
PHONE.................................317 919-0000
Daniel Connors, *Managing Member*
EMP: 2 EST: 2017
SALES (est): 162.41K **Privately Held**
SIC: **3448** Prefabricated metal buildings and components

(G-4508)
ECOLAB INC
Also Called: Ecolab Equipment Care
11973 Exit 5 Pkwy (46037-7939)
PHONE.................................317 567-2876
Linda Boser, *Adm/Asst*
EMP: 3
SALES (corp-wide): 15.32B **Publicly Held**
Web: www.ecolab.com
SIC: **2841** Soap and other detergents
PA: Ecolab Inc.
   1 Ecolab Pl
   Saint Paul MN 55102
   800 232-6522

(G-4509)
ELAN CORP PLC
11237 Wedgefield Ct (46037-8862)
PHONE.................................317 442-1502
EMP: 4 EST: 2017
SALES (est): 74.42K **Privately Held**
SIC: **2834** Pharmaceutical preparations

(G-4510)
ELENGAS CUSTOMWEAR
12463 Norman Pl (46037-3710)
PHONE.................................317 577-1677
Mike Tittle, *Owner*
EMP: 5 EST: 2007
SALES (est): 107.32K **Privately Held**
Web: www.elegan.com
SIC: **2759** Screen printing

(G-4511)
ELI LILLY AND COMPANY
Also Called: Elanco Animal Health
12023 Quarry Ct (46037-3926)
PHONE.................................317 748-1622
Adam M Fivush, *Prin*
EMP: 4
SALES (corp-wide): 34.12B **Publicly Held**
Web: www.lilly.com
SIC: **2834** Pharmaceutical preparations
PA: Eli Lilly And Company
   1 Lilly Corporate Ctr
   Indianapolis IN 46285
   317 276-2000

(G-4512)
EMP SOLUTIONS INC
11650 Lantern Rd Ste 105 (46038-3095)
PHONE.................................937 608-0283
Fernanda Eaton, *Dir*
Jay Kothari, *CEO*
EMP: 1 EST: 2016
SALES (est): 149.19K **Privately Held**
Web: www.empsolutionsinc.com
SIC: **3643** Lightning protection equipment

(G-4513)
EMPLIFY LLC
8626 E 116th St (46038-2853)
PHONE.................................800 580-5344
Santiago Jaramillo, *CEO*
Mitch Shields, *
David Sears, *
EMP: 49 EST: 2013
SALES (est): 4.29MM **Privately Held**
Web: www.15five.com
SIC: **7372** Application computer software

(G-4514)
ENGINRING CNCPTS UNLIMITED INC
Also Called: Ecu
8950 Technology Dr (46038-2834)
P.O. Box 250 (46038-0250)
PHONE.................................317 849-8470
Adam Suchko, *Pr*
Susan Suchko, *Sec*
EMP: 4 EST: 1975
SQ FT: 10,000
SALES (est): 969.61K **Privately Held**
Web: www.ecu-engine-controls.com
SIC: **3625** Control equipment, electric

(G-4515)
ENROLL HQ LLC
12175 Visionary Way Ste 710 (46038-3069)
PHONE.................................317 376-8282
EMP: 2 EST: 2017
SALES (est): 45K **Privately Held**
Web: go.afterschoolhq.com
SIC: **7372** Educational computer software

(G-4516)
ENTERPRISE MARKING PDTS INC
Also Called: Emp
12840 Ford Dr (46038-2894)
PHONE.................................317 867-7600
Chris Fread, *Pr*
Carol R Fread, *Marketing**
EMP: 25 EST: 1989
SQ FT: 5,000
SALES (est): 4.55MM **Privately Held**
Web: www.emp4labels.com
SIC: **2754** Intaglio printing

(G-4517)
ESAOTE NORTH AMERICA INC
11907 Exit 5 Pkwy (46037-7939)
P.O. Box 6152 (46038-6152)
PHONE.................................317 813-6000
Glenn Davis, *Pr*
Kim Akers, *
Lorenzo Eadadlio Board Mbnr, *Prin*
▲ EMP: 69 EST: 1979
SALES (est): 34MM **Privately Held**
Web: www.esaote.com
SIC: **3845** 3699 3841 Ultrasonic medical equipment, except cleaning; Electrical equipment and supplies, nec; Surgical and medical instruments
HQ: Esaote Spa
   Via Di Caciolle 15
   Firenze FI 50127

(G-4518)
ETCETERA PRESS
11480 E 111th St (46037-3610)
PHONE.................................317 845-9999
Nils Nordell, *Prin*
EMP: 9 EST: 2018
SALES (est): 72.83K **Privately Held**
SIC: **2741** Miscellaneous publishing

(G-4519)
EVENT ODYSSEY INC
11549 Yard St (46037-0018)
PHONE.................................317 483-0027
Michael Ewen, *CEO*
EMP: 1
SALES (est): 74.32K **Privately Held**
SIC: **7372** Prepackaged software

(G-4520)
F D DESKINS COMPANY INC
12554 Spire View Dr (46037-3701)
PHONE.................................317 284-4014
David Deskins, *Pr*
EMP: 10 EST: 1986
SALES (est): 447.39K **Privately Held**
SIC: **3569** 8748 Filters; Environmental consultant

(G-4521)
FAIRWAY CUSTOM GOLF
12500 Brooks School Rd (46037-9745)
PHONE.................................317 842-0017
Randy Campbell, *Owner*
Diana Campbell, *Admn*
EMP: 2 EST: 1994
SALES (est): 148.96K **Privately Held**
Web: www.fairwaycustomgolf.co
SIC: **3949** 7699 5941 Shafts, golf club; Golf club and equipment repair; Golf goods and equipment

(G-4522)
FISHERS FIRE STATION 92
11595 Brooks School Rd (46037-9404)
PHONE.................................317 595-3292
Ed Sorg, *Prin*
EMP: 2 EST: 2000
SALES (est): 120.9K **Privately Held**
Web: www.fishersin.gov
SIC: **3711** Fire department vehicles (motor vehicles), assembly of

(G-4523)
FISHERS LASER CARVERS LLC
11918 Halla Pl (46038-2768)
PHONE.................................317 845-0500
EMP: 2
SALES (est): 130.84K **Privately Held**
SIC: **3479** Etching and engraving

(G-4524)
FLAT ELECTRONICS LLC (PA)
9783 E 116th St Pmb 3040 (46037-2822)
PHONE.................................765 414-6635
EMP: 2 EST: 2016
SALES (est): 48.63K
SALES (corp-wide): 48.63K **Privately Held**
SIC: **7371** 3629 5065 Computer software development and applications; Battery chargers, rectifying or nonrotating; Mobile telephone equipment

(G-4525)
FORRO PRESS INC
12210 Driftstone Dr (46037-8407)
PHONE.................................317 576-1797
Suzanne L Abram, *Prin*
EMP: 1 EST: 2007
SALES (est): 51.52K **Privately Held**
SIC: **2741** Miscellaneous publishing

(G-4526)
FREEZE DRIED PARTNERS LLC
Also Called: Funky Monkey Snacks
11650 Olio Rd Ste 1000 (46037)
PHONE.................................800 783-1326
Matthew Herzog, *Managing Member*
▲ EMP: 1 EST: 2006
SALES (est): 122.22K **Privately Held**
SIC: **2099** Tortillas, fresh or refrigerated

(G-4527)
FREIJE TREATMENT SYSTEMS INC
Also Called: Easywater
9910 N By Northeast Blvd Ste 200 (46037-8507)
PHONE.................................888 766-7258
William Freije Iii, *Pr*
Sandra M Freije, *
EMP: 25 EST: 1986
SALES (est): 4.93MM **Privately Held**
Web: www.easywater.com
SIC: **3589** Water treatment equipment, industrial

(G-4528)
FRONT END DIGITAL INC
Also Called: Pyrimont Operating Solutions
11899 Stepping Stone Dr (46037-3918)
PHONE.................................317 652-6134
Matthew David Welch, *CEO*
Kc Cohen, *Sec*
Sean Reiche, *Ex VP*
EMP: 4 EST: 2000
SQ FT: 2,500
SALES (est): 900K **Privately Held**
Web: www.pyrimont.com
SIC: **3578** Point-of-sale devices

(G-4529)
FURTRIEVE LLC
9783 E 116th St Pmb 67 (46037)
PHONE.................................317 325-8010
Jordan Hetlund, *CEO*
EMP: 5 EST: 2017
SALES (est): 48.13K **Privately Held**
Web: www.furtrieve.com
SIC: **0752** 3663 4812 Animal specialty services; Global positioning systems (GPS) equipment; Cellular telephone services

(G-4530)
GENERAL MILLS INC
Also Called: General Mills
12222 Bedrock Ct (46037-3921)
PHONE.................................317 509-3709
EMP: 4
SALES (corp-wide): 19.86B **Publicly Held**
Web: www.generalmills.com

Fishers - Hamilton County (G-4531)   GEOGRAPHIC SECTION

SIC: 2043 Cereal breakfast foods
PA: General Mills, Inc.
1 General Mills Blvd
Minneapolis MN 55426
763 764-7600

(G-4531)
GLIDEPATH COM LLC
12175 Visionary Way (46038-3069)
PHONE.................................317 288-4459
Mark Anderson, *VP*
EMP: 7 EST: 2015
SALES (est): 281.65K **Privately Held**
SIC: 7372 Business oriented computer software

(G-4532)
GRACIES PAW PRINTS
10053 Parkshore Dr (46038-6858)
PHONE.................................317 910-9969
EMP: 5 EST: 2010
SALES (est): 84.23K **Privately Held**
SIC: 2752 Commercial printing, lithographic

(G-4533)
GRAFFITI DEFENSE LLC
12488 Brandamore Ln (46037-7519)
PHONE.................................317 284-1788
Jeannette Brennan, *Prin*
EMP: 6 EST: 2016
SALES (est): 187.98K **Privately Held**
SIC: 3812 Defense systems and equipment

(G-4534)
GRANDPAS BEEF JERKY LLC
12310 Eddington Pl (46037-5402)
PHONE.................................317 258-3209
EMP: 5 EST: 2019
SALES (est): 224.51K **Privately Held**
Web: www.grandpasjerky.net
SIC: 2013 Snack sticks, including jerky: from purchased meat

(G-4535)
GRAPHIC EXPRESSIONS INC
13025 New Britton Dr (46038-1073)
PHONE.................................317 577-9622
Erin Goodwin, *Owner*
EMP: 2 EST: 2001
SALES (est): 178.33K **Privately Held**
Web: www.graphicexpressionsinc.com
SIC: 2752 Offset printing

(G-4536)
HAMMER MARKETING
9635 Woodlands Dr (46037-9309)
PHONE.................................317 841-1567
Jeffery White, *Owner*
EMP: 1 EST: 2009
SALES (est): 50.55K **Privately Held**
Web: www.hammermarketing.com
SIC: 2741 Business service newsletters: publishing and printing

(G-4537)
HAWAIIAN SMOOTHIE LLC
12395 Eddington Pl (46037-5400)
PHONE.................................317 881-7290
Hyon Kim, *Admn*
EMP: 6 EST: 2016
SALES (est): 159.89K **Privately Held**
SIC: 2037 Frozen fruits and vegetables

(G-4538)
HETZLER OCULAR PROSTHETICS INC (PA)
10173 Allisonville Rd Ste 200 (46038)
PHONE.................................317 598-6298
Kathy J Hetzler, *Pr*
J R Hetzler, *VP*

EMP: 2 EST: 1979
SQ FT: 1,950
SALES (est): 492.13K
SALES (corp-wide): 492.13K **Privately Held**
Web: www.hetzlerocular.com
SIC: 3851 Eyes, glass and plastic

(G-4539)
HJR OIL INC
11361 Rainbow Falls Ln (46037-4086)
PHONE.................................317 849-4503
Darshan S Darar, *Prin*
EMP: 2 EST: 2011
SALES (est): 100K **Privately Held**
SIC: 1382 Oil and gas exploration services

(G-4540)
HYMNS2GO LLC
Also Called: Hymns To Go
10315 Stonebridge Ct (46037-9482)
PHONE.................................317 577-0730
EMP: 1 EST: 2012
SALES (est): 153.73K **Privately Held**
Web: www.hymns2go.com
SIC: 3679 Recording and playback apparatus, including phonograph

(G-4541)
I4 IDENTITY LLC
12463 Duval Dr (46037-8272)
PHONE.................................317 662-0448
Jodee Thompson, *Prin*
EMP: 1 EST: 2014
SALES (est): 72K **Privately Held**
SIC: 2754 5112 Cards, except greeting: gravure printing; Office supplies, nec

(G-4542)
IDONIX SOLUTIONS INC ◊
12377 Berry Patch Ln (46037-4494)
PHONE.................................317 544-8171
Rohail Ali Sohail, *Pr*
EMP: 4 EST: 2023
SALES (est): 180.77K **Privately Held**
SIC: 3663 7389 Radio and t.v. communications equipment; Business Activities at Non-Commercial Site

(G-4543)
INCOG BIOPHARMA SERVICES INC
12050 Exit 5 Pkwy (46037)
PHONE.................................812 320-4236
EMP: 15
SALES (corp-wide): 10.39MM **Privately Held**
Web: www.incogbiopharma.com
SIC: 2834 Pharmaceutical preparations
PA: Incog Biopharma Services, Inc.
600 E 96th St Ste 600
Indianapolis IN 46240
812 320-4236

(G-4544)
INDIANA BEVEL INC
8605 South St (46038-2907)
PHONE.................................317 596-0001
EMP: 4 EST: 2000
SALES (est): 345.79K **Privately Held**
Web: www.indianabevel.com
SIC: 3211 5231 Flat glass; Glass, leaded or stained

(G-4545)
INDIANA RMNCE WRITERS AMER INC
11807 Allisonville Rd 552 (46038-2313)
PHONE.................................317 695-5255
Tipani Hickey, *Prin*
EMP: 5 EST: 2009

SALES (est): 55.74K **Privately Held**
Web: www.indianarwa.com
SIC: 2741 Miscellaneous publishing

(G-4546)
INDIANAPOLIS WOODWORKING
6745 Barrington Pl (46038-2780)
PHONE.................................317 345-4180
EMP: 6 EST: 2019
SALES (est): 103.02K **Privately Held**
Web: www.iwimillwork.com
SIC: 2431 Millwork

(G-4547)
INFO PUBLISHING IMPACT LLC
9869 Worthington Blvd (46038-3068)
PHONE.................................317 912-3642
Kimberly Roach, *Prin*
EMP: 4 EST: 2015
SALES (est): 112.34K **Privately Held**
SIC: 2711 Newspapers, publishing and printing

(G-4548)
INSULPEDIA LLC
11430 Idlewood Dr (46037-4194)
PHONE.................................317 459-4030
Chad Rebholz, *Prin*
EMP: 4 EST: 2019
SALES (est): 104.31K **Privately Held**
Web: www.insulpedia.com
SIC: 3999 Manufacturing industries, nec

(G-4549)
JCS TECHNOLOGIES INC
13872 Wendessa Dr (46038-6681)
PHONE.................................317 201-5064
Steve Schulenberg, *Prin*
EMP: 6 EST: 2012
SALES (est): 270.74K **Privately Held**
Web: www.jcs-technologies.com
SIC: 3999 Manufacturing industries, nec

(G-4550)
JEDA EQUIPMENT SERVICES INC
13270 Summerwood Ln (46038)
PHONE.................................317 842-9377
Dave Cortner, *Pr*
Jeannie Cortner, *Treas*
EMP: 4 EST: 1989
SALES (est): 896.18K **Privately Held**
Web: www.888jedainc.com
SIC: 5084 3531 7699 2611 Plastic products machinery; Crushers, grinders, and similar equipment; Industrial machinery and equipment repair; Pulp mills, mechanical and recycling processing

(G-4551)
JOHNSON & JOHNSON
10284 Seagrave Dr (46037)
PHONE.................................732 524-0400
Joyce Kordusky, *Brnch Mgr*
EMP: 5
SALES (corp-wide): 85.16B **Publicly Held**
Web: www.jnj.com
SIC: 2676 Feminine hygiene paper products
PA: Johnson & Johnson
1 Johnson & Johnson Plz
New Brunswick NJ 08933
732 524-0400

(G-4552)
KALDEWEI USA INC
14074 Trade Center Dr Ste 148 (46038-4575)
P.O. Box 2701 (47402-2701)
PHONE.................................866 822-2527
Chad Novinger, *Mgr*
▲ EMP: 6 EST: 2014

SALES (est): 217.48K **Privately Held**
Web: www.kaldewei.us
SIC: 3842 Whirlpool baths, hydrotherapy equipment

(G-4553)
KC MIG WELDING LLC
189 S Sunblest Blvd (46038-1382)
PHONE.................................317 739-1051
EMP: 4 EST: 2015
SALES (est): 38.95K **Privately Held**
SIC: 7692 Welding repair

(G-4554)
KEVIN M WALTERS
Also Called: Airborne Services
11220 Hearthstone Dr (46037-4277)
PHONE.................................317 565-9564
Kevin Walters, *Owner*
EMP: 1 EST: 2014
SALES (est): 71.61K **Privately Held**
SIC: 2752 Offset printing

(G-4555)
LEAF HUT SOFTWARE LLC
8430 Weaver Woods Pl (46038-5203)
PHONE.................................317 770-3632
Charles E Perry Iii, *Prin*
EMP: 5 EST: 2012
SALES (est): 130.32K **Privately Held**
SIC: 7372 Prepackaged software

(G-4556)
LIFOAM INDUSTRIES LLC
9999 E 121st St (46037-9727)
PHONE.................................410 889-1023
EMP: 53
SALES (corp-wide): 1.86B **Privately Held**
Web: www.lifoam.com
SIC: 3086 Plastics foam products
HQ: Lifoam Industries, Llc
1303 S Batesville Rd
Greer SC 29650
410 889-1023

(G-4557)
LONDON HAIR BUNDLES LLC
Also Called: London Hair Bundles
13813 Wendessa Dr (46038-6681)
PHONE.................................317 953-3888
Teisha Dias, *Owner*
EMP: 1 EST: 2021
SALES (est): 36.3K **Privately Held**
SIC: 7231 7389 3999 Hairdressers; Styling, wigs; Hair and hair-based products

(G-4558)
LOTS OF SOFTWARE LLC
13534 Kelsey Ln (46038-4423)
PHONE.................................317 578-8120
EMP: 2 EST: 2014
SALES (est): 74.67K **Privately Held**
Web: www.lotsofsoftware.com
SIC: 7372 Prepackaged software

(G-4559)
LUCKY MAN WDWKG HNDYMAN SVCS L
13011 Blalock Dr (46037-7704)
PHONE.................................810 247-3099
Daniel Borzymowski, *Owner*
EMP: 6 EST: 2018
SALES (est): 59.54K **Privately Held**
SIC: 2431 Millwork

(G-4560)
MAJESTIC BLOCK & SUPPLY INC
7711 Loma Ct (46038-2524)
PHONE.................................317 842-6602
Kent Earls, *Prin*

GEOGRAPHIC SECTION
Fishers - Hamilton County (G-4589)

EMP: 8 EST: 1983
SALES (est): 731.12K **Privately Held**
SIC: 5032 3271 Lime, except agricultural; Concrete block and brick

(G-4561)
MANTRA ENTERPRISE LLC
12694 Balbo Pl (46037-8674)
P.O. Box 7206 (46038-7306)
PHONE..................201 428-8709
EMP: 1 EST: 2013
SALES (est): 35.86K **Privately Held**
Web: www.mantra-ent.com
SIC: 7699 7389 3713 3561 Industrial machinery and equipment repair; Business Activities at Non-Commercial Site; Truck bodies and parts; Industrial pumps and parts

(G-4562)
MAY FIRST INC
Also Called: Glassic Design
10497 Silver Ridge Cir (46038-4035)
PHONE..................317 330-1000
Anthony Sandlin, *Pr*
EMP: 1 EST: 2000
SALES (est): 73K **Privately Held**
SIC: 3231 Decorated glassware: chipped, engraved, etched, etc.

(G-4563)
MCL WINDOW COVERINGS INC (PA)
11815 Technology Ln (46038-2890)
PHONE..................317 577-2670
Timothy Mc Laughlin, *Pr*
Geraldyne T Mc Laughlin, *Sec*
EMP: 12 EST: 1972
SALES (est): 2.41MM
SALES (corp-wide): 2.41MM **Privately Held**
Web: www.mclwindowcoverings.com
SIC: 5714 7359 2221 1799 Draperies; Equipment rental and leasing, nec; Upholstery, tapestry, and wall covering fabrics; Drapery track installation

(G-4564)
MENON BEARINGS LIMITED
10849 Windermere Blvd (46037-8986)
PHONE..................866 556-3666
EMP: 2
Web: www.menonbearings.in
SIC: 3562 Ball and roller bearings
PA: Menon Bearings Limited
G-1, Midc, Gokul Shirgaon,
Kolhapur MH 41623

(G-4565)
METAKITE SOFTWARE LLC
8430 Weaver Woods Pl (46038-5203)
PHONE..................317 441-7385
EMP: 2 EST: 2013
SALES (est): 102.6K **Privately Held**
Web: www.metakite.com
SIC: 7372 Prepackaged software

(G-4566)
MID-STATE TRUCK EQUIPMENT INC
Also Called: Retail Truck and Turf Eqp
11020 Allisonville Rd (46038-2631)
PHONE..................317 849-4903
TOLL FREE: 800
Michael Eby, *Pr*
EMP: 26 EST: 1981
SQ FT: 18,500
SALES (est): 4.51MM **Privately Held**
Web: www.mid-statetruck.com
SIC: 5012 5013 1799 5531 Truck bodies; Truck parts and accessories; Welding on site; Truck equipment and parts

(G-4567)
MOBIL TRACKR LLC
Also Called: Mobil Trackr
12175 Visionary Way (46038-3069)
PHONE..................888 504-2074
EMP: 1 EST: 2016
SALES (est): 36.05K **Privately Held**
Web: www.mobiltrackr.com
SIC: 7372 Business oriented computer software

(G-4568)
MYCLOUD LLC
8595 Babson Ct (46038-4428)
PHONE..................317 570-8999
EMP: 5 EST: 2014
SALES (est): 61.67K **Privately Held**
Web: www.micloudforce.com
SIC: 7372 8999 Application computer software; Cloud seeding

(G-4569)
NO FAN CLOTHING LLC
12610 Misty Ridge Ct (46037)
PHONE..................312 371-7648
Charles Laster, *Managing Member*
EMP: 1
SALES (est): 69.27K **Privately Held**
SIC: 2389 Apparel and accessories, nec

(G-4570)
OHANA DONUTS AND ICE CREAM LLC (PA)
11640 Brooks School Rd Ste 100 (46037-4354)
PHONE..................317 288-0922
Nate Haugh, *Pr*
EMP: 6 EST: 2020
SALES (est): 519.96K
SALES (corp-wide): 519.96K **Privately Held**
Web: www.eatohanalulu.com
SIC: 2051 Bread, cake, and related products

(G-4571)
OPTICAL SOLUTIONS LLC LLC
P.O. Box 115 (46038-0115)
PHONE..................317 525-8308
Doug Martin, *Prin*
EMP: 4 EST: 2010
SALES (est): 64.57K **Privately Held**
SIC: 3827 Optical instruments and lenses

(G-4572)
PATRIA PRESS LLC
7117 Koldyke Dr (46038-2739)
PHONE..................317 508-7239
Carol Tully Harrison, *Prin*
EMP: 5 EST: 2018
SALES (est): 93.59K **Privately Held**
SIC: 2741 Miscellaneous publishing

(G-4573)
PERSONAL RECORD MEDIA LLC
9760 Highpoint Ridge Dr Unit 102 (46037)
PHONE..................317 507-4459
William Hartman, *Prin*
EMP: 4 EST: 2017
SALES (est): 58.7K **Privately Held**
SIC: 2741 Miscellaneous publishing

(G-4574)
PHARMA FORM FINDERS LLC
11164 Muirfield Trce (46037-8830)
PHONE..................317 362-1191
Gregory Stephenson, *Prin*
EMP: 5 EST: 2017
SALES (est): 94.14K **Privately Held**
SIC: 2834 Pharmaceutical preparations

(G-4575)
PIRO SHOES LLC
Also Called: Piro
8327 Weaver Woods Pl (46038-5202)
PHONE..................888 849-0916
EMP: 16
SALES (est): 1.07MM **Privately Held**
SIC: 3021 Rubber and plastics footwear

(G-4576)
PLAQUEMAKER PLUS INC
Also Called: P M P Design
10080 E 121st St Ste 118 (46037-4211)
PHONE..................317 594-5556
EMP: 7 EST: 1995
SQ FT: 3,500
SALES (est): 607.65K **Privately Held**
Web: www.plaquemakerplus.com
SIC: 3999 8743 Plaques, picture, laminated; Sales promotion

(G-4577)
PLATINUM INDUSTRIES LLC
11625 Suncatcher Dr (46037-7891)
P.O. Box 333 (47383-0333)
PHONE..................765 744-8323
Heather Ane Zeto, *Pr*
EMP: 5 EST: 2010
SALES (est): 61.51K **Privately Held**
SIC: 3999 Manufacturing industries, nec

(G-4578)
POLAR INFORMATION TECH LLC
7083 Koldyke Dr (46038-2737)
PHONE..................303 725-8015
EMP: 4 EST: 2013
SALES (est): 125.69K **Privately Held**
Web: www.websqltraining.com
SIC: 3999 Manufacturing industries, nec

(G-4579)
PORCHLIGHT GROUP INC
Also Called: Porchlight
7 Launch Way Ste 610 (46038-1559)
PHONE..................317 804-1166
James Brown, *CEO*
EMP: 5 EST: 2014
SQ FT: 18,000
SALES (est): 103.38K **Privately Held**
Web: www.porchlightgroup.com
SIC: 2741 Internet publishing and broadcasting

(G-4580)
POWER WALL SYSTEMS LLC
11253 Tall Trees Dr (46038-4651)
PHONE..................317 348-1260
EMP: 2 EST: 2009
SALES (est): 112.16K **Privately Held**
SIC: 3511 Turbines and turbine generator sets

(G-4581)
PPG INDUSTRIES INC
10564 E 96th St Ste 6 (46037-9643)
PHONE..................317 598-9448
Ben Kunkel, *Mgr*
EMP: 2
SALES (corp-wide): 17.65B **Publicly Held**
Web: www.ppg.com
SIC: 2851 Paints and allied products
PA: Ppg Industries, Inc.
1 Ppg Pl
Pittsburgh PA 15272
412 434-3131

(G-4582)
PPG INDUSTRIES INC
Also Called: PPG 9259
7275 E 116th St (46038-2301)
PHONE..................317 577-2344
George Merner, *Brnch Mgr*
EMP: 4
SALES (corp-wide): 17.65B **Publicly Held**
Web: www.ppg.com
SIC: 2851 Paints and allied products
PA: Ppg Industries, Inc.
1 Ppg Pl
Pittsburgh PA 15272
412 434-3131

(G-4583)
PRECISION STMPING SLUTIONS LLC
10823 Turne Grv (46037-9006)
PHONE..................317 501-4436
EMP: 5 EST: 2017
SALES (est): 61.83K **Privately Held**
SIC: 3469 Stamping metal for the trade

(G-4584)
PROJECT FIELD SOLUTIONS INC
11 Municipal Dr Ste 200 (46038-1634)
PHONE..................317 590-7678
Tiffany Garner, *CEO*
EMP: 5 EST: 2014
SALES (est): 517.42K **Privately Held**
SIC: 1389 7349 8742 6531 Construction, repair, and dismantling services; Janitorial service, contract basis; Management consulting services; Real estate managers

(G-4585)
PULSE ANALYTICS LLC
12764 Tamworth Dr (46037-7395)
PHONE..................260 615-8016
Lisa Mitchell, *Prin*
Marlin Jackson, *Prin*
EMP: 2 EST: 2020
SALES (est): 57.88K **Privately Held**
Web: www.pulseanalyticsapp.com
SIC: 7372 Prepackaged software

(G-4586)
QUALITY DATA PRODUCTS INC
10142 Brooks School Rd Ste 210 (46037-3839)
PHONE..................317 595-0700
Dan Falls, *Pr*
EMP: 2 EST: 1997
SALES (est): 147.88K **Privately Held**
SIC: 7372 Prepackaged software

(G-4587)
QUALITY INFORMATION TECH INC
10142 Brooks School Rd Ste 210 (46037-3840)
PHONE..................317 595-0700
EMP: 6 EST: 2016
SALES (est): 129.87K **Privately Held**
Web: www.qit-software.com
SIC: 7372 Prepackaged software

(G-4588)
QUEEN CITY PRESS
9623 Wandering Woods Ct (46037-8009)
PHONE..................317 840-1135
EMP: 4 EST: 2019
SALES (est): 70.31K **Privately Held**
SIC: 2741 Miscellaneous publishing

(G-4589)
QUEST ENERGY INC
8856 South St (46038-2911)
P.O. Box 606 (46038-0606)
PHONE..................317 318-5737
Mark Jensen, *CEO*
Thomas Sauve, *Pr*
EMP: 10 EST: 2015
SALES (est): 843.63K **Privately Held**
Web: www.questenergy.com

SIC: 1389 Oil and gas field services, nec

(G-4590)
QUMULEX INC
9059 Technology Ln (46038-2828)
PHONE..............................317 207-0520
Libby Ball, *Pr*
Dan Rittman, *
Libby Ball, *CFO*
EMP: 30 EST: 2018
SALES (est): 2.8MM **Privately Held**
Web: www.qumulex.com
SIC: 3699 Security devices

(G-4591)
RECOVERY FORCE LLC
10022 Lantern Rd Ste 100 (46037)
PHONE..............................866 604-6458
EMP: 6 EST: 2013
SALES (est): 947.79K **Privately Held**
Web: www.recoveryforceusa.com
SIC: 7699 3842 Life saving and survival equipment, non-medical; repair; Surgical appliances and supplies

(G-4592)
RECREATION INSITES LLC
12237 Westmorland Dr (46038-4406)
PHONE..............................317 578-0588
EMP: 2 EST: 2012
SALES (est): 152.72K **Privately Held**
Web: www.recreationinsites.com
SIC: 3949 2531 3069 2273 Playground equipment; Picnic tables or benches, park; Flooring, rubber: tile or sheet; Floor coverings: paper, grass, reed, coir, sisal, jute, etc.

(G-4593)
REDLIN CUSTOM WOODWORKING LLC
8507 Barstow Dr (46038-4448)
PHONE..............................317 578-1852
David Redlin, *Prin*
EMP: 2 EST: 2010
SALES (est): 87.9K **Privately Held**
SIC: 2431 Millwork

(G-4594)
REELEMENT TECHNOLOGIES CORP
12115 Visionary Way (46038-3069)
P.O. Box 606 (46038-0606)
PHONE..............................317 855-9926
EMP: 7 EST: 2020
SALES (est): 100K **Privately Held**
Web: www.reelementtech.com
SIC: 1099 Rare-earth ores mining

(G-4595)
RELX INC
9737 Pine Ridge East Dr (46038-2166)
PHONE..............................317 849-9806
Beverly Hogan, *Mgr*
EMP: 1
SALES (corp-wide): 11.42B **Privately Held**
Web: www.lexisnexis.com
SIC: 2721 Periodicals
HQ: Relx Inc.
    230 Park Ave Ste 700
    New York NY 10169
    212 309-8100

(G-4596)
RGR MEDICAL SOLUTIONS INC
11807 Allisonville Rd Ste 137 (46038)
PHONE..............................317 285-9703
Ronald Reed, *CEO*
Greg Hughes Managing, *Prin*
EMP: 113 EST: 2014
SALES (est): 9.71MM **Privately Held**

SIC: 5047 3841 Medical equipment and supplies; Inhalation therapy equipment

(G-4597)
ROBERT M KOLARICH
Also Called: A R. Martin Woodworks
10688 Adam Ct (46037-9050)
PHONE..............................317 596-9753
Robert M Kolarich, *Owner*
EMP: 1 EST: 2004
SALES (est): 110.54K **Privately Held**
Web: www.rmartinwoodworks.com
SIC: 2521 Wood office furniture

(G-4598)
ROEBIC LABORATORIES INC
8280 Courtney Dr (46038-4417)
PHONE..............................317 578-0135
EMP: 13
SALES (corp-wide): 4.22MM **Privately Held**
Web: www.roebic.com
SIC: 2842 Polishes and sanitation goods
PA: Roebic Laboratories, Inc.
    25 Connair Rd
    Orange CT 06477
    203 795-1283

(G-4599)
ROOST
7371 E 116th St (46038-2304)
PHONE..............................317 842-3735
Scott Pipe, *Pt*
Ed Sahm, *Pt*
EMP: 3 EST: 1999
SALES (est): 216.1K **Privately Held**
Web: www.theroostindiana.com
SIC: 7389 3556 Restaurant reservation service; Ovens, bakery

(G-4600)
RT SOFTWARE
13534 Kelsey Ln (46038-4423)
PHONE..............................317 578-8518
Brad Jones, *Prin*
EMP: 2 EST: 2010
SALES (est): 107.42K **Privately Held**
SIC: 7372 Prepackaged software

(G-4601)
RUSSELL METAL PRODUCTS
9238 Alton Ct (46037-8909)
PHONE..............................317 841-9003
Alex Russell, *Owner*
▲ EMP: 13 EST: 1962
SQ FT: 5,000
SALES (est): 202.17K **Privately Held**
Web: www.russellmetalproducts.com
SIC: 3599 Machine shop, jobbing and repair

(G-4602)
RVA LLC
Also Called: Housz of Drake
11393 Hawkshead Ln Apt 201 (46037-4731)
PHONE..............................317 800-9800
Valarie Von Drake, *Managing Member*
EMP: 1 EST: 2020
SALES (est): 105.69K **Privately Held**
SIC: 8322 2591 3161 5961 Travelers' aid; Curtain and drapery rods, poles, and fixtures; Traveling bags; Catalog sales

(G-4603)
SAGAMORE READY-MIX LLC (PA)
9170 E 131st St (46038-3545)
PHONE..............................317 570-6201
Mike Shumaker, *Prin*
John Schilling, *
Chris Beaver, *Prin*

Gus B Nuckols Iii, *Prin*
EMP: 9 EST: 2012
SALES (est): 4.31MM
SALES (corp-wide): 4.31MM **Privately Held**
Web: www.sagamorereadymix.com
SIC: 3273 Ready-mixed concrete

(G-4604)
SHARP PRINTING SERVICES INC
Also Called: Sharp Printing
11100 Allisonville Rd (46038-1835)
PHONE..............................317 842-5159
Steven Sharp, *Pr*
Walter Sharp, *Treas*
EMP: 7 EST: 1982
SALES (est): 974.61K **Privately Held**
Web: www.sharp-printing.com
SIC: 2752 7334 Offset printing; Photocopying and duplicating services

(G-4605)
SNYDERS-LANCE INC
10100 Lantern Rd (46037-9651)
PHONE..............................317 270-7599
EMP: 7
SALES (corp-wide): 9.36B **Publicly Held**
Web: www.campbellsoupcompany.com
SIC: 2052 Cookies
HQ: Snyder's-Lance, Inc.
    One Campbell Place
    Camden NJ 08103
    704 554-1421

(G-4606)
STATIC MEDIA INC (PA)
79 Madison Ave Fl 2 (46038)
PHONE..............................212 366-4500
Reginald Renner, *Pr*
EMP: 1 EST: 2015
SALES (est): 2.8MM
SALES (corp-wide): 2.8MM **Publicly Held**
SIC: 2711 Newspapers, publishing and printing

(G-4607)
STORAGEWORKS INC
12000 Exit 5 Pkwy (46037-7940)
PHONE..............................317 577 3511
David P Williams, *Pr*
Tom O'neil, *VP*
Jack Fidger, *Prin*
Lee Leo Allison, *Sec*
EMP: 9 EST: 1993
SALES (est): 1.86MM **Privately Held**
Web: www.storageworksinc.com
SIC: 5046 3537 7699 5084 Commercial equipment, nec; Industrial trucks and tractors; Industrial equipment services; Industrial machinery and equipment

(G-4608)
SUNROOMS OF INDIANA INC
115 Shadowlawn Dr (46038-2432)
PHONE..............................317 891-3232
R Douglas Smith, *CFO*
George Faerber, *
David Maersch, *
Pam Faerber, *
EMP: 40 EST: 2001
SALES (est): 6MM **Privately Held**
SIC: 3448 Sunrooms, prefabricated metal

(G-4609)
T N D PRINTING
Also Called: T & D Printing
12634 Walrond Rd (46037-6632)
PHONE..............................260 493-4949
Gary Swaidner, *Owner*
EMP: 4 EST: 1983
SALES (est): 228.36K **Privately Held**

SIC: 2752 Offset printing

(G-4610)
TC4 LLC
9217 Muir Ln (46037-7959)
PHONE..............................317 709-5429
James Croft, *Prin*
Richard Collins, *Prin*
EMP: 2 EST: 2013
SALES (est): 193.98K **Privately Held**
SIC: 5199 3993 7389 Decals; Signs and advertising specialties; Business Activities at Non-Commercial Site

(G-4611)
TELIX PHARMACEUTICALS US INC (HQ)
11700 Exit 5 Pkwy Ste 200 (46037)
PHONE..............................317 588-9700
Bernard Lambert, *Pr*
Nannette Rich, *VP*
EMP: 80 EST: 2017
SALES (est): 11.46MM **Privately Held**
Web: www.telixpharma.com
SIC: 2834 Pharmaceutical preparations
PA: Telix Pharmaceuticals Limited
    55 Flemington Road
    North Melbourne VIC 3051

(G-4612)
THOMSON REUTERS CORPORATION
8670 Harrison Pkwy (46038-4456)
PHONE..............................317 570-9387
James Hickerson, *Brnch Mgr*
EMP: 19
SALES (corp-wide): 10.66B **Publicly Held**
Web: www.thomsonreuters.com
SIC: 2741 Miscellaneous publishing
HQ: Thomson Reuters Corporation
    333 Bay St
    Toronto ON M5H 2
    416 687-7500

(G-4613)
TLC CANDLE CO LLC
11650 Olio Rd Ste 1000 (46037-7621)
PHONE..............................317 313-3029
Tamara Crawford, *CEO*
EMP: 5 EST: 2018
SALES (est): 208.23K **Privately Held**
Web: www.tlccandleco.com
SIC: 3999 Candles

(G-4614)
TOPICS NEWSPAPERS INC
Also Called: Fishers Sun Herald
13095 Publishers Dr (46038-8826)
PHONE..............................888 357-7827
Tom Jeckel, *Mgr*
EMP: 14 EST: 1869
SQ FT: 40,000
SALES (est): 188.43K **Privately Held**
SIC: 2711 Newspapers, publishing and printing

(G-4615)
TRANE US INC
Also Called: Trane
8100 E 106th St (46038-2542)
PHONE..............................317 255-8777
James Fischer, *Brnch Mgr*
EMP: 90
Web: www.trane.com
SIC: 3585 Refrigeration and heating equipment
HQ: Trane U.S. Inc.
    800-E Beaty St
    Davidson NC 28036
    704 655-4000

GEOGRAPHIC SECTION

Fishers - Hancock County (G-4644)

(G-4616)
TREAT AMERICA ROCHE DIAGNOSTIC
10300 Kincaid Dr (46037-8508)
PHONE..................317 521-1490
EMP: 2 EST: 2012
SALES (est): 291.78K Privately Held
SIC: 2834 Pharmaceutical preparations

(G-4617)
TRUE YOU NATURALLY INC
Also Called: USA
107 Northwood Dr (46038-1152)
PHONE..................317 518-2268
Janet Beckett, Prin
EMP: 5 EST: 2016
SALES (est): 46.58K Privately Held
SIC: 2299 Jute and flax textile products

(G-4618)
TUTTLE ALUMINUM & BRONZE INC
Also Called: Tuttle Railing Systems
120 Shadowlawn Dr (46038-2433)
P.O. Box 6090 (46038-6090)
PHONE..................317 842-2420
▲ EMP: 65
Web: www.tuttlehandrailings.com
SIC: 3446 5039 7692 3444 Railings, banisters, guards, etc: made from metal pipe; Architectural metalwork; Welding repair; Sheet metalwork

(G-4619)
U WANT ICECREAM LLC
8320 Shoe Overlook Dr (46038-1085)
PHONE..................317 577-4057
EMP: 1 EST: 2009
SALES (est): 41.77K Privately Held
SIC: 5812 2024 Family restaurants; Ice cream, bulk

(G-4620)
UNITED TURF ALLIANCE LLC
Also Called: Accounting Department
12840 Ford Dr (46038-2894)
PHONE..................770 335-3015
Tim Zech, Brnch Mgr
EMP: 1
Web: www.utaarmortech.com
SIC: 2879 Fungicides, herbicides
PA: United Turf Alliance, Llc
   8014 Cumming Hwy Ste 403
   Canton GA

(G-4621)
UNIVERSAL TOOL & ENGRG CO
105 Rush Ct (46038-1374)
PHONE..................317 842-8999
Carl A Grummann, CEO
Francis Jenkins, *
Robert Rossiter, *
EMP: 22 EST: 1941
SQ FT: 45,000
SALES (est): 390.29K Privately Held
Web: www.universaltool.com
SIC: 3599 Machine shop, jobbing and repair

(G-4622)
UNJUST LLC
10854 Nature Trail Dr Apt 101 (46038-4251)
PHONE..................317 443-2584
Tristan Pittmon, Pr
EMP: 2 EST: 2020
SALES (est): 85.31K Privately Held
SIC: 5611 2211 2389 Clothing, sportswear, men's and boys'; Apparel and outerwear fabrics, cotton; Apparel for handicapped

(G-4623)
UNPLUG SOY CANDLES
16250 Remington Dr (46037-7416)
PHONE..................217 520-2658
Jennifer Sturgill, Prin
EMP: 5 EST: 2015
SALES (est): 129.11K Privately Held
Web: www.unplugsoycandles.com
SIC: 3999 Candles

(G-4624)
USA TODAY
13095 Publishers Dr (46038-8826)
PHONE..................212 715-2188
EMP: 7 EST: 2018
SALES (est): 62.99K Privately Held
Web: www.usatoday.com
SIC: 2711 Newspapers, publishing and printing

(G-4625)
USA VISION SYSTEMS INC
12550 Promise Creek Ln Ste 116 (46038-7717)
PHONE..................949 583-1519
Joseph Leonard, Sls Mgr
EMP: 1
SQ FT: 8,725
Web: www.geovision.com.tw
SIC: 3699 Security control equipment and systems
HQ: Usa Vision Systems Inc.
   9301 Irvine Blvd
   Irvine CA 92618
   949 583-1519

(G-4626)
UVA SOFTWARE LLC
11650 Olio Rd Ste 1000 (46037-7621)
PHONE..................877 927-1115
EMP: 4 EST: 2019
SALES (est): 115.95K Privately Held
SIC: 7372 Prepackaged software

(G-4627)
VALGOTECH LLC
11079 Village Square Ln (46038-4552)
PHONE..................850 339-8877
David Olawale, Pr
EMP: 2 EST: 2018
SALES (est): 230.93K Privately Held
Web: www.valgotech.com
SIC: 3825 Energy measuring equipment, electrical

(G-4628)
VERISTA INC
9100 Fall View Dr (46037)
PHONE..................317 849-0330
Manish Soman, CEO
Jeff Kinell, *
EMP: 700 EST: 2019
SALES (est): 47.33MM Privately Held
Web: www.verista.com
SIC: 3841 2834 Surgical and medical instruments; Pharmaceutical preparations

(G-4629)
VETERANS FABRICATION LLC
12655 Federal Pl (46037-7833)
PHONE..................317 604-7704
Christopher S Hauk, Managing Member
EMP: 2 EST: 2020
SALES (est): 117.57K Privately Held
SIC: 3441 3743 5051 Fabricated structural metal; Railroad equipment; Metals service centers and offices

(G-4630)
VOCEL INC
10240 Summerlin Way (46037-9579)
PHONE..................858 774-2063
Carl Washburn, Prin
EMP: 4 EST: 2016
SALES (est): 65.16K Privately Held
SIC: 2741 Miscellaneous publishing

(G-4631)
WASH SYSTEMS LLC (PA)
Also Called: Wash.systems
11088 Plum Hollow Cir (46037-9139)
PHONE..................317 201-2625
John Booth, Managing Member
EMP: 2 EST: 2014
SALES (est): 166.93K
SALES (corp-wide): 166.93K Privately Held
Web: www.wash.systems
SIC: 7372 Application computer software

(G-4632)
WESLEYAN CHURCH CORPORATION (PA)
Also Called: Wesley Publishing House, The
13300 Olio Rd Ste X (46037)
PHONE..................317 774-7900
Kevin Batman, CFO
Jo Anne Lyon, *
Wayne A Macbeth, *
EMP: 47 EST: 1843
SQ FT: 15,000
SALES (est): 20.12MM
SALES (corp-wide): 20.12MM Privately Held
Web: www.wesleyan.org
SIC: 8661 2731 Methodist Church; Books, publishing and printing

(G-4633)
WILEY
12162 Talon Trce (46037-4063)
PHONE..................317 794-6765
Katie Mohr, Prin
EMP: 5 EST: 2017
SALES (est): 47.42K Privately Held
Web: www.wiley.com
SIC: 2731 Books, publishing only

(G-4634)
WOLFGANG SOFTWARE
10401 Cotton Blossom Dr (46038-6564)
PHONE..................317 443-5147
John Dimmett, Prin
EMP: 3 EST: 2010
SALES (est): 124.64K Privately Held
Web: www.wolfgangsoftware.com
SIC: 7372 Prepackaged software

(G-4635)
WPR SERVICES LLC
9059 Technology Ln (46038-2828)
PHONE..................317 513-5269
Christopher Harris, Owner
EMP: 1 EST: 2016
SALES (est): 217.32K Privately Held
Web: www.wprservices.net
SIC: 8711 3613 Engineering services; Control panels, electric

(G-4636)
WYRCO LLC
13603 E 131st St (46037-6304)
PHONE..................317 691-2832
EMP: 3 EST: 2017
SALES (est): 122.55K Privately Held
SIC: 3541 Machine tools, metal cutting type

(G-4637)
ZING POLYMER FORMATIONS LLC
8907 Tynan Way (46038-3032)
PHONE..................317 598-0480
Craig Myers, Managing Member
EMP: 3 EST: 2014
SALES (est): 100K Privately Held
SIC: 3089 3299 5023 Injection molding of plastics; Nonmetallic mineral statuary and other decorative products; Decorating supplies

Fishers
Hancock County

(G-4638)
A PAGE BEYOND LLC
13009 Fairfax Ct (46055-9624)
PHONE..................317 589-8218
Amy Waninger, CEO
EMP: 1 EST: 2019
SALES (est): 85.01K Privately Held
SIC: 8748 2731 Publishing consultant; Books, publishing only

(G-4639)
AMERICAN ELITE PRINTING LLC
15541 Slip Anchor Ln (46040-6604)
PHONE..................765 513-0889
EMP: 4 EST: 2019
SALES (est): 82.98K Privately Held
SIC: 2752 Commercial printing, lithographic

(G-4640)
BUSHWOOD VENTURES HTC LLC
9693 Reston Ln (46055-9642)
PHONE..................317 523-0991
David A Glessner, Prin
EMP: 6 EST: 2007
SALES (est): 191.5K Privately Held
SIC: 2499 Wood products, nec

(G-4641)
GREEN AIR LLC
13967 Hawkstone Dr (46040-9441)
PHONE..................317 335-1706
Dhanashree Chakola, CEO
EMP: 2
SALES (est): 80K Privately Held
Web: www.greenairenv.com
SIC: 3822 Switches, thermostatic

(G-4642)
INFRONT SOFTWARE LLC
10785 Harbor Bay Ct (46040-9017)
PHONE..................317 501-1871
Daniel Coppersmith, Prin
EMP: 4 EST: 2010
SALES (est): 113.08K Privately Held
Web: www.infrontsoftware.com
SIC: 7372 Prepackaged software

(G-4643)
INNERPRINT INC
12940 Rocky Pointe Rd (46055-9580)
P.O. Box 30442 (28230-0442)
PHONE..................317 509-6511
EMP: 3 EST: 2010
SALES (est): 224.43K Privately Held
SIC: 2752 Commercial printing, lithographic

(G-4644)
LUMEN CACHE INCORPORATED
13402 Chrisfield Ln (46055-9646)
PHONE..................317 739-4218
Derek Cowburn, CEO
Derek Cownburn, CEO
Lynn Shinkel, Prin

Fishers - Hancock County (G-4645) GEOGRAPHIC SECTION

▲ EMP: 2 EST: 2014
SALES (est): 156.4K **Privately Held**
Web: www.reneta.lighting
SIC: 3699 7373 Electrical equipment and supplies, nec; Office computer automation systems integration

(G-4645)
OAKLEAF INDUSTRIES INC
9914 Soaring Eagle Ln (46055-6191)
PHONE..................................317 414-2040
EMP: 1 EST: 2011
SALES (est): 88.75K **Privately Held**
SIC: 2511 5021 7389 Unassembled or unfinished furniture, household: wood; Household furniture; Business Activities at Non-Commercial Site

(G-4646)
PANTERA MFG CORPORATION
10609 Serra Vista Pt (46040-8117)
PHONE..................................317 435-0422
Luis Gomez, *CEO*
Patricia Gomez, *CFO*
EMP: 2 EST: 2020
SALES (est): 57.88K **Privately Held**
SIC: 3671 Electron tubes

(G-4647)
POLITAN STEEL FABRICATION INC
15133 Clove Hitch Ct (46040-9127)
PHONE..................................317 714-6800
Gary Politan, *CEO*
EMP: 5 EST: 2017
SALES (est): 222.58K **Privately Held**
SIC: 3999 Manufacturing industries, nec

(G-4648)
PRIMARY RECORD INC
9678 Reston Ln (46055-9642)
PHONE..................................317 270-8327
Jean Ross, *CEO*
EMP: 1 EST: 2020
SALES (est): 92.36K **Privately Held**
Web: www.primaryrecord.com
SIC: 7372 Application computer software

(G-4649)
RHINO SHIPPING SOLUTIONS LLC
Also Called: Rhino Shipping Solutions
10432 Crestmoor Ln (46040-8101)
PHONE..................................317 721-9476
Deangelo Richey Senior, *Owner*
EMP: 1 EST: 2021
SALES (est): 40K **Privately Held**
SIC: 2448 Pallets, wood and metal combination

(G-4650)
SCHATZI PRESS
10004 Springstone Rd (46055-9630)
PHONE..................................317 335-2335
Joseph Krauter Junior, *Prin*
EMP: 2 EST: 2006
SALES (est): 87.01K **Privately Held**
SIC: 2741 Miscellaneous publishing

(G-4651)
SEPRACOR INC
13923 Ash Stone Ct (46040-9434)
PHONE..................................317 513-6257
Kimb Winfrey Holmes, *Prin*
EMP: 5 EST: 2016
SALES (est): 155.71K **Privately Held**
Web: us.sumitomo-pharma.com
SIC: 2834 Pharmaceutical preparations

(G-4652)
SOMERSAULTS LLC
Also Called: Somersaults Life Archives

10285 Normandy Ct (46040-1348)
PHONE..................................317 747-7496
EMP: 7 EST: 2006
SALES (est): 152.27K **Privately Held**
SIC: 2834 Pharmaceutical preparations

(G-4653)
VK STUDIOS
10251 Landis Blvd (46040-5501)
PHONE..................................317 224-6867
Michael Van Koevering, *Prin*
EMP: 5 EST: 2019
SALES (est): 54.13K **Privately Held**
SIC: 2431 Millwork

Flat Rock
Shelby County

(G-4654)
LLC WARD STONE
1610 W State Road 252 (47234-7716)
P.O. Box 193 (47234-0193)
PHONE..................................812 587-0272
EMP: 20 EST: 2003
SALES (est): 1.68MM **Privately Held**
SIC: 1422 Crushed and broken limestone

(G-4655)
MCCLURE CONCRETE
3139 E Vandalia Rd (47234-9717)
PHONE..................................765 525-6098
Nathan Mcclure, *Owner*
EMP: 3 EST: 2002
SALES (est): 263.18K **Privately Held**
SIC: 3273 Ready-mixed concrete

(G-4656)
MOCO FRAGRANCES LLC
1756 W 850 S (47234-9775)
PHONE..................................317 642-9014
EMP: 5 EST: 2021
SALES (est): 140.06K **Privately Held**
Web: www.mocofragrances.com
SIC: 3999 Candles

Flora
Carroll County

(G-4657)
CARROLL PAPERS INC (PA)
Also Called: Carroll County Comet
14 E Main St (46929-1351)
P.O. Box 26 (46929-0026)
PHONE..................................574 967-4135
Susan Scholl, *Pr*
Joe Moss, *Dir*
EMP: 4 EST: 1973
SQ FT: 2,000
SALES (est): 727.07K
SALES (corp-wide): 727.07K **Privately Held**
Web: www.carrollcountycomet.com
SIC: 2711 Newspapers: publishing only, not printed on site

(G-4658)
FLORA WASTEWATER TREATMENT
507 N Division St (46929)
PHONE..................................574 967-3005
Bill Mccarty, *Superintnt*
EMP: 3 EST: 2005
SALES (est): 150.61K **Privately Held**
SIC: 3589 Water treatment equipment, industrial

(G-4659)
HOG SLAT INCORPORATED
315 S Sycamore St Ste 11 (46929-1288)
PHONE..................................574 967-3776
EMP: 20
SALES (corp-wide): 538.94MM **Privately Held**
Web: www.hogslat.com
SIC: 3523 Farm machinery and equipment
PA: Hog Slat, Incorporated
    206 Fayetteville St
    Newton Grove NC 28366
    800 949-4647

(G-4660)
LAND OLAKES INC
Also Called: Land O'Lakes
95 S 200 E (46929-9324)
PHONE..................................574 967-3064
Jeff W Simmons, *Mgr*
EMP: 10
SALES (corp-wide): 2.89B **Privately Held**
Web: www.landolakes-ingredients.com
SIC: 2048 Prepared feeds, nec
PA: Land O'lakes, Inc.
    4001 Lexington Ave N
    Arden Hills MN 55112
    651 375-2222

(G-4661)
MIDWEST METER INC
200 Commercial Dr (46929-1528)
PHONE..................................574 967-0175
Joe Ropes, *Mgr*
EMP: 5 EST: 2004
SALES (est): 471.08K **Privately Held**
Web: www.midwest-meter.com
SIC: 3824 Water meters

(G-4662)
MUEHLHAUSEN SPRING COMPANY
488 N 705 E (46929-9360)
PHONE..................................574 859-2481
George Muehlhausen Ii, *Pr*
EMP: 8 EST: 1993
SQ FT: 2,400
SALES (est): 605.04K **Privately Held**
SIC: 3493 Steel springs, except wire

(G-4663)
PARRETTS MEAT PROC & CATRG INC
Also Called: Parretts Mt Proc Hog Roasting
603 Railroad St (46929-1502)
PHONE..................................574 967-3711
Gary Parrett, *Owner*
EMP: 12 EST: 1969
SALES (est): 945.55K **Privately Held**
Web: www.parrettscatering.com
SIC: 5421 5812 7299 2013 Meat markets, including freezer provisioners; Caterers; Butcher service, processing only - does not sell meat; Sausages and other prepared meats

(G-4664)
QGRAPHICS INC
103 W Walnut St (46929-1061)
PHONE..................................574 967-3733
Sarah Hanaway, *Mgr*
EMP: 5
SALES (corp-wide): 848.39K **Privately Held**
Web: www.qgraphicsinc.com
SIC: 2791 Typesetting
PA: Qgraphics, Inc.
    108 E Main St
    Delphi IN 46923
    765 564-2314

(G-4665)
SISSON & SON MFG JEWELERS
7 W Main St (46929-1354)
P.O. Box 187 (46929-0187)
PHONE..................................574 967-4331
Scott D Sisson, *Pr*
Eva Sisson, *Sec*
EMP: 3 EST: 1950
SQ FT: 2,500
SALES (est): 279.13K **Privately Held**
SIC: 5944 3961 7631 Jewelry, precious stones and precious metals; Costume jewelry, ex. precious metal and semiprecious stones; Jewelry repair services

Florence
Switzerland County

(G-4666)
PROCESS SYSTEMS & SERVICES (PA)
13395 Innovation Dr (47020-9531)
PHONE..................................812 427-2331
Deither Volk, *Owner*
EMP: 3 EST: 2003
SALES (est): 397.98K
SALES (corp-wide): 397.98K **Privately Held**
Web: www.pssplastics.com
SIC: 2821 Plastics materials and resins

(G-4667)
TRENWA INC
13268 Innovation Dr (47020-9530)
PHONE..................................812 427-2217
James Crockett, *Dir*
EMP: 16
SALES (corp-wide): 19.25MM **Privately Held**
Web: www.trenwa.com
SIC: 3272 Concrete products, precast, nec
PA: Trenwa, Inc.
    1419 Alexandria Pike
    Fort Thomas KY 41075
    859 781-0831

Floyds Knobs
Floyd County

(G-4668)
AMERICAN EAGLE HEALTH LLC
2572 Campion Rd (47119-8928)
PHONE..................................812 921-9224
Marina Kanare, *Asst Sec*
EMP: 2 EST: 2021
SALES (est): 86.67K **Privately Held**
SIC: 3842 3844 5047 5049 Surgical appliances and supplies; X-ray apparatus and tubes; Medical and hospital equipment; Professional equipment, nec

(G-4669)
AUTOMATION CONSULTANTS INC
4003 Kendall Ct (47119-9337)
P.O. Box 577 (47119-0577)
PHONE..................................502 552-4995
John Robbins, *Pr*
EMP: 5 EST: 1997
SQ FT: 2,000
SALES (est): 228.29K **Privately Held**
Web: www.shoprag.com
SIC: 7699 3699 Industrial equipment services; Electronic training devices

GEOGRAPHIC SECTION

(G-4670)
B & B SIGNS
5060 Buck Creek Rd (47119-9251)
P.O. Box 7 (47119-0007)
PHONE..................................812 282-5366
Freddie Brennenstuhl, *Owner*
EMP: 3 **EST:** 1989
SQ FT: 2,100
SALES (est): 154.14K **Privately Held**
SIC: 3993 Signs and advertising specialties

(G-4671)
CHILLERS MICROCREAMERY LLC
P.O. Box 603 (47119-0603)
PHONE..................................812 987-1298
Dottie Rosenbarger, *Prin*
EMP: 13 **EST:** 2009
SALES (est): 111.62K **Privately Held**
Web: www.ilovechillers.com
SIC: 2021 Creamery butter

(G-4672)
CITIVIEW PUBLICATIONS LLC
132 Lee Dr (47119)
P.O. Box 70281 (40270-0281)
PHONE..................................502 296-1623
EMP: 2 **EST:** 2010
SALES (est): 189.67K **Privately Held**
Web: www.thecitiview.com
SIC: 2711 Commercial printing and newspaper publishing combined

(G-4673)
CLINIWAVE INC
5605 Featheringill Rd (47119-9583)
PHONE..................................812 923-9591
Gary Coulter, *Pr*
▲ **EMP:** 2 **EST:** 2005
SALES (est): 160K **Privately Held**
SIC: 3845 Electromedical equipment

(G-4674)
CLOVIS LLC
3333 Buffalo Trl (47119-9725)
PHONE..................................812 944-4791
Philip Sanders, *Pr*
EMP: 3 **EST:** 1998
SALES (est): 215.4K **Privately Held**
SIC: 3577 Computer peripheral equipment, nec

(G-4675)
COMPLETE CMPT SOLUTIONS INC
4801 Paoli Pike Ste 104 (47119-9681)
PHONE..................................812 923-0910
EMP: 3 **EST:** 1992
SALES (est): 254.83K **Privately Held**
Web: www.rpmccs.com
SIC: 7379 7372 Computer related consulting services; Prepackaged software

(G-4676)
DESIGNERS TOUCH
5008 Lakeview Dr (47119-9350)
PHONE..................................812 944-2267
EMP: 1 **EST:** 1999
SALES (est): 70.87K **Privately Held**
Web: www.designers-touch.com
SIC: 5714 2391 Drapery and upholstery stores; Curtains and draperies

(G-4677)
FIX-UR-6 LLC
3330 Old Hill Rd (47119-9711)
PHONE..................................812 989-4310
EMP: 5 **EST:** 2016
SALES (est): 60.1K **Privately Held**
SIC: 3999 Manufacturing industries, nec

(G-4678)
FOSTROM PRESS LLC
2234 Balmer Fenwick Rd (47119-8801)
PHONE..................................812 945-0071
Barbara G Foster, *Owner*
EMP: 1 **EST:** 2011
SALES (est): 59.55K **Privately Held**
SIC: 2741 Miscellaneous publishing

(G-4679)
GETTELFINGER HOLDINGS LLC
Also Called: Logo Apparel Plus
5773 Scottsville Rd (47119)
PHONE..................................812 923-9065
Dennis R Gettelfinger, *Managing Member*
EMP: 4 **EST:** 2000
SALES (est): 237.94K **Privately Held**
SIC: 2759 2395 Screen printing; Embroidery and art needlework

(G-4680)
GIFFORD MFG ADVISORS LLC
3570 Lafayette Pkwy (47119-9760)
PHONE..................................918 809-4116
James R Gifford, *Prin*
EMP: 5 **EST:** 2018
SALES (est): 115.74K **Privately Held**
Web: www.giffordmanufacturingadvisors.com
SIC: 3999 Manufacturing industries, nec

(G-4681)
HIGHLAND MACHINE TOOL INC
3461 E Luther Rd (47119-8001)
P.O. Box 156 (47119-0156)
PHONE..................................812 923-8884
James E Bezy, *Pr*
Alan Gahlinger, *
EMP: 22 **EST:** 1961
SQ FT: 6,000
SALES (est): 930.11K **Privately Held**
Web: www.highlandmachinetool.com
SIC: 3599 7692 3544 Machine shop, jobbing and repair; Welding repair; Special dies, tools, jigs, and fixtures

(G-4682)
JACK MIX
3400 Lawrence Banet Rd (47119-9605)
PHONE..................................812 923-8679
Jack W Mix, *Prin*
EMP: 6 **EST:** 2006
SALES (est): 79.3K **Privately Held**
SIC: 3273 Ready-mixed concrete

(G-4683)
KES LLC
5013 Lakeview Dr (47119-9351)
PHONE..................................812 728-8101
Christopher Powell, *Prin*
EMP: 4 **EST:** 2016
SALES (est): 69.63K **Privately Held**
SIC: 3949 Hunting equipment

(G-4684)
LANG CAPITAL LLC
4100 Sylvan Dr (47119-9603)
PHONE..................................812 325-2177
John Lang, *Prin*
EMP: 4 **EST:** 2019
SALES (est): 39.69K **Privately Held**
SIC: 3999 Manufacturing industries, nec

(G-4685)
LILA J ATHLETIC WEAR
3415 Royal Lake Dr (47119-9807)
PHONE..................................502 619-2898
EMP: 5 **EST:** 2018
SALES (est): 76.8K **Privately Held**
Web: www.lilaj.com

SIC: 2759 Screen printing

(G-4686)
NEW IMAGE CABINET COATING
5506 Briarhill Dr (47119-9569)
PHONE..................................812 228-4666
EMP: 3 **EST:** 2019
SALES (est): 71.33K **Privately Held**
Web: www.newimagecabinetcoatings.com
SIC: 2434 Wood kitchen cabinets

(G-4687)
PEAS IN A POD PUBLICATIONS LLC
3909 Knable Ct (47119-9613)
PHONE..................................812 923-5365
Nancy Platt, *Owner*
EMP: 1 **EST:** 2009
SALES (est): 48.29K **Privately Held**
SIC: 2741 Miscellaneous publishing

(G-4688)
POTORTI ENTERPRISES INC
4618 Shadyview Dr (47119-9333)
PHONE..................................812 989-8528
Robert Potorti, *Pr*
EMP: 5
SALES (est): 235.78K **Privately Held**
SIC: 3999 7389 Manufacturing industries, nec; Business Activities at Non-Commercial Site

(G-4689)
PRINTING SOLUTIONS INC
6220 Sarles Creek Rd (47119-9407)
PHONE..................................812 923-0756
Richard Chin, *Owner*
EMP: 4 **EST:** 1996
SALES (est): 472.75K **Privately Held**
Web: www.printingsolutions.us
SIC: 2752 5199 Offset printing; Advertising specialties

(G-4690)
PROTON MOLD TOOL INC
6126 Saint Marys Rd (47119-9129)
PHONE..................................812 923-7263
David Gettelfinger, *Owner*
EMP: 2 **EST:** 2002
SALES (est): 169.11K **Privately Held**
SIC: 3544 Special dies and tools

(G-4691)
ROAD WIDENER LLC
4620 Williamsburg Sta (47119-9670)
PHONE..................................844 494-3363
EMP: 8 **EST:** 2006
SALES (est): 939.11K **Privately Held**
Web: www.roadwidenerllc.com
SIC: 3531 Finishers and spreaders (construction equipment)

(G-4692)
S&A TOOLING
300 Lafollette Sta S Ste 302 # 283 (47119-8300)
PHONE..................................502 836-3886
Michael Hunt, *Owner*
EMP: 1 **EST:** 2003
SALES (est): 200.48K **Privately Held**
Web: www.satoolingllc.com
SIC: 3599 Machine shop, jobbing and repair

(G-4693)
SIDNEY & JANICE BOND
4424 Erin Dr (47119-9301)
PHONE..................................812 366-8160
Sidney Bond, *Prin*
EMP: 2 **EST:** 2007
SALES (est): 131.35K **Privately Held**

SIC: 2452 8049 Log cabins, prefabricated, wood; Physical therapist

(G-4694)
STROHBECK CABINET INSTALL
4339 Country View Dr (47119-9313)
PHONE..................................812 923-5013
Herman Strohbeck, *Prin*
EMP: 2 **EST:** 2003
SALES (est): 75.22K **Privately Held**
SIC: 2434 Wood kitchen cabinets

(G-4695)
TECHSHOT LIGHTING LLC
5605 Featheringill Rd Ste 102 (47119-9583)
PHONE..................................812 923-9591
EMP: 2 **EST:** 2010
SALES (est): 235.3K **Privately Held**
Web: www.techshotlighting.com
SIC: 3647 Vehicular lighting equipment

(G-4696)
TETRAFAB CORPORATION
3429 Knobs Valley Dr (47119-9665)
PHONE..................................812 258-0000
▲ **EMP:** 13 **EST:** 2007
SALES (est): 418.18K **Privately Held**
Web: www.tetrafab.com
SIC: 3161 Clothing and apparel carrying cases

(G-4697)
VANESSA COLLINS LLC
2015 Leanders Rd (47119-9263)
PHONE..................................219 985-5705
EMP: 1 **EST:** 2010
SALES (est): 11K **Privately Held**
Web: www.vanessacollinsllc.com
SIC: 2731 8748 Book publishing; Publishing consultant

(G-4698)
WARD FORGING COMPANY INC
3311 E Luther Rd (47119-9679)
P.O. Box 328 (47119-0328)
PHONE..................................812 923-7463
Charles Becht Junior, *Pr*
Carla Becht, *Sec*
EMP: 5 **EST:** 1920
SQ FT: 14,000
SALES (est): 481.52K **Privately Held**
Web: www.wardforging.com
SIC: 3545 3316 Angle rings; Bars, steel, cold finished, from purchased hot-rolled

Fontanet
Vigo County

(G-4699)
GREEN LEAF INC
9490 N Baldwin St (47851)
P.O. Box 88 (47851-0088)
PHONE..................................812 877-1546
Pete A Goda, *Pr*
Curt Owens, *
Angela Vikstko, *
Michael A Goda, *
Linda K Goda, *
▲ **EMP:** 144 **EST:** 1980
SQ FT: 60,000
SALES (est): 24.89MM **Privately Held**
Web: www.green-leaf.us
SIC: 3089 3498 Fittings for pipe, plastics; Fabricated pipe and fittings

Forest
Clinton County

(G-4700)
EMBROIDERY BY JACKIE
11489 E County Road 600 N (46039-9602)
PHONE..................765 438-6240
Jacqueline Mitchell, Prin
EMP: 4 EST: 2018
SALES (est): 23.23K Privately Held
SIC: 2395 Pleating and stitching

Fort Branch
Gibson County

(G-4701)
A & T CONCRETE SUPPLY INC
81 E State Road 168 (47648-8041)
P.O. Box 23 (47648-0023)
PHONE..................812 753-4252
Patricia Pohl, Pr
James Pohl, VP
EMP: 20 EST: 1964
SQ FT: 13,000
SALES (est): 2.62MM Privately Held
Web: www.at-concrete.com
SIC: 3273 Ready-mixed concrete

(G-4702)
BARRETT MANUFACTURING INC
Also Called: Tri Star Embroidery
901 E John St (47648-9711)
PHONE..................812 753-5808
EMP: 3 EST: 1993
SQ FT: 10,000
SALES (est): 199.8K Privately Held
SIC: 2395 2392 Embroidery products, except Schiffli machine; Cushions and pillows

(G-4703)
GRANITE TEE SIGNS LLC
7913 S Andee Ln (47648-1548)
PHONE..................317 670-4967
Brad Lamborne, Prin
EMP: 5 EST: 2015
SALES (est): 55.76K Privately Held
SIC: 3993 Signs and advertising specialties

(G-4704)
IMI RIVING MATERIALS INC
79 E State Road 168 (47648-8041)
PHONE..................812 753-4201
Wayne Carter, Mgr
EMP: 1 EST: 2013
SALES (est): 128.2K Privately Held
SIC: 3273 Ready-mixed concrete

(G-4705)
JDH LOGISTICS LLC
313 E Park St (47648)
PHONE..................573 529-2005
Joshua Hemmings, CEO
EMP: 1 EST: 2020
SALES (est): 62.68K Privately Held
SIC: 1389 4213 8748 Construction, repair, and dismantling services; Trucking, except local; Business consulting, nec

(G-4706)
NICHOLS OPERATING LLC
8157 S 100 W (47648-8105)
PHONE..................812 753-3600
Ives Preston, Prin
EMP: 4 EST: 2006
SALES (est): 485.65K Privately Held
SIC: 1311 Crude petroleum production

(G-4707)
SOUTH GIBSON STAR-TIMES INC
203 S Mccreary St (47648-1317)
PHONE..................812 753-3553
EMP: 10 EST: 1990
SALES (est): 505.16K Privately Held
Web: www.pdclarion.com
SIC: 2711 Newspapers, publishing and printing

Fort Wayne
Allen County

(G-4708)
101 TOOL & DIE LLC
3418 Delray Dr (46815-6009)
PHONE..................260 203-2981
EMP: 8 EST: 2012
SALES (est): 493.06K Privately Held
Web: www.101toolanddie.com
SIC: 3312 Tool and die steel

(G-4709)
11/18 PRO ALUMINUM LLC
817 W Berry St Apt 3 (46802-3914)
PHONE..................260 204-3577
EMP: 1 EST: 2021
SALES (est): 39.74K Privately Held
SIC: 3291 Polishing wheels

(G-4710)
18 THREADS LLC
6121 W Jefferson Blvd (46804-3072)
PHONE..................260 409-2923
Chad Bushee, Prin
EMP: 16 EST: 2017
SALES (est): 531.94K Privately Held
Web: www.18threads.com
SIC: 2759 Screen printing

(G-4711)
1ST CHOICE SAFETY LLC
4642 Pleasant Valley Dr (46825-6812)
P.O. Box 8157 (46898-8157)
PHONE..................260 797-5338
Ronald V Chidester, Prin
EMP: 7 EST: 2013
SALES (est): 210.24K Privately Held
Web: www.1stchoicesafetyllc.com
SIC: 3842 Clothing, fire resistant and protective

(G-4712)
3RIVERS SOAP COMPANY LLC
1935 E State Blvd (46805-4617)
PHONE..................260 418-0241
EMP: 1 EST: 2018
SALES (est): 47.23K Privately Held
SIC: 2841 Soap and other detergents

(G-4713)
6 TWENTY-SIX INC
1907 Production Rd (46808-3647)
P.O. Box 15944 (46885-5944)
PHONE..................260 471-2002
Mark Overhiser, Pr
EMP: 11 EST: 2013
SALES (est): 375.56K Privately Held
SIC: 3449 Fabricated bar joists and concrete reinforcing bars

(G-4714)
6605 E STATE LLC
2311 Forest Glade (46845-9761)
PHONE..................260 433-7007
EMP: 2 EST: 2010
SALES (est): 218.88K Privately Held
SIC: 3641 Electric light bulbs, complete

(G-4715)
A BETTER U LLC
3419 Bass Rd (46808-2927)
PHONE..................260 704-3309
Amy Markley, Admn
EMP: 5 EST: 2013
SALES (est): 97.24K Privately Held
SIC: 3949 Sporting and athletic goods, nec

(G-4716)
AB ENGINEERING INC
5822 Kruse Dr (46818-9351)
PHONE..................260 489-2845
Alan Bell, Pr
EMP: 1 EST: 1995
SALES (est): 7K Privately Held
Web: www.abengineeringinc.com
SIC: 3827 Telescopes: elbow, panoramic, sighting, fire control, etc.

(G-4717)
ABSOLUTE MACHINING LLC
3834 Vanguard Dr (46809-3300)
PHONE..................260 747-4568
EMP: 4 EST: 1989
SQ FT: 2,000
SALES (est): 504.91K Privately Held
Web: www.absolutemachiningllc.com
SIC: 3599 Machine shop, jobbing and repair

(G-4718)
ACCESS ONE BY MSG INC
5120 Speedway Dr (46825-5247)
PHONE..................260 485-7007
Mark Gawel, Pr
EMP: 1 EST: 2005
SALES (est): 331.01K Privately Held
Web: www.accessonebymsg.com
SIC: 3842 Technical aids for the handicapped

(G-4719)
ACCRA PAC HOLDING CO LLC
6435 W Jefferson Blvd Ste 151 (46804-6203)
PHONE..................765 326-0005
EMP: 2 EST: 2018
SALES (est): 79.63K Privately Held
Web: www.accrapacindia.net
SIC: 3999 Manufacturing industries, nec

(G-4720)
ACCU-LABEL INC
2021 Research Dr (46808-3623)
PHONE..................260 482-5223
David J Manning Junior, Pr
EMP: 30 EST: 1987
SQ FT: 22,000
SALES (est): 4.96MM Privately Held
Web: www.acculabel.com
SIC: 2759 2752 2672 2671 Flexographic printing; Commercial printing, lithographic; Paper; coated and laminated, nec; Paper; coated and laminated packaging

(G-4721)
ACCUGEAR INC
6710 Innovation Blvd (46818-1334)
PHONE..................260 497-6600
Richard E Dauch, Ch
David C Dauch, *
Mark S Barrett, *
▲ EMP: 126 EST: 1994
SQ FT: 50,000
SALES (est): 24.99MM
SALES (corp-wide): 6.08B Publicly Held
Web: www.aam.com
SIC: 3462 Automotive forgings, ferrous: crankshaft, engine, axle, etc.
HQ: American Axle & Manufacturing, Inc.
One Dauch Dr
Detroit MI 48211

(G-4722)
ACCUTECH MOLD & MACHINE INC
2817 Goshen Rd (46808-1446)
PHONE..................260 471-6102
EMP: 130 EST: 1996
SQ FT: 8,000
SALES (est): 20.65MM Privately Held
Web: www.accutechmoldinc.com
SIC: 3544 3541 Special dies and tools; Grinding machines, metalworking

(G-4723)
ACTIVE TRADING INTL INC
6015 2 Highway Drive Ste G (46818)
PHONE..................260 637-1990
Gary Buschman, Pr
EMP: 3 EST: 2004
SALES (est): 143.71K Privately Held
Web: www.activetradinginc.com
SIC: 3949 Sporting and athletic goods, nec

(G-4724)
ADVANCE MACHINE WORKS CORP
2620 Independence Dr (46808-4403)
P.O. Box 8708 (46898-8708)
PHONE..................260 483-1183
Bryan Neireiter, Pr
EMP: 29 EST: 1971
SQ FT: 10,000
SALES (est): 514.43K Privately Held
SIC: 3599 Machine shop, jobbing and repair

(G-4725)
ADVANCED CUTTING SYSTEMS INC
3700 E Pontiac St (46803)
P.O. Box 10634 (46853)
PHONE..................260 423-3394
EMP: 22 EST: 1993
SALES (est): 4.03MM Privately Held
Web: www.advancedcuttingsystems.com
SIC: 3291 Abrasive products

(G-4726)
ADVANCED DIGITAL SIGNS LLC
5031 Charlotte Ave (46815-6837)
P.O. Box 5281 (46895-5281)
PHONE..................260 704-0319
Kenneth Graham, Prin
EMP: 4 EST: 2015
SALES (est): 56.67K Privately Held
SIC: 3993 Signs and advertising specialties

(G-4727)
ADVANCED MACHINE & TOOL CORP (PA)
Also Called: A M T
3706 Transportation Dr (46818-1388)
PHONE..................260 489-3572
Kyle Koob, Pr
▲ EMP: 50 EST: 1970
SQ FT: 70,000
SALES (est): 23.3MM
SALES (corp-wide): 23.3MM Privately Held
Web: www.amt-corp.com
SIC: 3599 Machine shop, jobbing and repair

(G-4728)
ADVANCED SYSTEMS INTGRTION LLC
4534 Allen Martin Dr (46806-2801)
PHONE..................260 447-5555
Heidi Albertson, Mgr
EMP: 5

GEOGRAPHIC SECTION
Fort Wayne - Allen County (G-4754)

Web: www.asifabrication.com
SIC: 3441 Fabricated structural metal
PA: Advanced Systems & Integration, Llc
8512 Mangum Hollow Dr
Wake Forest NC 27587

(G-4729)
ADVANCED TCTCAL ORD SYSTEMS LL
2713 W Ferguson Rd (46809-3202)
PHONE.................858 228-1439
John Stiska, Prin
▼ **EMP:** 5 **EST:** 2014
SALES (est): 90.86K **Privately Held**
SIC: 3489 Ordnance and accessories, nec

(G-4730)
ADVANTAGE CARTRIDGE CO INC
10319 Liberty Mills Rd (46804-6339)
PHONE.................260 747-9941
Gregory Eshelman, Pr
Rebecca Eshelman, Sec
EMP: 16 **EST:** 2001
SALES (est): 745.28K **Privately Held**
Web: www.advantagecartridge.com
SIC: 3699 7629 Electrical equipment and supplies, nec; Electrical repair shops

(G-4731)
AEGIS SALES AND ENGINEERING
5411 Industrial Rd (46825-5121)
PHONE.................260 483-4160
Joyce Armstrong, CEO
Dorsey Roth, Pr
EMP: 18 **EST:** 1962
SQ FT: 18,000
SALES (est): 2.42MM **Privately Held**
Web: www.aegiscnc.com
SIC: 3599 3451 Machine shop, jobbing and repair; Screw machine products

(G-4732)
AG APPAREL AND SCREEN PRTG LLC
5515 Planeview Dr (46825-5103)
PHONE.................260 483-3817
Andy Goodman, Owner
EMP: 4 **EST:** 2011
SALES (est): 479.23K **Privately Held**
Web: www.fortwaynescreenprinting.com
SIC: 2752 Offset printing

(G-4733)
AIRGAS USA LLC
4935 New Haven Ave (46803-3020)
PHONE.................260 749-9576
Scott Latta, Brnch Mgr
EMP: 10
SALES (corp-wide): 114.13MM **Privately Held**
Web: www.airgas.com
SIC: 5085 2813 Welding supplies; Industrial gases
HQ: Airgas Usa, Llc
259 N Radnor Chester Rd
Radnor PA 19087
216 642-6600

(G-4734)
AIRMAN PROFICIENCY LLC
210 Grove St (46805-1934)
PHONE.................260 602-5788
David Ehrman, Prin
EMP: 1 **EST:** 2010
SALES (est): 111.83K **Privately Held**
SIC: 3728 Link trainers (aircraft training mechanisms)

(G-4735)
AJAX TOOL INC
2828 Commercial Rd (46809-2924)
P.O. Box 9724 (46899-9724)
PHONE.................260 747-7482
William Osterholt, Pr
EMP: 7 **EST:** 1963
SQ FT: 12,000
SALES (est): 844.08K **Privately Held**
Web: www.ajaxtoolinc.com
SIC: 3544 Special dies and tools

(G-4736)
ALBRECHT INCORPORATED (PA)
Also Called: Albright's Raw Dog Food
1025 Osage St (46808-3401)
PHONE.................260 422-9440
Lee Albright, Pr
Karen Albright, Prin
EMP: 4 **EST:** 1987
SALES (est): 954.81K **Privately Held**
Web: www.albrechtinc.com
SIC: 2047 Dog food

(G-4737)
ALCONEX SPECIALTY PRODUCTS
Also Called: Alconex Specialty Products
4201 Piper Dr (46809-3153)
PHONE.................260 744-3446
EMP: 26
SALES (corp-wide): 19.47MM **Privately Held**
Web: www.alconex.com
SIC: 3355 Aluminum rolling and drawing, nec
PA: Alconex Specialty Products Inc
7255 Chalfant Rd
Fort Wayne IN 46818
260 744-3446

(G-4738)
ALCONEX SPECIALTY PRODUCTS (PA)
7255 Chalfant Rd (46818-1337)
PHONE.................260 744-3446
C David Mc Bane, Pr
Mark A Wilkins, *
▲ **EMP:** 39 **EST:** 1987
SQ FT: 75,000
SALES (est): 19.47MM
SALES (corp-wide): 19.47MM **Privately Held**
Web: www.alconex.com
SIC: 3355 3357 3354 3351 Extrusion ingot, aluminum: made in rolling mills; Magnet wire, nonferrous; Tube, extruded or drawn, aluminum; Copper rolling and drawing

(G-4739)
ALL GLASS LLC
221 Grandstand Way (46825-6326)
PHONE.................260 969-1839
EMP: 6 **EST:** 2005
SALES (est): 323.29K **Privately Held**
Web: www.allglassfw.com
SIC: 3231 Products of purchased glass

(G-4740)
ALL THINGS JCHARI LLC
6937 Huguenard Rd Apt 101 (46818-9401)
PHONE.................260 414-4065
EMP: 1
SALES (est): 69.27K **Privately Held**
SIC: 2389 7389 Apparel and accessories, nec; Business Activities at Non-Commercial Site

(G-4741)
ALLEN APR PLASTICS REPAIR INC
3685 Lima Rd (46805-1741)
PHONE.................260 482-8523

Dan Allen, Pr
Mark Allen, *
EMP: 35 **EST:** 1985
SQ FT: 50,000
SALES (est): 4.66MM **Privately Held**
Web: www.aprplasticrepair.com
SIC: 3089 Air mattresses, plastics

(G-4742)
ALLEN FABRICATORS INC
10106 Smith Rd (46809-9771)
PHONE.................260 458-0008
Bob Meriwether, Pr
Gregg Owens, Pr
EMP: 12 **EST:** 1998
SQ FT: 56,000
SALES (est): 1.94MM **Privately Held**
Web: www.allenfab.com
SIC: 3441 Fabricated structural metal

(G-4743)
ALLIANCE TOOL & EQUIPMENT INC
3919 Engle Rd (46804-4414)
PHONE.................260 432-2909
James Tomson, Pr
Jane Tomson, Sec
▲ **EMP:** 18 **EST:** 1983
SQ FT: 12,000
SALES (est): 466.83K **Privately Held**
Web: www.alliancetool.net
SIC: 3599 Machine shop, jobbing and repair

(G-4744)
ALLIANCE WINDING EQUIPMENT (PA)
Also Called: Goyal Products
3939 Vanguard Dr (46809-3305)
PHONE.................260 478-2200
Michael C Khorshid, CEO
Patricia A Shields, *
▲ **EMP:** 32 **EST:** 1986
SQ FT: 50,000
SALES (est): 9.01MM
SALES (corp-wide): 9.01MM **Privately Held**
Web: www.alliance-winding.com
SIC: 3559 Refinery, chemical processing, and similar machinery

(G-4745)
ALLIED MFG PARTNERS INC
Also Called: Tippmann Ordnance
4410 New Haven Ave (46803-1650)
PHONE.................260 428-2670
EMP: 3 **EST:** 1998
SQ FT: 15,840
SALES (est): 424.22K **Privately Held**
Web: www.alliedmfg.com
SIC: 3699 3489 Electronic training devices; Ordnance and accessories, nec

(G-4746)
ALUMINUM DYNAMICS LLC (HQ) ✪
7575 W Jefferson Blvd (46804-4131)
PHONE.................260 969-3500
EMP: 5 **EST:** 2022
SALES (est): 36.6MM **Publicly Held**
SIC: 3354 Aluminum extruded products
PA: Steel Dynamics, Inc.
7575 W Jefferson Blvd
Fort Wayne IN 46804

(G-4747)
AMALGAMATED INCORPORATED
6211 Discount Dr (46818-1231)
P.O. Box 8977 (46898-8977)
PHONE.................260 489-2549
Gary Pipenger, Pr
Paula Pipenger, Sec
▲ **EMP:** 8 **EST:** 1994
SQ FT: 15,000

SALES (est): 1.44MM **Privately Held**
Web: www.amalgamatedinc.com
SIC: 2899 Chemical preparations, nec

(G-4748)
AMANDA ELIZABETH LLC
Also Called: Ae Sport
3711 Vanguard Dr Ste C (46809-3301)
PHONE.................602 317-9633
Amy Blumenherst, Pr
Joan Abrams, TRS
EMP: 5 **EST:** 2011
SQ FT: 2,500
SALES (est): 341.48K **Privately Held**
Web: www.aesport.us
SIC: 3171 Women's handbags and purses

(G-4749)
AMBANDASH
3826 Walden Run (46815-5260)
PHONE.................260 415-1709
David Freon, Prin
EMP: 5 **EST:** 2010
SALES (est): 185.61K **Privately Held**
SIC: 2869 Freon

(G-4750)
AMERIBRACE ORTHOPEDIC LLC
14504 Lima Rd (46818-9537)
PHONE.................260 704-6027
Kristopher Carroll, Prin
EMP: 2 **EST:** 2021
SALES (est): 104.27K **Privately Held**
SIC: 3829 3821 Thermometers, including digital: clinical; Incubators, laboratory

(G-4751)
AMERICA WILD LLC
Also Called: Recon Power Bikes
327 Ley Rd (46825-5219)
PHONE.................888 485-2589
Jeffrey Fuze, Managing Member
EMP: 6 **EST:** 2011
SALES (est): 518.68K **Privately Held**
Web: www.reconpowerbikes.com
SIC: 3751 5091 Bicycles and related parts; Bicycles

(G-4752)
AMERICAN BOTTLING COMPANY
2711 Independence Dr (46808-1331)
PHONE.................260 484-4177
Pete Hoffman, Mgr
EMP: 71
Web: www.keurigdrpepper.com
SIC: 2086 5149 Soft drinks: packaged in cans, bottles, etc.; Groceries and related products, nec
HQ: The American Bottling Company
6425 Hall Of Fame Ln
Frisco TX 75034

(G-4753)
AMERICAN EQUIPMENT CORP
Also Called: American Cook Systems
10827 La Cabreah Ln (46845-2134)
PHONE.................888 321-0117
Richard Lay, Pr
Troy Holder, CEO
EMP: 9 **EST:** 2013
SQ FT: 8,000
SALES (est): 221.6K **Privately Held**
Web: www.americanequipmentgroup.com
SIC: 3556 Food products machinery

(G-4754)
AMERICAN FLAME LLC
9230 Conservation Way (46809-9642)
PHONE.................260 459-1703

Fort Wayne - Allen County (G-4755) GEOGRAPHIC SECTION

▲ EMP: 65 EST: 1996
SQ FT: 2,000
SALES (est): 8.86MM **Privately Held**
Web: www.skytechpg.com
SIC: 3429 7699 Fireplace equipment, hardware: andirons, grates, screens; Gas appliance repair service

(G-4755)
AMERICAN HYDRO SYSTEMS INC
7201 Engle Rd (46804-2228)
PHONE..................866 357-5063
Marshall Craig, *Pr*
EMP: 10 EST: 1985
SQ FT: 6,000
SALES (est): 941.65K **Privately Held**
Web: www.ridorust.net
SIC: 2842 3589 Rust removers; Sewage and water treatment equipment

(G-4756)
AMERICAN HYDROFORMERS INC
4410 New Haven Ave (46803-1650)
PHONE..................260 428-2660
Jack Tippmann, *Pr*
Jay Tippmann, *VP*
David Miller, *Sec*
William J Federspiel, *Treas*
Renee Dillon, *AD Manager*
EMP: 24 EST: 2008
SALES (est): 8.41MM **Privately Held**
Web: www.americanhydroformers.com
SIC: 3317 Tubing, mechanical or hypodermic sizes: cold drawn stainless

(G-4757)
AMERICAN SEALANTS INC (HQ)
9190 Yeager Ln (46809-9649)
PHONE..................800 325-7040
Christopher Zaremba, *Pr*
Linda Zaremba, *
EMP: 36 EST: 1987
SQ FT: 15,000
SALES (est): 22.36MM
SALES (corp-wide): 93.47MM **Privately Held**
Web: www.americansealantsinc.com
SIC: 2891 5169 Adhesives and sealants; Sealants
PA: Meridian Adhesives Group Llc
15720 Brxham Hl Ave Ste 5
Charlotte NC

(G-4758)
AMERICAN TOOL SERVICE INC (PA)
7007 Trafalgar Dr (46803-3288)
PHONE..................260 493-6351
Todd Gibson, *CEO*
Robert Gibson, *Prin*
EMP: 10 EST: 2000
SALES (est): 2.45MM
SALES (corp-wide): 2.45MM **Privately Held**
Web: www.archcuttingtools.com
SIC: 3541 Machine tool replacement & repair parts, metal cutting types

(G-4759)
AMERICAN WIRE ROPE SLING OF IN
3122 Engle Rd (46809-1110)
PHONE..................260 478-4700
EMP: 1
SALES (corp-wide): 169.95MM **Privately Held**
Web: info.lifting.com
SIC: 3496 Miscellaneous fabricated wire products
HQ: American Wire Rope & Sling Of Indianapolis Inc
5760 Dividend Rd
Indianapolis IN 46241
877 634-2545

(G-4760)
AMPAC INTERNATIONAL INC
1118 Cedar St (46803-1232)
PHONE..................260 424-2964
EMP: 1 EST: 1993
SALES (est): 210.76K **Privately Held**
Web: www.ampac-intl.com
SIC: 3825 Test equipment for electronic and electrical circuits

(G-4761)
AMT PRECISION PARTS INC
Also Called: Amt Parts International
3606 Transportation Dr (46818-1374)
PHONE..................260 490-0223
◆ EMP: 31 EST: 1994
SQ FT: 28,500
SALES (est): 5.37MM
SALES (corp-wide): 23.3MM **Privately Held**
Web: www.amt-corp.com
SIC: 3599 Machine shop, jobbing and repair
PA: Advanced Machine & Tool Corporation
3706 Transportation Dr
Fort Wayne IN 46818
260 489-3572

(G-4762)
ANTHONY WYNE RHBLTTION CTR FOR (PA)
Also Called: Awrc
8515 Bluffton Rd (46809-3022)
PHONE..................260 744-6145
William J Swiss, *Pr*
Shannon K Rhoton, *
Mark Flegge, *
EMP: 100 EST: 1959
SQ FT: 15,000
SALES (est): 46.79MM
SALES (corp-wide): 46.79MM **Privately Held**
Web: www.benchmarkhs.com
SIC: 8331 7331 3441 3412 Vocational rehabilitation agency; Mailing service; Fabricated structural metal; Metal barrels, drums, and pails

(G-4763)
APOLLO DESIGN TECHNOLOGY INC
4012 Merchant Rd (46818-1246)
PHONE..................260 497-9191
Joel Nichols, *Pr*
Keersten Nichols, *
Caryn Myrice, *
▲ EMP: 75 EST: 1992
SALES (est): 17.52MM **Privately Held**
Web: www.apollodesign.net
SIC: 3229 Pressed and blown glass, nec

(G-4764)
APPLIED COATING CONVERTING LLC
Also Called: A C C
3736 N Wells St (46808-4007)
PHONE..................260 436-4455
Rick Narramore, *Owner*
▲ EMP: 9 EST: 2008
SALES (est): 942.6K **Privately Held**
Web: www.appliedconverting.com
SIC: 2679 Paper products, converted, nec

(G-4765)
APPLIED ELECTRONIC MTLS LLC
9609 Ardmore Ave (46809-9625)
PHONE..................260 438-8632
EMP: 6 EST: 2015
SALES (est): 421.71K **Privately Held**
SIC: 3559 Semiconductor manufacturing machinery

(G-4766)
APPLIED METALS & MCH WORKS INC
1036 Saint Marys Ave (46808-2815)
PHONE..................260 424-4834
Gary Ecenbarger, *Pr*
EMP: 32 EST: 1959
SQ FT: 23,000
SALES (est): 4.74MM **Privately Held**
Web: www.appliedmetals.com
SIC: 3542 3479 3599 7692 Rebuilt machine tools, metal forming types; Coating of metals and formed products; Machine shop, jobbing and repair; Brazing

(G-4767)
APPLIED TECHNOLOGY GROUP INC
Also Called: A T G
2230 W Coliseum Blvd (46808-3651)
PHONE..................260 482-2844
Mark Gilpin, *Pr*
EMP: 10 EST: 1996
SALES (est): 2.4MM **Privately Held**
Web: www.atgfw.com
SIC: 3699 7382 Security devices; Confinement surveillance systems maintenance and monitoring

(G-4768)
APR PLASTIC FABRICATING INC
3685 Lima Rd (46805-1741)
PHONE..................260 482-8523
EMP: 50 EST: 1985
SQ FT: 15,000
SALES (est): 5.33MM **Privately Held**
Web: www.aprtanks.com
SIC: 3089 Injection molding of plastics

(G-4769)
APTERA SOFTWARE INC
113 W Berry St Ste 3 (46802-2324)
PHONE..................260 969-1410
T K Herman, *Pr*
Conrad Ehiner, *
EMP: 100 EST: 2003
SALES (est): 10.58MM **Privately Held**
Web: www.apterainc.com
SIC: 7372 Business oriented computer software

(G-4770)
ARDEN COMPANIES LLC
Also Called: Arden/Benhar Mills
3510 Piper Dr (46809-3196)
PHONE..................260 747-1657
Stacey Martin, *Mgr*
EMP: 58
SALES (corp-wide): 3.31B **Publicly Held**
Web: www.ardencompanies.com
SIC: 2392 3635 2842 Cushions and pillows; Household vacuum cleaners; Cleaning or polishing preparations, nec
HQ: Arden Companies, Llc
30400 Telg Rd Ste 200
Bingham Farms MI 48025
248 415-8500

(G-4771)
ARISTOLINE CABINETS INC
5803 Industrial Rd (46825-5129)
PHONE..................260 482-9719
Timothy D Molter, *Pr*
Rebecca Molter, *Sec*
EMP: 20 EST: 2000
SALES (est): 2.06MM **Privately Held**
Web: www.aristoline.com
SIC: 2434 Wood kitchen cabinets

(G-4772)
ARNEYS FREEZE-DRIED TREATS LLC
7312 Mill Run Rd Apt B (46819-1811)
PHONE..................812 801-1386
EMP: 1
SALES (est): 69.27K **Privately Held**
SIC: 2034 Dried and dehydrated fruits, vegetables and soup mixes

(G-4773)
ARTEK INC
3311 Enterprise Rd (46808)
P.O. Box 8975 (46898)
PHONE..................260 484-4222
Dennis Dammeyer, *CEO*
▼ EMP: 45 EST: 1985
SQ FT: 55,000
SALES (est): 9.31MM **Privately Held**
Web: www.artek-inc.com
SIC: 3089 Injection molded finished plastics products, nec

(G-4774)
ARTEMIS INTERNATIONAL INC
3711 Vanguard Dr Ste A (46809-3301)
PHONE..................260 436-6899
▲ EMP: 12 EST: 1995
SQ FT: 4,000
SALES (est): 1.29MM **Privately Held**
Web: www.artemis-nutraceuticals.com
SIC: 2834 Extracts of botanicals: powdered, pilular, solid, or fluid

(G-4775)
ASPHALT EQUIPMENT COMPANY INC (PA)
Also Called: Almix
13333 Us Highway 24 W (46814-7457)
PHONE..................260 672-3004
Michael A Shurtz, *Pr*
Grant Shurtz, *VP*
Kathern Shurtz, *Sec*
◆ EMP: 20 EST: 1952
SALES (est): 4.51MM
SALES (corp-wide): 4.51MM **Privately Held**
Web: www.almix.com
SIC: 3531 5084 3448 3443 Mixers, nec: ore, plaster, slag, sand, mortar, etc.; Industrial machinery and equipment; Prefabricated metal buildings and components; Fabricated plate work (boiler shop)

(G-4776)
ASSURED GENERAL CONTG LLC
Also Called: Construction
3907 Evergreen Ln (46815-4709)
PHONE..................260 740-4744
Eric Gillespie, *Managing Member*
EMP: 2 EST: 2020
SALES (est): 76.12K **Privately Held**
SIC: 1799 8741 8742 1521 Special trade contractors, nec; Construction management; Construction project management consultant; Patio and deck construction and repair

(G-4777)
ATHENA CHAMPION INC
2621 Corrinado Ct (46808-4406)
PHONE..................260 373-1917
Steve Yaggy, *CFO*
EMP: 29 EST: 1999
SQ FT: 5,000
SALES (est): 6.53MM
SALES (corp-wide): 191.04MM **Privately Held**
Web: www.athenachampion.com

SIC: 3843 Dental equipment
PA: Young Innovations, Inc.
2260 Wendt St
Algonquin IL 60102
847 458-5400

(G-4778)
ATHLETIC EDGE INC
Also Called: Custom Expressions
1133 Old Bridge Pl (46825-3563)
PHONE..................260 489-6613
Matt P Kostoff, *Pr*
Gary Nead, *Sec*
Michelle Nead, *Stockholder*
Cindy Kostoff, *Stockholder*
EMP: 10 **EST:** 1990
SALES (est): 622.65K **Privately Held**
Web: www.athleticedgeinc.com
SIC: 7389 2396 3993 Embroidery advertising; Screen printing on fabric articles; Advertising novelties

(G-4779)
AUGUST GILL APPAREL LLC
5534 Saint Joe Rd (46835-3328)
PHONE..................317 342-2800
EMP: 1 **EST:** 2020
SALES (est): 25.15K **Privately Held**
Web: www.augustgillapparel.com
SIC: 2331 Women's and misses' blouses and shirts

(G-4780)
AUTO BUMPER EXCHANGE INC
2321 Bremer Rd (46803-3010)
PHONE..................260 493-4408
Jerry R Grossman Senior, *Pr*
Charles Lake, *Sec*
Ralph Grossman, *Stockholder*
Charles W Lehman, *Sec*
◆ **EMP:** 9 **EST:** 1954
SQ FT: 8,500
SALES (est): 761.23K **Privately Held**
Web: www.abefw.com
SIC: 5013 5015 3714 Bumpers; Automotive parts and supplies, used; Motor vehicle parts and accessories

(G-4781)
AUTOMATED LASER CORPORATION
14224 Plank St (46818-9092)
PHONE..................260 637-4140
Joseph Deprisco, *Pr*
Mike Gigli, *OF MFG**
EMP: 9 **EST:** 1998
SQ FT: 4,800
SALES (est): 202.79K **Privately Held**
Web: www.autolase.com
SIC: 3699 8741 Laser systems and equipment; Management services

(G-4782)
AVALIGN TECHNOLOGIES INC
Avalign Technologies
8727 Clinton Park Dr (46825-3170)
PHONE..................260 484-1500
Kevin Countryman, *Prin*
EMP: 1
Web: www.aligntech.com
SIC: 3841 Surgical and medical instruments
PA: Avalign Technologies, Inc.
10275 W Higgins Rd # 920
Rosemont IL 60018

(G-4783)
AVERY DENNISON CORPORATION
Also Called: Fasson Roll North America Div
3011 Independence Dr (46808-1390)
PHONE..................260 481-4500
Philip Neal, *Ch*
EMP: 147

SALES (corp-wide): 8.36B **Publicly Held**
Web: www.averydennison.com
SIC: 2672 Adhesive papers, labels, or tapes: from purchased material
PA: Avery Dennison Corporation
8080 Norton Pkwy
Mentor OH 44060
440 534-6000

(G-4784)
AVID OPERATIONS INC
1210 Lynn Ave (46805-3552)
PHONE..................260 220-2001
Matthew P Rasbury, *Pr*
EMP: 8 **EST:** 2019
SALES (est): 302.55K **Privately Held**
SIC: 1731 1623 3825 Computer installation; Cable laying construction; Network analyzers

(G-4785)
AXIS CONTROLS INCORPORATED
6100 Lower Huntington Rd (46809-9617)
PHONE..................260 414-4028
Mark Dalman, *Pr*
John Auer, *Treas*
EMP: 2 **EST:** 1998
SALES (est): 226.22K **Privately Held**
Web: www.axiscontrols.com
SIC: 3625 Industrial controls: push button, selector switches, pilot

(G-4786)
BAALS LLC
118 W Columbia St Ste 402 (46802-1729)
PHONE..................260 993-0350
EMP: 2 **EST:** 2014
SALES (est): 87.75K **Privately Held**
Web: www.itsbaals.com
SIC: 7372 Prepackaged software

(G-4787)
BAE SYSTEMS CONTROLS INC
Also Called: Commercial Aircraft
4250 Airport Expy (46809)
P.O. Box 2232 (46801)
PHONE..................260 434-5195
EMP: 1037
SALES (corp-wide): 28.77B **Privately Held**
SIC: 3721 3812 Aircraft; Search and navigation equipment
HQ: Bae Systems Controls Inc.
1098 Clark St
Endicott NY 13760
607 770-2000

(G-4788)
BAIR WELDING LLC
7745 Trier Rd (46815-5647)
PHONE..................260 485-1452
Tom Bair, *Owner*
EMP: 1 **EST:** 1946
SALES (est): 41.04K **Privately Held**
SIC: 7692 Welding repair

(G-4789)
BEACH HOUSE BEVERAGES LLC
624 W Wayne St (46802-2126)
PHONE..................260 969-1064
Connie Hunt, *Acctg Dir*
EMP: 5 **EST:** 2018
SALES (est): 450K **Privately Held**
Web: www.beachhousebevs.com
SIC: 2082 Beer (alcoholic beverage)

(G-4790)
BEAR ARMS HOLSTERS
1149 Grant Ave (46803-1312)
PHONE..................260 310-2376
EMP: 3 **EST:** 2012

SALES (est): 58.67K **Privately Held**
Web: www.beararmsholsters.com
SIC: 3199 Holsters, leather

(G-4791)
BEAZER EAST INC
1820 W Washington Center Rd (46818-1416)
PHONE..................260 490-9006
Tom Meeker, *Brnch Mgr*
EMP: 1
SALES (corp-wide): 23.02B **Privately Held**
SIC: 3272 Concrete products, nec
HQ: Beazer East, Inc.
600 River Ave Ste 200
Pittsburgh PA 15212
412 428-9407

(G-4792)
BECKYS DIE CUTTING INC
701 Sherman Blvd (46808-2824)
PHONE..................260 467-1714
EMP: 4 **EST:** 1993
SALES (est): 478.91K **Privately Held**
Web: beckysdci.squarespace.com
SIC: 3544 Special dies and tools

(G-4793)
BEE KIND CANDLES
1409 Sinclair St (46808-2653)
PHONE..................765 618-5819
Crystal Parsons, *Prin*
EMP: 4 **EST:** 2019
SALES (est): 64.98K **Privately Held**
SIC: 3999 Candles

(G-4794)
BELLAHAUSS DISTRIBUTERS
4767 Evard Rd (46835-1926)
PHONE..................260 485-4343
Laura Johnson, *Owner*
EMP: 1 **EST:** 2009
SALES (est): 43.48K **Privately Held**
SIC: 3053 Gaskets; packing and sealing devices

(G-4795)
BENS CREATIVE VENTURES LLC
5534 Saint Joe Rd (46835-3328)
PHONE..................574 279-1057
EMP: 1
SALES (est): 69.27K **Privately Held**
SIC: 2261 Printing of cotton broadwoven fabrics

(G-4796)
BEST BLINDS
8534 Fritz Rd (46818-9307)
PHONE..................260 490-4422
EMP: 6 **EST:** 2019
SALES (est): 248.23K **Privately Held**
Web: www.bestblindsfortwayne.com
SIC: 2591 Window blinds

(G-4797)
BHAR INCORPORATED
6509 Moeller Rd (46806-1677)
PHONE..................260 749-5168
Richard B Kelly, *CEO*
Melissa Smith, *
Jeff Baker, *
EMP: 239 **EST:** 1976
SQ FT: 57,000
SALES (est): 3.87MM **Privately Held**
Web: www.bharinc.com
SIC: 3089 Injection molding of plastics
HQ: Sanko Gosei Technologies Usa, Inc.
6509 Moeller Rd
Fort Wayne IN 46806
260 749-5168

(G-4798)
BHAURA INC
4226 Lafayette St (46806-1740)
PHONE..................260 745-5700
Balbir Singh, *Pr*
EMP: 9 **EST:** 2010
SALES (est): 259.76K **Privately Held**
SIC: 3089 Injection molding of plastics

(G-4799)
BIG BRICK HOUSE BAKERY LLP
Also Called: Red Rover Wholesale
4322 Marvin Dr (46806-2596)
P.O. Box 13392 (46868-3392)
PHONE..................260 563-1071
Kevin Rowan, *Pt*
Virginia Leigh Rowan, *Pt*
EMP: 4 **EST:** 2007
SALES (est): 223.4K **Privately Held**
SIC: 2099 2041 7389 Pasta, rice, and potato, packaged combination products; Wheat flour; Business Activities at Non-Commercial Site

(G-4800)
BILLS INTERNATIONAL LLC
3330 S Anthony Blvd (46806-3815)
PHONE..................260 226-6004
EMP: 10 **EST:** 2020
SALES (est): 50K **Privately Held**
SIC: 3537 Trucks, tractors, loaders, carriers, and similar equipment

(G-4801)
BIODYNE-MIDWEST LLC
Also Called: Biodyne-Usa
3850 Concept Ct Ste 101 (46808-1498)
PHONE..................888 970-0955
EMP: 11 **EST:** 2012
SQ FT: 1,000
SALES (est): 2.51MM **Privately Held**
Web: www.biodyne-usa.com
SIC: 5191 2869 Chemicals, agricultural; Industrial organic chemicals, nec

(G-4802)
BIOPOLY LLC
7136 Gettysburg Pike (46804-5680)
PHONE..................260 999-6135
Herbert Schwartz, *Managing Member*
EMP: 14 **EST:** 2006
SALES (est): 1.16MM **Privately Held**
Web: www.biopolyortho.com
SIC: 3842 8731 Orthopedic appliances; Medical research, commercial

(G-4803)
BIRCH WOOD
8151 Glencarin Blvd (46804-5799)
PHONE..................260 432-0011
Jeffery Birch, *Prin*
EMP: 8 **EST:** 2013
SALES (est): 91.75K **Privately Held**
SIC: 2491 Structural lumber and timber, treated wood

(G-4804)
BIRD AND CLEAVER LLC
4036 Fernbank Dr (46815-5410)
PHONE..................260 579-2799
Lindsay Cheesebrew, *Prin*
EMP: 5 **EST:** 2016
SALES (est): 170.23K **Privately Held**
Web: www.birdandcleaver.com
SIC: 3421 Cutlery

(G-4805)
BISHOP LIFTING PRODUCTS INC
3122 Engle Rd (46809-1110)
PHONE..................260 478-4700

Fort Wayne - Allen County (G-4806)

GEOGRAPHIC SECTION

EMP: 1
SALES (corp-wide): 169.95MM **Privately Held**
Web: www.lifting.com
SIC: 1799 3531 Rigging and scaffolding; Crane carriers
PA: Bishop Lifting Products, Inc.
2301 Commerce St Ste 110
Houston TX
713 674-2266

(G-4806)
BLEACHERPRO LLC
4703 Collbran Ct (46835)
P.O. Box 15837 (46885)
PHONE.................................813 394-5316
Ricardo Vasquez, *Managing Member*
EMP: 3 **EST:** 2021
SALES (est): 105.54K **Privately Held**
Web: www.bleacher-pro.com
SIC: 1799 2531 1751 7389 Athletic and recreation facilities construction; Bleacher seating, portable; Lightweight steel framing (metal stud) installation; Business services, nec

(G-4807)
BLOOM PHARMACEUTICAL
Also Called: Erbeco
2831 Union Chapel Rd (46845-9271)
PHONE.................................260 615-2633
Cortney Schwartz, *Pr*
Jerra Myers, *VP*
EMP: 3 **EST:** 2016
SALES (est): 164.09K **Privately Held**
SIC: 2834 Ointments

(G-4808)
BLUE BELL MATTRESS COMPANY LLC
3434 S Maplecrest Rd (46803-3230)
PHONE.................................260 749-9393
EMP: 184
SALES (corp-wide): 53.78MM **Privately Held**
Web: www.bluebellmattress.com
SIC: 2515 Mattresses, innerspring or box spring
HQ: Blue Bell Mattress Company, Llc
24 Thompson Rd
East Windsor CT 06088
860 292-6372

(G-4809)
BLUE RING STENCILS LLC
Also Called: Metal Etching Tech Associates
2248 Research Dr (46808-3628)
PHONE.................................260 203-5461
Robert Hall, *Prin*
EMP: 14
SALES (corp-wide): 3.03MM **Privately Held**
Web: www.blueringstencils.com
SIC: 3672 Circuit boards, television and radio printed
PA: Blue Ring Stencils Llc
7345 Greendale Rd
Windsor CO 80550
866 763-3873

(G-4810)
BLUEHIVE HEALTH LLC
1690 Broadway Ste 550 (46802)
PHONE.................................260 217-5328
EMP: 8
SALES (est): 322.27K **Privately Held**
SIC: 7372 Business oriented computer software

(G-4811)
BODYCOTE THERMAL PROC INC
Also Called: Metallurgical Processing
3715 E Washington Blvd (46803-1547)
PHONE.................................260 423-1691
Tom Evans, *Brnch Mgr*
EMP: 37
SALES (corp-wide): 1B **Privately Held**
Web: www.bodycote.com
SIC: 3398 Metal heat treating
HQ: Bodycote Thermal Processing, Inc.
12750 Merit Dr Ste 1400
Dallas TX 75251
214 904-2420

(G-4812)
BORDNERS AUT SERV
3510 Eleanor Ave Apt A (46805-1844)
PHONE.................................260 483-4084
Steve Bordner, *Prin*
EMP: 5 **EST:** 2010
SALES (est): 87.47K **Privately Held**
SIC: 7692 Welding repair

(G-4813)
BOWMAR LLC
8000 Bluffton Rd (46809-3018)
PHONE.................................260 747-3121
EMP: 40 **EST:** 2010
SQ FT: 75,000
SALES (est): 7.77MM **Privately Held**
Web: www.bowmarllc.com
SIC: 3575 3674 3643 Computer terminals, monitors and components; Semiconductors and related devices; Current-carrying wiring services

(G-4814)
BRANIK INC
3626 Illinois Rd (46804-2062)
PHONE.................................260 467-1808
Stanley J Haynes, *Pr*
Stanley Haynes, *Pr*
EMP: 2 **EST:** 2003
SALES (est): 492.16K **Privately Held**
Web: www.branikmotorsports.com
SIC: 2431 Moldings, wood: unfinished and prefinished

(G-4815)
BRC RUBBER & PLASTICS INC (PA)
Also Called: BRC Rubber Group
1029a W State Blvd (46808-3165)
PHONE.................................260 693-2171
Charles Chaffee, *CEO*
Clifford Chaffee, *
Mike Meyer, *
Karen J Chaffee, *
Paul Bouza, *
▲ **EMP:** 250 **EST:** 1973
SQ FT: 90,000
SALES (est): 95.9MM
SALES (corp-wide): 95.9MM **Privately Held**
Web: www.brcrp.com
SIC: 3061 3714 3053 Automotive rubber goods (mechanical); Motor vehicle parts and accessories; Gaskets; packing and sealing devices

(G-4816)
BRENMEER LLC
Also Called: Nsignia Screenprinting
5716 Wald Rd (46818-9746)
PHONE.................................260 267-0249
EMP: 2 **EST:** 2014
SALES (est): 80.61K **Privately Held**
Web: www.nsigniascreenprinting.com
SIC: 2759 Promotional printing

(G-4817)
BRIGHT SIGNS AND MORE
2410 W Jefferson Blvd (46802-4639)
PHONE.................................260 203-2444
Aaron Keebler, *Prin*
EMP: 7 **EST:** 2019
SALES (est): 241.87K **Privately Held**
Web: www.brightsigns.marketing
SIC: 3993 Signs and advertising specialties

(G-4818)
BRISTOL-MYERS SQUIBB COMPANY
Also Called: Bristol-Myers Squibb
7527 Aboite Center Rd (46804)
PHONE.................................260 432-2764
Steve Brace, *Mgr*
EMP: 4
SALES (corp-wide): 45.01B **Publicly Held**
Web: www.bms.com
SIC: 2834 Pharmaceutical preparations
PA: Bristol-Myers Squibb Company
Route 206/Prvince Line Rd
Princeton NJ 08540
609 252-4621

(G-4819)
BROOKWOOD CABINET COMPANY INC
5912 Old Maumee Rd (46803-1705)
PHONE.................................260 749-5012
Jerry Kurtz, *Pr*
Gene L Ruse, *VP*
EMP: 10 **EST:** 1948
SALES (est): 745.57K **Privately Held**
Web: www.brookwoodcompany.com
SIC: 2434 Wood kitchen cabinets

(G-4820)
BRUCE PAYNE
Also Called: Payne's Die Cutting
810 Lakeridge Pl (46819-1468)
PHONE.................................260 492-2259
Bruce Payne, *Owner*
EMP: 3 **EST:** 1931
SQ FT: 2,400
SALES (est): 194.06K **Privately Held**
SIC: 2675 2759 Paper die-cutting; Embossing on paper

(G-4821)
BRUNSWICK CORPORATION
Also Called: Harris Kayot
1111 N Hadley Rd (46804-5540)
PHONE.................................260 459-8200
James R Poiry, *Pr*
EMP: 88
SALES (corp-wide): 6.4B **Publicly Held**
Web: www.brunswick.com
SIC: 3519 3471 3732 Outboard motors; Anodizing (plating) of metals or formed products; Pontoons, except aircraft and inflatable
PA: Brunswick Corporation
26125 N Rvrwoods Blvd Ste
Mettawa IL 60045
847 735-4700

(G-4822)
BUCHANAN COMPANY INC
4610 Industrial Rd (46825-5206)
PHONE.................................317 919-2025
EMP: 2 **EST:** 2010
SALES (est): 105.25K **Privately Held**
SIC: 3799 Transportation equipment, nec

(G-4823)
BUILDING TEMP SOLUTIONS LLC
3811 Fourier Dr (46825)
P.O. Box 508 (46947)
PHONE.................................260 449-9201

John Gilbert, *Managing Member*
EMP: 10 **EST:** 2009
SALES (est): 2.75MM
SALES (corp-wide): 5.21B **Publicly Held**
Web: www.dillinggroup.com
SIC: 3822 Temperature controls, automatic
PA: Comfort Systems Usa, Inc.
675 Bering Dr Ste 400
Houston TX 77057
713 830-9600

(G-4824)
C & B INDUSTRIES LLC
9009 Coldwater Rd (46825-2072)
PHONE.................................260 490-3000
EMP: 8 **EST:** 2009
SALES (est): 261.19K **Privately Held**
Web: www.tippmanngroup.com
SIC: 3999 Manufacturing industries, nec

(G-4825)
C & C INDUSTRIES
10214 Chestnut Plaza Dr (46814-8970)
PHONE.................................260 804-6518
Ben Truesdale, *Owner*
EMP: 5 **EST:** 2017
SALES (est): 136.95K **Privately Held**
SIC: 3999 Manufacturing industries, nec

(G-4826)
C & J SERVICES & SUPPLIES INC
Also Called: C & J Security Solutions
5201 Investment Dr (46808-3650)
P.O. Box 80605 (46898-0605)
PHONE.................................317 569-7222
EMP: 28 **EST:** 2004
SALES (est): 4.63MM **Privately Held**
Web: www.cjssinc.com
SIC: 3715 Truck trailers

(G-4827)
C & P MACHINE SERVICE INC
Also Called: C&P Machine
445 Council Dr (46825-5158)
PHONE.................................260 484-7723
Edwin R Baker, *Pr*
David R Baker, *
Charlene Randolph, *
Hilda Baker, *
Brian Baker, *
EMP: 17 **EST:** 1965
SQ FT: 20,000
SALES (est): 631.59K **Privately Held**
Web: www.cpmachine.com
SIC: 3599 5013 5531 7538 Machine shop, jobbing and repair; Automotive servicing equipment; Auto and home supply stores; Engine rebuilding: automotive

(G-4828)
C-POINT INC
Also Called: Craftline Printing
3522 W Ferguson Rd Ste A (46809-3164)
PHONE.................................260 478-9551
▲ **EMP:** 225
Web: www.craftlineprinting.com
SIC: 2732 2752 Book music: printing and binding, not published on site; Advertising posters, lithographed

(G-4829)
CALICO PRECISION MOLDING LLC
Also Called: Polytec Packaging Solution
1211 Progress Rd (46808-1261)
PHONE.................................260 484-4500
Ted Hayes, *
▲ **EMP:** 40 **EST:** 1970
SQ FT: 45,000
SALES (est): 7.73MM **Privately Held**
Web: www.calicopm.com

GEOGRAPHIC SECTION

Fort Wayne - Allen County (G-4855)

SIC: 3089 Synthetic resin finished products, nec

(G-4830)
CALIENTE LLC
315 E Wallace St (46803-2342)
PHONE..................260 426-3800
EMP: 25 EST: 2000
SQ FT: 40,000
SALES (est): 4.59MM **Privately Held**
Web: www.calientellc.com
SIC: 3585 3443 3822 Heating equipment, complete; Air coolers, metal plate; Pressure controllers, air-conditioning system type

(G-4831)
CANDLES BY DAR INC (PA)
Also Called: Darlite Designs
8308 Riveroak Dr (46825-7122)
PHONE..................260 482-2099
Darwin E Highlen Junior, Pr
▲ EMP: 10 EST: 1973
SALES (est): 1.75MM
SALES (corp-wide): 1.75MM **Privately Held**
SIC: 5021 5023 5193 3999 Household furniture; Homefurnishings; Florists' supplies; Novelties, bric-a-brac, and hobby kits

(G-4832)
CAPEABLE SENSORY PRODUCTS LLC
Also Called: Capeable Weighted Products
6411 Highview Dr (46818-1385)
PHONE..................260 387-5939
Marna Pacheco, CEO
EMP: 6 EST: 2016
SQ FT: 5,400
SALES (est): 385.37K **Privately Held**
Web: www.capeable.com
SIC: 2392 Blankets, comforters and beddings

(G-4833)
CAPRICE BOYB
Also Called: Hautefirebeauty
702 Tennessee Ave (46805-4122)
PHONE..................260 442-1736
Caprice Boyb, Owner
EMP: 1 EST: 2020
SALES (est): 40K **Privately Held**
SIC: 3634 Massage machines, electric, except for beauty/barber shops

(G-4834)
CAROL BUTLER
8324 Lamplighter Ct (46835-4498)
PHONE..................201 292-4364
Carol Butler, Prin
EMP: 4 EST: 2017
SALES (est): 75.49K **Privately Held**
Web: www.lamplighterpondmjk.com
SIC: 2741 Miscellaneous publishing

(G-4835)
CARTERS LLC
2200 Lafontaine St (46802-6967)
PHONE..................260 432-3568
EMP: 11 EST: 2016
SALES (est): 314.07K **Privately Held**
Web: www.masolite.com
SIC: 3272 Concrete products, nec

(G-4836)
CARTERS CONCRETE BLOCK INC (PA)
Also Called: Frankfort Masonry & Supply
2200 Lafontain St (46802-6967)
PHONE..................574 722-2644
Steve Carter, Pr
David Carter, VP

Linda Carter, Sec
EMP: 20 EST: 1943
SALES (est): 2.46MM
SALES (corp-wide): 2.46MM **Privately Held**
SIC: 3272 5211 Concrete structural support and building material; Brick

(G-4837)
CASTLETON VILLAGE CENTER INC (PA)
Also Called: Hightech Signs
6321 Huguenard Rd Ste A (46818-1503)
PHONE..................260 471-5959
Doug Abramowski, Pr
Stanley A Abramowski, Pr
Marjorie Abramowski, Ch Bd
▲ EMP: 11 EST: 1993
SALES (est): 2.31MM **Privately Held**
Web: www.hightech-signs.com
SIC: 3993 Signs, not made in custom sign painting shops

(G-4838)
CAT PEOPLE PRESS LLC
1836 Glenwood Ave (46805-2732)
PHONE..................260 750-8652
Rebecca Stockert, Managing Member
EMP: 1 EST: 2017
SALES (est): 57.49K **Privately Held**
Web: www.catpeoplepress.com
SIC: 2741 Miscellaneous publishing

(G-4839)
CENTERLINE MANUFACTURING INC
4611 Newaygo Rd Ste E (46808-4117)
PHONE..................260 348-7400
Chris Croy, Pr
EMP: 1 EST: 2009
SALES (est): 10.53K **Privately Held**
Web: www.clmanufacturing.com
SIC: 3999 Manufacturing industries, nec

(G-4840)
CENTRAL COCA-COLA BTLG CO INC
Coca-Cola
5010 Airport Expy (46809-9644)
PHONE..................260 478-2978
EMP: 60
SQ FT: 200,000
SALES (corp-wide): 45.75B **Publicly Held**
Web: www.coca-cola.com
SIC: 2086 Bottled and canned soft drinks
HQ: Central Coca-Cola Bottling Company, Inc.
555 Taxter Rd Ste 550
Elmsford NY 10523
914 789-1100

(G-4841)
CERTIFIED CHOICE TRUCKERS LLC
1211 Bethany Ln (46825-4607)
PHONE..................260 615-3437
EMP: 6 EST: 2021
SALES (est): 322.34K **Privately Held**
SIC: 3537 7389 Trucks, tractors, loaders, carriers, and similar equipment; Business Activities at Non-Commercial Site

(G-4842)
CFN 260 LLC
5625 Breconshire Dr (46804-1601)
PHONE..................260 241-5678
EMP: 1
SALES (est): 69.25K **Privately Held**
SIC: 7389 2389 Business Activities at Non-Commercial Site; Apparel and accessories, nec

(G-4843)
CHARLIE N83 INC
12207 Illinois Rd (46814-9103)
PHONE..................260 625-4211
Gary Probst, Pr
EMP: 1 EST: 1987
SALES (est): 264.17K **Privately Held**
SIC: 3721 Aircraft

(G-4844)
CHEM-DRY OF ALLEN COUNTY
Also Called: Chem-Dry
10214 Chestnut Plaza Dr (46814-8970)
PHONE..................260 490-2705
EMP: 5 EST: 2006
SALES (est): 20.74K **Privately Held**
Web: www.cdallencounty.com
SIC: 7349 2842 Building maintenance services, nec; Polishes and sanitation goods

(G-4845)
CHESSEX MANUFACTURING CO LLC
Also Called: Chessex
3415 Centennial Dr (46808-4515)
P.O. Box 80255 (46898-0255)
PHONE..................260 471-9511
▲ EMP: 13 EST: 1998
SALES (est): 2.41MM **Privately Held**
Web: www.chessex.com
SIC: 3944 Dice and dice cups

(G-4846)
CHUCK BIVENS SERVICES INC
Also Called: States Engineering
10216 Airport Dr (46809-3025)
P.O. Box 9590 (46899-9590)
PHONE..................260 747-6195
Chuck Bivens, Pr
▼ EMP: 13 EST: 1946
SQ FT: 48,000
SALES (est): 1.77MM **Privately Held**
Web: www.statesengineeringinc.com
SIC: 3559 Foundry machinery and equipment

(G-4847)
CI PUBLISHING ECOMM LLC ✪
5534 Saint Joe Rd (46835-3328)
PHONE..................317 679-1866
Candy Irven, Managing Member
EMP: 1 EST: 2023
SALES (est): 69.27K **Privately Held**
SIC: 2721 Periodicals, publishing only

(G-4848)
CINDA B USA LLC
Also Called: Cinda B
1530 Progress Rd (46808-1181)
PHONE..................260 469-0803
Jon Adams, Pr
▲ EMP: 5 EST: 2008
SALES (est): 923.44K **Privately Held**
Web: www.cindab.com
SIC: 5137 3161 Handbags; Traveling bags

(G-4849)
CITY OF FORT WAYNE
Also Called: Street Department
1701 Lafayette St (46803-2320)
PHONE..................260 427-1235
Brad Baumgartner, Commsnr
EMP: 44
SALES (corp-wide): 427.84MM **Privately Held**
Web: www.cityoffortwayne.org
SIC: 3991 Street sweeping brooms, hand or machine
PA: City Of Fort Wayne
200 East Berry St Ste 425
Fort Wayne IN 46802

260 427-1111

(G-4850)
CK PRODUCTS LLC
Also Called: CK Products
6230 Innovation Blvd (46818-1399)
PHONE..................260 484-2517
◆ EMP: 95 EST: 1965
SQ FT: 55,000
SALES (est): 17.22MM **Privately Held**
Web: www.ckproducts.com
SIC: 2064 Candy and other confectionery products
PA: Central Investment Llc
7265 Kenwood Rd Ste 240
Cincinnati OH 45236

(G-4851)
CLARIOS LLC
Also Called: Johnson Controls
6010 Brandy Chase Cv (46815-7601)
PHONE..................260 485-9999
EMP: 30
SALES (corp-wide): 69.83B **Privately Held**
Web: www.clarios.com
SIC: 2531 Seats, automobile
HQ: Clarios, Llc
5757 N Green Bay Ave Flor
Glendale WI 53209

(G-4852)
CLARIOS LLC
8710 Indianapolis Rd (46809-9793)
PHONE..................260 479-4400
Bruce Beach, Mgr
EMP: 150
SALES (corp-wide): 69.83B **Privately Held**
Web: www.clarios.com
SIC: 2531 Seats, automobile
HQ: Clarios, Llc
5757 N Green Bay Ave Flor
Glendale WI 53209

(G-4853)
CLASSIC GRAPHICS INC
Also Called: Copy Quick
4211 Earth Dr (46809-1513)
PHONE..................260 482-3487
James T Meier, Pr
Victoria Meier, VP
EMP: 11 EST: 1971
SALES (est): 517.8K **Privately Held**
Web: www.classicgraphicsprinting.com
SIC: 2752 7336 2791 2789 Offset printing; Commercial art and graphic design; Typesetting; Bookbinding and related work

(G-4854)
CLASSIC LLC
11512 Carroll Lynn Dr (46818-9567)
PHONE..................260 241-4353
Zachary J Weidler, CEO
EMP: 4 EST: 2020
SALES (est): 87.42K **Privately Held**
SIC: 2752 Commercial printing, lithographic

(G-4855)
CLASSIC PRODUCTS CORP (PA)
Also Called: Classic
4617 Industrial Rd (46825-5268)
PHONE..................260 484-2695
Mikel S Eid, Pr
Mike S Eid, *
Bob F Jesse, *
Bob Gudorf, *
▲ EMP: 50 EST: 1987
SQ FT: 38,500
SALES (est): 45.77MM
SALES (corp-wide): 45.77MM **Privately Held**
Web: bowl2.classicproducts.com

Fort Wayne - Allen County (G-4856) GEOGRAPHIC SECTION

SIC: **5091** 2262 2395 5044 Bowling equipment; Screen printing: manmade fiber and silk broadwoven fabrics; Embroidery and art needlework; Photocopy machines

(G-4856)
CLASSIC ROCK FACE BLOCK INC
520 Southview Ave (46806-3032)
PHONE..................260 704-3113
Bart Babis, *Sls Dir*
EMP: 7 **EST:** 2010
SALES (est): 123.39K **Privately Held**
Web: www.classicrockfaceblock.com
SIC: **1499** Precious stones mining, nec

(G-4857)
CLEAN BY DESIGN INC
1509 Holly Ridge Run (46845-2028)
PHONE..................260 414-4444
Karry Hook, *Pr*
EMP: 1 **EST:** 2011
SALES (est): 64.67K **Privately Held**
SIC: **7389** 7349 3089 Design services; Cleaning service, industrial or commercial; Organizers for closets, drawers, etc.: plastics

(G-4858)
CLEAR WATERS SERENITY CENTER
3207 Covington Rd (46802-4440)
PHONE..................260 459-9200
Julie Peters, *Owner*
EMP: 1 **EST:** 2006
SALES (est): 119.39K **Privately Held**
Web: www.fortwayneserenitycenter.com
SIC: **3829** Stress, strain, and flaw detecting/ measuring equipment

(G-4859)
CLEAVER ENTERPRISES INC
11334 Bay Pines Ct (46814-9041)
PHONE..................260 625-5822
EMP: 1 **EST:** 2007
SALES (est): 60K **Privately Held**
SIC: **3421** Cleavers

(G-4860)
CLIFF A OSTERMEYER
Also Called: Music Town Distributors
1727 N Glendale Dr (46804-5853)
PHONE..................615 361-7902
Cliff A Ostermeyer, *Owner*
EMP: 8 **EST:** 1951
SALES (est): 486.55K **Privately Held**
SIC: **2711** 6794 3652 7389 Newspapers: publishing only, not printed on site; Copyright buying and licensing; Prerecorded records and tapes; Music and broadcasting services

(G-4861)
CMA STEEL & FABRICATION INC
3333 Independence Dr (46808-4516)
PHONE..................260 207-9000
Roger Dammeier, *VP*
EMP: 11 **EST:** 2006
SALES (est): 263.4K **Privately Held**
SIC: **3449** Bars, concrete reinforcing: fabricated steel

(G-4862)
CMA SUPPLY CO FORT WAYNE INC
Also Called: CMA Supply
3333 Independence Dr (46808-4516)
PHONE..................260 471-9000
Bill Updike, *Pr*
Jeffery Degitz, *VP*
Roger Dammeier, *VP*
Jeffery T Degitz, *VP*
Elizabeth Updike, *Sec*
EMP: 23 **EST:** 1992
SQ FT: 15,000
SALES (est): 988K **Privately Held**
Web: www.whitecap.com
SIC: **5032** 3444 Concrete building products; Concrete forms, sheet metal

(G-4863)
CNC INDUSTRIES INC
3810 Fourier Dr (46818-9381)
PHONE..................260 490-5700
EMP: 45 **EST:** 1995
SQ FT: 40,000
SALES (est): 9.18MM **Privately Held**
Web: www.cncind.com
SIC: **3469** 3599 3728 Machine parts, stamped or pressed metal; Machine shop, jobbing and repair; Aircraft parts and equipment, nec

(G-4864)
COCOALOCA COSMETICS LLC
5337 Stonehedge Blvd (46835-3005)
PHONE..................352 246-6629
EMP: 1 **EST:** 2021
SALES (est): 47.23K **Privately Held**
SIC: **2844** Cosmetic preparations

(G-4865)
COFFEE LOMONT & MOYER INC
Also Called: Gensic Creative Metals
1205 W Main St (46808-3334)
PHONE..................260 422-7825
Jeannine Moyer, *CFO*
Jeannine Moyer, *Treas*
Daniel Lomont, *Ex VP*
Kathleen Lomont, *Sec*
EMP: 19 **EST:** 1959
SQ FT: 9,000
SALES (est): 980.83K **Privately Held**
Web: www.gensic.com
SIC: **3449** 3446 3444 3443 Miscellaneous metalwork; Architectural metalwork; Sheet metalwork; Fabricated plate work (boiler shop)

(G-4866)
COMMERCIAL SIGNS INC
Also Called: Commercial School of Lettering
513 E Hawthorne St (46806-3025)
PHONE..................260 745-2678
Garry Merrills, *Pr*
Diana Chamber, *VP*
EMP: 7 **EST:** 1953
SQ FT: 5,000
SALES (est): 871.01K **Privately Held**
Web: www.commercialsigns1.com
SIC: **3993** 5085 Signs, not made in custom sign painting shops; Signmaker equipment and supplies

(G-4867)
COMMERCIAL TECHNICAL SVCS INC
Also Called: Ctsi
2809 Carrington Dr (46804-6062)
PHONE..................260 436-9898
Vernon C Torres, *Pr*
EMP: 3 **EST:** 1997
SALES (est): 118.95K **Privately Held**
SIC: **3999** Manufacturing industries, nec

(G-4868)
COMPLETE CONTROLS INC
3923 Option Pass (46818-1275)
PHONE..................260 489-0852
Mark A Lewis, *Pr*
EMP: 5 **EST:** 1988
SALES (est): 970.65K **Privately Held**
Web: www.completecontrolsinc.com

SIC: **3823** 7699 1731 Temperature measurement instruments, industrial; Boiler and heating repair services; Electronic controls installation

(G-4869)
COMPLETE DRIVES INC (PA)
Also Called: C D I
6419 Discount Dr (46818-1235)
PHONE..................260 489-6033
Gregory D Hale, *Pr*
John Klopfenstein, *VP*
Steve King, *VP*
David Happel, *VP*
Dan Crozier, *Sec*
EMP: 16 **EST:** 1987
SQ FT: 14,000
SALES (est): 5.98MM
SALES (corp-wide): 5.98MM **Privately Held**
Web: www.completedrivesinc.com
SIC: **3566** Bushings and bearings

(G-4870)
COMPOSITES SYNDICATE LLC
Also Called: Plastic Composites Co.
8301 Clinton Park Dr (46825-3164)
PHONE..................260 484-3139
EMP: 12 **EST:** 2014
SQ FT: 34,000
SALES (est): 846.38K **Privately Held**
Web: www.buckettruckparts.com
SIC: **3089** Plastics and fiberglass tanks

(G-4871)
COOPER TRANSIT LLC
14105 Aloes Psge (46845-0036)
PHONE..................260 797-3003
EMP: 1
SALES (est): 65.99K **Privately Held**
SIC: **3537** 7389 Trucks: freight, baggage, etc.: industrial, except mining; Business Activities at Non-Commercial Site

(G-4872)
COOPER-STANDARD AUTOMOTIVE INC
Also Called: Cooper
9910 Dupont Circle Dr E (46825-0042)
PHONE..................260 247-7703
EMP: 24
SALES (corp-wide): 2.82B **Publicly Held**
Web: www.cooperstandard.com
SIC: **3714** Motor vehicle parts and accessories
HQ: Cooper-Standard Automotive Inc.
40300 Traditions Dr
Northville MI 48168
248 596-5900

(G-4873)
COPPER KTTLE FUDGE POPCORN LLC
4714 Union Chapel Rd (46845-9217)
PHONE..................260 417-1036
Carl Weaver, *Prin*
EMP: 6 **EST:** 2010
SALES (est): 213.99K **Privately Held**
Web: www.copperkettlepopcorn.com
SIC: **2064** Fudge (candy)

(G-4874)
COPY SOLUTIONS INC
6338 W Jefferson Blvd (46804)
PHONE..................260 436-2679
James Matthews, *Pr*
Kathy L Matthews, *Pr*
James Matthews, *VP*
EMP: 8 **EST:** 1991
SALES (est): 929.15K **Privately Held**
Web: www.yourcopysolution.com
SIC: **7334** 2752 Blueprinting service; Commercial printing, lithographic

(G-4875)
CORE BIOLOGIC LLC
3201 Stellhorn Rd (46815-4697)
PHONE..................888 390-8838
EMP: 6 **EST:** 2014
SALES (est): 231.5K **Privately Held**
SIC: **2835** Microbiology and virology diagnostic products

(G-4876)
CORE LABORATORIES LP
1726 Saint Joe River Dr (46805-1436)
PHONE..................260 312-0455
EMP: 4
Web: www.corelab.com
SIC: **1389** Oil field services, nec
PA: Core Laboratories Lp
6316 Windfern Rd
Houston TX 77040

(G-4877)
CORE-TECH INC
6000 Maumee Rd (46803-1750)
PHONE..................260 748-4477
▲ **EMP:** 65 **EST:** 1991
SQ FT: 40,000
SALES (est): 5.09MM **Privately Held**
Web: www.coretech1.com
SIC: **3543** Industrial patterns

(G-4878)
COREBIOLOGIC LLC
4415 Winding Brook Rd (46814-9449)
PHONE..................260 437-0353
EMP: 6 **EST:** 2016
SALES (est): 238.9K **Privately Held**
Web: www.corebiologic.com
SIC: **2836** Biological products, except diagnostic

(G-4879)
COURAGIO PRESS LLC
2226 Lawndale Dr (46805-3727)
PHONE..................260 471-5603
Larry Merino, *Owner*
EMP: 5 **EST:** 2014
SALES (est): 73.98K **Privately Held**
SIC: **2741** Miscellaneous publishing

(G-4880)
COX CLEANING SERVICES
6435 W Jefferson Blvd Num 140 (46804-6203)
PHONE..................260 804-9001
EMP: 1 **EST:** 2017
SALES (est): 70.05K **Privately Held**
Web: www.coxcleaningservices.com
SIC: **3589** 7699 High pressure cleaning equipment; Cleaning services

(G-4881)
CPI CARD GROUP - INDIANA INC
613 High St (46808-3440)
P.O. Box 10748 (46853-0748)
PHONE..................260 424-4920
Steve Montross, *Prin*
Anna Rossetti, *
Jerry Dreiling, *
Diane Jackson, *
Docia Myer, *
▲ **EMP:** 130 **EST:** 1947
SQ FT: 28,800
SALES (est): 22.89MM
SALES (corp-wide): 444.55MM **Publicly Held**
Web: www.cpicardgroup.com

GEOGRAPHIC SECTION
Fort Wayne - Allen County (G-4905)

SIC: 3089 Identification cards, plastics
HQ: Cpi Card Group - Colorado, Inc.
10368 W Centennial Rd A
Littleton CO 80127
720 681-6304

(G-4882)
CRAFT LABORATORIES INC
1901 Lakeview Dr (46803-3919)
PHONE.............................260 432-9467
R William Munsie, Sec
EMP: 24 EST: 1968
SQ FT: 35,000
SALES (est): 4.93MM Privately Held
Web: www.craftlabs.com
SIC: 2841 5169 2819 5084 Soap and other detergents; Chemicals and allied products, nec; Industrial inorganic chemicals, nec; Industrial machinery and equipment

(G-4883)
CRAFTSMAN SPECIALTIES
6535 Felger Rd (46818-9450)
PHONE.............................260 705-5388
Steve Dillman, Prin
EMP: 1 EST: 2008
SALES (est): 156.5K Privately Held
Web: www.craftsmanspec.com
SIC: 3553 Cabinet makers' machinery

(G-4884)
CREATIVE POWDER COATINGS LLC
Also Called: Creative Coatings
7505 Freedom Way (46818-2164)
PHONE.............................260 489-3580
Don Harper, Managing Member
Richard Lain, *
EMP: 60 EST: 2005
SQ FT: 106,000
SALES (est): 8.81MM Privately Held
Web: www.creativecoatingsinc.com
SIC: 3399 Powder, metal

(G-4885)
CREATIVE SIGN RESOURCES LLC (PA)
4707 E Washington Blvd (46803)
P.O. Box 10743 (46853)
PHONE.............................260 425-9618
EMP: 20 EST: 2001
SQ FT: 16,000
SALES (est): 2.35MM
SALES (corp-wide): 2.35MM Privately Held
Web: www.creativesignresources.com
SIC: 3993 Signs and advertising specialties

(G-4886)
CREATIVE SIGNS
4117 Merchant Rd (46818-1247)
PHONE.............................260 438-6352
EMP: 5 EST: 2019
SALES (est): 94.5K Privately Held
Web: www.creativesignresources.com
SIC: 3993 Signs and advertising specialties

(G-4887)
CREATIVE WOODWORKS LLC
9771 Maysville Rd (46815-4419)
PHONE.............................260 450-1742
EMP: 2 EST: 2001
SQ FT: 2,500
SALES (est): 163.58K Privately Held
Web: www.creativewoodllc.com
SIC: 2599 Cabinets, factory

(G-4888)
CROWN BATTERY MANUFACTURING CO
3000 E Washington Blvd (46803-1534)
PHONE.............................260 423-3358
Kenneth Talbert, Prin
EMP: 5
SALES (corp-wide): 105.99MM Privately Held
Web: www.crownbattery.com
SIC: 3691 Storage batteries
PA: Crown Battery Manufacturing Company
1445 Majestic Dr
Fremont OH 43420
419 334-7181

(G-4889)
CROWN EQUIPMENT CORPORATION
Also Called: Crown Lift Trucks-Ft Wayne
9110 Avionics Dr (46809-9657)
PHONE.............................260 484-0055
Troy Boyer, Mgr
EMP: 80
SQ FT: 11,000
SALES (corp-wide): 7.12B Privately Held
Web: www.crown.com
SIC: 3537 Lift trucks, industrial: fork, platform, straddle, etc.
PA: Crown Equipment Corporation
44 S Washington St
New Bremen OH 45869
419 629-2311

(G-4890)
CROWN GROUP CO
4301 Engle Ridge Dr (46804-4440)
PHONE.............................260 432-6900
EMP: 48
SALES (corp-wide): 17.65B Publicly Held
Web: www.thecrowngrp.com
SIC: 3479 Coating of metals and formed products
HQ: The Crown Group Co
1340 Neubrecht Rd
Lima OH 45801
586 575-9800

(G-4891)
CRS-DRS CORPORATION
Also Called: Dunham Rbr Blting Corp A Belt
4004 Lower Huntington Rd (46809-9710)
PHONE.............................260 478-7555
Crystal Hues, Brnch Mgr
EMP: 5
SALES (corp-wide): 17.08MM Privately Held
Web: www.dunhamrubber.com
SIC: 5085 5162 5251 3052 Rubber goods, mechanical; Plastics materials and basic shapes; Hardware stores; Rubber and plastics hose and beltings
PA: Crs-Drs Corporation
682 Commerce Pkwy W Dr
Greenwood IN 46143
317 888-3002

(G-4892)
CUMBERLAND MILLWORK & SUPPLY
Also Called: CUMBERLAND MILLWORK & SUPPLY INC
5736 Industrial Rd (46825-5128)
PHONE.............................260 471-6936
Jeff Lane, Sls Mgr
EMP: 4
Web: www.cumberlandtdd.com
SIC: 2431 Millwork
PA: Cumberland Millwork & Supply, Inc.
3025 Highway 90
Bronston KY 42518

(G-4893)
CUMMINGS HOLDINGS LLC
Also Called: Cummings Production Machining
1432 E Gump Rd (46845-9795)
PHONE.............................260 493-4405
EMP: 35
SIC: 3499 Machine bases, metal

(G-4894)
CUMMINS CROSSPOINT LLC
Also Called: Cummins
3415 W Coliseum Blvd (46808-1026)
PHONE.............................260 482-3691
Steve Gregg, Brnch Mgr
EMP: 37
SALES (corp-wide): 34.06B Publicly Held
Web: www.cummins.com
SIC: 5084 3519 Engines and parts, diesel; Internal combustion engines, nec
HQ: Cummins Crosspoint Llc
111 Monument Cir Ste 601
Indianapolis IN 46204
317 243-7979

(G-4895)
CUMMINS INC
Also Called: Cummins
3415 W Coliseum Blvd (46808-1026)
PHONE.............................260 482-3691
EMP: 5
SALES (corp-wide): 34.06B Publicly Held
Web: www.cummins.com
SIC: 5063 3714 Electrical apparatus and equipment; Motor vehicle parts and accessories
PA: Cummins Inc.
500 Jackson St
Columbus IN 47201
812 377-5000

(G-4896)
CUMMINS SALES SVC
3415 W Coliseum Blvd (46808-1026)
PHONE.............................260 482-3691
EMP: 4 EST: 2019
SALES (est): 71.73K Privately Held
SIC: 3714 Motor vehicle parts and accessories

(G-4897)
CUSTOM CREATIONS MGT LLC ✪
Also Called: Hard Workin Hard Livin
5534 Saint Joe Rd (46835)
PHONE.............................765 491-8434
EMP: 1 EST: 2022
SALES (est): 60K Privately Held
Web: www.hardworkinhardlivin.com
SIC: 3993 Signs and advertising specialties

(G-4898)
CUSTOM ENGRG & FABRICATION INC
2211 Freeman St (46802-6926)
PHONE.............................260 745-9299
Bob Hatfield, Prin
Todd Walter, Prin
James Davis, Prin
John Wilson, Prin
Deb Parker, Prin
EMP: 28 EST: 1998
SQ FT: 38,000
SALES (est): 4.15MM Privately Held
Web: www.ceandf.com
SIC: 3599 Machine shop, jobbing and repair

(G-4899)
CUSTOM SIGNS UNLIMITED CO
1410 Goshen Ave (46808-2036)
PHONE.............................260 483-4444
Dan Cameron, Owner
EMP: 2 EST: 2009
SALES (est): 208.65K Privately Held
Web: www.fortwaynecustomsigns.com
SIC: 3993 Electric signs

(G-4900)
CUSTOM SOFTWARE SOLUTIONS INC
1737 Traders Xing (46845-1535)
PHONE.............................260 637-8393
Michael Muzzillo, Prin
Mike Muzzill, Owner
EMP: 1 EST: 2000
SALES (est): 104.84K Privately Held
Web: www.css-oc.com
SIC: 7371 7372 Computer software development; Prepackaged software

(G-4901)
D & M ENTERPRISES LLC
Also Called: Custom Poly Packaging
3216 Congressional Pkwy (46808-4417)
PHONE.............................260 483-4008
Kim Schmidt, Mng Pt
EMP: 13 EST: 1957
SQ FT: 13,000
SALES (est): 2.07MM Privately Held
Web: www.custompoly.com
SIC: 2673 3081 Plastic bags: made from purchased materials; Unsupported plastics film and sheet

(G-4902)
D&W FINE PACK LLC
Also Called: C&M Fine Pack
7707 Vicksburg Pike (46804-5549)
P.O. Box 12347 (46863-2347)
PHONE.............................260 432-3027
Darrin Claussin, Genl Mgr
EMP: 75
SALES (corp-wide): 506.9MM Privately Held
Web: www.dwfinepack.com
SIC: 3089 Plastics containers, except foam
HQ: D&W Fine Pack Llc
777 Mark St
Wood Dale IL 60191

(G-4903)
DANA INCORPORATED
2100 W State Blvd (46808-1998)
PHONE.............................260 481-3597
EMP: 222
Web: www.dana.com
SIC: 3714 Motor vehicle parts and accessories
PA: Dana Incorporated
3939 Technology Dr
Maumee OH 43537

(G-4904)
DANA LIGHT AXLE PRODUCTS LLC (DH)
Also Called: Dana Light Axle Products
2100 W State Blvd (46808-1937)
PHONE.............................260 483-7174
◆ EMP: 16 EST: 2007
SALES (est): 38.37MM Publicly Held
Web: www.dana.com
SIC: 3714 Motor vehicle parts and accessories
HQ: Dana Automotive Systems Group, Llc
3939 Technology Dr
Maumee OH 43537

(G-4905)
DATA PRINT INITIATIVES LLC
1710 Dividend Rd (46808-1131)
PHONE.............................260 489-2665
Daniel T Foster, CEO
Jim Cawvey, VP
EMP: 9 EST: 2004
SALES (est): 1.15MM Privately Held
Web: www.dataprintusa.com
SIC: 2752 Offset printing

Fort Wayne - Allen County (G-4906)   GEOGRAPHIC SECTION

(G-4906)
DAUENHAUER GLASS COMPANY INC
12230 Chesterbrook Ct (46845-1966)
PHONE..................260 433-5876
Leo Dauenhauer, *Ch*
EMP: 1 EST: 2003
SALES (est): 55.63K **Privately Held**
Web: www.okinawanflatbellytonic.com
SIC: 5961 3949 Catalog sales; Shafts, golf club

(G-4907)
DAVIS VACHON ARTWORKS
227 W Wallen Rd (46825-2223)
PHONE..................260 489-9160
Davis Vachon, *Owner*
EMP: 2 EST: 1988
SALES (est): 57.91K **Privately Held**
Web: www.vachonarts.com
SIC: 3269 Stoneware pottery products

(G-4908)
DEAD END SKATEBOARDS LLC
7713 Placer Run (46815-8241)
PHONE..................970 699-6410
EMP: 3 EST: 2018
SALES (est): 47.08K **Privately Held**
Web: www.deadendskateboards.com
SIC: 3949 Skateboards

(G-4909)
DEBRAND INC (PA)
Also Called: Debrand Fine Chocolates
10105 Auburn Park Dr (46825-2388)
PHONE..................260 969-8333
Cathy Brand Beere, *Pr*
Timothy L Beere, *
▲ EMP: 90 EST: 1987
SQ FT: 3,000
SALES (est): 16.27MM **Privately Held**
Web: www.debrand.com
SIC: 2064 2066 Chocolate candy, except solid chocolate; Chocolate and cocoa products

(G-4910)
DEFINING TRNDSTTING CSTM PRINT
2050 Lafayette St (46803-3324)
PHONE..................260 755-1038
EMP: 1 EST: 2018
SALES (est): 46.75K **Privately Held**
SIC: 2759 Commercial printing, nec

(G-4911)
DEISTER CONCENTRATOR NA LLC
◆
Also Called: Deister Concentrator
3210 Freeman St (46802-4433)
PHONE..................260 747-2700
Matthew Wojewuczki, *Pr*
EMP: 12 EST: 2022
SALES (est): 1.52MM
SALES (corp-wide): 57.3MM **Privately Held**
Web: www.deisterconcentrator.com
SIC: 3462 Construction or mining equipment forgings, ferrous
PA: Na Holding Corp.
    4220 Angela Way
    Canandaigua NY 14424
    260 918-6041

(G-4912)
DEISTER MACHINE COMPANY INC
1604 E Berry St (46803-1021)
PHONE..................260 422-0354
EMP: 25
SALES (corp-wide): 46.7MM **Privately Held**
Web: www.deistermachine.com
SIC: 3444 3441 3532 Sheet metalwork; Fabricated structural metal; Separating machinery, mineral
PA: Deister Machine Company Inc
    1933 E Wayne St
    Fort Wayne IN 46803
    260 426-7495

(G-4913)
DEISTER MACHINE COMPANY INC
901 Glasgow Ave (46803-1308)
PHONE..................260 426-7495
Greg Wood, *Brnch Mgr*
EMP: 25
SALES (corp-wide): 46.7MM **Privately Held**
Web: www.deistermachine.com
SIC: 3532 Separating machinery, mineral
PA: Deister Machine Company Inc
    1933 E Wayne St
    Fort Wayne IN 46803
    260 426-7495

(G-4914)
DEISTER MACHINE COMPANY INC (PA)
1933 E Wayne St (46803-1332)
P.O. Box 1 (46801-0001)
PHONE..................260 426-7495
Irwin F Deister Junior, *Ch Bd*
E Mark Deister, *
▼ EMP: 200 EST: 1912
SQ FT: 65,000
SALES (est): 46.7MM
SALES (corp-wide): 46.7MM **Privately Held**
Web: www.deistermachine.com
SIC: 3532 Separating machinery, mineral

(G-4915)
DENTISSE INC
10542 Coldwater Rd Ste B (46845-1269)
PHONE..................260 444-3046
Michael Moore, *Pr*
Mark Putt, *VP*
David Dimberio, *Sec*
Nate Reusser, *Treas*
EMP: 5 EST: 2007
SALES (est): 249.25K **Privately Held**
Web: www.dentisse.com
SIC: 2844 Toothpastes or powders, dentifrices

(G-4916)
DEPRISCO VENTURES INC
Also Called: Adaptek Systems
14224 Plank St (46818-9092)
PHONE..................260 637-8660
Joseph G Deprisco, *Pr*
EMP: 35 EST: 1989
SQ FT: 14,000
SALES (est): 5.63MM
SALES (corp-wide): 43.58MM **Privately Held**
Web: www.adapteksystems.com
SIC: 3569 3699 3829 Assembly machines, non-metalworking; Electrical equipment and supplies, nec; Physical property testing equipment
PA: Huizenga Manufacturing Group, Inc.
    3755 36th St Se Ste 200
    Grand Rapids MI 49512
    616 957-0398

(G-4917)
DIRECT POINT LLC
200 6th St (46808-3286)
PHONE..................260 705-2279
EMP: 7 EST: 2011
SALES (est): 292.1K **Privately Held**
SIC: 2732 Book printing

(G-4918)
DISKEY ARCHITECTURAL SIGNAGE
450 E Brackenridge St (46802-3521)
P.O. Box 12100 (46862-2100)
PHONE..................260 424-0233
Mike Butler, *Pr*
Catherine Butler, *VP*
EMP: 10 EST: 1924
SQ FT: 2,000
SALES (est): 1.03MM **Privately Held**
Web: www.diskeysign.com
SIC: 3993 Signs, not made in custom sign painting shops

(G-4919)
DIVERSIFIED TOOLS AND MCHS INC
2701 W Wallen Rd (46818-2240)
PHONE..................260 489-0272
Richard Eversole, *Pr*
Ty Deveau, *CEO*
EMP: 7 EST: 1990
SQ FT: 5,700
SALES (est): 948.02K **Privately Held**
Web: www.diversifiedtoolsinc.com
SIC: 3544 Special dies and tools

(G-4920)
DKM EMBROIDERY INC
Also Called: Sg Trading Post
3203 Caprice Ct (46803)
P.O. Box 8895 (46898)
PHONE..................260 471-4070
Deborah K Mattox, *Pr*
▲ EMP: 8 EST: 1996
SALES (est): 994.13K **Privately Held**
Web: www.dkmembroidery.com
SIC: 2395 Embroidery products, except Schiffli machine

(G-4921)
DOELL DESIGNS
5211 Stellhorn Rd (46815-5057)
PHONE..................260 486-4504
Dave Doell, *Owner*
EMP: 2 EST: 1979
SQ FT: 3,000
SALES (est): 113.88K **Privately Held**
Web: www.doelldesigns.com
SIC: 7389 3993 Lettering and sign painting services; Signs, not made in custom sign painting shops

(G-4922)
DOMAIN INDUSTRIES LLC
Also Called: Aa Truck Sleeper LLC
3900 Transportation Dr (46818-1237)
P.O. Box 8099 (46898-8099)
PHONE..................800 227-5337
EMP: 8 EST: 2018
SALES (est): 266.04K **Privately Held**
Web: www.domainindustries.com
SIC: 3999 Manufacturing industries, nec

(G-4923)
DON R FRUCHEY INC
PWC Fabrication
2121 Wayne Haven St (46803-3280)
PHONE..................260 493-3626
Chuck Brewster, *Brnch Mgr*
EMP: 26
SALES (corp-wide): 20.09MM **Privately Held**
Web: www.donrfruchey.com
SIC: 3443 Fabricated plate work (boiler shop)
PA: Don R Fruchey Inc
    5608 Maumee Rd
    Fort Wayne IN 46803
    260 749-8502

(G-4924)
DONALD PAPE
3327 Collegiate Ct Rear (46805-1601)
PHONE..................260 484-6088
Donald Pape, *Owner*
EMP: 1 EST: 1999
SALES (est): 88.42K **Privately Held**
SIC: 3825 Network analyzers

(G-4925)
DONS SPECIALTY WELDING LLC
924 Mildred Ave (46808-2041)
PHONE..................260 557-3492
Donald L Pletcher, *Prin*
EMP: 4 EST: 2018
SALES (est): 77.66K **Privately Held**
SIC: 7692 Welding repair

(G-4926)
DOUBLE ENVELOPE CORP
10804 Lake Shasta Ct (46804-6907)
PHONE..................260 434-0500
Julie Shackley, *Pr*
EMP: 2 EST: 2008
SALES (est): 109.79K **Privately Held**
Web: www.double-envelope.com
SIC: 5112 2677 Envelopes; Envelopes

(G-4927)
DR PEPPER SNAPPLE GROUP I
2711 Independence Dr (46808-1331)
PHONE..................260 484-4177
EMP: 5 EST: 2014
SALES (est): 151.36K **Privately Held**
SIC: 2086 Soft drinks: packaged in cans, bottles, etc.

(G-4928)
DREYERS GRAND ICE CREAM INC
Also Called: Edys Grd Ice Cream
3426 N Wells St (46808-4001)
PHONE..................260 483-3102
Julia Zirpoli, *Mgr*
EMP: 256
SALES (corp-wide): 2.67MM **Privately Held**
Web: www.icecream.com
SIC: 5812 2024 Ice cream stands or dairy bars; Ice cream and frozen deserts
HQ: Dreyer's Grand Ice Cream, Inc.
    590 Ygnacio Valley Rd # 300
    Walnut Creek CA 94596
    510 594-9466

(G-4929)
DRY INC
Also Called: Dry Cleaners Secret
7201 Engle Rd (46804-2228)
PHONE..................503 977-9204
Scott Heim, *Pr*
EMP: 25 EST: 1997
SALES (est): 923.9K **Privately Held**
Web: www.summitbrands.com
SIC: 2842 Drycleaning preparations

(G-4930)
DUD(E)S N ROSES LLC
4325 Oakhurst Dr (46815-5249)
PHONE..................260 739-9053
EMP: 4 EST: 2020
SALES (est): 162.21K **Privately Held**
SIC: 3444 Sheet metal specialties, not stamped

(G-4931)
DUESENBURG INC
3330 Congressional Pkwy (46808-4439)
P.O. Box 50311 (46805-0311)
PHONE..................260 496-9650
Hunar Sakri, *Pr*

Renee Sakri, *Treas*
EMP: 8 **EST:** 2001
SQ FT: 27,000
SALES (est): 988.12K **Privately Held**
Web: www.duesenburg.com
SIC: 8711 3625 3569 Electrical or electronic engineering; Electric controls and control accessories, industrial; Liquid automation machinery and equipment

(G-4932)
DUPONT AND TONKEL PARTNERS LLC
10501 Day Lily Dr (46825-2763)
PHONE..............................260 444-2264
EMP: 5 **EST:** 2013
SALES (est): 186.39K **Privately Held**
SIC: 2879 Agricultural chemicals, nec

(G-4933)
DUPONT CIRCLE III
9910 Dupont Circle Dr E (46825-1617)
PHONE..............................260 489-9508
EMP: 2 **EST:** 2016
SALES (est): 74.42K **Privately Held**
SIC: 2879 Agricultural chemicals, nec

(G-4934)
DUPONT COMMONS LLC
10050 Bent Creek Blvd (46825-0023)
PHONE..............................260 637-3215
Hugh W Johnston Senior, *Prin*
EMP: 2 **EST:** 2012
SALES (est): 153.09K **Privately Held**
SIC: 2879 Agricultural chemicals, nec

(G-4935)
DX 4 LLC
Also Called: Proform
3518 S Maplecrest Rd (46806)
PHONE..............................260 749-0632
David Tippmann, *Managing Member*
EMP: 15 **EST:** 2005
SALES (est): 2.1MM **Privately Held**
Web: www.proformmfg.com
SIC: 3599 3443 7389 7699 Machine and other job shop work; Weldments; Metal cutting services; Welding equipment repair

(G-4936)
E & M TIRE SALVAGE INC
2609 S Clinton St (46803-3341)
PHONE..............................260 745-3016
Thomas Morgan, *Mgr*
EMP: 2 **EST:** 1961
SQ FT: 2,000
SALES (est): 180K **Privately Held**
SIC: 5531 5015 7534 Automotive tires; Tires, used: retail only; Tire recapping

(G-4937)
EAGLE FLOORING BROKERS INC
Also Called: Eagle Tile
220 Fernhill Ave (46805-1017)
PHONE..............................260 422-6100
Brady Wiggins, *Pr*
▲ **EMP:** 6 **EST:** 1986
SQ FT: 25,000
SALES (est): 942.5K **Privately Held**
Web: www.eagletileonline.com
SIC: 3996 Hard surface floor coverings, nec

(G-4938)
EASTERN ENGINEERING SUPPLY INC
1239 N Wells St (46808-2791)
PHONE..............................260 426-3119
Mark Langdon, *Prin*
EMP: 14
SALES (corp-wide): 6.55MM **Privately Held**

Web: www.easternengineering.com
SIC: 2759 5049 7334 Commercial printing, nec; Drafting supplies; Blueprinting service
PA: Eastern Engineering Supply, Inc.
2810 N Wheeling Ave
Muncie IN 47303
765 284-3119

(G-4939)
EBENEZER PRESS LLC
2121 Kenwood Ave (46805-2770)
PHONE..............................260 482-2864
Jeanne M Burger, *Prin*
EMP: 1 **EST:** 2007
SALES (est): 57.67K **Privately Held**
Web: www.ebenezerpress.com
SIC: 2741 Miscellaneous publishing

(G-4940)
EBONY & CO INC
3721 Plaza Dr (46806-4348)
P.O. Box 6656 (46896-0656)
PHONE..............................260 246-4691
Ebony E Sullivan, *Ch*
EMP: 6 **EST:** 2016
SALES (est): 77.63K **Privately Held**
SIC: 2711 Newspapers, publishing and printing

(G-4941)
ECP AMERICAN STEEL LLC (HQ)
Also Called: Engineered Products
3122 Engle Rd (46809)
PHONE..............................260 478-9101
Janneth Rusher, *Managing Member*
Eric Stetzel, *Managing Member*
EMP: 22 **EST:** 1933
SQ FT: 21,000
SALES (est): 23.7MM
SALES (corp-wide): 169.95MM **Privately Held**
Web: www.ecpamericansteel.com
SIC: 3496 Miscellaneous fabricated wire products
PA: Bishop Lifting Products, Inc.
2301 Commerce St Ste 110
Houston TX
713 674-2266

(G-4942)
EDELWEISS EDGE LLC
5316 Hopkinton Dr (46814-7549)
PHONE..............................260 399-6692
Erik Magner, *Prin*
EMP: 2 **EST:** 2009
SALES (est): 205.87K **Privately Held**
Web: www.meistercook.com
SIC: 3589 Food warming equipment, commercial

(G-4943)
EL MEXICANO INC
Also Called: El Mexicano Newspaper
2301 Fairfield Ave Ste 102 (46807-1247)
PHONE..............................260 456-6843
Fernando Zapari, *Pr*
EMP: 4 **EST:** 1994
SALES (est): 195.51K **Privately Held**
Web: www.elmexicanonews.com
SIC: 2741 2711 Miscellaneous publishing; Newspapers

(G-4944)
ELECTRICAL MOTOR PRODUCTS INC
15009 Dunton Rd (46845-9380)
PHONE..............................877 455-1599
Chuck Koehl, *Prin*
EMP: 2 **EST:** 2001
SALES (est): 221.54K **Privately Held**
Web: www.empinc.biz

SIC: 7694 Electric motor repair

(G-4945)
ELEKTRSOLA DR GERD SCHLDBACH G
Also Called: REA Magnet Wire
4300 New Haven Ave (46803)
PHONE..............................260 421-5400
Mike Shannon, *Mgr*
EMP: 400
SALES (corp-wide): 1.88MM **Privately Held**
Web: www.reawire.com
SIC: 3357 Nonferrous wiredrawing and insulating
HQ: Elektrisola Dr. Gerd Schildbach Gmbh & Co. Kg
Zur Steinagger 3
Reichshof NW 51580
2265120

(G-4946)
ELLISON BAKERY LLC
Also Called: Darlington Farms
4108 W Ferguson Rd (46809-3141)
PHONE..............................800 711-8091
▼ **EMP:** 150 **EST:** 1945
SALES (est): 24.62MM **Privately Held**
Web: www.ebakery.com
SIC: 2052 Cookies

(G-4947)
ELRINGKLINGER MFG IND INC
Also Called: Ekmi
2677 Persistence Dr (46808-1496)
PHONE..............................734 788-1776
Jurgen Weingartner, *Pr*
EMP: 50 **EST:** 2018
SALES (est): 10MM
SALES (corp-wide): 355.83K **Privately Held**
Web: www.elringklinger.de
SIC: 3711 Automobile assembly, including specialty automobiles
HQ: Elringklinger Ag
Max-Eyth-Str. 2
Dettingen An Der Erms BW 72581
71237240

(G-4948)
EMBOSSTEK
7525 Maplecrest Rd (46835-1897)
P.O. Box 15456 (46885-5456)
PHONE..............................260 484-7700
EMP: 1 **EST:** 1994
SALES (est): 147.59K **Privately Held**
Web: www.embosstek.com
SIC: 3993 Signs and advertising specialties

(G-4949)
EMBROIDERY DESIGN INC
2205 Braemar Dr (46814-9372)
PHONE..............................260 625-5538
EMP: 7 **EST:** 1985
SALES (est): 411.73K **Privately Held**
Web: www.baby-burps.com
SIC: 2395 Embroidery products, except Schiffli machine

(G-4950)
EMPIRICAL THEMES LLC
12103 Thornapple Cv (46845-6937)
PHONE..............................260 431-1437
Abdullah Bakhsh, *Pt*
EMP: 1 **EST:** 2013
SALES (est): 75.86K **Privately Held**
SIC: 7372 7389 Application computer software; Business Activities at Non-Commercial Site

(G-4951)
ENDURING ENDEAVORS LLC
13033 Sutters Pkwy (46845-9063)
PHONE..............................260 410-1025
EMP: 1 **EST:** 2015
SALES (est): 56.36K **Privately Held**
SIC: 2211 7389 Underwear fabrics, cotton; Business services, nec

(G-4952)
ENVELOPE SERVICE INC
7101 Lincoln Pkwy (46804-5673)
P.O. Box 392 (46748-0392)
PHONE..............................260 432-6277
Gary Hilgeman, *Pr*
EMP: 50 **EST:** 1978
SQ FT: 36,000
SALES (est): 4.89MM **Privately Held**
SIC: 2677 2752 Envelopes; Business form and card printing, lithographic

(G-4953)
ENVIRO INK
6926 Quemetco Ct Ste A (46803-3394)
PHONE..............................260 748-0636
Tony Williams, *Owner*
EMP: 3 **EST:** 2004
SALES (est): 217.59K **Privately Held**
Web: www.myenviroink.com
SIC: 2893 Printing ink

(G-4954)
ENVMTL FRANKE SYSTEMS LLC
1303 Big Horn Pl (46825-3420)
PHONE..............................260 710-6491
Michael Edward Franke, *Managing Member*
Sara Jane Franke, *Sec*
EMP: 2 **EST:** 2010
SALES (est): 121.5K **Privately Held**
SIC: 3589 Water treatment equipment, industrial

(G-4955)
ENZYME SOLUTIONS INC
10219 River Rapids Run (46845-8950)
PHONE..............................800 523-1323
Jared Hochstedler, *Brnch Mgr*
EMP: 2
SALES (corp-wide): 3.48MM **Privately Held**
Web: www.enzymesolutions.com
SIC: 2869 Enzymes
PA: Enzyme Solutions, Inc.
2105 Forrest Park Dr
Garrett IN 46738
260 553-9100

(G-4956)
EPCO PRODUCTS INC
3736 Vanguard Dr (46809-3303)
P.O. Box 9250 (46899-9250)
PHONE..............................260 747-8888
Fredric J Aichele, *Pr*
Sally A Aichele, *Sec*
▼ **EMP:** 20 **EST:** 1980
SQ FT: 25,200
SALES (est): 3.73MM **Privately Held**
Web: www.epcomarineproducts.com
SIC: 3451 3429 3541 3494 Screw machine products; Marine hardware; Machine tools, metal cutting type; Valves and pipe fittings, nec

(G-4957)
EPS ENTERPRISES INC
Also Called: Electric Power Service
5423 State Road 930 (46803-1771)
PHONE..............................260 493-4913
Pete Limkemann, *Pr*

Fort Wayne - Allen County (G-4958) GEOGRAPHIC SECTION

EMP: 4 EST: 1981
SQ FT: 6,000
SALES (est): 283.64K **Privately Held**
SIC: 7694 5063 Electric motor repair; Motors, electric

(G-4958)
ERIE-HAVEN INC
4708 Industrial Rd (46825-5208)
PHONE..................................260 483-3865
Randy Adams, *Mgr*
EMP: 9
SALES (corp-wide): 6.22MM **Privately Held**
Web: www.eriehaven.com
SIC: 3273 Ready-mixed concrete
PA: Erie-Haven Inc
3909 Limestone Dr
Fort Wayne IN 46809
260 478-1674

(G-4959)
ERIE-HAVEN INC (PA)
Also Called: Erie Haven Concrete
3909 Limestone Dr (46809-9709)
PHONE..................................260 478-1674
Larry D Gerig, *Pr*
John Leedy, *
EMP: 75 EST: 1961
SALES (est): 6.22MM
SALES (corp-wide): 6.22MM **Privately Held**
Web: www.eriehaven.com
SIC: 3273 3272 Ready-mixed concrete; Concrete products, nec

(G-4960)
ES DEICING
3500 Meyer Rd (46806-1582)
PHONE..................................260 422-2020
EMP: 2 EST: 2010
SALES (est): 100.37K **Privately Held**
Web: www.esdeicing.com
SIC: 2899 Salt

(G-4961)
ESSEX BROWNELL LLC
Also Called: Essex Brownell Llc
1601 Wall St (46802-4352)
PHONE..................................260 424-1708
Kenneth Beahrs, *Mgr*
EMP: 345
Web: www.essexbrownell.com
SIC: 3357 Nonferrous wiredrawing and insulating
HQ: Essex Brownell Inc.
5770 Powers Ferry Rd # 30
Atlanta GA 30327
205 591-8956

(G-4962)
ESSEX FRKAWA MGNT WIRE USA LLC
Also Called: Telecommunications Pdts Div
1700 Taylor (46802)
PHONE..................................260 461-4000
Chris Mapes, *Brnch Mgr*
EMP: 30
Web: www.essexfurukawa.com
SIC: 3357 3351 Building wire and cable, nonferrous; Copper and copper alloy pipe and tube
HQ: Essex Furukawa Magnet Wire Usa Llc
5770 Pwr Frry Rd Nw Ste 3
Atlanta GA 30327
770 657-6000

(G-4963)
ESSEX FRKAWA MGNT WIRE USA LLC
1601 Wall St (46802-4352)
PHONE..................................260 461-4000
Peter Seiser, *Mgr*
EMP: 2
Web: www.superioressex.com
SIC: 3357 Magnet wire, nonferrous
HQ: Essex Furukawa Magnet Wire Usa Llc
5770 Pwr Frry Rd Nw Ste 3
Atlanta GA 30327
770 657-6000

(G-4964)
ESSEX FRKAWA MGNT WIRE USA LLC
Also Called: Superior Essex
1700 Taylor St (46802)
PHONE..................................260 461-4183
Shafiq Jadallah, *Off Mgr*
EMP: 6
Web: www.essexfurukawa.com
SIC: 3357 Magnet wire, nonferrous
HQ: Essex Furukawa Magnet Wire Usa Llc
5770 Pwr Frry Rd Nw Ste 3
Atlanta GA 30327
770 657-6000

(G-4965)
ESSEX SERVICES INC
1601 Wall St (46802-4352)
PHONE..................................260 461-4000
Stephen Kanup, *CEO*
EMP: 359 EST: 2003
SALES (est): 4.04MM **Privately Held**
SIC: 3357 Nonferrous wiredrawing and insulating
HQ: Superior Essex International Inc.
5770 Pwers Frry Rd Ste 40
Atlanta GA 30327
770 657-6000

(G-4966)
EUROPEAN CONCEPTS LLC
Also Called: Anton Alexander
5607 Newland Pl (46835-3880)
PHONE..................................888 797-9005
Anton Babich, *Pr*
EMP: 2 EST: 2008
SALES (est): 206.6K **Privately Held**
Web: www.antonalexander.com
SIC: 2321 7389 Men's and boys' dress shirts ; Business services, nec

(G-4967)
EXCELL COLOR GRAPHICS INC
2623 Camino Ct (46808)
P.O. Box 80547 (46898)
PHONE..................................260 482-2720
Thomas Parrot Junior, *Pr*
Jerry Blaising, *
Tom Parrot, *Prin*
Jim Reutebuch, *Prin*
EMP: 35 EST: 1990
SQ FT: 40,000
SALES (est): 4.51MM **Privately Held**
Web: www.excellcg.com
SIC: 2759 2796 2791 2752 Screen printing; Platemaking services; Typesetting; Commercial printing, lithographic

(G-4968)
EXPRESSIONS BRAIDS BY GWEN LLC
3442 Stellhorn Rd Ste 4 (46815-4630)
PHONE..................................260 312-6037
Gwendolyn Walker, *CEO*
EMP: 1 EST: 2002
SALES (est): 54.37K **Privately Held**
SIC: 3999 Hair and hair-based products

(G-4969)
EXTENSIVE DESIGN LLC
10007 Northbrook Valley Dr Apt 3 (46825-2377)
PHONE..................................260 267-6752
EMP: 1
SALES (est): 60.62K **Privately Held**
SIC: 7389 2759 Business Activities at Non-Commercial Site; Screen printing

(G-4970)
F G METAL
721 Runnion Ave (46808-3743)
PHONE..................................260 580-0361
Antonio Garcia, *Owner*
EMP: 1 EST: 2009
SALES (est): 73.83K **Privately Held**
Web: www.sbhowardsurgery.com
SIC: 3446 Architectural metalwork

(G-4971)
FABCORE INDUSTRIES LLC
928 Pencross Dr (46845-1219)
PHONE..................................260 438-3431
Jason Mueller, *Prin*
EMP: 3 EST: 2013
SALES (est): 172.88K **Privately Held**
Web: www.fabcoreplastics.com
SIC: 3999 Manufacturing industries, nec

(G-4972)
FAES CABINET LLC
916 W Coliseum Blvd Ste 4 (46808-1291)
PHONE..................................567 259-8571
Byron Tribolet-ward, *Prin*
EMP: 4 EST: 2017
SALES (est): 107.94K **Privately Held**
Web: www.faescabinet.com
SIC: 2434 Wood kitchen cabinets

(G-4973)
FAIRFIELD GAS WAY
Also Called: Marathon Oil
4230 Fairfield Ave (46807-2740)
PHONE..................................260 744-2186
EMP: 3 EST: 2009
SALES (est): 272.85K **Privately Held**
Web: www.marathonoil.com
SIC: 5541 3578 Gasoline service stations; Automatic teller machines (ATM)

(G-4974)
FANROLL LLC (PA) ✪
Also Called: Metallic Dice Games
3236 Illinois Rd (46802-4938)
PHONE..................................617 909-6325
EMP: 4 EST: 2022
SALES (est): 325.54K
SALES (corp-wide): 325.54K **Privately Held**
SIC: 7372 Application computer software

(G-4975)
FASHION CITY
1108 E Pontiac St Ste 2 (46803-3400)
PHONE..................................260 744-6753
Hassan Nassor, *Pr*
EMP: 2 EST: 2005
SALES (est): 203.94K **Privately Held**
SIC: 2329 Riding clothes: men's, youths', and boys'

(G-4976)
FAST PRINT INCORPORATED
3050 E State Blvd (46805-4737)
PHONE..................................260 484-5487
Carolyn Plein, *Pr*
Caroline Cline, *Pr*
Stanley Cline, *Sec*
Dan Metzger, *VP*

EMP: 8 EST: 1975
SQ FT: 5,400
SALES (est): 945.98K **Privately Held**
Web: www.fastprintinc.com
SIC: 2752 Offset printing

(G-4977)
FASTSIGNS
3014 N Clinton St (46805-1912)
PHONE..................................260 373-0911
Frank Shepler, *Owner*
EMP: 2 EST: 2000
SALES (est): 216.65K **Privately Held**
Web: www.fastsigns.com
SIC: 3993 Signs and advertising specialties

(G-4978)
FAURECIA EMSSONS CTRL TECH USA
4510 Airport Express Way (46809-9658)
PHONE..................................248 758-8160
Michael Manson, *Brnch Mgr*
EMP: 100
SALES (corp-wide): 100.93MM **Privately Held**
Web: www.faurecia.com
SIC: 3714 Exhaust systems and parts, motor vehicle
HQ: Faurecia Emissions Control Technologies Usa, Llc
2800 High Meadow Cir
Auburn Hills MI 48326

(G-4979)
FAZTEK LLC
12788 Bluffton Rd (46809)
PHONE..................................260 482-7544
Mark Rupp, *Pt*
EMP: 30 EST: 2001
SALES (est): 5.01MM **Privately Held**
Web: www.faztek.net
SIC: 3599 Machine shop, jobbing and repair

(G-4980)
FENRIS FORGE LLC
706 Lawton Pl (46805-4132)
PHONE..................................260 422-9044
Steve L Sells, *Prin*
EMP: 3 EST: 2019
SALES (est): 106.38K **Privately Held**
Web: www.fenrisforge.com
SIC: 3999 Manufacturing industries, nec

(G-4981)
FFD PUBLISHING LLC
1730 Kensington Blvd (46805-5121)
PHONE..................................260 423-2119
Anthony Deutsch, *Owner*
EMP: 1 EST: 2013
SALES (est): 51.43K **Privately Held**
SIC: 2741 Miscellaneous publishing

(G-4982)
FILL-RITE COMPANY
8825 Aviation Dr (46809-9630)
PHONE..................................260 747-7529
EMP: 36
SALES (corp-wide): 659.51MM **Publicly Held**
Web: www.fillrite.com
SIC: 3561 Pumps and pumping equipment
HQ: Fill-Rite Company
600 S Airport Rd
Mansfield OH 44903
419 755-1011

(G-4983)
FILTER SCIENCES LLC
327 Ley Rd (46825-5219)
PHONE..................................260 387-7709

EMP: 1
SALES (est): 87.9K **Privately Held**
SIC: 3589 Water treatment equipment, industrial

(G-4984)
FIRST GEAR INC
Also Called: First Gear Engineering & Tech
4321 Goshen Rd (46818-1201)
PHONE.................................260 490-3238
Greg Leffler, *Pr*
Cynthia Leffler, *
EMP: 24 **EST:** 1987
SQ FT: 16,280
SALES (est): 4.04MM **Privately Held**
Web: www.first-gear.com
SIC: 3559 3728 3812 3841 Automotive related machinery; Gears, aircraft power transmission; Acceleration indicators and systems components, aerospace; Surgical and medical instruments

(G-4985)
FLARE PRECISION LLC
6210 Discount Dr (46818-1232)
PHONE.................................260 490-1101
Tyler Haber, *Pr*
Allen Collins, *Pr*
Cherie Collins, *Sec*
▲ **EMP:** 20 **EST:** 1976
SALES (est): 2.42MM **Privately Held**
Web: www.flareprecision.com
SIC: 3599 7692 3544 Machine shop, jobbing and repair; Welding repair; Special dies, tools, jigs, and fixtures

(G-4986)
FLICKINGER INDUSTRIES INC
1801 Carlton Ave (46802-4576)
PHONE.................................260 432-4527
Ronald Flickinger, *Pr*
Karen Flickinger, *
John Flickinger, *
EMP: 45 **EST:** 1960
SQ FT: 40,000
SALES (est): 5.2MM **Privately Held**
SIC: 3561 Cylinders, pump

(G-4987)
FLP WOODWORKS
1510 Boone St (46808-3708)
PHONE.................................260 424-3904
Philip Koher, *Prin*
EMP: 2 **EST:** 2005
SALES (est): 155.14K **Privately Held**
SIC: 2431 Millwork

(G-4988)
FLUID-TECH INTERNATIONAL CORP
820 Schick St (46803-1073)
P.O. Box 15426 (46885-5426)
PHONE.................................260 420-5000
John C Moran, *Pr*
EMP: 9 **EST:** 1982
SQ FT: 10,000
SALES (est): 783.42K **Privately Held**
SIC: 3589 Sewage and water treatment equipment

(G-4989)
FMT LLC
1525 Mayfield Rd (46825-3242)
PHONE.................................260 417-5613
EMP: 2 **EST:** 2009
SALES (est): 205.37K **Privately Held**
Web: www.forksmt.com
SIC: 3599 Machine shop, jobbing and repair

(G-4990)
FOAMEX LP
Also Called: Foamex
8520 Temple Drive (46809)
PHONE.................................800 417-4257
EMP: 49
Web: www.fxi.com
SIC: 3086 Plastics foam products
PA: Foamex L.P.
100 W Matsonford Rd # 5
Wayne PA 19087

(G-4991)
FORT WAYNE DIAMOND PDTS INC
2625 E Pontiac St (46803-3666)
PHONE.................................260 747-1681
Dwight Bieberich, *Pr*
Donald Bieberich, *VP*
Letha Scherer, *Sec*
Bradley Scherer, *Sec*
EMP: 4 **EST:** 1947
SQ FT: 30,000
SALES (est): 250.24K **Privately Held**
Web: www.fwwd.com
SIC: 7389 1481 Grinding, precision: commercial or industrial; Nonmetallic mineral services

(G-4992)
FORT WAYNE FABRICATION
3303 Freeman St (46802-4436)
PHONE.................................260 459-8848
Ed Morken, *Pr*
EMP: 4 **EST:** 2001
SALES (est): 400.72K **Privately Held**
Web: www.fortwaynefab.com
SIC: 3444 Sheet metalwork

(G-4993)
FORT WAYNE FABRICATION INC
1624 Simons St (46803-2573)
PHONE.................................260 704-6618
EMP: 9 **EST:** 2019
SALES (est): 246.03K **Privately Held**
Web: www.fortwaynefab.com
SIC: 3599 Machine shop, jobbing and repair

(G-4994)
FORT WAYNE METALS RES PDTS
Also Called: FORT WAYNE METALS RESEARCH PRODUCTS CORP
3401 Mcarthur Dr (46809-2884)
PHONE.................................260 747-4154
EMP: 1
SALES (corp-wide): 112.25MM **Privately Held**
Web: www.fwmetals.com
SIC: 3315 Steel wire and related products
PA: Fort Wayne Metals Research Products, Llc
9609 Ardmore Ave
Fort Wayne IN 46809
260 747-4154

(G-4995)
FORT WAYNE METALS RES PDTS LLC
Also Called: Fort Wayne Metals
9823 Ardmore Ave (46809-9626)
PHONE.................................260 747-4154
Scott Glaze, *Brnch Mgr*
EMP: 1
SALES (corp-wide): 112.25MM **Privately Held**
Web: www.fwmetals.com
SIC: 3315 Wire, steel: insulated or armored
PA: Fort Wayne Metals Research Products, Llc
9609 Ardmore Ave
Fort Wayne IN 46809
260 747-4154

(G-4996)
FORT WAYNE METALS RES PDTS LLC (PA)
Also Called: Fort Wayne Metals
9609 Ardmore Ave (46809-9625)
P.O. Box 9040 (46899-9040)
PHONE.................................260 747-4154
Scott Glaze, *CEO*
Mark Michael, *
▲ **EMP:** 505 **EST:** 1970
SQ FT: 50,000
SALES (est): 112.25MM
SALES (corp-wide): 112.25MM **Privately Held**
Web: www.fwmetals.com
SIC: 3315 Wire, steel: insulated or armored

(G-4997)
FORT WAYNE METALS RES PDTS LLC
9307 Avionics Dr (46809-9631)
P.O. Box 9040 (46899-9040)
PHONE.................................260 747-4154
Scott Glaze, *CEO*
EMP: 1
SALES (corp-wide): 112.25MM **Privately Held**
Web: www.fwmetals.com
SIC: 3315 3842 Wire, steel: insulated or armored; Surgical appliances and supplies
PA: Fort Wayne Metals Research Products, Llc
9609 Ardmore Ave
Fort Wayne IN 46809
260 747-4154

(G-4998)
FORT WAYNE MOLD & ENGRG INC
4501 Earth Dr (46809-1519)
PHONE.................................260 747-9168
Richard A Schmidt, *Pr*
Roger Marley, *
Brad Fiedler, *
Darell Beverly, *
EMP: 44 **EST:** 1978
SQ FT: 25,000
SALES (est): 5.24MM **Privately Held**
Web: www.fortwaynemold.com
SIC: 3544 Special dies and tools

(G-4999)
FORT WAYNE NEWSPAPERS INC
Also Called: News-Sentinel
600 W Main St (46802-1498)
PHONE.................................260 461-8444
Lori Fritz, *Pr*
Greg Johnson, *
EMP: 457 **EST:** 1833
SQ FT: 146,000
SALES (est): 39.17MM
SALES (corp-wide): 709.52MM **Privately Held**
Web: www.journalgazette.net
SIC: 2711 2721 2759 Newspapers, publishing and printing; Magazines: publishing and printing; Commercial printing, nec
HQ: News Publishing Company Inc
600 W Main St
Fort Wayne IN 46802
260 461-8444

(G-5000)
FORT WAYNE PLASTICS INC
Also Called: Fwp
510 Sumpter St (46804-5626)
PHONE.................................260 432-2520
Robb Robertson, *Pr*
Ray Linkhart, *
Phillip Swihart, *
◆ **EMP:** 120 **EST:** 1997
SQ FT: 160,000
SALES (est): 25.64MM
SALES (corp-wide): 494.03MM **Privately Held**
Web: www.fwderm.com
SIC: 3089 Blow molded finished plastics products, nec
HQ: Ftw Holdings Inc.
11840 Westline Indus Dr
Saint Louis MO

(G-5001)
FORT WAYNE POOLS
6930 Gettysburg Pike (46804-5614)
PHONE.................................260 459-4100
Manuel J Perez De La Mesa, *CEO*
Craig Hubbard, *
EMP: 227 **EST:** 1967
SALES (est): 46.6MM **Publicly Held**
Web: www.tredwaypools.com
SIC: 5091 3949 Swimming pools, equipment and supplies; Swimming pools, plastic
PA: Pool Corporation
109 Northpark Blvd
Covington LA 70433

(G-5002)
FORT WAYNE WIRE DIE INC (PA)
2424 American Way (46809-3098)
PHONE.................................260 747-1681
Dwight P Bieberich, *Pr*
Letha E Scherer, *
Donald E Bieberich, *
Brad Scherer, *
Eric Bieberich, *
▲ **EMP:** 177 **EST:** 1946
SQ FT: 50,000
SALES (est): 45.66MM
SALES (corp-wide): 45.66MM **Privately Held**
Web: www.fwwd.com
SIC: 3544 Diamond dies, metalworking

(G-5003)
FORT WYNE RDLGY ASSN FUNDATION
Also Called: Breast Diagnostic Center
3707 New Vision Dr (46845-1702)
PHONE.................................260 266-8120
Marita Dwight-smith, *Mgr*
EMP: 12
SALES (corp-wide): 4.99MM **Privately Held**
Web: www.fw-breastdiagnosticcenter.com
SIC: 3841 8011 Diagnostic apparatus, medical; Radiologist
PA: Fort Wayne Radiology Association Foundation Inc
3707 New Vision Dr
Fort Wayne IN 46845
260 484-0850

(G-5004)
FOXXIE PLANNER L L C ✪
1416 Rosemont Dr (46808-2241)
PHONE.................................260 247-6303
EMP: 1 **EST:** 2022
SALES (est): 69.27K **Privately Held**
SIC: 2678 7389 Stationery: made from purchased materials; Business Activities at Non-Commercial Site

(G-5005)
FRANKE PLATING WORKS INC
1918 E Wayne St (46803)
PHONE.................................260 422-8477
Warren T Franke, *Pr*
EMP: 56 **EST:** 1930
SALES (est): 8.61MM **Privately Held**
Web: www.frankeplatingworks.com

Fort Wayne - Allen County (G-5006)   GEOGRAPHIC SECTION

SIC: 3471 Plating of metals or formed products

(G-5006)
FRANKLIN ELECTRIC CO INC (PA)
Also Called: FRANKLIN ELECTRIC
9255 Coverdale Rd (46809)
PHONE.................260 824-2900
Joseph Ruzynski, *CEO*
Gregg C Sengstack, *
Jeffery L Taylor, *VP*
Jonathan M Grandon, *CAO*
Brent L Spikes V, *President Global Manufacturing*
◆ EMP: 268 EST: 1944
SALES (est): 2.07B
SALES (corp-wide): 2.07B **Publicly Held**
Web: www.franklin-electric.com
SIC: 3621 3561 Motors, electric; Pumps and pumping equipment

(G-5007)
FRANKLIN ELECTRIC INTL (HQ)
9255 Coverdale Rd (46809-9613)
PHONE.................260 824-2900
Jess B Ford, *Pr*
John B Lindsay, *Ex VP*
Greg Sinstack, *Sec*
William Lawson, *Ch Bd*
EMP: 12 EST: 1982
SALES (est): 53.09MM
SALES (corp-wide): 2.07B **Publicly Held**
Web: www.franklin-electric.com
SIC: 3621 Motors and generators
PA: Franklin Electric Co., Inc.
   9255 Coverdale Rd
   Fort Wayne IN 46809
   260 824-2900

(G-5008)
FRANKLIN GARAGE LTD
1312 Franklin Ave (46808-2684)
PHONE.................260 442-2439
Colby Metz, *Owner*
EMP: 1 EST: 2017
SALES (est): 53.35K **Privately Held**
SIC: 2431 Woodwork, interior and ornamental, nec

(G-5009)
FRECKER OPTICAL INC
7115 Old Trail Rd (46826-2715)
P.O. Box 9028 (46899-9028)
PHONE.................260 747-9653
Terry Frecker, *Pr*
Allan Frecker, *VP*
Brian Frecker, *Sec*
Bryan Frecker, *Treas*
EMP: 10 EST: 1971
SQ FT: 18,000
SALES (est): 683.22K **Privately Held**
Web: frecker-optical-inc.hub.biz
SIC: 3851 5048 Eyeglasses, lenses and frames; Optometric equipment and supplies

(G-5010)
FREEPORT MINERALS CORPORATION
Also Called: Phelps Dodge
2131 S Coliseum Blvd (46803-2933)
PHONE.................260 421-5400
Larry Mcdonald, *Brnch Mgr*
EMP: 4
SALES (corp-wide): 22.86B **Publicly Held**
Web: www.fcx.com
SIC: 1382 Oil and gas exploration services
HQ: Freeport Minerals Corporation
   333 N Central Ave
   Phoenix AZ 85004
   602 366-8100

(G-5011)
FRESH FENIX LLC (PA) ✪
1627 Short St (46808-3228)
PHONE.................260 385-2584
Brent James Helmkamp, *Pr*
EMP: 6 EST: 2022
SALES (est): 62.01K
SALES (corp-wide): 62.01K **Privately Held**
SIC: 2099 Food preparations, nec

(G-5012)
FRESH FENIX LLC
1620 Broadway (46802-4457)
PHONE.................260 385-2584
Brent Helmkamp, *Mgr*
EMP: 8
SALES (corp-wide): 62.01K **Privately Held**
SIC: 2099 Food preparations, nec
PA: Fresh Fenix Llc
   1627 Short St
   Fort Wayne IN 46808
   260 385-2584

(G-5013)
FRIENDS OF THIRD WORLD INC (PA)
Also Called: CO-OP TRADING
611 W Wayne St (46802)
PHONE.................260 422-6821
James Goetsch, *Pr*
Howard Traxmor, *Ch*
EMP: 3 EST: 1970
SQ FT: 9,000
SALES (est): 189.83K
SALES (corp-wide): 189.83K **Privately Held**
Web: www.friendsofthethirdworld.org
SIC: 8299 2752 5947 Educational services; Commercial printing, lithographic; Gift shop

(G-5014)
FT WAYNE READER
1301 Lafayette St Ste 202 (46802-3555)
PHONE.................260 420-8580
Michael Summers, *Owner*
EMP: 5 EST: 2006
SALES (est): 155K **Privately Held**
Web: www.fortwaynerecovery.com
SIC: 2711 Newspapers, publishing and printing

(G-5015)
FXI INC
Also Called: Foamex
3005 Commercial Rd (46809-2927)
PHONE.................260 747-7485
William Banks, *Brnch Mgr*
EMP: 1
SQ FT: 270,000
Web: www.fxi.com
SIC: 3086 Packaging and shipping materials, foamed plastics
HQ: Fxi, Inc.
   100 W Matsonford Rd
   Radnor PA 19087

(G-5016)
GCG INDUSTRIES INC
4636 Newaygo Rd (46808-4103)
PHONE.................260 482-7454
Terry A Gardner, *Pr*
Tamara Gardner, *Sec*
EMP: 27 EST: 1988
SQ FT: 12,000
SALES (est): 2.79MM **Privately Held**
Web: www.gcgindustries.com
SIC: 3544 Special dies, tools, jigs, and fixtures

(G-5017)
GDP INDUSTRIES LLC
7431 Regina Dr (46815-8244)
PHONE.................260 414-4003
Gary Boyd, *Prin*
EMP: 2 EST: 2010
SALES (est): 106.23K **Privately Held**
SIC: 3999 Manufacturing industries, nec

(G-5018)
GEN-TWELVE CORPORATION
10917 Smokey Ridge Pl (46818-8893)
PHONE.................260 483-7075
Renee S Bloom, *Acctg Mgr*
EMP: 7 EST: 2016
SALES (est): 83.48K **Privately Held**
SIC: 2752 Offset printing

(G-5019)
GENERAL DYNAMICS CORPORATION
1124 Falcon Creek Pkwy (46845-9043)
PHONE.................260 637-4773
EMP: 4
SALES (corp-wide): 42.27B **Publicly Held**
Web: www.gd.com
SIC: 3731 Shipbuilding and repairing
PA: General Dynamics Corporation
   11011 Sunset Hills Rd
   Reston VA 20190
   703 876-3000

(G-5020)
GENERAL DYNMICS MSSION SYSTEMS
1700 Magnavox Way Ste 200 (46804-1552)
PHONE.................260 434-9500
Rich Sargiano, *Mgr*
EMP: 12
SALES (corp-wide): 42.27B **Publicly Held**
Web: www.gdmissionsystems.com
SIC: 3571 Electronic computers
HQ: General Dynamics Mission Systems, Inc.
   12450 Fair Lakes Cir
   Fairfax VA 22033
   877 449-0600

(G-5021)
GENEVA MANUFACTURING INC
Also Called: Vgmc
6120 Highview Dr (46818-1378)
P.O. Box 219 (46740-0219)
PHONE.................260 368-7555
Terrill Vieth, *Pr*
Larry J Miller, *
Julie A Miller, *Sec*
Scott Miller, *
◆ EMP: 22 EST: 1953
SQ FT: 34,000
SALES (est): 2.45MM **Privately Held**
Web: www.genevamfgcorp.com
SIC: 3429 Casket hardware

(G-5022)
GENTEC LLC
3905 Goeglein Rd (46815-5731)
PHONE.................260 436-7333
Gene Tippmann, *Pr*
EMP: 8 EST: 2003
SQ FT: 2,000
SALES (est): 632.15K **Privately Held**
SIC: 3469 Household cooking and kitchen utensils, metal

(G-5023)
GESCO GROUP LLC (PA)
4422 Earth Dr (46809-1518)
P.O. Box 10474 (46852-0474)
PHONE.................260 747-5088
Timothy Hartigan, *Managing Member*
EMP: 5 EST: 2017
SALES (est): 6.27MM
SALES (corp-wide): 6.27MM **Privately Held**
Web: www.gasolineequipment.com
SIC: 3533 7353 5999 Gas field machinery and equipment; Oil equipment rental services; Business machines and equipment

(G-5024)
GIESECK+DVRENT EPYMNTS AMER IN
2621 Corrinado Ct (46808-4406)
PHONE.................866 484-0611
Ryan Wulpi, *Brnch Mgr*
EMP: 5
SALES (corp-wide): 2.62B **Privately Held**
SIC: 3089 7374 Identification cards, plastics; Data processing and preparation
HQ: Giesecke+Devrient Epayments America, Inc.
   1011 Warrenville Rd # 450
   Lisle IL 60532
   630 852-8200

(G-5025)
GKB HOLDINGS INC
909 Production Rd (46808-1270)
PHONE.................260 471-7744
Gary Bastin, *Pr*
Kimberley Bastin, *Treas*
EMP: 28 EST: 1902
SQ FT: 14,000
SALES (est): 891.72K **Privately Held**
Web: www.fortwayneprinting.com
SIC: 2752 2791 Offset printing; Typesetting

(G-5026)
GLADIEUX TRADING MFG CO
6414 Popp Rd (46845-9477)
PHONE.................260 417-6774
Robert Hayes, *Prin*
EMP: 4 EST: 2018
SALES (est): 39.69K **Privately Held**
SIC: 3999 Manufacturing industries, nec

(G-5027)
GLICKS MIRACLES INC
5732 Glendale Rd (46804-6636)
PHONE.................260 436-6671
Alfred Glick, *Pr*
EMP: 1 EST: 2005
SALES (est): 41.83K **Privately Held**
SIC: 7692 Welding repair

(G-5028)
GMI LLC
Also Called: Global Medical Industries
1830 Wayne Trce Ste 110 (46803-2657)
PHONE.................260 209-6676
Victor Lopez, *Pr*
EMP: 1 EST: 2015
SALES (est): 187.4K **Privately Held**
Web: www.globalmedicalind.com
SIC: 3841 3728 3541 Surgical and medical instruments; Aircraft parts and equipment, nec; Machine tools, metal cutting type

(G-5029)
GOOSE GRAPHICS L L C
4943 Coventry Pkwy (46804-7115)
PHONE.................260 563-4516
▲ EMP: 5 EST: 1996
SQ FT: 10,000
SALES (est): 400K **Privately Held**
SIC: 2759 Screen printing

▲ = Import ▼ = Export
◆ = Import/Export

GEOGRAPHIC SECTION
Fort Wayne - Allen County (G-5056)

(G-5030)
GORGANITE PUBLISHING LLC ✪
5534 Saint Joe Rd (46835)
PHONE.................................812 480-2787
Amos Grogan, *Managing Member*
EMP: 1 **EST:** 2022
SALES (est): 75.6K **Privately Held**
SIC: 2741 Miscellaneous publishing

(G-5031)
GOVPARTS LLC
1810 S Anthony Blvd (46803-3606)
PHONE.................................260 449-9741
EMP: 4 **EST:** 2017
SALES (est): 684.12K **Privately Held**
Web: www.govpartsllc.com
SIC: 3429 Aircraft hardware

(G-5032)
GRACIE INDUSTRIES LLC
Also Called: Bolt Custom Trucks
3900 Transportation Dr (46818-1237)
P.O. Box 8099 (46898-8099)
PHONE.................................260 748-0314
Brian Callan, *Pr*
EMP: 1 **EST:** 2013
SQ FT: 55,000
SALES (est): 1.55MM **Privately Held**
Web: www.boltcustom.com
SIC: 3711 Truck and tractor truck assembly

(G-5033)
GRAPHIC 2000 FORMS LABELS
8327 Norwood Ct (46835-9687)
PHONE.................................260 387-5943
Dave Pufahl, *Owner*
EMP: 3 **EST:** 2018
SALES (est): 97.36K **Privately Held**
SIC: 2759 Commercial printing, nec

(G-5034)
GRAPHICS SYSTEMS INC
8421 Mayhew Rd (46835-1003)
PHONE.................................260 485-9667
Kurt Leffers, *Pr*
EMP: 3 **EST:** 1975
SQ FT: 1,300
SALES (est): 247.4K **Privately Held**
Web: www.graphicsystemsinc.com
SIC: 3993 Signs and advertising specialties

(G-5035)
GRAPHIK MECHANIX INC
1716 S Harrison St (46802-5211)
PHONE.................................260 426-7001
William Wright, *CEO*
Sigrid Wright, *Sec*
Gary Gamble, *Admn*
EMP: 6 **EST:** 1991
SALES (est): 518.14K **Privately Held**
SIC: 2796 7384 Lithographic plates, positives or negatives; Film developing services

(G-5036)
GRAPHITE CUSTOMS LLC
9323 Parkway Dr (46804-4731)
PHONE.................................260 402-8690
Casey Spurgeon, *Admn*
EMP: 6 **EST:** 2014
SALES (est): 162.71K **Privately Held**
Web: www.graphitecustoms.com
SIC: 3624 Carbon and graphite products

(G-5037)
GRAYCRAFT SIGNS PLUS INC (PA)
2428 Getz Rd (46804-1632)
PHONE.................................260 432-3760
Mark A Gray, *Pr*
Nanette M Gray, *Sec*
EMP: 4 **EST:** 1993
SQ FT: 2,100
SALES (est): 655.38K **Privately Held**
Web: www.graycraftsigns.com
SIC: 3993 Signs, not made in custom sign painting shops

(G-5038)
GREAT LAKES PREFABRICATION LLC
4334 Ardmore Ave (46802-4246)
PHONE.................................260 489-1575
EMP: 6 **EST:** 2019
SALES (est): 365.44K **Privately Held**
Web: www.greatlakesprefabrication.com
SIC: 3499 Fabricated metal products, nec

(G-5039)
GREAT PANES GLASS CO
1307 N Wells St (46808-2793)
PHONE.................................260 426-0203
Judy Wire, *Pr*
EMP: 6 **EST:** 1991
SQ FT: 1,800
SALES (est): 404.16K **Privately Held**
Web: www.greatpanesglass.com
SIC: 5231 3231 Glass, leaded or stained; Products of purchased glass

(G-5040)
GREATBATCH LTD
Also Called: Greatbatch Medical
4545 Kroemer Rd (46818-9770)
PHONE.................................260 755-7300
Thomas Hook, *Pr*
EMP: 5 **EST:** 2012
SALES (est): 746.9K **Privately Held**
Web: www.greatbatchmedical.com
SIC: 3841 Surgical and medical instruments

(G-5041)
GREM USA CORPORATION
315 E Wallace St (46803-2342)
PHONE.................................260 456-2354
Edward Miers, *CAO*
Edward Miers, *CAO*
EMP: 1 **EST:** 1999
SQ FT: 40,000
SALES (est): 71.98K **Privately Held**
Web: www.gremusa.com
SIC: 3931 Musical instruments

(G-5042)
GROUP DEKKO INC (DH)
7310 Innovation Blvd # 104 (46818-1370)
PHONE.................................260 357-3621
John R May, *CEO*
Jon Jensen, *
Gerald J Whiteford, *
▲ **EMP:** 94 **EST:** 2015
SALES (est): 164.64MM
SALES (corp-wide): 4.41B **Publicly Held**
Web: www.dekko.com
SIC: 3479 3469 3643 3315 Coating of metals and formed products; Metal stampings, nec; Current-carrying wiring services; Wire and fabricated wire products
HQ: Group Dekko Holdings, Inc.
7310 Innovation Blvd
Fort Wayne IN 46818

(G-5043)
GROUP DEKKO HOLDINGS INC (HQ)
7310 Innovation Blvd Ste 104 (46818-1370)
PHONE.................................800 829-3101
David Burnworth, *CEO*
EMP: 2 **EST:** 2006
SALES (est): 478.09MM
SALES (corp-wide): 4.41B **Publicly Held**
Web: www.dekko.com

(G-5044)
GTA ENTERPRISES INC
Also Called: Gt Automation Group
9305 Yeager Ln (46809)
PHONE.................................260 478-7800
Steve Gildea, *CEO*
Steve Gildea, *Pr*
Mike Motter, *
◆ **EMP:** 34 **EST:** 2005
SQ FT: 62,000
SALES (est): 3.49MM **Privately Held**
Web: www.gtautomation.com
SIC: 3544 7373 Special dies and tools; Computer integrated systems design

(G-5045)
H & E MACHINED SPECIALTIES
1321 E Wallace St (46803-2559)
P.O. Box 669 (46725-0669)
PHONE.................................260 424-2527
Nick Knappenberger, *Pr*
Carl Ehinger, *Pr*
Teresa D Bauer, *Sec*
EMP: 15 **EST:** 1973
SQ FT: 33,000
SALES (est): 2.13MM **Privately Held**
SIC: 3599 3451 7539 Machine shop, jobbing and repair; Screw machine products; Machine shop, automotive

(G-5046)
H & M BAY INC
3410 Meyer Rd (46803-2923)
PHONE.................................410 463-5430
Dennis Jones, *Brnch Mgr*
EMP: 10
SALES (corp-wide): 99.65MM **Privately Held**
Web: www.hmbayinc.com
SIC: 2448 Cargo containers, wood and metal combination
PA: H & M Bay, Inc.
1800 Industrial Park Rd
Federalsburg MD 21632
800 932-7521

(G-5047)
H A KING CO INC
3210 Clairmont Ct (46808-4513)
PHONE.................................260 482-6376
EMP: 9
SALES (corp-wide): 2.37MM **Privately Held**
Web: www.ha-king.com
SIC: 3069 Molded rubber products
PA: H. A. King Co., Inc.
5038 Leafdale Blvd
Royal Oak MI 48073
248 280-0006

(G-5048)
HAIRD SALON LLC
420 Lillian Ave (46808-2136)
PHONE.................................260 804-7609
EMP: 1
SALES (est): 69.27K **Privately Held**
SIC: 3999 Hair curlers, designed for beauty parlors

(G-5049)
HAMPTON EQUIPMENT LLC
7127 Hessen Cassel Rd (46816-2116)
PHONE.................................260 740-8704
Erica Frey, *Prin*
EMP: 2 **EST:** 2007
SALES (est): 161.74K **Privately Held**
Web: www.hamptonequipmentllc.com
SIC: 7353 3523 1629 Heavy construction equipment rental; Farm machinery and equipment; Dams, waterways, docks, and other marine construction

(G-5050)
HARRIS FLOTEBOTE
1111 N Hadley Rd (46804-5540)
PHONE.................................260 432-4555
Dave Becker, *VP*
EMP: 6 **EST:** 2017
SALES (est): 144.1K **Privately Held**
Web: www.harrisboats.com
SIC: 3732 Boatbuilding and repairing

(G-5051)
HB CONNECT INC
Also Called: Excellon Technologies
2701 S Coliseum Blvd (46803-2950)
PHONE.................................855 503-9159
Heather Banks, *Pr*
EMP: 5 **EST:** 2018
SALES (est): 224.11K **Privately Held**
SIC: 3671 3679 3728 Light sensing and emitting tubes; Harness assemblies, for electronic use: wire or cable; Adapter assemblies, hydromatic propeller

(G-5052)
HB CONNECT INC
Also Called: Excellon Technologies
1105 Sherman Blvd (46808-3430)
PHONE.................................260 422-1212
Heather Backs, *Pr*
EMP: 60 **EST:** 2001
SQ FT: 27,000
SALES (est): 9.84MM **Privately Held**
Web: www.excellontech.com
SIC: 3671 3679 3728 Light sensing and emitting tubes; Harness assemblies, for electronic use: wire or cable; Adapter assemblies, hydromatic propeller

(G-5053)
HD WOODWORKING
7950 Rothman Rd (46835-9757)
PHONE.................................260 310-9327
Hunter Claycomb, *Prin*
EMP: 5 **EST:** 2019
SALES (est): 54.13K **Privately Held**
SIC: 2431 Millwork

(G-5054)
HEART STRUGGLE LLC
5534 Saint Joe Rd (46835-3328)
PHONE.................................812 480-2580
EMP: 4 **EST:** 2021
SALES (est): 50K **Privately Held**
SIC: 2329 Athletic clothing, except uniforms: men's, youths' and boys'

(G-5055)
HEARTCARE LLC
7806 W Jefferson Blvd Ste D (46804-4180)
PHONE.................................260 432-7000
Subhash K Reddy, *Prin*
EMP: 5 **EST:** 2011
SALES (est): 493.94K **Privately Held**
SIC: 3715 Trailers or vans for transporting horses

(G-5056)
HEAVY DUTY MANUFACTURING INC
4317 Clubview Dr (46804-4404)
PHONE.................................260 432-2480
Michael Miller, *Mgr*
EMP: 10

Fort Wayne - Allen County (G-5057)   **GEOGRAPHIC SECTION**

SALES (corp-wide): 5.99MM Privately Held
Web: www.heavydutymfg.com
SIC: 3714 Exhaust systems and parts, motor vehicle
PA: Heavy Duty Manufacturing, Inc.
1605 Indian Brook Way # 500
Norcross GA 30093
800 241-0551

(G-5057)
HEBRON VENTURES NORTH AMERICA
Also Called: Hebron Ventures Global
344 Field St (46805-1932)
PHONE..................260 437-7733
Reverend William Cp, Pr
EMP: 4 EST: 2014
SALES (est): 145.97K Privately Held
Web: www.hebronventuresglobal.com
SIC: 3312 Stainless steel

(G-5058)
HECKLEY PRINTING INC
6134 Constitution Dr (46804-1526)
PHONE..................260 434-1370
Bill Heckley, Owner
EMP: 6 EST: 2008
SALES (est): 340.52K Privately Held
Web: www.printingservicefortwayne.com
SIC: 2752 Offset printing

(G-5059)
HEDGEHOG MANUFACTURING LLC
1031 Columbia Ave (46805-4309)
PHONE..................260 424-9600
Kris Hartwig, Owner
EMP: 1 EST: 2002
SALES (est): 70.9K Privately Held
SIC: 3599 Machine and other job shop work

(G-5060)
HEDGEHOG PRESS LLC
1136 Columbia Ave (46805-4312)
PHONE..................260 387-5237
Julie Wall Toles, Admn
EMP: 7 EST: 2013
SALES (est): 281.01K Privately Held
Web: www.hedgehogpressfw.com
SIC: 2741 Miscellaneous publishing

(G-5061)
HEIDELBERG MTLS MDWEST AGG INC
6100 Ardmore Ave (46809-9501)
PHONE..................260 747-3105
Peggy Folgel, Brnch Mgr
EMP: 1
SQ FT: 5,000
SALES (corp-wide): 23.02B Privately Held
SIC: 3273 Ready-mixed concrete
HQ: Heidelberg Materials Midwest Agg, Inc.
300 E John Carpenter Fwy
Irving TX

(G-5062)
HEIDELBERG MTLS STHWEST AGG LL
Also Called: HEIDELBERG MATERIALS SOUTHWEST AGG LLC
7320 Lower Huntington Rd (46809-9762)
PHONE..................260 747-5011
Mike Roberts, Mgr
EMP: 1
SALES (corp-wide): 23.02B Privately Held
Web: www.heidelbergmaterials.us
SIC: 3273 Ready-mixed concrete
HQ: Hanson Aggregates Llc
8505 Freport Pkwy Ste 500
Irving TX 75063
469 417-1200

(G-5063)
HENTZ MFG LLC
1530 Progress Rd (46808-1181)
PHONE..................260 469-0800
EMP: 3 EST: 2008
SALES (est): 359.18K Privately Held
Web: www.hentzmfg.com
SIC: 3639 Sewing equipment

(G-5064)
HER MAJESTY CROWN LLC
429 E Dupont Rd # 1118 (46825-2051)
PHONE..................260 218-2255
EMP: 1 EST: 2021
SALES (est): 39.69K Privately Held
SIC: 3999 Hair and hair-based products

(G-5065)
HIGH TECH FABRICATORS INC
1211 E Wallace St (46803-2557)
PHONE..................260 744-4467
EMP: 37 EST: 1992
SALES (est): 5MM Privately Held
Web: www.hightechfabfw.com
SIC: 3469 Metal stampings, nec

(G-5066)
HIGHMARK TECHNOLOGIES LLC
Also Called: Highmark Pack Systems
8343 Clinton Park Dr (46825-3164)
PHONE..................260 483-0012
Debbie Parrot, Pr
Christopher Lake, VP
Michael Parrot, Managing Member
Kurt Moore, VP
EMP: 20 EST: 2006
SQ FT: 22,000
SALES (est): 10.74MM Privately Held
Web: www.highmarktech.com
SIC: 3355 Aluminum rail and structural shapes

(G-5067)
HILLSHIRE BRANDS COMPANY
1108 E Pontiac St (46803-3400)
PHONE..................260 456-4802
EMP: 2
SALES (corp-wide): 52.88B Publicly Held
Web: www.tysonfoods.com
SIC: 2013 Sausages and other prepared meats
HQ: The Hillshire Brands Company
400 S Jefferson St Ste 1n
Chicago IL 60607
312 614-6000

(G-5068)
HINSEYS PRO PAINT INC
Also Called: Custom Motorcycles
6931 Quemetco Ct (46803-3290)
PHONE..................260 407-2000
Derk J Hinsey, Pr
EMP: 3 EST: 1979
SALES (est): 389.98K Privately Held
Web: www.baddad.com
SIC: 3089 5231 Automotive parts, plastic; Paint and painting supplies

(G-5069)
HIS WORD IS MY SWORD LLC
7719 Allison Ave (46819-2205)
PHONE..................260 433-9911
Teresa Strader, Prin
EMP: 5 EST: 2016
SALES (est): 65.8K Privately Held
SIC: 3421 Cutlery

(G-5070)
HOFFMASTER GROUP INC
Also Called: Aardvark Straws
2701 S Coliseum Blvd Ste 1148 (46803-2950)
PHONE..................855 230-5281
EMP: 78
Web: www.hoffmaster.com
SIC: 2656 Straws, drinking: made from purchased material
HQ: Hoffmaster Group, Inc.
2920 N Main St
Oshkosh WI 54901
800 558-9300

(G-5071)
HOLSUM OF FORT WAYNE INC (HQ)
136 Murray St (46803)
P.O. Box 11468 (46858)
PHONE..................260 456-2130
Lewis Jr Jack, Pr
Rodger Lesh, *
Jeffery J Sankovitch, *
Peggy S Lewis, *
EMP: 160 EST: 1900
SQ FT: 34,000
SALES (est): 9.76MM
SALES (corp-wide): 9.76MM Privately Held
Web: www.holsum.com
SIC: 2051 Bread, all types (white, wheat, rye, etc); fresh or frozen
PA: Lewis Brothers Bakeries Inc
500 N Fulton Ave
Evansville IN 47710
812 425-4642

(G-5072)
HOME RESERVE LLC
Also Called: Home Reserve.com
3015 Cannongate Dr (46808-4508)
PHONE..................260 969-6939
Blaine Wieland, Managing Member
▼ EMP: 12 EST: 2000
SQ FT: 16,500
SALES (est): 2.41MM Privately Held
Web: www.homereserve.com
SIC: 2512 Upholstered household furniture

(G-5073)
HOOK & ARROW
7536 Winchester Rd (46819-2243)
PHONE..................260 739-6661
EMP: 2 EST: 2012
SALES (est): 146.53K Privately Held
Web: www.hookandarrow.net
SIC: 3949 Sporting and athletic goods, nec

(G-5074)
HOOK DEVELOPMENT INC
2731 Brooklyn Ave (46802-3801)
PHONE..................260 432-7771
Tom Hook, Pr
Kenneth Hook, Sec
EMP: 2 EST: 1979
SALES (est): 139.32K Privately Held
Web: www.hookindustrialsales.com
SIC: 3544 Special dies, tools, jigs, and fixtures

(G-5075)
HOOK INDUSTRIAL SALES INC (PA)
2731 Brooklyn Ave (46802)
P.O. Box 9177 (46899)
PHONE..................260 432-9441
Thomas G Hook, Pr
Kenneth Hook, *
EMP: 65 EST: 1970
SQ FT: 79,000
SALES (est): 7.75MM
SALES (corp-wide): 7.75MM Privately Held
Web: www.hookindustrialsales.com

SIC: 3569 5085 Filter elements, fluid, hydraulic line; Seals, industrial

(G-5076)
HOOSIER BOX LLC
7909 Grassland Ct (46825-3153)
PHONE..................260 210-3757
Rolando R Perez, Owner
EMP: 6 EST: 2018
SALES (est): 85.58K Privately Held
SIC: 3599 Machine shop, jobbing and repair

(G-5077)
HOOSIER ETHANOL ENERGY LLC
110 W Berry St Ste 1200 (46802-2366)
PHONE..................260 407-6161
EMP: 2 EST: 2007
SALES (est): 222.38K Privately Held
SIC: 2869 Ethyl alcohol, ethanol

(G-5078)
HOOSIER MANUFACTURING LLC
9312 Avionics Dr (46809-9631)
PHONE..................260 493-9990
EMP: 8 EST: 2011
SALES (est): 125.09K Privately Held
Web: www.hoosier-inc.com
SIC: 3544 Special dies and tools

(G-5079)
HOOSIER PRIDE PLASTICS INC
Also Called: Hpp Mold & Tool
6120 Highview Dr (46818-1378)
PHONE..................260 497-7080
Mike Hoeppner, Pr
Linda Hoeppner, VP
EMP: 20 EST: 1988
SQ FT: 30,000
SALES (est): 2.56MM Privately Held
Web: www.hoosierprideplastics.com
SIC: 3089 Injection molding of plastics

(G-5080)
HOOSIER PROCESSING LLC ◆
Also Called: Albrights Raw Pet Food
1025 Osage St (46803-3401)
P.O. Box 11707 (46860-1707)
PHONE..................260 422-9440
Joseph Monahan, Managing Member
EMP: 10 EST: 2022
SALES (est): 1.07MM Privately Held
Web: www.albrightsrawdogfood.com
SIC: 5149 5999 2048 Pet foods; Pet food; Canned pet food (except dog and cat)

(G-5081)
HOOSIER TOOLMAKING & ENGRG INC
6930 Derek Dr (46803-3299)
PHONE..................260 493-9990
EMP: 7 EST: 2017
SALES (est): 83.2K Privately Held
SIC: 3544 Special dies and tools

(G-5082)
HORNECO FABRICATION INC
13020 Redding Dr (46814-9773)
PHONE..................260 672-2064
Bruce Horne, Pr
Gail Fisher, Sec
EMP: 2 EST: 2005
SALES (est): 120.24K Privately Held
SIC: 3462 Ornamental metal forgings, ferrous

(G-5083)
HORNER INDUSTRIAL SERVICES INC
Also Called: Horner Electric
4421 Ardmore Ave (46809-9722)
PHONE..................260 434-1189
Troy Elder, Mgr

▲ = Import ▼ = Export
◆ = Import/Export

GEOGRAPHIC SECTION
Fort Wayne - Allen County (G-5108)

EMP: 4
SALES (corp-wide): 55.43MM **Privately Held**
Web: www.hornerindustrial.com
SIC: 3625 7694 7699 5063 Electric controls and control accessories, industrial; Electric motor repair; Pumps and pumping equipment repair; Electrical apparatus and equipment
PA: Horner Industrial Services, Inc.
1521 E Washington St
Indianapolis IN 46201
317 639-4261

(G-5084)
HOSETRACT INDUSTRIES LTD
6433 Discount Dr (46818)
P.O. Box 80008 (46898)
PHONE..................260 489-8828
James M Schaller, *Pr*
▲ **EMP:** 15 **EST:** 1985
SQ FT: 12,000
SALES (est): 1.93MM **Privately Held**
Web: www.hosetract.com
SIC: 3499 Reels, cable: metal

(G-5085)
HUTH TOOL
6930 Derek Dr (46803-3299)
PHONE..................260 749-9411
David D Richards, *Prin*
EMP: 2 **EST:** 2011
SALES (est): 118.62K **Privately Held**
Web: www.huthtool.net
SIC: 7389 3599 Grinding, precision: commercial or industrial; Machine shop, jobbing and repair

(G-5086)
HUTH TOOL & MACHINE CORP
6930 Derek Dr (46803-3299)
PHONE..................260 749-9411
David D Richards, *Pr*
EMP: 8 **EST:** 1923
SQ FT: 6,000
SALES (est): 946.83K **Privately Held**
Web: www.huthtool.com
SIC: 3544 7389 Industrial molds; Grinding, precision: commercial or industrial

(G-5087)
HY-TEC FIBERGLASS INC
2201 Suppliers Ct (46818-1172)
PHONE..................260 489-6601
Gary Onz, *Pr*
Rick Witzigreuter, *VP*
EMP: 7 **EST:** 1983
SQ FT: 14,000
SALES (est): 704.27K **Privately Held**
Web: www.solo-boat.com
SIC: 3296 3537 Fiberglass insulation; Industrial trucks and tractors

(G-5088)
HYDRO SYSTEMS MFG INC
3632 Illinois Rd Ofc (46804-2062)
PHONE..................260 436-4476
Michael Duff, *Pr*
Shannon Duff, *Sec*
EMP: 3 **EST:** 2006
SALES (est): 333.35K **Privately Held**
SIC: 3492 Control valves, fluid power: hydraulic and pneumatic

(G-5089)
HYNDMAN INDUSTRIAL PDTS INC
Also Called: Resistance Wire
4031 Merchant Rd Ste A (46818-1266)
PHONE..................260 483-6042
▲ **EMP:** 46 **EST:** 1983
SQ FT: 14,000
SALES (est): 4.85MM **Privately Held**
Web: www.resistancewire.com
SIC: 3634 Electric household cooking appliances

(G-5090)
IASA GROUP LLC (PA)
Also Called: Integrated Custom Components
1905 Production Rd (46808-3647)
P.O. Box 92488 (76092-0488)
PHONE..................260 484-1322
Imtiaz Ahmed, *Managing Member*
EMP: 1 **EST:** 2005
SALES (est): 567.24K
SALES (corp-wide): 567.24K **Privately Held**
Web: www.iasagrp.com
SIC: 3728 Aircraft assemblies, subassemblies, and parts, nec

(G-5091)
ICON INTERNATIONAL INC
Also Called: Displaysource
8333 Clinton Park Dr (46825-3164)
PHONE..................260 482-8700
▲ **EMP:** 52
SIC: 3993 Signs and advertising specialties

(G-5092)
ILLINOIS LUBRICANTS LLC
Also Called: Jiffy Lube
1300 Airport North Office Park Ste A (46825)
PHONE..................260 436-2444
Steve Sanner, *Pr*
EMP: 6 **EST:** 2008
SALES (est): 476.45K **Privately Held**
Web: www.jiffylube.com
SIC: 7549 2992 Lubrication service, automotive; Lubricating oils and greases

(G-5093)
IM INDIANA HOLDINGS INC
Also Called: Trans-Flo
6300 Ardmore Ave (46809-9502)
PHONE..................260 478-1674
Larry Schaefer, *Mgr*
EMP: 6
SQ FT: 40,000
SALES (corp-wide): 4.28MM **Privately Held**
SIC: 3273 Ready-mixed concrete
PA: Indiana Im Holdings Inc
13415 Coldwater Rd
Fort Wayne IN 46845
260 637-3101

(G-5094)
IMAGE LLC
6838 Covington Creek Trl (46804-2872)
PHONE..................260 436-6125
Irving M Adler, *Prin*
EMP: 1 **EST:** 2005
SALES (est): 56K **Privately Held**
SIC: 3299 Images, small: gypsum, clay, or papier mache

(G-5095)
IMI SOUTHWEST INC
201 S Thomas Rd (46808-2900)
PHONE..................260 432-3973
Bill Wittenmyer, *Brnch Mgr*
EMP: 15
SALES (corp-wide): 814.09MM **Privately Held**
SIC: 2411 Rails, fence: round or split
HQ: Imi Southwest, Inc.
1816 W Lloyd Expy
Evansville IN 47712
812 424-3554

(G-5096)
IMPERIAL TROPHY & AWARDS CO
2405 W Jefferson Blvd (46802-4640)
P.O. Box 10862 (46854-0862)
PHONE..................260 432-8161
Tom Loy, *Owner*
Rick Loy, *Pr*
EMP: 6 **EST:** 1966
SQ FT: 7,000
SALES (est): 499.15K **Privately Held**
Web: www.imperialtrophyawards.com
SIC: 5999 5094 3993 3446 Trophies and plaques; Trophies; Signs and advertising specialties; Architectural metalwork

(G-5097)
IN CLOUDBRST LAWN SPRNKLR SVCS
1707 Brandywine Trl (46845-1511)
PHONE..................260 492-8400
Marc Zahn, *Pr*
Michael Worman, *VP*
EMP: 10 **EST:** 2004
SALES (est): 982.61K **Privately Held**
SIC: 3432 1711 Lawn hose nozzles and sprinklers; Irrigation sprinkler system installation

(G-5098)
INDIANA BAKING CO
9025 Sunburst Ln (46804-3453)
PHONE..................260 483-5997
Ronald W Rice, *CEO*
Margaret N Rice, *Sec*
Thomas J Casaburo, *Pr*
EMP: 12 **EST:** 1989
SALES (est): 999.63K **Privately Held**
Web: www.indianabaking.com
SIC: 2051 Bakery: wholesale or wholesale/retail combined

(G-5099)
INDIANA BARRIER WALL LLC
7107 Smith Rd (46809-9789)
PHONE..................260 747-5777
Scott Fredrick, *Prin*
EMP: 2 **EST:** 2004
SALES (est): 180.53K **Privately Held**
SIC: 3272 Wall and ceiling squares, concrete

(G-5100)
INDIANA HANDPIECE REPAIR INC
9530 Old Grist Mill Pl (46835-9303)
PHONE..................260 436-0765
John Ball, *Pr*
EMP: 2 **EST:** 1994
SALES (est): 139.86K **Privately Held**
SIC: 3541 7699 Machine tool replacement & repair parts, metal cutting types; Professional instrument repair services

(G-5101)
INDIANA IM HOLDINGS INC (PA)
13415 Coldwater Rd (46845-9515)
PHONE..................260 637-3101
EMP: 25 **EST:** 1926
SALES (est): 4.28MM
SALES (corp-wide): 4.28MM **Privately Held**
SIC: 3273 3535 Ready-mixed concrete; Pneumatic tube conveyor systems

(G-5102)
INDIANA REFRACTORIES INC
1815 S Anthony Blvd (46803)
P.O. Box 12111 (46862)
PHONE..................260 426-3286
EMP: 44 **EST:** 1997
SQ FT: 33,000
SALES (est): 4.91MM **Privately Held**
Web: www.indianarefractories.com
SIC: 3297 Nonclay refractories

(G-5103)
INDIANA STAMP CO INC
Also Called: Indiana Signworks
1319 Production Rd (46808-1164)
PHONE..................260 407-4165
John Peirce, *Prin*
EMP: 3
SALES (corp-wide): 4.15MM **Privately Held**
Web: www.indianastamp.com
SIC: 3993 Signs and advertising specialties
PA: Indiana Stamp Co., Inc.
1319 Production Rd
Fort Wayne IN 46808
260 424-8973

(G-5104)
INDIANA STAMP CO INC (PA)
Also Called: United Ribtype Company
1319 Production Rd (46808-1164)
P.O. Box 8887 (46898-8887)
PHONE..................260 424-8973
Olivia Warner, *Pr*
Sarah Chesebrough, *
EMP: 37 **EST:** 1947
SQ FT: 32,000
SALES (est): 4.15MM
SALES (corp-wide): 4.15MM **Privately Held**
Web: www.indianastamp.com
SIC: 3953 3993 Embossing seals and hand stamps; Signs and advertising specialties

(G-5105)
INDUSTRIAL ENGINEERING INC
Also Called: Industrial Engineering NC
4430 Tielker Rd (46809-1500)
PHONE..................260 478-1514
Harry P Laffkas, *Pr*
Margaret Hyde, *
EMP: 23 **EST:** 1969
SQ FT: 13,500
SALES (est): 763.42K **Privately Held**
Web: www.ind-eng.com
SIC: 3599 3544 Machine shop, jobbing and repair; Special dies, tools, jigs, and fixtures

(G-5106)
INFOBIND SYSTEMS INC
3619 Centennial Dr (46808-4514)
PHONE..................260 248-4989
Stanley Needham Iii, *Pr*
Stanley Needham, *Pr*
Carol J Needham, *Sec*
EMP: 2 **EST:** 1990
SALES (est): 174.54K **Privately Held**
Web: www.maryjaneluxuryrobes.com
SIC: 2789 Bookbinding and related work

(G-5107)
INK SPOT
215 W State Blvd (46808-3189)
PHONE..................260 482-4492
Jon Slate, *Owner*
EMP: 2 **EST:** 1981
SQ FT: 1,700
SALES (est): 190.18K **Privately Held**
Web: www.inkspot.net
SIC: 2752 Offset printing

(G-5108)
INNOTEK CUSTOM SOLUTIONS LLC
429 E Dupont Rd Ste 49 (46825-2051)
PHONE..................260 341-8691
Alton Liu Md, *Managing Member*
EMP: 4 **EST:** 2021
SALES (est): 64.19K **Privately Held**
Web: www.innotekcustomsolutions.com

Fort Wayne - Allen County (G-5109)

GEOGRAPHIC SECTION

SIC: 3841 Surgical and medical instruments

(G-5109)
INNOVATIONS BY
Also Called: Silva Military Solutions
2611 Lincroft Dr (46845-1918)
PHONE.....................................260 413-1869
John Taller, Prin
Noel Hupp, Prin
EMP: 2 EST: 2014
SALES (est): 89.92K Privately Held
SIC: 3731 7389 Shipbuilding and repairing; Business Activities at Non-Commercial Site

(G-5110)
INNOVATIVE BATTERY POWER INC
10827 Middleford Pl (46818-8896)
PHONE.....................................260 267-6582
Jeremy Aker, Pr
EMP: 2 EST: 2013
SALES (est): 156.79K Privately Held
Web: www.innovativebatterypower.com
SIC: 3625 Truck controls, industrial battery

(G-5111)
INNOVTIVE TOLING SOLUTIONS INC
6225 Commodity Ct (46818-1221)
P.O. Box 8458 (46898-8458)
PHONE.....................................260 487-9970
Joseph Dunn, Pr
Joan Wheelock, Sec
▲ EMP: 10 EST: 2002
SQ FT: 10,000
SALES (est): 1.21MM Privately Held
Web: www.innovativetoolingsolutions.com
SIC: 3599 Machine shop, jobbing and repair

(G-5112)
INSTATE WELDING SERVICE INC
4911 Industrial Rd (46825-5211)
PHONE.....................................260 437-2894
EMP: 5 EST: 2016
SALES (est): 40.41K Privately Held
SIC: 7692 Welding repair

(G-5113)
INSUL-COUSTIC CORPORATION
2701 S Coliseum Blvd Ste 1286 (46803-2950)
PHONE.....................................260 420-1480
Wade Cunningham, Pr
Naomi Cunningham, *
Steve Alvey, *
Stephen D Alvey, *
EMP: 50 EST: 1999
SQ FT: 40,000
SALES (est): 4.79MM Privately Held
Web: www.insulcoustic.com
SIC: 3296 Fiberglass insulation

(G-5114)
INTEGER HOLDINGS CORPORATION
Also Called: Greatbatch Medical
4545 Kroemer Rd (46818)
PHONE.....................................260 373-1664
EMP: 9
SALES (corp-wide): 1.6B Publicly Held
Web: www.integer.net
SIC: 3675 3692 3691 Electronic capacitors; Primary batteries, dry and wet; Storage batteries
PA: Integer Holdings Corporation
2595 Dallas Pkwy Ste 310
Frisco TX 75034
214 618-5243

(G-5115)
INTERNATIONAL PAPER COMPANY
Also Called: International Paper
3904 W Ferguson Rd (46809-3150)
PHONE.....................................260 747-9111
Charles Vaughn, Brnch Mgr
EMP: 103
SALES (corp-wide): 18.92B Publicly Held
Web: www.internationalpaper.com
SIC: 2621 Paper mills
PA: International Paper Company
6400 Poplar Ave
Memphis TN 38197
901 419-7000

(G-5116)
INTRATEK INC
Also Called: Intratek Engineering
3209 Clearfield Ct (46808-4517)
P.O. Box 80188 (46898-0188)
PHONE.....................................260 484-3377
John Fanning Junior, Pr
EMP: 8 EST: 1980
SQ FT: 1,500
SALES (est): 767.87K Privately Held
SIC: 3479 Painting, coating, and hot dipping

(G-5117)
IPFW STUDENT HOUSING
2101 E Coliseum Blvd Ste 100 (46805-1499)
PHONE.....................................260 481-4180
Ray Hammond, Prin
EMP: 8 EST: 2008
SALES (est): 414.86K Privately Held
Web: www.pfw.edu
SIC: 3621 Motor housings

(G-5118)
IRON OUT INC
Also Called: Summit Brands
3404 Conestoga Dr (46808-4410)
PHONE.....................................260 483-2519
EMP: 7
SALES (corp-wide): 15.78MM Privately Held
Web: www.summitbrands.com
SIC: 2899 Water treating compounds
PA: Iron Out, Inc.
6714 Pointe Inverness Way
Fort Wayne IN 46804
800 654-0791

(G-5119)
IRON OUT INC (PA)
Also Called: Summit Brands
6714 Pointe Inverness Way Ste 200 (46804-7936)
PHONE.....................................800 654-0791
Joel Harter, CEO
Joel Harter, Pr
Charlotte Simonis, *
EMP: 43 EST: 1960
SALES (est): 15.78MM
SALES (corp-wide): 15.78MM Privately Held
Web: www.summitbrands.com
SIC: 2899 2891 2842 Water treating compounds; Adhesives and sealants; Polishes and sanitation goods

(G-5120)
IRVING MATERIALS INC
6300 Ardmore Ave (46809-9502)
PHONE.....................................317 326-3101
EMP: 11
SALES (corp-wide): 814.09MM Privately Held
Web: www.irvmat.com
SIC: 3273 Ready-mixed concrete
PA: Irving Materials, Inc.
8032 N State Road 9
Greenfield IN 46140
317 326-3101

(G-5121)
IRWIN HODSON GROUP INDIANA LLC
2980 E Coliseum Blvd Ste 102 (46805-1500)
PHONE.....................................260 482-8052
Brad Barondeau, Owner
EMP: 9 EST: 2015
SALES (est): 621.97K Privately Held
SIC: 3469 Automobile license tags, stamped metal
PA: Irwin Hodson Group Llc
12067 Ne Glenn Widing Dr # 103
Portland OR 97220

(G-5122)
ITT LLC
Also Called: ITT Communications Systems
1919 W Cook Rd (46818-1115)
P.O. Box 3700 (46801-3700)
PHONE.....................................260 451-6000
A Coleman, Brnch Mgr
EMP: 2
SALES (corp-wide): 3.28B Publicly Held
Web: www.itt.com
SIC: 3625 Control equipment, electric
HQ: Itt Llc
1133 Westchester Ave
White Plains NY 10604
914 641-2000

(G-5123)
J B TOOL DIE & ENGINEERING CO
1509 Dividend Rd (46808-1159)
PHONE.....................................260 483-9586
David Bear, Pr
David Thompson, *
Rick Zorger, *
Gregory Beer, *
▲ EMP: 115 EST: 1962
SQ FT: 65,000
SALES (est): 20.16MM Privately Held
Web: www.jbtool.com
SIC: 3544 3599 Special dies and tools; Machine shop, jobbing and repair

(G-5124)
J R SIGN COMPANY AND SERVICES
2811 Autumn Leaf Ln (46808-1842)
PHONE.....................................260 414-0510
EMP: 5 EST: 2014
SALES (est): 60.84K Privately Held
Web: www.jandrcompany.com
SIC: 3993 Signs and advertising specialties

(G-5125)
J T D SPIRAL INC
6212 Highview Dr (46818-1375)
P.O. Box 8007 (46898-8007)
PHONE.....................................260 497-1300
Tim Morris, Pr
James Morris, VP
Dan Morris, Sec
EMP: 8 EST: 2001
SQ FT: 48,000
SALES (est): 2.15MM
SALES (corp-wide): 104.56MM Publicly Held
Web: www.morrissheetmetal.com
SIC: 3444 Pipe, sheet metal
PA: Alpine 4 Holdings, Inc.
2525 E Ariz Bltmore Cir S
Phoenix AZ 85016
480 702-2431

(G-5126)
J-N SHEET METAL COMPANY INC
2828 Covington Rd (46802-6914)
P.O. Box 9201 (46899-9201)
PHONE.....................................260 436-7916
Nancy Galuoppo, Pr
Anthony Galuoppo, Sec
EMP: 9 EST: 1972
SQ FT: 4,000
SALES (est): 600K Privately Held
SIC: 3444 Sheet metalwork

(G-5127)
J4 PRINTING LLC
1008 Orlando Dr (46825-4040)
PHONE.....................................260 417-5382
Jeffrey S Junkin, Admn
EMP: 5 EST: 2009
SALES (est): 117.43K Privately Held
SIC: 2752 Commercial printing, lithographic

(G-5128)
JACYL TECHNOLOGY INC (PA)
Also Called: Jacyl Web Design
6020 Huguenard Rd (46818-1547)
PHONE.....................................260 471-6067
Rhonda Huebner, CEO
Joel Huebner, Pr
EMP: 4 EST: 2002
SQ FT: 3,400
SALES (est): 571.56K
SALES (corp-wide): 571.56K Privately Held
Web: www.domainhero.com
SIC: 3571 Electronic computers

(G-5129)
JAE ENTERPRISES INC (PA)
Also Called: Custom Tube Co
7707 Freedom Way (46818-2169)
PHONE.....................................260 489-6249
Dave Seybert, Pr
EMP: 1 EST: 1998
SALES (est): 2.51MM
SALES (corp-wide): 2.51MM Privately Held
Web: www.jaeeagle.com
SIC: 3498 Tube fabricating (contract bending and shaping)

(G-5130)
JAE ENTERPRISES INC
Also Called: Custom Tube Co
8000 Baer Rd (46809-9781)
PHONE.....................................260 747-0568
Dave Seybert, Brnch Mgr
EMP: 28
SALES (corp-wide): 2.51MM Privately Held
Web: www.jaeeagle.com
SIC: 3498 Tube fabricating (contract bending and shaping)
PA: Jae Enterprises, Inc.
7707 Freedom Way
Fort Wayne IN 46818
260 489-6249

(G-5131)
JAMES E TROWBRIDGE
Also Called: Kustom Tool
2629 Carroll Rd (46818-9803)
PHONE.....................................260 341-1952
James E Trowbridge, Owner
EMP: 1 EST: 2020
SALES (est): 60K Privately Held
SIC: 3599 Machine shop, jobbing and repair

(G-5132)
JAMES SMITH
1320 Goshen Ave (46808-2034)
PHONE.....................................260 414-1237
James Smith, Prin
EMP: 4 EST: 2016
SALES (est): 92.36K Privately Held
SIC: 2711 Newspapers, publishing and printing

▲ = Import ▼ = Export
◆ = Import/Export

GEOGRAPHIC SECTION
Fort Wayne - Allen County (G-5159)

(G-5133)
JEFF GOSHERT
11301 Us Highway 24 W (46814-8110)
PHONE..................260 672-3737
Jeff Goshert, *Owner*
Jeff Goghert, *Owner*
EMP: 1 **EST:** 1973
SALES (est): 69.68K **Privately Held**
SIC: 3861 Cameras and related equipment

(G-5134)
JENSEN CABINET INC
205 Murray St (46803-2334)
P.O. Box 10599 (46853-0599)
PHONE..................260 456-2131
Thomas L Dedrick, *Pr*
Jane Franklin, *
Daniel D Rohloff, *
David M Wester, *
Jane A Franklin, *
EMP: 40 **EST:** 1945
SQ FT: 80,000
SALES (est): 5.11MM **Privately Held**
Web: www.jensencabinet.com
SIC: 2541 Cabinets, except refrigerated: show, display, etc.: wood

(G-5135)
JEWELS HAIR & ACCESSORIES LLC
3215 Bowser Ave (46806-3748)
PHONE..................260 310-9915
EMP: 2 **EST:** 2021
SALES (est): 62.54K **Privately Held**
SIC: 3999 Hair, dressing of, for the trade

(G-5136)
JINNINGS EQUIPMENT LLC
4434 Allen Martin Dr (46806-2802)
PHONE..................260 447-4343
◆ **EMP:** 6 **EST:** 2000
SQ FT: 8,000
SALES (est): 1.28MM **Privately Held**
Web: www.jinnings.com
SIC: 3531 Pile drivers (construction machinery)

(G-5137)
JM FITTINGS LLC
Also Called: L & L Fittings Mfg
7815 Inverness Glens Dr (46804-3839)
PHONE..................260 747-9200
▲ **EMP:** 30
Web: www.llfittings.com
SIC: 3494 3463 3498 3492 Pipe fittings; Nonferrous forgings; Fabricated pipe and fittings; Fluid power valves and hose fittings

(G-5138)
JOHNNY WHITE
Also Called: Johnny White Signs
6607 Hanna St (46816-1180)
PHONE..................260 441-0077
Johnny White, *Owner*
EMP: 1 **EST:** 1966
SALES (est): 8.85K **Privately Held**
SIC: 3993 Signs and advertising specialties

(G-5139)
JPT ENTERPRISES INC
6435 W Jefferson Blvd (46804-6203)
PHONE..................260 672-1605
Paul Tweet, *CEO*
EMP: 6 **EST:** 2000
SALES (est): 555.08K **Privately Held**
SIC: 2911 Oils, fuel

(G-5140)
JW SIGNS INC
2511 Alma Ave (46809-2903)
PHONE..................260 747-5168
John Walker, *Pr*
Nancy Woosely, *Sec*
EMP: 9 **EST:** 1983
SQ FT: 6,000
SALES (est): 551.36K **Privately Held**
Web: www.signsbyjw.com
SIC: 3993 1799 Signs, not made in custom sign painting shops; Sign installation and maintenance

(G-5141)
K & S PALLET INC
Also Called: K and S Pallets
1025 Osage St (46808-3401)
PHONE..................260 422-1264
Steve Lefebvre, *Pr*
EMP: 30 **EST:** 1991
SQ FT: 7,000
SALES (est): 4.07MM **Privately Held**
Web: www.indianapallets.com
SIC: 2448 5031 4953 Pallets, wood; Pallets, wood; Refuse systems

(G-5142)
KAISER TOOL COMPANY INC
Also Called: Laser Images
3620 Centennial Dr (46808-4514)
P.O. Box 80430 (46898-0430)
PHONE..................260 484-3620
Lenore E Perry, *Pr*
Douglas Perry, *
EMP: 48 **EST:** 1955
SQ FT: 20,000
SALES (est): 5.21MM **Privately Held**
Web: www.thinbit.com
SIC: 3545 5085 3541 3423 Machine tool attachments and accessories; Industrial supplies; Machine tools, metal cutting type; Hand and edge tools, nec

(G-5143)
KAMAN CORPORATION
Also Called: Kaman Automation
213 W Wayne St (46802-3605)
PHONE..................714 696-3750
Steven J Smidler, *Brnch Mgr*
EMP: 58
SALES (corp-wide): 775.85MM **Privately Held**
Web: www.kaman.com
SIC: 3491 Industrial valves
PA: Kaman Corporation
1332 Blue Hills Ave
Bloomfield CT 06002
860 243-7100

(G-5144)
KEEFER PRINTING COMPANY INC
3824 Transportation Dr (46818-1223)
PHONE..................260 424-4543
Richard F Keefer, *Pr*
James M Keefer, *
EMP: 27 **EST:** 1926
SQ FT: 43,000
SALES (est): 2.27MM **Privately Held**
Web: www.keeferprinting.com
SIC: 2752 Offset printing

(G-5145)
KELLY BOX AND PACKAGING CORP (PA)
2801 Covington Rd (46802-6969)
PHONE..................260 432-4570
Thomas J Kelly, *Pr*
EMP: 86 **EST:** 1955
SQ FT: 120,000
SALES (est): 21.53MM
SALES (corp-wide): 21.53MM **Privately Held**
Web: www.kellybox.com
SIC: 2653 5199 Boxes, corrugated: made from purchased materials; Packaging materials

(G-5146)
KERHAM INC
Also Called: Markfore Shurtz Unlimited
205 E Collins Rd (46825-5303)
PHONE..................260 483-5444
Kevin Gould, *Pr*
EMP: 21 **EST:** 1980
SQ FT: 23,000
SALES (est): 717.97K **Privately Held**
Web: www.markforesales.com
SIC: 5941 5091 2396 2395 Bowling equipment and supplies; Bowling equipment ; Automotive and apparel trimmings; Pleating and stitching

(G-5147)
KEY MILLWORK INC
1830 Wayne Trce (46803-2657)
PHONE..................260 426-6501
EMP: 9 **EST:** 1995
SQ FT: 6,500
SALES (est): 996.79K **Privately Held**
SIC: 2434 Wood kitchen cabinets

(G-5148)
KEYSIGHT TECHNOLOGIES INC
1200 Airport North Office Park Ste D (46825)
PHONE..................260 203-2179
EMP: 9
SALES (corp-wide): 5.46B **Publicly Held**
Web: www.keysight.com
SIC: 3825 Instruments to measure electricity
PA: Keysight Technologies, Inc.
1400 Fountaingrove Pkwy
Santa Rosa CA 95403
800 829-4444

(G-5149)
KIEN INDUSTRIES LLP
4752 Trier Rd (46815-4969)
PHONE..................260 471-1098
Alexander Kien, *Prin*
EMP: 4 **EST:** 2018
SALES (est): 39.69K **Privately Held**
SIC: 3999 Manufacturing industries, nec

(G-5150)
KIMMEL FABRICATION STUDIO LLC
2727 Lofty Dr Ste 4 (46808-3941)
PHONE..................260 403-5691
EMP: 6 **EST:** 2017
SALES (est): 183.57K **Privately Held**
Web: www.kimmelfab.com
SIC: 3999 Manufacturing industries, nec

(G-5151)
KLOTZ SYNTHETIC LUBRICANTS LLC
7424 Freedom Way (46818)
PHONE..................260 490-0489
Brad Kruckenberg, *Pr*
EMP: 11 **EST:** 2020
SALES (est): 2.34MM **Privately Held**
Web: www.klotzlube.com
SIC: 2992 Lubricating oils and greases
PA: Cometic Gasket Inc.
8090 Auburn Rd
Concord Township OH

(G-5152)
KMM CREATIVE LLC
5534 Saint Joe Rd (46835)
PHONE..................813 764-9294
Katrina Miller, *Prin*
EMP: 1
SALES (est): 69.27K **Privately Held**
SIC: 2731 Books, publishing only

(G-5153)
KOKOMO PRESS LLC
5534 Saint Joe Rd (46835-3328)
P.O. Box 3593 (46082-3593)
PHONE..................317 575-9903
EMP: 5 **EST:** 2014
SALES (est): 65.16K **Privately Held**
Web: www.kokomopress.com
SIC: 2741 Miscellaneous publishing

(G-5154)
KONECRANES INC
3939 Fourier Dr Ste D (46818-9382)
PHONE..................260 451-2016
Joe Pucel, *Mgr*
EMP: 7
Web: www.konecranes.com
SIC: 3536 Hoists, cranes, and monorails
HQ: Konecranes, Inc.
4401 Gateway Blvd
Springfield OH 45502

(G-5155)
KOOMLER & SONS INC
3820 Superior Ridge Dr (46808-4423)
PHONE..................260 482-7641
Dennis Koomler, *Pr*
Mark Koomler, *VP*
Brad Koomler, *Treas*
EMP: 10 **EST:** 1990
SALES (est): 988.89K **Privately Held**
Web: www.koomlersheetmetal.com
SIC: 3444 Ducts, sheet metal

(G-5156)
KORE OUTDOOR (US) INC
4230 Lake Ave (46815-7220)
PHONE..................800 724-6822
Billy Cernaski, *CEO*
EMP: 30 **EST:** 2020
SALES (est): 3.72MM **Privately Held**
Web: www.koreoutdoor.com
SIC: 3484 Small arms

(G-5157)
KORTE BROS INC
620 W Cook Rd (46825-3324)
PHONE..................260 497-0500
EMP: 10
SIC: 3531 5032 Concrete plants; Aggregate

(G-5158)
KPC MEDIA GROUP INC
Also Called: Fort Wayne Business Weekly
6418 Lima Rd (46818-1424)
PHONE..................260 426-2640
EMP: 16
SALES (corp-wide): 23.55MM **Privately Held**
Web: www.fwbusiness.com
SIC: 2711 2791 2752 Newspapers, publishing and printing; Typesetting; Commercial printing, lithographic
PA: Kpc Media Group Inc.
102 N Main St
Kendallville IN 46755
260 347-0400

(G-5159)
KPRIME TECHNOLOGIES LLC
9318 Airport Dr Ste F (46809-3047)
PHONE..................260 399-1337
EMP: 6 **EST:** 2018
SALES (est): 78.5K **Privately Held**
Web: www.kprime.net
SIC: 3826 Analytical instruments

Fort Wayne - Allen County (G-5160)

(G-5160)
KREATIVE CONCEPTS LLC
Also Called: Construction
808 Colerick St (46806-3771)
PHONE.....................260 579-0922
Kenneth Clark, Admn
EMP: 1 EST: 2019
SALES (est): 154.24K **Privately Held**
Web: www.kreativeconcepts4you.com
SIC: 1389 Construction, repair, and dismantling services

(G-5161)
KRONMILLER MACHINE & TOOL INC
2230 Lakeview Dr (46808-3926)
PHONE.....................260 436-1355
Michael D Kronmiller, Pr
EMP: 7 EST: 1986
SQ FT: 4,000
SALES (est): 651.86K **Privately Held**
SIC: 3544 Special dies, tools, jigs, and fixtures

(G-5162)
KT INDUSTRIES LLC
3925 Ardmore Ave (46802-4237)
PHONE.....................260 432-0027
Dan Alt, Prin
▼ EMP: 5 EST: 2010
SALES (est): 134.7K **Privately Held**
Web: www.ktindustries.net
SIC: 3999 Manufacturing industries, nec

(G-5163)
KTI CUTTING TOOLS INC
Also Called: KTI Cutting Tool
7007 Trafalgar Dr (46803-3288)
PHONE.....................260 749-1465
Kevin Miguel, Pr
Todd Gibson, VP
EMP: 3 EST: 2003
SQ FT: 1,000
SALES (est): 276.28K **Privately Held**
Web: www.ktitools.com
SIC: 3545 Cutting tools for machine tools

(G-5164)
KUEHNERT DAIRY INC
6532 W Cook Rd (46818-9164)
PHONE.....................260 489-3766
EMP: 2 EST: 1971
SALES (est): 484.94K **Privately Held**
Web: www.kuehnertdairy.com
SIC: 0241 2022 Milk production; Processed cheese

(G-5165)
L H CARBIDE CORPORATION (HQ)
4420 Clubview Dr (46804-4407)
PHONE.....................260 432-5563
Bruce Emerick, Ch Bd
Bruce Emerick, Pr
Leon O Habegger, Ch Bd
Dan Brehm, Sec
Bradley N Habeger, Dir
▲ EMP: 90 EST: 1966
SQ FT: 92,000
SALES (est): 32.54MM
SALES (corp-wide): 54.91MM **Privately Held**
Web: www.lhindustries.com
SIC: 3469 Metal stampings, nec
PA: L.H. Industries Corp.
4420 Clubview Dr
Fort Wayne IN 46804
260 432-5563

(G-5166)
L H CONTROLS INC
4420 Clubview Dr (46804-4407)
PHONE.....................260 432-9020
Leon Habegger, Ch Bd
Bruce Emerick, Pr
Bradley N Habegger, VP
Dan Brehm, CFO
EMP: 16 EST: 1990
SALES (est): 1.6MM
SALES (corp-wide): 54.91MM **Privately Held**
Web: www.lhindustries.com
SIC: 3625 Relays and industrial controls
HQ: L H Carbide Corporation
4420 Clubview Dr
Fort Wayne IN 46804
260 432-5563

(G-5167)
L H STAMPING CORPORATION (HQ)
4420 Clubview Dr (46804-4407)
PHONE.....................260 432-5563
Leon Habegger, Ch
Bruce Emerick, *
Bradley Habegger, *
Dan Brehm, *
EMP: 32 EST: 1984
SQ FT: 20,000
SALES (est): 22.37MM
SALES (corp-wide): 54.91MM **Privately Held**
Web: www.lhindustries.com
SIC: 3469 Stamping metal for the trade
PA: L.H. Industries Corp.
4420 Clubview Dr
Fort Wayne IN 46804
260 432-5563

(G-5168)
L-SOURCE LTD LLC
4630 W Jefferson Blvd Ste 6 (46804-6856)
PHONE.....................260 459-1971
EMP: 3 EST: 1996
SALES (est): 204.43K **Privately Held**
SIC: 3355 Cable, aluminum: made in rolling mills

(G-5169)
L3HARRIS TECHNOLOGIES INC
ITT Corporation Space Systems
1919 W Cook Rd (46818-1115)
P.O. Box 3700 (46801-3700)
PHONE.....................260 451-5597
Ken Peterson, Brnch Mgr
EMP: 7
SALES (corp-wide): 19.42B **Publicly Held**
Web: www.l3harris.com
SIC: 3812 3669 3823 Search and navigation equipment; Burglar alarm apparatus, electric ; Process control instruments
PA: L3harris Technologies, Inc.
1025 W Nasa Blvd
Melbourne FL 32919
321 727-9100

(G-5170)
L3HARRIS TECHNOLOGIES INC
Also Called: Electonic Systems Division
1919 W Cook Rd (46818-1115)
P.O. Box 3700 (46801-3700)
PHONE.....................260 451-6180
Dave Melcher, Brnch Mgr
EMP: 99
SALES (corp-wide): 19.42B **Publicly Held**
Web: www.l3harris.com
SIC: 3669 Intercommunication systems, electric
PA: L3harris Technologies, Inc.
1025 W Nasa Blvd
Melbourne FL 32919
321 727-9100

(G-5171)
L3HARRIS TECHNOLOGIES INC
Harris
7310 Innovation Blvd (46818-1370)
P.O. Box 371 (46801)
PHONE.....................260 451-6000
Nick Bobay, Brnch Mgr
EMP: 8
SALES (corp-wide): 19.42B **Publicly Held**
Web: www.l3harris.com
SIC: 3625 Control equipment, electric
PA: L3harris Technologies, Inc.
1025 W Nasa Blvd
Melbourne FL 32919
321 727-9100

(G-5172)
LAKEVIEW ENGINEERED PDTS INC
2500 W Jefferson Blvd (46802-4641)
PHONE.....................260 432-3479
Donald J Akey, Pr
Alberta Akey, VP
EMP: 7 EST: 1993
SALES (est): 779.08K **Privately Held**
Web: www.lakeviewengineered.com
SIC: 3443 Fabricated plate work (boiler shop)

(G-5173)
LAMAR ADVERTISING COMPANY
4511 Executive Blvd (46808-1136)
PHONE.....................260 482-9566
Michelle Raney-millard, Brnch Mgr
EMP: 10
Web: www.lamar.com
SIC: 7312 3993 Billboard advertising; Neon signs
PA: Lamar Advertising Company
5321 Corporate Blvd
Baton Rouge LA 70808

(G-5174)
LAMBERT METAL FINISHING INC
Also Called: Smith Metal Finishing
6912 Derek Dr (46803-3299)
PHONE.....................260 493-0529
EMP: 19 EST: 2010
SALES (est): 1.93MM **Privately Held**
Web: www.americananodizingco.com
SIC: 3471 Electroplating of metals or formed products

(G-5175)
LASSUS BROS OIL INC
10225 Illinois Rd (46814-8971)
PHONE.....................260 625-4003
Andy Carmichael, Brnch Mgr
EMP: 16
SALES (corp-wide): 152.54MM **Privately Held**
Web: www.lassus.com
SIC: 1311 Crude petroleum and natural gas
PA: Lassus Bros Oil Inc
1800 Magnavox Way
Fort Wayne IN 46804
260 436-1415

(G-5176)
LAUER LOG HOMES INC
6630 Reed Rd (46835-2271)
PHONE.....................260 486-7010
Connie Lauer, Owner
EMP: 2 EST: 1995
SALES (est): 224.11K **Privately Held**
Web: www.lauerloghomes.com
SIC: 2452 Log cabins, prefabricated, wood

(G-5177)
LAWRENCE INDUSTRIES INC
10403 Arbor Trl (46804-4607)
PHONE.....................260 432-9693
Kerry L Mcatee, Pr
EMP: 2 EST: 2002
SALES (est): 224.9K **Privately Held**
Web: www.lawrenceindustriesnow.com
SIC: 3353 Aluminum sheet, plate, and foil

(G-5178)
LAYSHIAS CLAWED MADAM LLC
1415 Sinclair St (46808-2653)
PHONE.....................260 257-7633
EMP: 3 EST: 2021
SALES (est): 39.69K **Privately Held**
SIC: 3999 Fingernails, artificial

(G-5179)
LCF ENTERPRISES LLC
10050 Bent Creek Blvd (46825-0023)
PHONE.....................260 483-3248
EMP: 5 EST: 1993
SALES (est): 496.9K **Privately Held**
Web: www.lcfhomes.com
SIC: 2451 Mobile homes

(G-5180)
LEEPOXY PLASTICS INC
3706 W Ferguson Rd (46809-3199)
PHONE.....................260 747-7411
Lawrence H Lee, Pr
EMP: 5 EST: 1965
SQ FT: 14,400
SALES (est): 756.57K **Privately Held**
Web: www.leepoxy.com
SIC: 2821 Epoxy resins

(G-5181)
LH INDUSTRIES CORP (PA)
4420 Clubview Dr (46804-4407)
PHONE.....................260 432-5563
Leon O Habegger, Ch
Bruce Emerick, Pr
Dan Brehm, Sec
EMP: 22 EST: 1991
SQ FT: 10,000
SALES (est): 54.91MM
SALES (corp-wide): 54.91MM **Privately Held**
Web: www.lhindustries.com
SIC: 3469 3544 8741 Stamping metal for the trade; Special dies, tools, jigs, and fixtures; Management services

(G-5182)
LH INDUSTRIES CORP
Also Called: Lh Stamping
4503 Ardon Ct (46816-4150)
PHONE.....................260 432-5563
EMP: 7
SALES (est): 51.52K **Privately Held**
Web: www.lhindustries.com
SIC: 3999 Manufacturing industries, nec

(G-5183)
LH MEDICAL CORPORATION
6932 Gettysburg Pike (46804-5614)
PHONE.....................260 387-5194
Bruce Emerick, Pr
Bradley N Habegger, *
Leon Habegger, *
Warren Brehm, *
Scott Nine, *
EMP: 80 EST: 2007
SQ FT: 64,000
SALES (est): 20.44MM
SALES (corp-wide): 54.91MM **Privately Held**
Web: www.lhindustries.com
SIC: 5047 3841 Orthopedic equipment and supplies; Surgical instruments and apparatus
HQ: L H Carbide Corporation
4420 Clubview Dr

GEOGRAPHIC SECTION
Fort Wayne - Allen County (G-5208)

Fort Wayne IN 46804
260 432-5563

(G-5184)
LICENSED ELIQUID MFG LLC
6746 E State Blvd (46815-7762)
PHONE...................260 245-6442
Shawn Anderson, *Prin*
Richard Evans, *Prin*
Steven Mavity, *Prin*
Adam Congdon, *Prin*
Lassus Brothers, *Prin*
EMP: 10 **EST:** 2016
SALES (est): 623.38K **Privately Held**
SIC: 3999 Manufacturing industries, nec

(G-5185)
LIFE MANAGEMENT INC
Also Called: Airomat
2916 Engle Rd (46809-1106)
PHONE...................260 747-7408
Joanne K Feasel, *Pr*
Jody Feasel, *VP*
Pamela J Peters, *VP*
EMP: 8 **EST:** 1958
SQ FT: 6,000
SALES (est): 1.64MM **Privately Held**
Web: www.mymatting.com
SIC: 3089 Plastics hardware and building products

(G-5186)
LINCOLN PRINTING CORPORATION
Also Called: Lincoln Printing
10351 Dawsons Creek Blvd Ste D (46825-1904)
PHONE...................260 424-5200
Billy Bradberry, *Pr*
Todd Wiedemann, *
Liz Hartmann, *
Joe Mcgrath, *Contrlr*
EMP: 2398 **EST:** 1959
SALES (est): 2.37MM
SALES (corp-wide): 292.19MM **Privately Held**
Web: www.printlinc.net
SIC: 2752 2791 2789 2761 Offset printing; Typesetting; Bookbinding and related work; Manifold business forms
PA: R.R. Donnelley Printing Company L.P.
35 W Wacker Dr Ste 3650
Chicago IL 60601
800 782-4892

(G-5187)
LINDE GAS & EQUIPMENT INC
Also Called: Praxair
1725 Edsall Ave (46803-2725)
PHONE...................260 423-4468
EMP: 4
Web: www.lindeus.com
SIC: 5084 5999 2813 Welding machinery and equipment; Welding supplies; Carbon dioxide
HQ: Linde Gas & Equipment Inc.
10 Riverview Dr
Danbury CT 06810
844 445-4633

(G-5188)
LOADING DOCK MAINTENANCE LLC
5032 Moeller Rd (46806-1504)
PHONE...................260 424-3635
EMP: 3 **EST:** 1994
SALES (est): 302.89K **Privately Held**
Web: www.loadingdockmaintenance.net
SIC: 3599 7692 Machine shop, jobbing and repair; Welding repair

(G-5189)
LOGIKOS OVERVIEW LLC
9812 Dawsons Creek Blvd (46825-1960)
PHONE...................260 483-3638
EMP: 6 **EST:** 2012
SALES (est): 223.32K **Privately Held**
Web: www.logikosoverview.com
SIC: 3663 Global positioning systems (GPS) equipment

(G-5190)
LONE STAR INDUSTRIES INC
4805 Investment Dr (46808-3609)
PHONE...................260 482-4559
Ken Squires, *Mgr*
EMP: 2
SALES (corp-wide): 4.69B **Privately Held**
Web: www.buzziunicemusa.com
SIC: 3241 Portland cement
HQ: Lone Star Industries Inc
10401 N Meridian St # 120
Carmel IN 46290
317 706-3314

(G-5191)
LONG TAIL CORPORATION (PA)
Also Called: Codeclouds
4630 W Jefferson Blvd Ste 1 (46804)
PHONE...................260 918-0489
Brian Hill, *Pr*
EMP: 5 **EST:** 2012
SALES (est): 486.71K
SALES (corp-wide): 486.71K **Privately Held**
SIC: 7373 7372 7374 Computer integrated systems design; Application computer software; Computer graphics service

(G-5192)
LUBE-LINE CORPORATION (PA)
906 Carroll Rd (46845-9778)
P.O. Box 38 (62947-0038)
PHONE...................260 637-3779
Thomas Luchies, *Pr*
EMP: 3 **EST:** 1980
SQ FT: 4,000
SALES (est): 484.29K **Privately Held**
Web: www.lubeline.com
SIC: 3569 Lubricating systems, centralized

(G-5193)
LUXURYLINKS LLC
848 Dolphin Dr (46816-1186)
PHONE...................260 258-2814
EMP: 3 **EST:** 2020
SALES (est): 83.91K **Privately Held**
SIC: 3999 Hair and hair-based products

(G-5194)
M & J SHELTON ENTERPRISES INC
Also Called: Shelton Enterprises
2131 Fairfield Ave (46802-5160)
PHONE...................260 745-1616
Mike Shelton, *Pr*
Norma Shelton, *VP*
EMP: 8 **EST:** 1988
SQ FT: 20,000
SALES (est): 942.4K **Privately Held**
SIC: 3999 1799 Dock equipment and supplies, industrial; Dock equipment installation, industrial

(G-5195)
MACALLISTER MACHINERY CO INC
Also Called: Caterpillar Authorized Dealer
2500 W Coliseum Blvd (46808-3640)
PHONE...................260 483-6469
Dennis Sawcett, *Brnch Mgr*
EMP: 104
SALES (corp-wide): 658.13MM **Privately Held**
Web: www.macallister.com
SIC: 3492 5082 5084 7699 Hose and tube fittings and assemblies, hydraulic/pneumatic; Contractor's materials; Engines and parts, diesel; Hydraulic equipment repair
PA: Macallister Machinery Co Inc
6300 Southeastern Ave
Indianapolis IN 46203
317 545-2151

(G-5196)
MACEDNIAN PTRTIC ORGNZTION OF
Also Called: MACEDONIAN TRIBUNE
124 W Wayne St Ste 204 (46802-2505)
PHONE...................260 422-5900
Maria T Makowski, *Pr*
Steve Petroff, *Treas*
Lois Levihn, *Ex Dir*
EMP: 1 **EST:** 1922
SQ FT: 15,000
SALES (est): 142.87K **Privately Held**
Web: www.macedonian.org
SIC: 2711 Newspapers, publishing and printing

(G-5197)
MACHINE REBUILDERS & SERVICE
Also Called: Mrs International
646 Pentolina Dr (46845)
PHONE...................260 482-8168
Willi Breuning, *Pr*
Don Taube, *VP*
EMP: 17 **EST:** 1979
SALES (est): 680.94K **Privately Held**
SIC: 3599 7694 Machine shop, jobbing and repair; Armature rewinding shops

(G-5198)
MAD DASHER INC
Also Called: I E Products
4410 Tielker Rd (46809-1543)
PHONE...................260 747-0545
Harry P Laffkas, *Pr*
Margaret Hyde, *
EMP: 30 **EST:** 1976
SQ FT: 13,500
SALES (est): 2.15MM **Privately Held**
Web: www.maddasher.com
SIC: 3089 2385 3081 Plastics containers, except foam; Waterproof outerwear; Unsupported plastics film and sheet

(G-5199)
MAGIC COMPANY
Also Called: Magic Premium Snacks
405 Lower Huntington Rd (46819-1522)
PHONE...................260 747-1502
James Godschalk, *Pr*
▲ **EMP:** 20 **EST:** 1987
SQ FT: 37,000
SALES (est): 175.21K **Privately Held**
SIC: 2096 2099 Potato chips and other potato-based snacks; Food preparations, nec

(G-5200)
MAKINGMOVES TRANSPORTS LLC
6322 Millhollow Ln (46815-6287)
PHONE...................260 579-5584
EMP: 1
SALES (est): 69.27K **Privately Held**
SIC: 3669 7389 Transportation signaling devices; Business Activities at Non-Commercial Site

(G-5201)
MAMA FOX TEE COMPANY
1712 Glen Elm Dr (46845-9672)
PHONE...................260 438-4054
Kayla Fox, *Prin*
EMP: 4 **EST:** 2019
SALES (est): 83.67K **Privately Held**
SIC: 2759 Screen printing

(G-5202)
MANTECH MANIFOLD
9105 Clubridge Dr (46809-3045)
P.O. Box 9070 (46899-9070)
PHONE...................260 479-2383
Joe Oberlin, *Pr*
EMP: 6 **EST:** 2015
SALES (est): 167.15K **Privately Held**
SIC: 3511 Turbines and turbine generator sets

(G-5203)
MARSHALL G SMITH SIGN PAINTING
Also Called: Smith, M G Sign Painting
472 Wiebke St (46806-4145)
PHONE...................260 744-9492
Marshall Smith, *Owner*
EMP: 1 **EST:** 1976
SALES (est): 66.76K **Privately Held**
SIC: 7389 3993 Sign painting and lettering shop; Signs and advertising specialties

(G-5204)
MASSEY-NULL INC
4519 Allen Martin Dr (46806)
PHONE...................260 447-7900
Beverly Rectenwald, *CEO*
James Daniel Rectenwald, *Pr*
Walter Rectenwald, *VP*
Brad Wolfe, *Sec*
EMP: 23 **EST:** 1976
SQ FT: 10,000
SALES (est): 1.08MM **Privately Held**
Web: www.industrialtruckbeds.com
SIC: 3441 Fabricated structural metal

(G-5205)
MASTERS HAND BBQ LLC
2753 Freeman St (46802-4424)
PHONE...................260 247-5807
Steve Beers, *Managing Member*
Joshua Beers, *Managing Member*
Amanda Johnson, *Managing Member*
EMP: 4 **EST:** 2010
SALES (est): 275.85K **Privately Held**
Web: www.mastershandbbq.com
SIC: 5812 2035 Barbecue restaurant; Seasonings, meat sauces (except tomato and dry)

(G-5206)
MASTERSPAS LLC (PA)
Also Called: Master Spas
6927 Lincoln Pkwy (46804-5623)
PHONE...................260 436-9100
◆ **EMP:** 85 **EST:** 1996
SQ FT: 185,000
SALES (est): 45.44MM **Privately Held**
Web: www.masterspas.com
SIC: 3999 5999 Hot tubs; Spas and hot tubs

(G-5207)
MASTERSPAS LLC
510 Sumpter St (46804-5626)
PHONE...................260 436-9100
Robert Lauter, *Brnch Mgr*
EMP: 201
Web: www.masterspas.com
SIC: 3999 5999 Hot tubs; Spas and hot tubs
PA: Masterspas, Llc
6927 Lincoln Pkwy
Fort Wayne IN 46804

(G-5208)
MAXWELL ENGINEERING INC
616 E Wallace St (46803-2368)
P.O. Box 10540 (46852-0540)

PHONE..................260 745-4991
Matt Maxwell, Pr
EMP: 9 EST: 1920
SQ FT: 16,000
SALES (est): 933.12K Privately Held
Web: www.maxwellengine.com
SIC: 3543 3544 3999 Foundry patternmaking; Industrial molds; Models, general, except toy

(G-5209)
MAY SUU MON LLC
5125 Standish Dr (46806-5236)
PHONE..................786 556-8295
EMP: 2 EST: 2021
SALES (est): 62.38K Privately Held
SIC: 2051 Bakery: wholesale or wholesale/retail combined

(G-5210)
MC COY BOLT WORKS INC
2811 Congressional Pkwy (46808-1389)
PHONE..................260 482-4476
Robert M Mc Ardle, Pr
Beverly Mc Ardle, *
Mark Brown, *
Timothy Houston, *
Lisa Houston, *
▲ EMP: 55 EST: 1944
SQ FT: 40,000
SALES (est): 5.69MM Privately Held
Web: www.mccoybolt.com
SIC: 3452 Bolts, metal

(G-5211)
MCCRORY PUBLISHING
2530 Deerwood Dr (46825-3918)
PHONE..................260 485-1812
Greg Mccrory, Owner
EMP: 2 EST: 2005
SALES (est): 121.98K Privately Held
Web: www.mccpub.com
SIC: 2752 Offset printing

(G-5212)
MCMILLAN EXPRESS
3505 Wayne Trce (46806-4557)
PHONE..................260 447-7648
J Singh, Owner
EMP: 4 EST: 2006
SALES (est): 273.94K Privately Held
SIC: 2741 Miscellaneous publishing

(G-5213)
MDL WOODWORKING LLC
1011 W Packard Ave (46807-1753)
PHONE..................260 242-1824
Michael Liechty, Admn
EMP: 5 EST: 2015
SALES (est): 79.69K Privately Held
SIC: 2431 Woodwork, interior and ornamental, nec

(G-5214)
MERIWETHER TOOL & ENGRG INC
10108 Smith Rd (46809-9771)
PHONE..................260 744-6955
Bob Meriwether, Pr
▲ EMP: 20 EST: 1990
SQ FT: 8,000
SALES (est): 972.03K Privately Held
SIC: 3312 3549 Tool and die steel; Metalworking machinery, nec

(G-5215)
MET-PAK SPECIALTIES CORP
9910 Airport Dr (46809-3041)
PHONE..................260 420-2217
Doug Schisler, Pr
Doug Schisler, Prin
Monty Oakes, *
▲ EMP: 28 EST: 1996
SALES (est): 4.48MM Privately Held
Web: www.metpak.com
SIC: 2653 Boxes, corrugated: made from purchased materials

(G-5216)
METFORM TOOL CORPORATION
2424 American Way (46809-3005)
PHONE..................260 745-1436
Dwight Bieberich, Pr
Donald E Bieberich, *
Letha Scherer, *
Bradley Scherer, *
EMP: 25 EST: 1981
SQ FT: 250
SALES (est): 3.89MM
SALES (corp-wide): 45.66MM Privately Held
SIC: 3544 Special dies, tools, jigs, and fixtures
PA: Fort Wayne Wire Die, Inc.
2424 American Way
Fort Wayne IN 46809
260 747-1681

(G-5217)
METTLE HOLDINGS INCORPORATED (PA)
Also Called: Bruco Industries
4630 Allen Martin Dr (46806-2800)
PHONE..................260 447-3880
Mark Webb, Pr
EMP: 47 EST: 1976
SQ FT: 48,000
SALES (est): 9.45MM
SALES (corp-wide): 9.45MM Privately Held
Web: www.quikcutinc.com
SIC: 3441 Fabricated structural metal

(G-5218)
METTLE HOLDINGS INCORPORATED
4532 Allen Martin Dr (46806-2801)
PHONE..................260 447-3880
Mark Webb, Pr
EMP: 3
SALES (corp-wide): 9.45MM Privately Held
Web: www.quikcutinc.com
SIC: 3443 Fabricated plate work (boiler shop)
PA: Mettle Holdings Incorporated
4630 Allen Martin Dr
Fort Wayne IN 46806
260 447-3880

(G-5219)
MEYER PLASTICS INC
Also Called: Plastic Works
3410 Congressional Pkwy (46808-4440)
PHONE..................260 482-4595
Tom Warner, Mgr
EMP: 19
SALES (corp-wide): 23.11MM Privately Held
Web: www.meyerplastics.com
SIC: 2821 Plastics materials and resins
PA: Meyer Plastics Inc
5968 Sunnyside Rd
Indianapolis IN 46236
317 259-4131

(G-5220)
MICHIANA BUS PUBLICATIONS INC
Also Called: Business Pple Mag Grter Fort W
7729 Westfield Dr (46825-8313)
PHONE..................260 497-0433
Daniel Copeland, Pr
EMP: 7 EST: 1987
SALES (est): 954.55K Privately Held
Web: www.businesspeople.com
SIC: 2721 Magazines: publishing only, not printed on site

(G-5221)
MICROTECH HOLDING CORP
3601 Focus Dr (46818)
PHONE..................260 490-4005
Matthew Wojewuczki, Pr
EMP: 1 EST: 2017
SALES (est): 104.31K Privately Held
SIC: 3548 Electric welding equipment

(G-5222)
MICROTECH WELDING CORP (PA)
3601 Focus Dr (46818-9394)
PHONE..................260 490-4005
EMP: 19 EST: 1999
SQ FT: 1,400
SALES (est): 916.08K Privately Held
Web: www.microtechwelding.com
SIC: 7692 Welding repair

(G-5223)
MID AMERICA SIGN CORPORATION (PA)
1319 Production Rd (46808-1164)
PHONE..................260 744-2200
Richard D Middleton, Pr
EMP: 18 EST: 1980
SQ FT: 18,000
SALES (est): 1.8MM
SALES (corp-wide): 1.8MM Privately Held
Web: www.mid-americasign.net
SIC: 3993 Signs, not made in custom sign painting shops

(G-5224)
MIDWEST COMM SOLUTIONS LLP ◆
4801 Hartman Rd (46807-2919)
PHONE..................800 880-5847
Tyler Smith Ptrn, Prin
Jeff Kuhn Ptrn, Prin
EMP: 1 EST: 2024
SALES (est): 78.52K Privately Held
SIC: 3663 Satellites, communications

(G-5225)
MIDWEST PRECISION MACHINING
3626 Illinois Rd (46804-2062)
PHONE..................260 459-6866
Jeff Bernath, Pr
EMP: 5 EST: 1999
SALES (est): 499.61K Privately Held
Web: www.midwest-brokers.com
SIC: 3599 Machine shop, jobbing and repair

(G-5226)
MIDWEST TOOL & DIE CORP
Also Called: Mtd
1126 Sunset Lake Cv (46845-9009)
PHONE..................260 414-1506
Victor Felger, Pr
David Venderly, *
EMP: 24 EST: 1974
SQ FT: 40,000
SALES (est): 444.2K Privately Held
Web: www.midwest-tool.com
SIC: 3544 Special dies and tools

(G-5227)
MIGHTIER PRESS
10088 Chapmans Cv (46835-9263)
PHONE..................260 609-6582
EMP: 5 EST: 2018
SALES (est): 89.2K Privately Held
Web: www.mightier.com
SIC: 2741 Miscellaneous publishing

(G-5228)
MIGHTY-QUIP INDUSTRIES
921 E Dupont Rd 894 (46825-1551)
PHONE..................260 615-1899
Harlan Wheeler, Owner
EMP: 2 EST: 2008
SALES (est): 166.56K Privately Held
SIC: 3621 Motors and generators

(G-5229)
MILSTRATA MANUFACTURING LLC
7525 Maplecrest Rd Ste 156 (46835-1897)
PHONE..................260 209-4415
Nathan Crawford, Prin
EMP: 4 EST: 2019
SALES (est): 90.29K Privately Held
Web: www.milstrata.com
SIC: 3999 Manufacturing industries, nec

(G-5230)
MINNICH MANUFACTURING INC
2421 W Wallen Rd (46818-2249)
PHONE..................260 489-5357
Robert J Minnich Junior, Pr
Robert Minnich, *
Sharon A Minnich, Sec
EMP: 6 EST: 1979
SQ FT: 2,400
SALES (est): 489.92K Privately Held
Web: www.minnichmfg.com
SIC: 3599 Machine shop, jobbing and repair

(G-5231)
MINNICK SERVICES CORP (PA)
Also Called: Minnick Services
222 N Thomas Rd (46808)
P.O. Box 11100 (46855)
PHONE..................260 432-5031
Mark Minnick, Pr
Alice Minnick, *
Rick Schaefer, *
EMP: 24 EST: 1981
SQ FT: 45,000
SALES (est): 4.99MM
SALES (corp-wide): 4.99MM Privately Held
Web: www.minnickservices.com
SIC: 3272 5032 Burial vaults, concrete or precast terrazzo; Concrete building products

(G-5232)
MIRTEQ HOLDINGS INC
2246 Research Dr (46808-3628)
PHONE..................260 490-3706
Thomas Lavin, CEO
EMP: 3 EST: 2015
SALES (est): 149.78K Privately Held
SIC: 2869 Industrial organic chemicals, nec

(G-5233)
MITSUBISHI CHEMICAL ADVNCD MTR
Also Called: Quadrant Engrg Plastic Pdts
2710 American Way (46809-3011)
PHONE..................260 479-4100
Glen Steady, Brnch Mgr
EMP: 250
Web: www.quadrantplastics.com
SIC: 2824 3082 2821 3052 Nylon fibers; Unsupported plastics profile shapes; Nylon resins; Plastic hose
HQ: Mitsubishi Chemical Advanced Materials Inc.
2120 Fairmont Ave
Reading PA 19612
610 320-6600

(G-5234)
MITSUBSHI CHEM ADVNCED MTLS IN

4115 Polymer Pl (46809-1140)
PHONE.........................260 479-4700
Harold Etts, Brnch Mgr
EMP: 75
Web: www.quadrantplastics.com
SIC: 2824 3082 2821 3052 Nylon fibers; Unsupported plastics profile shapes; Nylon resins; Plastic hose
HQ: Mitsubishi Chemical Advanced Materials Inc.
2120 Fairmont Ave
Reading PA 19612
610 320-6600

(G-5235)
MKMCLAIN INC
7105 Ardmore Ave (46809-9541)
PHONE.........................260 478-1636
Mel K Mcclain, Pr
Karen S Mc Clain, Sec
EMP: 9 EST: 1980
SQ FT: 5,000
SALES (est): 657.25K Privately Held
Web: www.fortwayneawning.com
SIC: 2394 Canvas awnings and canopies

(G-5236)
MOBILE DISPOSAL
5310 Oak Chase Run (46845-9435)
P.O. Box 594 (46774-0594)
PHONE.........................260 267-6348
Larry Lamb, Owner
EMP: 1 EST: 2013
SALES (est): 80.18K Privately Held
SIC: 3443 Dumpsters, garbage

(G-5237)
MOBILITY SVM LLC
505 Avenue Of Autos (46804-1195)
PHONE.........................260 434-4777
Peter Kelley, *
Rick Schoenian, *
EMP: 25 EST: 2012
SALES (est): 2.31MM Privately Held
Web: www.mobilitysvm.com
SIC: 3999 Wheelchair lifts

(G-5238)
MOCKENHAUPT PUBLISHING INC
1901 Pemberton Dr (46805-4623)
PHONE.........................315 778-0067
EMP: 5 EST: 2012
SALES (est): 71.26K Privately Held
SIC: 2741 Miscellaneous publishing

(G-5239)
MODBAR LLC
628 Leesburg Rd (46808-2500)
PHONE.........................206 450-4743
Corey Waldron, Mgr
EMP: 15 EST: 2012
SQ FT: 10,000
SALES (est): 2.05MM Privately Held
Web: www.modbar.com
SIC: 3494 Steam fittings and specialties

(G-5240)
MOMENTIVE PERFORMANCE MTLS INC
3206 Teramo Cv (46814-2501)
PHONE.........................612 499-3902
Timothy Higgins, Brnch Mgr
EMP: 50
Web: www.momentive.com
SIC: 2869 Industrial organic chemicals, nec
HQ: Momentive Performance Materials Inc.
2750 Balltown Rd
Niskayuna NY 12309

(G-5241)
MOORE SHIRTS LLC ✪
5534 Saint Joe Rd (46835-3328)
PHONE.........................317 350-4342
EMP: 1 EST: 2022
SALES (est): 68.86K Privately Held
SIC: 2211 Apparel and outerwear fabrics, cotton

(G-5242)
MOOSE LAKE PRODUCTS CO INC
Also Called: First Flash Line
6528 Constitution Dr (46804-1550)
PHONE.........................260 432-2768
EMP: 10 EST: 1993
SQ FT: 5,000
SALES (est): 820.37K Privately Held
Web: www.firstflash.com
SIC: 7336 2759 Graphic arts and related design; Promotional printing

(G-5243)
MORGAN COMMERCIAL LETTERING
434 Merkler St (46825-5228)
PHONE.........................260 482-6430
Gary Morgan, Owner
EMP: 2 EST: 1984
SALES (est): 146.07K Privately Held
SIC: 3993 Signs and advertising specialties

(G-5244)
MORRIS SHEET METAL CORP
6212 Highview Pl (46818-1375)
P.O. Box 8007 (46898-8007)
PHONE.........................260 497-1300
Thomas Laubhan, Pr
Terry Protto, *
Dan Morris, *
Tim Morris, *
EMP: 68 EST: 1992
SQ FT: 50,000
SALES (est): 15.74MM
SALES (corp-wide): 104.56MM Publicly Held
Web: www.morrissheetmetal.com
SIC: 3444 Sheet metalwork
PA: Alpine 4 Holdings, Inc.
2525 E Ariz Bltmore Cir S
Phoenix AZ 85016
480 702-2431

(G-5245)
MOSES LEATHERS
810 Schick St (46803-1073)
PHONE.........................260 203-8799
Moses Leathers, Prin
EMP: 6 EST: 2016
SALES (est): 127.89K Privately Held
SIC: 3172 Personal leather goods, nec

(G-5246)
MOSSBERG & COMPANY INC
3202 Clearfield Ct (46808-4517)
PHONE.........................260 755-6283
Charles W Hillman, Brnch Mgr
EMP: 14
SALES (corp-wide): 32.28MM Privately Held
Web: www.mossbergco.com
SIC: 5999 2759 Packaging materials: boxes, padding, etc.; Commercial printing, nec
PA: Mossberg & Company Inc
301 E Sample St
South Bend IN 46601
574 289-9253

(G-5247)
MOTOROLA SOLUTIONS INC
Also Called: Motorola
3304 Mallard Cove Ln (46804-2884)
PHONE.........................260 436-5331
Thomas M King, Brnch Mgr
EMP: 5
SALES (corp-wide): 9.98B Publicly Held
Web: www.motorolasolutions.com
SIC: 3663 Radio and t.v. communications equipment
PA: Motorola Solutions, Inc.
500 W Monroe St Ste 4400
Chicago IL 60661
847 576-5000

(G-5248)
MPP INC
Also Called: Metal Plate Polishing
2413 Meyer Rd (46803-2911)
PHONE.........................260 422-5426
James Mccall, Pr
EMP: 40 EST: 1985
SQ FT: 30,000
SALES (est): 4.47MM Privately Held
Web: www.metalplatepolishing.com
SIC: 3471 3599 Finishing, metals or formed products; Machine shop, jobbing and repair

(G-5249)
MSD GROUP LLC
9025 Coldwater Rd Ste 400 (46825)
PHONE.........................260 444-4658
EMP: 6 EST: 2020
SALES (est): 128.4K Privately Held
Web: www.msd.com
SIC: 2834 Pharmaceutical preparations

(G-5250)
MULTIMATIC INDIANA INC
2808 S Maplecrest Rd (46803-3218)
PHONE.........................260 749-3700
Peter Czapka, Brnch Mgr
EMP: 165
SALES (corp-wide): 9.14B Privately Held
SIC: 3465 Automotive stampings
HQ: Multimatic Indiana Inc.
201 Re Jones Rd
Butler IN 46721

(G-5251)
MURPAC OF FORT WAYNE LLC
3405 Meyer Rd Ste 135 (46803-2983)
PHONE.........................260 424-2299
EMP: 7 EST: 2010
SALES (est): 912.97K Privately Held
SIC: 3499 Reels, cable: metal

(G-5252)
MURRAY EQUIPMENT INC
Also Called: Total Control Systems
2515 Charleston Pl (46808-1397)
PHONE.........................260 484-0382
Daniel Murray, Pr
Martha Murray, *
Forest David Musselman Iii, CFO
▲ EMP: 145 EST: 1960
SQ FT: 90,000
SALES (est): 50.99MM Privately Held
Web: www.murrayequipment.com
SIC: 5084 3594 Materials handling machinery; Fluid power pumps and motors

(G-5253)
MUZFEED INC
6304 Tanbark Trl (46835-1852)
PHONE.........................815 252-7676
Tyler Berggren, Prin
Tyler Berggren, CEO
Justin Rix, VP
Dave Sanders, VP
EMP: 3 EST: 2017
SALES (est): 96.85K Privately Held

SIC: 2721 7389 Periodicals, publishing only; Business Activities at Non-Commercial Site

(G-5254)
NA HOLDING-LIME CITY LLC ✪
3601 Focus Dr (46818)
PHONE.........................260 212-2294
Matthew Wojewuczki, Managing Member
EMP: 10 EST: 2023
SALES (est): 680.61K Privately Held
SIC: 3469 Metal stampings, nec

(G-5255)
NATIONAL ATHC SPORTSWEAR INC
3911 Option Pass (46818-1275)
PHONE.........................260 436-2248
EMP: 10 EST: 1995
SQ FT: 10,000
SALES (est): 311.23K Privately Held
Web: www.nasinc.biz
SIC: 2395 Embroidery products, except Schiffli machine

(G-5256)
NATIONAL RCREATION SYSTEMS INC
Also Called: N R S
1300 Airport North Office Park Ste D (46825)
PHONE.........................260 482-6023
Bob Farnsworth, Pr
Karen R Hagan, Sec
▼ EMP: 15 EST: 1989
SQ FT: 90,000
SALES (est): 4.75MM Privately Held
Web: www.bleachers.net
SIC: 2531 Bleacher seating, portable
HQ: Playcore Wisconsin, Inc.
544 Chestnut St
Chattanooga TN 37402
423 265-7529

(G-5257)
NATIONAL TUBE FORM LLC
Also Called: N T F
3405 Engle Rd (46809-1115)
PHONE.........................260 478-2363
EMP: 150
SIC: 3498 Tube fabricating (contract bending and shaping)

(G-5258)
NATIONWIDE PUBLISHING COMPANY
12110 Glen Lake Dr (46814-4569)
PHONE.........................260 312-3924
Michael Kay, Brnch Mgr
EMP: 4
SALES (corp-wide): 4.32MM Privately Held
SIC: 2741 Telephone and other directory publishing
PA: Nationwide Publishing Company Inc
537 Deltona Blvd
Deltona FL 32725
352 253-0017

(G-5259)
NEFF GROUP DISTRIBUTORS INC (PA)
Also Called: Neff Engineering
7114 Innovation Blvd (46818)
P.O. Box 8604 (46898)
PHONE.........................260 489-6007
John J Neff, Pr
Daniel W Neff, VP
Harry M Neff, Treas
James T Neff, Sec
EMP: 19 EST: 1952
SQ FT: 4,500

Fort Wayne - Allen County (G-5260)   GEOGRAPHIC SECTION

SALES (est): 51.21MM
SALES (corp-wide): 51.21MM **Privately Held**
Web: www.neffautomation.com
SIC: 3492 Fluid power valves and hose fittings

(G-5260)
NEIL SILKE ◊
Also Called: Laser Welder LLC
5534 Saint Joe Rd (46835)
PHONE...............................574 999-4866
EMP: 1 EST: 2023
SALES (est): 69.7K **Privately Held**
SIC: 7692 Welding repair

(G-5261)
NELSON GLOBAL PRODUCTS INC
Also Called: National Tube Form
3405 Engle Rd (46809-1115)
PHONE...............................608 719-1752
EMP: 122
Web: www.nelsongp.com
SIC: 3498 Tube fabricating (contract bending and shaping)
PA: Nelson Global Products, Inc.
1560 Williams Dr
Stoughton WI 53589

(G-5262)
NEMCO FOOD EQUIPMENT LTD
5316 Hopkinton Dr (46814-7549)
PHONE...............................260 399-6692
Kenny Moffatt, *Brnch Mgr*
EMP: 2
SALES (corp-wide): 26.28MM **Privately Held**
Web: www.nemcofoodequip.com
SIC: 3556 Food products machinery
PA: Nemco Food Equipment, Ltd.
301 Meuse Argonne St
Hicksville OH 43526
419 542-7751

(G-5263)
NEMCO MEDICAL LTD
8727 Clinton Park Dr (46825-3170)
P.O. Box 263 (43526-0263)
PHONE...............................260 484-1500
Kevin Countryman, *Pt*
EMP: 23 EST: 2006
SALES (est): 1.46MM **Privately Held**
Web: www.nemcomedical.com
SIC: 3841 Surgical and medical instruments

(G-5264)
NEMCOMED FW LLC
Also Called: Avalign Instrs & Implants Div
8727 Clinton Park Dr (46825-3170)
PHONE...............................260 480-5226
Forrest Whittaker, *Managing Member*
EMP: 27 EST: 2005
SALES (est): 10.27MM **Privately Held**
Web: www.nemcomed.com
SIC: 3842 Implants, surgical

(G-5265)
NEMCOMED INSTRS & IMPLANTS
8727 Clinton Park Dr (46825-3170)
PHONE...............................800 255-4576
Forrest R Whittaker, *CEO*
Tony Oneill, *Sr VP*
Mcneil Mac Brown, *VP*
Scott Gareiss, *VP*
Barbara Sullivan, *CFO*
EMP: 14 EST: 2015
SALES (est): 1.31MM **Privately Held**
Web: www.nemcomed.com
SIC: 3999 3842 Atomizers, toiletry; Surgical appliances and supplies

(G-5266)
NEW IMAGE PRTG & DESIGN INC
3233 Lafayette St (46806-4049)
PHONE...............................260 969-0410
Sharon Miller, *Pr*
Timothy Spradling, *Dir*
EMP: 14 EST: 2007
SALES (est): 484.95K **Privately Held**
Web: www.newimageprinting.net
SIC: 2752 Offset printing

(G-5267)
NEW MLLENNIUM BLDG SYSTEMS LLC (HQ)
1690 Broadway Ste 19 (46802)
PHONE...............................260 969-3500
Gary Heasley, *Genl Mgr*
Troy Bayman, *Contrlr*
Bert Hollman, *Prin*
▼ EMP: 4 EST: 1999
SQ FT: 225,000
SALES (est): 463.01MM **Publicly Held**
Web: www.newmill.com
SIC: 3441 Joists, open web steel: long-span series
PA: Steel Dynamics, Inc.
7575 W Jefferson Blvd
Fort Wayne IN 46804

(G-5268)
NEW PROCESS GRAPHICS LLC
Also Called: New Process
310 W Cook Rd (46825-3320)
PHONE...............................260 489-1700
EMP: 20 EST: 2012
SALES (est): 2.36MM **Privately Held**
Web: www.newprocesscorp.com
SIC: 2759 Screen printing

(G-5269)
NEWCOMED INC
8727 Clinton Park Dr (46825-3170)
PHONE...............................260 484-1500
Kevin Countryman, *Owner*
EMP: 8 EST: 2011
SALES (est): 207.75K **Privately Held**
Web: www.nemcomed.com
SIC: 3841 Surgical and medical instruments

(G-5270)
NEWS PUBLISHING COMPANY INC (DH)
600 W Main St (46802-1408)
P.O. Box 100 (46801-0100)
PHONE...............................260 461-8444
Scott Mc Gehee, *Pr*
Robert Nutting, *VP*
Duane Wittman, *VP*
William Nutting, *VP*
EMP: 1 EST: 1904
SQ FT: 146,000
SALES (est): 152.29MM
SALES (corp-wide): 709.52MM **Privately Held**
SIC: 2711 Newspapers, publishing and printing
HQ: Jck Legacy Company
1601 Alhmbra Blvd Ste 100
Sacramento CA 95816
916 321-1844

(G-5271)
NISHIKAWA COOPER LLC
2785 Persistence Dr (46808-1491)
PHONE...............................260 593-2156
Steve Folden, *Brnch Mgr*
EMP: 107
Web: www.niscoseals.com
SIC: 3069 Weather strip, sponge rubber
HQ: Nishikawa Cooper Llc
324 Morrow St
Topeka IN 46571
260 593-2156

(G-5272)
NISHIKAWA COOPER LLC
5120 Investment Dr (46808-3600)
PHONE...............................248 978-6953
EMP: 250
Web: www.niscoseals.com
SIC: 3069 Weather strip, sponge rubber
HQ: Nishikawa Cooper Llc
324 Morrow St
Topeka IN 46571
260 593-2156

(G-5273)
NK WELDING PRODUCTS INC
302 W Superior St (46802-1112)
PHONE...............................260 424-1901
Douglas M Kline, *Prin*
EMP: 2 EST: 2010
SALES (est): 118.89K **Privately Held**
SIC: 7692 Welding repair

(G-5274)
NORTH COAST ORGANICS LLC
629 E Washington Blvd (46802)
PHONE...............................260 246-0289
Nathan Morin, *Managing Member*
Debbie Morin, *Managing Member*
EMP: 5 EST: 2012
SQ FT: 7,000
SALES (est): 253.06K **Privately Held**
Web: www.northcoastorganics.us
SIC: 2844 5122 5999 7389 Perfumes, cosmetics and other toilet preparations; Toiletries; Toiletries, cosmetics, and perfumes; Business Activities at Non-Commercial Site

(G-5275)
NORTHEAST ENTERPRISES INC
Also Called: Northeast Welding
6428 Saint Joe Center Rd Ste A (46835-3899)
PHONE...............................260 485-8011
Jim Love, *CEO*
EMP: 1 EST: 1966
SALES (est): 156.46K **Privately Held**
Web: www.newelding.net
SIC: 7692 Welding repair

(G-5276)
NORTHWEST NEWS & PRINTING
Also Called: Northwest News
3306 Independence Dr (46808-4510)
P.O. Box 663 (46748-0663)
PHONE...............................260 637-9003
Bob Allman, *Owner*
Ryan Swab, *Mgr*
EMP: 2 EST: 1997
SALES (est): 62.95K **Privately Held**
Web: www.kpcnews.com
SIC: 2711 Newspapers, publishing and printing

(G-5277)
NOVAMATIQ INC
Also Called: Guide Engineering
1515 Dividend Rd (46808-1126)
PHONE...............................260 483-1153
Gopi Ganta, *CEO*
Craig S Taylor, *
Andy Tyler, *
EMP: 45 EST: 1960
SQ FT: 18,000
SALES (est): 9.42MM **Privately Held**
Web: www.guideeng.com
SIC: 3599 Custom machinery

(G-5278)
NSIGNIA SCREEN PRINTING
Also Called: Subterranean Mbf
512 W Superior St (46802-1021)
PHONE...............................260 420-0500
Tim Straley, *Pr*
EMP: 9 EST: 1994
SALES (est): 114.6K **Privately Held**
SIC: 2395 2759 Embroidery products, except Schiffli machine; Screen printing

(G-5279)
OASIS SOFTWARE SOLUTIONS
1910 Saint Joe Center Rd (46825-5000)
PHONE...............................620 515-1240
EMP: 5 EST: 2015
SALES (est): 181.12K **Privately Held**
SIC: 7372 Prepackaged software

(G-5280)
OCE CORPORATE PRINTING DIV
6915 Innovation Blvd (46818-1372)
PHONE...............................260 436-7395
Ed O'reilly, *Prin*
EMP: 4 EST: 2010
SALES (est): 305.87K **Privately Held**
SIC: 2752 Offset printing

(G-5281)
ODB INC
Also Called: Our Daily Brew
7203 Wintergreen Dr (46814-8138)
PHONE...............................260 673-0062
Lee E Pomerantz, *Prin*
EMP: 6 EST: 2014
SALES (est): 112.38K **Privately Held**
SIC: 2711 Newspapers, publishing and printing

(G-5282)
OFFSET ONE INC
1609 S Calhoun St (46802-5255)
PHONE...............................260 456-8828
Kent Whiting, *Pr*
Margaret Konger, *Prin*
Bernard Konger, *Prin*
EMP: 10 EST: 1981
SQ FT: 18,000
SALES (est): 790.03K **Privately Held**
Web: www.offset1.com
SIC: 2752 2791 2789 2759 Offset printing; Typesetting; Bookbinding and related work; Commercial printing, nec

(G-5283)
OLD FORT TEE COMPANY LLC
4930 Woodhurst Blvd (46807-3132)
PHONE...............................248 506-3762
Melissa Hitzemann, *Mgr*
EMP: 4 EST: 2017
SALES (est): 92.36K **Privately Held**
Web: www.oldfortteeco.com
SIC: 2759 Screen printing

(G-5284)
OLDE YORK POTATO CHIPS INC
918 W Cook Rd (46825-3270)
▲ EMP: 30 EST: 2003
SQ FT: 45,000
SALES (est): 3.82MM
SALES (corp-wide): 3.23MM **Privately Held**
SIC: 2096 Potato chips and similar snacks
PA: Tomato Express Ltd
230 Deerhurst Dr
Brampton ON L6T 5
905 458-4100

GEOGRAPHIC SECTION
Fort Wayne - Allen County (G-5309)

(G-5285)
OMNIMAX INTERNATIONAL LLC
Amerimax Building Products
5201 Investment Dr (46808-3650)
PHONE....................574 848-7432
Mitchell B Lewis, *CEO*
EMP: 55
Web: www.omnimax.com
SIC: 3444 Sheet metalwork
HQ: Omnimax International, Llc
30 Technlogy Pkwy S Ste 4
Peachtree Corners GA 30092
770 449-7066

(G-5286)
OMNISOURCE LLC (HQ)
Also Called: Omni Auto Parts
7575 W Jefferson Blvd (46804)
PHONE....................260 422-5541
Russell Rinn, *Pr*
Denny Luma, *VP*
Jason Redden, *VP*
Mike Hausfeld, *VP*
Rick Poinsatte, *VP*
◆ **EMP:** 220 **EST:** 1946
SQ FT: 30,000
SALES (est): 860.15MM **Publicly Held**
Web: www.omnisource.com
SIC: 5093 3462 3399 Ferrous metal scrap and waste; Iron and steel forgings; Metal powders, pastes, and flakes
PA: Steel Dynamics, Inc.
7575 W Jefferson Blvd
Fort Wayne IN 46804

(G-5287)
ONE BODY SOFTWARE LLC
12022 Waterside Ct (46814-3274)
PHONE....................260 494-8354
Joseph Landrigan, *Prin*
EMP: 4 **EST:** 2014
SALES (est): 44.83K **Privately Held**
SIC: 7372 Prepackaged software

(G-5288)
OTIS DYNAMIC ENTERPRISES LLC (PA) ✪
5534 Saint Joe Rd (46835-3328)
PHONE....................860 978-6003
EMP: 1 **EST:** 2024
SALES (est): 75.31K
SALES (corp-wide): 75.31K **Privately Held**
SIC: 2731 Books, publishing only

(G-5289)
OTTENWELLER CO INC (PA)
3011 Congressional Pkwy (46808-4415)
PHONE....................260 484-3166
Ottenweller Michael, *Pr*
Michael Ottenweller, *
Gary Ottenweller, *
David Ottenweller, *
Nancy Dwire, *
▲ **EMP:** 127 **EST:** 1916
SQ FT: 75,000
SALES (est): 28.75MM
SALES (corp-wide): 28.75MM **Privately Held**
Web: www.ottenweller.com
SIC: 3443 3441 3444 Tanks, standard or custom fabricated: metal plate; Fabricated structural metal; Sheet metalwork

(G-5290)
OTTENWELLER COMPANY LLC
2321 Bremer Rd (46803-3010)
PHONE....................260 245-0197
EMP: 9 **EST:** 2013
SALES (est): 156.49K **Privately Held**
Web: www.ottenweller.com

(G-5291)
P H C INDUSTRIES INC
3115 Pittsburg St (46803-2259)
EMP: 6 **EST:** 1967
SQ FT: 12,500
SALES (est): 1.11MM **Privately Held**
Web: www.phcindustries.com
SIC: 5085 3492 7694 Power transmission equipment and apparatus; Hose and tube fittings and assemblies, hydraulic/pneumatic; Electric motor repair

(G-5292)
PAINT TOWN GRAPHICS INC
1828 W Main St (46808-3760)
PHONE....................260 422-9152
EMP: 20 **EST:** 1986
SQ FT: 5,000
SALES (est): 2.32MM **Privately Held**
Web: www.pttgi.com
SIC: 3993 Signs and advertising specialties

(G-5293)
PANA-PACIFIC
918 E State Blvd (46805-3405)
PHONE....................260 482-6607
EMP: 3 **EST:** 2018
SALES (est): 67.01K **Privately Held**
Web: www.panapacific.com
SIC: 3714 Motor vehicle parts and accessories

(G-5294)
PANORAMIC RENTAL CORP
4321 Goshen Rd (46818-1242)
PHONE....................800 654-2027
Steve Yaggy, *VP*
Carey Sipe, *
Matthew Kline, *
▲ **EMP:** 35 **EST:** 1986
SQ FT: 18,000
SALES (est): 5.66MM
SALES (corp-wide): 191.04MM **Privately Held**
Web: www.pancorp.com
SIC: 3843 Dental equipment and supplies
PA: Young Innovations, Inc.
2260 Wendt St
Algonquin IL 60102
847 458-5400

(G-5295)
PARAGON TUBE CORPORATION
1605 Winter St (46803-2513)
PHONE....................260 424-1266
Jerome F Henry Junior, *Pr*
Thomas M Carter, *VP*
▲ **EMP:** 22 **EST:** 1990
SQ FT: 91,250
SALES (est): 4.71MM **Privately Held**
Web: www.paragontube.com
SIC: 3317 Steel pipe and tubes

(G-5296)
PARCO INCORPORATED
9100 Front St (46818-2209)
PHONE....................260 451-0810
Phillip Roser, *Pr*
Lisa Roser, *VP*
EMP: 18 **EST:** 2001
SQ FT: 60,000
SALES (est): 4.96MM **Privately Held**
Web: www.parco-inc.com
SIC: 3354 Aluminum extruded products

(G-5297)
PARKER-HANNIFIN CORPORATION
Also Called: Climate Systems Division
5417 State Road 930 (46803-1771)
PHONE....................260 748-6000
Darryl Miller, *Brnch Mgr*
EMP: 600
SALES (corp-wide): 19.93B **Publicly Held**
Web: www.parker.com
SIC: 3492 3585 3494 3429 Hose and tube fittings and assemblies, hydraulic/pneumatic; Refrigeration and heating equipment; Valves and pipe fittings, nec; Hardware, nec
PA: Parker-Hannifin Corporation
6035 Parkland Blvd
Cleveland OH 44124
216 896-3000

(G-5298)
PARROT PRESS INC
520 Spring St (46808-3232)
P.O. Box 8297 (46898-8297)
PHONE....................260 422-6402
EMP: 30
Web: www.parrotpress.com
SIC: 2759 2789 2752 Letterpress printing; Bookbinding and related work; Commercial printing, lithographic

(G-5299)
PBP PUBLISHING LLC ✪
5534 Saint Joe Rd (46835)
PHONE....................574 707-1010
Pamela B Primrose, *Prin*
EMP: 1 **EST:** 2024
SALES (est): 65.99K **Privately Held**
SIC: 2741 Miscellaneous publishing

(G-5300)
PEG PEREGO USA INC
3625 Independence Dr (46808-4504)
PHONE....................800 671-1701
Lucio Perego, *Pr*
Nicola Perego, *
Deanna Mohre, *
◆ **EMP:** 70 **EST:** 1949
SQ FT: 415,000
SALES (est): 26.73MM
SALES (corp-wide): 114.01MM **Privately Held**
Web: us.pegperego.com
SIC: 5099 3944 Baby carriages, strollers and related products; Baby carriages and restraint seats
PA: Peg Perego Spa
Via Alcide De Gasperi 50
Arcore MB 20862
03960881

(G-5301)
PEPSI BEVERAGES COMPANY
Also Called: Pepsi Beverages Co.
4433 Gulfstream Dr (46809-0004)
PHONE....................260 428-9156
Dawn Borgan, *Brnch Mgr*
EMP: 47
SALES (corp-wide): 86.39B **Publicly Held**
Web: www.pepsico.com
SIC: 2086 Carbonated soft drinks, bottled and canned
HQ: Pepsi Beverages Company
110 S Byhalia Rd
Collierville TN 38017
901 853-5736

(G-5302)
PEPSICO
4692 Craftsbury Cir Apt A (46818)
PHONE....................260 750-9106
Corey Morton, *Prin*
EMP: 4 **EST:** 2019
SALES (est): 67.33K **Privately Held**
Web: www.pepsico.com
SIC: 2086 Carbonated soft drinks, bottled and canned

(G-5303)
PEPSICO INC
Also Called: Pepsico
3939 N Wells St (46808-4008)
PHONE....................260 579-3461
EMP: 20 **EST:** 2017
SALES (est): 5.04MM **Privately Held**
Web: www.pepsico.com
SIC: 2086 Carbonated soft drinks, bottled and canned

(G-5304)
PERDUE PRINTED PRODUCTS INC
1707 S Harrison St (46802-5210)
P.O. Box 10924 (46854-0924)
PHONE....................260 456-7575
Matthew J Erb, *Pr*
Judith L Erb, *Sec*
EMP: 7 **EST:** 1966
SALES (est): 972.85K **Privately Held**
Web: www.perdueink.com
SIC: 2752 5112 2759 2395 Offset printing; Business forms; Screen printing; Embroidery products, except Schiffli machine

(G-5305)
PERFECT WORLD DENIM LLC
212 Pearl St (46802-1610)
PHONE....................260 449-9099
EMP: 6 **EST:** 2011
SALES (est): 23.5K **Privately Held**
SIC: 2211 Denims

(G-5306)
PERFECTION BAKERIES INC (PA)
Also Called: Aunt Millie's Bakeries
6230 Bluffton Rd (46809)
PHONE....................260 424-8245
John F Popp, *Pr*
Judy Bobilya-feher, *VP*
▼ **EMP:** 230 **EST:** 1901
SQ FT: 400,000
SALES (est): 486.65MM
SALES (corp-wide): 486.65MM **Privately Held**
Web: www.auntmillies.com
SIC: 2051 Bread, all types (white, wheat, rye, etc); fresh or frozen

(G-5307)
PETE D LIMKEMANN
724 S Doyle Rd (46803)
PHONE....................260 403-4297
Pete D Limkemann, *Prin*
Pete D Limkemann, *Managing Member*
EMP: 6 **EST:** 2004
SALES (est): 360.64K **Privately Held**
SIC: 3621 Motors, electric

(G-5308)
PHAN GEAR PRINTS LLC
2301 Fairfield Ave Apt 702 (46807-1253)
PHONE....................260 450-2539
Cory Rowe, *Owner*
EMP: 5 **EST:** 2018
SALES (est): 92.18K **Privately Held**
SIC: 2752 Commercial printing, lithographic

(G-5309)
PHD INC
9030 Clubridge Dr (46809-3000)
PHONE....................260 747-6151
EMP: 9
Web: www.phdinc.com
SIC: 3593 Fluid power cylinders and actuators

(PA)=Parent Co (HQ)=Headquarters
✪ = New Business established in last 2 years

Fort Wayne - Allen County (G-5310)   GEOGRAPHIC SECTION

HQ: Phd, Inc.
9009 Clubridge Dr
Fort Wayne IN 46809
260 747-6151

(G-5310)
PHD INC (HQ)
9009 Clubridge Dr (46809-3000)
P.O. Box 9070 (46899-9070)
PHONE..................................260 747-6151
EMP: 220 **EST:** 1957
SALES (est): 39.39MM **Privately Held**
Web: www.phdinc.com
SIC: 3593 Fluid power actuators, hydraulic or pneumatic
PA: International Automation Inc
9009 Clubridge Dr
Fort Wayne IN 46809

(G-5311)
PHOENIX AMERICA LLC
4717 Clubview Dr (46804-4448)
PHONE..................................260 432-9664
Scott Mentzer, *Managing Member*
EMP: 50 **EST:** 2019
SALES (est): 11.91MM
SALES (corp-wide): 554.6MM **Privately Held**
Web: www.phoenixamerica.com
SIC: 3824 Gasoline dispensing meters
PA: Discoverie Group Plc
2 Chancellor Court
Guildford GU2 7
148 354-4500

(G-5312)
PHOENIX AMERICA INC
4717 Clubview Dr (46804-4448)
PHONE..................................260 432-9664
▲ **EMP:** 44
Web: www.phoenixamerica.com
SIC: 3824 Tachometer, centrifugal

(G-5313)
PHOENIX INFINITI LLC
9723 W Cove Ct (46804-5915)
PHONE..................................260 443-2782
EMP: 2
SALES (est): 74.03K **Privately Held**
SIC: 1389 Construction, repair, and dismantling services

(G-5314)
PHOENIX STAMPING GROUP LLC
2701 S Coliseum Blvd Ste 1326 (46803-2990)
PHONE..................................404 699-2882
EMP: 50
Web: www.phoenixstamping.com
SIC: 3469 Stamping metal for the trade
PA: Phoenix Stamping Group, Llc
6100 Emmanuel Dr Sw
Atlanta GA 30336

(G-5315)
PIN OAK GROUP LLC
3150 Mallard Cove Ln (46804-2882)
PHONE..................................260 637-7778
Rosaura Martinez, *Prin*
EMP: 1 **EST:** 2010
SALES (est): 101.6K **Privately Held**
SIC: 3452 Pins

(G-5316)
PIN-UP CURLS LLC
1835 Marietta Dr (46804-5727)
PHONE..................................260 241-5871
EMP: 6 **EST:** 2011
SALES (est): 153.44K **Privately Held**
Web: www.pin-upcurls.com

SIC: 3452 Pins

(G-5317)
PLASTIC CARDZ LLC
12721 Us Highway 24 W (46814-7445)
PHONE..................................260 431-6380
Ryan Messmann, *Prin*
EMP: 5 **EST:** 2014
SALES (est): 87.41K **Privately Held**
Web: www.plasticcardz.com
SIC: 2752 Commercial printing, lithographic

(G-5318)
PLASTIC RECYCL EXPORT LTD LLC
6167 Stoney Creek Dr (46825-4409)
PHONE..................................301 758-6885
EMP: 2 **EST:** 2021
SALES (est): 77.45K **Privately Held**
Web: www.plasticrecyclingandexportltd.com
SIC: 3085 5162 5093 3999 Plastics bottles; Plastics materials and basic shapes; Scrap and waste materials; Manufacturing industries, nec

(G-5319)
PLAYFAIR SHUFFLEBOARD COMPANY
7021 Bluffton Rd (46809-2705)
PHONE..................................260 747-7288
Brian G Crowl, *Pr*
EMP: 10 **EST:** 1984
SQ FT: 4,500
SALES (est): 752.44K **Privately Held**
Web: www.playfairgroup.com
SIC: 3949 5091 5046 Shuffleboards and shuffleboard equipment; Billiard equipment and supplies; Commercial equipment, nec

(G-5320)
POCKET PRESS LLC
4101 S Harrison St (46807-2421)
PHONE..................................888 237-2110
Kyle Brittain, *Pr*
Laura West, *VP*
EMP: 2 **EST:** 2018
SALES (est): 45.48K **Privately Held**
Web: www.pocketpress.com
SIC: 2741 Miscellaneous publishing

(G-5321)
POIRY PARTNERS LLC
7337 W Jefferson Blvd (46804-6284)
PHONE..................................260 436-7070
EMP: 1 **EST:** 2004
SALES (est): 487.19K **Privately Held**
SIC: 3471 Plating and polishing
PA: Poiry Partners Llc
2535 Wayne Trce
Fort Wayne IN 46803

(G-5322)
POIRY PARTNERS LLC (PA)
Also Called: Poiry Partners
2535 Wayne Trce (46803-3785)
PHONE..................................260 424-1030
Thomas B Poiry, *Pr*
James Poiry, *VP*
EMP: 49 **EST:** 1995
SALES (est): 6.25MM **Privately Held**
Web: www.fortwayneanodizing.com
SIC: 3471 Electroplating of metals or formed products

(G-5323)
POLAR KING INTERNATIONAL INC
4424 New Haven Ave (46803-1650)
PHONE..................................260 428-2530
David C Schenkel, *Pr*
Barry Tippmann, *VP*

William J Federspiel, *Treas*
Dave Miller, *Sec*
▼ **EMP:** 40 **EST:** 1982
SQ FT: 120,000
SALES (est): 9.69MM **Privately Held**
Web: www.polarking.com
SIC: 3585 Coolers, milk and water: electric

(G-5324)
POLY HI SOLIDUR INC
2710 American Way (46809)
PHONE..................................260 479-4100
▲ **EMP:** 100 **EST:** 1971
SQ FT: 60,000
SALES (est): 2.04MM
SALES (corp-wide): 110.43MM **Privately Held**
SIC: 3089 Injection molding of plastics
PA: Professional Plastics, Inc.
1810 E Valencia Dr
Fullerton CA 92831
714 446-6500

(G-5325)
POLYMOD TECHNOLOGIES INC
4146 Engleton Dr (46804-3162)
P.O. Box 10180 (46850-0180)
PHONE..................................260 436-1322
Ron Zielinski, *Pr*
EMP: 12 **EST:** 1992
SQ FT: 10,000
SALES (est): 1.57MM **Privately Held**
Web: www.polymod.com
SIC: 8731 2821 5085 Commercial physical research; Plastics materials and resins; Gaskets and seals

(G-5326)
POMPS TIRE SERVICE INC
2720 Goshen Rd (46808-1445)
PHONE..................................260 489-5252
Jesse Salsar, *Mgr*
EMP: 20
SALES (corp-wide): 918.27MM **Privately Held**
Web: www.pompstire.com
SIC: 5531 5014 7534 Automotive tires; Tires and tubes; Tire retreading and repair shops
PA: Pomp's Tire Service, Inc.
1122 Cedar St
Green Bay WI 54301
920 435-8301

(G-5327)
POWER FREIGHT LLC
Also Called: Power Freight
4825 Devonshire Dr (46806-3419)
PHONE..................................260 258-6012
EMP: 2 **EST:** 2021
SALES (est): 50K **Privately Held**
SIC: 3799 Transportation equipment, nec

(G-5328)
POWER PLANT SERVICE INC
2500 W Jefferson Blvd (46802-4641)
PHONE..................................260 432-6716
Donald J Akey, *Pr*
Alberta Akey, *
EMP: 44 **EST:** 1911
SQ FT: 70,000
SALES (est): 2.55MM **Privately Held**
Web: www.powerplantserviceinc.com
SIC: 7699 3567 5074 3714 Boiler repair shop; Fuel-fired furnaces and ovens; Plumbing and hydronic heating supplies; Motor vehicle parts and accessories

(G-5329)
POWERCLEAN INC (PA)
Also Called: Powerclean Industrial Services
6808 Metro Park Dr E (46818-9393)

P.O. Box 80345 (46898-0345)
PHONE..................................260 483-1375
Steven J Barber, *Pr*
Sue Pollit, *
EMP: 21 **EST:** 1996
SALES (est): 7.02MM
SALES (corp-wide): 7.02MM **Privately Held**
Web: www.powercleanindustrial.com
SIC: 1521 1799 2842 Patio and deck construction and repair; Exterior cleaning, including sandblasting; Specialty cleaning

(G-5330)
PPG ARCHITECTURAL FINISHES INC
Also Called: Glidden Professional Paint Ctr
826 Lawrence Dr (46804-1192)
PHONE..................................260 436-1854
Eric Barber, *Brnch Mgr*
EMP: 6
SALES (corp-wide): 17.65B **Publicly Held**
Web: www.ppgpaints.com
SIC: 2851 Paints and allied products
HQ: Ppg Architectural Finishes, Inc.
1 Ppg Pl
Pittsburgh PA 15272
412 434-3131

(G-5331)
PPG ARCHITECTURAL FINISHES INC
Also Called: Glidden Professional Paint Ctr
826 Lawrence Dr (46804-1192)
PHONE..................................260 436-1854
Todd Harriman, *Mgr*
EMP: 6
SALES (corp-wide): 17.65B **Publicly Held**
Web: www.ppgpaints.com
SIC: 2851 Paints and allied products
HQ: Ppg Architectural Finishes, Inc.
1 Ppg Pl
Pittsburgh PA 15272
412 434-3131

(G-5332)
PPG ARCHITECTURAL FINISHES INC
Also Called: Porter Paints
2510 Independence Dr (46808-1324)
PHONE..................................260 373-2373
Mike Nichols, *Mgr*
EMP: 6
SALES (corp-wide): 17.65B **Publicly Held**
Web: www.ppgpaints.com
SIC: 2851 Paints and allied products
HQ: Ppg Architectural Finishes, Inc.
1 Ppg Pl
Pittsburgh PA 15272
412 434-3131

(G-5333)
PPG INDUSTRIES INC
Also Called: PPG 4383
2510 Independence Dr (46808-1324)
PHONE..................................260 373-2373
Mike Nichols, *Brnch Mgr*
EMP: 4
SALES (corp-wide): 17.65B **Publicly Held**
Web: www.ppgpaints.com
SIC: 2851 Paints and allied products
PA: Ppg Industries, Inc.
1 Ppg Pl
Pittsburgh PA 15272
412 434-3131

(G-5334)
PPG INDUSTRIES INC
Also Called: Indiana Coatings Division
4301 Engle Rd (46804-4422)
PHONE..................................260 432-6900
Bart Alexander, *Mgr*
EMP: 49
SQ FT: 56,000

GEOGRAPHIC SECTION
Fort Wayne - Allen County (G-5358)

SALES (corp-wide): 17.65B **Publicly Held**
Web: www.ppg.com
SIC: **2851** Paints and allied products
PA: Ppg Industries, Inc.
1 Ppg Pl
Pittsburgh PA 15272
412 434-3131

(G-5335)
PRECISION COLORS LLC
2617 Meyer Rd (46803-2915)
PHONE..................260 969-6402
Bob Mann, *Managing Member*
EMP: 15 EST: 2014
SQ FT: 9,500
SALES (est): 2.05MM **Privately Held**
Web: www.precision-colors.com
SIC: **2821** Plastics materials and resins

(G-5336)
PRECISION DIE TECHNOLOGIES LLC
4716 Speedway Dr (46825-5239)
PHONE..................260 482-5001
John Frieburger, *Pr*
Josef Geisler, *
Brad Frieburger, *
EMP: 19 EST: 1989
SQ FT: 5,000
SALES (est): 3.17MM **Privately Held**
Web: www.pdtinc.com
SIC: **3544** Wire drawing and straightening dies

(G-5337)
PRECISION FABRICATION INC
710 Hanover St (46803-1042)
PHONE..................260 422-4448
Julia R Isch, *Pr*
Fred Hagadorn, *VP*
EMP: 10 EST: 1970
SQ FT: 12,000
SALES (est): 1.49MM **Privately Held**
Web: www.prefabfw.com
SIC: **3441** Fabricated structural metal

(G-5338)
PRECISION HEAT TREATING CORP
2711 Adams Center Rd (46803-3283)
P.O. Box 6162 (46896-0162)
PHONE..................260 749-5125
Kenneth Vandre Senior, *Pr*
Mark Vandre, *VP*
Kenneth Vandre Junior, *VP*
Mary Vandre, *Sec*
EMP: 21 EST: 1972
SQ FT: 29,000
SALES (est): 2.12MM **Privately Held**
Web: www.phtc.net
SIC: **3398** Metal heat treating

(G-5339)
PRECISION LASER SERVICES INC
14730 Lima Rd (46818-9585)
PHONE..................260 744-4375
Eward Ferrier, *Pr*
Ed Ferrier, *
▼ EMP: 32 EST: 1941
SQ FT: 30,000
SALES (est): 4.36MM **Privately Held**
Web: www.plsmfg.com
SIC: **3599** Machine shop, jobbing and repair

(G-5340)
PRECISION PRODUCTS GROUP INC
Also Called: Paramount Tube Division
1430 Progress Rd (46803-1179)
P.O. Box 80400 (46898-0400)
PHONE..................260 484-4111
Ken Seifert, *Mgr*
EMP: 49
SQ FT: 30,000

Web: www.ppgintl.com
SIC: **2655** 3498 Fiber cans, drums, and similar products; Fabricated pipe and fittings
PA: Precision Products Group, Inc.
8770 Guion Rd Ste A
Indianapolis IN 46268

(G-5341)
PRECISION PRODUCTS GROUP INC
Also Called: Phenix
2701 S Coliseum Blvd Ste 1148 (46803-2950)
PHONE..................260 424-3734
EMP: 8
Web: www.ppgintl.com
SIC: **2655** Tubes, fiber or paper: made from purchased material
PA: Precision Products Group, Inc.
8770 Guion Rd Ste A
Indianapolis IN 46268

(G-5342)
PRECISION UTILITIES GROUP INC
5916 E State Blvd (46815-7637)
PHONE..................260 485-8300
Dave Schmaucg, *Pr*
Rich Hamilton, *
Jim Samples, *
EMP: 65 EST: 2009
SALES (est): 4.63MM **Privately Held**
Web: www.precisionug.net
SIC: **3357** Fiber optic cable (insulated)

(G-5343)
PREMIER CONSULTING INC (PA)
Also Called: Premier Wire Die
1415 Profit Dr (46808-1170)
PHONE..................260 496-9300
Vincent Griffin, *Pr*
Tammy L Griffin, *VP*
▼ EMP: 10 EST: 2003
SALES (est): 1.01MM
SALES (corp-wide): 1.01MM **Privately Held**
Web: www.premierwiredie.com
SIC: **3544** Wire drawing and straightening dies

(G-5344)
PREMIER HYDRAULIC AUGERS INC
2707 Lofty Dr (46808-3927)
PHONE..................260 456-8518
Greg Seifert, *Pr*
Bob Meriwether, *
Gregg Owens, *
EMP: 26 EST: 2002
SQ FT: 80,000
SALES (est): 4.24MM **Privately Held**
Web: www.premierattach.com
SIC: **3531** Construction machinery attachments

(G-5345)
PREMIER MFG GROUP INC
Also Called: Electri-Cable Assemblies
7310 Innovation Blvd Ste 104 (46818-1370)
PHONE..................203 924-6617
EMP: 60 EST: 1975
SALES (est): 10MM
SALES (corp-wide): 4.41B **Publicly Held**
SIC: **3645** 2541 Residential lighting fixtures; Office fixtures, wood
HQ: Group Dekko, Inc.
7310 Innovation Blvd # 104
Fort Wayne IN 46818

(G-5346)
PRENTICE PRODUCTS HOLDINGS LLC
Also Called: Prentice Products
310 W Cook Rd (46825-3320)

PHONE..................260 747-3195
Mark Hagar, *Pr*
Mark Lewis, *VP*
EMP: 21 EST: 2015
SALES (est): 2.38MM **Privately Held**
Web: www.prenticeproducts.com
SIC: **2759** Screen printing

(G-5347)
PRENTICE PRODUCTS INC
4236 W Ferguson Rd (46809-3198)
PHONE..................260 747-3195
◆ EMP: 21
SIC: **3993** 2752 2759 2396 Signs and advertising specialties; Commercial printing, lithographic; Commercial printing, nec; Automotive and apparel trimmings

(G-5348)
PRESS A DENT
614 Constance Ave (46805-1834)
PHONE..................260 760-1585
Maurice Taulman, *Prin*
EMP: 4 EST: 2017
SALES (est): 76.53K **Privately Held**
SIC: **2741** Miscellaneous publishing

(G-5349)
PRESS-SEAL CORPORATION
2801 W State Blvd (46808-1801)
PHONE..................260 436-0521
James W Skinner, *Pr*
EMP: 1
SALES (corp-wide): 45.71MM **Privately Held**
Web: www.press-seal.com
SIC: **3053** Oil seals, rubber
PA: Press-Seal Corporation
2424 W State Blvd
Fort Wayne IN 46808
260 436-0521

(G-5350)
PRESS-SEAL CORPORATION (PA)
2424 W State Blvd (46808-3934)
P.O. Box 10482 (46852-0482)
PHONE..................260 436-0521
James W Skinner, *Pr*
M Anne Skinner, *
▼ EMP: 145 EST: 1954
SQ FT: 150,000
SALES (est): 45.71MM
SALES (corp-wide): 45.71MM **Privately Held**
Web: www.press-seal.com
SIC: **3053** 5085 Oil seals, rubber; Gaskets and seals

(G-5351)
PREVAIL PRSTHTICS ORTHTICS INC
7735 W Jefferson Blvd # C (46804-4135)
PHONE..................765 668-0890
John Lee, *Mgr*
EMP: 3
SALES (corp-wide): 3.05MM **Privately Held**
Web: www.prevailpando.com
SIC: **3842** Prosthetic appliances
PA: Prevail Prosthetics & Orthotics, Inc.
7735 W Jefferson Blvd
Fort Wayne IN 46804
260 483-5219

(G-5352)
PROAPSE SOFTWARE
604 Constance Ave (46805-1834)
PHONE..................260 615-9839
Don Ashley, *Owner*
EMP: 1 EST: 2009
SALES (est): 72.58K **Privately Held**
Web: www.proapsesoftware.com

SIC: **7372** 7389 Prepackaged software; Business Activities at Non-Commercial Site

(G-5353)
PROFESSIONAL METAL REFINISHING
Also Called: Pro-Blast Equip
2415 W State Blvd (46808-3933)
PHONE..................260 436-2828
Joseph Bruck, *Pr*
Tonya Vojtkofsky, *Sec*
EMP: 7 EST: 1985
SQ FT: 12,000
SALES (est): 829.54K **Privately Held**
Web: www.prostrip.com
SIC: **3471** Cleaning and descaling metal products

(G-5354)
PROTECTIVE COATINGS INC
Also Called: Proco
1602 Birchwood Ave (46803-2797)
PHONE..................260 424-2900
Michael Murrell, *Pr*
Robert Kaufman, *
EMP: 40 EST: 1958
SQ FT: 100,000
SALES (est): 4.45MM **Privately Held**
Web: www.proco-fwi.com
SIC: **3069** Molded rubber products

(G-5355)
PRP TECHNOLOGIES LLC
3201 Stellhorn Rd (46815-4697)
PHONE..................260 433-3769
John Finch, *Admn*
EMP: 6 EST: 2013
SALES (est): 232.61K **Privately Held**
Web: www.prptech.net
SIC: **3841** Surgical and medical instruments

(G-5356)
PURE CREATIVE PUBLISHING LLC ✪
5534 Saint Joe Rd (46835)
PHONE..................765 860-8999
Samantha D Runge, *CEO*
EMP: 1 EST: 2024
SALES (est): 65.99K **Privately Held**
SIC: **2741** Miscellaneous publishing

(G-5357)
PWT GROUP LLC
Also Called: Precision Wire Technologies
6320 Highview Dr (46818-1382)
PHONE..................260 490-6477
EMP: 29 EST: 2001
SQ FT: 24,900
SALES (est): 4.32MM **Privately Held**
Web: www.precisionwiretech.com
SIC: **3496** 3315 Miscellaneous fabricated wire products; Steel wire and related products

(G-5358)
PYROMATION LLC
5211 Industrial Rd (46825-5152)
PHONE..................260 484-2580
Dennis Tichio, *Managing Member*
Peter C Wilson, *
Mark Beckman, *
Melani Wilson, *
EMP: 205 EST: 1962
SQ FT: 30,000
SALES (est): 40.55MM **Privately Held**
Web: www.pyromation.com

Fort Wayne - Allen County (G-5359)   GEOGRAPHIC SECTION

SIC: 3823 3829 3822 3812 Temperature instruments: industrial process type; Temperature sensors, except industrial process and aircraft; Environmental controls; Search and navigation equipment

(G-5359)
QBOTIX LLC
1355 Getz Rd Ste E (46804)
PHONE..................................562 526-5725
Ashok Kumar Jg, *Prin*
Ashok Kumar Jg, *Managing Member*
EMP: 5 **EST:** 2019
SALES (est): 93.5K **Privately Held**
SIC: 7372 Application computer software

(G-5360)
QTR INDUSTRIES LLC
1035 Sutton Dr Unit B (46804-1141)
PHONE..................................260 416-8981
Trevor Spencer, *Managing Member*
EMP: 6 **EST:** 2021
SALES (est): 293.86K **Privately Held**
Web: www.qtrindustries.com
SIC: 3484 Small arms

(G-5361)
QUAD/GRAPHICS INC
Also Called: QUAD/GRAPHICS INC.
6502 Nelson Rd (46803-1920)
PHONE..................................260 748-5300
EMP: 3
SALES (corp-wide): 2.96B **Publicly Held**
Web: www.quad.com
SIC: 2752 Offset printing
PA: Quad/Graphics, Inc.
  N61 W23044 Harry's Way
  Sussex WI 53089
  414 566-6000

(G-5362)
QUAKE MANUFACTURING INC
3923 Engle Rd (46804-4414)
PHONE..................................260 432-8023
Paul Quake, *CEO*
Hermann Quake, *Pr*
Sally Quake, *Sec*
EMP: 11 **EST:** 1989
SQ FT: 5,000
SALES (est): 1.82MM **Privately Held**
Web: www.quakemfg.com
SIC: 3599 Machine shop, jobbing and repair

(G-5363)
QUIKCUT LLC
4630 Allen Martin Dr (46806-2800)
PHONE..................................260 447-3880
Mark Webb, *Managing Member*
EMP: 40 **EST:** 2021
SALES (est): 1.01MM **Privately Held**
Web: www.quikcutinc.com
SIC: 3441 Fabricated structural metal

(G-5364)
R & R WELDING
1238 E Lewis St (46803-2066)
PHONE..................................260 424-3635
Rod Sebring, *Prin*
EMP: 6 **EST:** 2013
SALES (est): 91.04K **Privately Held**
Web: www.all-stardoor.com
SIC: 7692 Welding repair

(G-5365)
R O I SYSTEMS INC
9181 Lima Rd (46818-1803)
PHONE..................................260 413-6307
Gregory T Pelosi, *Prin*
EMP: 1 **EST:** 2013
SALES (est): 60.54K **Privately Held**

SIC: 7372 Prepackaged software

(G-5366)
RAYTHEON COMPANY
Also Called: Raytheon
5001 Us Highway 30 W (46818-9815)
PHONE..................................310 647-9438
Thomas Kennedy, *CEO*
EMP: 3000
SALES (corp-wide): 68.92B **Publicly Held**
Web: www.rtx.com
SIC: 3812 Search and navigation equipment
HQ: Raytheon Company
  870 Winter St
  Waltham MA 02451
  781 522-3000

(G-5367)
RAYTHEON COMPANY
Also Called: Raytheon
1320 Production Rd (46808-1165)
PHONE..................................260 429-6000
EMP: 1
SALES (corp-wide): 68.92B **Publicly Held**
Web: www.rtx.com
SIC: 3812 Sonar systems and equipment
HQ: Raytheon Company
  870 Winter St
  Waltham MA 02451
  781 522-3000

(G-5368)
RAYTHEON COMPANY
Also Called: Raytheon
1010 Production Rd (46808-4106)
PHONE..................................260 429-6000
Albert Perry, *CEO*
EMP: 700
SALES (corp-wide): 68.92B **Publicly Held**
Web: www.rtx.com
SIC: 3812 3489 Sonar systems and equipment; Ordnance and accessories, nec
HQ: Raytheon Company
  870 Winter St
  Waltham MA 02451
  781 522-3000

(G-5369)
RAYTHEON COMPANY
Also Called: Raytheon
1010 Production Rd (46808-4106)
PHONE..................................310 647-9438
EMP: 5
SQ FT: 1,000
SALES (corp-wide): 68.92B **Publicly Held**
Web: www.rtx.com
SIC: 3812 3663 3761 Defense systems and equipment; Space satellite communications equipment; Guided missiles and space vehicles, research and development
HQ: Raytheon Company
  870 Winter St
  Waltham MA 02451
  781 522-3000

(G-5370)
REA MAGNET WIRE COMPANY INC (PA)
3400 E Coliseum Blvd Ste 200 (46805)
PHONE..................................800 732-9473
◆ **EMP:** 60 **EST:** 1933
SALES (est): 220.53MM
SALES (corp-wide): 220.53MM **Privately Held**
Web: www.reawire.com
SIC: 3357 Magnet wire, nonferrous

(G-5371)
REBAR CORP OF INDIANA
Also Called: Rebar
5601 Industrial Rd (46825-5125)

P.O. Box 15944 (46885-5944)
PHONE..................................260 471-2002
EMP: 7
SIC: 3449 Fabricated bar joists and concrete reinforcing bars

(G-5372)
RECKON PLATING INC
5300 Hanna St (46806-3135)
PHONE..................................260 744-4339
Kashem Sarker, *Pr*
Cindy Sarker, *Treas*
EMP: 22 **EST:** 1993
SQ FT: 6,800
SALES (est): 2.27MM **Privately Held**
Web: www.reckonplating.com
SIC: 3471 Electroplating of metals or formed products

(G-5373)
RED EARTH LLC
Also Called: Red Earth Industrial
P.O. Box 5138 (46895-5138)
PHONE..................................260 338-1439
Adam Connelly, *Managing Member*
EMP: 4 **EST:** 2010
SALES (est): 243.45K **Privately Held**
SIC: 1799 3999 Dock equipment installation, industrial; Dock equipment and supplies, industrial

(G-5374)
REDMASTER FUSION LLC
9308 Madina Pkwy (46825-1133)
PHONE..................................260 273-5819
EMP: 2 **EST:** 2012
SALES (est): 51.95K **Privately Held**
Web: www.redmasterfusion.com
SIC: 2844 3999 Lotions, shaving; Candles

(G-5375)
REFLECTIVE COATING LLC
Also Called: Reflective Coating
1240 W Main St (46808-3335)
PHONE..................................260 414-1245
David Height, *Prin*
EMP: 1 **EST:** 2016
SALES (est): 53.09K **Privately Held**
Web: www.reflectivecoatingsllc.com
SIC: 3479 Metal coating and allied services

(G-5376)
REFRACTORY SPECIALISTS LLC
3525 Metro Dr N (46818-9388)
PHONE..................................260 969-1099
Larry Snell, *Managing Member*
EMP: 3 **EST:** 2011
SALES (est): 187.25K **Privately Held**
SIC: 3255 Glasshouse refractories

(G-5377)
REGAL BELOIT AMERICA INC
Also Called: Genteq
1946 W Cook Rd (46818-1166)
PHONE..................................260 416-5400
EMP: 19
SALES (corp-wide): 6.25B **Publicly Held**
SIC: 3621 Motors and generators
HQ: Regal Beloit America, Inc.
  111 W Michigan St
  Milwaukee WI 53203
  608 364-8800

(G-5378)
REGAL REXNORD CORPORATION
1946 W Cook Rd (46818-1166)
PHONE..................................608 364-8800
EMP: 26
SALES (corp-wide): 6.25B **Publicly Held**
Web: www.regalrexnord.com

SIC: 3621 3566 Motors and generators; Speed changers, drives, and gears
PA: Regal Rexnord Corporation
  111 W Michigan St
  Milwaukee WI 53203
  608 364-8800

(G-5379)
REGAL-BELOIT ELECTRIC MOTORS INC
1946 W Cook Rd (46818-1166)
PHONE..................................260 416-5400
▲ **EMP:** 506
SIC: 3621 Motors and generators

(G-5380)
RENEGADE DISPATCHING LLC
2737 W Washington Center Rd (46818-1469)
PHONE..................................260 797-5423
EMP: 1
SALES (est): 69.27K **Privately Held**
SIC: 3537 7389 Trucks: freight, baggage, etc.: industrial, except mining; Business Activities at Non-Commercial Site

(G-5381)
RESIDUAL PAYS DAILY
2313 Florida Dr Apt C15 (46805-3557)
PHONE..................................260 267-1617
Maye Shondiqua, *Prin*
EMP: 6 **EST:** 2017
SALES (est): 90.74K **Privately Held**
SIC: 2911 Residues

(G-5382)
RIC CORPORATION D/B/A
6215 Constitution Dr (46804-1517)
PHONE..................................260 432-0799
Rick Kriscka, *Pr*
EMP: 1 **EST:** 2010
SALES (est): 66.07K **Privately Held**
SIC: 3999 Manufacturing industries, nec

(G-5383)
RICHARDS BAKERY
1130 N Wells St (46808-3470)
PHONE..................................260 424-4012
Michelle Moore, *Pt*
Dick Moore, *Pt*
EMP: 10 **EST:** 1976
SQ FT: 1,500
SALES (est): 816.16K **Privately Held**
SIC: 2051 5461 Bakery: wholesale or wholesale/retail combined; Retail bakeries

(G-5384)
RITE-WAY ARMS LLC
6911 Trafalgar Dr (46803-3281)
PHONE..................................260 493-4517
EMP: 4 **EST:** 2016
SALES (est): 81.6K **Privately Held**
SIC: 3489 Ordnance and accessories, nec

(G-5385)
RITS LTD BROKERS INC
3339 Stone Blvd (46802-4452)
PHONE..................................260 348-0786
Peter Tsuleff, *Pr*
EMP: 2 **EST:** 2003
SQ FT: 3,200
SALES (est): 171.97K **Privately Held**
Web: www.ritsltdbrokers.com
SIC: 3053 3452 5072 5085 Gaskets; packing and sealing devices; Bolts, nuts, rivets, and washers; Bolts, nuts, and screws; Gaskets and seals

GEOGRAPHIC SECTION
Fort Wayne - Allen County (G-5412)

(G-5386)
RIVERSIDE MFG LLC
14510 Lima Rd (46818-9537)
PHONE..................260 637-4470
Fred Merritt, *CEO*
EMP: 375 **EST:** 2007
SQ FT: 35,000
SALES (est): 57.39MM
SALES (corp-wide): 83.33MM **Privately Held**
Web: www.riversidemfg.com
SIC: 3625 Industrial electrical relays and switches
PA: Riverside Mfg. Inc.
   14510 Lima Rd
   Fort Wayne IN 46818
   260 637-4470

(G-5387)
RIVERSIDE MFG INC (PA)
14510 Lima Rd (46818)
PHONE..................260 637-4470
Fred Merritt, *CEO*
▲ **EMP:** 160 **EST:** 1947
SQ FT: 35,000
SALES (est): 83.33MM
SALES (corp-wide): 83.33MM **Privately Held**
Web: www.riversidemfg.com
SIC: 3714 Motor vehicle parts and accessories

(G-5388)
ROBOCFI LLC ✪
505 Roxbury Ct (46807-3116)
PHONE..................317 612-7889
EMP: 1 **EST:** 2024
SALES (est): 68.7K **Privately Held**
Web: www.robocfi.io
SIC: 7372 7371 Prepackaged software; Software programming applications

(G-5389)
ROSE & PETAL LLC ✪
6625 Pointe Inverness Way (46804-7908)
PHONE..................260 704-5731
S Chipasula-perry, *Prin*
Schauntrice Chipasula-perry, *Prin*
EMP: 1 **EST:** 2024
SALES (est): 54.05K **Privately Held**
SIC: 2678 7389 Notebooks: made from purchased paper; Business services, nec

(G-5390)
RUGGED STEEL WORKS LLC
Also Called: Ameri-Kan
4325 Meyer Rd (46806-2817)
PHONE..................260 444-4241
Doug Gunsaullus, *Pr*
EMP: 10 **EST:** 2014
SQ FT: 93,000
SALES (est): 472.04K **Privately Held**
Web: www.ruggedsteelcontainers.com
SIC: 7539 3443 Trailer repair; Industrial vessels, tanks, and containers

(G-5391)
RUSHER MEDICAL LLC
6028 Heywood Cv (46815-6270)
PHONE..................260 341-6514
Michael Rusher, *Managing Member*
EMP: 1 **EST:** 2011
SALES (est): 5.21K **Privately Held**
SIC: 3841 Inhalation therapy equipment

(G-5392)
RYAN FUELLING
6928 Nighthawk Dr (46835-9217)
PHONE..................260 403-6450
Ryan J Fuelling, *Prin*

EMP: 7 **EST:** 2010
SALES (est): 245.67K **Privately Held**
SIC: 2869 Fuels

(G-5393)
S S & E ENTERPRISES
1906 Kendawa Dr (46815-7939)
PHONE..................260 749-0026
Gary R Gill, *Owner*
EMP: 1 **EST:** 1968
SALES (est): 48K **Privately Held**
Web: www.etsenterprises.com
SIC: 3089 Engraving of plastics

(G-5394)
SABERT CORPORATION
8510 Ardmore Ave (46809)
PHONE..................260 222-0758
Marc Yazel, *Brnch Mgr*
EMP: 40
SALES (corp-wide): 615.82MM **Privately Held**
Web: www.sabert.com
SIC: 3089 Trays, plastics
PA: Sabert Corporation
   2288 Main St
   Sayreville NJ 08872
   800 722-3781

(G-5395)
SABERT CORPORATION
3511 Engle Rd (46809-1117)
PHONE..................260 747-3149
EMP: 5
SALES (corp-wide): 615.82MM **Privately Held**
Web: www.sabert.com
SIC: 2671 Plastic film, coated or laminated for packaging
PA: Sabert Corporation
   2288 Main St
   Sayreville NJ 08872
   800 722-3781

(G-5396)
SANCO INDUSTRIES
409 E Cook Rd Ste 200 (46825-3656)
P.O. Box 11384 (46857-1384)
PHONE..................219 426-3922
Todd Chambers, *Prin*
EMP: 5 **EST:** 2017
SALES (est): 39.69K **Privately Held**
SIC: 3999 Manufacturing industries, nec

(G-5397)
SANCO INDUSTRIES INC
Also Called: Pond Champs
1819 S Calhoun St (46802-5259)
PHONE..................260 467-1791
Brett Zachary, *Brnch Mgr*
EMP: 4
Web: www.sancoind.com
SIC: 2899 1629 Chemical preparations, nec; Pond construction
PA: Sanco Industries, Inc.
   1819 S Calhoun St
   Fort Wayne IN 46802

(G-5398)
SANCO INDUSTRIES INC (PA)
1819 S Calhoun St (46802-5259)
P.O. Box 11617 (46859-1617)
PHONE..................260 426-6281
Brett Zachary, *CEO*
Kevin Appenzeller, *Pr*
EMP: 22 **EST:** 2001
SQ FT: 46,000
SALES (est): 5.86MM **Privately Held**
Web: www.sancoind.com
SIC: 2899 1629 Chemical preparations, nec; Pond construction

(G-5399)
SAND DCL LLC
5618 W Jefferson Blvd (46804-1671)
P.O. Box 307 (46936-0307)
PHONE..................260 459-9565
Micah Mouser, *Pt*
EMP: 2 **EST:** 2020
SALES (est): 74.42K **Privately Held**
SIC: 2842 Laundry cleaning preparations

(G-5400)
SANSHER CORPORATION
8005 N Clinton St (46825-3115)
PHONE..................260 484-2000
Phillip W Bradley, *Pr*
EMP: 4 **EST:** 1967
SQ FT: 14,000
SALES (est): 340K **Privately Held**
Web: www.sansher.com
SIC: 2851 Paint removers

(G-5401)
SCADATA VENTURES LLC
Also Called: Scadata Scientific, LLC
1700 Magnavox Way Ste 100 (46804-1552)
PHONE..................260 373-0100
Kevin Stock, *CEO*
EMP: 10 **EST:** 2003
SQ FT: 5,000
SALES (est): 927.89K **Privately Held**
Web: www.scadata.net
SIC: 3823 Process control instruments

(G-5402)
SCHMUCKERS WOOD SHOP
9966 Eby Rd (46835-9570)
PHONE..................260 485-1434
Dan Schmucker, *Owner*
EMP: 6 **EST:** 2000
SALES (est): 495.56K **Privately Held**
SIC: 2499 Decorative wood and woodwork

(G-5403)
SCHOLASTIC EDUCATION
1120 Lake Pointe Cv (46845-6411)
PHONE..................260 437-1485
Randee Salisbury, *Prin*
EMP: 4 **EST:** 2018
SALES (est): 68.03K **Privately Held**
Web: www.scholastic.com
SIC: 2741 Miscellaneous publishing

(G-5404)
SCOTIA CORPORATION
Also Called: Amercan
7707 Freedom Way (46818-2169)
PHONE..................260 479-8800
David Seybert, *Pr*
EMP: 14 **EST:** 2000
SALES (est): 488.61K **Privately Held**
SIC: 3444 Canopies, sheet metal

(G-5405)
SEAL PRODUCTS LLC
3702 Vanguard Dr (46809-3303)
PHONE..................260 436-5628
Jeff S Huntine, *Managing Member*
▲ **EMP:** 7 **EST:** 2007
SALES (est): 792.52K **Privately Held**
Web: www.sealproducts.net
SIC: 3053 Gaskets; packing and sealing devices

(G-5406)
SEASONED SOFTWARE LLC
13030 Callison Ct (46845-2344)
PHONE..................260 431-5666
EMP: 3 **EST:** 2015
SALES (est): 77.52K **Privately Held**

SIC: 7372 Prepackaged software

(G-5407)
SEAVAC (USA) LLC
9304 Yeager Ln (46809-9646)
PHONE..................260 747-7123
Masahiro Imoto, *Ex Dir*
EMP: 15 **EST:** 2005
SALES (est): 1.94MM **Privately Held**
Web: www.seavacusa.com
SIC: 3479 Coating of metals and formed products

(G-5408)
SELKING INTERNATIONAL LLC (HQ)
2807 Goshen Rd (46808-1446)
P.O. Box 80040 (46898-0040)
PHONE..................260 482-3000
Jerry Selking, *Pr*
James Selking, *VP*
Joseph Selking, *Treas*
EMP: 45 **EST:** 1997
SALES (est): 24.72MM
SALES (corp-wide): 29.7MM **Privately Held**
Web: www.selkinginternational.com
SIC: 5012 7538 3537 Trucks, commercial; General automotive repair shops; Industrial trucks and tractors
PA: Decatur Truck & Tractor Inc
   1850 W Us Highway 224
   Decatur IN 46733
   260 482-3000

(G-5409)
SENSORTEC INC
7620 Disalle Blvd (46825-3373)
PHONE..................260 497-8811
Grant Passwater, *Pr*
EMP: 27 **EST:** 1992
SQ FT: 15,000
SALES (est): 1.1MM **Privately Held**
Web: www.sensortecinc.com
SIC: 3829 Thermometers and temperature sensors

(G-5410)
SHAKLEE AUTHORIZED DISTRIBUTOR
3330 Thames Dr (46815-5994)
PHONE..................260 471-8232
Rita Musser, *Owner*
EMP: 1 **EST:** 2014
SALES (est): 112.89K **Privately Held**
Web: us.shaklee.com
SIC: 5023 3471 2048 Homefurnishings; Cleaning and descaling metal products; Feed supplements

(G-5411)
SHANK BROTHERS INC
Also Called: Apsco of Indiana
3710 Piper Dr (46809-3159)
PHONE..................260 744-4802
Thomas J Shank, *Pr*
Michael J Shank, *VP*
James Shank, *Sec*
EMP: 12 **EST:** 1969
SQ FT: 2,500
SALES (est): 1.75MM **Privately Held**
Web: www.shankbrothers.com
SIC: 1711 3431 Warm air heating and air conditioning contractor; Metal sanitary ware

(G-5412)
SHAR SYSTEMS INC
3210 Freeman St (46802)
P.O. Box P.O. Box 9196 (46899)
PHONE..................260 432-5312
▲ **EMP:** 22 **EST:** 1994
SQ FT: 28,000

Fort Wayne - Allen County (G-5413)

GEOGRAPHIC SECTION

SALES (est): 3.71MM **Privately Held**
Web: www.sharsystems.com
SIC: 3559 Chemical machinery and equipment

(G-5413)
SHILLING SALES INC
414 E Wayne St (46802-2895)
PHONE.................260 426-2626
Carol Shilling Nole, *Pr*
EMP: 23 **EST:** 1949
SQ FT: 6,000
SALES (est): 2.54MM **Privately Held**
Web: www.shillingsales.com
SIC: 5199 7311 2395 Advertising specialties; Advertising agencies; Pleating and stitching

(G-5414)
SHOEMAKER INC
12120 Yellow River Rd (46818-9702)
PHONE.................260 625-4321
John C Shoemaker, *Pr*
John C Shoemaker Ii, *VP*
Ruby Shoemaker, *Sec*
Gena R Hamby, *Asst Tr*
Lora Slates, *Sec*
EMP: 11 **EST:** 1974
SQ FT: 11,500
SALES (est): 941.88K **Privately Held**
Web: www.shoemakerinc.com
SIC: 3491 Valves, automatic control

(G-5415)
SIGN PRO OF FORT WAYNE INC
Also Called: Sign Pro
7710 Lima Rd (46818-2163)
PHONE.................260 497-8484
EMP: 4 **EST:** 1994
SALES (est): 389.04K **Privately Held**
Web: www.signprofw.com
SIC: 3993 Signs, not made in custom sign painting shops

(G-5416)
SIGNS IN TIME BY GREG INC
Also Called: Signs In Time
4306 Lake Ave (46815-7222)
PHONE.................260 749-7446
EMP: 3 **EST:** 1992
SALES (est): 365.92K **Privately Held**
Web: www.signsintimeinc.com
SIC: 3993 Signs and advertising specialties

(G-5417)
SIMAN PROMOTIONS INC
904 Mill Pointe (46845-6420)
PHONE.................260 637-5621
Joseph R Siman, *Pr*
EMP: 3 **EST:** 1991
SALES (est): 269.45K **Privately Held**
SIC: 2759 Letterpress and screen printing

(G-5418)
SIMPLE GLOW CANDLE CO
9501 Chapmans Blvd (46835-9112)
PHONE.................260 435-0062
EMP: 3 **EST:** 2018
SALES (est): 97.51K **Privately Held**
Web: www.simpleglowcandleco.com
SIC: 3999 Candles

(G-5419)
SJ SALES INC
6715 Wood Glen Ct (46814-4566)
PHONE.................260 433-5947
S J Sales, *Prin*
EMP: 2 **EST:** 2001
SALES (est): 122.42K **Privately Held**
SIC: 3751 Motorcycle accessories

(G-5420)
SKY HIGH GRAPHIX LLC
1501 S Clinton St (46866)
PHONE.................260 267-0724
EMP: 4 **EST:** 2019
SALES (est): 147.1K **Privately Held**
Web: www.skyhighgraphix.com
SIC: 3993 Signs and advertising specialties

(G-5421)
SKYTECH II LLC
9230 Conservation Way (46809-9642)
PHONE.................260 459-1703
Henry O Hall, *Managing Member*
▲ **EMP:** 25 **EST:** 2001
SALES (est): 3.43MM **Privately Held**
Web: www.skytechpg.com
SIC: 3651 3679 Video triggers (remote control TV devices); Video triggers, except remote control TV devices

(G-5422)
SKYTECH-SYSTEMS INC
9230 Conservation Way (46809-9642)
PHONE.................260 459-1703
Christopher Flick, *Pr*
Corbit W Beasey, *Sec*
▲ **EMP:** 13 **EST:** 1996
SALES (est): 2.41MM **Privately Held**
Web: www.skytechpg.com
SIC: 3651 3679 Video triggers (remote control TV devices); Video triggers, except remote control TV devices

(G-5423)
SMOKED Q LLC
921 E Dupont Rd (46825-1551)
PHONE.................260 494-5029
Michael Rauch, *Pr*
EMP: 1 **EST:** 2021
SALES (est): 20K **Privately Held**
Web: shop.smokedq.com
SIC: 2033 Barbecue sauce: packaged in cans, jars, etc.

(G-5424)
SOLFIRE CONTRACT MFG INC
Also Called: Solfire
4939 Decatur Rd (46806)
PHONE.................260 755-2115
Otzo Solis, *Pr*
EMP: 10 **EST:** 2012
SALES (est): 1.11MM **Privately Held**
Web: www.solfire-inc.us
SIC: 3639 Major kitchen appliances, except refrigerators and stoves

(G-5425)
SOLID ROCK LLC
6201 Discount Dr (46818-1231)
PHONE.................260 755-2687
EMP: 1 **EST:** 2005
SALES (est): 242.43K **Privately Held**
Web: www.solidrockllc.net
SIC: 7389 3825 Inspection and testing services; Test equipment for electronic and electric measurement

(G-5426)
SORBASHOCK LLC
204 Barouche Pl (46845-2110)
PHONE.................574 520-9784
EMP: 2 **EST:** 2007
SALES (est): 143.65K **Privately Held**
SIC: 3996 Hard surface floor coverings, nec

(G-5427)
SORG MILLWORK
10744 S Us Highway 27 (46816-3418)
PHONE.................260 639-3223
Don L Sorg, *Pt*
Phil Sorg, *Pt*
Cindy Sorg, *Pt*
EMP: 4 **EST:** 1969
SQ FT: 1,248
SALES (est): 280.92K **Privately Held**
SIC: 2431 Millwork

(G-5428)
SPECIALIZED PRINTED PRODUCTS (PA)
6716 Metro Park Dr E (46818-9396)
PHONE.................260 483-7075
Mark Hager, *Pr*
EMP: 7 **EST:** 1981
SALES (est): 942.93K **Privately Held**
SALES (corp-wide): 942.93K **Privately Held**
Web: www.sppdirect.com
SIC: 2752 7389 2791 2789 Offset printing; Printing broker; Typesetting; Bookbinding and related work

(G-5429)
SPEEDWAY CONSTRUCTION PDTS LLC
4817 Industrial Rd (46825-5209)
P.O. Box 9530 (46899-9530)
PHONE.................260 203-9806
Peter Schenkel, *Pr*
EMP: 2 **EST:** 2012
SALES (est): 335.84K **Privately Held**
Web: www.speedwaycp.com
SIC: 3531 Construction machinery

(G-5430)
SPEEDWAY REDI-MIX INC (PA)
4820 Industrial Rd (46825-5210)
PHONE.................260 496-8877
EMP: 16 **EST:** 2000
SALES (est): 6.22MM **Privately Held**
Web: www.speedwayredimix.com
SIC: 3273 Ready-mixed concrete

(G-5431)
SPORTS PLUS INC
Also Called: Sports Plus
4201 Coldwater Rd (46805-1113)
PHONE.................260 482-8261
EMP: 62
SALES (corp-wide): 847.53K **Privately Held**
Web: www.sportsplus.app
SIC: 3949 Sporting and athletic goods, nec
PA: Sports Plus, Inc.
4120 Douglas Blvd
Granite Bay CA 95746
916 797-5377

(G-5432)
SPORTSCENTER INC
5511 Coventry Ln (46804-7144)
PHONE.................260 436-6198
Kevin Rodenbeck, *Pr*
Tom Rodenbeck, *VP*
EMP: 6 **EST:** 1992
SQ FT: 3,000
SALES (est): 579.43K **Privately Held**
Web: www.expiredwixdomain.com
SIC: 5941 2396 Team sports equipment; Screen printing on fabric articles

(G-5433)
SS CUSTOM CHOPPERS LLC
804 W Wildwood Ave (46807-1643)
PHONE.................260 415-3793
David Stauffer, *Prin*
EMP: 6 **EST:** 2015
SALES (est): 179.14K **Privately Held**
SIC: 3751 Motorcycles and related parts

(G-5434)
ST LENZER LLC
4520 Ellenwood Dr (46806-2850)
PHONE.................260 441-9300
Donna Lenzer, *Pt*
EMP: 3 **EST:** 2004
SALES (est): 247.28K **Privately Held**
Web: www.streamtekllc.com
SIC: 3599 Machine shop, jobbing and repair

(G-5435)
STANDARD PATTERN COMPANY INC
2136 Lafayette St (46803-3373)
PHONE.................260 456-4870
Keith Peters, *Pr*
David Wagner, *Sec*
EMP: 5 **EST:** 1939
SALES (est): 463.99K **Privately Held**
Web: www.standardpattern.com
SIC: 3543 Industrial patterns

(G-5436)
STATE BEAUTY SUPPLY
3822 Lafayette St (46806-4140)
PHONE.................260 755-6361
Yong Yang, *Pr*
EMP: 2 **EST:** 2012
SALES (est): 178.12K **Privately Held**
Web: www.statebeautystores.com
SIC: 5087 3999 Beauty parlor equipment and supplies; Barber and beauty shop equipment

(G-5437)
STEEL DYNAMICS INC
6714 Pointe Inverness Way (46804-7936)
PHONE.................260 969-3500
EMP: 5
Web: www.steeldynamics.com
SIC: 3312 Blast furnaces and steel mills
PA: Steel Dynamics, Inc.
7575 W Jefferson Blvd
Fort Wayne IN 46804

(G-5438)
STEEL DYNAMICS INC (PA)
Also Called: SDI
7575 W Jefferson Blvd (46804)
PHONE.................260 969-3500
Mark D Millett, *Ch Bd*
Barry T Schneider, *
Theresa E Wagler, *Corporate Secretary**
Richard A Poinsatte, *
Miguel Alvarez, *
◆ **EMP:** 480 **EST:** 1993
SALES (est): 18.8B **Publicly Held**
Web: www.steeldynamics.com
SIC: 3312 3316 7389 Blast furnaces and steel mills; Cold finishing of steel shapes; Scrap steel cutting

(G-5439)
STEEL DYNAMICS COLUMBUS LLC
7575 W Jefferson Blvd (46804-4131)
PHONE.................260 969-3500
EMP: 461
Web: www.steeldynamics.com
SIC: 3312 Blast furnaces and steel mills
HQ: Steel Dynamics Columbus, Llc
1945 Airport Rd
Columbus MS 39701

(G-5440)
STEEL DYNAMICS SLS N AMER INC (HQ)
7575 W Jefferson Blvd (46804-4131)
PHONE.................260 969-3500
Theresa W Wagler, *Pr*

Bill Brown, *Pr*
Mark Millett, *VP*
Richard Teets Junior, *VP*
Kent Weber, *Sec*
EMP: 46 **EST:** 2002
SALES (est): 163.62MM **Publicly Held**
Web: www.steeldynamics.com
SIC: 3312 Blast furnaces and steel mills
PA: Steel Dynamics, Inc.
7575 W Jefferson Blvd
Fort Wayne IN 46804

(G-5441)
STERITECH-USA INC
2007 Bremer Rd (46803-3004)
P.O. Box 10816 (46854-0816)
PHONE..............................260 745-7272
Samih Abouhalkah, *Pr*
EMP: 5 **EST:** 2013
SALES (est): 196.05K **Privately Held**
SIC: 2842 Sanitation preparations, disinfectants and deodorants

(G-5442)
STERLING MANUFACTURING LLC
144 E Collins Rd (46825-5302)
PHONE..............................260 451-9760
EMP: 5 **EST:** 2014
SALES (est): 1.03MM **Privately Held**
Web: www.sterlingsteamers.com
SIC: 3631 Household cooking equipment

(G-5443)
STITCH N FRAME
4220 Bluffton Rd (46809-1752)
PHONE..............................260 478-1301
Paul Schoppman, *Owner*
EMP: 6 **EST:** 1969
SQ FT: 1,800
SALES (est): 456.5K **Privately Held**
Web: www.stitchnframes.com
SIC: 5999 5945 2499 Artists' supplies and materials; Arts and crafts supplies; Picture and mirror frames, wood

(G-5444)
STONCOR GROUP INC
Also Called: Stonehard
4115 Polymer Pl (46809-1140)
PHONE..............................260 747-9724
Bob Fox, *Brnch Mgr*
EMP: 1
SALES (corp-wide): 7.34B **Publicly Held**
Web: www.stonhard.com
SIC: 2851 Coating, air curing
HQ: Stoncor Group, Inc.
1000 E Park Ave
Maple Shade NJ 08052
800 257-7953

(G-5445)
STONE CUSTOM DRUM LLC
2701 S Coliseum Blvd (46803-2950)
PHONE..............................260 403-7519
Bernie Stone, *Pr*
EMP: 2 **EST:** 2013
SALES (est): 222.82K **Privately Held**
Web: www.stonecustomdrum.com
SIC: 3931 Percussion instruments and parts

(G-5446)
STOTLAR HILL LLC
4723 E Washington Blvd (46803-1684)
PHONE..............................260 497-0808
Tisha Stotlar, *Prin*
EMP: 10 **EST:** 2010
SALES (est): 258.98K **Privately Held**
SIC: 3271 Paving blocks, concrete

(G-5447)
STRYKERIL INDUSTRIES LLC
5534 Saint Joe Rd (46835)
PHONE..............................219 321-0400
Jeffrey Manibusan, *Owner*
EMP: 1 **EST:** 2021
SALES (est): 65.93K **Privately Held**
SIC: 3999 Manufacturing industries, nec

(G-5448)
STUART MANUFACTURING INC
Also Called: Stuart Integrated Systems
1830 Wayne Trce Unit 407 (46803-2657)
PHONE..............................260 403-2003
Lionel Tobin, *Pr*
EMP: 31 **EST:** 1992
SQ FT: 3,000
SALES (est): 1MM **Privately Held**
Web: www.stuartmfg.com
SIC: 3679 Electronic switches

(G-5449)
SUB BLANKS SOCIETY LLC
429 E Dupont Rd Ste 1078 (46825-2051)
PHONE..............................877 405-6406
EMP: 1 **EST:** 2021
SALES (est): 10K **Privately Held**
SIC: 3944 Craft and hobby kits and sets

(G-5450)
SUGAR TREE INCORPORATED
Also Called: Camo Diva
9185 Lima Rd (46818-1803)
PHONE..............................260 417-3362
Dawn Merriman, *Pr*
Joanna Uttertack, *Mgr*
EMP: 5 **EST:** 2011
SALES (est): 180.65K **Privately Held**
SIC: 5699 2311 2335 Formal wear; Tailored suits and formal jackets; Gowns, formal

(G-5451)
SUMMIT CY PRECISION MACHINING
815 Lawrence Dr (46804-1193)
PHONE..............................260 258-0855
Cary Straley, *Pr*
EMP: 9 **EST:** 2020
SALES (est): 843K **Privately Held**
Web: www.goscpm.com
SIC: 3841 Surgical instruments and apparatus

(G-5452)
SUMMIT FOUNDRY SYSTEMS INC
2100 Wayne Haven St (46803-3279)
PHONE..............................260 749-7740
Richard L Meyer, *Pr*
Sharon Meyer, *Sec*
EMP: 14 **EST:** 1981
SQ FT: 18,000
SALES (est): 2.35MM **Privately Held**
Web: www.summitfoundrysystems.com
SIC: 3559 Foundry machinery and equipment

(G-5453)
SUMMIT MANUFACTURING CORP
2320 Meyer Rd (46803-2910)
PHONE..............................260 428-2600
Alan Zemen, *Pr*
Vincent Tippmann, *
William J Federspiel, *
Renee Dillon, *AD Manager*
EMP: 25 **EST:** 1984
SQ FT: 95,000
SALES (est): 946.24K **Privately Held**
Web: www.summitmc.com
SIC: 3443 3444 3353 Metal parts; Sheet metalwork; Aluminum sheet, plate, and foil

(G-5454)
SUMMIT PEDORTHICS LLC
6207 Monarch Dr (46815-7633)
PHONE..............................260 348-7268
Steven Bumgarder, *Prin*
Steven Bumgardner, *Prin*
EMP: 1 **EST:** 2016
SALES (est): 63.44K **Privately Held**
Web: www.summitpedorthics.com
SIC: 3842 Limbs, artificial

(G-5455)
SUMMT OUTDOORS
6714 Pointe Inverness Way Ste 200 (46804-7936)
PHONE..............................260 483-2519
John Didier, *Prin*
EMP: 5 **EST:** 2019
SALES (est): 201.93K **Privately Held**
Web: www.shadowhunterblinds.com
SIC: 3949 Sporting and athletic goods, nec

(G-5456)
SUN CONTROL CENTER LLC
6032 Highview Dr Ste E (46818-1390)
PHONE..............................260 490-9902
Wayne M Shive, *Owner*
Becky Pack, *Sec*
EMP: 10 **EST:** 1976
SALES (est): 962.42K **Privately Held**
Web: www.suncontrolcenter.com
SIC: 3442 1799 5719 Storm doors or windows, metal; Window treatment installation; Window furnishings

(G-5457)
SUN POLYMERS
2415 Pennsylvania St (46803-2227)
PHONE..............................219 426-1220
EMP: 4 **EST:** 2018
SALES (est): 74.42K **Privately Held**
Web: www.sunpolymers.com
SIC: 2821 Plastics materials and resins

(G-5458)
SUPERIOR ESSEX INC
3405 Meyer Rd Ste 170 (46803-2982)
PHONE..............................260 420-1565
EMP: 123
Web: www.superioressex.com
SIC: 3357 Nonferrous wiredrawing and insulating
HQ: Superior Essex Inc.
5770 Pwers Frry Rd Nw Ste
Atlanta GA 30327
770 657-6000

(G-5459)
SUPERIOR ESSEX INTL LP
Also Called: SUPERIOR ESSEX INTERNATIONAL LP
1700 Swinney Ave (46802-4388)
PHONE..............................260 461-4000
EMP: 222
Web: www.superioressex.com
SIC: 3357 Nonferrous wiredrawing and insulating
HQ: Superior Essex International Inc.
5770 Pwers Frry Rd Ste 40
Atlanta GA 30327
770 657-6000

(G-5460)
SUPERIOR MACHINE & TOOL CO
6911 Trafalgar Dr (46803-3281)
PHONE..............................260 493-4517
Michael S Perkins, *Pr*
EMP: 19 **EST:** 1946
SQ FT: 15,000
SALES (est): 1.91MM **Privately Held**
Web: www.superiormachineandtool.com
SIC: 3599 Machine shop, jobbing and repair

(G-5461)
SUSHIYA-US
14328 Brafferton Pkwy (46814-2304)
PHONE..............................260 444-4263
Yong Lee, *Prin*
EMP: 5 **EST:** 2011
SALES (est): 59.58K **Privately Held**
Web: www.sushiya-us.com
SIC: 3421 Table and food cutlery, including butchers'

(G-5462)
SW WATKINS LIMITED
Also Called: Dirig Sheet Metal
918 W Cook Rd (46825-3270)
PHONE..............................260 484-4844
EMP: 100 **EST:** 1925
SALES (est): 8.66MM **Privately Held**
Web: www.dirigsheetmetal.com
SIC: 3444 7692 1761 Sheet metalwork; Welding repair; Sheet metal work, nec

(G-5463)
SWEETWATER SOUND LLC (PA)
Also Called: Sweetwater Productions
5501 Us Highway 30 W (46818-8998)
PHONE..............................260 432-8176
EMP: 1 **EST:** 2008
SALES (est): 996.33K **Privately Held**
Web: www.sweetwater.com
SIC: 7822 3931 Motion picture and tape distribution; Musical instruments

(G-5464)
SWVA KENTUCKY LLC
7575 W Jefferson Blvd (46804-4131)
PHONE..............................260 969-3500
EMP: 16 **EST:** 2018
SALES (est): 2.56MM **Publicly Held**
Web: www.swvaky.com
SIC: 3312 Blast furnaces and steel mills
PA: Steel Dynamics, Inc.
7575 W Jefferson Blvd
Fort Wayne IN 46804

(G-5465)
SYSTEM SCIENCE INSTITUTE
Also Called: Ssi
4710 Arden Dr Fl 1 (46804-4400)
PHONE..............................260 436-6096
EMP: 8 **EST:** 1995
SQ FT: 22,000
SALES (est): 808.58K **Privately Held**
Web: www.systsci.com
SIC: 3599 Machine shop, jobbing and repair

(G-5466)
SYSTEMS ENGINEERING AND SLS CO
Also Called: Sesco
3805 E Pontiac St (46803-3898)
PHONE..............................260 422-1671
James J Stout, *Pr*
EMP: 8 **EST:** 1968
SQ FT: 21,000
SALES (est): 1.84MM **Privately Held**
Web: www.sesco-inc.com
SIC: 3559 3569 5084 3563 Petroleum refinery equipment; Lubricating equipment; Industrial machinery and equipment; Air and gas compressors

(G-5467)
TAB SOFTWARE CORP
8118 Victoria Woods Pl (46825-6505)
PHONE..............................260 490-7132
Thomas Olinger, *Pr*

Fort Wayne - Allen County (G-5468) GEOGRAPHIC SECTION

EMP: 2 **EST:** 1995
SALES (est): 200K **Privately Held**
Web: www.tabsoftware.com
SIC: 7372 Application computer software

(G-5468)
TARGAMITE LLC
6917 Innovation Blvd (46818-1372)
PHONE.................260 489-0046
EMP: 2 **EST:** 2013
SALES (est): 164.08K **Privately Held**
Web: www.targamite.com
SIC: 3699 Electronic training devices

(G-5469)
TARGET PRINTING INC
3233 Lafayette St (46806-4049)
PHONE.................260 744-6038
Jay Daniel Crance, *Pr*
Jay Daniel Dan Crance, *Pr*
EMP: 7 **EST:** 1963
SQ FT: 6,000
SALES (est): 892K **Privately Held**
Web: www.targetprinting.net
SIC: 2752 Offset printing

(G-5470)
TEAM HILLMAN LLC
414 E Wayne St (46802-2815)
PHONE.................260 426-2626
EMP: 5 **EST:** 2010
SALES (est): 66.86K **Privately Held**
SIC: 3993 Signs and advertising specialties

(G-5471)
TECH TRONIC LLC ◇
2100 Saint Marys Ave Apt 308
(46808-2362)
PHONE.................260 750-7992
Shaquille Mcghee, *CEO*
EMP: 1 **EST:** 2022
SALES (est): 62.01K **Privately Held**
SIC: 3999 Manufacturing industries, nec

(G-5472)
TECHNICAL EQUIPMENT SALES LLC
4501 Earhart Dr Ste A (46809-9648)
PHONE.................260 445-1008
Mike Schalper, *Mgr*
EMP: 5
Web: www.techequip.com
SIC: 3599 Machine shop, jobbing and repair
HQ: Technical Equipment Sales, Llc
10165 International Blvd
Cincinnati OH 45246
513 874-0160

(G-5473)
TEK COAT AND SPRAY LLC
3900 Transportation Dr (46818-1237)
PHONE.................260 748-0314
Brian Callan, *Admn*
EMP: 9 **EST:** 2017
SALES (est): 380.21K **Privately Held**
Web: www.tekcoatandspray.com
SIC: 3452 Bolts, nuts, rivets, and washers

(G-5474)
TELECTRO-MEK INC
2700 Nuttman Ave (46802-4210)
P.O. Box 11289 (46857-1289)
PHONE.................260 747-0586
Ruth Russ, *Pr*
Scott Aldridge, *Sr VP*
EMP: 7 **EST:** 1965
SQ FT: 32,000
SALES (est): 746.25K **Privately Held**
Web: telectro-mek-inc.sbcontract.com

SIC: 3663 Radio broadcasting and communications equipment

(G-5475)
TEREX ADVANCE MIXER INC
7727 Freedom Way (46818)
PHONE.................260 497-0728
EMP: 96 **EST:** 1995
SALES (est): 6.1MM
SALES (corp-wide): 5.15B **Publicly Held**
Web: www.terex.com
SIC: 3531 Construction machinery
PA: Terex Corporation
45 Glover Ave Fl 4
Norwalk CT 06850
203 222-7170

(G-5476)
TEREX CORPORATION
Terex Advance Mixer
7727 Freedom Way (46818-2169)
PHONE.................260 497-0728
Gary Dennis, *Mgr*
EMP: 220
SALES (corp-wide): 5.15B **Publicly Held**
Web: www.terex.com
SIC: 3531 Construction machinery
PA: Terex Corporation
45 Glover Ave Fl 4
Norwalk CT 06850
203 222-7170

(G-5477)
TERRAPIN MFG
4109 Evard Rd (46835-1914)
PHONE.................717 339-6007
Jason Moyer, *Prin*
EMP: 5 **EST:** 2010
SALES (est): 59.24K **Privately Held**
Web: www.terrapinmfg.com
SIC: 3999 Manufacturing industries, nec

(G-5478)
TFS INC
Also Called: O'SULLIVANS ITALIAN PUB
1808 W Main St (46808)
PHONE.................260 422-5896
Tom F Sokolik, *Pr*
Frank Casagrande, *VP*
Louis Lecoque, *Mgr*
EMP: 9 **EST:** 1978
SQ FT: 2,500
SALES (est): 32.83K **Privately Held**
SIC: 2599 2531 Bar, restaurant and cafeteria furniture; Public building and related furniture

(G-5479)
THAT BEVERAGE COMPANY LLC
810 Donnell Ave Ste 102 (46808-1296)
PHONE.................260 413-9660
Thomas Brookshire, *Pr*
Robert A Johnson, *Prin*
EMP: 1 **EST:** 2016
SALES (est): 80.78K **Privately Held**
Web: www.thatbeveragecompany.com
SIC: 2099 Tea blending

(G-5480)
THE BALDUS COMPANY INC
440 E Brackenridge St (46802-3598)
PHONE.................260 424-2366
George H Baldus, *CEO*
EMP: 8 **EST:** 1950
SQ FT: 25,000
SALES (est): 889.3K **Privately Held**
Web: www.balduscompany.com
SIC: 3993 Electric signs

(G-5481)
THE PRO SHEAR CORPORATION CORP
3405 Meyer Rd Ste 100 (46803-2982)
PHONE.................260 408-1010
Tony Stewart, *CEO*
Timothy Albertson, *Sec*
EMP: 7 **EST:** 2008
SALES (est): 1.65MM **Privately Held**
Web: www.proshearcorp.com
SIC: 3714 Motor vehicle parts and accessories

(G-5482)
THERMODYNE FOOD SVC PDTS INC
4418 New Haven Ave (46803-1650)
PHONE.................260 428-2535
Tim Tippmann, *Pr*
Dave Miller, *VP*
Todd Ellinger, *Sec*
William J Federspiel, *Treas*
Renee Dillon, *AD Manager*
EMP: 22 **EST:** 1987
SQ FT: 50,000
SALES (est): 4.91MM **Privately Held**
Web: www.tdyne.com
SIC: 3589 5046 3631 Cooking equipment, commercial; Commercial equipment, nec; Household cooking equipment

(G-5483)
THREE RIVERS DISTILLING CO LLC
220 E Wallace St (46803-2341)
PHONE.................260 745-9355
Travis Kraick, *Prin*
EMP: 30 **EST:** 2013
SALES (est): 1.62MM **Privately Held**
Web: www.3rdistilling.com
SIC: 2085 Distilled and blended liquors

(G-5484)
TINT MASTERS
5015 Speedway Dr (46825-5264)
PHONE.................260 704-2676
EMP: 2
SALES (est): 130.57K **Privately Held**
SIC: 3211 Window glass, clear and colored

(G-5485)
TIPPMANN ARMS COMPANY LLC
2955 S Maplecrest Rd (46803-3219)
PHONE.................260 245-0602
▼ **EMP:** 6 **EST:** 1980
SQ FT: 6,000
SALES (est): 969.75K **Privately Held**
Web: www.tippmannarms.com
SIC: 3484 Small arms

(G-5486)
TIPPMANN BROTHERS LLC
8834 Mayhew Rd (46835-1012)
PHONE.................260 403-1911
Joseph Tippmann, *Prin*
EMP: 4 **EST:** 2016
SALES (est): 81.15K **Privately Held**
Web: www.tippmann.com
SIC: 3949 Sporting and athletic goods, nec

(G-5487)
TIPPMANN PRODUCTS LLC
3905 Goeglein Rd (46815-5731)
PHONE.................260 438-7946
Gene Tippmann, *Pr*
EMP: 3 **EST:** 2013
SALES (est): 138.96K **Privately Held**
Web: www.tippmann.com
SIC: 2299 Textile goods, nec

(G-5488)
TIPPMANN SPORTS LLC (DH)
Also Called: Tippmann
4230 Lake Ave (46815)
PHONE.................800 533-4831
David Sieradzk, *Managing Member*
Joseph Trustey, *
Howard A Kosick, *
◆ **EMP:** 92 **EST:** 2004
SALES (est): 24.36MM
SALES (corp-wide): 11.24MM **Privately Held**
Web: www.tippmann.com
SIC: 3546 Guns, pneumatic: chip removal
HQ: Tippmann Us Holdco Inc.
4230 Lake Ave
Fort Wayne IN 46815
260 749-6022

(G-5489)
TIPPMANN US HOLDCO INC (HQ)
4230 Lake Ave (46815-7220)
PHONE.................260 749-6022
David Sieradzk, *Dir*
EMP: 33 **EST:** 2019
SALES (est): 52.71MM
SALES (corp-wide): 11.24MM **Privately Held**
Web: www.tippmann.com
SIC: 8742 3546 5091 Management consulting services; Guns, pneumatic: chip removal; Sporting and recreation goods
PA: Fulcrum Capital Partners Inc.
1020-885 Georgia St W
Vancouver BC V6C 3
604 631-8088

(G-5490)
TITAN METAL WORX LLC
5225 New Haven Ave (46803-3026)
PHONE.................260 422-4433
Justin Reed, *Pr*
EMP: 28 **EST:** 2015
SALES (est): 3.78MM
SALES (corp-wide): 20.32MM **Privately Held**
Web: www.hmc-us.com
SIC: 3599 Machine shop, jobbing and repair
PA: Entegra Attachments, Llc
Saint Charles IL 60174
734 983-8443

(G-5491)
TM SHADOW PUBLISHING LLC
5534 Saint Joe Rd (46835-3328)
PHONE.................502 794-8435
EMP: 1
SALES (est): 65.99K **Privately Held**
SIC: 2741 Miscellaneous publishing

(G-5492)
TODD K HOCKEMEYER INC
Also Called: K & N Carpet
12108 S Us Highway 27 (46816-9423)
PHONE.................260 639-3591
Todd K Hockemeyer, *Pr*
Kristina Smith, *Mgr*
EMP: 5 **EST:** 1961
SQ FT: 18,000
SALES (est): 980.77K **Privately Held**
Web: www.kncarpet.com
SIC: 5023 5713 2273 Floor coverings; Floor covering stores; Carpets and rugs

(G-5493)
TONYA GERHARDT
6134 Constitution Dr (46804-1526)
PHONE.................260 434-1370
Tonya Gerhardt, *Ofcr*
EMP: 4 **EST:** 2018
SALES (est): 83.91K **Privately Held**

GEOGRAPHIC SECTION

Fort Wayne - Allen County (G-5517)

SIC: 2752 Commercial printing, lithographic

(G-5494)
TOOLCRAFT LLC
Also Called: Cnc Metalworking
2620 S Maplecrest Rd (46803)
PHONE..................260 749-0454
Bruce Meyer, *Pr*
Bruce Meyer, *Managing Member*
EMP: 22 **EST:** 1960
SQ FT: 28,000
SALES (est): 2.33MM **Privately Held**
Web: www.toolcraftfw.com
SIC: 3544 3545 7692 Special dies and tools; Machine tool accessories; Welding repair

(G-5495)
TOOMUCHFUN RUBBERSTAMPS INC
11738 Winchester Rd (46819-9714)
PHONE..................260 557-4808
Steve Lindeman, *Pr*
EMP: 5 **EST:** 2008
SALES (est): 128.9K **Privately Held**
Web: www.toomuchfunrubberstamps.com
SIC: 3953 Canceling stamps, hand: rubber or metal

(G-5496)
TOTAL CLEANING SOLUTIONS LLC
4620 Lima Rd (46808-1202)
PHONE..................260 471-7761
EMP: 2 **EST:** 2005
SALES (est): 244.31K **Privately Held**
Web: www.totalcleaningsolutionsfortwayne.com
SIC: 2899 Chemical preparations, nec

(G-5497)
TOUCHPLATE TECHNOLOGIES INC
Also Called: Touch Plate Led
4822 Projects Dr (46825-5377)
PHONE..................260 426-1565
Doug Ford, *Pr*
◆ **EMP:** 26 **EST:** 1995
SQ FT: 8,500
SALES (est): 2.45MM **Privately Held**
Web: www.touchplateled.com
SIC: 3625 3648 3699 3643 Control equipment, electric; Lighting equipment, nec; Electrical equipment and supplies, nec; Current-carrying wiring services

(G-5498)
TRANE US INC
Also Called: Trane
6602 Innovation Blvd (46818-1389)
PHONE..................260 489-0884
Randy Katz, *Mgr*
EMP: 14
Web: www.trane.com
SIC: 3585 Refrigeration and heating equipment
HQ: Trane U.S. Inc.
    800-E Beaty St
    Davidson NC 28036
    704 655-4000

(G-5499)
TRANSCEND ORTHTICS PRSTHTICS L
417 Fernhill Ave (46805-1039)
PHONE..................574 233-3352
Bernie Veldman, *CEO*
EMP: 8
SALES (corp-wide): 25.64MM **Privately Held**
Web: www.hangerclinic.com
SIC: 3842 Surgical appliances and supplies
HQ: Transcend Orthotics & Prosthetics, Llc
    17530 Dugdale Dr
    South Bend IN 46635
    574 233-3352

(G-5500)
TRANSFORMATIONS BY WIELAND INC
Also Called: Transformations
310 Racquet Dr (46825-4229)
PHONE..................800 440-9337
Brenda Wieland, *Pr*
Jaret Wieland, *
Brace T Wieland, *
Stuart Reynolds, *
Brenda Wieland, *Prin*
EMP: 55 **EST:** 1997
SQ FT: 76,000
SALES (est): 8.2MM **Privately Held**
Web: www.transformationsfurniture.com
SIC: 2512 Upholstered household furniture

(G-5501)
TRANSWORKS INC
9910 Dupont Circle Dr E Ste 200 (46825-1617)
P.O. Box 716 (91916-0716)
PHONE..................619 441-0133
Tim Minnich, *Pr*
Bruce Cox, *VP*
Eric Laundrie, *Owner*
EMP: 3 **EST:** 1990
SALES (est): 1.24MM
SALES (corp-wide): 12.16B **Publicly Held**
SIC: 3714 4011 Rebuilding engines and transmissions, factory basis; Railroads, line-haul operating
PA: Norfolk Southern Corporation
    650 W Peachtree St Nw
    Atlanta GA 30308
    855 667-3655

(G-5502)
TRELLBORG SLING SLTIONS US INC
Also Called: Trelleborg Sealing Solutions
2531 Bremer Rd (46803-3014)
PHONE..................260 748-5895
Ray Cristman, *Brnch Mgr*
EMP: 250
SALES (corp-wide): 45.02B **Privately Held**
Web: www.trelleborg.com
SIC: 2891 Sealing compounds, synthetic rubber or plastic
HQ: Trelleborg Sealing Solutions Us, Inc.
    2531 Bremer Rd
    Fort Wayne IN 46803
    260 749-9631

(G-5503)
TRELLBORG SLING SLTIONS US INC (DH)
Also Called: Busakshamban
2531 Bremer Rd (46803-3014)
PHONE..................260 749-9631
Linda Muroski, *Pr*
Henning Jensen, *
Kevin Alofs, *
Per Danielsson, *
Adam H Bloomenstein, *
◆ **EMP:** 30 **EST:** 1985
SQ FT: 9,370
SALES (est): 512.51MM
SALES (corp-wide): 45.02B **Privately Held**
Web: www.trelleborg.com
SIC: 3089 Plastics processing
HQ: Trelleborg Corporation
    200 Veterans Blvd Ste 3
    South Haven MI 49090
    269 639-9891

(G-5504)
TRELLIS GROWING SYSTEMS LLC
Also Called: Tgs
2427 S Hadley Rd (46804-1511)
PHONE..................260 241-3128
EMP: 1 **EST:** 2007
SALES (est): 183.37K **Privately Held**
Web: www.trellisgrowingsystems.com
SIC: 3999 Manufacturing industries, nec

(G-5505)
TRI-STATE MACHINING INC
2515 Mcdonald St (46803-1561)
PHONE..................260 422-2508
Gary Nuhauf, *Pr*
Abe Nurser, *VP*
EMP: 3 **EST:** 2002
SALES (est): 430.02K **Privately Held**
Web: www.tristatemachining.com
SIC: 3599 Machine shop, jobbing and repair

(G-5506)
TRI-STATE MECHANICAL INC
4530 Secretary Dr (46808-1199)
PHONE..................260 471-0345
Marshall Loveless, *Pr*
Donna Loveless, *VP*
EMP: 10 **EST:** 1985
SQ FT: 3,000
SALES (est): 984.69K **Privately Held**
SIC: 1711 3441 Mechanical contractor; Fabricated structural metal

(G-5507)
TRI-STATE SHTMTL & MFG LLC
1738 Traders Xing (46845-1536)
PHONE..................260 402-8831
EMP: 5 **EST:** 2017
SALES (est): 110.92K **Privately Held**
SIC: 3999 Manufacturing industries, nec

(G-5508)
TRINITY CMMNICATIONS GROUP INC
2524 Merivale St (46805-1532)
P.O. Box 5021 (46895-5021)
PHONE..................260 484-1029
Robert Willey, *Pr*
Donald Willey, *VP*
Leone Willey, *Sec*
Ann Willey, *Sec*
EMP: 2 **EST:** 1982
SALES (est): 505.36K **Privately Held**
Web: www.trinitymusicfest.com
SIC: 5999 8732 7922 2759 Wheelchair lifts; Market analysis or research; Concert management service; Tickets: printing, nsk

(G-5509)
TRIVECTOR MANUFACTURING INC
Also Called: Only Alpha
4404 Engle Ridge Dr (46804-4443)
PHONE..................260 637-0141
Thomas Epple, *CEO*
Timothy Saxer, *
EMP: 45 **EST:** 2010
SALES (est): 15.59MM **Privately Held**
Web: www.onlyalpha.com
SIC: 5033 3469 Fiberglass building materials; Metal stampings, nec

(G-5510)
TRUE ROYALTY BOUTIQUE LLC
513 E Jefferson Blvd (46802-3203)
PHONE..................260 706-5121
Shantell Salter-boone, *CEO*
EMP: 11 **EST:** 2020
SALES (est): 717.43K **Privately Held**
Web: www.trueroyaltyboutique.com
SIC: 2339 Women's and misses' athletic clothing and sportswear

(G-5511)
TT2 LLC
Also Called: Yudu
14516 Lima Rd (46818-9537)
PHONE..................260 438-4575
Tim Burns, *Managing Member*
Tyler G Eifert, *Managing Member*
EMP: 2 **EST:** 2016
SALES (est): 51.47K **Privately Held**
SIC: 5961 2269 7389 Clothing, mail order (except women's); Labels, cotton: printed; Business Activities at Non-Commercial Site

(G-5512)
TUFF TOOL INC
6003 Highgate Pl (46815-7614)
PHONE..................262 612-8300
John Schultz, *Prin*
EMP: 6 **EST:** 2012
SALES (est): 74.61K **Privately Held**
SIC: 3544 Special dies, tools, jigs, and fixtures

(G-5513)
TUGGLE PUBLISHING
5904 Meadows Dr (46804-7653)
PHONE..................678 702-2139
Anne Ueber, *Prin*
EMP: 4 **EST:** 2017
SALES (est): 71.67K **Privately Held**
SIC: 2741 Miscellaneous publishing

(G-5514)
TUTHILL CORPORATION
Also Called: Tuthill Transfer Systems
8825 Aviation Dr (46809-9630)
PHONE..................260 747-7529
Tom Carmazzi, *Sec*
David P Groeber, *Treas*
◆ **EMP:** 5 **EST:** 1966
SALES (est): 2.66MM **Privately Held**
Web: www.fillrite.com
SIC: 3561 Pumps and pumping equipment

(G-5515)
TUTHILL CORPORATION
Also Called: Fill-Rite Division
8825 Aviation Dr (46809-9630)
P.O. Box 9100 (46899-9100)
PHONE..................260 747-7529
John Gould, *Brnch Mgr*
EMP: 185
SQ FT: 100,000
SALES (corp-wide): 234.05MM **Privately Held**
Web: www.fillrite.com
SIC: 3561 4813 Pumps and pumping equipment; Telephone communication, except radio
PA: Tuthill Corporation
    8500 S Madison St
    Burr Ridge IL 60527
    630 382-4900

(G-5516)
TV EXCEL INC
3215 Stellhorn Rd (46815-4697)
PHONE..................323 797-8538
EMP: 53 **EST:** 2019
SALES (est): 700K **Privately Held**
Web: www.tvexcel.com
SIC: 2741 Internet publishing and broadcasting

(G-5517)
TWE NONWOVENS US INC
9403 Avionics Dr (46809-9632)
PHONE..................260 747-0990
EMP: 50
SALES (corp-wide): 391.92MM **Privately Held**

Fort Wayne - Allen County (G-5518) — GEOGRAPHIC SECTION

Web: www.twenonwovensus.com
SIC: 2297 Nonwoven fabrics
HQ: Twe Nonwovens Us, Inc.
2215 Shore St
High Point NC 27263
336 431-7187

(G-5518)
TWO B ENTERPRISES INC
Also Called: Graphics Output
6926 Quemetco Ct (46803)
PHONE..................260 245-0119
Richard J Byanski, *Pr*
Michael D Burgess, *VP*
Sharon Schiffbauer, *VP Opers*
EMP: 10 EST: 2005
SALES (est): 964.55K Privately Held
Web: www.gographicsoutput.com
SIC: 2752 Offset printing

(G-5519)
UNIQUE OUTDOOR PRODUCTS LLC
4211 Chetham Dr (46835-4635)
PHONE..................260 486-4955
William Dietsch, *Prin*
EMP: 5 EST: 2012
SALES (est): 231.63K Privately Held
Web: www.uniqueoutdoorproducts.com
SIC: 3949 Sporting and athletic goods, nec

(G-5520)
UNITED MACHINE & TOOL LLC
5431 New Haven Ave (46803-3158)
PHONE..................260 749-8880
Terry Johnson, *Mng Pt*
EMP: 3 EST: 2000
SALES (est): 241.72K Privately Held
SIC: 3599 Machine shop, jobbing and repair

(G-5521)
UNITED OIL CORP
Also Called: Fort Meyers
Hwy 33 And Washington Center Rd (46808)
PHONE..................260 489-3511
EMP: 5
SALES (corp-wide): 13.24MM Privately Held
Web: www.natloil.com
SIC: 1389 Oil field services, nec
PA: United Oil Corp
1609 E Business 30
Columbia City IN 46725
260 244-6000

(G-5522)
US SILICONES LLC
623 Airport North Office Park (46825-6706)
PHONE..................260 497-0819
Daniel T Arnold, *Brnch Mgr*
EMP: 1
Web: www.ussilicones.com
SIC: 2869 Silicones
PA: U.S. Silicones, Llc
3508 Independence Dr
Fort Wayne IN 46808

(G-5523)
US SILICONES LLC (PA)
3508 Independence Dr (46808-4509)
PHONE..................260 480-0171
EMP: 19 EST: 2008
SALES (est): 4.4MM Privately Held
Web: www.ussilicones.com
SIC: 2869 Silicones

(G-5524)
USV OPTICAL INC
Also Called: J C Penney Optical
4201 Coldwater Rd Ste 4 (46805-1187)
PHONE..................260 482-5033
Janet King, *Mgr*
EMP: 5
Web: www.jcpenneyoptical.com
SIC: 5995 3851 Eyeglasses, prescription; Frames and parts, eyeglass and spectacle
HQ: Usv Optical, Inc.
1 Harmon Dr
Blackwood NJ 08012

(G-5525)
UTOPIAN COFFEE COMPANY LLC
2001 S Calhoun St (46802-6411)
PHONE..................888 558-8674
Brendon Maxwell, *CEO*
EMP: 6 EST: 2007
SALES (est): 675.15K Privately Held
Web: www.utopiancoffee.com
SIC: 2095 5499 Coffee roasting (except by wholesale grocers); Coffee

(G-5526)
VALVE SERVE LLC
2020 E Washington Blvd Ste 550 (46803-1367)
PHONE..................260 421-1927
Stephen M Mishler, *Prin*
EMP: 7 EST: 2008
SALES (est): 91.26K Privately Held
SIC: 3592 Valves

(G-5527)
VANDERBILT LUXURY PONTOONS LLC
4422 Airport Expy Ste 220 (46809-9634)
PHONE..................260 478-7227
Patrick M Delaney, *Pr*
Andrew Brickman, *Managing Member*
EMP: 15 EST: 2021
SALES (est): 1.21MM Privately Held
Web: www.vanderbiltpontoons.com
SIC: 3732 Motorized boat, building and repairing

(G-5528)
VANILLA BEAN LLC
7513 Leswood Ct (46816-2659)
PHONE..................260 415-4652
Sandra Wharton, *VP*
EMP: 5 EST: 2015
SALES (est): 191.27K Privately Held
Web: vanillabeanchefs.wordpress.com
SIC: 2051 Bread, cake, and related products

(G-5529)
VDK PRINTING LLC
3822 Live Oak Blvd (46804-3938)
PHONE..................260 602-8212
Brian Vandekeere, *Prin*
EMP: 5 EST: 2017
SALES (est): 133.4K Privately Held
SIC: 2752 Offset printing

(G-5530)
VEE ENGINEERING INC
3805 Reynolds St (46803-1682)
P.O. Box 11705 (46860-1705)
PHONE..................260 424-6635
EMP: 86
SQ FT: 30,000
SALES (corp-wide): 9.88MM Privately Held
Web: www.plant4.com
SIC: 3089 3714 Injection molded finished plastics products, nec; Motor vehicle parts and accessories
PA: Vee Engineering Inc
3620 W 73rd St
Anderson IN 46011
765 778-7895

(G-5531)
VERTICAL SALE
3838 Sherman Blvd (46808-4017)
PHONE..................260 438-4299
EMP: 6 EST: 2013
SALES (est): 153.49K Privately Held
SIC: 2591 Blinds vertical

(G-5532)
VIKING BUSINESS VENTURES INC
Also Called: Proforma Viking
7530 Disalle Blvd (46825-3368)
PHONE..................260 489-7787
Lisa Sandstrom, *Pr*
Jack C Sandstrom, *CEO*
Caroline R Sandstrom, *Sec*
EMP: 4 EST: 1979
SQ FT: 10,000
SALES (est): 386.81K Privately Held
Web: viking.proforma.com
SIC: 2754 Forms, business: gravure printing

(G-5533)
VINTAGE CHEMICAL INC
2007 Bremer Rd (46803-3004)
P.O. Box 10816 (46854-0816)
PHONE..................260 745-7272
Samih Abouhalkah, *Pr*
▲ EMP: 6 EST: 1998
SALES (est): 600K Privately Held
Web: www.vintagechemical.com
SIC: 5999 2841 Medical apparatus and supplies; Soap and other detergents

(G-5534)
VIVID DRAGONFLY PRESS LLC
5534 Saint Joe Rd (46835-3328)
PHONE..................609 954-1010
EMP: 1 EST: 2020
SALES (est): 33.35K Privately Held
Web: www.vividdragonfly.com
SIC: 2731 Book publishing

(G-5535)
VLC SERVICES LLC
Also Called: Lighting
4807 Willow Brook Dr (46835)
PHONE..................260 459-9501
Janette Chowdhury, *CEO*
EMP: 15 EST: 2021
SALES (est): 1.15MM Privately Held
SIC: 1389 Construction, repair, and dismantling services

(G-5536)
VOSS AUTOMOTIVE INC (DH)
4640 Hillegas Rd (46818-1903)
PHONE..................260 373-2277
Eduardo Vultorius, *Pr*
Carsten Beissel, *
▲ EMP: 91 EST: 1997
SALES (est): 28.86MM
SALES (corp-wide): 355.83K Privately Held
Web: www.vossusa.com
SIC: 5013 3089 Automotive servicing equipment; Automotive parts, plastic
HQ: Voss Automotive Gmbh
Leiersmuhle 2-6
Wipperfurth NW 51688
2267630

(G-5537)
W W WILLIAMS COMPANY LLC
Also Called: Midwest Division - Bluffton
5415 State Road 930 (46803-1771)
PHONE..................260 827-0553
Alan Gatlin, *CEO*
EMP: 34
SALES (corp-wide): 1.47B Privately Held
Web: www.wwwilliams.com
SIC: 3621 Motor generator sets
HQ: The W W Williams Company Llc
400 Metro Pl N Ste 201
Dublin OH 43017
614 228-5000

(G-5538)
WAGNER ELECTRIC FORT WAYNE INC
3610 N Clinton St (46805-1898)
PHONE..................260 484-5532
Peter Bell, *Pr*
Andrew Bell, *VP*
Mary Bell, *Sec*
EMP: 9 EST: 1938
SQ FT: 11,000
SALES (est): 2.13MM Privately Held
Web: www.wagnerelectricfw.com
SIC: 5063 7694 Motors, electric; Electric motor repair

(G-5539)
WAGNER TOOL GRINDING INC
419 High St (46808-3436)
PHONE..................260 426-5145
Gregory I Geyer, *Pr*
Charlene Geyer, *Sec*
EMP: 3
SQ FT: 1,600
SALES (est): 255.77K Privately Held
Web: www.wagner-tool-grinding.com
SIC: 3599 Machine shop, jobbing and repair

(G-5540)
WAGNER ZIP-CHANGE INC
913 Arbordale Pl (46825-4673)
PHONE..................708 681-4100
Georgene A Bercier, *Pr*
Gary Delaquila, *
Donald Kolkebeck, *
▲ EMP: 40 EST: 1930
SALES (est): 4.63MM Privately Held
Web: www.wagnerzip.com
SIC: 5099 3993 3953 3444 Signs, except electric; Letters for signs, metal; Marking devices; Sheet metalwork

(G-5541)
WAGNERS PLASTI CRAFT CO
5705 Union Chapel Rd (46845-9614)
PHONE..................260 627-3147
Mike Wagner, *Owner*
EMP: 2 EST: 1970
SALES (est): 136.07K Privately Held
SIC: 2541 Cabinets, except refrigerated: show, display, etc.: wood

(G-5542)
WALL CONTROL SERVICES INC
2826 Longwood Ct (46845-1631)
PHONE..................260 450-6411
David Wall, *Pr*
Yan Wall, *Acctg Mgr*
EMP: 3 EST: 2011
SALES (est): 246.16K Privately Held
SIC: 3569 3589 7371 7699 Robots, assembly line: industrial and commercial; Asbestos removal equipment; Software programming applications; Industrial machinery and equipment repair

(G-5543)
WALTER OSTERMEYER
Also Called: Basket Buddy
6210 Beaver Creek Ct (46814-8202)
PHONE..................260 705-1960
Walter Ostermeyer, *Owner*
EMP: 1 EST: 2020
SALES (est): 3K Privately Held

GEOGRAPHIC SECTION
Fort Wayne - Allen County (G-5566)

SIC: 2542 Racks, merchandise display or storage: except wood

(G-5544)
WALTERS DEVELOPMENT CO LLC
6600 Ardmore Ave (46809-9703)
PHONE..................260 747-7531
Peggy Walters, *Managing Member*
EMP: 3 EST: 1998
SALES (est): 219.54K **Privately Held**
SIC: 2951 Asphalt paving mixtures and blocks

(G-5545)
WARD CORPORATION (PA)
Also Called: Ward Production Machine
642 Growth Ave (46808-3712)
PHONE..................260 426-8700
Vern Ward, *Ch Bd*
Marion Ward, *
Chris Ward, *Quality Vice President*
Don Ward, *
Mary J Atkins, *
▲ EMP: 140 EST: 1975
SQ FT: 91,675
SALES (est): 24.61MM
SALES (corp-wide): 24.61MM **Privately Held**
Web: www.permanentmoldcasting.com
SIC: 3365 3544 3369 Aluminum foundries; Special dies, tools, jigs, and fixtures; Nonferrous foundries, nec

(G-5546)
WARD CORPORATION
Also Called: Ward Heat Treating
7603 Opportunity Dr (46825-3364)
PHONE..................260 489-2281
Bill Jennings, *Mgr*
EMP: 13
SALES (corp-wide): 24.61MM **Privately Held**
Web: www.permanentmoldcasting.com
SIC: 3398 3544 Metal heat treating; Special dies, tools, jigs, and fixtures
PA: Ward Corporation
642 Growth Ave
Fort Wayne IN 46808
260 426-8700

(G-5547)
WARD PATTERN & ENGINEERING INC
Also Called: Ward
642 Growth Ave (46808-3712)
PHONE..................260 426-8700
▲ EMP: 170
Web: www.workcorp.com
SIC: 3365 3543 Aluminum foundries; Foundry patternmaking

(G-5548)
WATER SCIENCES INC
3208 Caprice Ct (46808-4506)
PHONE..................260 485-4655
Kevin Fuze, *Pr*
Michael A Fuze, *Pr*
EMP: 7 EST: 1979
SALES (est): 847.69K **Privately Held**
Web: www.filtersciences.com
SIC: 2899 Water treating compounds

(G-5549)
WATERFURNACE INTERNATIONAL INC
Also Called: Waterfurnace Renewable Energy
9000 Conservation Way (46809)
PHONE..................260 478-5667
EMP: 276 EST: 1992
SALES (est): 114MM
SALES (corp-wide): 4.57MM **Privately Held**
Web: www.waterfurnace.com
SIC: 3585 5084 4961 Heat pumps, electric; Heat exchange equipment, industrial; Steam supply systems, including geothermal
PA: Nibe Industrier Ab
Jarnvagsgatan 40
Markaryd 285 3
43373000

(G-5550)
WAYNE BLACK OXIDE INC
4505 Executive Blvd (46808-1136)
PHONE..................260 484-0280
Kent Flaig, *Pr*
John Flaig, *Pr*
Arlene Flaig, *Treas*
EMP: 7 EST: 1961
SQ FT: 6,000
SALES (est): 852.23K **Privately Held**
Web: www.wayneblackoxide.com
SIC: 3471 Electroplating of metals or formed products

(G-5551)
WAYNE CHEMICAL INC
7114 Homestead Rd (46814-4678)
PHONE..................260 432-1120
William E Spindler, *Pr*
EMP: 25 EST: 1969
SQ FT: 12,000
SALES (est): 2.83MM **Privately Held**
Web: www.waynechemical.com
SIC: 3559 2819 2842 Chemical machinery and equipment; Industrial inorganic chemicals, nec; Polishes and sanitation goods

(G-5552)
WAYNE CONCEPT MFG INC
5005 Speedway Dr (46825-5244)
PHONE..................260 482-8615
James Gast, *Pr*
Kenneth Gast, *VP*
EMP: 8 EST: 1983
SQ FT: 10,000
SALES (est): 958.7K **Privately Held**
Web: www.cleanwithperoxide.com
SIC: 2841 Detergents, synthetic organic or inorganic alkaline

(G-5553)
WAYNE PRESS INCORPORATED
Also Called: Garphik Mechanix
1716 S Harrison St (46802-5211)
PHONE..................260 744-3022
Bill Wright, *Pr*
Fred S Mertz, *Mgr*
EMP: 5 EST: 1924
SQ FT: 2,000
SALES (est): 385.98K **Privately Held**
SIC: 2752 2759 Offset printing; Letterpress printing

(G-5554)
WAYNE STEEL SUPPLY INC
7707 Freedom Way (46818-2169)
PHONE..................260 489-6249
David Seybert, *Pr*
EMP: 29 EST: 1984
SQ FT: 19,200
SALES (est): 4.23MM **Privately Held**
Web: www.waynesteel.us
SIC: 3441 Fabricated structural metal

(G-5555)
WAYNE/SCOTT FETZER COMPANY
Also Called: Wayne Combustion Systems
801 Glasgow Ave (46803)
PHONE..................260 425-9200
Kenneth Kuczmanski, *Pr*
Kenneth J Semelsberger, *
David C Lamb, *
◆ EMP: 52 EST: 1928
SQ FT: 350,000
SALES (est): 10.87MM
SALES (corp-wide): 226 **Privately Held**
Web: www.waynecombustion.com
SIC: 3433 Oil burners, domestic or industrial
PA: The Scott Fetzer Company
28800 Clemens Rd
Westlake OH 44145
440 892-3000

(G-5556)
WAYNEDALE NEWS INC
2505 Lower Huntington Rd Ste A (46809-2692)
PHONE..................260 747-4535
Robert L Stark, *Pr*
Cindy Cornwell, *Ex Dir*
EMP: 3 EST: 1932
SALES (est): 234.63K **Privately Held**
Web: www.waynedalenews.com
SIC: 2711 Newspapers, publishing and printing

(G-5557)
WB AUTOMOTIVE HOLDINGS INC
3405 Meyer Rd (46803-2981)
PHONE..................734 604-8962
Mike Hayes, *Dir Opers*
EMP: 1
SIC: 5013 3711 Automotive hardware; Chassis, motor vehicle
PA: Wb Automotive Holdings, Inc.
3033 Excelsior Blvd # 300
Minneapolis MN 55416

(G-5558)
WEB INDUSTRIES DALLAS INC
Also Called: Web Converting
3925 Ardmore Ave (46802)
PHONE..................260 432-0027
Don Romine, *CEO*
Robert A Fulton, *Ch Bd*
Donald Romine, *Pr*
Carl Rubin, *CFO*
Dennis Latimer, *Ex VP*
▲ EMP: 79 EST: 1987
SQ FT: 40,000
SALES (est): 3.61MM
SALES (corp-wide): 104.33MM **Privately Held**
Web: www.webindustries.com
SIC: 2679 Paper products, converted, nec
PA: Web Industries Inc.
293 Bston Post Rd W Ste 5
Marlborough MA 01752
508 898-2988

(G-5559)
WEB INDUSTRIES FORT WAYNE INC
Also Called: Web Converting of Fort Wayne
3925 Ardmore Ave (46802-4237)
PHONE..................260 432-0027
Don Romine, *
Blake Batley, *
Carl Rubin, *
Mark Pihl, *
▲ EMP: 47 EST: 2004
SQ FT: 110,000
SALES (est): 3.97MM **Privately Held**
Web: www.steppac.com
SIC: 7389 2241 Tape slitting; Electric insulating tapes and braids, except plastic

(G-5560)
WEB PRINTING CONNECTION INC
11706 Trails End Ct (46845-1307)
PHONE..................260 637-4037
Dick Gannon, *Pr*
Kaye Gannon, *Sec*
EMP: 2 EST: 2000
SALES (est): 192.69K **Privately Held**
Web: www.webprintingconnection.com
SIC: 2752 Offset printing

(G-5561)
WELBILT FDSRVICE COMPANIES LLC
1111 N Hadley Rd (46804-5540)
PHONE..................260 459-8200
Stephen M Amos, *Brnch Mgr*
EMP: 281
SALES (corp-wide): 4.8B **Privately Held**
Web: direct.welbilt.us
SIC: 3585 Refrigeration and heating equipment
HQ: Welbilt Foodservice Companies, Llc
2227 Welbilt Blvd
Trinity FL 34655

(G-5562)
WHATZUP LLC
5501 Us Highway 30 W (46818-8998)
PHONE..................260 407-3198
EMP: 3 EST: 2018
SALES (est): 195K **Privately Held**
Web: www.whatzup.com
SIC: 2711 Newspapers, publishing and printing

(G-5563)
WHIPP IN HOLDINGS LLC (PA)
Also Called: National Tube Form
3405 Engle Rd (46809-1115)
PHONE..................260 478-2363
Adam Whipp, *Pr*
Richard Whipp, *
Fred Whipp, *
Rhett Burgess, *
▲ EMP: 5 EST: 2001
SALES (est): 51.4MM
SALES (corp-wide): 51.4MM **Privately Held**
SIC: 3498 Tube fabricating (contract bending and shaping)

(G-5564)
WHITCRAFT ENTERPRISES INC
Also Called: Precise Manufacturing
4323 Merchant Rd (46818-1257)
PHONE..................260 422-6518
John E Whitcraft, *Pr*
James E Whitcraft, *VP*
EMP: 18 EST: 1971
SQ FT: 20,000
SALES (est): 4.55MM **Privately Held**
Web: www.precisemfginc.com
SIC: 3599 Machine shop, jobbing and repair

(G-5565)
WHITE CAP LP
Also Called: White Cap 153
3333 Independence Dr (46804-4516)
PHONE..................260 471-7619
Eric Solyom, *Brnch Mgr*
EMP: 23
SALES (corp-wide): 7.35B **Privately Held**
Web: www.whitecap.com
SIC: 3272 Concrete products, nec
HQ: White Cap, L.P.
6250 Brook Hollow Pkwy # 100
Norcross GA 30071
800 944-8322

(G-5566)
WHITE SURGICAL INC
14520 Egrets Ct (46814-7581)
PHONE..................260 755-5800

Fort Wayne - Allen County (G-5567)

EMP: 6 EST: 1995
SALES (est): 470.32K **Privately Held**
Web: www.whitesurgical.com
SIC: 3841 5047 Surgical and medical instruments; Instruments, surgical and medical

(G-5567)
WHYTE HAUS
1629 Channel Pl (46825-5936)
PHONE..................260 484-5666
Dana M White, *Owner*
EMP: 2 EST: 1992
SALES (est): 111.25K **Privately Held**
SIC: 3577 Computer peripheral equipment, nec

(G-5568)
WILDEBEEST LLC
4128 S Calhoun St (46807-2451)
PHONE..................812 391-5631
S T Sasidharan, *Prin*
EMP: 1 EST: 2013
SALES (est): 49.83K **Privately Held**
SIC: 7371 7372 7389 Computer code authors ; Prepackaged software; Business Activities at Non-Commercial Site

(G-5569)
WILLIAMS SCOTSMAN INC
5314 Maumee Rd (46803-1727)
PHONE..................260 749-6611
David Staadt, *Brnch Mgr*
EMP: 37
SALES (corp-wide): 2.36B **Publicly Held**
Web: www.mobilemini.com
SIC: 3448 Prefabricated metal buildings and components
HQ: Williams Scotsman, Inc.
4646 E Van Bren St Ste 40
Phoenix AZ 85008
480 894-6311

(G-5570)
WILLOWGREEN INC
2209 Saint Joe Center Rd Apt 166 (46825-5095)
PHONE..................260 490-2222
James Miller, *Pr*
Bernie Miller, *VP*
EMP: 3 EST: 1982
SALES (est): 225.58K **Privately Held**
Web: www.willowgreen.com
SIC: 2741 Miscellaneous publishing

(G-5571)
WIREAMERICA INC
1613 E Wallace St (46803-2564)
PHONE..................260 969-1700
Lionell Tobin, *Pr*
Ted Jamison, *Ex VP*
EMP: 9 EST: 1988
SQ FT: 45,000
SALES (est): 255.39K **Privately Held**
Web: www.wiredsoul.com
SIC: 4226 3357 Special warehousing and storage, nec; Communication wire

(G-5572)
WISE BUSINESS FORMS INC
4301 Merchant Rd (46818-1251)
P.O. Box 8550 (46898-8550)
PHONE..................260 489-1561
Sally Spur, *Brnch Mgr*
EMP: 85
SQ FT: 30,000
SALES (corp-wide): 82.12MM **Privately Held**
Web: www.wbf.com

SIC: 2761 2759 2752 Manifold business forms; Commercial printing, nec; Commercial printing, lithographic
PA: Wise Business Forms Incorporated
555 Mcfarland 400 Dr
Alpharetta GA 30004
770 442-1060

(G-5573)
WNT
Also Called: W N T
3009 Parnell Ave (46805-2550)
PHONE..................260 440-0485
James Swan, *Owner*
EMP: 1 EST: 1992
SALES (est): 99K **Privately Held**
SIC: 3441 Fabricated structural metal

(G-5574)
WOLF CORPORATION
3434 Maplecrest Rd (46803)
P.O. Box 11306 (46857)
PHONE..................260 749-9393
Anthony Wolf, *Pr*
Richard Wolf, *
◆ EMP: 40 EST: 1873
SQ FT: 95,000
SALES (est): 4.64MM **Privately Held**
Web: www.wolfmattress.com
SIC: 2515 2299 Mattresses, innerspring or box spring; Padding and wadding, textile

(G-5575)
WOODWARD TIRE SALES & SVC INC
Also Called: Woodward Tire Service
3111 Covington Rd (46802-6919)
PHONE..................260 432-0694
Michael Woodward, *Pr*
Mary M Woodward, *Sec*
Paul J Woodward, *VP*
EMP: 7 EST: 1976
SQ FT: 8,000
SALES (est): 834.21K **Privately Held**
Web: www.woodwardtirefortwayne.com
SIC: 5531 7534 7538 Automotive tires; Tire repair shop; General automotive repair shops

(G-5576)
WORKRITE MACHINE & TOOL INC
6319 Discount Dr (46818-1261)
P.O. Box 8069 (46898-8069)
PHONE..................260 489-4778
Charles Hagan, *Pr*
Herbert A Beltz Junior, *Pr*
EMP: 22 EST: 1986
SQ FT: 17,400
SALES (est): 2.46MM **Privately Held**
Web: hwww.aerostarmfg.com
SIC: 3599 Machine shop, jobbing and repair

(G-5577)
WPTA TELEVISION INC
3401 Butler Rd (46808-3811)
PHONE..................217 221-3353
Ralph Oakley, *CEO*
Brad Eaton, *
EMP: 90 EST: 2015
SALES (est): 2.91MM
SALES (corp-wide): 3.28B **Publicly Held**
Web: www.21alivenews.com
SIC: 2711 Newspapers, publishing and printing
PA: Gray Television, Inc.
4370 Pchtree Rd Ne Ste 40
Atlanta GA 30319
404 504-9828

(G-5578)
WYNN WIRE DIE SERVICES INC
1919 Lakeview Dr (46808-3919)
PHONE..................260 471-1395
Rick A Wynn, *Pr*
Jayne L Wynn V, *Sec*
EMP: 4 EST: 1983
SQ FT: 1,200
SALES (est): 480.96K **Privately Held**
Web: www.wynnwiredie.com
SIC: 3544 Wire drawing and straightening dies

(G-5579)
YAGER & ASSOCIATES LLC
2601 E Gump Rd (46845-9740)
PHONE..................260 413-9571
EMP: 2 EST: 2012
SALES (est): 350K **Privately Held**
SIC: 3841 Medical instruments and equipment, blood and bone work

(G-5580)
YELLOW CUP LLC
228 E Collins Rd Ste C (46825-5394)
PHONE..................260 403-3489
EMP: 5 EST: 2017
SALES (est): 144.46K **Privately Held**
Web: www.yellowcuproasters.com
SIC: 3999 Barber and beauty shop equipment

(G-5581)
YOSIRA LLC
14017 Pendleton Mills Ct (46814-8801)
PHONE..................260 241-1203
EMP: 1 EST: 2020
SALES (est): 55K **Privately Held**
SIC: 3841 Medical instruments and equipment, blood and bone work

(G-5582)
YOURSPACE LLC
6320 Highview Dr (46818-1382)
PHONE..................260 702-9595
Jimmie Eggleston, *Managing Member*
EMP: 1 EST: 2020
SALES (est): 137.08K **Privately Held**
Web: www.yourspaceinc.com
SIC: 2541 Wood partitions and fixtures

(G-5583)
ZEHRHAUS INC
8516 Samantha Dr (46835-1033)
PHONE..................260 486-3198
David Zehr, *Pr*
EMP: 4 EST: 1966
SQ FT: 5,600
SALES (est): 314.8K **Privately Held**
SIC: 2449 2541 Boxes, wood: wirebound; Cabinets, except refrigerated: show, display, etc.: wood

(G-5584)
ZIMMER BIOMET
6016 Highview Dr (46818-1392)
PHONE..................574 453-1326
EMP: 16 EST: 2018
SALES (est): 294.81K **Privately Held**
Web: www.zimmerbiomet.com
SIC: 3842 Orthopedic appliances

Fortville
Hancock County

(G-5585)
3C COMAN LTD
800 W Ohio St (46040-1241)

PHONE..................317 650-5156
Thomas Cook, *Pr*
EMP: 3 EST: 2015
SALES (est): 214.7K **Privately Held**
SIC: 1799 1541 3444 Coating of metal structures at construction site; Steel building construction; Metal roofing and roof drainage equipment

(G-5586)
ABBOO CANDLE CO LLC
10091 N Balfer Dr W (46040-9335)
PHONE..................317 395-4404
Michelle Schreiber, *Owner*
EMP: 4 EST: 2017
SALES (est): 192.75K **Privately Held**
Web: www.abboocandleco.com
SIC: 3999 Candles

(G-5587)
ABRASIVE PROCESSING & TECH LLC (PA)
712 E Ohio St (46040-1552)
P.O. Box 309 (46040-0309)
PHONE..................317 485-5157
Mike Riggs, *Managing Member*
EMP: 8 EST: 2005
SALES (est): 2.13MM **Privately Held**
Web: www.abrasiveprocessing.com
SIC: 3471 Sand blasting of metal parts

(G-5588)
CENTRAL TOOL CO INC
767 W Garden St (46040-1448)
PHONE..................317 485-5344
James Cooper, *Pr*
William Cooper, *Treas*
Mary Louis, *Sec*
Fred Cooper, *VP*
EMP: 6 EST: 1946
SALES (est): 483.74K **Privately Held**
Web: www.centraltoolco.com
SIC: 3599 Machine shop, jobbing and repair

(G-5589)
CLM PALLET RECYCLING INC (PA)
3103 W 1000 N (46040-9705)
P.O. Box 19184 (46219-0184)
PHONE..................317 485-4080
Charles L Mong Iii, *Prin*
Charles L Mong Iii, *Prin*
Mark L Loughery, *Pr*
Cody M Welch, *Prin*
EMP: 6 EST: 1992
SALES (est): 8.79MM **Privately Held**
Web: www.clmpallet.com
SIC: 7699 2499 Pallet repair; Mulch, wood and bark

(G-5590)
D & D BRAKE SALES INC
Also Called: Honeywell Friction Materials
State Road 234 & County Rd 200 W (46040)
PHONE..................317 485-5177
Charles E Stewart, *Pr*
▲ EMP: 31 EST: 1966
SQ FT: 130,000
SALES (est): 799.37K **Privately Held**
SIC: 3714 Motor vehicle brake systems and parts

(G-5591)
DEATONS WATERFRONT SVCS LLC
3253 W 1000 N (46040-9705)
PHONE..................317 336-7180
Paul Deaton, *Prin*
EMP: 15 EST: 2011
SALES (est): 2.26MM **Privately Held**
Web: www.deatonsdocks.com
SIC: 3536 Boat lifts

GEOGRAPHIC SECTION

Fowler - Benton County (G-5618)

(G-5592)
DSN CABINETRY INC
1373 W 850 N (46040-9552)
PHONE..................317 747-4740
David Shepherd, Prin
EMP: 1 EST: 2011
SALES (est): 247.37K Privately Held
Web: www.dsncabinetry.com
SIC: 3553 Cabinet makers' machinery

(G-5593)
ENERLINC INC
315 N Madison St (46040-1160)
PHONE..................317 574-1009
Michael Hale, Pr
EMP: 7
SALES (est): 545.14K Privately Held
SIC: 3634 Fans, exhaust and ventilating, electric: household

(G-5594)
FORTVILLE AUTOMOTIVE SUP INC
Also Called: NAPA Autoparts Fortville
305 W Broadway St (46040-1408)
PHONE..................317 485-5114
Aaron Vail, Pr
EMP: 5 EST: 2008
SALES (est): 449.66K Privately Held
Web: www.napaonline.com
SIC: 3542 5531 Machine tools, metal forming type; Automotive parts

(G-5595)
FORTVILLE FEEDERS INC (PA)
750 E Broadway St (46040-1550)
P.O. Box 70 (46040-0070)
PHONE..................317 485-5195
Jason Crouse, Pr
Michael A Crouse, *
Jacqueline Crouse, *
EMP: 53 EST: 1981
SQ FT: 55,000
SALES (est): 9.5MM Privately Held
Web: www.fortvillefeeders.com
SIC: 3599 Custom machinery

(G-5596)
FULL TANK FREEDOM INC
720 E Broadway St (46040-1550)
PHONE..................317 485-7887
Tom Ryder, Pr
Robert C Smith, *
▲ EMP: 30 EST: 1992
SQ FT: 15,000
SALES (est): 6.4MM Privately Held
Web: www.genesisplasticswelding.com
SIC: 3089 Plastics containers, except foam

(G-5597)
GUARDIAN FIRE SYSTEMS INC
435 W Broadway St (46040-1410)
PHONE..................317 752-2768
Mychal S Nation, Pr
Christian Geiger, VP
EMP: 9 EST: 2006
SALES (est): 342.32K Privately Held
Web: www.guardianfiresystemsinc.com
SIC: 3569 Sprinkler systems, fire: automatic

(G-5598)
HALE INDUSTRIES INC
Also Called: Advanced Radiant Systems
315 N Madison St (46040-1160)
PHONE..................317 577-0337
Craig Hale, Pr
◆ EMP: 17 EST: 1991
SQ FT: 36,000
SALES (est): 4.9MM Privately Held
Web: www.haleindustriesinc.com

SIC: 5084 3255 3433 3443 Heat exchange equipment, industrial; Heater radiants, clay; Room and wall heaters, including radiators; Heat exchangers: coolers (after, inter), condensers, etc.

(G-5599)
HOLLOWAY HOUSE INC
309 Business Park Dr (46040)
P.O. Box 158 (46040)
PHONE..................317 485-4272
Christopher G Eck, CEO
Cameron N Eckv, *
▲ EMP: 27 EST: 1962
SQ FT: 27,000
SALES (est): 4.69MM Privately Held
Web: www.quickshinefloors.com
SIC: 2842 2841 Cleaning or polishing preparations, nec; Soap and other detergents

(G-5600)
INDIANA AIRCRAFT HARDWARE CO
221 S Main St (46040-1514)
PHONE..................317 485-6500
Robert Ferrell, Pr
EMP: 9 EST: 1976
SQ FT: 3,475
SALES (est): 1.31MM Privately Held
Web: www.indianaaircraft.com
SIC: 5088 3728 Aircraft and space vehicle supplies and parts; Aircraft parts and equipment, nec

(G-5601)
KLABUNDE LLC ✪
9662 S State Road 13 (46040-9208)
PHONE..................765 635-1101
Cole Elijah Klabunde, Pr
EMP: 1 EST: 2022
SALES (est): 62.01K Privately Held
SIC: 2048 Hay, cubed

(G-5602)
KOMODO PHARMACEUTICALS INC
8064 W 1000 S (46040-9224)
PHONE..................317 485-0023
Jarold Mcveigh, CEO
Robin Mcveigh, VP
EMP: 11 EST: 2005
SALES (est): 477.38K Privately Held
SIC: 2834 5122 Pharmaceutical preparations; Pharmaceuticals

(G-5603)
LGENIA INC
412 S Maple St Ste 104 (46040-1680)
PHONE..................317 861-8850
Laura Lee Hipskind, Prin
EMP: 16 EST: 2018
SALES (est): 191.89K Privately Held
Web: www.lgenia.com
SIC: 2834 Pharmaceutical preparations

(G-5604)
PERSONAL IMPRESSIONS INC
325 W Broadway St (46040-1800)
PHONE..................317 485-4409
Jeremy Chastain, Owner
EMP: 1 EST: 1984
SQ FT: 1,200
SALES (est): 125.05K Privately Held
Web: www.personalimpressions.com
SIC: 2759 Screen printing

(G-5605)
REGISTRATION SYSTEM LLC
Also Called: Trs
412 S Maple St Ste 230 (46040-0117)
PHONE..................317 966-6919

Florence May, Pr
EMP: 6 EST: 2008
SALES (est): 493.91K Privately Held
Web: www.my-trs.com
SIC: 7372 7379 8748 Application computer software; Computer related services, nec; Business consulting, nec

(G-5606)
SUPERIOR RADIANT PRODUCTS INC
315 N Madison St (46040-1160)
PHONE..................800 527-4328
Kevin Merritt, Pr
EMP: 12 EST: 2012
SALES (est): 763.49K Privately Held
Web: www.superiorradiant.com
SIC: 3255 Heater radiants, clay

(G-5607)
THURSDAY POOLS LLC
840 Commerce Pkwy Ste 2 (46040-1278)
PHONE..................317 973-0200
William H Khamis, Prin
EMP: 6 EST: 2010
SALES (est): 1.07MM Privately Held
Web: www.thursdaypools.com
SIC: 1799 3949 3088 Swimming pool construction; Swimming pools, except plastic; Hot tubs, plastics or fiberglass

(G-5608)
UNPLUG SOY CANDLES LLC
1360 E Broadway St Ste C (46040-9271)
PHONE..................317 650-5776
EMP: 8 EST: 2018
SALES (est): 546.41K Privately Held
Web: www.unplugsoycandles.com
SIC: 3999 Candles

Fountain City
Wayne County

(G-5609)
B2 MANUFACTURING LLC
606 Century Dr (47341-9440)
PHONE..................765 993-4519
Brandon E Blanford, Admn
EMP: 2 EST: 2013
SALES (est): 138.94K Privately Held
SIC: 3999 Manufacturing industries, nec

(G-5610)
D & H THURSTON FARMS LP
8307 Gifford Rd (47341-9705)
PHONE..................765 847-2304
EMP: 5 EST: 2011
SALES (est): 130K Privately Held
SIC: 3523 Driers (farm): grain, hay, and seed

(G-5611)
FOUNTAIN ACRES FOODS
1140 W Whitewater Rd (47341-9540)
PHONE..................765 847-1897
Stevie Miller, Owner
EMP: 9 EST: 2006
SALES (est): 402.84K Privately Held
SIC: 2051 Bakery: wholesale or wholesale/retail combined

(G-5612)
STARLINE MFG LLC
11262 Arba Pike (47341-9748)
PHONE..................765 847-1306
Ivan Esch, Managing Member
EMP: 7 EST: 2020
SALES (est): 406.35K Privately Held
SIC: 3229 Lenses, lantern, flashlight, headlight, etc.: glass

Fountaintown
Shelby County

(G-5613)
ASH-LIN INC
Also Called: Crates & Pallets
386 E Brookville Rd (46130-9631)
P.O. Box 49 (46130-0049)
PHONE..................317 861-1540
EMP: 11 EST: 1971
SQ FT: 14,500
SALES (est): 377.37K Privately Held
Web: www.cratesandpalletsindy.com
SIC: 2448 2441 Pallets, wood; Boxes, wood

(G-5614)
FOUNTAINTOWN FORGE INC
5513 S 100 E (46130-9441)
P.O. Box 139 (46130-0139)
PHONE..................317 861-5403
John H Konzen, CEO
Jerry Hill, VP
Jeff Kommann, CFO
Jenny Gipson, VP
EMP: 20 EST: 1967
SQ FT: 25,000
SALES (est): 2.19MM Privately Held
Web: www.fountaintownforge.com
SIC: 3462 3463 Iron and steel forgings; Machinery forgings, nonferrous

(G-5615)
KEYSTONE COOPERATIVE INC
1124 W Railroad St (46130-9456)
P.O. Box 73 (46129)
PHONE..................317 861-5080
Ray Kerkhof, Mgr
EMP: 5
SALES (corp-wide): 570.05MM Privately Held
Web: www.keystonecoop.com
SIC: 5261 2875 Fertilizer; Fertilizers, mixing only
PA: Keystone Cooperative, Inc.
770 N High School
Indianapolis IN 46214
800 525-0272

(G-5616)
SOLUTIONS FOR PRINT LLC
9530 N 100 W (46130-9780)
PHONE..................812 584-2701
EMP: 3 EST: 2018
SALES (est): 89.94K Privately Held
Web: www.solutionsforprint.com
SIC: 2752 Commercial printing, lithographic

Fowler
Benton County

(G-5617)
AMERICAN GARDENWORKS INC
407 S Adeway (47944-8410)
PHONE..................765 869-4033
EMP: 24 EST: 2009
SALES (est): 2.2MM Privately Held
Web: www.americangardenworks.com
SIC: 3524 Lawn and garden mowers and accessories

(G-5618)
ARCHER-DANIELS-MIDLAND COMPANY
Also Called: ADM Grain
203 E Railroad St (47944-8413)
PHONE..................765 299-1672
EMP: 3

Fowler - Benton County (G-5619)

SALES (corp-wide): 93.94B **Publicly Held**
Web: www.adm.com
SIC: **2046** 2041 2075 2074 Wet corn milling; Wheat flour; Soybean oil mills; Cottonseed oil, cake or meal
PA: Archer-Daniels-Midland Company
77 W Wacker Dr Ste 4600
Chicago IL 60601
312 634-8100

(G-5619)
BENTON REVIEW NEWSPAPER
204 N Adams Ave (47944-1161)
P.O. Box 527 (47944-0527)
PHONE..................................765 884-1902
EMP: 4 **EST:** 1995
SQ FT: 2,500
SALES (est): 169.3K **Privately Held**
SIC: **2711** Newspapers, publishing and printing

(G-5620)
BP ALTERNATIVE ENERGY NA INC
91 S 100 E (47944-8201)
PHONE..................................765 884-1000
Scott Tomtkins, *Prin*
EMP: 4 **EST:** 2009
SALES (est): 403.39K
SALES (corp-wide): 171.22B **Privately Held**
SIC: **3523** Windmills for pumping water, agricultural
PA: Bp P.L.C.
1 St. James's Square
London SW1Y
207 496-4000

(G-5621)
BP WIND ENERGY NORTH AMER INC
91 S 100 E (47944-8201)
PHONE..................................765 884-1000
Scott Tomtkins, *Brnch Mgr*
EMP: 4
SALES (corp-wide): 171.22B **Privately Held**
SIC: **2282** Throwing and winding mills
HQ: Bp Wind Energy North America Inc.
700 Louisiana St Fl 33
Houston TX 77002

(G-5622)
BROUILLETTE HTG COOLG PLBG LLC
403 W 5th St (47944-1413)
PHONE..................................765 884-0176
Victor Brouillette, *Owner*
EMP: 3 **EST:** 1987
SALES (est): 242.72K **Privately Held**
Web: www.brouillettehvac.com
SIC: **1711** 3567 Warm air heating and air conditioning contractor; Industrial furnaces and ovens

(G-5623)
DAILY II LARRY
702 N Lincoln Ave (47944-1300)
PHONE..................................765 884-9355
Larry Daily, *Prin*
EMP: 1 **EST:** 2003
SALES (est): 87.21K **Privately Held**
SIC: **2711** Newspapers, publishing and printing

(G-5624)
FOWLER RIDGE IV WIND FARM LLC
2870 W State Road 18 (47944-8306)
PHONE..................................765 884-1029
Ryan Logan, *Prin*
EMP: 5 **EST:** 2018
SALES (est): 139.87K **Privately Held**
SIC: **2448** Skids, wood

(G-5625)
HOLSCHER PRODUCTS INC
Also Called: Powder Cting / Hlscher Pwdr Ct
407 W Main St (47944)
P.O. Box 247 (47944)
PHONE..................................765 884-8021
Joseph Holscher, *Pr*
Marilyn Holscher, *
▲ **EMP:** 45 **EST:** 1985
SQ FT: 75,000
SALES (est): 6.04MM **Privately Held**
Web: www.holscherproductsinc.com
SIC: **3479** Painting of metal products

(G-5626)
LOD LLC
1153 N Us Highway 41 (47944-8309)
PHONE..................................765 385-0631
EMP: 1 **EST:** 2007
SALES (est): 236.41K **Privately Held**
Web: www.lodoffroad.com
SIC: **3714** Bumpers and bumperettes, motor vehicle

(G-5627)
MID STATE WATER TREATMENT
1009 E 5th St (47944-1521)
PHONE..................................765 884-1220
Lisa Cosby, *Owner*
EMP: 4 **EST:** 2002
SALES (est): 236.44K **Privately Held**
SIC: **3589** Water treatment equipment, industrial

(G-5628)
MILLENNIUM SUPPLY INC
407 S Adeway (47944-8410)
P.O. Box 127 (47918-0127)
PHONE..................................765 764-7000
L Gene Mcgowen, *Pr*
EMP: 9 **EST:** 2003
SQ FT: 78,000
SALES (est): 1.66MM **Privately Held**
Web: www.millenniumsupply.com
SIC: **3568** Joints and couplings

(G-5629)
OXFORD HOUSE INCORPORATED
Also Called: Oxford House
606 W State Road 18 (47944-8300)
PHONE..................................765 884-3265
Polet W Senesac, *Pr*
Polet Senesac, *
▲ **EMP:** 65 **EST:** 1989
SQ FT: 34,000
SALES (est): 4.93MM **Privately Held**
Web: www.oxford-house.com
SIC: **2591** 5521 Blinds vertical; Used car dealers

(G-5630)
POWELL SYSTEMS INC
83 S Meridian Rd (47944-8405)
P.O. Box 345 (47944-0345)
PHONE..................................765 884-0980
Larry Fording, *Mgr*
EMP: 31
SALES (corp-wide): 5.33MM **Privately Held**
Web: www.powellsystems.com
SIC: **3537** 3596 3565 3412 Skids, metal; Scales and balances, except laboratory; Packaging machinery; Metal barrels, drums, and pails
PA: Powell Systems, Inc.
162 Churchill Hubbard Rd
Youngstown OH
330 759-9220

(G-5631)
POWELL SYSTEMS INC
Fowler Division
604 E 9th St (47944-1652)
P.O. Box 345 (47944-0345)
PHONE..................................765 884-0613
Jay Davis, *Brnch Mgr*
EMP: 7
SALES (corp-wide): 5.33MM **Privately Held**
Web: www.powellsystems.com
SIC: **3444** 3537 2448 3412 Sheet metalwork ; Skids, metal; Skids, wood; Metal barrels, drums, and pails
PA: Powell Systems, Inc.
162 Churchill Hubbard Rd
Youngstown OH
330 759-9220

(G-5632)
PRAIRIE PRESERVATION GUILD LTD
111 E 5th St (47944)
P.O. Box 527 (47944)
PHONE..................................765 884-1902
Karen Moyars, *Pr*
Karen Kemme, *Treas*
EMP: 1 **EST:** 2001
SALES (est): 155.46K **Privately Held**
Web: www.fowlertheater.com
SIC: **2711** Newspapers

(G-5633)
SLON INC
206 N Harrison Ave (47944-1032)
P.O. Box 67 (47944-0067)
PHONE..................................765 884-1792
Darrell R Sloniger, *Pr*
Beverly Sloniger, *Sec*
Marlys Vanderwall, *Off Mgr*
EMP: 21 **EST:** 1972
SQ FT: 30,000
SALES (est): 2.42MM **Privately Held**
Web: www.sloninc.com
SIC: **3281** 3272 3271 Stone, quarrying and processing of own stone products; Concrete products, nec; Concrete block and brick

(G-5634)
TIPPECANOE TIRE SERVICE INC
Also Called: Etter Tire Service
219 E 5th St (47944-1445)
PHONE..................................765 884-0920
David Etter, *Pr*
Eleanore Etter, *Sec*
EMP: 4 **EST:** 1960
SQ FT: 7,200
SALES (est): 513.7K **Privately Held**
Web: etter-tire-services.edan.io
SIC: **5531** 7534 Automotive tires; Tire repair shop

Francesville
Pulaski County

(G-5635)
ADAPTASOFT INC
106 E Montgomery St (47946-8087)
P.O. Box 68 (47959-0068)
PHONE..................................219 567-2547
Timothy C Troxel, *Pr*
Joel Troxel, *CFO*
EMP: 25 **EST:** 1996
SQ FT: 7,500
SALES (est): 1.33MM **Privately Held**
Web: www.cyberpay.com
SIC: **7372** Business oriented computer software

(G-5636)
ALAN SUTTON GRAPHIC DESIGN
4635 S 1450 W (47946-8215)
PHONE..................................219 567-2764
Al Sutton, *Owner*
EMP: 2 **EST:** 2001
SALES (est): 105.07K **Privately Held**
Web: www.alsuttongraphics.com
SIC: **3993** Signs and advertising specialties

(G-5637)
CLEAR DECISION FILTRATION INC
4571 S 1450 W (47946-8215)
PHONE..................................219 567-2008
Anthony Holliday, *Pr*
Melanie K Holliday, *Sec*
EMP: 8 **EST:** 2008
SQ FT: 4,000
SALES (est): 498K **Privately Held**
Web: www.cdfilter.com
SIC: **3569** Filters

(G-5638)
DISINGER MACHINE SHOP
4045 S 1450 W (47946)
P.O. Box 483 (47946-0483)
PHONE..................................219 567-2357
Douglas R Disinger, *Owner*
EMP: 4 **EST:** 1988
SALES (est): 294.38K **Privately Held**
Web: www.disingerrp.com
SIC: **3599** Machine shop, jobbing and repair

(G-5639)
ELVIN L NUEST SALES AND SERVIC
420 S Bill St (47946-8073)
PHONE..................................219 863-5216
Elvin L Nuest, *Owner*
EMP: 5 **EST:** 2014
SALES (est): 79.19K **Privately Held**
SIC: **2875** Compost

(G-5640)
FRANCESVILLE VULCAN MATERIALS
14530 W 700 S (47946-8009)
PHONE..................................219 567-9155
Kevin Cox, *Pr*
EMP: 6 **EST:** 2007
SALES (est): 221.07K **Privately Held**
SIC: **1422** Crushed and broken limestone

(G-5641)
FRATCO INC
4385 S 1450 W (47946)
PHONE..................................800 854-7120
EMP: 8
SALES (corp-wide): 11.1MM **Privately Held**
Web: www.fratco.com
SIC: **3312** Blast furnaces and steel mills
PA: Fratco, Inc.
105 W Broadway St
Monticello IN 47960
800 854-7120

(G-5642)
FTC PRODUCTS CORP
Hwy 421 N One Half Mile (47946)
PHONE..................................219 567-2441
Douglas Gutwein, *Pr*
Mary F Gutwein, *Sec*
EMP: 5 **EST:** 1963
SQ FT: 15,000
SALES (est): 963.38K **Privately Held**
Web: www.ftcenterprisesinc.com
SIC: **3714** Motor vehicle wheels and parts

GEOGRAPHIC SECTION

Frankfort - Clinton County (G-5666)

(G-5643)
LEGACY VULCAN LLC
Also Called: Midwest Division
14530 W 700 S (47946-8009)
PHONE......................219 567-9155
Todd Schultz, *Superintnt*
EMP: 4
Web: www.vulcanmaterials.com
SIC: 3273 Ready-mixed concrete
HQ: Legacy Vulcan, Llc
1200 Urban Center Dr
Birmingham AL 35242
205 298-3000

(G-5644)
RDB ENVIRONMENTAL LLC (PA)
2953 In-14 (47946)
PHONE......................708 362-3618
EMP: 1 EST: 2021
SALES (est): 168.22K
SALES (corp-wide): 168.22K **Privately Held**
SIC: 1321 Natural gas liquids production

(G-5645)
SCHLATTERS INC
16179 W 500 S (47946-8636)
P.O. Box 548 (47946-0548)
PHONE......................219 567-9158
Ronald Schlatter, *Pr*
Jody Schlatter, *VP*
Nanci Schlatter, *Off Mgr*
EMP: 6 EST: 1952
SQ FT: 12,960
SALES (est): 624.57K **Privately Held**
Web: www.schlattersinc.com
SIC: 3599 5082 5083 Machine shop, jobbing and repair; General construction machinery and equipment; Agricultural machinery and equipment

Francisco
Gibson County

(G-5646)
PEABODY MIDWEST MINING LLC
Also Called: Francisco Mining
County Rd 850 E (47649)
PHONE......................812 782-3209
EMP: 437
SALES (corp-wide): 4.95B **Publicly Held**
SIC: 1221 Bituminous coal surface mining
HQ: Peabody Midwest Mining, Llc
566 Dickeyville Rd
Lynnville IN 47619

Frankfort
Clinton County

(G-5647)
421 PALLET & CRATE
888 S Us Highway 421 (46041-8944)
PHONE......................765 249-5088
Frankie Smith, *Owner*
EMP: 1 EST: 2005
SALES (est): 79.89K **Privately Held**
SIC: 2448 Pallets, wood

(G-5648)
A-ROSE CONSULTANTS LLC
805 E Washington St (46041-2062)
PHONE......................765 650-8700
Fabrizzio Vargas, *Managing Member*
EMP: 10 EST: 2019
SALES (est): 299.58K **Privately Held**
SIC: 1081 Metal mining exploration and development services

(G-5649)
ARCHER-DANIELS-MIDLAND COMPANY
Also Called: ADM
2191 W County Road 0 N/S (46041)
P.O. Box 249 (46041-0249)
PHONE......................765 654-4411
Matt Hartman, *Mgr*
EMP: 28
SQ FT: 75,000
SALES (corp-wide): 93.94B **Publicly Held**
Web: www.adm.com
SIC: 5153 2099 Grains; Food preparations, nec
PA: Archer-Daniels-Midland Company
77 W Wacker Dr Ste 4600
Chicago IL 60601
312 634-8100

(G-5650)
ARION ROOFING & SHTMTL INC
1686 S Hiland Dr (46041-6826)
PHONE......................317 525-1984
EMP: 7 EST: 2019
SALES (est): 246.45K **Privately Held**
SIC: 3444 Sheet metalwork

(G-5651)
AZAMI PRESS
859 N Main St (46041-1442)
PHONE......................765 242-7988
EMP: 3 EST: 2019
SALES (est): 104.59K **Privately Held**
Web: www.azamipress.com
SIC: 2741 Miscellaneous publishing

(G-5652)
BELL MACHINE COMPANY INC
Also Called: Basteel Perimeter Systems
1400 Magnolia Ave (46041-1028)
PHONE......................765 654-5225
Marshall Bell, *Pr*
Ron Bell, *VP*
Brenda Bell, *Sec*
▲ EMP: 22 EST: 1946
SQ FT: 5,400
SALES (est): 2.31MM **Privately Held**
Web: www.basteel.com
SIC: 3544 Wire drawing and straightening dies

(G-5653)
CF GUNWORKS LLC
1157 S County Road 1000 E (46041-8949)
PHONE......................317 538-1122
EMP: 2 EST: 2012
SALES (est): 233.77K **Privately Held**
Web: www.cfgunworks.com
SIC: 3484 Guns (firearms) or gun parts, 30 mm. and below

(G-5654)
CM WELDING INC
238 W County Road 425 N (46041-7856)
PHONE......................765 258-4024
Don Estes, *Owner*
EMP: 2 EST: 2010
SALES (est): 132.93K **Privately Held**
Web: www.cmweldinginc.com
SIC: 7692 Welding repair

(G-5655)
COOMER & SONS SAWMILL INC
Also Called: Coomer & Sons Sawmill
184 Roy Scott Pkwy (46041-8757)
PHONE......................765 659-2846
Charles Coomer, *Owner*
EMP: 60 EST: 1978
SALES (est): 4.51MM **Privately Held**
Web: www.coomersawmill.com
SIC: 2448 2421 Pallets, wood; Sawmills and planing mills, general

(G-5656)
COVESTRO LLC
3110 W State Road 28 (46041-8718)
PHONE......................765 659-4721
Steven Dalton, *Brnch Mgr*
EMP: 1
SALES (corp-wide): 15.63B **Privately Held**
Web: www.covestro.com
SIC: 2821 Plastics materials and resins
HQ: Covestro Llc
1 Covestro Cir
Pittsburgh PA 15205
412 413-2000

(G-5657)
CTB INC
Brock Grain Systems
1750 W State Road 28 (46041-9146)
PHONE......................765 654-8517
Blain Buttermore, *Mgr*
EMP: 30
SALES (corp-wide): 364.48B **Publicly Held**
Web: www.brockgrain.com
SIC: 3535 3523 Pneumatic tube conveyor systems; Driers (farm): grain, hay, and seed
HQ: Ctb, Inc.
611 N Higbee St
Milford IN 46542
574 658-4191

(G-5658)
CTB MN INVESTMENT CO INC
Brock Grain Conditioning Group
1750 W State Road 28 (46041-9146)
PHONE......................765 654-8517
Bill Crosby, *Mgr*
EMP: 1115
SALES (corp-wide): 364.48B **Publicly Held**
Web: www.ctbinc.com
SIC: 3523 3535 Driers (farm): grain, hay, and seed; Pneumatic tube conveyor systems
HQ: Ctb Mn Investment Co., Inc.
611 N Higbee St
Milford IN 46542

(G-5659)
CUSTOM BUILDING PRODUCTS LLC
3800 W State Road 28 (46041-8701)
PHONE......................765 656-0234
Mike Bilek Senior, *Mgr*
EMP: 121
Web: www.custombuildingproducts.com
SIC: 5085 2899 2891 Adhesives, tape and plasters; Chemical preparations, nec; Adhesives and sealants
HQ: Custom Building Products Llc
7711 Center Ave Ste 500
Huntington Beach CA 92647
800 272-8786

(G-5660)
DONALDSON COMPANY INC
3260 W State Road 28 (46041-8721)
PHONE......................765 659-4766
Rich Lewis, *Brnch Mgr*
EMP: 693
SQ FT: 120,000
SALES (corp-wide): 3.43B **Publicly Held**
Web: www.donaldson.com
SIC: 3714 3564 Cleaners, air, motor vehicle; Blowers and fans
PA: Donaldson Company, Inc.
1400 W 94th St
Minneapolis MN 55431
952 887-3131

(G-5661)
ESKAPE PRESS LLC
2587 S County Road 180 E (46041-8652)
PHONE......................765 659-1237
Kimberly Bowman, *Owner*
EMP: 1 EST: 2014
SALES (est): 53.84K **Privately Held**
SIC: 2741 Miscellaneous publishing

(G-5662)
FEDERAL-MOGUL POWERTRAIN LLC
Also Called: Federal-Mogul
2845 W State Road 28 (46041-8779)
PHONE......................765 659-7207
Chuck Hinshaw, *Brnch Mgr*
EMP: 1
SQ FT: 175,000
SALES (corp-wide): 18.04B **Privately Held**
Web: www.tenneco.com
SIC: 3714 Motor vehicle parts and accessories
HQ: Federal-Mogul Powertrain Llc
15701 Technology Dr
Northville MI 48168

(G-5663)
FOG FOUNDRY FRANKFORT
58 W Clinton St (46041-1914)
PHONE......................765 670-6445
EMP: 4 EST: 2019
SALES (est): 108.21K **Privately Held**
SIC: 3366 Copper foundries

(G-5664)
FONTANA FASTENERS INC (DH)
Also Called: Lep Special Fasteners
3595 W State Road 28 (46041)
PHONE......................765 654-0477
Giuseppe Zichella, *CEO*
▲ EMP: 150 EST: 2006
SQ FT: 250,000
SALES (est): 45.14MM **Privately Held**
Web: www.fontanagruppoagtna.com
SIC: 3452 Bolts, metal
HQ: Fontana America Incorporated
6125 Eighteen Mile Road
Sterling Heights MI 48314
586 997-5600

(G-5665)
FOREST PRODUCTS GROUP INC
Also Called: Forest Products Group Ind Div
901 Blinn Ave (46041-1585)
PHONE......................765 659-1807
Jeff Reinke, *Brnch Mgr*
EMP: 11
SQ FT: 1,000
SALES (corp-wide): 10.33MM **Privately Held**
Web: www.forestproductsgroup.com
SIC: 5031 2431 2426 2421 Lumber: rough, dressed, and finished; Millwork; Hardwood dimension and flooring mills; Sawmills and planing mills, general
PA: The Forest Products Group Inc
1269 Grandview Ave
Columbus OH 43212
614 488-9743

(G-5666)
FRANKFORT NEWSPAPER
251 E Clinton St (46041-1906)
PHONE......................859 254-2385
Jay Frizzo, *Prin*
EMP: 6 EST: 2016
SALES (est): 92.73K **Privately Held**
Web: www.frankfort-indiana.com
SIC: 2711 Newspapers, publishing and printing

Frankfort - Clinton County (G-5667)

GEOGRAPHIC SECTION

(G-5667)
FRANKFORT PLASTICS INC
2021 W County Road 0 Ns (46041-8745)
PHONE.....................................931 510-0525
Sasi Noothalapati, *Pr*
EMP: 11 **EST:** 2017
SALES (est): 490.74K **Privately Held**
SIC: 3089 Prefabricated plastics buildings

(G-5668)
FRITO-LAY NORTH AMERICA INC
Also Called: Frito-Lay
2611 W County Road 0 Ns (46041-8703)
PHONE.....................................765 659-4517
EMP: 34
SALES (corp-wide): 86.39B **Publicly Held**
Web: www.fritolay.com
SIC: 2096 2099 Potato chips and similar snacks; Food preparations, nec
HQ: Frito-Lay North America, Inc.
7701 Legacy Dr
Plano TX 75024

(G-5669)
FRITO-LAY NORTH AMERICA INC
Also Called: Frito-Lay
323 S County Road 300 W (46041-8780)
PHONE.....................................765 659-1831
Frank Armetta, *Mgr*
EMP: 500
SALES (corp-wide): 86.39B **Publicly Held**
Web: www.fritolay.com
SIC: 2096 2099 2032 Potato chips and similar snacks; Food preparations, nec; Canned specialties
HQ: Frito-Lay North America, Inc.
7701 Legacy Dr
Plano TX 75024

(G-5670)
GEM CITY JUNCTION LLC
63 E Clinton St (46041-2797)
PHONE.....................................765 659-6733
Ryan Prather, *Pr*
EMP: 5 **EST:** 2019
SALES (est): 101.84K **Privately Held**
Web: www.gemcityjunction.com
SIC: 2099 Food preparations, nec

(G-5671)
GLOVERS ICE CREAM INC
705 W Clinton St (46041-1824)
P.O. Box 504 (46041-0504)
PHONE.....................................765 654-6712
TOLL FREE: 800
R Stephen Glover, *Pr*
EMP: 8 **EST:** 1923
SQ FT: 3,000
SALES (est): 999K **Privately Held**
Web: www.gloversicecream.com
SIC: 2024 Ice cream, bulk

(G-5672)
HARNESS MACHINE & FAB LLC
7734 S 500 E (46041-9600)
PHONE.....................................765 652-2831
Kyle Harness, *Managing Member*
EMP: 12 **EST:** 2017
SALES (est): 882.22K **Privately Held**
SIC: 3498 Tube fabricating (contract bending and shaping)

(G-5673)
HI-TECH LABEL INC
357 E Washington St (46041-1946)
P.O. Box 765 (46041-0765)
PHONE.....................................765 659-1800
TOLL FREE: 800
Dan W Scott, *Pr*
Pat Scott, *VP*
EMP: 16 **EST:** 1989
SQ FT: 10,000
SALES (est): 970.49K **Privately Held**
Web: www.hitechlabel.com
SIC: 2679 2759 2672 Labels, paper: made from purchased material; Commercial printing, nec; Paper; coated and laminated, nec

(G-5674)
HINSHAW ROOFING & SHEET METAL CO INC
2452 S State Road 39 (46041-7658)
P.O. Box 636 (46041-0636)
PHONE.....................................765 659-3311
EMP: 50 **EST:** 1947
SALES (est): 4.91MM **Privately Held**
Web: www.hinshawroofing.com
SIC: 1761 3444 Roofing contractor; Sheet metalwork

(G-5675)
IRVING MATERIALS INC
28 W St Rd (46041-7121)
PHONE.....................................765 654-5333
Ron Knowles, *Mgr*
EMP: 10
SALES (corp-wide): 814.09MM **Privately Held**
Web: www.irvmat.com
SIC: 3273 Ready-mixed concrete
PA: Irving Materials, Inc.
8032 N State Road 9
Greenfield IN 46140
317 326-3101

(G-5676)
JBS UNITED INC
3503 W County Road 300 N (46041-7371)
PHONE.....................................765 296-4539
EMP: 5 **EST:** 2019
SALES (est): 82.18K **Privately Held**
Web: www.unitedanh.com
SIC: 2834 Pharmaceutical preparations

(G-5677)
KAY COMPANY INC
Also Called: Kayco
509 W Barner St (46041)
P.O. Box 2286 (47996)
PHONE.....................................765 659-3388
Michael S Kay, *Pr*
EMP: 41 **EST:** 1961
SQ FT: 150,000
SALES (est): 4.97MM **Privately Held**
Web: www.thekaycompany.com
SIC: 3993 2493 5031 Displays and cutouts, window and lobby; Fiberboard, wood; Particleboard

(G-5678)
KEYSTONE COOPERATIVE INC
Also Called: Impact
411b Eb Kellyb Road (46041)
PHONE.....................................765 659-2596
Jack Barett, *Mgr*
EMP: 6
SALES (corp-wide): 570.05MM **Privately Held**
Web: www.keystonecoop.com
SIC: 2873 5191 Nitrogenous fertilizers; Farm supplies
PA: Keystone Cooperative, Inc.
770 N High School
Indianapolis IN 46214
800 525-0272

(G-5679)
LEAHY ADOLOGY HEARING AIDS LLC ◆
1303 S Jackson St (46041)
PHONE.....................................765 601-4003
Ryan David Leahy, *Dir*
EMP: 7 **EST:** 2023
SALES (est): 75.6K **Privately Held**
SIC: 3842 Hearing aids

(G-5680)
LONGHORN MARKETING GROUP
1950 E Walnut St (46041-2721)
PHONE.....................................765 650-4430
EMP: 6 **EST:** 2019
SALES (est): 358.21K **Privately Held**
Web: www.youradvisorteam.com
SIC: 2752 Commercial printing, lithographic

(G-5681)
MASBEZ LLC
509 W Barner St (46041-1606)
P.O. Box 202344 (80220-8344)
PHONE.....................................855 962-7239
Samuel Neri, *Pr*
Samuel Neri D.o.s., *Prin*
EMP: 7 **EST:** 2015
SALES (est): 866.46K **Privately Held**
Web: www.masbez.com
SIC: 5082 3699 5699 3542 General construction machinery and equipment; Electrical welding equipment; Uniforms and work clothing; Punching and shearing machines

(G-5682)
MATHEWS WIRE INC
358 N Columbia St (46041-1600)
PHONE.....................................765 659-3542
Mike Mathews, *Pr*
Martin Mathews, *
EMP: 13 **EST:** 1984
SQ FT: 200,000
SALES (est): 305.11K **Privately Held**
Web: www.whsl.net
SIC: 3496 5947 Woven wire products, nec; Gift, novelty, and souvenir shop

(G-5683)
NHK SEATING OF AMERICA INC
2195 W Barner St (46041)
PHONE.....................................765 605-2443
EMP: 1
Web: www.nhkseating.com
SIC: 2531 Seats, automobile
HQ: Nhk Seating Of America, Inc.
2298 W State Rd 28
Frankfort IN 46041
765 659-4781

(G-5684)
NHK SEATING OF AMERICA INC (DH)
2298 W State Road 28 (46041)
PHONE.....................................765 659-4781
Tatsuro Ono, *Pr*
▲ **EMP:** 22 **EST:** 1987
SQ FT: 80,000
SALES (est): 24.24MM **Privately Held**
Web: www.nhkseating.com
SIC: 2531 Seats, automobile
HQ: Nhk International Corporation
46855 Magellan Dr
Novi MI 48377

(G-5685)
NORTH AMERICAN INK
2642 W State Road 28 (46041-9193)
PHONE.....................................765 659-6000
Tom Butera, *Mgr*
EMP: 2 **EST:** 2010
SALES (est): 101.24K **Privately Held**
SIC: 2893 Printing ink

(G-5686)
NORTH-SIDE MACHINE & TOOL INC
1604 N County Road 0 Ew (46041-7804)
PHONE.....................................765 654-4538
Dan Stokes, *Pr*
EMP: 19 **EST:** 2007
SALES (est): 884.71K **Privately Held**
Web: www.northsidemt.com
SIC: 3544 3599 5031 Special dies and tools; Machine shop, jobbing and repair; Lumber: rough, dressed, and finished

(G-5687)
NTK PRECISION AXLE CORPORATION
741 S County Road 200 W (46041-8704)
PHONE.....................................765 656-1000
Tadao Okamura, *Pr*
Takashi Tanaka, *
▲ **EMP:** 252 **EST:** 2003
SQ FT: 200,000
SALES (est): 49.76MM **Privately Held**
Web: www.ntkaxle.com
SIC: 3312 Axles, rolled or forged: made in steel mills
PA: Ntn Corporation
3-6-32, Nakanoshima, Kita-Ku
Osaka OSK 530-0

(G-5688)
OSTLER ENTERPRISES INC
Also Called: Landscape Products
1624 W Armstrong Rd (46041-8272)
PHONE.....................................765 656-1275
Gary G Ostler, *Pr*
Gary Ostler, *Pr*
Melissa Ostler, *Sec*
EMP: 7 **EST:** 1997
SALES (est): 996.63K **Privately Held**
SIC: 2499 2875 Mulch, wood and bark; Potting soil, mixed

(G-5689)
PADDACK BROTHERS INC
Also Called: Country Estate Mobile Home Pk
4410 W Old State Road 28 (46041-7245)
PHONE.....................................765 659-4777
Jack W Paddack, *Pr*
Lynn A Paddack, *Sec*
EMP: 8 **EST:** 1957
SQ FT: 3,400
SALES (est): 433.18K **Privately Held**
SIC: 4212 1442 6515 Local trucking, without storage; Gravel mining; Mobile home site operators

(G-5690)
PEPSI BOTTLING VENTURES LLC
Also Called: Pepsi-Cola
2611 W County Road 0 Ns (46041-8751)
PHONE.....................................765 659-7313
Randy Haggard, *Brnch Mgr*
EMP: 49
Web: www.pepsibottlingventures.com
SIC: 2086 Carbonated soft drinks, bottled and canned
HQ: Pepsi Bottling Ventures Llc
4141 Parklake Ave Ste 600
Raleigh NC 27612
919 865-2300

(G-5691)
PRO-TECH TOOL & STAMPING INC
890 E County Road 600 N (46041-7613)
PHONE.....................................765 258-3613
Kevin Wilhelm, *Pr*
EMP: 7 **EST:** 1995
SQ FT: 11,000
SALES (est): 982.41K **Privately Held**
Web: www.pro-techtool.com

SIC: 5084 5051 3465 Tool and die makers equipment; Stampings, metal; Automotive stampings

(G-5692)
PURINA ANIMAL NUTRITION LLC
2472 W State Road 28 (46041-8773)
PHONE..................................765 659-4791
Troy Smith, *Mgr*
EMP: 1
SALES (corp-wide): 2.89B Privately Held
Web: www.purinamills.com
SIC: 2048 Prepared feeds, nec
HQ: Purina Animal Nutrition Llc
100 Danforth Dr
Gray Summit MO 63039

(G-5693)
RICHEY M A MFG CO SPRTNG GDS
401 S Prairie Ave (46041-9144)
PHONE..................................765 659-5389
EMP: 4 **EST:** 2013
SALES (est): 87.82K Privately Held
SIC: 3999 Manufacturing industries, nec

(G-5694)
SMITH BUSINESS SUPPLY INC
Also Called: Express Print
358 N Columbia St (46041-1600)
PHONE..................................765 654-4442
Eric Smith, *Pr*
EMP: 4 **EST:** 1991
SQ FT: 2,700
SALES (est): 400K Privately Held
Web: www.expressprint.com
SIC: 2752 Offset printing

(G-5695)
SUN CHEMICAL CORPORATION
Also Called: U S Ink Division
2642 W State Road 28 (46041-8774)
PHONE..................................972 270-6735
Steven Bill, *Brnch Mgr*
EMP: 25
Web: www.sunchemical.com
SIC: 2893 Printing ink
HQ: Sun Chemical Corporation
35 Waterview Blvd
Parsippany NJ 07054
973 404-6000

(G-5696)
SUN CHEMICAL CORPORATION
General Printing Ink
2642 W State Road 28 (46041-8774)
PHONE..................................765 659-6000
Tom Butera, *Mgr*
EMP: 33
Web: www.sunchemical.com
SIC: 2893 Printing ink
HQ: Sun Chemical Corporation
35 Waterview Blvd
Parsippany NJ 07054
973 404-6000

(G-5697)
TAYLOR WELDING
3342 Washington Ave (46041-8216)
PHONE..................................765 659-2955
James E Taylor, *Owner*
James E Taylor, *Prin*
EMP: 1 **EST:** 1961
SALES (est): 53.92K Privately Held
SIC: 7692 Welding repair

(G-5698)
TIMES
Also Called: Paxton Media Group
62 N Main St Ste 104 (46041-2795)
PHONE..................................765 659-4622

David Paxton, *Pr*
David Mathis, *
Richard Welch, *
Karen Turner, *
Jay Frizzo, *
EMP: 28 **EST:** 1894
SALES (est): 754.05K
SALES (corp-wide): 147.64MM Privately Held
Web: www.ftimes.com
SIC: 2711 4841 2791 2752 Newspapers, publishing and printing; Cable television services; Typesetting; Commercial printing, lithographic
PA: Paxton Media Group, Llc
100 Television Ln
Paducah KY 42003
270 575-8630

(G-5699)
TORDILLERIA DEL VALLE
905 Walnut Ave (46041-1847)
PHONE..................................765 654-9590
Alphonso Ruic, *Owner*
EMP: 3 **EST:** 2002
SALES (est): 119.41K Privately Held
SIC: 2099 Tortillas, fresh or refrigerated

(G-5700)
VICKSMETAL ARMCO ASSOCIATES (PA)
150 S County Road 300 W (46041-8765)
PHONE..................................765 659-5555
Henery Kato, *Pt*
EMP: 40 **EST:** 1990
SQ FT: 64,000
SALES (est): 2.16MM Privately Held
SIC: 7389 3312 Metal slitting and shearing; Blast furnaces and steel mills

(G-5701)
WEST PHRM SVCS AZ INC
2810 W State Road 28 (46041-9197)
PHONE..................................765 650-2300
Robert Hargesheimer, *Pr*
EMP: 1
SALES (corp-wide): 2.95B Publicly Held
Web: www.westpharma.com
SIC: 3089 Injection molding of plastics
HQ: West Pharmaceutical Services Az, Inc.
14677 N 74th St
Scottsdale AZ 85260
480 281-4500

(G-5702)
WINSKI BROTHERS INC
751 W Washington St (46041-1895)
PHONE..................................765 654-5323
Sherman Winski, *Pr*
Joel Stiller, *VP*
EMP: 7 **EST:** 1937
SQ FT: 10,000
SALES (est): 470.08K Privately Held
Web: www.winskibrothers.com
SIC: 5093 5051 4953 3341 Ferrous metal scrap and waste; Steel; Hazardous waste collection and disposal; Secondary nonferrous metals

---

Franklin
Johnson County

(G-5703)
AGRI-TRONIX CORP
Also Called: Pro Traument Scale
2001 N Morton St (46131-9628)
PHONE..................................317 738-4474
Terry L Clarkson, *Pr*
Jim Beswick, *VP*

EMP: 12 **EST:** 1982
SQ FT: 10,000
SALES (est): 2.23MM Privately Held
Web: www.agritronixcorp.com
SIC: 3823 7629 Computer interface equipment, for industrial process control; Electrical equipment repair services

(G-5704)
AIM MEDIA INDIANA OPER LLC
Daily Journal
30 S Water St Ste A (46131-2316)
P.O. Box 699 (46131-0699)
PHONE..................................317 736-7101
Chris Cosner, *Brnch Mgr*
EMP: 26
SALES (corp-wide): 26.88MM Privately Held
Web: www.aimmediaindiana.com
SIC: 7313 2752 2711 Newspaper advertising representative; Commercial printing, lithographic; Newspapers, publishing and printing
PA: Aim Media Indiana Operating, Llc
2980 N National Rd # A
Columbus IN 47201
812 372-7811

(G-5705)
AIM MEDIA INDIANA OPER LLC
South Magazine
30 S Water St Ste A (46131-2316)
P.O. Box 699 (46131-0699)
PHONE..................................812 736-7101
Chris Cosner, *Brnch Mgr*
EMP: 2
SALES (corp-wide): 26.88MM Privately Held
Web: www.aimmediaindiana.com
SIC: 2711 Commercial printing and newspaper publishing combined
PA: Aim Media Indiana Operating, Llc
2980 N National Rd # A
Columbus IN 47201
812 372-7811

(G-5706)
AIRTOMIC LLC
75 Linville Way (46131-5600)
PHONE..................................317 738-0148
Daniel Bergeron, *CEO*
EMP: 32 **EST:** 2018
SALES (est): 5.69MM
SALES (corp-wide): 1.56B Publicly Held
Web: www.sargentaerospace.com
SIC: 3728 Aircraft parts and equipment, nec
PA: Rbc Bearings Incorporated
1 Tribiology Ctr
Oxford CT 06478
203 267-7001

(G-5707)
AIRTOMIC REPAIR STATION
Also Called: Sargent Controls & Aerospace
75 Linville Way (46131-5600)
PHONE..................................317 738-0148
EMP: 6 **EST:** 2010
SALES (est): 114.27K Privately Held
SIC: 3728 Aircraft parts and equipment, nec

(G-5708)
AMCOR RIGID PACKAGING USA LLC
Also Called: Schmalbach-Lubeca
3201 Bearing Dr (46131-7415)
PHONE..................................317 736-4313
Tom Balk, *Brnch Mgr*
EMP: 5
SALES (corp-wide): 14.69B Privately Held
SIC: 3089 Plastics containers, except foam
HQ: Amcor Rigid Packaging Usa, Llc

10521 S Hwy M-52
Manchester MI 48158

(G-5709)
ANNUAL REPORTS INC
Also Called: Annual Reports Services
1250 Park Ave (46131-8868)
P.O. Box 607 (46131-0607)
PHONE..................................317 736-8838
Christopher Doyle, *Pr*
Jay P Doyle, *
Gloria L Doyle, *
Cynthia Doyle, *Product Vice President**
EMP: 6 **EST:** 1969
SQ FT: 1,600
SALES (est): 175.31K Privately Held
Web: www.annualreportsinc.com
SIC: 7336 8743 2791 Graphic arts and related design; Public relations services; Typesetting, computer controlled

(G-5710)
APEX ENGINEERED ENTPS LLC
2590 E 200 S (46131)
PHONE..................................317 346-7148
Timothy Flynn, *Owner*
EMP: 3 **EST:** 2015
SALES (est): 37.24K Privately Held
Web: www.apexep.com
SIC: 3443 Fabricated plate work (boiler shop)

(G-5711)
AXIS INDUSTRIES USA LLC
1400 Commerce Pkwy (46131)
PHONE..................................317 739-3390
EMP: 12
SALES (corp-wide): 397.85K Privately Held
Web: www.axisindustriesusa.com
SIC: 3826 Laser scientific and engineering instruments
PA: Axis Industries Usa, Llc
817 Mohr Ave
Waterford WI 53185
317 739-3390

(G-5712)
BALL INC
1900 Commerce Pkwy (46131-6965)
PHONE..................................317 736-8236
EMP: 3475
SALES (corp-wide): 13.81B Publicly Held
Web: www.rexam.com
SIC: 3411 Metal cans
HQ: Ball Inc.
4201 Congress St Ste 340
Charlotte NC 28209

(G-5713)
BEARDS WELDING & FABRICATION
8321 W Shelby 250 S (46131-9209)
PHONE..................................317 374-4779
EMP: 4 **EST:** 2018
SALES (est): 137.72K Privately Held
SIC: 7692 Welding repair

(G-5714)
BERRY GLOBAL INC
1900 Commerce Pkwy (46131-6965)
PHONE..................................812 421-3136
EMP: 8
Web: www.berryglobal.com
SIC: 3089 3081 Bottle caps, molded plastics; Unsupported plastics film and sheet
HQ: Berry Global, Inc.
101 Oakley St
Evansville IN 47710

Franklin - Johnson County (G-5715) GEOGRAPHIC SECTION

(G-5715)
BEST TIRES & WHEELS
320 N Morton St (46131-1648)
PHONE..................317 306-3379
Colleen Mckinnel, *Prin*
EMP: 10 **EST:** 2011
SALES (est): 358.48K **Privately Held**
SIC: 3312 Wheels

(G-5716)
BIG SHOT OUTFITTERS LLC
2777 N Morton St (46131-8888)
P.O. Box 467 (46131-0467)
PHONE..................317 736-4867
EMP: 1 **EST:** 2013
SALES (est): 79.14K **Privately Held**
SIC: 3949 5091 Sporting and athletic goods, nec; Hunting equipment and supplies

(G-5717)
BLEHM PLASTICS
2140 Earlywood Dr (46131)
P.O. Box 327 (46131)
PHONE..................317 736-4090
Roger Brunette, *Owner*
EMP: 7 **EST:** 2017
SALES (est): 123.94K **Privately Held**
Web: www.polytek.com
SIC: 2821 Plastics materials and resins

(G-5718)
CATERPILLAR REMN POWRTRN INDNA (HQ)
751 International Dr (46131-9637)
PHONE..................317 738-2117
James W Owens, *CEO*
▲ **EMP:** 298 **EST:** 2007
SQ FT: 115,000
SALES (est): 90.59MM
SALES (corp-wide): 67.06B **Publicly Held**
SIC: 3714 Rebuilding engines and transmissions, factory basis
PA: Caterpillar Inc.
5205 N Ocnnor Blvd Ste 10
Irving TX 75039
972 891-7700

(G-5719)
CHART LIFECYCLE INC
1725 N Graham Rd (46131-9726)
PHONE..................317 535-4315
EMP: 11 **EST:** 2018
SALES (est): 1.41MM **Privately Held**
Web: www.chartindustries.com
SIC: 3443 Fabricated plate work (boiler shop)

(G-5720)
CL HOLDING LLC
Also Called: Pro Industies
1441 Amy Ln (46131-1491)
PHONE..................317 736-4414
Chris Lynch, *Managing Member*
Shawn Taylor, *Managing Member*
EMP: 8 **EST:** 1989
SALES (est): 877.1K **Privately Held**
Web: www.proindustries.com
SIC: 3949 Exercise equipment

(G-5721)
CLASSIQUE HAIR STYLE
50 S Water St (46131-2316)
PHONE..................317 738-2104
Sandy Brown, *Pt*
Gloria Crofts, *Pt*
EMP: 8 **EST:** 1980
SALES (est): 95.12K **Privately Held**
SIC: 7231 2844 Unisex hair salons; Shampoos, rinses, conditioners: hair

(G-5722)
CORPORATE SHIRTS DIRECT INC
2141 Holiday Ln (46131-2600)
PHONE..................317 474-6033
Matthew Mccall, *Prin*
EMP: 3 **EST:** 2008
SALES (est): 234.31K **Privately Held**
Web: www.corporateshirtsdirect.com
SIC: 2395 Embroidery products, except Schiffli machine

(G-5723)
COUNTERTOP CONNECTIONS INC
3042 Hudson St (46131-7203)
PHONE..................317 822-9858
Rocky Caudill, *Pr*
EMP: 9 **EST:** 1994
SQ FT: 3,600
SALES (est): 990.48K **Privately Held**
Web: www.countertopconnectionsinc.com
SIC: 2434 2541 Wood kitchen cabinets; Table or counter tops, plastic laminated

(G-5724)
CREATIVE COMPUTER SERVICES
4223 S Shelby 750 W (46131-9205)
PHONE..................317 729-5779
Sharon Romine-west, *Pr*
James West, *Mgr*
EMP: 6 **EST:** 1988
SALES (est): 400K **Privately Held**
Web: www.ccservices.com
SIC: 7389 2752 Mapmaking services; Maps, lithographed

(G-5725)
DIRECT CONVEYORS LLC
551 Earlywood Dr (46131-9712)
PHONE..................317 346-7777
John Van Kooten, *Pr*
Tyler Wood, *
◆ **EMP:** 30 **EST:** 2006
SALES (est): 4.86MM **Privately Held**
Web: www.directconveyors.com
SIC: 3535 Conveyors and conveying equipment

(G-5726)
DRANSFIELD & ASSOCIATES WLDG
8955 W Shelby (46131)
PHONE..................317 736-6281
Richard Dransfield, *Owner*
EMP: 1 **EST:** 1970
SALES (est): 49K **Privately Held**
SIC: 7692 Welding repair

(G-5727)
DUALTECH INC
Also Called: Innovative Casting Tech
450 Blue Chip Ct (46131-8825)
P.O. Box 476 (46131-0476)
PHONE..................317 738-9043
Jack Laugle, *Pr*
Sandy Laugle, *
Jason Best, *
EMP: 25 **EST:** 2002
SQ FT: 10,000
SALES (est): 4.48MM **Privately Held**
Web: www.innovative-castings.com
SIC: 3365 Aluminum foundries

(G-5728)
ELECTRO-SPEC INC
1800 Commerce Pkwy (46131-6964)
PHONE..................317 738-9199
Jeffrey D Smith, *Pr*
EMP: 85 **EST:** 1959
SQ FT: 20,500
SALES (est): 11.42MM **Privately Held**
Web: www.electro-spec.com
SIC: 3471 Electroplating of metals or formed products

(G-5729)
ESSEX FRKAWA MGNT WIRE USA LLC
Also Called: Superioir Essex
3200 Essex Dr (46131-9669)
PHONE..................317 738-4365
Dave Mackerel, *Brnch Mgr*
EMP: 27
Web: www.essexfurukawa.com
SIC: 3357 Magnet wire, nonferrous
HQ: Essex Furukawa Magnet Wire Usa Llc
5770 Pwr Frry Rd Nw Ste 3
Atlanta GA 30327
770 657-6000

(G-5730)
FAULKENBERG PRINTING CO INC
1670 Amy Ln (46131-1562)
PHONE..................317 638-1359
Thomas L Faulkenberg, *Pr*
James Eugene Faulkenberg, *Pr*
EMP: 17 **EST:** 1948
SQ FT: 5,300
SALES (est): 1.66MM **Privately Held**
Web: www.hightowergraphics.com
SIC: 2752 2789 2759 Offset printing; Bookbinding and related work; Commercial printing, nec

(G-5731)
G & H WIRE COMPANY INC (PA)
Also Called: G&H Orthodontics
40 Linville Way (46131)
PHONE..................317 346-6655
John Voskuil, *CEO*
Kevin Mcnulty, *Pr*
EMP: 60 **EST:** 2009
SALES (est): 10.14MM **Privately Held**
Web: www.ghorthodontics.com
SIC: 3843 Dental equipment and supplies

(G-5732)
GLOBAL
600 Ironwood Dr Ste N (46131-8324)
PHONE..................317 494-6174
Ken Smith, *Prin*
▲ **EMP:** 2 **EST:** 2011
SALES (est): 106.69K **Privately Held**
SIC: 5051 5021 3365 2522 Miscellaneous nonferrous products; Office and public building furniture; Aluminum foundries; Office furniture, except wood

(G-5733)
GMI CORPORATION
Also Called: GMI
700 International Dr (46131-9733)
PHONE..................317 736-5116
Fred Mcwilliams, *CEO*
Fred Mcwilliams, *Pr*
Loraine Mc Williams, *
EMP: 65 **EST:** 1989
SQ FT: 68,000
SALES (est): 9.68MM **Privately Held**
Web: www.gmicorp.com
SIC: 3599 Machine shop, jobbing and repair

(G-5734)
GOLDEN PRESS STUDIO
98 W Adams St (46131-1702)
PHONE..................765 318-7936
Jonathan Overmyer, *Prin*
EMP: 6 **EST:** 2016
SALES (est): 88.17K **Privately Held**
Web: www.goldenpressstudio.com

SIC: 2741 Miscellaneous publishing

(G-5735)
GOOD SIGNS
368 S Main St Ste 1 (46131-2414)
PHONE..................317 738-4663
Jim Crocker, *Owner*
EMP: 5 **EST:** 1984
SQ FT: 1,400
SALES (est): 200.03K **Privately Held**
Web: www.goodsignqc.com
SIC: 3993 Signs and advertising specialties

(G-5736)
GRAYSON THERMAL SYSTEMS CORP
Also Called: Grayson Automotive Systems
980 Hurricane Rd (46131-9501)
PHONE..................317 739-3290
Helene Cornils, *CEO*
EMP: 250 **EST:** 2015
SALES (est): 22.53MM
SALES (corp-wide): 45.95MM **Privately Held**
Web: www.graysonts.com
SIC: 3585 7699 Heating and air conditioning combination units; Thermostat repair
PA: Grayson Automotive Services Limited
Wharfdale House, 257 Wharfdale Road
Birmingham W MIDLANDS B11 2
121 700-5600

(G-5737)
HAGEMIER PRODUCTS
6181 S 550 E (46131-8001)
PHONE..................812 526-0377
Carolyn Hagemier, *Owner*
EMP: 9 **EST:** 1984
SALES (est): 566.78K **Privately Held**
SIC: 2448 Pallets, wood

(G-5738)
HENRY STREET LLC
1001 Hurricane St Ste 5 (46131)
PHONE..................317 788-7225
Carrie Lawrenece, *Admn*
EMP: 100 **EST:** 2007
SALES (est): 4.64MM **Privately Held**
SIC: 2448 Pallets, wood and metal combination

(G-5739)
HMI INVESTMENTS LLC
Also Called: Holbrook Manufacturing
291 Province Rd (46131-1453)
P.O. Box 95 (46131-0095)
PHONE..................317 736-9387
Jeffery M Pitcher, *Pr*
EMP: 30 **EST:** 1966
SQ FT: 16,400
SALES (est): 4.39MM **Privately Held**
Web: www.holbrookmfg.com
SIC: 3444 3599 Sheet metalwork; Machine shop, jobbing and repair

(G-5740)
HOBSON TOOL AND MACHINE CO
3061 N Morton St (46131-9662)
PHONE..................317 736-4203
Earl Hobson, *Pr*
EMP: 10 **EST:** 2007
SALES (est): 1.85MM **Privately Held**
Web: www.hobsontoolandmachine.com
SIC: 3599 Machine shop, jobbing and repair

(G-5741)
HONEY AND ME
2908 N Graham Rd # A (46131-9652)
PHONE..................317 668-3924
Tonya Pumey, *Prin*

GEOGRAPHIC SECTION

Franklin - Johnson County (G-5765)

▲ EMP: 7 EST: 2013
SALES (est): 462.21K **Privately Held**
Web: www.honeyandme.com
SIC: 5092 3944 Arts and crafts equipment and supplies; Games, toys, and children's vehicles

(G-5742)
HOVAIR AUTOMOTIVE LLC
Also Called: Hovair Automotive
211 Province St (46131-1453)
P.O. Box 474 (46131-0474)
PHONE..................317 738-0485
Jim Edwards, CEO
James M Edwards, *
David Benham, *
Jeff Hupke, *
▲ EMP: 40 EST: 2000
SQ FT: 60,000
SALES (est): 7.23MM **Privately Held**
Web: www.hovairauto.com
SIC: 3535 Conveyors and conveying equipment

(G-5743)
IBC US HOLDINGS INC
Also Called: IBC Advanced Alloys
401 Arvin Rd (46131-1549)
PHONE..................317 738-2558
Mark Wolma, Pr
David Anderson, Treas
Simon John Anderson, Dir
Anthony Dutton, Dir
▲ EMP: 7 EST: 2008
SALES (est): 1.25MM **Privately Held**
Web: www.ibcadvancedalloys.com
SIC: 3325 Steel foundries, nec

(G-5744)
INDIANA SCTION OF THE PROF GLF
2625 Hurricane Rd (46131-9263)
P.O. Box 26159 (46226-0159)
PHONE..................317 738-9696
EMP: 11 EST: 2010
SALES (est): 1.08MM **Privately Held**
Web: www.indianagolf.org
SIC: 3949 Shafts, golf club

(G-5745)
INDY TUBE FABRICATION LLC
398 Cincinnati St (46131-1415)
P.O. Box 98 (46131-0098)
PHONE..................317 883-2000
Brian Russle, Owner
EMP: 4 EST: 2007
SQ FT: 1,290
SALES (est): 373.64K **Privately Held**
Web: www.indytubefab.com
SIC: 3498 Tube fabricating (contract bending and shaping)

(G-5746)
INK - LLC
290 Fairway Lakes Dr (46131-8317)
P.O. Box 966 (46131-0966)
PHONE..................317 502-6473
EMP: 1 EST: 2005
SALES (est): 26.57K **Privately Held**
Web: www.introducingnewkoncepts.com
SIC: 3479 2899 5169 Rust proofing (hot dipping) of metals and formed products; Fuel tank or engine cleaning chemicals; Industrial chemicals

(G-5747)
INNOVATIVE 3D MFG LLC
600 International Dr (46131-9756)
PHONE..................317 560-5080
EMP: 3 EST: 2017
SALES (est): 251.23K **Privately Held**
Web: www.innovative3dm.com

SIC: 3599 3499 Machine shop, jobbing and repair; Friction material, made from powdered metal

(G-5748)
INNOVATIVE CASTING TECH INC
Also Called: Ict
2100 Earlywood Dr (46131-8870)
P.O. Box 462 (46131-0462)
PHONE..................317 738-5966
Jack W Laugle, Pr
Sandy Laugle, Sec
Bryan Lee Ciyou, Prin
EMP: 10 EST: 1997
SQ FT: 9,000
SALES (est): 2.43MM **Privately Held**
Web: www.innovative-castings.com
SIC: 3365 Aluminum foundries

(G-5749)
INTERNATIONAL FUEL SYSTEMS
751 International Dr (46131-9637)
PHONE..................317 345-3302
Patrick Boffo, Prin
EMP: 1 EST: 2010
SALES (est): 104.25K **Privately Held**
SIC: 2869 Fuels

(G-5750)
KYB AMERICAS CORPORATION (HQ)
2625 N Morton St (46131)
PHONE..................317 736-7774
Hiroaki Hirayama, Pr
A Tanaka, *
▲ EMP: 492 EST: 1987
SQ FT: 185,000
SALES (est): 196.27MM **Privately Held**
Web: www.kyb.com
SIC: 3714 8711 Shock absorbers, motor vehicle; Engineering services
PA: Kyb Corporation
2-4-1, Hamamatsucho
Minato-Ku TKY 105-0

(G-5751)
KYLE FABRICATION & WELDING LLC
200 W King St (46131-1634)
PHONE..................317 627-8537
EMP: 3 EST: 2019
SALES (est): 25.09K **Privately Held**
SIC: 7692 Welding repair

(G-5752)
LESHA AND WADE PRINTING SVCS
Also Called: L & W Printing Services
4242 E 500 S (46131-8167)
P.O. Box 116 (46131-0116)
PHONE..................317 738-4992
Lesha Lederman, Pr
Wade Lederman, VP
EMP: 4 EST: 1995
SALES (est): 260.44K **Privately Held**
Web: www.landwprinting.com
SIC: 2752 Offset printing

(G-5753)
LIFT WORKS INC
1726 S Centerline Rd (46131-8455)
PHONE..................812 797-0479
Zacheriah Cole, Pr
EMP: 4 EST: 2016
SALES (est): 228.12K **Privately Held**
Web: www.lift.works
SIC: 3728 Aircraft parts and equipment, nec

(G-5754)
MANN MADE MICROWAVE LLC
240 N Forsythe St (46131-1534)
PHONE..................317 407-1223
David K Mann, Admn

David Mann, Pr
EMP: 1 EST: 2016
SALES (est): 65.08K **Privately Held**
SIC: 3679 3678 Microwave components; Electronic connectors

(G-5755)
MCGINN TOOL & ENGINEERING CO
1001 Yandes St (46131-1468)
PHONE..................317 736-5512
Joseph L Hudson, Pr
Jacqueline Hudson, Sec
Joseph Alt, VP
EMP: 10 EST: 1974
SQ FT: 5,200
SALES (est): 819.75K **Privately Held**
Web: www.mcginntool.com
SIC: 3544 7692 Special dies and tools; Welding repair

(G-5756)
MICROWAVE DEVICES INC
240 N Forsythe St (46131)
PHONE..................317 868-8833
David Mann, Pr
Saralee Mann, Sec
EMP: 7 EST: 1981
SQ FT: 3,000
SALES (est): 550.62K **Privately Held**
Web: www.mwdevices.com
SIC: 3679 3663 Microwave components; Radio and t.v. communications equipment

(G-5757)
MILLER CHEMICAL TECH & MGT INC
Also Called: Miller Chemical Tech & MGT
980 Hurricane Rd Ste B (46131-9501)
PHONE..................317 560-5437
Anthony Mccullough, Pr
Patricia Mccullough, Sec
Michael Mccullough, VP
EMP: 7 EST: 1991
SALES (est): 727.6K **Privately Held**
SIC: 2899 Chemical preparations, nec

(G-5758)
MITSUBSHI TRBCHRGER ENG AMER I
1200 N Mitsubishi Pkwy Ste A (46131-7560)
PHONE..................317 346-5291
Yoshifumi Nuruyu, Contrlr
EMP: 28
Web: www.mitsubishi-turbo.com
SIC: 3566 Speed changers (power transmission equipment), except auto
HQ: Mitsubishi Turbocharger And Engine America, Inc.
2 Pierce Pl Ste 1100
Itasca IL 60143
630 268-0750

(G-5759)
NF INDUSTRIES INC
401 Arvin Rd (46131-1549)
PHONE..................317 738-2558
Denis B Brady, Pr
EMP: 9 EST: 1945
SALES (est): 402.07K **Privately Held**
SIC: 3999 Atomizers, toiletry

(G-5760)
NITREX INC
350 Blue Chip Ct (46131-8824)
PHONE..................317 346-7700
Chris Morawski, Pr
EMP: 21 EST: 2002
SQ FT: 16,000
SALES (est): 4.56MM **Privately Held**
Web: www.nitrex.com

SIC: 3398 Metal heat treating

(G-5761)
NONFERROUS PRODUCTS INC
Also Called: IBC Advanced Alloys Copper
401 Arvin Rd (46131-1549)
P.O. Box 349 (46131-0349)
PHONE..................317 738-2558
Mark Wolma, Pr
▼ EMP: 40 EST: 1994
SQ FT: 75,000
SALES (est): 8.59MM
SALES (corp-wide): 28.55MM **Privately Held**
Web: www.nonferrousproducts.com
SIC: 3312 3369 Blast furnaces and steel mills; Nonferrous foundries, nec
PA: Ibc Advanced Alloys Corp
1200-570 Granville St
Vancouver BC V6C 3
604 685-6263

(G-5762)
NSK PRECISION AMERICA INC
Also Called: NSK Prcsion Amer Bllscrew Plan
3450 Bearing Dr (46131-9660)
PHONE..................317 738-5000
Christopher Swartwout, Pr
EMP: 84
Web: www.nsk.com
SIC: 3562 3714 3568 3452 Ball and roller bearings; Motor vehicle parts and accessories; Power transmission equipment, nec; Bolts, nuts, rivets, and washers
HQ: Nsk Precision America, Inc.
3450 Bearing Dr
Franklin IN 46131
317 738-5000

(G-5763)
ORTHODONTIC DESIGN & PROD INC (PA)
Also Called: O D P
40 Linville Way (46131-5600)
PHONE..................317 346-6655
▲ EMP: 38 EST: 1992
SQ FT: 13,000
SALES (est): 2.56MM **Privately Held**
Web: www.ghorthodontics.com
SIC: 3843 3369 5047 Orthodontic appliances; Nonferrous foundries, nec; Dental equipment and supplies

(G-5764)
PALMARY AMERICA LLC
1880 Northwood Plz (46131-1037)
PHONE..................317 494-1415
EMP: 6
SALES (est): 262.96K **Privately Held**
Web: www.palmaryamerica.com
SIC: 3541 Machine tools, metal cutting type

(G-5765)
PATRIOT PRODUCTS LLC
Also Called: Patriot Products
2011 Earlywood Dr (46131-8871)
P.O. Box 747 (46131-0747)
PHONE..................317 736-8007
Kathleen M Johnson, CEO
Jerry Johnson, Pr
Daniel Johnson, Contract Member
Mike Saunders, VP
▲ EMP: 12 EST: 2008
SALES (est): 3.49MM **Privately Held**
Web: www.patriotproductsllc.com
SIC: 3599 Machine shop, jobbing and repair

Franklin - Johnson County (G-5766)

GEOGRAPHIC SECTION

(G-5766)
PILKINGTON NORTH AMERICA INC
1001 Hurricane St (46131-1550)
PHONE..................317 346-0621
Susan Gilbert, *Mgr*
EMP: 8
Web: www.pilkington.com
SIC: 3211 Construction glass
HQ: Pilkington North America, Inc.
    811 Madison Ave
    Toledo OH 43604
    419 247-3731

(G-5767)
POLYTEK DEVELOPMENT CORP
2140 Earlywood Dr (46131-8870)
PHONE..................317 494-6420
EMP: 1
SALES (corp-wide): 55.55MM **Privately Held**
Web: www.polytek.com
SIC: 3087 2851 2821 Custom compound purchased resins; Paints and allied products; Plastics materials and resins
PA: Polytek Development Corp.
    55 Hilton St
    Easton PA 18042
    610 559-8620

(G-5768)
POWDER METAL TECHNICIANS INC
1565 Graham St (46131-9722)
P.O. Box 358 (46142-0358)
PHONE..................317 353-2812
Riley Bennett, *Prin*
EMP: 3 EST: 2001
SALES (est): 311.19K **Privately Held**
Web: www.pmtpress.com
SIC: 3599 Machine shop, jobbing and repair

(G-5769)
PREFERRED SHTMTL FBRCATION LLC
299 Cincinnati St (46131-1438)
PHONE..................317 494-6232
Richard Parks, *Prin*
EMP: 6 EST: 2019
SALES (est): 125.97K **Privately Held**
Web: www.sheet-metal-fabrication.com
SIC: 3444 Sheet metalwork

(G-5770)
PRIDGEON & CLAY INC
150 Arvin Rd (46131-1485)
PHONE..................317 738-4885
Doug Hooyer, *Mgr*
EMP: 4
SALES (corp-wide): 99.72MM **Privately Held**
Web: www.pridgeonandclay.com
SIC: 4225 3714 3465 3429 General warehousing and storage; Motor vehicle parts and accessories; Automotive stampings; Hardware, nec
PA: Pridgeon & Clay, Inc.
    50 Cottage Grove St Sw
    Grand Rapids MI 49507
    616 241-5675

(G-5771)
RCO-REED CORPORATION
Also Called: Reed Manufacturing Services
1050 Eastview Dr (46131-9588)
PHONE..................317 736-8014
Samuel Reed, *Pr*
▲ EMP: 25 EST: 1965
SQ FT: 30,000
SALES (est): 3.67MM **Privately Held**
Web: www.reedmfgservices.com

SIC: 3451 Screw machine products

(G-5772)
REDHEAD PUBLISHING LLC
4129 N 75 W (46131-8343)
PHONE..................317 535-7400
Kathy Mueller, *Prin*
EMP: 6 EST: 2014
SALES (est): 127.37K **Privately Held**
SIC: 2741 Miscellaneous publishing

(G-5773)
REDI/CONTROLS INC
161 R J Pkwy (46131-7399)
PHONE..................317 494-6600
Mark Key, *CEO*
Lenora Key, *Sec*
Walter Key, *Treas*
EMP: 6 EST: 1989
SQ FT: 30,000
SALES (est): 1.05MM **Privately Held**
Web: www.redicontrols.com
SIC: 3585 Refrigeration and heating equipment

(G-5774)
RMO INC (PA)
Also Called: Rocky Mountain Orthodontics
2165 Earlywood Dr (46131-8879)
P.O. Box 17085 (80217-0085)
PHONE..................303 592-8200
Jody Whitson, *Pr*
Martin Brusse, *
Mary Wingert, *
Susan Hiatt, *
EMP: 200 EST: 1930
SALES (est): 24.14MM
SALES (corp-wide): 24.14MM **Privately Held**
Web: www.rmortho.com
SIC: 3843 Orthodontic appliances

(G-5775)
ROY UMBARGER AND SONS INC
186 S 600 E (46131-6501)
PHONE..................317 422-5195
Roy Martin Umbarger, *Pr*
Thomas Umbarger, *Sec*
Umbarger Jackson, *Sec*
EMP: 14 EST: 1939
SALES (est): 5.26MM **Privately Held**
Web: www.umbargerandsons.com
SIC: 5153 5191 2879 2875 Grain elevators; Fertilizer and fertilizer materials; Agricultural chemicals, nec; Fertilizers, mixing only

(G-5776)
SHELBY GRAVEL INC
451 Arvin Rd (46131-1549)
PHONE..................317 738-3445
Gary Simpson, *Brnch Mgr*
EMP: 16
SALES (corp-wide): 74.83MM **Privately Held**
Web: www.shelbymaterials.com
SIC: 3273 3271 1442 Ready-mixed concrete; Blocks, concrete or cinder: standard; Construction sand and gravel
PA: Shelby Gravel, Inc
    157 E Rampart St
    Shelbyville IN 46176
    317 398-4485

(G-5777)
SMART TECHNOLOGIES LLC
317 E Creekside Ct W (46131-8993)
PHONE..................317 738-4338
EMP: 3
SQ FT: 5,000
SALES (est): 253.53K **Privately Held**

SIC: 3714 5013 Fuel systems and parts, motor vehicle; Automotive brakes

(G-5778)
STEM POINT LLC
4828 E 300 N (46131-8735)
PHONE..................352 870-0122
EMP: 2
SALES (est): 97.4K **Privately Held**
SIC: 2836 7389 Veterinary biological products; Business Activities at Non-Commercial Site

(G-5779)
STEVES MACHINING & REWORK
1299 Paris Dr (46131-8559)
PHONE..................317 500-4627
Steve Woodcock, *Prin*
EMP: 6 EST: 2010
SALES (est): 71.22K **Privately Held**
SIC: 3599 Machine shop, jobbing and repair

(G-5780)
SWISS LABS MACHINE & ENGRG INC
2854 N Graham Rd (46131-7676)
PHONE..................317 346-6190
Joe Bowman, *Pr*
EMP: 6 EST: 2004
SQ FT: 4,000
SALES (est): 929.84K **Privately Held**
Web: www.swisslabinc.com
SIC: 3599 Machine shop, jobbing and repair

(G-5781)
TEST RITE SYSTEMS & MFG CO LLC
1650 N 800 E (46131-7307)
P.O. Box 372 (46131-0372)
PHONE..................317 736-9192
Michael Kaiser, *Owner*
EMP: 2 EST: 1986
SQ FT: 7,050
SALES (est): 220.09K **Privately Held**
SIC: 3599 Machine shop, jobbing and repair

(G-5782)
THERMAX INC
1725 N Graham Rd (46131-9726)
PHONE..................978 844-2528
Adam Gawley, *Pdt Mgr*
EMP: 1
Web: www.chartindustries.com
SIC: 3443 Fabricated plate work (boiler shop)
HQ: Thermax, Inc.
    407 7th St Nw
    New Prague MN 56071
    508 999-1231

(G-5783)
TOMLINSON MANUFACTURING CO
1421 Amy Ln (46131-1491)
PHONE..................765 719-3700
Tom Tomlinson, *Prin*
EMP: 7 EST: 2019
SALES (est): 598.65K **Privately Held**
Web: www.tomlinsonmfg.com
SIC: 3444 Sheet metal specialties, not stamped

(G-5784)
W T BOONE ENTERPRISES INC
159 Cincinnati St (46131-1751)
P.O. Box 344 (46131-0344)
PHONE..................317 738-0275
William T Boone, *Pr*
Paula S Boone, *VP*
EMP: 7 EST: 1993
SALES (est): 862.17K **Privately Held**
Web: www.wtboone.com

SIC: 3599 7371 Machine shop, jobbing and repair; Computer software systems analysis and design, custom

(G-5785)
WAYNE DAVID INCORPORATED
2441 S 25 W (46131-8450)
PHONE..................317 417-7165
David Bleke, *Pr*
EMP: 2 EST: 2008
SALES (est): 252.83K **Privately Held**
Web: www.davidbleke.com
SIC: 3714 Motor vehicle parts and accessories

(G-5786)
WENDELL DENTON
4257 S 200 E (46131-8978)
PHONE..................317 736-8397
Wendell Denton, *Owner*
EMP: 4 EST: 2001
SALES (est): 187.6K **Privately Held**
SIC: 3399 Primary metal products

(G-5787)
WESLEYS PALLETS & HEAT TREAT
6181 S 550 E (46131-8001)
PHONE..................812 526-0377
Eugene Harrell Wesley, *Prin*
Joshua E F Wesley, *Prin*
Joshua Wesley, *VP*
EMP: 1 EST: 2006
SALES (est): 187.51K **Privately Held**
SIC: 3398 Metal heat treating

(G-5788)
WK-RPE INC
1424 Commerce Pkwy (46131)
PHONE..................317 739-3543
EMP: 8 EST: 1996
SALES (est): 870.4K **Privately Held**
Web: www.rpemachining.com
SIC: 3599 Machine shop, jobbing and repair

(G-5789)
XL GRAPHICS INC
Also Called: Spotlight Strategies
170 Commerce Dr (46131-7312)
P.O. Box 155 (46131-0155)
PHONE..................317 738-3434
Susan Mccarty, *Pr*
Erin Smith, *VP*
EMP: 10 EST: 1993
SQ FT: 15,000
SALES (est): 2.08MM **Privately Held**
Web: www.spotlight-strategies.com
SIC: 2759 3993 2791 2752 Promotional printing; Signs and advertising specialties; Typographic composition, for the printing trade; Offset printing

Frankton
Madison County

(G-5790)
E & M MACHINING
204 S Washington St (46044)
PHONE..................765 754-3613
Eric G Erwman, *Owner*
EMP: 1 EST: 1998
SALES (est): 8.53K **Privately Held**
Web: www.emmachining.com
SIC: 3599 Machine shop, jobbing and repair

(G-5791)
FOUR STAR PRINTING
1001 E Sigler St (46044-9344)
PHONE..................765 620-9728
EMP: 4 EST: 2017

SALES (est): 112.95K **Privately Held**
Web: www.fourstarprinting.com
SIC: 2752 Offset printing

(G-5792)
INTERSTATE STEEL ERECTORS INC (PA)
Also Called: Interstate Steel Fabricating
1110 E Sigler St (46044)
P.O. Box 455 (46001)
PHONE.................................765 754-7508
James K Harris, *Pr*
EMP: 13 EST: 1995
SQ FT: 10,000
SALES (est): 4.68MM
SALES (corp-wide): 4.68MM **Privately Held**
Web: www.interstatesteelfab.com
SIC: 3441 Fabricated structural metal

Fredericksburg
Washington County

(G-5793)
FIRST MIRACLE LLC
8518 S Kays Chapel Rd (47120-8501)
PHONE.................................812 472-3527
Jean Sickels, *Prin*
EMP: 6 EST: 2010
SALES (est): 228.09K **Privately Held**
SIC: 2084 Wines

(G-5794)
JONES MACHINE & TOOL INC
14710 N Crossroad Nw (47120)
PHONE.................................812 364-4588
Danny Jones, *Pr*
EMP: 45 EST: 1993
SQ FT: 12,000
SALES (est): 8.67MM **Privately Held**
Web: www.jmttool.com
SIC: 3089 3544 3545 3599 Injection molded finished plastics products, nec; Industrial molds; Machine tool accessories; Machine shop, jobbing and repair

(G-5795)
P&C PRIME LLC
9879 S Bullington Rd (47120-8721)
PHONE.................................231 420-3650
George Marks, *Managing Member*
EMP: 12 EST: 2018
SALES (est): 1.6MM **Privately Held**
Web: www.pandctesting.com
SIC: 3825 4911 7389 Engine electrical test equipment; Electric services; Business Activities at Non-Commercial Site

(G-5796)
SCREENS
Also Called: Cervantes-Screens
6750 W Nesmith Rd (47120-8818)
PHONE.................................812 472-3274
Mary Cervantes, *Owner*
EMP: 1 EST: 1987
SALES (est): 57.97K **Privately Held**
SIC: 2395 2759 Embroidery products, except Schiffli machine; Screen printing

Freedom
Owen County

(G-5797)
AXTROM INDS PALLET DIV LLC
Also Called: Axtrom Industries/Pallat Div
170 Mt Calvery Rd (47431-7216)
PHONE.................................812 859-4873
Thomas E Chandler, *CEO*
EMP: 7 EST: 1990
SALES (est): 232.07K **Privately Held**
SIC: 2448 Pallets, wood

(G-5798)
AYNES UPHOLSTERY LLC
Also Called: Aynes Custom Upholstery
3220 Dunn Rd (47431-7092)
PHONE.................................812 829-1321
EMP: 2 EST: 2009
SALES (est): 181.5K **Privately Held**
Web: www.aynes.biz
SIC: 1799 2521 Home/office interiors finishing, furnishing and remodeling; Wood office furniture

(G-5799)
ELIZABETH A TAYLOR
7675 Ault Rd (47431-7009)
PHONE.................................815 353-4798
Elizabeth Taylor, *Owner*
EMP: 1 EST: 2014
SALES (est): 51.14K **Privately Held**
SIC: 2299 0279 7999 0752 Preparing textile fibers for spinning (scouring and combing); Domestic animal farms; Arts and crafts instruction; Breeding services, pet and animal specialties (not horses)

(G-5800)
FREEDOM VALLEY CABINETS
7483 Old Glory Ln (47431-7226)
PHONE.................................717 606-2811
EMP: 8 EST: 1992
SALES (est): 879.67K **Privately Held**
Web: www.fvcabinets.com
SIC: 2541 1751 Cabinets, except refrigerated: show, display, etc.: wood; Cabinet and finish carpentry

(G-5801)
HESSIT WORKS INC
4181 S Us Highway 231 (47431-7329)
PHONE.................................812 829-6246
Friedrich Naether, *Pr*
Idella Naether, *VP*
▲ EMP: 6 EST: 1982
SALES (est): 482.1K **Privately Held**
Web: www.hessit.net
SIC: 3271 3272 Paving blocks, concrete; Concrete products, precast, nec

(G-5802)
LAKESIDE WOODWORKING
10915 Hauser Rd (47431-7181)
PHONE.................................812 687-7901
Leroy Graber, *Owner*
EMP: 4 EST: 2006
SALES (est): 151.11K **Privately Held**
Web: www.lakesidewoodworking.ca
SIC: 2434 Wood kitchen cabinets

Freelandville
Knox County

(G-5803)
M & M SERVICE CO WLDG & REPR
Also Called: M & M Service Co
Hwy 159 S (47535)
P.O. Box 323 (47535-0323)
PHONE.................................812 328-6195
Michael Moore, *Owner*
EMP: 1 EST: 1980
SALES (est): 44K **Privately Held**
SIC: 7692 Welding repair

Freetown
Jackson County

(G-5804)
MCPHEETERS AND ASSOCIATES INC
7517 Becks Grove Rd (47235-9656)
PHONE.................................812 988-2840
Charles Mcpheeters, *Prin*
EMP: 5 EST: 2016
SALES (est): 149.82K **Privately Held**
Web: www.realtycapitallg.com
SIC: 3999 Manufacturing industries, nec

(G-5805)
TWIN WILLOWS LLC
Also Called: Salt Creek Winery
7603 W County Road 925 N (47235-8530)
PHONE.................................812 497-0254
Adrian Lee, *Prin*
Nichole Lee, *Prin*
EMP: 2 EST: 2010
SALES (est): 158.06K **Privately Held**
Web: www.saltcreekwinery.com
SIC: 2084 Wines

Fremont
Steuben County

(G-5806)
ACS GRAPHICS INC
103 N Wayne St (46737-2083)
P.O. Box 330 (46737-0330)
PHONE.................................260 495-7446
Andy Stroh, *Owner*
EMP: 1 EST: 1995
SALES (est): 95.15K **Privately Held**
Web: www.acsgraphics.com
SIC: 3993 Signs, not made in custom sign painting shops

(G-5807)
ALLEGHENY COATINGS RE LLC
Also Called: Allegheny Coatings
302 E Mcswain Dr (46737-2102)
PHONE.................................260 495-4445
Steve Quinn, *Managing Member*
EMP: 16 EST: 2014
SALES (est): 2.31MM **Privately Held**
Web: www.all-coat.com
SIC: 3479 Coating of metals and formed products

(G-5808)
AMERICAN AXLE & MFG INC
Also Called: AAM Powertrain
307 S Tillotson St (46737-2157)
PHONE.................................260 495-4315
EMP: 21
SALES (corp-wide): 6.08B **Publicly Held**
Web: www.aam.com
SIC: 3714 Rear axle housings, motor vehicle
HQ: American Axle & Manufacturing, Inc.
One Dauch Dr
Detroit MI 48211

(G-5809)
BARRY A WILCOX
207 S Wayne St (46737-2089)
P.O. Box 121 (46737-0121)
PHONE.................................260 495-3677
Melissa A Wilcox, *Prin*
Melissa A Wilcox, *Owner*
EMP: 2 EST: 2012
SALES (est): 147.8K **Privately Held**
SIC: 2511 Wood household furniture

(G-5810)
BATTLE CREEK EQUIPMENT CO (PA)
Also Called: Battle Creek Health Eqp Co
702 S Reed Rd (46737-2098)
P.O. Box 629 (46737-0629)
PHONE.................................260 495-3472
David Underhill, *Pr*
Joyce Underhill, *
▲ EMP: 40 EST: 1957
SQ FT: 28,000
SALES (est): 4.75MM
SALES (corp-wide): 4.75MM **Privately Held**
Web: www.battlecreekequipment.com
SIC: 3949 3842 3634 Sporting and athletic goods, nec; Surgical appliances and supplies; Electric housewares and fans

(G-5811)
BERRY GLOBAL INC
701 E Depot St (46737-2119)
PHONE.................................260 495-2000
EMP: 7
Web: www.berryglobal.com
SIC: 3089 Plastics containers, except foam
HQ: Berry Global, Inc.
101 Oakley St
Evansville IN 47710

(G-5812)
BRIALI VINEYARDS LLC
Also Called: Briali Vineyards
102 W State Road 120 (46737-8875)
PHONE.................................260 316-5156
Bronislaw Sarosek, *Bd of Dir*
EMP: 3 EST: 2011
SALES (est): 223.65K **Privately Held**
Web: www.brialivineyards.com
SIC: 2084 Wines

(G-5813)
CARDINAL GLASS INDUSTRIES INC
Also Called: Cardina L G
301 E Mcswain Dr (46737-2102)
P.O. Box 99 (46737-0099)
PHONE.................................260 495-4105
Jim Devaney, *Genl Mgr*
EMP: 331
SALES (corp-wide): 1B **Privately Held**
Web: www.cardinalcorp.com
SIC: 3231 5031 Products of purchased glass; Lumber, plywood, and millwork
PA: Cardinal Glass Industries Inc
775 Pririe Ctr Dr Ste 200
Eden Prairie MN 55344
952 229-2600

(G-5814)
CARVER NON-WOVEN INDIANA LLC ✪
706 E Depot St (46737-2119)
PHONE.................................260 627-0033
Mark Glidden, *Managing Member*
EMP: 4 EST: 2022
SALES (est): 62.01K **Privately Held**
Web: www.carvernonwoven.com
SIC: 2297 Nonwoven fabrics

(G-5815)
CARVER NON-WOVEN TECH LLC
706 E Depot St (46737-2119)
PHONE.................................260 627-0033
Mark Glidden, *Pr*
EMP: 149 EST: 2015
SALES (est): 26.04MM
SALES (corp-wide): 27.54MM **Privately Held**
Web: www.r3composites.com
SIC: 2297 Nonwoven fabrics
PA: R3 Composites Corp.
14123 Roth Rd

Grabill IN 46741
260 627-0033

(G-5816)
COLD HEADING CO
900 S Cassell St (46737-2116)
P.O. Box 947 (46737-0947)
PHONE..................................260 495-7003
Ryan Boekhout, *Brnch Mgr*
EMP: 35
SALES (corp-wide): 78.82MM **Privately Held**
Web: www.coldheading.com
SIC: 3452 Bolts, metal
HQ: The Cold Heading Co
21777 Hoover Rd
Warren MI 48089
586 497-7000

(G-5817)
COLD HEADING CO
401 E Sidel St (46737-2138)
P.O. Box 394 (46737-0394)
PHONE..................................260 495-4222
Dominic Blasutti, *Brnch Mgr*
EMP: 35
SALES (corp-wide): 78.82MM **Privately Held**
Web: www.coldheading.com
SIC: 3452 Bolts, metal
HQ: The Cold Heading Co
21777 Hoover Rd
Warren MI 48089
586 497-7000

(G-5818)
DALTECH ENTERPRISES INC
Also Called: Daltech Force
810 S Broad St (46737-2113)
P.O. Box 66 (46737-0066)
PHONE..................................260 527-4590
Alex Dallas, *Pr*
Alexander Dallas, *Pr*
EMP: 8 EST: 2015
SALES (est): 705.02K **Privately Held**
Web: www.daltechenterprises.com
SIC: 3199 Holsters, leather

(G-5819)
DAVENPORT MFG GROUP LLC ✪
301 W Water St (46737-2162)
PHONE..................................260 495-1818
Michael Owen Miller, *Pr*
EMP: 43 EST: 2023
SALES (est): 5.11MM **Privately Held**
SIC: 3441 7389 Fabricated structural metal; Business services, nec

(G-5820)
DEXTER AXLE COMPANY
Also Called: Dexter Axle
301 W Pearl St (46737-2049)
PHONE..................................260 495-5100
Jerry Nusbaum, *Mgr*
EMP: 100
SALES (corp-wide): 1.41B **Privately Held**
Web: www.dexteraxle.com
SIC: 3714 Axle housings and shafts, motor vehicle
HQ: Dexter Axle Company Llc
2900 Industrial Pkwy E
Elkhart IN 46516

(G-5821)
FREMONT COATINGS DIV
302 E Mcswain Dr (46737-2102)
P.O. Box 659 (46737-0659)
PHONE..................................260 495-4445
Tammy Zarate, *Contrlr*
EMP: 6 EST: 2017
SALES (est): 210.1K **Privately Held**

SIC: 3398 Metal heat treating

(G-5822)
GENERAL ALUMINUM MFG COMPANY
Metalloy Fremont Division
303 E Swager St (46737-2148)
P.O. Box 757 (46737-0757)
PHONE..................................260 495-2600
Thomas Abernathey, *Mgr*
EMP: 124
Web: www.generalaluminum.com
SIC: 3363 3545 3365 Aluminum die-castings; Machine tool accessories; Aluminum foundries
HQ: General Aluminum Mfg. Llc
5159 S Prospect St
Ravenna OH 44266
330 297-1225

(G-5823)
INDUSTRIAL REP INC
1184 E State Road 120 (46737-9686)
P.O. Box 830 (46703-0830)
PHONE..................................260 316-4973
EMP: 1 EST: 2010
SQ FT: 2,400
SALES (est): 239.09K **Privately Held**
Web: www.mrotracking.com
SIC: 3599 Machine shop, jobbing and repair

(G-5824)
JAMES LAKE VINEYARD INC
Also Called: Satek Winery
6208 N Van Guilder Rd (46737-9340)
PHONE..................................260 495-9463
Larry Satek, *Pt*
Pam Satek, *Pt*
EMP: 9 EST: 2001
SALES (est): 976.05K **Privately Held**
Web: www.satekwinery.com
SIC: 2084 5921 Wines; Wine

(G-5825)
KOESTER METALS INC
Also Called: K M I
301 W Water St (46737-2162)
PHONE..................................260 495-1818
EMP: 50
Web: www.kmienclosures.com
SIC: 3469 3699 3444 Electronic enclosures, stamped or pressed metal; Electrical equipment and supplies, nec; Sheet metalwork

(G-5826)
LAGRANGE PRODUCTS INC
607 S Wayne St (46737-2170)
P.O. Box 658 (46737-0658)
PHONE..................................260 495-3025
Lynn Blue, *CEO*
EMP: 105 EST: 1962
SQ FT: 60,000
SALES (est): 18.79MM **Privately Held**
Web: www.lagrangeproducts.com
SIC: 3443 Tanks, lined: metal plate

(G-5827)
MOYER PROCESS & CONTROLS CO
105 N Wayne St (46737-2083)
P.O. Box 935 (46737-0935)
PHONE..................................260 495-2405
Jeffrey Duguid, *Pr*
EMP: 4 EST: 1985
SQ FT: 2,400
SALES (est): 433.3K **Privately Held**
Web: www.moyercompanies.com
SIC: 3829 Physical property testing equipment

(G-5828)
NEW HORIZONS BAKING CO LLC
700 W Water St (46737-2165)
P.O. Box 695 (46737-0695)
PHONE..................................260 495-7055
Mark Duke, *Brnch Mgr*
EMP: 116
SALES (corp-wide): 57.51MM **Privately Held**
Web: www.newhorizonsbaking.com
SIC: 2051 Bakery: wholesale or wholesale/retail combined
PA: New Horizons Baking Company, Llc
211 Woodlawn Ave
Norwalk OH 44857
419 668-8226

(G-5829)
NOB HILL VINEYARDS LLC
844 S Clear Lake Dr (46737-8866)
PHONE..................................260 402-6070
Kay Kummer, *Managing Member*
EMP: 4 EST: 2007
SALES (est): 111.46K **Privately Held**
SIC: 2084 Wines, brandy, and brandy spirits

(G-5830)
NORTHERN TOOL & DIE LLC
501 E Depot St (46737-2117)
P.O. Box 941 (46737-0941)
PHONE..................................260 495-7314
Carl Coburn, *Owner*
EMP: 4 EST: 1987
SQ FT: 4,000
SALES (est): 400.82K **Privately Held**
SIC: 3544 Special dies and tools

(G-5831)
PFC FARM SERVICES INC ✪
3204 N 250 E (46737-9789)
PHONE..................................260 235-0817
EMP: 5 EST: 2022
SALES (est): 78.58K **Privately Held**
Web: www.pfcfarmservices.com
SIC: 2411 0851 1629 Logging; Forestry services; Land clearing contractor

(G-5832)
REES INC
405 S Reed Rd (46737-2129)
P.O. Box 652 (46737-0652)
PHONE..................................260 495-9811
Debra Kolbow, *Pr*
EMP: 15 EST: 1970
SQ FT: 32,400
SALES (est): 2.33MM **Privately Held**
Web: www.reesinc.com
SIC: 5211 3822 3643 Electrical construction materials; Environmental controls; Current-carrying wiring services

(G-5833)
RICHTERS MACHINE & TOOL
4395 E 300 N (46737-9780)
PHONE..................................260 495-5327
Michael P Richter, *Owner*
EMP: 3 EST: 1999
SALES (est): 286.43K **Privately Held**
SIC: 3599 Machine shop, jobbing and repair

(G-5834)
RICKLES PICKLES LLC
103 W Toledo St (46737-2069)
P.O. Box 490 (46737-0490)
PHONE..................................260 495-9024
EMP: 4 EST: 2008
SALES (est): 202.64K **Privately Held**
Web: www.ricklespickles.com
SIC: 2035 Pickles, vinegar

(G-5835)
SONOCO TEQ LLC
Also Called: Fremont Plastics
500 W Water St (46737-2163)
PHONE..................................260 495-9842
Lyndon Tucker, *Pr*
EMP: 8
SALES (corp-wide): 6.78B **Publicly Held**
Web: www.teqnow.com
SIC: 3089 Injection molding of plastics
HQ: Sonoco Teq Llc
11320 Main St
Huntley IL 60142

(G-5836)
SUR-LOC INC
501 E Swager St (46737-2149)
P.O. Box 750 (46737-0750)
PHONE..................................260 495-4065
Tim Swager, *Pr*
Lee Swager, *Sec*
EMP: 10 EST: 1987
SQ FT: 5,000
SALES (est): 801.26K **Privately Held**
Web: www.sur-loc.com
SIC: 3429 3444 Hardware, nec; Sheet metalwork

(G-5837)
SWAGER COMMUNICATIONS INC
501 E Swager St (46737)
P.O. Box 656 (46737)
PHONE..................................260 495-2515
Lee Swager, *Pr*
Dan J Swager, *Pr*
Lee Swager, *VP*
Tim Swager, *Sec*
EMP: 22 EST: 1985
SQ FT: 40,000
SALES (est): 4.9MM **Privately Held**
Web: www.swager.com
SIC: 3441 1623 Tower sections, radio and television transmission; Transmitting tower (telecommunication) construction

(G-5838)
V & P PRINTING
3655 N 300 E (46737-9784)
PHONE..................................260 495-3741
Vernon Strang, *Owner*
EMP: 2 EST: 1979
SALES (est): 74.13K **Privately Held**
SIC: 2759 2752 Commercial printing, nec; Commercial printing, lithographic

(G-5839)
WENZEL ACQUISITION INC
5610 N West St (46737)
P.O. Box 708 (46737-0708)
PHONE..................................260 495-9898
Matt Trubergen, *Pr*
EMP: 8 EST: 2004
SALES (est): 108.37K **Privately Held**
SIC: 3469 Spinning metal for the trade

(G-5840)
WENZEL METAL SPINNING INC (PA)
Also Called: Wenzel Metal Spinning
701 W Water St (46737-2165)
P.O. Box 708 (46737-0708)
PHONE..................................260 495-9898
Matthew Tubergen, *Pr*
Mark H Quinlivan, *
EMP: 58 EST: 1982
SQ FT: 70,000
SALES (est): 8.71MM **Privately Held**
Web: www.wenzelmetalspinning.com
SIC: 3469 Stamping metal for the trade

GEOGRAPHIC SECTION

Garrett - Dekalb County (G-5863)

(G-5841)
WENZEL METAL SPINNING INC IND
Also Called: Wenzel Metal Spinning
701 W Water St (46737-2165)
P.O. Box 708 (46737-0708)
PHONE..................260 495-9898
Thomas J Wenzel, Pr
James Hornbacher, Marketing*
EMP: 17 EST: 1982
SQ FT: 70,000
SALES (est): 318.18K Privately Held
Web: www.wenzelmetalspinning.com
SIC: 3469 Spinning metal for the trade

(G-5842)
WESTERN CONSOLIDATED TECH INC (DH)
700 W Swager St (46737-2145)
P.O. Box 657 (46737-0657)
PHONE..................260 495-9866
Michael J Kelly, Ch
Kevin Kelly, *
EMP: 75 EST: 1983
SQ FT: 185,000
SALES (est): 14.18MM
SALES (corp-wide): 142.12MM Privately Held
Web: www.kelcoind.com
SIC: 3089 3544 3643 3625 Plastics processing; Forms (molds), for foundry and plastics working machinery; Current-carrying wiring services; Relays and industrial controls
HQ: Guardian Electric Manufacturing Co.
1425 Lake Ave
Woodstock IL 60098
815 334-3600

French Lick
Orange County

(G-5843)
AHF INDUSTRIES INC
Also Called: Pluto
8647 W State Road 56 (47432-9390)
P.O. Box 391 (47432-0391)
PHONE..................812 936-9988
Michael J Kelley, Pr
Alan J Friedman, *
Bernice Friedman, *
▲ EMP: 210 EST: 1913
SQ FT: 120,000
SALES (est): 24.66MM Privately Held
Web: www.plutocorp.com
SIC: 7389 3085 Packaging and labeling services; Plastics bottles

(G-5844)
BEAR HOLLOW WOOD CARVERS
469 S Maple St (47432-1006)
PHONE..................812 936-3030
EMP: 3 EST: 2010
SALES (est): 243.65K Privately Held
Web: www.bearhollowwoodcarvers.com
SIC: 2431 Millwork

(G-5845)
FRENCH LICK AUTO SIGNS (PA)
9451 W State Road 56 (47432-8102)
P.O. Box 222 (47469-0222)
PHONE..................812 936-7777
Larry Kalb, Owner
EMP: 4 EST: 2005
SALES (est): 1.03MM
SALES (corp-wide): 1.03MM Privately Held
Web: www.visitfrenchlickwestbaden.com
SIC: 3993 Signs and advertising specialties

(G-5846)
INDIANA IMPRINT LLC
7352 S Meadows Ln (47432-9238)
PHONE..................812 704-2773
Kari Mcgilvra, Admn
EMP: 6 EST: 2010
SALES (est): 102.87K Privately Held
Web: www.indianaimprint.com
SIC: 3555 Printing presses

(G-5847)
JASPER SEATING COMPANY INC
Also Called: Jsi
8084 W County Road 25 S (47432-9022)
P.O. Box 31 (47432-0031)
PHONE..................812 936-9977
Michael Eckstein, Brnch Mgr
EMP: 169
SALES (corp-wide): 198.33MM Privately Held
Web: jaspergroup.us.com
SIC: 2521 Chairs, office: padded, upholstered, or plain: wood
PA: Jasper Seating Company Inc
225 Clay St
Jasper IN 47546
812 482-3204

(G-5848)
RANDALL LOWE SONS SAWMILL LLC
6543 W County Road 875 S (47432-9327)
PHONE..................812 936-2254
Carl Randall Lowe, Pt
EMP: 12 EST: 1976
SALES (est): 411.53K Privately Held
SIC: 2421 2426 Sawmills and planing mills, general; Hardwood dimension and flooring mills

(G-5849)
SAMUEL POWELL
Also Called: Insane Wayne's Metal Art
395 N County Road 1075 W (47432-9785)
PHONE..................812 887-6813
Samuel Powell, Owner
EMP: 1
SALES (est): 38K Privately Held
SIC: 3499 7389 Metal household articles; Business Activities at Non-Commercial Site

Fulda
Spencer County

(G-5850)
WANINGER KNNETH SONS LOG TMBER
Also Called: Waninger & Sons Timber Co
Hwy 545 (47536)
P.O. Box 85 (47536-0085)
PHONE..................812 357-5200
Kenneth Waninger, Owner
EMP: 7 EST: 1971
SALES (est): 539.16K Privately Held
SIC: 5031 2411 Lumber: rough, dressed, and finished; Logging

Galveston
Cass County

(G-5851)
ANDERSONS AGRICULTURE GROUP LP
8086 E 900 (46932)
PHONE..................574 626-2522
Joe Johnson, Mgr
EMP: 1
SALES (corp-wide): 14.75B Publicly Held
Web: www.andersonsinc.com
SIC: 2874 2873 2899 5191 Ammonium phosphate; Fertilizers: natural (organic), except compost; Deicing or defrosting fluid; Fertilizer and fertilizer materials
HQ: The Andersons Agriculture Group L P
1947 Briarfield Blvd
Maumee OH 43537
419 893-5050

(G-5852)
DOYLE PITNER
Also Called: Dp Construction
201 S California St (46932-5003)
P.O. Box 546 (46932-0546)
PHONE..................574 699-6046
EMP: 1 EST: 1980
SALES (est): 49.3K Privately Held
SIC: 2394 Sails: made from purchased materials

(G-5853)
ROGER BABER PORTABLE WLDG LLC
9132 County Rd 50 S (46932)
PHONE..................574 859-4520
Roger Baber, Prin
EMP: 6 EST: 2005
SALES (est): 152.33K Privately Held
Web: www.rbportablewelding.com
SIC: 7692 Welding repair

Garrett
Dekalb County

(G-5854)
ASSMANN CORPORATION AMERICA (PA)
Also Called: Assmann
300 N Taylor Rd (46738-1844)
PHONE..................260 357-3181
David L Crager, Pr
Vickie S Elliott, *
Mary Monce, *
EMP: 32 EST: 1980
SQ FT: 51,000
SALES (est): 9.6MM
SALES (corp-wide): 9.6MM Privately Held
Web: www.assmann-usa.com
SIC: 3089 Plastics containers, except foam

(G-5855)
CENTURION INDUSTRIES INC (PA)
Also Called: A-Lert Construction Service
1107 N Taylor Rd (46738-1880)
PHONE..................260 357-6665
Kenneth L Tharp, Ch Bd
Bradley S Parish, *
Randy Shinkle, *
Loren R Troyer, *
EMP: 60 EST: 1975
SQ FT: 80,000
SALES (est): 242.37MM
SALES (corp-wide): 242.37MM Privately Held
Web: www.centurionind.com
SIC: 3444 1796 Canopies, sheet metal; Millwright

(G-5856)
CORNERSTONE MILL WORK
106 N Randolph St (46738-1138)
PHONE..................260 357-0754
Shawn Koble, Owner
Shawn Koble, Prin
EMP: 2 EST: 2007
SALES (est): 207.01K Privately Held
Web: www.cornerstoneinteriorwood.com
SIC: 2431 Millwork

(G-5857)
COUNTRYSIDE TOOL
1723 South Rd (46738-1853)
PHONE..................260 357-3839
Thomas Griffin, Pt
EMP: 2 EST: 1999
SALES (est): 151.59K Privately Held
SIC: 3469 Machine parts, stamped or pressed metal

(G-5858)
DEKALB TOOL AND ENGRG LLC
700 E Quincy St (46738-1617)
PHONE..................260 357-1500
EMP: 15 EST: 2006
SALES (est): 1.48MM Privately Held
Web: www.dekalbtooleng.com
SIC: 3599 Machine shop, jobbing and repair

(G-5859)
E-COLLAR TECHNOLOGIES INC
2120 Forrest Park Dr (46738-1882)
PHONE..................260 357-0051
▲ EMP: 8 EST: 2011
SQ FT: 56,000
SALES (est): 1.23MM Privately Held
Web: www.ecollar.com
SIC: 3545 Collars (machine tool accessories)

(G-5860)
ELECTRIC MOTORS AND SPC
Also Called: EM&s
701 W King St (46738-1396)
P.O. Box 180 (46738-0180)
PHONE..................260 357-4141
Judy Morrill, Pr
Keith Bradtmiller, *
EMP: 155 EST: 1947
SQ FT: 13,000
SALES (est): 24.04MM Privately Held
Web: www.emsmotors.com
SIC: 3621 Motors, electric

(G-5861)
ENZYME SOLUTIONS INC (PA)
Also Called: E S I
2105 Forrest Park Dr (46738-1882)
PHONE..................260 553-9100
Timothy Beck, CEO
Edwin Fisher Junior, Sec
◆ EMP: 12 EST: 1993
SQ FT: 39,000
SALES (est): 3.48MM
SALES (corp-wide): 3.48MM Privately Held
Web: www.enzymesolutions.com
SIC: 2869 Industrial organic chemicals, nec

(G-5862)
GARRETT PRODUCTS
1605 Dekko Dr (46738-1877)
PHONE..................260 357-5988
Tom Wilcoxson, Prin
EMP: 2 EST: 2010
SALES (est): 151.05K Privately Held
Web: www.bandcip.com
SIC: 3479 Metal coating and allied services

(G-5863)
GRACE ISLAND SPCALTY FOODS INC
5840 County Road 11 (46738-9743)
PHONE..................260 357-3336
Kalista A Johnston, Pr
EMP: 3 EST: 2004
SALES (est): 162.61K Privately Held
SIC: 2096 2052 Potato chips and similar snacks; Cookies and crackers

(PA)=Parent Co (HQ)=Headquarters
✪ = New Business established in last 2 years

(G-5864)
GRIFFITH RBR MILLS OF GARRETT (HQ)
Also Called: Bauman Harnish Rubber Co
400 N Taylor Rd (46738-1846)
PHONE..................................260 357-3125
Howard Laney, *Pr*
Donna Laney, *
Richard D Hahnert, *
Jill D Laney, *
▲ **EMP:** 27 **EST:** 1948
SQ FT: 98,000
SALES (est): 25.32MM
SALES (corp-wide): 48.48MM **Privately Held**
Web: www.griffithrubber.com
SIC: 3061 Appliance rubber goods (mechanical)
PA: Griffith Rubber Mills
2625 Nw Indul St
Portland OR 97210
503 226-6971

(G-5865)
GRIFFITH RBR MILLS OF GARRETT
Also Called: Microwave Plant
507 N Lee St (46738-1045)
PHONE..................................260 357-0876
Max Gregory, *Mgr*
EMP: 137
SALES (corp-wide): 48.48MM **Privately Held**
Web: www.griffithrubber.com
SIC: 3069 3053 Molded rubber products; Packing, rubber
HQ: Griffith Rubber Mills Of Garrett Inc
400 N Taylor Rd
Garrett IN 46738
260 357-3125

(G-5866)
GROUP DEKKO INC
1605 Dekko Dr (46738-1877)
PHONE..................................260 357-5988
Craig Rumsey, *Manager*
EMP: 1
SALES (corp-wide): 4.41B **Publicly Held**
Web: www.dekko.com
SIC: 3699 Electrical equipment and supplies, nec
HQ: Group Dekko, Inc.
7310 Innovation Blvd # 104
Fort Wayne IN 46818

(G-5867)
J & A MACHINE INC
219 E Quincy St (46738-1116)
P.O. Box 89 (46738-0089)
PHONE..................................260 637-6215
Michael Blomberg, *Pr*
Steve Blomberg, *VP*
◆ **EMP:** 6 **EST:** 1976
SQ FT: 6,624
SALES (est): 513.86K **Privately Held**
SIC: 3599 Machine shop, jobbing and repair

(G-5868)
J & P MACHINE INC
1213 S Franklin St (46738-2025)
PHONE..................................260 357-5157
James C Fike, *Pr*
Paula J Fike, *Sec*
EMP: 11 **EST:** 1980
SQ FT: 6,000
SALES (est): 383.1K **Privately Held**
SIC: 3599 Machine shop, jobbing and repair

(G-5869)
M & S STEEL CORP
217 E Railroad St (46738-1085)
P.O. Box 299 (46738-0299)
PHONE..................................260 357-5184
Walter G Fuller, *Pr*
Michael Fuller, *
Kent L York, *
◆ **EMP:** 27 **EST:** 1971
SQ FT: 35,000
SALES (est): 2.49MM **Privately Held**
Web: www.mssteelcorp.com
SIC: 3441 3443 Building components, structural steel; Fabricated plate work (boiler shop)

(G-5870)
MJS APPAREL EMB SCREENPRINTING
1308 S Randolph St (46738-1994)
PHONE..................................260 357-0199
Mark Stebing, *Owner*
EMP: 3 **EST:** 2011
SALES (est): 232.44K **Privately Held**
SIC: 2395 Embroidery products, except Schiffli machine

(G-5871)
MOLARGIK WOODWORKING INC
1116 S Hamsher St (46738-9628)
PHONE..................................260 357-6625
James Molargik, *Pr*
EMP: 4 **EST:** 2005
SALES (est): 402.44K **Privately Held**
SIC: 2431 2541 Millwork; Table or counter tops, plastic laminated

(G-5872)
MOMENTIVE PERFORMANCE MTLS INC
Also Called: Momentive Performance Mtls
420 N Taylor Rd (46738-1846)
PHONE..................................260 357-2000
Tom Lapsley, *Brnch Mgr*
EMP: 282
Web: www.momentive.com
SIC: 2869 3479 Silicones; Coating of metals with silicon
HQ: Momentive Performance Materials Inc.
2750 Balltown Rd
Niskayuna NY 12309

(G-5873)
MOSSBERG INDUSTRIES INC (HQ)
204 N 2nd St (46738-1600)
P.O. Box 37 (46738-0037)
PHONE..................................260 357-5141
James Khorshid, *Pr*
EMP: 60 **EST:** 1863
SQ FT: 80,000
SALES (est): 12.87MM
SALES (corp-wide): 52.79MM **Privately Held**
Web: www.mossbergindustries.com
SIC: 3089 3086 Hardware, plastics; Plastics foam products
PA: Khorporate Holdings, Inc.
6492 State Road 205
Laotto IN 46763
260 357-3365

(G-5874)
PRINCE MANUFACTURING CORP
Also Called: Prince Manufacturing
320 N Taylor Rd (46738-1844)
P.O. Box En Dr (46710)
PHONE..................................260 357-4484
Bernard Talwin, *Off Mgr*
EMP: 81
SALES (corp-wide): 274.85MM **Privately Held**
Web: www.princemanufacturing.com
SIC: 2759 3479 Commercial printing, nec; Coating of metals and formed products
HQ: Prince Manufacturing Corporation
203 W Main St Ste A3
Lexington SC 29072
803 708-4789

(G-5875)
RD RUBBER PRODUCTS INC
1600 South Rd (46738-1726)
P.O. Box 149 (46738-0149)
PHONE..................................260 357-3571
EMP: 4 **EST:** 1994
SALES (est): 494.25K **Privately Held**
Web: www.rdrubberinc.com
SIC: 3061 8711 Mechanical rubber goods; Engineering services

(G-5876)
SCOTT CULBERTSON
Also Called: Garrett Printing
1202 S Hamsher St (46738-9664)
PHONE..................................260 357-6430
Scott Culbertson, *Owner*
EMP: 2 **EST:** 2001
SQ FT: 1,800
SALES (est): 163.59K **Privately Held**
SIC: 2754 5943 Stationery and invitation printing, gravure; Office forms and supplies

(G-5877)
SUPERIOR WOODCRAFTS LLC
1111 S Franklin St (46738-2023)
PHONE..................................260 357-3743
EMP: 4 **EST:** 2015
SALES (est): 111.69K **Privately Held**
SIC: 2511 Wood household furniture

(G-5878)
TR MANUFACTURING LLC
1106 S Cowen St (46738-1910)
PHONE..................................260 357-4679
Matt Mason, *Managing Member*
EMP: 6 **EST:** 2004
SALES (est): 908.62K **Privately Held**
Web: www.trmanufacturing.com
SIC: 3599 Machine shop, jobbing and repair

(G-5879)
TRISTATE BOLT COMPANY
1110 Fuller Dr (46738-1873)
PHONE..................................260 357-5541
James M Getz, *Pr*
Kinjal V Amin, *Pr*
EMP: 12 **EST:** 2003
SALES (est): 1.93MM **Privately Held**
SIC: 3452 3479 Bolts, metal; Galvanizing of iron, steel, or end-formed products

(G-5880)
WHEELOCK MANUFACTURING INC
2505 Dekko Dr (46738-1886)
PHONE..................................219 285-8540
EMP: 25
Web: www.wheelockmfg.com
SIC: 3679 3643 Harness assemblies, for electronic use: wire or cable; Current-carrying wiring services

(G-5881)
ZF ACTIVE SAFETY & ELEC US LLC
817 N Taylor Rd (46738-1885)
PHONE..................................260 357-6327
EMP: 100
SALES (corp-wide): 144.19K **Privately Held**
SIC: 3714 Motor vehicle parts and accessories
HQ: Zf Active Safety & Electronics Us Llc
34605 W 12 Mile Rd
Farmington Hills MI 48331
765 429-1936

(G-5882)
ZF AUTOMOTIVE
817 N Taylor Rd (46738-1885)
PHONE..................................260 357-1148
EMP: 18 **EST:** 2019
SALES (est): 390.64K **Privately Held**
Web: www.zf.com
SIC: 3714 Motor vehicle parts and accessories

Gary
Lake County

(G-5883)
7TH LEADERSHIP ORGANIZATION
Also Called: 7lo
6775 Ash Pl (46403-3911)
PHONE..................................219 938-6906
Anthony Brown, *CEO*
EMP: 1
SALES (est): 63K **Privately Held**
SIC: 7389 8711 3711 3812 Interior designer; Mechanical engineering; Universal carriers, military, assembly of; Aircraft/aerospace flight instruments and guidance systems

(G-5884)
A SNACK ABOVE REST LLC
466 Johnson St (46402-1042)
PHONE..................................219 455-3335
EMP: 1
SALES (est): 60.62K **Privately Held**
SIC: 7389 3581 Business Activities at Non-Commercial Site; Automatic vending machines

(G-5885)
A2 SALES LLC (PA)
Also Called: Alliance Steel
2700 E 5th Ave (46402-1606)
PHONE..................................708 924-1200
Andrew Gross, *Pr*
William Vorderer, *
EMP: 44 **EST:** 2000
SALES (est): 23.27MM
SALES (corp-wide): 23.27MM **Privately Held**
Web: www.alliancesteel.net
SIC: 3399 5051 Metal powders, pastes, and flakes; Steel

(G-5886)
AARON COMPANY INC
Also Called: Family Design
4835 W 45th Ave (46408-3539)
PHONE..................................219 838-0852
Gerald A Gearhart, *Pr*
Henrietta Gearhart, *Sec*
EMP: 16 **EST:** 1976
SQ FT: 3,800
SALES (est): 409.02K **Privately Held**
Web: www.aarons.com
SIC: 7359 2512 7641 Home appliance, furniture, and entertainment rental services; Upholstered household furniture; Reupholstery

(G-5887)
ABUNDANT LIFE PUBLICATIONS LLC
320 Roosevelt St (46404-1150)
P.O. Box 641015 (46401-1015)
PHONE..................................219 730-7621
Tavetta Patterson, *Pr*
EMP: 2 **EST:** 2006
SALES (est): 59.16K **Privately Held**

GEOGRAPHIC SECTION

Gary - Lake County (G-5915)

SIC: 8748 2731 5999 2741 Business consulting, nec; Book publishing; Educational aids and electronic training materials; Business service newsletters: publishing and printing

(G-5888)
ALL PET SUPPLIES INC
3982 Broadway (46408-2705)
PHONE.............................219 885-9670
Gary M Carlton, *Prin*
EMP: 9 **EST:** 2013
SALES (est): 73.37K **Privately Held**
Web: www.allpetsuppliestore.com
SIC: 3999 Pet supplies

(G-5889)
ALLIANCE STEEL LLC
2700 E 5th Ave (46402-1606)
PHONE.............................219 427-5400
Andrew Gross, *Managing Member*
EMP: 150 **EST:** 1998
SALES (est): 18.73MM **Privately Held**
Web: www.alliancesteel.net
SIC: 3498 Coils, pipe: fabricated from purchased pipe

(G-5890)
ALLIANCE STEEL CORPORATION
2700 E 5th Ave (46402-1606)
PHONE.............................708 924-1200
Andrew Gross, *Pr*
Andy Gross, *
Andrew Sandberg, *
Mike Durby, *
▼ **EMP:** 30 **EST:** 1970
SQ FT: 80,000
SALES (est): 4.94MM **Privately Held**
Web: www.alliancesteel.net
SIC: 3441 3471 Fabricated structural metal; Plating and polishing

(G-5891)
ALPHA & OMEGA MFG LLC
1408 W 47th Ave (46408-4436)
PHONE.............................219 344-8738
EMP: 1 **EST:** 2003
SALES (est): 8.62K **Privately Held**
SIC: 3599 Machine shop, jobbing and repair

(G-5892)
AMERICAN PRECISION SVCS INC
7110 W 21st Ave (46406-2406)
PHONE.............................219 977-4451
Robert Migliorini, *Pr*
John Teefel, *
Jeffery Keith, *
EMP: 48 **EST:** 2002
SQ FT: 8,000
SALES (est): 9.13MM **Privately Held**
Web: www.amprservices.com
SIC: 3599 Machine shop, jobbing and repair

(G-5893)
ANCHOR SEALS INCORPORATED
Also Called: Anchor Seals Incorporated
219 Virginia St (46402-1337)
PHONE.............................412 299-6900
Bill Adams, *Brnch Mgr*
EMP: 4
Web: www.anchorseals.com
SIC: 3053 Gaskets; packing and sealing devices
PA: Anchor Seals Llc
   920 2nd Ave Ste 1
   Coraopolis PA 15108

(G-5894)
ANDERSON SHYKIA
Also Called: Kia Dos

4025 Kentucky St (46409-1837)
PHONE.............................773 304-6852
Shykia Anderson, *Owner*
EMP: 1 **EST:** 2020
SALES (est): 45K **Privately Held**
SIC: 7231 7929 1389 3663 Beauty shops; Entertainers and entertainment groups; Construction, repair, and dismantling services; Studio equipment, radio and television broadcasting

(G-5895)
AREA WELDING INNOVATIONS LLC
4705 Roosevelt St (46408-3747)
PHONE.............................219 789-2209
EMP: 4 **EST:** 2018
SALES (est): 75.35K **Privately Held**
SIC: 7692 Welding repair

(G-5896)
ARMSTRONGS
1189 Gerry St (46406-2165)
PHONE.............................219 977-8368
Darryl S Armstrong, *Prin*
EMP: 4 **EST:** 2005
SALES (est): 59.47K **Privately Held**
Web: www.armstrongsgroup.com
SIC: 3273 Ready-mixed concrete

(G-5897)
BADA BOOM FIREWORKS LLC
4601 Cleveland St (46408-3716)
PHONE.............................219 472-6700
EMP: 5 **EST:** 2017
SALES (est): 74.42K **Privately Held**
Web: shop.badaboomfireworkspa.com
SIC: 2899 Fireworks

(G-5898)
BEAUTYBYNEYADIOR LLC
2007 Harrison St (46407-2438)
PHONE.............................800 988-2592
Ronesha Latrese Nailon, *CEO*
EMP: 1 **EST:** 2021
SALES (est): 69.22K **Privately Held**
Web: www.beautybyneyadior.com
SIC: 7231 3999 Beauty shops; Hair and hair-based products

(G-5899)
BEH IL CORP
201 Mississippi St (46402-1546)
PHONE.............................219 886-2710
William R Wilson, *Brnch Mgr*
EMP: 1
SIC: 3448 Prefabricated metal components
PA: Beh Il Corp.
   15 Salt Creek Ln Ste 412
   Hinsdale IL 60521

(G-5900)
BIVETTES
3636 W 19th Ave (46404-2679)
PHONE.............................219 949-1742
Willie N Scales, *Prin*
EMP: 1 **EST:** 2001
SALES (est): 54.57K **Privately Held**
SIC: 3961 Costume jewelry

(G-5901)
BLACK ROSE PASTRIES LLC
1315 Marshall Pl (46404-2029)
PHONE.............................773 708-3650
EMP: 1 **EST:** 2016
SALES (est): 85.12K **Privately Held**
Web: www.blackrosepastries.com
SIC: 5461 2051 5999 7999 Retail bakeries; Bakery: wholesale or wholesale/retail combined; Cake decorating supplies; Cake or pastry decorating instruction

(G-5902)
BLACKMON METAL FABRICATION LLC
840 E 44th Ave (46409-2313)
PHONE.............................346 254-9500
EMP: 1
SALES (est): 54.1K **Privately Held**
SIC: 3548 7389 Welding apparatus; Business Activities at Non-Commercial Site

(G-5903)
BMI REFRACTORY SERVICES INC
201 Mississippi St (46402-1546)
PHONE.............................219 885-2209
Bill Schleizer, *Mgr*
EMP: 1
SALES (corp-wide): 2.41B **Privately Held**
SIC: 3255 Glasshouse refractories
HQ: Bmi Refractory Services, Inc.
   250 Parkwest Dr
   Pittsburgh PA 15275
   412 429-1800

(G-5904)
BODYCOTE TESTING GROUP INC
2090 E 15th Ave (46402-3005)
PHONE.............................219 882-4283
Gary Richter, *Mgr*
EMP: 9 **EST:** 2016
SALES (est): 80.61K **Privately Held**
Web: www.bodycote.com
SIC: 3398 Metal heat treating

(G-5905)
BOEING COMPANY
Also Called: Boeing
6309 Airport Rd (46406)
PHONE.............................219 977-4354
EMP: 5
SALES (corp-wide): 77.79B **Publicly Held**
Web: www.boeing.com
SIC: 3721 Aircraft
PA: The Boeing Company
   929 Long Bridge Dr
   Arlington VA 22202
   703 465-3500

(G-5906)
BREADMANSRT LLC
3500 W 22nd Ave (46404-2955)
PHONE.............................219 238-9169
EMP: 1 **EST:** 2021
SALES (est): 38.27K **Privately Held**
SIC: 2741 Internet publishing and broadcasting

(G-5907)
BURST OF BEAUTY LLC
1329 Williams St (46404-1667)
PHONE.............................708 970-2181
EMP: 1 **EST:** 2021
SALES (est): 47.23K **Privately Held**
SIC: 2844 Cosmetic preparations

(G-5908)
BUSINESS SYSTEMS MGT CORP
Also Called: B S M
8414 Maple Ave (46403-1419)
PHONE.............................219 938-0166
Geraldine Barron-simpson, *Pr*
Shaun Butler, *VP*
Steve Simpson Md, *Sec*
EMP: 6 **EST:** 1993
SQ FT: 1,600
SALES (est): 798.12K **Privately Held**
Web: www.bsmproducts.com

SIC: 5731 5044 5961 5045 Consumer electronic equipment, nec; Office equipment ; Computers and peripheral equipment, mail order; Computers, peripherals, and software

(G-5909)
CALIFORNIA SUGARS LLC ✿
911 Virginia St (46402-2705)
PHONE.............................219 886-9151
EMP: 10 **EST:** 2022
SALES (est): 692.13K **Privately Held**
Web: www.sugars.com
SIC: 2099 Sugar

(G-5910)
CALUMET WILBERT VAULT CO INC
1920 W 41st Ave (46408-2399)
PHONE.............................219 980-1173
Edward H Carroll Junior, *Pr*
Nancy Eggbali, *Sec*
EMP: 10 **EST:** 1948
SQ FT: 30,000
SALES (est): 857.72K **Privately Held**
Web: www.calwilbert.com
SIC: 3272 Burial vaults, concrete or precast terrazzo

(G-5911)
CAPTURED BEAUTY ETC LLC
1809 Chase St (46404-2057)
PHONE.............................219 801-2572
Tameka Fowler, *Prin*
EMP: 1 **EST:** 2021
SALES (est): 41.02K **Privately Held**
SIC: 3961 Costume jewelry

(G-5912)
CARMEUSE LIME INC
Also Called: Carmeuse Lime & Stone
1 N Carmeuse Ln (46406-1279)
PHONE.............................219 949-1450
Thomas A Buck, *CEO*
EMP: 53
SALES (corp-wide): 2.67MM **Privately Held**
Web: www.carmeuse.com
SIC: 1422 Crushed and broken limestone
HQ: Carmeuse Lime, Inc.
   11 Stanwix St Fl 21
   Pittsburgh PA 15222
   412 995-5500

(G-5913)
CATHERINE J BERGREN ✿
Also Called: Fancy Bee Clothing Co.
862 Floyd St (46403)
PHONE.............................219 225-2819
Catherine J Bergren, *Owner*
EMP: 4 **EST:** 2024
SALES (est): 125.42K **Privately Held**
SIC: 2339 7389 Athletic clothing: women's, misses', and juniors'; Business services, nec

(G-5914)
CEADOGS LLC-S
100 N Montgomery St (46403-3922)
PHONE.............................219 779-1352
EMP: 1
SALES (est): 69.27K **Privately Held**
SIC: 2099 Food preparations, nec

(G-5915)
CENTRAL ILLINOIS STEEL COMPANY
50 N Bridge St (46404-1074)
P.O. Box 78 (62626-0078)
PHONE.............................219 882-1026
Dan Fleig, *Dir*
EMP: 5

Gary - Lake County (G-5916) GEOGRAPHIC SECTION

SALES (corp-wide): 20.04MM **Privately Held**
SIC: 3441 5051 Fabricated structural metal; Steel
PA: Central Illinois Steel Company
21050 Rte 4
Carlinville IL 62626
217 854-3251

(G-5916)
CHEMCOATERS LLC
700 Chase St (46404-1246)
PHONE....................219 977-1929
Connor Mcmenamin, *Pr*
Bill Capizziano, *
EMP: 35 EST: 1999
SQ FT: 80,000
SALES (est): 5.23MM **Privately Held**
Web: www.chemcoaters.com
SIC: 3479 Coating or wrapping steel pipe

(G-5917)
CHICAGO CRUSADER NEWS GROUP
Also Called: Gary Crusader
1549 Broadway (46407-2240)
PHONE....................219 885-4357
FAX: 219 883-3317
EMP: 2
SALES (corp-wide): 350K **Privately Held**
SIC: 2711 Newspapers
PA: Chicago Crusader News Group
6429 S King Dr
Chicago IL 60637
773 752-2500

(G-5918)
CHICAGO STEEL LTD PARTNERSHIP
700 Chase St (46404-1246)
PHONE....................219 949-1111
Bruce Mannakee, *Pt*
Ted Katsahnias, *VP Opers*
William Boak, *S&M/VP*
EMP: 29 EST: 1991
SQ FT: 285,000
SALES (est): 2.27MM **Privately Held**
Web: www.upgllc.com
SIC: 7389 5051 3312 Metal cutting services; Metals service centers and offices; Blast furnaces and steel mills

(G-5919)
CLOVERLEAF FARMS DAIRY
6401 Melton Rd (46403-3010)
PHONE....................219 938-5140
R Curtis, *Owner*
EMP: 9 EST: 1999
SALES (est): 143.89K **Privately Held**
SIC: 2024 Ice cream and frozen deserts

(G-5920)
CRAFTED VANITY COMPANY
1933 Hendricks St (46404-2647)
PHONE....................219 293-6063
Michael Bingham, *Prin*
EMP: 1 EST: 2016
SALES (est): 82.54K **Privately Held**
Web: www.craftedvanity.com
SIC: 3231 Reflecting glass

(G-5921)
D S CUSTOM TEES
2548 Marshalltown Dr (46407-1858)
PHONE....................219 802-3127
EMP: 3 EST: 2019
SALES (est): 85.6K **Privately Held**
SIC: 2759 Screen printing

(G-5922)
DIANNE FORREST WELDING COMPANY
5101 Vermont St (46409-2988)
PHONE....................219 381-1667
Consandra Jimerson, *Prin*
EMP: 1 EST: 2010
SALES (est): 39.52K **Privately Held**
SIC: 7692 Welding repair

(G-5923)
DIVINE GRACE HOMECARE
4224 Connecticut St (46409-2106)
PHONE....................219 290-5911
Cleveneatha Lloyd, *Owner*
EMP: 5 EST: 1965
SALES (est): 140K **Privately Held**
SIC: 2656 7389 Sanitary food containers; Business Activities at Non-Commercial Site

(G-5924)
DROPSHIP MY BUNDLES LLC
1021 Willard St (46404-1723)
PHONE....................219 381-8061
EMP: 2 EST: 2019
SALES (est): 62.54K **Privately Held**
SIC: 3999 Hair and hair-based products

(G-5925)
EDSAL INC
700 Chase St Ste 400 (46404-1274)
PHONE....................219 427-1294
▲ EMP: 10 EST: 2015
SALES (est): 479.08K **Privately Held**
Web: www.edsal.com
SIC: 3999 Manufacturing industries, nec

(G-5926)
EDSAL MANUFACTURING CO LLC
700 Chase St Ste 400 (46404-1274)
PHONE....................773 254-0600
EMP: 115
SALES (corp-wide): 279.66MM **Privately Held**
Web: www.edsal.com
SIC: 2599 2542 2522 Factory furniture and fixtures; Shelving, office and store, except wood; Office furniture, except wood
PA: Edsal Manufacturing Company, Llc
1555 W 44th St
Chicago IL 60609
773 475-3000

(G-5927)
EGG INNVTONS ORGANIC FEEDS LLC
578 Jefferson St (46402-1913)
PHONE....................800 337-1951
EMP: 1 EST: 2003
SALES (est): 231.24K **Privately Held**
SIC: 2048 Chicken feeds, prepared
PA: Egg Innovations, Llc
4799 W 100 N
Warsaw IN 46580

(G-5928)
ENVIRI CORPORATION
7100 W 9th Ave (46406-1924)
PHONE....................219 944-6250
Dave Wollehgan, *Mgr*
EMP: 18
SALES (corp-wide): 2.07B **Publicly Held**
Web: www.enviri.com
SIC: 3295 3291 Roofing granules; Abrasive products
PA: Enviri Corporation
100-120 N 18th St # 17
Philadelphia PA 19103
267 857-8715

(G-5929)
ENVIRO FILTRATION INC (PA)
Also Called: Enviro Filters
4719 Roosevelt St (46408-3747)
PHONE....................815 469-2871
Tim Rucinski, *Pr*
EMP: 3 EST: 1992
SQ FT: 4,200
SALES (est): 978.57K **Privately Held**
SIC: 3569 Filters, general line: industrial

(G-5930)
EPIC GRAPHICS AND PRINTING
201 E 5th Ave (46402-1315)
PHONE....................219 545-1240
EMP: 4 EST: 2012
SALES (est): 89.74K **Privately Held**
SIC: 7336 2759 Graphic arts and related design; Commercial printing, nec

(G-5931)
EXTRASURPLUS LLC
504 Broadway Ste 316 (46402-1943)
P.O. Box 811 (46312-1511)
PHONE....................252 619-8604
Anthony Thomas, *Pr*
EMP: 1 EST: 2015
SALES (est): 83.41K **Privately Held**
SIC: 3312 3613 Wire products, steel or iron; Switchgear and switchboard apparatus

(G-5932)
FASI COATINGS LLC
Also Called: Fasi Coatings
3905 W Ridge Rd (46408-1847)
PHONE....................219 985-0788
Timothy Kuiper, *Prin*
James Robshaw, *Prin*
EMP: 4 EST: 2016
SALES (est): 250.5K **Privately Held**
Web: www.fasicoatings.com
SIC: 3479 Coating of metals and formed products

(G-5933)
FIRE APPARATUS SERVICE INC
Also Called: Fasi Codings
3905 W Ridge Rd (46408-1847)
PHONE....................219 985-0788
EMP: 4 EST: 1996
SALES (est): 515.62K **Privately Held**
SIC: 5012 7699 3823 Fire trucks; Industrial truck repair; Thermal conductivity instruments, industrial process type

(G-5934)
FRAZIER COMFORT DETAILS
1500 W 46th Ave (46408-3835)
PHONE....................219 276-2288
Raffiel Frazier, *CEO*
EMP: 1
SALES (est): 60.08K **Privately Held**
SIC: 3532 Cars, mining

(G-5935)
GARCO GRAPHICS
4730 Broadway (46408-4508)
P.O. Box 2118 (46409-0118)
PHONE....................219 980-1113
Jeannine B Pavic, *Owner*
EMP: 1 EST: 1976
SQ FT: 3,750
SALES (est): 141.49K **Privately Held**
Web: www.garcographics.net
SIC: 2752 5199 2759 Offset printing; Advertising specialties; Letterpress printing

(G-5936)
GARY BRIDGE AND IRON CO INC
3700 Roosevelt St (46408-2034)
PHONE....................219 884-3792
Stephan Truchan Junior, *Pr*
Jean Truchan, *Sec*
EMP: 5 EST: 1942
SQ FT: 45,000
SALES (est): 463.51K **Privately Held**
Web: www.gbi1.com
SIC: 3441 3599 7699 4225 Building components, structural steel; Machine shop, jobbing and repair; Industrial machinery and equipment repair; General warehousing

(G-5937)
GARY METAL MFG LLC
2700 E 5th Ave (46402-1606)
PHONE....................219 885-3232
David J Strilich, *Managing Member*
EMP: 24 EST: 2002
SQ FT: 350,000
SALES (est): 463.96K **Privately Held**
SIC: 3444 Sheet metal specialties, not stamped

(G-5938)
GARY PRINTING INC
1950 W 11th Ave (46404-2406)
PHONE....................219 886-1767
Patricia L Eaton, *Pr*
Helen J Danko, *Sec*
EMP: 4 EST: 1946
SQ FT: 925
SALES (est): 296.96K **Privately Held**
Web: www.garyprintingcompany.com
SIC: 2752 2791 2796 2759 Offset printing; Typesetting; Platemaking services; Engraving, nec

(G-5939)
GENERTONAL OUTREACH GAMING LLC ◆
1934 W 5th Ave Apt 202 (46404)
PHONE....................872 777-6882
EMP: 1 EST: 2022
SALES (est): 60.08K **Privately Held**
SIC: 3537 Trucks: freight, baggage, etc.: industrial, except mining

(G-5940)
GENOA HEALTHCARE LLC
1100 W 6th Ave (46402-1711)
PHONE....................219 427-1837
EMP: 4
SALES (corp-wide): 371.62B **Publicly Held**
Web: www.genoahealthcare.com
SIC: 5912 2834 Drug stores and proprietary stores; Pharmaceutical preparations
HQ: Genoa Healthcare Llc
707 S Grady Way Ste 700
Renton WA 98057

(G-5941)
GEORGES WELDING & MECH SVC
2630 Colfax St (46406-3034)
PHONE....................219 989-0781
George Sporting, *Owner*
EMP: 1 EST: 1968
SALES (est): 60.94K **Privately Held**
SIC: 7692 Welding repair

(G-5942)
GINGER WHITE LLC
7429 Ash Ave (46403-2116)
PHONE....................773 818-8740
Christopher Jaroscak, *Prin*
EMP: 7 EST: 2014
SALES (est): 496.85K **Privately Held**
Web: www.whitegingerchicago.com
SIC: 3999 Manufacturing industries, nec

GEOGRAPHIC SECTION

Gary - Lake County (G-5970)

(G-5943)
GLASS CITY INC
Also Called: Glass City
4980 Broadway (46408-4605)
PHONE..............................219 887-2100
EMP: 4 **EST:** 1986
SALES (est): 665.32K Privately Held
Web: www.glasscityinc.com
SIC: 5039 5521 5231 2821 Glass construction materials; Automobiles, used cars only; Glass; Plastics materials and resins

(G-5944)
GRODIN TRANSPORTATION
307 Marshall St (46404-1055)
PHONE..............................773 614-7062
John Grodin, *CEO*
EMP: 8 **EST:** 2021
SALES (est): 200.49K Privately Held
SIC: 3799 Transportation equipment, nec

(G-5945)
HARBISONWALKER INTL INC
76 N Bridge St (46404-1074)
PHONE..............................219 881-4440
Carol Jackson, *Brnch Mgr*
EMP: 4
SALES (corp-wide): 367.49K Privately Held
Web: www.thinkhwi.com
SIC: 3255 Clay refractories
HQ: Harbisonwalker International, Inc.
  1305 Cherrington Pkwy # 1
  Moon Township PA 15108

(G-5946)
HAYMONS PUBLISHING LLC
5100 Vermont St (46409-2963)
PHONE..............................219 484-8510
Orlando Haymon, *Admn*
EMP: 1 **EST:** 2013
SALES (est): 52.94K Privately Held
SIC: 2741 Miscellaneous publishing

(G-5947)
HEARTS RMNED LIFESTYLE CIR LLC
Also Called: Hearts Remained
1052 N County Line Rd (46403-1735)
PHONE..............................800 807-0485
EMP: 7 **EST:** 2015
SALES (est): 314.53K Privately Held
Web: www.heartsremained.com
SIC: 2311 7389 Tailored suits and formal jackets; Business Activities at Non-Commercial Site

(G-5948)
HEAVEN SENT GURMET COOKIES INC
3745 Broadway (46409-1501)
P.O. Box 1796 (46409-0796)
PHONE..............................219 980-1066
EMP: 6 **EST:** 2003
SQ FT: 2,000
SALES (est): 434.38K Privately Held
SIC: 2052 5812 Cookies and crackers; Caterers

(G-5949)
HELLMANS AUTO SUPPLY CO INC
Also Called: Hellman's Tire Service
612 E 5th Ave (46402-1404)
PHONE..............................219 885-7655
Robert Chiabai, *Pr*
Jeff Chiabai, *Sec*
Ronald L Chiabai Junior, *VP*
Helen Chiabai, *Stockholder*
EMP: 7 **EST:** 1938
SQ FT: 6,000
SALES (est): 934.63K Privately Held
Web: www.hellmantire.com
SIC: 5014 5531 7534 Truck tires and tubes; Truck equipment and parts; Tire retreading and repair shops

(G-5950)
HERALD MACHINE WERKS LLC ✪
7100 Industrial Hwy (46406-1045)
PHONE..............................219 949-0580
EMP: 18 **EST:** 2023
SALES (est): 1.16MM Privately Held
SIC: 3599 Machine shop, jobbing and repair

(G-5951)
HESSVILLE CABLE & SLING CO
1601 Cline Ave (46406-2296)
PHONE..............................773 768-8181
George Randall, *Pr*
Tom Randall, *
D Kenneth Randall, *
▲ **EMP:** 35 **EST:** 1960
SQ FT: 12,000
SALES (est): 4.92MM Privately Held
Web: www.hessvillecable.com
SIC: 5063 2298 3496 Wire and cable; Nets, seines, slings and insulator pads; Miscellaneous fabricated wire products

(G-5952)
HOMEOWNERS EQUITY & RLTY CORP
306 W Ridge Rd Bldg 300 (46408-2735)
PHONE..............................219 981-1700
Allan Fefferman, *Prin*
Allan Fefferman, *VP*
Felipa Ortiz, *Asst Sec*
EMP: 6 **EST:** 1996
SQ FT: 2,500
SALES (est): 286.42K Privately Held
SIC: 3272 Building materials, except block or brick: concrete

(G-5953)
HORTON LOGISTICS LLC
3758 Polk St (46408-2240)
PHONE..............................219 290-2910
EMP: 1 **EST:** 2020
SALES (est): 54.62K Privately Held
SIC: 3743 Freight cars and equipment

(G-5954)
HUMBLE INDUSTRIES LLC
772 Buchanan St (46402-2108)
PHONE..............................219 702-6607
Aliceya Anderson, *Prin*
EMP: 1 **EST:** 2020
SALES (est): 27.98K Privately Held
Web: www.humbleindustries.com
SIC: 3599 Machine shop, jobbing and repair

(G-5955)
HUSSLEAIRE LLC
3960 Southeastern Ave (46404-1045)
PHONE..............................312 889-4866
Andre Morris, *CEO*
EMP: 2 **EST:** 2021
SALES (est): 64.64K Privately Held
SIC: 2731 Books, publishing only

(G-5956)
IFC FENCE LLC
3245 W 46th Ave (46408-3653)
PHONE..............................219 977-4000
Luigi Biancardi, *Managing Member*
EMP: 5 **EST:** 2016
SALES (est): 266.63K Privately Held
SIC: 3315 Chain link fencing

(G-5957)
IGETPAID LLC
4645 Buchanan St (46408-3838)
PHONE..............................708 916-2967
Cordarro Garrett, *Managing Member*
EMP: 2
SALES (est): 92.67K Privately Held
SIC: 2389 Apparel and accessories, nec

(G-5958)
IMMA JERK LLC
1742 Hayes St (46404-2739)
PHONE..............................219 885-8613
EMP: 1
SALES (est): 69.25K Privately Held
SIC: 7389 2099 Business Activities at Non-Commercial Site; Food preparations, nec

(G-5959)
IMS SURFACE CONDITIONING
1 N Buchanan St (46402-1060)
P.O. Box 2353 (46368-5853)
PHONE..............................219 881-0155
Pascal Martin, *Prin*
EMP: 1 **EST:** 1991
SALES (est): 89.41K Privately Held
SIC: 3312 Blast furnaces and steel mills

(G-5960)
INDUSTRIAL COMBUSTN ENGINEERS
Also Called: Industrial Combustion Engnrs
7000 W 21st Ave (46406-2404)
PHONE..............................219 949-5066
Leonard G Nowak, *Pr*
EMP: 20 **EST:** 1954
SQ FT: 12,000
SALES (est): 2.18MM Privately Held
Web: www.indcomb.com
SIC: 3585 3567 8711 Refrigeration and heating equipment; Industrial furnaces and ovens; Industrial engineers

(G-5961)
INDUSTRIAL CONTROLS CORP
3821 Vermont St (46409-1635)
P.O. Box 8 (46374-0008)
PHONE..............................219 884-1141
Richard Cannon, *Pr*
EMP: 6 **EST:** 1989
SQ FT: 7,000
SALES (est): 685.13K Privately Held
Web: www.industrialcontrolsonline.com
SIC: 3625 3536 7699 Industrial controls: push button, selector switches, pilot; Hoists, cranes, and monorails; Industrial machinery and equipment repair

(G-5962)
INDUSTRIAL STEEL CNSTR INC
86 N Bridge St (46404-1074)
PHONE..............................219 885-5610
Daniel Moore, *Mgr*
EMP: 200
SALES (corp-wide): 23.48MM Privately Held
SIC: 3441 3444 3443 3312 Fabricated structural metal; Sheet metalwork; Fabricated plate work (boiler shop); Blast furnaces and steel mills
PA: Industrial Steel Construction, Inc.
  413 Old Kirk Rd
  Geneva IL 60134
  630 232-7473

(G-5963)
INTERNATIONAL MILL SERVICE INC
1 N Broadway (46402-3101)
P.O. Box 64824 (46401-0824)
PHONE..............................219 881-0155
EMP: 1 **EST:** 2008
SALES (est): 224.15K Privately Held
SIC: 3312 Blast furnaces and steel mills

(G-5964)
INTERSTATE POWER SYSTEMS INC
Also Called: Interstate Powersystems
2601 E 15th Ave (46402)
PHONE..............................952 854-2044
Mark Goverg, *Brnch Mgr*
EMP: 1
SALES (corp-wide): 465.85MM Privately Held
Web: www.istate.com
SIC: 3714 5084 Motor vehicle parts and accessories; Industrial machinery and equipment
HQ: Interstate Power Systems, Inc.
  1340 Corporate Ctr Curv
  Saint Paul MN 55121
  952 854-2044

(G-5965)
INX LLC
4491 Roosevelt St (46408-3151)
PHONE..............................219 779-0508
Christopher Deinert Senior, *Admn*
EMP: 9 **EST:** 2019
SALES (est): 152.55K Privately Held
Web: www.inxinternational.com
SIC: 2893 Printing ink

(G-5966)
JACKIE COLLECTION LLC ✪
1400 E 51st Pl (46409-2937)
PHONE..............................219 678-8176
Jacqueline Meredith, *Mgr*
EMP: 2 **EST:** 2022
SALES (est): 94.12K Privately Held
SIC: 2389 Apparel and accessories, nec

(G-5967)
JACKSON VISION QUEST
Also Called: Vision Quest
521 Broadway (46402-1910)
PHONE..............................219 882-9397
Alexander Koukiakis, *Pr*
Doctor Dick D Jackson, *Pr*
EMP: 3 **EST:** 1929
SALES (est): 291.77K Privately Held
SIC: 3851 5995 Eyeglasses, lenses and frames; Optical goods stores
PA: A & K Kouklakis, O.D., P.C.
  2294 W 81st Ave
  Merrillville IN 46410

(G-5968)
JANELS BODY BAR LLC
1116 Broadway (46407-1307)
PHONE..............................219 455-4888
EMP: 2
SALES (est): 88.38K Privately Held
SIC: 3634 Massage machines, electric, except for beauty/barber shops

(G-5969)
JASZY DRINKS LLC ✪
1572 Ralston St (46406-2347)
PHONE..............................219 742-5013
Jasmine Barfield, *CEO*
EMP: 1 **EST:** 2022
SALES (est): 39.59K Privately Held
SIC: 2082 7389 Malt beverages; Business Activities at Non-Commercial Site

(G-5970)
JENSTAR ASPHALT LLC
3003 E 15th Pl (46403)
PHONE..............................219 963-6263
W Douglas Robinson, *Prin*

Gary - Lake County (G-5971)

EMP: 10 EST: 2016
SALES (est): 236.46K **Privately Held**
Web: www.jenstarasphalt.com
SIC: 2951 Asphalt paving mixtures and blocks

(G-5971)
JONES INTERNATIONAL INC
Also Called: Senoj
437 Connecticut St (46402-1312)
PHONE..............................219 746-1478
Charles V Jones, *Pr*
EMP: 1 EST: 1992
SQ FT: 1,575
SALES (est): 243.13K **Privately Held**
Web: www.senoj-usa.com
SIC: 3674 Integrated circuits, semiconductor networks, etc.

(G-5972)
KATH ENTERPRISE LLC
4308 E 6th Ave (46403-2711)
PHONE..............................877 641-6990
EMP: 1 EST: 2020
SALES (est): 250K **Privately Held**
SIC: 3537 Trucks: freight, baggage, etc.: industrial, except mining

(G-5973)
KAYS WAY ◊
5058 Massachusetts St (46409-2734)
PHONE..............................219 290-0782
Kays Way, *CEO*
EMP: 1 EST: 2022
SALES (est): 39.69K **Privately Held**
SIC: 3999 Fingernails, artificial

(G-5974)
KIDSTUFF PLAYSYSTEMS INC
5400 Miller Ave (46403-2844)
PHONE..............................219 938-3331
Richard Hagelberg, *CEO*
George Mc Guan, *
▲ EMP: 53 EST: 1982
SQ FT: 28,000
SALES (est): 4.65MM **Privately Held**
Web: www.kidstuffplaysystems.com
SIC: 3949 5941 Playground equipment; Playground equipment

(G-5975)
KORE INDUSTRIES LLC ◊
518 S Hancock St Unit 2671 (46403-6001)
PHONE..............................773 343-5966
EMP: 3 EST: 2022
SALES (est): 80.37K **Privately Held**
Web: www.koreindustries.com
SIC: 3999 Manufacturing industries, nec

(G-5976)
LAKE RIDGE VLNTR FIRE DEPT INC
2301 W 47th Ave (46408-3642)
PHONE..............................219 980-8620
Donald Stojakovich, *Pr*
EMP: 24 EST: 1941
SALES (est): 287.63K **Privately Held**
SIC: 3711 Fire department vehicles (motor vehicles), assembly of

(G-5977)
LAMONICOS CNSTR & MAINT LLC
1173 Van Buren St (46407-1124)
PHONE..............................219 951-8554
EMP: 1 EST: 2021
SALES (est): 41.07K **Privately Held**
Web: construction.altg.com
SIC: 1389 Construction, repair, and dismantling services

(G-5978)
LOVES ENTERPRISE LLC ◊
3589 Delaware St (46409-1340)
PHONE..............................219 307-9191
EMP: 1 EST: 2022
SALES (est): 39.59K **Privately Held**
SIC: 2051 7389 Bakery: wholesale or wholesale/retail combined; Business Activities at Non-Commercial Site

(G-5979)
MAGNECO/METREL INC
201 Mississippi St (46402-1546)
PHONE..............................219 885-4190
Tom Colander, *Brnch Mgr*
EMP: 87
SALES (corp-wide): 45.46MM **Privately Held**
Web: www.magneco-metrel.com
SIC: 5085 3297 Refractory material; Nonclay refractories
PA: Magneco/Metrel, Inc.
740 Waukegan Rd Ste 212
Deerfield IL 60015
630 543-6660

(G-5980)
MAKE IT BLACK SEAL COATING
3764 Louisiana St (46409-1611)
PHONE..............................219 629-6230
Thomas Ross Junior, *Owner*
EMP: 6 EST: 2017
SALES (est): 102.93K **Privately Held**
SIC: 3479 Metal coating and allied services

(G-5981)
MHP DISTRIBUTION LLC
300 S Henry St (46403-2385)
PHONE..............................312 731-8380
Maurice Pruitt, *CEO*
EMP: 12 EST: 2007
SALES (est): 873.37K **Privately Held**
SIC: 5199 3537 Nondurable goods, nec; Trucks: freight, baggage, etc.: industrial, except mining

(G-5982)
MILLER RACEWAY
4900 Melton Rd (46403-2872)
PHONE..............................219 939-9688
Lakhwinder P Singh, *Prin*
EMP: 3 EST: 2010
SALES (est): 186.78K **Privately Held**
SIC: 3644 Raceways

(G-5983)
MILLWRIGHT MACHINE INC
899 Grant St (46404-1528)
PHONE..............................219 845-9200
Kathy Krukowski, *Pr*
EMP: 18 EST: 2000
SALES (est): 2.06MM **Privately Held**
Web: www.millwrightmachine.com
SIC: 3599 Machine shop, jobbing and repair

(G-5984)
MINTEQ INTERNATIONAL INC
1 N Broadway (46402-3101)
PHONE..............................219 886-9555
Don Cochran, *Mgr*
EMP: 2
Web: www.mineralstech.com
SIC: 3297 Nonclay refractories
HQ: Minteq International Inc.
35 Highland Ave
Bethlehem PA 18017

(G-5985)
MODRAK PRODUCTS COMPANY INC
3700 Clark Rd (46408-1308)
PHONE..............................219 838-0308
Larry Modrak, *Pr*
Judy Modrak, *VP*
EMP: 10 EST: 1948
SQ FT: 15,000
SALES (est): 1.07MM **Privately Held**
Web: www.modrakproducts.com
SIC: 2842 5087 5999 Polishes and sanitation goods; Janitors' supplies; Cleaning equipment and supplies

(G-5986)
MULTI-WALL PACKAGING CORP
1 N Bridge St (46404-1073)
PHONE..............................219 882-0070
Charlie Dunn, *Pr*
EMP: 75 EST: 2017
SALES (est): 9.14MM **Privately Held**
Web: www.signode.com
SIC: 2671 Resinous impregnated paper for packaging

(G-5987)
NSPIRE LLC
1325 Bigger St (46404-1839)
PHONE..............................219 301-2446
EMP: 5 EST: 2020
SALES (est): 74.42K **Privately Held**
SIC: 2844 Cosmetic preparations

(G-5988)
OLD DUTCH SAND CO INC
4600 E 15th Ave (46403-3699)
PHONE..............................219 938-7020
Gary Goldberg, *VP*
Bernice Gray, *Pr*
EMP: 5 EST: 1961
SQ FT: 500
SALES (est): 821.7K **Privately Held**
Web: www.jackgray.com
SIC: 5032 1442 Sand, construction; Construction sand mining

(G-5989)
ONE EIGHT SEVEN INCORPORATED
Also Called: One Eight Seven
1050 Michigan St (46402-3009)
PHONE..............................219 886-2060
Dan Luce, *Mgr*
EMP: 6
SALES (corp-wide): 881.27K **Privately Held**
Web: www.187basics.com
SIC: 3297 Nonclay refractories
PA: One Eight Seven Incorporated
10485 Frankstown Rd
Pittsburgh PA
412 243-7365

(G-5990)
ONE LINEAGE TRUCKING CORP
636 Mckinley St (46404-1423)
PHONE..............................708 257-6333
Derrick Grant, *Pr*
EMP: 12 EST: 2021
SALES (est): 200K **Privately Held**
SIC: 3537 Trucks, tractors, loaders, carriers, and similar equipment

(G-5991)
ORGANIC BREAD OF HEAVEN LLC
Also Called: Organic Bread of Heaven
2700 W 5th Ave (46404-1248)
PHONE..............................219 883-5126
Ronald J Bruno, *Managing Member*
Pamela Sue Bruno, *Managing Member*
Jessica Bruno, *Acctnt*
EMP: 15 EST: 2014
SQ FT: 2,800
SALES (est): 4.22MM **Privately Held**
Web: www.ovenfreshdelivery.com
SIC: 5149 5461 2051 Crackers, cookies, and bakery products; Retail bakeries; Bread, cake, and related products

(G-5992)
OWENS PROPERTY SOLUTIONS LLC
1308 Delaware St (46407-1419)
PHONE..............................708 374-2626
Darrius Owens, *Pr*
EMP: 1 EST: 2021
SALES (est): 144.21K **Privately Held**
SIC: 1389 0783 7389 Construction, repair, and dismantling services; Removal services, bush and tree; Business Activities at Non-Commercial Site

(G-5993)
OZINGA INDIANA RDYMX CON INC
400 Blaine St (46406-1252)
PHONE..............................219 949-9800
EMP: 10
SALES (est): 1.11MM **Privately Held**
SIC: 3273 5032 Ready-mixed concrete; Brick, stone, and related material

(G-5994)
PHIPPS SONS WELDING
2126 W Ridge Rd (46408-2057)
PHONE..............................219 776-3810
EMP: 4 EST: 2017
SALES (est): 43.64K **Privately Held**
SIC: 7692 Welding repair

(G-5995)
PRES-DEL ELECTRIC INC
4172 Broadway (46408-2809)
PHONE..............................219 884-3146
Ron Price, *Pr*
EMP: 6 EST: 1948
SQ FT: 18,000
SALES (est): 475.96K **Privately Held**
Web: www.presdel.com
SIC: 7694 5999 Electric motor repair; Motors, electric

(G-5996)
PRO PALLET LLC
1584 Blaine St (46406-2220)
PHONE..............................219 292-3389
Matthew Collins, *Prin*
EMP: 7 EST: 2016
SALES (est): 476.88K **Privately Held**
Web: www.collinspallet.com
SIC: 2448 Pallets, wood

(G-5997)
PROFIT OVER ROMANCE LLC
1400 W 19th Pl (46407-2403)
PHONE..............................219 900-3592
Antonio Dominguez, *CEO*
EMP: 3 EST: 2021
SALES (est): 69.69K **Privately Held**
SIC: 7389 2284 5999 5611 Embroidery advertising; Embroidery thread; Miscellaneous retail stores, nec; Clothing, sportswear, men's and boys'

(G-5998)
QME LLC
2262 W 17th Ave (46404-2301)
PHONE..............................773 263-9830
EMP: 2 EST: 2021
SALES (est): 95.58K **Privately Held**
SIC: 3537 Trucks: freight, baggage, etc.: industrial, except mining

(G-5999)
RAMO & CO LLC
2572 Van Buren St (46407-3916)
PHONE..............................219 381-1843

GEOGRAPHIC SECTION

Gary - Lake County (G-6024)

Raquel Young, *CEO*
EMP: 1 **EST:** 2021
SALES (est): 49.15K **Privately Held**
SIC: 3161 Clothing and apparel carrying cases

(G-6000)
RAY KAMMER
Also Called: Midwest Water Controls
6805 Forest Ave (46403-1280)
PHONE..................219 938-1708
Ray Kammer, *Owner*
EMP: 3 **EST:** 1997
SALES (est): 159.1K **Privately Held**
SIC: 3823 Water quality monitoring and control systems

(G-6001)
REED MINERALS
7100 W 9th Ave (46406-1924)
PHONE..................219 944-6250
Derek Hathaway, *Prin*
EMP: 7 **EST:** 2010
SALES (est): 106.23K **Privately Held**
SIC: 3295 Minerals, ground or treated

(G-6002)
REFAX INC
Also Called: Imperial Steel Tank
3240 W 5th Ave (46406-1724)
P.O. Box 9018 (46402-9018)
PHONE..................219 977-0414
Richard A Oliver, *Pr*
EMP: 180 **EST:** 1983
SQ FT: 20,000
SALES (est): 24.49MM
SALES (corp-wide): 47.52MM **Privately Held**
Web: www.refaxinc.com
SIC: 3441 Fabricated structural metal
PA: Gi Properties, Inc.
    6610 Melton Rd
    Portage IN 46368
    219 763-1177

(G-6003)
REFAX WEAR PRODUCTS INC
3240 W 5th Ave (46406-1724)
PHONE..................219 977-0414
Richard Oliver, *Prin*
EMP: 18 **EST:** 1983
SALES (est): 208.72K **Privately Held**
Web: www.refaxinc.com
SIC: 3441 3446 Fabricated structural metal; Architectural metalwork

(G-6004)
RHYNE ENGINES INC
Also Called: Rhyne Competition Engines
5733 W 25th Ave (46406-3127)
PHONE..................219 845-1218
Joe Rhyne, *Pr*
EMP: 7 **EST:** 1972
SQ FT: 7,000
SALES (est): 502.6K **Privately Held**
Web: www.rhynecompetitionengines.com
SIC: 3599 7549 Machine shop, jobbing and repair; High performance auto repair and service

(G-6005)
RIETH-RILEY CNSTR CO INC
7500 W 5th Ave (46406-1238)
PHONE..................574 875-5183
Doug Robinson, *Mgr*
EMP: 25
SALES (corp-wide): 174.41MM **Privately Held**
Web: www.rieth-riley.com

SIC: 1611 2951 Surfacing and paving; Asphalt paving mixtures and blocks
PA: Rieth-Riley Construction Co., Inc.
    3626 Elkhart Rd
    Goshen IN 46526
    574 875-5183

(G-6006)
S AND SM ACHINE USA LLC
3110 W 5th Ave (46406-1722)
PHONE..................708 758-8300
EMP: 5 **EST:** 2019
SALES (est): 137.53K **Privately Held**
SIC: 3537 Industrial trucks and tractors

(G-6007)
S M SMITH LLC - S STNGEL MNGED
3098 Hanley St (46406-3433)
PHONE..................219 802-6064
Allen Stangel, *Mgr*
EMP: 4 **EST:** 2020
SALES (est): 110K **Privately Held**
SIC: 1389 Construction, repair, and dismantling services

(G-6008)
SEDUCTIVE LIFESTYLE LLC
1128 Burr St (46406-2158)
PHONE..................708 990-0720
EMP: 1 **EST:** 2021
SALES (est): 59.58K **Privately Held**
SIC: 5999 2844 5122 Toiletries, cosmetics, and perfumes; Suntan lotions and oils; Cosmetics, perfumes, and hair products

(G-6009)
SHANXI-INDIANA LLC
Also Called: Dvs Refractories
201 Mississippi St (46402-1546)
PHONE..................219 885-2209
EMP: 15 **EST:** 2008
SALES (est): 820.17K **Privately Held**
SIC: 3559 Kilns

(G-6010)
SKIPS BUMPER REPAIR
520 W Ridge Rd (46408-2747)
PHONE..................773 289-2255
EMP: 4 **EST:** 2013
SALES (est): 46.6K **Privately Held**
SIC: 7699 3083 Repair services, nec; Laminated plastics plate and sheet

(G-6011)
SMITHS MEDICAL ASD INC
5700 W 23rd Ave (46406-2617)
PHONE..................219 554-2196
Jackie Gerner, *Brnch Mgr*
EMP: 46
SALES (corp-wide): 2.26B **Publicly Held**
SIC: 3841 Surgical and medical instruments
HQ: Smiths Medical Asd, Inc.
    6000 Nathan Ln N
    Plymouth MN 55442
    763 383-3000

(G-6012)
SMS GROUP INC
Also Called: SMS Technical Services
201 Mississippi St Ste 12a (46402)
PHONE..................219 880-0256
Steve Winger, *Prin*
EMP: 50
SALES (corp-wide): 144.19K **Privately Held**
Web: www.sms-group.com
SIC: 3441 3443 Fabricated structural metal; Fabricated plate work (boiler shop)
HQ: Sms Group Inc.
    100 Sandusky St

Pittsburgh PA 15212
412 231-1200

(G-6013)
SOUTHLAKE LIFT TRUCK
3601 Arizona St (46405-3121)
PHONE..................219 962-4695
Don Glorioso, *Owner*
EMP: 5 **EST:** 2002
SALES (est): 360.75K **Privately Held**
Web: www.forkliftdealerlakestation.com
SIC: 3537 4213 Forklift trucks; Trucking, except local

(G-6014)
SOYFUL FRAGRANT CANDLES LLC
1129 Baker St (46404-1629)
PHONE..................219 588-2685
Richard M Williams, *Prin*
EMP: 6 **EST:** 2014
SALES (est): 63.28K **Privately Held**
Web: soyfulfragrantcandles.webs.com
SIC: 3999 Candles

(G-6015)
SSSI INC
1 N Broadway (46402-3101)
P.O. Box 64771 (46401-0771)
PHONE..................219 880-0818
Rich Soohey, *Brnch Mgr*
EMP: 13
SALES (corp-wide): 50.92MM **Privately Held**
Web: www.songerservices.com
SIC: 1611 3312 4925 General contractor, highway and street construction; Blast furnaces and steel mills; Coke oven gas, production and distribution
PA: Sssi, Inc.
    100 Houston Sq Ste 200
    Canonsburg PA 15317
    724 743-5815

(G-6016)
SUPERIOR TRUSS & PANEL INC
7592 Melton Rd (46403-3147)
PHONE..................708 339-1200
William Welty, *Pr*
EMP: 50 **EST:** 1997
SQ FT: 40,000
SALES (est): 9.53MM **Privately Held**
Web: www.superior-truss.com
SIC: 2439 Trusses, wooden roof

(G-6017)
T K SALES & SERVICE
Also Called: T B K Tarp Sales & Service
669 S Grand Blvd (46403-2901)
P.O. Box 2497 (46403-0497)
PHONE..................219 962-8982
Anthony J Kettwig, *Owner*
EMP: 4 **EST:** 1982
SQ FT: 3,796
SALES (est): 182.68K **Privately Held**
SIC: 2394 5199 7692 5251 Tarpaulins, fabric: made from purchased materials; Tarpaulins; Automotive welding; Hardware stores

(G-6018)
THATCHER ENGINEERING CORP
7100 Industrial Hwy (46406-1099)
PHONE..................219 949-2084
R Stephen Parkison, *Pr*
Thomas Wysockey, *Stockholder*
EMP: 90 **EST:** 1932
SQ FT: 12,000
SALES (est): 4.37MM **Privately Held**
Web: www.thatcherfoundations.com

SIC: 1741 1629 3822 1794 Foundation and retaining wall construction; Pile driving contractor; Environmental controls; Excavation work

(G-6019)
TIRES ENTERPRISES CORP
3716 W Ridge Rd (46408-1844)
PHONE..................866 807-4930
Guadalupe Navarro, *Pr*
EMP: 13 **EST:** 2017
SALES (est): 6.2MM **Privately Held**
SIC: 7534 Tire repair shop

(G-6020)
TMS INTERNATIONAL LLC
Truck Stop 749 (46402)
PHONE..................219 881-0155
EMP: 10
Web: www.tmsinternational.com
SIC: 3312 Blast furnaces and steel mills
HQ: Tms International, Llc
    Southside Wrks Bldg 1 3f
    Pittsburgh PA 15203
    412 678-6141

(G-6021)
TMS INTERNATIONAL LLC
1 N Broadway (46402-3101)
PHONE..................219 881-0266
EMP: 35
Web: www.tmsinternational.com
SIC: 3312 Blast furnaces and steel mills
HQ: Tms International, Llc
    Southside Wrks Bldg 1 3f
    Pittsburgh PA 15203
    412 678-6141

(G-6022)
TRIM-A-SEAL OF INDIANA INC (PA)
Also Called: Styled-Rite
1500 Polk St (46407-1999)
PHONE..................219 883-2180
TOLL FREE: 888
Howard B Weiss, *Pr*
Lawrence S Weiss, *VP*
Marlene Weiss, *Treas*
Pamela Weiss, *Sec*
EMP: 15 **EST:** 1947
SQ FT: 4,000
SALES (est): 2.24MM
SALES (corp-wide): 2.24MM **Privately Held**
Web: www.trimaseal.com
SIC: 3442 3444 Storm doors or windows, metal; Sheet metalwork

(G-6023)
UNITED STATES STEEL CORP
Also Called: U. S. Steel
1 N Broadway (46402-3199)
PHONE..................219 888-2000
James P Mcnamara, *Mgr*
EMP: 1
SALES (corp-wide): 18.05B **Publicly Held**
Web: www.ussteel.com
SIC: 3325 3441 3312 Steel foundries, nec; Fabricated structural metal; Blast furnaces and steel mills
PA: United States Steel Corp
    600 Grant St
    Pittsburgh PA 15219
    412 433-1121

(G-6024)
UNIVERSAL EXPORT PARTNR LLC
5528 Melton Rd (46403-2958)
PHONE..................219 939-9529
EMP: 2 **EST:** 2011
SALES (est): 105.39K **Privately Held**
Web: www.darnaillyles.com

SIC: 3253 Ceramic wall and floor tile

(G-6025)
UPG ENTERPRISES LLC
Also Called: Lexington Steel
700 Chase St (46404-1246)
PHONE.................................708 594-9200
Christopher Hutter, *Brnch Mgr*
EMP: 85
SALES (corp-wide): 557.04MM **Privately Held**
Web: www.lexingtonsteel.net
SIC: 5051 3312 Steel; Blast furnaces and steel mills
PA: Upg Enterprises Llc
   1400 16th St Ste 250
   Oak Brook IL 60523
   630 822-7000

(G-6026)
VAN GARD VAULT CO INC
4401 W Ridge Rd (46408-1329)
PHONE.................................219 980-6233
EMP: 3 EST: 2010
SALES (est): 213.49K **Privately Held**
SIC: 3272 Burial vaults, concrete or precast terrazzo

(G-6027)
VAN GARD VAULT COMPANY INC
Also Called: Van Guard Vault
5100 Industrial Hwy (46406-1124)
P.O. Box 629 (46319-0629)
PHONE.................................219 949-7723
Robert Williams, *Pr*
EMP: 15 EST: 1970
SQ FT: 16,000
SALES (est): 842.45K **Privately Held**
Web: www.vangardvault.com
SIC: 3272 Burial vaults, concrete or precast terrazzo

(G-6028)
WES GROUP INC
1225 Martin Luther King Dr (46402-3013)
PHONE.................................219 932-5200
EMP: 201
SIC: 3743 Freight cars and equipment

(G-6029)
ZIMCO MATERIALS INC
2555 E 15th Ave (46402-3021)
PHONE.................................219 883-0870
Scott Zimmer, *Genl Mgr*
EMP: 8 EST: 2005
SALES (est): 193.38K **Privately Held**
SIC: 3273 5051 5211 Ready-mixed concrete; Concrete reinforcing bars; Cement

Gas City
Grant County

(G-6030)
AMERICAN CRANE & MILLWRIGHT
6132 Industrial Dr (46933-9205)
PHONE.................................765 452-5000
EMP: 3 EST: 2019
SALES (est): 149.68K **Privately Held**
Web: www.americancranekokomo.com
SIC: 3441 Fabricated structural metal

(G-6031)
AMERICAN WOODMARK CORPORATION
5300 Eastside Parkway Dr (46933-1648)
PHONE.................................765 677-1690
Pete Palpant, *Mgr*
EMP: 400
SALES (corp-wide): 1.85B **Publicly Held**

Web: www.americanwoodmark.com
SIC: 2434 Wood kitchen cabinets
PA: American Woodmark Corporation
   561 Shady Elm Rd
   Winchester VA 22602
   540 665-9100

(G-6032)
ARTISTIC EXPRESSIONS PUBG INC
111 E South C St (46933-1736)
P.O. Box 308 (46933-0308)
PHONE.................................317 502-6213
EMP: 4 EST: 2012
SALES (est): 92.83K **Privately Held**
Web: www.billpattisonstudio.com
SIC: 2741 Miscellaneous publishing

(G-6033)
AVG NORTH AMERICA INC
5133 Eastside Parkway Dr (46933-1601)
PHONE.................................765 748-3162
Karim Suleman, *Pr*
EMP: 10 EST: 2017
SALES (est): 848.58K **Privately Held**
SIC: 3714 Motor vehicle parts and accessories

(G-6034)
BUTTERWORTH INDUSTRIES INC
5050 Eastside Parkway Dr (46933-1645)
P.O. Box 107 (46933-0107)
PHONE.................................765 677-6725
Frank W Butterworth Iii, *Pr*
Frank L Butterworth Iii, *Pr*
Alice Butterworth, *
Julie Hawkins, *
EMP: 50 EST: 1968
SQ FT: 32,000
SALES (est): 7.58MM **Privately Held**
Web: www.butterworthindustries.com
SIC: 3535 Robotic conveyors

(G-6035)
DAVE TURNER
Also Called: Ebenezer Sportswear
109 E South D St (46933-1741)
PHONE.................................765 674-3360
Dave L Turner, *Owner*
EMP: 6 EST: 1989
SALES (est): 122.73K **Privately Held**
SIC: 7299 7336 2396 2395 Stitching services; Silk screen design; Automotive and apparel trimmings; Pleating and stitching

(G-6036)
EARTHWISE PLASTICS INC
Also Called: Earthwise Plastics
100 Earthwise Way (46933-2008)
PHONE.................................765 673-0308
Roger Dyson, *Pr*
Rocci Decamp, *
Andy Miller, *
EMP: 45 EST: 2009
SQ FT: 10,000
SALES (est): 7.45MM **Privately Held**
Web: www.earthwiseplastics.com
SIC: 3089 Plastics processing

(G-6037)
GAS CITY B & K INC
928 E Main St (46933-1549)
PHONE.................................765 674-9651
John Thompson, *Pr*
EMP: 9 EST: 2002
SALES (est): 121.6K **Privately Held**
Web: www.gcpowdercoat.com
SIC: 1389 Cementing oil and gas well casings

(G-6038)
HEARTLAND HARVEST PROC LLC (PA)
Also Called: Floral Beverages
4861 S 600 E Bldg A (46933-9547)
PHONE.................................260 228-0736
EMP: 5 EST: 2019
SALES (est): 563.66K
SALES (corp-wide): 563.66K **Privately Held**
SIC: 2079 Oil, hydrogenated: edible

(G-6039)
PACKAGING CORPORATION AMERICA
Also Called: PCA/Gas City 323
520 S 1st St (46933-1727)
PHONE.................................765 674-9781
Paul Olsen, *Brnch Mgr*
EMP: 95
SALES (corp-wide): 8.48B **Publicly Held**
Web: www.packagingcorp.com
SIC: 2653 Boxes, corrugated: made from purchased materials
PA: Packaging Corporation Of America
   1 N Field Ct
   Lake Forest IL 60045
   847 482-3000

(G-6040)
TURNING OVER A NEW LEAF LLC
313 W Main St (46933-1073)
PHONE.................................765 573-3366
Rebecca R Banks, *Managing Member*
EMP: 1 EST: 2011
SALES (est): 71.29K **Privately Held**
SIC: 3999 8748 Artificial flower arrangements; Business consulting, nec

(G-6041)
TWIN CITY JOURNAL REPORTER
Also Called: Journal Reporter
407 E Main St (46933-1532)
PHONE.................................765 674-0070
Greg Lenaze, *Owner*
EMP: 2
SALES (est): 67.22K **Privately Held**
SIC: 2711 Newspapers: publishing only, not printed on site

(G-6042)
WRIGHT REPAIRS INC
5900 Eastside Parkway Dr (46933-1656)
PHONE.................................765 674-3300
Thomas Wright, *Pr*
Dale Johnson, *VP*
EMP: 14 EST: 1991
SQ FT: 5,000
SALES (est): 2.26MM **Privately Held**
Web: www.wrightrepairs.com
SIC: 7694 Electric motor repair

Gaston
Delaware County

(G-6043)
AGBEST COOPERATIVE INC
430 S Sycamore St (47342-9441)
P.O. Box 398 (47342-0398)
PHONE.................................765 358-3388
Marty Clock, *Brnch Mgr*
EMP: 8
SALES (corp-wide): 42.4MM **Privately Held**
Web: www.agbest.com
SIC: 5261 2875 Fertilizer; Fertilizers, mixing only
PA: Agbest Cooperative Inc
   2101 N Granville Ave

   Muncie IN 47303
   765 288-5001

(G-6044)
C & C MAILBOX PRODUCTS
18100 N County Road 925 W (47342-9062)
PHONE.................................765 358-4880
Gerald Clock, *Prin*
EMP: 2 EST: 2007
SALES (est): 132.84K **Privately Held**
Web: www.ccmailboxes.com
SIC: 5021 3444 2441 Outdoor and lawn furniture, nec; Mail (post office) collection or storage boxes, sheet metal; Nailed wood boxes and shook

(G-6045)
G AND G PEPPERS LLC
12245 N County Road 450 W (47342-9423)
P.O. Box 326 (46063-0326)
PHONE.................................765 358-4519
Gary Reichart, *Pt*
Michell Reichart, *Pt*
Greg Cox, *Pt*
EMP: 20 EST: 2000
SALES (est): 1.68MM **Privately Held**
Web: www.gandgpeppers.com
SIC: 2099 Chili pepper or powder

(G-6046)
GREAT DEALS RACING
8081 W Mccolm Rd (47342-9258)
PHONE.................................765 288-4608
EMP: 5 EST: 2010
SALES (est): 69.56K **Privately Held**
SIC: 2711 Newspapers

Geneva
Adams County

(G-6047)
ADVANCED MANUFACTURING IN
500 W Line St (46740-9202)
PHONE.................................260 273-9669
Robert W Raugh, *Pr*
EMP: 2 EST: 2010
SALES (est): 84.02K **Privately Held**
SIC: 3999 Barber and beauty shop equipment

(G-6048)
BAUMBAUER SIGNS
Also Called: Highway Sign Service
967 Sw High St (46740-9069)
PHONE.................................260 368-7537
John Baumbauer, *Owner*
EMP: 1 EST: 1972
SALES (est): 62.34K **Privately Held**
SIC: 3993 Signs and advertising specialties

(G-6049)
ETI LLC (HQ)
Also Called: Elkhart Tri-Went Industrial
700 Rainbow Rd (46740-9700)
PHONE.................................260 368-7246
Dave Thompson, *CEO*
Joe Headdy, *Pr*
EMP: 14 EST: 2019
SALES (est): 13.26MM
SALES (corp-wide): 193.09MM **Privately Held**
Web: www.elkharttriwent.com
SIC: 3494 Valves and pipe fittings, nec
PA: Lion Equity Holdings Ii, Llc
   260 Josephine St Ste 220
   Denver CO 80206
   303 847-4100

GEOGRAPHIC SECTION

Georgetown - Floyd County (G-6076)

(G-6050)
RED GOLD INC
Red Gold/Geneva
705 Williams St (46740-1061)
P.O. Box 247 (46740-0247)
PHONE.....................260 368-9017
Richard Jones, *Mgr*
EMP: 214
SALES (corp-wide): 451.21MM **Privately Held**
Web: www.redgoldfoods.com
SIC: 2033 2035 Canned fruits and specialties; Pickles, sauces, and salad dressings
PA: Red Gold, Inc.
1520 S 22nd St
Elwood IN 46036
765 557-5500

(G-6051)
RED GOLD INC
901 W 1200 S (46740-9263)
PHONE.....................765 557-5500
Beau Reichart, *COO*
EMP: 215
SALES (corp-wide): 451.21MM **Privately Held**
Web: www.redgoldfoods.com
SIC: 2033 2035 Tomato products, packaged in cans, jars, etc.; Pickles, sauces, and salad dressings
PA: Red Gold, Inc.
1520 S 22nd St
Elwood IN 46036
765 557-5500

(G-6052)
SERVICES EVERYONE NEEDS TODAY
11725 S 650 W (46740-9234)
PHONE.....................260 368-9262
Barb Smith, *Owner*
EMP: 1 **EST:** 1999
SALES (est): 61.26K **Privately Held**
SIC: 2221 Broadwoven fabric mills, manmade

Gentryville
Spencer County

(G-6053)
STAHL EQUIPMENT INC
14094 N Base Rd (47537-9763)
P.O. Box 130 (47610-0130)
PHONE.....................812 925-3341
Norbert Stahl, *Pr*
Bobbie Stahl, *
EMP: 10 **EST:** 1959
SALES (est): 325.17K **Privately Held**
SIC: 3441 3537 3535 3444 Building components, structural steel; Industrial trucks and tractors; Conveyors and conveying equipment; Sheet metalwork

Georgetown
Floyd County

(G-6054)
APPAREL PLUS INC
1175 Copperfield Dr (47122-9083)
PHONE.....................812 951-2111
Carol Richmer, *Pr*
EMP: 1 **EST:** 1999
SALES (est): 280.78K **Privately Held**
Web: www.apparelplusinc.com
SIC: 5199 2395 Advertising specialties; Embroidery products, except Schiffli machine

(G-6055)
AREVA PHARMACEUTICALS INC
7112 Areva Dr Ne (47122-7953)
P.O. Box 336 (47122-0336)
PHONE.....................855 853-4760
Irene Swaminathan, *CEO*
Tom Murphy, *Pr*
Greg Olson, *COO*
EMP: 15 **EST:** 2010
SALES (est): 1.71MM **Privately Held**
Web: www.arevapharma.com
SIC: 2834 Pharmaceutical preparations

(G-6056)
DESK CODER LLC
6170 Park St (47122-9285)
PHONE.....................812 406-5367
EMP: 1 **EST:** 2012
SALES (est): 80.86K **Privately Held**
Web: www.deskcoder.com
SIC: 7372 Application computer software

(G-6057)
DESTINY SOLUTIONS INC
8265 State Road 64 (47122-9056)
PHONE.....................502 384-0031
EMP: 7 **EST:** 2010
SALES (est): 980.87K **Privately Held**
Web: www.destinysolutions.us
SIC: 3663 8742 Radio and t.v. communications equipment; Management consulting services

(G-6058)
DIVERSE WOODWORKING LLC
505 Maplewood Blvd (47122-9261)
PHONE.....................812 366-3000
EMP: 3 **EST:** 2012
SALES (est): 420.2K **Privately Held**
Web: www.diversewoodworking.com
SIC: 2431 Millwork

(G-6059)
EXHALE FANS LLC
6370 Forest Grove Dr Ne (47122-7764)
PHONE.....................812 366-3351
EMP: 5 **EST:** 2012
SALES (est): 235.01K **Privately Held**
Web: www.exhalefans.com
SIC: 3634 Electric housewares and fans

(G-6060)
FABTRATION LLC
526 Maplewood Blvd (47122-9261)
PHONE.....................812 989-6730
Rick Keenan, *Managing Member*
▼ **EMP:** 12 **EST:** 2011
SQ FT: 10,000
SALES (est): 1.45MM **Privately Held**
Web: www.fabtration.com
SIC: 3449 3613 Bars, concrete reinforcing: fabricated steel; Control panels, electric

(G-6061)
GEORGETOWN TRUSS COMPANY INC
9627 State Road 64 (47122-8842)
P.O. Box 1 (47122-0001)
PHONE.....................812 951-2647
Tim Youtsey, *Pr*
Cindy Youtsey, *
EMP: 28 **EST:** 1984
SQ FT: 14,000
SALES (est): 711.4K **Privately Held**
SIC: 2439 Trusses, except roof: laminated lumber

(G-6062)
HENDRIX CO
3025 E Whiskey Run Rd Ne (47122-7426)
PHONE.....................812 366-4333
Danny Hendrix, *Owner*
EMP: 1 **EST:** 1986
SALES (est): 53.05K **Privately Held**
Web: www.hendrix.com
SIC: 3915 Jewel preparing: instruments, tools, watches, and jewelry

(G-6063)
JC MOAG CORPORATION
4835 Research Blvd Ne (47122-7954)
P.O. Box 1415 (47131-1415)
PHONE.....................812 284-8400
John T Moag, *CEO*
James C Moag, *
▲ **EMP:** 75 **EST:** 1946
SQ FT: 80,000
SALES (est): 8.57MM **Privately Held**
Web: www.moagglass.com
SIC: 2541 3231 Store fixtures, wood; Products of purchased glass

(G-6064)
KAZE ENERGY LLC
Also Called: Kaze
6108 Deer Trace Ct (47122-0119)
PHONE.....................502 664-5519
EMP: 1 **EST:** 2008
SALES (est): 123.36K **Privately Held**
SIC: 2899 Chemical preparations, nec

(G-6065)
KENTUCKIANA MACHINE & TOOL INC
Also Called: Kellco
518 Maplewood Blvd (47122-9261)
PHONE.....................502 593-3975
Scott Patterson, *Pr*
EMP: 5 **EST:** 1995
SQ FT: 5,500
SALES (est): 449.9K **Privately Held**
Web: www.kellcomachine.com
SIC: 3599 Machine shop, jobbing and repair

(G-6066)
KS KREATIONS
7700 Greenbrier Rd Ne (47122-9617)
PHONE.....................574 514-7366
EMP: 4 **EST:** 2014
SALES (est): 81.97K **Privately Held**
Web: www.kskreations.com
SIC: 3999 Candles

(G-6067)
LIBERTY GREEN RENEWABLES LLP
5019 Georges Hill Rd Ne (47122-2001)
PHONE.....................812 951-3143
EMP: 3 **EST:** 2008
SALES (est): 138.28K **Privately Held**
SIC: 3621 Generating apparatus and parts, electrical

(G-6068)
MARTIN GRGORY CNVYOR ENGRG LLC
1549 Pirtle Dr (47122-9109)
P.O. Box 246 (47122-0246)
PHONE.....................812 923-9814
Pamela A Villiger, *Managing Member*
EMP: 3 **EST:** 2003
SALES (est): 240.73K **Privately Held**
Web: www.martingregoryconveyor.com
SIC: 3535 Unit handling conveying systems

(G-6069)
MARYS GIFT BASKETS LLC
9039 Richland Dr (47122-8831)
PHONE.....................502 819-3022
EMP: 1 **EST:** 2013
SALES (est): 88.78K **Privately Held**
SIC: 2449 Baskets: fruit and vegetable, round stave, till, etc.

(G-6070)
MIKES METAL DECTORS
9350 Indian Bluff Rd Ne (47122-7353)
PHONE.....................812 366-3558
Michael Byrn, *Asstg*
EMP: 6 **EST:** 2004
SALES (est): 186.55K **Privately Held**
SIC: 3669 Metal detectors

(G-6071)
NATALIE ANDERSON LLC
2007 Brookstone Way (47122-9440)
PHONE.....................812 951-3532
Natalie Anderson, *Owner*
EMP: 2 **EST:** 2007
SALES (est): 100K **Privately Held**
Web: www.natalie-anderson.com
SIC: 2741 Miscellaneous publishing

(G-6072)
ODYSSEY MACHINE INC
Also Called: Odyssey Machine
9627 State Road 64 (47122-8842)
PHONE.....................812 951-1160
Robert E Kiper, *Prin*
EMP: 6 **EST:** 2014
SALES (est): 496.14K **Privately Held**
Web: vortexcomp.wixsite.com
SIC: 7699 3599 3089 Industrial machinery and equipment repair; Crankshafts and camshafts, machining; Automotive parts, plastic

(G-6073)
PARAKLESE TECHNOLOGIES LLC
Also Called: Ground Pounder of Indiana
7600 State Rd 64 Ste Alpha 2 (47122-9073)
PHONE.....................502 357-0735
EMP: 11 **EST:** 2002
SQ FT: 1,200
SALES (est): 905.17K **Privately Held**
Web: www.paraklesetechnologies.com
SIC: 3482 3949 Small arms ammunition; Targets, archery and rifle shooting

(G-6074)
SDN SPECIALTY WALLCOVERIN
9219 Dawn Dr (47122-8917)
PHONE.....................812 736-1806
Steven Nealy, *Owner*
EMP: 1 **EST:** 1999
SALES (est): 104.08K **Privately Held**
SIC: 2522 Wallcases, office: except wood

(G-6075)
SMOKED BROS LLC
7007 Windsong Ct (47122-9099)
PHONE.....................360 440-6948
Michael Beaven, *Managing Member*
EMP: 2 **EST:** 2020
SALES (est): 27K **Privately Held**
Web: www.smokedbros.com
SIC: 2099 Spices, including grinding

(G-6076)
UTZ QUALITY FOODS LLC
9595 State Road 64 (47122-8840)
PHONE.....................812 430-5751
Adam Bost, *Mgr*
EMP: 1

(PA)=Parent Co (HQ)=Headquarters
✪ = New Business established in last 2 years

SALES (corp-wide): 732.3MM **Privately Held**
Web: www.utzsnacks.com
SIC: 2096 Potato chips and other potato-based snacks
PA: Utz Quality Foods, Llc
900 High St
Hanover PA 17331
800 367-7629

Goodland
Newton County

(G-6077)
3D MACHINE INC
215 S Newton St (47948-8189)
P.O. Box 465 (47948-0465)
PHONE......................219 297-3674
Tim Deno, *Pr*
Kelly Deno, *
EMP: 35 **EST:** 1996
SQ FT: 72,000
SALES (est): 7.58MM **Privately Held**
Web: www.3dmach.com
SIC: 3599 Machine shop, jobbing and repair

(G-6078)
ADKEV INC (PA)
664 S Iroquois St (47948-8167)
P.O. Box 390 (47948-0390)
PHONE......................219 297-4484
▲ **EMP:** 91 **EST:** 1986
SALES (est): 81.2MM **Privately Held**
Web: www.adkev.com
SIC: 3089 Molding primary plastics

(G-6079)
BEASLEY FABRICATING & MCHNNG
11237 S State Road 55 (47948-8020)
PHONE......................219 297-4000
EMP: 4 **EST:** 2018
SALES (est): 53.42K **Privately Held**
SIC: 7692 Welding repair

(G-6080)
BUTLER TOOL & DESIGN INC
641 S Newton St (47948-8128)
PHONE......................219 297-4531
James Butler, *Pr*
R Kay Butler, *VP*
EMP: 13 **EST:** 1980
SQ FT: 7,000
SALES (est): 498.7K **Privately Held**
Web: www.butlertoolanddesign.com
SIC: 3545 3544 3599 8711 Tools and accessories for machine tools; Special dies and tools; Machine shop, jobbing and repair; Engineering services

(G-6081)
GENERATION FOUR MACHINE &
319 N Newton St (47948-8119)
P.O. Box 257 (47948-0257)
PHONE......................219 297-3003
Eric Geravsen, *Prin*
EMP: 2 **EST:** 2006
SALES (est): 178.24K **Privately Held**
SIC: 3599 Machine shop, jobbing and repair

(G-6082)
JANETS EMBROIDERY
9515 W 1600 S (47948-8621)
PHONE......................219 261-2812
Janet Alter, *Owner*
EMP: 1 **EST:** 1996
SALES (est): 62.14K **Privately Held**
SIC: 2395 Embroidery and art needlework

(G-6083)
USEFUL PRODUCTS LLC
429 W Jasper St (47948)
P.O. Box 377 (47948)
PHONE......................877 304-9036
Donald Ringer, *Managing Member*
EMP: 33 **EST:** 1973
SQ FT: 60,000
SALES (est): 2.2MM **Privately Held**
Web: www.usefulproducts.com
SIC: 2759 3086 Flexographic printing; Packaging and shipping materials, foamed plastics

Goshen
Elkhart County

(G-6084)
A AMP R WOODWORKING
15006 County Road 28 (46528-9655)
PHONE......................574 849-1477
EMP: 4 **EST:** 2019
SALES (est): 54.13K **Privately Held**
SIC: 2431 Millwork

(G-6085)
A&J WOODWORKING LLC
12263 County Road 36 (46528-6964)
PHONE......................574 642-4551
EMP: 9 **EST:** 2010
SALES (est): 565.51K **Privately Held**
SIC: 2431 Millwork

(G-6086)
A/C FABRICATING CORP
1821 Century Dr (46528-5044)
P.O. Box 774 (46527-0774)
PHONE......................574 534-1415
Gerie Mast, *Pr*
Melody Biddle, *Sec*
EMP: 20 **EST:** 1975
SQ FT: 20,000
SALES (est): 2.17MM **Privately Held**
Web: www.acfabricating.com
SIC: 3498 3542 3355 Tube fabricating (contract bending and shaping); Headers; Extrusion ingot, aluminum: made in rolling mills

(G-6087)
ACCU-BUILT TOOLING AND WELD
17821 County Road 14 (46528-8624)
PHONE......................574 825-7878
Robert Lievore, *Pr*
EMP: 1 **EST:** 1991
SALES (est): 76K **Privately Held**
SIC: 7692 7699 1799 Welding repair; Industrial machinery and equipment repair; Welding on site

(G-6088)
ADVANCE GREEN MFG CO INC
2482 E Kercher Rd (46526-6466)
PHONE......................574 457-2695
EMP: 6 **EST:** 2007
SQ FT: 1,000
SALES (est): 570.87K **Privately Held**
SIC: 3999 Coin-operated amusement machines

(G-6089)
ADVANCE MCS ELECTRONICS INC (PA)
67928 Us Highway 33 (46526-8549)
PHONE......................574 642-3501
Michael Snavely, *Pr*
Charlene Snavely, *Sec*
◆ **EMP:** 9 **EST:** 1993
SQ FT: 2,200

SALES (est): 775.78K **Privately Held**
Web: www.advancemcs.com
SIC: 5961 3613 Electronic kits and parts, mail order; Control panels, electric

(G-6090)
ADVANCED LF SPPORT INNVTONS LL
59125 County Road 21 (46528-7715)
PHONE......................574 538-1688
EMP: 1 **EST:** 2013
SALES (est): 61.65K **Privately Held**
Web: www.alsiconsultinggov.com
SIC: 7389 5999 3569 3842 Divers, commercial; Safety supplies and equipment; Firefighting and related equipment; Respiratory protection equipment, personal

(G-6091)
ADVANCING GEOMETRICS
20544 County Road 138 (46526-9110)
PHONE......................574 831-6480
EMP: 1 **EST:** 1991
SALES (est): 69.81K **Privately Held**
SIC: 7372 Prepackaged software

(G-6092)
AMERICAN PRINTING COMPANY (PA)
2331 Eisenhower Dr N (46526-8805)
PHONE......................574 533-5399
Jim Magnus, *Pr*
EMP: 5 **EST:** 1990
SALES (est): 296.42K
SALES (corp-wide): 296.42K **Privately Held**
Web: www.americanspeedy.com
SIC: 2752 Offset printing

(G-6093)
B T BTTERY CHARGER SYSTEMS INC
17189 County Road 22 (46528-6612)
PHONE......................574 533-6030
Tom Jewell, *Prin*
EMP: 3 **EST:** 2007
SALES (est): 234.09K **Privately Held**
SIC: 3691 5063 5084 Storage batteries; Storage batteries, industrial; Materials handling machinery

(G-6094)
B T DOOR
1206 Abbington Ct (46526-5596)
PHONE......................574 534-1726
Brad Daniels, *Owner*
EMP: 1 **EST:** 2000
SALES (est): 112.66K **Privately Held**
SIC: 2431 Doors, wood

(G-6095)
B&M WOOD INC
2108 Eisenhower Dr N (46528-8836)
PHONE......................574 535-0024
Brian Roe, *Pr*
Mark Wert, *VP*
EMP: 2 **EST:** 2004
SQ FT: 40,000
SALES (est): 1.86MM **Privately Held**
Web: www.brimarwood.com
SIC: 2431 Millwork

(G-6096)
BARRETT CUSTOM KNIVES
18943 County Road 18 (46528-7001)
PHONE......................574 533-4297
Rick Barrett, *Owner*
EMP: 1 **EST:** 2000
SALES (est): 66.43K **Privately Held**
Web: www.barrettcustomknives.com

SIC: 3421 Knives: butchers', hunting, pocket, etc.

(G-6097)
BEARCAT ANODIZING LLC
2431 E Kercher Rd (46526-6465)
PHONE......................574 533-0448
EMP: 1 **EST:** 2016
SALES (est): 186K **Privately Held**
Web: www.bearcatcorp.com
SIC: 3471 Anodizing (plating) of metals or formed products

(G-6098)
BEARCAT CORP
Also Called: Conversions By Bearcat
2431 E Kercher Rd (46526-6465)
P.O. Box 613 (46527-0613)
PHONE......................574 533-0448
Donald Cowan, *Pr*
Cassandra Cowan, *
EMP: 35 **EST:** 1971
SALES (est): 2.3MM **Privately Held**
Web: www.bearcatcorp.com
SIC: 3444 7532 Sheet metal specialties, not stamped; Customizing services, nonfactory basis

(G-6099)
BELLS TRUCKING LLC
531 Broadmore Est (46528-6342)
PHONE......................574 263-6030
EMP: 1 **EST:** 2019
SALES (est): 69.27K **Privately Held**
SIC: 3715 Truck trailers

(G-6100)
BRISTOL PALLET
64466 State Road 19 (46526-9421)
PHONE......................574 862-1862
EMP: 6 **EST:** 2014
SALES (est): 164.29K **Privately Held**
SIC: 2448 Pallets, wood

(G-6101)
BRUNK LLC (PA)
Also Called: Brunk Plastic Services
803 Logan St (46528-3508)
PHONE......................800 227-4156
Larry Barkowski, *Pr*
Patricia Hankila, *
Sandy Hochstetler, *
EMP: 80 **EST:** 1957
SQ FT: 125,000
SALES (est): 11.2MM
SALES (corp-wide): 11.2MM **Privately Held**
Web: www.brunkus.com
SIC: 3999 5162 Grinding and pulverizing of materials, nec; Plastics materials and basic shapes

(G-6102)
BRYAN SNYDER INC
2213 Cambridge Dr (46528-5714)
PHONE......................574 238-4481
Bryan Snyder, *Owner*
EMP: 6 **EST:** 2017
SALES (est): 105.84K **Privately Held**
Web: www.snyderartdesign.com
SIC: 2431 Millwork

(G-6103)
BUD LLC
Also Called: Foremost Fabricators
3352 Maple City Dr (46526-6807)
P.O. Box 638 (46526)
PHONE......................574 534-5300
▲ **EMP:** 35

GEOGRAPHIC SECTION

Goshen - Elkhart County (G-6132)

SIC: 3365 Aluminum and aluminum-based alloy castings

(G-6104)
BULLY PRODUCTS INC
2701 Lismore Dr (46526-6113)
PHONE.................................574 312-0511
EMP: 4 **EST:** 2016
SALES (est): 56.75K **Privately Held**
SIC: 3423 Hand and edge tools, nec

(G-6105)
BURKHOLDER MACHINE LLC
25354 County Road 40 (46526-7433)
PHONE.................................574 862-2004
EMP: 2 **EST:** 1989
SQ FT: 3,700
SALES (est): 165.57K **Privately Held**
SIC: 3599 Machine shop, jobbing and repair

(G-6106)
BUSH PILOT BEARD BALM
217 S Cottage Ave (46528-3320)
PHONE.................................574 535-4949
EMP: 5 **EST:** 2017
SALES (est): 52.27K **Privately Held**
Web: www.meanbeardco.com
SIC: 2844 Perfumes, cosmetics and other toilet preparations

(G-6107)
BYLER FAMILY WOOD WORKING
60845 State Road 13 (46528-6581)
PHONE.................................574 825-3339
EMP: 5 **EST:** 2008
SALES (est): 183.73K **Privately Held**
SIC: 2431 Millwork

(G-6108)
C IS FOR COOKIE LLP
67209 County Road 27 (46526-8599)
PHONE.................................574 538-9841
Tracy Mullins, *Pt*
EMP: 1
SALES (est): 68.54K **Privately Held**
SIC: 2051 Bakery, for home service delivery

(G-6109)
CAA INC
16255 County Road 22 (46526-9165)
PHONE.................................574 537-0933
Dawn Maes, *CEO*
EMP: 1 **EST:** 2002
SALES (est): 72.48K **Privately Held**
Web: www.caa.com
SIC: 2395 Embroidery and art needlework

(G-6110)
CENTRAL RUBBER & PLASTICS INC
17416 County Road 34 (46528)
P.O. Box 821 (46527)
PHONE.................................574 534-6411
EMP: 24 **EST:** 1994
SQ FT: 20,000
SALES (est): 2.15MM **Privately Held**
Web: www.centralrubberinc.com
SIC: 3069 Rubber automotive products

(G-6111)
CENTRUM FORCE FABRICATION
204 W Clinton St (46526-3216)
PHONE.................................574 295-5367
EMP: 2 **EST:** 2013
SALES (est): 119.93K **Privately Held**
Web: www.centrumforce.com
SIC: 3446 Ornamental metalwork

(G-6112)
CLINTON CUSTOM WOOD TURNING
62172 County Road 33 (46528-9609)
PHONE.................................574 535-0543
Lavern Yoder, *Owner*
EMP: 5 **EST:** 2015
SALES (est): 127.39K **Privately Held**
SIC: 2431 Millwork

(G-6113)
CLINTON HARNESS SHOP LLC
13705 State Road 4 (46528-9650)
PHONE.................................574 533-9797
Lloyd Miller, *Owner*
EMP: 2 **EST:** 1994
SALES (est): 108.77K **Privately Held**
SIC: 2386 3111 Leather and sheep-lined garments; Equestrian leather products

(G-6114)
COLBY L STANGER
Also Called: Stanger Excavating
15504 County Road 42 (46528-6945)
PHONE.................................574 536-5835
Colby L Stanger, *Owner*
EMP: 3 **EST:** 2004
SALES (est): 244.61K **Privately Held**
SIC: 3531 Construction machinery

(G-6115)
COMMERCIAL STRUCTURES CORP
Speed Space
65213 County Road 31 (46528-9250)
PHONE.................................574 773-7931
EMP: 3
SALES (corp-wide): 4.93MM **Privately Held**
Web: www.comstruc.com
SIC: 2451 Mobile buildings: for commercial use
PA: Commercial Structures Corp.
    655 N Tomahawk Trl
    Nappanee IN 46550
    574 773-7931

(G-6116)
COUNTRY VIEW CABINETS LLC
11770 County Road 32 (46528-9646)
PHONE.................................574 825-3150
Mervin L Yoder, *Admn*
EMP: 2 **EST:** 2010
SALES (est): 117.49K **Privately Held**
SIC: 2434 Wood kitchen cabinets

(G-6117)
COUNTRY WOODSHOP LLC
Also Called: Fusion Designs
62870 County Road 43 (46528-6846)
PHONE.................................574 642-3681
EMP: 20 **EST:** 2002
SALES (est): 2.26MM **Privately Held**
Web: www.fusiondesign.us
SIC: 2511 5031 5021 Kitchen and dining room furniture; Kitchen cabinets; Dining room furniture

(G-6118)
CRANE COMPOSITES INC
2424 E Kercher Rd (46526-6466)
PHONE.................................815 467-8600
Paul Margherio, *Mgr*
EMP: 1
SALES (corp-wide): 2.09B **Publicly Held**
Web: www.cranecomposites.com
SIC: 3089 Panels, building: plastics, nec
HQ: Crane Composites, Inc.
    23525 W Eames St
    Channahon IL 60410
    815 467-8600

(G-6119)
DAVID W IMHOFF
Also Called: Imhoff's Leather Works
62480 County Road 9 (46526-7167)
PHONE.................................574 862-4375
David W Imhoff, *Owner*
EMP: 1 **EST:** 1973
SQ FT: 1,026
SALES (est): 93.48K **Privately Held**
SIC: 3199 Straps, leather

(G-6120)
DELORO STELLITE HOLDINGS CORPORATION
1201 Eisenhower Dr N (46526-5311)
PHONE.................................574 534-2585
◆ **EMP:** 1000
SIC: 3479 Coating of metals and formed products

(G-6121)
DIGISTITCH
16123 County Road 40 (46526-6916)
PHONE.................................574 538-3960
EMP: 2 **EST:** 2012
SALES (est): 103.01K **Privately Held**
Web: www.digistitchcustomapparel.net
SIC: 2395 7389 Embroidery products, except Schiffli machine; Business Activities at Non-Commercial Site

(G-6122)
DIVINE CONFIDENCE LLC
2932 Elkhart Rd Apt 308 (46526-1038)
PHONE.................................574 218-1279
Tiffani Nicole Dawson, *Mgr*
EMP: 1 **EST:** 2021
SALES (est): 69.27K **Privately Held**
SIC: 3999 Hair and hair-based products

(G-6123)
DMI HOLDING CORP (HQ)
2164 Caragana Ct (46526-9149)
PHONE.................................574 534-1224
David Hoefer, *Pr*
Richard W Florea, *
Steve Paul, *
Bill Maki, *
Larry R Schrock, *
▲ **EMP:** 120 **EST:** 1988
SQ FT: 200,000
SALES (est): 205.54MM
SALES (corp-wide): 11.12B **Publicly Held**
SIC: 5012 3792 Recreational vehicles, motor homes, and trailers; Travel trailer chassis
PA: Thor Industries, Inc.
    601 E Beardsley Ave
    Elkhart IN 46514
    574 970-7460

(G-6124)
DOMETIC CORPORATION
2482 Century Dr (46528-5021)
PHONE.................................574 389-3759
Tony Short, *Brnch Mgr*
EMP: 109
SALES (corp-wide): 2.84B **Privately Held**
Web: www.dometic.com
SIC: 3634 Personal electrical appliances
HQ: Dometic Corporation
    5600 N River Rd Ste 250
    Rosemont IL 60018

(G-6125)
DOORS & DRAWERS INC
2302 Dierdorff Rd (46526-6928)
PHONE.................................574 533-3509
Mark Botts, *Pr*
Kim Botts, *VP*
EMP: 10 **EST:** 1980
SQ FT: 8,000
SALES (est): 453.9K **Privately Held**
Web: www.doorsanddrawersinc.com
SIC: 2431 2434 Doors and door parts and trim, wood; Wood kitchen cabinets

(G-6126)
DOUBLE L WOODWORKING LLC
12478 County Road 34 (46528-6837)
PHONE.................................260 768-3155
Melvin Slabach, *Prin*
EMP: 10 **EST:** 2010
SALES (est): 483.83K **Privately Held**
SIC: 2431 Millwork

(G-6127)
DUTCH PARK HOMES INC
2249 Lincolnway E (46526-6429)
PHONE.................................574 642-0150
Omer Kropf, *CEO*
Omer Kropf, *CEO*
Kermit Kropf, *
EMP: 21 **EST:** 1999
SQ FT: 32,000
SALES (est): 527.14K **Privately Held**
Web: www.dutchpark.com
SIC: 3799 All terrain vehicles (ATV)

(G-6128)
EAGLE PACKAGING INC
2301 W Wilden Ave (46528-1026)
PHONE.................................260 281-2333
Michael Johnson, *Pr*
Stephen Holle, *VP*
EMP: 3 **EST:** 2000
SALES (est): 367.79K **Privately Held**
SIC: 2671 Paper; coated and laminated packaging

(G-6129)
ECONOMY OFFSET PRINTERS INC
2516 Industrial Park Dr Ste A (46526-5372)
PHONE.................................574 534-6270
Roy Beaupain, *Pr*
EMP: 3 **EST:** 1994
SQ FT: 5,000
SALES (est): 494.14K **Privately Held**
SIC: 2752 Offset printing

(G-6130)
ELDORADO NATIONAL KANSAS INC (HQ)
2367 Century Dr (46528-5002)
P.O. Box 3260 (67402-3260)
PHONE.................................785 827-1033
Andrew Imanse, *Pr*
Walter L Bennett, *
Peter B Orthwein, *
▼ **EMP:** 113 **EST:** 1988
SALES (est): 23.97MM **Publicly Held**
Web: www.eldorado-bus.com
SIC: 3711 Buses, all types, assembly of
PA: Rev Group, Inc.
    245 S Exec Dr Ste 100
    Brookfield WI 53005

(G-6131)
EXPRESS CONTROLS
24471 County Road 142 (46526-7232)
PHONE.................................574 831-3497
EMP: 4 **EST:** 2014
SALES (est): 217.76K **Privately Held**
SIC: 3674 Semiconductors and related devices

(G-6132)
EXTON INC
Also Called: Travel Star Products
2134 Dierdorff Rd 27 (46526-6940)
P.O. Box 513 (46527-0513)

Goshen - Elkhart County (G-6133)

PHONE.................................574 533-0447
Terry Truex, *Pr*
EMP: 11 **EST:** 1989
SQ FT: 15,000
SALES (est): 2.37MM **Privately Held**
Web: www.travelstarproducts.com
SIC: 3089 Injection molded finished plastics products, nec

(G-6133)
FARM FAB
65511 County Road 9 (46526-9236)
PHONE.................................574 862-4775
Isaac Ramer, *Owner*
EMP: 2 **EST:** 2003
SALES (est): 123.21K **Privately Held**
SIC: 3441 Fabricated structural metal

(G-6134)
FIBER BY-PRODUCTS CORP
61801 County Road 127 (46528-9603)
EMP: 6
Web: www.fiberby-products.com
SIC: 2421 Sawmills and planing mills, general
PA: Fiber By-Products Corp.
70721 Us Highway 131
White Pigeon MI 49099

(G-6135)
FIEDEKE VINYL COVERINGS INC
811 Eisenhower Dr N (46526-5303)
PHONE.................................574 534-3408
Jackie Fiedeke, *Pr*
EMP: 11 **EST:** 1975
SQ FT: 10,500
SALES (est): 371.79K **Privately Held**
SIC: 2396 3429 7532 Automotive trimmings, fabric; Hardware, nec; Van conversion

(G-6136)
FILTER FABRICS INC
63023 Lakeside Dr (46528-6877)
EMP: 11 **EST:** 1944
SALES (est): 979.14K **Privately Held**
Web: www.filterfabricsinc.com
SIC: 3569 Filters, general line: industrial

(G-6137)
FLAIR INTERIORS INC
1010 Eisenhower Dr S (46526-5353)
PHONE.................................574 534-2163
▲ **EMP:** 100
Web: www.flairsandbox.com
SIC: 2531 Vehicle furniture

(G-6138)
FLJ TRANSPORT LLC
1025 Lantern Ln (46526-2510)
PHONE.................................574 642-0200
EMP: 4 **EST:** 2007
SALES (est): 491.25K **Privately Held**
SIC: 3799 Trailers and trailer equipment

(G-6139)
FOAMCRAFT INC
2506 Industrial Park Dr (46526-5370)
PHONE.................................574 534-4343
Curtis Elliot, *Brnch Mgr*
EMP: 50
SQ FT: 22,000
SALES (corp-wide): 92.24MM **Privately Held**
Web: www.foamcraftinc.com
SIC: 3069 3086 2821 5199 Foam rubber; Plastics foam products; Plastics materials and resins; Foams and rubber
PA: Foamcraft Inc
9230 Harrison Park Ct
Indianapolis IN 46216

317 545-3626

(G-6140)
FOREST RIVER INC
Also Called: Starcraft Bus
2367 Century Dr (46528-5002)
PHONE.................................574 642-3112
Daid Wright, *Brnch Mgr*
EMP: 600
SALES (corp-wide): 364.48B **Publicly Held**
Web: www.starcraftbus.com
SIC: 3792 Travel trailers and campers
HQ: Forest River, Inc.
900 County Rd 1 N
Elkhart IN 46514

(G-6141)
FOREST RIVER INC
3010 College Ave (46528-5050)
P.O. Box 3030 (46528)
PHONE.................................574 533-5934
Michael Schoeffler, *Mgr*
EMP: 120
SALES (corp-wide): 364.48B **Publicly Held**
Web: www.forestriverinc.com
SIC: 5561 3792 5012 Recreational vehicle dealers; Travel trailers and campers; Recreational vehicles, motor homes, and trailers
HQ: Forest River, Inc.
900 County Rd 1 N
Elkhart IN 46514

(G-6142)
FOREST RIVER CUSTOM EXTRUSIONS
712 Eisenhower Dr S (46526-5347)
PHONE.................................574 975-0206
Don Parsons, *Mgr*
EMP: 7 **EST:** 2010
SALES (est): 175.68K **Privately Held**
SIC: 3792 Travel trailers and campers

(G-6143)
GDC INC (PA)
Also Called: G D C
815 Logan St (46528-3508)
P.O. Box 98 (46527-0098)
PHONE.................................574 533-3128
Loretta Miller, *Pr*
Maury Miller, *
Aury Miller, *
Lonnie Abney, *
▲ **EMP:** 180 **EST:** 1955
SQ FT: 100,000
SALES (est): 73.86MM
SALES (corp-wide): 73.86MM **Privately Held**
Web: www.gdc-corp.com
SIC: 3086 3069 2891 2869 Plastics foam products; Medical and laboratory rubber sundries and related products; Adhesives and sealants; Industrial organic chemicals, nec

(G-6144)
GENERAL CRAFTS CORP
602 E Madison St (46526-3436)
P.O. Box 515 (46527-0515)
PHONE.................................574 533-1936
Thomas Wilhelm, *Pr*
Michael Wilhelm, *VP*
Anna Mary Wilhelm, *Stockholder*
EMP: 9 **EST:** 1959
SQ FT: 20,000
SALES (est): 995.93K **Privately Held**
Web: www.gcfab.net

SIC: 3449 3545 3446 3444 Miscellaneous metalwork; Tools and accessories for machine tools; Architectural metalwork; Sheet metalwork

(G-6145)
GENESIS PRODUCTS LLC
1846 Eisenhower Dr S (46526-6154)
PHONE.................................574 533-5089
Bahri Benguesmia, *CFO*
EMP: 366
SALES (corp-wide): 114.8MM **Privately Held**
Web: www.genesisproductsinc.com
SIC: 2431 Millwork
PA: Genesis Products, Llc
1853 Eisenhower Dr S
Goshen IN 46526
877 266-8292

(G-6146)
GENESIS PRODUCTS LLC (PA)
1853 Eisenhower Dr S (46526)
PHONE.................................877 266-8292
Jonathan Wenger, *Pr*
▲ **EMP:** 120 **EST:** 2002
SQ FT: 200,000
SALES (corp-wide): 114.8MM
SALES (corp-wide): 114.8MM **Privately Held**
Web: www.genesisproductsinc.com
SIC: 7389 2431 Laminating service; Doors, wood

(G-6147)
GET PRINTING INC
432 Blackport Dr (46528)
PHONE.................................574 533-6827
Marvin Beachy, *Pr*
Ray Gerber, *Mgr*
EMP: 5 **EST:** 1982
SQ FT: 2,600
SALES (est): 502.34K
SALES (corp-wide): 1.31MM **Privately Held**
SIC: 2752 Offset printing
PA: Gospel Echoes Team Association Inc
1809 E Monroe St Ste C
Goshen IN 46528
574 533-0221

(G-6148)
GET RIGHT HOME SOLUTIONS LLC
275 Winchester Trl (46526-6161)
PHONE.................................574 374-2001
EMP: 1
SALES (est): 82.9K **Privately Held**
SIC: 1389 7389 Construction, repair, and dismantling services; Business Activities at Non-Commercial Site

(G-6149)
GINDOR INC
66101 Us Highway 33 (46526-9483)
PHONE.................................574 642-4004
Ginny Nichols, *Pr*
Dorn Nichols, *VP*
EMP: 6 **EST:** 1987
SQ FT: 8,000
SALES (est): 476.59K **Privately Held**
Web: www.gindor.com
SIC: 3053 3993 2672 Gaskets, all materials; Signs and advertising specialties; Paper; coated and laminated, nec

(G-6150)
GLEASON CORPORATION
612 E Reynolds St (46526-4097)
PHONE.................................574 533-1141
EMP: 116
SALES (corp-wide): 36.7MM **Privately Held**

Web: www.gleasoncorporation.com
SIC: 3499 3444 Wheels: wheelbarrow, stroller, etc.: disc, stamped metal; Sheet metalwork
PA: Gleason Corporation
10474 Santa Monica Blvd # 400
Los Angeles CA 90025
310 470-6001

(G-6151)
GOCKEL INC
Also Called: Gockle
62360 County Road 33 (46528-9609)
PHONE.................................574 402-0220
Joseph Yoder, *CEO*
EMP: 1
SALES (est): 41.07K **Privately Held**
SIC: 1389 5999 7359 Construction, repair, and dismantling services; Sales barn; Rental store, general

(G-6152)
GOSHEN MFG CO INC
612 E Reynolds St (46526-4050)
PHONE.................................574 533-1357
A L Kotler, *Pr*
EMP: 1 **EST:** 2003
SALES (est): 78.55K **Privately Held**
Web: www.goshen.org
SIC: 3999 Manufacturing industries, nec

(G-6153)
GOSPEL ECHOES TEAM ASSOCIATION (PA)
1809 E Monroe St Ste C (46528)
P.O. Box 555 (46527)
PHONE.................................574 533-0221
Marvin Beachy, *Pr*
Kathy Yoder, *Mgr*
EMP: 9 **EST:** 1969
SQ FT: 5,000
SALES (est): 1.31MM
SALES (corp-wide): 1.31MM **Privately Held**
Web: www.gospelechoes.com
SIC: 2752 8661 Offset printing; Religious organizations

(G-6154)
GREEN COW POWER LLC
24130 County Road 40 (46526-9210)
P.O. Box 402 (47980-0402)
PHONE.................................219 984-5915
EMP: 5 **EST:** 2012
SALES (est): 262.92K **Privately Held**
SIC: 1311 Natural gas production

(G-6155)
GREEN WAY CANDLE COMPANY LLC
63 Greenway Dr (46526-1543)
PHONE.................................574 536-3802
Dianne Martin, *Prin*
EMP: 4 **EST:** 2017
SALES (est): 62.54K **Privately Held**
SIC: 3999 Candles

(G-6156)
GROUPER WILD LLC
Also Called: Shiloh Industries Hot Stamping
910 Eisenhower Dr S (46526-5351)
PHONE.................................574 534-1499
Ed Steinebach, *Brnch Mgr*
EMP: 150
SALES (corp-wide): 2.37B **Privately Held**
SIC: 3465 3714 5012 Automotive stampings; Motor vehicle parts and accessories; Automobiles
HQ: Grouper Wild, Llc
1780 Pond Run
Auburn Hills MI 48326
248 299-7500

GEOGRAPHIC SECTION
Goshen - Elkhart County (G-6182)

(G-6157)
GT STAMPING INC
1025 S 10th St (46526-4401)
PHONE.....................574 533-4108
Gerald A Trolz, *Ch Bd*
Wayne Hart, *
EMP: 70 **EST:** 1923
SQ FT: 100,000
SALES (est): 8.26MM **Privately Held**
Web: www.goshenstamping.com
SIC: 3469 Stamping metal for the trade

(G-6158)
GUTIERREZ MEXICAN BKY MKT INC
122 S Main St (46526-3702)
PHONE.....................574 534-9979
German Gutierrez, *Pt*
Isabel Gutierrez, *Pt*
EMP: 2 **EST:** 2001
SALES (est): 207.36K **Privately Held**
SIC: 2051 Bread, cake, and related products

(G-6159)
H-C LIQUIDATING CORP
Also Called: Homecrest Cabinetry
1002 Eisenhower Dr N (46526-5308)
PHONE.....................574 535-9300
Warner R S, *Pr*
John Goebel, *
▲ **EMP:** 1753 **EST:** 1969
SALES (est): 4.48MM
SALES (corp-wide): 2.73B **Publicly Held**
SIC: 2434 Vanities, bathroom: wood
HQ: Omega Cabinets, Ltd.
1 Masterbrand Cabinets Dr
Jasper IN 47546
319 235-5700

(G-6160)
HAMILTON IRON WORKS INC
208 W Lincoln Ave (46526-3219)
P.O. Box 232 (46527-0232)
PHONE.....................574 533-3784
Philip M Daub, *Pr*
EMP: 5 **EST:** 1917
SQ FT: 9,700
SALES (est): 464.13K **Privately Held**
Web: www.hamiltoniron.com
SIC: 3446 3441 Ornamental metalwork; Fabricated structural metal

(G-6161)
HARDER WOODS
64844 County Road 35 (46528-6809)
PHONE.....................402 572-0433
Stan Harder, *Owner*
EMP: 1 **EST:** 2002
SALES (est): 55.12K **Privately Held**
Web: www.harderwoods.com
SIC: 2499 Decorative wood and woodwork

(G-6162)
HARRISON HAULING INC
Also Called: Yellow Creek Gravel Service
64341 County Road 11 (46526-9426)
PHONE.....................574 862-3196
Burnell Weaver, *Pr*
Lincoln Graybill, *VP*
Shada Weaver, *Treas*
EMP: 3 **EST:** 1997
SALES (est): 596.87K **Privately Held**
SIC: 1442 Construction sand and gravel

(G-6163)
HEARTFELT CREATIONS INC
2147 Eisenhower Dr N (46526)
PHONE.....................574 773-3088
Linda M Bontrager, *CEO*
Linda M Bontrager, *Pr*
Richard A Beechy, *
EMP: 32 **EST:** 2008
SQ FT: 24,000
SALES (est): 5.94MM **Privately Held**
Web: www.heartfeltcreations.us
SIC: 3953 Time stamps, hand: rubber or metal

(G-6164)
HERITAGE UNLIMITED LLC (PA)
11641 County Road 30 (46528-9626)
PHONE.....................574 538-8021
Mervin D Hostetler, *Pr*
EMP: 7 **EST:** 2011
SALES (est): 1.47MM
SALES (corp-wide): 1.47MM **Privately Held**
SIC: 2435 Hardwood plywood, prefinished

(G-6165)
HOOGIES SPORTS HOUSE INC
Also Called: Hoogie's
825 Logan St (46528-3508)
PHONE.....................574 533-9875
John Hoogewerf, *Pr*
Lilli Hoogewerf, *Sec*
EMP: 4 **EST:** 1984
SQ FT: 2,000
SALES (est): 396.75K **Privately Held**
SIC: 5699 5137 2321 2339 Customized clothing and apparel; Women's and children's clothing; Men's and boy's furnishings; Women's and misses' outerwear, nec

(G-6166)
HOOSIER HOUSE FURNISHINGS LLC
220 Blackport Dr (46528-3650)
PHONE.....................574 975-0357
Dennis Yoder, *Managing Member*
EMP: 9 **EST:** 2009
SALES (est): 494.38K **Privately Held**
Web: www.hoosierhouse.us
SIC: 2434 Wood kitchen cabinets

(G-6167)
HOOSIER INDUSTRIAL SUPPLY
2516 Industrial Park Dr (46526-5372)
P.O. Box 929 (46527-0929)
PHONE.....................574 535-0712
Susan Smith, *Pr*
EMP: 2 **EST:** 2011
SALES (est): 246.68K **Privately Held**
Web: hoosier-industrial-supply-inc.sbcontract.com
SIC: 5085 3812 3721 3599 Bearings; Aircraft/aerospace flight instruments and guidance systems; Aircraft; Industrial machinery, nec

(G-6168)
HOOSIER INDUSTRIAL SUPPLY INC
1223 N Chicago Ave Ste 2 (46526-1910)
P.O. Box 929 (46527-0929)
PHONE.....................574 533-8565
Jennifer Mishler, *Pr*
Bruce Barker, *Sec*
EMP: 15 **EST:** 1991
SQ FT: 20,000
SALES (est): 8.39MM **Privately Held**
SIC: 5085 5082 5088 3714 Industrial supplies; Contractor's materials; Marine supplies; Motor vehicle parts and accessories

(G-6169)
HOOSIER INTERIOR DOORS INC
523 E Lincoln Ave (46528-3362)
PHONE.....................574 534-3072
Enos Yost Miller, *Pr*
EMP: 7 **EST:** 1992
SQ FT: 8,400
SALES (est): 964.38K **Privately Held**
Web: www.hoosierinteriordoorinc.com
SIC: 2431 5211 Doors, wood; Door and window products

(G-6170)
IMAGELAZ LLC
Also Called: Photograv
2106 Lisa Ct (46528-8806)
PHONE.....................574 534-0906
Jerald Troyer, *Pr*
EMP: 1 **EST:** 2016
SALES (est): 39.65K **Privately Held**
SIC: 7372 Application computer software

(G-6171)
IMAGINE METALS
2102 E Lincoln Ave (46528)
PHONE.....................574 971-3902
EMP: 4 **EST:** 2020
SALES (est): 56.76K **Privately Held**
Web: www.i-metals.net
SIC: 3441 Fabricated structural metal

(G-6172)
INDEPENDENT PROTECTION CO (PA)
Also Called: Turtle Top
1607 S Main St (46526-4721)
PHONE.....................574 533-4116
Robert E Cripe, *Pr*
Richard D Cripe, *VP*
Robert E Cripe Junior, *VP*
Phillip Tom Junior, *VP*
Betty J Cripe, *Sec*
▼ **EMP:** 20 **EST:** 1934
SQ FT: 22,000
SALES (est): 42.61MM
SALES (corp-wide): 42.61MM **Privately Held**
Web: www.ipclp.com
SIC: 3643 7532 3711 3446 Lightning protection equipment; Van conversion; Buses, all types, assembly of; Architectural metalwork

(G-6173)
INDIANA GRAVEL LLC
66541 Us Highway 33 (46526-9700)
PHONE.....................574 538-7152
EMP: 4 **EST:** 2019
SALES (est): 333.83K **Privately Held**
SIC: 1442 Construction sand and gravel

(G-6174)
INDUSTRIAL MOTOR & TOOL LLC
60282 County Road 21 (46528)
PHONE.....................574 534-8282
Luke Hoover, *Pr*
Nelba Hoover, *VP*
EMP: 6 **EST:** 2013
SALES (est): 474.39K **Privately Held**
Web: www.imtdirect.com
SIC: 7694 Electric motor repair

(G-6175)
INNOVATIVE WELDING LLC
64640 County Road 37 (46528-9350)
PHONE.....................574 642-4537
EMP: 4 **EST:** 2020
SALES (est): 66.78K **Privately Held**
SIC: 7692 Welding repair

(G-6176)
INVIGN LLC
2514 Messick Dr S (46526-5393)
PHONE.....................574 971-5498
Evan Bontrager, *CEO*
Steven Brenneman, *Pr*
EMP: 2 **EST:** 2020
SALES (est): 57.88K **Privately Held**
Web: www.invign.com
SIC: 3442 Window and door frames

(G-6177)
IRON BALUSTER LLC
Also Called: Viewrail
1722 Eisenhower Dr N # B (46526)
PHONE.....................574 975-0288
Len Morris, *Managing Member*
◆ **EMP:** 6 **EST:** 2003
SALES (est): 2.22MM **Privately Held**
Web: www.stairsupplies.com
SIC: 3446 Architectural metalwork

(G-6178)
J & J REPAIR
22064 County Road 142 (46526-9201)
PHONE.....................574 831-3075
Elias Martin, *Owner*
EMP: 3 **EST:** 1988
SALES (est): 243.52K **Privately Held**
Web: www.jnjrepair.com
SIC: 7692 1799 3444 7359 Welding repair; Welding on site; Sheet metalwork; Lawn and garden equipment rental

(G-6179)
JEC STEEL COMPANY
57587 County Road 29 (46528-8603)
PHONE.....................574 326-3829
Jeremy Seniff, *Pr*
EMP: 3
SALES (corp-wide): 1.14MM **Privately Held**
Web: www.jecsteelcompany.com
SIC: 3325 5051 Steel foundries, nec; Iron and steel (ferrous) products
PA: Jec Steel Company
1151 Bloomingdale Dr
Bristol IN 46507
574 326-3829

(G-6180)
JTD ENTERPRISES INC
Also Called: Inventure Electronics
609 N Harrison St (46528-1912)
PHONE.....................574 533-9438
Jennifer Ducheteau, *Pr*
EMP: 10 **EST:** 2015
SQ FT: 15,000
SALES (est): 1.12MM **Privately Held**
Web: www.inventuredesign.com
SIC: 3672 Printed circuit boards

(G-6181)
JZJ SERVICES LLC
63410 County Road 33 (46528-7563)
PHONE.....................574 642-3182
EMP: 1
SALES (corp-wide): 2.12MM **Privately Held**
Web: www.protexall.com
SIC: 2842 5087 Polishes and sanitation goods; Janitors' supplies
PA: Jzj Services, Llc
210 S Morton Ave
Evansville IN 47713
812 424-8268

(G-6182)
K & D CUSTOM COACH INC
408 High Park Ave (46526-4814)
PHONE.....................574 537-1716
Ray Lichty, *Pr*
Pamela Lichty, *VP*
EMP: 20 **EST:** 1998
SALES (est): 941.71K **Privately Held**
Web: www.kdspecialtyvehicles.com

Goshen - Elkhart County (G-6183) **GEOGRAPHIC SECTION**

SIC: **7549** 3711 Automotive customizing services, nonfactory basis; Automobile assembly, including specialty automobiles

(G-6183)
K2 MOLD LLC ◐
60232 State Road 15 Lot 12 (46528-9579)
PHONE..............................574 293-4613
EMP: 1 EST: 2022
SALES (est): 62.01K **Privately Held**
SIC: **3089** Injection molding of plastics

(G-6184)
KELWOOD DESIGNS LLC
25440 County Road 138 (46526-7453)
PHONE..............................574 862-2472
EMP: 8 EST: 2010
SALES (est): 500.16K **Privately Held**
Web: www.kelwoodcabinetry.com
SIC: **2434** 7389 Wood kitchen cabinets; Business Activities at Non-Commercial Site

(G-6185)
KENNAMETAL INC
1201 Eisenhower Dr N (46526-5311)
PHONE..............................574 534-2585
Mike Omalley, *Brnch Mgr*
EMP: 22
SALES (corp-wide): 2.05B **Publicly Held**
Web: www.kennametal.com
SIC: **3545** 3548 Cutting tools for machine tools; Welding apparatus
PA: Kennametal Inc.
    525 Wlliam Penn Pl Ste 33
    Pittsburgh PA 15219
    412 248-8000

(G-6186)
KENNAMETAL STELLITE LP
Also Called: Kennametal Stellite
1201 Eisenhower Dr N (46526-5311)
PHONE..............................574 534-9532
John Pawlikowski, *Pt*
◆ EMP: 80 EST: 1979
SQ FT: 56,000
SALES (est): 17.54MM
SALES (corp-wide): 2.05B **Publicly Held**
Web: www.stellite.com
SIC: **3479** Coating of metals and formed products
PA: Kennametal Inc.
    525 Wlliam Penn Pl Ste 33
    Pittsburgh PA 15219
    412 248-8000

(G-6187)
KEVIN KOCH
Also Called: Koch House of Design
211 E Washington St (46528-3322)
PHONE..............................574 971-8094
Kevin A Koch, *Owner*
EMP: 1 EST: 2015
SALES (est): 86.35K **Privately Held**
Web: www.kochhouseofdesign.com
SIC: **2395** 2311 Embroidery products, except Schiffli machine; Tailored suits and formal jackets

(G-6188)
KEYSTONE RV COMPANY
2164 Caragana Ct (46526-9149)
PHONE..............................574 537-0600
Troy James, *Brnch Mgr*
EMP: 88
SALES (corp-wide): 11.12B **Publicly Held**
Web: www.keystonerv.com
SIC: **3792** Travel trailers and campers
HQ: Keystone Rv Company
    2642 Hackberry Dr
    Goshen IN 46526

(G-6189)
KEYSTONE RV COMPANY
2425 Davis Dr (46526-6938)
P.O. Box 2000 (46527-2000)
PHONE..............................574 535-2100
EMP: 258
SALES (corp-wide): 11.12B **Publicly Held**
Web: www.keystonerv.com
SIC: **3792** Travel trailers and campers
HQ: Keystone Rv Company
    2642 Hackberry Dr
    Goshen IN 46526

(G-6190)
KEYSTONE RV COMPANY
17400 Hackberry Dr (46526-6468)
PHONE..............................574 535-2100
Tonja Lucchese, *Brnch Mgr*
EMP: 338
SALES (corp-wide): 11.12B **Publicly Held**
Web: www.keystonerv.com
SIC: **3792** Travel trailers and campers
HQ: Keystone Rv Company
    2642 Hackberry Dr
    Goshen IN 46526

(G-6191)
KEYSTONE RV COMPANY (HQ)
2642 Hackberry Dr (46526)
P.O. Box 2000 (46527)
PHONE..............................574 534-9430
EMP: 70 EST: 1995
SQ FT: 66,000
SALES (est): 425.22MM
SALES (corp-wide): 11.12B **Publicly Held**
Web: www.keystonerv.com
SIC: **3792** Travel trailer chassis
PA: Thor Industries, Inc.
    601 E Beardsley Ave
    Elkhart IN 46514
    574 970-7460

(G-6192)
KROPF INDUSTRIES INC
58647 State Road 15 (46528)
P.O. Box 30 (46527)
PHONE..............................574 533-2171
Don Kropf, *Pr*
Curt Yoder, *
EMP: 45 EST: 1946
SQ FT: 55,600
SALES (est): 5.37MM **Privately Held**
Web: www.kropfind.com
SIC: **3792** 2451 House trailers, except as permanent dwellings; Mobile homes

(G-6193)
KUERT CONCRETE INC
18370 Us Highway 20 (46528-9014)
PHONE..............................574 293-0430
Jim Miller, *Mgr*
EMP: 11
SALES (corp-wide): 13.04MM **Privately Held**
Web: www.kuert.com
SIC: **3273** 5032 Ready-mixed concrete; Concrete building products
PA: Kuert Concrete Inc
    5909 Nimtz Pkwy
    South Bend IN 46628
    574 232-9911

(G-6194)
L M CORPORATION
416 Steury Ave (46528-3007)
P.O. Box 98 (46527-0098)
PHONE..............................574 535-0581
Loretta Miller, *Pr*
Maury Miller, *
EMP: 30 EST: 1987
SALES (est): 1.5MM **Privately Held**

SIC: **7389** 3399 Packaging and labeling services; Laminating steel

(G-6195)
L R NISLEY & SONS
Also Called: Nisley, L R & Sons
62724 County Road 35 (46528-6814)
PHONE..............................574 642-1245
Leroy R Nisley, *Owner*
EMP: 9 EST: 1983
SQ FT: 11,000
SALES (est): 416.86K **Privately Held**
SIC: **2511** Wood household furniture

(G-6196)
LAKEVIEW WOODWORKING
10190 County Road 34 (46528-9639)
PHONE..............................574 642-1335
Felty Lambright, *Prin*
EMP: 5 EST: 2008
SALES (est): 60.85K **Privately Held**
SIC: **2431** Millwork

(G-6197)
LCM REALTY IV LLC
2469 E Kercher Rd (46526-6465)
PHONE..............................574 312-6182
EMP: 1 EST: 2018
SALES (est): 397.57K
SALES (corp-wide): 3.78B **Publicly Held**
SIC: **3465** Automotive stampings
PA: Lci Industries
    3501 County Rd 6 E
    Elkhart IN 46514
    574 535-1125

(G-6198)
LINDE GAS & EQUIPMENT INC
Also Called: Praxair Distribution
2502 Dierdorff Rd (46526-6930)
PHONE..............................574 537-1366
EMP: 5
Web: www.lindedirect.com
SIC: **2813** Industrial gases
HQ: Linde Gas & Equipment Inc.
    10 Riverview Dr
    Danbury CT 06810
    844 445-4633

(G-6199)
LIONSHEAD ALLOYS LLC (PA)
305 Steury Ave (46528-3004)
PHONE..............................574 533-6169
EMP: 8 EST: 2020
SALES (est): 7.15MM
SALES (corp-wide): 7.15MM **Privately Held**
Web: www.lionsheadtireandwheel.com
SIC: **3355** Aluminum rod and bar

(G-6200)
LIONSHEAD SPECIALTY TIRE & WHE (PA)
305 Steury Ave (46528-3004)
PHONE..............................574 533-6169
◆ EMP: 14 EST: 2007
SQ FT: 13,000
SALES (est): 25.06MM **Privately Held**
Web: www.lionsheadtireandwheel.com
SIC: **5531** 3011 Automotive tires; Tires and inner tubes

(G-6201)
LIPPERT COMPONENTS INC
Also Called: Lippert Interior Solutions
2602 College Ave (46528-5014)
PHONE..............................574 534-8177
EMP: 85
SALES (corp-wide): 3.78B **Publicly Held**
Web: www.lci1.com

SIC: **2531** Vehicle furniture
HQ: Lippert Components, Inc.
    3501 County Rd 6 E
    Elkhart IN 46514
    574 535-1125

(G-6202)
LIPPERT COMPONENTS INC
Also Called: Lipper Components
2703 College Ave (46528-5040)
PHONE..............................574 535-1125
Carl Owens, *Mgr*
EMP: 84
SALES (corp-wide): 3.78B **Publicly Held**
Web: www.lci1.com
SIC: **3469** 3711 3444 3714 Stamping metal for the trade; Chassis, motor vehicle; Metal roofing and roof drainage equipment; Motor vehicle parts and accessories
HQ: Lippert Components, Inc.
    3501 County Rd 6 E
    Elkhart IN 46514
    574 535-1125

(G-6203)
LIPPERT COMPONENTS INC
1701 Century Dr (46528-5048)
PHONE..............................574 537-8900
EMP: 10
SALES (corp-wide): 3.78B **Publicly Held**
Web: www.lci1.com
SIC: **3441** Fabricated structural metal
HQ: Lippert Components, Inc.
    3501 County Rd 6 E
    Elkhart IN 46514
    574 535-1125

(G-6204)
LIPPERT COMPONENTS INC
Also Called: Trazcor
1302 Eisenhower Dr N (46526-5341)
PHONE..............................574 536-7803
Michael Koronkiewicz, *Brnch Mgr*
EMP: 9
SALES (corp-wide): 3.78B **Publicly Held**
Web: corporate.lippert.com
SIC: **3444** Metal roofing and roof drainage equipment
HQ: Lippert Components, Inc.
    3501 County Rd 6 E
    Elkhart IN 46514
    574 535-1125

(G-6205)
LIPPERT COMPONENTS INC
2703 College Ave (46528-5040)
PHONE..............................574 537-8900
Jason Lippert, *CEO*
EMP: 113
SALES (corp-wide): 3.78B **Publicly Held**
Web: www.lci1.com
SIC: **3711** Chassis, motor vehicle
HQ: Lippert Components, Inc.
    3501 County Rd 6 E
    Elkhart IN 46514
    574 535-1125

(G-6206)
LIPPERT COMPONENTS INC
65781 Sourwood (46526-9146)
PHONE..............................574 849-0869
Rob Nelson, *Brnch Mgr*
EMP: 9
SALES (corp-wide): 3.78B **Publicly Held**
Web: www.lci1.com
SIC: **3711** 3469 3444 3714 Chassis, motor vehicle; Stamping metal for the trade; Metal roofing and roof drainage equipment; Motor vehicle parts and accessories
HQ: Lippert Components, Inc.
    3501 County Rd 6 E

GEOGRAPHIC SECTION

Goshen - Elkhart County (G-6231)

Elkhart IN 46514
574 535-1125

(G-6207)
LIPPERT COMPONENTS INC
16840 Skyview Rd (46526-6552)
PHONE..................574 971-4320
EMP: 11
SALES (corp-wide): 3.78B Publicly Held
Web: www.lci1.com
SIC: 3711 3469 3444 3714 Chassis, motor vehicle; Stamping metal for the trade; Metal roofing and roof drainage equipment; Motor vehicle parts and accessories
HQ: Lippert Components, Inc.
3501 County Rd 6 E
Elkhart IN 46514
574 535-1125

(G-6208)
M&M PERFORMANCE INC
16077 Prairie Rose Ave (46528-7304)
PHONE..................574 536-6103
Bruce Mcdonald, Pr
EMP: 3 EST: 2000
SALES (est): 249.99K Privately Held
Web: www.mandmperformance.com
SIC: 3089 Automotive parts, plastic

(G-6209)
MAGNASPHERE CORPORATION
2556 Southside Park Dr (46526)
PHONE..................574 533-1310
EMP: 6 EST: 2017
SALES (est): 69.59K Privately Held
SIC: 3699 Security control equipment and systems

(G-6210)
MAGNUM VENUS PRODUCTS INC
Also Called: Magnum Industries
320 N Main St (46528-2826)
PHONE..................727 573-2955
Stephen E Ciesielski, Brnch Mgr
EMP: 9
SALES (corp-wide): 50.37MM Privately Held
Web: www.mvpind.com
SIC: 5084 3563 Processing and packaging equipment; Spraying outfits: metals, paints, and chemicals (compressor)
PA: Magnum Venus Products, Inc.
2030 Flling Wters Rd Ste
Knoxville TN 37922
865 686-5670

(G-6211)
MAPLE CITY MACHINE INC
1762 E Kercher Rd (46526-6308)
PHONE..................574 533-6742
Phillip Shank, Pr
Becka Shank, Sec
EMP: 14 EST: 1975
SQ FT: 18,000
SALES (est): 519.38K Privately Held
SIC: 3599 Machine shop, jobbing and repair

(G-6212)
MAPLE LEAF PRINTING CO INC
301 W Lincoln Ave (46526-3227)
PHONE..................574 534-7790
Regan S Lehman, Pr
Terry Kercher, VP
EMP: 8 EST: 2006
SALES (est): 939.17K Privately Held
Web: www.mapleleafprinting.us
SIC: 2752 Offset printing

(G-6213)
MARKETING KREATIVO
22541 Briarhill Dr (46528-8411)
PHONE..................574 370-5410
Lisa Alford Collio, Prin
EMP: 5 EST: 2018
SALES (est): 72.24K Privately Held
SIC: 2752 Commercial printing, lithographic

(G-6214)
MARTINS MINI BARNS LLC
25707 State Road 119 (46526-7456)
PHONE..................574 238-0045
EMP: 4 EST: 2018
SALES (est): 161.99K Privately Held
Web: www.mmbarns.com
SIC: 3448 Prefabricated metal buildings and components

(G-6215)
MARTINS WOOD WORKS
66227 County Road 9 (46526-9237)
PHONE..................574 862-4080
Carlyle Martin, Owner
EMP: 4 EST: 1984
SALES (est): 190.24K Privately Held
SIC: 2511 5712 5021 Wood household furniture; Custom made furniture, except cabinets; Furniture

(G-6216)
MASTERBRAND CABINETS LLC
Also Called: Master Brand Cabinets
1002 Eisenhower Dr N (46526-5308)
PHONE..................574 535-9300
Christa Guife, Brnch Mgr
EMP: 7
SALES (corp-wide): 2.73B Publicly Held
Web: www.masterbrand.com
SIC: 2434 Wood kitchen cabinets
HQ: Masterbrand Cabinets Llc
3300 Entp Pkwy Ste 300
Beachwood OH 44122
812 482-2527

(G-6217)
MASTERS APPS LLC
2807 S Main St (46526-5418)
PHONE..................574 312-5233
EMP: 1 EST: 2015
SALES (est): 46.33K Privately Held
SIC: 7372 7389 Application computer software; Business Activities at Non-Commercial Site

(G-6218)
MICA SHOP INC
2122 Lincolnway E (46526-6426)
PHONE..................574 533-1102
Verlin Chupp, Pr
Karen Chupp, Sec
EMP: 26 EST: 1969
SQ FT: 40,000
SALES (est): 2.42MM Privately Held
Web: www.micashop.com
SIC: 2541 Counters or counter display cases, wood

(G-6219)
MICHIANA CARWASH SYSTEMS LLC
15228 County Road 22 (46528-9188)
PHONE..................574 320-2331
EMP: 2 EST: 1998
SALES (est): 177.31K Privately Held
Web: www.michianacws.com
SIC: 3589 Car washing machinery

(G-6220)
MICHIANA COLUMN & TRUSS LLC
27608 County Road 36 # A (46526-7143)

PHONE..................574 862-2828
EMP: 5 EST: 2002
SALES (est): 455.27K Privately Held
Web: www.michianacolumnandtruss.com
SIC: 2493 Reconstituted wood products

(G-6221)
MIDE PRODUCTS LLC
22420 Forsythia Dr (46528-8332)
PHONE..................574 333-5906
EMP: 2 EST: 2008
SQ FT: 3,000
SALES (est): 148.39K Privately Held
Web: www.mideproducts.com
SIC: 3089 Fences, gates, and accessories: plastics

(G-6222)
MILLER BROTHERS BUILDERS INC
1819 E Monroe St (46528-9260)
PHONE..................574 533-8602
Daniel B Miller, Pr
D Bradley Plett, VP
EMP: 48 EST: 1961
SQ FT: 5,000
SALES (est): 881.11K Privately Held
Web: www.millerbrothersbuilders.com
SIC: 1521 1522 1542 3448 New construction, single-family houses; Multi-family dwelling construction, nec; Commercial and office building contractors; Prefabricated metal buildings and components

(G-6223)
MILLER CREATIONS
62909 Fairview Dr (46528-7508)
PHONE..................574 903-9961
Brent Miller, Prin
EMP: 7 EST: 2011
SALES (est): 58.85K Privately Held
Web: www.millerdoorandtrim.com
SIC: 2499 Decorative wood and woodwork

(G-6224)
MILLER DISTRIBUTIONS INC
Also Called: Dutch Maid Bakery
508 W Lincoln Ave Ste D (46526)
PHONE..................574 533-1940
Lyle E Miller, Pr
Gretchen Miller, VP
Marlin Schwartz, Prin
Rudy Helmuth, Prin
EMP: 16 EST: 2014
SALES (est): 750K Privately Held
SIC: 2051 Bread, cake, and related products

(G-6225)
MILLER DOOR & TRIM INC
2249 Lincolnway E (46526-6429)
PHONE..................574 533-8141
Nathan D Miller, Pr
EMP: 4 EST: 1961
SQ FT: 30,000
SALES (est): 486.16K Privately Held
Web: www.millerdoorandtrim.com
SIC: 2431 Doors, wood

(G-6226)
MO TRAILER CORPORATION
Also Called: MO Trailers
2211 W Wilden Ave (46528-1147)
P.O. Box 486 (46527-0486)
PHONE..................574 533-0824
Jeff Mitschelen, Pr
Phil Vail, VP
EMP: 10 EST: 1971
SQ FT: 10,000
SALES (est): 930.58K Privately Held
Web: www.motrailers.com

SIC: 3799 3621 Trailers and trailer equipment; Electric motor and generator parts

(G-6227)
NIBCO INC
Goshen Division
701 Eisenhower Dr N (46526-5301)
PHONE..................574 296-1240
Steve Seevers, Mgr
EMP: 101
SQ FT: 89,000
SALES (corp-wide): 509.67MM Privately Held
Web: www.nibco.com
SIC: 3089 3432 3088 5162 Fittings for pipe, plastics; Plumbing fixture fittings and trim; Plastics plumbing fixtures; Plastics products, nec
PA: Nibco Inc.
1516 Middlebury St
Elkhart IN 46516
574 295-3000

(G-6228)
NOBLE COMPOSITES INC
2424 E Kercher Rd (46526-6466)
PHONE..................574 533-1462
Larry Farver, Pr
John Gardner, CFO
Roger Gowdy, VP
EMP: 1 EST: 2000
SALES (est): 3.69MM
SALES (corp-wide): 2.09B Publicly Held
Web: www.noblecomposites.com
SIC: 3492 Control valves, fluid power: hydraulic and pneumatic
HQ: Crane Composites, Inc.
23525 W Eames St
Channahon IL 60410
815 467-8600

(G-6229)
NORINE S HERBS
14746 County Road 34 (46528-7576)
PHONE..................574 642-4272
EMP: 4 EST: 2018
SALES (est): 79.33K Privately Held
Web: www.importantlocalbusinesses.com
SIC: 3999 Manufacturing industries, nec

(G-6230)
OLYMPIA CANDY KITCHEN LLC
136 N Main St (46526-3207)
PHONE..................574 533-5040
Kathy Andersen, Owner
EMP: 8 EST: 1912
SQ FT: 1,000
SALES (est): 376.44K Privately Held
Web: www.olympiacandykitchen.com
SIC: 2064 5812 5441 2066 Candy and other confectionery products; Eating places; Candy; Chocolate and cocoa products

(G-6231)
OPERATION 1 VETERAN INC
Also Called: Op1vet
20201 Eagle Hill Ln (46528-6253)
PHONE..................574 536-5536
Edward Christner, Pr
EMP: 4 EST: 2018
SALES (est): 1.5MM Privately Held
Web: www.op1vet.vet
SIC: 5651 5699 3842 7389 Family clothing stores; Military goods and regalia; Wheelchairs; Business Activities at Non-Commercial Site

Goshen - Elkhart County (G-6232)

(G-6232)
ORCHARD LANE CABINETS
14425 County Road 126 (46528-9666)
PHONE.....................574 825-7568
Toby Borntrager, Prin
EMP: 7 EST: 2008
SALES (est): 250.86K Privately Held
SIC: 2434 Wood kitchen cabinets

(G-6233)
OZINGA BROS INC
Also Called: Ozinga Bros
1700 Egbert Ave (46528-4214)
PHONE.....................574 971-8239
EMP: 23
SALES (corp-wide): 552.21MM Privately Held
Web: www.ozinga.com
SIC: 3273 Ready-mixed concrete
PA: Ozinga Bros., Inc.
19001 Old Lagrange Rd # 3
Mokena IL 60448
708 326-4200

(G-6234)
OZINGA BROS INC
Also Called: Ozinga
65723 Us Highway 33 (46526-6924)
PHONE.....................574 642-4455
EMP: 35
SALES (corp-wide): 552.21MM Privately Held
Web: www.ozinga.com
SIC: 3273 Ready-mixed concrete
PA: Ozinga Bros., Inc.
19001 Old Lagrange Rd # 3
Mokena IL 60448
708 326-4200

(G-6235)
PAPERS INC
134 S Main St (46526-3794)
P.O. Box 188 (46542-0188)
PHONE.....................574 534-2591
Marilyn Yoder, Mgr
EMP: 7
SALES (corp-wide): 20.23MM Privately Held
Web: www.the-papers.com
SIC: 2711 Newspapers: publishing only, not printed on site
PA: The Papers Inc
206 S Main St
Milford IN 46542
574 658-4111

(G-6236)
PARKER-HANNIFIN CORPORATION
Also Called: Techseal Division
1525 S 10th St (46526-4505)
P.O. Box 517 (46527-0517)
PHONE.....................574 533-1111
Joseph Lotter, Brnch Mgr
EMP: 60
SALES (corp-wide): 19.93B Publicly Held
Web: www.parker.com
SIC: 3053 3061 3544 2822 Gaskets, all materials; Mechanical rubber goods; Special dies, tools, jigs, and fixtures; Synthetic rubber
PA: Parker-Hannifin Corporation
6035 Parkland Blvd
Cleveland OH 44124
216 896-3000

(G-6237)
PATRICK INDUSTRIES INC
Also Called: Foremost Fabricators
3352 Maple City Dr (46526-6807)
PHONE.....................574 534-5300
Ryan Berger, Business Director
EMP: 150
SALES (corp-wide): 3.47B Publicly Held
Web: www.patrickind.com
SIC: 3354 Aluminum extruded products
PA: Patrick Industries, Inc.
107 W Franklin St
Elkhart IN 46516
574 294-7511

(G-6238)
PINE MANOR INC
321 S 3rd St (46526)
PHONE.....................574 533-4186
EMP: 6 EST: 2020
SALES (est): 250.41K Privately Held
SIC: 5191 2048 0254 Farm supplies; Prepared feeds, nec; Poultry hatcheries

(G-6239)
PLANET GOSHEN LLC
2616 Peddlers Village Rd (46526-1002)
PHONE.....................574 830-5797
EMP: 6 EST: 2017
SALES (est): 253.67K Privately Held
SIC: 2711 Newspapers, publishing and printing

(G-6240)
PLANKS PRINTING SERVICE INC
Also Called: Rapid Ribbons
505 S 9th St (46526-3446)
P.O. Box 222 (46527-0222)
PHONE.....................574 533-1739
David Plank, Pr
David A Plank, Pr
EMP: 9 EST: 1946
SQ FT: 2,500
SALES (est): 649.7K Privately Held
Web: new.rapidribbons.com
SIC: 2759 Commercial printing, nec

(G-6241)
PLYMOUTH OIL AND GAS INC
57592 Hearthstone Ct (46528-7852)
PHONE.....................574 875-4808
Onkar Singh, Prin
EMP: 2 EST: 2012
SALES (est): 174.32K Privately Held
SIC: 1382 Oil and gas exploration services

(G-6242)
PREMIERE SIGNS CO INC
Also Called: Premiere Services
400 N Main St (46528-2828)
PHONE.....................574 533-8585
TOLL FREE: 800
Michael Brown, Pr
Cynthia Brown, Sec
EMP: 9 EST: 1990
SQ FT: 16,000
SALES (est): 237.18K Privately Held
Web: www.premieresigns.com
SIC: 3993 1799 5999 Electric signs; Sign installation and maintenance; Banners, flags, decals, and posters

(G-6243)
PROMOTOR ENGINES & COMPONENTS
Also Called: Pro-Motor Engines
1814 Lincolnway E (46526-6411)
PHONE.....................574 533-9898
Doug Tarman, Pr
EMP: 3 EST: 1984
SQ FT: 8,000
SALES (est): 437.31K Privately Held
Web: www.gopromotor.com
SIC: 5531 3599 5013 Automotive parts; Machine shop, jobbing and repair; Automotive supplies and parts

(G-6244)
QUALITY CONCEPTS
14206 State Road 4 (46528-9658)
PHONE.....................574 215-6391
Kirk Miller, Owner
EMP: 1 EST: 1990
SALES (est): 82.5K Privately Held
Web: www.qualityconcepts.com
SIC: 3716 3799 Motor homes; Recreational vehicles

(G-6245)
R & D METAL FABRICATING INC
414 N Main St Ste 414 (46528-2828)
PHONE.....................574 533-2424
Jeff Gruntman, Pr
Laura Gruntman, Sec
EMP: 3 EST: 2008
SALES (est): 52K Privately Held
SIC: 3499 Fabricated metal products, nec

(G-6246)
RECREATIONAL CUSTOMS INC
67928 Us Highway 33 (46526-8549)
PHONE.....................574 642-0632
Anita Carpenter, Pr
EMP: 6 EST: 2005
SALES (est): 517.97K Privately Held
Web: www.rciwave.com
SIC: 3799 Recreational vehicles

(G-6247)
RIEGSECKER WOODWORKS INC
15600 County Road 38 (46528-9353)
PHONE.....................574 642-3504
Timothy J Riegsecker, Pr
Larry Riegsecker, Treas
EMP: 3 EST: 1997
SALES (est): 364.31K Privately Held
SIC: 2499 Decorative wood and woodwork

(G-6248)
ROANN PUBLISHERS
22425 County Road 42 (46526-9215)
PHONE.....................574 831-2795
Roy Zimmerman, Owner
EMP: 5 EST: 2001
SALES (est): 27.4K Privately Held
SIC: 2721 Magazines: publishing only, not printed on site

(G-6249)
ROTH BIOSCIENCE LLC
1303 Eisenhower Dr S (46526-5360)
P.O. Box 340 (46527-0340)
PHONE.....................574 533-3351
EMP: 9 EST: 1986
SALES (est): 933.63K Privately Held
Web: www.micrologylabs.com
SIC: 2836 Culture media

(G-6250)
ROYERS GENERAL WLDG & REPR LLC
26354 County Road 38 (46526)
PHONE.....................574 862-2707
Thomas Royer, Owner
EMP: 1 EST: 1976
SALES (est): 97.85K Privately Held
SIC: 7692 Welding repair

(G-6251)
SCHLABACH HARDWOODS LLC
11186 County Road 34 (46528-9628)
PHONE.....................574 642-1157
La Verne Schlabach, Pt
John Schlabach Junior, Pt
EMP: 5 EST: 1976
SQ FT: 3,500
SALES (est): 489.07K Privately Held
SIC: 2431 Planing mill, millwork

(G-6252)
SCOTT SIGNS LLC
600 E Jackson St (46526-4001)
PHONE.....................574 533-7524
EMP: 4 EST: 2019
SALES (est): 297.12K Privately Held
Web: www.scottsignsonline.com
SIC: 3993 Signs and advertising specialties

(G-6253)
SEATING TECHNOLOGY INC
Also Called: Seat Tech
2703 College Ave (46526-5040)
PHONE.....................574 971-4100
Rick Finnigan, Pr
Marlene Finnigan, VP
Matthew Troyer, CFO
▲ EMP: 53 EST: 1989
SQ FT: 32,000
SALES (est): 2.51MM
SALES (corp-wide): 3.78B Publicly Held
SIC: 2512 2514 2515 Recliners: upholstered on wood frames; Household furniture: upholstered on metal frames; Sofa beds (convertible sofas)
HQ: Lippert Components, Inc.
3501 County Rd 6 E
Elkhart IN 46514
574 535-1125

(G-6254)
SIDELINE EQUIPMENT INC
64701 Cr35 (46528-6806)
P.O. Box 449 (46543-0449)
PHONE.....................574 202-0525
Jeff Troyer, Pr
EMP: 1 EST: 2003
SALES (est): 201.47K Privately Held
SIC: 3552 Opening machinery and equipment

(G-6255)
SIGNTECH SIGN SERVICES INC
Also Called: Signtech
1508 Bashor Rd (46528-1903)
P.O. Box 835 (46527-0835)
PHONE.....................574 537-8080
TOLL FREE: 800
Todd Lehman, Pr
Jan Plummer, Prin
EMP: 4 EST: 2002
SALES (est): 469.33K Privately Held
Web: www.signtechsigns.com
SIC: 3993 Signs and advertising specialties

(G-6256)
SOUTH BEND TRIBUNE CORP
114 S Main St (46526-3702)
PHONE.....................574 971-5651
EMP: 18
SALES (corp-wide): 3.28B Publicly Held
Web: www.southbendtribune.com
SIC: 2711 Newspapers, publishing and printing
HQ: South Bend Tribune Corp
225 W Colfax Ave
South Bend IN 46626
574 235-6161

(G-6257)
STABILITY AMERICA INC
Also Called: Parent Co. Glassteel
2928 Elder Dr (46526-8926)
PHONE.....................574 642-3029
EMP: 2 EST: 2011
SALES (est): 81.74K Privately Held
SIC: 3229 Glass fiber products

Goshen - Elkhart County (G-6279)

(G-6258)
STAMINA METAL PRODUCTS INC
901 E Madison St (46528-3510)
PHONE..................574 534-7410
Randy Huber, *Pr*
Mary Huber, *VP*
EMP: 2 **EST:** 1992
SQ FT: 2,500
SALES (est): 283.13K **Privately Held**
Web: www.wielanddesigns.com
SIC: 3469 3544 3599 Stamping metal for the trade; Special dies and tools; Machine and other job shop work

(G-6259)
STARCRAFT CORPORATION
Also Called: Starcraft Accessories
2006 Century Dr (46528-5000)
P.O. Box 12 (46540-0012)
PHONE..................574 534-7705
Sherry Roberts, *Prin*
EMP: 6
SQ FT: 30,000
Web: www.starcraftbus.com
SIC: 3714 Motor vehicle parts and accessories
HQ: Starcraft Corporation
1123 S Indiana Ave
Goshen IN 46526

(G-6260)
STARCRAFT CORPORATION (HQ)
Also Called: Starcraft
1123 S Indiana Ave (46526)
P.O. Box 12 (46540)
PHONE..................574 534-7827
Kelly L Rose, *Ch Bd*
Joseph E Katona Iii, *CFO*
Douglass C Goad, *Ex VP*
Michael H Schoeffler, *CEO*
▼ **EMP:** 7 **EST:** 1903
SQ FT: 5,000
SALES (est): 13.51MM **Privately Held**
Web: www.starcraftbus.com
SIC: 3714 3792 3716 3713 Motor vehicle parts and accessories; Travel trailers and campers; Motor homes; Truck and bus bodies
PA: Qf Liquidation, Inc.
25242 Arctic Ocean Dr
Lake Forest CA 92630

(G-6261)
SUPERIOR LAMINATING INC
60894 County Road 19 (46528-7409)
PHONE..................574 361-7266
Elroy Bontrager, *Pr*
Andrea Rosevelle, *Sec*
EMP: 7 **EST:** 1984
SQ FT: 19,820
SALES (est): 980.55K **Privately Held**
Web: www.superiorlaminatinginc.com
SIC: 5031 2434 Kitchen cabinets; Wood kitchen cabinets

(G-6262)
SUPREME CORPORATION
2581 Kercher Rd (46528-7556)
PHONE..................574 642-4888
Mark Weber, *CEO*
EMP: 1
SALES (corp-wide): 2.54B **Publicly Held**
Web: www.supremecorp.com
SIC: 3713 Truck bodies (motor vehicles)
HQ: Supreme Corporation
2581 Kercher Rd
Goshen IN 46528
574 642-4888

(G-6263)
SUPREME CORPORATION (DH)
2581 Kercher Rd (46528-7556)
P.O. Box 463 (46527-0463)
PHONE..................574 642-4888
Robert W Wilson, *Pr*
Omer G Kropf, *Vice Chairman**
Herbert M Gardner, *
William J Barrett, *
Christy Miller, *
◆ **EMP:** 172 **EST:** 1974
SQ FT: 280,000
SALES (est): 38.68MM
SALES (corp-wide): 2.54B **Publicly Held**
Web: www.supremecorp.com
SIC: 3713 3792 3585 Truck bodies (motor vehicles); Travel trailers and campers; Refrigeration and heating equipment
HQ: Supreme Industries, Inc.
2581 Kercher Rd
Goshen IN 46528
574 642-3070

(G-6264)
SUPREME CORPORATION GEORGIA
2581 Kercher Rd (46528-7556)
PHONE..................574 228-4130
Mark D Weber, *Pr*
EMP: 1 **EST:** 2013
SALES (est): 2.13MM
SALES (corp-wide): 2.54B **Publicly Held**
SIC: 3713 Truck bodies (motor vehicles)
HQ: Supreme Corporation
2581 Kercher Rd
Goshen IN 46528
574 642-4888

(G-6265)
SUPREME INDUSTRIES INC (HQ)
Also Called: Supreme
2581 Kercher Rd (46528-7556)
P.O. Box 463 (46527-0463)
PHONE..................574 642-3070
Brent L Yeagy, *Pr*
Erin J Roth, *Sec*
◆ **EMP:** 154 **EST:** 1974
SQ FT: 26,000
SALES (est): 860.29MM
SALES (corp-wide): 2.54B **Publicly Held**
Web: www.onewabash.com
SIC: 3537 3713 3799 Industrial trucks and tractors; Truck and bus bodies; Trailers and trailer equipment
PA: Wabash National Corporation
3900 Mccarty Ln
Lafayette IN 47905
765 771-5310

(G-6266)
SWARTZNDRBER HRDWOOD CREAT LLC
17229 County Road 18 (46528-8681)
PHONE..................574 534-2502
EMP: 6 **EST:** 1971
SQ FT: 30,000
SALES (est): 272.93K **Privately Held**
Web: www.swartzendruber.com
SIC: 2426 2511 2521 Furniture stock and parts, hardwood; Wood household furniture; Wood office furniture

(G-6267)
T & M RUBBER INC
1102 S 10th St (46526-4487)
P.O. Box 516 (46527-0516)
PHONE..................574 533-3173
Martina Dawson, *Pr*
Jerry Bernard, *
Martina Dawson, *VP*
Karl Shively, *
◆ **EMP:** 30 **EST:** 1948
SQ FT: 62,000
SALES (est): 4.84MM **Privately Held**
Web: www.tmrubber.com
SIC: 3061 2822 3053 Mechanical rubber goods; Synthetic rubber; Oil seals, rubber

(G-6268)
TECHKNOWLEDGEY INC
1711 W Clinton St (46526-1613)
PHONE..................574 202-0362
Krista Smith, *Brnch Mgr*
EMP: 1
SALES (corp-wide): 1.47MM **Privately Held**
Web: www.techknowledgeyinc.com
SIC: 3572 Computer storage devices
PA: Techknowledgey, Inc.
1840 W Lincoln Ave
Goshen IN 46526
574 971-4267

(G-6269)
TECHKNOWLEDGEY INC (PA)
1840 W Lincoln Ave (46526-5918)
P.O. Box 391 (46527-0391)
PHONE..................574 971-4267
Boyd Smith, *Pr*
Krista L Smith, *VP*
EMP: 7 **EST:** 2006
SALES (est): 1.47MM
SALES (corp-wide): 1.47MM **Privately Held**
Web: www.techknowledgeyinc.com
SIC: 3572 7371 Computer storage devices; Custom computer programming services

(G-6270)
TMI
14578 State Road 4 (46528-9653)
PHONE..................574 533-4741
Trent Miller, *Owner*
EMP: 1 **EST:** 2001
SALES (est): 133.55K **Privately Held**
SIC: 3432 8748 Lawn hose nozzles and sprinklers; Agricultural consultant

(G-6271)
TRIANGLE RUBBER CO LLC
1801 Eisenhower Dr N (46526-5386)
PHONE..................574 533-3118
Kevin Gerwells, *Mgr*
EMP: 1
SQ FT: 36,500
SALES (corp-wide): 32MM **Privately Held**
Web: www.trianglerubberco.com
SIC: 2821 Plastics materials and resins
PA: Triangle Rubber Co., Llc
1924 Elkhart Rd
Goshen IN 46526
574 533-3118

(G-6272)
TRIANGLE RUBBER CO LLC (PA)
Also Called: Thermoplastic Division
1924 Elkhart Rd (46526-1174)
P.O. Box 95 (46527-0095)
PHONE..................574 533-3118
Kevin Gerwells, *Managing Member*
Charles H Gerwels, *
Paul Gerwels, *
Edward V Gerwels, *
◆ **EMP:** 120 **EST:** 1950
SQ FT: 68,000
SALES (est): 32MM
SALES (corp-wide): 32MM **Privately Held**
Web: www.trianglerubberco.com
SIC: 2821 3053 3061 3083 Elastomers, nonvulcanizable (plastics); Gaskets and sealing devices; Mechanical rubber goods; Laminated plastics plate and sheet

(G-6273)
TRIPLE CROWN MEDIA LLC
Also Called: The Goshen News
114 S Main St (46526-3702)
P.O. Box 569 (46527-0569)
PHONE..................574 533-2151
John Reynolds, *Prin*
EMP: 1
SALES (corp-wide): 26.91MM **Privately Held**
Web: www.rockdalenewtoncitizen.com
SIC: 2711 2791 2759 2752 Commercial printing and newspaper publishing combined; Typesetting; Commercial printing, nec; Commercial printing, lithographic
HQ: Triple Crown Media, Llc
725 Old Norcross Rd
Lawrenceville GA 30046

(G-6274)
VIEWRAIL
1722 Eisenhower Dr N (46526-5383)
PHONE..................574 742-1030
EMP: 21
SALES (est): 5.73MM **Privately Held**
Web: www.viewrail.com
SIC: 3441 Fabricated structural metal

(G-6275)
WAVE EXPRESS
67952 Us Highway 33 (46526-8549)
P.O. Box 67 (46567-0067)
PHONE..................574 642-0630
Anita Carpenter, *Prin*
EMP: 3 **EST:** 2008
SALES (est): 462.93K **Privately Held**
Web: www.waveexpress.com
SIC: 3711 Motor vehicles and car bodies

(G-6276)
WIELAND DESIGNS INC
Also Called: Logic Furniture
901 E Madison St (46528-3510)
P.O. Box 179 (46527-0179)
PHONE..................574 533-2168
▲ **EMP:** 225 **EST:** 1976
SALES (est): 23.9MM **Privately Held**
Web: www.wielanddesigns.com
SIC: 2531 Public building and related furniture

(G-6277)
WILDWOOD MILLWORK LLC
2408 Lincolnway E (46526-6424)
PHONE..................574 535-9104
EMP: 8 **EST:** 2004
SALES (est): 1MM **Privately Held**
SIC: 2431 Millwork

(G-6278)
WOOD & MORE LLC
20386 County Road 38 (46526-9136)
PHONE..................260 350-1537
Timothy A Randolph, *Admn*
EMP: 5 **EST:** 2015
SALES (est): 89.95K **Privately Held**
Web: www.flip-in-hinge.com
SIC: 3429 Hardware, nec

(G-6279)
ZIEMAN MANUFACTURING COMPANY INC (HQ)
Also Called: Seating Technologies
2703 College Ave (46528-5040)
PHONE..................574 535-1125
▲ **EMP:** 250 **EST:** 1946
SALES (est): 97.95MM
SALES (corp-wide): 3.78B **Publicly Held**
Web: www.seatingtechnologyinc.com

SIC: 3715 3441 2451 3799 Truck trailer chassis; Fabricated structural metal; Mobile homes; Trailers and trailer equipment
PA: Lci Industries
3501 County Rd 6 E
Elkhart IN 46514
574 535-1125

(G-6280)
ZIMMER METAL SALES LLC
64470 State Road 19 (46526-9421)
PHONE...................................574 862-1800
David Zimmerman, *Managing Member*
Marv Zimmerman, *Managing Member*
EMP: 5 EST: 2011
SQ FT: 9,600
SALES (est): 501.8K **Privately Held**
Web: www.zimmermetalsales.com
SIC: 3444 5211 Siding, sheet metal; Siding

Gosport
Owen County

(G-6281)
4 BAR M INC
9825 W Mount Carmel Rd (47433-9641)
PHONE...................................765 653-7119
Matthew Edward Barnes, *Pr*
Misti Barnes, *VP*
EMP: 5 EST: 2020
SALES (est): 294.06K **Privately Held**
SIC: 2011 Meat packing plants

(G-6282)
ALEXANDER MACHINE INC
7847 Jones Rd (47433-7712)
PHONE...................................812 879-4982
Mark Alexander, *Owner*
EMP: 4 EST: 1994
SQ FT: 10,000
SALES (est): 349.83K **Privately Held**
Web: www.alexandermachine.com
SIC: 3678 Electronic connectors

(G-6283)
BIG CREEK LLC
8636 W Mount Carmel Rd (47433-9642)
P.O. Box 607 (47429-0607)
PHONE...................................812 876-0835
EMP: 10 EST: 2002
SALES (est): 895.04K **Privately Held**
Web: www.bigcreekstone.com
SIC: 1422 Limestones, ground

(G-6284)
GOSPORT MANUFACTURING CO INC
Also Called: King of Tarpaulins The
11 Lousisa St (47433)
P.O. Box 26 (47433)
PHONE...................................800 457-4406
Joseph B King, *Pr*
Alyssa K Rice, *
▲ EMP: 35 EST: 1981
SQ FT: 22,000
SALES (est): 1.57MM **Privately Held**
Web: www.gosportmanufacturing.com
SIC: 2394 Tarpaulins, fabric: made from purchased materials

(G-6285)
KINSER TIMBER PRODUCTS INC
Also Called: Kinser Trucking
8283 W Hedrick Rd (47433-9515)
PHONE...................................812 876-4775
Jerry Kinser, *Pr*
Julia Kinser, *Sec*
EMP: 7 EST: 1976
SALES (est): 575.78K **Privately Held**
SIC: 2411 2421 5211 5031 Logging camps and contractors; Sawmills and planing mills, general; Lumber products; Lumber: rough, dressed, and finished

(G-6286)
LEONARDS AUTO SERVICE
7566 Smith Rd (47433-7983)
PHONE...................................812 879-4802
EMP: 1 EST: 1990
SALES (est): 164.23K **Privately Held**
Web: www.case-5-19-cv-07071.info
SIC: 7534 7538 Tire retreading and repair shops; General automotive repair shops

(G-6287)
LIBERTY CUT STONE INC
9921 N Liberty Hollow Rd (47433-9521)
PHONE...................................812 935-5515
Phil Wampler, *Pr*
Mike Wampler, *VP*
Marybeth Wampler, *Treas*
EMP: 3 EST: 2001
SQ FT: 5,000
SALES (est): 190.24K **Privately Held**
SIC: 3281 Cut stone and stone products

(G-6288)
OHM ENTERPRISE LLC
Also Called: Custom Manufacturing Solutions
2534 State Highway 67 (47433-7722)
PHONE...................................812 879-5455
Sonny Shah, *VP*
Ami Shah, *Pr*
EMP: 4 EST: 2014
SALES (est): 322.97K **Privately Held**
SIC: 3599 Tubing, flexible metallic

Grabill
Allen County

(G-6289)
BRANDENBERGER DOOR MFG
14633 Antwerp Rd (46741-9799)
PHONE...................................260 657-1494
Willis Brandenberger, *Owner*
EMP: 1 EST: 2000
SALES (est): 144.53K **Privately Held**
Web: www.brandenbergercustom.com
SIC: 2434 Wood kitchen cabinets

(G-6290)
BRINDLE PRODUCTS INC (PA)
13633 David Dr (46741)
P.O. Box 227 (46741-0227)
PHONE...................................260 627-2156
Fred Gage, *Ch Bd*
Joseph F Gage, *Pr*
EMP: 17 EST: 1951
SQ FT: 38,000
SALES (est): 5.08MM
SALES (corp-wide): 5.08MM **Privately Held**
Web: www.brindleproducts.com
SIC: 3714 3715 3713 Motor vehicle parts and accessories; Truck trailers; Truck bodies (motor vehicles)

(G-6291)
CEDAR CREEK SAWMILL LLC
15010 Page Rd (46741-9680)
P.O. Box 605 (46741-0605)
PHONE...................................260 627-3985
Benjamin S Graber, *Owner*
EMP: 25 EST: 2009
SALES (est): 2.2MM **Privately Held**
SIC: 2421 Sawmills and planing mills, general

(G-6292)
CHRIS SCHWARTZ
Also Called: Schwartz's Custom Woodworking
13631 Spencerville Rd (46741-9675)
PHONE...................................260 615-9574
Chris Schwartz, *Prin*
EMP: 2 EST: 2010
SALES (est): 103.56K **Privately Held**
SIC: 2431 5712 Woodwork, interior and ornamental, nec; Furniture stores

(G-6293)
COURIER PRINTING CO ALLEN CNTY
13720 Main St (46741-2011)
P.O. Box 77 (46741-0077)
PHONE...................................260 627-2728
Charles A Dick, *Pr*
Waldo P Dick, *Sec*
Judy Dick, *VP*
EMP: 9 EST: 1949
SQ FT: 6,400
SALES (est): 987.29K **Privately Held**
Web: www.courierprinting.biz
SIC: 2711 2791 2789 2759 Job printing and newspaper publishing combined; Typesetting; Bookbinding and related work; Commercial printing, nec

(G-6294)
DUTCH MADE INC (PA)
10415 Roth Rd (46741-9637)
P.O. Box 310 (46741-0310)
PHONE...................................260 657-3311
Lester R Zehr, *Pr*
Martin Graber, *
EMP: 105 EST: 1968
SQ FT: 11,000
SALES (est): 8.85MM
SALES (corp-wide): 8.85MM **Privately Held**
Web: www.dutchmade.com
SIC: 2434 Wood kitchen cabinets

(G-6295)
FIBERGLASS PDTS & BOAT REPR
12401 Bay Heights Blvd (46741-9605)
PHONE...................................260 627-3209
Thomas J Miller, *Prin*
EMP: 2 EST: 2001
SALES (est): 152.05K **Privately Held**
SIC: 3732 Boatbuilding and repairing

(G-6296)
GRABER BOX PLLET FMLY LTD PRTN
16301 Trammel Rd (46741-9769)
PHONE...................................260 657-5657
Joshua Graber, *
Norman Graber, *
EMP: 27 EST: 1999
SALES (est): 947.69K **Privately Held**
Web: www.graberboxandpallet.com
SIC: 2448 7389 Pallets, wood; Business services, nec

(G-6297)
GRABER CABINETRY LLC
Also Called: Cabinets & Furniture
15210 Grabill Rd (46741-9719)
PHONE...................................260 627-2243
Chris Graber, *Pr*
Solomon Graber, *VP*
Vincent Tipman Senior, *Prin*
EMP: 24 EST: 1981
SQ FT: 10,500
SALES (est): 2.76MM **Privately Held**
Web: www.grabercabinetry.com

SIC: 2541 2517 2521 2434 Cabinets, except refrigerated: show, display, etc.: wood; Home entertainment unit cabinets, wood; Wood office furniture; Wood kitchen cabinets

(G-6298)
GRABER MANUFACTURING LLC
12836 Cuba Rd (46741-9721)
PHONE...................................260 657-3400
EMP: 3 EST: 2000
SALES (est): 325.16K **Privately Held**
Web: www.grabermanufacturing.com
SIC: 3089 2511 Window frames and sash, plastics; Storage chests, household: wood

(G-6299)
GRABILL CANNING COMPANY LLC
Also Called: Grabill Country Meats
13211 West St (46741-2031)
PHONE...................................815 692-6036
EMP: 9 EST: 2021
SQ FT: 13,000
SALES (est): 530.98K **Privately Held**
Web: www.grabillmeats.com
SIC: 2099 Food preparations, nec

(G-6300)
GRABILL COUNTRY MEAT 1 INC
Also Called: Grabill Home Food Service
13211 West St (46741-2031)
P.O. Box 190 (46741-0190)
PHONE...................................260 627-3691
Patrick Fonner, *Pr*
Dennis Fonner, *Sec*
EMP: 10 EST: 1950
SQ FT: 10,000
SALES (est): 818.15K **Privately Held**
Web: www.grabillmeats.com
SIC: 5149 2038 2013 Canned goods: fruit, vegetables, seafood, meats, etc.; Frozen specialties, nec; Sausages and other prepared meats

(G-6301)
GRABILL TRUSS INCORPORATED
Also Called: Grabill Truss Manufacturing
14005 David Ln (46741)
P.O. Box 250 (46741-0250)
PHONE...................................260 627-0933
William Kaufman, *Pr*
EMP: 6 EST: 2000
SQ FT: 12,800
SALES (est): 975.79K **Privately Held**
Web: www.grabilltruss.net
SIC: 3443 Truss plates, metal

(G-6302)
HOME GUARD INDUSTRIES INC
13101 Main St (46741-2021)
P.O. Box 39 (46741-0039)
PHONE...................................260 627-6060
Brian G Barbieri, *Pr*
Joseph Barbieri Junior, *VP*
▲ EMP: 100 EST: 1983
SQ FT: 170,000
SALES (est): 19.76MM **Privately Held**
Web: www.homeguardindustries.com
SIC: 3442 3089 Metal doors; Windows, plastics

(G-6303)
J L WICKEY CORP
10107 Graber Rd (46741-9414)
P.O. Box 407 (46741-0407)
PHONE...................................260 627-3109
EMP: 1 EST: 1993
SALES (est): 171.97K **Privately Held**
Web: www.heirsofabraham.net
SIC: 3089 Automotive parts, plastic

GEOGRAPHIC SECTION

Granger - St. Joseph County (G-6331)

(G-6304)
J M WOODWORKING CO INC
10832 Witmer Rd (46741-9752)
PHONE.................260 627-8362
EMP: 2 EST: 1991
SALES (est): 336.07K Privately Held
SIC: 2499 Decorative wood and woodwork

(G-6305)
JOHNNY GRABER WOODWORKING
11522 Notestine Rd (46741-9735)
PHONE.................260 466-4957
Johnny Graber, Owner
EMP: 5 EST: 2016
SALES (est): 142.53K Privately Held
SIC: 2434 1799 7389 Wood kitchen cabinets; Kitchen cabinet installation; Business services, nec

(G-6306)
JR GRABER & SONS LLC (PA)
Also Called: J.R. Graber Wood Box Division
15822 Trammel Rd (46741-9752)
PHONE.................260 657-1071
EMP: 6 EST: 1965
SQ FT: 14,000
SALES (est): 1.52MM
SALES (corp-wide): 1.52MM Privately Held
SIC: 2449 Boxes, wood: wirebound

(G-6307)
JR GRBER SONS FMLY LTD PRTNR
Also Called: Jrxgra-50
15822 Trammel Rd (46741-9767)
PHONE.................260 657-1071
Ruben Graber, Pt
Joseph Graber Junior, Mng Pt
EMP: 9 EST: 1984
SALES (est): 1.52MM
SALES (corp-wide): 1.52MM Privately Held
SIC: 2441 2448 Boxes, wood; Pallets, wood
PA: J.R. Graber & Sons, Llc
15822 Trammel Rd
Grabill IN 46741
260 657-1071

(G-6308)
LENGACHER MACHINE INC
17305 Grabill Rd (46741-9538)
PHONE.................260 657-3114
Eli Lengacher, Pr
Anna Lengacher, Sec
EMP: 10 EST: 1973
SQ FT: 13,000
SALES (est): 796.78K Privately Held
SIC: 3599 Machine shop, jobbing and repair

(G-6309)
LENGACHER MEATS LLC
13601 Antwerp Rd (46741-9716)
PHONE.................260 627-8060
Dan Lengacher, Owner
EMP: 4 EST: 2006
SALES (est): 399.34K Privately Held
SIC: 2011 Meat packing plants

(G-6310)
LENGACHERS WELDING LLC
13817 Antwerp Rd (46741-9716)
PHONE.................260 438-9033
EMP: 4 EST: 2016
SALES (est): 72.71K Privately Held
SIC: 7692 Welding repair

(G-6311)
LSM MANUFACTURING LLC
15303 Roth Rd (46741-9618)
PHONE.................260 409-4030
Sheryl Lyons, Prin
EMP: 3 EST: 2009
SALES (est): 310.23K Privately Held
Web: www.lsmmanufacturing.com
SIC: 3999 Bleaching and dyeing of sponges

(G-6312)
M & D WOODWORKING
11522 Antwerp Rd (46741-9715)
PHONE.................260 450-0484
EMP: 4 EST: 2017
SALES (est): 63.93K Privately Held
SIC: 2431 Millwork

(G-6313)
MAPLE LANE METALS LLC
13428 Springfield Center Rd (46741-9679)
PHONE.................260 627-0987
Benjamin D Graber, Managing Member
EMP: 18 EST: 2009
SQ FT: 100,000
SALES (est): 2.63MM Privately Held
SIC: 2952 Roofing materials

(G-6314)
MIDWEST LEATHER LLC
10914 Page Rd (46741-9792)
PHONE.................435 257-7880
Marcus Plank, Pt
EMP: 6 EST: 1990
SALES (est): 347.75K Privately Held
SIC: 3111 Accessory products, leather

(G-6315)
MILLER CABINETRY & FURN LLC
16016 Trammel Rd (46741-9723)
PHONE.................260 657-5052
EMP: 2 EST: 1995
SALES (est): 231.69K Privately Held
Web: www.millercabinetry.com
SIC: 2434 Wood kitchen cabinets

(G-6316)
MONOGRAM METAL SHOP LLC
11213 Witmer Rd (46741-9410)
PHONE.................260 797-3307
Menno Lengacher, Prin
EMP: 7 EST: 2019
SALES (est): 305.64K Privately Held
Web: www.monogrammetalshop.com
SIC: 7692 Welding repair

(G-6317)
OLD FORT DISTILLERY INC
12311 Saint Joe Rd (46741-9411)
PHONE.................260 705-5128
Paul Grush, Pr
Kristal Grush, Sec
EMP: 2
SALES (est): 62.38K Privately Held
SIC: 2085 Distilled and blended liquors

(G-6318)
OUR COUNTRY HOME ENTPS INC
Also Called: Our Country Home
13101 Main St (46741-2021)
PHONE.................260 657-5605
EMP: 72
Web: www.ochinc.com
SIC: 2541 Wood partitions and fixtures
PA: Our Country Home Enterprises, Inc.
12120 Water St
Harlan IN 46743

(G-6319)
OUTMAN INDUSTRIES INC
13737 Main St (46741-2037)
PHONE.................260 467-1576
Tom Outman, Pr
EMP: 9 EST: 1998
SQ FT: 3,000
SALES (est): 963.74K Privately Held
Web: www.outmaninc.com
SIC: 3643 Connectors and terminals for electrical devices

(G-6320)
PERFORMANCE BRAKE PARTS INC
10709 Steury Ln (46741-9700)
PHONE.................260 410-1404
Robert Sawgle, Prin
EMP: 3 EST: 2010
SALES (est): 140.54K Privately Held
SIC: 3714 Motor vehicle parts and accessories

(G-6321)
R3 COMPOSITES CORP (PA)
14123 Roth Rd (46741-9678)
PHONE.................260 627-0033
Mark Glidden, Pr
Kirk Klein, *
EMP: 94 EST: 2000
SQ FT: 235,000
SALES (est): 27.54MM
SALES (corp-wide): 27.54MM Privately Held
Web: www.r3composites.com
SIC: 3089 Injection molding of plastics

(G-6322)
RITE PRODUCTS INC
13601 Roth Rd (46741-9631)
P.O. Box 23 (46741-0023)
PHONE.................260 627-6465
Mark L Sauder, Pr
EMP: 6 EST: 2017
SALES (est): 246.52K Privately Held
Web: www.riteproductsinc.com
SIC: 3089 Plastics products, nec

(G-6323)
S L MANUFACTURING LLC
18535 Hurshtown Rd (46741)
PHONE.................260 657-3392
EMP: 3 EST: 2020
SALES (est): 39.69K Privately Held
SIC: 3999 Manufacturing industries, nec

(G-6324)
SCHERTZ CRAFTSMEN INC
Also Called: Grabill Cabinet Co
13844 Sawmill Rd (46741)
P.O. Box 40 (46741)
PHONE.................877 472-2782
Martin Heiny, Pr
David Carnahan, *
▼ EMP: 210 EST: 1946
SQ FT: 105,000
SALES (est): 24.7MM Privately Held
Web: www.grabillcabinets.com
SIC: 2431 2434 2511 Panel work, wood; Wood kitchen cabinets; Wood household furniture

(G-6325)
TEIJIN AUTOMOTIVE TECH INC
13811 Roth Rd (46741-9003)
PHONE.................260 627-0890
Rod Swann, Mgr
EMP: 108
Web: www.teijinautomotive.com
SIC: 3089 Injection molding of plastics
HQ: Teijin Automotive Technologies, Inc.
255 Rex Blvd
Auburn Hills MI 48326
248 237-7800

(G-6326)
WOOD TECHNOLOGIES LLC
13804 Antwerp Rd (46741-9716)
PHONE.................260 627-8858
Benjamin E Lengacher, Managing Member
▼ EMP: 25 EST: 2001
SQ FT: 40,000
SALES (est): 5.52MM Privately Held
Web: www.woodtechlp.com
SIC: 5046 2541 Store fixtures and display equipment; Store and office display cases and fixtures

Grandview
Spencer County

(G-6327)
CORN ISLAND SHIPYARD INC
9447 Indiana 66 (47615)
P.O. Box 125 (47550-0125)
PHONE.................812 362-8808
Don Foertsch, Pr
David Foertsch, VP
Linda Foertsch, Sec
▲ EMP: 4 EST: 1988
SALES (est): 2.02MM Privately Held
Web: www.cornislandshipyard.com
SIC: 3731 Barges, building and repairing

(G-6328)
GRANDVIEW ALUMINUM PRODUCTS
110 W 4th St (47615-9483)
P.O. Box 687 (47615-0687)
PHONE.................812 649-2569
Harold L Banks, Pr
Georgia Lee Banks, *
Leslie Banks, *
Brett Banks, *
▲ EMP: 18 EST: 1965
SQ FT: 13,000
SALES (est): 1.2MM Privately Held
Web: www.gapalum.com
SIC: 3363 3993 3366 3365 Aluminum die-castings; Signs and advertising specialties; Copper foundries; Aluminum foundries

Granger
St. Joseph County

(G-6329)
AAM-EQUIPCO INC (PA)
12838 Loop Ct (46530-9289)
PHONE.................574 272-8886
John Finks, Pr
Nancy Finks, Sec
EMP: 3 EST: 1975
SALES (est): 1.03MM Privately Held
SIC: 5084 3549 Industrial machinery and equipment; Metalworking machinery, nec

(G-6330)
ADLINK PROMOTIONS
52074 N Lakeshore Dr (46530-7847)
PHONE.................574 271-7003
Todd Zaseck, Pr
EMP: 1 EST: 1995
SALES (est): 153.15K Privately Held
Web: www.adlinkpromo.com
SIC: 2759 3993 Promotional printing; Signs and advertising specialties

(G-6331)
ALLEGIANCE TOOL AND DIE INC
12888 Industrial Park Dr (46530-8868)
PHONE.................574 277-1819
Donald Litznerski, Pr
EMP: 7 EST: 1989
SQ FT: 5,600

Granger - St. Joseph County (G-6332)

SALES (est): 608.05K **Privately Held**
SIC: 3544 Special dies and tools

(G-6332)
ASHLEY WORLDWIDE INC (PA)
Also Called: Gerber Manufacturing
13388 State Road 23 (46530-8621)
PHONE..........................574 259-2481
Terry L Gerber, *Ch Bd*
Nancy D Gerber, *Sec*
Deron Gerber, *Pr*
▲ **EMP:** 5 **EST:** 1924
SQ FT: 1,500
SALES (est): 4.3MM
SALES (corp-wide): 4.3MM **Privately Held**
Web: ashleyworldwide.openfos.com
SIC: 2311 Men's and boys' uniforms

(G-6333)
B & B SPECIALTIES INC
14234 Cleveland Rd (46530-9653)
PHONE..........................574 277-0499
Richard Bennett, *Pr*
EMP: 2 **EST:** 1979
SALES (est): 156.49K **Privately Held**
Web: www.bennettbuilt.com
SIC: 3944 5945 Airplane models, toy and hobby; Models, toy and hobby

(G-6334)
B C WELDING INC
12801 Industrial Park Dr (46530-8868)
P.O. Box 257 (46530-0257)
PHONE..........................574 272-9008
William Carnes, *Pr*
EMP: 6 **EST:** 1980
SQ FT: 15,000
SALES (est): 778.09K **Privately Held**
Web: www.bcwelding.net
SIC: 7692 Welding repair

(G-6335)
B Y M ELECTRONICS INC
10288 Anderson Rd (46530-7263)
PHONE..........................574 674-5096
Brian Y Mccay, *CEO*
Brian Y Mc Cay, *Pr*
Suzanne M Mc Cay, *VP*
EMP: 2 **EST:** 1980
SALES (est): 249.46K **Privately Held**
SIC: 3699 Welding machines and equipment, ultrasonic

(G-6336)
BAWAENTERPRISES LLC
30836 Oakcrest Dr (46530-9304)
PHONE..........................269 228-1258
EMP: 1
SALES (est): 49.15K **Privately Held**
SIC: 3061 7389 Automotive rubber goods (mechanical); Business Activities at Non-Commercial Site

(G-6337)
BIRDS NEST INC
Also Called: Wild Birds Unlimited
421 E University Dr (46530-4499)
PHONE..........................574 247-0201
David Gunter, *Pr*
Kathy Gunter, *Owner*
EMP: 2 **EST:** 1997
SALES (est): 150K **Privately Held**
Web: www.birdsnestresort.com
SIC: 5999 2048 Pets and pet supplies; Bird food, prepared

(G-6338)
BT&F LLC
Also Called: Grip-Tite
12441 Beckley St Ste 8 (46530-9660)
PHONE..........................574 272-6128
▲ **EMP:** 7 **EST:** 2004
SQ FT: 23,000
SALES (est): 986.03K **Privately Held**
Web: www.griptitetools.com
SIC: 3423 Hand and edge tools, nec

(G-6339)
CITY PATTERN AND FOUNDRY COMPANY INC
Also Called: C-P Industries
12767 Industrial Park Dr (46530-6874)
P.O. Box 690 (46530-0690)
PHONE..........................574 273-3000
EMP: 75 **EST:** 1937
SALES (est): 9.1MM **Privately Held**
Web: www.cpind.com
SIC: 3544 3599 Jigs and fixtures; Machine shop, jobbing and repair

(G-6340)
CUSTOM CANDY WRAPPERS COMPANY
52092 Larkspur Cir (46530-8956)
PHONE..........................574 247-0756
Beth Anne Jackson, *Owner*
EMP: 2 **EST:** 2000
SALES (est): 87.59K **Privately Held**
SIC: 2759 5947 Wrappers: printing, nsk; Gift, novelty, and souvenir shop

(G-6341)
CUSTOM FAB & WELD INC (PA)
16915 Cleveland Rd (46530)
PHONE..........................574 277-8877
Andrew Helfrich, *Pr*
EMP: 8 **EST:** 2021
SALES (est): 966.05K
SALES (corp-wide): 966.05K **Privately Held**
SIC: 7692 Welding repair

(G-6342)
CYNTHIA BERGSTRAND
50648 Glen Meadow Ln (46530-9044)
PHONE..........................574 277-6160
EMP: 1 **EST:** 1993
SALES (est): 42.84K **Privately Held**
SIC: 5963 2211 Home related products, direct sales; Broadwoven fabric mills, cotton

(G-6343)
DAUGHERTY CABINETS
51719 Gumwood Rd (46530-3304)
PHONE..........................574 272-9205
Douglas Daugherty, *Prin*
EMP: 5 **EST:** 2011
SALES (est): 74.28K **Privately Held**
SIC: 2434 Wood kitchen cabinets

(G-6344)
DAVID ASKEW
Also Called: Daves Custom Design
51931 Pennyroyal Ln (46530-9418)
PHONE..........................574 273-0184
EMP: 1 **EST:** 1996
SALES (est): 78.53K **Privately Held**
SIC: 3571 Electronic computers

(G-6345)
DONALD LESLIE
Also Called: Leslie Lathe Tool Co
16780 Brick Rd (46530-9632)
PHONE..........................574 272-3537
Donald Leslie, *Owner*
EMP: 1 **EST:** 1971
SALES (est): 84.81K **Privately Held**
SIC: 3599 Machine shop, jobbing and repair

(G-6346)
DURUSA LLC
12980-F Ste 310 (46530)
PHONE..........................574 312-0923
▼ **EMP:** 7 **EST:** 2009
SALES (est): 332.35K **Privately Held**
Web: www.durusa.com
SIC: 3479 Coating of metals and formed products

(G-6347)
FULTON INDUSTRIES INC (PA)
51565 Bittersweet Rd Ste B (46530-8859)
PHONE..........................574 968-3222
John D Razzano, *Pr*
▲ **EMP:** 30 **EST:** 1978
SALES (est): 19.9MM
SALES (corp-wide): 19.9MM **Privately Held**
Web: www.fultonindustries.com
SIC: 3599 Machine shop, jobbing and repair

(G-6348)
GBI AIR SYSTEMS INC
50867 Post Rd (46530-6853)
PHONE..........................574 272-0600
Ray Ritchey, *Pr*
Diane Ritchey, *VP*
EMP: 2 **EST:** 1949
SALES (est): 308.34K **Privately Held**
Web: www.gbiairsystems.com
SIC: 4961 3564 Air conditioning supply services; Purification and dust collection equipment

(G-6349)
GILLIS COMPANY
51093 Bittersweet Rd (46530)
P.O. Box 65 (46530-0065)
PHONE..........................574 273-9086
Greg Gillis, *Pr*
Brian Gillis, *VP*
▲ **EMP:** 7 **EST:** 1989
SQ FT: 2,600
SALES (est): 797.45K **Privately Held**
Web: www.gillissales.com
SIC: 2842 5094 Cleaning or polishing preparations, nec; Jewelers' findings

(G-6350)
GRANGER GAZETTE INC
50841 Stonebridge Dr (46530-8268)
P.O. Box 16 (46530-0016)
PHONE..........................574 277-2679
Kerry Byler, *Pr*
EMP: 5 **EST:** 1997
SALES (est): 334.99K **Privately Held**
SIC: 2711 2791 2789 2752 Newspapers, publishing and printing; Typesetting; Bookbinding and related work; Commercial printing, lithographic

(G-6351)
GREAT LAKES WATERJET INC
53100 Corydon Ct (46530-5838)
P.O. Box 902 (46530-0902)
PHONE..........................574 651-2158
Stacey E Curtiss, *Pr*
David Curtiss, *General MRG*
EMP: 2 **EST:** 2007
SALES (est): 136.34K **Privately Held**
Web: www.greatlakeswaterjetandlaser.com
SIC: 3999 7389 Manufacturing industries, nec; Metal cutting services

(G-6352)
HESTAD INDUSTRIES INC
52265 Wood Haven Dr (46530-5605)
PHONE..........................574 271-7609
Ron Hestad, *Pr*
EMP: 5 **EST:** 2001
SALES (est): 88.4K **Privately Held**
SIC: 3999 Manufacturing industries, nec

(G-6353)
IN DEFENSE OF WOMEN INC
52075 Avanelle St (46530-9590)
PHONE..........................574 855-1864
Anthony Pearson, *Owner*
EMP: 6 **EST:** 2013
SALES (est): 77.45K **Privately Held**
SIC: 3812 Defense systems and equipment

(G-6354)
INTERACTIVE ENGINEERING INC
15925 Fair Banks Ct (46530-7067)
PHONE..........................574 272-5851
Thomas E Henry, *Pr*
Sarah Henry, *Sec*
EMP: 3 **EST:** 1992
SQ FT: 2,000
SALES (est): 310.48K **Privately Held**
SIC: 3089 Injection molded finished plastics products, nec

(G-6355)
ITALMAC USA INC
12743 Heather Park Dr Ste 104 (46530-4318)
PHONE..........................574 243-0217
Mattia Marchiotto, *Pr*
▲ **EMP:** 7 **EST:** 2013
SALES (est): 160.39K **Privately Held**
Web: www.italmac.it
SIC: 3444 Sheet metalwork

(G-6356)
KAIZEN WOODWORKS
13371 Kingsfield Ct (46530-9130)
P.O. Box 44803 (46244-0803)
PHONE..........................714 350-6281
Kyle Divine, *Prin*
EMP: 5 **EST:** 2016
SALES (est): 79.01K **Privately Held**
Web: www.kaizendiygym.com
SIC: 2431 Millwork

(G-6357)
KARK WELDING
51285 Bittersweet Rd Ste F (46530-7817)
PHONE..........................574 400-3989
EMP: 3 **EST:** 2016
SALES (est): 30.36K **Privately Held**
Web: www.karkwelding.com
SIC: 7692 Welding repair

(G-6358)
LAZAR SCIENTIFIC INCORPORATED
Also Called: LSI
12692 Sandy Dr Ste 116 (46530-4340)
P.O. Box 1128 (46530-1128)
PHONE..........................574 271-7020
Gregory G Lazarczyk, *Pr*
Michael J Finn, *S&M/Mgr*
Susan Y Lazarczyk, *Sec*
EMP: 4 **EST:** 1998
SQ FT: 1,400
SALES (est): 2.25MM **Privately Held**
Web: www.lazarsci.com
SIC: 5049 3826 Analytical instruments; Petroleum product analyzing apparatus

(G-6359)
MARCOTTE CABINETS
51286 Ironwood Rd (46530-7622)
PHONE..........................574 520-1342
Faye Marcotte, *CFO*
EMP: 2 **EST:** 2002
SALES (est): 176.8K **Privately Held**

SIC: 2434 Wood kitchen cabinets

(G-6360)
MICRO TOOL & MACHINE CO INC
51836 Purdue Ct (46530-9566)
PHONE..................574 272-9141
Michael Casini, Pr
Joseph Kertes, VP
Thomas Pauwels, Sec
EMP: 8 **EST:** 1980
SQ FT: 6,000
SALES (est): 589.95K **Privately Held**
Web: www.mtmmachines.ca
SIC: 3544 3541 Industrial molds; Machine tools, metal cutting type

(G-6361)
MIDWEST FABRICATION LLC
16100 Branchwood Ln (46530-8986)
PHONE..................574 276-5041
EMP: 2 **EST:** 2010
SALES (est): 101.53K **Privately Held**
SIC: 3569 General industrial machinery, nec

(G-6362)
MISHAWAKA BREWING COMPANY
408 W Cleveland Rd (46530-9577)
PHONE..................574 256-9993
Tom R Schmidt Senior, Pr
Sally J Foster, Sec
EMP: 9 **EST:** 1992
SQ FT: 1,800
SALES (est): 236.29K **Privately Held**
SIC: 2082 5181 5813 5812 Beer (alcoholic beverage); Beer and ale; Drinking places; Eating places

(G-6363)
MOLDED ACSTCAL PDTS EASTON INC
13065 Anderson Rd (46530-9283)
P.O. Box 4027 (18043-4027)
PHONE..................574 968-3124
Robert Snyder, Bmch Mgr
EMP: 50
Web: www.mapeaston.com
SIC: 3269 Cookware: stoneware, coarse earthenware, and pottery
PA: Molded Acoustical Products Of Easton, Inc.
3 Danforth Dr
Easton PA 18045

(G-6364)
MORSE METAL FAB INC
51111 Bittersweet Rd (46530-7880)
P.O. Box 648 (46530-0648)
PHONE..................574 674-6237
Kevin Montague, Pr
Troy Turnock, Sec
EMP: 14 **EST:** 1994
SQ FT: 28,000
SALES (est): 879.27K **Privately Held**
Web: www.morsemetalfab.com
SIC: 3444 3441 Sheet metalwork; Fabricated structural metal

(G-6365)
NEELY PUBLISHING LLC
17145 Barryknoll Way (46530-9748)
PHONE..................574 271-7978
Keith Neely, Prin
EMP: 1 **EST:** 2003
SALES (est): 62.76K **Privately Held**
SIC: 2741 Miscellaneous publishing

(G-6366)
NEETA SWEET CUPCAKES N MINIS
52101 Goldenrod Ln (46530-7150)
PHONE..................574 286-7032
EMP: 4 **EST:** 2013
SALES (est): 90.21K **Privately Held**
SIC: 2051 Bread, cake, and related products

(G-6367)
NIELSEN ENTERPRISES INC
Also Called: Proforma Corporate Solutions
51950 Chicory Ln (46530-7587)
P.O. Box 719 (46530-0719)
PHONE..................574 277-3748
TOLL FREE: 800
Jon R Nielsen, Pr
EMP: 2 **EST:** 1996
SALES (est): 162.29K **Privately Held**
Web: www.nielsens.com
SIC: 2759 Promotional printing

(G-6368)
PAIGE MARSCHALL
Also Called: Paige's Custom Lettering
12622 Alexander Dr (46530-9619)
P.O. Box 412 (46530-0412)
PHONE..................574 277-1631
Paige Marschall, Owner
EMP: 9 **EST:** 1990
SQ FT: 6,000
SALES (est): 496.49K **Privately Held**
Web: www.paigeslettering.com
SIC: 7389 2395 Textile and apparel services; Embroidery products, except Schiffli machine

(G-6369)
PGI MFG LLC (PA)
Also Called: Fulton Industries
51565 Bittersweet Rd # B (46530-8859)
PHONE..................574 968-3222
Dave Razzano, *
EMP: 31 **EST:** 2002
SALES (est): 24.81MM
SALES (corp-wide): 24.81MM **Privately Held**
Web: www.pgimfg.com
SIC: 3599 Machine shop, jobbing and repair

(G-6370)
PLASTIC DYNAMICS INC (PA)
52060 Larkspur Cir (46530-8956)
PHONE..................574 272-4576
Steve Plumhoff, Pr
EMP: 1 **EST:** 1979
SALES (est): 395.63K **Privately Held**
Web: www.plasticsdynamics.com
SIC: 3089 Injection molding of plastics

(G-6371)
PRECISION SHEET METAL INC
51963 Bellflower Ln (46530-7146)
PHONE..................269 663-8810
Joe Fetnor, Pr
EMP: 12
SALES (est): 525.89K **Privately Held**
Web: www.precsheetmetal.com
SIC: 3564 Dust or fume collecting equipment, industrial

(G-6372)
PREMIER PRINT & SVCS GROUP INC
6910 N Main St Unit 11 (46530-9681)
PHONE..................574 273-2525
EMP: 10
SALES (corp-wide): 8.69MM **Privately Held**
Web: www.premierprint.com
SIC: 2759 5943 Business forms: printing, nsk; Office forms and supplies
PA: Premier Print & Services Group, Inc.
311 S Wacker Dr Ste 2250
Chicago IL 60606
312 648-2266

(G-6373)
PSL RHEOTEK USA INC
12692 Sandy Dr Ste 115 (46530-4340)
PHONE..................574 271-9417
Gregory Lazarczyk, Prin
EMP: 8 **EST:** 2014
SALES (est): 196.65K **Privately Held**
Web: www.psl-rheotek.com
SIC: 3829 Measuring and controlling devices, nec

(G-6374)
RC FUN PARKS LLC
12990 Adams Rd (46530-7895)
PHONE..................574 217-7715
Donna Shearer, Owner
EMP: 2 **EST:** 2012
SALES (est): 249.81K **Privately Held**
Web: www.rcfunpark.com
SIC: 3944 Electronic toys

(G-6375)
SALON CANVAS LLC
52245 Woodsedge Dr (46530-8233)
PHONE..................574 703-7018
Ae-young Schaetzle, Prin
EMP: 6 **EST:** 2017
SALES (est): 56.36K **Privately Held**
SIC: 2211 Canvas

(G-6376)
SENTINEL SERVICES INC
Also Called: Chikol Equities
51618 Autumn Ridge Dr (46530-7009)
P.O. Box 774 (46530-0774)
PHONE..................574 360-5279
David Kebrdle, Pr
Trixie Hawley, Admn
EMP: 28 **EST:** 2006
SALES (est): 235.06K **Privately Held**
Web: www.chikol.com
SIC: 7389 7322 8742 8748 Financial services; Adjustment and collection services; Financial consultant; Business consulting, nec

(G-6377)
SIMPLY SWANK HM DCOR SIGNS LLC
12650 Adams Rd (46530-6828)
PHONE..................574 204-2339
Lester R Anderson, CEO
EMP: 5 **EST:** 2021
SALES (est): 75.6K **Privately Held**
Web: www.simplyswankhd.com
SIC: 3993 Signs and advertising specialties

(G-6378)
SINCERELY DIFFERENT LLC
51860 Sharon Ct (46530-6823)
PHONE..................574 292-1727
Sarah Dwigans, Admn
EMP: 6 **EST:** 2014
SALES (est): 97.66K **Privately Held**
Web: www.sincerelydifferent.com
SIC: 2844 Perfumes, cosmetics and other toilet preparations

(G-6379)
SIR GRAPHICS INC
Also Called: Screen Printing
12599 Industrial Park Dr (46530-6872)
P.O. Box 1452 (46530-1452)
PHONE..................574 272-9330
EMP: 6 **EST:** 1993
SQ FT: 10,000
SALES (est): 498.27K **Privately Held**
Web: sir-graphics-inc.business.site
SIC: 2759 2396 Screen printing; Automotive and apparel trimmings

(G-6380)
SPECTRUM SERVICES INC
Also Called: Spectrum Service
12911 Industrial Park Dr Unit 7 (46530-4603)
P.O. Box 363 (46530-0363)
PHONE..................574 272-7605
Dan Courtney, Pr
EMP: 4 **EST:** 1985
SALES (est): 318.94K **Privately Held**
Web: www.spectrumservicescorp.com
SIC: 3545 7699 Machine tool accessories; Sewing machine repair shop

(G-6381)
SPORTCRAFTERS INC (PA)
Also Called: Spin Zone Cycling
51345 Bittersweet Rd (46530-6204)
P.O. Box 452 (46530-0452)
PHONE..................574 243-2453
EMP: 1 **EST:** 1995
SQ FT: 2,500
SALES (est): 399.12K **Privately Held**
Web: www.spinzonecycling.com
SIC: 5941 3429 5091 Bicycle and bicycle parts; Bicycle racks, automotive; Bicycle equipment and supplies

(G-6382)
SR PETROLEUM INC
15482 Bryanton Ct (46530-8212)
PHONE..................574 383-5879
Sarwan Singh, Prin
EMP: 9 **EST:** 2015
SALES (est): 378.81K **Privately Held**
SIC: 1381 Drilling oil and gas wells

(G-6383)
STANTON AND ASSOCIATES INC
6910 N Main St Unit 15 (46530-9681)
PHONE..................574 247-5522
Brian J Milnamow, Pr
Jeffrey B Rothermel, VP
EMP: 3 **EST:** 1988
SALES (est): 792.33K **Privately Held**
Web: www.stantonrefrigeration.com
SIC: 3585 5078 Refrigeration equipment, complete; Refrigeration equipment and supplies

(G-6384)
SYSGENOMICS LLC
51210 Lexingham Dr (46530-8256)
PHONE..................574 302-5396
Steven Buechler, Managing Member
Yesim Gokmen-polar, Managing Member
Sunil Dadve, Managing Member
EMP: 3 **EST:** 2014
SALES (est): 170.27K **Privately Held**
SIC: 2835 2834 In vitro diagnostics; Pharmaceutical preparations

(G-6385)
TEAM ONEWAY
12911 Industrial Park Dr Unit 9 (46530-4603)
PHONE..................574 387-5417
Josh Holt, Pr
EMP: 5 **EST:** 2018
SALES (est): 109.15K **Privately Held**
SIC: 3714 Motor vehicle parts and accessories

(G-6386)
TECHNICAL WATER TREATMENT INC
51431 Autumn Ridge Dr (46530-7006)
PHONE..................574 277-1949
EMP: 2 **EST:** 2000
SALES (est): 171.97K **Privately Held**
Web: www.technicalwater.com

Granger - St. Joseph County (G-6387)   GEOGRAPHIC SECTION

SIC: 5084 3589 Industrial machinery and equipment; Sewage and water treatment equipment

(G-6387)
UFP GRANGER LLC
Also Called: U F P
50415 Herbert St (46530-9161)
P.O. Box 129 (46530-0129)
PHONE.................................574 277-7670
David A Tutas, Managing Member
EMP: 23 EST: 2010
SALES (est): 20.97MM
SALES (corp-wide): 7.22B Publicly Held
SIC: 5031 2448 2421 2439 Lumber: rough, dressed, and finished; Wood pallets and skids; Building and structural materials, wood; Structural wood members, nec
HQ: Ufp Factory Built, Llc
 2801 E Beltline Ave Ne
 Grand Rapids MI 49525
 616 364-6161

(G-6388)
UNIVERSAL FREST PDTS IND LTD P
51070 Bittersweet Rd (46530-7929)
P.O. Box 129 (46530-0129)
PHONE.................................574 273-6326
Dick Mcbride, Genl Pt
EMP: 25 EST: 1996
SALES (est): 917.97K Privately Held
SIC: 2491 2435 2431 2426 Wood preserving ; Hardwood veneer and plywood; Millwork; Hardwood dimension and flooring mills

(G-6389)
VTI PACKAGING SPECIALTIES
12912 Industrial Park Dr (46530-8837)
P.O. Box 320 (46530-0320)
PHONE.................................574 277-4119
Margaret Anne Lavanture, Pr
EMP: 7 EST: 2015
SALES (est): 99.95K Privately Held
SIC: 2671 Paper; coated and laminated packaging

(G-6390)
VYTEC INC
12912 Industrial Park Dr (46530-8837)
P.O. Box 1148 (46530-1148)
PHONE.................................574 277-4295
Margaret A Lavanture, Pr
Robert W Lavanture, *
EMP: 30 EST: 1982
SQ FT: 30,000
SALES (est): 2.47MM Privately Held
Web: www.vytecinc.com
SIC: 3089 Extruded finished plastics products, nec

(G-6391)
XYLEM VUE INC
12441 Beckley St Ste 6 (46530-9660)
PHONE.................................574 360-1093
Luis Montestruque, Brnch Mgr
EMP: 45
SIC: 3825 Instruments to measure electricity
HQ: Xylem Vue Inc.
 3725 Foundation Ct
 South Bend IN 46628
 574 855-1012

Greencastle
Putnam County

(G-6392)
A&M COMMERCIAL CLEANING LLC
1138 Avenue D St (46135-1840)
PHONE.................................765 720-3737

EMP: 5 EST: 2010
SALES (est): 280K Privately Held
SIC: 3589 Commercial cleaning equipment

(G-6393)
BUZZI UNICEM USA INC
3301 S County Road 150 W (46135)
P.O. Box 482 (46135-0482)
PHONE.................................765 653-9766
John Kass, Mgr
EMP: 175
SALES (corp-wide): 4.69B Privately Held
Web: www.buzziunicemusa.com
SIC: 3241 Portland cement
HQ: Buzzi Unicem Usa Inc
 100 Brodhead Rd Ste 230
 Bethlehem PA 18017
 610 882-5000

(G-6394)
CASH CONCRETE PRODUCTS INC
State Road 240 (46135)
PHONE.................................765 653-4887
EMP: 2
SALES (corp-wide): 3.37MM Privately Held
Web: www.cashconcrete.com
SIC: 3273 Ready-mixed concrete
PA: Cash Concrete Products Inc
 1541 S County Road 450 E
 Greencastle IN 46135
 765 653-4007

(G-6395)
CASH CONCRETE PRODUCTS INC (PA)
1541 S County Road 450 E (46135-7951)
PHONE.................................765 653-4007
Thomas C Cash, Pr
Tim Cash, Sec
EMP: 14 EST: 1918
SQ FT: 13,000
SALES (est): 3.37MM
SALES (corp-wide): 3.37MM Privately Held
Web: www.cashconcrete.com
SIC: 3273 3271 3272 Ready-mixed concrete ; Blocks, concrete or cinder: standard; Concrete products, nec

(G-6396)
CHIYODA USA CORPORATION
2200 E State Road 240 (46135)
P.O. Box 494 (46135)
PHONE.................................765 653-9098
Michihiro Oe, Dir
Kevin Redding, *
Koichiro Nose, *
Dayne Kono, *
▲ EMP: 180 EST: 2005
SALES (est): 45.19MM Privately Held
Web: www.chiyoda-usa.com
SIC: 5013 3714 Automotive supplies and parts; Motor vehicle parts and accessories
HQ: Chiyoda Manufacturing Corporation
 126-2, Nishishinmachi
 Ota GNM 373-0

(G-6397)
COLLETT PARTNERS LLC
944 W County Road 350 N (46135-8597)
PHONE.................................812 298-4451
Steve Stewart, Genl Mgr
EMP: 7 EST: 2013
SALES (est): 221.72K Privately Held
Web: www.dnemachine.com
SIC: 3599 Machine shop, jobbing and repair

(G-6398)
CONCEPT CABINET SHOP
Also Called: CONCEPT CABINET SHOP
508 S Bloomington St (46135-2114)
PHONE.................................765 653-1080
Aaron Albers, Brnch Mgr
EMP: 1
SALES (corp-wide): 985.05K Privately Held
Web: www.conceptsthecabinetshop.com
SIC: 2434 Wood kitchen cabinets
PA: Concepts The Cabinet Shop, Inc.
 7599 E Us Highway 36
 Avon IN 46123
 317 272-7430

(G-6399)
CROWN EQUIPMENT CORPORATION
Also Called: Crown Lift Trucks
2600 State Rd 240 E (46135)
P.O. Box 840 (46135-0840)
PHONE.................................765 653-4240
EMP: 469
SALES (corp-wide): 7.12B Privately Held
Web: www.crown.com
SIC: 3537 Lift trucks, industrial: fork, platform, straddle, etc.
PA: Crown Equipment Corporation
 44 S Washington St
 New Bremen OH 45869
 419 629-2311

(G-6400)
CUSHMAN PERFORMANCE PARTS LLC
1556 N County Road 175 W (46135-9295)
PHONE.................................765 653-3054
EMP: 3
SALES (est): 40K Privately Held
Web: www.cushmanperformanceparts.com
SIC: 3714 Motor vehicle parts and accessories

(G-6401)
CYCLONE CUSTOM PROUDUCTS LLC
4982 E County Road 325 S (46135-7932)
PHONE.................................765 246-6523
EMP: 1
SALES (est): 39K Privately Held
SIC: 7336 3993 5131 5999 Graphic arts and related design; Electric signs; Flags and banners; Banners, flags, decals, and posters

(G-6402)
D & E MACHINE INC
944 W County Road 350 N (46135-8597)
PHONE.................................765 653-8919
Dennis Flora, Pr
EMP: 7 EST: 1976
SQ FT: 5,000
SALES (est): 638.72K Privately Held
Web: www.dnemachine.com
SIC: 3599 3544 Machine shop, jobbing and repair; Special dies and tools

(G-6403)
DISCOVER PUTNAM COUNTY
20 S Jackson St (46135-1514)
PHONE.................................765 653-4026
EMP: 5 EST: 2019
SALES (est): 103.9K Privately Held
Web: www.discoverputnamcounty.com
SIC: 2752 Commercial printing, lithographic

(G-6404)
GARDNER GRAPHICS & SIGNS
1221 S Bloomington St (46135-2205)
PHONE.................................765 630-8475
EMP: 4 EST: 2019
SALES (est): 46.08K Privately Held
SIC: 3993 Signs and advertising specialties

(G-6405)
GRAPHIC SHACK SIGNS
3216 S County Road 675 E (46135-7525)
PHONE.................................765 721-4317
EMP: 4 EST: 2019
SALES (est): 93.55K Privately Held
Web: www.graphicshacksign.com
SIC: 3993 Signs and advertising specialties

(G-6406)
GREENCASTLE OFFSET INC
Also Called: Greencastle Offset Printing
20 S Jackson St (46135-1514)
PHONE.................................765 653-4026
Terry Mc Carter, Pr
Pat Mc Carter, VP
EMP: 2 EST: 1961
SQ FT: 7,200
SALES (est): 256.61K Privately Held
Web: www.greencastleoffsetprinting.com
SIC: 2752 2789 2721 Offset printing; Bookbinding and related work; Periodicals

(G-6407)
HARRIS SUGAR BUSH LLC (PA)
999 E County Road 325 N (46135-8025)
PHONE.................................765 653-5108
Arthur Harris, Prin
EMP: 4 EST: 2007
SALES (est): 285.54K Privately Held
Web: www.harrissugarbush.com
SIC: 2099 Sugar, industrial maple

(G-6408)
HARTMAN LOGGING
1158 W Us Highway 40 (46135-8794)
PHONE.................................765 653-3889
Darrell Minor, Pt
Daryle Minor, Pt
EMP: 3 EST: 1991
SALES (est): 310.75K Privately Held
SIC: 2411 Logging camps and contractors

(G-6409)
HEARTLAND AUTOMOTIVE INC
300 S Warren Dr (46135)
P.O. Box P.O. Box 648 (46135)
PHONE.................................765 653-4263
Atsuo Shoda, CEO
Ronan Miot, *
▲ EMP: 600 EST: 1987
SQ FT: 132,000
SALES (est): 93.66MM Privately Held
Web: www.hauto.net
SIC: 3714 Motor vehicle parts and accessories

(G-6410)
HEARTLAND AUTOMOTIVE LLC
Also Called: Heartland Automotive
300 S Warren Dr (46135-7573)
P.O. Box 648 (46135-0648)
PHONE.................................765 653-4263
Atsuo Shoda, Dir
Kaji Sawabe, Dir
Ronan Miot, Sec
Yusuke Sakuma, Treas
EMP: 41 EST: 1997
SALES (est): 6.31MM Privately Held
Web: www.hauto.net
SIC: 3714 Motor vehicle parts and accessories

▲ = Import ▼ = Export
◆ = Import/Export

GEOGRAPHIC SECTION Greencastle - Putnam County (G-6435)

(G-6411)
HEIDELBERG MTLS MDWEST AGG INC
70 Veterans Memorial Hwy (46135)
PHONE...................................765 653-1956
Jack Thompson, *Brnch Mgr*
EMP: 10
SALES (corp-wide): 23.02B **Privately Held**
SIC: 3273 1422 5032 Ready-mixed concrete; Crushed and broken limestone; Stone, crushed or broken
HQ: Heidelberg Materials Midwest Agg, Inc.
300 E John Carpenter Fwy
Irving TX

(G-6412)
HENDERSHOT SERVICE CENTER INC
711 N Jackson St (46135-1036)
P.O. Box 56 (46135-0056)
PHONE...................................765 653-2600
EMP: 10 EST: 2005
SQ FT: 40,000
SALES (est): 905.58K **Privately Held**
Web: www.hendershotsservice.com
SIC: 7538 7549 3621 General automotive repair shops; Towing services; Generating apparatus and parts, electrical

(G-6413)
HOMESTEAD BARNS LLC
2794 N County Road 50 E (46135-8588)
PHONE...................................740 624-0997
EMP: 32
SALES (corp-wide): 284.04K **Privately Held**
Web: www.homesteadbarnsllc.com
SIC: 2452 Chicken coops, prefabricated, wood
PA: Homestead Barns Llc
724 Westbrook Rd
Hickory KY 42051
270 623-6878

(G-6414)
JAMES BILLINGSLEY
101 Percy L Julian Dr (46135-2452)
PHONE...................................765 301-9171
James Billingsley, *Owner*
EMP: 1 EST: 2009
SALES (est): 113.37K **Privately Held**
SIC: 3544 Special dies, tools, jigs, and fixtures

(G-6415)
JTN SERVICES INC
4421 S Us Highway 231 (46135-8711)
PHONE...................................765 653-7158
Bill Newgent, *Pr*
Tammy Newgetn, *Sec*
EMP: 4 EST: 2005
SALES (est): 509.96K **Privately Held**
Web: www.jtnservices.com
SIC: 5261 3647 Lawn and garden equipment; Flasher lights, automotive

(G-6416)
K C CMPONENTS WLDG FABRICATION
Also Called: Solid Base Waterproofing
5334 E County Road 600 S (46135-9016)
PHONE...................................317 539-6067
Kent Christian, *Owner*
EMP: 1 EST: 1992
SALES (est): 47.06K **Privately Held**
SIC: 7692 3599 1799 3711 Welding repair; Custom machinery; Waterproofing; Motor vehicles and car bodies

(G-6417)
LEAR CORPORATION
750 S Fillmore Rd (46135-7322)
P.O. Box 491 (46135-0491)
PHONE...................................765 653-2511
Carl Beckwith, *Mgr*
EMP: 4
SALES (corp-wide): 23.47B **Publicly Held**
Web: www.lear.com
SIC: 3714 Motor vehicle parts and accessories
PA: Lear Corporation
21557 Telegraph Rd
Southfield MI 48033
248 447-1500

(G-6418)
LEWIS JERRY CNSTR & EXCVTG
Also Called: Jerry Lewis Cnstr & Excvtg
1249 N Jackson St (46135-8929)
PHONE...................................765 653-2800
Jerry Lewis, *Pr*
Barbara Lewis, *Sec*
EMP: 8 EST: 1969
SQ FT: 11,000
SALES (est): 988.49K **Privately Held**
SIC: 1794 1771 3273 Excavation work; Concrete work; Ready-mixed concrete

(G-6419)
LONE STAR INDUSTRIES INC
3301 S County Road 150 W (46135)
P.O. Box 482 (46135-0482)
PHONE...................................765 653-9766
John Kass, *Mgr*
EMP: 7
SALES (corp-wide): 4.69B **Privately Held**
Web: www.lonestarind.com
SIC: 3241 Portland cement
HQ: Lone Star Industries Inc
10401 N Meridian St # 120
Carmel IN 46290
317 706-3314

(G-6420)
LOST HOLLOW BEER CO LLC
102 E Franklin St (46135)
PHONE...................................317 796-9516
Curtis Eaker, *CEO*
Curtis Alexander Eaker, *Prin*
EMP: 6 EST: 2020
SALES (est): 501.84K **Privately Held**
SIC: 5921 2082 Beer (packaged); Beer (alcoholic beverage)

(G-6421)
MBPC PROGRESSIVE CONSULTANTS
401 Longcastle Dr Apt 3 (46135-2447)
PHONE...................................765 301-1864
Schantell B Wharton, *CEO*
EMP: 1 EST: 2021
SALES (est): 33.35K **Privately Held**
SIC: 2731 Books, publishing and printing

(G-6422)
OBRIEN JACK & PAT ENTERPRISES
Also Called: Jack O'Brien Welding Service
1208 W County Road 125 S (46135-8479)
PHONE...................................765 653-5070
Jack O'brien, *Pr*
Pat O'brien, *VP*
Joyce Obrian, *Sec*
EMP: 2 EST: 1978
SALES (est): 60K **Privately Held**
SIC: 7692 Welding repair

(G-6423)
PARIS BLACK FASHION LLC
3084 W Us Highway 40 (46135-8652)
PHONE...................................317 529-7119
EMP: 1
SALES (est): 60.62K **Privately Held**
SIC: 7389 2329 Business Activities at Non-Commercial Site; Men's and boy's clothing, nec

(G-6424)
PHOENIX CLOSURES INC
2000 S Jackson St (46135-2050)
PHONE...................................765 658-1800
Stacie Gannon, *CFO*
EMP: 17
SALES (corp-wide): 54.2MM **Privately Held**
Web: www.phxpkg.com
SIC: 3069 3089 5031 Molded rubber products; Injection molding of plastics; Molding, all materials
PA: Phoenix Closures, Inc.
975 Meridian Lake Dr Fl 1
Aurora IL 60504
630 420-4750

(G-6425)
PINGLETON LOGGING INC
525 S County Road 550 W (46135-8362)
PHONE...................................765 653-2878
EMP: 6 EST: 2019
SALES (est): 415.52K **Privately Held**
SIC: 2411 Logging

(G-6426)
PINGLETON SAWMILL INC
525 S County Road 550 W (46135-8362)
PHONE...................................765 653-2878
Lee Pingleton, *Pr*
Robert Pingleton, *VP*
Linda Pingleton, *Treas*
Ardell Pingleton, *Sec*
EMP: 24 EST: 1943
SALES (est): 2.35MM **Privately Held**
Web: www.pingletonsawmillinc.com
SIC: 2421 2426 2411 Sawmills and planing mills, general; Hardwood dimension and flooring mills; Logging

(G-6427)
PROGRESSIVE PRINTING CO INC
115 N Jackson St Ste 1 (46135-1233)
P.O. Box 4 (46135-0004)
PHONE...................................765 653-3814
Gary Gram, *Pr*
Cathy Lowery, *VP*
S James Gram, *Stockholder*
EMP: 3 EST: 1949
SQ FT: 6,000
SALES (est): 242.85K **Privately Held**
SIC: 2752 2791 2789 2759 Offset printing; Typesetting; Bookbinding and related work; Commercial printing, nec

(G-6428)
RB ANNIS INSTRUMENTS INC
117 W Franklin St (46135-1223)
PHONE...................................765 848-1621
Michael E Scott, *Pr*
Sylvia M Scott, *Sec*
EMP: 8 EST: 1928
SQ FT: 6,000
SALES (est): 895.53K **Privately Held**
Web: www.rbannis.com
SIC: 3629 3695 3677 3651 Electronic generation equipment; Magnetic and optical recording media; Electronic coils and transformers; Household audio and video equipment

(G-6429)
RUST PUBLISHING IN LLC
100 N Jackson St (46135-1240)
PHONE...................................765 653-5151
EMP: 4 EST: 2010
SALES (est): 210.06K **Privately Held**
SIC: 2741 Miscellaneous publishing

(G-6430)
SEEDLINE INTERNATIONAL INC
5409 S County Road 250 E (46135-8733)
PHONE...................................765 795-2500
Keith Davidson, *Pr*
Wanda Sue Thompson, *Sec*
Jamie Davidson, *Sec*
▼ EMP: 1 EST: 1995
SALES (est): 383.43K **Privately Held**
Web: www.seedline.org
SIC: 2759 Commercial printing, nec

(G-6431)
SPECKIN SIGN SERVICE INC
845 Indianapolis Rd (46135-1451)
PHONE...................................317 539-5133
EMP: 3 EST: 1996
SALES (est): 224.68K **Privately Held**
SIC: 3993 Signs and advertising specialties

(G-6432)
STEVE STAMPER
Also Called: Silverwood Signs
210 Elizabeth St (46135-1000)
PHONE...................................765 653-8786
EMP: 1 EST: 1982
SQ FT: 2,400
SALES (est): 80K **Privately Held**
SIC: 3993 Signs and advertising specialties

(G-6433)
TAYLOR MADE ENTERPRISES INC
Also Called: Taylor Made Awards
1292 N Jackson St (46135-8929)
P.O. Box 492 (46135-0492)
PHONE...................................765 653-8481
Lawrence Taylor Junior, *Pr*
EMP: 6 EST: 1968
SALES (est): 969.04K **Privately Held**
Web: www.taylormadeawards.com
SIC: 3353 Plates, aluminum

(G-6434)
TRUTH PUBLISHING COMPANY INC
Also Called: Banner Graphic
100 N Jackson St (46135-1240)
P.O. Box 509 (46135-0509)
PHONE...................................765 653-5151
Steve Hendershot, *Brnch Mgr*
EMP: 1
SALES (corp-wide): 9.23MM **Privately Held**
Web: www.bannergraphic.com
SIC: 2711 2791 2752 Newspapers: publishing only, not printed on site; Typesetting; Commercial printing, lithographic
PA: Truth Publishing Company Inc
421 S 2nd St Ste 100
Elkhart IN 46516
574 294-1661

(G-6435)
WASSER BREWING COMPANY LLC
102 E Franklin St (46135-1220)
PHONE...................................765 653-3240
EMP: 11 EST: 2014
SALES (est): 456.5K **Privately Held**
Web: www.wasserbrewing.com
SIC: 2082 5812 Beer (alcoholic beverage); Eating places

Greendale
Dearborn County

(G-6436)
A ONE PALLET INC
100 Brown St (47025-2909)
PHONE..................................859 282-6137
EMP: 7
SIC: 2448 Pallets, wood
PA: A One Pallet, Inc.
7435 Industrial Rd
Florence KY 41042

(G-6437)
ANCHOR GLASS CONTAINER CORP
200 Belleview Dr (47025-1485)
PHONE..................................812 537-1655
Randy Becker, *Mgr*
EMP: 73
Web: www.anchorglass.com
SIC: 3221 Glass containers
PA: Anchor Glass Container Corporation
3001 N Rocky Point Dr E # 300
Tampa FL 33607

(G-6438)
AUDUBON WORKSHOP
5200 Schenley Pl (47025-2182)
PHONE..................................812 537-3583
Niles Kinerk, *Owner*
EMP: 1 **EST:** 1997
SALES (est): 83.95K **Privately Held**
SIC: 2048 Bird food, prepared

(G-6439)
B/C PRECISION TOOL INC
1000b Schenley Pl (47025-1571)
PHONE..................................812 577-0642
Glenn Bryant, *Pr*
EMP: 2 **EST:** 2009
SALES (est): 167.98K **Privately Held**
Web: www.bcprecisiontool.com
SIC: 3544 Special dies and tools

(G-6440)
BJH ENTERPRISES LLC
Also Called: Cargo Towing Solutions
890 Rudolph Way (47025-8312)
PHONE..................................812 655-4544
Wendell Hansel, *CEO*
EMP: 15 **EST:** 2012
SALES (est): 8.65MM **Privately Held**
Web: www.cargotowingsolutions.com
SIC: 3593 Fluid power cylinders and actuators

(G-6441)
CATALENT WELLNESS LLC (DH)
601 Rudolph Way (47025)
PHONE..................................800 344-6225
John Swift, *Genl Mgr*
Alessandro Maselli, *Pr*
Thomas Castellano, *Sr VP*
Steven L Fasman, *Sr VP*
Jose Ibietatorremendia, *VP*
EMP: 17 **EST:** 2017
SALES (est): 36.19MM **Publicly Held**
Web: consumerhealth.catalent.com
SIC: 2834 Vitamin, nutrient, and hematinic preparations for human use
HQ: Catalent Wellness Holdings, Llc
601 Rudolph Way
Greendale IN 47025
800 344-6225

(G-6442)
CATALENT WELLNESS HOLDINGS LLC (HQ)
601 Rudolph Way (47025-8377)
PHONE..................................800 344-6225
Alessandro Maselli, *Pr*
Thomas Castellano, *Sr VP*
Steven L Fasman, *Sr VP*
Jose Ibietatorremendia, *VP*
EMP: 87 **EST:** 2017
SALES (est): 266.59MM **Publicly Held**
SIC: 2834 Pharmaceutical preparations
PA: Catalent, Inc.
14 Schoolhouse Rd
Somerset NJ 08873

(G-6443)
CATALENT WELLNESS INDIANA LLC
Also Called: Queen City Candy, LLC
601 Rudolph Way (47025-8377)
PHONE..................................812 537-5203
Vince Klee, *Pr*
EMP: 10 **EST:** 2018
SALES (est): 2.63MM **Publicly Held**
Web: www.queencitycandy.com
SIC: 2064 7336 Chewing candy, not chewing gum; Package design
HQ: Catalent Wellness, Llc
601 Rudolph Way
Greendale IN 47025
800 344-6225

(G-6444)
CM REED LLC (PA)
Also Called: Pur-SE
18463 Running Deer Ln (47025-8246)
PHONE..................................517 546-4100
Carolyn Reed, *Managing Member*
EMP: 3 **EST:** 2007
SQ FT: 1,800
SALES (est): 247.89K
SALES (corp-wide): 247.89K **Privately Held**
SIC: 3171 2339 5621 Women's handbags and purses; Women's and misses' accessories; Women's specialty clothing stores

(G-6445)
GILES CHEMICAL CORPORATION
Also Called: Giles Manufacturing
200 Brown St (47025-1583)
PHONE..................................812 537-4852
Rick Skipton, *Prin*
EMP: 4
SALES (corp-wide): 335.68MM **Privately Held**
Web: www.premiermagnesia.com
SIC: 2899 2819 Salt; Magnesium compounds or salts, inorganic
HQ: Giles Chemical Corporation
102 Commerce St
Waynesville NC 28786
828 452-4784

(G-6446)
GILES MANUFACTURING COMPANY
200 Brown St (47025-1583)
PHONE..................................812 537-4852
Richard Wrenn, *Pr*
EMP: 3 **EST:** 1988
SALES (est): 336.62K **Privately Held**
SIC: 2834 2819 Pharmaceutical preparations; Industrial inorganic chemicals, nec

(G-6447)
HREZO INDUSTRIAL EQP & ENGRG
Also Called: Hrezo Engineering
1025 Ridge Ave (47025-1324)
PHONE..................................812 537-4700
Bob Hrezo, *Owner*
EMP: 12 **EST:** 1983
SQ FT: 6,000
SALES (est): 2.44MM **Privately Held**
Web: www.hrezoengineering.com
SIC: 5084 5074 3585 8711 Pumps and pumping equipment, nec; Convectors; Heating equipment, complete; Consulting engineer

(G-6448)
MGPI PROCESSING INC
7 Ridge Ave (47025-1637)
PHONE..................................812 532-4100
EMP: 19
SALES (corp-wide): 836.52MM **Publicly Held**
Web: www.mgpingredients.com
SIC: 2085 Distilled and blended liquors
HQ: Mgpi Processing, Inc.
100 Commercial St
Atchison KS 66002
913 367-1480

(G-6449)
OMNI TECH INTRMDATE HLDNGS LLC (PA)
779 Rudolph Way (47025-8378)
PHONE..................................786 201-2094
EMP: 1 **EST:** 2019
SALES (est): 88.58K
SALES (corp-wide): 88.58K **Privately Held**
Web: www.omnitechnologies.com
SIC: 3089 Injection molding of plastics

(G-6450)
OMNI TECHNOLOGIES INC (PA)
779 Rudolph Way (47025-8378)
PHONE..................................812 537-4102
Donald Culbertson, *Pr*
EMP: 53 **EST:** 1979
SQ FT: 50,000
SALES (est): 9.18MM
SALES (corp-wide): 9.18MM **Privately Held**
Web: www.omnitechnologies.com
SIC: 3089 Injection molding of plastics

(G-6451)
OMNI TECHNOLOGIES INC
80 Brown St (47025-1502)
PHONE..................................812 539-4144
EMP: 12
SALES (corp-wide): 9.18MM **Privately Held**
Web: www.omnitechnologies.com
SIC: 2821 Plastics materials and resins
PA: Omni Technologies, Inc.
779 Rudolph Way
Greendale IN 47025
812 537-4102

(G-6452)
POLYCRAFT PRODUCTS INC (PA)
897 Rudolph Way (47025)
PHONE..................................812 577-3401
▼ **EMP:** 47 **EST:** 1982
SALES (est): 6.4MM
SALES (corp-wide): 6.4MM **Privately Held**
Web: www.polycraftproducts.com
SIC: 3724 3061 Aircraft engines and engine parts; Mechanical rubber goods

(G-6453)
PRIORITY STEEL INDUS CONTG LLC
777 E Eads Pkwy (47025-8506)
PHONE..................................937 626-4361
James Stutts, *Managing Member*
EMP: 31 **EST:** 2021
SALES (est): 2.05MM **Privately Held**
SIC: 3441 3548 Fabricated structural metal; Soldering equipment, except hand soldering irons

(G-6454)
PROFESSIONAL PALLETS LLC
100 Brown St (47025-2909)
PHONE..................................859 393-4328
Brian Bush, *Managing Member*
EMP: 11 **EST:** 2021
SALES (est): 1.35MM **Privately Held**
Web: www.professionalpallets.com
SIC: 2448 Pallets, wood

(G-6455)
REFRESCO BEVERAGES US INC
Also Called: Refresco Beverages
2000 Schenley Pl (47025-1593)
PHONE..................................812 537-7300
EMP: 18
Web: www.refresco-na.com
SIC: 2086 Soft drinks: packaged in cans, bottles, etc.
HQ: Refresco Beverages Us Inc.
8112 Woodland Center Blvd
Tampa FL 33614

(G-6456)
TY BOWELLS FARRIER SERVICE
Also Called: Bowell Ty & Michelle
170 Us Highway 50 E (47025-8401)
PHONE..................................812 537-3990
Ty Bowell, *Owner*
Michelle Bowell, *Mng Pt*
EMP: 2 **EST:** 1988
SALES (est): 107.8K **Privately Held**
SIC: 3462 Horseshoes

Greenfield
Hancock County

(G-6457)
AARON DICKINSON
1789 W 200 N (46140-8612)
PHONE..................................317 503-0922
Aaron Dickinson, *Prin*
EMP: 4 **EST:** 2013
SALES (est): 167.29K **Privately Held**
Web: www.dickinsonwoodworking.com
SIC: 2431 Millwork

(G-6458)
AIM MEDIA INDIANA OPER LLC
Daily Reporter
22 W New Rd (46140-1090)
P.O. Box 279 (46140-0279)
PHONE..................................317 462-5528
John Senger, *Brnch Mgr*
EMP: 21
SALES (corp-wide): 26.88MM **Privately Held**
Web: www.aimmediaindiana.com
SIC: 2711 2791 2752 Newspapers, publishing and printing; Typesetting; Commercial printing, lithographic
PA: Aim Media Indiana Operating, Llc
2980 N National Rd # A
Columbus IN 47201
812 372-7811

(G-6459)
AIM MEDIA INDIANA OPER LLC
New Palestine Press
22 W New Rd (46140-1090)
PHONE..................................317 462-5528
John Senger, *Brnch Mgr*
EMP: 2
SALES (corp-wide): 26.88MM **Privately Held**
Web: www.aimmediaindiana.com
SIC: 2711 Commercial printing and newspaper publishing combined
PA: Aim Media Indiana Operating, Llc

GEOGRAPHIC SECTION

Greenfield - Hancock County (G-6484)

2980 N National Rd # A
Columbus IN 47201
812 372-7811

(G-6460)
AIM MEDIA INDIANA OPER LLC
Aim Media Printing
22 W New Rd (46140-1090)
PHONE.................................317 462-5528
Larry Ham, *Brnch Mgr*
EMP: 43
SALES (corp-wide): 26.88MM **Privately Held**
Web: www.aimmediaindiana.com
SIC: 2711 Commercial printing and newspaper publishing combined
PA: Aim Media Indiana Operating, Llc
2980 N National Rd # A
Columbus IN 47201
812 372-7811

(G-6461)
AMERICAS CABINET CO IND INC
7367 E Us Highway 40 (46140-9411)
PHONE.................................317 788-9533
Wilford Listenfelt, *VP*
EMP: 17 **EST:** 2015
SALES (est): 978.93K **Privately Held**
SIC: 2434 Wood kitchen cabinets

(G-6462)
APEX ELECTRIC & SIGN INC
4328 E State Road 234 (46140-9043)
PHONE.................................317 326-1325
Gregory L Heuer, *Brnch Mgr*
EMP: 2
SALES (corp-wide): 488.25K **Privately Held**
Web: www.apexelectricandsign.com
SIC: 3993 Signs and advertising specialties
PA: Apex Electric & Sign Inc
500 N Range Line Rd
Morristown IN 46161
317 326-1325

(G-6463)
API INTERNATIONAL INC
6219 W Stoner Dr (46140-7307)
PHONE.................................317 894-1100
Shawn Merrill, *Mgr*
EMP: 11
SALES (corp-wide): 17.59MM **Privately Held**
Web: www.apiint.com
SIC: 3541 Flange facing machines
PA: Api International, Inc.
12505 Sw Herman Rd
Tualatin OR 97062
503 692-3800

(G-6464)
APPLICATION SOFTWARE
117 Wood St (46140-2164)
PHONE.................................317 814-8010
William Hodson, *Prin*
EMP: 2 **EST:** 1999
SALES (est): 114.98K **Privately Held**
SIC: 7372 Prepackaged software

(G-6465)
APPLIED FABRICATORS INC
Also Called: Circle City Copperworks
7185 W 200 N (46140-9633)
P.O. Box 241 (46055-0241)
PHONE.................................317 284-0685
Brandon Reeve, *Pr*
Julie Reeve, *Treas*
EMP: 7 **EST:** 1984
SQ FT: 8,500
SALES (est): 2.23MM **Privately Held**
Web: www.appliedfabricators.com

SIC: 3444 Sheet metalwork

(G-6466)
ARATANA THERAPEUTICS INC (HQ)
Also Called: Aratana
2500 Innovation Way N (46140)
PHONE.................................913 353-1000
Craig Tooman, *Pr*
Wendy L Yarno, *
Brent Standridge, *COO*
Ernst Heinen, *CDO*
Rhonda Hellums, *CFO*
EMP: 61 **EST:** 2010
SALES (est): 10.36MM
SALES (corp-wide): 4.42B **Publicly Held**
Web: investor.elanco.com
SIC: 2834 2836 Pharmaceutical preparations; Veterinary biological products
PA: Elanco Animal Health Incorporated
2500 Innovation Way N
Greenfield IN 46140
877 352-6261

(G-6467)
AVERY DENNISON CORPORATION
Also Called: Avery Dennison Fasson
870 Anderson Blvd (46140-7997)
PHONE.................................317 462-1988
EMP: 99
SALES (corp-wide): 8.36B **Publicly Held**
Web: www.averydennison.com
SIC: 2672 Adhesive backed films, foams and foils
PA: Avery Dennison Corporation
8080 Norton Pkwy
Mentor OH 44060
440 534-6000

(G-6468)
BASTIAN AUTOMATION ENGRG LLC
Also Called: Bastian Solutions
315 W New Rd (46140-3000)
PHONE.................................317 467-2583
William A Bastian Ii, *CEO*
EMP: 60 **EST:** 2003
SALES (est): 22.53MM **Privately Held**
Web: www.bastianautomation.com
SIC: 3579 7699 Forms handling equipment; Industrial equipment services
HQ: Bastian Solutions, Llc
10585 N Meridian St # 300
Carmel IN 46290
317 575-9992

(G-6469)
BATH & BODY WORKS LLC
Also Called: Bath & Body Works
1519 N State St (46140-1066)
PHONE.................................317 468-0834
Phyllis Ficorilli, *Mgr*
EMP: 11
SALES (corp-wide): 7.43B **Publicly Held**
Web: www.bathandbodyworks.com
SIC: 5999 2844 Perfumes and colognes; Perfumes, cosmetics and other toilet preparations
HQ: Bath & Body Works, Llc
7 Limited Pkwy E
Reynoldsburg OH 43068

(G-6470)
BELLTONE HEARING CARE CENTER
1789 N State St (46140-1085)
PHONE.................................317 462-9999
Jason Cooper, *Mgr*
EMP: 1 **EST:** 2010
SALES (est): 43.52K **Privately Held**
Web: www.beltone.com
SIC: 5999 5047 3842 Hearing aids; Hearing aids; Hearing aids

(G-6471)
BIZCARD
1253 N Blue Spruce Ct (46140-7937)
PHONE.................................317 436-8649
EMP: 6 **EST:** 2013
SALES (est): 152.14K **Privately Held**
Web: www.instantimprints.com
SIC: 2752 Offset printing

(G-6472)
BRIGHTTANY POLLITT
Also Called: Encouragement Today
2181 N West Bay Dr Apt D (46140-7623)
P.O. Box 919 (46140-0919)
PHONE.................................217 597-1624
Brighttany Pollitt, *Owner*
EMP: 1
SALES (est): 39.69K **Privately Held**
SIC: 3999 Candles

(G-6473)
BROMIRE TECHNOLOGY
120 Lake View Ct N (46140-1355)
PHONE.................................317 294-9083
Walter Brown, *Owner*
EMP: 5 **EST:** 2015
SALES (est): 219.94K **Privately Held**
Web: www.bromiretechnology.com
SIC: 3571 Electronic computers

(G-6474)
BW ENERGY & INNOVATION LLC (PA) ✪
1752 Fields Blvd (46140-3039)
PHONE.................................214 223-2459
Andrea Mccann Reeder, *Prin*
EMP: 6 **EST:** 2023
SALES (est): 65.62K
SALES (corp-wide): 65.62K **Privately Held**
SIC: 3691 Storage batteries

(G-6475)
BWI INDIANA INC
Also Called: Bwi Group
989 Opportunity Pkwy (46140-0010)
PHONE.................................937 260-2460
Thomas P Gold, *Pr*
Zijian Zhao, *
Karen Hendricks, *
EMP: 42 **EST:** 2017
SALES (est): 10.8MM **Privately Held**
SIC: 3714 Motor vehicle brake systems and parts
HQ: Bwi North America Inc.
3100 Res Blvd Ste 240
Kettering OH 45420

(G-6476)
CATERPILLAR INC
Also Called: Caterpillar
6719 W 350 N (46140-9617)
PHONE.................................630 743-4094
Jim Owens, *CEO*
Tim Huston Epoc, *Prin*
▲ **EMP:** 26 **EST:** 2008
SALES (est): 506.24K **Privately Held**
Web: www.caterpillar.com
SIC: 3531 5082 Construction machinery; Construction and mining machinery

(G-6477)
CEMEX MATERIALS LLC
Also Called: Rinker Materials
6662 W 350 N (46140-9617)
PHONE.................................317 891-7500
Tom Hartley, *Brnch Mgr*
EMP: 217
SIC: 3273 Ready-mixed concrete
HQ: Cemex Materials Llc
1720 Cntrpark Dr E Ste 10

West Palm Beach FL 33401
561 833-5555

(G-6478)
CERTIFIED CLIPPER INC
Also Called: Indiana Clipper Blade Co
6790 W 300 N (46140-8473)
PHONE.................................317 894-3787
Bob Harold, *Pr*
EMP: 5 **EST:** 1989
SALES (est): 77.54K **Privately Held**
SIC: 7699 3421 Knife, saw and tool sharpening and repair; Scissors, shears, clippers, snips, and similar tools

(G-6479)
CHAMELEON LIFESTYLES LLC
1678 E Grey Feather Trl (46140-7155)
PHONE.................................317 468-3246
Matt Mueller, *Mgr*
EMP: 6 **EST:** 2012
SALES (est): 153.36K **Privately Held**
Web: chameleonlifestyles.webs.com
SIC: 2752 Commercial printing, lithographic

(G-6480)
CHERISHED WOODCRAFT
627 W South St (46140-2269)
PHONE.................................317 502-4451
Eric Cummings, *Owner*
EMP: 5 **EST:** 2013
SALES (est): 108.35K **Privately Held**
Web: www.cherishedwoodcraft.com
SIC: 2511 Wood household furniture

(G-6481)
CITADEL ARCHITECTURAL PDTS LLC ✪
6198 W Airport Blvd (46140-9119)
PHONE.................................800 446-8828
Anthony Mallinger, *CEO*
Bob Hintz, *
EMP: 35 **EST:** 2022
SALES (est): 9.42MM
SALES (corp-wide): 50.63MM **Privately Held**
SIC: 3444 Roof deck, sheet metal
PA: Metal-Era, Llc
1600 Airport Rd
Waukesha WI 53188
262 549-6900

(G-6482)
COMMON SENSE PRODUCING LLC
1041 N Village Greene Dr (46140-8288)
PHONE.................................317 622-1682
John Sifferlen, *Prin*
EMP: 5 **EST:** 2015
SALES (est): 200.23K **Privately Held**
SIC: 1311 Crude petroleum and natural gas

(G-6483)
COPELAND LP
Also Called: Emerson Climate Technologies
6579 W 350 N Ste A (46140-7233)
PHONE.................................317 968-4250
EMP: 2
SALES (corp-wide): 4.71B **Privately Held**
Web: www.copeland.com
SIC: 3823 Process control instruments
PA: Copeland Lp
1675 W Campbell Rd
Sidney OH 45365
937 498-3011

(G-6484)
CORROSION TECHNOLOGIES INC
6268 W Stoner Dr Ste C (46140-7306)
PHONE.................................317 894-0627
Kay Squires, *CEO*

Greenfield - Hancock County (G-6485)

Kevin Squires, *Pr*
EMP: 3 **EST:** 1999
SQ FT: 2,500
SALES (est): 414.92K **Privately Held**
Web: www.corrosiontech.com
SIC: 3084 Plastics pipe

(G-6485)
D & V PRECISION SHEETMETAL
205 S 400 W (46140-8500)
PHONE.................................317 462-2601
Dan Mattingly Senior, *CEO*
Vicki Mattingly, *Sec*
Dan Mattingly Junior, *Pr*
EMP: 20 **EST:** 1981
SQ FT: 14,000
SALES (est): 2.37MM **Privately Held**
Web: www.dvsheetmetal.com
SIC: 3444 Sheet metal specialties, not stamped

(G-6486)
DAED TOOLWORKS
3255 W Birdsong Ct (46140-9298)
PHONE.................................317 861-7419
Raney Nelson, *Prin*
EMP: 6 **EST:** 2012
SALES (est): 109.22K **Privately Held**
Web: www.daedtoolworks.com
SIC: 2499 Decorative wood and woodwork

(G-6487)
DANIELS VINEYARD LLC
6311 W Stoner Dr (46140-7413)
PHONE.................................317 894-6860
Randy Degan, *Admn*
EMP: 10 **EST:** 2013
SALES (est): 669.89K **Privately Held**
Web: www.danielsvineyard.com
SIC: 2084 Wines

(G-6488)
DEAN CO INC
Also Called: Spitzer Enterprises
6153 W 400 N (46140-9641)
PHONE.................................317 891-2518
Mike Spitzer, *Owner*
EMP: 4 **EST:** 2004
SALES (est): 294.88K **Privately Held**
SIC: 2895 Carbon black

(G-6489)
DIAPER STONE OPCO LLC ✪
Also Called: Made of
7284 W 200 N (46140)
PHONE.................................866 221-2145
Pierre Abousleiman, *CEO*
EMP: 2 **EST:** 2022
SALES (est): 92.92K **Privately Held**
SIC: 2676 5137 Infant and baby paper products; Baby goods

(G-6490)
DICKINSON WOODWORKING LLC
1789 W 200 N (46140-8612)
PHONE.................................317 519-5254
EMP: 3 **EST:** 2019
SALES (est): 222.73K **Privately Held**
Web: www.dickinsonwoodworking.com
SIC: 2431 Millwork

(G-6491)
DORMA
215 W New Rd (46140-1095)
PHONE.................................317 468-6742
EMP: 5 **EST:** 2017
SALES (est): 73.45K **Privately Held**
Web: www.modernfold.com
SIC: 3429 Hardware, nec

(G-6492)
EDWARDS STEEL INC
Also Called: Custom Metal Industries
2042 E Main St (46140-8130)
PHONE.................................317 462-9451
Skylar T Edwards, *Pr*
EMP: 10 **EST:** 1970
SQ FT: 22,600
SALES (est): 977.28K **Privately Held**
Web: www.custommetalindustries.com
SIC: 3444 Sheet metalwork

(G-6493)
ELANCO ANIMAL HEALTH INC (PA)
Also Called: Elanco Animal Health
2500 Innovation Way N (46140)
PHONE.................................877 352-6261
Jeffrey N Simmons, *Pr*
R David Hoover, *Non-Executive Chairman of the Board*
Todd S Young, *Ex VP*
Shiv O'neill, *Corporate Secretary*
James M Meer, *CAO*
EMP: 569 **EST:** 1954
SALES (est): 4.42B
SALES (corp-wide): 4.42B **Publicly Held**
Web: www.elanco.com
SIC: 2834 0742 5191 5122 Veterinary pharmaceutical preparations; Veterinarian, animal specialties; Animal feeds; Animal medicines

(G-6494)
ELANCO INTERNATIONAL INC (HQ)
2500 Innovation Way N (46140-9163)
PHONE.................................877 352-6261
Ms. Amy E Porter, *Pr*
EMP: 52 **EST:** 2018
SALES (est): 37.21MM
SALES (corp-wide): 4.42B **Publicly Held**
Web: www.elanco.com
SIC: 0742 2834 5191 Veterinarian, animal specialties; Veterinary pharmaceutical preparations; Animal feeds
PA: Elanco Animal Health Incorporated
   2500 Innovation Way N
   Greenfield IN 46140
   877 352-6261

(G-6495)
ELANCO US INC (HQ)
2500 Innovation Way N (46140)
PHONE.................................877 352-6261
◆ **EMP:** 202 **EST:** 1996
SALES (est): 101.82MM
SALES (corp-wide): 4.42B **Publicly Held**
Web: www.elanco.com
SIC: 2834 Pharmaceutical preparations
PA: Elanco Animal Health Incorporated
   2500 Innovation Way N
   Greenfield IN 46140
   877 352-6261

(G-6496)
EMGE FOODS LLC
5593 W Us Highway 40 (46140-8793)
PHONE.................................317 894-7777
EMP: 55 **EST:** 1998
SQ FT: 3,700
SALES (est): 495.38K
SALES (corp-wide): 54.3MM **Privately Held**
SIC: 2011 Meat packing plants
PA: Peer Foods Group, Inc.
   1200 W 35th St Fl 3
   Chicago IL 60609
   773 927-1440

(G-6497)
ENERFUEL INC
3023 N Distribution Way # 100 (46140)
EMP: 22 **EST:** 2004
SALES (est): 1.82MM **Privately Held**
Web: www.enerfuel.com
SIC: 3629 Electronic generation equipment

(G-6498)
ENGINEERED MACHINED PDTS INC
Also Called: Emp
317 462-8894 (46140)
PHONE.................................317 462-8894
Ted Ochs, *Manager*
EMP: 1
SQ FT: 60,000
SALES (corp-wide): 4.18MM **Privately Held**
Web: www.emp-corp.com
SIC: 3714 3519 Motor vehicle parts and accessories; Internal combustion engines, nec
HQ: Engineered Machined Products, Inc.
   3111 N 28th St
   Escanaba MI 49829

(G-6499)
ENGINEERED MACHINED PDTS INC
Also Called: E M P
125 N Blue Rd (46140-8900)
PHONE.................................317 462-8894
Ted Ochs, *Brnch Mgr*
EMP: 100
SQ FT: 60,000
SALES (corp-wide): 4.18MM **Privately Held**
Web: www.emp-corp.com
SIC: 3714 Oil pump, motor vehicle
HQ: Engineered Machined Products, Inc.
   3111 N 28th St
   Escanaba MI 49829

(G-6500)
ENVIGO RMS INC
6825 W 400 N Ste 170 (46140-6606)
PHONE.................................317 806-6080
EMP: 4
Web: www.inotivco.com
SIC: 0279 2048 2836 3821 Laboratory animal farm; Prepared feeds, nec; Veterinary biological products; Laboratory apparatus and furniture
HQ: Envigo Rms, Inc.
   8520 Allison Pointe Blvd
   Indianapolis IN 46250
   317 806-6080

(G-6501)
ENVIGO RMS INC
671 S Meridian Rd (46140-8501)
PHONE.................................317 806-6060
EMP: 1
Web: www.inotivco.com
SIC: 0279 2048 3821 Laboratory animal farm ; Prepared feeds, nec; Laboratory apparatus and furniture
HQ: Envigo Rms, Inc.
   8520 Allison Pointe Blvd
   Indianapolis IN 46250
   317 806-6080

(G-6502)
EXCEL MACHINE COMPANY LLC
3103 W Us Highway 40 (46140-8320)
PHONE.................................317 467-0299
EMP: 4 **EST:** 1996
SQ FT: 3,000
SALES (est): 274.21K **Privately Held**
SIC: 3599 Machine shop, jobbing and repair

(G-6503)
EXECUTIVE AUTOMTN SYSTEMS INC
Also Called: Moorfeed Corporation
4162 N Ems Blvd (46140-5502)
P.O. Box 501818 (46250-6818)
PHONE.................................317 545-7171
EMP: 30 **EST:** 2011
SALES (est): 2.29MM **Privately Held**
Web: www.moorfeed.com
SIC: 3549 Assembly machines, including robotic

(G-6504)
FRUGAL TIMES
2309 W 100 N (46140-8487)
P.O. Box 925 (46140-0925)
PHONE.................................317 326-4165
M Babcock, *Supervisor*
EMP: 2 **EST:** 2001
SALES (est): 83.09K **Privately Held**
Web: www.frugaltimes.com
SIC: 2731 Books, publishing only

(G-6505)
GEM ELEVATOR INC
768 N 400 W (46140-8545)
PHONE.................................317 894-7722
Richard Merlau, *Pr*
Charles Merlau Junior, *VP*
Raymond Merlau, *Sec*
EMP: 5 **EST:** 1985
SQ FT: 700
SALES (est): 852.24K **Privately Held**
SIC: 5153 2048 Grain elevators; Feed premixes

(G-6506)
GREENFIELD GRAVEL INC
2605 W 200 N (46140-8466)
PHONE.................................317 326-4003
Jeary Smith, *Pr*
EMP: 7 **EST:** 2016
SALES (est): 169.98K **Privately Held**
SIC: 1442 Construction sand and gravel

(G-6507)
GREENFIELD SIGNS INC
716 W Main St (46140-2061)
PHONE.................................317 469-3095
EMP: 7 **EST:** 2013
SALES (est): 349.1K **Privately Held**
Web: www.greenfieldsigns.com
SIC: 3993 Electric signs

(G-6508)
HANGER BOLT & STUD CO INC
165 W New Rd (46140-1093)
PHONE.................................317 462-4477
◆ **EMP:** 19
SIC: 3452 Bolts, nuts, rivets, and washers

(G-6509)
HITACHI ASTEMO INDIANA INC (HQ)
400 W New Rd (46140)
PHONE.................................317 462-3015
Greg York, *Pr*
Koki Onuma, *
Gregory S Young, *
Masami Watanabe, *
Sosuke Sese, *
◆ **EMP:** 1768 **EST:** 1988
SALES (est): 497.75MM **Privately Held**
Web: www.hitachi-automotive.us
SIC: 3714 Fuel systems and parts, motor vehicle
PA: Hitachi, Ltd.
   1-6-6, Marunouchi
   Chiyoda-Ku TKY 100-0

GEOGRAPHIC SECTION
Greenfield - Hancock County (G-6533)

(G-6510)
HYDRO CONDUIT
6662 W 350 N (46140-9617)
PHONE..................561 651-7177
EMP: 6 EST: 2019
SALES (est): 83.11K Privately Held
SIC: 5211 5032 3271 Lumber and other building materials; Brick, stone, and related material; Concrete block and brick

(G-6511)
INDIANA AUTOMOTIVE FAS INC
1300 Anderson Blvd (46140-7934)
PHONE..................317 467-0100
▲ EMP: 401 EST: 1996
SQ FT: 849,780
SALES (est): 73.47MM Privately Held
Web: www.iafi.com
SIC: 3452 3714 Screws, metal; Motor vehicle parts and accessories
PA: Aoyama Seisakusho Co.,Ltd.
1-8, Takahashi, Oguchicho
Niwa-Gun AIC 480-0

(G-6512)
INDIANA BOX COMPANY
2200 Royal Dr (46140-7441)
P.O. Box 307 (46140-0307)
PHONE..................317 462-7743
Johnnie Jones, Mgr
EMP: 35
SALES (corp-wide): 573.33MM Privately Held
Web: theroyalgroup.wpengine.com
SIC: 2653 Boxes, corrugated: made from purchased materials
HQ: Indiana Box Company
1200 Riverfork Dr
Huntington IN 46750
260 356-9660

(G-6513)
INDIANA KNITWEAR CORPORATION (PA)
230 E Osage St (46140-2423)
P.O. Box 309 (46140-0309)
PHONE..................317 462-4413
Gene Bate, CEO
Patrick Jeffers, CFO
◆ EMP: 28 EST: 1930
SQ FT: 85,000
SALES (est): 5.2MM
SALES (corp-wide): 5.2MM Privately Held
Web: www.indyknit.com
SIC: 2329 2369 Shirt and slack suits: men's, youths', and boys'; Girl's and children's outerwear, nec

(G-6514)
INDIANA PRECISION TECHNOLOGY
400 W New Rd (46140-3001)
PHONE..................317 462-3015
Sosuke Sese, Pr
EMP: 4 EST: 2006
SALES (est): 484.76K Privately Held
Web: www.ipt-inc.com
SIC: 3714 Motor vehicle parts and accessories

(G-6515)
INDIANA SOAP COMPANY
3252 W Sunset Dr N (46140-9526)
PHONE..................317 448-5295
Jeri Reichanadter, Prin
EMP: 5 EST: 2018
SALES (est): 51.76K Privately Held
Web: www.indianasoapco.com
SIC: 2844 Perfumes, cosmetics and other toilet preparations

(G-6516)
INFRARED TECHNOLOGIES LLC
6531 E 200 N (46140-9450)
PHONE..................317 326-2019
EMP: 32 EST: 2010
SALES (est): 201.56K Privately Held
Web: www.infraredtechnologies.net
SIC: 3567 Infrared ovens, industrial

(G-6517)
IRON HAWG
5191 E Us Highway 40 (46140-9407)
PHONE..................317 462-0991
EMP: 2 EST: 1981
SQ FT: 3,780
SALES (est): 197.5K Privately Held
SIC: 3751 5571 7699 Motorcycles and related parts; Motorcycle parts and accessories; Motorcycle repair service

(G-6518)
IRVING MATERIALS INC (PA)
Also Called: I M I
8032 N State Road 9 (46140-9097)
PHONE..................317 326-3101
Earl G Brinker, Pr
Pete Irving, *
Shawn Burgess, *
EMP: 60 EST: 1946
SQ FT: 36,000
SALES (est): 814.09MM
SALES (corp-wide): 814.09MM Privately Held
Web: www.irvmat.com
SIC: 3273 3271 5032 2951 Ready-mixed concrete; Concrete block and brick; Sand, construction; Asphalt paving blocks (not from refineries)

(G-6519)
IT SYNERGISTICS
1283 S Harmony Trl (46140-9700)
PHONE..................317 627-6858
Timothy Bryant, Prin
EMP: 9 EST: 2015
SALES (est): 61.81K Privately Held
Web: www.itsynergistics.com
SIC: 7372 Business oriented computer software

(G-6520)
J & J ENGINEERING INC
610 W Osage St (46140-2396)
PHONE..................317 462-2309
EMP: 15 EST: 1991
SALES (est): 1.18MM Privately Held
Web: www.jandjengineering.com
SIC: 3559 Vibratory parts handling equipment

(G-6521)
J SQUARED INC (PA)
Also Called: University Loft Company
2588 Jannetides Blvd (46140)
PHONE..................317 866-5638
◆ EMP: 87 EST: 1988
SALES (est): 18.61MM Privately Held
Web: www.uloft.com
SIC: 2511 2521 2531 5021 Wood household furniture; Wood office furniture; Public building and related furniture; Furniture

(G-6522)
JOB SHOP COATINGS INC
18 E Pierson St (46140-2442)
P.O. Box 923 (46140-0923)
PHONE..................317 462-9714
Joseph Strodtman, Pr
EMP: 11 EST: 1985
SQ FT: 15,500
SALES (est): 444.98K Privately Held
Web: www.jobshopcoatings.net
SIC: 3479 Coating of metals with plastic or resins

(G-6523)
KBC MACHINE
408 Woodland East Dr (46140-8887)
PHONE..................317 446-6163
Keith Coleman, Owner
EMP: 2 EST: 2000
SALES (est): 232.89K Privately Held
Web: www.kbcmachine.com
SIC: 3555 Printing presses

(G-6524)
KINDRED BIOSCIENCES INC (HQ)
2500 Innovation Way N (46140-9163)
PHONE..................650 701-7901
Katja Buhrer, Chief of Staff
Wendy Wee, CFO
Normand Brown, Regulatory Affairs Vice President
Russell Radefeld, Information Technology Vice President
EMP: 81 EST: 2012
SALES (est): 42.16MM
SALES (corp-wide): 4.42B Publicly Held
Web: www.elanco.com
SIC: 2834 Veterinary pharmaceutical preparations
PA: Elanco Animal Health Incorporated
2500 Innovation Way N
Greenfield IN 46140
877 352-6261

(G-6525)
LOGOWEAR LLC
910 Meadow Ln (46140-1053)
PHONE..................317 462-3376
Alan Davis, Owner
EMP: 1 EST: 2001
SALES (est): 99.07K Privately Held
Web: www.elogowear.com
SIC: 2759 Screen printing

(G-6526)
LUBRICATION SPECIALIST INC
5231 N Sugar Hills Dr (46140-8654)
PHONE..................317 326-4296
Greg Landuyt, Owner
EMP: 1
Web: www.lubricationspecialist.com
SIC: 3569 Lubricating systems, centralized
PA: Lubrication Specialist Inc
370 W Cocoa Beach Cswy
Cocoa Beach FL 32931

(G-6527)
MG ELECTRIC AND SIGN LLC
3885 W 100 S (46140-8347)
PHONE..................317 538-0455
EMP: 5 EST: 2016
SALES (est): 46.08K Privately Held
SIC: 3993 Electric signs

(G-6528)
MID-AMERICA SOUND CORPORATION
Also Called: Mid-America Sound
6643 W 400 N (46140-9116)
PHONE..................317 947-9880
Robert Williams, CEO
Jason Wells, Prin
EMP: 17 EST: 2016
SQ FT: 25,000
SALES (est): 2.1MM Privately Held
Web: www.midamericasound.com
SIC: 7922 3648 Concert management service; Lighting equipment, nec

(G-6529)
MITCHELL-FLEMING PRINTING INC
420 W Osage St (46140-2231)
P.O. Box 477 (46140-0477)
PHONE..................317 462-5467
Rodney Fleming, Ch Bd
John Fleming, Pr
Roger Fleming, VP
Douglas Fleming, Sec
EMP: 10 EST: 1954
SQ FT: 37,500
SALES (est): 539.19K Privately Held
Web: www.mitchell-fleming.com
SIC: 2732 2789 2752 Book printing; Binding only: books, pamphlets, magazines, etc.; Offset printing

(G-6530)
MOAN RACING PRODUCTS LLC
Also Called: Www.psychmxgrafix.com
4812 S 50 W (46140-9243)
PHONE..................317 644-3100
EMP: 4 EST: 2010
SQ FT: 8,500
SALES (est): 234.21K Privately Held
Web: www.psychmxgrafix.com
SIC: 2752 Poster and decal printing, lithographic

(G-6531)
MODERNFOLD INC (DH)
Also Called: Modernfold of Nevada
215 W New Rd (46140-1095)
PHONE..................800 869-9685
Lewis N Stryke, Pr
Brian Hurley, *
Daniel P Connor, *
▲ EMP: 204 EST: 1990
SQ FT: 200,000
SALES (est): 97.07MM Privately Held
Web: www.modernfold.com
SIC: 2542 2522 Partitions for floor attachment, prefabricated: except wood; Panel systems and partitions, office: except wood
HQ: Dormakaba Usa Inc.
100 Dorma Dr
Reamstown PA 17567
717 336-3881

(G-6532)
MOORFEED CORPORATION
4162 N Ems Blvd (46140-5502)
PHONE..................317 545-7171
Domenic Angelicchio, Pr
Dennis O'donnell, VP
Brian Bego, *
EMP: 40 EST: 1945
SQ FT: 56,000
SALES (est): 4.3MM Privately Held
Web: www.moorfeed.com
SIC: 3559 Electronic component making machinery

(G-6533)
MOSELEY LABORATORIES INC
6108 W Stoner Dr (46140-7383)
PHONE..................317 866-8460
Wesley D Sing, Pr
Ethel P Sing, Sec
Francine Sing-borsa, Asst VP
Wesley Sing, Asst VP
EMP: 10 EST: 1969
SQ FT: 10,000
SALES (est): 239.47K Privately Held
Web: www.vivolac.com
SIC: 8734 2087 Product testing laboratories; Flavoring extracts and syrups, nec

(PA)=Parent Co (HQ)=Headquarters
✪ = New Business established in last 2 years

Greenfield - Hancock County (G-6534)

(G-6534)
OBELISK RE-PLAY OPCO LLC
Also Called: Re-Play
7284 W 200 N (46140)
PHONE...........................866 228-1485
Pierre Abousleiman, *CEO*
EMP: 1 **EST:** 2021
SALES (est): 253.56K **Privately Held**
SIC: 3069 Sponge rubber and sponge rubber products

(G-6535)
PATRIOT INC
343 N Windswept Rd (46140-7992)
PHONE...........................317 462-5172
Timothy Colip, *Prin*
EMP: 5 **EST:** 2016
SALES (est): 56.82K **Privately Held**
SIC: 2711 Newspapers, publishing and printing

(G-6536)
PEBBLE NATURSUTTEN LLC
Also Called: Natursutten
7284 W 200 N (46140)
PHONE...........................866 228-1473
Pierre Abousleiman, *Managing Member*
EMP: 6 **EST:** 2021
SALES (est): 1.33MM **Privately Held**
SIC: 1442 Gravel and pebble mining

(G-6537)
PEER FOODS GROUP INC
Also Called: Peer Foods
5593 W Us Highway 40 (46140-8793)
PHONE...........................317 894-7777
EMP: 8
SALES (corp-wide): 54.3MM **Privately Held**
Web: www.peerfoods.com
SIC: 2011 Meat packing plants
PA: Peer Foods Group, Inc.
1200 W 35th St Fl 3
Chicago IL 60609
773 927-1440

(G-6538)
PHOTON AUTOMATION INC
275 Center St (46140-2289)
PHONE...........................844 574-6866
Rick Mudd, *Pr*
EMP: 10
SALES (corp-wide): 9.6MM **Privately Held**
Web: www.photonautomation.com
SIC: 3599 Electrical discharge machining (EDM)
PA: Photon Automation, Inc.
501 W New Rd
Greenfield IN 46140
844 574-6866

(G-6539)
PHOTON AUTOMATION INC (PA)
501 W New Rd (46140-3004)
PHONE...........................844 574-6866
William Huffman, *CEO*
Rick Mudd, *
Jason Webster, *
EMP: 103 **EST:** 2000
SQ FT: 5,000
SALES (est): 9.6MM
SALES (corp-wide): 9.6MM **Privately Held**
Web: www.photonautomation.com
SIC: 3599 Electrical discharge machining (EDM)

(G-6540)
POPE STEEL
4496 E 100 N (46140-9405)
PHONE...........................317 498-0504
Donna Pope, *Owner*
EMP: 1 **EST:** 2009
SALES (est): 78.27K **Privately Held**
SIC: 3312 Stainless steel

(G-6541)
POSTNET POSTAL & BUSINESS SVCS
Also Called: PostNet
1547 N State St (46140-1066)
PHONE...........................317 462-7118
EMP: 3 **EST:** 1995
SALES (est): 245.19K **Privately Held**
Web: locations.postnet.com
SIC: 7389 2754 Mailbox rental and related service; Business form and card printing, gravure

(G-6542)
PRECOAT METALS CORP (DH)
1950 E Main St (46140-8128)
PHONE...........................317 462-7761
Gerard Dombek, *Pr*
Gerard M Dombek, *Pr*
Steven R Lowson, *Sec*
▲ **EMP:** 50 **EST:** 2011
SALES (est): 107.97MM
SALES (corp-wide): 1.54B **Publicly Held**
Web: www.azz.com
SIC: 3479 Painting of metal products
HQ: Precoat Metals Corp.
635 Mryvlle Cntre Dr Ste
Saint Louis MO 63141

(G-6543)
PUNJAB EMPIRE INC
981 Sheets Ct (46140-7234)
PHONE...........................765 987-8786
Benny Khera, *Managing Member*
EMP: 3 **EST:** 2011
SALES (est): 152.91K **Privately Held**
SIC: 3421 Table and food cutlery, including butchers'

(G-6544)
ROSE-WALL MFG INC
5827 W Us Highway 40 (46140-8881)
PHONE...........................317 894-4497
Theodore Rossell, *VP*
Brad Rosell, *VP*
Chris Rossell, *Sec*
Brad Rossell, *Pr*
EMP: 6 **EST:** 1985
SQ FT: 7,200
SALES (est): 1.01MM **Privately Held**
Web: www.rose-wall.com
SIC: 1781 3533 5999 Water well drilling; Water well drilling equipment; Business machines and equipment

(G-6545)
ROYAL BOX GROUP LLC
2200 Royal Dr (46140-7441)
PHONE...........................317 462-7743
Johnny Jones, *COO*
EMP: 173
SALES (corp-wide): 573.33MM **Privately Held**
Web: theroyalgroup.wpengine.com
SIC: 2653 Boxes, corrugated: made from purchased materials
HQ: Royal Box Group, Llc
1301 S 47th Ave
Cicero IL 60804
708 656-2020

(G-6546)
RPH ON CALL LLC
1115 N 300 W (46140-8488)
PHONE...........................317 622-4800
Brian Durham, *Managing Member*
EMP: 6 **EST:** 2012
SALES (est): 108.24K **Privately Held**
SIC: 2834 Pharmaceutical preparations

(G-6547)
RWH WOODWORKING LLC
1166 S 25 E # F (46140-5018)
PHONE...........................317 714-5179
Ronny W Holliday, *Owner*
EMP: 2 **EST:** 2004
SALES (est): 114.86K **Privately Held**
SIC: 2426 Carvings, furniture: wood

(G-6548)
SAFEGUARD SOLUTIONS LLC ◆
635 N State St (46140-1400)
PHONE...........................317 519-0255
EMP: 7 **EST:** 2023
SALES (est): 334.7K **Privately Held**
SIC: 1799 3829 Fence construction; Turnstiles, equipped with counting mechanisms

(G-6549)
SEALWRAP SYSTEMS LLC
325 E Main St (46140-2307)
PHONE...........................317 462-3310
Melvin C Brewer, *Managing Member*
Curtis D Wilson, *CEO*
EMP: 4 **EST:** 1997
SQ FT: 5,000
SALES (est): 461.01K **Privately Held**
Web: www.sealwrapsystems.com
SIC: 2822 Silicone rubbers

(G-6550)
SERVICE ENGINEERING INC
2190 W Main St (46140-2715)
P.O. Box 5001 (46140-5001)
PHONE...........................317 467-2000
▲ **EMP:** 76 **EST:** 1967
SALES (est): 8.66MM **Privately Held**
Web: www.serviceengineering.com
SIC: 3559 Vibratory parts handling equipment

(G-6551)
SIGN-A-RAMA
1302 W Main St (46140)
PHONE...........................317 477-2400
Cheryl Edon, *Owner*
EMP: 3 **EST:** 2010
SALES (est): 195.82K **Privately Held**
Web: www.signarama.com
SIC: 3993 Signs and advertising specialties

(G-6552)
SIMPLY GOOD FOODS USA INC
3023 N Distribution Way Unit 200 (46140)
PHONE...........................317 622-4154
Joseph E Scalzo, *CEO*
EMP: 2
SALES (corp-wide): 1.24B **Publicly Held**
Web: www.thesimplygoodfoodscompany.com
SIC: 2099 Food preparations, nec
HQ: Simply Good Foods Usa, Inc.
1225 17th St Ste1000
Denver CO 80202

(G-6553)
SIMS-LOHMAN INC
725 E Main St (46140-2618)
PHONE...........................317 467-0710
EMP: 4
SALES (corp-wide): 96.65MM **Privately Held**
Web: www.sims-lohman.com
SIC: 5031 2435 Kitchen cabinets; Hardwood veneer and plywood
PA: Sims-Lohman, Inc.
6325 Este Ave
Cincinnati OH 45232
513 651-3510

(G-6554)
SMITHFIELD FOODS INC
Also Called: Smithfield Foods
3271 N Distribution Way (46140-6619)
PHONE...........................317 891-1888
EMP: 38
Web: www.smithfieldfoods.com
SIC: 2011 Meat packing plants
HQ: Smithfield Foods, Inc.
200 Commerce St
Smithfield VA 23430
757 365-3000

(G-6555)
SOFTWARE INFORMATICS GROUP LLC
869 N 300 W (46140-7996)
PHONE...........................317 326-2598
Larry Myers, *Prin*
EMP: 2 **EST:** 2004
SALES (est): 82.61K **Privately Held**
SIC: 7372 Business oriented computer software

(G-6556)
SONICU LLC
11 American Legion Pl (46140-2317)
PHONE...........................317 468-2345
Christopher Smith, *Managing Member*
EMP: 3 **EST:** 2007
SALES (est): 1.46MM **Privately Held**
Web: www.sonicu.com
SIC: 3677 Filtration devices, electronic

(G-6557)
SPECTRA PRMIUM MBLITY SLTONS L (PA)
3052 N Distribution Way (46140)
PHONE...........................800 628-5442
Josh Gordon, *Managing Member*
EMP: 18 **EST:** 2021
SALES (est): 6.51MM
SALES (corp-wide): 6.51MM **Privately Held**
SIC: 3694 Distributors, motor vehicle engine

(G-6558)
SPECTRA PRMIUM MBLITY SLTONS U
3052 N Distribution Way (46140)
PHONE...........................800 628-5442
Josh Gordon, *CEO*
EMP: 1 **EST:** 2021
SALES (est): 422.77K
SALES (corp-wide): 6.51MM **Privately Held**
SIC: 3462 Automotive and internal combustion engine forgings
PA: Spectra Premium Mobility Solutions, Llc
3052 N Distribution Way
Greenfield IN 46140
800 628-5442

(G-6559)
SPITZER RACING ENTERPRISES
6135 W 400 N (46140)
PHONE...........................317 894-9533
Michael D Spitzer, *Pr*
Karen Spitzer, *Sec*
EMP: 12 **EST:** 1972
SQ FT: 30,000
SALES (est): 1.99MM **Privately Held**
Web: www.gospitzer.com

SIC: 3711 3714 Automobile assembly, including specialty automobiles; Motor vehicle parts and accessories

(G-6560)
SUBMICRON LLC
1434 Hedge Ct (46140-7803)
PHONE..............................800 609-1390
EMP: 2 EST: 2020
SALES (est): 175K Privately Held
SIC: 3564 Air purification equipment

(G-6561)
SUMMERVILLE MINIATURE WORK SP
Also Called: Summerville Miniature Workshop
2145 Melody Ln (46140-9587)
PHONE...............................317 326-8355
Nancy S Summers, Owner
EMP: 1 EST: 1976
SALES (est): 107.4K Privately Held
Web: www.summerviileminiatureworkshop.com
SIC: 5092 5961 3999 Toy novelties and amusements; Mail order house, nec; Miniatures

(G-6562)
TEAM IMAGE
18 W South St (46140-2327)
PHONE...............................317 477-0027
Phil Morris, Prin
EMP: 1 EST: 2007
SALES (est): 86.53K Privately Held
Web: www.teamimage.org
SIC: 2395 Embroidery products, except Schiffli machine

(G-6563)
TEAM IMAGE LLC (PA)
121 S Pennsylvania St (46140-2478)
PHONE...............................317 468-0802
EMP: 22 EST: 2004
SALES (est): 4.89MM Privately Held
Web: www.teamimage.org
SIC: 2759 Screen printing

(G-6564)
TEAM IMAGE LLC
212 E Main St (46140-2305)
PHONE...............................317 477-7468
EMP: 28
Web: www.teamimage.org
SIC: 2759 Screen printing
PA: Team Image, Llc
121 S Pennsylvania St
Greenfield IN 46140

(G-6565)
THUNDER PRO
1439 W Us Highway 40 (46140-8883)
PHONE...............................317 498-0241
EMP: 4 EST: 2019
SALES (est): 84.24K Privately Held
Web: www.thunderproperformance.com
SIC: 3732 Boatbuilding and repairing

(G-6566)
TLC METALS INC
Also Called: MCB Accessories
2155 Fields Blvd (46140)
PHONE...............................317 894-8684
Dennis R Cowan, Pr
EMP: 60 EST: 1969
SALES (est): 8.14MM Privately Held
Web: www.monroebodies.com
SIC: 3713 3469 Specialty motor vehicle bodies; Boxes: tool, lunch, mail, etc.: stamped metal

(G-6567)
TSUDA USA CORPORATION
2934 Jannetides Blvd (46140-9334)
PHONE...............................317 468-9177
Tatsuya Kinoshita, Pr
▲ EMP: 12 EST: 2012
SALES (est): 3.12MM Privately Held
Web: www.tsuda-usa.com
SIC: 3714 Transmissions, motor vehicle

(G-6568)
UPANAWAY LLC
Also Called: Blooming Bath
7284 W 200 N (46140)
PHONE..............................866 218-7143
Pierre Abousleiman, Managing Member
EMP: 2 EST: 2011
SALES (est): 243.67K Privately Held
Web: www.bloomingbath.com
SIC: 2399 5719 5999 3088 Infant carriers; Bath accessories; Baby carriages and strollers; Tubs (bath, shower, and laundry), plastics

(G-6569)
VIVOLAC CULTURES CORPORATION
6108 W Stoner Dr (46140-7383)
PHONE..............................317 866-9528
Wesley D Sing, Pr
David Jaramillo, *
EMP: 40 EST: 2005
SALES (est): 9.7MM Privately Held
Web: www.vivolac.com
SIC: 2099 Baking powder and soda, yeast, and other leavening agents

(G-6570)
WARBURTON WOOD WORKS LLC
1347 Pauls Dr (46140-1131)
PHONE...............................317 318-9113
Erik Warburton, Owner
EMP: 5 EST: 2017
SALES (est): 87.48K Privately Held
SIC: 2431 Millwork

(G-6571)
WETHINGTON
Also Called: Oger
4162 N Ems Blvd (46140-5502)
PHONE..............................317 594-6000
Dave Bego, Owner
EMP: 7 EST: 2011
SALES (est): 239.77K Privately Held
SIC: 3711 2656 Automobile assembly, including specialty automobiles; Ice cream containers: made from purchased material

(G-6572)
ZACHARY T LAFFIN
2181 N West Bay Dr Apt A (46140-7622)
PHONE..............................317 480-2248
Zachary Laffin, Owner
EMP: 1
SALES (est): 54.05K Privately Held
SIC: 2741 7389 Internet publishing and broadcasting; Business Activities at Non-Commercial Site

(G-6573)
ZIG-ZAG CRNR QILTS BASKETS LLC
7872 N Troy Rd (46140-9028)
PHONE..............................317 326-3115
EMP: 2 EST: 2002
SQ FT: 1,200
SALES (est): 219.35K Privately Held
Web: www.zigzagcorner.com
SIC: 2395 2211 7299 Quilting: for the trade; Basket weave fabrics, cotton; Quilting for individuals

Greens Fork
Wayne County

(G-6574)
A&R SAWMILL LLC
9450 Clyde Oler Rd (47345-9731)
PHONE..............................765 238-8829
EMP: 4 EST: 2016
SALES (est): 55.04K Privately Held
SIC: 2421 Sawmills and planing mills, general

(G-6575)
L & S LUMBER
7501 State Road 38 (47345-9708)
PHONE..............................765 886-1452
Stephen Stoltzfus, Owner
EMP: 10 EST: 2017
SALES (est): 430.15K Privately Held
SIC: 3429 Builders' hardware

(G-6576)
PINETREE WOODCRAFT LLC
3734 Sugar Grove Rd (47345-9732)
PHONE..............................765 886-1177
EMP: 4 EST: 2019
SALES (est): 64.3K Privately Held
SIC: 2511 Wood household furniture

Greensburg
Decatur County

(G-6577)
A & A INDUSTRIES INC
201 S Monfort St (47240-1922)
PHONE..............................812 663-5584
Walter Allen, Owner
EMP: 1 EST: 1947
SQ FT: 3,200
SALES (est): 236.94K Privately Held
SIC: 3441 7692 Fabricated structural metal; Welding repair

(G-6578)
ABM ADVANCED BEARING MTLS LLC
1515 W Main St (47240-9585)
PHONE..............................812 663-3401
Rob Ewing, Managing Member
▲ EMP: 1 EST: 2005
SALES (est): 356.38K Privately Held
SIC: 3339 Antifriction bearing metals, lead-base

(G-6579)
ACRO ENGINEERING INC
1120 W Washington St (47240-9504)
PHONE..............................812 663-6236
Rollin N Harpring, Pr
Sonny Neisius, VP
Christopher L Harpring, Sec
▲ EMP: 23 EST: 2000
SQ FT: 13,000
SALES (est): 451.7K Privately Held
Web: www.acroeng.com
SIC: 3599 7692 3544 Machine shop, jobbing and repair; Welding repair; Special dies, tools, jigs, and fixtures

(G-6580)
ADVANCED BEARING MATERIALS LLC
1515 W Main St (47240-9585)
PHONE..............................812 663-3401
EMP: 36 EST: 2005
SALES (est): 3.02MM Privately Held
Web: www.miba.com

SIC: 3568 Bearings, bushings, and blocks

(G-6581)
BLASDEL ENTERPRISES INC
Also Called: Blasdel Enterprises
495 W Mckee St (47240-2067)
PHONE..............................812 663-3213
William Blasdel, Pr
Elizabeth Blasdel, VP
EMP: 10 EST: 1982
SQ FT: 30,000
SALES (est): 2.5MM Privately Held
Web: www.blasdel.net
SIC: 3567 3565 Infrared ovens, industrial; Bag opening, filling, and closing machines

(G-6582)
BODYCOTE THERMAL PROC INC
1930 N Montgomery Rd (47240-1276)
PHONE..............................812 662-0500
Martin Swan, Prin
EMP: 27
SALES (corp-wide): 1B Privately Held
Web: www.bodycote.com
SIC: 3398 Metal heat treating
HQ: Bodycote Thermal Processing, Inc.
12750 Merit Dr Ste 1400
Dallas TX 75251
214 904-2420

(G-6583)
BROTHERS INDUSTRIES LLC
803 E Washington St (47240-2214)
PHONE..............................812 560-6224
EMP: 3 EST: 2014
SALES (est): 49.21K Privately Held
SIC: 3999 Manufacturing industries, nec

(G-6584)
CIRCLE PRINTING LLC
130 W Main St (47240-1601)
PHONE..............................812 663-7367
Jan Gunter, Managing Member
EMP: 2 EST: 1984
SQ FT: 2,000
SALES (est): 238.53K Privately Held
Web: www.circleprinting.net
SIC: 5331 2752 Variety stores; Offset printing

(G-6585)
COMMUNITY HOLDINGS INDIANA INC
Also Called: Greensburg Daily News
135 S Franklin St (47240-2023)
P.O. Box 106 (47240-0106)
PHONE..............................812 663-3111
EMP: 1
SALES (corp-wide): 34.97B Privately Held
Web: www.greensburgdailynews.com
SIC: 2711 2791 2752 Newspapers, publishing and printing; Typesetting; Commercial printing, lithographic
HQ: Community Holdings Of Indiana, Inc.
3500 Colonnade Pkwy # 600
Birmingham AL 35243

(G-6586)
CREATIVE FINISHING LLC
6417 S County Road 220 Sw (47240-7425)
PHONE..............................812 591-8111
David Cherry, Prin
EMP: 2 EST: 2002
SALES (est): 199.16K Privately Held
Web: www.creativefinishing.com
SIC: 3479 Coating of metals and formed products

(G-6587)
CUSTOM CONTROLS & ENGRG INC
346 E North St (47240-1718)

Greensburg - Decatur County (G-6588)

PHONE.................................812 663-0755
EMP: 2 EST: 1995
SQ FT: 4,000
SALES (est): 199.34K **Privately Held**
SIC: 3824 1731 Controls, revolution and timing instruments; Computerized controls installation

(G-6588)
CUSTOM CONVEYOR INC
4858 E State Road 46 (47240-8668)
PHONE.................................812 663-2023
▲ EMP: 15
Web: www.customconveyorcorp.com
SIC: 3535 3536 Conveyors and conveying equipment; Cranes, overhead traveling

(G-6589)
DANCE WORLD BAZAAR CORPORATION
Also Called: McLean's Screen Printing
1553 N Commerce East Dr (47240-1291)
PHONE.................................812 663-7679
Sandy Mclean, Pr
EMP: 9 EST: 1986
SQ FT: 9,000
SALES (est): 916.85K **Privately Held**
Web: www.dawobaz.com
SIC: 2396 2759 Screen printing on fabric articles; Commercial printing, nec

(G-6590)
DEC CO ECUMENICAL AGAPE CENTER
1533 N Commerce West Dr (47240)
PHONE.................................812 222-0392
EMP: 4 EST: 2018
SALES (est): 114.86K **Privately Held**
SIC: 3571 Electronic computers

(G-6591)
DENIM AND HONEY
217 N Broadway St (47240-1701)
PHONE.................................812 222-2009
Jada Ogle, Owner
EMP: 1 EST: 2009
SALES (est): 47K **Privately Held**
Web: www.denimandhoney.com
SIC: 2211 5261 Denims; Retail nurseries and garden stores

(G-6592)
FILMTECH INC
3830 E County Road 200 S (47240-7728)
P.O. Box 32 (47240-0032)
PHONE.................................888 399-7442
Michael Scott Theobald, CEO
Michael Sturges, Dir Opers
EMP: 6 EST: 1984
SALES (est): 453.45K **Privately Held**
Web: www.filmtech-inc.com
SIC: 2671 Paper; coated and laminated packaging

(G-6593)
FIVE STAR FAB & ERECTORS LLC
806 E Randall St (47240)
PHONE.................................812 614-9558
John Grimes, Managing Member
EMP: 6 EST: 2020
SALES (est): 315.31K **Privately Held**
Web: www.fivestarfabricators.com
SIC: 3441 Fabricated structural metal

(G-6594)
FOREMOST FLEXIBLE FABRICATING
Also Called: Foremost Flexible Products
824 N Michigan Ave (47240-1484)
PHONE.................................812 663-4756
Adam Huffmeyer, Pr
Daniel Wenning, Pr
Deanna Wenning, VP
Dam Huffmeyer, VP
EMP: 12 EST: 1985
SQ FT: 8,000
SALES (est): 892.75K **Privately Held**
Web: www.foremostflex.com
SIC: 2299 2399 Batting, wadding, padding and fillings; Emblems, badges, and insignia

(G-6595)
G E C O M CORP (DH)
1025 E Barachel Ln (47240)
PHONE.................................812 663-2270
Makoto Sakamoto, Pr
Hiromasa Iwaya, *
Harusumi Sakai, *
Hidekazu Urushibara, *
Toru Shibata, *
◆ EMP: 900 EST: 1987
SQ FT: 210,000
SALES (est): 257.62MM **Privately Held**
Web: www.gecomcorp.com
SIC: 3714 3429 Motor vehicle body components and frame; Keys, locks, and related hardware
HQ: Mitsui Kinzoku Act Corporation
1-1-2, Takashima, Nishi-Ku
Yokohama KNG 220-0

(G-6596)
GAME PLAN GRAPHICS LLC
102 E Washington St (47240-1715)
PHONE.................................812 663-3238
Angie Willson, Pr
Keith Greiwe, VP
EMP: 3 EST: 1974
SALES (est): 255.92K **Privately Held**
Web: www.gameplangraphics.com
SIC: 5661 5941 2396 5999 Footwear, athletic ; Sporting goods and bicycle shops; Screen printing on fabric articles; Trophies and plaques

(G-6597)
GREEN SIGN CO INC
Also Called: Greensignco.com
1045 E Freeland Rd (47240-9435)
PHONE.................................812 663-2550
Shawn C Green, Pr
Rose Perdue, VP
Bud Perdue, Sec
EMP: 11 EST: 1971
SQ FT: 10,000
SALES (est): 1.04MM **Privately Held**
Web: www.greensignco.com
SIC: 3993 Electric signs

(G-6598)
GREENSBURG PRINTING CO INC
116 N Franklin St (47240-2046)
PHONE.................................812 663-8265
Wayne Peetz, Pr
John Wenning, VP
EMP: 3 EST: 1971
SQ FT: 3,000
SALES (est): 247.73K **Privately Held**
Web: www.greensburgprinting.com
SIC: 2752 2791 2789 2759 Offset printing; Typesetting; Bookbinding and related work; Commercial printing, nec

(G-6599)
H AND M TOOL & DIE INC
242 W Mckee St (47240-1999)
PHONE.................................812 663-8252
La Donna Hoeing, Sec
Norbert Hoeing, Pr
EMP: 10 EST: 1971
SQ FT: 11,200
SALES (est): 963.27K **Privately Held**
Web: www.hm-tool.com
SIC: 3544 Special dies and tools

(G-6600)
HARRISON SAND AND GRAVEL CO (PA)
992 S County Road 800 E (47240-8854)
PHONE.................................812 663-2021
Kenneth T Wanstrath, Pr
John R Wanstrath, Sec
EMP: 9 EST: 1954
SQ FT: 2,800
SALES (est): 1.84MM
SALES (corp-wide): 1.84MM **Privately Held**
SIC: 1442 Common sand mining

(G-6601)
HERBERTS SAWMILL INC
Also Called: Herbert Vernon Sawmill
3438 E County Road 700 S (47240-9645)
PHONE.................................812 663-9347
Vernon Herbert, Owner
EMP: 10 EST: 1926
SQ FT: 12,160
SALES (est): 890.8K **Privately Held**
SIC: 2421 2426 Sawmills and planing mills, general; Hardwood dimension and flooring mills

(G-6602)
HH RELLIM INC
Also Called: Streetscape Products Limited
3494 E Base Rd (47240-7967)
PHONE.................................812 662-9944
Jeff Miller, Pr
EMP: 2 EST: 2004
SALES (est): 164.35K **Privately Held**
Web: www.streetscapeltd.com
SIC: 3229 Glass furnishings and accessories

(G-6603)
HOMETOWN ENERGY LLC
1430 W Main St (47240-9730)
PHONE.................................812 663-3391
Lori Pilz, Prin
EMP: 9 EST: 2007
SALES (est): 133.25K **Privately Held**
SIC: 2911 Gases and liquefied petroleum gases

(G-6604)
HONDA DEV & MFG AMER LLC
2755 N Michigan Ave (47240-9341)
PHONE.................................812 222-6000
EMP: 1293
Web: www.honda.com
SIC: 3714 Motor vehicle parts and accessories
HQ: Honda Development & Manufacturing Of America, Llc
24000 Honda Pkwy
Marysville OH 43040
937 642-5000

(G-6605)
HOTMIX INC
992 S County Road 800 E (47240-8854)
PHONE.................................812 663-2020
Randy Wanstrath, Mgr
EMP: 2
SALES (corp-wide): 592.25K **Privately Held**
Web: www.hotmixparts.com
SIC: 2951 Asphalt and asphaltic paving mixtures (not from refineries)
PA: Hotmix Inc
110 Forest Ave
Aurora IN 47001
812 926-1471

(G-6606)
HOUCK INDUSTRIES INC
814 E Randall St (47240-2311)
P.O. Box 8 (47240-0008)
PHONE.................................812 663-5675
Richard C Fayette, Pr
Vicky Ostendorf, *
EMP: 19 EST: 1959
SALES (est): 1.02MM **Privately Held**
Web: www.houckind.com
SIC: 3429 2434 Cabinet hardware; Wood kitchen cabinets

(G-6607)
INDIANA ASSEMBLIES LLC
1424 W Main St (47240-9730)
P.O. Box 47 (47240-0047)
PHONE.................................812 662-2173
Billy R Vickers, Pr
EMP: 2 EST: 2007
SALES (est): 2.49MM
SALES (corp-wide): 45.05MM **Privately Held**
Web: www.modularai.com
SIC: 3711 Automobile assembly, including specialty automobiles
PA: Modular Assembly Innovations Llc
600 Stnhnge Pkwy Ste 100a
Dublin OH 43017
614 389-4860

(G-6608)
INDIANA WIRE PRODUCTS INC
915 N Ireland St (47240-1136)
P.O. Box 169 (47240-0169)
PHONE.................................812 663-7441
Jerry C Westhafer, Ch Bd
Steven Westhafer, Pr
William Burr, VP
Julie Kuehl, Sec
Carlie Burr, Stockholder
EMP: 13 EST: 1960
SQ FT: 24,000
SALES (est): 2.49MM **Privately Held**
Web: www.indianawireproducts.com
SIC: 3496 Fencing, made from purchased wire

(G-6609)
INTERNTNAL MTL HDLG SYSTEMS IN
806 E Randall St (47240-2311)
PHONE.................................812 222-4488
Timothy Stapp, CEO
Angela Stapp, Prin
▲ EMP: 10 EST: 2014
SALES (est): 974.32K **Privately Held**
Web: www.internationalmaterialhandling.com
SIC: 3449 3535 Miscellaneous metalwork; Conveyors and conveying equipment

(G-6610)
K & S FARM MACHINE SHOP INC
4620 S County Road 550 E (47240-8638)
PHONE.................................812 663-8567
Kenny Peters, Pr
Rita Peters, Sec
EMP: 10 EST: 1985
SQ FT: 15,000
SALES (est): 494.08K **Privately Held**
SIC: 7699 3449 Agricultural equipment repair services; Miscellaneous metalwork

(G-6611)
K-FAB INC
1940 N Montgomery Rd (47240-1276)
PHONE.................................812 663-6299
EMP: 3 EST: 1994
SQ FT: 11,000
SALES (est): 1.09MM **Privately Held**

Greensburg - Decatur County (G-6636)

Web: www.kfabinc.com
SIC: 3599 Machine shop, jobbing and repair

(G-6612)
KLENE PIPE STRUCTURES INC
515 N Anderson St (47240-1410)
PHONE..................812 663-6445
Robin Klene, *Pr*
EMP: 6 **EST:** 1953
SQ FT: 10,500
SALES (est): 540.43K **Privately Held**
Web: www.klenepipe.com
SIC: 3498 Fabricated pipe and fittings

(G-6613)
KOVA FERTILIZER INC (PA)
1330 N Anderson St (47240)
PHONE..................812 663-5081
Bradley Reed, *Pr*
Brain Reed, *VP*
Todd Reed, *VP*
EMP: 20 **EST:** 1947
SQ FT: 50,000
SALES (est): 22.84MM
SALES (corp-wide): 22.84MM **Privately Held**
Web: www.ekova.com
SIC: 5191 2875 Fertilizer and fertilizer materials; Fertilizers, mixing only

(G-6614)
LANGELAND FARMS INC
3806 S County Road 550 E (47240-8644)
PHONE..................812 663-9546
Patty Lange Fischer, *Pr*
Nathan Reding, *Prin*
EMP: 4 **EST:** 1984
SALES (est): 759.06K **Privately Held**
Web: www.lfgrain.com
SIC: 5153 0723 2099 Grains; Grain cleaning services; Food preparations, nec

(G-6615)
LOWES PELLETS AND GRAIN INC (PA)
2372 W State Road 46 (47240-9056)
PHONE..................812 663-7863
Floyd Alan Lowe, *Pr*
Don Lowe, *
Regina Lowe, *
Kristi Lowe, *
EMP: 26 **EST:** 1963
SQ FT: 10,000
SALES (est): 9.07MM
SALES (corp-wide): 9.07MM **Privately Held**
Web: www.lowespellets.com
SIC: 5153 2048 1542 Grains; Cereal-, grain-, and seed-based feeds; Farm building construction

(G-6616)
MAYASARIS LLC (PA)
213 N Broadway St (47240-1701)
PHONE..................812 222-6292
Richard Mays, *Managing Member*
EMP: 3 **EST:** 2012
SALES (est): 239.38K
SALES (corp-wide): 239.38K **Privately Held**
Web: www.mayasaritempeh.com
SIC: 5812 2034 Barbecue restaurant; Dried and dehydrated vegetables

(G-6617)
MAYASARIS LLC
1570 W Commerce Dr Ste 302 (47240)
PHONE..................812 593-2881
EMP: 2
SALES (corp-wide): 239.38K **Privately Held**

Web: www.mayasaritempeh.com
SIC: 2034 Dried and dehydrated vegetables
PA: Mayasari's Llc
213 N Broadway St
Greensburg IN 47240
812 222-6292

(G-6618)
MESCO MANUFACTURING LLC
900 E Randall St (47240-2328)
PHONE..................812 663-3870
Bryan Messer, *Managing Member*
Greg Mason, *
Larry Rogers, *
EMP: 65 **EST:** 2011
SQ FT: 77,000
SALES (est): 9.86MM **Privately Held**
Web: www.mescomfg.com
SIC: 3599 Machine shop, jobbing and repair

(G-6619)
MEYER ENGINEERING INC
1420 W Main St (47240-9730)
PHONE..................812 663-6535
John S Meyer, *Pr*
Pam Meyer, *Treas*
EMP: 12 **EST:** 1979
SQ FT: 6,000
SALES (est): 998.57K **Privately Held**
Web: www.meyereng.net
SIC: 3599 Machine shop, jobbing and repair

(G-6620)
MSSH INC
Also Called: Ashley Machine
901 N Carver St (47240-1014)
P.O. Box 2 (47240-0002)
PHONE..................812 663-2180
E Thomas Barnes, *Pr*
EMP: 7 **EST:** 1958
SQ FT: 9,000
SALES (est): 684.85K **Privately Held**
Web: www.ashleymachine.com
SIC: 3523 3556 3444 Poultry brooders, feeders and waterers; Food products machinery; Sheet metalwork

(G-6621)
MY PNEUMATIC TOOLS AND SERVICE
7032 E Shelby County Road 1100 S (47240)
PHONE..................317 364-3324
Michael Young, *Owner*
EMP: 2 **EST:** 2008
SALES (est): 97.6K **Privately Held**
SIC: 3544 Special dies, tools, jigs, and fixtures

(G-6622)
NEW POINT STONE CO INC (PA)
Also Called: Harris City Stone Company
992 S County Road 800 E (47240-8854)
PHONE..................812 663-2021
Kenneth T Wanstrath, *Pr*
Steven Wanstrath, *VP*
Dan Wanstrath, *VP*
Russell Wanstrath, *Prin*
James Wanstrath, *Prin*
▲ **EMP:** 17 **EST:** 1924
SQ FT: 2,800
SALES (est): 8.86MM
SALES (corp-wide): 8.86MM **Privately Held**
Web: www.newpointstone.com
SIC: 1422 Crushed and broken limestone

(G-6623)
PLATINUM FEEDS AND SUPPLY LLC
✪
6140 W County Road 240 Nw (47240-9322)

PHONE..................812 593-7232
EMP: 1 **EST:** 2023
SALES (est): 84.62K **Privately Held**
SIC: 2048 Pulverized oats, prepared as animal feed

(G-6624)
PORTER SIGNS
305 E 5th St (47240-1232)
PHONE..................812 222-0283
EMP: 1
SALES (est): 49.31K **Privately Held**
SIC: 3993 Signs and advertising specialties

(G-6625)
PRINTPACK INC
Flexible Packaging Group
930 E Barachel Ln Ste 200 (47240-3254)
PHONE..................812 663-5091
Bob Wangsley, *Mgr*
EMP: 115
SQ FT: 80,000
SALES (corp-wide): 1.3B **Privately Held**
Web: www.printpack.com
SIC: 2673 3081 2759 Bags: plastic, laminated, and coated; Plastics film and sheet; Commercial printing, nec
HQ: Printpack, Inc.
2800 Overlook Pkwy Ne
Atlanta GA 30339
404 460-7000

(G-6626)
PROWLER INDUSTRIES LLC
1220 N Liberty Cir E (47240-6682)
PHONE..................877 477-6953
◆ **EMP:** 13 **EST:** 2013
SALES (est): 483.96K **Privately Held**
Web: www.prowlertracks.com
SIC: 3999 Manufacturing industries, nec

(G-6627)
REMMLER WELL DRILLING LLC
Also Called: Remmler Drilling & Pump Svc
3970 N County Rd 500 N (47240)
PHONE..................812 663-8178
John Remmler, *Owner*
EMP: 2 **EST:** 1975
SALES (est): 230.64K **Privately Held**
Web: www.remmlerdrilling.com
SIC: 1381 1781 Drilling oil and gas wells; Water well drilling

(G-6628)
RESONAC POWDERED METALS AMERIC (DH)
1024 E Barachel Ln (47240)
P.O. Box 588 (47240)
PHONE..................812 663-5058
Gregory Owens, *Pr*
Hiroyasu Yoshikawa, *
Yasushi Kamata, *
Martha Swango Ctrl, *Prin*
▲ **EMP:** 25 **EST:** 1987
SQ FT: 148,000
SALES (est): 48.17MM **Privately Held**
Web: pa.showadenko.com
SIC: 3714 Motor vehicle parts and accessories
HQ: Resonac America, Inc.
2150 N 1st St Ste 350
San Jose CA 95131
408 873-2200

(G-6629)
S & J MANUFACTURING LLC
712 S Christy Rd (47240-2386)
PHONE..................812 662-6640
Steve Fasnacht, *Owner*
EMP: 4 **EST:** 1998
SALES (est): 221.39K **Privately Held**

SIC: 3496 Miscellaneous fabricated wire products

(G-6630)
SCHEIDLER MACHINE INCORPORATED
3551 N Old Us Highway 421 (47240-9371)
PHONE..................812 662-6555
Jerome Scheidler, *CEO*
EMP: 2 **EST:** 1993
SALES (est): 178.7K **Privately Held**
Web: www.mountainembroidery.com
SIC: 3545 Precision tools, machinists'

(G-6631)
SIGN EXCHANGE
3242 S Us Highway 421 (47240-8017)
PHONE..................812 662-9469
EMP: 3 **EST:** 2019
SALES (est): 115.75K **Privately Held**
SIC: 3993 Signs and advertising specialties

(G-6632)
STANDARD FERTILIZER COMPANY
2006 S County Road 60 Sw (47240-8299)
PHONE..................812 663-8391
TOLL FREE: 800
Sheldon J Roberts Senior, *Pr*
Danny Bausback, *VP*
Kendra Trenkamtp, *Off Mgr*
EMP: 17 **EST:** 1925
SQ FT: 4,000
SALES (est): 2.35MM **Privately Held**
Web: www.standardfertilizer.com
SIC: 2077 Meat meal and tankage, except as animal feed

(G-6633)
STEEL TECHNOLOGIES LLC
1811 N Montgomery Rd (47240-2519)
PHONE..................812 663-9704
Ronda Lee, *Brnch Mgr*
EMP: 53
Web: www.steeltechnologies.com
SIC: 3312 Blast furnaces and steel mills
HQ: Steel Technologies Llc
700 N Hurstbourne Pkwy # 400
Louisville KY 40222
502 245-2110

(G-6634)
TAYLOR MADE CANDLES
7864 W County Road 80 N (47240-7910)
PHONE..................812 663-6634
James Taylor, *Pt*
Eileen Taylor, *Pt*
EMP: 2 **EST:** 1986
SALES (est): 150.36K **Privately Held**
SIC: 5999 3999 Candle shops; Candles

(G-6635)
TOP NOTCH TOOL AND ENGRG INC
930 E Main St (47240-2305)
PHONE..................812 663-2184
Chris Bruns, *Pr*
Donald Lecher, *VP*
Roger Meyer, *Sec*
EMP: 6 **EST:** 1996
SQ FT: 4,500
SALES (est): 516.29K **Privately Held**
Web: www.weugenerussell.com
SIC: 3599 Machine shop, jobbing and repair

(G-6636)
TREE CITY SAW MILL
Also Called: Tree City Sawmill
2663 E County Road 500 S (47240-7877)
PHONE..................812 663-6363
Paul Stuehrenberg, *Owner*
EMP: 8 **EST:** 1956

Greensburg - Decatur County (G-6637)

SQ FT: 3,200
SALES (est): 815.63K **Privately Held**
SIC: **2421** Sawmills and planing mills, general

(G-6637)
TREE CITY TOOL & ENGRG CO INC
1954 N Montgomery Rd (47240-1276)
P.O. Box 409 (47240-0409)
PHONE.................................812 663-4196
Steve Simmonds, *Pr*
▼ EMP: 26 EST: 1966
SALES (est): 10.01MM **Privately Held**
Web: www.treecitytool.com
SIC: **3599** 3544 Custom machinery; Special dies, tools, jigs, and fixtures

(G-6638)
VALEO ENGINE COOLING INC
1100 E Barachel Ln (47240-1200)
PHONE.................................812 663-8541
◆ EMP: 600
SIC: **3714** Motor vehicle parts and accessories

(G-6639)
VALEO NORTH AMERICA INC
Also Called: Valeo Eng Coolant Aftermarket
1580 E Commerce Dr (47240)
PHONE.................................800 677-6004
EMP: 215
SALES (corp-wide): 2.67MM **Privately Held**
SIC: **3714** Motor vehicle parts and accessories
HQ: Valeo North America, Inc.
150 Stephenson Hwy
Troy MI 48083

(G-6640)
VALEO NORTH AMERICA INC
Also Called: Valeo Engine Cooling
1100 E Barachel Ln (47240-1200)
PHONE.................................812 663-8541
Arthur Connelly, *Brnch Mgr*
EMP: 493
SALES (corp-wide): 2.67MM **Privately Held**
SIC: **3714** Radiators and radiator shells and cores, motor vehicle
HQ: Valeo North America, Inc.
150 Stephenson Hwy
Troy MI 48083

(G-6641)
WINTERS PUBLISHING
330 E Central Ave (47240-1704)
P.O. Box 501 (47240-0501)
PHONE.................................812 663-4948
Tracy Winters, *Owner*
▲ EMP: 2 EST: 1984
SALES (est): 111.35K **Privately Held**
Web: www.winterspublishing.com
SIC: **2731** Books, publishing only

(G-6642)
WOOD-MIZER HOLDINGS INC
Also Called: Woodmizer Products
8829 E State Road 46 (47240-7449)
PHONE.................................812 663-5257
Jeff Heidlage, *Brnch Mgr*
EMP: 80
SQ FT: 43,000
SALES (corp-wide): 133.23MM **Privately Held**
Web: www.woodmizer.com
SIC: **3553** 3546 Sawmill machines; Power-driven handtools
PA: Wood-Mizer Holdings, Inc.
8180 W 10th St
Indianapolis IN 46214

317 271-1542

(G-6643)
WORTHINGTON INDUSTRIES INC
Worthington Steelpac Systems
1445 N Michigan Ave (47240-1400)
PHONE.................................219 465-6107
Patrick J Cotter Gen'l, *Mgr*
EMP: 26
SALES (corp-wide): 1.25B **Publicly Held**
Web: www.worthingtonenterprises.com
SIC: **3441** Building components, structural steel
PA: Worthington Enterprises, Inc.
200 W Old Wlson Bridge Rd
Worthington OH 43085
614 438-3210

Greentown
Howard County

(G-6644)
ACCENT WIRE PRODUCTS
324 Shamrock Ave (46936-9302)
PHONE.................................765 628-3587
EMP: 2 EST: 2008
SALES (est): 138.47K **Privately Held**
SIC: **3496** Miscellaneous fabricated wire products

(G-6645)
BLONDIES COOKIES INC (PA)
100 W Main St (46936-1115)
PHONE.................................765 628-3978
Brenda Coffman, *Pr*
Beverly Austin, *VP*
Mark A Coffman, *Sec*
EMP: 12 EST: 1985
SALES (est): 8.44MM
SALES (corp-wide): 8.44MM **Privately Held**
Web: www.blondiescookies.com
SIC: **2052** 5461 Cookies; Cookies

(G-6646)
FLODDER SAWMILL LLC
10861 E 100 N (46936-9595)
PHONE.................................765 628-0280
Ross Flodder, *Pr*
EMP: 9 EST: 2008
SALES (est): 560.14K **Privately Held**
Web: www.specialinspectors.net
SIC: **2421** Sawmills and planing mills, general

(G-6647)
HENSLER FARM INC
652 Villa Manor Ct (46936-1439)
PHONE.................................765 628-3411
Max Custer, *Pr*
Mira S Custer, *VP*
Carol S Hensler, *Sec*
EMP: 3 EST: 1999
SALES (est): 231.16K **Privately Held**
SIC: **3523** Driers (farm): grain, hay, and seed

(G-6648)
RAVEN LAKE ORIGINALS CANDLES
489 S 950 E (46936-1367)
PHONE.................................765 419-1473
Laura Lanning, *Prin*
EMP: 4 EST: 2016
SALES (est): 77.71K **Privately Held**
Web: www.ravenlakecandles.com
SIC: **3999** Candles

(G-6649)
SUPERIOR CONCEPTS INDUS LLC
11763 E 300 S (46936-9436)
PHONE.................................765 628-2956
Shane Campbell, *Pr*
EMP: 14 EST: 1992
SQ FT: 15,000
SALES (est): 761.87K **Privately Held**
SIC: **3199** Safety belts, leather

Greenville
Floyd County

(G-6650)
502 MOLD POLISHING LLC
1007 Wagon Trl (47124-8614)
PHONE.................................502 436-0239
Richard Cochran, *Prin*
EMP: 6 EST: 2014
SALES (est): 168.18K **Privately Held**
SIC: **3471** Polishing, metals or formed products

(G-6651)
EMBROIDERY SOLUTIONS LLC
8301 Pekin Rd Ste 1 (47124-9403)
PHONE.................................812 923-9152
John Schillingberger, *Owner*
Anita Schillingberber, *Mgr*
EMP: 2 EST: 1995
SALES (est): 102.29K **Privately Held**
SIC: **2395** Embroidery products, except Schiffli machine

(G-6652)
MADDOX ENGINEERING INC
6670 Buttontown Rd (47124-9699)
P.O. Box 67 (47165-0067)
PHONE.................................812 903-0048
EMP: 18 EST: 2005
SALES (est): 2.4MM **Privately Held**
Web: www.maddengineering.com
SIC: **8711** 3089 7389 5087 Consulting engineer; Engraving of plastics; Engraving service; Engraving equipment and supplies

(G-6653)
REDWIRE SPACE TECHNOLOGIES INC
Also Called: Techshot
7200 Highway 150 (47124-9515)
PHONE.................................812 923-9591
Peter Cannito, *Pr*
John Vellinger, *
EMP: 28 EST: 1989
SQ FT: 20,000
SALES (est): 9.53MM
SALES (corp-wide): 243.8MM **Publicly Held**
Web: www.redwirespace.com
SIC: **3679** Electronic circuits
PA: Redwire Corporation
8226 Philips Hwy Ste 101
Jacksonville FL 32256
650 701-7722

(G-6654)
RICHARDS PRINTERY
9357 Arthur Coffman Rd (47124-9436)
PHONE.................................812 406-0295
Rich Mullins, *Owner*
EMP: 2 EST: 2013
SALES (est): 82.39K **Privately Held**
SIC: **2752** Offset printing

(G-6655)
ROL PUBLICATIONS
3600 Amy Ln Ne (47124-7802)
PHONE.................................812 366-4154

Larry Rol, *Prin*
EMP: 2 EST: 2001
SALES (est): 151.72K **Privately Held**
Web: www.rolstudio.com
SIC: **2741** Miscellaneous publishing

(G-6656)
STACY PUBLISHING INC
6901 Georgetown Greenville Rd (47124-9659)
PHONE.................................812 923-1111
Thomas Brimm, *Owner*
EMP: 2 EST: 2001
SALES (est): 197.21K **Privately Held**
Web: www.stacypublishing.com
SIC: **2741** Miscellaneous publishing

(G-6657)
STANDARD ISSUE ARMORY LLC
8600 Highway 150 (47124)
PHONE.................................812 364-1466
Jc Cheshire, *CEO*
EMP: 10 EST: 2020
SALES (est): 541.52K **Privately Held**
Web: www.standardissuearmory.com
SIC: **5091** 3484 5941 Sporting and recreation goods; Small arms; Ammunition

Greenwood
Johnson County

(G-6658)
ABELL TOOL CO INC
446 Park 800 Dr (46143-9525)
P.O. Box 1014 (46142-0968)
PHONE.................................317 887-0021
Jeffery Abell, *Pr*
A Donna Abell, *VP*
EMP: 8 EST: 1973
SQ FT: 7,500
SALES (est): 804.69K **Privately Held**
Web: www.abelltool.com
SIC: **3549** Metalworking machinery, nec

(G-6659)
ADVANTAGE ELECTRONICS INC
525 E Stop 18 Rd (46143-9808)
P.O. Box 407 (46142-0407)
PHONE.................................317 888-1946
Steven E Wash, *Pr*
Harold R Short, *Sec*
EMP: 15 EST: 1984
SQ FT: 5,000
SALES (est): 4.34MM **Privately Held**
Web: www.advantageelectronics.com
SIC: **3625** 3825 Control equipment, electric; Test equipment for electronic and electric measurement

(G-6660)
ADVANTAGE ENGINEERING INC (PA)
525 E Stop 18 Rd (46142)
P.O. Box 407 (46142)
PHONE.................................317 887-0729
Jon Gunderson, *
Susan Schaub, *
Randy Goode, *
Ron Wolfe, *
EMP: 94 EST: 1977
SQ FT: 60,000
SALES (est): 24.43MM
SALES (corp-wide): 24.43MM **Privately Held**
Web: www.advantageengineering.com
SIC: **3822** 3585 3443 Temperature controls, automatic; Refrigeration equipment, complete; Cooling towers, metal plate

(G-6661)
ADVANTIS MEDICAL INC
Also Called: Advantis
2121 Southtech Dr Ste 600 (46143-6395)
PHONE.................................317 859-2300
Forrest Whittaker, Pr
Barbara Sullivan, *
Michael Bettini, *
Brian Mcroberts, VP
Sue Fawbush, *
▼ **EMP:** 129 **EST:** 2004
SQ FT: 400,000
SALES (est): 21.71MM **Privately Held**
Web: www.advantismedical.com
SIC: 3841 Surgical and medical instruments
PA: Avalign Technologies, Inc.
10275 W Higgins Rd # 920
Rosemont IL 60018

(G-6662)
AFRAA EYEBROWS
888 N Us Highway 31 N (46142-4401)
PHONE.................................317 881-6200
Afraa Alshdidi, Pr
EMP: 1 **EST:** 2009
SALES (est): 59.95K **Privately Held**
Web: eyebrows-by-afraa.edan.io
SIC: 3999 Eyelashes, artificial

(G-6663)
AIRFEET LLC
Also Called: Airfeet Insoles
191 Us Highway 31 S Ste C (46142-3575)
PHONE.................................317 441-1817
EMP: 7 **EST:** 2011
SALES (est): 456.76K **Privately Held**
Web: www.myairfeet.com
SIC: 3131 Inner parts for shoes

(G-6664)
ALLAN DEFENSE LLC
2828 Coventry Ln (46143-7184)
PHONE.................................317 525-1244
EMP: 4 **EST:** 2014
SALES (est): 76K **Privately Held**
SIC: 3812 Defense systems and equipment

(G-6665)
ALPINE ELECTRONICS MANUFACTURING OF AMERICA INC
421 N Emerson Ave (46143-9704)
P.O. Box 2859 (90509-2859)
PHONE.................................956 217-3200
◆ **EMP:** 550
SIC: 3651 3679 Speaker systems; Harness assemblies, for electronic use: wire or cable

(G-6666)
AMCOR RIGID PACKAGING USA LLC
Also Called: Amcor Pet Packaging NA
800 Commerce Parkway West Dr (46143-6100)
PHONE.................................317 736-4313
Michael Schmitt, Pr
EMP: 1
SALES (corp-wide): 14.69B **Privately Held**
SIC: 3085 Plastics bottles
HQ: Amcor Rigid Packaging Usa, Llc
10521 S Hwy M-52
Manchester MI 48158

(G-6667)
AMERICAN CLASSIFIEDS
Also Called: Thrifty Nickel Want ADS
1776 Windward Dr (46143-8408)
PHONE.................................317 782-8111
Minni Dhanjal, Pr
Daljit Dhanjal, VP
EMP: 6 **EST:** 1987
SALES (est): 255.58K **Privately Held**
SIC: 2741 2711 Miscellaneous publishing; Newspapers

(G-6668)
AMERICAN INDUSTRIAL CO LLC
1400 American Way (46143-8466)
P.O. Box 859 (46142-0859)
PHONE.................................317 859-9900
Bill Canady, CEO
EMP: 50 **EST:** 1969
SQ FT: 64,000
SALES (est): 9.58MM
SALES (corp-wide): 11.2MM **Privately Held**
Web: www.otcindustrial.com
SIC: 3531 Finishers and spreaders (construction equipment)
PA: Otc Industrial Technologies
1900 Jetway Blvd
Columbus OH 43219
800 837-6827

(G-6669)
ANTHONY GROUP LLC
2011 Southtech Dr Ste 100 (46143-6948)
PHONE.................................317 536-7445
Todd Anthony, CEO
Tyler Dishman, *
Reed Barich, *
◆ **EMP:** 47 **EST:** 2003
SQ FT: 68,000
SALES (est): 8.04MM **Privately Held**
Web: www.ntsupply.com
SIC: 5075 3564 Air filters; Filters, air: furnaces, air conditioning equipment, etc.

(G-6670)
ANTHONYJEAN LLC
Also Called: N2 Publishing
2000 Dockside Dr (46143-8237)
PHONE.................................317 513-4981
Deena Nystrom, Prin
EMP: 6 **EST:** 2017
SALES (est): 86.67K **Privately Held**
Web: www.strollmag.com
SIC: 2741 Miscellaneous publishing

(G-6671)
ARROYO INDUSTRIES LLC
Also Called: Direct Path Alliance
5324 Crooked Stick Ct (46142-9105)
PHONE.................................317 605-4163
EMP: 1 **EST:** 2004
SALES (est): 895.37K **Privately Held**
SIC: 8711 8742 3499 3353 Engineering services; Management consulting services; Machine bases, metal; Aluminum sheet, plate, and foil

(G-6672)
AVALIGN TECHNOLOGIES INC
2121 Southtech Dr Ste 600 (46143-6395)
PHONE.................................317 865-6436
Tony O'neil, VP Opers
EMP: 1
Web: www.avaligntech.com
SIC: 3829 Thermometers, including digital: clinical
PA: Avalign Technologies, Inc.
10275 W Higgins Rd # 920
Rosemont IL 60018

(G-6673)
AVALIGN TECHNOLOGIES INC
Also Called: Avalign Delivery Systems Div
2121 Southtech Dr Ste 600 (46143-6395)
PHONE.................................888 625-4697
EMP: 1
Web: www.avalign.com

SIC: 3841 Surgical and medical instruments
PA: Avalign Technologies, Inc.
10275 W Higgins Rd # 920
Rosemont IL 60018

(G-6674)
AVON SPORTS APPAREL CORP
3115 Meridian Parke Dr Ste D (46142-9414)
PHONE.................................317 887-2673
Phil Orlando, Brnch Mgr
EMP: 2
SALES (corp-wide): 2.16MM **Privately Held**
Web: www.avonsportsapparel.com
SIC: 2395 5941 Embroidery products, except Schiffli machine; Soccer supplies
PA: Avon Sports Apparel Corp.
7710 E Us Highway 36
Avon IN 46123
317 272-3831

(G-6675)
BEMIS DISTILLERS LLC
3374 Shore Dr (46143-8822)
PHONE.................................317 619-0711
EMP: 4 **EST:** 2016
SALES (est): 80.67K **Privately Held**
SIC: 2085 Distilled and blended liquors

(G-6676)
BINARIE LLC
Also Called: Binarie
863 Silverleaf Dr (46143-7236)
PHONE.................................317 496-8836
Scott Dial, Managing Member
EMP: 1 **EST:** 2020
SALES (est): 68.41K **Privately Held**
Web: www.binarie.net
SIC: 8711 7379 3575 7371 Engineering services; Computer related consulting services; Computer terminals, monitors and components; Software programming applications

(G-6677)
BSB TRANS INC
711 Legacy Blvd (46143-6437)
PHONE.................................317 919-8778
Baljit Singh Boparai, Pr
EMP: 2 **EST:** 2011
SALES (est): 236.63K **Privately Held**
SIC: 3715 Truck trailers

(G-6678)
BW WHOLESALE LLC ✪
336 N Windsong Ln (46142)
PHONE.................................775 856-3522
Charles Bradley West, CEO
EMP: 6 **EST:** 2024
SALES (est): 87.96K **Privately Held**
SIC: 2231 Apparel and outerwear broadwoven fabrics

(G-6679)
C R GRAPHICS
485 E Pearl St (46143-1348)
PHONE.................................317 881-6192
Russel Poamey, Owner
EMP: 2 **EST:** 1987
SALES (est): 90.44K **Privately Held**
SIC: 2752 Offset printing

(G-6680)
CHRISTYS DESIGN & SIGN INC
500 Polk St Ste 17 (46143-1629)
P.O. Box 703 (46142-0703)
PHONE.................................317 882-5444
Christine Holt, Pr
EMP: 2 **EST:** 1980

SQ FT: 5,000
SALES (est): 182.08K **Privately Held**
Web: www.christysdesignandsign.com
SIC: 3993 7389 Signs, not made in custom sign painting shops; Sign painting and lettering shop

(G-6681)
COFFEY CONNECTION LLC
1000 S Morgantown Rd (46143-8851)
PHONE.................................317 300-9639
EMP: 5 **EST:** 2017
SALES (est): 139.14K **Privately Held**
Web: www.connectiongraphics.net
SIC: 2759 Screen printing

(G-6682)
CORNER CABINET
405 E Main St (46143-1363)
PHONE.................................317 859-6336
Ross Agresta, Owner
EMP: 4 **EST:** 2004
SALES (est): 244.55K **Privately Held**
Web: corner-cabinet.business.site
SIC: 2434 Wood kitchen cabinets

(G-6683)
D-10 SERVICES INC
887 Jennifer Dr (46143-8457)
PHONE.................................317 889-7235
Jeffrey Lowry, Pr
EMP: 2 **EST:** 2002
SALES (est): 190K **Privately Held**
SIC: 3444 Sheet metalwork

(G-6684)
DEM GUYS LLC ✪
2945 Sentiment Ln (46143-6797)
PHONE.................................708 552-3056
EMP: 2 **EST:** 2022
SALES (est): 92.67K **Privately Held**
SIC: 2099 7389 Food preparations, nec; Business Activities at Non-Commercial Site

(G-6685)
DHGRAPHIX AND APPAREL CO LLC
500 Polk St Ste 13 (46143)
PHONE.................................317 908-2634
EMP: 6
SALES (est): 269.03K **Privately Held**
SIC: 2397 Schiffli machine embroideries

(G-6686)
DISTANCE LEARNING SYSTEMS IND
Also Called: Distance Learning Systems
107 N State Road 135 Ste 302 (46142-1351)
PHONE.................................888 955-3276
David Christy, Pr
EMP: 40 **EST:** 1999
SQ FT: 10,000
SALES (est): 6.04MM **Privately Held**
Web: www.dlsii.com
SIC: 2731 7389 Book publishing; Personal service agents, brokers, and bureaus

(G-6687)
DISTINCTIVE KITCHEN & BATH INC
1480 Olive Branch Parke Ln Ste 500 (46143-6252)
PHONE.................................317 882-7100
Marianne Alsphch, VP
Jim Smith, VP
Chris Alspach, Pr
EMP: 3 **EST:** 1999
SALES (est): 482.75K **Privately Held**
Web: www.distinctivekb.com
SIC: 2434 Wood kitchen cabinets

Greenwood - Johnson County (G-6688)   GEOGRAPHIC SECTION

(G-6688)
DK CARRIER INC
777 Fireside Dr (46143-6471)
PHONE.................................317 374-1835
Jamsher Singh, *Prin*
EMP: 1 **EST:** 2013
SALES (est): 148.76K **Privately Held**
SIC: 3537 Trucks, tractors, loaders, carriers, and similar equipment

(G-6689)
DOOR SERVICE SUPPLY
4075 Primrose Path (46142-8391)
PHONE.................................317 496-0391
Pat Fischer, *Owner*
EMP: 2 **EST:** 2005
SALES (est): 92.86K **Privately Held**
Web: www.geutherelectrical.com
SIC: 3442 Window and door frames

(G-6690)
DRAGON PRINTING LLC
5075 Olive Branch Rd (46143-8801)
PHONE.................................317 919-9619
Thom Garcia, *Pr*
EMP: 5 **EST:** 2017
SALES (est): 235.99K **Privately Held**
Web: www.thedragonsigns.com
SIC: 2752 Offset printing

(G-6691)
DURHAT TRANSPORTATION LLC
335 Lake Ridge Ln (46142-2112)
PHONE.................................463 204-9119
Corliss Durham, *CEO*
Sandra Durham, *Owner*
EMP: 6 **EST:** 2020
SALES (est): 63.8K **Privately Held**
SIC: 8711 8731 3799 2813 Pollution control engineering; Energy research; Transportation equipment, nec; Hydrogen

(G-6692)
ELEGANT EYES LLC
1271 Barngate Cir (46142-1273)
PHONE.................................317 640-1995
EMP: 1
SALES (est): 60.62K **Privately Held**
SIC: 7389 3999 Business Activities at Non-Commercial Site; Eyelashes, artificial

(G-6693)
ELITE PROTECTIVE COATINGS
3632 Woodland Streams Dr (46143-9462)
PHONE.................................317 476-1712
Mark Whitaker, *Prin*
EMP: 6 **EST:** 2017
SALES (est): 81.52K **Privately Held**
SIC: 3479 Metal coating and allied services

(G-6694)
EMMANUEL MICHAEL
2027 Prairie Sky Ln (46143-6646)
PHONE.................................806 559-5673
Emmanuel Michael, *Owner*
EMP: 2
SALES (est): 70.89K **Privately Held**
SIC: 3571 7389 Electronic computers; Business Activities at Non-Commercial Site

(G-6695)
ENDRESS + HAUSER INC
2413 Endress Pl (46143-8683)
PHONE.................................317 535-7138
EMP: 1
Web: us.endress.com
SIC: 3823 Process control instruments
HQ: Endress + Hauser Inc
2350 Endress Pl
Greenwood IN 46143
317 535-7138

(G-6696)
ENDRESS + HAUSER INC
Infoserv Division
2350 Endress Pl (46143-9672)
PHONE.................................317 535-2159
Stephen Baehr, *Mgr*
EMP: 1
Web: us.endress.com
SIC: 3823 Process control instruments
HQ: Endress + Hauser Inc
2350 Endress Pl
Greenwood IN 46143
317 535-7138

(G-6697)
ENDRESS + HAUSER INC (DH)
Also Called: Endresshauser USA
2350 Endress Pl (46143-9672)
PHONE.................................317 535-7138
Klaus Endress, *Pr*
Nancy Winter, *
Jon E Williams, *
Todd Lucey, *
▲ **EMP:** 200 **EST:** 1970
SQ FT: 250,000
SALES (est): 135.56MM **Privately Held**
Web: www.endressdirect.us
SIC: 3823 Process control instruments
HQ: Endress+Hauser Management Ag
Kagenstrasse 2
Reinach BL 4153

(G-6698)
ENDRESS + HSER FLWTEC AG DIV U
Also Called: Endresshauser
2330 Endress Pl (46143-9772)
PHONE.................................317 535-7138
Gerhard Jost, *CEO*
Hans-peter Blaser, *Dir*
Frank Steinhoff, *
Joerg Herwig, *
Jon E Williams, *
◆ **EMP:** 120 **EST:** 1995
SALES (est): 41.45MM **Privately Held**
SIC: 3823 Flow instruments, industrial process type
HQ: Endress+Hauser Management Ag
Kagenstrasse 2
Reinach BL 4153

(G-6699)
ENDRESS+HAUSER (USA) AUTOMATIO
Also Called: (SISTER COMPANY OF ENDRESS + HAUSER INC, GREENWOOD, IN)
2340 Endress Pl (46143-9772)
PHONE.................................317 535-2121
Jason Baker, *Sec*
Jon Mccullum, *Contrlr*
EMP: 120 **EST:** 2007
SALES (est): 20.82MM **Privately Held**
Web: us.endress.com
SIC: 3823 Process control instruments
HQ: Endress + Hauser Inc
2350 Endress Pl
Greenwood IN 46143
317 535-7138

(G-6700)
ENDRESS+HAUSER INFOSERVE INC
2350 Endress Pl (46143-9672)
P.O. Box 246 (46142-0246)
PHONE.................................888 363-7377
Pieter De Koning, *Pr*
EMP: 1 **EST:** 2011
SALES (est): 2.3MM **Privately Held**
Web: us.endress.com
SIC: 3823 Process control instruments
HQ: Endress + Hauser Infoserve Gmbh + Co. Kg
Colmarer Str. 6
Weil Am Rhein BW 79576

(G-6701)
ENDRESS+HAUSER WETZER USA INC
2413 Endress Pl (46143-8683)
PHONE.................................317 535-1362
Patrick Ncglothen, *Genl Mgr*
Jayson Norris, *Contrlr*
◆ **EMP:** 1 **EST:** 2008
SQ FT: 2,000
SALES (est): 1.69MM **Privately Held**
Web: us.endress.com
SIC: 3823 Process control instruments
HQ: Endress + Hauser Inc
2350 Endress Pl
Greenwood IN 46143
317 535-7138

(G-6702)
ENVIRO GROUP INC
290 Noble St Ste A (46142-3677)
PHONE.................................317 882-9360
John Garver, *Pr*
EMP: 1 **EST:** 1991
SQ FT: 3,600
SALES (est): 350K **Privately Held**
Web: www.envirogroup.com
SIC: 3295 Clay, ground or otherwise treated

(G-6703)
EQUIPPE ADVANCED MOBILITY
Also Called: Equippe Mobility Resources
3209 W Smith Valley Rd Ste 146 (46142)
PHONE.................................317 807-6789
David Dokmanovich, *Prin*
EMP: 2 **EST:** 2016
SQ FT: 220
SALES (est): 195.44K **Privately Held**
Web: www.advancedmobilityofbend.com
SIC: 3842 Wheelchairs

(G-6704)
FIRE STAR INDUSTRIES LLC
4644 Brentridge Pkwy (46143-9360)
PHONE.................................317 432-3212
Jason Stits, *CEO*
EMP: 9 **EST:** 2010
SALES (est): 464.15K **Privately Held**
Web: www.firestarindy.com
SIC: 3999 Manufacturing industries, nec

(G-6705)
FRANKLIN PUBLISHING INC
Also Called: Road Runner Expediting
5373 Ashby Ct (46143-6268)
PHONE.................................800 634-1993
Michael Jones, *Pr*
▲ **EMP:** 5 **EST:** 1994
SALES (est): 386.23K **Privately Held**
Web: www.generalcode.com
SIC: 2732 Pamphlets: printing and binding, not published on site

(C-6700)
FULLY PROMOTED
996 S State Road 135 Ste B (46143-7366)
PHONE.................................317 884-9290
EMP: 5 **EST:** 2018
SALES (est): 137.59K **Privately Held**
Web: www.fullypromoted.com
SIC: 2395 Embroidery and art needlework

(G-6707)
GLANDER
1678 Ashwood Dr (46143-8823)
PHONE.................................317 889-1039
Karl Glander, *Prin*
EMP: 6 **EST:** 2005
SALES (est): 86.14K **Privately Held**
Web: www.glanderrochfordorthodontics.com
SIC: 3579 Shorthand machines

(G-6708)
GLEAM ELECTRICAL LLC
1313 Millstone Ct (46143-0014)
PHONE.................................317 968-0927
Ashley Martin, *Pr*
John Martin, *VP*
EMP: 20 **EST:** 2018
SALES (est): 2.32MM **Privately Held**
Web: www.gleamlightingexperts.com
SIC: 3645 Residential lighting fixtures

(G-6709)
GRAFTON PEEK INCORPORATED
Also Called: Hartwell's Premium Products
410 E Main St (46143-1364)
PHONE.................................317 557-8377
Jason West, *CEO*
EMP: 19 **EST:** 2010
SALES (est): 383.89K **Privately Held**
Web: www.graftonpeek.com
SIC: 5812 7299 2035 Caterers; Banquet hall facilities; Dressings, salad: raw and cooked (except dry mixes)

(G-6710)
GREENWOOD MODELS INC
350 Commerce Parkway West Dr (46143-7046)
PHONE.................................317 859-2988
Val J Weakley, *Pr*
John Weakley, *Sec*
EMP: 7 **EST:** 1973
SQ FT: 14,000
SALES (est): 858.15K **Privately Held**
Web: www.greenwoodmodels.com
SIC: 3444 3599 7692 2396 Sheet metalwork; Machine shop, jobbing and repair; Welding repair; Automotive and apparel trimmings

(G-6711)
HETSCO
2620 Endress Pl (46143-8678)
PHONE.................................317 530-5331
EMP: 4 **EST:** 2019
SALES (est): 25.09K **Privately Held**
SIC: 7692 Welding repair

(G-6712)
HORIZON BIOTECHNOLOGIES LLC
1740 S Morgantown Rd (46143-8348)
PHONE.................................317 534-2540
EMP: 2 **EST:** 2005
SALES (est): 177.96K **Privately Held**
SIC: 2834 Pharmaceutical preparations

(G-6713)
HUBBARD SERVICES INC
Also Called: Fastsigns
1280 Us Highway 31 N Ste T (40142-4525)
PHONE.................................317 881-2828
John Hubbard, *Pr*
Marilyn Hubbard, *Sec*
EMP: 7 **EST:** 1990
SQ FT: 850
SALES (est): 484.16K **Privately Held**
Web: www.fastsigns.com
SIC: 3993 Signs and advertising specialties

(G-6714)
IKE NEWTON LLC
949 Fry Rd (46142-1822)
PHONE.................................317 902-1772

GEOGRAPHIC SECTION
Greenwood - Johnson County (G-6741)

EMP: 2 EST: 2012
SALES (est): 89.41K **Privately Held**
Web: www.ikenewton.com
SIC: **8742** 7372 7389 Marketing consulting services; Application computer software; Business services, nec

(G-6715)
INDIGO INDUSTRIES LLC
3209 Smith Valley Rd (46142-8495)
PHONE.................480 747-4560
EMP: 3 EST: 2018
SALES (est): 39.87K **Privately Held**
Web: www.indigo.industries
SIC: **8711** 8748 3728 7363 Aviation and/or aeronautical engineering; Systems analysis and engineering consulting services; Target drones; Pilot service, aviation

(G-6716)
INTERNATIONAL RESOURCES INC
Also Called: Just Phone Rentals.com
545 Christy Dr Ofc 7304 (46143-1086)
PHONE.................317 813-5300
▲ EMP: 7 EST: 1993
SALES (est): 648.54K **Privately Held**
SIC: **3661** 5063 Telephone and telegraph apparatus; Telephone and telegraph wire and cable

(G-6717)
IRVING MATERIALS INC
Also Called: IMI Irving Material
6695 W Smith Valley Rd (46142)
PHONE.................317 888-0157
EMP: 7
SALES (corp-wide): 814.09MM **Privately Held**
Web: www.irvmat.com
SIC: **3273** Ready-mixed concrete
PA: Irving Materials, Inc.
  8032 N State Road 9
  Greenfield IN 46140
  317 326-3101

(G-6718)
JBS WELDING
1350 N Harvey Rd (46143-8691)
PHONE.................317 946-8676
Robert Daoust, *Prin*
EMP: 5 EST: 2008
SALES (est): 75.09K **Privately Held**
SIC: **7692** Welding repair

(G-6719)
JULIE STERGEN
157 Sycamore Ln (46142-4148)
PHONE.................317 888-6146
Julie Stergen, *Owner*
EMP: 1 EST: 1996
SALES (est): 56.06K **Privately Held**
SIC: **2721** Trade journals: publishing only, not printed on site

(G-6720)
K & P INDUSTRIES LLC
1200 Tanglewood Dr (46142-5225)
PHONE.................317 881-9245
Kenneth Fair, *Prin*
EMP: 2 EST: 2007
SALES (est): 73.7K **Privately Held**
SIC: **3999** Manufacturing industries, nec

(G-6721)
KAWNEER COMPANY INC
1040 Sierra Dr Ste 1500 (46143-7022)
PHONE.................317 882-2314
Jeff Hance, *Mgr*
EMP: 52
SALES (corp-wide): 8.96B **Privately Held**
Web: www.kawneer.us
SIC: **3446** Architectural metalwork
HQ: Kawneer Company, Inc.
  555 Guthridge Ct
  Norcross GA 30092
  770 449-5555

(G-6722)
KENNEY ORTHPDICS INDNPOLIS LLC (HQ)
521 E County Line Rd Ste B (46143-1065)
PHONE.................317 300-0814
John M Kenney, *Managing Member*
EMP: 2 EST: 2014
SALES (est): 914.04K
SALES (corp-wide): 23.4MM **Privately Held**
Web: www.kenneyorthopedics.com
SIC: **3842** Surgical appliances and supplies
PA: Kenney Ortho Group, Inc.
  208 Normandy Ct
  Nicholasville KY 40356
  859 241-1015

(G-6723)
KING SIGNS
722 N Hawey Rd (46142)
PHONE.................317 882-0785
Thomas King, *Owner*
EMP: 1 EST: 2002
SALES (est): 84.65K **Privately Held**
SIC: **3993** Signs and advertising specialties

(G-6724)
KONECRANES INC
Also Called: Crane Pro Services
134 S Park Blvd (46143-8837)
PHONE.................317 546-8122
EMP: 18
Web: www.konecranes.com
SIC: **3536** Hoists, cranes, and monorails
HQ: Konecranes, Inc.
  4401 Gateway Blvd
  Springfield OH 45502

(G-6725)
KORTZENDORF MACHINE & TOOL
646 Macy Way (46142-7489)
PHONE.................317 783-5449
Robert Kortzendorf, *Sec*
Tom Kortzendorf, *Pr*
EMP: 19 EST: 1956
SALES (est): 1.74MM **Privately Held**
Web: www.kortzendorf.com
SIC: **3599** 7692 3544 Machine shop, jobbing and repair; Welding repair; Special dies, tools, jigs, and fixtures

(G-6726)
KYB AMERICAS CORPORATION
850 N Graham Rd Ste C (46143-4601)
PHONE.................317 881-7772
Kazumi Fujikawa, *CEO*
EMP: 461
Web: www.kyb.com
SIC: **3714** 4225 Motor vehicle parts and accessories; General warehousing and storage
HQ: Kyb Americas Corporation
  2625 N Morton St
  Franklin IN 46131
  317 736-7774

(G-6727)
L&E ENGINEERING LLC
Also Called: Ferco Aerospace
254 N Graham Rd (46143-7829)
PHONE.................937 746-6696
Millagros Blance, *CEO*
EMP: 795 EST: 2016
SALES (est): 10.82MM
SALES (corp-wide): 55.53MM **Privately Held**
Web: www.fercoaerospacegroup.com
SIC: **3728** Aircraft parts and equipment, nec
PA: Novaria Holdings, Llc
  809 W Vickery Blvd
  Fort Worth TX 76104
  817 381-3810

(G-6728)
LEAP FROGZ INK LLC
872 N State Road 135 # D (46142-1358)
PHONE.................317 786-2441
Todd S Kenzig, *Pr*
EMP: 5 EST: 2018
SALES (est): 233.55K **Privately Held**
SIC: **2759** Screen printing

(G-6729)
LIONSHEAD PRECISION METALS LLC
1222 S Graham Rd (46143-9711)
PHONE.................317 787-6358
Brian Smith, *Pr*
EMP: 75 EST: 2017
SALES (est): 10.18MM **Privately Held**
Web: www.lionsheadmetals.com
SIC: **3444** 3542 3541 Sheet metalwork; Presses: forming, stamping, punching, sizing (machine tools); Lathes

(G-6730)
LOGICAL CONCEPTS
494 S Emerson Ave Ste E1 (46143-1913)
PHONE.................317 885-6330
Tom Ward, *Pr*
EMP: 15 EST: 1979
SALES (est): 753.5K **Privately Held**
SIC: **3669** 5063 Burglar alarm apparatus, electric; Electrical apparatus and equipment

(G-6731)
MAGICAL MOMENTS LLC
1687 Honey Ln (46143-7209)
PHONE.................463 209-5766
EMP: 1
SALES (est): 69.27K **Privately Held**
SIC: **2754** 7389 Stationery and invitation printing, gravure; Business Activities at Non-Commercial Site

(G-6732)
MAILGATE INTERNATIONAL INC ✪
Also Called: Mailgate SC
3209 W Smith Valley Rd (46142-8495)
PHONE.................866 843-1990
Jake Nardone, *Ch*
Kyle Fisher, *CFO*
EMP: 6 EST: 2022
SALES (est): 250.06K **Privately Held**
Web: www.mailgatesc.com
SIC: **7372** Application computer software

(G-6733)
MARTELL & CO
1674 Harvest Meadow Dr (46143-6773)
PHONE.................317 752-2847
Sean Fagan, *Pr*
EMP: 5 EST: 2017
SALES (est): 55.13K **Privately Held**
Web: www.martellandco.com
SIC: **2431** Millwork

(G-6734)
MAXIMUM LOGISTICS LLC
1237 Southlake Ave E (46143-6406)
PHONE.................317 488-1010
EMP: 5 EST: 2021
SALES (est): 202.26K **Privately Held**

SIC: **3799** Transportation equipment, nec

(G-6735)
MAY AND CO INC
Also Called: Scandinavian Sleep Products
3210 Greensview Dr (46143-9579)
PHONE.................317 236-6500
Lawrence T May, *CEO*
Robert G May, *Pr*
Maria May, *Sec*
EMP: 39 EST: 1952
SQ FT: 74,000
SALES (est): 618.48K **Privately Held**
SIC: **2515** Mattresses and foundations

(G-6736)
MCNEIL COATINGS CONS INC
1132 Kay Dr (46122-2204)
PHONE.................317 885-1557
Malcom Mcneil, *Pr*
Lenora Mcneil, *Genl Mgr*
EMP: 2 EST: 1993
SALES (est): 136.6K **Privately Held**
Web: www.mcneilcoatingsconsulting.com
SIC: **8742** 3479 Industrial consultant; Painting, coating, and hot dipping

(G-6737)
MD LAIRD INC
Also Called: PIP Printing
2947 S Emerson Ave (46143-7324)
PHONE.................317 842-6338
Mike Laird, *Pr*
EMP: 2 EST: 2001
SALES (est): 237K **Privately Held**
Web: www.pip.com
SIC: **2752** Offset printing

(G-6738)
METRO PRINTED PRODUCTS INC
1001 Commerce Parkway South Dr Ste H (46143-6442)
PHONE.................317 885-0077
Marlo Webb, *Pr*
EMP: 6 EST: 1990
SQ FT: 3,600
SALES (est): 893.26K **Privately Held**
Web: www.metroprintedproducts.com
SIC: **2752** Commercial printing, lithographic

(G-6739)
MICHAEL HAZELTINE
2704 Monarchy Ln (46143-6949)
PHONE.................317 750-5091
Michael Hazeltine, *Owner*
EMP: 10
SALES (est): 364.04K **Privately Held**
SIC: **3484** 7389 Guns (firearms) or gun parts, 30 mm. and below; Business Activities at Non-Commercial Site

(G-6740)
MIDWEST PURIFICATION LLC
2011 Southtech Dr # 130 (46143-6948)
PHONE.................317 536-7445
Todd Anthony, *CEO*
Tyler Dishman, *Pr*
Dan Moering, *COO*
EMP: 3 EST: 2013
SALES (est): 243.85K **Privately Held**
SIC: **3564** Air purification equipment

(G-6741)
MILD TO WILD PEPPER & HERB CO
Also Called: Franklin Cornucopia
305 Sunbeam Ln (46143-7721)
PHONE.................317 736-8300
James Campbell, *Owner*
EMP: 1 EST: 1995

Greenwood - Johnson County (G-6742)

SALES (est): 66.93K **Privately Held**
Web: www.wildpepper.com
SIC: 2035 5149 Seasonings and sauces, except tomato and dry; Groceries and related products, nec

(G-6742)
MILWAUKEE ELECTRIC TOOL CORP
Also Called: Milwaukee Tool
2198 Southtech Dr (46143-6725)
PHONE.................800 729-3878
EMP: 38
Web: www.milwaukeetool.com
SIC: 3546 3425 Power-driven handtools; Saw blades, for hand or power saws
HQ: Milwaukee Electric Tool Corporation
    13135 W Lisbon Rd
    Brookfield WI 53005
    800 729-3878

(G-6743)
NACHI AMERICA INC (HQ)
715 Pushville Rd (46143-9782)
PHONE.................877 622-4487
Tony Inoue, *Pr*
Sue Deaton, *
◆ **EMP:** 25 **EST:** 1962
SQ FT: 53,000
SALES (est): 63.05MM **Privately Held**
Web: www.nachiamerica.com
SIC: 3545 3568 3542 3569 Machine tool accessories; Bearings, bushings, and blocks; Machine tools, metal forming type; Robots, assembly line: industrial and commercial
PA: Nachi-Fujikoshi Corp.
    1-9-2, Higashishimbashi
    Minato-Ku TKY 105-0

(G-6744)
NACHI TECHNOLOGY INC
Also Called: Nachi
713 Pushville Rd (46143-9782)
PHONE.................317 535-5000
Robert Komasara, *Pr*
◆ **EMP:** 150 **EST:** 1974
SQ FT: 137,000
SALES (est): 24.9MM **Privately Held**
Web: www.nachitech.com
SIC: 3562 Ball and roller bearings
HQ: Nachi America Inc.
    715 Pushville Rd
    Greenwood IN 46143
    877 622-4487

(G-6745)
NACHI TOOL AMERICA INC
717 Pushville Rd (46143-9782)
PHONE.................317 535-0320
Kirk Blumemstock, *Mgr*
EMP: 27 **EST:** 2005
SALES (est): 2.15MM **Privately Held**
Web: www.nachiamerica.com
SIC: 3545 Drills (machine tool accessories)

(G-6746)
NELSON GLOBAL PRODUCTS INC
Also Called: Ctp Division Nelson Globl Pdts
2615 Endress Pl (46143-8684)
PHONE.................317 787-5747
EMP: 15 **EST:** 2011
SALES (est): 2.46MM **Privately Held**
SIC: 2836 Tuberculins

(G-6747)
NU LED LIGHTING
1147 Old Vines Ct (46143-3811)
PHONE.................317 989-7352
Shane Jardine, *Admn*
EMP: 5 **EST:** 2013
SALES (est): 170.11K **Privately Held**
SIC: 3648 Lighting equipment, nec

(G-6748)
OAKEN BARREL BREWING CO INC
Also Called: Oakenbarrel.com
50 Airport Pkwy Ste L (46143-1438)
PHONE.................317 887-2287
EMP: 26 **EST:** 1994
SQ FT: 7,700
SALES (est): 1MM **Privately Held**
Web: www.oakenbarrel.com
SIC: 5813 2082 Bars and lounges; Malt beverages

(G-6749)
PAR DIGITAL IMAGING INC
1134 Sweetbriar Dr (46143-7779)
PHONE.................317 787-3330
Ray Wilkisin, *Pr*
Vaughn Rathburn, *Prin*
EMP: 4 **EST:** 1982
SALES (est): 324.14K **Privately Held**
Web: www.pardigitalimage.com
SIC: 2752 Offset printing

(G-6750)
PERFECT PLASTIC PRINTING CORP
3967 Woodmore Dr (46142-9761)
PHONE.................317 888-9447
Joe Renforth, *Mgr*
EMP: 2 **EST:** 1992
SALES (est): 129.59K **Privately Held**
Web: www.perfectplastic.com
SIC: 2759 Commercial printing, nec

(G-6751)
PHOENIX ASSEMBLY LLC (HQ)
164 S Park Blvd (46143-8837)
PHONE.................317 884-3600
Harry Sherman, *CEO*
Gary Sherman, *
Patrick Sherman, *
▲ **EMP:** 91 **EST:** 2010
SQ FT: 9,106
SALES (est): 19.53MM **Privately Held**
Web: www.falcon-manufacturing.com
SIC: 5013 3569 4731 8741 Motor vehicle supplies and new parts; Assembly machines, non-metalworking; Freight transportation arrangement; Industrial management
PA: The Phoenix Group Inc
    164 S Park Blvd
    Greenwood IN 46143

(G-6752)
PLASTER SHAK
1797 Old State Road 37 (46143-9186)
PHONE.................317 881-6518
Don Weaver, *Owner*
EMP: 3 **EST:** 1970
SQ FT: 6,200
SALES (est): 133.6K **Privately Held**
SIC: 3843 3299 5032 3272 Plaster, dental; Plaques: clay, plaster, or papier mache; Drywall materials; Concrete products, nec

(G-6753)
POYNTER SHEET METAL INC
Also Called: Poynter
775 Commerce Parkway West Dr (46143-7535)
PHONE.................317 893-1193
Joseph Lanstell, *CEO*
EMP: 275 **EST:** 2000
SQ FT: 72,000
SALES (est): 60.4MM **Privately Held**
Web: www.poyntersheetmetal.com
SIC: 5075 3444 7349 Fans, heating and ventilation equipment; Sheet metalwork; Air duct cleaning

(G-6754)
PRECISION PRODUCTS INC (PA)
1701 Industrial Dr (46143-9678)
PHONE.................317 882-1852
EMP: 43 **EST:** 1974
SALES (est): 9MM
SALES (corp-wide): 9MM **Privately Held**
Web: www.prec-prod.com
SIC: 3544 Special dies, tools, jigs, and fixtures

(G-6755)
PREMIER CUSTOM COATINGS LLC
4676 Rainmaker Row (46143-7433)
PHONE.................317 557-7841
Chris Foutz, *Prin*
EMP: 8 **EST:** 2016
SALES (est): 141.38K **Privately Held**
SIC: 3479 Metal coating and allied services

(G-6756)
QUALITY REPAIR SERVICES INC
411 Knight Dr (46142-9372)
PHONE.................317 881-0205
Larry Jordan, *Pr*
EMP: 15 **EST:** 1979
SQ FT: 6,768
SALES (est): 1.54MM **Privately Held**
Web: www.qualityrepairservicellc.com
SIC: 7694 Electric motor repair
PA: Straeffer Pump & Supply, Inc.
    8055 State Route 62 W
    Chandler IN 47610

(G-6757)
R J SMITHEY LLC
2213 Running Brook Pl (46143-9252)
PHONE.................317 435-8473
EMP: 1 **EST:** 2011
SALES (est): 97.23K **Privately Held**
SIC: 2834 Pharmaceutical preparations

(G-6758)
RAYBURN AUTOMOTIVE INC
1120 Meriman Dr (46143-6922)
PHONE.................317 535-8232
Carl J Rayburn, *Pr*
Royce Johnson, *Frmn Supr*
EMP: 7 **EST:** 1975
SALES (est): 640.56K **Privately Held**
SIC: 3711 3714 Automobile assembly, including specialty automobiles; Motor vehicle engines and parts

(G-6759)
RBC HOLDING INC
Also Called: Ultimate Bowling Products
1006 Old Eagle Way (46143-7653)
P.O. Box 327 (46131-0327)
PHONE.................317 340-3845
Roger Brunette Senior, *CEO*
Roger Brunette Junior, *Pr*
Pauline Brunette, *Treas*
Catherine Brunette, *Sec*
▲ **EMP:** 14 **EST:** 1974
SALES (est): 2.4MM **Privately Held**
Web: www.ultimatebowling.com
SIC: 3087 2851 2821 6719 Custom compound purchased resins; Paints and allied products; Plastics materials and resins; Investment holding companies, except banks

(G-6760)
ROGERS ENTERPRISES INC
Also Called: Rogers & Hollands Jewelers
1251 Us Highway 31 N (46142-4503)
PHONE.................317 851-5500
Gina Anapachelli, *Mgr*
EMP: 5
SALES (corp-wide): 77.04MM **Privately Held**
Web: www.rogersandhollands.com
SIC: 5944 7631 3911 Jewelry, precious stones and precious metals; Jewelry repair services; Jewelry mountings and trimmings
PA: Rogers Enterprises, Inc.
    20821 S Cicero Ave
    Matteson IL 60443
    708 679-7588

(G-6761)
ROWE CONVEYOR LLC (PA)
1729 Us Highway 31 S Ste F (46143-4100)
PHONE.................317 602-1024
EMP: 5 **EST:** 2012
SALES (est): 213.27K
SALES (corp-wide): 213.27K **Privately Held**
Web: www.roweconveyor.com
SIC: 3535 3537 3499 Conveyors and conveying equipment; Stacking machines, automatic; Strapping, metal

(G-6762)
RUBBER PRODUCTS DISTRS INC (PA)
1741 Keaton Way Ste C (46143)
PHONE.................317 883-6700
EMP: 11 **EST:** 1993
SALES (est): 2.78MM **Privately Held**
SIC: 3069 Bags, rubber or rubberized fabric

(G-6763)
RUNNING COMPANY LLC
1251 N Us Highway 31 N Spc 112 (46142-4558)
PHONE.................317 887-0606
EMP: 1
SALES (corp-wide): 523.44K **Privately Held**
SIC: 3949 Sporting and athletic goods, nec
PA: Running Company, Llc
    1079 Broad Ripple Ave
    Indianapolis IN 46220
    317 202-0202

(G-6764)
RYAN OSBORNE INC
3667 Woodland Streams Dr (46143-8878)
PHONE.................317 535-4881
Ryan Osborne, *Owner*
EMP: 5 **EST:** 2015
SALES (est): 67.69K **Privately Held**
Web: www.ryanosborne.com
SIC: 3993 Signs and advertising specialties

(G-6765)
SABCO SIGN CO INC
1620 W Smith Valley Rd Ste C (46142-1550)
PHONE.................317 882-3380
Richard Simpson, *Pr*
EMP: 3 **EST:** 1980
SQ FT: 4,000
SALES (est): 232.29K **Privately Held**
Web: www.signsindiana.net
SIC: 3993 Signs, not made in custom sign painting shops

(G-6766)
SAN JO STEEL INC
610 W Main St (46142-2098)
PHONE.................317 888-6227
Jeffrey T Cave, *Pr*
Dean Martin, *VP*
Brad Pugh, *Treas*
David Martin, *Stockholder*
Ray Wickham, *Stockholder*
EMP: 18 **EST:** 1979
SQ FT: 10,000

GEOGRAPHIC SECTION

Griffith - Lake County (G-6790)

SALES (est): 3.95MM **Privately Held**
Web: www.sanjosteel.com
SIC: 3446 3441 Architectural metalwork; Fabricated structural metal

(G-6767)
SIGN GUYS INC
Also Called: Next Day Signs
80 S Serenity Way (46142-8429)
PHONE..................317 875-7446
Mike Ford, *Pr*
Chris Nash, *Pr*
EMP: 5 EST: 1990
SALES (est): 230.61K **Privately Held**
Web: www.nextdaysignsindy.com
SIC: 3993 5999 Signs and advertising specialties; Banners, flags, decals, and posters

(G-6768)
SIGN SOLUTIONS INC
505 Commerce Parkway West Dr (46143-6483)
PHONE..................317 881-1818
EMP: 14 EST: 1994
SALES (est): 1.07MM **Privately Held**
Web: www.signsolution.com
SIC: 3993 Electric signs

(G-6769)
SPEAR INDUSTRIES INC
943 Maple Stone Dr (46143-3830)
PHONE..................317 717-1957
EMP: 5 EST: 2009
SALES (est): 12.13K **Privately Held**
SIC: 3999 Manufacturing industries, nec

(G-6770)
SPRING VENTURES INFOVATION LLC
1846 Saratoga Dr (46143-6879)
PHONE..................317 847-1117
EMP: 4 EST: 2010
SALES (est): 218.44K **Privately Held**
SIC: 8742 7379 8748 7371 Management consulting services; Computer related consulting services; Systems analysis and engineering consulting services; Custom computer programming services

(G-6771)
T ORGANIZATION INC
Also Called: T Logistics
624 Nicole Dr Apt D (46143-2023)
PHONE..................463 204-5118
Tanbeer Brar, *Pr*
Tanbeer Brar, *CEO*
Lakhvir Singh Dhillon, *Pr*
EMP: 20 EST: 2018
SQ FT: 900
SALES (est): 945.68K **Privately Held**
SIC: 4213 4731 3444 6531 Trucking, except local; Freight transportation arrangement; Housings for business machines, sheet metal; Real estate leasing and rentals

(G-6772)
T&S GROUP LLC
1141 Paradise Way N Unit B (46143-2128)
PHONE..................219 310-0364
EMP: 2
SALES (est): 83.76K **Privately Held**
SIC: 7389 3743 Business Activities at Non-Commercial Site; Freight cars and equipment

(G-6773)
TEMPTEK INC
525 E Stop 18 Rd (46143-9808)
P.O. Box 1152 (46142-0276)

PHONE..................317 887-6352
Jon Gunderson, *Pr*
Susan Schaub, *Ex VP*
Randy Goode, *VP*
Ron Wolfe, *VP*
EMP: 5 EST: 1987
SQ FT: 20,000
SALES (est): 948.96K **Privately Held**
Web: www.temptek.com
SIC: 3822 1711 3443 3433 Temperature controls, automatic; Plumbing, heating, air-conditioning; Fabricated plate work (boiler shop); Heating equipment, except electric

(G-6774)
TNEMEC COMPANY INC
458 Park 800 Dr (46143-9525)
PHONE..................317 884-1806
Jeff Payton, *Brnch Mgr*
EMP: 3
SALES (corp-wide): 129.58MM **Privately Held**
Web: www.tnemec.com
SIC: 2851 Coating, air curing
PA: Tnemec Company, Inc.
123 W 23rd Ave
Kansas City MO 64116
816 483-3400

(G-6775)
TOCO INC
4307 Blackwood Ct (46143-7909)
PHONE..................317 627-8854
Laura Mcintosh, *Pr*
EMP: 3 EST: 2009
SALES (est): 181.66K **Privately Held**
SIC: 3559 Special industry machinery, nec

(G-6776)
TRANSCEND ORTHTICS PRSTHTICS L
595 S Emerson Ave Ste 300 (46143-1951)
PHONE..................317 300-9016
Bernie Veldman, *CEO*
EMP: 8
SALES (corp-wide): 25.64MM **Privately Held**
Web: www.hangerclinic.com
SIC: 3842 Surgical appliances and supplies
HQ: Transcend Orthotics & Prosthetics, Llc
17530 Dugdale Dr
South Bend IN 46635
574 233-3352

(G-6777)
TRUE CHEM INC
283 Innisbrooke Ave (46142-9215)
P.O. Box 1424 (46142-6324)
PHONE..................317 769-2701
Leslie Sherry, *Pr*
EMP: 4 EST: 2006
SALES (est): 373.95K **Privately Held**
Web: www.truechem.net
SIC: 3589 7389 Water purification equipment, household type; Business services, nec

(G-6778)
VISION AID SYSTEMS INC
Also Called: Low Vision Store
916 E Main St Ste 114 (46143-1500)
P.O. Box 1369 (46142-6269)
PHONE..................317 888-0323
James Fortman, *Pr*
Lisa Preston, *Sec*
EMP: 2 EST: 1986
SQ FT: 750
SALES (est): 212.04K **Privately Held**
Web: www.visionaidsystem.com

SIC: 3827 4841 Optical instruments and apparatus; Cable and other pay television services

(G-6779)
WB FROZEN US LLC
1760 Industrial Dr (46143-9526)
PHONE..................317 858-9000
Mike Swanson, *Brnch Mgr*
EMP: 616
SALES (corp-wide): 1.22B **Privately Held**
SIC: 2051 Bakery: wholesale or wholesale/retail combined
HQ: Wb Frozen Us, Llc
50 Maplehurst Dr
Brownsburg IN 46112
317 858-9000

(G-6780)
WESSELS COMPANY
101 Tank St (46143-1203)
PHONE..................317 888-9800
James Fuller, *Pr*
Guy Kirk Junior, *VP*
◆ EMP: 80 EST: 1908
SQ FT: 103,000
SALES (est): 20.88MM
SALES (corp-wide): 174.69MM **Privately Held**
Web: www.westank.com
SIC: 3443 Tanks, standard or custom fabricated: metal plate
PA: Nm Group Global, Llc
161 Greenfield St
Tiffin OH 44883
419 447-5211

(G-6781)
WILSON WELDING & PIPING LLC
4774 Olive Branch Rd (46143-8603)
PHONE..................317 397-4865
Don Lee Wilson Ii, *Pr*
EMP: 4 EST: 2018
SALES (est): 104.56K **Privately Held**
Web: www.wilsonweldingandpiping.com
SIC: 7692 Welding repair

(G-6782)
WURTH ADDITIVE GROUP INC
598 Chaney Ave (46143-0112)
PHONE..................551 269-7695
Aj Strandquist, *CEO*
Achim W Grenner, *CFO*
EMP: 10 EST: 2021
SALES (est): 2.35MM
SALES (corp-wide): 22.17B **Privately Held**
Web: www.wurthadditive.com
SIC: 2851 Paints and paint additives
HQ: Wurth Group Of North America Inc.
93 Grant St
Ramsey NJ 07446

(G-6783)
YARD SIGNS INC
1444 Demaree Rd (46143-8672)
PHONE..................317 535-7000
Tracey Kramer, *Prin*
EMP: 1 EST: 2007
SALES (est): 112.42K **Privately Held**
Web: www.storksandmoreyardsigns.com
SIC: 3993 Signs and advertising specialties

Griffin
Posey County

(G-6784)
REEVES FEED & GRAIN LLC
12407 Upper Griffin Rd (47616)
PHONE..................812 453-3313

EMP: 4 EST: 2009
SALES (est): 279.62K **Privately Held**
SIC: 2099 Food preparations, nec

Griffith
Lake County

(G-6785)
ACME CABINET CORPORATION
1331 E Main St (46319-2932)
PHONE..................219 924-1800
Donald Elman, *Pr*
Richard Elman, *Sec*
EMP: 8 EST: 1959
SQ FT: 5,400
SALES (est): 886.61K **Privately Held**
Web: www.acmecabinetcorp.net
SIC: 2434 Wood kitchen cabinets

(G-6786)
ACS TECHNICAL PRODUCTS INC
Also Called: ACS
420 S Colfax St (46319-3446)
P.O. Box 190 (46319-0190)
PHONE..................219 924-4370
EMP: 25 EST: 1955
SALES (est): 7.88MM **Privately Held**
Web: www.acstech.com
SIC: 2869 Plasticizers, organic: cyclic and acyclic

(G-6787)
AEROMET INDUSTRIES INC
739 S Arbogast St (46319-3149)
PHONE..................219 924-7442
TOLL FREE: 800
Fred Wahlberg, *Pr*
Gus Sitaras, *
Drew Wahlberg, *
Susan Wahlberg, *Stockholder**
▲ EMP: 55 EST: 1971
SQ FT: 25,500
SALES (est): 9.39MM **Privately Held**
Web: www.aerometindustries.com
SIC: 3599 3545 Machine shop, jobbing and repair; Machine tool attachments and accessories

(G-6788)
AHEPA 157
1400 S Broad St (46319-3212)
PHONE..................219 864-3255
Anthony Matlon, *Prin*
EMP: 1 EST: 2008
SALES (est): 62.66K **Privately Held**
Web: www.ahepa157bingo.com
SIC: 3944 Bingo boards (games)

(G-6789)
ALLIED MINERAL PRODUCTS INC
Also Called: ALLIED MINERAL PRODUCTS, INC.
1950 N Griffith Blvd Ste D (46319-1050)
PHONE..................219 923-5875
Bob Kuhn, *Mgr*
EMP: 10
SALES (corp-wide): 91.72MM **Privately Held**
Web: www.alliedmineral.com
SIC: 3297 Nonclay refractories
PA: Allied Mineral Products, Llc
2700 Scioto Pkwy
Columbus OH 43221
614 876-0244

(G-6790)
AMERICAN NATURAL RESOURCES LLC
Also Called: American Natural Resources Str

(PA)=Parent Co (HQ)=Headquarters
✪ = New Business established in last 2 years

Griffith - Lake County (G-6791) GEOGRAPHIC SECTION

120 N Broad St (46319-2219)
PHONE..................................219 922-6444
Edward Leep, *Managing Member*
EMP: 15 **EST:** 1986
SALES (est) 659.8K **Privately Held**
Web:
www.americannaturalresources.com
SIC: 7699 2599 5021 5712 Taxidermists; Boards: planning, display, notice; Furniture; Furniture stores

(G-6791)
ATCO-GARY METAL TECH LLC
1931 E Main St (46319-2921)
PHONE..................................219 885-3232
David A Strilich, *Managing Member*
EMP: 10 **EST:** 2012
SALES (est): 792.09K **Privately Held**
SIC: 3444 Sheet metalwork

(G-6792)
B K & M INC
210 S Lindberg St (46319-2694)
PHONE..................................219 924-0184
Vince Gwiazda, *VP*
Toni Gwiazda, *Pr*
EMP: 3 **EST:** 1975
SALES (est): 242.56K **Privately Held**
SIC: 3452 Bolts, metal

(G-6793)
BAXTER PRINTING INCORPORATED
311 N Broad St (46319-2222)
PHONE..................................219 923-1999
Betty Turoci, *Pr*
David Turoci, *Head SALES*
EMP: 7 **EST:** 1950
SALES (est): 973.32K **Privately Held**
Web: www.baxterprint.com
SIC: 2759 2752 2789 Screen printing; Offset printing; Bookbinding and related work

(G-6794)
BEARING SERVICE COMPANY PA
1951 N Griffith Blvd (46319-1043)
PHONE..................................773 734-5132
Janet July, *Mgr*
EMP: 4
SALES (corp-wide): 89.93MM **Privately Held**
Web: www.bearing-service.com
SIC: 3568 5085 Power transmission equipment, nec; Bearings
PA: Bearing Service Company Of Pennsylvania
630 Alpha Dr
Pittsburgh PA 15238
412 963-7710

(G-6795)
BLYTHES SPORT SHOP INC (PA)
138 N Broad St (46319-2287)
P.O. Box 539 (46319-0539)
PHONE..................................219 924-4403
Rodger Blythe, *Pr*
Michael Blythe, *VP*
Lester Blythe, *Sec*
EMP: 15 **EST:** 1952
SQ FT: 6,000
SALES (est): 3.97MM
SALES (corp-wide): 3.97MM **Privately Held**
Web: www.blythesgungear.com
SIC: 3484 5099 3482 Guns (firearms) or gun parts, 30 mm. and below; Firearms and ammunition, except sporting; Cores, bullet: 30 mm. and below

(G-6796)
BM CREATIONS INC
1313 E Main St (46319-2932)
PHONE..................................219 922-8935
EMP: 40 **EST:** 2013
SALES (est): 15MM **Privately Held**
Web: www.berylmartin.com
SIC: 2759 Commercial printing, nec

(G-6797)
BRIGHT CORP
1313 E Main St (46319-2932)
P.O. Box 403 (46015-0403)
PHONE..................................765 642-3114
William D Bowser, *Pr*
Steven J Bowser, *VP*
Edward L Bowser, *Sec*
EMP: 18 **EST:** 1946
SALES (est): 711.88K **Privately Held**
Web: www.brightcorporation.com
SIC: 2741 2731 2752 Miscellaneous publishing; Books, publishing only; Commercial printing, lithographic

(G-6798)
CALUMET WELDING CENTER INC
1947 N Griffith Blvd (46319-1043)
P.O. Box 1510 (46322-0510)
PHONE..................................219 923-9353
EMP: 3 **EST:** 2010
SALES (est): 237.16K **Privately Held**
Web: www.calumetweldingcenter.com
SIC: 7692 Welding repair

(G-6799)
CCMP INC
Also Called: Beryl Martin
1313 E Main St (46319-2932)
PHONE..................................219 922-8935
J Kim Sorenson, *Pr*
J Kim Sorenson, *Pr*
Brian Tucker, *
EMP: 24 **EST:** 2003
SQ FT: 50,000
SALES (est): 2.05MM **Privately Held**
Web: www.berylmartin.com
SIC: 2759 Commercial printing, nec

(G-6800)
CHEMICAL CONTROL SYSTEMS INC (PA)
403 Industrial Dr (46319-3811)
PHONE..................................219 465-5103
Mike Walker, *Pr*
Jim Flannery, *VP*
Susy Walker, *Sec*
EMP: 3 **EST:** 1991
SQ FT: 8,000
SALES (est): 684.03K **Privately Held**
SIC: 3589 3586 Water treatment equipment, industrial; Measuring and dispensing pumps

(G-6801)
D TO 3-DIMENSION
633 N Colfax St (46319-2528)
PHONE..................................219 793-6123
Michael Carlson, *Prin*
EMP: 8 **EST:** 2018
SALES (est): 320.59K **Privately Held**
Web: www.dto3dimension.com
SIC: 3599 Machine shop, jobbing and repair

(G-6802)
DJS CYLINDER SERVICE INC
223 S Lindberg St (46319-2694)
PHONE..................................219 922-4819
Daniel Joy, *Pr*
EMP: 1 **EST:** 1998
SALES (est): 160K **Privately Held**
SIC: 3593 3599 Fluid power cylinders, hydraulic or pneumatic; Machine and other job shop work

(G-6803)
EASON MANUFACTURING INC
601 Industrial Dr Ste B (46319-2695)
PHONE..................................312 310-9430
Earl Hokens Junior, *Pr*
EMP: 3 **EST:** 1974
SQ FT: 4,200
SALES (est): 210K **Privately Held**
SIC: 3599 Machine shop, jobbing and repair

(G-6804)
GORDON LUMBER COMPANY
806 W Avenue H (46319-3012)
PHONE..................................219 924-0500
Vincent Gwiazda, *Pr*
Conrad Swalwell, *VP*
Louis Piattoni, *Sec*
EMP: 4 **EST:** 1940
SQ FT: 7,500
SALES (est): 973.14K
SALES (corp-wide): 973.14K **Privately Held**
Web: www.gordonlumber.com
SIC: 2449 5031 Wood containers, nec; Lumber: rough, dressed, and finished
PA: Continental Custom Crate Inc
806 W Avenue H
Griffith IN

(G-6805)
GREENWOOD TOOL AND DIE CO INC
231 S Lindberg St (46319-2694)
PHONE..................................219 924-9663
Myron Kurth, *Pr*
David Kurth, *Treas*
Gail Kurth, *Sec*
EMP: 2 **EST:** 1963
SQ FT: 6,000
SALES (est): 204.58K **Privately Held**
SIC: 3599 3544 Machine shop, jobbing and repair; Special dies, tools, jigs, and fixtures

(G-6806)
HD MECHANICAL INC
507 Industrial Dr (46319-2696)
PHONE..................................219 924-6050
Erik Hansen, *Pr*
Keith Best, *Sec*
EMP: 17 **EST:** 2013
SQ FT: 10,000
SALES (est): 5.59MM **Privately Held**
Web: www.hdmechanicalinc.com
SIC: 1623 3498 3317 Pipe laying construction; Fabricated pipe and fittings; Steel pipe and tubes

(G-6807)
HUDEC CONSTRUCTION COMPANY
Also Called: Hudec Woodworking Company
148 N Ivanhoe Ct (46319-3457)
PHONE..................................219 922-9811
EMP: 20 **EST:** 1987
SALES (est): 3.41MM **Privately Held**
Web: www.hudecwoodworking.com
SIC: 2431 1521 Millwork; General remodeling, single-family houses

(G-6808)
ICE CREAM ON WHEELS INC
2011 N Griffith Blvd (46319-1009)
PHONE..................................800 884-9793
Thomas Benedict Renwald, *Ch*
EMP: 8 **EST:** 2017
SALES (est): 218.9K **Privately Held**
Web: www.icecreamonwheels.com
SIC: 2024 5451 Ice cream, packaged: molded, on sticks, etc.; Ice cream (packaged)

(G-6809)
J MAKES INCORPORATED
1820 Norwood Dr (46319-1132)
PHONE..................................773 610-9867
Jeremi Murray, *CEO*
EMP: 1 **EST:** 2021
SALES (est): 54.36K **Privately Held**
SIC: 3499 Fabricated metal products, nec

(G-6810)
KEYWEST METAL
2034 N Griffith Blvd (46319-1009)
PHONE..................................219 513-8429
EMP: 3 **EST:** 2012
SALES (est): 239.41K **Privately Held**
SIC: 3399 Primary metal products

(G-6811)
LEGACY HEAT TREATMENT LLC
Also Called: Heat Treatment
801 E Main St Ste 16 (46319)
PHONE..................................219 237-4500
Christopher Brown, *Pr*
Christopher Brown, *Managing Member*
Nicole Tarnowski, *
EMP: 60 **EST:** 2021
SALES (est): 500K **Privately Held**
Web: www.legacyheattreatment.com
SIC: 3398 Metal heat treating

(G-6812)
LINEAR SOLUTIONS INC
149 S Colfax St (46319)
PHONE..................................219 237-2399
Patrick Fay, *Pr*
EMP: 15 **EST:** 2018
SALES (est): 16.48MM **Privately Held**
Web: www.linearsolutionsinc.com
SIC: 3644 Electric conduits and fittings

(G-6813)
MARGARET MACHINE AND TOOL CO
206 S Lindberg St (46319-2694)
PHONE..................................219 924-0859
Vincent G Wiazda, *Pr*
EMP: 9 **EST:** 1977
SQ FT: 10,000
SALES (est): 813.12K **Privately Held**
SIC: 3599 Machine shop, jobbing and repair

(G-6814)
MIDWEST MACHINING & FABG
711 W Main St (46319-2634)
P.O. Box D (46319-0498)
PHONE..................................219 924-0206
Ronald W Stassin, *Pr*
Stanley Majkowski, *Sec*
EMP: 10 **EST:** 1973
SQ FT: 5,000
SALES (est): 990K **Privately Held**
SIC: 3599 7692 Machine shop, jobbing and repair; Welding repair

(G-6815)
PREMIUM VINYL MFG
231 S Lindberg St (46319-2694)
PHONE..................................219 922-6501
EMP: 4 **EST:** 2020
SALES (est): 194.91K **Privately Held**
SIC: 3999 Manufacturing industries, nec

(G-6816)
RAILWAY UNLOADING SERVICES LLC
2001 N Cline Ave (46319-1008)
PHONE..................................219 989-7700

Hagerstown - Wayne County (G-6839)

EMP: 6 EST: 2011
SALES (est): 143.04K **Privately Held**
Web: www.railwayunloading.com
SIC: 3621 Railway motors and control equipment, electric

(G-6817)
SWEET MOON MACARON LLC
109 N Broad St (46319-2218)
PHONE.................................219 484-9851
EMP: 7 EST: 2020
SALES (est): 247.57K **Privately Held**
Web: www.sweetmoonmacaron.com
SIC: 2024 Ice cream and frozen deserts

(G-6818)
TEC HOIST LLC
1349 E Main St (46319-2932)
PHONE.................................708 598-2300
▲ EMP: 30 EST: 2007
SQ FT: 10,000
SALES (est): 317.54K
SALES (corp-wide): 24.3MM **Privately Held**
SIC: 3534 3536 Elevators and moving stairways; Hoisting slings
PA: Imperial Crane Services, Inc.
7500 Imperial Dr
Bridgeview IL 60455
708 598-2300

(G-6819)
TECHNICAL WEIGHING SVCS INC (PA)
Also Called: Tech Weigh Manufacturing
1004 Reder Rd (46319-3116)
PHONE.................................219 924-3366
Jack L Clark, *Pr*
Sandra L Clark, *
▲ EMP: 32 EST: 1986
SQ FT: 30,000
SALES (est): 6.92MM
SALES (corp-wide): 6.92MM **Privately Held**
Web: www.techweigh.com
SIC: 5046 7699 3596 3825 Scales, except laboratory; Scale repair service; Weighing machines and apparatus; Electrical energy measuring equipment

(G-6820)
TFP INC
1950 N Griffith Blvd Ste A (46319-1050)
PHONE.................................219 513-9572
Tim Joyce, *Mgr*
EMP: 5 EST: 2015
SALES (est): 83.78K **Privately Held**
Web: www.truweldstudwelding.com
SIC: 7692 Welding repair

(G-6821)
UPRIGHT IRON WORKS INC
1941 N Woodlawn Ave (46319-1047)
PHONE.................................219 922-1994
Elizabeth Matelundin, *Pr*
Elizabeth Mate-lundin, *Pr*
EMP: 9 EST: 1989
SALES (est): 1.85MM **Privately Held**
Web: www.uprightiron.com
SIC: 3446 Ornamental metalwork

(G-6822)
VALPARISO AREA APPRNTCSHIP ADV
739 S Arbogast St (46319-3102)
PHONE.................................219 613-6226
EMP: 6 EST: 2017
SALES (est): 106.94K **Privately Held**
Web: www.aerometindustries.com

SIC: 3599 Machine shop, jobbing and repair

Grovertown
Starke County

(G-6823)
DACK BLOWER MANUFACTURING INC
10660 E Us Highway 30 (46531-9540)
PHONE.................................574 867-2025
Melvin R Divine, *Pr*
M Ross Divine, *Pr*
Gail Divine, *Sec*
Chris Divine, *VP*
EMP: 6 EST: 1985
SQ FT: 10,000
SALES (est): 532.16K **Privately Held**
SIC: 3564 Blowers and fans

(G-6824)
TECHNICOAT LLC
4421 N 1150 E (46531-9491)
PHONE.................................574 339-1745
EMP: 1 EST: 2006
SALES (est): 103.45K **Privately Held**
Web: www.technicoat.net
SIC: 3479 Coating of metals and formed products

(G-6825)
WHITCRAFT WELDING
7915 E 300 N (46531-9452)
PHONE.................................574 867-6021
James Whitcraft, *Owner*
EMP: 1 EST: 1972
SALES (est): 85.54K **Privately Held**
SIC: 7699 3523 Farm machinery repair; Farm machinery and equipment

Guilford
Dearborn County

(G-6826)
ADVANCED COMMUNITY ENHANCEMENT
19412 Collier Ridge Rd (47022-9634)
P.O. Box 142 (45041-0142)
PHONE.................................513 615-6730
Jordan M Wayne, *Pr*
EMP: 5 EST: 2011
SALES (est): 156.17K **Privately Held**
Web: www.enhancedbyadvanced.com
SIC: 8322 1389 Community center; Construction, repair, and dismantling services

(G-6827)
BES RACING ENGINES INC
27545 State Route 1 (47022-9334)
PHONE.................................812 576-2371
Anthony Bischoff, *Pr*
EMP: 10 EST: 2005
SALES (est): 980.36K **Privately Held**
Web: www.besracing.com
SIC: 3519 Internal combustion engines, nec

(G-6828)
DOWN TO FABRICATE LLC
5016 Main St (47022-9167)
PHONE.................................812 249-1825
Scott Damico, *Prin*
EMP: 6 EST: 2019
SALES (est): 87.78K **Privately Held**
Web: www.downtofabricate.com
SIC: 3999 Manufacturing industries, nec

(G-6829)
EVERS WELDING COMPANY INC
7218 Wolf Creek Rd (47022-9159)
PHONE.................................812 576-2232
Timothy Virgin, *Prin*
EMP: 1 EST: 2010
SALES (est): 50K **Privately Held**
SIC: 7692 Welding repair

(G-6830)
TIN MAN SHTMTL & ROOFG LLC
26170 Sawdon Ridge Rd (47022-9769)
PHONE.................................513 276-1716
Dainiel Fey, *Prin*
EMP: 6 EST: 2019
SALES (est): 205.11K **Privately Held**
SIC: 3444 Sheet metalwork

Gwynneville
Shelby County

(G-6831)
PEARL CSTM PLASTIC MOLDING INC
Also Called: Pearl Custom Plastic
7072 E Mulberry St (46144-5502)
P.O. Box 149 (46144-0149)
PHONE.................................765 763-6961
Nancy J Grimes, *Owner*
EMP: 9 EST: 1987
SQ FT: 5,000
SALES (est): 719.6K **Privately Held**
SIC: 3843 Dental equipment and supplies

Hagerstown
Wayne County

(G-6832)
ABBOTTS CANDY AND GIFTS INC (PA)
Also Called: Abbott's Candy Shop
48 E Walnut St (47346-1542)
PHONE.................................765 489-4442
Suanna Goodnight, *Pr*
Gordon Goodnight, *VP*
Richard Federico, *Sec*
EMP: 20 EST: 1890
SQ FT: 12,000
SALES (est): 2.45MM
SALES (corp-wide): 2.45MM **Privately Held**
Web: www.abbottscandy.com
SIC: 2064 5947 5441 2066 Candy and other confectionery products; Gift shop; Candy; Chocolate and cocoa products

(G-6833)
AUTOCAR LLC (DH)
Also Called: Autocar Trucks
551 S Washington St (47346)
PHONE.................................765 489-5499
Jim Johnston, *
James M Johnston, *
Ryan Billet, *
◆ EMP: 26 EST: 2002
SQ FT: 200,000
SALES (est): 151.03MM **Privately Held**
Web: www.autocartruck.com
SIC: 3713 Garbage, refuse truck bodies
HQ: Gvw Group, Llc
625 Roger Williams Ave
Highland Park IL 60035
847 681-8417

(G-6834)
BRIAN BEX REPORT INC
Also Called: AMERICAN COMMUNICATIONS NETWOR

100 N Woodpecker Rd (47346-1431)
P.O. Box 111 (47346-0111)
PHONE.................................765 489-5566
Brian Bex, *Pr*
Kristopher Bex, *VP*
EMP: 3 EST: 1966
SQ FT: 15,000
SALES (est): 124.58K **Privately Held**
Web: www.thethreefoldacademy.com
SIC: 2721 Periodicals, publishing only

(G-6835)
CUSTOM MTAL FNSHNG-INDIANA LLC
9705 State Road 38 (47346-9520)
PHONE.................................765 489-4089
James M Canfield, *Owner*
EMP: 3 EST: 2004
SALES (est): 238.74K **Privately Held**
Web: www.chromeplatingin.com
SIC: 3471 Electroplating of metals or formed products

(G-6836)
DAVIS CABINET AND FLOORING LLC
Also Called: Davis Cabinet & Design
10 Paul R Foulke Pkwy (47346-1626)
PHONE.................................765 530-8170
EMP: 7 EST: 2017
SALES (est): 424.71K **Privately Held**
Web: www.daviscabinetanddesign.com
SIC: 2434 Wood kitchen cabinets

(G-6837)
HEART BREAKER SALES LLC
Also Called: Heart Breaker Video Dis Jockey
10094 Lacy Rd (47346-9700)
PHONE.................................765 489-4048
TOLL FREE: 800
Larry Black, *Managing Member*
EMP: 1 EST: 1978
SQ FT: 1,000
SALES (est): 186.03K **Privately Held**
Web: www.cargotrailer.com
SIC: 7929 7812 3792 Disc jockey service; Video production; Travel trailers and campers

(G-6838)
KEYSTONE COOPERATIVE INC
4379 Jacksonburg Rd (47346-9624)
PHONE.................................765 489-4141
Butch Shiebla, *Mgr*
EMP: 1
SALES (corp-wide): 570.05MM **Privately Held**
Web: www.keystonecoop.com
SIC: 5191 2879 2875 2048 Fertilizers and agricultural chemicals; Agricultural chemicals, nec; Fertilizers, mixing only; Prepared feeds, nec
PA: Keystone Cooperative, Inc.
770 N High School
Indianapolis IN 46214
800 525-0272

(G-6839)
MANCHESTER INDUSTRIES INC VA
63 Paul R Foulke Pkwy (47346-1632)
P.O. Box 229 (47346-0229)
PHONE.................................765 489-4521
Ranse Mckinney, *Mgr*
EMP: 38
Web: www.manind.com
SIC: 2679 Paperboard products, converted, nec
HQ: Manchester Industries Inc. Of Virginia
200 Orleans St
Richmond VA 23231
804 226-4250

Hagerstown - Wayne County (G-6840)

(G-6840)
MAXWELL MILLING INDIANA INC
4359 N State Road 1 (47346-9620)
P.O. Box 230 (47346-0230)
PHONE.................765 489-3506
James L Maxwell Iii, *Pr*
J Walter Pelletier Iii, *Treas*
EMP: 7 **EST:** 2006
SALES (est): 800.09K **Privately Held**
SIC: 3541 Milling machines

(G-6841)
PB METAL WORKS
50 Paul R Foulke Pkwy (47346-1626)
PHONE.................765 489-1311
Melvin Teachey, *Owner*
EMP: 2 **EST:** 2013
SALES (est): 120.59K **Privately Held**
Web: www.pbmetalworks.com
SIC: 1761 5719 5031 3443 Sheet metal work, nec; Metalware; Trim, sheet metal; Cupolas, metal plate

(G-6842)
PRECISION WIRE ASSEMBLIES INC
551 E Main St (47346-1421)
PHONE.................765 489-6302
Penny Wickes, *Pr*
William M Wickes, *
Mike Wickes, *
EMP: 75 **EST:** 1987
SQ FT: 265,000
SALES (est): 9.28MM **Privately Held**
Web: www.pwawire.com
SIC: 3679 Harness assemblies, for electronic use; wire or cable

(G-6843)
SYLTECH EXPERIMENTAL
13931 Clyde Oler Rd (47346-9764)
PHONE.................765 489-1777
Ray Rigaud, *Owner*
EMP: 5 **EST:** 2015
SALES (est): 166.03K **Privately Held**
SIC: 3599 Machine shop, jobbing and repair

(G-6844)
T & I TOOL LLC
99 N Sycamore St (47346-1329)
PHONE.................765 489-6293
Todd Morris, *Managing Member*
EMP: 1 **EST:** 1996
SALES (est): 187.24K **Privately Held**
SIC: 3544 Special dies and tools

(G-6845)
TEDCO INC
303 W Main St (47346-1143)
PHONE.................765 489-5807
Mark Marlat, *Mgr*
EMP: 2
SALES (corp-wide): 2.02MM **Privately Held**
Web: www.tedcotoys.com
SIC: 3089 Injection molding of plastics
PA: Tedco Inc
498 S Washington St
Hagerstown IN 47346
765 489-4527

(G-6846)
TEDCO INC (PA)
Also Called: Tedco Toys
498 S Washington St (47346-1596)
PHONE.................765 489-4527
Ralph R Meyer, *Pr*
Marjorie T Meyer, *Sec*
◆ **EMP:** 13 **EST:** 1982
SQ FT: 9,000
SALES (est): 2.02MM

SALES (corp-wide): 2.02MM **Privately Held**
Web: www.tedcotoys.com
SIC: 3944 Games, toys, and children's vehicles

(G-6847)
WHITE WATER TRUSS LLC
79 Paul R Foulke Pkwy (47346-1632)
PHONE.................765 489-6261
Dan Lapp, *Managing Member*
EMP: 8 **EST:** 2010
SALES (est): 992.57K **Privately Held**
Web: www.whitewatertrusses.com
SIC: 2439 Trusses, wooden roof

(G-6848)
WILLOW WAY LLC
520 W Main St (47346-1126)
PHONE.................765 886-4642
EMP: 7 **EST:** 2016
SALES (est): 327.96K **Privately Held**
Web: www.soapequipment.com
SIC: 2841 5046 Soap and other detergents; Commercial equipment, nec

(G-6849)
WILLOW WAY LLC
Also Called: Soapequipment.com
12873 We Oler Rd (47346-9716)
PHONE.................765 886-4640
Ron Jonas, *CEO*
▼ **EMP:** 9 **EST:** 2008
SALES (est): 943.24K **Privately Held**
Web: www.soapequipment.com
SIC: 3556 Cutting, chopping, grinding, mixing, and similar machinery

Hamilton
Steuben County

(G-6850)
AAA GALVANIZING - JOLIET INC
Also Called: Azz Galvanizing Hamilton
7825 S Homestead Dr (46742-9622)
PHONE.................260 488-4477
Jeff Reynolds, *Brnch Mgr*
EMP: 10
SALES (corp-wide): 1.54B **Publicly Held**
SIC: 3479 Hot dip coating of metals or formed products
HQ: Aaa Galvanizing - Joliet, Inc.
625 Mills Rd
Joliet IL 60433

(G-6851)
CHUCKS CLEANERS LLC
3820 E Bellefontaine Rd (46742-9363)
P.O. Box 433 (46742-0433)
PHONE.................260 488-3362
Charles J Ott, *Owner*
EMP: 2 **EST:** 1988
SALES (est): 108.98K **Privately Held**
SIC: 7216 3582 Cleaning and dyeing, except rugs; Ironers, commercial laundry and drycleaning

(G-6852)
E M F CORP
Also Called: Indiana Wire Assembly
7335 S Enterprise Dr (46742-9662)
P.O. Box 484 (46742-0484)
PHONE.................260 488-2479
Richard Poe, *Pr*
EMP: 26
SALES (corp-wide): 24.52MM **Privately Held**
Web: www.emfusa.com
SIC: 3643 3351 3694 Current-carrying wiring services; Wire, copper and copper alloy; Engine electrical equipment
PA: E M F Corp
505 Pokagon Trl
Angola IN 46703
260 665-9541

(G-6853)
EICHERS SAWMILL
6395 E 450 S (46742-9249)
PHONE.................260 624-5882
Joseph A Eicher, *Owner*
EMP: 5 **EST:** 2014
SALES (est): 500K **Privately Held**
Web: www.eicherssawmill.com
SIC: 2421 Lath, made in sawmills and lathmills

(G-6854)
G & L MACHINE LLP
5920 County Road 4 (46742-9743)
P.O. Box 314 (46742-0314)
PHONE.................260 488-2100
EMP: 5 **EST:** 2006
SALES (est): 417.3K **Privately Held**
SIC: 3334 Primary aluminum

(G-6855)
HAMILTON INDUSTRIAL INC
6610 S State Road 1 (46742-9519)
PHONE.................260 488-3662
Lloyd J Bartels, *CEO*
EMP: 6 **EST:** 1999
SALES (est): 97.29K **Privately Held**
Web: www.hicom.ca
SIC: 3599 Machine shop, jobbing and repair

(G-6856)
INDUSTRIAL STEERING PDTS INC (PA)
7790 S Homestead Dr (46742-9622)
P.O. Box 868 (43506-0868)
PHONE.................260 488-1880
Terri Freudenberger, *Pr*
John Freudenberger, *VP*
EMP: 15 **EST:** 1980
SQ FT: 100,000
SALES (est): 10.2MM
SALES (corp-wide): 10.2MM **Privately Held**
Web: www.tritonmetalproducts.com
SIC: 3714 Steering mechanisms, motor vehicle

(G-6857)
JD ENGINEERED PRODUCTS LLC
2725 E 500 S (46742-9010)
PHONE.................260 316-2907
Jay Wetzel, *Managing Member*
EMP: 2 **EST:** 2021
SALES (est): 88.97K **Privately Held**
SIC: 3089 Extruded finished plastics products, nec

(G-6858)
MAGITEK LLC
5618 County Road 6 (46742-9730)
PHONE.................260 488-2226
EMP: 8 **EST:** 2009
SALES (est): 513.73K **Privately Held**
Web: www.magitek.com
SIC: 3841 Diagnostic apparatus, medical

(G-6859)
PITTSFIELD PRODUCTS INC
Also Called: Pittsfield of Indiana
7365 S Enterprise Dr (46742-9662)
P.O. Box 126 (46742-0126)
PHONE.................260 488-2124

Charles Ackman, *Brnch Mgr*
EMP: 64
SALES (corp-wide): 19.88MM **Privately Held**
Web: www.pittsfieldproducts.com
SIC: 3569 Filters, general line: industrial
PA: Pittsfield Products, Inc.
160 Dino Dr
Ann Arbor MI 48103
734 665-3771

(G-6860)
PLASTIC PROCESSORS INC
7450 S Homestead Dr (46742-9361)
P.O. Box 508 (46742-0508)
PHONE.................260 488-3999
Jackson Wetzel, *Pr*
Jay Wetzel, *VP*
EMP: 13 **EST:** 1969
SQ FT: 30,000
SALES (est): 2.49MM **Privately Held**
SIC: 3089 Injection molding of plastics

(G-6861)
SCOTT FETZER COMPANY
Also Called: Kirby
7715 S Homestead Dr (46742-9622)
PHONE.................260 488-3531
John Obrien, *Mgr*
EMP: 1
SALES (corp-wide): 226 **Privately Held**
Web: www.scottfetzer.com
SIC: 3634 Personal electrical appliances
PA: The Scott Fetzer Company
28800 Clemens Rd
Westlake OH 44145
440 892-3000

(G-6862)
SUPERIOR CANOPY CORPORATION
2435 E Bellefontaine Rd (46742-9619)
PHONE.................260 488-4065
George Stamper, *Pr*
Ralph Lingo, *Prin*
EMP: 21 **EST:** 1997
SALES (est): 2.4MM **Privately Held**
Web: www.superiorcanopy.com
SIC: 3444 3281 Canopies, sheet metal; Building stone products

(G-6863)
TRITON METAL PRODUCTS INC
7790 S Homestead Dr (46742-9622)
PHONE.................260 488-1800
EMP: 35 **EST:** 2010
SALES (est): 10.2MM
SALES (corp-wide): 10.2MM **Privately Held**
Web: www.tritonmetalproducts.com
SIC: 3441 Fabricated structural metal
PA: Industrial Steering Products, Inc.
7790 S Homestead Dr
Hamilton IN 46742
260 488-1880

Hamlet
Starke County

(G-6864)
NORTON PACKAGING INC
5190 N Industrial Pkwy (46532-9596)
PHONE.................574 867-6002
EMP: 26
SALES (corp-wide): 56.46MM **Privately Held**
Web: www.nortonpackaging.com
SIC: 3089 3411 Plastics containers, except foam; Metal cans
PA: Norton Packaging, Inc.

20670 Corsair Blvd
Hayward CA 94545
510 786-1922

Hammond
Lake County

(G-6865)
18TH STREET DISTILLERY LLC
5417 Oakley Ave Ste 1 (46320)
PHONE..............................219 803-0820
Drew Fox, *Prin*
EMP: 18 **EST:** 2016
SALES (est): 283.76K **Privately Held**
Web: www.18thstreetdistillery.com
SIC: 2085 Distilled and blended liquors

(G-6866)
2 EZ PRICE LLC
4126 Towle Ave (46327-1260)
PHONE..............................312 912-4084
EMP: 1
SALES (est): 69.27K **Privately Held**
SIC: 3743 Freight cars and equipment

(G-6867)
ACCUCRAFT IMAGING INC
5920 Hohman Ave (46320-2423)
PHONE..............................219 933-3007
Leon Dombrowski, *Pr*
EMP: 6 **EST:** 2010
SALES (est): 805.02K **Privately Held**
Web: www.accucraftimaging.com
SIC: 2796 Color separations, for printing

(G-6868)
ADVANTAGE SIGNS INC
6223 Hohman Ave (46324-1055)
PHONE..............................219 853-1427
Bill O'brien, *Prin*
EMP: 8 **EST:** 2009
SALES (est): 72.98K **Privately Held**
SIC: 3993 Signs, not made in custom sign painting shops

(G-6869)
AFFORDABLE SIGN & NEON INC
534 Conkey St Ste 1 (46324-1146)
PHONE..............................219 853-1855
EMP: 3 **EST:** 1995
SALES (est): 244.92K **Privately Held**
Web: www.a1affordablesigns.com
SIC: 3993 Signs and advertising specialties

(G-6870)
ALEXANDER THOMPSON
3348 169th St G137 (46323-2492)
PHONE..............................218 577-7627
Alexander Thompson, *Owner*
EMP: 1 **EST:** 2019
SALES (est): 45K **Privately Held**
SIC: 1389 1522 Construction, repair, and dismantling services; Residential construction, nec

(G-6871)
ALLIN PLASTIC ENGRAVING INC
2845 Garfield Ave (46322-1639)
PHONE..............................219 972-2223
Jacqueline A Jarecki, *Owner*
EMP: 2 **EST:** 1964
SALES (est): 144.07K **Privately Held**
Web: www.allinplasticengraving.com
SIC: 3089 Engraving of plastics

(G-6872)
ALMIRAS BAKERY
2635 169th St (46323-1507)
PHONE..............................219 844-4334
Frank Vantil, *Pr*
Ronald Karner, *
EMP: 10 **EST:** 1949
SQ FT: 4,000
SALES (est): 206.38K **Privately Held**
SIC: 5461 2052 2051 Cakes; Cookies and crackers; Bread, cake, and related products

(G-6873)
AMERICAN FABRICATORS INC
5832 Cline Ave (46323)
P.O. Box 531 (46312)
PHONE..............................219 844-4744
Joseph Fraley, *Pr*
Michael Fraley, *Sec*
EMP: 20 **EST:** 1971
SQ FT: 18,000
SALES (est): 2.4MM **Privately Held**
Web: www.americanfabricators.com
SIC: 3441 Fabricated structural metal

(G-6874)
AMERICAN PRINTING & ADVG INC (PA)
5324 Hohman Ave (46320-1808)
PHONE..............................219 937-1844
Carla Yerga, *Pr*
John Yerga, *VP*
EMP: 15 **EST:** 1980
SQ FT: 12,000
SALES (est): 1.78MM
SALES (corp-wide): 1.78MM **Privately Held**
Web: www.americanprinting4usa.com
SIC: 2752 Offset printing

(G-6875)
AMERICAN STAIR CORP
3510 Calumet Ave (46320-1123)
PHONE..............................815 886-9600
EMP: 6 **EST:** 2019
SALES (est): 281.24K **Privately Held**
Web: www.americanstair.com
SIC: 3441 Fabricated structural metal

(G-6876)
AMERICAN STAIR CORPORATION INC
3510 Calumet Ave (46320-1123)
PHONE..............................800 872-7824
Gordon Fitzsimmons, *Pr*
Ross Johnson, *
EMP: 90 **EST:** 1956
SQ FT: 66,000
SALES (est): 11.34MM **Privately Held**
Web: www.americanstair.com
SIC: 3446 Railings, banisters, guards, etc: made from metal pipe

(G-6877)
AMSTED GRAPHITE MATERIALS LLC
Also Called: Asf Keystones
4831 Hohman Ave (46327-1579)
PHONE..............................219 931-1900
Bob Cantwell, *VP*
EMP: 100
SALES (corp-wide): 3.96B **Privately Held**
Web: www.amstedrail.com
SIC: 3743 Railroad equipment
HQ: Amsted Rail Company, Inc.
311 S Wacker Dr Ste 5300
Chicago IL 60606

(G-6878)
AMSTED RAIL INTERNATIONAL INC
4831 Hohman Ave (46327-1579)
PHONE..............................800 621-8442
EMP: 8 **EST:** 2008
SALES (est): 58.45K **Privately Held**
Web: www.amsted.com
SIC: 3443 Fabricated plate work (boiler shop)

(G-6879)
ANDRE RENEE WRITES PUBG CO LLC
P.O. Box 2246 (46323-0246)
PHONE..............................219 746-4329
EMP: 3 **EST:** 2017
SALES (est): 62.99K **Privately Held**
Web: www.arwrites.com
SIC: 2711 Newspapers

(G-6880)
ART BOOKBINDERS OF AMERICA
5920 Hohman Ave (46320-2423)
PHONE..............................312 226-4100
Joseph Ahner, *Pr*
Mario Poulet, *Pr*
Louis B Poulet, *VP*
Greg Poulet, *Marketing*
EMP: 12 **EST:** 1966
SALES (est): 1.05MM **Privately Held**
Web: www.abofa.com
SIC: 7334 2789 Photocopying and duplicating services; Bookbinding and related work

(G-6881)
BAR PROCESSING CORPORATION
Also Called: Bar Processing of Indiana
4527 Columbia Ave (46327)
PHONE..............................219 931-0702
Dave Johnson, *Mgr*
EMP: 14
SALES (corp-wide): 39.93MM **Privately Held**
Web: www.barprocessingcorp.com
SIC: 3471 5051 3444 Finishing, metals or formed products; Metals service centers and offices; Sheet metalwork
HQ: Bar Processing Corporation
26601 W Huron River Dr
Flat Rock MI 48134
734 782-4454

(G-6882)
BEATTY INTERNATIONAL INC (PA)
940 150th St (46327-1805)
PHONE..............................219 931-3000
William C Beatty, *Pr*
Phyllis Henkelmann, *
Phillip Beatty, *
Brian Beatty, *
Deborah Wilson, *
EMP: 25 **EST:** 1917
SQ FT: 180,000
SALES (est): 8.76MM **Privately Held**
Web: www.scrapintl.com
SIC: 3599 3542 3569 5084 Machine shop, jobbing and repair; Punching and shearing machines; Bridge or gate machinery, hydraulic; Metalworking machinery

(G-6883)
BEATTY MACHINE & MFG CO
940 150th St (46327-1805)
PHONE..............................219 931-3000
William C Beatty, *Pr*
Brian Beatty, *VP*
Deborah Wilson, *Asst Tr*
EMP: 25 **EST:** 1917
SQ FT: 125,000
SALES (est): 2.34MM **Privately Held**
Web: www.beattymachine.com
SIC: 3599 3542 Machine shop, jobbing and repair; Punching and shearing machines
PA: Beatty International, Inc
940 150th St
Hammond IN 46327

(G-6884)
BEEMSTERBOER SLAG CORP (PA)
3411 Sheffield Ave (46327)
PHONE..............................773 785-6000
Alan Beemsterboer, *Prin*
Alan Beemsterboer, *Pr*
Simon Beemsterboer, *
Michael Beemsterboer, *
Peter Beemsterboer, *
EMP: 25 **EST:** 1953
SALES (est): 20.99MM
SALES (corp-wide): 20.99MM **Privately Held**
Web: www.beemcompanies.com
SIC: 3295 Minerals, ground or treated

(G-6885)
BEMCOR INC
940 150th St (46327-1805)
PHONE..............................219 937-1600
Willian C Beatty, *CEO*
Daniel J Lazar, *Pr*
Brian Beatty, *VP*
Phyllis Henkelmann, *Sec*
Deborah Wilson, *Asst Tr*
EMP: 15 **EST:** 1981
SQ FT: 18,000
SALES (est): 4.99MM **Privately Held**
Web: www.bemcor.com
SIC: 3569 3599 5084 3542 Bridge or gate machinery, hydraulic; Machine shop, jobbing and repair; Metalworking machinery ; Machine tools, metal forming type
PA: Beatty International, Inc
940 150th St
Hammond IN 46327

(G-6886)
BERGREN & ASSOCIATES
481 Fayette St (46320-1841)
PHONE..............................219 852-1500
Bob Bergren, *Prin*
EMP: 1 **EST:** 2013
SALES (est): 62.97K **Privately Held**
SIC: 7692 Welding repair

(G-6887)
BLUE DOLPHIN FFY LLC
3348 169th St Ste G137 (46323-2492)
PHONE..............................773 255-3591
Teia Thompson, *Managing Member*
EMP: 2 **EST:** 2021
SALES (est): 148.35K **Privately Held**
SIC: 2051 7389 Bakery: wholesale or wholesale/retail combined; Business services, nec

(G-6888)
BRITTANY HORNSBY
Also Called: Bear Enterprise
7240 Northcote Ave (46324-2229)
PHONE..............................219 789-0984
Brittany Hornsby, *Owner*
EMP: 1 **EST:** 2020
SALES (est): 42.55K **Privately Held**
SIC: 2389 Apparel and accessories, nec

(G-6889)
CADE CARRIER SOLUTIONS INC
6430 Moraine Ave (46324-1037)
PHONE..............................312 953-5154
Debra L Armand-cade, *CEO*
EMP: 2 **EST:** 2019
SALES (est): 190.99K **Privately Held**
Web: www.ccs4transport.com
SIC: 3537 Trucks, tractors, loaders, carriers, and similar equipment

Hammond - Lake County (G-6890)

(G-6890)
CALBRITE INDUSTRIES
2207 165th St (46320-2904)
PHONE...............................219 844-6800
EMP: 8 EST: 2016
SALES (est): 90.89K **Privately Held**
Web: www.unitedfruit.org
SIC: 3312 Stainless steel

(G-6891)
CALUMET BREWERIES INC
6535 Osborne Ave (46320-2998)
PHONE...............................219 845-2242
John J Kiernan, *Pr*
Mark J Kiernan, *
▲ EMP: 45 EST: 1930
SQ FT: 80,000
SALES (est): 5.25MM **Privately Held**
Web: www.calbrew.com
SIC: 2082 5149 5181 Beer (alcoholic beverage); Groceries and related products, nec; Beer and ale

(G-6892)
CANDICE JEFFERSON
Also Called: Heads Up Bundles
220 Wildwood Rd Apt 201 (46324-1050)
PHONE...............................219 315-8629
Candice Jefferson, *Owner*
EMP: 3 EST: 2020
SALES (est): 83.91K **Privately Held**
SIC: 3999 Hair and hair-based products

(G-6893)
CAPRICORN FOODS LLC
6412 Forest Ave (46324-1015)
PHONE...............................219 670-1872
Gregory Lawson Stephan, *Pr*
EMP: 5 EST: 2015
SALES (est): 402.86K **Privately Held**
Web: www.capricornfoods.com
SIC: 2023 Condensed, concentrated, and evaporated milk products

(G-6894)
CAPS INC
6945 Forest Ave (46324-1423)
PHONE...............................773 859-0111
EMP: 7 EST: 2010
SALES (est): 167.03K **Privately Held**
SIC: 3089 Injection molding of plastics

(G-6895)
CARGILL INCORPORATED
Also Called: Cargill
1100 Indianapolis Blvd (46320-1019)
PHONE...............................402 533-4227
Jim Fritz, *Prin*
EMP: 260
SALES (corp-wide): 159.59B **Privately Held**
Web: www.cargill.com
SIC: 2048 2075 2046 2011 Prepared feeds, nec; Soybean oil, cake or meal; Corn oil, refined; Meat packing plants
PA: Cargill, Incorporated
   15407 Mcginty Rd W
   Wayzata MN 55391
   800 227-4455

(G-6896)
CASSIE CAKES LLC
3824 170th St (46323-2528)
PHONE...............................219 308-3320
EMP: 1 EST: 2021
SALES (est): 39.59K **Privately Held**
SIC: 2051 Cakes, bakery: except frozen

(G-6897)
CENTER FOR ETHCAL RBTICS A NNT ◆
5530 Sohl Ave (46320-9998)
PHONE...............................219 741-9374
EMP: 4 EST: 2023
SALES (est): 60.98K **Privately Held**
Web: www.cerain2023.org
SIC: 7371 3699 8299 Software programming applications; Security control equipment and systems; Educational service, nondegree granting: continuing educ.

(G-6898)
CENTRIFUGE CHICAGO CORPORATION
Also Called: Centrifuge Chicago
6015 Hump Rd (46320)
PHONE...............................219 852-5200
Douglas E Rivich, *Pr*
John Bargoz, *VP*
EMP: 7 EST: 2000
SQ FT: 3,500
SALES (est): 991.05K **Privately Held**
Web: www.centrifugechicago.com
SIC: 3569 Centrifuges, industrial

(G-6899)
CITRINE DISPATCH LLC
7603 Catalpa Ave (46324-3116)
PHONE...............................219 689-8293
EMP: 2 EST: 2020
SALES (est): 95.58K **Privately Held**
SIC: 3537 Trucks: freight, baggage, etc.: industrial, except mining

(G-6900)
CJ PRINTING
9445 Indianapolis Blvd Ste F (46322-2648)
PHONE...............................219 924-1685
Chuck Pease, *Owner*
EMP: 4 EST: 2008
SALES (est): 255.04K **Privately Held**
Web: www.cjprinting.com
SIC: 2752 Offset printing

(G-6901)
CJS MUZIC COMPANY-THE SPOT LLC
5258 Hohman Ave (46320-1722)
PHONE...............................219 487-9873
Charles Parker Junior, *CEO*
EMP: 2 EST: 2018
SALES (est): 41.08K **Privately Held**
SIC: 7389 3931 7929 8999 Music recording producer; Musical instruments; Musician; Music arranging and composing

(G-6902)
CKMT ASSOCIATES INC
Also Called: Calumet Press, The
6405 Olcott St (46320-2835)
PHONE...............................219 924-2820
Philip E Cartwright Ph.d., *Pr*
Philip E Cartwright Ph.d., *Pr*
Cean Cartwright, *
Konnie Kuiper, *Stockholder*
Randy Minas, *Stockholder*
EMP: 16 EST: 1938
SQ FT: 6,200
SALES (est): 232.27K **Privately Held**
Web: www.wjobcalpress.com
SIC: 2711 2791 2789 2752 Commercial printing and newspaper publishing combined; Typesetting; Bookbinding and related work; Commercial printing, lithographic

(G-6903)
CLINTON PARKER
Also Called: White ARC Welding
6341 Indianapolis Blvd (46320-2230)
PHONE...............................219 877-5096
Clinton Parker, *Owner*
EMP: 1 EST: 2011
SALES (est): 79K **Privately Held**
Web: www.whitearcwelding.com
SIC: 7692 Welding repair

(G-6904)
CONOPCO INC
1200 Calumet Ave (46320-1015)
PHONE...............................219 659-3200
Louie Gibuffone, *Mgr*
EMP: 73
SQ FT: 25,000
SALES (corp-wide): 64.79B **Privately Held**
Web: www.conopco.com
SIC: 2844 Perfumes, cosmetics and other toilet preparations
HQ: Conopco, Inc.
   700 Sylvan Ave
   Englewood Cliffs NJ 07632
   201 894-7760

(G-6905)
CONTROL CONSULTANTS OF AMERICA (PA)
Also Called: Ccoa of Indiana
3800 179th St (46323-3035)
PHONE...............................219 989-3311
▼ EMP: 5 EST: 1996
SALES (est): 612.99K **Privately Held**
SIC: 3613 3625 Control panels, electric; Control equipment, electric

(G-6906)
CR PUBLICATIONS
640 Conkey St (46324-1142)
P.O. Box 2097 (46323-0097)
PHONE...............................219 931-6700
Jake Jacobs, *Mgr*
EMP: 5 EST: 2007
SALES (est): 263.74K **Privately Held**
Web: www.crpubnwi.com
SIC: 2721 2731 8748 Magazines: publishing only, not printed on site; Book publishing; Business consulting, nec

(G-6907)
CR PUBLICATIONS
7103 Kennedy Ave (46323)
PHONE...............................219 931-6700
EMP: 3 EST: 2020
SALES (est): 106.89K **Privately Held**
Web: www.crpubnwi.com
SIC: 2741 Miscellaneous publishing

(G-6908)
CSA RACKING LLC ◆
6650 Arizona Ave (46323-1619)
PHONE...............................414 241-3585
Yonie Castillanos, *Pr*
EMP: 5 EST: 2022
SALES (est): 62.01K **Privately Held**
SIC: 1541 1799 1389 5046 Warehouse construction; Welding on site; Construction, repair, and dismantling services; Shelving, commercial and industrial

(G-6909)
CUSTOM DRAPERIES OF INDIANA
Also Called: Hammond Drapery
7205 Calumet Ave (46324-2407)
PHONE...............................219 924-2500
Samuel R Gershman, *Pr*
EMP: 9 EST: 1945
SALES (est): 509.23K **Privately Held**
SIC: 2391 2591 2431 Draperies, plastic and textile: from purchased materials; Drapery hardware and window blinds and shades; Millwork

(G-6910)
D & D INDUSTRIES INC
Also Called: Calumet Surface Hardening
6805 Mccook Ave (46323-1554)
PHONE...............................219 844-5600
Don Doffin, *Pr*
Don Doffin Junior, *VP*
EMP: 9 EST: 1962
SQ FT: 12,500
SALES (est): 817.42K **Privately Held**
SIC: 3398 Brazing (hardening) of metal

(G-6911)
DAVIES-IMPERIAL COATINGS INC
1275 State St (46320-1633)
P.O. Box 790 (46325-0790)
PHONE...............................219 933-0877
Imes Todd, *Pr*
Davies Donn T, *
Adele Davies, *
Joann Davies, *
▲ EMP: 25 EST: 1968
SQ FT: 55,000
SALES (est): 4.47MM **Privately Held**
Web: www.daviesimperial.com
SIC: 2851 2819 2891 Paints and paint additives; Industrial inorganic chemicals, nec; Adhesives and sealants

(G-6912)
DEBRA M LEWIS
Also Called: Bake-A-Batch
6630 Jefferson Ave (46324-1542)
P.O. Box 3312 (46321-0312)
PHONE...............................219 937-4240
Debra Lewis, *Prin*
EMP: 1 EST: 2004
SALES (est): 64.6K **Privately Held**
SIC: 2052 Cookies

(G-6913)
DIETRICH INDUSTRIES INC
1435 165th Street (46320-2816)
PHONE...............................219 931-6344
Tim Short, *Mgr*
EMP: 150
SALES (corp-wide): 1.25B **Publicly Held**
SIC: 3316 3312 3444 3443 Cold finishing of steel shapes; Blast furnaces and steel mills; Sheet metalwork; Fabricated plate work (boiler shop)
HQ: Dietrich Industries, Inc.
   200 W Old Wlson Bridge Rd
   Worthington OH 43085
   800 873-2604

(G-6914)
DOVER CHEMICAL CORPORATION
Also Called: Hammond Works
3000 Sheffield Ave (46327-1013)
PHONE...............................219 852-0042
Robert Glaze, *Prin*
EMP: 3
SALES (corp-wide): 2.03B **Privately Held**
Web: www.doverchem.com
SIC: 2819 2869 Industrial inorganic chemicals, nec; Industrial organic chemicals, nec
HQ: Dover Chemical Corporation
   3676 Davis Rd Nw
   Dover OH 44622
   330 343-7711

GEOGRAPHIC SECTION

Hammond - Lake County (G-6941)

(G-6915)
DOW THEORY FORECASTS INC
7412 Calumet Ave (46324-2692)
PHONE...................................219 931-6480
Charles Carlson, *CEO*
Cheryl Evans, *
EMP: 29 **EST:** 1946
SQ FT: 17,000
SALES (est): 202.51K **Privately Held**
Web: www.horizoninvestment.com
SIC: 2741 7311 Business service newsletters: publishing and printing; Advertising agencies
PA: Horizon Management Services, Inc.
 7412 Calumet Ave
 Hammond IN 46324

(G-6916)
DSM PUBLICATIONS
5430 White Oak Ave (46320-1441)
PHONE...................................312 730-7375
EMP: 4 **EST:** 2018
SALES (est): 68.16K **Privately Held**
SIC: 2741 Miscellaneous publishing

(G-6917)
E Z CHOICE
5529 Calumet Ave (46320-2019)
PHONE...................................219 852-4281
EMP: 2 **EST:** 2007
SALES (est): 233.44K **Privately Held**
SIC: 1389 Excavating slush pits and cellars

(G-6918)
EARTHLY-LOVE
267 Dyer Blvd (46320-3011)
PHONE...................................708 896-0191
EMP: 5 **EST:** 2016
SALES (est): 48.86K **Privately Held**
Web: www.earthlyloveimports.com
SIC: 2844 Perfumes, cosmetics and other toilet preparations

(G-6919)
ECO SERVICES OPERATIONS CORP
2000 Michigan St (46320-1462)
PHONE...................................219 932-7651
Greg Yates, *Brnch Mgr*
EMP: 42
SALES (corp-wide): 691.12MM **Publicly Held**
Web: www.pqcorp.com
SIC: 2819 2812 2865 2869 Boric acid; Soda ash, sodium carbonate (anhydrous); Phenol, alkylated and cumene; Fluorinated hydrocarbon gases
HQ: Eco Services Operations Corp.
 300 Lindenwood Dr
 Malvern PA 19355
 610 251-9118

(G-6920)
ECONOMY SIGNS INCORPORATED
Also Called: Economy Signs
546 Conkey St (46324-1153)
PHONE...................................219 932-1233
Walt Swets, *Pr*
▲ **EMP:** 7 **EST:** 1983
SALES (est): 839.45K **Privately Held**
Web: www.economysignsinc.com
SIC: 5099 3993 Signs, except electric; Signs and advertising specialties

(G-6921)
EDS TEEZ LLC
6312 Madison Ave Apt 2 (46324-1266)
PHONE...................................224 518-3388
Charde Woods, *CEO*
EMP: 1 **EST:** 2018
SALES (est): 45.04K **Privately Held**

SIC: 2396 Fabric printing and stamping

(G-6922)
ELECTRIC MOTOR SERVICES INC (PA)
6350 Indianapolis Blvd (46320-2231)
PHONE...................................219 931-2850
Joseph Kotso, *Pr*
Michael Kotso, *
Hector Graciano, *
Albert Burgos, *
EMP: 36 **EST:** 2005
SQ FT: 40,000
SALES (est): 10.56MM
SALES (corp-wide): 10.56MM **Privately Held**
Web: www.electricmotorservices.net
SIC: 7694 Electric motor repair

(G-6923)
ELECTRO-TECH INC
5334 Sohl Ave (46320-1615)
PHONE...................................219 937-0826
Pete Bambic, *Pr*
Rudy Bambic, *VP*
EMP: 8 **EST:** 1998
SALES (est): 934.77K **Privately Held**
Web: www.electro-tech-inc.com
SIC: 3599 Machine shop, jobbing and repair

(G-6924)
ELEVATED CNSTR GROUP LLC
405 Florence St (46324-1329)
PHONE...................................708 731-7232
EMP: 1 **EST:** 2020
SALES (est): 61.64K **Privately Held**
SIC: 1389 Construction, repair, and dismantling services

(G-6925)
FAITH NICOLE PUBLICATIONS LLC
477 Roosevelt Ct (46320-1259)
P.O. Box 515 (46325-0515)
PHONE...................................708 238-3101
Faith Nicole Hardy, *Prin*
EMP: 4 **EST:** 2019
SALES (est): 75.6K **Privately Held**
Web: www.purplediamondsinc.com
SIC: 2741 Miscellaneous publishing

(G-6926)
FATHER SON SANDERS TRNSPT LLC
7925 Belmont Ave (46324-3314)
PHONE...................................773 899-8078
EMP: 1
SALES (est): 54.62K **Privately Held**
SIC: 3799 7389 Transportation equipment, nec; Business Activities at Non-Commercial Site

(G-6927)
FELICIA FR8 LLC ✪
3831 Hohman Ave Pmb 1058 (46327-1160)
PHONE...................................312 597-9282
Lance Taylor, *Admn*
EMP: 1 **EST:** 2023
SALES (est): 69.27K **Privately Held**
SIC: 3799 3537 Transportation equipment, nec; Trucks, tractors, loaders, carriers, and similar equipment

(G-6928)
FIBERX INCORPORATED
Also Called: Fiberx Products
7150 Indianapolis Blvd (46324-2245)
PHONE...................................317 501-5619
EMP: 6
SALES (est): 78.58K **Privately Held**

SIC: 3533 Oil and gas field machinery

(G-6929)
FLAGSHIP SIGN SUPPLY LLC
Also Called: Flagship Sign Supply
532 Conkey St (46324-1153)
PHONE...................................708 474-9521
Stephen Hinds, *VP*
EMP: 5 **EST:** 2011
SALES (est): 120.28K **Privately Held**
Web: www.flagshipsignsupply.com
SIC: 3643 Lamp sockets and receptacles (electric wiring devices)

(G-6930)
FLAGSTONE VILLAGE LLC
1402 173rd St (46324-2861)
PHONE...................................219 989-3265
EMP: 6 **EST:** 2014
SALES (est): 243.27K **Privately Held**
Web: www.flagstonevillage.net
SIC: 3281 Flagstones

(G-6931)
FLAT ROCK
6732 Calumet Ave (46324-1646)
PHONE...................................219 852-5262
EMP: 4 **EST:** 2007
SALES (est): 219.24K **Privately Held**
Web: www.flatrockymca.org
SIC: 2599 Bar, restaurant and cafeteria furniture

(G-6932)
FLYING TURTLE PUBLISHING INC
7216 Birch Ave (46324-2449)
PHONE...................................219 221-8488
Mari L Barnes, *Admn*
EMP: 2 **EST:** 2010
SALES (est): 109.64K **Privately Held**
Web: www.flyingturtlepublishing.com
SIC: 2741 Miscellaneous publishing

(G-6933)
FUENTES DISTRIBUTING INC
6811 New Hampshire Ave (46323-1959)
PHONE...................................219 808-2147
Dave Fuentes, *Owner*
EMP: 2 **EST:** 1996
SALES (est): 192.39K **Privately Held**
SIC: 3537 Trucks: freight, baggage, etc.: industrial, except mining

(G-6934)
GALLOWELD LLC
3831 Hohman Ave (46327-1160)
PHONE...................................219 215-2006
Tyrone Galloway Senior, *CEO*
EMP: 6 **EST:** 2021
SALES (est): 66.9K **Privately Held**
SIC: 7692 Welding repair

(G-6935)
GOGOLAKS ENGRAVING
8620 Beech Ave (46321-2605)
PHONE...................................219 972-3995
Joe Gogolak, *Owner*
EMP: 1 **EST:** 2000
SALES (est): 64.23K **Privately Held**
SIC: 2759 Engraving, nec

(G-6936)
GRACE TO GROW PUBLICATIONS
507 State St (46320-1533)
PHONE...................................219 932-0711
EMP: 6 **EST:** 2019
SALES (est): 102.8K **Privately Held**
Web: www.gracetogrow.com
SIC: 2741 Miscellaneous publishing

(G-6937)
H A INDUSTRIES
4527 Columbia Ave (46327-1666)
PHONE...................................219 931-6304
Dick Mork, *Pr*
◆ **EMP:** 8 **EST:** 2003
SALES (est): 909.23K **Privately Held**
Web: www.castlemetals.com
SIC: 3999 Barber and beauty shop equipment

(G-6938)
HAMMOND GROUP INC (PA)
Also Called: Halstab
2901 Carlson Dr Ste 200 (46323-1191)
P.O. Box 6408 (46325-6408)
PHONE...................................219 931-9360
Terry Murphy, *Pr*
Stephen A Bolanowski Junior, *Sec*
Gordon C Beckley, *VP*
Gerry Kaoukis, *CFO*
◆ **EMP:** 15 **EST:** 1930
SALES (est): 106.52MM
SALES (corp-wide): 106.52MM **Privately Held**
Web: www.hammondglobal.com
SIC: 2819 Lead compounds or salts, inorganic, not used in pigments

(G-6939)
HAMMOND GROUP INC
Also Called: Halstab Division
3100 Michigan St (46323-1268)
PHONE...................................219 931-9360
Mark Labovitz, *Brnch Mgr*
EMP: 1
SALES (corp-wide): 106.52MM **Privately Held**
Web: www.amstabilizers.com
SIC: 3499 3356 2865 Stabilizing bars (cargo), metal; Nonferrous rolling and drawing, nec; Cyclic crudes and intermediates
PA: Hammond Group, Inc.
 2901 Carlson Dr Ste 200
 Hammond IN 46323
 219 931-9360

(G-6940)
HAMMOND GROUP INC
Also Called: Hammond Lead Products
2323 165th St (46320-2906)
P.O. Box 6408 (46325-6408)
PHONE...................................219 845-0031
EMP: 21
SALES (corp-wide): 106.52MM **Privately Held**
Web: www.hammondglobal.com
SIC: 3441 3356 Expansion joints (structural shapes), iron or steel; Nonferrous rolling and drawing, nec
PA: Hammond Group, Inc.
 2901 Carlson Dr Ste 200
 Hammond IN 46323
 219 931-9360

(G-6941)
HAMMOND LEAD PRODUCTS LLC
2901 Carlson Dr (46323-1191)
PHONE...................................219 931-9360
▲ **EMP:** 31 **EST:** 2001
SALES (est): 323.49K
SALES (corp-wide): 106.52MM **Privately Held**
Web: www.hammondglobal.com
SIC: 3356 Lead and lead alloy: rolling, drawing, or extruding
PA: Hammond Group, Inc.
 2901 Carlson Dr Ste 200
 Hammond IN 46323
 219 931-9360

(PA)=Parent Co (HQ)=Headquarters
✪ = New Business established in last 2 years

Hammond - Lake County (G-6942)

(G-6942)
HAMMOND MACHINE WORKS INC
5047 Columbia Ave (46327-1760)
PHONE.....................................219 933-0479
EMP: 35 EST: 1908
SALES (est): 8.95MM Privately Held
Web: www.hammondmachine.com
SIC: 3599 7692 3443 Machine shop, jobbing and repair; Welding repair; Fabricated plate work (boiler shop)

(G-6943)
HAMMOND STEEL COMPONENTS LLC
3200 Sheffield Ave (46327-1001)
PHONE.....................................630 816-1343
EMP: 10 EST: 2017
SALES (est): 605.81K Privately Held
Web: www.berlinmetals.com
SIC: 3315 Steel wire and related products

(G-6944)
HANGER PRSTHETCS & ORTHO INC
7324 Indianapolis Blvd (46324-2908)
PHONE.....................................219 844-2021
Brian Steinbeger, Mgr
EMP: 10
SALES (corp-wide): 1.12B Privately Held
Web: corporate.hanger.com
SIC: 3842 5999 Limbs, artificial; Orthopedic and prosthesis applications
HQ: Hanger Prosthetics & Orthotics, Inc.
10910 Domain Dr Ste 300
Austin TX 78758
512 777-3800

(G-6945)
HETTY INCORPORATED
Also Called: Miss Print
6937 Calumet Ave (46324-2045)
PHONE.....................................219 933-0833
Rick Baltensberger, Prin
EMP: 5
SALES (corp-wide): 925.39K Privately Held
Web: www.missprintindiana.com
SIC: 2752 7336 2791 2789 Offset printing; Graphic arts and related design; Typesetting; Bookbinding and related work
PA: Hetty Incorporated
8244 Calumet Ave
Munster IN 46321
219 836-2517

(G-6946)
HOLBA TRUCKING AND TRANSPORT
3241 176th St (46323-2718)
PHONE.....................................219 381-4236
Joemarre Holba, Pr
EMP: 1 EST: 2021
SALES (est): 50K Privately Held
SIC: 3537 Trucks, tractors, loaders, carriers, and similar equipment

(G-6947)
HOOSIER ROLL SHOP SERVICES LLC
7020 Cline Ave (46323-2502)
PHONE.....................................219 844-8077
EMP: 14 EST: 2004
SALES (est): 1.21MM Privately Held
SIC: 3547 Rolling mill machinery

(G-6948)
HORIZON MANAGEMENT SVCS INC (PA)
7412 Calumet Ave (46324-2656)
PHONE.....................................219 852-3200
EMP: 1 EST: 1995
SQ FT: 18,000
SALES (est): 2.43MM Privately Held
Web: www.horizoninvestment.com
SIC: 2741 Business service newsletters: publishing and printing

(G-6949)
HORIZON PUBLISHING COMPANY LLC
Also Called: Horizon Publishing Co
7412 Calumet Ave Ste 1 (46324-2657)
PHONE.....................................219 852-3200
Robert T Evans, Pr
EMP: 10 EST: 1998
SALES (est): 2.87MM Privately Held
Web: www.horizonpublishing.com
SIC: 6282 2731 2721 2741 Investment advice; Book publishing; Periodicals; Miscellaneous publishing

(G-6950)
HUHTAMAKI INC
Also Called: Huhtamaki Foodservice
6629 Indianapolis Blvd (46320-2833)
PHONE.....................................219 972-4264
Rich Blastic, Brnch Mgr
EMP: 110
SQ FT: 26,000
SALES (corp-wide): 4.53B Privately Held
Web: www.huhtamaki.com
SIC: 2621 2823 2671 Molded pulp products; Cellulosic manmade fibers; Paper; coated and laminated packaging
HQ: Huhtamaki, Inc.
9201 Packaging Dr
De Soto KS 66018
913 583-3025

(G-6951)
ICL SPECIALTY PRODUCTS INC
Also Called: Halox Division
6530 Schneider St (46320-2900)
PHONE.....................................219 933-1560
Ray Rex, Brnch Mgr
EMP: 1
Web: www.hammondglobal.com
SIC: 2816 2865 2851 Inorganic pigments; Cyclic crudes and intermediates; Paints and allied products
HQ: Icl Specialty Products Inc.
622 Emerson Rd Ste 500
Saint Louis MO 63141
314 983-7500

(G-6952)
ICL SPECIALTY PRODUCTS INC
Halox
1326 Summer St (46320-2240)
PHONE.....................................219 933-1560
Micheal Wagner, Brnch Mgr
EMP: 47
Web: www.halox.com
SIC: 2819 Lead compounds or salts, inorganic, not used in pigments
HQ: Perimeter Solutions Lp
8000 Maryland Ave Ste 350
Saint Louis MO 63105
314 983-7500

(G-6953)
IES SUBSIDIARY HOLDINGS INC
1825 Summer St (46320-2237)
PHONE.....................................219 937-0100
Fran Finn, Off Mgr
EMP: 1
Web: www.iesci.net
SIC: 3264 7694 Magnets, permanent: ceramic or ferrite; Motor repair services
HQ: Ies Subsidiary Holdings, Inc
5433 Westheimer Rd # 500
Houston TX 77056
713 860-1500

(G-6954)
ILLIANA REMEDIAL ACTION INC
6550 Osborne Ave (46320-2913)
PHONE.....................................219 844-4862
James Hough, Pr
EMP: 9 EST: 1989
SQ FT: 4,500
SALES (est): 1.09MM Privately Held
SIC: 1442 Sand mining

(G-6955)
INDUSTRIAL TOOL & MFG CO
4901 Calumet Ave (46327-1898)
PHONE.....................................219 932-8670
Stanley Sobilo Junior, Pr
EMP: 7 EST: 1947
SQ FT: 14,000
SALES (est): 880K Privately Held
SIC: 3599 Machine shop, jobbing and repair

(G-6956)
INSULATION FABRICATORS INC (DH)
2501 165th St Ste 3 (46320-2933)
PHONE.....................................219 845-2008
Ted Mcnabb, Pr
EMP: 70 EST: 1979
SQ FT: 15,000
SALES (est): 9.86MM
SALES (corp-wide): 5.19B Publicly Held
Web: www.distributioninternational.com
SIC: 5033 3296 Mineral wool insulation materials; Fiberglass insulation
HQ: Distribution International, Inc.
601 Jefferson St Ste 600
Houston TX 77002
800 231-3454

(G-6957)
INTEREBAR FABRICATORS LLC
4531 Columbia Ave Ste C (46327-1666)
PHONE.....................................630 701-9204
EMP: 14
SALES (corp-wide): 2.42MM Privately Held
Web: www.interebar.com
SIC: 3441 Fabricated structural metal
PA: Interebar Fabricators, Llc
10800 Biscayne Blvd # 830
Miami FL 33161
305 705-0208

(G-6958)
INTERNATIONAL LIGHTING LLC
Also Called: Interlight
7939 New Jersey Ave (46323-3040)
PHONE.....................................219 989-0060
◆ EMP: 15 EST: 1992
SALES (est): 5.05MM Privately Held
Web: www.interlightus.com
SIC: 5063 3641 Light bulbs and related supplies; Electric lamps and parts for generalized applications

(G-6959)
INTERNATIONAL PAPER COMPANY
Also Called: International Paper
2501 165th St Ste 3 (46320-2933)
PHONE.....................................219 844-6509
Phil Glenn, Mgr
EMP: 6
SALES (corp-wide): 18.02B Publicly Held
Web: www.internationalpaper.com
SIC: 2621 Paper mills
PA: International Paper Company
6400 Poplar Ave
Memphis TN 38197
901 419-7000

(G-6960)
ITS FAMILY TRUCKING LLC ✪
7121 Alexander Ave (46323-2110)
PHONE.....................................219 277-7162
EMP: 1 EST: 2022
SALES (est): 69.27K Privately Held
SIC: 3537 7389 Trucks: freight, baggage, etc.: industrial, except mining; Business services, nec

(G-6961)
JANETTE WALKER
1050 Eaton St (46320-2613)
PHONE.....................................219 937-9160
Jeanette Walker, Prin
EMP: 2 EST: 2007
SALES (est): 77.18K Privately Held
SIC: 3911 Jewelry, precious metal

(G-6962)
JUPITER ALUMINUM CORPORATION (PA)
1745 165th St Ste 6 (46320)
PHONE.....................................219 932-3322
Paul-henri Chevalier, Pr
Loren Jahn, *
Erika Gross Same, Sec
▲ EMP: 162 EST: 1992
SQ FT: 7,000
SALES (est): 77.49MM Privately Held
Web: www.jupiteraluminum.com
SIC: 3353 3354 Aluminum sheet, plate, and foil; Coils, rod, extruded, aluminum

(G-6963)
JVI INC
47 Ruth St Apt 2 (46320-2335)
PHONE.....................................872 276-0823
John Eric Vinson, CEO
EMP: 1 EST: 2020
SALES (est): 150K Privately Held
Web: www.jvi-inc.com
SIC: 3537 Trucks, tractors, loaders, carriers, and similar equipment

(G-6964)
K&D&S TRUCKING AND REALITY LLC
823 174th Pl (46324-2717)
PHONE.....................................847 791-6848
Kevin Mcdowell Junior, Pr
EMP: 5 EST: 2021
SALES (est): 125.41K Privately Held
SIC: 1389 Construction, repair, and dismantling services

(G-6965)
KAZMIER TOOLING INC
3039 169th Pl (46323-2346)
PHONE.....................................773 586-0300
Shawn J Ofarrell, Pr
Brian O Farrell, Sec
EMP: 8 EST: 1990
SALES (est): 890.67K Privately Held
Web: www.kazmiertooling.com
SIC: 3544 Special dies and tools

(G-6966)
KEIL CHEMICAL CORPORATION
3000 Sheffield Ave (46327-1013)
PHONE.....................................219 931-2630
Dwain Colvin, Pr
EMP: 47 EST: 2003
SALES (est): 3.9MM
SALES (corp-wide): 2.03B Privately Held
Web: www.doverchem.com
SIC: 2911 2992 Fuel additives; Lubricating oils and greases
HQ: Dover Chemical Corporation
3676 Davis Rd Nw

GEOGRAPHIC SECTION

Hammond - Lake County (G-6993)

Dover OH 44622
330 343-7711

(G-6967)
L AND P BROTHERS
7238 Oakdale Ave (46324-2446)
PHONE..............................219 313-6946
EMP: 3 **EST:** 2018
SALES (est): 83.91K **Privately Held**
SIC: 2752 Commercial printing, lithographic

(G-6968)
LANSING MTLLIZING GRINDING INC
Also Called: Lansing Metalizing & Grinding
4742 Calumet Ave (46327-1610)
PHONE..............................219 931-1785
Thomas Alb, *Pr*
Cheryl Alb, *VP*
Rayn Alb, *Sec*
EMP: 2 **EST:** 1968
SQ FT: 6,200
SALES (est): 217.78K **Privately Held**
Web: www.lansingmetallizing.com
SIC: 3479 3599 Coating of metals and formed products; Machine shop, jobbing and repair

(G-6969)
LEAR CORPORATION
2204 Michigan St (46320-1463)
PHONE..............................219 852-0014
EMP: 500
SALES (corp-wide): 23.47B **Publicly Held**
Web: www.lear.com
SIC: 3714 2531 Motor vehicle parts and accessories; Public building and related furniture
PA: Lear Corporation
21557 Telegraph Rd
Southfield MI 48033
248 447-1500

(G-6970)
LEE REED HOLDINGS LLC
Also Called: Lee Reed Embroidery
4737 Towle Ave (46327)
PHONE..............................219 255-0555
Jacob Reed, *Owner*
Jacob Reed, *Managing Member*
EMP: 1 **EST:** 2019
SALES (est): 54.26K **Privately Held**
Web: www.leereedembroidery.com
SIC: 2397 2759 3552 2211 Schiffli machine embroideries; Screen printing; Embroidery machines; Apparel and outerwear fabrics, cotton

(G-6971)
LEWIS & LEE PRESENTS LLC
3916 Torrence Ave (46327-1144)
PHONE..............................219 484-5298
EMP: 1
SALES (est): 65.99K **Privately Held**
SIC: 2517 7389 Wood television and radio cabinets; Business Activities at Non-Commercial Site

(G-6972)
LIONS QUARTER LLC
635 165th St (46324-1336)
PHONE..............................219 932-5531
EMP: 1 **EST:** 2010
SALES (est): 67.29K **Privately Held**
Web: lionsquarterstore.company.site
SIC: 2731 7929 7389 Books, publishing only; Popular music groups or artists; Music recording producer

(G-6973)
LMR INDUSTRIES LLC
930 165th St (46324-1325)
PHONE..............................219 765-4157
EMP: 1 **EST:** 2016
SALES (est): 80.51K **Privately Held**
SIC: 3541 Vertical turning and boring machines (metalworking)

(G-6974)
M-FAMOUZ LOGISTICS LLC
6616 Jefferson Ave (46324-1542)
PHONE..............................219 501-1921
EMP: 3 **EST:** 2020
SALES (est): 110K **Privately Held**
SIC: 3537 Trucks: freight, baggage, etc.: industrial, except mining

(G-6975)
MAGNETECH INDUSTRIAL SVCS INC
1825 Summer St (46320-2237)
PHONE..............................219 937-0100
Fran Finn, *Mgr*
EMP: 6 **EST:** 2010
SALES (est): 774.46K **Publicly Held**
Web: www.magnetech.com
SIC: 7694 Electric motor repair
PA: ies Holdings, Inc.
2 Riverway Ste 1730
Houston TX 77056

(G-6976)
MALLANG SPA ESSENTIALS
923 Field St (46320-2537)
PHONE..............................219 902-9788
EMP: 4 **EST:** 2013
SALES (est): 39.69K **Privately Held**
SIC: 3999 Candles

(G-6977)
MARI MANU CORP ✪
2929 Carlson Dr (46323)
PHONE..............................219 804-3294
Shomari Wright, *Pr*
EMP: 1 **EST:** 2023
SALES (est): 78.58K **Privately Held**
SIC: 3999 Manufacturing industries, nec

(G-6978)
MAXIMUM BUSINESS SOLUTIONS INC
5930 Hohman Ave Ste 201 (46320-3051)
PHONE..............................219 933-1809
Robert C Brown, *Pr*
Milton Reed Junior, *VP*
EMP: 3 **EST:** 2003
SALES (est): 316.94K **Privately Held**
Web: www.maxbss.com
SIC: 2752 Commercial printing, lithographic

(G-6979)
MEATS BY LINZ INC (PA)
628 Hoffman St (46327)
P.O. Box 6008 (46325)
PHONE..............................708 862-0830
Robert Linz, *Pr*
Frederick Linz, *
▼ **EMP:** 43 **EST:** 1961
SQ FT: 10,000
SALES (est): 29.8MM
SALES (corp-wide): 29.8MM **Privately Held**
Web: www.meatsbylinz.com
SIC: 5147 5812 2013 2011 Meats, cured or smoked; Eating places; Sausages and other prepared meats; Meat packing plants

(G-6980)
MG IRON WELDING INC
809 May St (46320-2153)
PHONE..............................708 916-1344
EMP: 4 **EST:** 2018
SALES (est): 25.09K **Privately Held**
SIC: 7692 Welding repair

(G-6981)
MIDLAND METAL PRODUCTS CO
Also Called: Midland Metal Products
1401 165th St (46320-2816)
PHONE..............................773 927-5700
Suzanne Z Mc Donald, *Pr*
EMP: 75 **EST:** 1925
SALES (est): 9.7MM **Privately Held**
Web: www.midlandmetalproducts.com
SIC: 3449 Miscellaneous metalwork

(G-6982)
MILLS ELECTRIC CO INC
4828 Calumet Ave (46327-1899)
PHONE..............................219 931-3114
Richard Mills Junior, *Pr*
Richard Mills Iii, *VP*
EMP: 9 **EST:** 1936
SQ FT: 10,000
SALES (est): 526.01K **Privately Held**
Web: www.mills-electric.net
SIC: 7694 5084 Rewinding services; Pumps and pumping equipment, nec

(G-6983)
MR TINTZ
6806 Indianapolis Blvd Ste D (46324-1739)
PHONE..............................219 844-5500
John Mancilla, *Prin*
EMP: 6 **EST:** 2009
SALES (est): 125.33K **Privately Held**
SIC: 3211 Window glass, clear and colored

(G-6984)
MUNSTER STEEL CO INC
1501 Huehn St (46327-0001)
PHONE..............................219 924-5198
Jeanne Robbins, *Pr*
Patricia Martin, *
EMP: 43 **EST:** 1958
SQ FT: 200,000
SALES (est): 4.8MM **Privately Held**
Web: www.munstersteel.com
SIC: 3441 Building components, structural steel

(G-6985)
MURO PALLETS CORPORATION
141 141st St (46327-1902)
PHONE..............................219 803-0500
EMP: 5 **EST:** 2019
SALES (est): 219.72K **Privately Held**
SIC: 2448 Pallets, wood

(G-6986)
NIAGARA LASALLE CORPORATION (HQ)
1412 150th St (46327-1743)
PHONE..............................219 853-6000
Michael Salamon, *CEO*
Michael Ivetich, *
Tony Verkruyse, *
David Ascher, *
▲ **EMP:** 97 **EST:** 1986
SALES (est): 136.75MM
SALES (corp-wide): 475.75MM **Privately Held**
Web: www.niagaralasalle.com
SIC: 3316 Cold finishing of steel shapes
PA: Specialty Steel Works Incorporated
1412 150th St
Hammond IN 46327

877 289-2277

(G-6987)
NORTHWEST ALUM FABRICATORS INC
6103 Kennedy Ave (46323-1045)
PHONE..............................219 844-4354
George Heldt Junior, *Pr*
EMP: 8 **EST:** 2003
SALES (est): 965.05K **Privately Held**
SIC: 3441 Fabricated structural metal

(G-6988)
O-M DISTRIBUTORS INC
Also Called: Tortillas Nuevo Leon
724 Hoffman St (46327-1827)
PHONE..............................219 853-1900
Oscar Martinez, *Pr*
Maria S Martinez, *
◆ **EMP:** 35 **EST:** 1979
SQ FT: 50,000
SALES (est): 4.22MM **Privately Held**
SIC: 2099 Tortillas, fresh or refrigerated

(G-6989)
ON-TIME LLC
Also Called: Ernestine's Food Gallery
6507 Ohio Ave (46323-1911)
PHONE..............................708 890-0230
Melvin Loggins, *CEO*
Ernestine Loggins, *CFO*
Chastidy Dix, *Mgr*
EMP: 7 **EST:** 2007
SQ FT: 2,000
SALES (est): 238.59K **Privately Held**
SIC: 2051 Pies, bakery: except frozen

(G-6990)
P & H IRON & SUPPLY INC
1435 Summer St (46320-2213)
PHONE..............................219 853-0240
Richard Hughes, *Mgr*
Lori Kovacich, *Sec*
EMP: 10 **EST:** 1963
SALES (est): 946.05K **Privately Held**
SIC: 5093 3341 Ferrous metal scrap and waste; Secondary nonferrous metals

(G-6991)
PHOENIX CORPORATION
Also Called: Phoenix Metals
1821 165th St (46320-2824)
PHONE..............................513 727-4763
Josh Gorham, *Brnch Mgr*
EMP: 16
SALES (corp-wide): 14.81B **Publicly Held**
Web: www.phoenixmetals.com
SIC: 3291 Abrasive metal and steel products
HQ: Phoenix Corporation
4685 Buford Hwy
Peachtree Corners GA 30071
770 447-4211

(G-6992)
PICKLE BITES LLC
7451 Olcott Ave (46323-2610)
PHONE..............................773 780-7559
David Hardy, *Owner*
EMP: 1 **EST:** 2015
SALES (est): 123.14K **Privately Held**
SIC: 2035 Pickled fruits and vegetables

(G-6993)
QUAD PLUS LLC
3535 165th St (46323-1226)
PHONE..............................219 844-9214
Raul Torres, *Brnch Mgr*
EMP: 2
Web: www.quadplus.com

Hammond - Lake County (G-6994)

SIC: **3566** Speed changers, drives, and gears
PA: Quad Plus Llc
2200 Ellis Rd
New Lenox IL 60451

(G-6994)
QUALITY GRAPHICS CORP
7801 Northcote Ave (46324-3337)
PHONE..................................219 845-7084
John Harrigan, *Pr*
Wiliam Harrigan, *VP*
EMP: 5 **EST:** 1993
SALES (est): 306.03K **Privately Held**
SIC: **2752** Offset printing

(G-6995)
RAW BARBERS AND COMPANY LLC
7450 California Ave (46323-2734)
PHONE..................................925 383-6212
Elizabeth Medina, *CFO*
EMP: 4 **EST:** 2021
SALES (est): 69.53K **Privately Held**
SIC: **3999** Barber and beauty shop equipment

(G-6996)
REFRACTORY SERVICE CORPORATION
4902 Calumet Ave (46327-1817)
P.O. Box 2276 (46312-7276)
PHONE..................................219 853-0885
Jeff Tianchi, *Brnch Mgr*
EMP: 20
SALES (corp-wide): 5.91MM **Privately Held**
Web: www.refractoryservice.net
SIC: **5085 3297** Refractory material; Nonclay refractories
PA: Refractory Service Corporation Inc
4900 Cline Ave
East Chicago IN 46312
219 397-7108

(G-6997)
RESCO PRODUCTS INC
5501 Kennedy Ave (46323-1168)
P.O. Box 2128 (46323-0128)
PHONE..................................219 844-7830
Frank Stumpo, *Prin*
EMP: 11
SALES (corp-wide): 99.85MM **Privately Held**
Web: www.rescoproducts.com
SIC: **3255** Clay refractories
PA: Resco Products, Inc.
1 Robinson Plz Ste 300
Pittsburgh PA 15205
412 494-4491

(G-6998)
RHI MAGNESITA
2929 Carlson Dr Ste 201 (46323-0018)
PHONE..................................219 237-2420
Stefan Borgas, *CEO*
EMP: 7 **EST:** 2019
SALES (est): 333.87K **Privately Held**
Web: www.rhimagnesita.com
SIC: **3255** Brick, clay refractory

(G-6999)
RMG CABINETRY INC
6809 Columbia Ave Ste C (46324-1653)
PHONE..................................219 712-6129
Robert M Gates, *Pr*
EMP: 5 **EST:** 2013
SALES (est): 198.14K **Privately Held**
SIC: **2434** Wood kitchen cabinets

(G-7000)
ROADWIN PARTS INC
3640 179th St (46323)
PHONE..................................630 742-4098
Diana Popovaite Zilys, *CEO*
EMP: 6 **EST:** 2019
SALES (est): 364.57K **Privately Held**
SIC: **3714** Motor vehicle engines and parts

(G-7001)
RPM
3142 174th Ct (46323-2731)
PHONE..................................309 798-1856
EMP: 4 **EST:** 2018
SALES (est): 107.2K **Privately Held**
SIC: **3999** Manufacturing industries, nec

(G-7002)
S TEC GROUP INC (PA)
2345 167th St (46323)
PHONE..................................219 844-7030
Thomas Gyure, *CEO*
William Hills, *CEO*
EMP: 16 **EST:** 1962
SALES (est): 27.1MM
SALES (corp-wide): 27.1MM **Privately Held**
Web: www.superiorengineering.com
SIC: **8711 3535** Consulting engineer; Unit handling conveying systems

(G-7003)
SCREW CONVEYOR CORPORATION (PA)
700 Hoffman St (46327-1827)
PHONE..................................219 931-1450
Garry M Abraham, *CEO*
Curtis F Abraham, *
Walter W Geisler, *VP Engg*
Randy Block, *VP*
Richard G Young, *Sec*
▼ **EMP:** 34 **EST:** 1933
SQ FT: 90,000
SALES (est): 32.4MM
SALES (corp-wide): 32.4MM **Privately Held**
Web: www.screwconveyor.com
SIC: **3535** Conveyors and conveying equipment

(G-7004)
SCREW CONVEYOR PACIFIC CORP (PA)
Also Called: Screw Conveyor
700 Hoffman St (46327-1827)
PHONE..................................219 931-1450
Garry M Abraham, *CEO*
Curtis F Abraham, *
Randolph Block, *
Richard G Young, *
EMP: 36 **EST:** 1932
SALES (est): 11.48MM
SALES (corp-wide): 11.48MM **Privately Held**
Web: www.screwconveyor.com
SIC: **3535** Conveyors and conveying equipment

(G-7005)
SDGS RUBS & SPICES LLC
1722 171st St (46324-2116)
PHONE..................................773 531-5497
EMP: 1 **EST:** 2021
SALES (est): 39.59K **Privately Held**
SIC: **2099** Seasonings and spices

(G-7006)
SILGAN CONTAINERS MFG CORP
Also Called: Silgan
2501 165th St Ste 2 (46320-2933)
PHONE..................................219 845-1500
EMP: 31
Web: www.silgancontainers.com
SIC: **3411** Metal cans
HQ: Silgan Containers Manufacturing Corporation
21600 Oxnard St Ste 1600
Woodland Hills CA 91367

(G-7007)
SIMKO & SONS INC
4545 Ash Ave (46327-1622)
P.O. Box 2919 (46312-7919)
PHONE..................................219 933-9100
Daniel Simko, *Pr*
Jon Simko, *Stockholder*
Elaine Simko, *Stockholder*
EMP: 18 **EST:** 1982
SQ FT: 50,000
SALES (est): 498.09K **Privately Held**
SIC: **3297** Nonclay refractories

(G-7008)
SIMKO INDUSTRIAL FABRICATORS
4545 Ash Ave (46327-1622)
P.O. Box 2919 (46312-7919)
PHONE..................................219 933-9100
Daniel Simko, *Pr*
EMP: 30 **EST:** 1968
SQ FT: 25,000
SALES (est): 4.91MM **Privately Held**
Web: www.simkofab.com
SIC: **3441** Fabricated structural metal

(G-7009)
SMART MACHINE INC
9941 Express Dr (46322-2610)
PHONE..................................219 922-0706
Michael Rohder, *Pr*
EMP: 6 **EST:** 2005
SALES (est): 297.79K **Privately Held**
Web: www.smartmachine.com
SIC: **3965** Fasteners

(G-7010)
SOUTH SHORE SLAG LLC (PA)
3411 Sheffield Ave (46327-1004)
PHONE..................................219 881-6544
EMP: 20 **EST:** 2008
SALES (est): 7.97MM **Privately Held**
Web: www.beemcompanies.com
SIC: **3295** Slag, crushed or ground

(G-7011)
SOUTHERN ELECTRIC COIL LLC
5025 Columbia Ave (46327-1759)
PHONE..................................219 931-5500
Ron Rossetto, *Managing Member*
Rich Skurka, *
Greg Dubrick, *
Dennis Nardoni, *
▲ **EMP:** 50 **EST:** 1952
SQ FT: 64,000
SALES (est): 7.34MM **Privately Held**
Web: www.southernelectriccoil.com
SIC: **3621 3677** Coils, for electric motors or generators; Electronic coils and transformers

(G-7012)
SPARKS BELTING COMPANY INC
3420 179th St # 3b (46323-3050)
PHONE..................................800 451-4537
Jim Staley, *Rgnl Mgr*
EMP: 6
SALES (corp-wide): 1.02B **Privately Held**
Web: www.sparksbelting.com
SIC: **3535 3568 3429** Conveyors and conveying equipment; Power transmission equipment, nec; Hardware, nec
HQ: Sparks Belting Company, Inc.
5005 Kraft Ave Se
Grand Rapids MI 49512

(G-7013)
SPECIALTY STEEL HOLDCO INC
1412 150th St (46327-1743)
PHONE..................................877 289-2277
Joel Hawthorne, *CEO*
Michael Salamon, *
Anthony J Verkruyse, *
EMP: 932 **EST:** 2017
SALES (est): 51.25MM **Privately Held**
Web: www.specialtysteelworks.com
SIC: **3317 6719** Tubes, seamless steel; Personal holding companies, except banks

(G-7014)
SPECIALTY STEEL WORKS INC (PA)
1412 150th St (46327)
PHONE..................................877 289-2277
Michael Salamon, *Pr*
Anthony Verkruyse, *CFO*
EMP: 5 **EST:** 2008
SALES (est): 475.75MM
SALES (corp-wide): 475.75MM **Privately Held**
Web: www.specialtysteelworks.com
SIC: **3317** Tubes, seamless steel

(G-7015)
STRIKE & WALK DA CUP WLDG LLC
Also Called: Welding Services/Training
6333 Kennedy Ave (46323-1000)
PHONE..................................219 455-4683
EMP: 5 **EST:** 2020
SALES (est): 106.65K **Privately Held**
SIC: **7692 8249** Welding repair; Trade school

(G-7016)
SUPER SPA XCLUSIVES LLC
7616 Jarnecke Ave (46324-3029)
PHONE..................................219 448-1486
EMP: 4 **EST:** 2019
SALES (est): 50K **Privately Held**
SIC: **3999** Manufacturing industries, nec

(G-7017)
SWANEL INC (PA)
Also Called: Swanel Beverage
6044 Erie Ave (46320-2532)
P.O. Box 1186 (46325-1186)
PHONE..................................219 932-7676
Edward Roviaro, *Pr*
EMP: 25 **EST:** 1942
SQ FT: 10,000
SALES (est): 9.4MM
SALES (corp-wide): 9.4MM **Privately Held**
Web: www.swanel.com
SIC: **5078 5169 5145 2086** Beverage coolers ; Carbon dioxide; Syrups, fountain; Soft drinks: packaged in cans, bottles, etc.

(G-7018)
TAP-A-LITE INC
820 165th St (46324-1394)
PHONE..................................219 932-8067
William Hayden, *Pr*
Margaret Schmidt, *
EMP: 47 **EST:** 1966
SQ FT: 10,000
SALES (est): 1.1MM
SALES (corp-wide): 5.63B **Publicly Held**
SIC: **3679 3643 3699 3641** Harness assemblies, for electronic use: wire or cable ; Plugs, electric; Electrical equipment and supplies, nec; Electric lamps
HQ: U-Haul International, Inc.
2727 N Central Ave
Phoenix AZ 85004
602 263-6011

GEOGRAPHIC SECTION

Hanover - Jefferson County (G-7044)

(G-7019)
THOMAS CUBIT INC
110 Brunswick St (46327-1553)
P.O. Box 625 (46303-0625)
PHONE..............................219 933-0566
Thomas E Cubit Ii, *Pr*
Rosemarie Roesel, *VP*
EMP: 5 **EST:** 1946
SQ FT: 3,600
SALES (est): 399.73K **Privately Held**
SIC: 3599 3441 7692 3444 Machine shop, jobbing and repair; Fabricated structural metal; Welding repair; Sheet metalwork

(G-7020)
THOMASVILLE FURNITURE INDS INC
442 165th St (46324-1328)
PHONE..............................336 476-2175
Salvador Balderas, *Prin*
EMP: 5 **EST:** 2016
SALES (est): 67.17K **Privately Held**
SIC: 2511 Wood household furniture

(G-7021)
TMS INTERNATIONAL LLC
2901 Carlson Dr # 100 (46323-1191)
PHONE..............................219 762-2176
EMP: 15
Web: www.tmsinternational.com
SIC: 3312 Blast furnaces and steel mills
HQ: Tms International, Llc
Southside Wrks Bldg 1 3f
Pittsburgh PA 15203
412 678-6141

(G-7022)
TRAINED THOUGHTS PUBG LLC
4028 Hohman Ave (46327-1239)
PHONE..............................773 661-7237
Almondo Scott, *CEO*
EMP: 1 **EST:** 2019
SALES (est): 77.01K **Privately Held**
SIC: 2741 Miscellaneous publishing

(G-7023)
TRI-STATE INDUSTRIES INC
4923 Columbia Ave (46327-1853)
PHONE..............................219 933-1710
Donald Keller, *Pr*
Donald Keller, *Pr*
Frances Keller, *
▲ **EMP:** 62 **EST:** 1980
SQ FT: 35,000
SALES (est): 9.92MM **Privately Held**
Web: www.tsi-tsa.com
SIC: 3545 3548 3599 3541 Machine tool attachments and accessories; Gas welding equipment; Machine and other job shop work; Plasma process metal cutting machines

(G-7024)
TRIFAB & CONSTRUCTION INC (PA)
2433 167th St (46323-1422)
P.O. Box 68 (60442-0068)
PHONE..............................219 845-1300
William O Stott, *Pr*
Robert Wajda, *Sec*
Leonard Pysh, *VP*
▼ **EMP:** 6 **EST:** 1984
SQ FT: 6,800
SALES (est): 7.78MM
SALES (corp-wide): 7.78MM **Privately Held**
SIC: 1541 3053 7699 Renovation, remodeling and repairs: industrial buildings; Gaskets and sealing devices; Tank repair

(G-7025)
UNILEVER UNITED STATES INC
Also Called: Unilever Hpc USA
1200 Calumet Ave (46320-1097)
PHONE..............................219 659-3200
Brad Tieke, *Mgr*
EMP: 5172
SALES (corp-wide): 64.79B **Privately Held**
Web: www.unileverusa.com
SIC: 2841 Soap and other detergents
HQ: Unilever United States, Inc.
800 Sylvan Ave
Englewood Cliffs NJ 07632
201 735-9661

(G-7026)
UNITED SEAMS APPAREL CNSTR LLC
7231 Northcote Ave (46324-2228)
PHONE..............................773 397-3831
Kia Outlaw, *Managing Member*
EMP: 2 **EST:** 2020
SALES (est): 67.05K **Privately Held**
SIC: 2311 Men's and boys' uniforms

(G-7027)
US METALS INC
940 150th St (46327-1805)
PHONE..............................219 802-8465
EMP: 6
SALES (corp-wide): 40.97MM **Privately Held**
Web: www.usmetals.com
SIC: 5074 3432 1711 Plumbing fittings and supplies; Plumbing fixture fittings and trim; Plumbing contractors
PA: U.S. Metals, Inc.
19102 Gundle Rd
Houston TX 77073
281 443-7473

(G-7028)
VANS INDUSTRIAL INC
231 Condit St (46320-1923)
PHONE..............................219 931-4881
Donald Van Camp, *Pr*
Renee Vancamp, *
Frances V Camp, *
EMP: 25 **EST:** 1964
SQ FT: 33,000
SALES (est): 4.97MM **Privately Held**
Web: www.vansindustrial.com
SIC: 1711 3441 1611 Mechanical contractor; Fabricated structural metal; General contractor, highway and street construction

(G-7029)
VIDICOM CORPORATION
124 Sibley St (46320-1726)
P.O. Box 1632 (46322-0632)
PHONE..............................219 923-7475
EMP: 4 **EST:** 1948
SALES (est): 68.84K **Privately Held**
Web: www.vidicomcctv.com
SIC: 3651 1731 Television receiving sets; Closed circuit television installation

(G-7030)
VIRAGO LOGISTIX LLC
5233 Hohman Ave Ste 202 (46320-1700)
PHONE..............................800 767-2090
EMP: 2 **EST:** 2021
SALES (est): 87.26K **Privately Held**
SIC: 3715 7389 Semitrailers for truck tractors; Business Activities at Non-Commercial Site

(G-7031)
WDB ENTERPRISES INC
7917 New Jersey Ave (46323-3040)
PHONE..............................219 844-4224
EMP: 10
SIC: 5084 7699 3629 Hydraulic systems equipment and supplies; Hydraulic equipment repair; Electronic generation equipment

(G-7032)
WELDERS CHOICE
5713 Pointe Dr (46320-2398)
PHONE..............................219 880-5470
Marc Manns, *Prin*
EMP: 5 **EST:** 2011
SALES (est): 28.12K **Privately Held**
SIC: 7692 Welding repair

(G-7033)
WICONE
7604 Mccook Ave (46323-2634)
PHONE..............................219 218-5199
EMP: 2 **EST:** 2017
SALES (est): 96.03K **Privately Held**
Web: www.wicone.com
SIC: 3999 Candles

(G-7034)
WILD HUNNITS GROUP INC
6945 Patricia Ln (46323-2468)
PHONE..............................312 609-9433
Alexis Brewer, *Pr*
EMP: 1 **EST:** 2020
SALES (est): 60.08K **Privately Held**
SIC: 3537 Trucks: freight, baggage, etc.: industrial, except mining

(G-7035)
WM EXPRESS LLP
1111 Merrill St (46320-2640)
PHONE..............................773 647-5305
Franchon Shields, *Pt*
EMP: 2 **EST:** 2021
SALES (est): 86.61K **Privately Held**
SIC: 3799 7389 Transportation equipment, nec; Business Activities at Non-Commercial Site

Hanna
Laporte County

(G-7036)
AUTO WOOD RESTORATION
Also Called: Rodman's Auto Wood Restoration
24 S Pennsylvania St (46340-9600)
P.O. Box 86 (46340-0086)
PHONE..............................219 797-3775
James Rodman, *Owner*
EMP: 2 **EST:** 1974
SQ FT: 1,000
SALES (est): 167.93K **Privately Held**
Web: www.autowood.net
SIC: 2431 Millwork

(G-7037)
BARKSDALE PERFORMANCE
4655 W Volk Rd (46340-9741)
P.O. Box 11 (65679-0011)
PHONE..............................219 916-5671
EMP: 1 **EST:** 2009
SALES (est): 59.04K **Privately Held**
Web: www.barksdale.com
SIC: 3599 Machine shop, jobbing and repair

(G-7038)
PICTURE THIS & STITCH THAT
2222 W 1200 S (46340-9751)
PHONE..............................219 797-4006
Traci Heironimus, *Prin*
EMP: 5 **EST:** 2017
SALES (est): 74.39K **Privately Held**
SIC: 2395 Embroidery and art needlework

Hanover
Jefferson County

(G-7039)
BARKER KITCHEN & BATH CABINETS
4240 S Carmel Rd (47243-9172)
PHONE..............................812 493-4693
Travis Barker, *Prin*
EMP: 4 **EST:** 2019
SALES (est): 75.19K **Privately Held**
Web: www.barkerkitchen.com
SIC: 2434 Wood kitchen cabinets

(G-7040)
BULK TRUCK & TRANSPORT SERVICE
659 W Lagrange Rd (47243-9433)
P.O. Box 28 (47243-0028)
PHONE..............................812 866-2155
Maurice Auxier, *Pr*
Dave Auxier, *
Warren Auxier, *
Patrick Auxier, *
Darrell Auxier, *Stockholder*
EMP: 28 **EST:** 1976
SQ FT: 13,400
SALES (est): 3.83MM **Privately Held**
Web: www.btandt.com
SIC: 3443 5012 7699 Tanks, standard or custom fabricated: metal plate; Trucks, commercial; Tank repair

(G-7041)
FAS PLASTIC ENTERPRISES INC
3408 W State Road 56 (47243-9063)
PHONE..............................812 265-2928
Frank G Mingione, *Pr*
Frank J Mingione, *
L Steve Ball, *
Carol L Lee, *
▲ **EMP:** 47 **EST:** 1985
SQ FT: 25,000
SALES (est): 4.25MM **Privately Held**
Web: www.fasplastics.com
SIC: 3089 Injection molding of plastics

(G-7042)
HANOVER MACHINE & TOOL INC
3408 W State Road 56 (47243)
PHONE..............................812 265-6265
Frank G Mingione, *Pr*
Frank J Mingione, *Sec*
EMP: 5 **EST:** 2001
SQ FT: 4,000
SALES (est): 500.5K **Privately Held**
Web: www.hanovermachineandtool.com
SIC: 3599 Machine shop, jobbing and repair

(G-7043)
HI-DEF COATINGS
6607 W State Road 56 (47243-9369)
PHONE..............................812 801-4895
EMP: 5 **EST:** 2017
SALES (est): 143.61K **Privately Held**
Web: www.hi-defcoatings.com
SIC: 3999 Manufacturing industries, nec

(G-7044)
PATES PROCESSING LLC
Also Called: Kent Mercantile
4251 S 850 W (47243-9154)
PHONE..............................812 866-4710
Tim Morrison, *Pr*
Iva Pate, *Prin*
EMP: 8 **EST:** 2009

SALES (est): 248.78K **Privately Held**
SIC: 3421 Table and food cutlery, including butchers'

(G-7045)
PATES SLAUGHTERING & PROC
Off Hwy 62 (47243)
PHONE..............................812 866-4710
Tim Morrison, *Owner*
EMP: 6 EST: 1975
SALES (est): 261.91K **Privately Held**
SIC: 0751 2011 2013 Slaughtering: custom livestock services; Meat packing plants; Sausages and other prepared meats

(G-7046)
TIMBERS CUSTOM SIGNS
3660 W State Road 56 (47243-9065)
PHONE..............................812 866-6655
Tim Harmon, *Owner*
EMP: 1 EST: 1997
SALES (est): 96.01K **Privately Held**
SIC: 3993 Signs, not made in custom sign painting shops

Hardinsburg
Washington County

(G-7047)
AUTOMATION CONTROL SERVICE
8349 W Radcliff Rd (47125-8905)
PHONE..............................812 472-3292
EMP: 1 EST: 1996
SALES (est): 65.47K **Privately Held**
SIC: 3613 1731 Control panels, electric; Electrical work

(G-7048)
PENNER TIRE & SERVICE LLC
390 E Us Highway 150 (47125-8558)
PHONE..............................812 653-0029
Mahlon L Penner, *Owner*
EMP: 1 EST: 2012
SALES (est): 222.98K **Privately Held**
Web: www.pennertireservice.com
SIC: 5531 7534 Automotive tires; Tire repair shop

Harlan
Allen County

(G-7049)
BA ROMINES SHEETMETAL INC
11827 Hood St (46743)
P.O. Box 242 (46743)
PHONE..............................260 657-5500
Brent Romines, *Pr*
EMP: 35 EST: 2005
SQ FT: 3,000
SALES (est): 9.39MM **Privately Held**
Web: www.rominessheetmetal.com
SIC: 3444 Ducts, sheet metal

(G-7050)
BR TOOL LLC
14310 State Road 101 (46743-7460)
PHONE..............................260 452-9487
EMP: 1 EST: 2018
SALES (est): 65.2K **Privately Held**
SIC: 3552 Dyeing, drying, and finishing machinery and equipment

(G-7051)
CAC WALLPANELS LLC
14329 Rupert Rd (46743-7412)
PHONE..............................260 437-4003
EMP: 5 EST: 1999

SALES (est): 504.96K **Privately Held**
SIC: 2431 Panel work, wood

(G-7052)
CLOVER PRINTING LLC
16840 State Road 37 (46743-9789)
P.O. Box 224 (46743-0224)
PHONE..............................260 657-3003
Troy Gunder, *Prin*
EMP: 5 EST: 2015
SALES (est): 239.56K **Privately Held**
Web: www.cloverprintingllc.com
SIC: 2759 Commercial printing, nec

(G-7053)
CUMMINS REPAIR INC
Also Called: Cummins
11110 Scipio Rd (46743-9708)
PHONE..............................260 632-4800
James Cummins, *Pr*
EMP: 3 EST: 1997
SALES (est): 235.69K **Privately Held**
SIC: 7699 3519 Industrial machinery and equipment repair; Internal combustion engines, nec

(G-7054)
DUTCH MADE INC
Also Called: Kitchen/Bath Design Center
16836 State Road 37 (46743-9789)
PHONE..............................260 657-3331
Martin Graber, *Brnch Mgr*
EMP: 4
SALES (corp-wide): 8.85MM **Privately Held**
Web: www.dutchmade.com
SIC: 5399 2434 2431 2426 Catalog showroom stores; Wood kitchen cabinets; Millwork; Hardwood dimension and flooring mills
PA: Dutch Made Inc
   10415 Roth Rd
   Grabill IN 46741
   260 657-3311

(G-7055)
FISHER SPECIALTIES INC
Also Called: Fisher Specialties
11515 Roberts Rd (46743)
PHONE..............................260 385-8251
Joseph A Fisher, *Pr*
Terri L Fisher, *Sec*
EMP: 8 EST: 1989
SALES (est): 771.9K **Privately Held**
Web: www.fisherspecialties.com
SIC: 2541 Counter and sink tops

(G-7056)
HARLAN CABINETS INC
12707 Spencerville Rd (46743-7497)
P.O. Box 307 (46743-0307)
PHONE..............................260 657-5154
Simon Wagler, *Pr*
Omer Wagler, *
Ray Wagler, *
EMP: 18 EST: 1955
SQ FT: 100,000
SALES (est): 3.32MM **Privately Held**
Web: www.harlancabinets.com
SIC: 2434 Wood kitchen cabinets

(G-7057)
KENT BRENNEKE
Also Called: Maumee Machine & Tool
14038 Scipio Rd (46743-9711)
PHONE..............................260 446-5383
Kent Brenneke, *Owner*
EMP: 2 EST: 2000
SALES (est): 131.89K **Privately Held**

SIC: 3545 3451 3452 Cutting tools for machine tools; Screw machine products; Bolts, nuts, rivets, and washers

(G-7058)
OUR COUNTRY HOME ENTPS INC (PA)
Also Called: Sunequinox
12120 Water St (46743-5415)
P.O. Box 250 (46742-0250)
PHONE..............................260 657-5605
Thomas Blake Senior, *Pr*
Micheal Campo, *
▲ EMP: 44 EST: 1985
SQ FT: 24,000
SALES (est): 35MM **Privately Held**
Web: www.ochinc.com
SIC: 2541 3433 5074 Wood partitions and fixtures; Solar heaters and collectors; Heating equipment and panels, solar

Harmony
Clay County

(G-7059)
LAWSON WELDING SHOP
10516 North County 200e (47853)
P.O. Box 26 (47853-0026)
PHONE..............................812 448-8984
Ronald Lawson, *Owner*
EMP: 2 EST: 1969
SQ FT: 7,000
SALES (est): 202.94K **Privately Held**
Web: www.lawsonwelding.com
SIC: 7692 Welding repair

Hartford City
Blackford County

(G-7060)
3M COMPANY
3M
304 S 075 E (47348-9796)
PHONE..............................765 348-3200
Ray Lorenv, *Brnch Mgr*
EMP: 50
SALES (corp-wide): 32.68B **Publicly Held**
Web: www.3m.com
SIC: 3291 2672 2671 Abrasive products; Paper; coated and laminated, nec; Paper; coated and laminated packaging
PA: 3m Company
   3m Center
   Saint Paul MN 55144
   651 733-1110

(G-7061)
ADM CUSTOM CREATIONS LLC
6 Belfast Ct (47348-9755)
PHONE..............................765 499-0584
Allen D Johnson, *Pr*
EMP: 3 EST: 2014
SALES (est): 74.37K **Privately Held**
Web: www.admcustomcreations.com
SIC: 3993 Signs and advertising specialties

(G-7062)
BINGO BUGLE
2301 N 100 E (47348-8974)
PHONE..............................765 348-2859
M Phillips, *Prin*
EMP: 1 EST: 1994
SALES (est): 47.27K **Privately Held**
Web: www.bingobugle.com
SIC: 2711 Newspapers, publishing and printing

(G-7063)
D J INVESTMENTS INC (PA)
Also Called: Hearing Aid Outlet
0660 E 200 S (47348-9733)
PHONE..............................765 348-4381
Danny L Ahrens, *Pr*
B Joann Ahrens, *Treas*
EMP: 1 EST: 1967
SQ FT: 2,600
SALES (est): 574.23K
SALES (corp-wide): 574.23K **Privately Held**
Web: www.sonushearing.com
SIC: 5999 3842 Hearing aids; Hearing aids

(G-7064)
D J INVESTMENTS INC
Also Called: Hearing Aid Outlet
1608 N Cherry St (47348-1356)
PHONE..............................765 348-3558
Dan Ahrens, *Brnch Mgr*
EMP: 3
SALES (corp-wide): 574.23K **Privately Held**
Web: www.amplifon.com
SIC: 5999 3842 Hearing aids; Hearing aids
PA: D J Investments Inc
   0660 E 200 S
   Hartford City IN 47348
   765 348-4381

(G-7065)
G & S RURAL WOODWORKING
1102 S 200 E (47348-8884)
PHONE..............................765 348-7781
EMP: 5 EST: 2014
SALES (est): 82.66K **Privately Held**
SIC: 2431 Millwork

(G-7066)
GENTIS TIRE & SERVICE INC
219 N Walnut St (47348-2026)
PHONE..............................765 348-2400
William K Gentis, *Pr*
Kurt Gentis, *VP*
Ann Dunwiddie, *Sec*
Kelly Gentis, *Mgr*
Robin Gentis, *Sec*
EMP: 20 EST: 1981
SALES (est): 1.7MM **Privately Held**
SIC: 5531 7534 5014 Automotive tires; Tire repair shop; Automobile tires and tubes

(G-7067)
HAROLD PRECISION PRODUCTS INC
Also Called: H P Products
1600 Gilkey Ave (47348-9549)
P.O. Box 350 (47348-0350)
PHONE..............................765 348-2710
Michael Baughey, *CEO*
Dan Baughey, *Pr*
Mark Baughey, *VP*
EMP: 22 EST: 1947
SQ FT: 70,000
SALES (est): 2.08MM **Privately Held**
Web: www.hp4stamping.com
SIC: 3469 Stamping metal for the trade

(G-7068)
HARTFORD TEC GLASS CO INC (PA)
735 E Water St (47348-2264)
P.O. Box 613 (47348-0613)
PHONE..............................765 348-1282
George M Reidy, *Pr*
Michael Patrick Reidy, *Sec*
EMP: 20 EST: 1939
SQ FT: 40,000
SALES (est): 2.4MM
SALES (corp-wide): 2.4MM **Privately Held**
Web: www.hartfordglass.com

GEOGRAPHIC SECTION

Hazleton - Gibson County (G-7094)

SIC: 3231 5039 1793 Stained glass: made from purchased glass; Glass construction materials; Glass and glazing work

(G-7069)
HEARTLAND HARVEST PROC LLC
1532 N 325 W (47348-9541)
PHONE..................260 228-0736
EMP: 5
SALES (corp-wide): 563.66K Privately Held
SIC: 2079 Oil, hydrogenated: edible
PA: Heartland Harvest Processing, Llc
   4861 S 600 E Bldg A
   Gas City IN 46933
   260 228-0736

(G-7070)
MAYCO INTERNATIONAL LLC
Also Called: Mayco Intl Hartford Cy
1701 W Mcdonald St (47348-9599)
PHONE..................765 348-5780
EMP: 1
Web: www.maycointernational.com
SIC: 3089 Injection molding of plastics
PA: Mayco International Llc
   42400 Merrill Rd
   Sterling Heights MI 48314

(G-7071)
MIDDLETOWN ENTERPRISES INC
Also Called: Sinclair Glass
105 N Wabash Ave (47348-2366)
P.O. Box 527 (47348-0527)
PHONE..................765 348-3100
Gavin Mair, Pr
▲ EMP: 40 EST: 1986
SQ FT: 65,000
SALES (est): 3.16MM Privately Held
Web: www.sinclairglass.com
SIC: 3231 Ornamental glass: cut, engraved or otherwise decorated

(G-7072)
MILL CREEK LUMBER CO
729 E Water St (47348-2264)
PHONE..................765 347-8546
EMP: 4 EST: 2018
SALES (est): 124.2K Privately Held
SIC: 2431 Millwork

(G-7073)
NEW-INDY HARTFORD CITY LLC (DH)
Also Called: New-Indy Containerboard
501 S Spring St (47348)
P.O. Box 30 (47348)
PHONE..................765 348-5440
Philip Freel, Genl Mgr
EMP: 86 EST: 1998
SALES (est): 55.34MM
SALES (corp-wide): 679.24MM Privately Held
Web: www.newindycontainerboard.com
SIC: 2621 Wrapping and packaging papers
HQ: New-Indy Containerboard Llc
   3500 Porsche Wy Ste 150
   Ontario CA 91764
   909 296-3400

(G-7074)
PETOSKEY PLASTICS INC
1100 W Grant St (47348-1970)
PHONE..................765 348-9808
EMP: 72
SQ FT: 208,000
SALES (corp-wide): 102.38MM Privately Held
Web: www.petoskeyplastics.com

SIC: 3089 Injection molding of plastics
PA: Petoskey Plastics, Inc.
   1 Petoskey St
   Petoskey MI 49770
   231 347-2602

(G-7075)
QUALITY PALLET
1506 W Park Ave (47348-8739)
PHONE..................765 348-4840
Ding Goodnight, Owner
Matt Goodnight, Manager
EMP: 6 EST: 2011
SALES (est): 245.22K Privately Held
Web: www.h-cqualitypallet.com
SIC: 2448 Pallets, wood

(G-7076)
SINCERELY NAIYA LLC
213 E Kickapoo St (47348-2116)
PHONE..................602 518-3870
Naiya Kinder, Pr
EMP: 4 EST: 2021
SALES (est): 64.19K Privately Held
SIC: 3914 Silverware and plated ware

(G-7077)
STAN CLAMME
725 E Water St (47348-2264)
PHONE..................765 348-0008
EMP: 10 EST: 2007
SALES (est): 603.03K Privately Held
SIC: 3523 Sprayers and spraying machines, agricultural

(G-7078)
TRU-FORM STEEL & WIRE INC (PA)
1204 Gilkey Ave (47348-9549)
P.O. Box 266 (47348-0266)
PHONE..................765 348-5001
Jeffrey Tuttle, Pr
Monty Tuttle, *
▲ EMP: 30 EST: 1935
SALES (est): 9.71MM
SALES (corp-wide): 9.71MM Privately Held
Web: www.tru-formsteel.com
SIC: 3089 3315 3441 3412 Plastics processing; Wire and fabricated wire products; Fabricated structural metal; Metal barrels, drums, and pails

(G-7079)
TRU-FORM STEEL & WIRE INC
1822 Joe Bonham Dr (47348-9265)
P.O. Box 266 (47348-0266)
PHONE..................765 348-5001
Keith Rodarnel, Mgr
EMP: 13
SALES (corp-wide): 9.71MM Privately Held
Web: www.tru-formsteel.com
SIC: 3441 3089 Fabricated structural metal; Plastics processing
PA: Tru-Form Steel & Wire, Inc.
   1204 Gilkey Ave
   Hartford City IN 47348
   765 348-5001

(G-7080)
TWISTED STITCHER
7681 E 100 S (47348-9029)
PHONE..................765 330-1083
Kelly Willmann, Prin
EMP: 4 EST: 2017
SALES (est): 50.75K Privately Held
SIC: 2395 Embroidery and art needlework

(G-7081)
VISABLE VINYL
4635 E 250 N (47348-9241)
PHONE..................765 717-9678
Andrew Wilson, Owner
EMP: 1 EST: 2008
SALES (est): 46.08K Privately Held
Web: www.visablevinyl.com
SIC: 3993 7389 Signs and advertising specialties; Business services, nec

Hartsville
Bartholomew County

(G-7082)
HARTLEY J COMPANY INC
110 S 1000 E (47244)
P.O. Box 423 (47202)
PHONE..................812 376-9708
Brent S Hartley, Pr
EMP: 5 EST: 1937
SALES (est): 387.35K Privately Held
Web: www.jhartleyco.com
SIC: 2499 2759 Decorative wood and woodwork; Letterpress printing

Haubstadt
Gibson County

(G-7083)
DEWIG BROS PACKING CO INC
100 E Maple St (47639)
P.O. Box 186 (47639-0186)
PHONE..................812 768-6208
Thomas Dewig, Pr
Janet Dewig, *
EMP: 20 EST: 1915
SQ FT: 8,000
SALES (est): 1.88MM Privately Held
Web: www.dewigmeats.com
SIC: 5421 2011 Meat markets, including freezer provisioners; Pork products, from pork slaughtered on site

(G-7084)
EDS WOOD CRAFT
300 E Gibson St (47639-8203)
P.O. Box 362 (47639-0362)
PHONE..................812 768-6617
Edward C May, Owner
EMP: 3 EST: 1981
SALES (est): 209.33K Privately Held
SIC: 2521 1752 2541 2517 Cabinets, office: wood; Carpet laying; Wood partitions and fixtures; Wood television and radio cabinets

(G-7085)
GIBSON COUNTY SAND & GRAV INC
2997 W State Road 68 (47639-8631)
PHONE..................812 851-5800
EMP: 5 EST: 2008
SALES (est): 176.84K Privately Held
SIC: 1442 Construction sand and gravel

(G-7086)
HILLTOP MCH SP HAUBSTADT LLC
4958 E 1200 S (47639-7907)
PHONE..................812 768-5717
Kenneth I Langford, Prin
EMP: 3 EST: 2008
SALES (est): 244.02K Privately Held
SIC: 3599 Machine shop, jobbing and repair

(G-7087)
KINGS CUSTOM MACHINE LLC
1832 E Sierra Dr (47639-7975)
PHONE..................812 477-5262

William King, Owner
EMP: 8 EST: 1970
SALES (est): 644.64K Privately Held
Web: kings-custom-machine-llc.business.site
SIC: 3599 Machine shop, jobbing and repair

(G-7088)
PRODIGY MOLD & TOOL INC
88 E 1100 S (47639-8836)
PHONE..................812 753-3029
Shawn Mcgrew, Pr
Darrin Schmitt, *
EMP: 30 EST: 1996
SQ FT: 14,500
SALES (est): 2.93MM Privately Held
Web: www.prodigymold.com
SIC: 3599 3451 3089 Custom machinery; Screw machine products; Injection molding of plastics

(G-7089)
SCHMITT BENNETT
20101 Old Princeton Rd (47639-9277)
PHONE..................812 459-8523
Bennett Schmitt, Owner
EMP: 1 EST: 1998
SALES (est): 84.98K Privately Held
SIC: 2084 Wines

(G-7090)
TNT TRUCK ACCESSORIES LLC
152 W 1275 S (47639-8712)
PHONE..................812 305-0714
EMP: 2 EST: 2010
SALES (est): 221.76K Privately Held
SIC: 3714 Motor vehicle parts and accessories

(G-7091)
VOGLER COPPERWORKS LLC
308 S Vine St (47639-8151)
PHONE..................812 630-9010
EMP: 3 EST: 2007
SALES (est): 209.51K Privately Held
Web: www.voglermetaldesign.com
SIC: 3444 Sheet metalwork

(G-7092)
VOGLER METALWORK & DESIGN INC
1944 E 1200 S (47639-7931)
PHONE..................812 615-0042
Aaron Vogler, Pr
EMP: 1 EST: 2013
SALES (est): 239.43K Privately Held
Web: www.voglermetaldesign.com
SIC: 3444 Sheet metalwork

(G-7093)
WESTSIDE AUTOMATION INC
78 W 1100 S (47639-8837)
PHONE..................812 768-6878
Lanny Schmidt, Owner
Kathy Schmidt, Sec
EMP: 24 EST: 1998
SQ FT: 4,000
SALES (est): 2.12MM Privately Held
SIC: 3625 Relays and industrial controls

Hazleton
Gibson County

(G-7094)
ELLIS MACHINE SHOP LLC
1318 E 870 N (47640-9248)
PHONE..................812 779-7477
Chad Ellis, Prin
EMP: 6 EST: 2016

SALES (est): 89.64K **Privately Held**
SIC: 3599 Machine shop, jobbing and repair

(G-7095)
PAUL E POTTS
8689 W Private Road 375 N (47640-9631)
PHONE..............................812 354-3241
Paul E Potts, *Owner*
EMP: 3 **EST:** 1988
SALES (est): 417.96K **Privately Held**
SIC: 1311 Crude petroleum production

Hebron
Porter County

(G-7096)
ASH WELDING
296 W State Road 8 (46341-8854)
PHONE..............................219 808-7139
EMP: 4 **EST:** 2010
SALES (est): 56.88K **Privately Held**
SIC: 7692 Welding repair

(G-7097)
ASSALYS HOUSE GARLIC LLC
8529 E 181st Ave (46341-9345)
PHONE..............................219 310-5934
Elie Abou Assaly, *Managing Member*
EMP: 1 **EST:** 2021
SALES (est): 64.19K **Privately Held**
SIC: 2035 Spreads, garlic

(G-7098)
DAVID M PSZONKA
93 S 695 W (46341-9722)
PHONE..............................219 988-2235
David M Pszonka, *Owner*
EMP: 2 **EST:** 2013
SALES (est): 105.88K **Privately Held**
SIC: 2064 7389 Lollipops and other hard candy; Business Activities at Non-Commercial Site

(G-7099)
DOUGLAS ESTES
783 S 250 W (46341-8857)
PHONE..............................219 718-0911
Douglas Estes, *Prin*
EMP: 6 **EST:** 2010
SALES (est): 150.01K **Privately Held**
SIC: 2741 Miscellaneous publishing

(G-7100)
HOCHBAUM MACHINE SERVICES INC
11 Wood Ct (46341-9064)
PHONE..............................219 996-6830
Jamie Hochbaum, *Pr*
EMP: 20 **EST:** 1991
SQ FT: 5,000
SALES (est): 2.47MM **Privately Held**
Web: www.hmsprecisionmachining.com
SIC: 3599 Machine shop, jobbing and repair

(G-7101)
LAKE AIR BALANCE
639 W 250 S (46341-9226)
PHONE..............................219 988-2449
Wanda Vajner, *Prin*
EMP: 7 **EST:** 2005
SALES (est): 113.53K **Privately Held**
SIC: 3444 Sheet metalwork

(G-7102)
LENNON INDUSTRIES
1102 Norbeh Dr (46341-8511)
PHONE..............................219 996-6024
EMP: 8 **EST:** 2007
SALES (est): 576.32K **Privately Held**
Web: www.lennonindustries.com
SIC: 3999 Manufacturing industries, nec

(G-7103)
NATHAN MILLIS TOOLS LLC
115 Poplar Ct (46341-8890)
PHONE..............................219 996-3305
Nathan A Millis, *Prin*
EMP: 5 **EST:** 2016
SALES (est): 81.49K **Privately Held**
SIC: 3599 Industrial machinery, nec

(G-7104)
PORTER COUNTY IR & MET RECYCLE
552 S 600 W Ste 1 (46341-8822)
PHONE..............................219 996-7630
John Perzee, *Pr*
Janet Perzee, *Sec*
EMP: 15 **EST:** 1988
SQ FT: 2,640
SALES (est): 638.92K **Privately Held**
SIC: 5093 3341 Ferrous metal scrap and waste; Secondary nonferrous metals

(G-7105)
PREMIER COMPONENTS LLC
346 S 725 W (46341-9709)
PHONE..............................219 776-9372
Michael Williams, *Managing Member*
EMP: 5 **EST:** 2008
SALES (est): 336.96K **Privately Held**
SIC: 3547 Steel rolling machinery

(G-7106)
RUSS PRINT SHP/HBRON ADVRTSER
Also Called: Advertiser
131 N Main St (46341-8972)
P.O. Box 2 (46341-0002)
PHONE..............................219 996-3142
Russ Franzman Senior, *Pr*
EMP: 10 **EST:** 1978
SQ FT: 1,856
SALES (est): 941.03K **Privately Held**
SIC: 2752 2741 2791 2711 Offset printing; Newsletter publishing; Typesetting; Newspapers

(G-7107)
VAN SCHOUWEN FARMS LLC
19306 Clay St (46341-9347)
PHONE..............................219 696-0877
Jacob Van Schouwen, *Pt*
Marvin Van Schouwen, *Pt*
EMP: 5 **EST:** 1967
SALES (est): 555.77K **Privately Held**
SIC: 2035 Onions, pickled

(G-7108)
VAUTERBUILT INC
16448 Clay St (46341-9006)
PHONE..............................219 712-2384
EMP: 2 **EST:** 1995
SALES (est): 249.26K **Privately Held**
Web: www.vauterbuilt.com
SIC: 3559 Automotive related machinery

Heltonville
Lawrence County

(G-7109)
APPLIANCE PROS LLC
3730 State Road 58 E (47436-8688)
PHONE..............................812 329-2669
Michael Helgesen, *Prin*
EMP: 5 **EST:** 2019
SALES (est): 61.69K **Privately Held**
SIC: 3639 Household appliances, nec

(G-7110)
DWIGHT SMITH LOGGING
815 Roberts Ln (47436-8674)
PHONE..............................812 834-5546
Dwight Smith, *Pr*
EMP: 6 **EST:** 2003
SALES (est): 472.25K **Privately Held**
SIC: 2411 Logging camps and contractors

(G-7111)
SPECIAL IDEAS INCORPORATED
Also Called: Interfaith Resources
511 Diamond Rd (47436-8503)
PHONE..............................812 834-5691
Jusitce St Rain, *Owner*
Karen St Rain, *Owner*
EMP: 2 **EST:** 1981
SALES (est): 166.04K **Privately Held**
Web: www.special-ideas.com
SIC: 2711 Newspapers

Henryville
Clark County

(G-7112)
3SEVENS LLC
Also Called: Better Surplus
110 Ash St (47126-9704)
PHONE..............................502 594-2312
EMP: 4 **EST:** 2017
SALES (est): 180K **Privately Held**
SIC: 7389 5722 5064 5963 Business Activities at Non-Commercial Site; Appliance parts; Appliance parts, household ; Home related products, direct sales

(G-7113)
LAWSON DESIGN INC
2109 S Casey Rd (47126-9304)
PHONE..............................812 967-2810
Todd Lawson, *Pr*
EMP: 3 **EST:** 2003
SALES (est): 230.4K **Privately Held**
SIC: 3089 Plastics processing

(G-7114)
PROPHALT SEALCOATING LLC
331 Vest Rd (47126-9731)
P.O. Box 183 (47126-0183)
PHONE..............................502 356-3238
Robert Wardlow, *Prin*
EMP: 7 **EST:** 2020
SALES (est): 75.6K **Privately Held**
Web: www.prophaltsealcoating.com
SIC: 2952 Asphalt felts and coatings

(G-7115)
S & M PRECAST INC
16700 Sima Gray Rd (47126-8626)
PHONE..............................812 246-6258
Becky Graf, *Pr*
Raymond Grass, *
Becky A Graf, *
EMP: 73 **EST:** 1995
SALES (est): 8.21MM **Privately Held**
Web: www.smprecast.net
SIC: 3272 Concrete products, precast, nec

(G-7116)
SULLIVAN ENGINEERED SERVICES
Also Called: S.E.S.
316 Mount Zion Rd (47126-8657)
P.O. Box 410 (47126-0410)
PHONE..............................812 294-1724
EMP: 6 **EST:** 1993
SQ FT: 2,000
SALES (est): 565.36K **Privately Held**
SIC: 3613 3542 7371 Control panels, electric ; Machine tools, metal forming type; Custom computer programming services

Highland
Lake County

(G-7117)
5 STAR LOGISTICS LLC
3105 Amy Ct (46322-2920)
PHONE..............................708 926-4251
EMP: 1 **EST:** 2021
SALES (est): 60.08K **Privately Held**
SIC: 3537 Trucks: freight, baggage, etc.: industrial, except mining

(G-7118)
AC PRINTING INC
2647 Highway Ave (46322-1614)
PHONE..............................708 418-9100
Lee F Simmons, *Pr*
William Simmons, *VP*
EMP: 5 **EST:** 1957
SQ FT: 1,500
SALES (est): 482.47K **Privately Held**
Web: www.acgraphixhouse.com
SIC: 2752 Offset printing

(G-7119)
ADAMS SIGNS INC
9020 Ohio Pl (46322-2210)
PHONE..............................219 972-0700
Ernest Adams, *Pr*
EMP: 1 **EST:** 1986
SALES (est): 99.23K **Privately Held**
Web: www.adamsigns.com
SIC: 7389 3993 Sign painting and lettering shop; Signs and advertising specialties

(G-7120)
ALL THINGS KINGDOM LLC
9409 Southmoor Ave Apt 19 (46322-3604)
PHONE..............................312 200-4569
EMP: 5
SALES (est): 78.58K **Privately Held**
SIC: 2253 7389 T-shirts and tops, knit; Business Activities at Non-Commercial Site

(G-7121)
AMORLAI ORGANICS LLC
9445 Indianapolis Blvd Ste 1272 (46322-2648)
PHONE..............................219 595-9102
Lajanea Boswell, *Mgr*
EMP: 1 **EST:** 2021
SALES (est): 47.23K **Privately Held**
SIC: 2844 Hair preparations, including shampoos

(G-7122)
APPLE-LY EVER AFTER INC
3542 Highway Ave (46322-1712)
PHONE..............................219 838-9397
Lori A Sitter, *Pr*
EMP: 6 **EST:** 2008
SALES (est): 87.08K **Privately Held**
SIC: 3571 Electronic computers

(G-7123)
B & W SPECIALIZED DRILLING
9002 Indianapolis Blvd Ste B (46322-2501)
PHONE..............................219 746-9463
Thomas K Witherow, *Pr*
Neal E Witherow, *Treas*
Carl Bowling, *VP*
EMP: 5 **EST:** 2001
SQ FT: 2,500
SALES (est): 475.44K **Privately Held**

GEOGRAPHIC SECTION

Highland - Lake County (G-7152)

SIC: 3545 Boring machine attachments (machine tool accessories)

(G-7124)
BECKYS ORGNL PPPTS GS CLS
9326 Idlewild Dr (46322-3752)
PHONE...............................219 934-0895
EMP: 1 EST: 2000
SALES (est): 98.81K Privately Held
SIC: 3999 Candles

(G-7125)
BONZELL COMBS
Also Called: Gud Wazh Laundromat
9445 Indianapolis Blvd (46322-2648)
PHONE...............................872 248-4123
Bonzell Combs, Owner
EMP: 1 EST: 2021
SALES (est): 56.09K Privately Held
SIC: 3633 Laundry dryers, household or coin-operated

(G-7126)
C E R METAL MARKING CORP
2224 Industrial Dr Ste C (46322-2652)
PHONE...............................219 924-9710
EMP: 5 EST: 1999
SQ FT: 1,500
SALES (est): 479.71K Privately Held
Web: www.cermetalmarking.com
SIC: 3469 Stamping metal for the trade

(G-7127)
C J P CORPORATION
9445 Indianapolis Blvd Ste A (46322-2648)
PHONE...............................219 924-1685
Charles J Pease, Pr
David Dahms, Sec
EMP: 8 EST: 1978
SQ FT: 4,500
SALES (est): 928.07K Privately Held
Web: www.cjprinting.com
SIC: 2752 2791 2789 Offset printing; Typesetting; Bookbinding and related work

(G-7128)
CENTER FOR ORTHTIC PRSTHTIC EX
2213 Main St Unit 1c-102 (46322-3514)
PHONE...............................219 365-0248
Amit Bhanti, Prin
EMP: 4 EST: 2019
SALES (est): 67.67K Privately Held
SIC: 3842 Surgical appliances and supplies

(G-7129)
CHICAGO BIFOLD
2640 Condit St (46322-1601)
PHONE...............................708 532-4365
Mike Wallace, Pr
EMP: 8 EST: 2011
SALES (est): 74.03K Privately Held
Web: www.chicagobifold.com
SIC: 3211 Flat glass

(G-7130)
CLM EXPRESS TRUCKING LLC
9445 Indianapolis Blvd Ste 1148 (46322-2648)
PHONE...............................219 237-4646
EMP: 2 EST: 2020
SALES (est): 318.77K Privately Held
Web: www.clmexpresstrucking.com
SIC: 3537 Trucks, tractors, loaders, carriers, and similar equipment

(G-7131)
CUSTOM URETHANES INC
10010 Express Dr (46322-2612)
PHONE...............................219 924-1644
Jerry Lawhorn, Pr
Marie Lawhorn, Sec
EMP: 7 EST: 1971
SQ FT: 10,000
SALES (est): 716.35K Privately Held
SIC: 3089 Injection molded finished plastics products, nec

(G-7132)
DOCK BUMPERS INC ✪
9445 Indianapolis Blvd (46322-2648)
PHONE...............................312 597-9282
Lance Taylor, Managing Member
EMP: 1 EST: 2023
SALES (est): 77.54K Privately Held
SIC: 3711 8742 3715 Truck tractors for highway use, assembly of; Transportation consultant; Semitrailers for truck tractors

(G-7133)
DXD SIGNS
9231 Spring St (46322-2538)
PHONE...............................219 588-4403
Tracy Day, Prin
EMP: 5 EST: 2010
SALES (est): 58.4K Privately Held
SIC: 3993 Signs and advertising specialties

(G-7134)
ECONOMY ELECTRIC HTG & COOLG
9031 Grace St (46322-2166)
PHONE...............................219 923-4441
David Rivera, Owner
EMP: 2 EST: 2005
SALES (est): 168.67K Privately Held
Web: www.4ajobdoneright.com
SIC: 1711 3699 Heating systems repair and maintenance; Electrical equipment and supplies, nec

(G-7135)
EMMA PEARLS CREATIONS LLC
2158 45th St (46322-3742)
PHONE...............................219 200-2277
EMP: 1 EST: 2020
SALES (est): 143.24K Privately Held
SIC: 3999 5999 Candles; Candle shops

(G-7136)
FINK INDUSTRIES LLC
8750 Johnston St (46322-2035)
PHONE...............................219 923-2015
Charles Fink, Prin
EMP: 4 EST: 2010
SALES (est): 110.85K Privately Held
SIC: 3999 Manufacturing industries, nec

(G-7137)
GBJ HOLDINGS LLC
9445 Indianapolis Blvd Ste 1092 (46322-2648)
PHONE...............................317 483-1896
Gerald Bennett, Managing Member
EMP: 4 EST: 2018
SIC: 6719 5088 6531 3714 Holding companies, nec; Transportation equipment and supplies; Real estate agent, commercial; Dump truck lifting mechanism

(G-7138)
GERARD
9311 Southmoor Ave (46322-2518)
PHONE...............................219 924-6388
Sarah Mcmahon, Prin
EMP: 6 EST: 2010
SALES (est): 91.13K Privately Held
SIC: 3355 Structural shapes, rolled, aluminum

(G-7139)
GROWLERS
2816 Highway Ave (46322-1629)
PHONE...............................219 924-0245
Myron Chapman, Owner
EMP: 2 EST: 2007
SALES (est): 180.09K Privately Held
Web: www.901growlers.com
SIC: 2599 Bar, restaurant and cafeteria furniture

(G-7140)
HEADCO INDUSTRIES INC
Also Called: Bearing Headquarters Co
9922 Express Dr (46322-2609)
PHONE...............................219 924-7758
Carl Kator, Mgr
EMP: 4
SALES (corp-wide): 162MM Privately Held
Web: www.bearingheadquarters.com
SIC: 5085 5084 3599 Bearings; Hydraulic systems equipment and supplies; Machine shop, jobbing and repair
PA: Headco Industries, Inc.
2601 Parkes Dr
Broadview IL 60155
708 681-4400

(G-7141)
K2 INDUSTRIAL SERVICES INC (DH)
2552 Industrial Dr (46322-2625)
PHONE...............................219 933-1100
Ted L Mansfield, CEO
Rich Bartell, CFO
Rick Napier, COO
EMP: 10 EST: 1995
SALES (est): 321.11MM
SALES (corp-wide): 2.72B Privately Held
Web: www.k2industrial.com
SIC: 2842 1799 Specialty cleaning; Coating, caulking, and weather, water, and fireproofing
HQ: Asrc Industrial Services, Llc
1501 W Fntnhead Pkwy Ste
Tempe AZ 85282
707 644-7455

(G-7142)
LAKESIDE FOODS
9130 O Day Dr (46322-2849)
PHONE...............................219 924-4860
Edward R Mikula, Owner
EMP: 1 EST: 2001
SALES (est): 91.4K Privately Held
Web: www.lakesidefoods.com
SIC: 2033 Canned fruits and specialties

(G-7143)
MACHINING & REPR RESOURCE INC
3236 Strong St (46322-1452)
PHONE...............................219 588-7395
L David Kristoff, Pr
EMP: 5 EST: 2018
SALES (est): 287.94K Privately Held
Web: www.mrr-inc.com
SIC: 8742 3599 Industrial and labor consulting services; Machine shop, jobbing and repair

(G-7144)
MICKA CABINETS
8328 Kennedy Ave (46322-1137)
PHONE...............................219 838-5450
EMP: 6 EST: 2019
SALES (est): 130.35K Privately Held
Web: www.mickacabinets.com
SIC: 2434 Wood kitchen cabinets

(G-7145)
MIDWEST DACHSHUND RESCUE INC
2023 Ridgewood St (46322-1531)
PHONE...............................815 260-6734
EMP: 6 EST: 2010
SALES (est): 68.14K Privately Held
Web: www.mwdr.org
SIC: 3999 Pet supplies

(G-7146)
MODELE LLC
9445 Indianapolis Blvd (46322-2648)
PHONE...............................219 300-6929
Ann Gault, Managing Member
EMP: 1
SALES (est): 69.27K Privately Held
SIC: 2389 Apparel and accessories, nec

(G-7147)
NATURAL ANSWERS
2300 Ramblewood Dr Ste C (46322-3627)
PHONE...............................219 922-3663
Sarah Leep, Prin
EMP: 3 EST: 2007
SALES (est): 195.41K Privately Held
SIC: 2099 5149 8049 Food preparations, nec; Health foods; Nutritionist

(G-7148)
NWHOODTALES CORP
2436 Wicker Ave (46322-1842)
PHONE...............................708 858-0598
Nichelle Walker, CEO
EMP: 3 EST: 2020
SALES (est): 200K Privately Held
SIC: 2711 Newspapers, publishing and printing

(G-7149)
ONE LITTLE TRUCK LLC
2343 81st St (46322-1002)
PHONE...............................872 276-0014
EMP: 1 EST: 2020
SALES (est): 60.08K Privately Held
SIC: 3537 Trucks: freight, baggage, etc.: industrial, except mining

(G-7150)
P C COMMUNICATIONS INC
2301 Ridgewood St (46322-1537)
PHONE...............................219 838-2546
EMP: 5 EST: 1977
SALES (est): 157.29K Privately Held
SIC: 7291 3829 Tax return preparation services; Measuring and controlling devices, nec

(G-7151)
PASSIONS FRUITOPIA LLC
9445 Indianapolis Blvd Ste 1026 (46322-2648)
PHONE...............................800 515-1891
Rasheida Bennett, Pr
EMP: 5 EST: 2021
SALES (est): 361.58K Privately Held
Web: passionsfruitopia.constantcontactsites.com
SIC: 5149 7389 2099 5812 Specialty food items; Business Activities at Non-Commercial Site; Ready-to-eat meals, salads, and sandwiches; Contract food services

(G-7152)
REACHPOINT INDUSTRIES CORP
2419 81st St (46322-1004)
PHONE...............................219 707-3514
Gilbert Montoya, Prin
EMP: 1 EST: 2011
SALES (est): 44.79K Privately Held

Highland - Lake County (G-7153)

GEOGRAPHIC SECTION

SIC: 3999 Barber and beauty shop equipment

(G-7153)
SEMINOLE ENERGY SERVICES
8244 Kennedy Ave (46322-1133)
PHONE..................................219 923-2131
EMP: 5 EST: 2018
SALES (est): 77.7K Privately Held
SIC: 3822 Environmental controls

(G-7154)
SHEET METAL SERVICES INC
9944 Express Dr (46322-2688)
PHONE..................................219 924-1206
Robin Longfellow, Pr
Terry Longfellow, VP
EMP: 15 EST: 1973
SQ FT: 7,210
SALES (est): 779.28K Privately Held
SIC: 3444 Sheet metalwork

(G-7155)
SILHOUETTE BODY SCULPT LLC
9219 Indianapolis Blvd Ste 200 (46322)
PHONE..................................219 237-2391
Sandra Bowden, Managing Member
EMP: 5 EST: 2021
SALES (est): 245.92K Privately Held
Web: www.silhouettebodysculpt.com
SIC: 3299 Architectural sculptures: gypsum, clay, papier mache, etc.

(G-7156)
SMILES MOTORS LLC
2646 Highway Ave (46322-1661)
PHONE..................................219 801-5255
Nosakhare Oghafua, Managing Member
EMP: 5 EST: 2020
SALES (est): 529.11K Privately Held
SIC: 3537 4231 Truck trailers, used in plants, docks, terminals, etc.; Trucking terminal facilities

(G-7157)
TASCO INDUSTRIES INC
10018 Express Dr (46322)
PHONE..................................219 922-6100
Yucel Turan, Pr
Nalan Turan, VP
EMP: 5 EST: 1991
SQ FT: 6,000
SALES (est): 399.03K Privately Held
SIC: 3599 Machine shop, jobbing and repair

(G-7158)
TYLAYCULTURE LLC
Also Called: Tylayculture
9445 Indianapolis Blvd (46322-2648)
PHONE..................................219 678-8359
EMP: 4 EST: 2011
SALES (est): 104.88K Privately Held
SIC: 8999 7991 2741 6531 Music arranging and composing; Spas; Music, sheet: publishing only, not printed on site; Real estate leasing and rentals

(G-7159)
WOODHOLLOW LLC
9603 Spring St Rear (46322-2636)
PHONE..................................219 384-2802
Daniel Elzinga, Prin
EMP: 5 EST: 2016
SALES (est): 85.8K Privately Held
SIC: 2499 Wood products, nec

(G-7160)
XPEDITED BULK CARRIERS LLC
2043 Martha St (46322-2399)
PHONE..................................708 490-7539

EMP: 4 EST: 2021
SALES (est): 60K Privately Held
SIC: 3537 Truck trailers, used in plants, docks, terminals, etc.

Hillsboro
Fountain County

(G-7161)
NICHOLAS BRYANT
Also Called: Bryant's LP Gas
2539 E School House Rd (47949-8028)
PHONE..................................765 366-0108
Nicholas Bryant, Prin
EMP: 8 EST: 2014
SALES (est): 454.18K Privately Held
SIC: 1321 Natural gas liquids

(G-7162)
WALLACE PROCESSING LLC
3737 S State Road 341 (47949-8016)
PHONE..................................765 397-3363
Roy Smith, Owner
EMP: 2 EST: 1982
SALES (est): 130.02K Privately Held
SIC: 2011 Meat packing plants

Hillsdale
Vermillion County

(G-7163)
NEWPORT PALLET INC
1110 W Industrial Dr (47854-8117)
PHONE..................................765 505-9463
Adam Winland, Pr
EMP: 20 EST: 2014
SALES (est): 1.02MM Privately Held
Web: www.newportpallet.com
SIC: 2448 Pallets, wood

(G-7164)
SCOTT PET PRODUCTS INC
370 W Vermillion Rise Run (47854-8118)
PHONE..................................765 569-4702
Tj Clinkenbeard, Brnch Mgr
EMP: 60
SALES (corp-wide): 62.37MM Privately Held
Web: www.scottpet.com
SIC: 2047 Dog food
PA: Scott Pet Products, Inc.
1543 N Us Highway 41
Rockville IN 47872
765 569-4636

Hoagland
Allen County

(G-7165)
AMBROSIA ORCHARD INC
14025 Us Highway 27 (46745-9721)
PHONE..................................260 639-4101
EMP: 8 EST: 2019
SALES (est): 378.46K Privately Held
Web: www.ambrosiaorchardfw.com
SIC: 2084 Wines

(G-7166)
DAVAUS LLC
14508 Bruick Ln (46745-9623)
PHONE..................................260 245-5006
W Randall Kammeyer, Prin
EMP: 6 EST: 2018
SALES (est): 151.11K Privately Held
Web: www.davaus.com

SIC: 3523 Farm machinery and equipment

(G-7167)
DWD INDUSTRIES LLC
Also Called: Decatur Wire Die
11117 English St (46745-7402)
P.O. Box 65 (46745-0065)
PHONE..................................260 639-3254
EMP: 2
Web: www.estevesgroup.com
SIC: 3544 Wire drawing and straightening dies
HQ: Dwd Industries, Llc
1921 Patterson St
Decatur IN 46733
260 728-9272

(G-7168)
GARY E ELLSWORTH
14221 Franke Rd (46745-9746)
PHONE..................................260 639-3078
Gary Ellsworth, Prin
EMP: 1 EST: 2007
SALES (est): 75.45K Privately Held
SIC: 1751 2431 Carpentry work; Millwork

(G-7169)
KNAPKE & SONS INC
Also Called: Woodworking By Design
14525 Bruick Ln (46745-9623)
PHONE..................................260 639-0112
▲ EMP: 20 EST: 1993
SQ FT: 40,000
SALES (est): 2.05MM Privately Held
Web: www.woodworkingbydesign.net
SIC: 2431 Moldings, wood: unfinished and prefinished

(G-7170)
MADISON CABINETS INC
14727 Bruick Dr (46745-1500)
P.O. Box 188 (46745-0188)
PHONE..................................260 639-3915
Herman Guenin, Pr
Heath Guenin, VP
Craig Guenin, Sec
EMP: 8 EST: 1972
SQ FT: 4,000
SALES (est): 654.41K Privately Held
Web: www.madisoncabinets.com
SIC: 2434 2517 2511 Wood kitchen cabinets; Wood television and radio cabinets; Wood household furniture

(G-7171)
STONE-STREET QUARRIES INC
5536 Hoagland Rd (46745-9619)
P.O. Box 9246 (46899-9246)
PHONE..................................260 639-6511
William Sovers, Pr
Larry Gerig, VP
EMP: 19 EST: 1917
SQ FT: 1,000
SALES (est): 4.46MM Privately Held
SIC: 1422 3281 Limestones, ground; Cut stone and stone products

Hobart
Lake County

(G-7172)
AIRTEK LLC
Also Called: Catco
4410 W 37th Ave Frnt (46342-1654)
P.O. Box 428 (46342-0428)
PHONE..................................219 947-1664
▲ EMP: 120 EST: 1990
SALES (est): 9.84MM Privately Held
Web: www.catcoairtek.com

SIC: 3714 7533 Motor vehicle parts and accessories; Catalytic conversion

(G-7173)
ARISTO LLC
Also Called: Aristo Catalyst Technology
4410 W 37th Ave Frnt (46342-1654)
▲ EMP: 50 EST: 1991
SALES (est): 4.73MM Privately Held
Web: www.aristoglobal.com
SIC: 3694 3714 Armatures, automotive; Motor vehicle parts and accessories

(G-7174)
BAXTER HEALTHCARE CORPORATION
428 N Liberty St (46342-2418)
PHONE..................................219 942-8136
John Hammersmith, Pr
EMP: 1
SALES (corp-wide): 14.81B Publicly Held
Web: www.baxter.com
SIC: 3841 Surgical and medical instruments
HQ: Baxter Healthcare Corporation
1 Baxter Pkwy
Deerfield IL 60015
224 948-2000

(G-7175)
CAL PIPE MANUFACTURING INC
6451 Northwind Pkwy (46342-2496)
PHONE..................................219 844-6800
Bob Westerfield, Mgr
EMP: 8
SALES (corp-wide): 5.34MM Privately Held
Web: www.atkore.com
SIC: 3317 Steel pipe and tubes
PA: Cal Pipe Manufacturing, Inc.
12160 Woodruff Ave
Downey CA 90241
562 803-4388

(G-7176)
CALPIPE INDUSTRIES LLC
Calbrite
6451 Northwind Pkwy (46342-2496)
PHONE..................................219 844-6800
Daniel J Markus, CEO
EMP: 38
Web: www.atkore.com
SIC: 5051 3498 Metals service centers and offices; Fabricated pipe and fittings
HQ: Calpipe Industries, Llc
16100 Lathrop Ave
Harvey IL 60426

(G-7177)
CALUMET ORTHPD PROSTHETICS CO
7554 Grand Blvd (46342-6672)
PHONE..................................219 942-2148
Ronald Pawlowski, Pr
Micalea Pawlowski, VP
EMP: 9 EST: 1953
SALES (est): 962.96K Privately Held
Web: www.calumetoandp.com
SIC: 3842 Braces, orthopedic

(G-7178)
CARCAPSULE USA INC
4590 W 61st Ave (46342-6474)
PHONE..................................219 945-9493
▲ EMP: 10 EST: 2012
SALES (est): 527.08K Privately Held
Web: www.carcapsule.com
SIC: 2399 Automotive covers, except seat and tire covers

GEOGRAPHIC SECTION

Hobart - Lake County (G-7205)

(G-7179)
CATER TO YOU CATERING LLC
994 Deer Cross Trl (46342-5358)
PHONE..................219 301-1091
EMP: 4 **EST:** 2021
SALES (est): 116.15K **Privately Held**
SIC: 2099 7389 Food preparations, nec; Business Activities at Non-Commercial Site

(G-7180)
CBF FORENSICS LLC
201 N Linda St (46342-3249)
PHONE..................708 383-8320
Charles Steele, *Managing Member*
EMP: 5 **EST:** 2020
SALES (est): 194.16K **Privately Held**
SIC: 5734 3821 Software, business and non-game; Laboratory apparatus, except heating and measuring

(G-7181)
CHAPPOS INC
101 N Wabash St (46342-4031)
PHONE..................219 942-8101
Martin T Chappo, *Pr*
Judith Chappo, *Sec*
EMP: 4 **EST:** 1986
SALES (est): 222.94K **Privately Held**
SIC: 7692 7538 Automotive welding; Engine rebuilding: automotive

(G-7182)
COIL-TRAN LLC (HQ)
Also Called: Hobart Electronics
160 S Illinois St (46342-4512)
PHONE..................219 942-8511
Nicholas N Kriadis, *CEO*
Gary N Kriadis, *
Demetra Kriadis, *
▲ **EMP:** 90 **EST:** 1969
SQ FT: 30,000
SALES (est): 27.41MM
SALES (corp-wide): 554.6MM **Privately Held**
Web: www.hobart-electronics.com
SIC: 3677 5065 3621 3612 Electronic coils and transformers; Electronic parts and equipment, nec; Motors and generators; Transformers, except electric
PA: Discoverie Group Plc
 2 Chancellor Court
 Guildford GU2 7
 148 354-4500

(G-7183)
CONNIES SATIN STITCH INC
829 E 3rd St (46342-4501)
PHONE..................219 942-1887
Harry Decausemaker, *Pr*
Connie Decausemaker, *Pt*
EMP: 5 **EST:** 1982
SQ FT: 2,500
SALES (est): 358.95K **Privately Held**
SIC: 7389 2395 Sewing contractor; Pleating and stitching

(G-7184)
CRR INDUSTRIES LLC
8414 Old Lincoln Hwy (46342-7044)
PHONE..................219 947-2052
Cal Rueben Ramirez, *Pr*
EMP: 5 **EST:** 2015
SALES (est): 142.37K **Privately Held**
SIC: 3999 Atomizers, toiletry

(G-7185)
CRUZ ELECTRIC & HANDY SVC LLC
541 N Wisconsin St (46342)
P.O. Box 107 (46342)
PHONE..................219 308-7117
Steven Cruz, *Managing Member*
EMP: 5 **EST:** 2005
SALES (est): 325K **Privately Held**
Web: www.cruzelectricandhandysvc.com
SIC: 3643 7299 Electric connectors; Handyman service

(G-7186)
DAIFUKU INTRLGISTICS AMER CORP (DH)
6300 Northwind Pkwy (46342)
PHONE..................219 777-2220
Christoph Schenk, *Pr*
Clint Lasher, *
Michael J Farley, *
Anthony J Caruso, *
Scott Shepherd, *
▲ **EMP:** 100 **EST:** 1972
SQ FT: 350,000
SALES (est): 264.14MM **Privately Held**
Web: www.daifukuia.com
SIC: 1796 3535 8711 Machinery installation; Conveyors and conveying equipment; Engineering services
HQ: Daifuku North America Inc.
 30100 Cabot Dr
 Novi MI 48377
 248 553-1000

(G-7187)
EASTONS LETTERING SERVICE
514 E 3rd St (46342-4418)
PHONE..................219 942-5101
Mark Easton, *Owner*
EMP: 2 **EST:** 1960
SQ FT: 1,600
SALES (est): 152.65K **Privately Held**
SIC: 3999 Novelties, bric-a-brac, and hobby kits

(G-7188)
FLOWERS BAKING CO OHIO LLC
1601 W 37th Ave (46342-1909)
PHONE..................502 350-4700
Jamie Wilson, *Mgr*
EMP: 1
SALES (corp-wide): 5.09B **Publicly Held**
SIC: 2051 Bread, all types (white, wheat, rye, etc); fresh or frozen
HQ: Flowers Baking Co. Of Ohio, Llc
 325 W Alexis Rd Ste 1
 Toledo OH 43612
 419 269-9202

(G-7189)
HIELO SERVICES LLC
3011 Crabapple Ln (46342-3815)
PHONE..................219 973-1952
EMP: 3 **EST:** 2004
SALES (est): 174.88K **Privately Held**
SIC: 2711 Newspapers

(G-7190)
HOMELAND SPORTS LLC
4697 E 36th Ave (46342-1001)
PHONE..................219 962-2315
EMP: 1 **EST:** 2008
SALES (est): 52.84K **Privately Held**
SIC: 2741 7389 Miscellaneous publishing; Business services, nec

(G-7191)
INDIANA BOTANIC GARDENS INC
Also Called: Botanic Choice
3401 W 37th Ave (46342-1751)
PHONE..................219 947-4040
Harvey Cleland, *Ch Bd*
Timothy D Cleland, *
David Meyer, *
Tamara Cleland, *Prin*
◆ **EMP:** 157 **EST:** 1910
SQ FT: 50,000
SALES (est): 21.14MM **Privately Held**
Web: www.botanicchoice.com
SIC: 5961 2833 Mail order house, nec; Botanical products, medicinal: ground, graded, or milled

(G-7192)
INDIANNA
1931 Northwind Pkwy (46342-6550)
PHONE..................219 947-9533
EMP: 6 **EST:** 2019
SALES (est): 80.86K **Privately Held**
SIC: 3398 Metal heat treating

(G-7193)
ITR AMERICA LLC (PA)
Also Called: Bulldog
6301 Northwind Pkwy (46342-2495)
PHONE..................219 947-8230
◆ **EMP:** 55 **EST:** 2008
SQ FT: 100,000
SALES (est): 101.47MM
SALES (corp-wide): 101.47MM **Privately Held**
Web: www.itramerica.com
SIC: 5082 3531 General construction machinery and equipment; Construction machinery

(G-7194)
J J P ENTERPRISE
Also Called: American Hosiery
442 Quail Dr (46342-2373)
PHONE..................219 947-3154
Jannes F Johnson, *Owner*
EMP: 1 **EST:** 1992
SALES (est): 58.95K **Privately Held**
SIC: 2252 Hosiery, nec

(G-7195)
KALUSTYAN CORPORATION ✪
1650 Northwind Pkwy (46342-6564)
PHONE..................908 688-6111
Fernando Porras, *COO*
EMP: 10 **EST:** 2023
SALES (est): 545.66K **Privately Held**
SIC: 2099 Seasonings and spices

(G-7196)
KARBACH HOLDINGS CORPORATION
1701 Northwind Pkwy (46342-6549)
PHONE..................219 924-2454
Kevin Huseman, *Pr*
Connie Huseman, *Sec*
EMP: 19 **EST:** 1990
SQ FT: 10,000
SALES (est): 925.74K **Privately Held**
SIC: 3993 Signs and advertising specialties

(G-7197)
KEYWEST METAL
6338 E 35th Ave (46342-1463)
PHONE..................219 654-4063
Michael Clark, *Admn*
EMP: 5 **EST:** 2015
SALES (est): 157.39K **Privately Held**
SIC: 5051 3399 Metals service centers and offices; Primary metal products

(G-7198)
KNITTING MILL INC
Also Called: Kms
291 N County Line Rd (46342-7103)
PHONE..................219 942-8031
Fred Karrle, *Pr*
EMP: 5 **EST:** 1963
SQ FT: 2,000
SALES (est): 306.67K **Privately Held**
Web: www.knittingmillinc.com
SIC: 3843 Dental materials

(G-7199)
LINDAS GONE BUGGIE
28 E 36th Pl (46342-1031)
PHONE..................219 299-0174
EMP: 4 **EST:** 2012
SALES (est): 79.57K **Privately Held**
Web: www.lindasgonebuggie.com
SIC: 3531 Concrete buggies, powered

(G-7200)
LJ MOTIVE LLC
6163 Oregon St (46342-6418)
PHONE..................219 588-5480
EMP: 10 **EST:** 2020
SALES (est): 491.81K **Privately Held**
SIC: 2335 7389 Women's, junior's, and misses' dresses; Business Activities at Non-Commercial Site

(G-7201)
MELLON TAX SERVICE
101 Center St (46342-4425)
PHONE..................219 947-1660
James Mellon, *Pt*
Pamela Mellon, *Pt*
EMP: 3 **EST:** 1983
SALES (est): 251.95K **Privately Held**
Web: www.mellontaxservice.com
SIC: 7389 7372 Legal and tax services; Prepackaged software

(G-7202)
NOBLE PROJECT SERVICES LLC
Also Called: Construction
822 W 39th Pl (46342-2130)
PHONE..................219 484-9669
Dan Granquist, *Admn*
EMP: 3 **EST:** 2021
SALES (est): 237.49K **Privately Held**
SIC: 1389 Construction, repair, and dismantling services

(G-7203)
PAPPAS CONSTRUCTION LLC
2310 Pembroke Dr N (46342-3472)
PHONE..................219 314-7068
EMP: 1
SALES (est): 64.69K **Privately Held**
SIC: 1389 7389 Construction, repair, and dismantling services; Business Activities at Non-Commercial Site

(G-7204)
RUWALDT PACKING COMPANY INC
6510 E Ridge Rd (46342-2302)
P.O. Box 563 (46342-0563)
PHONE..................219 942-2911
Edward Oedzes, *Pr*
EMP: 14 **EST:** 1957
SQ FT: 1,000
SALES (est): 482.23K **Privately Held**
SIC: 2011 2013 Lamb products, from lamb slaughtered on site; Sausages and other prepared meats

(G-7205)
SAMS TECH TIRE LLC
Also Called: Sam's Tech Supply
435 S Shelby St (46342-4731)
PHONE..................219 942-7317
Jason Baldwin, *Managing Member*
EMP: 4 **EST:** 2021
SALES (est): 253.08K **Privately Held**
SIC: 3011 7389 Tire and inner tube materials and related products; Business Activities at Non-Commercial Site

Hobart - Lake County (G-7206)

(G-7206)
SAPPERS MARKET AND GREENHOUSES
Also Called: Sapper's Farm Market
1155 S Lake Park Ave (46342)
PHONE.................................219 942-4995
Janet Kraynik, *Owner*
EMP: 9 **EST:** 1923
SALES (est): 241.62K **Privately Held**
Web: www.sappersmarket.com
SIC: 0181 0161 2048 5261 Ornamental nursery products; Vegetables and melons; Bird food, prepared; Christmas trees (natural)

(G-7207)
SIGN ART QUALITY ADVERTISING
Also Called: Sign Art
5474 Us Hwy 6 (46342)
PHONE.................................219 763-6122
Timothy R Bruns, *Owner*
EMP: 1 **EST:** 1977
SALES (est): 86.17K **Privately Held**
SIC: 2759 3993 Letterpress and screen printing; Signs and advertising specialties

(G-7208)
SIGN SOURCE ONE GROUP INC
3429 Michigan St (46342-1170)
PHONE.................................219 736-5865
Scott Billeck, *Pr*
EMP: 3 **EST:** 1997
SQ FT: 2,500
SALES (est): 233.81K **Privately Held**
Web: www.signsourceone.com
SIC: 3993 Electric signs

(G-7209)
SMOKE SMOKE SMOKE
1165 W 37th Ave (46342-2012)
PHONE.................................219 942-3331
Omar Alburei, *Owner*
EMP: 3 **EST:** 2005
SALES (est): 242.49K **Privately Held**
Web: www.smokepipeshops.com
SIC: 3999 Cigarette and cigar products and accessories

(G-7210)
STORK NEWS NORTHWEST INDIANA
2880 Tulip Ln (46342-7521)
PHONE.................................219 808-5221
David Parsanko, *Prin*
EMP: 5 **EST:** 2008
SALES (est): 44.04K **Privately Held**
SIC: 2721 Periodicals, publishing and printing

(G-7211)
THOMPSON
421 Driftwood Dr (46342-3909)
PHONE.................................219 942-8133
Harold Thompson, *Mgr*
EMP: 3 **EST:** 2008
SALES (est): 220.72K **Privately Held**
SIC: 3841 Veterinarians' instruments and apparatus

(G-7212)
TITANIUM RAILS NUTRITION LLC
1709 E 37th Ave (46342-2576)
PHONE.................................219 940-3704
Martin Amaya, *Mgr*
EMP: 6 **EST:** 2014
SALES (est): 193.69K **Privately Held**
SIC: 3356 Titanium

(G-7213)
VINZANT SOFTWARE INC
904 W Old Ridge Rd Ste 1 (46342-2957)
P.O. Box 2907 (46403-0907)
PHONE.................................219 942-9544
David Vinzant, *Pr*
John Vinzant, *Ex VP*
EMP: 21 **EST:** 1988
SQ FT: 5,000
SALES (est): 465.43K **Privately Held**
Web: www.vinzantsoftware.com
SIC: 7372 Prepackaged software

Holland
Dubois County

(G-7214)
BRATCO INC
502 N 2nd St (47541-9675)
P.O. Box 157 (47541-0157)
PHONE.................................812 536-4071
EMP: 9 **EST:** 1978
SALES (est): 528.51K **Privately Held**
SIC: 2431 Millwork

(G-7215)
WOODS PRINTING COMPANY INC
601 W Main St (47541-9687)
P.O. Box 99 (47541-0099)
PHONE.................................812 536-2261
David Springston, *Pr*
Maurice C Woods, *CEO*
Sharon Springston, *VP*
Emma Lou Woods, *Sec*
EMP: 16 **EST:** 1971
SQ FT: 8,800
SALES (est): 2.17MM **Privately Held**
Web: www.brandedbywoods.com
SIC: 2752 Offset printing

Holton
Ripley County

(G-7216)
GUYS WOOD N THINGS
340 N County Road 300 W (47023-8508)
PHONE.................................812 689-0433
Sara Lee, *Owner*
EMP: 2 **EST:** 2003
SALES (est): 66.65K **Privately Held**
SIC: 2431 Woodwork, interior and ornamental, nec

(G-7217)
HOLMAN SPTIC TANK SLS RDYMIX I
Also Called: Holman's Septic Tank Sales
4896 S Old Michigan Rd (47023-9115)
PHONE.................................812 689-1913
Harry Holman, *Pr*
Bernette Holman, *VP*
EMP: 18 **EST:** 1972
SQ FT: 7,500
SALES (est): 572.63K **Privately Held**
SIC: 3272 Septic tanks, concrete

(G-7218)
IWP LLC
7207 W Versailles St (47023-8614)
PHONE.................................812 756-0303
Brian Oliver, *Admn*
EMP: 6 **EST:** 2013
SALES (est): 82.03K **Privately Held**
Web: www.iwpllc.com
SIC: 7692 Welding repair

(G-7219)
OTTER CREEK CANDLE LLC
2303 N Old Michigan Rd (47023-8599)
PHONE.................................812 750-4129
Robin L Reeves, *Pr*
EMP: 3 **EST:** 2015
SALES (est): 43.66K **Privately Held**
Web: www.ottercreekcandle.com
SIC: 3999 Candles

(G-7220)
ROHRS CUSTOM METAL
2426 N Old Michigan Rd (47023-8400)
PHONE.................................812 689-3764
Dean Rohr, *Owner*
EMP: 1 **EST:** 1993
SALES (est): 85.32K **Privately Held**
Web: rohrs-custom-metal-steel-fabricator.business.site
SIC: 3444 Ducts, sheet metal

Homer
Rush County

(G-7221)
SAMPLER INC (PA)
7138 W 235 S (46146-9812)
PHONE.................................765 663-2233
Avis Brown, *Pr*
Bruce Levi, *Mgr*
EMP: 14 **EST:** 1946
SQ FT: 10,000
SALES (est): 1MM
SALES (corp-wide): 1MM **Privately Held**
Web: www.samplercherryfurniture.com
SIC: 5719 2511 Housewares, nec; Wood bedroom furniture

Hope
Bartholomew County

(G-7222)
ACTION FILTRATION INC (PA)
221 Raymond St (47246-9356)
PHONE.................................812 546-6262
Les Benesh, *Pr*
Paul M Trotta Junior, *VP*
▼ **EMP:** 5 **EST:** 1989
SQ FT: 12,000
SALES (est): 3.99MM
SALES (corp-wide): 3.99MM **Privately Held**
Web: www.actionfiltration.com
SIC: 3569 Filters, general line: industrial

(G-7223)
ECLIPSE MOLDING COMPANY LLC
Also Called: Air Support Medical Company
199 Raymond St (47246-9382)
PHONE.................................812 546-0050
Scott Hartwell, *Managing Member*
EMP: 6 **EST:** 2019
SALES (est): 880K **Privately Held**
Web: www.eclipsemolding.com
SIC: 3089 Injection molding of plastics

(G-7224)
FLW PLASTICS INC
Also Called: Air Support Medical
199 Raymond St (47246-9382)
P.O. Box 99 (47246-0099)
PHONE.................................812 546-0050
Kathy Walters, *Pr*
EMP: 12 **EST:** 1986
SQ FT: 12,000
SALES (est): 377.2K **Privately Held**
Web: www.airsupportmedical.com
SIC: 3089 3841 Injection molding of plastics; Anesthesia apparatus

(G-7225)
FOURMAN ENTERPRISES INC
701 South St (47246-9345)
PHONE.................................812 546-5734
Gary Bailey, *Pr*
EMP: 14 **EST:** 1974
SQ FT: 7,200
SALES (est): 1.85MM **Privately Held**
Web: www.fourmanenterprises.com
SIC: 3599 7699 Custom machinery; Hydraulic equipment repair

(G-7226)
HOPE HARDWOODS INC
1006 Seminary St (47246-1427)
P.O. Box 37 (47246-0037)
PHONE.................................812 546-4427
D Thomas Miller, *Pr*
Gary M Miller, *VP*
Lowell Miller, *Sec*
Ben Miller, *VP*
EMP: 10 **EST:** 1972
SQ FT: 13,000
SALES (est): 2.01MM **Privately Held**
Web: www.goodhopehardwoods.com
SIC: 5084 2421 Sewing machines, industrial; Sawmills and planing mills, general

(G-7227)
INDIANA CUSTOM FABRICATION INC
113 High St (47246-1568)
PHONE.................................812 727-8900
Stephanie Long, *Pr*
EMP: 3 **EST:** 2017
SALES (est): 294.52K **Privately Held**
Web: www.indianacustomfab.com
SIC: 3441 Fabricated structural metal

(G-7228)
INDIANA NEWS MEDIA LLC (PA)
Also Called: Hope Star Journal
645 Harrison St (47246-1203)
PHONE.................................812 546-4940
Larry D Simpson, *Prin*
EMP: 3 **EST:** 2008
SALES (est): 84.94K **Privately Held**
Web: www.alabamapersonalinjurylawyers.org
SIC: 2711 Job printing and newspaper publishing combined

(G-7229)
MOTORSPORT PRICE ENGINEERING
205 Main St (47246-1524)
PHONE.................................812 546-4220
Mary K Price, *Pr*
William F Price, *Sec*
EMP: 5 **EST:** 1982
SALES (est): 435.48K **Privately Held**
Web: www.pricemotorsport.com
SIC: 3519 3714 5531 Internal combustion engines, nec; Motor vehicle parts and accessories; Speed shops, including race car supplies

(G-7230)
PACE TOOL & ENGINEERING INC
19905 E County Road 640 N (47246-9370)
PHONE.................................812 373-9885
Todd Burbrink, *Pr*
Mark Thomson, *Sec*
Don Coombs, *VP*
EMP: 5 **EST:** 2001
SALES (est): 485.39K **Privately Held**
Web: www.pacetool.com
SIC: 3544 Special dies and tools

(G-7231)
PLASTIC PROJECT RESOURCE LLC
3302 N Meadow Dr (47246-9481)
PHONE.................................812 390-9790
EMP: 1 **EST:** 2017
SALES (est): 62.11K **Privately Held**
SIC: 3089 Plastics products, nec

GEOGRAPHIC SECTION

Huntertown - Allen County (G-7257)

(G-7232)
RUSACH INTERNATIONAL INC
100 Raymond St (47246-9382)
PHONE.................................317 638-0298
Rudi Sachs, *Ex VP*
▲ **EMP:** 15 **EST:** 1983
SQ FT: 24,000
SALES (est): 2.49MM **Privately Held**
Web: www.rusach.com
SIC: 3545 5085 Machine tool attachments and accessories; Industrial tools

Howe
Lagrange County

(G-7233)
D RV LUXURY SUITES LLC
1000 Interchange Dr (46746)
P.O. Box 235 (46746-0235)
PHONE.................................260 562-1075
David Fought, *Managing Member*
EMP: 14 **EST:** 2008
SALES (est): 385.11K **Privately Held**
Web: www.drvsuites.com
SIC: 3799 Recreational vehicles

(G-7234)
ELMERS SERVICE LLC
1880 W 300 N (46746)
PHONE.................................260 463-8287
Elmer Eash, *Managing Member*
EMP: 1 **EST:** 2016
SALES (est): 735K **Privately Held**
SIC: 1381 Drilling oil and gas wells

(G-7235)
EXO-S US LLC (DH)
Also Called: Camoplast Crocker
6505 N State Road 9 (46746)
P.O. Box 69 (46746)
PHONE.................................260 562-4100
Emmanuel Duchesne, *CEO*
Sylvain Dupuis, *
Daniel Denault, *
◆ **EMP:** 112 **EST:** 2005
SQ FT: 725
SALES (est): 50.27MM
SALES (corp-wide): 1.06B **Privately Held**
Web: www.exo-s.com
SIC: 3089 Injection molding of plastics
HQ: Exo-S Inc.
  2100 Rue King O Bureau 240
  Sherbrooke QC J1J 2
  819 346-3967

(G-7236)
HENSCHEN SAND AND GRAVEL
4635 N 800 E (46746-9767)
PHONE.................................260 367-2636
EMP: 3 **EST:** 2012
SALES (est): 193.74K **Privately Held**
SIC: 1442 Construction sand and gravel

(G-7237)
JAG MOBILE SOLUTIONS INC
770 E State Road 120 (46746-9218)
P.O. Box 100 (46746-0100)
PHONE.................................260 562-1045
William E Gibson, *Pr*
Bill Gibson, *
EMP: 30 **EST:** 2006
SQ FT: 90,000
SALES (est): 8.98MM **Privately Held**
Web: www.jagmobilesolutions.com
SIC: 5561 3259 Motor homes; Clay sewer and drainage pipe and tile

(G-7238)
LGIN LLC
6825 N 375 E (46746-9684)
PHONE.................................260 562-2233
John Larimer, *Prin*
EMP: 3 **EST:** 2008
SALES (est): 138.04K **Privately Held**
SIC: 2068 Salted and roasted nuts and seeds

(G-7239)
MAKE IT MOBILE LLC
770 E State Road 120 (46746-9218)
P.O. Box 10 (46746-0010)
PHONE.................................260 562-1045
EMP: 9 **EST:** 2010
SALES (est): 233.53K **Privately Held**
SIC: 3714 Motor vehicle parts and accessories

(G-7240)
MICHIANA LAMINATED PRODUCTS
7130 N 050 E (46746-9706)
PHONE.................................260 562-2871
Matthew R Sutter, *Pr*
Michael R Sutter, *CEO*
Matthew Sutter, *Pr*
EMP: 24 **EST:** 1978
SQ FT: 20,000
SALES (est): 986.52K **Privately Held**
Web: www.michianalaminated.com
SIC: 2542 Partitions and fixtures, except wood

(G-7241)
RAPID SENSORS INC
6060 N 160 W (46746-9436)
P.O. Box 188 (46746-0188)
PHONE.................................260 499-0079
Larry Hedeen, *Pr*
EMP: 6 **EST:** 2000
SALES (est): 496.13K **Privately Held**
Web: www.rapidsensors.com
SIC: 3674 Ultra-violet sensors, solid state

(G-7242)
SHOPHOUSE FABRICATION LLC
4925 N 900 E (46746-9357)
PHONE.................................260 367-2156
Tim Johnson, *Prin*
EMP: 5 **EST:** 2015
SALES (est): 82.95K **Privately Held**
SIC: 3999 Manufacturing industries, nec

(G-7243)
THERMA-TRU CORP
8055 N State Road 9 (46746-9822)
PHONE.................................260 562-1009
EMP: 16
SALES (corp-wide): 4.63B **Publicly Held**
Web: www.thermatru.com
SIC: 5031 3442 Windows; Metal doors, sash, and trim
HQ: Therma-Tru Corp.
  1750 Indian Wood Cir # 100
  Maumee OH 43537
  800 843-7628

Hudson
Steuben County

(G-7244)
COLD HEADING CO
103 W State Road 4 (46747-9336)
PHONE.................................260 587-3231
EMP: 35
SALES (corp-wide): 78.82MM **Privately Held**
Web: www.coldheading.com
SIC: 3452 Bolts, metal
HQ: The Cold Heading Co
  21777 Hoover Rd
  Warren MI 48089
  586 497-7000

(G-7245)
COMMERCIAL PALLET RECYCL INC
7430 S 800 W (46747-9508)
PHONE.................................260 668-6208
Sam Campbell, *Brnch Mgr*
EMP: 1
SALES (corp-wide): 951.21K **Privately Held**
Web: www.commercialpalletinc.com
SIC: 2448 5031 Pallets, wood; Pallets, wood
PA: Commercial Pallet Recycling, Inc.
  5235 N State Road 327
  Orland IN 46776
  260 829-1021

(G-7246)
HUDSON INDUSTRIES INC
105 W State Road 4 (46747-9336)
P.O. Box 426 (46747-0426)
PHONE.................................260 587-3288
EMP: 150 **EST:** 1986
SALES (est): 49.61MM **Privately Held**
SIC: 3465 Automotive stampings
PA: Midway Products Group, Inc.
  1 Lyman E Hoyt Dr
  Monroe MI 48161

(G-7247)
KZ WELDING
7754 W 400 S (46747-9728)
PHONE.................................260 350-7397
Kenneth Zweracker, *Owner*
EMP: 5 **EST:** 2014
SALES (est): 47.77K **Privately Held**
SIC: 7692 Welding repair

(G-7248)
MIDWAY PRODUCTS GROUP INC
105 W State Road 4 (46747-9336)
PHONE.................................734 241-7242
EMP: 10
Web: www.midwayproducts.com
SIC: 3469 Metal stampings, nec
PA: Midway Products Group, Inc.
  1 Lyman E Hoyt Dr
  Monroe MI 48161

Huntertown
Allen County

(G-7249)
ASPHALT DRUM MIXERS LLC
Also Called: ADM
1 Adm Pkwy (46748)
PHONE.................................260 637-5729
Wayne Boyd, *CEO*
Michael Devine, *
Linda Boyd, *
▼ **EMP:** 50 **EST:** 1983
SQ FT: 45,000
SALES (est): 8.93MM
SALES (corp-wide): 34.69MM **Privately Held**
Web: www.admasphaltplants.com
SIC: 3531 Mixers, nec: ore, plaster, slag, sand, mortar, etc.
PA: Fayat
  137 Rue Du Palais Gallien
  Bordeaux 33000
  556002100

(G-7250)
CLUTE ENTERPRISES INC
Also Called: O3 Solutions
18706 Coldwater Rd (46748-9732)
PHONE.................................260 413-0810
Kevin Clute, *Pr*
EMP: 2 **EST:** 1995
SALES (est): 238.7K **Privately Held**
Web: www.o3solutions.net
SIC: 3589 Sewage and water treatment equipment

(G-7251)
CREATIVE TOOL INC
2403 W Shoaff Rd (46748-9549)
PHONE.................................260 338-1222
Thomas Lowe, *Pr*
EMP: 4 **EST:** 1999
SQ FT: 3,000
SALES (est): 486.89K **Privately Held**
SIC: 3541 Machine tool replacement & repair parts, metal cutting types

(G-7252)
CS PRECISION MACHINING INC
16335 Lima Rd Ste 6a (46748-9302)
PHONE.................................260 338-1081
Craig Sanford, *Pr*
Tracy Conrad, *VP*
Brian Simpson, *Sec*
EMP: 6 **EST:** 2005
SQ FT: 7,000
SALES (est): 556.41K **Privately Held**
Web: www.cspmachining.com
SIC: 3599 Machine shop, jobbing and repair

(G-7253)
DIAMOND J CONSTRUCTION LLC
14910 Towne Gardens Dr (46748-9102)
PHONE.................................260 433-5571
EMP: 1 **EST:** 2016
SALES (est): 57.22K **Privately Held**
Web: www.diamondjconstruction.com
SIC: 1389 Construction, repair, and dismantling services

(G-7254)
EAGLE PRECISION LLC ✪
2420 W Shoaff Rd (46748)
PHONE.................................260 637-4649
EMP: 14 **EST:** 2022
SALES (est): 556.73K **Privately Held**
SIC: 3545 Tools and accessories for machine tools

(G-7255)
EAGLE PRECISION MACHINING INC
2420 W Shoaff Rd (46748)
PHONE.................................260 637-4649
EMP: 8 **EST:** 1995
SQ FT: 4,700
SALES (est): 607.48K **Privately Held**
SIC: 3541 Machine tool replacement & repair parts, metal cutting types

(G-7256)
FITCH INC
3708 Mccomb Rd (46748-9448)
PHONE.................................260 637-0835
Richard Fitch, *Brnch Mgr*
EMP: 17
SALES (corp-wide): 18.5B **Privately Held**
Web: www.landor.com
SIC: 3491 Industrial valves
HQ: Fitch Inc
  585 Suth Front St Ste 300
  Columbus OH 43215
  614 885-3453

(G-7257)
H & H SALES COMPANY INC
16339 Lima Rd (46748-9756)
PHONE.................................260 637-3177

(PA)=Parent Co (HQ)=Headquarters
✪ = New Business established in last 2 years

Huntertown - Allen County (G-7258)

John Hawkins, CEO
Phil Randall, Pr
Tom Hiser, VP
Rex Yant, VP
◆ **EMP:** 16 **EST:** 1951
SQ FT: 23,000
SALES (est): 2.29MM **Privately Held**
Web: www.hhsalescompany.com
SIC: 3713 3715 3499 Truck bodies (motor vehicles); Trailer bodies; Aerosol valves, metal

(G-7258)
JOE MAY INDUSTRIES LLC
2650 Stonecrop Rd (46748-9516)
PHONE..................................260 494-8735
Joseph May, *Prin*
EMP: 4 **EST:** 2018
SALES (est): 43.66K **Privately Held**
SIC: 3999 Manufacturing industries, nec

(G-7259)
NEXT PHASE GRAPHICS
16825 Lima Rd (46748-9712)
P.O. Box 403 (46765-0403)
PHONE..................................260 627-6259
EMP: 1 **EST:** 1999
SALES (est): 95.78K **Privately Held**
Web: www.nxphase.biz
SIC: 2759 2395 Screen printing; Embroidery and art needlework

(G-7260)
PARAMETRIC MACHINING INC
16335 Lima Rd Ste 3 (46748-9302)
PHONE..................................260 338-1564
Michael Sutton, *Pr*
Sandra Sutton, *Sec*
EMP: 13 **EST:** 2001
SQ FT: 16,000
SALES (est): 1.12MM **Privately Held**
Web: www.pmifw.com
SIC: 3599 Machine shop, jobbing and repair

(G-7261)
PRECISION WELDING CORP
16403 Lima Rd (46748-9756)
P.O. Box 511 (46748-0511)
PHONE..................................260 637-5514
Janice Hantz, *Sec*
Orville E Hantz, *Pr*
EMP: 4 **EST:** 1972
SQ FT: 10,000
SALES (est): 350.03K **Privately Held**
Web: www.precisionweldingcorp.com
SIC: 7692 3544 Welding repair; Special dies, tools, jigs, and fixtures

(G-7262)
PREVAIL DESIGN SYSTEMS LLC
5130 Willow Bluff Trl (46748-9798)
PHONE..................................260 245-1245
Aaron Engle, *Pr*
EMP: 5 **EST:** 2011
SALES (est): 415.91K **Privately Held**
Web: www.prevaildesignsystems.com
SIC: 3571 Computers, digital, analog or hybrid

(G-7263)
PRICE MACHINE & TOOL INC (PA)
16335 Lima Rd Ste 9a (46748-9302)
PHONE..................................260 338-1081
Stevan Price, *Pr*
Joyce M Price, *Sec*
EMP: 1 **EST:** 1978
SQ FT: 4,000
SALES (est): 486.06K
SALES (corp-wide): 486.06K **Privately Held**

SIC: 3544 Special dies and tools

(G-7264)
PRIMAL PRINTS LLC
15115 Hidden Oaks Run (46748-9340)
PHONE..................................260 494-8435
EMP: 6 **EST:** 2019
SALES (est): 312.71K **Privately Held**
Web: www.primalprints.us
SIC: 2752 Commercial printing, lithographic

(G-7265)
RMT INC
2420 W Shoaff Rd (46748-9484)
P.O. Box 431 (46748-0431)
PHONE..................................260 637-4649
Paul Russell, *Pr*
Timothy Pease, *VP*
EMP: 11 **EST:** 1990
SQ FT: 1,800
SALES (est): 578.85K **Privately Held**
Web: www.rmt-tooling.com
SIC: 3599 Machine shop, jobbing and repair

(G-7266)
SOMMER LETTER COMPANY LLC
3916 E North County Line Rd (46748-9486)
PHONE..................................260 414-6686
Kyle Sommer, *Prin*
EMP: 5 **EST:** 2015
SALES (est): 62.99K **Privately Held**
Web: www.sommerletterco.com
SIC: 2711 Newspapers

(G-7267)
US AUTOMATION LLC
7143 State Road 3 (46748-9605)
PHONE..................................260 338-1100
Dale Duncan, *Managing Member*
Dee Duncan, *Managing Member*
EMP: 8 **EST:** 2003
SQ FT: 10,000
SALES (est): 1.22MM **Privately Held**
Web: www.usautomationllc.com
SIC: 3599 Machine shop, jobbing and repair

(G-7268)
WETWILLIES BUBBLES LLC
15486 Bears Breech Ct (46748-9153)
PHONE..................................260 633-0064
Willie Buffenbarger, *CEO*
EMP: 1 **EST:** 2019
SALES (est): 55.37K **Privately Held**
SIC: 3714 Cleaners, air, motor vehicle

(G-7269)
WILLIAMS QUALITY PALLETS INC
15414 Delphinium Pl (46748)
PHONE..................................770 265-1030
Marsha Siha, *Prin*
Morgan Williams, *Prin*
EMP: 1 **EST:** 2016
SALES (est): 70.88K **Privately Held**
Web: www.williamsqualitypallets.com
SIC: 2448 Pallets, wood

Huntingburg
Dubois County

(G-7270)
B & A CNSTR & DESIGN INC
772 W 3rd St (47542-1206)
P.O. Box 135 (47542-0135)
PHONE..................................812 683-4600
Roger Thacker, *Pr*
EMP: 15 **EST:** 2002
SQ FT: 12,500
SALES (est): 2.35MM **Privately Held**
Web: www.banda-construction.com

SIC: 3448 Trusses and framing, prefabricated metal

(G-7271)
BY THE SWORD INC
304 E Sunset Dr (47542-9317)
P.O. Box 7282 (33919-0282)
PHONE..................................877 433-9368
David Rothgeb, *Pr*
EMP: 10 **EST:** 2009
SALES (est): 782.54K **Privately Held**
Web: www.bytheswordinc.com
SIC: 3312 Armor plate

(G-7272)
C & L LUMBER INC
8836 W State Road 64 (47542-9759)
PHONE..................................812 536-2171
Chuck Jones, *CEO*
Chuck Jones, *Pr*
Larry Jones, *VP*
EMP: 6 **EST:** 1991
SALES (est): 525.18K **Privately Held**
Web: www.cllumber.com
SIC: 2421 Sawmills and planing mills, general

(G-7273)
CECILS PRINTING & OFF SUPS INC
319 E 4th St (47542-1337)
PHONE..................................812 683-4416
Sue Fraze, *Pr*
Jeff Fraze, *VP*
EMP: 3 **EST:** 1978
SQ FT: 1,000
SALES (est): 253.21K **Privately Held**
SIC: 2759 2752 5943 2796 Letterpress printing; Offset printing; Office forms and supplies; Platemaking services

(G-7274)
CHARLES E OBRYAN
8999 S 500w (47542-9653)
PHONE..................................812 536-2399
Charles E Obryan, *Owner*
EMP: 1 **EST:** 1997
SALES (est): 85.73K **Privately Held**
SIC: 3543 Industrial patterns

(G-7275)
COVIA HOLDINGS CORPORATION
Also Called: COVIA HOLDINGS CORPORATION
1405 Industrial Park Dr (47542-9818)
P.O. Box 194 (47542-0194)
PHONE..................................812 683-2179
Kevin Heckel, *Mgr*
EMP: 8
SALES (corp-wide): 1.6B **Privately Held**
Web: www.coviacorp.com
SIC: 1455 3295 3281 Ball clay mining; Minerals, ground or treated; Cut stone and stone products
PA: Covia Holdings Llc
3 Summit Park Dr Ste 700
Independence OH 44131
800 255-7263

(G-7276)
DUBOIS COUNTY FREE PRESS LLC
4288 W 630s (47542-9660)
P.O. Box 46 (47542-0046)
PHONE..................................812 639-9651
EMP: 2 **EST:** 2011
SALES (est): 80.37K **Privately Held**
Web: www.duboiscountyfreepress.com
SIC: 2711 Newspapers: publishing only, not printed on site

(G-7277)
DUBOIS WOOD PRODUCTS INC (PA)
707 E 6th St (47542-1131)
P.O. Box 386 (47542-0386)
PHONE..................................812 683-3613
Jack B Parker, *CEO*
Bryan Meyerholtz, *
Phil Lueken, *
Paul Lueken, *
Vickie Meyerholtz, *
EMP: 160 **EST:** 1979
SQ FT: 200,000
SALES (est): 633.98K
SALES (corp-wide): 633.98K **Privately Held**
Web: www.duboiswood.com
SIC: 2511 Novelty furniture: wood

(G-7278)
DURCHOLZ EXCVTG & CNSTR CO INC
Also Called: Durcholz Excvtg & Cnstr Co In
4308 S State Road 162 (47542-9467)
PHONE..................................812 634-1764
Robert Anthony Durcholz, *Pr*
Mary Jane Durcholz, *Sec*
EMP: 6 **EST:** 1967
SQ FT: 1,200
SALES (est): 852.52K **Privately Held**
SIC: 1794 3715 Excavation work; Trailer bodies

(G-7279)
FARBEST FARMS INC
4689 S 400w (47542-9199)
P.O. Box 480 (47542-0480)
PHONE..................................812 481-1034
Theodore Seger, *Pr*
Gerald Jones, *Sec*
EMP: 10 **EST:** 1998
SALES (est): 2.17MM **Privately Held**
Web: www.farbestfoods.com
SIC: 2015 Poultry slaughtering and processing

(G-7280)
FARBEST FOODS INTL INC
4689 S 400w (47542-9199)
PHONE..................................812 683-4200
Ted J Seger, *Pr*
EMP: 7 **EST:** 2014
SALES (est): 126.41K **Privately Held**
Web: www.farbestfoods.com
SIC: 2015 Turkey, processed, nsk

(G-7281)
HUCKS FOOD FUEL
Also Called: Citgo
601 N Main St (47542-1043)
PHONE..................................812 683-5566
Mike Tubbs, *Mgr*
EMP: 11 **EST:** 2010
SALES (est): 179.18K **Privately Held**
Web: www.hucks.com
SIC: 2869 Fuels

(G-7282)
HUNTINGBURG MACHINE WORKS INC
309 N Main St (47542-1344)
PHONE..................................812 683-3531
Mark Gasser, *Pr*
EMP: 16 **EST:** 1918
SQ FT: 7,100
SALES (est): 2.23MM **Privately Held**
Web: www.huntingburgmachineworks.com
SIC: 1711 5074 3599 Plumbing contractors; Plumbing and hydronic heating supplies; Machine shop, jobbing and repair

GEOGRAPHIC SECTION

Huntington - Huntington County (G-7306)

(G-7283)
HURST CUSTOM CABINETS INC
1003 S Cherry St (47542-9493)
PHONE..............................812 683-3378
John Hurst, *Pr*
Janice Hurst, *Sec*
EMP: 5 **EST:** 1983
SALES (est): 374.18K **Privately Held**
Web: www.huntingburgcabinets.com
SIC: 2434 Wood kitchen cabinets

(G-7284)
IRVING MATERIALS INC
Also Called: I M I
615 W 12th St (47542-9335)
PHONE..............................812 683-4444
Calvin Cash, *Brnch Mgr*
EMP: 6
SALES (corp-wide): 814.09MM **Privately Held**
Web: www.irvmat.com
SIC: 3273 Ready-mixed concrete
PA: Irving Materials, Inc.
8032 N State Road 9
Greenfield IN 46140
317 326-3101

(G-7285)
KNIES SAWMILL INC
Also Called: Charles W Knies Sawmill
2238 E 550s (47542-9417)
PHONE..............................812 683-3402
Charles Knies, *Pr*
Chad Knies, *Prin*
Rachel Knies, *Prin*
Carla Knies, *Prin*
David Knies, *Prin*
EMP: 8 **EST:** 1974
SQ FT: 20,000
SALES (est): 715K **Privately Held**
SIC: 2426 Flooring, hardwood

(G-7286)
LOEWENSTEIN FURNITURE INC
1204 E 6th St (47542-9375)
PHONE..............................800 521-5381
Bruce Albertson, *Pr*
EMP: 10 **EST:** 2016
SALES (est): 131.32K **Privately Held**
Web: www.ofs.com
SIC: 2519 2515 Furniture, household: glass, fiberglass, and plastic; Chair and couch springs, assembled

(G-7287)
MASTERBRAND CABINETS LLC
Also Called: Production Systems Assoc
1009 N Geiger St (47542-8914)
P.O. Box 420 (47547-0420)
PHONE..............................812 482-2527
Travis Lane, *Brnch Mgr*
EMP: 80
SALES (corp-wide): 2.73B **Publicly Held**
Web: www.masterbrand.com
SIC: 2434 Wood kitchen cabinets
HQ: Masterbrand Cabinets Llc
3300 Entp Pkwy Ste 300
Beachwood OH 44122
812 482-2527

(G-7288)
NORTHSIDE MACHINING INC
304 W 12th St (47542-9350)
PHONE..............................812 683-3500
Paul Betz, *Pr*
Joseph A Betz, *Sec*
EMP: 6 **EST:** 1979
SQ FT: 4,500
SALES (est): 494.39K **Privately Held**
SIC: 3599 7692 3544 Machine shop, jobbing and repair; Welding repair; Special dies, tools, jigs, and fixtures

(G-7289)
OFS BRANDS HOLDINGS INC (PA)
Also Called: Ofs Brands
1204 E 6th St (47542-9375)
P.O. Box 100 (47542-0100)
PHONE..............................800 521-5381
Robert H Menke Junior, *Pr*
Joseph Bellino, *
Jim Huebner, *
Michael Wagner, *
Jeff Eckert, *
▲ **EMP:** 100 **EST:** 1937
SQ FT: 1,600,000
SALES (est): 228.87MM
SALES (corp-wide): 228.87MM **Privately Held**
Web: www.ofs.com
SIC: 2521 2522 2511 2599 Wood office furniture; Office furniture, except wood; Wood household furniture; Hospital furniture, except beds

(G-7290)
SCHNELL SERVICE CENTER
209 N Cherry St (47542-1443)
PHONE..............................812 683-2461
Kenneth Schnell, *Owner*
EMP: 1 **EST:** 1976
SALES (est): 87.98K **Privately Held**
SIC: 3585 7538 Air conditioning, motor vehicle; General automotive repair shops

(G-7291)
SOUTHERN INDIANA HARDWOODS INC
2739 S Saint Anthony Rd W (47542-8802)
PHONE..............................812 326-2053
Gene Merkley, *Pr*
Richard Merkley, *Stockholder**
Joe Merkley, *Stockholder**
Frank Merkley, *Stockholder**
EMP: 23 **EST:** 1981
SQ FT: 9,500
SALES (est): 2.98MM **Privately Held**
Web: www.sihlumb.com
SIC: 2421 2449 Lumber: rough, sawed, or planed; Wood containers, nec

(G-7292)
STEINKAMP WAREHOUSES INC
Also Called: Southern Indiana Treating
1000 N Main St (47542-1050)
P.O. Box 535 (47542-0535)
PHONE..............................812 683-3860
Scott A Steinkamp, *Pr*
Tony Bailey, *
EMP: 45 **EST:** 1885
SQ FT: 18,000
SALES (est): 6.44MM **Privately Held**
Web: www.steinkamphomecenter.com
SIC: 2491 5211 Preserving (creosoting) of wood; Lumber and other building materials

(G-7293)
TOP CAT PRINTING INC
6636 S 585w (47542-9233)
PHONE..............................812 683-2773
Thomas Meyer, *CEO*
EMP: 1 **EST:** 2001
SALES (est): 118.72K **Privately Held**
Web: www.topcatprinting.com
SIC: 2759 Screen printing

(G-7294)
UNITED MINERALS INC
409 N Van Buren St (47542-1404)
P.O. Box 13 (47542-0013)
PHONE..............................812 683-5024
Olinger Gregory, *Pr*
J Kenneth Merten, *VP*
Merten J Kenneth, *Sec*
EMP: 4 **EST:** 1979
SQ FT: 1,750
SALES (est): 2.23MM **Privately Held**
Web: www.unitedmineralsllc.com
SIC: 1382 Oil and gas exploration services

(G-7295)
ZEISING WINERY
8715 S 500w (47542-9653)
P.O. Box 305 (47542-0305)
PHONE..............................812 518-0607
EMP: 1 **EST:** 2010
SALES (est): 35.98K **Privately Held**
SIC: 2084 Wines

Huntington
Huntington County

(G-7296)
ADVANCED ENGINEERING INC
5299 N Mishler Rd (46750-8322)
PHONE..............................260 356-8077
Phillip Layman, *Pr*
Dan Thompson, *Sec*
John Layman, *Treas*
EMP: 11 **EST:** 1982
SQ FT: 10,000
SALES (est): 1.87MM **Privately Held**
Web: www.aeinc1.net
SIC: 3312 Tool and die steel

(G-7297)
ALTERNATIVE FUEL SOLUTIONS LLC
8380 N 200 W (46750-9724)
PHONE..............................260 224-1965
EMP: 10 **EST:** 2008
SALES (est): 1.03MM **Privately Held**
Web: www.alternativefuelsolutionsllc.com
SIC: 2869 Fuels

(G-7298)
ARMOR COAT LLC
328 Hauenstein Rd (46750-4424)
P.O. Box 1005 (46750-1005)
PHONE..............................260 210-1307
Dustin Smith, *Pr*
EMP: 5 **EST:** 2021
SALES (est): 452.22K **Privately Held**
SIC: 2951 Asphalt paving mixtures and blocks

(G-7299)
AUTO TRUCK GROUP LLC
1640 Riverfork Dr (46750-8445)
PHONE..............................260 356-1610
Brandon Fruechte, *Manager*
EMP: 1
SALES (corp-wide): 2.54B **Privately Held**
Web: www.holman.com
SIC: 3599 7692 3444 Machine shop, jobbing and repair; Welding repair; Sheet metalwork
HQ: Auto Truck Group, Llc
1420 Brewster Creek Blvd
Bartlett IL 60103
630 860-5600

(G-7300)
BECKLER POWER EQUIPMENT
1255 S Jefferson St (46750-3824)
PHONE..............................260 356-1188
Timothy J Beckler, *Owner*
EMP: 2 **EST:** 1993
SALES (est): 125K **Privately Held**
SIC: 5261 3546 Lawnmowers and tractors; Saws and sawing equipment

(G-7301)
BENDIX COML VHCL SYSTEMS LLC
Bendix Wpdc
1850 Riverfork Dr (46750-9004)
PHONE..............................260 356-9720
Mike Pogoreic, *Brnch Mgr*
EMP: 22
SQ FT: 102,000
SALES (corp-wide): 2.67MM **Privately Held**
Web: www.bendix.com
SIC: 3714 4225 Motor vehicle parts and accessories; General warehousing and storage
HQ: Bendix Commercial Vehicle Systems Llc
35500 Chester Rd
Avon OH 44011
440 329-9000

(G-7302)
BRAD SCHER
Also Called: Scher Machine
1910 William St (46750-3187)
PHONE..............................260 356-1515
Brad Scher, *Owner*
EMP: 1 **EST:** 1983
SQ FT: 3,500
SALES (est): 106.56K **Privately Held**
SIC: 3599 Machine shop, jobbing and repair

(G-7303)
BRYAN MACHINE SERVICES INC
345 Commerce Dr (46750-9098)
PHONE..............................260 356-5530
Steven Bryan, *Pr*
EMP: 8 **EST:** 1983
SQ FT: 12,000
SALES (est): 715.87K **Privately Held**
Web: www.bryanmachine.com
SIC: 3599 3544 Machine shop, jobbing and repair; Special dies, tools, jigs, and fixtures

(G-7304)
CARRIER CORPORATION
3650 W 200 N (46750-9002)
P.O. Box 969 (46750-0969)
PHONE..............................260 358-0888
Joel Jerabek, *Mgr*
EMP: 18
SALES (corp-wide): 22.1B **Publicly Held**
Web: www.carrier.com
SIC: 3672 Printed circuit boards
HQ: Carrier Corporation
13995 Pasteur Blvd
Palm Beach Gardens FL 33418
561 365-2000

(G-7305)
CAUSE PRINTING COMPANY
2812 Theater Ave (46750-7978)
PHONE..............................765 573-3330
Valerie Jullierat, *Pr*
EMP: 6 **EST:** 2016
SALES (est): 111.1K **Privately Held**
Web: www.causeprintingnetwork.com
SIC: 2759 Screen printing

(G-7306)
COACHS CONNECTION INC
200 E Park Dr (46750-2718)
P.O. Box 1123 (46750-1123)
PHONE..............................260 356-0400
James L Schroeder, *Pr*
Linda Schroeder, *Sec*
EMP: 7 **EST:** 1984
SALES (est): 740K **Privately Held**

Huntington - Huntington County (G-7307)

SIC: **5091 5941 2759 2752** Sporting and recreation goods; Sporting goods and bicycle shops; Commercial printing, nec; Commercial printing, lithographic

(G-7307)
D K ENTERPRISES LLC
1675 Riverfork Dr (46750-8427)
P.O. Box 151 (46750-0151)
PHONE..............................260 356-9011
Daniel M Drummond, *Admn*
EMP: 6 **EST:** 2007
SALES (est): 168.8K **Privately Held**
SIC: **2295** Metallizing of fabrics

(G-7308)
ECOLAB INC
970 E Tipton St (46750-1611)
PHONE..............................260 359-3280
EMP: 46
SALES (corp-wide): 15.32B **Publicly Held**
Web: www.ecolab.com
SIC: **2841 2842** Soap and other detergents; Disinfectants, household or industrial plant
PA: Ecolab Inc.
 1 Ecolab Pl
 Saint Paul MN 55102
 800 232-6522

(G-7309)
EL SHADDAI INC
2819 Wal Mart Dr Ste D (46750)
PHONE..............................260 359-9080
Randy Fields, *Pr*
Jason Fields, *VP*
Linda Fields, *Treas*
EMP: 5 **EST:** 2002
SALES (est): 486.68K **Privately Held**
Web: www.elshaddaiwear.com
SIC: **2759** Screen printing

(G-7310)
FOIL DIE INTERNATIONAL INC
Also Called: Foil Die International
1054 W 900 N (46750-9772)
PHONE..............................260 359-9011
EMP: 14 **EST:** 1993
SQ FT: 3,600
SALES (est): 1.93MM **Privately Held**
Web: www.foildie.com
SIC: **3544** Special dies and tools

(G-7311)
FOIL FORM INC
1054 W 900 N (46750-9772)
PHONE..............................260 359-9011
Lanie Creech, *Pr*
Christopher Eckert, *Sec*
EMP: 5 **EST:** 2002
SALES (est): 498.63K **Privately Held**
Web: www.foildie.com
SIC: **3544** Special dies and tools

(G-7312)
FUTURE MANUFACTURING INC
1700 Riverfork Dr (46750-8443)
PHONE..............................260 454-0222
Chris Wilson, *Pr*
EMP: 9 **EST:** 2010
SALES (est): 446.99K **Privately Held**
SIC: **3999** Manufacturing industries, nec

(G-7313)
FWD TECHNOLOGIES LLC
7872 N 100 E (46750-9660)
PHONE..............................360 907-9755
EMP: 3 **EST:** 2019
SALES (est): 80.91K **Privately Held**
SIC: **3999** Manufacturing industries, nec

(G-7314)
GENERAL ALUMINUM MFG COMPANY
Also Called: Park Ohio
1345 Henry St (46750-3837)
P.O. Box 709 (46750-0709)
PHONE..............................260 356-3900
Gary Barlow, *Prin*
EMP: 108
Web: www.generalaluminum.com
SIC: **3365** Aluminum and aluminum-based alloy castings
HQ: General Aluminum Mfg. Llc
 5159 S Prospect St
 Ravenna OH 44266
 330 297-1225

(G-7315)
GERDAU MACSTEEL INC
Heat Treating Division
25 Commercial Rd (46750-8805)
PHONE..............................260 356-9520
Ron Kensky, *Brnch Mgr*
EMP: 48
Web: www.gerdau.com
SIC: **3398** Metal heat treating
HQ: Gerdau Macsteel, Inc.
 5591 Morrill Rd
 Jackson MI 49201

(G-7316)
HEARTLAND ALUMINUM INC
1750 Riverfork Dr (46750-8443)
PHONE..............................260 375-4652
▲ **EMP:** 26
Web: www.heartlandaluminum.com
SIC: **3365** Aluminum foundries

(G-7317)
HELENA AGRI-ENTERPRISES LLC
321 Thurman Poe Way (46750-4317)
PHONE..............................574 268-4762
EMP: 1
Web: www.helenaagri.com
SIC: **5191 2879** Chemicals, agricultural; Agricultural chemicals, nec
HQ: Helena Agri-Enterprises, Llc
 225 Schilling Blvd
 Collierville TN 38017
 901 761-0050

(G-7318)
HERITAGE TOOL AND DIE INC
Also Called: Heritage Arms
679 W Markle Rd (46750-9369)
PHONE..............................260 359-8121
John Wegmann, *Pr*
Jerry Smith, *VP*
Kevin Scheiber, *Sec*
EMP: 5 **EST:** 1993
SQ FT: 7,200
SALES (est): 454.56K **Privately Held**
SIC: **3544** Special dies and tools

(G-7319)
HITTLER INSURANCE LLC
301 Erie Stone Rd (46750-9607)
PHONE..............................260 519-1275
Zechariah Hittler, *CEO*
EMP: 1
SALES (est): 59.56K **Privately Held**
Web: www.krishittlerinsurance.com
SIC: **3444** Sheet metalwork

(G-7320)
HOOP-IT EMBROIDERY
3869 W 608 N (46750-8039)
PHONE..............................260 224-6571
EMP: 5 **EST:** 2014
SALES (est): 47.01K **Privately Held**
SIC: **2395** Embroidery products, except Schiffli machine

(G-7321)
HUNTINGTON COUNTY TAB INC
1670 Etna Ave (46750-4132)
P.O. Box 744 (47960-0744)
PHONE..............................260 356-1107
Scott Trauner, *Pr*
EMP: 9 **EST:** 1985
SALES (est): 223.63K **Privately Held**
Web: www.huntingtoncountytab.com
SIC: **2711** Newspapers, publishing and printing

(G-7322)
HUNTINGTON EXTERIORS INC
Also Called: W.A. Zimmer Company
1700 N Broadway St (46750-4311)
PHONE..............................260 356-1621
TOLL FREE: 800
William Zimmer, *Pr*
Marcia S Zimmer, *VP*
EMP: 15 **EST:** 1975
SQ FT: 11,000
SALES (est): 1.77MM **Privately Held**
Web: www.wazimmer.com
SIC: **3448 1761 1751 5712** Sunrooms, prefabricated metal; Siding contractor; Window and door (prefabricated) installation ; Outdoor and garden furniture

(G-7323)
HUNTINGTON SHEET METAL INC (PA)
1675 Riverfork Dr (46750-8427)
P.O. Box 151 (46750-0151)
PHONE..............................260 356-9011
Dan Drummond, *Pr*
David Drummond, *
Barbara Drummond, *
EMP: 75 **EST:** 1984
SQ FT: 90,000
SALES (est): 24.72MM
SALES (corp-wide): 24.72MM **Privately Held**
Web: www.hsmetal.com
SIC: **3444 7692** Sheet metal specialties, not stamped; Welding repair

(G-7324)
HUNTINGTON SHEET METAL INC
2060 Old Us Highway 24 (46750-1679)
PHONE..............................260 356-9011
Dan Drummond, *Brnch Mgr*
EMP: 10
SALES (corp-wide): 24.72MM **Privately Held**
Web: www.hsmetal.com
SIC: **3441** Fabricated structural metal
PA: Huntington Sheet Metal Inc
 1675 Riverfork Dr
 Huntington IN 46750
 260 356-9011

(G-7325)
INCIPIO DEVICES LLC
3650 W 200 N (46750-9002)
PHONE..............................260 200-1970
Troy Johnson, *Pr*
EMP: 81 **EST:** 2013
SALES (est): 26.08MM **Privately Held**
Web: www.incipiodevices.com
SIC: **5047 3999** Orthopedic equipment and supplies; Atomizers, toiletry

(G-7326)
INDIANA BOX COMPANY (DH)
1200 Riverfork Dr (46750-9054)
PHONE..............................260 356-9660
Robert L Mcilvane, *CEO*
Jay King, *
J Jordan Nerenberg, *
Scott M Clary, *
EMP: 40 **EST:** 1953
SQ FT: 2,500
SALES (est): 10.23MM
SALES (corp-wide): 573.33MM **Privately Held**
Web: theroyalgroup.wpengine.com
SIC: **2653** Boxes, corrugated: made from purchased materials
HQ: Royal Box Group, Llc
 1301 S 47th Ave
 Cicero IL 60804
 708 656-2020

(G-7327)
INDUSTRIAL CONTROL SERVICE INC
Also Called: I C S
1321 W Park Dr (46750-8028)
P.O. Box 1141 (46750-1141)
PHONE..............................260 356-4698
Mark Reust, *Pr*
EMP: 1 **EST:** 1992
SQ FT: 3,000
SALES (est): 22.85K **Privately Held**
Web: www.icscontrolnet.com
SIC: **3599** Machine shop, jobbing and repair
HQ: Motion & Control Enterprises Llc
 100 Williams Dr
 Zelienople PA 16063
 724 452-6000

(G-7328)
INFINITE LIFTS LLC
615 Arthur St (46750-2213)
PHONE..............................260 388-2868
EMP: 4 **EST:** 2016
SALES (est): 57.97K **Privately Held**
SIC: **3999** Manufacturing industries, nec

(G-7329)
INNOVATIVE PACKAGING INC
1312 Flaxmill Rd (46750-1370)
PHONE..............................260 356-6577
Gene Fleek, *Pr*
Brien Blackburn, *
EMP: 49 **EST:** 1988
SALES (est): 4.28MM **Privately Held**
Web: www.innpac.com
SIC: **2653** Boxes, corrugated: made from purchased materials

(G-7330)
INNOVATIVE PACKAGING ASSOC INC
1312 Flaxmill Rd (46750-1370)
PHONE..............................260 356-6577
Eugene Fleck, *CEO*
Brien Blackburn, *
Chris Fleck, *
EMP: 35 **EST:** 1988
SQ FT: 130,000
SALES (est): 3.16MM **Privately Held**
Web: www.innpac.com
SIC: **2653 3086** Boxes, corrugated: made from purchased materials; Packaging and shipping materials, foamed plastics

(G-7331)
IRVING MATERIALS INC
Also Called: I M I
500 Erie Stone Rd (46750-9682)
PHONE..............................260 356-7214
EMP: 10
SALES (corp-wide): 814.09MM **Privately Held**
Web: www.irvmat.com
SIC: **3273** Ready-mixed concrete
PA: Irving Materials, Inc.
 8032 N State Road 9

GEOGRAPHIC SECTION

Huntington - Huntington County (G-7355)

Greenfield IN 46140
317 326-3101

(G-7332)
IRVING MATERIALS INC
500 Erie Stone Rd (46750-9682)
PHONE..................260 356-7214
Fred Irving, *Pr*
Earl Brinker, *CFO*
EMP: 25 **EST:** 1946
SALES (est): 867.58K **Privately Held**
Web: www.irvmat.com
SIC: 3273 Ready-mixed concrete

(G-7333)
J O WOLF TOOL & DIE INC
550 Condit St (46750-2506)
P.O. Box 6 (46783-0006)
PHONE..................260 672-2605
Keith Miller, *Pr*
Dawn L Miller, *VP*
EMP: 6 **EST:** 1979
SQ FT: 4,800
SALES (est): 493.09K **Privately Held**
Web: www.wolftool.com
SIC: 3544 Special dies and tools

(G-7334)
KNORR BRAKE TRUCK SYSTEMS CO
1230 Sabine St (46750-2427)
PHONE..................260 356-9720
Chris Camp, *Brnch Mgr*
▲ **EMP:** 2
SALES (corp-wide): 2.67MM **Privately Held**
Web: www.knorr-bremse.us
SIC: 2499 Shoe and boot products, wood
HQ: Knorr Brake Truck Systems Company
748 Starbuck Ave
Watertown NY 13601

(G-7335)
KOCH INDUSTRIES INC
Also Called: KOCH INDUSTRIES, INC.
502 E Hosler Rd (46750-9501)
PHONE..................260 356-7191
Shawn Kimberly, *Mgr*
EMP: 4
SALES (corp-wide): 64.37B **Privately Held**
Web: www.kochindusinc.com
SIC: 2879 Agricultural disinfectants
HQ: Koch Industries, Llc
4111 E 37th St N
Wichita KS 67220
316 828-5500

(G-7336)
LEAGUE OF FANCY HATS LLC
8588 N 100 E (46750-9656)
P.O. Box 281 (46750-0281)
PHONE..................260 355-7115
Alex Hoffman, *Prin*
EMP: 4 **EST:** 2016
SALES (est): 52.82K **Privately Held**
Web: www.fancyhats.com
SIC: 2353 Hats, caps, and millinery

(G-7337)
LILLSUN MANUFACTURING CO INC
1350 Harris St (46750-4302)
P.O. Box 767 (46750-0767)
PHONE..................260 356-6514
William Sunderman, *VP*
Sharon Sunderman Ulrich, *Sec*
Lillian Sunderman, *Pr*
EMP: 9 **EST:** 1951
SALES (est): 907.11K **Privately Held**
Web: www.lillsun.com

SIC: 2499 Woodenware, kitchen and household

(G-7338)
LOON CREEK LEATHER LLC
750 N Marion Rd (46750-7813)
PHONE..................260 356-0726
Robert E Glessner, *Pr*
Patricia Glessner, *Sec*
EMP: 1 **EST:** 2001
SALES (est): 125.4K **Privately Held**
Web: www.looncreekleather.com
SIC: 3111 Saddlery leather

(G-7339)
M & S INDUS MET FBRICATORS INC
Also Called: M & S Indus Met Fabricators
5 Commercial Rd (46750-8805)
PHONE..................260 356-0300
Gary Mickley, *Ch Bd*
Jason Mickley, *
Nancy Mickley, *
EMP: 100 **EST:** 1966
SQ FT: 72,000
SALES (est): 16MM **Privately Held**
Web: www.msfab.com
SIC: 3441 Fabricated structural metal

(G-7340)
M S POWDER COATING
5 Commercial Rd (46750)
PHONE..................260 356-0300
EMP: 8 **EST:** 2008
SALES (est): 159.81K **Privately Held**
Web: www.msfab.com
SIC: 3479 Coating of metals and formed products

(G-7341)
MEMCOR INC
Also Called: Memcor-Truohm
1320 Flaxmill Rd (46750-4405)
PHONE..................260 356-4300
Jeffrey R Crawford, *Pr*
EMP: 24 **EST:** 1986
SQ FT: 7,000
SALES (est): 2.19MM **Privately Held**
Web: www.memcorinc.com
SIC: 3824 Mechanical and electromechanical counters and devices

(G-7342)
MIDWEST INDUS MET FBRCTION INC
281 Thurman Poe Way (46750-4319)
P.O. Box 903 (46750-0903)
PHONE..................260 356-5262
Blaine Kaylor, *Pr*
EMP: 45 **EST:** 1998
SQ FT: 75,000
SALES (est): 4.84MM **Privately Held**
Web: www.midwestimf.com
SIC: 3441 Fabricated structural metal

(G-7343)
MIDWEST INDUSTRIAL METAL
2080 Old Us Highway 24 (46750-1679)
PHONE..................260 358-0373
Blaine Kaylor, *Pr*
EMP: 7 **EST:** 1999
SALES (est): 868.26K **Privately Held**
Web: www.midwestimf.com
SIC: 3441 Fabricated structural metal

(G-7344)
MIGNONE COMMUNICATIONS INCORPORATED
Also Called: Phillips Brothers Printers
880 E State St (46750-2956)
PHONE..................260 358-0266
EMP: 155

SIC: 2791 2752 2789 Photocomposition, for the printing trade; Commercial printing, lithographic; Bookbinding and related work

(G-7345)
NORTHERN INDIANA PACKG CO INC (DH)
1200 Riverfork Dr (46750-9054)
PHONE..................260 356-9660
Tim Tootle, *Pr*
EMP: 26 **EST:** 1998
SALES (est): 3.45MM
SALES (corp-wide): 573.33MM **Privately Held**
SIC: 2653 Boxes, corrugated: made from purchased materials
HQ: Schwarz Partners Packaging, Llc
10 W Carmel Dr Ste 300 In
Carmel IN 46032
317 290-1140

(G-7346)
ONWARD MANUFACTURING COMPANY (DH)
1000 E Market St (46750-2576)
PHONE..................260 358-4111
Ted Witzel, *Pr*
◆ **EMP:** 20 **EST:** 2006
SALES (est): 44.26MM
SALES (corp-wide): 84.87MM **Privately Held**
SIC: 3631 5023 Barbecues, grills, and braziers (outdoor cooking); Homefurnishings
HQ: Onward Manufacturing Company Limited
585 Kumpf Dr
Waterloo ON
519 885-4540

(G-7347)
ORTON-MCCULLOUGH CRANE COMPANY
Also Called: Orton Crane
1244 E Market St (46750-2582)
P.O. Box 824 (46750-0824)
PHONE..................260 356-7900
Martin W Mccullough, *Pr*
John M Mccullough, *Ch*
Eileen R Mccullough, *VP*
EMP: 1 **EST:** 1963
SALES (est): 242.74K **Privately Held**
SIC: 3531 7699 Cranes, locomotive; Aircraft and heavy equipment repair services

(G-7348)
OSTERHOLT CONSTRUCTION INC
Also Called: Osterholt Truss
3648 N Norwood Rd (46750-8052)
PHONE..................260 672-3493
Steven Osterholt, *Pr*
Janet Osterholt, *Sec*
EMP: 6 **EST:** 1980
SQ FT: 9,000
SALES (est): 489.12K **Privately Held**
SIC: 1761 2439 Roofing contractor; Structural wood members, nec

(G-7349)
OUR SUNDAY VISITOR APPS LLC
200 Noll Plz (46750-4304)
PHONE..................800 348-2440
Kyle Hamilton, *CEO*
EMP: 23 **EST:** 2015
SALES (est): 187.06K **Privately Held**
Web: www.oursundayvisitor.com
SIC: 2731 2677 Books, publishing and printing; Envelopes

(G-7350)
OUR SUNDAY VISITOR INC (PA)
200 Noll Plz (46750-4304)
PHONE..................260 359-2564
◆ **EMP:** 290 **EST:** 1937
SALES (est): 53.39MM
SALES (corp-wide): 53.39MM **Privately Held**
Web: www.osv.com
SIC: 2721 Periodicals

(G-7351)
OWENS FUEL CENTER
2718 Guilford St (46750-9701)
PHONE..................260 358-1211
Dave Weaver, *Mgr*
EMP: 7 **EST:** 2010
SALES (est): 186.18K **Privately Held**
SIC: 2869 Fuels

(G-7352)
P-KELCO INC
465 N Broadway St (46750)
PHONE..................260 356-1376
EMP: 40
SALES (corp-wide): 4.73MM **Privately Held**
SIC: 3444 3699 Sheet metalwork; Electrical equipment and supplies, nec
PA: P-Kelco, Inc.
245 Erie St
Huntington IN 46750
260 356-6326

(G-7353)
P-KELCO INC (PA)
Also Called: Premier Powder Coating
245 Erie St (46750)
PHONE..................260 356-6326
James L Foster, *Pr*
Marla A Foster, *CEO*
Dena M Kellam, *VP*
EMP: 22 **EST:** 1959
SQ FT: 100,000
SALES (est): 4.73MM
SALES (corp-wide): 4.73MM **Privately Held**
SIC: 2522 3444 Office cabinets and filing drawers, except wood; Culverts, sheet metal

(G-7354)
PATHFINDER SERVICES INC (PA)
Also Called: RESOURCE CONNECTION
2824 Theater Ave (46750)
P.O. Box 1001 (46750)
PHONE..................260 356-0500
John J Niederman, *Pr*
Diana Laux, *
Brooks Fetters Cmdo, *Prin*
EMP: 50 **EST:** 1966
SQ FT: 10,000
SALES (est): 28.69MM
SALES (corp-wide): 28.69MM **Privately Held**
Web: www.pathfinderservices.org
SIC: 8331 7389 2652 Vocational rehabilitation agency; Packaging and labeling services; Setup paperboard boxes

(G-7355)
PERFECTION WHEEL LLC
255 N Briant St (46750-2957)
PHONE..................260 358-9239
Roger Mcclellan, *Managing Member*
EMP: 1 **EST:** 2010
SALES (est): 1.16MM
SALES (corp-wide): 34.11MM **Privately Held**
Web: shop.perfectionwheel.com
SIC: 3714 Motor vehicle parts and accessories

Huntington - Huntington County (G-7356)

(G-7356)
PHD INC
4763 N Us Highway 24 E (46750-9617)
PHONE..................................260 356-0120
Ron Cardin, Brnch Mgr
EMP: 10
Web: www.phdinc.com
SIC: 3561 3494 Cylinders, pump; Valves and pipe fittings, nec
HQ: Phd, Inc.
9009 Clubridge Dr
Fort Wayne IN 46809
260 747-6151
PA: All Star Auto Lights, Inc.
300 W Grant St
Orlando FL 32806
407 271-8949

(G-7357)
POLAR SEAL INC
4461 W 500 N (46750-8941)
PHONE..................................260 356-2369
Joyce Rethlake, Pr
David Rethlake, VP
EMP: 3 EST: 2001
SALES (est): 422.05K Privately Held
Web: www.polarsealinc.com
SIC: 2952 Roofing materials

(G-7358)
QUANEX HEAT TREAT
25 Commercial Rd (46750-8999)
PHONE..................................260 356-9520
Ron Kensky, Mgr
EMP: 8 EST: 2008
SALES (est): 81.77K Privately Held
Web: www.quanex.com
SIC: 3433 Heating equipment, except electric

(G-7359)
QUICKBLADES
1640 Riverfork Dr Ste A (46750-8445)
PHONE..................................260 359-2072
Tim Delong, Mgr
EMP: 4 EST: 2007
SALES (est): 87.74K Privately Held
Web: www.quickblades.net
SIC: 3479 Painting, coating, and hot dipping

(G-7360)
REBER ENTERPRISES LLC
Also Called: Lime City Manufacturing
1470 Etna Ave (46750)
PHONE..................................260 356-6826
Mandy Reber, CEO
Cory Reber, Sec
EMP: 3 EST: 2017
SALES (est): 1.29MM
SALES (corp-wide): 57.3MM Privately Held
Web: www.limecitymfg.com
SIC: 3469 Stamping metal for the trade
PA: Na Holding Corp.
4220 Angela Way
Canandaigua NY 14424
260 918-6041

(G-7361)
ROYAL BOX GROUP LLC
Indiana Box Company
1200 Riverfork Dr (46750-9054)
PHONE..................................765 728-2416
EMP: 101
SALES (corp-wide): 573.33MM Privately Held
Web: theroyalgroup.wpengine.com
SIC: 2653 Boxes, corrugated: made from purchased materials
HQ: Royal Box Group, Llc
1301 S 47th Ave
Cicero IL 60804
708 656-2020

(G-7362)
ROYER ENTERPRISES INC
Also Called: Indiana Wire Die Co
6780 N 362 W (46750-8882)
PHONE..................................260 359-0689
Brian Royer, Pr
Brian Royer, Pr
Nancy Carpenter, Mgr
EMP: 9 EST: 1941
SQ FT: 12,000
SALES (est): 159.84K Privately Held
Web: www.royerenterprises.com
SIC: 3544 3291 Wire drawing and straightening dies; Abrasive products

(G-7363)
RPDM SOLUTIONS INC
925 Poplar St (46750-2055)
PHONE..................................317 608-2938
EMP: 4 EST: 2016
SALES (est): 68.31K Privately Held
Web: www.rpdmsolutions.com
SIC: 3652 Prerecorded records and tapes

(G-7364)
RTX CORPORATION
3650 W 200 N (46750-9002)
PHONE..................................260 358-0888
Joel Jerabek, Mgr
EMP: 5
SALES (corp-wide): 68.92B Publicly Held
Web: www.rtx.com
SIC: 3724 Aircraft engines and engine parts
PA: Rtx Corporation
1000 Wilson Blvd
Arlington VA 22209
781 522-3000

(G-7365)
SCHACHT-PFISTER INC
232 E Washington St Ste 3 (46750-2749)
PHONE..................................260 356-9775
Steve Pfister, Pr
Jane Young, Sec
▲ EMP: 5 EST: 1988
SQ FT: 5,000
SALES (est): 383.58K Privately Held
SIC: 3069 Molded rubber products

(G-7366)
SCHNEIDER ELECTRIC USA INC
Also Called: Schneider Electric
6 Commercial Rd (46750-8805)
PHONE..................................260 356-2060
Jim Harden, Mgr
EMP: 98
SQ FT: 45,000
SALES (corp-wide): 82.05K Privately Held
Web: www.se.com
SIC: 5063 3612 Electrical supplies, nec; Transformers, except electric
HQ: Schneider Electric Usa, Inc.
One Boston Pl Ste 2700
Boston MA 02108
978 975-9600

(G-7367)
SHAW MACHINE WORKS
Also Called: Shaw Machine Shop
1024 2nd St (46750-2332)
PHONE..................................260 356-4297
Francis Shaw Iii, Owner
EMP: 1 EST: 1939
SALES (est): 70K Privately Held
SIC: 3599 Machine shop, jobbing and repair

(G-7368)
SHUTTLEWORTH LLC (DH)
Also Called: Shuttleworth North America
10 Commercial Rd (46750-8805)
PHONE..................................260 356-8500
Ken Tinnell, Genl Mgr
Bret Ranc, *
Mark W Anderson, *
James D Bonahoom, *
Breton Ranc, *
▲ EMP: 75 EST: 1962
SQ FT: 50,700
SALES (est): 19.8MM Privately Held
Web: www.shuttleworth.com
SIC: 3535 Conveyors and conveying equipment
HQ: Pro Mach, Inc.
50 E Rvrcnter Blvd Ste 18
Covington KY 41011
513 831-8778

(G-7369)
SPECIALTY ENGRG TL & DIE LLC
875 E State St (46750-2927)
P.O. Box 5171 (46750-5171)
PHONE..................................260 356-2678
David Goodpasture, Managing Member
EMP: 5 EST: 1992
SQ FT: 8,000
SALES (est): 495.81K Privately Held
Web: www.setooldie.com
SIC: 3544 Special dies and tools

(G-7370)
SPEEDWAY REDI-MIX INC
1217 W Park Dr (46750-8027)
PHONE..................................260 356-5600
Steve Turner, Mgr
EMP: 5
Web: www.speedwaycp.com
SIC: 3273 Ready-mixed concrete
PA: Speedway Redi-Mix Inc
4820 Industrial Rd
Fort Wayne IN 46825

(G-7371)
STINES PRINTING INC
549 Warren St (46750-2723)
PHONE..................................260 356-5994
Rodney Stine, Pr
Kay Stine, VP
EMP: 3 EST: 1979
SALES (est): 284.21K Privately Held
SIC: 2759 2752 2791 2789 Envelopes: printing, nsk; Commercial printing, lithographic; Typesetting; Bookbinding and related work

(G-7372)
STOFFEL BROTHERS INC
6195 N 200 W (46750-9777)
PHONE..................................260 356-6844
Dan Stoffel, Pr
EMP: 1 EST: 1996
SALES (est): 218.6K Privately Held
SIC: 3523 Driers (farm): grain, hay, and seed

(G-7373)
TEIJIN AUTOMOTIVE TECH INC
1890 Riverfork Dr (46750-9004)
PHONE..................................260 355-4011
EMP: 266
Web: www.teijinautomotive.com
SIC: 3089 Injection molding of plastics
HQ: Teijin Automotive Technologies, Inc.
255 Rex Blvd
Auburn Hills MI 48326
248 237-7800

(G-7374)
TRANSWHEEL CORPORATION (HQ)
Also Called: Coast To Coast
3000 Yeoman Way (46750-9003)
PHONE..................................260 358-8660
Jim Devlin, Pr
Roger Mcclellan, VP
▲ EMP: 195 EST: 1992
SQ FT: 53,000
SALES (est): 28.46MM
SALES (corp-wide): 13.87B Publicly Held
Web: www.wheelbuyer.com
SIC: 3714 5521 Wheels, motor vehicle; Used car dealers
PA: Lkq Corporation
500 W Madison St Ste 2800
Chicago IL 60661
312 621-1950

(G-7375)
TWO EES WINERY
6808 N Us Highway 24 E (46750-9690)
PHONE..................................260 672-2000
Eric Harris, Prin
EMP: 11 EST: 2012
SALES (est): 833.61K Privately Held
Web: www.twoees.com
SIC: 2084 Wines

(G-7376)
USMPC BUYER INC
Also Called: Isolatek International
701 N Broadway St (46750-2577)
P.O. Box 5006 (46750-5006)
PHONE..................................260 356-2040
Tom Lund, Brnch Mgr
EMP: 42
SQ FT: 1,000
SALES (corp-wide): 18.76MM Privately Held
Web: www.isolatek.com
SIC: 3296 Mineral wool
PA: Usmpc Buyer Inc.
41 Furnace St
Stanhope NJ 07874
973 347-1200

(G-7377)
UTEC INC
Also Called: UT Electronic Controls
3650 W 200 N (46750)
PHONE..................................260 359-3514
Donald Cawley, Pr
Kelly A Romano, *
Ronald Bruehlman, *
Joseph Gest, *
Theresa Mackinnon, *
▲ EMP: 550 EST: 1987
SALES (est): 271.12MM
SALES (corp-wide): 22.1B Publicly Held
Web: www.uteccontrols.com
SIC: 3822 Environmental controls
HQ: Carrier Corporation
13995 Pasteur Blvd
Palm Beach Gardens FL 33418
561 365-2000

(G-7378)
VINTAGE AVI PUBLICATIONS LLC (PA)
1355 Waco Dr (46750-0008)
P.O. Box 1057 (46750-1057)
PHONE..................................260 440-3144
EMP: 5 EST: 2017
SALES (est): 139.91K
SALES (corp-wide): 139.91K Privately Held
Web: www.warbirddigest.com
SIC: 2741 Miscellaneous publishing

(G-7379)
VINTAGE AVI PUBLICATIONS LLC
442 N Jefferson St (46750-2745)
PHONE.................................260 440-3144
EMP: 33
SALES (corp-wide): 139.91K **Privately Held**
Web: www.warbirddigest.com
SIC: 2741 Miscellaneous publishing
PA: Vintage Aviation Publications, Llc
1355 Waco Dr
Huntington IN 46750
260 440-3144

(G-7380)
WILSON BURIAL VAULT INC
446 W Markle Rd (46750-9363)
P.O. Box 429 (46750-0429)
PHONE.................................260 356-5722
Garland Wilson, *Pr*
Everett Wilson, *VP*
Greg L Wilson, *Sec*
EMP: 5 **EST:** 1970
SQ FT: 25,000
SALES (est): 482.93K **Privately Held**
Web: www.wilsonburialvault.com
SIC: 3272 1799 Burial vaults, concrete or precast terrazzo; Grave excavation

(G-7381)
WOOD SHOPPE
2107 S 600 E (46750)
PHONE.................................260 758-3453
Stephen T Emely, *Owner*
Stephen Thomas Emely, *Owner*
EMP: 1 **EST:** 1978
SALES (est): 79.22K **Privately Held**
SIC: 2434 Wood kitchen cabinets

Indianapolis
Hamilton County

(G-7382)
EMPIRE LACROSS & SPORTS LLC
9700 Lake Shore Dr E B (46280-1997)
PHONE.................................317 497-8918
EMP: 2
SALES (est): 105.48K **Privately Held**
SIC: 3949 Lacrosse equipment and supplies, general

Indianapolis
Marion County

(G-7383)
12-05 DISTILLERY LLC
636 Virginia Ave (46203-1756)
PHONE.................................317 402-4818
EMP: 7 **EST:** 2013
SALES (est): 284.33K **Privately Held**
Web: www.1205distillery.com
SIC: 2085 Distilled and blended liquors

(G-7384)
1500 SOUTH TIBBS LLC
Also Called: Vertellus Intgrted Pyrdnes LLC
201 N Illinois St Ste 1800 (46204-1904)
PHONE.................................317 247-8141
John Van Hulle, *Pr*
Anne Frye, *
David Schwind, *
EMP: 128 **EST:** 2016
SALES (est): 46.2MM
SALES (corp-wide): 688.33MM **Privately Held**
Web: www.aurorium.com

SIC: 5191 5169 2833 Chemicals, agricultural; Industrial chemicals; Medicinal chemicals
PA: Ppc Investment Partners Lp
110 N Wacker Dr Ste 4400
Chicago IL 60606
312 447-6050

(G-7385)
1ST CHOICE CONTRACTORS LLC
3510 Delmar Rd (46220-5570)
PHONE.................................317 628-4721
Bryce Hill, *Managing Member*
EMP: 1 **EST:** 2016
SALES (est): 198.27K **Privately Held**
Web: www.1stchoiceroof.com
SIC: 3537 7389 Trucks, tractors, loaders, carriers, and similar equipment; Business Activities at Non-Commercial Site

(G-7386)
250OK LLC
9247 N Meridian St Ste 301 (46260-1879)
PHONE.................................855 250-6529
Greg Kraios, *CEO*
EMP: 22 **EST:** 2010
SALES (est): 817.38K **Privately Held**
Web: www.250ok.com
SIC: 7372 Business oriented computer software

(G-7387)
3 MICRON LASER TECHNOLOGY LLC
8174 E 21st St (46219-2514)
PHONE.................................317 677-8958
Laryssa Skolnik, *Prin*
Thong Nguyen, *Prin*
EMP: 2 **EST:** 2021
SALES (est): 60.69K **Privately Held**
Web: www.3micronlasers.com
SIC: 3674 Semiconductors and related devices

(G-7388)
3M COMPANY
Also Called: 3M
5457 W 79th St (46268-1675)
PHONE.................................317 692-6666
Denise Rutherford, *Pr*
EMP: 332
SALES (corp-wide): 32.68B **Publicly Held**
Web: www.acelity.com
SIC: 3841 3842 3291 2842 Surgical instruments and apparatus; Bandages and dressings; Abrasive products; Polishes and sanitation goods
PA: 3m Company
3m Center
Saint Paul MN 55144
651 733-1110

(G-7389)
3STAX PRINTING & EMB LLC ✪
5699 E 71st St (46220)
PHONE.................................317 612-7122
Isaac D Avant, *CEO*
EMP: 2 **EST:** 2022
SALES (est): 83.91K **Privately Held**
SIC: 2752 Commercial printing, lithographic

(G-7390)
4 LENS PARTNERSHIPS LLC
7242 Crest Ln (46256-2014)
PHONE.................................317 490-1389
Bryan Erdmann, *Pr*
EMP: 1 **EST:** 2017
SALES (est): 87.82K **Privately Held**
Web: www.4lenspartnerships.com
SIC: 3999 Manufacturing industries, nec

(G-7391)
4BOARD LLC
802 N Meridian St (46204-1118)
PHONE.................................317 997-3354
EMP: 3 **EST:** 2014
SALES (est): 140.92K **Privately Held**
SIC: 3499 Novelties and specialties, metal

(G-7392)
55 WEST LLC ✪
Also Called: Solas Ray Lighting
5935 W 84th St Ste D (46278-1350)
EMP: 12 **EST:** 2022
SALES (est): 711.08K **Privately Held**
Web: www.sargentlundy.com
SIC: 3646 Commercial lighting fixtures

(G-7393)
80OF80 GROUP LLC
7022 W 10th St (46214-3501)
PHONE.................................812 814-1167
EMP: 1
SALES (est): 69,27K **Privately Held**
SIC: 2389 Apparel and accessories, nec

(G-7394)
8TH DAY DISTILLERY LLC
1080 E Beechwood Ln (46227-2102)
PHONE.................................317 690-2202
EMP: 5 **EST:** 2017
SALES (est): 222.94K **Privately Held**
Web: www.8thdaydistillery.com
SIC: 2085 Distilled and blended liquors

(G-7395)
A & E PUBLICATIONS LLC
125 E 86th St (46240-1501)
PHONE.................................317 795-4308
EMP: 2 **EST:** 2019
SALES (est): 52.55K **Privately Held**
SIC: 2731 Books, publishing only

(G-7396)
A AND R ERECTORS INCORPORATED
1605 Country Club Rd (46234-1826)
PHONE.................................317 271-3429
Rick Warrum, *Pr*
EMP: 14 **EST:** 1991
SQ FT: 6,000
SALES (est): 2.53MM **Privately Held**
Web: www.arerectors.com
SIC: 3441 Fabricated structural metal

(G-7397)
A C MALLORY CAPACITORS LLC (PA)
4411 S High School Rd (46241-6404)
PHONE.................................317 612-1000
Ronald Voegele, *CFO*
EMP: 3 **EST:** 2002
SQ FT: 45,000
SALES (est): 6.91MM
SALES (corp-wide): 6.91MM **Privately Held**
Web: www.mspindy.com
SIC: 3675 Electronic capacitors

(G-7398)
A DIVINE IMAGE ENTERPRISE LLC
9114 Key Ln (46234-1546)
PHONE.................................317 397-8132
EMP: 3 **EST:** 2021
SALES (est): 276.82K **Privately Held**
SIC: 3537 Trucks: freight, baggage, etc.: industrial, except mining

(G-7399)
A G A GAS INC
5825 Elmwood Ave (46203-6032)
PHONE.................................317 783-2331
Bob Hilliard, *Pr*
EMP: 6 **EST:** 2010
SALES (est): 92.19K **Privately Held**
SIC: 2813 Industrial gases

(G-7400)
A HARRIS VERL INC
Also Called: Sign-A-Rama
112 W Saint Clair St (46204-1139)
PHONE.................................317 736-4680
Verl Allen Harris, *Pr*
Judith Caroline Harris, *VP*
EMP: 4 **EST:** 1992
SALES (est): 295.84K **Privately Held**
Web: www.signarama.com
SIC: 3993 Signs and advertising specialties

(G-7401)
A PALLET COMPANY
1305 Bedford St (46221-1409)
PHONE.................................317 687-9020
Sa Mencer, *Pr*
EMP: 8 **EST:** 2011
SALES (est): 814.39K **Privately Held**
Web: www.apalletcompany.com
SIC: 2448 Pallets, wood

(G-7402)
A SIGN OF TYMES
2881 E 56th St (46220)
PHONE.................................317 251-0792
EMP: 3 **EST:** 2018
SALES (est): 46.08K **Privately Held**
Web: www.signofthetymessalon.com
SIC: 3993 Signs and advertising specialties

(G-7403)
A T SYSTEMS TECHNOLOGIES INC
68 N Gale St (46201-3507)
P.O. Box 19817 (46219-0817)
PHONE.................................317 352-1030
EMP: 1 **EST:** 2009
SALES (est): 88.28K **Privately Held**
SIC: 3578 Coin counters

(G-7404)
A&J DEVELOPMENT GROUP LLC
633 N Livingston Ave (46222-3305)
PHONE.................................317 767-1182
EMP: 1
SALES (est): 41.07K **Privately Held**
SIC: 1389 7389 Construction, repair, and dismantling services; Business Activities at Non-Commercial Site

(G-7405)
A+ IMAGES INC
5700 W Minnesota St Ste A5 (46241-3855)
PHONE.................................317 405-8955
EMP: 6 **EST:** 2000
SALES (est): 937.99K **Privately Held**
Web: www.aplusimages.com
SIC: 2759 Screen printing

(G-7406)
A-1 AWARDS INC
2500 N Ritter Ave (46218-3294)
PHONE.................................317 546-9000
Stephen L Capper, *Pr*
Nora Capper, *Sec*
▲ **EMP:** 15 **EST:** 1958
SQ FT: 15,000
SALES (est): 2.31MM **Privately Held**
Web: www.a-1awards.com

Indianapolis - Marion County (G-7407)   GEOGRAPHIC SECTION

SIC: 3914 2789 2396 2395 Trophies, silver; Bookbinding and related work; Automotive and apparel trimmings; Pleating and stitching

(G-7407)
A-1VET LLC
4411 Dunn St (46226-3935)
PHONE..............................317 498-1804
Nicholas Biddy, *Pr*
EMP: 3 EST: 2016
SALES (est): 149.74K **Privately Held**
SIC: 3679 7389 Harness assemblies, for electronic use: wire or cable; Business Activities at Non-Commercial Site

(G-7408)
A1 DELIVERIES LLC
2926 Medford Ave (46222-2254)
PHONE..............................317 828-3951
EMP: 2
SALES (est): 80.88K **Privately Held**
SIC: 2759 7389 Schedules, transportation: printing, nsk; Business Activities at Non-Commercial Site

(G-7409)
AAR CORP
Also Called: AAR Aircraft Services
2825 West Perimeter Rd Ste 101 (46241-3613)
PHONE..............................317 227-5000
EMP: 1
SALES (corp-wide): 2.32B **Publicly Held**
Web: www.aarcorp.com
SIC: 3728 Aircraft parts and equipment, nec
PA: Aar Corp.
 1100 N Wood Dale Rd
 Wood Dale IL 60191
 630 227-2000

(G-7410)
AAR SUPPLY CHAIN INC
Also Called: AAR Defense Systems Logistics
2825 West Perimeter Rd (46241-3612)
PHONE..............................317 227-5000
William Elyea, *Brnch Mgr*
EMP: 10
SQ FT: 1,600,000
SALES (corp-wide): 2.32B **Publicly Held**
Web: www.aarcorp.com
SIC: 3728 Aircraft parts and equipment, nec
HQ: Aar Supply Chain, Inc.
 1100 N Wood Dale Rd
 Wood Dale IL 60191
 630 227-2000

(G-7411)
AARVEE ASSOCIATES LLC
Also Called: Signs By Tmrrow Indianapolis NW
9541 Valparaiso Ct (46268-1130)
PHONE..............................312 222-5665
EMP: 2 EST: 2012
SALES (est): 155.59K **Privately Held**
Web: www.aarvee.com
SIC: 3993 Signs and advertising specialties

(G-7412)
ABACUS PRINTINGNGRAPHICS INC ✪
425 Blue Spring Dr Ste 103 (46239-8880)
PHONE..............................915 223-5166
Bernetta Curtis, *Pr*
EMP: 24 EST: 2022
SALES (est): 1.35MM **Privately Held**
SIC: 3555 7389 Printing presses; Business Activities at Non-Commercial Site

(G-7413)
ABB ENTERPRISE SOFTWARE INC
Also Called: ABB ENTERPRISE SOFTWARE INC.
6530 Corporate Dr (46278-2915)
PHONE..............................317 876-9090
Berry Wadley, *Brnch Mgr*
EMP: 39
Web: new.abb.com
SIC: 3612 Transformers, except electric
HQ: Abb Inc.
 305 Gregson Dr
 Cary NC 27511

(G-7414)
ABB FLEXIBLE AUTOMATION INC
Also Called: ABB Robotics
8401 Northwest Blvd (46278-1382)
PHONE..............................317 876-9090
Edward Gross, *Brnch Mgr*
EMP: 3
SIC: 3569 3625 3563 Robots, assembly line: industrial and commercial; Relays and industrial controls; Air and gas compressors
HQ: Abb Flexible Automation Inc.
 1250 Brown Rd
 Auburn Hills MI 48326
 248 391-9000

(G-7415)
ABBOTT CONTROLS INC
Also Called: Honeywell Authorized Dealer
5777 W 74th St (46278-1755)
PHONE..............................317 697-7102
Dave Abbott, *Pr*
Kristi Abbott, *VP*
EMP: 4 EST: 2010
SALES (est): 461.34K **Privately Held**
Web: www.abbottcontrols.com
SIC: 3822 Temperature controls, automatic

(G-7416)
ABDA INCORPORATED
1159 Country Club Rd (46224-0036)
PHONE..............................317 273-8343
▼ EMP: 5 EST: 1998
SALES (est): 297.27K **Privately Held**
Web: www.abdawindowfashions.com
SIC: 8611 5719 1799 2591 Manufacturers' institute; Venetian blinds; Window treatment installation; Drapery hardware and window blinds and shades

(G-7417)
ABS FREIGHT LINES LLC
1138 W 33rd St (46208-4513)
PHONE..............................317 691-6846
EMP: 1
SALES (est): 60.08K **Privately Held**
SIC: 3537 Trucks: freight, baggage, etc.: industrial, except mining

(G-7418)
ABSTRAKT GROUP LLC
7022 W 10th St Ste A (46214)
PHONE..............................800 200-8994
Terry Henton, *Prin*
EMP: 1
SALES (est): 66.12K **Privately Held**
SIC: 1389 Construction, repair, and dismantling services

(G-7419)
AC WELDING MSCELLANEOUS IR INC
2625 S Lockburn St (46241-5709)
PHONE..............................317 491-2898
EMP: 4 EST: 2013
SALES (est): 96.01K **Privately Held**
SIC: 7692 Welding repair

(G-7420)
ACCURATE MNFCTRED PDTS GROUP I
Also Called: Accurate Manufactured Products
8090 Woodland Dr (46278-1349)
PHONE..............................317 472-9000
Matthew Goldberg, *Pr*
Richard Jacobs, *
Linda Thompson, *
▲ EMP: 40 EST: 1987
SALES (est): 8.87MM **Privately Held**
Web: www.ampg.com
SIC: 3451 Screw machine products

(G-7421)
ACE MOBILITY INC
9850 E 30th St (46229-3608)
PHONE..............................317 241-2444
Tim Roberts, *Pr*
◆ EMP: 10 EST: 2003
SQ FT: 16,000
SALES (est): 465.66K **Privately Held**
Web: www.acemobility.us
SIC: 3089 Automotive parts, plastic

(G-7422)
ACI CONSTRUCTION COMPANY INC
5108 Topp Dr (46218-3259)
PHONE..............................317 549-1833
EMP: 20 EST: 1996
SALES (est): 814.22K **Privately Held**
Web: www.aciindiana.com
SIC: 2851 Paints, asphalt or bituminous

(G-7423)
ACS SIGN SOLUTION
Also Called: ACS Sign Systems
115 E 21st St (46202-1423)
PHONE..............................317 201-4838
Richard Lutin, *Brnch Mgr*
EMP: 25
SALES (corp-wide): 251.65K **Privately Held**
Web: www.acssigns.com
SIC: 3993 Signs and advertising specialties
PA: Acs Sign Solution
 1110 E 22nd St
 Indianapolis IN 46202
 317 925-2835

(G-7424)
ACS SIGN SOLUTION (PA)
1110 E 22nd St (46202-1848)
PHONE..............................317 925-2835
Joseph Lehner, *Prin*
EMP: 4 EST: 2010
SALES (est): 251.65K
SALES (corp-wide): 251.65K **Privately Held**
Web: www.acssigns.com
SIC: 3993 Electric signs

(G-7425)
ACTERNA LLC
5808 Churchman Byp (46203-6109)
PHONE..............................317 788-9351
EMP: 50
SALES (corp-wide): 1B **Publicly Held**
SIC: 3669 7379 3825 5065 Intercommunication systems, electric; Computer related consulting services; Instruments to measure electricity; Electronic parts and equipment, nec
HQ: Acterna Llc
 20250 Cntury Blvd Ste 100
 Germantown MD 20874
 301 353-1550

(G-7426)
ACWELDING & MISC IRON INC
2209 E Beecher St Ste B (46203-2961)
PHONE..............................317 491-2898
Archie Harrington, *Pr*
EMP: 1 EST: 2013
SALES (est): 75.56K **Privately Held**
SIC: 7692 Welding repair

(G-7427)
ADAFILL GLOBAL LLC
735 Shelby St Ste 33 (46203-1167)
PHONE..............................317 798-5378
EMP: 2 EST: 2021
SALES (est): 63.66K **Privately Held**
SIC: 3679 5999 8742 Electronic loads and power supplies; Miscellaneous retail stores, nec; Real estate consultant

(G-7428)
ADALPHI CORP
9668 Spruance Ct (46256-9622)
PHONE..............................847 624-3301
Alexander Newman, *Sec*
EMP: 1
SALES (est): 75K **Privately Held**
SIC: 7372 Application computer software

(G-7429)
ADAPTIVE MOBILITY INC
7040 Guion Rd (46268-4812)
PHONE..............................317 347-6400
TOLL FREE: 800
F Keith Conaway, *CEO*
Janice Conaway, *Pr*
EMP: 13 EST: 1985
SQ FT: 24,000
SALES (est): 544.21K **Privately Held**
Web: www.pridemobility.com
SIC: 3999 5047 Wheelchair lifts; Medical equipment and supplies

(G-7430)
ADDENDA LLC (HQ)
5929 Lakeside Blvd (46278-1996)
P.O. Box 423 (47834-0423)
PHONE..............................317 290-5007
Gary R Mitchener, *Pr*
Mark S Mccaughey, *VP*
EMP: 17 EST: 1999
SALES (est): 12.34MM
SALES (corp-wide): 24.81MM **Privately Held**
Web: www.addendallc.com
SIC: 2819 Industrial inorganic chemicals, nec
PA: Metals And Additives, Llc
 5929 Lakeside Blvd
 Indianapolis IN 46278
 317 290-5007

(G-7431)
ADEMCO INC
Also Called: ADI Global Distribution
3160 N Shadeland Ave (46226-6292)
PHONE..............................317 359-9505
Richard Groves, *Mgr*
EMP: 5
SALES (corp-wide): 6.24B **Publicly Held**
Web: www.adiglobaldistribution.us
SIC: 5063 3669 Electrical apparatus and equipment; Emergency alarms
HQ: Ademco Inc.
 275 Bradhollow Rd Ste 400
 Melville NY 11747
 631 692-1000

(G-7432)
ADHESIVE PRODUCTS INC
8736 E 33rd St (46226-6516)
P.O. Box 6434 (46038-6434)

GEOGRAPHIC SECTION

Indianapolis - Marion County (G-7456)

PHONE.....................317 899-0565
David Rebholz, *Pr*
EMP: 5 **EST:** 1994
SALES (est): 485.67K **Privately Held**
Web: www.adhesivemanufacturers.net
SIC: 2672 5169 Adhesive backed films, foams and foils; Chemicals and allied products, nec

(G-7433)
ADJUST YOUR CROWN HAIR CARE PD
5332 Penway St (46224-1437)
PHONE.....................317 970-1144
Samikian Ingram, *CEO*
EMP: 1 **EST:** 2020
SALES (est): 85.01K **Privately Held**
Web: www.adjustyourcrownhaircare.com
SIC: 2844 Hair preparations, including shampoos

(G-7434)
ADRIAN ORCHARDS INC
500 W Epler Ave (46217-3620)
PHONE.....................317 784-0550
George J Adrian, *Pr*
Janet Adrian-nixon, *Sec*
EMP: 6 **EST:** 1925
SQ FT: 2,000
SALES (est): 479.73K **Privately Held**
Web: www.hmbcoastsidetours.com
SIC: 0175 0171 2099 Apple orchard; Berry crops; Cider, nonalcoholic

(G-7435)
ADVANCE PRTECTIVE COATINGS INC
Also Called: Line-X of Indy
8448 Moller Rd (46268-1507)
PHONE.....................317 228-0123
EMP: 8 **EST:** 2007
SQ FT: 10,000
SALES (est): 965.1K **Privately Held**
Web: www.linex-indy.com
SIC: 2821 3714 5531 Plastics materials and resins; Pickup truck bed liners; Truck equipment and parts

(G-7436)
ADVANCE STORES COMPANY INC
Also Called: Advance Auto Parts
5125 N Keystone Ave (46205-1559)
PHONE.....................317 253-5034
Jessica Christensen, *Brnch Mgr*
EMP: 9
SALES (corp-wide): 11.29B **Publicly Held**
Web: shop.advanceautoparts.com
SIC: 5531 3825 Auto and truck equipment and parts; Battery testers, electrical
HQ: Advance Stores Company Incorporated
4200 Six Forks Rd
Raleigh NC 27609
540 362-4911

(G-7437)
ADVANCED CONTROL TECH INC
Also Called: Act
6805 Hillsdale Ct (46250-2039)
P.O. Box 40965 (46240-0965)
PHONE.....................317 806-2750
Gary Colip, *Pr*
Judith Colip, *VP*
▲ **EMP:** 5 **EST:** 1987
SQ FT: 16,000
SALES (est): 876.49K **Privately Held**
SIC: 3822 3674 3643 3625 Thermostats and other environmental sensors; Semiconductors and related devices; Current-carrying wiring services; Relays and industrial controls

(G-7438)
ADVANCED DRAINAGE SYSTEMS INC
420 S Belmont Ave (46222-4269)
PHONE.....................317 917-7960
EMP: 4
SALES (corp-wide): 2.87B **Publicly Held**
Web: www.adspipe.com
SIC: 3084 Plastics pipe
PA: Advanced Drainage Systems, Inc.
4640 Trueman Blvd
Hilliard OH 43026
614 658-0050

(G-7439)
ADVANCED ORTHOPRO INC (HQ)
1820 N Illinois St (46202-1318)
PHONE.....................317 924-4444
TOLL FREE: 800
Mohamad Mansoori, *Pr*
Karen Mansoori, *VP*
Aboul Mansoori, *Sec*
EMP: 21 **EST:** 1983
SQ FT: 7,600
SALES (est): 3.31MM
SALES (corp-wide): 1.12B **Privately Held**
Web: www.hangerclinic.com
SIC: 3842 8011 Braces, orthopedic; Offices and clinics of medical doctors
PA: Hanger, Inc.
10910 Domain Dr Ste 300
Austin TX 78758
512 777-3800

(G-7440)
ADVANCED RACG SUSPENSIONS INC
1698 Midwest Blvd (46214-2281)
PHONE.....................317 896-3306
Corey Fillip, *Pr*
EMP: 15 **EST:** 1990
SQ FT: 2,500
SALES (est): 833.16K **Privately Held**
Web: www.advancedracingsuspensions.com
SIC: 3714 Shock absorbers, motor vehicle

(G-7441)
ADVANCED SERVICES LLC
5426 Elmwood Ave (46203-6025)
PHONE.....................317 780-6909
Paul Clark, *Managing Member*
EMP: 10 **EST:** 2003
SALES (est): 429.83K **Privately Held**
Web: www.advsvcindy.com
SIC: 2273 Carpets and rugs

(G-7442)
ADVANCED TEST CONCEPTS LLC
4037 Guion Ln (46268-2564)
PHONE.....................317 328-8492
EMP: 30
Web: usa.pfeiffer-vacuum.com
SIC: 3829 Liquid leak detection equipment

(G-7443)
ADVANCED WELDING AND ENGRG
8155 Crawfordsville Rd (46214-1471)
PHONE.....................317 820-3595
EMP: 4 **EST:** 2016
SALES (est): 43.85K **Privately Held**
SIC: 8711 7692 Engineering services; Welding repair

(G-7444)
ADVANTAGE MANUFACTURING LLC
1802 W 10th St (46222-3804)
PHONE.....................317 237-4289
Richard Bryant, *Owner*
EMP: 4 **EST:** 1990

SQ FT: 8,000
SALES (est): 330.62K **Privately Held**
SIC: 3444 Sheet metalwork

(G-7445)
ADVENT PRECISION INC
1740 Industry Dr Ste E (46219)
PHONE.....................317 908-6937
Timothy Brenamen, *Pr*
Mark Earls, *VP*
EMP: 4 **EST:** 2016
SALES (est): 478.71K **Privately Held**
Web: www.adventprecision.com
SIC: 3545 Precision tools, machinists'

(G-7446)
AEARO TECHNOLOGIES LLC (DH)
Also Called: Aearo Company
7911 Zionsville Rd (46268)
P.O. Box 33331 (55133)
PHONE.....................612 284-1232
Matt Gualdoni, *Managing Member*
John R Castellano, *
▲ **EMP:** 600 **EST:** 1978
SQ FT: 200,000
SALES (est): 298.44MM
SALES (corp-wide): 32.68B **Publicly Held**
Web: www.aearotechnologies.com
SIC: 3842 3851 3643 Ear plugs; Protective eyeware; Plugs, electric
HQ: Aearo Llc
7911 Zionsville Rd
Indianapolis IN

(G-7447)
AEARO TECHNOLOGIES LLC
E-A-R Specialty Composites
7911 Zionsville Rd (46268-1650)
PHONE.....................317 692-6666
Randy Mallitz, *Brnch Mgr*
EMP: 200
SALES (corp-wide): 32.68B **Publicly Held**
Web: www.aearotechnologies.com
SIC: 3086 3444 3443 3296 Plastics foam products; Sheet metalwork; Fabricated plate work (boiler shop); Mineral wool
HQ: Aearo Technologies Llc
7911 Zionsville Rd
Indianapolis IN 46268

(G-7448)
AERO INDUSTRIES INC (PA)
4243 W Bradbury Ave (46241-5253)
PHONE.....................317 244-2433
James R Tuerk, *CEO*
Robert P Tuerk, *
Paul Tuerk, *
Don Cross, *
David L Boyd, *
▲ **EMP:** 100 **EST:** 1946
SQ FT: 46,000
SALES (est): 47.72MM
SALES (corp-wide): 47.72MM **Privately Held**
Web: www.aeroindustries.com
SIC: 3714 Motor vehicle parts and accessories

(G-7449)
AERO-MED LLC
5110 W 74th St (46268-4160)
PHONE.....................740 412-3855
Paul Schechter, *Brnch Mgr*
EMP: 1
SALES (corp-wide): 226.83B **Publicly Held**
Web: www.aero-med.com
SIC: 3843 Dental equipment and supplies
HQ: Aero-Med, Llc
65 Olde Roberts St
East Hartford CT 06108
860 659-0602

(G-7450)
AERODINE COMPOSITES LLC
1755 Midwest Blvd (46214)
PHONE.....................317 271-1207
Craig Mccarthy, *Pr*
Craig Mccarthy, *Managing Member*
EMP: 42 **EST:** 1989
SALES (est): 7.78MM **Privately Held**
Web: www.aerodinecomposites.com
SIC: 3624 Carbon and graphite products

(G-7451)
AERODYN ENGINEERING LLC (PA)
Also Called: A E I
1919 S Girls School Rd (46241-3636)
PHONE.....................317 334-1523
David Lawrence, *Pr*
David Lawrence, *Ex Dir*
Nicole Abernathy, *
EMP: 42 **EST:** 2002
SQ FT: 33,500
SALES (est): 24.72MM
SALES (corp-wide): 24.72MM **Privately Held**
Web: www.aerodyn-global.com
SIC: 8711 3724 Aviation and/or aeronautical engineering; Aircraft engines and engine parts

(G-7452)
AEROFAB CORP
3750 Shelby St (46227-3361)
PHONE.....................317 787-6438
Mike Gill, *Owner*
EMP: 6 **EST:** 2000
SALES (est): 52.71K **Privately Held**
Web: www.aerofab-corp.com
SIC: 3599 Machine shop, jobbing and repair

(G-7453)
AEROMIND LLC
Also Called: Silca
835 N Capitol Ave (46204)
PHONE.....................800 905-2157
EMP: 2 **EST:** 2013
SALES (est): 556.22K **Privately Held**
Web: www.silca.cc
SIC: 2891 2252 3561 7389 Sealants; Socks; Industrial pumps and parts; Business services, nec

(G-7454)
AESTHTCALLY PLEASING SKIN SOAK
2454 Wigeon Ct (46234-8801)
PHONE.....................317 551-0156
Rivee Brown, *CEO*
EMP: 1 **EST:** 2021
SALES (est): 49.15K **Privately Held**
SIC: 7389 2844 5122 5999 Business Activities at Non-Commercial Site; Cosmetic preparations; Cosmetics; Candle shops

(G-7455)
AF OHAB COMPANY INC
Also Called: Afequip.com
2346 S Lynhurst Dr Ste 302 (46241-5171)
PHONE.....................317 225-4740
Abdul Feroze Ohab, *CEO*
EMP: 45 **EST:** 1990
SALES (est): 5.13MM **Privately Held**
Web: 0460a8a.netsolhost.com
SIC: 5082 3531 General construction machinery and equipment; Graders, road (construction machinery)

(G-7456)
AFFORDABLE NEON SERVICES
7051 Crawfordsville Rd (46214-2104)

Indianapolis - Marion County (G-7457)   GEOGRAPHIC SECTION

P.O. Box 34375 (46234-0375)
PHONE..........................317 299-6061
Clark Bennet, *Owner*
EMP: 1 **EST:** 2000
SALES (est): 111.61K **Privately Held**
Web:
affordable-neon-services.business.site
SIC: 3993 Neon signs

(G-7457)
AFTER ACTION MED DNTL SUP LLC
4444 Decatur Blvd Ste 100 (46241-9626)
PHONE..........................800 892-5352
EMP: 6 **EST:** 2011
SALES (est): 1.5MM **Privately Held**
Web: www.afteractionmedical.com
SIC: 5047 3841 Medical equipment and supplies; Surgical and medical instruments

(G-7458)
AGI INTERNATIONAL INC
Also Called: Agi Logistics
2525 N Shadeland Ave Ste D5 (46219)
P.O. Box 31791 (28231)
PHONE..........................317 536-2415
E Jerome Agnew, *Pr*
▲ **EMP:** 17 **EST:** 2006
SQ FT: 1,200
SALES (est): 1.18MM **Privately Held**
Web: www.agiintl.com
SIC: 4225 8741 8748 3569 General warehousing and storage; Management services; Business consulting, nec; Assembly machines, non-metalworking

(G-7459)
AGILE ENGINEERING & MFG LLC
3902 E 16th St Ste A (46201-1562)
PHONE..........................317 359-3360
EMP: 11 **EST:** 2003
SALES (est): 2.29MM **Privately Held**
Web: www.aem-mfg.com
SIC: 3599 Machine shop, jobbing and repair

(G-7460)
AIR ENERGY SYSTEMS INC (PA)
4790 W 73rd St (46268-2115)
PHONE..........................317 290-8500
William C Maher, *Pr*
Dorothy G Maher, *VP*
EMP: 6 **EST:** 1986
SQ FT: 24,000
SALES (est): 2.44MM
SALES (corp-wide): 2.44MM **Privately Held**
Web: www.aesrack.com
SIC: 5075 3634 Warm air heating equipment and supplies; Electric household fans, heaters, and humidifiers

(G-7461)
AIR IN MOTION PUBLISHERS LLC
1963 Clark Rd (46224-5330)
PHONE..........................317 850-0149
Randy M Williams, *Prin*
EMP: 1 **EST:** 2011
SALES (est): 62.43K **Privately Held**
SIC: 2741 Miscellaneous publishing

(G-7462)
AIRCOM MANUFACTURING INC
6205 E 30th St (46219-1084)
P.O. Box 18054 (46218-0054)
PHONE..........................317 545-5383
▲ **EMP:** 300
Web: www.aircommfg.com
SIC: 3089 3544 3499 3469 Injection molded finished plastics products, nec; Special dies, tools, jigs, and fixtures; Metal household articles; Metal stampings, nec

(G-7463)
AIRGAS INC
Also Called: Airgas
1441 Bates St (46201-3943)
PHONE..........................317 632-7106
Scott Neeton, *Mgr*
EMP: 2
SALES (corp-wide): 114.13MM **Privately Held**
Web: www.airgas.com
SIC: 2813 2097 2911 Dry ice, carbon dioxide (solid); Manufactured ice; Petroleum refining
HQ: Airgas, Inc.
 259 N Rdnor Chster Rd Ste
 Radnor PA 19087
 610 687-5253

(G-7464)
AIRGAS USA LLC
Also Called: Airgas Puritan Medical
5430 W Morris St (46241-3429)
PHONE..........................317 248-8072
Keany Earl, *Mgr*
EMP: 5
SALES (corp-wide): 114.13MM **Privately Held**
Web: www.airgas.com
SIC: 3842 3841 2813 Respirators; Surgical and medical instruments; Industrial gases
HQ: Airgas Usa, Llc
 259 N Radnor Chester Rd
 Radnor PA 19087
 216 642-6600

(G-7465)
AK SUPPLY INC
6321 E 30th St Ste 206 (46219-1081)
PHONE..........................317 895-0410
Kevin Drake, *Pr*
Areli Drake, *VP*
EMP: 9 **EST:** 2009
SALES (est): 239.39K **Privately Held**
SIC: 2394 Shades, canvas: made from purchased materials

(G-7466)
AL DISHNO NEON
5249 Hickory Rd (46239-1834)
PHONE..........................317 862-5374
EMP: 1 **EST:** 1987
SALES (est): 81.85K **Privately Held**
Web:
hstrial-dishnossignsa.intuitwebsites.com
SIC: 3993 Signs, not made in custom sign painting shops

(G-7467)
ALE ENTERPRISES INC
4623 S High School Rd (46241-7652)
PHONE..........................317 856-2981
Anthony L Elrod, *Owner*
EMP: 5 **EST:** 1973
SALES (est): 993.08K **Privately Held**
SIC: 1521 1542 2511 2521 General remodeling, single-family houses; Commercial and office building, new construction; Wood household furniture; Cabinets, office: wood

(G-7468)
ALEBRO LLC
Also Called: Davis Wholesale Supply
7690 Zionsville Rd (46268-2173)
PHONE..........................317 876-9212
Gino Lucchese, *Prin*
EMP: 10 **EST:** 2007
SALES (est): 925.05K **Privately Held**
Web: www.claritysalt.com
SIC: 2899 Salt

(G-7469)
ALEXANDER SCREW PRODUCTS INC
Also Called: Stiffler Handy Product
8750 Pendleton Pike (46226)
P.O. Box 26084 (46226)
PHONE..........................317 898-5313
Larry Alexander, *CEO*
Oren D Alexander, *
Jesse Alexander, *
EMP: 49 **EST:** 1961
SQ FT: 50,000
SALES (est): 9.51MM **Privately Held**
Web: www.alexanderscrew.com
SIC: 3451 3449 Screw machine products; Miscellaneous metalwork

(G-7470)
ALEXANDRIA EXTRSION MDMRICA LL
4925 Aluminum Dr (46218-3156)
PHONE..........................317 545-1221
Joe Schabel, *CEO*
Steve Schabel, *Pr*
EMP: 2 **EST:** 2012
SALES (est): 11.26MM
SALES (corp-wide): 214.24MM **Privately Held**
Web: www.alexandriaindustries.com
SIC: 3354 Aluminum extruded products
PA: Alexandria Extrusion Company
 401 County Road 22 Nw
 Alexandria MN 56308
 320 763-6537

(G-7471)
ALGALCO LLC
6532 Castle Knoll Ct (46250-1439)
PHONE..........................317 361-2787
Kc Cohen, *Admn*
EMP: 2 **EST:** 2007
SALES (est): 238.99K **Privately Held**
Web: www.algalco.com
SIC: 3399 Aluminum atomized powder

(G-7472)
ALL AMERICAN EX SOLUTIONS LLC
5101 Decatur Blvd Ste W (46241-9529)
PHONE..........................317 789-3070
EMP: 45 **EST:** 2014
SALES (est): 2.48MM **Privately Held**
Web: www.all-american-solutions.com
SIC: 4212 1771 2869 7389 Local trucking, without storage; Concrete work; Fuels; Courier or messenger service

(G-7473)
ALL GUSSIED UP EMBROIDERY
12207 Beckley Rd (46229-3205)
PHONE..........................317 517-1557
EMP: 3 **EST:** 2016
SALES (est): 97.98K **Privately Held**
SIC: 2759 Screen printing

(G-7474)
ALL PRO PROPERTY SERVICES LLC
9175 Harrison Park Ct (46216-2108)
PHONE..........................317 721-1227
Katrina Smith, *Managing Member*
EMP: 1 **EST:** 2012
SALES (est): 2.2MM **Privately Held**
Web: www.callallproindy.com
SIC: 6512 3585 1711 Nonresidential building operators; Heating equipment, complete; Heating systems repair and maintenance

(G-7475)
ALL PRO SHEARING INC
1905 Lawton Ave (46203-2994)
P.O. Box 1744 (46546-1744)

PHONE..........................317 691-1005
Danny Fey, *Pr*
EMP: 18 **EST:** 2003
SQ FT: 87,120
SALES (est): 600.08K **Privately Held**
SIC: 3341 Secondary nonferrous metals

(G-7476)
ALL SHPPERS ARE PRRITY TRCKG L ◊
5953 Wixson Ct (46254-2337)
PHONE..........................317 525-6954
EMP: 1 **EST:** 2022
SALES (est): 60.08K **Privately Held**
SIC: 3537 Trucks: freight, baggage, etc.: industrial, except mining

(G-7477)
ALL TIME LOW MAGAZINE LLC
9996 Olympic Cir (46234-5056)
PHONE..........................317 286-7221
EMP: 3
SALES (est): 127.59K **Privately Held**
SIC: 2711 Newspapers

(G-7478)
ALLEGION S&S HOLDING CO INC
8506 E 30th St (46219-1423)
PHONE..........................317 429-2299
EMP: 34
Web: www.allegion.com
SIC: 3561 Pumps and pumping equipment
HQ: Allegion S&S Holding Company Inc.
 11819 N Penn St
 Carmel IN 46032
 317 810-3700

(G-7479)
ALLEGRA MARKETING PRINT MAIL
8025 Castleway Dr Ste 103 (46278-1753)
PHONE..........................317 643-6248
EMP: 5 **EST:** 2019
SALES (est): 92.3K **Privately Held**
Web: www.allegramarketingprint.com
SIC: 2752 Offset printing

(G-7480)
ALLEN MONUMENT CO
Also Called: Allen Monument Co
5234 Madison Ave (46227-4242)
PHONE..........................317 941-7047
EMP: 1
SALES (corp-wide): 878.9K **Privately Held**
Web: www.allenmonuments.com
SIC: 5999 3272 3281 Monuments and tombstones; Monuments and grave markers, except terrazzo; Monument or burial stone, cut and shaped
PA: Allen Monument Company
 212 Hamilton St
 Crawfordsville IN 47933
 765 362-8886

(G-7481)
ALLENS THERAPUETIC SERVICES
450 E 96th St Ste 500 (46240-3760)
PHONE..........................317 820-3600
Allen M Rader, *Owner*
EMP: 5 **EST:** 2016
SALES (est): 190.94K **Privately Held**
SIC: 3724 Aircraft engines and engine parts

(G-7482)
ALLFAB LLC
1414 Sadlier Circle West Dr (46239-1058)
PHONE..........................317 359-3539
Scott A Spicklemire, *Managing Member*
EMP: 7 **EST:** 2011
SALES (est): 243.62K **Privately Held**
Web: www.allfab-llc.com

▲ = Import ▼ = Export
◊ = Import/Export

GEOGRAPHIC SECTION

Indianapolis - Marion County (G-7506)

SIC: 3542 7389 7692 3546 Machine tools, metal forming type; Metal slitting and shearing; Welding repair; Drills and drilling tools

(G-7483)
ALLIANCE STUDIOS LLC
5634 Nuckols Ct (46237-8472)
PHONE.................317 525-8487
Mackenzie Jackson, *Mgr*
EMP: 5 EST: 2019
SALES (est): 90.98K **Privately Held**
SIC: 3999 Manufacturing industries, nec

(G-7484)
ALLIED STEEL RULE DIES INC
5811 W Minnesota St (46241-3845)
PHONE.................317 634-9835
Kelly Russell, *Pr*
EMP: 15 EST: 1982
SQ FT: 17,000
SALES (est): 1.47MM **Privately Held**
Web: www.allieddies.com
SIC: 3544 Dies, steel rule

(G-7485)
ALLISON PYMNT SYSTEMS LLC DBA (HQ)
2200 Production Dr (46241-4912)
P.O. Box 102 (46206-0102)
PHONE.................317 808-2400
EMP: 160 EST: 1888
SQ FT: 60,000
SALES (est): 45.59MM
SALES (corp-wide): 64.6MM **Privately Held**
Web: www.apsllc.com
SIC: 2752 5112 Offset printing; Business forms
PA: Doxim Solutions Ulc
102-1380 Rodick Rd
Markham ON L3R 4
866 475-9876

(G-7486)
ALLISON TRANSM HOLDINGS INC (PA)
Also Called: Allison Transmission
1 Allison Way (46222)
PHONE.................317 242-5000
EMP: 1583 EST: 1915
SALES (est): 3.04B **Publicly Held**
Web: www.allisontransmission.com
SIC: 3714 Motor vehicle transmissions, drive assemblies, and parts

(G-7487)
ALLISON TRANSMISSION INC
Also Called: Allison Transmission Division
901 Grande Ave (46222-3276)
P.O. Box 894 (46206-0894)
PHONE.................317 242-5000
EMP: 207
Web: www.allisontransmission.com
SIC: 3714 Motor vehicle parts and accessories
HQ: Allison Transmission, Inc.
1 Allison Way
Indianapolis IN 46222

(G-7488)
ALLISON TRANSMISSION INC
Also Called: Allison Parts Distribution
5902 Decatur Blvd (46241-9579)
PHONE.................317 821-5104
EMP: 239
Web: www.allisontransmission.com
SIC: 3714 3511 Motor vehicle parts and accessories; Turbines and turbine generator sets

HQ: Allison Transmission, Inc.
1 Allison Way
Indianapolis IN 46222

(G-7489)
ALLISON TRANSMISSION INC
6040 W 62nd St (46278-2909)
PHONE.................317 280-6206
Terence Molloy, *Brnch Mgr*
EMP: 116
Web: www.allisontransmission.com
SIC: 3714 3728 Motor vehicle parts and accessories; Aircraft power transmission equipment
HQ: Allison Transmission, Inc.
1 Allison Way
Indianapolis IN 46222

(G-7490)
ALLISON TRANSMISSION INC
Also Called: Allison Transmission
2840 Fortune Cir W Ste A (46241)
PHONE.................317 242-2080
EMP: 94
Web: www.allisontransmission.com
SIC: 3714 Transmissions, motor vehicle
HQ: Allison Transmission, Inc.
1 Allison Way
Indianapolis IN 46222

(G-7491)
ALLISON TRANSMISSION INC
Allison Transmission
1 Allison Way (46222-3271)
P.O. Box 894 (46206-0894)
PHONE.................317 242-5000
Paul Nicholas, *Brnch Mgr*
EMP: 2600
Web: www.allisontransmission.com
SIC: 3511 3714 3724 Turbines and turbine generator sets; Transmissions, motor vehicle; Turbines, aircraft type
HQ: Allison Transmission, Inc.
1 Allison Way
Indianapolis IN 46222

(G-7492)
ALOCIT USA
1128 S West St (46225-1463)
PHONE.................317 631-9111
Kenny Boehm, *Pr*
▲ EMP: 3 EST: 2013
SALES (est): 150.9K **Privately Held**
Web: www.alocitusa.com
SIC: 3479 Coating of metals and formed products

(G-7493)
ALTEC INDUSTRIES INC
Also Called: Northern Division
5201 W 84th St (46268-1532)
P.O. Box 681308 (46268-7308)
PHONE.................317 872-3460
Hugh Cate, *Brnch Mgr*
EMP: 164
SALES (corp-wide): 1.21B **Privately Held**
Web: www.altec.com
SIC: 3531 Aerial work platforms: hydraulic/elec. truck/carrier mounted
HQ: Altec Industries, Inc.
210 Inverness Center Drv
Birmingham AL 35242
205 991-7733

(G-7494)
AMA USA INC
5350 Lakeview Parkway South Dr Ste D (46268)
PHONE.................317 329-6590
Giuliano Cacucci, *Pr*
◆ EMP: 4 EST: 2006

SQ FT: 10,000
SALES (est): 527.65K **Privately Held**
Web: www.amausainc.com
SIC: 3531 Construction machinery

(G-7495)
AMAZING WELL DRILL PUMP PLBG
3015 Radford Dr (46226-6225)
PHONE.................317 384-9132
Dee Hughes, *Pr*
EMP: 4 EST: 2020
SALES (est): 207.04K **Privately Held**
SIC: 1381 Drilling oil and gas wells

(G-7496)
AMBRE BLENDS
7825 E 89th St (46256-1239)
PHONE.................317 257-0202
Amber Crocket, *Owner*
EMP: 7 EST: 2013
SALES (est): 280.21K **Privately Held**
Web: www.ambreblends.com
SIC: 2844 Perfumes, cosmetics and other toilet preparations

(G-7497)
AMERAWHIP INC
1735 W 18th St (46202-1056)
PHONE.................317 639-5248
John Clifford, *Pr*
▲ EMP: 8 EST: 2013
SALES (est): 493.72K **Privately Held**
Web: www.amerawhip.com
SIC: 3629 Electronic generation equipment

(G-7498)
AMERIBRIDGE LLC
5425 Poindexter Dr (46235-9040)
P.O. Box 1253 (55337-0253)
PHONE.................317 826-2000
Dustin Sloan, *Pr*
Gary Sloan, *
Tim Keyes, *
EMP: 53 EST: 2012
SALES (est): 9.69MM **Privately Held**
Web: www.ameribridge.us
SIC: 3531 Airport construction machinery

(G-7499)
AMERICAN ART CLAY CO INC (PA)
Also Called: A M A C O
6060 Guion Rd (46254-1222)
PHONE.................317 244-6871
Lester B Sandoe Junior, *Ch*
Valri P Sandoe, *Vice Chairman**
William E Berry, *
◆ EMP: 116 EST: 1919
SALES (est): 38.15MM
SALES (corp-wide): 38.15MM **Privately Held**
Web: www.amaco.com
SIC: 3295 3559 5092 3083 Clay, ground or otherwise treated; Pottery making machinery; Toys and hobby goods and supplies; Plastics finished products, laminated

(G-7500)
AMERICAN BOTTLING COMPANY
Also Called: 7 Up Bottling Co
5430 W 81st St (46268-1611)
PHONE.................317 875-4900
TOLL FREE: 800
Bill Murray, *Mgr*
EMP: 150
Web: www.keurigdrpepper.com
SIC: 2086 5149 Soft drinks: packaged in cans, bottles, etc.; Groceries and related products, nec
HQ: The American Bottling Company
6425 Hall Of Fame Ln

Frisco TX 75034

(G-7501)
AMERICAN BRONZE CRAFT INC (PA)
5520 Kopetsky Dr Ste A (46217-9003)
PHONE.................501 729-3018
Fred W Meyer Junior, *Pr*
Jean H Meyer, *VP*
Durwin L Foisey, *Treas*
Edith Mcgaughey, *Sec*
EMP: 15 EST: 1975
SQ FT: 18,000
SALES (est): 2.32MM
SALES (corp-wide): 2.32MM **Privately Held**
Web: www.americanbronzecraft.com
SIC: 3543 3281 Foundry cores; Cut stone and stone products

(G-7502)
AMERICAN DIABETES ASSOCIATION
8604 Allisonville Rd Ste 140 (46250)
P.O. Box 7023 (22116-7023)
PHONE.................859 268-9129
EMP: 2
SALES (corp-wide): 146.77MM **Privately Held**
Web: www.diabetes.org
SIC: 8699 3731 Charitable organization; Shipbuilding and repairing
PA: American Diabetes Association
2451 Crystal Dr Ste 900
Arlington VA 22202
703 549-1500

(G-7503)
AMERICAN FAMILY PHARMACY LLC
Also Called: AFP
3250 N Post Rd Ste 285 (46226-6541)
PHONE.................317 334-1933
▲ EMP: 7 EST: 2002
SALES (est): 754.79K **Privately Held**
Web: www.afpharmacy.com
SIC: 2834 Pills, pharmaceutical

(G-7504)
AMERICAN HERITAGE SHUTTERS LLC
Also Called: Mk Interiors
9450 Timberline Dr (46256-4722)
PHONE.................317 598-6908
EMP: 2 EST: 1986
SALES (est): 164.86K **Privately Held**
Web: www.ahshutters.com
SIC: 2431 Windows and window parts and trim, wood

(G-7505)
AMERICAN LEGION NATIONAL HEADQUARTERS (PA)
Also Called: NATIONAL EMBLEM SALES DIV
700 N Pennsylvania St (46204-1172)
P.O. Box 1055 (46206-1055)
PHONE.................317 630-1200
EMP: 75 EST: 1919
SALES (est): 28.46MM
SALES (corp-wide): 28.46MM **Privately Held**
Web: www.legion.org
SIC: 8641 5961 2721 Veterans' organization; Catalog sales; Magazines: publishing and printing

(G-7506)
AMERICAN RIGGING RENTAL
1717 W 10th St (46222-5351)
PHONE.................317 721-9553
Mike Griggs, *Brnch Mgr*
EMP: 2 EST: 2011

Indianapolis - Marion County (G-7507) GEOGRAPHIC SECTION

SALES (est): 109.11K **Privately Held**
SIC: **3496** Miscellaneous fabricated wire products

(G-7507)
AMERICAN SENIOR HOMECARE
4519 E 82nd St Ofc (46250-5641)
PHONE...................317 849-4968
Diane Anderson, *Dir*
EMP: 5 EST: 2002
SALES (est): 73.5K **Privately Held**
SIC: **2711** Newspapers, publishing and printing

(G-7508)
AMERICAN WIRE ROPE SLING OF IN (HQ)
Also Called: American Wire Rope & Sling
5760 Dividend Rd (46241-4304)
PHONE...................877 634-2545
Eric Stetzel, *Pr*
EMP: 19 EST: 1985
SALES (est): 8.52MM
SALES (corp-wide): 169.95MM **Privately Held**
SIC: **3496** Miscellaneous fabricated wire products
PA: Bishop Lifting Products, Inc.
2301 Commerce St Ste 110
Houston TX
713 674-2266

(G-7509)
AMERIFAB INC
3501 E 9th St (46201-2509)
PHONE...................317 231-0100
Gabe Carinci, *Pr*
Joseph P Hochgesang, *
▲ EMP: 70 EST: 1992
SQ FT: 85,000
SALES (est): 9.84MM **Privately Held**
Web: www.amerifabinc.com
SIC: **3441** Fabricated structural metal

(G-7510)
AMERIFLO INC
4496 Saguaro Trl (46268-2554)
PHONE...................317 844-2019
Rebecca Voege, *Pr*
Jim Voege, *Pr*
EMP: 12 EST: 1997
SALES (est): 740.12K **Privately Held**
Web: www.ameriflo.com
SIC: **3494** Valves and pipe fittings, nec

(G-7511)
AMERIFLO2 INC
Also Called: Medical Manufacturing
4496 Saguaro Trl (46268-2554)
PHONE...................317 844-2019
Rebecca Voege, *CEO*
Rebecca Voege, *Pr*
Jim Voege, *VP*
EMP: 15 EST: 2014
SALES (est): 1.07MM **Privately Held**
Web: www.ameriflo2.com
SIC: **3841** Surgical and medical instruments

(G-7512)
AMG ENGINEERING MACHINING INC
4030 Guion Ln (46268)
P.O. Box 681245 (46268)
PHONE...................317 329-4000
Theaodis Gary, *Pr*
Helen Randolph, *Sec*
▲ EMP: 20 EST: 1989
SQ FT: 30,000
SALES (est): 3.78MM **Privately Held**
Web: www.amgindy.com

SIC: **3599** Machine shop, jobbing and repair

(G-7513)
AMG LLC
Also Called: Regin Manufacturing
4030 Guion Ln (46268-2564)
P.O. Box 781108 (46278-8108)
PHONE...................317 329-4004
Theaodis Gary Junior, *Managing Member*
EMP: 15 EST: 2001
SALES (est): 952.72K **Privately Held**
Web: www.amgindy.com
SIC: **3823** 3491 Flow instruments, industrial process type; Industrial valves

(G-7514)
ANATOLIA GROUP LTD PARTNERSHIP
640 E Michigan St (46202-0008)
PHONE...................203 343-7808
Arif Ugur, *Mng Pt*
EMP: 4 EST: 2015
SQ FT: 1,650
SALES (est): 399.53K **Privately Held**
SIC: **3559** Semiconductor manufacturing machinery

(G-7515)
ANCIENT CELLARS
360 W 63rd St (46260-4718)
PHONE...................503 437-4827
EMP: 5 EST: 2010
SALES (est): 111.01K **Privately Held**
SIC: **2084** Wines

(G-7516)
ANDON SPECIALTIES INC
5736 W 79th St (46278-1708)
PHONE...................317 983-1700
EMP: 5
SALES (corp-wide): 20.76MM **Privately Held**
Web: www.andon.com
SIC: **3677** Filtration devices, electronic
PA: Andon Specialties, Inc.
2720 Reed Rd Ste 280
Houston TX 77051
713 791-9800

(G-7517)
ANDRETTI TECHNOLOGIES LLC
7615 Zionsville Rd (46268-2174)
PHONE...................317 872-2700
EMP: 3 EST: 2015
SALES (est): 234.94K **Privately Held**
Web: www.andretti-global.com
SIC: **3711** Automobile assembly, including specialty automobiles

(G-7518)
ANDYS GLOBAL INC
8445 Castlewood Dr Ste C (46250-4582)
PHONE...................317 595-8825
Arvind Mistry, *Pr*
Jyoti A Mistry, *VP*
Shital A Mistry, *Treas*
▲ EMP: 4 EST: 1999
SQ FT: 2,400
SALES (est): 357.38K **Privately Held**
Web: www.andysglobal.com
SIC: **3421** Scissors, shears, clippers, snips, and similar tools

(G-7519)
ANNDYS PARADISE LLC
7105 Knobwood Dr Apt A (46260-3593)
PHONE...................317 258-7531
EMP: 1
SALES (est): 69.27K **Privately Held**

SIC: **2499** Food handling and processing products, wood

(G-7520)
ANNS BOBA TEA LLC ✪
3827 N Mitthoefer Rd Ste B7 Pmb B8 (46235-1810)
PHONE...................317 681-3143
Paula Kuria, *CEO*
EMP: 5 EST: 2022
SALES (est): 62.01K **Privately Held**
Web: www.annsbobatea.com
SIC: **2099** 5812 Tea blending; Cafe

(G-7521)
ANODIZING TECHNOLOGIES INC
5868 N New Jersey St (46220-2535)
P.O. Box 502770 (46250-7770)
PHONE...................317 253-5725
EMP: 3 EST: 1996
SALES (est): 470.44K **Privately Held**
Web: www.anodizingtechnologies.com
SIC: **3559** Metal finishing equipment for plating, etc.

(G-7522)
ANTHONY WYNE RHBLTTION CTR FOR
Also Called: Postmasters
2762 Rand Rd (46241-5506)
PHONE...................317 972-1000
Gary Johloz, *Mgr*
EMP: 118
SALES (corp-wide): 46.79MM **Privately Held**
Web: www.thinktandem.com
SIC: **7331** 2759 Mailing service; Laser printing
PA: Anthony Wayne Rehabilitation Center For Handicapped And Blind, Inc
8515 Bluffton Rd
Fort Wayne IN 46809
260 744-6145

(G-7523)
ANTREASIAN DESIGN INC
3124 Ridgeview Dr (46226-6152)
PHONE...................317 546-3234
Mark B Antreasian, *Pr*
Cris Antreasian, *VP*
EMP: 18 EST: 1990
SQ FT: 17,000
SALES (est): 501.88K **Privately Held**
Web: www.adiarchwood.com
SIC: **2511** 2521 2431 Wood household furniture; Wood office furniture; Millwork

(G-7524)
AON(ALL OR NOTHING) LLC
Also Called: AON
2003 Lisa Walk Dr (46227)
PHONE...................219 405-0163
EMP: 1 EST: 2021
SALES (est): 100K **Privately Held**
Web: www.aon.com
SIC: **2211** 4789 7336 2842 Press cloth; Transportation services, nec; Graphic arts and related design; Laundry cleaning preparations

(G-7525)
APOLLO OTDOOR CSTM DESIGNS INC
1848 Stout Field East Dr (46241-4009)
P.O. Box 90233 (46290-0233)
PHONE...................317 430-1373
Brent Mason, *Pr*
EMP: 10 EST: 2000
SQ FT: 7,500
SALES (est): 1.55MM **Privately Held**

SIC: **2522** Office chairs, benches, and stools, except wood

(G-7526)
APOTEX CORP
5110 W 74th St (46268-4160)
PHONE...................317 334-1314
EMP: 10 EST: 2019
SALES (est): 230.82K **Privately Held**
SIC: **2836** Biological products, except diagnostic

(G-7527)
APP ENGINEERING INCORPORATED
5234 Elmwood Ave (46203-5915)
PHONE...................317 536-5300
Greg Bradley, *Pr*
Wing-kin Wai, *VP*
EMP: 10 EST: 2005
SQ FT: 6,000
SALES (est): 2.25MM **Privately Held**
Web: www.appengineering.com
SIC: **3825** Instruments to measure electricity

(G-7528)
APP PRESS LLC
435 Virginia Ave Unit 607 (46203-1967)
PHONE...................317 661-4759
EMP: 2 EST: 2010
SALES (est): 248.35K **Privately Held**
Web: www.app-press.com
SIC: **7372** 7371 Business oriented computer software; Computer software development

(G-7529)
APPEXTREMES LLC
Also Called: Conga
54 Monument Cir Ste 200 (46204-2943)
PHONE...................317 550-0148
EMP: 55
Web: www.conga.com
SIC: **7372** 8742 Prepackaged software; Marketing consulting services
HQ: Appextremes, Llc
13699 Via Varra
Broomfield CO 80020
303 465-1616

(G-7530)
APPLE PRESS INC
6327 Ferguson St (46220-1707)
PHONE...................317 253-7752
Mark Finch, *Pr*
EMP: 4 EST: 1984
SQ FT: 10,000
SALES (est): 236.61K **Privately Held**
Web: www.branches.com
SIC: **2752** Offset printing

(G-7531)
APPLICATION SOFTWARE INC
9801 Fall Creek Rd Ste 101 (46256-4802)
PHONE...................317 823-3525
Roger Welter, *Pr*
EMP: 2 EST: 2011
SALES (est): 139.88K **Privately Held**
Web: www.erebar.com
SIC: **7372** Business oriented computer software

(G-7532)
APPLICON COMPANY INCORPORATED
450 N Somerset Ave (46222-4926)
PHONE...................317 635-7843
EMP: 10 EST: 1979
SALES (est): 925.64K **Privately Held**
Web: www.appliconco.com

GEOGRAPHIC SECTION
Indianapolis - Marion County (G-7556)

SIC: 3535 5084 Conveyors and conveying equipment; Materials handling machinery

(G-7533)
APPLIED COMPOSITES ENGRG INC
705 S Girls School Rd (46231-1131)
PHONE.................................317 243-4225
Leigh R Sargent, *Pr*
EMP: 44 EST: 1982
SQ FT: 45,000
SALES (est): 11.35MM
SALES (corp-wide): 189.21MM **Privately Held**
Web: www.appliedcomposites.com
SIC: 3544 3624 3083 2823 Industrial molds; Fibers, carbon and graphite; Laminated plastics plate and sheet; Cellulosic manmade fibers
HQ: Ac&A Enterprises, Llc
   25671 Commercentre Dr
   Lake Forest CA 92630
   949 716-3511

(G-7534)
APPLIED LOGIC ELECTRONICS LLC
2525 N Shadeland Ave Ste C6 (46219-1787)
PHONE.................................317 633-7300
Gerald Peterson, *Pr*
EMP: 9 EST: 2019
SALES (est): 800.43K **Privately Held**
Web: www.a-l-e.us
SIC: 3353 Aluminum sheet, plate, and foil

(G-7535)
APRIMO INC
135 N Pennsylvania St Ste 2300 (46204-4403)
PHONE.................................317 663-6556
William M Godfrey, *CEO*
Darryl Mcdonald, *Pr*
George J Lawrence, *Corporate Secretary**
Umesh Singh, *
Alex Meyer, *
EMP: 400 EST: 2000
SQ FT: 49,000
SALES (est): 54.66MM **Publicly Held**
SIC: 7372 Prepackaged software
PA: Teradata Corporation
    17095 Via Del Campo
    San Diego CA 92127

(G-7536)
APS KREATIVE KUSTOMZ LLC
3709 N Shadeland Ave (46226)
PHONE.................................317 384-1267
Aariel Porter, *CEO*
EMP: 1 EST: 2020
SALES (est): 135.61K **Privately Held**
SIC: 2211 Print cloths, cotton

(G-7537)
AR SHOT IT LLC ✪
5409 Ashbourne Ln (46226-3232)
PHONE.................................317 654-0187
EMP: 1 EST: 2023
SALES (est): 69.27K **Privately Held**
SIC: 2752 Offset and photolithographic printing

(G-7538)
ARCAMED LLC
5101 Decatur Blvd Ste A (46241-9529)
PHONE.................................317 375-7733
Jon Desalvo, *Managing Member*
▼ EMP: 42 EST: 2011
SQ FT: 20,000
SALES (est): 8.13MM **Privately Held**
Web: www.arcamed.com
SIC: 3841 Medical instruments and equipment, blood and bone work

(G-7539)
ARCHER INDUSTRIES LLC
3245 N College Ave (46205-3856)
PHONE.................................317 418-1260
Sarah G C Bilek, *Admn*
EMP: 5 EST: 2014
SALES (est): 52.4K **Privately Held**
SIC: 3999 Manufacturing industries, nec

(G-7540)
ARCHER PRODUCTS INC
8756 E 33rd St (46226-6516)
PHONE.................................317 899-0700
Perry A Benson, *Pr*
EMP: 4 EST: 1984
SQ FT: 2,021
SALES (est): 490.05K **Privately Held**
Web: www.archerblades.com
SIC: 3425 Saw blades and handsaws

(G-7541)
ARCHITURA CORPORATION
9880 Westpoint Dr Ste 400 (46256-3390)
PHONE.................................317 348-1000
Charles A Kotterman, *VP*
Michael F Conley, *Pr*
EMP: 6 EST: 2000
SQ FT: 4,500
SALES (est): 949.96K **Privately Held**
Web: www.archituracorp.com
SIC: 8712 2421 Architectural engineering; Building and structural materials, wood

(G-7542)
ARDAGH GLASS INC (HQ)
Also Called: Verallia North America
10194 Crosspoint Blvd Ste 410 (46256)
P.O. Box 50487 (46250-0487)
PHONE.................................317 558-1002
◆ EMP: 299 EST: 1995
SQ FT: 60,000
SALES (est): 513.74MM
SALES (corp-wide): 2.67MM **Privately Held**
Web: www.ardaghgroup.com
SIC: 3221 Bottles for packing, bottling, and canning: glass
PA: Ard Holdings S.A.
    Rue Charles Martel 56
    Luxembourg
    26258555

(G-7543)
ARDAGH GLASS PACKAGING INC
10194 Crosspoint Blvd Ste 410 (46256)
PHONE.................................317 558-1002
EMP: 6 EST: 2021
SALES (est): 271.44K **Privately Held**
Web: www.ardaghgroup.com
SIC: 3221 Glass containers

(G-7544)
ARIZONA SPORT SHIRTS INC
100 Gasoline Aly Ste Az (46222-5916)
PHONE.................................317 481-2160
Karl Korbacher, *Pr*
Cheryl Korbacher, *
EMP: 30 EST: 1974
SQ FT: 10,000
SALES (est): 5.33MM **Privately Held**
Web: www.arizonasportshirts.com
SIC: 5136 5137 3993 2396 Sportswear, men's and boys'; Sportswear, women's and children's; Signs and advertising specialties; Automotive and apparel trimmings

(G-7545)
ARKLEY BIOTEK LLC
4444 Decatur Blvd Ste 300 (46241-9539)
PHONE.................................317 331-7580
EMP: 1 EST: 2009
SQ FT: 3,000
SALES (est): 241.14K **Privately Held**
Web: www.arkleybiotek.com
SIC: 2836 Biological products, except diagnostic

(G-7546)
ARM KANDY LLC
6100 N Keystone Ave Ste 459 (46220-2452)
PHONE.................................317 975-1576
Aaliyah Brown, *CEO*
EMP: 1 EST: 2015
SALES (est): 47.7K **Privately Held**
SIC: 3171 5632 Women's handbags and purses; Handbags

(G-7547)
ARRAYED ADDITIVE INC
6119 Guion Rd (46254-1223)
PHONE.................................317 981-5982
EMP: 6
SALES (est): 78.58K **Privately Held**
SIC: 3499 Friction material, made from powdered metal

(G-7548)
ARROW CONTAINER LLC
6550 E 30th St Ste 130 (46219-1145)
PHONE.................................317 882-6444
Walter Gill, *
James R La Sarre, *
EMP: 100 EST: 1982
SALES (est): 24.31MM **Privately Held**
Web: www.arrowpackagingsolutions.com
SIC: 2653 Boxes, corrugated: made from purchased materials

(G-7549)
ASD SIGNS & GRAPHICS LLC
2020 Churchman Ave (46203-3043)
PHONE.................................317 437-6921
EMP: 1 EST: 2013
SALES (est): 157.89K **Privately Held**
Web: www.asd-signs.com
SIC: 3993 Signs and advertising specialties

(G-7550)
ASH & ELM CIDER COMPANY LLC
2112 E Washington St (46201-4131)
PHONE.................................317 600-3164
EMP: 5 EST: 2016
SALES (est): 643.48K **Privately Held**
Web: www.ashandelmcider.com
SIC: 5084 2082 Brewery products manufacturing machinery, commercial; Ale (alcoholic beverage)

(G-7551)
ASPHALT MATERIALS INC
Heritage Research Group
7901 W Morris St (46231-1366)
P.O. Box 68123 (46268-0123)
PHONE.................................317 243-8304
Tony Kriech, *Mgr*
EMP: 1
SALES (corp-wide): 894.43MM **Privately Held**
Web: www.asphalt-materials.com
SIC: 2951 Asphalt paving mixtures and blocks
HQ: Asphalt Materials, Inc.
    8720 Robbins Rd
    Indianapolis IN 46268
    317 872-6010

(G-7552)
ASPHALT MATERIALS INC (HQ)
8720 Robbins Rd (46268)
P.O. Box 68123 (46268)
PHONE.................................317 872-6010
Fred M Fehsenfeld Junior, *Dir*
David N Blackburn, *
Deborah C Edwards, *
John P Vercruysse, *
Amy M Schumacher, *
EMP: 370 EST: 1957
SQ FT: 2,500
SALES (est): 221.66MM
SALES (corp-wide): 894.43MM **Privately Held**
Web: www.asphalt-materials.com
SIC: 2951 1442 Asphalt and asphaltic paving mixtures (not from refineries); Sand mining
PA: Heritage Group Inc
    6320 Intech Way
    Indianapolis IN 46278
    317 872-6010

(G-7553)
ASPHALT MATERIALS INC
Also Called: Heritage Group Safety
5400 W 86th St (46268-1537)
PHONE.................................317 875-4670
Mike Kelly, *Pr*
EMP: 9
SALES (corp-wide): 894.43MM **Privately Held**
Web: www.asphalt-materials.com
SIC: 2951 1442 8748 5099 Asphalt and asphaltic paving mixtures (not from refineries); Sand mining; Safety training service; Safety equipment and supplies
HQ: Asphalt Materials, Inc.
    8720 Robbins Rd
    Indianapolis IN 46268
    317 872-6010

(G-7554)
ASSOCIATED CNSTR PUBLICATIONS
1028 Shelby St (46203-1152)
PHONE.................................317 660-2395
EMP: 29 EST: 2018
SALES (est): 781.92K **Privately Held**
Web: www.acppubs.com
SIC: 2741 Miscellaneous publishing

(G-7555)
ASSURED WATER CARE COMPANY
304 Crosby Dr (46227-2808)
PHONE.................................317 997-5790
Christopher Coppock, *Prin*
EMP: 6 EST: 2017
SALES (est): 146.02K **Privately Held**
Web: www.assuredwatercare.com
SIC: 3589 Water treatment equipment, industrial

(G-7556)
ASTBURY WATER TECHNOLOGY INC (PA)
Also Called: A W T
5940 W Raymond St (46241-4349)
PHONE.................................317 328-7153
Daniel T Astbury, *CEO*
Kathryn B Astbury, *
EMP: 79 EST: 1979
SQ FT: 16,000
SALES (est): 10.12MM
SALES (corp-wide): 10.12MM **Privately Held**
Web: www.astburygroup.com
SIC: 3589 1629 Water filters and softeners, household type; Waste water and sewage treatment plant construction

Indianapolis - Marion County (G-7557)   GEOGRAPHIC SECTION

(G-7557)
ASTEC CORP
7750 Zionsville Rd Ste 650 (46268-5126)
PHONE..................317 872-7550
James J Arlington, *Pr*
Robert A Salem, *VP*
EMP: 6 EST: 1988
SQ FT: 8,600
SALES (est): 555.62K **Privately Held**
Web: www.asteccorp.com
SIC: 2842 2819 Cleaning or polishing preparations, nec; Industrial inorganic chemicals, nec

(G-7558)
ATC PLASTICS LLC (PA)
450 E 96th St Ste 500 (46240)
PHONE..................317 469-7552
Tom Stevning, *Managing Member*
EMP: 1 EST: 1976
SQ FT: 1,000
SALES (est): 10.14MM
SALES (corp-wide): 10.14MM **Privately Held**
Web: www.atcplastics.com
SIC: 2821 Plastics materials and resins

(G-7559)
ATHLETES MANAGEMENT & SERVICES
3750 Guion Rd Ste 315 (46222-1669)
P.O. Box 931 (46158-0931)
PHONE..................317 925-8200
Garry H Donna, *Pr*
EMP: 2 EST: 1976
SALES (est): 91.41K **Privately Held**
SIC: 7941 2721 Sports clubs, managers, and promoters; Magazines: publishing and printing

(G-7560)
ATI
6635 E 30th St (46219-1138)
PHONE..................317 238-3073
Ken Hammond, *Prin*
▲ EMP: 17 EST: 2010
SALES (est): 458.31K **Privately Held**
Web: www.atiinc.com
SIC: 3312 Stainless steel

(G-7561)
AUBRY LANE LLC
120 E Market St Ste 100 (46204-3259)
PHONE..................317 644-6372
EMP: 4 EST: 2016
SALES (est): 239.17K **Privately Held**
SIC: 3171 Handbags, women's

(G-7562)
AUDIO-VIDEO BY FLYNN
Also Called: Avbf
4911 Carrollton Ave (46205-1125)
PHONE..................317 408-6269
Jj Flynn, *Owner*
EMP: 1 EST: 2009
SALES (est): 59.7K **Privately Held**
SIC: 3663 Radio and t.v. communications equipment

(G-7563)
AURORIUM FOREIGN HOLDINGS LLC (PA)
201 N Illinois St Ste 1800 (46204-1904)
PHONE..................317 247-8141
John Van Hulle, *CEO*
EMP: 3 EST: 2016
SALES (est): 888.37K
SALES (corp-wide): 888.37K **Privately Held**
Web: www.aurorium.com

SIC: 2869 Industrial organic chemicals, nec

(G-7564)
AURORIUM HOLDINGS LLC (PA)
Also Called: Vertellus Agrculture Ntrtn Spc
201 N Illinois St Ste 1800 (46204)
PHONE..................317 247-8141
John Van Hulle, *Pr*
EMP: 1 EST: 2016
SALES (est): 636.82MM
SALES (corp-wide): 636.82MM **Privately Held**
Web: www.aurorium.com
SIC: 2869 Industrial organic chemicals, nec

(G-7565)
AURORIUM LLC
201 N Illinois St (46204)
PHONE..................317 247-8141
EMP: 1
SALES (corp-wide): 636.82MM **Privately Held**
Web: www.aurorium.com
SIC: 2869 Industrial organic chemicals, nec
HQ: Aurorium Llc
    201 N Ill St Ste 1800
    Indianapolis IN 46204
    317 247-8141

(G-7566)
AURORIUM LLC (HQ)
Also Called: Aurorium
201 N Illinois St Ste 1800 (46204)
PHONE..................317 247-8141
John Van Hulle, *Pr*
EMP: 45 EST: 2016
SALES (est): 454.96MM
SALES (corp-wide): 636.82MM **Privately Held**
Web: www.aurorium.com
SIC: 2869 2865 Industrial organic chemicals, nec; Cyclic crudes and intermediates
PA: Aurorium Holdings Llc
    201 N Ill St Ste 1800
    Indianapolis IN 46204
    317 247-8141

(G-7567)
AURORIUM PPC HOLDINGS LLC
201 N Illinois St Ste 1800 (46204-1904)
PHONE..................317 247-8141
EMP: 8 EST: 2020
SALES (est): 2.57MM **Privately Held**
Web: www.aurorium.com
SIC: 2869 Industrial organic chemicals, nec

(G-7568)
AUS EMBROIDERY INC
8745 Rawles Ave Ste C (46219-7831)
PHONE..................317 899-1225
Jay Conway, *Pr*
Richard Conway, *Treas*
Carla Conway, *Sec*
EMP: 4 EST: 1980
SQ FT: 1,200
SALES (est): 245.63K **Privately Held**
Web: www.indianapolisembroidery.com
SIC: 3999 Embroidery kits

(G-7569)
AUSTIN-WESTRAN LLC (PA)
2876 Wooded Glen Ct (46268-4246)
P.O. Box 802990 (60680-2990)
PHONE..................815 234-2811
Bill Diemel, *Pr*
Chris Osterholz, *
◆ EMP: 35 EST: 2001
SQ FT: 200,000
SALES (est): 11.31MM
SALES (corp-wide): 11.31MM **Privately Held**

SIC: 3567 3444 2514 Industrial furnaces and ovens; Sheet metalwork; Tables, household: metal

(G-7570)
AUTHENTICX INC
9405 Delegates Row (46240-3805)
PHONE..................317 296-6238
Kip Zurcher, *Admn*
Kip Zurcher, *Pr*
EMP: 62 EST: 2018
SALES (est): 4.67MM **Privately Held**
Web: www.authenticx.com
SIC: 7389 7371 7372 Business services, nec; Software programming applications; Prepackaged software

(G-7571)
AUTO CENTER INC
Also Called: Pre-Owned Auto Center
5461 Massachusetts Ave (46218-2463)
PHONE..................317 545-3360
Gus Rajabi, *Pr*
David Brumley, *VP*
EMP: 2 EST: 1980
SQ FT: 20,000
SALES (est): 185.9K **Privately Held**
SIC: 7538 3599 Engine repair; Machine shop, jobbing and repair

(G-7572)
AUTO EXPRESS VALE
9065 Pendleton Pike (46236-3205)
PHONE..................317 897-6618
Miguel Nemjia, *Pr*
EMP: 21 EST: 2004
SALES (est): 379.34K **Privately Held**
Web: www.autoexpressvale.com
SIC: 7538 7534 General automotive repair shops; Tire repair shop

(G-7573)
AUTO-CHLOR SYSTEM WASH INC
6040 W 79th St (46278-1727)
PHONE..................317 334-0430
Bill Ballock, *Prin*
EMP: 1
SALES (corp-wide): 285.79MM **Privately Held**
Web: www.autochlor.com
SIC: 3639 Dishwashing machines, household
PA: Auto-Chlor System Of Washington, Inc.
    450 Ferguson Dr
    Mountain View CA 94043
    650 967-3085

(G-7574)
AUTOMATED WEAPON SECURITY INC
9324 E 10th St (46229-2505)
PHONE..................860 559-7176
Charles Phersele, *Pr*
EMP: 2 EST: 2011
SALES (est): 90.02K **Privately Held**
Web: www.estesaws.com
SIC: 3842 Linemen's safety belts

(G-7575)
AUTOMATIC FASTNER TOOLS
3250 Payne Dr (46227-7680)
PHONE..................317 784-4111
Kay Ralston, *Owner*
EMP: 6 EST: 1988
SALES (est): 361.01K **Privately Held**
Web: www.aboutair.com
SIC: 3559 Automotive related machinery

(G-7576)
AUTOMOBILE DEALERS ASSN OF IND (PA)

150 W Market St Ste 812 (46204-2886)
PHONE..................317 635-1441
Timothy Dowling, *Ex VP*
EMP: 4 EST: 1937
SQ FT: 2,068
SALES (est): 380.62K
SALES (corp-wide): 380.62K **Privately Held**
Web: www.adai-inc.org
SIC: 8611 2741 5943 8748 Trade associations; Business service newsletters: publishing and printing; Office forms and supplies; Business consulting, nec

(G-7577)
AUTOSAVVY OF INDIANAPOLIS LLC ✪
5333 W Pike Plaza Rd (46254-3008)
PHONE..................463 900-4685
Cory Stephen Goodfellow, *CFO*
EMP: 13 EST: 2022
SALES (est): 999.16K **Privately Held**
SIC: 3743 Interurban cars and car equipment

(G-7578)
AV SOLUTIONS INDY LLC ✪
4929 Evanston Ave (46205-1362)
PHONE..................317 509-5930
EMP: 5 EST: 2022
SALES (est): 250.5K **Privately Held**
SIC: 3699 Security control equipment and systems

(G-7579)
AWNING PARTNERS MFG GROUP LLC
Also Called: Sommer Awning Group
1160 W 16th St (46202)
PHONE..................317 644-3793
EMP: 27 EST: 2010
SALES (est): 4.79MM **Privately Held**
Web: www.apsigngroup.com
SIC: 3993 2394 Electric signs; Canvas awnings and canopies

(G-7580)
AXON NETWORK SERVICES LLC
9245 N Meridian St Ste 225 (46260-1832)
PHONE..................317 818-9000
Jerad Dalton, *Prin*
EMP: 6 EST: 2016
SALES (est): 390.45K **Privately Held**
SIC: 3577 Computer peripheral equipment, nec

(G-7581)
AYTCH LOGISTICS LLC
2304 E 34th St (46218-2007)
PHONE..................317 443-9812
EMP: 1 EST: 2021
SALES (est): 60.08K **Privately Held**
SIC: 3537 Trucks, tractors, loaders, carriers, and similar equipment

(G-7582)
B Q PRODUCTS INC
6233 Brookville Rd (46219-8213)
P.O. Box 430 (46107-0430)
PHONE..................317 786-5500
Dennis Laswell, *Pr*
EMP: 12 EST: 1991
SQ FT: 8,000
SALES (est): 200.68K **Privately Held**
Web: www.bqproducts.com
SIC: 3679 Electronic circuits

(G-7583)
B WORD LLC
8818 Cardinal Flower Ln (46231-5287)
PHONE..................317 654-6873

GEOGRAPHIC SECTION
Indianapolis - Marion County (G-7609)

EMP: 1
SALES (est): 65.99K **Privately Held**
SIC: 3161 Clothing and apparel carrying cases

(G-7584)
B&B URBAN EATS CORPORATION ✪
3445 Welch Dr (46224-1634)
PHONE...............317 998-9848
Vickie Brewer, *Prin*
EMP: 1 **EST:** 2022
SALES (est): 57.39K **Privately Held**
SIC: 2599 Food wagons, restaurant

(G-7585)
B&C DISTRIBUTOR INC (PA) ✪
3950 Culligan Ave Ste A (46218-5509)
PHONE...............609 293-3257
Binalkumar Patel, *CEO*
EMP: 2 **EST:** 2022
SALES (est): 103.88K
SALES (corp-wide): 103.88K **Privately Held**
SIC: 2393 7389 Canvas bags; Business Activities at Non-Commercial Site

(G-7586)
B&D LIGHTING LLC
5635 Hickory Rd (46239-1842)
P.O. Box 39089 (46239-0089)
PHONE...............317 414-8056
Brian Distel, *Prin*
EMP: 5 **EST:** 2008
SALES (est): 405.58K **Privately Held**
SIC: 3648 Lighting equipment, nec

(G-7587)
B6 MANUFACTURING LLC
4701 Massachusetts Ave (46218)
PHONE...............317 549-4290
Allan Bir Junior, *CEO*
Steven Hedges, *CFO*
EMP: 8 **EST:** 2016
SQ FT: 10,000
SALES (est): 850.3K **Privately Held**
SIC: 3499 Friction material, made from powdered metal

(G-7588)
BACKYARD COMPANY
5621 Woodland Trace Blvd (46237-3186)
PHONE...............317 727-0298
John Hingle, *Prin*
EMP: 7 **EST:** 2010
SALES (est): 217.44K **Privately Held**
Web: www.thebyco.com
SIC: 3446 Fences, gates, posts, and flagpoles

(G-7589)
BAD BOYS BLLARD PRDUCTIONS LLC
9041 Matterhorn Rd (46234-2079)
PHONE...............702 738-4950
EMP: 2 **EST:** 2010
SALES (est): 115.05K **Privately Held**
Web: www.badboysbp.com
SIC: 3949 Billiard and pool equipment and supplies, general

(G-7590)
BAG CORPORATION
3039 E 38th St (46218-1233)
PHONE...............317 699-5523
Jenkins Reese, *CEO*
EMP: 5 **EST:** 2019
SALES (est): 55.65K **Privately Held**
SIC: 3161 Clothing and apparel carrying cases

(G-7591)
BAKED WITH BILLIE LLC
653 Temperance Ave (46203-1656)
PHONE...............317 517-1575
EMP: 1 **EST:** 2021
SALES (est): 39.59K **Privately Held**
SIC: 2051 Bakery products, partially cooked (except frozen)

(G-7592)
BAND BROTHERS TRANSPORT LLC
2415 Penny Ct (46229-1452)
PHONE...............317 709-4415
EMP: 1 **EST:** 2016
SALES (est): 67K **Privately Held**
SIC: 3715 4212 Demountable cargo containers; Local trucking, without storage

(G-7593)
BANDAG WARRANTY
9302 E 30th St (46229-1078)
PHONE...............800 523-6366
EMP: 6 **EST:** 2015
SALES (est): 173.14K **Privately Held**
Web: www.bandag.com
SIC: 7534 Tire retreading and repair shops

(G-7594)
BANE-CLENE CORP
4533 Millersville Rd (46205-2599)
PHONE...............317 546-5448
William Bane, *Brnch Mgr*
EMP: 1
SALES (corp-wide): 941.48K **Privately Held**
Web: www.carpet-cleaning-indianapolis.com
SIC: 5087 5169 7217 2842 Carpet and rug cleaning equipment and supplies, commercial; Chemicals and allied products, nec; Carpet and upholstery cleaning; Polishes and sanitation goods
PA: Bane-Clene Corp
 3940 N Keystone Ave
 Indianapolis IN 46205
 317 546-5448

(G-7595)
BANE-CLENE CORP (PA)
Also Called: William F Bane Co
3940 N Keystone Ave (46205-2911)
PHONE...............317 546-5448
TOLL FREE: 800
William F Bane Junior, *Pr*
William F Bane Senior, *Ch*
Donald A Bane, *Treas*
Elizabeth Ann Bane, *Sec*
EMP: 19 **EST:** 1962
SQ FT: 27,000
SALES (est): 941.48K
SALES (corp-wide): 941.48K **Privately Held**
Web: www.carpet-cleaning-indianapolis.com
SIC: 7217 5169 5087 2842 Carpet and upholstery cleaning on customer premises; Chemicals and allied products, nec; Carpet and rug cleaning equipment and supplies, commercial; Polishes and sanitation goods

(G-7596)
BANTAM INDUSTRIES INC
2346 S Lynhurst Dr Ste 601 (46241-8621)
PHONE...............714 561-6122
EMP: 5 **EST:** 2018
SALES (est): 77.07K **Privately Held**
SIC: 3999 Manufacturing industries, nec

(G-7597)
BATTLE BOARDS LLC
4851 W Minnesota St (46241-4450)
PHONE...............317 518-7245
Charles Gaddy Junior, *Prin*
EMP: 4 **EST:** 2019
SALES (est): 97.76K **Privately Held**
Web: www.battleboard.us
SIC: 3949 Sporting and athletic goods, nec

(G-7598)
BAXTER HEALTHCARE CORPORATION
6812 Corporate Dr (46278-1935)
PHONE...............317 291-0620
David Hoffman, *Mgr*
EMP: 5
SALES (corp-wide): 14.81B **Publicly Held**
Web: www.baxter.com
SIC: 3841 Surgical and medical instruments
HQ: Baxter Healthcare Corporation
 1 Baxter Pkwy
 Deerfield IL 60015
 224 948-2000

(G-7599)
BBLISS & JUS BE ZANY
446 Blue Spring Dr (46239-8868)
PHONE...............215 251-9235
Kimberly Barnett, *CEO*
EMP: 1 **EST:** 2017
SALES (est): 85.01K **Privately Held**
Web: www.bblissspa.com
SIC: 3161 Clothing and apparel carrying cases

(G-7600)
BC COUNTERTOPS INC
Also Called: Beyond The Countertops
1343 Sadlier Circle South Dr (46239-1059)
PHONE...............317 637-4427
John T Thompson, *Pr*
Clay Hargitt, *VP*
EMP: 20 **EST:** 1983
SALES (est): 1.26MM **Privately Held**
Web: www.beyondcountertops.com
SIC: 1542 2431 Commercial and office buildings, renovation and repair; Millwork

(G-7601)
BCD AND ASSOCIATES LLC
8904 Bash St Ste M (46256-1286)
PHONE...............317 873-5394
Duane Durkos, *Owner*
EMP: 5 **EST:** 1988
SALES (est): 475.84K **Privately Held**
Web: www.bcdandassociates.com
SIC: 3841 3599 Diagnostic apparatus, medical; Custom machinery

(G-7602)
BE BODY BUTTERS LLC
5345 Brendon Park Dr (46226-1723)
PHONE...............317 362-9248
EMP: 1 **EST:** 2021
SALES (est): 47.23K **Privately Held**
SIC: 2844 Face creams or lotions

(G-7603)
BEADS TO FEED LLC
8888 Keystone Xing Ste 1300 (46240-4609)
PHONE...............816 299-8118
EMP: 5
SALES (est): 78.58K **Privately Held**
SIC: 3911 Jewelry apparel

(G-7604)
BECKMAN COULTER INC
7451 Winton Dr (46268-5103)
PHONE...............317 808-4200
Scott Atkin, *Mgr*
EMP: 10
SALES (corp-wide): 23.89B **Publicly Held**
Web: www.beckman.com
SIC: 3826 Analytical instruments
HQ: Beckman Coulter, Inc.
 250 S Kraemer Blvd
 Brea CA 92821
 714 993-5321

(G-7605)
BECKMAN COULTER INC
5350 Lakeview Parkway South Dr Ste A (46268)
PHONE...............317 808-4200
Scott Atkin, *Brnch Mgr*
EMP: 82
SALES (corp-wide): 23.89B **Publicly Held**
Web: www.beckmancoulter.com
SIC: 3826 Analytical instruments
HQ: Beckman Coulter, Inc.
 250 S Kraemer Blvd
 Brea CA 92821
 714 993-5321

(G-7606)
BECKMAN COULTER INC
5355 W 76th St (46268-4166)
PHONE...............317 471-8029
Coulter Beckman, *Brnch Mgr*
EMP: 82
SALES (corp-wide): 23.89B **Publicly Held**
Web: www.beckmancoulter.com
SIC: 3826 3821 2869 Analytical instruments; Chemical laboratory apparatus, nec; Laboratory chemicals, organic
HQ: Beckman Coulter, Inc.
 250 S Kraemer Blvd
 Brea CA 92821
 714 993-5321

(G-7607)
BECKMAN COULTER LIFE SCIENCES
5350 Lakeview Pkwy S Dr (46268-5129)
PHONE...............408 747-2000
Suzanne Foster, *Pr*
EMP: 53 **EST:** 2019
SALES (est): 11.5MM
SALES (corp-wide): 23.89B **Publicly Held**
Web: www.beckman.com
SIC: 3826 Analytical instruments
PA: Danaher Corporation
 2200 Pa Ave Nw Ste 800w
 Washington DC 20037
 202 828-0850

(G-7608)
BECOMING HER LLC
8319 Michigan Rd (46268-3635)
PHONE...............317 200-0165
EMP: 1 **EST:** 2021
SALES (est): 39.69K **Privately Held**
SIC: 3999 Hair and hair-based products

(G-7609)
BEECHER HAIRSTON HAIRSTON LLC
3621 N Drexel Ave (46218-1608)
PHONE...............317 714-6703
Robert Beecher, *Managing Member*
EMP: 4 **EST:** 2021
SALES (est): 65.5K **Privately Held**
SIC: 1389 Construction, repair, and dismantling services

Indianapolis - Marion County (G-7610)   GEOGRAPHIC SECTION

(G-7610)
BELL TRANSPORTATION LLC
11333 Fairweather Pl (46229-4983)
PHONE.....................317 833-0745
EMP: 1
SALES (est): 69.27K Privately Held
Web: www.mycitytransportation.com
SIC: 3537 7389 Trucks: freight, baggage, etc.: industrial, except mining; Business Activities at Non-Commercial Site

(G-7611)
BELLS OF STEEL USA INC
6002 Corporate Way (46278-2923)
PHONE.....................317 981-5586
Kaevon Khoozani, CEO
Bryan Chu, CFO
EMP: 6 EST: 2019
SALES (est): 289.59K Privately Held
Web: www.bellsofsteel.us
SIC: 3949 Sporting and athletic goods, nec

(G-7612)
BEN TIRE DISTRIBUTORS LTD (PA)
Also Called: Neal Tire & Auto Service
9465 Counselors Row Ste 112 (46240-6423)
P.O. Box 158 (62468-0158)
PHONE.....................317 798-2013
James Laneve, CEO
Burnham Neal, Pr
Nancy Shupe, Sec
Cerry Carlinn, VP
Terry Carlon, VP
▲ EMP: 20 EST: 1969
SQ FT: 72,000
SALES (est): 133.06MM
SALES (corp-wide): 133.06MM Privately Held
Web: www.bentiredistributors.com
SIC: 5013 5531 7534 Automotive supplies and parts; Automotive tires; Tire repair shop

(G-7613)
BENCHMARK CHEMICAL CORP
8425 Zionsville Rd (46268-1525)
PHONE.....................317 875-0051
EMP: 5 EST: 2019
SALES (est): 141.94K Privately Held
SIC: 2819 Industrial inorganic chemicals, nec

(G-7614)
BERGER TABLE PADS INC
1501 W Market St (46222-4421)
PHONE.....................317 631-2577
Tim Perry, Pr
▲ EMP: 40 EST: 2004
SQ FT: 22,500
SALES (est): 5.12MM Privately Held
Web: www.tablepads.com
SIC: 2392 Pads and padding, table: except asbestos, felt, or rattan

(G-7615)
BEST BOY PRODUCTS LLC
Also Called: Best Boy & Co.
7337 Glenview Dr E (46250-2453)
P.O. Box 502864 (46250-7864)
PHONE.....................317 442-9735
EMP: 1 EST: 2007
SALES (est): 405.31K Privately Held
SIC: 2099 7389 Food preparations, nec; Business services, nec

(G-7616)
BEST EQUIPMENT & WELDING CO
1960 Midwest Blvd (46214-2337)
PHONE.....................317 271-8563
Glenn N Foy, Pr
Richard Gilbert, *
Richard B Gilbert Junior, Sec
EMP: 30 EST: 1983
SQ FT: 17,000
SALES (est): 4.24MM Privately Held
Web: www.bewinc.com
SIC: 3548 7692 Welding apparatus; Welding repair

(G-7617)
BEST EQUIPMENT CO INC (PA)
5550 Poindexter Dr (46235-9041)
PHONE.....................317 823-3050
Mike Dahlmann, Pr
Maria Dahlmann, *
Adam Bowen, *
EMP: 28 EST: 1964
SALES (est): 18.48MM
SALES (corp-wide): 18.48MM Privately Held
Web: www.bestequipmentco.com
SIC: 5084 7629 3699 Waste compactors; Electrical equipment repair services; Welding machines and equipment, ultrasonic

(G-7618)
BEUNERFARM PUBLISHING INC
418 S Sheridan Ave (46219-7433)
PHONE.....................317 514-1505
Aaron Boe, Prin
EMP: 1 EST: 2006
SALES (est): 70.09K Privately Held
SIC: 2741 Miscellaneous publishing

(G-7619)
BEVERLY HARRIS ◆
Also Called: Touch 4 Life
8401 Moller Rd Unit 681161 (46268)
PHONE.....................317 910-0542
Beverly Harris, Owner
EMP: 1 EST: 2023
SALES (est): 54.05K Privately Held
SIC: 2899 Distilled water

(G-7620)
BEX SCREEN PRINTING INC
5602 Elmwood Ave Ste 214 (46203-6072)
PHONE.....................317 791-0375
EMP: 3 EST: 1995
SQ FT: 1,400
SALES (est): 257.29K Privately Held
Web: www.bexscreenprinting.com
SIC: 2759 Screen printing

(G-7621)
BEYOND DISTRIBUTIONS LLC
10427 Hornton St (46236-7036)
PHONE.....................631 960-1745
EMP: 1
SALES (est): 69.27K Privately Held
SIC: 3537 7389 Trucks: freight, baggage, etc.: industrial, except mining; Business Activities at Non-Commercial Site

(G-7622)
BHAR PRINTING INCORPORATED
929 W 16th St (46202-2214)
PHONE.....................317 899-1020
Madhu Bhargava, Pr
Ram Bhargava, Pr
EMP: 7 EST: 1983
SALES (est): 833.76K Privately Held
Web: www.bharprinting.com
SIC: 2752 Offset printing

(G-7623)
BIG GUY SIGNS LLC
5575 Elmwood Ave Ste C (46203-6046)
PHONE.....................317 780-6000
Angel Crawford, Managing Member
EMP: 5 EST: 2010
SALES (est): 418.49K Privately Held
Web: www.bigguysigns.com
SIC: 3993 Signs, not made in custom sign painting shops

(G-7624)
BIGG DAWG CONSTRUCTION LLC
3330 N Bancroft St (46218-2339)
PHONE.....................317 506-1436
Antonio Mcfarland, Pr
Antonio Mcfarland, Prin
Antwuan Mcfarland, Prin
EMP: 2 EST: 2020
SALES (est): 159.13K Privately Held
SIC: 1521 1389 Single-family housing construction; Construction, repair, and dismantling services

(G-7625)
BILBEES SERVICE AND SUPPLY INC
8777 E 16th St (46219-1901)
PHONE.....................317 895-8288
Dallas Bilbee, Pr
Martha Bilbee, Sec
EMP: 1 EST: 2000
SALES (est): 147.33K Privately Held
SIC: 5099 2451 5561 Mobile home parts and accessories; Mobile homes; Recreational vehicle parts and accessories

(G-7626)
BILLY R PHILLIPS
Also Called: Neon Services
1844 Winton Ave (46224-5624)
PHONE.....................317 828-5058
Billy R Phillips, Prin
EMP: 1 EST: 2010
SALES (est): 79.93K Privately Held
SIC: 3993 Neon signs

(G-7627)
BIMBO BAKERIES USA INC
Also Called: Bimbo Bakeries USA, Inc
6935 Lake Plaza Dr Ste D (46220-4088)
PHONE.....................317 570-1741
EMP: 1
Web: www.arnoldbread.com
SIC: 2051 Bakery: wholesale or wholesale/retail combined
HQ: Bimbo Bakeries Usa, Inc.
355 Business Center Drive
Horsham PA 19044
215 347-5500

(G-7628)
BIONODE LLC
7987 Clearwater Pkwy (46240-4902)
PHONE.....................317 292-7686
Murray Firestone, CEO
EMP: 4
SALES (est): 164.44K Privately Held
Web: www.bionode.net
SIC: 3845 Electrotherapeutic apparatus

(G-7629)
BIOSAFE ENGINEERING LLC
5750 W 80th St (46278-1340)
PHONE.....................317 858-8099
Phillip Mervis, CEO
EMP: 20 EST: 2007
SQ FT: 16,000
SALES (est): 2.63MM Privately Held
Web: www.biosafeeng.com
SIC: 8711 2836 Mechanical engineering; Biological products, except diagnostic

(G-7630)
BIRCH AND STITCH LLC
1701 Redbay Dr (46234-0167)
PHONE.....................317 353-7786
EMP: 4 EST: 2017
SALES (est): 66.28K Privately Held
SIC: 3999 Candles

(G-7631)
BISHOP LIFTING PRODUCTS INC
5760 Dividend Rd (46241-4304)
PHONE.....................317 634-2545
EMP: 1
SALES (corp-wide): 169.95MM Privately Held
Web: www.lifting.com
SIC: 3496 Miscellaneous fabricated wire products
PA: Bishop Lifting Products, Inc.
2301 Commerce St Ste 110
Houston TX
713 674-2266

(G-7632)
BITTERSWEET LLC
1912 Broad Ripple Ave (46220-2328)
PHONE.....................317 254-0677
Nicole Anderson, Prin
EMP: 6 EST: 2010
SALES (est): 78.65K Privately Held
SIC: 2431 Millwork

(G-7633)
BITUMINOUS MATERIALS & SUP LP
5400 W 86th St (46268-1502)
PHONE.....................317 228-8203
EMP: 9 EST: 2011
SALES (est): 341.51K Privately Held
Web: www.asphalt-materials.com
SIC: 2951 Asphalt paving mixtures and blocks

(G-7634)
BIZNESS AS USUAL PUBG LLC ◆
3524 Bodelva Ln (46228-2892)
PHONE.....................463 701-6433
EMP: 1 EST: 2023
SALES (est): 69.27K Privately Held
SIC: 2741 7389 Miscellaneous publishing; Business Activities at Non-Commercial Site

(G-7635)
BJ CORPORATION OF INDIANA LLC
3605 Commercial Dr (46222-1681)
PHONE.....................317 507-6672
EMP: 5 EST: 2018
SALES (est): 202.1K Privately Held
Web: www.ibj.com
SIC: 2711 Newspapers, publishing and printing

(G-7636)
BLACK & DECKER (US) INC
10475 Crosspoint Blvd Ste 400 (46256-3386)
PHONE.....................860 225-5111
Nolan D Archibald, Pr
EMP: 16
SALES (corp-wide): 15.78B Publicly Held
Web: www.blackanddecker.com
SIC: 3546 Power-driven handtools
HQ: Black & Decker (U.S.) Inc.
1000 Stanley Dr
New Britain CT 06053
860 225-5111

(G-7637)
BLACK ACRE BREWING COMPANY LLC
5632 E Washington St (46219-6428)
PHONE.....................317 207-6266
▲ EMP: 30 EST: 2011
SQ FT: 48,000

SALES (est): 3.34MM **Privately Held**
Web: www.90phutr.tv
SIC: 5181 2082 Ale; Beer (alcoholic beverage)

(G-7638)
BLACK HUSTLE HOLDINGS CORP
838 N Delaware St Ste 191090 (46204-1127)
PHONE..............................800 988-7067
Cletus Green, *Pr*
EMP: 4
SALES (est): 180.77K **Privately Held**
SIC: 2759 Commercial printing, nec

(G-7639)
BLACK LAVISH ESSENTIALS LLC
8888 Keystone Xing Ste 1300 (46240-4609)
PHONE..............................800 214-8664
Joshua Reed, *Prin*
EMP: 4 **EST:** 2019
SALES (est): 327.24K **Privately Held**
Web: www.blacklavishessentials.com
SIC: 5961 5122 5999 2841 Cosmetics and perfumes, mail order; Cosmetics, perfumes, and hair products; Toiletries, cosmetics, and perfumes; Soap and other detergents

(G-7640)
BLACK PLATE CATERING
6033 Moon Shadow Dr (46259-6828)
PHONE..............................317 255-8030
EMP: 12 **EST:** 2013
SALES (est): 859.8K **Privately Held**
Web: www.indinfratrust.com
SIC: 3312 Black plate

(G-7641)
BLINDS AT HOME LLC
4709 N Capitol Ave (46208-3517)
PHONE..............................317 489-8133
EMP: 4 **EST:** 2019
SALES (est): 235.18K **Privately Held**
Web: www.blinds-at-home.com
SIC: 2591 Window blinds

(G-7642)
BLINKLESS POWER EQUIPMENT LLC
8802 Bash St Ste F (46256-1288)
PHONE..............................317 844-7328
EMP: 8 **EST:** 2011
SALES (est): 377.92K **Privately Held**
Web: www.blinklesspower.com
SIC: 3613 3621 Control panels, electric; Phase or rotary converters (electrical equipment)

(G-7643)
BLOOMERS WOODWORKING INC
1834 N Shortridge Rd (46219-2302)
PHONE..............................317 502-9360
EMP: 6 **EST:** 2013
SALES (est): 59.54K **Privately Held**
SIC: 2431 Millwork

(G-7644)
BLUE J LOGISTICS LLC
4859 Leone Dr (46226-2575)
PHONE..............................317 721-1784
EMP: 4 **EST:** 2020
SALES (est): 187K **Privately Held**
SIC: 3537 Trucks, tractors, loaders, carriers, and similar equipment

(G-7645)
BLUE MARBLE COCKTAILS INC
6008 Corporate Way (46278-2923)
PHONE..............................888 400-3090
Alan Miller, *Pr*
EMP: 30 **EST:** 2016
SALES (est): 3.69MM **Privately Held**
Web: www.lovebluemarble.com
SIC: 2085 Cocktails, alcoholic

(G-7646)
BLUE OCTOPUS PRINTING COMPANY
2431 Directors Row (46241-4972)
PHONE..............................317 247-1997
Gary Johnloz, *VP*
EMP: 10 **EST:** 2009
SALES (est): 148.65K **Privately Held**
Web: www.thinktandem.com
SIC: 2759 Screen printing

(G-7647)
BLUE PILLAR INC
9025 River Rd Ste 150 (46240-6447)
PHONE..............................317 723-6601
EMP: 57 **EST:** 2006
SALES (est): 12.04MM **Publicly Held**
Web: www.bluepillar.com
SIC: 7372 Application computer software
HQ: Generac Power Systems, Inc.
S45 W29290 Hwy 59
Waukesha WI 53189
262 544-4811

(G-7648)
BLUE RIBBON PRODUCTS INC
8188 Allison Ave (46268-1615)
P.O. Box 781043 (46278-8043)
PHONE..............................317 972-7970
EMP: 5 **EST:** 1996
SQ FT: 10,000
SALES (est): 792.38K **Privately Held**
Web: www.blueribboninc.com
SIC: 2842 Cleaning or polishing preparations, nec

(G-7649)
BLUE SUN VENTURES LTD
Also Called: Bakesmart
525 S Meridian St (46225-1108)
P.O. Box 2343 (46206-2343)
PHONE..............................317 426-0001
Michael Clements, *Pr*
EMP: 3 **EST:** 2013
SALES (est): 263.24K **Privately Held**
Web: www.bakesmart.com
SIC: 7372 Application computer software

(G-7650)
BLUEPRINT RESTORATION LLC
3320 Montgomery Dr (46227-9675)
PHONE..............................301 730-4727
EMP: 1
SALES (est): 69.27K **Privately Held**
SIC: 2842 7389 Specialty cleaning; Business Activities at Non-Commercial Site

(G-7651)
BO-MAR INDUSTRIES INC
3838 S Arlington Ave (46203-6107)
PHONE..............................317 899-1240
Robert Buchanan, *Pr*
Mark Buchanan, *
Jill Buchanan, *
EMP: 45 **EST:** 1991
SQ FT: 42,000
SALES (est): 9.14MM **Privately Held**
Web: www.bomarind.com
SIC: 3444 3993 2514 Sheet metal specialties, not stamped; Signs and advertising specialties; Metal household furniture

(G-7652)
BOARDER MAGIC BY J & A
902 W Banta Rd (46217)
PHONE..............................317 545-4401
Jim Ault, *Mgr*
EMP: 5 **EST:** 2014
SALES (est): 165.07K **Privately Held**
Web: www.bordermagic.com
SIC: 3531 Construction machinery

(G-7653)
BODYCARE BODEGA LLC
Also Called: Bodycare Bodega, The
3960 Southeastern Ave (46203-1500)
PHONE..............................317 643-3562
Brittney Tyler, *CEO*
EMP: 1 **EST:** 2020
SALES (est): 58.05K **Privately Held**
SIC: 2844 5499 Cosmetic preparations; Health foods

(G-7654)
BODYCOTE THERMAL PROC INC
500 W 21st St (46202-1195)
P.O. Box 1226 (46206-1226)
PHONE..............................317 924-4321
Ray Thompson, *Brnch Mgr*
EMP: 46
SALES (corp-wide): 1B **Privately Held**
Web: www.bodycote.com
SIC: 3398 Metal heat treating
HQ: Bodycote Thermal Processing, Inc.
12750 Merit Dr Ste 1400
Dallas TX 75251
214 904-2420

(G-7655)
BOEHRNGER MNNHEIM PHRMCTCALS C
9115 Hague Rd (46256-1025)
PHONE..............................317 521-2000
Dennis Taschek, *Prin*
EMP: 16 **EST:** 2010
SALES (est): 1.33MM **Privately Held**
Web: diagnostics.roche.com
SIC: 2833 Medicinals and botanicals

(G-7656)
BOEING COMPANY
Also Called: Boeing
2745 S Hoffman Rd (46241-3623)
P.O. Box 51200 (46251)
PHONE..............................317 484-1363
Barbara Dubowsky, *Mgr*
EMP: 2
SALES (corp-wide): 77.79B **Publicly Held**
Web: www.boeing.com
SIC: 3721 Airplanes, fixed or rotary wing
PA: The Boeing Company
929 Long Bridge Dr
Arlington VA 22202
703 465-3500

(G-7657)
BOLINGER MACHINE LLC
23 N Alton Ave (46222-3908)
PHONE..............................317 241-2989
Alan Bolinger, *Owner*
Jerry Bolinger, *Owner*
EMP: 7 **EST:** 1971
SQ FT: 13,000
SALES (est): 166.84K **Privately Held**
SIC: 3599 Machine shop, jobbing and repair

(G-7658)
BOLLYGOOD INC
1075 Broad Ripple Ave Pmb 334 (46220)
PHONE..............................317 215-5616
Maxine Henderson, *CEO*
EMP: 3 **EST:** 2017

SALES (est): 25.2K **Privately Held**
Web: www.bollygood.com
SIC: 2086 Soft drinks: packaged in cans, bottles, etc.

(G-7659)
BOMBTRACK FABRICATION LLC
11058 Mallard Way (46278-9510)
PHONE..............................317 518-9509
Joe Barszcz, *Prin*
EMP: 5 **EST:** 2016
SALES (est): 161.76K **Privately Held**
Web: www.bombtrackfabrication.com
SIC: 3599 Machine shop, jobbing and repair

(G-7660)
BORDER MGIC BY WLDEN ENTPS INC
2532 W Morris St (46221)
PHONE..............................317 628-2314
Dean Walden, *Owner*
EMP: 5 **EST:** 2017
SALES (est): 64.61K **Privately Held**
Web: www.bordermagic.com
SIC: 3531 Construction machinery

(G-7661)
BORRV CONCEPTS LLC (PA)
6420 Cotton Bay Dr N (46254-4529)
PHONE..............................317 405-9121
EMP: 2
SALES (est): 69.04K
SALES (corp-wide): 69.04K **Privately Held**
SIC: 8082 7389 3842 Home health care services; Business Activities at Non-Commercial Site; Surgical appliances and supplies

(G-7662)
BOSS BATTLE GAMES
10202 E Washington St Ste 500 (46229-2645)
PHONE..............................317 875-1446
EMP: 5 **EST:** 2015
SALES (est): 133.38K **Privately Held**
Web: bossbattlegames.weebly.com
SIC: 3944 Games, toys, and children's vehicles

(G-7663)
BOSTON SCIENTIFIC CORP
111 Monument Cir Ste 2900 (46204-5405)
PHONE..............................951 914-2400
EMP: 9 **EST:** 2018
SALES (est): 139.51K **Privately Held**
Web: www.guidant.com
SIC: 3841 Surgical and medical instruments

(G-7664)
BOUDOIR LASH PARLOR LLC
1534 Lancashire Ct (46260-2124)
PHONE..............................330 259-5696
EMP: 2
SALES (est): 62.54K **Privately Held**
SIC: 3999 7389 Hair curlers, designed for beauty parlors; Business Activities at Non-Commercial Site

(G-7665)
BOWERS ENVELOPE COMPANY INC
Also Called: Bowers Record Sleeve Bag Div
5331 N Tacoma Ave (46220-3671)
P.O. Box 66854 (46205)
PHONE..............................317 253-4321
EMP: 7 **EST:** 1928
SALES (est): 2.12MM
SALES (corp-wide): 219.99MM **Privately Held**
Web: www.supremex.com

Indianapolis - Marion County (G-7666)   GEOGRAPHIC SECTION

SIC: 2677 2678 2671 Envelopes; Stationery: made from purchased materials; Plastic film, coated or laminated for packaging
PA: Supremex Inc
7213 Rue Cordner
Lasalle QC H8N 2
514 595-0555

(G-7666)
BOWTIE WOODWORKS LLC
4820 Broadway St (46205-1856)
PHONE.................................765 667-1934
EMP: 4 EST: 2019
SALES (est): 57.83K Privately Held
SIC: 2431 Millwork

(G-7667)
BOYCE INDUSTRIES GROUP LLC
5373 W 86th St (46268-1501)
PHONE.................................317 409-3235
Al Lowe, Prin
EMP: 10 EST: 2019
SALES (est): 521.51K Privately Held
Web: www.boyceindustries.com
SIC: 3599 Machine shop, jobbing and repair

(G-7668)
BPAC INC
9025 River Rd Ste 150 (46240-6447)
PHONE.................................317 723-7427
EMP: 10 EST: 2019
SALES (est): 481.97K Privately Held
SIC: 7372 Prepackaged software

(G-7669)
BRADEN SUTPHIN INK CO
1340 Sadlier Circle East Dr (46239-1052)
PHONE.................................317 352-8781
Brian Chronister, Prin
EMP: 2 EST: 2008
SALES (est): 193.82K Privately Held
SIC: 2893 Printing ink

(G-7670)
BRAINSTORM PRINT LLC
Also Called: Brainstorm Print
2603 55th Pl (46220-3527)
PHONE.................................317 466-1600
EMP: 8 EST: 2010
SALES (est): 711.09K Privately Held
Web: www.brainstormprint.com
SIC: 2752 Offset printing

(G-7671)
BRAMA INC
Also Called: Big Red
5855 Kopetsky Dr Ste I (46217-9636)
PHONE.................................317 786-7770
Dennis Blong, Pr
▲ EMP: 14 EST: 1986
SALES (est): 438.91K Privately Held
SIC: 3563 Air and gas compressors

(G-7672)
BRANDYWINE CREEK
12524 Southeastern Ave (46259-1152)
PHONE.................................317 868-0563
EMP: 4 EST: 2018
SALES (est): 177.13K Privately Held
Web: www.brandywinecreekvineyards.com
SIC: 2084 Wines

(G-7673)
BREDENSTEINER & ASSOCIATES
1920 Dr Martin Luther King Jr St Ste A (46202-1108)
PHONE.................................317 921-2226
Jim Bredenstein, Pr
EMP: 2 EST: 2001

SALES (est): 164.39K Privately Held
SIC: 2759 Commercial printing, nec

(G-7674)
BREDENSTEINER IMAGING INC
1920 Dr Martin Luther King Jr St Ste A (46202)
P.O. Box 1451 (46206)
PHONE.................................317 921-1900
James Bredensteiner, Prin
Roy Bredensteiner, Prin
EMP: 6 EST: 1993
SQ FT: 25,000
SALES (est): 503.94K Privately Held
Web: www.bredensteiner.biz
SIC: 2752 Offset printing

(G-7675)
BREG INC
3055 N Meridian St (46208-4750)
PHONE.................................760 505-0521
EMP: 8 EST: 2012
SALES (est): 88.53K Privately Held
Web: www.breg.com
SIC: 3841 Surgical and medical instruments

(G-7676)
BREG INC
2835 Fortune Cir W (46241-5565)
PHONE.................................317 559-0479
EMP: 26
Web: www.breg.com
SIC: 3841 Surgical and medical instruments
HQ: Breg, Inc.
2382 Faraday Ave
Carlsbad CA 92008

(G-7677)
BRENDACURTIS RECIPE BOOKS LLC
425 Blue Spring Dr Ste 101 (46239-8880)
PHONE.................................574 216-2261
EMP: 25
SALES (est): 998.56K Privately Held
SIC: 2731 Books, publishing and printing

(G-7678)
BRICKHOUSE ELECTRONICS LLC
Also Called: Brickhouse Security
5718 W 79th St (46278-1708)
PHONE.................................212 643-7449
Todd Morris, CEO
EMP: 17 EST: 2005
SALES (est): 3.37MM Privately Held
Web: www.brickhousesecurity.com
SIC: 5999 5065 3663 Alarm and safety equipment stores; Security control equipment and systems; Global positioning systems (GPS) equipment

(G-7679)
BRICKYARD CROSSING
2572 Moller Rd (46224-3381)
PHONE.................................317 492-6573
EMP: 6 EST: 2010
SALES (est): 156.01K Privately Held
Web: www.brickyardcrossing.com
SIC: 3949 Shafts, golf club

(G-7680)
BRICS
901 E 64th St (46220-1101)
PHONE.................................317 257-5757
David Gabovitch, Owner
EMP: 12 EST: 2010
SALES (est): 188.66K Privately Held
Web: www.bricsindy.com
SIC: 2024 Ice cream, bulk

(G-7681)
BRIDGESTONE RET OPERATIONS LLC
Also Called: Firestone
1300 E 86th St Ste 2 (46240-1990)
PHONE.................................317 846-6516
Sara Smith, Mgr
EMP: 8
Web: www.bridgestoneamericas.com
SIC: 5531 7534 Automotive tires; Rebuilding and retreading tires
HQ: Bridgestone Retail Operations, Llc
200 4th Ave S Ste 100
Nashville TN 37201
630 259-9000

(G-7682)
BRIDGESTONE RET OPERATIONS LLC
Also Called: Firestone
6020 E 82nd St Ofc (46250-5528)
PHONE.................................317 849-9120
Elizabeth Kelly, Mgr
EMP: 8
Web: www.bridgestoneamericas.com
SIC: 5531 7534 Automotive tires; Tire repair shop
HQ: Bridgestone Retail Operations, Llc
200 4th Ave S Ste 100
Nashville TN 37201
630 259-9000

(G-7683)
BRIGHT SHEET METAL COMPANY INC
Also Called: Snodgrass Sheet Metal
1930 S State Ave (46203-4185)
PHONE.................................317 783-3181
Philip Meyers, Pr
EMP: 55
Web: www.brightsheetmetal.com
SIC: 1761 3444 Sheet metal work, nec; Sheet metalwork
PA: Bright Sheet Metal Company, Inc.
4212 W 71st St Ste A
Indianapolis IN 46268

(G-7684)
BRIGHT SHEET METAL COMPANY INC (PA)
Also Called: A To Z Sheet Metal
4212 W 71st St Ste A (46268-2274)
PHONE.................................317 291-7600
Phil Meyers, Pr
Gary Aletto, *
EMP: 90 EST: 1958
SQ FT: 35,500
SALES (est): 26.25MM Privately Held
Web: www.brightsheetmetal.com
SIC: 1761 3444 Sheet metal work, nec; Sheet metalwork

(G-7685)
BRIGHTLAMP INC
1230 Hoyt Ave (46203-1103)
PHONE.................................317 285-9287
Kurtis Sluss, CEO
Craig Wilhite, Development
Michael Heims, CFO
EMP: 1 EST: 2015
SALES (est): 47.98K Privately Held
Web: www.brightlamp.org
SIC: 7372 Prepackaged software

(G-7686)
BRINKMAN PRESS INC
6945 Hawthorn Park Dr (46220-3910)
PHONE.................................317 722-0305
Thomas Brinkman, Pr
Sandra L Brinkman, Sec

EMP: 9 EST: 1990
SQ FT: 2,800
SALES (est): 1.5MM Privately Held
Web: www.brinkmanpress.com
SIC: 2752 Offset printing

(G-7687)
BROAD RIPPLE CHIP CO LLC
5060 E 62nd St Ste 124 (46220-5353)
PHONE.................................317 590-7687
Mark Mcswiney, Managing Member
EMP: 5 EST: 2013
SALES (est): 360.9K Privately Held
Web: www.broadripplechip.com
SIC: 2096 Potato chips and other potato-based snacks

(G-7688)
BROOKS PUBLICATIONS INC
Also Called: Urban Times
305 N East St (46202-3610)
P.O. Box 441166 (46244-1166)
PHONE.................................317 756-9830
William Brooks, Pr
EMP: 1 EST: 2005
SALES (est): 69.86K Privately Held
Web: www.urbantimesonline.com
SIC: 2741 Newsletter publishing

(G-7689)
BROWMI BY MISHA LLC ◆
8022 E 46th St (46226-3905)
PHONE.................................317 801-3911
Tamisha Mcdowell, CEO
EMP: 1 EST: 2022
SALES (est): 42.55K Privately Held
SIC: 2326 7389 Service apparel (baker, barber, lab, etc.), washable: men's; Business Activities at Non-Commercial Site

(G-7690)
BROWNSBURG CUSTOM CABINETS INC
1747 Country Club Rd (46234-1828)
P.O. Box 198 (46112-0198)
PHONE.................................317 271-1887
Robert Overman, Pr
David Roberts, VP
EMP: 6 EST: 1987
SQ FT: 10,000
SALES (est): 895.76K Privately Held
SIC: 3083 Plastics finished products, laminated

(G-7691)
BRULIN & COMPANY INC
Also Called: Brulin
2920 Dr Andrew J Brown Ave (46205-4066)
P.O. Box 270 (46206-0270)
PHONE.................................317 923-3211
◆ EMP: 100
Web: www.brulin.com
SIC: 2842 2841 Cleaning or polishing preparations, nec; Soap: granulated, liquid, cake, flaked, or chip

(G-7692)
BRULIN HOLDING COMPANY INC (PA)
Also Called: Brulin
2920 Dr Andrew J Brown Ave (46205-4066)
PHONE.................................317 923-3211
Charles Pollnow, Ch Bd
Dean Pollnow, *
Kim Essenburg, *
Liesl Mcwilliams, Sec
EMP: 34 EST: 2008
SALES (est): 23.44MM
SALES (corp-wide): 23.44MM Privately Held

GEOGRAPHIC SECTION

Indianapolis - Marion County (G-7717)

Web: www.brulin.com
SIC: **2842** Cleaning or polishing preparations, nec

(G-7693)
BRUNO CB INC
9465 Counselors Row Ste 200 (46240-6423)
PHONE..................317 619-7467
EMP: 9 EST: 1995
SALES (est): 472.54K **Privately Held**
SIC: **2672** Cellophane adhesive tape: made from purchased materials

(G-7694)
BRYTON CORPORATION
4001 Methanol Ln (46268-4855)
P.O. Box 68177 (46268-0177)
PHONE..................317 334-8700
Bob Samuels, *Pr*
Martha Samuels, *VP*
R T Samuels, *Prin*
◆ EMP: 15 EST: 1981
SALES (est): 4.77MM **Privately Held**
Web: www.steris.com
SIC: **5047** 3842 Medical equipment and supplies; Surgical appliances and supplies

(G-7695)
BTS DISPATCHING LLC ✪
988 N Boehning St (46219-5529)
PHONE..................317 300-4594
EMP: 1 EST: 2022
SALES (est): 60.08K **Privately Held**
SIC: **3537** 7389 Trucks, tractors, loaders, carriers, and similar equipment; Business Activities at Non-Commercial Site

(G-7696)
BUCKAROOS INC (PA)
9800 Crosspoint Blvd (46256-3569)
PHONE..................317 899-9100
Jeffrey Rebholz, *Pr*
Arnold Rebholz, *Sec*
EMP: 8 EST: 1991
SALES (est): 2.98MM **Privately Held**
Web: www.buckaroos.com
SIC: **3444** 2499 3432 5072 Metal housings, enclosures, casings, and other containers; Dowels, wood; Plastic plumbing fixture fittings, assembly; Hand tools

(G-7697)
BUCKEYE CORRUGATED INC
CRA-Wal Container
4001 S High School Rd (46241-6448)
PHONE..................317 856-3701
David Haba, *Brnch Mgr*
EMP: 100
SALES (corp-wide): 196.62MM **Privately Held**
Web: www.bcipkg.com
SIC: **2653** Boxes, corrugated: made from purchased materials
PA: Buckeye Corrugated, Inc.
822 Kumho Dr Ste 400
Fairlawn OH 44333
330 576-0590

(G-7698)
BUCKEYE DIAMOND LOGISTICS INC
Also Called: Bdl Supply
217 S Belmont Ave Ste E (46222-4286)
PHONE..................317 524-9304
Todd Davis, *Brnch Mgr*
EMP: 1
SALES (corp-wide): 32.81MM **Privately Held**
Web: www.bdlsupply.com
SIC: **2448** Pallets, wood
PA: Buckeye Diamond Logistics, Inc.

15 Sprague Rd
South Charleston OH 45368
937 462-8361

(G-7699)
BUCKNER INC (PA)
Also Called: Sundae's
9922 E 79th St (46256-4824)
PHONE..................317 570-0533
David Bucker, *Pr*
Steve Buckner, *VP*
EMP: 26 EST: 1983
SQ FT: 1,600
SALES (est): 2.22MM
SALES (corp-wide): 2.22MM **Privately Held**
Web: www.sundaeshomemade.com
SIC: **5812** 2024 5149 Restaurant, family: independent; Ice cream, bulk; Coffee and tea

(G-7700)
BUNNY FLAMING INDUSTRIES
1741 S Delaware St (46225-1760)
PHONE..................317 554-7143
Kirsten Cleveland, *Prin*
EMP: 4 EST: 2017
SALES (est): 55.22K **Privately Held**
SIC: **3999** Manufacturing industries, nec

(G-7701)
BURRIS ENGINEERING INC
5430 S Franklin Rd (46239-9646)
PHONE..................317 862-1046
Mark Burris, *Pr*
David Smith, *Sec*
EMP: 18 EST: 1979
SQ FT: 15,000
SALES (est): 493.48K **Privately Held**
Web: www.burrisengineering.com
SIC: **3599** Machine shop, jobbing and repair

(G-7702)
BURTON DEBICEIOUS (PA) ✪
Also Called: Your Mane Nails
3827 N Mitthoefer Rd Unit C9 (46235-1810)
PHONE..................317 495-0123
Debiceious Burton, *Owner*
EMP: 1 EST: 2022
SALES (est): 64.49K
SALES (corp-wide): 64.49K **Privately Held**
SIC: **2844** 5051 Manicure preparations; Nails

(G-7703)
BUSINESS FORMS DESIGNS INC
1333 N Huber St (46219-3811)
PHONE..................317 353-6647
Harry E Mumaug Ii, *Pr*
EMP: 3 EST: 1995
SALES (est): 120K **Privately Held**
SIC: **2759** Fashion plates: printing, nsk

(G-7704)
BUTLER-MACDONALD INC
5955 W 80th St (46278-1322)
PHONE..................317 872-5115
J Scott Johnson, *Pr*
Tim Cash, *
Susan B Johnson, *
▲ EMP: 70 EST: 1983
SQ FT: 120,000
SALES (est): 9.65MM **Privately Held**
Web: www.butlermacdonald.com
SIC: **3089** Plastics processing

(G-7705)
BUZZI UNICEM USA INC
1112 W Thompson Rd (46217-9264)
PHONE..................317 780-9860
Mike Glaze, *Mgr*

EMP: 25
SALES (corp-wide): 4.69B **Privately Held**
Web: www.buzziunicemusa.com
SIC: **3241** Portland cement
HQ: Buzzi Unicem Usa Inc
100 Brodhead Rd Ste 230
Bethlehem PA 18017
610 882-5000

(G-7706)
C & W INKD
6300 Brookville Rd Bldg B (46219-8251)
PHONE..................317 352-1000
Tommy L Cooper, *Pr*
EMP: 16 EST: 2007
SQ FT: 10,000
SALES (est): 1.76MM **Privately Held**
Web: www.cwaif.com
SIC: **3554** 2789 2675 7319 Die cutting and stamping machinery, paper converting; Binding only: books, pamphlets, magazines, etc.; Die-cut paper and board; Distribution of advertising material or sample services

(G-7707)
C H ELLIS LLC
Also Called: C. H. Ellis
2432 Southeastern Ave (46201)
PHONE..................317 636-3351
Jeffrey Hale, *Pr*
Clay Barnes, *CEO*
Robert Able, *VP*
EMP: 6 EST: 2015
SALES (est): 85.85K **Privately Held**
Web: www.chellis.com
SIC: **3161** Luggage

(G-7708)
C JOHNSON GROUP LLC
Also Called: CJ Sweets
8734 Navigator Dr Apt 1305 (46237-2992)
PHONE..................219 512-0619
Cura Johnson, *Managing Member*
EMP: 1 EST: 2021
SALES (est): 64.19K **Privately Held**
SIC: **2051** 7389 Bakery: wholesale or wholesale/retail combined; Business Activities at Non-Commercial Site

(G-7709)
C N J WELL DRILLING
1721 Laurel St (46203-4007)
P.O. Box 747 (46112-0747)
PHONE..................317 892-2100
Josh Abdnour, *Pr*
EMP: 10 EST: 1971
SALES (est): 964.06K **Privately Held**
Web: www.cj4water.com
SIC: **1381** Drilling oil and gas wells

(G-7710)
C&R RACING INCORPORATED (HQ)
Also Called: C & R
6950 Guion Rd (46268-2576)
PHONE..................317 293-4100
Chris B Paulsen, *Pr*
Debra Paulsen, *
▲ EMP: 30 EST: 1988
SQ FT: 35,000
SALES (est): 19.18MM **Privately Held**
Web: www.crracing.com
SIC: **3599** Machine shop, jobbing and repair
PA: Pwr Holdings Limited
103 Lahrs Rd
Ormeau QLD 4208

(G-7711)
CA INC
Also Called: CA
250 E 96th St Ste 375 (46240)

PHONE..................317 844-7221
Trenli Bacon, *Brnch Mgr*
EMP: 50
SALES (corp-wide): 35.82B **Publicly Held**
Web: www.broadcom.com
SIC: **3674** Semiconductors and related devices
HQ: Ca, Inc.
3421 Hillview Ave
Palo Alto CA 94304
800 225-5224

(G-7712)
CABINET AND STONE EXPO
8227 Northwest Blvd Ste 205 (46278-1386)
PHONE..................317 879-1688
EMP: 6 EST: 2020
SALES (est): 610.95K **Privately Held**
Web: www.cabinetstoneexpo.com
SIC: **2434** Wood kitchen cabinets

(G-7713)
CABINET AND STONE EXPO LLC
5775 W 79th St (46278-1712)
PHONE..................317 879-1688
Kowng Bun Lee, *Owner*
▲ EMP: 1 EST: 2013
SALES (est): 241K **Privately Held**
Web: www.cabinetstoneexpo.com
SIC: **2434** Wood kitchen cabinets

(G-7714)
CABINETRY IDEAS INC
6113 Allisonville Rd (46220-4607)
PHONE..................317 722-1300
Nancy L Barbee, *Prin*
EMP: 4 EST: 2008
SALES (est): 455.53K **Privately Held**
Web: www.cabinetryideas.com
SIC: **2434** Wood kitchen cabinets

(G-7715)
CABINETS TO GO LLC
Also Called: Cabinets To Go
3150 Rand Rd (46241-5408)
PHONE..................317 486-0888
EMP: 5
SALES (corp-wide): 99.82MM **Privately Held**
Web: www.cabinetstogo.com
SIC: **2434** Wood kitchen cabinets
PA: Cabinets To Go, Llc
2350 Wo Smith Dr
Lawrenceburg TN 38464
909 646-5900

(G-7716)
CAICOS SOLUTIONS LLC ✪
3410 N High School Rd Ste G Pmb 1017 (46224)
PHONE..................317 314-3776
Rose Darline Aristile, *CEO*
EMP: 2 EST: 2024
SALES (est): 65.6K **Privately Held**
SIC: **2834** Intravenous solutions

(G-7717)
CALUMET INC (PA)
2780 Waterfront Parkway East Dr Ste 200 (46214)
PHONE..................317 328-5660
Todd Borgmann, *CEO*
Stephen P Mawer, *Ch Bd*
David Lunin, *Ex VP*
Bruce Fleming, *MONTANA RENEWABLES CORP Development*
Scott Obermeier, *VP Sls*
EMP: 26 EST: 1919
SALES (est): 4.18B
SALES (corp-wide): 4.18B **Publicly Held**

(PA)=Parent Co (HQ)=Headquarters
✪ = New Business established in last 2 years

Indianapolis - Marion County (G-7718)   GEOGRAPHIC SECTION

SIC: 2911 Petroleum refining

(G-7718)
CALUMET FINANCE CORP
2780 Waterfront Parkway (46214)
PHONE...................................317 328-5660
EMP: 23 **EST:** 2013
SALES (est): 5.29MM
SALES (corp-wide): 4.18B **Publicly Held**
Web: www.calumet.com
SIC: 2911 Petroleum refining
HQ: Calumet Specialty Products Partners Lp
1060 N Cptol Ave Ste 6-40
Indianapolis IN 46204

(G-7719)
CALUMET GP LLC
2780 Waterfront Parkway East Dr Ste 200 (46214)
P.O. Box 24359 (46224-0359)
PHONE...................................317 328-5660
Stephen P Mawer, CEO
Fred M Fehsenfeld Junior, Ch Bd
L Todd Borgmann, Ex VP
Bruce A Fleming, Ex VP
Scott Obermeier, Ex VP
EMP: 23 **EST:** 2005
SALES (est): 1.67MM **Privately Held**
SIC: 2911 Petroleum refining

(G-7720)
CALUMET INTERNATIONAL INC
2780 Waterfront Parkway East Dr Ste 200 (46214-2044)
PHONE...................................317 328-5660
Bill Grube, Pr
Allan Moyes, VP
EMP: 2 **EST:** 2006
SALES (est): 673.33K
SALES (corp-wide): 4.18B **Publicly Held**
Web: www.calumet.com
SIC: 2911 Petroleum refining
HQ: Calumet Specialty Products Partners Lp
1060 N Cptol Ave Ste 6-40
Indianapolis IN 46204

(G-7721)
CALUMET KARNS CITY REF LLC (DH)
Also Called: Magie Brothers
2780 Waterfront Parkway East Dr Ste 300 (46214)
PHONE...................................317 328-5660
◆ **EMP:** 32 **EST:** 1974
SALES (est): 41.34MM
SALES (corp-wide): 4.18B **Publicly Held**
Web: www.calumet.com
SIC: 2911 Petroleum refining
HQ: Calumet Specialty Products Partners Lp
1060 N Cptol Ave Ste 6-40
Indianapolis IN 46204

(G-7722)
CALUMET MISSOURI LLC (DH)
Also Called: Calumet
2780 Waterfront Parkway East Dr (46214-2044)
PHONE...................................318 795-3800
David Volpe, Manager
Donna Meyers, Finance/Quality Lead*
▲ **EMP:** 26 **EST:** 1990
SQ FT: 958,320
SALES (est): 9.24MM
SALES (corp-wide): 4.18B **Publicly Held**
Web: www.calumet.com
SIC: 2911 Solvents

HQ: Calumet Specialty Products Partners Lp
1060 N Cptol Ave Ste 6-40
Indianapolis IN 46204

(G-7723)
CALUMET OPERATING LLC (DH)
2780 Waterfront Pkwy (46214)
PHONE...................................317 328-5660
R Patrick Murray Ii, VP
EMP: 19 **EST:** 2005
SALES (est): 353.18MM
SALES (corp-wide): 4.18B **Publicly Held**
Web: www.calumet.com
SIC: 2911 Petroleum refining
HQ: Calumet Specialty Products Partners Lp
1060 N Cptol Ave Ste 6-40
Indianapolis IN 46204

(G-7724)
CALUMET REFINING LLC (DH)
Also Called: Calumet Spcialty Pdts Partners
2780 Waterfront Parkway East Dr Ste 200 (46214-2044)
PHONE...................................317 328-5660
Philip Murphy, VP
◆ **EMP:** 47 **EST:** 1990
SQ FT: 10,000
SALES (est): 199.43MM
SALES (corp-wide): 4.18B **Publicly Held**
Web: www.calumet.com
SIC: 2911 Petroleum refining
HQ: Calumet Operating, L.L.C.
2780 Waterfront Pkwy
Indianapolis IN 46214
317 328-5660

(G-7725)
CALUMET SHREVEPORT LLC
2780 Waterfront Parkway East Dr (46214-2044)
PHONE...................................317 328-5660
Roy Jacobsen, Prin
EMP: 1 **EST:** 2004
SALES (est): 5.05MM
SALES (corp-wide): 4.18B **Publicly Held**
Web: www.calumet.com
SIC: 2911 Petroleum refining
HQ: Calumet Refining, Llc
2780 Wtrfront Pkwy E Dr S
Indianapolis IN 46214

(G-7726)
CALUMET SHREVEPORT FUELS LLC
2780 Waterfront Parkway East Dr (46214-2044)
PHONE...................................317 328-5660
EMP: 77
SIC: 5983 2999 Fuel oil dealers; Fuel briquettes and waxes

(G-7727)
CALUMET SHREVEPORT REF LLC (DH)
2780 Waterfront Parkway East Dr Ste 200 (46214-2044)
PHONE...................................317 328-5660
F Grube, CEO
EMP: 16 **EST:** 2004
SALES (est): 21.71MM
SALES (corp-wide): 4.18B **Publicly Held**
Web: www.calumet.com
SIC: 2911 Petroleum refining
HQ: Calumet Specialty Products Partners Lp
1060 N Cptol Ave Ste 6-40
Indianapolis IN 46204

(G-7728)
CALUMET SPCLTY PDTS PRTNERS LP (HQ)
Also Called: Calumet
1060 N Capitol Ave Ste 6-401 (46204)
PHONE...................................317 328-5660
Todd Borgmann, CEO
David Lunin, Ex VP
▼ **EMP:** 189 **EST:** 1916
SQ FT: 58,501
SALES (est): 4.18B
SALES (corp-wide): 4.18B **Publicly Held**
Web: www.calumet.com
SIC: 2911 Solvents
PA: Calumet, Inc.
2780 Wtrfront Pkwy E Dr S
Indianapolis IN 46214
317 328-5660

(G-7729)
CALUMET SUPERIOR LLC
2780 Waterfront Parkway East Dr Ste 200 (46214)
PHONE...................................317 328-5660
EMP: 200 **EST:** 2011
SALES (est): 28.54MM
SALES (corp-wide): 4.18B **Publicly Held**
Web: www.calumet.com
SIC: 5983 2999 Fuel oil dealers; Fuel briquettes and waxes
HQ: Calumet Specialty Products Partners Lp
1060 N Cptol Ave Ste 6-40
Indianapolis IN 46204

(G-7730)
CANARY BROTHERS LLC
Also Called: Herculean Meal Prep
900 N College Ave (46202-3403)
PHONE...................................317 954-1225
EMP: 5
SALES (corp-wide): 1.2MM **Privately Held**
Web: www.herculeanmealprep.com
SIC: 2038 Breakfasts, frozen and packaged
PA: Canary Brothers Llc
3832 E 82nd St
Indianapolis IN 46240
317 954-1225

(G-7731)
CANARY BROTHERS LLC (PA)
Also Called: Herculean Meal Prep
3832 E 82nd St (46240-4328)
PHONE...................................317 954-1225
Ben Canary, Managing Member
EMP: 9 **EST:** 2016
SQ FT: 1,600
SALES (est): 1.2MM
SALES (corp-wide): 1.2MM **Privately Held**
Web: www.herculeanmealprep.com
SIC: 2038 5411 Breakfasts, frozen and packaged; Grocery stores

(G-7732)
CANDIED CAKES
4415 Mountbatten Ct (46254-2139)
P.O. Box 50075 (46250-0075)
PHONE...................................800 261-0823
Jennie Parker, Owner
EMP: 4 **EST:** 2010
SALES (est): 244K **Privately Held**
Web: www.candiedcakes.com
SIC: 2064 Lollipops and other hard candy

(G-7733)
CAPITAL ENVMTL ENTPS INC
3440b S Post Rd (46239-8301)
PHONE...................................317 240-8085
Davies Batterton, Pr
EMP: 6 **EST:** 1990
SQ FT: 8,000

SALES (est): 510.21K **Privately Held**
Web: www.capitalenvironmentalenterprises.com
SIC: 3826 Analytical instruments

(G-7734)
CAPITAL MACHINE COMPANY INC
Also Called: Capital Machines International
2801 Roosevelt Ave (46218)
P.O. Box 18310 (46218)
PHONE...................................317 638-6661
William L Koss, Pr
Mary Joan Koss Rothenberger, Dir
EMP: 17 **EST:** 1887
SQ FT: 35,000
SALES (est): 2.26MM **Privately Held**
Web: www.capitalmachineco.com
SIC: 3553 3545 3541 Veneer mill machines; Machine tool accessories; Machine tools, metal cutting type

(G-7735)
CAPITOL CITY CONTAINER CORP
8240 Zionsville Rd (46268)
PHONE...................................317 875-0290
Richard Purcell, Pr
Joshua Bryant, *
Toni M Purcell, *
EMP: 43 **EST:** 1974
SQ FT: 75,000
SALES (est): 8.99MM **Privately Held**
Web: www.capcitycontainer.com
SIC: 2653 Boxes, corrugated: made from purchased materials

(G-7736)
CAPTIVE-AIRE SYSTEMS INC
1515 Brookville Crossing Way (46239)
PHONE...................................352 467-4439
EMP: 8 **EST:** 2018
SALES (est): 202.52K **Privately Held**
Web: www.captiveaire.com
SIC: 3444 Sheet metalwork

(G-7737)
CARBONITE INC (HQ)
8470 Allison Pointe Blvd Ste 300 (46250-4365)
PHONE...................................617 587-1100
Steve Munford, Interim Chief Executive Officer
Stephen Munford, Interim Chief Executive Officer*
Anthony Folger, *
Norman Guadagno, *
Paul Mellinger, Senior Vice President Global Sales*
EMP: 82 **EST:** 2005
SALES (est): 239.64MM
SALES (corp-wide): 5.77B **Privately Held**
Web: www.carbonite.com
SIC: 7372 7374 Prepackaged software; Data processing and preparation
PA: Open Text Corporation
275 Frank Tompa Dr
Waterloo ON N2L 0
519 888-7111

(G-7738)
CARDEN JENNINGS PUBLISHING
8363 Basswood Dr Apt 1a (46268-3581)
PHONE...................................317 490-7080
Jason Pearce, Prin
EMP: 1 **EST:** 2011
SALES (est): 63.04K **Privately Held**
SIC: 2741 Miscellaneous publishing

(G-7739)
CARDINAL CONTAINER CORP
750 S Post Rd (46239-9745)
PHONE...................................317 898-2715

GEOGRAPHIC SECTION

Indianapolis - Marion County (G-7764)

D E Ferguson, *CEO*
H Dale Farmer, *
Duane Stoots, *
Mark A Prosser, *
EMP: 40 **EST:** 1963
SQ FT: 60,000
SALES (est): 5.78MM **Privately Held**
Web: www.cardinalcontainercorp.com
SIC: 2653 Boxes, corrugated: made from purchased materials

(G-7740)
CARDINAL HEALTH 414 LLC
4343 W 62nd St (46268-2514)
PHONE..................317 981-4100
Alyssa Carter, *Brnch Mgr*
EMP: 11
SALES (corp-wide): 226.83B **Publicly Held**
SIC: 2834 2835 Pharmaceutical preparations; Diagnostic substances
HQ: Cardinal Health 414, Llc
7000 Cardinal Pl
Dublin OH 43017
614 757-5000

(G-7741)
CARDINAL MANUFACTURING CO INC
Also Called: Cardinal
1095 E 52nd St (46205-1204)
PHONE..................317 283-4175
Jim Mulligan, *Pr*
EMP: 10 **EST:** 2003
SALES (est): 911K **Privately Held**
Web: www.cardinalmfginc.com
SIC: 3993 3444 Signs, not made in custom sign painting shops; Sheet metalwork

(G-7742)
CARE TEST LAB LLC ✪
2346 S Lynhurst Dr Ste 606 (46241-8621)
PHONE..................574 326-1082
Lakara Murphy, *CEO*
EMP: 1 **EST:** 2022
SALES (est): 69.27K **Privately Held**
SIC: 3821 Clinical laboratory instruments, except medical and dental

(G-7743)
CARECYCLE LLC
8302 E 33rd St (46226-6503)
PHONE..................317 372-7444
EMP: 3 **EST:** 2014
SQ FT: 10,000
SALES (est): 117.43K **Privately Held**
SIC: 3841 Surgical instruments and apparatus

(G-7744)
CARGILL DRY CORN INGRDENTS INC
I C M Grain
1730 W Michigan St (46222-3855)
PHONE..................317 632-1481
Mike Smith, *Brnch Mgr*
EMP: 39
SALES (corp-wide): 159.59B **Privately Held**
Web: www.cargill.com
SIC: 2041 2048 Corn meal; Livestock feeds
HQ: Cargill Dry Corn Ingredients, Inc.
616 S Jefferson St
Paris IL 61944
217 465-5331

(G-7745)
CARL ABBOTT
Also Called: Armour Fire Protection
6725 Shelley St (46219-6233)
PHONE..................317 590-4143
Carl Abbott, *Owner*
EMP: 1 **EST:** 2014
SALES (est): 30.77K **Privately Held**
SIC: 7389 3999 5999 Fire extinguisher servicing; Fire extinguishers, portable; Fire extinguishers

(G-7746)
CARLTON VENTURES INC
Also Called: Ink Well
1815 N Meridian St Ste 100 (46202-1448)
P.O. Box 44366 (46244-0366)
PHONE..................317 637-2590
Karen Carlton, *Pr*
Lynn Carlton, *Sec*
EMP: 8 **EST:** 1991
SQ FT: 3,500
SALES (est): 787.98K **Privately Held**
Web: www.theinkwellusa.com
SIC: 2752 Offset printing

(G-7747)
CARMICHAEL SOLUTIONS LLC
Also Called: Carmichael Solutions
8227 Northwest Blvd Ste 130 (46278-1387)
PHONE..................317 356-2883
Pj Greco, *Pr*
EMP: 6 **EST:** 2013
SALES (est): 982.12K **Privately Held**
Web: www.carmichael.solutions
SIC: 2844 Perfumes, cosmetics and other toilet preparations

(G-7748)
CARPENTER CO INC
Also Called: Carpenter Realtors
5751 W 56th St (46254-1604)
PHONE..................317 297-2900
Regina Jones, *Prin*
EMP: 31
SALES (corp-wide): 45.22MM **Privately Held**
Web: www.callcarpenter.com
SIC: 3423 Carpenters' hand tools, except saws: levels, chisels, etc.
PA: Carpenter Co Inc
8901 S Meridian St
Indianapolis IN 46217
317 888-3303

(G-7749)
CARRIER CORPORATION
7310 W Morris St (46231-1355)
P.O. Box 70 (46206-0070)
PHONE..................317 243-0851
Halsey Cook, *Pr*
EMP: 80
SALES (corp-wide): 22.1B **Publicly Held**
Web: www.carrier.com
SIC: 3585 3433 Refrigeration and heating equipment; Heating equipment, except electric
HQ: Carrier Corporation
13995 Pasteur Blvd
Palm Beach Gardens FL 33418
561 365-2000

(G-7750)
CARSON MANUFACTURING CO INC
5451 N Rural St (46220-3691)
P.O. Box 20464 (46220-0464)
PHONE..................317 257-3191
Barbara S Ferguson, *Pr*
William H Carson, *Sec*
◆ **EMP:** 19 **EST:** 1946
SQ FT: 47,000
SALES (est): 4.79MM **Privately Held**
Web: www.carson-mfg.com
SIC: 3625 3679 3577 3669 Relays and industrial controls; Electronic circuits; Computer peripheral equipment, nec; Sirens, electric: vehicle, marine, industrial, and air raid

(G-7751)
CARTER & CARTER PUBLISHING LLC
7521 Gunyon Ct (46237-9378)
PHONE..................317 882-0748
Tammy L Carter, *Owner*
EMP: 3 **EST:** 2018
SALES (est): 37.59K **Privately Held**
SIC: 2741 Miscellaneous publishing

(G-7752)
CARTER-LEE BUILDING COMPONENTS
1717 W Washington St (46222-4542)
PHONE..................317 639-5431
Dave N Carter, *Ch Bd*
John Carter, *
EMP: 39 **EST:** 1996
SALES (est): 470.62K **Privately Held**
Web: www.bldr.com
SIC: 2439 3448 Trusses, wooden roof; Trusses and framing, prefabricated metal

(G-7753)
CASE INDY PRODUCTS INC
407 Ansley Ct (46234-2602)
PHONE..................317 677-0200
Jake Klemann, *Pr*
EMP: 5 **EST:** 1997
SALES (est): 403.48K **Privately Held**
Web: www.indycase.com
SIC: 2449 Shipping cases, wood: wirebound

(G-7754)
CASE LINEAGE MANAGEMENT ✪
12125 E 65th St Unit 36838 (46236)
PHONE..................317 721-1764
Krystina Wilson, *Pt*
EMP: 2 **EST:** 2024
SALES (est): 80.88K **Privately Held**
SIC: 3523 Farm machinery and equipment

(G-7755)
CASPER LLC
4310 Stout Field North Dr (46241-4002)
PHONE..................660 221-5906
EMP: 1 **EST:** 2012
SALES (est): 88.45K **Privately Held**
SIC: 7372 Publisher's computer software

(G-7756)
CAST STONE
5236 Basin Park Dr (46239-9027)
PHONE..................317 617-1088
Shannon Cook, *Prin*
EMP: 4 **EST:** 2016
SALES (est): 55.83K **Privately Held**
Web: www.customcaststone.com
SIC: 3272 Concrete products, nec

(G-7757)
CASTING COMPANY INC
8047 Raindance Trl (46239-9541)
PHONE..................317 509-4311
Brian Moore, *Pr*
EMP: 1 **EST:** 2011
SALES (est): 67.34K **Privately Held**
Web: www.thecastingcompanyinc.com
SIC: 3599 3999 Machine shop, jobbing and repair; Manufacturing industries, nec

(G-7758)
CASTLETON VILLAGE CENTER INC
Also Called: Hightech Signs
450 E 96th St (46240-5703)
PHONE..................317 577-1995
Doug Abramowski, *Prin*
EMP: 3
Web: www.hightech-signs.com
SIC: 3993 Signs and advertising specialties
PA: Castleton Village Center Inc
6321 Huguenard Rd Ste A
Fort Wayne IN 46818

(G-7759)
CATCHRS LLC
365 E 75th St (46240-2845)
PHONE..................310 902-9723
Jonathan Henrichsen, *Prin*
EMP: 8 **EST:** 2011
SALES (est): 219.09K **Privately Held**
Web: www.synergyrealty.com
SIC: 2076 Coconut oil

(G-7760)
CATHETER RESEARCH INC
Also Called: Thomas Medical
6102 Victory Way (46278-2934)
PHONE..................317 872-0074
Phil H Sheingold, *Pr*
John A Steen, *
Glenn Uhrich, *
Suzy Sunviling, *
John S Arnold, *
▲ **EMP:** 150 **EST:** 1987
SQ FT: 37,000
SALES (est): 20.29MM **Privately Held**
Web: www.thomasmedical.com
SIC: 3841 Surgical and medical instruments

(G-7761)
CAVITY FACTORY LLC
8144 Crackling Ln (46259-7683)
PHONE..................317 937-5385
Destinee Smith, *CEO*
EMP: 3 **EST:** 2021
SALES (est): 66.48K **Privately Held**
SIC: 2099 Food preparations, nec

(G-7762)
CBD REVOLUTION LLC
Also Called: Health and Wellness
10202 E Washington St Ste 446 (46229-2670)
PHONE..................463 888-2806
Frederick William Erdmann, *Pr*
EMP: 3 **EST:** 2018
SQ FT: 1,180
SALES (est): 246.95K **Privately Held**
Web: www.cbdrevolution2018.com
SIC: 3999

(G-7763)
CBFC LLC (PA)
Also Called: Kingmaker Foods
7698 Zionsville Rd (46268-2173)
P.O. Box 68618 (46268-0618)
PHONE..................317 677-1577
Geff Hays, *Managing Member*
EMP: 5 **EST:** 2007
SALES (est): 3.59MM
SALES (corp-wide): 3.59MM **Privately Held**
Web: www.kingmakerfoods.com
SIC: 2099 Ready-to-eat meals, salads, and sandwiches

(G-7764)
CBRK LLC
6025 W 46th St (46254-1905)
PHONE..................317 601-8546

Indianapolis - Marion County (G-7765)

EMP: 2 EST: 2021
SALES (est): 45K Privately Held
SIC: 7389 5661 1389 Business Activities at Non-Commercial Site; Shoe stores; Construction, repair, and dismantling services

(G-7765)
CCTS TECHNOLOGY GROUP INC
Also Called: CLEAN EXHAUST
8403 N Illinois St (46260-2319)
PHONE..................................305 209-5743
Theodore Sputh, Pr
EMP: 2 EST: 2003
SALES (est): 198.83K Privately Held
SIC: 3519 5084 7538 Diesel, semi-diesel, or duel-fuel engines, including marine; Engines and parts, diesel; Engine repair, except diesel: automotive

(G-7766)
CEMEX
1051 S Emerson Ave (46203-1606)
PHONE..................................317 351-9912
EMP: 10 EST: 2017
SALES (est): 226.36K Privately Held
SIC: 3273 Ready-mixed concrete

(G-7767)
CEMEX MATERIALS LLC
Also Called: Indianapolis - Pipe
1501 S Holt Rd (46241-4107)
PHONE..................................317 891-3015
John Susong, Brnch Mgr
EMP: 121
SIC: 3273 Ready-mixed concrete
HQ: Cemex Materials Llc
1720 Cntrpark Dr E Ste 10
West Palm Beach FL 33401
561 833-5555

(G-7768)
CENTERPOINT BREWING CO LLC
Also Called: Centerpoint Brewing
1125 Brookside Ave Ste B1 (46202-2779)
PHONE..................................317 602-8386
Jonathan Robinson, Managing Member
EMP: 10 EST: 2016
SALES (est): 433.62K Privately Held
Web: www.centerpointbrewing.com
SIC: 5813 2082 Bars and lounges; Beer (alcoholic beverage)

(G-7769)
CENTRAL BRACE & LIMB CO INC (PA)
1901 N Capitol Ave (46202-1265)
PHONE..................................317 925-4296
Miles A Hobbs, Pr
Michael Hobbs, Pr
Patricia Hobbs, Sec
Justin Hobbs, VP
EMP: 13 EST: 1961
SQ FT: 3,100
SALES (est): 2.38MM
SALES (corp-wide): 2.38MM Privately Held
Web: www.centralbraceandlimb.com
SIC: 3842 5999 Orthopedic appliances; Orthopedic and prosthesis applications

(G-7770)
CENTRAL COCA-COLA BTLG CO INC
Also Called: Coca-Cola
8351 Northwest Blvd (46278-1354)
PHONE..................................800 241-2653
EMP: 32
SALES (corp-wide): 45.75B Publicly Held
Web: www.coca-cola.com
SIC: 5149 2086 8741 Soft drinks; Soft drinks: packaged in cans, bottles, etc.; Management services
HQ: Central Coca-Cola Bottling Company, Inc.
555 Taxter Rd Ste 550
Elmsford NY 10523
914 789-1100

(G-7771)
CENTRAL COCA-COLA BTLG CO INC
Also Called: Coca-Cola
5000 W 25th St (46224-3378)
PHONE..................................317 398-0129
EMP: 52
SALES (corp-wide): 45.75B Publicly Held
Web: www.coca-cola.com
SIC: 2086 Bottled and canned soft drinks
HQ: Central Coca-Cola Bottling Company, Inc.
555 Taxter Rd Ste 550
Elmsford NY 10523
914 789-1100

(G-7772)
CENTRAL COCA-COLA BTLG CO INC
Also Called: Coca-Cola
3830 Hanna Cir (46241-7202)
PHONE..................................317 243-3771
EMP: 20
SALES (corp-wide): 45.75B Publicly Held
Web: www.coca-cola.com
SIC: 2086 5149 2087 Bottled and canned soft drinks; Groceries and related products, nec; Flavoring extracts and syrups, nec
HQ: Central Coca-Cola Bottling Company, Inc.
555 Taxter Rd Ste 550
Elmsford NY 10523
914 789-1100

(G-7773)
CENTRAL INDIANA WOODWORKERS
1702 Misty Lake Dr (46260-6124)
PHONE..................................317 407-9228
EMP: 4 EST: 2013
SALES (est): 110K Privately Held
SIC: 2431 Millwork

(G-7774)
CENTRAL VAN LINES INC
8010 Castleton Rd (46250-2005)
P.O. Box 50800 (46250-0800)
PHONE..................................317 849-7900
Mark Kirschner, CEO
EMP: 217 EST: 2004
SALES (est): 4.02MM
SALES (corp-wide): 99.87MM Privately Held
Web: www.arpin.com
SIC: 3812 Defense systems and equipment
PA: Wheaton Van Lines Inc
8010 Castleton Rd
Indianapolis IN 46250
317 849-7900

(G-7775)
CENTURY PHARMACEUTICALS INC
10377 Hague Rd (46256-3399)
PHONE..................................317 849-4210
Ross A Deardorff, Pr
Carol Deardorff, Opers Mgr
EMP: 29 EST: 1966
SQ FT: 28,000
SALES (est): 4.62MM Privately Held
Web: www.getdakins.com
SIC: 7389 3841 2844 2834 Packaging and labeling services; Surgical and medical instruments; Perfumes, cosmetics and other toilet preparations; Vitamin, nutrient, and hematinic preparations for human use

(G-7776)
CENTURY TOOL & ENGR INC
1330 Deloss St (46203-1159)
PHONE..................................317 685-0942
David J Yanasak, Pr
EMP: 6 EST: 1984
SQ FT: 4,500
SALES (est): 488.97K Privately Held
SIC: 3544 7692 3545 Special dies and tools; Welding repair; Machine tool accessories

(G-7777)
CERAMICA INC
6695 E 34th St (46226-6121)
PHONE..................................317 546-0087
Doug Light, Pr
Dick Light, Ch Bd
Keith Light, VP
Marianne Townley, Sec
▲ EMP: 16 EST: 1982
SQ FT: 6,000
SALES (est): 484.31K Privately Held
Web: www.ceramicainc.com
SIC: 3251 3281 3471 Structural brick and blocks; Cut stone and stone products; Plating and polishing

(G-7778)
CERTA CRAFT INC
3902 E 16th St Ste A (46201-1562)
PHONE..................................317 535-0226
Emil Kernel Iii, Pr
EMP: 7 EST: 2007
SALES (est): 931.7K Privately Held
Web: www.certacraft.com
SIC: 3599 Machine shop, jobbing and repair

(G-7779)
CERTIFIED AUTOMOTIVE & MCH SP
8340 E Washington St (46219)
PHONE..................................317 897-9724
EMP: 6 EST: 2016
SALES (est): 81.49K Privately Held
SIC: 3599 Machine shop, jobbing and repair

(G-7780)
CESARS WELDING LLC
1213 N Sherman Dr (46201-2331)
PHONE..................................317 938-8830
EMP: 5 EST: 2012
SALES (est): 81.92K Privately Held
SIC: 7692 Welding repair

(G-7781)
CGENETECH INC
7940 Crestway Dr Apt 1010 (46236-7925)
PHONE..................................317 295-1925
Qiang Yu, Pr
Fengping Wei, Sec
EMP: 2 EST: 2005
SALES (est): 231.98K Privately Held
Web: www.cgenetech.com
SIC: 2833 Medicinal chemicals

(G-7782)
CH ELLIS CO INC (PA)
Also Called: Howe Industries
2432 Southeastern Ave (46201-4161)
P.O. Box 1005 (46206-1005)
PHONE..................................317 636-3351
Robert N Able, CEO
Wanda K Cooney, *
▲ EMP: 40 EST: 1902
SQ FT: 53,000
SALES (est): 4.68MM
SALES (corp-wide): 4.68MM Privately Held
Web: www.chellis.com

SIC: 3161 2449 Cases, carrying, nec; Shipping cases and drums, wood: wirebound and plywood

(G-7783)
CHANCE IND STANDARDS LAB INC
Also Called: Indiana Standards Laboratory
2919 Shelby St (46203-5236)
PHONE..................................317 787-6578
Mark Cook, Pr
EMP: 14 EST: 2004
SQ FT: 4,000
SALES (est): 1MM Privately Held
Web: www.indianastandards.com
SIC: 7629 3825 Electrical measuring instrument repair and calibration; Test equipment for electronic and electric measurement

(G-7784)
CHANEL J LUXURY COLLECTION LLC
4407 Lakefield Trce (46254-4907)
PHONE..................................470 210-4706
EMP: 1
SALES (est): 47.23K Privately Held
SIC: 2844 Hair preparations, including shampoos

(G-7785)
CHANNEL 40 NETWORK LLC
4248 Royalty Dr Apt E (46254-6720)
PHONE..................................317 794-6150
Donnell Brian Dillon, CEO
EMP: 1 EST: 2021
SALES (est): 54.37K Privately Held
SIC: 3663 Television broadcasting and communications equipment

(G-7786)
CHARLES WNNGS DBA DASSAULT AVI
6871 Pierson Dr (46241-4226)
PHONE..................................928 276-4983
EMP: 5 EST: 2019
SALES (est): 62.38K Privately Held
SIC: 2082 Malt beverages

(G-7787)
CHASE SOUTHPORT EMERSON
7120 Emblem Dr (46237-8502)
PHONE..................................317 266-7470
Deanna Eagan, Prin
EMP: 2 EST: 2010
SALES (est): 122.29K Privately Held
SIC: 3578 Automatic teller machines (ATM)

(G-7788)
CHASIN PAPER LLC
5282 Jonathan Trce Apt 2c (46226-1847)
PHONE..................................317 429-6116
EMP: 2 EST: 2021
SALES (est): 92.67K Privately Held
SIC: 3669 Transportation signaling devices

(G-7789)
CHATTER HOUSE PRESS
7915 S Emerson Ave Ste B303 (46237-8556)
PHONE..................................317 514-4133
EMP: 4 EST: 2016
SALES (est): 40.51K Privately Held
Web: www.chatterhousepress.com
SIC: 2741 Miscellaneous publishing

(G-7790)
CHEDDAR STACKS INC
5875 Castle Creek Parkway North Dr Ste 310 (46250-4331)
PHONE..................................317 566-0425

GEOGRAPHIC SECTION
Indianapolis - Marion County (G-7815)

Aaron M Wilson, *CEO*
EMP: 3 **EST:** 2018
SALES (est): 95.76K **Privately Held**
Web: www.cheddarstacks.com
SIC: 7372 Prepackaged software

(G-7791)
CHEM-AQUA
8401 E 33rd St (46226-6504)
PHONE...................317 899-3660
Joe Fisher, *Prin*
EMP: 2 **EST:** 2010
SALES (est): 266.46K **Privately Held**
Web: www.chemaqua.com
SIC: 3589 Water treatment equipment, industrial

(G-7792)
CHEMICALS INC USA
8194 Allison Ave (46268-1615)
PHONE...................317 334-1000
EMP: 6 **EST:** 2020
SALES (est): 74.42K **Privately Held**
SIC: 2899 Chemical preparations, nec

(G-7793)
CHEMQUE INC
6107 Guion Rd (46254-1223)
PHONE...................800 268-6111
Curt Eikel, *Genl Mgr*
EMP: 5
SALES (corp-wide): 3.51B **Publicly Held**
Web: www.chemque.com
SIC: 2899 Chemical preparations, nec
HQ: Royal Adhesives & Sealants Canada Ltd.
266 Humberline Dr
Etobicoke ON M9W 5
416 679-5676

(G-7794)
CHEMTRADE SOLUTIONS LLC
Also Called: General Alum & Chemical
1598 S Senate Ave (46225-1516)
PHONE...................317 917-0319
Steve Combs, *Branch Mg*
EMP: 4
SALES (corp-wide): 1.34B **Privately Held**
SIC: 2819 Aluminum compounds
HQ: Chemtrade Solutions Llc
90 E Halsey Rd
Parsippany NJ 07054

(G-7795)
CHEP (USA) INC
606 W Troy Ave (46225-2238)
PHONE...................317 780-0700
Brian Cutcher, *Mgr*
EMP: 7
Web: www.chep.com
SIC: 3952 2448 Palettes, artists'; Cargo containers, wood and wood with metal
HQ: Chep (U.S.A.) Inc.
5897 Windward Pkwy
Alpharetta GA 30005
770 668-8100

(G-7796)
CHEYENNE ENTERPRISES LLC
6100 N Keystone Ave Ste 105 (46220-2452)
PHONE...................317 253-7795
Sheila Thomas, *Prin*
EMP: 6 **EST:** 2010
SALES (est): 110K **Privately Held**
SIC: 2741 Miscellaneous publishing

(G-7797)
CHG DEVELOPMENTS LLC
Also Called: Little Nugget
1075 Broad Ripple Ave # 202 (46220-2034)
PHONE...................720 480-0957
EMP: 1 **EST:** 2015
SALES (est): 32.77K **Privately Held**
SIC: 7372 7389 Application computer software; Business Activities at Non-Commercial Site

(G-7798)
CHIP GANASSI RACING TEAMS INC
7777 Woodland Dr (46278)
PHONE...................317 802-0000
Chip Ganassi, *CEO*
Steve Lauletta, *
EMP: 100 **EST:** 1980
SALES (est): 16.72MM **Privately Held**
Web: www.chipganassiracing.com
SIC: 7948 3949 Race car owners; Archery equipment, general

(G-7799)
CHISHOLM LUMBER & SUPPLY CO
3419 Roosevelt Ave (46218-3761)
P.O. Box 18280 (46218-0280)
PHONE...................317 547-3535
Douglas Chisholm Senior, *Pr*
Elizabeth Chisholm, *
Michael B Chisholm, *
EMP: 35 **EST:** 1870
SQ FT: 4,000
SALES (est): 22.35MM **Privately Held**
Web: www.chisholmmillwork.com
SIC: 5031 2431 3444 2435 Lumber: rough, dressed, and finished; Millwork; Sheet metalwork; Hardwood veneer and plywood

(G-7800)
CHRISTIAN CANDLE COMPANY
1509 Mary Dr (46241-2809)
PHONE...................317 427-8070
EMP: 3 **EST:** 2015
SALES (est): 62.54K **Privately Held**
SIC: 3999 Candles

(G-7801)
CHRISTIE MACHINE WORKS CO INC
Also Called: Indianapolis Welding Co
425 W Mccarty St (46225-1237)
PHONE...................317 638-8840
John R Humphrey, *Pr*
John R Humphrey Senior, *Pr*
Joseph H Humphrey, *Sec*
EMP: 5 **EST:** 1909
SQ FT: 7,300
SALES (est): 477.6K **Privately Held**
Web: www.christiemachineworks.com
SIC: 3599 1799 Machine shop, jobbing and repair; Welding on site

(G-7802)
CHRISTINA ANN CLARK
10547 Moqui Ct (46235-3484)
PHONE...................317 778-7832
Christina Clark, *Owner*
EMP: 1 **EST:** 2017
SALES (est): 29.18K **Privately Held**
SIC: 2035 Pickled fruits and vegetables

(G-7803)
CHUCK STACE-ALLEN INC
2246 W Minnesota St Ste 50 (46221-1842)
P.O. Box 21216 (46221-0216)
PHONE...................317 632-2401
Phil Grimes, *Sec*
Marcia Grimes, *Pr*
Larry E Grimes, *VP*
Tim Grimes, *Sec*
James Timmons, *VP Sls*
EMP: 20 **EST:** 1946
SQ FT: 12,000
SALES (est): 2.44MM **Privately Held**
Web: www.stace-allen.com
SIC: 3545 Chucks: drill, lathe, or magnetic (machine tool accessories)

(G-7804)
CINDYS CROSSSTITCH & PATTERNS
2265 Reformers Ave (46203-2982)
PHONE...................317 410-0764
EMP: 4 **EST:** 2014
SALES (est): 155.25K **Privately Held**
SIC: 3543 Industrial patterns

(G-7805)
CIRCLE CITY HEAT TREATING INC
Also Called: Circle City Cryogenics
2243 Massachusetts Ave (46218)
PHONE...................317 440-9102
Tom Dunn, *Pr*
Richard W Krug, *Pr*
Kathy S Krug, *Sec*
EMP: 16 **EST:** 1952
SQ FT: 14,000
SALES (est): 2.39MM **Privately Held**
Web: www.incertec.com
SIC: 3398 3471 Metal heat treating; Plating and polishing
PA: Innovative Certified Technical Plating, L.L.C.
500 73rd Ave Ne Ste 123
Fridley MN 55432

(G-7806)
CIRCLE CITY REBAR LLC
4002 Industrial Blvd (46254-2512)
PHONE...................317 917-8566
EMP: 12 **EST:** 2005
SALES (est): 1.76MM **Privately Held**
Web: www.circlecityrebar.com
SIC: 3441 Fabricated structural metal

(G-7807)
CIRCLE CITY SONORANS LLC
Also Called: Circle City Kombucha
1050 E Washington St (46202-3953)
PHONE...................317 395-3693
Matthew Whiteside, *CEO*
EMP: 3 **EST:** 2015
SALES (est): 535.06K **Privately Held**
Web: www.circlebev.com
SIC: 2086 Carbonated beverages, nonalcoholic: pkgd. in cans, bottles

(G-7808)
CIRCLE CITY WOODWORKING
5574 Alcott Ln (46221-4869)
PHONE...................765 637-6687
Kyle Mooneyhan, *Prin*
EMP: 4 **EST:** 2018
SALES (est): 61.46K **Privately Held**
SIC: 2431 Millwork

(G-7809)
CIRCLE MEDICAL PRODUCTS INC
8202 Indy Ln (46214-2326)
PHONE...................317 271-2626
Jon S Watson, *Pr*
EMP: 6 **EST:** 1995
SQ FT: 7,000
SALES (est): 500K **Privately Held**
SIC: 3841 4953 Surgical and medical instruments; Medical waste disposal

(G-7810)
CIS HOLDINGS INC
8888 Keystone Xing Ste 600 (46240-4609)
PHONE...................703 996-0500
Luke Phenicie, *Ch Bd*
EMP: 7 **EST:** 2021
SALES (est): 85.99K **Privately Held**
SIC: 3575 Computer terminals

(G-7811)
CITIZENS BY-PRODUCTS COAL CO (HQ)
2020 N Meridian St (46202-1306)
PHONE...................317 927-4738
Dave Griffiths, *Pr*
Kerry Lykins, *Pr*
EMP: 12 **EST:** 1951
SALES (est): 23.43MM
SALES (corp-wide): 552.56MM **Privately Held**
Web: info.citizensenergygroup.com
SIC: 1321 8742 Natural gas liquids; Marketing consulting services
PA: Citizens Energy Group
2020 N Meridian St
Indianapolis IN 46202
317 924-3341

(G-7812)
CITIZENS ENERGY GROUP
366 Kentucky Ave (46225-1165)
PHONE...................317 261-8794
David Tombs, *Genl Mgr*
EMP: 14
SALES (corp-wide): 552.56MM **Privately Held**
Web: info.citizensenergygroup.com
SIC: 4925 3312 Gas: mixed, natural and manufactured; Chemicals and other products derived from coking
PA: Citizens Energy Group
2020 N Meridian St
Indianapolis IN 46202
317 924-3341

(G-7813)
CITY OPTICAL CO INC (PA)
Also Called: Dr Tavel's One Hour Optical
2839 Lafayette Rd (46222-2147)
PHONE...................317 924-1300
Lawrence S Tavel Md, *Pr*
Lawrence S Tavel Md, *Pr*
Alan G Tavel O.d., *VP*
EMP: 60 **EST:** 1946
SQ FT: 21,000
SALES (est): 48.94MM
SALES (corp-wide): 48.94MM **Privately Held**
Web: www.drtavel.com
SIC: 5048 5049 5995 8042 Ophthalmic goods; Optical goods; Optical goods stores; Offices and clinics of optometrists

(G-7814)
CITY OPTICAL CO INC
Also Called: Dr Tavel Premium Optical
3636 S East St (46227-1239)
PHONE...................317 788-4243
Sue Miller, *Mgr*
EMP: 5
SALES (corp-wide): 48.94MM **Privately Held**
Web: www.drtavel.com
SIC: 5049 3851 Optical goods; Lens grinding, except prescription: ophthalmic
PA: City Optical Co., Inc.
2839 Lafayette Rd
Indianapolis IN 46222
317 924-1300

(G-7815)
CLAIRES CABINET REFINISHING
6207 Broadway St (46220-1836)
PHONE...................317 495-5406
EMP: 6 **EST:** 2018
SALES (est): 53.79K **Privately Held**
SIC: 2434 Wood kitchen cabinets

(PA)=Parent Co (HQ)=Headquarters
✪ = New Business established in last 2 years

Indianapolis - Marion County (G-7816) GEOGRAPHIC SECTION

(G-7816)
CLARIOS LLC
Johnson Controls
5920 Castleway West Dr (46250-1957)
PHONE.............................317 638-7611
Marke Roberts, *Genl Mgr*
EMP: 300
SALES (corp-wide): 69.83B **Privately Held**
Web: www.clarios.com
SIC: 2531 1711 Seats, automobile; Plumbing, heating, air-conditioning
HQ: Clarios, Llc
5757 N Green Bay Ave Flor
Glendale WI 53209

(G-7817)
CLARITY INDUSTRY CO LLC
827 Laclede St (46241-2309)
PHONE.............................678 389-5006
EMP: 2 **EST:** 2021
SALES (est): 350K **Privately Held**
SIC: 3911 Jewelry, precious metal

(G-7818)
CLARKS BIG DOG TRUCKING LLC
2701 Highland Pl (46208-5122)
PHONE.............................317 625-1388
EMP: 1 **EST:** 2020
SALES (est): 60.08K **Privately Held**
SIC: 3537 Trucks, tractors, loaders, carriers, and similar equipment

(G-7819)
CLASSIC CHEMICAL CORP
7750 Zionsville Rd Ste 700 (46268-5126)
P.O. Box 781493 (46278-8493)
PHONE.............................812 934-3289
Frank Desmond, *Pr*
▼ **EMP:** 4 **EST:** 2000
SQ FT: 9,000
SALES (est): 507.35K **Privately Held**
Web: www.degreaser.net
SIC: 2869 2843 Industrial organic chemicals, nec; Surface active agents

(G-7820)
CLASSICHYDROS
940 N Audubon Rd (46219-4509)
PHONE.............................317 352-1315
Douglas Campbell, *Owner*
EMP: 1 **EST:** 2003
SALES (est): 54.52K **Privately Held**
SIC: 3944 Boat and ship models, toy and hobby

(G-7821)
CLASSY STITCHES
5336 Honey Manor Dr (46221-3909)
PHONE.............................317 856-3261
EMP: 1 **EST:** 1991
SALES (est): 84K **Privately Held**
SIC: 2337 2399 Uniforms, except athletic: women's, misses', and juniors'; Flags, fabric

(G-7822)
CLIF BAR & COMPANY
Also Called: CLIF BAR & COMPANY
7575 Georgetown Rd (46268-4132)
PHONE.............................510 596-6451
Kevin Cleary, *CEO*
EMP: 66
Web: www.clifbar.com
SIC: 2052 Cookies and crackers
HQ: Clif Bar & Company, Llc
1451 66th St
Emeryville CA 94608

(G-7823)
CLINICAL SCRUBS LLC
9961 Ellis Dr (46235-1645)
PHONE.............................317 607-3991
EMP: 1 **EST:** 2021
SALES (est): 42.55K **Privately Held**
Web: www.scrubidentity.com
SIC: 2326 Medical and hospital uniforms, men's

(G-7824)
CLONDALKIN PHARMA & HEALTHCARE INC
Also Called: Keller Crescent Co
6454 Saguaro Ct (46268-2545)
P.O. Box 78005 (46278-0005)
PHONE.............................336 292-4555
◆ **EMP:** 850
Web: www.kellercrescentadvertising.com
SIC: 2752 2631 7311 Offset printing; Folding boxboard; Advertising agencies

(G-7825)
CLOSURE SYSTEMS INTL INC (HQ)
Also Called: C S I
7820 Innovation Blvd Ste 100 (46278-0016)
PHONE.............................317 390-5000
Malcolm P Bundey, *Pr*
Thomas Degnan, *
Barringto Owens, *
Ronald D Dickel, *
Lawrence R Purtell, *
◆ **EMP:** 163 **EST:** 1987
SQ FT: 64,000
SALES (est): 237.19MM **Privately Held**
Web: www.csiclosures.com
SIC: 3334 3565 Primary aluminum; Bottling machinery: filling, capping, labeling
PA: Closure Systems International Holdings Llc
7820 Innvtion Blvd Ste 10
Indianapolis IN 46278

(G-7826)
CLOVER INDUSTRIAL SERVICES LLC
1555 S Franklin Rd Ste D (46239-8575)
PHONE.............................317 879-5001
Troy Gamble, *Pr*
EMP: 8 **EST:** 2010
SQ FT: 21,000
SALES (est): 173.3K **Privately Held**
Web: www.clover-is.com
SIC: 3589 Vacuum cleaners and sweepers, electric: industrial

(G-7827)
CMG INC
455 Rawles Ct (46229-3147)
PHONE.............................317 890-1999
Chris Julka, *Genl Mgr*
EMP: 5
SALES (corp-wide): 21.98MM **Privately Held**
Web: www.cmgmetals.com
SIC: 3444 Metal roofing and roof drainage equipment
PA: Cmg, Inc.
301 Yard Dr
Verona WI 53593
608 826-0356

(G-7828)
CMOSS TRANSPORT LLC
3413 Luewan Dr (46235-2215)
PHONE.............................317 656-1846
EMP: 2
SALES (est): 95.58K **Privately Held**
SIC: 3537 Trucks: freight, baggage, etc.: industrial, except mining

(G-7829)
COACH MONAY PUBLISHING LLC
3250a W 86th St (46268-3605)
PHONE.............................463 256-5096
E Mason, *Admn*
EMP: 3 **EST:** 2020
SALES (est): 110.91K **Privately Held**
SIC: 2741 Miscellaneous publishing

(G-7830)
COBO INDUSTRIES
6831 Ridge Vale Pl Apt 2b (46237-7826)
PHONE.............................812 341-4318
Colin Bouillon, *Prin*
EMP: 3 **EST:** 2018
SALES (est): 67.08K **Privately Held**
SIC: 3999 Manufacturing industries, nec

(G-7831)
CODEWELD INC
905 E Edgewood Ave (46227-2037)
P.O. Box 17913 (46217-0913)
PHONE.............................317 784-4140
EMP: 4 **EST:** 1995
SALES (est): 360K **Privately Held**
Web: www.codeweldinc.com
SIC: 3443 Heat exchangers, condensers, and components

(G-7832)
COHDA WIRELESS AMERICA LLC
450 E 96th St Ste 500 (46240-3760)
PHONE.............................248 513-2105
EMP: 1 **EST:** 2013
SQ FT: 16,800
SALES (est): 1.34MM **Privately Held**
Web: www.cohdawireless.com
SIC: 3663 Carrier equipment, radio communications
PA: Cohda Wireless Pty Ltd
27 Greenhill Rd
Wayville SA 5034

(G-7833)
COHESANT TECHNOLOGIES INC
5845 W 82nd St Ste 102 (46278-1363)
PHONE.............................317 871-7611
EMP: 8 **EST:** 2019
SALES (est): 141.63K **Privately Held**
SIC: 3563 Air and gas compressors

(G-7834)
COLA VOCE MUSIC INC
4600 Sunset Ave (46208-3443)
PHONE.............................317 466-0624
Fred Hatfield, *Owner*
EMP: 2 **EST:** 2008
SALES (est): 113.59K **Privately Held**
Web: www.collavoce.com
SIC: 2741 Music book and sheet music publishing

(G-7835)
COLLEGE NETWORK INC (PA)
Also Called: Itestout.com
3815 River Crossing Pkwy Ste 260 (46240-7758)
P.O. Box 80016 (46280-0016)
PHONE.............................800 395-3276
EMP: 90 **EST:** 1996
SQ FT: 25,000
SALES (est): 9.08MM **Privately Held**
Web: www.collegenetwork.com
SIC: 2741 Guides: publishing only, not printed on site

(G-7836)
COLORCON INC
6585 E 30th St (46219-1101)
PHONE.............................317 545-6211

EMP: 8
SALES (corp-wide): 2.13B **Privately Held**
Web: www.colorcon.com
SIC: 2834 Pharmaceutical preparations
HQ: Colorcon, Inc.
420 Moyer Blvd
West Point PA 19486
215 699-7733

(G-7837)
COLORCON INC
Also Called: Colorcon
3702 E 21st St (46218-4487)
PHONE.............................317 545-6211
Steven Bennett, *Brnch Mgr*
EMP: 90
SALES (corp-wide): 2.13B **Privately Held**
Web: www.colorcon.com
SIC: 2834 2046 Pharmaceutical preparations; Wet corn milling
HQ: Colorcon, Inc.
420 Moyer Blvd
West Point PA 19486
215 699-7733

(G-7838)
COLORRUSH INC
1802 W 51st St (46228-2305)
PHONE.............................317 374-3494
EMP: 6 **EST:** 2014
SALES (est): 70.23K **Privately Held**
Web: www.colorrushprintshop.com
SIC: 2759 Screen printing

(G-7839)
COMFORT SUITES BATON ROUGE
5701 Progress Rd (46241-4334)
PHONE.............................317 247-5500
EMP: 2
SALES (est): 179.27K **Privately Held**
SIC: 3949 Batons

(G-7840)
COMMERCIAL FINISHING CORP
7199 English Ave (46219-7406)
PHONE.............................317 267-0377
Timothy B Hughes, *Pr*
EMP: 14 **EST:** 1971
SQ FT: 13,000
SALES (est): 452.2K **Privately Held**
Web: www.commercialfinishing.net
SIC: 3479 3471 Coating of metals and formed products; Plating and polishing

(G-7841)
COMMUNITY PAPERS INC
Also Called: West Side Community News
2191 Real Quiet Dr (46234-7637)
PHONE.............................317 241-7363
EMP: 4 **EST:** 1965
SALES (est): 249.6K **Privately Held**
SIC: 2711 2791 Newspapers: publishing only, not printed on site; Typesetting

(G-7842)
COMPANION PUBLICATIONS LLC
5640 Rawles Ave (46219-7120)
PHONE.............................317 294-8189
Phyllis Manfredi, *Prin*
EMP: 4 **EST:** 2016
SALES (est): 60.4K **Privately Held**
SIC: 2741 Miscellaneous publishing

(G-7843)
COMPASSIONATE PROCEDURES LLC
8140 Morningside Dr (46240-2531)
PHONE.............................317 259-4656
EMP: 7 **EST:** 2010
SALES (est): 255.57K **Privately Held**

GEOGRAPHIC SECTION

SIC: 3841 Surgical and medical instruments

(G-7844)
COMPETITION ELECTRONIC SYSTEMS
5706 Hollister Dr (46224-3037)
PHONE..................................317 291-2823
EMP: 1 **EST:** 2000
SALES (est): 110.08K **Privately Held**
SIC: 3679 Electronic circuits

(G-7845)
COMPONENT MACHINE INC
1631 Gent Ave (46202-2185)
PHONE..................................317 635-8929
Thomas Crowe Senior, *Pr*
Donna Crowe, *Sec*
Thomas Crowe Junior, *VP*
EMP: 7 **EST:** 1969
SQ FT: 14,400
SALES (est): 517.07K **Privately Held**
Web: www.componentmachine.com
SIC: 3599 5531 3714 Machine shop, jobbing and repair; Automotive parts; Motor vehicle parts and accessories

(G-7846)
COMPOSITECH INC
Also Called: Zipp Speed Weaponry
5315 Walt Pl (46254-5797)
PHONE..................................800 231-6755
Andrew Ording, *Pr*
Andrew Miller, *Stockholder**
James Mann, *Stockholder**
◆ **EMP:** 35 **EST:** 1988
SQ FT: 17,400
SALES (est): 8.48MM
SALES (corp-wide): 358.5MM **Privately Held**
Web: www.sram.com
SIC: 3949 3751 3714 Sporting and athletic goods, nec; Motorcycles, bicycles and parts; Motor vehicle parts and accessories
PA: Sram, Llc
  1000 W Fulton Market Fl 4
  Chicago IL 60607
  312 664-8800

(G-7847)
CONAGRA BRANDS INC
4300 W 62nd St (46268-2520)
PHONE..................................317 329-3700
EMP: 87
SALES (corp-wide): 12.05B **Publicly Held**
Web: www.conagrabrands.com
SIC: 2099 Food preparations, nec
PA: Conagra Brands, Inc.
  222 W Mdse Mart Plz Ste 1
  Chicago IL 60654
  312 549-5000

(G-7848)
CONAGRA BRANDS INC
7579 Georgetown Rd (46268-4132)
PHONE..................................402 240-5000
EMP: 103
SALES (corp-wide): 12.05B **Publicly Held**
Web: www.conagrabrands.com
SIC: 2038 2013 2099 Frozen specialties, nec; Sausages and other prepared meats; Dessert mixes and fillings
PA: Conagra Brands, Inc.
  222 W Mdse Mart Plz Ste 1
  Chicago IL 60654
  312 549-5000

(G-7849)
CONAGRA DAIRY FOODS COMPANY
4300 W 62nd St (46268-2520)
PHONE..................................317 329-3700
Michael Pfeiffer, *Brnch Mgr*
EMP: 1080
SQ FT: 30,000
SALES (corp-wide): 12.05B **Publicly Held**
Web: www.conagrabrands.com
SIC: 2099 Food preparations, nec
HQ: Conagra Dairy Foods Company Inc
  222 Merchandise Mart Plz
  Chicago IL 60654
  630 848-0975

(G-7850)
CONCEPT MACHINERY INC
1219 N Delaware St (46202-2530)
PHONE..................................317 845-5588
Jeff Tucker, *VP*
EMP: 5 **EST:** 2015
SALES (est): 320.93K **Privately Held**
Web: www.conceptmachinery.com
SIC: 3549 Metalworking machinery, nec

(G-7851)
CONCEPT PRINTS INC
6707 Guion Rd (46268-4810)
PHONE..................................317 290-1222
Thomas Hackett, *Pr*
▲ **EMP:** 16 **EST:** 1983
SQ FT: 15,000
SALES (est): 1.45MM **Privately Held**
Web: www.conceptprints.com
SIC: 2395 7389 2261 Embroidery and art needlework; Design services; Screen printing of cotton broadwoven fabrics

(G-7852)
CONNECTA CORPORATION
3363 Boulevard Pl (46208)
P.O. Box 88241 (46208)
PHONE..................................317 923-9282
Alan R Pyle, *Pr*
▲ **EMP:** 12 **EST:** 1988
SQ FT: 7,300
SALES (est): 2.01MM **Privately Held**
Web: www.connecta.com
SIC: 3643 Electric connectors

(G-7853)
CONOVER CUSTOM FABRICATION INC
2625 S Pennsylvania St (46225-2320)
PHONE..................................317 784-1904
John Conover, *Pr*
Claire Conover, *Sec*
EMP: 15 **EST:** 1990
SALES (est): 2.1MM **Privately Held**
Web: www.conofab.com
SIC: 1799 3444 Food service equipment installation; Sheet metalwork

(G-7854)
CONTAINMED INC (PA)
1841 Ludlow Ave (46201-1035)
PHONE..................................317 487-8800
Tyler Deal, *Pr*
EMP: 5 **EST:** 2005
SALES (est): 2.21MM **Privately Held**
Web: www.containmed.com
SIC: 3999 Barber and beauty shop equipment

(G-7855)
CONTAINMENT TECH GROUP INC (PA)
5460 Victory Dr Ste 300 (46203-5970)
PHONE..................................317 862-5945
Michelle Moore, *Pr*
Janet Rahe, *VP*
EMP: 5 **EST:** 1994
SQ FT: 10,000
SALES (est): 1.3MM
SALES (corp-wide): 1.3MM **Privately Held**
Web: www.mic4.com
SIC: 3829 Ion chambers

(G-7856)
CONTECH ENGNERED SOLUTIONS LLC
7164 Graham Rd Ste 120 (46250-2675)
PHONE..................................317 842-7766
Robert Trees, *Mgr*
EMP: 10
Web: www.conteches.com
SIC: 3443 Fabricated plate work (boiler shop)
HQ: Contech Engineered Solutions Llc
  9025 Centre Pointe Dr # 400
  West Chester OH 45069
  513 645-7000

(G-7857)
CONTEMPORARY BOOKS INC
7965 Mallard Lndg (46278-9521)
PHONE..................................317 753-5247
EMP: 1 **EST:** 1995
SALES (est): 34.19K **Privately Held**
Web: www.publishersarchive.com
SIC: 2741 Miscellaneous publishing

(G-7858)
CONTINNTAL BROADCAST GROUP LLC
Also Called: Wedj-FM
1800 N Meridian St Ste 201 (46202-1433)
PHONE..................................317 924-1071
Marvin Kososky, *Owner*
Jeffrey Warshaw, *Treas*
EMP: 22 **EST:** 2009
SALES (est): 472.91K **Privately Held**
Web: www.wedjfm.com
SIC: 4832 3651 Radio broadcasting stations; FM and AM radio tuners

(G-7859)
CONTINUOUS CARE TRNSP LLC ✪
10932 Freeman Ct (46234-9730)
PHONE..................................463 336-0555
EMP: 3 **EST:** 2022
SALES (est): 78.58K **Privately Held**
SIC: 2752 Schedules, transportation: lithographed

(G-7860)
CONTINUUM GAMES INCORPORATED
1240 Brookville Way Ste J (46239-1099)
PHONE..................................877 405-2662
▲ **EMP:** 4 **EST:** 2005
SALES (est): 902.12K **Privately Held**
Web: www.continuumgames.com
SIC: 5092 3944 Board games; Bingo boards (games)

(G-7861)
CONTOUR HARDENING INC (PA)
8401 Northwest Blvd (46278-1382)
PHONE..................................888 867-2184
John Storm, *Pr*
John M Storm, *
Sam Spenia, *
▲ **EMP:** 46 **EST:** 1990
SQ FT: 59,000
SALES (est): 9.98MM
SALES (corp-wide): 9.98MM **Privately Held**
Web: www.contourhardening.com
SIC: 3567 8731 5084 3621 Heating units and devices, industrial: electric; Commercial physical research; Metalworking machinery; Motors and generators

(G-7862)
CONTROL KEY PLUS
4015 E 82nd St (46250-1693)
PHONE..................................317 567-2194
EMP: 6 **EST:** 2012
SALES (est): 73.45K **Privately Held**
SIC: 3429 Keys, locks, and related hardware

(G-7863)
CONTROLS CENTER INC
Also Called: Johnson Controls
1125 Western Dr (46241-1438)
PHONE..................................317 634-2665
EMP: 2
SALES (corp-wide): 26.96MM **Privately Held**
Web: www.johnstonesolutions.com
SIC: 5722 3621 5063 Air conditioning room units, self-contained; Motors and generators; Electrical supplies, nec
PA: Controls Center, Inc.
  1640 E Kemper Rd Ste 2
  Cincinnati OH 45246
  513 772-2665

(G-7864)
CONVERGENT CONSULTING LLC
6226 N Delaware St (46220-1824)
PHONE..................................202 441-6453
Ryan Klitzsch, *Prin*
EMP: 1 **EST:** 2014
SALES (est): 87.87K **Privately Held**
SIC: 3674 Semiconductors and related devices

(G-7865)
CONVERSIGHTAI
1220 Waterway Blvd (46202-2157)
PHONE..................................201 294-1896
Ganesan Gandhieswara, *CEO*
Dharini Ganesan, *Prin*
Gayathri Arunachalam, *Prin*
EMP: 10 **EST:** 2017
SALES (est): 638.14K **Privately Held**
Web: www.conversight.ai
SIC: 7372 7371 Business oriented computer software; Computer software development and applications

(G-7866)
COOK GENERAL BIOTECHNOLOGY LLC
Also Called: Advanced Cryotechnology
1102 Indiana Ave (46202-3206)
PHONE..................................317 917-3450
EMP: 11 **EST:** 1997
SQ FT: 1,500
SALES (est): 2.56MM
SALES (corp-wide): 1.61B **Privately Held**
Web: www.cookgbt.com
SIC: 3841 Surgical and medical instruments
PA: Cook Group Incorporated
  750 Daniels Way
  Bloomington IN 47404
  812 339-2235

(G-7867)
COOKIE PLEASE
3444b Washington Blvd (46205-3717)
PHONE..................................317 879-6589
Judith Jones, *Owner*
EMP: 4 **EST:** 2017
SQ FT: 5,000
SALES (est): 223.44K **Privately Held**
Web: www.wearepleaseandthankyou.com
SIC: 5142 2051 Bakery products, frozen; Biscuits, baked; baking powder and raised

---

(PA)=Parent Co (HQ)=Headquarters
✪ = New Business established in last 2 years

Indianapolis - Marion County (G-7868) GEOGRAPHIC SECTION

(G-7868)
COOL PLANET LLC
Also Called: Cool Planet Awning Co
340 S Mitthoeffer Rd (46229-3065)
PHONE..................317 927-9000
Matthew Garvey, *Pr*
EMP: 7 **EST:** 1998
SALES (est): 649.34K **Privately Held**
Web: www.coolplanetawnings.com
SIC: 2394 Awnings, fabric: made from purchased materials

(G-7869)
COOPERS CANVAS
9355 Rawles Ave (46229-3020)
PHONE..................317 292-2165
Lacey Padgett, *Prin*
EMP: 5 **EST:** 2017
SALES (est): 46.58K **Privately Held**
SIC: 2211 Canvas

(G-7870)
COPIA VINEYARDS AND WINERY LLC
435 Virginia Ave Unit 707 (46203-1968)
PHONE..................805 835-6094
Varinder Sahi, *Pr*
EMP: 6 **EST:** 2017
SALES (est): 69.49K **Privately Held**
SIC: 2084 Wines

(G-7871)
COPIES PLUS LLC
5845 Lawton Loop East Dr Ste 201 (46216-1072)
PHONE..................317 545-5083
Edwin P Craig, *Pr*
EMP: 2 **EST:** 2005
SALES (est): 87.66K **Privately Held**
Web: www.copiesplususa.com
SIC: 2752 Offset printing

(G-7872)
COPPER MOUNTAIN TECH LLC (PA)
631 E New York St (46202-3706)
PHONE..................317 222-5400
Irena Goloschikin, *CEO*
EMP: 30 **EST:** 2011
SALES (est): 7.06MM
SALES (corp-wide): 7.06MM **Privately Held**
Web: www.coppermountaintech.com
SIC: 5065 3825 Electronic parts and equipment, nec; Instruments for measuring electrical quantities

(G-7873)
COPYFIRE TYPESETTING INC
1513 Touchstone Dr (46239-8864)
PHONE..................317 894-0408
EMP: 4 **EST:** 2010
SALES (est): 70.79K **Privately Held**
SIC: 2791 Typesetting

(G-7874)
CORANGE INTERNATIONAL
Also Called: Roche Diagnostics Puerto Rico
9115 Hague Rd (46256-1025)
P.O. Box 7085 (00732-7085)
▲ **EMP:** 1 **EST:** 2008
SALES (est): 207.28K **Privately Held**
SIC: 2834 Pharmaceutical preparations

(G-7875)
CORESLAB STRCTRES INDNPLIS INC
Also Called: Coreslab Structures
1030 S Kitley Ave (46203-2623)
PHONE..................317 353-2118
Mario Franciosa, *Pr*
Matt Ballain, *
Frank Franciosa, *
EMP: 60 **EST:** 2004
SALES (est): 21.05MM
SALES (corp-wide): 27.34MM **Privately Held**
Web: www.coreslab.com
SIC: 3272 Concrete products, precast, nec
HQ: Coreslab Structures (Ont) Inc
205 Coreslab Dr
Dundas ON L9H 0
905 689-3993

(G-7876)
CORNER STO LLC ◎
4725 Madison Ave Apt 56 (46227-4177)
PHONE..................219 798-2822
EMP: 5 **EST:** 2022
SALES (est): 139.9K **Privately Held**
SIC: 2099 7389 Food preparations, nec; Business Activities at Non-Commercial Site

(G-7877)
CORNERSTONE BREAD CO
840 N Meridian St (46204-1108)
PHONE..................317 897-9671
Cynthia Helmling, *Pr*
EMP: 1 **EST:** 2009
SALES (est): 171.55K **Privately Held**
Web: www.cornerstonebread.com
SIC: 5461 2051 Bread; Bakery: wholesale or wholesale/retail combined

(G-7878)
CORPORATE SYSTEMS ENGRG LLC
Also Called: Corporate Systems Engineering
1215 Brookville Way (46239-1049)
PHONE..................317 375-3600
Steve Taylor, *Pr*
John D Lutz, *CFO*
Angelo Kostarides, *Dir*
EMP: 65 **EST:** 1983
SQ FT: 10,000
SALES (est): 7.55MM **Privately Held**
Web: www.corporatesystems.com
SIC: 7379 3663 Computer related consulting services; Radio and t.v. communications equipment

(G-7879)
CORPORATESTARS INDUSTRIES LLC
5528 Grassy Bank Dr (46237-8498)
PHONE..................317 783-0614
Chavis Taylor, *Owner*
EMP: 1 **EST:** 2014
SALES (est): 39.69K **Privately Held**
SIC: 3999 Manufacturing industries, nec

(G-7880)
CORRUGATED CONCEPTS LLC
Also Called: Corrugated Concepts
7225 Woodland Dr Ste 200 (46278-1787)
PHONE..................317 290-1140
David Hunt, *Contrlr*
EMP: 1 **EST:** 2000
SALES (est): 259.02K **Privately Held**
SIC: 2653 Boxes, corrugated: made from purchased materials

(G-7881)
CORSI CABINET COMPANY INC
6111 Churchman Byp (46203-6116)
PHONE..................317 786-1434
EMP: 75 **EST:** 1973
SALES (est): 9.63MM **Privately Held**
Web: www.corsicabinet.com
SIC: 2434 Wood kitchen cabinets

(G-7882)
CORTEVA INC
Also Called: Corteva Agriscience
9146 Zionsville Rd (46268)
PHONE..................765 586-4077
Tom Monroe, *Mgr*
EMP: 9
SALES (corp-wide): 17.23B **Publicly Held**
Web: www.corteva.com
SIC: 0721 2879 7342 Crop protecting services; Fungicides, herbicides; Pest control in structures
PA: Corteva, Inc.
9330 Zionsville Rd
Indianapolis IN 46268
833 267-8382

(G-7883)
CORTEVA INC (PA)
Also Called: Corteva Agriscience
9330 Zionsville Rd (46268)
PHONE..................833 267-8382
Charles V Magro, *CEO*
Gregory R Page, *Non-Executive Chairman of the Board*
David J Anderson, *Ex VP*
Samuel Eathington, *CDO*
Cornel B Fuerer, *Sr VP*
EMP: 745 **EST:** 2018
SALES (est): 17.23B
SALES (corp-wide): 17.23B **Publicly Held**
Web: www.corteva.com
SIC: 0721 2879 7342 Crop protecting services; Fungicides, herbicides; Pest control in structures

(G-7884)
CORTEVA AGRISCIENCE LLC (HQ)
9330 Zionsville Rd (46268)
P.O. Box 1000 (50131)
PHONE..................317 337-3000
Chuck Magro, *CEO*
Dave Anderson, *
Sam Eathington, *Co-Vice President*
Tim Glenn, *
◆ **EMP:** 1200 **EST:** 1989
SQ FT: 1,205,000
SALES (est): 3.92MM
SALES (corp-wide): 17.23B **Publicly Held**
Web: www.corteva.com
SIC: 0721 5191 8731 2879 Crop protecting services; Seeds and bulbs; Agricultural research; Insecticides and pesticides
PA: Corteva, Inc.
9330 Zionsville Rd
Indianapolis IN 46268
833 267-8382

(G-7885)
COSMOPROF
9455 E Washington St (46229-3085)
PHONE..................317 897-0124
EMP: 4 **EST:** 2015
SALES (est): 118.25K **Privately Held**
Web: stores.cosmoprofbeauty.com
SIC: 5087 3999 Electrolysis equipment and supplies; Cigar and cigarette holders

(G-7886)
COSMOS SUPERIOR FOODS LLC
10611 E 59th St (46236-8334)
PHONE..................317 975-2747
Sean Litke, *CEO*
EMP: 25 **EST:** 2013
SALES (est): 1.45MM **Privately Held**
Web: www.cosmossuperior.com
SIC: 2013 Snack sticks, including jerky: from purchased meat

(G-7887)
COSWORTH LLC
5355 W 86th St (46268)
PHONE..................317 644-1037
Hal Reisiger, *CEO*
Pierre Wildman, *Managing Member*
▲ **EMP:** 88 **EST:** 1977
SQ FT: 60,000
SALES (est): 17.42MM
SALES (corp-wide): 124.7MM **Privately Held**
Web: www.cosworth.com
SIC: 3519 Parts and accessories, internal combustion engines
PA: Cosworth Group Holdings Limited
The Octagon
Northampton NORTHANTS NN5 5
160 459-8300

(G-7888)
COSWORTH ELECTRONICS LLC
Also Called: Cosworth
5355 W 86th St (46268-1501)
PHONE..................317 808-3800
Ryan Tindall, *Managing Member*
EMP: 5 **EST:** 1990
SQ FT: 3,000
SALES (est): 857.38K
SALES (corp-wide): 124.7MM **Privately Held**
Web: www.cosworth.com
SIC: 3823 Data loggers, industrial process type
PA: Cosworth Group Holdings Limited
The Octagon
Northampton NORTHANTS NN5 5
160 459-8300

(G-7889)
COUNTRY CLUB COMPUTER
8247 Indy Ct (46214-2300)
PHONE..................317 271-4000
Mark Genung, *Owner*
Mark Genung, *Prin*
EMP: 7 **EST:** 2007
SALES (est): 120.69K **Privately Held**
Web: asbi-100296.square.site
SIC: 7997 5734 5045 3571 Country club, membership; Computer and software stores; Computers, peripherals, and software; Electronic computers

(G-7890)
COURTNEY SIGNS
2410 Enterprise St (46219-1752)
PHONE..................317 653-5146
EMP: 11 **EST:** 2015
SALES (est): 164.11K **Privately Held**
Web: www.midwestsigns.com
SIC: 3993 Signs and advertising specialties

(G-7891)
COVERS OF INDIANA INC
5050 W Mooresville Rd (46221-2742)
PHONE..................317 244-0291
Boyd Warren Senior, *Pr*
Boyd Warren Junior, *VP*
Edith Warren, *Treas*
EMP: 6 **EST:** 1987
SALES (est): 489.27K **Privately Held**
Web: marine-upholstery-services.cmac.ws
SIC: 7641 2211 Reupholstery; Canvas

(G-7892)
COX INTERIOR INC
Also Called: Cox Interior
9333 Castlegate Dr (46256-1002)
PHONE..................317 896-2227
Joe Jodd, *Mgr*
EMP: 5

GEOGRAPHIC SECTION
Indianapolis - Marion County (G-7918)

SALES (corp-wide): 119.76MM **Privately Held**
Web: www.coxinterior.com
SIC: 2431 Millwork
HQ: Cox Interior, Inc.
   1751 Old Columbia Rd
   Campbellsville KY 42718
   270 789-3129

(G-7893)
COY & ASSOCIATES
2305 E Banta Rd (46227-4908)
PHONE.................317 787-5089
Chester Coy, *Owner*
EMP: 2 **EST:** 1978
SALES (est): 140K **Privately Held**
SIC: 5943 2791 5734 Office forms and supplies; Typesetting; Computer and software stores

(G-7894)
CPM CONVEYOR LLC
2260 Distributors Dr (46241-5005)
PHONE.................317 875-1919
EMP: 5 **EST:** 2018
SALES (est): 503.56K **Privately Held**
Web: www.cpmconveyor.com
SIC: 3535 Conveyors and conveying equipment

(G-7895)
CPS INC
Also Called: Corporate Packaging Solutions
5645 W 82nd St # 100 (46278-1323)
PHONE.................317 804-2300
EMP: 11 **EST:** 1996
SALES (est): 2.08MM **Privately Held**
Web: www.cpsindy.com
SIC: 2653 Boxes, corrugated: made from purchased materials

(G-7896)
CRA-WAL INC
Also Called: Crawal Division
4001 S High School Rd (46241-6448)
PHONE.................317 856-3701
EMP: 80
SIC: 2653 Boxes, corrugated: made from purchased materials

(G-7897)
CRAFT METAL PRODUCTS INC
2751 N Emerson Ave (46218-3267)
PHONE.................317 545-3252
Kenneth Knauss, *Pr*
Janet Knauss, *Sec*
▼ **EMP:** 9 **EST:** 1955
SQ FT: 17,000
SALES (est): 2.38MM **Privately Held**
Web: www.craftmetal.com
SIC: 3646 5023 5033 5021 Commercial lighting fixtures; Carpets; Fiberglass building materials; Office and public building furniture

(G-7898)
CRAFTMARK BAKERY LLC
5202 Exploration Dr (46241-9003)
PHONE.................317 548-3929
▲ **EMP:** 2 **EST:** 2013
SALES (est): 35.21MM **Privately Held**
Web: www.craftmarkbakery.com
SIC: 2051 5461 Breads, rolls, and buns; Retail bakeries
PA: Cic Partners I Lp
   3879 Maple Ave Ste 400
   Dallas TX 75219

(G-7899)
CREATEC CORPORATION
6835 Guion Rd Ste A (46268-6811)
PHONE.................317 566-0022
▲ **EMP:** 370
SIC: 3086 2821 Packaging and shipping materials, foamed plastics; Plastics materials and resins

(G-7900)
CREATIVE BLESSINGS CO LLC
4723 Round Lake Rd Apt H (46205-1597)
PHONE.................219 293-9595
EMP: 1 **EST:** 2021
SALES (est): 33.35K **Privately Held**
SIC: 2731 7389 Books, publishing only; Business services, nec

(G-7901)
CREATIVE MNDS WORK PBLCTONS LL
8063 Madison Ave Pmb 587 (46227)
PHONE.................317 759-1002
Tiana Mumford, *CEO*
EMP: 1 **EST:** 2015
SALES (est): 66.25K **Privately Held**
Web: www.creativemindswork.com
SIC: 2741 2326 2211 7379 Miscellaneous publishing; Medical and hospital uniforms, men's; Scrub cloths; Online services technology consultants

(G-7902)
CREATIVE WORKS INC
Also Called: Creative Works Theme Factory
5767 Dividend Rd (46241-4303)
PHONE.................317 834-4770
Jeff Schilling, *Pr*
Kimberly Schilling, *VP*
◆ **EMP:** 15 **EST:** 1997
SQ FT: 19,280
SALES (est): 4.76MM **Privately Held**
Web: www.wearecreativeworks.com
SIC: 2541 Showcases, except refrigerated: wood

(G-7903)
CRICHLOW INDUSTRIES INC
Also Called: Indianapolis Badge Name Plate
6848 Hawthorn Park Dr (46220-3909)
PHONE.................317 925-5178
David C Crichlow, *Pr*
EMP: 4 **EST:** 1949
SQ FT: 18,000
SALES (est): 493K **Privately Held**
Web: www.indybadge.com
SIC: 3999 2796 3993 3479 Badges, metal: policemen, firemen, etc.; Embossing plates, for printing; Signs, not made in custom sign painting shops; Name plates: engraved, etched, etc.

(G-7904)
CRITERION PRESS INC
Also Called: THE CRITERION NEWSPAPER
1400 N Meridian St (46202-2305)
P.O. Box 1410 (46206-1410)
PHONE.................317 236-1570
Daniel M Buechlein, *Pr*
EMP: 37 **EST:** 1953
SQ FT: 5,300
SALES (est): 1.1MM **Privately Held**
Web: www.archindy.org
SIC: 2711 2759 2741 Newspapers: publishing only, not printed on site; Commercial printing, nec; Directories, nec: publishing only, not printed on site

(G-7905)
CROSS MATCH TECHNOLOGIES INC
8440 Allison Pointe Blvd (46250-4352)
PHONE.................317 596-3260
John Carver, *Sr VP*
EMP: 6 **EST:** 2010
SALES (est): 123.65K **Privately Held**
SIC: 3999 Manufacturing industries, nec

(G-7906)
CROSS PRINTWEAR INC
3466 N Raceway Rd (46234-9201)
PHONE.................317 293-1776
Kenneth Mierke, *Pr*
Paul Summers, *Sec*
EMP: 8 **EST:** 1981
SQ FT: 3,500
SALES (est): 172.85K **Privately Held**
SIC: 2396 Screen printing on fabric articles

(G-7907)
CROSSPOINT POWER AND RFRGN LLC (PA)
4301 W Morris St (46241-2503)
PHONE.................317 240-1967
EMP: 11 **EST:** 2015
SALES (est): 11.44MM
SALES (corp-wide): 11.44MM **Privately Held**
Web: www.crosspointpowerandrefrigeration.com
SIC: 3585 Refrigeration and heating equipment

(G-7908)
CROSSPOINT SOLUTIONS LLC
2601 Fortune Cir E Ste 300c (46241-5567)
PHONE.................877 826-9399
▲ **EMP:** 30
SIC: 3585 Heating and air conditioning combination units

(G-7909)
CROSSRADS CNTRTOPS CBNETRY LLC
606 S Audubon Rd (46219-8112)
PHONE.................317 908-9254
John Dicken, *Prin*
EMP: 5 **EST:** 2018
SALES (est): 108.5K **Privately Held**
SIC: 2434 Wood kitchen cabinets

(G-7910)
CROSSRADS RHBILITATION CTR INC
Crossroads Industrial Services
8302 E 33rd St (46226-6503)
PHONE.................317 897-7320
Jack Costello, *Mgr*
EMP: 110
SQ FT: 18,000
SALES (corp-wide): 17.82MM **Privately Held**
Web: www.eastersealscrossroads.org
SIC: 7389 3599 7331 3469 Finishing services; Machine shop, jobbing and repair; Direct mail advertising services; Metal stampings, nec
PA: Crossroads Rehabilitation Center, Inc.
   4740 Kingsway Dr
   Indianapolis IN 46205
   317 466-1000

(G-7911)
CROSSROAD FREIGHT LLC
12255 Country Side Dr (46229-3084)
PHONE.................239 248-4058
EMP: 1
SALES (est): 60.08K **Privately Held**
SIC: 3537 Trucks, tractors, loaders, carriers, and similar equipment

(G-7912)
CROSSWIND PHARMACY ✿
4838 Fletcher Ave (46203-1642)
PHONE.................812 381-4815
EMP: 7 **EST:** 2022
SALES (est): 78.58K **Privately Held**
SIC: 2834 Pharmaceutical preparations

(G-7913)
CROW WELDING AND FABRICATION
2410 W County Line Rd (46217-4663)
PHONE.................317 619-3190
Robbie Crowley, *Prin*
EMP: 1 **EST:** 2017
SALES (est): 25.09K **Privately Held**
Web: www.crowwelding.com
SIC: 7692 3441 Welding repair; Fabricated structural metal

(G-7914)
CROWN TECHNOLOGY INC
7513 E 96th St (46256)
P.O. Box 50426 (46250)
PHONE.................317 845-0045
Joseph C Peterson, *Pr*
Marilyn L Peterson, *
▲ **EMP:** 35 **EST:** 1946
SQ FT: 65,000
SALES (est): 5.8MM **Privately Held**
Web: www.crowntech.com
SIC: 2899 2819 6794 Foam charge mixtures; Iron (ferric/ferrous) compounds or salts; Patent buying, licensing, leasing

(G-7915)
CRUST N MORE INC
6815 E 34th St (46226-6125)
PHONE.................317 890-7878
Mick R Holt, *Pr*
EMP: 14 **EST:** 1998
SQ FT: 19,000
SALES (est): 1.29MM **Privately Held**
SIC: 2041 Pizza mixes

(G-7916)
CRYOVAC LLC
Also Called: Cryovac Division
7950 Allison Ave (46268-1612)
PHONE.................317 876-4100
Dennis Nuhfer, *Prin*
EMP: 47
SALES (corp-wide): 5.49B **Publicly Held**
Web: www.sealedair.com
SIC: 3086 Packaging and shipping materials, foamed plastics
HQ: Cryovac, Llc
   2415 Cascade Pointe Blvd
   Charlotte NC 28208
   980 430-7000

(G-7917)
CS WARRIOR ENTERPRISE LLC
5868 E 71st St (46220-4075)
PHONE.................317 528-0152
EMP: 5
SALES (est): 303.83K **Privately Held**
SIC: 3799 Transportation equipment, nec

(G-7918)
CSR ASSOCIATES LLC
Also Called: Cynthia Rogers
5315 N Pennsylvania St (46220-3058)
PHONE.................317 255-2247
Cynthia S Rogers, *Managing Member*
EMP: 1 **EST:** 1987
SALES (est): 130.1K **Privately Held**
Web: www.rogershomeindiana.com
SIC: 2599 Hotel furniture

Indianapolis - Marion County (G-7919)

(G-7919)
CTB HAULING SERVICE LLC
6511 Crandall Cir (46260-4331)
PHONE.................................317 760-3308
EMP: 1 EST: 2021
SALES (est): 54.62K Privately Held
SIC: 3799 Transportation equipment, nec

(G-7920)
CUDA II INC (PA) ◆
1910 S Girls School Rd (46241-3637)
PHONE.................................317 514-0885
James Brown Senior, CEO
James Brown Junior, Sec
EMP: 6 EST: 2022
SALES (est): 2.57MM
SALES (corp-wide): 2.57MM Privately Held
SIC: 3365 Aerospace castings, aluminum

(G-7921)
CUDA II INC
Midwest Aircraft Machine & Tl
1910 S Girls School Rd (46241-3637)
PHONE.................................317 839-1515
Megan Hemmelgarn, Brnch Mgr
EMP: 15
SALES (corp-wide): 2.57MM Privately Held
Web: www.aerospaceproducts.com
SIC: 3724 3728 Aircraft engines and engine parts; Aircraft parts and equipment, nec
PA: Cuda Ii Inc.
  1910 S Girls School Rd
  Indianapolis IN 46241
  317 514-0885

(G-7922)
CUMMINS - ALLISON CORP
Also Called: Cummins-Allison
5696 W 74th St (46278-1752)
PHONE.................................317 872-6244
TOLL FREE: 800
Mark Winter, Mgr
EMP: 6
SALES (corp-wide): 1.39B Publicly Held
Web: www.cranepi.com
SIC: 5044 7629 3519 Office equipment; Business machine repair, electric; Internal combustion engines, nec
HQ: Cummins-Allison Corp.
  852 Feehanville Dr
  Mount Prospect IL 60056
  800 786-5528

(G-7923)
CUMMINS CROSSPOINT LLC
Also Called: OEM Solution Center
4557 W Bradbury Ave Ste 3 (46241-5236)
PHONE.................................317 484-2146
John Canellas, Brnch Mgr
EMP: 29
SALES (corp-wide): 34.06B Publicly Held
Web: www.cummins.com
SIC: 5084 3519 Engines and parts, diesel; Internal combustion engines, nec
HQ: Cummins Crosspoint Llc
  111 Monument Cir Ste 601
  Indianapolis IN 46204
  317 243-7979

(G-7924)
CUMMINS CROSSPOINT LLC
Also Called: Crosspoint Solutions
3621 W Morris St (46241-2703)
PHONE.................................317 244-7251
EMP: 44
SALES (corp-wide): 34.06B Publicly Held
Web: www.cummins.com
SIC: 5084 3519 Engines and parts, diesel; Internal combustion engines, nec
HQ: Cummins Crosspoint Llc
  111 Monument Cir Ste 601
  Indianapolis IN 46204
  317 243-7979

(G-7925)
CUMMINS CROSSPOINT LLC (HQ)
Also Called: Cummins
111 Monument Cir Ste 601 (46204-5136)
PHONE.................................317 243-7979
R David Smitson, Pr
Jay Goad, *
Mike Patterson, Prin
Edward Afriel, *
John R Smitson, *
EMP: 28 EST: 1981
SALES (est): 95.6MM
SALES (corp-wide): 34.06B Publicly Held
Web: www.cummins.com
SIC: 5084 7538 5063 3519 Engines and parts, diesel; Diesel engine repair: automotive; Generators; Internal combustion engines, nec
PA: Cummins Inc.
  500 Jackson St
  Columbus IN 47201
  812 377-5000

(G-7926)
CUMMINS CUMBERLAND INC
Also Called: Cummins
2601 Fortune Cir E Ste 300c (46241-5548)
P.O. Box 3005 (46206-3005)
PHONE.................................317 243-7979
▲ EMP: 330
SIC: 5084 7538 3519 Engines and parts, diesel; Diesel engine repair: automotive; Internal combustion engines, nec

(G-7927)
CUMMINS INC
Also Called: Cummins Sales and Service
301 E Market St (46204-2997)
PHONE.................................317 610-2493
Angela Harker, Brnch Mgr
EMP: 11
SALES (corp-wide): 34.06B Publicly Held
Web: www.cummins.com
SIC: 3714 3694 3621 3519 Motor vehicle parts and accessories; Engine electrical equipment; Generator sets: gasoline, diesel, or dual-fuel; Engines, diesel and semi-diesel or dual-fuel
PA: Cummins Inc.
  500 Jackson St
  Columbus IN 47201
  812 377-5000

(G-7928)
CUMMINS INC
3621 W Morris St (46241-2703)
PHONE.................................317 244-7251
Betty Gilbert, Brnch Mgr
EMP: 6
SALES (corp-wide): 34.06B Publicly Held
Web: www.cummins.com
SIC: 3519 3714 3694 3621 Internal combustion engines, nec; Motor vehicle parts and accessories; Engine electrical equipment; Generator sets: gasoline, diesel, or dual-fuel
PA: Cummins Inc.
  500 Jackson St
  Columbus IN 47201
  812 377-5000

(G-7929)
CURATED LUXE CO LLC
5928 Keensburg Dr (46228-1398)
PHONE.................................317 797-1531
EMP: 1
SALES (est): 69.27K Privately Held
SIC: 3999 Shades, lamp or candle

(G-7930)
CUSTOM INTERIOR DYNAMICS LLC
Also Called: Custom Interior Dynamics
3314 Prospect St (46203-2234)
PHONE.................................317 632-0477
EMP: 10 EST: 2003
SQ FT: 40,000
SALES (est): 951.27K Privately Held
Web: www.custominteriordynamics.com
SIC: 2431 3446 7389 Interior and ornamental woodwork and trim; Architectural metalwork; Interior decorating

(G-7931)
CUSTOM KEEPSAKES MACHINE EMB
915 Tanninger Dr (46239-9474)
PHONE.................................317 894-5506
Kathleen Harrison, Prin
EMP: 5 EST: 2015
SALES (est): 96.95K Privately Held
Web: www.customkeepsakes.com
SIC: 3599 Industrial machinery, nec

(G-7932)
CUSTOM OUTFITTED PROTECTION
9309 Memorial Park Dr 1b (46216-2262)
PHONE.................................317 373-2092
Jeffrey Weaver, Prin
EMP: 4 EST: 2013
SALES (est): 108.17K Privately Held
SIC: 3842 Ear plugs

(G-7933)
CUSTOM PACKAGING INC
7248 Haverhill Ct (46250-2442)
PHONE.................................317 876-9559
Bert Wilhoite, Pr
EMP: 13 EST: 1985
SQ FT: 44,800
SALES (est): 467.91K Privately Held
Web: www.brownandpratt.com
SIC: 2653 2759 2671 Boxes, corrugated: made from purchased materials; Commercial printing, nec; Paper; coated and laminated packaging

(G-7934)
CUSTOM PALLET RECYCL TRNSP LLC
2222 Hillside Ave (46218-3632)
PHONE.................................317 903-4447
Darian Coons, Prin
EMP: 2 EST: 2012
SALES (est): 175.16K Privately Held
Web: www.custompalletrecycling.com
SIC: 2448 Pallets, wood

(G-7935)
CUSTOM PRINTS AND TEES LLC
7915 S Emerson Ave (46237)
PHONE.................................317 891-4550
EMP: 4 EST: 2019
SALES (est): 249.42K Privately Held
SIC: 2759 Screen printing

(G-7936)
CUSTOM WOODWORK DESIGN LLC
6303 N Oakland Ave (46220-4430)
PHONE.................................317 254-1358
Andrew Bowers, Prin
EMP: 6 EST: 2015
SALES (est): 60.91K Privately Held
SIC: 2499 Wood products, nec

(G-7937)
CUTS INC ◆
830 Massachusetts Ave Ste 1500 (46204)
PHONE.................................408 334-3134
Josh Israel, Prin
EMP: 2 EST: 2023
SALES (est): 87.69K Privately Held
SIC: 7372 Prepackaged software

(G-7938)
CYBERIA LTD
Also Called: Club Cyberia
6800 E 30th St (46219-1104)
PHONE.................................317 721-2582
Jason Voyles, Ch
Jason Voyles, Ch Bd
David Norris, Pr
Franklin Robison, Treas
Austin Owens, Sec
EMP: 5 EST: 2011
SALES (est): 235.3K Privately Held
Web: www.clubcyberia.org
SIC: 8331 8322 3541 7371 Sheltered workshop; Community center; Home workshop machine tools, metalworking; Custom computer programming services

(G-7939)
CYBERNAUT INDUSTRIA LLC
7640 Gunyon Dr (46237-9388)
PHONE.................................317 664-5316
Ryan Eldridge, Pr
EMP: 6 EST: 2016
SALES (est): 508.57K Privately Held
SIC: 7379 5999 1731 3571 Computer related consulting services; Electronic parts and equipment; Computer installation; Personal computers (microcomputers)

(G-7940)
CZECH INDUSTRIES LLC
10 S New Jersey St Ste 300 (46204-2633)
PHONE.................................317 946-1380
Lena Hackett, Owner
EMP: 5 EST: 2018
SALES (est): 43.66K Privately Held
SIC: 3999 Manufacturing industries, nec

(G-7941)
D & S MACHINE INC
10640 Deme Dr Ste R (46236-4713)
PHONE.................................317 826-2900
Martin Patterson, Pr
Monet Patterson, VP
EMP: 7 EST: 1992
SQ FT: 4,000
SALES (est): 772.99K Privately Held
SIC: 3599 Machine shop, jobbing and repair

(G-7942)
D & S METAL FAB & WELDING LLC
6217 S Carroll Rd (46259-1019)
PHONE.................................317 862-2503
Karl Vanderbur, Prin
EMP: 1 EST: 2007
SALES (est): 80.97K Privately Held
SIC: 7692 Welding repair

(G-7943)
D D MCKAY AND ASSOCIATES
Also Called: Next Day Signs
4068 Pendleton Way (46226-5224)
PHONE.................................317 546-7446
David Mckay, Pr
EMP: 3 EST: 1988
SQ FT: 1,600
SALES (est): 205.72K Privately Held
Web: www.nextdaysignsindianapolis.com

GEOGRAPHIC SECTION

Indianapolis - Marion County (G-7969)

SIC: 3993 Signs, not made in custom sign painting shops

(G-7944)
D M SALES & ENGINEERING INC
1325 Sunday Dr (46217-9334)
PHONE..................................317 783-5493
David D Mickel, Pr
Richard Mickel, *
Patricia A Mickel, *
▼ EMP: 24 EST: 1973
SQ FT: 20,000
SALES (est): 1.76MM Privately Held
Web: www.dmsales-eng.com
SIC: 3089 Injection molding of plastics

(G-7945)
DACCO/DETROIT INDIANA INC
514 W Merrill St (46225-1129)
PHONE..................................317 545-5334
Pat Mills, Prin
EMP: 4 EST: 2003
SALES (est): 261.08K Privately Held
SIC: 3714 Motor vehicle parts and accessories

(G-7946)
DAECHANG SEAT CO LTD USA
8150 Woodland Dr (46278-1347)
PHONE..................................317 755-3663
Kyoung Min Cho, CEO
Wi-in Cho, Pr
EMP: 50 EST: 2016
SALES (est): 120.25MM Privately Held
SIC: 3714 Motor vehicle parts and accessories
PA: Daechang Seat Co., Ltd.
70-62 Munsan 2sandan 1-Ro, Oedong-Eup
Gyeongju 38206

(G-7947)
DAMOR & CO LLC
3812 Screech Owl Cir (46228-1512)
PHONE..................................317 790-8360
Tara Stubbs, CEO
EMP: 1 EST: 2019
SALES (est): 63.4K Privately Held
Web: www.damorandco.com
SIC: 2844 3999 2834 Face creams or lotions; Candles; Lip balms

(G-7948)
DANCE SOPHISTICATES INC
1605 Prospect St (46203-2024)
PHONE..................................317 634-7728
Denise L Dennis, Prin
EMP: 40 EST: 1983
SQ FT: 3,000
SALES (est): 2.98MM Privately Held
Web: www.dancesoph.com
SIC: 2389 2339 2326 Uniforms and vestments; Women's and misses' outerwear, nec; Men's and boy's work clothing

(G-7949)
DARDEN CORPORATION CORP
7847 Swallowtail Dr (46214-2410)
PHONE..................................317 376-5724
Gary A Darden, CEO
EMP: 1 EST: 2018
SALES (est): 48.48K Privately Held
Web: www.darden.com
SIC: 2844 Perfumes, cosmetics and other toilet preparations

(G-7950)
DARK SOURCE RECORDS LLC
5017 E 41st St (46226-4515)
PHONE..................................616 378-6060
Elijah Jackson, Admn
Elijah Jackson, Managing Member
Tim Clay, Treas
EMP: 2 EST: 2012
SALES (est): 74.65K Privately Held
SIC: 2741 7389 Music, sheet: publishing and printing; Business Activities at Non-Commercial Site

(G-7951)
DARLING INGREDIENTS INC
700 W Southern Ave (46225-2062)
P.O. Box 33639 (46203-0639)
PHONE..................................317 784-4486
Tony Croteau, Mgr
EMP: 24
SALES (corp-wide): 6.79B Publicly Held
Web: www.darlingii.com
SIC: 2077 Animal and marine fats and oils
PA: Darling Ingredients Inc.
5601 N Macarthur Blvd
Irving TX 75038
972 717-0300

(G-7952)
DARLINGTON COOKIE COMPANY (PA)
Also Called: Darlington Farms
10475 Crosspoint Blvd Ste 110 (46256)
PHONE..................................800 754-2202
EMP: 8 EST: 1995
SALES (est): 9.2MM Privately Held
Web: www.darlingtonsnacks.com
SIC: 2052 5149 Cookies; Crackers, cookies, and bakery products

(G-7953)
DASH CAM FUSION LLC
8465 Keystone Xing Ste 115 (46240-4355)
PHONE..................................708 365-8553
Gregory Trotter, CEO
EMP: 1 EST: 2021
SALES (est): 56.09K Privately Held
SIC: 7389 3651 4212 Business Activities at Non-Commercial Site; Video camera-audio recorders, household use; Delivery service, vehicular

(G-7954)
DAVID FLEMING
Also Called: FLEming&sonz
1409 Butternut Ln (46234-1912)
PHONE..................................414 202-6586
David Fleming, Owner
EMP: 5 EST: 2020
SALES (est): 187.69K Privately Held
SIC: 2599 Food wagons, restaurant

(G-7955)
DAVIS INDUSTRIES INC
4090 Westover Dr (46268-1843)
PHONE..................................317 871-0103
Thomas W Davis, Pr
EMP: 8 EST: 2006
SALES (est): 512.87K Privately Held
SIC: 3999 Manufacturing industries, nec

(G-7956)
DBC IMAGING
Also Called: Speedpro Imaging
5583 W 74th St (46268-4184)
PHONE..................................317 757-5298
Diane Cutter, Owner
EMP: 3 EST: 2012
SALES (est): 212.08K Privately Held
Web: www.speedpro.com
SIC: 3993 Signs and advertising specialties

(G-7957)
DBISP LLC (PA)
Also Called: Dbfederal
777 Beachway Dr Ste 102 (46224)
PHONE..................................317 222-1671
John Miller, Pr
EMP: 5 EST: 2005
SQ FT: 2,585
SALES (est): 3.99MM Privately Held
Web: www.dbispllc.com
SIC: 5072 4212 3577 5112 Hardware; Dump truck haulage; Computer peripheral equipment, nec; Office supplies, nec

(G-7958)
DC CONSTRUCTION SERVICES INC
9465 Counselors Row (46240)
PHONE..................................317 577-0276
Dustin Calhoun, Pr
Christopher M Wirth, *
EMP: 50 EST: 2013
SALES (est): 8.36MM Privately Held
Web: www.dccpaving.com
SIC: 1542 2951 Commercial and office buildings, renovation and repair; Asphalt paving mixtures and blocks

(G-7959)
DEBERRY MGT & CONSULTING LLC
10475 Crosspoint Blvd Ste 250 (46256)
PHONE..................................317 767-4703
Tamicka Deberry, Managing Member
EMP: 1 EST: 2018
SALES (est): 92.81K Privately Held
SIC: 8742 7372 Management consulting services; Application computer software

(G-7960)
DECO COATINGS INC
1428 W Henry St Ste B1 (46221-1272)
PHONE..................................317 889-9290
EMP: 20 EST: 1991
SALES (est): 2.49MM Privately Held
Web: www.decocoatings.com
SIC: 1721 2851 Residential painting; Coating, air curing

(G-7961)
DEEM & LOUREIRO INC
8111 Bayberry Ct (46250-1629)
PHONE..................................770 652-9871
Edwina Loureiro, Prin
Edwina Loureiro, CEO
Karen Deem, COO
EMP: 2 EST: 1999
SALES (est): 171.55K Privately Held
Web: www.dlicreative.com
SIC: 7389 2541 8712 7336 Interior design services; Cabinets, except refrigerated: show, display, etc.: wood; Architectural engineering; Art design services

(G-7962)
DEFLECTO LLC (DH)
7035 E 86th St (46250-1547)
P.O. Box 50057 (46250-0057)
PHONE..................................317 849-9555
Paul Thompson, CEO
Thomas H Quinn, Pr
Keith Huffman, VP Opers
Wayne Daege, Treas
Lisa M Ondrula, Sec
◆ EMP: 300 EST: 1960
SALES (est): 185.36MM
SALES (corp-wide): 475.79MM Privately Held
Web: www.deflecto.com
SIC: 3089 2542 Plastics hardware and building products; Office and store showcases and display fixtures
HQ: Jordan Specialty Plastics, Inc.
1751 Lake Cook Rd Ste 550
Deerfield IL 60015

(G-7963)
DELP PRINTING & MAILING INC
7750 Zionsville Rd Ste 200 (46268-2195)
PHONE..................................317 872-9744
Lorie Darland, Pr
EMP: 8 EST: 1968
SQ FT: 7,200
SALES (est): 466.93K Privately Held
Web: www.delpprintingandmailing.com
SIC: 7331 2752 Mailing service; Commercial printing, lithographic

(G-7964)
DENVER MARKETING CO LLC
8235 E 96th St Ste 110 (46256-1090)
P.O. Box 80202 (46280-0202)
PHONE..................................866 692-2326
EMP: 3 EST: 2018
SALES (est): 120.81K Privately Held
SIC: 8742 2023 Marketing consulting services; Dietary supplements, dairy and non-dairy based

(G-7965)
DEONTA WALKER
Also Called: Mis Amores
5528 Dollar Hide North Dr (46221-4108)
PHONE..................................317 970-3586
Deonta Walker, Owner
EMP: 5 EST: 2021
SALES (est): 209.53K Privately Held
SIC: 2099 2499 5963 5812 Food preparations, nec; Food handling and processing products, wood; Food services, direct sales; Contract food services

(G-7966)
DEPENDABLE MACHINE COMPANY
1846 E 30th St (46218-2699)
PHONE..................................317 924-5378
Cory Lowe, Pr
Cheryl Lowe, *
EMP: 25 EST: 1956
SQ FT: 32,000
SALES (est): 2.45MM Privately Held
Web: www.dependablemachineinc.com
SIC: 3599 Machine shop, jobbing and repair

(G-7967)
DETROIT SALT COMPANY LC
1575 W Senate Ave (46201)
PHONE..................................313 841-5144
EMP: 1
SALES (corp-wide): 5MM Privately Held
Web: www.detroitsalt.com
SIC: 1481 Nonmetallic mineral services
HQ: The Detroit Salt Company L C
12841 Sanders St
Detroit MI 48217
313 554-0456

(G-7968)
DEVELOPMENTAL NATURAL RES
8750 Sugar Pine Pt (46256-4350)
PHONE..................................317 543-4886
EMP: 9 EST: 1993
SQ FT: 15,000
SALES (est): 871.88K Privately Held
Web: www.dnrsite.com
SIC: 2833 Botanical products, medicinal: ground, graded, or milled

(G-7969)
DIALING INNOVATIONS LLC
6401 S East St Ste C (46227-2109)
PHONE..................................877 523-5384
EMP: 10 EST: 2011

Indianapolis - Marion County (G-7970) — GEOGRAPHIC SECTION

SALES (est): 929.19K **Privately Held**
Web: www.dialinginnovations.com
SIC: 7372 Prepackaged software

(G-7970)
DIAMOND MINING LEAD
929 Evening Dr Ste A (46201)
PHONE.................................317 340-7760
Brian D Williams, *Owner*
EMP: 2 EST: 2008
SALES (est): 170K **Privately Held**
SIC: 1081 Metal mining services

(G-7971)
DIAMOND STATE NATURALS LLC
10783 Caval Cade Ct (46234-7658)
PHONE.................................479 970-4755
EMP: 1 EST: 2021
SALES (est): 47.23K **Privately Held**
SIC: 2844 Cosmetic preparations

(G-7972)
DIAMONDS & PEARLS TRNSP LLC
4368 N Audubon Rd (46226-3321)
PHONE.................................504 295-2701
Colessie Halliburton, *CEO*
EMP: 2 EST: 2021
SALES (est): 95.58K **Privately Held**
SIC: 3537 Trucks: freight, baggage, etc.: industrial, except mining

(G-7973)
DIENG GROUP LLC
Also Called: Senefoods
3167 N Delaware St (46205-3918)
PHONE.................................317 699-1909
EMP: 3 EST: 2016
SALES (est): 57.09K **Privately Held**
SIC: 8748 5145 5149 2032 Business consulting, nec; Snack foods; Dried or canned foods; Ethnic foods, canned, jarred, etc.

(G-7974)
DIGIOP INC
9340 Priority Way West Dr (46240-1468)
PHONE.................................800 968-3606
Rich Mellott, *Pr*
EMP: 35 EST: 2009
SALES (est): 4.95MM **Privately Held**
Web: www.digiop.com
SIC: 3699 Electrical equipment and supplies, nec

(G-7975)
DIMPLEX NORTH AMERICA LIMITED
221 S Franklin Rd Ste 300 (46219-7735)
PHONE.................................317 890-0809
Martyn Camp, *Brnch Mgr*
EMP: 10
SALES (corp-wide): 115.07MM **Privately Held**
Web: www.glendimplexamericas.com
SIC: 3822 Electric heat controls
PA: Glen Dimplex Americas Limited
1367 Industrial Rd Unit 2
Cambridge ON N3H 4
888 346-7539

(G-7976)
DINTEC AGRICHEMICALS
9330 Zionsville Rd (46268-1053)
PHONE.................................317 337-7870
Dow Agrosciences, *Pt*
I Pi Ci, *Pt*
◆ EMP: 2 EST: 1994
SALES (est): 317.63K **Privately Held**
SIC: 2879 Agricultural chemicals, nec

(G-7977)
DISTINCT IMAGES INC
6830 Hawthorn Park Dr (46220-3909)
PHONE.................................317 613-4413
James Pike, *Pr*
EMP: 19 EST: 2001
SQ FT: 5,000
SALES (est): 2.2MM **Privately Held**
Web: www.distinctimages.net
SIC: 2759 Promotional printing

(G-7978)
DIVERS SUPPLY COMPANY INC
Also Called: Ikelite Underwater Systems
50 W 33rd St (46208-4638)
P.O. Box 88100 (46208-0100)
PHONE.................................317 923-4523
Jean M Brigham, *Pr*
Duane Brigham, *
Boyd J E, *
▼ EMP: 80 EST: 1959
SQ FT: 20,000
SALES (est): 8.78MM **Privately Held**
Web: www.ikelite.com
SIC: 3949 Skin diving equipment, scuba type

(G-7979)
DIVERSE FABRICATION SVCS LLC
1721 S Franklin Rd Ste 100 (46239-2170)
PHONE.................................317 781-8800
Kristofer C Deckard, *Prin*
EMP: 6 EST: 2010
SALES (est): 503.27K **Privately Held**
Web: www.diversefabrication.com
SIC: 3599 Machine shop, jobbing and repair

(G-7980)
DIVERSE MACHINE SERVICES LLC
2705 Chamberlin Dr (46227-4423)
PHONE.................................317 670-1381
Humberto Alejandro Moguel, *Pr*
EMP: 6 EST: 2020
SALES (est): 276.78K **Privately Held**
Web: www.diversemachineservices.com
SIC: 3599 7389 Machine shop, jobbing and repair; Business Activities at Non-Commercial Site

(G-7981)
DIVERSE SALES SOLUTIONS LLC
4947 Oakbrook Ct (46254-1116)
PHONE.................................317 514-2403
Sterling Davis, *Prin*
Peter Le, *Prin*
EMP: 4 EST: 2013
SALES (est): 177.87K **Privately Held**
Web: www.nfmindy.com
SIC: 2396 2752 2796 7389 Fabric printing and stamping; Offset printing; Engraving on copper, steel, wood, or rubber: printing plates; Business Activities at Non-Commercial Site

(G-7982)
DIVERSE TECH SERVICES INC
Also Called: Diverse Managed Services
7135 Waldemar Dr (46268-4158)
PHONE.................................317 432-6444
Clyde Harris, *Pr*
George Apgar, *Sec*
Rj Mcconnell, *Pr*
EMP: 43 EST: 2013
SALES (est): 5.42MM **Privately Held**
Web: www.diversetechservices.com
SIC: 7371 7372 7373 7378 Computer software systems analysis and design, custom; Business oriented computer software; Computer systems analysis and design; Computer peripheral equipment repair and maintenance

(G-7983)
DIVERSFIED CMMNCTONS GROUP INC
Also Called: Digital Color Graphics
5550 N Delaware St (46220)
PHONE.................................317 755-3191
EMP: 13 EST: 1984
SALES (est): 2.4MM **Privately Held**
Web: www.dcgindy.com
SIC: 2752 Offset printing

(G-7984)
DIVERSIFIED BUS SYSTEMS INC
1398 N Shadeland Ave Ste 2233 (46219-3619)
PHONE.................................317 254-8668
Joe Cremer, *Pr*
EMP: 4 EST: 1986
SALES (est): 832.04K **Privately Held**
Web: www.diversifiedbus.com
SIC: 5112 2732 2752 2759 Business forms; Book printing; Offset printing; Catalogs: printing, nsk

(G-7985)
DIVERSIFIED OPHTHALMICS INC
4555 Independence Sq (46203-5591)
PHONE.................................317 780-1677
EMP: 42
Web: www.abboptical.com
SIC: 5048 3851 3229 Ophthalmic goods; Ophthalmic goods; Pressed and blown glass, nec
HQ: Diversified Ophthalmics, Inc.
250 Mccullough St
Cincinnati OH
800 852-8089

(G-7986)
DIVERSITY PRESS LLC
4026 W 10th St (46222-3203)
PHONE.................................317 241-4234
EMP: 9 EST: 2011
SALES (est): 208.01K **Privately Held**
Web: www.diversity-press.com
SIC: 2752 Offset printing

(G-7987)
DIVSYS AEROSPACE & ENGRG LLC
Also Called: Divaero
8174 Zionsville Rd (46268-1625)
PHONE.................................317 941-7777
Stanley Bentley, *CEO*
Stanley Loren Bentley, *Prin*
Stanley Eric Bentley, *Prin*
EMP: 16 EST: 2018
SALES (est): 1.7MM **Privately Held**
Web: www.divaero.com
SIC: 7373 8734 3679 7389 Computer-aided design (CAD) systems service; Assaying service; Electronic components, nec; Brokers, contract services

(G-7988)
DIVSYS INTL - ICAPE LLC
8102 Zionsville Rd (46268-1625)
PHONE.................................317 405-9427
EMP: 40 EST: 2010
SQ FT: 20,000
SALES (est): 9.68MM
SALES (corp-wide): 5.51MM **Privately Held**
Web: www.icape-group.com
SIC: 3672 8734 Printed circuit boards; Testing laboratories
PA: Icape Holding
33 17 Avenue Du General Leclerc
Fontenay-Aux-Roses 92260
158183910

(G-7989)
DIXIE LEE DRAPERY CO INC
2434 Madison Ave (46225-2107)
PHONE.................................317 783-9869
Dixie Lee, *Pr*
EMP: 1 EST: 1990
SALES (est): 82.19K **Privately Held**
SIC: 5714 2391 Draperies; Curtains and draperies

(G-7990)
DIXIE METAL SPINNING CORP
4730 Industrial Pkwy (46226-2900)
PHONE.................................317 541-1330
David Terhune, *Pr*
Jack Proctor, *Sec*
EMP: 4 EST: 1945
SQ FT: 14,400
SALES (est): 354.27K **Privately Held**
Web: www.dixiemetalspinning.com
SIC: 3469 5051 Spinning metal for the trade; Ferrous metals

(G-7991)
DJ WREATH CREATIONS LLC
6829 Meadowgreen Dr (46236-8014)
PHONE.................................317 723-3268
Diane J Fischer, *Admn*
EMP: 5 EST: 2013
SALES (est): 147.2K **Privately Held**
SIC: 3999 Wreaths, artificial

(G-7992)
DLB TRANSPORTERS LLC
3043 N White River Parkway East Dr (46208)
PHONE.................................317 667-3368
EMP: 2 EST: 2021
SALES (est): 80.88K **Privately Held**
SIC: 3537 7389 Trucks, tractors, loaders, carriers, and similar equipment; Business Activities at Non-Commercial Site

(G-7993)
DMG MORI USA INC
6848 Hillsdale Ct (46250-2001)
PHONE.................................317 913-0978
Brian Mcgirk, *Pr*
EMP: 8
Web: en.dmgmori.com
SIC: 3541 Machine tools, metal cutting type
HQ: Dmg Mori Usa, Inc.
2400 Huntington Blvd
Hoffman Estates IL 60192
847 593-5400

(G-7994)
DOERR PRINTING CO
4222 E 18th St (46218-4576)
PHONE.................................317 568-0135
Jan Doerr, *Prin*
EMP: 3 EST: 1986
SALES (est): 256.8K **Privately Held**
Web: www.doerrprinting.com
SIC: 2752 2791 2789 2759 Offset printing; Typesetting; Bookbinding and related work; Commercial printing, nec

(G-7995)
DOG EAR PUBLISHING
8888 Keystone Xing Ste 1300 (46240-4600)
P.O. Box 3548 (46082-3548)
PHONE.................................317 228-3656
Nelson Miles, *Publisher*
EMP: 10 EST: 2018
SALES (est): 467.54K **Privately Held**
Web: www.dogearpublishing.net
SIC: 2741 Miscellaneous publishing

GEOGRAPHIC SECTION   Indianapolis - Marion County (G-8022)

(G-7996)
DONALD LLOYD
Also Called: Don's Truck -N- Go
2040 Theodore Dr (46214-4211)
PHONE.................................937 304-5683
Donald Lloyd, *Owner*
EMP: 1 **EST:** 2007
SALES (est): 78.04K **Privately Held**
SIC: 3792 Travel trailers and campers

(G-7997)
DORMAKABA USA INC
6161 E 75th St (46250)
PHONE.................................317 806-4605
Richard Monahan, *Brnch Mgr*
EMP: 750
Web: www.dormakaba.com
SIC: 3429 3446 Door locks, bolts, and checks; Railings, banisters, guards, etc. made from metal pipe
HQ: Dormakaba Usa Inc.
     100 Dorma Dr
     Reamstown PA 17567
     717 336-3881

(G-7998)
DOTSTAFF LLC
Also Called: Dotstaff
9800 Crosspoint Blvd (46256-3552)
PHONE.................................317 806-6100
Joseph Bielawski, *Managing Member*
Dave Stenger, *
EMP: 40 **EST:** 2005
SALES (est): 4.31MM **Privately Held**
Web: www.knowledgeservices.com
SIC: 7372 Prepackaged software

(G-7999)
DOVE PRINTING SERVICES INC
7410 E 33rd St (46226-6271)
PHONE.................................317 469-7546
Andrew Dove, *Owner*
EMP: 2 **EST:** 1997
SALES (est): 136.75K **Privately Held**
Web: www.doveprint.com
SIC: 2752 Offset printing

(G-8000)
DOW AGROSCIENCES LLC
Also Called: DOW AGROSCIENCES LLC
5110 E 69th St (46220-3830)
PHONE.................................317 252-5602
EMP: 42
SALES (corp-wide): 17.23B **Publicly Held**
Web: www.corteva.com
SIC: 2879 Agricultural chemicals, nec
HQ: Corteva Agriscience Llc
     9330 Zionsville Rd
     Indianapolis IN 46268

(G-8001)
DOW CHEMICAL COMPANY
Also Called: Dow Chemical
9330 Zionsville Rd (46268-1053)
PHONE.................................317 337-3819
Carl De Amicis, *CEO*
EMP: 197
SALES (corp-wide): 44.62B **Publicly Held**
Web: www.dow.com
SIC: 2899 Chemical preparations, nec
HQ: The Dow Chemical Company
     2211 H H Dow Way
     Midland MI 48674
     989 636-1000

(G-8002)
DOW ELANCO SCIENCES
9330 Zionsville Rd (46268-1080)
PHONE.................................317 337-3691
Jim Gidley, *Dir*

EMP: 2 **EST:** 2000
SALES (est): 493.17K **Privately Held**
Web: www.corteva.com
SIC: 2879 Agricultural chemicals, nec

(G-8003)
DOWNEY CREATIONS LLC
1811 Executive Dr Ste R (46241-4361)
PHONE.................................317 248-9888
Alan Heritier, *
EMP: 11 **EST:** 1993
SALES (est): 1.52MM **Privately Held**
SIC: 5094 3911 Diamonds (gems); Jewel settings and mountings, precious metal

(G-8004)
DPICT IMAGING INC
7400 N Shadeland Ave Ste 255 (46250-2084)
PHONE.................................317 436-8411
EMP: 5 **EST:** 2004
SALES (est): 769.2K **Privately Held**
Web: www.dpictimaging.com
SIC: 3672 Printed circuit boards

(G-8005)
DRAKE CORPORATION
9930 E 56th St (46236-2810)
PHONE.................................636 464-5070
Greg Harris, *Southern Regional Manager*
EMP: 10
SQ FT: 6,000
SALES (corp-wide): 6.04MM **Privately Held**
Web: www.drakescomeplay.com
SIC: 3545 3546 Drill bits, metalworking; Saws and sawing equipment
PA: Drake Corporation
     1180 Wernsing Rd
     Jasper IN 47546
     636 464-5070

(G-8006)
DRAPER MANUFACTURING LLC
Also Called: Draper Manufacturing
4008 W 10th St (46222-3203)
PHONE.................................317 347-5195
EMP: 9
Web: www.drapermfg.com
SIC: 3523 Cabs, tractors, and agricultural machinery

(G-8007)
DRIBOT LLC
203 W Morris St (46225-1440)
PHONE.................................317 885-6330
EMP: 1 **EST:** 2018
SALES (est): 235.3K **Privately Held**
Web: www.dribot.com
SIC: 2899 Distilled water

(G-8008)
DRINAN RACING PRODUCTS INC
100 Gasoline Aly Ste F (46222-5916)
PHONE.................................317 486-9710
Daniel J Drinan, *Pr*
EMP: 2 **EST:** 1990
SQ FT: 3,000
SALES (est): 226.99K **Privately Held**
Web: www.drinanindustries.com
SIC: 3711 3441 3444 Automobile assembly, including specialty automobiles; Fabricated structural metal; Sheet metalwork

(G-8009)
DRINKGP LLC
5707 Brockton Dr Apt 115 (46220-5476)
PHONE.................................317 410-4748
Erin Jones, *CEO*
James Edds, *COO*

EMP: 2 **EST:** 2016
SALES (est): 68.62K **Privately Held**
SIC: 2082 7389 Malt beverages; Business Activities at Non-Commercial Site

(G-8010)
DRIVERZ FOR LIFE(D 4 L) LLC
3151 N New Jersey St (46205-3922)
PHONE.................................317 619-4513
EMP: 3
SALES (est): 124.94K **Privately Held**
SIC: 7389 3799 Business Activities at Non-Commercial Site; Transportation equipment, nec

(G-8011)
DRS GRAPHIX GROUP INC
Also Called: PIP Printing
3855 E 96th St Ste P (46240-2070)
PHONE.................................317 569-1855
Carol Sandberg, *Pr*
EMP: 4 **EST:** 2015
SALES (est): 478.56K **Privately Held**
Web: www.pip.com
SIC: 2752 7336 7373 Offset printing; Graphic arts and related design; Systems integration services

(G-8012)
DRSHOPECOM LLC
5740 Thunderbird Rd Ste C (46236-3180)
PHONE.................................800 255-1510
EMP: 4 **EST:** 2017
SALES (est): 39.59K **Privately Held**
SIC: 2023 Dietary supplements, dairy and non-dairy based

(G-8013)
DRY HEAT COFFEE LLC ✪
6255 Carrollton Ave Ste 30091 (46220-1990)
PHONE.................................760 422-9865
Joseph Shoemaker, *Managing Member*
EMP: 1 **EST:** 2023
SALES (est): 60.62K **Privately Held**
SIC: 7371 2095 Computer software development and applications; Roasted coffee

(G-8014)
DS MGMT GROUP LLC
7533 Prairie View Dr (46256-8408)
PHONE.................................317 946-8646
EMP: 1
SALES (est): 69.27K **Privately Held**
SIC: 3581 7389 Automatic vending machines; Business Activities at Non-Commercial Site

(G-8015)
DTI SERVICES LTD LIABILITY CO
Also Called: RCA Commercial Electronics
5935 W 84th St Ste A (46278-1350)
PHONE.................................765 745-0261
Kent Wilson, *CEO*
Craig Pfeifer, *CFO*
▲ **EMP:** 1 **EST:** 2009
SALES (est): 89.98K
SALES (corp-wide): 104.56MM **Publicly Held**
SIC: 5064 5065 3674 Television sets; Electronic parts and equipment, nec; Light emitting diodes
PA: Alpine 4 Holdings, Inc.
     2525 E Ariz Bltmore Cir S
     Phoenix AZ 85016
     480 702-2431

(G-8016)
DTP TRUCKING LLC
11526 Stoeppelwerth Dr (46229-4241)
PHONE.................................463 701-8508
EMP: 1 **EST:** 2021
SALES (est): 40K **Privately Held**
SIC: 3799 Transportation equipment, nec

(G-8017)
DUAL MACHINE CORPORATION
Also Called: Klincher Locknut
1951 Bloyd Ave (46218-3590)
PHONE.................................317 921-9850
John A Bratt, *Pr*
Carol Schnyder, *Sec*
EMP: 10 **EST:** 1946
SQ FT: 18,000
SALES (est): 1MM **Privately Held**
Web: www.dualmachinecorp.com
SIC: 3451 Screw machine products

(G-8018)
DUEL TOOL & GAGE INC
1553 S Concord St (46241-4542)
PHONE.................................317 244-0129
Mike D Shively, *Pr*
Brad Collins, *Sr VP*
EMP: 4 **EST:** 1993
SALES (est): 376.27K **Privately Held**
Web: www.dueltoolandgage.net
SIC: 3544 Special dies and tools

(G-8019)
DUGDALE BEEF COMPANY INC
4224 W 71st St (46268-2259)
PHONE.................................317 291-9660
EMP: 40
Web: www.dugdalefoods.com
SIC: 5149 5143 2099 5146 Groceries and related products, nec; Cheese; Salads, fresh or refrigerated; Fish, fresh

(G-8020)
DUPLICAST METALWORKS INC
1809 Cornell Ave (46202-1823)
PHONE.................................317 926-0745
Charles Simpson, *Pr*
Linda Simpson, *Sec*
EMP: 6 **EST:** 1990
SQ FT: 12,800
SALES (est): 512.63K **Privately Held**
SIC: 3365 Aluminum foundries

(G-8021)
DURM VINEYARD INC
Also Called: Buck Creek Winery
11747 Indian Creek Rd S (46259-1056)
PHONE.................................317 862-9463
Jeffrey A Durm, *Pr*
Kelly Drum, *VP*
Josett Randolph, *Sec*
EMP: 8 **EST:** 1995
SQ FT: 2,400
SALES (est): 1.51MM **Privately Held**
Web: www.buckcreekwinery.com
SIC: 5182 2084 Wine; Wines, brandy, and brandy spirits

(G-8022)
DWD TRUCKING LLC
2715 Cabin Hill Rd (46229-4021)
PHONE.................................317 586-3484
EMP: 1 **EST:** 2018
SALES (est): 150K **Privately Held**
Web: www.dwdcompany.com
SIC: 3537 Truck trailers, used in plants, docks, terminals, etc.

(PA)=Parent Co (HQ)=Headquarters
✪ = New Business established in last 2 years

Indianapolis - Marion County (G-8023) — GEOGRAPHIC SECTION

(G-8023)
DYNAMARK GRAPHICS GROUP INC (PA)
Also Called: PIP Printing
7210 Zionsville Rd (46268-2165)
PHONE.................317 328-2555
Thomas D Fulner, *Pr*
Dianne Robinson, *Sec*
EMP: 23 EST: 1971
SQ FT: 25,000
SALES (est): 4.23MM
SALES (corp-wide): 4.23MM Privately Held
Web: www.dynamarkprinting.com
SIC: 7389 7334 2752 2791 Printing broker; Photocopying and duplicating services; Offset printing; Typesetting

(G-8024)
DYNAMARK GRAPHICS GROUP INC
Also Called: PIP Printing
3855 E 96th St Ste L (46240-2070)
PHONE.................317 569-1855
EMP: 4
SALES (corp-wide): 4.23MM Privately Held
Web: www.dggink.com
SIC: 2752 Offset printing
PA: Dynamark Graphics Group, Inc.
  7210 Zionsville Rd
  Indianapolis IN 46268
  317 328-2555

(G-8025)
DYNAMIC DIES INC
2801 Fortune Cir E Ste I (46241-5551)
PHONE.................419 861-5613
EMP: 27
SALES (corp-wide): 22.27MM Privately Held
Web: www.dynamicdies.com
SIC: 3544 Special dies and tools
PA: Dynamic Dies, Inc.
  1705 Commerce Rd
  Holland OH 43528
  419 865-0249

(G-8026)
DYNAMIC DIES INC
2321 Executive Dr (46241-5008)
PHONE.................317 247-4706
Doug Ringle, *Mgr*
EMP: 27
SQ FT: 4,500
SALES (corp-wide): 22.27MM Privately Held
Web: www.dynamicdies.com
SIC: 3544 2796 Paper cutting dies; Platemaking services
PA: Dynamic Dies, Inc.
  1705 Commerce Rd
  Holland OH 43528
  419 865-0249

(G-8027)
DZ INVESTMENTS LLC
Also Called: International Metals Proc
3131 N Franklin Rd Ste E (46226-6390)
PHONE.................317 895-4141
▲ EMP: 42
SIC: 3341 5051 Secondary nonferrous metals; Steel

(G-8028)
E & H INDUSTRIAL SERVICES INC
5671 Guion Rd (46254-1515)
PHONE.................317 670-4456
Phillip Knickrehm, *Pr*
EMP: 30 EST: 2014
SALES (est): 2.62MM Privately Held
Web: www.eh-industrialservices.com
SIC: 7692 Welding repair

(G-8029)
E FAB INC
513 National Ave Ste A (46227-1282)
PHONE.................317 786-9593
Gony Eldridde, *Pr*
EMP: 3 EST: 2002
SALES (est): 256.64K Privately Held
Web: www.efabinc.biz
SIC: 3444 Sheet metalwork

(G-8030)
E-TANK LTD
999 W Troy Ave (46225-2243)
PHONE.................317 296-0510
Williams Hallene, *Brnch Mgr*
EMP: 13
SALES (corp-wide): 9.99MM Privately Held
Web: www.etank.net
SIC: 3443 Industrial vessels, tanks, and containers
PA: E-Tank, Ltd.
  3150 Millennium Blvd Se
  Massillon OH 44646
  330 837-5100

(G-8031)
EAGLE CONSULTING INC
7968 Zionsville Rd (46268-1649)
PHONE.................317 590-0485
Alyce M Miller, *Prin*
Alyce M Miller, *Pr*
Raymond T Miller, *Pr*
EMP: 6 EST: 2001
SALES (est): 650.16K Privately Held
SIC: 3559 Automotive related machinery

(G-8032)
EAGLE MAGNETIC COMPANY INC
7417 Crawfordsville Rd (46214-1571)
PHONE.................317 297-1030
Alice Coddington, *Pr*
Jerry Burton, *
Michelle Burt, *
EMP: 43 EST: 1970
SQ FT: 35,000
SALES (est): 5.12MM Privately Held
Web: www.eaglemagnetic.com
SIC: 3444 Sheet metalwork

(G-8033)
EARTH MAMA COMPOST
10830 Lafayette Rd (46278-5029)
PHONE.................317 759-4589
EMP: 3 EST: 2018
SALES (est): 74.42K Privately Held
Web: www.earthmamacompost.com
SIC: 2875 Compost

(G-8034)
EARTHCHAIN MAGNETIC PRO
9930 E 56th St (46236-2810)
PHONE.................317 803-8034
Michael Harris, *Prin*
EMP: 7 EST: 2016
SALES (est): 236.49K Privately Held
Web: www.techniksusa.com
SIC: 3545 Machine tool accessories

(G-8035)
EARTHSMARTE WATER INDIANA INC
Also Called: Water Treatment Systems
8481 Bash St Ste 1200 (46250-4525)
PHONE.................317 800-8442
Heather Denton, *Pr*
EMP: 2 EST: 2017
SALES (est): 39.42K Privately Held
Web: www.healthywaterin.com
SIC: 3589 Water treatment equipment, industrial

(G-8036)
EASLEY ENTERPRISES INC
Also Called: Easley Winery
205 N College Ave (46202-3701)
PHONE.................317 636-4516
Mark Easley, *Pr*
EMP: 1 EST: 1974
SQ FT: 20,000
SALES (est): 1.64MM Privately Held
Web: www.easleywinery.com
SIC: 2084 2085 Wine cellars, bonded: engaged in blending wines; Distilled and blended liquors

(G-8037)
EAST HEAT WOOD PELLETS LLC
217 S Belmont Ave Ste E (46222-4286)
PHONE.................317 638-4840
EMP: 2 EST: 2012
SALES (est): 212.34K Privately Held
SIC: 2299 Wool waste processing

(G-8038)
EAST PENN MANUFACTURING CO
Also Called: Deka Battery
918 S Senate Ave (46225-1456)
PHONE.................317 236-6288
EMP: 5
SALES (corp-wide): 3.51B Privately Held
Web: www.eastpennmanufacturing.com
SIC: 3694 Battery cable wiring sets for internal combustion engines
PA: East Penn Manufacturing Co.
  102 Deka Rd
  Lyon Station PA 19536
  610 682-6361

(G-8039)
EAST SIDE WELDING INC
10148 Pendleton Pike (46236-2827)
PHONE.................317 823-4065
Joanne Sensney, *Pr*
EMP: 2 EST: 1975
SALES (est): 142.89K Privately Held
Web: www.eastsidewelding.com
SIC: 7692 Welding repair

(G-8040)
EASTSIDE MACHINE SHOP INC
4500 Dunn St (46226-3938)
PHONE.................317 549-2216
Jeannie Smith, *Pt*
Denver Smith, *Pt*
EMP: 8 EST: 1989
SQ FT: 2,000
SALES (est): 846.19K Privately Held
Web: www.eastsidemachineshop.com
SIC: 3599 Machine shop, jobbing and repair

(G-8041)
EASTSIDE VICE CMNTY NEWS MDIA
195 N Shortridge Rd (46219-8908)
PHONE.................317 356-2222
Paula Nicewanger, *Owner*
EMP: 4 EST: 2009
SALES (est): 223.61K Privately Held
SIC: 2711 Newspapers, publishing and printing

(G-8042)
EAT HERE INDY LLC (PA)
5255 Winthrop Ave Ste 110 (46220)
PHONE.................317 502-4419
Bradley Houser, *Managing Member*
EMP: 1 EST: 2016
SALES (est): 256.87K
SALES (corp-wide): 256.87K Privately Held
Web: eatherestag.wpengine.com
SIC: 7372 Application computer software

(G-8043)
EATON CORPORATION
Eaton Logistics Center
7365 Winton Dr (46268-5101)
PHONE.................317 704-2520
Rob Haynes, *Brnch Mgr*
EMP: 6
Web: www.dix-eaton.com
SIC: 5063 8111 3714 3713 Electrical apparatus and equipment; Legal services; Motor vehicle parts and accessories; Truck and bus bodies
HQ: Eaton Corporation
  1000 Eaton Blvd
  Cleveland OH 44122
  440 523-5000

(G-8044)
EBWA INDUSTRIES INC
Also Called: Electron Beam Welding
1556 Deloss St (46201-3904)
PHONE.................317 637-5860
Daniel Diehl, *Pr*
EMP: 10 EST: 2017
SALES (est): 536.67K Privately Held
Web: www.ebwelding.com
SIC: 7692 Welding repair

(G-8045)
ECHO ENGRG & PROD SUPS INC (PA)
Also Called: Echo Supply
7150 Winton Dr Ste 300 (46268-4398)
PHONE.................317 876-8848
Kingdon Offenbacker, *CEO*
John Offenbacker, *
Albert Chew, *
▲ EMP: 43 EST: 2001
SQ FT: 21,600
SALES (est): 49.93MM
SALES (corp-wide): 49.93MM Privately Held
Web: www.echosupply.com
SIC: 2821 Plastics materials and resins

(G-8046)
ECKHART & COMPANY INC
4011 W 54th St (46254-4789)
PHONE.................317 347-2665
Chris Eckhart, *Pr*
EMP: 45 EST: 1918
SQ FT: 60,000
SALES (est): 7.86MM
SALES (corp-wide): 78.34MM Privately Held
Web: www.eckhartandco.com
SIC: 2789 2782 Binding only: books, pamphlets, magazines, etc.; Blankbooks and looseleaf binders
HQ: Bindtech, Llc
  1232 Antioch Pike
  Nashville TN 37211
  615 834-0404

(G-8047)
ECO PARKING TECHNOLOGIES LLC
8001 Castleway Dr (46250-1946)
PHONE.................866 897-1234
Andrew D Teed, *CEO*
Jeff Pinyot, *Pr*
Dave Packard, *COO*
EMP: 10 EST: 2008
SALES (est): 1.8MM Privately Held
Web: www.ecoparkingtechnologies.com
SIC: 3646 Commercial lighting fixtures

GEOGRAPHIC SECTION

Indianapolis - Marion County (G-8073)

(G-8048)
ECO-BAT AMERICA LLC
Also Called: Quemetco
7870 W Morris St (46231-1365)
PHONE....................317 247-1303
Glen Harold, *Brnch Mgr*
EMP: 244
SALES (corp-wide): 7.66MM **Privately Held**
Web: www.ecobat.com
SIC: 3356 3341 3339 Nonferrous rolling and drawing, nec; Secondary nonferrous metals ; Lead smelting and refining (primary)
HQ: Eco-Bat America Llc
2777 N Stemmons Fwy # 185
Dallas TX 75207
214 631-6070

(G-8049)
ECOBAT RESOURCES CAL INC
7870 W Morris St (46231-1365)
PHONE....................317 247-1303
EMP: 394
SALES (corp-wide): 492.55MM **Privately Held**
Web: www.quemetco.com
SIC: 3341 4953 Secondary nonferrous metals; Refuse systems
HQ: Ecobat Resources California, Inc.
720 S 7th Ave
City Of Industry CA 91746
626 937-3290

(G-8050)
ECONOMY DUMPSTER
6116 Burlington Ave (46220-2410)
PHONE....................317 308-7774
Brandon Pullian, *Pr*
EMP: 4 **EST:** 2020
SALES (est): 128.35K **Privately Held**
Web: www.economydumpster.net
SIC: 3469 Metal stampings, nec

(G-8051)
ED SONS INC (PA)
Also Called: PIP Printing
8335 Pendleton Pike (46226-4017)
PHONE....................317 897-8821
Paul Edson, *Pr*
Lurette Edson, *VP*
Dale R Edson, *Sec*
EMP: 12 **EST:** 1969
SQ FT: 4,200
SALES (est): 991.48K
SALES (corp-wide): 991.48K **Privately Held**
Web: www.pip.com
SIC: 2752 7334 2791 2789 Offset printing; Photocopying and duplicating services; Typesetting; Bookbinding and related work

(G-8052)
EDCO WELDING AND HYDRAULIC INC
1815 Kentucky Ave (46221-1911)
PHONE....................317 783-2323
Melvin E Vanmeter, *Pr*
Donna Vanmeter, *Prin*
EMP: 10 **EST:** 2007
SALES (est): 503.21K **Privately Held**
Web: www.edcowelding.com
SIC: 7692 Welding repair

(G-8053)
EDGE TECHNOLOGIES INC
4455 W 62nd St (46268-2521)
PHONE....................317 408-0116
George Kim, *Pr*
Vada Kim, *VP*
EMP: 9 **EST:** 1983
SQ FT: 5,500

SALES (est): 965.55K **Privately Held**
Web: www.edgetechdiamondtools.com
SIC: 3541 Machine tools, metal cutting type

(G-8054)
EDITARTS
4503 N College Ave (46205-1935)
PHONE....................317 702-1215
Joyce Krauser, *Prin*
EMP: 4 **EST:** 2017
SALES (est): 57.88K **Privately Held**
Web: www.editarts.com
SIC: 2741 Miscellaneous publishing

(G-8055)
EDITIONS LTD GLLERY FINE ART I
838 E 65th St (46220-1896)
PHONE....................317 466-9940
Chris Mallen, *Mgr*
EMP: 4 **EST:** 2007
SALES (est): 240.23K **Privately Held**
Web: www.editionsltd.com
SIC: 2499 5023 5999 8412 Picture frame molding, finished; Frames and framing, picture and mirror; Art, picture frames, and decorations; Art gallery

(G-8056)
EDM SPECIALTIES INC
7746 Milhouse Rd (46241-9550)
PHONE....................317 856-4700
EMP: 4 **EST:** 1995
SALES (est): 486.21K **Privately Held**
SIC: 3541 Machine tools, metal cutting type

(G-8057)
EDWARD E PETRI COMPANY
20 N Meridian St Ste 206 (46204-3023)
PHONE....................317 636-5007
Charles Walker, *Pr*
EMP: 4 **EST:** 1922
SQ FT: 1,498
SALES (est): 248.64K **Privately Held**
Web: www.petrijewelers.com
SIC: 3911 5944 Jewelry, precious metal; Jewelry, precious stones and precious metals

(G-8058)
EFURNITUREMAX LLC
8070 Castleton Rd # 117 (46250-2005)
PHONE....................317 697-9504
Cameron Paterson, *Managing Member*
EMP: 2 **EST:** 2014
SALES (est): 251.08K **Privately Held**
Web:
www.americancommercialfurniture.com
SIC: 2511 7389 Wood household furniture; Business Activities at Non-Commercial Site

(G-8059)
EGENOLF CONTG & RIGGING II INC
350 Wisconsin St (46225-1536)
PHONE....................317 787-5301
Peter Egenolf, *Pr*
R Joseph Jansen, *
Michael Egenolf, *
EMP: 13 **EST:** 1990
SALES (est): 861.74K **Privately Held**
Web: www.egenolf-rigging.com
SIC: 1796 1541 3599 Machine moving and rigging; Industrial buildings and warehouses ; Catapults

(G-8060)
EGENOLF ENTERPRISE INC
Also Called: Capstone Commerce Company
2855 N Evanklin Rd Ste (46226)
PHONE....................317 501-5069
Pat Egenolf, *Pr*

EMP: 11 **EST:** 1983
SALES (est): 244.81K **Privately Held**
Web: www.egenolf-rigging.com
SIC: 3524 Lawn and garden tractors and equipment

(G-8061)
EGENOLF MACHINE INC
2916 Bluff Rd Ste A (46225-2296)
PHONE....................317 787-5301
James Egenolf, *Pr*
Joseph Egenolf, *Ex VP*
Eileen Egenolf, *Sec*
Mary T Egenolf, *Treas*
EMP: 17 **EST:** 1926
SQ FT: 55,000
SALES (est): 398.79K **Privately Held**
Web: www.egenolf-rigging.com
SIC: 1796 3599 7692 7629 Machine moving and rigging; Machine shop, jobbing and repair; Welding repair; Electrical repair shops

(G-8062)
EHOB LLC
250 N Belmont Ave (46222-4265)
PHONE....................317 972-4600
Scott D Rogers, *Pr*
Brian Conway, *
▲ **EMP:** 120 **EST:** 1985
SQ FT: 53,000
SALES (est): 49.74MM **Privately Held**
Web: www.ehob.com
SIC: 3842 Surgical appliances and supplies

(G-8063)
EHRGOTTS SIGNS & STAMPS INC
12001 E Washington St Ste B (46229-3980)
PHONE....................317 353-2222
Sarah Barker Clevenger, *Pr*
EMP: 2 **EST:** 2013
SALES (est): 124.47K **Privately Held**
Web: www.ehrgotts.com
SIC: 3993 Signs, not made in custom sign painting shops

(G-8064)
EIDP INC (HQ)
Also Called: CORTEVA AGRISCIENCE
974 Centre Rd Bldg 735 (46268)
PHONE....................833 267-8382
Charles V Magro, *CEO*
David J Anderson, *
Brian Titus, *VP*
◆ **EMP:** 6000 **EST:** 1802
SALES (est): 17.23B
SALES (corp-wide): 17.23B **Publicly Held**
Web: www.dupont.com
SIC: 2879 2824 2865 2821 Agricultural chemicals, nec; Nylon fibers; Dyes and pigments; Thermoplastic materials
PA: Corteva, Inc.
9330 Zionsville Rd
Indianapolis IN 46268
833 267-8382

(G-8065)
EIGHT TEN TWELVE LLC
954 Conner St (46201)
PHONE....................317 773-8532
Jamie Worline, *Pr*
EMP: 6 **EST:** 2017
SALES (est): 170.01K **Privately Held**
SIC: 2752 Commercial printing, lithographic

(G-8066)
EISELES HONEY LLC
8146 Zionsville Rd (46268-1625)
PHONE....................317 896-5830
EMP: 3 **EST:** 2013

SQ FT: 3,600
SALES (est): 152.66K **Privately Held**
Web: www.eiseleshoney.com
SIC: 2099 Honey, strained and bottled

(G-8067)
EJ USA INC
201 N Illinois St Ste 1900 (46204-1904)
PHONE....................765 744-1184
EMP: 7
Web: www.ejco.com
SIC: 3321 Manhole covers, metal
HQ: Ej Usa, Inc.
301 Spring St
East Jordan MI 49727
800 874-4100

(G-8068)
EKOS MANUFACTURING LLC ✪
365 S Post Rd (46219-7900)
PHONE....................847 630-9717
EMP: 7 **EST:** 2022
SALES (est): 78.58K **Privately Held**
SIC: 2082 Beer (alcoholic beverage)

(G-8069)
ELEKTRISOLA INCORPORATED
2400 N Shadeland Ave Ste B (46219-1737)
PHONE....................317 375-8192
EMP: 3
SALES (corp-wide): 26.2MM **Privately Held**
Web: www.elektrisola.com
SIC: 3496 Miscellaneous fabricated wire products
PA: Elektrisola Incorporated
126 High St
Boscawen NH 03303
603 796-2114

(G-8070)
ELEMENTS ELEARNING LLC
4543 Melbourne Rd (46228-2771)
PHONE....................317 986-2113
Constance Carlisle, *Prin*
EMP: 5 **EST:** 2014
SALES (est): 118.27K **Privately Held**
Web: www.elementselearning.com
SIC: 2819 Industrial inorganic chemicals, nec

(G-8071)
ELEVATOR ONE LLC
120 E Market St (46204-3250)
PHONE....................317 634-8001
Chance Felling, *Managing Member*
EMP: 8 **EST:** 2012
SALES (est): 603.16K **Privately Held**
Web: www.elevatorfirst.com
SIC: 3534 Elevators and equipment

(G-8072)
ELI LILLY AND COMPANY
Lilly Corporate Center (46285-0001)
PHONE....................317 276-2000
Daniel Boehm, *Brnch Mgr*
EMP: 4
SALES (corp-wide): 34.12B **Publicly Held**
Web: www.lilly.com
SIC: 2834 Pharmaceutical preparations
PA: Eli Lilly And Company
1 Lilly Corporate Ctr
Indianapolis IN 46285
317 276-2000

(G-8073)
ELI LILLY AND COMPANY
1280 S Dakota St (46225-1581)
PHONE....................317 276-7907
D Kyle Thompson, *Brnch Mgr*
EMP: 4

Indianapolis - Marion County (G-8074)

SALES (corp-wide): 34.12B **Publicly Held**
Web: www.lilly.com
SIC: 2834 Pharmaceutical preparations
PA: Eli Lilly And Company
1 Lilly Corporate Ctr
Indianapolis IN 46285
317 276-2000

(G-8074)
ELI LILLY AND COMPANY
Also Called: Elanco Animal Health
639 S Delaware St (46225-1392)
PHONE..................................317 276-2118
EMP: 4
SALES (corp-wide): 34.12B **Publicly Held**
Web: www.lilly.com
SIC: 2834 Pharmaceutical preparations
PA: Eli Lilly And Company
1 Lilly Corporate Ctr
Indianapolis IN 46285
317 276-2000

(G-8075)
ELI LILLY AND COMPANY
Also Called: Elanco Animal Health
2301 Executive Dr (46241-5008)
PHONE..................................317 276-2000
EMP: 4
SALES (corp-wide): 34.12B **Publicly Held**
Web: www.lilly.com
SIC: 2834 Pharmaceutical preparations
PA: Eli Lilly And Company
1 Lilly Corporate Ctr
Indianapolis IN 46285
317 276-2000

(G-8076)
ELI LILLY AND COMPANY
450 S Meridian St (46225-1103)
PHONE..................................317 276-2000
EMP: 5
SALES (corp-wide): 34.12B **Publicly Held**
Web: www.lilly.com
SIC: 2834 Pharmaceutical preparations
PA: Eli Lilly And Company
1 Lilly Corporate Ctr
Indianapolis IN 46285
317 276-2000

(G-8077)
ELI LILLY AND COMPANY
Also Called: Elanco Animal Health
1402 S Dakota St (46225)
PHONE..................................317 276-5925
EMP: 5
SALES (corp-wide): 34.12B **Publicly Held**
Web: www.lilly.com
SIC: 2834 Pharmaceutical preparations
PA: Eli Lilly And Company
1 Lilly Corporate Ctr
Indianapolis IN 46285
317 276-2000

(G-8078)
ELI LILLY AND COMPANY
427 S Illinois St (46225-1102)
PHONE..................................317 276-2000
Andreas Kaerner, *Brnch Mgr*
EMP: 10
SALES (corp-wide): 34.12B **Publicly Held**
Web: www.lilly.com
SIC: 2834 Pharmaceutical preparations
PA: Eli Lilly And Company
1 Lilly Corporate Ctr
Indianapolis IN 46285
317 276-2000

(G-8079)
ELI LILLY AND COMPANY
1223 S Harding St (46221-1616)
PHONE..................................317 651-7790

John Lechleiter, *Pr*
EMP: 11
SQ FT: 60,000
SALES (corp-wide): 34.12B **Publicly Held**
Web: www.lilly.com
SIC: 2834 Pharmaceutical preparations
PA: Eli Lilly And Company
1 Lilly Corporate Ctr
Indianapolis IN 46285
317 276-2000

(G-8080)
ELI LILLY AND COMPANY
Also Called: Elanco Animal Health
30 S Meridian St 5th Fl (46204-3564)
PHONE..................................317 277-0147
Monica Dickenson, *Brnch Mgr*
EMP: 11
SALES (corp-wide): 34.12B **Publicly Held**
Web: www.lilly.com
SIC: 2834 Pharmaceutical preparations
PA: Eli Lilly And Company
1 Lilly Corporate Ctr
Indianapolis IN 46285
317 276-2000

(G-8081)
ELI LILLY AND COMPANY
Also Called: Lilly Technology Center - N
1223 W Morris St (46221)
PHONE..................................317 276-2000
EMP: 12
SALES (corp-wide): 34.12B **Publicly Held**
Web: www.lilly.com
SIC: 2834 Pharmaceutical preparations
PA: Eli Lilly And Company
1 Lilly Corporate Ctr
Indianapolis IN 46285
317 276-2000

(G-8082)
ELI LILLY AND COMPANY
Also Called: Elanco Animal Health
2401 Directors Row (46241-4907)
PHONE..................................317 276-2000
Angela Bryant, *Brnch Mgr*
EMP: 14
SALES (corp-wide): 34.12B **Publicly Held**
Web: www.lilly.com
SIC: 2834 Pharmaceutical preparations
PA: Eli Lilly And Company
1 Lilly Corporate Ctr
Indianapolis IN 46285
317 276-2000

(G-8083)
ELI LILLY AND COMPANY
1400 W Raymond St (46221-2004)
PHONE..................................317 276-2000
Michael Broughton, *Mgr*
EMP: 15
SALES (corp-wide): 34.12B **Publicly Held**
Web: www.lilly.com
SIC: 2834 Pharmaceutical preparations
PA: Eli Lilly And Company
1 Lilly Corporate Ctr
Indianapolis IN 46285
317 276-2000

(G-8084)
ELI LILLY AND COMPANY
355 E Merrill St (46225-1340)
PHONE..................................317 276-7907
EMP: 16
SALES (corp-wide): 34.12B **Publicly Held**
Web: www.lilly.com
SIC: 2834 Pharmaceutical preparations
PA: Eli Lilly And Company
1 Lilly Corporate Ctr
Indianapolis IN 46285
317 276-2000

(G-8085)
ELI LILLY AND COMPANY
Also Called: Elanco Animal Health
1555 S Harding St (46221-1873)
PHONE..................................317 276-2000
EMP: 22
SALES (corp-wide): 34.12B **Publicly Held**
Web: www.lilly.com
SIC: 2834 Pharmaceutical preparations
PA: Eli Lilly And Company
1 Lilly Corporate Ctr
Indianapolis IN 46285
317 276-2000

(G-8086)
ELI LILLY AND COMPANY
Elanco Animal Health
1 Lilly Corporate Ctr (46285-0002)
PHONE..................................317 277-1307
EMP: 85
SALES (corp-wide): 34.12B **Publicly Held**
Web: www.lilly.com
SIC: 2834 Pharmaceutical preparations
PA: Eli Lilly And Company
1 Lilly Corporate Ctr
Indianapolis IN 46285
317 276-2000

(G-8087)
ELI LILLY AND COMPANY
Also Called: Elanco Animal Health
1200 Kentucky Ave (46221-1718)
PHONE..................................317 276-2000
EMP: 112
SALES (corp-wide): 34.12B **Publicly Held**
Web: www.lilly.com
SIC: 2834 Pharmaceutical preparations
PA: Eli Lilly And Company
1 Lilly Corporate Ctr
Indianapolis IN 46285
317 276-2000

(G-8088)
ELI LILLY AND COMPANY (PA)
Also Called: Lilly
Lilly Corporate Ctr (46285)
PHONE..................................317 276-2000
David A Ricks, *Ch Bd*
Anat Hakim, *Ex VP*
Eric Dozier, *DIVERSITY*
Diogo Rau, *INFORMATION DIGITAL*
Gordon Brooks, *CTRL*
EMP: 3877 EST: 1876
SALES (est): 34.12B
SALES (corp-wide): 34.12B **Publicly Held**
Web: www.lilly.com
SIC: 2834 Pharmaceutical preparations

(G-8089)
ELI LILLY AND COMPANY
Dista Products Company
893 S Delaware St (46225-1782)
PHONE..................................317 276-2000
EMP: 150
SALES (corp-wide): 34.12B **Publicly Held**
Web: www.lilly.com
SIC: 2834 5122 Pharmaceutical preparations
; Pharmaceuticals
PA: Eli Lilly And Company
1 Lilly Corporate Ctr
Indianapolis IN 46285
317 276-2000

(G-8090)
ELI LILLY INTERAMERICA INC (HQ)
Lilly Corporate Center (46285-0001)
PHONE..................................317 276-2000
Jacques Tapiero, *Pr*
David R Mcavoy, *Sec*
Jan C H Mertens, *Treas*
EMP: 10 EST: 1957

SALES (est): 58.93MM
SALES (corp-wide): 34.12B **Publicly Held**
SIC: 2834 Pharmaceutical preparations
PA: Eli Lilly And Company
1 Lilly Corporate Ctr
Indianapolis IN 46285
317 276-2000

(G-8091)
ELI LILLY INTERNATIONAL CORP (HQ)
893 S Delaware St (46225-1782)
PHONE..................................317 276-2000
David Ricks, *Pr*
David Mcavoy, *Sec*
James B Lootens, *Prin*
Richard Smith, *EASTERN CENT EUROPE*
J A Harper, *Global Marketing Vice President*
EMP: 15 EST: 1943
SALES (est): 97.78MM
SALES (corp-wide): 34.12B **Publicly Held**
Web: www.lilly.com
SIC: 8742 2834 8731 3841 Business management consultant; Pharmaceutical preparations; Commercial physical research ; Surgical and medical instruments
PA: Eli Lilly And Company
1 Lilly Corporate Ctr
Indianapolis IN 46285
317 276-2000

(G-8092)
ELITE INDUSTRIES LLC
6331 Muirfield Way (46237-9584)
PHONE..................................317 407-6869
Steven Eli, *Admn*
EMP: 11 EST: 2015
SALES (est): 257.32K **Privately Held**
SIC: 3999 Manufacturing industries, nec

(G-8093)
ELITE PRINTING INC
4239 Madison Ave (46227-1530)
PHONE..................................317 781-9701
Tim Derloshon, *Brnch Mgr*
EMP: 2
SALES (corp-wide): 470.61K **Privately Held**
Web: www.eliteprintingindy.com
SIC: 2752 Offset printing
PA: Elite Printing Inc.
2138 E 52nd St
Indianapolis IN 46205
317 257-2744

(G-8094)
ELITE PRINTING INC (PA)
2138 E 52nd St (46205-1408)
PHONE..................................317 257-2744
Jim V Renterghem, *Pr*
Jim Van Renterghem, *VP*
Suzy Van Renterghem, *Pr*
Suzette Van Renterghem, *Prin*
EMP: 3 EST: 1986
SQ FT: 2,200
SALES (est): 470.61K
SALES (corp-wide): 470.61K **Privately Held**
Web: www.eliteprintingindy.com
SIC: 2752 Offset printing

(G-8095)
ELITE TRANSIT LLC
9210 Tenor Dr (46231-4272)
PHONE..................................317 507-2126
EMP: 2
SALES (est): 80.88K **Privately Held**
Web: www.elitetransit.com
SIC: 2519 Household furniture, nec

GEOGRAPHIC SECTION
Indianapolis - Marion County (G-8118)

(G-8096)
ELLIOTT CO OF INDIANAPOLIS
Also Called: Elliott Company
9200 Zionsville Rd (46268-1081)
PHONE..................317 291-1213
Bryan C Elliott, *Pr*
Charles Elliott, *VP*
Linda M Elliott, *Sec*
EMP: 15 **EST:** 1957
SQ FT: 30,000
SALES (est): 4.15MM **Privately Held**
Web: www.elliottfoam.com
SIC: 3086 Insulation or cushioning material, foamed plastics

(G-8097)
ELLIOTT-WILLIAMS COMPANY INC
3500 E 20th St (46218-4485)
PHONE..................317 453-2295
Michael M Elliott Senior, *Pr*
Richard A Fiorelli, *
Michael M Elliott Junior, *VP Sls*
EMP: 44 **EST:** 1945
SQ FT: 110,000
SALES (est): 663.24K **Privately Held**
SIC: 3585 3822 5078 1799 Refrigeration equipment, complete; Air conditioning and refrigeration controls; Refrigeration equipment and supplies; Appliance installation

(G-8098)
ELWOOD FUEL AND CIGS LLC
1050 S High School Rd (46241-3120)
PHONE..................317 244-5744
Kevin Cleveland, *Prin*
EMP: 6 **EST:** 2010
SALES (est): 118.38K **Privately Held**
SIC: 2869 Fuels

(G-8099)
EMARSYS NORTH AMERICA INC
10 W Market St Ste 1350 (46204-2930)
PHONE..................630 395-2944
Josef Ahorner, *Ch*
Hagai Hartman, *
Sean Brady, *
EMP: 50 **EST:** 2015
SQ FT: 20,000
SALES (est): 10.34MM
SALES (corp-wide): 33.92B **Privately Held**
Web: www.emarsys.com
SIC: 7372 8742 Prepackaged software; Marketing consulting services
PA: Sap Se
Dietmar-Hopp-Allee 16
Walldorf BW 69190
622 774-7474

(G-8100)
EMBROIDERY PLUS INC
5514 W Washington St (46241-2103)
PHONE..................317 243-3445
Stan Wisehart, *Pr*
EMP: 6 **EST:** 1991
SALES (est): 456.42K **Privately Held**
Web: www.embplusindy.com
SIC: 2395 Embroidery products, except Schiffli machine

(G-8101)
EMBROIDERY SEW INTO IT LLC
9130 Otis Ave Ste C (46216-2032)
PHONE..................317 734-3891
Linda G Reynolds, *Mgr*
EMP: 4 **EST:** 2019
SALES (est): 33.77K **Privately Held**
Web: www.esii.biz
SIC: 2395 Embroidery products, except Schiffli machine

(G-8102)
EMC2
3539 N Colorado Ave (46218)
P.O. Box 18713 (46218)
PHONE..................317 435-8021
EMP: 5 **EST:** 2014
SALES (est): 155.38K **Privately Held**
Web: www.emergingmanufacturing.org
SIC: 3572 Computer storage devices

(G-8103)
EMCO GEARS INC
703 S Girls School Rd (46231-3129)
PHONE..................317 243-3836
Dan Cota, *Mgr*
EMP: 6
SALES (corp-wide): 3.88MM **Privately Held**
Web: www.emcogears.com
SIC: 3462 Gear and chain forgings
PA: Emco Gears, Inc.
160 King St
Elk Grove Village IL 60007
847 220-4327

(G-8104)
EMERGE CURRICULUM PUBG LLC
5330 E 38th St (46218-1764)
PHONE..................317 523-2687
Kenneth Sollivan, *Prin*
EMP: 1 **EST:** 2012
SALES (est): 93.42K **Privately Held**
Web: www.bliglobal.org
SIC: 2741 Miscellaneous publishing

(G-8105)
EMERSON ELECTRIC CO
Also Called: Emerson
8320 Brookville Rd Ste E (46239-8914)
PHONE..................317 322-2055
EMP: 5
SALES (corp-wide): 15.16B **Publicly Held**
Web: www.emerson.com
SIC: 3823 Process control instruments
PA: Emerson Electric Co.
8000 W Florissant Ave
Saint Louis MO 63136
314 553-2000

(G-8106)
EMMIS CORPORATION (PA)
Also Called: Emmis Communications
40 Monument Cir Ste 700 (46204)
PHONE..................317 266-0100
Jeffrey H Smulyan, *Ch Bd*
Patrick M Walsh, *
Gregory T Loewen, *CSO*
Ryan A Hornaday, *Ex VP*
J Scott Enright, *Ex VP*
EMP: 60 **EST:** 1981
SQ FT: 115,000
SALES (est): 39.71MM
SALES (corp-wide): 39.71MM **Privately Held**
Web: www.emmis.com
SIC: 4832 2721 Radio broadcasting stations; Periodicals, publishing and printing

(G-8107)
EMMIS OPERATING COMPANY (HQ)
40 Monument Cir Ste 700 (46204)
PHONE..................317 266-0100
Jefferey Smulyan, *CEO*
Jeff Snulyan, *
Richard F Cummings, *Auto Division President**
Gary Thoe, *President Publishing**
Michael Levitan, *
EMP: 32 **EST:** 2001
SQ FT: 142,000
SALES (est): 24.7MM
SALES (corp-wide): 39.71MM **Privately Held**
Web: www.emmis.com
SIC: 4832 4833 2721 Radio broadcasting stations; Television broadcasting stations; Magazines: publishing only, not printed on site
PA: Emmis Corporation
40 Monument Cir Ste 700
Indianapolis IN 46204
317 266-0100

(G-8108)
EMMIS PUBLISHING LP (HQ)
Also Called: Texas Monthly
40 Monument Cir Ste 100 (46204-3045)
PHONE..................317 266-0100
Greg Loewen, *Pt*
Barbara Brill, *Pt*
EMP: 46 **EST:** 1988
SALES (est): 28.36MM
SALES (corp-wide): 39.71MM **Privately Held**
Web: hourwp-p.innoscale.net
SIC: 2721 Magazines: publishing only, not printed on site
PA: Emmis Corporation
40 Monument Cir Ste 700
Indianapolis IN 46204
317 266-0100

(G-8109)
EMMIS PUBLISHING CORPORATION (HQ)
40 Monument Cir Ste 700 (46204-3017)
PHONE..................317 266-0100
Patrick M Walsh, *Pr*
Scott Enright, *Sec*
EMP: 32 **EST:** 1988
SALES (est): 3.9MM
SALES (corp-wide): 39.71MM **Privately Held**
Web: www.emmis.com
SIC: 2721 Periodicals, publishing and printing
PA: Emmis Corporation
40 Monument Cir Ste 700
Indianapolis IN 46204
317 266-0100

(G-8110)
EMPRO MANUFACTURING CO INC
10920 E 59th St (46236)
P.O. Box 26060 (46226)
PHONE..................317 823-3000
Gary J Graf, *Pr*
Gretchen E Graf, *Sec*
▲ **EMP:** 20 **EST:** 1950
SQ FT: 5,000
SALES (est): 2.48MM **Privately Held**
Web: www.emproshunts.com
SIC: 3825 3629 Test equipment for electronic and electrical circuits; Electronic generation equipment

(G-8111)
EMQUIP CORPORATION
4359 E 75th St (46250-2207)
PHONE..................317 849-3977
Donald Wilson, *Pr*
Shirley Wilson, *Sec*
EMP: 5 **EST:** 1965
SALES (est): 513.92K **Privately Held**
Web: www.emquipcorp.com
SIC: 3533 Oil field machinery and equipment

(G-8112)
ENCONCO INC
Also Called: Engineered Models
6450 Rucker Rd (46220-4841)
PHONE..................317 251-1251
EMP: 30
Web: www.engineeredmodels.com
SIC: 3444 Sheet metal specialties, not stamped

(G-8113)
ENCORR SHEETS LLC
3600 Woodview Trce Ste 300 (46268)
PHONE..................317 290-1140
Paula Finch, *Dir*
EMP: 1 **EST:** 2016
SALES (est): 231.25K **Privately Held**
Web: www.encorrsheetsllc.com
SIC: 2621 Paper mills

(G-8114)
ENDOWMENT DEVELOPMENT SERVICES
Also Called: EDS
921 E 86th St (46240-1841)
PHONE..................317 542-9829
James R Marshell, *Pr*
Judith Epperson, *VP*
EMP: 10 **EST:** 1981
SALES (est): 673.54K **Privately Held**
Web: www.endowdevelop.com
SIC: 2741 2721 Miscellaneous publishing; Periodicals

(G-8115)
ENERGY ACCESS INCORPORATED
5595 W 74th St (46268-4184)
PHONE..................317 329-1676
Thomas Peine, *Pr*
Malcolm Mcclure, *VP*
Catherine Mcclure, *Treas*
▲ **EMP:** 15 **EST:** 1998
SALES (est): 2.75MM **Privately Held**
Web: www.energyaccess.com
SIC: 3629 3699 Battery chargers, rectifying or nonrotating; Electrical equipment and supplies, nec

(G-8116)
ENERGY HARNESS CORPORATION
5225 Exploration Dr (46241-9003)
PHONE..................317 999-5561
EMP: 4
SALES (corp-wide): 2.7MM **Privately Held**
Web: www.energyharness.com
SIC: 3646 Commercial lighting fixtures
PA: Energy Harness Corporation
71 Mid Cape Ter Ste 8
Cape Coral FL 33991
239 790-3300

(G-8117)
ENERGY QUEST INC
8553 Bash St Ste 107 (46250-5534)
PHONE..................317 827-9212
Albert Hyde, *Mgr*
EMP: 4
Web: www.nrgqst.com
SIC: 2869 Industrial organic chemicals, nec
PA: Energy Quest, Inc.
103 Firetower Rd
Leesburg GA 31763

(G-8118)
ENERGY SAVER LIGHTS INC
2530 Brandywine Ct (46241-5199)
PHONE..................202 544-7868
Carlet Auguste, *Pr*
EMP: 10
SALES (est): 344.62K **Privately Held**
SIC: 3999 3641 Stage hardware and equipment, except lighting; Electric light bulbs, complete

Indianapolis - Marion County (G-8119)

(G-8119)
ENGHOUSE NETWORKS (US) INC (HQ)
333 N Alabama St Ste 240 (46204)
PHONE..................317 262-4666
Michael J Reinarts, *Ch Bd*
Manfred Hanuschek, *
Nathan Habegger, *
EMP: 43 **EST:** 1968
SQ FT: 15,931
SALES (est): 26.14MM
SALES (corp-wide): 335.89MM **Privately Held**
Web: www.downtownindy.org
SIC: 7372 Business oriented computer software
PA: Enghouse Systems Limited
800-80 Tiverton Crt
Markham ON L3R 0
905 946-3200

(G-8120)
ENGINEERED DOCK SYSTEMS INC
Also Called: Floating Docks Mfg Co
3010 W Morris St (46241-2717)
PHONE..................317 803-2443
Dennis S Gaughan, *Pr*
Christopher Gaughan, *Pr*
Brian Gaughan, *Sec*
EMP: 1 **EST:** 1984
SALES (est): 2.06MM **Privately Held**
Web: www.floatingdocks.com
SIC: 3429 2499 Hardware, nec; Floating docks, wood

(G-8121)
ENGINEERED INDUSTRIAL PRODUCTS
5652 W 74th St (46278-1752)
P.O. Box 114 (46206-0114)
PHONE..................317 684-4280
Steve Fink, *Pr*
Donald W Fink, *Ch Bd*
Thomas Kuhn, *VP*
EMP: 5 **EST:** 1967
SALES (est): 449.9K **Privately Held**
Web: www.finkandcompany.com
SIC: 3599 Hose, flexible metallic

(G-8122)
ENGINEERED MEDICAL SYSTEMS
Also Called: E M S
2055 Executive Dr (46241-4311)
PHONE..................317 246-5500
Jeffrey J Quinn, *Pr*
Brad H Quinn, *
Andrew Shurig, *
▲ **EMP:** 70 **EST:** 1986
SQ FT: 20,000
SALES (est): 9.61MM **Privately Held**
Web: www.engmedsys.com
SIC: 3841 Surgical and medical instruments

(G-8123)
ENPOWER INC
8740 Hague Rd Bldg 7 (46256)
PHONE..................463 213-3200
Annette Finsterbusch, *CEO*
Charudatta Galande, *CEO*
Adrian Yao, *VP*
EMP: 25 **EST:** 2014
SQ FT: 1,102
SALES (est): 3.42MM **Privately Held**
Web: www.enpowerinc.com
SIC: 3691 Batteries, rechargeable

(G-8124)
ENTOURAGE YEARBOOKS
5321 N College Ave (46220-3141)
PHONE..................317 552-2207
Shaun Stapleton, *Pr*
EMP: 8 **EST:** 2017
SALES (est): 55.54K **Privately Held**
Web: www.entourageyearbooks.com
SIC: 2741 Miscellaneous publishing

(G-8125)
ENVIGO RMS INC (DH)
Also Called: Teklad Diets
8520 Allison Pointe Blvd Ste 400 (46250-5700)
PHONE..................317 806-6080
Mark Bibi, *VP*
Dawn Griffin, *
Joseph Bondi, *
M G O'reilly, *VP*
Adrian Hardy, *
▲ **EMP:** 150 **EST:** 1962
SQ FT: 48,000
SALES (est): 46.85MM **Privately Held**
Web: www.inotivco.com
SIC: 0279 2048 2836 3821 Laboratory animal farm; Prepared feeds, nec; Veterinary biological products; Laboratory apparatus and furniture
HQ: Labcorp Early Development Laboratories Limited
Otley Road
Harrogate HG3 1
142 350-0011

(G-8126)
ENVIROPEEL USA
1128 S West St (46225-1463)
PHONE..................317 631-9100
Corey Pierce, *Rgnl Mgr*
Corey Pierce, *Mgr*
EMP: 6 **EST:** 2011
SALES (est): 467.09K **Privately Held**
Web: www.enviropeel.com
SIC: 1382 Oil and gas exploration services

(G-8127)
EORIGAMI PUBLISHING LLC
8614 Amy Ln (46256-1549)
PHONE..................317 842-9659
Brian K Webb, *Prin*
EMP: 1 **EST:** 2010
SALES (est): 51.22K **Privately Held**
Web: www.origamipublishing.com
SIC: 2741 Miscellaneous publishing

(G-8128)
EP OLD INC
520 S Post Rd (46239-9741)
P.O. Box 17463 (46217-0463)
PHONE..................317 782-8362
John F Wilson, *Pr*
EMP: 9 **EST:** 1995
SALES (est): 454.49K **Privately Held**
Web: www.eastmanproducts.com
SIC: 3499 Ladder assemblies, combination workstand: metal

(G-8129)
EPI PRINTERS INC
Also Called: E P I
7502 E 86th St (46256-1210)
PHONE..................317 579-4870
EMP: 71
SALES (corp-wide): 102.45MM **Privately Held**
Web: www.epiinc.com
SIC: 2752 2789 Offset printing; Bookbinding and related work
PA: Epi Printers, Inc.
5404 Wayne Rd
Battle Creek MI 49037
800 562-9733

(G-8130)
ESCO COMMUNICATIONS LLC (HQ)
8940 Vincennes Cir (46268-3036)
PHONE..................317 298-2975
EMP: 100 **EST:** 1963
SALES (est): 42.73MM
SALES (corp-wide): 243.37MM **Privately Held**
Web: www.neweratech.com
SIC: 3651 3669 3661 Sound reproducing equipment; Emergency alarms; Telephones and telephone apparatus
PA: New Era Technology, Inc.
1370 Ave Of The Amrcas Fl
New York NY 10019
973 253-7600

(G-8131)
ESCO ENTERPRISES INDIANA INC
Also Called: Earl's Indy
302 Gasoline Aly (46222-4076)
PHONE..................317 241-0318
Thomas Meko, *Pr*
Mark J Meko, *VP*
Sara A Meko, *Sec*
EMP: 13 **EST:** 1990
SQ FT: 15,000
SALES (est): 2MM **Privately Held**
Web: www.earlsindy.com
SIC: 3599 7549 Hose, flexible metallic; Automotive maintenance services

(G-8132)
ESII - EMBROIDERY SEW INTO IT
9130 Otis Ave Ste C (46216-2032)
PHONE..................317 734-3891
EMP: 3 **EST:** 2019
SALES (est): 46.91K **Privately Held**
Web: www.esii.biz
SIC: 2395 Embroidery products, except Schiffli machine

(G-8133)
ESSENCE IN HARMONY
438 W Stop 11 Rd (46217-4265)
PHONE..................317 727-6420
Mary Vannoy, *Prin*
EMP: 4 **EST:** 2010
SALES (est): 48.63K **Privately Held**
Web: www.essenceinharmony.com.au
SIC: 2844 Perfumes, cosmetics and other toilet preparations

(G-8134)
ESSENCE SCENTS LLC
10839 Teeter Ct (46236-7717)
PHONE..................317 679-5627
Tiffany Reece, *Prin*
EMP: 5 **EST:** 2018
SALES (est): 53.34K **Privately Held**
Web: www.essencescentsllc.com
SIC: 2844 Perfumes, cosmetics and other toilet preparations

(G-8135)
ESSENTIAL ARCHTCTRAL SIGNS INC
6464 Rucker Rd (46220-4841)
PHONE..................317 253-6000
Cynthia Hulen, *Owner*
O'brien Bassett, *VP*
EMP: 10 **EST:** 2002
SQ FT: 13,480
SALES (est): 1.53MM **Privately Held**
Web: www.essentialsigns.com
SIC: 3993 Signs and advertising specialties

(G-8136)
ESSEX
5105 Plantation Dr (46250-1640)
PHONE..................317 201-7099
EMP: 6 **EST:** 2019
SALES (est): 97.32K **Privately Held**
SIC: 2591 Window blinds

(G-8137)
ESTES AWS LLC
470 S Mitthoefer Rd (46229-3058)
PHONE..................317 995-9742
C Ryan Estes, *Mgr*
EMP: 8 **EST:** 2017
SALES (est): 268.09K **Privately Held**
Web: www.estesaws.com
SIC: 3999 Manufacturing industries, nec

(G-8138)
ESTES DESIGN AND MFG INC
470 S Mitthoeffer Rd (46229-3058)
PHONE..................317 899-2203
Larry Estes, *Pr*
Ron Estes, *
Diana Estes, *
EMP: 90 **EST:** 1976
SQ FT: 52,000
SALES (est): 19.92MM **Privately Held**
Web: www.estesdm.com
SIC: 3444 Sheet metal specialties, not stamped

(G-8139)
ETHELS KITCHEN LLC
3533 N Audubon Rd (46218-1831)
PHONE..................317 441-2712
EMP: 1
SALES (est): 69.27K **Privately Held**
SIC: 2099 Food preparations, nec

(G-8140)
EVANS HERRON
Also Called: Executive Polishing
702 Yosemite Dr (46217-3964)
PHONE..................317 492-1384
EMP: 1 **EST:** 1996
SALES (est): 92.04K **Privately Held**
SIC: 3471 7389 Polishing, metals or formed products; Business Activities at Non-Commercial Site

(G-8141)
EVANS ENTERPRISES LLC
7644 Bancaster Dr (46268-5716)
PHONE..................317 986-2073
Tara Evans, *Pr*
EMP: 5 **EST:** 2015
SALES (est): 38.16K **Privately Held**
SIC: 7694 Electric motor repair

(G-8142)
EVERYTHING UNDERGROUND INC
4410 Rhapsody Ln (46235-8225)
PHONE..................317 491-8148
Lashell Daniels, *CEO*
EMP: 8 **EST:** 2011
SALES (est): 112.19K **Privately Held**
Web: www.everythingunderground.com
SIC: 7372 Business oriented computer software

(G-8143)
EVOLVING TRANSPORT LLC
502 Bernard Ave (46208-3800)
PHONE..................317 794-4426
Clarence Barnett, *CEO*
EMP: 1 **EST:** 2020
SALES (est): 54.62K **Privately Held**
Web: www.pamtransport.com
SIC: 3799 Transportation equipment, nec

GEOGRAPHIC SECTION

Indianapolis - Marion County (G-8170)

(G-8144)
EVOQUA WATER TECHNOLOGIES LLC
6125 Guion Rd (46254-1223)
PHONE..................317 280-4251
Dave Fowler, *Mgr*
EMP: 50
Web: www.evoqua.com
SIC: 5074 2821 Water heaters and purification equipment; Plastics materials and resins
HQ: Evoqua Water Technologies Llc
210 6th Ave Ste 3300
Pittsburgh PA 15222
724 772-0044

(G-8145)
EVOQUA WATER TECHNOLOGIES LLC
6111 Guion Rd (46254-1223)
PHONE..................317 280-4255
EMP: 22
Web: www.evoqua.com
SIC: 3589 Sewage and water treatment equipment
HQ: Evoqua Water Technologies Llc
210 6th Ave Ste 3300
Pittsburgh PA 15222
724 772-0044

(G-8146)
EWING LIGHT METALS CO INC
Also Called: E L M
3451 Terrace Ave (46203-2247)
P.O. Box 33187 (46203-0187)
PHONE..................317 926-4591
Cayne Inocencio, *Pr*
Michelle Inocencio, *VP*
Carlos Inocencio, *VP*
EMP: 31 EST: 1943
SQ FT: 18,000
SALES (est): 2.35MM **Privately Held**
Web: www.ewinglightmetals.com
SIC: 3365 3366 3369 3322 Aluminum and aluminum-based alloy castings; Castings (except die), nec, brass; Nonferrous foundries, nec; Malleable iron foundries

(G-8147)
EXACTO MACHINE & TOOL INC
3402 W 79th St (46268-1912)
PHONE..................317 872-3136
George Lemcke, *Pr*
EMP: 5 EST: 1977
SQ FT: 1,800
SALES (est): 490.38K **Privately Held**
Web: www.exactomachine.com
SIC: 3599 Machine shop, jobbing and repair

(G-8148)
EXACTSEAL INC
7601 E 88th Pl Ste 3b (46256-1396)
PHONE..................317 559-2220
Hiren Jetani, *CEO*
EMP: 2 EST: 2016
SALES (est): 97.79K **Privately Held**
Web: www.exactseal.com
SIC: 3053 3052 3069 5085 Gaskets; packing and sealing devices; Rubber and plastics hose and beltings; Rubber automotive products; Rubber goods, mechanical

(G-8149)
EXCEL BUSINESS PRINTING INC
6302 Rucker Rd Ste A (46220-4853)
PHONE..................317 259-1075
Michael R Miller, *Pr*
EMP: 6 EST: 1991
SQ FT: 1,200
SALES (est): 480.89K **Privately Held**
SIC: 2752 5112 Offset printing; Business forms

(G-8150)
EXCEPT AS A CHILD PUBG LLC
6131 N Pershing Ave (46228-1181)
PHONE..................317 658-0075
EMP: 5 EST: 2016
SALES (est): 41.03K **Privately Held**
SIC: 2741 Miscellaneous publishing

(G-8151)
EXCLUSIVE STYLEZ LLC
2018 Winter Ave (46218-3555)
PHONE..................470 406-2804
EMP: 3 EST: 2021
SALES (est): 90K **Privately Held**
SIC: 3999 7389 Hair and hair-based products; Business Activities at Non-Commercial Site

(G-8152)
EXECUTIVE MGT SVCS IND INC
Also Called: EXECUTIVE MANAGEMENT SERVICES OF INDIANA, INC.
1605 Prospect St (46203-2024)
P.O. Box 501818 (46250-6818)
PHONE..................317 594-6000
Brian Wyatt, *Brnch Mgr*
EMP: 3
Web: www.emsinc.com
SIC: 3599 Machine and other job shop work
PA: Executive Management Services, Inc.
4177 N Ems Blvd
Indianapolis IN 46250

(G-8153)
EXELEAD INC (HQ)
6925 Guion Rd (46268)
PHONE..................317 347-2800
EMP: 28 EST: 2009
SALES (est): 65.26MM
SALES (corp-wide): 100.79MM **Privately Held**
Web: www.exeleadbiopharma.com
SIC: 2834 Pharmaceutical preparations
PA: Essetifin Spa
Via Sudafrica 20
Roma RM 00144
06542771

(G-8154)
EXELEAD INC
6102 Victory Way (46278)
PHONE..................317 612-2900
EMP: 97
SALES (corp-wide): 100.79MM **Privately Held**
Web: www.exeleadbiopharma.com
SIC: 2834 Pharmaceutical preparations
HQ: Exelead Inc.
6925 Guion Rd
Indianapolis IN 46268

(G-8155)
EXIDE TECHNOLOGIES LLC
5945 W 84th St Ste B (46278-1397)
PHONE..................317 876-7475
Rick King, *Mgr*
EMP: 3
SALES (corp-wide): 2.06B **Privately Held**
Web: www.exide.com
SIC: 3691 3629 Lead acid batteries (storage batteries); Battery chargers, rectifying or nonrotating
PA: Exide Technologies, Llc
13000 Drfeld Pkwy Bldg 20
Milton GA 30004
678 566-9000

(G-8156)
EXOTIC METAL TREATING INC
6234 E Hanna Ave (46203-6129)
PHONE..................317 784-8565
Kathy Susko, *Pr*
Keith Susko, *VP*
Kelli Hall, *Sec*
▲ EMP: 12 EST: 1973
SQ FT: 14,000
SALES (est): 969.76K **Privately Held**
Web: www.exoticmetaltreating.com
SIC: 3398 Brazing (hardening) of metal

(G-8157)
EXPRESS PRCSION COMPONENTS INC
2750 S Arlington Ave (46203-5703)
PHONE..................317 294-8138
Marlon R Casey, *Prin*
EMP: 8 EST: 2013
SALES (est): 130.55K **Privately Held**
SIC: 3599 Machine shop, jobbing and repair

(G-8158)
EXPRESSIONS CUSTOM TEES
12407 Rose Haven Dr (46235-6061)
PHONE..................317 205-6229
Howard Taylor, *Owner*
EMP: 5 EST: 2017
SALES (est): 121.19K **Privately Held**
SIC: 2759 Screen printing

(G-8159)
F HOFFMANN-LA ROCHE LTD (PA) ✪
Also Called: Hoffman La Roche
2701 Castle Hill Dr Apt 921 (46250)
PHONE..................317 370-8578
EMP: 7 EST: 2022
SALES (est): 1.1MM
SALES (corp-wide): 1.1MM **Privately Held**
Web: www.roche.com
SIC: 2834 Pharmaceutical preparations

(G-8160)
F HOFFMANN-LA ROCHE LTD ✪
Also Called: Hoffman La Roche
9115 Hague Rd (46256-1025)
PHONE..................317 370-8578
EMP: 10 EST: 2022
SALES (est): 1.3MM **Privately Held**
Web: www.roche.com
SIC: 2834 Pharmaceutical preparations

(G-8161)
F ROBERT GARDNER CO INC
1621 E New York St (46201-3095)
PHONE..................317 634-2333
Brian F Gardner, *Pr*
Bonnie Gardner, *Sec*
EMP: 5 EST: 1934
SQ FT: 12,000
SALES (est): 302.72K **Privately Held**
Web: www.rfgardner.com
SIC: 2752 3083 2759 2672 Offset printing; Laminated plastics plate and sheet; Commercial printing, nec; Paper; coated and laminated, nec

(G-8162)
FABRICATED STEEL CORPORATION
9809 Park Davis Dr (46235-2393)
PHONE..................317 899-0012
Derek Romeril, *Pr*
EMP: 7 EST: 1988
SQ FT: 20,000
SALES (est): 557.44K **Privately Held**
SIC: 3535 3441 Conveyors and conveying equipment; Fabricated structural metal

(G-8163)
FAM EXPRESS 1982 LLC ✪
1534 N Emerson Ave (46219-2938)
PHONE..................317 628-3901
EMP: 1 EST: 2023
SALES (est): 62.01K **Privately Held**
SIC: 3537 Truck trailers, used in plants, docks, terminals, etc.

(G-8164)
FAMILY LEISURECOM INC
11811 Pendleton Pike (46236-3910)
PHONE..................317 823-4448
Kevin Presontanie, *Pr*
EMP: 15 EST: 2011
SALES (est): 904.86K **Privately Held**
Web: www.familyleisure.com
SIC: 5021 3944 Furniture; Board games, puzzles, and models, except electronic

(G-8165)
FAMILY VINEYARD LLC
3944 N Delaware St (46205-2650)
PHONE..................812 322-1720
Eric B Weddle, *Prin*
EMP: 5 EST: 2016
SALES (est): 174.38K **Privately Held**
Web: www.family-vineyard.com
SIC: 2084 Wines

(G-8166)
FANATICS LIDS COLLEGE LLC
7676 Interactive Way Ste 300 (46278-2735)
PHONE..................888 814-4287
EMP: 26 EST: 2020
SALES (est): 487.11K **Privately Held**
SIC: 2329 2339 3949 Men's and boys' sportswear and athletic clothing; Women's and misses' athletic clothing and sportswear; Team sports equipment

(G-8167)
FARIS MAILING INC
701 N Holt Rd Ste 3 (46222-3455)
PHONE..................317 246-3315
Robert L Faris Junior, *Pr*
Jane Faris Parsons, *Treas*
EMP: 15 EST: 1967
SQ FT: 25,000
SALES (est): 1.72MM **Privately Held**
Web: www.farismailing.net
SIC: 7331 2752 Mailing service; Commercial printing, lithographic

(G-8168)
FARMERSMARKETCOM LLC
115 Pope Ave Apt O (46202-4062)
PHONE..................317 523-4025
EMP: 1 EST: 2011
SALES (est): 105.58K **Privately Held**
SIC: 7372 Business oriented computer software

(G-8169)
FASTSIGNS
9668 Allisonville Rd (46250)
PHONE..................317 280-3041
Justin Taylor, *Prin*
EMP: 8 EST: 2019
SALES (est): 201.36K **Privately Held**
Web: www.fastsigns.com
SIC: 3993 Signs and advertising specialties

(G-8170)
FEDERAL PROVIDER LLC
55 Monument Cir Ste 744 (46204-2910)
PHONE..................317 710-3997
EMP: 1 EST: 2017
SALES (est): 66.03K **Privately Held**
Web: www.federalprovider.com

Indianapolis - Marion County (G-8171)

SIC: 3577 Computer peripheral equipment, nec

(G-8171)
FEDERAL-MOGUL MOTORPARTS LLC
Also Called: Federal-Mogul
8325 N Norfolk St 100 (46268-1695)
PHONE..................317 875-7259
Chuck Kerschen, *Brnch Mgr*
EMP: 2
SALES (corp-wide): 18.04B **Privately Held**
Web: www.drivparts.com
SIC: 3714 Motor vehicle parts and accessories
HQ: Federal-Mogul Motorparts Llc
27300 W 11 Mile Rd
Southfield MI 48034
248 354-7700

(G-8172)
FEDEX OFFICE & PRINT SVCS INC
Also Called: Fedex
10 S West St (46204-2709)
PHONE..................317 974-0378
EMP: 1
SALES (corp-wide): 87.69B **Publicly Held**
Web: local.fedex.com
SIC: 7389 7334 5099 2752 Packaging and labeling services; Photocopying and duplicating services; Signs, except electric; Commercial printing, lithographic
HQ: Fedex Office And Print Services, Inc.
7900 Legacy Dr
Plano TX 75024
800 463-3339

(G-8173)
FEDEX OFFICE & PRINT SVCS INC
Also Called: Fedex
50 S Capitol Ave (46204-3435)
PHONE..................317 917-1529
EMP: 1
SALES (corp-wide): 87.69B **Publicly Held**
Web: local.fedex.com
SIC: 7389 7334 5099 2752 Packaging and labeling services; Photocopying and duplicating services; Signs, except electric; Commercial printing, lithographic
HQ: Fedex Office And Print Services, Inc.
7900 Legacy Dr
Plano TX 75024
800 463-3339

(G-8174)
FEDEX OFFICE & PRINT SVCS INC
Also Called: Fedex
4825 E 82nd St Ste 200 (46250-1673)
PHONE..................317 849-9683
EMP: 1
SALES (corp-wide): 87.69B **Publicly Held**
Web: local.fedex.com
SIC: 7334 2791 2789 Photocopying and duplicating services; Typesetting; Bookbinding and related work
HQ: Fedex Office And Print Services, Inc.
7900 Legacy Dr
Plano TX 75024
800 463-3339

(G-8175)
FEDEX OFFICE & PRINT SVCS INC
Also Called: Fedex
8231 Us 31 (46227-6228)
PHONE..................317 885-6480
EMP: 1
SALES (corp-wide): 87.69B **Publicly Held**
Web: local.fedex.com
SIC: 7334 2791 2789 Photocopying and duplicating services; Typesetting; Bookbinding and related work

HQ: Fedex Office And Print Services, Inc.
7900 Legacy Dr
Plano TX 75024
800 463-3339

(G-8176)
FEDEX OFFICE & PRINT SVCS INC
Also Called: Fedex
5030 W Pike Plaza Rd (46254-3001)
PHONE..................317 295-1063
EMP: 3
SALES (corp-wide): 87.69B **Publicly Held**
Web: local.fedex.com
SIC: 7334 2791 2789 Photocopying and duplicating services; Typesetting; Bookbinding and related work
HQ: Fedex Office And Print Services, Inc.
7900 Legacy Dr
Plano TX 75024
800 463-3339

(G-8177)
FEDEX OFFICE & PRINT SVCS INC
Also Called: Fedex
3269 W 86th St Ste A (46268-3822)
PHONE..................317 337-2679
EMP: 1
SALES (corp-wide): 87.69B **Publicly Held**
Web: local.fedex.com
SIC: 7334 2791 2789 2672 Photocopying and duplicating services; Typesetting; Bookbinding and related work; Paper; coated and laminated, nec
HQ: Fedex Office And Print Services, Inc.
7900 Legacy Dr
Plano TX 75024
800 463-3339

(G-8178)
FEDEX OFFICE & PRINT SVCS INC
Also Called: Fedex
120 Monument Cir Ste 107 (46204-4902)
PHONE..................317 631-6862
EMP: 1
SALES (corp-wide): 87.69B **Publicly Held**
Web: local.fedex.com
SIC: 7334 2791 2789 2752 Photocopying and duplicating services; Typesetting; Bookbinding and related work; Commercial printing, lithographic
HQ: Fedex Office And Print Services, Inc.
7900 Legacy Dr
Plano TX 75024
800 463-3339

(G-8179)
FEDEX OFFICE & PRINT SVCS INC
Also Called: Fedex
1050 Broad Ripple Ave (46220-2035)
PHONE..................317 251-2406
EMP: 1
SALES (corp-wide): 87.69B **Publicly Held**
Web: local.fedex.com
SIC: 7334 2791 2789 2759 Photocopying and duplicating services; Typesetting; Bookbinding and related work; Commercial printing, nec
HQ: Fedex Office And Print Services, Inc.
7900 Legacy Dr
Plano TX 75024
800 463-3339

(G-8180)
FELLERS INC
Also Called: FELLERS INC
7768 Moller Rd (46268-4163)
PHONE..................317 876-3008
Mike Mc Atee, *Mgr*
EMP: 1
SALES (corp-wide): 74.09MM **Privately Held**

Web: www.fellers.com
SIC: 3993 Signs and advertising specialties
PA: Fellers, Llc
6566 E Skelly Dr
Tulsa OK 74145
918 621-4400

(G-8181)
FESTIVE LIGHTS LLC
4617 E 16th St (46201-1730)
PHONE..................317 998-0627
EMP: 3 EST: 2015
SALES (est): 93.96K **Privately Held**
Web: www.festivelightsllc.com
SIC: 0782 3648 Lawn and garden services; Lighting equipment, nec

(G-8182)
FEX LLC
Also Called: Fex Labs
4909 Sunview Cir Apt 1218 (46237-4616)
PHONE..................317 308-8820
EMP: 1 EST: 2013
SALES (est): 64K **Privately Held**
SIC: 3944 7389 Electronic games and toys; Business Activities at Non-Commercial Site

(G-8183)
FIBERGLAS & PLASTIC FABG
2832 N Webster Ave (46219-1013)
PHONE..................317 549-1779
Karl A Spandau, *Pr*
George L Craig, *VP*
EMP: 34 EST: 1971
SQ FT: 21,000
SALES (est): 1.54MM **Privately Held**
Web: www.fpfinc.net
SIC: 3089 Injection molding of plastics

(G-8184)
FIBERGRATE COMPOSITE
8148 Castle Lake Rd (46256-1653)
PHONE..................317 752-2500
Scott Zink, *Brnch Mgr*
EMP: 1
SALES (corp-wide): 7.34B **Publicly Held**
Web: www.fibergrate.com
SIC: 3089 Plastics processing
HQ: Fibergrate Composite Structures Incorporated
5151 Belt Line Rd Ste 121
Dallas TX 75254

(G-8185)
FIDELITY DENTAL HANDPIECE SVC
Also Called: Dental Handpiece Service
4330 Black Oak Dr (46228-3110)
PHONE..................317 254-0277
Francis Feeney, *Owner*
EMP: 2 EST: 1989
SALES (est): 135.2K **Privately Held**
SIC: 7699 3843 Dental instrument repair; Hand pieces and parts, dental

(G-8186)
FIERCE PUBLISHING
501 Fletcher Ave Apt B (46203-1176)
PHONE..................765 251-3262
EMP: 4 EST: 2018
SALES (est): 68.57K **Privately Held**
SIC: 2741 Miscellaneous publishing

(G-8187)
FINELINE DIGITAL GROUP INC
8081 Zionsville Rd (46268-1624)
PHONE..................317 872-4490
Richard Miller, *Pr*
Dan Clark, *VP Opers*
Rich Mathiesen, *VP Sls*
Rick Kappel, *Pdt Mgr*

EMP: 20 EST: 1998
SALES (est): 533.51K **Privately Held**
Web: www.finelineprintinggroup.com
SIC: 2752 Offset printing

(G-8188)
FINELINE GRAPHICS INCORPORATED
Also Called: Fineline Printing Group
8081 Zionsville Rd (46268-1624)
PHONE..................317 872-4490
Richard Miller, *Pr*
Paul Doerfler, *
Guy Vreeman, *
Lisa Young, *
EMP: 56 EST: 1980
SQ FT: 48,000
SALES (est): 9.94MM **Privately Held**
Web: www.finelineprintinggroup.com
SIC: 2752 7331 2791 Offset printing; Mailing service; Typesetting

(G-8189)
FINISH ALTERNATIVES
705 Northfield Ct (46227-1617)
PHONE..................317 440-2899
Robert Lyle, *Owner*
EMP: 2 EST: 2011
SALES (est): 89.63K **Privately Held**
Web: www.finishalternatives.com
SIC: 2434 Wood kitchen cabinets

(G-8190)
FIRESMOKE ORG
323 N Delaware St (46204-1801)
PHONE..................317 690-2542
Jason Krusen, *VP*
EMP: 2 EST: 2011
SALES (est): 133.75K **Privately Held**
Web: www.firesmoke.org
SIC: 2515 Foundations and platforms

(G-8191)
FIRST AGE WOODWORKING LLC ◆
5725 Carry Back Dr (46237-2180)
PHONE..................765 667-1847
James Paul Hyatt, *Pr*
EMP: 1 EST: 2023
SALES (est): 75.6K **Privately Held**
SIC: 2431 Millwork

(G-8192)
FIRST CLASS PRINTING
6800 E 30th St (46219-1104)
PHONE..................317 808-2222
Mark Zainey, *Prin*
EMP: 2 EST: 2010
SALES (est): 117.52K **Privately Held**
SIC: 2759 Commercial printing, nec

(G-8193)
FIRST GENERATION TRUCKING LLC
8445 Country Meadows Dr (46234-1883)
PHONE..................317 654-6272
EMP: 1 EST: 2021
SALES (est): 60.08K **Privately Held**
SIC: 3537 Trucks, tractors, loaders, carriers, and similar equipment

(G-8194)
FIRST IMPRESSION TRNSP
2654 N Harding St (46208-5277)
P.O. Box 24493 (46224-0493)
PHONE..................317 682-8436
Latasha Freeman, *CEO*
EMP: 1 EST: 2018
SALES (est): 79.67K **Privately Held**
SIC: 3537 Trucks, tractors, loaders, carriers, and similar equipment

GEOGRAPHIC SECTION

Indianapolis - Marion County (G-8222)

(G-8195)
FIRST QUALITY PRINTING INC
5410 Radnor Rd (46226-2312)
PHONE..................317 506-8633
Keith Rand, Pr
Joyce Rand, VP
EMP: 3 EST: 1989
SALES (est): 252.23K Privately Held
Web: www.firstqualityprint.com
SIC: 2752 2791 Offset printing; Typesetting

(G-8196)
FIRST QUALITY PRINTING CENTER
5498 Emerson Way (46226-1408)
PHONE..................317 546-5531
Joyce Rand, Prin
EMP: 4 EST: 2013
SALES (est): 73.74K Privately Held
Web: www.firstqualityprint.com
SIC: 2752 Offset printing

(G-8197)
FISHER CLINICAL SERVICES INC
1220 W Morris St (46221-1710)
PHONE..................317 277-0337
Jen Griffith, Genl Mgr
EMP: 36
SALES (corp-wide): 42.86B Publicly Held
Web: www.patheon.com
SIC: 2834 Pharmaceutical preparations
HQ: Fisher Clinical Services Inc.
  7554 Schantz Rd
  Allentown PA 18106
  610 391-0800

(G-8198)
FIVE DMENSIONS RESTORATION LLC
7020 Pershing Rd (46268-2702)
PHONE..................347 490-8904
EMP: 1
SALES (est): 64.69K Privately Held
SIC: 1389 Construction, repair, and dismantling services

(G-8199)
FLAG & BANNER COMPANY INC
Also Called: Fabco Publishing
5450 Lafayette Rd Ste 5 (46254-1655)
PHONE..................317 299-4880
Karen E Bush, Pr
Clifton H Bush Iv, VP
Nancy Wood, Sec
EMP: 10 EST: 1971
SQ FT: 3,500
SALES (est): 1.67MM Privately Held
Web: www.fabco-usa.com
SIC: 5131 5999 5199 2396 Flags and banners; Flags; Advertising specialties; Screen printing on fabric articles

(G-8200)
FLAVOR IMPERIUM LLC
6139 Robin Run Apt A (46254-1150)
PHONE..................765 499-0854
Francis J Tremmel, Pr
EMP: 4 EST: 2019
SALES (est): 75.48K Privately Held
Web: www.flavorimperium.com
SIC: 2099 Food preparations, nec

(G-8201)
FLAWLESS UNITS LLC
6919 E 10th St (46219-4893)
PHONE..................317 833-5975
EMP: 1
SALES (est): 39.69K Privately Held
SIC: 3999 Hair and hair-based products

(G-8202)
FLEMING ASSOC CALIBRATION INC
Also Called: Fleming Air Flow
2318 E 45th St (46205-2226)
PHONE..................317 631-4605
Ronald J Fleming, Pr
EMP: 8 EST: 1972
SQ FT: 2,600
SALES (est): 909.65K Privately Held
Web: www.flemingairflow.com
SIC: 3829 Vibration meters, analyzers, and calibrators

(G-8203)
FLICKERS CANDLE SHOP
2310 E Loretta Dr (46227-4957)
PHONE..................317 403-5045
EMP: 4 EST: 2018
SALES (est): 80.02K Privately Held
SIC: 3999 Candles

(G-8204)
FLINT CPS INKS NORTH AMER LLC
4910 W 78th St (46268-4169)
PHONE..................317 870-4422
John Louvon, Brnch Mgr
EMP: 30
SALES (corp-wide): 1.91B Privately Held
Web: www.flintgrp.com
SIC: 2865 2893 Color pigments, organic; Printing ink
HQ: Flint Cps Inks North America Llc
  17177 N Laurel Park Dr # 300
  Livonia MI 48152
  734 781-4600

(G-8205)
FLIR SECURITY INC
Also Called: Db Schenker
5250 W 76th St (46268-4137)
PHONE..................443 936-9108
EMP: 5 EST: 2018
SALES (est): 67.77K Privately Held
Web: www.flir.eu
SIC: 3826 Analytical instruments

(G-8206)
FLOTEC INC
7625 W New York St (46214-4938)
PHONE..................317 273-6960
▲ EMP: 24 EST: 1983
SALES (est): 4.63MM Privately Held
Web: www.floteco2.com
SIC: 3494 Valves and pipe fittings, nec

(G-8207)
FLUID HANDLING TECHNOLOGY INC
7692 Zionsville Rd (46268-2173)
PHONE..................317 216-9629
EMP: 4 EST: 2005
SALES (est): 1.87MM Privately Held
Web: www.fhtindy.com
SIC: 5051 3069 Tubing, metal; Tubing, rubber

(G-8208)
FLUTES INC (PA)
8252 Zionsville Rd (46268-1627)
PHONE..................317 870-6010
Tony Reiley, Pr
Jeffrey Schwarz, *
Terry Walles, *
Jack Schwarz, *
EMP: 71 EST: 2006
SQ FT: 160,000
SALES (est): 23.14MM
SALES (corp-wide): 23.14MM Privately Held
Web: www.flutescorrugated.com
SIC: 2679 Corrugated paper: made from purchased material

(G-8209)
FLUTES INC
1102 W Hanna Ave (46217-5123)
PHONE..................844 317-2021
EMP: 100
SALES (corp-wide): 23.14MM Privately Held
Web: www.flutescorrugated.com
SIC: 2679 Corrugated paper: made from purchased material
PA: Flutes, Inc.
  8252 Zionsville Rd
  Indianapolis IN 46268
  317 870-6010

(G-8210)
FLYNN MEDIA LLC
Also Called: Flynn Interactive
9334 Champton Dr (46256-1061)
P.O. Box 503068 (46250-8068)
PHONE..................317 536-2972
Patrick Flynn, Managing Member
EMP: 3 EST: 2005
SALES (est): 162.75K Privately Held
Web: www.flynn-media.com
SIC: 7371 7372 7373 Computer software systems analysis and design, custom; Business oriented computer software; Computer integrated systems design

(G-8211)
FLYWITHME DELIVERY LLC
4350 Madison Ave Apt 110 (46227-1592)
PHONE..................219 614-9384
EMP: 1
SALES (est): 54.62K Privately Held
SIC: 3799 Transportation equipment, nec

(G-8212)
FOAMCRAFT INC (PA)
Also Called: Bestway Foam
9230 Harrison Park Ct (46216-1090)
PHONE..................317 545-3626
Robert W Elliott, Pr
Robert B Green, *
Jennifer E Chapman, *
Michael D Rich, *
▲ EMP: 30 EST: 1952
SQ FT: 48,000
SALES (est): 92.24MM
SALES (corp-wide): 92.24MM Privately Held
Web: www.foamcraftinc.com
SIC: 3086 Plastics foam products

(G-8213)
FOLK ART TO GO
8152 Meadow Bend Dr (46259-6731)
PHONE..................317 753-8553
Chris Michel, Owner
EMP: 1 EST: 2000
SALES (est): 57.83K Privately Held
SIC: 2741 Art copy and poster publishing

(G-8214)
FORECAST SALES INC
2719 Tobey Dr (46219-1417)
PHONE..................317 829-0147
Brian L Mccoy, Pr
Steven L Mccoy, VP
EMP: 17 EST: 2010
SALES (est): 2.91MM Privately Held
Web: www.forecastsalesinc.com
SIC: 3589 Sandblasting equipment

(G-8215)
FOREVER YOUNG TRCKG SVCS LLC
6444 Grandview Dr (46260-4424)
PHONE..................616 350-4053
EMP: 1 EST: 2021
SALES (est): 60.08K Privately Held
SIC: 3537 7389 Trucks: freight, baggage, etc.: industrial, except mining; Business services, nec

(G-8216)
FORTUNE DIVERSIFIED INDUSTRIES
6809 Corporate Dr (46278-1994)
PHONE..................317 532-3644
Doug May, Prin
EMP: 1 EST: 2013
SALES (est): 70.23K Privately Held
Web: www.fortunewirelessinc.com
SIC: 3999 Manufacturing industries, nec

(G-8217)
FOX STUDIOS INC
6027 Gladden Dr (46220-2567)
PHONE..................317 253-0135
Clare Fox Acheson, Pr
Ann Fox Clark, VP
Mary Fox, Sec
EMP: 10 EST: 1970
SQ FT: 5,500
SALES (est): 231.55K Privately Held
Web: www.americanringsource.com
SIC: 3231 3211 Products of purchased glass ; Plate and sheet glass

(G-8218)
FOY INDUSTRIES
6953 Dean Rd (46220-3809)
PHONE..................317 727-3905
Dave Strobel, Prin
EMP: 5 EST: 2018
SALES (est): 90.36K Privately Held
SIC: 3999 Manufacturing industries, nec

(G-8219)
FR CHINOOK LLC
7441 Chinook Cir (46219-7534)
PHONE..................317 356-1666
Adam Mcneal, Pt
EMP: 4 EST: 2011
SALES (est): 210.84K Privately Held
SIC: 2451 Mobile homes

(G-8220)
FRAKES ENGINEERING INC
7950 Castleway Dr Ste 160 (46250-1994)
PHONE..................317 577-3000
James L Frakes, Pr
Sheila Frakes, *
Lisa Frakes-bratcher, Sec
EMP: 30 EST: 1977
SQ FT: 22,000
SALES (est): 5.79MM Privately Held
Web: www.frakesengineering.com
SIC: 7373 3625 Systems integration services ; Relays and industrial controls

(G-8221)
FRANCES MONFORTE
Also Called: Fanfare Sales
8788 Robbins Rd (46268-1021)
PHONE..................317 875-0880
Frances Monforte, Owner
EMP: 1 EST: 1985
SQ FT: 7,500
SALES (est): 91.97K Privately Held
SIC: 3161 Cases, carrying, nec

(G-8222)
FRANK WISS RACG COMPONENTS INC

Indianapolis - Marion County (G-8223)

140 Gasoline Aly (46222-3965)
PHONE.................317 243-9585
Frank W Weiss, *Pr*
Wade Weiss, *VP*
Christina Weiss, *Sec*
Shawna Greves, *Sec*
EMP: 9 **EST:** 1980
SQ FT: 8,800
SALES (est): 453.13K **Privately Held**
Web: www.fwrc.com
SIC: 7539 3714 5013 Machine shop, automotive; Motor vehicle parts and accessories; Motor vehicle supplies and new parts

(G-8223)
FRANKE MOTORSPORTS INC
Also Called: Franke & Associates
6501 E Troy Ave (46203-6160)
PHONE.................317 357-6995
Steve Franke, *Pr*
EMP: 1 **EST:** 1992
SALES (est): 75.34K **Privately Held**
SIC: 3711 Motor vehicles and car bodies

(G-8224)
FRANKLIN BARRY GALLERY
Also Called: Frame Shop, The
617 Massachusetts Ave (46204-1606)
PHONE.................317 822-8455
Don Elliot, *Pr*
EMP: 2 **EST:** 2002
SALES (est): 191.49K **Privately Held**
Web: www.theframeshopindy.com
SIC: 5999 8999 2752 Art, picture frames, and decorations; Actuarial consultant; Advertising posters, lithographed

(G-8225)
FRANKLIN TOWNSHIP CIVIC LEAGUE
Also Called: FRANKLIN TOWNSHIP INFORMER
8822 Southeastern Ave (46239-1341)
PHONE.................317 862-1774
Kathy Burton, *Pr*
EMP: 4 **EST:** 1971
SALES (est): 46.29K **Privately Held**
Web: www.ftcivicleague.org
SIC: 2711 Newspapers, publishing and printing

(G-8226)
FREEBAND CUSTOM PAINT LLC
3156 Watergate Pl (46224-2558)
PHONE.................219 216-2553
Jayveon Daniels, *Managing Member*
EMP: 1 **EST:** 2019
SALES (est): 50K **Privately Held**
SIC: 2851 Paints: oil or alkyd vehicle or water thinned

(G-8227)
FREEDOM CORRUGATED LLC
5505 W 74th St (46268-4184)
PHONE.................317 290-1140
EMP: 5
SALES (est): 416.99K **Privately Held**
SIC: 2653 Corrugated and solid fiber boxes

(G-8228)
FREEDOM INTENTIONAL LLC
5690 Cheval Ln (46235-6081)
PHONE.................219 576-2699
EMP: 1 **EST:** 2017
SALES (est): 47.64K **Privately Held**
SIC: 2741 Miscellaneous publishing

(G-8229)
FREELANCE LETTERING INC
4 Gasoline Aly Ste A (46222-5930)
PHONE.................317 244-9272
EMP: 13 **EST:** 1982
SQ FT: 14,000
SALES (est): 483K **Privately Held**
SIC: 3993 Signs and advertising specialties

(G-8230)
FREIJE TREATMENT SYSTEMS INC
7435 E 86th St (46256-1207)
PHONE.................317 508-3848
Gregory Lloyd, *Prin*
EMP: 6 **EST:** 2018
SALES (est): 87.98K **Privately Held**
Web: www.easywater.com
SIC: 3589 Water treatment equipment, industrial

(G-8231)
FREMA HOLDINGS LLC
1030 E New York St (46202-3730)
P.O. Box 2005 (46206-2005)
PHONE.................317 822-8002
EMP: 12 **EST:** 2006
SQ FT: 17,000
SALES (est): 1.01MM **Privately Held**
Web: www.arrowpowder.com
SIC: 3479 Coating of metals and formed products

(G-8232)
FRESH BAKERY CANDLES LLC
Also Called: Fresh Bakery Candles
223 Belmar Ave (46219-5221)
PHONE.................317 899-2377
Cassandra Stone, *Managing Member*
EMP: 1 **EST:** 2005
SALES (est): 63K **Privately Held**
Web: www.freshbakerycandles.com
SIC: 3999 Candles

(G-8233)
FRICTION-FREE LLC
6520 Royal Oakland Pl (46236-4811)
PHONE.................317 385-6975
EMP: 1
SALES (est): 69.27K **Privately Held**
SIC: 2836 Culture media

(G-8234)
FRITZ DISTRIBUTION LLC
1015 W 31st St Apt 213 (46208)
PHONE.................463 207-8210
EMP: 4
SALES (est): 180.77K **Privately Held**
SIC: 2035 Seasonings and sauces, except tomato and dry

(G-8235)
FRONTIER ENGINEERING
12469 E 65th St (46236-9720)
PHONE.................317 823-6885
Steve Jourdan, *Owner*
Lila Jourdan, *Owner*
EMP: 2 **EST:** 1985
SALES (est): 109.3K **Privately Held**
Web: www.frontierengineering.com
SIC: 3559 3535 Vibratory parts handling equipment; Unit handling conveying systems

(G-8236)
FSI FILTRATION LLC (PA)
1550 Indiana Ave (46202-3220)
PHONE.................317 264-2123
Ernest Joseph Kelly, *Managing Member*
EMP: 2 **EST:** 2019
SALES (est): 5MM

SALES (corp-wide): 5MM **Privately Held**
Web: www.fsifiltration.com
SIC: 3564 Filters, air: furnaces, air conditioning equipment, etc.

(G-8237)
FTN LOGISTICS LLC
3622 Cedar Pine Pl (46235-5811)
PHONE.................317 488-7446
Adriann Moorman, *CEO*
EMP: 3 **EST:** 2020
SALES (est): 134.07K **Privately Held**
SIC: 4789 3537 Transportation services, nec ; Trucks: freight, baggage, etc.: industrial, except mining

(G-8238)
FUEL RECOVERY SERVICE INC
125 W South St Unit 2690 (46206-4696)
P.O. Box 2676 (89041-2676)
PHONE.................317 372-3029
EMP: 2 **EST:** 2011
SALES (est): 180.4K **Privately Held**
SIC: 2911 Oils, fuel

(G-8239)
FUEL VM LLC
P.O. Box 503025 (46250-8025)
PHONE.................317 828-6060
EMP: 7 **EST:** 2010
SALES (est): 349.59K **Privately Held**
Web: www.fuelvm.com
SIC: 2869 Fuels

(G-8240)
FULL THROTTLE ENTERPRISE INC
6115 Allisonville Rd (46220-4604)
PHONE.................317 779-3887
James Royal, *CEO*
EMP: 4 **EST:** 2021
SALES (est): 265.99K **Privately Held**
SIC: 3537 3711 4213 5088 Trucks, tractors, loaders, carriers, and similar equipment; Truck tractors for highway use, assembly of ; Heavy hauling, nec; Marine crafts and supplies

(G-8241)
FUNDEX GAMES LTD
Also Called: Great American Puzzle Factory
1901 W 16th St (46202-2034)
PHONE.................317 248-1080
Carl E Voigt Iv, *Pr*
Chip Voigt, *
Pete Voigt, *
◆ **EMP:** 25 **EST:** 1986
SQ FT: 10,000
SALES (est): 991.13K **Privately Held**
SIC: 3944 Board games, children's and adults'

(G-8242)
FUR BEE
6552 Cornell Ave (46220-1146)
PHONE.................317 259-9498
T Lee, *Prin*
EMP: 1 **EST:** 2009
SALES (est): 95.75K **Privately Held**
Web: www.fur-bee.com
SIC: 3999 Furs

(G-8243)
FURNITURE DISTRIBUTORS INC
6405 Brookville Rd (46219-8246)
PHONE.................317 357-8508
Thomas A Neu, *Pr*
Robert L Funke, *VP*
EMP: 10 **EST:** 1977
SQ FT: 60,000
SALES (est): 2.23MM **Privately Held**

Web: www.furnituredistributorsinc.biz
SIC: 2512 2511 5021 5712 Living room furniture: upholstered on wood frames; Wood bedroom furniture; Office furniture, nec; Mattresses

(G-8244)
FURNITURE SALES & MARKETING
7219 Knollvalley Ln (46256-2190)
PHONE.................317 849-1508
Don Morris, *Owner*
EMP: 2 **EST:** 2000
SALES (est): 113.58K **Privately Held**
SIC: 2512 Upholstered household furniture

(G-8245)
FUTON FACTORY INC (PA)
Also Called: Eclipse Imports
5920 E 34th St (46218-1809)
PHONE.................317 549-8639
Margaret Brady, *Pr*
Darwin Bostrom, *VP*
EMP: 12 **EST:** 1990
SQ FT: 49,000
SALES (est): 5MM **Privately Held**
Web: www.futonfactoryinc.com
SIC: 5712 2515 Bedding and bedsprings; Mattresses and bedsprings

(G-8246)
FUTURETEK
535 N Livingston Ave (46222-3401)
PHONE.................317 631-0098
Mitchell Lewis, *Owner*
EMP: 2 **EST:** 2005
SALES (est): 146.94K **Privately Held**
SIC: 3571 Electronic computers

(G-8247)
FUTUREWERKS LLC
9112 Sargent Rd (46256-1132)
PHONE.................305 926-3633
Michelle Coe, *Pr*
EMP: 1 **EST:** 2011
SALES (est): 130.92K **Privately Held**
Web: www.futurewerksllc.com
SIC: 4911 3621 3519 Generation, electric power; Motors and generators; Internal combustion engines, nec

(G-8248)
FUZION PRODUCTS LLC
6312 Southeastern Ave (46203-5828)
PHONE.................317 536-0745
Scott Brown, *CEO*
Chris Felger, *CFO*
EMP: 6 **EST:** 2014
SALES (est): 228.47K **Privately Held**
SIC: 3315 Nails, steel: wire or cut

(G-8249)
FUZZYS SPIRITS LLC
Also Called: Fuzzys Vodka
9455 Delegates Row (46240-3805)
PHONE.................317 489-6572
EMP: 9 **EST:** 2009
SALES (est): 257.65K **Privately Held**
Web: www.fuzzyvodka.com
SIC: 2085 Vodka (alcoholic beverage)

(G-8250)
G & G METAL SPINNERS INC
1717 Cornell Ave (46202-1898)
PHONE.................317 923-3225
Kenneth T Young, *Pr*
Linda J Young, *Sec*
EMP: 20 **EST:** 1949
SQ FT: 50,000
SALES (est): 3.32MM **Privately Held**
Web: www.ggmetalspinners.com

SIC: 3542 3444 Spinning machines, metal; Sheet metalwork

(G-8251)
G & H DIVERSIFIED MFG LP
1705 Midwest Blvd (46214-2378)
PHONE..................................713 849-2111
EMP: 50
SALES (corp-wide): 94.1MM Privately Held
Web: www.ghdiv.com
SIC: 3441 Fabricated structural metal
PA: G & H Diversified Mfg., L.P.
11927 Tanner Rd
Houston TX 77041
713 856-1600

(G-8252)
G C SOLUTIONS INC
Also Called: Fastsigns
3702 W 86th St Ste B (46268-1903)
PHONE..................................317 334-1149
EMP: 4 EST: 2011
SQ FT: 6,600
SALES (est): 391.26K Privately Held
Web: www.fastsigns.com
SIC: 3993 Signs and advertising specialties

(G-8253)
G L D INC (PA)
6427 N Ewing St (46220-4425)
PHONE..................................317 924-7981
David Combs, Pr
Larry Ostendorf, VP
EMP: 3 EST: 1996
SQ FT: 1,800
SALES (est): 420.41K
SALES (corp-wide): 420.41K Privately Held
SIC: 3949 Skin diving equipment, scuba type

(G-8254)
G THRAPP JEWELERS INC
3810 E 79th St (46240-3457)
PHONE..................................317 255-5555
Gary Thrapp, Pr
Barbara Thrapp, Sec
EMP: 9 EST: 1984
SALES (est): 439.58K Privately Held
Web: www.gthrapp.com
SIC: 5944 3911 Jewelry, precious stones and precious metals; Jewelry, precious metal

(G-8255)
GALE ENAMELING CO INC
10095 Old National Rd (46231-1990)
PHONE..................................317 839-7474
Curtis Ping, Pr
Samuel Ping, Treas
Doreen Ping, VP
EMP: 8 EST: 1971
SQ FT: 6,000
SALES (est): 810.02K Privately Held
SIC: 3479 Coating of metals and formed products

(G-8256)
GALE FORCE SOFTWARE CORP
8720 Castle Creek Parkway East Dr Ste 200 (46250-4315)
PHONE..................................317 695-7423
Fran Gale, Pr
Scott Rulong, Dir Fin
Marshall Parker, Eng/Dir
EMP: 10 EST: 2006
SALES (est): 420.79K Privately Held
Web: www.deviceiq.com
SIC: 7372 Business oriented computer software

(G-8257)
GAMETIME SPORTING EVENTS LLC ✪
8520 Allison Pointe Blvd Ste 223 (46250-5700)
PHONE..................................812 406-8281
EMP: 2 EST: 2023
SALES (est): 62.01K Privately Held
SIC: 7372 Prepackaged software

(G-8258)
GAMMONS METAL & MFG CO INC
Also Called: Colorworks
2900 N Richardt Ave (46219-1119)
PHONE..................................317 546-7091
Jeffery F Slipher, Pr
▲ EMP: 40 EST: 1969
SQ FT: 33,600
SALES (est): 5.64MM Privately Held
Web: www.gammonsmetal.com
SIC: 3444 3469 3479 7389 Sheet metalwork; Stamping metal for the trade; Coating of metals and formed products; Metal cutting services

(G-8259)
GAPCO INC
1817 Inisheer Ct (46217-5430)
PHONE..................................317 787-6440
Gary C Gray, Pr
EMP: 7 EST: 1952
SQ FT: 7,023
SALES (est): 395.63K Privately Held
SIC: 3451 Screw machine products

(G-8260)
GARDNER GLASS PRODUCTS INC
Also Called: Division 60
1705 Lafayette Rd (46222-2808)
PHONE..................................317 464-0881
Pamela Harris, Mgr
EMP: 9
SALES (corp-wide): 49.88MM Privately Held
Web: www.dreamwalls.com
SIC: 3231 Products of purchased glass
PA: Gardner Glass Products, Inc.
301 Elkin Hwy
North Wilkesboro NC 28659
336 651-9300

(G-8261)
GARDNER MIRROR CORP
1705 Lafayette Rd (46222-2808)
PHONE..................................317 464-0881
Cindy Mills, Prin
EMP: 1 EST: 2001
SALES (est): 51.88K Privately Held
Web: www.dreamwalls.com
SIC: 3231 Products of purchased glass

(G-8262)
GARMCO (USA) INC
300 N Meridian St Ste 1100 (46204-1736)
PHONE..................................352 404-8998
William Witherspoon, Pr
Graham Leel, Dir
EMP: 1 EST: 2011
SALES (est): 236.37K Privately Held
Web: www.garmco.com
SIC: 3353 Aluminum sheet, plate, and foil

(G-8263)
GARRITY STONE INC
3137 N Ritter Ave (46218-2502)
PHONE..................................317 546-0893
Brandon Garrity, Pr
Kenneth Kalal, VP
EMP: 3 EST: 1997
SALES (est): 534.75K Privately Held
Web: www.garritystoneinc.com
SIC: 1411 5032 Dimension stone; Aggregate

(G-8264)
GARRITY TOOL COMPANY LLC
3555 Developers Rd Ste A (46227-3577)
PHONE..................................317 541-1400
EMP: 1
Web: www.garritytoolcompany.com
SIC: 3599 Machine shop, jobbing and repair

(G-8265)
GCAM INC
5341 E Thompson Rd (46237-4094)
PHONE..................................714 738-6462
EMP: 2
SALES (corp-wide): 9.4MM Privately Held
Web: www.gcamplasma.com
SIC: 2836 Plasmas
PA: Gcam, Inc.
1561 E Orangethorpe Ave # 205
Fullerton CA 92831
714 738-6462

(G-8266)
GEIGER & PETERS INC
761 S Sherman Dr (46203-1584)
P.O. Box 33807 (46203-0807)
PHONE..................................317 322-7740
Stephen H Kitter, Pr
Carl Peters, *
James Colzani, *
Steve Knitter, *
Barry Hochstedler, *
EMP: 62 EST: 1905
SQ FT: 130,000
SALES (est): 22.52MM Privately Held
Web: www.gpsteel.com
SIC: 3441 Building components, structural steel

(G-8267)
GEMA USA INC
4141 W 54th St (46254)
PHONE..................................317 298-5000
David M Lowe, Pr
Joseph J Humke, VP
▲ EMP: 1 EST: 2010
SALES (est): 1.17MM
SALES (corp-wide): 2.2B Publicly Held
Web: www.gemapowdercoating.com
SIC: 3479 Aluminum coating of metal products
PA: Graco Inc.
88 11th Ave Ne
Minneapolis MN 55413
612 623-6000

(G-8268)
GEN DIGITAL INC
Also Called: Symantec
8888 Keystone Xing Ste 1300 (46240-4609)
PHONE..................................317 575-4010
Scott Berkel, Brnch Mgr
EMP: 6
SALES (corp-wide): 3.81B Publicly Held
Web: www.nortonlifelock.com
SIC: 3674 Semiconductors and related devices
PA: Gen Digital Inc.
60 E Rio Slado Pkwy Ste 1
Tempe AZ 85281
650 527-8000

(G-8269)
GENER8 LLC
1901 W 16th St (46202-2034)
PHONE..................................317 253-8737
Carl E Voigt, Pr
EMP: 8 EST: 2012
SALES (est): 1.3MM Privately Held
Web: www.gener8.net
SIC: 5092 3944 Toys and games; Games, toys, and children's vehicles

(G-8270)
GENERAL DEVICES CO INC
1410 S Post Rd Ste 100 (46239-9788)
P.O. Box 39100 (46239-0100)
PHONE..................................317 897-7000
Maxwell S Fall, Pr
Martin K Fall, *
Rebecca D Bryan, Prin
EMP: 32 EST: 1953
SQ FT: 143,500
SALES (est): 7.27MM Privately Held
Web: www.generaldevices.com
SIC: 3469 Metal stampings, nec

(G-8271)
GENERAL FABRICATORS INC
5230 S Harding St (46217-9572)
P.O. Box 17014 (46217-0014)
PHONE..................................317 787-9354
Mark Blackard, Pr
EMP: 8 EST: 1958
SQ FT: 21,500
SALES (est): 849.16K Privately Held
Web: www.generalfabricators.com
SIC: 3089 3083 Plastics hardware and building products; Laminated plastics plate and sheet

(G-8272)
GENERAL MATERIAL HANDLING CO
1302 Kings Cove Ct (46260-1671)
P.O. Box 47662 (46247-0662)
PHONE..................................317 888-5735
John M Drey, Pr
Ann Drey, VP
EMP: 2 EST: 1988
SALES (est): 344.71K Privately Held
SIC: 5084 3535 Materials handling machinery; Unit handling conveying systems

(G-8273)
GENERATION LOGISTICS LLC
201 N Illinois St Ste 1600 (46204-1904)
PHONE..................................877 238-7380
EMP: 1 EST: 2021
SALES (est): 100K Privately Held
Web: www.generationlogistics.net
SIC: 3537 Trucks: freight, baggage, etc.: industrial, except mining

(G-8274)
GENES TRANSPORT LLC
11266 Echo Grove Ct (46236-9074)
PHONE..................................404 227-5178
EMP: 1
SALES (est): 54.62K Privately Held
SIC: 3799 7389 Transportation equipment, nec; Business Activities at Non-Commercial Site

(G-8275)
GENESYS CLOUD SERVICES INC
Interactive Intelligence
7601 Interactive Way (46278-2727)
PHONE..................................317 872-3000
EMP: 849
SALES (corp-wide): 220.02MM Privately Held
Web: www.genesys.com
SIC: 7372 Business oriented computer software
HQ: Genesys Cloud Services, Inc.
1302 El Cmino Real Ste 30
Menlo Park CA 94025

Indianapolis - Marion County (G-8276) GEOGRAPHIC SECTION

(G-8276)
GENESYS TELECOM US INC
Also Called: Genesys
7601 Interactive Way (46278)
PHONE.................703 673-1773
Tony Bates, *Ch*
EMP: 254 EST: 2014
SALES (est): 9.28MM **Privately Held**
Web: www.genesys.com
SIC: 7372 Business oriented computer software

(G-8277)
GENRICH CUSTOM CABINETRY MLLWK
2525 N Shadeland Ave (46219-1787)
PHONE.................317 351-0991
Jeff Genrich, *Prin*
EMP: 13 EST: 2015
SALES (est): 715.31K **Privately Held**
Web: www.gccmionline.com
SIC: 2434 Wood kitchen cabinets

(G-8278)
GEORGE P STEWART PRINTING CO
Also Called: Indianapolis Recorder
2901 N Tacoma Ave (46218-2737)
P.O. Box 18499 (46218-0499)
PHONE.................317 924-5143
Caroleen Mays, *Pr*
Angie Kuhn, *Mgr*
EMP: 21 EST: 1896
SQ FT: 12,000
SALES (est): 26.92K **Privately Held**
Web: www.indianapolisrecorder.com
SIC: 2711 Commercial printing and newspaper publishing combined

(G-8279)
GEORGIA-PACIFIC CORRUGATED III LLC (DH)
5645 W 82nd St (46278-1323)
EMP: 5 EST: 1977
SALES (est): 129.65MM
SALES (corp-wide): 64.37B **Privately Held**
SIC: 2679 Corrugated paper: made from purchased material
HQ: Georgia-Pacific Llc
133 Peachtree St Nw
Atlanta GA 30303
404 652-4000

(G-8280)
GET LATHERED
5129 E 68th St (46220-3928)
PHONE.................317 201-7291
EMP: 5 EST: 2018
SALES (est): 96.91K **Privately Held**
Web: getlathered.indiemade.com
SIC: 2844 Perfumes, cosmetics and other toilet preparations

(G-8281)
GILES AGENCY INCORPORATED
7002 Graham Rd Ste 219 (46220-4057)
PHONE.................317 842-5546
EMP: 7 EST: 2006
SALES (est): 698.65K **Privately Held**
Web: www.thegilesagency.com
SIC: 8742 2752 Marketing consulting services; Promotional printing, lithographic

(G-8282)
GIRAFFE-X GRAPHICS INC
5746 Wheeler Rd (46216-1038)
PHONE.................317 546-4944
EMP: 9 EST: 1994
SQ FT: 3,000
SALES (est): 683.42K **Privately Held**
Web: www.itye-dye.com

SIC: 2759 2395 Screen printing; Embroidery products, except Schiffli machine

(G-8283)
GIVESTR INC
6198 Meridian Street West Dr (46208-1539)
PHONE.................202 997-5862
Kyle Brown, *Prin*
EMP: 2 EST: 2014
SALES (est): 71.67K **Privately Held**
Web: www.givestr.org
SIC: 7372 7389 Application computer software; Business Activities at Non-Commercial Site

(G-8284)
GLEANERS FOOD BANK OF IND INC
3737 Waldemere Ave (46241)
PHONE.................317 925-0191
John Elliott, *Pr*
Joe Slater, *CFO*
Melissa Hill, *Ch*
Catherine Keiner Cpc, *Prin*
Miguel Larry, *CPO*
EMP: 100 EST: 1980
SQ FT: 295,000
SALES (est): 187.4MM **Privately Held**
Web: www.gleaners.org
SIC: 7389 2099 Labeling bottles, cans, cartons, etc.; Box lunches, for sale off premises

(G-8285)
GLEN-GERY CORPORATION
5518 Shelby St (46227-4656)
PHONE.................317 784-2505
EMP: 14
Web: www.glengery.com
SIC: 3271 Blocks, concrete: landscape or retaining wall
HQ: Glen-Gery Corporation
1166 Spring St
Reading PA 19610
610 374-4011

(G-8286)
GLENS PACT LLC
7018 Patrick Pl (46256-2707)
PHONE.................317 540-5869
EMP: 1
SALES (est): 69.27K **Privately Held**
SIC: 2599 7389 Food wagons, restaurant; Business Activities at Non-Commercial Site

(G-8287)
GLOBAL AIR INC (PA)
913 Bates St (46202-4018)
PHONE.................317 634-5300
Jr Spitznogle, *Pr*
Arnold H Breeden, *Stockholder*
EMP: 5 EST: 1965
SQ FT: 35,000
SALES (est): 2.03MM
SALES (corp-wide): 2.03MM **Privately Held**
Web: www.global-air.us
SIC: 3599 Chemical milling job shop

(G-8288)
GLOBAL AIR INC
6450 Rucker Rd (46220-4841)
PHONE.................317 251-1251
Natasha Schriver, *School Co-ordinator*
EMP: 9
SALES (corp-wide): 2.03MM **Privately Held**
Web: www.global-air.us
SIC: 3599 Chemical milling job shop
PA: Global Air Inc.
913 Bates St

Indianapolis IN 46202
317 634-5300

(G-8289)
GLOBAL FORMING LLC
913 Bates St (46202-4018)
PHONE.................317 290-1000
▼ EMP: 25 EST: 2007
SALES (est): 4.78MM **Privately Held**
Web: www.globalforming.us
SIC: 3714 Motor vehicle parts and accessories

(G-8290)
GLOBAL PLASTICS INC
6739 Guion Rd (46268-4810)
PHONE.................317 299-2345
J R Spitznogle, *Pr*
James G Spitznogle, *
▲ EMP: 100 EST: 1992
SQ FT: 35,500
SALES (est): 27.06MM **Privately Held**
Web: www.global-plastics.com
SIC: 3089 3544 Injection molding of plastics; Special dies, tools, jigs, and fixtures

(G-8291)
GLOBAL TECHNOLOGY GROUP IMPORT
1209 S High School Rd (46241-3126)
PHONE.................317 987-6902
Sami Awad, *Pr*
EMP: 1 EST: 2019
SALES (est): 450K **Privately Held**
SIC: 3663 Radio and t.v. communications equipment

(G-8292)
GLOBAL WATER TECHNOLOGIES INC
351 W 10th St Ste 537 (46202-4103)
P.O. Box 702 (46206-0702)
PHONE.................317 452-4488
Erik Hromadka, *Pr*
Tony Sandlin, *Treas*
EMP: 5 EST: 1990
SQ FT: 3,000
SALES (est): 734K **Privately Held**
Web: www.gwtr.com
SIC: 3589 Water treatment equipment, industrial

(G-8293)
GLOBE ASPHALT PAVING CO INC
6445 E 30th St (46219-1006)
P.O. Box 19168 (46219-0168)
PHONE.................317 568-4344
William Shumaker, *Pr*
Jane P Shumaker, *
John Shumaker, *
EMP: 50 EST: 1983
SQ FT: 10,000
SALES (est): 9.6MM **Privately Held**
Web: www.globeasphalt.com
SIC: 1794 2951 1611 Excavation work; Asphalt paving blocks (not from refineries); Grading

(G-8294)
GMP HOLDINGS LLC
Also Called: Crossroads Lighting
2525 N Shadeland Ave Bldg 30 # 6 (46219-1787)
PHONE.................317 353-6580
Gerald Peterson, *Pr*
Nilza Gonzalez, *CMO*
EMP: 9 EST: 2015
SQ FT: 12,000
SALES (est): 1.62MM **Privately Held**
Web: www.parksidedev.com

SIC: 3433 3648 8711 Solar heaters and collectors; Lighting equipment, nec; Engineering services

(G-8295)
GNB STUDIO INC
5410 E Washington St (46219-6412)
PHONE.................317 356-4834
Garry Brown, *Pr*
EMP: 1 EST: 1980
SALES (est): 130K **Privately Held**
Web: www.azppa.com
SIC: 3915 7631 Jewelers' castings; Jewelry repair services

(G-8296)
GOLD N GEMS
10202 E Washington St Ste 1325 (46229-2599)
PHONE.................317 895-6002
Salim Ali, *Owner*
EMP: 2 EST: 1999
SALES (est): 93.97K **Privately Held**
SIC: 3911 Jewelry, precious metal

(G-8297)
GOLDEN BEAM METALS LLC
8122 Dean Rd (46240-2918)
P.O. Box 40965 (46240-0965)
PHONE.................317 806-2750
Gary Colip, *Pr*
Brad Smith, *Treas*
Jon Colip, *Contrlr*
▲ EMP: 7 EST: 2015
SALES (est): 405.53K **Privately Held**
Web: www.gb-metals.com
SIC: 3399 Iron ore recovery from open hearth slag

(G-8298)
GOLDEN PRIDE HAIR COMPANY LLC
7576 Ivywood Dr Apt B (46250-5114)
P.O. Box 40543 (46240-0543)
PHONE.................812 777-9604
EMP: 3 EST: 2018
SALES (est): 64.17K **Privately Held**
SIC: 2389 Apparel and accessories, nec

(G-8299)
GOLDEN SIGNWORKS LIGHTING
7019 Brookville Rd (46239-1005)
PHONE.................317 358-4791
C Golden, *Prin*
EMP: 5 EST: 2005
SALES (est): 49.88K **Privately Held**
Web: www.signworksthinks.com
SIC: 3993 Signs and advertising specialties

(G-8300)
GOLDEN VENTURES INC
7687 Winton Dr (46268-4142)
P.O. Box 781343 (46278-8343)
PHONE.................317 872-2705
EMP: 20 EST: 1992
SALES (est): 2.09MM **Privately Held**
Web: www.cerambryte.com
SIC: 2842 5719 Specialty cleaning; Housewares, nec

(G-8301)
GOLDENMARC LLC
10475 Crosspoint Blvd Ste 250 (46256)
PHONE.................317 855-1651
EMP: 5 EST: 2018
SALES (est): 247.28K **Privately Held**
SIC: 8748 7371 2741 7363 Business consulting, nec; Computer software systems analysis and design, custom; Business service newsletters: publishing and printing; Temporary help service

GEOGRAPHIC SECTION

Indianapolis - Marion County (G-8329)

(G-8302)
GOLDLEAF PROMOTIONAL PDTS INC
6630 Ferguson St (46220-1151)
PHONE.................317 202-2754
EMP: 5 EST: 1996
SQ FT: 2,000
SALES (est): 513.53K **Privately Held**
Web: www.goldleafpromotions.com
SIC: 7311 2759 Advertising agencies; Commercial printing, nec

(G-8303)
GONZALEZ PALLETS
105 S Denny St (46201)
PHONE.................317 644-1242
Arnulfa Tigre, Prin
EMP: 6 EST: 2016
SALES (est): 142.13K **Privately Held**
Web: www.gonzalez-pallets.com
SIC: 2448 Pallets, wood

(G-8304)
GOODLIFE INDUSTRIES INC
3925 E 26th St (46218-3074)
PHONE.................317 339-6341
Nathan E Oatts Ii, Prin
EMP: 2 EST: 2010
SALES (est): 125.03K **Privately Held**
SIC: 3999 Manufacturing industries, nec

(G-8305)
GOODLOE INDUSTRY SVC
3101 N Campbell Ave (46218-2553)
PHONE.................317 258-5534
Fred Goodloe, Mgr
EMP: 4 EST: 2018
SALES (est): 39.69K **Privately Held**
SIC: 3999 Manufacturing industries, nec

(G-8306)
GOODTIME TECHNOLOGY DEV LTD
5150 W 76th St (46268-4100)
P.O. Box 631 (46077-0631)
PHONE.................317 876-3661
▲ EMP: 1 EST: 2009
SALES (est): 311.07K
SALES (corp-wide): 26.52MM **Privately Held**
SIC: 3069 Rubber automotive products
PA: Suzhou Goodtime Technology Development Co., Ltd
No.2009, Zuanshiroad, Weitangtown, Xiangcheng District
Suzhou JS 21513

(G-8307)
GORILLA PLASTIC RBR GROUP LLC
3401 Newton Ave (46201-4340)
PHONE.................317 635-9616
Don Katz, Managing Member
EMP: 10 EST: 2000
SALES (est): 901.4K **Privately Held**
SIC: 3069 Molded rubber products

(G-8308)
GORREPATI SERVICE SYSTEMS
Also Called: Car-X Muffler & Brake
3653 Lafayette Rd (46222-1108)
PHONE.................317 299-7590
Brad Lukas, Brnch Mgr
EMP: 1
SALES (corp-wide): 10.89MM **Privately Held**
Web: www.carx.com
SIC: 7694 7549 Armature rewinding shops; Lubrication service, automotive
PA: Gorrepati Service Systems, Inc
11843 Kemper Springs Dr
Cincinnati OH 45240
513 825-2660

(G-8309)
GOULDING & WOOD INC
823 Massachusetts Ave (46204-1610)
PHONE.................317 637-5222
Jason Overall, Pr
Brandon Woods, VP
Mark Goulding, Sec
EMP: 14 EST: 1976
SQ FT: 10,500
SALES (est): 922.91K **Privately Held**
Web: www.gouldingandwood.com
SIC: 3931 7699 Pipes, organ; Organ tuning and repair

(G-8310)
GOV 6 CORP
450 E 96th St Ste 500 (46240-3760)
PHONE.................317 847-4942
Azeem Bade, CEO
EMP: 2 EST: 2012
SALES (est): 402.44K **Privately Held**
Web: www.gov6corp.com
SIC: 2621 2677 2678 2679 Paper mills; Envelopes; Stationery products; Adding machine rolls, paper: made from purchased material

(G-8311)
GRACE FTHS CLBRATORY SIGNS LLC
3713 Newcastle Ct (46235-0011)
PHONE.................463 701-7673
Shakeena Kimbrough, CEO
EMP: 1 EST: 2021
SALES (est): 46.08K **Privately Held**
Web: www.gandfcelebrate.com
SIC: 3993 Signs and advertising specialties

(G-8312)
GRAND PRODUCTS INC
1650 S Girls School Rd (46231-1308)
PHONE.................317 870-3122
EMP: 201
SALES (corp-wide): 24.03MM **Privately Held**
Web: www.grandproductsinc.com
SIC: 3999 Coin-operated amusement machines
PA: Grand Products, Inc.
1718 Hampshire Dr
Elk Grove Village IL 60007
800 621-6101

(G-8313)
GRAVEL DOCTOR INDIANAPOLIS LLC
7611 Dornock Dr (46237-9675)
PHONE.................317 399-4585
EMP: 4 EST: 2015
SALES (est): 181.63K **Privately Held**
Web: www.graveldoctorindianapolis.com
SIC: 1442 Construction sand and gravel

(G-8314)
GRAVES MEDIA & PUBG GROUP LLC
1312 Scotland Blvd (46231-5242)
PHONE.................317 679-4072
Faye Cox, Admn
EMP: 4 EST: 2016
SALES (est): 45.48K **Privately Held**
SIC: 2741 Miscellaneous publishing

(G-8315)
GRAVEYARDGARLIC LLC ✪
8888 Keystone Xing (46240)
PHONE.................502 523-8148
EMP: 2 EST: 2022
SALES (est): 92.67K **Privately Held**

SIC: 2099 Food preparations, nec

(G-8316)
GRAYBULL ORGANIC WINES INC
8435 Georgetown Rd Ste 600 (46268-5629)
PHONE.................317 797-2186
EMP: 6
SALES (est): 209.07K **Privately Held**
Web: www.graybull.com
SIC: 2084 Wines

(G-8317)
GREEN PLUS PLASTICS LLC
3131 N Franklin Rd Ste L (46226-6390)
PHONE.................317 672-2410
Kumar Aeneni, Managing Member
EMP: 7 EST: 2013
SALES (est): 160.86K **Privately Held**
SIC: 3089 Injection molding of plastics

(G-8318)
GREENCYCLE OF INDIANA INC
Also Called: Greencycle
1103 W Troy Ave (46225-2247)
PHONE.................317 780-8175
John Repenning, Brnch Mgr
EMP: 9
Web: www.greencycle.com
SIC: 2499 Mulch or sawdust products, wood
HQ: Greencycle Of Indiana, Inc.
400 Central Ave Ste 115
Northfield IL 60093

(G-8319)
GREENLEAF FOODS SPC INC ✪
8735 E 33rd St Bldg B (46226-6528)
PHONE.................317 554-4322
Adam Grogan, CEO
EMP: 60 EST: 2022
SALES (est): 8.41MM
SALES (corp-wide): 3.54B **Privately Held**
Web: www.greenleaffoods.com
SIC: 2033 Vegetables: packaged in cans, jars, etc.
PA: Maple Leaf Foods Inc
6897 Financial Dr
Mississauga ON L5N 0
519 900-8917

(G-8320)
GREENLIGHT LLC
Also Called: Greenlight Collectibles
5901 Lakeside Blvd (46278-1996)
PHONE.................317 287-0600
Russell Hughes, Managing Member
▲ EMP: 13 EST: 2002
SALES (est): 2.17MM **Privately Held**
Web: www.greenlighttoys.com
SIC: 3944 Automobile and truck models, toy and hobby

(G-8321)
GREENLINE SCREEN PRINTING
6830 Hawthorn Park Dr (46220-3909)
PHONE.................317 572-1155
Jim Pike, Pr
EMP: 2 EST: 2011
SALES (est): 119.97K **Privately Held**
Web: www.distinctimages.net
SIC: 2752 Offset printing

(G-8322)
GREENSBROOM
4555 W Bradbury Ave Ste 1 (46241-5209)
PHONE.................317 416-7818
EMP: 5 EST: 2018
SALES (est): 101.59K **Privately Held**
Web: www.greensbroom.com

SIC: 3523 Farm machinery and equipment

(G-8323)
GREENSGROOMER WORLDWIDE INC
3890 N Raceway Rd (46234-9226)
PHONE.................317 388-0695
EMP: 1
Web: www.greensgroomer.com
SIC: 3441 Fabricated structural metal
PA: Greensgroomer Worldwide Inc
10930 E Us Highway 136 A
Indianapolis IN 46234

(G-8324)
GREENSGROOMER WORLDWIDE INC (PA)
10930 E Us Highway 136 (46234-9095)
P.O. Box 34151 (46234-0151)
PHONE.................317 388-0695
EMP: 3 EST: 1996
SQ FT: 23,000
SALES (est): 910.5K **Privately Held**
Web: www.greensgroomer.com
SIC: 3441 Fabricated structural metal

(G-8325)
GREENWOOD LADIES AUXILIARY 252
4619 Anita Dr (46217-3401)
PHONE.................317 788-8458
Donna Miller, Prin
EMP: 5 EST: 2016
SALES (est): 62.25K **Privately Held**
SIC: 2499 Wood products, nec

(G-8326)
GREIF INC
3719 W 96th St (46268-3100)
PHONE.................740 657-6606
EMP: 5
SALES (corp-wide): 5.22B **Publicly Held**
Web: www.greif.com
SIC: 2655 Fiber cans, drums, and similar products
PA: Greif, Inc.
425 Winter Rd
Delaware OH 43015
740 549-6000

(G-8327)
GREYPAINT LLC
Also Called: Wood Shop
3055 Pawnee Dr (46235-2495)
PHONE.................765 407-6321
Tyrone Harley, Admn
EMP: 1 EST: 2021
SALES (est): 64.19K **Privately Held**
SIC: 3553 Furniture makers machinery, woodworking

(G-8328)
GREYS AUTOMOTIVE INC
1604 W Minnesota St (46221-1833)
PHONE.................317 632-3562
Charles Grey, Pr
Patricia Grey, Sec
EMP: 2 EST: 1952
SQ FT: 3,600
SALES (est): 253.78K **Privately Held**
SIC: 5531 3599 Automotive parts; Machine shop, jobbing and repair

(G-8329)
GRIDER & CO CONSTRUCTION LLC
5607 N Oxford St (46220-2904)
PHONE.................310 986-7533
Stephen J Grider, Managing Member
EMP: 1 EST: 2021
SALES (est): 100K **Privately Held**

Indianapolis - Marion County (G-8330)

SIC: 1389 Construction, repair, and dismantling services

(G-8330)
GRINDHARD PERFORMANCE LLC
6020 E 82nd St (46250-4746)
PHONE.................................317 334-5795
Justin Lamar Mcafee, *CEO*
EMP: 1 EST: 2021
SALES (est): 65.93K **Privately Held**
SIC: 3949 Sporting and athletic goods, nec

(G-8331)
GRINDING AND POLSG MCHY CORP
Also Called: G & P Machinery
2801 Tobey Dr (46219-1481)
PHONE.................................317 898-0750
James Reiman, *Pr*
Sarah Chaille, *Treas*
▲ EMP: 15 EST: 1952
SQ FT: 30,000
SALES (est): 2.48MM **Privately Held**
Web: www.gandpmachineryin.com
SIC: 3549 3541 3553 Metalworking machinery, nec; Machine tools, metal cutting type; Woodworking machinery

(G-8332)
GRINON INDUSTRIES LLC (PA)
7649 Winton Dr (46268-4142)
PHONE.................................317 388-5100
▲ EMP: 22 EST: 2008
SQ FT: 25,000
SALES (est): 3.93MM **Privately Held**
Web: www.bottomsupbeer.com
SIC: 3585 Beer dispensing equipment

(G-8333)
GRIT INTO GRACE INC
859 N Parker Ave (46201-2450)
PHONE.................................317 331-8334
Stefanie Jeffers, *Prin*
EMP: 3 EST: 2017
SALES (est): 125.34K **Privately Held**
Web: www.gritintograce.org
SIC: 3999 Manufacturing industries, nec

(G-8334)
GROUPONE HEALTH SOURCE INC
Also Called: Revele
11715 Fox Rd Ste 400 # 178 (46236-8431)
PHONE.................................800 769-5288
Arun Murali, *CEO*
Diane Swanson, *
EMP: 55 EST: 1999
SALES (est): 12.73MM **Privately Held**
Web: www.revelemd.com
SIC: 7372 8011 8721 Prepackaged software; Offices and clinics of medical doctors; Billing and bookkeeping service
PA: Gohs, Llc
  8275 Allison Pointe Trl
  Indianapolis IN 46250

(G-8335)
GROWING SMILES INC
7210 Madison Ave Apt O (46227-5227)
P.O. Box 56022 (46256-0022)
PHONE.................................317 787-6404
Ellen M Ahlers, *Mgr*
EMP: 4 EST: 2007
SALES (est): 231.18K **Privately Held**
Web: www.growingsmiles.com
SIC: 3843 Orthodontic appliances

(G-8336)
GRRK HOLDINGS INC
Also Called: Ds Smith Rapak
7430 New Augusta Rd (46268-2291)
PHONE.................................317 872-0172

Gary W Smith, *CEO*
Daniel A Cunningham, *
▲ EMP: 50 EST: 1960
SQ FT: 28,000
SALES (est): 8.03MM
SALES (corp-wide): 8.62B **Privately Held**
SIC: 3089 3565 2673 Injection molding of plastics; Packaging machinery; Plastic and pliofilm bags
PA: Ds Smith Plc
  Level 3
  London W2 1D
  754 542-9001

(G-8337)
GRUNDFOS PUMPS MFG CORP
2005 Dr Martin Luther King Jr St (46202-1165)
PHONE.................................317 925-9661
Andrew Warrington, *Mgr*
EMP: 7
SALES (corp-wide): 5.02B **Privately Held**
Web: www.grundfos.com
SIC: 3561 Industrial pumps and parts
HQ: Grundfos Pumps Manufacturing Corporation
  5900 E Shields Ave
  Fresno CA 93727

(G-8338)
GTC MACHINING LLC
3555 Developers Rd (46227-3586)
PHONE.................................317 541-1400
Scott Geller, *Pr*
EMP: 63 EST: 2019
SALES (est): 10.15MM
SALES (corp-wide): 24.04MM **Privately Held**
Web: www.gtcmachining.com
SIC: 3599 Machine shop, jobbing and repair
PA: Phx Holdings, Llc
  6100 Emmanuel Dr Sw
  Atlanta GA 30336
  404 699-2882

(G-8339)
GTC MACHINING LLC
Also Called: Garrity Tool Company, LLC
3555 Developers Rd Ste A (46227-3577)
PHONE.................................317 541-1400
Michael Pinkerton, *Managing Member*
EMP: 1 EST: 2018
SALES (est): 266.99K **Privately Held**
SIC: 3599 3441 Machine shop, jobbing and repair; Fabricated structural metal for ships

(G-8340)
GUARDIAN ENTERPRISES LLC
9465 Counselors Row Ste 200 (46240-6423)
PHONE.................................317 416-8926
EMP: 4
SALES (est): 101.26K **Privately Held**
SIC: 1389 Construction, repair, and dismantling services

(G-8341)
GUIDE BOOK PUBLISHING
5929 Haverford Ave (46220-2752)
PHONE.................................317 259-0599
Bob Vogt, *Prin*
EMP: 5 EST: 2016
SALES (est): 69.67K **Privately Held**
Web: www.guidebookpublishing.com
SIC: 2741 Miscellaneous publishing

(G-8342)
GUIDE TECHNOLOGIES LLC
Also Called: Administrative Office
250 E 96th St Ste 525 (46240-3736)
PHONE.................................317 844-3162

EMP: 4
SALES (corp-wide): 4.97MM **Privately Held**
Web: www.guidetechnologies.com
SIC: 7372 Prepackaged software
PA: Guide Technologies, Llc
  7363 E Kemper Rd Ste Ab
  Cincinnati OH 45249
  513 631-8800

(G-8343)
GUSA HOLDINGS INC
4925 Aluminum Dr (46218-3156)
PHONE.................................317 545-1221
Bill Witherspoon, *Pr*
EMP: 60 EST: 2001
SALES (est): 6.51MM **Privately Held**
SIC: 3354 3353 5051 Aluminum extruded products; Foil, aluminum; Aluminum bars, rods, ingots, sheets, pipes, plates, etc.
PA: Gulf Aluminium Rolling Mill B.S.C Closed
  Block 601, Building 462 North Sitra Industrial Area
  Sitra

(G-8344)
GUTTER ONE SUPPLY
8026 Woodland Dr (46278-1349)
PHONE.................................317 872-1257
EMP: 10 EST: 2016
SALES (est): 130.01K **Privately Held**
SIC: 5211 5031 2431 Lumber and other building materials; Composite board products, woodboard; Millwork

(G-8345)
GVS FILTER TECHNOLOGY INC
5353 W 79th St (46268-1699)
PHONE.................................317 471-3700
▲ EMP: 20
SIC: 5999 3569 Medical apparatus and supplies; Filters, general line: industrial

(G-8346)
GWIN ENTERPRISES
7294 S Delaware St (46227-2434)
PHONE.................................317 881-6401
Barry L Gwin, *Prin*
EMP: 4 EST: 2010
SALES (est): 230.32K **Privately Held**
Web: www.gwin-enterprises.com
SIC: 3663 Airborne radio communications equipment

(G-8347)
H C SCHUMACHER MACHINE CO IN
3619 S Arlington Ave (46203-6104)
PHONE.................................317 787-9361
Clair W Golay, *Pr*
Michael Hope, *VP*
Jackie Golay, *VP*
EMP: 16 EST: 1929
SQ FT: 20,000
SALES (est): 1.17MM **Privately Held**
SIC: 3559 Glass making machinery: blowing, molding, forming, etc.

(G-8348)
H&G LEGACY CO
Also Called: Hill and Griffith
3637 Farnsworth St (46241-5310)
PHONE.................................317 241-9233
Michael Lawry, *Mgr*
EMP: 7
SALES (corp-wide): 8.69MM **Privately Held**
Web: www.hillandgriffith.com
SIC: 2899 Chemical preparations, nec
PA: H&G Legacy Co.
  1085 Summer St

Cincinnati OH 45204
513 921-1075

(G-8349)
H3R GARAGE LLC ◊
11125 Baycreek Dr (46236-9103)
PHONE.................................317 519-1368
Ginnyla Cash, *CEO*
EMP: 1 EST: 2022
SALES (est): 62.01K **Privately Held**
SIC: 2396 Apparel and other linings, except millinery

(G-8350)
HACKETT PUBLISHING COMPANY
832 Pierson St (46204-1109)
P.O. Box 44937 (46244-0937)
PHONE.................................317 635-9250
Sherry Brown, *Mgr*
EMP: 6
SALES (corp-wide): 3.4MM **Privately Held**
Web: www.hackettpublishing.com
SIC: 2731 Books, publishing only
PA: Hackett Publishing Company Inc
  3333 Massachusetts Ave
  Indianapolis IN 46218
  317 635-9250

(G-8351)
HACKETT PUBLISHING COMPANY (PA)
3333 Massachusetts Ave (46218-3754)
P.O. Box 44937 (46244-0937)
PHONE.................................317 635-9250
James N Hullett, *CEO*
Frances Hackett, *Pr*
Cheri L Brown, *Sec*
Deborah D Wilkes, *Pr*
EMP: 19 EST: 1972
SQ FT: 51,000
SALES (est): 3.4MM
SALES (corp-wide): 3.4MM **Privately Held**
Web: www.hackettpublishing.com
SIC: 2731 Textbooks: publishing only, not printed on site

(G-8352)
HACKNEY HOME FURNISHINGS INC
Also Called: Volunteer Fabricators, Inc.
9420 E 33rd St (46235)
P.O. Box 238 (37901)
PHONE.................................317 895-4300
William B Sansom, *Pr*
B E France, *
Leonard Robinette, *
Tonia Roberts, *
Michael D Morton, *
▲ EMP: 200 EST: 1980
SQ FT: 3,000
SALES (est): 1.42MM
SALES (corp-wide): 25.63MM **Privately Held**
SIC: 2541 Table or counter tops, plastic laminated
PA: The H T Hackney Co
  502 S Gay St Ste 100
  Knoxville TN 37902
  865 546-1291

(G-8353)
HAMILTON BROS INC
1840 Midwest Blvd (46214-2376)
PHONE.................................317 241-2571
Larry Hamilton, *Pr*
EMP: 14 EST: 1949
SALES (est): 612.59K **Privately Held**
Web: www.hamiltonbrosinc.com
SIC: 7699 1381 Pumps and pumping equipment repair; Drilling water intake wells

GEOGRAPHIC SECTION

Indianapolis - Marion County (G-8379)

(G-8354)
HANSFORD PREVENT LLC
5658 Buck Pond Ct (46237-8423)
P.O. Box 39223 (46239-0223)
PHONE.....................317 985-2346
Michael Hansford, *Prin*
EMP: 5 **EST:** 2016
SALES (est): 86.66K **Privately Held**
SIC: 3582 Commercial laundry equipment

(G-8355)
HAPPY TEES LLC
628 E 63rd St (46220-1734)
PHONE.....................317 465-0122
EMP: 4 **EST:** 2014
SALES (est): 111.57K **Privately Held**
SIC: 2759 Screen printing

(G-8356)
HARDING GROUP LLC
Also Called: Hmi North
5145 E 96th St (46240-1440)
PHONE.....................317 846-7401
EMP: 4
SALES (corp-wide): 23.39MM **Privately Held**
Web: www.howardcompanies.com
SIC: 3531 Asphalt plant, including gravel-mix type
PA: Harding Group, Inc.
2916 Kentucky Ave
Indianapolis IN 46221
317 849-9666

(G-8357)
HARDING GROUP LLC
Also Called: Hmi South
1100 S Tibbs Ave (46241-2733)
PHONE.....................317 536-8364
EMP: 88
SALES (corp-wide): 23.39MM **Privately Held**
Web: www.howardcompanies.com
SIC: 2951 Asphalt paving mixtures and blocks
PA: Harding Group, Inc.
2916 Kentucky Ave
Indianapolis IN 46221
317 849-9666

(G-8358)
HARDING MATERIALS INC
10151 Hague Rd (46256-3319)
PHONE.....................317 849-9666
EMP: 5
SIC: 3531 Asphalt plant, including gravel-mix type

(G-8359)
HARDINGPOORMAN INC
Also Called: Full Court Press
4923 W 78th St (46268-4170)
PHONE.....................317 876-3355
David A Harding, *Pr*
Robert Poorman, *
Steve Ancalonea, *Stockholder**
Bob Poorman, *
Steve Anzalone, *
EMP: 134 **EST:** 1967
SQ FT: 52,800
SALES (est): 32.51MM **Privately Held**
Web: www.hardingpoorman.com
SIC: 2752 Offset printing

(G-8360)
HARDINGPOORMAN GROUP INC
Also Called: Full Court Press Printing
4923 W 78th St (46268-4170)
PHONE.....................317 876-3355
David A Harding, *Ch*
Steve Anzalone, *Pr*
Keith Craig, *VP*
Max Phillips, *VP*
EMP: 6 **EST:** 2000
SALES (est): 1.34MM **Privately Held**
Web: www.hardingpoorman.com
SIC: 2752 Offset printing

(G-8361)
HARLAN BAKERIES LLC
Also Called: Harlan Bakeries
404 S Kitley Ave (46219-7426)
PHONE.....................317 272-3600
Hugh Harlan, *Managing Member*
EMP: 120
Web: www.harlanfoods.com
SIC: 5149 2051 2045 Bakery products; Bread, cake, and related products; Prepared flour mixes and doughs
PA: Harlan Bakeries, Llc
7597 E Us Hwy 36
Avon IN 46123

(G-8362)
HARLAN DEVELOPMENT COMPANY
404 S Kitley Ave (46219-7426)
PHONE.....................317 352-1583
Hal Harlan, *Prin*
EMP: 3 **EST:** 2009
SALES (est): 494.61K **Privately Held**
Web: www.harlandevelopment.com
SIC: 2836 Biological products, except diagnostic
PA: Harlan Bakeries, Llc
7597 E Us Hwy 36
Avon IN 46123

(G-8363)
HARMAN EMBEDDED AUDIO LLC
6602 E 75th St Ste 520 (46250-2870)
PHONE.....................317 849-8175
Chris Welsh, *Managing Member*
▲ **EMP:** 11 **EST:** 1997
SQ FT: 5,000
SALES (est): 897.04K **Privately Held**
Web: www.harman.com
SIC: 5065 3651 Electronic parts and equipment, nec; Audio electronic systems
HQ: Harman International Industries Incorporated
400 Atlantic St Fl 15
Stamford CT 06901
203 328-3500

(G-8364)
HAROLD MAILAND
Also Called: Textile Conservation Services
928 N Alabama St (46202-3350)
PHONE.....................317 266-8398
Harold Mailand, *Owner*
EMP: 1 **EST:** 1986
SALES (est): 80.44K **Privately Held**
SIC: 2299 Recovering textile fibers from clippings and rags

(G-8365)
HARPERCOLLINS PUBLISHERS LLC
2700 N Richardt Ave (46219-1117)
PHONE.....................800 242-7737
EMP: 2
SALES (corp-wide): 10.09B **Publicly Held**
Web: www.harpercollins.com
SIC: 2731 Books, publishing only
HQ: Harpercollins Publishers L.L.C.
195 Broadway
New York NY 10007
212 207-7000

(G-8366)
HARRELL FAMILY LLC
Also Called: Window Makeover
6802 Hillsdale Ct (46250)
PHONE.....................317 770-4550
EMP: 17 **EST:** 2013
SALES (est): 2.07MM **Privately Held**
Web: www.windowmakeoverinc.com
SIC: 3531 3462 Subgraders (construction equipment); Construction or mining equipment forgings, ferrous

(G-8367)
HARRY & IZZYS NORTHSIDE LLC
4050 E 82nd St (46250-1620)
PHONE.....................317 915-8045
Jeff Smith, *Prin*
EMP: 4 **EST:** 2011
SALES (est): 437.07K **Privately Held**
Web: www.harryandizzys.com
SIC: 3421 Table and food cutlery, including butchers'

(G-8368)
HARRY J KLOEPPEL & ASSOCIATES
6974 Hillsdale Ct (46250-2040)
PHONE.....................317 578-1300
EMP: 7 **EST:** 2018
SALES (est): 122.79K **Privately Held**
Web: www.kloeppel.com
SIC: 3821 Laboratory apparatus and furniture

(G-8369)
HARVEST CAFE COFFEE & TEA LLC
2225 E 54th St Ste A (46220-3435)
P.O. Box 20603 (46220-0603)
PHONE.....................317 585-9162
Andy Wolf, *Managing Member*
Larry French, *Managing Member*
EMP: 5 **EST:** 2013
SALES (est): 202.97K **Privately Held**
Web: www.harvestcafecoffee.com
SIC: 5812 5149 2095 Cafe; Coffee and tea; Roasted coffee

(G-8370)
HAUS LOVE INC
5901 N College Ave (46220-2553)
PHONE.....................317 601-6521
EMP: 1 **EST:** 2013
SALES (est): 237K **Privately Held**
Web: www.heidiwoodmaninteriors.com
SIC: 2389 Men's miscellaneous accessories

(G-8371)
HAYABUSA LLC
5025 E 82nd St (46250-5600)
PHONE.....................317 594-1188
Shang Song, *Prin*
EMP: 8 **EST:** 2008
SALES (est): 180.25K **Privately Held**
SIC: 3421 Table and food cutlery, including butchers'

(G-8372)
HAYWOOD PRINTING CO INC
1801 W 18th St (46202-1015)
PHONE.....................765 742-4085
Donald Benham, *Pr*
Scott Benham, *VP*
Jeff Benham, *VP*
Warren Benham, *VP*
Dona Benham, *VP*
EMP: 25 **EST:** 1823
SALES (est): 970.85K **Privately Held**
SIC: 2759 2752 Letterpress printing; Offset printing

(G-8373)
HCO HOLDING I CORPORATION
Monsey Bakor
4351 W Morris St (46241-2503)
PHONE.....................317 248-1344
Rob Franklin, *Mgr*
EMP: 1
SALES (corp-wide): 254.17MM **Privately Held**
SIC: 2952 2951 2891 Roofing felts, cements, or coatings, nec; Asphalt paving mixtures and blocks; Adhesives and sealants
HQ: Hco Holding I Corporation
999 N Splveda Blvd Ste 80
El Segundo CA 90245
323 583-5000

(G-8374)
HDH MANFACTURING
1715 Expo Ln (46214-2334)
PHONE.....................317 918-4088
EMP: 3 **EST:** 2020
SALES (est): 43.66K **Privately Held**
SIC: 3999 Manufacturing industries, nec

(G-8375)
HDH MANUFACTURING INC
4008 W 10th St (46222-3203)
PHONE.....................317 918-4088
Austin Hall, *Pr*
EMP: 3
SALES (corp-wide): 272.5K **Privately Held**
Web: www.hdhmfg.com
SIC: 3599 Machine shop, jobbing and repair
PA: Hdh Manufacturing Inc.
3534 Nolen Dr
Indianapolis IN 46234
317 918-4088

(G-8376)
HDH MANUFACTURING INC (PA)
3534 Nolen Dr (46234-1410)
PHONE.....................317 918-4088
Austin Hall, *Pr*
Gabe Hall, *VP*
Roger Detmering, *VP*
EMP: 2 **EST:** 2015
SALES (est): 272.5K
SALES (corp-wide): 272.5K **Privately Held**
Web: www.hdhmfg.com
SIC: 3599 7389 Machine shop, jobbing and repair; Business Activities at Non-Commercial Site

(G-8377)
HEARTLAND FILM INC
1043 Virginia Ave Ste 2 (46203)
PHONE.....................317 464-9405
Stuart Lowry, *Pr*
EMP: 9 **EST:** 1991
SQ FT: 4,970
SALES (est): 2.85MM **Privately Held**
Web: www.heartlandfilm.org
SIC: 3861 Motion picture film

(G-8378)
HEARTLAND SHUTTER COMPANY LLC
4920 Mccray St (46224-5146)
PHONE.....................317 710-3350
Michael Burt, *Prin*
EMP: 5 **EST:** 2017
SALES (est): 238.39K **Privately Held**
SIC: 3442 Shutters, door or window: metal

(G-8379)
HEAT EXCHANGER DESIGN INC
901 E Beecher St (46203-3974)
P.O. Box 524 (46206-0524)
PHONE.....................317 686-9000

Indianapolis - Marion County (G-8380)

Hesham Derazi, *Pr*
◆ **EMP:** 35 **EST:** 1984
SQ FT: 114,000
SALES (est): 4.83MM **Privately Held**
Web: www.hed-inc.com
SIC: 3443 Heat exchangers: coolers (after, inter), condensers, etc.

(G-8380)
HEIDELBERG MTLS STHAST AGG LLC
4200 S Harding St (46217-9537)
PHONE.................................317 788-4086
Randy Jones, *Genl Mgr*
EMP: 38
SALES (corp-wide): 23.02B **Privately Held**
Web: www.heidelbergmaterials.us
SIC: 1442 1422 1429 Sand mining; Limestones, ground; Boulder, crushed and broken-quarrying
HQ: Heidelberg Materials Southeast Agg Llc
3237 Satellite Blvd # 30
Duluth GA 30096
770 491-2756

(G-8381)
HELIOS LLC
Also Called: Helios Software
8001 Woodland Dr (46278-1332)
PHONE.................................317 554-9911
Scott Bogden, *Managing Member*
EMP: 41 **EST:** 2001
SALES (est): 902.67K **Privately Held**
Web: www.gohelios.com
SIC: 7372 Application computer software

(G-8382)
HERCULES ACHIEVEMENT INC
4501 W 62nd St (46268-2587)
PHONE.................................317 297-3740
EMP: 73 **EST:** 2014
SALES (est): 2.09MM
SALES (corp-wide): 2.02B **Privately Held**
SIC: 3949 Sporting and athletic goods, nec
PA: Varsity Brands Holding Co., Llc
14460 Varsity Brand Way
Farmers Branch TX 75244
972 406-7162

(G-8383)
HERFF JONES LLC (HQ)
Also Called: Camera Art
4501 W 62nd St (46268)
PHONE.................................317 297-3741
Ronald Stoupa, *CEO*
Adam Blumenfeld, *Managing Member*
◆ **EMP:** 200 **EST:** 1985
SQ FT: 42,700
SALES (est): 472.92MM
SALES (corp-wide): 8.23B **Privately Held**
Web: www.herffjones.com
SIC: 3911 2741 2499 5699 Rings, finger: precious metal; Yearbooks: publishing and printing; Picture and mirror frames, wood; Caps and gowns (academic vestments)
PA: Atlas Holdings, Llc
100 Northfield St
Greenwich CT 06830
203 622-9138

(G-8384)
HERFF JONES LLC
4625 W 62nd St (46268-2546)
P.O. Box 36 (64658-0036)
PHONE.................................317 612-3400
Tom James, *Mgr*
EMP: 22
SALES (corp-wide): 8.23B **Privately Held**
Web: www.yearbookdiscoveries.com

SIC: 2741 2752 2732 2731 Yearbooks: publishing and printing; Commercial printing, lithographic; Book printing; Book publishing
HQ: Herff Jones, Llc
4501 W 62nd St
Indianapolis IN 46268
317 297-3741

(G-8385)
HERFF JONES CO INDIANA - INC
4625 W 62nd St (46268-2546)
PHONE.................................317 297-3740
Scott Cool, *Prin*
EMP: 45 **EST:** 2015
SALES (est): 5.99MM **Privately Held**
Web: www.herffjones.com
SIC: 3911 3452 Jewelry, precious metal; Pins

(G-8386)
HERITAGE AGGREGATES LLC
3719 W 96th St (46268-3100)
PHONE.................................317 434-4600
Robert J Simpson, *Ch Bd*
EMP: 2
SALES (corp-wide): 4.06MM **Privately Held**
Web: www.usagg.com
SIC: 1422 Limestones, ground
PA: Heritage Aggregates, Llc
5400 W 86th St
Indianapolis IN 46268
317 872-6010

(G-8387)
HERITAGE AGGREGATES LLC (PA)
Also Called: Meshberger Stone Inc
5400 W 86th St (46268-1502)
PHONE.................................317 872-6010
Robert J Simpson, *Ch Bd*
James C Fehsenfeld, *Pr*
Lewis L Davis, *Sec*
John P Vercruysse, *VP*
EMP: 9 **EST:** 1937
SQ FT: 4,000
SALES (est): 4.06MM
SALES (corp-wide): 4.06MM **Privately Held**
Web: www.usagg.com
SIC: 1422 Limestones, ground

(G-8388)
HERITAGE ASPHALT LLC
5400 W 86th St (46268-1502)
P.O. Box 68123 (46268-0123)
PHONE.................................317 872-6010
EMP: 9 **EST:** 2011
SALES (est): 379.94K **Privately Held**
SIC: 2951 Asphalt paving mixtures and blocks

(G-8389)
HERITAGE LDSCP SUP GROUP INC
5272 E 65th St (46220-4819)
PHONE.................................317 849-9100
Brad Smith, *Brnch Mgr*
EMP: 29
SALES (corp-wide): 152.67B **Publicly Held**
Web: www.heritagelandscapesupplygroup.com
SIC: 5211 3281 1411 5032 Masonry materials and supplies; Cut stone and stone products; Dimension stone; Building stone
HQ: Heritage Landscape Supply Group, Inc.
7440 State Highway 121
Mckinney TX 75070
214 491-4149

(G-8390)
HERITAGE-CRYSTAL CLEAN INC
3970 W 10th St (46222-3269)
PHONE.................................317 390-3642
Kevin Cesnik, *Prin*
EMP: 7
SALES (corp-wide): 709.33MM **Privately Held**
Web: www.crystal-clean.com
SIC: 2911 Petroleum refining
HQ: Heritage-Crystal Clean, Inc.
2000 Center Dr Ste E C300
Hoffman Estates IL 60192

(G-8391)
HF CHLOR-ALKALI LLC (PA)
9307 E 56th St (46216)
PHONE.................................317 591-0000
Timothy Harris, *Pr*
Ernest L Duncan, *Contrlr*
▲ **EMP:** 13 **EST:** 2012
SALES (est): 5.79MM
SALES (corp-wide): 5.79MM **Privately Held**
SIC: 2812 Caustic soda, sodium hydroxide

(G-8392)
HG METAL FABRICATION
1426 N Graham Ave (46219-3134)
PHONE.................................317 491-3381
Oscar Hilario, *Prin*
EMP: 6 **EST:** 2010
SALES (est): 161.61K **Privately Held**
Web: www.hgmetals.com
SIC: 3499 Fabricated metal products, nec

(G-8393)
HGL DYNAMICS INC
6979 Corporate Cir (46278-1957)
PHONE.................................317 782-3500
James Hone, *Pr*
Aliza Sparkman, *Mgr*
Robert Sparkman, *VP*
EMP: 5 **EST:** 2009
SALES (est): 895.75K **Privately Held**
Web: www.hgl-dynamics.com
SIC: 3825 8711 3829 Instruments to measure electricity; Engineering services; Vibration meters, analyzers, and calibrators

(G-8394)
HGMC SUPPLY INC
Also Called: Hg Metals
5402 Massachusetts Ave (46218-2451)
PHONE.................................317 351-9500
Cynthia B Gardner, *Pr*
Sean E Gardner, *VP*
EMP: 18 **EST:** 2005
SQ FT: 26,000
SALES (est): 9.15MM **Privately Held**
Web: www.hgmetals.com
SIC: 1541 8741 1791 3446 Industrial buildings and warehouses; Construction management; Structural steel erection; Stairs, fire escapes, balconies, railings, and ladders

(G-8395)
HI-PERFRMNCE SPERABRASIVES INC
9133 Pendleton Pike Ste G (46236-3244)
PHONE.................................317 899-1050
Travis L Rhoden Senior, *Pr*
Kevin Brown, *VP*
Bill West, *VP*
EMP: 9 **EST:** 2003
SQ FT: 3,000
SALES (est): 828.96K **Privately Held**
Web: www.hps-usa.com

SIC: 3599 Machine shop, jobbing and repair

(G-8396)
HI-TECH FOAM PRODUCTS LLC (PA)
550 Bell St (46202-3593)
P.O. Box 21280 (42304-1280)
PHONE.................................317 737-2298
John Metaxas, *Pr*
▲ **EMP:** 22 **EST:** 1992
SQ FT: 50,000
SALES (est): 2.34MM **Privately Held**
Web: www.hitechfoam.com
SIC: 3053 3086 3069 Gaskets and sealing devices; Packaging and shipping materials, foamed plastics; Foam rubber

(G-8397)
HIDEA OUTBOARD MOTOR USA INC
7043 Girls School Ave (46241-2821)
PHONE.................................317 286-3694
Huali Zheng, *Prin*
EMP: 6 **EST:** 2017
SALES (est): 185.04K **Privately Held**
Web: hideaoutboardmotors.a-zcompanies.com
SIC: 3519 Outboard motors

(G-8398)
HIGHLAND PARK SERVICES INC
5345 Winthrop Ave (46220-3278)
PHONE.................................317 954-0456
Christian J Franke, *Pr*
Robert J Mocek, *Sec*
Nicholas Guemes, *Prin*
EMP: 3 **EST:** 2014
SALES (est): 190K **Privately Held**
SIC: 3531 Construction machinery

(G-8399)
HIRATA CORPORATION OF AMERICA (HQ)
5625 Decatur Blvd (46241-9509)
PHONE.................................317 856-8600
Shawn Egger, *CEO*
Biagio Longo, *
Kenichiro Otomaru, *
Shigeru Maeda, *
Yukihiro Kawamoto, *
◆ **EMP:** 30 **EST:** 1980
SQ FT: 30,000
SALES (est): 27.14MM **Privately Held**
SIC: 3537 8711 3535 3559 Industrial trucks and tractors; Engineering services; Conveyors and conveying equipment; Semiconductor manufacturing machinery
PA: Hirata Corporation
111, Uekimachihitotsugi, Kita-Ku
Kumamoto KUM 861-0

(G-8400)
HIS LOVE KEPT ME PUBG LLC
2310 Fescue Pl Apt D (46260-2770)
PHONE.................................408 893-5908
Lydia Davis, *Prin*
EMP: 4 **EST:** 2013
SALES (est): 84.33K **Privately Held**
SIC: 2741 Miscellaneous publishing

(G-8401)
HOBBS TRANSPORT SERVICES LLC ✪
4450 N Vinewood Ave (46254-2322)
PHONE.................................317 607-5590
EMP: 1 **EST:** 2022
SALES (est): 54.62K **Privately Held**
SIC: 3799 7389 Trailers and trailer equipment; Business Activities at Non-Commercial Site

GEOGRAPHIC SECTION

Indianapolis - Marion County (G-8425)

(G-8402)
HOLE N WALL ENTERTAINMENT LLC
9165 Otis Ave Ste 225 (46216-2306)
PHONE..................317 586-1037
EMP: 1
SALES (est): 75.6K Privately Held
SIC: 3651 Music distribution apparatus

(G-8403)
HOLZER READY MIX LLC ✪
Also Called: Holzer Site Mix LLC
405 S Shortridge Rd (46219-7407)
PHONE..................317 306-9327
Carter Holzer, Managing Member
EMP: 12 EST: 2022
SALES (est): 1.1MM Privately Held
SIC: 3273 Ready-mixed concrete

(G-8404)
HOME CITY ICE COMPANY
2000 Dr Martin Luther King Jr St (46202-1156)
PHONE..................317 926-2451
Jim Serger, Brnch Mgr
EMP: 8
SALES (corp-wide): 100.42MM Privately Held
Web: www.homecityice.com
SIC: 2097 5999 Manufactured ice; Ice
PA: The Home City Ice Company
6045 Bridgetown Rd Ste 1
Cincinnati OH 45248
513 574-1800

(G-8405)
HOME CITY ICE COMPANY
Also Called: Polar Ice
3602 W Washington St (46241-1625)
PHONE..................317 926-2451
Scott Beil, Genl Mgr
EMP: 10
SALES (corp-wide): 100.42MM Privately Held
Web: www.homecityice.com
SIC: 2097 Block ice
PA: The Home City Ice Company
6045 Bridgetown Rd Ste 1
Cincinnati OH 45248
513 574-1800

(G-8406)
HOME PUBLISHING LLC
9465 Counselors Row Ste 200 (46240-6423)
PHONE..................317 886-1137
Tierney Toles, CEO
EMP: 1 EST: 2021
SALES (est): 75.12K Privately Held
SIC: 2741 Miscellaneous publishing

(G-8407)
HONEY & SALT LLC
309 Poplar Rd (46219-5643)
PHONE..................317 625-1135
EMP: 4 EST: 2013
SALES (est): 85.1K Privately Held
Web: www.honeyandsaltphoto.com
SIC: 2899 Chemical preparations, nec

(G-8408)
HONEYWELL INTERNATIONAL INC
Also Called: Honeywell
6826 Hillsdale Ct (46250-2001)
PHONE..................317 580-6165
Scott Maynard, Mgr
EMP: 16
Web: www.honeywell.com
SIC: 3724 Aircraft engines and engine parts
PA: Honeywell International Inc.
855 S Mint St
Charlotte NC 28202

(G-8409)
HOOSIER GASKET CORPORATION (PA)
2400 Enterprise Park Pl (46218-4291)
PHONE..................317 545-2000
Jeffery Jackson, Pr
Daniel Jackson, *
▲ EMP: 52 EST: 1960
SQ FT: 130,000
SALES (est): 24.07MM
SALES (corp-wide): 24.07MM Privately Held
Web: www.hgcindustries.com
SIC: 3452 3053 Washers; Gaskets, all materials

(G-8410)
HOOSIER MACHINE & WELDING INC
451 Arbor Ave (46221-1257)
P.O. Box 21204 (46221-0204)
PHONE..................317 638-6286
Randy Routier, Pr
Cecelia Routier, Sec
EMP: 12 EST: 1966
SQ FT: 8,000
SALES (est): 946.94K Privately Held
Web: www.hoosiermachinewelding.com
SIC: 7692 Welding repair

(G-8411)
HOOSIER PENN OIL CO INC (PA)
Also Called: H P Oil Co
4060 W 10th St (46222-3203)
P.O. Box 22669 (46222-0669)
PHONE..................317 390-5406
EMP: 25 EST: 1976
SALES (est): 10.31MM
SALES (corp-wide): 10.31MM Privately Held
Web: www.hpoil.com
SIC: 5172 2911 Petroleum products, nec; Solvents

(G-8412)
HOOSIER TRIM PRODUCTS LLC
1850 Expo Ln (46214-2335)
PHONE..................317 271-4007
Joshua Mellentine, *
Richard Hauser, *
Wallace Bryant, *
EMP: 25 EST: 1977
SQ FT: 50,000
SALES (est): 2.47MM Privately Held
Web: www.hoosiertrim.com
SIC: 3469 3354 3449 Metal stampings, nec; Shapes, extruded aluminum, nec; Custom roll formed products

(G-8413)
HORIZON ANIM LLC
7834 Gilmore Rd (46219-1220)
PHONE..................317 742-4917
EMP: 1
SALES (est): 39.69K Privately Held
SIC: 3999 7389 Framed artwork; Business Activities at Non-Commercial Site

(G-8414)
HORNER APG LLC (PA)
Also Called: Horner Advanced Products Group
59 S State Ave (46201-3876)
PHONE..................317 916-4274
Philip Horner, *
Mary Horner, *
Don Swan, *
Allen Horner, *
▲ EMP: 13 EST: 1999
SALES (est): 9.17MM Privately Held
Web: www.hornerlighting.com
SIC: 3625 5063 7694 Electric controls and control accessories, industrial; Electrical apparatus and equipment; Electric motor repair

(G-8415)
HORNER ELECTRIC INC
Also Called: Scherer Indus Group Horner Elc
1521 E Washington St (46201-3899)
PHONE..................317 639-4261
Mark Wolma, Dir
EMP: 31 EST: 2004
SALES (est): 3.11MM Privately Held
Web: www.hornerindustrial.com
SIC: 7694 5063 Motor repair services; Electrical apparatus and equipment

(G-8416)
HORNER INDUSTRIAL SERVICES INC (PA)
Also Called: Horner Industrial Group
1521 E Washington St (46201-3848)
PHONE..................317 639-4261
EMP: 117 EST: 1949
SALES (est): 55.43MM
SALES (corp-wide): 55.43MM Privately Held
Web: www.hornerindustrial.com
SIC: 3625 7694 7699 7629 Electric controls and control accessories, industrial; Electric motor repair; Pumps and pumping equipment repair; Electrical equipment repair, high voltage

(G-8417)
HORNER INDUSTRIAL SERVICES INC
940 S West St (46225-1461)
PHONE..................317 957-4244
EMP: 10
SALES (corp-wide): 55.43MM Privately Held
Web: www.hornerindustrial.com
SIC: 3625 Relays and industrial controls
PA: Horner Industrial Services, Inc.
1521 E Washington St
Indianapolis IN 46201
317 639-4261

(G-8418)
HORNER INDUSTRIAL SERVICES INC
Also Called: Indiana Fan & Fabrication
2045 E Washington St (46201-4184)
PHONE..................317 634-7165
Marc Dardeen, Mgr
EMP: 10
SALES (corp-wide): 55.43MM Privately Held
Web: www.hornerindustrial.com
SIC: 3564 3444 5084 5075 Blowing fans: industrial or commercial; Sheet metalwork; Industrial machinery and equipment; Warm air heating and air conditioning
PA: Horner Industrial Services, Inc.
1521 E Washington St
Indianapolis IN 46201
317 639-4261

(G-8419)
HOT CAKE
6845 Bluff Rd (46217-3926)
PHONE..................317 889-2253
EMP: 31
SALES (corp-wide): 264.81K Privately Held
Web: www.hotcakesemporiumpancakehouseandrestaurant.com
SIC: 7299 5949 2759 Tanning salon; Sewing and needlework; Screen printing
PA: Hot Cake

8555 Ditch Rd
Indianapolis IN 46260
317 254-5993

(G-8420)
HOT OFF PRESS
5838 Bonnie Brae St (46228-1842)
PHONE..................317 253-5987
Dave Overman, Pr
Rita Overman, Sec
EMP: 2 EST: 1994
SALES (est): 127.06K Privately Held
SIC: 2759 Commercial printing, nec

(G-8421)
HOT ROD CAR CARE LLC
Also Called: Indy Auto Graphics
7266 E 86th St (46250-3597)
PHONE..................317 660-2077
EMP: 9 EST: 2010
SALES (est): 803.74K Privately Held
Web: www.indyautographics.com
SIC: 3993 7532 7336 Signs and advertising specialties; Lettering, automotive; Creative services to advertisers, except writers

(G-8422)
HOTEL TANGO WHISKEY INC
Also Called: Hotel Tango Distillery
951 W Morris St Ste E (46221-1760)
PHONE..................317 653-1806
Travis Barnes, CEO
Travis Barnes, Pr
Brian Willsey, *
EMP: 28 EST: 2013
SQ FT: 3,500
SALES (est): 4.82MM Privately Held
Web: www.hoteltangodistillery.com
SIC: 2084 2085 Brandy and brandy spirits; Distilled and blended liquors

(G-8423)
HOTEL VANITIES INTL LLC
400 N Johnson Rd (46237)
PHONE..................317 787-2330
EMP: 1
SALES (corp-wide): 1.94MM Privately Held
Web: www.vanitiesinternational.com
SIC: 3088 Bathroom fixtures, plastics
PA: Hotel Vanities International Llc
5514 Stockwell Ct
Indianapolis IN 46237
317 787-2330

(G-8424)
HOTEL VANITIES INTL LLC (PA)
5514 Stockwell Ct (46237)
PHONE..................317 787-2330
Chris Dolne, Managing Member
▲ EMP: 11 EST: 1997
SALES (est): 1.94MM
SALES (corp-wide): 1.94MM Privately Held
Web: www.vanitiesinternational.com
SIC: 3088 Bathroom fixtures, plastics

(G-8425)
HOUGHTON MIFFLIN HARCOURT CO
Also Called: Hmh
2700 N Richardt Ave (46219-1117)
PHONE..................317 359-5585
Dennis Carey, Owner
EMP: 120
SALES (corp-wide): 1.97B Privately Held
Web: ir.hmhco.com
SIC: 3999 2731 Education aids, devices and supplies; Book publishing
HQ: Houghton Mifflin Harcourt Company
125 High St
Boston MA 02110
617 351-5000

Indianapolis - Marion County (G-8426)

(G-8426)
HOUGHTON MIFFLIN HARCOURT PUBG
2700 N Richardt Ave (46219-1117)
PHONE..................317 359-5585
EMP: 53
SALES (corp-wide): 1.97B Privately Held
Web: www.hmhco.com
SIC: 2731 Book publishing
HQ: Houghton Mifflin Harcourt Publishing Company
125 High St Ste 900
Boston MA 02110
617 351-5000

(G-8427)
HOUSE OF DELRENEE LLC
9052 Woodmoss Ln (46250-1035)
PHONE..................219 670-1153
EMP: 2 EST: 2021
SALES (est): 67.05K Privately Held
SIC: 2335 Women's, junior's, and misses' dresses

(G-8428)
HOVERSTREAM LLC
4801 Van Cleave St (46226-2942)
PHONE..................317 489-0075
Jason Kuehn, Owner
▲ EMP: 5 EST: 2015
SALES (est): 238.1K Privately Held
Web: www.hoverstream.com
SIC: 3599 Propellers, ship and boat: machined

(G-8429)
HOW YOU PERCEIVE EVER (PA)
Also Called: Hype Magazine, The
7399 N Shadeland Ave Ste 299 (46250-2052)
PHONE..................301 579-4973
Jameelah Wilkerson, Pr
EMP: 3 EST: 2001
SQ FT: 1,500
SALES (est): 994.03K
SALES (corp-wide): 994.03K Privately Held
Web: www.thehypemagazine.com
SIC: 2721 Magazines: publishing only, not printed on site

(G-8430)
HOWARD MATERIALS LLC
Also Called: Harding Group
2916 Kentucky Ave (46221-2102)
PHONE..................317 849-9666
Shelby D Howard Iv, CEO
EMP: 5 EST: 2018
SALES (est): 2.05MM Privately Held
Web: www.howardcompanies.com
SIC: 3531 Construction machinery

(G-8431)
HOWERTON RACECAR WORKS INC
Also Called: Howerton Racing Products
360 Gasoline Aly (46222-3967)
PHONE..................317 241-0868
Jack Howerton, Pr
EMP: 10 EST: 1976
SQ FT: 3,000
SALES (est): 1.02MM Privately Held
Web: www.howertonproducts.org
SIC: 3711 Automobile assembly, including specialty automobiles

(G-8432)
HOWMET AEROSPACE INC
2334 Production Dr (46241-4914)
PHONE..................317 241-9393
Gene Bleke, Mgr
EMP: 2
SALES (corp-wide): 6.64B Publicly Held
Web: www.howmet.com
SIC: 3353 Aluminum sheet and strip
PA: Howmet Aerospace Inc.
201 Isabella St Ste 200
Pittsburgh PA 15212
412 553-1950

(G-8433)
HUEHLS SALCOATING LAWNCARE LLC
312 E Epler Ave (46227-1927)
PHONE..................317 782-4069
Christopher Huehls, Managing Member
EMP: 2 EST: 2008
SALES (est): 135.11K Privately Held
SIC: 0782 1611 7692 Lawn care services; Surfacing and paving; Welding repair

(G-8434)
HUNGRY CANDLE LLC ◆
1243 S East St (46225-2529)
PHONE..................773 656-1774
Gail Scott, Prin
EMP: 1 EST: 2022
SALES (est): 69.27K Privately Held
SIC: 3999 Candles

(G-8435)
HURCO COMPANIES INC
7220 Winton Dr (46268-5142)
PHONE..................317 347-6208
Jason Strachman, Mgr
EMP: 7
SALES (corp-wide): 250.81MM Publicly Held
Web: www.hurco.com
SIC: 3823 Computer interface equipment, for industrial process control
PA: Hurco Companies, Inc.
1 Technology Way
Indianapolis IN 46268
317 293-5309

(G-8436)
HURCO COMPANIES INC (PA)
Also Called: HURCO
1 Technology Way (46268)
P.O. Box 68180 (46268)
PHONE..................317 293-5309
Gregory S Volovic, Pr
Michael Doar, *
Sonja K Mcclelland, VP
Haiquynh Jamison, Corporate Controller
Jonathon D Wright, Corporate Secretary
EMP: 182 EST: 1968
SQ FT: 165,000
SALES (est): 250.81MM
SALES (corp-wide): 250.81MM Publicly Held
Web: www.hurco.com
SIC: 3823 7372 Computer interface equipment, for industrial process control; Prepackaged software

(G-8437)
HURCO INTERNATIONAL HOLDINGS (HQ)
1 Technology Way (46268-5106)
PHONE..................317 293-5309
EMP: 7
SALES (est): 872.41K
SALES (corp-wide): 250.81MM Publicly Held
Web: www.hurco.com
SIC: 3599 Machine shop, jobbing and repair
PA: Hurco Companies, Inc.
1 Technology Way
Indianapolis IN 46268
317 293-5309

(G-8438)
HUSH CLOTHING 317 LLC ◆
5111 Kingman Dr (46226-2746)
PHONE..................317 935-2184
Anthony Wright Junior, Managing Member
EMP: 1 EST: 2023
SALES (est): 83.66K Privately Held
SIC: 2329 7389 Men's and boys' sportswear and athletic clothing; Business Activities at Non-Commercial Site

(G-8439)
HUTCHISON SIGNS & ELEC CO INC
215 S Munsie St (46229-2823)
PHONE..................317 894-8787
William P Hutchison Ii, Pr
EMP: 20 EST: 1980
SQ FT: 40,000
SALES (est): 2.48MM Privately Held
Web: www.hutchisonsigns.com
SIC: 3993 1799 Electric signs; Sign installation and maintenance

(G-8440)
HYDRATION TURBINE INC ◆
5433 Brendonridge Rd (46226-1511)
PHONE..................317 491-0656
John Corey Morgan, Pr
EMP: 2 EST: 2023
SALES (est): 92.67K Privately Held
SIC: 3511 7389 Hydraulic turbine generator set units, complete; Business Activities at Non-Commercial Site

(G-8441)
HYDRAULIC PRESS BRICK COMPANY (HQ)
3600 Woodview Trce Ste 300 (46268-3167)
PHONE..................317 290-1140
Jack W Schwarz, Ch Bd
Thomas E Bennett, Pr
Cheri Jones, Contrlr
EMP: 42 EST: 1868
SQ FT: 3,000
SALES (est): 2.49MM
SALES (corp-wide): 573.33MM Privately Held
Web: www.arcosalightweight.com
SIC: 3295 Shale, expanded
PA: Schwarz Partners, L.P.
10 W Carmel Dr Ste 300
Carmel IN 46032
317 290-1140

(G-8442)
HYDRO FIRE PROTECTION INC
8603 Bluff Rd (46217-4602)
PHONE..................317 780-6980
Robert Birk, Pr
Mary Birk, Sec
Tracy Branneman, Treas
EMP: 35 EST: 1983
SALES (est): 2.23MM Privately Held
Web: www.hydrofireprotectioninc.com
SIC: 1711 3569 Fire sprinkler system installation; Sprinkler systems, fire: automatic

(G-8443)
HYDRO VAC SERVICES LLC
Also Called: Groundbreakers
6435 E 30th St (46219-1006)
PHONE..................317 345-2120
Andrea Sloan, Prin
EMP: 27 EST: 2011
SALES (est): 3.3MM Privately Held
Web: www.groundbreakersllc.com
SIC: 1081 Metal mining exploration and development services

(G-8444)
HYDRO-GEAR INC
7330 Woodland Dr (46278-1736)
PHONE..................317 821-0477
EMP: 4
SALES (corp-wide): 11.6B Privately Held
Web: www.hydro-gear.com
SIC: 3594 Hydrostatic drives (transmissions)
HQ: Hydro-Gear Inc
1411 S Hamilton St
Sullivan IL 61951

(G-8445)
I F S CORP
Also Called: Fastsigns
9433 E Washington St (46229-3085)
PHONE..................317 898-6118
EMP: 3 EST: 1995
SALES (est): 485.45K Privately Held
Web: www.fastsigns.com
SIC: 3993 Signs and advertising specialties

(G-8446)
I RUN AMUCK LLC
8105 Halyard Way (46236-9569)
PHONE..................317 674-3339
EMP: 1 EST: 2012
SALES (est): 94.87K Privately Held
SIC: 3949 Sporting and athletic goods, nec

(G-8447)
IAIRE LLC (PA)
6805 Hillsdale Ct (46250-2039)
P.O. Box 40965 (46240-0965)
PHONE..................317 806-2750
Joe Finkan, Managing Member
EMP: 8 EST: 2014
SALES (est): 4.19MM
SALES (corp-wide): 4.19MM Privately Held
Web: www.myiaire.com
SIC: 3564 Air purification equipment

(G-8448)
IBJ CORPORATION
Also Called: Court & Commercial Records
1 Monument Cir Ste 300 (46204-3026)
PHONE..................317 634-6200
Michael Maurer, Pr
Robert Schloss, *
Jeff Basch, *
Greg Morris, Adviser*
EMP: 75 EST: 1980
SALES (est): 10.04MM Privately Held
Web: www.ibj.com
SIC: 2711 Newspapers: publishing only, not printed on site

(G-8449)
ICAPE-USA LLC (HQ)
Also Called: Icape Group
8102 Zionsville Rd (46268)
PHONE..................765 431-1271
▲ EMP: 3 EST: 2010
SQ FT: 1,000
SALES (est): 2.5MM
SALES (corp-wide): 5.51MM Privately Held
Web: www.icape-group.com
SIC: 3672 Printed circuit boards
PA: Icape Holding
33 17 Avenue Du General Leclerc
Fontenay-Aux-Roses 92260
158183910

(G-8450)
ICHINEN USA CORPORATION
Also Called: Toyoshima Special Steel USA
735 Saint Paul St (46203-1466)
PHONE..................317 638-3511

GEOGRAPHIC SECTION
Indianapolis - Marion County (G-8476)

Kathi Davidson, *CEO*
Yoshikazu Tanabe, *Pr*
Anthony York, *VP*
◆ EMP: 7 EST: 1920
SQ FT: 57,000
SALES (est): 1.87MM **Privately Held**
Web: www.tssu.com
SIC: 3537 Lift trucks, industrial: fork, platform, straddle, etc.

(G-8451)
ICP LIQUIDATING COMPANY
2050 S Harding St (46221-1948)
PHONE.................................419 841-3361
EMP: 100
SIC: 3272 Pipe, concrete or lined with concrete

(G-8452)
ICS INKS LLP
6101 Drawbridge Ln (46250-1329)
PHONE.................................317 690-9254
Alan Nave, *Prin*
EMP: 1 EST: 2011
SALES (est): 117.91K **Privately Held**
Web: www.icsinks.com
SIC: 2759 Screen printing

(G-8453)
IDEAL SAFETY & HYGIENE LLC
818 Canyon Rd (46217-3918)
PHONE.................................317 281-3921
Chris Scheib, *Prin*
EMP: 7 EST: 2010
SALES (est): 234.55K **Privately Held**
Web: www.ideal-safety.com
SIC: 3825 Instruments to measure electricity

(G-8454)
IDEAL TESTING AND SERVICES LLC
3410 N High School Rd Ste G (46224-1742)
PHONE.................................812 431-8500
EMP: 1
SALES (est): 69.27K **Privately Held**
SIC: 2899 Drug testing kits, blood and urine

(G-8455)
IFS COATINGS
5335 W 74th St (46268-4180)
PHONE.................................317 471-5122
EMP: 6 EST: 2020
SALES (est): 134.41K **Privately Held**
Web: www.ifscoatings.com
SIC: 2899 Chemical preparations, nec

(G-8456)
IHS CAMPAIGN FOR IND EXPRNCE
450 W Ohio St (46202-3269)
PHONE.................................317 234-5232
EMP: 2 EST: 2014
SALES (est): 59.23K **Privately Held**
SIC: 2741 Miscellaneous publishing

(G-8457)
IIIIMPRESSIONS THAT COUNT INC
917 Greer St (46203-1717)
PHONE.................................317 423-0581
Gregory Townsend, *Pr*
EMP: 3 EST: 1981
SALES (est): 168.64K **Privately Held**
SIC: 2752 Offset printing

(G-8458)
IKIO LED LIGHTING LLC
Also Called: Ikio Led Lighting
8470 Allison Pointe Blvd Ste 128 (46250)
P.O. Box 910529 (40591)
PHONE.................................765 414-0835
Ekamdeep Singh, *Managing Member*
Hardeep Singh, *
▲ EMP: 1000 EST: 2014
SQ FT: 55,000
SALES (est): 55.55MM **Privately Held**
Web: www.ikioledlighting.com
SIC: 3648 7349 Lighting equipment, nec; Lighting maintenance service

(G-8459)
ILAB LLC
5432 Wood Hollow Dr (46239-6899)
PHONE.................................317 218-3258
EMP: 54 EST: 2010
SALES (est): 9.57MM **Privately Held**
Web: www.ilabquality.com
SIC: 7371 7372 5045 Computer software development; Prepackaged software; Computer software

(G-8460)
ILLINOIS AGRI-NEWS
2575 55th Pl Ste A (46220-3511)
PHONE.................................317 726-5391
EMP: 5 EST: 2018
SALES (est): 73.26K **Privately Held**
Web: www.agrinews-pubs.com
SIC: 2711 Newspapers, publishing and printing

(G-8461)
ILLINOIS TOOL WORKS INC
Also Called: ITW Gema
4141 W 54th St (46254-3728)
PHONE.................................317 298-5000
Chris Merritt, *Genl Mgr*
EMP: 8
SQ FT: 63,000
SALES (corp-wide): 16.11B **Publicly Held**
Web: www.itw.com
SIC: 3549 3621 Assembly machines, including robotic; Control equipment for electric buses and locomotives
PA: Illinois Tool Works Inc.
155 Harlem Ave
Glenview IL 60025
847 724-7500

(G-8462)
IMAGE INKS COMPANY
7363 Red Rock Rd (46236-9358)
PHONE.................................317 432-5041
Zachary L Grider, *Pr*
EMP: 2 EST: 2007
SALES (est): 115.2K **Privately Held**
Web: www.yourimageink.com
SIC: 3861 Printing equipment, photographic

(G-8463)
IMAGE PLUS ORIGINAL LLC
5160 E 65th St Ste 100 (46220-4840)
PHONE.................................800 226-7316
EMP: 1 EST: 2018
SALES (est): 33K **Privately Held**
Web: www.imageplusoriginalllc.com
SIC: 2759 7699 Screen printing; Hobby and collectors services

(G-8464)
IMAGINEERING ENTERPRISES INC
2719 N Emerson Ave Ste A (46218-3283)
PHONE.................................317 635-8565
F James Hammer, *Pr*
EMP: 20
SQ FT: 50,000
SALES (corp-wide): 19.58MM **Privately Held**
Web: www.iftworldwide.com
SIC: 3479 8711 Coating of metals and formed products; Engineering services
PA: Imagineering Enterprises Inc
1302 W Sample St
South Bend IN 46619
574 287-2941

(G-8465)
IMH FABRICATION LLC
2073 Dr Andrew J Brown Ave (46202-1932)
P.O. Box 20814 (46220-0814)
PHONE.................................317 252-5566
EMP: 38
SALES (corp-wide): 23.71MM **Privately Held**
Web: www.imh.com
SIC: 3444 3469 Sheet metal specialties, not stamped; Metal stampings, nec
PA: Imh Fabrication Llc
1929 Columbia Ave
Indianapolis IN 46202
317 508-7462

(G-8466)
IMH FABRICATION LLC (PA)
Also Called: Imh Products
1929 Columbia Ave (46202-1924)
P.O. Box 20814 (46220-0814)
PHONE.................................317 508-7462
Eric Odmark, *Pr*
Mark Seger, *COO*
EMP: 10 EST: 1955
SQ FT: 25,000
SALES (est): 23.71MM
SALES (corp-wide): 23.71MM **Privately Held**
Web: www.imh.com
SIC: 3444 3469 Sheet metal specialties, not stamped; Stamping metal for the trade

(G-8467)
IMMUNOTEK BIO CENTERS LLC
3859 W Washington St (46241-1528)
PHONE.................................337 500-1294
Pam Farris, *Prin*
EMP: 1
SALES (corp-wide): 140.79MM **Privately Held**
Web: www.immunotek.com
SIC: 2836 Blood derivatives
PA: Immunotek Bio Centers, L.L.C.
1430 E Southlake Blvd # 200
Southlake TX 76092
337 500-1175

(G-8468)
IMPACT RACING INC
Also Called: Mastercraft Safety
7991 W 21st St Ste A2 (46214-4304)
PHONE.................................317 852-3067
Lorenzo Cucia, *CEO*
▲ EMP: 80 EST: 1981
SALES (est): 4.16MM **Privately Held**
Web: www.mastercraftsafety.com
SIC: 7692 2311 Welding repair; Tailored suits and formal jackets
PA: Sparco Spa
Via Leini' 524
Volpiano TO 10088

(G-8469)
IMPACT SAFETY INC
7991 W 21st St Ste D1 (46214-4304)
PHONE.................................317 852-3067
Robby Pierce, *CEO*
▲ EMP: 10 EST: 2015
SALES (est): 488.06K **Privately Held**
Web: www.impactraceproducts.com
SIC: 3949 Sporting and athletic goods, nec

(G-8470)
INCHROMATICS LLC
1545 Trace Ln (46260-2740)
PHONE.................................317 872-7401
EMP: 3 EST: 2010
SALES (est): 221.54K **Privately Held**
Web: www.inchromatics.com
SIC: 3826 Chromatographic equipment, laboratory type

(G-8471)
INDEPENDENT CONCRETE PIPE COMPANY
Also Called: Independent Concrete Pipe
2050 S Harding St (46221-1948)
PHONE.................................317 262-4920
EMP: 50
SIC: 3272 5074 Pipe, concrete or lined with concrete; Pipes and fittings, plastic

(G-8472)
INDEPENDENT RAIL CORPORATION
Also Called: Indierail
6233 Brookville Rd (46219-8213)
P.O. Box 430 (46107-0430)
PHONE.................................317 780-8480
Robert Driggers, *Pr*
Dennis L Laswell, *
EMP: 23 EST: 2001
SQ FT: 5,000
SALES (est): 3.66MM **Privately Held**
Web: www.indierailer.com
SIC: 3542 Mechanical (pneumatic or hydraulic) metal forming machines

(G-8473)
INDIANA AUTO DEALERS ASSN SVCS
150 W Market St Ste 812 (46204-2814)
PHONE.................................317 635-1441
Timothy J Dowling, *Ex VP*
Deborah Baker, *Prin*
EMP: 4 EST: 1946
SALES (est): 334.28K
SALES (corp-wide): 594.47K **Privately Held**
SIC: 2741 5943 8748 Business service newsletters: publishing and printing; Office forms and supplies; Business consulting, nec
PA: Automobile Dealers Association Of Indiana Inc
150 W Market St Ste 812
Indianapolis IN 46204
317 635-1441

(G-8474)
INDIANA BUSINESS PEOPLE LLC
7176 Lakeview Parkway West Dr (46268-4104)
PHONE.................................317 455-4040
EMP: 6 EST: 2013
SALES (est): 111.6K **Privately Held**
Web: www.insideindianabusiness.com
SIC: 2752 5734 Commercial printing, lithographic; Printers and plotters: computers

(G-8475)
INDIANA CAST METALS ASSN INC
P.O. Box 441743 (46244-1743)
PHONE.................................317 974-1830
Tim Street, *Pr*
EMP: 7 EST: 2001
SALES (est): 78.39K **Privately Held**
Web: www.incma.org
SIC: 7389 3441 5051 Automobile recovery service; Fabricated structural metal; Metals service centers and offices

(G-8476)
INDIANA CHEMICAL LLC
Also Called: Trademark
8070 Castleton Rd Unit 413-414 (46250-2005)

Indianapolis - Marion County (G-8477)

PHONE..................................317 912-3800
EMP: 1 **EST:** 2018
SALES (est): 30.77K **Privately Held**
SIC: 7389 2899 Business Activities at Non-Commercial Site; Chemical supplies for foundries

(G-8477)
INDIANA DEPARTMENT EDUCATIO
100 N Senate Ave Rm N248 (46204-2217)
PHONE..................................765 361-5247
EMP: 8 **EST:** 2019
SALES (est): 148.82K **Privately Held**
Web: doe.state.in.us
SIC: 3663 Radio and t.v. communications equipment

(G-8478)
INDIANA FIBER WORKS
625 E 11th St (46202-2727)
PHONE..................................317 524-5711
Rob Mcnabb, *Prin*
EMP: 11 **EST:** 2008
SALES (est): 282.22K **Privately Held**
Web: www.visitindiana.com
SIC: 3554 Paper industries machinery

(G-8479)
INDIANA INSTRUMENTS INC
8032 Gordon Dr (46278-1316)
P.O. Box 53731 (46253-0731)
PHONE..................................317 875-8032
Barry J Stern, *Pr*
Judy Stern, *Sec*
EMP: 3 **EST:** 1966
SALES (est): 284.54K **Privately Held**
Web: www.bbinstruments.com
SIC: 3823 Process control instruments

(G-8480)
INDIANA INTERACTIVE LLC
Also Called: Accessindiana
151 W Ohio St # 100 (46204-1960)
PHONE..................................317 233-2010
EMP: 43 **EST:** 1995
SQ FT: 6,848
SALES (est): 9.2MM
SALES (corp-wide): 1.95B **Publicly Held**
Web: www.indianainteractive.org
SIC: 2741 7374 7371 Internet publishing and broadcasting; Data processing and preparation; Custom computer programming services
HQ: Nicusa, Inc.
  7701 College Blvd Ste 200
  Overland Park KS 66210

(G-8481)
INDIANA LOGO SIGN GROUP
600 E 96th St Ste 460 (46240-3823)
PHONE..................................800 950-1093
EMP: 5 **EST:** 2015
SALES (est): 104.6K **Privately Held**
Web: www.indianalogo.com
SIC: 3993 Signs and advertising specialties

(G-8482)
INDIANA MASONRY LLC
955 Burbank Rd (46219-5022)
PHONE..................................317 937-4275
Jorge Moreno, *Prin*
EMP: 6 **EST:** 2019
SALES (est): 215.83K **Privately Held**
SIC: 2024 Yogurt desserts, frozen

(G-8483)
INDIANA MOBILE MARINE LLC
3720 Tade Ln (46234-1421)
PHONE..................................317 961-1881
Stephen Burgess, *Managing Member*
EMP: 7 **EST:** 2017
SALES (est): 105.56K **Privately Held**
Web: www.qualitycraftmobilemarine.com
SIC: 7538 3732 Diesel engine repair: automotive; Boatbuilding and repairing

(G-8484)
INDIANA MODEL COMPANY INC
Also Called: IMC
6136 E Hanna Ave (46203-6127)
PHONE..................................317 787-6358
Ernest E Huber, *Pr*
Paula M Huber, *
EMP: 63 **EST:** 1963
SQ FT: 50,000
SALES (est): 7.94MM **Privately Held**
SIC: 3444 3599 3544 Sheet metalwork; Machine shop, jobbing and repair; Special dies, tools, jigs, and fixtures

(G-8485)
INDIANA NANOTECH LLC
Also Called: Research
7750 Centerstone Dr (46259-1485)
PHONE..................................317 385-1578
Robert Karlinsey, *Managing Member*
EMP: 6 **EST:** 2006
SQ FT: 2,500
SALES (est): 487.28K **Privately Held**
Web: www.indianananotech.com
SIC: 2844 Perfumes, cosmetics and other toilet preparations

(G-8486)
INDIANA NEWSPAPERS LLC
Also Called: Indianapolis Star
8278 Georgetown Rd (46268-1622)
PHONE..................................317 444-3800
EMP: 80
SALES (corp-wide): 2.66B **Publicly Held**
Web: www.indystar.com
SIC: 2711 Commercial printing and newspaper publishing combined
HQ: Indiana Newspapers Llc
  130 S Meridian St
  Indianapolis IN 46225
  317 444-4000

(G-8487)
INDIANA NEWSPAPERS LLC (DH)
Also Called: Indianapolis Star, The
130 S Meridian St (46225-1046)
PHONE..................................317 444-4000
Karen Crotchfelt, *Pr*
Gracia C Martore, *
Michael A Hart, *
Craig A Dubow, *
Todd A Mayman, *
EMP: 900 **EST:** 1998
SQ FT: 324,000
SALES (est): 75.77MM
SALES (corp-wide): 2.66B **Publicly Held**
Web: www.indystar.com
SIC: 2711 2752 Commercial printing and newspaper publishing combined; Commercial printing, lithographic
HQ: Gannett Media Corp.
  7950 Jones Branch Dr
  Mclean VA 22102
  703 854-6000

(G-8488)
INDIANA OXYGEN COMPANY INC (PA)
6099 Corporate Way (46278)
P.O. Box 78588 (46278)
PHONE..................................317 290-0003
Walter L Brant, *Ch Bd*
Anne Hayes, *
Kathy W Brant, *
Gary Halter, *
Michael Gunnels, *
EMP: 55 **EST:** 1915
SQ FT: 31,000
SALES (est): 43.09MM
SALES (corp-wide): 43.09MM **Privately Held**
Web: www.indianaoxygen.com
SIC: 5169 5084 2813 Industrial gases; Welding machinery and equipment; Industrial gases

(G-8489)
INDIANA PQ STUCCO LLC
325 S Oakland Ave (46201-4362)
PHONE..................................317 685-0246
Proto Quinonez, *Prin*
EMP: 1 **EST:** 2008
SALES (est): 71K **Privately Held**
SIC: 3299 Stucco

(G-8490)
INDIANA PUB BRDCSTG STNS INC
1630 N Meridian St Ste 2105 (46202-1429)
PHONE..................................317 489-4477
Roger Rhodes, *Ex Dir*
Karen Schuman, *Dir*
Nichole Carie, *Pr*
EMP: 3
SALES (est): 1.69MM **Privately Held**
Web: www.ipbs.org
SIC: 3663 Radio and t.v. communications equipment

(G-8491)
INDIANA SEAL
9329 Castlegate Dr (46256-1002)
PHONE..................................317 841-3547
Brian Mcconnell, *Mgr*
EMP: 7 **EST:** 2012
SALES (est): 166.43K **Privately Held**
Web: www.indiana-seal.com
SIC: 3498 Fabricated pipe and fittings

(G-8492)
INDIANA SIGN & BARRICADE INC
5240 E 25th St (46218-3934)
PHONE..................................317 377-8000
EMP: 37 **EST:** 2007
SQ FT: 37,000
SALES (est): 9.54MM **Privately Held**
Web: www.indianasb.com
SIC: 3993 Signs and advertising specialties

(G-8493)
INDIANA STATE GOVERNMEN
101 W Ohio St Ste 500 (46204-4254)
PHONE..................................623 326-6826
EMP: 22 **EST:** 2019
SALES (est): 242.37K **Privately Held**
SIC: 3499 Fabricated metal products, nec

(G-8494)
INDIANA STATE MEDICAL ASSN
Also Called: I S M A Report
322 Canal Walk (46202-3265)
PHONE..................................317 261-2060
Richard R King, *Dir*
EMP: 34 **EST:** 1849
SQ FT: 11,585
SALES (est): 4.02MM **Privately Held**
Web: www.ismanet.org
SIC: 8621 2721 Medical field-related associations; Periodicals

(G-8495)
INDIANA STEEL FABRICATING INC (PA)
4545 W Bradbury Ave (46241-5210)
P.O. Box 421547 (46242-1547)
PHONE..................................317 247-4545
Michael Jordan, *CEO*
Steve Dowden, *
Barbara E Osborne, *
EMP: 31 **EST:** 1954
SQ FT: 36,000
SALES (est): 9.29MM
SALES (corp-wide): 9.29MM **Privately Held**
Web: www.indianasteelfabricating.com
SIC: 3441 Fabricated structural metal

(G-8496)
INDIANA STEEL RULE DIE INC
Also Called: Indiana Steel Rule & Die
6331 English Ave (46219-8267)
P.O. Box 33843 (46203-0843)
PHONE..................................317 352-9859
Rick Lee, *Pr*
EMP: 2 **EST:** 1990
SALES (est): 246.63K **Privately Held**
Web: www.marketingbloodwork.com
SIC: 3544 Dies and die holders for metal cutting, forming, die casting

(G-8497)
INDIANA THERMAL SOLUTIONS LLC
6872 Hillsdale Ct Bldg 375 (46250-2001)
PHONE..................................317 570-5400
EMP: 10 **EST:** 2007
SQ FT: 2,700
SALES (est): 3.21MM **Privately Held**
Web: www.its-indiana.com
SIC: 3823 Thermal conductivity instruments, industrial process type

(G-8498)
INDIANA UNIV SCHL MEDICINE ✪
980 W Walnut St (46202-5188)
PHONE..................................317 278-6518
EMP: 16 **EST:** 2023
SALES (est): 1.29MM **Privately Held**
SIC: 2834 Pharmaceutical preparations

(G-8499)
INDIANA VENEERS CORP
Also Called: Indiana Veneers
1121 E 24th St (46205-4425)
P.O. Box 55771 (46205-0771)
PHONE..................................317 926-2458
Peter Lorenz, *Pr*
Werner Lorenz, *
◆ **EMP:** 100 **EST:** 1892
SQ FT: 200,000
SALES (est): 10.07MM **Privately Held**
Web: www.indianaveneers.com
SIC: 2435 Veneer stock, hardwood

(G-8500)
INDIANA WHITESELL CORPORATION
5101 Decatur Blvd Ste W (46241-9529)
P.O. Box 2570 (35662-2570)
PHONE..................................317 279-3278
EMP: 400
SIC: 3399 5085 4212 4225 Metal fasteners; Industrial supplies; Delivery service, vehicular; General warehousing

(G-8501)
INDIANA WHL WINE & LQ CO INC
1240 Brookville Way Ste J (46239-1099)
PHONE..................................317 667-0231
▲ **EMP:** 5
SALES (corp-wide): 95.19K **Privately Held**
Web: www.johnsonbrothersofin.com
SIC: 5182 2084 Wine; Wines
PA: Indiana Wholesale Wine & Liquor Company, Inc.
  200 Lumber Center Rd
  Michigan City IN 46360
  219 879-8855

Indianapolis - Marion County (G-8529)

(G-8502)
INDIANAPOLIS IN ✪
Also Called: Distributor
8520 E 33rd St (46226)
PHONE.................................855 628-3458
Christopher Thompson, Pr
Christopher T Thompson, *
EMP: 25 **EST:** 2023
SALES (est): 1.29MM Privately Held
SIC: 3564 3569 5085 5013 Filters, air: furnaces, air conditioning equipment, etc.; Filters; Filters, industrial; Filters, air and oil

(G-8503)
INDIANAPOLIS CONTAINER COMPANY
P.O. Box 40006 (46240-0006)
PHONE.................................317 580-5000
EMP: 6 **EST:** 1958
SQ FT: 55,000
SALES (est): 249.24K Privately Held
Web: www.containerworks.com
SIC: 5113 3411 3221 2396 Boxes and containers; Metal cans; Glass containers; Automotive and apparel trimmings

(G-8504)
INDIANAPOLIS FABRICATIONS LLC
Also Called: Lfab
1125 Brookside Ave Ste G50 (46202-3587)
PHONE.................................317 600-3522
▲ **EMP:** 12 **EST:** 2009
SALES (est): 2.28MM Privately Held
Web: www.indianapolisfabrications.com
SIC: 3441 Fabricated structural metal

(G-8505)
INDIANAPOLIS GATORADE
5858 Decatur Blvd (46241-9575)
PHONE.................................317 821-6400
Lance Oxley, Dir
EMP: 9 **EST:** 2013
SALES (est): 227.19K Privately Held
SIC: 2086 Bottled and canned soft drinks

(G-8506)
INDIANAPOLIS INDUSTRIAL PDTS
Also Called: Matjack Division Indianapolis
2320 Duke St (46205-2240)
PHONE.................................317 359-3078
John Sweezy Junior, CEO
Bradley Sweezy, VP
Susan Sweezy, Sec
EMP: 7 **EST:** 1981
SQ FT: 6,000
SALES (est): 972.52K Privately Held
Web: www.matjack.com
SIC: 3069 Air-supported rubber structures

(G-8507)
INDIANAPOLIS METAL SPINNING CO
1924 Midwest Blvd (46214-2337)
PHONE.................................317 273-7440
James C Kaufman, Pr
▲ **EMP:** 12 **EST:** 1924
SQ FT: 50,000
SALES (est): 1.53MM Privately Held
Web: www.imspinning.com
SIC: 3469 Stamping metal for the trade

(G-8508)
INDIANAPOLIS SIGNWORKS INC
5349 W 86th St (46268-1501)
PHONE.................................317 872-8722
EMP: 22 **EST:** 1992
SQ FT: 15,000
SALES (est): 2.11MM Privately Held
Web: www.signworksthinks.com
SIC: 3993 7336 Signs and advertising specialties; Commercial art and illustration

(G-8509)
INDIANAPOLIS SOCIAL SEC OFF
5515 N Post Rd (46216-1000)
PHONE.................................800 772-1213
EMP: 7 **EST:** 2015
SALES (est): 54.2K Privately Held
Web: www.ssa.gov
SIC: 2741 Internet publishing and broadcasting

(G-8510)
INDIANPLIS LEGISLATIVE INSIGHT
Also Called: Insight Group
200 W Washington St Ste M12 (46204-2728)
P.O. Box 383 (46061-0383)
PHONE.................................317 955-9997
Edward D Feigenbaum, Owner
Edward F Feigenbaum, Owner
EMP: 1 **EST:** 1989
SALES (est): 76.18K Privately Held
Web: www.indianainsight.com
SIC: 2711 Newspapers, publishing and printing

(G-8511)
INDIANPLIS PRESS CLB FNDTION I
615 N Alabama St Ste 119 (46204-1431)
P.O. Box 40923 (46240-0923)
PHONE.................................317 701-1130
EMP: 9
SALES (est): 62.5K Privately Held
Web: www.indypressfoundation.org
SIC: 2741 Miscellaneous publishing

(G-8512)
INDIANPLIS WLDG FBRICATION LLC ✪
10565 E Southport Rd (46259-1431)
PHONE.................................317 999-7856
EMP: 6 **EST:** 2022
SALES (est): 25.09K Privately Held
Web: www.radfabrication.com
SIC: 7692 Welding repair

(G-8513)
INDIENGAGE LLC
634 E New York St (46202-3707)
PHONE.................................317 331-7781
EMP: 1 **EST:** 2011
SALES (est): 57.01K Privately Held
Web: www.indiengage.com
SIC: 7372 7389 Application computer software; Business services, nec

(G-8514)
INDIGO CANDLES
640 E 16th St (46202-2759)
PHONE.................................317 457-9814
Amari Martin, Prin
EMP: 4 **EST:** 2016
SALES (est): 39.69K Privately Held
SIC: 3999 Candles

(G-8515)
INDIWOODWORKS COMPANY
348 W 44th St (46208-3734)
PHONE.................................317 283-6931
James Wallihan, Admn
EMP: 5 **EST:** 2017
SALES (est): 80.72K Privately Held
SIC: 2499 Wood products, nec

(G-8516)
INDUSTRIAL ADHESIVES INDIANA
8202 Indy Ln (46214-2326)
PHONE.................................317 271-2100
Jon S Watson, Pr
Jon Scott Watson, Pr
Mary Jane Watson, VP
▲ **EMP:** 5 **EST:** 2004
SALES (est): 508.55K Privately Held
Web: www.targetandtactical.com
SIC: 2891 Adhesives

(G-8517)
INDUSTRIAL ANODIZING CO INC
1610 W Washington St (46222-4594)
P.O. Box 1363 (46206-1363)
PHONE.................................317 637-4641
William Wimmenauer Junior, Pr
EMP: 50 **EST:** 1963
SQ FT: 30,000
SALES (est): 5.23MM Privately Held
Web: www.industrialanodizing.com
SIC: 3471 Electroplating of metals or formed products

(G-8518)
INDUSTRIAL HYDRAULICS INC
1005 Western Dr (46241-1436)
PHONE.................................317 247-4421
Ronald P Dilley, Pr
Duane Harris, *
Audrey Pringle, *
William Duane Harris Junior, VP
Janet Mcclain, Sec
EMP: 24 **EST:** 1969
SQ FT: 18,000
SALES (est): 4.82MM Privately Held
Web: www.ihi-indy.com
SIC: 7699 3599 Hydraulic equipment repair; Custom machinery

(G-8519)
INDUSTRIAL SALES & SUPPLY INC
Also Called: Zoofari Gardens
5640 Professional Cir (46241-5015)
PHONE.................................317 240-0560
Patti Luc, Pr
EMP: 20 **EST:** 1994
SALES (est): 1.34MM Privately Held
Web: www.issindy.com
SIC: 3334 3545 Primary aluminum; Machine tool accessories

(G-8520)
INDUSTRIAL SOFTWARE LLC
7657 Stones River Ct (46259-6727)
PHONE.................................317 862-0650
EMP: 2 **EST:** 2009
SALES (est): 82.36K Privately Held
SIC: 7372 Prepackaged software

(G-8521)
INDUSTRIAL WATER MGT INC
5365 W Minnesota St (46241-3817)
P.O. Box 511 (46142-0511)
PHONE.................................317 889-0836
William Yost, Pr
EMP: 3 **EST:** 1994
SALES (est): 490K Privately Held
Web: www.industrial-water.com
SIC: 5084 2819 Chemical process equipment; Industrial inorganic chemicals, nec

(G-8522)
INDY AEROSPACE INC
2801 Fortune Cir E Ste J (46241-5551)
PHONE.................................817 521-6508
Jose Rodriguez, CEO
Austin Mielczarek, Prin
EMP: 5 **EST:** 2012
SALES (est): 949.86K Privately Held
Web: www.indyaerospaceinc.com
SIC: 4581 3499 1799 3429 Aircraft upholstery repair; Aerosol valves, metal; Renovation of aircraft interiors; Aircraft hardware

(G-8523)
INDY CBD PLUS LLP
10911 Parker Dr (46231-1082)
PHONE.................................317 600-6362
Josh Bennett, Genl Pt
EMP: 5 **EST:** 2018
SALES (est): 207.83K Privately Held
Web: www.indycbdplus.com
SIC: 3999

(G-8524)
INDY COLOR PRINTING LLC
6220 Hardegan St (46227-4907)
PHONE.................................317 371-8829
Jeanne Mccullough, Owner
EMP: 7 **EST:** 2011
SALES (est): 235.77K Privately Held
SIC: 2752 Commercial printing, lithographic

(G-8525)
INDY CUSTOM MACHINE INC
8267 Indy Ct (46214-2300)
PHONE.................................317 271-1544
EMP: 7 **EST:** 1996
SQ FT: 5,600
SALES (est): 852.62K Privately Held
Web: www.indycustommachine.com
SIC: 3599 Machine shop, jobbing and repair

(G-8526)
INDY CYLINDER HEAD INC
8621 Southeastern Ave Ste B (46239)
PHONE.................................317 862-3724
Russell E Flagle, Pr
◆ **EMP:** 22 **EST:** 1972
SQ FT: 3,000
SALES (est): 2.41MM Privately Held
Web: www.indyheads.com
SIC: 3714 Cylinder heads, motor vehicle

(G-8527)
INDY GLASS CENTER INC
6366 E 32nd Ct (46226-6168)
PHONE.................................317 591-5000
Paul Davis, Pr
Jack Ferrell, VP
EMP: 23 **EST:** 1989
SQ FT: 25,000
SALES (est): 999.9K Privately Held
SIC: 3211 5039 3231 Insulating glass, sealed units; Glass construction materials; Products of purchased glass

(G-8528)
INDY HIGH BTU LLC
2319 Kentucky Ave (46221-5002)
PHONE.................................317 749-0732
Casey Holsapple, Managing Member
EMP: 9 **EST:** 2018
SALES (est): 2.32MM Privately Held
SIC: 1311 Natural gas production

(G-8529)
INDY HOODS LLC
1367 Sadlier Circle South Dr (46239-1059)
PHONE.................................317 731-7170
Nancy Guzman, CEO
EMP: 10 **EST:** 2016
SALES (est): 1.19MM Privately Held
Web: www.indianapoliskitchenhoods.com
SIC: 1542 5046 3444 8711 Restaurant construction; Restaurant equipment and supplies, nec; Restaurant sheet metalwork; Fire protection engineering

Indianapolis - Marion County (G-8530)

(G-8530)
INDY IMAGING INC
1300 W 16th St (46202-2112)
PHONE.....................317 917-7938
Robert Gordon, *Pr*
▲ **EMP:** 43 **EST:** 2003
SALES (est): 4.78MM **Privately Held**
Web: www.indyimaging.com
SIC: 3993 Signs and advertising specialties

(G-8531)
INDY LASH AND BROW LLC
7404 Franklin Parke Ct (46259-9731)
PHONE.....................502 751-4947
EMP: 4 **EST:** 2017
SALES (est): 39.69K **Privately Held**
SIC: 3999 Eyelashes, artificial

(G-8532)
INDY PARTS INC
2 Gasoline Aly # A (46222-3963)
PHONE.....................317 243-7171
Scott Jasek, *Pr*
EMP: 6 **EST:** 2006
SALES (est): 142.79K **Privately Held**
Web: www.indyraceparts.com
SIC: 3089 Automotive parts, plastic

(G-8533)
INDY POWDER COATING INC
4300 W 10th St (46222-3208)
PHONE.....................317 244-2231
EMP: 5 **EST:** 1996
SALES (est): 911.59K **Privately Held**
Web: www.indypowdercoating.com
SIC: 3479 Coating of metals and formed products

(G-8534)
INDY SIDE PIECE LLC ◊
6015 E 34th St (46226-6109)
PHONE.....................317 426-3927
EMP: 1 **EST:** 2022
SALES (est): 46.61K **Privately Held**
SIC: 3423 Mechanics' hand tools

(G-8535)
INDY STUD WELDING INC
2654 Allen Ave (46203-5144)
PHONE.....................317 416-3617
Kenneth M Pologruto, *Owner*
EMP: 2 **EST:** 2003
SALES (est): 161.52K **Privately Held**
SIC: 3423 Ironworkers' hand tools

(G-8536)
INDY W EMB SILK SCREENING LLC
1417 E Riverside Dr (46202-2037)
PHONE.....................317 634-4906
Stephen B Kantner, *Pr*
EMP: 5 **EST:** 2018
SALES (est): 235.07K **Privately Held**
Web: www.indywestembroidery.com
SIC: 2395 Embroidery products, except Schiffli machine

(G-8537)
INDY WEB INC
3151 Madison Ave (46227-1160)
PHONE.....................317 536-1201
EMP: 4 **EST:** 1996
SQ FT: 2,400
SALES (est): 488.2K **Privately Held**
Web: www.indyweb.net
SIC: 4813 3571 8748 Internet connectivity services; Personal computers (microcomputers); Systems engineering consultant, ex. computer or professional

(G-8538)
INDY WIDE FORMAT
8905 Stonebriar Dr (46259-1322)
PHONE.....................317 912-1385
EMP: 5 **EST:** 2019
SALES (est): 80.7K **Privately Held**
Web: www.indywideformat.com
SIC: 3993 Signs and advertising specialties

(G-8539)
INDYS INFANT CENTER LLC
2842 Boulevard Pl (46208-5109)
PHONE.....................317 717-3622
EMP: 4 **EST:** 2014
SALES (est): 123.04K **Privately Held**
Web: www.indyschild.com
SIC: 2721 Magazines: publishing only, not printed on site

(G-8540)
INDYS SIGN SOURCE INC
5501 W 86th St Ste C (46268-1583)
P.O. Box 78064 (46278-0064)
PHONE.....................317 372-2260
EMP: 3 **EST:** 1993
SALES (est): 211.11K **Privately Held**
SIC: 3993 Signs and advertising specialties

(G-8541)
INFINIAS LLC
9340 Priority Way West Dr (46240-1468)
PHONE.....................317 348-1249
▼ **EMP:** 9 **EST:** 2009
SQ FT: 1,600
SALES (est): 870.66K **Privately Held**
Web: www.3xlogic.com
SIC: 3679 Electronic switches

(G-8542)
INFINITY PERFORMANCE INC
7002 N Park Ave (46220-1040)
PHONE.....................317 479-1017
George Atkinson, *Pr*
EMP: 43 **EST:** 1996
SQ FT: 30,000
SALES (est): 3.41MM **Privately Held**
Web: www.infinityperformance.com
SIC: 3069 Rubber floorcoverings/mats and wallcoverings

(G-8543)
INGENUS LLC
5664 Fen Ct (46220-7401)
PHONE.....................317 430-1855
EMP: 10 **EST:** 2009
SALES (est): 58.66K **Privately Held**
Web: www.ingenus.com
SIC: 2834 Pharmaceutical preparations

(G-8544)
INGREDION INCORPORATED
1050 W Raymond St (46221-2010)
P.O. Box 1084 (46206-1084)
PHONE.....................317 635-4455
Judy Wooden, *Mgr*
EMP: 30
SALES (corp-wide): 8.16B **Publicly Held**
Web: www.ingredion.com
SIC: 3999 Lawn ornaments
PA: Ingredion Incorporated
5 Westbrook Corporate Ctr
Westchester IL 60154
708 551-2600

(G-8545)
INGREDION INCORPORATED
1515 Drover St (46221-1735)
PHONE.....................317 635-4455
Bob Stefansic, *Mgr*
EMP: 71
SALES (corp-wide): 8.16B **Publicly Held**
Web: www.ingredion.com
SIC: 2046 Corn starch
PA: Ingredion Incorporated
5 Westbrook Corporate Ctr
Westchester IL 60154
708 551-2600

(G-8546)
INGREDION INCORPORATED
5521 W 74th St (46268-4184)
PHONE.....................317 295-4122
EMP: 267
SALES (corp-wide): 8.16B **Publicly Held**
Web: www.ingredion.com
SIC: 2046 Corn starch
PA: Ingredion Incorporated
5 Westbrook Corporate Ctr
Westchester IL 60154
708 551-2600

(G-8547)
INGROUP
200 W Washington St Ste M12 (46204-2728)
P.O. Box 383 (46061-0383)
PHONE.....................317 817-9997
Edward Feigenbaum, *Owner*
EMP: 2 **EST:** 1988
SQ FT: 120
SALES (est): 115.05K **Privately Held**
Web: ingroupassociates.aleragroup.com
SIC: 2741 8748 Newsletter publishing; Publishing consultant

(G-8548)
INHABIT INC
211 S Ritter Ave Ste B (46219-7151)
PHONE.....................317 636-1699
Jennifer Tuttle, *Pr*
Michael Tuttle, *VP*
▲ **EMP:** 9 **EST:** 2003
SQ FT: 6,500
SALES (est): 990.85K **Privately Held**
Web: www.inhabitliving.com
SIC: 2392 Household furnishings, nec

(G-8549)
INLAND CONTAINER
4030 Vincennes Rd (46268-3007)
PHONE.....................317 876-0768
EMP: 8 **EST:** 2019
SALES (est): 241.14K **Privately Held**
Web: www.inlandscorezone.com
SIC: 2653 Boxes, corrugated: made from purchased materials

(G-8550)
INLAND PAPER BOARD & PACKAGING
5461 W 79th St (46268-1675)
PHONE.....................317 879-9710
Steve Raine, *Prin*
EMP: 3 **EST:** 2009
SALES (est): 163.73K **Privately Held**
SIC: 2621 Wrapping and packaging papers

(G-8551)
INNOLEO LLC
6510 Telecom Dr Ste 165 (46278-6330)
PHONE.....................561 994-8905
Matthew Kriech, *CEO*
▲ **EMP:** 3 **EST:** 2011
SALES (est): 244.49K **Privately Held**
Web: www.innoleo.com
SIC: 2076 Castor oil and pomace

(G-8552)
INNOVATIONS AMPLIFIED LLC
2255 Colfax Ln (46260-6601)
PHONE.....................317 339-4685
Erik C Morris, *CMO*
EMP: 3 **EST:** 2017
SALES (est): 245.04K **Privately Held**
SIC: 8742 3087 2295 2821 Management consulting services; Custom compound purchased resins; Chemically coated and treated fabrics; Vinyl resins, nec

(G-8553)
INNOVATIVE CHEM RESOURCES INC
Also Called: I C R
6464 Rucker Rd (46220-4841)
PHONE.....................317 695-6001
John Hulen, *Pr*
Clay F Cox, *VP*
EMP: 5 **EST:** 2003
SQ FT: 1,000
SALES (est): 515.67K **Privately Held**
SIC: 2899 8999 Chemical preparations, nec; Chemical consultant

(G-8554)
INNOVATIVE CONCEPTS GROUP INC
8624 Quarterhorse Dr (46256-4322)
PHONE.....................317 408-0292
Robert Puma, *Pr*
EMP: 5 **EST:** 2003
SALES (est): 367.9K **Privately Held**
SIC: 2048 5199 Prepared feeds, nec; Pet supplies

(G-8555)
INNOVATIVE FABRICATION LLC
Also Called: Indy Hanger
1440 Brookville Way (46239-1066)
PHONE.....................317 215-5988
Roger A Crowder, *Managing Member*
Walt Smith, *
EMP: 70 **EST:** 2007
SALES (est): 13.83MM **Privately Held**
Web: www.indyhanger.com
SIC: 3315 Hangers (garment), wire

(G-8556)
INNOVATIVE MEDIA SCIENCES INC
Also Called: Technology
36 Parkview Ave (46201-3153)
PHONE.....................317 366-4371
Alan Scott Ealy, *CEO*
EMP: 1 **EST:** 2020
SALES (est): 91K **Privately Held**
Web: www.innovativei.com
SIC: 2711 Newspapers, publishing and printing

(G-8557)
INNOVATIVE MOLD & MACHINE INC
2702 Brill Rd (46225-2303)
PHONE.....................317 634-1177
Michael D Thomas, *Pr*
EMP: 3 **EST:** 1995
SQ FT: 2,000
SALES (est): 488.29K **Privately Held**
Web: www.innovativemachine.com
SIC: 3089 3549 Injection molding of plastics; Metalworking machinery, nec

(G-8558)
INNOVATIVE SLOTS LLC
2652 Brill Rd (46225-2301)
PHONE.....................317 520-7374
Michael D Thomas, *Owner*
EMP: 4 **EST:** 2016
SALES (est): 94.41K **Privately Held**
Web: www.innovativeslots.com
SIC: 3999 Manufacturing industries, nec

GEOGRAPHIC SECTION

Indianapolis - Marion County (G-8583)

(G-8559)
INNOVTIVE CATING SOLUTIONS INC
7950 Georgetown Rd Ste 200 (46268-1617)
PHONE.....................317 879-2222
▲ EMP: 43 EST: 2013
SALES (est): 7.51MM Privately Held
Web: www.innovative-coating-solutions.com
SIC: 2396 Automotive trimmings, fabric
HQ: Toyota Tsusho America, Inc.
825 3rd Ave Fl 10
New York NY 10022
212 355-3600

(G-8560)
INSERTEC INC (PA)
4011 W 54th St (46254-4789)
PHONE.....................800 556-1911
▲ EMP: 64 EST: 1994
SQ FT: 75,000
SALES (est): 3MM Privately Held
Web: www.insertec.com
SIC: 7372 7389 Prepackaged software; Packaging and labeling services

(G-8561)
INSIGN INC
Also Called: Real Estate Sign Services
5812 Linton Ln (46220-5355)
PHONE.....................317 251-0131
Laura J Tomlin, Pr
EMP: 2 EST: 2003
SALES (est): 234.95K Privately Held
Web: www.realestatesignservices.com
SIC: 3993 Signs and advertising specialties

(G-8562)
INSPIRE LLC
6503 Ferguson St (46220-1148)
PHONE.....................317 339-7718
Ellen Robinson, Admn
EMP: 7 EST: 2016
SALES (est): 156.42K Privately Held
Web: www.inspireautomation.com
SIC: 2834 Pharmaceutical preparations

(G-8563)
INSTANTWHIP-INDIANAPOLIS INC
9125 Burk Rd (46229-3083)
PHONE.....................317 899-1533
Ted Wadsworth, Mgr
EMP: 10
SALES (corp-wide): 9.74MM Privately Held
Web: www.instantwhip.com
SIC: 2026 5143 Whipped topping, except frozen or dry mix; Dairy products, except dried or canned
PA: Instantwhip-Indianapolis Inc
2200 Cardigan Ave
Columbus OH 43215
614 488-2536

(G-8564)
INSTY-PRINTS
930 E Hanna Ave (46227)
PHONE.....................317 788-1504
Robin Heldman, Prin
EMP: 6 EST: 2011
SALES (est): 76.4K Privately Held
Web: www.instyprints.com
SIC: 2752 Commercial printing, lithographic

(G-8565)
INSULTECH LLC
Also Called: Insultech
2681 Rand Rd (46241-5501)
PHONE.....................317 389-5134
EMP: 10
Web: www.insultech.com
SIC: 2899 Chemical preparations, nec
PA: Insultech, Llc
3530 W Garry Ave
Santa Ana CA 92704

(G-8566)
INTEGER HOLDINGS CORPORATION
Also Called: Greatbatch Medical
3737 N Arlington Ave (46218)
PHONE.....................317 454-8800
EMP: 16
SALES (corp-wide): 1.6B Publicly Held
Web: www.integer.net
SIC: 3841 Surgical and medical instruments
PA: Integer Holdings Corporation
2595 Dallas Pkwy Ste 310
Frisco TX 75034
214 618-5243

(G-8567)
INTEGRATED DE ICING SERVI
7899 S Service Rd Ste H (46241-4214)
PHONE.....................317 517-1643
EMP: 5 EST: 2013
SALES (est): 231.19K Privately Held
SIC: 3728 Aircraft parts and equipment, nec

(G-8568)
INTEGRATED INSTRUMENT SVCS INC
Also Called: I2s
5601 Fortune Cir S Ste A (46241-5533)
P.O. Box 51013 (46251-0013)
PHONE.....................317 248-1958
Al Chamen, Pr
Hasan Al Mahrovq, VP
Kassab Sayel, Genl Mgr
EMP: 10 EST: 1988
SQ FT: 10,000
SALES (est): 1.47MM Privately Held
Web: www.i2sinc.com
SIC: 8734 3821 Testing laboratories; Vacuum pumps, laboratory

(G-8569)
INTEGRATED TECH RESOURCES
2445 Directors Row Ste J (46241-4936)
PHONE.....................317 757-5432
William Derrer, Pr
Diane Fleete, Pr
EMP: 8 EST: 2014
SALES (est): 987.79K Privately Held
SIC: 3613 Control panels, electric

(G-8570)
INTEMPO SOFTWARE INC
8777 Purdue Rd Ste 340 (46268-3121)
PHONE.....................800 950-2221
Matt Hopp, Genl Mgr
EMP: 20 EST: 2008
SALES (est): 2.29MM Privately Held
Web: www.intemposoftware.com
SIC: 7372 Prepackaged software

(G-8571)
INTEPRINTATIONS
8909 Stonewall Dr (46231-2574)
PHONE.....................765 404-0887
Cari Bowersock, Owner
EMP: 5 EST: 2009
SALES (est): 6.66K Privately Held
SIC: 2754 5943 Invitations: gravure printing; Stationery stores

(G-8572)
INTERACTIVE INTELLIGENCE INC
7601 Interactive Way (46278-2727)
PHONE.....................317 872-3000
EMP: 3
SALES (corp-wide): 37.98MM Privately Held
SIC: 7372 Prepackaged software
HQ: Interactive Intelligence, Inc.
7601 Interactive Way
Indianapolis IN 46278

(G-8573)
INTERACTIVE INTELLIGENCE INC
7601 Interactive Way (46278-2727)
PHONE.....................803 699-7778
EMP: 3
SALES (corp-wide): 37.98MM Privately Held
SIC: 7372 Application computer software
HQ: Interactive Intelligence, Inc.
7601 Interactive Way
Indianapolis IN 46278

(G-8574)
INTERACTIVE INTELLIGENCE GROUP INC
7601 Interactive Way (46278-2727)
PHONE.....................317 872-3000
EMP: 2309
Web: www.genesys.com
SIC: 7372 Application computer software

(G-8575)
INTERACTIVE INTELLIGENCE INC
7601 Interactive Way (46278-2727)
PHONE.....................800 267-1364
EMP: 849
SIC: 7372 7371 Application computer software; Custom computer programming services

(G-8576)
INTERNATIONAL CODE COUNCIL INC
Also Called: Icbo
1223 S Richland St (46221-1604)
PHONE.....................317 879-1677
Brent Snyder, Off Mgr
EMP: 4
SALES (corp-wide): 96.46MM Privately Held
Web: www.iccsafe.org
SIC: 2741 Directories, nec: publishing only, not printed on site
PA: International Code Council, Inc.
200 Massachusetts Ave Nw # 250
Washington DC 20001
888 422-7233

(G-8577)
INTERNATIONAL GAME TECHNOLOGY
1302 N Meridian St (46202-2365)
PHONE.....................317 731-3791
EMP: 3
SALES (corp-wide): 4.31B Privately Held
Web: www.igt.com
SIC: 3999 Atomizers, toiletry
HQ: International Game Technology Inc
6355 S Buffalo Dr
Las Vegas NV 89113
702 669-7777

(G-8578)
INTERNATIONAL PAPER COMPANY
Also Called: International Paper
5012 W 79th St (46268-1645)
PHONE.....................317 870-0192
EMP: 5
SALES (corp-wide): 18.92B Publicly Held
Web: www.internationalpaper.com
SIC: 2621 Paper mills
PA: International Paper Company
6400 Poplar Ave
Memphis TN 38197
901 419-7000

(G-8579)
INTERNATIONAL PAPER COMPANY
Also Called: International Paper
7536 Miles Dr (46231-3344)
PHONE.....................317 481-4000
Mark Crevonis, Brnch Mgr
EMP: 10
SALES (corp-wide): 18.92B Publicly Held
Web: www.internationalpaper.com
SIC: 2621 Paper mills
PA: International Paper Company
6400 Poplar Ave
Memphis TN 38197
901 419-7000

(G-8580)
INTERNATIONAL PAPER COMPANY
Also Called: International Paper
8501 Moller Rd (46268-1510)
PHONE.....................317 715-9080
EMP: 12
SALES (corp-wide): 18.92B Publicly Held
Web: www.internationalpaper.com
SIC: 2621 Paper mills
PA: International Paper Company
6400 Poplar Ave
Memphis TN 38197
901 419-7000

(G-8581)
INTERNATIONAL PAPER COMPANY
Also Called: International Paper
4901 W 79th St (46268-1662)
PHONE.....................317 871-6999
John Falk, Mgr
EMP: 35
SALES (corp-wide): 18.92B Publicly Held
Web: www.internationalpaper.com
SIC: 2621 Paper mills
PA: International Paper Company
6400 Poplar Ave
Memphis TN 38197
901 419-7000

(G-8582)
INTERNATIONAL PAPER COMPANY
Also Called: International Paper
2135 Stout Field East Dr (46241-4014)
PHONE.....................317 390-3300
EMP: 76
SALES (corp-wide): 18.92B Publicly Held
Web: www.internationalpaper.com
SIC: 2653 Boxes, corrugated: made from purchased materials
PA: International Paper Company
6400 Poplar Ave
Memphis TN 38197
901 419-7000

(G-8583)
INTERNTNAL DAMND GOLD EXCH LTD
Also Called: Patora Fine Jewelers
6010 W 86th St Ste 114 (46278-1407)
PHONE.....................317 872-6666
Pamela Hickman, Pr
EMP: 7 EST: 1990
SQ FT: 3,200
SALES (est): 416.31K Privately Held
Web: www.patorajewelers.com
SIC: 5944 3911 7631 7389 Jewelry, precious stones and precious metals; Jewelry, precious metal; Jewelry repair services; Auction, appraisal, and exchange services

Indianapolis - Marion County (G-8584)

(G-8584)
INTERVENTION DIAGNOSTICS INC
6925 Hawthorn Park Dr (46220-3910)
PHONE..................317 432-6091
James Connolly, *Owner*
EMP: 8 EST: 2010
SALES (est): 229.08K **Privately Held**
Web: www.ivd-corp.com
SIC: 2835 Diagnostic substances

(G-8585)
INVENTORY SOLUTIONS INC
4305 Saguaro Trl (46268-2553)
PHONE..................212 749-5027
EMP: 6 EST: 2018
SALES (est): 95.34K **Privately Held**
Web: www.cryois.com
SIC: 3841 Surgical and medical instruments

(G-8586)
IOT TECHNOLOGIES INTL LLC
4525 Saguaro Trl (46268-2557)
PHONE..................317 824-4544
Bernard Hasten, *Prin*
EMP: 12 EST: 2019
SALES (est): 529.13K **Privately Held**
SIC: 3829 Measuring and controlling devices, nec

(G-8587)
IPHEION DEVELOPMENT CORP
Also Called: Ipheion Custom Technologies
3421 Breckenridge Dr (46228-2751)
PHONE..................240 281-1619
Elsa Rose Hoffmann, *Pr*
Dominik Hoffmann, *Engr*
EMP: 2 EST: 2013
SALES (est): 98.47K **Privately Held**
SIC: 8999 8748 8711 3826 Scientific consulting; Systems analysis and engineering consulting services; Engineering services; Analytical instruments

(G-8588)
IPS-INTEGRATED PRJ SVCS LLC
Also Called: Ips Indiana
320 N Meridian St Ste 212 (46204-1721)
PHONE..................317 247-1200
Michael Vitello, *Brnch Mgr*
EMP: 5
SALES (corp-wide): 364.48B **Publicly Held**
Web: www.ipsdb.com
SIC: 2834 Solutions, pharmaceutical
HQ: Ips-Integrated Project Services, Llc
    721 Arbor Way Ste 100
    Blue Bell PA 19422

(G-8589)
IRVING MATERIALS INC
Also Called: I M I
5244 E 96th St (46240-3747)
PHONE..................317 843-2944
EMP: 7
SALES (corp-wide): 814.09MM **Privately Held**
Web: www.irvmat.com
SIC: 3273 Ready-mixed concrete
PA: Irving Materials, Inc.
    8032 N State Road 9
    Greenfield IN 46140
    317 326-3101

(G-8590)
IRVING MATERIALS INC
Also Called: I M I
4700 W 96th St (46268-2917)
PHONE..................317 872-0152
EMP: 5
SALES (corp-wide): 814.09MM **Privately Held**
Web: www.irvmat.com
SIC: 3273 Ready-mixed concrete
PA: Irving Materials, Inc.
    8032 N State Road 9
    Greenfield IN 46140
    317 326-3101

(G-8591)
IRVING MATERIALS INC
Also Called: I M I
4200 S Harding St Ste X (46217-9593)
PHONE..................317 783-3381
EMP: 6
SALES (corp-wide): 814.09MM **Privately Held**
Web: www.irvmat.com
SIC: 3273 Ready-mixed concrete
PA: Irving Materials, Inc.
    8032 N State Road 9
    Greenfield IN 46140
    317 326-3101

(G-8592)
IRVING MATERIALS INC
4330 W Morris St (46241-2504)
PHONE..................317 243-7391
EMP: 6
SALES (corp-wide): 814.09MM **Privately Held**
Web: www.irvmat.com
SIC: 3273 Ready-mixed concrete
PA: Irving Materials, Inc.
    8032 N State Road 9
    Greenfield IN 46140
    317 326-3101

(G-8593)
IRVING MATERIALS INC
3130 N Post Rd (46226-6514)
PHONE..................317 899-2187
EMP: 6
SALES (corp-wide): 814.09MM **Privately Held**
Web: www.irvmat.com
SIC: 3273 Ready-mixed concrete
PA: Irving Materials, Inc.
    8032 N State Road 9
    Greenfield IN 46140
    317 326-3101

(G-8594)
ISF INC
Also Called: Sign Fab
6468 Rucker Rd (46220-4841)
PHONE..................317 251-1219
EMP: 24 EST: 1996
SQ FT: 12,000
SALES (est): 4.93MM **Privately Held**
Web: www.isfsigns.com
SIC: 3993 Electric signs

(G-8595)
ISI OF INDIANA INC
5342 W Vermont St (46224-8841)
PHONE..................317 241-2999
William Witchger, *Ch Bd*
Guy Driggers, *Pr*
EMP: 8 EST: 1974
SQ FT: 20,000
SALES (est): 2.05MM **Privately Held**
SIC: 5199 2295 Packaging materials; Tape, varnished: plastic, and other coated (except magnetic)

(G-8596)
ISSI ENGRG & MACHINING LLC
5640 Professional Cir (46241-5015)
PHONE..................317 240-0560
Brenton Rettig, *Managing Member*
EMP: 16 EST: 2021
SALES (est): 1.26MM **Privately Held**
Web: www.issindy.com
SIC: 3599 Machine shop, jobbing and repair

(G-8597)
ITECH HOLDINGS LLC
Also Called: Itech Digital
6330 E 75th St Ste 132 (46250)
PHONE..................317 567-5160
Ryan Schalk, *CEO*
Mark Nazarenus, *
Steve Spiech, *
Nicole Davis, *
◆ EMP: 25 EST: 1999
SQ FT: 10,000
SALES (est): 4.31MM **Privately Held**
Web: www.itechdigital.com
SIC: 3651 Video camera-audio recorders, household use

(G-8598)
ITW GEMA
Also Called: Gema
4141 W 54th St (46254-3728)
PHONE..................317 298-5000
Mark Fooksman, *Dir*
▲ EMP: 15 EST: 2007
SALES (est): 4.67MM **Privately Held**
Web: www.gemapowdercoating.com
SIC: 3399 Powder, metal

(G-8599)
J & K ASSOCIATES INC
6302 Rucker Rd Ste C (46220-4853)
P.O. Box 734 (46135-0734)
PHONE..................317 255-3588
John R Means, *Pt*
Howard Thomas, *Pt*
EMP: 3 EST: 1987
SQ FT: 2,600
SALES (est): 332.22K **Privately Held**
SIC: 3469 Machine parts, stamped or pressed metal

(G-8600)
J & T MARINE SPECIALISTS INC
810 S Mitthoeffer Rd (46239-9640)
PHONE..................317 890-9444
James Booe, *Pr*
Tinka Booe, *Sec*
▲ EMP: 2 EST: 1973
SALES (est): 261.2K **Privately Held**
SIC: 3324 3599 Commercial investment castings, ferrous; Machine and other job shop work

(G-8601)
J 2 SYSTEMS AND SUPPLY LLC
Also Called: J2 S&S
3820 N Keystone Ave (46205-2909)
PHONE..................317 602-3940
James Leonard, *Managing Member*
EMP: 6 EST: 2007
SALES (est): 2.01MM **Privately Held**
Web: www.j2systemsandsupply.com
SIC: 5169 2992 2842 2841 Industrial chemicals; Lubricating oils and greases; Polishes and sanitation goods; Soap and other detergents

(G-8602)
J B HINCHMAN INC
Also Called: Hinchman Racing Uniforms
100 Gasoline Aly Ste A (46222-5916)
PHONE..................317 359-1808
Nancy Chumbley, *Ch Bd*
EMP: 5 EST: 1925
SQ FT: 5,000
SALES (est): 369.05K **Privately Held**
Web: www.hinchmanindy.com
SIC: 5699 2326 Uniforms; Aprons, work, except rubberized and plastic: men's

(G-8603)
J C SIPE INC
Also Called: J C Sipe Jewelers
2949 River Bay Dr N (46240)
PHONE..................317 848-0215
Sam H Sipe, *Ch Bd*
Laura C Sipe, *Pr*
EMP: 5 EST: 1884
SALES (est): 488.23K **Privately Held**
Web: www.jcsipe.com
SIC: 5944 3911 Jewelry, precious stones and precious metals; Jewel settings and mountings, precious metal

(G-8604)
J COFFEY METAL MASTERS INC
Also Called: Metal Masters
2514 Bethel Ave (46203-3034)
P.O. Box 33001 (46203-0001)
PHONE..................317 780-1864
James L Coffey, *Pr*
William Rinnert, *VP*
Janet S Coffey, *Sec*
EMP: 75 EST: 1984
SQ FT: 35,000
SALES (est): 4.06MM **Privately Held**
Web: www.mmindy.com
SIC: 1761 3441 Sheet metal work, nec; Fabricated structural metal

(G-8605)
J HENRYS MACHINE SHOP LLC
1111 S East St (46225-1325)
PHONE..................317 917-1052
Michele Young, *Pr*
EMP: 2 EST: 2012
SALES (est): 90.8K **Privately Held**
SIC: 3599 Machine shop, jobbing and repair

(G-8606)
J L SQUARED INC
1347 Sadlier Circle South Dr (46239-1059)
P.O. Box 807 (46107-0807)
PHONE..................317 354-1513
Leann Jenkins, *Pr*
EMP: 2 EST: 2003
SQ FT: 8,100
SALES (est): 319.73K **Privately Held**
Web: www.jl2inc.com
SIC: 3441 Fabricated structural metal

(G-8607)
J M MCCORMICK
8214 Allison Ave (46268-1616)
PHONE..................317 874-4444
EMP: 2 EST: 2009
SALES (est): 108.85K **Privately Held**
SIC: 5031 2421 Lumber: rough, dressed, and finished; Sawmills and planing mills, general

(G-8608)
J PINTO WOOD AND VENEER CORP
68 N Gale St Ste B (46201-3508)
PHONE..................317 389-0440
Filipe Santos, *Pr*
EMP: 5 EST: 2015
SALES (est): 382.18K **Privately Held**
SIC: 2435 Veneer stock, hardwood

(G-8609)
J W MODEL & ENGINEERING INC
5508 Elmwood Ave Ste 406 (46203-6039)
PHONE..................317 788-7471
Larry Woempner, *Pr*
EMP: 8 EST: 1981
SQ FT: 14,300
SALES (est): 575.69K **Privately Held**
SIC: 3544 Special dies and tools

GEOGRAPHIC SECTION

Indianapolis - Marion County (G-8636)

(G-8610)
J&K YURTS INC
Also Called: Yurts of America
4375 Sellers St (46226-7109)
PHONE..........................317 377-9878
Kenneth Lawrence, *Prin*
EMP: 5 EST: 2007
SALES (est): 495.44K **Privately Held**
Web: www.yurtsofamerica.com
SIC: 3792 Tent-type camping trailers

(G-8611)
J&P CUSTOM DESIGNS INC
Also Called: Jnp Custom Designs
550 W 65th St (46260-4604)
P.O. Box 68854 (46268-0854)
PHONE..........................317 253-2198
Portia O Neal, *Pr*
John Oneal, *VP*
EMP: 2 EST: 1985
SALES (est): 175.15K **Privately Held**
Web: www.jpcustomdesigns.com
SIC: 2759 2395 Screen printing; Embroidery and art needlework

(G-8612)
JACK HOWARD
1915 S State Ave (46203-4184)
PHONE..........................317 788-7643
Jack Howard, *Owner*
EMP: 3 EST: 2003
SALES (est): 155.46K **Privately Held**
SIC: 3444 Sheet metalwork

(G-8613)
JACK LAURIE COML FLOORS INC
7998 Georgetown Rd (46268-5631)
PHONE..........................317 569-2095
John Laurie, *Brnch Mgr*
EMP: 3
SALES (corp-wide): 17.54MM **Privately Held**
Web: www.jacklauriegroup.com
SIC: 5713 3081 5198 Floor covering stores; Floor or wall covering, unsupported plastics; Paints, varnishes, and supplies
PA: Jack Laurie Commercial Floors, Inc.
430 W Coliseum Blvd
Fort Wayne IN 46805
317 704-1100

(G-8614)
JACKSON GROUP INC
5804 Churchman Byp (46203-6109)
PHONE..........................317 791-9000
EMP: 180 EST: 2006
SALES (est): 46.55MM
SALES (corp-wide): 15B **Privately Held**
Web: www.rrd.com
SIC: 2752 Commercial printing, lithographic
HQ: Consolidated Graphics, Inc.
5858 Westheimer Rd # 200
Houston TX 77057

(G-8615)
JACKSON SYSTEMS LLC
Also Called: Io Hvac Controls
5418 Elmwood Ave (46203-6025)
PHONE..........................888 359-0365
Eileen E Jackson, *
Thomas W Jackson, *
EMP: 120 EST: 1997
SQ FT: 10,000
SALES (est): 23.06MM **Privately Held**
Web: www.jacksonsystems.com
SIC: 8711 3585 3822 Heating and ventilation engineering; Heating equipment, complete; Temperature controls, automatic

(G-8616)
JACKSONS 33 TRANSPORTING LLC
3172 N Capitol Ave (46208-4626)
PHONE..........................901 628-7803
EMP: 1
SALES (est): 60.08K **Privately Held**
SIC: 3537 7389 Trucks: freight, baggage, etc.: industrial, except mining; Business Activities at Non-Commercial Site

(G-8617)
JAMES R MCNUTT
3130 N Mitthoefer Rd (46235-2400)
P.O. Box 36550 (46236-0550)
PHONE..........................317 899-6955
Jim Mcnutt Junior, *Owner*
EMP: 2 EST: 2002
SALES (est): 116.62K **Privately Held**
SIC: 3578 Change making machines

(G-8618)
JAY ORNER SONS BILLIARD CO INC (PA)
6333 Rockville Rd (46214-3920)
PHONE..........................317 243-0046
TOLL FREE: 800
Steve Orner, *Pr*
Tom Orner, *VP*
Daniele Orner, *Sec*
▲ EMP: 8 EST: 1968
SQ FT: 5,000
SALES (est): 1.67MM
SALES (corp-wide): 1.67MM **Privately Held**
Web: www.ornerbilliards.com
SIC: 3949 5091 7699 Billiard and pool equipment and supplies, general; Billiard equipment and supplies; Billiard table repair

(G-8619)
JCANTAVE TRANSIT LLC
7375 Mariner Way Apt 311 (46214-1733)
PHONE..........................855 608-2777
EMP: 1
SALES (est): 65.99K **Privately Held**
SIC: 3715 7389 Truck trailers; Business services, nec

(G-8620)
JDB MANUFACTURING LLC
1010 E Sumner Ave (46227-1348)
PHONE..........................317 752-8756
Jacob Bernard, *Prin*
EMP: 7 EST: 2017
SALES (est): 261.16K **Privately Held**
SIC: 3999 Manufacturing industries, nec

(G-8621)
JDSU ACTERNA HOLDINGS LLC
5808 Churchman Byp (46203-6109)
PHONE..........................317 788-9351
EMP: 5
SALES (corp-wide): 1B **Publicly Held**
SIC: 3674 Optical isolators
HQ: Jdsu Acterna Holdings Llc
1 Milestone Center Ct
Germantown MD 20876
240 404-1550

(G-8622)
JENSON INDUSTRIES INC
Also Called: Alternative Container
8219 Zionsville Rd (46268-1628)
PHONE..........................317 871-0122
Charles Jenson, *Pr*
EMP: 8 EST: 2002
SALES (est): 1.53MM **Privately Held**
Web: www.alternativecontainer.com
SIC: 2631 Container, packaging, and boxboard

(G-8623)
JET FAST CARRIERS LLC
8818 Cardinal Flower Ln (46231-5287)
PHONE..........................219 218-3021
EMP: 1 EST: 2021
SALES (est): 60.08K **Privately Held**
SIC: 3537 7389 Trucks, tractors, loaders, carriers, and similar equipment; Business Activities at Non-Commercial Site

(G-8624)
JEWELERS BOUTIQUE INC
3320 Madison Ave (46227-1130)
PHONE..........................317 788-7679
Charles Gardner, *Pr*
Elaine Gardner, *Sec*
EMP: 4 EST: 1970
SQ FT: 1,800
SALES (est): 380K **Privately Held**
Web: www.jewelersboutique.us
SIC: 3911 5944 Jewelry, precious metal; Jewelry stores

(G-8625)
JFW INDUSTRIES INCORPORATED
5134 Commerce Square Dr (46237-9705)
PHONE..........................317 887-1340
Fred D Walker, *Pr*
James W Leach, *
EMP: 105 EST: 1979
SQ FT: 14,000
SALES (est): 11.01MM **Privately Held**
Web: www.jfwindustries.com
SIC: 3825 Instruments to measure electricity

(G-8626)
JIMCO ENGINEERING CO
3315 Sutherland Ave (46218-1904)
PHONE..........................317 923-2290
Daniel Noland, *Owner*
EMP: 2 EST: 1957
SQ FT: 6,500
SALES (est): 222.18K **Privately Held**
Web: www.jimcoengineering.com
SIC: 3599 Machine shop, jobbing and repair

(G-8627)
JL 2 INCORPORATED
4109 Five Points Rd (46239-9611)
PHONE..........................317 783-3340
EMP: 10 EST: 2009
SALES (est): 907.82K **Privately Held**
SIC: 3441 Fabricated structural metal for ships

(G-8628)
JL WALTER & ASSOCIATES INC
2099 Montcalm St (46202-1128)
PHONE..........................317 524-3600
James L Walter, *Prin*
EMP: 75 EST: 2009
SALES (est): 10.81MM **Privately Held**
Web: www.jlwalt.com
SIC: 3441 7699 Fabricated structural metal; Metal reshaping and replating services

(G-8629)
JOEY CHESTNUT FOODS LLC
Also Called: Joey Chestnut Eats
101 W Washington St Ste 1250 (46204-3427)
PHONE..........................317 602-4830
James Blake, *CFO*
EMP: 1 EST: 2018
SALES (est): 144K **Privately Held**
Web: www.joeychestnut.com
SIC: 2035 5149 Seasonings and sauces, except tomato and dry; Sauces

(G-8630)
JOHN KING
6515 Olivia Ln (46226-6167)
PHONE..........................317 801-3080
John King, *Admn*
EMP: 6 EST: 2017
SALES (est): 141.29K **Privately Held**
SIC: 2084 Wines, brandy, and brandy spirits

(G-8631)
JOHN WILEY & SONS INC
Also Called: Wiley Publishing
9200 Keystone Xing Ste 800 (46240-4603)
PHONE..........................317 572-3000
Lou Peragallo, *Prin*
EMP: 19
SALES (corp-wide): 1.87B **Publicly Held**
Web: www.wiley.com
SIC: 2731 Books, publishing only
PA: John Wiley & Sons, Inc.
111 River St
Hoboken NJ 07030
201 748-6000

(G-8632)
JOHNCO CORP
8770 Commerce Park Pl Ste F (46268-3172)
PHONE..........................317 576-4417
Nadia Miller, *Pr*
EMP: 5 EST: 2012
SALES (est): 915.57K **Privately Held**
Web: www.johncocorp.com
SIC: 5112 5087 2521 5251 Stationery and office supplies; Janitors' supplies; Wood office furniture; Hardware stores

(G-8633)
JOHNSON CNTRLS FIRE PRTCTION L
1255 N Senate Ave (46202-2219)
PHONE..........................317 826-2130
TOLL FREE: 800
Terry Dollar, *Mgr*
EMP: 1
SIC: 1711 5999 1731 3498 Fire sprinkler system installation; Fire extinguishers; Fire detection and burglar alarm systems specialization; Fabricated pipe and fittings
HQ: Johnson Controls Fire Protection Lp
6600 Congress Ave
Boca Raton FL 33487
561 988-7200

(G-8634)
JOHNSON CNTRLS SEC SLTIONS LLC
Also Called: Johnson Controls SEC Solutions
10405 Crosspoint Blvd (46256-3323)
PHONE..........................800 238-2455
Anthony Mcgraw, *Mgr*
EMP: 3 EST: 1989
SALES (est): 297.23K **Privately Held**
SIC: 3699 Security control equipment and systems

(G-8635)
JOHNSON SAMYRA ✪
Also Called: Londynn Nailed You
11531 Planewood Ct (46235-3630)
PHONE..........................872 216-0551
Samyra Johnson, *Owner*
EMP: 1 EST: 2022
SALES (est): 54.05K **Privately Held**
SIC: 3999 Fingernails, artificial

(G-8636)
JOHNSONS BURIAL DESIGNS
3950 N Layman Ave (46226-4861)
P.O. Box 26753 (46226-0753)

Indianapolis - Marion County (G-8637) — GEOGRAPHIC SECTION

PHONE..........................317 549-2148
Janice Johnson, *Owner*
EMP: 1 **EST:** 2001
SALES (est): 131.57K **Privately Held**
SIC: 3272 Burial vaults, concrete or precast terrazzo

(G-8637)
JONES & WEBB ASSOCIATES INC
2544 Andy Dr (46229-1202)
PHONE..........................317 236-9755
Dave Webb, *Pr*
David Jones, *VP*
EMP: 4 **EST:** 1995
SALES (est): 342.32K **Privately Held**
SIC: 2759 Commercial printing, nec

(G-8638)
JORDAN SAFETY AND SUPPLY LLC (PA)
4614 Radnor Rd (46226-2154)
PHONE..........................513 315-6267
Gary Johnson Junior, *COO*
EMP: 6 **EST:** 2016
SALES (est): 57.58K
SALES (corp-wide): 57.58K **Privately Held**
Web: www.jordansafetyandsupply.com
SIC: 5999 7372 Alarm and safety equipment stores; Business oriented computer software

(G-8639)
JOSSEY-BASS PUBLISHERS
10475 Crosspoint Blvd (46256-3386)
PHONE..........................877 762-2974
EMP: 2
SALES (est): 84.01K **Privately Held**
SIC: 2741 Miscellaneous publishing

(G-8640)
JOURNAL OF TEACHING WRITING
425 University Blvd (46202-5148)
PHONE..........................317 274-0092
Barbara Cambrigie, *Prin*
EMP: 5
SALES (est): 16.57K **Privately Held**
SIC: 2711 Newspapers, publishing and printing

(G-8641)
JOYCE CONSULTING LLC
9132 Sargent Manor Ct (46256-1392)
PHONE..........................317 577-8504
James R Joyce, *Prin*
Christine Joyce, *Mng Pt*
◆ **EMP:** 2 **EST:** 2007
SQ FT: 6,000
SALES (est): 110.06K **Privately Held**
Web: www.joycecg.com
SIC: 3531 Bulldozers (construction machinery)

(G-8642)
JOYFUL SIGN COMPANY LLC
4205 Devon Court West Dr (46226-3152)
PHONE..........................317 529-1020
EMP: 5 **EST:** 2013
SALES (est): 59K **Privately Held**
SIC: 3993 Signs and advertising specialties

(G-8643)
JP OWNERSHIP GROUP INC
5804 Churchman Byp (46203-6109)
PHONE..........................317 791-1122
Patsy Koepke, *Pr*
EMP: 53 **EST:** 1980
SQ FT: 125,000
SALES (est): 4.93MM **Privately Held**
SIC: 2752 Offset printing

(G-8644)
JRP MACHINE CO
1607 Deloss St Ste B (46201-3968)
PHONE..........................317 955-1905
EMP: 2 **EST:** 1996
SQ FT: 4,800
SALES (est): 248.93K **Privately Held**
Web: www.jrpmachine.net
SIC: 3451 Screw machine products

(G-8645)
JT COMPOSITES LLC (PA)
312 Gasoline Aly Ste C (46222-3990)
PHONE..........................317 297-9520
Julian Bailey, *Genl Pt*
Tony Holl, *Mgr*
EMP: 2 **EST:** 2009
SALES (est): 457.81K
SALES (corp-wide): 457.81K **Privately Held**
Web: www.jtcomposites.com
SIC: 2813 2655 Carbon dioxide; Cans, composite: foil-fiber and other: from purchased fiber

(G-8646)
JT TRANSPORTS LLC
5625 N German Church Rd # 3194 (46235-8513)
PHONE..........................317 658-1523
Jasmine Jones, *Managing Member*
EMP: 2 **EST:** 2021
SALES (est): 75K **Privately Held**
SIC: 3711 Trucks, pickup, assembly of

(G-8647)
JTI INC
1801 S Lynhurst Dr (46241-4421)
PHONE..........................317 797-9698
Odis R Jeffers, *Pr*
EMP: 9 **EST:** 2009
SALES (est): 99.36K **Privately Held**
Web: www.jti.com
SIC: 1389 Pumping of oil and gas wells

(G-8648)
JULIE EDWARDS CERAMICS
957 N Graham Ave (46219-4537)
PHONE..........................317 681-9523
Julie Edwards, *Prin*
EMP: 1 **EST:** 2013
SALES (est): 41.82K **Privately Held**
Web: www.julieedwardsceramics.com
SIC: 3269 Pottery products, nec

(G-8649)
JUST FOR GRANITE LLC
5277 Emco Dr (46220-4850)
PHONE..........................317 842-8255
Pete Rusomaroff, *Owner*
EMP: 8 **EST:** 1994
SALES (est): 682.19K **Privately Held**
Web: www.justforgranite.com
SIC: 1799 3441 Counter top installation; Fabricated structural metal

(G-8650)
JUST PERFECTION LLC
6613 Meadowlark Dr (46226-3655)
PHONE..........................347 559-5878
EMP: 3
SALES (est): 78.58K **Privately Held**
SIC: 3471 7389 Plating and polishing; Business Activities at Non-Commercial Site

(G-8651)
JUST STANDOUT LLC
951 E 86th St Ste 200e (46240-2092)
PHONE..........................317 531-6956
Matthew Jones, *Managing Member*

Raymond Mack, *Managing Member*
EMP: 2 **EST:** 2017
SALES (est): 171.87K **Privately Held**
SIC: 2252 Socks

(G-8652)
K & K FENCE INC
6520 Brookville Rd (46219-8219)
PHONE..........................317 359-5425
Frederick C Poe, *Pr*
EMP: 25 **EST:** 1967
SQ FT: 2,500
SALES (est): 6.15MM **Privately Held**
Web: www.kkfence.com
SIC: 1799 5211 3446 Fence construction; Fencing; Fences or posts, ornamental iron or steel

(G-8653)
K C CREATIONS
11612 Breckenridge Ct (46236-3829)
PHONE..........................937 418-1859
Ken Cleveland, *Pr*
Sandra Love, *VP*
EMP: 3 **EST:** 1987
SQ FT: 10,000
SALES (est): 247.71K **Privately Held**
SIC: 7389 3499 Design, commercial and industrial; Novelties and giftware, including trophies

(G-8654)
K&A SHEET METAL LLC ✪
5333 Commerce Square Dr Ste E (46237)
PHONE..........................317 300-1518
EMP: 5 **EST:** 2023
SALES (est): 75.6K **Privately Held**
SIC: 3444 Sheet metalwork

(G-8655)
KAISER PRESS LLC
2525 E 91st St (46240-2064)
PHONE..........................317 619-7092
Nathan Hopman, *Prin*
EMP: 5 **EST:** 2015
SALES (est): 101.45K **Privately Held**
Web: www.kaiserpressllc.com
SIC: 2711 Newspapers

(G-8656)
KAL TRANSPORTATION LLC
1110 Aqua Vista Dr (46229-3408)
PHONE..........................317 615-9341
EMP: 4 **EST:** 2021
SALES (est): 88.38K **Privately Held**
SIC: 3669 Transportation signaling devices

(G-8657)
KALA MINDFULNESS LLC
2951 Cooperland Ct (46268-5052)
PHONE..........................720 351-9664
EMP: 1
SALES (est): 65.51K **Privately Held**
SIC: 7372 7389 Publisher's computer software; Business Activities at Non-Commercial Site

(G-8658)
KALEMS ENTERPRISES INC
Also Called: Metro Area Printing
8455 Castlewood Dr Ste H (46250-1565)
PHONE..........................317 399-1645
Karen Daniels, *Prin*
Lee Daniels, *Pr*
EMP: 3 **EST:** 2015
SALES (est): 242.7K **Privately Held**
Web: www.metroareaprinting.com
SIC: 2752 Offset printing

(G-8659)
KAMPS INC
1905 S Belmont Ave (46221-1924)
PHONE..........................317 634-8360
Matt Scott, *Brnch Mgr*
EMP: 26
SALES (corp-wide): 1.74B **Privately Held**
Web: www.kampspallets.com
SIC: 2448 Pallets, wood
HQ: Kamps, Inc.
665 Seward Ave Nw Ste 301
Grand Rapids MI 49504
616 453-9676

(G-8660)
KANE USA INC
7601 E 88th Pl Ste 888 (46256-1396)
PHONE..........................800 547-5740
EMP: 26
Web: www.ueitest.com
SIC: 5084 3825 3621 3677 Measuring and testing equipment, electrical; Instruments to measure electricity; Motors and generators; Electronic coils and transformers
HQ: Kane Usa, Inc.
8625 Sw Cascade Ave # 550
Beaverton OR 97008
503 644-8723

(G-8661)
KARTISTRY PRO LLC
5555 N Tacoma Ave Ste 208 (46220-3547)
PHONE..........................317 969-7075
Briana Dawson, *CEO*
EMP: 1 **EST:** 2018
SALES (est): 21.53K **Privately Held**
Web: www.kartistrypro.com
SIC: 7231 3999 Cosmetology and personal hygiene salons; Eyelashes, artificial

(G-8662)
KASTING PRINTING SERVICE
7146 S Meridian St (46217-4042)
PHONE..........................317 881-9411
Betty Kasting, *Owner*
EMP: 2 **EST:** 1993
SALES (est): 71.14K **Privately Held**
SIC: 2752 Commercial printing, lithographic

(G-8663)
KBK MAGIK LLC
730 Lansdowne Rd (46234-2247)
PHONE..........................219 512-4040
EMP: 1 **EST:** 2021
SALES (est): 10K **Privately Held**
SIC: 3944 Craft and hobby kits and sets

(G-8664)
KC ENGINEERING INC
5602 Elmwood Ave Ste 118 (46203-6071)
PHONE..........................317 352-9742
Thomas L Covington, *Pr*
Sue A Covington, *VP*
EMP: 8 **EST:** 1969
SQ FT: 11,000
SALES (est): 805.31K **Privately Held**
Web: www.zoemusic.com
SIC: 3544 Forms (molds), for foundry and plastics working machinery

(G-8665)
KCC INC
1511 Bates St (46201-3945)
PHONE..........................317 632-5258
EMP: 7 **EST:** 2018
SALES (est): 151.02K **Privately Held**
Web: www.kcccustomdesigns.com
SIC: 2211 Canvas

GEOGRAPHIC SECTION

Indianapolis - Marion County (G-8690)

(G-8666)
KECO ENGINEERED COATINGS INC (PA)
1030 S Kealing Ave (46203-1516)
PHONE..................317 356-7279
Michael Klinge, *Pr*
▲ EMP: 9 EST: 1979
SQ FT: 25,000
SALES (est): 3.08MM
SALES (corp-wide): 3.08MM Privately Held
Web: www.kecocoatings.com
SIC: 3479 Coating of metals and formed products

(G-8667)
KELCO STEEL FABRICATION INC
3827 W Troy Ave (46241-6011)
PHONE..................317 248-9229
Kurt Leis, *Pr*
EMP: 1 EST: 1993
SQ FT: 2,400
SALES (est): 156.41K Privately Held
Web: www.kelcosteel.com
SIC: 1799 3535 3444 3443 Welding on site; Conveyors and conveying equipment; Sheet metalwork; Fabricated plate work (boiler shop)

(G-8668)
KELLY BOX AND PACKAGING CORP
3035 N Shadeland Ave Ste 400 (46226-6281)
PHONE..................317 804-7044
Thomas J Kelly, *Pr*
EMP: 2
SALES (corp-wide): 21.53MM Privately Held
Web: www.kellybox.com
SIC: 2653 Boxes, corrugated: made from purchased materials
PA: Kelly Box And Packaging Corporation
2801 Covington Rd
Fort Wayne IN 46802
260 432-4570

(G-8669)
KELVION PRODUCTS INC
2401 Directors Row (46241-4907)
PHONE..................865 606-6027
Cathy Powers, *Brnch Mgr*
EMP: 230
SALES (corp-wide): 2.67MM Privately Held
Web: www.kelvion.com
SIC: 3443 Fabricated plate work (boiler shop)
HQ: Kelvion Products Inc.
5050 S National Dr
Knoxville TN 37914
866 535-8466

(G-8670)
KENNAMETAL INC
9217 Backwater Dr (46250-4134)
PHONE..................317 696-8798
EMP: 7
SALES (corp-wide): 2.05B Publicly Held
Web: www.kennametal.com
SIC: 3545 Machine tool accessories
PA: Kennametal Inc.
525 Wlliam Penn Pl Ste 33
Pittsburgh PA 15219
412 248-8000

(G-8671)
KENNEDY TANK & MFG CO
833 E Sumner Ave (46227-1345)
P.O. Box 47070 (46247-0070)
PHONE..................317 787-1311
Patrick W Kennedy, *Pr*
Gerald A Hemmelgarn, *
Paul Bolin, *
Scot W Evans, *
John Cochran, *
EMP: 130 EST: 1898
SQ FT: 51,000
SALES (est): 30.64MM Privately Held
Web: www.kennedytank.com
SIC: 3443 Tanks, standard or custom fabricated: metal plate

(G-8672)
KENNEY ORTHPDICS INDNPOLIS LLC
1801 Senate Blvd Ste 420 (46202-1228)
PHONE..................859 241-1015
John M Kenny, *Brnch Mgr*
EMP: 3
SALES (corp-wide): 23.4MM Privately Held
Web: www.kenneyorthopedics.com
SIC: 3842 Surgical appliances and supplies
HQ: Kenney Orthopedics Indianapolis, Llc
521 E County Line Rd B
Greenwood IN 46143
317 300-0814

(G-8673)
KENRA PROFESSIONAL LLC (HQ)
Also Called: Elucence Products
7445 Company Dr (46237-9296)
PHONE..................800 428-8073
Patrick Ludwig, *Managing Member*
EMP: 10 EST: 2010
SQ FT: 48,500
SALES (est): 22.84MM
SALES (corp-wide): 23.39B Privately Held
Web: www.kenraprofessional.com
SIC: 2844 7231 2899 Hair preparations, including shampoos; Beauty shops; Chemical preparations, nec
PA: Henkel Ag & Co. Kgaa
Henkelstr. 67
Dusseldorf NW 40589
2117970

(G-8674)
KERMIT USA INC
221 S Franklin Rd Ste 710 (46219-7718)
PHONE..................765 288-3334
EMP: 4 EST: 2013
SALES (est): 52.58K Privately Held
SIC: 3999 Manufacturing industries, nec

(G-8675)
KESSLER CONCEPTS INC
Also Called: National Screen Printing Co
225 E 10th St (46202-3303)
PHONE..................317 630-9901
William M Kessler, *Pr*
EMP: 10 EST: 1990
SQ FT: 7,000
SALES (est): 1.05MM Privately Held
SIC: 8743 2759 7389 Promotion service; Screen printing; Embroidery advertising

(G-8676)
KEY MADE NOW
317 N Kenyon St (46219-6109)
PHONE..................317 664-8582
EMP: 2 EST: 2012
SALES (est): 94.5K Privately Held
SIC: 3429 Keys, locks, and related hardware

(G-8677)
KEY SHEET METAL INC
1128 E Maryland St (46202-3975)
PHONE..................317 546-7151
EMP: 5 EST: 1994
SQ FT: 3,800
SALES (est): 731.15K Privately Held
Web: www.keysheetmetal.com
SIC: 3444 3546 Awnings, sheet metal; Drills and drilling tools

(G-8678)
KEYS COMPUTERS INC
8443 La Habra Ln Bldg 1 (46236-8832)
PHONE..................317 750-5071
Donna Keys, *CEO*
EMP: 10 EST: 2021
SALES (est): 506.81K Privately Held
SIC: 3571 Electronic computers

(G-8679)
KEYS R US
3210 E Thompson Rd (46227-6623)
PHONE..................317 616-0267
EMP: 2 EST: 2013
SALES (est): 85.56K Privately Held
SIC: 3429 Keys, locks, and related hardware

(G-8680)
KEYSTONE COOPERATIVE INC (PA)
770 N High School Rd (46214)
P.O. Box 560 (46122)
PHONE..................800 525-0272
Kevin Still, *Pr*
◆ EMP: 135 EST: 1920
SALES (est): 570.05MM
SALES (corp-wide): 570.05MM Privately Held
Web: www.keystonecoop.com
SIC: 5191 5171 5153 2875 Feed; Petroleum bulk stations and terminals; Grains; Fertilizers, mixing only

(G-8681)
KHAMIS FINE JEWELERS INC
9763 Fall Creek Rd (46256)
PHONE..................317 841-8440
Mary J Khamis, *Pr*
EMP: 2 EST: 1995
SQ FT: 1,600
SALES (est): 310.41K Privately Held
Web: www.khamisfinejewelers.com
SIC: 5944 7631 7389 3479 Jewelry, precious stones and precious metals; Jewelry repair services; Auction, appraisal, and exchange services; Engraving jewelry, silverware, or metal

(G-8682)
KILL HER SET LLC
6920 Eagle Highlands Way Ste 100 (46254-5609)
PHONE..................317 992-2220
Chauntanese Mitchell, *Managing Member*
EMP: 10 EST: 2021
SALES (est): 387.26K Privately Held
SIC: 3999 5087 Furniture, barber and beauty shop; Beauty salon and barber shop equipment and supplies

(G-8683)
KIM PRINT LLC
6604 Heron Neck Dr Apt N (46217-8733)
PHONE..................812 223-5333
Tristan Parmley, *Prin*
EMP: 1 EST: 2018
SALES (est): 63.57K Privately Held
Web: www.ibj.com
SIC: 2752 Commercial printing, lithographic

(G-8684)
KIMBALL ELEC INDIANAPOLIS INC
2950 N Catherwood Ave (46219-1011)
PHONE..................812 634-4000
Michael Sergesketter, *CFO*
EMP: 67 EST: 2016
SALES (est): 9.96MM
SALES (corp-wide): 1.71B Publicly Held
Web: www.kimballelectronics.com
SIC: 3672 Printed circuit boards
HQ: Kimball Electronics Group, Llc
1205 Kimball Blvd
Jasper IN 47546

(G-8685)
KIMBALL ELECTRONICS INC
2402 N Shadeland Ave (46219-1137)
PHONE..................317 357-3175
Curtis Bilbrey, *Brnch Mgr*
EMP: 48
SALES (corp-wide): 1.71B Publicly Held
Web: www.kimballelectronics.com
SIC: 3089 Injection molded finished plastics products, nec
PA: Kimball Electronics, Inc.
1205 Kimball Blvd
Jasper IN 47546
812 634-4000

(G-8686)
KIMBALL ELECTRONICS INC
6205 E 30th St (46219-1003)
PHONE..................317 545-5383
EMP: 100
SALES (corp-wide): 1.71B Publicly Held
Web: www.kimballelectronics.com
SIC: 3089 3544 3499 3469 Injection molded finished plastics products, nec; Special dies, tools, jigs, and fixtures; Metal household articles; Metal stampings, nec
PA: Kimball Electronics, Inc.
1205 Kimball Blvd
Jasper IN 47546
812 634-4000

(G-8687)
KINGERY GROUP INC
Also Called: National Printfast
6574 Breckenridge Dr (46236-3827)
PHONE..................317 823-9585
Pat Kingery, *Pr*
EMP: 9 EST: 2004
SQ FT: 24,000
SALES (est): 204.51K Privately Held
SIC: 2759 Commercial printing, nec

(G-8688)
KIPIN INDUSTRIES
2950 Prospect St (46203)
PHONE..................317 510-1181
EMP: 4 EST: 2019
SALES (est): 92.19K Privately Held
Web: www.kipin.com
SIC: 3999 Manufacturing industries, nec

(G-8689)
KITE & KEY LLC
5825 Alpine Ave (46224-2135)
PHONE..................317 654-7703
Chameleon Porter, *Prin*
EMP: 5 EST: 2014
SALES (est): 88.45K Privately Held
SIC: 3944 Kites

(G-8690)
KITE GREYHOUND LLC
30 S Meridian St (46204-3564)
PHONE..................317 577-5600
John A Kite, *CEO*
EMP: 1 EST: 2013
SALES (est): 2.25MM Publicly Held
Web: www.kiterealty.com
SIC: 1389 Construction, repair, and dismantling services
PA: Kite Realty Group Trust
30 S Meridian St Ste 1100
Indianapolis IN 46204

(PA)=Parent Co (HQ)=Headquarters
✪ = New Business established in last 2 years

Indianapolis - Marion County (G-8691) — GEOGRAPHIC SECTION

(G-8691)
KITLEY COMPANY
Also Called: Interstate Castings
3823 Massachusetts Ave (46218-3833)
PHONE.................................317 546-2427
EMP: 50 EST: 1883
SALES (est): 3.88MM **Privately Held**
SIC: 3321 Gray iron castings, nec

(G-8692)
KJS BEAUTY LOUNGE LLC
3639 N Raceway Rd (46234)
PHONE.................................317 426-0621
Kamryn Novotny, *Owner*
EMP: 1 EST: 2021
SALES (est): 55.21K **Privately Held**
SIC: 7231 3421 3999 Beauty shops; Clippers, fingernail and toenail; Fingernails, artificial

(G-8693)
KLH HOLDING CORPORATION (HQ)
2002 Lafayette Rd (46222-2325)
PHONE.................................317 634-3976
Kevin Neighbours, *Pr*
Bryan J Hite, *Sec*
EMP: 21 EST: 1976
SQ FT: 25,000
SALES (est): 4.55MM **Privately Held**
Web: www.rgausa.com
SIC: 3069 Rubber automotive products
PA: Rubber & Gasket Company Of America, Inc.
3905 E Progress St
North Little Rock AR 72114

(G-8694)
KLINGE ENAMELING COMPANY INC
Also Called: Klinge Coatings
5001 Prospect St (46203-2499)
PHONE.................................317 359-8291
Philip Klinge, *Pr*
Sheila Shaw, *
EMP: 45 EST: 1956
SQ FT: 30,000
SALES (est): 4.63MM **Privately Held**
Web: www.klingecoatings.com
SIC: 3479 2899 3471 8711 Enameling, including porcelain, of metal products; Chemical preparations, nec; Sand blasting of metal parts; Mechanical engineering

(G-8695)
KLIPSCH GROUP INC (HQ)
Also Called: Klipsch
3502 Woodview Trce Ste 200 (46268)
PHONE.................................317 860-8100
Paul Jacobs, *Pr*
Fred S Klipsch, *Ch Bd*
Michael F Klipsch, *Sec*
Frederick L Farrar, *Ex VP*
◆ EMP: 150 EST: 1951
SQ FT: 12,200
SALES (est): 47.27MM
SALES (corp-wide): 468.91MM **Publicly Held**
Web: www.klipsch.com
SIC: 3651 Loudspeakers, electrodynamic or magnetic
PA: Voxx International Corporation
2351 J Lawson Blvd
Orlando FL 32824
800 645-7750

(G-8696)
KLOSTERMAN BAKING CO
Also Called: KLOSTERMAN BAKING CO.
5867 Churchman Rd (46203-6012)
PHONE.................................317 359-5545
Steve Faulstich, *Prin*
EMP: 13
SALES (corp-wide): 190.57MM **Privately Held**
Web: www.klostermanbakery.com
SIC: 2051 Bread, cake, and related products
PA: Klosterman Baking Co., Llc
4760 Paddock Rd
Cincinnati OH 45229
513 242-1004

(G-8697)
KMUET LLC
2815 Ralston Ave (46218-2654)
PHONE.................................317 645-0421
Atsu Kpotufe, *Admn*
EMP: 5 EST: 2011
SALES (est): 65.13K **Privately Held**
Web: www.youarehappening.com
SIC: 7372 Prepackaged software

(G-8698)
KNOW WONDER PUBLISHING LLC
2844 Medford Ave (46222-2252)
PHONE.................................317 506-4611
Derrick S Slack, *Pr*
EMP: 5 EST: 2019
SALES (est): 41.35MM **Privately Held**
SIC: 2741 Miscellaneous publishing

(G-8699)
KNOX ENTERPRISES INC
1 Technology Way (46268-5106)
PHONE.................................317 714-3073
EMP: 8
SALES (est): 650K **Privately Held**
SIC: 3053 3069 3086 Gaskets; packing and sealing devices; Fabricated rubber products, nec; Plastics foam products

(G-8700)
KOCHS ELECTRIC INC
202 E Palmer St (46225-1640)
PHONE.................................317 639-5624
Kevin Koch, *Pr*
Kristi Williams, *VP*
Betty Koch, *Stockholder*
EMP: 22 EST: 1987
SQ FT: 1,500
SALES (est): 921.1K **Privately Held**
Web: www.kochselectric.com
SIC: 7699 7694 Pumps and pumping equipment repair; Electric motor repair

(G-8701)
KOMUN SCENTS
4635 Falcon Run Way (46254-2073)
PHONE.................................317 308-0714
Anthony Dix, *Prin*
EMP: 5 EST: 2010
SALES (est): 107.4K **Privately Held**
SIC: 2844 Perfumes, cosmetics and other toilet preparations

(G-8702)
KRAZY KLOTHES LTD (PA)
1101 S Illinois St (46225-1411)
PHONE.................................317 687-8310
Dan Murphy, *Pr*
EMP: 4 EST: 1987
SQ FT: 13,000
SALES (est): 504.76K **Privately Held**
Web: www.krazyklothes.com
SIC: 2341 2322 Pajamas and bedjackets: women's and children's; Nightwear, men's and boys': from purchased materials

(G-8703)
KROGER LIMITED PARTNERSHIP II
Also Called: Crossroads Farms Dairy
400 S Shortridge Rd (46219-7403)
PHONE.................................317 229-7600
Bob Scher, *Mgr*
EMP: 1
SALES (corp-wide): 150.04B **Publicly Held**
Web: www.thekrogerco.com
SIC: 2022 Natural cheese
HQ: Kroger Limited Partnership Ii
1014 Vine St
Cincinnati OH 45202
513 762-4000

(G-8704)
KROWNED BY QWAN LLC
6101 N Keystone Ave (46220-2488)
PHONE.................................317 813-9914
EMP: 1 EST: 2018
SALES (est): 74.64K **Privately Held**
SIC: 3999 Hair, dressing of, for the trade

(G-8705)
L R GREEN CO INC
Also Called: Poster Display Co
5650 Elmwood Ave (46203-6029)
PHONE.................................317 781-4200
Lawrence R Green, *Pr*
Patricia S Green, *
Karen Beckham, *Finance*
▲ EMP: 75 EST: 1974
SQ FT: 65,000
SALES (est): 4.94MM **Privately Held**
Web: www.poster-display.com
SIC: 2759 Commercial printing, nec

(G-8706)
L5 SOLUTIONS LLC
7950 Castleway Dr Ste 160 (46250-1994)
PHONE.................................317 436-1044
Frank Howard, *Managing Member*
EMP: 5 EST: 2006
SALES (est): 477.27K **Privately Held**
Web: www.l5solutions.com
SIC: 3571 5045 Electronic computers; Computers, peripherals, and software

(G-8707)
LA OLA LATINO AMERICANA
2401 W Washington St (46222-4178)
P.O. Box 22056 (46222-0056)
PHONE.................................317 822-0345
Ildefonso Carbajal, *Owner*
EMP: 10 EST: 1997
SALES (est): 497.03K **Privately Held**
SIC: 2711 Newspapers, publishing and printing

(G-8708)
LA VOZ DE INDIANA INC
6332 Hollister Dr Apt 2005 (46224-0068)
PHONE.................................317 636-7970
EMP: 5
SALES (est): 113.97K **Privately Held**
Web: www.lavozdeindiana.com
SIC: 2711 Newspapers, publishing and printing

(G-8709)
LA VOZ DE INDIANA INC
Also Called: La Voz De Ind Blingual Newsppr
2911 W Washington St Ste B (46222-5384)
P.O. Box 22122 (46222-0122)
PHONE.................................317 423-0957
Liliana Hamnik Parod, *CEO*
Jose Gonzalez, *VP*
EMP: 8 EST: 1999
SQ FT: 5,000
SALES (est): 563.15K **Privately Held**
Web: www.lavozdeindiana.com
SIC: 2711 Newspapers, publishing and printing

(G-8710)
LABOR NEWS INC
Also Called: Indiana Labor News
4280 Kessler Lane East Dr (46220-5204)
PHONE.................................317 251-1287
Fred Levin, *Pr*
EMP: 12 EST: 1965
SQ FT: 2,000
SALES (est): 582.19K **Privately Held**
SIC: 2711 Newspapers: publishing only, not printed on site

(G-8711)
LACED CAKE LLC
7408 Bentley Dr (46214)
PHONE.................................317 520-6235
Devin Thomas, *Owner*
EMP: 1 EST: 2019
SALES (est): 65.93K **Privately Held**
SIC: 2389 Apparel and accessories, nec

(G-8712)
LADY Q LLC-S
8520 Allison Pointe Blvd (46250-5700)
PHONE.................................219 304-8404
Marquita Pate, *CEO*
EMP: 1 EST: 2018
SALES (est): 29.09K **Privately Held**
SIC: 7349 7389 2396 Building and office cleaning services; Document and office record destruction; Screen printing on fabric articles

(G-8713)
LAIBE CORPORATION
1414 Bates St (46201-3944)
PHONE.................................317 231-2250
James R Hopkins, *Pr*
Mark Laibe, *
Martin Wright, *
Judy Laibe, *Stockholder*
Marcus Laibe, *Stockholder*
▲ EMP: 55 EST: 1966
SALES (est): 9.6MM **Privately Held**
Web: www.versa-drill.com
SIC: 3533 Oil and gas drilling rigs and equipment

(G-8714)
LAKE EFFECT PHARMA LLC
1800 N Capitol Ave Ste E504 (46202-1218)
PHONE.................................315 694-1111
EMP: 2 EST: 2014
SALES (est): 74.42K **Privately Held**
SIC: 2834 Drugs acting on the respiratory system

(G-8715)
LAMB MACHINE & TOOL CO
3619 S Arlington Ave (46203)
PHONE.................................317 780-9106
Kenneth Boehm, *Pr*
EMP: 7 EST: 2018
SALES (est): 475.09K **Privately Held**
Web: www.pcimachining.com
SIC: 3599 Machine shop, jobbing and repair

(G-8716)
LAMBEL CORPORATION
7902 E 88th St (46256-1236)
PHONE.................................317 849-6828
Richard M Cook, *Pr*
Susan Cook, *Treas*
EMP: 6 EST: 1965
SQ FT: 10,000
SALES (est): 461.41K **Privately Held**
Web: www.lambel.com
SIC: 2759 2672 Labels and seals: printing, nsk; Paper; coated and laminated, nec

Indianapolis - Marion County (G-8743)

(G-8717)
LAMCO FINISHERS INC
8260 Zionsville Rd (46268-1627)
P.O. Box 78258 (46278-0258)
PHONE..................317 471-1010
EMP: 35 EST: 1973
SQ FT: 33,000
SALES (est): 4.47MM Privately Held
Web: www.lamcofinishers.com
SIC: 3999 2759 7389 2789 Plaques, picture, laminated; Laser printing; Laminating service; Bookbinding and related work

(G-8718)
LAMON BREWSTER INDUSTRIES LLC
1248 Munsee Cir (46228-1327)
PHONE..................818 668-4298
EMP: 3 EST: 2019
SALES (est): 61.82K Privately Held
SIC: 3999 Manufacturing industries, nec

(G-8719)
LAMPLITER
9521 Valparaiso Ct (46268)
PHONE..................317 827-0250
EMP: 5 EST: 2020
SALES (est): 263.17K Privately Held
Web: www.thelampliter.com
SIC: 3641 Electric lamps and parts for specialized applications

(G-8720)
LANCE SNYDER
9040 Orly Rd Ste 100 (46241-9004)
PHONE..................717 632-4477
Lance Snyder, Prin
EMP: 5 EST: 2016
SALES (est): 209.05K Privately Held
SIC: 2052 Cookies

(G-8721)
LANDIS GYR INC
8002 N Shadeland Ave (46250-2043)
PHONE..................317 578-2200
Greg Hare, Brnch Mgr
EMP: 13 EST: 2015
SALES (est): 124.72K Privately Held
Web: www.landisgyr.eu
SIC: 3825 Instruments to measure electricity

(G-8722)
LANE WRIGHT LLC
1006 W 35th St (46208-4122)
PHONE..................317 473-4783
Kenneth Wright, Managing Member
EMP: 1 EST: 2021
SALES (est): 69.27K Privately Held
SIC: 3799 7389 Transportation equipment, nec; Business Activities at Non-Commercial Site

(G-8723)
LARRY ROBERTSON ASSOCIATES
Also Called: Beveled Glass & Ltg Designs
1056 Millwood Ct (46260-2230)
PHONE..................812 537-4090
Larry Robertson, Pr
Ronald Slagle, Sec
▲ EMP: 12 EST: 1970
SALES (est): 505.54K Privately Held
Web: www.beveledglassdesigns.com
SIC: 3231 2431 Leaded glass; Doors and door parts and trim, wood

(G-8724)
LARRYS TL HYDRLIC JACK SVC LLC
702 S Lynhurst Dr (46241-2135)
PHONE..................317 243-8666
Larry Dorris, Owner
EMP: 2 EST: 2006
SALES (est): 243.41K Privately Held
Web: www.larrystoolsandhydraulic.com
SIC: 3549 Cutting and slitting machinery

(G-8725)
LASTEC LLC
8180 W 10th St (46214-2430)
PHONE..................317 892-4444
Mark Thompson, Prin
Sheri Galloway, Mgr
Dave Baylif, Prin
EMP: 11 EST: 2012
SALES (est): 928.76K Privately Held
Web: www.lastec.com
SIC: 3524 Lawn and garden mowers and accessories

(G-8726)
LATICRETE INTERNATIONAL INC
4620 W 84th St Ste 200 (46268-3820)
PHONE..................317 298-8510
Ron Roach, Mgr
EMP: 8
SALES (corp-wide): 135.71MM Privately Held
Web: www.laticrete.com
SIC: 2891 Adhesives and sealants
PA: Laticrete International, Inc.
    91 Amity Rd
    Bethany CT 06524
    203 393-0010

(G-8727)
LAUCK MANUFACTURING CO INC
735 Bacon St (46227-1113)
PHONE..................317 787-6269
Dan Slightom, Pr
Laurie A Slightom, Sec
EMP: 13 EST: 1882
SQ FT: 12,000
SALES (est): 2.14MM Privately Held
Web: www.lauckmfg.com
SIC: 3444 7692 3496 3469 Sheet metal specialties, not stamped; Welding repair; Miscellaneous fabricated wire products; Metal stampings, nec

(G-8728)
LAVA LIPS
6821 Grosvenor Pl (46220-4136)
PHONE..................317 965-6629
Michael T Siemer, VP
EMP: 5 EST: 2013
SALES (est): 86.85K Privately Held
SIC: 2035 Pickles, sauces, and salad dressings

(G-8729)
LCA-VISION INC
Also Called: Lasikplus Vision Center
8930 Keystone Xing (46240-2179)
PHONE..................317 818-3980
Randy Poynter, Dir
EMP: 6
SALES (corp-wide): 154.83MM Privately Held
Web: www.lasikplus.com
SIC: 3841 8042 Ophthalmic lasers; Offices and clinics of optometrists
HQ: Lca-Vision Inc.
    7840 Montgomery Rd
    Cincinnati OH 45236
    513 792-9292

(G-8730)
LEAR CORPORATION
4409 W Morris St (46241-2401)
PHONE..................317 481-0530
EMP: 21
SALES (corp-wide): 23.47B Publicly Held
Web: www.lear.com
SIC: 3714 Motor vehicle electrical equipment
PA: Lear Corporation
    21557 Telegraph Rd
    Southfield MI 48033
    248 447-1500

(G-8731)
LEASENET INCORPORATED
8888 Keystone Xing Ste 1300 (46240-4609)
PHONE..................317 575-4098
EMP: 2 EST: 2007
SALES (est): 158.37K Privately Held
SIC: 3569 Lubrication equipment, industrial

(G-8732)
LEE CRAWFORD WELDING
2836 Newhart St (46217-9443)
PHONE..................317 490-8009
Lee Crawford, Owner
EMP: 1 EST: 2009
SALES (est): 95.54K Privately Held
SIC: 7692 Welding repair

(G-8733)
LEED THERMAL PROCESSING INC
1718 N Luett Ave (46222-2529)
PHONE..................317 637-5102
EMP: 7 EST: 1988
SALES (est): 664.72K Privately Held
SIC: 3312 3398 Blast furnaces and steel mills ; Metal heat treating

(G-8734)
LEGACY RESOURCES CO LP (PA)
Also Called: Legacy
2780 Waterfront Parkway East Dr Ste 200 (46214-2030)
PHONE..................317 328-5660
F W Grube, Genl Pt
EMP: 3 EST: 1993
SQ FT: 2,500
SALES (est): 2.38MM Privately Held
Web: www.legacyresourcesco.com
SIC: 1382 Oil and gas exploration services

(G-8735)
LEGENDS MAINGATE LLC
Also Called: Legends Global Merchandise
7900 Rockville Rd (46214-3112)
PHONE..................317 243-2000
Dan Smith, Pr
EMP: 10 EST: 2019
SALES (est): 5.46MM
SALES (corp-wide): 79.42MM Privately Held
Web: www.legends.net
SIC: 2339 2396 2395 6794 Women's and misses' athletic clothing and sportswear; Screen printing on fabric articles; Embroidery and art needlework; Copyright buying and licensing
HQ: Legends Hospitality, Llc
    61 Broadway Suite 2400
    New York NY 10006

(G-8736)
LEME INC (PA)
6107 Churchman Byp (46203)
PHONE..................317 788-4114
Robert E Behrens, CEO
Larry E Emery, *
EMP: 22 EST: 1991
SQ FT: 35,000
SALES (est): 4.94MM Privately Held
SIC: 3599 Machine shop, jobbing and repair

(G-8737)
LEMONWIRE LLC
5616 W 74th St Ste A (46278-1752)
PHONE..................317 243-1758
EMP: 1 EST: 2017
SQ FT: 200
SALES (est): 39.83K Privately Held
Web: www.lemonwire.com
SIC: 2741 Internet publishing and broadcasting

(G-8738)
LENEX STEEL COMPANY (PA)
450 E 96th St Ste 100 (46240-3784)
PHONE..................317 818-1622
Michael Berghoff, Pr
EMP: 5 EST: 2002
SQ FT: 20,000
SALES (est): 24.63MM
SALES (corp-wide): 24.63MM Privately Held
Web: www.lenexsteel.com
SIC: 3441 Fabricated structural metal

(G-8739)
LENNOX NAT ACCOUNT SVCS LLC
1345 Brookville Way Ste Q (46239-1125)
PHONE..................800 333-4001
EMP: 8
SALES (corp-wide): 4.98B Publicly Held
Web: www.lennoxnas.com
SIC: 3585 Refrigeration and heating equipment
HQ: Lennox National Account Services Llc
    3511 Ne 22nd Ave Ste 300
    Fort Lauderdale FL 33308
    954 537-5544

(G-8740)
LESSONLY INC
1129 E 16th St (46202-1943)
PHONE..................317 469-9194
John M Yoder, Pr
EMP: 106 EST: 2014
SALES (est): 11.08MM
SALES (corp-wide): 151.4MM Privately Held
Web: www.seismic.com
SIC: 7372 Educational computer software
PA: Seismic Software Holdings, Inc.
    11455 El Cmino Real Ste 3
    San Diego CA

(G-8741)
LETTERKENNY PRESS INC
5032 Beaumont Way South Dr (46250-1659)
PHONE..................317 752-4375
EMP: 5 EST: 2017
SALES (est): 56.38K Privately Held
SIC: 2741 Miscellaneous publishing

(G-8742)
LEWIS SEALING & CLEANING
1601 E Sumner Ave (46227-3277)
PHONE..................317 783-1424
EMP: 1 EST: 1994
SALES (est): 162.18K Privately Held
Web: www.lewissealing.com
SIC: 1611 2951 Surfacing and paving; Asphalt paving mixtures and blocks

(G-8743)
LEXINGTON PHARMACEUTICALS
8496 Georgetown Rd (46268-1672)
PHONE..................317 870-0370
Michael D Becker, Prin
EMP: 6 EST: 2010
SALES (est): 213.58K Privately Held

Indianapolis - Marion County (G-8744) — GEOGRAPHIC SECTION

SIC: 2834 Pharmaceutical preparations

(G-8744)
LIBERTY BOOK & BB MANUFACTURES (PA)
901 E Maryland St (46202-3931)
PHONE.................317 633-1450
Robert Van Horn, *Pr*
Henry Jones, *
Ted Pitrelli, *
Tom Ross, *
Marshall Gage, *
▲ EMP: 38 EST: 1983
SQ FT: 40,000
SALES (est): 2.58MM
SALES (corp-wide): 2.58MM **Privately Held**
Web: www.eckhartandco.com
SIC: 3111 2789 2759 Bookbinders' leather; Edging books, cards, or paper; Labels and seals: printing, nsk

(G-8745)
LIBRA ELITE LLC
9702 E Washington St Ste 400-116 (46229-3611)
PHONE.................706 831-5753
EMP: 3 EST: 2021
SALES (est): 75K **Privately Held**
SIC: 3944 Craft and hobby kits and sets

(G-8746)
LIFE LESS ORDINARY LLC
9032 Sargent Creek Dr (46256-1366)
PHONE.................317 727-4277
Scott Drake, *Managing Member*
EMP: 2 EST: 2016
SALES (est): 62.17K **Privately Held**
SIC: 7371 3949 Computer software development and applications; Sporting and athletic goods, nec

(G-8747)
LIFE PATH NUMEROLOGY CENTER
Also Called: Life Path Business Sevices
108 S Elder Ave (46222-4522)
PHONE.................317 638-9752
Daniel Hardt, *Pr*
Timothy Thipps, *VP*
Donna Winsted, *Sec*
Cynthia A Coplen, *Treas*
EMP: 3 EST: 1996
SALES (est): 243.94K **Privately Held**
Web: www.lifepathnumerology.com
SIC: 8742 2711 General management consultant; Commercial printing and newspaper publishing combined

(G-8748)
LIFTED LOADS LLC
Also Called: General Freight Trucking
7936 Bach Dr (46239-8969)
PHONE.................317 432-1542
Ronald Franklin, *CEO*
EMP: 2 EST: 2020
SALES (est): 41.52K **Privately Held**
SIC: 3537 Trucks: freight, baggage, etc.: industrial, except mining

(G-8749)
LIGHT ENGINEERING
Also Called: L E
7951 Zionsville Rd (46268-1650)
P.O. Box 582 (46122-0582)
PHONE.................317 471-1800
▲ EMP: 18 EST: 1998
SALES (est): 2.44MM **Privately Held**
SIC: 3621 Motors and generators

(G-8750)
LIGHTNING LOGISTICS ENTPS LLC ⊛
8520 Allison Pointe Blvd (46250-5700)
PHONE.................317 333-9563
EMP: 2 EST: 2023
SALES (est): 92.67K **Privately Held**
SIC: 3799 Transportation equipment, nec

(G-8751)
LIL GIRLS GLAM LLC
Also Called: Lil Girl's Glam Spa Bus
2333 Rostock Ct (46229-2397)
PHONE.................317 507-3443
Jenise Dunn, *CEO*
EMP: 5 EST: 2015
SALES (est): 71.34K **Privately Held**
Web: www.lilgirlsglam.com
SIC: 3999 Fingernails, artificial

(G-8752)
LIL MS ONE HUNDRED LLC
2515 Village Cir W (46229-1280)
PHONE.................765 609-9526
EMP: 1 EST: 2021
SALES (est): 39.69K **Privately Held**
SIC: 3999 Eyelashes, artificial

(G-8753)
LIL RED STUDIOS LLC
8113 States Bend Dr (46239-7673)
PHONE.................317 443-4932
Ashley Robertson, *Pr*
EMP: 3 EST: 2021
SALES (est): 100.62K **Privately Held**
SIC: 8721 3944 5947 Billing and bookkeeping service; Craft and hobby kits and sets; Gifts and novelties

(G-8754)
LILLY RESEARCH LABORATORIES
1 Lilly Corporate Ctr (46285-0001)
PHONE.................317 276-0127
John Hutchings Holcombe, *Prin*
EMP: 3 EST: 2010
SALES (est): 191.11K **Privately Held**
SIC: 2834 Pharmaceutical preparations

(G-8755)
LILLY USA LLC
Lilly Corporate Center (46285-0001)
PHONE.................317 276-2000
David Ricks, *Pr*
Michael Harrington, *
Terrence Lyons, *
▼ EMP: 153 EST: 2008
SALES (est): 25.07MM
SALES (corp-wide): 34.12B **Publicly Held**
Web: www.lilly.com
SIC: 2834 Pharmaceutical preparations
PA: Eli Lilly And Company
1 Lilly Corporate Ctr
Indianapolis IN 46285
317 276-2000

(G-8756)
LILLY VENTURES
Lilly Corporate Center Dc 10 (46285-0001)
PHONE.................317 651-3050
Lisa Belas, *Mgr*
EMP: 5 EST: 2006
SALES (est): 255.17K **Privately Held**
Web: www.lilly.com
SIC: 2834 Pharmaceutical preparations

(G-8757)
LIMON WOODWORKING LLC
4002 Bertrand Rd (46222-4610)
PHONE.................317 362-9179
Miguel Limon, *Admn*
EMP: 4 EST: 2013
SALES (est): 66.66K **Privately Held**
SIC: 2431 Millwork

(G-8758)
LINDE ADVANCED MATERIAL TECHNO (DH)
Also Called: Praxair
1500 Polco St (46222-3274)
PHONE.................317 240-2500
Pierre Luthi, *Pr*
Thomas Lewis, *
Dean Hackett, *
◆ EMP: 132 EST: 1988
SQ FT: 58,000
SALES (est): 564.95MM **Privately Held**
Web: www.linde-amt.com
SIC: 3479 3548 3563 Coating of metals and formed products; Electric welding equipment; Spraying outfits: metals, paints, and chemicals (compressor)
HQ: Linde Inc.
10 Riverview Dr
Danbury CT 06810
203 837-2000

(G-8759)
LINDE ADVANCED MTL TECH INC
Also Called: Praxair
1555 Main St (46224-6539)
PHONE.................317 240-2500
EMP: 180
Web: www.linde-amt.com
SIC: 3479 Coating of metals and formed products
HQ: Linde Advanced Material Technologies Inc.
1500 Polco St
Indianapolis IN 46222
317 240-2500

(G-8760)
LINDE GAS & EQUIPMENT INC
Also Called: Linde Gas North America
5720 Kopetsky Dr Ste N (46217-9281)
PHONE.................317 782-4661
Tom Poupa, *Brnch Mgr*
EMP: 7
Web: www.lindedirect.com
SIC: 2813 Nitrogen
HQ: Linde Gas & Equipment Inc.
10 Riverview Dr
Danbury CT 06810
844 445-4633

(G-8761)
LINDE GAS & EQUIPMENT INC
Also Called: Praxair
1400 Polco St (46222-5210)
PHONE.................317 481-4550
Neil Faucett, *Brnch Mgr*
EMP: 2
SQ FT: 1,900
Web: www.lindeus.com
SIC: 5084 5999 2813 Welding machinery and equipment; Welding supplies; Carbon dioxide
HQ: Linde Gas & Equipment Inc.
10 Riverview Dr
Danbury CT 06810
844 445-4633

(G-8762)
LINDE INC
Also Called: Praxair
5255 E Stop 11 Rd Ste 490 (46237-6346)
PHONE.................317 881-6825
EMP: 5
Web: www.lindeus.com
SIC: 2813 Industrial gases
HQ: Linde Inc.
10 Riverview Dr
Danbury CT 06810
203 837-2000

(G-8763)
LINEAR PUBLISHING CORP
Also Called: Midwest Parenting Publications
921 E 86th St Ste 108 (46240-1841)
PHONE.................317 722-8500
Gregory Wynne, *Pr*
EMP: 3 EST: 1984
SQ FT: 2,499
SALES (est): 484.38K **Privately Held**
Web: www.indyschild.com
SIC: 2721 Magazines: publishing only, not printed on site

(G-8764)
LINK PRINTING SERVICES LLC (PA)
7370 Royal Oakland Dr (46236)
PHONE.................317 826-9852
William L Cole Ii, *Prin*
EMP: 1 EST: 2012
SALES (est): 242.45K
SALES (corp-wide): 242.45K **Privately Held**
Web: www.linkprintandpromo.com
SIC: 2752 Offset printing

(G-8765)
LINK PRINTING SERVICES LLC
11216 Fall Creek Rd (46256-9406)
PHONE.................317 902-6374
EMP: 1
SALES (corp-wide): 242.45K **Privately Held**
Web: www.linkprintandpromo.com
SIC: 2752 Offset printing
PA: Link Printing Services, Llc
7370 Royal Oakland Dr
Indianapolis IN 46236
317 826-9852

(G-8766)
LIONFISH CYBER HLDNGS LLC-S LN
Also Called: Lionfish Cyber Security
101 W Ohio St Ste 2000 (46204-4204)
PHONE.................877 732-6772
Jeremy Miller, *CEO*
Matt Pitchford, *Prin*
EMP: 8 EST: 2018
SALES (est): 969.92K **Privately Held**
Web: www.lionfishcybersecurity.com
SIC: 3571 3575 8211 5065 Computers, digital, analog or hybrid; Computer terminals, monitors and components; Public elementary and secondary schools; Communication equipment

(G-8767)
LIT BY NEEK
10949 Minuteman Ct (46234-9770)
PHONE.................317 775-5574
Shanika Baskin, *Owner*
Shanika Baskin, *CEO*
EMP: 1 EST: 2020
SALES (est): 22K **Privately Held**
SIC: 3999 Candles

(G-8768)
LITE MAGNESIUM PRODUCTS INC ⊛
6119 Guion Rd (46254-1223)
PHONE.................765 299-3644
Arun Jeldi, *Pr*
EMP: 5 EST: 2022
SALES (est): 289.36K **Privately Held**
Web: www.litemagnesium.com
SIC: 3999 3369 3812 3621 Manufacturing industries, nec; Aerospace castings, nonferrous: except aluminum; Defense systems and equipment; Motor housings

▲ = Import ▼ = Export
◆ = Import/Export

GEOGRAPHIC SECTION
Indianapolis - Marion County (G-8796)

(G-8769)
LITEAUTO INC
10475 Crosspoint Blvd Ste 250 (46256)
PHONE..................................317 813-5045
Arun Jeldi, *Ex Dir*
EMP: 5
SALES (est): 234.61K **Privately Held**
Web: www.liteauto.com
SIC: 3356 Magnesium

(G-8770)
LITERATURE DISPLAY SYSTEMS
7035 E 86th St (46250-1547)
P.O. Box 501790 (46250-6790)
PHONE..................................317 841-4398
Teresa Reiasoner, *Prin*
EMP: 1 **EST:** 2010
SALES (est): 68.94K **Privately Held**
Web: www.deflecto.com
SIC: 3993 Signs and advertising specialties

(G-8771)
LITHO PRESS INC
1747 Massachusetts Ave (46201-1040)
PHONE..................................317 634-6468
Joseph B Lacy, *Pr*
Bernard Lacy, *
John Lacy, *
▲ **EMP:** 25 **EST:** 1953
SQ FT: 36,000
SALES (est): 4.78MM **Privately Held**
Web: www.lithopress.com
SIC: 2752 Offset printing

(G-8772)
LLC WHITE DIAMOND
5610 Crawfordsville Rd Ste 1904 (46224-3727)
PHONE..................................463 888-3585
EMP: 7 **EST:** 2020
SALES (est): 262.64K **Privately Held**
SIC: 3843 Teeth, artificial (not made in dental laboratories)

(G-8773)
LLOYD JR FRANK P AND ASSOC
4461 Sylvan Rd (46228-2844)
PHONE..................................317 388-9225
Frank P Lloyd Junior Md, *Prin*
EMP: 2 **EST:** 2005
SALES (est): 177.79K **Privately Held**
SIC: 3826 Analytical instruments

(G-8774)
LLOYDS OF INDIANA INC
2507 Roosevelt Ave (46218-3642)
PHONE..................................317 251-5430
Gary Jones, *Pr*
EMP: 6 **EST:** 1987
SQ FT: 2,400
SALES (est): 600K **Privately Held**
Web: www.lloydsofindiana.com
SIC: 3999 Plaques, picture, laminated

(G-8775)
LOCKERBIE SQUARE CAB CO INC
4350 W 10th St (46222-3208)
PHONE..................................317 635-1134
Tracy Godfrey, *Pr*
Cathy Burch, *Sec*
EMP: 5 **EST:** 1978
SQ FT: 7,000
SALES (est): 627.62K **Privately Held**
Web: www.lockerbiesquarecabinets.com
SIC: 2431 3083 2511 2434 Millwork; Laminated plastics plate and sheet; Wood household furniture; Wood kitchen cabinets

(G-8776)
LOCKHEED MARTIN CORPORATION
Also Called: Lockheed Martin
5101 Decatur Blvd Ste A (46241-9529)
PHONE..................................317 821-4000
David Jacobs, *Brnch Mgr*
EMP: 2
Web: www.lockheedmartin.com
SIC: 3812 Search and navigation equipment
PA: Lockheed Martin Corporation
6801 Rockledge Dr
Bethesda MD 20817

(G-8777)
LOGIC FURNITURE LLC
Also Called: Wieland Designs
1149 Monroe St (46229)
PHONE..................................574 975-0007
Ron Turk, *Managing Member*
EMP: 300 **EST:** 2003
SALES (est): 9.24MM **Privately Held**
Web: www.logicfurniture.com
SIC: 2511 Wood household furniture

(G-8778)
LONE STAR INDUSTRIES INC
1112 W Thompson Rd (46217-9264)
PHONE..................................317 780-9860
Michael Glave, *Brnch Mgr*
EMP: 2
SALES (corp-wide): 4.69B **Privately Held**
Web: www.lonestarind.com
SIC: 3241 Portland cement
HQ: Lone Star Industries Inc
10401 N Meridian St # 120
Carmel IN 46290
317 706-3314

(G-8779)
LONG JIM JAY JR
Also Called: Hoosier Sealing Supply Co
5822 Rahke Rd (46217-3678)
PHONE..................................317 446-4409
Jim J Long Junior, *Owner*
EMP: 2 **EST:** 2009
SALES (est): 38.13K **Privately Held**
SIC: 3053 Gaskets; packing and sealing devices

(G-8780)
LONG ITEM DEVELOPMENT CORP
Also Called: Lid
2210 National Ave (46227-3512)
PHONE..................................317 780-1077
Gregg H Wood, *Pr*
▲ **EMP:** 8 **EST:** 1974
SQ FT: 22,000
SALES (est): 1.17MM **Privately Held**
SIC: 3469 5064 Appliance parts, porcelain enameled; Electrical appliances, major

(G-8781)
LONN MANUFACTURING INC
5450 W 84th St (46268-1523)
PHONE..................................317 897-1440
Scott Guenther, *Pr*
Jim Russell, *VP*
▼ **EMP:** 4 **EST:** 2008
SQ FT: 30,000
SALES (est): 363.31K **Privately Held**
Web: www.lonn.net
SIC: 3589 Water purification equipment, household type

(G-8782)
LORD CORPORATION
Also Called: Thermoset Plastics Division
5101 E 65th St (46220-4816)
PHONE..................................317 259-4161
Joe Luchik, *Brnch Mgr*
EMP: 100
SALES (corp-wide): 19.93B **Publicly Held**
Web: www.lord.com
SIC: 2891 Adhesives
HQ: Lord Corporation
111 Lord Dr
Cary NC 27511
919 468-5979

(G-8783)
LORD FMS GAMES LLC
7244 Rooses Way (46217-7484)
PHONE..................................317 710-2253
EMP: 3 **EST:** 2014
SALES (est): 116.49K **Privately Held**
SIC: 7371 7372 7389 Computer software development; Home entertainment computer software; Business Activities at Non-Commercial Site

(G-8784)
LOUTSA INC
7435 W 10th St (46214-2517)
PHONE..................................317 273-0123
Toris Naples, *Pr*
EMP: 8 **EST:** 2011
SALES (est): 311.07K **Privately Held**
SIC: 2043 Cereal breakfast foods

(G-8785)
LOVE HANDLE LLC
11702 Maze Rd (46259)
PHONE..................................317 384-1102
Christopher Benedyk, *Prin*
EMP: 5 **EST:** 2016
SALES (est): 56.65K **Privately Held**
SIC: 2499 Handles, wood

(G-8786)
LOVE2READLOVE2WRITE PUBG LLC
5936 Copeland Lakes Dr (46221-4555)
PHONE..................................317 550-9755
Michele Harper, *Prin*
EMP: 6 **EST:** 2015
SALES (est): 71.06K **Privately Held**
Web: www.love2readlove2writepublishing.com
SIC: 2741 Miscellaneous publishing

(G-8787)
LOVETT PALLET RECYCLING LLC
217 S Belmont Ave Ste E (46222-4286)
PHONE..................................317 638-4840
Brad Lovett, *
EMP: 55 **EST:** 2001
SQ FT: 20,000
SALES (est): 5.63MM **Privately Held**
Web: www.lovettpallet.com
SIC: 2448 Pallets, wood

(G-8788)
LOYAL MFG CORP
1121 S Shortridge Rd (46239-1081)
PHONE..................................317 359-3185
Ronald Lambert, *Pr*
Todd Fox, *Genl Mgr*
EMP: 12 **EST:** 1975
SQ FT: 13,000
SALES (est): 1.76MM **Privately Held**
Web: www.loyalmfg.com
SIC: 3444 Sheet metal specialties, not stamped

(G-8789)
LSC COMMUNICATIONS BOOK LLC
Also Called: Lakeside Book Company
5532 W 74th St Ste 14 N (46268-4183)
PHONE..................................317 715-2406
EMP: 1
SALES (corp-wide): 8.23B **Privately Held**
SIC: 2731 Book publishing
HQ: Lsc Communications Book Llc
5550 W 74th St
Indianapolis IN 46268
317 715-2402

(G-8790)
LSC COMMUNICATIONS BOOK LLC
Also Called: Lakeside Book Company
5536 W 74th St (46268-4183)
PHONE..................................317 715-2406
EMP: 1
SALES (corp-wide): 8.23B **Privately Held**
SIC: 2731 Book publishing
HQ: Lsc Communications Book Llc
5550 W 74th St
Indianapolis IN 46268
317 715-2402

(G-8791)
LSC COMMUNICATIONS BOOK LLC (HQ)
Also Called: Lakeside Book Company
5550 W 74th St (46268)
PHONE..................................317 715-2402
David B Mccree, *CEO*
EMP: 41 **EST:** 2020
SALES (est): 99.77MM
SALES (corp-wide): 8.23B **Privately Held**
SIC: 2731 Book publishing
PA: Atlas Holdings, Llc
100 Northfield St
Greenwich CT 06830
203 622-9138

(G-8792)
LT METAL MASTERS INC
2514 Bethel Ave (46203-3034)
PHONE..................................317 780-1864
EMP: 13 **EST:** 2016
SALES (est): 539.51K **Privately Held**
Web: www.mmindy.com
SIC: 3441 Fabricated structural metal

(G-8793)
LUCAS OIL PRODUCTS INC (PA)
Also Called: Lucas Oil
1310 E 96th St (46240)
PHONE..................................951 270-0154
Morgan Lucas, *CEO*
Matthew Kimmick, *
Katie Lucas, *
◆ **EMP:** 150 **EST:** 1989
SALES (est): 182.35MM **Privately Held**
Web: www.lucasoil.com
SIC: 5169 2992 Oil additives; Lubricating oils and greases

(G-8794)
LUCKMANN INDUSTRIES
3135 Jackson St (46222-4039)
PHONE..................................317 464-0323
EMP: 4 **EST:** 2016
SALES (est): 83.22K **Privately Held**
SIC: 3999 Manufacturing industries, nec

(G-8795)
LUI PLUS
7933 Valley Stream Dr (46237-8540)
PHONE..................................812 309-9350
EMP: 4 **EST:** 2015
SALES (est): 119.87K **Privately Held**
SIC: 5021 2522 Office and public building furniture; Office furniture, except wood

(G-8796)
LUMEN CACHE INC
11216 Fall Creek Rd Ste 110 (46256-9406)
PHONE..................................317 222-1314

Indianapolis - Marion County (G-8797) — GEOGRAPHIC SECTION

Derek Cowburn, *Pr*
EMP: 10 **EST:** 2011
SALES (est): 199.57K **Privately Held**
Web: www.reneta.lighting
SIC: 3648 Lighting equipment, nec

(G-8797)
LUNA LOGISTICS LLC
8355 Weathervane Cir (46239-8595)
PHONE.................................317 721-2363
EMP: 3 **EST:** 2021
SALES (est): 80K **Privately Held**
Web: www.lunalogistics.net
SIC: 3537 Trucks, tractors, loaders, carriers, and similar equipment

(G-8798)
LUSH & LUXE CREATIONS LLC
4841 Industrial Pkwy (46226-2929)
PHONE.................................317 561-0574
EMP: 1
SALES (est): 49.15K **Privately Held**
SIC: 3087 Custom compound purchased resins

(G-8799)
LUXE FASHION PALACE LLC
11705 Sinclair Dr (46235-6019)
PHONE.................................317 379-1372
EMP: 4 **EST:** 2020
SALES (est): 50K **Privately Held**
SIC: 2331 Women's and misses' blouses and shirts

(G-8800)
LUXOTTICA OF AMERICA INC
Also Called: Lenscrafters
4020 Lafayette Rd (46254-2506)
PHONE.................................317 293-9999
Elizabeth Young, *Mgr*
EMP: 4
SALES (corp-wide): 2.55MM **Privately Held**
Web: www.luxottica.com
SIC: 5995 8042 3851 Eyeglasses, prescription; Offices and clinics of optometrists; Ophthalmic goods
HQ: Luxottica Of America Inc.
4000 Luxottica Pl
Mason OH 45040

(G-8801)
M & M SVC STN EQP SPCALIST INC
Also Called: Mid Valley Supply Co
2228 Yandes St (46205-4534)
PHONE.................................317 347-8001
John Childes, *Mgr*
EMP: 7
Web: www.mid-valleysupply.com
SIC: 3492 Hose and tube couplings, hydraulic/pneumatic
PA: M & M Service Station Equipment Specialist, Inc.
315 E 15th St
Covington KY 41011

(G-8802)
M & S CURTIS LLC
10015 Chester Dr (46240)
PHONE.................................317 946-8440
Michael D Curtis, *Managing Member*
EMP: 8 **EST:** 2011
SALES (est): 325.13K **Privately Held**
SIC: 3999 Manufacturing industries, nec

(G-8803)
M A C CORPORATION
4717 Massachusetts Ave (46218-3144)
PHONE.................................317 545-3341
Roger Hobbs, *Pr*
Ray Hobbs, *
A Kay Hobbs, *
Ida Young, *
EMP: 68 **EST:** 1975
SQ FT: 60,000
SALES (est): 4.94MM **Privately Held**
SIC: 3443 Dumpsters, garbage

(G-8804)
M AND M EMBROIDERY
3553 Lowry Rd (46222-1026)
PHONE.................................317 504-2235
Marcos Montes, *Admn*
EMP: 3 **EST:** 2017
SALES (est): 49.44K **Privately Held**
Web: www.mmembroidery.net
SIC: 2395 Embroidery products, except Schiffli machine

(G-8805)
M BRYANT DENISA
3650 W 86th St (46268-1901)
PHONE.................................317 350-3878
Denisa Bryant, *Owner*
EMP: 1
SALES (est): 56.53K **Privately Held**
SIC: 2517 Wood television and radio cabinets

(G-8806)
M2 WATER SOLUTIONS LLC
951 E 86th St Ste 200d (46240-2092)
P.O. Box 40337 (46240-0337)
PHONE.................................317 431-7941
EMP: 5 **EST:** 2016
SALES (est): 184.45K **Privately Held**
Web: www.m2watersolutions.com
SIC: 3599 Industrial machinery, nec

(G-8807)
M2M HOLDINGS INC
450 E 96th St Ste 300 (46240-3797)
PHONE.................................317 249-1700
Vincent Burkett, *Pr*
Jeff Tognoni, *
Kathy Kinder, *
Don Melton, *
Brenda Padgett, *
EMP: 96 **EST:** 2003
SALES (est): 1.45MM **Privately Held**
SIC: 7372 Prepackaged software

(G-8808)
MACHINE TOOL AFFILIATES INC
8401 E 75th St (46256-2128)
PHONE.................................317 846-3487
James Sweeney, *Pr*
Kathleen Ann Sweeney, *Sec*
EMP: 3 **EST:** 1959
SQ FT: 900
SALES (est): 280.13K **Privately Held**
Web: www.mtaindy.com
SIC: 3599 Machine shop, jobbing and repair

(G-8809)
MAGIC CANDLE INC
203 S Audubon Rd (46219-7214)
PHONE.................................317 357-1101
Janet Deferbrache, *Pr*
EMP: 2 **EST:** 2004
SALES (est): 99.1K **Privately Held**
Web: www.themagickcandle.com
SIC: 3999 Candles

(G-8810)
MAGNETIC INSTRUMENTATION LLC
Also Called: Kjs Associates
8431 Castlewood Dr (46250-1534)
PHONE.................................317 842-7500
David Miller, *Pr*
EMP: 27 **EST:** 2014
SQ FT: 40,000
SALES (est): 4.73MM **Privately Held**
Web: www.maginst.com
SIC: 3699 Electrical equipment and supplies, nec

(G-8811)
MAGNIFISCENTS
5207 E 38th St (46218-1718)
PHONE.................................317 549-3880
EMP: 2 **EST:** 1995
SALES (est): 254.91K **Privately Held**
Web: www.magnifiscents.net
SIC: 2899 Incense

(G-8812)
MAIN EVENT MDSG GROUP LLC
6880 Hillsdale Ct (46250-2001)
PHONE.................................317 570-8900
Brian Fahle, *Managing Member*
▲ **EMP:** 18 **EST:** 2002
SQ FT: 4,000
SALES (est): 2.25MM **Privately Held**
Web: www.yourcompanystore.com
SIC: 2262 7336 Screen printing: manmade fiber and silk broadwoven fabrics; Silk screen design

(G-8813)
MAIN1MEDIA LLC
Also Called: Main One Media
8459 Castlewood Dr Ste D (46250-4581)
PHONE.................................317 841-7000
EMP: 7 **EST:** 2001
SQ FT: 3,000
SALES (est): 586.97K **Privately Held**
Web: www.main1media.com
SIC: 2731 Pamphlets: publishing and printing

(G-8814)
MAINGATE LLC
7900 Rockville Rd Ste X (46214)
▲ **EMP:** 100 **EST:** 1963
SQ FT: 30,000
SALES (est): 47.85MM **Privately Held**
SIC: 2339 2396 2395 6794 Women's and misses' athletic clothing and sportswear; Screen printing on fabric articles; Embroidery and art needlework; Copyright buying and licensing

(G-8815)
MAJESTIC CREATIONS LLC
8094 Stonebranch East Dr (46256-4607)
PHONE.................................317 258-2794
EMP: 2
SALES (est): 74.03K **Privately Held**
SIC: 1389 Construction, repair, and dismantling services

(G-8816)
MAJESTIC MARBLE IMPORTS INC
1100 E Maryland St (46202-3975)
PHONE.................................317 237-4400
Jose Alejos, *Pr*
Barcia Alejos, *Sec*
▲ **EMP:** 12 **EST:** 1989
SQ FT: 6,200
SALES (est): 638.51K **Privately Held**
Web: www.majesticstoneimports.com
SIC: 3281 Cut stone and stone products

(G-8817)
MAJESTIC WATER COMPANY
3815 River Crossing Pkwy Ste 100 (46240-7746)
PHONE.................................317 790-2448
EMP: 3 **EST:** 2019
SALES (est): 159.34K **Privately Held**
Web: majesticwatercompany.wixsite.com
SIC: 2899 Distilled water

(G-8818)
MAJESTY HAIR CARE SYSTEM LLC
Also Called: Majesty Hair Care
4010 W 86th St Ste N (46268-1779)
PHONE.................................317 900-6789
Angela Constable, *Owner*
EMP: 1 **EST:** 2012
SALES (est): 68.24K **Privately Held**
Web: www.majestyhaircare.com
SIC: 2844 5999 7231 Hair preparations, including shampoos; Cosmetics; Beauty shops

(G-8819)
MAJOR TOOL AND MACHINE INC
2045 Doctor Andrew (46202)
PHONE.................................317 636-6433
EMP: 506
SALES (corp-wide): 155.26MM **Privately Held**
Web: www.majortool.com
SIC: 3599 Machine shop, jobbing and repair
HQ: Major Tool And Machine Inc.
1458 E 19th St
Indianapolis IN 46218
317 636-6433

(G-8820)
MAJOR TOOL AND MACHINE INC (HQ)
1458 E 19th St (46218-4289)
PHONE.................................317 636-6433
David Macmahon, *Pr*
◆ **EMP:** 130 **EST:** 1946
SQ FT: 450,000
SALES (est): 48.97MM
SALES (corp-wide): 155.26MM **Privately Held**
Web: www.majortool.com
SIC: 7692 3599 3769 3544 Welding repair; Machine and other job shop work; Space vehicle equipment, nec; Special dies, tools, jigs, and fixtures
PA: Maine Machine Products Company
79 Prospect Ave
South Paris ME 04281
207 743-6344

(G-8821)
MALIBU WELLNESS INC
Also Called: Malibu C
6050 E Hanna Ave Ste 1 (46203-6288)
PHONE.................................317 624-7560
Thomas G Porter, *CEO*
Debra Porter, *
▲ **EMP:** 45 **EST:** 1985
SQ FT: 97,000
SALES (est): 9.68MM **Privately Held**
Web: www.malibuc.com
SIC: 2844 Hair preparations, including shampoos

(G-8822)
MALLORY SONALERT PRODUCTS INC
Also Called: Mallory Sonalert
4411 S High School Rd (46241-6404)
P.O. Box 2064 (46206-2064)
PHONE.................................317 612-1000
Wayne Hodges, *Pr*
Wayne Hodges, *Pr*
Ronald L Voegele, *
▲ **EMP:** 35 **EST:** 2002
SQ FT: 22,500
SALES (est): 5.25MM **Privately Held**
Web: www.mspindy.com
SIC: 3679 Electronic circuits

GEOGRAPHIC SECTION

Indianapolis - Marion County (G-8849)

(G-8823)
MAMAS SOUL ROLLIN LLC
731 Lynn St (46222-3813)
PHONE.....................256 479-4171
EMP: 1 EST: 2021
SALES (est): 57.39K **Privately Held**
SIC: 2599 Food wagons, restaurant

(G-8824)
MAN CHILD PROPERTY DEV LLC
Also Called: Manchild Property Development
4035 Sunshine Ave (46228-6724)
PHONE.....................317 205-4109
Eric Potter, *Pr*
EMP: 1 EST: 2014
SALES (est): 175.68K **Privately Held**
SIC: 1389 Construction, repair, and dismantling services

(G-8825)
MANE RESERVED LLC
333 N Alabama St (46204-2034)
PHONE.....................219 516-5800
EMP: 1
SALES (est): 70.48K **Privately Held**
SIC: 3999 Manufacturing industries, nec

(G-8826)
MAR-KAN MARKETING INC
3402 W 79th St (46268-1912)
PHONE.....................317 228-9335
George A Lemcke, *Pr*
George A Lampki, *Pr*
EMP: 1 EST: 1993
SALES (est): 112.67K **Privately Held**
SIC: 3089 Plastics processing

(G-8827)
MARC WOODWORKING INC
Also Called: Marc Woodworking
1719 English Ave (46201-4006)
PHONE.....................317 635-9663
Joseph A Hirsch, *Pr*
EMP: 65 EST: 1972
SQ FT: 60,000
SALES (est): 4.73MM **Privately Held**
Web: www.marcwoodworking.com
SIC: 2431 Millwork

(G-8828)
MARGCO INTERNATIONAL LLC
6445 E 30th St (46219-1006)
PHONE.....................317 568-4274
▲ EMP: 6 EST: 2008
SQ FT: 3,500
SALES (est): 361.17K **Privately Held**
SIC: 2851 Paints and allied products

(G-8829)
MARIAN INC (HQ)
1011 E Saint Clair St (46202)
PHONE.....................317 638-6525
Eugene J Witchger, *Pr*
▲ EMP: 41 EST: 2011
SALES (est): 87.02MM
SALES (corp-wide): 281.83MM **Privately Held**
Web: www.marianinc.com
SIC: 3544 Special dies, tools, jigs, and fixtures
PA: Marian Worldwide, Inc.
1011 E Saint Clair St
Indianapolis IN 46202
317 638-6525

(G-8830)
MARIAN SUZHOU LLC (PA)
1011 E Saint Clair St (46202-3569)
PHONE.....................317 638-6525
EMP: 4 EST: 2011
SALES (est): 233.14K
SALES (corp-wide): 233.14K **Privately Held**
Web: www.marianinc.com
SIC: 3699 Electrical welding equipment

(G-8831)
MARIAN WORLDWIDE INC (PA)
1011 E Saint Clair St (46202-3569)
PHONE.....................317 638-6525
William J Witchger, *Pr*
Bill Witchger, *
Eugene J Witchger, *
Alan Leighton, *
Joseph Shikany, *
▲ EMP: 2681 EST: 1954
SQ FT: 200,000
SALES (est): 281.83MM
SALES (corp-wide): 281.83MM **Privately Held**
Web: www.marianinc.com
SIC: 3544 Special dies, tools, jigs, and fixtures

(G-8832)
MARIE COLLECTIVE LLC
7893 Hunters Path (46214-1534)
PHONE.....................317 683-0408
EMP: 2 EST: 2019
SALES (est): 92.36K **Privately Held**
SIC: 7389 5621 2389 Business Activities at Non-Commercial Site; Ready-to-wear apparel, women's; Men's miscellaneous accessories

(G-8833)
MARIE LASHAAYS LLC
2042 Titleist Ln (46229-4316)
PHONE.....................317 869-7939
Reather Gardner, *CEO*
EMP: 1 EST: 2021
SALES (est): 75.13K **Privately Held**
Web: www.marielashaays.com
SIC: 3911 Jewelry apparel

(G-8834)
MARIETTA MARTIN MATERIALS INC
Also Called: Belmont Sand
5620 S Belmont Ave (46217-9712)
P.O. Box 47217 (46247-0217)
PHONE.....................317 789-4020
EMP: 3
Web: www.martinmarietta.com
SIC: 1422 Crushed and broken limestone
PA: Martin Marietta Materials Inc
4123 Parklake Ave
Raleigh NC 27612

(G-8835)
MARION QUARTERS AT FORT
5747 N Post Rd (46216)
PHONE.....................317 672-4841
EMP: 4 EST: 2019
SALES (est): 86.81K **Privately Held**
SIC: 3131 Quarters

(G-8836)
MARK MILLER
Also Called: Mark Miller Backflow
249 Byrkit St (46217-3507)
PHONE.....................317 626-9441
Mark Miller, *Owner*
EMP: 1 EST: 1999
SALES (est): 86.38K **Privately Held**
Web: www.markmillerbackflow.com
SIC: 3432 Plumbing fixture fittings and trim

(G-8837)
MARKED LLC
4445 Greenmeadow Cir (46235-1209)
PHONE.....................317 777-3625
EMP: 1 EST: 2017
SALES (est): 42.55K **Privately Held**
SIC: 2389 Apparel and accessories, nec

(G-8838)
MARKETING SERVICES GROUP INC
2601 S Holt Rd (46241-5736)
P.O. Box 421268 (46242-1268)
PHONE.....................317 381-2268
Jennifer Rode Senior, *Mktg Dir*
EMP: 374 EST: 2014
SALES (est): 354.07K
SALES (corp-wide): 23.09B **Publicly Held**
SIC: 7336 2759 Commercial art and graphic design; Commercial printing, nec
HQ: Balkamp Inc
2601 Stout Heritage Pkwy # 200
Plainfield IN 46168
317 754-3900

(G-8839)
MARMON HIGHWAY TECH LLC
Also Called: Fontaine Truck Equipment Co
2770 Bluff Rd (46225-2205)
PHONE.....................317 787-0718
Joseph A Stoutner, *Mgr*
EMP: 23
SQ FT: 2,400
SALES (corp-wide): 364.48B **Publicly Held**
Web: www.marmonhitech.com
SIC: 5013 7538 7532 3713 Wheels, motor vehicle; General automotive repair shops; Top and body repair and paint shops; Truck and bus bodies
HQ: Marmon Highway Technologies Llc
5915 Chalkville Rd 300
Birmingham AL 35235
205 508-2000

(G-8840)
MARQUISE ENTERPRISES LTD
7330 E 86th St Ste 100 (46256-1252)
PHONE.....................317 578-3400
Mark Wolf, *Brnch Mgr*
EMP: 8
SALES (corp-wide): 4.6MM **Privately Held**
Web: www.woodcraft.com
SIC: 1751 2431 5084 Carpentry work; Millwork; Woodworking machinery
PA: Marquise Enterprises Ltd.
5248 Port Royal Rd
Springfield VA 22151
703 912-6727

(G-8841)
MARTIN MARIETTA MATERIALS INC
Also Called: Kentucky Ave Mine
2605 Kentucky Ave (46221-5005)
PHONE.....................317 244-4460
Matt Shwent, *Brnch Mgr*
EMP: 9
Web: www.martinmarietta.com
SIC: 1422 Crushed and broken limestone
PA: Martin Marietta Materials Inc
4123 Parklake Ave
Raleigh NC 27612

(G-8842)
MARTIN SIGNS & CRANE SERVICES
Also Called: Martin Signs
7204 E 46th St (46226-3800)
PHONE.....................317 908-9708
Fred Martin, *Pr*
EMP: 3 EST: 1917
SQ FT: 2,500
SALES (est): 247.71K **Privately Held**
Web: www.martincraneservice.com
SIC: 7532 3993 Truck painting and lettering; Electric signs

(G-8843)
MARTIN UNIFORMS LLC ✪
6057 Lakeside Manor Ave (46254-5988)
PHONE.....................317 408-9186
EMP: 1 EST: 2022
SALES (est): 42.55K **Privately Held**
SIC: 2386 7389 Garments, leather; Business Activities at Non-Commercial Site

(G-8844)
MARTINSVILLE MILLING CO INC
8510 Olde Mill Circle East Dr (46260-2367)
PHONE.....................317 253-2581
Elizabeth Carpenter, *Pr*
Sarah Lugar, *Sec*
▲ EMP: 2 EST: 1940
SALES (est): 152.85K **Privately Held**
SIC: 2041 Flour and other grain mill products

(G-8845)
MARY JONAS
Also Called: Df Global Mfg
2104 Dr Andrew J Brown Ave (46202-1935)
PHONE.....................317 500-0600
Mary Jonas, *Owner*
EMP: 12 EST: 2017
SALES (est): 506.14K **Privately Held**
SIC: 3089 3492 3444 Injection molded finished plastics products, nec; Hose and tube fittings and assemblies, hydraulic/pneumatic; Radiator shields or enclosures, sheet metal

(G-8846)
MASCO BATH CORPORATION
Also Called: Masco Bath South
8445 Keystone Xing (46240-2496)
PHONE.....................317 254-5959
◆ EMP: 1450
SIC: 3088 3842 Tubs (bath, shower, and laundry), plastics; Whirlpool baths, hydrotherapy equipment

(G-8847)
MASCO CORPORATION OF INDIANA
Also Called: Masco
300 S Carroll Rd (46229-3959)
PHONE.....................317 848-1812
EMP: 48
SALES (corp-wide): 8.38B **Publicly Held**
Web: www.masco.com
SIC: 2759 3993 2789 2752 Promotional printing; Signs and advertising specialties; Bookbinding and related work; Commercial printing, lithographic
HQ: Masco Corporation Of Indiana
55 E 111th St
Carmel IN 46280
317 848-1812

(G-8848)
MASSON INC
Also Called: M Ross Masson
567 N Highland Ave (46202-3545)
PHONE.....................317 632-8021
William Witchger, *Pr*
C Joseph Koehler, *General Vice President*
EMP: 12 EST: 1907
SQ FT: 22,000
SALES (est): 1.32MM **Privately Held**
Web: www.massoninc.com
SIC: 2241 3542 2851 5112 Strapping webs; Marking machines; Polyurethane coatings; Marking devices

(G-8849)
MASTER FILTER CORPORATION
Also Called: Master Enterprises
4195 Millersville Rd (46205-2966)
P.O. Box 18523 (46218-0523)

Indianapolis - Marion County (G-8850) GEOGRAPHIC SECTION

PHONE.........................317 545-3335
Darrin Orr, *Pr*
Ronald Orr, *VP*
EMP: 2 **EST:** 1984
SQ FT: 1,500
SALES (est): 5.5MM **Privately Held**
Web: www.odoo.com
SIC: 5039 3625 3585 3669 Structural assemblies, prefabricated: non-wood; Electric controls and control accessories, industrial; Heating and air conditioning combination units; Traffic signals, electric

(G-8850)
MASTER MACHINE CORP
3902 E 16th St Ste A (46201-1562)
PHONE.........................317 535-6526
John Underwood, *Owner*
EMP: 6 **EST:** 2001
SALES (est): 247.15K **Privately Held**
Web: www.mastermachine.com
SIC: 3599 Machine shop, jobbing and repair

(G-8851)
MATAM CORP
1434 N New Jersey St (46202-2624)
P.O. Box 44238 (46244-0238)
PHONE.........................317 264-9908
Joseph Mcintosh, *Pr*
▼ **EMP:** 3 **EST:** 2008
SQ FT: 1,700
SALES (est): 252.62K **Privately Held**
Web: www.mataminc.com
SIC: 2048 Kelp meal and pellets, prepared as animal feed

(G-8852)
MATTOX AND MOORE INC
1503 E Riverside Dr (46202-2097)
PHONE.........................317 632-7534
Richard Feigh, *Pr*
Greg Feigh, *Sec*
Brett Breht, *VP*
EMP: 6 **EST:** 1950
SQ FT: 4,000
SALES (est): 502.45K **Privately Held**
SIC: 2834 3841 3829 Veterinary pharmaceutical preparations; Surgical and medical instruments; Measuring and controlling devices, nec

(G-8853)
MAURY BOYD & ASSOCIATES INC
9900 Westpoint Dr Ste 120 (46256-3338)
PHONE.........................317 849-6110
Richard A Boyd, *Pr*
Thomas Hicks, *Sec*
EMP: 15 **EST:** 1949
SALES (est): 550.06K **Privately Held**
Web: www.mauryboyd.com
SIC: 7389 2796 2791 2789 Printing broker; Platemaking services; Typesetting; Bookbinding and related work

(G-8854)
MAUSER PACKAGING SOLUTIONS
Also Called: MAUSER PACKAGING SOLUTIONS
6061 Guion Rd (46254-1221)
PHONE.........................317 297-4638
Ron Bowman, *VP*
EMP: 1
Web: www.bwaycorp.com
SIC: 3089 Plastics containers, except foam
HQ: Bway Corporation
1515 W 22nd St Ste 1100
Oak Brook IL 60523

(G-8855)
MAX KATZ BAG COMPANY INC
235 S Lasalle St (46201-4334)
PHONE.........................317 635-9561
EMP: 70 **EST:** 1911
SALES (est): 13.26MM **Privately Held**
Web: www.maxkatzbag.com
SIC: 2671 Plastic film, coated or laminated for packaging

(G-8856)
MAXWELL POWER LLC
5868 E 71st St # 712 (46220-4075)
PHONE.........................317 998-5092
Hanniyyah Mustafaa, *CEO*
Hanniyyah Mustafaa, *Prin*
EMP: 1 **EST:** 2017
SALES (est): 41.52K **Privately Held**
SIC: 3629 Electrical industrial apparatus, nec

(G-8857)
MAYHAM MFIA CSTOMS TRNSPRTING ◊
3102 E Minnesota St (46203-3208)
PHONE.........................463 248-5181
Dennis Ahmad, *Managing Member*
EMP: 1 **EST:** 2024
SALES (est): 62.01K **Privately Held**
SIC: 3559 Automotive maintenance equipment

(G-8858)
MAYS+RED SPOT COATINGS LLC
5611 E 71st St (46220-3920)
PHONE.........................317 558-2024
EMP: 5 **EST:** 2000
SALES (est): 449.97K **Privately Held**
SIC: 3479 Coating, rust preventive

(G-8859)
MBV-MIDWEST LLC ◊
Also Called: Nna Beverages
7520 Georgetown Rd Bldg 131 (46268)
PHONE.........................800 400-3090
EMP: 1 **EST:** 2023
SALES (est): 78.58K **Privately Held**
SIC: 2087 Beverage bases

(G-8860)
MCBROOM ELECTRIC CO INC
Also Called: McBroom Industrial Services
800 W 16th St (46202-2202)
PHONE.........................317 926-3451
Richard Mcbroom, *Pr*
EMP: 65 **EST:** 1932
SQ FT: 46,800
SALES (est): 4.68MM **Privately Held**
Web: www.mcbroomservices.com
SIC: 7694 5063 3549 Rebuilding motors, except automotive; Motors, electric; Metalworking machinery, nec

(G-8861)
MCCALLISTER INDUSTRIES INC
Also Called: McCallister's Custom Iron
1417 N Harding St Ste C (46202-2009)
PHONE.........................317 417-7365
Kevin Mccallister, *Pr*
Christopher Mccallister, *VP*
EMP: 4 **EST:** 2003
SQ FT: 2,000
SALES (est): 470.56K **Privately Held**
SIC: 3462 Ornamental metal forgings, ferrous

(G-8862)
MCCLINTON LIFE SCIENCES INC
8110 Woodland Dr (46278-1347)
PHONE.........................317 903-4230
William Mcclinton, *Owner*
EMP: 4 **EST:** 2012
SALES (est): 137.56K **Privately Held**
Web: www.mlifesci.com
SIC: 3841 Surgical and medical instruments

(G-8863)
MCCULLUGH ARCHLOGICAL SVCS LLC
410 N Arsenal Ave (46201-3004)
PHONE.........................260 402-3462
EMP: 3 **EST:** 2020
SALES (est): 134.45K **Privately Held**
Web: www.archaeologicalservice.com
SIC: 1481 Nonmetallic mineral services

(G-8864)
MCELROY METAL MILL INC
Also Called: McElroy Metal Service Center
10504 E 59th St (46236-8333)
PHONE.........................317 823-6895
Dave Abel, *Brnch Mgr*
EMP: 1
SALES (corp-wide): 362.01MM **Privately Held**
Web: www.mcelroymetal.com
SIC: 3448 Prefabricated metal components
PA: Mcelroy Metal Mill, Inc.
1500 Hamilton Rd
Bossier City LA 71111
318 747-8000

(G-8865)
MCGINTY CONVEYORS INC
5002 W Washington St (46241-2299)
PHONE.........................317 240-4315
John W Mcginty Iii, *Pr*
John W Mc Ginty Iii, *Pr*
▲ **EMP:** 6 **EST:** 1972
SQ FT: 12,000
SALES (est): 2.43MM **Privately Held**
Web: www.mcgintyconveyors.com
SIC: 5084 3535 Materials handling machinery; Conveyors and conveying equipment

(G-8866)
MCGUIRES MAGIC CLEANING LLC
5344 Traditions Dr (46235-8526)
PHONE.........................317 504-7739
EMP: 1
SALES (est): 69.27K **Privately Held**
SIC: 3589 7389 Commercial cleaning equipment; Business Activities at Non-Commercial Site

(G-8867)
ME TIME CANDLE CO LLC
4928 E 62nd St Apt E (46220-5291)
P.O. Box 533034 (46253-3034)
PHONE.........................317 378-5533
Lagina Woodard, *Prin*
EMP: 4 **EST:** 2019
SALES (est): 108.84K **Privately Held**
SIC: 3999 Candles

(G-8868)
MECOM LTD INC
Also Called: Mecom
500 E 96th St Ste 360 (46240-3774)
PHONE.........................317 218-2600
Susan Adinamis Michael, *CEO*
Carol M Adinamis, *
Jeff Saunders, *
Michael Russel, *
EMP: 53 **EST:** 1988
SQ FT: 93,000
SALES (est): 7.19MM **Privately Held**
Web: www.mecomltd.com
SIC: 5111 2752 Printing and writing paper; Commercial printing, lithographic

(G-8869)
MED DEVICES LLC
6335 Old Orchard Rd (46226-1040)
PHONE.........................317 508-1699
Gabe Browne, *Pr*
EMP: 7 **EST:** 2010
SALES (est): 213.25K **Privately Held**
SIC: 3841 Surgical and medical instruments

(G-8870)
MED2950 LLC
2950 N Catherwood Ave (46219)
P.O. Box 18189 (46218)
PHONE.........................317 545-5383
▲ **EMP:** 42 **EST:** 2002
SQ FT: 8,000
SALES (est): 4.23MM **Privately Held**
SIC: 3841 Surgical and medical instruments

(G-8871)
MEDICAL DEVICE BUS SVCS INC
8904 Bash St Ste A (46256-1286)
PHONE.........................317 596-3320
Gay Davis, *Mgr*
EMP: 5
SALES (corp-wide): 85.16B **Publicly Held**
SIC: 3842 Surgical appliances and supplies
HQ: Medical Device Business Services, Inc.
700 Orthopaedic Dr
Warsaw IN 46582

(G-8872)
MEDICAL SYSTEMS CORP INDIANA
6352 Airway Dr (46241-6400)
PHONE.........................317 856-1340
Stephen M Skoronski, *Pr*
EMP: 22 **EST:** 1986
SQ FT: 28,000
SALES (est): 211.17K **Privately Held**
Web: www.engmedsys.com
SIC: 3841 Surgical and medical instruments

(G-8873)
MEJJM INC
Also Called: Crown Point Graphics
4371 Sellers St (46226)
PHONE.........................317 893-6929
Micheal Smith, *Pr*
EMP: 6 **EST:** 2019
SALES (est): 690.71K **Privately Held**
Web: www.crownpointgraphics.com
SIC: 2771 3944 Greeting cards; Puzzles

(G-8874)
MELISSA LAMBINO
Also Called: Plank & Stella
524 E 11th St Apt 2 (46202-2823)
PHONE.........................317 506-5274
Melissa Lambino, *Owner*
EMP: 1 **EST:** 2017
SALES (est): 52.22K **Privately Held**
SIC: 2269 7389 Dyeing: raw stock, yarn, and narrow fabrics; Business services, nec

(G-8875)
MELISSA TOWNSEND
Also Called: My Charisma
623 S Gerrard Dr (46241-2235)
PHONE.........................317 797-7992
Melissa Townsend, *Owner*
EMP: 1 **EST:** 2021
SALES (est): 60K **Privately Held**
SIC: 3944 Craft and hobby kits and sets

(G-8876)
MERCHANTS METALS LLC
Also Called: Merchants Metals
6701 Bluff Rd (46217-3986)
PHONE.........................317 783-7678
Ryan Riggins, *Brnch Mgr*

GEOGRAPHIC SECTION
Indianapolis - Marion County (G-8900)

EMP: 10
SALES (corp-wide): 1.06B **Privately Held**
Web: www.merchantsmetals.com
SIC: 3496 Miscellaneous fabricated wire products
HQ: Merchants Metals Llc
3 Ravinia Dr Ste 1750
Atlanta GA 30346
770 741-0300

(G-8877)
MERIN INTERIORS INDIANAPOLIS
1145 Woodmere Dr (46260-4003)
PHONE...................317 251-6603
Harry A Merin, *Owner*
EMP: 2 **EST:** 1971
SALES (est): 174.71K **Privately Held**
SIC: 2591 2391 Window blinds; Curtains and draperies

(G-8878)
MERRITT MANUFACTURING INC
1350c W Southport Rd Ste 218 (46217-5394)
P.O. Box 17152 (46217-0152)
PHONE...................317 409-0148
Jammie Shayne Merritt, *Pr*
Barbara G Merritt, *Sec*
EMP: 2 **EST:** 2006
SQ FT: 1,000
SALES (est): 434.06K **Privately Held**
Web: www.merrittcarseat.com
SIC: 3944 Child restraint seats, automotive

(G-8879)
MERSS CORPORATION
1017 W 23rd St (46208-5442)
PHONE...................317 632-7299
Robert Polk, *Pr*
Beverly Polk, *Sec*
Sharron Polk, *Stockholder*
Christopher Polk, *VP*
EMP: 6 **EST:** 1975
SQ FT: 20,000
SALES (est): 444K **Privately Held**
Web: www.mersscorporation.com
SIC: 3821 7699 5047 Sterilizers; Medical equipment repair, non-electric; Medical equipment and supplies

(G-8880)
MES LEGACY PC INC
5759 W 85th St (46278-1330)
P.O. Box 189 (46082-0189)
PHONE...................317 769-5503
Mark Sanders, *Pr*
Devon Moon, *
Belinda Cripe, *
EMP: 30 **EST:** 1998
SALES (est): 5.55MM
SALES (corp-wide): 338.37MM **Privately Held**
SIC: 3273 Ready-mixed concrete
PA: County Materials Corp.
205 North St
Marathon WI 54448
715 443-2434

(G-8881)
MESSER LLC
1045 Harding Ct (46217-9260)
PHONE...................908 464-8100
Jerry Petro, *Brnch Mgr*
EMP: 22
SALES (corp-wide): 1.63B **Privately Held**
Web: www.messeramericas.com
SIC: 2813 Nitrogen
HQ: Messer Llc
200 Smrst Corp Blvd # 7000
Bridgewater NJ 08807
800 755-9277

(G-8882)
MET-PRO TECHNOLOGIES LLC
Dean Pump Division
6040 Guion Rd (46254-1222)
PHONE...................317 293-2930
Jerry D'alterio, *Genl Mgr*
EMP: 1
Web: www.cecoenviro.com
SIC: 3561 3594 Pumps and pumping equipment; Fluid power pumps and motors
HQ: Met-Pro Technologies Llc
4625 Red Bank Rd
Cincinnati OH 45227
513 458-2600

(G-8883)
METAFAB
226 Lincoln St (46225-1818)
PHONE...................317 217-1546
EMP: 6 **EST:** 2018
SALES (est): 153.89K **Privately Held**
Web: www.meta-fab.com
SIC: 3441 Fabricated structural metal

(G-8884)
METAL FABRICATORS PLUS LLC
Also Called: Metal Fabricators Plus
4701 Rockville Rd Ste E (46222-5940)
PHONE...................317 757-3672
Sarah Ogara, *Managing Member*
EMP: 6 **EST:** 2021
SALES (est): 126.7K **Privately Held**
SIC: 3441 Fabricated structural metal

(G-8885)
METAL FINISHING CO INC
3901 E 26th St (46218-3003)
PHONE...................317 546-9004
Damian Mc Dowell, *Pr*
Ruth Mcclellan, *S*
EMP: 6 **EST:** 1941
SQ FT: 4,000
SALES (est): 933.4K **Privately Held**
Web: www.metalfinishingco.com
SIC: 3471 Electroplating of metals or formed products

(G-8886)
METAL IMPROVEMENT COMPANY LLC
5945 W 84th St Ste D (46278-1397)
PHONE...................317 875-6030
Dan Richardson, *Mgr*
EMP: 6
SALES (corp-wide): 2.85B **Publicly Held**
Web: www.imrtest.com
SIC: 3398 Shot peening (treating steel to reduce fatigue)
HQ: Metal Improvement Company, Llc
80 E Rte 4 Ste 310
Paramus NJ 07652
201 843-7800

(G-8887)
METAL POWDER PRODUCTS LLC
111 Monument Cir Ste 3200 (46204-0066)
PHONE...................317 214-8120
Donald Hicks, *Brnch Mgr*
EMP: 9
SALES (corp-wide): 154.49MM **Privately Held**
Web: www.mppinnovation.com
SIC: 3399 Powder, metal
PA: Metal Powder Products, Llc
14670 Cumberland Rd
Noblesville IN 46060
317 805-3764

(G-8888)
METAL SOLUTIONS INC
5756 Churchman Rd (46203-6009)
PHONE...................317 781-6734
Michael Burdine, *Pr*
EMP: 13 **EST:** 2002
SALES (est): 908.82K **Privately Held**
Web: www.indianametalroofing.com
SIC: 3441 Fabricated structural metal

(G-8889)
METALLIC SEALS INC
2735 Brill Rd (46225-2302)
PHONE...................317 780-0773
Virginia Allen, *Pr*
EMP: 3 **EST:** 1999
SQ FT: 3,500
SALES (est): 164.64K **Privately Held**
Web: www.metallicsealsinc.us
SIC: 3053 Gaskets, all materials

(G-8890)
METALS AND ADDITIVES LLC (PA)
Also Called: Omni Oxide
5929 Lakeside Blvd (46278-1996)
P.O. Box 423 (47834-0423)
PHONE...................317 290-5007
Greg Stevens, *Pr*
Mark Mc Caughey, *VP*
Gregg R Bennett, *CFO*
▼ **EMP:** 18 **EST:** 1999
SQ FT: 6,000
SALES (est): 24.81MM
SALES (corp-wide): 24.81MM **Privately Held**
Web: www.pagholdings.com
SIC: 2899 Chemical preparations, nec

(G-8891)
METALWORKING LUBRICANTS CO
1509 S Senate Ave (46225-1573)
PHONE...................317 269-2444
Garry Baize, *Mgr*
EMP: 168
SALES (corp-wide): 91.05MM **Privately Held**
Web: www.metalworkinglubricants.com
SIC: 2992 2899 2842 2841 Cutting oils, blending: made from purchased materials; Chemical preparations, nec; Polishes and sanitation goods; Soap and other detergents
PA: Metalworking Lubricants Company
25 W Silverdome Indus Pk
Pontiac MI 48342
248 332-3500

(G-8892)
METALWORKING MACHINERY LLC
11126 Baycreek Dr (46236-9102)
PHONE...................317 752-0981
EMP: 1 **EST:** 2020
SALES (est): 300K **Privately Held**
SIC: 3999 Manufacturing industries, nec

(G-8893)
METCALF ENGINEERING INC
Also Called: Hopkins & Woods
405 W Raymond St (46225-1944)
PHONE...................765 342-6792
Steve Metcalf, *Pr*
Julie Metcalf, *Sec*
EMP: 9 **EST:** 1942
SALES (est): 685.37K **Privately Held**
SIC: 3599 7692 Machine shop, jobbing and repair; Welding repair

(G-8894)
METERGENIUS INC
5621 Indianola Ave (46220-3336)
PHONE...................317 979-8257
Ty Benefiel, *Pr*
EMP: 4 **EST:** 2014
SQ FT: 400
SALES (est): 242.91K **Privately Held**
Web: www.metergenius.com
SIC: 7372 4911 Utility computer software; Electric power marketers

(G-8895)
MEYER PLASTICS INC (PA)
Also Called: Sila Seal
5968 Sunnyside Rd (46236-2859)
PHONE...................317 259-4131
Ralph R Meyer, *Pr*
Marjorie Meyer, *
Larry Pike, *
▲ **EMP:** 60 **EST:** 1950
SQ FT: 84,000
SALES (est): 23.11MM
SALES (corp-wide): 23.11MM **Privately Held**
Web: www.meyerplastics.com
SIC: 3089 5162 Thermoformed finished plastics products, nec; Plastics materials and basic shapes

(G-8896)
MGTC INC
5757 Kopetsky Dr Ste D (46217-9282)
PHONE...................317 780-0609
Tom Wilson, *Brnch Mgr*
EMP: 59
Web: www.motionwear.com
SIC: 2339 Sportswear, women's
HQ: Mgtc, Inc.
11541 Trail Ridge Pl
Zionsville IN 46077

(G-8897)
MICHAEL HOLLAND
1167 N Mitthoefer Rd (46229-2462)
PHONE...................317 538-1776
Michael Holland, *Owner*
EMP: 1
SALES (est): 49.02K **Privately Held**
SIC: 1389 7389 Construction, repair, and dismantling services; Business Activities at Non-Commercial Site

(G-8898)
MICHAEL MONTGOMERY
Also Called: P.sprayz
5340 Holly Springs Ct (46254-4283)
PHONE...................317 478-6080
Michael Montgomery, *Owner*
EMP: 1 **EST:** 2020
SALES (est): 20K **Privately Held**
SIC: 2842 Automobile polish

(G-8899)
MICHELE L GRAVEL
8607 Depot Dr (46217-5202)
PHONE...................317 889-0521
Michele Gravel, *Prin*
EMP: 5 **EST:** 2008
SALES (est): 91.66K **Privately Held**
SIC: 1442 Construction sand and gravel

(G-8900)
MICRO MOTION INC
Also Called: MICRO MOTION INC
8525 Northwest Blvd (46278-1384)
PHONE...................317 334-1893
Joe Almond, *Mgr*
EMP: 2
SALES (corp-wide): 15.16B **Publicly Held**
Web: www.emerson.com
SIC: 3823 Process control instruments
HQ: Micro Motion, Inc.
7060 Winchester Cir
Boulder CO 80301
303 530-8400

Indianapolis - Marion County (G-8901) GEOGRAPHIC SECTION

(G-8901)
MICROCHIP TECHNOLOGY INC
9114 Sargent Creek Dr (46256-1373)
PHONE..................................317 842-1676
EMP: 1
SALES (corp-wide): 7.63B **Publicly Held**
Web: www.microchip.com
SIC: 3674 Semiconductors and related devices
PA: Microchip Technology Inc
2355 W Chandler Blvd
Chandler AZ 85224
480 792-7200

(G-8902)
MICROMETL CORPORATION (PA)
3035 N Shadeland Ave Ste 300 (46226-6281)
PHONE..................................317 524-5400
Gerald E Schultz, *Pr*
Eugene Sikorovsky, *
Barbara E Schultz, *
EMP: 144 EST: 1965
SQ FT: 180,000
SALES (est): 148.23MM **Privately Held**
Web: www.micrometl.com
SIC: 3444 Sheet metalwork

(G-8903)
MICRONUTRIENTS USA LLC
Also Called: Micronutrients Division
1550 Research Way (46231-3350)
PHONE..................................317 486-5880
Bruce Crutcher, *CEO*
Fred Steward, *Pr*
▲ EMP: 60 EST: 1995
SQ FT: 30,000
SALES (est): 40.57MM **Privately Held**
Web: www.micro.net
SIC: 2048 Feed supplements
HQ: Trouw Nutrition Usa, Llc
115 Executive Dr
Highland IL 62249
618 654-2070

(G-8904)
MICROSOFT CORPORATION
Also Called: Microsoft
8702 Keystone Xing Ste 66 (46240-7621)
PHONE..................................317 705-6900
Steve Piper, *Prin*
EMP: 13
SALES (corp-wide): 245.12B **Publicly Held**
Web: www.microsoft.com
SIC: 7372 Application computer software
PA: Microsoft Corporation
1 Microsoft Way
Redmond WA 98052
425 882-8080

(G-8905)
MICROVOTE GENERAL CORP
7144 Lakeview Parkway West Dr (46268-4104)
PHONE..................................317 257-4900
Mandy Miller, *CEO*
EMP: 17 EST: 1997
SALES (est): 1.48MM **Privately Held**
Web: www.microvote.com
SIC: 3579 Voting machines

(G-8906)
MID AMERICA COOP EDUCATION
6302 Rucker Rd (46220-4886)
PHONE..................................317 726-6910
EMP: 2 EST: 2011
SALES (est): 125.49K **Privately Held**
SIC: 2754 Business form and card printing, gravure

(G-8907)
MIDDTRAN ENTERPRISES INC
7399 N Shadeland Ave Pmb 323 (46250-2052)
PHONE..................................317 869-5212
Eric Middleton, *Owner*
EMP: 4 EST: 2019
SALES (est): 275.88K **Privately Held**
SIC: 3537 Trucks, tractors, loaders, carriers, and similar equipment

(G-8908)
MIDWEST EMPIRE LLC
Also Called: ASG Unlimited
3747 S Meridian St (46217-3265)
PHONE..................................317 786-7446
Scott Femler, *Managing Member*
EMP: 2 EST: 2004
SALES (est): 287.71K **Privately Held**
Web: www.asgunlimited.com
SIC: 2752 Offset printing

(G-8909)
MIDWEST ENERGY PARTNERS LLC
Also Called: Midwest Energy Partners
201 S Capitol Ave Ste 510 (46225-1025)
PHONE..................................317 600-3235
EMP: 2 EST: 2009
SALES (est): 226.18K **Privately Held**
Web: www.midwestenergypartners.com
SIC: 1381 Drilling oil and gas wells

(G-8910)
MIDWEST GRAPHICS INC
5550 Elmwood Ct (46203-6043)
PHONE..................................317 780-4600
Michael L La Londe, *Pr*
John Hannon, *
James Timmerman, *
EMP: 50 EST: 1989
SQ FT: 30,000
SALES (est): 7.02MM **Privately Held**
Web: www.midwestgraphics.com
SIC: 2752 Offset printing

(G-8911)
MIDWEST MINIS LLC
Also Called: Midwest Minis
3116 Elizabeth St (46234-1617)
PHONE..................................317 500-3294
EMP: 1 EST: 2017
SALES (est): 56.47K **Privately Held**
SIC: 3446 Architectural metalwork

(G-8912)
MIDWEST NONWOVENS INDIANA LLC
4760 Kentucky Ave Ste A (46221-3530)
PHONE..................................317 241-8956
Bryan Speight, *Managing Member*
Christopher Look, *Managing Member*
EMP: 23 EST: 2011
SALES (est): 2.37MM **Privately Held**
Web: www.midwestnonwovens.com
SIC: 2297 Nonwoven fabrics

(G-8913)
MIDWEST SHADE & DRAPERY CO
1422 Sadlier Circle West Dr (46239-1058)
PHONE..................................317 849-2131
Michael Scott Reisinger, *Pr*
Lovette Dobson, *Prin*
EMP: 8 EST: 2020
SALES (est): 548.05K **Privately Held**
Web: www.msdco.net
SIC: 2591 Drapery hardware and window blinds and shades

(G-8914)
MIDWEST STL RULE CUTNG DIE INC
5570 Elmwood Ct (46203-6043)
PHONE..................................317 780-4600
Michael Lalonde, *Pr*
John Hannon, *
Robert A Morr, *
EMP: 28 EST: 1997
SQ FT: 19,000
SALES (est): 2.3MM **Privately Held**
Web: www.midwestgraphics.com
SIC: 3544 Dies, steel rule

(G-8915)
MIDWEST SURFACE PREP LLC
5835 White Oak Ct (46220-5229)
PHONE..................................317 726-1336
Christopher J Theriac, *Managing Member*
EMP: 5 EST: 2008
SALES (est): 226.13K **Privately Held**
Web: www.midwestafi.com
SIC: 3471 Sand blasting of metal parts

(G-8916)
MIKE JONES SOFTWARE
8903 Powderhorn Ln (46256-1350)
PHONE..................................317 845-7479
EMP: 5 EST: 2013
SALES (est): 60.55K **Privately Held**
SIC: 7372 Prepackaged software

(G-8917)
MIKE-SELLS WEST VIRGINIA INC
5767 Dividend Rd (46241-4303)
PHONE..................................317 241-7422
Larry Ore, *Mgr*
EMP: 1
SALES (corp-wide): 47.84MM **Privately Held**
Web: www.mikesells.com
SIC: 2052 2096 2099 Pretzels; Corn chips and other corn-based snacks; Food preparations, nec
PA: Mike-Sell's West Virginia, Inc.
333 Leo St
Dayton OH 45404
937 228-9400

(G-8918)
MIKESMOBIMECH LLC
3921 E Washington St (46201-4413)
PHONE..................................317 753-0492
Michael Vaal, *CEO*
EMP: 1 EST: 2016
SALES (est): 65.97K **Privately Held**
SIC: 7699 7537 7692 7539 Miscellaneous automotive repair services; Automotive transmission repair shops; Automotive welding; Automotive springs, rebuilding and repair

(G-8919)
MILES PRINTING CORPORATION
Also Called: Miles Printing
4923 W 78th St (46268)
PHONE..................................317 243-8571
Lynne A Churchill, *Pr*
EMP: 10 EST: 2004
SQ FT: 2,500
SALES (est): 1.88MM **Privately Held**
Web: www.milesprinting.com
SIC: 2752 Offset printing

(G-8920)
MILLCRAFT PAPER COMPANY
2735 Fortune Cir W Ste A (46241-5520)
PHONE..................................317 240-3500
Donald Chamness, *Brnch Mgr*
EMP: 5
Web: www.millcraft.com
SIC: 5111 5112 2789 2675 Printing paper; Envelopes; Bookbinding and related work; Die-cut paper and board
HQ: The Millcraft Paper Company
9010 Rio Nero Dr
Independence OH 44131

(G-8921)
MILLER INDUSTRIAL FLUIDS LLC
1751 W Raymond St (46221-2025)
PHONE..................................317 634-7300
EMP: 25
SIC: 2992 5172 Oils and greases, blending and compounding; Lubricating oils and greases

(G-8922)
MILLER MAID CABINETS INC
6815 S Emerson Ave Ste D (46237)
P.O. Box 47806 (46247)
PHONE..................................317 780-8280
EMP: 6
SALES (est): 159.17K **Privately Held**
Web: www.millercabs.com
SIC: 2434 Wood kitchen cabinets

(G-8923)
MILLER VENEERS INC
3724 E 13th St (46201-1502)
P.O. Box 11085 (46201-0085)
PHONE..................................317 638-2326
Thomas A Miller, *Pr*
Sally M Sando, *
Benjamin R Miller, *
▼ EMP: 140 EST: 1930
SQ FT: 12,000
SALES (est): 23.26MM **Privately Held**
Web: www.millerveneers.com
SIC: 2435 Hardwood veneer and plywood

(G-8924)
MILLER WASTE MILLS INC
Also Called: R T P Company
8111 Zionsville Rd (46268-1626)
PHONE..................................507 454-6900
Greg Whitten, *Mgr*
EMP: 5
SALES (corp-wide): 630.62MM **Privately Held**
Web: www.millerwastemills.com
SIC: 3087 3083 Custom compound purchased resins; Laminated plastics plate and sheet
PA: Miller Waste Mills, Incorporated
580 E Front St
Winona MN 55987
507 454-6906

(G-8925)
MILLIPORE SIGMA ✪
6925 Guion Rd (46268-2582)
PHONE..................................317 453-5490
EMP: 11 EST: 2023
SALES (est): 317.18K **Privately Held**
SIC: 2834 Pharmaceutical preparations

(G-8926)
MILLTRONICS MFG CO INC
2920 Fortune Cir W (46241-5514)
PHONE..................................952 442-1410
Gregory S Volovic, *Pr*
◆ EMP: 113 EST: 2007
SALES (est): 23.97MM
SALES (corp-wide): 250.81MM **Publicly Held**
Web: www.milltronics.com
SIC: 3541 3823 Numerically controlled metal cutting machine tools; Computer interface equipment, for industrial process control
HQ: Milltronics Usa, Inc.
1 Technology Way

▲ = Import ▼ = Export
◆ = Import/Export

GEOGRAPHIC SECTION

Indianapolis - Marion County (G-8952)

Indianapolis IN 46268
317 293-5309

(G-8927)
MILLTRONICS USA INC
2920 Fortune Cir W Ste C (46241-5516)
PHONE..............................317 293-5309
EMP: 1
SALES (corp-wide): 250.81MM **Publicly Held**
SIC: 3823 Process control instruments
HQ: Milltronics Usa, Inc.
1 Technology Way
Indianapolis IN 46268
317 293-5309

(G-8928)
MILLTRONICS USA INC
7220 Winton Dr (46268-5142)
PHONE..............................317 293-5309
EMP: 1
SALES (corp-wide): 250.81MM **Publicly Held**
SIC: 3823 Process control instruments
HQ: Milltronics Usa, Inc.
1 Technology Way
Indianapolis IN 46268
317 293-5309

(G-8929)
MILLTRONICS USA INC (HQ)
Also Called: Hurco Usa, Inc.
1 Technology Way (46268-5106)
PHONE..............................317 293-5309
Michael Doar, *CEO*
▲ **EMP:** 13 **EST:** 2015
SALES (est): 23.97MM
SALES (corp-wide): 250.81MM **Publicly Held**
SIC: 3823 7372 Computer interface equipment, for industrial process control; Prepackaged software
PA: Hurco Companies, Inc.
1 Technology Way
Indianapolis IN 46268
317 293-5309

(G-8930)
MINING MEDIA INC
6043 Primrose Ave (46220-2349)
PHONE..............................317 802-7116
Peter Johnson, *Brnch Mgr*
EMP: 2
SALES (corp-wide): 1.88MM **Privately Held**
Web: www.mining-media.com
SIC: 2741 Miscellaneous publishing
PA: Mining Media Inc.
8751 E Hampden Ave Ste B1
Denver CO 80231
303 283-0640

(G-8931)
MINUTEMAN PRESS
6377 Rockville Rd (46214)
PHONE..............................317 209-1677
Evan Walters, *Owner*
EMP: 10 **EST:** 2011
SALES (est): 249.06K **Privately Held**
Web: www.minutemanpress.com
SIC: 2752 2759 Commercial printing, lithographic; Commercial printing, nec

(G-8932)
MIRA VISTA DIAGNOSTICS LLC
4705 Decatur Blvd (46241-9603)
PHONE..............................317 856-2681
L Joseph Wheat, *Managing Member*
EMP: 34 **EST:** 2002
SALES (est): 6.72MM **Privately Held**
Web: www.miravistalabs.com

SIC: 8071 3841 Testing laboratories; IV transfusion apparatus

(G-8933)
MITCHEL & SCOTT MACHINE CO
Also Called: Bar Steel Service Center
1841 Ludlow Ave (46201-1035)
P.O. Box 336 (46082-0336)
PHONE..............................317 639-5331
Thomas L Mitchel, *Ch Bd*
Richard G Siler, *Pr*
David Mitchel, *VP Mfg*
Stephen Mitchel, *VP*
Gary Williams, *Contrlr*
EMP: 19 **EST:** 1933
SQ FT: 94,000
SALES (est): 414.64K **Privately Held**
SIC: 3451 Screw machine products

(G-8934)
MITCHEL GROUP INCORPORATED (PA)
Also Called: Mitchel & Scott Machine Co
1841 Ludlow Ave (46201-1035)
P.O. Box 336 (46082-0336)
PHONE..............................317 639-5331
Bradley Smith, *Pr*
▲ **EMP:** 200 **EST:** 1933
SQ FT: 120,000
SALES (est): 19.37MM
SALES (corp-wide): 19.37MM **Privately Held**
SIC: 3451 Screw machine products

(G-8935)
MITCHUM-SCHAEFER INC
Also Called: Schaefer Technologies
4901 W Raymond St (46241-4733)
PHONE..............................317 546-4081
Steven J Schaefer, *Pr*
Michael G Schaefer, *
Mike Rizzi, *General Vice President**
EMP: 36 **EST:** 1932
SQ FT: 60,000
SALES (est): 955.39K **Privately Held**
Web: www.schaefer-technologies.net
SIC: 3599 7692 Custom machinery; Welding repair

(G-8936)
MITO MATERIAL SOLUTIONS INC (PA)
8902 Vincennes Cir Ste B (46268-3019)
PHONE..............................855 344-6486
Haley Kurtz, *CEO*
Kevin Keith, *COO*
EMP: 3 **EST:** 2016
SALES (est): 1.16MM
SALES (corp-wide): 1.16MM **Privately Held**
Web: www.mitomaterials.com
SIC: 2655 2891 Cans, composite: foil-fiber and other: from purchased fiber; Epoxy adhesives

(G-8937)
MITTLER SUPPLY INC
6810 Guion Rd (46268-2535)
PHONE..............................317 290-0121
EMP: 5 **EST:** 2018
SALES (est): 81.96K **Privately Held**
SIC: 1311 Crude petroleum and natural gas

(G-8938)
MJS BUSINESSES LLC
Also Called: Sign Factory
8444 Castlewood Dr (46250-5531)
PHONE..............................317 845-1932
EMP: 2 **EST:** 1996
SALES (est): 219.9K **Privately Held**

Web: www.signfactoryco.com
SIC: 3993 Signs and advertising specialties

(G-8939)
MNBKC LLC
7953 E Southport Rd (46259-6740)
PHONE..............................317 956-6558
Amy Gibson, *Pr*
EMP: 10 **EST:** 2013
SALES (est): 653.72K **Privately Held**
SIC: 3471 7699 Cleaning, polishing, and finishing; Restaurant equipment repair

(G-8940)
MOBILE DRILL OPERATING CO LLC
Also Called: Mobile Drill Intl
3807 Madison Ave (46227-1372)
PHONE..............................317 260-8108
Tim Sabo, *Managing Member*
Mike Johnson, *
Brad Todd, *
▲ **EMP:** 42 **EST:** 2008
SALES (est): 9.77MM **Privately Held**
Web: www.mobiledrill.net
SIC: 3533 Oil and gas drilling rigs and equipment

(G-8941)
MOBILE KING
1638 Shelby St (46203-2761)
PHONE..............................317 835-9772
EMP: 7 **EST:** 2017
SALES (est): 97.59K **Privately Held**
Web: www.mobilekingindy.com
SIC: 3663 Radio and t.v. communications equipment

(G-8942)
MOBILI FIVER USA CORP ✪
135 N Pennsylvania St Ste 1610 (46204)
PHONE..............................219 900-3751
Ronny Gobbo, *CEO*
EMP: 1 **EST:** 2024
SALES (est): 78.58K **Privately Held**
SIC: 2421 Furniture dimension stock, softwood

(G-8943)
MODULAR DVCS ACQUISITION LLC
Also Called: Modular Devices
1515 Brookville Crossing Way (46239)
PHONE..............................317 818-4480
Greg Mink, *Pr*
EMP: 53 **EST:** 2021
SALES (est): 8.1MM **Privately Held**
SIC: 3821 Laboratory furniture

(G-8944)
MOELLER PRINTING CO INC
4401 E New York St (46201-3646)
P.O. Box 11288 (46201-0288)
PHONE..............................317 353-2224
David Moeller Senior, *Pr*
David Moeller Junior, *VP*
Charles T Moeller, *Sec*
EMP: 20 **EST:** 1931
SQ FT: 9,000
SALES (est): 2.25MM **Privately Held**
Web: www.moellerprinting.com
SIC: 2752 Offset printing

(G-8945)
MOHAWK LABORATORIES
8401 E 33rd St (46226-6504)
PHONE..............................317 899-3660
Lester Levy, *Pr*
▲ **EMP:** 4 **EST:** 2008
SALES (est): 517.04K **Privately Held**
SIC: 3589 Water treatment equipment, industrial

(G-8946)
MOLD REMOVERS LLC
1020 E 86th St (46240-1802)
PHONE..............................317 846-0977
Tom Marshall, *Managing Member*
EMP: 1 **EST:** 2005
SALES (est): 94K **Privately Held**
Web: www.themoldremovers.com
SIC: 2842 5999 7349 8734 Stain removers; Medical apparatus and supplies; Building maintenance services, nec; Pollution testing

(G-8947)
MONARCH DISTRIBUTING LLC
Also Called: Monarch Distributing Company
430 Fintail Dr (46219)
PHONE..............................800 382-9851
Kimberly Clift, *Managing Member*
EMP: 600 **EST:** 2020
SALES (est): 54.24MM **Privately Held**
Web: www.monarchdistributingllc.com
SIC: 2082 Beer (alcoholic beverage)

(G-8948)
MONITORING SOLUTIONS INC
4404 Guion Rd (46254-3113)
PHONE..............................317 856-9400
Tom Barr, *Mgr*
EMP: 21
Web: www.escspectrum.com
SIC: 3823 Water quality monitoring and control systems
PA: Monitoring Solutions, Incorporated
78 State Route 173 Ste 7
Hampton NJ 08827

(G-8949)
MONOGRAMMED MRS LLC
5415 N Pennsylvania St (46220-3021)
PHONE..............................317 605-8471
Matthew G Gabet, *Owner*
EMP: 4 **EST:** 2018
SALES (est): 101K **Privately Held**
SIC: 2395 Embroidery and art needlework

(G-8950)
MONROE MANUFACTURING TECH INC
Also Called: Manufacturing Technology
5508 Elmwood Ave Ste 422 (46203-6074)
P.O. Box 91 (46107-0091)
PHONE..............................317 782-1005
Anita Monroe, *Pr*
Joseph Monroe Junior, *Sec*
EMP: 5 **EST:** 1979
SQ FT: 3,600
SALES (est): 468.49K **Privately Held**
SIC: 3599 Machine shop, jobbing and repair

(G-8951)
MONTGOMERY TENT & AWNING CO
5054 E 10th St (46201-2864)
P.O. Box 11516 (46201-0516)
PHONE..............................317 357-9759
James W Montgomery, *Pr*
Kenneth Montgomery, *VP*
EMP: 10 **EST:** 1955
SALES (est): 844.74K **Privately Held**
Web: www.montgomerytent.com
SIC: 5999 2394 5941 Tents; Tents: made from purchased materials; Camping and backpacking equipment

(G-8952)
MONUMENT CHEMICAL LLC (PA)
6510 Telecom Dr Ste 425 (46278-6330)
PHONE..............................317 223-2630
Paul Raymond, *CEO*
Bill Grube Junior, *Ex VP*
▲ **EMP:** 62 **EST:** 2008

Indianapolis - Marion County (G-8953)

SALES (est): 218.14MM **Privately Held**
Web: www.monumentchemical.com
SIC: **2821** 2951 5033 Thermoplastic materials; Asphalt paving mixtures and blocks; Asphalt felts and coating

(G-8953)
MONUMENT LIGHTHOUSE CHART
8503 Summertree Ln (46256-3487)
PHONE.............................317 657-0160
EMP: 5 EST: 2018
SALES (est): 105.96K **Privately Held**
SIC: **3272** Monuments and grave markers, except terrazzo

(G-8954)
MORRIS MACHINE CO INC
6480 S Belmont Ave (46217-9767)
PHONE.............................317 788-0371
Robert J Chylaszek, *CEO*
Christopher D Morris, *
Cecil Williams, *
EMP: 70 EST: 1957
SQ FT: 24,000
SALES (est): 10.91MM **Privately Held**
Web: www.morrismachine.com
SIC: **3599** Machine shop, jobbing and repair

(G-8955)
MORRIS MOLD AND MACHINE CO
4015 Ferguson Rd (46239-1529)
PHONE.............................317 923-6653
Morris Fishburn Junior, *Pr*
Ray Fishburn, *Sec*
EMP: 6 EST: 1983
SALES (est): 746.57K **Privately Held**
Web: www.morrismold.com
SIC: **3544** 7699 3545 Industrial molds; Plastics products repair; Machine tool accessories

(G-8956)
MORRIS PRINTING COMPANY INC
1502 N College Ave (46202-2799)
P.O. Box 97 (46154-0097)
PHONE.............................317 639-5553
Daniel M Evard, *Pr*
EMP: 7 EST: 1877
SQ FT: 5,000
SALES (est): 564.48K **Privately Held**
Web: www.morrisprinting.com
SIC: **2752** Offset printing

(G-8957)
MOSS L GLASS CO INC
Also Called: Moss Glass
5265 E 82nd St (46250-1627)
PHONE.............................765 642-4946
Rickie B Moss, *Pr*
Ted Moss, *VP*
EMP: 19 EST: 1946
SQ FT: 30,000
SALES (est): 464.71K **Privately Held**
SIC: **1793** 5231 3231 Glass and glazing work ; Glass; Products of purchased glass

(G-8958)
MOTOROLA SOLUTIONS INC
Also Called: Motorola
2461 Directors Row Ste C (46241-4937)
PHONE.............................317 481-0914
Ronald Moe, *Mgr*
EMP: 10
SALES (corp-wide): 9.98B **Publicly Held**
Web: www.motorolasolutions.com
SIC: **3663** Radio and t.v. communications equipment
PA: Motorola Solutions, Inc.
    500 W Monroe St Ste 4400
    Chicago IL 60661
    847 576-5000

(G-8959)
MOTOROLA SOLUTIONS INC (PA)
2461 Directors Row Ste C (46241-4937)
PHONE.............................317 716-8064
EMP: 9 EST: 2013
SALES (est): 806.81K
SALES (corp-wide): 806.81K **Privately Held**
Web: www.motorolasolutions.com
SIC: **3663** Radio and t.v. communications equipment

(G-8960)
MOTSINGER AUTO SUPPLY INC
345 W Hanna Ave (46217-5107)
PHONE.............................317 782-8484
Jack Whitaker, *Pr*
Cynthia S Whitaker, *VP*
EMP: 6 EST: 1952
SQ FT: 2,500
SALES (est): 326.6K **Privately Held**
SIC: **3599** 5013 7692 Machine and other job shop work; Automotive supplies and parts; Welding repair

(G-8961)
MOUNTJOY WOODING
1221 Schleicher Ave (46229-2330)
PHONE.............................317 897-6792
Peter Mountjoy, *Owner*
EMP: 5 EST: 1994
SALES (est): 137.29K **Privately Held**
SIC: **2431** Millwork

(G-8962)
MOURON & COMPANY INC
1025 Western Dr (46241-1436)
P.O. Box 42129 (46242-0129)
PHONE.............................317 243-7955
Thomas Mouron, *Pr*
Gwenda R Mouron, *VP*
EMP: 15 EST: 1932
SQ FT: 15,000
SALES (est): 2.07MM **Privately Held**
Web: www.mouronstainless.com
SIC: **2521** 2541 2514 2434 Tables, office: wood; Counters or counter display cases, wood; Metal household furniture; Wood kitchen cabinets

(G-8963)
MP CONSTRUCTIONS LLC
8888 Keystone Xing (46240-4609)
PHONE.............................888 520-7005
EMP: 1
SALES (est): 41.07K **Privately Held**
SIC: **1389** Construction, repair, and dismantling services

(G-8964)
MPC GLOBAL LLC
6300 Southeastern Ave (46203)
PHONE.............................816 399-4710
EMP: 4
SALES (corp-wide): 2.08MM **Privately Held**
Web: www.mpc-global.com
SIC: **3519** 5082 Diesel, semi-diesel, or duel-fuel engines, including marine; Mining machinery and equipment, except petroleum
PA: Mpc Global Llc
    1800 E Adams St
    Springfield IL 62703
    816 399-4710

(G-8965)
MPICHE LLC (PA)
Also Called: Chicago Case Company
2432 Southeastern Ave (46201-4161)
P.O. Box 1005 (46206-1005)
PHONE.............................317 636-3351
Stanley Barrish, *Pr*
Mark Gewirtz, *VP*
◆ EMP: 10 EST: 2015
SQ FT: 18,750
SALES (est): 909.06K
SALES (corp-wide): 909.06K **Privately Held**
Web: www.chicagocase.com
SIC: **3949** Sporting and athletic goods, nec

(G-8966)
MPS INDIANAPOLIS INC
Also Called: Multi Packaging Solutions Ind
2020 Production Dr (46241-4325)
PHONE.............................317 241-2020
▲ EMP: 110 EST: 1999
SQ FT: 20,000
SALES (est): 42.28MM
SALES (corp-wide): 20.31B **Privately Held**
SIC: **2759** Advertising literature: printing, nsk
HQ: Mps Holdco, Inc.
    5800 W Grand River Ave
    Lansing MI 48906

(G-8967)
MRG ROBOTICS
6328 Moonstruck Pkwy (46259-6823)
PHONE.............................814 341-4334
Charles W Cliff, *Prin*
EMP: 7 EST: 2011
SALES (est): 183.92K **Privately Held**
SIC: **3541** Machine tools, metal cutting type

(G-8968)
MS SEDCO INC
7898 Zionsville Rd (46268)
PHONE.............................317 842-2545
EMP: 20 EST: 1968
SALES (est): 4.88MM **Privately Held**
Web: www.mssedco.com
SIC: **3613** Switches, electric power except snap, push button, etc.

(G-8969)
MS WHEELCHAIR INDIANA INC
9106 Tansel Ct (46234-1371)
PHONE.............................317 408-0947
Geraldine Padgett, *Owner*
EMP: 5 EST: 2016
SALES (est): 95.34K **Privately Held**
SIC: **3842** Wheelchairs

(G-8970)
MTD PRODUCTS INC
Also Called: Mtd Products
7868 Zionsville Rd (46268-2177)
PHONE.............................317 986-2042
EMP: 10
SALES (corp-wide): 15.78B **Publicly Held**
Web: www.mtdparts.com
SIC: **3524** Lawn and garden equipment
HQ: Mtd Products Inc
    5965 Grafton Rd
    Valley City OH 44280
    330 225-2600

(G-8971)
MULTI PACKAGING SOLUTIONS INC
Also Called: Ivy Hill Packaging Division
2020 Production Dr (46241-4325)
P.O. Box 3189 (47803-3189)
PHONE.............................317 241-2020
EMP: 1
SQ FT: 10,000
SALES (corp-wide): 20.31B **Privately Held**
Web: www.westrock.com
SIC: **2752** 2759 Commercial printing, lithographic; Commercial printing, nec
HQ: Multi Packaging Solutions, Inc.

1000 Abernathy Rd
Atlanta GA 30328

(G-8972)
MULTIPLE RESOURCE SOLUTION
6925 S Carroll Rd (46259-1067)
PHONE.............................317 862-2584
David B Fagel, *Sr VP*
EMP: 2 EST: 2005
SALES (est): 155.68K **Privately Held**
SIC: **3442** Molding, trim, and stripping

(G-8973)
MVK PHARMACEUTICALS LLC
1800 N Capitol Ave Ste E504 (46202-1218)
PHONE.............................317 374-2178
Michael Kubek, *Managing Member*
EMP: 1 EST: 2017
SQ FT: 500
SALES (est): 114.56K **Privately Held**
Web: www.mvkpharmaceuticals.com
SIC: **2834** Pharmaceutical preparations

(G-8974)
MVO USA INC
Also Called: Mvo USA
8804 Bash St Ste A (46256-1287)
P.O. Box 501910 (46250-6910)
PHONE.............................317 585-5785
Tammy Borden-dennis, *Pr*
John Naidus, *Pr*
Kelvin J Tiedman, *VP*
◆ EMP: 15 EST: 1985
SALES (est): 4.83MM
SALES (corp-wide): 2.52B **Privately Held**
Web: www.gmh-gruppe.de
SIC: **3559** 3714 3728 Automotive related machinery; Motor vehicle parts and accessories; Military aircraft equipment and armament
HQ: Gmh Stahlverarbeitung Gmbh
    Neue Huttenstr. 1
    Georgsmarienhutte NI 49124
    23029108080

(G-8975)
MY DAILY WEDDING DEALS LLC
4822 Crystal River Ct (46240-6435)
PHONE.............................812 603-6149
EMP: 4 EST: 2011
SALES (est): 97.78K **Privately Held**
Web: www.mydailyweddingdeals.com
SIC: **2711** Newspapers, publishing and printing

(G-8976)
MY OLD KY BLOG PRESENTS LLC
Also Called: Mokb Presents
1043 Virginia Ave Ste 217 (46203)
PHONE.............................317 602-6641
Josh Baker, *Managing Member*
EMP: 15 EST: 2019
SALES (est): 598.02K **Privately Held**
Web: www.mokbpresents.com
SIC: **7389** 7372 Advertising, promotional, and trade show services; Application computer software

(G-8977)
MYCOGEN CORPORATION (HQ)
9330 Zionsville Rd (46268)
PHONE.............................317 337-3000
Jerome Periberie, *Pr*
Geoffrey E Merszer, *Treas*
William W Wales, *VP*
W Pete Siggelko, *VP*
◆ EMP: 10 EST: 1986
SQ FT: 22,917
SALES (est): 100.51MM
SALES (corp-wide): 17.23B **Publicly Held**
Web: www.corteva.us

SIC: 5191 2879 0721 8731 Seeds: field, garden, and flower; Agricultural chemicals, nec; Crop protecting services; Agricultural research
PA: Corteva, Inc.
9330 Zionsville Rd
Indianapolis IN 46268
833 267-8382

(G-8978)
N ROLLS-ROYCE AMERCN TECH INC
Also Called: Libertyworks
2059 S Tibbs Ave Ste Sc (46241-4812)
P.O. Box 420 (46206-0420)
PHONE..................................317 230-4347
EMP: 72 EST: 1996
SALES (est): 23.3MM
SALES (corp-wide): 20.55B Privately Held
Web: www.rolls-royce.com
SIC: 3724 Aircraft engines and engine parts
HQ: Rolls-Royce Corporation
450 S Meridian St
Indianapolis IN 46225

(G-8979)
NAIL FACTORY LLC
1122 E 16th St Unit 110 (46202-1965)
PHONE..................................317 292-5637
EMP: 1 EST: 2021
SALES (est): 100K Privately Held
SIC: 3999 Fingernails, artificial

(G-8980)
NAKOMA PRODUCTS LLC
2855 N Franklin Rd Ste A7 (46219-1349)
PHONE..................................317 357-5715
EMP: 7 EST: 2017
SALES (est): 284.19K Privately Held
SIC: 3999 Manufacturing industries, nec

(G-8981)
NAMSOU LIMS LLC
2002 High Eagle Trl Apt 1025 (46224-4250)
PHONE..................................347 641-5886
EMP: 1
SALES (est): 39.59K Privately Held
SIC: 2051 Bakery: wholesale or wholesale/retail combined

(G-8982)
NANAS CAKES AND SWEETS LLC
3136 N Tacoma Ave (46218-2038)
PHONE..................................317 694-4271
EMP: 5 EST: 2020
SALES (est): 30K Privately Held
SIC: 2051 Cakes, bakery: except frozen

(G-8983)
NANOSONICS INC
7205 E 87th St (46256-1204)
PHONE..................................844 876-7466
Ron Bacskai, Pr
EMP: 40 EST: 2011
SQ FT: 5,000
SALES (est): 7.44MM Privately Held
Web: www.nanosonics.us
SIC: 3845 Ultrasonic scanning devices, medical
PA: Nanosonics Limited
7-11 Talavera Rd
Macquarie Park NSW 2113

(G-8984)
NAPORAMIC LLC ✪
11308 Narrowleaf Dr (46235-3594)
PHONE..................................463 249-8265
Ronald Spencer, Managing Member
EMP: 1 EST: 2022
SALES (est): 33.35K Privately Held

SIC: 2731 7389 Books, publishing only; Business Activities at Non-Commercial Site

(G-8985)
NATARE CORPORATION (PA)
Also Called: Natare
5905 W 74th St (46278-1786)
PHONE..................................317 290-8828
▼ EMP: 47 EST: 1992
SALES (est): 9.02MM Privately Held
Web: www.natare.com
SIC: 3949 5091 8711 Water sports equipment; Swimming pools, equipment and supplies; Engineering services

(G-8986)
NATIONAL CHIMNEY SUPPLY-VT INC
2147c Fletcher Ave (46203-1479)
PHONE..................................317 636-0552
Marty Fuller, CEO
EMP: 20 EST: 2015
SALES (est): 1.95MM Privately Held
Web: www.nationalchimney.com
SIC: 3251 Chimney blocks, radial: clay

(G-8987)
NATIONAL DENTEX LLC
Ndx Lumident
8840 Commerce Park Pl (46268-3171)
PHONE..................................317 849-5143
Vicky Rice, Brnch Mgr
EMP: 106
SALES (corp-wide): 339.71MM Privately Held
Web: www.nationaldentex.com
SIC: 8072 8021 3843 3842 Crown and bridge production; Offices and clinics of dentists; Dental equipment and supplies; Surgical appliances and supplies
HQ: National Dentex, Llc
1701 Military Trl Ste 150
Jupiter FL 33458
800 678-4140

(G-8988)
NATIONAL FDRTION STATE HIGH SC (PA)
690 W Washington St (46204)
PHONE..................................317 972-6900
Robert F Kanaby, Ex Dir
Kathleen Rodewald, *
Steve Savarese, *
EMP: 31 EST: 1920
SQ FT: 41,700
SALES (est): 17.62MM
SALES (corp-wide): 17.62MM Privately Held
Web: www.nfhs.org
SIC: 2731 7812 5136 5137 Books, publishing only; Video tape production; Uniforms, men's and boys'; Uniforms, women's and children's

(G-8989)
NATIONAL LIB BINDERY CO OF IND
55 S State Ave Ste 100 (46201-3800)
PHONE..................................317 636-5606
Joseph Cox, Pr
Janet Cox, Sec
Eric Lindseth, VP
EMP: 8 EST: 1938
SALES (est): 699.01K Privately Held
Web: www.nlbco.com
SIC: 2789 Binding only: books, pamphlets, magazines, etc.

(G-8990)
NATURAL ESSENTIALS
3812 Screech Owl Cir (46228-1512)
PHONE..................................310 493-6509
EMP: 6 EST: 2019

SALES (est): 56.05K Privately Held
Web: www.naturalessentialsinc.com
SIC: 2844 Perfumes, cosmetics and other toilet preparations

(G-8991)
NATURALLY LLC
1235 E 52nd St Apt A11 (46205-1282)
PHONE..................................317 667-5690
Shirley Postell, Managing Member
EMP: 1 EST: 2021
SALES (est): 39.69K Privately Held
SIC: 3999 Hair and hair-based products

(G-8992)
NATURESPIRE LLC
10301 Medallion Dr Apt 150 (46231)
PHONE..................................463 266-0395
Michelle Weatherspoon, Managing Member
EMP: 1 EST: 2017
SALES (est): 41.52K Privately Held
SIC: 7231 3999 5999 2844 Cosmetology and personal hygiene salons; Manufacturing industries, nec; Miscellaneous retail stores, nec; Cosmetic preparations

(G-8993)
NAVISTAR INC
Also Called: Navistar
1429 Harding Ct (46217-9538)
PHONE..................................317 787-3113
Bill Foster, Brnch Mgr
EMP: 9
SALES (corp-wide): 350.31B Privately Held
Web: www.navistar.com
SIC: 3711 Motor vehicles and car bodies
HQ: Navistar, Inc.
2701 Navistar Dr
Lisle IL 60532
331 332-5000

(G-8994)
NAVISTAR CMPONENT HOLDINGS LLC
5565 Brookville Rd (46219-7109)
PHONE..................................317 352-4500
William D Graf, *
Jerry Sweetland, *
▲ EMP: 700 EST: 1991
SQ FT: 500,000
SALES (est): 100.24MM
SALES (corp-wide): 350.31B Privately Held
SIC: 3321 6719 Gray iron castings, nec; Investment holding companies, except banks
HQ: Navistar, Inc.
2701 Navistar Dr
Lisle IL 60532
331 332-5000

(G-8995)
NAYA TRANS LLC ✪
7498 Rockleigh Ave Apt A (46214-3041)
PHONE..................................317 720-8602
EMP: 1 EST: 2022
SALES (est): 69.27K Privately Held
SIC: 3537 7389 Trucks, tractors, loaders, carriers, and similar equipment; Business Activities at Non-Commercial Site

(G-8996)
NCH CORPORATION
Chemsearch Division
8401 E 33rd St (46226-6504)
PHONE..................................317 899-3660
Joe Fisher, Prin
EMP: 14
SQ FT: 1,000

SALES (corp-wide): 1.45B Privately Held
Web: www.nch.com
SIC: 2842 Polishes and sanitation goods
PA: Nch Corporation
2727 Chemsearch Blvd
Irving TX 75062
972 438-0211

(G-8997)
NECHANNA ONE PRODUCTIONS CORP
11252 Redskin Ln Apt G (46235-9241)
PHONE..................................317 400-8908
Denise Harris, CEO
EMP: 2 EST: 2015
SALES (est): 85.22K Privately Held
SIC: 7372 8249 Business oriented computer software; Business training services

(G-8998)
NEENAH FOUNDRY COMPANY
5950 W 82nd St (46278-1326)
PHONE..................................317 875-7245
Jason App, Mgr
EMP: 4
SALES (corp-wide): 841.88MM Privately Held
Web: www.groupnei.com
SIC: 3366 Copper foundries
HQ: Neenah Foundry Company
2121 Brooks Ave
Neenah WI 54956
920 725-7000

(G-8999)
NELSON GLOBAL PRODUCTS INC
Also Called: Ctp Corporation
2840 Fortune Cir W Ste A (46241-5508)
PHONE..................................317 782-9486
Steve Scgalski, CEO
EMP: 117
Web: www.nelsongp.com
SIC: 3714 3317 Motor vehicle parts and accessories; Steel pipe and tubes
PA: Nelson Global Products, Inc.
1560 Williams Dr
Stoughton WI 53589

(G-9000)
NEU SCRAPBOOKING STORE LLC
Also Called: Neu Scrapbooking Store
5309 Kit Dr (46237-3000)
PHONE..................................317 781-7970
Elizabeth Neu, Admn
EMP: 1 EST: 2014
SALES (est): 120.13K Privately Held
SIC: 2782 Albums

(G-9001)
NEURAVA INC ✪
1220 Waterway Blvd (46202)
PHONE..................................281 995-8055
Jay Shah, CEO
Jay Vatsal Shah, Mgr
EMP: 3 EST: 2022
SALES (est): 88.92K Privately Held
Web: www.neurava.com
SIC: 3841 Diagnostic apparatus, medical

(G-9002)
NEW CARBON COMPANY LLC
Also Called: Ncd Indianapolis
1840 Executive Dr Bldg 21 (46241-4308)
PHONE..................................574 247-2270
Beth Morganti, Mgr
EMP: 1
SALES (corp-wide): 25.28MM Privately Held
Web: www.goldenmalted.com

Indianapolis - Marion County (G-9003)

SIC: **2045** Pancake mixes, prepared; from purchased flour
HQ: New Carbon Company, Llc
50 Applied Bank Blvd
Glen Mills PA 19342
574 247-2270

(G-9003)
NEW CENTURY PUBLISHING
1040 E 86th St Ste 42a (46240-1847)
PHONE.................................317 366-9691
David Caswell, *Prin*
EMP: 7 **EST:** 2006
SALES (est): 82.59K **Privately Held**
SIC: **2741** Miscellaneous publishing

(G-9004)
NEW DAY MEADERY LLC
1125 Brookside Ave Ste D1 (46202-2881)
PHONE.................................317 602-7030
Tia Agnew, *Pt*
EMP: 5 **EST:** 2013
SALES (est): 147.82K **Privately Held**
SIC: **2084** Wines

(G-9005)
NEW ENGLAND SHEETS LLC
3600 Woodview Trce Ste 300 (46268)
PHONE.................................978 487-2500
Fred Hamilton, *Managing Member*
EMP: 28
SALES (corp-wide): 9.89MM **Privately Held**
Web: www.newenglandsheets.com
SIC: **3444** Sheet metalwork
PA: New England Sheets, Llc
36 Saratoga Blvd
Devens MA 01434
978 487-2500

(G-9006)
NEWSLETTER EXPRESS LTD
3500 Depauw Blvd Ste 1000 (46268-1136)
PHONE.................................317 876-8916
Sue Wagner, *Prin*
EMP: 2 **EST:** 2008
SALES (est): 95.6K **Privately Held**
SIC: **2752** Offset printing

(G-9007)
NEWSLINK INC
Also Called: Howey Political Report, The
6255 Evanston Ave (46220-2111)
PHONE.................................317 202-0210
EMP: 4 **EST:** 1994
SALES (est): 210K **Privately Held**
Web: www.newslink.org
SIC: **2741** Newsletter publishing

(G-9008)
NEXT GNRTION DLRSHP WARSAW LLC ◆
Also Called: Model 1
9225 Priority Way West Dr Ste 300 (46240)
PHONE.................................463 234-9400
Anthony Matijevich Iii, *Managing Member*
EMP: 1 **EST:** 2024
SALES (est): 62.01K **Privately Held**
SIC: **7539** **3714** Automotive repair shops, nec; Motor vehicle parts and accessories

(G-9009)
NEXVOO INC
8517 Oakmont Ln (46260-5340)
PHONE.................................866 910-8366
John Gayman Pred, *Prin*
EMP: 3 **EST:** 2020
SALES (est): 377.81K **Privately Held**
Web: www.nexvoostore.com

SIC: **3661** Telephone and telegraph apparatus

(G-9010)
NIGHT LIGHTS COMPANY LLC
1323 Lemans Ct Apt 606 (46205-1263)
PHONE.................................574 606-4288
EMP: 5 **EST:** 2021
SALES (est): 72.65K **Privately Held**
Web: www.nightlightscompany.com
SIC: **3999** Candles

(G-9011)
NIGHTHAWK ENTERPRISES LLC
Also Called: XCEL Clean of Indiana
8658 Castle Park Dr Ste 101 (46256-1397)
P.O. Box 502441 (46250-7441)
PHONE.................................317 576-9235
Karen Dezelan, *Managing Member*
Daniel Dezelan, *Managing Member*
Kara Jones, *COO*
EMP: 20 **EST:** 2007
SALES (est): 5.5MM **Privately Held**
SIC: **3589** Commercial cleaning equipment

(G-9012)
NITAS SCRUBS ZONE LLC
11533 Signet Ln (46235-9792)
PHONE.................................317 204-6576
EMP: 1 **EST:** 2021
SALES (est): 75K **Privately Held**
SIC: **2326** Medical and hospital uniforms, men's

(G-9013)
NKG SALES
12136 Pepperwood Dr (46236-8357)
PHONE.................................317 626-6555
EMP: 3 **EST:** 2019
SALES (est): 53.99K **Privately Held**
SIC: **3949** Sporting and athletic goods, nec

(G-9014)
NO MORE BUGS
5008 Bonnie Brae St (46228-3034)
PHONE.................................317 658-6096
Kimberly Jones, *Prin*
EMP: 6 **EST:** 2014
SALES (est): 100K **Privately Held**
SIC: **2824** **7389** Organic fibers, noncellulosic; Business Activities at Non-Commercial Site

(G-9015)
NOAH WORCESTER DERM SOCIETY
8365 Keystone Xing (46240-2684)
PHONE.................................317 257-5907
James Ertle, *Prin*
EMP: 9 **EST:** 2014
SALES (est): 243.23K **Privately Held**
Web: www.noahderm.org
SIC: **2834** Dermatologicals

(G-9016)
NOBLE TRANSPORTATION LLC
3701 Rome Ter (46228)
PHONE.................................317 488-7710
EMP: 1 **EST:** 2020
SALES (est): 228.85K **Privately Held**
SIC: **4789** **3799** Transportation services, nec; Transportation equipment, nec

(G-9017)
NOBLEMAN LOGISTICS LLC ◆
4514 Brookhollow Blvd (46254-2278)
PHONE.................................317 340-7406
EMP: 2 **EST:** 2022
SALES (est): 77.45K **Privately Held**

SIC: **3086** **7389** Packaging and shipping materials, foamed plastics; Business Activities at Non-Commercial Site

(G-9018)
NOCHAR INC
1311 W 96th St Ste 240 (46260)
PHONE.................................317 613-3046
Carl Gehlhausen, *Pr*
Carolyn Gehlhausen, *Sec*
EMP: 3 **EST:** 1986
SALES (est): 518.75K **Privately Held**
Web: www.nochar.com
SIC: **5169** **2899** **2819** Industrial chemicals; Chemical preparations, nec; Industrial inorganic chemicals, nec

(G-9019)
NOEL STUDIO INC
8533 Zionsville Rd (46268-1511)
P.O. Box 248 (46077-0248)
PHONE.................................317 297-1117
Nancy Noel, *Pr*
▼ **EMP:** 13 **EST:** 1983
SALES (est): 495.91K **Privately Held**
Web: www.nanoel.com
SIC: **2741** **5199** **5999** Posters: publishing only, not printed on site; Art goods; Art dealers

(G-9020)
NOEL-SMYSER ENGINEERING CORP
4005 Industrial Blvd (46254-2511)
PHONE.................................317 293-2215
Jeff Noel, *Pr*
John Noel, *VP*
EMP: 20 **EST:** 1956
SQ FT: 20,000
SALES (est): 6.29MM **Privately Held**
Web: www.noel-smyser.com
SIC: **3694** **3825** Automotive electrical equipment, nec; Test equipment for electronic and electric measurement

(G-9021)
NORTH AMERICA PACKAGING CORP
Also Called: Nampac
6061 Guion Rd (46254-1221)
PHONE.................................317 291-2396
Bruce Smith, *Brnch Mgr*
EMP: 3
SIC: **3412** **3085** Barrels, shipping; metal; Plastics bottles
HQ: North America Packaging Corp
1515 W 22nd St Ste 550
Oak Brook IL 60523
630 203-4100

(G-9022)
NORTHERN INDIANA OIL LLC
Also Called: Pure Edible Oils
8553 Zionsville Rd (46268-1511)
PHONE.................................317 966-0288
EMP: 15 **EST:** 2016
SALES (est): 1.44MM **Privately Held**
Web: www.pureedibleoils.com
SIC: **2079** Edible oil products, except corn oil

(G-9023)
NORTHFIELD BLOCK COMPANY
901 E Troy Ave (46203-5135)
PHONE.................................800 424-0190
EMP: 1
SALES (corp-wide): 34.95B **Privately Held**
Web: www.northfieldblock.com
SIC: **3272** Concrete products, nec
HQ: Northfield Block Company
1 Hunt Ct
Mundelein IL 60060
847 816-9000

(G-9024)
NORTHWIND ELECTRONICS LLC
8875 Bash St (46256-1276)
PHONE.................................317 288-0787
EMP: 13 **EST:** 2009
SALES (est): 844.12K **Privately Held**
Web: www.northwindelectronics.com
SIC: **5999** **3714** **3679** Electronic parts and equipment; Automotive wiring harness sets; Harness assemblies, for electronic use: wire or cable

(G-9025)
NORTHWIND PHARMACEUTICALS LLC
9402 Uptown Dr Ste 1200 (46256-1042)
PHONE.................................317 436-8522
Phillip Berry, *Brnch Mgr*
EMP: 3
SALES (corp-wide): 4.64MM **Privately Held**
Web: www.nwpharma.com
SIC: **2834** Pharmaceutical preparations
PA: Northwind Pharmaceuticals, Llc
4838 Fletcher Ave # 1000
Indianapolis IN 46203
317 522-1637

(G-9026)
NORTHWIND PHARMACEUTICALS LLC
212 W 10th St Ste A310 (46202-5686)
PHONE.................................800 722-0772
Phillip Berry, *CEO*
EMP: 6
SQ FT: 918
SALES (corp-wide): 4.64MM **Privately Held**
Web: www.nwpharma.com
SIC: **2834** Pharmaceutical preparations
PA: Northwind Pharmaceuticals, Llc
4838 Fletcher Ave # 1000
Indianapolis IN 46203
317 522-1637

(G-9027)
NOV INC
9870 E 30th St (46229-3608)
PHONE.................................317 897-3099
Ryan Corn, *Mgr*
EMP: 3
SALES (corp-wide): 8.58B **Publicly Held**
Web: www.nov.com
SIC: **3533** Oil and gas field machinery
PA: Nov Inc.
10353 Richmond Ave
Houston TX 77042
346 223-3000

(G-9028)
NOVAPRINTS LLC
Also Called: Novaprints
7805 E 89th St (46256-1239)
PHONE.................................317 577-6682
EMP: 11 **EST:** 2012
SALES (est): 2.2MM **Privately Held**
Web: www.novaindy.com
SIC: **2752** **7334** Offset printing; Photocopying and duplicating services

(G-9029)
NOVO NRDISK RES CTR INDNPLIS I
5225 Exploration Dr (46241-9003)
PHONE.................................541 520-8030
EMP: 1 **EST:** 2015
SQ FT: 6,000
SALES (est): 2.35MM
SALES (corp-wide): 33.87B **Privately Held**
SIC: **2834** Pharmaceutical preparations
PA: Novo Nordisk A/S

Novo Alle 1
Bagsvard 2880
44448888

(G-9030)
NPS XOFIGO MFG PLANT 5889
4343 W 62nd St (46268-2514)
PHONE...................317 981-4129
EMP: 4 **EST:** 2017
SALES (est): 108.24K **Privately Held**
SIC: 3999 Manufacturing industries, nec

(G-9031)
NPX ONE LLC
Also Called: NPX One, LLC
7950 Allison Ave (46268-1612)
PHONE...................201 791-7600
Mike Vanatsky, Brnch Mgr
EMP: 64
SALES (corp-wide): 231.02MM **Privately Held**
Web: www.npxone.com
SIC: 2673 Plastic and pliofilm bags
PA: Npx One Llc
4275 Reading Crest Ave
Reading PA 19605
866 764-8338

(G-9032)
NUCLEAR MEASUREMENTS CORP
2460 N Arlington Ave (46239)
P.O. Box 18248 (46218)
PHONE...................317 546-2415
Donald Demoss, Pr
Lg Vaughn, Ch Bd
EMP: 4 **EST:** 1948
SALES (est): 452.97K **Privately Held**
Web: www.nuclearmeasurements.com
SIC: 3829 Nuclear radiation and testing apparatus

(G-9033)
NUEVOPOLY LLC
8481 Bash St Ste 700 (46250-0025)
PHONE...................317 260-0026
EMP: 4 **EST:** 2020
SALES (est): 224.28K **Privately Held**
Web: www.nuevopoly.com
SIC: 2431 Millwork

(G-9034)
NUMERICAL PRODUCTIONS INC
3901 S Arlington Ave (46203-6169)
PHONE...................317 783-1362
▲ **EMP:** 60
SIC: 3599 7539 Machine and other job shop work; Machine shop, automotive

(G-9035)
NUVO INC
Also Called: Nuvo Newsweekly
3951 N Meridian St Ste 200 (46208-4078)
PHONE...................317 254-2400
Kevin Mckinney, Pr
EMP: 30 **EST:** 1989
SQ FT: 6,090
SALES (est): 2.31MM **Privately Held**
Web: www.nuvo.net
SIC: 2711 Newspapers: publishing only, not printed on site

(G-9036)
NUWAVE MANUFACTURING
68 N Gale St Ste G (46201-3508)
PHONE...................317 987-8229
▲ **EMP:** 8 **EST:** 2011
SALES (est): 984.46K **Privately Held**
Web: www.nuwavescaffold.com
SIC: 3999 Barber and beauty shop equipment

(G-9037)
NVB PLAYGROUNDS INC
Also Called: AAA State of Play.com
10859 E Washington St # 100 (46229-2615)
PHONE...................317 826-2777
Nicolas Breedlove, Pr
Nancy Breedlove, Prin
▲ **EMP:** 6 **EST:** 2007
SALES (est): 1.23MM **Privately Held**
Web: www.aaastateofplay.com
SIC: 5941 2531 Playground equipment; Picnic tables or benches, park

(G-9038)
O C TANNER COMPANY
3850 Priority Way South Dr Ste 116 (46240-3813)
PHONE...................317 575-8553
Susan Popp, Brnch Mgr
EMP: 3
SALES (corp-wide): 566.42MM **Privately Held**
Web: www.octanner.com
SIC: 3911 Jewelry, precious metal
PA: O. C. Tanner Company
1930 S State St
Salt Lake City UT 84115
801 486-2430

(G-9039)
O&T ALLIANCE GROUP LLC
7432 River Walk Dr (46214-4637)
PHONE...................302 287-0953
EMP: 2
SALES (est): 92.67K **Privately Held**
SIC: 3537 Trucks: freight, baggage, etc.: industrial, except mining

(G-9040)
OAK SECURITY GROUP LLC
10640 E 59th St Ste 200 (46236-8512)
PHONE...................317 585-9830
Lawrence E Rogers, CEO
Lawrence Rogers, CEO
Travis Wilson, CFO
▲ **EMP:** 11 **EST:** 2005
SALES (est): 2.5MM **Privately Held**
Web: www.oaksecurity.com
SIC: 3429 Door opening and closing devices, except electrical

(G-9041)
ODIN CORPORATION
6736 E 82nd St (46250-1506)
P.O. Box 50187 (46250-0187)
PHONE...................317 849-3770
Kim Dahlstrand, Pr
Josef Y Dahlstrand Junior, Ch Bd
EMP: 5 **EST:** 1950
SQ FT: 8,775
SALES (est): 450.47K **Privately Held**
Web: www.odinproperties.com
SIC: 3568 Couplings, shaft: rigid, flexible, universal joint, etc.

(G-9042)
OFFSET HOUSE INC
Also Called: Offset House Printing
9374 Castlegate Dr (46256)
PHONE...................317 849-5155
Lois J Bonjour, Pr
Robert E Bon Jour Junior, VP
Renee E Bon Jour Weiberg, Sec
EMP: 13 **EST:** 1965
SQ FT: 11,000
SALES (est): 1.7MM **Privately Held**
Web: www.offsethouseinc.com
SIC: 2752 2759 2791 2789 Offset printing; Publication printing; Typesetting; Bookbinding and related work

(G-9043)
OIL PALACE LIMITED
Also Called: Oil Palace
4525 Lafayette Rd Ste L (46254-2011)
PHONE...................317 679-9187
Julia Pettigrew, Prin
Ismaila Ndiaye, Prin
EMP: 2 **EST:** 2010
SALES (est): 163.51K **Privately Held**
Web: www.oilpalacebodyoils.com
SIC: 2844 Perfumes and colognes

(G-9044)
OLDCASTLE BUILDINGENVELOPE INC
8441 Bearing Dr (46268-1686)
P.O. Box 68596 (46268-0596)
PHONE...................317 876-1155
Dwayne Pierson, Brnch Mgr
EMP: 81
SALES (corp-wide): 1.88B **Privately Held**
Web: www.obe.com
SIC: 5231 3231 Glass; Tempered glass: made from purchased glass
PA: Oldcastle Buildingenvelope, Inc.
5005 Lyndon B Jhnson Fwy
Dallas TX 75244
214 273-3400

(G-9045)
OLE MEXICAN FOODS INC
Also Called: Indiana Distribution Center
5945 W 84th St (46278-1396)
PHONE...................574 359-7262
Yolanda Ramos, Mgr
EMP: 6
Web: www.olemex.com
SIC: 2099 Tortillas, fresh or refrigerated
PA: Ole' Mexican Foods, Inc.
6585 Crescent Dr
Norcross GA 30071

(G-9046)
OLSON CUSTOM DESIGNS LLC
4825 W 79th St (46268-1664)
PHONE...................317 892-6400
EMP: 30 **EST:** 2014
SALES (est): 3.34MM **Privately Held**
Web: www.olsoncustomdesigns.com
SIC: 7389 3599 Design services; Machine and other job shop work

(G-9047)
OMEGA ENGINEERING LLC
6731 Winnock Dr (46220-4177)
PHONE...................317 995-1965
Thomas Pottschmidt, Pt
EMP: 1 **EST:** 2016
SALES (est): 150K **Privately Held**
Web: www.omega-mep.com
SIC: 3823 Process control instruments

(G-9048)
OMEGA ONE CONNECT INC
3825 E 78th St (46240-3401)
P.O. Box 40953 (46240-0953)
PHONE...................317 626-3445
Michael Falkner, Pr
Daniel Pierson, VP
EMP: 2 **EST:** 2012
SALES (est): 75.31K **Privately Held**
Web: www.omegaoneconnect.com
SIC: 2721 7389 Magazines: publishing and printing; Business Activities at Non-Commercial Site

(G-9049)
OMNION POWER INC
3148 E 48th St (46205-1623)
PHONE...................317 259-9264
EMP: 6
Web: www.omnionpower.com
SIC: 3661 Telephone and telegraph apparatus
HQ: Omnion Power Inc.
601 Shiloh Rd
Plano TX 75074
972 244-9288

(G-9050)
OMNISOURCE MARKETING GROUP INC
Also Called: Housefield Marketing
8925 N Meridian St Ste 150 (46260-5363)
PHONE...................317 575-3300
Janet Goldberg, Pr
Linda Maurer, *
Michael Rudy, *
◆ **EMP:** 43 **EST:** 1989
SALES (est): 15.97MM **Privately Held**
Web: www.omni.cc
SIC: 5199 2759 Advertising specialties; Commercial printing, nec

(G-9051)
ON CALL MCGRAW LLC
1507 N Downey Ave (46219-3036)
PHONE...................317 938-8777
Sheik Mcgraw, Owner
EMP: 1 **EST:** 2019
SALES (est): 50K **Privately Held**
SIC: 1389 7371 Construction, repair, and dismantling services; Computer software development and applications

(G-9052)
ON POINT PRECISION LLC
3633 N Grant Ave (46218-1427)
PHONE...................317 590-2510
EMP: 1
SALES (est): 60.62K **Privately Held**
SIC: 7389 3799 Business Activities at Non-Commercial Site; Transportation equipment, nec

(G-9053)
ON THE SPOT WELDING LLC
1936 S Lynhurst Dr Ste D (46241-4636)
PHONE...................317 746-6699
Josh Hurrle, Prin
EMP: 4 **EST:** 2018
SALES (est): 176.91K **Privately Held**
SIC: 7692 Welding repair

(G-9054)
ONESOURCE WATER
1060 N Capitol Ave Ste E230 (46204-1064)
PHONE...................866 917-7873
EMP: 4
Web: www.quenchwater.com
SIC: 3589 Water purification equipment, household type

(G-9055)
ONFIELD APPAREL GROUP LLC
8677 Impact Ct (46219-1424)
PHONE...................317 895-7249
Janie Lewis, CFO
EMP: 8 **EST:** 2014
SALES (est): 188.6K **Privately Held**
SIC: 3149 Athletic shoes, except rubber or plastic

(G-9056)
ONION ENTERPRISES INC
Also Called: Zvibleman, Barry
5705 W 73rd St (46278-1741)
PHONE...................317 762-6007
Barry Zvibleman, Brnch Mgr
EMP: 2

Indianapolis - Marion County (G-9057) — GEOGRAPHIC SECTION

SALES (corp-wide): 390.29K **Privately Held**
Web: www.onionenterprises.com
SIC: 3589 Water treatment equipment, industrial
PA: Onion Enterprises, Inc.
    14713 Reserve Ln
    Naples FL 34109
    239 272-6655

(G-9057)
ONLY GET BETTER LOGISTICS LLC
6022 Morning Dove Dr (46228-1501)
PHONE.............................317 835-5606
EMP: 1
SALES (est): 69.27K **Privately Held**
SIC: 3537 7389 Trucks, tractors, loaders, carriers, and similar equipment; Business Activities at Non-Commercial Site

(G-9058)
ONTIME TOYS INC (PA)
Also Called: Commodity Brokers Company
9190 Corporation Dr Ste 106 (46256)
PHONE.............................317 598-9333
Christopher S Thifault, *CEO*
Christopher S Thifault, *Pr*
Carrie A Thifault, *Stockholder*
EMP: 3 EST: 1985
SALES (est): 2.6MM **Privately Held**
Web: www.ontimetoys.com
SIC: 5137 7389 5092 5199 Women's and children's clothing; Credit card service; Toys and hobby goods and supplies; General merchandise, non-durable

(G-9059)
OOLEY PRODUCTS INC
Also Called: Indianapolis Thermal Proc
405 W Raymond St (46225)
PHONE.............................317 787-9351
Phillip Olley, *Pr*
EMP: 23 EST: 1960
SQ FT: 10,000
SALES (est): 2.72MM **Privately Held**
Web: www.indyhoneycomb.com
SIC: 3398 Metal heat treating

(G-9060)
OOSHIRTS INC
7800 Records St Ste C (46226-3986)
PHONE.............................317 246-9083
Raymond Lei, *Brnch Mgr*
EMP: 2
SALES (corp-wide): 44.61MM **Privately Held**
Web: www.ooshirts.com
SIC: 2759 Screen printing
PA: Ooshirts Inc.
    39899 Blentine Dr Ste 220
    Newark CA 94560
    866 660-8667

(G-9061)
OOTEN PATTERN WORKS
1101 N Eleanor St (46214-3440)
PHONE.............................317 244-7348
EMP: 2 EST: 1992
SALES (est): 82.85K **Privately Held**
SIC: 3543 Industrial patterns

(G-9062)
OPEN CONTROL SYSTEMS LLC
905 N Capitol Ave Ste 200 (46204-1004)
PHONE.............................317 429-0627
Anthony Wilkerson, *Managing Member*
EMP: 5 EST: 2005
SALES (est): 1.35MM **Privately Held**
Web: www.envelopgroup.com
SIC: 3822 Temperature controls, automatic

(G-9063)
OPEN KITCHEN LLC
4022 Shelby St (46227-3625)
PHONE.............................317 974-9966
Dexter Smith, *Prin*
EMP: 7 EST: 2020
SALES (est): 196.04K **Privately Held**
Web: www.opennkitchen.org
SIC: 2099 Food preparations, nec

(G-9064)
OPFLEX SOLUTIONS INC
Also Called: Opflex
733 S West St (46225-1253)
PHONE.............................800 568-7036
EMP: 17 EST: 2011
SALES (est): 598.24K **Privately Held**
SIC: 3086 Plastics foam products

(G-9065)
OPFLEX TECHNOLOGIES LLC (HQ)
Also Called: Opflex Environmental Tech
733 S West St (46225-1253)
PHONE.............................518 568-7036
Mitchell T Stoltz, *Pr*
John J Baker, *Sec*
Patrick A Trefun, *Treas*
James E Lacrosse, *Mgr*
EMP: 12 EST: 2012
SALES (est): 5.22MM
SALES (corp-wide): 5.22MM **Privately Held**
SIC: 3086 Plastics foam products
PA: Nws Holdings, Llc
    733 S West St
    Indianapolis IN 46225
    317 602-6644

(G-9066)
OPFLEX TECHNOLOGIES LLC
2525 N Shadeland Ave (46219-1787)
PHONE.............................317 731-6123
EMP: 23
SALES (corp-wide): 5.22MM **Privately Held**
SIC: 3086 Cups and plates, foamed plastics
HQ: Opflex Technologies, Llc
    733 S West St
    Indianapolis IN 46225
    518 568-7036

(G-9067)
ORB LLC
Also Called: Orb
8016 Sandi Ct (46260)
PHONE.............................833 946-4672
Jaron Sherard, *CEO*
EMP: 2 EST: 2021
SALES (est): 71.64K **Privately Held**
Web: www.officialorb.com
SIC: 3021 3143 3144 5139 Rubber and plastics footwear; Men's footwear, except athletic; Women's footwear, except athletic; Footwear

(G-9068)
ORDONEZ CONSTRUCCION SVCS LLC
825 S Fleming St (46241-2410)
PHONE.............................317 771-1213
Maria Ordonez, *Prin*
EMP: 5 EST: 2016
SALES (est): 83.91K **Privately Held**
SIC: 2752 Commercial printing, lithographic

(G-9069)
ORECA NORTH AMERICA INC
Also Called: Oreca
3950 Guion Ln (46268-2578)
PHONE.............................317 517-2948
Hugues De Chaumac, *Pr*
Renaud Chevalier, *Sec*
▲ EMP: 2 EST: 2015
SQ FT: 800
SALES (est): 479.13K **Privately Held**
Web: www.oreca.com
SIC: 3465 3711 Body parts, automobile: stamped metal; Automobile assembly, including specialty automobiles
PA: Oreca
    Cite Coriallo
    La Hague

(G-9070)
ORION SHIPPING SOLUTIONS CORP
201 N Illinois St Ste 1600 (46204-1904)
PHONE.............................800 410-4910
Robert Bowman, *CEO*
EMP: 1 EST: 2017
SALES (est): 243.71K **Privately Held**
SIC: 3537 Trucks, tractors, loaders, carriers, and similar equipment

(G-9071)
ORORA PACKAGING SOLUTIONS
Also Called: Landsberg Indianapolis Div 1015
4635 W 84th St Ste 500 (46268-1792)
PHONE.............................317 879-4628
Steve Pittler, *Brnch Mgr*
EMP: 14
Web: www.ororapackagingsolutions.com
SIC: 5113 2653 Paper, wrapping or coarse, and products; Boxes, corrugated: made from purchased materials
HQ: Orora Packaging Solutions
    6600 Valley View St
    Buena Park CA 90620
    714 562-6000

(G-9072)
ORTHOCONCEPTS INC
10947 Echo Grove Cir (46236-9069)
PHONE.............................317 727-0100
John Alley, *Pr*
EMP: 3 EST: 2004
SALES (est): 279.96K **Privately Held**
SIC: 3845 Ultrasonic scanning devices, medical

(G-9073)
OSCAR TELECOM INC
5812 Hartle Dr (46216-2133)
PHONE.............................317 359-7000
EMP: 2 EST: 2007
SALES (est): 184.35K **Privately Held**
Web: www.oscartelecom.net
SIC: 3651 Household video equipment

(G-9074)
OSI SPECIALTIES INC
6299 Guion Rd (46268-2530)
PHONE.............................317 293-4858
Debbie Williams, *Pr*
EMP: 10 EST: 1995
SALES (est): 208.61K **Privately Held**
Web: www.alliedosilabs.com
SIC: 3842 Surgical appliances and supplies

(G-9075)
OTTINGER MACHINE CO
Also Called: Ottinger Machine Shop
2900 N Richardt Ave (46219-1119)
PHONE.............................317 654-1700
Jeffrey Ottinger, *Pt*
Candy Buckmaster, *Pt*
EMP: 2 EST: 1950
SQ FT: 7,000
SALES (est): 156.69K **Privately Held**
Web: www.ottingermachine.com
SIC: 3599 Machine shop, jobbing and repair

(G-9076)
OUT OF BOX SOLUTIONS INC
755 Fletcher Ave (46203-1037)
PHONE.............................317 605-8719
Amanda Hadley, *Pr*
EMP: 1 EST: 2008
SALES (est): 87.89K **Privately Held**
SIC: 2542 Partitions and fixtures, except wood

(G-9077)
OXFORD INDUSTRIES INC
8701 Keystone Xing Ste 14b (46240-4641)
PHONE.............................317 569-0866
Terry Pillow, *Brnch Mgr*
EMP: 3
SALES (corp-wide): 1.57B **Publicly Held**
Web: www.oxfordinc.com
SIC: 3161 Clothing and apparel carrying cases
PA: Oxford Industries, Inc.
    999 Pchtree St Ne Ste 688
    Atlanta GA 30309
    404 659-2424

(G-9078)
P & J TOOL CO INC
3525 Massachusetts Ave (46218-3899)
PHONE.............................317 546-4858
Gerald Johnson, *Pr*
Charles W Johnson Junior, *VP*
Joanne Johnson, *VP*
Gerald Johnson, *Prin*
EMP: 5 EST: 1943
SQ FT: 15,000
SALES (est): 351.26K **Privately Held**
Web: www.pandjtoolco.com
SIC: 3599 7389 Machine shop, jobbing and repair; Grinding, precision: commercial or industrial

(G-9079)
P A ROGERS PRINTING SERVICE
10748 Oyster Bay Ct (46236)
PHONE.............................317 823-7627
EMP: 3 EST: 2019
SALES (est): 83.91K **Privately Held**
SIC: 2752 Offset printing

(G-9080)
P H DREW INCORPORATED
2450 N Raceway Rd (46234-9152)
P.O. Box 34295 (46234-0295)
PHONE.............................317 297-5152
Philip H Drew, *Pr*
Christopher Drew, *
EMP: 31 EST: 1982
SQ FT: 18,000
SALES (est): 4.36MM **Privately Held**
Web: www.phdrew.com
SIC: 3441 Building components, structural steel

(G-9081)
P-AMERICAS LLC
Also Called: Pepsico
1104 S Post Rd (46239-9832)
PHONE.............................765 289-0270
EMP: 1
SALES (corp-wide): 86.39B **Publicly Held**
Web: www.pepsico.com
SIC: 2086 5149 Carbonated soft drinks, bottled and canned; Soft drinks
HQ: P-Americas Llc
    1 Pepsi Way
    Somers NY 10589
    336 896-5740

▲ = Import ▼ = Export
◆ = Import/Export

(G-9082)
PACIFIC BEACH PEANUT BTR LLC
9402 Uptown Dr Ste 1200 (46256-1042)
PHONE.................................858 522-9297
Jean Mulvihill, *Managing Member*
EMP: 2 **EST:** 2011
SALES (est): 228.87K **Privately Held**
Web: www.pacificbeachpeanutbutter.com
SIC: 2099 Peanut butter

(G-9083)
PACK PRINTING LLC
1916 Haynes Ave (46240-3236)
PHONE.................................317 437-9779
Brian V Powers, *Prin*
EMP: 2 **EST:** 2013
SALES (est): 74.99K **Privately Held**
SIC: 2752 Commercial printing, lithographic

(G-9084)
PACKAGING CORPORATION AMERICA
Also Called: PCA
7752 W Morris St (46231-1363)
PHONE.................................317 247-0193
Rob Rop, *Mgr*
EMP: 5
SALES (corp-wide): 8.4BB **Publicly Held**
Web: www.packagingcorp.com
SIC: 2653 Boxes, corrugated: made from purchased materials
PA: Packaging Corporation Of America
1 N Field Ct
Lake Forest IL 60045
847 482-3000

(G-9085)
PACKRAT INDUSTRIES LLC
8464 Flatwood Ct (46278-9592)
PHONE.................................317 295-0208
Scott Decker, *Prin*
EMP: 5 **EST:** 2018
SALES (est): 39.69K **Privately Held**
SIC: 3999 Manufacturing industries, nec

(G-9086)
PACVAN INC
2995 S Harding St Ste 1 (46225-2231)
PHONE.................................317 791-2020
EMP: 9 **EST:** 2019
SALES (est): 363.29K **Privately Held**
Web: www.unitedrentals.com
SIC: 3443 Fabricated plate work (boiler shop)

(G-9087)
PAG HOLDINGS LLC (HQ)
Also Called: Pag Holdings, Inc.
5929 Lakeside Blvd (46278-1996)
P.O. Box 423 (47834-0423)
PHONE.................................317 290-5006
Greg Stevens, *Pr*
Stephen J Groves, *CEO*
Gregg Robert Bennett, *CFO*
◆ **EMP:** 4 **EST:** 2006
SALES (est): 5.48MM
SALES (corp-wide): 24.81MM **Privately Held**
Web: www.pagholdings.com
SIC: 2861 Gum and wood chemicals
PA: Metals And Additives, Llc
5929 Lakeside Blvd
Indianapolis IN 46278
317 290-5007

(G-9088)
PALLET DEPOT
9226 E 33rd St (46235-4200)
PHONE.................................317 897-1774
EMP: 5 **EST:** 2014
SALES (est): 174.64K **Privately Held**
Web: www.thepalletdepot.net
SIC: 2448 Pallets, wood

(G-9089)
PANTHER GRAPHICS LLC
5740 Decatur Blvd (46241)
P.O. Box 4330 (46082)
PHONE.................................317 223-3845
John Barnes, *Managing Member*
EMP: 3 **EST:** 2011
SALES (est): 222.98K **Privately Held**
Web: www.panthergraphics.net
SIC: 2752 Offset printing

(G-9090)
PAPERCHARM SCRPBKING STDIO LLC
6101 N Keystone Ave Ste 100 (46220-2488)
PHONE.................................317 624-2878
EMP: 1 **EST:** 2021
SALES (est): 46.43K **Privately Held**
SIC: 2782 Scrapbooks, albums, and diaries

(G-9091)
PARADISE MACHINE AND TOOL CORP
6820 W Minnesota St (46241-2943)
PHONE.................................317 247-4606
Francis N Paradise, *Pr*
Rita Paradise, *VP*
Dennis Paradise, *Stockholder*
Mark Paradise, *Stockholder*
EMP: 5 **EST:** 1973
SQ FT: 30,000
SALES (est): 439.86K **Privately Held**
Web: www.gammonsmetal.com
SIC: 3599 Machine shop, jobbing and repair

(G-9092)
PARAGON MEDICAL INC
Also Called: Indianapolis I&I
7350 E 86th St (46256-1206)
PHONE.................................317 570-5830
Sairajkiran Nagboth, *Brnch Mgr*
EMP: 224
SALES (corp-wide): 6.6B **Publicly Held**
Web: www.paragonmedical.com
SIC: 3842 Surgical appliances and supplies
HQ: Paragon Medical, Inc.
8 Matchett Dr
Pierceton IN 46562

(G-9093)
PARK 100 FOODS INC
Also Called: A & L Spcialty Foods H C Trnsp
6908 E 30th St (46219)
P.O. Box 19638 (46219)
PHONE.................................317 549-4545
Jim Washburn, *Brnch Mgr*
EMP: 36
SALES (corp-wide): 105.14MM **Privately Held**
Web: www.park100foods.com
SIC: 2013 2032 2035 Frozen meats, from purchased meat; Soups, except seafood: packaged in cans, jars, etc.; Pickles, sauces, and salad dressings
PA: Park 100 Foods Inc
326 E Adams St
Tipton IN 46072
765 675-3480

(G-9094)
PARK EMBROIDERY DESIGNS LLC
5230 Park Emerson Dr Ste L (46203-6936)
PHONE.................................317 780-1515
Amy Park, *Managing Member*
Steven Park, *Pt*
EMP: 3 **EST:** 2009
SALES (est): 233.13K **Privately Held**
Web: www.parkembroiderydesigns.com
SIC: 2395 Embroidery products, except Schiffli machine

(G-9095)
PARTS CLEANING TECH LLC
2263 Distributors Dr (46241-5004)
PHONE.................................317 243-4205
Roy Richards, *Mgr*
EMP: 3
SALES (corp-wide): 9.18MM **Privately Held**
Web: www.partscleaningtech.com
SIC: 2842 Cleaning or polishing preparations, nec
PA: Parts Cleaning Technologies, Llc
26400 Capitol
Redford MI 48239
313 952-2646

(G-9096)
PASTELERIA GRESIL LLC
5348 W 38th St (46254-2916)
PHONE.................................317 299-8801
Silvia Y Gordon, *Prin*
EMP: 8 **EST:** 2007
SALES (est): 425.73K **Privately Held**
Web: www.orderpasteleriagresilllc.com
SIC: 2051 Cakes, bakery: except frozen

(G-9097)
PATCHWORK COSTUMES LLC
Also Called: Patchwork Costumes
6091 Parrington Dr (46236-6312)
PHONE.................................317 750-6162
Andrew Spencer, *Managing Member*
EMP: 2 **EST:** 2019
SALES (est): 114.3K **Privately Held**
Web: www.patchworkcostumes.com
SIC: 8999 2389 7922 Services, nec; Costumes; Costume design, theatrical

(G-9098)
PATH BRIGHT PUBLICATIONS LLC
9801 Fall Creek Rd Ste 115 (46256-4802)
PHONE.................................888 505-6780
Tammy Leroy, *Pr*
EMP: 4 **EST:** 2017
SALES (est): 42.42K **Privately Held**
Web: www.brightpathpublications.com
SIC: 2741 Miscellaneous publishing

(G-9099)
PATHFINDER CUTTING TECH LLC
5623 W 74th St (46278-1753)
PHONE.................................424 342-9723
Martin Morison, *Pr*
EMP: 10 **EST:** 2015
SALES (est): 1.07MM **Privately Held**
Web: www.pathfindercut.com
SIC: 5084 3111 3541 Industrial machinery and equipment; Cutting of leather; Machine tool replacement & repair parts, metal cutting types

(G-9100)
PATHFINDER SCHOOL LLC (PA)
Also Called: Self Reliance Outfitters
6050 Churchman Byp (46203-6064)
PHONE.................................317 791-8777
EMP: 6 **EST:** 2010
SALES (est): 2.47MM
SALES (corp-wide): 2.47MM **Privately Held**
Web: www.selfrelianceoutfitters.com
SIC: 8211 3949 Public adult education school ; Camping equipment and supplies

(G-9101)
PATRIOT SOFTWARE SOLUTIONS INC
1311 W 96th St Ste 220 (46260-1173)
PHONE.................................317 573-5431
Scott Martin, *Pr*
Pamela Marra, *Corporate Secretary*
EMP: 5 **EST:** 2001
SQ FT: 1,500
SALES (est): 388.41K **Privately Held**
Web: www.sentinelmembership.com
SIC: 7372 Business oriented computer software

(G-9102)
PATTERN INC
941 N Meridian St (46204-1012)
PHONE.................................317 733-8302
Polina Osherov, *Ex Dir*
EMP: 1 **EST:** 2016
SALES (est): 451.62K **Privately Held**
Web: www.patternindy.com
SIC: 2741 Miscellaneous publishing

(G-9103)
PAVER RESCUE INC
9386 Castlegate Dr (46256-1001)
PHONE.................................317 259-4880
Parker Weber, *Prin*
EMP: 2 **EST:** 2011
SALES (est): 436.95K **Privately Held**
Web: www.paverrescue.com
SIC: 3531 Pavers

(G-9104)
PAVERS INC
2900 N County Road 900 E (46234)
PHONE.................................317 271-0823
EMP: 2
SIC: 3272 Concrete products, precast, nec
PA: Pavers Inc.
4181 S Us Highway 231
Freedom IN 47431

(G-9105)
PAVING PLUS COMPANY
3541 Brehob Rd (46217-3211)
PHONE.................................317 784-1857
EMP: 1 **EST:** 1993
SALES (est): 120.05K **Privately Held**
SIC: 1611 2951 1799 1629 Surfacing and paving; Asphalt paving mixtures and blocks ; Parking lot maintenance; Tennis court construction

(G-9106)
PAX CUSTOM WOODWORKING LLC
8418 Castle Farms Rd (46256-3447)
PHONE.................................805 300-3720
Robert Scott Leming Ii, *Prin*
EMP: 5 **EST:** 2019
SALES (est): 54.13K **Privately Held**
Web: www.paxwoodworking.com
SIC: 2431 Millwork

(G-9107)
PB & J FACTORY LLC
1220 Waterway Blvd (46202-2157)
PHONE.................................317 504-4714
Samuel Campbell, *Managing Member*
EMP: 3 **EST:** 2020
SALES (est): 93K **Privately Held**
Web: www.pbandjfactory.com
SIC: 2099 5812 Sandwiches, assembled and packaged: for wholesale market; Sandwiches and submarines shop

Indianapolis - Marion County (G-9108) GEOGRAPHIC SECTION

(G-9108)
PCA PUBLISHING INC
8845 Jackson St (46231-1147)
PHONE..................317 658-2055
John Lee Couch, *Owner*
EMP: 5 **EST:** 2011
SALES (est): 37.69K **Privately Held**
SIC: 2741 Music book and sheet music publishing

(G-9109)
PD KANGAROO INC
1241 N New Jersey St (46202-2619)
PHONE..................317 417-7143
EMP: 4 **EST:** 2018
SALES (est): 74.57K **Privately Held**
SIC: 2086 Bottled and canned soft drinks

(G-9110)
PEARSON EDUCATION INC
Also Called: Financial Times-Prentice Hall
800 E 96th St Ste 300 (46240-3759)
PHONE..................317 428-3049
EMP: 15
SALES (corp-wide): 4.58B **Privately Held**
Web: www.pearsonitcertification.com
SIC: 2731 Books, publishing and printing
HQ: Pearson Education, Inc.
221 River St
Hoboken NJ 07030
201 236-7000

(G-9111)
PEER FOODS GROUP INC
1825 Stout Field Ter (46241-4028)
PHONE..................317 735-4283
EMP: 3
SALES (corp-wide): 54.3MM **Privately Held**
Web: www.peerfoods.com
SIC: 2011 Meat packing plants
PA: Peer Foods Group, Inc.
1200 W 35th St Fl 3
Chicago IL 60609
773 927-1440

(G-9112)
PEERVIEW DATA INC
5255 Winthrop Ave (46220-3573)
PHONE..................317 238-3234
Glenn Dunlap, *CEO*
EMP: 7 **EST:** 2017
SALES (est): 281.13K **Privately Held**
Web: app.peerviewdata.com
SIC: 3652 Prerecorded records and tapes

(G-9113)
PEN & PINK
2435 Shelby St (46203-4286)
PHONE..................317 372-6465
EMP: 5 **EST:** 2016
SALES (est): 57.58K **Privately Held**
Web: penandpinkvintage.square.site
SIC: 2741 Miscellaneous publishing

(G-9114)
PENN & BEECH CANDLE CO
1219 N New Jersey St (46202-2619)
PHONE..................317 645-8732
EMP: 8 **EST:** 2017
SALES (est): 72.18K **Privately Held**
Web: www.pennandbeech.com
SIC: 3999 Candles

(G-9115)
PENN-MAR CAPITAL LLC
10475 Crosspoint Blvd Ste 250 (46256)
PHONE..................463 239-2632
Gregory Harris, *Ex Dir*
EMP: 1 **EST:** 2019
SALES (est): 355.1K **Privately Held**
SIC: 6799 6211 1389 Commodity investors; Syndicate shares (real estate, entertainment, equip.) sales; Oil consultants

(G-9116)
PENTERA GROUP INC
921 E 86th St Ste 100 (46240-1841)
PHONE..................317 543-2055
Judith Cohn, *Pr*
Kim Trittin, *Treas*
EMP: 22 **EST:** 1975
SQ FT: 2,500
SALES (est): 473.28K **Privately Held**
Web: www.pgiresources.com
SIC: 2741 Miscellaneous publishing

(G-9117)
PEPSI 3449
Also Called: Pepsico
5510 Exploration Dr (46241-9007)
PHONE..................317 760-7335
EMP: 11 **EST:** 2019
SALES (est): 2.84MM **Privately Held**
Web: www.pepsico.com
SIC: 2086 Carbonated soft drinks, bottled and canned

(G-9118)
PEPSICO
Also Called: Pepsico
5858 Decatur Blvd (46241-9575)
PHONE..................317 821-6400
▲ **EMP:** 140 **EST:** 1890
SALES (est): 48.33MM
SALES (corp-wide): 86.39B **Publicly Held**
Web: www.pepsico.com
SIC: 2086 Carbonated soft drinks, bottled and canned
PA: Pepsico, Inc.
700 Anderson Hill Rd
Purchase NY 10577
914 253-2000

(G-9119)
PEPSICO INC
9101 Orly Rd (46241-9605)
PHONE..................317 830-4011
EMP: 4
SALES (corp-wide): 86.39B **Publicly Held**
Web: www.pepsico.com
SIC: 2086 2096 2087 2037 Carbonated soft drinks, bottled and canned; Potato chips and similar snacks; Flavoring extracts and syrups, nec; Frozen fruits and vegetables
PA: Pepsico, Inc.
700 Anderson Hill Rd
Purchase NY 10577
914 253-2000

(G-9120)
PERFECT APPAREL LLC
8443 Flatwood Ct (46278-9593)
PHONE..................317 389-5553
EMP: 6 **EST:** 2018
SALES (est): 392.35K **Privately Held**
Web: www.perfectapparel.com
SIC: 2759 Letterpress and screen printing

(G-9121)
PERFECT IMPRESSIONS PRINTING
Also Called: Interchurch Print Shop
3901 N Meridian St Ste 15 (46208-4026)
P.O. Box 90311 (46290-0311)
PHONE..................317 923-1756
Debbie S Smith, *Owner*
EMP: 6 **EST:** 1979
SQ FT: 1,500
SALES (est): 484.72K **Privately Held**
SIC: 2752 7334 Offset printing; Photocopying and duplicating services

(G-9122)
PERFECT MANUFACTURING LLC
450 W 16th Pl (46202-1167)
PHONE..................317 924-5284
EMP: 6 **EST:** 2008
SALES (est): 1.05MM **Privately Held**
Web: www.perfectpallets.com
SIC: 3089 Pallets, plastics
PA: Perfect Pallets, Inc.
450 W 16th Pl
Indianapolis IN 46202

(G-9123)
PERFECT PALLETS INC (PA)
450 W 16th Pl (46202-1167)
PHONE..................888 553-5559
EMP: 19 **EST:** 1991
SQ FT: 50,000
SALES (est): 9.26MM **Privately Held**
Web: www.perfectpallets.com
SIC: 2448 Pallets, wood

(G-9124)
PERFECTA USA
Also Called: Absolute Printing Equipment
5505 S Franklin Rd (46239-9646)
PHONE..................317 862-7371
Paul Myer, *Pr*
Brett Stow, *Asst VP*
▲ **EMP:** 10 **EST:** 2004
SALES (est): 409.74K **Privately Held**
Web: www.perfectausa.com
SIC: 3555 Printing trades machinery

(G-9125)
PERFORMERS EDITION LLC
Also Called: Performer's Edition
230 E Ohio St (46204-2160)
PHONE..................317 429-1300
Mark Schuster, *Owner*
EMP: 1 **EST:** 2010
SALES (est): 21.88K **Privately Held**
Web: www.performersedition.com
SIC: 2731 2741 7389 Book music: publishing and printing; Music book and sheet music publishing; Business services, nec

(G-9126)
PERMA LUBRICATION
2346 S Lynhurst Dr Ste J (46241-8621)
PHONE..................317 241-0797
Exel Woodcock, *Mgr*
EMP: 3 **EST:** 2011
SALES (est): 132.78K **Privately Held**
Web: www.permausa.com
SIC: 7514 3569 Passenger car rental; Lubricating equipment

(G-9127)
PERQ CONVERT LLC ✪
5868 E 71st St Ste E-672 (46220-4075)
PHONE..................800 873-3117
Scott Hill, *Managing Member*
EMP: 90 **EST:** 2022
SALES (est): 2.67MM **Privately Held**
Web: www.perq.com
SIC: 7372 Prepackaged software

(G-9128)
PERQ MULTIFAMILY SOFTWARE LLC ✪
5868 E 71st St Ste E-672 (46220-4075)
PHONE..................800 873-3117
Scott Hill, *Managing Member*
EMP: 90 **EST:** 2022
SALES (est): 2.5MM **Privately Held**
SIC: 7372 Prepackaged software

(G-9129)
PETNET INDIANA LLC
1345 W 16th St Rm 1 (46202-2111)
PHONE..................865 218-2000
EMP: 23
SALES (est): 713.83K
SALES (corp-wide): 89.68B **Privately Held**
SIC: 2835 Radioactive diagnostic substances
HQ: Petnet Solutions, Inc.
810 Innovation Dr
Knoxville TN 37932
865 218-2000

(G-9130)
PETROCHOICE HOLDINGS INC
Also Called: Miller Industrial Fluids
1751 W Raymond St (46221-2025)
PHONE..................317 634-7300
Ross Smith, *Genl Mgr*
EMP: 25
SALES (corp-wide): 676.37MM **Privately Held**
Web: www.petrochoice.com
SIC: 2992 5172 Oils and greases, blending and compounding; Lubricating oils and greases
PA: Petrochoice Holdings, Inc.
933 1st Ave
King Of Prussia PA 19406
267 705-2015

(G-9131)
PFM CAR & TRUCK CASTLETON INC
Also Called: Pfm Car & Truck Care
9501 Corporation Dr (46256-1033)
PHONE..................317 577-7777
John S Neely, *Pr*
EMP: 28 **EST:** 2005
SQ FT: 12,000
SALES (est): 3.84MM **Privately Held**
Web: www.greatwater360autocare.com
SIC: 5013 7534 7538 Motor vehicle supplies and new parts; Tire retreading and repair shops; General automotive repair shops

(G-9132)
PFM ONSITE SERVICES INC
Also Called: Pfm Onsite
1402 W Hanna Ave (46217-5129)
PHONE..................317 784-7777
John Neely, *Pr*
EMP: 6 **EST:** 2017
SALES (est): 558.6K **Privately Held**
Web: www.greatwater360autocare.com
SIC: 5013 7534 7538 Motor vehicle supplies and new parts; Tire retreading and repair shops; Engine repair

(G-9133)
PFORTUNE ART & DESIGN INC
Also Called: Pfortune Art & Design
9549 Valparaiso Ct (46268-1130)
PHONE..................317 872-4123
EMP: 2 **EST:** 1996
SQ FT: 1,800
SALES (est): 200.43K **Privately Held**
Web: www.pfortuneart.com
SIC: 2499 5999 Picture frame molding, finished; Art dealers

(G-9134)
PHIL IRWIN ADVERTISING INC
Also Called: Ad-Sign & Display Division
5995 E 30th St (46218-3317)
PHONE..................317 547-5117
Phil Irwin, *Pr*
Phil Irwin Junior, *VP*
Pamela Polovich, *Off Mgr*
EMP: 10 **EST:** 1945
SQ FT: 12,000
SALES (est): 700K **Privately Held**

GEOGRAPHIC SECTION
Indianapolis - Marion County (G-9158)

SIC: **2759** 7359 Screen printing; Tent and tarpaulin rental

(G-9135)
PHILIPS ULTRASOUND INC
Also Called: A T L
7518 E 39th St (46226-5164)
PHONE.....................317 591-5242
Dan Tallent, *Prin*
EMP: 10
SALES (corp-wide): 18.51B **Privately Held**
Web: usa.philips.com
SIC: **3841** Surgical and medical instruments
HQ: Philips Ultrasound Llc
   22100 Bothell Everett Hwy
   Bothell WA 98021
   800 982-2011

(G-9136)
PHILLIP D KENNEDY PUBLISHING
Also Called: Phyllis Kennedy Hardware
9256 Holyoke Ct (46268-1237)
PHONE.....................317 872-6366
Phillip D Kennedy, *Prin*
EMP: 1 EST: 1989
SALES (est): 40.63K **Privately Held**
SIC: **2731** Books, publishing only

(G-9137)
PHILLIPS FEED SERVICE INC
Also Called: Phillips Pet Food & Supplies
1936 S Lynhurst Dr, Indianapolis, In 46241, United States. (46241)
PHONE.....................610 250-2099
EMP: 38
SALES (corp-wide): 471MM **Privately Held**
Web: www.phillipspet.com
SIC: **2047** Dog and cat food
PA: Phillips Feed Service, Inc.
   3747 Hecktown Rd
   Easton PA 18045
   800 451-2817

(G-9138)
PHOENIX BRANDS LLC (PA)
2601 Fortune Cir E Ste 102b (46241-5523)
PHONE.....................203 975-0319
Sanjiv Mehra, *Managing Member*
◆ EMP: 10 EST: 2003
SQ FT: 7,000
SALES (est): 5.71MM
SALES (corp-wide): 5.71MM **Privately Held**
SIC: **2841** Soap and other detergents

(G-9139)
PHOENIX SIGN WORKS INC
5345 Lexington Ave (46219-7025)
PHONE.....................317 432-4027
Hal Paul, *Pr*
EMP: 9 EST: 2010
SALES (est): 518.21K **Privately Held**
Web: www.phoenixsignworks.com
SIC: **3993** Electric signs

(G-9140)
PHOTO SCREEN SERVICE INC
1505 Southeastern Ave (46201-3980)
PHONE.....................317 636-7712
Brian M Chambers, *Pr*
Sebrina Chambers, *Sec*
EMP: 5 EST: 1948
SQ FT: 8,000
SALES (est): 381.54K **Privately Held**
Web: photo-screen-services-inc.business.site
SIC: **2759** Screen printing

(G-9141)
PIEZOTECH LLC (HQ)
Also Called: Meggitt Sensing Systems
8431 Georgetown Rd Ste 300 (46268-5628)
PHONE.....................317 876-4670
John Jaqua, *CEO*
Joseph Lehr, *VP*
Michael Phillips, *VP*
John Jaqua Junior, *Sec*
Richard D Barton, *CEO*
EMP: 30 EST: 1968
SQ FT: 30,000
SALES (est): 11.15MM
SALES (corp-wide): 12.55B **Publicly Held**
Web: www.piezotechnologies.com
SIC: **3829** Measuring and controlling devices, nec
PA: Amphenol Corporation
   358 Hall Ave
   Wallingford CT 06492
   203 265-8900

(G-9142)
PIN POINT AV LLC
8226 Kentallen Ct (46236-8380)
PHONE.....................317 750-3120
Dave Anderson, *Prin*
EMP: 6 EST: 2009
SALES (est): 60.28K **Privately Held**
SIC: **3452** Pins

(G-9143)
PINNACLE EQUIPMENT COMPANY INC
1616 Milburn St (46202)
P.O. Box 88637 (46208)
PHONE.....................317 259-1180
EMP: 10 EST: 1997
SQ FT: 11,000
SALES (est): 13.49MM **Privately Held**
Web: www.pinnaclequipment.com
SIC: **3444** Sheet metalwork

(G-9144)
PINNACLE OIL HOLDINGS LLC
8175 Allison Ave (46268-1648)
PHONE.....................317 875-9465
John Fought, *Mgr*
EMP: 105
SQ FT: 300,000
Web: www.pinnacleoil.com
SIC: **2992** 5172 8742 Lubricating oils and greases; Lubricating oils and greases; Marketing consulting services
PA: Pinnacle Oil Holdings, Llc
   5009 W 81st St
   Indianapolis IN 46268

(G-9145)
PINNACLE OIL HOLDINGS LLC (PA)
Also Called: Pinnacle Oil
5009 W 81st St (46268-1639)
PHONE.....................317 875-9465
EMP: 26 EST: 2008
SQ FT: 150,000
SALES (est): 96.03MM **Privately Held**
Web: www.pinnacleoil.com
SIC: **2992** 8742 5172 Lubricating oils and greases; Marketing consulting services; Lubricating oils and greases

(G-9146)
PINNACLE OIL INC
Also Called: Pinnacle Oil
5009 W 81st St (46268-1639)
PHONE.....................317 875-9465
▲ EMP: 101
SIC: **2992** Lubricating oils and greases

(G-9147)
PINNACLE OIL TRADING LLC
5009 W 81st St (46268-1639)
PHONE.....................317 875-9465
EMP: 24 EST: 2015
SALES (est): 12MM **Privately Held**
Web: www.pinnacleoil.com
SIC: **1389** Gas field services, nec
PA: Pinnacle Oil Holdings, Llc
   5009 W 81st St
   Indianapolis IN 46268

(G-9148)
PITNEY BOWES INC
Also Called: Pitney Bowes
5071 W 74th St (46268-5112)
PHONE.....................260 436-7395
Ed Oreily, *Mgr*
EMP: 8
SALES (corp-wide): 3.27B **Publicly Held**
Web: www.pitneybowes.com
SIC: **3579** 7359 Postage meters; Business machine and electronic equipment rental services
PA: Pitney Bowes Inc.
   3001 Summer St
   Stamford CT 06926
   203 356-5000

(G-9149)
PIZO OPERATING COMPANY LLC
7901 W Morris St (46231-1366)
PHONE.....................317 243-0811
EMP: 28 EST: 2007
SALES (est): 2.45MM
SALES (corp-wide): 452.34MM **Privately Held**
SIC: **3312** Hoops, iron and steel
HQ: Heritage Environmental Services, Llc
   6510 Telecom Dr Ste 400
   Indianapolis IN 46278
   317 243-0811

(G-9150)
PLASTIC ASSEMBLY TECH INC
8445 Castlewood Dr Ste B (46250-4570)
PHONE.....................317 841-1202
Gary Clodfelter, *Pr*
Mary Clodfelter, *VP*
EMP: 6 EST: 1986
SQ FT: 5,500
SALES (est): 1.09MM **Privately Held**
Web: www.patsonics.com
SIC: **5047** 3845 Medical equipment and supplies; Electromedical equipment

(G-9151)
PLASTIC RECYCLING INC (PA)
7601 Rockville Rd (46214-3102)
PHONE.....................317 780-6100
Alan R Shaw, *Pr*
Robert L Faris Junior, *Sec*
◆ EMP: 45 EST: 1988
SALES (est): 26.57MM **Privately Held**
Web: www.plastic-recycling.net
SIC: **4953** 2821 Recycling, waste materials; Plastics materials and resins

(G-9152)
PLASTIC TOP FABRICATORS INC
1302 W Troy Ave (46225-2252)
PHONE.....................317 786-4367
Mark Mounsey, *Pr*
EMP: 6 EST: 1974
SALES (est): 493.86K **Privately Held**
SIC: **2541** Table or counter tops, plastic laminated

(G-9153)
PLASTICS FAMILY HOLDINGS INC
Also Called: Laird Plastics
3439 N Shadeland Ave Ste 5 (46226)
PHONE.....................317 890-1808
Matthew Ward, *Brnch Mgr*
EMP: 6
Web: www.lairdplastics.com
SIC: **3089** 5162 Windows, plastics; Plastics film
HQ: Plastics Family Holdings, Inc.
   5800 Cmpus Cir Dr E Ste 1
   Irving TX 75063
   469 299-7000

(G-9154)
PLATINUM DISPLAY GROUP
5855 Kopetsky Dr (46217-9635)
PHONE.....................317 731-5026
Adam Lickliter, *Pr*
EMP: 5 EST: 2011
SALES (est): 400.36K **Privately Held**
SIC: **2541** Store fixtures, wood

(G-9155)
PLUM GROUP INC (HQ)
Also Called: Plum Voice
101 W Washington St (46204-3407)
PHONE.....................617 712-3000
Andrew Kuan, *CEO*
Matthew Ervin, *Pr*
Joel Fan, *Dir*
David Liptak, *Dir*
▲ EMP: 10 EST: 2000
SALES (est): 8.49MM
SALES (corp-wide): 11.67MM **Privately Held**
Web: www.plumvoice.com
SIC: **7299** 4813 8742 7372 Information services, consumer; Voice telephone communications; Automation and robotics consultant; Business oriented computer software
PA: Sharpen Technologies Inc.
   101 W Wa St Ste 600e
   Indianapolis IN 46204
   855 249-3357

(G-9156)
PLZ CORP
6501 Julian Ave (46219-6603)
PHONE.....................317 788-0750
David Moskal, *Brnch Mgr*
EMP: 58
SALES (corp-wide): 766.3MM **Privately Held**
Web: www.plzcorp.com
SIC: **2844** Perfumes, cosmetics and other toilet preparations
PA: Plz Corp.
   2651 Wrrnvlle Rd Stre 300 300 Stre
   Downers Grove IL 60515
   630 628-3000

(G-9157)
PODFAN LLC
6507 Carrollton Ave (46220-1877)
PHONE.....................317 771-0475
EMP: 1 EST: 2020
SALES (est): 32.77K **Privately Held**
SIC: **7372** Application computer software

(G-9158)
POINT BIOPHARMA GLOBAL INC (HQ)
4850 W 78th St (46268-2385)
PHONE.....................317 543-9957
Joe Mccann, *CEO*
Allan C Silber, *Ex Ch Bd*
Bill Demers, *CFO*
Neil Fleshner, *CMO*

Indianapolis - Marion County (G-9159)

Jessica Jensen, *Ex VP*
EMP: 10 **EST:** 2019
SQ FT: 10,500
SALES (est): 226.58MM
SALES (corp-wide): 34.12B **Publicly Held**
Web: www.lilly.com
SIC: 2834 Pharmaceutical preparations
PA: Eli Lilly And Company
  1 Lilly Corporate Ctr
  Indianapolis IN 46285
  317 276-2000

(G-9159)
POINT BIOPHARMA INC
4850 W 78th St (46268-2385)
PHONE.................................833 544-2637
Joe Mccann, *CEO*
EMP: 31 **EST:** 2020
SQ FT: 13,500
SALES (est): 7.5MM
SALES (corp-wide): 34.12B **Publicly Held**
Web: www.lilly.com
SIC: 2834 Pharmaceutical preparations
HQ: Point Biopharma Global Inc.
  4850 W 78th St
  Indianapolis IN 46268
  317 543-9957

(G-9160)
POINT BIOPHARMA USA INC
4850 W 78th St (46268-2385)
PHONE.................................317 543-9957
Joe Mccann, *CEO*
Bill Demers, *CFO*
EMP: 2 **EST:** 2020
SALES (est): 1.25MM
SALES (corp-wide): 34.12B **Publicly Held**
Web: www.pointbiopharma.com
SIC: 2834 Pharmaceutical preparations
HQ: Point Biopharma Global Inc.
  4850 W 78th St
  Indianapolis IN 46268
  317 543-9957

(G-9161)
POLYMATH PUBLISHING LLC
6043 N Oxford St (46220-2923)
PHONE.................................317 410-5551
Katherine Shoup, *Prin*
EMP: 5 **EST:** 2016
SALES (est): 76.92K **Privately Held**
SIC: 2741 Miscellaneous publishing

(G-9162)
POPCORN WEAVER MFG LLC (PA)
Also Called: Trail's End Popcorn Company
9365 Counselors Row (46240-6422)
PHONE.................................765 934-2101
Jason Kashman, *CEO*
Michael E Weaver, *
Rebecca Weaver, *
William M Weaver, *
Welcome I Weaver, *
◆ **EMP:** 150 **EST:** 1928
SALES (est): 472.42MM
SALES (corp-wide): 472.42MM **Privately Held**
Web: www.weaverpopcorn.com
SIC: 4213 5145 2096 Trucking, except local; Popcorn and supplies; Popcorn, already popped (except candy covered)

(G-9163)
POPGUNS INC
30 S Post Rd (46219-6808)
PHONE.................................317 897-8660
Michael Hilton, *Pr*
EMP: 8 **EST:** 2000
SALES (est): 131.97K **Privately Held**
SIC: 3949 5099 5941 Ammunition belts, sporting type; Ammunition, except sporting; Ammunition

(G-9164)
PORTABLE WELDING SOLUTIONS
805 Olin Ave (46222-3239)
PHONE.................................714 381-1690
Brenden Wethington, *Prin*
EMP: 4 **EST:** 2018
SALES (est): 25.09K **Privately Held**
Web: portableweldingsolutions.weebly.com
SIC: 7692 Welding repair

(G-9165)
POSTERS 2 PRINTS LLC (PA)
9900 Westpoint Dr Ste 138 (46256-3338)
PHONE.................................800 598-5837
EMP: 5 **EST:** 2008
SALES (est): 434.31K **Privately Held**
Web: www.posters2prints.com
SIC: 2752 Commercial printing, lithographic

(G-9166)
POSTERS 2 PRINTS LLC
10428 Starboard Way (46256-9514)
PHONE.................................317 414-8972
EMP: 22
Web: www.posters2prints.com
SIC: 2752 Commercial printing, lithographic
PA: Posters 2 Prints, Llc
  9900 Westpoint Dr Ste 138
  Indianapolis IN 46256

(G-9167)
POWER TRAIN CORP FORT WAYNE (PA)
2334 Production Dr (46241-4990)
PHONE.................................317 241-9393
TOLL FREE: 800
Lyle Bass, *Pr*
Joe Leffel, *Sec*
Bob Biggs, *VP*
EMP: 16 **EST:** 1984
SALES (est): 4.11MM
SALES (corp-wide): 4.11MM **Privately Held**
SIC: 5015 3714 3446 Motor vehicle parts, used; Motor vehicle parts and accessories; Architectural metalwork

(G-9168)
PPG ARCHITECTURAL FINISHES INC
Also Called: Glidden Professional Paint Ctr
1435 Brookville Way Ste E (46239-1037)
PHONE.................................317 634-2547
Steve Fink, *Dist Mgr*
EMP: 7
SALES (corp-wide): 17.65B **Publicly Held**
Web: www.ppgpaints.com
SIC: 2851 Paints and allied products
HQ: Ppg Architectural Finishes, Inc.
  1 Ppg Pl
  Pittsburgh PA 15272
  412 434-3131

(G-9169)
PPG ARCHITECTURAL FINISHES INC
Also Called: Glidden Professional Paint Ctr
7025 Madison Ave (46227-5203)
PHONE.................................317 787-9393
Ricky Mitchel, *Mgr*
EMP: 7
SALES (corp-wide): 17.65B **Publicly Held**
Web: www.ppgpaints.com
SIC: 2851 Paints and allied products
HQ: Ppg Architectural Finishes, Inc.
  1 Ppg Pl
  Pittsburgh PA 15272

(G-9170)
PPG HOLDINGS INC
Also Called: Precision Products Group
8770 Guion Rd Ste A (46268)
PHONE.................................317 663-4590
David Hooe, *CEO*
EMP: 9 **EST:** 2013
SALES (est): 714.48K **Privately Held**
Web: www.ppgintl.com
SIC: 2851 Paints and allied products

(G-9171)
PPG INDUSTRIES INC
Also Called: PPG 4363
2311 E 53rd St (46220-3429)
PHONE.................................317 251-9494
Roy Moore, *Brnch Mgr*
EMP: 2
SALES (corp-wide): 17.65B **Publicly Held**
Web: www.ppgpaints.com
SIC: 2851 Paints and allied products
PA: Ppg Industries, Inc.
  1 Ppg Pl
  Pittsburgh PA 15272
  412 434-3131

(G-9172)
PPG INDUSTRIES INC
Also Called: PPG 4361
952 N Delaware St (46202-3375)
PHONE.................................317 267-0511
Douglas Ve, *Brnch Mgr*
EMP: 4
SALES (corp-wide): 17.65B **Publicly Held**
Web: www.ppg.com
SIC: 2851 Paints and allied products
PA: Ppg Industries, Inc.
  1 Ppg Pl
  Pittsburgh PA 15272
  412 434-3131

(G-9173)
PPG INDUSTRIES INC
Also Called: PPG 4365
10009 E Washington St (46229-2623)
PHONE.................................317 897-3836
Jim Skweres, *Mgr*
EMP: 4
SALES (corp-wide): 17.65B **Publicly Held**
Web: www.ppg.com
SIC: 2851 Paints and allied products
PA: Ppg Industries, Inc.
  1 Ppg Pl
  Pittsburgh PA 15272
  412 434-3131

(G-9174)
PPG INDUSTRIES INC
Also Called: PPG 4364
7025 Madison Ave (46227-5203)
PHONE.................................317 787-9393
Kevin Lannan, *Brnch Mgr*
EMP: 4
SALES (corp-wide): 17.65B **Publicly Held**
Web: www.ppg.com
SIC: 2851 Paints and allied products
PA: Ppg Industries, Inc.
  1 Ppg Pl
  Pittsburgh PA 15272
  412 434-3131

(G-9175)
PPG INDUSTRIES INC
Also Called: PPG 5547
6951 E 30th St Ste E (46219-1190)
PHONE.................................317 546-5714
Nathan Pittman, *Mgr*
EMP: 4
SALES (corp-wide): 17.65B **Publicly Held**
Web: www.ppgpaints.com
SIC: 2851 Paints and allied products
PA: Ppg Industries, Inc.
  1 Ppg Pl
  Pittsburgh PA 15272
  412 434-3131

(G-9176)
PRATT VISUAL SOLUTIONS COMPANY
3035 N Shadeland Ave (46226-6200)
PHONE.................................800 428-7728
EMP: 50 **EST:** 2012
SQ FT: 50,000
SALES (est): 5.47MM
SALES (corp-wide): 258.06MM **Privately Held**
Web: www.pratt.com
SIC: 2759 Commercial printing, nec
PA: Vomela Specialty Company
  845 Minnehaha Ave E
  Saint Paul MN 55106
  651 228-2200

(G-9177)
PRC - DESOTO INTERNATIONAL INC
Also Called: PPG Aerospace
6022 Corporate Way (46278-2923)
PHONE.................................317 290-1600
Roald Johanssan, *Brnch Mgr*
EMP: 37
SALES (corp-wide): 17.65B **Publicly Held**
Web: guide13227.guidechem.com
SIC: 2891 3089 Sealing compounds, synthetic rubber or plastic; Plastics containers, except foam
HQ: Prc - Desoto International, Inc.
  24811 Ave Rockefeller
  Valencia CA 91355
  661 678-4209

(G-9178)
PRECISELY WRITE INC
9801 Fall Creek Rd # 202 (46256-4802)
PHONE.................................317 585-7701
Ruth Nickolich, *Pr*
EMP: 3 **EST:** 1996
SQ FT: 1,240
SALES (est): 352.21K **Privately Held**
Web: www.precisely.com
SIC: 2741 7338 8999 Technical manual and paper publishing; Editing service; Technical writing

(G-9179)
PRECISION CADCAM INCORPORATED
8446 Brookville Rd (46239-9491)
PHONE.................................317 353-8058
Darryl G Williams, *Pr*
EMP: 1 **EST:** 2004
SQ FT: 800
SALES (est): 184.92K **Privately Held**
Web: www.pccinc.org
SIC: 3599 Machine shop, jobbing and repair

(G-9180)
PRECISION CAMS INC
Also Called: State Gear Co.
522 S Harding St (46221-1137)
PHONE.................................317 634-3521
EMP: 5
SALES (corp-wide): 2.5MM **Privately Held**
Web: www.pcimachining.com
SIC: 3545 Cams (machine tool accessories)
PA: Precision Cams, Inc.
  3619 S Arlington Ave
  Indianapolis IN 46203
  317 631-9100

GEOGRAPHIC SECTION

Indianapolis - Marion County (G-9207)

(G-9181)
PRECISION CAMS INC (PA)
Also Called: Enviropeel USA
3510 E Raymond St (46203)
PHONE...................317 631-9100
Kenneth L Boehm, *Pr*
EMP: 15 **EST:** 1962
SALES (est): 2.5MM
SALES (corp-wide): 2.5MM **Privately Held**
Web: www.pcimachining.com
SIC: 3599 Machine shop, jobbing and repair

(G-9182)
PRECISION CRYOGENIC SYSTEMS
7804 Rockville Rd (46214-3105)
PHONE...................317 273-2800
Roy Larrison, *Pr*
Richard Gummer, *VP*
Paul Coverdale, *VP Opers*
EMP: 15 **EST:** 1982
SQ FT: 7,000
SALES (est): 2.07MM **Privately Held**
Web: www.precisioncryo.com
SIC: 3443 Cryogenic tanks, for liquids and gases

(G-9183)
PRECISION POLISHING & BUFFING
1038 S Kealing Ave (46203-1516)
PHONE...................317 352-0165
EMP: 8 **EST:** 1995
SQ FT: 17,850
SALES (est): 797.69K **Privately Held**
Web: www.precisionpolishingandbuffing.com
SIC: 3471 Electroplating of metals or formed products

(G-9184)
PRECISION PRODUCTS GROUP INC (PA)
Also Called: Paramount Tube Division
8770 Guion Rd Ste A (46268-3017)
PHONE...................317 663-4590
Chad Heathco, *Pr*
▲ **EMP:** 10 **EST:** 1992
SALES (est): 49.54MM **Privately Held**
Web: www.ppgintl.com
SIC: 3082 3565 5113 7389 Tubes, unsupported plastics; Packaging machinery ; Paper tubes and cores; Packaging and labeling services

(G-9185)
PRECISION RINGS INCORPORATED
5611 Progress Rd (46241-4332)
P.O. Box 421189 (46242-1189)
PHONE...................317 247-4786
Jay S Crannell, *Ch Bd*
Joseph L Crannell, *Pr*
Deedee Crannell, *Sec*
EMP: 50 **EST:** 1950
SQ FT: 49,000
SALES (est): 9.18MM **Privately Held**
Web: www.precisionrings.com
SIC: 3592 Pistons and piston rings

(G-9186)
PRECISION RUBBER PLATE CO INC
5620 Elmwood Ave (46203-6029)
PHONE...................317 783-3226
Lawrence R Green, *Pr*
Manuel S Green, *
James A Green, *
Susan Green, *
▲ **EMP:** 59 **EST:** 1938
SQ FT: 36,000
SALES (est): 9.51MM **Privately Held**
Web: www.prpgraphics.com
SIC: 3555 Printing plates

(G-9187)
PRECISION TUBES INC
Also Called: Penn Tool
5730 Kopetsky Dr Ste C (46217-9006)
PHONE...................317 783-2339
Richard E Warren, *Pr*
Patricia Warren, *Sec*
EMP: 5 **EST:** 1974
SALES (est): 400K **Privately Held**
Web: www.penntoolco.com
SIC: 3544 7692 3545 Special dies and tools; Welding repair; Machine tool accessories

(G-9188)
PREFERRED PPLTION HLTH MGT LLC
9951 Crosspoint Blvd Ste 300 (46256)
PHONE...................317 245-7482
James Vandagrifft, *CEO*
EMP: 1 **EST:** 2014
SALES (est): 58.05K **Privately Held**
Web: www.preferredphm.com
SIC: 7372 Business oriented computer software

(G-9189)
PREFERRED PRINT
6220 Hardegan St (46227-4907)
PHONE...................317 371-8829
EMP: 5 **EST:** 2011
SALES (est): 161.48K **Privately Held**
Web: www.preferredprint.com
SIC: 2752 Offset printing

(G-9190)
PREFERRED SEATING COMPANY LLC
633 Yosemite Dr (46217-3961)
P.O. Box 17622 (46217-0622)
PHONE...................317 782-3323
EMP: 2 **EST:** 2006
SALES (est): 411.79K **Privately Held**
Web: www.preferred-seating.com
SIC: 5021 2531 Theater seats; Stadium seating

(G-9191)
PREMIER SCRAP PROCESSING LLC
6051 Central Ave (46220-1809)
PHONE...................317 242-9502
EMP: 10 **EST:** 2019
SALES (est): 800K **Privately Held**
Web: www.premiersp.us
SIC: 2611 Pulp mills, mechanical and recycling processing

(G-9192)
PREMIER SIGN GROUP INC
740 E 52nd St Ste 7 (46205-1175)
PHONE...................317 613-4411
Jim Leahy, *Pr*
Greg Cunningham, *VP*
EMP: 7 **EST:** 1999
SQ FT: 3,500
SALES (est): 458.25K **Privately Held**
Web: www.premiersigngroup.com
SIC: 3993 Electric signs

(G-9193)
PREMIERE ADVERTISING
2704 E 62nd St Ste B (46220-2985)
PHONE...................317 722-2400
Andrew H Auch, *Pr*
EMP: 3 **EST:** 1989
SQ FT: 2,500
SALES (est): 500.15K **Privately Held**
Web: www.premiereadv.com
SIC: 5199 2759 Advertising specialties; Commercial printing, nec

(G-9194)
PRETTY CHIQUE LLC
4203 Millersville Rd Ste 300 (46205)
PHONE...................317 922-5899
Temeka Matthews, *CEO*
EMP: 8 **EST:** 2019
SALES (est): 214.28K **Privately Held**
SIC: 5699 2261 T-shirts, custom printed; Printing of cotton broadwoven fabrics

(G-9195)
PREVOUNCE HEALTH INC
Also Called: Pylo Health
3250 N Post Rd Ste 180 (46226-6535)
PHONE...................800 618-7738
Daniel Tashnek, *CEO*
Daniel Tashnek, *Prin*
Gary Tashnek, *Prin*
EMP: 14 **EST:** 2005
SALES (est): 1.14MM **Privately Held**
Web: www.prevounce.com
SIC: 3999 7371 Manufacturing industries, nec; Software programming applications

(G-9196)
PRIME TECH INC
3131 N Franklin Rd Ste B (46226-6390)
PHONE...................317 715-1162
A Desida, *Director of Information*
EMP: 11 **EST:** 2018
SALES (est): 118.69K **Privately Held**
Web: www.primetechint.com
SIC: 3511 Turbines and turbine generator sets

(G-9197)
PRIMED & READY LLC
5036 E 65th St (46220-4585)
PHONE...................317 694-2028
Paul Jesch, *Owner*
EMP: 2 **EST:** 2005
SALES (est): 207.62K **Privately Held**
SIC: 3273 Ready-mixed concrete

(G-9198)
PRINCESS PALAYSE
2829 Schofield Ave (46218-2621)
PHONE...................317 937-9394
Cierra Jones, *CEO*
EMP: 3 **EST:** 2019
SALES (est): 102.18K **Privately Held**
SIC: 2389 Apparel and accessories, nec

(G-9199)
PRINT IDEAS
2233 Country Club Rd (46234-1838)
PHONE...................317 299-8766
William Yount, *Owner*
EMP: 3 **EST:** 2005
SALES (est): 208.62K **Privately Held**
Web: www.printideas.net
SIC: 2752 Offset printing

(G-9200)
PRINT IT INC
7349 N Shadeland Ave (46250-2052)
PHONE...................317 774-6848
Theron I Keller, *Pr*
EMP: 3 **EST:** 2021
SALES (est): 78.58K **Privately Held**
Web: www.creativepanzee.com
SIC: 2752 7389 Commercial printing, lithographic; Business Activities at Non-Commercial Site

(G-9201)
PRINT QUEENS LLC
2004 Fernway St (46218-3574)
PHONE...................317 285-8934
EMP: 2 **EST:** 2021
SALES (est): 106.06K **Privately Held**
SIC: 3555 Printing presses

(G-9202)
PRINT RESOURCES INC
Also Called: Tactive
1500 E Riverside Dr (46202-2039)
PHONE...................317 833-7000
Timothy J Browning, *Pr*
Kurt Ellinger, *
Erin Marlow, *
Phil Dewitt, *
Robin Hartowicz, *
EMP: 76 **EST:** 2000
SQ FT: 18,000
SALES (est): 13.3MM **Privately Held**
Web: www.tactive.cc
SIC: 2752 Offset printing

(G-9203)
PRINT SHARP ENTERPRISES INC
Also Called: Minuteman Press
9105 E 56th St Ste E (46216-2231)
PHONE...................317 899-2754
Timothy Newberry, *Pr*
David L Ruse, *Sec*
EMP: 4 **EST:** 2004
SALES (est): 486.68K **Privately Held**
Web: indyeast.minutemanpress.com
SIC: 2752 Commercial printing, lithographic

(G-9204)
PRINTING CENTER INC
Also Called: Printing Complex, The
3503 N Shadeland Ave (46226-5708)
PHONE...................317 545-8518
Gregory Ernest, *Pr*
Doris Ernest, *Sec*
EMP: 7 **EST:** 1976
SQ FT: 2,400
SALES (est): 510.51K **Privately Held**
SIC: 2752 Offset printing

(G-9205)
PRINTING CONCEPTS INC
Also Called: Minuteman Press
4371 Sellers St (46226)
PHONE...................317 899-2754
Frank Endicott, *Pr*
EMP: 5 **EST:** 2015
SQ FT: 6,000
SALES (est): 463.92K **Privately Held**
Web: www.printingconcepts.com
SIC: 2752 Offset printing

(G-9206)
PRINTING PARTNERS INC (PA)
Also Called: Partners Marketing
929 W 16th St (46202-2214)
PHONE...................317 635-2282
Michael O Brien, *Pr*
Joel O Brien, *
Joe Brower, *
EMP: 92 **EST:** 1989
SQ FT: 53,000
SALES (est): 22.69MM
SALES (corp-wide): 22.69MM **Privately Held**
Web: www.printingpartners.net
SIC: 2752 7331 2759 Offset printing; Mailing service; Letterpress printing

(G-9207)
PRINTING PARTNERS EAST INC
Also Called: Insty-Prints
929 W 16th St (46202-2214)
PHONE...................317 356-2522
EMP: 6
SQ FT: 2,140
SALES (est): 558.58K **Privately Held**

Indianapolis - Marion County (G-9208)

SIC: **2752** 7334 Commercial printing, lithographic; Photocopying and duplicating services

(G-9208)
PRINTING SERVICES INC
5333 Commerce Square Dr (46237-8627)
PHONE..................................317 300-0363
EMP: **6** EST: 2011
SALES (est): **98.26K** Privately Held
SIC: **2759** Commercial printing, nec

(G-9209)
PRINTING TECHNOLOGIES INC
6266 Morenci Trl (46268)
PHONE..................................800 428-3786
EMP: **45** EST: 1994
SQ FT: 30,000
SALES (est): **8.92MM** Privately Held
Web: www.ptionaroll.com
SIC: **2752** Commercial printing, lithographic

(G-9210)
PRINTSOURCE
6139 Riverview Dr (46208-1542)
PHONE..................................317 507-6526
EMP: **3** EST: 2019
SALES (est): **83.91K** Privately Held
Web: www.printsourcenewyork.com
SIC: **2752** Commercial printing, lithographic

(G-9211)
PRIORITY PRESS INC (PA)
Also Called: Priority Business Forms
4026 W 10th St (46222-3282)
PHONE..................................317 241-4234
Joseph Straka, *Pr*
Robert Straka, *
EMP: **35** EST: 1980
SQ FT: 52,000
SALES (est): **9.15MM**
SALES (corp-wide): **9.15MM** Privately Held
Web: www.priority-press.com
SIC: **2759** 5112 5049 Commercial printing, nec; Computer paper; Engineers' equipment and supplies, nec

(G-9212)
PRIORITY PRESS INC
Press 96
4026 W 10th St (46222-3282)
PHONE..................................317 240-0103
Gary Weatherholt, *Brnch Mgr*
EMP: **3**
SALES (corp-wide): **9.15MM** Privately Held
Web: www.priority-press.com
SIC: **2759** 7334 2752 Commercial printing, nec; Photocopying and duplicating services; Offset printing
PA: Priority Press, Inc.
 4026 W 10th St
 Indianapolis IN 46222
 317 241-4234

(G-9213)
PRIORITY PRINTING LLC
4026 W 10th St (46222-3203)
PHONE..................................317 241-4234
EMP: **2** EST: 2013
SQ FT: 1,000
SALES (est): **175.49K** Privately Held
Web: www.priority-press.com
SIC: **2752** 2791 2732 Offset printing; Linotype composition, for the printing trade; Pamphlets: printing and binding, not published on site

(G-9214)
PRIZED POSSESSION
Also Called: Websters Tom Custom WD Turning
6606 Avalon Forest Dr (46250-2804)
PHONE..................................317 842-1498
Tom Webster, *Owner*
EMP: **3** EST: 1985
SALES (est): **175.21K** Privately Held
Web: www.prizepossessions.com
SIC: **2426** Turnings, furniture: wood

(G-9215)
PRO-KOTE INDY LLC
8813 Robbins Rd (46268-1024)
PHONE..................................317 872-0001
John Griffin, *Owner*
EMP: **4** EST: 2005
SALES (est): **319.87K** Privately Held
Web: www.prokoteindy.com
SIC: **3479** Coating of metals and formed products

(G-9216)
PRO-STRIP INDY LLC
4020 Millersville Rd (46205-2852)
PHONE..................................317 872-0001
EMP: **5** EST: 2018
SALES (est): **124.47K** Privately Held
Web: www.prostripindy.com
SIC: **3479** Coating of metals and formed products

(G-9217)
PROBOTECH INC
6848 Hawthorn Park Dr (46220-3909)
PHONE..................................317 849-6197
C Edward Poisel, *Pr*
Jeanette L Poisel, *Sec*
EMP: **5** EST: 1984
SQ FT: 2,400
SALES (est): **531.28K** Privately Held
Web: www.probotech.com
SIC: **3569** Robots, assembly line: industrial and commercial

(G-9218)
PROCOAT INC
920 E New York St (46202-3729)
PHONE..................................317 263-5071
Kenneth P Gootee, *Pr*
Penny L Gootee, *VP*
EMP: **3** EST: 1991
SALES (est): **269K** Privately Held
SIC: **3479** 5091 Coating of metals and formed products; Sporting and recreation goods

(G-9219)
PRODUCTION PLASTIC MOLDING
3402 W 79th St (46268-1912)
PHONE..................................317 872-4669
George A Lemcke, *Pr*
Suzanne Lemcke, *VP*
▲ EMP: **4** EST: 1983
SQ FT: 1,500
SALES (est): **427.6K** Privately Held
Web: www.winslowazrealestate.com
SIC: **3089** Injection molding of plastics

(G-9220)
PROFESSIONAL BOWLING BALL SVC
Also Called: Flying W Trophy Div
2630 Madison Ave (46225-2180)
PHONE..................................317 786-4329
Christa Guedel, *Pr*
Charles Guedel, *Pr*
Christopher Guedel, *VP*
Christa Dunham, *VP*
Linda Guedel, *VP*
EMP: **9** EST: 1969
SQ FT: 5,000
SALES (est): **850.94K** Privately Held
Web: www.flyingwawards.com
SIC: **3499** 3479 Trophies, metal, except silver; Engraving jewelry, silverware, or metal

(G-9221)
PROFESSIONAL GIFTING INC
6366 Guilford Ave # 300 (46220-1750)
PHONE..................................800 350-1796
Ken Reinstrom, *Prin*
EMP: **11** EST: 2008
SALES (est): **328.27K** Privately Held
Web: www.professionalgifting.com
SIC: **2253** 7319 5699 7389 T-shirts and tops, knit; Distribution of advertising material or sample services; Customized clothing and apparel; Advertising, promotional, and trade show services

(G-9222)
PROFESSIONAL GRADE SVCS LLC
Also Called: Professional Grade Services
10428 Windward Dr (46234-3667)
P.O. Box 531451 (46253-1451)
PHONE..................................317 688-8898
Damien Blain, *Prin*
EMP: **9** EST: 2013
SALES (est): **273.75K** Privately Held
Web: www.pgsindy.com
SIC: **7349** 0782 3646 Building maintenance services, nec; Lawn and garden services; Fluorescent lighting fixtures, commercial

(G-9223)
PROFIT FINDERS INCORPORATED
Also Called: Indiana Custom Embroidery
7750 Records St (46226-3961)
PHONE..................................317 251-7792
Kris Maynard, *Pr*
Karla J Maynard, *Sec*
EMP: **10** EST: 1992
SALES (est): **528.01K** Privately Held
Web: www.indianacustomembroidery.com
SIC: **2395** Embroidery products, except Schiffli machine

(G-9224)
PROFORMA PREMIER PRINTING
10252 Eastwind Ct (46256-9782)
PHONE..................................317 842-9181
Al Elskus, *Pr*
Lynn Elskus, *VP*
EMP: **2** EST: 2001
SALES (est): **212.42K** Privately Held
Web: www.proformapremierprinting.com
SIC: **2752** Offset printing

(G-9225)
PROGRESSIVE DESIGN APPAREL INC
Also Called: Sugar Abd Bruno
7260 Georgetown Rd (46268-4125)
PHONE..................................317 293-5888
Challen L Powers, *Pr*
Steven L Powers, *Sec*
EMP: **26** EST: 1989
SQ FT: 14,000
SALES (est): **844.62K** Privately Held
Web: www.pdacoolstuff.com
SIC: **3993** 2395 2396 Signs and advertising specialties; Embroidery and art needlework; Screen printing on fabric articles

(G-9226)
PROGRESSIVE PLATING COMPANY
Also Called: Production Plating
2064 Columbia Ave (46202-1994)
PHONE..................................317 923-2413
Allen L Williamson, *Pr*
Betty Williamson, *
EMP: **25** EST: 1928
SQ FT: 27,000
SALES (est): **928.27K** Privately Held
Web: www.progressiveplatingco.com
SIC: **3471** Electroplating of metals or formed products

(G-9227)
PROJECT HOUSE
9149 Lantern Ln (46256-2276)
PHONE..................................317 691-4237
Michael Vander Sande, *Pt*
EMP: **1** EST: 2012
SALES (est): **97.07K** Privately Held
SIC: **2721** Magazines: publishing only, not printed on site

(G-9228)
PROJECTIONE LLC
Also Called: Project One Studio
3151 Kirkbride Way Apt C (46222-5390)
PHONE..................................812 480-6006
EMP: **4** EST: 2011
SQ FT: 5,500
SALES (est): **264.17K** Privately Held
Web: www.p1-studio.com
SIC: **3446** Architectural metalwork

(G-9229)
PROLINE SPRAY FOAM INC ◆
3880 Pendleton Way Ste 700 (46226-7627)
PHONE..................................317 981-2158
Christopher G Serrott, *CEO*
EMP: **4** EST: 2023
SALES (est): **60.98K** Privately Held
SIC: **1742** 2493 Insulation, buildings; Insulation and roofing material, reconstituted wood

(G-9230)
PROMEX TECHNOLOGIES LLC
Also Called: US Biopsy
7510 E 82nd St (46256-1410)
PHONE..................................317 736-0128
EMP: **41** EST: 2000
SQ FT: 20,000
SALES (est): **1.63MM**
SALES (corp-wide): **205.12MM** Privately Held
SIC: **3841** Surgical and medical instruments
HQ: Argon Medical Devices, Inc.
 7800 Dallas Pkwy Ste 200
 Plano TX 75024
 903 675-9321

(G-9231)
PROSPECT DISTRIBUTION INC
Also Called: Southeastern Supply Co
6312 Southeastern Ave (46203-5828)
PHONE..................................317 359-9551
EMP: **50**
SIC: **5031** 2431 Lumber: rough, dressed, and finished; Millwork

(G-9232)
PROSPERER TRUCKING LLC
6620 Hollow Run Dr (46214)
PHONE..................................317 551-5691
EMP: **1** EST: 2020
SALES (est): **200K** Privately Held
SIC: **3537** Trucks: freight, baggage, etc.: industrial, except mining

Indianapolis - Marion County

(G-9233)
PROSPERUS LLC
Also Called: Test Gauge & Backflow Supply
5644 S Meridian St Ste E (46217-2759)
PHONE..................................317 786-8990
EMP: 4 EST: 2011
SALES (est): 553.36K Privately Held
Web: www.shopbackflow.com
SIC: 3824 Gauges for computing pressure temperature corrections

(G-9234)
PRP WINE INTERNATIONAL
8310 Allison Pointe Blvd Ste 205 (46250-1998)
P.O. Box 508 (47940-0508)
PHONE..................................317 288-0005
EMP: 11 EST: 2014
SALES (est): 152.88K Privately Held
Web: www.prpgraphics.com
SIC: 5921 5182 2084 Wine; Wine; Wines

(G-9235)
PRYSMIAN CBLES SYSTEMS USA LLC
Also Called: Indianapolis, In Plant
7950 Rockville Rd (46214-3107)
PHONE..................................317 271-8447
William Wright, Mgr
EMP: 80
SQ FT: 45,000
Web: na.prysmian.com
SIC: 3357 Nonferrous wiredrawing and insulating
HQ: Prysmian Cables And Systems Usa, Llc
4 Tesseneer Dr
Highland Heights KY 41076
859 572-8000

(G-9236)
PRYSMIAN CBLES SYSTEMS USA LLC
Also Called: In, Technology Center
7920 Rockville Rd (46214-3107)
PHONE..................................317 271-8447
Daniel Jessop, Brnch Mgr
EMP: 74
SQ FT: 50,000
Web: na.prysmian.com
SIC: 3357 7379 Communication wire; Online services technology consultants
HQ: Prysmian Cables And Systems Usa, Llc
4 Tesseneer Dr
Highland Heights KY 41076
859 572-8000

(G-9237)
PSC INDUSTRIES INC
Also Called: Glasrite Div
6790 E 32nd St (46226-6163)
PHONE..................................317 547-5439
Rick Harvey, Manager
EMP: 9
SALES (corp-wide): 1.71B Privately Held
Web: www.pscindustries.com
SIC: 1742 3296 2891 Insulation, buildings; Mineral wool; Adhesives and sealants
HQ: Psc Industries, Inc.
1100 W Market St
Louisville KY 40203
502 625-7700

(G-9238)
PSI GROUP INC
5071 W 74th St (46268-5112)
PHONE..................................317 297-3211
Troy Evans, VP
EMP: 2 EST: 2010
SALES (est): 221.91K Privately Held
Web: www.psigroupinc.com
SIC: 3444 Mail (post office) collection or storage boxes, sheet metal

(G-9239)
PUMPALARMCOM LLC
203 W Morris St (46225-1440)
PHONE..................................888 454-5051
EMP: 5 EST: 2013
SALES (est): 497.25K Privately Held
Web: www.pumpalarm.com
SIC: 3669 Signaling apparatus, electric

(G-9240)
PURE BEAUTEE BUNDLEZ INC ✪
6929 E 10th St Ste 200 (46219-4803)
PHONE..................................574 204-3979
Desiree Sanders, CEO
EMP: 1 EST: 2022
SALES (est): 39.69K Privately Held
SIC: 3999 Hair and hair-based products

(G-9241)
PURE ELEMENTS LLC
8415 Southern Springs Dr (46237-8403)
PHONE..................................317 503-0411
Tatpachuen Parker, Admn
EMP: 5 EST: 2013
SALES (est): 139.51K Privately Held
SIC: 2819 Industrial inorganic chemicals, nec

(G-9242)
PURE IMAGE LASER AND SPA LLC
8350 S Emerson Ave Ste 120 (46237-8744)
PHONE..................................317 306-6603
EMP: 2 EST: 2015
SALES (est): 172.86K Privately Held
Web: www.pureimagelaserandspa.com
SIC: 3999 Massage machines, electric: barber and beauty shops

(G-9243)
QFS HOLDINGS LLC
Also Called: Quality Fabricated Solutions
2457 E Washington St Ste B (46201-4179)
PHONE..................................317 634-2543
Charley Powers, Managing Member
EMP: 5 EST: 1883
SQ FT: 30,000
SALES (est): 857.2K Privately Held
SIC: 3449 Miscellaneous metalwork

(G-9244)
QTG PEPSI CO LARRY DAVI
9101 Orly Rd (46241-9605)
PHONE..................................317 830-4020
EMP: 7 EST: 2010
SALES (est): 216.61K Privately Held
SIC: 2086 Soft drinks: packaged in cans, bottles, etc.

(G-9245)
QUAKER OATS COMPANY
Also Called: Quaker Oats
5858 Decatur Blvd (46241-9575)
PHONE..................................317 821-6462
David Copeland, Mgr
EMP: 116
SALES (corp-wide): 86.39B Publicly Held
SIC: 2086 Bottled and canned soft drinks
HQ: The Quaker Oats Company
433 W Van Buren St Ste 3n
Chicago IL 60607
312 821-1000

(G-9246)
QUALITY IMAGINATION CORP
4405 Massachusetts Ave (46218-3142)
PHONE..................................317 753-0042
Jorge Senisse, Pr
EMP: 2 EST: 2010
SALES (est): 185.24K Privately Held
Web: www.qualityimagination.com
SIC: 2759 Commercial printing, nec

(G-9247)
QUALITY TANK TRUCKS & EQP INC
3301 Moore Ave (46201-4305)
PHONE..................................317 635-0000
Robert Bray, Pr
EMP: 7 EST: 1997
SQ FT: 1,000
SALES (est): 568.4K Privately Held
Web: www.qualitytanktrucks.net
SIC: 3713 3272 Truck and bus bodies; Septic tanks, concrete

(G-9248)
QUANTUMTECH LLC
5042 Brandywine Dr Apt 322 (46241-8612)
PHONE..................................786 512-0827
Jose Disotuar, Owner
EMP: 5 EST: 2017
SALES (est): 94.64K Privately Held
SIC: 3572 Computer storage devices

(G-9249)
QUICK WALK SYSTEMS INC
5315 N Pennsylvania St (46220-3058)
PHONE..................................317 255-2247
Sam Rogers, Pr
EMP: 2 EST: 2000
SALES (est): 144.25K Privately Held
SIC: 3996 Tile, floor: supported plastic

(G-9250)
QUICKSPACE TRANSPORTATION LLC
6701 N College Ave Apt 503 (46220-1687)
PHONE..................................812 585-2317
EMP: 1
SALES (est): 54.62K Privately Held
SIC: 3799 7389 Transportation equipment, nec; Business Activities at Non-Commercial Site

(G-9251)
QUIKRETE COMPANIES LLC
Also Called: Rinker Materials
1501 S Holt Rd (46241-4107)
PHONE..................................317 241-8237
John Finch, Brnch Mgr
EMP: 30
Web: www.quikrete.com
SIC: 3272 Concrete products, nec
HQ: The Quikrete Companies Llc
5 Concourse Pkwy Ste 1900
Atlanta GA 30328
404 634-9100

(G-9252)
QUIKRETE COMPANIES LLC
Also Called: Quikrete
3100 E 56th St (46220-3624)
PHONE..................................317 251-2281
EMP: 50
Web: www.quikrete.com
SIC: 3272 3273 3255 1442 Building materials, except block or brick: concrete; Ready-mixed concrete; Clay refractories; Construction sand and gravel
HQ: The Quikrete Companies Llc
5 Concourse Pkwy Ste 1900
Atlanta GA 30328
404 634-9100

(G-9253)
QUO VADIS AEROSPACE LLC
1951 W Edgewood Ave (46217-9678)
PHONE..................................575 621-2372
Steven Ross, Pr
EMP: 1 EST: 2018
SALES (est): 61.65K Privately Held
Web: www.quovadisaero.com
SIC: 3721 Aircraft

(G-9254)
R & R TRUCKING & FREIGHT LLC
6101 N Keystone Ave Ste 100 (46220-2488)
PHONE..................................888 477-8782
Ronald Williams, CEO
EMP: 2 EST: 2021
SALES (est): 142K Privately Held
SIC: 4212 3537 Local trucking, without storage; Trucks: freight, baggage, etc.: industrial, except mining

(G-9255)
R & S PLATING INC
2302 Bloyd Ave (46218-3527)
PHONE..................................317 925-2396
James Raymond, Pr
Joe Raymond, VP
EMP: 9 EST: 1946
SQ FT: 5,000
SALES (est): 980.92K Privately Held
Web: www.rsplating.com
SIC: 3471 Plating of metals or formed products

(G-9256)
R R DONNELLEY INC
Also Called: More Wallace
201 S Capitol Ave Ste 201 (46225-1095)
PHONE..................................317 614-2508
Mark Angelson, Pr
EMP: 10 EST: 2005
SALES (est): 430.13K Privately Held
Web: www.rrd.com
SIC: 2711 Commercial printing and newspaper publishing combined

(G-9257)
R W MORAN EXPRESS INC
6214 Morenci Trl Ste 200 (46268-4892)
PHONE..................................317 445-5861
Richard Moran, Pr
EMP: 6 EST: 2018
SALES (est): 51.33K Privately Held
SIC: 3993 Signs and advertising specialties

(G-9258)
RABB AND HOWE CABINET TOP CO
2571 Winthrop Ave (46205-4464)
PHONE..................................317 926-6442
Philip C Rabb, Pr
Philip C Rabb, Pt
Philip B Rabb, Pt
EMP: 14 EST: 1959
SQ FT: 18,000
SALES (est): 1.1MM Privately Held
Web: www.rabbhowecabinetry.com
SIC: 2521 2599 2541 2434 Cabinets, office: wood; Cabinets, factory; Wood partitions and fixtures; Wood kitchen cabinets

(G-9259)
RACKCOLLECTIONS LLC
317 N Hamilton Ave (46201-3125)
PHONE..................................317 779-4302
Lenzy Cortez Donnerson, Managing Member
EMP: 1 EST: 2020
SALES (est): 61.66K Privately Held
Web: www.rackcollections.com

Indianapolis - Marion County (G-9260) — GEOGRAPHIC SECTION

SIC: **1521 7299 1389 7389** Single-family home remodeling, additions, and repairs; Handyman service; Construction, repair, and dismantling services; Business services, nec

(G-9260)
RAD CUBE LLC (PA)
9449 Priority Way West Dr Ste 110 (46240-6425)
PHONE..............................317 456-7560
EMP: 12 EST: 2015
SALES (est): 1.2MM
SALES (corp-wide): 1.2MM **Privately Held**
Web: www.radcube.com
SIC: **7372 8748** Application computer software; Business consulting, nec

(G-9261)
RAD FABRICATION LLC
940 E Michigan St (46202-3626)
PHONE..............................317 903-0065
Robert Daly, *Managing Member*
EMP: 25 EST: 2007
SALES (est): 3.05MM **Privately Held**
Web: www.radfabrication.com
SIC: **3441** Fabricated structural metal

(G-9262)
RADIATION PHYSICS CNSLTING INC
7022 Warwick Rd (46220-1051)
PHONE..............................317 251-0193
EMP: 3 EST: 1988
SALES (est): 257.26K **Privately Held**
Web: www.radphysicsconsulting.com
SIC: **3845** Ultrasonic scanning devices, medical

(G-9263)
RAI LLC (PA) ✪
Also Called: Construction
3638 Lombardy Pl (46226-5960)
PHONE..............................765 227-0111
Clinton Hunter Iii, *Pr*
EMP: 1 EST: 2022
SALES (est): 434.08K
SALES (corp-wide): 434.08K **Privately Held**
SIC: **1389 7389** Construction, repair, and dismantling services; Business Activities at Non-Commercial Site

(G-9264)
RAM SERVICES RFRGN & MECH
5170 Atherton North Dr (46219-6904)
PHONE..............................317 679-8541
Debra Leach, *Sec*
David Leach, *Pr*
EMP: 5 EST: 2000
SALES (est): 350.39K **Privately Held**
SIC: **3585** Refrigeration and heating equipment

(G-9265)
RAND WORLDWIDE INC
8604 Allisonville Rd (46250-1546)
PHONE..............................317 572-1267
EMP: 1
SALES (corp-wide): 313.19MM **Privately Held**
Web: www.rand.com
SIC: **7372** Prepackaged software
PA: Rand Worldwide, Inc.
   11201 Dlfeld Blvd Ste 112
   Owings Mills MD 21117
   410 581-8080

(G-9266)
RAPPID MFG INC
8219 Indy Ct (46214-2300)
PHONE..............................317 440-8084
Tammy Powell, *Prin*
EMP: 2 EST: 2011
SALES (est): 96.68K **Privately Held**
SIC: **3999** Manufacturing industries, nec

(G-9267)
RAY ENVELOPE COMPANY INC
450 S Kitley Ave (46219-7488)
PHONE..............................317 353-6251
EMP: 42 EST: 1938
SALES (est): 5MM **Privately Held**
Web: www.rayenvelope.com
SIC: **2677** Envelopes

(G-9268)
RAYCO MCH & ENGRG GROUP INC
970 Western Dr (46241-1435)
PHONE..............................317 291-7848
Gregory A Cox, *Pr*
Angela Cox, *VP*
EMP: 21 EST: 2005
SQ FT: 7,500
SALES (est): 2.49MM **Privately Held**
SIC: **3599 3714 3728** Air intake filters, internal combustion engine, except auto; Motor vehicle parts and accessories; Aircraft parts and equipment, nec

(G-9269)
RAYCONN LLC
2122 Dr Martin Luther King Jr St Unit A3 (46202)
PHONE..............................317 809-5788
Dan Gibson, *Owner*
EMP: 1 EST: 2009
SALES (est): 129.97K **Privately Held**
Web: www.rayconn.com
SIC: **3679** Harness assemblies, for electronic use: wire or cable

(G-9270)
RAYES RPID RSLTS - MBL DRG ALC
532 Chase St (46221-1236)
PHONE..............................317 721-1065
EMP: 1
SALES (est): 47.23K **Privately Held**
SIC: **2899 7389** Drug testing kits, blood and urine; Business Activities at Non-Commercial Site

(G-9271)
RAYMOND LITTLE PRINT SHOP
2900 N Shadeland Ave Ste B1 (46218)
PHONE..............................317 246-9083
EMP: 8 EST: 2013
SALES (est): 282.26K **Privately Held**
SIC: **2759** Commercial printing, nec

(G-9272)
RAYMONE SANDERS FMLY TRCKG LLC
5414 Calder Way Apt 411 (46226-1766)
PHONE..............................317 400-3545
EMP: 1 EST: 2021
SALES (est): 66.29K **Privately Held**
SIC: **4212 3799** Local trucking, without storage; Transportation equipment, nec

(G-9273)
RAYTHEON COMPANY
Also Called: Raytheon
3939 Priority Way South Dr Ste 100 (46240-3833)
PHONE..............................317 306-8471
Steve Kaspar, *VP*
EMP: 117
SALES (corp-wide): 68.92B **Publicly Held**
Web: www.rtx.com
SIC: **3812** Search and navigation equipment
HQ: Raytheon Company
   870 Winter St
   Waltham MA 02451
   781 522-3000

(G-9274)
RAYTHEON COMPANY
Also Called: Raytheon
623 Midnight Ct (46239-9233)
PHONE..............................317 306-7492
EMP: 3
SALES (corp-wide): 68.92B **Publicly Held**
Web: www.rtx.com
SIC: **3812** Sonar systems and equipment
HQ: Raytheon Company
   870 Winter St
   Waltham MA 02451
   781 522-3000

(G-9275)
RAYTHEON COMPANY
Also Called: Raytheon
6125 E 21st St (46219-2058)
PHONE..............................317 306-4633
EMP: 3
SALES (corp-wide): 68.92B **Publicly Held**
Web: www.rtx.com
SIC: **3812 3663 3761** Defense systems and equipment; Space satellite communications equipment; Guided missiles and space vehicles, research and development
HQ: Raytheon Company
   870 Winter St
   Waltham MA 02451
   781 522-3000

(G-9276)
RCA CORPORATION
Also Called: RCA Commerical Electronics
5935 W 84th St Ste A (46278-1350)
PHONE..............................800 722-2161
Jeff Kingston, *CEO*
EMP: 157 EST: 1919
SALES (est): 1.35MM
SALES (corp-wide): 104.56MM **Publicly Held**
Web: www.rcacommercialtv.com
SIC: **3678 3663 5731** Electronic connectors; Radio and t.v. communications equipment; Radio, television, and electronic stores
PA: Alpine 4 Holdings, Inc.
   2525 E Ariz Bltmore Cir S
   Phoenix AZ 85016
   480 702-2431

(G-9277)
READING BAKERY SYSTEMS INC
7517 Winton Dr (46268-5105)
PHONE..............................317 337-0000
◆ EMP: 18 EST: 2010
SALES (est): 1.53MM **Privately Held**
Web: www.readingbakery.com
SIC: **3556** Bakery machinery

(G-9278)
RED LINE GRAPHICS INCORPORATED (PA)
6430 S Belmont Ave (46217-9767)
PHONE..............................317 784-3777
Michael W Wadsworth, *Pr*
Janet M Wadsworth, *
EMP: 30 EST: 1994
SQ FT: 19,000
SALES (est): 4.53MM **Privately Held**
Web: www.redlinegrp.com
SIC: **2752** Offset printing

(G-9279)
REED AUTO - INDY MICH LLC
Also Called: Midas Muffler
8530 Michigan Rd (46268-1940)
PHONE..............................317 872-1132
Michael Reed, *Pr*
EMP: 14 EST: 2011
SALES (est): 888.29K
SALES (corp-wide): 2.43MM **Privately Held**
Web: www.midas.com
SIC: **7533 7534 7538 5531** Muffler shop, sale or repair and installation; Tire repair shop; Engine repair; Automotive tires
PA: Reed Automotive Service, Inc.
   2439 Kessler Blvd E Dr
   Indianapolis IN 46220
   317 908-6854

(G-9280)
REFLEXALLEN USA INC
2655 Fortune Cir W Ste A (46241-5542)
PHONE..............................317 870-3610
Renzo Gibellini, *Pr*
▲ EMP: 40 EST: 2011
SALES (est): 10.5MM
SALES (corp-wide): 149.37MM **Privately Held**
Web: www.reflexallenusa.com
SIC: **3714** Motor vehicle parts and accessories
HQ: Reflexallen Spa
   Via Serravalle 283
   Guiglia MO 41052

(G-9281)
REFRACTORY ENGINEERS INC
1750 Midwest Blvd (46214-2377)
PHONE..............................317 273-2000
Rick Sauer, *Pr*
Jan E Sauer, *
◆ EMP: 23 EST: 1962
SQ FT: 60,000
SALES (est): 4.35MM **Privately Held**
Web: www.refractoryeng.com
SIC: **3255** Clay refractories

(G-9282)
REGENBOGEN WOODWORKS LLC
431 Rainbow Ln (46260-4607)
PHONE..............................317 902-8221
Lori Perdue, *Prin*
EMP: 5 EST: 2019
SALES (est): 101.01K **Privately Held**
SIC: **2431** Millwork

(G-9283)
REIBERG CERAMICS
5723 N Meridian St (46208-1563)
PHONE..............................317 283-8441
Robert Reiberg, *Prin*
EMP: 3 EST: 2008
SALES (est): 166.74K **Privately Held**
Web: www.reibergceramics.com
SIC: **3269** Pottery products, nec

(G-9284)
REILLY INDUSTRIES INC
1500 S Tibbs Ave (46241-4537)
PHONE..............................317 247-8141
EMP: 3 EST: 2008
SALES (est): 521.58K **Privately Held**
SIC: **2869** Industrial organic chemicals, nec

(G-9285)
REISS ORNA & STRUCTURALL PDTS
3739 N Illinois St (46208-4229)
PHONE..............................317 925-2371
Paul R Reiss, *Pr*
Waneta L Reiss, *Sec*

GEOGRAPHIC SECTION

Indianapolis - Marion County (G-9312)

EMP: 20 EST: 1886
SQ FT: 14,000
SALES (est): 2.21MM **Privately Held**
Web: www.reissornamental.com
SIC: 3441 Fabricated structural metal

(G-9286)
RELATIONAL GRAVITY INC
12623 Tealwood Dr (46236-8174)
PHONE.....................317 855-7685
Jeffrey D Hutson, *Prin*
EMP: 5 EST: 2008
SALES (est): 104.48K **Privately Held**
Web: www.relationalgravity.com
SIC: 7372 Prepackaged software

(G-9287)
RELAXURA LLC
5726 High Timber Ln (46235-6852)
PHONE.....................317 333-1324
EMP: 1 EST: 2020
SALES (est): 33.35K **Privately Held**
SIC: 2731 Book publishing

(G-9288)
RELIANT ENGINEERING INC
1329 Sadlier Circle West Dr (46239-1055)
PHONE.....................317 322-9084
Bill Wycoff, *Pr*
Sharon K Wycoff, *Sec*
EMP: 32 EST: 1986
SQ FT: 4,800
SALES (est): 982.2K **Privately Held**
Web: www.reliantengineering.com
SIC: 3599 Machine shop, jobbing and repair

(G-9289)
RELOADED ACTIVEWEAR LLC
4738 E 34th St (46218-2366)
PHONE.....................317 652-7394
EMP: 1
SALES (est): 42.55K **Privately Held**
SIC: 2339 7389 Athletic clothing: women's, misses', and juniors'; Business Activities at Non-Commercial Site

(G-9290)
RENAISSNCE ELECTRONIC SVCS LLC
Also Called: Premier Claim Services
6510 Telecom Dr Ste 300 (46278-6030)
PHONE.....................317 786-2235
Eric Joseph, *CEO*
EMP: 12 EST: 2001
SALES (est): 2.57MM
SALES (corp-wide): 4.96MM **Privately Held**
Web: www.rss-llc.com
SIC: 7372 Business oriented computer software
PA: Vyne Corporation
100 Ashford Ctr N Ste 300
Dunwoody GA 30338
800 782-5150

(G-9291)
REO-USA INC
8450 E 47th St (46226-2925)
PHONE.....................317 899-1395
Frediel Twellsieca, *Pr*
Barbara Miller, *VP*
◆ EMP: 11 EST: 2001
SALES (est): 2.26MM **Privately Held**
Web: www.reo-usa.com
SIC: 3677 Inductors, electronic

(G-9292)
REPEAL 1205 LLC
7254 Whitehall Dr (46256-2273)
PHONE.....................317 402-4818

William Webster, *Prin*
EMP: 5 EST: 2015
SALES (est): 111.97K **Privately Held**
Web: www.1205distillery.com
SIC: 2085 Distilled and blended liquors

(G-9293)
RESPECT DA FLAVA LLC ✪
5580 Revolutionary Dr (46254-1066)
PHONE.....................765 243-1629
Tisha Arberry, *CEO*
EMP: 4 EST: 2022
SALES (est): 125.42K **Privately Held**
SIC: 2599 7389 Food wagons, restaurant; Business Activities at Non-Commercial Site

(G-9294)
RETRO ATM LLC
5325 E 82nd St Pmb 145 (46250-4510)
PHONE.....................317 752-6915
EMP: 1 EST: 2021
SALES (est): 74.13K **Privately Held**
SIC: 6231 6099 3578 Commodity contract exchanges; Automated teller machine (ATM) network; Automatic teller machines (ATM)

(G-9295)
REVERE INDUSTRIES
111 Monument Cir Ste 3200 (46204-0066)
PHONE.....................317 638-1521
Julie Campbell, *Prin*
EMP: 7 EST: 2016
SALES (est): 230.26K **Privately Held**
Web: www.revereplasticssystems.com
SIC: 3999 Manufacturing industries, nec

(G-9296)
REVIVAL LLC
Also Called: Revival Food Co
4315 N Park Ave (46205-1832)
PHONE.....................812 345-4317
Rachel N Klein, *Managing Member*
EMP: 2 EST: 2014
SALES (est): 113.45K **Privately Held**
Web: www.revivalfoodco.com
SIC: 2099 5143 5451 Butter, renovated and processed; Butter; Butter

(G-9297)
RHEEM SALES COMPANY INC
1240 Brookville Way (46239-1041)
PHONE.....................479 648-4900
EMP: 2 EST: 2011
SALES (est): 2.4MM **Privately Held**
Web: www.rheem.com
SIC: 3585 Refrigeration and heating equipment
HQ: Rheem Manufacturing Company Inc
1100 Abrnathy Rd Ste 1700
Atlanta GA 30328
770 351-3000

(G-9298)
RHR CORPORATION
Also Called: Direct Cnnect Prtg Dgital Svcs
930 E Hanna Ave (46227-1306)
P.O. Box 47529 (46298-1529)
PHONE.....................317 788-1504
Robin K Heldman, *Pr*
EMP: 4 EST: 1973
SQ FT: 3,600
SALES (est): 448.7K **Privately Held**
Web: www.directconnectprinting.net
SIC: 2752 7334 2791 2789 Offset printing; Photocopying and duplicating services; Typesetting; Bookbinding and related work

(G-9299)
RHYNE & ASSOCIATES INC
Also Called: Rhyne, R E & Company
3560 Madison Ave (46227-1352)
PHONE.....................317 786-4459
Robert E Rhyne, *Pr*
Deborah Moore, *VP*
Mary A Rhyne, *Sec*
EMP: 10 EST: 1957
SQ FT: 12,500
SALES (est): 173.32K **Privately Held**
Web: www.neuroncabling.com
SIC: 7641 2392 Reupholstery; Slip covers: made of fabric, plastic, etc.

(G-9300)
RICH BURES
5108 W Vermont St (46224-8852)
PHONE.....................317 270-9360
EMP: 4 EST: 2016
SALES (est): 120.2K **Privately Held**
Web: www.mywaterpumpman.com
SIC: 3714 Motor vehicle parts and accessories

(G-9301)
RICHARDS COMPLETE MACHINE SHOP
6403 W Thompson Rd (46221-3620)
PHONE.....................317 856-9163
EMP: 5 EST: 1998
SALES (est): 81.49K **Privately Held**
Web: www.richardscylinderrepair.com
SIC: 3599 Machine shop, jobbing and repair

(G-9302)
RICHARDS ELECTRIC LLC
1949 Herford Dr (46229)
PHONE.....................317 253-1083
EMP: 7 EST: 2007
SALES (est): 130K **Privately Held**
SIC: 3699 Electrical equipment and supplies, nec

(G-9303)
RICHARDSON MOLDING LLC
Engineering Division
5601 S Meridian St Ste B (46217-2738)
PHONE.....................317 787-9463
EMP: 3
SALES (corp-wide): 8.23B **Privately Held**
Web: www.richardsonmolding.com
SIC: 3089 5211 Molding primary plastics; Lumber and other building materials
HQ: Richardson Molding Incorporated
2405 Norcross Dr
Columbus IN 30005
812 342-0139

(G-9304)
RICHESON CONTRACTING INC
Also Called: Richeson Cabinet
5325 Commerce Square Dr (46237-9743)
PHONE.....................317 889-5995
Kimberly Richeson, *Pr*
Dale Richeson, *
EMP: 30 EST: 1978
SALES (est): 2.12MM **Privately Held**
Web: www.richesoncabinets.com
SIC: 2434 Wood kitchen cabinets

(G-9305)
RICK WHITT
Also Called: Whitt Photo Service
316 N Kealing Ave (46201-3434)
P.O. Box 130 (46077-0130)
PHONE.....................317 873-5507
Rick Whitt, *Owner*
EMP: 1 EST: 1977
SQ FT: 1,500

SALES (est): 60K **Privately Held**
SIC: 2791 7371 Typesetting; Custom computer programming services

(G-9306)
RICS SOFTWARE INC
129 E Market St Ste 1100 (46204-3295)
PHONE.....................317 455-5338
Jason Becker, *CEO*
Mark Brown, *
EMP: 35 EST: 2007
SALES (est): 5.62MM **Privately Held**
Web: www.ricssoftware.com
SIC: 7372 Business oriented computer software

(G-9307)
RILEY SIGNS & SHEET METAL LLC
5800 Massachusetts Ave (46218-2567)
PHONE.....................317 359-7446
EMP: 4 EST: 2019
SALES (est): 230.63K **Privately Held**
Web: www.rileysignshop.com
SIC: 3993 Signs and advertising specialties

(G-9308)
RIMEDION INC
5742 W 74th St (46278-1754)
PHONE.....................415 513-5535
Erik Woods, *Managing Member*
EMP: 6 EST: 2017
SALES (est): 133.41K **Privately Held**
Web: www.rimedion.com
SIC: 2836 Vaccines and other immunizing products

(G-9309)
RIVARS INC
3925 River Crossing Pkwy Ste 300 (46240-2279)
PHONE.....................765 789-6119
Beth Slusher, *CEO*
Timothy Slusher, *
▲ EMP: 24 EST: 1977
SALES (est): 2.45MM **Privately Held**
Web: www.sepapparel.com
SIC: 2389 5699 Costumes; Costumes, masquerade or theatrical

(G-9310)
RIVERS RESOURCES LLC
7114 Lakeview Parkway West Dr (46268-4104)
PHONE.....................317 572-5029
Eddie Rivers Junior, *Mgr*
Eddie Rivers Junior, *Managing Member*
EMP: 4 EST: 2005
SQ FT: 3,000
SALES (est): 495K **Privately Held**
Web: www.riversresources.net
SIC: 5112 2522 Stationery and office supplies; Office furniture, except wood

(G-9311)
RJ PARTNERS OF INDIANA INC
2457 E Washington St (46201-4155)
EMP: 170
SIC: 2752 Offset printing

(G-9312)
RLR ASSOCIATES INC
1302 N Illinois St (46202-2321)
PHONE.....................317 632-1300
EMP: 8 EST: 1988
SQ FT: 4,000
SALES (est): 908.67K **Privately Held**
Web: www.rlr.biz
SIC: 7336 7389 3993 Graphic arts and related design; Interior design services; Signs and advertising specialties

Indianapolis - Marion County (G-9313) GEOGRAPHIC SECTION

(G-9313)
ROBERSON FIRE & SAFETY INC
5603 W 74th St (46278-1753)
PHONE..................................317 879-3119
David Roberson, *Pr*
Janette Roberson, *Sec*
EMP: 6 **EST:** 1992
SALES (est): 925.36K **Privately Held**
SIC: 5087 5999 3569 Firefighting equipment; Safety supplies and equipment; Firefighting and related equipment

(G-9314)
ROBERT PEREZ
Also Called: Neodyne Technologies
3945 Guion Ln Ste A (46268-2677)
PHONE..................................317 291-7311
Robert Perez, *Owner*
EMP: 5 **EST:** 2010
SALES (est): 261.44K **Privately Held**
Web: www.neodynetech.com
SIC: 3724 8711 Aircraft engines and engine parts; Mechanical engineering

(G-9315)
ROBINSON AUTO PARTS MFG
830 E 38th St (46205-2824)
PHONE..................................317 921-0076
EMP: 3 **EST:** 2019
SALES (est): 77.34K **Privately Held**
SIC: 3999 Manufacturing industries, nec

(G-9316)
ROCHE DIABETES CARE INC
9115 Hague Rd (46256-1025)
P.O. Box 50457 (46250-0457)
PHONE..................................317 521-2000
Tom Abkins, *Sr VP*
Edwin Sonnenschein, *
▲ **EMP:** 99 **EST:** 2014
SALES (est): 43.11B **Privately Held**
Web: www.accu-chekto.com
SIC: 2834 Pharmaceutical preparations
HQ: Roche Holdings, Inc.
 1 Dna Way
 South San Francisco CA 94080
 650 225-1000

(G-9317)
ROCHE DIAGNOSTICS CORP
9344 Castlegate Dr Bldg F (46256-1001)
PHONE..................................317 521-2000
EMP: 24 **EST:** 2018
SALES (est): 3.01MM **Privately Held**
Web: www.roche.com
SIC: 2834 Pharmaceutical preparations

(G-9318)
ROCHE DIAGNOSTICS CORPORATION
Also Called: Roche Applied Sciences
7988 Centerpoint Dr (46256-3377)
PHONE..................................317 521-2000
Ben Molter, *Brnch Mgr*
EMP: 180
Web: www.roche.com
SIC: 2834 Pharmaceutical preparations
HQ: Roche Diagnostics Corporation
 9115 Hague Rd
 Indianapolis IN 46256
 800 428-5076

(G-9319)
ROCHE DIAGNOSTICS CORPORATION (DH)
9115 Hague Rd (46256-1045)
P.O. Box 50457 (46250-0457)
PHONE..................................800 428-5076
Brad Moore, *Pr*
Scott Wilson, *
Steve A Oldham, *
Wayne Burris, *
Bridget Boyle, *
◆ **EMP:** 1000 **EST:** 1998
SQ FT: 700,000
SALES (est): 1.36B **Privately Held**
Web: www.roche.com
SIC: 2835 Diagnostic substances
HQ: Roche Holdings, Inc.
 1 Dna Way
 South San Francisco CA 94080
 650 225-1000

(G-9320)
ROCHE OPERATIONS LTD
9115 Hague Rd # C (46256-1025)
PHONE..................................787 285-0170
EMP: 100 **EST:** 1988
SALES (est): 8.4MM **Privately Held**
SIC: 2834 Pharmaceutical preparations
HQ: Roche Holding Ag
 Grenzacherstrasse 124
 Basel BS 4058

(G-9321)
ROI MARKETING COMPANY INC
Also Called: Roi Marketing and Safety
9511 Angola Ct Ste 261 (46268-1119)
P.O. Box 78092 (46278-0092)
PHONE..................................317 644-0797
Adell Means, *Pr*
▲ **EMP:** 3 **EST:** 2004
SALES (est): 511.67K **Privately Held**
Web: www.roimarketingcompany.com
SIC: 7389 8742 5946 3089 Advertising, promotional, and trade show services; Marketing consulting services; Camera and photographic supply stores; Identification cards, plastics

(G-9322)
ROKA URBAN AG LLC
Also Called: Roka Farms
6845 Massachusetts Ave (46226-5651)
PHONE..................................317 513-8828
Chad Brandenburg, *Managing Member*
EMP: 5 **EST:** 2016
SALES (est): 54.98K **Privately Held**
SIC: 0182 2099 Hydroponic crops, grown under cover; Vegetables, peeled for the trade

(G-9323)
ROLL COATER INC
9908 Blue Ridge Way (46234-5045)
PHONE..................................317 652-1102
Jennifer Radwin, *Prin*
EMP: 7 **EST:** 2010
SALES (est): 114.41K **Privately Held**
SIC: 3471 Electroplating of metals or formed products

(G-9324)
ROLLER-WILSON INDUSTRIES LLC
2730 Hillside Ave (46218)
PHONE..................................317 377-4900
Ronald Daniel Wilson, *Pr*
EMP: 3 **EST:** 2020
SALES (est): 83.91K **Privately Held**
SIC: 3999 5812 5963 Manufacturing industries, nec; Caterers; Bakery goods, house-to-house

(G-9325)
ROLLS-ROYCE CORPORATION
Also Called: Uaw/Rolls-Royce Training Ctr
2601 W Raymond St (46241-4806)
PHONE..................................317 230-2000
EMP: 41
SALES (corp-wide): 20.55B **Privately Held**
Web: www.rolls-roycemotorcars.com
SIC: 5511 3443 3462 3731 New and used car dealers; Industrial vessels, tanks, and containers; Nuclear power plant forgings, ferrous; Submarines, building and repairing
HQ: Rolls-Royce Corporation
 450 S Meridian St
 Indianapolis IN 46225

(G-9326)
ROLLS-ROYCE CORPORATION
Also Called: Contols and Data Services
7661 North Perimeter Rd Ste 1x (46241-3630)
PHONE..................................317 230-2000
Dennis Warner, *Mgr*
EMP: 66
SALES (corp-wide): 20.55B **Privately Held**
Web: www.rolls-roycemotorcars.com
SIC: 3724 Aircraft engines and engine parts
HQ: Rolls-Royce Corporation
 450 S Meridian St
 Indianapolis IN 46225

(G-9327)
ROLLS-ROYCE CORPORATION
Also Called: Rolls-Royce Performance Bldg
2359 S Tibbs Ave (46241-4818)
PHONE..................................317 230-4118
EMP: 40
SALES (corp-wide): 20.55B **Privately Held**
Web: www.rolls-roycemotorcars.com
SIC: 3724 Research and development on aircraft engines and parts
HQ: Rolls-Royce Corporation
 450 S Meridian St
 Indianapolis IN 46225

(G-9328)
ROLLS-ROYCE CORPORATION
1875 S Tibbs Ave (46241)
PHONE..................................317 230-4118
EMP: 172 **EST:** 1993
SALES (est): 3.2MM **Privately Held**
Web: www.rolls-roycemotorcars.com
SIC: 3724 Research and development on aircraft engines and parts

(G-9329)
ROLLS-ROYCE CORPORATION (DH)
450 S Meridian St (46225)
P.O. Box 420 (46206)
PHONE..................................317 230-2000
Warren East Cbe, *CEO*
Tom Bell, *
Chris Cholerton, *CIVIL AEROSPACE**
Stephen Daintith, *
Simon Kirby, *
▲ **EMP:** 4000 **EST:** 1915
SQ FT: 2,700,000
SALES (est): 1.74B
SALES (corp-wide): 20.55B **Privately Held**
Web: www.rolls-royce.com
SIC: 3724 Research and development on aircraft engines and parts
HQ: Rolls-Royce North America Holdings Inc.
 1900 Reston Metro Plz # 4
 Reston VA 20190
 703 834-1700

(G-9330)
ROLLS-ROYCE DEFENSE SVCS INC
450 S Meridian St (46225-1103)
P.O. Box 420 (46206-0420)
PHONE..................................317 230-5006
Kevin Mccarty, *Pr*
Todd Pepmeier, *VP Fin*
EMP: 100 **EST:** 2003
SALES (est): 4.78MM
SALES (corp-wide): 20.55B **Privately Held**
Web: www.rolls-royce.com
SIC: 3812 Acceleration indicators and systems components, aerospace
HQ: Rolls-Royce North America Holdings Inc.
 1900 Reston Metro Plz # 4
 Reston VA 20190
 703 834-1700

(G-9331)
RONLEWHORN INDUSTRIES LLC
4226 Sunset Ave (46208-3766)
PHONE..................................765 661-9343
Aaron Scamihorn, *Prin*
EMP: 4 **EST:** 2018
SALES (est): 74.42K **Privately Held**
Web: www.ronlewhorn.com
SIC: 3999 Manufacturing industries, nec

(G-9332)
ROSE BLACK
1357 W 18th St Ste 101 (46202-2173)
PHONE..................................317 636-7459
Rose Black, *Pr*
EMP: 1 **EST:** 2005
SALES (est): 90.83K **Privately Held**
SIC: 3499 Barricades, metal

(G-9333)
ROSE ENGINEERING COMPANY INC
1105 Martin St (46227-3198)
PHONE..................................317 788-4446
David Howard, *Pr*
Charles N Howard, *VP*
EMP: 9 **EST:** 1969
SQ FT: 10,000
SALES (est): 855.41K **Privately Held**
Web: www.rose-eng.com
SIC: 3599 3452 Machine shop, jobbing and repair; Lock washers

(G-9334)
ROSE SHARON ALL NATURALS LLC
1220 Waterway Blvd (46202-2157)
PHONE..................................317 500-4725
Nycole Lynetta Johnson, *CEO*
EMP: 1 **EST:** 2020
SALES (est): 15K **Privately Held**
Web: www.roseofsharonallnaturals.biz
SIC: 7389 5961 2023 5999 Business Activities at Non-Commercial Site; Catalog and mail-order houses; Dietary supplements, dairy and non-dairy based; Miscellaneous retail stores, nec

(G-9335)
ROSS-GAGE INC (PA)
4011 W 54th St (46254-4789)
P.O. Box 3321 (46082-3321)
PHONE..................................317 283-2323
Thomas W Ross, *Pr*
Bill Main, *
Paco Fernandez, *Stockholder**
◆ **EMP:** 39 **EST:** 1972
SALES (est): 5.28MM
SALES (corp-wide): 5.28MM **Privately Held**
Web: www.rossgage.com
SIC: 2675 Die-cut paper and board

(G-9336)
ROUND TABLE RECORDING CO LLP
6345 Carrollton Ave (46220-1754)
PHONE..................................317 981-5351
EMP: 7 **EST:** 2019
SALES (est): 124.62K **Privately Held**
Web: www.thertrc.com
SIC: 7372 Prepackaged software

GEOGRAPHIC SECTION

Indianapolis - Marion County (G-9362)

(G-9337)
ROUND TOWN BREWERY LLC
950 S White River Pky West Dr (46204)
PHONE.................317 657-6397
Mackenzie Schenk, *CEO*
Jerry Sutherlin, *VP*
Mitchell Schenk, *Bd of Dir*
David Castor, *Bd of Dir*
EMP: 2 **EST:** 2013
SQ FT: 12,000
SALES (est): 181.12K **Privately Held**
Web: www.roundtownbrewery.com
SIC: 2082 Beer (alcoholic beverage)

(G-9338)
ROWE CONVEYOR LLC
5719 Garden Dr (46217-3744)
PHONE.................317 602-1024
William Bill Rowe Junior, *Brnch Mgr*
EMP: 26
SALES (corp-wide): 213.27K **Privately Held**
Web: www.roweconveyor.com
SIC: 3535 Conveyors and conveying equipment
PA: Rowe Conveyor Llc
1729 Us Highway 31 S Fj
Greenwood IN 46143
317 602-1024

(G-9339)
ROWE TECH
4327 Carrollton Ave (46205-1913)
PHONE.................317 453-0015
EMP: 1 **EST:** 2014
SALES (est): 63.08K **Privately Held**
SIC: 3751 7389 Motorcycles, bicycles and parts; Business Activities at Non-Commercial Site

(G-9340)
ROYAL FOOD PRODUCTS INC
Also Called: Royal
7001 Hawthorn Park Dr Ste A (46220-3912)
PHONE.................317 782-2660
EMP: 74 **EST:** 1904
SQ FT: 84,000
SALES (est): 1.15MM **Privately Held**
Web: www.royalfoodproducts.com
SIC: 2035 2026 Seasonings and sauces, except tomato and dry; Cream, sour

(G-9341)
ROYAL SPA CORPORATION (PA)
Also Called: Royal Spa Manufacturing
2041 W Epler Ave (46217-9695)
PHONE.................317 781-0828
TOLL FREE: 800
Richard Bartlett, *Pr*
Robert Dapper, *
▲ **EMP:** 70 **EST:** 1981
SQ FT: 78,000
SALES (est): 8.8MM
SALES (corp-wide): 8.8MM **Privately Held**
Web: www.royalspa.com
SIC: 3949 3634 3088 Sporting and athletic goods, nec; Electric housewares and fans; Bathroom fixtures, plastics

(G-9342)
RPG ENERGY GROUP INC
5610 Dividend Rd (46241-4302)
PHONE.................317 614-0054
Jami Krynski, *CEO*
Richard E Johnson, *Pr*
Andy Cooper, *VP*
EMP: 18 **EST:** 2018
SALES (est): 498.23K **Privately Held**
Web: www.rpgenergygroup.com

SIC: 1711 3621 3646 7374 Solar energy contractor; Storage battery chargers, motor and engine generator type; Commercial lighting fixtures; Data processing service

(G-9343)
RRC CORPORATION
Also Called: King's Copies
1002 E Garfield Dr (46203-4216)
PHONE.................317 687-8325
Robert Cosby, *Pr*
◆ **EMP:** 10 **EST:** 1997
SALES (est): 263.9K **Privately Held**
Web: www.kingscopies.biz
SIC: 7334 2752 2791 Photocopying and duplicating services; Offset printing; Typesetting

(G-9344)
RST CUSTOM WOODWORKING LL
1015 E 42nd St (46205-2001)
PHONE.................317 602-2490
EMP: 8 **EST:** 2017
SALES (est): 291.66K **Privately Held**
SIC: 2431 Millwork

(G-9345)
RT SMART SOLUTIONS LLC
4901 W 36th St (46224-1605)
PHONE.................317 435-2200
EMP: 10 **EST:** 2021
SALES (est): 898.57K **Privately Held**
SIC: 1389 7389 Construction, repair, and dismantling services; Business services, nec

(G-9346)
RUBENSTEIN LLC
Also Called: Edibleindy
7982 Fishback Rd (46278-9717)
PHONE.................317 946-2752
EMP: 5 **EST:** 2010
SALES (est): 232.9K **Privately Held**
Web: edibleindy.ediblecommunities.com
SIC: 2759 7389 Magazines: printing, nsk; Business services, nec

(G-9347)
RUBICON FOODS LLC
7320 E 86th St Ste 400 (46256-1250)
PHONE.................317 826-8793
EMP: 10 **EST:** 2006
SALES (est): 967.41K **Privately Held**
Web: www.rubiconfoods.com
SIC: 2013 Sausages and other prepared meats

(G-9348)
RUSSELLS TUBE FORMING INC
220 Gasoline Aly (46222-3909)
PHONE.................317 241-4072
John Russell, *Pr*
Tim Russell, *VP*
Nancy Russell, *Sec*
EMP: 20 **EST:** 1971
SQ FT: 17,500
SALES (est): 4.37MM **Privately Held**
Web: www.russellstubeforming.com
SIC: 3498 Tube fabricating (contract bending and shaping)

(G-9349)
RUSTIC GLOW CANDLE CO LLC
7605 Indian Lake Rd (46236-9520)
PHONE.................317 696-4264
Brandyn Allen Hall, *Pr*
EMP: 5 **EST:** 2017
SALES (est): 67.75K **Privately Held**
SIC: 3999 Candles

(G-9350)
RX HELP CENTERS LLC
3905 Vincennes Rd Ste 200 (46268-3039)
P.O. Box 34555 (46234-0555)
PHONE.................866 478-9593
Jeffery Paul Christensen, *CEO*
William Lee Stafford, *Pr*
EMP: 2 **EST:** 2009
SALES (est): 644.34K **Privately Held**
Web: www.rxhelpcenters.com
SIC: 3841 Surgical and medical instruments

(G-9351)
RYAN LANE
5548 Broadway St (46220-3071)
PHONE.................317 475-9730
Ryan Lane, *Owner*
EMP: 1 **EST:** 2001
SALES (est): 70.66K **Privately Held**
Web: www.ryanlaneonline.com
SIC: 3599 Weather vanes

(G-9352)
RYOEI USA INC
5524 Fortune Cir S (46241-5540)
PHONE.................317 912-4498
Masaaki Sugiyama, *Ch Bd*
Hiroaki Ihara, *Pr*
Chiyoyoshi Oikawa, *Treas*
EMP: 15 **EST:** 2017
SALES (est): 2.94MM **Privately Held**
Web: www.ryoei-usa.com
SIC: 3569 Liquid automation machinery and equipment
PA: Ryoei Co.,Ltd.
4-52, Honjicho
Toyota AIC 471-0

(G-9353)
S & R WELDING INC
113 Pennsylvania Ct (46225-2327)
PHONE.................317 710-0360
Steve Rusomaroff, *Pr*
Terry Rusomaroff, *Sec*
EMP: 3 **EST:** 1987
SQ FT: 1,500
SALES (est): 376.23K **Privately Held**
SIC: 3052 7699 Rubber hose; Rubber product repair

(G-9354)
S C PRYOR INC
Also Called: Pryor Safe & Lock
5424 Brookville Rd (46219-7103)
PHONE.................317 352-1281
Stanley C Pryor, *Pr*
Mary Pryor, *VP*
▲ **EMP:** 10 **EST:** 1974
SQ FT: 1,500
SALES (est): 663.61K **Privately Held**
Web: www.pryorsafe.com
SIC: 5044 5099 1799 7699 Vaults and safes; Locks and lock sets; Safe or vault installation; Lock and key services

(G-9355)
S CJ INCORPORATED
2021 W Raymond St (46221-2013)
PHONE.................317 822-3477
Cathy Houston, *Owner*
EMP: 10 **EST:** 2008
SALES (est): 691.3K **Privately Held**
SIC: 3713 Dump truck bodies

(G-9356)
S S M INC
Also Called: Unit Step
4000 Southeastern Ave (46203-1563)
PHONE.................317 357-4552
James W Marten, *Pr*

◆ **EMP:** 5 **EST:** 1958
SQ FT: 12,000
SALES (est): 489.24K **Privately Held**
Web: www.unitstepind.com
SIC: 3446 3272 Architectural metalwork; Concrete products, precast, nec

(G-9357)
S T PRAXAIR TECHNOLOGY INC
1500 Polco St (46222-3274)
PHONE.................317 240-2500
EMP: 21 **EST:** 2014
SALES (est): 764.83K **Privately Held**
Web: www.linde-amt.com
SIC: 3479 3548 Coating of metals and formed products; Electric welding equipment
HQ: Linde Inc.
10 Riverview Dr
Danbury CT 06810
203 837-2000

(G-9358)
SA HEINEN LLC
Also Called: Greens Groomer
3890 N Raceway Rd (46234-9226)
PHONE.................317 416-7818
Shawn Heinen, *Managing Member*
EMP: 5 **EST:** 2017
SALES (est): 490.44K **Privately Held**
Web: www.greensgroomer.com
SIC: 3523 Turf and grounds equipment

(G-9359)
SAAM INC
55 Monument Cir Fl 7 (46204)
PHONE.................855 405-7773
Rob Qualls, *CEO*
Greg Stewart, *Pr*
Robert Qualls, *CEO*
Erik Deutsch, *Engr*
Phil Mccormack, *CFO*
EMP: 7 **EST:** 2001
SALES (est): 914.59K **Privately Held**
Web: saam.us.com
SIC: 3829 Measuring and controlling devices, nec

(G-9360)
SABRE HOLDINGS LLC
Also Called: Crazy Skates USA
2801 Fortune Cir E Ste B (46241-5551)
PHONE.................317 222-6150
Trent Carter, *Managing Member*
EMP: 17 **EST:** 2015
SALES (est): 500.57K **Privately Held**
Web: www.crazyskates.com
SIC: 5941 3949 Skating equipment; Skateboards

(G-9361)
SABRE INTEGRATED SERVICES
800 E 96th St (46240-3770)
PHONE.................317 844-9100
Dan Baker, *VP*
EMP: 1 **EST:** 2011
SALES (est): 2.39MM
SALES (corp-wide): 574.27MM **Privately Held**
SIC: 3441 Tower sections, radio and television transmission
PA: Sabre Industries, Inc.
8653 E Hwy 67
Alvarado TX 76009
817 852-1700

(G-9362)
SAFE BIRD EXPRESS LLC ✪
Also Called: Freight Transport
3039 N Post Rd (46226-6543)
PHONE.................607 376-7633
Ryan Henderson, *Pr*

Indianapolis - Marion County (G-9363) — GEOGRAPHIC SECTION

EMP: 2 EST: 2022
SALES (est): 92.67K **Privately Held**
SIC: 3537 Trucks, tractors, loaders, carriers, and similar equipment

(G-9363)
SAFE TRAVELS SOLUTIONS LLC ○
8939 New Church Blvd (46231-4221)
PHONE..................................317 640-4576
Dylan Allen, *CEO*
EMP: 2 EST: 2022
SALES (est): 117.31K **Privately Held**
SIC: 4724 3799 Travel agencies; Transportation equipment, nec

(G-9364)
SAFETY VEHICLE EMBLEM INC
5235 Commerce Cir (46237-9747)
PHONE..................................317 885-7565
Shelley Warrick, *Pr*
Rhonda Chatfield, *Sec*
Lynnette Deogracias, *Prin*
EMP: 10 EST: 1965
SQ FT: 6,000
SALES (est): 400.12K **Privately Held**
Web: www.safetyvehicle.com
SIC: 3993 2396 2395 Signs, not made in custom sign painting shops; Automotive and apparel trimmings; Pleating and stitching

(G-9365)
SALDANA RACING TANKS INC
Also Called: Saldana Racing Products
3754 N Raceway Rd (46234-9225)
PHONE..................................317 852-4193
Keith Wagoner, *Pr*
▼ EMP: 14 EST: 1994
SQ FT: 11,000
SALES (est): 2.49MM **Privately Held**
Web: www.saldanaracingproducts.com
SIC: 3714 Radiators and radiator shells and cores, motor vehicle

(G-9366)
SALESFORCE INC
111 Monument Cir Ste 2000 (46204-5180)
PHONE..................................317 370-5737
EMP: 53
SALES (corp-wide): 34.86B **Publicly Held**
Web: www.salesforce.com
SIC: 7372 Business oriented computer software
PA: Salesforce, Inc.
 415 Mission St Fl 3
 San Francisco CA 94105
 415 901-7000

(G-9367)
SALESFORCECOM INC
Also Called: SALESFORCE.COM, INC.
111 Monument Cir Ste 2000 (46204-5180)
PHONE..................................317 981-4924
EMP: 12
SALES (corp-wide): 26.49B **Publicly Held**
Web: www.salesforce.com
SIC: 7372 Business oriented computer software
PA: Salesforce, Inc.
 415 Mssion St Fl 3slsfrc Flr 3
 San Francisco CA 94105
 415 901-7000

(G-9368)
SAMS TECHNICAL PUBLISHING LLC
9850 E 30th St (46229-3608)
PHONE..................................800 428-7267
EMP: 15 EST: 2003
SALES (est): 916.29K **Privately Held**
Web: www.samswebsite.com

SIC: 2741 Miscellaneous publishing

(G-9369)
SANBAR OF INDIANA INC
Also Called: Hoover Sheet Metal
1721 S Franklin Rd Ste 100 (46239-2170)
PHONE..................................317 375-6220
John W Kraus, *Pr*
Allen Heyd, *VP*
Michael M Kraus, *Treas*
Sandra K Kraus, *Sec*
EMP: 4 EST: 1958
SQ FT: 4,750
SALES (est): 648.21K **Privately Held**
Web: www.nywf64photos.com
SIC: 3444 3441 Sheet metalwork; Fabricated structural metal

(G-9370)
SANOFI US SERVICES INC
5225 W 81st St (46268-1643)
PHONE..................................317 228-5750
David Groth, *Mgr*
EMP: 51
Web: www.sanofi.us
SIC: 2834 Pharmaceutical preparations
HQ: Sanofi Us Services Inc.
 55 Corporate Dr
 Bridgewater NJ 08807
 800 981-2491

(G-9371)
SANTAROSSA MOSAIC TILE CO INC (PA)
2707 Roosevelt Ave (46218-3646)
P.O. Box 18181 (46218-0181)
PHONE..................................317 632-9494
Ketchum Todd, *Pr*
David M Santarossa, *
Santarossa John, *
◆ EMP: 198 EST: 1924
SQ FT: 24,000
SALES (est): 22.39MM
SALES (corp-wide): 22.39MM **Privately Held**
Web: www.santarossa.com
SIC: 1743 5023 1752 3251 Terrazzo work; Carpets; Floor laying and floor work, nec; Flooring brick, clay

(G-9372)
SARAH JOHNSON NETTLES
Also Called: Esteem Style Wear
1226 N Illinois St # 404 (46202-2325)
PHONE..................................317 778-0023
Sarah Johnson Nettles, *Owner*
EMP: 6 EST: 2020
SALES (est): 236.56K **Privately Held**
SIC: 3161 Clothing and apparel carrying cases

(G-9373)
SARAN LP
820 S Post Rd (46239-9790)
EMP: 105 EST: 1998
SQ FT: 27,000
SALES (est): 2.42MM **Privately Held**
Web: www.saranindustries.com
SIC: 3479 3471 1721 1799 Coating of metals with plastic or resins; Plating and polishing; Industrial painting; Sandblasting of building exteriors

(G-9374)
SASAKI COATING NORTH AMER INC ○
6330 Corporate Dr Ste B (46278)
PHONE..................................317 956-2232
Akio Nakano, *Pr*
Akio Nakano, *CEO*
Ryuji Sawatani, *VP*

Hideki Ono, *Dir*
Yoichi Iguchi, *Genl Mgr*
EMP: 15 EST: 2023
SALES (est): 523.41K **Privately Held**
SIC: 3089 Automotive parts, plastic

(G-9375)
SASSY ORGANICS COLLECTION LLC
7840 Gilmore Rd (46219-1220)
PHONE..................................231 942-0751
EMP: 1
SALES (est): 69.27K **Privately Held**
Web: www.sassyorganicscollection.com
SIC: 2899 Oils and essential oils

(G-9376)
SASSY SCRUBZ LLC
7535 Bayview Club Dr Apt 1c (46250)
PHONE..................................463 224-5693
Manisha Brown, *Owner*
EMP: 4 EST: 2021
SALES (est): 75K **Privately Held**
SIC: 2211 Scrub cloths

(G-9377)
SATCO INC
4221 S High School Rd (46241-6452)
PHONE..................................317 856-0301
Robert Duvall, *Mgr*
EMP: 60
SALES (corp-wide): 56.12MM **Privately Held**
Web: www.satco-inc.com
SIC: 2448 Cargo containers, wood and metal combination
PA: Satco, Inc.
 1601 E El Segundo Blvd
 El Segundo CA 90245
 310 322-4719

(G-9378)
SATIN & STEMS
808 Canyon Rd (46217-3918)
PHONE..................................765 318-2211
Elizabeth Digiusto, *Prin*
EMP: 4 EST: 2018
SALES (est): 81.19K **Privately Held**
Web: www.satinandstems.com
SIC: 2221 Satins

(G-9379)
SATURDAY EVENING POST SOC INC
Also Called: CHILDREN'S BETTER HEALTH INSTI
3520 Guion Rd Ste 200 (46222-1672)
P.O. Box 37426 (50037-0426)
PHONE..................................317 634-1100
Joan Servaas, *Pr*
Dwight Lamb, *
Robert Silvers, *
EMP: 53 EST: 1976
SALES (est): 9.91MM **Privately Held**
Web: www.saturdayeveningpost.com
SIC: 2721 Magazines: publishing only, not printed on site

(G-9380)
SAUL GOODE INDUSTRIES LLC
2024 Bluff Rd (46225-1969)
PHONE..................................317 929-1111
Jeff Dunlap, *Owner*
EMP: 16 EST: 2018
SALES (est): 824.61K **Privately Held**
Web: www.saulgoodeindustries.com
SIC: 3999 Manufacturing industries, nec

(G-9381)
SAZZYS PLACE LLC
9124 Venona Way (46234-2357)

PHONE..................................317 414-6332
EMP: 4 EST: 2021
SALES (est): 147.33K **Privately Held**
SIC: 2844 Cosmetic preparations

(G-9382)
SB FINISHING
6844 Hawthorn Park Dr (46220-3909)
PHONE..................................317 598-0965
Anita Hays, *Prin*
EMP: 6 EST: 2008
SALES (est): 146.71K **Privately Held**
Web: www.powdercoatchicago.com
SIC: 3949 Playground equipment

(G-9383)
SCALABLE PRESS
7800 Records St (46226-3984)
PHONE..................................510 396-5226
EMP: 12 EST: 2017
SALES (est): 927.63K **Privately Held**
Web: www.scalablepress.com
SIC: 2741 Miscellaneous publishing

(G-9384)
SCALABLE PRESS INC
4805 Punjab Dr (46218)
PHONE..................................877 752-9060
EMP: 1
SALES (est): 78.58K **Privately Held**
SIC: 3555 Printing presses

(G-9385)
SCALE COMPUTING INC (PA)
525 S Meridian St Ste 3e (46225-1108)
PHONE..................................317 856-9959
Jeff Ready, *Pr*
Ehren Maedge, *
Dave Demlow, *
Jason Collier, *
Scott Loughmiller, *CPO*
EMP: 25 EST: 2008
SALES (est): 30.76MM
SALES (corp-wide): 30.76MM **Privately Held**
Web: www.scalecomputing.com
SIC: 3572 Computer storage devices

(G-9386)
SCANDIGITAL INC
9900 Westpoint Dr Ste 138 (46256-3338)
PHONE..................................888 333-2808
Anderson Schoenrock, *CEO*
▼ EMP: 5 EST: 2007
SALES (est): 711.23K **Privately Held**
Web: www.scandigital.com
SIC: 3825 Analog-digital converters, electronic instrumentation type

(G-9387)
SCHAEFER SIGN WORKS
5658 W 73rd St (46278-1738)
PHONE..................................317 292-9373
Charles Schaefer, *Mgr*
EMP: 5 EST: 2017
SALES (est): 194.37K **Privately Held**
Web: www.schaefersignworks.com
SIC: 3993 Signs and advertising specialties

(G-9388)
SCHAEFER TECHNOLOGIES INC
4901 W Raymond St (46241-4733)
PHONE..................................317 241-9444
Steven J Schaefer, *CEO*
Kevin Schaefer, *
Michael G Schaefer, *Stockholder*
EMP: 85 EST: 1995
SQ FT: 60,000
SALES (est): 9.16MM **Privately Held**
Web: www.schaefer-technologies.net

GEOGRAPHIC SECTION

Indianapolis - Marion County (G-9415)

SIC: 3599 Machine shop, jobbing and repair

(G-9389)
SCHAFFNER LLC
7016 Cricklewood Rd (46220-4119)
PHONE...................317 450-3956
Mary Schaffner, *Prin*
EMP: 5 EST: 2018
SALES (est): 83.21K Privately Held
Web: www.schaffner.com
SIC: 3612 Transformers, except electric

(G-9390)
SCHNEIDER ELC SYSTEMS USA INC
101 W Ohio St (46204-1906)
PHONE...................317 372-2839
EMP: 5
SALES (corp-wide): 82.05K Privately Held
Web: www.se.com
SIC: 3822 Temperature controls, automatic
HQ: Schneider Electric Systems Usa, Inc.
10900 Equity Dr
Houston TX 77041
713 329-1600

(G-9391)
SCHOUTEN METAL CRAFT INC
2211 E 44th St (46205-2204)
P.O. Box 58 (46064-0058)
PHONE...................317 546-2639
Ron Schouten, *Pr*
EMP: 6 EST: 1960
SQ FT: 4,300
SALES (est): 501.46K Privately Held
Web: www.schoutenmetalcraft.com
SIC: 3446 Ornamental metalwork

(G-9392)
SCOOP ENTERTAINMENT SOURCE
2021 E 52nd St Ste 204 (46205-1405)
PHONE...................317 475-0615
Cliff Robinson, *Owner*
EMP: 1 EST: 2005
SALES (est): 99.82K Privately Held
Web: www.scoopmg.com
SIC: 2759 Publication printing

(G-9393)
SCOOP LLC
241 N Pennsylvania St Ste 300 (46204-2408)
PHONE...................317 713-2141
EMP: 4 EST: 2019
SALES (est): 229.57K Privately Held
Web: www.scoopmg.com
SIC: 2741 Miscellaneous publishing

(G-9394)
SCOTT BILLMAN
5411 Maplewood Dr (46224-3329)
PHONE...................317 293-9921
Scott Billman, *Owner*
EMP: 2 EST: 2001
SALES (est): 90.65K Privately Held
SIC: 3577 Computer peripheral equipment, nec

(G-9395)
SCRAMBOOSAY LLC
5441 Kelvington Ln (46254-5449)
PHONE...................317 654-0595
EMP: 10 EST: 2020
SALES (est): 234.29K Privately Held
SIC: 2389 Apparel and accessories, nec

(G-9396)
SCREENPRINT SPECIAL TEES LLC
4353 W 96th St Ste 200 (46268-1439)
PHONE...................317 396-0349
EMP: 4 EST: 2005
SALES (est): 248.78K Privately Held
Web: www.screenprintspecialtees.com
SIC: 2759 Screen printing

(G-9397)
SCRUBS2THERESCUE LLC
5348 Crittenden Ave (46220-3441)
PHONE...................317 748-7677
EMP: 4 EST: 2021
SALES (est): 75K Privately Held
SIC: 2339 Women's and misses' athletic clothing and sportswear

(G-9398)
SECURED FTP HOSTING LLC
Also Called: Smartfile
525 S Meridian St # 3b (46225-1108)
PHONE...................877 336-3453
EMP: 21 EST: 2009
SQ FT: 6,000
SALES (est): 1.91MM Privately Held
Web: www.smartfile.com
SIC: 7372 Prepackaged software

(G-9399)
SEGO WOODWORKING
5839 Garden Dr (46217-3746)
PHONE...................317 431-9087
EMP: 4 EST: 2019
SALES (est): 54.13K Privately Held
SIC: 2431 Millwork

(G-9400)
SEGUNDO DELUXE LLC
2725 S Kenmore Rd (46203-5816)
PHONE...................260 414-7820
Victor Segundo, *CEO*
EMP: 1 EST: 2020
SALES (est): 46.43K Privately Held
SIC: 2782 Checkbooks

(G-9401)
SELEKTD WORX LLC
1453 Woodlawn Ave (46203-1232)
PHONE...................317 227-9337
EMP: 1
SALES (est): 69.27K Privately Held
SIC: 3949 7389 Sporting and athletic goods, nec; Business Activities at Non-Commercial Site

(G-9402)
SENTECH CORPORATION
8358 Masters Rd (46250-1538)
PHONE...................317 596-1988
Jerry W Spore, *CEO*
Jerry R Coonrod, *Pr*
EMP: 8 EST: 1987
SQ FT: 10,000
SALES (est): 1.07MM Privately Held
Web: www.sentechcorp.com
SIC: 3826 Gas testing apparatus

(G-9403)
SENTIMENTAL STITCHES
9722 Oakhaven Ct (46256-8101)
PHONE...................317 694-1244
EMP: 4 EST: 2016
SALES (est): 68.63K Privately Held
Web: www.sentimentalstitches.net
SIC: 2395 Embroidery and art needlework

(G-9404)
SERMATECH INTL CANADA CORP
1500 Polco St (46222-3274)
PHONE...................317 240-2500
George Bradley, *Pr*
EMP: 44 EST: 2014
SALES (est): 1.46MM Privately Held
SIC: 3479 Coating of metals and formed products
HQ: Linde Advanced Material Technologies Inc.
1500 Polco St
Indianapolis IN 46222
317 240-2500

(G-9405)
SERVAAS INC (PA)
3520 Guion Rd Ste 200 (46222-1672)
PHONE...................317 633-2020
Amy Servaas, *Pr*
Joan S Durham, *Sec*
EMP: 3 EST: 1949
SALES (est): 925.85K
SALES (corp-wide): 925.85K Privately Held
Web: www.servaasfactories.com
SIC: 3462 3069 2842 2721 Iron and steel forgings; Rubber automotive products; Polishes and sanitation goods; Magazines: publishing only, not printed on site

(G-9406)
SERVAAS LABORATORIES INC
Also Called: Bar Keepers Friend
5240 Walt Pl (46254-5795)
PHONE...................317 636-7760
Paul Servaas, *Pr*
Matthew Selig, *
Tony Patterson, *
Amy Reismeyer, *
◆ EMP: 50 EST: 1957
SALES (est): 18.65MM Privately Held
Web: www.barkeepersfriend.com
SIC: 2842 Cleaning or polishing preparations, nec

(G-9407)
SERVAAS MANUFACTURING CORP
Also Called: Floral-Guard
4897 Kessler Boulevard East Dr (46220-5348)
PHONE...................317 253-0454
David A Servaas, *Pr*
Lara B Servaas, *Sec*
EMP: 1 EST: 1979
SALES (est): 140.05K Privately Held
Web: www.floral-guard.com
SIC: 2819 Industrial inorganic chemicals, nec

(G-9408)
SERVICE GRAPHICS INC
Also Called: S G I
8350 Allison Ave (46268-1660)
PHONE...................317 471-8246
Michael P Burks, *Pr*
Jack Burns, *
Bernie Weitekamp, *
Thomas Dean, *
EMP: 65 EST: 1967
SQ FT: 200,000
SALES (est): 11.66MM Privately Held
Web: www.mysgi.com
SIC: 7389 7334 7331 2752 Packaging and labeling services; Multilithing; Mailing service; Lithographing on metal

(G-9409)
SHACKELFORD GRAPHICS
7522 Honnen Dr N (46256-3228)
PHONE...................317 783-3582
Paul J Shackelford, *Owner*
EMP: 2 EST: 1991
SALES (est): 128.16K Privately Held
SIC: 2752 Offset printing

(G-9410)
SHADE BY DESIGN INC
6321 E 30th St Ste 206 (46219-1081)
PHONE...................317 602-3513
Kevin Drake, *Pr*
Larry Marietta, *Prin*
EMP: 7 EST: 2006
SALES (est): 401.84K Privately Held
Web: www.shade-bydesign.com
SIC: 2394 1799 Canvas awnings and canopies; Awning installation

(G-9411)
SHADOW GRAPHIX INC
4703 W Vermont St (46222-3258)
PHONE...................317 481-9710
Daren Merkle, *Pr*
EMP: 7 EST: 1994
SQ FT: 6,400
SALES (est): 864.31K Privately Held
Web: www.shadowgraphix.com
SIC: 7373 2759 7336 Computer-aided manufacturing (CAM) systems service; Wrappers: printing, nsk; Commercial art and illustration

(G-9412)
SHADOW SIGNS
4703 W Vermont St (46222-3258)
PHONE...................317 481-9710
EMP: 4 EST: 1993
SQ FT: 900
SALES (est): 104.31K Privately Held
Web: www.shadowgraphix.com
SIC: 3993 Signs and advertising specialties

(G-9413)
SHARPEN TECHNOLOGIES INC (PA)
Also Called: Sharpen
101 W Washington St Ste 600e (46204-3494)
PHONE...................855 249-3357
Mike Simmons, *Ch*
Charlie Newark French, *CEO*
Pamela Hynes, *COO*
Ashley Vukovits, *CFO*
EMP: 35 EST: 2011
SQ FT: 12,846
SALES (est): 11.67MM
SALES (corp-wide): 11.67MM Privately Held
Web: www.sharpencx.com
SIC: 7371 7372 Computer software development; Prepackaged software

(G-9414)
SHE PUBLISHING LLC
5625 N German Church Rd (46235-8513)
P.O. Box 1912 (46322-0912)
PHONE...................219 515-8032
EMP: 1 EST: 2021
SALES (est): 130.5K Privately Held
Web: www.shepublishingllc.com
SIC: 2741 7389 Miscellaneous publishing; Business services, nec

(G-9415)
SHEET METAL MODELS INC
Also Called: Sheet Metal Models/Machine Tl
2702 National Ave (46227-3531)
P.O. Box 404 (46107-0404)
PHONE...................317 783-1303
Joseph A Gilliland, *Pr*
EMP: 15 EST: 1959
SQ FT: 12,500
SALES (est): 2.47MM Privately Held
Web: www.shtmod.com
SIC: 3444 Sheet metal specialties, not stamped

(PA)=Parent Co (HQ)=Headquarters
✿ = New Business established in last 2 years

Indianapolis - Marion County (G-9416)

(G-9416)
SHEET MTAL WKRS LCAL 20 APPRNT
2828 E 45th St Ste A (46205-2403)
PHONE..................317 541-0050
Michael D Patrick, *Prin*
EMP: 12 **EST:** 2008
SALES (est): 4.41MM **Privately Held**
Web: www.smw20training.com
SIC: 3444 Sheet metalwork

(G-9417)
SHELBY GRAVEL INC
2701 S Emerson Ave (46203-4822)
PHONE..................317 784-6678
John D Haehl Senior, *Brnch Mgr*
EMP: 18
SALES (corp-wide): 74.83MM **Privately Held**
Web: www.shelbymaterials.com
SIC: 3273 Ready-mixed concrete
PA: Shelby Gravel, Inc
    157 E Rampart St
    Shelbyville IN 46176
    317 398-4485

(G-9418)
SHELBY GRAVEL INC
Also Called: Shelby Materials
10770 E County Road 300 N (46234-9415)
PHONE..................317 216-7556
EMP: 10
SALES (corp-wide): 74.83MM **Privately Held**
Web: www.shelbymaterials.com
SIC: 5211 3273 Cement; Ready-mixed concrete
PA: Shelby Gravel, Inc
    157 E Rampart St
    Shelbyville IN 46176
    317 398-4485

(G-9419)
SHELBY WESTSIDE UPHOLSTERING
Also Called: Shelby Upholstering Interiors
3136 W 16th St (46222-2781)
PHONE..................317 631-8911
TOLL FREE: 800
Donald R Quass, *Pr*
Betty Quass, *Sec*
Donald P Quass, *Contrlr*
EMP: 7 **EST:** 1932
SQ FT: 4,800
SALES (est): 489.96K **Privately Held**
Web: www.shelbyupholstering.com
SIC: 7641 5713 5714 2512 Reupholstery; Carpets; Draperies; Living room furniture: upholstered on wood frames

(G-9420)
SHIMP OPTICAL CORP
Also Called: V J Shimp Optical
932 S Meridian St Ste 101 (46225-1307)
PHONE..................317 636-4448
Michael Shimp, *Pr*
Diane Shimp, *VP*
EMP: 2 **EST:** 1964
SALES (est): 254.72K **Privately Held**
Web: www.shimpoptical.com
SIC: 5995 3851 Eyeglasses, prescription; Lens grinding, except prescription: ophthalmic

(G-9421)
SHOBE CASES LLC
26 W Washington St Apt 1001 (46204-3437)
PHONE..................317 363-9006
Nickolas S Turner, *Owner*
EMP: 5 **EST:** 2016
SALES (est): 80.69K **Privately Held**
SIC: 3523 Farm machinery and equipment

(G-9422)
SHORT 9TH LLC
6453 Waterloo Ln (46268-8646)
PHONE..................270 313-5665
EMP: 2
SALES (est): 74.03K **Privately Held**
SIC: 1389 7389 Construction, repair, and dismantling services; Business services, nec

(G-9423)
SHURTRACK TRANSPORT LLC ◊
10417 Lookout Ln (46234)
PHONE..................317 779-5902
EMP: 1 **EST:** 2024
SALES (est): 69.27K **Privately Held**
SIC: 3799 7389 Transportation equipment, nec; Business services, nec

(G-9424)
SIEMENS ENERGY INC
201 S Capitol Ave Ste 910 (46225)
PHONE..................317 677-1340
EMP: 130
SALES (corp-wide): 33.81B **Privately Held**
Web: new.siemens.com
SIC: 3511 Gas turbine generator set units, complete
HQ: Siemens Energy, Inc.
    4400 N Alafaya Trl
    Orlando FL 32826
    407 736-2000

(G-9425)
SIEMENS INDUSTRY INC
7800 Col.H Weir Cook Mem Dr (46241-8003)
PHONE..................317 381-0734
EMP: 22
SALES (corp-wide): 84.48B **Privately Held**
Web: www.siemens.com
SIC: 3822 Air conditioning and refrigeration controls
HQ: Siemens Industry, Inc.
    100 Technology Dr
    Alpharetta GA 30005
    847 215-1000

(G-9426)
SIG MEDIA LLC
3750 Wallace Ave (46218-1679)
PHONE..................317 858-7624
James Byers, *Prin*
EMP: 10 **EST:** 2012
SALES (est): 227.99K **Privately Held**
Web: www.sigmediallc.com
SIC: 7312 7319 7336 3993 Outdoor advertising services; Transit advertising services; Graphic arts and related design; Advertising novelties

(G-9427)
SIGN ART LLC
2525 N Shadeland Ave Ste A9 (46219)
PHONE..................317 247-0333
EMP: 5 **EST:** 2015
SALES (est): 69.56K **Privately Held**
Web: www.sign-artindy.com
SIC: 3993 Signs and advertising specialties

(G-9428)
SIGN CRAFT INDUSTRIES INC
Also Called: Quicksign
8816 Corporation Dr (46256-1291)
PHONE..................317 842-8664
Greg Beyerl, *Pr*
Phil Sheingold, *
EMP: 49 **EST:** 1958
SQ FT: 43,000
SALES (est): 4.9MM **Privately Held**
Web: www.signcraftind.com
SIC: 3993 5999 5046 Electric signs; Alarm signal systems; Signs, electrical

(G-9429)
SIGN GROUP INC
Front Row Sports Technology
5370 W 84th St (46268-1517)
PHONE..................317 228-8049
EMP: 1
SALES (corp-wide): 2.31MM **Privately Held**
Web: www.thesigngroup.net
SIC: 3993 Scoreboards, electric
PA: The Sign Group Inc
    5370 W 84th St
    Indianapolis IN 46268
    317 875-6969

(G-9430)
SIGN GROUP INC (PA)
Also Called: S G I
5370 W 84th St (46268-1517)
PHONE..................317 875-6969
Robert Scherer, *Pr*
Danielle Wills, *VP*
EMP: 16 **EST:** 1981
SALES (est): 2.31MM
SALES (corp-wide): 2.31MM **Privately Held**
Web: www.thesigngroup.net
SIC: 1799 7629 3993 Sign installation and maintenance; Electrical equipment repair services; Electric signs

(G-9431)
SIGN HERE LTD
4444 Decatur Blvd Ste 1200 (46241-9537)
PHONE..................317 487-8001
Diana Scalph, *Owner*
EMP: 4 **EST:** 1999
SALES (est): 271.76K **Privately Held**
Web: www.uprintsolutions.com
SIC: 3993 Signs and advertising specialties

(G-9432)
SIGN SERVICES
1305 W 29th St (46208-4942)
PHONE..................317 546-1111
Mickey Levy, *Prin*
EMP: 6 **EST:** 2010
SALES (est): 480.5K **Privately Held**
Web: www.ssindy.com
SIC: 3993 Signs and advertising specialties

(G-9433)
SIGN UP 4 FUN
11729 Tidewater Dr S (46236-8580)
PHONE..................317 800-3535
EMP: 3 **EST:** 2019
SALES (est): 46.08K **Privately Held**
SIC: 3993 Signs and advertising specialties

(G-9434)
SIGNCRAFTERS INC
7602 E 88th Pl (46256-1261)
PHONE..................317 579-4800
EMP: 2
SALES (corp-wide): 5.08MM **Privately Held**
Web: www.signcrafters-inc.com
SIC: 3993 Electric signs
PA: Signcrafters Inc
    1508 Stringtown Rd
    Evansville IN 47711
    812 424-9011

(G-9435)
SIGNDOC IDENTITY LLC
3150 Rand Rd (46241-5408)
P.O. Box 42264 (46242-0264)
PHONE..................317 247-9670
EMP: 8 **EST:** 2008
SQ FT: 25,000
SALES (est): 973.76K **Privately Held**
Web: www.signdoc.com
SIC: 5046 3993 1799 1731 Signs, electrical; Electric signs; Sign installation and maintenance; Lighting contractor

(G-9436)
SIGNS BY TM LLC
6246 La Pas Trl (46268-2509)
PHONE..................317 872-3220
EMP: 5 **EST:** 2019
SALES (est): 120.8K **Privately Held**
SIC: 3993 Signs and advertising specialties

(G-9437)
SIGNS INC INTERNATIONAL
2525 N Shadeland Ave Ste A9 (46219-1787)
PHONE..................317 925-2835
Jeffrey Morgan, *CEO*
EMP: 1 **EST:** 2010
SALES (est): 135.43K **Privately Held**
SIC: 3993 Signs and advertising specialties

(G-9438)
SIGNWORKS LLC
5349 W 86th St (46268-1501)
PHONE..................317 872-8722
EMP: 11 **EST:** 2012
SALES (est): 1.14MM **Privately Held**
Web: www.signworksthinks.com
SIC: 3993 Signs and advertising specialties

(G-9439)
SIGSTR INC
20 N Meridian St Ste 400 # 4 (46204-3007)
PHONE..................317 960-3003
Bryan Wade, *CEO*
Dan Hanrahan, *Pr*
EMP: 27 **EST:** 2015
SALES (est): 776.07K **Privately Held**
Web: www.terminus.com
SIC: 7372 Business oriented computer software

(G-9440)
SIM2K INC
7160 Graham Rd (46250-2672)
PHONE..................317 251-7920
Mark Finegan, *Pr*
Christy Finegan, *CEO*
EMP: 26 **EST:** 1999
SALES (est): 3.02MM **Privately Held**
Web: www.sim2k.com
SIC: 7372 7379 Prepackaged software; Computer related maintenance services

(G-9441)
SIMONE-CHRISETTE PUBG LLC
10838 Tallow Wood Ln (46236-8307)
PHONE..................317 985-9851
Victoria Dinkins, *Prin*
EMP: 5 **EST:** 2018
SALES (est): 76.74K **Privately Held**
SIC: 2741 Miscellaneous publishing

(G-9442)
SIMPLY NATURAL BY J LLC
2269 Tradewinds Dr Apt H (46229-3832)
PHONE..................317 464-7299
EMP: 1 **EST:** 2020
SALES (est): 10K **Privately Held**

GEOGRAPHIC SECTION

Indianapolis - Marion County (G-9469)

SIC: 2841 Soap and other detergents

(G-9443)
SINDEN RACING SERVICE INC
1201 Main St (46224-6533)
PHONE..................317 243-7171
Jeff Sinden, *Pr*
Joseph Kennedy, *Sec*
EMP: 10 EST: 1987
SQ FT: 21,000
SALES (est): 782.25K **Privately Held**
Web: www.indyracingexperience.com
SIC: 3559 3949 3596 3441 Automotive related machinery; Sporting and athletic goods, nec; Scales and balances, except laboratory; Fabricated structural metal

(G-9444)
SITEWISE INC
Also Called: VA Optical Laboratory
4440 S High School Rd (46241-6401)
PHONE..................317 988-1630
EMP: 2
SALES (corp-wide): 679.04K **Privately Held**
Web: www.sitewiseinc.com
SIC: 3699 Security control equipment and systems
PA: Sitewise, Inc.
    306 E 3rd St Unit D
    Huntingburg IN 47542
    812 631-2374

(G-9445)
SKINNY & CO INC
Also Called: Apothecare Rx
5762 W 74th St Ste 117 (46278-1754)
P.O. Box 68445 (46268-0445)
PHONE..................888 865-4278
Luke Geddie, *CEO*
Matt Geddie, *Prin*
EMP: 21 EST: 2013
SALES (est): 4.41MM **Privately Held**
Web: www.skinnyandcompany.com
SIC: 2076 Coconut oil

(G-9446)
SL BEAUTY LLC
2212 Emrich Ln (46222-3280)
PHONE..................317 969-0341
EMP: 1
SALES (est): 39.69K **Privately Held**
SIC: 3999 7389 Eyelashes, artificial; Business Activities at Non-Commercial Site

(G-9447)
SL TERRASTAR GROUP LLC
55 S State Ave Ste 318 (46201-3898)
PHONE..................317 702-7240
Steven Lester, *CEO*
EMP: 1 EST: 2018
SALES (est): 20K **Privately Held**
SIC: 2741 Internet publishing and broadcasting

(G-9448)
SLEEGERS ENGINEERED PDTS INC
Also Called: Sleegers
5855 Kopetsky Dr Ste I (46217-9636)
PHONE..................317 786-7770
EMP: 1
SALES (corp-wide): 1.05MM **Privately Held**
Web: www.sleegers.ca
SIC: 3795 3443 Tanks and tank components; Industrial vessels, tanks, and containers
HQ: Sleegers Engineered Products Inc.
    5 Cuddy Blvd
    London ON N5V 3
    519 451-5480

(G-9449)
SMITH & NEPHEW INC
8434 Georgetown Rd (46268-1672)
PHONE..................800 357-6155
EMP: 3
SALES (corp-wide): 5.55B **Privately Held**
Web: www.smith-nephew.com
SIC: 3841 Surgical and medical instruments
HQ: Smith & Nephew, Inc.
    1450 E Brooks Rd
    Memphis TN 38116
    901 396-2121

(G-9450)
SMITH EXPEDITING RESOURCES LLC
8520 Allison Pointe Blvd Ste 220 (46250-5700)
PHONE..................317 935-1180
EMP: 4 EST: 2021
SALES (est): 75K **Privately Held**
SIC: 3799 Transportation equipment, nec

(G-9451)
SMITSON CMMNICATIONS GROUP LLC
Also Called: American Speedy Printing
3500 Depauw Blvd Ste 1000 (46268-1136)
PHONE..................317 876-8916
EMP: 6 EST: 2006
SALES (est): 651.56K **Privately Held**
Web: www.allegramarketingprint.com
SIC: 2752 Offset printing

(G-9452)
SMOCK MATERIALS HANDLING CO
3420 Park Davis Cir (46235-2397)
PHONE..................317 890-3200
William B Smock, *Pr*
John T Smock, *VP*
Robert M Smock, *Sec*
EMP: 18 EST: 1970
SQ FT: 20,000
SALES (est): 4.78MM **Privately Held**
Web: www.smockmh.com
SIC: 3535 5084 Conveyors and conveying equipment; Materials handling machinery

(G-9453)
SNA LLC
8309 Hampton Cir E (46256-9778)
PHONE..................317 931-1022
EMP: 6 EST: 2011
SALES (est): 70.52K **Privately Held**
Web: www.snadisplays.com
SIC: 3993 Signs and advertising specialties

(G-9454)
SNEAKY MICRO VIDEO DIVISIO
3216 N Pennsylvania St (46205-3414)
PHONE..................317 925-1496
EMP: 1 EST: 2008
SALES (est): 36.6K **Privately Held**
SIC: 5999 5065 3663 Alarm and safety equipment stores; Communication equipment; Television closed circuit equipment

(G-9455)
SNOWBIRD INDUSTRIES LLC
1116 N Linwood Ave (46201-2719)
PHONE..................716 481-1142
Lauren Madar, *Prin*
EMP: 4 EST: 2016
SALES (est): 50.85K **Privately Held**
SIC: 3999 Manufacturing industries, nec

(G-9456)
SNYDERS-LANCE INC
9040 Orly Rd (46241-9004)
PHONE..................317 858-2209
EMP: 1
SALES (corp-wide): 8.56B **Publicly Held**
Web: www.campbellsoupcompany.com
SIC: 2052 Pretzels
HQ: Snyder's-Lance, Inc.
    13515 Balntyn Corp Pl
    Charlotte NC 08103
    704 554-1421

(G-9457)
SNYKIN INC
Also Called: Fastsigns
3915 E 96th St (46240-1419)
PHONE..................317 845-5051
Wes Snyder, *Pr*
EMP: 7 EST: 1990
SALES (est): 500.69K **Privately Held**
Web: www.fastsigns.com
SIC: 3993 Signs and advertising specialties

(G-9458)
SOJANE TECHNOLOGIES INC
Also Called: Info-Lite
9002 N Meridian St Ste 210 (46260-5381)
PHONE..................317 915-1059
Rajesh J Shah, *Pr*
EMP: 7 EST: 2005
SALES (est): 676.43K **Privately Held**
Web: www.sojanetechnologies.com
SIC: 3993 Electric signs

(G-9459)
SOL MELANIN BEAUTY LLC
7801 Knue Rd (46250-2135)
PHONE..................317 354-3977
EMP: 1 EST: 2020
SALES (est): 85.01K **Privately Held**
SIC: 2899 Oils and essential oils

(G-9460)
SOMETHIN SWEET LLC
2717 Coldstream Ln Apt 2d (46220-1554)
PHONE..................317 804-4894
Keme Henderson, *Managing Member*
EMP: 5 EST: 2016
SALES (est): 77.57K **Privately Held**
Web: www.somethinsweetshop.com
SIC: 2052 Bakery products, dry

(G-9461)
SOUND MIND TREATS
7646 Sand Pt Apt B (46240-3351)
PHONE..................317 809-5832
EMP: 1 EST: 2017
SALES (est): 39.59K **Privately Held**
Web: www.sound-mind-treats.com
SIC: 2051 Cakes, pies, and pastries

(G-9462)
SOUND SYSTEM
5219 Five Points Rd (46239-9654)
PHONE..................317 407-4092
EMP: 1 EST: 2009
SALES (est): 29.57K **Privately Held**
SIC: 2731 Book publishing

(G-9463)
SOUTHEAST SPECIALTIES INC
2210 National Ave (46227-3512)
PHONE..................706 667-0422
Gregg Wood, *Pr*
John Lombardi, *Sec*
EMP: 4 EST: 1965
SALES (est): 302.62K **Privately Held**
Web: www.southeastspecialties.net

SIC: 3634 Heating units, for electric appliances

(G-9464)
SOUTHERN ALUM FINSHG CO INC
5302 W 78th St (46268-4147)
PHONE..................800 357-9016
James N Mcclatchey, *CEO*
EMP: 1
SALES (corp-wide): 49.04MM **Privately Held**
Web: www.saf.com
SIC: 3479 5051 3353 3471 Aluminum coating of metal products; Aluminum bars, rods, ingots, sheets, pipes, plates, etc.; Aluminum sheet, plate, and foil; Anodizing (plating) of metals or formed products
PA: Southern Aluminum Finishing Company, Inc.
    1581 Huber St Nw
    Atlanta GA 30318
    404 355-1560

(G-9465)
SOUTHSIDER
Also Called: Southside Publishing
6025 Madison Ave Ste B (46227-4722)
P.O. Box 17187 (46217-0187)
PHONE..................317 781-0023
Denise Summers, *Owner*
Denise Summers, *Prin*
Kelly Sawyers, *Prin*
EMP: 2 EST: 2009
SALES (est): 126.74K **Privately Held**
Web: www.southsidervoice.com
SIC: 2711 Commercial printing and newspaper publishing combined

(G-9466)
SPACE KRAFT
4901 W 79th St (46268-1662)
PHONE..................317 871-6999
Mark Jones, *Mgr*
▼ EMP: 18 EST: 2013
SALES (est): 2.36MM **Privately Held**
Web: www.spacekraft.com
SIC: 2621 Paper mills

(G-9467)
SPAGHEADY INC
6419 Hunters Green Ct (46278-2824)
PHONE..................317 499-6184
Marvin Rodriguez, *CFO*
Jasmine Rodrigues, *CEO*
EMP: 5 EST: 2020
SALES (est): 231.25K **Privately Held**
SIC: 3229 5961 7389 Art, decorative and novelty glassware; Electronic shopping; Business Activities at Non-Commercial Site

(G-9468)
SPARKLING ASHE LLC
4610 Karen Dr (46226-2617)
PHONE..................317 426-1824
EMP: 1 EST: 2019
SALES (est): 39.69K **Privately Held**
Web: www.sparklingashe.com
SIC: 3999 Eyelashes, artificial

(G-9469)
SPECIALTY COATING SYSTEMS INC (DH)
7645 Woodland Dr (46278-2707)
PHONE..................317 244-1200
▲ EMP: 11 EST: 1991
SQ FT: 60,224
SALES (est): 100.15MM **Privately Held**
Web: www.scscoatings.com
SIC: 3479 Coating of metals and formed products
HQ: Kisco (Taiwan) Ltd.

Rm. 1421, 14f, 144, Min Chuan E. Rd.,
Sec. 3,
Taipei City TAP 10540

(G-9470)
SPECIALTY COATING SYSTEMS INC
7645 Woodland Dr (46278-2707)
PHONE....................................317 244-1200
Peter Marinow, Brnch Mgr
EMP: 73
Web: www.scscoatings.com
SIC: 3479 Coating of metals and formed products
HQ: Specialty Coating Systems, Inc.
   7645 Woodland Dr
   Indianapolis IN 46278

(G-9471)
SPECIALTY TOOL LLC
6011 E Hanna Ave Ste D (46203-6120)
PHONE....................................260 493-6351
Tom Martin, Mgr
EMP: 12
SALES (corp-wide): 364.48B **Publicly Held**
SIC: 3541 5084 3545 Machine tools, metal cutting type; Industrial machinery and equipment; Machine tool accessories
HQ: Specialty Tool Llc
   6925 Trafalgar Dr
   Fort Wayne IN 46803
   260 493-6351

(G-9472)
SPECIFIED LTG SYSTEMS IND INC
8904 Bash St Ste B (46256-1286)
PHONE....................................317 577-8100
Paul Brock, Mgr
EMP: 11 EST: 2012
SALES (est): 1.29MM **Privately Held**
Web: www.slsindiana.com
SIC: 3646 Commercial lighting fixtures

(G-9473)
SPECILTY STNLESS STL FBRCTION
7626 Normandy Blvd (46278-1552)
PHONE....................................317 430-3490
Matt Dittemore, Brnch Mgr
EMP: 2
SALES (corp-wide): 807.86K **Privately Held**
Web: www.specialtystainlesssteel.net
SIC: 3441 Fabricated structural metal
PA: Specialty Stainless Steel Fabrication, Llc
   4337 W 96th St Ste 500
   Indianapolis IN 46268
   317 337-9800

(G-9474)
SPECILTY STNLESS STL FBRCTION (PA)
4337 W 96th St Ste 500 (46268-6122)
PHONE....................................317 337-9800
Matt Dittemore, Pr
EMP: 3 EST: 2003
SALES (est): 807.86K
SALES (corp-wide): 807.86K **Privately Held**
Web: www.specialtystainlesssteel.net
SIC: 3441 Fabricated structural metal

(G-9475)
SPECTACLES OF CARMEL INC
7945 Lieber Rd (46260-2834)
PHONE....................................317 475-9011
Bradley M Subrin, Pr
EMP: 2 EST: 2005
SALES (est): 150.81K **Privately Held**
Web: www.geckoshadesolutions.com
SIC: 3851 Spectacles

(G-9476)
SPECTRA METAL SALES INC
1711 W New York St (46222-4669)
PHONE....................................317 822-8291
Jim Dotson, Mgr
EMP: 6
SALES (corp-wide): 271.25MM **Privately Held**
Web: www.spectraguttersystems.com
SIC: 3355 5051 Aluminum rolling and drawing, nec; Aluminum bars, rods, ingots, sheets, pipes, plates, etc.
PA: Spectra Metal Sales, Inc.
   6104 Boat Rock Blvd
   Atlanta GA 30336
   404 344-4305

(G-9477)
SPEEDREAD TECHNOLOGIES LLC
Also Called: Speedread Technologies
4525 Saguaro Trl (46268-2557)
PHONE....................................317 824-4544
Bernard Hasten, Owner
EMP: 6 EST: 1999
SALES (est): 976.92K **Privately Held**
Web: www.speedreadtech.com
SIC: 3824 Water meters

(G-9478)
SPEEDY-SCREEN LLC
11109 Keough Dr (46236-9351)
PHONE....................................317 910-0724
Patrick J Lauer, Prin
EMP: 4 EST: 2019
SALES (est): 88.55K **Privately Held**
Web: www.speedy-screen.com
SIC: 2752 Commercial printing, lithographic

(G-9479)
SPOBRIC LLC
8911 Himebaugh Ln (46231-2585)
PHONE....................................302 249-1045
EMP: 1 EST: 2018
SALES (est): 42.21K **Privately Held**
SIC: 5961 2231 5699 2211 Electronic shopping; Apparel and outerwear broadwoven fabrics; Sports apparel; Apparel and outerwear fabrics, cotton

(G-9480)
SPOHN ASSOCIATES INC
3935 N Meridian St (46208-4011)
PHONE....................................317 921-2445
Jan Alston, CEO
EMP: 1
SALES (corp-wide): 11.27MM **Privately Held**
Web: www.spohnassociates.com
SIC: 5031 3211 2421 Building materials, exterior; Construction glass; Building and structural materials, wood
PA: Spohn Associates, Inc.
   7150 Winton Dr Ste 100
   Indianapolis IN 46268
   317 921-0021

(G-9481)
SPORTS LICENSED DIVISION
Also Called: Sld of The Adidas Group
8677 Logo Athletic Ct (46219-1424)
PHONE....................................317 895-7000
Debbie Wisenan, Mgr
EMP: 1100
SIC: 2329 2339 Men's and boys' sportswear and athletic clothing; Women's and misses' athletic clothing and sportswear
HQ: Sports Licensed Division Of The Adidas Group, Llc
   25 Drydock Ave Ste 110e
   Boston MA 02210

(G-9482)
SPORTS SELECT USA INC
1920 N Shadeland Ave (46219-1732)
PHONE....................................317 631-4011
▲ EMP: 4
SALES (est): 433.83K **Privately Held**
SIC: 3651 Household audio and video equipment

(G-9483)
SPRINTER XPRESS DELIVERY LLC
3654 Katelyn Ln (46228-7020)
PHONE....................................317 496-5959
EMP: 1
SALES (est): 69.27K **Privately Held**
SIC: 2519 7389 Household furniture, nec; Business services, nec

(G-9484)
ST CLAIR PRESS
1203 E Saint Clair St (46202-3590)
PHONE....................................317 612-9100
Judy Huntley, Prin
EMP: 6 EST: 2016
SALES (est): 163.06K **Privately Held**
Web: www.stclairpress.com
SIC: 2752 Offset printing

(G-9485)
ST LOUIS GROUP LLC
8888 Keystone Xing Ste 650 (46240)
PHONE....................................317 975-3121
▲ EMP: 1 EST: 2010
SALES (est): 2.25MM **Privately Held**
Web: www.thestlouisgroup.com
SIC: 3669 Smoke detectors

(G-9486)
ST REGIS INC (PA)
3233 N Post Rd (46226)
PHONE....................................317 591-3500
Richard Firkser, Pr
EMP: 12 EST: 1979
SALES (est): 10.08MM
SALES (corp-wide): 10.08MM **Privately Held**
Web: us.stregisgrp.com
SIC: 3499 3231 Novelties and giftware, including trophies; Products of purchased glass

(G-9487)
ST REGIS CULVERT INC
1101 S Kitley Ave (46203-2639)
PHONE....................................317 353-8065
Robert Mooney, Mgr
EMP: 15
SALES (corp-wide): 4.43MM **Privately Held**
Web: www.stregisculvert.com
SIC: 3498 3432 3272 Fabricated pipe and fittings; Plumbing fixture fittings and trim; Concrete products, nec
PA: St. Regis Culvert, Inc.
   202 Morrell St
   Charlotte MI 48813
   517 543-3430

(G-9488)
STAAB SHEET METAL INC
2720 S Tibbs Ave Ste 1x (46241-5301)
PHONE....................................317 241-2553
John Staab, Pr
Judy Staab, VP
EMP: 7 EST: 1929
SQ FT: 2,600
SALES (est): 561.14K **Privately Held**
SIC: 3441 Fabricated structural metal

(G-9489)
STACKMAN SIGNS/GRAPHICS INC
Also Called: United Sign Advertising
5520 S Harding St (46217-9578)
PHONE....................................317 784-6120
John Walker, Pr
Dana Walker, Sec
EMP: 13 EST: 1952
SQ FT: 6,800
SALES (est): 441.73K **Privately Held**
SIC: 3993 Electric signs

(G-9490)
STAGE NINJA LLC
707 E Murry St (46227-1139)
PHONE....................................317 829-1507
Brent Eskew, Managing Member
EMP: 6 EST: 2005
SQ FT: 1,000
SALES (est): 756.49K **Privately Held**
Web: www.stageninja.com
SIC: 3699 Electrical equipment and supplies, nec

(G-9491)
STANDARD CHANGE-MAKERS INC (PA)
Also Called: Distributeurs De Monnaie Std
3130 N Mitthoefer Rd (46235-2400)
P.O. Box 36550 (46236-0550)
PHONE....................................317 899-6955
James Robert Mcnutt, CEO
Michael Hassfurder, *
Alexander C Mcnutt, Sec
▲ EMP: 110 EST: 1955
SQ FT: 36,000
SALES (est): 19.87MM
SALES (corp-wide): 19.87MM **Privately Held**
Web: www.standardchange.com
SIC: 3578 3581 7359 Change making machines; Locks, coin-operated; Equipment rental and leasing, nec

(G-9492)
STANDARD CHANGE-MAKERS INC
Also Called: Nik-O-Lok Company
3130 N Mitthoefer Rd (46235-2400)
PHONE....................................317 899-6955
Jeff Kagan, Brnch Mgr
EMP: 10
SALES (corp-wide): 19.87MM **Privately Held**
Web: www.standardchange.com
SIC: 7699 5072 3578 Vending machine repair; Security devices, locks; Change making machines
PA: Standard Change-Makers, Inc.
   3130 N Mitthoefer Rd
   Indianapolis IN 46235
   317 899-6955

(G-9493)
STANDARD DIE SUPPLY OF INDIANA INC
927 S Pennsylvania St (46225-1395)
PHONE....................................317 236-6200
EMP: 68
SIC: 5085 3544 3452 Industrial supplies; Die sets for metal stamping (presses); Bolts, nuts, rivets, and washers

(G-9494)
STANDOUT SOCKS
3704 Ontario Cir (46268-1981)
PHONE....................................317 531-6950
EMP: 4 EST: 2017
SALES (est): 77.67K **Privately Held**
SIC: 2252 Socks

GEOGRAPHIC SECTION

Indianapolis - Marion County (G-9522)

(G-9495)
STANLEY BLACK & DECKER INC
Also Called: Stanley Hydraulic Tools AP
6161 E 75th St (46250-2701)
P.O. Box 50400 (46250-0400)
PHONE..................860 225-5111
Richard Vanderwielen, *Mgr*
EMP: 62
SALES (corp-wide): 15.78B **Publicly Held**
Web: www.stanleyblackanddecker.com
SIC: **5251** 7699 3423 3545 Tools; Industrial equipment services; Screw drivers, pliers, chisels, etc. (hand tools); Tools and accessories for machine tools
PA: Stanley Black & Decker, Inc.
1000 Stanley Dr
New Britain CT 06053
860 225-5111

(G-9496)
STANS SIGN DESIGN INC
6373 Rucker Rd (46220-4836)
PHONE..................317 251-3838
Stanley Charles, *Pr*
Caroline Charles, *VP*
EMP: 4 EST: 1984
SALES (est): 462.18K **Privately Held**
Web: www.classroll.net
SIC: **3993** Signs, not made in custom sign painting shops

(G-9497)
STAPERT TOOL & MACHINE CO INC
2958 Carson Ave (46203-5220)
PHONE..................317 787-2387
Steve Stapert, *Pr*
EMP: 8 EST: 1998
SQ FT: 6,600
SALES (est): 632.15K **Privately Held**
SIC: **3545** Precision tools, machinists'

(G-9498)
STAR PACKAGING COMPANY INC
6124 Brokenhurst Rd (46220)
PHONE..................317 357-3707
Jane H Morrison, *Pr*
William W Morrison, *VP*
EMP: 8 EST: 1975
SALES (est): 838.48K **Privately Held**
Web: www.starpackaging.net
SIC: **2655** Fiber spools, tubes, and cones

(G-9499)
STAR PIPE LLC
6119 Guion Rd (46254-1223)
PHONE..................317 428-7408
Greg Earnhart, *Mgr*
EMP: 8
Web: www.starpipeproducts.com
SIC: **3498** Fabricated pipe and fittings
PA: Star Pipe, L.L.C.
4018 Westhollow Pkwy
Houston TX 77082

(G-9500)
STATE CLEANING SOLUTIONS
8813 Boehning Ln (46219-1974)
PHONE..................812 336-4817
EMP: 2 EST: 2016
SALES (est): 83.91K **Privately Held**
SIC: **2752** Commercial printing, lithographic

(G-9501)
STEEL SERVICES INC
3551 S Lynhurst Dr (46241-6408)
PHONE..................317 783-5255
EMP: 8 EST: 1994
SALES (est): 3.21MM **Privately Held**
Web: www.steelservices.com
SIC: **3441** Fabricated structural metal

(G-9502)
STEPHEN L CAPPER & ASSOCIATES
2500 N Ritter Ave (46218-3202)
PHONE..................317 546-9000
EMP: 7 EST: 2019
SALES (est): 118.87K **Privately Held**
Web: www.stephenlcapper.com
SIC: **3914** Silverware and plated ware

(G-9503)
STERIS CORPORATION
6015 W 79th St (46278-1709)
PHONE..................440 354-2600
EMP: 51
Web: www.steris.com
SIC: **3842** Sterilizers, hospital and surgical
HQ: Steris Corporation
5960 Heisley Rd
Mentor OH 44060
440 354-2600

(G-9504)
STERLING CREEK SOFTWARE L L C
8888 Keystone Xing (46240-4609)
PHONE..................317 567-5060
George Jones, *Owner*
EMP: 5 EST: 2017
SALES (est): 86.26K **Privately Held**
SIC: **7372** Prepackaged software

(G-9505)
STERLING ELECTRIC INC (PA)
7997 Allison Ave (46268-1613)
PHONE..................317 872-0471
Kathryn H Jordan, *CEO*
Timothy Moellerm, *
▲ EMP: 43 EST: 1927
SQ FT: 80,000
SALES (est): 7.86MM
SALES (corp-wide): 7.86MM **Privately Held**
Web: www.sterlingelectric.com
SIC: **3566** 3621 Speed changers, drives, and gears; Motors, electric

(G-9506)
STERLING FLUID SYSTEMS USA LLC (DH)
Also Called: Peerless Pump Company
2005 Dr Martin Luther King Jr St (46202-1165)
PHONE..................317 925-9661
Francesco Cesare Magri, *Pr*
◆ EMP: 250 EST: 1923
SQ FT: 300,000
SALES (est): 151.95MM
SALES (corp-wide): 5.02B **Privately Held**
Web: www.peerlesspump.com
SIC: **3561** Pumps and pumping equipment
HQ: Grundfos Holding Ag
C/O Bratschi Ag, Zweigniederlassung Zug
Zug ZG 6300

(G-9507)
STERLING IMPRESSIONS INC
7016 Coffman Rd (46268-2507)
PHONE..................317 329-9773
Eric P Van Kersen, *Pr*
Alina Vankersen, *Mgr*
Phillip Vankersen, *VP*
EMP: 5 EST: 1989
SQ FT: 4,800
SALES (est): 373.43K **Privately Held**
Web: www.sterlingimpressions.com
SIC: **2759** Screen printing

(G-9508)
STEVE SCHMIDT RACING ENGINES
8560 E 30th St (46219-1423)
PHONE..................317 898-1831
Steve Schmidt, *Pr*
▲ EMP: 10 EST: 1998
SQ FT: 28,000
SALES (est): 217.78K **Privately Held**
Web: www.steveschmidtracing.com
SIC: **3599** Machine shop, jobbing and repair

(G-9509)
STG NETWORKS LLC
5536 W Raymond St (46241-4341)
PHONE..................317 667-0865
EMP: 6 EST: 2018
SALES (est): 321.82K **Privately Held**
SIC: **3661** Telephones and telephone apparatus

(G-9510)
STICKLE STEAM SPECIALTIES CO
2215 Valley Ave (46218-4388)
PHONE..................317 636-6563
Stickle Roger Harris, *Pr*
Chad Stickle, *VP*
Lynn Stickle, *Treas*
EMP: 19 EST: 1907
SQ FT: 10,000
SALES (est): 4.49MM **Privately Held**
Web: www.sticklesteam.com
SIC: **3554** Paper industries machinery

(G-9511)
STINGRAY SYSTEMS LLC
Also Called: Stingray Valves
5701 Elmwood Ave (46203-6014)
PHONE..................317 238-6508
EMP: 3 EST: 2010
SALES (est): 33.33K **Privately Held**
Web: www.buystingray.com
SIC: **3491** Industrial valves

(G-9512)
STONE ARTISANS LTD
7952 Zionsville Rd (46268-1649)
PHONE..................317 362-0107
Cory Kroger, *Pr*
EMP: 4 EST: 2010
SALES (est): 247.23K **Privately Held**
Web: www.stone-artisans.com
SIC: **3423** 3259 3281 Stonecutters' hand tools; Architectural clay products; Curbing, granite or stone

(G-9513)
STONE ARTISANS LTD
3820 E 62nd St (46220-4416)
PHONE..................847 219-7862
Thomas Romano, *Ch*
EMP: 2 EST: 2010
SQ FT: 5,000
SALES (est): 65.12K **Privately Held**
SIC: **1743** 3281 Terrazzo, tile, marble and mosaic work; Curbing, granite or stone

(G-9514)
STONECAST FINANCIAL LLC
Also Called: Hypeauditor
9165 Otis Ave Ste 238 (46216)
PHONE..................317 537-1707
Alexander Frolov, *CEO*
EMP: 5 EST: 2013
SALES (est): 398.37K **Privately Held**
Web: www.stonecast-vc.com
SIC: **8742** 7372 Planning consultant; Application computer software

(G-9515)
STOP N GO TRANSPORT LLC
7821 Palawan Dr (46239-2219)
PHONE..................317 902-0815
Cedrick T Edwards, *CEO*
EMP: 1 EST: 2019
SALES (est): 69.78K **Privately Held**
SIC: **4789** 3537 Transportation services, nec ; Trucks, tractors, loaders, carriers, and similar equipment

(G-9516)
STOUT FIELD IND PARTNERS
4001 E Minnesota St (46203-3440)
PHONE..................317 247-7486
EMP: 4 EST: 2016
SALES (est): 63.13K **Privately Held**
SIC: **3599** Machine shop, jobbing and repair

(G-9517)
STRAND DIAGNOSTICS LLC
5770 Decatur Blvd Ste A (46241-9902)
PHONE..................317 455-2100
Ted Schenberg, *CEO*
Laura Beggrow, *Pr*
Travis Morgan, *CFO*
EMP: 3 EST: 2012
SALES (est): 954.74K **Privately Held**
Web: www.knowerror.com
SIC: **2835** Diagnostic substances

(G-9518)
STURM HEAT TREATING INC
1110 S Drexel Ave (46203-2301)
PHONE..................317 357-2368
Eric Ambler, *Pr*
EMP: 10 EST: 1983
SQ FT: 15,000
SALES (est): 946.03K **Privately Held**
SIC: **3398** Metal heat treating

(G-9519)
STYLISH UNIQUE SALON LLC
935 N Pennsylvania St (46204-1020)
PHONE..................317 938-1273
EMP: 1
SALES (est): 69.27K **Privately Held**
SIC: **3999** Barber and beauty shop equipment

(G-9520)
SUGAR AND BRUNO INC
7260 Georgetown Rd (46268)
PHONE..................317 991-4422
Challen L Powers, *Prin*
EMP: 14 EST: 2017
SALES (est): 52.24K **Privately Held**
Web: www.sugarandbruno.com
SIC: **2323** Men's and boy's neckwear

(G-9521)
SUMCO LLC
1351 S Girls School Rd (46231-1352)
PHONE..................317 241-7600
Tom Brouillard, *Managing Member*
◆ EMP: 100 EST: 2009
SQ FT: 120,000
SALES (est): 11.41MM **Privately Held**
Web: www.sumco.com
SIC: **3471** Electroplating of metals or formed products

(G-9522)
SUMCO GROUP LLC
1351 S Girls School Rd (46231-1352)
PHONE..................317 241-7600
Will Hurrle, *Managing Member*
Shane Willis, *
EMP: 100 EST: 2020
SALES (est): 10.49MM **Privately Held**

(G-9523)
SUMMER COTTAGE INC
7750 Zionsville Rd Ste 850 (46268-5126)
PHONE..................317 873-4176
Beth Moorin, Pr
EMP: 1 EST: 1998
SALES (est): 99K Privately Held
Web: www.summercottage.com
SIC: 3429 Hardware, nec

(G-9524)
SUMMIT MANUFACTURING CORP
10586 E 59th St (46236-8333)
PHONE..................317 823-2848
Weldon Wright, Pr
Burch Johnson, VP
Linda Wright, Sec
Cliff Johnson, Off Mgr
EMP: 7 EST: 1974
SQ FT: 2,200
SALES (est): 654.87K Privately Held
Web: www.summithosereels.com
SIC: 3569 Lubricating equipment

(G-9525)
SUN KING BREWING COMPANY LLC
Also Called: Sk Beer
135 N College Ave (46202)
PHONE..................317 602-3702
Clayton Robinson, Managing Member
▲ EMP: 55 EST: 2008
SALES (est): 18.54MM Privately Held
Web: www.sunkingbrewing.com
SIC: 5181 2082 Beer and other fermented malt liquors; Beer (alcoholic beverage)

(G-9526)
SUNCOAST COFFEE INC (PA)
Also Called: Hubbard & Cravens Coffee
1114 E 52nd St (46205-1213)
PHONE..................317 251-3198
Rick Hubbard, Pr
Jerry Cravens, *
Marcy Hubbard, *
EMP: 25 EST: 1991
SQ FT: 2,500
SALES (est): 20.06MM Privately Held
Web: www.hubbardandcravens.com
SIC: 5149 7389 2095 Coffee, green or roasted; Coffee service; Coffee roasting (except by wholesale grocers)

(G-9527)
SUNRIGHT SOLAR INC
5342 W Vermont St (46224-8841)
PHONE..................317 503-9253
EMP: 6
SALES (est): 271.06K Privately Held
Web: www.sunright.solar
SIC: 3674 Solar cells

(G-9528)
SUPERIOR DISTRIBUTION
2570 N Shadeland Ave (46219-1739)
PHONE..................317 308-5525
Joe Vaal, Prin
EMP: 5 EST: 2009
SALES (est): 925.27K Privately Held
Web: www.teamindianavolleyball.com
SIC: 5075 3585 1711 Warm air heating equipment and supplies; Heating equipment, complete; Ventilation and duct work contractor

(G-9529)
SUPERIOR INDUS SOLUTIONS INC (PA)
Also Called: Superior Solvents and Chem
1411 Roosevelt Ave Ste 250 (46201-1006)
P.O. Box 186 (46206-0186)
PHONE..................317 781-4400
Robert W Andersen, Ch Bd
Robert W Andersen, CEO
Kurt A Hettinga, *
Bryan Teed, *
Douglas P Stewart, *
▲ EMP: 32 EST: 1932
SQ FT: 35,000
SALES (est): 306.28MM
SALES (corp-wide): 306.28MM Privately Held
Web: www.relyonsuperior.com
SIC: 5169 5162 2899 8711 Chemicals and allied products, nec; Plastics materials, nec; Chemical preparations, nec; Engineering services

(G-9530)
SUPERIOR METAL TECH LLC
Also Called: Morgan Francis Flagpoles & ACC
9850 E 30th St (46229-3608)
PHONE..................317 897-9850
Tim Gross, *
Curt Lamb, *
Steve Blackburn, *
Cherie D Smith, *
▲ EMP: 85 EST: 2002
SALES (est): 9.11MM Privately Held
Web: www.superiormetals.us
SIC: 3471 3479 Anodizing (plating) of metals or formed products; Painting of metal products

(G-9531)
SUPERNOVA INTERNATIONAL INC
Also Called: AP Lazer
4444 Decatur Blvd Ste 1200 (46241-9537)
PHONE..................317 969-8246
EMP: 5
Web: www.supernovaintl.com
SIC: 3699 Laser systems and equipment
PA: Supernova International, Inc.
4215 Legion Dr
Mason MI 48854

(G-9532)
SUPREMEX MIDWEST INC
Bowers Envelope Company
5331 N Tacoma Ave (46220-3613)
PHONE..................317 253-4321
EMP: 1
SALES (corp-wide): 219.99MM Privately Held
Web: www.supremex.com
SIC: 2621 Paper mills
HQ: Supremex Midwest Llc
5331 N Tacoma Ave
Indianapolis IN 46220
317 253-4321

(G-9533)
SUPREMEX MIDWEST LLC (HQ)
5331 N Tacoma Ave (46220-3613)
PHONE..................317 253-4321
Stewart Emerson, CEO
EMP: 50 EST: 2016
SQ FT: 76,000
SALES (est): 6.05MM
SALES (corp-wide): 219.99MM Privately Held
Web: www.supremex.com
SIC: 2621 Stationary, envelope and tablet papers
PA: Supremex Inc
7213 Rue Cordner
Lasalle QC H8N 2
514 595-0555

(G-9534)
SUPREMEX MIDWEST LLC
Vista Graphic Communications
7915 E 30th St (46219-1235)
PHONE..................317 898-2000
Stewart Emerson, CEO
EMP: 1
SALES (corp-wide): 219.99MM Privately Held
Web: www.supremex.com
SIC: 2671 Paper, coated or laminated for packaging
HQ: Supremex Midwest Llc
5331 N Tacoma Ave
Indianapolis IN 46220
317 253-4321

(G-9535)
SUPREMEX USA INC (HQ)
5331 N Tacoma Ave (46220-3613)
PHONE..................317 253-4321
Stewart Emerson, CEO
Mary Chronopoulos, Sec
EMP: 21 EST: 2015
SALES (est): 7.47MM
SALES (corp-wide): 219.99MM Privately Held
SIC: 2621 Stationary, envelope and tablet papers
PA: Supremex Inc
7213 Rue Cordner
Lasalle QC H8N 2
514 595-0555

(G-9536)
SUSTAINABLES LLC
6106 Evanston Ave (46220-2318)
PHONE..................502 741-4834
EMP: 5 EST: 2021
SALES (est): 64.19K Privately Held
SIC: 2656 Straws, drinking: made from purchased material

(G-9537)
SWAROVSKI NORTH AMERICA LTD
6020 E 82nd St Ste 430 (46250-5530)
PHONE..................317 841-0037
EMP: 7
SALES (corp-wide): 3.33B Privately Held
SIC: 3961 Costume jewelry
HQ: Swarovski North America Limited
1 Kenney Dr
Cranston RI 02920
401 463-6400

(G-9538)
SWEET TOOTH LLC
4543 E 38th St (46218-1579)
PHONE..................317 986-3764
EMP: 4 EST: 2020
SALES (est): 120K Privately Held
SIC: 2051 Cakes, bakery: except frozen

(G-9539)
SYNERGY COMPOSITES LLC
9034 Caminito Ct (46234-2517)
PHONE..................217 454-9711
EMP: 4 EST: 2013
SALES (est): 82.03K Privately Held
Web: www.synergycomposites.net
SIC: 3993 Signs and advertising specialties

(G-9540)
SYNTAG RFLD
602 N Park Ave (46204-1615)
PHONE..................317 685-5292
Peter Hanson, Prin

EMP: 6 EST: 2009
SALES (est): 77.48K Privately Held
SIC: 3577 Bar code (magnetic ink) printers

(G-9541)
SYNTHYPNION PRESS LLC
8144 S Pennsylvania St (46227-2651)
PHONE..................317 885-8394
Matthew E Gladden, Owner
EMP: 5 EST: 2015
SALES (est): 41.35K Privately Held
SIC: 2741 Miscellaneous publishing

(G-9542)
SYSTEC CORPORATION
Also Called: Systec Conveyors
3245 N Mitthoefer Rd (46235-3489)
PHONE..................317 890-9230
Richard D Harris, CEO
Christopher W Harris, *
Teresa L Harris, *
Michael F Harris, *
John Gould, *
EMP: 85 EST: 1992
SQ FT: 60,000
SALES (est): 19.54MM Privately Held
Web: www.systecconveyors.com
SIC: 3535 Unit handling conveying systems

(G-9543)
T & M EQUIPMENT COMPANY INC
6501 Guion Rd (46268-4808)
PHONE..................317 293-9255
Michael Malatestinic, Mgr
EMP: 13
SALES (corp-wide): 19.5MM Privately Held
Web: www.tmcranes.com
SIC: 7699 5013 5084 3536 Industrial equipment services; Motor vehicle supplies and new parts; Industrial machinery and equipment; Hoists, cranes, and monorails
PA: T & M Equipment Company Inc
2880 E 83rd Pl
Merrillville IN 46410
219 942-2299

(G-9544)
T AND J PRINTING SUPPLY
5739 W 85th St (46278-1330)
PHONE..................317 986-4765
EMP: 5 EST: 2016
SALES (est): 98.1K Privately Held
SIC: 2752 Commercial printing, lithographic

(G-9545)
T&T ELITE CONSTRUCTION LLC
4652 Falcon Run Way (46254-2000)
PHONE..................317 657-8898
EMP: 1 EST: 2019
SALES (est): 41.07K Privately Held
SIC: 1389 Construction, repair, and dismantling services

(G-9546)
TABLE THYME DESIGNS LLC
Also Called: Colored Threads
217 W 10th St Ste 125 (46202-4135)
PHONE..................317 634-0281
Laurie Rice, Prin
EMP: 5 EST: 2002
SALES (est): 499.56K Privately Held
Web: www.colored-threads.com
SIC: 2759 Screen printing

(G-9547)
TACTICAL WLDG FABRICATION LLC
3620 Developers Rd (46227-3520)
PHONE..................317 457-5340
EMP: 6 EST: 2018

GEOGRAPHIC SECTION

Indianapolis - Marion County (G-9574)

SALES (est): 310.24K **Privately Held**
SIC: 7692 Welding repair

(G-9548)
TAMWALL INC
Also Called: Tamwall Demountable Partitions
4362 Sellers St (46226-7107)
PHONE.................................317 546-5055
Thomas Mills, *Pr*
Susan Mills, *Sec*
EMP: 15 EST: 1978
SQ FT: 18,000
SALES (est): 960.83K **Privately Held**
Web: www.tamwall.com
SIC: 2542 Partitions for floor attachment, prefabricated: except wood

(G-9549)
TANGLEWOOD PUBLISHING INC
Also Called: Tanglewood Press
1060 N Capitol Ave Ste E395 (46204-1044)
PHONE.................................812 877-9488
Peggy Tierney, *Pr*
▲ EMP: 3 EST: 2003
SALES (est): 263.21K **Privately Held**
Web: www.tanglewoodpress.com
SIC: 2741 Miscellaneous publishing

(G-9550)
TANGOE US INC
Also Called: Tangoe
8888 Keystone Xing Ste 1300 (46240-4600)
PHONE.................................203 859-9300
Robert Irwin, *CEO*
EMP: 300
Web: www.tangoe.com
SIC: 7372 Prepackaged software
HQ: Tangoe Us, Inc.
8888 Kystne Xing Ste 1300
Indianapolis IN 46240
973 257-0300

(G-9551)
TANGOE US INC (DH)
8888 Keystone Xing Ste 1300 (46240)
PHONE.................................973 257-0300
Bob Irwin, *CEO*
Chris Taylor, *
Sidra Berman, *
Tom Flynn, *CAO**
Mike Sheridan, *
EMP: 120 EST: 2000
SALES (est): 479.28MM **Privately Held**
Web: www.tangoe.com
SIC: 7372 Application computer software
HQ: Tangoe, Llc
6410 Poplar Ave Ste 200
Memphis TN 38119
901 752-6200

(G-9552)
TAOTAO USA INC
Also Called: Tao Tao USA
8207 Zionsville Rd (46268-1628)
PHONE.................................317 856-8628
EMP: 2
Web: www.taomotor.com
SIC: 3711 Motor vehicles and car bodies
PA: Taotao Usa, Inc.
2201 Luna Rd
Carrollton TX 75006

(G-9553)
TARPENNING-LAFOLLETTE CO INC
4212 W 71st St Ste B (46268-2274)
PHONE.................................317 780-1500
Rex A Martin, *Pr*
Kim Martin, *
Chad G Martin, *
Rodney H Pittman, *

EMP: 41 EST: 1920
SALES (est): 2.34MM **Privately Held**
Web: www.tarp-laff.com
SIC: 3444 7699 Sheet metal specialties, not stamped; Industrial equipment services

(G-9554)
TARTAN PROPERTIES LLC
3419 Roosevelt Ave (46218-3761)
P.O. Box 18280 (46218-0280)
PHONE.................................317 714-7337
John D Chisholm, *Prin*
EMP: 4 EST: 2002
SALES (est): 412.16K **Privately Held**
Web: www.tartanproperties.com
SIC: 2431 6512 5251 5072 Trim, wood; Nonresidential building operators; Builders' hardware; Hand tools

(G-9555)
TASCON CORP
2213 Duke St (46205-2237)
PHONE.................................317 547-6127
Stephen E Schmidt, *Pr*
Eve Schmidt, *Sec*
EMP: 15 EST: 1981
SQ FT: 4,800
SALES (est): 420.69K **Privately Held**
Web: www.tascon.com
SIC: 3545 3541 Diamond cutting tools for turning, boring, burnishing, etc.; Machine tools, metal cutting type

(G-9556)
TASTY TREATS BAKERY LLC
8251 Dogwood Circle East Dr (46268-3812)
PHONE.................................317 622-8829
EMP: 1
SALES (est): 39.59K **Privately Held**
Web: tasty-treats-bakery.edan.io
SIC: 2051 Cakes, bakery: except frozen

(G-9557)
TAVISTOCK RESTAURANTS LLC
Also Called: Alcatraz Brewing Co.
49 W Maryland St Ste 104 (46204-3523)
PHONE.................................317 488-1230
EMP: 1
SALES (corp-wide): 195.01MM **Privately Held**
Web: www.tavistockrestaurantcollection.com
SIC: 2082 5181 5812 Beer (alcoholic beverage); Beer and ale; Eating places
PA: Tavistock Restaurants Llc
6900 Tvstock Lkes Blvd St
Orlando FL 32827
407 909-7101

(G-9558)
TAYLOR & FRANCIS
5500 W 74th St (46268-4183)
PHONE.................................765 364-1300
EMP: 9 EST: 2021
SALES (est): 67.74K **Privately Held**
Web: www.taylorandfrancis.com
SIC: 2741 Miscellaneous publishing

(G-9559)
TAYLOR TIRE TREADING CO INC
2101 Massachusetts Ave (46218-4339)
PHONE.................................317 634-9476
Carl E Taylor, *Pr*
Linda J Taylor, *VP*
EMP: 5 EST: 1972
SQ FT: 7,400
SALES (est): 354.65K **Privately Held**
Web: www.taylortireindy.com
SIC: 7534 Rebuilding and retreading tires

(G-9560)
TC HEARTLAND LLC
Also Called: Heartland Food Products Group
4635 W 84th St Ste 300 (46268-3721)
PHONE.................................317 876-7121
EMP: 1
Web: www.heartlandfpg.com
SIC: 2099 Sorghum syrups, for sweetening
PA: Tc Heartland Llc
14390 Clay Ter Blvd Ste 2
Carmel IN 46032

(G-9561)
TCB INTERNATIONAL LLC
12378 Bridgewater Rd (46256-9430)
PHONE.................................502 619-3191
Kenji Takada, *Prin*
EMP: 6 EST: 2015
SALES (est): 108.2K **Privately Held**
SIC: 3341 Secondary nonferrous metals

(G-9562)
TCLOGIC LLC
519 E Mccarty St (46203-1719)
PHONE.................................317 464-5152
Thomas Uhrig, *VP*
Thomas Uhrig, *Managing Member*
Cindy Uhrig, *VP Opers*
EMP: 8 EST: 1997
SALES (est): 732.47K **Privately Held**
Web: www.tclogic.com
SIC: 3695 5045 Computer software tape and disks: blank, rigid, and floppy; Computer software

(G-9563)
TCT TECHNOLOGIES LLC
Also Called: Tct Technologies
8435 Keystone Xing Ste 230 (46240-4357)
P.O. Box 501527 (46250-6527)
PHONE.................................317 833-6730
Tim O Connell, *Pr*
EMP: 11 EST: 2007
SALES (est): 3.16MM **Privately Held**
Web: www.tcttechnologies.com
SIC: 3669 Visual communication systems

(G-9564)
TE CUSTOM WOODWORK LLC
10480 Lookout Ln (46234-9855)
PHONE.................................317 910-6906
Terrence Ellis Senior, *Prin*
EMP: 5 EST: 2018
SALES (est): 54.13K **Privately Held**
SIC: 2431 Millwork

(G-9565)
TEAM GREEN INC
7615 Zionsville Rd (46268-2174)
PHONE.................................317 872-2700
EMP: 19 EST: 1992
SALES (est): 193.22K **Privately Held**
Web: www.andretti-global.com
SIC: 7948 3711 Motor vehicle racing and drivers; Automobile assembly, including specialty automobiles

(G-9566)
TECH INNOVATION LLC
8517 Oakmont Ln (46260-5340)
PHONE.................................317 506-8343
EMP: 11 EST: 2016
SALES (est): 937.69K **Privately Held**
Web: www.techinnovation.com
SIC: 7372 Application computer software

(G-9567)
TECH SOLUTIONS AND SALES INC
6898 Hawthorn Park Dr (46220-3909)
P.O. Box 3689 (46082-3689)
PHONE.................................317 536-5846
Dave Fellabaum, *Prin*
EMP: 5 EST: 2008
SALES (est): 114.69K **Privately Held**
Web: www.tricorfurniture.com
SIC: 3651 Audio electronic systems

(G-9568)
TECHNALYSIS INC
7172 Waldemar Dr (46268-2183)
P.O. Box 44316 (46244-0316)
PHONE.................................317 291-1985
Akin Ecer, *Pr*
Jason R Lemon, *
Hasan Akay, *
EMP: 8 EST: 1985
SQ FT: 13,500
SALES (est): 243.22K **Privately Held**
Web: www.technalysisresearch.com
SIC: 8711 7371 7372 Consulting engineer; Computer software development; Prepackaged software

(G-9569)
TECHNOLOGY DYNAMICS
9105 E 56th St Ste 2150 (46216-2233)
PHONE.................................317 524-6338
Brian Scott, *Prin*
EMP: 6 EST: 2016
SALES (est): 129.15K **Privately Held**
Web: www.techdyn.net
SIC: 3679 Electronic components, nec

(G-9570)
TECK USA INC
715 W Southern Ave (46225-2006)
PHONE.................................888 995-1972
Vaneet Pasricha, *Pr*
EMP: 1 EST: 2013
SALES (est): 43.81K **Privately Held**
SIC: 2741 Internet publishing and broadcasting

(G-9571)
TEDCO INC
5167 E 65th St (46220-4816)
PHONE.................................401 461-1118
EMP: 6 EST: 2019
SALES (est): 270.8K **Privately Held**
Web: www.tedcotoys.com
SIC: 3944 Games, toys, and children's vehicles

(G-9572)
TEEJAYS SWEET TOOTH LLC
8660 Purdue Rd Ste 8660-600 (46268-6126)
PHONE.................................219 208-5229
Taylor Debruce, *Prin*
EMP: 6 EST: 2018
SALES (est): 215.67K **Privately Held**
Web: www.teejayssweettooth.com
SIC: 2024 Ice cream and frozen deserts

(G-9573)
TEEKI HUT CUSTOM TEES INC
807 Broad Ripple Ave (46220-1960)
PHONE.................................317 205-3589
Matthew Stuart, *Owner*
EMP: 6 EST: 2005
SALES (est): 195.88K **Privately Held**
Web: www.teekihut.com
SIC: 2759 Screen printing

(G-9574)
TEMPLE-ISLAND
2135 Stout Field East Dr (46241-4014)
PHONE.................................901 419-9000
Bruce White, *Owner*
EMP: 6 EST: 2011

(PA)=Parent Co (HQ)=Headquarters
✪ = New Business established in last 2 years

Indianapolis - Marion County (G-9575)

SALES (est): 170.75K **Privately Held**
SIC: **2653** Boxes, corrugated: made from purchased materials

(G-9575)
TEMPLETON MYERS INC
Also Called: B C T
351 S Post Rd (46219-7900)
PHONE..................317 898-6688
Doug Keller, *Pr*
EMP: **48 EST:** 1982
SALES (est): 4.51MM **Privately Held**
Web: www.bctindy.com
SIC: **2752** Commercial printing, lithographic

(G-9576)
TEMPUS NOVA LLC (HQ)
111 Monument Cir Ste 202 (46204-2991)
PHONE..................877 379-7376
Didi Dellanno, *Pr*
Joseph Dellanno, *
EMP: **10 EST:** 2001
SALES (est): 4.48MM
SALES (corp-wide): 10.79MM **Privately Held**
Web: www.resultant.com
SIC: **7372** 7371 Business oriented computer software; Custom computer programming services
PA: Resultant, Llc
 111 Monument Cir Ste 202
 Indianapolis IN 46204
 317 452-1700

(G-9577)
TENNECO INC
Also Called: Tenneco
7002 Graham Rd Ste 128 (46220-4057)
PHONE..................317 842-5550
Gary Sentieri, *Mgr*
EMP: 2
SALES (corp-wide): 18.04B **Privately Held**
Web: www.tenneco.com
SIC: **3714** Motor vehicle parts and accessories
HQ: Tenneco Inc.
 7450 Mccormick Blvd
 Skokie IL 60076
 847 482-5000

(G-9578)
TERRECORP INC
2121 Hillside Ave (46218-3569)
PHONE..................317 951-8325
Michael Lanza, *Pr*
Kurt Cargnino, *VP*
EMP: **16 EST:** 1998
SQ FT: 25,000
SALES (est): 3.31MM
SALES (corp-wide): 114.12MM **Privately Held**
SIC: **3463** Bearing and bearing race forgings, nonferrous
PA: Cooper Machinery Services Llc
 16250 Port Nw Dr
 Houston TX 77041
 713 354-1900

(G-9579)
TESLA INC
8280 Castleton Corner Dr (46250-3598)
PHONE..................317 558-8431
EMP: 2
SALES (corp-wide): 96.77B **Publicly Held**
Web: www.tesla.com
SIC: **3711** Motor vehicles and car bodies
PA: Tesla, Inc.
 1 Tesla Rd
 Austin TX 78725
 512 516-8177

(G-9580)
TEXTRON AVIATION INC
Hawker Beechcraft Services
6911 Pierson Dr (46241)
P.O. Box 42307 (46242-0307)
PHONE..................317 241-2893
Tim Gray, *Brnch Mgr*
EMP: 29
SALES (corp-wide): 12.87B **Publicly Held**
Web: www.txtav.com
SIC: **3721** Aircraft
HQ: Textron Aviation Inc.
 1 Cessna Blvd
 Wichita KS 67215
 316 517-6000

(G-9581)
TEXTRON AVIATION INC
Also Called: Hawker Beechcraft Svcs
6911 Pierson Dr (46241-4208)
PHONE..................317 227-3621
EMP: 43
SALES (corp-wide): 12.87B **Publicly Held**
Web: www.txtav.com
SIC: **3721** Aircraft
HQ: Textron Aviation Inc.
 1 Cessna Blvd
 Wichita KS 67215
 316 517-6000

(G-9582)
TEXYS AMERICA LLC
7301 Georgetown Rd Ste 125 (46268-5124)
PHONE..................317 469-4828
Philippe Leuwers, *Managing Member*
Pierre Aucouturier, *Mgr*
EMP: **1 EST:** 2008
SQ FT: 600
SALES (est): 189.85K **Privately Held**
Web: www.texense.com
SIC: **3829** Measuring and controlling devices, nec

(G-9583)
TEXYS SENSORS LLC
8425 Woodfield Crossing Blvd Ste 100 (46240-7515)
PHONE..................317 469-4828
EMP: **1 EST:** 2009
SALES (est): 22.56K **Privately Held**
Web: www.texense.com
SIC: **3829** Measuring and controlling devices, nec

(G-9584)
TFP UNLIMITED LLC ◆
9433 E Washington St (46229-3085)
PHONE..................317 414-8819
Todd A Finnell, *Pr*
EMP: **2 EST:** 2022
SALES (est): 62.01K **Privately Held**
SIC: **3993** Signs and advertising specialties

(G-9585)
TGF ENTERPRISES LLC
Also Called: Bigasspizzacutter.com
11075 Woods Bay Ln (46236-9021)
PHONE..................440 840-9704
Thomas Faludy, *Managing Member*
EMP: **2 EST:** 2011
SALES (est): 146.72K **Privately Held**
Web: www.imetra.com
SIC: **8742** 8732 3556 7389 Business management consultant; Merger, acquisition, and reorganization research; Slicers, commercial, food; Business services, nec

(G-9586)
THANK YOU LORD LLC
9538 Oakley Dr (46260-1325)
PHONE..................317 319-1271
Jason L Flowers, *Prin*
EMP: **5 EST:** 2014
SALES (est): 51.59K **Privately Held**
SIC: **3829** Measuring and controlling devices, nec

(G-9587)
THAT PRINT LADY LLC
4517 Jamestown Ct Apt D (46226-3455)
PHONE..................317 339-7411
EMP: **3 EST:** 2018
SALES (est): 39.97K **Privately Held**
SIC: **2711** Commercial printing and newspaper publishing combined

(G-9588)
THE EMINENCE HAIR COLLECTN LLC
8404 Penbrooke Pl (46237)
PHONE..................317 300-6051
Brandi Spencer, *CEO*
EMP: **2 EST:** 2017
SALES (est): 69.17K **Privately Held**
Web: www.theeminencehaircollection.com
SIC: **3999** Hair and hair-based products

(G-9589)
THE KILLION CORPORATION
Also Called: Bentcil Company, The
1755 Midwest Blvd (46214-2378)
PHONE..................317 271-4536
▲ EMP: **80 EST:** 1973
SALES (est): 8.66MM **Privately Held**
Web: www.bentcil.com
SIC: **3089** 3951 3993 3952 Plastics processing; Pencils and pencil parts, mechanical; Signs and advertising specialties; Lead pencils and art goods

(G-9590)
THERMAL STRUCTURES INC
5705 W 80th St (46278-1319)
PHONE..................317 876-7213
Gavin Lemon, *Mgr*
EMP: 15
Web: www.thermalstructures.com
SIC: **3292** Blankets, insulating for aircraft asbestos
HQ: Thermal Structures, Inc.
 2362 Railroad St
 Corona CA 92878
 951 736-9911

(G-9591)
THIS THAT EMB SCREEN PRTG LLC
3724 N Dequincy St (46218-1641)
PHONE..................317 541-8548
Lorraine Johnson, *Prin*
EMP: **2 EST:** 2011
SALES (est): 79.88K **Privately Held**
SIC: **2752** Commercial printing, lithographic

(G-9592)
THOMAS & SKINNER INC (PA)
1120 E 23rd St (46205-4590)
P.O. Box 150 (46206-0150)
PHONE..................317 923-2501
Norris E Krall, *Ch Bd*
Vernon Detlef, *
Neil Moehring, *
EMP: **120 EST:** 1925
SQ FT: 28,000
SALES (est): 38.67MM
SALES (corp-wide): 38.67MM **Privately Held**
Web: www.thomas-skinner.com
SIC: **3499** Magnets, permanent: metallic

(G-9593)
THOMAS GREEN LLC
7517 Winton Dr (46268-5105)
PHONE..................317 337-0000
▲ EMP: **2 EST:** 2003
SALES (est): 553.39K **Privately Held**
Web: www.readingbakery.com
SIC: **3556** Food products machinery

(G-9594)
THOMAS MONUMENTS INC
7009 W Washington St (46241-2840)
PHONE..................317 244-6525
June Bolton, *Pr*
Glen Bolton, *VP*
EMP: **6 EST:** 1962
SQ FT: 1,500
SALES (est): 788.76K **Privately Held**
Web: www.thomasmonument.com
SIC: **5999** 3281 Monuments, finished to custom order; Monument or burial stone, cut and shaped

(G-9595)
THOMAS TAYLOR
Also Called: Year
3220 Halifax Dr (46222-2119)
PHONE..................317 557-3287
Thomas Taylor, *Owner*
EMP: **1 EST:** 2010
SALES (est): 66.35K **Privately Held**
SIC: **1389** Construction, repair, and dismantling services

(G-9596)
THOMAS/EUCLID INDUSTRIES INC
Also Called: Euclid Machine Co
2575 Bethel Ave (46203-3000)
P.O. Box 33459 (46203-0459)
PHONE..................317 783-7171
Billy R Thomas, *Pr*
Ron Merrill, *
Jeanette Thomas, *
Roynal Merrill, *
Jeanette J Thomas, *
▲ EMP: **78 EST:** 1946
SQ FT: 32,000
SALES (est): 8.67MM **Privately Held**
Web: www.thomaseuclid.com
SIC: **3599** Machine shop, jobbing and repair

(G-9597)
THOMCO INC
1414 Sadlier Circle West Dr (46239-1058)
P.O. Box 19753 (46219-0753)
PHONE..................317 359-3539
Tom Spicklemire, *Pr*
Tracey Gruell, *Sec*
Tom Yocum, *VP*
EMP: **4 EST:** 1990
SQ FT: 5,500
SALES (est): 483.2K **Privately Held**
Web: www.thomco1.com
SIC: **3444** Sheet metalwork

(G-9598)
THOMPSON PRINTING SERVICE INC
447 E Elbert St (46227-1656)
PHONE..................317 783-7448
Michael A Thompson, *Pr*
Mike Thompson, *Sec*
Mary R Thompson, *Sec*
Wesley H Thompson, *VP*
EMP: **3 EST:** 1982
SALES (est): 226.26K **Privately Held**
SIC: **2752** Offset printing

GEOGRAPHIC SECTION

Indianapolis - Marion County (G-9626)

(G-9599)
THOUGHTS ARE THINGS INC
Also Called: T A T Apparrel and Promotions
8035 Clearwater Dr (46256-4613)
PHONE..................................317 585-8053
Nancy Paul, *Owner*
EMP: 2 **EST:** 1995
SALES (est): 210.18K **Privately Held**
SIC: 2759 Promotional printing

(G-9600)
THREE CUPS LLC
310 W Michigan St Ste A (46202-3227)
PHONE..................................317 633-8082
EMP: 2 **EST:** 2007
SALES (est): 80.91K **Privately Held**
SIC: 2731 Books, publishing only

(G-9601)
THUGS INC CHOPPERS
735 N Lynhurst Dr (46224-6888)
PHONE..................................317 454-3762
Vince Ballard, *Owner*
EMP: 6 **EST:** 2009
SALES (est): 199.42K **Privately Held**
SIC: 3751 Motorcycles and related parts

(G-9602)
THUNDERBIRD AVIATION LLC
8623 E Washington St (46219-6823)
PHONE..................................847 303-3100
Robert P Thomas, *Admn*
EMP: 2 **EST:** 1998
SALES (est): 134.84K **Privately Held**
SIC: 3721 Aircraft

(G-9603)
TIMBER CREEK DESIGN CO INC
7230 Guion Rd (46268-4888)
PHONE..................................317 297-5336
EMP: 5 **EST:** 1988
SALES (est): 302.19K **Privately Held**
Web: www.timbercreekdesign.com
SIC: 2511 Wood household furniture

(G-9604)
TIMBERLIGHT MANUFACTURING CO
8146 Grassy Meadow Ct (46259-7728)
PHONE..................................317 694-1317
Robin R Livesay, *Pr*
EMP: 6 **EST:** 2002
SALES (est): 123.92K **Privately Held**
Web: www.timberlight.com
SIC: 3999 Candles

(G-9605)
TIMECPSUAL ANTIQ GL CLLCTABLES
6142 Crystal View Dr (46237-5011)
PHONE..................................317 902-6201
John Strangeway, *Prin*
EMP: 5 **EST:** 2016
SALES (est): 48.09K **Privately Held**
SIC: 3211 Antique glass

(G-9606)
TIMOTHY D GOIN
8240 E 75th St (46256-2104)
PHONE..................................317 771-0404
Timothy Goin, *Owner*
EMP: 1
SALES (est): 55.37K **Privately Held**
SIC: 3714 7389 Booster (jump-start) cables, automotive; Business Activities at Non-Commercial Site

(G-9607)
TIMS TEES
10310 Majestic Perch Ct (46234-3661)
PHONE..................................317 503-5736
EMP: 4 **EST:** 2016
SALES (est): 62.81K **Privately Held**
SIC: 2759 Screen printing

(G-9608)
TIRE CENTRAL AND SERVICE AVON
214 S Raceway Rd (46231-1300)
PHONE..................................317 966-0662
Brent Lockliear, *Pr*
Henry Tilford, *Brnch Mgr*
EMP: 7 **EST:** 2011
SALES (est): 342.34K **Privately Held**
Web: www.tirecentralandservice.com
SIC: 7534 7538 Tire repair shop; General truck repair

(G-9609)
TIS HOLDING INC
1132 Southeastern Ave (46202-3947)
P.O. Box 20894 (46220-0894)
PHONE..................................317 946-6354
Pat Roche, *Pr*
John Ferguson, *VP*
EMP: 3 **EST:** 2003
SALES (est): 640.18K **Privately Held**
Web: www.alliedinst.com
SIC: 3999 Dock equipment and supplies, industrial

(G-9610)
TISHLER INDUSTRIES INC
500 E 96th St Ste 475 (46240-3761)
P.O. Box 40008 (46240-0008)
PHONE..................................317 581-8811
Ravi Talwar, *Brnch Mgr*
EMP: 21
Web: www.tishlerindustries.com
SIC: 3443 Fabricated plate work (boiler shop)
PA: Tishler Industries Inc
    1810 S Macedonia Ave
    Muncie IN 47302

(G-9611)
TJ CONSTRUCTIONS LLC ✪
2020 Winter Ave (46218-3555)
PHONE..................................470 406-2804
EMP: 1 **EST:** 2022
SALES (est): 41.07K **Privately Held**
SIC: 1389 7389 Construction, repair, and dismantling services; Business services, nec

(G-9612)
TK ELEVATOR CORPORATION
8665 Bash St (46256-1202)
PHONE..................................317 595-1125
Rick Wilheite, *Brnch Mgr*
EMP: 67
SQ FT: 1,500
SALES (corp-wide): 2.67MM **Privately Held**
Web: www.tkelevator.com
SIC: 7699 1796 5084 3999 Elevators: inspection, service, and repair; Elevator installation and conversion; Elevators; Wheelchair lifts
HQ: Tk Elevator Corporation
    788 Crcle 75 Pkwy Se Ste
    Atlanta GA 30339
    678 319-3240

(G-9613)
TLS BY DESIGN LLC
Also Called: Furniture Manufacturer
10737 Sand Key Cir (46256-9533)
PHONE..................................765 683-1971
EMP: 35 **EST:** 2004
SALES (est): 2.25MM **Privately Held**
Web: www.tlsbydesign.com
SIC: 2531 2512 2599 Public building and related furniture; Upholstered household furniture; Restaurant furniture, wood or metal

(G-9614)
TMX HEALTHCARE TECH LLC (DH)
Also Called: Trimedx
5451 Lakeview Parkway South Dr (46268-4115)
PHONE..................................877 874-6339
Henry Hummel, *CEO*
Chris Dunkerley, *
Tim Mcgeath, *CCO*
Gene Schrecengost, *Chief Human Resource Officer*
Doug Folsom, *CIO*
EMP: 16 **EST:** 1980
SALES (est): 40.44MM
SALES (corp-wide): 3.7B **Privately Held**
Web: www.trimedx.com
SIC: 8713 3829 8742 Ariel digital imaging; Medical diagnostic systems, nuclear; Hospital and health services consultant
HQ: Trimedx, Llc
    5451 Lakeview Pkwy S Dr
    Indianapolis IN 46268
    877 874-6339

(G-9615)
TO A TEE INC
7125 Girls School Ave (46241-2805)
PHONE..................................317 757-8842
Barbara A Young, *Pr*
Richard Meyer, *VP*
William Gilbreath, *VP*
Richard Young, *VP*
EMP: 17 **EST:** 2005
SQ FT: 13,000
SALES (est): 566.17K **Privately Held**
Web: www.toatee.net
SIC: 2759 Screen printing

(G-9616)
TODDLER TIMER LLC
920 E 62nd St Apt U4 (46220-1917)
P.O. Box 161164 (44116-7164)
PHONE..................................216 282-7247
EMP: 1 **EST:** 2013
SALES (est): 59.18K **Privately Held**
SIC: 7372 Prepackaged software

(G-9617)
TOM DOHERTY COMPANY INC
Also Called: Cardinal Publishers Group
2402 N Shadeland Ave Ste A (46219-1137)
PHONE..................................317 352-8200
Thomas Doherty, *Pr*
Adrianne Doherty, *VP*
▲ **EMP:** 8 **EST:** 1999
SQ FT: 13,500
SALES (est): 839.07K **Privately Held**
Web: www.cardinalpub.com
SIC: 2741 2731 5192 Music, book: publishing and printing; Book publishing; Books

(G-9618)
TOO TUFT LLC
8465 Keystone Xing (46240-4355)
PHONE..................................317 719-2182
EMP: 1
SALES (est): 69.27K **Privately Held**
SIC: 2273 Rugs, hand and machine made

(G-9619)
TOOTIES ZENERGY CANDLES LLC
5941 Winston Dr (46226-2329)
PHONE..................................317 437-9936
EMP: 1
SALES (est): 39.69K **Privately Held**
SIC: 3999 7389 Candles; Business services, nec

(G-9620)
TOP SHELF ACOUSTICS LLC
8175 Ehlerbrook Rd (46237-9789)
PHONE..................................317 512-4569
Miranda Gahimer, *Prin*
EMP: 5 **EST:** 2015
SALES (est): 159.05K **Privately Held**
Web: www.topshelfacoustics.com
SIC: 3679 Electronic components, nec

(G-9621)
TOPNOTCH LOCS LLC
728 E 22nd St (46202-1727)
PHONE..................................260 557-9628
EMP: 3 **EST:** 2021
SALES (est): 50K **Privately Held**
Web: www.topnotchlocs.com
SIC: 3999 Hair and hair-based products

(G-9622)
TORALGEN INC
1220 Waterway Blvd Ste H123 (46202-2157)
PHONE..................................812 820-3374
Gerald Rea, *CEO*
EMP: 3 **EST:** 2017
SALES (est): 448.49K **Privately Held**
Web: www.toralgen.com
SIC: 2834 8071 Medicines, capsuled or ampuled; Biological laboratory

(G-9623)
TOTAL HOME CONTROL LLC
7369 Yorkshire Blvd N (46229-4230)
PHONE..................................317 430-3679
David Spanke, *Owner*
EMP: 4 **EST:** 2019
SALES (est): 60.53K **Privately Held**
Web: www.control4.com
SIC: 3651 Household audio and video equipment

(G-9624)
TOTAL QUALITY PALLETS INC
1401 Newman St (46201-1044)
P.O. Box 19870 (46219-0870)
PHONE..................................317 822-9888
EMP: 5 **EST:** 1995
SQ FT: 10,000
SALES (est): 350.4K **Privately Held**
Web: total-quality-pallets-inc.business.site
SIC: 2448 Pallets, wood

(G-9625)
TOWNE POST NETWORK INC
11216 Fall Creek Rd Ste 125 (46256-9406)
PHONE..................................317 288-7101
Tom Britt, *CEO*
EMP: 6 **EST:** 2005
SALES (est): 445.44K **Privately Held**
Web: www.townepost.com
SIC: 2721 Magazines: publishing only, not printed on site

(G-9626)
TPG MT VERNON MARINE LLC
Also Called: Mt. Vernon Barge Service
1341 N Capitol Ave (46202-2313)
PHONE..................................317 631-0234
Daniel B Altman, *CEO*
Don W Miller, *
Steve Siemers, *
Daniel O'leary, *CFO*
EMP: 175 **EST:** 2012
SALES (est): 19.18MM **Privately Held**
Web: www.mvbarge.com

(PA)=Parent Co (HQ)=Headquarters
✪ = New Business established in last 2 years

Indianapolis - Marion County (G-9627)

SIC: 4731 3731 Freight transportation arrangement; Shipbuilding and repairing

(G-9627)
TRAFFIC SIGN CO INC
9402 Uptown Dr Ste 1500 (46256-1076)
PHONE..................................317 845-9305
Doug Fehribach, *Pr*
EMP: 3 **EST:** 1970
SALES (est): 260K **Privately Held**
Web: www.streetscapellc.com
SIC: 5099 3993 Signs, except electric; Signs and advertising specialties

(G-9628)
TRAIL SOFTWARE INC
Also Called: Kindful
5724 Birtz Rd Ste 1 (46216)
P.O. Box 2865 (37024)
PHONE..................................888 854-0933
EMP: 17 **EST:** 2012
SALES (est): 2.47MM **Privately Held**
Web: www.kindful.com
SIC: 7372 Business oriented computer software

(G-9629)
TRANSCEND ORTHTICS PRSTHTICS L
3445 W 96th St (46268-1102)
PHONE..................................317 334-1114
Bernie Veldman, *CEO*
EMP: 8
SALES (corp-wide): 25.64MM **Privately Held**
Web: www.hangerclinic.com
SIC: 3842 Surgical appliances and supplies
HQ: Transcend Orthotics & Prosthetics, Llc
17530 Dugdale Dr
South Bend IN 46635
574 233-3352

(G-9630)
TRANSFOAM LLC
Also Called: Ourobio
1210 Waterway Blvd (46202-2167)
PHONE..................................631 747-0255
Alec Brewer, *Managing Member*
EMP: 5 **EST:** 2020
SALES (est): 431.25K **Privately Held**
Web: www.ourobio.com
SIC: 2821 Thermosetting materials

(G-9631)
TRANSTEX LLC
8219 Northwest Blvd Ste 100 (46278)
PHONE..................................877 960-2644
Mathieu Boivin, *Pr*
Sylvain Charbonneau, *CFO*
▲ **EMP:** 3 **EST:** 2005
SALES (est): 933.06K **Privately Held**
Web: www.transtex-llc.com
SIC: 3537 Trucks: freight, baggage, etc.: industrial, except mining

(G-9632)
TRAVIS BRITTON
Also Called: T1design
315 N Franklin Rd (46219-5213)
PHONE..................................317 762-6018
Travis Britton, *Owner*
EMP: 2 **EST:** 2017
SALES (est): 59.57K **Privately Held**
Web: www.travisbritton.com
SIC: 7389 2396 3993 5999 Design services; Screen printing on fabric articles; Signs, not made in custom sign painting shops; Banners, flags, decals, and posters

(G-9633)
TREMAIN CERAMIC TILE & FLR CVG
8105 E 47th St (46226-2970)
PHONE..................................317 542-1491
Jesse R Tremain Junior, *Pr*
Grover Kahler, *
Stephen M Winter, *
EMP: 25 **EST:** 1979
SQ FT: 2,000
SALES (est): 2.03MM **Privately Held**
SIC: 1743 5211 3281 2541 Tile installation, ceramic; Lumber and other building materials; Cut stone and stone products; Wood partitions and fixtures

(G-9634)
TREMIKE ENTERPRISES
5869 Meadowlark Dr (46226-3330)
PHONE..................................317 547-6308
John Davis, *Owner*
EMP: 1 **EST:** 1988
SALES (est): 82.95K **Privately Held**
SIC: 3993 7311 Advertising novelties; Advertising consultant

(G-9635)
TRENDSETTIN TEES LLC
1127 Ridgepointe Dr (46234-1944)
PHONE..................................219 201-1410
Ron Adams, *Admn*
EMP: 5 **EST:** 2017
SALES (est): 137.11K **Privately Held**
SIC: 2759 Screen printing

(G-9636)
TRI-STAR FILTRATION INC
5319 W 86th St (46268-1501)
PHONE..................................317 337-0940
Jeff Hangan, *Pr*
EMP: 4 **EST:** 2005
SALES (est): 437.62K **Privately Held**
Web: www.tristarfiltration.net
SIC: 3677 Filtration devices, electronic

(G-9637)
TRI-STATE FOREST PRODUCTS INC
6740 Guion Rd (46268-2547)
PHONE..................................317 328-1850
Tom Lathan, *Pr*
EMP: 10
Web: www.tsfpi.com
SIC: 2411 Logging
PA: Tri-State Forest Products Inc
2105 Sheridan Ave
Springfield OH 45505

(G-9638)
TRI-STATE VALVE LLC (PA) ◊
9355 Delegates Row (46240)
PHONE..................................901 388-1550
William Henson, *Pr*
Summer Couch, *Acctg Mgr*
EMP: 12 **EST:** 2023
SALES (est): 1.4MM
SALES (corp-wide): 1.4MM **Privately Held**
SIC: 3491 7699 Industrial valves; Valve repair, industrial

(G-9639)
TRIANGLE ENGINEERING CORP
2206 Production Dr (46241-4998)
PHONE..................................317 243-8549
Jon Reeves, *Pr*
Douglas Staten, *
David Golay, *
EMP: 51 **EST:** 1964
SQ FT: 31,500
SALES (est): 9.27MM **Privately Held**
Web: www.tecindy.com

SIC: 3599 Machine shop, jobbing and repair

(G-9640)
TRILITHIC
9027 Pinecreek Way (46256-1194)
PHONE..................................317 536-1071
EMP: 4 **EST:** 2018
SALES (est): 247.3K **Privately Held**
SIC: 3699 Electrical equipment and supplies, nec

(G-9641)
TRILITHIC INC
5808 Churchman Byp (46203-6109)
PHONE..................................317 895-3600
▲ **EMP:** 110
Web: www.viavisolutions.com
SIC: 3826 8999 1731 Analytical instruments; Communication services; Communications specialization

(G-9642)
TRILLIUM CABINET COMPANY INC
4357 W 96th St (46268-1178)
PHONE..................................317 471-8870
Steve Campbell, *Pr*
Steve Campbell, *Pr*
Scott Campbell, *VP*
EMP: 3 **EST:** 1999
SALES (est): 242.19K **Privately Held**
Web: www.trilliumcabinet.com
SIC: 2434 Wood kitchen cabinets

(G-9643)
TRINETTE CLARK AGENCY CORP
10733 Chenille Ct (46235-4790)
PHONE..................................317 671-6097
Trinette Clark, *Managing Member*
EMP: 6 **EST:** 2021
SALES (est): 235.45K **Privately Held**
SIC: 8748 2741 Publishing consultant; Music book and sheet music publishing

(G-9644)
TRINITY METALS LLC (PA)
6400 English Ave (46219-8227)
PHONE..................................317 358-8265
Wade Conner, *CEO*
◆ **EMP:** 7 **EST:** 2008
SALES (est): 6.35MM **Privately Held**
Web: www.trinitymetals.net
SIC: 3399 Tacks, nonferrous metal or wire

(G-9645)
TRINITY METALS LLC
2440 N Shadeland Ave (46219-1737)
PHONE..................................317 358-8265
EMP: 13
Web: www.trinitymetals.net
SIC: 3399 Tacks, nonferrous metal or wire
PA: Trinity Metals Llc
6400 English Ave
Indianapolis IN 46219

(G-9646)
TRIPLE JS EXPRESS TRANSPORT
4029 Congaree Dr (46235-8826)
PHONE..................................317 667-2368
Jeffrey Hardwick, *Owner*
EMP: 1
SALES (est): 54.62K **Privately Held**
SIC: 3743 Freight cars and equipment

(G-9647)
TROPICAL DELIGHTS LLC
3703 Commercial Dr (46222-1676)
PHONE..................................317 261-1001
EMP: 4 **EST:** 2021
SALES (est): 116.15K **Privately Held**
Web: www.tropicaldelightsmoothies.com

SIC: 2091 Juice, clam: packaged in cans, jars, etc.

(G-9648)
TROUW NUTRITION USA LLC
2601 Fortune Cir E Ste 200c (46241-5548)
PHONE..................................618 654-2070
EMP: 52
Web: www.trouwnutritionpets.com
SIC: 2048 Prepared feeds, nec
HQ: Trouw Nutrition Usa, Llc
115 Executive Dr
Highland IL 62249
618 654-2070

(G-9649)
TROYC-INDUSTRIES LLC
10947 Echo Grove Cir (46236-9069)
PHONE..................................317 531-1660
Troycine N Mitchell, *Prin*
EMP: 5 **EST:** 2019
SALES (est): 39.69K **Privately Held**
SIC: 3999 Barber and beauty shop equipment

(G-9650)
TRUCK LETTERING
5102 Sandhurst Dr (46217-9461)
PHONE..................................317 787-7875
Garry Vandeder, *Prin*
EMP: 1 **EST:** 2009
SALES (est): 64.54K **Privately Held**
Web: www.truckletteringindy.com
SIC: 3993 Signs and advertising specialties

(G-9651)
TRUE ESSENCE FOODS INC
Also Called: Sochatti
1125 Brookside Ave Ste D2 (46202)
PHONE..................................317 430-3156
Matthew Rubin, *CEO*
EMP: 12 **EST:** 2013
SALES (est): 3.08MM **Privately Held**
Web: www.sochatti.com
SIC: 2066 Chocolate and cocoa products

(G-9652)
TRUE STORIES PUBLISHING CO LLC
48 N Whitcomb Ave (46224-8727)
PHONE..................................765 425-8224
Rebecca Harbert, *Prin*
EMP: 4 **EST:** 2014
SALES (est): 61.81K **Privately Held**
SIC: 2741 Miscellaneous publishing

(G-9653)
TRUU CONFIDENCE LLC
456 N Meridian St Ste 44761 (46204-1795)
PHONE..................................317 795-0042
Pierre Hamilton, *CEO*
EMP: 2 **EST:** 2018
SALES (est): 81.14K **Privately Held**
SIC: 5611 2339 Clothing, sportswear, men's and boys'; Women's and misses' athletic clothing and sportswear

(G-9654)
TUBE PROCESSING CORP
Aerofab Division
604 E Legrande Ave (46203-3907)
PHONE..................................317 787-1321
EMP: 1
SALES (corp-wide): 91.39MM **Privately Held**
Web: www.tubeproc.com
SIC: 3498 Fabricated pipe and fittings
PA: Tube Processing Corp
604 E Legrande Ave
Indianapolis IN 46203
317 787-1321

GEOGRAPHIC SECTION

Indianapolis - Marion County (G-9680)

(G-9655)
TUBE PROCESSING CORP
604 E Legrande Ave (46203-3907)
PHONE....................317 787-5747
EMP: 208
SALES (corp-wide): 91.39MM **Privately Held**
Web: www.tubeproc.com
SIC: 3498 Tube fabricating (contract bending and shaping)
PA: Tube Processing Corp
604 E Legrande Ave
Indianapolis IN 46203
317 787-1321

(G-9656)
TUBE PROCESSING CORP
Ctp Division
2840 Fortune Cir W Ste A (46241-5508)
PHONE....................317 782-9486
Mike Gill, *Brnch Mgr*
EMP: 200
SALES (corp-wide): 91.39MM **Privately Held**
Web: www.tubeproc.com
SIC: 3498 3444 3441 3317 Tube fabricating (contract bending and shaping); Sheet metalwork; Fabricated structural metal; Steel pipe and tubes
PA: Tube Processing Corp
604 E Legrande Ave
Indianapolis IN 46203
317 787-1321

(G-9657)
TUBE PROCESSING CORP
Ctp Sheetmetal Division
2840 Fortune Cir W Ste A (46241-5508)
PHONE....................317 264-4760
Russ Chisham, *Brnch Mgr*
EMP: 1
SALES (corp-wide): 91.39MM **Privately Held**
Web: www.tubeproc.com
SIC: 3356 3469 7692 3444 Nickel and nickel alloy pipe, plates, sheets, etc.; Machine parts, stamped or pressed metal; Brazing; Sheet metalwork
PA: Tube Processing Corp
604 E Legrande Ave
Indianapolis IN 46203
317 787-1321

(G-9658)
TUBE PROCESSING CORP (PA)
Also Called: Aerofab
604 E Legrande Ave (46203-3907)
PHONE....................317 787-1321
George J Seybert, *Pr*
Steven R Dreyer, *
▲ EMP: 275 EST: 1939
SQ FT: 164,000
SALES (est): 91.39MM
SALES (corp-wide): 91.39MM **Privately Held**
Web: www.tubeproc.com
SIC: 3356 3469 7692 3444 Nickel and nickel alloy pipe, plates, sheets, etc.; Machine parts, stamped or pressed metal; Brazing; Sheet metalwork

(G-9659)
TUFF SHED INC
4250 W Morris St (46241-2502)
PHONE....................317 481-8388
Tom Saurey, *Brnch Mgr*
EMP: 2
SALES (corp-wide): 347.42MM **Privately Held**
Web: www.tuffshed.com
SIC: 2452 Prefabricated wood buildings
PA: Tuff Shed, Inc.
1777 S Harrison St # 600
Denver CO 80210
303 753-8833

(G-9660)
TULIP TREE CREAMERY LLC
6330 Corporate Dr Ste D (46278-2937)
PHONE....................317 331-5469
EMP: 15 EST: 2013
SALES (est): 1.05MM **Privately Held**
Web: www.tuliptreecreamery.com
SIC: 2022 2021 Processed cheese; Creamery butter

(G-9661)
TURNER MACHINE CO
Also Called: Manufacturing
1951 Bloyd Ave (46218-3534)
PHONE....................317 751-5105
Derek Turner, *Pr*
EMP: 3 EST: 2020
SALES (est): 315.04K **Privately Held**
Web: www.turnermachine.co
SIC: 3599 Machine shop, jobbing and repair

(G-9662)
TWAY COMPANY INCORPORATED
Also Called: Tway Lifting Products
1609 Oliver Ave (46221-1145)
P.O. Box 1525 (46206-1525)
PHONE....................317 636-2591
Robert S Hansen, *CEO*
Peter G Hansen, *Pr*
Stan R Deal, *VP*
K Arlene Hansen, *Sec*
EMP: 20 EST: 1944
SQ FT: 9,400
SALES (est): 7.89MM **Privately Held**
Web: www.twaylifting.com
SIC: 5051 3315 5084 5085 Cable, wire; Cable, steel: insulated or armored; Hoists; Rope, except wire rope

(G-9663)
TWIN COATINGS & FINISHES LLC
10216 E 25th St (46229-1326)
PHONE....................317 557-0633
EMP: 6 EST: 2017
SALES (est): 229.18K **Privately Held**
SIC: 3479 Coating of metals and formed products

(G-9664)
TWISTED JUTE LLC
41 National Ave (46227-1210)
PHONE....................317 885-4276
Marcus Griswold, *CEO*
EMP: 5 EST: 2020
SALES (est): 248.04K **Privately Held**
SIC: 2621 Rope or jute paper

(G-9665)
TWISTED KILTS TEES & SUCH INC
4627 Eagles Watch Ln (46254-9527)
PHONE....................317 413-8900
Larry White, *Pr*
EMP: 1 EST: 1997
SQ FT: 7,000
SALES (est): 135.77K **Privately Held**
Web: www.twistedkilts.com
SIC: 2397 Schiffli machine embroideries

(G-9666)
TWISTED STIXX LLC
8018 Witherington Rd (46268-2053)
PHONE....................317 435-5034
EMP: 2 EST: 2021
SALES (est): 90.43K **Privately Held**
SIC: 2599 Food wagons, restaurant

(G-9667)
TY SPECIALIZED LLC
11423 Narrowleaf Dr (46235-3614)
PHONE....................317 734-7900
Tiyrai Fuller, *CEO*
EMP: 1 EST: 2020
SALES (est): 64.2K **Privately Held**
SIC: 3711 Truck tractors for highway use, assembly of

(G-9668)
TYCOON LOGISTICS LLC
3620 Donald Ave (46224-1623)
PHONE....................317 749-1381
EMP: 1 EST: 2021
SALES (est): 56.09K **Privately Held**
SIC: 3669 Transportation signaling devices

(G-9669)
TYSON FOODS
Also Called: Tyson
1301 S Keystone Ave (46203)
PHONE....................317 791-8430
EMP: 150
SALES (corp-wide): 52.88B **Publicly Held**
Web: www.tyson.com
SIC: 2011 Meat packing plants
HQ: Tyson Foods
400 S Jefferson St
Chicago IL 60607

(G-9670)
TYSON SALES AND DIST INC
1301 S Keystone Ave (46203-2114)
PHONE....................479 290-7776
EMP: 113
SALES (corp-wide): 52.88B **Publicly Held**
Web: www.tyson.com
SIC: 2015 Chicken slaughtering and processing
HQ: Tyson Sales And Distribution, Inc.
2200 W Don Tyson Pkwy
Springdale AR 72762
479 290-4000

(G-9671)
U S FILTER
6125 Guion Rd (46254-1223)
PHONE....................317 280-4251
David Fowler, *Prin*
EMP: 2 EST: 2011
SALES (est): 249.4K **Privately Held**
SIC: 3569 Filters

(G-9672)
U S FILTER DISTRIBUTION
1680 Expo Ln (46214-2332)
PHONE....................317 271-1463
Larry Hanley, *Mgr*
EMP: 8 EST: 2010
SALES (est): 118.44K **Privately Held**
SIC: 3569 Filters

(G-9673)
UBACKOFF
7121 E 46th St (46226-3803)
PHONE....................317 557-3951
EMP: 3 EST: 2018
SALES (est): 121.24K **Privately Held**
Web: www.ubackoff.com
SIC: 3999 Manufacturing industries, nec

(G-9674)
UEBELHORS GOLF
Also Called: Custom Golf By Uebelhor
7611 S Meridian St (46217-4257)
PHONE....................317 881-4109
Robert N Uebelhor, *Pr*
EMP: 4 EST: 1972
SALES (est): 294.05K **Privately Held**
Web: www.ubiegolf.com
SIC: 3949 5091 5941 Golf equipment; Golf equipment; Golf goods and equipment

(G-9675)
ULRICH CHEMICAL INC
3111 N Post Rd (46226-6566)
PHONE....................317 898-8632
Edward M Pitkin, *Pr*
Stephen J Hiatt, *Ex VP*
James P Fohl, *Treas*
James W Collins, *VP*
Suzanne P Shaw, *VP*
▲ EMP: 27 EST: 1919
SQ FT: 103,000
SALES (est): 3.76MM **Privately Held**
SIC: 5169 2812 Chemicals, industrial and heavy; Chlorine, compressed or liquefied

(G-9676)
UNCLE ALBERTS AMPLIFIER INC
7709 Hague Rd (46256-1751)
PHONE....................317 845-3037
Kevin Silva, *Pr*
Jan Silva, *Treas*
EMP: 3 EST: 1990
SQ FT: 1,600
SALES (est): 194.34K **Privately Held**
Web: www.unclealberts.com
SIC: 3651 7699 Amplifiers: radio, public address, or musical instrument; Professional instrument repair services

(G-9677)
UNIQUE JEWELRY AND MORE LLC
9209 Mccarty St (46231-3113)
PHONE....................317 244-3732
EMP: 1 EST: 2015
SALES (est): 74.2K **Privately Held**
SIC: 3961 5632 Costume jewelry, ex. precious metal and semiprecious stones; Costume jewelry

(G-9678)
UNIQUELY DIVINE YONIS LLC
4050 Candy Apple Blvd (46235-4812)
PHONE....................317 918-9112
Keli Sargeant, *Mgr*
EMP: 1 EST: 2021
SALES (est): 30K **Privately Held**
SIC: 2431 Woodwork, interior and ornamental, nec

(G-9679)
UNITED COATINGS MFG CO
Also Called: United Coatings
5839 Barnstable Ct (46250-2750)
PHONE....................317 845-8830
EMP: 6
SALES (corp-wide): 60.04MM **Privately Held**
SIC: 2851 1761 2952 Paints and allied products; Roofing, siding, and sheetmetal work; Coating compounds, tar
HQ: United Coatings Manufacturing Company
19011 E Cataldo Ave
Greenacres WA 99016

(G-9680)
UNITED PRECISION GEAR CO INC
Also Called: United Precision Gear Co
4937 Camden St (46227-1683)
PHONE....................317 784-4665
Don Le Masters, *Pr*
Marilyn Le Masters, *Sec*
EMP: 3 EST: 1946
SQ FT: 2,000
SALES (est): 288.69K **Privately Held**

Indianapolis - Marion County (G-9681)   GEOGRAPHIC SECTION

SIC: 3566 Gears, power transmission, except auto

(G-9681)
UNITED TECHNOLOGY CORP
Also Called: Carrier
7304 W Morris St (46231-1355)
PHONE..................................317 481-5784
EMP: 19 EST: 2015
SALES (est): 5.7MM Privately Held
SIC: 3812 Aircraft/aerospace flight instruments and guidance systems

(G-9682)
UNIVERSAL DOOR CARRIER INC
1609 S Sigsbee St (46241-2903)
P.O. Box 42165 (46242-0165)
PHONE..................................317 241-3447
Daniel Y Shattuck Senior, Pr
Daniel Y Shattuck Junior, VP
Ruth Ann Shattuck, Sec
EMP: 7 EST: 1904
SQ FT: 10,000
SALES (est): 662.93K Privately Held
Web: www.universaldoor.com
SIC: 2431 3441 3567 3442 Millwork; Fabricated structural metal; Industrial furnaces and ovens; Metal doors, sash, and trim

(G-9683)
UNIVERSAL TRANSPARENT BAG INC
230 W Mccarty St (46225-1234)
P.O. Box 985 (46206-0985)
PHONE..................................317 634-6425
Needham S Hurst, Pr
William C Hurst, Sec
EMP: 4 EST: 1951
SQ FT: 45,000
SALES (est): 382.38K Privately Held
SIC: 2673 Plastic bags: made from purchased materials

(G-9684)
UPPER LEVEL SPORTS LLC
2303 E Riverside Dr (46208-5247)
PHONE..................................317 681-3754
Gregory Ash-buck, Prin
EMP: 3 EST: 2013
SALES (est): 190.63K Privately Held
SIC: 3131 Footwear cut stock

(G-9685)
UPRIZING LLC
5706 Vicksburg Dr (46254-5095)
PHONE..................................317 500-9359
Wesley Bailey, CEO
Wesley Bailey, Prin
Tameara Bailey, Prin
EMP: 6 EST: 2018
SALES (est): 417.25K Privately Held
SIC: 1389 1611 1795 Construction, repair, and dismantling services; Concrete construction: roads, highways, sidewalks, etc.; Demolition, buildings and other structures

(G-9686)
UPSHAW FREIGHT LLC
9702 E Washington St Ste 400 # 142 (46229-3611)
PHONE..................................317 200-8655
Travis Upshaw, Managing Member
EMP: 1 EST: 2020
SALES (est): 178.92K Privately Held
SIC: 3537 7389 Trucks, tractors, loaders, carriers, and similar equipment; Business services, nec

(G-9687)
URBAN LOGGING COMPANY LLC
404 W 44th St (46208-3736)
PHONE..................................317 710-4070
EMP: 9 EST: 2010
SQ FT: 2,000
SALES (est): 239.94K Privately Held
SIC: 2499 Decorative wood and woodwork

(G-9688)
US WATER SYSTEMS INC
1209 Country Club Rd (46234-1818)
PHONE..................................317 209-0889
Patricia Timmons, CEO
Mark Timmons, *
Patricia Anies, *
EMP: 46 EST: 2000
SALES (est): 8.93MM Privately Held
Web: www.uswatersystems.com
SIC: 3589 5046 5999 5074 Water purification equipment, household type; Restaurant equipment and supplies, nec; Water purification equipment; Water purification equipment

(G-9689)
USA MEDICAL SUPPLIERS LTD
9658 Oakhaven Ct (46256-2199)
PHONE..................................608 782-1855
Polly Ann Mihalovic, Pr
EMP: 2 EST: 2006
SQ FT: 2,500
SALES (est): 128.89K Privately Held
SIC: 3842 Surgical appliances and supplies

(G-9690)
USE WHAT YOUVE GOT MINISTRY
3549 Boulevard Pl (46208-4403)
P.O. Box 1521 (46206-1521)
PHONE..................................317 924-4124
Cecelia Whitfield, Pr
EMP: 2 EST: 1990
SALES (est): 183.57K Privately Held
Web: www.usewhatyouvegotministry.org
SIC: 3799 Recreational vehicles

(G-9691)
UTILITY PIPE SALES INDIANA INC
2821 N Catherwood Ave (46219)
PHONE..................................317 224-2300
William Zausch, Pr
EMP: 7 EST: 2007
SALES (est): 85.27K Privately Held
SIC: 3317 Steel pipe and tubes

(G-9692)
UTILITY SYSTEMS INC (PA)
Also Called: Magnetic Instrumentation
8431 Castlewood Dr (46250-1534)
PHONE..................................317 842-9000
Todd Mcmullen, CEO
EMP: 44 EST: 1978
SQ FT: 30,000
SALES (est): 10.85MM
SALES (corp-wide): 10.85MM Privately Held
Web: www.maginst.com
SIC: 3699 3825 Electrical equipment and supplies, nec; Test equipment for electronic and electric measurement

(G-9693)
UTZ QUALITY FOODS LLC
2801 Fortune Cir E Ste N-Q (46241)
PHONE..................................717 443-7230
Howard Friedman, Mgr
EMP: 1
SALES (corp-wide): 732.3MM Privately Held
Web: www.utzsnacks.com
SIC: 2096 Potato chips and other potato-based snacks
PA: Utz Quality Foods, Llc
900 High St
Hanover PA 17331
800 367-7629

(G-9694)
V ART GRAFIX LLC
5102 Sandhurst Dr (46217-9461)
P.O. Box 17008 (46217-1080)
PHONE..................................317 513-5522
V Grafix, Prin
EMP: 5 EST: 2011
SALES (est): 164.75K Privately Held
SIC: 3993 Signs and advertising specialties

(G-9695)
V GLOBAL HOLDINGS LLC (HQ)
Also Called: Vertellus
201 N Illinois St Ste 1800 (46204-1904)
PHONE..................................317 247-8141
Rich Preziotti, Pr
Philip Gillespie, *
Anne Frye, *
EMP: 47 EST: 2016
SALES (est): 96.05MM
SALES (corp-wide): 636.82MM Privately Held
Web: www.aurorium.com
SIC: 0711 2819 2821 2879 Soil chemical treatment services; Ammonium salts and compounds; Epoxy resins; Insecticides and pesticides
PA: Aurorium Holdings Llc
201 N Ill St Ste 1800
Indianapolis IN 46204
317 247-8141

(G-9696)
V M INTEGRATED
8501 Bash St Ste 1000 (46250-5505)
PHONE..................................877 296-0621
Adam Rolfsen, Pr
Linda Rolfsen, CFO
EMP: 11 EST: 2015
SALES (est): 200.57K Privately Held
Web: www.vmintegrated.com
SIC: 1761 3952 Roof repair; Chalk: carpenters', blackboard, marking, tailors', etc.

(G-9697)
VADENS FIREARMS & AMMUN LLC
4485 E 10th St (46201-2700)
PHONE..................................317 840-5799
Ryan Christopher Vaden, CEO
EMP: 5 EST: 2020
SALES (est): 473.72K Privately Held
Web: www.vadensfirearmsammunition.com
SIC: 5941 5099 3484 Firearms; Firearms and ammunition, except sporting; Guns (firearms) or gun parts, 30 mm. and below

(G-9698)
VAL ROLLERS INCORPORATED
2345 N Butler Ave (46218-3910)
PHONE..................................317 542-1968
William J Williams, Pr
Andrew Williams, Sec
EMP: 7 EST: 1962
SALES (est): 510.84K Privately Held
Web: www.valrollers.com
SIC: 3599 Machine shop, jobbing and repair

(G-9699)
VALIDATED CUSTOM SOLUTIONS LLC (PA)
905 N Capitol Ave # 200 (46204-1004)
PHONE..................................317 259-7604
Anthony Wilkerson, Pt
EMP: 2 EST: 2003
SALES (est): 5.31MM
SALES (corp-wide): 5.31MM Privately Held
Web: www.envelopgroup.com
SIC: 3585 Heating and air conditioning combination units

(G-9700)
VAN WESTRUM CORPORATION
1750 E 37th St (46218-1015)
PHONE..................................317 926-3200
Mark S Van Westrum, Pr
Mark S Westrum, Pr
Edith Westrum, Sec
EMP: 5 EST: 1946
SQ FT: 33,000
SALES (est): 447.29K Privately Held
Web: www.vanwestrum.com
SIC: 3479 Coating of metals and formed products

(G-9701)
VARIOTECH CORP
8804 Bash St Ste C (46256-1287)
PHONE..................................404 566-2935
Benedikt Fleig, CEO
Alexandre Holzheimer, CFO
Aaron Olin, Prin
EMP: 5 EST: 2019
SALES (est): 611.76K Privately Held
Web: www.variotech.de
SIC: 3089 Plastics containers, except foam

(G-9702)
VASMO INC
Also Called: Polymicrospheres Division
4101 E 30th St Ste 2 (46218-3068)
PHONE..................................317 549-3722
Doctor S Mohan, Dir
EMP: 10 EST: 1990
SQ FT: 45,000
SALES (est): 769.08K Privately Held
Web: www.polymicrospheres.com
SIC: 2836 3841 Biological products, except diagnostic; Surgical and medical instruments

(G-9703)
VDB CREATIVE PUBLISHING LLC
1240 W 75th Court Ter Apt G (46260-6304)
PHONE..................................317 441-9204
EMP: 1
SALES (est): 78.58K Privately Held
SIC: 2731 Books, publishing only

(G-9704)
VECTOR GRAPHICS INC
7409 Steinmeier Dr (46250-2568)
PHONE..................................317 255-9800
Terry Jacob, Pr
Mark Green, VP
EMP: 2 EST: 1988
SQ FT: 800
SALES (est): 240.25K Privately Held
Web: www.vectorgr.com
SIC: 3672 Printed circuit boards

(G-9705)
VENEER SERVICES LLC
5851 S Harding St (46217-9592)
PHONE..................................317 346-0711
Dane Floyd, Managing Member
◆ EMP: 16 EST: 2003
SALES (est): 3.46MM Privately Held
Web: www.veneerservices.com
SIC: 3553 Bandsaws, woodworking

GEOGRAPHIC SECTION

Indianapolis - Marion County (G-9734)

(G-9706)
VERBOTT TRUCKING & TRANSPORTAT
5883 Jamestown Square Ln (46234-3696)
PHONE..................317 363-9698
Jared Thomas, *Pr*
EMP: 1 **EST:** 2020
SALES (est): 79.46K **Privately Held**
SIC: 3537 7389 Trucks: freight, baggage, etc.: industrial, except mining; Business services, nec

(G-9707)
VERGENCE LLC
9365 Counselors Row (46240-6422)
PHONE..................317 547-4417
Gabriel Browne, *CEO*
Michael Gallagher, *Prin*
James Robertson, *Prin*
EMP: 10 **EST:** 2011
SALES (est): 1.07MM **Privately Held**
Web: www.vergencegroup.com
SIC: 7379 7361 7373 8082 Computer related consulting services; Labor contractors (employment agency); Systems engineering, computer related; Visiting nurse service

(G-9708)
VERONA LLC
2346 S Lynhurst Dr Ste C101 (46241-5169)
PHONE..................317 248-9888
EMP: 7 **EST:** 2010
SALES (est): 202.23K **Privately Held**
Web: www.veronaus.com
SIC: 3911 Shirt studs, precious and semiprecious metal or stone

(G-9709)
VERTELLUS HEALTH & SPECIALTY PRODUCTS LLC
201 N Illinois St Ste 1800 (46204-1904)
PHONE..................317 247-8141
◆ **EMP:** 1000
SIC: 2865 Coal tar: crudes, intermediates, and distillates

(G-9710)
VERTEX MDRNZTION SSTINMENT LLC
6125 E 21st St (46219)
PHONE..................601 607-6866
Bill Beard, *
Bob Sill, *
Rick Mendoz, *
EMP: 7200 **EST:** 2021
SALES (est): 91.08MM **Privately Held**
SIC: 3728 R and D by manuf., aircraft parts and auxiliary equipment

(G-9711)
VERTICAL STEEL MAINTENANCE LLC
Also Called: Telecommunications
8465 Keystone Xing Ste 115 (46240)
PHONE..................912 710-0626
EMP: 2 **EST:** 2021
SALES (est): 70.17K **Privately Held**
SIC: 3441 7629 Tower sections, radio and television transmission; Telecommunication equipment repair (except telephones)

(G-9712)
VESTA INGREDIENTS INC
5767 Thunderbird Rd (46236-2866)
PHONE..................317 895-9000
Sam Kwoen, *Pr*
EMP: 8 **EST:** 2005
SALES (est): 1.09MM **Privately Held**
Web: www.vestanutra.com
SIC: 2834 Druggists' preparations (pharmaceuticals)

(G-9713)
VESTA PHARMACEUTICALS INC
Also Called: Vesta
5767 Thunderbird Rd (46236-2866)
PHONE..................317 895-9000
Sam Kwon, *Pr*
▲ **EMP:** 20 **EST:** 1996
SQ FT: 6,000
SALES (est): 4.79MM **Privately Held**
Web: www.vestanutra.com
SIC: 2834 Pharmaceutical preparations

(G-9714)
VETERANS INDUSTRIES AND ARTS
5380 N College Ave (46220-3142)
PHONE..................317 730-1815
EMP: 5 **EST:** 2015
SALES (est): 96.06K **Privately Held**
SIC: 3999 Manufacturing industries, nec

(G-9715)
VETERANS PROMISE CNSTR LLC
10904 Tallow Wood Ln (46236-8311)
PHONE..................317 501-4570
EMP: 3 **EST:** 2019
SALES (est): 300K **Privately Held**
SIC: 1389 Construction, repair, and dismantling services

(G-9716)
VIANT
3735 N Arlington Ave (46218-1867)
PHONE..................317 788-7225
EMP: 19 **EST:** 2020
SALES (est): 2.6MM **Privately Held**
Web: www.viantmedical.com
SIC: 3841 Surgical and medical instruments

(G-9717)
VIANT MEDICAL LLC
3735 N Arlington Ave (46218)
PHONE..................317 454-8824
EMP: 35
SALES (corp-wide): 1.18B **Privately Held**
Web: www.viantmedical.com
SIC: 3841 Surgical and medical instruments
HQ: Viant Medical, Llc
2 Hampshire St
Foxborough MA 02035

(G-9718)
VIARILOC DISTRIBUTORS INC
1717 Expo Ln (46214-2334)
PHONE..................317 273-0089
Richard Pare, *Pr*
EMP: 2 **EST:** 1992
SALES (est): 159K **Privately Held**
Web: www.icpcitation.com
SIC: 3714 Motor vehicle parts and accessories

(G-9719)
VIAVI SOLUTIONS INC
5808 Churchman Byp (46203-6109)
PHONE..................317 788-9351
Joseph Banich, *Brnch Mgr*
EMP: 26
SALES (corp-wide): 1B **Publicly Held**
Web: www.viavisolutions.com
SIC: 3674 Optical isolators
PA: Viavi Solutions Inc.
1445 S Spctrum Blvd Ste 1
Chandler AZ 85286
408 404-3600

(G-9720)
VIN ELITE IMPORTS INC
55 S State Ave Ste 358 (46201-3896)
PHONE..................317 264-9250
▲ **EMP:** 2 **EST:** 1993
SQ FT: 1,800
SALES (est): 282.87K **Privately Held**
SIC: 5182 2086 Wine; Carbonated beverages, nonalcoholic: pkged. in cans, bottles

(G-9721)
VINEYARD FISHERY PRODUCTS LLC
3032 Ruckle St (46205-3968)
P.O. Box 881425 (46208-1425)
PHONE..................317 902-0753
EMP: 4 **EST:** 2014
SALES (est): 134.42K **Privately Held**
SIC: 2084 Wines

(G-9722)
VIRTU FINE ART SERVICES INC
Also Called: Heartland Printworks
212 W 10th St Ste B100 (46202-5418)
PHONE..................317 822-1800
Charles Knorp, *Prin*
Eileen Quinn, *Prin*
Robert Pierce Eagerton, *Treas*
EMP: 5 **EST:** 2005
SALES (est): 184.14K **Privately Held**
Web: www.virtufinearts.com
SIC: 2752 Offset printing

(G-9723)
VISPALEXO INC
450 E Vermont St (46202-3680)
PHONE..................330 323-4138
Ajay K Seth, *CEO*
Chandan Sen, *Pr*
EMP: 3 **EST:** 2020
SALES (est): 117.43K **Privately Held**
Web: www.vispalexo.com
SIC: 3842 Braces, orthopedic

(G-9724)
VITALSWAP TECHNOLOGIES LLC
6401 Gateway Dr (46253-5300)
PHONE..................725 234-0077
Akinsola Jegede, *Managing Member*
EMP: 3
SALES (est): 128.97K **Privately Held**
SIC: 7372 Application computer software

(G-9725)
VITRUVIAN COMPOSITION LLC
6330 Hythe Rd (46220-4215)
PHONE..................317 447-8383
Alison Duane, *Owner*
EMP: 5 **EST:** 2016
SALES (est): 51.07K **Privately Held**
SIC: 2791 Typesetting

(G-9726)
VIVID SOCIAL GROUP LLC ✪
6817 Ridge Vale Pl Apt 1f (46237-7825)
PHONE..................317 447-7319
Shaun Gordon, *Owner*
EMP: 1 **EST:** 2022
SALES (est): 63.99K **Privately Held**
Web: www.vividsocialgroup.com
SIC: 2759 8742 Screen printing; Marketing consulting services

(G-9727)
VIVINT INC
3902 Hanna Cir Ste A (46241-7207)
PHONE..................317 983-0112
EMP: 277
Web: www.vivint.com
SIC: 3822 Building services monitoring controls, automatic
HQ: Vivint, Inc.
4931 N 300 W
Provo UT 84604
801 377-9111

(G-9728)
VK PRESS LLC
930 Prospect St Apt 206 (46203-1877)
P.O. Box 78044 (46278-0044)
PHONE..................317 400-6883
Shavonne Holton, *Prin*
EMP: 5 **EST:** 2016
SALES (est): 75.81K **Privately Held**
Web: www.vkpresses.com
SIC: 2741 Miscellaneous publishing

(G-9729)
VON DUPRIN LLC
Also Called: Glynn Johnson
2720 Tobey Dr (46219)
PHONE..................317 429-2866
Randy Smith, *Pr*
Mike Cain, *VP*
Tim Eckersley, *Pr*
Barbara Santoro, *Sec*
◆ **EMP:** 522 **EST:** 1908
SQ FT: 225,000
SALES (est): 89.67MM **Privately Held**
Web: us.allegion.com
SIC: 3429 Builders' hardware
HQ: Schlage Lock Company Llc
11819 N Pennsylvania St
Carmel IN 46032
317 810-3700

(G-9730)
VSI ACQUISITION CORP
201 N Illinois St (46204-1904)
PHONE..................317 247-8141
Richard V Preziott, *Pr*
Anne M Frye, *Sec*
Craig Wian, *CFO*
◆ **EMP:** 200 **EST:** 2014
SALES (est): 19.75MM **Privately Held**
SIC: 2833 Organic medicinal chemicals: bulk, uncompounded

(G-9731)
VSI LIQUIDATING INC
Also Called: Vertellus Agriculture & Ntrtn
201 N Illinois St Ste 1800 (46204)
PHONE..................317 247-8141
◆ **EMP:** 2
SIC: 2869 Industrial organic chemicals, nec

(G-9732)
VXA APPAREL ✪
8465 Keystone Xing (46240-4355)
PHONE..................219 259-6279
Aisha Taylor, *CEO*
EMP: 2 **EST:** 2023
SALES (est): 92.67K **Privately Held**
SIC: 2389 Apparel and accessories, nec

(G-9733)
W W G INC
5602 Elmwood Ave Ste 222 (46203-6072)
PHONE..................317 783-6413
William Watson, *Pr*
Virgil Warren, *Sec*
EMP: 6 **EST:** 1981
SQ FT: 2,200
SALES (est): 557.14K **Privately Held**
SIC: 3544 Special dies and tools

(G-9734)
W/S PACKAGING GROUP INC
6231 Avalon Lane East Dr (46220-5077)

Indianapolis - Marion County (G-9735)

PHONE..................317 578-4454
Chris Doerr, Mgr
EMP: 3
SALES (corp-wide): 14.54B Privately Held
SIC: 2759 Labels and seals: printing, nsk
HQ: W/S Packaging Group, Inc.
2571 S Hemlock Rd
Green Bay WI 54229
800 818-5481

(G-9735)
WAGNER SIGNS INC
2802 E Troy Ave (46203-5585)
PHONE..................317 788-0202
Gene Wagner, Pr
EMP: 23 EST: 1962
SQ FT: 4,200
SALES (est): 1.36MM Privately Held
Web: www.wagner-signs.com
SIC: 7336 7389 3993 Silk screen design; Sign painting and lettering shop; Signs and advertising specialties

(G-9736)
WANAFEED CORPORATION
Also Called: Wanamaker Feed & Seed Company
4410 Northeastern Ave (46239-1659)
PHONE..................317 862-4032
James R Trimble, Pr
EMP: 5 EST: 1964
SQ FT: 12,000
SALES (est): 561.42K Privately Held
Web: www.wanamakerfs.com
SIC: 2048 5261 5191 Livestock feeds; Fertilizer; Seeds: field, garden, and flower

(G-9737)
WARM SOCKS INC
3545 Hollow Run Cir Apt 226 (46214)
PHONE..................309 868-3398
Natasha Faulkner, Prin
EMP: 5 EST: 2016
SALES (est): 57.03K Privately Held
SIC: 2252 Socks

(G-9738)
WASHINGTON AND SCOVILLE
450 E 96th St (46240-5703)
PHONE..................317 798-2911
EMP: 5 EST: 2015
SALES (est): 212.68K Privately Held
Web: www.domainmanage.com
SIC: 3441 Fabricated structural metal

(G-9739)
WATER PUMP SPECIALISTS
5108 W Vermont St (46224-8852)
PHONE..................317 270-9360
EMP: 3 EST: 2019
SALES (est): 119.6K Privately Held
Web: www.mywaterpumpman.com
SIC: 3714 Motor vehicle parts and accessories

(G-9740)
WATERJET CUTTING INDIANA INC
10760 E Us Highway 136 (46234-9093)
PHONE..................317 328-8444
Michael Trapp, Pr
Melinda Trapp, CFO
EMP: 4 EST: 2002
SQ FT: 2,200
SALES (est): 497.24K Privately Held
Web: www.waterjetcuttingofindiana.com
SIC: 3599 Machine shop, jobbing and repair

(G-9741)
WATERSHIPBLUE LLC
4021 Ruckle St (46205-2718)
PHONE..................317 910-8585
Thomas Estes, CEO
EMP: 6 EST: 2019
SALES (est): 280.5K Privately Held
SIC: 1623 3559 1731 Water and sewer line construction; Desalination equipment; Energy management controls

(G-9742)
WAYNE BURIAL VAULT COMPANY INC
602 S Emerson Ave (46203-1664)
PHONE..................317 357-4656
Donald C Davis, Pr
David L Preist, Sec
Philip Davis, Mgr
EMP: 8 EST: 1928
SQ FT: 10,000
SALES (est): 851.95K Privately Held
SIC: 3272 Burial vaults, concrete or precast terrazzo

(G-9743)
WB REFRACTORY SERVICE INC
826 E Sumner Ave (46227-1346)
PHONE..................317 450-7386
Loyd Wallace, Pr
EMP: 7 EST: 2014
SALES (est): 528.14K Privately Held
SIC: 3255 Foundry refractories, clay

(G-9744)
WE GREATER COURIER SVCS LLC
9165 Otis Ave Ste 263 (46216-2306)
PHONE..................317 966-1043
EMP: 2
SALES (est): 92.67K Privately Held
SIC: 3799 Transportation equipment, nec

(G-9745)
WEBBER MANUFACTURING COMPANY
8498 Brookville Rd (46239-9491)
P.O. Box 19449 (46219-0449)
PHONE..................317 357-8681
David E Lovett, Pr
Doug Nering, Treas
Sandra L Nering, Sec
EMP: 21 EST: 1946
SQ FT: 29,800
SALES (est): 2.17MM Privately Held
Web: www.webbermfg.com
SIC: 3569 3826 3535 3565 Testing chambers for altitude, temperature, ordnance, power; Environmental testing equipment; Conveyors and conveying equipment; Packaging machinery

(G-9746)
WELDING PLUS LLC
7239 Shelbyville Rd (46259-9721)
PHONE..................317 902-0883
Casey A Gaudin, Prin
EMP: 5 EST: 2012
SALES (est): 42.24K Privately Held
SIC: 7692 Welding repair

(G-9747)
WELL GROOMED MENS CARE LLC
1705 N Shadeland Ave (46219-2733)
PHONE..................317 908-4451
Denisha Cole, Managing Member
EMP: 4 EST: 2020
SALES (est): 64.48K Privately Held
Web: www.wgmcllc.com
SIC: 2844 Cosmetic preparations

(G-9748)
WELLINGTON GLOBAL LLC
2136 N Catherwood Ave Apt 2b (46219-2039)
PHONE..................317 590-1755
Brian Wellington, CEO
EMP: 1 EST: 2021
SALES (est): 41.52K Privately Held
SIC: 2879 Agricultural chemicals, nec

(G-9749)
WELLS ROBE SALES & RENTAL
Also Called: Wells Unlimited Robes Service
5702 E 40th St (46226-4865)
PHONE..................317 542-9062
Salathiel E Wells, Owner
EMP: 2 EST: 1979
SALES (est): 91.74K Privately Held
SIC: 2384 Robes and dressing gowns

(G-9750)
WELLS TRCKG A DIV WLLS ASSOC I
2901 N Euclid Ave (46218-3123)
PHONE..................317 250-2616
Macheo Wells Senior, CEO
EMP: 4 EST: 2008
SALES (est): 252.02K Privately Held
SIC: 1442 Construction sand and gravel

(G-9751)
WEST FORK WHISKEY CO
1660 Bellefontaine St (46202-1811)
PHONE..................812 583-9797
Julian Ross Jones, Pr
EMP: 3 EST: 2015
SALES (est): 494.09K Privately Held
Web: www.westforkwhiskey.com
SIC: 2085 Bourbon whiskey

(G-9752)
WESTERLEY INC
1300 E 86th St Ste 14 # 340 (46240-1990)
EMP: 30 EST: 1993
SQ FT: 50,000
SALES (est): 3.95MM Privately Held
Web: www.clowesfund.org
SIC: 3724 Aircraft engines and engine parts

(G-9753)
WESTFIELD OUTDOOR INC
8675 Purdue Rd (46268)
PHONE..................317 334-0364
Charlie Cai, CEO
Liping Yuan, *
Daoqing Yang, *
◆ EMP: 150 EST: 2004
SQ FT: 18,000
SALES (est): 19.53MM Privately Held
Web: www.westfieldoutdoors.com
SIC: 3949 Camping equipment and supplies

(G-9754)
WESTROCK MWV LLC
Envelope Division
6302 Churchman Byp (46203-6119)
PHONE..................317 787-3361
Bill Stinger, Genl Mgr
EMP: 54
SQ FT: 65,000
SALES (corp-wide): 20.31B Privately Held
Web: www.westrock.com
SIC: 2653 Boxes, corrugated: made from purchased materials
HQ: Westrock Mwv, Llc
3500 45th St Sw
Lanett AL 36863
804 444-1000

(G-9755)
WHATZTHAT VENDING LLC
5168 Alpine Violet Way (46254-7053)
PHONE..................317 362-9088
EMP: 2 EST: 2020
SALES (est): 58.81K Privately Held
Web: www.whatzthatvending.com
SIC: 5046 5962 3581 Vending machines, coin-operated; Food vending machines; Automatic vending machines

(G-9756)
WHEEL GROUP HOLDINGS LLC
Also Called: Wheel One
5720 Kopetsky Dr Ste I (46217-9281)
PHONE..................317 780-1661
Pam Goss, Brnch Mgr
EMP: 6
SALES (corp-wide): 51MM Privately Held
Web: www.thewheelgroup.com
SIC: 3714 Wheel rims, motor vehicle
PA: Wheel Group Holdings, Llc
1050 N Vineyard Ave
Ontario CA 91764
888 399-8885

(G-9757)
WHEELCHAIR OF INDIANA
4717 Boulevard Pl (46208-3501)
PHONE..................317 627-6560
Julie Fritz, Prin
EMP: 5 EST: 2016
SALES (est): 73.06K Privately Held
SIC: 3842 Wheelchairs

(G-9758)
WHIMSICAL GARDENS
5464 N Capitol Ave (46208-2632)
PHONE..................317 257-4704
David Giles, Prin
EMP: 1 EST: 2000
SALES (est): 62.56K Privately Held
Web: www.gherrli.com
SIC: 3251 Ceramic glazed brick, clay

(G-9759)
WHITE SAND & GRAVEL INC
7229 Lake Rd (46217-9417)
PHONE..................317 882-7791
Paul White, Owner
EMP: 1 EST: 2005
SALES (est): 149.16K Privately Held
Web: www.widebandtech.com
SIC: 1442 Construction sand mining

(G-9760)
WHITEHEAD SIGNS INC
1801 Deloss St (46201-4004)
PHONE..................317 632-1800
Charles S Whitehead, Pr
Charles Toby, VP
Steven T Whitehead, Sec
EMP: 10 EST: 1976
SQ FT: 8,000
SALES (est): 672K Privately Held
Web: www.whiteheadsigns.com
SIC: 3993 1799 7389 Neon signs; Sign installation and maintenance; Sign painting and lettering shop

(G-9761)
WIESE HOLDING COMPANY
Also Called: Wiese
4549 W Bradbury Ave (46241-5210)
P.O. Box 421009 (46242-1009)
PHONE..................317 241-8600
Don Turk, Brnch Mgr
EMP: 75
SALES (corp-wide): 102.39MM Privately Held
Web: www.wieseusa.com
SIC: 5084 3537 Materials handling machinery; Industrial trucks and tractors
PA: Wiese Holding Company
1435 Woodson Rd
Saint Louis MO 63132
314 997-4444

GEOGRAPHIC SECTION
Indianapolis - Marion County (G-9788)

(G-9762)
WILBERT BURIAL VAULT CO INC
Also Called: Wilbert Burial Vault Co
2165 N Sherman Dr (46218-3817)
P.O. Box 18126 (46218-0126)
PHONE.....................317 547-1387
Robert Rose, *Pr*
Judith Rose, *Treas*
▲ **EMP:** 20 **EST:** 1936
SQ FT: 28,000
SALES (est): 2.15MM **Privately Held**
Web: www.indywilbert.com
SIC: 3272 Burial vaults, concrete or precast terrazzo

(G-9763)
WILCO CORPORATION
5352 W 79th St (46268-1631)
PHONE.....................317 228-9320
Jerry Carroll, *Pr*
Roger D Carroll, *Sec*
EMP: 18 **EST:** 1953
SQ FT: 12,500
SALES (est): 1.1MM **Privately Held**
Web: www.wilcocorp.com
SIC: 3679 Electronic circuits

(G-9764)
WILCOXEN MACHINE & TOOL INC
4937 Camden St (46227-1683)
PHONE.....................317 784-4665
Mark Wilcoxen, *Prin*
EMP: 6 **EST:** 2020
SALES (est): 83.4K **Privately Held**
SIC: 3599 Machine shop, jobbing and repair

(G-9765)
WILD FLAVORS INC
6326 Calais Dr (46220-5088)
PHONE.....................859 991-5229
EMP: 6 **EST:** 2018
SALES (est): 104.34K **Privately Held**
Web: www.adm.com
SIC: 2087 Flavoring extracts and syrups, nec

(G-9766)
WILLIAM WSLEY PROF ORAL PRSTHT
5605 W 73rd St (46278-1739)
PHONE.....................317 635-1000
TOLL FREE: 800
William C Perkins, *Pr*
Wesley Spiller, *VP*
EMP: 8 **EST:** 1984
SALES (est): 233.69K **Privately Held**
SIC: 3843 8072 Teeth, artificial (not made in dental laboratories); Dental laboratories

(G-9767)
WILLIAMS DISTRIBUTION LLC
Also Called: Chemical Ingrdent Ppe Jn-San D
1642 Mccollough Ct (46260-5239)
P.O. Box 80095 (46280-0095)
PHONE.....................317 749-0006
Andre Williams, *CEO*
Andre Williams, *VP*
Marshall Williams, *Pr*
Rhonda Williams, *Mng Pt*
Sheryl Williams, *Mng Pt*
EMP: 4 **EST:** 2017
SALES (est): 479.14K **Privately Held**
Web: www.williamsdistllc.com
SIC: 2869 5049 5087 Ethyl alcohol, ethanol; Laboratory equipment, except medical or dental; Janitors' supplies

(G-9768)
WILLIAMS SCOTSMAN INC
2301 S Holt Rd (46241-4822)
PHONE.....................317 782-2463
Ibrahim Iilyas, *Brnch Mgr*
EMP: 10
SALES (corp-wide): 2.36B **Publicly Held**
Web: www.mobilemini.com
SIC: 3448 Buildings, portable: prefabricated metal
HQ: Williams Scotsman, Inc.
4646 E Van Bren St Ste 40
Phoenix AZ 85008
480 894-6311

(G-9769)
WILLIAMS WOODS PUBG SVCS LLC
3921 English Ave (46201-4571)
PHONE.....................317 270-0976
Deborah J Williams, *Admn*
EMP: 5 **EST:** 2008
SALES (est): 120.94K **Privately Held**
SIC: 2741 Miscellaneous publishing

(G-9770)
WILLOUGHBY INDUSTRIES INC
5105 W 78th St (46268-4138)
P.O. Box 21217 (46221)
PHONE.....................317 875-0830
EMP: 104 **EST:** 1947
SALES (est): 22.75MM **Privately Held**
Web: www.willoughby-ind.com
SIC: 3432 3441 Plumbing fixture fittings and trim; Fabricated structural metal

(G-9771)
WINBUSH REFRESHMENTS LLC
433 N Capitol Ave (46204-1234)
PHONE.....................317 762-8236
EMP: 2
SALES (est): 92.67K **Privately Held**
SIC: 3581 Automatic vending machines

(G-9772)
WINE AND CANVAS DEV LLC
6411 Kentucky Ave (46221-9705)
PHONE.....................765 278-0432
Troy Cooper, *Brnch Mgr*
EMP: 2
SALES (corp-wide): 805.52K **Privately Held**
Web: www.wineandcanvas.com
SIC: 2211 Canvas
PA: Wine And Canvas Development Llc
1760 Cholla Ter
Indianapolis IN 46240
317 345-1567

(G-9773)
WINE AND CANVAS DEV LLC (PA)
Also Called: Wine and Canvas
1760 Cholla Ter (46240-1933)
PHONE.....................317 345-1567
Steve Gentry, *Mgr*
EMP: 6 **EST:** 2013
SALES (est): 805.52K
SALES (corp-wide): 805.52K **Privately Held**
Web: www.wineandcanvas.com
SIC: 2211 Canvas

(G-9774)
WIPBEATZ LLC
5625 N German Church Rd (46235-8513)
PHONE.....................866 676-1465
Willie Stinson, *Managing Member*
EMP: 1 **EST:** 2021
SALES (est): 56.09K **Privately Held**
Web: www.wipbeatz.com
SIC: 3651 Music distribution apparatus

(G-9775)
WIRECUT TECHNOLOGIES INC
5328 Commerce Square Dr (46237-9742)
PHONE.....................317 885-9915
James Ditman, *Pr*
Valerie Ditman, *Sec*
Kimberly Young, *Off Mgr*
EMP: 8 **EST:** 1986
SQ FT: 5,400
SALES (est): 852K **Privately Held**
Web: www.wirecuttechnologies.com
SIC: 3599 Machine shop, jobbing and repair

(G-9776)
WISE ENERGY LLC
5999 Medora Dr (46228-1396)
PHONE.....................317 475-0305
Nathan Harris, *Managing Member*
EMP: 1 **EST:** 2011
SIC: 3822 1542 7349 Building services monitoring controls, automatic; Nonresidential construction, nec; Building maintenance services, nec

(G-9777)
WISE PRINTING INC (PA)
Also Called: Allegra Print & Imaging
1429 Sadlier Circle West Dr (46239-1057)
PHONE.....................317 351-9477
David Wise, *Pr*
Karen Wise, *Ex VP*
EMP: 1 **EST:** 1989
SQ FT: 3,600
SALES (est): 282.17K **Privately Held**
Web: www.allegramarketingprint.com
SIC: 2752 Offset printing

(G-9778)
WISEMED INC
Also Called: Victoza
1192 Chelsey Village Ct Unit D (46260)
PHONE.....................317 644-1169
Daniel Smith, *Pr*
EMP: 6 **EST:** 2010
SALES (est): 482.07K **Privately Held**
SIC: 2833 7389 Animal based products; Business services, nec

(G-9779)
WITH LOVE BATH BOMBS
7903 Wildcat Run Ln (46239-6923)
PHONE.....................317 523-9197
EMP: 3 **EST:** 2014
SALES (est): 60.31K **Privately Held**
SIC: 2844 Bath salts

(G-9780)
WNC OF DAYTON LLC
3969 E 82nd St (46240-2468)
PHONE.....................937 999-8868
Philip Davis, *Prin*
EMP: 2 **EST:** 2013
SALES (est): 140K **Privately Held**
SIC: 2211 Canvas

(G-9781)
WOLF TECHNICAL ENGINEERING LLC
9855 Crosspoint Blvd Ste 126 (46256)
PHONE.....................800 783-9653
EMP: 3 **EST:** 2012
SALES (est): 142.77K **Privately Held**
SIC: 8711 2399 2531 3728 Mechanical engineering; Seat belts, automobile and aircraft; Seats, aircraft; R and D by manuf.; aircraft parts and auxiliary equipment

(G-9782)
WOLFE AND SWICKARD MCH CO INC
1344 S Tibbs Ave (46241)
P.O. Box 42817 (46242)
PHONE.....................317 241-2589
Samuel W Swickard, *Pr*
Carolyn Swickard, *Stockholder**
EMP: 80 **EST:** 1945
SQ FT: 50,000
SALES (est): 7.32MM **Privately Held**
Web: www.wolfeandswickard.com
SIC: 3599 3625 Machine shop, jobbing and repair; Relays and industrial controls

(G-9783)
WOOD-MIZER LLC
Also Called: Wood-Mizer
8180 W 10th St (46214-2430)
PHONE.....................317 271-1542
Mark Thompson, *CFO*
EMP: 22 **EST:** 2012
SALES (est): 4.17MM
SALES (corp-wide): 133.23MM **Privately Held**
Web: www.woodmizer.com
SIC: 2421 Sawmills and planing mills, general
PA: Wood-Mizer Holdings, Inc.
8180 W 10th St
Indianapolis IN 46214
317 271-1542

(G-9784)
WOOD-MIZER HOLDINGS INC (PA)
Also Called: Lastec
8180 W 10th St (46214)
PHONE.....................317 271-1542
Richard Vivers, *Pr*
◆ **EMP:** 150 **EST:** 1972
SQ FT: 148,000
SALES (est): 133.23MM
SALES (corp-wide): 133.23MM **Privately Held**
Web: www.woodmizer.com
SIC: 3553 3524 3425 2431 Sawmill machines; Lawn and garden mowers and accessories; Saw blades and handsaws; Doors and door parts and trim, wood

(G-9785)
WOODBERRY FAMILY FREIGHT LLC
5919 Parkwood Ct Apt 8 (46254-2994)
PHONE.....................317 665-6917
EMP: 2
SALES (est): 77.36K **Privately Held**
SIC: 7389 3799 Business Activities at Non-Commercial Site; Transportation equipment, nec

(G-9786)
WOODEN SIGNS
2013 Beach Ave (46240-2763)
PHONE.....................317 506-6991
Chris Mc Cloud, *Prin*
EMP: 1 **EST:** 2013
SALES (est): 80.08K **Privately Held**
Web: www.woodsignsbychris.com
SIC: 3993 Signs and advertising specialties

(G-9787)
WORD 4 WORD LLC
218 W Morris St (46225-1441)
PHONE.....................317 601-3995
Desiree Flemming, *CEO*
EMP: 1 **EST:** 2021
SALES (est): 55.83K **Privately Held**
SIC: 3161 2211 2221 Clothing and apparel carrying cases; Apparel and outerwear fabrics, cotton; Apparel and outerwear fabric, manmade fiber or silk

(G-9788)
WORDPRO COMMUNICATION SERVICES
6525 Emerald Hill Ct (46237)
PHONE.....................847 296-3964

Lin Johnson, *Owner*
EMP: 1 **EST:** 1989
SALES (est): 149.34K **Privately Held**
Web: www.wordprocommunications.com
SIC: 2741 Miscellaneous publishing

(G-9789)
WORK FIELD COLLABORATIVE INC
2834 E Washington St (46201-4215)
PHONE..................360 581-9476
Dominic Senibaldi, *Pr*
EMP: 6 **EST:** 2016
SALES (est): 221.72K **Privately Held**
Web: www.catheadpress.com
SIC: 2752 Commercial printing, lithographic

(G-9790)
WORLD MEDIA GROUP INC
Also Called: W M G
2301 Whispering Dr (46239-9678)
PHONE..................317 549-8484
Jeff Mellentine, *Pr*
Julia Whistler, *Finance*
▲ **EMP:** 100 **EST:** 1988
SQ FT: 70,000
SALES (est): 5.57MM **Privately Held**
SIC: 3652 7336 Prerecorded records and tapes; Art design services

(G-9791)
WRIGHT COATINGS CORPORATION
8620 W 82nd St (46278-1009)
PHONE..................317 937-6768
Charles Seth Wright, *Prin*
EMP: 4 **EST:** 2013
SALES (est): 110.13K **Privately Held**
Web: www.thewrightcoatings.com
SIC: 3479 Coating of metals and formed products

(G-9792)
WRIT LABS INC
433 N Capitol Ave Ste 100 (46204-1234)
PHONE..................650 560-5008
Adam Weinstein, *Prin*
EMP: 1
SALES (est): 66.66K **Privately Held**
SIC: 7372 Business oriented computer software

(G-9793)
WRITEGUARD BUSINESS SYSTEMS
5102 E 65th St (46220-4817)
P.O. Box 20113 (46220-0113)
PHONE..................317 849-7292
Larry La Hue, *Pr*
EMP: 4 **EST:** 1978
SQ FT: 6,000
SALES (est): 477.2K **Privately Held**
Web: www.writeguard.com
SIC: 2761 2782 2791 2759 Computer forms, manifold or continuous; Checkbooks; Typesetting; Commercial printing, nec

(G-9794)
WRR INC
Also Called: State Plating
8908 Gary Pl (46256-1388)
PHONE..................317 577-1149
W R Railing, *Pr*
Randy Railing, *
EMP: 27 **EST:** 1962
SQ FT: 300,000
SALES (est): 528.1K **Privately Held**
SIC: 3471 Chromium plating of metals or formed products

(G-9795)
XCELERIX CORP
9000 Keystone Xing Ste 900 (46201)
PHONE..................317 208-2320
Christopher Dozier, *Pr*
David Layden, *Sec*
David Broadwin Esq, *Sec*
EMP: 18 **EST:** 1982
SALES (est): 1.4MM **Privately Held**
SIC: 7372 Prepackaged software

(G-9796)
XPRESSVENDING LLC
2228 Harbor Dr (46229-3301)
PHONE..................331 264-3541
EMP: 1
SALES (est): 50.76K **Privately Held**
SIC: 3581 7389 Automatic vending machines; Business services, nec

(G-9797)
XTRAC INC
6183 W 80th St (46278-1344)
PHONE..................317 472-2451
Andrew Hood, *VP*
EMP: 10
SALES (corp-wide): 105.3MM **Privately Held**
Web: www.xtrac.com
SIC: 3714 Motor vehicle parts and accessories
HQ: Xtrac Limited
Gables Way
Thatcham BERKS RG19
163 529-3800

(G-9798)
XTREME SIGNS & GRAPHICS LLC
Also Called: Xtreme Graphics
3350 N High School Rd Ste J (46224-2051)
PHONE..................317 299-5622
EMP: 8 **EST:** 2011
SALES (est): 222.54K **Privately Held**
Web: www.xtrmgraphics.com
SIC: 3993 Signs and advertising specialties

(G-9799)
YALEL UNBLAND LLC ◆
1075 Broad Ripple Ave 120 (46220-2034)
PHONE..................404 232-9139
Nicholas Mitchell, *CEO*
EMP: 2 **EST:** 2022
SALES (est): 62.01K **Privately Held**
SIC: 5699 5651 2389 Clothing, hand painted; Family clothing stores; Apparel and accessories, nec

(G-9800)
YAMAHA MOTOR CORPORATION USA
Also Called: Yamaha Mar Precision Propeller
2427 N Ritter Ave (46218)
PHONE..................317 545-9080
EMP: 26
SIC: 3366 Propellers
HQ: Yamaha Motor Corporation Usa
6555 Katella Ave
Cypress CA 90630
714 761-7300

(G-9801)
YES YES TRUCKING LLC
10475 Crosspoint Blvd Ste 250 (46256)
PHONE..................800 971-3633
EMP: 1 **EST:** 2020
SALES (est): 100K **Privately Held**
Web: www.yesyestrucking.com
SIC: 3537 Trucks: freight, baggage, etc.: industrial, except mining

(G-9802)
YESCO SIGN & LIGHTING SERVICE
8621 Bash St Ste A (46256-1202)
PHONE..................317 559-3374
EMP: 7 **EST:** 2019
SALES (est): 182.53K **Privately Held**
Web: www.yesco.com
SIC: 3993 Signs and advertising specialties

(G-9803)
YOLANDA DENISE LLC
6137 Crawfordsville Rd Ste F179 (46224-3730)
PHONE..................317 457-6831
Yolanda Davis, *Managing Member*
EMP: 1 **EST:** 2018
SALES (est): 54.62K **Privately Held**
SIC: 3743 Freight cars and equipment

(G-9804)
YONGS AUDIO CONNECTION LLC
3851 Kevin Way (46254-2993)
PHONE..................317 298-8333
EMP: 4 **EST:** 2013
SALES (est): 234.71K **Privately Held**
Web: www.yongaudio.com
SIC: 3651 5199 Audio electronic systems; General merchandise, non-durable

(G-9805)
YOURBODYGETSIT LLC
3354 Graceland Ave (46208-4622)
PHONE..................317 908-7445
James Arron Lee, *CEO*
EMP: 4 **EST:** 2021
SALES (est): 74.96K **Privately Held**
SIC: 3949 Golf equipment

(G-9806)
Z GRILLS INC
6161 Decatur Blvd Ste A (46241-9610)
PHONE..................909 295-5264
Kimmy Cao, *Mgr*
EMP: 7 **EST:** 2018
SALES (est): 519.04K **Privately Held**
Web: www.zgrills.com
SIC: 3631 Household cooking equipment

(G-9807)
ZAFFER INDUSTRIES LLC
854 Sunbow Cir (46231-1185)
PHONE..................317 910-4958
Jordan Von Essen, *Owner*
EMP: 4 **EST:** 2017
SALES (est): 39.69K **Privately Held**
SIC: 3999 Manufacturing industries, nec

(G-9808)
ZEBRA EXPRESS LLC
605 Summer Wood Ln Apt 4 (46229-2876)
P.O. Box 421423 (46242-1423)
PHONE..................317 828-9277
Patson Dubek, *Managing Member*
EMP: 2 **EST:** 2019
SALES (est): 200K **Privately Held**
SIC: 3537 Trucks, tractors, loaders, carriers, and similar equipment

(G-9809)
ZELLER LLC
Also Called: Zeller Polymer Solutions, LLC
8888 Keystone Xing Ste 650 (46240)
PHONE..................317 343-2930
Dagoberto Hornedo, *Pr*
EMP: 8 **EST:** 2017
SALES (est): 688.54K **Privately Held**
Web: www.zellersolutions.com
SIC: 2899 Chemical preparations, nec

(G-9810)
ZIMMER BIOMET HOLDINGS INC
Also Called: Zimmer Biomet Indiana
6825 Hillsdale Ct (46250-2039)
PHONE..................317 872-8484
EMP: 4
SALES (corp-wide): 7.39B **Publicly Held**
Web: www.zimmerbiomet.com
SIC: 3842 Orthopedic appliances
PA: Zimmer Biomet Holdings, Inc.
345 E Main St
Warsaw IN 46580
574 267-6131

(G-9811)
ZIMMER PAPER PRODUCTS DEL LLC (PA)
Also Called: Zimmer Custom-Made Packaging
1450 E 20th St (46218-3498)
PHONE..................317 263-3420
Colleen Bohn, *Pr*
Curt Lucas, *Pr*
Milan Milivojevic, *CFO*
▲ **EMP:** 81 **EST:** 1930
SQ FT: 110,000
SALES (est): 17.57MM
SALES (corp-wide): 17.57MM **Privately Held**
SIC: 2671 2759 2672 Waxed paper: made from purchased material; Commercial printing, nec; Paper; coated and laminated, nec

(G-9812)
ZIMMER WELDING LLC
16 N Harding St (46222-4400)
PHONE..................317 632-5212
Bob J Marshall, *Owner*
EMP: 4 **EST:** 1940
SQ FT: 1,600
SALES (est): 332.2K **Privately Held**
Web: www.zimmerwelding.com
SIC: 7692 1799 3444 Welding repair; Welding on site; Sheet metalwork

(G-9813)
ZOLLMAN PLASTIC SURGERY PC
Also Called: Zollman
6848 Fox Lake Dr N (46278-1220)
PHONE..................317 328-1100
Charles W Zollman, *Pr*
EMP: 16 **EST:** 2002
SALES (est): 372.06K **Privately Held**
Web: www.zollmansurgery.com
SIC: 8011 3842 Plastic surgeon; Implants, surgical

(G-9814)
ZOTIC SCENTS LLC
832 Park Central Ct (46260-4506)
PHONE..................317 766-6501
EMP: 1 **EST:** 2021
SALES (est): 49.15K **Privately Held**
SIC: 3161 Clothing and apparel carrying cases

(G-9815)
ZPS AMERICA LLC
4950 W 79th St (46268-1665)
PHONE..................317 452-4030
Olaf Tessarzyk, *Managing Member*
▲ **EMP:** 26 **EST:** 2008
SALES (est): 2.46MM **Privately Held**
Web: www.zpsamerica.com
SIC: 3545 3541 Milling machine attachments (machine tool accessories); Vertical turning and boring machines (metalworking)

GEOGRAPHIC SECTION

Jasper - Dubois County (G-9838)

Ireland
Dubois County

(G-9816)
LEED SELLING TOOLS CORP
5312 W Ireland Center St (47545)
P.O. Box 68 (47545-0068)
PHONE................................812 482-7888
Richard Edwards, *Mgr*
EMP: 233
SQ FT: 40,000
SALES (corp-wide): 18.9MM **Privately Held**
Web: www.leedsamples.com
SIC: 2782 3161 Blankbooks and looseleaf binders; Luggage
PA: Leed Selling Tools Corp
9700 Highway 57
Evansville IN 47725
812 867-4340

Jamestown
Boone County

(G-9817)
FUKAI TOYOTETSU INDIANA CORP
Also Called: Ftic
1100 N Lebanon St (46147-9381)
PHONE................................765 676-4800
Satoru Fukai, *Pr*
Takayuki Kubota, *Sec*
Kazuasa Fukuchi, *Dir*
Kazuhiko Takarada, *Dir*
Tomio Harada, *Dir*
EMP: 55 EST: 2014
SQ FT: 151,000
SALES (est): 29.32MM **Privately Held**
Web: www.fticna.com
SIC: 3465 Body parts, automobile: stamped metal

(G-9818)
JOKERR FABRICATION LLC
409 W Mill St (46147)
PHONE................................513 312-0408
Wetonah Sisk, *Admn*
EMP: 5 EST: 2014
SALES (est): 116.77K **Privately Held**
SIC: 3499 Fabricated metal products, nec

(G-9819)
MELVIN MCCULLOUGH
Also Called: Mels Guitars and Repair
52 W Jefferson St (46147-9500)
P.O. Box 121 (46147-0121)
PHONE................................765 577-0083
Melvin Mccullough, *Owner*
EMP: 1
SALES (est): 37K **Privately Held**
SIC: 3931 7389 Musical instruments, electric and electronic, nec; Business Activities at Non-Commercial Site

(G-9820)
SIGNS & STRIPES BY CARR
Also Called: Carr Custom Painted Mtcyc
8970 W Us Highway 136 (46147-9566)
PHONE................................317 432-9215
Paul J Carr, *Owner*
EMP: 2 EST: 1972
SQ FT: 3,200
SALES (est): 120.74K **Privately Held**
SIC: 3993 Signs and advertising specialties

(G-9821)
WILLIAMS TOOL & MACHINE CORP
54 W Main St (46147-9131)
P.O. Box 183 (46147-0183)
PHONE................................765 676-5859
Gary Williams, *Pr*
Louis Williams, *VP*
EMP: 10 EST: 1965
SQ FT: 50,000
SALES (est): 959.97K **Privately Held**
Web: www.williamstoolmachine.com
SIC: 3444 3599 Sheet metalwork; Machine shop, jobbing and repair

Jasonville
Greene County

(G-9822)
AYCO PANEL
4641 N County Road 825 E (47438-9025)
PHONE................................765 635-8106
Robert Ayres, *Owner*
EMP: 2 EST: 1991
SALES (est): 150K **Privately Held**
SIC: 3542 5084 3613 Machine tools, metal forming type; Machine tools and accessories; Control panels, electric

(G-9823)
ERC MINING INDIANA CORP
15127 W 700 N (47438-6160)
PHONE................................812 665-9780
Mark Jensen, *Pr*
EMP: 8 EST: 2015
SALES (est): 170.73K **Privately Held**
SIC: 1241 Mining services, nec: anthracite

Jasper
Dubois County

(G-9824)
ARISTOCRAT INC
1 Masterbrand Cabinets Dr (47546-2248)
PHONE................................812 634-0460
S Pfister, *Prin*
▲ EMP: 2 EST: 2005
SALES (est): 224.8K **Privately Held**
Web: www.aristocrat.com
SIC: 2434 Wood kitchen cabinets

(G-9825)
BROKEN TEE LLC ✪
904 Reyling Dr Unit 4 (47546)
PHONE................................812 559-0741
EMP: 5 EST: 2022
SALES (est): 75.6K **Privately Held**
SIC: 2759 Screen printing

(G-9826)
CELEBRATION ICE LLC
31 S Clay St (47546-2848)
P.O. Box 43 (47545-0043)
PHONE................................812 634-9801
EMP: 15 EST: 2007
SQ FT: 5,500
SALES (est): 1.36MM **Privately Held**
Web: www.celebration-ice.com
SIC: 2097 Manufactured ice

(G-9827)
CENTRAL COCA-COLA BTLG CO INC
Also Called: Coca-Cola
641 Wernsing Rd (47546-8137)
PHONE................................812 482-7475
EMP: 32
SALES (corp-wide): 45.75B **Publicly Held**
Web: www.coca-cola.com
SIC: 2086 8741 Bottled and canned soft drinks; Management services
HQ: Central Coca-Cola Bottling Company, Inc.
555 Taxter Rd Ste 550
Elmsford NY 10523
914 789-1100

(G-9828)
CENTRAL CONCRETE SUPPLY LLC
801 E 230s (47546-7300)
P.O. Box 249 (47586-0249)
PHONE................................812 481-2331
Brad Persohn, *Owner*
EMP: 14 EST: 1999
SALES (est): 851.45K **Privately Held**
Web: www.mulzer.com
SIC: 3273 Ready-mixed concrete

(G-9829)
CONCEPT DESIGN & FABRICATION
352 S Saint Charles St (47546-7807)
PHONE................................812 481-1142
Rick Fuhrman, *Mgr*
EMP: 1 EST: 2004
SALES (est): 192.99K **Privately Held**
SIC: 3714 Motor vehicle parts and accessories

(G-9830)
DADS ROOT BEER COMPANY LLC
950 S Saint Charles St (47546-2688)
P.O. Box 790 (47547-0790)
PHONE................................812 482-5352
EMP: 2 EST: 2007
SALES (est): 153.99K **Privately Held**
Web: www.dadsrootbeer.com
SIC: 2086 Carbonated soft drinks, bottled and canned

(G-9831)
DAVID EDWARD FURNITURE INC (DH)
1600 Royal St (47546-2256)
PHONE................................812 482-1600
Phyllis M Goetz, *CEO*
EMP: 147 EST: 2018
SQ FT: 125,000
SALES (est): 53.91MM
SALES (corp-wide): 2.43B **Publicly Held**
Web: www.kimballinternational.com
SIC: 2512 2522 2521 Upholstered household furniture; Office furniture, except wood; Wood office furniture
HQ: Kimball Furniture Group, Llc
1600 Royal St
Jasper IN 47546

(G-9832)
DITTO SALES INC (PA)
Also Called: Versteel
2332 Cathy Ln (47546-7705)
PHONE................................812 482-3043
G Scott Schwinghammer, *Pr*
Robert J John, *
▲ EMP: 25 EST: 1970
SQ FT: 90,000
SALES (est): 31.67MM
SALES (corp-wide): 31.67MM **Privately Held**
Web: www.dittosales.com
SIC: 3499 5072 Furniture parts, metal; Hardware

(G-9833)
DSTYLE INC
Also Called: Allan Copley Designs
1600 Royal St (47546-2256)
PHONE................................619 662-0560
Katherine S Sigler, *CEO*
Lonnie Nicholson, *VP*
▲ EMP: 10 EST: 1988
SALES (est): 2.76MM
SALES (corp-wide): 2.43B **Publicly Held**
Web: www.dstyleinc.com
SIC: 3499 5021 Furniture parts, metal; Furniture
HQ: Kimball International, Inc.
1600 Royal St
Jasper IN 47546
812 482-1600

(G-9834)
DUBOIS CNTY BLOCK & BRICK INC
Also Called: Dubois Co Block & Brick
2208 Newton St (47546-1501)
P.O. Box 1030 (47547-1030)
PHONE................................812 482-6293
Dennis Persohn, *Pr*
Roger Cox, *VP*
Steve Jahn, *Treas*
EMP: 17 EST: 1999
SALES (est): 3.65MM **Privately Held**
Web: www.dcblockbrick.com
SIC: 5032 3271 Brick, stone, and related material; Concrete block and brick

(G-9835)
DUBOIS COUNTY LINERS LLP
Also Called: Line-X
555 E 12th Ave (47546)
PHONE................................812 634-1294
Jason Neocum, *Pt*
Robert Rasche, *Pt*
EMP: 2 EST: 1998
SALES (est): 238.3K **Privately Held**
Web: www.linex.com
SIC: 5531 2821 Truck equipment and parts; Plastics materials and resins

(G-9836)
ERNY SHEET METAL INC
1020 2nd Ave (47546-3409)
PHONE................................812 482-1044
David Erny, *Pr*
Barbara Erny, *Sec*
EMP: 24 EST: 1940
SQ FT: 1,500
SALES (est): 4.24MM **Privately Held**
SIC: 3444 Sheet metalwork

(G-9837)
FARBEST FOODS INC
1155 W 12th Ave Ste B (47546-8195)
P.O. Box 480 (47542-0480)
PHONE................................812 683-4200
Ted J Segar, *Pr*
Gerald K Jones, *VP Fin*
Brian Hawkins, *VP*
Ronnie Parker, *Sec*
Phil Seger, *V Ch Bd*
EMP: 900 EST: 1998
SALES (est): 98.39MM **Privately Held**
Web: www.farbestfoods.com
SIC: 2015 Turkey, processed, nsk

(G-9838)
FOREST PRODUCTS MFG CO (PA)
51 E 30th St (47546-1300)
P.O. Box 606 (47547-0606)
PHONE................................812 482-5625
John Seng, *Pr*
Phil Gramelspacher, *
David Seng, *
Joseph Seng, *
EMP: 40 EST: 1940
SQ FT: 40,000
SALES (est): 8.8MM
SALES (corp-wide): 8.8MM **Privately Held**
Web: www.forestp.com
SIC: 2421 2426 Sawmills and planing mills, general; Furniture dimension stock, hardwood

Jasper - Dubois County (G-9839)   GEOGRAPHIC SECTION

(G-9839)
G & T INDUSTRIES INC
2741 Cathy Ln (47546-9463)
PHONE..................................812 634-2252
Paul Wise, *Mgr*
EMP: 1
SALES (corp-wide): 53.58MM **Privately Held**
Web: www.gtindustries.com
SIC: 5087 2821 2671 Upholsterers' equipment and supplies; Plastics materials and resins; Paper; coated and laminated packaging
PA: G & T Industries, Inc.
  1001 76th St Sw
  Byron Center MI 49315
  616 452-8611

(G-9840)
G & T INDUSTRIES INC
290 E 30th St (47546-1308)
PHONE..................................812 634-2252
Paul Wise, *Mgr*
EMP: 1
SALES (corp-wide): 53.58MM **Privately Held**
Web: www.gtindustries.com
SIC: 3086 Insulation or cushioning material, foamed plastics
PA: G & T Industries, Inc.
  1001 76th St Sw
  Byron Center MI 49315
  616 452-8611

(G-9841)
GEMINI MACHINE AND DESIGN LLC
1321 W Magnolia St (47546-9688)
PHONE..................................812 559-1727
Jarod Wendholt, *Pr*
EMP: 4 **EST:** 2019
SALES (est): 181.54K **Privately Held**
Web: www.geminimachineshop.com
SIC: 3599 Machine shop, jobbing and repair

(G-9842)
HELMING BROS INC
1030 Fairview Ave (47546-2407)
P.O. Box 103 (47547-0103)
PHONE..................................812 634-9797
Joseph Helming, *Pr*
Vincent Helming, *VP*
Jennifer Rasche, *Sec*
EMP: 5 **EST:** 1981
SQ FT: 7,500
SALES (est): 725.29K **Privately Held**
Web: www.helmingbrothers.com
SIC: 1761 1721 1799 1793 Sheet metal work, nec; Commercial painting; Steeple jacks; Glass and glazing work

(G-9843)
IMPRESSIONS PRINTING INC
508 Jackson St (47546-3128)
PHONE..................................812 634-2574
Kurt Mehringer, *CEO*
EMP: 4 **EST:** 1997
SALES (est): 489.31K **Privately Held**
Web: www.jasperprinter.com
SIC: 2752 Offset printing

(G-9844)
IMPULSE OF JASPER INC
613 Main St (47546-3040)
PHONE..................................812 481-2880
Brenda Buschkoetter, *Prin*
EMP: 8 **EST:** 2007
SALES (est): 57.38K **Privately Held**
Web: www.impulseofjasper.com
SIC: 2323 Men's and boy's neckwear

(G-9845)
INDIANA FURNITURE INDUSTRIES INC (PA)
Also Called: Indiana Furniture
1224 Mill St (47546-2852)
P.O. Box 270 (47547-0270)
PHONE..................................812 482-5727
▲ **EMP:** 100 **EST:** 1905
SALES (est): 40.25MM
SALES (corp-wide): 40.25MM **Privately Held**
Web: www.indianafurniture.com
SIC: 2521 2531 2512 5712 Desks, office: wood; School furniture; Chairs: upholstered on wood frames; Furniture stores

(G-9846)
INDUSTRIAL WOODKRAFT INC
251 E 30th St (47546-1309)
PHONE..................................812 827-6544
Thad Leinenbach, *Prin*
EMP: 1
SALES (corp-wide): 4.45MM **Privately Held**
Web: www.industrialwoodkraft.com
SIC: 2448 Pallets, wood
PA: Industrial Woodkraft, Inc.
  811 Hyrock Blvd
  Boonville IN 47601
  812 897-4893

(G-9847)
INWOOD OFFICE FURNITURE INC
Also Called: Inwood Office Environment
1108 E 15th St (47546-2227)
P.O. Box 646 (47547-0646)
PHONE..................................812 482-6121
EMP: 100
Web: www.inwood.net
SIC: 2521 2531 Wood office furniture; School furniture

(G-9848)
JASPER CHAIR COMPANY
534 E 8th St (47546-2953)
P.O. Box 331 (47547-0331)
PHONE..................................812 482-5239
Jeff S Barth, *Pr*
Fred A Barth, *
Chad Barth, *
▲ **EMP:** 100 **EST:** 1921
SQ FT: 75,000
SALES (est): 9MM **Privately Held**
Web: www.jasperchair.com
SIC: 2522 2521 2531 2512 Office furniture, except wood; Chairs, office: padded, upholstered, or plain: wood; School furniture ; Upholstered household furniture

(G-9849)
JASPER DESK COMPANY INC
415 E 6th St (47546-2918)
P.O. Box 111 (47547-0111)
PHONE..................................812 482-4132
James Arvin, *Pr*
John Wright, *
James Seifert, *
Phillip Gramelspacher, *
EMP: 82 **EST:** 1876
SQ FT: 2,000
SALES (est): 4.67MM **Privately Held**
Web: www.jasperdesk.com
SIC: 2521 Desks, office: wood

(G-9850)
JASPER ELECTRIC MOTOR INC (HQ)
815 Wernsing Rd (47546-8141)
P.O. Box 650 (47547-0650)
PHONE..................................812 482-1660
Doug Bawel, *Pr*
Mike Schwenk, *VP*
E Ray Bawel, *Sec*
Raymond Schwenk, *Treas*
Gervase Schwenk, *Ch Bd*
EMP: 10
SQ FT: 2,500
SALES (est): 5.52MM
SALES (corp-wide): 418.4MM **Privately Held**
Web: www.jasperelectric.com
SIC: 7694 5063 5999 Electric motor repair; Motors, electric; Motors, electric
PA: Jasper Engine Exchange, Inc.
  815 Wernsing Rd
  Jasper IN 47546
  812 482-1041

(G-9851)
JASPER ELECTRIC MOTOR INC
733 W Division Rd (47546-9711)
PHONE..................................812 482-1660
EMP: 15
SALES (corp-wide): 418.4MM **Privately Held**
Web: www.jasperelectric.com
SIC: 7694 5063 Electric motor repair; Motors, electric
HQ: Jasper Electric Motor Inc
  815 Wernsing Rd
  Jasper IN 47546
  812 482-1660

(G-9852)
JASPER EMB & SCREEN PRTG
Also Called: Jasper EMB & Screenprinting
310 Main St (47546-3315)
PHONE..................................812 482-4787
EMP: 6 **EST:** 1994
SQ FT: 3,000
SALES (est): 477.96K **Privately Held**
Web: www.jasperemb.com
SIC: 2395 2396 Embroidery products, except Schiffli machine; Screen printing on fabric articles

(G-9853)
JASPER ENGINE EXCHANGE INC (PA)
Also Called: Jasper Engines & Transmissions
815 Wernsing Rd (47546-8141)
P.O. Box 650 (47547-0650)
PHONE..................................812 482-1041
Douglas Bawel, *CEO*
Zachery Bawel, *Pr*
Mike Schwenk, *VP*
Raymond Schwenk, *Treas*
E Ray Bawel, *Sec*
◆ **EMP:** 900 **EST:** 1952
SQ FT: 220,000
SALES (est): 418.4MM
SALES (corp-wide): 418.4MM **Privately Held**
Web: www.jasperengines.com
SIC: 3714 7538 6512 Rebuilding engines and transmissions, factory basis; General automotive repair shops; Nonresidential building operators

(G-9854)
JASPER HOLDINGS INC (PA)
815 Wernsing Rd (47546-8141)
PHONE..................................812 482-1041
Zach Bawel, *Pr*
EMP: 16 **EST:** 2018
SALES (est): 28.4MM
SALES (corp-wide): 28.4MM **Privately Held**
Web: www.jasperengines.com
SIC: 3714 Motor vehicle parts and accessories

(G-9855)
JASPER RUBBER PRODUCTS INC
1093 1st Ave W (47546-3217)
PHONE..................................812 482-3242
Mike Hayden, *Ex VP*
EMP: 65
SALES (corp-wide): 8.28B **Privately Held**
Web: www.jasperrubber.com
SIC: 3061 Mechanical rubber goods
HQ: Jasper Rubber Products Inc
  1010 First Ave
  Jasper IN 47546
  812 482-3242

(G-9856)
JASPER RUBBER PRODUCTS INC (DH)
1010 1st Ave W (47546)
PHONE..................................812 482-3242
Jeffrey Geisler, *Ch Bd*
Douglas Mathias, *
Audrey Place Haas, *
Marcus Oxley, *
R Keith Wyatt, *
▲ **EMP:** 444 **EST:** 1949
SQ FT: 330,000
SALES (est): 68.32MM
SALES (corp-wide): 8.28B **Privately Held**
Web: www.jasperrubber.com
SIC: 3061 Mechanical rubber goods
HQ: Jasper Acquisition Corp.
  127 Public Sq Ste 5300
  Cleveland OH 44114
  216 978-2359

(G-9857)
JASPER SEATING COMPANY INC
932 Mill St (47546-2821)
PHONE..................................812 771-4500
EMP: 169
SALES (corp-wide): 198.33MM **Privately Held**
Web: jaspergroup.us.com
SIC: 2521 Wood office furniture
PA: Jasper Seating Company Inc
  225 Clay St
  Jasper IN 47546
  812 482-3204

(G-9858)
JASPER SEATING COMPANY INC (PA)
Also Called: Jasper Group Brands
225 Clay St (47546)
PHONE..................................812 482-3204
Michael S Wagner, *Pr*
Jason Lints, *
Nicholas Gramelspacher Ii, *Sec*
Christine Sander, *
◆ **EMP:** 128 **EST:** 1929
SQ FT: 207,000
SALES (est): 198.33MM
SALES (corp-wide): 198.33MM **Privately Held**
Web: jaspergroup.us.com
SIC: 2521 2531 Chairs, office: padded, upholstered, or plain: wood; School furniture

(G-9859)
JASPER VENEER INC
810 W 14th St (47546-1838)
PHONE..................................812 482-4245
George Gramelspacher, *Prin*
EMP: 10 **EST:** 2008
SALES (est): 308.05K **Privately Held**
Web: www.jasperveneermills.com
SIC: 2435 Veneer stock, hardwood

GEOGRAPHIC SECTION
Jasper - Dubois County (G-9880)

(G-9860)
JASPER WILLOW SPRINGS MO LLC
815 Wernsing Rd (47546-8141)
PHONE..................................800 827-7455
Raymond Schwenk, *Admn*
EMP: 5 **EST:** 2014
SALES (est): 193.95K **Privately Held**
Web: www.jasperengines.com
SIC: 3714 Motor vehicle parts and accessories

(G-9861)
JOFCO INC
Also Called: Jofco, International
225 Clay St (47546-3306)
PHONE..................................812 482-5154
◆ **EMP:** 221
Web: www.jsifurniture.com
SIC: 5021 2521 Office furniture, nec; Chairs, office: padded, upholstered, or plain: wood

(G-9862)
JUST MONOGRAMS LLC
535 University Dr (47546-8084)
PHONE..................................812 827-3693
Sherri Schwenk, *Prin*
EMP: 7 **EST:** 2016
SALES (est): 248.84K **Privately Held**
Web: www.justmonograms.com
SIC: 2395 Embroidery and art needlework

(G-9863)
KENNETH FUHRMAN
6711 N 550w (47546-8701)
PHONE..................................812 482-4612
Kenneth Fuhrman, *Pt*
EMP: 2 **EST:** 2001
SALES (est): 167.17K **Privately Held**
SIC: 3523 Driers (farm): grain, hay, and seed

(G-9864)
KEUSCH GLASS INC
403 E 23rd St (47546-8172)
P.O. Box 487 (47547-0487)
PHONE..................................812 482-2566
Timothy Keusch, *Pr*
Elisabeth R Anderson, *Sec*
Ronald C Keusch, *Stockholder*
EMP: 24 **EST:** 1966
SQ FT: 15,600
SALES (est): 3.61MM **Privately Held**
Web: www.keuschglass.com
SIC: 5039 3089 Glass construction materials; Windows, plastics

(G-9865)
KIMBALL ELECTRONICS INC
1038 E 15th St (47546-2225)
PHONE..................................812 634-4200
Bob Mc Kenzie, *Mgr*
EMP: 778
SALES (corp-wide): 1.71B **Publicly Held**
Web: www.kimballelectronics.com
SIC: 3571 3672 Electronic computers; Printed circuit boards
PA: Kimball Electronics, Inc.
1205 Kimball Blvd
Jasper IN 47546
812 634-4000

(G-9866)
KIMBALL ELECTRONICS INC (PA)
Also Called: Kimball Electronics
1205 Kimball Blvd (47546)
PHONE..................................812 634-4000
Richard D Phillips, *CEO*
Robert J Phillippy, *Non-Executive Chairman of the Board*
Jana T Croom, *CFO*
Steven T Korn, *COO*

Douglas A Hass, *Legal*
EMP: 283 **EST:** 1961
SQ FT: 42,000
SALES (est): 1.71B
SALES (corp-wide): 1.71B **Publicly Held**
Web: www.kimballelectronics.com
SIC: 3672 Printed circuit boards

(G-9867)
KIMBALL ELECTRONICS GROUP LLC
1600 Royal St (47546-2256)
PHONE..................................812 634-4200
EMP: 1
SALES (corp-wide): 1.71B **Publicly Held**
Web: www.kimballelectronics.com
SIC: 3672 Printed circuit boards
HQ: Kimball Electronics Group, Llc
1205 Kimball Blvd
Jasper IN 47546

(G-9868)
KIMBALL ELECTRONICS GROUP LLC (HQ)
Also Called: Kimball Corporate, The
1205 Kimball Blvd (47546-0017)
PHONE..................................812 634-4000
◆ **EMP:** 150 **EST:** 1999
SQ FT: 1,000,000
SALES (est): 491.19MM
SALES (corp-wide): 1.71B **Publicly Held**
Web: www.kimballelectronics.com
SIC: 3694 3699 Automotive electrical equipment, nec; Electrical equipment and supplies, nec
PA: Kimball Electronics, Inc.
1205 Kimball Blvd
Jasper IN 47546
812 634-4000

(G-9869)
KIMBALL ELECTRONICS MFG INC
1600 Royal St (47549)
PHONE..................................812 482-1600
Douglas Habig, *Ch Bd*
Don Charron, *
EMP: 825 **EST:** 1999
SALES (est): 380.04MM
SALES (corp-wide): 1.71B **Publicly Held**
Web: www.kimballinternational.com
SIC: 3672 Printed circuit boards
HQ: Kimball Electronics Group, Llc
1205 Kimball Blvd
Jasper IN 47546

(G-9870)
KIMBALL ELECTRONICS TAMPA INC (DH)
1205 Kimball Blvd (47546-0017)
PHONE..................................812 634-4000
Michelle R Schroeder, *VP*
John H Kahle, *
Michael K Sergesketter, *
Gregory R Kincer, *
R G Kincer, *
▲ **EMP:** 1 **EST:** 1973
SQ FT: 150,000
SALES (est): 101.2MM
SALES (corp-wide): 1.71B **Publicly Held**
Web: www.kimballelectronics.com
SIC: 3679 3672 Electronic circuits; Printed circuit boards
HQ: Kimball Electronics Group, Llc
1205 Kimball Blvd
Jasper IN 47546

(G-9871)
KIMBALL FURNITURE GROUP LLC
Also Called: Kimball Office
1620 Cherry St (47546-2238)
PHONE..................................812 482-8401

Greg Meunier, *Brnch Mgr*
EMP: 358
SQ FT: 72,000
SALES (corp-wide): 2.43B **Publicly Held**
Web: www.kimballinternational.com
SIC: 2436 2435 Softwood veneer and plywood; Hardwood veneer and plywood
HQ: Kimball Furniture Group, Llc
1600 Royal St
Jasper IN 47546

(G-9872)
KIMBALL FURNITURE GROUP LLC (DH)
1600 Royal St (47546-2256)
PHONE..................................812 482-1600
Kristine L Juster, *CEO*
James C Thyen, *
John H Kahle, *
Michelle R Schroeder, *
R Gregory Kincer, *
▲ **EMP:** 292 **EST:** 1988
SQ FT: 133,000
SALES (est): 606.75MM
SALES (corp-wide): 2.43B **Publicly Held**
Web: www.kimballinternational.com
SIC: 2521 2522 Wood office furniture; Office furniture, except wood
HQ: Kimball International, Inc.
1600 Royal St
Jasper IN 47546
812 482-1600

(G-9873)
KIMBALL FURNITURE GROUP LLC
1180 E 16th St (47546-2234)
PHONE..................................812 482-8517
EMP: 40
SALES (corp-wide): 2.43B **Publicly Held**
Web: www.kimballinternational.com
SIC: 2522 Office furniture, except wood
HQ: Kimball Furniture Group, Llc
1600 Royal St
Jasper IN 47546

(G-9874)
KIMBALL FURNITURE GROUP LLC
National Office Furniture
340 11th Ave (47546-2662)
PHONE..................................812 634-3526
Greg Meunier, *Brnch Mgr*
EMP: 250
SALES (corp-wide): 2.43B **Publicly Held**
Web: www.kimballinternational.com
SIC: 2522 Office furniture, except wood
HQ: Kimball Furniture Group, Llc
1600 Royal St
Jasper IN 47546

(G-9875)
KIMBALL HOSPITALITY INC
1180 E 16th St (47546-2234)
PHONE..................................812 482-8090
Katherine S Sigler, *Brnch Mgr*
EMP: 36
SALES (corp-wide): 2.43B **Publicly Held**
Web: www.kimballhospitality.com
SIC: 2521 Wood office furniture
HQ: Kimball Hospitality, Inc.
1600 Royal St
Jasper IN 47546

(G-9876)
KIMBALL HOSPITALITY INC (DH)
1600 Royal St (47546)
PHONE..................................812 482-8090
◆ **EMP:** 314 **EST:** 1965
SALES (est): 50.08MM
SALES (corp-wide): 2.43B **Publicly Held**
Web: www.kimballhospitality.com

SIC: 2522 Office furniture, except wood
HQ: Kimball Furniture Group, Llc
1600 Royal St
Jasper IN 47546

(G-9877)
KIMBALL INC
Also Called: Property Management
1600 Royal St (47546-2256)
PHONE..................................812 482-1600
Bob Fleck, *CEO*
Thomas L Habig, *V Ch Bd*
James C Thyen, *Pr*
◆ **EMP:** 600 **EST:** 1969
SQ FT: 195,000
SALES (est): 165.78MM
SALES (corp-wide): 2.43B **Publicly Held**
Web: www.kimballinternational.com
SIC: 2522 Office furniture, except wood
HQ: Kimball International, Inc.
1600 Royal St
Jasper IN 47546
812 482-1600

(G-9878)
KIMBALL INTERNATIONAL INC (HQ)
Also Called: Kimball International
1600 Royal St (47546)
PHONE..................................812 482-1600
Kristine L Juster, *CEO*
Kourtney L Smith, *WORKPLACE & HEALTH*
Gregory Meunier, *
Lonnie P Nicholson, *Chief Human Resource Officer*
Michael Roch, *CCO*
◆ **EMP:** 209 **EST:** 1939
SALES (est): 665.88MM
SALES (corp-wide): 2.43B **Publicly Held**
Web: www.kimballinternational.com
SIC: 2511 2512 2521 2522 Wood household furniture; Upholstered household furniture; Wood office furniture; Office furniture, except wood
PA: Hni Corporation
600 E 2nd St
Muscatine IA 52761
563 272-7400

(G-9879)
KIMBALL INTERNATIONAL INC
Kimball Intl Logistics Svcs
1600 Royal St (47546-2256)
PHONE..................................812 937-3284
EMP: 28
SALES (corp-wide): 2.43B **Publicly Held**
Web: www.kimballinternational.com
SIC: 2522 Office furniture, except wood
HQ: Kimball International, Inc.
1600 Royal St
Jasper IN 47546
812 482-1600

(G-9880)
KIMBALL INTERNATIONAL TRANSIT (DH)
1001 Hrj Ln (47546-3061)
PHONE..................................812 634-3346
Mark Merder, *Dir*
Douglas A Habig, *Ch Bd*
Thomas L Habig, *V Ch Bd*
James C Thyen, *Pr*
EMP: 206 **EST:** 1972
SALES (est): 59.4MM
SALES (corp-wide): 2.43B **Publicly Held**
Web: www.kimballinternational.com
SIC: 2522 Office furniture, except wood
HQ: Kimball International, Inc.
1600 Royal St
Jasper IN 47546
812 482-1600

Jasper - Dubois County (G-9881)   GEOGRAPHIC SECTION

(G-9881)
KIMBALL INTL BRANDS INC (DH)
1600 Royal St (47546-2256)
PHONE.................812 482-1600
Kourtney L Smith, *Pr*
Douglas A Habig, *
Thomas L Habig, *
Ronald J Thyen, *
John T Thyen, *
▲ **EMP:** 500 **EST:** 1986
SQ FT: 195,000
SALES (est): 358.28MM
SALES (corp-wide): 2.43B **Publicly Held**
Web: www.kimballinternational.com
SIC: 2522 Office desks and tables, except wood
HQ: Kimball Furniture Group, Llc
1600 Royal St
Jasper IN 47546

(G-9882)
LECLERE MANUFACTURING INC
2905 Newton St (47546-1335)
P.O. Box 846 (47547-0846)
PHONE.................812 683-5627
James M Le Clere, *Pr*
Rhonda K Le Clere, *Sec*
EMP: 9 **EST:** 1997
SALES (est): 831.23K **Privately Held**
SIC: 2448 2441 Pallets, wood; Nailed wood boxes and shook

(G-9883)
LOVE UPHOLSTERY LLC
5265 W Oak Ridge Dr (47546-8097)
PHONE.................812 639-3789
EMP: 1 **EST:** 2015
SQ FT: 1,000
SALES (est): 46.52K **Privately Held**
SIC: 7641 2512 2426 7532 Upholstery work; Upholstered household furniture; Frames for upholstered furniture, wood; Upholstery and trim shop, automotive

(G-9884)
LUND INTERNATIONAL HOLDING CO
2415 Cathy Ln (47546-7708)
PHONE.................888 477-3729
Mark Wolf, *Brnch Mgr*
EMP: 1
SALES (corp-wide): 829.18MM **Privately Held**
Web: www.roadworksmfg.com
SIC: 3714 Motor vehicle parts and accessories
HQ: Lund International Holding Company
4325 Hmlton Mill Rd Ste 4
Buford GA 30518

(G-9885)
M & C LLC
Also Called: Mailboxes and Parcel Depot
3626 N Newton St (47546-9601)
PHONE.................812 482-7447
EMP: 3 **EST:** 1998
SQ FT: 1,500
SALES (est): 216.27K **Privately Held**
SIC: 3086 Packaging and shipping materials, foamed plastics

(G-9886)
MAGNOLIA
311 W 36th St (47546-9521)
PHONE.................317 831-3220
Cherryl A Jedele, *Prin*
EMP: 6 **EST:** 2007
SALES (est): 89.46K **Privately Held**
Web: www.magnolia.com
SIC: 3842 Prosthetic appliances

(G-9887)
MASTERBRAND INC (PA)
1 Masterbrand Cabinets Dr (47546)
PHONE.................812 482-2527
R David Banyard Junior, *CEO*
David D Petratis, *Non-Executive Chairman of the Board*
Andrea H Simon, *Ex VP*
Bruce A Kendrick, *Chief Human Resources Officer*
Navi Grewal, *DIGITAL*
EMP: 324 **EST:** 1986
SALES (est): 2.73B
SALES (corp-wide): 2.73B **Publicly Held**
Web: www.masterbrand.com
SIC: 2434 Wood kitchen cabinets

(G-9888)
MASTERBRAND CABINETS LLC
Also Called: Decora Cabinets
1491 S Meridian Rd (47546-3831)
P.O. Box 420 (47547-0420)
PHONE.................812 482-2513
Joe Schaffer, *Mgr*
EMP: 51
SALES (corp-wide): 2.73B **Publicly Held**
Web: www.masterbrand.com
SIC: 2434 Wood kitchen cabinets
HQ: Masterbrand Cabinets Llc
3300 Entp Pkwy Ste 300
Beachwood OH 44122
812 482-2527

(G-9889)
MASTERBRAND US HOLDINGS CORP
1 Masterbrand Cabinets Dr (47546-2248)
PHONE.................812 482-2527
EMP: 234 **EST:** 2019
SALES (est): 534.2K
SALES (corp-wide): 2.73B **Publicly Held**
Web: www.masterbrandcabinets.com
SIC: 2434 Wood kitchen cabinets
PA: Masterbrand, Inc.
1 Masterbrand Cabinets Dr
Jasper IN 47546
812 482-2527

(G-9890)
MERKLEY & SONS INC
Also Called: Merkley Packing Co
3994 W 180n (47546-8498)
PHONE.................812 482-7020
Selma Merkley, *Treas*
James Merkley, *
David Merkley, *
Karen Altmann, *
EMP: 30 **EST:** 1950
SQ FT: 21,000
SALES (est): 2.19MM **Privately Held**
SIC: 5421 5147 2011 2013 Meat markets, including freezer provisioners; Meats, fresh; Meat packing plants; Sausages and other prepared meats

(G-9891)
MID CONTINENT CABINETRY
1 Masterbrand Cabinets Dr (47546-2248)
PHONE.................866 527-0141
EMP: 6 **EST:** 2019
SALES (est): 269.28K **Privately Held**
Web: www.midcontinentcabinetry.com
SIC: 2434 Wood kitchen cabinets

(G-9892)
MO-WOOD PRODUCTS INC (HQ)
51 E 30th St (47546-1300)
P.O. Box 606 (47547-0606)
PHONE.................812 482-5625
John W Seng, *Pr*
EMP: 3 **EST:** 1977
SQ FT: 3,200
SALES (est): 4.62MM
SALES (corp-wide): 8.8MM **Privately Held**
Web: www.forestp.com
SIC: 2431 Millwork
PA: Forest Products Manufacturing Company
51 E 30th St
Jasper IN 47546
812 482-5625

(G-9893)
MORTON BUILDINGS INC
Us-231 (47546)
PHONE.................800 447-7436
EMP: 10
SALES (corp-wide): 213.04MM **Privately Held**
Web: www.mortonbuildings.com
SIC: 3448 Prefabricated metal buildings and components
PA: Morton Buildings, Inc.
252 W Adams St
Morton IL 61550
800 447-7436

(G-9894)
NAP ASSET HOLDINGS LTD (PA)
Also Called: Peak Toolworks
1180 Wernsing Rd (47546)
PHONE.................812 482-2000
Bradley Stack, *Pr*
Jeannot Perron, *Sec*
◆ **EMP:** 75 **EST:** 1941
SQ FT: 55,000
SALES (est): 43.28MM
SALES (corp-wide): 43.28MM **Privately Held**
Web: www.peaktoolworks.com
SIC: 7699 3541 3545 Knife, saw and tool sharpening and repair; Saws, power (metalworking machinery); Tools and accessories for machine tools

(G-9895)
NEWSNOW DUBOIS COUNTY
511 Newton St (47546-3160)
PHONE.................812 827-6131
EMP: 8 **EST:** 2016
SALES (est): 121.72K **Privately Held**
Web: www.newsnowdc.com
SIC: 2711 Newspapers, publishing and printing

(G-9896)
NORCRAFT COMPANIES INC (DH)
1 Masterbrand Cabinets Dr (47546-2248)
PHONE.................800 297-0661
Mark Buller, *CEO*
Kurt Wanninger, *MID CONTINENT*
John Press-starmark Swedeen, *Prin*
Leigh Ginter, *CFO*
EMP: 51 **EST:** 1966
SALES (est): 46.89MM
SALES (corp-wide): 2.73B **Publicly Held**
Web: www.masterbrandcabinets.com
SIC: 2434 Vanities, bathroom: wood
HQ: Masterbrand Cabinets Llc
3300 Entp Pkwy Ste 300
Beachwood OH 44122
812 482-2527

(G-9897)
NORCRAFT COMPANIES LP (DH)
Also Called: Mid Continent Cabinetry
1 Masterbrand Cabinets Dr (47546-2248)
PHONE.................812 482-2527
Mark Buller, *Pr*
Leigh Ginter, *
◆ **EMP:** 263 **EST:** 1966
SALES (est): 475.47MM

SALES (corp-wide): 2.73B **Publicly Held**
SIC: 2434 Vanities, bathroom: wood
HQ: Masterbrand Cabinets Llc
3300 Entp Pkwy Ste 300
Beachwood OH 44122
812 482-2527

(G-9898)
NORCRAFT HOLDING LLC
1 Masterbrand Cabinets Dr (47546-2248)
PHONE.................812 482-2527
EMP: 198 **EST:** 2019
SALES (est): 450.76K
SALES (corp-wide): 2.73B **Publicly Held**
SIC: 2531 Public building and related furniture
PA: Masterbrand, Inc.
1 Masterbrand Cabinets Dr
Jasper IN 47546
812 482-2527

(G-9899)
NSK SERVICES INC
5384 N Kellerville Rd (47546-8641)
PHONE.................812 695-2004
Dave Ferguson, *Prin*
EMP: 6 **EST:** 2008
SALES (est): 533.13K **Privately Held**
Web: www.nsk.com
SIC: 3714 Motor vehicle parts and accessories

(G-9900)
OMEGA CABINETS LTD (HQ)
Also Called: Omega Cabinetry
1 Masterbrand Cabinets Dr (47546)
PHONE.................319 235-5700
Greg Stoner, *Pr*
Robert J Bertch, *
Mary H Bertch, *
◆ **EMP:** 647 **EST:** 1977
SQ FT: 500,000
SALES (est): 98.89MM
SALES (corp-wide): 2.73B **Publicly Held**
Web: www.omegacabinetry.com
SIC: 5211 2434 Lumber and other building materials; Vanities, bathroom: wood
PA: Masterbrand, Inc.
1 Masterbrand Cabinets Dr
Jasper IN 47546
812 482-2527

(G-9901)
PACKAGING CORPORATION AMERICA
Also Called: PCA
240 S Truman Rd (47546-9768)
PHONE.................812 482-4598
EMP: 7
SALES (corp-wide): 8.48B **Publicly Held**
Web: www.packagingcorp.com
SIC: 2653 Boxes, corrugated: made from purchased materials
PA: Packaging Corporation Of America
1 N Field Ct
Lake Forest IL 60045
847 482-3000

(G-9902)
PEPSI-COLA
Also Called: Pepsico
2811 Market St (47546-1409)
PHONE.................812 634-1844
EMP: 6 **EST:** 2018
SALES (est): 102.46K **Privately Held**
Web: www.pepsico.com
SIC: 2086 Carbonated soft drinks, bottled and canned

GEOGRAPHIC SECTION
Jeffersonville - Clark County (G-9926)

(G-9903)
PHOENIX NATURAL RESOURCES INC (HQ)
Rte 5 (47546)
P.O. Box 207 (47542-0207)
PHONE..............................636 537-0283
Larry J Walls, *Pr*
Hal J Finefield, *Treas*
John Shaal, *Sec*
EMP: 4 **EST:** 1992
SQ FT: 2,000
SALES (est): 3.76MM **Privately Held**
SIC: 1221 Bituminous coal surface mining
PA: Phoenix Resources Holding Company, Inc.
16409 Farmers Mill Ln
Chesterfield MO 63005

(G-9904)
PUZZLES PADLOCKS ESCAPE RM LLC
402 Mccrillus St (47546-2924)
PHONE..............................812 559-0767
EMP: 3 **EST:** 2021
SALES (est): 64.65K **Privately Held**
Web: www.puzzlesandpadlocks.com
SIC: 3944 Puzzles

(G-9905)
ROBERT L WEHR
Also Called: Wehr Welding & Repair Shop
1527 W 100s (47546-8204)
PHONE..............................812 482-2673
Robert L Wehr, *Owner*
EMP: 2 **EST:** 1975
SALES (est): 118.45K **Privately Held**
SIC: 7692 Welding repair

(G-9906)
ROLLIE WILLIAMS PAINT SPOT
1391 Cherry St (47546-2214)
PHONE..............................812 827-2488
EMP: 1
SALES (corp-wide): 23.12MM **Privately Held**
Web: www.rolliewilliams.com
SIC: 2851 Paints and allied products
PA: Rollie Williams Paint Spot Inc
1179 Kent St
Elkhart IN 46514
574 264-3174

(G-9907)
RT ACQUISITION CORP
Also Called: Air Ride Technologies
350 S Saint Charles St (47546-7807)
PHONE..............................812 482-2932
▲ **EMP:** 55 **EST:** 1996
SQ FT: 12,000
SALES (est): 10.42MM
SALES (corp-wide): 1.46B **Publicly Held**
Web: www.ridetech.com
SIC: 3714 Motor vehicle parts and accessories
PA: Fox Factory Holding Corp.
2055 Sgarloaf Cir Ste 300
Duluth GA 30097
831 274-6500

(G-9908)
SCHMIDT CONTRACTING INC
1111 Maurice St (47546-3748)
PHONE..............................812 482-3923
Phillip A Schmidt, *Pr*
Thomas R Schmidt, *Sec*
Carol L Schmidt, *VP*
EMP: 23 **EST:** 1948
SQ FT: 10,200
SALES (est): 501.07K **Privately Held**
Web: www.schmidtcontractingjasper.com
SIC: 1711 1761 3441 3433 Warm air heating and air conditioning contractor; Roofing contractor; Fabricated structural metal; Heating equipment, except electric

(G-9909)
SEMINOLE STONE INC
1503 S Meridian Rd (47546-3832)
PHONE..............................812 634-7115
Joseph R Knies, *Pr*
Jeff Knies, *Sec*
EMP: 10 **EST:** 1997
SQ FT: 800
SALES (est): 751.26K **Privately Held**
SIC: 1422 Limestones, ground

(G-9910)
SERVANTS INC (PA)
3145 Lottes Dr (47546-3264)
P.O. Box 848 (47547-0848)
PHONE..............................812 634-2201
Sharon Montgomery, *Pr*
John Besaw, *
EMP: 60 **EST:** 1973
SQ FT: 106,000
SALES (est): 9.55MM
SALES (corp-wide): 9.55MM **Privately Held**
Web: www.servants.com
SIC: 2653 5113 5031 2448 Boxes, corrugated: made from purchased materials; Industrial and personal service paper; Lumber, plywood, and millwork; Wood pallets and skids

(G-9911)
SHAMROCK CABINETS INC
5785 W 150n (47546-9733)
P.O. Box 724 (47545-0724)
PHONE..............................812 482-7969
Clara M Braunecker, *Pr*
Jeff Braunecker, *
Debbie Wickman, *Stockholder**
Dennis Wickman, *
Julie Braunecker, *
EMP: 33 **EST:** 1962
SALES (est): 3.11MM **Privately Held**
Web: www.shamrockcabinets.com
SIC: 2431 2511 2542 2521 Mantels, wood; Bookcases, household: wood; Partitions and fixtures, except wood; Wood office furniture

(G-9912)
SMOKER FRIENDLY
1925 Newton St (47546-1607)
PHONE..............................812 556-0244
Susan Garloch, *Genl Mgr*
Susan Garloch, *Mgr*
EMP: 9 **EST:** 2013
SALES (est): 81.89K **Privately Held**
Web: www.collettenterprises.com
SIC: 5993 5194 2111 Cigarette store; Smoking tobacco; Cigarettes

(G-9913)
SNAPPY MINDS LLC
1330 Cobblestone Rd (47546-8050)
PHONE..............................812 661-8506
Bill Heyman, *Pt*
EMP: 2 **EST:** 2013
SALES (est): 99.62K **Privately Held**
Web: www.snappyminds.com
SIC: 7372 7389 Business oriented computer software; Business services, nec

(G-9914)
SOUTHERN INDIANA SUPPLY INC
1059 Wernsing Rd (47546-7911)
PHONE..............................812 482-2267
Jim Ruhe, *Pr*
EMP: 10 **EST:** 1996
SALES (est): 1.26MM **Privately Held**
Web: www.southernindianasupply.com
SIC: 3272 Building materials, except block or brick: concrete

(G-9915)
UNITED CABINET CORPORATION NIT
1 Masterbrand Cabinets Dr (47546-2248)
PHONE..............................812 482-2561
Martin V Doren, *Prin*
EMP: 7 **EST:** 2007
SALES (est): 155.13K **Privately Held**
SIC: 2599 Cabinets, factory

(G-9916)
WERNER SAWMILL INC
3545 N 550w (47546-9797)
PHONE..............................812 482-7565
Kevin Werner, *Pr*
Mary J Werner, *
EMP: 35 **EST:** 1984
SQ FT: 21,000
SALES (est): 2.4MM **Privately Held**
SIC: 2421 2426 Sawmills and planing mills, general; Hardwood dimension and flooring mills

(G-9917)
WHITE OAK LAND & TIMBER LLC
560 E 25th St (47546-8117)
PHONE..............................812 482-5102
Michael K Braun, *Prin*
EMP: 3 **EST:** 2008
SALES (est): 172.2K **Privately Held**
SIC: 2411 Timber, cut at logging camp

(G-9918)
WOODCRAFTERS HOME PRODUCTS LLC
1 Masterbrand Cabinets Dr (47546-2248)
PHONE..............................812 482-2527
EMP: 594 **EST:** 2019
SALES (est): 2MM
SALES (corp-wide): 2.73B **Publicly Held**
SIC: 2531 Public building and related furniture
PA: Masterbrand, Inc.
1 Masterbrand Cabinets Dr
Jasper IN 47546
812 482-2527

Jeffersonville
Clark County

(G-9919)
1ST SOURCE PRODUCTS INC
2822 Sable Mill Ln (47130-9247)
PHONE..............................812 288-7466
Donald L Sandusky, *Pr*
B Scott Sparks, *VP*
▲ **EMP:** 12 **EST:** 2000
SALES (est): 2.49MM **Privately Held**
Web: www.1stsourceproducts.com
SIC: 3535 3315 Conveyors and conveying equipment; Fence gates, posts, and fittings: steel

(G-9920)
323INK LLC
2818 Sable Mill Ln (47130-9247)
PHONE..............................812 282-3620
Doug Comingore, *Managing Member*
EMP: 5 **EST:** 1968
SQ FT: 1,500
SALES (est): 383.85K **Privately Held**
Web: www.323ink.com
SIC: 2752 2261 Offset printing; Screen printing of cotton broadwoven fabrics

(G-9921)
ACBL HOLDING CORPORATION (PA)
Also Called: Platinum Equity
1701 E Market St (47130)
PHONE..............................310 712-1850
EMP: 2575 **EST:** 2010
SALES (est): 1.38B **Privately Held**
Web: www.acbl.net
SIC: 4449 3731 4491 Canal barge operations; Barges, building and repairing; Marine terminals

(G-9922)
ACL PROFESSIONAL SERVICES INC
1701 Utica Pike (47130-4747)
PHONE..............................812 288-0100
Mike Ryan, *CEO*
EMP: 120 **EST:** 2008
SALES (est): 2.3MM **Privately Held**
SIC: 4491 3731 Marine cargo handling; Shipbuilding and repairing
HQ: Commercial Barge Line Company
1701 E Market St
Jeffersonville IN 47130

(G-9923)
ACL SALES CORPORATION
1701 E Market St (47130-4755)
PHONE..............................812 288-0100
EMP: 1 **EST:** 2006
SALES (est): 1.12MM **Privately Held**
Web: www.bargeacbl.com
SIC: 4449 3731 4491 Canal barge operations; Barges, building and repairing; Marine terminals
HQ: Acbl Transportation Services Llc
1701 E Market St
Jeffersonville IN 47130
812 288-0100

(G-9924)
ACOUSTICAL AUDIO DESIGNS LLC
2008 Coopers Ln (47130-9225)
PHONE..............................812 282-7522
EMP: 13 **EST:** 2011
SALES (est): 1.1MM **Privately Held**
Web: www.faroutmusicstore.com
SIC: 3663 Radio and t.v. communications equipment

(G-9925)
ACTIVE ANKLE SYSTEMS INC
233 Quartermaster Ct (47130-3669)
P.O. Box 1001 (66030-1001)
PHONE..............................812 258-0663
Glen R Snow, *Pr*
Henry H Porter Junior, *Ch*
Scott Morton, *COO*
Diane Lilly, *Treas*
Doug Stetner, *Stockholder*
EMP: 15 **EST:** 1989
SQ FT: 4,480
SALES (est): 900.86K **Privately Held**
Web: www.activeankle.com
SIC: 3842 5047 Supports: abdominal, ankle, arch, kneecap, etc.; Medical equipment and supplies

(G-9926)
ALAN SWORD LLC
2908 River Heritage Trl (47130-6844)
PHONE..............................812 913-1412
Alan Sword, *Owner*
EMP: 7 **EST:** 2018

(PA)=Parent Co (HQ)=Headquarters
✪ = New Business established in last 2 years

Jeffersonville - Clark County (G-9927)

SALES (est): 241.71K **Privately Held**
SIC: 3421 Cutlery

(G-9927)
ALANI NUTRITION LLC
Also Called: Alaninu
351 Logistics Ave (47130)
PHONE..................502 509-4922
Trey Steiger, *Managing Member*
EMP: 1
SALES (corp-wide): 33.31MM **Privately Held**
Web: www.alaninu.com
SIC: 2023 Dietary supplements, dairy and non-dairy based
PA: Alani Nutrition Llc
13551 Triton Park Blvd
Louisville KY 40223
502 509-4922

(G-9928)
ALTEC LLC
Also Called: Alumnitec
242 America Pl (47130-4272)
PHONE..................812 282-8256
EMP: 91 EST: 1996
SALES (est): 19.45MM
SALES (corp-wide): 6.29MM **Privately Held**
Web: www.altecextrusions.com
SIC: 3354 3471 Aluminum extruded products; Plating and polishing
HQ: Matalco Shelbyville, Llc
1100 Brooks Industrial Rd
Shelbyville KY 40065
502 633-2783

(G-9929)
AMATROL INC
1638 Production Rd (47130-9604)
PHONE..................800 264-8285
EMP: 1
SALES (corp-wide): 43.92MM **Privately Held**
Web: www.amatrol.com
SIC: 3569 Robots, assembly line: industrial and commercial
PA: Amatrol Inc
2400 Centennial Blvd
Jeffersonville IN 47130
812 288-8285

(G-9930)
AMERICAN BARGE LINE COMPANY (DH)
1701 E Mkt St (47130)
PHONE..................812 288-0100
Mark Holden, *Pr*
EMP: 1 EST: 2004
SALES (est): 143.65MM **Privately Held**
Web: www.aclines.com
SIC: 4449 3731 4491 Canal barge operations; Barges, building and repairing; Marine terminals
HQ: American Commercial Lines, Inc.
1701 E Market St
Jeffersonville IN 47130

(G-9931)
AMERICAN COML BARGE LINE LLC (DH)
1701 E Market St (47130)
PHONE..................812 288-0100
Mike Ellis, *CEO*
Christopher A Black, *
Jerry R Linzey, *
Kevin S Boyle, *
Paul F Brotzge, *
EMP: 190 EST: 2004
SQ FT: 165,000
SALES (est): 494.07MM **Privately Held**
Web: www.bargeacbl.com
SIC: 4449 3731 4491 Canal barge operations; Barges, building and repairing; Marine terminals
HQ: American Commercial Lines, Inc.
1701 E Market St
Jeffersonville IN 47130

(G-9932)
AMERICAN COMMERCIAL LINES INC (HQ)
Also Called: American Commercial Barge Line
1701 E Market St (47130-4755)
P.O. Box 610 (47131-0610)
PHONE..................812 288-0100
Mark K Knoy, *CEO*
David J Huls, *Sr VP*
Thomas R Pilholski, *Sr VP*
Dawn R Landry, *Sr VP*
Paul A Tobin, *Sr VP*
EMP: 170 EST: 1953
SQ FT: 165,000
SALES (est): 1.35B **Privately Held**
Web: www.aclines.com
SIC: 4449 3731 4491 Canal barge operations; Barges, building and repairing; Marine terminals
PA: Acbl Holding Corporation
1701 E Market St
Jeffersonville IN 47130

(G-9933)
ANCHOR ENTERPRISES
10 Arctic Spgs (47130-4701)
PHONE..................812 282-7220
Judy Lloyd, *Owner*
EMP: 2 EST: 1984
SALES (est): 100K **Privately Held**
Web: www.anchor-enterprises.com
SIC: 2759 2761 2752 Letterpress printing; Manifold business forms; Offset printing

(G-9934)
APOLLO AMERICA
701 Port Rd (47130-8425)
PHONE..................812 284-3700
EMP: 8 EST: 2019
SALES (est): 271.1K **Privately Held**
Web: www.apolloamerica.com
SIC: 2911 Petroleum refining

(G-9935)
AS YOU WISH CUSTOM
2100 Elk Pointe Blvd (47130-6782)
PHONE..................502 216-3144
Steven Mcstoots, *Prin*
EMP: 5 EST: 2017
SALES (est): 49.8K **Privately Held**
SIC: 2759 Screen printing

(G-9936)
ATKINS QUARRY
1415 Quarry Rd (47130-6377)
PHONE..................972 653-5550
Sally Stock, *Dir Fin*
EMP: 7 EST: 2014
SALES (est): 100.36K **Privately Held**
SIC: 3273 Ready-mixed concrete

(G-9937)
AUTONEUM NORTH AMERICA INC
100 River Ridge Pkwy (47130-7762)
PHONE..................248 848-0100
John Lenga, *Brnch Mgr*
EMP: 2
Web: www.autoneum.com
SIC: 3714 Motor vehicle parts and accessories
HQ: Autoneum North America, Inc.
34705 W 12 Mile Rd Ste 10
Farmington Hills MI 48331
248 848-0100

(G-9938)
BADD LLC
4750 New Middle Rd (47130-8539)
PHONE..................812 280-1854
EMP: 29
Web: www.baddinc.com
SIC: 3599 Machine and other job shop work

(G-9939)
BASSETT SIGNS LLC
5812 Bates Ct (47130-8894)
PHONE..................812 946-0017
Robert Bassett, *Prin*
EMP: 4 EST: 2016
SALES (est): 229.65K **Privately Held**
Web: www.bassettsigns.com
SIC: 3993 Signs and advertising specialties

(G-9940)
BENJAMIN CARRIER
6 Fay Ave (47130-5235)
PHONE..................337 366-2603
Benjamin Carrier, *Owner*
EMP: 1
SALES (est): 54.05K **Privately Held**
SIC: 2389 7371 Apparel and accessories, nec; Computer software development

(G-9941)
BEST-ONE KENTUCKIANA INC (PA)
3215 Industrial Pkwy (47130-9666)
P.O. Box 365 (47131-0365)
PHONE..................812 285-5400
Thomas Sander, *Pr*
Paul W Zurcher, *VP*
EMP: 35 EST: 1979
SQ FT: 22,000
SALES (est): 21.41MM
SALES (corp-wide): 21.41MM **Privately Held**
Web: www.bestone.tires
SIC: 5014 7534 Truck tires and tubes; Tire repair shop

(G-9942)
BEST-ONE KENTUCKIANA INC
1402 Truckers Blvd (47130-9623)
PHONE..................812 282-4799
EMP: 1
SALES (corp-wide): 21.41MM **Privately Held**
Web: www.bestone.tires
SIC: 7534 Rebuilding and retreading tires
PA: Best-One Kentuckiana, Inc.
3215 Industrial Pkwy
Jeffersonville IN 47130
812 285-5400

(G-9943)
BK ROYSTON PUBLISHING LLC
3117 Wooded Way (47130-5937)
PHONE..................502 802-5385
EMP: 1 EST: 2016
SALES (est): 59.07K **Privately Held**
Web: www.bkroystonpublishing.com
SIC: 2731 2741 Books, publishing only; Miscellaneous publishing

(G-9944)
BLITZ MANUFACTURING CO IND
Also Called: Blitz
263 America Pl (47130-4285)
P.O. Box 846 (47131-0846)
PHONE..................812 284-2548
Howard Sturm, *Pr*
Robert Solensky, *
◆ EMP: 60 EST: 1912
SQ FT: 4,000
SALES (est): 9.32MM **Privately Held**
Web: www.blitzinc.com
SIC: 3471 2842 Cleaning, polishing, and finishing; Metal polish

(G-9945)
BOWLES MATTRESS COMPANY INC (PA)
1220 Watt St (47130-3893)
PHONE..................812 288-8614
EMP: 9 EST: 1975
SALES (est): 2.55MM
SALES (corp-wide): 2.55MM **Privately Held**
Web: www.bowlesmattress.com
SIC: 2515 5712 Mattresses, innerspring or box spring; Mattresses

(G-9946)
BRENT MORRIS
Also Called: Morris Machine Shop
508 Hemlock Rd (47130-5533)
PHONE..................812 282-6945
EMP: 1 EST: 1964
SALES (est): 60K **Privately Held**
SIC: 7539 3599 Machine shop, automotive; Machine shop, jobbing and repair

(G-9947)
BRINLY-HARDY COMPANY (PA)
3230 Industrial Pkwy (47130-9632)
PHONE..................812 218-7200
Jane W Hardy, *CEO*
Michael Schmitt, *
◆ EMP: 100 EST: 1839
SALES (est): 48.92MM
SALES (corp-wide): 48.92MM **Privately Held**
Web: www.brinly.com
SIC: 3423 3524 Hand and edge tools, nec; Carts or wagons for lawn and garden

(G-9948)
BUDGET PRINTING CENTERS INC (PA)
Also Called: Budget Instant Print
902 E 10th St (47130-4141)
PHONE..................812 282-8832
Lisa Green, *Mgr*
Roger W Fisher, *Pr*
EMP: 5 EST: 1981
SQ FT: 2,000
SALES (est): 836.99K
SALES (corp-wide): 836.99K **Privately Held**
Web: www.budgetprintcenter.net
SIC: 2752 7384 Offset printing; Film processing and finishing laboratory

(G-9949)
C&W FABRICATION LLC
Also Called: G.F. Munich Welding
211 Eastern Blvd (47130-2801)
PHONE..................812 282-0488
W Dean Collins, *CEO*
Jordan Walker, *
EMP: 59 EST: 2018
SQ FT: 85,000
SALES (est): 9.71MM **Privately Held**
Web: www.munichwelding.com
SIC: 3441 7692 Fabricated structural metal; Welding repair

(G-9950)
CARMAN INDUSTRIES INC (PA)
1005 W Riverside Dr (47130-3143)
P.O. Box 579 (47131-0579)
PHONE..................812 288-4710
C James Hyslop, *CEO*

GEOGRAPHIC SECTION
Jeffersonville - Clark County (G-9974)

David E Wantland, *
William Wetherton, *
Ising J L, *
EMP: 50 **EST:** 1961
SQ FT: 60,000
SALES (est): 8.95MM
SALES (corp-wide): 8.95MM **Privately Held**
Web: www.carmanindustries.com
SIC: 3535 Conveyors and conveying equipment

(G-9951)
CHEMTRUSION INC
Also Called: Chemtrusion-Indiana
1403 Port Rd (47130-8411)
PHONE....................812 280-2910
EMP: 50
SALES (corp-wide): 23.48MM **Privately Held**
Web: www.chemtrusion.com
SIC: 2821 3714 Thermoplastic materials; Motor vehicle parts and accessories
PA: Chemtrusion, Inc.
  7115 Clinton Dr
  Houston TX 77020
  713 675-1616

(G-9952)
CLARCOR AIR FILTRATION PRODUCTS INC
100 River Ridge Cir (47130-8974)
PHONE....................502 969-2304
◆ **EMP:** 1100
Web: www.clcair.com
SIC: 3564 Air cleaning systems

(G-9953)
CLARKE HARLAND CORP
237 America Pl (47130-4272)
PHONE....................812 283-9598
EMP: 1
Web: www.harlandclarke.com
SIC: 2782 Blankbooks and looseleaf binders
HQ: Harland Clarke Corp.
  15955 La Cantera Pkwy
  San Antonio TX 78256
  830 609-5500

(G-9954)
CLARKE HARLAND CORP
240 America Pl (47130-4272)
PHONE....................812 283-9598
Ronald Ryder, *Brnch Mgr*
EMP: 1
Web: www.harlandclarke.com
SIC: 2782 Checkbooks
HQ: Harland Clarke Corp.
  15955 La Cantera Pkwy
  San Antonio TX 78256
  830 609-5500

(G-9955)
CNHI LLC
Also Called: New Albany Tribune
221 Spring St (47130-3353)
PHONE....................812 944-6481
Steve Kozarovich, *Mgr*
EMP: 1
SALES (corp-wide): 34.97B **Privately Held**
Web: www.cnhi.com
SIC: 2711 2791 2752 Newspapers, publishing and printing; Typesetting; Commercial printing, lithographic
HQ: Cnhi, Llc
  445 Dexter Ave
  Montgomery AL 36104

(G-9956)
COMMERCIAL BARGE LINE COMPANY (DH)
1701 E Market St (47130)
PHONE....................812 288-0100
Mark K Knoy, *Pr*
David J Huls, *Sr VP*
Dawn R Landry, *Sr VP*
Robert M Blocker, *Customer Service*
Paul Tobin, *COO*
EMP: 43 **EST:** 1975
SALES (est): 143.65MM **Privately Held**
Web: www.aclines.com
SIC: 4491 3731 4449 Marine terminals; Barges, building and repairing; Canal barge operations
HQ: American Barge Line Company
  1701 E Mkt St
  Jeffersonville IN 47130

(G-9957)
COMPLETE METAL FABRICATION INC
801 Trey St (47130-7751)
PHONE....................812 284-4470
Hugh Willeford, *Pr*
Roger A Harshey Junior, *Sec*
EMP: 48 **EST:** 1997
SALES (est): 1.14MM **Privately Held**
SIC: 3599 Machine shop, jobbing and repair

(G-9958)
COMPLETE PRTG SOLUTIONS INC
2199 Hamburg Pike (47130-6317)
PHONE....................812 285-9200
David H Leuhart, *CEO*
Shan Leuhart, *Pr*
EMP: 3 **EST:** 2005
SQ FT: 15,000
SALES (est): 331.95K **Privately Held**
Web: www.completeprintingsolutions.com
SIC: 2752 Offset printing

(G-9959)
COMPUTER TECHNOLOGY
1101 Watt St (47130-3843)
P.O. Box 2774 (47131-2774)
PHONE....................812 283-5094
Neal Altman, *Pr*
EMP: 4 **EST:** 1995
SALES (est): 365.49K **Privately Held**
SIC: 3469 Machine parts, stamped or pressed metal

(G-9960)
COOK COMPRESSION LLC
2540 Centennial Blvd (47130-8535)
PHONE....................502 515-6900
EMP: 4
SALES (corp-wide): 8.44B **Publicly Held**
Web: www.cookcompression.com
SIC: 3563 Air and gas compressors
HQ: Cook Compression, Llc
  11951 North Spectrum Blvd
  Houston TX 77047

(G-9961)
CORBETTS CUSTOM CABINETRY LLC
6104 Carr Cir (47130-9244)
PHONE....................812 670-6211
EMP: 4 **EST:** 2014
SALES (est): 71.33K **Privately Held**
SIC: 2434 Wood kitchen cabinets

(G-9962)
CORONADO STONE INC
Also Called: Coronado Stone
4306 Charlestown Pike (47130-8702)
PHONE....................812 284-2845
TOLL FREE: 800
EMP: 45 **EST:** 1992
SALES (est): 6.55MM **Privately Held**
Web: www.coronado.com
SIC: 3281 1752 Furniture, cut stone; Vinyl floor tile and sheet installation

(G-9963)
COVINGTON AND MARTIN LLC
1513 Clairview Dr (47130-4531)
PHONE....................812 946-3846
EMP: 1
SALES (est): 60.62K **Privately Held**
SIC: 7389 2395 Business Activities at Non-Commercial Site; Embroidery and art needlework

(G-9964)
CREATIVE CONCEPT VENTURES INC
Also Called: Insty-Prints
590 Missouri Ave (47130-3083)
P.O. Box 812 (47131-0812)
PHONE....................812 282-9442
Mike Rich, *Pr*
Carlotta Simpson, *VP*
Denise Freville, *VP*
EMP: 5 **EST:** 1976
SQ FT: 3,000
SALES (est): 493.03K **Privately Held**
Web: www.allegramarketingprint.com
SIC: 2752 7334 2791 2789 Offset printing; Photocopying and duplicating services; Typesetting; Bookbinding and related work

(G-9965)
CRS-SPV INC
4555 New Middle Rd (47130)
PHONE....................502 805-0143
Scott Massie, *CEO*
EMP: 50 **EST:** 2017
SALES (est): 4.74MM **Privately Held**
SIC: 3823 Fluidic devices, circuits, and systems for process control

(G-9966)
CUSTOM KRAFT PACK LLC
100 Technology Way (47130-9644)
PHONE....................502 595-8146
David Brown, *Managing Member*
EMP: 10 **EST:** 2021
SALES (est): 440.41K **Privately Held**
SIC: 2631 Packaging board

(G-9967)
CYLICRON LLC
5171 Maritime (47130-8452)
P.O. Box 4185 (47131-4185)
PHONE....................812 283-4600
Adam Gabbard, *
Karen Cane, *
Jacob Kuerzi, *
▲ **EMP:** 63 **EST:** 1983
SQ FT: 140,000
SALES (est): 9.06MM **Privately Held**
Web: www.cylicron.com
SIC: 2796 Plates and cylinders for rotogravure printing

(G-9968)
DALLAS GROUP OF AMERICA INC
Magnesol Div
1402 Fabricon Blvd (47130-9607)
PHONE....................812 283-6675
Walter Mulflur, *Prin*
EMP: 269
SQ FT: 6,000
SALES (corp-wide): 97.38MM **Privately Held**
Web: www.dallasgrp.com
SIC: 2819 3339 Magnesium compounds or salts, inorganic; Primary nonferrous metals, nec
PA: The Dallas Group Of America Inc
  374 Rte 22
  Whitehouse NJ 08888
  908 534-7800

(G-9969)
DELACO KASLE PROC IND LLC
5146 Maritime (47130-8452)
PHONE....................812 280-8800
Jim Jaggers, *Manager*
EMP: 58 **EST:** 2003
SALES (est): 8.86MM
SALES (corp-wide): 112.35MM **Privately Held**
SIC: 3312 Blast furnaces and steel mills
PA: Delaco Steel Corporation
  8111 Tireman Ave Ste 1
  Dearborn MI 48126
  313 491-1200

(G-9970)
DIAMOND BILLIARD PRODUCTS INC
4700 New Middle Rd (47130-8539)
PHONE....................812 288-7665
Robert G Sullivan, *Pr*
Chad Scharlow, *
Julie Creamer, *
▲ **EMP:** 70 **EST:** 1993
SQ FT: 71,000
SALES (est): 820K **Privately Held**
Web: www.diamondbilliards.com
SIC: 5091 3949 Billiard equipment and supplies; Billiard and pool equipment and supplies, general

(G-9971)
DUPRE CAPITAL LLC
Also Called: Fastsigns
215 Quartermaster Ct (47130-3669)
PHONE....................812 291-1141
Aaron Dupre, *Prin*
EMP: 12 **EST:** 2016
SALES (est): 277.26K **Privately Held**
Web: www.fastsigns.com
SIC: 3993 Signs and advertising specialties

(G-9972)
DUSTEX
3428 Charlestown Pike (47130-8168)
PHONE....................812 725-0808
Dale Arvin, *Mgr*
EMP: 6 **EST:** 2014
SALES (est): 114.15K **Privately Held**
Web: www.ldxsolutions.com
SIC: 3564 Blowers and fans

(G-9973)
EAGLE INDUSTRIES INC
Also Called: Nolan Co
131 E Court Ave Ste 200 (47130-3603)
P.O. Box 1059 (47131-1059)
PHONE....................812 282-1393
Chris Nolan, *Pr*
EMP: 10 **EST:** 1991
SQ FT: 3,500
SALES (est): 1.06MM **Privately Held**
Web: www.eagleindustries.com
SIC: 2673 Plastic bags: made from purchased materials

(G-9974)
ELECTRIC MTR REPR & REWIND INC
1502 Research Dr (47130-9613)
PHONE....................812 284-5059
Candace Stroud, *CEO*
Frank Hardin, *COO*
EMP: 9 **EST:** 1986
SQ FT: 12,000

Jeffersonville - Clark County (G-9975)

GEOGRAPHIC SECTION

SALES (est): 930.01K Privately Held
Web: www.emotorrepair.com
SIC: 7694 5999 Electric motor repair; Motors, electric

(G-9975)
ELITE PACKAGING LLC
100 Technology Way (47130-9644)
P.O. Box 36062 (40233-6062)
PHONE..................................502 232-2596
EMP: 2 EST: 2015
SQ FT: 7,000
SALES (est): 526.86K Privately Held
Web: www.elitepackgroup.com
SIC: 2631 7389 2671 2653 Container, packaging, and boxboard; Cosmetic kits, assembling and packaging; Paper; coated and laminated packaging; Corrugated and solid fiber boxes

(G-9976)
EM GLOBAL LLC
Also Called: Eiler Marketing
326 E Court Ave (47130-3412)
PHONE..................................812 258-9993
Jeremy Eiler, Pr
Jeremy Eiler, Managing Member
EMP: 9 EST: 2015
SALES (est): 962.19K Privately Held
Web: www.emglobalgroup.com
SIC: 8742 7311 7389 2759 Marketing consulting services; Advertising agencies; Embroidery advertising; Screen printing

(G-9977)
ENERGY DELIVERY SOLUTIONS LLC
Also Called: EDS
3315 Industrial Pkwy (47130-9633)
PHONE..................................502 271-8753
William Ehringer, Managing Member
EMP: 5 EST: 2012
SQ FT: 7,500
SALES (est): 742.72K Privately Held
Web: www.energy-delivery-solutions.com
SIC: 2834 2844 Pharmaceutical preparations; Cosmetic preparations

(G-9978)
ENJOY LIFE NATURAL BRANDS LLC
Also Called: Enjoy Life Foods
301 Salem Rd (47130-7764)
PHONE..................................844 624-7162
EMP: 8
Web: www.enjoylifefoods.com
SIC: 2046 2051 Wheat gluten; Bread, cake, and related products
HQ: Enjoy Life Natural Brands, Llc
8770 W Bryn Mawr Ave Ste
Chicago IL 60631
773 632-2163

(G-9979)
EPIC WELDING LLC
5815 New Chapel Rd (47130-8645)
PHONE..................................502 554-6326
Frank A Hoskins Iii, Owner
EMP: 6 EST: 2018
SALES (est): 208.47K Privately Held
Web: www.epicweldingllc.com
SIC: 7692 Welding repair

(G-9980)
ERNEST A COOPER
Also Called: Competitive Pallet Service
1502 Production Rd (47130-9604)
PHONE..................................812 284-0436
Ernest Cooper, Owner
EMP: 12 EST: 1984
SQ FT: 9,600
SALES (est): 521.8K Privately Held
Web: www.competitivepallet.com
SIC: 2448 Pallets, wood

(G-9981)
ERNSTBERGER ENTERPRISES INC
211 Eastern Blvd (47130-2801)
PHONE..................................812 282-0488
▲ EMP: 70
SIC: 3441 7692 Fabricated structural metal; Welding repair

(G-9982)
ESTES WASTE SOLUTIONS LLC
5005 Hamburg Pike (47130-9203)
P.O. Box 578 (47119-0578)
PHONE..................................812 283-6400
EMP: 16 EST: 2014
SALES (est): 962.66K Privately Held
Web: www.esteswaste.com
SIC: 3443 Dumpsters, garbage

(G-9983)
ESTILL SMITH MARINE SVCS INC
4210 E Hwy 62 (47130)
PHONE..................................812 282-7944
Estill Smith, Pr
Helen Smith, Sec
EMP: 2 EST: 1992
SALES (est): 199.48K Privately Held
SIC: 3731 Barges, building and repairing

(G-9984)
FLEXIBLE MATERIALS INC (PA)
3101 Hamburg Pike Ste B (47130-9645)
PHONE..................................812 280-7000
Ronald W Humin, CEO
Rodney Beyl, *
Edward J Krawiec, *
▲ EMP: 87 EST: 1957
SQ FT: 25,000
SALES (est): 16.3MM
SALES (corp-wide): 16.3MM Privately Held
Web: www.flexwood.com
SIC: 2435 Hardwood veneer and plywood

(G-9985)
FLOW INTERNATIONAL CORPORATION
A S I Robotic Systems
1635 Production Rd (47130-9624)
PHONE..................................253 850-3500
Kent Eubank, Brnch Mgr
EMP: 11
SQ FT: 25,000
SALES (corp-wide): 543.3MM Privately Held
Web: www.flowwaterjet.com
SIC: 3569 Robots, assembly line: industrial and commercial
HQ: Flow International Corporation
23500 64th Ave S
Kent WA 98032
253 850-3500

(G-9986)
FORM WOOD INDUSTRIES INC
1601 Production Rd (47130)
PHONE..................................812 284-3676
Todd Smith, Pr
▲ EMP: 40 EST: 1987
SQ FT: 80,000
SALES (est): 9.13MM Privately Held
Web: www.formwood.com
SIC: 2435 3469 Veneer stock, hardwood; Architectural panels or parts, porcelain enameled

(G-9987)
FREUDENBERG MEDICAL MIS INC (DH)
Also Called: Medventure Technology
2301 Centennial Blvd (47130-8975)
PHONE..................................812 280-2400
Mark Ostwald, CEO
Mitch Moeller, *
Robert Grable, *
EMP: 124 EST: 2005
SQ FT: 100,000
SALES (est): 83.79MM
SALES (corp-wide): 12.23B Privately Held
Web: www.freudenbergmedical.com
SIC: 3841 Medical instruments and equipment, blood and bone work
HQ: Freudenberg Medical, Llc
1110 Mark Ave
Carpinteria CA 93013
805 684-3304

(G-9988)
FULL METAL SOLUTIONS LLC
295a America Pl (47130-4286)
PHONE..................................812 725-9660
Chad Webb, Managing Member
EMP: 10 EST: 2011
SALES (est): 463.53K Privately Held
Web: new.fullmetalsolutions.com
SIC: 3448 Ramps, prefabricated metal

(G-9989)
GABRIEL PRODUCTS INC
2303 Cypress Pt (47130-6775)
PHONE..................................502 291-5388
Gabriel Appiah, Pr
EMP: 6 EST: 2010
SALES (est): 66.15K Privately Held
SIC: 2899 Corrosion preventive lubricant

(G-9990)
GENESIS PLASTICS SOLUTIONS LLC
2200 Centennial Blvd (47130-8533)
PHONE..................................812 283-4435
Jim Gladden, CEO
EMP: 2 EST: 2006
SALES (est): 323.97K Privately Held
SIC: 3089 Injection molding of plastics

(G-9991)
GENPAK LLC
251 Paul Garrett Ave (47130-4674)
PHONE..................................812 256-7040
James Mcintyre, Mgr
EMP: 10
Web: www.genpak.com
SIC: 3089 Plastics containers, except foam
HQ: Genpak Llc
10601 Westlake Dr
Charlotte NC 28273
800 626-6695

(G-9992)
GEO PFAUS SONS COMPANY INC
800 Wall St (47130-3619)
P.O. Box 7 (47131-0007)
PHONE..................................800 732-8645
Norman E Pfau Junior, Pr
Sue D Pfau, *
Kari Pfau Hall, *
EMP: 50 EST: 1869
SALES (est): 9.52MM Privately Held
Web: www.pfauoil.com
SIC: 2077 Animal and marine fats and oils

(G-9993)
GOODRICH CORPORATION
Collins Aerospace
510 Patrol Rd (47130)
PHONE..................................812 704-5200
EMP: 53
SALES (corp-wide): 68.92B Publicly Held
Web: www.collinsaerospace.com
SIC: 7372 3724 3728 Prepackaged software; Aircraft engines and engine parts; Aircraft parts and equipment, nec
HQ: Goodrich Corporation
2730 W Tyvola Rd
Charlotte NC 28217
704 423-7000

(G-9994)
HERITAGE HARDWOODS KY INC (PA)
1507 Production Rd (47130-9624)
PHONE..................................812 288-5855
Maurice Smith, Ch Bd
Todd Smith, *
EMP: 70 EST: 1977
SALES (est): 8.77MM
SALES (corp-wide): 8.77MM Privately Held
Web: www.heritagehardwoodsky.com
SIC: 2435 2426 Veneer stock, hardwood; Hardwood dimension and flooring mills

(G-9995)
HI TECH VENEER LLC
Also Called: Diversified Wood Products
276 America Pl (47130-4286)
PHONE..................................812 284-9775
Tim Griffin, Pr
Jason Crapo, *
▲ EMP: 50 EST: 2014
SALES (est): 5.7MM Privately Held
Web: www.diversifiedwp.com
SIC: 2436 Softwood veneer and plywood

(G-9996)
HIGHWAY PRESS INC
2199 Hamburg Pike (47130-6397)
PHONE..................................812 283-6462
Jack Leuthart, Pr
Robert Leuthart, VP
Jo Ann Leuthart, Sec
EMP: 6 EST: 1947
SQ FT: 5,500
SALES (est): 483.24K Privately Held
SIC: 2752 2759 Offset printing; Letterpress printing

(G-9997)
HOME PHONE INC
414 Spring St (47130-3452)
PHONE..................................812 941-8551
Kenneth Calkins, Pr
EMP: 2 EST: 2003
SALES (est): 124.11K Privately Held
SIC: 2451 Mobile homes

(G-9998)
HOOSIER PENN OIL CO INC
Also Called: H P Oil
2990 Industrial Pkwy (47130)
P.O. Box 22669 (46222)
PHONE..................................812 284-9433
Jack Hedges, Mgr
EMP: 7
SALES (corp-wide): 10.31MM Privately Held
Web: www.hpoil.com
SIC: 5171 2869 Petroleum bulk stations; Solvents, organic
PA: Hoosier Penn Oil Co Inc.
4060 W 10th St
Indianapolis IN 46222
317 390-5406

GEOGRAPHIC SECTION
Jeffersonville - Clark County (G-10022)

(G-9999)
HORIZON TERRA INCORPORATED (DH)
Also Called: Idx - Louisville
101 River Ridge Cir (47130-8974)
PHONE..............................812 280-0000
Terrence Schultz, *Pr*
Fritz Baumgartner, *
◆ **EMP:** 80 **EST:** 1998
SQ FT: 150,000
SALES (est): 8.53MM
SALES (corp-wide): 7.22B **Publicly Held**
SIC: 1793 2541 Glass and glazing work; Cabinets, lockers, and shelving
HQ: Idx Corporation
2801 E Beltline Ave Ne
Grand Rapids MI 49525
844 249-4633

(G-10000)
IDEMITSU LUBRICANTS AMER CORP (DH)
701 Port Rd (47130-8425)
PHONE..............................812 284-3300
Kazumi Kikuchi, *Pr*
Tammi Walts, *
Shukichi Shimoda, *
Shinji Otsubo, *
◆ **EMP:** 55 **EST:** 1991
SQ FT: 150,000
SALES (est): 257.61MM **Privately Held**
Web: www.ilacorp.com
SIC: 2992 Lubricating oils and greases
HQ: Idemitsu Apollo Corporation
1831 16th St
Sacramento CA 95811
916 443-0890

(G-10001)
IGP NORTH AMERICA LLC
702 N Shore Dr Ste 500 (47130-3104)
PHONE..............................812 670-3483
EMP: 5 **EST:** 2016
SALES (est): 86.33K **Privately Held**
Web: www.igp-powder.com
SIC: 3714 Motor vehicle parts and accessories

(G-10002)
IMMUNOTEK BIO CENTERS LLC
1665 E 10th St (47130-6276)
PHONE..............................337 500-1294
Pam Farris, *Prin*
EMP: 1
SALES (corp-wide): 140.79MM **Privately Held**
Web: www.immunotek.com
SIC: 2836 Blood derivatives
PA: Immunotek Bio Centers, L.L.C.
1430 E Southlake Blvd # 200
Southlake TX 76092
337 500-1175

(G-10003)
JDC VENEERS INC
Also Called: HI Tech Veneer
276 America Pl (47130)
PHONE..............................812 284-9775
Jason Crapo, *Prin*
Jason Crato, *
Chris Totten, *
▲ **EMP:** 63 **EST:** 1998
SQ FT: 30,000
SALES (est): 1.07MM **Privately Held**
Web: www.diversifiedwp.com
SIC: 2436 Plywood, softwood

(G-10004)
KAPSCH TRAFFICCOM USA INC
107 Quartermaster Ct (47130-3627)
PHONE..............................812 258-5905
EMP: 110
SALES (corp-wide): 593.49MM **Privately Held**
Web: www.kapsch.net
SIC: 3625 Relays and industrial controls
HQ: Kapsch Trafficcom Usa, Inc.
2855 Premiere Pkwy Ste F
Duluth GA 30097
678 473-6400

(G-10005)
KENTUCKIANA WIRE ROPE & SUPPLY
3335 Industrial Pkwy (47130-9619)
PHONE..............................812 282-3667
John P Fireovid, *Pr*
Fireovid L Patricia, *Sec*
EMP: 13 **EST:** 1980
SQ FT: 15,500
SALES (est): 4.16MM **Privately Held**
Web: www.kwrinc.com
SIC: 5051 2298 3496 5072 Rope, wire (not insulated); Rope, except asbestos and wire; Wire chain; Chains

(G-10006)
KENTUCKIANA WOOD PRODUCTS INC
1275 Meigs Ave (47130-3811)
PHONE..............................812 288-7989
Connie Poole, *Pr*
Janet Puckett, *
EMP: 26 **EST:** 1978
SQ FT: 15,700
SALES (est): 2.46MM **Privately Held**
Web: www.kentuckianawoodproducts.com
SIC: 2448 Pallets, wood

(G-10007)
KENTUCKIANA YACHT SERVICES LLC
Also Called: Kys
700 E Market St (47130-3924)
PHONE..............................812 282-7579
EMP: 7 **EST:** 2012
SQ FT: 25,000
SALES (est): 996.48K **Privately Held**
Web: www.kys.com
SIC: 3732 5561 Yachts, building and repairing; Recreational vehicle parts and accessories

(G-10008)
KENTUCKY CONCRETE INDIANA LLC
Also Called: Ohio Valley Ready Mix
2220 Hamburg Pike (47130-6320)
PHONE..............................812 282-6671
Sharon H Schlatter, *Pr*
Fred Schlatter, *VP*
EMP: 20 **EST:** 2007
SALES (est): 2.06MM **Privately Held**
SIC: 3273 Ready-mixed concrete

(G-10009)
KEY ELECTRONICS INC
2533 Centennial Blvd (47130)
PHONE..............................812 206-2500
David Meece, *Pr*
Thomas Hardy, *
▲ **EMP:** 150 **EST:** 1976
SQ FT: 104,000
SALES (est): 23.19MM **Privately Held**
Web: www.keyelectronics.com
SIC: 3672 Printed circuit boards

(G-10010)
KEY ENHANCEMENT LLC
3310 E 10th St Ste 4 (47130-7285)
PHONE..............................502 403-5661
EMP: 1
SALES (est): 69.27K **Privately Held**
SIC: 3581 Automatic vending machines

(G-10011)
KITCHEN KOMPACT INC
911 E 11th St (47130-4172)
P.O. Box 868 (47130-1868)
PHONE..............................812 282-6681
Walter Dwight Gahm, *Ch Bd*
Walter Dwight Gahm Junior, *Pr*
Gordon Gahm, *
Phillip Gahm, *
Robert G Wilson, *
EMP: 200 **EST:** 1937
SQ FT: 390,000
SALES (est): 21.95MM **Privately Held**
Web: www.kitchenkompact.com
SIC: 2434 Vanities, bathroom: wood

(G-10012)
LICAR AMERICA LLC
600 Patrol Rd Ste 300 (47130)
PHONE..............................812 256-6400
EMP: 22 **EST:** 2018
SALES (est): 5.23MM **Privately Held**
SIC: 2431 Door frames, wood

(G-10013)
LINK ELECTRICAL SERVICE
1018 E 7th St (47130-4451)
PHONE..............................812 288-8184
Susan Link, *Prin*
EMP: 5 **EST:** 2008
SALES (est): 144.43K **Privately Held**
SIC: 5099 3993 1731 Signs, except electric; Signs and advertising specialties; General electrical contractor

(G-10014)
M2 INDUSTRIES LLC
2200 Utica Pike Apt 4 (47130-5082)
P.O. Box 145 (47131-0145)
PHONE..............................812 246-0651
Dale Mills, *Prin*
EMP: 5 **EST:** 2015
SALES (est): 155.27K **Privately Held**
SIC: 3999 Manufacturing industries, nec

(G-10015)
MACPACTOR INC
414 Spring St (47130-3452)
P.O. Box 145 (47131-0145)
PHONE..............................502 643-7845
Dale Mills, *VP*
EMP: 4 **EST:** 2013
SALES (est): 393.04K **Privately Held**
Web: www.macpactor.com
SIC: 3496 Miscellaneous fabricated wire products

(G-10016)
MARINE BUILDERS INC
5821 Utica Pike (47130-8408)
P.O. Box 2215 (47131-2215)
PHONE..............................812 283-7932
David A Evanczyk, *Pr*
David W Evanczyk, *
Sarah Evanczyk, *
Byron Evanczyk, *
EMP: 92 **EST:** 1972
SQ FT: 18,000
SALES (est): 9.12MM **Privately Held**
SIC: 3731 3441 Towboats, building and repairing; Fabricated structural metal

(G-10017)
MARWOOD SALES CO
2901 Hamburg Pike (47130-6722)
PHONE..............................812 288-8344
EMP: 6
SALES (est): 369.87K **Privately Held**
SIC: 2435 Veneer stock, hardwood

(G-10018)
MATA CUSTOM WOODWORKING
923 Penn St (47130-4160)
PHONE..............................812 987-2676
Eddie Mata, *Prin*
EMP: 1 **EST:** 2007
SALES (est): 110.99K **Privately Held**
Web: www.woodfloorrefinishinglouisville.com
SIC: 2431 Millwork

(G-10019)
MIDWEST MOLD REMEDIATION INC
912 Webster Blvd (47130-6530)
PHONE..............................502 386-6559
Terry Tuggle, *Pr*
EMP: 6 **EST:** 2004
SALES (est): 340.88K **Privately Held**
SIC: 3544 Industrial molds

(G-10020)
MIXER DIRECT LLC
Also Called: Mixer Direct
4650 New Middle Rd (47130-8540)
PHONE..............................812 202-4047
Mark Franco, *CEO*
Mark Franco, *Pr*
Bart Anderson, *
Charles R Marcum Stockhldr, *Prin*
Edward Stogner, *
EMP: 51 **EST:** 2010
SALES (est): 17.89MM **Privately Held**
Web: www.mixerdirect.com
SIC: 5084 3599 3569 Chemical process equipment; Machine and other job shop work; Liquid automation machinery and equipment

(G-10021)
MYTEX POLYMERS US CORP (DH)
Also Called: Mytex Polymers
1403 Port Rd (47130)
PHONE..............................812 280-2900
Masayuki Arai, *Pr*
Mamoru Hirasawa, *VP*
▲ **EMP:** 22 **EST:** 1987
SQ FT: 235,000
SALES (est): 15.63MM **Privately Held**
Web: www.mytexpolymers.com
SIC: 3089 Plastics containers, except foam
HQ: Mitsubishi Chemical Corporation
1-1-1, Marunouchi
Chiyoda-Ku TKY 100-8

(G-10022)
NEW HOPE SERVICES INC (PA)
Also Called: ABERDEEN WOODS APARTMENTS
725 Wall St (47130)
PHONE..............................812 288-8248
James A Bosley, *CEO*
EMP: 50 **EST:** 1958
SQ FT: 30,000
SALES (est): 8.94MM
SALES (corp-wide): 8.94MM **Privately Held**
Web: www.newhopeservices.org
SIC: 8322 2396 8331 3993 Child related social services; Automotive and apparel trimmings; Sheltered workshop; Signs and advertising specialties

Jeffersonville - Clark County (G-10023) GEOGRAPHIC SECTION

(G-10023)
NEWS AND TRIBUNE
221 Spring St (47130-3353)
PHONE.....................812 206-2168
E Newland, *Mgr*
EMP: 13 **EST:** 2017
SALES (est): 444.05K **Privately Held**
Web: www.newsandtribune.com
SIC: 2711 Newspapers, publishing and printing

(G-10024)
NEWSPAPER HOLDING INC
Also Called: Glasgow Daily Times
221 Spring St (47130-3353)
P.O. Box 1179 (42142-1179)
PHONE.....................270 678-5171
Cindy Green, *Brnch Mgr*
EMP: 1
SALES (corp-wide): 34.97B **Privately Held**
Web: www.tribdem.com
SIC: 2711 7313 Newspapers, publishing and printing; Newspaper advertising representative
HQ: Newspaper Holding, Inc.
425 Locust St
Johnstown PA 15901
814 532-5102

(G-10025)
NIAGARA BOTTLING LLC
350 Logistics Ave (47130-4676)
PHONE.....................909 230-5000
EMP: 6
SALES (corp-wide): 120MM **Privately Held**
Web: www.niagarawater.com
SIC: 2086 Water, natural: packaged in cans, bottles, etc.
PA: Niagara Bottling, Llc
1440 Bridgegate Dr
Diamond Bar CA 91765
909 230-5000

(G-10026)
NICHOLSON AND SONS PRTG INC
Also Called: Nicholson Printing
209 Eastern Blvd (47130-2801)
PHONE.....................812 283-1200
Martha Nicholson, *Pr*
Mike Nicholson, *VP*
Chris Nicholson, *VP*
Marvin Nicholson, *Sec*
EMP: 26 **EST:** 1979
SQ FT: 10,500
SALES (est): 799.86K **Privately Held**
Web: www.nicholsonprinting.com
SIC: 2752 Offset printing

(G-10027)
OFFICE SUP OF SOUTHERN IND INC (PA)
Also Called: Kopy Kat
417 Spring St (47130-3451)
P.O. Box 1148 (47131-1148)
PHONE.....................812 283-5523
Jeffery E Frey, *Pr*
EMP: 6 **EST:** 1970
SQ FT: 5,000
SALES (est): 1.36MM
SALES (corp-wide): 1.36MM **Privately Held**
SIC: 5112 2752 5044 Office supplies, nec; Offset printing; Office equipment

(G-10028)
OHIO VALLEY READY MIX INC
2220 Hamburg Pike (47130-6398)
P.O. Box 9 (42702-0009)
PHONE.....................812 282-6671
Gerald Ayres, *Pr*
Todd Ayres, *
Marsha Gardner, *
EMP: 46 **EST:** 1971
SQ FT: 2,000
SALES (est): 863.34K **Privately Held**
SIC: 3273 Ready-mixed concrete

(G-10029)
OLD JB LLC
1701 E Market St (47130-4755)
P.O. Box 610 (47131-0610)
PHONE.....................812 288-0200
Barker Price, *Managing Member*
Mark K Knoy, *
David J Huls, *
Paul A Tobin, *
Robert M Blocker, *
▲ **EMP:** 117 **EST:** 1915
SALES (est): 46.13MM **Privately Held**
Web: www.aclines.com
SIC: 3531 Marine related equipment
HQ: Commercial Barge Line Company
1701 E Market St
Jeffersonville IN 47130

(G-10030)
OLON INDUSTRIES INC (US)
600 Patrol Rd (47130-7700)
PHONE.....................812 256-6400
Louis Cajka, *Dir*
EMP: 8
SALES (corp-wide): 38.47MM **Privately Held**
Web: www.olon.ca
SIC: 2426 Furniture dimension stock, hardwood
HQ: Olon Industries Inc. (Us)
411 Union St
Geneva IL 60134
630 232-4705

(G-10031)
OPTUM PHARMACY 702 LLC
1050 Patrol Rd (47130-7750)
PHONE.....................812 256-8600
Jake Ward, *Mgr*
EMP: 85 **EST:** 2014
SALES (est): 10.42MM
SALES (corp-wide): 371.62B **Publicly Held**
Web: www.optum.com
SIC: 2834 Pharmaceutical preparations
PA: Unitedhealth Group Incorporated
9900 Bren Rd E
Minnetonka MN 55343
952 936-1300

(G-10032)
OXINAS PARTNERS LLC
607 N Shore Dr Ste 101 (47130-3131)
PHONE.....................812 725-8649
EMP: 5 **EST:** 2018
SALES (est): 247.65K **Privately Held**
Web: www.oxinaspartners.com
SIC: 7389 7372 Financial services; Application computer software

(G-10033)
PACKAGING LGSTICS SLUTIONS LLC
Also Called: Pls
300 Missouri Ave (47130-3010)
PHONE.....................502 807-8346
EMP: 6 **EST:** 2013
SALES (est): 195.33K **Privately Held**
Web: www.packerslogistics.com
SIC: 2653 Boxes, corrugated: made from purchased materials

(G-10034)
PARKER-HANNIFIN CORPORATION
Also Called: Parker Hvac Filtration
100 River Ridge Cir (47130-8974)
PHONE.....................866 247-4827
Jonathan Gallisdorfer, *Genl Mgr*
EMP: 47
SALES (corp-wide): 19.93B **Publicly Held**
Web: www.parker.com
SIC: 3594 Fluid power pumps and motors
PA: Parker-Hannifin Corporation
6035 Parkland Blvd
Cleveland OH 44124
216 896-3000

(G-10035)
PEYTONS BARRICADE SIGN CO LLC
814 Spring St (47130-3637)
PHONE.....................812 283-6461
Darrell L Peyton, *Pr*
Debbie Peyton, *VP*
EMP: 8 **EST:** 2006
SALES (est): 731.28K **Privately Held**
Web: www.peytonsbarricade.com
SIC: 3993 Signs and advertising specialties

(G-10036)
PGP CORP
Also Called: Voss Industries
701 Loop Rd (47130-8428)
PHONE.....................812 285-7700
Joseph Rhodea, *Brnch Mgr*
EMP: 90
SQ FT: 180,000
SALES (corp-wide): 82.43MM **Privately Held**
Web: www.vossindustries.com
SIC: 3559 7389 5051 Metal pickling equipment; Metal slitting and shearing; Steel
PA: Pgp Corp.
7925 Beech Daly Rd
Taylor MI 48180
313 291-7500

(G-10037)
PHANTOM INDUSTRIES LLC
734 Spring St (47130-3556)
PHONE.....................812 276-5956
Sean Fitzgerald, *Pr*
EMP: 5 **EST:** 2015
SALES (est): 183.01K **Privately Held**
Web: www.phantomautobody.com
SIC: 3999 Manufacturing industries, nec

(G-10038)
PHOTOPROSE PRODUCTIONS INC
1528 Scott St (47130-9614)
PHONE.....................316 371-4634
Dave Higdon, *Pr*
EMP: 2 **EST:** 1995
SALES (est): 110.65K **Privately Held**
SIC: 2741 Business service newsletters: publishing and printing

(G-10039)
PLEASANT HILL VENEER CORP
Also Called: Edgeband USA
278c America Pl Ste C (47130-4286)
PHONE.....................812 725-8924
Darren Selkus, *Pr*
Chas Boyle, *Ex VP*
◆ **EMP:** 7 **EST:** 1980
SQ FT: 20,000
SALES (est): 1.52MM
SALES (corp-wide): 25.37MM **Privately Held**
Web: www.edgebandusa.com
SIC: 2435 2436 Veneer stock, hardwood; Veneer stock, softwood
PA: Uv Group Plc
20b Rigg Approach Leabridge Road
London E10 7
208 556-8866

(G-10040)
PREMIER PRINTS LLC
3018 Seminole Dr (47130-5866)
PHONE.....................812 987-1129
Reganel Burgess, *Prin*
EMP: 8 **EST:** 2013
SALES (est): 216.22K **Privately Held**
Web: www.premierprintsinc.com
SIC: 2752 Offset printing

(G-10041)
PRINTING INC LOUISVILLE KY
Also Called: Pretty Incredible
1600 Dutch Ln Ste A (47130-6302)
P.O. Box 5343 (40255-0343)
PHONE.....................800 237-5894
Kelly Abney, *Pr*
Ken Minogue, *VP*
◆ **EMP:** 18 **EST:** 1971
SQ FT: 75,000
SALES (est): 2.48MM **Privately Held**
Web: www.workwithmira.com
SIC: 2759 3993 8742 7371 Promotional printing; Signs and advertising specialties; Management consulting services; Custom computer programming services

(G-10042)
PROCARD INC
Also Called: Tsys Isolutions
1 Heartland Way (47130-5870)
PHONE.....................303 279-2255
Ian Hill, *Prin*
EMP: 98 **EST:** 1989
SALES (est): 30.27MM
SALES (corp-wide): 9.65B **Publicly Held**
SIC: 6153 7371 7372 Credit card services, central agency collection; Computer software development and applications; Prepackaged software
PA: Global Payments Inc.
3550 Lenox Rd Ne
Atlanta GA 30326
770 829-8000

(G-10043)
PUROLATOR PDTS A FILTRATION CO (PA)
Also Called: Air Filters Sales & Service
100 River Ridge Cir (47130-8974)
PHONE.....................866 925-2247
Bill Pappas, *Pr*
Alan H Spicer, *VP*
◆ **EMP:** 250 **EST:** 1999
SQ FT: 250,000
SALES (est): 42.69MM
SALES (corp-wide): 42.69MM **Privately Held**
SIC: 3564 3433 Filters, air: furnaces, air conditioning equipment, etc.; Heating equipment, except electric

(G-10044)
R C SYSTEMS INC
Also Called: RC Systems
P.O. Box 721 (47131-0721)
PHONE.....................812 282-4898
Bob Shields, *Prin*
Bob Clark, *Prin*
Bob Johnston, *Prin*
EMP: 8 **EST:** 1976
SQ FT: 5,000
SALES (est): 2.5MM **Privately Held**
Web: www.rcsystemsco.com
SIC: 3679 7629 Electronic circuits; Electronic equipment repair

Jeffersonville - Clark County (G-10070)

(G-10045)
REVERE PLASTICS SYSTEMS LLC
5171 Maritime (47130-8452)
PHONE..........................812 670-2240
EMP: 195
SALES (corp-wide): 33.16MM Privately Held
Web: www.revereplasticssystems.com
SIC: 3089 Injection molding of plastics
HQ: Revere Plastics Systems, Llc
  39555 Orchard Hill Pl # 155
  Novi MI 48375

(G-10046)
RFC LLC
1205 N Access Dr (47130-8477)
PHONE..........................812 284-0650
Chad Shaffer, Brnch Mgr
EMP: 55
SALES (corp-wide): 19.29B Privately Held
Web: www.rfccorp.com
SIC: 3449 Custom roll formed products
HQ: Rfc Llc
  1070 Brooks Industrial Rd
  Shelbyville KY 40065
  502 633-4435

(G-10047)
RIGHT DIRECTION TRCKG EX LLC
1250 Veterans Pkwy (47129-2394)
PHONE..........................502 912-2504
EMP: 4
SALES (est): 180.77K Privately Held
SIC: 3537 Trucks: freight, baggage, etc.: industrial, except mining

(G-10048)
RIVER CEMENT SALES COMPANY
Also Called: RIVER CEMENT SALES COMPANY
1350 Bates Bowyer Ave (47130-3888)
PHONE..........................812 285-1003
Rick Bryan, Brnch Mgr
EMP: 3
SALES (corp-wide): 4.69B Privately Held
Web: www.buzziunicemusa.com
SIC: 3241 Portland cement
HQ: Buzzi Unicem Usa Inc
  100 Brodhead Rd Ste 230
  Bethlehem PA 18017
  610 882-5000

(G-10049)
RO-VIC WOOD PRODUCTS INC
254c America Pl (47130-4285)
P.O. Box 1014 (47131-1014)
PHONE..........................812 283-9199
Robert Mondun, Pr
Vickie Mondun, *
EMP: 13 EST: 1986
SQ FT: 53,200
SALES (est): 536.17K Privately Held
Web: www.kentuckianawoodproducts.com
SIC: 2511 2431 Bookcases, household: wood ; Millwork

(G-10050)
SAMPAN GROUP LLC
202 Ash St (47130-9408)
PHONE..........................812 280-6094
Elaine M Kittrell, Prin
EMP: 5 EST: 2009
SALES (est): 55.94K Privately Held
Web: www.sampanscreenprint.com
SIC: 2759 Screen printing

(G-10051)
SAMPAN SCREEN PRINT NEW IMAGE
Also Called: Sampan Screen Print
202 Ash St (47130-9408)
PHONE..........................812 282-8499
Lynn Murchy, Owner
EMP: 5 EST: 1980
SQ FT: 4,800
SALES (est): 476.8K Privately Held
Web: www.sampanscreenprint.com
SIC: 2759 Screen printing

(G-10052)
SCHIMPFFS CONFECTIONERY LLC
347 Spring St (47130-3449)
PHONE..........................812 283-8367
Warren Schimpff, Owner
Warren Schimpff, Pt
EMP: 14 EST: 1891
SQ FT: 5,000
SALES (est): 412.39K Privately Held
Web: www.schimpffs.com
SIC: 5441 2064 5812 Candy; Candy and other confectionery products; Restaurant, lunch counter

(G-10053)
SEAL TEC INC
Also Called: Strobel Technologies
3131 Industrial Pkwy (47130-9631)
PHONE..........................812 282-4388
EMP: 30 EST: 1991
SQ FT: 40,000
SALES (est): 3.43MM Privately Held
Web: www.seal-tec.com
SIC: 2515 Mattresses, containing felt, foam rubber, urethane, etc.

(G-10054)
SIGNS NOW JEFFERSONVILLE
590 Missouri Ave Ste 104 (47130-3085)
PHONE..........................812 282-2440
EMP: 5 EST: 2020
SALES (est): 65.26K Privately Held
Web: www.signsnow.com
SIC: 3993 Signs and advertising specialties

(G-10055)
SNYDERS-LANCE INC
125 Peacely St (47130-6459)
PHONE..........................812 285-0939
EMP: 3
SALES (corp-wide): 9.36B Publicly Held
Web: www.campbellsoupcompany.com
SIC: 2052 Cookies
HQ: Snyder's-Lance, Inc.
  One Campbell Place
  Camden NJ 08103
  704 554-1421

(G-10056)
SOUTHERN INDIANA BUS SOURCE
Also Called: News & Tribune
221 Spring St (47130-3353)
PHONE..........................812 206-6397
Janice Ashby, Prin
EMP: 8 EST: 2010
SALES (est): 144.64K Privately Held
Web: www.newsandtribune.com
SIC: 2711 Newspapers, publishing and printing

(G-10057)
SPENCER MACHINE AND TL CO INC
Also Called: Spencer Strainer Systems
6205 Gheens Mill Rd (47130-9214)
PHONE..........................812 282-6300
Glenn Spencer, Pr
Bradley Spencer, VP
Betty J Spencer, Sec
EMP: 20 EST: 1985
SQ FT: 24,000
SALES (est): 2.86MM Privately Held
Web: www.spencerstrainer.com
SIC: 3569 3599 Filters; Machine shop, jobbing and repair

(G-10058)
STADRY ENCLOSURE CO
213 Riverwood Dr (47130-5641)
PHONE..........................812 284-2244
EMP: 3 EST: 2010
SALES (est): 254.47K Privately Held
Web: www.stadry.com
SIC: 3444 Metal housings, enclosures, casings, and other containers

(G-10059)
STEEL DYNAMICS INC
Also Called: Flat Roll Div - Jeffersonville
5134 Loop Rd (47130-8412)
PHONE..........................812 218-1490
Chris Winger, Brnch Mgr
EMP: 100
Web: www.steeldynamics.com
SIC: 3312 3479 Plate, sheet and strip, except coated products; Galvanizing of iron, steel, or end-formed products
PA: Steel Dynamics, Inc.
  7575 W Jefferson Blvd
  Fort Wayne IN 46804

(G-10060)
STEWART GRAPHICS INC (PA)
Also Called: Voluforms
1419 Fabricon Blvd (47130-9603)
P.O. Box 402 (47172-0402)
PHONE..........................812 283-0455
Charles H Stewart, CEO
C Michael Stewart, Prin
Jeff Waiz, *
Mark T Stewart, Prin
Jane Stewart, *
EMP: 34 EST: 1987
SALES (est): 18.17MM
SALES (corp-wide): 18.17MM Privately Held
Web: www.voluforms.com
SIC: 5112 2761 7384 Business forms; Manifold business forms; Photographic services

(G-10061)
STROBEL MFG INC
6516 Longview Beach Rd (47130-8432)
PHONE..........................812 282-4388
Mark Strobel, Pr
EMP: 5 EST: 2020
SALES (est): 42.55K Privately Held
Web: www.strobel.com
SIC: 3999 Manufacturing industries, nec

(G-10062)
SWEET PROPERTIES LLC
347 Spring St (47130-3449)
PHONE..........................812 283-8367
Warren Schimpff, Prin
EMP: 2 EST: 2008
SALES (est): 84.4K Privately Held
Web: www.sweetpropertiesllc.com
SIC: 2064 Candy and other confectionery products

(G-10063)
TC PALLETS & PEDDLER SWEET LLC
1414 E 10th St (47130-4205)
PHONE..........................812 283-1090
EMP: 5 EST: 2016
SALES (est): 318.96K Privately Held
SIC: 2448 Pallets, wood

(G-10064)
TIMOTHY HOOVER INDUSTRIES LLC
1701 Village Green Blvd (47130-5173)
PHONE..........................812 987-6342
Timothy Hoover, Prin
EMP: 5 EST: 2017
SALES (est): 42.83K Privately Held
SIC: 3999 Manufacturing industries, nec

(G-10065)
TRIDENT ENGRAVING INC
3114 New Chapel Rd (47130-8916)
PHONE..........................812 282-2098
Ronald Woodward, Prin
EMP: 5 EST: 2015
SALES (est): 95.76K Privately Held
SIC: 2759 Commercial printing, nec

(G-10066)
TRUCKIN4YA LLC
Also Called: Trucking
4001 Williams Crossing Way (47130-8003)
PHONE..........................812 225-2640
EMP: 2 EST: 2021
SALES (est): 95.58K Privately Held
SIC: 3537 Trucks: freight, baggage, etc.: industrial, except mining

(G-10067)
TWIN HILL ACQUISITION CO INC
Also Called: Twin Hill
401 Salem Rd (47130)
PHONE..........................888 206-0699
Scott Silverstein, Pr
▲ EMP: 35 EST: 2001
SALES (est): 9.48MM
SALES (corp-wide): 9.48MM Privately Held
Web: www.twinhill.com
SIC: 2326 Work uniforms
PA: Th Holdco Inc
  6380 Rogerdale Rd
  Houston TX 77072
  888 206-0699

(G-10068)
UNITED SERVICES INC
Also Called: U.S.I. Custom Blinds
2626 America Place (47130)
PHONE..........................812 989-3320
EMP: 1
SQ FT: 22,000
SIC: 2591 Window blinds
PA: United Services Inc.
  118 W Lewis & Clark Pkwy
  Clarksville IN 47129

(G-10069)
VOICE OF GOD RECORDINGS INC
5911 Charlestown Pike (47130)
P.O. Box 950 (47130)
PHONE..........................812 246-2137
Joseph M Branham, Pr
William P Branham Senior, VP
▼ EMP: 84 EST: 1980
SQ FT: 60,000
SALES (est): 28.78MM Privately Held
Web: www.branham.org
SIC: 5961 3652 2791 2789 Record and/or tape (music or video) club, mail order; Prerecorded records and tapes; Typesetting ; Bookbinding and related work

(G-10070)
VPI ACQUISITION LLC
2200 Centennial Blvd (47130-8533)
PHONE..........................812 283-4435
EMP: 5
Web: www.vikingplastics.com

Jeffersonville - Clark County (G-10071)

(G-10071 cont.)
SIC: 3089 Injection molding of plastics
PA: Vpi Acquisition, Llc
1 Viking St
Corry PA 16407

(G-10071)
WATER ENERGIZERS INC
Also Called: Water Energizers
3008 Middle Rd Ste A (47130-5500)
PHONE..................812 288-6900
Rhonda Harris, Pr
C L Harris, Ch Bd
Rhonda R Harris, Pr
Doctor Robert E Harris, Ex VP
Ronald D Harris, Stockholder
EMP: 10 EST: 1987
SQ FT: 12,000
SALES (est): 990.43K **Privately Held**
Web: www.waterenergizers.com
SIC: 3589 Water treatment equipment, industrial

(G-10072)
WELBILT FDSRVICE COMPANIES LLC
Also Called: Manitowoc Kitchencare
600 Patrol Rd Ste 500 (47130-7700)
PHONE..................812 406-4527
EMP: 281
SALES (corp-wide): 4.8B **Privately Held**
Web: direct.welbilt.us
SIC: 3585 Refrigeration and heating equipment
HQ: Welbilt Foodservice Companies, Llc
2227 Welbilt Blvd
Trinity FL 34655

(G-10073)
WENDELL CONGER
Also Called: Conger Signs
3018 Grand Pointe (47130-8300)
PHONE..................812 282-2564
Wendell Conger, Owner
EMP: 2 EST: 1956
SALES (est): 136.49K **Privately Held**
SIC: 3993 Electric signs

(G-10074)
WENTWORTH SOFTWARE
3410 Lakewood Blvd (47130-9727)
PHONE..................812 218-0052
Steven Driver, Owner
EMP: 1 EST: 1991
SALES (est): 65.26K **Privately Held**
SIC: 7372 Prepackaged software

(G-10075)
WHITESELL PRCSION CMPNENTS INC
100 Technology Way (47130-9644)
PHONE..................812 282-4014
Neil L Whitesell, CEO
Hart Vogt, *
Bob Wiese, *
EMP: 150 EST: 2011
SQ FT: 286,000
SALES (est): 22.85MM **Privately Held**
Web: www.whitesellprecision.com
SIC: 3541 Machine tools, metal cutting type

(G-10076)
XTREME GRAPHICS
3301 Justinian (47130-8631)
P.O. Box 1452 (47131-1452)
PHONE..................812 989-6948
Tonya Nolan, Prin
EMP: 5 EST: 2007
SALES (est): 90.13K **Privately Held**
Web: www.branded.ink

SIC: 2759 5699 5941 5949 Screen printing; Sports apparel; Sporting goods and bicycle shops; Sewing, needlework, and piece goods

(G-10077)
YELLOW FELLOW SAFETY SIGNS LLC
1415 E 8th St (47130-4462)
PHONE..................813 557-6428
Eddie Green, Prin
EMP: 5 EST: 2016
SALES (est): 46.08K **Privately Held**
SIC: 3993 Signs and advertising specialties

Jonesboro
Grant County

(G-10078)
EXEON PROCESSORS LLC (PA)
232 W Pearl St (46938-1054)
PHONE..................765 674-2266
Jason Kozin, Managing Member
EMP: 16 EST: 2014
SQ FT: 30,000
SALES (est): 4.52MM
SALES (corp-wide): 4.52MM **Privately Held**
Web: www.exeoninc.com
SIC: 5093 3356 Scrap and waste materials; Nonferrous rolling and drawing, nec

(G-10079)
H A P INDUSTRIES INC
Also Called: Rich Glas Products
7220 S 200 W (46938-9769)
PHONE..................765 948-3385
Allen J Fox, Pr
Paul Fox, Sec
▲ EMP: 6 EST: 1973
SALES (est): 494.85K **Privately Held**
SIC: 3089 3431 Plastics kitchenware, tableware, and houseware; Metal sanitary ware

(G-10080)
JROTTEN CHOPPER INC
6563 Wheeling Pike (46938-9702)
PHONE..................765 517-1779
John Armes, Prin
EMP: 2 EST: 2010
SALES (est): 189.01K **Privately Held**
Web: www.jrottenchoppers.com
SIC: 3751 Motorcycles and related parts

(G-10081)
TEAGUE CONCRETE BACKHOE
105 W 3rd St (46938-1102)
PHONE..................765 674-4692
John Teague, Owner
EMP: 1 EST: 1992
SALES (est): 67.26K **Privately Held**
SIC: 1794 3545 Excavation and grading, building construction; Tools and accessories for machine tools

Jonesville
Bartholomew County

(G-10082)
BRICK
309 Walnut St (47247-4718)
PHONE..................812 522-8636
Bill Jefferies, Owner
EMP: 2 EST: 2001
SALES (est): 99.45K **Privately Held**
Web: www.thebrick.com

SIC: 2599 Bar, restaurant and cafeteria furniture

(G-10083)
C & G TOOL INC
706 W Chestnut St (47247-4724)
PHONE..................812 524-7061
Curt Price, Pr
Greg Price, VP
EMP: 6 EST: 2000
SALES (est): 493.6K **Privately Held**
Web: www.cgtool.com
SIC: 3544 Special dies and tools

(G-10084)
CARL FOX CABINETS INC
704 W Chestnut St (47247-4724)
PHONE..................812 342-3020
Dan Newell, Pr
Izetta Fox, Sec
Blake Everroad, VP
EMP: 6 EST: 1956
SALES (est): 600K **Privately Held**
Web: www.foxcabinets.com
SIC: 2541 Cabinets, except refrigerated: show, display, etc.: wood

(G-10085)
L & P MANUFACTURING COMPANY
207 Rodgers Ln (47247-4731)
PHONE..................812 405-2093
Roselyn Long, CEO
James Long, Pr
Jason Patrick, Mgr
EMP: 5 EST: 2015
SALES (est): 664.63K **Privately Held**
Web: www.lpmfg.net
SIC: 3599 Machine shop, jobbing and repair

Kempton
Tipton County

(G-10086)
DRAGONWOOD LLC
11965 W 150 N (46049-9249)
PHONE..................765 947-0097
Michael Gerig, Managing Member
Abigail Gerig, Managing Member
EMP: 8 EST: 2013
SALES (est): 220K **Privately Held**
Web: www.dragonwood.online
SIC: 2099 Syrups

Kendallville
Noble County

(G-10087)
AFFORDABLE SIGNS INCORPORATED
700 S Orchard St (46755-2022)
P.O. Box 503 (46755-0503)
PHONE..................260 349-1710
Brian Anderson, Owner
EMP: 2 EST: 1997
SALES (est): 177.9K **Privately Held**
Web: www.hoosiersigns.com
SIC: 3993 Signs and advertising specialties

(G-10088)
ALUM-ELEC STRUCTURES INC
250 W Grove St (46755-1409)
PHONE..................260 347-9362
Joseph Taylor, Pr
Nancy Taylor, Sec
EMP: 6 EST: 1972
SQ FT: 7,600
SALES (est): 882.07K **Privately Held**

Web: www.alumelec.com
SIC: 3441 Building components, structural steel

(G-10089)
APPLE TERRACE LLC
515 Professional Way (46755-2928)
P.O. Box 633 (46755-0633)
PHONE..................260 347-9400
Michael M Yoder, Prin
EMP: 8 EST: 2012
SALES (est): 561.75K **Privately Held**
SIC: 3571 Electronic computers

(G-10090)
ARCHIMEDES INC (DH)
2705 Marion Dr (46755-3280)
PHONE..................260 347-3903
Steve Paddock, Pr
EMP: 14 EST: 2000
SALES (est): 27.62MM
SALES (corp-wide): 811.52MM **Privately Held**
Web: www.boellhoff.com
SIC: 3965 Fasteners
HQ: Bollhoff Beteiligungsges. Mbh
Archimedesstr. 1-4
Bielefeld NW 33649
521448201

(G-10091)
ARTISTIC CARTON
301 S Progress Dr E (46755-3266)
PHONE..................260 925-6060
EMP: 10 EST: 2020
SALES (est): 2.19MM **Privately Held**
Web: www.graphicpkg.com
SIC: 2652 Setup paperboard boxes

(G-10092)
ASHLEY INDUSTRIAL MOLDING INC
100 S Progress Dr W (46755-3261)
PHONE..................260 349-1982
Rod Schoon, Brnch Mgr
EMP: 48
SALES (corp-wide): 41.43MM **Privately Held**
Web: www.ashinmold.com
SIC: 3089 Injection molding of plastics
PA: Ashley Industrial Molding Inc
310 S Wabash St
Ashley IN 46705
260 587-9155

(G-10093)
AWOL METAL CONTORSION LLC
439 Prospect Ave (46755-2250)
PHONE..................260 909-0411
EMP: 4 EST: 2015
SALES (est): 91.77K **Privately Held**
SIC: 3441 7538 Fabricated structural metal; General automotive repair shops

(G-10094)
B & J MEDICAL LLC
4268 E Us Highway 6 (46755-9343)
PHONE..................260 349-1275
John Wicker, Pr
Scott Sizemore, *
EMP: 50 EST: 2011
SALES (est): 4.87MM **Privately Held**
Web: www.bjmedicalinc.com
SIC: 3841 Surgical and medical instruments

(G-10095)
B & J SPECIALTY INC
B & J Medical
4268 E Us Highway 6 (46755-9343)
PHONE..................260 636-2067
John Wicker, Brnch Mgr

EMP: 4
Web: www.bjspecialtyinc.com
SIC: 3845 Electromedical equipment
PA: B & J Specialty, Inc.
7919 N 100 E
Wawaka IN 46794

(G-10096)
BANCO INDUSTRIES INC
11542 N State Road 3 (46755-9732)
P.O. Box 5191 (46755-5191)
PHONE.................................260 347-9524
Marvin Nagel, *Pr*
Brenda Nagel, *VP*
EMP: 9 **EST:** 1992
SQ FT: 6,000
SALES (est): 937K **Privately Held**
Web: www.bancoindustries.com
SIC: 3599 Machine shop, jobbing and repair

(G-10097)
BOLLHOFF INC (DH)
2705 Marion Dr (46755)
PHONE.................................260 347-3903
Steve Paddock, *Pr*
▲ **EMP:** 63 **EST:** 1992
SQ FT: 100,000
SALES (est): 21.76MM
SALES (corp-wide): 811.52MM **Privately Held**
Web: www.bollhoff-usa.com
SIC: 3452 3965 Bolts, nuts, rivets, and washers; Fasteners
HQ: Archimedes, Inc.
2705 Marion Dr
Kendallville IN 46755
260 347-3903

(G-10098)
CHARMARAN COMPANY LLC
1451 Stonebraker Dr (46755-1027)
PHONE.................................260 347-3347
Terry Smith, *Pr*
EMP: 13 **EST:** 1989
SQ FT: 30,000
SALES (est): 969.21K **Privately Held**
Web: www.charmaran.com
SIC: 3466 3469 3444 2655 Closures, stamped metal; Machine parts, stamped or pressed metal; Culverts, flumes, and pipes; Fiber spools, tubes, and cones

(G-10099)
COLWELL INC (HQ)
2605 Marion Dr (46755)
P.O. Box 308 (46755)
PHONE.................................260 347-1981
William V Byars, *CEO*
Patrick Van Arnam, *
Donovan Freeland, *
Kevin C Gurney, *
John Olson, *
▲ **EMP:** 108 **EST:** 1949
SQ FT: 200,000
SALES (est): 49.92MM
SALES (corp-wide): 53.5MM **Privately Held**
Web: www.colwellcolour.com
SIC: 2752 Cards, lithographed
PA: Colwell Industries, Inc.
1611 County Road B W # 315
Saint Paul MN 55113
612 340-0365

(G-10100)
COLWELL INC
231 S Progress Dr E (46755-3269)
P.O. Box 308 (46755-0308)
PHONE.................................260 347-1981
David Brayton, *Mgr*
EMP: 115

SALES (corp-wide): 53.5MM **Privately Held**
Web: www.colwellcolour.com
SIC: 2752 Cards, lithographed
HQ: Colwell, Inc.
2605 Marion Dr
Kendallville IN 46755
260 347-1981

(G-10101)
CONLEY WELDING SPECIALTIES INC
605 S Orchard St (46755-2011)
PHONE.................................260 343-9051
Latesa Conley, *Pr*
Jeffrey Conley, *Sec*
EMP: 3 **EST:** 2004
SALES (est): 263.25K **Privately Held**
SIC: 7692 Welding repair

(G-10102)
CORNERSTONE FLLWSHIP KNDLLVLLE
110 S Oak St (46755-1755)
PHONE.................................260 347-0615
Marlena Smith, *Sec*
EMP: 5 **EST:** 2017
SALES (est): 128.48K **Privately Held**
Web: www.kpcnews.com
SIC: 2711 Newspapers, publishing and printing

(G-10103)
COUNTRY SEWING
8929 E 1125 N (46755-9745)
PHONE.................................260 347-9733
Homer Morgan, *Owner*
Pam Morgan, *Owner*
EMP: 2 **EST:** 1997
SALES (est): 61.31K **Privately Held**
SIC: 7219 2399 Garment alteration and repair shop; Fabricated textile products, nec

(G-10104)
CREATIVE LIQUID COATINGS INC
Also Called: Dan St. Germain
221 S Progress Dr W (46755-3264)
PHONE.................................260 349-1862
Randy Geist, *Pr*
EMP: 1
Web: www.creativeliquidcoatings.com
SIC: 3479 Painting, coating, and hot dipping
PA: Creative Liquid Coatings, Inc.
2620 Marion Dr
Kendallville IN 46755

(G-10105)
CREATIVE LIQUID COATINGS INC (PA)
Also Called: CLC
2620 Marion Dr (46755)
P.O. Box 369 (46755)
PHONE.................................260 349-1862
◆ **EMP:** 392 **EST:** 1996
SQ FT: 200,000
SALES (est): 107.77MM **Privately Held**
Web: www.creativeliquidcoatings.com
SIC: 1721 3479 3714 Industrial painting; Coating of metals and formed products; Motor vehicle body components and frame

(G-10106)
CRUNCHTECH HOLDINGS LLC
Also Called: Atomic Filament
6928 N 400 E (46755-9346)
PHONE.................................818 583-0004
John Maly, *Managing Member*
EMP: 6 **EST:** 2021
SALES (est): 475.18K **Privately Held**
Web: www.atomicfilament.com

SIC: 3555 Printing trades machinery

(G-10107)
DA-MAR INDUSTRIES INC (PA)
Also Called: Lewger Machine & Tool
201 W Ohio St (46755-2015)
PHONE.................................260 347-1662
David Vangessel, *Pr*
EMP: 10 **EST:** 1951
SQ FT: 25,000
SALES (est): 2.4MM
SALES (corp-wide): 2.4MM **Privately Held**
Web: www.lewger.com
SIC: 3599 3549 3469 7692 Machine shop, jobbing and repair; Assembly machines, including robotic; Stamping metal for the trade; Welding repair

(G-10108)
DALTON CORP KNDLLVLLE MFG FCLT
200 W Ohio St (46755-2016)
PHONE.................................260 637-6047
Joseph L Derita, *Pr*
▼ **EMP:** 136 **EST:** 1927
SQ FT: 210,000
SALES (est): 1.83MM
SALES (corp-wide): 110.99MM **Privately Held**
SIC: 3321 Gray iron castings, nec
HQ: The Dalton Corporation
1900 E Jefferson St
Warsaw IN 46580
574 267-8111

(G-10109)
DEKKO ACQUISITION PARENT INC (PA)
6928 N 400 E (46755-9346)
PHONE.................................260 347-0700
Robert Bergmann, *Pr*
Gerald Whiteford, *VP*
Michael Schnabel, *Sec*
▲ **EMP:** 6 **EST:** 2006
SALES (est): 48.7MM **Privately Held**
SIC: 3496 Wire fasteners

(G-10110)
DEPENDABLE METAL TREATING INC
902 Dowling St (46755-9401)
P.O. Box 276 (46755-0276)
PHONE.................................260 347-5744
Ross L Noble, *Pr*
EMP: 18 **EST:** 1995
SQ FT: 23,600
SALES (est): 2.08MM **Privately Held**
Web: www.dependablemetaltreating.com
SIC: 3398 Metal heat treating

(G-10111)
FLINT & WALLING INC (HQ)
Also Called: Star Water Systems
95 N Oak St (46755-1736)
PHONE.................................800 345-9422
John A Zoeller, *CEO*
Eric B Rimmel, *Pr*
Dwight C Newton, *Sec*
Thomas Howard, *Treas*
◆ **EMP:** 50 **EST:** 1866
SQ FT: 232,080
SALES (est): 99.97MM
SALES (corp-wide): 197.28MM **Privately Held**
Web: www.flintandwailing.com
SIC: 3561 Industrial pumps and parts
PA: Zoeller Company
3649 Cane Run Rd
Louisville KY 40211
502 778-2731

(G-10112)
FRYE WELDING LLC
6065 E Leighty Rd (46755-9768)
PHONE.................................260 908-4766
Stephanie R Frye, *Mgr*
EMP: 1 **EST:** 2011
SALES (est): 99.56K **Privately Held**
SIC: 7692 Welding repair

(G-10113)
GPI MIDWEST LLC
301 S Progress Dr E (46755-3266)
PHONE.................................260 925-6060
Michael P Doss, *Pr*
EMP: 1 **EST:** 2014
SALES (est): 575.96K **Publicly Held**
Web: www.graphicpkg.com
SIC: 2611 Pulp manufactured from waste or recycled paper
HQ: Graphic Packaging International, Llc
1500 Rvredge Pkwy Ste 100
Atlanta GA 30328

(G-10114)
GROUP DEKKO INC
6928 N 400e Dock 101 (46755-9346)
PHONE.................................260 599-3405
Jamie Prescott, *Brnch Mgr*
EMP: 1
SALES (corp-wide): 4.41B **Publicly Held**
Web: www.dekko.com
SIC: 3841 Surgical and medical instruments
HQ: Group Dekko, Inc.
7310 Innovation Blvd # 104
Fort Wayne IN 46818

(G-10115)
HENDRICKSON INTERNATIONAL
101 S Progress Dr W (46755-3262)
PHONE.................................260 349-6400
Joseph Ross, *Pr*
EMP: 25 **EST:** 2008
SALES (est): 1.88MM **Privately Held**
Web: www.hendrickson-intl.com
SIC: 3714 Motor vehicle parts and accessories

(G-10116)
HENDRICKSON INTERNATIONAL CORP
Also Called: Hendrickson Truck Suspension
220 S Progress Dr W (46755)
PHONE.................................260 349-6400
EMP: 24 **EST:** 1967
SALES (est): 1.02MM **Privately Held**
SIC: 3714 Motor vehicle parts and accessories

(G-10117)
HENDRICKSON INTERNATIONAL CORP
Hendrickson Truck Suspension
101 S Progress Dr W (46755-3262)
PHONE.................................260 349-6400
Randy Alwless, *Mgr*
EMP: 123
SALES (corp-wide): 758.84MM **Privately Held**
Web: www.hendrickson-intl.com
SIC: 3714 3713 Motor vehicle parts and accessories; Truck and bus bodies
HQ: Hendrickson International Corporation
840 S Frontage Rd
Woodridge IL 60517

(G-10118)
HIDINGHILDA LLC
1511 Brookview Blvd (46755-2777)
PHONE.................................260 760-7093
Dawn Hillyer, *Managing Member*

Kendallville - Noble County (G-10119)

EMP: 3 EST: 2015
SALES (est): 209.76K **Privately Held**
Web: www.hidinghilda.com
SIC: **2339** 5632 Women's and misses' accessories; Women's accessory and specialty stores

(G-10119)
HONEY POT DEVELOPMENT
730 E Mitchell St (46755-1831)
PHONE..................................260 318-0001
Kristen Johnson, *Prin*
EMP: 5 EST: 2018
SALES (est): 48.82K **Privately Held**
Web: www.fop126.com
SIC: **2844** Perfumes, cosmetics and other toilet preparations

(G-10120)
JEFF SNYDER
Also Called: Hometown Food Service
3273 N Old State Road 3 (46755-9200)
PHONE..................................260 349-0405
Jeff Snyder, *Owner*
EMP: 1 EST: 2001
SALES (est): 7.79K **Privately Held**
Web: www.snyderfoodservices.com
SIC: **2099** Food preparations, nec

(G-10121)
JO MORY INC
621 Professional Way (46755-2930)
PHONE..................................260 347-3753
Gary Worman, *Brnch Mgr*
EMP: 1
SALES (corp-wide): 16.4MM **Privately Held**
Web: www.jomory.com
SIC: **1711** 1731 3444 Ventilation and duct work contractor; Electrical work; Sheet metalwork
PA: J.O. Mory, Inc.
    7470 S State Road 3
    South Milford IN 46786
    260 351-2221

(G-10122)
KAMMERER DYNAMICS INC
5780 E Concrete Dr (46755-9395)
PHONE..................................260 349-9098
Klint Kammerer, *Pr*
Kelly Kammerer, *Prin*
EMP: 18 EST: 2014
SQ FT: 5,000
SALES (est): 2.67MM **Privately Held**
Web: www.kammerer-kdi.com
SIC: **3441** Fabricated structural metal

(G-10123)
KAMMERER INC (PA)
2348 E Kammerer Rd (46755-3067)
PHONE..................................260 347-0389
Kelly Kammerer, *Mgr*
Sherril Kammerer, *Owner*
EMP: 12 EST: 1946
SALES (est): 2.34MM
SALES (corp-wide): 2.34MM **Privately Held**
Web: www.kammerer-inc.com
SIC: **7692** 3444 3443 3441 Welding repair; Sheet metalwork; Fabricated plate work (boiler shop); Fabricated structural metal

(G-10124)
KAMMERER INC
303 W Wayne St (46755-1484)
PHONE..................................260 349-9098
Kelly Kammerer, *Brnch Mgr*
EMP: 81
SALES (corp-wide): 2.34MM **Privately Held**

Web: www.kammerer-inc.com
SIC: **7692** 5051 3312 1542 Welding repair; Steel; Blast furnaces and steel mills; Nonresidential construction, nec
PA: Kammerer Inc.
    2348 E Kammerer Rd
    Kendallville IN 46755
    260 347-0389

(G-10125)
KENDALLVILLE CUSTOM PRINTING
1307 N Lima Rd (46755-2319)
P.O. Box 932 (46755-0932)
PHONE..................................260 347-9233
Duane Targgart, *Pr*
Henry Freistroffer, *Sec*
EMP: 10 EST: 1991
SQ FT: 14,000
SALES (est): 198.16K **Privately Held**
Web: www.kendallvilleglass.com
SIC: **2752** 2791 2789 2761 Commercial printing, lithographic; Typesetting; Bookbinding and related work; Manifold business forms

(G-10126)
KENDALLVILLE IRON & METAL INC
243 E Lisbon Rd (46755-3618)
P.O. Box 69 (46755-0069)
PHONE..................................260 347-1958
Gary Spidel, *Pr*
Lynn R Spidel, *
Susan Norris, *
EMP: 16 EST: 1964
SALES (est): 892.65K **Privately Held**
Web: www.kendallvilleiron.com
SIC: **5093** 4212 3341 Metal scrap and waste materials; Local trucking, without storage; Secondary nonferrous metals

(G-10127)
KENDALLVILLE PUBLISHING CO INC
102 N Main St (46755-1714)
P.O. Box 39 (46755-0039)
PHONE..................................260 347-0400
EMP: 5 EST: 2019
SALES (est): 40.55K **Privately Held**
Web: www.kpcnews.net
SIC: **2741** Miscellaneous publishing

(G-10128)
KIMMEL MUSIC
221 S Morton St (46755-1636)
PHONE..................................260 302-3082
William L Kimmel, *Owner*
EMP: 1 EST: 2019
SALES (est): 96.5K **Privately Held**
Web: www.kimmel-music.com
SIC: **3931** Musical instruments

(G-10129)
KITCHEN-QUIP INC
Also Called: Americhef USA
338 S Oak St (46755-1759)
P.O. Box 548 (46755-0548)
PHONE..................................260 837-8311
Stephen B Sparling, *Pr*
Winston B Sparling, *
Treva E Sparling, *
Jeffery Musick, *
EMP: 45 EST: 1946
SQ FT: 70,000
SALES (est): 2.32MM **Privately Held**
Web: www.kqcasting.com
SIC: **3363** 3369 3556 Aluminum die-castings ; Nonferrous foundries, nec; Food products machinery

(G-10130)
KPC MEDIA GROUP INC (PA)
Also Called: Advance Leader
102 N Main St (46755-1714)
PHONE..................................260 347-0400
Lou Phelps, *CEO*
Terry Housholder, *
George B Witwer, *
Violet Wysong, *
Grace Householder, *
EMP: 110 EST: 1911
SQ FT: 40,000
SALES (est): 23.55MM
SALES (corp-wide): 23.55MM **Privately Held**
Web: www.kpcnews.com
SIC: **2711** 2791 2752 Commercial printing and newspaper publishing combined; Typesetting; Commercial printing, lithographic

(G-10131)
KRAFT HEINZ FOODS COMPANY
Also Called: Kraft Foods
151 W Ohio St (46755-2033)
PHONE..................................260 347-1300
Bob Bortner, *Mgr*
EMP: 89
SALES (corp-wide): 26.64B **Publicly Held**
Web: www.kraftheinzcompany.com
SIC: **2033** Canned fruits and specialties
HQ: Kraft Heinz Foods Company
    1 Ppg Pl Ste 3400
    Pittsburgh PA 15222
    412 456-5700

(G-10132)
LBW PRINTING & DTP
1219 N Lima Rd (46755-2661)
P.O. Box 154 (46755-0154)
PHONE..................................260 347-9053
Laurie Way, *Owner*
EMP: 1 EST: 1997
SALES (est): 49.25K **Privately Held**
SIC: **2752** Offset printing

(G-10133)
LEGGETT & PLATT INCORPORATED
Kendallville 5801
2225 Production Rd (46755-3255)
PHONE..................................260 347-2600
Russell Dunton, *Brnch Mgr*
EMP: 69
SALES (corp-wide): 5.15B **Publicly Held**
Web: www.leggett.com
SIC: **3495** 2515 Mechanical springs, precision; Mattresses and bedsprings
PA: Leggett & Platt, Incorporated
    1 Leggett Rd
    Carthage MO 64836
    417 358-8131

(G-10134)
MAHONEY FOUNDRIES INC (PA)
Also Called: Vermont Foundry Company
209 W Ohio St (46755-2015)
PHONE..................................260 347-1768
Stephen Patrick Mahoney, *Pr*
Joan Mahoney, *
Christine M Krehl, *
Christine Krehl, *
EMP: 50 EST: 1946
SQ FT: 29,000
SALES (est): 14.17MM
SALES (corp-wide): 14.17MM **Privately Held**
Web: www.aluminumsandcastingsfoundry.com
SIC: **3366** 3365 Castings (except die), nec, brass; Aluminum and aluminum-based alloy castings

(G-10135)
MAINTENANCE SOLUTIONS INC
313 W Rush St (46755-1646)
P.O. Box 174 (46788-0174)
EMP: 14
Web: www.maintenancesolutions.net
SIC: **3549** Assembly machines, including robotic

(G-10136)
MD MOXIE LLC
Also Called: Advantage Thermal Service
5966 E Concrete Dr (46755-9361)
P.O. Box 876 (46755-0876)
PHONE..................................260 347-1203
Michael Moxie, *Managing Member*
EMP: 12 EST: 2005
SALES (est): 985.09K **Privately Held**
Web: www.advantagethermal1.com
SIC: **3585** Heating and air conditioning combination units

(G-10137)
MURPHYS TOWNHOUSE CANDLES LLC
226 S Park Ave (46755-2273)
PHONE..................................260 318-0504
Kimberly Murphy, *Prin*
EMP: 3 EST: 2018
SALES (est): 41.99K **Privately Held**
SIC: **3999** Candles

(G-10138)
MURRAYS TIN CUP
2004 W North St (46755-2856)
PHONE..................................260 349-1002
Wendy Potter, *Mgr*
EMP: 6 EST: 2009
SALES (est): 205.84K **Privately Held**
SIC: **3356** Tin

(G-10139)
NORTHEAST BOTTLING CO
250 W Vine St (46755-2020)
PHONE..................................260 343-0208
Jerry Anderson, *Prin*
EMP: 1 EST: 2005
SALES (est): 74.84K **Privately Held**
SIC: **2086** Bottled and canned soft drinks

(G-10140)
P & T MANUFACTURING CORP
1451 Stonebraker Dr (46755-1027)
PHONE..................................260 442-9304
EMP: 4 EST: 2019
SALES (est): 39.69K **Privately Held**
SIC: **3999** Manufacturing industries, nec

(G-10141)
PENT ASSEMBLIES
6928 N 400 E (46755-9346)
P.O. Box 246 (46755-0246)
PHONE..................................260 347-5828
Steve Hankins, *Pr*
Charles Schrimper, *
Dianne Gerencser, *
Robert Kozlowski, *
EMP: 23 EST: 1952
SQ FT: 10,000
SALES (est): 706.28K **Privately Held**
SIC: **3679** 3643 3089 Harness assemblies, for electronic use: wire or cable; Current-carrying wiring services; Injection molding of plastics

(G-10142)
PENT PLASTICS INC (PA)
6928 N 400 E (46755-9346)
PHONE..................................260 897-3775
Rick Nowels, *Pr*

Charles Schrimper, *
Robert Kozlowski, COO
Dianne Gerencser, Sec
▲ EMP: 118 EST: 1968
SQ FT: 50,000
SALES (est): 15.84MM
SALES (corp-wide): 15.84MM **Privately Held**
SIC: 3089 3641 3469 Molding primary plastics; Electric lamps; Metal stampings, nec

(G-10143)
PONDEROSA CABINET COMPANY LLC
7817 E Cree Lake Dr N (46755-9729)
PHONE.................................260 349-2509
Joseph Schrorder, Prin
EMP: 4 EST: 2009
SALES (est): 240.47K **Privately Held**
Web: www.ponderosacabinetcompany.com
SIC: 2434 Wood kitchen cabinets

(G-10144)
PRECISION MACHINED PDTS LLC
6065 E Leighty Rd (46755-9768)
PHONE.................................260 908-4766
EMP: 2 EST: 2016
SALES (est): 211.9K **Privately Held**
Web: www.precisionmachineproducts.com
SIC: 3599 Machine and other job shop work

(G-10145)
QUICK TANKS INC
545 Krueger St (46755-1420)
PHONE.................................260 347-3850
EMP: 6 EST: 1951
SALES (est): 194.68K **Privately Held**
Web: www.quicktanks.com
SIC: 3443 Fabricated plate work (boiler shop)

(G-10146)
QUICK TANKS INC
522 Krueger St (46755-1421)
P.O. Box 338 (46755-0338)
PHONE.................................260 347-3850
Thomas R Quick, Pr
EMP: 65 EST: 1950
SQ FT: 3,000
SALES (est): 10.3MM **Privately Held**
Web: www.quicktanks.com
SIC: 3443 3479 Tanks, standard or custom fabricated: metal plate; Galvanizing of iron, steel, or end-formed products

(G-10147)
RACEWAY HAND CAR WASH LLC
606 Fairview Blvd (46755-2924)
PHONE.................................260 242-9866
Sateesh Rachamadugu, Pr
EMP: 6 EST: 2011
SALES (est): 212.79K **Privately Held**
Web: racewayhandcarwash.wordpress.com
SIC: 3644 Raceways

(G-10148)
RELIABLE TOOL & MACHINE CO
902 S Main St (46755-2025)
PHONE.................................260 347-4000
EMP: 11
SALES (corp-wide): 16.95MM **Privately Held**
Web: www.reliabletool.com
SIC: 3599 Machine shop, jobbing and repair
PA: Reliable Tool & Machine Company Inc
    301 W Ohio St
    Kendallville IN 46755
    260 343-7150

(G-10149)
RELIABLE TOOL & MACHINE CO
800 Weston Ave (46755-2041)
PHONE.................................260 347-4000
EMP: 11
SALES (corp-wide): 16.95MM **Privately Held**
Web: www.reliabletool.com
SIC: 3599 Machine shop, jobbing and repair
PA: Reliable Tool & Machine Company Inc
    301 W Ohio St
    Kendallville IN 46755
    260 343-7150

(G-10150)
RELIABLE TOOL & MACHINE CO (PA)
Also Called: Reliable Prod Machining & Wldg
301 W Ohio St (46755-2017)
P.O. Box 757 (46755-0757)
PHONE.................................260 343-7150
Charles Drerup, Pr
Tom Walterhouse, *
Owen Drerup, *
Chuck Drerup, *
EMP: 48 EST: 1946
SALES (est): 16.95MM
SALES (corp-wide): 16.95MM **Privately Held**
Web: www.reliabletool.com
SIC: 3714 3599 Wheels, motor vehicle; Machine shop, jobbing and repair

(G-10151)
SACRED SELECTIONS
Also Called: RE Winset Music
112 N Shore Dr (46755-2632)
P.O. Box 5145 (46755-5145)
PHONE.................................260 347-3758
EMP: 3 EST: 1956
SALES (est): 246.46K **Privately Held**
Web: www.asacredselections.com
SIC: 2731 5961 Book music: publishing only, not printed on site; Catalog and mail-order houses

(G-10152)
SLATER CONCRETE PRODUCTS INC
322 E Wayne St (46755-1458)
PHONE.................................260 347-0164
Jeff Slater, Pr
Joe Schroeder, VP
Marylin Slater, Sec
EMP: 7 EST: 1923
SQ FT: 10,000
SALES (est): 596.4K **Privately Held**
Web: www.slatersconcrete.com
SIC: 3271 5211 5032 Blocks, concrete or cinder: standard; Concrete and cinder block ; Concrete and cinder block

(G-10153)
STIEN DESIGNS & GRAPHICS INC
106 S Main St (46755-1716)
PHONE.................................260 347-9136
Diann Stienbarger, Pr
Doug Younce, VP
Pam Younce, Sec
Gerry Stienbarger, Treas
EMP: 3 EST: 1993
SALES (est): 334.7K **Privately Held**
SIC: 2754 7336 7389 3089 Commercial printing, gravure; Silk screen design; Embroidery advertising; Engraving of plastics

(G-10154)
WAUSEON MCHNE&MFG-KNDLVLLE DIV
708 S Orchard St (46755-2022)
PHONE.................................260 347-5095
Douglas A Weddelman, Pr
EMP: 20 EST: 2003
SALES (est): 1.88MM **Privately Held**
SIC: 3599 Machine shop, jobbing and repair

(G-10155)
WOLFPACK CHASSIS LLC
800 Weston Ave (46755)
PHONE.................................260 349-1887
Steve Hawk Junior, Pr
EMP: 30 EST: 2011
SALES (est): 2.56MM
SALES (corp-wide): 3.78B **Publicly Held**
Web: www.wolfpackchassis.com
SIC: 3315 3792 Steel wire and related products; Camping trailers and chassis
HQ: Lippert Components, Inc.
    3501 County Rd 6 E
    Elkhart IN 46514
    574 535-1125

(G-10156)
YANFENG US AUTO INTR SYSTEMS I
Also Called: YANFENG US AUTOMOTIVE INTERIOR SYSTEMS I LLC
300 S Progress Dr E (46755-3266)
PHONE.................................260 347-0500
Bart Alexander, Mgr
EMP: 68
SQ FT: 60,000
Web: www.yanfeng.com
SIC: 3089 Injection molding of plastics
HQ: Yanfeng International Automotive Technology Us I Llc
    41935 W 12 Mile Rd
    Novi MI 48377
    248 319-7333

Kentland
Newton County

(G-10157)
BONNELL ALUMINUM INC
508 Wilson St (47951-9700)
P.O. Box 106 (47951-0106)
PHONE.................................815 351-6802
David Asher, Brnch Mgr
EMP: 760
SQ FT: 120,000
Web: www.bonnellaluminum.com
SIC: 3354 3471 3444 Aluminum extruded products; Plating and polishing; Sheet metalwork
HQ: Bonnell Aluminum, Inc.
    25 Bonnell St
    Newnan GA 30263
    770 253-2020

(G-10158)
CONTINENTAL MACHINING PDTS INC
306 S 3rd St (47951-1311)
PHONE.................................219 474-5061
Garry Hixson, Pr
Brad Hixson, VP
Alan Adwell, Sec
EMP: 4 EST: 1990
SQ FT: 3,000
SALES (est): 250K **Privately Held**
Web: www.continental.com
SIC: 3544 Special dies and tools

(G-10159)
CPX INC
410 E Kent St (47951-8625)
PHONE.................................219 474-5280
Michael Sanders, Pr
Douglas K Miller, *
Mike Miller, *
▲ EMP: 350 EST: 1983
SQ FT: 40,000
SALES (est): 29.48MM **Privately Held**
Web: www.cpxinc.com
SIC: 3089 3694 Molding primary plastics; Harness wiring sets, internal combustion engines

(G-10160)
HOOSIER METAL POLISH INC
Also Called: Lehman Manufacturing
304 N Fairground Rd (47951)
P.O. Box 85 (47951-0085)
PHONE.................................219 474-6011
Luanne Watt, Pr
Keith E Watt, VP
Eric G Watt, CFO
EMP: 15 EST: 2005
SALES (est): 1.89MM **Privately Held**
Web: www.llc-equipment.com
SIC: 5084 3567 Industrial machinery and equipment; Ceramic kilns and furnaces

(G-10161)
PHILLIP WESTRICK
Also Called: Pw Apparel
101 E Lincoln St (47951-1130)
PHONE.................................219 232-8337
Phillip Westrick, Owner
EMP: 1 EST: 2008
SALES (est): 52.99K **Privately Held**
SIC: 2759 Commercial printing, nec

(G-10162)
PRMI 1 INC
Also Called: Ace Hardware
102 S 4th St (47951-1373)
P.O. Box 70 (60970-0070)
PHONE.................................219 474-5022
Daniel Martin, Pr
Samuel Martin Ii, Sec
Richard Martin, Ch
EMP: 7 EST: 1956
SQ FT: 3,000
SALES (est): 915.38K **Privately Held**
Web: www.peopleslbm.com
SIC: 3273 Ready-mixed concrete

(G-10163)
ROGERS GROUP INC
Also Called: Newton County Stone Co
235 E Us Highway 24 (47951-8623)
PHONE.................................219 474-5125
Tom Goyett, Superintnt
EMP: 57
SALES (corp-wide): 1.05B **Privately Held**
Web: www.rogersgroupincint.com
SIC: 1422 5032 3274 Limestones, ground; Stone, crushed or broken; Lime
PA: Rogers Group, Inc.
    421 Great Cir Rd
    Nashville TN 37228
    615 242-0585

(G-10164)
TRILL MACHINE LLC
104 W Washington St (47951-1154)
PHONE.................................219 730-0744
Joanne Mendes, Pt
Sean Patwell, Pt
EMP: 2 EST: 2013
SALES (est): 105.32K **Privately Held**
SIC: 7372 7389 Application computer software; Business Activities at Non-Commercial Site

Kewanna
Fulton County

(G-10165)
INDUSTRIAL MLDING CNSLTING DSI
Also Called: Manitou Plastics
630 E Main St (46939)
P.O. Box 506 (46939-0506)
PHONE..................574 653-2772
Terry Hobbs, *Pr*
Vida Kathryn Hobbs, *Sec*
EMP: 3 **EST:** 1995
SQ FT: 6,500
SALES (est): 298.3K **Privately Held**
Web: www.imcdinc.com
SIC: 3544 Special dies and tools

(G-10166)
KEWANNA METAL SPECIALTIES INC (PA)
419 W Main St (46939-9527)
P.O. Box 367 (46939-0367)
PHONE..................574 653-2554
Allen Finke, *Pr*
James B Finke, *
Jeffrey A Finke, *
EMP: 65 **EST:** 1959
SQ FT: 160,000
SALES (est): 9.15MM
SALES (corp-wide): 9.15MM **Privately Held**
Web: www.kmswire.com
SIC: 3496 Grilles and grillework, woven wire

(G-10167)
KEWANNA SCREEN PRINTING INC
109 Toner St (46939)
P.O. Box 397 (46939-0397)
PHONE..................574 653-2683
Carol J Hickle, *Pr*
Benjamin Fehrer, *VP*
Tammy Sue Fehrer, *Sec*
▼ **EMP:** 9 **EST:** 1961
SALES (est): 842.52K **Privately Held**
Web: www.ksprints.com
SIC: 2759 2396 Screen printing; Automotive and apparel trimmings

(G-10168)
WINAMAC COIL SPRING INC
512 N Smith St (46939-2039)
P.O. Box 278 (46939-0278)
PHONE..................574 653-2186
Daniel Pesaresi Senior, *Ch Bd*
Joseph Pesaresi, *
Gene Huber Junior, *VP Sls*
Daniel Pesaresi Senior, *Dir*
Barbara Huber, *
EMP: 194 **EST:** 1948
SQ FT: 120,000
SALES (est): 24.32MM **Privately Held**
Web: www.winamaccoilspring.com
SIC: 3495 3496 3493 Mechanical springs, precision; Miscellaneous fabricated wire products; Steel springs, except wire

Kimmell
Noble County

(G-10169)
BOYD MACHINE AND REPAIR CO
Also Called: Bmr Group
3794 W 50 S (46760)
P.O. Box 93 (46796)
PHONE..................260 635-2195
Larry L Boyd, *Pr*
Carolyn Boyd, *
Mark Boyd, *
Matthew J Boyd Sed, *Prin*
EMP: 30 **EST:** 1974
SQ FT: 50,000
SALES (est): 2.45MM **Privately Held**
Web: www.bmrgroup.net
SIC: 7699 3398 Industrial machinery and equipment repair; Metal heat treating

(G-10170)
LIGHT BEAM TECHNOLOGY INC
3794 W 50 S (46760-9766)
P.O. Box 308 (46796-0308)
PHONE..................260 635-2195
Larry L Boyd, *Pr*
EMP: 5 **EST:** 2005
SALES (est): 546.5K **Privately Held**
Web: www.bmrgroup.net
SIC: 3567 Industrial furnaces and ovens

(G-10171)
METZGER DAIRY INC
4837 W 100 S (46760-9679)
PHONE..................260 564-5445
Jack D Metzger, *Pr*
Jack J Metzger, *Pr*
John Metzger, *VP*
Susan Metzger, *Treas*
Kimery Metzger, *Sec*
EMP: 10 **EST:** 1994
SALES (est): 1.53MM **Privately Held**
SIC: 3556 Dairy and milk machinery

Kingman
Fountain County

(G-10172)
JRS WOOD SHOP
6950 W 1025 N (47952-7240)
PHONE..................765 498-2663
Kenneth Asbury, *Owner*
Kenneth Asbury Junior, *Owner*
EMP: 5 **EST:** 1999
SALES (est): 221.33K **Privately Held**
SIC: 2431 Trim, wood

(G-10173)
RIBBE WELDING & MFG INC
4526 S Odd St (47952-8335)
PHONE..................765 390-4044
Daniel L Ribbe, *Prin*
EMP: 1 **EST:** 2013
SALES (est): 60.55K **Privately Held**
SIC: 7692 3999 Welding repair; Manufacturing industries, nec

(G-10174)
STEEL GRIP INC
Also Called: Steel Grip Safety Apparel
42233 S Kingman Rd (47952)
P.O. Box 247 (47952-0247)
PHONE..................765 397-3344
Dick Minnette, *Mgr*
EMP: 3
SALES (corp-wide): 15.25MM **Privately Held**
Web: www.steelgripinc.com
SIC: 3842 2381 2326 Personal safety equipment; Fabric dress and work gloves; Men's and boy's work clothing
PA: Steel Grip, Inc.
1501 E Voorhees St
Danville IL 61832
217 442-6240

(G-10175)
YORK TANK AND MFG LLC
4438 S Roberts St (47952-8402)
PHONE..................765 401-0667
EMP: 11 **EST:** 2016
SALES (est): 937.08K **Privately Held**
SIC: 3999 Manufacturing industries, nec

Kingsbury
Laporte County

(G-10176)
D & M PRECISION MACHINING INC
1 Kingsbury Industrial Park, 7111 Union Center Road (46345)
P.O. Box 46 (46345-0046)
PHONE..................219 393-5132
Tonya Gross, *VP*
Ron Gross, *Pr*
EMP: 4 **EST:** 2008
SALES (est): 229.19K **Privately Held**
SIC: 3599 Machine shop, jobbing and repair

(G-10177)
ELECTRO CORP
1st Rd Kingsbury Industrial Park (46345)
P.O. Box 387 (46345-0387)
PHONE..................219 393-5571
Mitch Juszkiewicz, *Pr*
Linda Juszkiewicz, *Sec*
EMP: 13 **EST:** 1980
SQ FT: 15,000
SALES (est): 645.21K **Privately Held**
SIC: 7694 5063 3625 3621 Electric motor repair; Motors, electric; Relays and industrial controls; Motors and generators

(G-10178)
ENVIRONMENTAL PRODUCTS INC
Also Called: E P I
Fourth Road Kingsbury (46345)
P.O. Box 6 (46352-0006)
PHONE..................219 393-3446
Tom Robinson, *Pr*
◆ **EMP:** 10 **EST:** 1971
SALES (est): 944.7K **Privately Held**
SIC: 2522 2521 Chairs, office: padded or plain: except wood; Wood office furniture

(G-10179)
INDUSTRIAL MINT WLDG MACHINING (PA)
Also Called: Imw
2nd & Hupp Rd (46345)
PHONE..................219 393-5531
Matthew Sularski, *Pr*
Gene Berchem, *
Matthew Sularski, *VP*
Robert Sularski, *
Stephen Sularski, *
▲ **EMP:** 50 **EST:** 1972
SQ FT: 85,000
SALES (est): 24.79MM
SALES (corp-wide): 24.79MM **Privately Held**
Web: www.imwnet.com
SIC: 3569 3599 4212 7692 Assembly machines, non-metalworking; Machine shop, jobbing and repair; Heavy machinery transport, local; Welding repair

(G-10180)
MAYFIELD - GLENN GROUP INC
3999 Hupp Rd Bldg R23 (46345)
P.O. Box 388 (46345-0388)
PHONE..................219 393-7117
Rodney E Mayfield, *Pr*
Jim D Glenn, *Sec*
EMP: 17 **EST:** 1998
SQ FT: 11,000
SALES (est): 2.17MM **Privately Held**
SIC: 3599 Machine shop, jobbing and repair

(G-10181)
MC WLDG & MACHINING CO INC
I Kingsbury Industrial Park (46345)
PHONE..................219 393-5718
Marian Cetera, *Pr*
Martha Cetera, *VP*
EMP: 4 **EST:** 1995
SQ FT: 13,000
SALES (est): 441.71K **Privately Held**
Web: www.mcwelding.net
SIC: 3599 Machine shop, jobbing and repair

(G-10182)
NATIONAL PRODUCTS LLC
1st Rd Kingsbury Industrial Pk (46345)
P.O. Box 1701 (46352-1701)
PHONE..................219 393-5536
EMP: 5 **EST:** 1974
SALES (est): 219.71K **Privately Held**
Web: www.rammount.com
SIC: 7389 2842 Packaging and labeling services; Rug, upholstery, or dry cleaning detergents or spotters

(G-10183)
ON POINT MACHINING INC
7111 Union Center Rd (46345)
P.O. Box 46 (46345-0046)
PHONE..................219 393-5132
Matthew R Kalucki, *Pr*
EMP: 5 **EST:** 2015
SQ FT: 5,000
SALES (est): 387.16K **Privately Held**
Web: www.onpointmachining.net
SIC: 3599 Machine shop, jobbing and repair

(G-10184)
OPTA (USA) INC
5th Rd Bldg 4 (46345)
PHONE..................716 446-8888
EMP: 31
SALES (corp-wide): 4.67MM **Privately Held**
Web: www.optagroupllc.com
SIC: 2899 Metal treating compounds
HQ: Opta (Usa) Inc.
300 Corporate Pkwy 118n
Amherst NY 14226
716 446-8914

(G-10185)
R & R PLASTICS INC
4th Rd Kingsbury Industrial Park (46345)
P.O. Box 303 (46345-0303)
PHONE..................219 393-5505
Robert Jackson, *Pr*
Maynard Searing, *VP*
EMP: 52 **EST:** 1979
SQ FT: 72,000
SALES (est): 4.75MM **Privately Held**
SIC: 3089 Injection molding of plastics

Kingsford Heights
Laporte County

(G-10186)
PROTERO CORPORATION
Also Called: Dental Enterprises
605 Grayton Rd (46346-3330)
P.O. Box 600 (46346-0600)
PHONE..................219 393-5591
Jeffrey A Maki, *Pr*
EMP: 23 **EST:** 1988
SQ FT: 14,000
SALES (est): 2.48MM **Privately Held**
Web: www.dentalmodelsplus.com
SIC: 3843 Orthodontic appliances

Kirklin
Clinton County

(G-10187)
CARMEL ENGINEERING INC
413 E Madison St (46050-9028)
P.O. Box 67 (46050-0067)
PHONE..................................765 279-8955
Paul Weaver, *CEO*
Sonny Brunes, *Pr*
Randy Weaver, *VP*
Arlene Weaver, *Sec*
EMP: 12 EST: 1979
SQ FT: 1,200
SALES (est): 2.3MM **Privately Held**
Web: www.carmeleng.com
SIC: 1799 3599 3556 3443 Food service equipment installation; Custom machinery; Food products machinery; Fabricated plate work (boiler shop)

(G-10188)
E & R MFG CO INC
504 N Illinois St (46050)
P.O. Box 68 (46050-0068)
PHONE..................................765 279-8826
Paul Mangis, *Pr*
Ronald E Neese, *Sec*
Martha Mangis, *Ch*
EMP: 8 EST: 1954
SQ FT: 13,000
SALES (est): 674.56K **Privately Held**
SIC: 3559 Stone working machinery

(G-10189)
EXCEL TOOL & ENGINEERING LLC
307 S Main St (46050-9735)
P.O. Box 5 (46050-0005)
PHONE..................................765 279-8528
EMP: 6 EST: 1997
SQ FT: 7,000
SALES (est): 789.34K **Privately Held**
Web: www.exceltoolandengineering.com
SIC: 3599 Machine shop, jobbing and repair

(G-10190)
KIRKLIN WASTE WATER TREATMENT
800 North Main Street (46050)
P.O. Box 147 (46050-0147)
PHONE..................................765 279-5251
EMP: 4 EST: 2007
SALES (est): 132.64K **Privately Held**
Web: www.kirklinindiana.org
SIC: 3589 Water treatment equipment, industrial

(G-10191)
KNOTHOLE WOODWORKS LLC
223 W Henry Rd (46050-9413)
PHONE..................................317 600-8151
Bryan Essex, *Owner*
EMP: 2 EST: 2011
SALES (est): 135.64K **Privately Held**
SIC: 2431 Millwork

(G-10192)
STOWERS WLDG INDUS PIPING LLC
6103 S County Road 980 E (46050-9029)
PHONE..................................765 279-5002
Mark Stowers, *Prin*
EMP: 1 EST: 2013
SALES (est): 32.38K **Privately Held**
SIC: 7692 Welding repair

Knightstown
Henry County

(G-10193)
BASTINS CUSTOM FABRICATING LLC
5002 W County Road 450 S (46148-9583)
PHONE..................................765 987-8385
Ron Bastin, *Owner*
EMP: 2 EST: 2005
SALES (est): 225.24K **Privately Held**
Web: www.bastinscustomfab.com
SIC: 3441 Fabricated structural metal

(G-10194)
BEVER WLDG & FABRICATION LLC
9653 S County Road 575 W (46148-9602)
PHONE..................................765 524-4597
EMP: 4 EST: 2016
SALES (est): 223.73K **Privately Held**
SIC: 7692 Welding repair

(G-10195)
GREENSBORO SAND & GRAVEL LLC
4497 W County Road 350 S (46148-9525)
PHONE..................................765 624-9342
EMP: 5 EST: 2005
SQ FT: 809,365
SALES (est): 800K **Privately Held**
Web: www.greensboro-sand-gravel.com
SIC: 1442 Gravel mining

(G-10196)
HARMONY WINERY
18 N Jefferson St (46148-1243)
PHONE..................................317 585-9463
Tatyana Croak, *Owner*
EMP: 4 EST: 2011
SALES (est): 175.67K **Privately Held**
Web: www.harmonywinery.com
SIC: 2084 Wines

(G-10197)
HOOSIER CONVEYOR COMPANY LLC
100 W Morgan St (46148-9363)
PHONE..................................765 445-3337
Greg Schombert, *Prin*
EMP: 7 EST: 2019
SALES (est): 369.28K **Privately Held**
Web: www.hoosierconveyorcompany.com
SIC: 3535 Conveyors and conveying equipment

(G-10198)
HY-FLEX CORPORATION
8774 In 109 (46148)
PHONE..................................765 571-5125
Ben Mills, *Pr*
Allen Mills, *
Esther Mills, *
EMP: 35 EST: 1964
SQ FT: 18,000
SALES (est): 5.46MM **Privately Held**
Web: www.hyflexcorp.com
SIC: 3561 3444 Industrial pumps and parts; Sheet metalwork

(G-10199)
MAYHILL PUBLICATIONS INC (PA)
Also Called: Farmweek
27 N Jefferson St (46148-1242)
PHONE..................................765 345-5133
R Thomas Mayhill, *CEO*
Margaret A Mayhill, *
Gary A Thoe, *
Merry Thoe, *Stockholder**
EMP: 35 EST: 1867
SQ FT: 39,924
SALES (est): 4.81MM
SALES (corp-wide): 4.81MM **Privately Held**
Web: www.antiqueweek.com
SIC: 2711 Newspapers, publishing and printing

(G-10200)
MIDCOUNTRY MEDIA INC
27 N Jefferson St (46148)
P.O. Box 90 (46148)
PHONE..................................765 345-5133
EMP: 70 EST: 2009
SQ FT: 10,500
SALES (est): 4.15MM **Privately Held**
Web: www.midcountrymedia.com
SIC: 2711 2721 Job printing and newspaper publishing combined; Periodicals, publishing and printing

(G-10201)
PEPSICO INC
Also Called: Pepsico
7870 W County Road 850 S (46148-9511)
PHONE..................................765 345-7668
Marc Vaught, *Brnch Mgr*
EMP: 3
SALES (corp-wide): 86.39B **Publicly Held**
Web: www.pepsico.com
SIC: 2086 Carbonated soft drinks, bottled and canned
PA: Pepsico, Inc.
700 Anderson Hill Rd
Purchase NY 10577
914 253-2000

Knightsville
Clay County

(G-10202)
INTERIOR FIXS & MLLWK CO INC
995 E Barnett St (47857-8012)
P.O. Box 157 (47857-0157)
PHONE..................................812 446-0933
Ray Jones, *CEO*
EMP: 9 EST: 1973
SQ FT: 12,000
SALES (est): 996.08K **Privately Held**
Web: interiorfixtures.weebly.com
SIC: 2434 2431 Wood kitchen cabinets; Millwork

Knox
Starke County

(G-10203)
CARTERS MANUFACTURING & WELD
3270 S County Road 210 (46534-7965)
PHONE..................................630 464-1520
Carter Comella, *Prin*
EMP: 6 EST: 2012
SALES (est): 78.58K **Privately Held**
SIC: 3999 Manufacturing industries, nec

(G-10204)
DAUBERT VCI INC
1805 Pacific Ave (46534-9489)
PHONE..................................574 772-9310
M Lawrence Garman, *Pr*
EMP: 39
SALES (corp-wide): 54.68MM **Privately Held**
Web: www.daubertcromwell.com
SIC: 2672 Paper; coated and laminated, nec
HQ: Daubert Vci, Inc.
1333 Burr Ridge Pkwy # 200
Burr Ridge IL 60527
630 203-6800

(G-10205)
DRAGON INDUSTRIES INC
2180 E 400 S (46534-9760)
PHONE..................................574 772-2243
Michael J Bailey, *Prin*
EMP: 1 EST: 2005
SALES (est): 103.06K **Privately Held**
SIC: 3999 Manufacturing industries, nec

(G-10206)
DRAGON INDUSTRIES INCORPORATED
2120 E State Road 10 (46534-8512)
PHONE..................................574 772-3508
Mike Bailey, *Owner*
EMP: 3 EST: 2007
SALES (est): 141.65K **Privately Held**
SIC: 3999 Manufacturing industries, nec

(G-10207)
FIBER FORGED COMPOSITES LLC
1517 S 100 W (46534-9693)
PHONE..................................574 772-0107
Zachary Ingram, *Mgr*
EMP: 6 EST: 2019
SALES (est): 211.44K **Privately Held**
Web: www.fiberforgedcomposites.com
SIC: 3714 Motor vehicle parts and accessories

(G-10208)
FONTAINE TRAILER COMPANY
Also Called: Fontaine Trailer Company
1201 W Culver Rd (46534-8558)
PHONE..................................574 772-6673
EMP: 3
SALES (corp-wide): 364.48B **Publicly Held**
Web: www.fontainetrailer.com
SIC: 3715 Trailer bodies
HQ: Fontaine Commercial Trailer, Inc.
430 Sam Letson Indus Rd
Haleyville AL 35565
205 486-5251

(G-10209)
GARY POPPINS LLC
Also Called: Gary Poppins Popcorn
4055 E 250 N (46534-9605)
P.O. Box 5153 (85261-5153)
PHONE..................................866 354-1300
Brian Lipner, *Managing Member*
EMP: 25 EST: 2003
SALES (est): 2.98MM **Privately Held**
Web: www.garypoppins.com
SIC: 2096 2064 Popcorn, already popped (except candy covered); Popcorn balls or other treated popcorn products

(G-10210)
HOOSIER CUSTOM PLASTICS LLC
Also Called: Eco Golf
201 Hamilton Dr (46534-8118)
PHONE..................................574 772-2120
Gordon Schenk, *Managing Member*
Mike Tetzlofs, *
Craig Dulworth, *
▲ EMP: 35 EST: 2004
SQ FT: 16,000
SALES (est): 4.55MM **Privately Held**
Web: www.hcplastic.com
SIC: 3089 Injection molding of plastics

Knox - Starke County (G-10211)   GEOGRAPHIC SECTION

(G-10211)
INDIANA FINE BLANKING
1200 Kloeckner Dr (46534-7500)
P.O. Box 409 (46534-0409)
PHONE..................574 772-3850
Alex Weisheit, *Manager*
EMP: 2 **EST:** 2010
SALES (est): 160.77K **Privately Held**
SIC: 3469 Stamping metal for the trade

(G-10212)
JW HICKS INC
20 Kloeckner Dr (46534-8107)
PHONE..................574 772-7755
James W Hicks, *Pr*
James W Hicks, *Pr*
Jillayne Hicks, *
▲ **EMP:** 35 **EST:** 1992
SQ FT: 20,000
SALES (est): 2.06MM **Privately Held**
SIC: 3297 Castable refractories, nonclay

(G-10213)
KNOX FERTILIZER COMPANY INC
Also Called: Knox
2660 E 100 S (46534-8768)
P.O. Box 248 (46534-0248)
PHONE..................574 772-6275
Robert Shaw Junior, *Pr*
Mark C Shaw, *Sec*
◆ **EMP:** 115 **EST:** 1950
SALES (est): 49.92MM **Privately Held**
Web: www.knoxfert.com
SIC: 0782 2873 Lawn and garden services; Nitrogenous fertilizers

(G-10214)
KRUZ INC (PA)
Also Called: Kruz
1201 W Culver Rd (46534-8558)
P.O. Box 129 (46534-0129)
PHONE..................574 772-6673
Kent P Kruzick, *Pr*
Diane K Kruzick Secrt, *Prin*
Kent Kruzick, *Prin*
▲ **EMP:** 40 **EST:** 1998
SQ FT: 63,000
SALES (est): 9.7MM
SALES (corp-wide): 9.7MM **Privately Held**
Web: www.kruzinc.com
SIC: 3713 3715 Dump truck bodies; Truck trailers

(G-10215)
MPI ENGINEERED TECH LLC
1200 Kloeckner Dr (46534-7500)
PHONE..................574 772-3850
Susana Lewis, *Corporate Controller*
EMP: 350 **EST:** 2019
SALES (est): 24.58MM **Privately Held**
SIC: 3469 Machine parts, stamped or pressed metal

(G-10216)
MPI ENGINEERED TECH WIN LLC
Also Called: Indiana Fine Blanking
1200 Kloeckner Dr (46534-7500)
PHONE..................574 772-3850
Trevor Myers, *Pr*
EMP: 3
SQ FT: 50,000
SALES (corp-wide): 447.38MM **Privately Held**
SIC: 3469 3465 Stamping metal for the trade; Automotive stampings
HQ: Mpi Engineered Technologies Win Llc
101 N Grand Ave
Deerfield WI 53531

(G-10217)
MPI PRODUCTS HOLDINGS LLC (DH)
1200 Kloeckner Dr (46534-7500)
PHONE..................248 237-3007
Steven Crain, *Pr*
Mike Putz, *CFO*
EMP: 6 **EST:** 2012
SALES (est): 266.85MM
SALES (corp-wide): 447.38MM **Privately Held**
SIC: 3448 Prefabricated metal components
HQ: Mpi Global Holdings Corp.
1351 Silhavy Rd Ste 201
Valparaiso IN 46383
248 237-3007

(G-10218)
MPI PRODUCTS LLC
1200 Kloeckner Dr (46534)
PHONE..................248 237-3007
Trevor Meyers, *Managing Member*
EMP: 45 **EST:** 1969
SALES (est): 5.97MM **Privately Held**
Web: www.mpiproducts.com
SIC: 3365 Machinery castings, aluminum

(G-10219)
PHILIP KONRAD & SONS INC
1315 E State Road 10 (46534-8506)
PHONE..................574 772-3966
Phillip W Konrad, *Pr*
Donald P Konrad, *VP*
Dennis P Konrad, *Sec*
Carole Konrad, *VP*
EMP: 11 **EST:** 1957
SQ FT: 16,000
SALES (est): 393.37K **Privately Held**
SIC: 2431 2434 Millwork; Wood kitchen cabinets

(G-10220)
REAGENT CHEMICAL & RES INC
Also Called: Reagent Chemical & Research, Inc.
317 Kloeckner Dr (46534-7720)
PHONE..................574 772-7424
EMP: 100
SALES (corp-wide): 384.87MM **Privately Held**
Web: www.reagentchemical.com
SIC: 2819 Industrial inorganic chemicals, nec
HQ: Reagent Chemical & Research, Llc
115 Us Hwy 202
Ringoes NJ 08551
908 284-2800

(G-10221)
REAGENT CHEMICAL & RES INC
REAGENT CHEMICAL & RESEARCH, INC.
1705 Pacific Ave (46534-1001)
PHONE..................574 772-7424
EMP: 2
SALES (corp-wide): 384.87MM **Privately Held**
Web: www.reagentchemical.com
SIC: 3949 2819 Targets, archery and rifle shooting; Sulfur, recovered or refined, incl. from sour natural gas
HQ: Reagent Chemical & Research, Llc
115 Us Hwy 202
Ringoes NJ 08551
908 284-2800

(G-10222)
SABRE MANUFACTURING LLC
5420 E State Road 8 (46534-9696)
PHONE..................574 772-5380
EMP: 130
Web: www.sabremfg.com
SIC: 3443 Containers, shipping (bombs, etc.): metal plate

(G-10223)
SCP BUILDING PRODUCTS LLC
Also Called: Barber & Ross of Indiana
1001 W Culver Rd (46534-8553)
PHONE..................574 772-2955
EMP: 5 **EST:** 2006
SALES (est): 652.34K **Privately Held**
Web: www.rockwellwindows.com
SIC: 2431 Millwork

(G-10224)
SILLS CUSTOM WORKS & FAB LLC
6082 E 25 N (46534-8730)
PHONE..................219 200-9813
EMP: 1
SALES (est): 70.37K **Privately Held**
SIC: 2514 7389 Metal household furniture; Business services, nec

(G-10225)
SPECIALTY SHOPPE
640 S 800 E (46534-9656)
PHONE..................574 772-7873
Robin Marshall, *Owner*
Susan A Marshall, *Mgr*
EMP: 2
SALES (est): 111.53K **Privately Held**
SIC: 5999 2396 7389 Trophies and plaques; Fabric printing and stamping; Engraving service

(G-10226)
SPORTS UNLIMITED PRINTED AP
6 S Cleveland St (46534-2402)
PHONE..................574 772-4239
Albert Einstein, *Owner*
EMP: 6 **EST:** 2001
SALES (est): 159.67K **Privately Held**
SIC: 2759 Screen printing

(G-10227)
V & H FIBERGLASS REPAIR
680 N Us Highway 35 (46534-8932)
PHONE..................574 772-4920
EMP: 2 **EST:** 1984
SALES (est): 92.14K **Privately Held**
SIC: 3229 Glass fiber products

(G-10228)
WESTROCK CP LLC
Also Called: Rocktenn-Knox
6595 E State Road 10 (46534-8462)
PHONE..................574 772-5545
Wes Lenig, *Genl Mgr*
EMP: 34
SQ FT: 50,000
SALES (corp-wide): 20.31B **Privately Held**
Web: www.westrock.com
SIC: 2653 Boxes, corrugated: made from purchased materials
HQ: Westrock Cp, Llc
1000 Abernathy Rd Ste 125
Atlanta GA 30328

(G-10229)
Z RODZ & CUSTOMS LLC
4015 E 200 N (46534-8920)
PHONE..................574 806-5774
EMP: 5 **EST:** 2011
SALES (est): 68.96K **Privately Held**
Web: www.zrodz.com
SIC: 7641 3449 5084 Antique furniture repair and restoration; Bars, concrete reinforcing: fabricated steel; Metal refining machinery and equipment

Kokomo
Howard County

(G-10230)
4EVER CHOSEN LLC
2300 S Berkley Rd (46902-8021)
PHONE..................765 431-7548
EMP: 1
SALES (est): 60.62K **Privately Held**
SIC: 7389 3161 Business Activities at Non-Commercial Site; Clothing and apparel carrying cases

(G-10231)
A D I SCREEN PRINTING
6776 W 00 Ns (46901)
PHONE..................765 457-8580
Larry Amthauer, *Owner*
EMP: 7 **EST:** 1980
SALES (est): 446.37K **Privately Held**
Web: adi.imprintableapparel.com
SIC: 2261 2395 Screen printing of cotton broadwoven fabrics; Embroidery and art needlework

(G-10232)
ALLIED TUBE & CONDUIT CORP
101 E Broadway St (46901-2919)
PHONE..................765 459-8811
Richard Paul, *Mgr*
EMP: 10
Web: www.atkore.com
SIC: 3312 3498 Tubes, steel and iron; Fabricated pipe and fittings
HQ: Allied Tube & Conduit Corporation
16100 S Center Ave
Harvey IL 60426
708 339-1610

(G-10233)
APTIV SERVICES US LLC
Also Called: Delphi
2705 S Goyer Rd (46902-7403)
P.O. Box 9005 (46904-9005)
PHONE..................765 451-5011
EMP: 572
SALES (corp-wide): 20.05B **Privately Held**
Web: www.aptiv.com
SIC: 3714 Motor vehicle parts and accessories
HQ: Aptiv Services Us, Llc
5725 Innovation Dr
Troy MI 48098

(G-10234)
B & D MANUFACTURING INC
2100 E Carter St (46901-5660)
PHONE..................765 452-2761
Mike Green, *Pr*
EMP: 6 **EST:** 1967
SQ FT: 10,000
SALES (est): 917.76K **Privately Held**
Web: www.bdmfgmolds.com
SIC: 3544 Special dies and tools

(G-10235)
BEACHY MACHINE INC
Also Called: Beachy Performance Parts
175 E North St (46901-2958)
PHONE..................765 452-9051
Ezra M Beachy, *Pr*
Michael Beachy, *VP*
EMP: 5 **EST:** 1970
SQ FT: 1,800
SALES (est): 352.22K **Privately Held**
SIC: 3714 Motor vehicle engines and parts

Kokomo - Howard County (G-10263)

(G-10236)
BEACHY MACHINE SHOP LLC
3884 E 400 N (46901-9359)
PHONE..................................765 452-9051
Ezra Beachy, Pr
EMP: 6 EST: 1990
SALES (est): 464.69K Privately Held
SIC: 3462 Automotive forgings, ferrous: crankshaft, engine, axle, etc.

(G-10237)
BEACON MANUFACTURING INC
2200 N Calumet St (46901-1673)
PHONE..................................765 753-0265
Brian Dehaven, CEO
EMP: 1 EST: 2014
SALES (est): 82.32K Privately Held
SIC: 3599 Machine shop, jobbing and repair

(G-10238)
BELCHER TOBIAH
Also Called: Push Enterprises
906 Danbury Dr (46901-1566)
PHONE..................................765 513-2211
Tobiah Belcher, Owner
EMP: 1 EST: 2014
SALES (est): 26K Privately Held
SIC: 2841 Soap and other detergents

(G-10239)
BLUE CREEK TRAIL MAP CO
3506 Hawthorne Ln (46902-4521)
PHONE..................................765 455-9867
Archie Wills, Prin
EMP: 2 EST: 2008
SALES (est): 162.76K Privately Held
SIC: 2752 Maps, lithographed

(G-10240)
BORGWARNER NOBLESVILLE LLC
Also Called: Production Plant
2151 E Lincoln Rd (46902-3773)
PHONE..................................765 451-0400
EMP: 7
SALES (corp-wide): 14.2B Publicly Held
Web: www.phinia.com
SIC: 3714 Motor vehicle parts and accessories
HQ: Borgwarner Noblesville Llc
3850 Hamlin Rd
Auburn Hills MI

(G-10241)
BORGWARNER PROPULSION II LLC
Also Called: Kokomo Power Electronics
1501 E 200 N (46901-8909)
PHONE..................................765 236-0025
Lisa Hardwick, Brnch Mgr
EMP: 1
SALES (corp-wide): 14.2B Publicly Held
Web: www.phinia.com
SIC: 3714 Motor vehicle parts and accessories
HQ: Borgwarner Propulsion Ii Llc
3850 Hamlin Rd
Auburn Hills MI 48326
248 754-9200

(G-10242)
BRYANT ICE CO INC
824 S Armstrong St (46901-5328)
PHONE..................................765 459-4543
Daniel J Bryant, Pr
EMP: 3 EST: 2000
SALES (est): 232.94K Privately Held
SIC: 2097 Ice cubes

(G-10243)
CENTRAL BRACE & LIMB CO INC
802 S Berkley Rd Ste B (46901-5110)
PHONE..................................765 457-4868
Ann Vent, Brnch Mgr
EMP: 3
SALES (corp-wide): 2.38MM Privately Held
Web: www.centralbraceandlimb.com
SIC: 3842 Limbs, artificial
PA: Central Brace & Limb Co., Inc.
1901 N Capitol Ave
Indianapolis IN 46202
317 925-4296

(G-10244)
CIL ELECTRONICS LLC
Also Called: Csi Electronics
1942 S Elizabeth St (46902-2432)
PHONE..................................765 457-3894
Dave Newcomer, CFO
EMP: 28 EST: 2019
SALES (est): 3.25MM Privately Held
Web: www.csielectronics.com
SIC: 3672 Printed circuit boards

(G-10245)
CLIFFORD SIGNS INC
3040 S Lafountain St (46902-3708)
PHONE..................................765 453-0745
Patrick Clifford, Pr
EMP: 18 EST: 1997
SALES (est): 1.28MM Privately Held
Web: www.cliffordsigns.com
SIC: 3993 Signs and advertising specialties

(G-10246)
COAN ENGINEERING LLC
2277 E North St (46901)
PHONE..................................765 456-3957
EMP: 30 EST: 1976
SALES (est): 3.89MM Privately Held
Web: www.coanracing.com
SIC: 3714 Power transmission equipment, motor vehicle

(G-10247)
COAST OEM LLC
2500 N Union St (46901-5836)
PHONE..................................765 553-5904
EMP: 6 EST: 2017
SALES (est): 220K Privately Held
SIC: 3261 Vitreous plumbing fixtures

(G-10248)
COCA COLA BTLG CO KOKOMO IND (PA)
Also Called: Coca-Cola
2305 Davis Rd (46901)
P.O. Box 1049 (46901)
PHONE..................................765 457-4421
Edmond P Severns Junior, Pr
Virginia Severns, *
▲ EMP: 72 EST: 1915
SQ FT: 70,000
SALES (est): 885.15K
SALES (corp-wide): 885.15K Privately Held
Web: www.cckokomo.com
SIC: 2086 Bottled and canned soft drinks

(G-10249)
COMMUNITY HOLDINGS INDIANA INC
620 S Berkley Rd (46901-5144)
PHONE..................................765 457-4130
EMP: 1
SALES (corp-wide): 34.97B Privately Held
Web: www.heraldbulletin.com
SIC: 2711 Newspapers: publishing only, not printed on site
HQ: Community Holdings Of Indiana, Inc.
3500 Colonnade Pkwy # 600
Birmingham AL 35243

(G-10250)
COUNTY LINE COMPANIES LLC
4815 S 100 W (46902-9552)
PHONE..................................866 959-7866
Amanda Steinbrunner, Prin
EMP: 1 EST: 2017
SALES (est): 237.46K Privately Held
SIC: 3599 Amusement park equipment

(G-10251)
CTO PUBLISHING LLC
306 S Main St Apt 207 (46901-5872)
P.O. Box 5 (46903-0005)
PHONE..................................765 210-8290
EMP: 2 EST: 2008
SALES (est): 72.12K Privately Held
Web: www.ctobooks.com
SIC: 2741 Miscellaneous publishing

(G-10252)
CUMULUS INTRMDATE HOLDINGS INC
Also Called: Sign Pro
4834 N Parkway (46901-3970)
PHONE..................................765 452-5704
Bob Wall, Brnch Mgr
EMP: 3
Web: www.cumulusmedia.com
SIC: 3993 Signs and advertising specialties
PA: Cumulus Intermediate Holdings Llc
3280 Peachtree Rd Ne # 23
Atlanta GA 30305

(G-10253)
CUSTOM BUILT BARNS INC (PA)
Also Called: Custom Built Storage Sheds
2312 N Plate St (46901-1692)
PHONE..................................765 457-9037
John D Bass, Pr
EMP: 2 EST: 1975
SQ FT: 2,300
SALES (est): 524.97K
SALES (corp-wide): 524.97K Privately Held
Web: www.cbbarns.com
SIC: 2452 2511 Prefabricated buildings, wood; Wood lawn and garden furniture

(G-10254)
CUSTOM WOOD CREATIONS LLC
2913 E Center Rd (46902-9795)
PHONE..................................765 860-1983
Larry L Baker, Owner
EMP: 4 EST: 2018
SALES (est): 120.84K Privately Held
Web: www.kokomowoodcreations.com
SIC: 2431 Millwork

(G-10255)
DELCO ELECTRONICS
3700 Orleans Dr (46902-4344)
PHONE..................................765 455-9713
Pete Moody, Engr
EMP: 6 EST: 2017
SALES (est): 134.47K Privately Held
Web: www.aecouncil.com
SIC: 3714 Motor vehicle parts and accessories

(G-10256)
DELPHI ELECTRONICS SAFETY
1705 Greenacres Dr (46901-9549)
PHONE..................................765 883-7795
EMP: 7 EST: 2019
SALES (est): 146.06K Privately Held
Web: www.borgwarner.com
SIC: 3714 Motor vehicle parts and accessories

(G-10257)
DELPHI TECHNOLOGIES
5514 Four Mile Dr (46901-3893)
PHONE..................................765 451-0670
EMP: 10 EST: 2018
SALES (est): 136.24K Privately Held
Web: www.phinia.com
SIC: 3714 Motor vehicle parts and accessories

(G-10258)
DELPHI TECHNOLOGIES
1008 Pinoak Dr (46901-6437)
PHONE..................................765 480-1993
EMP: 25 EST: 2018
SALES (est): 119.25K Privately Held
Web: www.phinia.com
SIC: 3714 Motor vehicle parts and accessories

(G-10259)
DROPEM GAME CALLS
1003 N Forest Dr (46901-1875)
PHONE..................................765 513-7667
Frank Sears, Prin
EMP: 4 EST: 2017
SALES (est): 56.1K Privately Held
SIC: 3949 Game calls

(G-10260)
DUPOUY ENTERPRISES LLC
Also Called: Jet Black
2215 Carr Dr (46902-9543)
PHONE..................................765 453-1466
EMP: 2 EST: 2003
SQ FT: 1,800
SALES (est): 165.82K Privately Held
SIC: 2952 Asphalt felts and coatings

(G-10261)
ECHELBARGER MACHINING CO LLC
Also Called: Echelbrger Precision Machining
2614 Precision Dr (46902)
PHONE..................................765 252-1965
Brian Echelbarger, Managing Member
EMP: 7 EST: 2010
SQ FT: 8,000
SALES (est): 630.76K Privately Held
Web: www.epm-emc.com
SIC: 3599 Machine shop, jobbing and repair

(G-10262)
ELECTRONIC SERVICES LLC
1942 S Elizabeth St (46902-2432)
PHONE..................................765 457-3894
Shep Beyland, Mng Pt
Patricia A Beyland, VP
EMP: 32 EST: 1990
SQ FT: 11,600
SALES (est): 4.95MM Privately Held
Web: www.csielectronics.com
SIC: 1731 3679 General electrical contractor; Electronic circuits

(G-10263)
ENGINEERED CONVEYORS INC (PA)
1055 Home Ave (46902-1624)
P.O. Box 1112 (46903-1112)
PHONE..................................765 459-4545
Eric Puckebaum, Ch Bd
EMP: 16 EST: 1983
SQ FT: 12,500
SALES (est): 4.82MM
SALES (corp-wide): 4.82MM Privately Held
Web: www.engineeredconveyors.com
SIC: 1796 3441 Machinery installation; Fabricated structural metal

Kokomo - Howard County (G-10264)

(G-10264)
FCA NORTH AMERICA HOLDINGS LLC
Also Called: Chrysler Foundry
1947 S Elizabeth St (46902-2431)
PHONE...............................765 454-0018
Bob Bowers, Brnch Mgr
EMP: 263
Web: www.stellantis.com
SIC: 3365 3714 3519 3325 Aluminum foundries; Motor vehicle parts and accessories; Internal combustion engines, nec; Steel foundries, nec
HQ: Fca Us Llc
1000 Chrysler Dr
Auburn Hills MI 48326

(G-10265)
FCA NORTH AMERICA HOLDINGS LLC
Also Called: Chrysler Transmission
2401 S Reed Rd (46902-7902)
P.O. Box 9007 (46904-9007)
PHONE...............................765 454-1705
Dan Grizzle, Prin
EMP: 53
Web: www.stellantis.com
SIC: 3714 Motor vehicle transmissions, drive assemblies, and parts
HQ: Fca Us Llc
1000 Chrysler Dr
Auburn Hills MI 48326

(G-10266)
FCA NORTH AMERICA HOLDINGS LLC
3660 State Rd 931 (46901)
PHONE...............................765 854-4234
Jeremy Keaping, Brnch Mgr
EMP: 1
Web: www.stellantis.com
SIC: 3714 Transmissions, motor vehicle
HQ: Fca North America Holdings Llc
1000 Chrysler Dr
Auburn Hills MI 48326

(G-10267)
FCA US LLC
Also Called: Kokomo Casting Plant
1001 E Boulevard (46902-5740)
P.O. Box 9007 (46904-9007)
PHONE...............................765 454-1005
EMP: 217
Web: www.stellantis.com
SIC: 3714 3365 3363 Motor vehicle parts and accessories; Aluminum foundries; Aluminum die-castings
HQ: Fca Us Llc
1000 Chrysler Dr
Auburn Hills MI 48326

(G-10268)
G & J
Also Called: Handle Bar, The
1252 N Main St (46901-2849)
PHONE...............................765 457-9889
Sherri Dewitt, Mgr
EMP: 3 EST: 1995
SALES (est): 228.74K Privately Held
SIC: 2499 Handles, wood

(G-10269)
GM COMPONENTS HOLDINGS LLC
Gmch Kokomo Fab 3
2150 E Lincoln Rd (46902-3774)
P.O. Box 9005 (46904-9005)
PHONE...............................765 451-5011
EMP: 5
SIC: 3694 Automotive electrical equipment, nec

HQ: Gm Components Holdings, Llc
300 Renaissance Ctr
Detroit MI 48243

(G-10270)
GM COMPONENTS HOLDINGS LLC
Also Called: Kokomo Electronic Assembly
2100 E Lincoln Rd (46902-3774)
PHONE...............................765 451-8440
Steve Hartwig, Manager
EMP: 1
Web: www.gm.com
SIC: 3714 Motor vehicle parts and accessories
HQ: Gm Components Holdings, Llc
300 Renaissance Ctr
Detroit MI 48243

(G-10271)
GOUDY BROS BOILER CO INC
100 W Spraker St (46901-2240)
P.O. Box 537 (46903-0537)
PHONE...............................765 459-4416
Vicki Spall, Pr
Donald Spall, Sec
Jeffrey Spall Ii, Stockholder
EMP: 9 EST: 1919
SQ FT: 10,000
SALES (est): 239.02K Privately Held
SIC: 7699 3446 3444 3443 Gas appliance repair service; Architectural metalwork; Sheet metalwork; Fabricated plate work (boiler shop)

(G-10272)
GRAPHICS LAB UV PRINTING INC
Also Called: Throttle Jockey
1041 S Union St (46902-1630)
PHONE...............................765 457-5784
Robert Davis, Pr
Matthew Davis, VP
Jamie Lubben, Sec
EMP: 10 EST: 1983
SALES (est): 852.99K Privately Held
Web: www.graphicslab.com
SIC: 2759 5571 Screen printing; Motorcycle dealers

(G-10273)
GREEN CUBES TECHNOLOGY LLC (PA)
Also Called: Green Cubes Tech
2121 E Boulevard (46902-2402)
PHONE...............................502 416-1060
Keith Washington, Pr
Mohammed Alobaidi, *
◆ EMP: 47 EST: 2007
SALES (est): 34.51MM Privately Held
Web: www.greencubestech.com
SIC: 3679 Electronic loads and power supplies

(G-10274)
H & H PARTNERSHIP INC
Also Called: Fast Land Food
174 E North St (46901-2959)
PHONE...............................765 513-4739
Charnpreet Kaur, Pr
Inderjit Singh, VP
EMP: 5 EST: 2009
SQ FT: 3,000
SALES (est): 318.33K Privately Held
SIC: 7215 2032 2092 Laundry, coin-operated; Chicken broth: packaged in cans, jars, etc.; Prepared fish or other seafood cakes and sticks

(G-10275)
H & R INDUSTRIAL LLC
Also Called: H & R Industrial
832 S Berkley Rd (46901-5110)

PHONE...............................765 868-8408
Steve Hearn, Managing Member
Scott Ronk, *
EMP: 72 EST: 2006
SALES (est): 9.89MM Privately Held
Web: www.hrindust.com
SIC: 3441 Fabricated structural metal

(G-10276)
HARVEY HINKLEMEYERS
1554 S Dixon Rd (46902-5997)
PHONE...............................765 452-1942
Harvey Hinklemeyers, Owner
Harvey Hinklemeyers, Prin
EMP: 2 EST: 2004
SALES (est): 72.34K Privately Held
Web: www.harveyhinklemeyers.com
SIC: 5812 2099 Family restaurants; Food preparations, nec

(G-10277)
HAYNES INTERNATIONAL INC
2000 W Defenbaugh St (46902-6015)
P.O. Box 9013 (46904-9013)
PHONE...............................765 457-3790
August Cigan, VP
EMP: 308
SALES (corp-wide): 589.96MM Publicly Held
Web: www.haynesintl.com
SIC: 3356 Gold and gold alloy: rolling, drawing, or extruding
PA: Haynes International, Inc.
1020 W Park Ave
Kokomo IN 46904
765 456-6000

(G-10278)
HAYNES INTERNATIONAL INC (PA)
Also Called: Haynes
1020 W Park Ave (46904)
P.O. Box 9013 (46904)
PHONE...............................765 456-6000
Michael L Shor, Pr
Robert H Getz, Non-Executive Chairman of the Board*
Daniel W Maudlin, VP Fin
Gregory W Tipton, CIO
David S Van Bibber, CAO
▲ EMP: 748 EST: 1912
SALES (est): 589.96MM
SALES (corp-wide): 589.96MM Publicly Held
Web: www.haynesintl.com
SIC: 3312 3356 Blast furnaces and steel mills; Nickel

(G-10279)
HAYNES INTERNATIONAL INC
527 E Lincoln Rd (46902-3742)
PHONE...............................765 450-4310
Lee Mumaw, Mgr
EMP: 7
SALES (corp-wide): 589.96MM Publicly Held
Web: www.haynesintl.com
SIC: 3312 Blast furnaces and steel mills
PA: Haynes International, Inc.
1020 W Park Ave
Kokomo IN 46904
765 456-6000

(G-10280)
HMH MANUFACTURING LLC
832 S Berkley Rd (46901-5110)
PHONE...............................765 553-5447
Derek Miller, Prin
EMP: 4 EST: 2018
SALES (est): 94.68K Privately Held
SIC: 3999 Manufacturing industries, nec

(G-10281)
HOOSIER SPLINE BROACH CORP
1401 Touby Pike (46902-2503)
P.O. Box 538 (46903-0538)
PHONE...............................765 452-8273
Gilbert Larison, Pr
Jeff Larison, VP
Mary Larison, Sec
Linda Lovell, Admn
EMP: 22 EST: 1971
SQ FT: 15,000
SALES (est): 1.61MM Privately Held
Web: www.hoosierbroach.com
SIC: 3545 7692 3541 Machine tool attachments and accessories; Welding repair; Machine tools, metal cutting type

(G-10282)
HOROHO PRINTING COMPANY INC
500 N Philips St (46901-4259)
PHONE...............................765 452-8862
Merrill L Horoho, Pr
Gregory E Horoho, VP
Marjorie Horoho, Sec
Linda Beachy, Treas
EMP: 4 EST: 1979
SQ FT: 2,016
SALES (est): 331.05K Privately Held
Web: www.horohoprinting.com
SIC: 2752 Offset printing

(G-10283)
HOWARD PRINT SHOP LLC
2111 W Alto Rd (46902-4810)
PHONE...............................765 453-6161
David Howard, Owner
EMP: 6 EST: 1987
SQ FT: 2,000
SALES (est): 550K Privately Held
Web: www.howardps.com
SIC: 2752 2791 2789 Offset printing; Typesetting; Bookbinding and related work

(G-10284)
IDEAL INC
Also Called: Ideal Janitor Supply
1037 S Union St (46902-1630)
P.O. Box 203 (46903-0203)
PHONE...............................765 457-6222
TOLL FREE: 800
Brad Bourff, Pr
EMP: 7 EST: 1961
SQ FT: 6,000
SALES (est): 834.43K Privately Held
Web: www.idealjanitor.com
SIC: 5087 2842 Janitors' supplies; Dusting cloths, chemically treated

(G-10285)
IDRA NORTH AMERICA INC
1510 Ann St (46901-2242)
PHONE...............................765 459-0085
Ricardo Ferario, Pr
EMP: 4 EST: 2007
SALES (est): 790.63K Privately Held
Web: www.idragroup.com
SIC: 3542 Die casting machines

(G-10286)
INDALEX INC
1500 E Murden St (46901-5667)
PHONE...............................765 457-1117
Tim Stubbs, CEO
EMP: 6 EST: 2017
SALES (est): 145.14K Privately Held
SIC: 3354 Aluminum extruded products

(G-10287)
INDIANA TRANSMISSION
3660 Us Highway 31 N (46901-5956)

GEOGRAPHIC SECTION   Kokomo - Howard County (G-10312)

PHONE..................765 854-4201
Jim Mullins, Prin
▲ EMP: 2 EST: 1997
SALES (est): 378.75K Privately Held
SIC: 3714 Motor vehicle parts and accessories

(G-10288)
INFINEON TECH AMERICAS CORP
2529 Commerce Dr Ste H (46902-7815)
PHONE..................866 951-9519
John Bartow, Mgr
EMP: 3
SALES (corp-wide): 17.72B Privately Held
Web: www-blue.infineon.com
SIC: 3674 Semiconductors and related devices
HQ: Infineon Technologies Americas Corp.
  101 N Pacific Coast Hwy
  El Segundo CA 90245
  310 726-8200

(G-10289)
INVESTWELL ELECTRONICS INC
329 E Firmin St (46902-2240)
PHONE..................765 457-1911
Bradley A Johnson, Pr
EMP: 4 EST: 2004
SQ FT: 6,000
SALES (est): 412.49K Privately Held
Web: www.investwellelectronics.com
SIC: 3679 Electronic circuits

(G-10290)
IRVING MATERIALS INC
Also Called: I M I
1315 S Dixon Rd (46902-6056)
PHONE..................765 452-4044
Gary Jones, Brnch Mgr
EMP: 7
SALES (corp-wide): 814.09MM Privately Held
Web: www.irvmat.com
SIC: 3273 Ready-mixed concrete
PA: Irving Materials, Inc.
  8032 N State Road 9
  Greenfield IN 46140
  317 326-3101

(G-10291)
IRVING MATERIALS INC
I M I
1420 S Union St (46902-1619)
PHONE..................765 922-7285
EMP: 10
SALES (corp-wide): 814.09MM Privately Held
Web: www.irvmat.com
SIC: 3273 1442 1611 3295 Ready-mixed concrete; Construction sand and gravel; Resurfacing contractor; Minerals, ground or treated
PA: Irving Materials, Inc.
  8032 N State Road 9
  Greenfield IN 46140
  317 326-3101

(G-10292)
KOKOMO METAL FABRICATORS INC
1931 E North St (46901-3169)
PHONE..................765 459-8173
Jeff Jones, Pr
Terry Etchison, VP
EMP: 4 EST: 1960
SQ FT: 5,000
SALES (est): 381.18K Privately Held
Web: www.kometfab.net
SIC: 3599 3444 3443 3441 Custom machinery; Sheet metalwork; Fabricated plate work (boiler shop); Fabricated structural metal

(G-10293)
KOKOMO OPTICAL COMPANY INC
501 E Lincoln Rd (46902-3742)
P.O. Box 2132 (46904-2132)
PHONE..................765 459-5137
Jill Reeb, Owner
Jack Ellis, Pr
EMP: 5 EST: 1951
SQ FT: 4,000
SALES (est): 536.86K Privately Held
SIC: 5995 3851 5048 Eyeglasses, prescription; Eyeglasses, lenses and frames ; Ophthalmic goods

(G-10294)
KOKOMO SPRING COMPANY INC
320 Rainbow Dr (46902-3796)
PHONE..................765 459-5156
Sheila Rossman, Pr
Douglas G Bailey, Stockholder
Ralph E Bailey, Stockholder
Richard H Rossmann, Stockholder
William J Drake, Stockholder
EMP: 10 EST: 1800
SQ FT: 110,000
SALES (est): 469.48K Privately Held
Web: www.kokomospring.com
SIC: 3493 Coiled flat springs

(G-10295)
KOKOMO THRIFT & GIFT LLC
1016 S Main St (46902-1609)
PHONE..................765 553-5973
Bruce Grimes, Pr
EMP: 5 EST: 2021
SALES (est): 145.43K Privately Held
SIC: 3993 Signs and advertising specialties

(G-10296)
KOKOMO TRUCK STORE
901 E Markland Ave (46901-6218)
PHONE..................765 459-5118
Kenny Pollard, Owner
EMP: 4 EST: 2007
SALES (est): 250K Privately Held
Web: www.kokomotruckstore.com
SIC: 3537 Trucks, tractors, loaders, carriers, and similar equipment

(G-10297)
LINDE INC
Also Called: Praxair
2100 E Lincoln Rd (46902-3774)
PHONE..................765 456-1128
EMP: 2
Web: www.lindeus.com
SIC: 2813 Industrial gases
HQ: Linde Inc.
  10 Riverview Dr
  Danbury CT 06810
  203 837-2000

(G-10298)
LINK ENGINEERING LLC (PA)
Also Called: Shotmizer Unit Dose Packaging
1719 N Main St (46901-2268)
PHONE..................765 457-1166
EMP: 5 EST: 2009
SQ FT: 24,000
SALES (est): 940.89K Privately Held
Web: www.linkeng.com
SIC: 3089 Injection molding of plastics

(G-10299)
LITTLE CREATIONS LLC
800 N Washington St (46901-3312)
PHONE..................765 868-9656
Scott Little, Owner
EMP: 1 EST: 1997
SALES (est): 58.06K Privately Held

SIC: 7692 Welding repair

(G-10300)
LORENTSON MANUFACTURING CO (PA)
1111 Rank Pkwy (46901-3124)
P.O. Box 932 (46903-0932)
PHONE..................765 452-4425
Christian Sawyer, *
Creda J Lorentson, *
▲ EMP: 45 EST: 1949
SQ FT: 15,000
SALES (est): 12.55MM
SALES (corp-wide): 12.55MM Privately Held
Web: www.lorentson.com
SIC: 3089 3544 Injection molding of plastics; Industrial molds

(G-10301)
M J MARKIEWICZ & ASSOCIATES
1768 N 300 W (46901-1788)
P.O. Box 6615 (46904-6615)
PHONE..................765 452-6562
Mark J Markiewicz, Pr
EMP: 1 EST: 2001
SALES (est): 108.41K Privately Held
SIC: 3589 Water treatment equipment, industrial

(G-10302)
M PRO LLC
4812 N Parkway (46901-3941)
PHONE..................765 459-4750
Michael Polk, Prin
EMP: 6 EST: 2005
SALES (est): 109.88K Privately Held
SIC: 3535 Conveyors and conveying equipment

(G-10303)
MACS EXPRESS INC
428 E Center Rd (46902-5321)
PHONE..................765 865-9700
Maria Farrington, Prin
EMP: 4 EST: 2005
SALES (est): 244.65K Privately Held
SIC: 2741 Miscellaneous publishing

(G-10304)
MARIETTA MARTIN MATERIALS INC
Also Called: Martin Marietta Aggregates
2400 W 50 S (46902-5964)
PHONE..................765 459-3194
Dan Yentis, Mgr
EMP: 13
Web: www.martinmarietta.com
SIC: 1422 Crushed and broken limestone
PA: Martin Marietta Materials Inc
  4123 Parklake Ave
  Raleigh NC 27612

(G-10305)
MAX OF ALL TRADES LLC
Also Called: General Contractor
801 N Mccann St (46901-3259)
PHONE..................317 703-4242
Maxwell Hughey, Managing Member
EMP: 1 EST: 2019
SALES (est): 130.52K Privately Held
SIC: 1389 1542 1743 2599 Construction, repair, and dismantling services; Commercial and office building contractors; Tile installation, ceramic; Food wagons, restaurant

(G-10306)
MERVIS INDUSTRIES INC
Also Called: Mervis & Sons
990 E Carter St (46901-4919)

P.O. Box 827 (61834-0827)
PHONE..................765 454-5800
TOLL FREE: 800
Michael Mervis, Mgr
EMP: 7
SALES (corp-wide): 99.07MM Privately Held
Web: www.mervis.com
SIC: 5093 3341 Ferrous metal scrap and waste; Secondary nonferrous metals
PA: Mervis Industries, Inc.
  3295 E Main St Ste C
  Danville IL 61834
  217 442-5300

(G-10307)
MIER PRODUCTS INC
Also Called: Bw Manufacturing
1500 Ann St (46901-2242)
PHONE..................765 457-0223
Robert Hullinger, Pr
C Scott Hullinger, *
EMP: 25 EST: 1987
SQ FT: 30,000
SALES (est): 4.04MM Privately Held
Web: www.mierproducts.com
SIC: 3469 3679 Electronic enclosures, stamped or pressed metal; Electronic circuits

(G-10308)
MILLER SIGN & DESIGN
1820 N Purdum St (46901-2475)
PHONE..................765 457-6592
Dean Miller, Owner
EMP: 1 EST: 1985
SALES (est): 82.83K Privately Held
SIC: 3993 Signs, not made in custom sign painting shops

(G-10309)
MILLER WELDING
3305 N 700 E (46901-8499)
PHONE..................765 628-2463
EMP: 4 EST: 2019
SALES (est): 203.09K Privately Held
SIC: 7692 Welding repair

(G-10310)
MILLWOOD BOX & PALLET
4665 E 600 N (46901-9241)
PHONE..................765 628-7330
Homer Miller, Owner
EMP: 6 EST: 2014
SALES (est): 243.4K Privately Held
SIC: 2448 Pallets, wood

(G-10311)
MOBILE DYNAMOMETER LLC
1309 E Markland Ave (46901-6226)
PHONE..................765 271-5080
Mark Harrell, Prin
EMP: 4 EST: 2015
SALES (est): 207.64K Privately Held
Web: www.mobiledynamometer.com
SIC: 3714 Motor vehicle parts and accessories

(G-10312)
MOON FABRICATING CORP
700 W Morgan St (46901-2159)
P.O. Box 567 (46903-0567)
PHONE..................765 459-4194
Greg Veach, Pr
EMP: 43 EST: 1923
SQ FT: 60,000
SALES (est): 5.33MM Privately Held
Web: www.moontanks.com
SIC: 3443 Fabricated plate work (boiler shop)

(PA)=Parent Co (HQ)=Headquarters
✪ = New Business established in last 2 years

Kokomo - Howard County (G-10313) — GEOGRAPHIC SECTION

(G-10313)
MOONLIGHT MOLD & MACHINE INC
924 Millbrook Ln (46901-5127)
PHONE.....................765 868-9860
Timothy Skaggs, *Pr*
Rusty Ritchie, *VP*
EMP: 5 EST: 1998
SQ FT: 1,080
SALES (est): 840.89K **Privately Held**
Web: www.moonlightmold.com
SIC: 3544 Industrial molds

(G-10314)
MOORES PIE SHOP INC
115 W Elm St (46901-2839)
PHONE.....................765 457-2428
Greg Lukas, *Pr*
Patty A Parrett, *Pr*
EMP: 6 EST: 1946
SQ FT: 3,000
SALES (est): 481.91K **Privately Held**
SIC: 2051 2053 Pies, bakery: except frozen; Pies, bakery; frozen

(G-10315)
MY SISTERS DOLL CLOTHES
1038 Springwater Rd (46902-4899)
PHONE.....................765 459-7977
EMP: 3 EST: 2017
SALES (est): 175.87K **Privately Held**
Web: mysistersdollclothes.patternbyetsy.com
SIC: 3942 Clothing, doll

(G-10316)
NELSON SALOMON CRUZ RAMOS LLC
821 W Park Ave (46901-6328)
PHONE.....................765 863-2885
EMP: 1 EST: 2020
SALES (est): 41.07K **Privately Held**
SIC: 1389 Construction, repair, and dismantling services

(G-10317)
NO LIMIT OUTDOOR SIGN CO LLC
2501 N Apperson Way (46901-1454)
PHONE.....................765 457-1877
Michael Lovely, *Prin*
EMP: 6 EST: 2010
SALES (est): 120.25K **Privately Held**
SIC: 3993 Signs and advertising specialties

(G-10318)
NXP USA INC
Also Called: Nxp Semiconductors
2733 Albright Rd (46902-3996)
PHONE.....................765 459-5355
Larry Freiburger, *Brnch Mgr*
EMP: 6
SALES (corp-wide): 13.28B **Privately Held**
Web: www.nxp.com
SIC: 3674 Semiconductors and related devices
HQ: Nxp Usa, Inc.
   6501 W William Cannon Dr
   Austin TX 78735
   512 933-8214

(G-10319)
PEPKA SPRING COMPANY INC
810 S Waugh St (46901-5502)
P.O. Box 2825 (46904-2825)
PHONE.....................765 459-3114
John V Pepka, *Pr*
Rita S Pepka, *Treas*
Paul C Pepka, *VP*
EMP: 10 EST: 1946
SQ FT: 9,000
SALES (est): 937.36K **Privately Held**
Web: www.pepkaspring.com
SIC: 3495 3493 Precision springs; Steel springs, except wire

(G-10320)
PERFORMANCE POWDER COATING
1124 S Union St (46902-1676)
PHONE.....................765 438-5224
Danny Miller, *Owner*
EMP: 5 EST: 2009
SALES (est): 308.16K **Privately Held**
SIC: 3471 Sand blasting of metal parts

(G-10321)
PJKELLYNET
4814 N Parkway (46901-3941)
PHONE.....................765 457-5864
Joann Kelly, *CEO*
EMP: 1 EST: 2001
SALES (est): 42.19K **Privately Held**
SIC: 3229 Christmas tree ornaments, from glass produced on-site

(G-10322)
PLATING PRODUCTS INC
1020 S Main St (46902-1609)
P.O. Box 699 (89403-0699)
PHONE.....................775 241-0416
David Young, *Pr*
Richard Hamilton, *Sec*
Jane Young, *Stockholder*
EMP: 4 EST: 1949
SQ FT: 20,000
SALES (est): 412.06K **Privately Held**
Web: www.platingproducts.in
SIC: 3559 Metal finishing equipment for plating, etc.

(G-10323)
PREMIER PRINTING
1708 W Taylor St (46901-4218)
PHONE.....................765 459-8339
Keith Krzeminski, *Owner*
EMP: 4 EST: 2002
SALES (est): 174.29K **Privately Held**
SIC: 2752 Offset printing

(G-10324)
PRINTCRAFT PRESS INC
524 S Union St (46901-5498)
PHONE.....................765 457-2141
David Pelgen, *Pr*
Peggy Debard, *Sec*
Kevin Debard, *VP*
EMP: 5 EST: 1956
SQ FT: 2,000
SALES (est): 470.62K **Privately Held**
Web: www.printcraftpress.com
SIC: 2752 Offset printing

(G-10325)
RAAD CUSTOM WOODWORKING LLC
2651 Sea Biscuit Ln (46901-4956)
PHONE.....................765 432-1385
Ronald Brantley, *Prin*
EMP: 4 EST: 2018
SALES (est): 54.13K **Privately Held**
Web: www.raadcustomwoodworking.com
SIC: 2431 Millwork

(G-10326)
REED CONTRACTING COMPANY
113 W Jefferson St (46901-4538)
P.O. Box 329 (46903-0329)
PHONE.....................765 452-2638
Charlie Reed, *Owner*
EMP: 25 EST: 1974
SQ FT: 30,000
SALES (est): 795.48K **Privately Held**
Web: www.reedcontractingco.com
SIC: 1542 1541 3479 1799 Commercial and office buildings, renovation and repair; Renovation, remodeling and repairs: industrial buildings; Coating of metals and formed products; Sandblasting of building exteriors

(G-10327)
REED SIGN SERVICE INC
113 W Jefferson St (46901-4538)
PHONE.....................765 459-4033
Jay Reed, *Pr*
Charlie Reed, *VP*
EMP: 5 EST: 1947
SQ FT: 28,000
SALES (est): 464.24K **Privately Held**
SIC: 3993 7389 Signs and advertising specialties; Sign painting and lettering shop

(G-10328)
REX BYERS HTG & COOLG SYSTEMS
4108 Cartwright Dr (46902-4388)
PHONE.....................765 459-8858
Rex A Byers, *Pr*
EMP: 13 EST: 1978
SALES (est): 531.68K **Privately Held**
Web: www.cjsheatingandair.com
SIC: 1711 3432 1731 Warm air heating and air conditioning contractor; Plumbing fixture fittings and trim; Electronic controls installation

(G-10329)
SANGSIN INDIANA INC
700 E Firmin St (46902)
PHONE.....................765 432-4143
Byung Lee, *CEO*
EMP: 6
SALES (est): 271.06K **Privately Held**
SIC: 3411 Metal cans

(G-10330)
SEARCHLIGHT SOCIAL LLC
1694 S 200 E (46902-4142)
PHONE.....................317 983-3802
EMP: 4 EST: 2018
SALES (est): 88.38K **Privately Held**
SIC: 3648 Searchlights

(G-10331)
SECOND CYCLE LLC
1233 W Jackson St Ste A (46901-4582)
PHONE.....................765 432-8178
Bo Linton, *Pr*
EMP: 1 EST: 2013
SALES (est): 213.13K
SALES (corp-wide): 2.5MM **Privately Held**
Web: www.secondcyclerecycling.com
SIC: 2679 Paper products, converted, nec
PA: Calipharms Inc.
   3001 N Rcky Pt Rd Ste 200
   Tampa FL 33607
   949 800-6645

(G-10332)
SELBY PUBLISHING & PRINTING
3405 Zartman Rd (46902-2979)
PHONE.....................765 453-5417
Phyllis Selby, *Pt*
Robert Selby, *Pt*
EMP: 2 EST: 1995
SALES (est): 120.61K **Privately Held**
SIC: 2759 7299 Commercial printing, nec; Genealogical investigation service

(G-10333)
SEMICNDCTOR CMPONENTS INDS LLC
Also Called: On Semiconductor
1708 Mollee Ct (46902-4484)
PHONE.....................765 868-5015
Brad Yount, *Mgr*
EMP: 8
SALES (corp-wide): 8.25B **Publicly Held**
Web: www.onsemi.com
SIC: 3674 Semiconductors and related devices
HQ: Semiconductor Components Industries, Llc
   5701 N Pima Rd
   Scottsdale AZ 85250
   602 244-6600

(G-10334)
SHEARER PRINTING SERVICE INC
Also Called: Shearer Business Products
107 W Markland Ave (46901-6102)
P.O. Box 668 (46903-0668)
PHONE.....................765 457-3274
Brian G Shearer, *Pr*
Stephen K Shupperd, *
EMP: 25 EST: 1937
SQ FT: 7,800
SALES (est): 2.18MM **Privately Held**
Web: www.shearerpos.com
SIC: 2752 5712 5943 7629 Offset printing; Office furniture; Office forms and supplies; Business machine repair, electric

(G-10335)
SLATE MECHANICAL INC
4602 W 100 N (46901-3889)
PHONE.....................765 452-9611
Ted Slate, *Pr*
Miriam Slate, *Sec*
Rick Slate, *VP*
EMP: 13 EST: 1970
SQ FT: 7,000
SALES (est): 368.86K **Privately Held**
Web: www.slatemechanical.net
SIC: 1711 3444 Mechanical contractor; Sheet metalwork

(G-10336)
SOULBRAIN MI INC
2141 Touby Pike (46901)
PHONE.....................248 869-3079
Admiral Betty Szarama, *Prin*
EMP: 10
SALES (est): 593.47K **Privately Held**
SIC: 2819 Chemicals, high purity: refined from technical grade

(G-10337)
SPECIALTY TOOL & DIE COMPANY
1614 Rank Parkway Ct (46901-3123)
PHONE.....................765 452-9209
Gordon L Riley, *Pr*
Brian Riley, *VP*
Gordon B Riley, *Sec*
EMP: 14 EST: 1983
SQ FT: 10,000
SALES (est): 2.1MM **Privately Held**
Web: www.specialtytoolddie.com
SIC: 3544 Special dies and tools

(G-10338)
STAR NAIL
1500 E Markland Ave (46901-6229)
PHONE.....................765 453-0743
Chris Phan, *Owner*
EMP: 2 EST: 2005
SALES (est): 150.25K **Privately Held**
Web: www.starnailsbeautysalonkokomo.com

GEOGRAPHIC SECTION

SIC: 2844 Manicure preparations

(G-10339)
STELLANTIS ✪
3660 Us Highway 31 N (46901-5956)
PHONE..............................765 854-4201
EMP: 24 EST: 2022
SALES (est): 3.97MM **Privately Held**
Web: media.stellantisnorthamerica.com
SIC: 3711 Automobile assembly, including specialty automobiles

(G-10340)
STEPHENS DYNAMICS INC
1600 Dodge St (46902-2407)
PHONE..............................765 459-4451
EMP: 9 EST: 2019
SALES (est): 278.52K **Privately Held**
Web: www.stephensdynamics.com
SIC: 3599 Machine shop, jobbing and repair

(G-10341)
STEPHENS MACHINE INC (PA)
Also Called: SD
1600 Dodge St (46902-2407)
PHONE..............................765 459-4017
Gregory A Stephens, Pr
Stephens Greg, *
EMP: 17 EST: 1984
SQ FT: 14,400
SALES (est): 9.59MM
SALES (corp-wide): 9.59MM **Privately Held**
Web: www.stephensmachine.com
SIC: 3599 Machine shop, jobbing and repair

(G-10342)
STEPHENS MACHINE INC
1801 S Berkley Rd (46902-6085)
PHONE..............................765 459-9770
Richard Stephens, Mgr
EMP: 38
SALES (corp-wide): 9.59MM **Privately Held**
Web: www.stephensmachine.com
SIC: 3599 Machine shop, jobbing and repair
PA: Stephens Machine Inc
    1600 Dodge St
    Kokomo IN 46902
    765 459-4017

(G-10343)
STITCHERY GARDEN LLC
4410 S 00 Ew Ste A (46902-5209)
PHONE..............................765 450-4695
EMP: 7 EST: 2009
SALES (est): 133.53K **Privately Held**
Web: www.thestitchgarden.com
SIC: 2395 Embroidery and art needlework

(G-10344)
SUV PARTS & ACCESSORIES INC
2109 N Wabash Ave (46901-2001)
PHONE..............................765 457-1345
EMP: 9 EST: 2011
SALES (est): 479.7K **Privately Held**
Web: www.maxxmotor.com
SIC: 3621 Electric motor and generator auxiliary parts

(G-10345)
SYNDICATE SALES INC (PA)
2025 N Wabash Ave (46901-2063)
PHONE..............................765 457-7277
Delmar Demaree, Ch Bd
Laura Shinall, Prin
John Demaree, Prin
Linda Utter, Prin
Thomas Lunsford, Prin
◆ EMP: 400 EST: 1955
SQ FT: 85,000
SALES (est): 96.83MM
SALES (corp-wide): 96.83MM **Privately Held**
Web: www.syndicatesales.com
SIC: 3089 Injection molding of plastics

(G-10346)
T L TATE MANUFACTURING INC
1500 N Webster St (46901-2123)
PHONE..............................765 452-8283
Timothy L Tate, Pr
EMP: 7 EST: 2000
SQ FT: 18,500
SALES (est): 754.98K **Privately Held**
Web: www.tltate.com
SIC: 3599 Machine shop, jobbing and repair

(G-10347)
TATE SOAPS & SURFACTANTS INC
1500 N Webster St (46901-2123)
PHONE..............................765 868-4488
Troy L Tate, Pr
Michael F Hartz, VP
Thomas J Kronk, VP
EMP: 7 EST: 2003
SQ FT: 64,000
SALES (est): 736.52K **Privately Held**
Web: www.tatesoaps.com
SIC: 2842 Cleaning or polishing preparations, nec

(G-10348)
TGR INC
Also Called: T G R Finishings
1257 E Morgan St (46901-2557)
PHONE..............................765 452-8225
Timothy Ryberg, Pr
Gayle Ryberg, Sec
EMP: 15 EST: 1970
SQ FT: 25,000
SALES (est): 448.41K **Privately Held**
Web: www.tgrfinishing.com
SIC: 3479 3993 Coating of metals and formed products; Signs and advertising specialties

(G-10349)
TITANIUM LLC
847 N 300 E (46901-5768)
PHONE..............................765 236-6906
Eric Newman, Prin
EMP: 6 EST: 2017
SALES (est): 247.73K **Privately Held**
Web: www.titaniumllc.com
SIC: 3356 Titanium

(G-10350)
TOPPAN PHOTOMASKS INC
Also Called: Dupont
1901 E Morgan St (46901)
P.O. Box 4088 (46904)
PHONE..............................765 854-7500
Larry Mckinnley, Mgr
EMP: 170
Web: www.photomask.com
SIC: 3679 3674 3544 3229 Electronic circuits; Semiconductors and related devices; Special dies, tools, jigs, and fixtures; Pressed and blown glass, nec
HQ: Toppan Photomasks, Inc.
    8911 N Cpitl Of Texas Hwy
    Austin TX 78759
    512 310-6500

(G-10351)
TOUCH OF CLASS INTERIORS
802 E Sycamore St (46901-4874)
PHONE..............................765 452-5879
Julia Sawyer, Owner
EMP: 1 EST: 1975
SALES (est): 123.78K **Privately Held**
Web: www.touchofclass.com
SIC: 5713 5231 2391 7389 Carpets; Paint; Draperies, plastic and textile: from purchased materials; Interior decorating

(G-10352)
TRUE PRECISION TECH INC
1602 E Havens St (46901-3176)
PHONE..............................765 432-2177
Andrew Jay, Pr
Andrew I Jay, Prin
Derek H Krause, Prin
EMP: 3 EST: 2013
SALES (est): 235.39K **Privately Held**
Web: www.trueprecisiontechnologies.com
SIC: 3999 3599 3312 Atomizers, toiletry; Machine shop, jobbing and repair; Tool and die steel

(G-10353)
USEFUL HOME PRODUCTS LLC
186 Champagne Ct (46901-9565)
PHONE..............................765 459-0095
EMP: 9 EST: 2002
SQ FT: 720
SALES (est): 833.45K **Privately Held**
SIC: 2519 Furniture, household: glass, fiberglass, and plastic

(G-10354)
VICKERS GRAPHICS INC
329 S 00 Ew (46902-5102)
P.O. Box 2525 (46904-2525)
PHONE..............................765 868-4646
EMP: 6 EST: 2007
SQ FT: 12,000
SALES (est): 524.32K **Privately Held**
Web: www.vickersgraphics.com
SIC: 2759 2395 Screen printing; Embroidery and art needlework

(G-10355)
WALTERS CABINET SHOP
Also Called: Walters'
471 E 1300 S (46901-7629)
PHONE..............................765 452-9634
Jim Walters, Owner
▲ EMP: 3 EST: 1990
SALES (est): 164.59K **Privately Held**
SIC: 2434 2541 2517 2511 Wood kitchen cabinets; Wood partitions and fixtures; Wood television and radio cabinets; Wood household furniture

(G-10356)
WEB SOFTWARE LLC
Also Called: 1 Up
2115 W Alto Rd Ste A (46902-5398)
P.O. Box 6553 (46904-6553)
PHONE..............................765 452-3936
David Mcchesney, Pt
EMP: 11 EST: 1998
SALES (est): 1.06MM **Privately Held**
SIC: 7372 7371 Prepackaged software; Computer software systems analysis and design, custom

(G-10357)
WEBER VINTAGE SOUND TECH INC
329 E Firmin St (46902-2240)
PHONE..............................765 452-1249
T A Weber, Pr
▲ EMP: 6 EST: 1998
SALES (est): 492.01K **Privately Held**
Web: www.tedweber.com
SIC: 3651 Speaker systems

(G-10358)
WILLIAM DONSON
7636 E 300 N (46901-9348)
PHONE..............................765 628-3236
William Donson, Owner
EMP: 1 EST: 1962
SALES (est): 71.46K **Privately Held**
SIC: 2026 0115 0111 Farmers' cheese; Corn; Wheat

(G-10359)
WILSON MEDIA GROUP INC
Also Called: Kokomo Perspective Wilson Advg
515 W Sycamore St (46901-4547)
PHONE..............................765 452-0055
Don Wilson, Pr
William Eldridge, VP
Joyce Addison, Sec
EMP: 13 EST: 1989
SALES (est): 443.64K **Privately Held**
Web: www.wilsonmedia.com
SIC: 2711 Newspapers, publishing and printing

Kouts
Porter County

(G-10360)
ACTION WELDING & MACHINE SVCS
1101 W Daumer Rd (46347-9540)
PHONE..............................219 766-0406
Robert Westfall, Owner
EMP: 1 EST: 2001
SALES (est): 67.1K **Privately Held**
Web: www.actionweldingandmachiningservice.com
SIC: 7692 Welding repair

(G-10361)
BELSTRA MILLING CO INC
207 E Mentor St (46347-7010)
PHONE..............................219 766-2284
Tracy Lane, Off Mgr
EMP: 5
SALES (corp-wide): 8.38MM **Privately Held**
Web: www.belstramilling.com
SIC: 2048 Prepared feeds, nec
PA: Belstra Milling Co Inc
    424 15th St Se
    Demotte IN 46310
    219 987-4343

(G-10362)
C D C P INC
Also Called: Heinold Feeds
207 E Mentor St (46347-7010)
P.O. Box 639 (46347-0639)
PHONE..............................219 766-2284
EMP: 25
SIC: 2048 Prepared feeds, nec

(G-10363)
LEGGETT & PLATT INCORPORATED
Also Called: Leggett & Platt 0714
State Road 8 (46347)
P.O. Box 609 (46347-0609)
PHONE..............................219 766-2261
EMP: 27
SALES (corp-wide): 5.15B **Publicly Held**
Web: www.leggett.com
SIC: 2515 Mattresses and bedsprings
PA: Leggett & Platt, Incorporated
    1 Leggett Rd
    Carthage MO 64836
    417 358-8131

La Crosse
Laporte County

(G-10364)
CANNON TIMBER LLC
418 E Oneida St (46348-9551)
PHONE..................................219 754-1088
Jesse Cannon, *Prin*
EMP: 3 **EST:** 2008
SALES (est): 248.81K **Privately Held**
SIC: 2411 Timber, cut at logging camp

(G-10365)
KIEL MEDIA LLC
16 E Main St (46348-9515)
P.O. Box 53 (46348-0053)
PHONE..................................219 544-2060
Justin Kiel, *Managing Member*
Kelly Kiel, *Managing Member*
EMP: 2 **EST:** 2014
SALES (est): 57.83K **Privately Held**
Web: www.kielmedia.com
SIC: 2741 Miscellaneous publishing

(G-10366)
LA BRAID INC
Also Called: Country Maid
9404 W 2100 S (46348-9745)
PHONE..................................219 754-2501
EMP: 5 **EST:** 1992
SQ FT: 1,800
SALES (est): 488.05K **Privately Held**
Web: www.labraidfundraising.com
SIC: 2053 Pastries, e.g. danish; frozen

La Fontaine
Wabash County

(G-10367)
CHUCK CABLE
Also Called: Cable Sign Painting
1 Rennaker St (46940-9181)
PHONE..................................765 981-2800
Chuck Cable, *Owner*
EMP: 1 **EST:** 1970
SQ FT: 2,800
SALES (est): 80.51K **Privately Held**
SIC: 3993 Electric signs

(G-10368)
LA FONTAINE GENERATOR EXCHANGE
202 Logan St (46940-2825)
P.O. Box 308 (46940-0308)
PHONE..................................765 981-4561
Michael Loschiavo, *Pr*
Linda E Loschiavo, *Treas*
Jeremy Steel, *Mgr*
EMP: 7 **EST:** 1973
SQ FT: 10,000
SALES (est): 724.46K **Privately Held**
SIC: 3694 Breaker point sets, internal combustion engine

(G-10369)
LAFONTAINE GRAVEL INC
1244 E 1050 S (46940-9196)
P.O. Box 416 (46940-0416)
PHONE..................................765 981-4849
James Derck, *Pr*
Andrew King, *VP*
EMP: 3 **EST:** 2000
SALES (est): 474.59K **Privately Held**
Web: www.lafontainegravelinc.com
SIC: 1442 Gravel mining

La Porte
Laporte County

(G-10370)
104 WELDING
2721 S State Road 104 (46350-9046)
PHONE..................................219 393-0801
Warren Pease, *Owner*
EMP: 1 **EST:** 2013
SALES (est): 45.28K **Privately Held**
SIC: 7692 Welding repair

(G-10371)
A & A SHEET METAL PRODUCTS (PA)
Also Called: Se-Cur-All Cabinets
5122 N State Road 39 (46350)
P.O. Box 1848 (46350)
PHONE..................................219 326-1288
Ben Williams, *Pr*
David E Williams, *
Michael H Williams, *
Jack Williams, *
▼ **EMP:** 72 **EST:** 1950
SQ FT: 155,000
SALES (est): 11.22MM
SALES (corp-wide): 11.22MM **Privately Held**
Web: www.securallproducts.com
SIC: 3442 2542 Fire doors, metal; Lockers (not refrigerated): except wood

(G-10372)
A PACKAGING SYSTEMS LLC
Also Called: A Packs
1500 Lake St (46350-3173)
PHONE..................................219 369-4141
▲ **EMP:** 19
Web: www.apacks.com
SIC: 3565 Bag opening, filling, and closing machines

(G-10373)
ACCURATE CASTINGS INC (PA)
Also Called: Hiler Industries
118 Koomler Dr (46350-2596)
P.O. Box 639 (46352-0639)
PHONE..................................219 362-8531
EMP: 55 **EST:** 1964
SALES (est): 21.81MM
SALES (corp-wide): 21.81MM **Privately Held**
Web: www.hilerindustries.com
SIC: 3364 Nonferrous die-castings except aluminum

(G-10374)
ACCURATE CASTINGS INC
Also Called: Kingsbury Castings Div
3232 3rd Rd (46350)
P.O. Box 639 (46352-0639)
PHONE..................................219 393-3122
William Lange, *Brnch Mgr*
EMP: 24
SALES (corp-wide): 21.81MM **Privately Held**
Web: www.hilerindustries.com
SIC: 3321 3369 3322 Ductile iron castings; Nonferrous foundries, nec; Malleable iron foundries
PA: Accurate Castings Inc
118 Koomler Dr
La Porte IN 46350
219 362-8531

(G-10375)
ACTION PRINTING SIGN CO
238 W Johnson Rd (46350-2027)
PHONE..................................219 362-9729
EMP: 4 **EST:** 2020
SALES (est): 50.69K **Privately Held**
Web: www.actionprintingsignandclockrepair.com
SIC: 3993 Signs and advertising specialties

(G-10376)
ADVANTAGE PRODUCTIONS
Also Called: Everyone's News
7256 W Oakmeadow Dr (46350-7009)
P.O. Box 321 (46361-0321)
PHONE..................................219 879-6892
EMP: 1 **EST:** 1980
SALES (est): 51.97K **Privately Held**
SIC: 2791 Typesetting

(G-10377)
AERO METALS INC (PA)
1201 E Lincolnway (46350-3955)
PHONE..................................219 326-1976
Robert Stowell, *CEO*
James Fleming, *
Linda Stowell, *
Patricia Graham, *
Pamela Fleming, *
▲ **EMP:** 324 **EST:** 1960
SQ FT: 76,000
SALES (est): 35.62MM
SALES (corp-wide): 35.62MM **Privately Held**
Web: www.aerometals.com
SIC: 3324 3364 Commercial investment castings, ferrous; Brass and bronze die-castings

(G-10378)
AERO-FLO INDUSTRIES INC
3999 E Hupp Rd Bldg R34 (46350-7694)
PHONE..................................219 393-3555
Jack Rich Junior, *Pr*
Margaret E Rich, *Sec*
▲ **EMP:** 9 **EST:** 1991
SQ FT: 25,000
SALES (est): 999.17K **Privately Held**
Web: www.aero-flo.com
SIC: 3564 5075 Blowers and fans; Air conditioning and ventilation equipment and supplies

(G-10379)
ALEXANDRIA MW LLC
Also Called: Alex Mid West
4747 W State Road 2 Ste B (46350-6561)
P.O. Box 164 (46352-0164)
PHONE..................................219 324-9541
Marty Hurlbut, *Managing Member*
♦ **EMP:** 5 **EST:** 2005
SALES (est): 2.34MM
SALES (corp-wide): 752.98MM **Privately Held**
SIC: 2431 Moldings, wood: unfinished and prefinished
HQ: U.S. Lumber Group, Llc
2160 Satellite Blvd # 450
Duluth GA 30097
678 474-4577

(G-10380)
ALLEN STREET ROASTERS LLC ✪
415 Allen St (46350)
P.O. Box 1945 (46352)
PHONE..................................815 955-7872
EMP: 2 **EST:** 2022
SALES (est): 62.01K **Privately Held**
Web: www.allenstreetroasters.com
SIC: 2095 5149 5499 Coffee roasting (except by wholesale grocers); Coffee and tea; Coffee

(G-10381)
ALPHA BAKING CO INC
360 N Fail Rd (46350-7051)
PHONE..................................219 324-7440
Larry Mitchell, *Pr*
EMP: 170
SALES (corp-wide): 323.59MM **Privately Held**
Web: www.alphabaking.com
SIC: 2051 2053 Breads, rolls, and buns; Frozen bakery products, except bread
PA: Alpha Baking Co., Inc.
5001 W Polk St
Chicago IL 60639
773 261-6000

(G-10382)
AMERICAN LICORICE COMPANY (PA)
1914 Happiness Way (46350)
P.O. Box 119 (46352-0119)
PHONE..................................219 324-1400
John R Kretchmer, *CEO*
Timothy R Walsh, *
▲ **EMP:** 35 **EST:** 1914
SQ FT: 3,500
SALES (est): 156.19MM
SALES (corp-wide): 156.19MM **Privately Held**
Web: www.americanlicorice.com
SIC: 2064 Candy and other confectionery products

(G-10383)
AMERICAN RENOLIT CORP LA
Also Called: American Renolit
1207 E Lincolnway (46350-3987)
PHONE..................................856 241-4901
Fred Breidenbach, *Genl Mgr*
EMP: 7
SALES (corp-wide): 2.67MM **Privately Held**
Web: www.laminatefinder.com
SIC: 3081 Vinyl film and sheet
HQ: Solvay Draka, Inc.
6900 Elm St
Commerce CA 90040
323 725-7010

(G-10384)
AMERICAN RENOLIT CORPORATION (DH)
Also Called: Renolit
1207 E Lincolnway (46350-3987)
PHONE..................................219 324-6886
Nils Dietz, *Pr*
Melissa Gruber, *Sec*
♦ **EMP:** 171 **EST:** 1991
SQ FT: 125,000
SALES (est): 56.66MM
SALES (corp-wide): 2.67MM **Privately Held**
Web: www.laminatefinder.com
SIC: 3081 5162 Plastics film and sheet; Plastics film
HQ: Renolit Se
Horchheimer Str. 50
Worms RP 67547
62413030

(G-10385)
AMI DEFENSE INC
1201 E Lincolnway (46350-3955)
PHONE..................................219 326-1976
EMP: 12 **EST:** 2016
SALES (est): 65.42K **Privately Held**
Web: www.aerometals.com
SIC: 3599 Machine shop, jobbing and repair

La Porte - Laporte County (G-10411)

(G-10386)
APPLETON GRP LLC
Also Called: Appleton Electric Division
2362 N Us Highway 35 (46350-8380)
PHONE................................219 326-5936
Claudette Harrison, *Brnch Mgr*
EMP: 5
SALES (corp-wide): 15.16B **Publicly Held**
Web: appleton.emerson.com
SIC: 3644 Noncurrent-carrying wiring devices
HQ: Appleton Grp Llc
    9377 W Higgins Rd
    Rosemont IL 60018
    847 268-6000

(G-10387)
B & B MANUFACTURING INC
Also Called: B&B Manufacturing
712 N Fail Rd (46350-9020)
PHONE................................219 324-0247
Bob Hamilton, *Pr*
Brian Mulligan, *
Dave Lee, *
Rick Talbert, *
▲ EMP: 80 EST: 1998
SQ FT: 35,000
SALES (est): 23.86MM **Privately Held**
Web: www.bbman.com
SIC: 3714 Motor vehicle parts and accessories

(G-10388)
BEV CAN PRINTERS LLC
1705 State St Bldg B (46350-3118)
PHONE................................219 617-6181
Dave Strupeck, *Pr*
EMP: 2 EST: 2014
SQ FT: 12,500
SALES (est): 124.93K **Privately Held**
SIC: 2759 Commercial printing, nec

(G-10389)
BLANEY SEALCOATING
6752 W Forrester Rd (46350-7802)
PHONE................................219 241-3622
Vern Blaney, *Owner*
EMP: 1 EST: 2010
SALES (est): 89.98K **Privately Held**
SIC: 2951 Asphalt paving mixtures and blocks

(G-10390)
BOSS INDUSTRIES LLC
1761 Genesis Dr (46350-2492)
PHONE................................219 324-7776
Paul Wilkins, *CEO*
Todd Hudson, *
▲ EMP: 32 EST: 1988
SQ FT: 50,000
SALES (est): 7.45MM **Privately Held**
Web: www.bossair.com
SIC: 3563 Air and gas compressors

(G-10391)
BOTTI STDIO ARCHTCTRAL ARTS IN (PA)
1500 Lake St (46350-3173)
PHONE................................847 869-5933
Ettore C Botti, *CEO*
EMP: 40 EST: 1864
SALES (est): 4.68MM
SALES (corp-wide): 4.68MM **Privately Held**
Web: www.bottistudio.com
SIC: 3231 3446 3281 2431 Stained glass: made from purchased glass; Architectural metalwork; Marble, building: cut and shaped ; Ornamental woodwork: cornices, mantels, etc.

(G-10392)
C FABCO/L INC
9811 W State Road 2 Ste 1 (46350-7061)
PHONE................................219 785-4181
EMP: 11 EST: 1992
SQ FT: 30,000
SALES (est): 746.3K **Privately Held**
Web: www.fabcolc.com
SIC: 3441 Fabricated structural metal

(G-10393)
CADDO CONNECTIONS INC
2833 N Goldring Rd (46350-7134)
PHONE................................219 874-8119
John Taddeucci, *Pr*
Joseph Demorrow, *
Ronald Caddo, *
EMP: 23 EST: 1979
SQ FT: 13,500
SALES (est): 5.81MM **Privately Held**
Web: www.caddoconnections.com
SIC: 3679 3613 3694 Harness assemblies, for electronic use: wire or cable; Control panels, electric; Engine electrical equipment

(G-10394)
CJ MAGERS ENTERPRISES LLC
5505 N 300 E (46350-8950)
PHONE................................219 778-4884
EMP: 5 EST: 2016
SALES (est): 160.46K **Privately Held**
SIC: 3564 Blowers and fans

(G-10395)
CLEAR STAMP INC
24 Industrial Pkwy (46350-7055)
PHONE................................219 324-3800
EMP: 3 EST: 2019
SALES (est): 41.02K **Privately Held**
Web: www.craffiti.com
SIC: 3953 Marking devices

(G-10396)
COUNTRY STITCHES EMBROIDERY
606 E 400 N (46350-4470)
PHONE................................219 324-7625
Norm Eggert, *Pr*
Maxine Eggert, *VP*
Kathy Johnson, *Sec*
Michelle Eggert, *Treas*
EMP: 8 EST: 1998
SALES (est): 515.18K **Privately Held**
SIC: 5699 5611 2395 T-shirts, custom printed ; Hats, men's and boys'; Embroidery and art needlework

(G-10397)
CREATIONS IN GLASS
725 Pine Lake Ave (46350-2320)
PHONE................................219 326-7941
Al Gardner, *Owner*
Carolyn Gardner, *Mgr*
EMP: 2 EST: 1980
SALES (est): 70K **Privately Held**
Web: www.creationsinglass.net
SIC: 3229 5947 Pressed and blown glass, nec; Gift, novelty, and souvenir shop

(G-10398)
DANTA INC
Also Called: Danta Welding
3202 E 400 S (46350-9179)
PHONE................................219 369-9190
Daniel Tarnow, *Pr*
Linda Tarnow, *Sec*
EMP: 1 EST: 1979
SQ FT: 4,000
SALES (est): 101.59K **Privately Held**
SIC: 3714 Motor vehicle parts and accessories

(G-10399)
DANWOOD INDUSTRIES
7606 S Young Rd (46350-9252)
PHONE................................219 369-1484
William "bill" Dankert, *Owner*
EMP: 4 EST: 1983
SQ FT: 11,000
SALES (est): 439.86K **Privately Held**
SIC: 2448 Wood pallets and skids

(G-10400)
DEATH STUDIOS
431 Pine Lake Ave (46350-2303)
PHONE................................219 362-4321
Jeff Keim, *Owner*
EMP: 4 EST: 1979
SQ FT: 1,200
SALES (est): 250.33K **Privately Held**
Web: www.deathstudios.com
SIC: 2389 Masquerade costumes

(G-10401)
DIEDRICH DRILL INC
5 Fisher St (46350-4768)
PHONE................................219 326-7788
Thomas S Ledonne, *Prin*
James E Lange, *Prin*
Jean F Lange, *
▲ EMP: 35 EST: 1973
SQ FT: 25,000
SALES (est): 8.02MM **Privately Held**
Web: www.diedrichdrill.com
SIC: 3533 3546 Drill rigs; Drills and drilling tools

(G-10402)
DWYER INSTRUMENTS INC
Also Called: EMC Stamping
3999 E Hupp Rd (46350-7692)
P.O. Box 291 (46345-0291)
PHONE................................219 393-5250
Jeff Belkiewitz, *Mgr*
EMP: 7
SALES (corp-wide): 653.43MM **Privately Held**
Web: intl.dwyer-inst.com
SIC: 3679 3469 Electronic switches; Metal stampings, nec
HQ: Dwyer Instruments, Llc
    102 Indiana Hwy 212
    Michigan City IN 46360
    219 879-8868

(G-10403)
E-PAK MACHINERY INC
1535 S State Road 39 (46350-6301)
PHONE................................219 393-5541
Ronald Sarto, *CEO*
Greg Simsa, *
Tony Swedersky, *
◆ EMP: 50 EST: 2001
SQ FT: 52,000
SALES (est): 9.7MM **Privately Held**
Web: www.epakmachinery.com
SIC: 3565 Bottling machinery: filling, capping, labeling

(G-10404)
ELECTRIK CONNECTION INC
Also Called: S & W Electric
106 Washington St (46350-2426)
PHONE................................219 362-4581
John T Barnhart, *Pr*
Lola N Barnhart, *Sec*
EMP: 4 EST: 1949
SQ FT: 9,700
SALES (est): 631.26K **Privately Held**
Web: www.swelectriclaporte.com
SIC: 5063 7694 Motors, electric; Electric motor repair

(G-10405)
ELF MACHINERY LLC
1535 S State Road 39 (46350-6301)
PHONE................................219 393-5541
Rick Allegretti, *Pr*
Tracy Connors, *
EMP: 25 EST: 1981
SQ FT: 80,000
SALES (est): 452.59K **Privately Held**
Web: www.epakmachinery.com
SIC: 3565 Bottling machinery: filling, capping, labeling

(G-10406)
EMPROTECH STEEL SERVICES LLC
3234 N State Road 39 (46350-8605)
PHONE................................219 326-6900
Ron Johnson, *Contrlr*
EMP: 25 EST: 2001
SALES (est): 769.93K **Privately Held**
SIC: 3599 Machine shop, jobbing and repair

(G-10407)
EXTREME TOOL SUPPLY
6348 W 100 S (46350-9711)
PHONE................................219 362-5129
Ron Mccarty, *Owner*
EMP: 1 EST: 2005
SALES (est): 116.21K **Privately Held**
SIC: 3541 Machine tools, metal cutting: exotic (explosive, etc.)

(G-10408)
FINZER ROLLER INC
Also Called: Rotation Dynamics
1164 E 150 N (46350-9119)
PHONE................................219 325-8808
Steve Aker, *Mgr*
EMP: 1
SALES (corp-wide): 83.27MM **Privately Held**
Web: www.finzerroller.com
SIC: 3555 2796 Printing trades machinery; Platemaking services
PA: Finzer Roller, Inc.
    880 W Thorndale Ave
    Itasca IL 60143
    847 390-6200

(G-10409)
FINZER ROLLER INC
Also Called: Rotadyne
235 Factory St (46350-2624)
PHONE................................219 325-8808
EMP: 9 EST: 2014
SALES (est): 53.93K **Privately Held**
Web: www.finzerroller.com
SIC: 3069 Fabricated rubber products, nec

(G-10410)
GRAPHIC PACKAGING HOLDING CO
115 Koomler Dr (46350)
PHONE................................219 324-6160
EMP: 1
Web: www.graphicpkg.com
SIC: 2631 Container, packaging, and boxboard
PA: Graphic Packaging Holding Company
    1500 Rvredge Pkwy Ste 100
    Atlanta GA 30328

(G-10411)
GREAT LAKE SALES & MARKETING
3735 W Pawnee Dr (46350-7955)
PHONE................................219 325-0637
Jim Pritz, *Mgr*
EMP: 1 EST: 1999
SALES (est): 114.88K **Privately Held**
SIC: 3842 Personal safety equipment

(PA)=Parent Co (HQ)=Headquarters
✪ = New Business established in last 2 years

2024 Harris Indiana Industrial Directory

La Porte - Laporte County (G-10412) — GEOGRAPHIC SECTION

(G-10412)
GREGORY THOMAS INC (PA)
Also Called: Gti Static Solutions
1823 N Circle View Ln (46350-2132)
PHONE..................................219 324-3801
Thomas G Smith, *Pr*
EMP: 1 **EST:** 2006
SALES (est): 666.64K
SALES (corp-wide): 666.64K **Privately Held**
SIC: 5063 3629 Electrical apparatus and equipment; Static elimination equipment, industrial

(G-10413)
GTW ENTERPRISES INC
1164 E 150 N (46350-9119)
PHONE..................................219 362-2278
George Wroblewski, *Pr*
Vera Wroblewski, *VP*
EMP: 15 **EST:** 1992
SALES (est): 1.2MM **Privately Held**
Web: www.gtwenterprises.com
SIC: 3554 Paper industries machinery

(G-10414)
H J J INC
Also Called: Art Gallery, The
1533 Weller Ave (46350-4657)
PHONE..................................219 362-4421
Judy Jorgenson, *Secretary of Treasurer*
Harry Jorgenson, *Pr*
EMP: 2 **EST:** 1975
SQ FT: 800
SALES (est): 167.23K **Privately Held**
SIC: 5999 2499 Art dealers; Picture and mirror frames, wood

(G-10415)
HARPERCOLLINS PUBLISHERS LLC
Also Called: Harpercollins Return Center
2205 E Lincolnway (46350-8732)
PHONE..................................219 324-4880
Harper Collins, *Owner*
EMP: 66
SALES (corp-wide): 10.09B **Publicly Held**
Web: www.harpercollins.com
SIC: 2731 Books, publishing only
HQ: Harpercollins Publishers L.L.C.
195 Broadway
New York NY 10007
212 207-7000

(G-10416)
HARRIS PRECAST INC (PA)
Also Called: Kovenz Memorial Shop
1877 W Severs Rd (46350-6915)
P.O. Box 321 (46352-0321)
PHONE..................................219 362-2457
Jeffery Scott Harris, *Pr*
EMP: 2 **EST:** 1937
SQ FT: 6,820
SALES (est): 421.82K
SALES (corp-wide): 421.82K **Privately Held**
Web: www.harrisprecast.com
SIC: 5999 3272 Monuments, finished to custom order; Burial vaults, concrete or precast terrazzo

(G-10417)
HARRIS PRECAST INC
703 N Fail Rd (46350-9021)
PHONE..................................219 362-9671
EMP: 6 **EST:** 2020
SALES (est): 248.41K **Privately Held**
Web: www.harrisprecast.com
SIC: 3272 Burial vaults, concrete or precast terrazzo

(G-10418)
HAYNES INTERNATIONAL INC
3238 N State Road 39 (46350)
PHONE..................................219 326-8530
Dave Mahan, *Mgr*
EMP: 15
SALES (corp-wide): 589.96MM **Publicly Held**
Web: www.haynesintl.com
SIC: 3356 3341 Nickel; Secondary nonferrous metals
PA: Haynes International, Inc.
1020 W Park Ave
Kokomo IN 46904
765 456-6000

(G-10419)
HICKMAN WILLIAMS & COMPANY
Also Called: Hickman Williams & Co
2321 W Progress Dr (46350-7782)
PHONE..................................219 379-5199
John Kalinowski, *Mgr*
EMP: 6
SQ FT: 132,000
SALES (corp-wide): 50.64MM **Privately Held**
Web: www.hicwilco.com
SIC: 1221 4225 3624 Coal preparation plant, bituminous or lignite; General warehousing; Carbon and graphite products
PA: Hickman, Williams & Company
250 E 5th St Ste 300
Cincinnati OH 45202
513 621-1946

(G-10420)
HLB1 LLC
Also Called: Manufacturing
9977 N State Road 39 (46350-8700)
PHONE..................................219 575-7534
Hitesh Bhatt, *Pr*
EMP: 10 **EST:** 2020
SALES (est): 680.68K **Privately Held**
SIC: 3999 Manufacturing industries, nec

(G-10421)
HOLSUM OF FORT WAYNE INC
Also Called: Lewis Bakeries
800 Boyd Blvd (46350-4419)
P.O. Box 426 (46352-0426)
PHONE..................................219 362-4561
Jim Hudock, *Mgr*
EMP: 2340
SQ FT: 69,000
SALES (corp-wide): 9.76MM **Privately Held**
Web: www.holsum.com
SIC: 2051 Bread, cake, and related products
HQ: Holsum Of Fort Wayne Inc
136 Murray St
Fort Wayne IN 46803
260 456-2130

(G-10422)
HOUSE OF FARA INCORPORATED
4747 W State Road 2 Ste A (46350-6561)
P.O. Box 337 (46352-0337)
PHONE..................................219 362-8544
◆ **EMP:** 78
Web: www.houseoffara.com
SIC: 2431 3442 Moldings, wood: unfinished and prefinished; Metal doors, sash, and trim

(G-10423)
HOWMET AEROSPACE INC
1110 E Lincolnway (46350-3954)
PHONE..................................219 326-7400
Chris Kraynak, *Brnch Mgr*
EMP: 645
SQ FT: 160,000
SALES (corp-wide): 6.64B **Publicly Held**
Web: www.howmet.com
SIC: 3324 3369 3341 Steel investment foundries; Nonferrous foundries, nec; Secondary nonferrous metals
PA: Howmet Aerospace Inc.
201 Isabella St Ste 200
Pittsburgh PA 15212
412 553-1950

(G-10424)
HOWMET CORPORATION
926 E Lincolnway (46350-3950)
PHONE..................................219 325-4143
EMP: 8 **EST:** 1975
SALES (est): 116.21K **Privately Held**
SIC: 2891 Adhesives and sealants

(G-10425)
HRR ENTERPRISES INC
1755 Genesis Dr (46350)
PHONE..................................219 362-9050
W D Tarpley, *Pr*
EMP: 30 **EST:** 1975
SQ FT: 13,000
SALES (est): 18.37MM
SALES (corp-wide): 45.62MM **Privately Held**
Web: www.hrrenterprises.com
SIC: 2077 2011 Animal and marine fats and oils; Meat packing plants
PA: Kane-Miller Corp.
1515 Rngling Blvd Ste 840
Sarasota FL 34236
941 346-2003

(G-10426)
HULL AIRCRAFT SUPPORT LLC
602 Lakeside St (46350-2210)
P.O. Box 1637 (46352-1637)
PHONE..................................219 324-6247
Eric Hull, *Prin*
EMP: 2 **EST:** 2001
SALES (est): 197.9K **Privately Held**
SIC: 3721 Airplanes, fixed or rotary wing

(G-10427)
INDUSTRIAL LUMBER PRODUCTS INC
251 N State Road 39 (46350-2052)
PHONE..................................219 324-7697
Everett Atwood, *Pr*
Debora Atwood, *Sec*
EMP: 9 **EST:** 1989
SQ FT: 10,000
SALES (est): 2.36MM **Privately Held**
Web: www.industriallp.com
SIC: 2448 5031 Cargo containers, wood; Lumber, plywood, and millwork

(G-10428)
INDUSTRIAL PATTERN WORKS INC
119 Koomler Dr (46350-2545)
P.O. Box 341 (46352-0341)
PHONE..................................219 362-4547
Frank Pinkepank, *Pr*
EMP: 10 **EST:** 1958
SQ FT: 17,500
SALES (est): 965.4K **Privately Held**
SIC: 3599 Machine shop, jobbing and repair

(G-10429)
J & J INDUSTRIAL SERVICE INC
2204 E Lincolnway Bldg D (46350-6556)
P.O. Box 1737 (46352-1737)
PHONE..................................219 362-4973
James Jablonski, *Pr*
Scott Kessler, *Prin*
EMP: 2 **EST:** 1985
SQ FT: 800
SALES (est): 204.29K **Privately Held**

Web:
www.directcontrollerreplacement.com
SIC: 3823 3613 Panelboard indicators, recorders and controllers: receiver; Panel and distribution boards and other related apparatus

(G-10430)
J & L DIMENSIONAL SERVICES INC
16 Industrial Pkwy (46350-7055)
P.O. Box 1629 (46352-1629)
PHONE..................................219 325-3588
Lisa Corey, *Pr*
Lisa Corey, *Pr*
Larry Corey, *
EMP: 45 **EST:** 1990
SQ FT: 20,000
SALES (est): 5.8MM **Privately Held**
Web: www.j-ldimensional.com
SIC: 3471 7334 Cleaning, polishing, and finishing; Blueprinting service

(G-10431)
JAEGER-NTEK SLING SLUTIONS INC
115 Koomler Dr (46350-2545)
PHONE..................................219 324-1111
◆ **EMP:** 60 **EST:** 2010
SQ FT: 132,000
SALES (est): 14.83MM
SALES (corp-wide): 199.95MM **Privately Held**
Web: www.jaeger-unitek.com
SIC: 3083 Laminated plastics plate and sheet
PA: Arnold Jager Holding Gmbh
Lohweg 1
Hannover NI 30559
51153580

(G-10432)
KELLERS LIMESTONE SERVICE INC
2074 N 50 W (46350-8009)
PHONE..................................219 326-1688
Larry Keller, *Pr*
Jane L Keller, *Sec*
EMP: 6 **EST:** 1947
SQ FT: 6,000
SALES (est): 523.9K **Privately Held**
SIC: 4212 1794 1422 Dump truck haulage; Excavation work; Crushed and broken limestone

(G-10433)
KENCO PLASTICS INC
Also Called: Train Co
809 Pine Lake Ave (46350-2322)
PHONE..................................219 324-6621
Connie Coates, *Mgr*
EMP: 14
SALES (corp-wide): 8.82MM **Privately Held**
Web: www.kenco.net
SIC: 3089 3559 Injection molded finished plastics products, nec; Plastics working machinery
PA: Kenco Plastics Inc
2022 W 450 N
La Porte IN 46350
219 362-7565

(G-10434)
KENCO PLASTICS INC (PA)
2022 W 450 N (46350-8324)
P.O. Box 364 (46352-0364)
PHONE..................................219 362-7565
Kenneth W Coates Iii, *Pr*
Barbara Coates, *Sec*
EMP: 18 **EST:** 1972
SQ FT: 5,500
SALES (est): 8.82MM
SALES (corp-wide): 8.82MM **Privately Held**

GEOGRAPHIC SECTION
La Porte - Laporte County (G-10459)

Web: www.kenco.net
SIC: 3089 Injection molding of plastics

(G-10435)
KENNAMETAL INC
Also Called: Casting Service
300 Philadelphia St (46350-3927)
P.O. Box 488 (46352-0488)
PHONE..............................219 362-1000
Joe Walker, VP
EMP: 9
SALES (corp-wide): 2.05B **Publicly Held**
Web: www.kennametal.com
SIC: 2819 Tungsten carbide powder, except abrasive or metallurgical
PA: Kennametal Inc.
525 Wlliam Penn Pl Ste 33
Pittsburgh PA 15219
412 248-8000

(G-10436)
KFC COMPOSITE ENGINEERING CO
3451 S State Road 104 (46350-6808)
PHONE..............................219 369-9093
Todd Hornig, Pr
Mary Hornig, Sec
EMP: 3 EST: 1983
SQ FT: 6,800
SALES (est): 250K **Privately Held**
Web: www.kfccomposite.com
SIC: 3711 Automobile bodies, passenger car, not including engine, etc.

(G-10437)
KT SOAP PRODUCTS LLC
1709 Genesis Dr (46350-2492)
PHONE..............................219 344-5871
William Dan Tarpley, Managing Member
EMP: 15 EST: 2019
SALES (est): 913K **Privately Held**
Web: www.ktsoap.com
SIC: 2841 Soap and other detergents

(G-10438)
KTOOL & FIRE LLC
1503 Monroe St (46350-5187)
PHONE..............................219 575-1428
Kyle Andrew Kozlowski, Managing Member
EMP: 1 EST: 2011
SQ FT: 7,000
SALES (est): 187.34K **Privately Held**
Web: www.ktoolfirellc.com
SIC: 3568 Couplings, shaft: rigid, flexible, universal joint, etc.

(G-10439)
LA PORTE DEFENSE TECH CORP
300 Philadelphia St (46350-3927)
PHONE..............................219 362-1000
Kenji Scott, Prin
EMP: 1 EST: 2017
SALES (est): 947.73K
SALES (corp-wide): 2.49MM **Privately Held**
SIC: 3812 Defense systems and equipment
PA: La Porte Technologies Llc
300 Philadelphia St
La Porte IN 46350
219 362-1000

(G-10440)
LA PORTE PRCSION MCH WORKS LLC
1756 Genesis Dr (46350-2492)
PHONE..............................219 326-7000
EMP: 6 EST: 2013
SQ FT: 6,000
SALES (est): 658.31K **Privately Held**
Web: www.lpmachineworks.com

SIC: 3599 Machine shop, jobbing and repair

(G-10441)
LA PORTE SMOKES AND BEVERAGES
609 E Lincolnway (46350-3835)
PHONE..............................219 575-7754
Ashokkumar S Patel, Prin
EMP: 2 EST: 2010
SALES (est): 248.36K **Privately Held**
Web: www.laportelibrary.org
SIC: 2131 Smoking tobacco

(G-10442)
LA PORTE TECHNOLOGIES LLC (PA)
300 Philadelphia St (46350-3927)
PHONE..............................219 362-1000
Joe Walker, Manager
EMP: 12 EST: 2015
SALES (est): 2.49MM
SALES (corp-wide): 2.49MM **Privately Held**
Web: www.laportech.com
SIC: 3321 Gray and ductile iron foundries

(G-10443)
LAKE EFFECT EMBROIDERY
6313 W 450 S (46350-9559)
PHONE..............................219 785-4551
Patricia Yocom, Owner
EMP: 6 EST: 2010
SALES (est): 214.32K **Privately Held**
SIC: 2395 Embroidery and art needlework

(G-10444)
LAKESHORE FOODS CORP
Also Called: Al's
702 E Lincolnway Ste 1 (46350-3890)
PHONE..............................219 362-8513
TOLL FREE: 800
Donald Gonser, Mgr
EMP: 51
SALES (corp-wide): 36.31MM **Privately Held**
Web: www.alssupermarkets.com
SIC: 5411 5912 2051 Grocery stores, chain; Drug stores and proprietary stores; Bread, cake, and related products
PA: Lakeshore Foods Corp.
100 Commerce Square
Michigan City IN 46360
219 326-7500

(G-10445)
LAKESIDE MANOR
196 W Mcclung Rd (46350-2054)
PHONE..............................219 362-3956
EMP: 37 EST: 2020
SALES (est): 248.35K **Privately Held**
Web: www.santefortneighborhoods.com
SIC: 6519 6515 2452 Real property lessors, nec; Mobile home site operators; Prefabricated wood buildings

(G-10446)
LINDE INC
Also Called: Praxair
3076 N State Road 39 (46350-8604)
PHONE..............................219 326-7808
Roy Downs, Pr
EMP: 13
Web: www.lindeus.com
SIC: 2813 Oxygen, compressed or liquefied
HQ: Linde Inc.
10 Riverview Dr
Danbury CT 06810
203 837-2000

(G-10447)
MAKI PRECISION MACHINING LLC ✪
720 Boyd Blvd (46350-4417)
PHONE..............................219 575-7995
Jeffrey Maki, Mgr
EMP: 6 EST: 2022
SALES (est): 2.09MM **Privately Held**
Web: www.makicnc.com
SIC: 3599 Machine shop, jobbing and repair

(G-10448)
MASTER ROLL MANUFACTURING INC
3999 Hupp Rd Bldg R-2-3 (46350-7693)
PHONE..............................219 393-7117
Mark Brashem, Pr
Jon Ferguson, Prin
EMP: 7 EST: 2016
SALES (est): 194.47K **Privately Held**
Web: www.master-roll.com
SIC: 3599 Machine shop, jobbing and repair

(G-10449)
MECHANOVENT CORPORATION
171 Factory St (46350-2622)
PHONE..............................219 326-1767
Dana Wade, Dir
EMP: 5 EST: 1981
SQ FT: 32,000
SALES (est): 2.05MM
SALES (corp-wide): 69.24MM **Privately Held**
Web: www.nyb.com
SIC: 3564 Blowers and fans
PA: The New York Blower Company
7660 Quincy St
Willowbrook IL 60527
630 794-5700

(G-10450)
MESSER LLC
7996 N State Road 39 (46350-8607)
PHONE..............................219 324-0498
Tom Zolvinski, Brnch Mgr
EMP: 54
SALES (corp-wide): 1.63B **Privately Held**
Web: www.messeramericas.com
SIC: 2813 Nitrogen
HQ: Messer Llc
200 Smrst Corp Blvd # 7000
Bridgewater NJ 08807
800 755-9277

(G-10451)
METALIZED COATINGS LLC
1540 Genesis Dr (46350-2593)
PHONE..............................219 851-0683
Jeff Maki, Managing Member
EMP: 3 EST: 2014
SALES (est): 496.24K **Privately Held**
Web: www.metalizedcoatings.com
SIC: 3479 Coating of metals and formed products

(G-10452)
METALTEC INC
11 Pine Lake Ave Ste C (46350-3076)
P.O. Box 1187 (46384-1187)
PHONE..............................219 362-9811
▲ EMP: 6 EST: 1994
SQ FT: 35,000
SALES (est): 498.83K **Privately Held**
Web: www.metaltecinc.com
SIC: 3599 3441 Custom machinery; Fabricated structural metal

(G-10453)
MILLWORK SPECIALTIES CO INC
Also Called: MSC Property Management Div

1405 Lake St (46350-3168)
PHONE..............................219 362-2960
Willard Dorman, Pr
June Dorman, Sec
EMP: 3 EST: 1957
SQ FT: 5,000
SALES (est): 245.62K **Privately Held**
SIC: 6531 2421 Real estate managers; Planing mills, nec

(G-10454)
MONOSOL LLC
1609 Genesis Dr (46350-2493)
PHONE..............................219 324-9459
Tim Boyle, Brnch Mgr
EMP: 5
Web: www.monosol.com
SIC: 2671 Plastic film, coated or laminated for packaging
HQ: Monosol, Llc
707 E 80th Pl Ste 301
Merrillville IN 46410
219 762-3165

(G-10455)
MOOSE LODGE
Also Called: Moose Lodge No 492
925 Boyd Blvd (46350-4420)
PHONE..............................219 362-2446
Edward Pace, Admn
Ed Pays, Admn
EMP: 3 EST: 2001
SALES (est): 234.9K **Privately Held**
Web: www.findmooselodgelocations.com
SIC: 2389 Lodge costumes

(G-10456)
NEW BEGINNINGS ART FOUNDRY
57 Keston Elm Dr (46350-6641)
PHONE..............................219 326-7059
Mark Swanson, Mgr
EMP: 1 EST: 2015
SALES (est): 118.32K **Privately Held**
SIC: 3366 Copper foundries

(G-10457)
NEW YORK BLOWER COMPANY
Also Called: N Y B
171 Factory St (46350)
PHONE..............................217 347-3233
EMP: 200
SALES (corp-wide): 69.24MM **Privately Held**
Web: www.nyb.com
SIC: 3564 Ventilating fans: industrial or commercial
PA: The New York Blower Company
7660 Quincy St
Willowbrook IL 60527
630 794-5700

(G-10458)
NEXT LEVEL LOGO STORE INC
811 Fairfield Ave (46350-3002)
PHONE..............................219 344-5141
Daniel Beerwart, Owner
EMP: 1 EST: 2013
SALES (est): 102.23K **Privately Held**
Web: www.nextlevellogo.com
SIC: 5699 2759 Sports apparel; Screen printing

(G-10459)
NRP JONES LLC
28 Industrial Pkwy (46350-7055)
PHONE..............................219 362-9908
EMP: 2
SALES (corp-wide): 14.44MM **Privately Held**
Web: www.nrpjones.com

(PA)=Parent Co (HQ)=Headquarters
✪ = New Business established in last 2 years

2024 Harris Indiana Industrial Directory

La Porte - Laporte County (G-10460) GEOGRAPHIC SECTION

SIC: 3492 Fluid power valves and hose fittings
PA: Nrp Jones, Llc
302 Philadelphia St
La Porte IN 46350
800 348-8868

(G-10460)
NRP JONES LLC (PA)
Also Called: Screw Machine Products
302 Philadelphia St (46350-3927)
P.O. Box 310 (46352-0310)
PHONE..................800 348-8868
Mark Prast, VP Opers
▲ EMP: 63 EST: 1945
SQ FT: 15,000
SALES (est): 14.44MM
SALES (corp-wide): 14.44MM Privately Held
Web: www.nrpjones.com
SIC: 3492 3533 3829 Control valves, aircraft: hydraulic and pneumatic; Oil field machinery and equipment; Testing equipment: abrasion, shearing strength, etc.

(G-10461)
OZINGA INC
708 N Fail Rd (46350-9020)
PHONE..................219 324-2286
EMP: 7 EST: 2019
SALES (est): 108.76K Privately Held
Web: www.ozinga.com
SIC: 3273 Ready-mixed concrete

(G-10462)
P M FABRICATING INCORPORATED
2008 Ohio St (46350-8053)
PHONE..................219 362-9926
Van Risley, Pr
Patrick Meaney, Ch
Kathleen Meaney, Sec
EMP: 9 EST: 1987
SQ FT: 13,125
SALES (est): 941.84K Privately Held
Web: www.pmfabricating.com
SIC: 3599 Machine and other job shop work

(G-10463)
PLI LLC ✪
Also Called: Packaging Logic
239 Factory St (46350-2624)
PHONE..................219 326-1350
William C Akers Ii, Pr
EMP: 39 EST: 2022
SALES (est): 8.62MM
SALES (corp-wide): 74.17MM Privately Held
Web: www.packaginglogic.com
SIC: 2653 Boxes, corrugated: made from purchased materials
PA: Akers Packaging Service, Inc.
2820 Lefferson Rd
Middletown OH 45044
513 422-6312

(G-10464)
PRECISIONAIR LLC
Also Called: Precisionair
1828 N Summit Dr (46350-2107)
PHONE..................219 380-9267
EMP: 2 EST: 2010
SALES (est): 95.37K Privately Held
Web: www.vanair.com
SIC: 3563 Air and gas compressors

(G-10465)
PRECOAT METALS CORP
858 E Hupp Rd (46350-7691)
PHONE..................219 393-3561
Todd Ryan, Brnch Mgr
EMP: 233

SQ FT: 155,000
SALES (corp-wide): 1.54B Publicly Held
Web: www.azz.com
SIC: 3479 Painting of metal products
HQ: Precoat Metals Corp.
1950 E Main St
Greenfield IN 46140
317 462-7761

(G-10466)
PREMIUM MANUFACTURING LLC
28 Richmond St (46350-2564)
PHONE..................219 258-0141
EMP: 1 EST: 2020
SALES (est): 35K Privately Held
SIC: 3999 Manufacturing industries, nec

(G-10467)
PROTECT PLUS INDUSTRIES
229 Factory St (46350-2624)
PHONE..................219 324-8482
EMP: 6 EST: 2015
SALES (est): 146.9K Privately Held
Web: www.protectplusair.com
SIC: 3564 Air cleaning systems

(G-10468)
QUALITY INDUSTRIAL SUPPLIES
Also Called: Quality Industrial Services
517 Brighton St (46350-2612)
P.O. Box 1702 (46352-1702)
PHONE..................219 324-2654
John Blind, Ch Bd
Richard Weller, Pr
EMP: 9 EST: 1984
SQ FT: 7,000
SALES (est): 412.91K Privately Held
Web: www.qisautomate.com
SIC: 3613 3823 3549 Control panels, electric ; Process control instruments; Metalworking machinery, nec

(G-10469)
QUALITY TOOL & DIE INC
521 Brighton St (46350-2612)
PHONE..................219 324-2511
EMP: 5 EST: 1992
SALES (est): 495.44K Privately Held
Web: www.qualitymanufacturinggroup.com
SIC: 3544 Special dies and tools

(G-10470)
R & B MOLD AND DIE INC
1560 Lake St (46350-3173)
PHONE..................219 324-4176
David Brantley, Pr
EMP: 11 EST: 1989
SQ FT: 4,560
SALES (est): 1MM Privately Held
Web: www.rbmoldanddie.com
SIC: 3599 Machine shop, jobbing and repair

(G-10471)
REGION DESIGN CO LLC
1334 W 300 N (46350-7021)
PHONE..................219 851-1308
EMP: 4 EST: 2016
SALES (est): 43.82K Privately Held
SIC: 2741 Miscellaneous publishing

(G-10472)
REUER MACHINE & TOOL INC
1733 E State Road 2 (46350-4490)
PHONE..................219 362-2894
Robert Reuer, Pr
Dean Tuholski, VP
EMP: 8 EST: 1980
SQ FT: 6,000
SALES (est): 718.56K Privately Held

SIC: 3599 Machine shop, jobbing and repair

(G-10473)
RIDEN INC
Also Called: Hawkins Print Shop
315 Lincolnway (46350-2412)
PHONE..................219 362-5511
Christopher Hawkins, Pr
Greg Hawkins, VP
EMP: 5 EST: 1980
SQ FT: 20,000
SALES (est): 481.33K Privately Held
Web: www.hawkinsprintshop.com
SIC: 2752 2791 2789 Offset printing; Typesetting; Bookbinding and related work

(G-10474)
ROGER MILLER
Also Called: Radio Resources
230 Whispering Blvd (46350-3592)
PHONE..................219 531-2566
Roger Miller, Owner
EMP: 1 EST: 2006
SALES (est): 167.57K Privately Held
Web: www.novarealtypro.com
SIC: 3663 Radio and t.v. communications equipment

(G-10475)
RS PRECISION MACHINING
7909 N Wilhelm Rd (46350-8631)
PHONE..................219 362-4560
Rudy Schlager, Owner
EMP: 2 EST: 2007
SALES (est): 91.98K Privately Held
Web: www.rsprecisionmachining.com
SIC: 3599 Machine shop, jobbing and repair

(G-10476)
SALIWNCHIK SONS WLDG FBRCTION
3707 N Us Highway 35 (46350-8383)
P.O. Box 68 (46352-0068)
PHONE..................219 362-9009
Ted Saliwanchik, Owner
EMP: 2 EST: 1992
SALES (est): 208.32K Privately Held
SIC: 7692 Welding repair

(G-10477)
SCHMIDT MARKEN DESIGNS
3403 S Wozniak Rd (46350-7820)
PHONE..................219 785-4238
Karen Marken, Pt
Douglas Schmidt, Pt
EMP: 3 EST: 1987
SALES (est): 227.51K Privately Held
Web: www.heart-of-art.com
SIC: 5719 3269 Pottery; Pottery household articles, except kitchen articles

(G-10478)
SEALS & COMPONENTS INC
Also Called: Seal Jet Unlimited
6436 W Laura Ln (46350-8251)
PHONE..................708 895-5222
EMP: 5
SALES (est): 325.85K Privately Held
Web: www.sealjetofchicago.com
SIC: 3053 3089 3492 Gaskets, all materials; Extruded finished plastics products, nec; Fluid power valves and hose fittings

(G-10479)
SEMCOR INC
Also Called: Semcor Manufacturing
1500 Genesis Dr (46350-2593)
PHONE..................219 362-0222
Scott Siefker, Pr
Mark Siefker, VP

EMP: 26 EST: 1997
SQ FT: 50,000
SALES (est): 2.84MM Privately Held
Web: www.semcor-mfg.com
SIC: 3613 3621 3646 Panel and distribution boards and other related apparatus; Generator sets: gasoline, diesel, or dual-fuel ; Commercial lighting fixtures

(G-10480)
SEVENOKS INC
Also Called: Sterno Delivery
3539 Monroe St (46350-6178)
P.O. Box 870 (46352-0870)
PHONE..................800 523-8715
Don Hinshaw, Pr
EMP: 8 EST: 2011
SALES (est): 2.62MM Publicly Held
Web: www.sternodelivery.com
SIC: 3086 Cups and plates, foamed plastics
HQ: The Sterno Group Companies Llc
6900 Dallas Pkwy Ste 870
Plano TX 75024
951 682-9600

(G-10481)
SHADOWHOUSE JIU-JITSU INC
Also Called: Contact Concealment
3707 N Promenade Cir (46350-8287)
PHONE..................219 873-4556
Bruce Weiler, Pr
EMP: 2 EST: 2010
SALES (est): 132.54K Privately Held
SIC: 3089 Cases, plastics

(G-10482)
SILCOTEC INC
Also Called: Silcotec
707 Boyd Blvd (46350)
PHONE..................219 324-4411
Brian Sauers, CEO
Clifford E Myers, Pr
Charles B Sauers, Sec
▲ EMP: 10 EST: 1991
SQ FT: 22,000
SALES (est): 4.84MM Publicly Held
Web: www.silcotec.com
SIC: 2821 Plastics materials and resins
PA: Avient Corporation
33587 Walker Rd
Avon Lake OH 44012

(G-10483)
SILGAN CONTAINERS MFG CORP
Also Called: Silgan
300 N Fail Rd (46350-7051)
PHONE..................219 362-7002
EMP: 26
Web: www.silgancontainers.com
SIC: 3411 Metal cans
HQ: Silgan Containers Manufacturing Corporation
21600 Oxnard St Ste 1600
Woodland Hills CA 91367

(G-10484)
SKYWAY FUELS INC
1131 S Redbud Dr (46350-9454)
PHONE..................219 575-7624
EMP: 1 EST: 2013
SALES (est): 58.51K Privately Held
SIC: 2869 Fuels

(G-10485)
STRATIKORE INC
1714 E Lincolnway (46350-4479)
P.O. Box 689 (46352-0689)
PHONE..................574 807-0028
Ray Wolff, Pr
▲ EMP: 4 EST: 2004
SALES (est): 440.88K Privately Held

GEOGRAPHIC SECTION

Lafayette - Tippecanoe County (G-10512)

Web: www.stratikore.com
SIC: **3082** 8711 Rods, unsupported plastics; Consulting engineer

(G-10486)
TALL COTTON MARKETING LLC
Also Called: Soap Guy, The
3522 S State Road 104 (46350-6806)
PHONE.................................312 320-5862
Jeffrey Dorrian, *CEO*
EMP: 2 **EST:** 2016
SALES (est): 432.41K **Privately Held**
Web: www.thesoapguy.com
SIC: **5122** 2841 Toilet soap; Soap: granulated, liquid, cake, flaked, or chip

(G-10487)
TALON TERRA LLC
399 E Hupp Rd (46350-9296)
PHONE.................................219 393-1400
EMP: 5 **EST:** 2010
SALES (est): 496.49K **Privately Held**
SIC: **3524** Lawn and garden equipment

(G-10488)
TERAS SPORTY INK
515 Lincolnway (46350)
PHONE.................................219 369-6276
EMP: 5 **EST:** 2018
SALES (est): 183.28K **Privately Held**
SIC: **2759** Screen printing

(G-10489)
TERRY LIQUIDATION III INC (PA)
Also Called: Hytek Hose & Coupling Div
210 Philadelphia St (46350-3925)
P.O. Box 310 (46352-0310)
PHONE.................................219 362-9908
Terry Jones, *VP*
Terry H Jones, *
Brian K Jones, *
Lois Weeden, *
▲ **EMP:** 60 **EST:** 1977
SQ FT: 60,000
SALES (est): 4.94MM
SALES (corp-wide): 4.94MM **Privately Held**
SIC: **3492** 5085 Hose and tube fittings and assemblies, hydraulic/pneumatic; Industrial supplies

(G-10490)
TERRY LIQUIDATION III INC
Hy-Tek Hose & Coupling
28 Industrial Pkwy (46350-7055)
P.O. Box 130 (46352-0130)
PHONE.................................219 362-3557
Kelly Donahoe, *Mgr*
EMP: 10
SALES (corp-wide): 4.94MM **Privately Held**
SIC: **5084** 3594 3451 3429 Hydraulic systems equipment and supplies; Fluid power pumps and motors; Screw machine products; Hardware, nec
PA: Terry Liquidation Iii, Inc.
210 Philadelphia St
La Porte IN 46350
219 362-9908

(G-10491)
TFCO INCORPORATED (PA)
2606 N State Road 39 (46350-2034)
P.O. Box 339 (46352-0339)
PHONE.................................219 324-4166
Brad M Childress, *Pr*
▲ **EMP:** 4 **EST:** 2000
SALES (est): 1.13MM
SALES (corp-wide): 1.13MM **Privately Held**
Web: www.tfcoinc.com

SIC: **3053** Gasket materials

(G-10492)
TFCO INCORPORATED
207 N State Road 39 (46350-2052)
PHONE.................................219 324-4166
EMP: 4
SALES (corp-wide): 1.13MM **Privately Held**
Web: www.tfcoinc.com
SIC: **3053** Gasket materials
PA: Tfco Incorporated
2606 N State Road 39
La Porte IN 46350
219 324-4166

(G-10493)
THERMCO INSTRUMENT CORPORATION
1201 W Us Highway 20 (46350-8613)
P.O. Box 309 (46352-0309)
PHONE.................................219 362-6258
Dennis Richardson, *Pr*
Kent Richardson, *Prin*
Glen Richardson, *Sec*
EMP: 14 **EST:** 1951
SQ FT: 24,670
SALES (est): 2.33MM **Privately Held**
Web: www.thermco.com
SIC: **3823** On-stream gas/liquid analysis instruments, industrial

(G-10494)
TP ORTHODONTICS INC (PA)
100 Center Plz (46350-9672)
P.O. Box 73 (46352-0073)
PHONE.................................219 785-2591
EMP: 300 **EST:** 1942
SALES (est): 36.7MM
SALES (corp-wide): 36.7MM **Privately Held**
Web: www.tportho.com
SIC: **3843** Orthodontic appliances

(G-10495)
TRUE BLUE COMPANY LLC
229 Factory St (46350-2624)
PHONE.................................219 324-8482
EMP: 44 **EST:** 1999
SQ FT: 300,000
SALES (est): 2.16MM **Privately Held**
SIC: **3599** Air intake filters, internal combustion engine, except auto

(G-10496)
TRUSSLINK
512 Washington St (46350-3334)
PHONE.................................219 362-3968
Pat South, *Owner*
EMP: 3 **EST:** 1976
SALES (est): 186.39K **Privately Held**
SIC: **2439** Structural wood members, nec

(G-10497)
WAGNERS TREE SERVICE
Also Called: Wagners Tree Svc & Clean Up
1511 E State Road 2 (46350-8070)
P.O. Box 825 (46350-0825)
PHONE.................................219 608-1525
EMP: 1 **EST:** 2010
SALES (est): 86.84K **Privately Held**
Web: www.wagnerstreeservices.com
SIC: **3999** Manufacturing industries, nec

(G-10498)
WEB PRODUCTS
229 Factory St (46350-2624)
PHONE.................................816 777-3735
EMP: 7 **EST:** 2019
SALES (est): 213.69K **Privately Held**

Web: www.airfilters.com
SIC: **3569** Filters

(G-10499)
WILLIAMS PRPRTY PRSRVATION LLC
548 Circle Dr (46350-5836)
PHONE.................................219 336-3047
Sade Williams, *CEO*
EMP: 2 **EST:** 2021
SALES (est): 65.5K **Privately Held**
SIC: **1389** Construction, repair, and dismantling services

(G-10500)
WILLOW CREEK CROSSING INC
3574 W Us Highway 20 (46350-8355)
P.O. Box 205 (60126-0205)
PHONE.................................219 809-8952
Sherry Segnitz, *Pr*
EMP: 5 **EST:** 2015
SALES (est): 305.67K **Privately Held**
Web: www.wilowcreekcrossing.com
SIC: **2451** 5271 Mobile homes, personal or private use; Mobile home dealers

(G-10501)
WINN MACHINE INC
1712 Genesis Dr (46350-2492)
PHONE.................................219 324-2978
Damon Gasaway, *Pr*
Dina Gasaway, *Treas*
Virginia Winn, *Sec*
EMP: 8 **EST:** 1979
SALES (est): 895.75K **Privately Held**
Web: www.winndeavor.com
SIC: **3599** 3451 Machine shop, jobbing and repair; Screw machine products

(G-10502)
WINNDEAVOR LLC ✪
1712 Genesis Dr (46350-2492)
PHONE.................................219 324-2978
EMP: 1 **EST:** 2022
SALES (est): 265.26K **Privately Held**
SIC: **3541** Machine tools, metal cutting type

(G-10503)
YANDT BOAT WORKS LLC
308 Grayson Rd (46350-2249)
PHONE.................................219 851-8311
Andrew F Yandt, *Owner*
EMP: 5 **EST:** 2015
SALES (est): 171.41K **Privately Held**
Web: www.yandtboatworks.com
SIC: **3732** Boatbuilding and repairing

Laconia
Harrison County

(G-10504)
A NEW COVENANT WOODWORK LLC
4305 Hooptown Rd Se (47135-9132)
PHONE.................................812 737-2929
Ken Buzek, *Managing Member*
Debbie Buzek, *Managing Member*
EMP: 5 **EST:** 1997
SALES (est): 348.25K **Privately Held**
SIC: **2426** Hardwood dimension and flooring mills

(G-10505)
GRACE AMAZING GRAPHICS
250 W Old Highway 11 Sw (47135-8902)
PHONE.................................812 737-2841
Edward Farrow, *Prin*
EMP: 5 **EST:** 2017
SALES (est): 83.91K **Privately Held**

SIC: **2752** Commercial printing, lithographic

(G-10506)
LACONIA LASER ENGRAVING
2825 Mosquito Creek Rd Se (47135-9070)
PHONE.................................812 786-3641
Jeffrey W Lehman, *Owner*
EMP: 2 **EST:** 2002
SALES (est): 66.18K **Privately Held**
SIC: **2759** Commercial printing, nec

Ladoga
Montgomery County

(G-10507)
EMERALD CAST RNEWABLE FUEL LLC
Also Called: ECR Fuel
329 W College St (47954-7307)
PHONE.................................765 942-5019
EMP: 7 **EST:** 2014
SALES (est): 619.04K **Privately Held**
Web: www.ecrfuels.com
SIC: **2911** Diesel fuels

(G-10508)
MICHAEL GREENE
Also Called: Mvgreene Distributing
1001 E Main St Unit 12 (47954-9304)
P.O. Box 528 (47954-0528)
PHONE.................................317 753-7226
Michael Greene, *Owner*
EMP: 1 **EST:** 2009
SALES (est): 55K **Privately Held**
SIC: **2051** Bakery: wholesale or wholesale/retail combined

(G-10509)
RON MENDENHALL
Also Called: Mendenhall Powder Coating
751 W 1150 S (47954-8032)
PHONE.................................765 866-8283
Ron Mendenhall, *Owner*
EMP: 1 **EST:** 2002
SALES (est): 45.31K **Privately Held**
SIC: **7692** Welding repair

(G-10510)
STULLS MACHINING CENTER INC
209 E College St (47954-7041)
P.O. Box 353 (47954-0353)
PHONE.................................765 942-2717
Ryan Stull, *Pr*
Warren Boling, *Stockholder*
EMP: 2 **EST:** 1993
SALES (est): 203.59K **Privately Held**
SIC: **3549** Wiredrawing and fabricating machinery and equipment, ex. die

(G-10511)
STULLS MCH & FABRICATION INC
213 E Locust St (47954-7045)
P.O. Box 646 (47933-0646)
PHONE.................................765 942-2717
Ryan Stull, *Pr*
Scott Stull, *VP*
EMP: 2 **EST:** 2007
SALES (est): 243.82K **Privately Held**
SIC: **3599** 3499 Machine shop, jobbing and repair; Machine bases, metal

Lafayette
Tippecanoe County

(G-10512)
20 MINUTE SIGNS PLUS INC
3032 E 800 S (47909-9124)

Lafayette - Tippecanoe County (G-10513)

PHONE.....................765 413-1046
Mike Moll, *Pr*
Terri A Moll, *Sec*
EMP: 2 **EST:** 2010
SALES (est): 116.48K **Privately Held**
SIC: 3993 Signs and advertising specialties

(G-10513)
A PINCH OF SWEETNESS LLC
2415 Sagamore Pkwy S (47905)
PHONE.....................765 838-2358
Tyreeka L Wilburn, *Admn*
EMP: 1 **EST:** 2020
SALES (est): 85.01K **Privately Held**
SIC: 5461 2051 5963 Retail bakeries; Cakes, bakery: except frozen; Bakery goods, house-to-house

(G-10514)
ACELL INC
3589 Sagamore Pkwy N Ste 220 (47904)
PHONE.....................765 464-8198
Sherry Dibro, *Pr*
EMP: 193
Web: marketing.integralife.com
SIC: 2833 Medicinals and botanicals
HQ: Acell, Inc.
6640 Eli Whitney Dr # 200
Columbia MD 21046
800 826-2926

(G-10515)
ADVANCE REPAIR & MACHINING INC
3311 Imperial Pkwy Ste B (47909-5114)
P.O. Box 6154 (47903-6154)
PHONE.....................765 474-8000
Kyle D Garrett, *Pr*
EMP: 7 **EST:** 2007
SALES (est): 630.53K **Privately Held**
Web: www.armindiana.com
SIC: 3599 Machine shop, jobbing and repair

(G-10516)
ADVANCED VSCULAR THERAPIES INC
1125 N 13th St (47904-2012)
PHONE.....................765 423-1720
Kerry Logan, *Pr*
Kathryn Logan, *Pr*
EMP: 2 **EST:** 2010
SALES (est): 157.08K **Privately Held**
Web: www.avtcare.com
SIC: 3841 Surgical and medical instruments

(G-10517)
AG PRINTING SPECIALISTS LLC
2880 Us Highway 231 S Ste 200 (47909-2874)
PHONE.....................866 445-6824
EMP: 4 **EST:** 2005
SALES (est): 247.87K **Privately Held**
Web: www.agprinters.com
SIC: 2752 Offset printing

(G-10518)
ALL DAY CARPET BINDING LLC
3814 Rushgrove Dr (47909-8438)
PHONE.....................219 851-8071
EMP: 1
SALES (est): 69.27K **Privately Held**
SIC: 2273 7389 Carpets and rugs; Business services, nec

(G-10519)
ALLIED PRECISION MACHINE INC
3900 E 450 S (47909-7726)
PHONE.....................765 418-7607
Toby L Lamb, *Prin*
EMP: 9 **EST:** 2010
SALES (est): 117.44K **Privately Held**
Web: www.alliedprecisionusa.com
SIC: 3599 Machine shop, jobbing and repair

(G-10520)
ALLOY CUSTOM PRODUCTS LLC
9701 Old State Road 25 N (47905-9734)
P.O. Box 198 (46923-0198)
PHONE.....................765 564-4684
Edward Leon, *Prin*
Ted Boatman, *
Edward Leon, *Pr*
▼ **EMP:** 80 **EST:** 1992
SQ FT: 101,000
SALES (est): 16.05MM
SALES (corp-wide): 891.34MM **Publicly Held**
Web: www.alloycustomproducts.com
SIC: 3443 3715 Cryogenic tanks, for liquids and gases; Truck trailers
PA: Plug Power Inc.
968 Albany Shaker Rd
Latham NY 12110
518 782-7700

(G-10521)
AMERICAN FIBERTECH CORPORATION
Also Called: Industrial Pallet
250 Main St (47901-1287)
PHONE.....................219 261-3586
Rob Meister, *CEO*
EMP: 75
SALES (corp-wide): 49.88MM **Privately Held**
Web: www.ind-pallet-corp.com
SIC: 2448 2449 2441 Pallets, wood; Wood containers, nec; Nailed wood boxes and shook
PA: American Fibertech Corporation
4 N New York St
Remington IN 47977
219 261-3586

(G-10522)
ANITA MACHINE AND TOOL INC
510 Elston Rd (47909-6317)
PHONE.....................765 477-6054
Anita Williams, *Owner*
EMP: 4 **EST:** 1999
SALES (est): 511.61K **Privately Held**
Web: www.anitamachine.com
SIC: 3599 Machine shop, jobbing and repair

(G-10523)
ANTIQUE CANDLE WORKS INC
1611 Schuyler Ave (47904-1117)
PHONE.....................765 250-8481
Brittany Whitenack, *Pr*
EMP: 25 **EST:** 2017
SALES (est): 2.63MM **Privately Held**
Web: www.antiquecandleco.com
SIC: 3999 5199 Candles; Candles

(G-10524)
ARCONIC US LLC
160 N 36th St (47905-4701)
PHONE.....................765 447-1707
Greg Clayton, *Mgr*
EMP: 1
SALES (corp-wide): 8.96B **Privately Held**
Web: www.arconic.com
SIC: 3353 Aluminum sheet and strip
HQ: Arconic Us Llc
201 Isabella St
Pittsburgh PA 15212
412 992-2500

(G-10525)
ARCONIC US LLC
Also Called: Arconic Forgings & Extrusions
3131 Main St (47905-2272)
PHONE.....................765 771-3600
Brad Blomberg, *Brnch Mgr*
EMP: 850
SALES (corp-wide): 8.96B **Privately Held**
Web: www.arconic.com
SIC: 3354 Tube, extruded or drawn, aluminum
HQ: Arconic Us Llc
201 Isabella St
Pittsburgh PA 15212
412 992-2500

(G-10526)
ARCONIC US LLC
3131 Main St (47905-2272)
PHONE.....................412 553-2500
EMP: 854
SALES (corp-wide): 8.96B **Privately Held**
Web: www.arconic.com
SIC: 3355 3353 Aluminum rolling and drawing, nec; Aluminum sheet and strip
HQ: Arconic Us Llc
201 Isabella St
Pittsburgh PA 15212
412 992-2500

(G-10527)
ARROW VAULT CO INC
1312 Underwood St (47904-1122)
PHONE.....................765 742-1704
Robert Burris, *Pr*
Kathleen Burris, *Sec*
EMP: 6 **EST:** 1946
SQ FT: 6,000
SALES (est): 482.46K **Privately Held**
SIC: 3272 Burial vaults, concrete or precast terrazzo

(G-10528)
ASH ACCESS TECHNOLOGY INC
3601 Sagamore Pkwy N Ste B (47904)
PHONE.....................765 742-4813
Robert B Truitt, *Pr*
Stephen R Ash Md, *Ch Bd*
Nels Bergmark, *Treas*
Roland Winger, *VP*
Carmine J Durham, *VP*
EMP: 9 **EST:** 1983
SQ FT: 8,500
SALES (est): 929.99K **Privately Held**
Web: www.ashaccess.com
SIC: 8733 3841 Medical research; Surgical and medical instruments

(G-10529)
AUDIO DIAGNOSTICS INC
Also Called: Audiodiagnostics
2320 Concord Rd Ste A (47909-2710)
PHONE.....................765 477-7016
Susan Berner, *Pr*
Shari Haillsamer, *Sec*
EMP: 2 **EST:** 1984
SALES (est): 234.82K **Privately Held**
Web: www.audiodiagnosticsii.com
SIC: 3842 8099 8049 Hearing aids; Hearing testing service; Audiologist

(G-10530)
AUTO ART & SIGNS
420 Sagamore Pkwy N (47904-2826)
PHONE.....................765 448-6800
Ken Klim, *Prin*
EMP: 4 **EST:** 2010
SALES (est): 146.93K **Privately Held**
Web: www.klimsigns.com
SIC: 3993 Signs and advertising specialties

(G-10531)
AUTO SPECIALTY LAFAYETTE INC
313 Teal Rd (47905-2310)
PHONE.....................765 446-2311
Connie Budreau, *Pr*
Greg Budreau, *VP*
EMP: 9 **EST:** 1989
SALES (est): 821.18K **Privately Held**
Web: www.autospecialtyoflafayette.com
SIC: 7538 7549 7539 7533 General automotive repair shops; Inspection and diagnostic service, automotive; Brake repair, automotive; Muffler shop, sale or repair and installation

(G-10532)
AWARDS UNLIMITED INC
3031 Union St (47904-2756)
PHONE.....................765 447-9413
Stacey Shirar, *Pr*
Darrel Shirar, *Sec*
EMP: 7 **EST:** 1977
SQ FT: 5,180
SALES (est): 877.4K **Privately Held**
Web: www.awardsunlimitedinc.net
SIC: 5999 5199 3993 Trophies and plaques; Advertising specialties; Signs and advertising specialties

(G-10533)
B & M ELECTRICAL COMPANY INC
710 Navco Dr (47905-4719)
P.O. Box 4795 (47903-4795)
PHONE.....................765 448-4532
Mark J Buche, *Pr*
Kathleen S Buche, *Sec*
▼ **EMP:** 11 **EST:** 1979
SQ FT: 8,400
SALES (est): 501.88K **Privately Held**
Web: www.repairshopwebsites.com
SIC: 3625 3694 7539 Starter, electric motor; Alternators, automotive; Automotive repair shops, nec

(G-10534)
BACKWOODS VYNL WERKS LLC
2008 S 22nd St (47905)
PHONE.....................765 607-1292
EMP: 6 **EST:** 2021
SALES (est): 85.87K **Privately Held**
Web: backwoods-vynl-werks.business.site
SIC: 2299 Textile goods, nec

(G-10535)
BASK AROMA CO LLC
8600 Patience Ln (47905-7737)
PHONE.....................765 404-7582
Brett Henrikson, *Prin*
EMP: 5 **EST:** 2018
SALES (est): 114.3K **Privately Held**
Web: www.hairspalafayette.com
SIC: 3999 Candles

(G-10536)
BEUTLER MEAT PROCESSING CO
802 Wabash Ave (47905-1055)
PHONE.....................765 742-7285
Stephen Beutler, *Pr*
EMP: 5 **EST:** 1953
SALES (est): 81.99K **Privately Held**
Web: www.beutlermeat.com
SIC: 2011 7299 Meat packing plants; Butcher service, processing only - does not sell meat

(G-10537)
BILLS GAR & AUTO REFINISHING
Also Called: Bill's Garage & Hot Rod Parts
5219 S 900 E (47905-9397)
PHONE.....................765 296-4978
William Blevins, *Owner*
EMP: 1 **EST:** 2000
SALES (est): 106.06K **Privately Held**
Web: www.billshotrodparts.com

GEOGRAPHIC SECTION
Lafayette - Tippecanoe County (G-10562)

SIC: 3441 7538 Fabricated structural metal; General automotive repair shops

(G-10538)
BIONIC PROSTHETICS AND ORTHO
5 Executive Dr Ste D-2 (47905-3832)
PHONE..................................765 838-8222
EMP: 2
Web: www.bionicpo.com
SIC: 3842 Surgical appliances and supplies
PA: Bionic Prosthetics And Orthotics Group Llc
8695 Connecticut St Ste E
Merrillville IN 46410

(G-10539)
BLUE PRINT SPECIALTIES INC
1500 Union St (47904-2156)
PHONE..................................765 742-6976
Neil Klinker, *Pr*
Carolyn Schnelle, *Sec*
EMP: 3 EST: 1958
SALES (est): 284.76K **Privately Held**
Web: www.blueprintspecialties.net
SIC: 7334 5049 2752 Blueprinting service; Engineers' equipment and supplies, nec; Commercial printing, lithographic

(G-10540)
BLUMLING DESIGN & GRAPHICS INC
3228 Olympia Dr Ste C (47909-5116)
PHONE..................................765 477-7446
Thomas K Blumling, *Pr*
EMP: 5 EST: 1998
SQ FT: 2,500
SALES (est): 406.55K **Privately Held**
Web: www.blumlingdesigngroup.com
SIC: 3993 5198 Signs, not made in custom sign painting shops; Wallcoverings

(G-10541)
BOLLOCK INTERPRISES INC
900 Farabee Ct (47905-5922)
PHONE..................................765 448-6000
Alfred A Bollock Junior, *Pr*
Carol Bollock, *VP*
Sharon Bollock, *Treas*
Steve Young, *Stockholder*
Stewart Bollock, *Mktg Mgr*
EMP: 10 EST: 1961
SQ FT: 21,000
SALES (est): 717.19K **Privately Held**
Web: www.bollocktops.com
SIC: 2599 5712 Factory furniture and fixtures ; Furniture stores

(G-10542)
BRIDGESTONE RET OPERATIONS LLC
Also Called: Firestone
2415 Sagamore Pkwy S (47905-5124)
PHONE..................................765 447-5041
Danny Smith, *Mgr*
EMP: 8
Web: www.bridgestoneamericas.com
SIC: 5531 7534 Automotive tires; Rebuilding and retreading tires
HQ: Bridgestone Retail Operations, Llc
200 4th Ave S Ste 100
Nashville TN 37201
630 259-9000

(G-10543)
BRIGHT LINE STRIPING LLC
1620 N 15th St (47904-1323)
PHONE..................................765 404-1402
John Held, *Managing Member*
EMP: 5 EST: 2016
SALES (est): 217.51K **Privately Held**
Web: www.brightlinelafayette.com

SIC: 3559 Parking facility equipment and supplies

(G-10544)
BRIGHTER DESIGN INC
Also Called: Lighting Studio, The
1650 Skyline Rd (47905-5550)
PHONE..................................765 447-9494
Stephanie Richeson, *Pr*
EMP: 1 EST: 2009
SALES (est): 89.01K **Privately Held**
SIC: 3648 Lighting equipment, nec

(G-10545)
BROWELL BELLHOUSING INC
711 N 31st St (47904-2709)
PHONE..................................765 447-2292
EMP: 5 EST: 2019
SALES (est): 136.8K **Privately Held**
Web: www.browellbellhousing.com
SIC: 3999 Manufacturing industries, nec

(G-10546)
BROWELL ENTERPRISES INC
Also Called: Custom Machine Shop
711 N 31st St (47904-2709)
PHONE..................................765 447-2292
Debra Browell, *Pr*
Brian Browell, *Pr*
Rick Chester, *Sec*
EMP: 18 EST: 1975
SQ FT: 7,500
SALES (est): 2.42MM **Privately Held**
Web: www.browellbellhousing.com
SIC: 3599 Machine shop, jobbing and repair

(G-10547)
BUC CONSTRUCTION SUPPLY INC
2304 Brothers Dr Ste E (47909-2292)
P.O. Box 4153 (47903-4153)
PHONE..................................574 532-9345
Teresa Butler, *Pr*
EMP: 3 EST: 2017
SALES (est): 323.07K **Privately Held**
SIC: 3089 5039 Plastics hardware and building products; Structural assemblies, prefabricated: non-wood

(G-10548)
CARTESIAN CORP
230 Walnut St (47905-1001)
PHONE..................................765 742-0293
Stephen M Rush, *Pr*
Jim Peters, *VP*
EMP: 20 EST: 1937
SQ FT: 60,000
SALES (est): 2.4MM **Privately Held**
Web: www.cartcorp.com
SIC: 3444 Sheet metal specialties, not stamped

(G-10549)
CATERPILLAR INC
Also Called: Caterpillar
3701 South St (47905-4856)
PHONE..................................765 448-5000
Rodd Bussell, *Mgr*
EMP: 120
SQ FT: 30,000
SALES (corp-wide): 67.06B **Publicly Held**
Web: www.caterpillar.com
SIC: 3531 Construction machinery
PA: Caterpillar Inc.
5205 N Ocnnor Blvd Ste 10
Irving TX 75039
972 891-7700

(G-10550)
CATERPILLAR INC
Also Called: Caterpillar

1451 Veterans Memorial Pkwy E (47905-8917)
PHONE..................................765 447-6816
EMP: 3
SALES (corp-wide): 67.06B **Publicly Held**
Web: www.caterpillar.com
SIC: 3531 3519 3511 6531 Construction machinery; Engines, diesel and semi-diesel or dual-fuel; Gas turbine generator set units, complete; Fiduciary, real estate
PA: Caterpillar Inc.
5205 N Ocnnor Blvd Ste 10
Irving TX 75039
972 891-7700

(G-10551)
CATHOLIC MOMENT
610 Lingle Ave (47901-1740)
P.O. Box 260 (47902-0260)
PHONE..................................765 742-2050
Thomas Russel, *Mgr*
Thomas Russel, *Prin*
EMP: 5 EST: 1945
SALES (est): 223.38K **Privately Held**
Web: www.thecatholicmoment.org
SIC: 2711 Newspapers

(G-10552)
CBD SOLUTIONS LLC
2469 State St (47905-2274)
PHONE..................................765 477-1900
EMP: 7 EST: 2018
SALES (est): 213.85K **Privately Held**
Web: www.cbdsolutionsllc.com
SIC: 3999

(G-10553)
COLEMAN CABLE LLC
3400 Union St (47905-4448)
PHONE..................................765 449-7227
John Semyen, *Mgr*
EMP: 96
SALES (corp-wide): 1.7B **Privately Held**
Web: www.colemancable.com
SIC: 3061 3548 2891 2822 Mechanical rubber goods; Welding apparatus; Adhesives and sealants; Synthetic rubber
HQ: Coleman Cable, Llc
1 Overlook Pt
Lincolnshire IL 60069
847 672-2300

(G-10554)
CONCORD REALSTATE CORP
Also Called: Concord Window Manufacturing
308 Erie St (47904-2553)
PHONE..................................765 423-5555
E G Kenworthy, *Pr*
Merle Kenworthy, *VP*
EMP: 10 EST: 1965
SALES (est): 1.24MM **Privately Held**
Web: www.bestwindowanddoor.com
SIC: 2431 5211 1751 1521 Windows and window parts and trim, wood; Door and window products; Window and door (prefabricated) installation; Single-family home remodeling, additions, and repairs

(G-10555)
COPPER MOON COFFEE LLC (PA)
Also Called: Copper Moon World Coffees
1503 Veterans Memorial Pkwy E (47905-8917)
PHONE..................................317 541-9000
Cary B Gutwein, *✪*
EMP: 100 EST: 2007
SQ FT: 35,000
SALES (est): 10.94MM **Privately Held**
Web: www.coppermooncoffee.com
SIC: 5499 2095 Coffee; Roasted coffee

(G-10556)
COPY-PRINT SHOP INC
Also Called: National Group, The
627 S Earl Ave Ste A (47905-3600)
PHONE..................................765 447-6868
Leo S Farrell, *Pr*
EMP: 21 EST: 1972
SQ FT: 12,000
SALES (est): 4.38MM **Privately Held**
Web: www.thenational-group.com
SIC: 2752 7334 Offset printing; Photocopying and duplicating services

(G-10557)
COPYMAT SERVICES INC
20 N Salisbury St (47906-3027)
PHONE..................................765 743-5995
Donald Steele, *Pr*
EMP: 4 EST: 1989
SQ FT: 2,400
SALES (est): 333.36K **Privately Held**
Web: www.copymatservices.com
SIC: 7334 2752 2791 Photocopying and duplicating services; Offset printing; Typesetting

(G-10558)
COUNTER COLUMN LLC
1000 Sagamore Pkwy N Ste 102 (47904-2461)
PHONE..................................815 564-7569
Johnick Petry, *Prin*
EMP: 5 EST: 2016
SALES (est): 61.84K **Privately Held**
Web: www.countercolumnthemovie.com
SIC: 2741 Miscellaneous publishing

(G-10559)
COZY CAT INC
2101 Indian Trail Dr (47906-2030)
P.O. Box 2823 (47996-2823)
PHONE..................................765 463-1254
Linda Stafford, *Pr*
EMP: 4 EST: 1998
SALES (est): 311.82K **Privately Held**
Web: www.petsitterwestlafayette.com
SIC: 7331 7338 2759 1542 Mailing service; Resume writing service; Invitations: printing, nsk; Agricultural building contractors

(G-10560)
CPP FILTER CORPORATION
730 Farabee Ct (47905-5917)
P.O. Box 5602 (47903-5602)
PHONE..................................765 446-8416
John Gleason, *Pr*
Milo Reinhardt, *VP*
EMP: 5 EST: 2000
SQ FT: 3,700
SALES (est): 718.3K **Privately Held**
Web: www.cppfilter.com
SIC: 3569 Filters

(G-10561)
CREATIVE INC
Also Called: Sign Experts
150 N 36th St (47905-4701)
PHONE..................................765 447-3500
EMP: 8 EST: 1989
SALES (est): 886.23K **Privately Held**
Web: www.thinkbigci.com
SIC: 3993 Signs and advertising specialties

(G-10562)
CROSSROADS BIOLOGICALS LLC
331 Cromwell Ct (47909-8153)
PHONE..................................765 239-9113
Tim Priebe, *Prin*
EMP: 5 EST: 2013

(PA)=Parent Co (HQ)=Headquarters
✪ = New Business established in last 2 years

2024 Harris Indiana Industrial Directory

Lafayette - Tippecanoe County (G-10563)

SALES (est): 126.32K **Privately Held**
Web: www.crossroadsbiologicals.com
SIC: 2834 Pharmaceutical preparations

(G-10563)
CROSSROADS GALVANIZING LLC
4877 E Old 350 S (47905-7723)
PHONE..................................765 421-6741
Brent Williams, *Brnch Mgr*
EMP: 12
SALES (corp-wide): 1.88MM **Privately Held**
Web: www.crossroadsgalvanizing.com
SIC: 3479 Galvanizing of iron, steel, or end-formed products
PA: Crossroads Galvanizing, Llc
    400 Industrial Dr
    Glasgow MO 65254
    660 338-2242

(G-10564)
CRYOGENIC INDUS SOLUTIONS LLC
Also Called: Alloy Custom Products
9701 Old State Road 25 N (47905)
PHONE..................................765 564-4684
Edward Leon, *Managing Member*
EMP: 12 EST: 2018
SALES (est): 1.94MM **Privately Held**
Web: www.cryoindsolutions.com
SIC: 3715 Truck trailers

(G-10565)
CUSTOM FORMS INC
1400 Canal Rd Ste B (47904-4031)
P.O. Box 2277 (47996-2277)
PHONE..................................765 463-6162
Maria E Goble, *Pr*
Gary R Goble, *VP*
▲ EMP: 14 EST: 1980
SQ FT: 4,000
SALES (est): 2.19MM **Privately Held**
Web: www.customforms.com
SIC: 5112 2752 Business forms; Offset printing

(G-10566)
CUTTING EDGE INDUS TECH LLC
3323 Concord Rd Ste 2 (47905-5118)
P.O. Box 4793 (47903-4793)
PHONE..................................765 471-7007
Marcus Mcgowen, *Prin*
EMP: 1 EST: 2010
SALES (est): 198.27K **Privately Held**
Web: www.cuttingedgeindustrial.com
SIC: 3599 Crankshafts and camshafts, machining

(G-10567)
CYBER INFORM LLC
5536 Lux Blvd (47905-8903)
PHONE..................................219 688-1183
Rachel A Sitarz, *Admn*
Rachel Sitarz, *CEO*
EMP: 1 EST: 2016
SALES (est): 39.65K **Privately Held**
SIC: 7372 Application computer software

(G-10568)
DANA INCORPORATED
2400 Sagamore Pkwy S (47903)
PHONE..................................765 772-4000
EMP: 9
Web: www.dana.com
SIC: 3714 Motor vehicle parts and accessories
PA: Dana Incorporated
    3939 Technology Dr
    Maumee OH 43537

(G-10569)
DEPENDABLE RUBBER INDUSTRIAL
201 Farabee Dr S (47905-4703)
P.O. Box 6081 (47903-6081)
PHONE..................................765 447-5654
Paul Swinford, *Pr*
EMP: 3 EST: 1991
SQ FT: 2,400
SALES (est): 939.99K **Privately Held**
Web: www.dripsinc.net
SIC: 5085 7699 3599 3492 Valves, pistons, and fittings; Hydraulic equipment repair; Flexible metal hose, tubing, and bellows; Hose and tube fittings and assemblies, hydraulic/pneumatic

(G-10570)
DESIRABLE SCENTS
3843 Daisy Dr (47905-4904)
PHONE..................................317 504-4976
EMP: 4 EST: 2013
SALES (est): 72.13K **Privately Held**
SIC: 2844 Perfumes, cosmetics and other toilet preparations

(G-10571)
DILDEN BROTHERS INC
Also Called: Dilden Bros Well & Drilling
1426 Canal Rd (47904-1832)
P.O. Box 1538 (47902-1538)
PHONE..................................765 742-1717
Wayne Findlay, *Pr*
Don Findlay, *Sec*
Dottie Findlay, *Mgr*
EMP: 29 EST: 1946
SQ FT: 9,000
SALES (est): 2.36MM **Privately Held**
Web: www.dildendrilling.com
SIC: 3533 1781 Water well drilling equipment; Servicing, water wells

(G-10572)
DUNCAN SUPPLY CO INC
Also Called: Johnson Contrls Authorized Dlr
510 Morland Dr (47905-4716)
PHONE..................................765 446-0105
Todd Brumley, *Mgr*
EMP: 5
SALES (corp-wide): 102.73MM **Privately Held**
Web: www.duncansupply.com
SIC: 5722 5078 3585 Household appliance stores; Commercial refrigeration equipment; Refrigeration equipment, complete
PA: Duncan Supply Co Inc
    910 N Illinois St
    Indianapolis IN 46204
    317 634-1335

(G-10573)
E-BEAM SERVICES INC
3400 Union St (47905-4448)
PHONE..................................765 447-6755
Robb Huff, *Brnch Mgr*
EMP: 2
SALES (corp-wide): 11.85MM **Privately Held**
Web: www.ebeamservices.com
SIC: 3999 Sterilizers, barber and beauty shop
PA: E-Beam Services, Inc.
    270 Duffy Ave Ste H
    Hicksville NY 11801
    516 622-1422

(G-10574)
ELEKTRSOLA DR GERD SCHLDBACH G
Also Called: REA Magnet Wire
2800 Concord Rd (47909)
PHONE..................................765 477-8000
John Hake, *Brnch Mgr*
EMP: 290
SALES (corp-wide): 1.88MM **Privately Held**
Web: www.reawire.com
SIC: 3351 3643 3357 3355 Wire, copper and copper alloy; Current-carrying wiring services; Nonferrous wiredrawing and insulating; Aluminum rolling and drawing, nec
HQ: Elektrisola Dr. Gerd Schildbach Gmbh & Co. Kg
    Zur Steinagger 3
    Reichshof NW 51580
    2265120

(G-10575)
EVONIK CORPORATION
Also Called: Tippecanoe Laboratories
1650 Lilly Rd (47909-9201)
PHONE..................................765 477-4300
Larry Mcshane, *Brnch Mgr*
EMP: 650
SALES (corp-wide): 2.27B **Privately Held**
Web: corporate.evonik.com
SIC: 2869 Industrial organic chemicals, nec
HQ: Evonik Corporation
    2 Turner Pl
    Piscataway NJ 08854
    732 982-5000

(G-10576)
FAIRFIELD MANUFACTURING CO INC (HQ)
Also Called: Dana Fairfield
2400 Sagamore Pkwy S (47903)
P.O. Box 7940 (47903)
PHONE..................................765 772-4000
David Evans, *Pr*
Garry Francis, *
Dave Martin, *
◆ EMP: 800 EST: 1919
SQ FT: 600,000
SALES (est): 189.67MM **Publicly Held**
Web: www.fairfieldmfg.com
SIC: 3462 3714 5085 7389 Gear and chain forgings; Gears, motor vehicle; Gears; Business services, nec
PA: Dana Incorporated
    3939 Technology Dr
    Maumee OH 43537

(G-10577)
FAIRFIELD MANUFACTURING CO INC
Also Called: Dana Fairfield
2309 Concord Rd (47909-2707)
PHONE..................................815 508-7353
Jeff Potrzebowski, *CFO*
EMP: 1
Web: www.oerlikon.com
SIC: 3714 3568 3545 Differentials and parts, motor vehicle; Power transmission equipment, nec; Machine tool accessories
HQ: Fairfield Manufacturing Company, Inc.
    2400 Sagamore Pkwy S
    Lafayette IN 47903

(G-10578)
FCA LLC
Also Called: FCA Packaging
3517 Crouch St (47905-4477)
PHONE..................................765 448-1775
Bryan Henry, *Brnch Mgr*
EMP: 1
Web: www.fcapackaging.com
SIC: 2448 Pallets, wood
PA: Fca, Llc
    7601 John Deere Pkwy
    Moline IL 61266

(G-10579)
FEDEX OFFICE & PRINT SVCS INC
Also Called: Fedex
3520 South St (47905-4724)
PHONE..................................765 449-4950
EMP: 10
SALES (corp-wide): 87.69B **Publicly Held**
Web: local.fedex.com
SIC: 7334 2796 2791 2789 Photocopying and duplicating services; Platemaking services; Typesetting; Bookbinding and related work
HQ: Fedex Office And Print Services, Inc.
    7900 Legacy Dr
    Plano TX 75024
    800 463-3339

(G-10580)
FOUR QUARTERS RE LLC
728 Cherokee Ave (47905-1872)
PHONE..................................765 474-2295
Lisa V Schrader, *Owner*
EMP: 1 EST: 2012
SALES (est): 98.84K **Privately Held**
SIC: 3131 Footwear cut stock

(G-10581)
FRECKLES GRPHICS LAFAYETTE INC
3835 Fortune Dr (47905-4879)
PHONE..................................765 448-4692
EMP: 15 EST: 1994
SQ FT: 20,000
SALES (est): 1.77MM **Privately Held**
Web: www.frecklesgraphics.com
SIC: 7389 7336 2759 2395 Sewing contractor; Commercial art and graphic design; Screen printing; Embroidery products, except Schiffli machine

(G-10582)
FREDDIE POWELL
339 S 30th St (47904-3138)
PHONE..................................574 658-3345
Powell Freddie, *Owner*
EMP: 1 EST: 2001
SALES (est): 102.31K **Privately Held**
SIC: 2621 Newsprint paper

(G-10583)
GALE INDUSTRIES INSLTN MATL
150 N 36th St (47905-4701)
PHONE..................................765 447-1191
EMP: 4 EST: 2012
SALES (est): 70.34K **Privately Held**
SIC: 3999 Hair and hair-based products

(G-10584)
GANNETT CO INC
Journal and Courier
1501 Veterans Memorial Pkwy E (47905-8917)
PHONE..................................765 423-5511
EMP: 1
SALES (corp-wide): 2.66B **Publicly Held**
Web: www.gannett.com
SIC: 2711 7375 Newspapers, publishing and printing; Information retrieval services
HQ: Gannett Media Corp.
    7950 Jones Branch Dr
    Mclean VA 22102
    703 854-6000

(G-10585)
GANNETT MEDIA CORP
Also Called: Journal and Courier
300 Main St Ste 314 (47901-1328)
PHONE..................................765 423-5512

Lafayette - Tippecanoe County (G-10610)

Gary M Suisman, *Publisher*
EMP: 217
SALES (corp-wide): 2.66B **Publicly Held**
Web: www.jconline.com
SIC: 2711 2752 Newspapers: publishing only, not printed on site; Commercial printing, lithographic
HQ: Gannett Media Corp.
7950 Jones Branch Dr
Mclean VA 22102
703 854-6000

(G-10586)
GARDINER RENTALS BILL
510 Veterans Memorial Pkwy E (47905-8790)
PHONE....................765 447-5111
Bill Gardiner, *Prin*
EMP: 4 **EST:** 2011
SALES (est): 249.57K **Privately Held**
Web: www.billgardinerrv.com
SIC: 3799 Recreational vehicles

(G-10587)
GARY RATCLIFF
Also Called: Ratcliff Enterprises
9950 Us Highway 231 S (47909-9050)
PHONE....................765 538-3170
Gary Ratcliff, *Owner*
EMP: 2 **EST:** 1986
SALES (est): 163.03K **Privately Held**
SIC: 3441 Fabricated structural metal

(G-10588)
GE AVIATION SYSTEMS LLC
Also Called: GE
3700 Us Highway 52 S (47905-7768)
PHONE....................765 432-5917
Eric Matteson, *Brnch Mgr*
EMP: 1
SALES (corp-wide): 67.95B **Publicly Held**
Web: www.geaerospace.com
SIC: 3724 Aircraft engines and engine parts
HQ: Ge Aviation Systems Llc
1 Neumann Way
Cincinnati OH 45215
937 898-9600

(G-10589)
GIBBS SUSIE FRAMING & ART
514 Main St (47901-1445)
PHONE....................765 428-2434
Susie Gibbs, *Owner*
EMP: 2 **EST:** 1984
SALES (est): 131.33K **Privately Held**
Web: www.susiegibbsframingandartgallery.com
SIC: 2499 8999 5999 Picture frame molding, finished; Artist; Art dealers

(G-10590)
GLGRAPHIX
311 Sagamore Pkwy N Ste 6 (47904-2800)
PHONE....................765 446-8600
EMP: 5 **EST:** 2019
SALES (est): 103.91K **Privately Held**
Web: www.glgraphix.com
SIC: 3993 Signs and advertising specialties

(G-10591)
GOLDDEN CORPORATION (PA)
Also Called: Crowd Factor
3601 Sagamore Pkwy N Ste E (47904-5041)
PHONE....................765 423-4366
Gary E Edmondson, *Pr*
EMP: 11 **EST:** 1980
SQ FT: 12,000
SALES (est): 2.34MM
SALES (corp-wide): 2.34MM **Privately Held**
Web: www.goldencorral.com
SIC: 5947 5699 2759 Souvenirs; Sports apparel; Screen printing

(G-10592)
GOLDEN LION INC
Also Called: Golden Lion Jewelers
3416 State Road 38 E (47905-5120)
PHONE....................765 446-9557
Millie Nelson, *Prin*
Paul Nelson, *Prin*
EMP: 2 **EST:** 1993
SALES (est): 156.83K **Privately Held**
Web: www.goldenlionengagementrings.com
SIC: 3911 5944 7631 5932 Jewelry, precious metal; Jewelry stores; Jewelry repair services; Pawnshop

(G-10593)
GRATEFUL HEART ENTERPRISES LLC
Also Called: Grateful Heart Gallery & Gifts
5082 Glacier Way (47909-9189)
PHONE....................765 838-2266
Diane L Gee, *Prin*
EMP: 9 **EST:** 2008
SQ FT: 2,400
SALES (est): 359.42K **Privately Held**
SIC: 3269 Art and ornamental ware, pottery

(G-10594)
HANDSTITCHED MEMORIES
56 Jester Ct (47905-7608)
PHONE....................765 430-4346
Linda Barlow, *Prin*
EMP: 5 **EST:** 2010
SALES (est): 49.28K **Privately Held**
SIC: 2395 Embroidery and art needlework

(G-10595)
HEARTLAND AUTOMOTIVE
3700 David Howarth Dr (47909-9360)
PHONE....................765 446-2311
Dave Percefull, *Prin*
▲ **EMP:** 1 **EST:** 2003
SALES (est): 2.42MM **Privately Held**
Web: www.hauto.net
SIC: 3714 Motor vehicle parts and accessories

(G-10596)
HEMOCLEANSE INC (PA)
3601 Sagamore Pkwy N Ste B (47904-5033)
PHONE....................765 742-4813
Robert B Truitt, *Pr*
Stephen R Ash Md, *Ch*
EMP: 13 **EST:** 1989
SQ FT: 10,000
SALES (est): 1.5MM **Privately Held**
Web: www.hemocleanse.com
SIC: 3841 Surgical and medical instruments

(G-10597)
HI-TECH CONCRETE INC
3691 S 500 E (47905-0510)
PHONE....................765 477-5550
Tom Berhammer, *Pr*
Ned Derhammer, *VP*
EMP: 8 **EST:** 2000
SALES (est): 547.84K **Privately Held**
SIC: 3272 Concrete products, nec

(G-10598)
HIGH QUALITY FLASKS LLC
3732 Navarre Ct (47905-4371)
PHONE....................765 357-6392
Matthew Hoon, *Pr*
Matthew Edward Hoon, *Managing Member*
EMP: 5 **EST:** 2021
SALES (est): 289.14K **Privately Held**
SIC: 3429 5999 Vacuum bottles or jugs; Miscellaneous retail stores, nec

(G-10599)
HIGHWAY SAFETY SERVICES INC
4121 S 500 E (47905-9314)
PHONE....................765 474-1000
Michael Madrid, *Pr*
EMP: 54 **EST:** 2005
SALES (est): 2.12MM **Privately Held**
Web: www.highwaysafetyservicesindiana.com
SIC: 7389 3669 7359 Flagging service (traffic control); Pedestrian traffic control equipment; Work zone traffic equipment (flags, cones, barrels, etc.)

(G-10600)
HOLDER BEDDING INC (PA)
Also Called: HB
230 Farabee Dr N (47905-5912)
PHONE....................765 447-7907
Daphine Holder, *Pr*
Scott Holder, *VP*
Allen Holder, *VP*
Gary Holder, *VP*
Carol Holder, *Sec*
EMP: 4 **EST:** 1986
SQ FT: 6,200
SALES (est): 1MM
SALES (corp-wide): 1MM **Privately Held**
Web: www.holderbeddingoflafayette.com
SIC: 5712 2515 Mattresses; Mattresses and foundations

(G-10601)
HOMER BANES
Also Called: Banes Machine Shop
520 S Earl Ave (47904-3262)
PHONE....................765 449-8551
Homer Banes, *Owner*
EMP: 2 **EST:** 1990
SALES (est): 229.21K **Privately Held**
SIC: 3569 General industrial machinery, nec

(G-10602)
HOWE HOUSE LTD EDITIONS INC (PA)
Also Called: Howe House Limited Editions
624 South St (47901-1469)
PHONE....................765 742-6831
William H Baugh, *Pr*
Rick Spies, *VP*
EMP: 3 **EST:** 2000
SALES (est): 491.62K
SALES (corp-wide): 491.62K **Privately Held**
Web: www.howehouse.com
SIC: 5199 2656 Gifts and novelties; Paper cups, plates, dishes, and utensils

(G-10603)
ICE CREAM SPECIALTIES INC
Also Called: North Star Distributing
2600 Concord Rd (47909-2773)
P.O. Box 679 (47902-0679)
PHONE....................765 474-2989
Robert Burkey, *Ltd Pt*
EMP: 100
SALES (corp-wide): 1.63B **Privately Held**
Web: www.northstarfrozentreats.com
SIC: 2024 Ice cream and frozen desserts
HQ: Ice Cream Specialties, Inc.
8419 Hanley Industrial Ct
Saint Louis MO 63144
314 962-2550

(G-10604)
IMPRESSIONS LLC
3007 1/2 Kossuth St (47904-3252)
PHONE....................765 490-2575
EMP: 6 **EST:** 1998
SALES (est): 177.11K **Privately Held**
Web: www.impressions.dental
SIC: 2752 Commercial printing, lithographic

(G-10605)
IN SPACE LLC
820 Roberts St (47904-1841)
PHONE....................765 775-2107
Amy Austin, *Mgr*
EMP: 9 **EST:** 2003
SALES (est): 769.96K **Privately Held**
Web: www.inspacellc.com
SIC: 8711 3764 Consulting engineer; Space propulsion units and parts

(G-10606)
INDIANA STEEL FABRICATING INC
925 S 1st St (47905-1034)
P.O. Box 748 (47902-0748)
PHONE....................765 742-1031
Stephen Porter, *Pr*
EMP: 12
SALES (corp-wide): 9.29MM **Privately Held**
Web: www.indianasteelfabricating.com
SIC: 3312 3441 Structural shapes and pilings, steel; Fabricated structural metal
PA: Indiana Steel Fabricating Inc
4545 W Bradbury Ave
Indianapolis IN 46241
317 247-4545

(G-10607)
INDUSTRIAL PLATING INC
120 N 36th St (47905-4786)
PHONE....................765 447-5036
Darrell Uerkwitz, *Pr*
William Uerkwitz, *
Charles Williams, *
EMP: 57 **EST:** 1955
SQ FT: 50,000
SALES (est): 4.93MM **Privately Held**
Web: www.industrialplatinginc.com
SIC: 3471 Electroplating of metals or formed products

(G-10608)
INSPIRED FIRE GL STDIO GLLERY
2124 State Road 25 W (47909-9229)
PHONE....................765 474-1981
Sharon Owens, *Owner*
EMP: 2 **EST:** 2003
SALES (est): 144.94K **Privately Held**
Web: www.inspiredfire.com
SIC: 3229 Glassware, art or decorative

(G-10609)
INTELLECTUAL QUALITY LLC
5004 Trotter Dr (47905-0710)
PHONE....................708 979-3127
EMP: 3
SALES (est): 121.77K **Privately Held**
SIC: 3161 Clothing and apparel carrying cases

(G-10610)
IRVING MATERIALS INC
Also Called: I M I
2903 Old State Road 25 N (47905-7891)
P.O. Box 2220 (47996-2220)
PHONE....................765 423-2533
Ron Knowles, *Brnch Mgr*
EMP: 6
SALES (corp-wide): 814.09MM **Privately Held**

Lafayette - Tippecanoe County (G-10611)   GEOGRAPHIC SECTION

Web: www.irvmat.com
SIC: 3273 Ready-mixed concrete
PA: Irving Materials, Inc.
   8032 N State Road 9
   Greenfield IN 46140
   317 326-3101

(G-10611)
J & K SUPPLY INC
3515 Coleman Ct (47905-4484)
PHONE..................765 448-1188
EMP: 9 EST: 1990
SALES (est): 993.58K Privately Held
Web: www.jandksupply.com
SIC: 3273 5169 Ready-mixed concrete; Chemicals, industrial and heavy

(G-10612)
J ROBERT SWITZER
1020 Beck Ln (47909-3067)
PHONE..................765 474-1307
EMP: 2 EST: 1970
SALES (est): 131.74K Privately Held
SIC: 2411 Logging

(G-10613)
JACOBS MFG LLC
218 Trowbridge Dr (47909-6925)
PHONE..................765 490-6111
EMP: 5 EST: 2009
SALES (est): 71.2K Privately Held
SIC: 3999 Manufacturing industries, nec

(G-10614)
JAMES A ANDREW INC
Also Called: Home Works
665 Maple Point Dr (47904)
PHONE..................765 269-9807
James Andrew, Brnch Mgr
EMP: 9
SALES (corp-wide): 11.88MM Privately Held
Web: www.henrypoor.com
SIC: 2426 Flooring, hardwood
PA: James A Andrew Inc
   3315 Brady Ln
   Lafayette IN 47909
   765 474-1388

(G-10615)
JESSUP PAPER BOX LLC
4775 Dale Dr (47905-7770)
PHONE..................765 588-9137
John D Huber Junior, Pr
EMP: 14 EST: 2002
SALES (est): 238.23K Privately Held
Web: www.jessuppaperbox.com
SIC: 2652 Setup paperboard boxes

(G-10616)
JKS MUSIC PUBLISHING LLC ◆
3817 Maplewood Dr (47905-4171)
PHONE..................888 461-8703
Dewayne Moffitt, CEO
EMP: 1 EST: 2022
SALES (est): 75.6K Privately Held
Web: www.jksmusicpublishing.com
SIC: 2741 Miscellaneous publishing

(G-10617)
K M DAVIS INC
Also Called: Drapery Gallery
919b Main St (47901-1465)
PHONE..................765 426-9227
Kathryn M Davis, Pr
EMP: 2 EST: 1981
SQ FT: 2,400
SALES (est): 167.16K Privately Held

SIC: 5713 5719 5231 5712 Floor covering stores; Window shades, nec; Wallpaper; Furniture stores

(G-10618)
KALEIDOSCOPE INC
1214 North St (47904-2561)
PHONE..................765 423-1951
Susan Delong, Pr
Susan De Long, Pr
EMP: 4 EST: 1974
SQ FT: 1,600
SALES (est): 292.57K Privately Held
Web: www.stainedglass4you.com
SIC: 3231 1793 Stained glass: made from purchased glass; Glass and glazing work

(G-10619)
KARMA INDUSTRIES INC
525 Wabash Ave (47905-1048)
PHONE..................765 742-9200
Adriana Corbin, Prin
EMP: 7 EST: 2017
SALES (est): 182.4K Privately Held
Web: www.karmaindustriesinc.com
SIC: 3999 Manufacturing industries, nec

(G-10620)
KINKOS INC
Also Called: Kinko's
3520 South St (47905-4724)
PHONE..................765 449-4950
Sylvia Zerbes, Mgr
EMP: 2 EST: 2010
SALES (est): 96.76K Privately Held
SIC: 2752 Commercial printing, lithographic

(G-10621)
KIRBY RISK CORPORATION
Also Called: Kirby Risk Servicenter
3574 Mccarty Ln (47905-4895)
P.O. Box 5089 (47903-5089)
PHONE..................765 447-1402
Kurt Jenkins, Mgr
EMP: 53
SALES (corp-wide): 501.02MM Privately Held
Web: www.kirbyrisk.com
SIC: 5063 3825 3714 3694 Electrical supplies, nec; Instruments to measure electricity; Motor vehicle parts and accessories; Engine electrical equipment
PA: Kirby Risk Corporation
   1815 Sagamore Pkwy N
   Lafayette IN 47904
   765 448-4567

(G-10622)
KIRBY RISK CORPORATION
Also Called: Kirby Risk Electric Motor Repr
714 S 1st St (47905-1009)
PHONE..................765 423-4205
Marty Guy, Mgr
EMP: 55
SALES (corp-wide): 501.02MM Privately Held
Web: www.kirbyrisk.com
SIC: 5063 7694 Electrical supplies, nec; Electric motor repair
PA: Kirby Risk Corporation
   1815 Sagamore Pkwy N
   Lafayette IN 47904
   765 448-4567

(G-10623)
KIRBY RISK CORPORATION (PA)
Also Called: Kirby Risk Electrical Supply
1815 Sagamore Pkwy N (47904-1765)
P.O. Box 5089 (47903-5089)
PHONE..................765 448-4567
James K Risk Iii, Pr

Jason J Bricker, *
Mary Jo Risk, *
Robert B Truitt, *
▲ EMP: 100 EST: 1926
SQ FT: 55,000
SALES (est): 501.02MM
SALES (corp-wide): 501.02MM Privately Held
Web: www.kirbyrisk.com
SIC: 5063 7694 3599 3679 Electrical supplies, nec; Electric motor repair; Machine shop, jobbing and repair; Harness assemblies, for electronic use: wire or cable

(G-10624)
KNOY APPAREL
1164 S Creasy Ln (47905-4959)
PHONE..................765 448-1031
EMP: 3 EST: 2007
SALES (est): 142.66K Privately Held
SIC: 2759 5941 Screen printing; Sporting goods and bicycle shops

(G-10625)
LAFAYETTE FURNITURE
3812 Fortune Dr (47905-4879)
PHONE..................765 446-9777
EMP: 4 EST: 2018
SALES (est): 90.43K Privately Held
Web: www.lafayettefurniture.com
SIC: 2599 Furniture and fixtures, nec

(G-10626)
LAFAYETTE INSTRUMENT CO LLC (PA)
Also Called: LI
3700 Sagamore Pkwy N (47904-1066)
P.O. Box 5729 (47903-5729)
PHONE..................765 423-1505
Jennifer Rider, Pr
Steve Rider, VP Opers
▲ EMP: 42 EST: 1995
SQ FT: 43,000
SALES (est): 10.58MM
SALES (corp-wide): 10.58MM Privately Held
Web: www.lafayetteinstrument.com
SIC: 3829 Polygraph devices

(G-10627)
LAFAYETTE MATERIALS MGT CO INC
Also Called: Lammco
635 Erie St (47904)
P.O. Box 6187 (47903)
PHONE..................765 447-7400
Daniel G Carmody, Pr
Abri A Camody, Sec
EMP: 4 EST: 1991
SQ FT: 1,920
SALES (est): 2.99MM Privately Held
Web: www.lammco.net
SIC: 5046 5211 5084 2599 Shelving, commercial and industrial; Closets, interiors and accessories; Materials handling machinery; Factory furniture and fixtures

(G-10628)
LAFAYETTE QUALITY PRODUCTS INC
111 Farabee Dr S (47905-4704)
P.O. Box 5827 (47903-5827)
PHONE..................765 446-0890
Roland Kuntz, Pr
EMP: 14 EST: 1961
SQ FT: 41,600
SALES (est): 1.91MM Privately Held
Web: www.lqp-mfg.com
SIC: 3599 Machine shop, jobbing and repair

(G-10629)
LAFAYETTE SIGN GUY LLC
310 Farabee Dr S (47905-4709)
PHONE..................765 771-9900
Philip Obrien, Admn
EMP: 4 EST: 2016
SALES (est): 99.35K Privately Held
Web: www.lafayettesignguy.com
SIC: 3993 Signs and advertising specialties

(G-10630)
LAFAYETTE TENTS & EVENTS LLC
3320 S 460 E (47905-7727)
PHONE..................765 742-4277
Benjamin Anderson, Prin
Henry Ebershoff, *
Craig Ebershoff, *
Sarah Ebershoff, *
Scott Ebershoff, *
EMP: 25 EST: 1913
SQ FT: 65,000
SALES (est): 4.22MM Privately Held
Web: www.lafayettetents.com
SIC: 2394 5999 Awnings, fabric: made from purchased materials; Tents

(G-10631)
LAFAYETTE TOOL & DIE INC
1836 Monon Ave (47904-1150)
PHONE..................765 429-6362
Larry W Skinner, Pr
Judy Skinner, Treas
EMP: 6 EST: 1995
SQ FT: 5,000
SALES (est): 455.37K Privately Held
Web: www.lafayettetoolanddie.com
SIC: 3544 Special dies and tools

(G-10632)
LAFAYETTE WIRE PRODUCTS INC
2700 Concord Rd (47909-2775)
P.O. Box 4552 (47903-4552)
PHONE..................765 474-7896
John S Castell, Ch Bd
Sam Newton,
Patricia C Castell, *
▲ EMP: 65 EST: 1979
SQ FT: 100,000
SALES (est): 9.73MM Privately Held
Web: www.lafayettewire.com
SIC: 3496 3537 Shelving, made from purchased wire; Industrial trucks and tractors

(G-10633)
LANDIS GYR UTILITIES SVCS INC
2800 Duncan Rd (47904-5012)
PHONE..................765 742-1001
John Grad, Pr
EMP: 55 EST: 1993
SALES (est): 3.96MM Privately Held
Web: www.landisgyr.com
SIC: 3613 Metering panels, electric

(G-10634)
LANDIS+GYR TECHNOLOGY INC
2800 Duncan Rd (47904-5012)
PHONE..................765 742-1001
EMP: 1
Web: www.landisgyr.com
SIC: 3825 Meters: electric, pocket, portable, panelboard, etc.
HQ: Landis+Gyr Technology, Inc.
   30000 Mill Creek Ave # 100
   Alpharetta GA 30022
   678 258-1295

(G-10635)
LAZY DOG PRESS LLC
Also Called: Lazy Dog Press

GEOGRAPHIC SECTION
Lafayette - Tippecanoe County (G-10661)

815 Wabash Ave (47905-1054)
PHONE..................510 227-9404
Jennifer Yeandle, *Managing Member*
EMP: 2 **EST:** 2019
SALES (est): 59.23K **Privately Held**
Web: www.lazydog.eu
SIC: 2741 Miscellaneous publishing

(G-10636)
LIGHT HOUSE CENTER INC (PA)
3918 Harry Ave (47905-5285)
PHONE..................765 448-4502
James Tarvin, *Pr*
Harry Van Der Noord, *Stockholder*
Tom Santefort, *Stockholder*
EMP: 15 **EST:** 1983
SQ FT: 2,400
SALES (est): 2.39MM
SALES (corp-wide): 2.39MM **Privately Held**
SIC: 5271 5211 3241 2452 Mobile home dealers; Modular homes; Cement, hydraulic; Prefabricated wood buildings

(G-10637)
LIONS PRIDE CUSTOMS LLC
6598 E 900 S (47909-9195)
PHONE..................765 490-8296
Chase T Woodrow, *Prin*
EMP: 4 **EST:** 2019
SALES (est): 65.93K **Privately Held**
SIC: 2431 Millwork

(G-10638)
LIQUIDSPRING LLC
4899 E 400 S (47905-9371)
PHONE..................765 474-7816
EMP: 6 **EST:** 2004
SQ FT: 2,000
SALES (est): 2.15MM **Privately Held**
Web: www.liquidspring.com
SIC: 3446 Acoustical suspension systems, metal

(G-10639)
LOUIES COMPANIES INC
2415 Sagamore Pkwy S (47905-5124)
PHONE..................765 448-4300
EMP: 1
SALES (corp-wide): 1.9MM **Privately Held**
Web: www.louiestuxshop.com
SIC: 7299 5699 2759 Tuxedo rental; Formal wear; Commercial printing, nec
PA: The Louie's Companies Inc
716 Lincoln Way W
South Bend IN 46616
574 234-1061

(G-10640)
LUDO FACT USA LLC (DH)
4775 Dale Dr (47905)
PHONE..................765 588-9137
EMP: 25 **EST:** 2016
SALES (est): 9.94MM
SALES (corp-wide): 115.96MM **Privately Held**
Web: www.ludofact.de
SIC: 3944 Board games, children's and adults'
HQ: Ludo Fact Usa Inc.
1000 Essington Rd
Joliet IL 60435

(G-10641)
LUND INTERNATIONAL HOLDING CO
Also Called: Roadworks Manufacturing
3565 E 300 N (47905-8819)
PHONE..................765 742-7200
EMP: 20
SALES (corp-wide): 829.18MM **Privately Held**
Web: www.roadworksmfg.com
SIC: 3647 3713 Headlights (fixtures), vehicular; Truck and bus bodies
HQ: Lund International Holding Company
4325 Hmlton Mill Rd Ste 4
Buford GA 30518

(G-10642)
MAPLE HILL NATURALS LLC
508 Fairington Ave (47905-3813)
PHONE..................765 427-9413
EMP: 1 **EST:** 2013
SALES (est): 75.24K **Privately Held**
SIC: 2844 Perfumes, cosmetics and other toilet preparations

(G-10643)
MAST SERVICES LAFAYETTE LLC ✪
Also Called: Construction
14 Torchwood Ct (47905-5214)
PHONE..................765 464-6940
Casey Mast, *Pr*
Casey L Mast, *Managing Member*
EMP: 7 **EST:** 2022
SALES (est): 408.69K **Privately Held**
Web: www.msllaf.com
SIC: 7389 7299 1389 Business Activities at Non-Commercial Site; Handyman service; Construction, repair, and dismantling services

(G-10644)
MCKINNEY CORPORATION
4710 Fastline Dr (47905-7914)
PHONE..................765 448-4800
Lawrence Mckinney, *Pr*
EMP: 20 **EST:** 1981
SALES (est): 2.35MM **Privately Held**
Web: www.mckinneycorp.com
SIC: 3599 Machine shop, jobbing and repair

(G-10645)
MEDTRIC LLC
4129 Nauset Dr (47909-8269)
PHONE..................765 427-7234
Jianming Li, *Mgr*
EMP: 3 **EST:** 2010
SQ FT: 600
SALES (est): 240.28K **Privately Held**
Web: www.medtricbiotech.com
SIC: 2833 Medicinals and botanicals

(G-10646)
MENTAL REHABILITATION
1322 Fairfax Dr (47909-7312)
P.O. Box 4456 (47903-4456)
PHONE..................765 414-5590
Russell W Burry, *Pr*
EMP: 6 **EST:** 2005
SALES (est): 485.68K **Privately Held**
SIC: 7372 Prepackaged software

(G-10647)
MID AMERICA PRINT COUNCIL INC
2217 Miami Trl (47906-1923)
PHONE..................765 463-3971
Michal Hathaway, *Prin*
EMP: 2 **EST:** 2000
SALES (est): 115.27K **Privately Held**
Web: www.midamericaprintcouncil.org
SIC: 2752 Commercial printing, lithographic

(G-10648)
MIDWEST COIL LLC
2304 Brothers Dr Ste A (47909-2292)
PHONE..................765 807-5429
Michael E Corcoran, *Managing Member*
▲ **EMP:** 8 **EST:** 2007
SALES (est): 530.4K **Privately Held**
Web: www.midwestcoil.com
SIC: 3677 Electronic coils and transformers

(G-10649)
MIDWEST FADE CONTROL
4901 Tazer Dr (47905-4696)
PHONE..................219 926-5043
Joel Meyers, *Prin*
EMP: 1 **EST:** 2010
SALES (est): 130K **Privately Held**
SIC: 3211 Window glass, clear and colored

(G-10650)
MILESTONE CONTRACTORS LP
3301 S 460 E (47905-7727)
P.O. Box 6246 (47903-6246)
PHONE..................765 772-7500
EMP: 70
SALES (corp-wide): 894.43MM **Privately Held**
Web: www.milestonelp.com
SIC: 1611 2951 Highway and street paving contractor; Asphalt paving mixtures and blocks
HQ: Milestone Contractors, L.P.
5757 Decatur Blvd Ste 250
Indianapolis IN 46241
317 788-6885

(G-10651)
MITCHELL FABRICS INC
3532 Coleman Ct Ste B (47905-4455)
PHONE..................309 674-8631
Mitchell Favus, *Pr*
EMP: 30 **EST:** 1945
SALES (est): 4.79MM **Privately Held**
Web: www.mitchellfabrics.com
SIC: 5131 2591 Drapery material, woven; Blinds vertical

(G-10652)
MODERN BIOLOGY INCORPORATED
2211 South St (47904-2968)
PHONE..................765 523-3338
Martha J Anderson, *Pr*
EMP: 4 **EST:** 1987
SALES (est): 300.4K **Privately Held**
Web: www.modernbio.com
SIC: 3999 Education aids, devices and supplies

(G-10653)
MONSANTO COMPANY
Also Called: MONSANTO COMPANY
6025 W 300 S (47909-9278)
PHONE..................323 265-1025
Elizabeth Hawkins, *Brnch Mgr*
EMP: 6
SALES (corp-wide): 51.78B **Privately Held**
Web: www.monsanto.com
SIC: 2879 Agricultural chemicals, nec
HQ: Monsanto Technology Llc.
800 N Lindbergh Blvd
Saint Louis MO 63167
314 694-1000

(G-10654)
MR-LINK LLC
408 Brunswick Dr Apt 13 (47909-6983)
PHONE..................512 297-4582
Nishant Babaria, *CEO*
Zhongming Liu, *Pr*
Ranajay Mandal, *VP*
EMP: 2 **EST:** 2017
SALES (est): 79.02K **Privately Held**
Web: www.expiredwixdomain.com
SIC: 3845 Electromedical equipment

(G-10655)
MTA TECHNOLOGY LLC
2624 Salem St (47904-2726)
PHONE..................765 447-2221
Maung Than, *Managing Member*
EMP: 10 **EST:** 2016
SALES (est): 483.86K **Privately Held**
SIC: 3089 7389 Corrugated panels, plastics; Business services, nec

(G-10656)
NACJAM INTERIOR BLINDS INC
5021 Saddle Dr (47905-7695)
PHONE..................765 449-8035
EMP: 5 **EST:** 2016
SALES (est): 66.81K **Privately Held**
SIC: 2591 Window blinds

(G-10657)
NANSHAN AMER ADVNCED ALUM TECH
3600 Us Highway 52 S (47905-7706)
PHONE..................765 838-8645
John Linson, *Pr*
Hunzian Zhao, *
◆ **EMP:** 230 **EST:** 2011
SQ FT: 600,000
SALES (est): 110MM **Privately Held**
Web: www.nanshanusa.com
SIC: 3334 3341 Primary aluminum; Aluminum smelting and refining (secondary)
PA: Shandong Nanshan Aluminium Co.,Ltd.
Nanshan Village,Dongjiang Town, Longkou
Yantai SD 26570

(G-10658)
NEW CONCEPT METAL DETECTOR
511 N Earl Ave (47904-2818)
PHONE..................765 447-2681
Iris Perez, *Owner*
EMP: 7 **EST:** 2005
SALES (est): 972.16K **Privately Held**
Web: www.newconceptflooringin.com
SIC: 3669 Metal detectors

(G-10659)
NKA CABINET DESIGNS LLC ✪
90 Professional Ct (47905-5152)
PHONE..................765 490-4661
Nathan Allen, *Managing Member*
EMP: 4 **EST:** 2022
SALES (est): 68.7K **Privately Held**
SIC: 7389 2434 Design services; Wood kitchen cabinets

(G-10660)
OLIVE BRANCH ETC INC
Also Called: Sign Art Etc
181 Sagamore Pkwy S Ste B (47905-4744)
PHONE..................765 449-1884
Doug Ellenberger, *Pr*
▲ **EMP:** 9 **EST:** 2003
SQ FT: 8,000
SALES (est): 980.21K **Privately Held**
Web: www.signartetc.com
SIC: 3993 7389 Signs, not made in custom sign painting shops; Advertising, promotional, and trade show services

(G-10661)
PACKAGING SYSTEMS INDIANA INC (PA)
3532 Crouch St (47905-4476)
PHONE..................765 449-1011
Patrick J Tharp, *Pr*
Robert A Tharp, *Sec*
EMP: 9 **EST:** 1989
SQ FT: 10,500
SALES (est): 8.63MM **Privately Held**
Web: www.packaging-systems.com
SIC: 3565 Packaging machinery

(PA)=Parent Co (HQ)=Headquarters
✪ = New Business established in last 2 years

Lafayette - Tippecanoe County (G-10662)

(G-10662)
PALMER CANING
3204 Olympia Dr Ste A (47909-5111)
PHONE.................................773 394-4913
EMP: 5 EST: 2015
SALES (est): 146.32K **Privately Held**
SIC: 3556 Food products machinery

(G-10663)
PATTERSON ENGRG & MFG LLC
517 N Admirals Pointe Dr (47909-8201)
PHONE.................................217 260-1415
Donald Patterson, *Owner*
EMP: 2 EST: 2002
SALES (est): 208.51K **Privately Held**
SIC: 3699 Electrical equipment and supplies, nec

(G-10664)
PAUL MILLER
Also Called: Rock N' Roll Alley
1516 Sherwood Dr (47909-3746)
PHONE.................................765 449-4893
Paul Miller, *Owner*
EMP: 5 EST: 1986
SALES (est): 340.76K **Privately Held**
SIC: 3552 5699 Silk screens for textile industry; T-shirts, custom printed

(G-10665)
PAYNES FINE CABRINETRY
7705 E 300 N (47905-9624)
PHONE.................................765 589-9176
EMP: 3 EST: 1984
SALES (est): 183.5K **Privately Held**
SIC: 2434 Wood kitchen cabinets

(G-10666)
PEERLESS PATTERN & MACHINE CO
3521 Coleman Ct (47905-4484)
PHONE.................................765 477-7719
Nathan D Scaggs, *Pr*
Joyce Scaggs, *Treas*
EMP: 9 EST: 1967
SQ FT: 10,000
SALES (est): 835.12K **Privately Held**
Web: www.peerlesspattern.com
SIC: 7692 3599 3543 Welding repair; Machine and other job shop work; Industrial patterns

(G-10667)
PERRY FOAM PRODUCTS INC (PA)
Also Called: Diskit Sales Division
2335 S 30th St (47909)
PHONE.................................765 474-3404
Richard Landrum, *Pr*
Scott Kempin, *
David P Holder, *
▲ EMP: 34 EST: 1960
SQ FT: 40,000
SALES (est): 5.38MM
SALES (corp-wide): 5.38MM **Privately Held**
Web: www.perryfoam.com
SIC: 3089 Injection molding of plastics

(G-10668)
PHOENIX INT PUBLICATIONS
4792 E 400 S Ste B (47905-9371)
PHONE.................................317 796-2375
EMP: 5 EST: 2018
SALES (est): 202.64K **Privately Held**
SIC: 2741 Miscellaneous publishing

(G-10669)
PPG ARCHITECTURAL FINISHES INC
Also Called: Glidden Professional Paint Ctr
15 N Earl Ave (47904-2812)
PHONE.................................765 447-9334
Tim Johnston, *Mgr*
EMP: 5
SALES (corp-wide): 17.65B **Publicly Held**
Web: www.ppgpaints.com
SIC: 2851 Paints and allied products
HQ: Ppg Architectural Finishes, Inc.
    1 Ppg Pl
    Pittsburgh PA 15272
    412 434-3131

(G-10670)
PRIMARY PDTS INGRDNTS AMRCAS L
2245 Sagamore Pkwy N (47904-1620)
P.O. Box 1398 (47902-1398)
PHONE.................................765 448-7123
Jayne Rockhill, *Brnch Mgr*
EMP: 86
SALES (corp-wide): 1.16B **Privately Held**
Web: www.tateandlyle.com
SIC: 2046 Wet corn milling
HQ: Primary Products Ingredients
    Americas Llc
    2200 E Eldorado St
    Decatur IL 62521
    217 423-4411

(G-10671)
PRIMARY PDTS INGRDNTS AMRCAS L
Also Called: Primmient
3300 Us Highway 52 S (47905-7701)
P.O. Box 7977 (47903-7977)
PHONE.................................765 474-5474
Keith Oliger, *Brnch Mgr*
EMP: 262
SALES (corp-wide): 1.16B **Privately Held**
Web: www.tateandlyle.com
SIC: 2046 Wet corn milling
HQ: Primary Products Ingredients
    Americas Llc
    2200 E Eldorado St
    Decatur IL 62521
    217 423-4411

(G-10672)
PURDY CONCRETE INC (PA)
3633 Old Us Highway 231 S (47909-2422)
PHONE.................................765 477-7687
Carol A Purdy, *Pr*
Edward Purdy, *Sec*
EMP: 5 EST: 1958
SALES (est): 4.97MM
SALES (corp-wide): 4.97MM **Privately Held**
Web: www.purdyconcrete.com
SIC: 3273 Ready-mixed concrete

(G-10673)
PURDY MATERIALS INC
3633 Us Highway 231 S (47909-2422)
PHONE.................................765 474-8993
Edward Purdy, *Pr*
Carol Purdy, *Prin*
EMP: 25 EST: 1997
SALES (est): 1.03MM **Privately Held**
Web: www.purdymaterials.com
SIC: 3273 Ready-mixed concrete

(G-10674)
PYRAMID SIGN & DESIGN INC
515 Farabee Dr S (47905-4712)
PHONE.................................765 447-4174
Rex Deaton, *Pr*
Robert Vandergraff Ii, *VP*
Brian Roark, *Sec*
EMP: 4 EST: 1982
SQ FT: 3,600
SALES (est): 340.6K **Privately Held**
Web: www.pyramidsignanddesign.com
SIC: 3993 7532 5999 Signs and advertising specialties; Lettering, automotive; Decals

(G-10675)
RADIAN RESEARCH INC
Also Called: Utility Test Equipment Company
3852 Fortune Dr (47905-4879)
PHONE.................................765 449-5500
Timothy C Everidge, *Pr*
Martin Rogers, *
◆ EMP: 60 EST: 1982
SQ FT: 22,000
SALES (est): 20.66MM **Privately Held**
Web: www.radianresearch.com
SIC: 3825 8748 Power measuring equipment, electrical; Systems analysis or design

(G-10676)
RALPH PRIVOZNIK JEWELRY ART
1010 Main St (47901-1541)
PHONE.................................765 742-4904
Ralph Privoznik, *Owner*
EMP: 1 EST: 1971
SQ FT: 200
SALES (est): 72.66K **Privately Held**
Web: www.ralphprivoznikjewelryart.com
SIC: 3911 5944 Jewelry, precious metal; Jewelry stores

(G-10677)
RAYNE WATER CONDITIONING
2706 Elk St (47904)
PHONE.................................765 742-8967
EMP: 6 EST: 2019
SALES (est): 35.66K **Privately Held**
Web: www.raynewater.com
SIC: 5999 3589 Water purification equipment; Service industry machinery, nec

(G-10678)
RED STORM ATHLETICS INC
156 Sagamore Pkwy W (47906-1569)
PHONE.................................765 464-3336
Greg Tudor, *Owner*
EMP: 6 EST: 2006
SALES (est): 120K **Privately Held**
Web: www.wlredstorm.org
SIC: 2329 Athletic clothing, except uniforms: men's, youths' and boys'

(G-10679)
REPROCOMM INC
Lafayette Printing
1400 Teal Rd Ste 1 (47905-2463)
PHONE.................................765 423-2578
EMP: 1
SALES (corp-wide): 8.82MM **Privately Held**
Web: www.marketing.com
SIC: 2752 2789 Offset printing; Bookbinding and related work
PA: Reprocomm Inc
    179 N Miami St
    Peru IN 46970
    765 472-5700

(G-10680)
RICK BLACK ASSOCIATES LLC
Also Called: Wildcat Creek Winery
3233 E 200 N (47905-8801)
PHONE.................................765 838-3498
Richard Black, *Managing Member*
EMP: 7 EST: 2008
SALES (est): 477.72K **Privately Held**
Web: www.wildcatcreekwinery.com
SIC: 2084 Wines

(G-10681)
ROYAL BARBIE BLINKS LLC
408 Brunswick Dr (47909-6980)
PHONE.................................765 400-6205
EMP: 1
SALES (est): 39.69K **Privately Held**
SIC: 3999 7389 Eyelashes, artificial; Business Activities at Non-Commercial Site

(G-10682)
S & S PROGRAMMING INC
625 S Earl Ave Ste D (47904-3602)
PHONE.................................765 423-4472
Keith Schuman, *Pr*
EMP: 6 EST: 1981
SALES (est): 474.93K **Privately Held**
Web: www.sspro.com
SIC: 7372 5045 Business oriented computer software; Computers, peripherals, and software

(G-10683)
SANOH AMERICA INC
3701 David Howarth Dr Ste C (47909-9388)
PHONE.................................419 425-2600
Ronald Frisch, *Dir Fin*
EMP: 1
Web: www.sanoh-america.com
SIC: 3465 Body parts, automobile: stamped metal
HQ: Sanoh America, Inc.
    1849 Industrial Dr
    Findlay OH 45840
    419 425-2600

(G-10684)
SCAGGS MOTO DESIGNS
3521 Coleman Ct (47905-4484)
PHONE.................................765 426-2526
Jared Scaggs, *Prin*
EMP: 5 EST: 2015
SALES (est): 104.33K **Privately Held**
Web: www.scaggsracks.com
SIC: 3999 Manufacturing industries, nec

(G-10685)
SCALAR DESIGN ENGRG & DIST LLC
836 Shawnee Ave (47905-1456)
PHONE.................................765 429-5545
EMP: 2 EST: 2001
SALES (est): 218.26K **Privately Held**
Web: www.sded.co
SIC: 3824 8711 Mechanical and electromechanical counters and devices; Designing: ship, boat, machine, and product

(G-10686)
SCHUG AWARDS LLC
229 S 30th St (47909)
PHONE.................................765 447-0002
Sharon A Schug, *Managing Member*
EMP: 4 EST: 2014
SALES (est): 217.64K **Privately Held**
Web: www.engravelafayette.com
SIC: 5999 2499 Trophies and plaques; Trophy bases, wood

(G-10687)
SCHUMAKER TECHNICAL ASSEMBLY
681 N 36th St (47905-4475)
P.O. Box 439 (47902-0439)
PHONE.................................765 742-7176
Daniel A Schumaker, *Owner*
EMP: 8 EST: 1988
SQ FT: 3,500
SALES (est): 686.06K **Privately Held**
Web: www.schumakertech.com

GEOGRAPHIC SECTION
Lafayette - Tippecanoe County (G-10714)

SIC: 3679 Electronic circuits

(G-10688)
SCOTTORSVILLE SALES AND SVC
602 S Earl Ave (47904-3264)
PHONE.................................765 250-5245
EMP: 5 EST: 2012
SALES (est): 26.55K Privately Held
SIC: 3621 Motors, electric

(G-10689)
SDI INNOVATIONS INC (PA)
Also Called: School Datebooks
2880 Us Highway 231 S Ste 200 (47909-2874)
PHONE.................................765 471-8883
Timothy J Powers, Pr
Jeff Bapst, *
Scott Brady, *
▲ EMP: 117 EST: 1985
SQ FT: 10,000
SALES (est): 22.81MM Privately Held
Web: www.schooldatebooks.com
SIC: 2731 Textbooks: publishing and printing

(G-10690)
SERAPHIM COFFEE
1 Berwick Dr (47909)
PHONE.................................765 409-1942
EMP: 2 EST: 2020
SALES (est): 62.38K Privately Held
SIC: 2095 Coffee roasting (except by wholesale grocers)

(G-10691)
SMG GLOBAL INC
3701 David Howarth Dr Ste B (47909-9387)
PHONE.................................765 250-0081
Yaolu Jia, Owner
EMP: 7 EST: 2018
SALES (est): 142.74K Privately Held
SIC: 3679 Electronic circuits

(G-10692)
SMR MANAGEMENT INC
Also Called: SMR MANAGEMENT INC
2139 Klondike Rd (47906-5124)
PHONE.................................765 252-0257
Tom Houck, Brnch Mgr
EMP: 2
SALES (corp-wide): 1.57MM Privately Held
SIC: 3714 Motor vehicle parts and accessories
PA: Smr Management Inc.
    1728 Coral Way
    Coral Gables FL 33145
    305 529-2488

(G-10693)
SOUTHWIRE COMPANY LLC
3400 Union St (47905-4448)
PHONE.................................765 449-7227
EMP: 46
SALES (corp-wide): 1.7B Privately Held
Web: www.southwire.com
SIC: 3351 Copper rolling and drawing
PA: Southwire Company, Llc
    One Southwire Dr
    Carrollton GA 30119
    770 832-4529

(G-10694)
SOY MAGNIFISCENTS
651 N 7th St Apt 2 (47901-2409)
PHONE.................................765 746-6358
Cathy Collins, Prin
EMP: 4 EST: 2017
SALES (est): 78.99K Privately Held
SIC: 3999 Candles

(G-10695)
SPEEDPRO IMAGING
311 Sagamore Pkwy N Ste 6 (47904-2800)
PHONE.................................765 446-8600
Mark Sweval, Prin
EMP: 6 EST: 2012
SALES (est): 233.33K Privately Held
Web: www.speedpro.com
SIC: 3993 Signs and advertising specialties

(G-10696)
SQUAREFRAME INDUSTRIES LLC
25 Executive Dr Ste G (47905-4880)
PHONE.................................765 430-3301
EMP: 1 EST: 2013
SALES (est): 92.67K Privately Held
Web: www.ironcloudtech.com
SIC: 3999 Atomizers, toiletry

(G-10697)
STACKS LIMITED
4570 Duckhorn Ln (47909-8413)
PHONE.................................765 409-5081
Jason Murray, Prin
EMP: 1 EST: 2017
SALES (est): 55K Privately Held
Web: www.borrowmypickup.com
SIC: 4213 7372 Automobiles, transport and delivery; Business oriented computer software

(G-10698)
STALL & KESSLER INC
Also Called: Stall Kessler's Diamond Center
333 Columbia St (47901-1315)
P.O. Box 938 (47902-0938)
PHONE.................................765 742-1259
Jeffery Kessler, Pr
EMP: 7 EST: 1979
SQ FT: 2,000
SALES (est): 897.31K Privately Held
Web: www.stallandkessler.com
SIC: 5944 3911 7631 Watches; Jewelry, precious metal; Watch, clock, and jewelry repair

(G-10699)
STATIC PEN PUBLISHING LLC
10 N Tahoe Ct (47909-2643)
P.O. Box 5742 (47903-5742)
PHONE.................................765 609-0202
Amanda Hardebeck, Brnch Mgr
EMP: 6
SALES (corp-wide): 61.24K Privately Held
SIC: 2741 Miscellaneous publishing
PA: Static Pen Publishing Llc
    Lafayette IN

(G-10700)
STEINER ENTERPRISES INC
3532 Coleman Ct Ste B (47905-4455)
PHONE.................................765 429-6409
Ed Steiner, Pr
Thomas P Hicks, Pr
▲ EMP: 18 EST: 1991
SQ FT: 4,500
SALES (est): 4.98MM Privately Held
Web: www.steineronline.com
SIC: 3824 Mechanical and electromechanical counters and devices

(G-10701)
STYLES KITCHEN LLC ✪
3117 Coppergate Dr Apt 8 (47909-0909)
PHONE.................................765 405-6875
Prystal Hale, CEO
EMP: 2 EST: 2023
SALES (est): 80.88K Privately Held
SIC: 3089 Kitchenware, plastics

(G-10702)
STYLES VERSATILITY LLC ✪
1601 Vinton St (47904)
PHONE.................................765 270-2217
Blake Hale, Owner
EMP: 1 EST: 2023
SALES (est): 54.05K Privately Held
SIC: 3581 Automatic vending machines

(G-10703)
SUBARU INDIANA AUTOMOTIVE INC (HQ)
5500 State Road 38 E (47905)
P.O. Box 5689 (47903)
PHONE.................................765 449-1111
Nobuyuki Bando, Ch Bd
Scott Brand, *
Tatsuya Nishizawa, *
◆ EMP: 5500 EST: 1987
SQ FT: 2,700,000
SALES (est): 874.98MM Privately Held
Web: www.subaru-sia.com
SIC: 5511 3711 Automobiles, new and used; Automobile assembly, including specialty automobiles
PA: Subaru Corporation
    1-20-8, Ebisu
    Shibuya-Ku TKY 150-0

(G-10704)
SUGARCUBE SYSTEMS INC
2746 Margesson Xing (47909-8092)
PHONE.................................765 543-6709
Jason Clark, Pr
EMP: 2 EST: 2013
SALES (est): 126.42K Privately Held
SIC: 3559 7389 Semiconductor manufacturing machinery; Business Activities at Non-Commercial Site

(G-10705)
SUITABLE STYLEZ
2660 Hastings Ct Apt C (47905-5782)
PHONE.................................765 409-9375
Angelique Warren, Owner
EMP: 1
SALES (est): 39.69K Privately Held
SIC: 3999 7389 Eyelashes, artificial; Business Activities at Non-Commercial Site

(G-10706)
SUNDANCE SIGNS
1116b S 4th St (47905-1756)
PHONE.................................765 420-7446
John Boehm, Owner
EMP: 2 EST: 1997
SALES (est): 11.5K Privately Held
Web: www.sundancesigncompany.com
SIC: 3993 Signs and advertising specialties

(G-10707)
SURPLUS STORE AND EXCHANGE
Also Called: Vierks Fine Jewelry
1650 Main St (47904-2919)
PHONE.................................765 447-0200
Dan Vierk, Pr
EMP: 14 EST: 1946
SQ FT: 10,000
SALES (est): 827.12K Privately Held
Web: www.vierks.com
SIC: 5094 5944 3911 Jewelry; Jewelry, precious stones and precious metals; Jewel settings and mountings, precious metal

(G-10708)
T-H LICENSING INC
2400 Sagamore Pkwy S (47905-5116)
PHONE.................................765 772-4128
Michael Blinn, Sec
EMP: 36 EST: 1989
SALES (est): 671.87K Privately Held
SIC: 3462 Gear and chain forgings
PA: Oc Oerlikon Corporation Ag, Pfaffikon
    Churerstrasse 120
    PfAffikon SZ 8808

(G-10709)
TACTILE ENGINEERING INC
3601 Sagamore Pkwy N Ste C (47904-5033)
PHONE.................................765 233-6620
David Schleppenbac, CEO
David Schleppenbach, Pr
EMP: 21 EST: 2019
SALES (est): 1.55MM Privately Held
Web: www.tactile-engineering.com
SIC: 3089 Hardware, plastics

(G-10710)
TRW COMMERCIAL STEERING
800 Heath St (47904-1863)
P.O. Box 60 (47902-0060)
PHONE.................................765 423-5377
Lynn Honsey, VP
◆ EMP: 40 EST: 1906
SALES (est): 2.24MM Privately Held
SIC: 3714 Motor vehicle parts and accessories

(G-10711)
TWIN PRINTS INC
Also Called: Instant Copy
701 Main St (47901-1459)
PHONE.................................765 742-8656
William Freeman, VP
James Speed, Pr
EMP: 6 EST: 1985
SQ FT: 6,000
SALES (est): 784.09K Privately Held
Web: www.instantcopyprinting.com
SIC: 2752 Offset printing

(G-10712)
VICTORIAN HOUSE SCONES LLC
1305 Richards St (47904-2658)
P.O. Box 8094 (47903-8094)
PHONE.................................765 586-6295
Deborah Anderson, Managing Member
EMP: 2 EST: 2003
SALES (est): 121.62K Privately Held
Web: www.victorianhousescones.com
SIC: 2052 Bakery products, dry

(G-10713)
WABASH NATIONAL LP (HQ)
1000 Sagamore Pkwy S (47905-4727)
P.O. Box 6129 (47903-6129)
PHONE.................................765 771-5300
▲ EMP: 45 EST: 1999
SALES (est): 47.46MM
SALES (corp-wide): 2.54B Publicly Held
Web: www.onewabash.com
SIC: 3715 3792 Truck trailers; Travel trailers and campers
PA: Wabash National Corporation
    3900 Mccarty Ln
    Lafayette IN 47905
    765 771-5310

(G-10714)
WABASH NATIONAL CORPORATION
3550 Veterans Memorial Pkwy S (47909-9374)
PHONE.................................800 937-4784
EMP: 83
SALES (corp-wide): 2.54B Publicly Held
Web: www.onewabash.com
SIC: 3715 Truck trailers
PA: Wabash National Corporation
    3900 Mccarty Ln
    Lafayette IN 47905

Lafayette - Tippecanoe County (G-10715)

765 771-5310

(G-10715)
WABASH NATIONAL CORPORATION
3000 Main St (47904-3356)
PHONE.................765 771-5300
EMP: 47
SALES (corp-wide): 2.54B Publicly Held
Web: www.onewabash.com
SIC: 3715 3714 5012 Truck trailers; Motor vehicle parts and accessories; Automobiles and other motor vehicles
PA: Wabash National Corporation
3900 Mccarty Ln
Lafayette IN 47905
765 771-5310

(G-10716)
WABASH NATIONAL CORPORATION (PA)
Also Called: Wabash
3900 Mccarty Ln Ste 202 (47905)
P.O. Box 6129 (47903)
PHONE.................765 771-5310
Brent L Yeagy, Pr
Larry J Magee, *
Michael N Pettit, Sr VP
Dustin T Smith, Sr VP
Kevin J Page, CCO
▲ EMP: 502 EST: 1985
SALES (est): 2.54B
SALES (corp-wide): 2.54B Publicly Held
Web: www.onewabash.com
SIC: 3715 3714 5012 Truck trailers; Motor vehicle parts and accessories; Automobiles and other motor vehicles

(G-10717)
WABASH NATIONAL MFG LP
1000 Sagamore Pkwy S (47905-4727)
P.O. Box 6129 (47903-6129)
PHONE.................765 771-5310
EMP: 441
SALES (est): 5.07MM
SALES (corp-wide): 2.54B Publicly Held
Web: www.onewabash.com
SIC: 3715 Truck trailers
PA: Wabash National Corporation
3900 Mccarty Ln
Lafayette IN 47905
765 771-5310

(G-10718)
WASTE 1
3304 Concord Rd (47909-5128)
PHONE.................765 477-9138
Tom Mcdonald, Prin
EMP: 10 EST: 2007
SALES (est): 433.18K Privately Held
SIC: 3089 Garbage containers, plastics

(G-10719)
WORWAG COATINGS
2330 S 30th St (47909)
PHONE.................765 746-6037
EMP: 6 EST: 2018
SALES (est): 109.91K Privately Held
Web: www.woerwag.com
SIC: 2851 Paints and allied products

(G-10720)
XEROX CORP
698 Ahlers Dr (47907-2113)
PHONE.................765 494-6511
EMP: 10 EST: 2019
SALES (est): 410.05K Privately Held
Web: www.xerox.com
SIC: 3577 Computer peripheral equipment, nec

(G-10721)
ZF ACTIVE SAFETY & ELEC US LLC
4820 Dale Dr (47905-7770)
PHONE.................765 429-1984
EMP: 60
SALES (corp-wide): 144.19K Privately Held
SIC: 3469 3679 3089 Metal stampings, nec; Electronic switches; Plastics processing
HQ: Zf Active Safety & Electronics Us Llc
34605 W 12 Mile Rd
Farmington Hills MI 48331
765 429-1936

(G-10722)
ZF ACTIVE SAFETY & ELEC US LLC
9th & Greenbush (47904)
PHONE.................765 429-1678
Brian Kipp, Brnch Mgr
EMP: 32
SALES (corp-wide): 144.19K Privately Held
SIC: 3714 Motor vehicle parts and accessories
HQ: Zf Active Safety & Electronics Us Llc
34605 W 12 Mile Rd
Farmington Hills MI 48331
765 429-1936

(G-10723)
ZF ACTIVE SAFETY & ELEC US LLC
1450 N 9th St (47904)
PHONE.................765 429-1936
EMP: 59
SALES (corp-wide): 144.19K Privately Held
SIC: 3714 Motor vehicle parts and accessories
HQ: Zf Active Safety & Electronics Us Llc
34605 W 12 Mile Rd
Farmington Hills MI 48331
765 429-1936

(G-10724)
ZF ACTIVE SAFETY & ELEC US LLC
Also Called: TRW Atmtive Coml String System
800 Heath St (47904-1863)
P.O. Box 60 (47902-0060)
PHONE.................765 423-5377
Brian Kipp, Brnch Mgr
EMP: 655
SALES (corp-wide): 144.19K Privately Held
SIC: 3714 Motor vehicle parts and accessories
HQ: Zf Active Safety & Electronics Us Llc
34605 W 12 Mile Rd
Farmington Hills MI 48331
765 429-1936

(G-10725)
ZF NORTH AMERICA INC
1450 N 9th St (47904)
PHONE.................765 429-1622
Marina Brouillette, Brnch Mgr
EMP: 38
SALES (corp-wide): 144.19K Privately Held
Web: www.zf.com
SIC: 3714 Motor vehicle parts and accessories
HQ: Zf North America, Inc.
15811 Centennial Dr
Northville MI 48168

(G-10726)
ZOJILA LTD LIABILITY COMPANY
2004 N 9th St (47904-1036)
PHONE.................765 404-3767
▲ EMP: 2 EST: 2002
SALES (est): 114.75K Privately Held
Web: www.zojila.com
SIC: 7389 3469 Design services; Kitchen fixtures and equipment: metal, except cast aluminum

(G-10727)
ZS SYSTEMS LLC
675 N 36th St (47905-4475)
PHONE.................765 588-4528
▲ EMP: 2 EST: 2007
SQ FT: 1,000
SALES (est): 409.83K Privately Held
Web: www.zsinstruments.com
SIC: 3823 Process control instruments

Lagrange
Lagrange County

(G-10728)
ANR PIPELINE COMPANY
2255 W Us Highway 20 (46761-8626)
PHONE.................260 463-3342
Myron Pschyoda, Mgr
EMP: 5
SALES (corp-wide): 11.6B Privately Held
Web: www.anrpl.com
SIC: 4922 1311 1221 Pipelines, natural gas; Crude petroleum and natural gas; Bituminous coal and lignite-surface mining
HQ: Anr Pipeline Company
700 Louisiana St Ste 700
Houston TX 77002
832 320-2000

(G-10729)
AUTOMATED PRODUCTS INTL LLC
Also Called: API
2840 N State Road 9 (46761-9346)
P.O. Box 9 (46746-0009)
PHONE.................260 463-2515
EMP: 15 EST: 2002
SQ FT: 18,000
SALES (est): 2.32MM Privately Held
Web: www.apiclamps.com
SIC: 3714 Pickup truck bed liners

(G-10730)
BONTRAGER WELDING
3035 W 100 S # B (46761-9474)
PHONE.................260 463-8950
John Bountrager, Prin
EMP: 1 EST: 2008
SALES (est): 69K Privately Held
SIC: 7692 Welding repair

(G-10731)
CENTERLINE WOODWORKING
695 S 600 W (46761-8633)
PHONE.................260 768-4116
EMP: 4 EST: 2017
SALES (est): 62.92K Privately Held
SIC: 2431 Millwork

(G-10732)
COUNTY OF LAGRANGE
Also Called: La Grange County
300 E Factory St (46761-1507)
PHONE.................260 499-6353
Jeff Brill, Mgr
EMP: 10
Web: www.lagrangecounty.org
SIC: 4959 3531 Road, airport, and parking lot maintenance services; Road construction and maintenance machinery
PA: County Of Lagrange
114 W Michigan St Ste 1
Lagrange IN 46761
260 499-6380

(G-10733)
D W STEWART
104 E Wayne St (46761-1847)
PHONE.................260 463-2607
D W Stewart, Owner
EMP: 2 EST: 1995
SALES (est): 101.68K Privately Held
SIC: 3559 Automotive related machinery

(G-10734)
DUTCH COUNTRY WOODWORKING INC
Also Called: Shur Ply
200 Industrial Pkwy (46761-1144)
PHONE.................260 499-4847
Delbert Schrock, Pr
EMP: 2 EST: 2004
SALES (est): 254.72K Privately Held
Web: www.shurply.com
SIC: 2499 1751 Decorative wood and woodwork; Carpentry work

(G-10735)
DUTCHCRAFT CORPORATION
50 S 375 W (46761-9470)
PHONE.................260 463-8366
EMP: 5
SQ FT: 17,000
SALES (est): 564.51K Privately Held
SIC: 2431 Millwork

(G-10736)
E & S WOOD CREATIONS LLC
Also Called: Excell
2030 N 450 W (46761-8611)
PHONE.................260 768-3033
EMP: 10 EST: 2003
SALES (est): 916.91K Privately Held
Web: www.indianawoodcrafters.com
SIC: 2434 2511 Wood kitchen cabinets; Wood bedroom furniture

(G-10737)
EXCEL FINISHINGS LLC
4510 W 200 N (46761)
PHONE.................260 768-7667
EMP: 5 EST: 2020
SALES (est): 187.6K Privately Held
SIC: 3479 Metal coating and allied services

(G-10738)
F & N WOODWORKING LLC
Also Called: F & N Woodworking
2105 W 450 S (46761-9726)
PHONE.................260 463-8938
Freeman P Miller, Managing Member
EMP: 9 EST: 1995
SALES (est): 461.55K Privately Held
SIC: 2511 Chairs, household, except upholstered: wood

(G-10739)
FRONTIER WOODWORKS
3350 E 200 S (46761-9052)
PHONE.................260 463-2049
Vernon Bontrager, Prin
EMP: 1 EST: 2008
SALES (est): 82.62K Privately Held
SIC: 2431 Millwork

(G-10740)
GREEN TECH
2305 W 200 S (46761-9057)
PHONE.................260 350-0089
Jeremiah Miller, Pr
EMP: 5 EST: 2017
SALES (est): 92.36K Privately Held
SIC: 2869 Industrial organic chemicals, nec

Lagrange - Lagrange County (G-10768)

(G-10741)
HOCHSTETLER WELDING
2520 W 350 N (46761-9449)
PHONE..................260 463-2793
EMP: 6 EST: 2009
SALES (est): 147.25K Privately Held
SIC: 7692 Welding repair

(G-10742)
HOSTETLER CARRIAGE
3200 W 300 S (46761-9481)
PHONE..................260 463-9920
Marvin Hostetler, Owner
EMP: 5 EST: 2004
SALES (est): 354.55K Privately Held
SIC: 3799 Carriages, horse drawn

(G-10743)
INDIANA INTERSTATE ENTPS LLC
Also Called: Cross Rv Sales
1695 E Us Highway 20 (46761-8783)
PHONE..................260 463-8100
Paul Cross, Managing Member
EMP: 9 EST: 2005
SALES (est): 538.04K Privately Held
Web: www.crossrv.com
SIC: 3792 Campers, for mounting on trucks

(G-10744)
JAG WIRE LLC
130 E 200 N (46761-9345)
P.O. Box 218 (46761-0218)
PHONE..................260 463-8537
Kevin M Myers, Managing Member
EMP: 12 EST: 2000
SQ FT: 20,000
SALES (est): 2.14MM Privately Held
Web: www.jagwirellc.net
SIC: 3679 Harness assemblies, for electronic use: wire or cable

(G-10745)
KCH SERVICES INC
202 W Central Ave (46761-2283)
PHONE..................260 463-3100
Renee Marlor, Contrlr
EMP: 1 EST: 2005
SALES (est): 96.19K Privately Held
Web: www.kchservices.com
SIC: 3564 Blowers and fans

(G-10746)
KUNTRY LUMBER AND FARM SUP LTD
2875 S 00 E W (46761-8844)
P.O. Box 126 (46761-0126)
PHONE..................260 463-3242
William Connelly, Pr
Bryant Gilliland, VP
EMP: 15 EST: 1993
SALES (est): 908.77K Privately Held
SIC: 5211 2431 5191 Lumber and other building materials; Millwork; Farm supplies

(G-10747)
LA GRANGE PUBLISHING CO INC
Also Called: Waddell Printing Co
State Rte 9 S (46761)
PHONE..................260 463-3243
William Connelly, Pr
Eugene N Marten, VP
Charlette Connelly, Sec
Joyce Marten, Sec
EMP: 10 EST: 1856
SALES (est): 391.92K Privately Held
Web: www.lagrangepublishing.com
SIC: 2711 2791 2789 2759 Commercial printing and newspaper publishing combined; Typesetting; Bookbinding and related work; Commercial printing, nec

(G-10748)
LAGWANA PRINTING INC (PA)
Also Called: People's Exchange, The
4425 W Us Highway 20 Ste 3 (46761-8408)
P.O. Box 70 (46565-0070)
PHONE..................260 463-4901
Daniel Byler, Pr
Roger Wenger, VP
Jerry Hostetler, Treas
Justin R Geigley, Sec
EMP: 8 EST: 2006
SALES (est): 5.91MM
SALES (corp-wide): 5.91MM Privately Held
Web: www.lagwana.com
SIC: 2752 Offset printing

(G-10749)
LAKESTREET ENTERPRISES LLC
75 N 700 W (46761-8687)
PHONE..................260 768-7991
EMP: 2 EST: 2004
SALES (est): 175.71K Privately Held
SIC: 2399 Horse and pet accessories, textile

(G-10750)
LAMBRIGHTS INC
2450 W Us Highway 20 (46761-8772)
P.O. Box 295 (46761-0295)
PHONE..................260 463-2178
Richard Lambright, Pr
Joe Walter, *
EMP: 8 EST: 1949
SQ FT: 90,000
SALES (est): 937.03K Privately Held
Web: www.darylelambright.com
SIC: 5144 5191 2048 2015 Eggs; Animal feeds; Prepared feeds, nec; Poultry slaughtering and processing

(G-10751)
LARRYS CANVAS CLEANING
909 S Poplar St (46761-2412)
PHONE..................260 463-2220
Larry Bontrager, Owner
EMP: 2 EST: 2004
SALES (est): 206.32K Privately Held
Web: www.lccovers.com
SIC: 2394 Awnings, fabric: made from purchased materials

(G-10752)
LC COVERS LLC
909 S Poplar St (46761-2412)
PHONE..................260 463-2220
Larry D Bontrager, Admn
EMP: 8 EST: 2016
SALES (est): 446.55K Privately Held
Web: www.lccovers.com
SIC: 2394 Canvas and related products

(G-10753)
LILLICH SIGN CO INC
1333 Industrial Dr N (46761-1159)
P.O. Box 240 (46761-0240)
PHONE..................260 463-3930
Joe Lillich, Pr
EMP: 10 EST: 1979
SALES (est): 640.26K Privately Held
SIC: 3993 Displays and cutouts, window and lobby

(G-10754)
MARTIN DIESEL SERVICES LLC
214 E Marquis Rd N (46761)
PHONE..................570 837-6101
Paul Martin, Owner
EMP: 1 EST: 1991
SALES (est): 180.91K Privately Held
Web: www.martindieselservices.com
SIC: 3621 Generator sets: gasoline, diesel, or dual-fuel

(G-10755)
MASTERCRAFT INC (PA)
711 S Poplar St (46761-2407)
P.O. Box 97 (46761-0097)
PHONE..................260 463-8702
Clifton D Reynolds, Pr
Doug Cline, *
Dave Toney, *
EMP: 150 EST: 1971
SALES (est): 22.94MM
SALES (corp-wide): 22.94MM Privately Held
Web: www.mastercraftincorporated.com
SIC: 2512 2514 2515 Upholstered household furniture; Metal household furniture; Mattresses, innerspring or box spring

(G-10756)
NELSON J HOCHSTETLER
Also Called: Ban Transit
2080 E 050 N (46761-9698)
PHONE..................260 499-0315
Nelson Hochstetler, Owner
Elizabeth Hochstetler, Sec
EMP: 2 EST: 2004
SALES (est): 157.55K Privately Held
SIC: 3537 7389 Industrial trucks and tractors ; Business services, nec

(G-10757)
PENN CENTRAL WELDING LLC
1245 S 100 E (46761-9810)
PHONE..................260 463-2490
EMP: 5 EST: 2015
SALES (est): 93.35K Privately Held
SIC: 7692 Welding repair

(G-10758)
PICTURE IT INC
Also Called: Wear Haus Designs
4425 W Us Highway 20 Ste 1 (46761-8407)
PHONE..................260 463-7373
EMP: 10 EST: 1992
SQ FT: 1,800
SALES (est): 423.44K Privately Held
Web: www.wearhaus.net
SIC: 2395 Embroidery products, except Schiffli machine

(G-10759)
SIX MILE WELDING LLC
40 S 600 W (46761-9428)
PHONE..................260 768-3126
Norman J Mishler, Owner
EMP: 9 EST: 2008
SALES (est): 448.65K Privately Held
Web: www.sixmileweldingllc.com
SIC: 7692 Welding repair

(G-10760)
SOLAR FREEZE LLC
214 E Marquis Rd N (46761-6100)
PHONE..................260 499-4973
Andrew Mishler, Pt
▲ EMP: 25 EST: 2011
SALES (est): 1.35MM Privately Held
Web: sunstarappliance.com
SIC: 3639 Household appliances, nec

(G-10761)
SOLAR FREEZE LLC
214 E Marquis Rd N (46761-6100)
PHONE..................260 499-4973
EMP: 25
SALES (est): 880.16K Privately Held

SIC: 3999 Manufacturing industries, nec

(G-10762)
SPECTRUM FINISHING LLC
1340 Industrial Dr N (46761-1143)
PHONE..................260 463-7300
EMP: 8 EST: 2006
SQ FT: 37,000
SALES (est): 470.86K Privately Held
Web: www.preferredcolorlist.com
SIC: 2431 5021 Millwork; Furniture

(G-10763)
SPREUER & SON INC
115 E Spring St (46761-1897)
PHONE..................260 463-3513
Ron Troyer, Pr
Ronald Troyer, Pr
Roberta Craig, Sec
EMP: 18 EST: 1944
SQ FT: 1,000
SALES (est): 6.47MM Privately Held
Web: www.hoosiertrailer.com
SIC: 3799 3441 3444 3443 Boat trailers; Fabricated structural metal; Sheet metalwork; Fabricated plate work (boiler shop)

(G-10764)
STANLEY OLIVER PRODUCTS LLC
3545 E 100 N (46761-9696)
P.O. Box 243 (46761-0243)
PHONE..................260 499-3506
EMP: 5 EST: 1996
SALES (est): 370.48K Privately Held
SIC: 3431 3432 Bathroom fixtures, including sinks; Plumbing fixture fittings and trim

(G-10765)
SUNRISE WOOD PRODUCTS LLC
3565 S 300 W (46761-8819)
PHONE..................260 463-4822
EMP: 4 EST: 2006
SQ FT: 130
SALES (est): 299.8K Privately Held
SIC: 2431 7699 Moldings, wood: unfinished and prefinished; Horseshoeing

(G-10766)
SUPER BLEND INC
105 S 500 E (46761-9511)
PHONE..................260 463-7486
Rose Miller, Pr
Phil Miller, VP
Helen Mischler, Sec
EMP: 6 EST: 1970
SALES (est): 459.48K Privately Held
Web: www.superblendinc.com
SIC: 2048 8611 Feed supplements; Business associations

(G-10767)
SUTTON CUSTOM MOLDS INC
4770 E 100 N (46761)
PHONE..................260 463-2772
Benjamin Sutton, Pr
Dale Claar, VP
EMP: 9 EST: 1995
SALES (est): 759.91K Privately Held
SIC: 3544 Industrial molds

(G-10768)
W & M WOODWORKING
3180 E 450 S (46761-9782)
PHONE..................260 854-3126
William Bontrager, Prin
EMP: 6 EST: 2008
SALES (est): 67.56K Privately Held
SIC: 2431 Millwork

(G-10769)
WEAVERS DTCH CNTRY SSNINGS LLC
7450 W 050 N (46761-8754)
PHONE..................260 768-7550
David J Weaver, *Managing Member*
EMP: 3 **EST:** 2010
SALES (est): 215.89K **Privately Held**
Web: www.weaversseasonings.com
SIC: 2099 Food preparations, nec

Lagro
Wabash County

(G-10770)
VICE BROS PATTERN SP & FNDRY
1010 W State Road 524 (46941-5416)
P.O. Box 327 (46941-0327)
PHONE..................260 782-2585
Stanley K Bowman, *Pr*
Phyllis Bowman, *CEO*
▲ **EMP:** 2 **EST:** 1939
SQ FT: 8,700
SALES (est): 260.81K **Privately Held**
Web: www.vicebrothers.com
SIC: 3365 Aluminum and aluminum-based alloy castings

Lake Station
Lake County

(G-10771)
A SIGN ODYSSEY LLC
727 Central Ave (46405-1511)
PHONE..................219 962-1247
Rick Besmehn, *Pr*
Cheryl Hullinger, *Mgr*
Dee Tucker, *VP*
EMP: 3 **EST:** 2002
SALES (est): 127.06K **Privately Held**
Web: www.asignodyssey.com
SIC: 3993 Signs and advertising specialties

(G-10772)
E D H INC
925 Central Ave Rm D (46405-1689)
PHONE..................219 712-5145
EMP: 8 **EST:** 2013
SALES (est): 327.22K **Privately Held**
SIC: 2752 Offset printing

(G-10773)
LOPEZ TIRES & WHEELS LLC
3020 Fairview Ave (46405-2225)
PHONE..................219 654-4586
EMP: 4 **EST:** 2020
SALES (est): 65.2K **Privately Held**
SIC: 7534 Tire retreading and repair shops

(G-10774)
MSF EXPRESS INC
1242 E 28th Ave (46405-1563)
P.O. Box 641178 (46401-1178)
PHONE..................561 413-4545
Mantas Ramanauskas, *Pr*
EMP: 1 **EST:** 2017
SALES (est): 109.44K **Privately Held**
SIC: 3537 Trucks, tractors, loaders, carriers, and similar equipment

(G-10775)
PRO-CHEM-CO INC
2319 Ripley St (46405-2398)
PHONE..................219 962-8554
EMP: 15 **EST:** 1971
SALES (est): 2.54MM **Privately Held**
Web: www.pro-chem-co.com

SIC: 2992 Lubricating oils and greases

(G-10776)
SMALL WORLD ENTERPRISES LLC
3822 Central Ave (46405-2324)
PHONE..................312 550-1717
Yolanda Martinez, *Pr*
Elbert Flowers, *Prin*
Yolanda Martinez, *Prin*
EMP: 2 **EST:** 2019
SALES (est): 152.1K **Privately Held**
SIC: 3711 5046 Truck tractors for highway use, assembly of; Vending machines, coin-operated

(G-10777)
SOUND & GRAPHICS
925 Central Ave Rm D (46405-1689)
P.O. Box 5064 (46405-0064)
PHONE..................219 963-7293
Henry Delbre, *CEO*
EMP: 2 **EST:** 2019
SALES (est): 176K **Privately Held**
Web: www.sounds-graphics.com
SIC: 2752 Offset printing

(G-10778)
SUN ENGINEERING INC
950 Marquette Rd (46405-1548)
PHONE..................219 962-1191
Walter E Williams, *Pr*
Melinda Rhodes, *
EMP: 50 **EST:** 1959
SQ FT: 85,000
SALES (est): 7.66MM **Privately Held**
Web: www.sun-engineering-inc.com
SIC: 3599 7692 3443 Machine shop, jobbing and repair; Welding repair; Fabricated plate work (boiler shop)

(G-10779)
WUNDER COMPANY INC
3200 E 37th Ave (46405-3001)
P.O. Box 5272 (46405-0272)
PHONE..................219 962-8573
Rick Tubbs, *Pr*
EMP: 15 **EST:** 1946
SQ FT: 2,000
SALES (est): 2.25MM **Privately Held**
Web: www.fenceandgarage.com
SIC: 5211 3089 Fencing; Fences, gates, and accessories: plastics

Lake Village
Newton County

(G-10780)
EXPERT WOODWORKS
9126 N 200 E (46349-9389)
PHONE..................219 345-2705
Linda Phelps, *Prin*
EMP: 5 **EST:** 2008
SALES (est): 67.76K **Privately Held**
SIC: 2431 Millwork

(G-10781)
JAYS WOODWORKING DIRECT LLC
387 E 800 N (46349-9224)
PHONE..................219 345-3335
EMP: 4 **EST:** 2017
SALES (est): 77.19K **Privately Held**
SIC: 2431 Millwork

(G-10782)
REESE FORGE ORNA IRONWORK
6873 W 700 N (46349-9520)
PHONE..................219 775-1039
David Reese, *Prin*
EMP: 5 **EST:** 2008

SALES (est): 321K **Privately Held**
Web: www.reeseforge.com
SIC: 1791 3446 3699 Iron work, structural; Gates, ornamental metal; Security devices

(G-10783)
RING INDUSTRIES INC
3572 W State Road 10 Lot 13 (46349-9483)
PHONE..................219 204-1577
EMP: 2 **EST:** 2011
SALES (est): 109.66K **Privately Held**
Web: www.ringindustries.com
SIC: 3999 Manufacturing industries, nec

(G-10784)
TJ MAINTENANCE LLC
8591 N 300 W (46349)
P.O. Box 277 (46349-0277)
PHONE..................219 776-8427
EMP: 9 **EST:** 2013
SALES (est): 895.84K **Privately Held**
Web: www.tanksnliners.com
SIC: 3089 3443 1791 Plastics and fiberglass tanks; Industrial vessels, tanks, and containers; Storage tanks, metal: erection

(G-10785)
WORLDWIDE DOOR CMPNNTS IND INC
8218 N 279 W (46349-9498)
PHONE..................219 992-9225
Jerry Monts De Oca, *Pr*
Jerry M Deoca, *Pr*
▲ **EMP:** 2 **EST:** 1997
SQ FT: 15,000
SALES (est): 200.59K **Privately Held**
SIC: 3442 Metal doors, sash, and trim

(G-10786)
WROUGHT IRON WERKS LLC
6873 W 700 N (46349)
PHONE..................219 779-7476
EMP: 3 **EST:** 2018
SALES (est): 109.34K **Privately Held**
SIC: 3446 Ornamental metalwork

Laketon
Wabash County

(G-10787)
LAKETON REFINING CORPORATION
2784 W Lukens Lake Rd (46943-0198)
P.O. Box 231 (46943)
PHONE..................260 982-0703
Lewis L Davis, *Ex VP*
EMP: 10
SALES (corp-wide): 894.43MM **Privately Held**
SIC: 5171 2951 Petroleum terminals; Asphalt paving mixtures and blocks
HQ: Laketon Refining Corporation
5400 W 86th St
Indianapolis IN 46268
260 982-2171

Lakeville
St. Joseph County

(G-10788)
BRANIFF GAME BIRDS
67510 Mulberry Rd (46536-9450)
PHONE..................574 784-3919
Beverly Braniff, *Owner*
EMP: 5 **EST:** 1989
SALES (est): 187.18K **Privately Held**

SIC: 3949 Decoys, duck and other game birds

(G-10789)
CREED & DYER PRECAST INC
68186 Us Highway 31 (46536-9738)
PHONE..................574 784-3361
Keith Dyer, *Pr*
EMP: 3 **EST:** 1996
SALES (est): 260.77K **Privately Held**
Web: www.creedanddyerprecastinc.com
SIC: 3272 5039 Septic tanks, concrete; Septic tanks

(G-10790)
DKD MFG INC
64695 Us Highway 31 (46536-9332)
PHONE..................574 298-9592
David Skeen, *Pr*
EMP: 1 **EST:** 2006
SALES (est): 83.08K **Privately Held**
SIC: 3999 Manufacturing industries, nec

(G-10791)
EDM SERVICES INC
18599 Osborne Rd (46536-9311)
PHONE..................574 784-3042
Edward D Miley, *Prin*
EMP: 1 **EST:** 2009
SALES (est): 22.28K **Privately Held**
Web: www.edmsvc.com
SIC: 3599 Machine shop, jobbing and repair

(G-10792)
HOOSIER RACING TIRE CORP (DH)
Also Called: Hoosier Tire
65465 State Road 931 (46536)
PHONE..................574 784-3152
Joyce L Newton, *CEO*
Joerg Burfien, *Pr*
◆ **EMP:** 6 **EST:** 1979
SALES (est): 44.77MM
SALES (corp-wide): 45.02B **Privately Held**
Web: www.hoosierracingtire.com
SIC: 5531 5014 3011 5699 Automotive tires; Automobile tires and tubes; Tires and inner tubes; Sports apparel
HQ: Continental Tire The Americas, Llc
1830 Macmillan Park Dr
Fort Mill SC 29707
800 847-3349

(G-10793)
ULTRA/GLAS OF LAKEVILLE INC
520 Industrial Dr (46536-9557)
P.O. Box 407 (46536-0407)
PHONE..................574 784-8958
Herbert Davidson, *Pr*
Ronald Davidson, *VP*
EMP: 18 **EST:** 1969
SQ FT: 8,000
SALES (est): 474.59K **Privately Held**
Web: www.ultraglas.com
SIC: 3088 Shower stalls, fiberglass and plastics

Lamar
Spencer County

(G-10794)
ALPHA MATRIX LLC
9946 N County Road 475 E (47550-7411)
PHONE..................812 686-1640
EMP: 1
SALES (est): 39.69K **Privately Held**
SIC: 3999 7389 Manufacturing industries, nec; Business Activities at Non-Commercial Site

(G-10795)
CHERI-THEREE INC
Also Called: Criss, Charles
P.O. Box 29 (47550-0029)
PHONE................................812 529-8132
Charles Criss, *Pr*
Cheryl Taylor, *Sec*
EMP: 2 **EST:** 1961
SALES (est): 190K **Privately Held**
SIC: 1389 7231 Pumping of oil and gas wells; Beauty shops

(G-10796)
COSOLOGY LLC
11573 N State Road 245 (47550)
PHONE................................812 630-3084
EMP: 4 **EST:** 2018
SALES (est): 39.69K **Privately Held**
Web: www.cosology.com
SIC: 3999 Manufacturing industries, nec

Lanesville
Harrison County

(G-10797)
GABRIEL V FULKERSON
5498 Ponderosa Rd Ne (47136-8210)
PHONE................................502 727-0038
Gabriel V Fulkerson, *Prin*
Gabriel Fulkerson, *Owner*
EMP: 1 **EST:** 2016
SALES (est): 44.52K **Privately Held**
SIC: 1389 Testing, measuring, surveying, and analysis services

(G-10798)
GRAPHIC BARN LLC
6636 Riley Ridge Rd (47136-9607)
PHONE................................812 952-3826
EMP: 1 **EST:** 2014
SALES (est): 120.1K **Privately Held**
SIC: 3999 Novelties, bric-a-brac, and hobby kits

(G-10799)
JBS POWDER COATING LLC
7320 Thomas Ave Ne (47136-8638)
PHONE................................812 952-1204
John Butler, *Managing Member*
EMP: 2 **EST:** 2006
SALES (est): 86.95K **Privately Held**
Web: www.jbspowdercoating.com
SIC: 3399 Powder, metal

(G-10800)
KENTUCKIANA MACHINE AND TL INC
4550 Lazy Creek Rd Ne (47136-8812)
PHONE................................502 301-9005
H Cobb, *Pr*
EMP: 2 **EST:** 2001
SALES (est): 246.37K **Privately Held**
Web: www.customqualityprinting.com
SIC: 3531 Construction machinery

(G-10801)
LAMBERT WOOD WORKS LLC
3745 Crandall Lanesville Rd Ne (47136-8963)
PHONE................................812 952-4204
Gary Lambert, *Owner*
EMP: 1 **EST:** 2014
SALES (est): 73.73K **Privately Held**
SIC: 2431 Millwork

(G-10802)
LARRY ZOELLER
7509 Geswein Rd (47136-9521)
PHONE................................502 439-0812
EMP: 4 **EST:** 2016
SALES (est): 155.67K **Privately Held**
Web: www.zoellerforge.com
SIC: 3999 Manufacturing industries, nec

Laotto
Noble County

(G-10803)
COUNTRY HRITG WNERY VINYRD INC
185 County Road 68 (46763-9614)
P.O. Box 371 (46763-0371)
PHONE................................260 637-2980
EMP: 10 **EST:** 2007
SALES (est): 557.2K **Privately Held**
Web: www.countryheritagewinery.com
SIC: 2084 Wines

(G-10804)
COUNTRY MILL CABINET CO INC
7590 E 400 S (46763-9786)
PHONE................................260 693-9289
Robert B Green, *Pr*
Richard Green, *VP*
Dianne Green, *Sec*
EMP: 10 **EST:** 1984
SQ FT: 6,560
SALES (est): 691.11K **Privately Held**
Web: www.countrymillcabinets.com
SIC: 2599 1751 Cabinets, factory; Cabinet building and installation

(G-10805)
GROUP DEKKO INC
Also Called: Dekko Techinal Center
11913 E 450 S (46763-9750)
PHONE................................260 637-3964
Robert Einhaus, *Mgr*
EMP: 1
SALES (corp-wide): 4.41B **Publicly Held**
Web: www.dekko.com
SIC: 3643 Current-carrying wiring services
HQ: Group Dekko, Inc.
7310 Innovation Blvd # 104
Fort Wayne IN 46818

(G-10806)
HOLBROOK FABRICATION REPR INC
10447 E Swan Rd (46763-9743)
PHONE................................260 348-4996
Daniel Holbrook, *Pr*
EMP: 2 **EST:** 2020
SALES (est): 85.67K **Privately Held**
SIC: 3498 Fabricated pipe and fittings

(G-10807)
KHORPORATE HOLDINGS INC (PA)
Also Called: Mossberg Industries
6492 State Road 205 (46763-9609)
P.O. Box 217 (46763-0217)
PHONE................................260 357-3365
Michael Khorshid, *Pr*
▲ **EMP:** 102 **EST:** 1950
SQ FT: 20,000
SALES (est): 52.79MM
SALES (corp-wide): 52.79MM **Privately Held**
Web: www.xytoolrtc.com
SIC: 3496 3676 3089 5084 Cable, uninsulated wire: made from purchased wire; Electronic resistors; Injection molding of plastics; Tool and die makers equipment

(G-10808)
KML INC (PA)
108 S Main St (46763-4818)
P.O. Box 380 (46763-0380)
PHONE................................260 897-3723
Andrew W Peterson, *Pr*
EMP: 7 **EST:** 1979
SQ FT: 16,000
SALES (est): 4.49MM
SALES (corp-wide): 4.49MM **Privately Held**
Web: www.kmlinc.com
SIC: 2819 5169 Chemicals, high purity: refined from technical grade; Industrial chemicals

(G-10809)
LANCON ELECTRIC INC
101 S Main St (46763-4818)
PHONE................................260 897-3285
Andrew J Langohr Senior, *Pr*
EMP: 6 **EST:** 2014
SALES (est): 486.65K **Privately Held**
SIC: 5063 3699 1731 Generators; Electrical equipment and supplies, nec; Electrical work

(G-10810)
STRONG STITCHES
503 S Main St (46763-4827)
PHONE................................260 450-1456
Rick Strong, *Prin*
EMP: 5 **EST:** 2016
SALES (est): 48.69K **Privately Held**
SIC: 2395 Embroidery and art needlework

(G-10811)
WAYNE MANUFACTURING LLC
Also Called: Wayne Tool Design
6505 State Road 205 (46763-9618)
P.O. Box 188 (46763-0188)
PHONE................................260 637-5586
EMP: 75 **EST:** 1963
SALES (est): 19MM **Privately Held**
Web: www.waynetool.net
SIC: 3469 Stamping metal for the trade

(G-10812)
X-Y TOOL AND DIE INC
6492 State Road 205 (46763-9609)
P.O. Box 217 (46763-0217)
PHONE................................260 357-3365
EMP: 93 **EST:** 1971
SALES (est): 15.5MM
SALES (corp-wide): 52.79MM **Privately Held**
Web: www.xytoolrtc.com
SIC: 3549 3544 7692 Metalworking machinery, nec; Special dies, tools, jigs, and fixtures; Welding repair
PA: Khorporate Holdings, Inc.
6492 State Road 205
Laotto IN 46763
260 357-3365

(G-10813)
ZRP LLC
Also Called: Triple A Sporting Goods
11750 E State Road 205 (46763-9754)
PHONE................................888 824-5587
Zachary R Pfafman, *Managing Member*
EMP: 6 **EST:** 2018
SALES (est): 270.39K **Privately Held**
SIC: 3484 Rifles or rifle parts, 30 mm. and below

Lapaz
Marshall County

(G-10814)
A HOMESTEAD SHOPPE INC (PA)
Also Called: Homestead Shoppe
330 E Vandalia St (46537)
P.O. Box 254 (46537-0254)
PHONE................................574 784-2307
Bruce Albert, *Pr*
▲ **EMP:** 33 **EST:** 1972
SQ FT: 85,000
SALES (est): 2.61MM
SALES (corp-wide): 2.61MM **Privately Held**
Web: www.ahomesteadshoppe.com
SIC: 3645 5063 Lamp and light shades; Lighting fixtures

(G-10815)
INJECTION PLASTICS
12798 2a Road (46537)
PHONE................................574 784-2070
EMP: 6 **EST:** 2013
SALES (est): 292.22K **Privately Held**
Web: www.injectionplasticsmfg.com
SIC: 3089 Injection molding of plastics

(G-10816)
INJECTION PLASTICS & MFG CO
12140 Us Hwy 6 E (46537)
P.O. Box 380 (46537-0380)
PHONE................................574 784-2070
Robert Strang Junior, *Pr*
John Strang, *VP*
Gail Strang, *Sec*
Bunni Strang, *Treas*
EMP: 23 **EST:** 1968
SQ FT: 12,000
SALES (est): 949.24K **Privately Held**
Web: www.injectionplasticsmfg.com
SIC: 3544 3089 3599 Special dies and tools; Injection molding of plastics; Custom machinery

(G-10817)
J & L FUTURE FIBERGLASS CO
Also Called: Future Fiberglass
211 W Randolph St (46537)
PHONE................................574 784-2900
FAX: 574 784-2169
EMP: 6
SQ FT: 10,100
SALES (est): 600K **Privately Held**
Web: www.futurefiberglass.com
SIC: 3714 Motor vehicle body components and frame

Lapel
Madison County

(G-10818)
WESTLUND CONCEPTS
806 N Woodward St (46051-5564)
P.O. Box 1051 (46051-1051)
PHONE................................317 819-0611
Doug Westlund, *Pt*
Dan Westlund, *Pt*
EMP: 17 **EST:** 2005
SQ FT: 10,000
SALES (est): 1.59MM **Privately Held**
Web: www.westlundconcepts.com
SIC: 7389 3993 3441 Design services; Signs and advertising specialties; Fabricated structural metal

Larwill
Whitley County

(G-10819)
INDIANA FACTORY OUTLET MAR INC
3450 S 1100 W-57 (46764-9601)
PHONE................................260 799-4764
Dan Lees, *Pr*
EMP: 5 **EST:** 2010

SALES (est): 447.59K **Privately Held**
Web: www.everythingpontoon.com
SIC: 3069 Pontoons, rubber

(G-10820)
J G CABINET & COUNTER INC
2571 S State Road 5 (46764-9766)
PHONE.............................260 723-4275
Jerry Grube, *Pr*
Sandra Grube, *Sec*
EMP: 5 **EST:** 1977
SQ FT: 12,000
SALES (est): 437.6K **Privately Held**
Web: www.jgcabinet.com
SIC: 2434 Wood kitchen cabinets

(G-10821)
PYRAMID PLASTIC GROUP INC
1560 N State Road 5 (46764-9791)
PHONE.............................260 327-3145
Karen Buesching, *Prin*
EMP: 2 **EST:** 2011
SALES (est): 102.35K **Privately Held**
SIC: 3089 Injection molding of plastics

(G-10822)
RED STAR CONTRACT MFG INC
Also Called: Red Star
1560 N State Road 5 (46764-9791)
PHONE.............................260 327-3145
EMP: 22 **EST:** 2009
SQ FT: 17,000
SALES (est): 5.16MM
SALES (corp-wide): 5.81MM **Privately Held**
SIC: 3089 Molding primary plastics
PA: Wishbone Medical, Inc.
  100 Capital Dr
  Warsaw IN 46582
  574 306-4006

Laurel
Franklin County

(G-10823)
A SIGN ABOVE
25033 Us Highway 52 (47024-9644)
PHONE.............................317 392-2144
Milton Cain, *Owner*
EMP: 2 **EST:** 2011
SALES (est): 170.83K **Privately Held**
SIC: 3993 Signs and advertising specialties

(G-10824)
AFR EQUIPMENT LLC
13046 Bulltown Rd (47024-9410)
PHONE.............................888 519-9899
EMP: 2
SALES (est): 92.67K **Privately Held**
SIC: 3537 7389 Platforms, stands, tables, pallets, and similar equipment; Business Activities at Non-Commercial Site

(G-10825)
NEW POINT STONE CO INC
Also Called: Harris City Stone Co
24031 Derbyshire Rd (47024-9757)
PHONE.............................765 698-2227
Nathan Wanstrath, *Brnch Mgr*
EMP: 8
SALES (corp-wide): 8.86MM **Privately Held**
Web: www.newpointstone.com
SIC: 3281 1422 Stone, quarrying and processing of own stone products; Crushed and broken limestone
PA: New Point Stone Co Inc
  992 S County Road 800 E
  Greensburg IN 47240

812 663-2021

(G-10826)
TREEHUGGER MAPLE SYRUP LLC
15203 Ott Rd (47024-9744)
PHONE.............................765 698-3728
Deirdre Schirmer, *Owner*
EMP: 6 **EST:** 2018
SALES (est): 140.95K **Privately Held**
Web: www.treehuggermaplesyrup.com
SIC: 2099 Maple syrup

Lawrenceburg
Dearborn County

(G-10827)
ALL ABOUT ORGANIZING
253 Charles A Liddle Dr Ste 1 (47025-2987)
PHONE.............................513 238-8157
Mark Grismore, *Owner*
EMP: 3 **EST:** 2006
SQ FT: 5,000
SALES (est): 205.3K **Privately Held**
Web: www.all-aboutorganizing.com
SIC: 1799 5047 2434 Closet organizers, installation and design; Medical and hospital equipment; Wood kitchen cabinets

(G-10828)
AMERICRAFT CARTON INC
Also Called: AMERICRAFT CARTON, INC.
102 Industrial Dr (47025-1116)
PHONE.............................812 537-1784
Todd Butcher, *VP Sls*
EMP: 592
Web: www.americraft.com
SIC: 2657 Folding paperboard boxes
HQ: Americraft Associates, Inc.
  7400 State Line Rd Ste 20
  Prairie Village KS 66208
  913 387-3700

(G-10829)
AT THE BARN WINERY
1726 Einsel Rd (47025-8773)
PHONE.............................513 310-8810
Debby Stutz, *Prin*
EMP: 5 **EST:** 2017
SALES (est): 83.18K **Privately Held**
Web: www.atthebarnwinery.com
SIC: 2084 Wines

(G-10830)
B N OIL LLC
622 Arch St (47025-1710)
PHONE.............................859 816-2244
Devanshi Patel, *Prin*
EMP: 8 **EST:** 2014
SALES (est): 1.74MM **Privately Held**
SIC: 1311 Crude petroleum and natural gas

(G-10831)
BATESVILLE PRODUCTS INC (PA)
434 Margaret St (47025-1747)
PHONE.............................513 381-2057
Richard E Weber, *Pr*
Tim Weber, *
Justin C Weber Junior, *Treas*
Terry Mc Carthy, *
Thomas Kersting, *
▲ **EMP:** 63 **EST:** 1945
SQ FT: 24,000
SALES (est): 9.1MM
SALES (corp-wide): 9.1MM **Privately Held**
Web: www.batesvilleproducts.com

SIC: 3429 3544 3471 3443 Hardware, nec; Special dies, tools, jigs, and fixtures; Plating and polishing; Fabricated plate work (boiler shop)

(G-10832)
DEARBORN COATINGS LLC
25768 Mount Pleasant Rd (47025-9729)
PHONE.............................513 600-9580
Michael Robert Schallick, *Admn*
EMP: 6 **EST:** 2013
SALES (est): 213.73K **Privately Held**
SIC: 3479 Metal coating and allied services

(G-10833)
DELPHOS HERALD OF INDIANA INC (HQ)
Also Called: Register Publication
126 W High St (47025-1908)
P.O. Box 4128 (47025-4128)
PHONE.............................812 537-0063
Murray Cohen, *Pr*
John Reiniger, *
EMP: 50 **EST:** 1825
SQ FT: 9,000
SALES (est): 18.4MM
SALES (corp-wide): 23.87MM **Privately Held**
Web: www.registerpublications.com
SIC: 2711 2752 Commercial printing and newspaper publishing combined; Commercial printing, lithographic
PA: Herald Delphos Inc
  405 N Main St
  Delphos OH 45833
  419 695-0015

(G-10834)
DOUBLE J WOODWORKING
1184 Carroll Ave (47025-1228)
PHONE.............................812 290-8877
Jim Laugle, *Prin*
EMP: 5 **EST:** 2017
SALES (est): 58.21K **Privately Held**
Web: www.jbussewoodworking.com
SIC: 2431 Millwork

(G-10835)
FAMILY BRACELETS DIRECT
21939 Wilbur Dr (47025-7424)
PHONE.............................513 312-5446
EMP: 3 **EST:** 2017
SALES (est): 61.53K **Privately Held**
Web: www.familybraceletsdirect.com
SIC: 3961 Bracelets, except precious metal

(G-10836)
FILCA LLC
22806 Stateline Rd (47025-9128)
PHONE.............................812 637-3559
Jonathon Wood, *Prin*
EMP: 5 **EST:** 2015
SALES (est): 96.56K **Privately Held**
SIC: 3599 Industrial machinery, nec

(G-10837)
FRAMERY
84 E High St (47025-1891)
PHONE.............................812 537-4319
Mary Crook, *Owner*
EMP: 1 **EST:** 1976
SALES (est): 104.81K **Privately Held**
Web: www.framerystudio.com
SIC: 8412 3952 Art gallery; Artists' equipment

(G-10838)
GC FULLER MFG CO INC
1 Shurlite Dr (47025-2945)
PHONE.............................812 539-2831

Richard C Haneberg, *Pr*
Robert Haneberg, *Treas*
Roman Welter, *Sec*
▲ **EMP:** 11 **EST:** 1917
SQ FT: 30,000
SALES (est): 2.08MM **Privately Held**
Web: www.shurlite.com
SIC: 3548 Welding apparatus

(G-10839)
HARRISON PRESS
126 W High St (47025)
P.O. Box 610 (45030)
PHONE.............................513 367-4582
EMP: 6 **EST:** 2018
SALES (est): 181.09K **Privately Held**
Web: www.theharrison-press.com
SIC: 2711 Newspapers, publishing and printing

(G-10840)
HOOSIER WALLBEDS INCORPORATED
23036 Stateline Rd (47025-7799)
PHONE.............................812 747-7154
Daniel J Badinghaus, *Pr*
EMP: 7 **EST:** 2015
SALES (est): 230.92K **Privately Held**
Web: www.hoosierwallbeds.com
SIC: 2679 Wallboard, decorated: made from purchased material

(G-10841)
HUBER INDUSTRIES
434 Margaret St (47025-1747)
PHONE.............................812 537-2275
Rick Weber, *Pr*
EMP: 5 **EST:** 2018
SALES (est): 107K **Privately Held**
Web: www.gobeaconnews.com
SIC: 3999 Manufacturing industries, nec

(G-10842)
J T WOODWORKING LLC
20531 Heather Ct (47025-9396)
PHONE.............................513 543-1130
James Timerding, *Owner*
EMP: 6 **EST:** 2015
SALES (est): 59.54K **Privately Held**
SIC: 2431 Millwork

(G-10843)
KOI ENTERPRISES INC
Also Called: Federated Auto Parts
601 Saint Clair St (47025-1760)
PHONE.............................812 537-2335
Dave Eldridge, *Brnch Mgr*
EMP: 89
SALES (corp-wide): 525.52MM **Privately Held**
Web: www.koiautoparts.com
SIC: 5531 5015 5013 3599 Automotive parts; Motor vehicle parts, used; Automotive supplies and parts; Machine shop, jobbing and repair
HQ: K.O.I. Enterprises, Inc.
  2701 Spring Grove Ave
  Cincinnati OH 45225
  513 357-2400

(G-10844)
LAWRENCEBURG MINI BARNS
535 W Eads Pkwy (47025-1157)
PHONE.............................513 290-5794
EMP: 4 **EST:** 2018
SALES (est): 86.73K **Privately Held**
Web: www.sheds-minibarns.com
SIC: 2452 Prefabricated wood buildings

Lebanon - Boone County (G-10872)

(G-10845)
LEISURE POOL & SPA LLC
159 Florence Dr (47025-1198)
PHONE..................812 537-0071
Thomas Cheek, *Managing Member*
EMP: 4 **EST:** 2005
SALES (est): 240.61K **Privately Held**
Web: www.leisurepoolnspa.net
SIC: 3949 5091 5999 Water sports equipment; Swimming pools, equipment and supplies; Swimming pool chemicals, equipment, and supplies

(G-10846)
MCCORD SIGNS LLC (PA)
1090 W Eads Pkwy (47025-1167)
PHONE..................812 537-5516
EMP: 23 **EST:** 2008
SALES (est): 2.51MM
SALES (corp-wide): 2.51MM **Privately Held**
SIC: 3993 Signs and advertising specialties

(G-10847)
NEON ACCENTS
Also Called: Custom Signs
101 W Eads Pkwy (47025-1174)
PHONE..................812 537-0102
EMP: 2 **EST:** 1988
SQ FT: 2,700
SALES (est): 130.14K **Privately Held**
SIC: 3993 Signs, not made in custom sign painting shops

(G-10848)
OHIO VALLEY ELECTRIC
800 Aep Dr (47025-2510)
PHONE..................812 532-5288
EMP: 7 **EST:** 2016
SALES (est): 104.86K **Privately Held**
SIC: 3699 1731 Electrical equipment and supplies, nec; Electrical work

(G-10849)
OHIO VALLEY PRECISION INC
42 Doughty Rd (47025-2939)
P.O. Box 3652 (47025-3652)
PHONE..................812 539-3687
Scott Allen, *Pr*
David E Miller, *VP*
Thomas Bipes, *Treas*
EMP: 15 **EST:** 2006
SALES (est): 941.72K **Privately Held**
Web: www.ohiovp.com
SIC: 3599 Machine shop, jobbing and repair

(G-10850)
OHIO VLY SCREEN PRTRS EMB ENGR
139 W Tate St Ste 3 (47025-1996)
PHONE..................812 539-3307
EMP: 2 **EST:** 1995
SQ FT: 1,500
SALES (est): 211.58K **Privately Held**
Web: www.ohiovalleyscreenprinting.com
SIC: 2759 Screen printing

(G-10851)
OVER TOP ROOFING AND RMDLG LLC
254 Charles A Liddle Dr Ste 5 (47025-2903)
PHONE..................513 704-5422
Christopher Schwab, *Pr*
Christopher Allen Schwab, *Pr*
EMP: 4 **EST:** 2017
SALES (est): 416.99K **Privately Held**
Web: www.overthetopcincy.com

SIC: 1761 3444 1542 Gutter and downspout contractor; Gutters, sheet metal; Commercial and office building contractors

(G-10852)
OVIDEON LLC
135 Short St Side (47025-2007)
PHONE..................812 577-3274
Tony Wiggins, *Pt*
EMP: 5 **EST:** 2011
SALES (est): 405.89K **Privately Held**
Web: www.ovideon.com
SIC: 3823 Digital displays of process variables

(G-10853)
PLANET PETS
1099 W Eads Pkwy (47025-1162)
PHONE..................812 539-7316
Mac Renburen, *Owner*
EMP: 5 **EST:** 2014
SALES (est): 243.81K **Privately Held**
Web: www.planet-pets.com
SIC: 3999 Pet supplies

(G-10854)
PRINTING IMPRESSION
21073 Alpine Dr (47025-9036)
PHONE..................812 537-4077
EMP: 1
SALES (est): 75.39K **Privately Held**
SIC: 2752 Offset printing

(G-10855)
PROXIMO DISTILLERS LLC
Also Called: Proximo Distillers Indiana
220 Shipping St (47025-2043)
PHONE..................201 204-1718
EMP: 69
SIC: 2082 Malt beverage products
HQ: Proximo Distillers, Llc
200 S Kalamath St
Denver CO 80223
201 204-1718

(G-10856)
QUILTERS GARDEN
9 E Center St (47025-1849)
PHONE..................812 539-4939
Betty Warwick, *Prin*
EMP: 2 **EST:** 2012
SALES (est): 146.12K **Privately Held**
Web: www.quiltersgarden.net
SIC: 2395 Quilting and quilting supplies

(G-10857)
RIX LASER PROCESSING
252 Charles A Liddle Dr (47025-2978)
PHONE..................812 537-9230
Richard Rees, *Prin*
EMP: 7 **EST:** 2002
SALES (est): 125.59K **Privately Held**
SIC: 3599 Machine shop, jobbing and repair

(G-10858)
RON OSBORNE MACHINING INC
25660 Mount Pleasant Rd (47025-9721)
PHONE..................812 637-1045
Ron Osborne, *Pr*
EMP: 5 **EST:** 2001
SALES (est): 418.84K **Privately Held**
SIC: 3599 Machine shop, jobbing and repair

(G-10859)
SCHEINER ART & FABRICATION LLC
998 Geneva Ct (47025-9202)
PHONE..................800 998-9345
EMP: 2 **EST:** 2008
SALES (est): 81.49K **Privately Held**

SIC: 3599 Industrial machinery, nec

(G-10860)
SIGN A RAMA
Also Called: Sign-A-Rama
1090 W Eads Pkwy (47025-1167)
PHONE..................812 537-5516
EMP: 9 **EST:** 2014
SALES (est): 494.75K **Privately Held**
Web: www.signarama.com
SIC: 3993 Signs and advertising specialties

(G-10861)
SIGN STORE INC
101 W Eads Pkwy (47025-1174)
PHONE..................812 537-0102
EMP: 4 **EST:** 2019
SALES (est): 144.97K **Privately Held**
Web: www.yourlocalsignstore.com
SIC: 3993 Signs and advertising specialties

(G-10862)
TRADELINE FABRICATING INC
22422 Stateline Rd (47025-7306)
PHONE..................812 637-1444
Eric Klem, *Sec*
Kurt Klem, *
Mark Klem, *
James Klem, *
EMP: 22 **EST:** 1984
SQ FT: 27,000
SALES (est): 2.15MM **Privately Held**
Web: www.tradelinefabricating.com
SIC: 3599 7692 3444 3441 Machine shop, jobbing and repair; Welding repair; Sheet metalwork; Fabricated structural metal

(G-10863)
TRI-STATE POWER SUPPLY LLC
48 Doughty Rd (47025-2939)
PHONE..................812 537-2500
Terry Miller, *Managing Member*
EMP: 5 **EST:** 2010
SALES (est): 711.41K **Privately Held**
Web: tristatebatterysupply.powerdealer.honda.com
SIC: 5531 3691 5085 Batteries, automotive and truck; Storage batteries; Industrial supplies

(G-10864)
TRINITY WOODWORKING
23036 Stateline Rd (47025-7799)
PHONE..................513 535-1964
Dan Badinghaus, *Prin*
EMP: 5 **EST:** 2014
SALES (est): 433.79K **Privately Held**
Web: www.trinitywoodworking.com
SIC: 2431 Millwork

(G-10865)
W & M ENTERPRISES INC
370 Industrial Dr (47025-2988)
PHONE..................812 537-4656
EMP: 12 **EST:** 1994
SQ FT: 30,000
SALES (est): 346.54K **Privately Held**
Web: www.wmtrailers.com
SIC: 3537 2449 Containers (metal), air cargo; Wood containers, nec

(G-10866)
WINGATE ENTERPRISE LLC
278 Ivy Hill Dr (47025-8913)
PHONE..................513 293-9833
EMP: 5 **EST:** 2012
SALES (est): 193.4K **Privately Held**
Web: www.wingate.com
SIC: 7372 Prepackaged software

(G-10867)
WOODYS HOT RODZ LLC
23950 Salt Fork Rd (47025-9177)
PHONE..................812 637-1933
Christopher Sondles, *Pr*
EMP: 8 **EST:** 2004
SALES (est): 1.08MM **Privately Held**
Web: www.woodyshotrodz.com
SIC: 3714 Propane conversion equipment, motor vehicle

(G-10868)
YESCO SING LIGHTING SERVICE
1090 W Eads Pkwy (47025-1167)
PHONE..................812 577-0904
EMP: 6 **EST:** 2016
SALES (est): 248.78K **Privately Held**
Web: www.yesco.com
SIC: 3993 Signs and advertising specialties

Leavenworth
Crawford County

(G-10869)
CRAWFORD COUNTY CONCRETE
7172 S Tower Rd (47137-8304)
PHONE..................812 739-2707
EMP: 2 **EST:** 2003
SALES (est): 131.35K **Privately Held**
SIC: 5032 3273 Stone, crushed or broken; Ready-mixed concrete

(G-10870)
JASPER ENGINE EXCHANGE INC
6400 E Industrial Ln (47137-8316)
PHONE..................812 482-1041
Michele Harris, *Brnch Mgr*
EMP: 1
SALES (corp-wide): 418.4MM **Privately Held**
Web: www.jasperengines.com
SIC: 3714 Rebuilding engines and transmissions, factory basis
PA: Jasper Engine Exchange, Inc.
815 Wernsing Rd
Jasper IN 47546
812 482-1041

(G-10871)
MULZER CRUSHED STONE INC
Also Called: Cape Sandy Quarry
19925 S Alton Fredonia Rd (47137-7209)
PHONE..................812 739-4777
Mart A Tarr, *Brnch Mgr*
EMP: 34
SALES (corp-wide): 34.95B **Privately Held**
Web: www.mulzer.com
SIC: 1422 Crushed and broken limestone
HQ: Mulzer Crushed Stone Inc
534 Mozart St
Tell City IN 47586
812 547-7921

Lebanon
Boone County

(G-10872)
A SIGN-BY-DESIGN INC
501 W Noble St (46052-2761)
P.O. Box 691 (46077-0691)
PHONE..................317 876-7900
Beverly Miller, *Pr*
Charles Miller, *VP*
EMP: 15 **EST:** 1988
SQ FT: 12,000
SALES (est): 2.38MM **Privately Held**
Web: www.asignbydesign.com
SIC: 3993 Electric signs

Lebanon - Boone County (G-10873) — GEOGRAPHIC SECTION

(G-10873)
AIR SYSTEMS COMPENTS LP
Also Called: ASC
843 Indianapolis Ave (46052-2829)
PHONE..................................765 483-5841
Thomas Kristin, *COO*
EMP: 4 **EST:** 2008
SALES (est): 1.04MM **Privately Held**
Web: www.pennbarry.com
SIC: 3585 Refrigeration and heating equipment

(G-10874)
AMERICAN ULTRAVIOLET COMPANY (PA)
212 S Mount Zion Rd (46052-9479)
PHONE..................................765 483-9514
TOLL FREE: 800
Meredith C Stines, *Pr*
◆ **EMP:** 40 **EST:** 1960
SQ FT: 70,000
SALES (est): 14.7MM
SALES (corp-wide): 14.7MM **Privately Held**
Web: www.americanultraviolet.com
SIC: 3674 3641 Ultra-violet sensors, solid state; Ultraviolet lamps

(G-10875)
ARC OF GREATER BOONE CNTY INC
Also Called: ARC Rehab Services
912 W Main St (46052-2318)
PHONE..................................765 482-0051
Brit Cartin, *Ex Dir*
EMP: 11
Web: www.thearcgbc.org
SIC: 8322 8331 3999 Rehabilitation services ; Job training and related services; Atomizers, toiletry
PA: Arc Of Greater Boone County, The Inc.
900 W Main St
Lebanon IN 46052

(G-10876)
ARTISANZ FABRICATION AND MCH
1209 W South St (46052-2365)
PHONE..................................765 859-5118
EMP: 7 **EST:** 2017
SALES (est): 197.39K **Privately Held**
SIC: 3441 Fabricated structural metal

(G-10877)
ATP WELDING INC
Also Called: Atp Steel & Welding Supplies
930 Hendricks Dr (46052-2973)
P.O. Box 822 (46052-0822)
PHONE..................................765 483-9273
Rick Scott, *Pr*
EMP: 9 **EST:** 1992
SALES (est): 767.82K **Privately Held**
Web: www.atpweldinginc.com
SIC: 7692 Welding repair

(G-10878)
AVT COMPOSITES
2970 S 500 W (46052-9440)
PHONE..................................219 742-0865
EMP: 4 **EST:** 2017
SALES (est): 67.69K **Privately Held**
SIC: 3728 Aircraft parts and equipment, nec

(G-10879)
B & K BEVERAGE SERVICE INC
3005 E 100 N (46052-8874)
PHONE..................................317 209-9842
EMP: 1 **EST:** 1989
SALES (est): 145.01K **Privately Held**
SIC: 3585 Refrigeration and heating equipment

(G-10880)
BOONE COUNTY ELECTRIC INC
2607 Viceroy Ln (46052-8895)
PHONE..................................765 482-1430
Bill Zimmerman, *Pr*
Dixie Zimmerman, *Sec*
Mike Zimmerman, *VP*
EMP: 8 **EST:** 1976
SALES (est): 861.04K **Privately Held**
Web: www.boonecountyelectric.com
SIC: 1731 5999 7694 General electrical contractor; Motors, electric; Electric motor repair

(G-10881)
CASE NEW HOLLAND LLC
420 S Enterprise Blvd (46052-8888)
PHONE..................................765 482-5446
Jeffrey Case, *Prin*
▲ **EMP:** 26 **EST:** 2010
SALES (est): 2.63MM **Privately Held**
SIC: 3523 Farm machinery and equipment

(G-10882)
CEDAR PLASTICS INC
Also Called: Gator Buckets
1016 W Main St Rear (46052-3208)
P.O. Box 603 (46052-0603)
PHONE..................................765 483-3260
Steven Busenbark, *Owner*
Steven Busenbark, *Pr*
Hugh L Busenbark, *Stockholder*
EMP: 10 **EST:** 1989
SQ FT: 16,000
SALES (est): 690.21K **Privately Held**
SIC: 3089 5941 Injection molded finished plastics products, nec; Sporting goods and bicycle shops

(G-10883)
CENTRE TOWNSHIP
525 Ransdell Rd (46052-2372)
PHONE..................................765 482-1729
Pat Mcginley, *Chief*
EMP: 30
SIC: 9224 1389 Fire department, not including volunteer; Fire fighting, oil and gas field
PA: Centre Township
320 N East St
Lebanon IN 46052

(G-10884)
CNH INDUSTRIAL AMERICA LLC
Also Called: Cnh Industrial Parts and Svc
400 S Enterprise Blvd (46052-8888)
PHONE..................................765 482-5409
Keith Hansen, *Mgr*
EMP: 208
Web: www.caseih.com
SIC: 3523 Farm machinery and equipment
HQ: Cnh Industrial America Llc
711 Jorie Blvd
Oak Brook IL 60523
630 887-2233

(G-10885)
COMMUNITY HOLDINGS INDIANA INC
Also Called: Lebanon Reporter, The
117 E Washington St (46052-2209)
PHONE..................................765 482-4650
Greta Sanderson, *Mgr*
EMP: 1
SALES (corp-wide): 34.97B **Privately Held**
Web: www.reporter.net
SIC: 2711 2791 2752 Newspapers: publishing only, not printed on site; Typesetting; Commercial printing, lithographic
HQ: Community Holdings Of Indiana, Inc.
3500 Colonnade Pkwy # 600
Birmingham AL 35243

(G-10886)
COMMUNITY HOLDINGS INDIANA INC
Also Called: Zionsville Times Sentinel
117 E Washington St (46052-2209)
PHONE..................................317 873-6397
EMP: 7
SALES (corp-wide): 34.97B **Privately Held**
Web: www.reporter.net
SIC: 2711 Newspapers, publishing and printing
HQ: Community Holdings Of Indiana, Inc.
3500 Colonnade Pkwy # 600
Birmingham AL 35243

(G-10887)
CROSSROADS IMPRINTS INC
107 W Main St (46052-2522)
PHONE..................................765 482-2931
Steve Horton, *Pr*
EMP: 6 **EST:** 2013
SALES (est): 158.32K **Privately Held**
SIC: 2752 Commercial printing, lithographic

(G-10888)
CUSTOM COVERS INC
4548 W 50 S (46052-9465)
PHONE..................................765 481-7800
Todd Stewart, *CEO*
Jodi Kinsler, *Pr*
EMP: 5 **EST:** 2003
SQ FT: 2,400
SALES (est): 486.59K **Privately Held**
SIC: 3081 Floor or wall covering, unsupported plastics

(G-10889)
CUSTOM FIBER COMPOSITES LLC
7285 S State Road 267 (46052-9774)
PHONE..................................765 376-1360
Luka Hilgardt, *Prin*
EMP: 5 **EST:** 2018
SALES (est): 86.11K **Privately Held**
Web: www.customfibercomposites.co
SIC: 2821 Plastics materials and resins

(G-10890)
D-A LUBRICANT COMPANY INC (PA)
Also Called: D-A Lubricant Company
801 Edwards Dr (46052-8896)
P.O. Box 769 (46052-0769)
PHONE..................................317 923-5321
Mike Protegere, *Ch Bd*
John Mccall, *CFO*
▲ **EMP:** 40 **EST:** 1919
SQ FT: 70,000
SALES (est): 111.61MM
SALES (corp-wide): 111.61MM **Privately Held**
Web: www.dalube.com
SIC: 5172 2992 Lubricating oils and greases ; Lubricating oils and greases

(G-10891)
DONALDSONS CHOCOLATES INC
Also Called: Donaldson Country Home
600 S State Road 39 (46052-9401)
PHONE..................................765 482-3334
George Donaldson, *Pr*
EMP: 8 **EST:** 1966
SALES (est): 221.25K **Privately Held**
Web: www.donaldsonschocolates.com
SIC: 2064 2066 Candy bars, including chocolate covered bars; Chocolate and cocoa products

(G-10892)
DSM ENTERPRISES LLC
3025 N 550 E (46052-9239)
PHONE..................................317 698-3317
Daniel Miller, *Prin*
EMP: 6 **EST:** 2017
SALES (est): 65.82K **Privately Held**
Web: www.dsm.com
SIC: 2834 Pharmaceutical preparations

(G-10893)
FALL CREEK CORPORATION
Also Called: Fall Creek Enterprises
917 E Walnut St (46052-2870)
P.O. Box 92 (46075-0092)
PHONE..................................765 482-1861
A J Fulks, *Pr*
EMP: 6 **EST:** 1978
SQ FT: 3,000
SALES (est): 925.12K **Privately Held**
Web: www.fcsutler.com
SIC: 2389 5932 Uniforms and vestments; Used merchandise stores

(G-10894)
HACHETTE BOOK GROUP INC
121 N Enterprise Blvd (46052-8193)
PHONE..................................765 483-9900
Alisha Fisher, *Mgr*
EMP: 250
Web: www.hachettebookgroup.com
SIC: 2731 5192 Books, publishing only; Books, periodicals, and newspapers
HQ: Hachette Book Group, Inc.
1290 6th Ave
New York NY 10104
800 759-0190

(G-10895)
HASTY WELDING
104 E Superior St (46052-2535)
PHONE..................................765 482-8925
Dan Hasty, *Prin*
EMP: 1 **EST:** 2001
SALES (est): 41.23K **Privately Held**
SIC: 7692 Welding repair

(G-10896)
HENDRICKSON INTERNATIONAL CORP
Also Called: Hendrickson Trailer Suspension
180 N Mount Zion Rd (46052-8329)
PHONE..................................765 483-5350
EMP: 250
SALES (corp-wide): 758.84MM **Privately Held**
Web: www.hendrickson-intl.com
SIC: 3715 3714 3713 Truck trailers; Motor vehicle parts and accessories; Truck and bus bodies
HQ: Hendrickson International Corporation
840 S Frontage Rd
Woodridge IL 60517

(G-10897)
HENDRICKSON INTERNATIONAL CORP
Also Called: Hendrickson Trailer
210 N Enterprise Blvd (46052-8192)
PHONE..................................765 483-7217
EMP: 6
SALES (corp-wide): 758.84MM **Privately Held**
Web: www.hendrickson-intl.com
SIC: 3714 Motor vehicle parts and accessories
HQ: Hendrickson International Corporation
840 S Frontage Rd
Woodridge IL 60517

GEOGRAPHIC SECTION
Lebanon - Boone County (G-10924)

(G-10898)
IBC COATINGS TECHNOLOGIES LTD
902 Hendricks Dr (46052-2973)
PHONE..................................317 418-3725
Solomon Berman, *Pr*
Elaine Kinsler, *Admn*
▲ **EMP:** 20 **EST:** 1996
SALES (est): 4.47MM **Privately Held**
Web: www.ibccoatings.com
SIC: 3479 Coating of metals and formed products

(G-10899)
IBC MATERIALS & TECH LLC
823 Hendricks Dr (46052-2972)
PHONE..................................765 481-2900
Solomon Berman, *Pr*
EMP: 44 **EST:** 2002
SALES (est): 10.97MM **Privately Held**
Web: www.ibcmaterials.com
SIC: 3479 8731 3724 Coating of metals and formed products; Commercial physical research; Aircraft engines and engine parts

(G-10900)
IBC-SPUTTEK INC
902 Hendricks Dr (46052-2973)
PHONE..................................765 482-9802
Solomon Berman, *Prin*
EMP: 9 **EST:** 2008
SALES (est): 107.31K **Privately Held**
SIC: 3479 Coating of metals and formed products

(G-10901)
IGH STEEL FABRICATION INC
1001 Ransdell Rd (46052-2352)
PHONE..................................765 482-7534
Scott Nirider, *Pr*
EMP: 60 **EST:** 2009
SALES (est): 6.59MM **Privately Held**
Web: www.ighsteel.com
SIC: 3441 Fabricated structural metal

(G-10902)
INDIANA BATON TWIRLING ASSOC
6920 S 280 E (46052-9780)
PHONE..................................317 769-6826
Larry Leap, *Prin*
EMP: 2 **EST:** 2008
SALES (est): 125.78K **Privately Held**
Web: www.indianatwirling.com
SIC: 3949 Sporting and athletic goods, nec

(G-10903)
IRVING MATERIALS INC
417 Sw St (46052)
PHONE..................................765 482-5620
EMP: 7
SALES (corp-wide): 814.09MM **Privately Held**
Web: www.irvmat.com
SIC: 3273 Ready-mixed concrete
PA: Irving Materials, Inc.
8032 N State Road 9
Greenfield IN 46140
317 326-3101

(G-10904)
JDLD ENTERPRISES INC
507 Indianapolis Ave (46052-2634)
P.O. Box 602 (46052-0602)
PHONE..................................765 481-2210
Jason Deakins, *CEO*
EMP: 1 **EST:** 2015
SALES (est): 168.13K **Privately Held**
SIC: 3537 Trucks, tractors, loaders, carriers, and similar equipment

(G-10905)
JJ ENERGY INC
621 Indianapolis Ave (46052-2636)
PHONE..................................630 401-7026
EMP: 2
SALES (est): 173.58K **Privately Held**
SIC: 3561 Pumps, oil well and field

(G-10906)
K & M TOOL & DIE INC
Also Called: K & M Tool & Die
406 S Patterson St (46052-2334)
P.O. Box 645 (46052-0645)
PHONE..................................765 482-9464
John Kouns, *CEO*
Steven Kouns, *VP Engg*
Norma Kouns, *Pr*
EMP: 6 **EST:** 1984
SQ FT: 72,000
SALES (est): 994.59K **Privately Held**
Web: www.km-tool.com
SIC: 3544 Special dies and tools

(G-10907)
KAUFFMAN ENGINEERING LLC
202 S Mount Zion Rd (46052-9479)
PHONE..................................765 482-5640
Gary Hake, *Brnch Mgr*
EMP: 59
SALES (corp-wide): 140.92MM **Privately Held**
Web: www.kewire.com
SIC: 3679 Harness assemblies, for electronic use; wire or cable
PA: Kauffman Engineering, Llc
595 Bond St
Lincolnshire IL 60069
765 482-5640

(G-10908)
KENS FOODS INC
917 Edwards Dr (46052-9032)
PHONE..................................765 505-7900
EMP: 64
SALES (corp-wide): 476.41MM **Privately Held**
Web: www.kensfoods.com
SIC: 2033 Barbecue sauce: packaged in cans, jars, etc.
PA: Ken's Foods, Inc.
1 Dangelo Dr
Marlborough MA 01752
508 229-1100

(G-10909)
LEBANON BERG VAULT CO INC
Also Called: Lebanon Berg Vault Co
730 E Elm St (46052-2620)
PHONE..................................765 482-0302
Marion Galvin, *Pr*
EMP: 5 **EST:** 1952
SQ FT: 8,000
SALES (est): 409.45K **Privately Held**
SIC: 3272 5087 Burial vaults, concrete or precast terrazzo; Concrete burial vaults and boxes

(G-10910)
LEBANON CORP
Also Called: David Alan Chocolatier
1700 N Lebanon St (46052-1501)
P.O. Box 588 (46052-0588)
PHONE..................................765 482-7273
David Honan, *Pr*
Kathleen Honan, *Sec*
Paul R Honan Junior, *VP*
Jon Silverderg, *VP*
EMP: 5 **EST:** 1976
SQ FT: 5,750
SALES (est): 445.65K **Privately Held**
Web: lebanontheg.mfgpages.com

(G-10911)
LOGOS EXPRESS INC
1225 Ransdell Ct (46052-2377)
PHONE..................................317 272-1200
Mark A Scott, *Pr*
Matthew Beem, *VP*
EMP: 3 **EST:** 1988
SALES (est): 292.02K **Privately Held**
Web: www.logosexpress.com
SIC: 2759 Screen printing

(G-10912)
MAINSTREET MARKETING ENTPS LLC ✪
900 W Main St (46052-2318)
PHONE..................................765 482-6815
Pamela Verbarg, *CEO*
EMP: 2 **EST:** 2023
SALES (est): 92.67K **Privately Held**
SIC: 2048 Prepared feeds, nec

(G-10913)
MARSHALL COMPANIES INDIANA
Also Called: Marshall Crane
6850 S 280 E (46052-9780)
PHONE..................................317 769-2666
TOLL FREE: 866
Jim Marshall, *Pr*
Rod Marshall, *VP*
EMP: 8 **EST:** 1997
SQ FT: 7,800
SALES (est): 930.13K **Privately Held**
SIC: 3531 1542 Cranes, nec; Commercial and office building contractors

(G-10914)
MARVELOUS WOODWORKING LLC
5475 S 175 W (46052-9740)
PHONE..................................317 679-5890
Douglas S Marvel, *Admn*
EMP: 5 **EST:** 2009
SALES (est): 211.46K **Privately Held**
Web: www.marvelouswoodworking.com
SIC: 2431 Millwork

(G-10915)
MC GINLEY FIRE APPARATUS
901 W Washington St (46052-2082)
PHONE..................................765 482-3152
James Mcginley, *Owner*
James Mc Ginley, *Owner*
EMP: 4 **EST:** 1975
SALES (est): 245.41K **Privately Held**
SIC: 3711 7539 Fire department vehicles (motor vehicles), assembly of; Automotive repair shops, nec

(G-10916)
MINUTE PRINT IT INC
312 W South St (46052-2458)
PHONE..................................765 482-9019
Yancy Stults, *Pr*
EMP: 8 **EST:** 1981
SQ FT: 7,200
SALES (est): 755.32K **Privately Held**
Web: www.minuteprint.com
SIC: 2791 2752 8743 Typesetting; Offset printing; Sales promotion

(G-10917)
MODELS LLC (PA)
2275 S 500 W (46052-8948)
P.O. Box 624 (46052-0624)
PHONE..................................765 676-6700
▲ **EMP:** 20 **EST:** 1961
SQ FT: 4,000
SALES (est): 2.49MM

SALES (corp-wide): 2.49MM **Privately Held**
Web: models-llc.business.site
SIC: 3089 3444 3599 Injection molding of plastics; Sheet metalwork; Machine shop, jobbing and repair

(G-10918)
MONOSOL LLC
155 S Mount Zion Rd (46052-8186)
PHONE..................................765 485-5400
EMP: 1
Web: www.monosol.com
SIC: 2821 Plastics materials and resins
HQ: Monosol, Llc
707 E 80th Pl Ste 301
Merrillville IN 46410
219 762-3165

(G-10919)
MOSSMAN METAL WORKS
3595 W 200 S (46052-8936)
PHONE..................................765 676-6055
Matthew Mossman, *Owner*
EMP: 3 **EST:** 1983
SALES (est): 187.62K **Privately Held**
SIC: 3444 Sheet metalwork

(G-10920)
MOUNT GRAPHICS & SIGNS INC
1101 S Lebanon St (46052-2718)
PHONE..................................765 483-1435
John Mount, *Owner*
EMP: 1 **EST:** 2001
SALES (est): 95.14K **Privately Held**
Web: www.mount-signs.com
SIC: 3993 Signs, not made in custom sign painting shops

(G-10921)
MR2 PERFORMANCE LLC
722 W Pearl St (46052-2454)
PHONE..................................765 483-9371
Mike Roth, *Owner*
EMP: 1 **EST:** 2005
SQ FT: 3,000
SALES (est): 191.95K **Privately Held**
Web: www.mr2performance.com
SIC: 3441 Building components, structural steel

(G-10922)
MUSTARD SEED WOODWORKING LLC
325 Lafayette Ave (46052-2030)
PHONE..................................765 336-4423
EMP: 3 **EST:** 2020
SALES (est): 54.13K **Privately Held**
SIC: 2431 Millwork

(G-10923)
MWI VETERINARY SUPPLY CO
Also Called: Mwi Animal Health- Lebanon
5025 In-267 Ste 100 (46052)
PHONE..................................317 769-7771
EMP: 6
SALES (corp-wide): 262.17B **Publicly Held**
Web: www.mwiah.com
SIC: 5047 2834 Veterinarians' equipment and supplies; Veterinary pharmaceutical preparations
HQ: Mwi Veterinary Supply Co.
3041 W Pasadena Dr
Boise ID 83705
208 955-8930

(G-10924)
MWI VETERINARY SUPPLY CO
Also Called: Mwi Animal Health

Lebanon - Boone County (G-10925) — GEOGRAPHIC SECTION

5025 S State Road 267 Rm 100 (46052)
PHONE.....................317 769-7771
Tom Wakefield, *Mgr*
EMP: 4
SALES (corp-wide): 262.17B **Publicly Held**
Web: www.mwiah.com
SIC: 5047 2834 2835 2836 Veterinarians' equipment and supplies; Veterinary pharmaceutical preparations; Veterinary diagnostic substances; Vaccines
HQ: Mwi Veterinary Supply Co.
3041 W Pasadena Dr
Boise ID 83705
208 955-8930

(G-10925)
NAYS CUSTOM CANVAS
104 Sawgrass Ct (46052-8183)
PHONE.....................317 523-4279
EMP: 4 EST: 2017
SALES (est): 46.58K **Privately Held**
SIC: 2211 Canvas

(G-10926)
NFI INDUSTRIES INC
510 S Enterprise Blvd (46052-8307)
PHONE.....................765 483-9741
EMP: 3
SALES (corp-wide): 1.26B **Privately Held**
Web: www.nfiindustries.com
SIC: 3999 Atomizers, toiletry
PA: Nfi Industries, Inc.
Triad1828, 2 Cooper St
Camden NJ 08102
877 634-3777

(G-10927)
OLD FOUNDRY TOY WORKS
6325 N 500 E (46052-8998)
PHONE.....................765 742-1020
Jason Spangle, *Owner*
EMP: 1 EST: 1999
SALES (est): 79.09K **Privately Held**
Web: www.oldfoundry.com
SIC: 3944 Games, toys, and children's vehicles

(G-10928)
PALMOR PRODUCTS INC
1990 John Bart Rd (46052-1212)
PHONE.....................800 872-2822
Deborah M Crum, *Pr*
Stanley Morton, *Pr*
Karen L Morton, *Treas*
Morton Stanley G, *Sec*
EMP: 26 EST: 1975
SQ FT: 56,000
SALES (est): 807.19K **Privately Held**
Web: www.trac-vac.com
SIC: 3524 3444 Blowers and vacuums, lawn; Sheet metalwork

(G-10929)
PEARSON EDUCATION INC
150 Pearson Parkway (46052-2798)
PHONE.....................765 483-6738
EMP: 5
SALES (corp-wide): 4.58B **Privately Held**
Web: www.pearson.com
SIC: 2721 Periodicals
HQ: Pearson Education, Inc.
221 River St
Hoboken NJ 07030
201 236-7000

(G-10930)
PENGUIN RANDOM HOUSE LLC
199 Pearson Pkwy (46052-2798)
PHONE.....................800 672-7836
David Shanks, *CEO*
EMP: 8
SALES (corp-wide): 54.57MM **Privately Held**
Web: www.prhspeakers.com
SIC: 2731 Books, publishing only
HQ: Penguin Random House Llc
1745 Broadway
New York NY 10019
212 782-9000

(G-10931)
PERDUE FARMS INC
Also Called: Perdue Farms
5490 N 500 E (46052-8214)
PHONE.....................765 325-2997
EMP: 9
SALES (corp-wide): 1.24B **Privately Held**
Web: www.perdue.com
SIC: 2015 Chicken, processed: fresh
PA: Perdue Farms Incorporated
31149 Old Ocean City Rd
Salisbury MD 21804
800 473-7383

(G-10932)
PERFECTION PRODUCTS INC
1320 Indianapolis Ave (46052)
PHONE.....................765 482-7786
John Vickery, *Pr*
EMP: 30 EST: 1971
SQ FT: 32,000
SALES (est): 4.86MM **Privately Held**
Web: www.perfection-products.com
SIC: 3674 Semiconductor diodes and rectifiers

(G-10933)
PICTURE PERFECT PRINTING
1301 Ashley Dr (46052-1081)
PHONE.....................765 482-4241
Robert Patterson, *Prin*
EMP: 2 EST: 2000
SALES (est): 114.18K **Privately Held**
Web: www.pictureperfectprinting.com
SIC: 2752 Offset printing

(G-10934)
PRYSMIAN CBLES SYSTEMS USA LLC
Also Called: Lebanon In Distribution Center
311 S Enterprise Blvd (46052-8858)
PHONE.....................765 483-1760
Manny Gomes, *Mgr*
EMP: 70
Web: na.prysmian.com
SIC: 3357 Nonferrous wiredrawing and insulating
HQ: Prysmian Cables And Systems Usa, Llc
4 Tesseneer Dr
Highland Heights KY 41076
859 572-8000

(G-10935)
PSI LLC (PA)
Also Called: Phoenix Safe International
382 N Mount Zion Rd (46052)
P.O. Box 608 (46052)
PHONE.....................765 483-0954
Alfred Mcqueen, *Pr*
Janet Pape, *Ex VP*
Penny Cooper, *VP*
◆ EMP: 4 EST: 2001
SQ FT: 2,150
SALES (est): 1.27MM
SALES (corp-wide): 1.27MM **Privately Held**
Web: www.phoenixsafeusa.com
SIC: 3499 Safe deposit boxes or chests, metal

(G-10936)
QUALITY DRAPERY CORPORATION
1334 W Main St (46052-2326)
PHONE.....................765 481-2370
EMP: 8 EST: 1994
SQ FT: 24,000
SALES (est): 246.95K **Privately Held**
SIC: 2391 5023 Curtains and draperies; Draperies

(G-10937)
RICH MANUFACTURING INC
1990 John Bart Rd (46052-1212)
P.O. Box 145 (46071-0145)
PHONE.....................765 436-2744
EMP: 6 EST: 1996
SALES (est): 712.31K **Privately Held**
Web: www.convertiblemower.com
SIC: 3524 3423 Lawn and garden equipment ; Hand and edge tools, nec

(G-10938)
SAINT ADRIAN MEATS SAUSAGE LLC
6115 E State Road 47 (46052-9227)
PHONE.....................317 403-3305
EMP: 2 EST: 2014
SALES (est): 208.5K **Privately Held**
Web: www.saintadrianmeats.com
SIC: 2013 Sausages and related products, from purchased meat

(G-10939)
SANDWABI WOODWORKING LLC
1416 Victoria Dr (46052-1062)
PHONE.....................765 891-0774
Jacob Sanders, *Prin*
EMP: 5 EST: 2018
SALES (est): 111.8K **Privately Held**
Web: www.sandwabiwoodworking.com
SIC: 2431 Millwork

(G-10940)
SEWER OPTICAL SERVICES INC
1825 John Bart Rd (46052-1211)
PHONE.....................765 242-3768
Lanell Flanagan, *Pr*
EMP: 7 EST: 2002
SALES (est): 470.67K **Privately Held**
SIC: 7389 3589 Sewer inspection service; Sewer cleaning equipment, power

(G-10941)
SHARK-CO MFG LLC
1231 Indianapolis Ave (46052-2932)
PHONE.....................317 670-6397
Monica Sharkey, *Prin*
Jason Sharkey, *Prin*
Ryan Walden, *Prin*
EMP: 5 EST: 2016
SALES (est): 479.27K **Privately Held**
Web: www.shark-co.com
SIC: 3999 Manufacturing industries, nec

(G-10942)
SKJODT-BARRETT FOODS INC
401 S Enterprise Blvd (46052-8888)
PHONE.....................765 482-6856
Dan Skjodt, *Pr*
EMP: 39 EST: 2006
SALES (est): 5.76MM **Privately Held**
Web: www.sbfoods.com
SIC: 2099 Food preparations, nec

(G-10943)
SMART MANUFACTURING INC
228 W 700 S (46052-9485)
PHONE.....................765 482-7481
Dale W Thompson, *Pr*
Gary Cummins, *VP*
EMP: 8 EST: 2003
SALES (est): 550.68K **Privately Held**
Web: www.smartmfginc.com
SIC: 3728 1799 Deicing equipment, aircraft; Welding on site

(G-10944)
STEEL GREEN MANUFACTURING LLC
824 S State Road 39 (46052)
PHONE.....................765 481-2890
Brent Mills, *Managing Member*
EMP: 20 EST: 2018
SALES (est): 2.25MM **Privately Held**
Web: www.steelgreenmfg.com
SIC: 3999 Barber and beauty shop equipment

(G-10945)
TEMPERATURE CONTROL SVCS LLC
4240 W 50 S (46052-9508)
P.O. Box 95 (46102-0095)
PHONE.....................765 325-2439
EMP: 3 EST: 2007
SALES (est): 577.05K **Privately Held**
Web: www.tcsbas.com
SIC: 3822 Temperature controls, automatic

(G-10946)
THREE K RACING ENTERPRISES
Also Called: 3-K Racing
2685 S 25 W (46052-9748)
PHONE.....................765 482-4273
Melvin Kenyon, *Pr*
Donald Kenyon, *Sec*
EMP: 2 EST: 1969
SALES (est): 161.97K **Privately Held**
Web: www.kenyonmidgetracing.com
SIC: 7538 3799 Engine rebuilding: automotive; Midget autos, power driven

(G-10947)
TRIANGLE ASPHALT PAVING CORP
501 Sam Ralston Rd (46052-1339)
PHONE.....................765 482-5701
Steven L Day, *Pr*
Elizabeth Lewis, *
John Day, *
EMP: 25 EST: 1961
SQ FT: 4,200
SALES (est): 3.83MM **Privately Held**
Web: www.triangleasphalt.com
SIC: 1611 2951 2952 Surfacing and paving; Asphalt and asphaltic paving mixtures (not from refineries); Asphalt felts and coatings

(G-10948)
TRUCKPRO LLC
Also Called: Power Train
450 N Enterprise Blvd (46052-8185)
PHONE.....................765 482-6525
EMP: 10
SALES (corp-wide): 1.12B **Privately Held**
Web: www.truckpro.com
SIC: 7537 3714 3315 Automotive transmission repair shops; Motor vehicle parts and accessories; Steel wire and related products
HQ: Truckpro, Llc
1900 Chrles Bryan Rd Ste
Cordova TN 38016
901 252-4200

(G-10949)
UNITED STATES COLD STORAGE INC
415 S Mount Zion Rd (46052-8897)
PHONE.....................765 482-2653
Adam Ashley, *Brnch Mgr*
EMP: 21

GEOGRAPHIC SECTION

Lexington - Scott County (G-10975)

SALES (corp-wide): 18.29B **Privately Held**
Web: www.uscold.com
SIC: **4222** 2097 Warehousing, cold storage or refrigerated; Block ice
HQ: United States Cold Storage, Inc.
2 Aquarium Dr Ste 400
Camden NJ 08103
856 354-8181

(G-10950)
WHITAKER GLASS & MIRROR LLC
104 E Superior St (46052)
PHONE.................................765 482-1500
EMP: 8
Web: www.whitglass.com
SIC: **3231** 5231 Products of purchased glass ; Glass, leaded or stained
PA: Whitaker Glass & Mirror Llc
7485 N Sugar Creek Rd
Thorntown IN 46071

Leesburg
Kosciusko County

(G-10951)
BRICK STREET EMBROIDERY
205 E Prairie St (46538-7719)
P.O. Box 193 (46538-0193)
PHONE.................................574 453-3729
Helen Smoker, *Owner*
EMP: 2 EST: 1990
SALES (est): 60K **Privately Held**
SIC: **3993** Signs and advertising specialties

(G-10952)
CLUNETTE ELEVATOR CO INC
4316 W 600 N (46538-9210)
PHONE.................................574 858-2281
John Anglin, *Pr*
John Anglin Junior, *Pr*
Dan Anglin, *VP*
Tom Anglin, *Sec*
EMP: 15 EST: 1951
SQ FT: 25,000
SALES (est): 4.61MM **Privately Held**
Web: www.clunetteelevator.com
SIC: **5191** 5153 2041 2875 Fertilizer and fertilizer materials; Grain elevators; Flour and other grain mill products; Fertilizers, mixing only

(G-10953)
COMPOSITE DESIGNS INC
Also Called: C D I
306 School St (46538-7726)
P.O. Box 176 (46538-0176)
PHONE.................................574 453-2902
Raymond Doss, *Pr*
Karl Schmucker, *Sec*
Sean Alderfer, *Prin*
EMP: 11 EST: 2008
SALES (est): 791.82K **Privately Held**
Web: www.compositedesigns.biz
SIC: **2439** Arches, laminated lumber

(G-10954)
GALLOWAY FABRICATING
3776 E 750 N (46538-9161)
PHONE.................................574 453-3802
Larry A Galloway, *Owner*
EMP: 4 EST: 1970
SQ FT: 8,000
SALES (est): 419.21K **Privately Held**
SIC: **3469** Spinning metal for the trade

(G-10955)
J L HARRIS MACHINE CO INC
4953 N 700 E (46538-8940)
PHONE.................................574 834-2866

James L Harris, *Pr*
Sandra Harris, *Sec*
EMP: 3 EST: 1974
SALES (est): 249.43K **Privately Held**
SIC: **3599** Machine shop, jobbing and repair

(G-10956)
LEESBURG STOP-N-GO LLC
101 S Main St (46538-9200)
PHONE.................................574 453-3004
EMP: 7 EST: 2018
SALES (est): 396.12K **Privately Held**
SIC: **2911** Petroleum refining

(G-10957)
LOMATT DYNAMICS LLC
106 W Van Buren St (46538-3800)
P.O. Box 156 (46538-0156)
PHONE.................................574 500-2517
Jeffrey Allen Long Ii, *CEO*
EMP: 1 EST: 2021
SALES (est): 41.52K **Privately Held**
Web: www.lomattdynamics.com
SIC: **7699** 3482 5091 3483 Gun parts made to individual order; Small arms ammunition; Firearms, sporting; Ammunition components

(G-10958)
MAPLE LEAF INC (PA)
Also Called: Maple Leaf Farms
101 E Church St (46538)
P.O. Box 167 (46538)
PHONE.................................574 453-4455
Mike Turk, *LIVE PROD*
John Tucker, *
Scott Reinholt, *
Sandra Tucker, *Stockholder*
◆ EMP: 455 EST: 1958
SALES (est): 218.89MM
SALES (corp-wide): 218.89MM **Privately Held**
Web: www.mapleleaffarms.com
SIC: **0259** 2015 5159 Duck farm; Ducks, processed, nsk; Feathers

(G-10959)
PRAIRIE WELDING & REPAIR
3360 W 700 N (46538-9229)
PHONE.................................574 858-0509
EMP: 7 EST: 2018
SALES (est): 229.12K **Privately Held**
SIC: **7692** Welding repair

(G-10960)
ROOKSTOOLS PIER SHOP INC
2931 E Armstrong Rd (46538-8824)
PHONE.................................574 453-4771
Kerry Rookstool, *Pr*
EMP: 24 EST: 1955
SQ FT: 13,000
SALES (est): 2.15MM **Privately Held**
Web: www.rookstoolspiershop.com
SIC: **2499** 3089 3429 3317 Fencing, docks, and other outdoor wood structural products; Plastics boats and other marine equipment; Marine hardware; Steel pipe and tubes

(G-10961)
STONEBRAKER WELDING SERVI
38 Ems T32c Ln (46538-9137)
PHONE.................................574 453-7630
EMP: 4 EST: 2009
SALES (est): 67.5K **Privately Held**
SIC: **7692** Welding repair

(G-10962)
TIPPY CREEK WINERY LLC
5998 N 200 E (46538-9535)
PHONE.................................574 253-1862
EMP: 8 EST: 2016

SALES (est): 491.56K **Privately Held**
Web: www.tippycreekwinery.com
SIC: **2084** Wines

Leo
Allen County

(G-10963)
BETTER VISIONS PC
Also Called: City Vision Center
10529 Hosler Rd Ste A (46765-0417)
PHONE.................................260 627-2669
Andrew B Hogue, *Pr*
Dennis D Sutton, *Prin*
EMP: 10 EST: 1999
SALES (est): 500.59K **Privately Held**
SIC: **5995** 3827 Contact lenses, prescription; Aiming circles (fire control equipment)

(G-10964)
BLACKPOINT DISTRIBUTION CO LLC
15718 Viberg Rd (46765)
P.O. Box 25606 (46825)
PHONE.................................260 414-9096
Mathew J Konkler, *
EMP: 35 EST: 2019
SALES (est): 2.73MM **Privately Held**
Web: www.blackpointdistribution.com
SIC: **2079** 2011 5147 2033 Edible fats and oils; Beef products, from beef slaughtered on site; Meats and meat products; Vegetables and vegetable products, in cans, jars, etc.

(G-10965)
C&M WOODWORKING LLC
10225 Donald Ave (46765-9507)
PHONE.................................260 403-4555
Charles A Biller, *Admn*
EMP: 6 EST: 2014
SALES (est): 70.57K **Privately Held**
SIC: **2431** Millwork

(G-10966)
CEDAR CREEK STUDIOS INC
7030 Hosler Rd (46765-9547)
P.O. Box 480 (46765-0480)
PHONE.................................260 627-7320
Nancy Walters, *Pr*
Jim Walters, *VP*
EMP: 2 EST: 1985
SQ FT: 1,200
SALES (est): 151.74K **Privately Held**
Web: www.cedarcreekstudios.com
SIC: **3089** 3714 3053 Injection molding of plastics; Motor vehicle parts and accessories; Gaskets; packing and sealing devices

(G-10967)
DAVID KECHEL
Also Called: Miltec Circuits
12921 Leo Rd (46765-9656)
PHONE.................................260 627-2749
David Kechel, *Owner*
EMP: 9 EST: 1988
SQ FT: 6,000
SALES (est): 1.08MM **Privately Held**
Web: www.2miltec.com
SIC: **3672** Printed circuit boards

(G-10968)
K GRIMMER INDUSTRIES INC
Also Called: Hurricane Compressor Company
17301 Juniper Ln (46765-9340)
PHONE.................................317 736-3800
◆ EMP: 160

SIC: **3563** 4924 Air and gas compressors including vacuum pumps; Natural gas distribution

(G-10969)
MOORES WELDING SERVICE INC
13131 Leo Rd (46765-9628)
PHONE.................................260 627-2177
Michael B Moore, *Pr*
Anne Moore, *VP*
▲ EMP: 5 EST: 1940
SQ FT: 3,500
SALES (est): 677.73K **Privately Held**
Web: www.mooreswelsingservice.com
SIC: **7692** 1799 Welding repair; Welding on site

(G-10970)
PEANUT BUTTER MINISTRIES INC
13631 Leo Rd (46765-9608)
PHONE.................................260 627-0777
EMP: 6 EST: 2012
SALES (est): 53K **Privately Held**
Web: www.peanutbutterministries.org
SIC: **2099** Peanut butter

(G-10971)
POCO A POCO LLC
7611 Hursh Rd (46765-9538)
PHONE.................................317 443-5753
EMP: 5 EST: 2016
SALES (est): 65.67K **Privately Held**
SIC: **2084** Wines, brandy, and brandy spirits

(G-10972)
SDBD INCORPORATED
10211 Hosler Rd (46765-9357)
PHONE.................................260 376-1134
Steve Dunning, *Prin*
EMP: 9 EST: 2010
SALES (est): 238.83K **Privately Held**
SIC: **3052** Rubber and plastics hose and beltings

Leroy
Lake County

(G-10973)
COPE BROTHERS MACHINE SHOP
5301 East State Rd 231 (46355)
PHONE.................................219 663-5561
Larry Cope, *Pr*
Sheryl Cope, *VP*
EMP: 4 EST: 1946
SQ FT: 4,000
SALES (est): 372.16K **Privately Held**
SIC: **3599** Machine shop, jobbing and repair

Lexington
Scott County

(G-10974)
BARGERS WELDING SHOP
6791 E State Road 362 (47138-8306)
PHONE.................................812 889-2095
EMP: 1 EST: 1970
SALES (est): 44.32K **Privately Held**
SIC: **7692** Welding repair

(G-10975)
BURTON LUMBER CO INC
13980 W Polk Rd (47138-6924)
PHONE.................................812 866-4438
Bobby Burton, *Pr*
Henry L Burton, *VP*
Christine Burton, *Sec*
EMP: 18 EST: 1955

Lexington - Scott County (G-10976)

SALES (est): 2.5MM **Privately Held**
Web: www.burtonlumbercompany.com
SIC: 2448 2426 2421 2411 Pallets, wood; Furniture dimension stock, hardwood; Sawmills and planing mills, general; Logging

(G-10976)
GLDN RULE TRUSS & METAL SALES
4886 S 850 W (47138-7620)
PHONE..................................812 866-1800
Milt Kinsinder, *Owner*
EMP: 2 EST: 2013
SALES (est): 184.14K **Privately Held**
SIC: 5051 3443 Plates, metal; Truss plates, metal

(G-10977)
HEIDELBERG MTLS MDWEST AGG INC
313 S State Road 203 (47138-9002)
P.O. Box 130 (47170-0130)
PHONE..................................812 889-2120
EMP: 1
SALES (corp-wide): 23.02B **Privately Held**
SIC: 1422 3281 3274 Limestones, ground; Cut stone and stone products; Lime
HQ: Heidelberg Materials Midwest Agg, Inc.
300 E John Carpenter Fwy
Irving TX

(G-10978)
KEITH BIXLER
Also Called: Bixlers Logging
352 S Getty Rd (47138-8403)
PHONE..................................812 866-1637
EMP: 4 EST: 1981
SALES (est): 238.16K **Privately Held**
SIC: 2411 Logging camps and contractors

(G-10979)
NIELSEN COMPANY
1602 S 1066 W (47138-7064)
PHONE..................................812 889-3493
EMP: 8 EST: 2017
SALES (est): 72.11K **Privately Held**
Web: www.nielsen.com
SIC: 2752 Commercial printing, lithographic

(G-10980)
RBG INC
Also Called: Clown Room, The
9186 W Henry Rd (47138-7933)
PHONE..................................812 866-3983
Ron Gregory, *Owner*
EMP: 3 EST: 2010
SALES (est): 167.02K **Privately Held**
SIC: 3949 Bowling balls

(G-10981)
SCHAFER POWER WASHING
8420 W Polk Rd (47138-7728)
PHONE..................................812 866-1956
Anita Schafer, *Owner*
EMP: 1 EST: 2007
SALES (est): 68K **Privately Held**
SIC: 3452 Washers

(G-10982)
WAGLER MACHINING LLC
11778 W State Road 256 (47138-6817)
PHONE..................................812 866-2904
Joshua Wagler Mng Mng, *Prin*
EMP: 4 EST: 2008
SQ FT: 1,200
SALES (est): 447.06K **Privately Held**
SIC: 3599 Machine shop, jobbing and repair

Liberty
Union County

(G-10983)
ADAM L HOSKINS
3922 N County Road 250 W (47353-8759)
PHONE..................................765 580-0345
Adam L Hoskins, *Prin*
EMP: 8 EST: 2010
SALES (est): 169.28K **Privately Held**
SIC: 3482 Small arms ammunition

(G-10984)
C & F INDUSTRIES LLC
5282 W Booth Rd (47353-8477)
PHONE..................................765 580-0378
EMP: 5 EST: 2012
SALES (est): 172.33K **Privately Held**
SIC: 3999 Manufacturing industries, nec

(G-10985)
CHARLES KOLB LOGGING
7096 S Snowden Rd (47353-8972)
PHONE..................................765 458-7766
Charles F Kolb, *Pt*
Thomas Kolb, *Pt*
James Kolb, *Pt*
EMP: 3 EST: 1957
SALES (est): 338.89K **Privately Held**
Web: www.charleskolblogging.com
SIC: 2411 Logging camps and contractors

(G-10986)
COLEMAN LOGGING
2529 S Us Highway 27 (47353-9798)
PHONE..................................765 458-7219
EMP: 1 EST: 1973
SALES (est): 88.45K **Privately Held**
SIC: 2411 Logging camps and contractors

(G-10987)
D & L INDUSTRIAL FINISHES INC
215 Brownsville Ave (47353)
P.O. Box 215 (47353)
PHONE..................................765 458-5157
Emanuele Bomben, *CEO*
Wayne Reed, *Pr*
EMP: 1 EST: 1973
SQ FT: 25,000
SALES (est): 145.25K **Privately Held**
SIC: 2851 Paints and paint additives

(G-10988)
GORDON D BROWNING
1617 E Swain Rd (47353-8438)
PHONE..................................765 458-7792
Gordon Browning, *Prin*
EMP: 2 EST: 2005
SALES (est): 166.11K **Privately Held**
SIC: 2411 Logging camps and contractors

(G-10989)
JAMES E BARNHIZER
Also Called: Barnhizer Machining and Wldg
2302 Omar Fields Dr (47353-9620)
PHONE..................................765 458-9344
James E Barnhizer, *Owner*
EMP: 5 EST: 1999
SALES (est): 484.19K **Privately Held**
SIC: 3544 Special dies, tools, jigs, and fixtures

(G-10990)
LARRY G BYRD
Also Called: B & B Washer Assemblies
2312 W County Road 250 S (47353-9056)
PHONE..................................765 458-7285
Larry G Byrd, *Owner*
EMP: 10 EST: 1982
SALES (est): 554.78K **Privately Held**
SIC: 3069 Washers, rubber

(G-10991)
LIBERTY HERALD
10 N Market St (47353-1122)
P.O. Box 10 (47353-0010)
PHONE..................................765 458-5114
Gary Wolf, *Pr*
EMP: 6 EST: 1851
SALES (est): 321.2K **Privately Held**
Web: libertyheraldblog.wordpress.com
SIC: 2711 Newspapers, publishing and printing

(G-10992)
NAPIER & NAPIER
2369 S Us Highway 27 (47353-9796)
PHONE..................................765 580-9116
Theresa Schwegman, *Pt*
Tara Mc Creary, *Pt*
Robert D Napier, *Pt*
EMP: 5 EST: 1925
SQ FT: 10,000
SALES (est): 450K **Privately Held**
SIC: 3644 3471 3444 3354 Insulators and insulation materials, electrical; Plating and polishing; Sheet metalwork; Aluminum extruded products

(G-10993)
NSK CORPORATION
Also Called: NSK Corporation, Liberty Plant
1112 E Kitchel Rd (47353-8985)
PHONE..................................765 458-5000
Brian Grissom, *Manager*
EMP: 94
Web: www.nsk.com
SIC: 3562 5085 3714 3568 Ball bearings and parts; Bearings; Motor vehicle parts and accessories; Power transmission equipment, nec
HQ: Nsk Corporation
4200 Goss Rd
Ann Arbor MI 48105
734 913-7500

(G-10994)
OUTDOOR PERFORMANCE
2920 S Us Highway 27 (47353-8516)
PHONE..................................765 732-3335
Travis Walters, *Owner*
EMP: 10 EST: 2009
SALES (est): 470.06K **Privately Held**
SIC: 3751 Motorcycles and related parts

(G-10995)
OXFORD CABINET COMPANY LLC
141 S Us Highway 27 (47353-9076)
P.O. Box 285 (45003-0285)
PHONE..................................765 223-2101
EMP: 7 EST: 2016
SALES (est): 220.15K **Privately Held**
Web: www.oxfordcabinetco.com
SIC: 2434 Wood kitchen cabinets

(G-10996)
PROLINE BOWSTRINGS
1957 S Hubble Rd (47353-9622)
PHONE..................................513 259-3738
Joe Hamilton, *Owner*
EMP: 5 EST: 2011
SALES (est): 162.45K **Privately Held**
SIC: 3949 Archery equipment, general

(G-10997)
PROTECH POWDER COATINGS INC
215 Brownsville Ave (47353-1002)
PHONE..................................814 456-1243
Thoma Dietsch, *Brnch Mgr*
◆ EMP: 7
SALES (corp-wide): 202.63K **Privately Held**
Web: www.theprotechgroup.com
SIC: 2851 Paints and allied products
HQ: Protech Powder Coatings, Inc.
21 Audrey Pl
Fairfield NJ 07004

(G-10998)
RPC MACHINERY INC
424 N Industrial Park Rd (47353-8575)
PHONE..................................765 458-5655
Edmond Reaser, *Pr*
EMP: 4 EST: 1994
SQ FT: 3,000
SALES (est): 465.05K **Privately Held**
Web: www.rpcmachinery.com
SIC: 3554 1796 Paper industries machinery; Installing building equipment

(G-10999)
TED BOSTICK
Also Called: Liberty Forge
2230 W Snake Hill Rd (47353-8973)
PHONE..................................765 458-6555
EMP: 1 EST: 1992
SALES (est): 87.58K **Privately Held**
SIC: 7692 Welding repair

(G-11000)
WINSLOW-BROWNING INC
Also Called: W B I
215 Brownsville Ave (47353-1002)
P.O. Box 215 (47353-0215)
PHONE..................................765 458-5157
W John Browning, *Pr*
Ronald Herring, *VP*
EMP: 20 EST: 2006
SQ FT: 28,000
SALES (est): 2.44MM **Privately Held**
Web: www.winslowbrowning.com
SIC: 2851 Coating, air curing

Ligonier
Noble County

(G-11001)
ACADIA
1201 Gerber St (46767-2420)
PHONE..................................260 894-7125
Ken Wiese, *Mgr*
EMP: 7 EST: 2007
SALES (est): 119.8K **Privately Held**
Web: www.acadia.com
SIC: 3714 Motor vehicle parts and accessories

(G-11002)
ADVANCE MCS ELECTRONICS INC
11034 County Rd (46767)
PHONE..................................574 642-3501
Michael Snavely, *Pr*
EMP: 1
Web: www.advancemcs.com
SIC: 5961 3613 Electronic kits and parts, mail order; Control panels, electric
PA: Advance Mcs Electronics, Inc.
67928 Us Highway 33
Goshen IN 46526

(G-11003)
ADVANCED METAL ETCHING INC
801 Gerber St (46767-2412)
PHONE..................................260 894-4189
Blake Geer, *Pr*
Scott Seniff, *
EMP: 26 EST: 1993

SQ FT: 22,000
SALES (est): 4.67MM **Privately Held**
Web: www.metaletching.com
SIC: 3599 3678 3699 Chemical milling job shop; Electronic connectors; Laser welding, drilling, and cutting equipment

(G-11004)
ANNIE OAKLEY ENTERPRISES INC
300 Johnson St (46767-2309)
P.O. Box 203 (46767-0203)
PHONE..................................260 894-7100
Renee Gabet, *Pr*
Charles Gabet, *VP*
▲ EMP: 12 EST: 1971
SQ FT: 2,400
SALES (est): 927.34K **Privately Held**
Web: www.annieoakley.com
SIC: 3961 2844 Costume jewelry, ex. precious metal and semiprecious stones; Perfumes, natural or synthetic

(G-11005)
BEELINE WOODWORKING
9687 N 700 W (46767-9569)
PHONE..................................260 894-3806
EMP: 4 EST: 2019
SALES (est): 54.13K **Privately Held**
SIC: 2431 Millwork

(G-11006)
BLACKPOINT ENGINEERING LLC
Also Called: Jet City Specialties
494 W Us Highway 6 (46767-1263)
PHONE..................................765 884-4100
Steve Wygant, *Managing Member*
EMP: 7 EST: 1996
SALES (est): 511.18K **Privately Held**
Web: www.partdaddy.com
SIC: 3599 Machine shop, jobbing and repair

(G-11007)
BRC RUBBER & PLASTICS INC
Ligonier Rubber
1497 Gerber St (46767-2422)
P.O. Box 71 (46767-0071)
PHONE..................................260 894-4121
Richard Nieno, *Mgr*
EMP: 21
SQ FT: 32,000
SALES (corp-wide): 95.9MM **Privately Held**
Web: www.brcrp.com
SIC: 3061 3714 3053 Mechanical rubber goods; Motor vehicle parts and accessories; Gaskets; packing and sealing devices
PA: Brc Rubber & Plastics, Inc.
    1029a W State Blvd
    Fort Wayne IN 46808
    260 693-2171

(G-11008)
BRC RUBBER PLASTICS INC
502 N Cavin St (46767)
PHONE..................................260 894-7263
EMP: 6 EST: 2020
SALES (est): 109.65K **Privately Held**
Web: www.brcrp.com
SIC: 3061 Mechanical rubber goods

(G-11009)
CARLEX GLASS AMERICA LLC
Carlex Glass Ind Inc-Ligonier
860 W Us Highway 6 (46767-2543)
PHONE..................................260 894-7750
Russell Ebeid, *Mgr*
EMP: 470
Web: www.carlex.com
SIC: 3211 Plate and sheet glass
PA: Carlex Glass America, Llc
    7200 Centennial Blvd
    Nashville TN 37209

(G-11010)
CREATIVE WOOD DESIGNS INC
710 Gerber St (46767-2409)
PHONE..................................260 894-4533
EMP: 40
SIC: 2431 2511 Interior and ornamental woodwork and trim; Tables, household: wood

(G-11011)
EMERGENCY RADIO SERVICE LLC
Also Called: Ers-Oci Wireless
9144 N 900 W (46767-9236)
P.O. Box 110 (46767-0110)
PHONE..................................800 377-2929
EMP: 1
SALES (corp-wide): 26.84MM **Privately Held**
Web: www.erswireless.com
SIC: 5065 3441 Communication equipment; Tower sections, radio and television transmission
PA: Emergency Radio Service, Llc
    592 W Perry Rd
    Ligonier IN 46767
    206 894-4145

(G-11012)
EMERGENCY RADIO SERVICE LLC (PA)
Also Called: Ers-Oci Wireless
592 W Perry Rd (46767-9590)
P.O. Box 110 (46767-0110)
PHONE..................................206 894-4145
Brian T Hull, *Pr*
John Hull, *
Mark T Hull, *
Kaye Hull, *
EMP: 35 EST: 1948
SQ FT: 6,000
SALES (est): 26.84MM
SALES (corp-wide): 26.84MM **Privately Held**
Web: www.erswireless.com
SIC: 5065 3441 Communication equipment; Tower sections, radio and television transmission

(G-11013)
ERS HOLDING COMPANY INC (PA)
9144 N 900 W (46767-9236)
PHONE..................................260 894-4145
Brian T Hull, *Pr*
EMP: 6 EST: 2014
SALES (est): 4.93MM
SALES (corp-wide): 4.93MM **Privately Held**
Web: www.mission1communications.com
SIC: 3441 Tower sections, radio and television transmission

(G-11014)
ERS TOWER LLC
Also Called: Mission 1 Communications
9144 N 900 W (46767-9236)
P.O. Box 110 (46767-0110)
PHONE..................................260 894-4145
Jon Shultz, *Genl Mgr*
EMP: 25 EST: 2012
SALES (est): 4.88MM
SALES (corp-wide): 4.93MM **Privately Held**
Web: www.ers-towers.com
SIC: 3441 Tower sections, radio and television transmission
PA: Ers Holding Company, Inc.
    9144 N 900 W
    Ligonier IN 46767
    260 894-4145

(G-11015)
FREUDENBERG-NOK GENERAL PARTNR
Also Called: Automotive Vibration Division
1497 Gerber St (46767-2422)
P.O. Box 150 (46767-0150)
PHONE..................................260 894-7183
Steve Sperlazza, *Brnch Mgr*
EMP: 155
SALES (corp-wide): 12.23B **Privately Held**
Web: www.fst.com
SIC: 3714 3594 3444 Motor vehicle engines and parts; Fluid power pumps and motors; Sheet metalwork
HQ: Freudenberg-Nok General Partnership
    47774 W Anchor Ct
    Plymouth MI 48170
    734 451-0020

(G-11016)
GROTRIAN TOOL & DIE
300 Sroufe St (46767-1246)
P.O. Box 171 (46767-0171)
PHONE..................................260 894-3558
Mark Grotrian, *Owner*
EMP: 3 EST: 1985
SQ FT: 1,000
SALES (est): 197.35K **Privately Held**
SIC: 3544 5084 5251 Special dies and tools; Metalworking tools, nec (such as drills, taps, dies, files); Tools

(G-11017)
HITACHI ASTEMO AMERICAS INC
925 N Main St (46767-2060)
PHONE..................................859 734-9451
EMP: 65
Web: www.hitachi-automotive.us
SIC: 3694 3714 3699 3625 Alternators, automotive; Motor vehicle parts and accessories; Electrical equipment and supplies, nec; Relays and industrial controls
HQ: Hitachi Astemo Americas, Inc.
    955 Warwick Rd
    Harrodsburg KY 40330
    859 734-9451

(G-11018)
KREIDER MANUFACTURING
405 Gerber St (46767-2404)
PHONE..................................260 894-7120
FAX: 260 894-3863
EMP: 2 EST: 2010
SALES (est): 95.32K **Privately Held**
SIC: 3999 Manufacturing industries, nec

(G-11019)
LIGONIER WOODWORKING
1068 E Perry Rd (46767-9568)
PHONE..................................260 894-9969
EMP: 7 EST: 1999
SALES (est): 450K **Privately Held**
SIC: 2431 7389 Millwork; Business services, nec

(G-11020)
OUTLAND CUSTOM COATINGS LLC
4310 N 750 W (46767-9613)
PHONE..................................260 894-4818
Carol Hagerman, *Prin*
EMP: 6 EST: 2019
SALES (est): 377.41K **Privately Held**
SIC: 3479 Metal coating and allied services

(G-11021)
P & J INDUSTRIES INC
1494 Gerber St (46767-2421)
PHONE..................................260 894-7143
260 894-4145
Chris Judt, *Mgr*
EMP: 40
SALES (corp-wide): 8.83MM **Privately Held**
Web: www.pjind.com
SIC: 3471 Chromium plating of metals or formed products
PA: P & J Industries, Inc.
    4934 Lewis Ave
    Toledo OH 43612
    419 726-2675

(G-11022)
PRECISION TANK & EQUIPMENT CO
215 Heckner Dr (46767-2064)
PHONE..................................260 894-4002
Harry Nichols, *Brnch Mgr*
EMP: 2
SALES (corp-wide): 17.42MM **Privately Held**
Web: www.precisiontank.com
SIC: 3443 Fabricated plate work (boiler shop)
PA: Precision Tank & Equipment Co.
    2935 S Koke Mill Rd # 100
    Springfield IL 62711
    217 452-7228

(G-11023)
SILGAN PLASTICS LLC
Also Called: Silgan
910 Gerber St (46767-2425)
PHONE..................................260 894-7814
Lawrence Winkler, *Prin*
EMP: 100
Web: www.silganplastics.com
SIC: 3089 Plastics containers, except foam
HQ: Silgan Plastics Llc
    14515 N Oter 40 Rd Ste 21
    Chesterfield MO 63017
    800 274-5426

(G-11024)
STRUCTURAL COMPOSITES IND INC
Also Called: SCI
1118 Gerber St (46767-2417)
PHONE..................................260 894-4083
Jim Fearnow, *Pr*
Ken Baranowski, *
Lynette Gerard, *
EMP: 100 EST: 1999
SQ FT: 40,000
SALES (est): 9.29MM
SALES (corp-wide): 3.47B **Publicly Held**
Web: www.scindiana.com
SIC: 2221 3799 Fiberglass fabrics; Recreational vehicles
PA: Patrick Industries, Inc.
    107 W Franklin St
    Elkhart IN 46516
    574 294-7511

(G-11025)
SUPERIOR SAMPLE CO INC
520 Gerber St (46767-2405)
P.O. Box 550 (46767-0550)
PHONE..................................260 894-3136
Rex Hagen, *Ch*
Nancy Hagen, *
Peggy Daniels, *
▲ EMP: 40 EST: 1952
SQ FT: 120,000
SALES (est): 2.49MM **Privately Held**
Web: www.superiorsample.com
SIC: 2789 Swatches and samples

(G-11026)
SUPREME CORPORATION
Also Called: Tower Structural Laminating
1491 Gerber St (46767-2422)
PHONE..................................260 894-9191
Al Schroeder, *Brnch Mgr*

Ligonier - Noble County (G-11027)

EMP: 1
SALES (corp-wide): 2.54B **Publicly Held**
Web: www.supremecorp.com
SIC: 3713 3792 3585 Truck bodies (motor vehicles); Travel trailers and campers; Refrigeration and heating equipment
HQ: Supreme Corporation
2581 Kercher Rd
Goshen IN 46528
574 642-4888

(G-11027)
TENNECO AUTOMOTIVE OPER CO INC
Tenneco
1490 Gerber St (46767-2421)
PHONE.................................260 894-9214
Tim Holland, *Brnch Mgr*
EMP: 204
SALES (corp-wide): 18.04B **Privately Held**
Web: www.tenneco.com
SIC: 3714 Mufflers (exhaust), motor vehicle
HQ: Tenneco Automotive Operating Company, Inc.
500 N Field Dr
Lake Forest IL 60045
847 482-5000

(G-11028)
TI AUTOMOTIVE LIGONIER CORP
925 N Main St (46767-2060)
PHONE.................................260 894-3163
William Kozyra, *Pr*
◆ EMP: 600 EST: 1990
SQ FT: 160,000
SALES (est): 49.02MM
SALES (corp-wide): 3.82B **Privately Held**
SIC: 3714 Motor vehicle parts and accessories
HQ: Ti Group Automotive Systems, Llc
2020 Taylor Rd
Auburn Hills MI 48326
248 296-8000

(G-11029)
WELDING SHOP
5157 W 1100 N (46767-9560)
PHONE.................................260 593-2544
Dennis A Miller, *Prin*
EMP: 1 EST: 2008
SALES (est): 52.35K **Privately Held**
Web: www.theweldingshop.com
SIC: 7692 Welding repair

Linden
Montgomery County

(G-11030)
CARLSON MOTORSPORTS
Also Called: Carlson Racing
215 N High St (47955-8108)
P.O. Box 153 (47955-0153)
PHONE.................................765 339-4407
Brian Carlson, *Pt*
Sarah Carlson, *Pt*
EMP: 2 EST: 1989
SALES (est): 205.32K **Privately Held**
Web: www.carlsonmotorsports.com
SIC: 3519 5599 Internal combustion engines, nec; Go-carts

(G-11031)
LINDEN MACHINE SHOP LLC
Also Called: Linden Machine Shop
220 N Main St (47955-8091)
P.O. Box 382 (47955-0382)
PHONE.................................765 339-7244
EMP: 4 EST: 1994
SQ FT: 9,200
SALES (est): 449.73K **Privately Held**
Web: linden.in.gov
SIC: 3599 7692 3471 Machine shop, jobbing and repair; Welding repair; Plating and polishing

(G-11032)
SPURLINO MTLS INDIANAPOLIS LLC
11528 N Us Highway 231 (47955-8004)
PHONE.................................765 339-4055
EMP: 5 EST: 2007
SALES (est): 76.33K **Privately Held**
SIC: 3273 Ready-mixed concrete

(G-11033)
TYSON FRESH MEATS INC
Also Called: I B P Hog Buying Station
38 E 900 N (47955-8006)
P.O. Box 321 (47955-0321)
PHONE.................................765 339-4512
EMP: 1
SALES (corp-wide): 52.88B **Publicly Held**
Web: www.tysonfreshmeats.com
SIC: 2011 Meat packing plants
HQ: Tyson Fresh Meats, Inc.
2200 W Don Tyson Pkwy
Springdale AR 72765
479 290-4000

Linton
Greene County

(G-11034)
D & M PRINTING INC
Also Called: Smith Printing
1089 1st St Se (47441)
P.O. Box 142 (47441)
PHONE.................................812 847-4837
Mike Smith, *Pr*
EMP: 2 EST: 1969
SALES (est): 227.21K **Privately Held**
SIC: 2752 2791 Offset printing; Typesetting

(G-11035)
INDIANA OPERATIONS LLC
Also Called: Advanced Building Concepts
325 Se 12th Street (47441-9532)
PHONE.................................812 847-8924
EMP: 25 EST: 2004
SQ FT: 198,000
SALES (est): 1.6MM **Privately Held**
SIC: 2452 Modular homes, prefabricated, wood

(G-11036)
JACKSON BROTHERS LUMBER CO
59 State Rd S (47441)
PHONE.................................812 847-7812
Rick Destrom, *Pr*
Bobbie Ferguson, *Sec*
EMP: 12 EST: 1946
SALES (est): 363.93K **Privately Held**
SIC: 2421 2431 2426 Lumber: rough, sawed, or planed; Millwork; Hardwood dimension and flooring mills

(G-11037)
LANDIS EQUIPMENT & TOOL RENTAL
Also Called: A Rental Center
390 S Main St (47441-2116)
P.O. Box 212 (47441-0212)
PHONE.................................812 847-2582
Scott Landis, *Owner*
EMP: 3 EST: 2005
SALES (est): 175.39K **Privately Held**

(G-11038)
MARKLE MUSIC
Also Called: Markle Classic Signs
1796 S State Road 59 (47441-5235)
PHONE.................................812 847-2103
Fred Markle, *Owner*
EMP: 3 EST: 1978
SALES (est): 248.03K **Privately Held**
Web: www.marklemusic.com
SIC: 5736 7699 3993 String instruments; Musical instrument repair services; Signs and advertising specialties

(G-11039)
MCMILLIN HEARING AID INC
2160 E State Highway 54 (47441-9460)
PHONE.................................812 847-2470
EMP: 4 EST: 2016
SALES (est): 75.43K **Privately Held**
SIC: 3842 Hearing aids

(G-11040)
MOODYS LOGISTICS SERVICES LLC
609 A St Ne (47441-1909)
PHONE.................................812 512-2772
Chad Moody, *CEO*
EMP: 1 EST: 2021
SALES (est): 60.08K **Privately Held**
SIC: 3537 7389 Trucks: freight, baggage, etc.: industrial, except mining; Business Activities at Non-Commercial Site

(G-11041)
OLD PLASTICS COMPANY INC
12759 W 300 N (47441-6112)
PHONE.................................812 699-0379
Jason Habich, *Prin*
EMP: 2 EST: 2015
SALES (est): 118.42K **Privately Held**
SIC: 3089 Injection molding of plastics

(G-11042)
PITTMAN MINE SERVICE LLC
2878 N State Road 59 (47441-6199)
PHONE.................................812 847-2340
Raymond Pittman, *Owner*
Victor Daiber, *
EMP: 7 EST: 2003
SALES (est): 968.9K **Privately Held**
Web: www.pittmanms.com
SIC: 1241 7353 8741 Bituminous coal mining services, contract basis; Heavy construction equipment rental; Construction management

(G-11043)
PRO-MARK BLDG SOLUTIONS LLC
575 N 1000 W (47441-5297)
PHONE.................................812 798-1178
Elmer Sensenig, *Prin*
EMP: 11 EST: 2017
SALES (est): 893.51K **Privately Held**
Web: www.promarkbuildingsolutions.com
SIC: 2952 Roofing materials

(G-11044)
ROLLING HILLS SPRINGS LLC
2897 N 1375 W (47441-6533)
PHONE.................................844 454-6866
Jody Todd, *Managing Member*
Jennifer Sons, *Administrator Sales*
EMP: 4 EST: 2017
SALES (est): 249.46K **Privately Held**
Web: www.rollinghillssprings.com

SIC: 3599 5084 7513 Machine shop, jobbing and repair; Industrial machinery and equipment; Truck rental and leasing, no drivers

(G-11045)
RUSS PUBLISHING
Also Called: Linton Daily Citizen
79 S Main St (47441-1818)
P.O. Box 129 (47441-0129)
PHONE.................................812 847-4487
Randy Lift, *CEO*
Chris Pruett, *Publisher*
EMP: 11 EST: 1973
SQ FT: 10,000
SALES (est): 239.7K **Privately Held**
Web: www.gcdailyworld.com
SIC: 2711 Commercial printing and newspaper publishing combined

(G-11046)
SHADS SIGNS
60 S Main St (47441-1819)
PHONE.................................812 512-6066
EMP: 4 EST: 2018
SALES (est): 46.08K **Privately Held**
SIC: 3993 Signs and advertising specialties

(G-11047)
TAULMAN3D LLC
1600 A St Ne Ste 18 (47441-1626)
PHONE.................................401 996-8868
Zach Lichaa, *Managing Member*
EMP: 3 EST: 2013
SALES (est): 236.4K
SALES (corp-wide): 470.59MM **Privately Held**
SIC: 2759 Commercial printing, nec
PA: Braskem America, Inc.
1735 Market St 28th Fl
Philadelphia PA 19103
215 841-3100

Lizton
Hendricks County

(G-11048)
BEDLAM BEARD COMPANY LLC
Also Called: E-Commerce
6427 N County Road 200 W (46149-9433)
PHONE.................................317 800-9631
Joshua Tolen, *Pr*
EMP: 1 EST: 2017
SALES (est): 52.12K **Privately Held**
Web: www.gotbedlam.com
SIC: 5087 2899 Beauty salon and barber shop equipment and supplies; Oils and essential oils

(G-11049)
INDUSTRIAL TUBE COMPONENTS INC
6114 N County Road 50 W (46149-9485)
PHONE.................................317 431-2188
Kimberly Russell, *Prin*
Matt Russell, *Prin*
EMP: 8 EST: 2014
SALES (est): 236.15K **Privately Held**
Web: www.industrialtubecomponents.com
SIC: 3498 Tube fabricating (contract bending and shaping)

(G-11050)
JJ MACHINE
921 Walnut Grove Ct (46149-9577)
PHONE.................................765 366-8258
EMP: 3 EST: 2018
SALES (est): 109.49K **Privately Held**
Web: www.jjonesmachinellc.com

SIC: 2086 5149 Mineral water, carbonated: packaged in cans, bottles, etc.; Mineral or spring water bottling

GEOGRAPHIC SECTION

Logansport - Cass County (G-11074)

SIC: 3599 Machine shop, jobbing and repair

(G-11051)
WG MACHINE & TOOL
317 W Main St (46149-9221)
P.O. Box 167 (46149-0167)
PHONE..............................317 994-5556
Scott Glidewell, *Pt*
Craig Walton, *Pt*
EMP: 2 EST: 1999
SALES (est): 211.63K **Privately Held**
Web: www.wandgmachine.com
SIC: 3599 Machine shop, jobbing and repair

(G-11052)
WOOD-MIZER HOLDINGS INC
Also Called: Lastec
7865 N County Road 100 E (46149)
PHONE..............................317 892-4444
Scott Dufek, *Brnch Mgr*
EMP: 10
SALES (corp-wide): 133.23MM **Privately Held**
Web: www.woodmizer.com
SIC: 3524 Lawn and garden mowers and accessories
PA: Wood-Mizer Holdings, Inc.
    8180 W 10th St
    Indianapolis IN 46214
    317 271-1542

Logansport
Cass County

(G-11053)
3B PHOTONICS LLC
2721 E County Road 650 N (46947-6664)
PHONE..............................574 702-2620
EMP: 2 EST: 2019
SALES (est): 315.73K **Privately Held**
Web: www.3bphotonics.com
SIC: 2851 Paints and allied products

(G-11054)
ADVANCED HARN & ASSEMBLY LLC ✪
830 Old State Rd 25 (46947)
PHONE..............................574 722-4040
Lewis Dowal Delinger, *Mgr*
EMP: 14 EST: 2023
SALES (est): 1.07MM **Privately Held**
SIC: 3679 Harness assemblies, for electronic use; wire or cable

(G-11055)
AMERI-TEK MANUFACTURING INC
3332 Billiard Dr (46947-8272)
P.O. Box 359 (46947-0359)
PHONE..............................574 753-8058
Joe B Bowyer, *Pr*
Steven E Bowyer, *VP*
Debbie Bowyer, *Sec*
EMP: 14 EST: 1991
SQ FT: 17,600
SALES (est): 1.89MM **Privately Held**
Web: www.ameri-tekmfg.com
SIC: 3469 3544 Stamping metal for the trade; Special dies and tools

(G-11056)
ANDERSONS AGRICULTURE GROUP LP
2345 S 400 E (46947)
PHONE..............................574 753-4974
EMP: 1
SALES (corp-wide): 14.75B **Publicly Held**
Web: www.andersonsinc.com
SIC: 2874 2873 2875 Phosphatic fertilizers; Nitrogenous fertilizers; Fertilizers, mixing only
HQ: The Andersons Agriculture Group L P
    1947 Briarfield Blvd
    Maumee OH 43537
    419 893-5050

(G-11057)
ANDERSONS CLYMERS ETHANOL LLC
3389 W County Road 300 S (46947-8924)
PHONE..............................574 722-2627
EMP: 9 EST: 2020
SALES (est): 2.77MM **Privately Held**
Web: www.andersonsinc.com
SIC: 2869 Ethyl alcohol, ethanol

(G-11058)
ARAYMOND MFG CTR N AMER INC
Also Called: A Raymond Tinnerman
800 W County Road 250 S (46947-8269)
PHONE..............................574 722-5168
Keith Holmes, *Brnch Mgr*
EMP: 240
SALES (corp-wide): 355.83K **Privately Held**
SIC: 3471 3495 3469 3429 Plating and polishing; Wire springs; Metal stampings, nec; Hardware, nec
HQ: Araymond Manufacturing Center North America, Inc.
    3091 Research Dr
    Rochester Hills MI 48309
    248 260-2121

(G-11059)
BACCHUS WINERY GOLF VINYRD LLC
14 Golfview Dr (46947-4104)
PHONE..............................574 732-4663
Amanda Crain, *Admn*
EMP: 7 EST: 2014
SALES (est): 257.1K **Privately Held**
SIC: 2084 Wines

(G-11060)
BACCHUS WINERY LLC
820 Golden Bear Ter (46947-4153)
PHONE..............................574 722-1416
EMP: 4 EST: 2018
SALES (est): 150.63K **Privately Held**
SIC: 2084 Wines

(G-11061)
BEATTYS CUSTOM WOODS
824 14th St (46947-4402)
PHONE..............................574 722-2752
Jarel Beatty, *Owner*
EMP: 1 EST: 1979
SALES (est): 59.6K **Privately Held**
SIC: 2434 Wood kitchen cabinets

(G-11062)
BHJ USA LLC
Also Called: Cass County Byproducts
81 E Industrial Blvd (46947-6712)
PHONE..............................574 722-3933
EMP: 5
SALES (corp-wide): 192.23MM **Privately Held**
Web: www.bhj.com
SIC: 5149 2047 Pet foods; Dog and cat food
HQ: Bhj Usa, Llc
    2510 Edward Babe Gmez Ave
    Omaha NE 68107
    402 734-8030

(G-11063)
BOOMERANG KIDZ CLOTHING
825 18th St (46947-4422)
PHONE..............................574 992-2233
EMP: 3 EST: 2019
SALES (est): 47.08K **Privately Held**
SIC: 3949 Boomerangs

(G-11064)
CARTER FUEL SYSTEMS LLC (DH)
Also Called: Carter Engineered Quality
101 E Industrial Blvd (46947)
PHONE..............................800 342-6125
Robert Henderson, *Managing Member*
▲ EMP: 270 EST: 2013
SALES (est): 395.15MM
SALES (corp-wide): 8.28B **Privately Held**
Web: www.carterengineered.com
SIC: 5989 3714 Coal; Fuel pumps, motor vehicle
HQ: First Brands Group, Llc
    127 Public Sq
    Cleveland OH 44114
    248 371-1700

(G-11065)
CARTER FUEL SYSTEMS LLC
91 E Industrial Blvd (46947-6712)
PHONE..............................574 735-0235
Brad Angel, *Manager*
EMP: 6
SALES (corp-wide): 8.28B **Privately Held**
Web: www.carterengineered.com
SIC: 3714 Motor vehicle parts and accessories
HQ: Carter Fuel Systems, Llc
    101 E Industrial Blvd
    Logansport IN 46947
    800 342-6125

(G-11066)
CASS COUNTY MACHINE INC
2915 Green Hills Dr (46947-1311)
P.O. Box 596 (46947-0596)
PHONE..............................574 722-5714
Larry David Bruck, *Pr*
Larry D Bruck, *Pr*
EMP: 10 EST: 1947
SQ FT: 7,500
SALES (est): 113.78K **Privately Held**
SIC: 3599 Machine shop, jobbing and repair

(G-11067)
CGF ENTERPRISES LLC
5438 N County Road 75 W (46947-6509)
PHONE..............................574 889-2074
EMP: 5 EST: 2011
SALES (est): 132.51K **Privately Held**
SIC: 3482 Small arms ammunition

(G-11068)
COMMUNITY HOLDINGS INDIANA INC
Also Called: Pharos Tribune
517 E Broadway (46947-3154)
P.O. Box 210 (46947-0210)
PHONE..............................574 722-5000
Robyn Mcclosky, *Brnch Mgr*
EMP: 1
SALES (corp-wide): 34.97B **Privately Held**
Web: www.pharostribune.com
SIC: 2711 2752 Newspapers, publishing and printing; Commercial printing, lithographic
HQ: Community Holdings Of Indiana, Inc.
    3500 Colonnade Pkwy # 600
    Birmingham AL 35243

(G-11069)
COMPAL ELECTRONICS NA INC ✪
1 Technology Way (46947)
PHONE..............................574 992-8793
Arthur Wang, *CEO*
Nicholas Ferry, *
EMP: 50 EST: 2023
SALES (est): 1.5MM **Privately Held**
SIC: 3679 Electronic circuits
PA: Compal Electronics, Inc.
    No. 581, 581-1, Ruiguang Rd.
    Taipei City TAP 11406

(G-11070)
COMPAL USA (INDIANA) INC
Also Called: Compal USA
1 Technology Way (46947)
PHONE..............................574 739-2929
Ta Chun Wang, *CEO*
Cheng Chiang Wang, *
Nicholas Ferry, *
Jui Tsung Chen, *
▲ EMP: 400 EST: 2003
SQ FT: 72,000
SALES (est): 84.06MM **Privately Held**
SIC: 3672 Circuit boards, television and radio printed
PA: Cal-Comp Electronics (Thailand) Public Company Limited
    191/54, 191/57 Ratchadaphisek Road
    Khlong Toei 10110

(G-11071)
EIS FIBERCOATING INC
616 E Main St (46947-5003)
PHONE..............................574 722-5192
Paul Rossomme, *Pr*
Linda Rossomme, *
EMP: 50 EST: 1983
SQ FT: 8,000
SALES (est): 4.39MM **Privately Held**
Web: www.fibercoating.com
SIC: 3069 3089 Hard rubber and molded rubber products; Plastics processing

(G-11072)
EIS PACKAGING MACHINERY INC
Also Called: Manufacturing
4754 E County Road 75 N (46947-6636)
PHONE..............................574 870-0087
Mark Neher, *Pr*
EMP: 5 EST: 2010
SALES (est): 238.43K **Privately Held**
SIC: 7699 3999 Industrial machinery and equipment repair; Manufacturing industries, nec

(G-11073)
ENGINEERING AND INDUSTRIAL SERVICES LLC
Also Called: Inline Cleaning Systems
2095 S County Road 150 E (46947-8006)
PHONE..............................574 722-3714
EMP: 25 EST: 1977
SALES (est): 2.11MM **Privately Held**
Web: www.eislogan.com
SIC: 3559 3999 3496 Rubber working machinery, including tires; Flocking metal products; Conveyor belts

(G-11074)
GALBREATH INDUSTRIAL SVCS LLC
801 Erie Ave (46947-3513)
P.O. Box 121 (46947-0121)
PHONE..............................574 737-8159
Anthony Suter, *Prin*
EMP: 1 EST: 2007
SALES (est): 78.58K **Privately Held**
Web: www.galbreathindustrial.com
SIC: 7692 Welding repair

Logansport - Cass County (G-11075)

(G-11075)
GRABLE BURIAL VAULT SVC INC
322 Highland St (46947-4936)
P.O. Box 1079 (46947-0979)
PHONE..................574 753-4514
EMP: 3 EST: 1987
SALES (est): 327.16K Privately Held
SIC: 3272 Burial vaults, concrete or precast terrazzo

(G-11076)
HEIDELBERG MTLS US CEM LLC
3084 W County Road 225 S (46947-8476)
PHONE..................574 753-5121
Ken Gillespie, Brnch Mgr
EMP: 110
SALES (corp-wide): 23.02B Privately Held
Web: www.heidelbergmaterials.us
SIC: 3241 2899 Portland cement; Chemical preparations, nec
HQ: Heidelberg Materials Us Cement Llc
    300 E John Carpenter Fwy
    Irving TX 75062
    877 534-4442

(G-11077)
HOPPER DEVELOPMENT INC
Also Called: H D I
1332 18th St (46947-4464)
P.O. Box 296 (46947-0296)
PHONE..................574 753-6621
John Hopper, Pr
Joan Hopper, Sec
Jhon Hopper, Pr
Jason Hopper, VP
EMP: 17 EST: 1970
SQ FT: 14,000
SALES (est): 2.37MM Privately Held
Web: www.teamhdi.com
SIC: 3089 3544 Injection molding of plastics; Forms (molds), for foundry and plastics working machinery

(G-11078)
HTI
500 W Clinton St Ste 2 (46947-4684)
P.O. Box 741 (46947-0741)
PHONE..................574 722-2814
Chico Rodriguez, Genl Mgr
EMP: 18 EST: 1976
SQ FT: 27,000
SALES (est): 2.33MM Privately Held
Web: www.callhti.com
SIC: 3398 Metal heat treating

(G-11079)
HUMPHREY TOOL CO INC
120 Water St (46947-1874)
P.O. Box 48 (46947-0048)
PHONE..................574 753-3853
Ron Bunger, Pr
EMP: 4 EST: 1976
SQ FT: 3,600
SALES (est): 380.49K Privately Held
SIC: 3469 3544 Stamping metal for the trade; Special dies and tools

(G-11080)
I N C O M WHOLESALE SUPPLY
2865 E Market St (46947-2070)
PHONE..................574 722-2442
Mike Mccord, Owner
Stephanie Tatacsil, Mgr
EMP: 3 EST: 2001
SALES (est): 292.45K Privately Held
SIC: 2899 Chemical supplies for foundries

(G-11081)
ICAN SOLUTIONS LLC
Also Called: Ican Mobile Canning
5294 E Division Rd (46947-7966)
PHONE..................574 355-6500
EMP: 1 EST: 2013
SALES (est): 150.88K Privately Held
SIC: 3411 Beer cans, metal

(G-11082)
INDIANA DIMENSION INC
Also Called: I D I
1621 W Market St (46947-9728)
P.O. Box 568 (46947-0568)
PHONE..................574 739-2319
Byron Roy Rentschler, Pr
William M Cole, *
Jeremy Rentschler, *
John A Land, *
James K Cole, Stockholder*
▲ EMP: 55 EST: 1991
SQ FT: 180,000
SALES (est): 7.03MM Privately Held
Web: www.indianadimension.com
SIC: 2431 Panel work, wood

(G-11083)
INTERACTIONS INCORPORATED
Also Called: Pepsi-Cola
1031 N 3rd St (46947-2619)
P.O. Box 449 (46947-0449)
PHONE..................574 722-6207
Curtis R Vander Meer, Pr
Gary L Enders, VP
EMP: 75 EST: 1985
SQ FT: 66,000
SALES (est): 4.84MM Privately Held
Web: www.pepsico.com
SIC: 2086 Soft drinks: packaged in cans, bottles, etc.

(G-11084)
IRVING MATERIALS INC
Also Called: I M I
2245 S County Road 150 E (46947-8007)
P.O. Box 842 (46947-0842)
PHONE..................574 722-3420
EMP: 4
SALES (corp-wide): 814.09MM Privately Held
Web: www.irvmat.com
SIC: 3273 Ready-mixed concrete
PA: Irving Materials, Inc.
    8032 N State Road 9
    Greenfield IN 46140
    317 326-3101

(G-11085)
JC PRINTING
301 Burlington Ave (46947-4834)
PHONE..................574 721-9000
Jorge Ceron, Prin
EMP: 7 EST: 2013
SALES (est): 168.84K Privately Held
SIC: 2752 Commercial printing, lithographic

(G-11086)
KAUFFMAN ENGINEERING INC
Also Called: KAUFFMAN ENGINEERING INC
830 S State Road 25 (46947-4682)
P.O. Box 658 (46947-0658)
PHONE..................574 722-3800
EMP: 90
SALES (corp-wide): 140.92MM Privately Held
Web: www.kewire.com
SIC: 3679 Harness assemblies, for electronic use: wire or cable
PA: Kauffman Engineering, Llc
    595 Bond St
    Lincolnshire IL 60069
    765 482-5640

(G-11087)
KENT NUTRITION GROUP INC
2407 S 400 E (46947)
PHONE..................574 722-5368
Dave Mayhill, Brnch Mgr
EMP: 11
SQ FT: 60,000
SALES (corp-wide): 515.77MM Privately Held
Web: www.kentfeeds.com
SIC: 2048 Livestock feeds
HQ: Kent Nutrition Group, Inc.
    2905 N Highway 61
    Muscatine IA 52761
    866 647-1212

(G-11088)
KEP CHEM INC
616 Center Ave (46947-2936)
P.O. Box 1141 (46947-7141)
PHONE..................574 739-0501
EMP: 5 EST: 1995
SALES (est): 373.27K Privately Held
SIC: 2879 Agricultural chemicals, nec

(G-11089)
LOGAN STAMPINGS INC (PA)
40 E Industrial Blvd (46947-6712)
P.O. Box 298 (46947-0298)
PHONE..................574 722-3101
Robert Baker, Pr
EMP: 48 EST: 1969
SQ FT: 76,000
SALES (est): 8.79MM
SALES (corp-wide): 8.79MM Privately Held
Web: www.loganstampings.com
SIC: 3469 Stamping metal for the trade

(G-11090)
LOGANSPORT MACHINE CO INC
Also Called: LMC Workholding
1200 W Linden Ave (46947-2950)
P.O. Box 7006 (46947-7006)
PHONE..................574 735-0225
▲ EMP: 40 EST: 1937
SQ FT: 60,000
SALES (est): 9.64MM Privately Held
Web: www.lmcworkholding.com
SIC: 3545 3593 5084 Machine tool attachments and accessories; Fluid power cylinders and actuators; Industrial machinery and equipment

(G-11091)
LOGO ZONE INC
731 Lakeview Dr (46947-2204)
PHONE..................574 753-7569
Tim Senesac, Pr
EMP: 2 EST: 2005
SALES (est): 148.98K Privately Held
Web: www.logozoneinc.com
SIC: 2759 Screen printing

(G-11092)
LSI METAL FABRICATION INC
1100 E Main St (46947-5013)
PHONE..................574 722-3101
Robert Breaker, CEO
EMP: 30 EST: 2006
SALES (est): 3.88MM Privately Held
Web: www.loganstampings.com
SIC: 3441 Fabricated structural metal

(G-11093)
MATTHEW WARREN INC
Also Called: Matthew Warren Spring
500 E Ottawa St (46947-2610)
PHONE..................574 722-8200
William Marcum, Brnch Mgr
EMP: 76
SALES (corp-wide): 1.05B Privately Held
Web: www.mwcomponents.com
SIC: 3493 Steel springs, except wire
HQ: Matthew Warren, Inc.
    3426 Toringdon Way # 100
    Charlotte NC 28277
    704 837-0331

(G-11094)
MOUNTVILLE MATS
5270 E Country Club Rd (46947-8451)
PHONE..................574 753-8858
EMP: 2 EST: 2000
SALES (est): 85.29K Privately Held
Web: www.mountville.com
SIC: 2273 Mats and matting

(G-11095)
MYERS DESIGN INC
6061 Logansport Rd (46947-8866)
PHONE..................317 955-2450
Jason Myers, Pr
EMP: 2 EST: 2002
SALES (est): 248.39K Privately Held
Web: www.myersdesigninc.com
SIC: 2519 Furniture, household: glass, fiberglass, and plastic

(G-11096)
MYERS SPRING CO INC
720 Water St (46947-1735)
P.O. Box 450 (46947-0450)
PHONE..................574 753-5105
Todd A Miller, Pr
Craig L Miller, *
Gretchen G Miller, *
EMP: 40 EST: 1946
SQ FT: 28,800
SALES (est): 9.37MM Privately Held
Web: www.myersspring.com
SIC: 3495 3496 3493 Mechanical springs, precision; Miscellaneous fabricated wire products; Steel springs, except wire

(G-11097)
NELSON ACQUISITION LLC
Also Called: Nelson Tube Company
130 E Industrial Blvd (46947-6994)
PHONE..................574 753-6377
EMP: 25 EST: 1947
SQ FT: 40,000
SALES (est): 499.54K Privately Held
Web: www.tubefabricationindustries.com
SIC: 3312 Tubes, steel and iron

(G-11098)
NF FRICTION COMPOSITES INC
1441 Holland St (46947-1720)
PHONE..................574 516-1131
Joyce Butzen, Pr
R Christopher Butzen, VP
EMP: 5 EST: 2011
SQ FT: 100,000
SALES (est): 447.69K Privately Held
Web: www.nffriction.com
SIC: 3299 Mica products, built-up or sheet

(G-11099)
NICK-EM BUILDERS LLC
Also Called: Foppers Pet Treat Bakery
501 N Park Ave (46947)
PHONE..................574 992-8313
EMP: 12
SALES (corp-wide): 4.71MM Privately Held
Web: www.foppers.com
SIC: 2047 Dog and cat food
PA: Nick-Em Builders, Llc
    1005 W Broadway
    Logansport IN 46947

GEOGRAPHIC SECTION

Long Beach - Laporte County (G-11122)

574 516-1060

(G-11100)
NICK-EM BUILDERS LLC (PA)
Also Called: Foppers Gourmet Pet Treat Bky
1005 W Broadway (46947)
PHONE..................................574 516-1060
Michelle Leffert, *CEO*
Clark Leffert, *General Vice President*
EMP: 20 **EST:** 2002
SQ FT: 75,000
SALES (est): 4.71MM
SALES (corp-wide): 4.71MM **Privately Held**
Web: www.foppers.com
SIC: 2047 Dog and cat food

(G-11101)
NORTHWEST INDIANA NEWSPPR INC
Also Called: Pharos-Tribune
517 E Broadway (46947-3154)
P.O. Box 210 (46947-0210)
PHONE..................................574 722-5000
Arden Draeger, *Pr*
EMP: 1 **EST:** 1913
SQ FT: 12,000
SALES (est): 2.11MM
SALES (corp-wide): 691.14MM **Publicly Held**
Web: www.pharostribune.com
SIC: 2711 Newspapers, publishing and printing
HQ: Lee Publications, Inc.
4600 E 53rd St
Davenport IA 52807
563 383-2100

(G-11102)
PETROLEUM JOBBERS DATA CONTROL
2938 N County Road 275 E (46947-8072)
PHONE..................................574 722-4477
Michael Young, *Owner*
EMP: 1 **EST:** 1981
SQ FT: 1,200
SALES (est): 77K **Privately Held**
SIC: 7374 7372 Data processing and preparation; Prepackaged software

(G-11103)
PROFESSIONAL SNDBLST & WLDG
4747 E Division Rd (46947-7961)
PHONE..................................574 355-9825
EMP: 3 **EST:** 2019
SALES (est): 34.2K **Privately Held**
Web: www.prosandblast.com
SIC: 7692 Welding repair

(G-11104)
QUALITY DIE SET CORP
600 Water St (46947-1804)
PHONE..................................574 967-4411
Jerry Shank, *Pr*
Christi Shank, *
Raymond Shank, *
EMP: 32 **EST:** 1969
SQ FT: 60,000
SALES (est): 4.97MM **Privately Held**
Web: www.lawsonproducts.net
SIC: 3469 3542 7692 3544 Stamping metal for the trade; Rebuilt machine tools, metal forming types; Welding repair; Special dies, tools, jigs, and fixtures

(G-11105)
ROGERS CABINETRY
2527 N County Road 925 E (46947-7794)
PHONE..................................574 664-9931
William Cassidy, *Prin*

EMP: 2 **EST:** 2006
SALES (est): 172.34K **Privately Held**
Web: www.rogerscabinetry.com
SIC: 2434 Wood kitchen cabinets

(G-11106)
SMALL PARTS INC
112 E Mildred St (46947-4979)
P.O. Box 7002 (46947-7002)
PHONE..................................574 739-6236
Carl Methner, *Prin*
EMP: 3
SALES (corp-wide): 146.79MM **Privately Held**
Web: www.smallpartsinc.com
SIC: 3469 Metal stampings, nec
HQ: Small Parts, Inc.
600 Humphrey St
Logansport IN 46947
574 753-6323

(G-11107)
SMALL PARTS INC (HQ)
600 Humphrey St (46947-4999)
P.O. Box 7002 (46947-7002)
PHONE..................................574 753-6323
John E Barnes, *CEO*
Clay Jackson, *
John Farmani, *
Clay T Barnes, *HOLDING COMPANY**
Jim Bauer, *
◆ **EMP:** 335 **EST:** 1958
SQ FT: 135,000
SALES (est): 93.54MM
SALES (corp-wide): 146.79MM **Privately Held**
Web: www.smallpartsinc.com
SIC: 3443 Metal parts
PA: Materials Processing, Inc.
3500 Depauw Blvd
Indianapolis IN 46268
317 803-3010

(G-11108)
SUMMIT/EMS CORPORATION
Also Called: Summit
1509 Woodlawn Ave (46947-4459)
PHONE..................................574 722-1317
Larry Graf, *Prin*
▲ **EMP:** 31 **EST:** 2005
SQ FT: 10,000
SALES (est): 1.08MM **Privately Held**
Web: www.kewire.com
SIC: 3621 Generating apparatus and parts, electrical

(G-11109)
SUS CAST PRODUCTS INC
Also Called: S U S
1825 W Market St (46947-1746)
P.O. Box 268 (46947-0268)
PHONE..................................574 753-4111
Kenneth Merlau, *Pr*
Kenneth Jr Merlau, *CEO*
Jeff Todd, *
Randall G Martin, *
▲ **EMP:** 100 **EST:** 1946
SQ FT: 80,000
SALES (est): 8.96MM **Privately Held**
Web: www.suscastproducts.com
SIC: 3363 3365 Aluminum die-castings; Aluminum foundries

(G-11110)
T & L TOOL & DIE II INC
911 Calla St (46947-1705)
PHONE..................................574 722-6246
Kirby Dillon, *Pr*
Margaret L Dillon, *Sec*
EMP: 5 **EST:** 1955
SQ FT: 9,075

SALES (est): 460.12K **Privately Held**
Web: www.tltool.com
SIC: 3544 Special dies and tools

(G-11111)
TRANSCO RAILWAY PRODUCTS INC
1331 S 18th St (46947)
P.O. Box 706 (46947-0706)
PHONE..................................574 753-6227
Eric Nichols, *Mgr*
EMP: 41
SQ FT: 10,000
SALES (corp-wide): 364.48B **Publicly Held**
Web: www.transcorailway.com
SIC: 3743 Railroad equipment
HQ: Transco Railway Products Inc.
200 N La Salle St Lbby 5
Chicago IL 60601
312 427-2818

(G-11112)
TRIBINE INDUSTRIES LLC
6991 E 750 N (46947-9301)
PHONE..................................316 282-8011
Ben Dillon, *Pr*
EMP: 7 **EST:** 2012
SALES (est): 75.48K **Privately Held**
Web: www.tribine.com
SIC: 2041 Grain mills (except rice)

(G-11113)
TUBE FABRICATION INDS INC
130 E Industrial Blvd (46947-6994)
PHONE..................................574 753-6377
Peter A Ferentinos, *CEO*
Julie Ellis, *
Troy Zimmerman, *
▲ **EMP:** 42 **EST:** 2006
SALES (est): 5.17MM **Privately Held**
Web: www.tubefabricationindustries.com
SIC: 3312 Blast furnaces and steel mills

(G-11114)
TYSON FRESH MEATS INC
Also Called: Tyson
2125 S County Road 125 W (46947-8477)
PHONE..................................574 753-6121
Daryell Schmidt, *Mgr*
EMP: 103
SQ FT: 800,000
SALES (corp-wide): 52.88B **Publicly Held**
Web: www.tysonfoods.com
SIC: 2011 Boxed beef, from meat slaughtered on site
HQ: Tyson Fresh Meats, Inc.
2200 W Don Tyson Pkwy
Springdale AR 72765
479 290-4000

(G-11115)
TYSON FRESH MEATS INC
Also Called: I B P
Hwy 35 S (46947)
PHONE..................................574 753-6134
Darrell Schmidt, *Mgr*
EMP: 1
SALES (corp-wide): 52.88B **Publicly Held**
Web: www.tysonfreshmeats.com
SIC: 2011 Pork products, from pork slaughtered on site
HQ: Tyson Fresh Meats, Inc.
2200 W Don Tyson Pkwy
Springdale AR 72765
479 290-4000

(G-11116)
ULERYS FIREWORKS INC
1030 N 3rd St (46947-2618)
PHONE..................................574 722-9119
EMP: 6 **EST:** 1992

SALES (est): 130K **Privately Held**
SIC: 2899 Fireworks

(G-11117)
VALLEY TOOL & DIE STAMPINGS
6408 W Us Highway 24 (46947-6901)
PHONE..................................574 722-4566
Norman E Miller, *Pr*
Michael A Holcomb, *
Lynn Burton, *
EMP: 24 **EST:** 1973
SQ FT: 32,600
SALES (est): 2.47MM **Privately Held**
Web: www.valleystampings.com
SIC: 3469 3544 3496 3495 Stamping metal for the trade; Special dies, tools, jigs, and fixtures; Miscellaneous fabricated wire products; Wire springs

(G-11118)
VERSATILE CAB SOLID SURFC INC
108 E Ottawa St (46947-2629)
PHONE..................................574 753-2359
EMP: 4 **EST:** 1998
SALES (est): 492.41K **Privately Held**
Web: www.versatilecabinets.com
SIC: 2434 Wood kitchen cabinets

(G-11119)
WAELZ SUSTAINABLE PRODUCTS LLC
3440 W Co Rd 300 S (46947)
P.O. Box 630 (46947-0630)
PHONE..................................317 334-7067
Nigel Morrison, *Managing Member*
EMP: 22 **EST:** 2018
SALES (est): 5.13MM **Privately Held**
Web: www.waelzsp.com
SIC: 2611 Pulp manufactured from waste or recycled paper

(G-11120)
WP BEVERAGES LLC
Also Called: Pepsico
1031 N 3rd St (46947-2619)
PHONE..................................574 722-6207
EMP: 15
SALES (corp-wide): 238.46MM **Privately Held**
Web: www.wpbpepsi.com
SIC: 2086 Carbonated soft drinks, bottled and canned
HQ: Wp Beverages, Llc
6176 Pepsi Way
Windsor WI 53598
608 846-1200

Long Beach
Laporte County

(G-11121)
CAINE PUBLISHING LLC
2721 Floral Trl (46360-1671)
PHONE..................................312 215-5253
Francesca Caine, *Prin*
EMP: 5 **EST:** 2011
SALES (est): 100.89K **Privately Held**
SIC: 2741 Miscellaneous publishing

(G-11122)
KOLOSSOS INC
Also Called: Kolossos
2715 Duffy Ln (46360-1552)
P.O. Box 309 (46361-0309)
PHONE..................................312 952-6991
Edward Billys, *Pr*
Giorgios Karayannis, *VP*
Michael Karayannis, *Sec*
▲ **EMP:** 3 **EST:** 2011

Long Beach - Laporte County (G-11123)

GEOGRAPHIC SECTION

SALES (est): 198.68K **Privately Held**
Web: www.kolossoslife.com
SIC: **2035** 5169 Seasonings, seafood sauces (except tomato and dry); Food additives and preservatives

(G-11123)
LANGLEY FINE ART PRINTS
2019 Somerset Rd (46360-1432)
PHONE..............................219 872-0087
Joan Langley, *Prin*
EMP: **5** EST: 2009
SALES (est): 151.25K **Privately Held**
SIC: **2752** Commercial printing, lithographic

(G-11124)
MCCULLAGH CORPORATION
2302 Florimond Dr (46360-1628)
P.O. Box 9267 (46361-9267)
PHONE..............................877 645-7676
▲ EMP: **10** EST: 2011
SALES (est): 504.51K **Privately Held**
SIC: **3569** Filters

(G-11125)
MOLDEN ASSOCIATES INC
1804 Lake Shore Dr (46360-1462)
P.O. Box 545 (46361-0545)
PHONE..............................219 879-8425
Teodore Craig Molden, *Pr*
Patricia K Molden, *Sec*
Francis Molden, *Treas*
EMP: **4** EST: 1976
SALES (est): 272.95K **Privately Held**
SIC: **3589** 3651 Water treatment equipment, industrial; Public address systems

(G-11126)
PAGELS-KELLEY ENTERPRISES LLC
Also Called: Mc Kay Printing Services
2718 Roslyn Trl (46360-1624)
PHONE..............................219 872-8552
EMP: **16** EST: 1950
SALES (est): 2.41MM **Privately Held**
SIC: **2752** 2759 Offset printing; Publication printing

(G-11127)
PHOENIX PURE HOLDINGS LLC
2511 Fairway Dr (46360-1516)
PHONE..............................219 448-0142
Ricky Lutterbach, *Managing Member*
EMP: **1** EST: 2015
SALES (est): 67.56K **Privately Held**
SIC: **3589** Water treatment equipment, industrial

(G-11128)
PRINT CENTER INC
2016 Oriole Trl (46360-1424)
PHONE..............................219 874-9683
Jennifer Rucinski, *Owner*
EMP: **2** EST: 2013
SALES (est): 118.97K **Privately Held**
Web: www.1printcenter.com
SIC: **2752** Offset printing

Loogootee
Martin County

(G-11129)
CRICKYS COUNTRY CABINETS LLC
1831 N 950 E (47553-5408)
PHONE..............................812 486-3705
Darvin Knepp, *Owner*
EMP: **1** EST: 2013
SALES (est): 92.67K **Privately Held**
SIC: **2434** Wood kitchen cabinets

(G-11130)
CUSTOM DOOR MANUFACTURING
8076 N 1100 E (47553-5630)
PHONE..............................812 636-3667
Dave Graber, *Owner*
EMP: **4** EST: 2008
SALES (est): 252.62K **Privately Held**
SIC: **2431** Doors and door parts and trim, wood

(G-11131)
DELMAR KNEPP LOGGING
10293 E 600 N (47553-5581)
PHONE..............................812 486-2565
Delmar Knepp, *Prin*
EMP: **2** EST: 2007
SALES (est): 156.8K **Privately Held**
SIC: **2411** Logging camps and contractors

(G-11132)
DG TIMBER INC
15562 Half Moon Rd (47553-4623)
PHONE..............................812 295-9876
EMP: **7** EST: 2019
SALES (est): 188.46K **Privately Held**
Web: www.dgtimber.com
SIC: **2421** Sawmills and planing mills, general

(G-11133)
DUTCHLAND LLC
1099 Seals Rd (47553-5112)
PHONE..............................812 254-5400
EMP: **7** EST: 2000
SALES (est): 74.27K **Privately Held**
Web: www.dutchland.com
SIC: **3089** Injection molding of plastics

(G-11134)
E & D TIRE & REPAIR LLC
11326 E 600 N (47553-5587)
PHONE..............................812 486-6493
EMP: **5** EST: 2019
SALES (est): 100K **Privately Held**
SIC: **3011** Tire and inner tube materials and related products

(G-11135)
EDS MACHINE & TOOL
1250 Mount Pleasant Rd (47553-4964)
PHONE..............................812 295-7264
Ed Searl, *Owner*
EMP: **5** EST: 2017
SALES (est): 94.53K **Privately Held**
Web: www.northernempire.com
SIC: **3599** Machine shop, jobbing and repair

(G-11136)
GRABER FURNITURE
6377 N 1200 E (47553-5607)
PHONE..............................812 295-4939
Enos Graber, *Owner*
EMP: **9** EST: 1977
SALES (est): 504.09K **Privately Held**
SIC: **2426** 5712 2434 Furniture stock and parts, hardwood; Furniture stores; Wood kitchen cabinets

(G-11137)
GREENWELL SOFTWARE LLC
9750 N 1300 E (47553-5176)
PHONE..............................812 709-0214
Tyler Wagler, *Owner*
EMP: **6** EST: 2013
SALES (est): 110.17K **Privately Held**
SIC: **7372** Prepackaged software

(G-11138)
HICKORY VALLEY WOODWORKING LLC
10432 E 625 N (47553-5583)
PHONE..............................812 486-2857
EMP: **6** EST: 2009
SALES (est): 454.72K **Privately Held**
SIC: **2431** Millwork

(G-11139)
J & R TOOL INC
1444 Us Highway 50 (47553-5006)
P.O. Box 123 (47553-0123)
PHONE..............................812 295-2557
EMP: **13** EST: 1994
SQ FT: 3,200
SALES (est): 1.36MM **Privately Held**
Web: www.jrtoolinc.com
SIC: **3599** Machine shop, jobbing and repair

(G-11140)
K Q SERVICING LLC
22383 Third Rd (47553-4683)
PHONE..............................812 486-9244
Kyla Quick, *Managing Member*
EMP: **5** EST: 2013
SALES (est): 148.94K **Privately Held**
SIC: **1241** 1542 Coal mining services; Commercial and office building contractors

(G-11141)
KC INNOVATIONS LLC
Also Called: Energy House
11720 W 250n (47553)
PHONE..............................888 290-8920
Ferman Miller, *CEO*
EMP: **12** EST: 2012
SALES (est): 823.68K **Privately Held**
SIC: **3648** Public lighting fixtures

(G-11142)
KNEPP LOGGING LLC
2946 N 900 E (47553-5423)
PHONE..............................812 486-3741
David Knepp, *Owner*
EMP: **6** EST: 2008
SALES (est): 323.49K **Privately Held**
SIC: **2411** Timber, cut at logging camp

(G-11143)
LOOGOOTEE TRIBUNE INC
514 N John F Kennedy Ave (47553-1102)
P.O. Box 277 (47553-0277)
PHONE..............................812 295-2500
Larry D Hatmbree, *Pr*
EMP: **7** EST: 1959
SQ FT: 1,200
SALES (est): 454.3K **Privately Held**
Web: www.loogooteetribune.com
SIC: **2711** Newspapers: publishing only, not printed on site

(G-11144)
LOUGHMILLER MCH TL DESIGN INC
12851 E 150 N (47553-5385)
PHONE..............................812 295-3903
Jason Loughmiller, *Pr*
Pamela Loughmiller, *
Richard Hoke, *
EMP: **50** EST: 1985
SQ FT: 3,600
SALES (est): 5.06MM **Privately Held**
Web: www.lmtdonline.com
SIC: **3441** Fabricated structural metal

(G-11145)
MAIN MUSIC
12958 E Us Highway 50 (47553-5211)
PHONE..............................812 295-2020
Chris Main, *Mgr*
EMP: **2** EST: 2003
SALES (est): 150.76K **Privately Held**
Web: www.mainmusicin.com
SIC: **3931** Musical instruments

(G-11146)
MIDWEST COUNTRY CABINETS
5973 N 1200 E (47553-5603)
P.O. Box 66 (47553-0066)
PHONE..............................812 486-8580
Mark Knepp, *Mgr*
EMP: **5** EST: 2017
SALES (est): 56.92K **Privately Held**
SIC: **2434** Wood kitchen cabinets

(G-11147)
PRECISION LASER
11919 E 250 N (47553-5489)
P.O. Box 144 (47553-0144)
PHONE..............................812 295-2200
Jamie Bell, *Owner*
EMP: **1** EST: 2006
SALES (est): 72.26K **Privately Held**
Web: www.plsmfg.com
SIC: **3599** Machine shop, jobbing and repair

(G-11148)
R & M WELDING & FABRICATING SP (PA)
1192 State Road 550 (47553-4755)
PHONE..............................812 295-9130
Robert Wathen, *Owner*
EMP: **4** EST: 1985
SALES (est): 328.75K **Privately Held**
SIC: **1799** 3411 7692 3444 Welding on site; Metal cans; Welding repair; Sheet metalwork

(G-11149)
REGAL MILLS ODON
2805 N 1200 E (47553-5493)
P.O. Box 95 (47553-0095)
PHONE..............................812 295-2299
Jerome Ginerich, *Prin*
EMP: **6** EST: 2011
SALES (est): 80.75K **Privately Held**
SIC: **2048** Prepared feeds, nec

(G-11150)
RONALD LEE ALLEN
8271 S 1125 E (47553-5335)
PHONE..............................812 644-7649
Ronald Lee Allen, *Prin*
Ronald Lee Allen, *Owner*
EMP: **3** EST: 2010
SALES (est): 175.98K **Privately Held**
SIC: **2411** 7389 Logging; Business Activities at Non-Commercial Site

(G-11151)
ROSE TRUE GRAPHICS
4432 Upper South Point Dr (47553-5523)
PHONE..............................812 844-1559
Rosy Truex, *Owner*
EMP: **1** EST: 2004
SALES (est): 50.98K **Privately Held**
SIC: **2759** Invitations: printing, nsk

(G-11152)
VALESCO MANUFACTURING INC
7857 N 1100 E (47553-5628)
PHONE..............................812 636-6001
Ammon Weaver, *Brnch Mgr*
EMP: **2**
SALES (corp-wide): 658.85K **Privately Held**
Web: www.silo-matic.com
SIC: **3523** Weeding machines, agricultural
PA: Valesco Manufacturing Inc.
9875 N County Road 600 E

GEOGRAPHIC SECTION

Lowell - Lake County (G-11180)

Roachdale IN 46172
765 522-2740

(G-11153)
W & S WOODWORKING LLC
6460 N 1100 E (47553-5591)
PHONE..............................812 486-3673
Willard F Toll, *Owner*
EMP: 6 **EST:** 2007
SALES (est): 420.02K **Privately Held**
SIC: 2499 Decorative wood and woodwork

(G-11154)
WAGLER WOODWORKING
19866 Us Highway 231 (47553-4652)
PHONE..............................812 486-6357
Jason Wagler, *Prin*
EMP: 9 **EST:** 2010
SALES (est): 246.28K **Privately Held**
SIC: 2431 Millwork

Lowell
Lake County

(G-11155)
AVERY DENNISON CORPORATION
270 Westmeadow Pl (46356-1678)
PHONE..............................219 696-7777
Keith Barstow, *Mgr*
EMP: 95
SALES (corp-wide): 8.36B **Publicly Held**
Web: www.averydennison.com
SIC: 2672 3081 3497 2678 Adhesive papers, labels, or tapes: from purchased material; Unsupported plastics film and sheet; Metal foil and leaf; Stationery products
PA: Avery Dennison Corporation
8080 Norton Pkwy
Mentor OH 44060
440 534-6000

(G-11156)
BLUMENAU ALPACAS
19950 Austin St (46356-9691)
PHONE..............................219 713-6171
EMP: 4 **EST:** 2012
SALES (est): 138.59K **Privately Held**
SIC: 2231 Alpacas, mohair: woven

(G-11157)
BUTCHER BLOCK INC
17918 Grant Pl (46356-9511)
PHONE..............................219 696-9111
Robert Reed, *Pr*
Diana Reed, *VP*
EMP: 7 **EST:** 1977
SQ FT: 3,168
SALES (est): 233.34K **Privately Held**
Web: www.butcherblock.com
SIC: 0751 2013 2011 Slaughtering: custom livestock services; Sausages and other prepared meats; Meat packing plants

(G-11158)
CCD NORTHWOODS LLC
12805 W 159th Ave (46356-9489)
PHONE..............................219 690-1868
Sue Smetana, *Prin*
EMP: 5 **EST:** 2016
SALES (est): 41.52K **Privately Held**
SIC: 2499 Wood products, nec

(G-11159)
CUSTOM STITCHER
19504 Clark St (46356-9537)
PHONE..............................219 306-7784
Ron Butchart, *Prin*
EMP: 1 **EST:** 2010

SALES (est): 56.14K **Privately Held**
SIC: 2395 Embroidery and art needlework

(G-11160)
DOCUTECH DOCUMENT SERVICE
1601 Northview Dr (46356-2598)
PHONE..............................219 690-3038
EMP: 4 **EST:** 2017
SALES (est): 122.78K **Privately Held**
SIC: 2759 Publication printing

(G-11161)
GRAPHEX INTERNATIONAL
792 W 181st Ave (46356-9529)
PHONE..............................219 696-4849
Ellen Bowers, *Pr*
EMP: 3 **EST:** 2005
SALES (est): 229.56K **Privately Held**
SIC: 3993 Signs and advertising specialties

(G-11162)
HELPING HANDS
516 Michigan Ave (46356-1845)
P.O. Box 223 (46356-0223)
PHONE..............................219 696-4564
Sandra S Schantz, *Owner*
EMP: 1 **EST:** 2001
SALES (est): 51K **Privately Held**
Web: www.helpinghandsmanchesternh.com
SIC: 2731 Books, publishing and printing

(G-11163)
INDIANA NATURAL INFUSIONS LLC (PA) ✪
287 Westmeadow Pl (46356-1679)
PHONE..............................847 754-9277
Marta Majewski, *Managing Member*
EMP: 1 **EST:** 2023
SALES (est): 75.31K
SALES (corp-wide): 75.31K **Privately Held**
SIC: 2085 Distilled and blended liquors

(G-11164)
JRS CUSTOM CABINETS CO
16855 Mississippi St (46356-9521)
PHONE..............................219 696-7205
EMP: 22 **EST:** 1991
SQ FT: 8,000
SALES (est): 927.77K **Privately Held**
Web: www.jrscustomcabinets.com
SIC: 2434 Wood kitchen cabinets

(G-11165)
JTM HOME & BUILDING
16005 Chestnut St (46356-9326)
PHONE..............................219 690-1445
EMP: 3 **EST:** 1996
SALES (est): 229.64K **Privately Held**
SIC: 1389 Construction, repair, and dismantling services

(G-11166)
KOZS QUALITY PRINTING INC
17934 Grant Pl # A (46356-9511)
PHONE..............................219 696-6711
John Kozlowski, *Pr*
Debbie Kozlowski, *VP*
EMP: 5 **EST:** 1977
SQ FT: 1,000
SALES (est): 411.14K **Privately Held**
Web: www.kqpinc.com
SIC: 2759 2752 Letterpress printing; Offset printing

(G-11167)
LEGACY VULCAN LLC
Also Called: Lowell Quarry
9331 W 205th Ave (46356-9606)
PHONE..............................219 696-5467

Kevin Cox, *Mgr*
EMP: 4
Web: www.vulcanmaterials.com
SIC: 3273 Ready-mixed concrete
HQ: Legacy Vulcan, Llc
1200 Urban Center Dr
Birmingham AL 35242
205 298-3000

(G-11168)
LIFE SPICE AND INGREDIENTS LLC
Also Called: Lifespice Ingredients
260 Westmeadow Pl (46356-1678)
PHONE..............................708 301-0447
EMP: 34
Web: www.lifespiceingredients.com
SIC: 2099 Spices, including grinding
PA: Life Spice And Ingredients Llc
213 W Institute Pl # 601
Chicago IL 60610

(G-11169)
LOWELL CONCRETE PRODUCTS INC
9312 W 181st Ave (46356-9452)
P.O. Box 247 (46356-0247)
PHONE..............................219 696-3339
William Austgen, *Pr*
Linda Savage, *
EMP: 31 **EST:** 1945
SQ FT: 2,000
SALES (est): 2.08MM **Privately Held**
SIC: 3272 Concrete products, precast, nec

(G-11170)
M&C WNDRINK RVERSIDE FARMS INC
24121 Whitcomb St (46356-9730)
PHONE..............................928 897-0061
Cathy Wunderink, *Prin*
EMP: 7 **EST:** 2019
SALES (est): 62.38K **Privately Held**
SIC: 2045 Prepared flour mixes and doughs

(G-11171)
MATTS REPAIR INC
9412 W 181st Ave (46356-9651)
P.O. Box 373 (46356-0373)
PHONE..............................219 696-6765
Roberta Bryant, *Pr*
EMP: 10 **EST:** 1940
SQ FT: 5,000
SALES (est): 1.08MM **Privately Held**
Web: www.mattsrepair.net
SIC: 3599 7692 Machine shop, jobbing and repair; Welding repair

(G-11172)
MIDWEST ACCURATE GRINDING SVC
17211 Morse St (46356-1432)
PHONE..............................219 696-4060
John Conley Senior, *Pr*
Carolyn Conley, *VP*
Cathy Womack, *Sec*
EMP: 10 **EST:** 1969
SQ FT: 8,500
SALES (est): 783.07K **Privately Held**
Web: www.midwestaccurate.com
SIC: 7389 3599 Grinding, precision: commercial or industrial; Machine shop, jobbing and repair

(G-11173)
MIDWEST AEROSPACE LTD
10653 W 181st Ave (46356-9451)
PHONE..............................219 365-7250
Lou Giannini, *Pr*
Joe Giannini, *Sec*
Michael R Lippner, *Prin*

▲ **EMP:** 10 **EST:** 2011
SALES (est): 2.32MM **Privately Held**
Web: www.midwestaeroltd.com
SIC: 3728 Aircraft parts and equipment, nec

(G-11174)
NICHOLS MFG CO INC
1006 W 203rd Ave (46356-9747)
PHONE..............................219 696-8577
James Nichols, *Pr*
William J Nichols, *Pr*
EMP: 10 **EST:** 1937
SQ FT: 13,300
SALES (est): 479.27K **Privately Held**
SIC: 7692 3523 Welding repair; Sprayers and spraying machines, agricultural

(G-11175)
PLUM GROVE STRINGS LLC
Also Called: Plum Grove Music
1107 E 181st Ave (46356-9526)
PHONE..............................219 696-5401
EMP: 1 **EST:** 2010
SALES (est): 245.12K **Privately Held**
Web: www.plumgrovemusic.com
SIC: 3931 8299 Violas and parts; Musical instrument lessons

(G-11176)
PRECISION AGRONOMY
23305 Whitcomb St (46356-7504)
PHONE..............................219 552-0032
Garrett Corning, *Prin*
EMP: 7 **EST:** 2016
SALES (est): 217.32K **Privately Held**
SIC: 3599 Industrial machinery, nec

(G-11177)
PURPLE DOOR PRESS
8833 W 156th Ct (46356-9438)
PHONE..............................219 690-1046
Jean Lahm, *Prin*
EMP: 5 **EST:** 2009
SALES (est): 75.26K **Privately Held**
SIC: 2741 Miscellaneous publishing

(G-11178)
SACO INDUSTRIES INC
17151 Morse St (46356-1433)
P.O. Box 342 (46356-0342)
PHONE..............................219 690-9900
Ronald Bergstrom, *Pr*
Paulette Bergstrom, *
EMP: 370 **EST:** 1952
SQ FT: 200,000
SALES (est): 49.75MM **Privately Held**
Web: www.sacoindustries.com
SIC: 2434 Vanities, bathroom: wood

(G-11179)
V N C INC
Also Called: Better Built Products
585 N Nichols St (46356-1649)
P.O. Box 305 (46356-0305)
PHONE..............................219 696-5031
Vincent Anderson, *Pr*
Cindy Anderson, *Sec*
EMP: 17 **EST:** 1990
SQ FT: 22,000
SALES (est): 813.37K **Privately Held**
SIC: 3353 3089 3444 Aluminum sheet, plate, and foil; Shutters, plastics; Sheet metalwork

(G-11180)
WELL DONE INDUSTRIES LLC
1679 Jonquil Dr (46356-2499)
PHONE..............................219 838-5201
Adam Wells, *Owner*
EMP: 4 **EST:** 2020
SALES (est): 66.01K **Privately Held**

Lynn
Randolph County

SIC: 3999 Manufacturing industries, nec

(G-11181)
ASTRAL CARRIER INC
7375 S Us Highway 27 (47355-9364)
P.O. Box 638 (47355-0638)
PHONE.................................765 874-1406
Charles Shaw, *CEO*
David Hazelett, *Pr*
EMP: 20 **EST:** 2019
SALES (est): 510.94K
SALES (corp-wide): 364.48B **Publicly Held**
Web: www.astralindustries.com
SIC: 3995 Burial caskets
HQ: Astral Industries Inc
7375 S Us Highway 27
Lynn IN 47355
765 874-2525

(G-11182)
ASTRAL INDUSTRIES INC (DH)
7375 S Us Highway 27 (47355-9364)
P.O. Box 638 (47355-0638)
PHONE.................................765 874-2525
EMP: 200 **EST:** 1972
SALES (est): 48.64MM
SALES (corp-wide): 364.48B **Publicly Held**
Web: www.astralindustries.com
SIC: 3995 Burial caskets
HQ: Wilbert Funeral Services, Inc.
10965 Granada Ln Ste 300
Overland Park KS 66211
913 345-2120

(G-11183)
ENVIRONMENTAL MGT & DEV INC
105 West Sherman Street (47355)
P.O. Box 126 (47355-0126)
PHONE.................................765 874-1539
EMP: 3 **EST:** 1999
SALES (est): 248.33K **Privately Held**
SIC: 3589 Water treatment equipment, industrial

(G-11184)
KABERT INDUSTRIES INC
Also Called: KABERT INDUSTRIES INC
514 W Church St (47355-9624)
PHONE.................................765 874-2335
Lucille Gibson, *Mgr*
EMP: 60
SALES (corp-wide): 4.69MM **Privately Held**
Web: www.kabert.com
SIC: 2221 3564 Fiberglass fabrics; Blowers and fans
PA: Kabert Industries, Inc.
321 W Saint Charles Rd
Villa Park IL 60181
630 833-2115

(G-11185)
LYNN TOOL COMPANY INC
107 Elm St (47355)
P.O. Box 366 (47355-0366)
PHONE.................................765 874-2471
Stephen Baker, *Pr*
EMP: 8 **EST:** 1966
SQ FT: 3,000
SALES (est): 987.51K **Privately Held**
SIC: 3599 3469 3443 Custom machinery; Metal stampings, nec; Weldments

(G-11186)
POWERHOUSE ENGINES LLC
10771 S 100 E (47355-9432)
PHONE.................................765 576-1418
EMP: 2 **EST:** 2013
SQ FT: 2,400
SALES (est): 160.31K **Privately Held**
SIC: 3519 Internal combustion engines, nec

(G-11187)
SIFFORD CUSTOM WELDING
246 W 1000 S (47355-9436)
PHONE.................................765 969-3473
Matthew Sifford, *Prin*
EMP: 4 **EST:** 2019
SALES (est): 52.8K **Privately Held**
SIC: 7692 Welding repair

(G-11188)
T F & T INC
Also Called: Hinshaw Tool & Die
603 W Linden St (47355-1000)
P.O. Box 615 (47355-0615)
PHONE.................................765 874-1628
Fred Green, *Pr*
Todd Green, *VP*
EMP: 7 **EST:** 1989
SQ FT: 9,000
SALES (est): 560K **Privately Held**
SIC: 3599 Machine shop, jobbing and repair

Lynnville
Warrick County

(G-11189)
DOUG WILCOX
Also Called: Custom Polishing
1188 W State Route 68 (47619-8273)
PHONE.................................812 476-1957
Doug Wilcox, *Owner*
EMP: 2 **EST:** 1994
SALES (est): 75.8K **Privately Held**
SIC: 3471 Polishing, metals or formed products

(G-11190)
MYSTIQUE WINERY AND VINYRD LLC
13000 Gore Rd (47619-8026)
PHONE.................................812 922-5612
Steven Clutter, *Prin*
EMP: 5 **EST:** 2009
SALES (est): 374.42K **Privately Held**
SIC: 2084 Wines

(G-11191)
PEABODY ENERGY CORPORATION
566 Dickeyville Rd (47619-8257)
PHONE.................................314 342-3400
Chad Wirthwein, *Brnch Mgr*
EMP: 5
SALES (corp-wide): 4.95B **Publicly Held**
Web: www.peabodyenergy.com
SIC: 1241 Coal mining services
PA: Peabody Energy Corporation
701 Market St
Saint Louis MO 63101
314 342-3400

(G-11192)
PEABODY MIDWEST MINING LLC (HQ)
Also Called: Black Beauty Mining Div
566 Dickeyville Rd (47619-8257)
P.O. Box 400 (47542-0400)
PHONE.................................812 297-7661
Steven Chancellor, *Managing Member*
C A Burggraf, *
J F Quinn, *

K L Wagner, *
W L Hawkins Junior, *Treas*
EMP: 50 **EST:** 2006
SALES (est): 484.04MM
SALES (corp-wide): 4.95B **Publicly Held**
SIC: 1221 1222 1241 Bituminous coal surface mining; Bituminous coal-underground mining; Coal mining services
PA: Peabody Energy Corporation
701 Market St
Saint Louis MO 63101
314 342-3400

(G-11193)
WILD BOAR MINE
2277 Tecumseh Rd (47619-8249)
PHONE.................................812 922-1015
Tom Peck, *Mgr*
EMP: 2 **EST:** 2011
SALES (est): 184.66K **Privately Held**
SIC: 1479 Mineral pigment mining

Macy
Miami County

(G-11194)
BERNARD BURNS
Also Called: Burns Tire Service
6093 S Old Us Highway 31 (46951-8584)
PHONE.................................574 382-5019
Bernard Burns, *Owner*
EMP: 2 **EST:** 1968
SALES (est): 231.22K **Privately Held**
SIC: 5014 5531 7534 Automobile tires and tubes; Automotive tires; Tire repair shop

(G-11195)
BURNS CONSTRUCTION INC
Also Called: Burns Buldings
6676 S Old Us Highway 31 (46951-8639)
PHONE.................................574 382-2315
TOLL FREE: 800
Dan Burns, *Pr*
EMP: 28 **EST:** 1969
SQ FT: 1,500
SALES (est): 2.4MM **Privately Held**
Web: www.burnspostbuildings.com
SIC: 1542 3448 2452 Commercial and office building, new construction; Prefabricated metal buildings and components; Prefabricated wood buildings

(G-11196)
TRIJENT LLC
1774 W 1000 N (46951-7807)
PHONE.................................502 544-4250
Jordan Laycock, *Prin*
EMP: 5 **EST:** 2016
SALES (est): 65.47K **Privately Held**
Web: www.trijent.com
SIC: 3489 Guns, howitzers, mortars, and related equipment

Madison
Jefferson County

(G-11197)
AJ EXPRESS BROKER SERVICE
73 N Rogers Rd (47250-7781)
PHONE.................................812 866-1380
Andrew Le Grand, *Prin*
EMP: 2 **EST:** 2006
SALES (est): 143.34K **Privately Held**
SIC: 2741 Miscellaneous publishing

(G-11198)
ALAN W LONG
Also Called: Gifts That Last
120 E Main St (47250-3411)
PHONE.................................812 265-6717
Alan Long, *Owner*
EMP: 2 **EST:** 1986
SQ FT: 2,600
SALES (est): 146.87K **Privately Held**
Web: www.giftsthatlastmadison.com
SIC: 5944 3911 5947 Jewelry, precious stones and precious metals; Jewelry apparel; Gift shop

(G-11199)
ALL GOOD THINGS LLC
5997 E Risks Ridge Rd (47250-8206)
PHONE.................................812 871-2844
Sonia Folkner, *Prin*
EMP: 2 **EST:** 2006
SALES (est): 204.01K **Privately Held**
Web: www.fountainalleybc.com
SIC: 2844 Perfumes, cosmetics and other toilet preparations

(G-11200)
ALL GOOD THINGS SOAPS AND
318 W Main St (47250-3716)
PHONE.................................812 801-4700
EMP: 5 **EST:** 2014
SALES (est): 150.84K **Privately Held**
Web: www.allgoodthingshandmade.com
SIC: 2844 Perfumes, cosmetics and other toilet preparations

(G-11201)
ALLIED TUBE & CONDUIT CORP
Also Called: Century Tube
4004 N Us 421 (47250-9800)
P.O. Box 1219 (47250-1219)
PHONE.................................812 265-9255
Mark A Acosta, *Brnch Mgr*
EMP: 12
Web: www.atkore.com
SIC: 3317 3714 3498 Welded pipe and tubes ; Motor vehicle parts and accessories; Fabricated pipe and fittings
HQ: Allied Tube & Conduit Corporation
16100 S Center Ave
Harvey IL 60426
708 339-1610

(G-11202)
ARMOR PRODUCTS INC
Also Called: Armor Metal Group Madison Inc
4600 N Mason Montgomery Rd (47250)
PHONE.................................502 228-1458
David Schmitt, *Pr*
Dennis Barbeau, *
EMP: 209 **EST:** 1999
SQ FT: 160,000
SALES (est): 44.88MM **Privately Held**
Web: www.thearmorgroup.com
SIC: 3443 3441 3444 3412 Containers, shipping (bombs, etc.); metal plate; Fabricated structural metal; Sheet metalwork; Metal barrels, drums, and pails
PA: The Armor Group, Inc.
4600 N Masn Montgomery Rd
Mason OH 45040

(G-11203)
ARVIN SANGO INC (HQ)
Also Called: A S I
2905 Wilson Ave (47250)
PHONE.................................812 265-2888
Masayuki Hirako, *Pr*
Scott Hubbard, *VP*
Kevin Orrill, *VP*
Greg Edwards, *VP*
◆ **EMP:** 600 **EST:** 1986

Madison - Jefferson County (G-11229)

SQ FT: 323,000
SALES (est): 192.94MM **Privately Held**
Web: www.arvinsango.com
SIC: 3714 Exhaust systems and parts, motor vehicle
PA: Sango Co.,Ltd.
　1-3-1, Mutsuno, Atsuta-Ku
　Nagoya AIC 456-0

(G-11204)
BAGBARN CO
975 Industrial Dr Ste 11 (47250-3900)
PHONE: 847 850-2592
Nathan Stormer, *Pr*
EMP: 10 **EST:** 2003
SALES (est): 978.16K **Privately Held**
SIC: 2673 Plastic bags: made from purchased materials

(G-11205)
CARL HUGNESS PUBLISHING
318 Mulberry St (47250-3498)
P.O. Box 225 (47250-0225)
PHONE: 812 273-2472
Carl Hungness, *Prin*
EMP: 5 **EST:** 2013
SALES (est): 125.47K **Privately Held**
SIC: 2741 Miscellaneous publishing

(G-11206)
CENTURY TUBE LLC
4004 N Us 421 (47250-9800)
PHONE: 812 265-9255
EMP: 125
SIC: 3317 Steel pipe and tubes

(G-11207)
CHARLES STEWART
Also Called: Madison Iron and Wood
3519 N Shun Pike Rd (47250-7859)
PHONE: 812 801-9694
Charles Stewart, *Owner*
EMP: 7 **EST:** 2017
SALES (est): 455.35K **Privately Held**
Web: www.madisonironandwood.com
SIC: 3431 Metal sanitary ware

(G-11208)
CHRISTMAN LOGGING
7641 N Bacon Ridge Rd (47250-9367)
PHONE: 502 525-2649
Tara Richmond, *Prin*
EMP: 8 **EST:** 2016
SALES (est): 207.09K **Privately Held**
SIC: 2411 Logging

(G-11209)
CHURCHILL CIGARS
605 W 2nd St (47250-3747)
PHONE: 812 273-2249
Edward Roszczynski, *Prin*
EMP: 2 **EST:** 2006
SALES (est): 61.41K **Privately Held**
Web: www.setmed.net
SIC: 3999 Cigarette and cigar products and accessories

(G-11210)
CLIFTY ENGINEERING AND TOOL CO
2949 Clifty Dr (47250-1680)
PHONE: 812 273-3272
Robert D Hughes, *CEO*
Raymond H Combs, *
Arnold W Curry, *
James F Scott, *
Cecil Dunn, *
EMP: 105 **EST:** 1961
SQ FT: 57,000
SALES (est): 9.55MM **Privately Held**
Web: www.cliftyengineering.com
SIC: 3599 Special dies and tools; Electrical discharge machining (EDM)

(G-11211)
COLLINS TL & DIE LTD LBLTY CO
2902 Wilson Ave (47250-1831)
PHONE: 812 273-4765
Ronnie Collins, *Pr*
Diann Collins, *Sec*
EMP: 9 **EST:** 1984
SQ FT: 6,000
SALES (est): 861.92K **Privately Held**
SIC: 3544 7692 Special dies and tools; Welding repair

(G-11212)
CRESTWOOD EQUITY PARTNERS LP
Also Called: Blue Flame
3625 Clifty Dr (47250-1649)
PHONE: 812 265-3313
Ted Klopfenstein, *Mgr*
EMP: 5
Web: www.crestwoodlp.com
SIC: 5984 3589 Propane gas, bottled; Water treatment equipment, industrial
HQ: Crestwood Equity Partners Lp
　811 Main St Ste 3400
　Houston TX 77002
　832 519-2200

(G-11213)
DIE-MENSIONAL METAL STAMPG INC
Also Called: Die-Mensional Metal Stampings
1404 W Niblo Rd Jpg (47250)
P.O. Box 756 (47250-0756)
PHONE: 812 265-3946
Fred Swinney, *Pr*
Dianna Swinney, *Sec*
EMP: 10 **EST:** 1991
SQ FT: 12,000
SALES (est): 890.82K **Privately Held**
Web: www.diemensional.com
SIC: 3469 3441 3542 3444 Stamping metal for the trade; Fabricated structural metal; Machine tools, metal forming type; Sheet metalwork

(G-11214)
DIGITAL PRINTING INCORPORATED
Also Called: Dpi
7122 W Interstate Block Rd (47250-8063)
PHONE: 812 265-2205
George Jackson, *Pr*
Julie Hoskins, *Sec*
Orme Wilson, *Prin*
EMP: 5 **EST:** 1994
SALES (est): 403.19K **Privately Held**
Web: www.dpimad.com
SIC: 2752 2791 2789 Offset printing; Typesetting; Bookbinding and related work

(G-11215)
DOE RUN TOOLING INC
8550 E Doe Run Rd (47250-8541)
PHONE: 812 265-3057
Jerry Hunter, *Pr*
Laura Hunter, *VP*
EMP: 2 **EST:** 1979
SALES (est): 137.76K **Privately Held**
SIC: 3544 Special dies and tools

(G-11216)
EAST INDUSTRIES LLC
831 W Main St (47250-3131)
P.O. Box 162 (47250-0162)
PHONE: 812 273-4358
Joshua Nichter, *Prin*
EMP: 6 **EST:** 2008
SALES (est): 154.95K **Privately Held**
Web: www.east-industries.com
SIC: 3999 Barber and beauty shop equipment

(G-11217)
EMBROIDERED PLANET
314 E 1st St (47250-3508)
PHONE: 812 599-7951
Kathryn Sauer, *Prin*
EMP: 5 **EST:** 2010
SALES (est): 58.62K **Privately Held**
SIC: 2395 Embroidery and art needlework

(G-11218)
EMBROIDERY UNLIMITED
220 E Main St (47250-3496)
PHONE: 812 265-4575
William Adams, *Owner*
EMP: 1 **EST:** 2010
SALES (est): 48.74K **Privately Held**
SIC: 2395 Embroidery products, except Schiffli machine

(G-11219)
EXTREME PRECISION PRODUCTS LLC
Also Called: 1st Choice Machining & Tooling
11388 N West Fork Rd (47250-7326)
PHONE: 812 839-0101
EMP: 2 **EST:** 2007
SALES (est): 268.49K **Privately Held**
SIC: 3599 Machine shop, jobbing and repair

(G-11220)
FORCE CNC LLC
940 Lanier Dr (47250-2014)
PHONE: 812 273-0218
Greg Goldsmith, *Pr*
Allen Wingham, *Genl Pt*
EMP: 6 **EST:** 2002
SQ FT: 8,000
SALES (est): 618.14K **Privately Held**
Web: www.forcecnc.com
SIC: 3599 Machine shop, jobbing and repair

(G-11221)
FORWARD LIFT / A DOVER COMPANY
996 Industrial Dr (47250-3901)
PHONE: 812 273-7325
Charles Thurman, *Pt*
EMP: 1 **EST:** 2008
SALES (est): 81K **Privately Held**
Web: www.forwardlift.com
SIC: 3495 Precision springs

(G-11222)
GROTE INDUSTRIES INC (PA)
2600 Lanier Dr (47250)
PHONE: 812 273-2121
William D Grote Iii, *Ch Bd*
William Dominic Grote Iv, *Pr*
John R Grote, *
Michael R Grote, *
Brian Blanton, *
◆ **EMP:** 822 **EST:** 1901
SQ FT: 435,000
SALES (est): 289.4MM
SALES (corp-wide): 289.4MM **Privately Held**
Web: www.grote.com
SIC: 3231 3647 Mirrors, truck and automobile: made from purchased glass; Vehicular lighting equipment

(G-11223)
GROTE INDUSTRIES LLC
2600 Lanier Dr (47250-1797)
PHONE: 812 265-8273
William Grote Iv, *Pr*
James Braun, *
John Grote, *
EMP: 1200 **EST:** 1996
SQ FT: 435,000
SALES (est): 48.93MM **Privately Held**
Web: www.grote.com
SIC: 3647 3231 Vehicular lighting equipment; Mirrors, truck and automobile: made from purchased glass

(G-11224)
HI DEF MACHINING LLC
3508 N Sr 7 (47250-7961)
PHONE: 812 493-9943
EMP: 6 **EST:** 2016
SALES (est): 554.53K **Privately Held**
SIC: 3549 Wiredrawing and fabricating machinery and equipment, ex. die

(G-11225)
HILLTOP WOOD WORKING
4406 W County Road 1050 S (47250)
PHONE: 270 604-1962
Caesar Stoltzfus, *Owner*
EMP: 6 **EST:** 2008
SALES (est): 342.35K **Privately Held**
SIC: 2499 Applicators, wood

(G-11226)
HK PETROLEUM LTD
606 E Main St (47250-4708)
P.O. Box 224 (47250-0224)
PHONE: 229 366-1313
Rick Kay, *Pt*
EMP: 5 **EST:** 2012
SQ FT: 1,800
SALES (est): 326.52K **Privately Held**
Web: www.hkpetroleum.com
SIC: 2911 Fractionation products of crude petroleum, hydrocarbons, nec

(G-11227)
HOUSE OF SOCCER INC
Also Called: HOUSE OF SOCCER, INC.
404 E Main St (47250-3539)
PHONE: 812 265-5196
Ed Huntsinger, *Pr*
EMP: 2
Web: www.houseofsoccer.com
SIC: 3949 Soccer equipment and supplies
PA: House Of Soccer, Inc.
　6611 W Highway 22
　Crestwood KY 40014

(G-11228)
HYPERBOLE SOFTWARE LLC
Also Called: Hyperbole Creations
9383 E Tate Ridge Rd (47250-8754)
P.O. Box 104 (47250-0104)
PHONE: 812 839-6635
Carl W Reynolds, *Owner*
EMP: 8 **EST:** 1983
SALES (est): 365.06K **Privately Held**
Web: www.thefiberartist.com
SIC: 7372 Business oriented computer software

(G-11229)
IMI SOUTH LLC
3650 N Sr 7 (47250)
PHONE: 812 273-1428
Edward Campbol, *Brnch Mgr*
EMP: 4
SALES (corp-wide): 814.09MM **Privately Held**
Web: www.irvmat.com
SIC: 3273 Ready-mixed concrete
HQ: Imi South, Llc
　1440 Selinda Ave
　Louisville KY 40213
　502 456-6930

Madison - Jefferson County (G-11230)   GEOGRAPHIC SECTION

(G-11230)
INTERSTATE BLOCK CORPORATION
3148 Clifty Dr (47250-1645)
P.O. Box 566 (47202-0566)
PHONE..................................812 273-1742
Harry E Horn, Pr
EMP: 7 EST: 2013
SALES (est): 62.77K Privately Held
Web: www.interstateblock.com
SIC: 3273 Ready-mixed concrete

(G-11231)
J & J BOAT WORKS INC
502 Miles Ridge Rd (47250-2420)
PHONE..................................812 667-5902
Joe Breek, Pr
EMP: 1 EST: 1997
SALES (est): 248.52K Privately Held
SIC: 3732 3441 Boatbuilding and repairing; Boat and barge sections, prefabricated metal

(G-11232)
JPG MACHINE & TOOL LLC
1263 W Jpg Woodfill Rd Ste 212 (47250-9731)
PHONE..................................812 265-4512
EMP: 6 EST: 2010
SALES (est): 477.11K Privately Held
Web: jpg-machine-tool-llc.business.site
SIC: 3544 Special dies and tools

(G-11233)
KOEHLER WELDING SUPPLY INC
2352 Michigan Rd (47250-2443)
PHONE..................................812 574-4103
David J Ungru, Pr
Suzanna Ungru, VP
◆ EMP: 14 EST: 2006
SQ FT: 8,300
SALES (est): 5.84MM Privately Held
Web: www.koehlerweld.com
SIC: 5085 3535 5999 5172 Welding supplies; Conveyors and conveying equipment; Alarm and safety equipment stores; Petroleum products, nec

(G-11234)
LANTHIER WINERY LLC
2612 Franks Dr (47250-2417)
PHONE..................................502 663-2399
EMP: 6 EST: 2019
SALES (est): 162.98K Privately Held
Web: www.lanthierwinery.com
SIC: 2084 Wines

(G-11235)
LANTHIER WINERY & RESTAURANT
123 Mill St (47250-3132)
PHONE..................................812 273-2409
EMP: 8 EST: 1997
SALES (est): 85.01K Privately Held
Web: www.lanthierwinery.com
SIC: 2084 5812 5947 Wines; Eating places; Gift, novelty, and souvenir shop

(G-11236)
LIBERTY SCREEN PRINTING
831 W Main St (47250-3131)
P.O. Box 162 (47250-0162)
PHONE..................................812 273-4358
EMP: 4 EST: 2007
SALES (est): 88.67K Privately Held
Web: www.libertyscreenprint.com
SIC: 2759 Screen printing

(G-11237)
MADISON COURIER
Also Called: Weekly Herald, The
310 Courier Sq (47250-9919)
PHONE..................................812 265-3641
Jane Wallis Jacobs, Pr
Curtis Jacobs Junior, Sec
Don Wallis Junior, VP
Jane Wallis Jacobs Prestreas, Prin
EMP: 36 EST: 1837
SQ FT: 4,480
SALES (est): 860.16K Privately Held
Web: www.madisoncourier.com
SIC: 2711 2752 Newspapers: publishing only, not printed on site; Commercial printing, lithographic

(G-11238)
MADISON PRECISION PRODUCTS INC
94 E 400 N (47250-9599)
PHONE..................................812 273-4702
Michihiko Kato, CEO
Kazuyoshi Matsushita, *
Randy Boyd, *
Ken Degler, *
David A Sutherland, *
▲ EMP: 500 EST: 1987
SQ FT: 176,500
SALES (est): 95.55MM Privately Held
Web: www.madisonprecision.com
SIC: 3363 3365 Aluminum die-castings; Aluminum foundries
HQ: Metts Corporation
    1620, Matoba
    Kawagoe STM 350-1

(G-11239)
MADISON TOOL AND DIE INC
3000 Michigan Rd (47250-1801)
PHONE..................................812 273-2250
Terry Sparks, Pr
Gary Sparks, *
▲ EMP: 75 EST: 1966
SQ FT: 75,000
SALES (est): 7.13MM Privately Held
Web: www.madisontoolinc.com
SIC: 3544 3451 Special dies and tools; Screw machine products

(G-11240)
MAYORS OFFICE CITY OF MADISON
Also Called: Madison Railroad
950 Industrial Dr (47250-3903)
PHONE..................................812 273-4248
EMP: 6
Web: www.madison-in.gov
SIC: 3312 Railroad crossings, steel or iron
PA: Mayors Office City Of Madison
    101 W Main St
    Madison IN 47250
    812 265-8300

(G-11241)
MEESE INC (HQ)
Also Called: Modroto
1745 Cragmont St (47250-2807)
PHONE..................................800 829-4535
John Ryan, Pr
John H Hurst, CFO
▼ EMP: 10 EST: 1931
SQ FT: 35,000
SALES (est): 8.56MM Privately Held
Web: www.meese-inc.com
SIC: 3089 2394 3443 Plastics containers, except foam; Canvas and related products; Containers, shipping (bombs, etc.): metal plate
PA: Tank Holding Corp.
    6400 N 60th St
    Lincoln NE 68507

(G-11242)
MIDWEST GYM SUPPLY INC (PA)
775 Scott Ct (47250-1829)
PHONE..................................812 265-4099
Paul Kemp, Pr
▼ EMP: 14 EST: 1983
SQ FT: 32,000
SALES (est): 1.9MM Privately Held
Web: www.midwestgymsupply.com
SIC: 3949 5091 Gymnasium equipment; Athletic goods

(G-11243)
MIDWEST TUBE MILLS INC (PA)
2906 Clifty Dr (47250-1641)
P.O. Box 830 (47250-0830)
PHONE..................................812 265-1553
Richard L Russell, Pr
EMP: 85 EST: 1993
SQ FT: 10,000
SALES (est): 21.55MM Privately Held
Web: www.midwesttubemills.com
SIC: 3312 Tubes, steel and iron

(G-11244)
MILLENNIUM TOOL INC
619 Thomas Hill Rd (47250-2537)
PHONE..................................812 701-5761
Cheryl Lyon, Pr
EMP: 35 EST: 1999
SQ FT: 17,000
SALES (est): 3.5MM Privately Held
Web: www.millenniumtoolinc.com
SIC: 3544 Special dies and tools

(G-11245)
MPS PRINTING INCORPORATED
339 Clifty Dr (47250-1605)
PHONE..................................812 273-4446
Jeff Daghir, Pr
Sharon Daghir, Treas
EMP: 4 EST: 1988
SQ FT: 3,000
SALES (est): 469.51K Privately Held
Web: www.mpsprinting.com
SIC: 2752 7334 2759 Offset printing; Photocopying and duplicating services; Commercial printing, nec

(G-11246)
NUCOR TUBULAR PRODUCTS
4004 N Us 421 (47250-9800)
PHONE..................................812 265-7548
EMP: 30 EST: 2018
SALES (est): 13.74MM
SALES (corp-wide): 34.71B Publicly Held
Web: www.nucortubular.com
SIC: 3317 Steel pipe and tubes
PA: Nucor Corporation
    1915 Rexford Rd
    Charlotte NC 28211
    704 366-7000

(G-11247)
RESOURCEMFG
220 Clifty Dr Ste P (47250-1669)
PHONE..................................812 574-5500
EMP: 8 EST: 2017
SALES (est): 117.87K Privately Held
Web: www.resourcemfg.com
SIC: 3999 Manufacturing industries, nec

(G-11248)
RKO ENTERPRISES LLC
2850 Clifty Dr (47250-1699)
PHONE..................................812 273-8813
◆ EMP: 8 EST: 2000
SQ FT: 16,000
SALES (est): 954.6K Privately Held
Web: www.rkoenterprises.com
SIC: 3499 Fire- or burglary-resistive products

(G-11249)
ROYER CORPORATION
805 East St (47250)
PHONE..................................800 457-8997
Roger Williams, Pr
Pat Berry, *
▲ EMP: 65 EST: 1976
SQ FT: 62,000
SALES (est): 9.67MM Privately Held
Web: www.royercorp.com
SIC: 3089 Novelties, plastics

(G-11250)
S L THOMAS FAMILY WINERY INC
208 E 2nd St (47250-3420)
PHONE..................................812 273-3755
EMP: 2 EST: 1995
SALES (est): 229.4K Privately Held
Web: www.thomasfamilywinery.us
SIC: 2084 Wines

(G-11251)
SAUERS RACING AUTO MACHINES
1532 E Telegraph Hill Rd (47250-8792)
PHONE..................................812 265-2803
Cris Sauers, Owner
EMP: 2 EST: 1981
SQ FT: 2,200
SALES (est): 84.85K Privately Held
SIC: 7538 3599 Engine rebuilding: automotive; Machine shop, jobbing and repair

(G-11252)
STAR QUALITY AWARDS INC
322 Crestwood Dr (47250-2353)
P.O. Box 1077 (47250-1077)
PHONE..................................812 273-1740
TOLL FREE: 888
Pamela Moon, Pr
EMP: 2 EST: 1996
SALES (est): 242.59K Privately Held
Web: pizzaoasis.home.mindspring.com
SIC: 7389 2396 5199 3479 Engraving service; Screen printing on fabric articles; Advertising specialties; Etching and engraving

(G-11253)
TAUNYAS CREATIVE CUTS
220 Clifty Dr (47250-1696)
PHONE..................................812 574-7722
EMP: 2 EST: 2008
SALES (est): 82.88K Privately Held
SIC: 3999 Barber and beauty shop equipment

(G-11254)
TRIUMPHANT JRNEY MBL NTARY SVC
Also Called: Tj Mobile Service
923 W Main St (47250)
PHONE..................................608 208-5604
Loren Washington, CEO
EMP: 5 EST: 2018
SALES (est): 214.47K Privately Held
SIC: 7389 8111 2759 8741 Notary publics; Real estate law; Financial note and certificate printing and engraving; Financial management for business

(G-11255)
VEHICLE SERVICE GROUP LLC
Also Called: Chief Automotive Technologies
996 Industrial Dr (47250-3901)
PHONE..................................800 445-9262
EMP: 21
SALES (corp-wide): 8.44B Publicly Held

GEOGRAPHIC SECTION

Marion - Grant County (G-11279)

Web: www.chieftechnology.com
SIC: 3714 Motor vehicle parts and accessories
HQ: Vehicle Service Group, Llc
2700 Lanier Dr
Madison IN 47250

(G-11256)
VEHICLE SERVICE GROUP LLC (HQ)
Also Called: Chief Automotive Technologies
2700 Lanier Dr (47250-1753)
PHONE..................................800 640-5438
Niclas Ytterdahl, *Managing Member*
James Wysinski, *Managing Member*
◆ **EMP:** 125 **EST:** 2007
SALES (est): 344.87MM
SALES (corp-wide): 8.44B **Publicly Held**
Web: www.rotarylift.com
SIC: 3711 Chassis, motor vehicle
PA: Dover Corporation
3005 Highland Pkwy
Downers Grove IL 60515
630 541-1540

(G-11257)
VEHICLE SERVICE GROUP LLC
Rotary Lift
2700 Lanier Dr (47250-1753)
P.O. Box 1560 (47250-0560)
PHONE..................................812 273-1622
Lawrence Chase, *Brnch Mgr*
EMP: 127
SALES (corp-wide): 8.44B **Publicly Held**
Web: www.rotarylift.com
SIC: 3711 Chassis, motor vehicle
HQ: Vehicle Service Group, Llc
2700 Lanier Dr
Madison IN 47250

Magnet
Perry County

(G-11258)
ANTHONY D ETIENNE LOGGING
Also Called: Doyle Logging Etienne
15502 N State Road 66 (47520-5069)
PHONE..................................812 843-5872
Anthony D Etienne, *Owner*
EMP: 7 **EST:** 1977
SALES (est): 463.64K **Privately Held**
SIC: 2411 Logging camps and contractors

Manilla
Rush County

(G-11259)
A SHUTTER IN TIME LLC
9780 W 450 S (46150-9565)
PHONE..................................317 512-6753
Dawna Branson, *Admn*
EMP: 5 **EST:** 2014
SALES (est): 202.49K **Privately Held**
Web: www.ashutterintimellc.com
SIC: 3442 Shutters, door or window: metal

(G-11260)
E & L CONSTRUCTION INC
Also Called: Log Home Construction Indiana
1375 N 800 E (46150-9609)
PHONE..................................765 525-7081
Paul Weaver Junior, *Pr*
Pansy Weaver, *VP*
EMP: 3 **EST:** 1983
SALES (est): 411.76K **Privately Held**
SIC: 1521 2452 New construction, single-family houses; Log cabins, prefabricated, wood

Marengo
Crawford County

(G-11261)
BENZ CUSTOM METAL LLC
4640 E Valeene Rd (47140-8902)
PHONE..................................812 365-2613
Kirk Benz, *Managing Member*
EMP: 1 **EST:** 2014
SALES (est): 109.71K **Privately Held**
SIC: 2514 3499 5023 Metal household furniture; Fabricated metal products, nec; Decorative home furnishings and supplies

(G-11262)
EASTERN RED CEDAR PRODUCTS LLC (PA)
9611 S County Road 425 E (47140-7305)
PHONE..................................812 365-2495
EMP: 4 **EST:** 1984
SALES (est): 907.38K **Privately Held**
Web: www.cedarusa.com
SIC: 2421 Sawmills and planing mills, general

(G-11263)
GABHART LOGGING LLC
4532 E Goodman Ridge Rd (47140-8501)
PHONE..................................812 365-2425
EMP: 4 **EST:** 2019
SALES (est): 89.89K **Privately Held**
SIC: 2411 Logging

(G-11264)
MARENGO CANDY BARN INC
376 S Bradley St (47140-3173)
PHONE..................................812 365-2141
William Burch, *Pr*
EMP: 5 **EST:** 2016
SALES (est): 53.49K **Privately Held**
SIC: 2064 Candy and other confectionery products

(G-11265)
SIL PUBLISHING CO LLC
Also Called: Sil Magazine
2176 Ne Trestle Lane (47140-8911)
P.O. Box 145 (47140-0145)
PHONE..................................812 989-8871
EMP: 6 **EST:** 2013
SALES (est): 63.34K **Privately Held**
Web: www.silivingmag.com
SIC: 2621 Catalog, magazine, and newsprint papers

(G-11266)
VANMETER AND SON LURES LLC
5341 E County Road 875 S (47140-7245)
PHONE..................................812 653-0497
Jason Vanmeter, *Prin*
EMP: 4 **EST:** 2018
SALES (est): 99.79K **Privately Held**
SIC: 3949 Lures, fishing: artificial

(G-11267)
WALTON LOGGING
991 S State Road 66 (47140-8419)
PHONE..................................812 365-9635
EMP: 5 **EST:** 2008
SALES (est): 73.37K **Privately Held**
SIC: 2411 Logging

Marion
Grant County

(G-11268)
ADVANCED CABINET SYSTEMS INC
1629 S Joaquin Dr (46953-9635)
P.O. Box 167 (46952-0167)
PHONE..................................765 677-8000
EMP: 65 **EST:** 2011
SQ FT: 70,000
SALES (est): 4.4MM **Privately Held**
Web: www.advancedcabinetsystems.com
SIC: 2434 Wood kitchen cabinets

(G-11269)
AGRICOR INC
Also Called: Grain Millers
1626 S Joaquin Dr (46953-9633)
P.O. Box 807 (46952-0807)
PHONE..................................765 662-0606
Steve Wickes, *Pr*
▼ **EMP:** 52 **EST:** 1983
SQ FT: 3,200
SALES (est): 12.06MM
SALES (corp-wide): 105.99MM **Privately Held**
Web: www.agricor.org
SIC: 2041 Oat flour
PA: Grain Millers, Inc.
10400 Viking Dr Ste 301
Eden Prairie MN 55344
952 829-8821

(G-11270)
ARDAGH GLASS INC
Also Called: Ardagh Is Services
123 E Mckinley St (46952-2271)
PHONE..................................765 662-1172
Gordon Love, *VP*
EMP: 1
SALES (corp-wide): 2.67MM **Privately Held**
Web: www.ardaghgroup.com
SIC: 3221 Bottles for packing, bottling, and canning: glass
HQ: Ardagh Glass Inc
10194 Crsspint Blvd Ste 4
Indianapolis IN 46256

(G-11271)
ASTECH SEATS
314 S Washington St (46952-4003)
PHONE..................................765 674-7448
EMP: 1 **EST:** 2011
SALES (est): 72.9K **Privately Held**
Web: www.astechseat.com
SIC: 3751 Saddles and seat posts, motorcycle and bicycle

(G-11272)
ATLAS FOUNDRY COMPANY INC
601 N Henderson Ave (46952-3348)
PHONE..................................765 662-2525
William Gartland, *Pr*
James M Gartland Junior, *Ch*
William F Gartland, *
Joseph C Gartland, *
EMP: 125 **EST:** 1900
SALES (est): 100.75K **Privately Held**
Web: www.atlasfdry.com
SIC: 3321 Gray iron castings, nec

(G-11273)
AVIONIC STRUCTURES INDIANA INC
4589 N Wabash Rd (46952-9738)
P.O. Box 1246 (46952-7646)
PHONE..................................765 671-7865
Charles E Herriman, *Prin*
EMP: 16 **EST:** 2010
SALES (est): 468.06K **Privately Held**
SIC: 3714 Motor vehicle parts and accessories

(G-11274)
BAHR BROS MFG INC
Also Called: Bahr Brothers Manufacturing
2545 S Lincoln Blvd (46953-3802)
P.O. Box 411 (46952-0411)
PHONE..................................765 664-6235
Jefferey P Jackson, *Ch Bd*
Jeffrey P Jackson, *
Timothy Street, *
Scott Bratcher, *
EMP: 48 **EST:** 1909
SQ FT: 45,000
SALES (est): 9.81MM **Privately Held**
Web: www.bahrbros.com
SIC: 3325 3554 3321 3312 Steel foundries, nec; Paper industries machinery; Gray iron castings, nec; Stainless steel

(G-11275)
CAMPUS INC
1500 S Western Ave (46953-1542)
PHONE..................................765 674-9530
Darren Campbell, *CEO*
EMP: 8 **EST:** 2019
SALES (est): 50K **Privately Held**
Web: www.campusedu.com
SIC: 7372 Educational computer software

(G-11276)
CANINES CHOICE INC
Also Called: Doglicious
1019 E 26th St (46953)
PHONE..................................765 662-2633
Robert Kramer, *Pr*
Barb Kinzie, *VP*
▲ **EMP:** 7 **EST:** 1982
SQ FT: 23,000
SALES (est): 946K **Privately Held**
Web: www.canineschoice.com
SIC: 2047 Dog food

(G-11277)
CENTRAL INDIANA ETHANOL LLC (PA)
Also Called: Cie
2955 W Delphi Pike (46952)
PHONE..................................765 384-4001
Ryan Drook, *Pr*
Steve Berry, *
EMP: 22 **EST:** 2004
SALES (est): 65.49MM
SALES (corp-wide): 65.49MM **Privately Held**
Web: www.cie.us
SIC: 2819 Nuclear fuel and cores, inorganic

(G-11278)
COMPUTER AGE ENGINEERING INC
Also Called: C A E
867 E 38th St (46953-4402)
P.O. Box 3268 (46953-0268)
PHONE..................................765 674-8551
Michael Bartrom, *Pr*
Sherri A Bartrom, *
EMP: 30 **EST:** 1982
SQ FT: 12,500
SALES (est): 4.49MM **Privately Held**
Web: www.caeweb.com
SIC: 8711 3559 Electrical or electronic engineering; Automotive related machinery

(G-11279)
D E KEY MACHINE SHOP
1442 E 450 N (46952-9020)
PHONE..................................765 664-1720
EMP: 6 **EST:** 2008

Marion - Grant County (G-11280)

SALES (est): 60.93K **Privately Held**
SIC: 3599 Machine shop, jobbing and repair

(G-11280)
DANA DRIVESHAFT PRODUCTS LLC
400 S Miller Ave (46953-1137)
PHONE.....................260 432-2903
Sam Simons, *Brnch Mgr*
EMP: 2
Web: www.dana.com
SIC: 3713 3714 Truck and bus bodies; Motor vehicle parts and accessories
HQ: Dana Driveshaft Products, Llc
3939 Technology Dr
Maumee OH 43537

(G-11281)
DOUBLE H MANUFACTURING CORP
Also Called: Double H Plastics
2548 W 26th St (46953-9414)
PHONE.....................215 674-4100
Joseph Harp, *Pr*
▲ EMP: 70
Web: www.doubleplastics.com
SIC: 3544 Special dies and tools
PA: Double H Manufacturing Corporation
50 W Street Rd
Warminster PA 18974

(G-11282)
DOUBLE H PLASTICS INC
2548 W 26th St (46953-9414)
PHONE.....................765 664-9090
EMP: 10 EST: 2019
SALES (est): 556.11K **Privately Held**
Web: www.doubleplastics.com
SIC: 2821 Plastics materials and resins

(G-11283)
DREAM BEAUTY LAB ◆
1023 S Maple St (46953)
PHONE.....................773 571-1817
Dominique Jones, *CEO*
EMP: 1 EST: 2024
SALES (est): 59.55K **Privately Held**
SIC: 2389 5961 5122 Apparel and accessories, nec; General merchandise, mail order; Cosmetics, perfumes, and hair products

(G-11284)
E & B PAVING INC
3888 S Garthwaite Rd (46953-5621)
PHONE.....................765 674-5848
Dave Coverdale, *Mgr*
EMP: 39
SALES (corp-wide): 814.09MM **Privately Held**
Web: www.irvmat.com
SIC: 1611 2951 1771 Highway and street paving contractor; Asphalt paving mixtures and blocks; Concrete work
HQ: E & B Paving, Inc.
286 W 300 N
Anderson IN 46012
765 643-5358

(G-11285)
EXPERT ELECTRICAL SERVICES LLC
2916 E Bocock Rd (46952-8665)
PHONE.....................765 664-6642
Chad Dixon, *Prin*
EMP: 8 EST: 2010
SALES (est): 229.51K **Privately Held**
Web: www.expertelectricity.net
SIC: 7623 3699 1731 1711 Refrigeration service and repair; Electrical equipment and supplies, nec; Electrical work; Warm air heating and air conditioning contractor

(G-11286)
FLOWERS BAKING CO OHIO LLC
1006 E 22nd St (46953)
PHONE.....................502 350-4700
Jamie Wilson, *Mgr*
EMP: 1
SALES (corp-wide): 5.09B **Publicly Held**
SIC: 2051 Bread, all types (white, wheat, rye, etc); fresh or frozen
HQ: Flowers Baking Co. Of Ohio, Llc
325 W Alexis Rd Ste 1
Toledo OH 43612
419 269-9202

(G-11287)
GENERAL MOTORS LLC
General Motors
2400 W 2nd St (46952-3249)
PHONE.....................765 668-2000
Joel Piatt, *Mgr*
EMP: 277
Web: www.gm.com
SIC: 5511 3711 3544 3469 Automobiles, new and used; Motor vehicles and car bodies; Special dies, tools, jigs, and fixtures; Metal stampings, nec
HQ: General Motors Llc
300 Rnaissance Ctr Ste L1
Detroit MI 48243

(G-11288)
GILLESPIE MRRELL GEN CONTG LLC
1240 S Adams St (46953-2327)
PHONE.....................765 618-4084
Andrew Morrell, *Pr*
Charles E Gillespie, *VP*
EMP: 7 EST: 2011
SALES (est): 120.07K **Privately Held**
Web: www.gillespiemorrellcontracting.com
SIC: 5211 3567 3822 Roofing material; Metal melting furnaces, industrial: electric; Air conditioning and refrigeration controls

(G-11289)
GRACE HENDERSON
Also Called: Lighthuse Cstm Frmng Fine Art
204 S Nebraska St (46952-3814)
PHONE.....................765 661-9063
Grace Henderson, *CEO*
EMP: 1 EST: 2009
SALES (est): 79.62K **Privately Held**
SIC: 2499 8999 7336 Picture and mirror frames, wood; Art restoration; Graphic arts and related design

(G-11290)
GRANT COUNTY STEEL INC
Also Called: Grant County Steel
2201 S Branson St (46953-3258)
P.O. Box 1285 (46952-7685)
PHONE.....................765 668-7547
Dinh Ngo, *Pr*
Hai Nguyen, *VP*
EMP: 15 EST: 1980
SQ FT: 15,000
SALES (est): 2.35MM **Privately Held**
Web: www.grantcountysteel.com
SIC: 5051 3441 3444 3443 Steel; Fabricated structural metal; Sheet metalwork; Fabricated plate work (boiler shop)

(G-11291)
HARTSON-KENNEDY CABINET TOP CO (PA)
522 W 22nd St (46953-2926)
P.O. Box 3095 (46953-0095)
PHONE.....................765 668-8144
William Kennedy, *Pr*
Michael R Kennedy, *
Christopher L Kennedy, *
EMP: 279 EST: 1948
SQ FT: 121,435
SALES (est): 58.43MM
SALES (corp-wide): 58.43MM **Privately Held**
Web: www.hartson-kennedy.com
SIC: 3083 Laminated plastics plate and sheet

(G-11292)
HELVIE AND SONS INC
5418 S Lincoln Blvd (46953-6203)
PHONE.....................765 674-1372
Jim Helvie, *Pr*
Kenneth Helvie, *VP*
EMP: 5 EST: 1953
SALES (est): 554.54K **Privately Held**
Web: www.helvieandsons.com
SIC: 1389 1781 Oil and gas wells: building, repairing and dismantling; Servicing, water wells

(G-11293)
HUHTAMAKI INC
1001 E 38th St Ste B (46953-4477)
P.O. Box 189 (46952-0189)
PHONE.....................765 677-0395
Clay Dunn, *CEO*
EMP: 69
SALES (corp-wide): 4.53B **Privately Held**
Web: www.huhtamaki.com
SIC: 5199 2823 Packaging materials; Acetate fibers, triacetate fibers
HQ: Huhtamaki, Inc.
9201 Packaging Dr
De Soto KS 66018
913 583-3025

(G-11294)
INDIANA EMERGENCY LIGHTING LLC
10709 E 100 S (46953-9698)
P.O. Box 44 (46989-0044)
PHONE.....................260 463-1277
Ryan N Troyer, *CEO*
EMP: 3 EST: 2015
SALES (est): 120.76K **Privately Held**
Web: www.indianaemergencylighting.com
SIC: 3648 Lighting equipment, nec

(G-11295)
INDIANA OXYGEN COMPANY INC
2215 S Western Ave (46953-2826)
PHONE.....................765 662-8700
Gary Morrison, *Brnch Mgr*
EMP: 4
SALES (corp-wide): 43.09MM **Privately Held**
Web: www.indianaoxygen.com
SIC: 3541 5084 5169 Machine tools, metal cutting type; Welding machinery and equipment; Industrial gases
PA: Indiana Oxygen Company Inc
6099 W Corporate Way
Indianapolis IN 46278
317 290-0003

(G-11296)
IRVING MATERIALS INC
Also Called: I M I
3892 S Garthwaite Rd (46953-5621)
PHONE.....................765 674-2271
EMP: 6
SALES (corp-wide): 814.09MM **Privately Held**
Web: www.irvmat.com
SIC: 3273 Ready-mixed concrete
PA: Irving Materials, Inc.
8032 N State Road 9
Greenfield IN 46140
317 326-3101

(G-11297)
J G BOWERS INC
Also Called: Advanced Cabinet Systems
1629 S Joaquin Dr (46953-9635)
P.O. Box 167 (46952-0167)
PHONE.....................765 677-1000
Greg Bowers, *Pr*
Jane Bowers, *
EMP: 30 EST: 1981
SQ FT: 15,000
SALES (est): 8.26MM **Privately Held**
Web: www.jgbowers.com
SIC: 1542 2541 Commercial and office building, new construction; Showcases, except refrigerated: wood

(G-11298)
J R NEWBY
405 N Henderson Ave (46952-3303)
P.O. Box 374 (46991-0374)
PHONE.....................765 664-3501
J R Newby, *Prin*
EMP: 5 EST: 2009
SALES (est): 244.4K **Privately Held**
SIC: 2499 Wood products, nec

(G-11299)
JBD MACHINING
1702 W Jeffras Ave (46952-3345)
PHONE.....................765 671-9050
Jerzy Radomski, *Owner*
EMP: 6 EST: 2005
SALES (est): 85.69K **Privately Held**
SIC: 3599 Machine shop, jobbing and repair

(G-11300)
JENNERJAHN MACHINE INC
701 N Miller Ave (46952)
P.O. Box 379 (46957)
PHONE.....................765 998-2733
Chris Jennerjahn, *Pr*
Kris Kimmerling, *
▲ EMP: 54 EST: 1979
SQ FT: 30,000
SALES (est): 20.55MM **Privately Held**
Web: www.jennerjahn.com
SIC: 3554 3599 Paper industries machinery; Custom machinery

(G-11301)
JODO INVESTMENTS INC
3112 S Boots St (46953-4016)
P.O. Box 1508 (46952-7908)
PHONE.....................765 651-0200
John Long, *Pr*
EMP: 49 EST: 1979
SQ FT: 200,000
SALES (est): 2.52MM **Privately Held**
SIC: 2621 2448 Wrapping and packaging papers; Pallets, wood

(G-11302)
K DIAMOND SHEET METAL
934 S Nebraska St (46953-1873)
PHONE.....................765 671-9847
Doug Holder, *Owner*
EMP: 7 EST: 2000
SALES (est): 912.47K **Privately Held**
Web: www.wileymetal.com
SIC: 3444 Sheet metalwork

(G-11303)
KEN DUIKHOFF
3112 S Washington St (46953-4022)
PHONE.....................765 668-8697
Ken Duikhoff, *Owner*
Ardeth Duikoff, *Sec*
EMP: 1 EST: 1980

GEOGRAPHIC SECTION

Marion - Grant County (G-11328)

SALES (est): 51.68K **Privately Held**
SIC: 2499 Decorative wood and woodwork

(G-11304)
KIRBY RISK CORPORATION
1221 S Adams St (46953-2328)
PHONE.................................765 664-5185
Tim Smith, *Mgr*
EMP: 10
SQ FT: 10,000
SALES (corp-wide): 501.02MM **Privately Held**
Web: www.kirbyrisk.com
SIC: 5063 5085 7694 Electrical supplies, nec ; Industrial sewing thread; Electric motor repair
PA: Kirby Risk Corporation
    1815 Sagamore Pkwy N
    Lafayette IN 47904
    765 448-4567

(G-11305)
L & L PRESS INC
Also Called: Hoosier Jiffy Print
1417 W Kem Rd (46952-1856)
P.O. Box 802 (46952-0802)
PHONE.................................765 664-3162
Rob Wilson, *Pr*
Lori Mcgillem, *VP*
EMP: 12 EST: 1987
SQ FT: 2,000
SALES (est): 972.4K **Privately Held**
Web: www.hoosierjiffyprint.com
SIC: 2752 2791 2789 2759 Offset printing; Typesetting; Bookbinding and related work; Commercial printing, nec

(G-11306)
LEE FARMS ENTERPRISES INC
10912 W 1000 S 90 (46952-8821)
PHONE.................................260 375-3319
EMP: 1 EST: 2004
SALES (est): 184.51K **Privately Held**
SIC: 3523 Driers (farm): grain, hay, and seed

(G-11307)
LEIN CORPORATION
3301 S Hamaker St (46953-4229)
P.O. Box 3064 (46953-0064)
PHONE.................................765 674-6950
David Compton, *Pr*
Lisa E Compton, *Sec*
EMP: 21 EST: 1991
SQ FT: 14,000
SALES (est): 916.26K **Privately Held**
Web: www.leincorporation.com
SIC: 3479 Coating of metals and formed products

(G-11308)
LGNDZ CUSTOMS LLC ✪
3402 S Landess St (46953-4225)
PHONE.................................765 293-9303
EMP: 1 EST: 2022
SALES (est): 42.55K **Privately Held**
SIC: 2329 7389 Men's and boy's clothing, nec; Business Activities at Non-Commercial Site

(G-11309)
LIFEDATA LLC
1800 N Wabash Rd Ste 300 (46952-1300)
PHONE.................................925 800-3381
Kevin Eklund, *CEO*
Kevin Eklund, *Prin*
Timothy Steenbergh, *Prin*
EMP: 2 EST: 2012
SALES (est): 258.16K **Privately Held**
Web: www.lifedatacorp.com

SIC: 3652 7371 Prerecorded records and tapes; Software programming applications

(G-11310)
LINDA HARMON DE SIGN STUDI
407 S Washington St (46953-1960)
PHONE.................................765 573-6138
EMP: 4 EST: 2018
SALES (est): 46.08K **Privately Held**
SIC: 3993 Signs and advertising specialties

(G-11311)
M2I LLC
3809 N 400 W (46952-9786)
PHONE.................................765 618-2162
Mark A Middlesworth, *Prin*
EMP: 7 EST: 2006
SALES (est): 73.61K **Privately Held**
SIC: 1389 Oil and gas field services, nec

(G-11312)
MARION GLASS EQUIPMENT AND TECHNOLOGY COMPANY INC
Also Called: Gps America
123 E Mckinley St (46952-2271)
P.O. Box 406 (46952-0406)
PHONE.................................765 662-1172
◆ EMP: 61
Web: www.gps-america.biz
SIC: 3559 Glass making machinery: blowing, molding, forming, etc.

(G-11313)
MARION METAL PRODUCTS INC
401 N Henderson Ave (46952-3303)
PHONE.................................765 662-8333
Tom Brubaker, *Pr*
Mark Brubaker, *
Jerri Henderson, *
EMP: 13 EST: 1990
SQ FT: 20,000
SALES (est): 945.87K **Privately Held**
Web: www.marionmetalproductsinc.com
SIC: 3441 Boat and barge sections, prefabricated metal

(G-11314)
MARION PAPER BOX COMPANY
600 E 18th St (46953-3304)
P.O. Box 276 (46952-0276)
PHONE.................................765 664-6435
David Wilson, *Pr*
David Wilson, *Prin*
Joseph Mccoy, *Prin*
Margaret Wilson, *VP*
EMP: 10 EST: 1895
SQ FT: 15,000
SALES (est): 936.7K **Privately Held**
Web: www.marionpaperboxco.com
SIC: 2653 Boxes, corrugated: made from purchased materials

(G-11315)
MARION STEEL FABRICATION INC
1819 S Branson St (46953-3237)
P.O. Box 1478 (46952-7878)
PHONE.................................765 664-1478
James Swan, *Pr*
EMP: 30
Web: www.sss2020.com
SIC: 3441 3444 3443 Building components, structural steel; Sheet metalwork; Fabricated plate work (boiler shop)
PA: Marion Steel Fabrication, Inc.
    333 W 4th St
    Marion IN 46952

(G-11316)
MARION STEEL FABRICATION INC (PA)

333 W 4th St (46952-4013)
P.O. Box 1478 (46952-7878)
PHONE.................................765 664-1478
EMP: 18 EST: 1990
SALES (est): 8.29MM **Privately Held**
Web: www.sss2020.com
SIC: 3441 3444 3443 Fabricated structural metal; Sheet metalwork; Fabricated plate work (boiler shop)

(G-11317)
MARION TENT & AWNING CO
225 W Swayzee St (46952-2709)
PHONE.................................765 664-7722
Roger Krumel, *Owner*
EMP: 3 EST: 1936
SALES (est): 141.77K **Privately Held**
SIC: 2394 3444 Awnings, fabric: made from purchased materials; Awnings, sheet metal

(G-11318)
MIDWEST CABINET SOLUTIONS INC
1001 E 24th St (46953-3324)
PHONE.................................765 664-3938
Jeremey E Mccord, *Managing Member*
EMP: 25 EST: 2003
SQ FT: 14,000
SALES (est): 927.34K **Privately Held**
Web: www.midwestcabinetsolutions.com
SIC: 2519 3083 Radio cabinets, plastic; Laminated plastics sheets

(G-11319)
MILLWRIGHT RIGGERS INC (MRI)
2703 W 9th St (46953-1000)
PHONE.................................765 673-4000
Roger Dyson, *Pr*
Jeff Dyson, *
John Dyson, *
EMP: 30 EST: 1990
SQ FT: 8,500
SALES (est): 3MM **Privately Held**
Web: www.millwrightriggers.com
SIC: 1796 3441 Millwright; Fabricated structural metal

(G-11320)
NEWS-HERALD INC
Also Called: News Herald Newspaper
120 E 4th St (46952-4000)
P.O. Box 744 (47960-0744)
PHONE.................................765 425-8903
Ruth Cartwright, *Pr*
J Michael Cartwright, *Dir*
EMP: 5 EST: 1972
SALES (est): 282.63K **Privately Held**
Web: www.newsherald.org
SIC: 2711 Newspapers, publishing and printing

(G-11321)
NOVA PACKAGING GROUP INC
Also Called: Nova Pak
2409 W 2nd St (46952-3248)
PHONE.................................765 651-2600
William Craig Dobbs, *CEO*
John R Irving, *
Gilbert Mcdaniel, *Genl Mgr*
EMP: 22 EST: 1999
SQ FT: 214,000
SALES (est): 493.67K **Privately Held**
SIC: 2653 3412 Boxes, corrugated: made from purchased materials; Metal barrels, drums, and pails

(G-11322)
OAKES
2728 N 500 W (46952-9770)
PHONE.................................765 384-5317
Robert Oakes, *Owner*
EMP: 1 EST: 1997

SALES (est): 85.28K **Privately Held**
SIC: 7692 Welding repair

(G-11323)
PAGES EDITORIAL SERVICES INC
Also Called: Pages
113 E Old Kokomo Rd (46953-6005)
PHONE.................................765 674-4212
Shirley Planck, *Pr*
Jae Berry, *VP*
EMP: 10 EST: 1983
SQ FT: 1,400
SALES (est): 503.22K **Privately Held**
SIC: 2721 8231 Magazines: publishing and printing; Libraries

(G-11324)
PAXTON MEDIA GROUP LLC
Also Called: Chronicle-Tribune
610 S Adams St (46953-2041)
P.O. Box 309 (46952-0309)
PHONE.................................765 664-5111
Amy Eads, *Brnch Mgr*
EMP: 7
SALES (corp-wide): 147.64MM **Privately Held**
Web: www.paducahsun.com
SIC: 2711 Commercial printing and newspaper publishing combined
PA: Paxton Media Group, Llc
    100 Television Ln
    Paducah KY 42003
    270 575-8630

(G-11325)
PEARSON PRINTING COMPANY
3239 S Washington St (46953-4025)
PHONE.................................765 664-8769
Kevin Pearson, *Owner*
EMP: 5 EST: 1938
SALES (est): 247.65K **Privately Held**
Web: www.pearsonprinting.com
SIC: 2752 Offset printing

(G-11326)
PEERLESS MACHINE & TOOL CORP
1804 W 2nd St (46952-3362)
P.O. Box 385 (46952-0385)
PHONE.................................765 662-2586
Jeffrey D Carson, *Pr*
Robert D Carson, *
Barry Conrad, *
▲ EMP: 60 EST: 1922
SQ FT: 75,000
SALES (est): 9.73MM **Privately Held**
Web: www.peerlessmachine.com
SIC: 3554 3559 Paper industries machinery; Plastics working machinery

(G-11327)
PEERLESS PRINTING CORPORATION
Also Called: Peerless Printing & Off Sups
513 S Washington St (46953-1962)
P.O. Box 962 (46952-0962)
PHONE.................................765 664-8341
Kurt Kohlmorgen, *Pr*
Ann Kohlmorgen, *VP*
Jane Kohlmorgen, *Sec*
EMP: 9 EST: 1910
SQ FT: 5,800
SALES (est): 880.35K **Privately Held**
Web: www.ppcprint.com
SIC: 5112 2752 Office supplies, nec; Offset printing

(G-11328)
PIPE DREAM INNOVATIONS LLC
4201 S Washington St # 3269 (46953-4974)
PHONE.................................503 910-8815

Marion - Grant County (G-11329)

Jonathan Berger, *CEO*
EMP: 1 **EST:** 2016
SALES (est): 56.29K **Privately Held**
SIC: 3949 2834 Sporting and athletic goods, nec; Analgesics

(G-11329)
PPI ACQUISITION LLC
Also Called: Pro Prints Gear
1424 W 35th St (46953-3454)
PHONE..............................765 674-8627
Steve Turner, *Pr*
EMP: 27 **EST:** 2013
SALES (est): 2.47MM **Privately Held**
Web: www.proprintsgear.com
SIC: 5091 2759 Athletic goods; Screen printing

(G-11330)
PRECISION TOOL & DIE INC
1735 W Factory Ave (46952-2424)
P.O. Box 808 (46952-0808)
PHONE..............................765 664-4786
Dennis Florek, *Pr*
C Greg Hearn, *Sec*
EMP: 6 **EST:** 1998
SQ FT: 5,900
SALES (est): 684.88K **Privately Held**
Web: www.precisiontoolanddie.us
SIC: 3544 Special dies and tools

(G-11331)
PRYSMIAN CBLES SYSTEMS USA LLC
Also Called: Marion, In Plant
440 E 8th St (46953-2088)
PHONE..............................765 664-2321
Jay Buehler, *Manager*
EMP: 250
SQ FT: 1,000,000
Web: na.prysmian.com
SIC: 3357 Communication wire
HQ: Prysmian Cables And Systems Usa, Llc
4 Tesseneer Dr
Highland Heights KY 41076
859 572-8000

(G-11332)
QUAKER CHEMICAL CORP
2400 W 2nd St (46952-3249)
PHONE..............................765 668-2441
Jim Greemy, *Mgr*
EMP: 3 **EST:** 1999
SALES (est): 263.32K **Privately Held**
Web: home.quakerhoughton.com
SIC: 4226 2899 Petroleum and chemical bulk stations and terminals for hire; Chemical preparations, nec

(G-11333)
RACING FUEL IGNITE
2950 W Delphi Pike (46952-9265)
PHONE..............................765 733-0833
EMP: 4 **EST:** 2015
SALES (est): 88.36K **Privately Held**
Web: www.igniteracingfuel.com
SIC: 2869 Fuels

(G-11334)
RC PROPERTY PRESERVATION LLC
3117 S Adams St (46953-4029)
PHONE..............................765 660-3808
EMP: 3 **EST:** 2019
SALES (est): 81.4K **Privately Held**
SIC: 1389 Construction, repair, and dismantling services

(G-11335)
REALITY MOTOR SPORTS INC
2021 S Western Ave (46953-2824)
PHONE..............................765 662-3000
Warren Thomas, *Pr*
Lori Thomas, *Sec*
EMP: 5 **EST:** 1999
SALES (est): 368.06K **Privately Held**
Web: www.realitymotorsports.co
SIC: 3751 Motorcycles and related parts

(G-11336)
RONALD L MILLER
1102 N Wabash Ave (46952-2510)
PHONE..............................765 662-3881
EMP: 6 **EST:** 2010
SALES (est): 113.13K **Privately Held**
SIC: 3843 Enamels, dentists'

(G-11337)
SCOTTS GRANT COUNTY ASP INC
2686 S 300 W (46953-9706)
PHONE..............................765 664-2754
Don Scott, *Pr*
EMP: 8 **EST:** 1997
SALES (est): 921.19K **Privately Held**
Web: www.chuaphatgiaovietnam.com
SIC: 2951 5032 1611 Asphalt paving mixtures and blocks; Paving materials; Surfacing and paving

(G-11338)
SIGN PROS OF MARION
4260 S 400 W (46953-9733)
PHONE..............................765 677-1234
Lee Cabe, *Owner*
EMP: 5 **EST:** 2008
SALES (est): 198.72K **Privately Held**
SIC: 3993 Signs and advertising specialties

(G-11339)
SUN ENERGY SERVICES LLC
213 E 33rd St (46953-4065)
PHONE..............................765 251-1526
Ronald Skinner, *Prin*
EMP: 2 **EST:** 2018
SALES (est): 126.67K **Privately Held**
SIC: 1382 Oil and gas exploration services

(G-11340)
SUNS OUT INC
1000 N Park Ave (46952-1721)
PHONE..............................765 205-5645
Diane J Skilling, *Pr*
Dl Hurd, *VP*
EMP: 21 **EST:** 1992
SQ FT: 2,000
SALES (est): 2.37MM **Privately Held**
Web: www.sunsout.com
SIC: 3944 5092 Puzzles; Toys and games

(G-11341)
SWAN REAL ESTATE MGMT INC
815 N Western Ave (46952-2507)
P.O. Box 1478 (46952-7878)
PHONE..............................765 664-1478
EMP: 5 **EST:** 2018
SALES (est): 173.26K **Privately Held**
Web: swan.managebuilding.com
SIC: 3441 Fabricated structural metal

(G-11342)
TJR FABRICATION LLC
2749 W 2nd St (46952-3247)
PHONE..............................765 384-4455
Jeanna Sue Riddle, *Pr*
EMP: 13 **EST:** 2006
SALES (est): 1.44MM **Privately Held**
SIC: 3399 Iron ore recovery from open hearth slag

(G-11343)
TREVARES D SMITH ◆
Also Called: Tads Construction Clean Up
1426 W 2nd St (46952-3559)
PHONE..............................765 603-0468
Trevares D Smith, *Owner*
EMP: 4 **EST:** 2023
SALES (est): 89.41K **Privately Held**
SIC: 1389 7389 Construction, repair, and dismantling services; Business Activities at Non-Commercial Site

(G-11344)
TRIANGLE PUBLISHING
4201 S Washington St (46953-4974)
PHONE..............................765 677-2544
Nathan Birky, *Mgr*
EMP: 2 **EST:** 2006
SALES (est): 136.7K **Privately Held**
Web: www.trianglepublishing.com
SIC: 2741 Miscellaneous publishing

(G-11345)
TULOX PLASTICS CORPORATION
1007 W Overlook Rd (46952-1330)
PHONE..............................765 664-5155
John C Sciaudone, *Pr*
William E Patuzzi, *
Thomas P Glynn, *
▲ **EMP:** 18 **EST:** 1983
SQ FT: 36,000
SALES (est): 962.85K **Privately Held**
Web: www.tulox.com
SIC: 3089 Injection molding of plastics

(G-11346)
ULTIMATE MFG
4794 S Lincoln Blvd (46953-5508)
PHONE..............................765 517-1160
EMP: 3 **EST:** 2018
SALES (est): 84.79K **Privately Held**
SIC: 3999 Manufacturing industries, nec

(G-11347)
VIA DEVELOPMENT CORP
867 E 38th St (46953-4402)
PHONE..............................888 225-5842
Michael Bartrom, *Pr*
Sherri Bartrom, *
EMP: 60 **EST:** 1988
SQ FT: 14,000
SALES (est): 7MM **Privately Held**
Web: www.viadevelopment.com
SIC: 3569 7371 Robots, assembly line: industrial and commercial; Custom computer programming services

(G-11348)
WELCH PACKAGING MARION LLC
Also Called: Welch Packaging
2409 W 2nd St (46952-3248)
PHONE..............................765 651-2600
EMP: 1 **EST:** 2012
SALES (est): 5.49MM
SALES (corp-wide): 457.79MM **Privately Held**
Web: www.welchpkg.com
SIC: 2653 Boxes, corrugated: made from purchased materials
HQ: Welch Packaging, Llc
1130 Herman St
Elkhart IN 46516
574 295-2460

(G-11349)
WILEY METAL FABRICATING INC
816 W 34th St (46953-4256)
P.O. Box 1246 (46952-7646)
PHONE..............................765 674-9707
Robert Wiley, *Brnch Mgr*
EMP: 1
SALES (corp-wide): 49.5MM **Privately Held**
Web: www.wileymetal.com
SIC: 3444 Sheet metalwork
PA: Wiley Metal Fabricating Inc
4589 N Wabash Rd
Marion IN 46952
765 671-7865

(G-11350)
WILEY METAL FABRICATING INC (PA)
4589 N Wabash Rd (46952-9738)
P.O. Box 1246 (46952-7646)
PHONE..............................765 671-7865
Edward M Wiley, *Pr*
Robert Wiley, *
Tom Reto, *
Rob Wiley, *
Joe Mcphearson, *Dir*
EMP: 159 **EST:** 1982
SQ FT: 110,000
SALES (est): 49.5MM
SALES (corp-wide): 49.5MM **Privately Held**
Web: www.wileymetal.com
SIC: 3444 Sheet metalwork

(G-11351)
WOOD PILE PALLET COMPANY LLC
637 S Lincoln Blvd (46953-2523)
PHONE..............................317 750-9272
Domenic Brankle, *Prin*
EMP: 13 **EST:** 2012
SALES (est): 704.59K **Privately Held**
SIC: 2448 Pallets, wood and wood with metal

(G-11352)
WWS FABRICATING INC
506 S Lenfesty Ave (46953-1223)
PHONE..............................765 506-7341
Amber Mechling, *Pr*
EMP: 8 **EST:** 2020
SALES (est): 285.46K **Privately Held**
SIC: 7692 Welding repair

Markle
Wells County

(G-11353)
AFFORDABLE LUXURY HOMES INC
Also Called: Alh Building Systems
49 S 500 E (46770-5448)
PHONE..............................260 758-2141
Kevin Cossairt, *Pr*
David Cossairt, *
EMP: 100 **EST:** 1976
SQ FT: 12,000
SALES (est): 9.65MM **Privately Held**
Web: www.alh-building.com
SIC: 2452 5031 Prefabricated wood buildings; Lumber, plywood, and millwork

(G-11354)
AMERIMACHINE LLC
10415 N 300 W-90 (46770-9745)
PHONE..............................260 414-1703
Derrick Feigel, *Prin*
EMP: 4 **EST:** 2016
SALES (est): 52.18K **Privately Held**
Web: www.amerimachine.com
SIC: 3599 Machine shop, jobbing and repair

(G-11355)
ELMOTEC-STATOLMAT
10214 Chestnut Dr Ste 211 (46770)
PHONE..............................260 758-8300
Keith Witwer, *Sec*

GEOGRAPHIC SECTION

Keith Witwer Secreatry, *Treas*
EMP: 1 **EST:** 2012
SALES (est): 68.23K **Privately Held**
SIC: 2282 Throwing and winding mills

(G-11356)
K-K TOOL AND DESIGN INC
50 Countryside Dr (46770-9563)
P.O. Box 456 (46770-0456)
PHONE.....................260 758-2940
Jim Blake, *Owner*
Kim Kinline, *Treas*
EMP: 20 **EST:** 1980
SALES (est): 2.47MM **Privately Held**
Web: www.kktooldesign.com
SIC: 3544 7692 3545 3444 Special dies and tools; Welding repair; Machine tool accessories; Sheet metalwork

(G-11357)
LATHER UP LLC
2040 W 900 N-90 (46770-9742)
PHONE.....................260 638-4978
Jean Bayless, *Owner*
EMP: 2 **EST:** 2007
SALES (est): 89.15K **Privately Held**
Web: www.latherupsoaps.com
SIC: 2841 Soap and other detergents

(G-11358)
MARKLE WATER TREATMENT PLANT
460 Parkview Dr (46770)
PHONE.....................260 758-3482
Stephen Jeffers, *Mgr*
Stephen Jeffers, *Prin*
EMP: 8 **EST:** 2007
SALES (est): 129.54K **Privately Held**
Web: www.markleindiana.com
SIC: 3589 5999 7389 Water treatment equipment, industrial; Water purification equipment; Water softener service

(G-11359)
NC2 LLC
1 Novae Pkwy (46770-9087)
PHONE.....................260 758-9838
EMP: 9 **EST:** 2010
SALES (est): 971.25K **Privately Held**
SIC: 3537 Trucks, tractors, loaders, carriers, and similar equipment

(G-11360)
NOSE AND MUSTACHE LLC
Also Called: Hare Canvas Products
300 N Tracy St (46770-9557)
PHONE.....................260 758-8800
Stacy Schoef, *Managing Member*
EMP: 4 **EST:** 1955
SQ FT: 3,000
SALES (est): 246.78K **Privately Held**
SIC: 5999 2394 Canvas products; Canvas and related products

(G-11361)
NOVAE LLC (PA)
Also Called: I-69 Trailer Center
1 Novae Pkwy (46770-9087)
PHONE.....................260 758-9838
▲ **EMP:** 50 **EST:** 1994
SQ FT: 30,000
SALES (est): 102.85MM **Privately Held**
Web: www.novaecorp.com
SIC: 5084 3524 Trailers, industrial; Lawn and garden mowers and accessories

(G-11362)
SORTERA TECHNOLOGIES INC
5224 E Asher Dr (46770-7002)
PHONE.....................260 330-7100

Michael Siemer, *CEO*
EMP: 20 **EST:** 2020
SALES (est): 4.08MM **Privately Held**
Web: www.sorteratechnologies.com
SIC: 3559 Recycling machinery

(G-11363)
STRUCTURAL IRON & FAB INC
480 W Scott St (46770-5401)
P.O. Box 166 (46770-0166)
PHONE.....................260 758-2273
Garland K Smith, *Pr*
EMP: 4 **EST:** 2006
SALES (est): 553.78K **Privately Held**
Web: www.smitherectors.com
SIC: 3441 Fabricated structural metal

(G-11364)
WAYNE METALS LLC (PA)
400 E Logan St (46770-9514)
PHONE.....................260 758-3121
Jerome Henry, *
Rollyn Coverdale, *
Kris Morrison, *
John Berish, *
EMP: 100 **EST:** 2001
SQ FT: 170,000
SALES (est): 47.35MM
SALES (corp-wide): 47.35MM **Privately Held**
Web: www.waynemetals.com
SIC: 3443 Metal parts

Markleville
Madison County

(G-11365)
2ND AMENDMENT CUSTOMS LLC
1572 E Us Highway 36 (46056-9711)
PHONE.....................765 716-5636
EMP: 1 **EST:** 2021
SALES (est): 10K **Privately Held**
SIC: 3484 Small arms

(G-11366)
BAGS BY BRENDA
3674 E 575 S (46056-9793)
PHONE.....................765 779-4287
Brenda L Lewis, *Owner*
EMP: 2 **EST:** 2000
SALES (est): 52.98K **Privately Held**
SIC: 2392 Bags, garment storage: except paper or plastic film

(G-11367)
BECKS BIRD FEEDERS
8909 S State Road 109 (46056-9784)
PHONE.....................765 874-1496
David Reed, *Owner*
EMP: 3 **EST:** 1975
SALES (est): 134.27K **Privately Held**
SIC: 3999 0211 Pet supplies; Beef cattle feedlots

(G-11368)
D&M REPAIR AND WELDING LLC
10261 E 1100 N (46056-9614)
PHONE.....................765 533-4565
EMP: 4 **EST:** 2019
SALES (est): 27.6K **Privately Held**
SIC: 7692 Welding repair

(G-11369)
MARK TOOL & DIE INC
50 W Main St (46056-9454)
PHONE.....................765 533-4932
Jeffrey Davis, *Pr*
EMP: 10 **EST:** 1963
SQ FT: 5,500

SALES (est): 865.9K **Privately Held**
SIC: 3544 Special dies and tools

(G-11370)
REFLECTIX INC
1 School St (46056)
P.O. Box 108 (46056)
PHONE.....................765 533-4332
Dale Tokarski, *Pr*
Lamont Millspaugh, *
◆ **EMP:** 100 **EST:** 1984
SQ FT: 10,000
SALES (est): 23.53MM
SALES (corp-wide): 5.49B **Publicly Held**
Web: www.reflectixinc.com
SIC: 2679 1711 Insulating paper: batts, fills, and blankets; Plumbing, heating, air-conditioning
PA: Sealed Air Corporation
2415 Cascade Pointe Blvd
Charlotte NC 28208
980 221-3235

Marshall
Parke County

(G-11371)
COUNTRYSIDE CABINETRY LLC
2881 E Lucas Rd (47859-8875)
PHONE.....................765 597-2391
Alfred Stoltzfus, *Prin*
EMP: 2 **EST:** 2010
SALES (est): 170.63K **Privately Held**
Web: www.countrysidecabinetryllc.com
SIC: 2434 Wood kitchen cabinets

(G-11372)
CROSSROADS MFG LLC
1882 E State Road 236 (47859-8832)
PHONE.....................765 592-6456
Dane Engle, *Prin*
EMP: 5 **EST:** 2016
SALES (est): 43.81K **Privately Held**
SIC: 3999 Manufacturing industries, nec

(G-11373)
FUTUREX INDUSTRIES INC
Futurex Automotive
101 E Guion St (47859)
P.O. Box 56 (47859-0056)
PHONE.....................765 597-2221
Richard Kremer, *Owner*
EMP: 35
SALES (corp-wide): 48.34MM **Privately Held**
Web: www.futurexind.com
SIC: 3081 5521 Plastics film and sheet; Used car dealers
PA: Futurex Industries, Inc.
70 N Main St
Bloomingdale IN 47832
765 498-3900

(G-11374)
IRON BULL MANUFACTURING LLC
5947 N 350 E (47859-8827)
PHONE.....................765 597-2480
Emmanuel King, *Managing Member*
EMP: 5 **EST:** 2013
SALES (est): 547.53K **Privately Held**
Web: www.ibullmfg.com
SIC: 3535 Unit handling conveying systems

(G-11375)
UWAY EXTRUSION LLC
48 N Parke Ave (47859)
P.O. Box 92 (47859-0092)
PHONE.....................765 592-6089
Dustin Kremer, *Pr*

EMP: 7 **EST:** 2013
SQ FT: 6,000
SALES (est): 190.21K **Privately Held**
Web: www.uwayextrusion.com
SIC: 3599 Custom machinery

Martinsville
Morgan County

(G-11376)
AAA BLACK SIGNS LLC
347 E Mahalasville Rd (46151-6456)
PHONE.....................765 315-9569
EMP: 4 **EST:** 2017
SALES (est): 143.62K **Privately Held**
SIC: 3993 Signs and advertising specialties

(G-11377)
ADVANTAGE MANUFACTURING LLC
30 Robb Hill Rd (46151-8871)
PHONE.....................317 831-2902
Richard M Bryant, *Owner*
EMP: 1 **EST:** 2014
SALES (est): 239.46K **Privately Held**
SIC: 3999 Manufacturing industries, nec

(G-11378)
AEROGAGE INC
1010 N Park Ave (46151-1072)
PHONE.....................978 422-8224
Wayne Haase, *Pr*
EMP: 2 **EST:** 1994
SALES (est): 187.65K **Privately Held**
SIC: 3812 Search and navigation equipment

(G-11379)
ALPHA LOOP INC
5950 Lincoln Rd (46151-7919)
PHONE.....................317 710-0076
Eddie Phelps Ii, *Pr*
EMP: 2 **EST:** 2001
SALES (est): 90.43K **Privately Held**
SIC: 2395 Embroidery products, except Schiffli machine

(G-11380)
ALWAYS FRESH BAKED GOODS INC
560 E Washington St (46151-1658)
PHONE.....................317 319-4747
EMP: 26 **EST:** 2011
SALES (est): 2.21MM **Privately Held**
Web: www.afbginc.com
SIC: 2051 5461 Biscuits, baked; baking powder and raised; Bread

(G-11381)
ANDERSON FAB LLC
9199 Huggin Hollow Rd (46151-7399)
PHONE.....................317 534-7306
EMP: 1 **EST:** 2015
SALES (est): 63.86K **Privately Held**
SIC: 3449 1799 Bars, concrete reinforcing: fabricated steel; Welding on site

(G-11382)
C & R WOODWORKS
8880 Huggin Hollow Rd (46151-7675)
PHONE.....................317 422-9603
Roger Anders, *Owner*
EMP: 2 **EST:** 1994
SALES (est): 69.29K **Privately Held**
SIC: 2434 Wood kitchen cabinets

(G-11383)
CARRIAGE HOUSE WOODWORKING
439 E Morgan St (46151)
PHONE.....................765 352-8514
EMP: 4 **EST:** 2020

Martinsville - Morgan County (G-11384)

SALES (est): 99K **Privately Held**
SIC: 2431 Millwork

(G-11384)
CEDAR CREEK DISTILLERY LLC
3820 Leonard Rd (46151-5600)
PHONE.................................765 342-9000
EMP: 6 EST: 2020
SALES (est): 100K **Privately Held**
SIC: 3556 Distillery machinery

(G-11385)
CEDAR CREEK WINERY
3820 Leonard Rd (46151-5600)
PHONE.................................765 342-9000
Bryce Elsner, *Admn*
EMP: 7 EST: 2010
SALES (est): 507.89K **Privately Held**
Web: www.drinkatthecreek.com
SIC: 2084 Wines

(G-11386)
CRONE LOGGING LLC
4005 Parker Rd (46151-6133)
PHONE.................................765 346-0025
EMP: 5 EST: 2016
SALES (est): 69.56K **Privately Held**
SIC: 2411 Logging

(G-11387)
CRONE LUMBER CO INC
501 N Park Ave (46151-1093)
P.O. Box 1171 (46151-0171)
PHONE.................................765 342-1160
Harmon Crone, *Pr*
Steve Crone, *
Nancy Crone, *
EMP: 32 EST: 1972
SQ FT: 27,000
SALES (est): 2.51MM **Privately Held**
Web: www.cronelbr.com
SIC: 2421 Lumber: rough, sawed, or planed

(G-11388)
DIGITAL DYNAMICS LLC
5660 Perry Rd (46151-8243)
PHONE.................................317 407-9658
Michael Pflum, *Admn*
EMP: 1 EST: 2015
SALES (est): 65.16K **Privately Held**
SIC: 3993 Electric signs

(G-11389)
DRP MOLD INC
70 James Baldwin Dr (46151-8080)
PHONE.................................765 349-3355
Donald L Parker, *Pr*
Linda Parker, *Sec*
EMP: 5 EST: 1976
SALES (est): 443.37K **Privately Held**
Web: www.drpmold.net
SIC: 3544 Special dies and tools

(G-11390)
EXPRESS STEEL INC
9240 N Waverly Park Rd (46151-7662)
PHONE.................................317 657-5017
Michael Ardizzone, *Pr*
Amanda Ardizzone, *Dir*
EMP: 12 EST: 2014
SALES (est): 4.4MM **Privately Held**
Web: www.expresssteelinc.com
SIC: 3531 Snow plow attachments

(G-11391)
FIDELI PUBLISHING
119 W Morgan St (46151-1449)
PHONE.................................888 343-3542
Robin Surface, *Owner*
EMP: 3 EST: 2008
SALES (est): 162.1K **Privately Held**
Web: www.fidelipublishing.com
SIC: 2741 Miscellaneous publishing

(G-11392)
FINE WOODWORKS
4045 Cramer Rd (46151-9415)
PHONE.................................765 346-2630
EMP: 3 EST: 2018
SALES (est): 75.54K **Privately Held**
SIC: 2431 Millwork

(G-11393)
FOR BARE FEET LLC ✪
1201 S Ohio St (46151)
PHONE.................................812 322-9317
Justin Fredericks, *CEO*
EMP: 1 EST: 2022
SALES (est): 503.15K **Privately Held**
Web: www.forbarefeet.com
SIC: 2252 Socks

(G-11394)
FOREST COMMODITIES INC (PA)
1789 S Old State Road 67 (46151-6252)
PHONE.................................765 349-3291
Daniel T Wooley, *Pr*
EMP: 1 EST: 1997
SALES (est): 468.81K
SALES (corp-wide): 468.81K **Privately Held**
Web: www.forestcommodities.com
SIC: 3524 Lawn and garden equipment

(G-11395)
FORM/TEC PLASTICS INCORPORATED
Also Called: Shields Designs
1000 Industrial Dr (46151-8095)
P.O. Box 1672 (46151-0672)
PHONE.................................765 342-2300
Jacqueline Shields, *CEO*
William D Shields, *
Jacqueline K Shields, *
EMP: 38 EST: 1985
SQ FT: 18,000
SALES (est): 4.65MM **Privately Held**
Web: www.racingshields.com
SIC: 3089 Injection molding of plastics

(G-11396)
FRANKLIN OLIN
Also Called: Electrical Technology Service
6425 Hall School Rd (46151-9749)
PHONE.................................765 342-9040
EMP: 1 EST: 1979
SALES (est): 213.29K **Privately Held**
Web: www.aquaprosystemsllc.com
SIC: 3523 Farm machinery and equipment

(G-11397)
GILL CARBIDE SAW & TL SVC LLC
8471 Waverly Rd (46151-7616)
PHONE.................................317 698-6787
Karyn Cleveland, *Prin*
EMP: 7 EST: 2017
SALES (est): 208.25K **Privately Held**
SIC: 2819 Carbides

(G-11398)
HAM ENTERPRISE LLC
160 E Morgan St (46151-1543)
PHONE.................................317 831-2902
EMP: 9 EST: 2008
SQ FT: 1,500
SALES (est): 752.11K **Privately Held**
SIC: 3599 Amusement park equipment

(G-11399)
HAM ENTERPRISES MACHINE CO
4590 Jordan Rd (46151-6544)
PHONE.................................765 342-7966
Opal Ham, *Pr*
EMP: 7 EST: 1973
SQ FT: 2,500
SALES (est): 509.33K **Privately Held**
SIC: 3451 Screw machine products

(G-11400)
HILEVEL TECHNOLOGY INC
Also Called: HILEVEL TECHNOLOGY INC.
4529 E Hacker Creek Rd (46151-9357)
PHONE.................................765 349-1650
Bjorn Dahlberg, *CEO*
EMP: 1
SALES (corp-wide): 978.34K **Privately Held**
Web: www.hilevel.com
SIC: 3825 Test equipment for electronic and electric measurement
PA: Hilevel Technology, Inc.
17805 Sky Park Cir Ste E
Irvine CA 92614
949 263-8998

(G-11401)
HILLTOP LEATHER
1820 Observatory Rd (46151-7128)
PHONE.................................317 508-3404
Thomas Thompson, *Owner*
EMP: 5 EST: 1972
SALES (est): 131.33K **Privately Held**
SIC: 2386 5699 Garments, leather; Leather garments

(G-11402)
HOOSIER TIMES INC
60 S Jefferson St (46151-1968)
P.O. Box 1636 (46151-0636)
PHONE.................................765 342-3311
Mayer Maloney, *Mgr*
EMP: 131
SALES (corp-wide): 3.28B **Publicly Held**
Web: www.heraldtimesonline.com
SIC: 2711 Newspapers, publishing and printing
HQ: Hoosier Times, Inc.
1840 S Walnut St
Bloomington IN 47401
812 331-4270

(G-11403)
IMPRESSION PRINTING
389 E Walnut St (46151-2060)
PHONE.................................765 342-6977
Randy Foley, *Owner*
EMP: 6 EST: 1978
SALES (est): 346.42K **Privately Held**
Web: www.impressionsprintingco.com
SIC: 2752 Offset printing

(G-11404)
INDIANA GRATINGS INC
210 W Douglas St (46151-1001)
P.O. Box 1762 (46151-0762)
PHONE.................................765 342-7191
TOLL FREE: 800
Debra Lenahan, *Pr*
Debra S Lenahan, *CEO*
Charles Maginn, *Pr*
Beverly Maginn, *Treas*
Douglas Maginn, *VP*
▼ EMP: 19 EST: 1976
SQ FT: 32,000
SALES (est): 2.39MM **Privately Held**
Web: www.indianagratingsinc.com

SIC: 3444 3441 3364 3354 Sheet metalwork ; Fabricated structural metal; Nonferrous die-castings except aluminum; Aluminum extruded products

(G-11405)
INDIANAPOLIS POWER
6075 High St (46151-8734)
PHONE.................................317 834-3871
Paula Wildt, *Prin*
EMP: 5 EST: 2012
SALES (est): 56.8K **Privately Held**
SIC: 2711 Newspapers, publishing and printing

(G-11406)
INSTANT WAREHOUSE
1290 Morton Ave (46151-3029)
PHONE.................................765 342-3430
Robert Bennet, *Pr*
EMP: 2 EST: 2000
SALES (est): 125.48K **Privately Held**
Web: www.maximamakeupartistry.com
SIC: 2752 Commercial printing, lithographic

(G-11407)
INTEGRITY QNTUM INNVATIONS LLC
6830 Hancock Ridge Rd (46151-9679)
PHONE.................................765 537-9037
Timothy J Spear, *Owner*
EMP: 5 EST: 2013
SALES (est): 117.54K **Privately Held**
SIC: 3572 Computer storage devices

(G-11408)
IRVING MATERIALS INC
1502 Rogers Rd (46151-3250)
PHONE.................................765 342-3369
EMP: 5
SALES (corp-wide): 814.09MM **Privately Held**
Web: www.irvmat.com
SIC: 3273 Ready-mixed concrete
PA: Irving Materials, Inc.
8032 N State Road 9
Greenfield IN 46140
317 326-3101

(G-11409)
JERRY HILLENBURG CO
8365 Woodlawn Dr (46151-7629)
PHONE.................................317 422-8884
EMP: 4 EST: 2018
SALES (est): 82.9K **Privately Held**
SIC: 2434 Wood kitchen cabinets

(G-11410)
MAHAN TECHNICAL DESIGN LLC
Also Called: Mtek Weapon Systems
400 E Mahalasville Rd (46151-5833)
PHONE.................................765 341-0533
Benjamin V Mahan, *Dir*
EMP: 6 EST: 2004
SALES (est): 518.48K **Privately Held**
Web: www.mtekweaponsystems.com
SIC: 3469 Helmets, steel

(G-11411)
MARIETTA MARTIN MATERIALS INC
Also Called: Martin Marietta Aggregates
8520 N Waverly Park Rd (46151-8339)
PHONE.................................317 831-7391
Keith Hurlbert, *Mgr*
EMP: 7
Web: www.martinmarietta.com
SIC: 1422 1442 Crushed and broken limestone; Construction sand and gravel
PA: Martin Marietta Materials Inc
4123 Parklake Ave
Raleigh NC 27612

GEOGRAPHIC SECTION

Mauckport - Harrison County (G-11439)

(G-11412)
MATCHLESS MACHINE & TOOL CO
55 James Baldwin Dr (46151-8081)
P.O. Box 1733 (46151-0733)
PHONE..................765 342-4550
Gerald L Etter, *Pr*
▲ **EMP:** 25 **EST:** 1977
SQ FT: 21,500
SALES (est): 1.42MM **Privately Held**
Web: www.matchlessmachine.com
SIC: 3544 Industrial molds

(G-11413)
MICHAEL CARY ROSS
Also Called: Ross Solutions
805 Riverview Dr (46151-8866)
PHONE..................765 631-2565
Michael Ross, *Owner*
EMP: 1 **EST:** 2017
SALES (est): 57.72K **Privately Held**
SIC: 2541 7389 Cabinets, lockers, and shelving; Business Activities at Non-Commercial Site

(G-11414)
MIDWEST LOGGING & VENEER
50 Rose St (46151-8055)
P.O. Box 1146 (46151-0146)
PHONE..................765 342-2774
Mike Dow, *Owner*
EMP: 3 **EST:** 1996
SALES (est): 165.09K **Privately Held**
SIC: 2411 Logging camps and contractors

(G-11415)
MOORESVILLE TIMES
Also Called: Times, The
78 N Main St (46151-1415)
PHONE..................317 831-0280
Sharon Billingsby, *Prin*
EMP: 24 **EST:** 1889
SALES (est): 367.6K
SALES (corp-wide): 3.28B **Publicly Held**
Web: www.reporter-times.com
SIC: 2711 Newspapers, publishing and printing
HQ: Schurz Communications, Inc.
1301 E Douglas Rd Ste 200
Mishawaka IN 46545
574 247-7237

(G-11416)
MTEK ARMOR GROUP LLC
Also Called: Mtek
501 Rogers Rd (46151)
PHONE..................765 341-0933
Michael Bowser, *Prin*
Vance Mahan, *Prin*
EMP: 7 **EST:** 2017
SALES (est): 496.34K **Privately Held**
Web: www.mtekusa.com
SIC: 3842 Surgical appliances and supplies

(G-11417)
MY FELICITY CREATIONS LLC
1125 Robb Hill Rd (46151-9193)
PHONE..................317 363-3269
EMP: 1 **EST:** 2012
SALES (est): 76.09K **Privately Held**
SIC: 2844 Perfumes, cosmetics and other toilet preparations

(G-11418)
MYERS CABINET COMPANY
409 E Pike St (46151-1624)
PHONE..................765 342-7781
EMP: 5 **EST:** 2010
SALES (est): 217.58K **Privately Held**
SIC: 2434 Wood kitchen cabinets

(G-11419)
OLIVER MACHINE & TL CORP
110 Industrial Dr (46151-8083)
PHONE..................765 349-2271
Eric Strahmayer, *Pr*
EMP: 10 **EST:** 2008
SALES (est): 467.04K **Privately Held**
Web: www.olivermachineandtool.com
SIC: 3599 Machine shop, jobbing and repair

(G-11420)
ONEAL WOOD PRODUCTS INC
1120 Lenvoil Rd (46151-8639)
PHONE..................765 342-2709
Marvin O'neal, *Pr*
Judy O'neall, *VP*
EMP: 6 **EST:** 1992
SALES (est): 727.64K **Privately Held**
SIC: 2421 Sawmills and planing mills, general

(G-11421)
PAUL NELSON
4009 E Rembrandt Dr (46151-6033)
PHONE..................765 352-0698
Paul Nelson, *Owner*
EMP: 9 **EST:** 2008
SALES (est): 467.44K **Privately Held**
Web: www.nelassoc.com
SIC: 3674 Solid state electronic devices, nec

(G-11422)
PRECISION WLDG SOLUTIONS LLC ✪
1369 Crabapple Ct (46151-9077)
PHONE..................317 698-7522
EMP: 1 **EST:** 2022
SALES (est): 54.1K **Privately Held**
Web: www.precisionweldingsolutions.com
SIC: 3548 Welding apparatus

(G-11423)
R H MARLIN EXCAVATING LLC
2502 W Clover Ln (46151)
PHONE..................765 913-4041
Charles F Robertson, *Pr*
EMP: 11 **EST:** 2007
SALES (est): 528.13K **Privately Held**
SIC: 3531 Plows: construction, excavating, and grading

(G-11424)
ROGERS GROUP INC
Also Called: Morgan County Sand & Gravel Co
1500 Rogers Rd (46151-3250)
PHONE..................765 342-6898
Donnie Campble, *Superintnt*
EMP: 8
SQ FT: 2,400
SALES (corp-wide): 1.05B **Privately Held**
Web: www.rogersgroupincint.com
SIC: 1442 3274 3272 2951 Construction sand and gravel; Lime; Concrete products, nec; Asphalt paving mixtures and blocks
PA: Rogers Group, Inc.
421 Great Cir Rd
Nashville TN 37228
615 242-0585

(G-11425)
SCURVY PALACE PUBLISHING LLC
6149 New Harmony Rd (46151-7519)
PHONE..................317 809-4591
EMP: 4 **EST:** 2013
SALES (est): 56.04K **Privately Held**
SIC: 2741 Miscellaneous publishing

(G-11426)
SEMICONDUCTOR TEST SUPPLY LLC
Also Called: Semiconductor Test Supply
400 E Mahalasville Rd (46151-5833)
PHONE..................317 513-7393
EMP: 4 **EST:** 2010
SQ FT: 2,500
SALES (est): 473.66K **Privately Held**
Web: semiconductor-test-supply-llc.business.site
SIC: 3672 Printed circuit boards

(G-11427)
SHARON K UTTER
Also Called: Utter's
140 Hammans St (46151-1354)
PHONE..................765 349-8991
Sharon K Utter, *Owner*
Sharon Utter, *Owner*
EMP: 2 **EST:** 1998
SALES (est): 18.22K **Privately Held**
SIC: 2752 2395 Commercial printing, lithographic; Pleating and stitching

(G-11428)
STEVES WOODWORKING LLC
5500 Lincoln Rd (46151-9136)
PHONE..................317 507-4194
EMP: 5 **EST:** 2016
SALES (est): 70.34K **Privately Held**
SIC: 2431 Millwork

(G-11429)
STRUCTRAL CMPNNTS FBRCTION INC
60 James Baldwin Dr (46151-8080)
PHONE..................765 342-9188
EMP: 15 **EST:** 1995
SALES (est): 3.8MM **Privately Held**
Web: www.scfab.net
SIC: 3449 3441 Miscellaneous metalwork; Fabricated structural metal

(G-11430)
TERRY L RAY
Also Called: Ray's Wood Products
340 S Sycamore St (46151-2246)
PHONE..................765 342-3180
Terry L Ray, *Owner*
EMP: 3 **EST:** 2004
SALES (est): 157.16K **Privately Held**
SIC: 2421 Sawmills and planing mills, general

(G-11431)
TWIGG CORPORATION (PA)
Also Called: Twigg
659 E York St (46151)
PHONE..................765 342-7126
Roy W Rapp Ii, *Ch Bd*
Roy W Rapp Iv, *Pr*
Cheryl L Rapp, *
EMP: 1 **EST:** 1971
SQ FT: 110,000
SALES (est): 13.82MM
SALES (corp-wide): 13.82MM **Privately Held**
Web: www.twiggcorp.com
SIC: 3724 7699 Aircraft engines and engine parts; Engine repair and replacement, non-automotive

(G-11432)
TWISOD WICK CANDLE COMPANY
1115 Twin Br (46151-8501)
PHONE..................317 490-4789
Richard Scheve, *Pt*
EMP: 5 **EST:** 2015
SALES (est): 74.49K **Privately Held**
Web: www.twistedwick.com
SIC: 3999 Candles

(G-11433)
USA TRAVEL MAGAZINE
7213 Bethany Park (46151-7820)
PHONE..................317 834-3683
Melody Schubert, *Owner*
EMP: 2 **EST:** 2007
SALES (est): 54.06K **Privately Held**
SIC: 2721 Magazines: publishing only, not printed on site

(G-11434)
WALLACE CONSTRUCTION INC
Also Called: W A P Company
9790 Old State Road 37 N (46151-8342)
P.O. Box 1432 (46151-0432)
PHONE..................317 422-5356
Richard E Wallace Junior, *Pr*
Roger Huff, *Sec*
EMP: 15 **EST:** 1986
SALES (est): 3.55MM **Privately Held**
Web: www.wallaceconstructioninc.com
SIC: 1611 2951 1442 Highway and street paving contractor; Paving mixtures; Construction sand and gravel

(G-11435)
WHITES WOODWORKS
1835 Pumpkinvine Hill Rd (46151-7402)
PHONE..................765 341-6678
James White, *Prin*
EMP: 5 **EST:** 2016
SALES (est): 62.87K **Privately Held**
SIC: 2431 Millwork

Marysville
Clark County

(G-11436)
SOLOMON M EICHER
Also Called: Ace Metal Sales
7809 Henderson Rd (47141-9765)
PHONE..................812 289-1252
Solomon M Eicher, *Owner*
EMP: 2 **EST:** 2005
SALES (est): 129.4K **Privately Held**
SIC: 3541 Home workshop machine tools, metalworking

Mauckport
Harrison County

(G-11437)
DEER RUN SAWMILL LLC
8242 Valley City Mauckport Rd Sw (47142)
PHONE..................812 732-4608
Chris Schneider, *Prin*
EMP: 7 **EST:** 2012
SALES (est): 179.19K **Privately Held**
SIC: 2421 Sawmills and planing mills, general

(G-11438)
MICHAEL SKAGGS
Also Called: Timber & Logging
Rr 1 (47142)
PHONE..................812 732-8809
Micheal Skaggs, *Owner*
EMP: 2 **EST:** 2002
SALES (est): 105.68K **Privately Held**
SIC: 2411 Logging

(G-11439)
MILLENNIAL FIREWORKS
10645 Highway 135 Sw (47142-9306)

Mauckport - Harrison County (G-11440)

PHONE..................812 732-5126
Michael Lagrange, *Prin*
EMP: 3 **EST:** 2001
SALES (est): 184.35K **Privately Held**
SIC: 2899 Fireworks

(G-11440)
MULZER CRUSHED STONE INC
9610 River Rd Sw (47142-8616)
PHONE..................812 732-1002
Jesse Pekinpaugh, *Prin*
EMP: 34
SALES (corp-wide): 34.95B **Privately Held**
Web: www.mulzer.com
SIC: 1422 Crushed and broken limestone
HQ: Mulzer Crushed Stone Inc
534 Mozart St
Tell City IN 47586
812 547-7921

(G-11441)
NORSTAM VENEERS INC
2990 Overlook Dr Sw (47142-9284)
P.O. Box 32 (47142-0032)
PHONE..................812 732-4391
Mark Fitzgerald, *Pr*
Dana Mc Carty, *
◆ **EMP:** 88 **EST:** 1970
SQ FT: 89,700
SALES (est): 8.07MM **Privately Held**
Web: www.norstam.com
SIC: 2421 2435 2426 Lumber: rough, sawed, or planed; Veneer stock, hardwood; Hardwood dimension and flooring mills

(G-11442)
WILLIAMS BROS LOGGING LLC
2880 Overlook Dr Sw (47142-9232)
PHONE..................270 547-0266
Rick Williams, *Prin*
EMP: 6 **EST:** 2005
SALES (est): 93.4K **Privately Held**
SIC: 2411 Logging camps and contractors

Maxwell
Hancock County

(G-11443)
COUNTY MATERIALS CORP
119 N Main St (46154-9718)
PHONE..................317 323-6000
Tim Sonnentag, *Pr*
EMP: 50
SALES (corp-wide): 338.37MM **Privately Held**
Web: www.countymaterials.com
SIC: 3272 Pipe, concrete or lined with concrete
PA: County Materials Corp.
205 North St
Marathon WI 54448
715 443-2434

(G-11444)
KLINE CABINET MAKERS LLC
16 S Main St (46154-9720)
P.O. Box 12 (46154-0012)
PHONE..................317 326-3049
Doug Dayhoff, *Managing Member*
EMP: 14 **EST:** 1976
SQ FT: 12,000
SALES (est): 473.24K **Privately Held**
Web: www.klinecabinets.com
SIC: 2434 2541 5211 Wood kitchen cabinets; Wood partitions and fixtures; Counter tops

Mays
Rush County

(G-11445)
P O C INDUSTRIES INC
8944 N Crossway (46155-9800)
PHONE..................765 645-5015
Paris O Cross Junior, *Pr*
John Wooldridge, *Treas*
Donna Trout, *Sec*
EMP: 8 **EST:** 1969
SQ FT: 15,000
SALES (est): 972.66K **Privately Held**
Web: www.pocindustries.com
SIC: 3599 Machine shop, jobbing and repair

Mccordsville
Hancock County

(G-11446)
CHAMPION RACING ENGINES LLC
5002 W State Road 234 (46055-9595)
PHONE..................317 335-2491
Richard Fox, *Owner*
EMP: 3 **EST:** 1975
SQ FT: 5,400
SALES (est): 257.6K **Privately Held**
Web: www.gochampion.com
SIC: 7539 3714 3519 Machine shop, automotive; Motor vehicle engines and parts; Internal combustion engines, nec

(G-11447)
FABRI-TECH INC
8236 N 600 W (46055-9802)
PHONE..................317 849-7755
Donald L Menchhofer, *CEO*
Jeffrey C Menchhofer, *
◆ **EMP:** 45 **EST:** 1971
SQ FT: 30,000
SALES (est): 2.59MM **Privately Held**
Web: www.fabri-tech.com
SIC: 2399 3429 Horse and pet accessories, textile; Saddlery hardware

(G-11448)
FFESAR INC
6564 W Black Tail Way (46055-4456)
P.O. Box 1497 (47202-1497)
PHONE..................812 378-4220
Roger Eng, *CEO*
▲ **EMP:** 3 **EST:** 1993
SALES (est): 242K **Privately Held**
Web: www.ffesar.com
SIC: 3469 5021 Furniture components, porcelain enameled; Furniture

(G-11449)
FOUNDERS WEST INC
8049 N 600 W (46055-9399)
PHONE..................812 936-7446
Jamie Chowning, *Admn*
EMP: 5 **EST:** 2001
SALES (est): 349.29K **Privately Held**
Web: www.wholesalemagneticsigns.com
SIC: 7336 3993 Graphic arts and related design; Signs and advertising specialties

(G-11450)
G L D INC
13206 Fairwood Dr (46055-9600)
PHONE..................317 335-2760
Larry Ostendorf, *Brnch Mgr*
EMP: 2
SALES (corp-wide): 420.41K **Privately Held**
SIC: 3949 Sporting and athletic goods, nec
PA: G. L. D., Inc.
6427 N Ewing St
Indianapolis IN 46220
317 924-7981

(G-11451)
IMAGE ONE LLC (PA)
Also Called: Awning Innovations
7795 N 200 W (46055-9545)
PHONE..................317 576-2700
Frank I Green, *Managing Member*
Brett Hodges, *
Todd Hayes, *
EMP: 73 **EST:** 1999
SQ FT: 25,000
SALES (est): 43.41MM
SALES (corp-wide): 43.41MM **Privately Held**
Web: www.awninginnovations.com
SIC: 5039 3993 Awnings; Advertising artwork

(G-11452)
INK TRAX PROMOTIONAL SOLUTIONS
6157 Terra Ln (46055-9436)
PHONE..................317 336-6921
Melissa Anderson, *Pr*
EMP: 1 **EST:** 2013
SALES (est): 104.23K **Privately Held**
Web: www.inktraxps.com
SIC: 3993 Signs and advertising specialties

(G-11453)
KEITH SMITH
6516 W Deer Crossing Blvd (46055-9297)
PHONE..................317 336-6746
Keith Smith, *Prin*
EMP: 5 **EST:** 2005
SALES (est): 72.41K **Privately Held**
Web: www.keith-smith.com
SIC: 2741 Miscellaneous publishing

(G-11454)
PROPORTION-AIR INC (PA)
8250 N 600 W (46055-9367)
P.O. Box 218 (46055-0218)
PHONE..................317 335-2602
Daniel E Cook, *Pr*
Amy Cook, *Corporate Secretary**
EMP: 59 **EST:** 1985
SQ FT: 115,000
SALES (est): 11MM
SALES (corp-wide): 11MM **Privately Held**
Web: www.proportionair.com
SIC: 3492 3491 Fluid power valves and hose fittings; Industrial valves

(G-11455)
SIGNATURE METALS INC
6315 Pin Oak Dr (46055-9418)
PHONE..................317 335-2207
Steven Duhamell, *Pr*
EMP: 2 **EST:** 2001
SALES (est): 126.39K **Privately Held**
Web: www.signaturemetalsinc.com
SIC: 3446 Ornamental metalwork

(G-11456)
SOUTHWARK METAL MFG CO
Also Called: Indianapolis Division
5671 W 600 N (46055-9715)
PHONE..................317 823-5300
EMP: 230
SALES (corp-wide): 86.69MM **Privately Held**
Web: www.southwarkmetal.com
SIC: 3444 3498 3433 Ducts, sheet metal; Fabricated pipe and fittings; Heating equipment, except electric
PA: Southwark Metal Manufacturing Company
2800 Red Lion Rd
Philadelphia PA 19154
215 735-3401

(G-11457)
TITAN GRAPHICS LLC
10036 Olio Rd (46055-9601)
PHONE..................317 496-2188
Dale Hensley, *Pr*
EMP: 1 **EST:** 2015
SALES (est): 111.63K **Privately Held**
Web: www.titan-graphics.com
SIC: 3993 2741 7336 2396 Letters for signs, metal; Posters: publishing and printing; Commercial art and graphic design; Fabric printing and stamping

Medaryville
Pulaski County

(G-11458)
HIVELY WELDING COMPANY INC
14695 W State Road 14 (47957-8150)
PHONE..................219 843-5111
Rex Hively, *Pr*
Debra Hively, *Sec*
EMP: 2 **EST:** 1990
SQ FT: 6,250
SALES (est): 191.63K **Privately Held**
Web: sites.hively.com
SIC: 7692 Welding repair

(G-11459)
JOHN F SEMRAU
Also Called: Best Barn Pizza
2617 N Us Highway 421 (47957-8003)
PHONE..................765 337-8831
John F Semrau, *Owner*
EMP: 1 **EST:** 2012
SALES (est): 65.5K **Privately Held**
SIC: 2045 7389 Bread and bread type roll mixes: from purchased flour; Business Activities at Non-Commercial Site

Medora
Jackson County

(G-11460)
AH MEDORA LFG LLC ✪
546 S County Road 870 W (47260-9525)
PHONE..................346 440-1416
EMP: 1 **EST:** 2022
SALES (est): 64.69K **Privately Held**
SIC: 1311 Natural gas production

(G-11461)
BENNETT PRINTING
1245 S County Road 925 W (47260-9550)
PHONE..................812 966-2917
EMP: 2 **EST:** 1987
SALES (est): 70.19K **Privately Held**
SIC: 2759 Commercial printing, nec

(G-11462)
BUNDY BROS AND SONS INC
3 David St (47260)
P.O. Box 278 (47260-0278)
PHONE..................812 966-2551
Leland R Bundy Junior, *Pr*
Leora Gossman, *VP*
Virginia Robertson, *Sec*
EMP: 12 **EST:** 1909
SQ FT: 1,350
SALES (est): 2.54MM **Privately Held**

GEOGRAPHIC SECTION

SIC: **5153** 5191 2875 2048 Grain elevators; Feed; Fertilizers, mixing only; Prepared feeds, nec

(G-11463)
MICHAEL L REYNOLDS
8274 W County Road 425 S (47260-9704)
PHONE.................................812 528-7844
Michael Reynolds, *Prin*
EMP: 6 **EST:** 2002
SALES (est): 106.05K **Privately Held**
SIC: **2411** Logging camps and contractors

Memphis
Clark County

(G-11464)
HEATHERWOOD ENTERPRISES INC
1210 Harvest Ridge Blvd (47143-9474)
PHONE.................................812 294-7270
Robert Scheff, *Prin*
EMP: 5 **EST:** 2019
SALES (est): 70.38K **Privately Held**
SIC: **3732** Boatbuilding and repairing

(G-11465)
INDEPENDENT CABINETS
12910 Highway 60 (47143-9608)
PHONE.................................502 594-6026
Jerry Longest, *Prin*
EMP: 5 **EST:** 2011
SALES (est): 104.92K **Privately Held**
SIC: **2434** Wood kitchen cabinets

(G-11466)
PRATHER MACHINING INC
13403 Columbus Mann Rd (47143-9548)
PHONE.................................812 401-7556
EMP: 7 **EST:** 2008
SALES (est): 257.9K **Privately Held**
SIC: **3599** Machine shop, jobbing and repair

(G-11467)
STRICKER WELDING LLC
506 Fairview Rd (47143-9504)
P.O. Box 87 (47143-0087)
PHONE.................................812 207-3800
EMP: 1 **EST:** 2010
SALES (est): 97.38K **Privately Held**
Web: www.strickerwelding.com
SIC: **7692** Welding repair

Mentone
Kosciusko County

(G-11468)
A & B FABRICATING & MAINT INC
Also Called: A & B Fabricating
516 N Morgan St (46539-9293)
P.O. Box 665 (46539-0665)
PHONE.................................574 353-1012
Jeff Beasley, *Pr*
EMP: 15 **EST:** 1990
SQ FT: 12,000
SALES (est): 446.87K **Privately Held**
SIC: **3441** 3444 3443 Fabricated structural metal; Sheet metalwork; Fabricated plate work (boiler shop)

(G-11469)
BARNWOOD MASTERS LLC
207 N Tucker St (46539-7719)
P.O. Box 104 (46539-0104)
PHONE.................................260 414-9790
Micah Bradley, *Managing Member*
EMP: 2 **EST:** 2018
SALES (est): 62.54K **Privately Held**
Web: www.barnwoodmasters.com
SIC: **3999** Manufacturing industries, nec

(G-11470)
CARGILL INCORPORATED
Cargill
104 N Etna St (46539-9115)
PHONE.................................574 353-7623
Larry Whipple, *Genl Mgr*
EMP: 4
SQ FT: 20,000
SALES (corp-wide): 159.59B **Privately Held**
Web: www.cargill.com
SIC: **2048** Prepared feeds, nec
PA: Cargill, Incorporated
  15407 Mcginty Rd W
  Wayzata MN 55391
  800 227-4455

(G-11471)
CARGILL INCORPORATED
Also Called: Cargill
104 N Etna St (46539-9115)
P.O. Box 336 (46539-0336)
PHONE.................................574 353-7621
Larry Whipple, *Mgr*
EMP: 2
SALES (corp-wide): 159.59B **Privately Held**
Web: www.cargill.com
SIC: **2048** 2041 Prepared feeds, nec; Flour and other grain mill products
PA: Cargill, Incorporated
  15407 Mcginty Rd W
  Wayzata MN 55391
  800 227-4455

(G-11472)
CRAIG WELDING AND MFG INC
5158 N 825 E (46539-9605)
PHONE.................................574 353-7912
TOLL FREE: 800
Donald K Craig, *Pr*
John Craig, *
Thomas Evans, *
Terry J Craig, *
Chris Peterson, *
EMP: 47 **EST:** 1971
SQ FT: 75,000
SALES (est): 4.38MM **Privately Held**
Web: www.craigwelding.com
SIC: **7692** 3441 Welding repair; Fabricated structural metal

(G-11473)
MID-WEST SPRING MFG CO (PA)
Also Called: Mid-West Spring and Stamping
105 N Etna St (46539-9116)
P.O. Box 337 (46539-0337)
PHONE.................................800 424-0244
Jeffery Ellison, *Pr*
Michael Curran, *CFO*
Cj Overmyer, *VP Mfg*
EMP: 4 **EST:** 1983
SQ FT: 2,000
SALES (est): 23.29MM
SALES (corp-wide): 23.29MM **Privately Held**
Web: www.mwspring.com
SIC: **3493** 3495 Torsion bar springs; Wire springs

(G-11474)
MID-WEST SPRING MFG CO
Also Called: Midwest Spring & Stamping
105 N Etna St (46539-9116)
P.O. Box 337 (46539-0337)
PHONE.................................574 353-1409
C J Overmyer, *Brnch Mgr*
EMP: 98
SALES (corp-wide): 23.29MM **Privately Held**
Web: www.mwspring.com
SIC: **3495** 3469 3496 3423 Wire springs; Stamping metal for the trade; Miscellaneous fabricated wire products; Hand and edge tools, nec
PA: Spring Mid-West Manufacturing Company
  105 N Etna St
  Mentone IN 46539
  800 424-0244

Merrillville
Lake County

(G-11475)
8105 GEORGIA LLC
8105 Georgia St (46410-6224)
PHONE.................................219 757-3532
Larry G Alt, *Prin*
EMP: 4 **EST:** 2012
SALES (est): 258.11K **Privately Held**
Web: www.8105georgia.com
SIC: **3993** Signs and advertising specialties

(G-11476)
AALAND GEM COMPANY INC
8102 Georgia St (46410-6225)
PHONE.................................219 769-4492
Thomas Moriarty, *Pr*
Virginia Moriarty, *Sec*
EMP: 4 **EST:** 1970
SQ FT: 900
SALES (est): 454.62K **Privately Held**
Web: www.wulfdiamondjewelers.com
SIC: **3911** 3915 Jewelry apparel; Gems, real and imitation: preparation for settings

(G-11477)
ADVANCE ENERGY LLC
Also Called: Advance Energy
8650 Mississippi St (46410-6322)
P.O. Box 646 (46342-0646)
PHONE.................................312 665-0022
Vance Kenney, *CEO*
EMP: 2 **EST:** 2012
SQ FT: 4,000
SALES (est): 2.26MM **Privately Held**
Web: www.advanceegy.com
SIC: **5172** 2911 Engine fuels and oils; Oils, fuel

(G-11478)
ADVANCING CHRSTS KNGDOM GLOBL
6220 Broadway (46410-3004)
PHONE.................................219 765-3586
James Randall, *Pr*
Sharon Randall, *VP*
Loretta Bly, *Sec*
Patricia Simes, *Treas*
EMP: 4 **EST:** 2016
SALES (est): 300K **Privately Held**
Web: www.ackmglobal.org
SIC: **8661** 7372 Non-denominational church; Application computer software

(G-11479)
ALBANESE CONF GROUP INC
Also Called: Albanese Candy Retail
5441 E Lincoln Hwy (46410-5947)
PHONE.................................219 947-3070
Scott Albanese, *Area Director*
EMP: 24
SALES (corp-wide): 83.76MM **Privately Held**
Web: www.albanesecandy.com
SIC: **5141** 2064 Groceries, general line; Candy and other confectionery products
PA: Albanese Confectionery Group, Inc.
  5441 E Lincoln Hwy
  Merrillville IN 46410
  219 947-3070

(G-11480)
ALBANESE CONF GROUP INC (PA)
5441 E Lincoln Hwy (46410)
PHONE.................................219 947-3070
Teresa Albanese, *Pr*
Dominique D Albanese, *
Bethany E Albanese, *
Dorothy Albanese, *
Daniel Caithamer, *
◆ **EMP:** 75 **EST:** 1983
SQ FT: 12,000
SALES (est): 83.76MM
SALES (corp-wide): 83.76MM **Privately Held**
Web: www.albanesecandy.com
SIC: **2064** 5141 Candy and other confectionery products; Groceries, general line

(G-11481)
ALL AROUND CONSTRUCTION LLC
5807 Hayes St (46410-2370)
PHONE.................................219 902-0742
Tracey Annette Sims, *CEO*
EMP: 1 **EST:** 2019
SALES (est): 250K **Privately Held**
SIC: **1389** Construction, repair, and dismantling services

(G-11482)
AMERICAN EAGLE SECURITY INC
6111 Harrison St Ste 126 (46410-2971)
PHONE.................................219 980-1177
Rose Ann Colon, *Pr*
Daniel R Colon, *Technology*
EMP: 6 **EST:** 2006
SQ FT: 1,259
SALES (est): 928.26K **Privately Held**
Web: www.aes-inc.us
SIC: **4841** 4899 7389 3669 Closed circuit television services; Data communication services; Fire extinguisher servicing; Emergency alarms

(G-11483)
AMERICAN INDUSTRIAL MCHY INC
4015 W 83rd Pl (46410-6054)
PHONE.................................219 755-4090
EMP: 17 **EST:** 1996
SQ FT: 7,500
SALES (est): 4.22MM **Privately Held**
Web: www.aimmachinery.com
SIC: **3599** 3537 Custom machinery; Trucks, tractors, loaders, carriers, and similar equipment

(G-11484)
APPLIED SCIENTIFIC RES INC
2036 W 86th Ln (46410-6460)
PHONE.................................219 776-4623
Lucretia Biancardi, *Pr*
EMP: 3 **EST:** 1988
SALES (est): 72.2K **Privately Held**
SIC: **8732** 3634 Research services, except laboratory; Immersion heaters, electric: household

(G-11485)
ARMCO
6071 Broadway (46410-2619)
PHONE.................................219 981-8864
Larry Rizer, *Owner*
EMP: 2 **EST:** 2004
SALES (est): 115.22K **Privately Held**

Merrillville - Lake County (G-11486)

Web: www.armcobuilders.com
SIC: 3312 Blast furnaces and steel mills

(G-11486)
ATKORE INC
2400 E 69th Ave (46410)
PHONE...............................219 844-6800
EMP: 6
Web: www.atkore.com
SIC: 3699 Electrical equipment and supplies, nec
PA: Atkore Inc.
16100 S Lathrop Ave
Harvey IL 60426

(G-11487)
BEA MA BKES SPCLTY DSSERTS LLC
3329 E 73rd Ave (46410-4076)
PHONE...............................219 302-6716
EMP: 2 EST: 2020
SALES (est): 95K **Privately Held**
SIC: 2051 Pies, bakery: except frozen

(G-11488)
BIONIC PRSTHTICS ORTHTICS GROU (PA)
Also Called: Bionic Prosthetics & Orthotics
8695 Connecticut St Ste E (46410-6240)
PHONE...............................219 791-9200
Sumesh Saxena, *Managing Member*
EMP: 4 EST: 2007
SALES (est): 2.43MM **Privately Held**
Web: www.bionicpo.com
SIC: 3842 Prosthetic appliances

(G-11489)
BIONIC PRSTHTICS ORTHTICS GROU
3803 E Lincoln Hwy (46410-5809)
PHONE...............................219 940-3104
EMP: 1
Web: www.bionicpo.com
SIC: 3842 Surgical appliances and supplies
PA: Bionic Prosthetics And Orthotics Group Llc
8695 Connecticut St Ste E
Merrillville IN 46410

(G-11490)
BLESSED HUMBLED BEGINNINGS LLC
Also Called: Wholebody Wholesoul
5164 E 81st Ave Ste 183 (46410-5852)
P.O. Box 719 (46312-0719)
PHONE...............................219 255-3820
Tanisha Stokes, *CEO*
Brenda Hughes, *Ex Dir*
EMP: 4 EST: 2020
SALES (est): 10K **Privately Held**
SIC: 5961 2844 Electronic shopping; Cosmetic preparations

(G-11491)
BLESSING ENTERPRISES INC
Also Called: Merrillville Awning & Tent
1420 E 91st Dr (46410-7174)
PHONE...............................219 736-9800
Mike Blessing, *Pr*
Nita Blessing, *Sec*
EMP: 19 EST: 1987
SQ FT: 10,000
SALES (est): 372.84K **Privately Held**
Web: www.awningguy.com
SIC: 2394 Awnings, fabric: made from purchased materials

(G-11492)
BOLD SOLUTIONS LLC
7452 Hendricks St (46410-4452)
PHONE...............................708 740-8577
EMP: 2 EST: 2020
SALES (est): 36K **Privately Held**
SIC: 3999 Hair and hair-based products

(G-11493)
BROADWAY AUTO GLASS LLC
6491 Broadway (46410-3007)
PHONE...............................219 884-5277
EMP: 17 EST: 2001
SALES (est): 1.03MM **Privately Held**
SIC: 7536 7699 3993 5531 Automotive glass replacement shops; China and glass repair; Signs and advertising specialties; Automotive accessories

(G-11494)
BT MANAGEMENT INC
Also Called: Custom Imprint
8605 Indiana Pl (46410-6369)
PHONE...............................219 794-9546
John Immordino, *Pr*
Tammy Immordino, *Sec*
EMP: 7 EST: 1992
SQ FT: 2,520
SALES (est): 890.24K **Privately Held**
Web: www.custom-imprint.net
SIC: 2759 Screen printing

(G-11495)
C & C IRON INC
6409 Hendricks St (46410-2805)
PHONE...............................219 769-2511
Michael R Crist, *Pr*
Lorenzo J Crist, *
Sharon Crist, *
EMP: 26 EST: 1963
SQ FT: 12,400
SALES (est): 917.59K **Privately Held**
Web: www.cnciron.com
SIC: 3441 Building components, structural steel

(G-11496)
CAMBRIDGE ENTERPRISE INC
Also Called: Web Design and Developer
5931 Roosevelt Pl (46410-2250)
PHONE...............................765 544-3402
Terry Bland, *CEO*
EMP: 4 EST: 2020
SALES (est): 212.27K **Privately Held**
SIC: 3571 1731 Computers, digital, analog or hybrid; Computer power conditioning

(G-11497)
CIVIC PRESS INC
8520 Broadway (46410-7032)
PHONE...............................219 750-9361
John Brant, *Pr*
EMP: 5 EST: 2013
SQ FT: 1,200
SALES (est): 500K **Privately Held**
SIC: 2741 Miscellaneous publishing

(G-11498)
COMPLEX STRUCTURES GROUP LLC
Also Called: Csg
4433 E 83rd Ave (46410)
PHONE...............................219 947-3939
Joel Spalding, *CEO*
Jon Hollowell, *Pr*
Nikole Aponte Byerman, *CFO*
Nick Bhambri, *Prin*
EMP: 20 EST: 2007
SALES (est): 1.36MM **Privately Held**
Web: www.csgllc.com

SIC: 3449 Miscellaneous metalwork

(G-11499)
CROWN PACKAGING INTERNATIONAL INC (PA)
8919 Colorado St (46410-7208)
PHONE...............................219 738-1000
▲ EMP: 72 EST: 1947
SALES (est): 43.8MM
SALES (corp-wide): 43.8MM **Privately Held**
Web: www.crownpolycon.com
SIC: 5085 3085 Commercial containers; Plastics bottles

(G-11500)
CROWN TRAINING AND DEV INC
2642 E 84th Pl (46410-6424)
PHONE...............................219 947-0845
Dave Maksimovich, *Pr*
Dawn Maksimovich, *
EMP: 18 EST: 1999
SQ FT: 6,600
SALES (est): 848.05K **Privately Held**
Web: www.crowntraining.com
SIC: 8748 2741 7373 8249 Business consulting, nec; Miscellaneous publishing; Computer integrated systems design; Vocational schools, nec

(G-11501)
CUSTOM EMBROIDERIES LLC
2109 Southlake Mall (46410-6438)
PHONE...............................708 257-0415
EMP: 4 EST: 2016
SALES (est): 92.52K **Privately Held**
SIC: 2395 Embroidery and art needlework

(G-11502)
CUSTOM IMPRINT CORPORATION
8605 Indiana Pl (46410-6369)
PHONE...............................800 378-3397
Tamara Immordino, *Pr*
John Immordino, *VP*
EMP: 16 EST: 2015
SALES (est): 996.02K **Privately Held**
Web: www.custom-imprint.net
SIC: 2395 2396 Embroidery products, except Schiffli machine; Screen printing on fabric articles

(G-11503)
D I HAIR EXTENSIONS LLC
7450 Noble St (46410-4351)
PHONE...............................219 742-3611
EMP: 1
SALES (est): 39.69K **Privately Held**
SIC: 3999 7389 Hair and hair-based products; Business Activities at Non-Commercial Site

(G-11504)
DEATH ENN LLC
2264 W 60th Dr (46410-2220)
PHONE...............................219 402-4436
EMP: 1
SALES (est): 49.15K **Privately Held**
SIC: 3161 7389 Clothing and apparel carrying cases; Business Activities at Non-Commercial Site

(G-11505)
DENTAL PROFESSIONAL LABORATORY
8040 Cleveland Pl (46410-5302)
PHONE...............................219 769-6225
Michael Suris, *Pr*
Dorothy Suris, *
EMP: 25 EST: 1969
SALES (est): 2MM **Privately Held**

Web: www.dentalprofessionallab.com
SIC: 8072 3843 Crown and bridge production; Dental equipment and supplies

(G-11506)
DIAMOND LUSH EXTENSIONS LLC
5164 E 81st Ave (46410-5852)
PHONE...............................773 984-1003
Tieanna Walker, *Admn*
EMP: 2 EST: 2018
SALES (est): 85.31K **Privately Held**
SIC: 3999 Hair and hair-based products

(G-11507)
DIVALICIOUS BY YOURS TRULY LLC
759 E 81st Ave (46410-5538)
PHONE...............................219 359-6335
EMP: 6 EST: 2012
SALES (est): 17.4K **Privately Held**
SIC: 3999 Hair curlers, designed for beauty parlors

(G-11508)
DOCU-TECH SERVICES INC (PA)
1442 E 86th Pl (46410-6342)
PHONE...............................219 769-7115
Richard Short, *Pr*
EMP: 2 EST: 1998
SALES (est): 280.36K
SALES (corp-wide): 280.36K **Privately Held**
Web: www.docutechdocuments.com
SIC: 2752 Offset printing

(G-11509)
EAGLE FREIGHT INC
6111 Harrison St Ste 119 (46410)
PHONE...............................646 634-5870
Marko Dordevic, *Pr*
EMP: 3
SALES (est): 202.15K **Privately Held**
SIC: 3799 Transportation equipment, nec

(G-11510)
EAT DA CAKE LLC
3764 W 92nd Ct (46410-5932)
PHONE...............................765 479-4985
Stella Morland, *Managing Member*
EMP: 2 EST: 2020
SALES (est): 69.32K **Privately Held**
Web: www.eatdacakellc.com
SIC: 5461 2051 Retail bakeries; Bakery: wholesale or wholesale/retail combined

(G-11511)
ED NICKELS
5793 Taney Pl (46410-2167)
PHONE...............................219 887-6128
Ed Nickels, *Prin*
EMP: 6 EST: 2010
SALES (est): 110.13K **Privately Held**
SIC: 3356 Nickel

(G-11512)
ELITE CONSTRUCTION NORTHWEST ◊
5164 E 81st Ave Ste 13 (46410-5852)
PHONE...............................888 811-0212
Ru Zheng, *Pr*
EMP: 11 EST: 2022
SALES (est): 251.48K **Privately Held**
SIC: 1389 7389 Construction, repair, and dismantling services; Business Activities at Non-Commercial Site

(G-11513)
ENTERPRISE MGT SOLUTIONS LLC (PA)
1900 W 62nd Ave (46410-2372)
PHONE...............................219 545-8544

GEOGRAPHIC SECTION

Merrillville - Lake County (G-11539)

Tasha Figueroa, *CEO*
Tina Mahone, *COO*
EMP: 1 **EST:** 2016
SALES (est): 246.1K
SALES (corp-wide): 246.1K Privately Held
Web: www.entmgmtsoln.com
SIC: 8711 8748 8111 8742 Engineering services; Business consulting, nec; Legal services; Management consulting services

(G-11514)
EROSION & CNSTR SOLUTIONS INC
Also Called: Erosion Construction Services
4088 W 82nd Ct (46410)
PHONE..............................219 885-9676
Daniel Moore, *CEO*
Joseph L Moore, *
Rexford Polovitch, *
EMP: 34 **EST:** 2017
SALES (est): 7.97MM Privately Held
Web: www.siltworm.com
SIC: 3999 5039 1731 Hydroponic equipment; Soil erosion control fabrics; Environmental system control installation

(G-11515)
EVELYNS ENTERPRISE
2525 W 59th Pl (46410-2137)
PHONE..............................219 980-8799
Evelyn B Wallace, *Prin*
EMP: 6 **EST:** 2009
SALES (est): 133.17K Privately Held
SIC: 3581 Automatic vending machines

(G-11516)
EXHAUST PRODUCTIONS INC
Also Called: E P I
2777 E 83rd Pl (46410)
PHONE..............................219 942-0069
Terry L Daniel, *Ch Bd*
Louis Pringle, *
◆ **EMP:** 70 **EST:** 1993
SQ FT: 40,000
SALES (est): 7.76MM Privately Held
Web: www.rushracingproducts.com
SIC: 3714 Exhaust systems and parts, motor vehicle

(G-11517)
FIRST IMAGE
1447 E 86th Pl (46410-6341)
PHONE..............................219 791-9900
Joanne Nary, *Prin*
EMP: 2 **EST:** 2009
SALES (est): 273.46K Privately Held
SIC: 2842 Laundry cleaning preparations

(G-11518)
GANAWAY SOLUTIONS LLC
5475 Broadway (46410-1647)
PHONE..............................219 359-7850
Eric Ganaway, *Managing Member*
EMP: 1
SALES (est): 69.27K Privately Held
SIC: 3575 Computer terminals, monitors and components

(G-11519)
GRANDMA IRMA SAUCES CORP
417 W 81st Ave (46410-5317)
PHONE..............................773 688-9029
Nicole Fleming, *CEO*
EMP: 1 **EST:** 2020
SALES (est): 50K Privately Held
Web: www.grandmairmasauces.com
SIC: 2035 Pickles, sauces, and salad dressings

(G-11520)
GRAPHIC EXPRESSIONS
6707 Broadway (46410-3531)
PHONE..............................219 663-2085
Rich Lambie, *Owner*
EMP: 3 **EST:** 1988
SALES (est): 159.75K Privately Held
Web: www.graphic-expressions.net
SIC: 2752 Commercial printing, lithographic

(G-11521)
HAIRE MACHINE CORPORATION
3019 E 84th Pl (46410)
P.O. Box 11030 (46411)
PHONE..............................219 947-4545
Michael J Mulroe, *Pr*
Bill Heintz, *
◆ **EMP:** 26 **EST:** 1978
SQ FT: 25,000
SALES (est): 4.31MM Privately Held
Web: www.hairegroup.com
SIC: 3554 Corrugating machines, paper

(G-11522)
HMT LLC
4100 W 82nd Ave (46410-6065)
PHONE..............................219 736-9901
E Lusk, *Brnch Mgr*
EMP: 1
SALES (corp-wide): 108.74MM Privately Held
Web: www.hmttank.com
SIC: 7699 3443 7389 1791 Tank repair; Fuel tanks (oil, gas, etc.), metal plate; Industrial and commercial equipment inspection service; Storage tanks, metal: erection
PA: Hmt Llc
19241 Dvid Mem Dr Ste 170
The Woodlands TX 77385
281 681-7000

(G-11523)
ICE CREAM SPECIALTIES INC
Also Called: North Star Distributing
6510 Broadway (46410-3010)
PHONE..............................219 980-0800
EMP: 10
SALES (corp-wide): 1.63B Privately Held
Web: www.northstarfrozentreats.com
SIC: 2024 Ice cream and frozen deserts
HQ: Ice Cream Specialties, Inc.
8419 Hanley Industrial Ct
Saint Louis MO 63144
314 962-2550

(G-11524)
INDIANA ULTRASOUND LLC
Also Called: Baby Gender Plus
2055 W 64th Pl (46410-3114)
PHONE..............................219 746-6662
Grace Smith, *Managing Member*
EMP: 2 **EST:** 2012
SALES (est): 217.97K Privately Held
Web: www.nwimobileultrasound.com
SIC: 3829 Measuring and controlling devices, nec

(G-11525)
INDIANA WRAP COMPANY LLC
6200 Broadway (46410-3004)
PHONE..............................219 902-4997
Michael Clark, *Pr*
EMP: 1 **EST:** 2019
SALES (est): 63.4K Privately Held
Web: www.indianawrapco.com
SIC: 3993 Signs and advertising specialties

(G-11526)
J W HICKS INC (PA)
8955 Louisiana St (46410-7114)
PHONE..............................219 736-2212
James W Hicks, *Pr*
James R Hicks, *
Jillayne Hicks, *
▲ **EMP:** 25 **EST:** 1985
SQ FT: 30,000
SALES (est): 8.89MM
SALES (corp-wide): 8.89MM Privately Held
Web: www.jwhicks.com
SIC: 3297 Castable refractories, nonclay

(G-11527)
KITCHENS BY GREGORY LTD
8680 Louisiana St (46410-6349)
PHONE..............................219 769-1551
Donald Gregory Hulls, *Pr*
EMP: 5 **EST:** 1988
SALES (est): 447.5K Privately Held
Web: www.kitchensbygregory.com
SIC: 2434 Wood kitchen cabinets

(G-11528)
LAKE COUNTY SAND & GRAVEL LLC
2115 W Lincoln Hwy (46410-5334)
PHONE..............................219 988-4540
Gerald M Bishop, *Prin*
EMP: 7 **EST:** 2014
SALES (est): 215.45K Privately Held
SIC: 1442 Construction sand and gravel

(G-11529)
LAZZARO COMPANIES INC
5880 Broadway (46410-2616)
PHONE..............................219 980-0860
EMP: 33 **EST:** 1956
SALES (est): 4.54MM Privately Held
Web: www.lazcos.com
SIC: 3444 5031 3231 3442 Sheet metalwork; Metal doors, sash and trim; Products of purchased glass; Metal doors, sash, and trim

(G-11530)
LEEPS SUPPLY CO INC (PA)
Also Called: Do It Best
8001 Tyler St (46410-5345)
PHONE..............................219 756-5337
John Hamstra, *Pr*
EMP: 30 **EST:** 1954
SQ FT: 24,500
SALES (est): 33.83MM
SALES (corp-wide): 33.83MM Privately Held
Web: www.leeps.com
SIC: 5074 3261 5251 Plumbing fittings and supplies; Vitreous plumbing fixtures; Hardware stores

(G-11531)
LEGACY ENTERPRISES INC
903 W 67th Pl (46410-3346)
PHONE..............................219 484-9483
Rolonda Bartnicki, *Prin*
EMP: 1 **EST:** 2014
SALES (est): 142.36K Privately Held
Web: www.legacyenterprises.net
SIC: 2844 5944 2311 5699 Perfumes and colognes; Jewelry, precious stones and precious metals; Men's and boy's suits and coats; Designers, apparel

(G-11532)
LENNOX INTERNATIONAL INC
Also Called: Lennox
3977 W 83rd Pl (46410-6059)
PHONE..............................219 756-3709
Jon Beal, *Brnch Mgr*
EMP: 29
SALES (corp-wide): 4.98B Publicly Held
Web: www.lennox.com
SIC: 3585 Refrigeration and heating equipment
PA: Lennox International Inc.
2140 Lake Park Blvd
Richardson TX 75080
972 497-5000

(G-11533)
LIFE43 LLC ✪
5162 E 81st Ave (46410-5876)
PHONE..............................708 335-7329
Donald Washington, *Managing Member*
EMP: 10 **EST:** 2023
SALES (est): 525.63K Privately Held
SIC: 3999 Manufacturing industries, nec

(G-11534)
LUX BEAUTY DEN LLC
5164 E 81st Ave Pmb 2022 (46410-5852)
PHONE..............................708 793-0871
EMP: 1
SALES (est): 60.62K Privately Held
SIC: 7389 3999 Business Activities at Non-Commercial Site; Fingernails, artificial

(G-11535)
LUXOTTICA OF AMERICA INC
Also Called: Lenscrafters
2212 Southlake Mall (46410-6441)
PHONE..............................219 736-0141
Sherry Merriman, *Brnch Mgr*
EMP: 4
SALES (corp-wide): 2.55MM Privately Held
Web: www.luxottica.com
SIC: 5995 3851 Eyeglasses, prescription; Ophthalmic goods
HQ: Luxottica Of America Inc.
4000 Luxottica Pl
Mason OH 45040

(G-11536)
MARKET PLACE PUBLICATIONS
7091 Broadway Ste D (46410-3537)
PHONE..............................219 769-7733
Steven Gallovick, *Owner*
EMP: 3 **EST:** 1992
SALES (est): 184.31K Privately Held
SIC: 5411 2721 Grocery stores; Magazines: publishing and printing

(G-11537)
MENDOZAS INCORPORATED
7425 Madison St (46410-4607)
PHONE..............................219 791-9034
Mellonie A Mendoza, *Pr*
EMP: 8 **EST:** 2004
SALES (est): 209.38K Privately Held
SIC: 3273 Ready-mixed concrete

(G-11538)
MILANI CUSTOM HOMES LLC
5222 Connecticut St (46410-1545)
PHONE..............................219 455-5804
EMP: 3 **EST:** 2008
SALES (est): 201.58K Privately Held
SIC: 6514 1542 1742 1541 Residential building, four or fewer units: operation; Nonresidential construction, nec; Plaster and drywall work; Renovation, remodeling and repairs: industrial buildings

(G-11539)
MILESTONE CABINETRY
2916 E 83rd Pl (46410-6414)
PHONE..............................219 947-0600
EMP: 10 **EST:** 2013
SALES (est): 277.51K Privately Held
Web: www.milestonecabinets.com

(PA)=Parent Co (HQ)=Headquarters
✪ = New Business established in last 2 years

Merrillville - Lake County (G-11540)

SIC: 2434 Wood kitchen cabinets

(G-11540)
MLA PRINTING INC
6331 Cleveland St (46410-3152)
PHONE.................................219 398-8888
Malcolm Adams, *CEO*
EMP: 1 EST: 2019
SALES (est): 83.91K **Privately Held**
SIC: 2752 Offset printing

(G-11541)
MODERN DROP FORGE COMPANY LLC (PA)
8757 Colorado St (46410-7204)
PHONE.................................708 489-4208
Gregory Heim, *CEO*
Richard Heim, *
Patrick Thompson, *
▲ EMP: 430 EST: 1913
SQ FT: 250,000
SALES (est): 82.77MM
SALES (corp-wide): 82.77MM **Privately Held**
Web: www.moderngroupusa.com
SIC: 3544 3462 Special dies and tools; Iron and steel forgings

(G-11542)
MODERN FORGE COMPANIES LLC (PA)
8757 Colorado St (46410)
PHONE.................................708 388-1806
EMP: 543 EST: 2004
SALES (est): 47.15MM
SALES (corp-wide): 47.15MM **Privately Held**
Web: www.moderngroupusa.com
SIC: 3429 8711 3312 Hardware, nec; Engineering services; Forgings, iron and steel

(G-11543)
MODERN FORGE INDIANA LLC
8757 Colorado St (46410-7204)
PHONE.................................219 945-5945
EMP: 30 EST: 2011
SALES (est): 5.44MM **Privately Held**
Web: www.moderngroupusa.com
SIC: 3462 Iron and steel forgings

(G-11544)
MOMS POUND CAKES LLC
7713 Colorado St (46410-4826)
PHONE.................................773 220-3822
Patricia Tyson, *CEO*
EMP: 2 EST: 2018
SALES (est): 36.81K **Privately Held**
Web: www.momspoundcakes.com
SIC: 5461 2053 Cakes; Frozen bakery products, except bread

(G-11545)
MONARCH ELITE NATURALS LLC ◊
2692 W 60th Dr (46410-2147)
PHONE.................................219 201-1816
Crystal Williams, *Managing Member*
EMP: 1 EST: 2022
SALES (est): 47.23K **Privately Held**
Web: www.monarchelitenaturals.com
SIC: 2844 Perfumes, cosmetics and other toilet preparations

(G-11546)
MONOSOL LLC (DH)
707 E 80th Pl Ste 301 (46410-5683)
PHONE.................................219 762-3165
P Scott Bening, *CEO*
▲ EMP: 19 EST: 1953
SALES (est): 96.48MM **Privately Held**
Web: www.monosol.com
SIC: 2821 Plastics materials and resins
HQ: Kuraray America, Inc.
3700 Bay Area Blvd
Houston TX 77058

(G-11547)
NEW BEGINNING LOGISTICS LLC
5164 E 81st Ave (46410-5852)
PHONE.................................773 457-0325
EMP: 3
SALES (est): 136.08K **Privately Held**
SIC: 3537 Trucks, tractors, loaders, carriers, and similar equipment

(G-11548)
NORTHWEST IND FABRICATION LLC
8900 Mississippi St Ste C (46410-7121)
PHONE.................................219 613-7461
Joseph L Ponziano, *Prin*
EMP: 11 EST: 2018
SALES (est): 939.31K **Privately Held**
Web: www.northwestindianafabrication.com
SIC: 3441 Fabricated structural metal

(G-11549)
PARKER-HANNIFIN CORPORATION
Also Called: Medical Systems Division
1201 E 86th Pl Ste H (46410-6377)
PHONE.................................219 736-0400
William Depel, *Prin*
EMP: 19
SALES (corp-wide): 19.93B **Publicly Held**
Web: www.parker.com
SIC: 3594 Fluid power pumps and motors
PA: Parker-Hannifin Corporation
6035 Parkland Blvd
Cleveland OH 44124
216 896-3000

(G-11550)
PHILIP PINS
3701 W 79th Pl (46410-5011)
PHONE.................................219 769-1059
Philip Pins, *Prin*
EMP: 6 EST: 2010
SALES (est): 68.32K **Privately Held**
SIC: 3452 Pins

(G-11551)
POLYCON INDUSTRIES INC
8919 Colorado St (46410-7208)
PHONE.................................219 738-1000
Berle Blitstein, *Pr*
Anne Blitstein, *Sec*
William Hansen, *CFO*
EMP: 250 EST: 1969
SQ FT: 200,000
SALES (est): 42.95MM
SALES (corp-wide): 43.8MM **Privately Held**
Web: www.crownpolycon.com
SIC: 3089 3085 Plastics containers, except foam; Plastics bottles
PA: Crown Packaging International, Inc.
8919 Colorado St
Merrillville IN 46410
219 738-1000

(G-11552)
PRIME CONVEYOR INC
8903 Louisiana St (46410-7114)
PHONE.................................219 736-1994
James Robinson, *Pr*
Dennis Armstrong, *
EMP: 35 EST: 1989
SQ FT: 28,000
SALES (est): 5.06MM **Privately Held**
Web: www.primeconveyor.com
SIC: 3535 Conveyors and conveying equipment

(G-11553)
RELIABLE DIAGNSTC BUS LAB LLC
5164 E 81st Ave (46410-5852)
PHONE.................................219 401-3122
EMP: 1
SALES (est): 69.27K **Privately Held**
SIC: 2899 Drug testing kits, blood and urine

(G-11554)
ROCK HARD STNES CSTM PRTG RHNS
9242 Bigger St (46410-5926)
PHONE.................................219 613-0112
Maurice Tisby, *CEO*
EMP: 2 EST: 2015
SALES (est): 56.53K **Privately Held**
SIC: 2752 Commercial printing, lithographic

(G-11555)
ROMANART INCORPORATED
7302 Taft St (46410-4549)
P.O. Box 879 (46308-0879)
PHONE.................................219 736-9150
Roman Perez, *Pr*
Kurt Pack, *VP*
EMP: 6 EST: 1996
SALES (est): 497.46K **Privately Held**
SIC: 2759 Screen printing

(G-11556)
SAVAGE YET CIVILIZED LLC
5475 Broadway (46410)
PHONE.................................855 560-9223
Kevin Lopez, *Owner*
EMP: 6 EST: 2018
SALES (est): 68.64K **Privately Held**
Web: www.sycapparel.com
SIC: 5621 2211 Ready-to-wear apparel, women's; Apparel and outerwear fabrics, cotton

(G-11557)
SERAPHIM LUX LLC
8714 Polk St (46410-8516)
PHONE.................................872 201-8273
EMP: 3 EST: 2020
SALES (est): 42.55K **Privately Held**
SIC: 2389 Apparel and accessories, nec

(G-11558)
SHARON SPERRY
Also Called: Sharon's Tolebooth
1106 W 73rd Ave (46410-3818)
PHONE.................................219 736-0121
Sharon Sperry, *Owner*
EMP: 2 EST: 1991
SALES (est): 78.05K **Privately Held**
SIC: 2499 Decorative wood and woodwork

(G-11559)
SHOP LULU BEAN LLC
Also Called: Retail
2032 W 81st Ave (46410-5337)
PHONE.................................219 525-5336
Latoya Carter, *CEO*
EMP: 3 EST: 2019
SALES (est): 243.21K **Privately Held**
Web: www.shoplulubean.com
SIC: 2361 5999 5641 5961 T-shirts and tops: girls', children's, and infants'; Miscellaneous retail stores, nec; Children's and infants' wear stores; Electronic shopping

(G-11560)
SITEONE LANDSCAPE SUPPLY LLC
Also Called: John Deere Landscapes
4068 W 82nd Ct (46410-6473)
PHONE.................................219 769-2351
EMP: 4
SALES (corp-wide): 4.3B **Publicly Held**
Web: www.lesco.com
SIC: 5261 5083 3432 Lawn and garden equipment; Lawn and garden machinery and equipment; Lawn hose nozzles and sprinklers
HQ: Siteone Landscape Supply, Llc
10291 Ophir Rd
Newcastle CA 95658

(G-11561)
SONLITE PALLET SERVICES INC
2404 E 73rd Ave (46410-4846)
PHONE.................................219 798-5003
Cheryl Brown, *Owner*
EMP: 1 EST: 2011
SALES (est): 74.89K **Privately Held**
SIC: 2448 Pallets, wood and wood with metal

(G-11562)
SUE & KIMS PIES LLC
5409 Dexter Dr (46410-1744)
PHONE.................................219 779-2140
Kimberly Penro, *Mgr*
EMP: 1 EST: 2019
SALES (est): 43.55K **Privately Held**
Web: www.sueandkimspies.com
SIC: 2053 Frozen bakery products, except bread

(G-11563)
T & M EQUIPMENT COMPANY INC (PA)
Also Called: T & M
2880 E 83rd Pl (46410-6412)
PHONE.................................219 942-2299
TOLL FREE: 800
William Malatestinic, *Pr*
Peter Turek, *
EMP: 37 EST: 1975
SQ FT: 35,000
SALES (est): 19.5MM
SALES (corp-wide): 19.5MM **Privately Held**
Web: www.tmcranes.com
SIC: 5084 3536 7699 Materials handling machinery; Hoists, cranes, and monorails; Industrial machinery and equipment repair

(G-11564)
TASTE OF JOY LLC
2031 Arrowhead Dr Apt 1a (46410-4979)
PHONE.................................219 501-0157
EMP: 2
SALES (est): 92.67K **Privately Held**
SIC: 3581 Automatic vending machines

(G-11565)
TECHNOLOGY CONS GROUP LLC
1500 E 89th Ave Bldg B (46410-7168)
PHONE.................................219 525-4064
EMP: 4 EST: 2006
SALES (est): 255.23K **Privately Held**
Web: www.tcgdesigns.com
SIC: 3651 5999 7812 Household audio and video equipment; Audio-visual equipment and supplies; Audio-visual program production

(G-11566)
TERRYS SEWER SERVICE
8235 Lincoln St (46410-6132)
PHONE.................................219 756-5238
Tammie Kilburn, *Pt*
Terry Kilburn, *Pt*
EMP: 2 EST: 2005
SALES (est): 136.78K **Privately Held**
Web: www.terrysewerservice.com

GEOGRAPHIC SECTION

Michigan City - Laporte County (G-11589)

SIC: **3272** Sewer pipe, concrete

(G-11567)
TORRID LLC
Also Called: Torrid
2109 Southlake Mall Spc 324 (46410-6438)
PHONE.....................219 769-1192
Angie Tantios, *Mgr*
EMP: 10
Web: www.torrid.com
SIC: **2329** 5651 Riding clothes: men's, youths', and boys'; Unisex clothing stores
HQ: Torrid Llc
  18501 E San Jose Ave
  City Of Industry CA 91748
  626 667-1002

(G-11568)
TRADEBE ENVIRONMENTAL SVCS LLC (DH)
1433 E 83rd Ave Ste 200 (46410)
PHONE.....................800 388-7242
EMP: 44 EST: 1986
SALES (est): 272.28MM **Privately Held**
Web: www.tradebeusa.com
SIC: **4953** 7699 1389 Hazardous waste collection and disposal; Ship boiler and tank cleaning and repair, contractors; Lease tanks, oil field: erecting, cleaning, and repairing
HQ: Tradebe Capital Corporation
  1433 E 83rd Ave Ste 200
  Merrillville IN 46410
  800 388-7242

(G-11569)
TRANSCEND ORTHTICS PRSTHTICS L
112 E 90th Dr (46410-7160)
PHONE.....................219 736-9960
Bernie Veldman, *Prin*
EMP: 5
SALES (corp-wide): 25.64MM **Privately Held**
Web: www.hangerclinic.com
SIC: **3842** Orthopedic appliances
HQ: Transcend Orthotics & Prosthetics, Llc
  17530 Dugdale Dr
  South Bend IN 46635
  574 233-3352

(G-11570)
UPS STORE 5219
417 W 81st Ave (46410-5317)
PHONE.....................219 750-9597
Adele Molinaro, *Pr*
EMP: 3 EST: 2010
SQ FT: 2,000
SALES (est): 181.75K **Privately Held**
Web: locations.theupsstore.com
SIC: **4215** 2752 Package delivery, vehicular; Calendar and card printing, lithographic

(G-11571)
VICTORY CRUNCH GRANOLA SNACKS
7003 Broadway (46410-3537)
PHONE.....................219 613-3594
Veronica Flournoy, *Owner*
EMP: 4 EST: 2017
SALES (est): 39.59K **Privately Held**
SIC: **2043** Granola and muesli, except bars and clusters

(G-11572)
WHITECO INDUSTRIES INC (PA)
Also Called: Celebration Station
701 E 83rd Ave Ste 17 (46410-7911)
PHONE.....................219 769-6601
Dean White, *Pr*

Dennis Kackos, *
John Peterman, *
Bill Wellman, *
EMP: 1000 EST: 1935
SALES (est): 49.46MM
SALES (corp-wide): 49.46MM **Privately Held**
Web: courtyard.marriott.com
SIC: **7011** 7922 6552 7374 Hotels and motels; Theatrical production services; Land subdividers and developers, commercial; Data processing service

Mexico
Miami County

(G-11573)
TOWNSENDS DISPOSAL
2444 W Main St (46958-2046)
P.O. Box 182 (46958-0182)
PHONE.....................765 985-2126
Patrick Townsend, *Owner*
EMP: 1 EST: 2004
SALES (est): 83.08K **Privately Held**
SIC: **3713** Garbage, refuse truck bodies

Michigan City
Laporte County

(G-11574)
A&E KLASSIC DETAILING LLC
1620 E Michigan Blvd (46360-4961)
PHONE.....................219 363-6671
EMP: 6 EST: 2019
SALES (est): 84K **Privately Held**
SIC: **3589** Car washing machinery

(G-11575)
ADIDAS NORTH AMERICA INC
Also Called: Adidas Outlet Store Mich Cy
601 Wabash St Ste 1205 (46360-3415)
PHONE.....................219 878-5822
Jaimi Dudzik-bolz, *Mgr*
EMP: 8
SALES (corp-wide): 23.29B **Privately Held**
SIC: **2329** Athletic clothing, except uniforms: men's, youths' and boys'
HQ: Adidas North America, Inc.
  3449 N Anchor St Ste 500
  Portland OR 97217
  971 234-2300

(G-11576)
ALEXSON LLC
Also Called: Sonya V Glutenfree
292 E Us Highway 20 (46360-7359)
PHONE.....................219 210-3642
EMP: 4 EST: 2019
SALES (est): 100K **Privately Held**
Web: www.expiredwixdomain.com
SIC: **2051** Bakery: wholesale or wholesale/retail combined

(G-11577)
ALTRA INDUSTRIAL MOTION CORP
Also Called: Guardian Industries
300 Indiana Highway 212 (46360-2859)
PHONE.....................219 874-5248
EMP: 40
SALES (corp-wide): 6.25B **Publicly Held**
Web: www.guardiancouplings.com
SIC: **3568** 5085 3542 3625 Power transmission equipment, nec; Power transmission equipment and apparatus; Brakes, metal forming; Brakes, electromagnetic
HQ: Altra Industrial Motion Corp.
  300 Granite St Ste 201
  Braintree MA 02184
  781 917-0600

(G-11578)
APEX FILLING SYSTEMS INC
1001 Eastwood Rd (46360-2850)
PHONE.....................219 575-7493
Marc Cannon, *Managing Member*
EMP: 8 EST: 2017
SALES (est): 1.82MM **Privately Held**
Web: www.apexfilling.com
SIC: **3565** Packaging machinery

(G-11579)
ARMORED LOCKS INC
6841 W Bleck Rd (46360-7896)
PHONE.....................219 798-6502
Gerald Bishop, *Admn*
EMP: 2 EST: 2021
SALES (est): 500K **Privately Held**
SIC: **3429** Locks or lock sets

(G-11580)
ASHLEY F WARD INC
Also Called: Fitech Divison
2031 Tryon Rd (46360-2813)
PHONE.....................219 879-4177
Todd Tirotta, *Opers Mgr*
EMP: 1
SQ FT: 27,000
SALES (corp-wide): 3.38K **Privately Held**
Web: www.ashleyward.com
SIC: **3451** 3494 3462 3452 Screw machine products; Valves and pipe fittings, nec; Iron and steel forgings; Bolts, nuts, rivets, and washers
PA: Ashley F. Ward, Inc.
  7490 Easy St
  Mason OH 45040
  513 398-1414

(G-11581)
BIELA PRINTING
1004 Kentucky St (46360-4034)
PHONE.....................219 874-8094
David Biela, *Owner*
EMP: 3 EST: 1970
SALES (est): 198.19K **Privately Held**
SIC: **2752** Offset printing

(G-11582)
BIONIC PROSTHETICS AND ORTHO
1200 S Woodland Ave Ste A (46360-7389)
PHONE.....................219 221-6119
EMP: 2
Web: www.bionicpo.com
SIC: **3842** Prosthetic appliances
PA: Bionic Prosthetics And Orthotics Group Llc
  8695 Connecticut St Ste E
  Merrillville IN 46410

(G-11583)
BOYCE INDUSTRIES
1655 N 500 E (46360-9508)
PHONE.....................708 345-0455
Robert Boyce, *Pr*
EMP: 6 EST: 1962
SALES (est): 93.57K **Privately Held**
SIC: **3498** Fabricated pipe and fittings

(G-11584)
CALUMET PALLET COMPANY INC
4333 Ohio St (46360-7743)
P.O. Box 736 (46361-0736)
PHONE.....................219 932-4550
Jeffery Bridegroom, *Pr*
Bridegroom Allison L, *
Carol Bridegroom, *
EMP: 72 EST: 1982

SQ FT: 35,000
SALES (est): 9.27MM **Privately Held**
Web: www.calumetpallet.com
SIC: **2448** Pallets, wood

(G-11585)
CANVAS MW LLC (DH)
Also Called: Marley-Wylain Company, The
500 Blaine St (46360)
PHONE.....................630 560-3703
Tom Blashill, *Pr*
Dan Watanapongse, *CFO*
Tony Curran, *VP Sls*
April Johnson, *Mktg Dir*
Greg Brennxcke, *Supply Chain Vice President*
▲ EMP: 97 EST: 1981
SALES (est): 97.83MM
SALES (corp-wide): 1.71B **Privately Held**
Web: www.weil-mclain.com
SIC: **3433** Boilers, low-pressure heating: steam or hot water
HQ: Canvas Sx, Llc
  6325 Ardrey Kell Rd Ste 4
  Charlotte NC 28277
  980 474-3700

(G-11586)
CENTRAL STATES MFG INC
2051 Tryon Rd (46360-2813)
PHONE.....................219 879-4770
Debbie Jordan, *Brnch Mgr*
EMP: 150
SALES (corp-wide): 148.14MM **Privately Held**
Web: www.centralstatesco.com
SIC: **3448** 3444 3441 2952 Panels for prefabricated metal buildings; Sheet metalwork; Fabricated structural metal; Asphalt felts and coatings
PA: Central States Manufacturing, Inc.
  171 Naples St
  Tontitown AR 72762
  800 356-2733

(G-11587)
CHANCE ABRASIVES
217 Twilight Dr (46360-1250)
PHONE.....................219 871-0977
Diane Kendrick, *Owner*
EMP: 5 EST: 2005
SALES (est): 74.17K **Privately Held**
SIC: **3291** Abrasive products

(G-11588)
CLEAN LINES PAINTING LLC
Also Called: Construction
120 Poplar St (46360-4748)
PHONE.....................708 200-2210
Patrick Luckett, *CEO*
EMP: 2 EST: 2019
SALES (est): 111.18K **Privately Held**
SIC: **1721** 1389 1742 1541 Painting and paper hanging; Construction, repair, and dismantling services; Drywall; Renovation, remodeling and repairs: industrial buildings

(G-11589)
CLOUDMAKER STUDIO INC
Also Called: Cloudmaker Glass Studio
4987 W Us Highway 20 (46360-6638)
PHONE.....................219 879-1724
Crystal Taylor, *Pr*
EMP: 3 EST: 1999
SQ FT: 2,750
SALES (est): 18.6K **Privately Held**
SIC: **3211** Window glass, clear and colored

(PA)=Parent Co (HQ)=Headquarters
✪ = New Business established in last 2 years

Michigan City - Laporte County (G-11590) — GEOGRAPHIC SECTION

(G-11590)
COLLINS CAVIAR COMPANY
113 York St (46360-3653)
PHONE..................................269 231-5100
Rachel Collins, *Owner*
EMP: 4 **EST:** 2005
SALES (est): 310.9K **Privately Held**
Web: www.collinscaviar.com
SIC: 2092 Seafoods, frozen: prepared

(G-11591)
CURRENT ELECTRIC INC
301 Chapala Pkwy (46360)
P.O. Box 8802 (46361)
PHONE..................................219 872-7736
Duane Seifert, *Pr*
Beth Seifert, *Sec*
EMP: 10 **EST:** 1989
SQ FT: 7,600
SALES (est): 465.3K **Privately Held**
Web: www.currentelectricmc.com
SIC: 1731 3569 General electrical contractor; Gas generators

(G-11592)
CUSTOM COMPRESSOR SVCS CORP
104 Woodland Ct Ste A (46360-7391)
P.O. Box 326 (46361-0326)
PHONE..................................219 879-4966
Scott Schermer, *Pr*
EMP: 6 **EST:** 1999
SALES (est): 783.33K **Privately Held**
SIC: 3563 Air and gas compressors

(G-11593)
CVG SPRAGUE DEVICES LLC (HQ)
527 W Us Highway 20 (46360-6835)
PHONE..................................614 289-5360
Ronald Seufert, *Pr*
▲ **EMP:** 121 **EST:** 1941
SQ FT: 80,000
SALES (est): 23.34MM
SALES (corp-wide): 994.68MM **Publicly Held**
Web: www.sprague-devices.com
SIC: 3714 3829 3231 Windshield wiper systems, motor vehicle; Aircraft and motor vehicle measurement equipment; Mirrors, truck and automobile: made from purchased glass
PA: Commercial Vehicle Group, Inc.
7800 Walton Pkwy
New Albany OH 43054
614 289-5360

(G-11594)
D & J CUSTOM EMBROIDERY
Also Called: D&J Custom Embroidery
707 E 11th St (46360-3619)
PHONE..................................219 874-9061
EMP: 2 **EST:** 1994
SALES (est): 80.81K **Privately Held**
SIC: 2395 Embroidery products, except Schiffli machine

(G-11595)
D MARTIN ENTERPRISES INC
310 Commerce Sq (46360-3288)
PHONE..................................219 872-8211
Csr Jennifer, *Brnch Mgr*
EMP: 5
SALES (corp-wide): 27.9MM **Privately Held**
Web: www.dmartinent.com
SIC: 3544 Special dies, tools, jigs, and fixtures
PA: D. Martin Enterprises, Inc.
320 Commerce Sq
Michigan City IN 46360
219 872-8211

(G-11596)
D MARTIN ENTERPRISES INC (PA)
320 Commerce Sq (46360-3288)
PHONE..................................219 872-8211
◆ **EMP:** 10 **EST:** 1975
SALES (est): 27.9MM
SALES (corp-wide): 27.9MM **Privately Held**
Web: www.dmartinent.com
SIC: 5085 5093 3315 3444 Refractory material; Metal scrap and waste materials; Steel wire and related products; Furnace casings, sheet metal

(G-11597)
DAGE-MTI MICHIGAN CITY INC
Also Called: Dage-MTI
106 Woodside Dr (46360-7418)
PHONE..................................219 872-5514
John B Moore, *Pr*
Peggy Moore, *VP*
James Kyle, *Stockholder*
EMP: 8 **EST:** 1953
SALES (est): 892.12K **Privately Held**
Web: www.dagemti.com
SIC: 3651 Household video equipment

(G-11598)
DEKKER VACUUM TECHNOLOGIES INC
935 S Woodland Ave (46360-5672)
PHONE..................................219 861-0661
Rick Jan Dekker, *CEO*
Charles Mitchell, *Pr*
▲ **EMP:** 70 **EST:** 1998
SQ FT: 45,000
SALES (est): 24.13MM **Privately Held**
Web: www.dekkervacuum.com
SIC: 5084 3563 Pumps and pumping equipment, nec; Vacuum (air extraction) systems, industrial
PA: Atlas Copco Ab
Sickla Industrivag 19
Nacka 131 5
87438000

(G-11599)
DELAURENCE COMPANY
Also Called: Banyan Tree, The
223 W 6th St (46360-3322)
PHONE..................................219 878-8712
Michelle M Sipich, *Pr*
Velo Edward Lawrence, *VP*
EMP: 6 **EST:** 1890
SALES (est): 466.81K **Privately Held**
Web: www.delaurencecompany.com
SIC: 3911 Jewelry apparel

(G-11600)
DIAMOND MANUFACTURING COMPANY
Also Called: Diamond Mfg Co Midwest
600 Royal Rd (46360-2744)
PHONE..................................219 874-2374
Phil Guba, *Brnch Mgr*
EMP: 61
SALES (corp-wide): 14.81B **Publicly Held**
Web: www.diamondman.com
SIC: 3469 3471 3479 3089 Perforated metal, stamped; Cleaning, polishing, and finishing; Coating of metals and formed products; Plastics processing
HQ: Diamond Manufacturing Company
243 W Eigth St
Wyoming PA 18644
570 693-0300

(G-11601)
DME MANUFACTURING PA INC ✪
310 Commerce Sq (46360-3288)
PHONE..................................219 872-8211
Bradley John Wartman, *Pr*
EMP: 13 **EST:** 2022
SALES (est): 1.23MM **Privately Held**
Web: www.dme.net
SIC: 3544 Industrial molds

(G-11602)
DUNELAND ALPACAS LTD
1394 N County Line Rd (46360-9522)
PHONE..................................219 877-4417
Michael W Small, *Prin*
EMP: 6 **EST:** 2008
SALES (est): 73.56K **Privately Held**
SIC: 2231 Alpacas, mohair: woven

(G-11603)
DWYER INSTRUMENTS LLC
Mercoid Division Dwyer Instrs
102 Indiana Highway 212 (46360-1956)
P.O. Box 373 (46361-0373)
PHONE..................................219 879-8000
Steven Clark, *Pr*
EMP: 27
SALES (corp-wide): 653.43MM **Privately Held**
Web: intl.dwyer-inst.com
SIC: 3823 Process control instruments
HQ: Dwyer Instruments, Llc
102 Indiana Hwy 212
Michigan City IN 46360
219 879-8868

(G-11604)
DWYER INSTRUMENTS LLC (HQ)
Also Called: Proximity Controls
102 Indiana Highway 212 (46360)
P.O. Box 373 (46361)
PHONE..................................219 879-8868
◆ **EMP:** 150 **EST:** 1966
SALES (est): 170.72MM
SALES (corp-wide): 653.43MM **Privately Held**
Web: intl.dwyer-inst.com
SIC: 3823 3824 3822 3829 Process control instruments; Fluid meters and counting devices; Hardware for environmental regulators; Anamometers
PA: Arcline Investment Management Lp
4 Embrcadero Ctr Ste 3460
San Francisco CA 94111
415 801-4570

(G-11605)
DYNAMIC DESIGNS SCOTTYS
3409 Franklin St (46360-7008)
PHONE..................................219 809-7268
Scott Roberts, *Prin*
EMP: 3 **EST:** 2007
SALES (est): 237.38K **Privately Held**
SIC: 2499 Trophy bases, wood

(G-11606)
EDWARD EMMONS
Also Called: Emmons Model Aircraft Company
11576 W 400 N (46360-9475)
PHONE..................................209 352-1475
Edward Emmons, *Owner*
EMP: 1
SALES (corp-wide): 145.06K **Privately Held**
SIC: 3999 Airplane models, except toy
PA: Edward Emmons
3600 Carol Kennedy Dr
San Andreas CA 95249
209 352-1475

(G-11607)
ELKHART PLASTICS INC
316 Lake Shore Dr (46360-2356)
PHONE..................................574 370-1079
Bonnie Turner, *Prin*
EMP: 8 **EST:** 2016
SALES (est): 250.93K **Privately Held**
Web: www.epi-roto.com
SIC: 3089 Injection molding of plastics

(G-11608)
EXPLODING BRAIN PRESS
607 Franklin St (46360-3411)
PHONE..................................219 393-0796
Nichole Sheaffer, *Prin*
EMP: 5 **EST:** 2014
SALES (est): 65.04K **Privately Held**
Web: www.explodingbrainpress.com
SIC: 2741 Miscellaneous publishing

(G-11609)
FABRICATED METALS CORP (PA)
4991a W Us Highway 20 (46360-6638)
PHONE..................................219 871-0230
William Moore, *Pr*
EMP: 5 **EST:** 1999
SQ FT: 12,000
SALES (est): 938.67K **Privately Held**
Web: www.fabricatedmetals.com
SIC: 3441 Fabricated structural metal

(G-11610)
FAITH WALKERS
Also Called: Faith Walkers Screen Printing
7358 W Johnson Rd (46360-2926)
PHONE..................................219 873-1900
Donald Brooks, *Pt*
Mary Brooks, *Pt*
EMP: 5 **EST:** 1994
SALES (est): 339.26K **Privately Held**
Web: www.4faithwalkers.com
SIC: 2759 Screen printing

(G-11611)
FEDERAL-MOGUL MOTORPARTS LLC
Also Called: Federal-Mogul
402 Royal Rd (46360-2769)
PHONE..................................219 872-5150
Mark Dranchak, *Brnch Mgr*
EMP: 2
SALES (corp-wide): 18.04B **Privately Held**
Web: www.drivparts.com
SIC: 3714 3713 Wipers, windshield, motor vehicle; Truck and bus bodies
HQ: Federal-Mogul Motorparts Llc
27300 W 11 Mile Rd
Southfield MI 48034
248 354-7700

(G-11612)
FILTRATION PLUS INC
4208 N 900 W (46360-9346)
PHONE..................................219 879-0663
William Ruckel, *Pr*
Donna Stich, *
EMP: 11 **EST:** 1979
SQ FT: 8,500
SALES (est): 898.85K **Privately Held**
Web: www.filtplus.com
SIC: 5085 3569 Filters, industrial; Filters, general line: industrial

(G-11613)
FITECH INC
2031 Tryon Rd (46360-2813)
PHONE..................................513 398-1414
Thomas Fitzgerald, *Pr*
Dan Wilson, *VP*
EMP: 20 **EST:** 1984

SQ FT: 25,000
SALES (est): 2.42MM **Privately Held**
Web: www.ashleyward.com
SIC: 3599 3451 Machine shop, jobbing and repair; Screw machine products

(G-11614)
FRECH U S A INC
6000 Ohio St (46360-7757)
PHONE...................................219 874-2812
Ioannis Ioannidis, *Ch Bd*
Norbert Erhard, *Treas*
▲ **EMP:** 14 **EST:** 1979
SQ FT: 30,000
SALES (est): 3.69MM
SALES (corp-wide): 13.75MM **Privately Held**
Web: www.frechusa.com
SIC: 3542 Machine tools, metal forming type
PA: Oskar Frech Gmbh + Co. Kg
Schorndorfer Str. 32
Schorndorf BW 73614
71817020

(G-11615)
FREEZING SYSTEMS AND SVC INC
107 Freyer Rd (46360-2224)
PHONE...................................219 879-6236
Christopher Redlarczyk, *Pr*
EMP: 16 **EST:** 2005
SQ FT: 60,000
SALES (est): 2.1MM **Privately Held**
Web: www.freezingsystems.com
SIC: 3632 Household refrigerators and freezers

(G-11616)
GAF
Also Called: GAF
505 N Roeske Ave (46360-2668)
PHONE...................................219 872-1111
EMP: 1
SALES (corp-wide): 6.35B **Privately Held**
Web: www.gaf.com
SIC: 2493 Reconstituted wood products
HQ: Building Materials Manufacturing Corporation
1 Campus Dr
Parsippany NJ 07054

(G-11617)
GUARDIAN COUPLINGS LLC
300 Indiana Highway 212 (46360-2859)
PHONE...................................219 874-5248
Carl R Christenson, *Managing Member*
◆ **EMP:** 40 **EST:** 2014
SALES (est): 10.1MM
SALES (corp-wide): 6.25B **Publicly Held**
Web: www.guardiancouplings.com
SIC: 3714 3568 Differentials and parts, motor vehicle; Power transmission equipment, nec
HQ: Altra Industrial Motion Corp.
300 Granite St Ste 201
Braintree MA 02184
781 917-0600

(G-11618)
GUARDIAN IND INC
Also Called: Guardian Industries
300 Indiana Highway 212 (46360-2859)
PHONE...................................219 874-5248
▲ **EMP:** 40
SIC: 3429 3568 Clamps and couplings, hose ; Couplings, shaft: rigid, flexible, universal joint, etc.

(G-11619)
HANSON PIPE PRECAST
302 Elmwood Dr (46360-1943)
PHONE...................................219 873-9509
Lorie Anderson, *Prin*
EMP: 7 **EST:** 2010
SALES (est): 117.75K **Privately Held**
SIC: 3272 Precast terrazzo or concrete products

(G-11620)
HARRISON ELECTRIC INC
10855 W 400 N (46360-9474)
PHONE...................................219 879-0444
Thomas E Walma, *Pr*
Jonathan T Walma, *VP*
Patricia A Walma, *Sec*
Michelle Walma, *Sec*
EMP: 19 **EST:** 1946
SQ FT: 17,500
SALES (est): 2.4MM **Privately Held**
Web: www.spina-enterprises.com
SIC: 7694 5063 Electric motor repair; Motors, electric

(G-11621)
HARRY S WATTS
10585 W 100 N (46360-8313)
PHONE...................................219 879-1606
Harry S Watts, *Prin*
EMP: 1 **EST:** 2009
SALES (est): 59.44K **Privately Held**
SIC: 2741 Miscellaneous publishing

(G-11622)
HEARTHSIDE FOOD SOLUTIONS LLC
Also Called: Michigan City Baking
502 W Us Highway 20 (46360-6836)
PHONE...................................219 878-1522
Dave Dolan, *Manager*
EMP: 300
Web: www.hearthsidefoods.com
SIC: 2052 2051 Cookies; Bread, cake, and related products
PA: Hearthside Food Solutions, Llc
333 Finley Road Ste 800
Downers Grove IL 60515

(G-11623)
HERALD ARGUS
422 Franklin St Ste B (46360-3386)
PHONE...................................219 362-2161
David Paxton, *Pr*
EMP: 1 **EST:** 2006
SALES (est): 60.55K **Privately Held**
Web: www.lpheralddispatch.com
SIC: 2711 Commercial printing and newspaper publishing combined

(G-11624)
HIGHTEC SOLAR INC
1000 Indiana Highway 212 (46360-3001)
PHONE...................................219 814-4279
Fred Mcneeley, *Pr*
▲ **EMP:** 13 **EST:** 2011
SALES (est): 488.94K **Privately Held**
Web: www.hightecsolar.com
SIC: 1711 3089 Solar energy contractor; Thermoformed finished plastics products, nec

(G-11625)
HITACHI GLOBAL AIR PWR US LLC
Also Called: Sullair Training Center
1100 Kieffer Rd (46360-7759)
PHONE...................................219 861-5207
EMP: 7
Web: www.sullair.com
SIC: 3563 Air and gas compressors including vacuum pumps
HQ: Hitachi Global Air Power Us, Llc
1 Sullair Way
Michigan City IN 46360
219 879-5451

(G-11626)
HITACHI GLOBAL AIR PWR US LLC (HQ)
1 Sullair Way (46360-0028)
PHONE...................................219 879-5451
Masakazu Aoki, *
Araya Yutaka, *
Michael Guido, *
Susumu Sakamoto, *
◆ **EMP:** 126 **EST:** 1965
SQ FT: 138,600
SALES (est): 181.29MM **Privately Held**
Web: www.sullair.com
SIC: 3563 3569 Air and gas compressors including vacuum pumps; Filters, general line: industrial
PA: Hitachi, Ltd.
1-6-6, Marunouchi
Chiyoda-Ku TKY 100-0

(G-11627)
J & J WELDING
Also Called: J&J Welding
4100 W 700 N (46360-9761)
PHONE...................................219 872-7282
EMP: 2 **EST:** 1996
SALES (est): 49.27K **Privately Held**
SIC: 7692 Welding repair

(G-11628)
JOSAM COMPANY (HQ)
525 W Us Highway 20 (46360-6835)
P.O. Box T (46361-0360)
PHONE...................................219 872-5531
B Scott Holloway Senior, *CEO*
Scott Holloway Junior, *CEO*
Steven J Holloway, *
Barry J Hodgekins, *
Marie B Holloway, *
◆ **EMP:** 51 **EST:** 1914
SQ FT: 120,000
SALES (est): 11.55MM
SALES (corp-wide): 2.06B **Publicly Held**
Web: www.josam.com
SIC: 3431 3432 3444 3423 Plumbing fixtures: enameled iron, cast iron,or pressed metal; Plumbing fixture fittings and trim; Sheet metalwork; Hand and edge tools, nec
PA: Watts Water Technologies, Inc.
815 Chestnut St
North Andover MA 01845
978 688-1811

(G-11629)
KTR CORPORATION
122 Anchor Rd (46360-2802)
P.O. Box 9065 (46361-9065)
PHONE...................................219 872-9100
Doctor Joseph Gerstner, *Ch Bd*
▲ **EMP:** 35 **EST:** 1989
SQ FT: 35,000
SALES (est): 9.95MM
SALES (corp-wide): 345.06MM **Privately Held**
Web: www.ktr.com
SIC: 3568 Power transmission equipment, nec
HQ: Ktr Systems Gmbh
Carl-Zeiss-Str. 25
Rheine NW 48432
59717980

(G-11630)
LANDMARK HOME & LAND COMPANY (PA)
1902 Washington St (46360-4476)
PHONE...................................219 874-4065
EMP: 3 **EST:** 1994
SALES (est): 471.21K **Privately Held**
Web: www.lhlc.com
SIC: 1799 2452 1521 Building site preparation; Prefabricated wood buildings; Single-family housing construction

(G-11631)
LEGACY SCREEN PRTG PRMTONS LLC
100 Anchor Rd Ste 5 (46360-2802)
PHONE...................................219 262-4000
Crystal Jones, *Managing Member*
EMP: 11 **EST:** 2016
SALES (est): 834.61K **Privately Held**
Web: www.legacyscreenprinting.net
SIC: 2752 Commercial printing, lithographic

(G-11632)
LESAC CORPORATION (PA)
700 W Michigan Blvd (46360-3285)
PHONE...................................219 879-3215
Richard D Kirsgalvis, *Pr*
▼ **EMP:** 38 **EST:** 1981
SALES (est): 5.25MM
SALES (corp-wide): 5.25MM **Privately Held**
SIC: 3569 2674 Filters, general line: industrial; Bags: uncoated paper and multiwall

(G-11633)
LIGHTHOUSE INDUSTRIES INC
Also Called: East Coast Plastics
107 Eastwood Rd Ste D (46360-2403)
PHONE...................................772 429-1774
Todd Holloway, *Pr*
EMP: 13
SALES (corp-wide): 4.96MM **Privately Held**
Web: www.lighthouseindustries.com
SIC: 3089 Injection molding of plastics
PA: Lighthouse Industries, Inc.
107 Eastwood Rd Ste D
Michigan City IN 46360
219 879-1550

(G-11634)
LIGHTHOUSE INDUSTRIES INC (PA)
107 Eastwood Rd Ste B (46360-2403)
P.O. Box 8905 (46361-8905)
PHONE...................................219 879-1550
Todd J Holloway Senior, *Pr*
John Wojcik, *Pr*
▲ **EMP:** 21 **EST:** 2000
SQ FT: 25,000
SALES (est): 4.96MM
SALES (corp-wide): 4.96MM **Privately Held**
Web: www.lighthouseindustries.com
SIC: 3089 Injection molding of plastics

(G-11635)
LITERATURE SALES
613 Franklin St (46360-3411)
PHONE...................................219 873-3093
Debra Strelesky, *Prin*
EMP: 2 **EST:** 2009
SALES (est): 111.67K **Privately Held**
Web: www.literature-sales.com
SIC: 2721 Magazines: publishing and printing

(G-11636)
MAGAZINE FULFILLMENT CORP
613 Franklin St (46360-3411)
PHONE...................................219 874-4245
Robert W Lake, *Pr*
Ruth Mokrycki, *VP*
EMP: 10 **EST:** 1975
SALES (est): 466.92K **Privately Held**
Web: www.mag-full.com

Michigan City - Laporte County (G-11637)   GEOGRAPHIC SECTION

SIC: 5192 2721 Magazines; Periodicals

(G-11637)
MICHIGAN CITY BREWING CO INC
208 Wabash St (46360-3244)
PHONE..................................219 879-4677
C David Strupeck, *Prin*
EMP: 1 EST: 2006
SALES (est): 124.77K **Privately Held**
Web: www.burnembrewing.com
SIC: 2082 Malt beverages

(G-11638)
MICHIGAN CITY PAPER BOX CO
1206 Pine St (46360-3732)
P.O. Box 275 (46361-0275)
PHONE..................................219 872-8383
Albert A Hoodwin, *CEO*
Linda Hardesty, *
◆ EMP: 70 EST: 1904
SQ FT: 25,000
SALES (est): 8.62MM **Privately Held**
Web: www.buyabox.com
SIC: 2653 Boxes, corrugated: made from purchased materials

(G-11639)
MIDWEST CUSTOM FINISHING INC
800 Royal Rd (46360-2746)
PHONE..................................219 874-0099
Rich Hamm, *VP*
EMP: 18
SIC: 3479 Coating of metals and formed products
PA: Midwest Custom Finishing, Inc.
1906 Clover Rd
Mishawaka IN 46545

(G-11640)
MIDWEST WHEELCOATERS LLC
800 Royal Rd (46360-2746)
PHONE..................................219 874-0099
Richard Hamm, *Managing Member*
EMP: 30 EST: 2006
SALES (est): 2.57MM **Privately Held**
Web: www.wheelcoaters.com
SIC: 3479 Coating of metals and formed products

(G-11641)
MONTGOMERY & ASSOCIATES INC
Also Called: Beacher Business Printers
911 Franklin St (46360)
PHONE..................................219 879-0088
Donald Montgomery, *Pr*
G A Montgomery, *Ch Bd*
Sally Montgomery, *Sec*
Thomas Montgomery, *VP*
EMP: 11 EST: 1976
SQ FT: 3,000
SALES (est): 422.11K **Privately Held**
Web: www.thebeacher.com
SIC: 2752 2711 2789 Offset printing; Newspapers, publishing and printing; Bookbinding and related work

(G-11642)
MTM MACHINING INC
Also Called: Peters & Marske
311 Indiana Highway 212 (46360-2858)
P.O. Box 9348 (46361-9348)
PHONE..................................219 872-8677
Todd Weist, *Pr*
Donna Weist, *Sec*
EMP: 10 EST: 1996
SQ FT: 15,000
SALES (est): 968.29K **Privately Held**
SIC: 3599 7692 3444 Machine shop, jobbing and repair; Welding repair; Sheet metalwork

(G-11643)
MULHERN BELTING INC
910 Indiana Highway 212 (46360-3025)
PHONE..................................201 337-5700
Dan Jonker, *Mgr*
EMP: 6
SALES (corp-wide): 18.1MM **Privately Held**
Web: www.mulhernbelting.com
SIC: 3052 Rubber and plastics hose and beltings
PA: Mulhern Belting, Inc.
148 Bauer Dr
Oakland NJ 07436
201 337-5700

(G-11644)
MYFOODMIXER LLC
Also Called: Chef Mikes Private Chef Catrg
3212 Salem Ct Apt 3 (46360-8044)
PHONE..................................219 229-7036
EMP: 1 EST: 2013
SALES (est): 53.58K **Privately Held**
SIC: 2099 7389 Food preparations, nec; Business Activities at Non-Commercial Site

(G-11645)
NEWS DISPATCH (HQ)
Also Called: Michigan City News Dispatch
422 Franklin St Ste B (46360-3267)
PHONE..................................219 874-7211
J Fred Paxton, *Pr*
▲ EMP: 110 EST: 1919
SQ FT: 25,000
SALES (est): 9.55MM
SALES (corp-wide): 147.64MM **Privately Held**
Web: www.lpheralddispatch.com
SIC: 2711 Newspapers, publishing and printing
PA: Paxton Media Group, Llc
100 Television Ln
Paducah KY 42003
270 575-8630

(G-11646)
NIKE INC
Also Called: Nike
917 Lighthouse Pl (46360-3462)
PHONE..................................219 879-1320
Katie Mcgarry, *Mgr*
EMP: 5
SALES (corp-wide): 51.36B **Publicly Held**
Web: www.nike.com
SIC: 3021 Rubber and plastics footwear
PA: Nike, Inc.
1 Sw Bowerman Dr
Beaverton OR 97005
503 671-6453

(G-11647)
OAK BROOK FOOT ANKLE SPCLSTS P
Also Called: Momentum Foot & Ankle Clinics
10176 W 400 N Ste D (46360-9009)
PHONE..................................219 214-2047
Aamir Mahmood, *Pr*
EMP: 5 EST: 2018
SALES (est): 121.07K **Privately Held**
Web: www.momentumfac.com
SIC: 3842 Supports: abdominal, ankle, arch, kneecap, etc.

(G-11648)
ONLINE PACKAGING INCORPORATED
124 Tri Quad Dr (46360-3182)
PHONE..................................219 872-0925
Tim Wyman, *Brnch Mgr*
EMP: 26

Web: www.onlinepackaging.org
SIC: 5169 2842 Specialty cleaning and sanitation preparations; Polishes and sanitation goods
PA: Online Packaging, Incorporated
4311 Liberty Ln
Plover WI 54467

(G-11649)
PACKAGING GROUP CORP (PA)
2125 E Us Highway 12 Ste C (46360-2198)
PHONE..................................219 879-2500
Elliott Weller, *Pr*
Daniel Goolsby, *VP*
EMP: 19 EST: 1985
SQ FT: 35,000
SALES (est): 2.44MM
SALES (corp-wide): 2.44MM **Privately Held**
Web: www.packaginggroupcorp.com
SIC: 2992 4783 Oils and greases, blending and compounding; Packing and crating

(G-11650)
PANICCIA HEATING & COOLING INC
Also Called: Honeywell Authorized Dealer
5076 N Bleck Rd (46360-9142)
PHONE..................................219 872-2198
EMP: 3 EST: 1993
SALES (est): 485.75K **Privately Held**
Web: www.panicciaheating.com
SIC: 3444 1711 Sheet metalwork; Heating and air conditioning contractors

(G-11651)
PHM BRANDS LLC
1700 E Us Highway 12 (46360-2076)
PHONE..................................219 879-7356
Darren Salyer, *Genl Mgr*
EMP: 26
SALES (corp-wide): 8.32MM **Privately Held**
Web: www.phmbrands.com
SIC: 2041 Wheat flour
PA: Phm Brands, Llc
730 17th St Ste 600
Denver CO 80202
303 927-0762

(G-11652)
PUBLISHERS CONSULTING CORP
613 Franklin St (46360-3411)
PHONE..................................219 874-4245
TOLL FREE: 800
Robert W Lake Junior, *Pr*
EMP: 17 EST: 1979
SQ FT: 25,000
SALES (est): 236.85K **Privately Held**
SIC: 2741 2791 2752 Miscellaneous publishing; Typesetting; Commercial printing, lithographic

(G-11653)
PYRAMID METALLIZING INC
3155 W Dunes Hwy (46360-6764)
PHONE..................................219 879-9967
Bill Cristea, *Pr*
Roger Growden, *Sec*
Kevin Downing, *Treas*
EMP: 7 EST: 1997
SQ FT: 12,000
SALES (est): 758.17K **Privately Held**
SIC: 3479 Coating of metals and formed products

(G-11654)
QUIET STORM PRODUCTIONS LLC
2320 Normandy Dr Apt 3d (46360-7559)
PHONE..................................219 448-1998
EMP: 1 EST: 2017
SALES (est): 39.69K **Privately Held**

SIC: 3999 Manufacturing industries, nec

(G-11655)
R & E PALLET INC
1843 E Us Highway 12 (46360-2075)
PHONE..................................219 873-9671
Salvador Gomez, *Pr*
Isaias Gomez, *VP*
EMP: 4 EST: 2007
SALES (est): 687.39K **Privately Held**
SIC: 2448 Pallets, wood

(G-11656)
RAYS JUICE COMPANY
Also Called: Cold Pressed Juice
1555 Delaware St (46360-6707)
PHONE..................................219 809-7400
Bradly Ray Sheets, *CEO*
EMP: 8 EST: 2021
SALES (est): 150K **Privately Held**
SIC: 2033 Fruits and fruit products, in cans, jars, etc.

(G-11657)
REXFORD RAND CORP (PA)
2123 E Us Highway 12 (46360-2153)
P.O. Box 9005 (46361-9005)
PHONE..................................219 872-5561
Albert I Ancel, *Pr*
Selwyn J Ancel, *Ch Bd*
Doris A Ancel, *Sec*
EMP: 22 EST: 1982
SQ FT: 16,000
SALES (est): 2.1MM
SALES (corp-wide): 2.1MM **Privately Held**
Web: www.rexfordrand.com
SIC: 2842 Specialty cleaning

(G-11658)
RONARD INDUSTRIES INC
Also Called: Olken Company
1005 E Michigan Blvd (46360-2503)
P.O. Box 708 (46361-0708)
PHONE..................................219 874-4801
Leonard Olken, *Pr*
Ruth Olken, *Sec*
EMP: 13 EST: 1965
SALES (est): 499.22K **Privately Held**
Web: www.ronard.com
SIC: 3499 3678 3663 3644 Novelties and giftware, including trophies; Electronic connectors; Radio and t.v. communications equipment; Noncurrent-carrying wiring devices

(G-11659)
SAGER METAL STRIP COMPANY LLC
100 Boone Dr (46360-7703)
PHONE..................................219 874-3609
Michael Brennan, *
◆ EMP: 35 EST: 1976
SQ FT: 88,000
SALES (est): 4.6MM **Privately Held**
Web: www.sagermetal.net
SIC: 3535 Conveyors and conveying equipment

(G-11660)
SAMCO GROUP INC (PA)
Also Called: Peepers Reading Glasses
9935 N Us Highway 12 E (46360-1315)
P.O. Box 739 (46361-0739)
PHONE..................................219 872-4413
Paul Sammann, *Pr*
Teress Sammann, *Sec*
◆ EMP: 4 EST: 1951
SQ FT: 8,500
SALES (est): 4.73MM
SALES (corp-wide): 4.73MM **Privately Held**

Michigan City - Laporte County (G-11684)

Web: www.peepers.com
SIC: 3851 3421 Eyeglasses, lenses and frames; Scissors, shears, clippers, snips, and similar tools

(G-11661)
SAMMANN COMPANY INC
Also Called: Peepers By Peeperspecs
9935 E Us Highway 12 (46360)
PHONE.............................219 872-4413
Alexander Sammann, Pr
Lindsay Sammann, Prin
▲ EMP: 3 EST: 2010
SALES (est): 4.72MM
SALES (corp-wide): 4.73MM Privately Held
Web: www.peepers.com
SIC: 3851 Eyeglasses, lenses and frames
PA: Samco Group, Inc.
9935 E Us Highway 12
Michigan City IN 46360
219 872-4413

(G-11662)
SANDIN MFG LLC
250 Indiana Highway 212 (46360)
PHONE.............................219 872-2253
Keith Sandin, Pr
Helen Sandlin, *
Nat Demaj, *
◆ EMP: 61 EST: 2009
SQ FT: 87,000
SALES (est): 9.94MM Privately Held
Web: www.sandinmanufacturing.com
SIC: 3496 3357 Miscellaneous fabricated wire products; Aircraft wire and cable, nonferrous

(G-11663)
SANDUSKY ABRASIVE WHEEL CO
Also Called: Sandusky-Chicago Abrasive Whl
532 W 4th St (46360)
P.O. Box 9233 (46361)
PHONE.............................219 879-6601
Anthony Llorens, Pr
EMP: 40 EST: 1895
SQ FT: 35,000
SALES (est): 2.53MM Privately Held
Web: www.sanduskychicago.com
SIC: 3291 Wheels, abrasive

(G-11664)
SANLO INC
Also Called: Central Wire Industries
400 Indiana Highway 212 (46360-2821)
PHONE.............................219 879-0241
Paul From, CEO
Christopher Charron, *
◆ EMP: 100 EST: 1957
SQ FT: 100,000
SALES (est): 23.02MM
SALES (corp-wide): 36.28MM Privately Held
Web: www.sanlo.com
SIC: 3315 3496 3357 Cable, steel: insulated or armored; Miscellaneous fabricated wire products; Nonferrous wiredrawing and insulating
HQ: Central Wire, Inc.
6509 Olson Rd
Union IL 60180
800 435-8317

(G-11665)
SANLO MANUFACTURING
400 Indiana Highway 212 (46360)
PHONE.............................219 879-0241
EMP: 8 EST: 2020
SALES (est): 253.77K Privately Held
Web: www.sanlo

SIC: 3999 Manufacturing industries, nec

(G-11666)
SHADY CREEK VINEYARD LLC
2030 Tryon Rd (46360-2814)
PHONE.............................219 874-9463
Tim Anderson, Prin
EMP: 8 EST: 2010
SALES (est): 521.61K Privately Held
Web: www.shadycreekwinery.com
SIC: 2084 Wines

(G-11667)
SHELL CATALYSTS & TECH LP
Also Called: Criterion Catalyst Technologys
1800 E Us Highway 12 (46360-2074)
PHONE.............................219 874-6211
Mik Burke, Mgr
EMP: 113
SALES (corp-wide): 316.62B Privately Held
SIC: 2819 Catalysts, chemical
HQ: Shell Catalysts & Technologies Lp
910 Louisiana St Fl 29
Houston TX 77002
888 737-2377

(G-11668)
SHORELINE EAST INC
301 W Us Highway 20 Ste C (46360-7499)
PHONE.............................219 878-9991
EMP: 4 EST: 1990
SALES (est): 4MM Privately Held
Web: www.shorelineaggregate.com
SIC: 3273 Ready-mixed concrete

(G-11669)
SPECIAL PROJECTS CORP
1 Buckingham Ct (46360-1532)
PHONE.............................219 874-7184
John Bluzma, Owner
EMP: 1 EST: 1990
SALES (est): 83.09K Privately Held
SIC: 2499 Decorative wood and woodwork

(G-11670)
SPINA ENTERPRISES INC ✪
10855 W 400 N (46360)
PHONE.............................219 879-0444
EMP: 7 EST: 2022
SALES (est): 344.14K Privately Held
SIC: 7694 Electric motor repair

(G-11671)
SPX CORPORATION
Marley
500 Blaine St (46360-2387)
PHONE.............................219 879-6561
Rick Millar, Brnch Mgr
EMP: 67
SQ FT: 460,000
SALES (corp-wide): 1.71B Privately Held
Web: www.spx.com
SIC: 3443 Cooling towers, metal plate
HQ: Canvas Sx, Llc
6325 Ardrey Kell Rd Ste 4
Charlotte NC 28277
980 474-3700

(G-11672)
STANDARD INDUSTRIES INC
Also Called: GAF Materials
505 N Roeske Ave (46360-2668)
PHONE.............................219 872-1111
Dwain Dodson, Mgr
EMP: 1
SALES (corp-wide): 6.35B Privately Held
Web: www.gaf.com

SIC: 2493 2952 Insulation and roofing material, reconstituted wood; Asphalt felts and coatings
HQ: Standard Building Solutions Inc.
1 Campus Dr
Parsippany NJ 07054

(G-11673)
STRANCO INC
1306 W Us Highway 20 (46360-6899)
PHONE.............................219 874-5221
Steve Depalma, Pr
EMP: 14 EST: 1954
SQ FT: 25,000
SALES (est): 2.46MM Privately Held
Web: www.strancoinc.com
SIC: 2759 Labels and seals: printing, nsk

(G-11674)
SULLAIR CORPORATION
1000 Kieffer Rd (46360-0008)
PHONE.............................219 861-5005
EMP: 9 EST: 2017
SALES (est): 654.18K Privately Held
Web: europe.sullair.com
SIC: 3563 Air and gas compressors

(G-11675)
SULLIVAN-PALATEK INC
1201 W Us Highway 20 (46360-6851)
PHONE.............................219 874-2497
Robert Mcfee, Pr
◆ EMP: 145 EST: 1988
SQ FT: 180,000
SALES (est): 45.62MM
SALES (corp-wide): 45.62MM Privately Held
Web: www.sullivan-palatek.com
SIC: 3563 Air and gas compressors including vacuum pumps
PA: G.H.S. Corporation
2813 Wilbur St
Springfield MI 49037
800 388-4447

(G-11676)
TEACO INC
2117 Ohio St (46360-5830)
P.O. Box E (46361-0290)
PHONE.............................219 874-6234
Ross Terry, Pr
Margaret Terry, VP
EMP: 5 EST: 1976
SQ FT: 5,600
SALES (est): 467.47K Privately Held
Web: www.teacoinc.com
SIC: 7629 7389 3825 3672 Electronic equipment repair; Inspection and testing services; Test equipment for electronic and electrical circuits; Printed circuit boards

(G-11677)
TEMPESTA MEDIA LLC
315 Washington Park Blvd (46360-2379)
PHONE.............................312 371-0555
EMP: 1 EST: 2011
SALES (est): 182.53K Privately Held
Web: www.tempestamedia.com
SIC: 2741 Internet publishing and broadcasting

(G-11678)
THOMAS MADISON
Also Called: Madison Printing & Mailing
450 St John Rd Ste 201-5 (46360-7354)
PHONE.............................312 625-9152
Thomas Madison, Owner
EMP: 5 EST: 2013
SQ FT: 1,300
SALES (est): 233.65K Privately Held

SIC: 2752 Commercial printing, lithographic

(G-11679)
TMAK INC
Also Called: Quality Industrial Service
200 Winski Dr (46360-4174)
P.O. Box 738 (46361-0738)
PHONE.............................219 874-7661
Timothy Johnson, Pr
Michelle Bazin-johnson, VP
▼ EMP: 27 EST: 1983
SQ FT: 10,700
SALES (est): 2.4MM Privately Held
Web: www.qisautomate.com
SIC: 3544 3599 Special dies and tools; Custom machinery

(G-11680)
TRIPLEX PLATING INC
1555 E Us Highway 12 (46360-2002)
PHONE.............................219 874-3209
James A Baldwin, CEO
Debra Sydrow, *
EMP: 40 EST: 1939
SQ FT: 28,200
SALES (est): 4.37MM Privately Held
Web: www.triplexplating.com
SIC: 3471 Electroplating of metals or formed products

(G-11681)
TT MACHINING & FABRICATING LLC
228 Indiana Highway 212 (46360-2857)
PHONE.............................219 878-0399
Thomas Lynch, Mgr
EMP: 11 EST: 2015
SALES (est): 476.13K Privately Held
Web: www.ttmachfab.com
SIC: 3599 Machine shop, jobbing and repair

(G-11682)
USALCO MICHIGAN CITY PLANT LLC
1750 E Us Highway 12 (46360-2076)
PHONE.............................219 873-0914
Peter Askew, Mgr
EMP: 7
SALES (corp-wide): 243.29MM Privately Held
Web: www.usalco.com
SIC: 2819 Industrial inorganic chemicals, nec
PA: Usalco Michigan City Plant, Llc
2601 Cannery Ave
Baltimore MD 21226
410 918-2230

(G-11683)
VACUUM TECHNIQUE LLC (HQ)
Also Called: Atlas Copco Vacuum
935 S Woodland Ave (46360-5672)
PHONE.............................800 848-4511
Jerry Geenen, Mgr
EMP: 25 EST: 2020
SALES (est): 20.37MM Privately Held
Web: www.atlascopco.us
SIC: 3563 Vacuum pumps, except laboratory
PA: Atlas Copco Ab
Sickla Industrivag 19
Nacka 131 5
87438000

(G-11684)
VANAIR MANUFACTURING INC (PA)
Also Called: Vanair
10896 W 300 N (46360)
PHONE.............................219 879-5100
Ralph Kokot, CEO
Greg Kokot, *
Ralph Kokot Iii, VP
Sara Tilden, *
John Graun Senior, VP
◆ EMP: 161 EST: 1972

(PA)=Parent Co (HQ)=Headquarters
✪ = New Business established in last 2 years

Michigan City - Laporte County (G-11685)

SQ FT: 18,000
SALES (est): 29.12MM
SALES (corp-wide): 29.12MM **Privately Held**
Web: www.vanair.com
SIC: **3713** 3563 3621 3566 Truck and bus bodies; Air and gas compressors including vacuum pumps; Motors and generators; Speed changers, drives, and gears

(G-11685)
VANITY FAIR BRANDS LP
1500 Lighthouse Pl (46360-3449)
PHONE...............................219 861-0205
EMP: 27
SALES (corp-wide): 364.48B **Publicly Held**
Web: www.fotlinc.com
SIC: **2341** Nightgowns and negligees: women's and children's
HQ: Vanity Fair Brands, Lp
    1 Fruit Of The Loom Dr
    Bowling Green KY 42103
    270 781-6400

(G-11686)
VITAMINS INC
1700 E Us Highway 12 (46360-2076)
PHONE...............................219 879-7356
Darin Salyer, *Brnch Mgr*
EMP: 46
SALES (corp-wide): 7.29MM **Privately Held**
Web: www.vitamins-inc.com
SIC: **2041** 2833 5122 2087 Wheat germ; Vitamins, natural or synthetic: bulk, uncompounded; Drugs, proprietaries, and sundries; Flavoring extracts and syrups, nec
PA: Vitamins, Inc.
    315 Fullerton Ave
    Carol Stream IL 60188

(G-11687)
WILLIAMS WEST & WITTS PDTS CO
Also Called: Integrative Flavors
3501 W Dunes Hwy (46360)
P.O. Box 61 (46361)
PHONE...............................219 879-8236
Georgeann Quealy, *Pr*
Brian Quealy, *Ex VP*
EMP: 9 EST: 1945
SALES (est): 1.25MM **Privately Held**
Web: www.integrativeflavors.com
SIC: **2034** 2099 Dried and dehydrated soup mixes; Sauce, gravy, dressing, and dip mixes

(G-11688)
WOODLAND LBOR RLTONS CNSLTING
15 Bristol Dr (46360-1977)
PHONE...............................219 879-6095
Douglas Bobillo, *Prin*
EMP: 5 EST: 2015
SALES (est): 50.24K **Privately Held**
SIC: **2499** Wood products, nec

Michigantown
Clinton County

(G-11689)
CRENSHAW PAVING INCORPORATED
Also Called: Crenshaw Paving
7304 E County Road 100 N (46057-9774)
PHONE...............................765 249-2342
Robert Crenshaw, *Pr*
Janet Crenshaw, *Sec*
Bryan Crenshaw, *VP*
EMP: 8 EST: 1965
SALES (est): 849.12K **Privately Held**
Web: www.crenshawpaving.com
SIC: **3272** Paving materials, prefabricated concrete

(G-11690)
ENGINEERING AGGREGATES CORP
Also Called: Michigan Stone Company Div
803 Main St (46057-9567)
PHONE...............................765 249-3073
Gary Thompson, *Mgr*
EMP: 2
SALES (corp-wide): 2.5MM **Privately Held**
Web: www.engagg.com
SIC: **1442** Construction sand and gravel
PA: Engineering Aggregates Corp
    2413 S County Road 150 E
    Logansport IN 46947
    574 722-3040

(G-11691)
KEYSTONE COOPERATIVE INC
805 East St (46057-9558)
P.O. Box 26 (46057-0026)
PHONE...............................765 249-2233
Joe Rule, *Brnch Mgr*
EMP: 8
SALES (corp-wide): 570.05MM **Privately Held**
Web: www.keystonecoop.com
SIC: **5153** 5171 5191 2875 Grains; Petroleum bulk stations and terminals; Feed ; Fertilizers, mixing only
PA: Keystone Cooperative, Inc.
    770 N High School
    Indianapolis IN 46214
    800 525-0272

Middlebury
Elkhart County

(G-11692)
A & R MACHINE SHOP LLP
14719 County Road 20 (46540-9649)
PHONE...............................574 825-5686
Rudy J Miller, *Pt*
Delbert R Miller, *Pt*
Wayne Miller, *Pt*
Wilbur Miller, *Pt*
Calvin Miller, *Pt*
EMP: 22 EST: 1969
SQ FT: 34,000
SALES (est): 943.08K **Privately Held**
SIC: **3599** Machine shop, jobbing and repair

(G-11693)
ALL AMERICAN GROUP INC
All American Specialty Vehicle
51165 Greenfield Pkwy (46540-8220)
PHONE...............................574 825-1720
Don Roberts, *Off Mgr*
EMP: 1
Web: www.arbocsv.com
SIC: **3716** Motor homes
HQ: All American Group, Inc.
    2831 Dexter Dr
    Elkhart IN 46514
    574 262-0123

(G-11694)
ALL AMERICAN GROUP INC
Coachmen Recreational Vehicle
423 N Main St (46540-9218)
P.O. Box 30 (46540-0030)
PHONE...............................574 825-5821
Michael Terlep, *Mgr*
EMP: 1
Web: www.coachmenrv.com
SIC: **3716** 3792 5012 Motor homes; Travel trailers and campers; Recreational vehicles, motor homes, and trailers
HQ: All American Group, Inc.
    2831 Dexter Dr
    Elkhart IN 46514
    574 262-0123

(G-11695)
ALL AMERICAN GROUP INC
Shasta Industries
14489 Us Highway 20 (46540-9733)
P.O. Box 30 (46540-0030)
PHONE...............................574 825-8555
Robert Adasiak, *Brnch Mgr*
EMP: 1
SQ FT: 80,000
Web: www.shastarving.com
SIC: **3792** 5012 Travel trailers and campers; Recreational vehicles, motor homes, and trailers
HQ: All American Group, Inc.
    2831 Dexter Dr
    Elkhart IN 46514
    574 262-0123

(G-11696)
APEX DOORS PLUS LLC
420 N Main St (46540-8985)
PHONE...............................574 370-0906
Mitchell Hawkins, *Managing Member*
EMP: 5 EST: 2020
SALES (est): 460.74K **Privately Held**
SIC: **3599** Machine and other job shop work

(G-11697)
ARBOC SPECIALTY VEHICLES LLC
51165 Greenfield Pkwy (46540)
PHONE...............................574 825-1720
John Proven, *Pr*
EMP: 99 EST: 2011
SALES (est): 21.03MM
SALES (corp-wide): 2.05B **Privately Held**
Web: www.arbocsv.com
SIC: **3713** Truck and bus bodies
PA: Nfi Group Inc
    711 Kernaghan Ave
    Winnipeg MB R2C 3
    204 224-1251

(G-11698)
ARBOR INDUSTRIES INC
117 14th Ave (46540-9222)
P.O. Box 313 (46540-0313)
PHONE...............................574 825-2375
David Sheeley, *Pr*
David Baylis, *VP*
EMP: 30 EST: 1974
SQ FT: 24,000
SALES (est): 881.06K **Privately Held**
Web: www.arborindustriesinc.com
SIC: **2421** Custom sawmill

(G-11699)
ARTISAN INTERIORS INC (PA)
526 S Main St (46540-9701)
P.O. Box 165 (46550-0165)
PHONE...............................574 825-9494
Jane E Yoder, *Pr*
Eli Yoder, *Sec*
EMP: 55 EST: 1971
SQ FT: 30,000
SALES (est): 2.4MM
SALES (corp-wide): 2.4MM **Privately Held**
Web: www.artisaninteriorsinc.com
SIC: **2391** 2392 Draperies, plastic and textile: from purchased materials; Bedspreads and bed sets: made from purchased materials

(G-11700)
B&J ROCKET AMERICA INC
325 N Main St (46540-9003)
PHONE...............................574 825-5802
Andreas Muller, *CEO*
▲ EMP: 20 EST: 1982
SQ FT: 38,000
SALES (est): 2.49MM **Privately Held**
Web: www.bj-rocket.com
SIC: **3469** 3599 3544 3398 Stamping metal for the trade; Machine shop, jobbing and repair; Special dies and tools; Metal heat treating

(G-11701)
BANNERS UNLIMITED
509 S Main St (46540-9004)
P.O. Box 538 (46540-0538)
PHONE...............................574 825-8070
David Kimmell, *Owner*
EMP: 3 EST: 1994
SALES (est): 100K **Privately Held**
Web: flag-and-banner-dealers.cmac.ws
SIC: **3993** Signs and advertising specialties

(G-11702)
BAWLING ACRES WOODWORKING LLC
155 S 1000 W (46540-9374)
PHONE...............................260 768-3214
EMP: 4 EST: 2018
SALES (est): 54.13K **Privately Held**
SIC: **2431** Millwork

(G-11703)
CLASSEE VINYL WINDOWS LLC
59323 County Road 35 (46540-8850)
PHONE...............................574 825-7863
EMP: 6 EST: 1992
SALES (est): 941.14K **Privately Held**
SIC: **3442** 5211 Louver windows, metal; Windows, storm: wood or metal

(G-11704)
COACHMEN RECRTL VHCL CO LLC
423 N Main St (46540-9218)
P.O. Box 30 (46540-0030)
PHONE...............................574 825-5821
Michael Terlep, *Managing Member*
EMP: 1 EST: 2000
SALES (est): 21.82MM **Privately Held**
Web: www.coachmenrv.com
SIC: **5012** 3716 3792 Automobiles and other motor vehicles; Motor homes; Travel trailers and campers
HQ: All American Group, Inc.
    2831 Dexter Dr
    Elkhart IN 46514
    574 262-0123

(G-11705)
CORNERSTONE BUSINESS PRTG LLC
801 Wayne St Ste 11 (46540-9074)
PHONE...............................574 642-4060
EMP: 6 EST: 2017
SALES (est): 287.53K **Privately Held**
Web: www.cornerstonebusinessprinting.com
SIC: **2752** Offset printing

(G-11706)
COUNTRY CORNER WOODWORKS LLC
13775 County Road 22 (46540-9104)
PHONE...............................574 825-6782
Lavern Lambright, *Managing Member*
EMP: 3 EST: 2002
SALES (est): 212.45K **Privately Held**

GEOGRAPHIC SECTION
Middlebury - Elkhart County (G-11731)

SIC: 2599 1751 Cabinets, factory; Cabinet building and installation

(G-11707)
COUNTY LINE CABINETRY LLC
705 N 1200 W (46540-9301)
PHONE.....................574 642-1202
Verlin Lehman, *Prin*
EMP: 4 **EST:** 2010
SALES (est): 248.85K **Privately Held**
SIC: 2434 Wood kitchen cabinets

(G-11708)
CSI MANUFACTURING INC
209 York Dr (46540-9101)
PHONE.....................574 825-7891
EMP: 10 **EST:** 1984
SQ FT: 24,000
SALES (est): 2.28MM **Privately Held**
Web: www.coulterone.com
SIC: 1721 3499 Commercial painting; Aerosol valves, metal

(G-11709)
CULVER DUCK FARMS INC
Also Called: Culver
12215 County Road 10 (46540-9694)
PHONE.....................574 825-9537
Joe Jurgielewicz, *Pr*
▼ **EMP:** 235 **EST:** 1977
SQ FT: 35,000
SALES (est): 41.78MM **Privately Held**
Web: www.culverduck.com
SIC: 2015 Duck slaughtering and processing

(G-11710)
D & M SALES LLC
Also Called: D&M Plywood Sales
13487 County Road 22 (46540-9076)
PHONE.....................574 825-9024
EMP: 5 **EST:** 2002
SQ FT: 150
SALES (est): 675.33K **Privately Held**
SIC: 2435 Plywood, hardwood or hardwood faced

(G-11711)
DIAMOND COMPONENTS INC
Also Called: Diamond Specialty Vehicles
109 14th Ave Ste 1 (46540)
PHONE.....................574 358-0452
Eric J Stutzman, *CEO*
EMP: 40 **EST:** 2017
SALES (est): 4.76MM **Privately Held**
Web: www.elkharttrailers.com
SIC: 3715 Truck trailers

(G-11712)
DIRTY SQUEEGEE SCREEN PRTG LLC
57319 County Road 35 (46540-9720)
PHONE.....................574 358-0003
Amy Miller, *Prin*
EMP: 8 **EST:** 2012
SALES (est): 277.96K **Privately Held**
Web: www.dirtysqueegee.com
SIC: 2759 Screen printing

(G-11713)
DUTCH COUNTRY ORGANICS LLC
407 N Main St (46540-9218)
PHONE.....................574 536-7403
Lamar Bontrager, *Managing Member*
▲ **EMP:** 36 **EST:** 2012
SALES (est): 2.66MM **Privately Held**
Web: www.dcollc.com
SIC: 2015 Egg processing

(G-11714)
ELKHART COUNTY GRAVEL INC
56570 County Road 35 (46540-8755)
PHONE.....................574 825-7913
EMP: 3
SALES (corp-wide): 4.21MM **Privately Held**
Web: www.elkhartcountygravel.com
SIC: 3273 Ready-mixed concrete
PA: Elkhart County Gravel Inc
19242 Us Highway 6
New Paris IN 46553
574 831-2815

(G-11715)
ESSENHAUS INC
Also Called: Essenhaus Foods
240 W Us Highway 20 (46540-9713)
PHONE.....................574 825-6790
Robert Miller, *Ch Bd*
Lance Miller, *
Joel Miller, *
EMP: 300 **EST:** 1971
SQ FT: 65,000
SALES (est): 24.07MM **Privately Held**
Web: www.essenhaus.com
SIC: 5812 2098 Restaurant, family: independent; Noodles (e.g. egg, plain, and water), dry

(G-11716)
FOUR STAR WELDING
11400 W 300n (46540)
PHONE.....................574 825-3856
EMP: 4 **EST:** 2013
SALES (est): 111.12K **Privately Held**
SIC: 7692 Welding repair

(G-11717)
GBO CORPORATION
Also Called: Steelmaster
106 Industrial Pkwy E (46540)
PHONE.....................574 825-7670
Paul Culp, *Pr*
Kathy Culp, *Sec*
EMP: 18 **EST:** 1984
SALES (est): 746.61K **Privately Held**
Web: www.steelmastercorp.com
SIC: 3469 Stamping metal for the trade

(G-11718)
GOHN BROS MANUFACTURING CO
105 S Main St (46540-4001)
P.O. Box 1110 (46540-1110)
PHONE.....................574 825-2400
John Swartzentruber, *Owner*
EMP: 8 **EST:** 1902
SQ FT: 6,000
SALES (est): 546.38K **Privately Held**
Web: www.gohnbrothers.com
SIC: 2326 5611 5331 5949 Work apparel, except uniforms; Clothing accessories: men's and boys'; Variety stores; Fabric stores piece goods

(G-11719)
GRAND DESIGN RV LLC (HQ)
Also Called: Black Bear Recrtl Vehicles
11333 County Road 2 (46540-9632)
PHONE.....................574 825-8000
Donald Clark, *Pr*
EMP: 150 **EST:** 2012
SALES (est): 99.78MM
SALES (corp-wide): 3.49B **Publicly Held**
Web: www.granddesignrv.com
SIC: 7519 3799 Recreational vehicle rental; Recreational vehicles
PA: Winnebago Industries, Inc.
13200 Pioneer Trl
Eden Prairie MN 55347
952 829-8600

(G-11720)
HELPING HRTS HELPING HANDS INC
411 E Warren St (46540-9546)
PHONE.....................248 980-5090
Nancy Sebring-cale, *Prin*
EMP: 6 **EST:** 2010
SALES (est): 55.9K **Privately Held**
Web: www.helpingheartshelpinghands.org
SIC: 2515 Foundations and platforms

(G-11721)
HICKORY HILL SOAP
13993 County Road 12 (46540-8703)
PHONE.....................574 825-9853
Lori Lyles, *Mgr*
EMP: 5 **EST:** 1989
SALES (est): 82.03K **Privately Held**
Web: www.hickoryhillsoap.com
SIC: 2841 Soap and other detergents

(G-11722)
IDEAL COATINGS LLC
11431 County Road 10 (46540-8927)
PHONE.....................574 358-0182
EMP: 12 **EST:** 2017
SALES (est): 1.05MM **Privately Held**
Web: www.idealcoatings.com
SIC: 3479 Metal coating and allied services

(G-11723)
INDIANA GALVANIZING LLC
51702 Lovejoy Dr (46540-9591)
PHONE.....................574 822-9102
John Monnig, *Pr*
EMP: 35 **EST:** 2012
SQ FT: 95
SALES (est): 2.51MM **Privately Held**
Web: www.indianagalvanizing.com
SIC: 3479 Coating of metals and formed products

(G-11724)
INDIANA WOOD PRODUCTS INC
58228 County Road 43 (46540-9555)
P.O. Box 1168 (46540-1168)
PHONE.....................574 825-2129
Daniel Sherman, *Ch Bd*
Mary Lou Hetler, *
Rick Hetler, *General Vice President*
Sarah Mc Cann, *
Jennifer Davis, *
EMP: 85 **EST:** 1954
SQ FT: 55,000
SALES (est): 5.33MM **Privately Held**
SIC; 2426 2448 2421 2441 Lumber, hardwood dimension; Pallets, wood; Sawmills and planing mills, general; Nailed wood boxes and shook

(G-11725)
INTEPLAST BUILDING PRODUCTS
219 W Us Highway 20 (46540-9713)
PHONE.....................574 825-5845
Ty Scopel, *Genl Mgr*
EMP: 17 **EST:** 2016
SALES (est): 2.25MM **Privately Held**
Web: www.inteplast.com
SIC: 3089 Plastics products, nec

(G-11726)
IP MOULDING INC
219 W Us Highway 20 (46540-9713)
PHONE.....................574 825-5845
John Young, *CEO*
EMP: 83 **EST:** 2013
SALES (est): 9.09MM **Privately Held**
Web: temp.inteplast.com

SIC: 2821 Plastics materials and resins
PA: Inteplast Group Corporation
9 Peach Tree Hill Rd
Livingston NJ 07039

(G-11727)
JAYCO INC (HQ)
Also Called: Bottom Line Rv
903 S Main St (46540)
P.O. Box 460 (46540)
PHONE.....................574 825-5861
Derald Bontrager, *Pr*
Derald Bontrager, *Pr*
Ken Walters, *
◆ **EMP:** 1550 **EST:** 1968
SQ FT: 700,000
SALES (est): 473.94MM
SALES (corp-wide): 11.12B **Publicly Held**
Web: www.jayco.com
SIC: 5013 3716 3792 Trailer parts and accessories; Motor homes; House trailers, except as permanent dwellings
PA: Thor Industries, Inc.
601 E Beardsley Ave
Elkhart IN 46514
574 970-7460

(G-11728)
JOMAR MACHINING & FABG INC
13393 County Road 22 (46540-9039)
PHONE.....................574 825-9837
Lavon Detweiler, *Pr*
Geff Fisher, *
Matt Troyer, *
EMP: 30 **EST:** 2007
SQ FT: 15,700
SALES (est): 4.81MM **Privately Held**
Web: www.4jomar.com
SIC: 3599 7692 3594 1799 Machine shop, jobbing and repair; Welding repair; Fluid power pumps and motors; Welding on site

(G-11729)
JOYFULLY SAID SIGNS LLC
402 E Warren St (46540-9546)
PHONE.....................574 596-9949
Chelsea Gorsuch, *Prin*
EMP: 8 **EST:** 2016
SALES (est): 475.52K **Privately Held**
Web: www.joyfullysaid.com
SIC: 3993 Signs and advertising specialties

(G-11730)
L & W ENGINEERING INC
107 Industrial Pkwy E (46540-8511)
PHONE.....................574 825-5351
Roger Huffman, *Pr*
Wilbur Bontrager, *
Kennard Weaver, *
Robert M Sutter, *
Ashley May, *
EMP: 200 **EST:** 1968
SQ FT: 100,000
SALES (est): 27.31MM **Privately Held**
Web: www.lw-eng.com
SIC: 3714 3429 3499 3498 Motor vehicle body components and frame; Hardware, nec; Metal ladders; Fabricated pipe and fittings

(G-11731)
LA WOODWORKING LLC ✪
10328 County Road 24 (46540-9791)
PHONE.....................574 825-5580
EMP: 5 **EST:** 2022
SALES (est): 54.13K **Privately Held**
SIC: 2431 Millwork

Middlebury - Elkhart County (G-11732) — GEOGRAPHIC SECTION

(G-11732)
LANE SHADY WELDING LLC
56322 Cr35 (46540-8753)
P.O. Box 1135 (46540-1135)
PHONE.................574 825-5553
James E Miller, Admn
EMP: 6 EST: 2010
SALES (est): 99.11K Privately Held
Web: www.importantlocalbusinesses.com
SIC: 7692 Welding repair

(G-11733)
LGS INDUSTRIES LLC (HQ)
Also Called: Look Trailers
11550 Harter Dr (46540-9663)
P.O. Box 339 (46507-0339)
PHONE.................574 848-5665
EMP: 21 EST: 2010
SQ FT: 50,000
SALES (est): 29.05MM Privately Held
Web: www.looktrailers.com
SIC: 5599 3715 Utility trailers; Truck trailers
PA: Novae Llc
    1 Novae Pkwy
    Markle IN 46770

(G-11734)
LIPPERT COMPONENTS INC
51040 Greenfield Pkwy (46540-8981)
PHONE.................574 312-7445
EMP: 26
SALES (corp-wide): 3.78B Publicly Held
Web: www.lci1.com
SIC: 3711 3469 3444 3714 Chassis, motor vehicle; Stamping metal for the trade; Metal roofing and roof drainage equipment; Motor vehicle parts and accessories
HQ: Lippert Components, Inc.
    3501 County Rd 6 E
    Elkhart IN 46514
    574 535-1125

(G-11735)
LOUISIANA-PACIFIC CORPORATION
Also Called: LP Middlebury
219 W Us Highway 20 (46540-9713)
PHONE.................574 825-5845
Mercer Dave, CEO
EMP: 53
SALES (corp-wide): 4.55B Publicly Held
Web: www.lpcorp.com
SIC: 2431 Moldings and baseboards, ornamental and trim
PA: Louisiana-Pacific Corporation
    1610 West End Ave Ste 200
    Nashville TN 37203
    615 986-5600

(G-11736)
MHP HOLDINGS INC (HQ)
Also Called: Middlebury Hardwood Pdts Inc
101 Joan Dr (46540)
PHONE.................574 825-9524
Charles E Lamb, Pr
Chuck Lamb, *
Mike Wagner, *
▲ EMP: 135 EST: 1985
SQ FT: 2,000
SALES (est): 19.6MM
SALES (corp-wide): 3.47B Publicly Held
Web: www.mhpi.us
SIC: 2431 2541 2511 1751 Doors and door parts and trim, wood; Cabinets, except refrigerated: show, display, etc.: wood; Chairs, household, except upholstered: wood; Cabinet and finish carpentry
PA: Patrick Industries, Inc.
    107 W Franklin St
    Elkhart IN 46516
    574 294-7511

(G-11737)
MIDDLEBURY CHEESE COMPANY LLC (HQ)
Also Called: Deutsch Kase Haus Inc
11275 W 250 N (46540-7708)
PHONE.................574 825-9511
Richard Guggisber, Pr
EMP: 12 EST: 1978
SQ FT: 40,000
SALES (est): 4.85MM
SALES (corp-wide): 18.44MM Privately Held
Web: www.mimilk.com
SIC: 2022 Cheese spreads, dips, pastes, and other cheese products
PA: Guggisberg Cheese, Inc.
    5060 State Route 557
    Millersburg OH 44654
    330 893-2550

(G-11738)
MILLERS MILL
55514 County Road 8 (46540-9539)
PHONE.................574 825-2010
Alta Miller, Owner
EMP: 6 EST: 1977
SALES (est): 241.63K Privately Held
Web: www.millerswindmillservice.com
SIC: 2099 2033 Cider, nonalcoholic; Canned fruits and specialties

(G-11739)
MILLERS WINDMILL SERVICE
Also Called: Sam's Windmill Service
14386 County Road 14 (46540-9527)
PHONE.................574 825-2877
EMP: 4 EST: 1993
SALES (est): 286.24K Privately Held
Web: www.millerswindmillservice.com
SIC: 3523 Windmills for pumping water, agricultural

(G-11740)
MILLERS WOODNTHINGS INC
11894 County Rd 14 (46540)
P.O. Box 725 (46540-0725)
PHONE.................574 825-2996
Jerry Miller, Pr
EMP: 10 EST: 1982
SALES (est): 447.97K Privately Held
SIC: 2511 2499 End tables: wood; Decorative wood and woodwork

(G-11741)
NORTH CENTRAL EQUIPMENT C
59871 E County Line Rd (46540-9790)
PHONE.................574 825-2006
EMP: 1 EST: 2010
SQ FT: 144
SALES (est): 244.57K Privately Held
SIC: 5046 3537 Commercial equipment, nec; Forklift trucks

(G-11742)
NRC MODIFICATIONS INC
51045 Greenfield Pkwy (46540-8982)
PHONE.................574 825-3646
Nick Cook, Pr
J Michael Lapp, VP
EMP: 14 EST: 1993
SQ FT: 20,000
SALES (est): 1.41MM Privately Held
Web: www.nrcmod.com
SIC: 3713 3711 Truck bodies (motor vehicles); Motor vehicles and car bodies

(G-11743)
OLD HOOSIER MEATS
101 Wayne St (46540-9221)
PHONE.................574 825-2940
Len Miller, Owner
EMP: 5 EST: 1945
SALES (est): 246.01K Privately Held
SIC: 2011 Meat by-products, from meat slaughtered on site

(G-11744)
PACE AMERICAN ENTERPRISES INC (HQ)
11550 Harter Dr (46540-9663)
PHONE.................800 247-5767
James R Tennant, CEO
Jack Cordan, *
Richard J Mullin, *
Peter Y Lee, *
EMP: 83 EST: 1986
SQ FT: 400,000
SALES (est): 55.42MM
SALES (corp-wide): 3.46B Privately Held
Web: www.paceamerican.com
SIC: 3715 Demountable cargo containers
PA: Sun Capital Partners, Inc.
    5200 Town Ctr Cr Fl 4
    Boca Raton FL 33486
    561 394-0550

(G-11745)
PARKLAND PLASTICS INC
104 Yoder Dr (46540)
P.O. Box 339 (46540-0339)
PHONE.................574 825-4336
◆ EMP: 30
Web: www.parklandplastics.com
SIC: 5162 3083 Plastics sheets and rods; Plastics finished products, laminated

(G-11746)
PATRICK INDUSTRIES INC
Also Called: Parkland Plastics
104 Yoder Dr (46540)
PHONE.................574 825-4336
EMP: 30
SALES (corp-wide): 3.47B Publicly Held
Web: www.patrickind.com
SIC: 5561 3083 Recreational vehicle dealers; Plastics finished products, laminated
PA: Patrick Industries, Inc.
    107 W Franklin St
    Elkhart IN 46516

(G-11747)
PUMPKIN PATCH MARKET INC
10532 Us Highway 20 (46540-9557)
PHONE.................574 825-3312
EMP: 5 EST: 1994
SALES (est): 451.83K Privately Held
Web: www.pumpkinpatchmarket.com
SIC: 2491 2434 2499 Wood products, creosoted; Wood kitchen cabinets; Decorative wood and woodwork

(G-11748)
SCHROCK METAL FAB LLC
54039 County Road 43 (46540-9617)
PHONE.................574 825-5653
EMP: 4 EST: 2008
SALES (est): 110K Privately Held
SIC: 3441 Fabricated structural metal

(G-11749)
SCHROEDER LOG HOME SUPPLY INC
409 W Berry St (46540-8621)
P.O. Box 264 (46540-0264)
PHONE.................574 825-1054
EMP: 1
SALES (corp-wide): 2.21MM Privately Held
Web: www.loghelp.com
SIC: 2452 Log cabins, prefabricated, wood
PA: Schroeder Log Home Supply Inc
    1101 Se 7th Ave
    Grand Rapids MN 55744
    218 326-4434

(G-11750)
SCHULT HOMES CORP
221 W Us Highway 20 (46540-7201)
P.O. Box 1218 (46540-1218)
PHONE.................574 825-5880
Tracy Smith, Prin
EMP: 10 EST: 2004
SALES (est): 222.32K Privately Held
SIC: 2451 Mobile homes

(G-11751)
SHOWHAULERS TRUCKS INC
Also Called: Showhaulers
114 Industrial Pkwy E (46540-8510)
P.O. Box 9 (46540-0009)
PHONE.................574 825-6764
Kermit L Troyer, Pr
Chad Troyer, *
EMP: 35 EST: 2000
SQ FT: 23,500
SALES (est): 4.55MM Privately Held
Web: www.showhauler.com
SIC: 3799 Recreational vehicles

(G-11752)
SHOWTIME CONVERSIONS INC
116 Industrial Pkwy E (46540-8510)
P.O. Box 810 (46540-0810)
PHONE.................574 825-1130
EMP: 50 EST: 1995
SALES (est): 2.01MM Privately Held
Web: www.showtimeconversions.com
SIC: 7532 3537 5012 Customizing services, nonfactory basis; Industrial trucks and tractors; Recreational vehicles, motor homes, and trailers

(G-11753)
T K T INC
Also Called: Woodie's Coverup
420 N Main St (46540-8985)
P.O. Box 25 (46540-0025)
PHONE.................574 825-5233
Todd Taylor, Pr
EMP: 4 EST: 1982
SALES (est): 402.8K Privately Held
SIC: 2399 3714 3011 Tire covers; Motor vehicle parts and accessories; Tires and inner tubes

(G-11754)
TCB ENTERPRISES LLC
51165 Greenfield Pkwy (46540-8220)
PHONE.................574 522-3971
▲ EMP: 10 EST: 2010
SALES (est): 2.57MM
SALES (corp-wide): 2.05B Privately Held
SIC: 3743 3647 3498 Trackless trolley buses; Vehicular lighting equipment; Tube fabricating (contract bending and shaping)
PA: Nfi Group Inc
    711 Kernaghan Ave
    Winnipeg MB R2C 3
    204 224-1251

(G-11755)
UPCYCLE INDUSTRIAL INC
221 W Us Highway 20 Ste B (46540-7200)
PHONE.................574 825-4990
Jeremy Wingard, Prin
EMP: 8 EST: 2015
SALES (est): 258.7K Privately Held
SIC: 3999 Manufacturing industries, nec

▲ = Import ▼ = Export
◆ = Import/Export

GEOGRAPHIC SECTION

Milan - Ripley County (G-11781)

(G-11756)
WARD INDUSTRIES INC
58582 State Road 13 (46540-8805)
PHONE...................574 825-2548
Derek G Ward, Pr
EMP: 11 EST: 1980
SQ FT: 20,000
SALES (est): 850.92K **Privately Held**
Web: www.wardindustries.com
SIC: 3648 3645 3446 3993 Lanterns: electric, gas, carbide, kerosene, or gasoline; Residential lighting fixtures; Lamp posts, metal; Signs and advertising specialties

(G-11757)
WASHBURN HEATING & AC
Also Called: Honeywell Authorized Dealer
54761 County Road 8 (46540-9516)
P.O. Box 1428 (46540-1428)
PHONE...................574 825-7697
EMP: 4 EST: 1994
SALES (est): 365.25K **Privately Held**
Web: www.washburnheatingandcooling.com
SIC: 3585 1711 Heating and air conditioning combination units; Heating and air conditioning contractors

(G-11758)
WHITETAIL HEARTBEAT
61755 State Road 13 (46540-9758)
PHONE...................260 336-1052
Faron Yoder, Prin
EMP: 3 EST: 2011
SALES (est): 171.03K **Privately Held**
SIC: 2721 Periodicals, publishing only

(G-11759)
WINNEBAGO OF INDIANA LLC
Also Called: Sunnybrook Rv
201 14th Ave (46540-9647)
PHONE...................574 825-5250
▼ EMP: 200 EST: 2010
SALES (est): 49.66MM
SALES (corp-wide): 3.49B **Publicly Held**
Web: www.winnebago.com
SIC: 3792 Trailer coaches, automobile
PA: Winnebago Industries, Inc.
   13200 Pioneer Trl
   Eden Prairie MN 55347
   952 829-8600

(G-11760)
WOODLAND PARK INC
111 Crystal Heights Blvd (46540-8553)
P.O. Box 1309 (46540-1309)
PHONE...................574 825-2104
Ernie Yoder, Pr
Derald Bontrager, *
Nancy Kauffman, *
Edna Yoder, *
EMP: 25 EST: 1983
SQ FT: 25,000
SALES (est): 1.51MM **Privately Held**
Web: www.woodland-park.com
SIC: 2451 Mobile homes, personal or private use

(G-11761)
WOODWORKING
900 S 1075 W (46540-9368)
PHONE...................574 825-5858
Daniel Yoder, Prin
EMP: 6 EST: 2008
SALES (est): 110K **Privately Held**
SIC: 2431 Millwork

(G-11762)
YODER WOODWORKING
60157 County Road 35 (46540-9750)
PHONE...................574 825-0402
Lavon Yoder, Prin
EMP: 5 EST: 2008
SALES (est): 175.63K **Privately Held**
SIC: 2431 Millwork

(G-11763)
ZEPPS PREDATOR CALLS LLC
11935 W 710 N (46540-9305)
PHONE...................574 971-8371
Mark Zepp, Brnch Mgr
EMP: 8
SALES (corp-wide): 115.23K **Privately Held**
Web: www.markzepp.com
SIC: 3949 Sporting and athletic goods, nec
PA: Zepp's Predator Calls, Llc
   10334 State Road 120
   Middlebury IN 46540
   574 971-8371

(G-11764)
ZEPPS PREDATOR CALLS LLC (PA)
10334 State Road 120 (46540-8906)
PHONE...................574 971-8371
EMP: 10 EST: 2020
SALES (est): 115.23K
SALES (corp-wide): 115.23K **Privately Held**
Web: www.markzepp.com
SIC: 3949 Sporting and athletic goods, nec

(G-11765)
ZIGGITY SYSTEMS INC
101 Industrial Pkwy E (46540-8549)
PHONE...................574 825-5849
Dale Hostetler, Pr
Robert Hostetler, VP
EMP: 40 EST: 1976
SALES (est): 4.7MM **Privately Held**
Web: www.ziggity.com
SIC: 3523 Poultry brooders, feeders and waterers

Middletown
Henry County

(G-11766)
BCW DIVERSIFIED INC
Also Called: Bcw Supplies
8984 W Sr236 (47356)
P.O. Box P.O. Box 970 (46015)
PHONE...................765 644-2033
▲ EMP: 35 EST: 1995
SQ FT: 78,000
SALES (est): 9.57MM **Privately Held**
Web: www.bcwsupplies.com
SIC: 5999 3081 Packaging materials: boxes, padding, etc.; Unsupported plastics film and sheet

(G-11767)
BELGIAN HORSE WINERY LLC
7122 W County Road 625 N (47356-9750)
PHONE...................765 779-3002
Harry Harter, Prin
EMP: 2 EST: 2012
SALES (est): 124.95K **Privately Held**
Web: www.belgianhorsewinery.com
SIC: 2084 Wines

(G-11768)
CONTACT FABRICATORS IND INC
8896 W State Road 236 (47356-9326)
PHONE...................317 366-7274
Rachel Batthauer, Pr
Sarah Beth Wattenbarger, Prin
EMP: 5 EST: 1987
SALES (est): 479.44K **Privately Held**
SIC: 3643 Contacts, electrical

(G-11769)
EVART ENGINEERING COMPANY INC
1340 State St (47356-9357)
P.O. Box 10 (47356-0010)
PHONE...................765 354-2232
Maurice Kemerly, Pr
Brett J Kemerly, VP
Carol Kemerly, Sec
EMP: 11 EST: 1953
SQ FT: 18,400
SALES (est): 653.22K **Privately Held**
SIC: 3599 3544 Custom machinery; Special dies and tools

(G-11770)
HOLIC LLC
710 Norfleet Dr W (47356-9551)
PHONE...................765 444-8115
Frances Torres, Pr
Frances Torres, Managing Member
Antony Torres, *
EMP: 30 EST: 2013
SQ FT: 36,000
SALES (est): 2.51MM **Privately Held**
Web: www.holicfoods.com
SIC: 8742 2033 2035 Marketing consulting services; Chili sauce, tomato: packaged in cans, jars, etc.; Pickles, sauces, and salad dressings

(G-11771)
JEFF GOODNIGHT
Also Called: J T Custom Woodcraft
5444 S County Road 350 E (47356-9507)
PHONE...................765 779-4867
Jeff Goodnight, Owner
EMP: 1 EST: 1994
SALES (est): 94K **Privately Held**
SIC: 2431 Moldings, wood: unfinished and prefinished

(G-11772)
LIBERTY TOOL AND ENGRG INC
277 N 11th St (47356-1707)
P.O. Box 67 (47356-0067)
PHONE...................765 354-9550
EMP: 5 EST: 1996
SQ FT: 3,000
SALES (est): 402.6K **Privately Held**
Web: www.libertycomp.com
SIC: 3599 3545 3544 Machine shop, jobbing and repair; Machine tool accessories; Special dies, tools, jigs, and fixtures

(G-11773)
LLOYD WERKING SIGN PAINTING
243 High St (47356-1419)
PHONE...................765 354-2881
Lloyd Werking, Owner
EMP: 1 EST: 1950
SALES (est): 56K **Privately Held**
SIC: 3993 Signs and advertising specialties

(G-11774)
METAL ART INC
7730 N Raider Rd (47356-9401)
P.O. Box 191 (47356-0191)
PHONE...................765 354-4571
EMP: 5 EST: 1993
SALES (est): 884.08K **Privately Held**
Web: www.metalartinc.net
SIC: 3444 Sheet metalwork

(G-11775)
MUDHOLE MACHINE SHOP LLC
5121 N County Road 200 W (47356-9417)
PHONE...................765 533-4228
Steven Province, Prin
EMP: 6 EST: 2015
SALES (est): 106.05K **Privately Held**
SIC: 3599 Machine shop, jobbing and repair

(G-11776)
NYXPERIMENTAL LLC
580 Locust St (47356-1435)
PHONE...................765 684-7077
Frank Magaletti, Managing Member
Noelle Rigud, Managing Member
EMP: 7 EST: 2017
SALES (est): 2.5K **Privately Held**
Web: www.nyxperimental.com
SIC: 3089 Injection molding of plastics

(G-11777)
TRACE ENGINEERING INC
400 Locust St (47356-1433)
P.O. Box 159 (47356-0159)
PHONE...................765 354-4351
Kaye Stephenson, Pr
Beth Dunkin, Sec
Edgar Dunkin, VP
EMP: 8 EST: 1975
SQ FT: 7,500
SALES (est): 861.35K **Privately Held**
Web: www.traceengineering.com
SIC: 3544 Special dies and tools

(G-11778)
TUFF STUFF SALES AND SVC INC
8520 W State Road 236 (47356-9326)
PHONE...................765 354-4151
Robert Butterfield, Prin
EMP: 10 EST: 2016
SALES (est): 397.24K **Privately Held**
Web: www.tuffstuffsales.com
SIC: 3499 Safes and vaults, metal

(G-11779)
U S ACCU-MET INC
6949 N County Road 400 W (47356-9477)
PHONE...................765 533-4219
EMP: 2 EST: 1987
SQ FT: 4,000
SALES (est): 85.31K **Privately Held**
SIC: 7699 3599 Industrial machinery and equipment repair; Machine shop, jobbing and repair

Milan
Ripley County

(G-11780)
H&S DEFENSE LLC
1455 N County Road 525 E (47031-9395)
PHONE...................812 654-2314
Richard A Hooker, Prin
EMP: 5 EST: 2013
SALES (est): 169.06K **Privately Held**
Web: www.hsdefense.com
SIC: 3812 Defense systems and equipment

(G-11781)
MILAN FOOD BANK
Also Called: Wayne Meats
201 Josephine St (47031-1107)
P.O. Box 648 (47031-0648)
PHONE...................812 654-3682
Wayne Worhrig, Owner
EMP: 6 EST: 1991
SALES (est): 898.98K **Privately Held**
Web: www.waynesmeats.com
SIC: 2011 5812 Meat packing plants; Caterers

Milan - Ripley County (G-11782) GEOGRAPHIC SECTION

(G-11782)
OUTDOOR TECHNOLOGIES LLC
2780 N County Road 450 E (47031-9428)
P.O. Box 30 (47006-0030)
PHONE.................................812 654-4399
Keith Pittman, *Prin*
EMP: 5 **EST:** 2017
SALES (est): 114.94K **Privately Held**
SIC: 3812 Search and navigation equipment

(G-11783)
ROEDER INDUSTRIES
406 W Carr St (47031-1114)
P.O. Box 728 (47031-0728)
PHONE.................................812 654-3322
Russ Roeder, *Owner*
EMP: 6 **EST:** 1985
SQ FT: 14,000
SALES (est): 507.38K **Privately Held**
Web: www.roederindustries.com
SIC: 3541 3542 5084 Machine tools, metal cutting type; Presses: forming, stamping, punching, sizing (machine tools); Machine tools and accessories

(G-11784)
SIGN EXCHANGE
1022 S County Road 625 E (47031-9579)
PHONE.................................812 621-2527
Cheryl Boggs, *Owner*
EMP: 4 **EST:** 2017
SALES (est): 46.08K **Privately Held**
SIC: 3993 Signs and advertising specialties

Milford
Kosciusko County

(G-11785)
AGILE MFG INC
720 Industrial Park Road (46542)
P.O. Box 2000 (46542-2000)
PHONE.................................417 845-6065
▲ **EMP:** 5 **EST:** 2005
SALES (est): 140.26K **Privately Held**
SIC: 3999 Manufacturing industries, nec

(G-11786)
ASCOT ENTERPRISES INC
1002 N Old State Road 15 (46542-9140)
PHONE.................................574 658-3000
EMP: 1
SALES (corp-wide): 41.85MM **Privately Held**
Web: www.ascotent.com
SIC: 2391 Curtains and draperies
PA: Ascot Enterprises Inc
  503 S Main St
  Nappanee IN 46550
  877 773-7751

(G-11787)
BISON COACH LLC
1002 N Old State Road 15 (46542-9140)
PHONE.................................574 658-4161
Scott Tuttle, *Pr*
EMP: 40 **EST:** 1984
SALES (est): 4.2MM
SALES (corp-wide): 11.12B **Publicly Held**
Web: www.bisontrailer.com
SIC: 3792 Travel trailers and campers
PA: Thor Industries, Inc.
  601 E Beardsley Ave
  Elkhart IN 46514
  574 970-7460

(G-11788)
BISON HORSE TRAILERS LLC
804 S Higbee St (46542-9608)
PHONE.................................574 658-4161
Joshua Chipps, *Prin*
EMP: 8 **EST:** 2014
SALES (est): 610.64K **Privately Held**
Web: www.bisontrailer.com
SIC: 3716 Motor homes

(G-11789)
CTB INC
Chore Time
410 N Higbee St (46542-9147)
P.O. Box 2000 (46542-2000)
PHONE.................................574 658-4191
EMP: 5
SALES (corp-wide): 364.48B **Publicly Held**
Web: www.ctbinc.com
SIC: 3443 Bins, prefabricated metal plate
HQ: Ctb, Inc.
  611 N Higbee St
  Milford IN 46542
  574 658-4191

(G-11790)
CTB INC (HQ)
Also Called: Brock Grain Systems
611 N Higbee St (46542-9752)
P.O. Box 2000 (46542-2000)
PHONE.................................574 658-4191
Victor A Mancinelli, *CAO*
Douglas J Niemeyer, *Pr*
Randy S Eveler, *VP*
William Mabee, *VP*
Robert Janek, *CIO*
◆ **EMP:** 700 **EST:** 1995
SQ FT: 600,000
SALES (est): 388.9MM
SALES (corp-wide): 364.48B **Publicly Held**
Web: www.brockgrain.com
SIC: 3443 3523 Bins, prefabricated metal plate; Hog feeding, handling, and watering equipment
PA: Berkshire Hathaway Inc.
  3555 Farnam St Ste 1440
  Omaha NE 68131
  402 346-1400

(G-11791)
CTB INC
Also Called: Chore-Time Plty Prod Systems
410 N Higbee St (46542-9147)
P.O. Box 2000 (46542-2000)
PHONE.................................574 658-4191
Chris Stoler, *Sls Mgr*
EMP: 25
SALES (corp-wide): 364.48B **Publicly Held**
Web: www.brockgrain.com
SIC: 3523 Farm machinery and equipment
HQ: Ctb, Inc.
  611 N Higbee St
  Milford IN 46542
  574 658-4191

(G-11792)
CTB INC EMPLOYEE BENEFIT TR A
P.O. Box 2000 (46542-2000)
PHONE.................................574 658-5132
EMP: 13 **EST:** 2010
SALES (est): 141.86M **Privately Held**
Web: www.ctbinc.com
SIC: 3443 Fabricated plate work (boiler shop)

(G-11793)
CTB INTERNATIONAL CORP
State Road 15 North (46542)
P.O. Box 2000 (46542-2000)
PHONE.................................574 658-9431
Victor Manscinelli, *CEO*
Thomas Hamilton, *VP*
Susan Hight, *Genl Mgr*
Larry Cripe, *Prin*
◆ **EMP:** 5 **EST:** 1972
SQ FT: 600
SALES (est): 2.17MM
SALES (corp-wide): 364.48B **Publicly Held**
Web: www.ctbinc.com
SIC: 3443 Fabricated plate work (boiler shop)
PA: Berkshire Hathaway Inc.
  3555 Farnam St Ste 1440
  Omaha NE 68131
  402 346-1400

(G-11794)
CTB MN INVESTMENT CO INC (HQ)
611 N Higbee St (46542-9752)
P.O. Box 2000 (46542-2000)
PHONE.................................574 658-4191
◆ **EMP:** 50 **EST:** 1985
SQ FT: 611,000
SALES (est): 52.07MM
SALES (corp-wide): 364.48B **Publicly Held**
Web: www.ctbinc.com
SIC: 3443 3523 3564 3556 Farm storage tanks, metal plate; Farm machinery and equipment; Blowers and fans; Food products machinery
PA: Berkshire Hathaway Inc.
  3555 Farnam St Ste 1440
  Omaha NE 68131
  402 346-1400

(G-11795)
JM WOODWORKING ENTERPRISE LLC
3701 W 1350 N (46542-9643)
PHONE.................................574 773-0444
James L Slabaugh, *Owner*
EMP: 2 **EST:** 2011
SALES (est): 113.12K **Privately Held**
SIC: 2431 Millwork

(G-11796)
LEMAR INDUSTRIES CORPORAT
611 N Higbee St (46542-9752)
P.O. Box 2000 (46542-2000)
PHONE.................................515 266-7264
EMP: 11 **EST:** 2017
SALES (est): 1.1MM **Privately Held**
Web: www.brockgrain.com
SIC: 3443 Fabricated plate work (boiler shop)

(G-11797)
M M PRINTING PLUS
634 E Beer Rd (46542-9057)
PHONE.................................574 658-9345
Michelle Hurst, *Owner*
EMP: 6 **EST:** 2010
SALES (est): 82.07K **Privately Held**
Web: www.mmprintingplus.com
SIC: 2759 Screen printing

(G-11798)
MAPLE LEAF FARMS INC (HQ)
Also Called: Serenade Foods
9166 N 200 E (46542-9722)
P.O. Box 167 (46538-0167)
PHONE.................................574 453-4500
Scott Reinholt, *CEO*
Terry L Tucker, *
Scott Tucker, *Prin*
John Tucker, *
John Kidiger, *
◆ **EMP:** 650 **EST:** 1958
SALES (est): 198.43MM
SALES (corp-wide): 218.89MM **Privately Held**
Web: www.mapleleaffarms.com
SIC: 0259 2015 Duck farm; Duck slaughtering and processing
PA: Maple Leaf, Inc.
  101 E Church St
  Leesburg IN 46538
  574 453-4455

(G-11799)
MAPLE LEAF FARMS INC
Also Called: Serenade Foods
9179 N 200 E (46542-9722)
PHONE.................................574 658-4121
EMP: 103
SALES (corp-wide): 218.89MM **Privately Held**
Web: www.mapleaffarms.com
SIC: 2015 Duck slaughtering and processing
HQ: Maple Leaf Farms, Inc.
  9166 N 200 E
  Milford IN 46542
  574 453-4500

(G-11800)
MILLERS CUSTOM CARE CANDES
12711 N 400 W (46542-9644)
PHONE.................................574 658-4976
Willis Miller, *Owner*
EMP: 6 **EST:** 2008
SALES (est): 136.87K **Privately Held**
SIC: 2211 Canvas

(G-11801)
NORRIS ARMS CO LLC
405 N Old State Road 15 (46542-9612)
PHONE.................................574 658-4163
EMP: 4 **EST:** 2016
SALES (est): 64.69K **Privately Held**
SIC: 3489 Ordnance and accessories, nec

(G-11802)
PHEND AND BROWN INC (PA)
367 E 1250 N (46542-9052)
P.O. Box 150 (46542-0150)
PHONE.................................574 658-4166
TOLL FREE: 800
Daniel F Brown, *Pr*
Douglas V Brown, *
Andrew J Brown, *
Gary M Price, *
EMP: 41 **EST:** 1922
SQ FT: 17,084
SALES (est): 13.38MM
SALES (corp-wide): 13.38MM **Privately Held**
Web: www.phend-brown.com
SIC: 1611 1442 1623 1794 Highway and street paving contractor; Gravel and pebble mining; Water, sewer, and utility lines; Excavation work

(G-11803)
PRECISION BENDERS INCORPORATED
411 N Old State Road 15 (46542-9612)
P.O. Box 239 (46542-0239)
PHONE.................................574 658-9317
Richard G Bohnstedt, *Pr*
Dan Bohnstedt, *VP*
EMP: 3 **EST:** 1974
SALES (est): 247.03K **Privately Held**
SIC: 3599 Machine shop, jobbing and repair

(G-11804)
PURINA ANIMAL NUTRITION LLC
346 W 1350 N (46542-9187)
PHONE.................................574 658-4137
Larry Moorman, *Mgr*
EMP: 1
SALES (corp-wide): 2.89B **Privately Held**
Web: www.purinamills.com
SIC: 2048 Prepared feeds, nec
HQ: Purina Animal Nutrition Llc
  100 Danforth Dr

GEOGRAPHIC SECTION

Gray Summit MO 63039

(G-11805)
PURINA MILLS LLC
Also Called: Purina Mills
346 W 1350 N (46542)
PHONE..................574 658-4137
Larry G Moorman, *Mgr*
EMP: 36
SALES (corp-wide): 2.89B **Privately Held**
Web: www.purina.com
SIC: 2047 Dog and cat food
HQ: Purina Mills, Llc
555 Mryvlle Univ Dr Ste 2
Saint Louis MO 63141

(G-11806)
SLABAUGH WELDING LLC
3942 W 1350 N (46542-9643)
PHONE..................574 773-5410
EMP: 5 **EST:** 2002
SALES (est): 167.18K **Privately Held**
SIC: 7692 Welding repair

(G-11807)
THE PAPERS INC (PA)
Also Called: Senior Lf Auto Rv Publications
206 S Main St (46542-3004)
P.O. Box 188 (46542-0188)
PHONE..................574 658-4111
EMP: 180 **EST:** 1939
SALES (est): 20.23MM
SALES (corp-wide): 20.23MM **Privately Held**
Web: www.the-papers.com
SIC: 2711 Newspapers, publishing and printing

(G-11808)
VANS CABINET SHOP INC
1704 E Mock Rd (46542-9732)
PHONE..................574 658-9625
Steve Van Laningham, *Pr*
Steve Vanlaningham, *Pr*
Susan Vanlaningham, *Sec*
EMP: 4 **EST:** 1972
SQ FT: 3,200
SALES (est): 435.53K **Privately Held**
SIC: 2434 5712 Wood kitchen cabinets; Cabinet work, custom

Mill Creek
Laporte County

(G-11809)
RICKS MOTORCYCLE TIRE SVC LLC
7117 E Division Rd (46365-9769)
PHONE..................219 369-1028
Richard J Kinas, *Owner*
EMP: 1 **EST:** 2011
SALES (est): 60.52K **Privately Held**
Web: www.ricksmotorcycletireservice.com
SIC: 7534 Tire retreading and repair shops

Millersburg
Elkhart County

(G-11810)
A & M WOODWORKING
5545 S 1125 W (46543-9546)
PHONE..................574 642-4555
EMP: 5 **EST:** 2013
SALES (est): 417.63K **Privately Held**
SIC: 2431 Millwork

(G-11811)
COUNTRY LANE WOODWORKING LLC
66991 County Road 43 (46543-9706)
PHONE..................574 642-0662
EMP: 4 **EST:** 1994
SALES (est): 236.19K **Privately Held**
SIC: 2511 Wood lawn and garden furniture

(G-11812)
FOREST RIVER INC
201 W Elm St (46543-7703)
P.O. Box 333 (46543-0333)
PHONE..................574 642-2640
Floyd Miller, *Mgr*
EMP: 140
SALES (corp-wide): 364.48B **Publicly Held**
Web: www.forestriverinc.com
SIC: 3792 3716 5012 Tent-type camping trailers; Motor homes; Recreational vehicles, motor homes, and trailers
HQ: Forest River, Inc.
900 County Rd 1 N
Elkhart IN 46514

(G-11813)
HERSHBERGER WELDING
11520 W 700 S (46543-9573)
PHONE..................574 642-3994
David Hershberger, *Prin*
EMP: 1 **EST:** 2008
SALES (est): 54K **Privately Held**
SIC: 7692 Welding repair

(G-11814)
HOOSIER CUSTOM WOODWORKING
67348 County Road 33 (46543-9407)
PHONE..................574 642-3764
Myron Slabach, *Owner*
EMP: 8 **EST:** 2010
SALES (est): 240.89K **Privately Held**
SIC: 2431 Millwork

(G-11815)
LAWNCREATIONS LLC
10592 County Rd (46543)
PHONE..................574 536-1546
EMP: 2 **EST:** 2010
SALES (est): 119.83K **Privately Held**
SIC: 3648 Decorative area lighting fixtures

(G-11816)
ROCK RUN INDUSTRIES LLC
11665 W 600 S (46543-9611)
PHONE..................574 361-0848
Gary Yoder, *
EMP: 45 **EST:** 2009
SALES (est): 4.03MM **Privately Held**
Web: www.rockruncabinetry.com
SIC: 3446 Architectural metalwork

(G-11817)
SCHWARTZ WOODWORKING
4810 S 950 W (46543-9607)
PHONE..................260 593-3193
Marvin Schwartz, *Owner*
EMP: 6 **EST:** 2010
SALES (est): 227.62K **Privately Held**
SIC: 2431 Millwork

(G-11818)
STONEY CREEK WASH MACHINE SHOP
66365 E County Line Rd (46543-9742)
PHONE..................574 642-1155
EMP: 4 **EST:** 2010
SALES (est): 62.88K **Privately Held**
SIC: 3599 Machine shop, jobbing and repair

(G-11819)
STONEY CREEK WINERY LLC
10315 County Road 146 (46543-9711)
PHONE..................574 642-4454
Gary Plank, *Ofcr*
EMP: 4 **EST:** 2011
SALES (est): 126.11K **Privately Held**
Web: www.stoneycreekwinery.com
SIC: 2084 Wines

Milltown
Crawford County

(G-11820)
ROBERTSON CRUSHED STONE INC
6300 Hwy 64 Nw (47145)
P.O. Box 97 (47145-0097)
PHONE..................812 633-4881
Charlie Robertson, *Pr*
Kathy Robertson Shank, *VP*
William Robertson, *VP*
EMP: 20 **EST:** 1970
SQ FT: 300
SALES (est): 2.44MM **Privately Held**
Web: www.robertsoncrushedstone.com
SIC: 1422 Crushed and broken limestone

Milroy
Rush County

(G-11821)
BILLS INDUSTRIES LLC
7794 S 175 W (46156-9003)
P.O. Box 274 (46156-0274)
PHONE..................765 629-0227
EMP: 6 **EST:** 2000
SALES (est): 237.6K **Privately Held**
SIC: 2759 Engraving, nec

(G-11822)
CANNON FABRICATION COMPANY
7957 S State Road 3 (46156)
P.O. Box 218 (46156)
PHONE..................765 629-2277
John Mcdaniel, *Pr*
Tom Simasko, *VP*
▲ **EMP:** 10 **EST:** 1998
SQ FT: 12,000
SALES (est): 839.51K **Privately Held**
Web: www.canfab.com
SIC: 3053 Gaskets, all materials

(G-11823)
DETWEILERS CABINET SHOP
6053 W State Road 244 (46156-9704)
PHONE..................765 629-2698
Levi Detweiler, *Owner*
EMP: 2 **EST:** 1979
SALES (est): 93.76K **Privately Held**
SIC: 2499 Woodenware, kitchen and household

(G-11824)
HARCOURT INDUSTRIES INC
Also Called: Harcourt Outlines
7765 S 175 W (46156-9003)
P.O. Box 128 (46156-0128)
PHONE..................765 629-2625
Jean Ann Harcourt, *Pr*
Joseph Harcourt, *
Rick Bills, *
Brad Sizemore, *
Joseph C Harcourt, *
▲ **EMP:** 45 **EST:** 1956
SQ FT: 70,000
SALES (est): 4.79MM **Privately Held**
Web: www.harcourtoutlines.com
SIC: 3952 5112 2782 2759 Pencils and leads, including artists'; Pens and/or pencils; Blankbooks and looseleaf binders; Commercial printing, nec

(G-11825)
HOOSIER PALLET LLC
4126 W 900 S (46156-9505)
PHONE..................765 629-2899
Abe Keim, *Owner*
EMP: 3 **EST:** 1996
SALES (est): 446.78K **Privately Held**
Web: www.hoosierpallet.com
SIC: 2448 Pallets, wood

(G-11826)
MIDWEST GASKET CORPORATION
100 S Railroad St (46156)
P.O. Box 125 (46156-0125)
PHONE..................765 629-2221
Robert Tobian, *Pr*
▲ **EMP:** 20 **EST:** 1976
SQ FT: 15,000
SALES (est): 2.06MM **Privately Held**
Web: www.midwestgasket.com
SIC: 3053 Gaskets, all materials

(G-11827)
MILROY CANNING COMPANY
100 S Railroad St (46156)
P.O. Box 125 (46156-0125)
PHONE..................765 629-2221
Bob Tovian, *Pr*
EMP: 5 **EST:** 1925
SQ FT: 25,000
SALES (est): 459.73K **Privately Held**
SIC: 2033 0191 Tomato products, packaged in cans, jars, etc.; General farms, primarily crop

(G-11828)
MILROY PALLET INC
Also Called: H & M Pallet
3018 W 1050 S (46156-9511)
PHONE..................765 629-2919
Steve Keim, *Pr*
Abe Keim, *VP*
Olivia Atherton, *Sec*
EMP: 3 **EST:** 1996
SQ FT: 12,000
SALES (est): 450.95K **Privately Held**
SIC: 2448 Pallets, wood

(G-11829)
MILROY SPINDLE SHOP
2221 W 1000 S (46156-9736)
PHONE..................765 629-2176
Bill Miller, *Owner*
EMP: 1 **EST:** 1994
SALES (est): 88.22K **Privately Held**
SIC: 2452 Modular homes, prefabricated, wood

(G-11830)
RUSH COUNTY STONE CO INC
5814 W State Road 244 (46156-9568)
PHONE..................765 629-2211
TOLL FREE: 800
Joe S Columbe, *Pr*
EMP: 6 **EST:** 1941
SALES (est): 685.81K **Privately Held**
SIC: 1411 3281 3274 Limestone, dimension-quarrying; Cut stone and stone products; Lime

(G-11831)
RUSH COUNTY WOOD PRODUCTS
2437 W 900 S (46156-9699)
PHONE..................765 629-0603
Richard Schrock, *Owner*

Milton - Wayne County (G-11832)   GEOGRAPHIC SECTION

EMP: 3 EST: 2005
SALES (est): 192.32K **Privately Held**
SIC: 2434 Wood kitchen cabinets

Milton
Wayne County

(G-11832)
DIMENSIONAL IMPRINTING INC
13579 Whitaker Dr (47357-9703)
PHONE..................................260 417-0202
EMP: 2 EST: 1992
SALES (est): 183.29K **Privately Held**
SIC: 2759 Promotional printing

Mishawaka
St. Joseph County

(G-11833)
123CARPORTZ
1321 E Jefferson Blvd (46545-7109)
PHONE..................................574 376-0470
EMP: 5 EST: 2011
SALES (est): 82.82K **Privately Held**
Web: www.123carportz.com
SIC: 3448 Prefabricated metal buildings and components

(G-11834)
ACCU-MOLD LLC
1702 E 7th St (46544-3213)
PHONE..................................269 323-0388
David Felicijan, Pr
EMP: 23 EST: 2012
SALES (est): 4.63MM
SALES (corp-wide): 24.41MM **Privately Held**
Web: www.accu-moldinc.com
SIC: 3544 3089 3678 3841 Forms (molds), for foundry and plastics working machinery; Injection molding of plastics; Electronic connectors; Surgical and medical instruments
HQ: Mno-Bmadsen
    415 E Prairie Ronde St
    Dowagiac MI 49047
    269 783-4111

(G-11835)
ADVANCED METAL FABRICATORS INC
1204 E 6th St (46544-2822)
PHONE..................................574 259-1263
John Ford, Dir
EMP: 10 EST: 2000
SALES (est): 929.47K **Privately Held**
Web: www.michianametalfab.com
SIC: 3469 Stamping metal for the trade

(G-11836)
AK TOOL AND DIE INC
13990 Early Rd (46545-4527)
P.O. Box 523 (46554-0523)
PHONE..................................574 286-9010
Kenny Beckham, Pr
EMP: 6 EST: 2009
SALES (est): 315.02K **Privately Held**
SIC: 3423 2675 Hand and edge tools, nec; Die-cut paper and board

(G-11837)
ALLEN-DAVIS ENTERPRISES INC
920 Brook Run Dr Apt 3b (46544-9009)
P.O. Box 1484 (46546-1484)
PHONE..................................574 303-2173
William W Allen, Pr
William C Davis, VP

▲ EMP: 2 EST: 1997
SALES (est): 139.82K **Privately Held**
SIC: 3421 Scissors, hand

(G-11838)
ALLIED SPECIALTY PRECISION INC
815 E Lowell Ave (46545-6480)
P.O. Box 543 (46546-0543)
PHONE..................................574 255-4718
Pam Rubenstein, CEO
Eric Kurzhal, *
Larry De Later, *
EMP: 65 EST: 1954
SQ FT: 26,000
SALES (est): 9.22MM **Privately Held**
Web: www.aspi-nc.com
SIC: 3599 Machine shop, jobbing and repair

(G-11839)
ALPHAJAK LLC
118 N Race St (46544-1429)
P.O. Box 1945 (46515-1945)
PHONE..................................574 800-4810
Andre Jackson, CEO
EMP: 2 EST: 2020
SALES (est): 111.81K **Privately Held**
Web: www.alphajak.com
SIC: 2952 Asphalt felts and coatings

(G-11840)
AM GENERAL LLC
13200 Mckinley Hwy (46545-7530)
P.O. Box 650 (46546-0650)
PHONE..................................574 258-7523
Adare Fritz, Mgr
EMP: 800
SQ FT: 16,200
SALES (corp-wide): 3.44B **Privately Held**
Web: www.amgeneral.com
SIC: 3711 3795 3537 7381 Military motor vehicle assembly; Tanks and tank components; Industrial trucks and tractors; Security guard service
HQ: Am General Llc
    105 N Niles Ave
    South Bend IN 46617
    574 237-6222

(G-11841)
AMERICAN WIRE ROPE SLING OF IN
5005 Lincolnway E (46544-4250)
PHONE..................................574 257-9424
EMP: 1
SALES (corp-wide): 169.95MM **Privately Held**
SIC: 3496 Miscellaneous fabricated wire products
HQ: American Wire Rope & Sling Of Indianapolis Inc
    5760 Dividend Rd
    Indianapolis IN 46241
    877 634-2545

(G-11842)
AN-MAR WIRING SYSTEMS INC
711 E Grove St (46545-6863)
PHONE..................................574 255-5523
Dean W Johnson, Pr
Ann Mary Johnson, Treas
EMP: 10 EST: 1981
SQ FT: 6,000
SALES (est): 969.87K **Privately Held**
Web: www.anmarwiring.com
SIC: 3621 3566 3643 3089 Motors and generators; Speed changers, drives, and gears; Current-carrying wiring services; Injection molding of plastics

(G-11843)
ART WORKS SIGN CO INC
Also Called: Art Works
55581 Currant Rd (46545-4741)
PHONE..................................574 360-9290
Steve Depositar, Pr
Shelly Depositar, Sec
EMP: 7 EST: 1989
SQ FT: 5,200
SALES (est): 738.18K **Privately Held**
Web: www.artworkssign.com
SIC: 3993 Signs, not made in custom sign painting shops

(G-11844)
AUNT LINDAS EMBROIDERY
621 E Broadway St # C (46545-6742)
PHONE..................................574 256-0508
Linda Howell, Prin
EMP: 5 EST: 2009
SALES (est): 78.58K **Privately Held**
Web: www.playninjagolf.com
SIC: 2395 Embroidery products, except Schiffli machine

(G-11845)
B & B MOLDERS LLC
58471 Fir Rd (46544-5834)
PHONE..................................574 259-7838
▲ EMP: 65 EST: 1963
SQ FT: 60,000
SALES (est): 10.18MM **Privately Held**
Web: www.bandbmolders.com
SIC: 3089 Injection molding of plastics

(G-11846)
BAYER HEALTHCARE LLC
4100 Edison Lakes Pkwy (46545-3465)
PHONE..................................574 252-4735
Dianne Nagy, Mgr
EMP: 21
SALES (corp-wide): 51.78B **Privately Held**
Web: www.bayercare.com
SIC: 2834 Pharmaceutical preparations
HQ: Bayer Healthcare Llc
    100 Bayer Blvd
    Whippany NJ 07981
    862 404-3000

(G-11847)
BAYER HEALTHCARE LLC
3930 Edison Lakes Pkwy (46545-3474)
PHONE..................................574 252-4734
Bayer Care, Brnch Mgr
EMP: 44
SALES (corp-wide): 51.78B **Privately Held**
Web: www.bayercare.com
SIC: 2834 Pharmaceutical preparations
HQ: Bayer Healthcare Llc
    100 Bayer Blvd
    Whippany NJ 07981
    862 404-3000

(G-11848)
BBS ENTERPRISES INC
Also Called: F & F Machine Specialties
55980 Russell Industrial Pkwy (46545-7545)
PHONE..................................574 255-3173
David A Behrens, Pr
Karen M Behrens, *
EMP: 66 EST: 1967
SQ FT: 16,000
SALES (est): 11.27MM **Privately Held**
SIC: 3841 3599 Diagnostic apparatus, medical; Machine shop, jobbing and repair

(G-11849)
BELLA FOOD SALES LLC
Also Called: Woof and Purr Naturals

56288 Erickson Dr (46545-7804)
PHONE..................................574 229-8803
▲ EMP: 2
Web: www.bellafoodsales.com
SIC: 2034 Dried and dehydrated fruits, vegetables and soup mixes

(G-11850)
BELLO CUSTOM WOODCRAFTS
4014 Fir Rd (46545)
PHONE..................................574 314-5973
EMP: 5 EST: 2019
SALES (est): 41.52K **Privately Held**
SIC: 2499 Wood products, nec

(G-11851)
BENDER MOLD & MACHINE INC
55951 Russell Industrial Pkwy (46545-5198)
PHONE..................................574 255-5176
Richard Bender, Pr
EMP: 10 EST: 1970
SALES (est): 977.27K **Privately Held**
SIC: 3089 Injection molding of plastics

(G-11852)
BENDER PRODUCTS INC
Also Called: Bender Plastics
55951 Russell Industrial Pkwy (46545-7544)
PHONE..................................574 255-5350
Nevin Siqueira, Pr
EMP: 50 EST: 2004
SQ FT: 40,000
SALES (est): 6.55MM **Privately Held**
Web: www.benderproducts.com
SIC: 3089 3714 3643 3496 Injection molding of plastics; Motor vehicle parts and accessories; Current-carrying wiring services; Miscellaneous fabricated wire products

(G-11853)
BRADFORD PRESS INC
302 W 3rd St (46544-1922)
PHONE..................................574 876-3601
Ruth J Smith, Prin
EMP: 5 EST: 2011
SALES (est): 76.16K **Privately Held**
Web: www.bradford-press.com
SIC: 2741 Miscellaneous publishing

(G-11854)
BUILDERS IRON WORKS INC
1016 E 12th St (46544-5706)
PHONE..................................574 254-1553
Elvis Balentine, Pr
Mary Wunder, Sec
EMP: 24 EST: 1932
SQ FT: 15,500
SALES (est): 928.22K **Privately Held**
SIC: 3441 3446 Fabricated structural metal; Architectural metalwork

(G-11855)
BUY BULK DISPLAYS
3505 N Home St (46545)
P.O. Box 703 (46561)
PHONE..................................574 855-3522
EMP: 6 EST: 2018
SALES (est): 488.56K **Privately Held**
Web: www.buybulkdisplays.com
SIC: 3993 Signs and advertising specialties

(G-11856)
C & J CABINETS
3203 York St (46544-3729)
PHONE..................................574 255-5812
Brent Lidgard, Owner
EMP: 1 EST: 1983

SALES (est): 105.04K **Privately Held**
SIC: 2434 Wood kitchen cabinets

(G-11857)
C & P DISTRIBUTING LLC
2500 Miracle Ln Ste D (46545-3017)
P.O. Box 220 (46546-0220)
PHONE.............................574 256-1138
John Pierce, *Pr*
EMP: 14 EST: 1984
SQ FT: 24,000
SALES (est): 1.76MM **Privately Held**
Web: www.cpdist.com
SIC: 3575 3999 5045 5099 Computer terminals, monitors and components; Coin-operated amusement machines; Computers, nec; Coin-operated machines and mechanisms

(G-11858)
CARDCARECOM
16540 Jackson Rd (46544-9315)
PHONE.............................574 315-5294
Jen Smoker, *Prin*
EMP: 5 EST: 2017
SALES (est): 54.64K **Privately Held**
Web: www.cardcare.com
SIC: 2752 Offset printing

(G-11859)
CAST PRODUCTS LP
Colorimeteric Division
1711 Clover Rd (46545-7248)
P.O. Box 1368 (46515-1368)
PHONE.............................574 255-9619
Roy Strong, *Genl Mgr*
EMP: 3
SALES (corp-wide): 3.47B **Publicly Held**
Web: www.castproducts.com
SIC: 2891 Caulking compounds
HQ: Cast Products, L.P.
5400 Beck Dr
Elkhart IN 46516
574 294-2684

(G-11860)
CHESTNUT LAND COMPANY
Also Called: Auntie Anne's
6501 Grape Rd Ste 670a (46545-1039)
PHONE.............................574 271-8740
Tracy Vervynckt, *Brnch Mgr*
EMP: 8
Web: www.auntieannes.com
SIC: 5461 2052 Pretzels; Pretzels
PA: Chestnut Land Company
100 Debartolo Pl Ste 300
Youngstown OH 44512

(G-11861)
CITY SUPPLY INC
1807 N Cedar St (46545-6467)
PHONE.............................574 259-6028
Pat Dailey, *Mgr*
EMP: 3
SALES (corp-wide): 2.16MM **Privately Held**
Web: www.citysupply.com
SIC: 3432 Plumbing fixture fittings and trim
PA: City Supply Inc
4301 Ohio St
Michigan City IN 46360
219 879-8304

(G-11862)
COLORIMETRIC INC
1711 Clover Rd (46545-7248)
P.O. Box 1368 (46515-1368)
PHONE.............................574 255-9619
John Hendricks, *Pr*
Gregory Querry, *VP*
EMP: 17 EST: 1977

SQ FT: 47,000
SALES (est): 838.91K
SALES (corp-wide): 3.47B **Publicly Held**
SIC: 2891 Caulking compounds
HQ: Cast Products, L.P.
5400 Beck Dr
Elkhart IN 46516
574 294-2684

(G-11863)
CONCEPT ASSEMBLY SOLUTIONS LLC
55625 Currant Rd (46545-4801)
PHONE.............................574 855-2534
Larry Geisel, *Off Mgr*
Kathryn Widmeyer, *Prin*
EMP: 14 EST: 2011
SQ FT: 2,000
SALES (est): 1.22MM **Privately Held**
Web: www.conceptassembly.com
SIC: 3089 Injection molded finished plastics products, nec

(G-11864)
CONCRETE & ASPHALT RECYCL INC (DH)
2010 Went Ave (46545-6447)
PHONE.............................574 237-1928
David L Schrock, *Pr*
EMP: 4 EST: 1991
SALES (est): 4.18MM
SALES (corp-wide): 24.72MM **Privately Held**
Web: www.mishawakaconcreteasphalt.com
SIC: 2951 4953 Concrete, asphaltic (not from refineries); Recycling, waste materials
HQ: Schrock Aggregate Company Inc
111 Industrial Dr
Wakarusa IN 46573

(G-11865)
COR-A-VENT INC
945 E 6th St (46544-2825)
PHONE.............................574 258-6161
EMP: 14
SALES (corp-wide): 4.04MM **Privately Held**
Web: www.cor-a-vent.com
SIC: 3089 3564 Plastics hardware and building products; Blowers and fans
PA: Cor-A-Vent Inc
2529 Lincolnway W
Mishawaka IN 46544
574 255-1910

(G-11866)
COR-A-VENT INC (PA)
2529 Lincolnway W (46544-1523)
P.O. Box 428 (46546-0428)
PHONE.............................574 255-1910
Gary L Sells, *Ch Bd*
Shirley Sells, *Sec*
Mark Keller, *COO*
◆ EMP: 12 EST: 1976
SQ FT: 6,000
SALES (est): 4.04MM
SALES (corp-wide): 4.04MM **Privately Held**
Web: www.cor-a-vent.com
SIC: 3089 1711 Extruded finished plastics products, nec; Ventilation and duct work contractor

(G-11867)
COVENTURE I LLC
Also Called: Showersleeve & Castcover Co
5776 Grape Rd (46545-8460)
PHONE.............................800 570-0072
EMP: 1 EST: 2006
SQ FT: 2,800

SALES (est): 136.72K **Privately Held**
Web: www.showersleeve.com
SIC: 3842 Surgical appliances and supplies

(G-11868)
CRESSY MEMORIAL GROUP INC
3925 Glaser Ct (46545-4539)
PHONE.............................574 258-1800
Steve Lyons, *Prin*
Mary Cressy, *Pr*
EMP: 2 EST: 2006
SALES (est): 239.99K **Privately Held**
Web: www.cressymemorial.com
SIC: 3995 Burial vaults, fiberglass

(G-11869)
CUMMINS CROSSPOINT LLC
Also Called: Cummins
3025 N Home St (46545-4439)
PHONE.............................574 252-2154
Carrie Buisman Op'ns Lead, *Brnch Mgr*
EMP: 37
SALES (corp-wide): 34.06B **Publicly Held**
Web: www.cummins.com
SIC: 5084 3519 Engines and parts, diesel; Internal combustion engines, nec
HQ: Cummins Crosspoint Llc
111 Monument Cir Ste 601
Indianapolis IN 46204
317 243-7979

(G-11870)
CUMMINS SALES SVC
3025 N Home St (46545-4439)
PHONE.............................574 252-2154
EMP: 6 EST: 2019
SALES (est): 124.44K **Privately Held**
SIC: 3714 Motor vehicle parts and accessories

(G-11871)
CUSTOM CREATIONS BY HEATHER
210 E 13th St (46544-5311)
PHONE.............................574 302-7525
Heather Lisenko, *Prin*
EMP: 1 EST: 2011
SALES (est): 62.63K **Privately Held**
SIC: 3421 Table and food cutlery, including butchers'

(G-11872)
CUSTOM FAB & WELD INC
1030 N Merrifield Ave (46545)
PHONE.............................574 255-9689
Andrew Helfrich, *Pr*
EMP: 2
SALES (corp-wide): 966.05K **Privately Held**
SIC: 3599 Machine shop, jobbing and repair
PA: Custom Fab & Weld, Inc.
16915 Cleveland Rd
Granger IN 46530
574 277-8877

(G-11873)
CUSTOM METAL FABRICATION LLC
603 W 9th St (46544-4916)
PHONE.............................574 257-8851
Kris Kruger, *Prin*
EMP: 2 EST: 2008
SALES (est): 134.81K **Privately Held**
Web: www.michianametalfab.com
SIC: 3499 Fabricated metal products, nec

(G-11874)
CUSTOM PLASTICS LLC
1950 E Mckinley Ave (46545-7206)
PHONE.............................574 259-2340
EMP: 23
SALES (corp-wide): 2.53MM **Privately Held**

Web: www.spinwelding.com
SIC: 3089 Injection molding of plastics
PA: Custom Plastics, Llc
1305 Brooks St
Ontario CA 91762
909 984-0200

(G-11875)
D AND D CUSTOM CONCRETE INC
14369 Douglas Rd (46545-1804)
PHONE.............................574 274-6013
EMP: 5 EST: 2018
SALES (est): 62.63K **Privately Held**
SIC: 3241 Cement, hydraulic

(G-11876)
DAISY TEES LLC
4224 Anchor Dr (46544-9143)
PHONE.............................574 259-1933
Kelly Jobin, *Prin*
EMP: 5 EST: 2018
SALES (est): 80.61K **Privately Held**
SIC: 2759 Screen printing

(G-11877)
DAMAGE INDUSTRIES II LLC
55685 Currant Rd (46545-4811)
PHONE.............................574 256-7006
EMP: 2 EST: 2016
SQ FT: 3,700
SALES (est): 70.58K **Privately Held**
Web: www.damageindustriesllc.com
SIC: 3999 Manufacturing industries, nec

(G-11878)
DAMAGE INDUSTRIES LLC
55685 Currant Rd Ste D (46545-4812)
PHONE.............................574 256-7006
EMP: 4 EST: 2011
SALES (est): 100.75K **Privately Held**
Web: www.damageindustriesllc.com
SIC: 3999 Manufacturing industries, nec

(G-11879)
DAMPING TECHNOLOGIES INC (PA)
55656 Currant Rd (46545)
PHONE.............................574 258-7916
Adam Parin, *Pr*
Michael L Parin, *
Marilyn J Parin, *
Mark Engdahl, *
EMP: 25 EST: 1989
SQ FT: 40,000
SALES (est): 7.63MM **Privately Held**
Web: www.damping.com
SIC: 8711 3625 Engineering services; Noise control equipment

(G-11880)
DAMPING TECHNOLOGIES INC
12970 Mckinley Hwy Ste 1 (46545-7500)
PHONE.............................574 258-7916
Joe Herman, *Brnch Mgr*
EMP: 15
Web: www.damping.com
SIC: 8711 3829 3823 3651 Engineering services; Measuring and controlling devices, nec; Process control instruments; Household audio and video equipment
PA: Damping Technologies, Inc.
55656 Currant Rd
Mishawaka IN 46545

(G-11881)
DAVE JONES MACHINISTS LLC
1212 N Merrifield Ave (46545-6709)
PHONE.............................574 256-5500
Davis P Jones, *Managing Member*
◆ EMP: 4 EST: 1969
SQ FT: 4,500

Mishawaka - St. Joseph County (G-11882)

SALES (est): 499.08K **Privately Held**
Web: www.sight-pipe.com
SIC: 3827 Optical instruments and apparatus

(G-11882)
DEARBORN CRANE AND ENGRG CO (PA)
Also Called: Dearborn Overhead Crane
1133 E 5th St (46544)
PHONE...................574 259-2444
Yatish Joshi, *Pr*
Joan Joshi, *
Debra Wilson, *
EMP: 28 **EST:** 1955
SQ FT: 43,000
SALES (est): 4.82MM
SALES (corp-wide): 4.82MM **Privately Held**
Web: www.dearborncrane.com
SIC: 3536 7389 Hoists, cranes, and monorails; Industrial and commercial equipment inspection service

(G-11883)
DECO CHEM INC
Also Called: Davis Chocolate
3502 N Home St (46545-4399)
PHONE...................574 255-2366
◆ **EMP:** 12 **EST:** 1972
SALES (est): 2.34MM **Privately Held**
Web: www.decochem.com
SIC: 2066 Chocolate

(G-11884)
DOEHLER DRY INGRDENT SLTONS LL
Also Called: Doehler Dry Ingrdent Solutions
1852 N Home St (46545-7268)
P.O. Box 853 (46546-0853)
PHONE...................574 797-0364
Garry Beckett, *Managing Member*
EMP: 11 **EST:** 2017
SALES (est): 1.26MM **Privately Held**
Web: www.doehler.com
SIC: 2034 Fruits, freeze-dried

(G-11885)
DRIKE INC
Also Called: It's Tops
315 Union St (46544-2163)
PHONE...................574 259-8822
Marty Dunmire, *Pr*
Cathy Stachowiak, *Off Mgr*
EMP: 13 **EST:** 2005
SALES (est): 841.49K **Privately Held**
Web: www.itstops.net
SIC: 2759 2395 2752 Screen printing; Pleating and stitching; Promotional printing, lithographic

(G-11886)
DRK GLOBAL MANUFACTURING LLC
1921 N Cedar St (46545-6466)
P.O. Box 13 (46530-0013)
PHONE...................574 387-6264
Dan Kuntz, *Prin*
EMP: 4 **EST:** 2009
SALES (est): 120K **Privately Held**
Web: www.drkglobalmfg.com
SIC: 3999 Manufacturing industries, nec

(G-11887)
DULEY PRESS INC
2906 N Home St (46545-4491)
P.O. Box 484 (46546-0484)
PHONE...................574 259-5203
Michael Lowenhar, *Pr*
Judd Lowenhar, *
EMP: 30 **EST:** 1936
SQ FT: 14,000
SALES (est): 2.51MM **Privately Held**
Web: www.duleypress.com
SIC: 2752 Offset printing

(G-11888)
EAGLE PET PRODUCTS INC
1025 W 11th St (46544-4818)
PHONE...................574 259-7834
◆ **EMP:** 82
SIC: 2047 Dog food

(G-11889)
ECKCO PLASTICS INC
56599 Twin Branch Dr (46545-7476)
PHONE...................574 258-5552
Gary Eck, *Pr*
▲ **EMP:** 1 **EST:** 2005
SALES (est): 911.58K **Privately Held**
Web: www.eckcoplastics.com
SIC: 3089 Injection molding of plastics

(G-11890)
ECP AMERICAN STEEL LLC
American Wire Rope
5005 Lincolnway E Ste B (46544-4250)
PHONE...................574 257-9424
Frank Becker, *Mgr*
EMP: 3
SALES (corp-wide): 169.95MM **Privately Held**
Web: www.ecpamericansteel.com
SIC: 3496 Miscellaneous fabricated wire products
HQ: Ecp American Steel, Llc
3122 Engle Rd
Fort Wayne IN 46809
260 478-9101

(G-11891)
ELECTRONICS INCORPORATED
56790 Magnetic Dr (46545-7493)
PHONE...................574 256-5001
EMP: 30 **EST:** 1974
SALES (est): 4.65MM **Privately Held**
Web: www.electronics-inc.com
SIC: 3625 3491 Control equipment, electric; Industrial valves

(G-11892)
ELIXIR INDUSTRIES
5201 Lincolnway E (46544-4213)
PHONE...................574 259-7133
EMP: 10 **EST:** 2020
SALES (est): 248.82K **Privately Held**
Web: www.elixirext.com
SIC: 3441 Fabricated structural metal

(G-11893)
ELLINGER MFG TECH LLC
55015 Currant Rd (46545-4715)
PHONE...................574 303-2086
Nathan D Ellinger, *Prin*
EMP: 5 **EST:** 2019
SALES (est): 91.41K **Privately Held**
SIC: 3999 Manufacturing industries, nec

(G-11894)
ENERPAC TOOL GROUP CORP
Also Called: Power Gear
1217 E 7th St (46544-2851)
P.O. Box 2888 (46515-2888)
PHONE...................574 254-1428
Tari Blazei, *Finance Leader*
EMP: 20
SALES (corp-wide): 598.2MM **Publicly Held**
Web: www.enerpactoolgroup.com
SIC: 3593 Fluid power cylinders, hydraulic or pneumatic
PA: Enerpac Tool Group Corp.
N86 W12500 Wstbrook Crssi
Menomonee Falls WI 53051
262 293-1500

(G-11895)
ERJ COMPOSITES LLC
1600 W 6th St (46544-1639)
PHONE...................574 360-3517
EMP: 7 **EST:** 2017
SALES (est): 557.85K **Privately Held**
Web: www.erjcomposites.com
SIC: 2821 Plastics materials and resins

(G-11896)
FENCING ADVISORY ASSOC INC
Also Called: Indiana Fencing Academy
109 Lincolnway W (46544-2010)
PHONE...................574 256-0111
Louise Leighton, *Mgr*
EMP: 1 **EST:** 1997
SALES (est): 73.14K **Privately Held**
Web: www.edlfencing.com
SIC: 3949 Fencing equipment (sporting goods)

(G-11897)
FOREFRONT FOAM LLC
1015 Saint Jerome St (46544)
PHONE...................574 343-1146
Ryan T Van Dyke, *Pr*
EMP: 13 **EST:** 2019
SALES (est): 1.85MM **Privately Held**
Web: www.forefrontfoam.com
SIC: 3086 3479 Plastics foam products; Rust proofing (hot dipping) of metals and formed products

(G-11898)
GARYRAE INC
Also Called: Precision Wood Products
800 Cleveland St (46544-4861)
PHONE...................574 255-7141
Gary Matt, *Pr*
Rae Matt, *VP*
EMP: 15 **EST:** 1975
SQ FT: 10,000
SALES (est): 361.31K **Privately Held**
SIC: 2541 2431 Wood partitions and fixtures; Doors and door parts and trim, wood

(G-11899)
GENESIS MOLDING INC
55901 Currant Rd (46545-4803)
PHONE...................574 256-9271
James Deren, *CEO*
James Deren, *Pr*
Brandon Geisel, *
Tim Morris, *
▲ **EMP:** 75 **EST:** 1989
SQ FT: 20,000
SALES (est): 15.33MM **Privately Held**
Web: www.genesismolding.com
SIC: 3089 Injection molded finished plastics products, nec

(G-11900)
GENESYS GROUP LLC
713 N Main St (46545-6617)
PHONE...................574 850-9435
Wesley Butler, *Managing Member*
EMP: 3 **EST:** 2018
SALES (est): 91.98K **Privately Held**
SIC: 7372 Business oriented computer software

(G-11901)
GLOBAL MOLD SOLUTIONS INC
1702 E 7th St (46544-3213)
PHONE...................574 259-6262
Michael A Vaughn, *Pr*
EMP: 16 **EST:** 2003
SQ FT: 35,000
SALES (est): 500.98K **Privately Held**
Web: www.mgmold.com
SIC: 3544 Industrial molds

(G-11902)
GREAT LAKES STEEL CORPORATION
4100 Edison Lakes Pkwy (46545)
PHONE...................574 273-7000
EMP: 9 **EST:** 2002
SALES (est): 201.56K **Privately Held**
SIC: 3312 Sheet or strip, steel, hot-rolled

(G-11903)
GUMENA LLC
13738 Jefferson Blvd (46545-7345)
PHONE...................574 339-6510
Claudio Diaz, *Managing Member*
EMP: 2 **EST:** 2010
SALES (est): 470.68K **Privately Held**
Web: www.gumenallc.com
SIC: 2822 Silicone rubbers

(G-11904)
HAMMER PLASTICS INCORPORATED
1015 E 12th St (46544-5705)
P.O. Box 446 (46546-0446)
PHONE...................574 255-7230
Michael E Hammer, *Pr*
Colette Russell, *
EMP: 33 **EST:** 2001
SQ FT: 40,000
SALES (est): 4.32MM **Privately Held**
Web: www.hammerplastics.com
SIC: 3089 Injection molding of plastics

(G-11905)
HARD SURFACE FABRICATIONS INC
2302 E 3rd St (46544-3330)
PHONE...................574 259-4843
Everett H Behnke, *Pr*
Constance Behnke, *Sec*
EMP: 7 **EST:** 1989
SALES (est): 509.58K **Privately Held**
Web: www.hardsurfacekormax.com
SIC: 2221 Acrylic broadwoven fabrics

(G-11906)
HEATHER SOUND AMPLIFICATION
1717 E 6th St (46544-3208)
PHONE...................574 255-6100
Richard Johnson, *Pr*
EMP: 3 **EST:** 1972
SQ FT: 3,200
SALES (est): 243.38K **Privately Held**
Web: www.hsarolltops.com
SIC: 3679 2517 Electronic circuits; Wood television and radio cabinets

(G-11907)
HENSLEY COMPOSITES LLC
1927 N Cedar St (46545-6466)
PHONE...................574 202-3840
EMP: 5 **EST:** 2009
SALES (est): 80.41K **Privately Held**
SIC: 3999 Manufacturing industries, nec

(G-11908)
HOOSIER BOX AND SKID INC
2401 Schumacher Dr (46545-3343)
P.O. Box 8123 (46660-8123)
PHONE...................574 256-2111
Neal Stanfield, *Pr*
Suzanne Stanfield, *Sec*
James Hansen, *General Vice President*
EMP: 8 **EST:** 1982

GEOGRAPHIC SECTION
Mishawaka - St. Joseph County (G-11935)

SQ FT: 45,000
SALES (est): 884.94K **Privately Held**
Web: www.hoosierboxandskid.com
SIC: 2448 2441 Pallets, wood; Nailed wood boxes and shook

(G-11909)
HOOSIER ROASTER LLC
2212 Lincolnway W (46544-1617)
PHONE..................................574 257-1415
Chris Skodinski, *Owner*
EMP: 2 EST: 2005
SALES (est): 164.46K **Privately Held**
Web: www.hoosierroaster.com
SIC: 3634 2095 Roasters, electric; Roasted coffee

(G-11910)
INDIANA MICRO MET ETCHING INC
1906 Clover Rd (46545-7245)
PHONE..................................574 293-3342
Leanne Brekke, *Pr*
Steve Zimmerman, *Off Mgr*
EMP: 10 EST: 1987
SALES (est): 1.39MM **Privately Held**
Web: www.met-mfg.com
SIC: 3599 Chemical milling job shop

(G-11911)
INDIANA RUG COMPANY
900 Cleveland St (46544-4859)
PHONE..................................574 252-4653
Pam Richards, *Owner*
EMP: 3 EST: 1983
SALES (est): 445.93K **Privately Held**
Web: www.indianarugco.com
SIC: 2273 5713 Carpets and rugs; Floor covering stores

(G-11912)
INGLESIDE HOLDINGS L P
4100 Edison Lakes Pkwy (46545)
PHONE..................................574 273-7000
EMP: 9 EST: 2002
SALES (est): 198.68K **Privately Held**
SIC: 3312 Sheet or strip, steel, hot-rolled

(G-11913)
IP CORPORATION
Also Called: North American Composites
1460 E 12th St (46544-5824)
PHONE..................................574 259-1505
Floyd Linch, *Brnch Mgr*
EMP: 15
SALES (corp-wide): 608.16MM **Privately Held**
Web: www.interplastic.com
SIC: 2821 Plastics materials and resins
PA: Ip Corporation
1225 Willow Lake Blvd
Saint Paul MN 55110
651 481-6860

(G-11914)
J H J INC
Also Called: Madison, The
15314 Harrison Rd (46544-5721)
PHONE..................................574 256-6966
Craig Nowicki, *Pr*
John J Hoffman, *
Paul Schuchman, *
EMP: 50 EST: 1972
SQ FT: 45,000
SALES (est): 11.26MM **Privately Held**
Web: www.jackel.com
SIC: 3089 Injection molding of plastics

(G-11915)
JACKSON HEWITT TAX SERVICE
Also Called: Access Cell Phones
922 S Beiger St (46544)
PHONE..................................574 255-2200
Tony Magaldi, *Pr*
EMP: 10 EST: 1996
SALES (est): 494.03K **Privately Held**
Web: www.jacksonhewitt.com
SIC: 7291 2899 Tax return preparation services; Fireworks

(G-11916)
JAMES F REILLY 3 ENT
1969 E Mckinley Ave (46545-7205)
PHONE..................................574 277-8267
James Reilly, *Pr*
EMP: 2 EST: 2000
SALES (est): 124.21K **Privately Held**
SIC: 1081 Mine development, metal

(G-11917)
JAMIL PACKAGING CORPORATION (PA)
1420 Industrial Dr (46544-5720)
P.O. Box 684 (46546-0684)
PHONE..................................574 256-2600
David A Diroll, *Pr*
Mary E Diroll, *
▲ EMP: 50 EST: 1973
SQ FT: 160,000
SALES (est): 15.79MM
SALES (corp-wide): 15.79MM **Privately Held**
Web: www.jamilpkg.com
SIC: 2653 5199 Boxes, corrugated: made from purchased materials; Packaging materials

(G-11918)
JANCO ENGINEERED PRODUCTS LLC
1217 E 7th St (46544-2851)
PHONE..................................574 255-3169
◆ EMP: 140 EST: 2011
SQ FT: 80,000
SALES (est): 22.96MM **Privately Held**
Web: www.jancoengineeredproducts.com
SIC: 3089 Injection molding of plastics

(G-11919)
JC METAL FABRICATION LLC
15393 Kelly Rd (46544-9204)
PHONE..................................574 340-1109
Joseph R Campoli, *Admn*
EMP: 2 EST: 2008
SALES (est): 244.18K **Privately Held**
SIC: 3499 Fabricated metal products, nec

(G-11920)
JEDEU INDUSTRIES LLC
154 Eastgate Cir (46544-3450)
P.O. Box 11322 (46634-0322)
PHONE..................................317 660-5526
Johnathan Snyder, *Prin*
EMP: 1 EST: 2013
SALES (est): 44.9K **Privately Held**
SIC: 3999 Manufacturing industries, nec

(G-11921)
KANOFF ENTERPRISES
928 W Berry Ave (46545-8842)
PHONE..................................574 575-6787
EMP: 3 EST: 1981
SALES (est): 182.73K **Privately Held**
SIC: 3312 3462 Pipes and tubes; Gears, forged steel

(G-11922)
KENDRION (MISHAWAKA) LLC
56733 Magnetic Dr (46545-7481)
PHONE..................................574 257-2422
EMP: 30 EST: 1997
SQ FT: 22,000
SALES (est): 8.27MM
SALES (corp-wide): 563.59MM **Privately Held**
Web: www.kendrion.com
SIC: 3679 3677 3089 3824 Electronic circuits; Electronic coils and transformers; Plastics processing; Mechanical and electromechanical counters and devices
PA: Kendrion N.V.
Herikerbergweg 213
Amsterdam NH 1101
850731500

(G-11923)
KRA INTERNATIONAL LLC (PA)
1810 Clover Rd (46545-7247)
PHONE..................................574 259-3550
Hari Agarwal, *Pr*
▲ EMP: 59 EST: 1978
SQ FT: 28,000
SALES (est): 8.76MM
SALES (corp-wide): 8.76MM **Privately Held**
Web: www.krainternational.com
SIC: 3679 Harness assemblies, for electronic use: wire or cable

(G-11924)
KRAIGS CUSTOM WOODWORKING
1810 E 12th St (46544-5928)
PHONE..................................574 904-7501
Kraig Pehling, *Prin*
EMP: 6 EST: 2010
SALES (est): 184.04K **Privately Held**
SIC: 2431 Millwork

(G-11925)
LAIDIG INC
14535 Dragoon Trl (46544-6814)
PHONE..................................574 256-0204
Daniel Laidig, *Prin*
Sonja Laidig, *
Wyn Laidig, *
Daniel Laidig, *VP*
EMP: 50 EST: 1959
SQ FT: 45,000
SALES (est): 9.3MM **Privately Held**
Web: www.laidig.com
SIC: 3523 3537 3448 3423 Silo fillers and unloaders; Industrial trucks and tractors; Prefabricated metal buildings and components; Hand and edge tools, nec

(G-11926)
LARCK INDUSTRIES LLC
55685 Currant Rd Ste D (46544-4812)
P.O. Box 1534 (46530-1534)
PHONE..................................574 993-5502
Amy Robison, *Prin*
EMP: 1 EST: 2017
SALES (est): 46.23K **Privately Held**
SIC: 3999 Manufacturing industries, nec

(G-11927)
LE-HUE MACHINE AND TOOL CO
1915 N Cedar St (46545-6466)
PHONE..................................574 255-8404
Dale Le Hue, *Pr*
Susan Le Hue, *Sec*
EMP: 7 EST: 1985
SQ FT: 12,200
SALES (est): 713.9K **Privately Held**
SIC: 3544 3599 Special dies and tools; Machine shop, jobbing and repair

(G-11928)
LEONI LLC
1015 W 7th St (46544-4852)
PHONE..................................574 315-0503
Leoni Lowery, *Owner*
EMP: 5 EST: 2018
SALES (est): 52.94K **Privately Held**
Web: www.leoni.com
SIC: 3679 Electronic circuits

(G-11929)
LIGHT OF LIFE GEL CANDLES
819 Kline St (46544-3735)
PHONE..................................574 310-3777
Debbie Erickson, *Prin*
EMP: 5 EST: 2018
SALES (est): 39.69K **Privately Held**
SIC: 3999 Candles

(G-11930)
LIPPERT COMPONENTS INC
Also Called: Duncan Systems
408 S Byrkit St (46544-3012)
PHONE..................................800 551-9149
Brent Watson, *Mgr*
EMP: 25
SALES (corp-wide): 3.78B **Publicly Held**
Web: www.lci1.com
SIC: 3711 3469 3444 3714 Chassis, motor vehicle; Stamping metal for the trade; Metal roofing and roof drainage equipment; Motor vehicle parts and accessories
HQ: Lippert Components, Inc.
3501 County Rd 6 E
Elkhart IN 46514
574 535-1125

(G-11931)
LIPPERT COMPONENTS INC
401 S Beiger St (46544-3206)
PHONE..................................574 537-8900
EMP: 54 EST: 1997
SALES (est): 384.33K **Privately Held**
Web: www.lippertcomponents.eu
SIC: 3714 Motor vehicle parts and accessories

(G-11932)
LOGO BOYS INC
3102 N Home St (46545-4438)
PHONE..................................574 256-6844
Dean A Himelick, *Pr*
Bob Nicol, *Sec*
EMP: 8 EST: 2000
SQ FT: 2,400
SALES (est): 962.96K **Privately Held**
Web: www.logoboys.net
SIC: 7336 2395 Silk screen design; Embroidery products, except Schiffli machine

(G-11933)
LULULEMON
6501 Grape Rd Spc 289 (46545-1007)
PHONE..................................574 271-3260
EMP: 5 EST: 1998
SALES (est): 42.55K **Privately Held**
SIC: 2389 Apparel and accessories, nec

(G-11934)
LURE VENTURES INC
532 Ballard Ave (46544-3810)
PHONE..................................219 313-5325
EMP: 7 EST: 2012
SALES (est): 86K **Privately Held**
SIC: 3949 Lures, fishing: artificial

(G-11935)
MACOR
1025 W 11th St (46544-4818)
PHONE..................................574 255-2658
Jim Cocquyt, *Owner*
EMP: 2 EST: 2010
SALES (est): 111.11K **Privately Held**

Mishawaka - St. Joseph County (G-11936) GEOGRAPHIC SECTION

SIC: 2047 Dog and cat food

(G-11936)
MAKS PLASTIC LLC ◊
13077 Mckinley Hwy (46545-7528)
PHONE...................................574 215-1800
Kristian Stankiewicz, *Managing Member*
EMP: 12 EST: 2022
SALES (est): 2.41MM **Privately Held**
Web: www.maksplastics.com
SIC: 3089 Plastics products, nec

(G-11937)
MARON PRODUCTS INC
1015 Saint Jerome St (46544-5735)
PHONE...................................574 254-0840
EMP: 8 EST: 2018
SALES (est): 39.69K **Privately Held**
Web: www.maronproducts.com
SIC: 3999 Manufacturing industries, nec

(G-11938)
MARON PRODUCTS INCORPORATED
1301 Industrial Dr (46544-5799)
PHONE...................................574 259-1971
Paul Mc Mahon, *Pr*
EMP: 85 EST: 1957
SQ FT: 200,000
SALES (est): 8.54MM **Privately Held**
Web: www.maronproducts.com
SIC: 3444 3469 Sheet metalwork; Stamping metal for the trade

(G-11939)
MATRIX TOOL INC
1210 S Merrifield Ave (46544-5711)
PHONE...................................574 259-3093
Andrew Bryant, *Pr*
EMP: 10 EST: 1991
SALES (est): 313.89K **Privately Held**
Web: www.matrixtoolinc.com
SIC: 2821 3544 Molding compounds, plastics ; Special dies, tools, jigs, and fixtures

(G-11940)
MAURER SPECIALTY POOLS AND CON
1310 E 6th St (46544-2820)
PHONE...................................574 320-2429
EMP: 7
SALES (est): 541.35K **Privately Held**
SIC: 3429 Hardware, nec

(G-11941)
MC METALCRAFT INC
Also Called: Reliable Metalcraft
1210 Willow St (46545-6762)
PHONE...................................574 259-8101
Scott Chakan, *Pr*
Blair Melvin, *COO*
EMP: 8 EST: 2015
SQ FT: 20,000
SALES (est): 1.29MM **Privately Held**
Web: www.reliablemetalcraft.com
SIC: 3469 Stamping metal for the trade

(G-11942)
MERRILL CORPORATION
Also Called: Merrill Pharmacy
606 N Main St (46545-6620)
PHONE...................................574 255-2988
Marc O Merrill, *Pr*
Christopher Merrill, *Sec*
EMP: 24 EST: 1959
SQ FT: 7,500
SALES (est): 2.43MM **Privately Held**
Web: www.merrillpharmacy.com
SIC: 5912 5047 2834 Drug stores; Medical and hospital equipment; Ointments

(G-11943)
MICHIANA EXECUTIVE JOURNAL
Also Called: Business To Business
203 N Main St (46544-1410)
PHONE...................................574 256-6666
EMP: 5 EST: 1992
SALES (est): 85.07K **Privately Held**
SIC: 2721 Trade journals: publishing and printing

(G-11944)
MICHIANA GLOBAL MOLD INC
1702 E 7th St (46544-3213)
PHONE...................................574 259-6262
Eric Seigel, *Pr*
▲ EMP: 14 EST: 2014
SALES (est): 1.99MM **Privately Held**
Web: www.mgmold.com
SIC: 3544 Industrial molds

(G-11945)
MICHIANA PLASTICS INC
1702 E 7th St (46544-3219)
PHONE...................................574 259-6262
James Orszulak, *Pr*
Michael A Vaughn, *
▲ EMP: 23 EST: 1964
SQ FT: 34,450
SALES (est): 902.45K **Privately Held**
Web: www.mgmold.com
SIC: 3544 Special dies and tools

(G-11946)
MICHIANA SIGNS AND LIGHTING
1035 E Mckinley Ave (46545-4113)
PHONE...................................574 520-1254
EMP: 4 EST: 2019
SALES (est): 46.08K **Privately Held**
Web: www.michianasignsandlighting.com
SIC: 3993 Signs and advertising specialties

(G-11947)
MIDWEST BLIND & SHADE CO
4115 Grape Rd (46545-2609)
PHONE...................................574 271-0770
Charles Prichard, *Owner*
June S Prichard, *Sec*
EMP: 5 EST: 1990
SQ FT: 2,500
SALES (est): 479.58K **Privately Held**
Web: www.midwestblindandshadeco.com
SIC: 2591 5719 5023 Window blinds; Window furnishings; Vertical blinds

(G-11948)
MIDWEST CUSTOM FINISHING INC (PA)
1906 Clover Rd (46545-7245)
PHONE...................................574 258-0099
EMP: 2 EST: 1995
SQ FT: 23,000
SALES (est): 2.36MM **Privately Held**
SIC: 3479 Coating of metals and formed products

(G-11949)
MIDWEST FINISHING SYSTEMS INC
55770 Evergreen Plaza Dr (46545-7964)
PHONE...................................574 257-0099
EMP: 40 EST: 1994
SALES (est): 9.64MM **Privately Held**
Web: www.midwestfinishing.com
SIC: 3991 8711 3567 3563 Brooms and brushes; Industrial engineers; Industrial furnaces and ovens; Air and gas compressors

(G-11950)
MIDWEST MWI INC
1201 Industrial Dr (46544-5724)
PHONE...................................574 288-6573
EMP: 8 EST: 2015
SALES (est): 94.1K **Privately Held**
Web: www.mwi-inc.com
SIC: 3599 Machine shop, jobbing and repair

(G-11951)
MILITARY NEON SIGNS
3304 Wild Cherry Rdg W (46544-6901)
PHONE...................................574 258-9804
Ted Spear, *Owner*
EMP: 2 EST: 2005
SALES (est): 79.75K **Privately Held**
SIC: 3993 Neon signs

(G-11952)
MISHAWAKA LLC
609 E Jefferson Blvd (46545-6524)
PHONE...................................574 259-1981
EMP: 12 EST: 2004
SALES (est): 927.93K **Privately Held**
Web: www.mishawakacommerciallandscaping.com
SIC: 3542 Magnetic forming machines

(G-11953)
MISHAWAKA ART & FRAME GALLERY
110 N Main St (46544-1413)
PHONE...................................574 259-9320
Peggy Oneil, *Pr*
EMP: 2 EST: 1976
SQ FT: 3,000
SALES (est): 149.91K **Privately Held**
Web: www.shopmishawaka.com
SIC: 3499 5945 5947 5999 Picture frames, metal; Arts and crafts supplies; Gift shop; Picture frames, ready made

(G-11954)
MISHAWAKA DOOR LLC
58743 Executive Dr (46544-6845)
PHONE...................................574 259-2822
Martin Madden, *Managing Member*
EMP: 4 EST: 2002
SALES (est): 644.81K **Privately Held**
Web: www.1800overhead.com
SIC: 2431 Door frames, wood

(G-11955)
MISHAWAKA FOOD PANTRY INC
315 Lincolnway W (46544-1903)
PHONE...................................574 220-6213
Michael Hayes, *Dir*
EMP: 3 EST: 2012
SALES (est): 384.6K **Privately Held**
Web: www.mishawakafoodpantry.org
SIC: 2099 Food preparations, nec

(G-11956)
MISHAWAKA FROZEN CUSTARD
Also Called: Ritter's Frozen Custard
3921 N Main St (46545-3107)
PHONE...................................574 255-8000
Bob Jaques, *Owner*
EMP: 7 EST: 1996
SALES (est): 228.31K **Privately Held**
Web: www.ritters.com
SIC: 2024 8322 5451 5812 Ice cream and frozen deserts; Hotline; Ice cream (packaged); Eating places

(G-11957)
MISHAWAKA WHSE & DISTRG LLC
2017 Elder Rd (46545-7323)
PHONE...................................574 259-6011
EMP: 2 EST: 1935

SQ FT: 28,300
SALES (est): 233.33K **Privately Held**
Web: www.mw-d.biz
SIC: 2541 Sink tops, plastic laminated

(G-11958)
NATIONAL CASTER ACQUISITION
4100 Edison Lakes Pkwy (46545-3465)
PHONE...................................574 273-7000
EMP: 9 EST: 2002
SALES (est): 102.34K **Privately Held**
SIC: 3312 Sheet or strip, steel, hot-rolled

(G-11959)
NATIONAL CASTING CORPORATION
4100 Edison Lakes Pkwy (46545-3465)
PHONE...................................574 273-7000
EMP: 9 EST: 2002
SALES (est): 150.47K **Privately Held**
Web: www.natlcasting.com
SIC: 3312 Sheet or strip, steel, hot-rolled

(G-11960)
NATIONAL COATING LINE CORP
4100 Edison Lakes Pkwy (46545-3465)
PHONE...................................574 273-7000
EMP: 11 EST: 2002
SALES (est): 102.34K **Privately Held**
SIC: 3312 Sheet or strip, steel, hot-rolled

(G-11961)
NATIONAL MTLS PROCUREMENT CORP
4100 Edison Lakes Pkwy (46545)
PHONE...................................574 273-7000
EMP: 9 EST: 2002
SALES (est): 198.68K **Privately Held**
SIC: 3312 Sheet or strip, steel, hot-rolled

(G-11962)
NATIONAL STEEL FUNDING CORP
4100 Edison Lakes Pkwy (46545-3468)
PHONE...................................574 273-7000
EMP: 6 EST: 2002
SALES (est): 106.95K **Privately Held**
SIC: 3312 Sheet or strip, steel, hot-rolled

(G-11963)
NATIONAL STEEL PELLET COMPANY
4100 Edison Lakes Pkwy (46545)
PHONE...................................574 273-7000
John Davis, *Pr*
EMP: 4 EST: 1983
SALES (est): 232.11K **Privately Held**
SIC: 1011 Iron ore mining

(G-11964)
NCP COATINGS INC
Also Called: Mishawaka Devision
1413 Clover Rd (46545-7271)
PHONE...................................574 255-9678
Sherman Drew, *Mgr*
EMP: 6
SALES (corp-wide): 24.82MM **Privately Held**
Web: www.ncpcoatings.com
SIC: 2851 2899 Paints and allied products; Core oil or binders
PA: Ncp Coatings, Inc.
225 Fort St
Niles MI 49120
269 683-3377

(G-11965)
NEXT DAY SIGNS
Also Called: Next Day Signs & Images
13565 Us 20 (46545)
PHONE...................................574 259-7446
EMP: 2 EST: 1995
SQ FT: 2,000

GEOGRAPHIC SECTION

Mishawaka - St. Joseph County (G-11991)

SALES (est): 140.26K **Privately Held**
Web:
www.nextdaysignsindianapolis.com
SIC: 3993 Signs and advertising specialties

(G-11966)
NS HOLDINGS CORPORATION
4100 Edison Lakes Pkwy (46545-3465)
PHONE..................574 273-7000
EMP: 9 EST: 2002
SALES (est): 102.34K **Privately Held**
SIC: 3312 Sheet or strip, steel, hot-rolled

(G-11967)
NS LAND COMPANY
4100 Edison Lakes Parkway (46545-3465)
PHONE..................574 273-7000
EMP: 9 EST: 2002
SALES (est): 11.19K **Privately Held**
SIC: 3312 Sheet or strip, steel, hot-rolled

(G-11968)
NYX FORT WAYNE LLC
Also Called: N Y X
616 W Mckinley Ave (46545-5518)
PHONE..................260 484-0595
▲ EMP: 85
SIC: 3089 Automotive parts, plastic

(G-11969)
PALLATIN MACHINE LLC
1902 W 6th St (46544-1633)
PHONE..................574 703-7505
William Pallatin, *Owner*
EMP: 5 EST: 2014
SALES (est): 186.18K **Privately Held**
SIC: 3599 Machine shop, jobbing and repair

(G-11970)
PATRICK INDUSTRIES INC
Also Called: West Executive Offices
5020 Lincolnway E (46544-4206)
PHONE..................574 255-9692
Dale Smith, *Brnch Mgr*
EMP: 7
SALES (corp-wide): 3.47B **Publicly Held**
Web: www.patrickind.com
SIC: 2295 Coated fabrics, not rubberized
PA: Patrick Industries, Inc.
107 W Franklin St
Elkhart IN 46516
574 294-7511

(G-11971)
PATRICK INDUSTRIES INC
Metals Division
5020 Lincolnway E (46544-4206)
PHONE..................574 255-9692
EMP: 5
SALES (corp-wide): 3.47B **Publicly Held**
Web: www.patrickind.com
SIC: 3354 5031 Aluminum extruded products; Lumber, plywood, and millwork
PA: Patrick Industries, Inc.
107 W Franklin St
Elkhart IN 46516
574 294-7511

(G-11972)
PAUL TIROTTA
Also Called: Maverick Molding
1701 E 6th St (46544-3208)
PHONE..................574 255-4101
EMP: 10 EST: 1996
SQ FT: 14,000
SALES (est): 984.07K **Privately Held**
SIC: 3089 Injection molding of plastics

(G-11973)
PENNPLASTICS LLC
945 E 6th St (46544-2825)
PHONE..................574 286-0705
Terry Pennington, *Managing Member*
EMP: 4 EST: 2018
SALES (est): 240.93K **Privately Held**
SIC: 2671 Paper; coated and laminated packaging

(G-11974)
PENZ INC
1320 S Merrifield Ave (46544)
PHONE..................574 255-4736
David A Penzenik, *Pr*
Gregory Penzenik, *
Richard Penzenik, *
▲ EMP: 40 EST: 1956
SQ FT: 70,000
SALES (est): 8.81MM
SALES (corp-wide): 174.22MM **Privately Held**
Web: hd.tramec.com
SIC: 3441 3089 Fabricated structural metal; Plastics processing
HQ: Tramec Sloan, L.L.C.
534 E 48th St
Holland MI 49423
800 336-7778

(G-11975)
PLASTIMATIC ARTS CORP
Also Called: Pac Banner Works
3622 N Home St (46545-4316)
PHONE..................574 254-9000
Timothy Rink, *Pr*
Lisa Rink, *
Michaelene Rink, *Prin*
EMP: 40 EST: 1961
SQ FT: 30,000
SALES (est): 4.32MM **Privately Held**
Web: www.pacbannerworks.com
SIC: 2759 Screen printing

(G-11976)
POWER COMPONENTS OF MIDWEST
56641 Twin Branch Dr (46545-7479)
P.O. Box 1348 (46546-1348)
PHONE..................574 256-6990
Todd Webster, *Pr*
Larry Jante, *
Gary Holvoet, *
James D Waters, *
EMP: 30 EST: 1980
SQ FT: 84,000
SALES (est): 771.19K **Privately Held**
SIC: 3625 3674 5063 Switches, electric power; Semiconductors and related devices; Switchgear

(G-11977)
PRECISION ELECTRIC INC
Also Called: Precision Electronics
1508 W 6th St (46544-1640)
P.O. Box 451 (46546-0451)
PHONE..................574 256-1000
Joe Chamberlin, *Pr*
Kerry R Dodd, *VP*
▲ EMP: 22 EST: 1987
SQ FT: 28,000
SALES (est): 4.26MM **Privately Held**
Web: www.precision-elec.com
SIC: 7694 3599 Electric motor repair; Machine shop, jobbing and repair

(G-11978)
PRECISION PIECE PARTS INC
712 S Logan St (46544-4892)
PHONE..................574 255-3185
Gregory C Rogers, *Pr*
EMP: 60 EST: 1943
SQ FT: 25,000
SALES (est): 5.27MM **Privately Held**
Web: www.ppp-inc.com
SIC: 3728 3842 3451 Aircraft parts and equipment, nec; Surgical appliances and supplies; Screw machine products

(G-11979)
PRINT MY MERCH LLC
14208 Dragoon Trl (46544-6831)
PHONE..................765 269-6772
Jacob Dobransky, *CEO*
EMP: 4 EST: 2017
SALES (est): 71.53K **Privately Held**
SIC: 2752 Commercial printing, lithographic

(G-11980)
PRODUCTION PARTNERS INC
1710 Clover Rd Ste 3 (46545-7273)
PHONE..................574 229-5960
Robert Roose, *Pr*
Michael Vanzant, *VP*
EMP: 10 EST: 2011
SALES (est): 825.17K **Privately Held**
Web: www.productionpartners.com
SIC: 3443 3089 Metal parts; Plastics processing

(G-11981)
PROFESSIONAL PERMITS
2319 Lincolnway E (46544-3314)
PHONE..................574 257-2954
Doug Merritt, *Owner*
EMP: 3 EST: 2006
SALES (est): 121.14K **Privately Held**
Web: www.professionalpermits.com
SIC: 3993 Signs and advertising specialties

(G-11982)
PULLIAM ENTERPRISES INC
Also Called: Pull Rite
13790 Jefferson Blvd (46545-7345)
PHONE..................574 259-1520
Andrew Pulliam, *Ch Bd*
Randall A Pulliam, *
Linda Hampton, *
Leota Pulliam, *
EMP: 50 EST: 1978
SQ FT: 25,000
SALES (est): 8.77MM **Privately Held**
Web: www.pullrite.com
SIC: 3714 Trailer hitches, motor vehicle

(G-11983)
R & D MOLD AND ENGINEERING INC
1710 Clover Rd (46545-7272)
PHONE..................574 257-1070
EMP: 8 EST: 1996
SQ FT: 6,400
SALES (est): 810.51K **Privately Held**
SIC: 3544 Industrial molds

(G-11984)
RAVENS
605 W Edison Rd Ste F (46545-8823)
PHONE..................269 362-4489
EMP: 4 EST: 2019
SALES (est): 122.4K **Privately Held**
SIC: 3715 Truck trailers

(G-11985)
RICHARDS LIQUIDATION CORP
Also Called: Starcraft Tire and Wheel
1655 E 12th St (46544)
PHONE..................574 807-8588
Bradley R M Richards, *Pr*
Joe Katona, *Genl Mgr*
▲ EMP: 14 EST: 1991
SQ FT: 25,000
SALES (est): 3.64MM

SALES (corp-wide): 1.41B **Privately Held**
Web: www.hispecwheel.com
SIC: 3312 3011 Wheels; Truck or bus tires, pneumatic
HQ: Dexter Axle Company Llc
2900 Industrial Pkwy E
Elkhart IN 46516

(G-11986)
RICK SINGLETON
Also Called: Studio A Advertising
203 N Main St (46544-1410)
P.O. Box 21 (46546-0021)
PHONE..................574 259-5555
Rick Singleton, *Owner*
EMP: 10 EST: 1981
SQ FT: 20,000
SALES (est): 379.69K **Privately Held**
Web: www.studioaadvertising.com
SIC: 7311 2721 Advertising agencies; Magazines: publishing only, not printed on site

(G-11987)
RIM MOLDING AND ENGRG INC
56855 Ferrettie Ct (46545)
PHONE..................574 294-1932
Brian Jagla, *CEO*
Phil Roth, *VP*
EMP: 15 EST: 2010
SALES (est): 2.25MM **Privately Held**
Web: www.rmemolding.com
SIC: 3089 Injection molding of plastics

(G-11988)
RIVER VALLEY SHEET METAL INC
Also Called: Air & Energy
58785 Executive Dr (46544-6845)
PHONE..................574 259-2538
Kurt Siebert, *Ex VP*
Kurt Siebert, *Stockholder*
Marlene Siebert, *VP*
Mark Siebert, *Pr*
Kurt Jeff Siebert, *Sec*
EMP: 14 EST: 1970
SQ FT: 27,000
SALES (est): 343.78K **Privately Held**
SIC: 1761 3444 5039 Roofing, siding, and sheetmetal work; Sheet metalwork; Air ducts, sheet metal

(G-11989)
RX HONING MACHINE CORP
1301 E 5th St (46544-2899)
PHONE..................574 259-1606
R J Watson, *Pr*
Vickie Watson, *Sec*
EMP: 4 EST: 1968
SQ FT: 6,000
SALES (est): 460.74K **Privately Held**
Web: www.rxhoning.com
SIC: 3541 7699 Honing and lapping machines; Knife, saw and tool sharpening and repair

(G-11990)
SAMPSON FIBERGLASS INC
2424 N Home St (46545-4426)
PHONE..................574 255-4356
Edwin Sampson, *Pr*
Konnie Sampson, *VP*
EMP: 36 EST: 1995
SALES (est): 982.62K **Privately Held**
Web: www.sampsonfiberglass.com
SIC: 2221 Fiberglass fabrics

(G-11991)
SC SUPPLY COMPANY LLC
14396 Sage Ct (46545-1860)
P.O. Box 11531 (46634-0531)
PHONE..................574 287-0252

Susan Caldwell, *Pr*
EMP: 3 **EST:** 2001
SALES (est): 360.17K **Privately Held**
Web: www.trafficsafetysuppliers.com
SIC: 3669 Traffic signals, electric

(G-11992)
SCHURZ COMMUNICATIONS INC (HQ)
1301 E Douglas Rd Ste 200 (46545-1732)
PHONE..............................574 247-7237
Todd Schurz, *Pr*
Gary N Hoipkemier, *CFO*
Ramona Heine, *Prin*
David Olivencia, *Prin*
EMP: 15 **EST:** 1872
SQ FT: 1,500
SALES (est): 311.5MM
SALES (corp-wide): 3.28B **Publicly Held**
Web: www.schurz.com
SIC: 4833 2711 Television broadcasting stations; Newspapers, publishing and printing
PA: Gray Television, Inc.
4370 Pchtree Rd Ne Ste 40
Atlanta GA 30319
404 504-9828

(G-11993)
SIGN CREATIONS
919 Saint Jerome St (46544)
PHONE..............................574 204-2179
Tim Grontkowski, *Owner*
EMP: 1 **EST:** 2006
SALES (est): 192K **Privately Held**
Web: www.signcreations1.net
SIC: 3993 Signs and advertising specialties

(G-11994)
SIGN FACTORY
55811 Elder Rd (46544-4605)
PHONE..............................574 255-7446
EMP: 4 **EST:** 2009
SALES (est): 118.86K **Privately Held**
SIC: 3993 Signs and advertising specialties

(G-11995)
SIGNS UNLIMITED
4121 Lincolnway E (46544-4022)
PHONE..............................574 255-0500
Mike Stowe, *Owner*
EMP: 3 **EST:** 2007
SALES (est): 182.84K **Privately Held**
Web: www.pwcgraphics.com
SIC: 3993 Signs and advertising specialties

(G-11996)
SLB CORPORATION
Also Called: Hose Assemblies
1906 E Mckinley Ave (46545-7206)
PHONE..............................574 255-9774
Matthew B Veldman, *Pr*
▲ **EMP:** 18 **EST:** 1997
SALES (est): 4.34MM **Privately Held**
Web: www.hoseassem.com
SIC: 3052 3492 3429 Rubber hose; Fluid power valves and hose fittings; Hardware, nec

(G-11997)
SMART SYSTEMS
303 S Byrkit St (46544-2904)
PHONE..............................800 348-0823
Michael Miller, *Pr*
EMP: 9 **EST:** 2008
SALES (est): 585.86K **Privately Held**
Web: www.smart-4.com
SIC: 2842 Sanitation preparations

(G-11998)
SMART TEMPS LLC
435 Park Place Cir Ste 100 (46545-3576)
PHONE..............................574 217-7202
John Miller, *Pr*
Michael Mckay, *COO*
EMP: 5 **EST:** 2009
SALES (est): 2.47MM
SALES (corp-wide): 444.85MM **Publicly Held**
Web: www.smartsense.co
SIC: 3822 Refrigeration thermostats
PA: Digi International Inc.
9350 Exclsior Blvd Ste 70
Hopkins MN 55343
952 912-3444

(G-11999)
SMITH SIGNS INC
Also Called: Smith Graphics & Design
317 Capital Ave (46544-3343)
P.O. Box 103 (46546-0103)
PHONE..............................574 255-6446
Douglas Smith, *Pr*
EMP: 9 **EST:** 2002
SALES (est): 892.07K **Privately Held**
Web: www.smithgraphics.net
SIC: 3993 Signs, not made in custom sign painting shops

(G-12000)
SNOW MANAGEMENT GROUP
14009 Jefferson Blvd (46545-7338)
PHONE..............................574 252-5253
Thomas Lovisa, *Prin*
EMP: 3 **EST:** 2006
SALES (est): 207.46K **Privately Held**
Web: www.mishawakasnowplow.com
SIC: 2851 Removers and cleaners

(G-12001)
SNYDERS PRTBLE WLDG FBRICATION
P.O. Box 1233 (46546-1233)
PHONE..............................574 258-4015
EMP: 1
SALES (est): 37.38K **Privately Held**
SIC: 7692 Welding repair

(G-12002)
SOUTH BEND CLUTCH INC
709 W Jefferson Blvd (46545-5843)
PHONE..............................574 256-5064
Walter Pyfer, *Pr*
Andrew Pyfer, *
Peter Pyfer, *
Mary A Bauer, *
▲ **EMP:** 25 **EST:** 1969
SQ FT: 6,000
SALES (est): 5.17MM **Privately Held**
Web: www.southbendclutch.com
SIC: 3714 Clutches, motor vehicle

(G-12003)
SOUTH BEND SCREEN PROCESS INC (PA)
Also Called: Shape Man
3622 N Home St (46544-4316)
PHONE..............................574 254-9000
Robert Kistler, *Pr*
Sue Kistler, *Sec*
EMP: 6 **EST:** 1954
SQ FT: 11,000
SALES (est): 607.3K
SALES (corp-wide): 607.3K **Privately Held**
Web: www.pacbannerworks.com
SIC: 2759 Screen printing

(G-12004)
SOUTHLAND METALS INC
4042 Southampton Dr (46544-9139)
PHONE..............................574 252-4441
Keith Crawford, *Pr*
EMP: 5
SALES (corp-wide): 4.92MM **Privately Held**
Web: www.smetals.com
SIC: 3325 Steel foundries, nec
PA: Southland Metals, Inc.
115 Carnahan Dr Ste 2
Maumelle AR 72113
501 851-1700

(G-12005)
SPARTAN TRAILER MFG INC
1207 Lincolnway W (46544-1709)
PHONE..............................574 309-3035
Laura Helman, *Pr*
EMP: 6 **EST:** 2016
SALES (est): 521.03K **Privately Held**
SIC: 3715 Truck trailers

(G-12006)
SPRINKGUARD LLC
5776 Grape Rd Ste 51 (46545-8460)
P.O. Box 161 (46546-0161)
PHONE..............................877 274-7976
Matt Hunsberger, *Pr*
Megan Hunsberger, *VP*
EMP: 18 **EST:** 2011
SALES (est): 991.09K **Privately Held**
Web: www.sprinkguard.com
SIC: 7389 1711 3569 Fire protection service other than forestry or public; Fire sprinkler system installation; Sprinkler systems, fire: automatic

(G-12007)
STANDARD MOTOR PRODUCTS INC
Also Called: Ristance
1718 N Home St (46545-7237)
PHONE..............................574 259-6253
Gerald Anton, *Mgr*
EMP: 85
SALES (corp-wide): 1.36B **Publicly Held**
Web: www.smpcorp.com
SIC: 3714 Motor vehicle parts and accessories
PA: Standard Motor Products, Inc.
3718 Northern Blvd
Long Island City NY 11101
718 392-0200

(G-12008)
STEEL AVENUE INC
3848 Cottage Ave (46544-3857)
EMP: 2 **EST:** 2000
SALES (est): 227.24K **Privately Held**
SIC: 3312 Slabs, steel

(G-12009)
STYRENE SOLUTIONS LLC
317 Capital Ave (46544-3343)
PHONE..............................270 317-2427
EMP: 5 **EST:** 2016
SALES (est): 119.75K **Privately Held**
SIC: 2865 Styrene

(G-12010)
SUBSTRATE TREATMENTS & LUBR
Also Called: ST&l
1309 S Byrkit Ave (46544-5837)
PHONE..............................574 258-0904
Robert Kvietkus, *Pr*
EMP: 16 **EST:** 1997
SALES (est): 2.47MM **Privately Held**
Web: www.stlchemicals.com
SIC: 2819 5169 Industrial inorganic chemicals, nec; Industrial chemicals

(G-12011)
SUPERIOR PIECE PARTS INC
54015 Fir Rd (46545-1701)
PHONE..............................574 277-4236
Harvey Ludwig, *Pr*
Gale Meisner, *VP*
EMP: 10 **EST:** 1965
SQ FT: 14,900
SALES (est): 224.47K **Privately Held**
SIC: 3599 Machine shop, jobbing and repair

(G-12012)
T PRODUCTIONS INC
504 S Byrkit St (46544-3010)
PHONE..............................574 257-8610
Tony Kozlowski, *Pr*
Deanna Kozlowski, *VP*
EMP: 9 **EST:** 1999
SALES (est): 399.8K **Privately Held**
Web: www.t-productions.com
SIC: 2759 Screen printing

(G-12013)
TEAL LAKE IRON MINING COMPANY
4100 Edison Lakes Pkwy (46545)
PHONE..............................574 273-7000
EMP: 9 **EST:** 2002
SALES (est): 198.68K **Privately Held**
SIC: 3312 Sheet or strip, steel, hot-rolled

(G-12014)
TOOLMASTERS INC
1203 E 6th St (46544-2896)
PHONE..............................574 256-1881
Ron Newcomer, *Pr*
Donald Barbour, *VP*
EMP: 8 **EST:** 1972
SQ FT: 10,000
SALES (est): 854.35K **Privately Held**
Web: www.diebuilders.com
SIC: 3544 3542 Special dies and tools; Machine tools, metal forming type

(G-12015)
TP REMAINCO IN INC (HQ)
Also Called: Techniplas
616 W Mckinley Ave (46545)
PHONE..............................574 256-1521
Robert Brzozowski, *Pr*
Steve Smith, *
◆ **EMP:** 357 **EST:** 2001
SQ FT: 165,000
SALES (est): 169.77MM
SALES (corp-wide): 483MM **Privately Held**
Web: www.techniplas.com
SIC: 3089 Injection molding of plastics
PA: Tp Remainco, Llc
N44 W33341 Wtrtown Plank
Nashotah WI 53058
262 369-5555

(G-12016)
TRIM-A-DOOR CORPORATION (PA)
Also Called: Advance Cabinetry and Millwork
1824 N Home St (46545-7268)
PHONE..............................574 254-0300
Keith Hatkevich, *Pr*
Shelli Hatkevich, *
Linda Leblanc, *
▲ **EMP:** 20 **EST:** 2000
SALES (est): 4.35MM
SALES (corp-wide): 4.35MM **Privately Held**
Web: www.trimadoor.com
SIC: 2431 Millwork

GEOGRAPHIC SECTION

Mitchell - Lawrence County (G-12040)

(G-12017)
TRIPLEX INDUSTRIES INC
55901 Currant Rd (46545-4803)
PHONE..................574 256-9253
James Deren, *Pr*
Kevin Geisel, *Pr*
Larry Geisel, *VP*
Kathleen Geisel, *Stockholder*
▲ **EMP:** 5 **EST:** 1983
SQ FT: 8,000
SALES (est): 760.42K **Privately Held**
Web: www.genesismolding.com
SIC: 3544 Industrial molds

(G-12018)
TRUE NORTH GROUP LLC
Also Called: North Woods Village
1409 E Day Rd (46545-3671)
PHONE..................574 247-1866
North Woods, *Prin*
EMP: 78 **EST:** 2013
SALES (est): 2.35MM **Privately Held**
Web: www.northwoodsmemorycare.com
SIC: 2499 Wood products, nec

(G-12019)
UNITED TOOL & ENGINEERING INC
337 Campbell St (46544-2898)
PHONE..................574 259-1953
Richard Penn, *Pr*
John R Penn, *
EMP: 42 **EST:** 1972
SQ FT: 40,000
SALES (est): 5.29MM **Privately Held**
Web: www.unitedtleng.com
SIC: 3544 Special dies and tools

(G-12020)
VALLEY SCREEN PROCESS CO INC
58740 Executive Dr (46544-6898)
PHONE..................574 256-0901
Jerome E Bauer, *CEO*
Karen M Barnett, *
Martin Hess, *
Carol Bauer, *
▲ **EMP:** 77 **EST:** 1967
SQ FT: 60,000
SALES (est): 8.66MM **Privately Held**
Web: www.valleyscreen.com
SIC: 2752 Commercial printing, lithographic

(G-12021)
VAN CO
1030 N Merrifield Ave (46545-6713)
PHONE..................574 271-8432
Godelieve O B Vandevoorde, *Prin*
EMP: 10 **EST:** 1992
SALES (est): 70.27K **Privately Held**
SIC: 3599 Machine shop, jobbing and repair

(G-12022)
VISION MACHINE WORKS INC
Also Called: K & P Products
56641 Twin Branch Dr (47545-7479)
PHONE..................574 259-6500
James Niemier, *Pr*
Michael Szymczak, *VP*
EMP: 14 **EST:** 1957
SALES (est): 1.8MM **Privately Held**
Web: www.vmwinc.net
SIC: 3599 7692 3544 Machine shop, jobbing and repair; Welding repair; Special dies, tools, jigs, and fixtures

(G-12023)
VISION TRAINING PRODUCTS INC
Also Called: Bernell
4016 N Home St (46545-4308)
PHONE..................574 259-2070
Craig Andrews, *Ch Bd*
Chris Andrews, *Pr*
Judy Andrews, *Sec*
Misti Horvath, *Treas*
▲ **EMP:** 16 **EST:** 1997
SQ FT: 12,000
SALES (est): 2.94MM **Privately Held**
Web: www.bernell.com
SIC: 5049 5048 3841 Optical goods; Ophthalmic goods; Ophthalmic instruments and apparatus

(G-12024)
VMW TOOLING GROUP LLC
56641 Twin Branch Dr (46545-7479)
PHONE..................574 293-5090
EMP: 6 **EST:** 2019
SALES (est): 245.89K **Privately Held**
Web: www.vmwtooling.com
SIC: 3089 Injection molding of plastics

(G-12025)
WAKA MANUFACTURING INC
945 E 5th St (46544-2835)
PHONE..................574 258-0019
Joseph J Gyarmati Senior, *Pr*
Joseph J Gyarmati Junior, *VP*
EMP: 5 **EST:** 1969
SQ FT: 8,000
SALES (est): 458.58K **Privately Held**
SIC: 3441 Fabricated structural metal

(G-12026)
WELLNESS PET LLC
1025 W 11th St (46544-4818)
PHONE..................574 259-7834
EMP: 20
SALES (corp-wide): 101.78MM **Privately Held**
Web: www.wellnesspet.com
SIC: 2047 Dog and cat food
PA: Wellness Pet, Llc
  77 S Bedford St
  Burlington MA 01803
  877 869-2971

(G-12027)
WESTROCK CP LLC
1925 Stone Ct (46545-4441)
PHONE..................574 256-0318
Bob Feeney, *Brnch Mgr*
EMP: 1
SALES (corp-wide): 20.31B **Privately Held**
Web: www.westrock.com
SIC: 2653 5113 Boxes, corrugated: made from purchased materials; Corrugated and solid fiber boxes
HQ: Westrock Cp, Llc
  1000 Abernathy Rd Ste 125
  Atlanta GA 30328

(G-12028)
ZIPP PRINTING LLC
Also Called: Zipp Print
235 E Mckinley Ave Ste 2 (46545-6260)
PHONE..................574 256-0059
Kyle Johnson, *CEO*
Mark Sirok, *Mgr*
EMP: 5 **EST:** 1967
SALES (est): 499.32K **Privately Held**
Web: www.zippprinting.com
SIC: 2752 2791 Lithographing on metal; Typesetting

Mitchell
Lawrence County

(G-12029)
ADKINS SAWMILL INC
2929 Fleenor Rd (47446-8062)
PHONE..................812 849-4036
Paul Adkin, *Owner*
EMP: 2 **EST:** 1997
SALES (est): 238.54K **Privately Held**
SIC: 2421 Sawmills and planing mills, general

(G-12030)
AKKA PLASTICS INC
1100 Teke Burton Dr (47446-5398)
P.O. Box 525 (47446-0525)
PHONE..................812 849-9256
Marvin Stahl, *Pr*
EMP: 25 **EST:** 1982
SQ FT: 25,000
SALES (est): 4.85MM **Privately Held**
Web: www.akkainc.net
SIC: 3089 Injection molded finished plastics products, nec

(G-12031)
AMERICAN FIBERTECH CORPORATION
Also Called: Industrial Pallet
3159 Fleenor Rd (47446-8063)
PHONE..................812 849-6095
Jack Faubion, *Brnch Mgr*
EMP: 75
SALES (corp-wide): 49.88MM **Privately Held**
Web: www.ind-pallet-corp.com
SIC: 2421 Sawmills and planing mills, general
PA: American Fibertech Corporation
  4 N New York St
  Remington IN 47977
  219 261-3586

(G-12032)
BASIN MATERIAL HANDLING LLC
240 S Meridian Rd (47446)
PHONE..................812 849-0124
Mark Suvak, *Managing Member*
EMP: 6
SALES (est): 75.6K **Privately Held**
SIC: 3999 Manufacturing industries, nec

(G-12033)
BEYOND WELDING INSPECTION INC
2041 Clover Ln (47446-7715)
PHONE..................812 849-4410
Brian S Gerkin, *Owner*
EMP: 4 **EST:** 2017
SALES (est): 82.55K **Privately Held**
Web: www.beyondweldinginspectioninc.com
SIC: 7692 Welding repair

(G-12034)
C&M CONVEYOR INC
Also Called: Automated Systems Technology
4598 State Road 37 (47446-5388)
PHONE..................812 849-5647
Don Laipple, *CEO*
Randy Grube, *
EMP: 160 **EST:** 1982
SQ FT: 84,000
SALES (est): 45.94MM
SALES (corp-wide): 94.9MM **Privately Held**
Web: www.innoveyance.com
SIC: 3535 5084 Conveyors and conveying equipment; Conveyor systems
PA: Hammond, Kennedy, Whitney & Company, Inc.
  420 Lexington Ave Ste 402
  New York NY 10170
  212 867-1010

(G-12035)
CAROUSEL WINERY
6058 Lawrenceport Rd (47446-6038)
PHONE..................812 849-1005
EMP: 3 **EST:** 2014
SALES (est): 135.08K **Privately Held**
Web: www.carouselwinery.com
SIC: 2084 Wines

(G-12036)
CONTECH ENGNERED SOLUTIONS LLC
Metric Industrial Pk (47446)
PHONE..................812 849-3933
Joe Behne, *Superintnt*
EMP: 3
Web: www.conteches.com
SIC: 3443 Fabricated plate work (boiler shop)
HQ: Contech Engineered Solutions Llc
  9025 Centre Pointe Dr # 400
  West Chester OH 45069
  513 645-7000

(G-12037)
CONTECH ENGNERED SOLUTIONS LLC
200 John R Williams Ave (47446-8021)
PHONE..................812 849-3933
TOLL FREE: 800
Joseph Behne, *Brnch Mgr*
EMP: 19
Web: www.conteches.com
SIC: 3443 3444 Fabricated plate work (boiler shop); Sheet metalwork
HQ: Contech Engineered Solutions Llc
  9025 Centre Pointe Dr # 400
  West Chester OH 45069
  513 645-7000

(G-12038)
DREWS DEER PROCESSING
8122 Us Highway 50 W (47446-5439)
PHONE..................812 279-6246
Denny Perkins, *Prin*
EMP: 6 **EST:** 2013
SALES (est): 70.79K **Privately Held**
SIC: 2011 Meat packing plants

(G-12039)
FOAMCRAFT INC
100 N Industrial Pkwy (47446-8037)
PHONE..................812 849-3350
Dick Yerington, *Brnch Mgr*
EMP: 50
SQ FT: 32,000
SALES (corp-wide): 92.24MM **Privately Held**
Web: www.foamcraftinc.com
SIC: 3086 Plastics foam products
PA: Foamcraft Inc
  9230 Harrison Park Ct
  Indianapolis IN 46216
  317 545-3626

(G-12040)
HEIDELBERG MTLS US CEM LLC
180 N Meridian Rd (47446-1144)
P.O. Box 97 (47446-0097)
PHONE..................812 849-2191
Ed Epping, *Brnch Mgr*
EMP: 274
SALES (corp-wide): 23.02B **Privately Held**
Web: www.heidelbergmaterials.us
SIC: 3273 3241 Ready-mixed concrete; Cement, hydraulic
HQ: Heidelberg Materials Us Cement Llc
  300 E John Carpenter Fwy
  Irving TX 75062
  877 534-4442

Mitchell - Lawrence County (G-12041)

(G-12041)
JOSEPH MATTHEW BIASO
Also Called: Service/Sales
615 W Warren St # A (47446-1445)
PHONE.................................812 277-6871
Joseph Biaso, *Owner*
EMP: 4 EST: 2019
SALES (est): 181.99K **Privately Held**
SIC: 5961 8243 1731 3571 Catalog sales; Repair training, computer; Computer installation; Computers, digital, analog or hybrid

(G-12042)
KLEIHEGE WELDING MACHINE
746 Parks Implement Rd (47446-7657)
PHONE.................................812 849-5056
John W Kleihege, *Prin*
EMP: 1 EST: 2008
SALES (est): 49.78K **Privately Held**
SIC: 7692 Welding repair

(G-12043)
LAWRENCE CNTY FABRICATION CORP
240 S Meridian Rd (47446-8015)
PHONE.................................812 849-0124
Melissa Barnes, *Pr*
Dean Barnes, *
▲ EMP: 23 EST: 1996
SQ FT: 15,000
SALES (est): 1.56MM **Privately Held**
SIC: 3441 Fabricated structural metal

(G-12044)
MAMMOTH HATS INC
1773 Huron Williams Rd (47446-7470)
PHONE.................................812 849-2772
Charles Clifford, *Pr*
EMP: 11 EST: 2014
SALES (est): 524.84K **Privately Held**
Web: www.mammothhats.com
SIC: 5611 7389 2353 2253 Hats, men's and boys'; Business services, nec; Hats, caps, and millinery; Hats and headwear, knit

(G-12045)
NOVELS BY NELLOTIE
393 Sonny Dorsett Rd (47446-7355)
PHONE.................................812 583-1196
Nellotie Chastain, *Prin*
EMP: 4 EST: 2015
SALES (est): 56.41K **Privately Held**
SIC: 2741 Miscellaneous publishing

(G-12046)
RED BULL ARMORY LLC
440 Peaceful Valley Rd (47446-6822)
PHONE.................................757 287-7738
Christopher Higgins, *CEO*
EMP: 7 EST: 2013
SALES (est): 249.01K **Privately Held**
SIC: 3484 7389 Guns (firearms) or gun parts, 30 mm. and below; Inspection and testing services

(G-12047)
ROGERS GROUP INC
Also Called: Mitchell Crushed Stone
3020 State Road 60 W (47446-7556)
PHONE.................................812 849-3530
Danny Powell, *Mgr*
EMP: 72
SALES (corp-wide): 1.05B **Privately Held**
Web: www.rogersgroupincint.com
SIC: 1442 5032 3295 3274 Construction sand and gravel; Stone, crushed or broken; Minerals, ground or treated; Lime
PA: Rogers Group, Inc.
    421 Great Cir Rd
    Nashville TN 37228
    615 242-0585

(G-12048)
SPX CORPORATION
Also Called: SPX CORPORATION
4598 State Road 37 (47446-5388)
P.O. Box 379 (47446-0379)
PHONE.................................812 849-5647
Jeff Smithers, *Pr*
EMP: 6
SALES (corp-wide): 1.71B **Privately Held**
Web: www.spx.com
SIC: 3443 Cooling towers, metal plate
HQ: Canvas Sx, Llc
    6325 Ardrey Kell Rd Ste 4
    Charlotte NC 28277
    980 474-3700

(G-12049)
STEELTECH PARTNERS LLC
240 S Meridian Rd (47446-8015)
PHONE.................................812 849-0124
Mark Suvak, *CEO*
Dean Barnes, *COO*
Dan Brown, *CFO*
▲ EMP: 3 EST: 2014
SALES (est): 533K **Privately Held**
SIC: 3441 Fabricated structural metal

Modoc
Randolph County

(G-12050)
BICKELS GARAGE & WELDING
5520 W 900 S (47358-9433)
PHONE.................................765 853-5457
Stewart Bickel, *Owner*
EMP: 1 EST: 1976
SALES (est): 248.67K **Privately Held**
SIC: 5083 5039 7699 3523 Grain elevators equipment and supplies; Grain storage bins; Farm machinery repair; Grain stackers

(G-12051)
GRO-TEC INC
10324 W Us Highway 36 (47358-9371)
PHONE.................................765 853-1246
Richard Martin, *Pr*
Penny Martin, *Sec*
Tyler Martin, *VP*
EMP: 14 EST: 1989
SQ FT: 9,000
SALES (est): 1.73MM **Privately Held**
Web: www.gro-tec.com
SIC: 2048 Feed premixes

(G-12052)
HARRIS FARMS INC
10575 W 400 S (47358-9522)
PHONE.................................765 468-6264
EMP: 1 EST: 1958
SALES (est): 96.29K **Privately Held**
SIC: 3523 0291 Driers (farm): grain, hay, and seed; Livestock farm, general

(G-12053)
M & S SCREW MACHINE PRODUCTS
S Main St (47358)
P.O. Box 223 (47355-0223)
PHONE.................................765 853-5022
Richard Million, *Pr*
EMP: 7 EST: 1965
SQ FT: 15,000
SALES (est): 500K **Privately Held**
SIC: 3599 Machine shop, jobbing and repair

Monon
White County

(G-12054)
CIMC REEFER TRAILER INC
285 E Water Tower Dr (47959-8160)
PHONE.................................219 253-2000
EMP: 180
SALES (corp-wide): 4.85MM **Privately Held**
SIC: 3537 Truck trailers, used in plants, docks, terminals, etc.
PA: Cimc Reefer Trailer, Inc.
    22101 Alessandro Blvd
    Moreno Valley CA 92553
    951 218-1414

(G-12055)
DEERWOOD GROUP
792 E State Road 16 (47959-8503)
PHONE.................................219 866-5521
Harold A Smith, *Owner*
EMP: 4 EST: 1990
SQ FT: 1,500
SALES (est): 378.65K **Privately Held**
SIC: 2522 2599 Cabinets, office: except wood; Cabinets, factory

(G-12056)
LEGACY VULCAN LLC
Midwest Division
6857 N Us Highway 421 (47959-8000)
PHONE.................................219 253-6686
Bob Agley, *Mgr*
EMP: 4
Web: www.vulcanmaterials.com
SIC: 3273 Ready-mixed concrete
HQ: Legacy Vulcan, Llc
    1200 Urban Center Dr
    Birmingham AL 35242
    205 298-3000

(G-12057)
MONON MEAT PACKING COMPANY
402 N Railroad St (47959-8177)
P.O. Box 776 (47959-0776)
PHONE.................................219 253-6363
Scott Wiggins, *Pr*
Sandy Wiggins, *VP*
EMP: 6 EST: 1963
SQ FT: 10,000
SALES (est): 506.27K **Privately Held**
SIC: 2011 Meat packing plants

(G-12058)
VANGUARD NATIONAL TRAILER CORP (DH)
289 Water Tower Dr (47959)
P.O. Box 748 (47960)
PHONE.................................219 253-2000
Charles Mudd, *Pr*
Flora Mao, *
◆ EMP: 45 EST: 2003
SQ FT: 400,000
SALES (est): 218.97MM **Privately Held**
Web: www.vanguardtrailer.com
SIC: 3715 3713 Truck trailers; Truck bodies and parts
HQ: China International Marine Containers (Group) Co.,Ltd.
    Floor 8, Zhongji Group Yanfa Center, No.2, Shekou Gangwan Avenue
    GD

(G-12059)
WHISTLE STOP
10012 N Us Highway 421 (47959-8253)
PHONE.................................219 253-4100
Dale Ward, *Owner*
EMP: 2 EST: 2007
SALES (est): 122.32K **Privately Held**
SIC: 3999 Whistles

Monroe
Adams County

(G-12060)
ECKHART WOODWORKING INC
424 S Van Buren St (46772-9308)
PHONE.................................260 692-6218
Joe Eckhart, *Pr*
Tim Eckhart, *
EMP: 29 EST: 1989
SQ FT: 11,000
SALES (est): 2.3MM **Privately Held**
Web: www.woodworkingmadeinamerica.com
SIC: 2431 Moldings and baseboards, ornamental and trim

(G-12061)
PHAZPAK INC
Also Called: Pems
259 N Van Buren St (46772-9700)
PHONE.................................260 692-6416
Kenneth Parrish, *Pr*
Ruth Parrish, *Treas*
John Parrish, *VP*
Tina Parrish, *Sec*
▲ EMP: 6 EST: 1961
SQ FT: 10,000
SALES (est): 1.12MM **Privately Held**
Web: www.phazpak.com
SIC: 5063 7694 Motors, electric; Electric motor repair

(G-12062)
STRICK CORPORATION
301 N Polk St (46772-9703)
PHONE.................................260 692-6121
Les Quay, *Genl Mgr*
EMP: 350
SALES (corp-wide): 49.64MM **Privately Held**
Web: www.stricktrailers.com
SIC: 3715 Truck trailers
PA: Strick Corporation
    448 Lincoln Hwy
    Fairless Hills PA 19030
    215 949-3600

(G-12063)
STRICK TRAILERS LLC
301 N Polk St (46772-9703)
PHONE.................................260 692-6121
EMP: 20 EST: 2009
SALES (est): 3.65MM **Privately Held**
Web: www.stricktrailers.com
SIC: 3715 Trailer bodies

(G-12064)
SWISS METAL SPINNING CO
2301 W 200 S (46772-9765)
PHONE.................................260 692-1401
Amos Schwartz, *Prin*
EMP: 7 EST: 2008
SALES (est): 241.07K **Privately Held**
SIC: 3469 Spinning metal for the trade

Monroe City
Knox County

(G-12065)
SHOUSE SAWMILL INC
4679 S State Road 241 (47557-7034)
PHONE.................................812 743-2017
Gerald Shouse, *Owner*

GEOGRAPHIC SECTION

Montgomery - Daviess County (G-12090)

EMP: 10 **EST:** 2008
SALES (est): 267.56K **Privately Held**
SIC: 2421 Sawmills and planing mills, general

Monroeville
Allen County

(G-12066)
AG PLUS INC
306 W South St (46773-9390)
PHONE.................................260 623-6121
Ron Roy, *Brnch Mgr*
EMP: 3
SALES (corp-wide): 51.74MM **Privately Held**
Web: www.agplusinc.com
SIC: 5191 2041 5153 Fertilizer and fertilizer materials; Flour and other grain mill products; Grain elevators
PA: Ag Plus, Inc.
  401 N Main St
  South Whitley IN 46787
  260 723-5141

(G-12067)
CME LLC
21600 Monroeville Rd (46773-9623)
PHONE.................................260 623-3700
Marlene Dehner, *Mgr*
▲ **EMP:** 20 **EST:** 2006
SALES (est): 1.02MM **Privately Held**
SIC: 3643 Current-carrying wiring services

(G-12068)
DUX SIGNAL KITS LLC
23132 Monroeville Rd (46773-9647)
PHONE.................................260 623-3017
Neil Ternet, *Managing Member*
EMP: 2 **EST:** 2009
SALES (est): 118.61K **Privately Held**
Web: www.duxsignalkits.com
SIC: 3669 7389 5063 Signaling apparatus, electric; Business services, nec; Signaling equipment, electrical

(G-12069)
GERARDOT PERFORMANCE PDTS INC
108 W Barnhart St (46773-9392)
P.O. Box 223 (46773-0223)
PHONE.................................260 623-3048
Donald Gerardot, *Owner*
EMP: 5 **EST:** 1967
SALES (est): 488.8K **Privately Held**
Web: www.gerardot.com
SIC: 2399 Seat belts, automobile and aircraft

(G-12070)
JBJ CUSTOM WOODWORKING INC
22221 S County Line Rd E (46773-9522)
PHONE.................................260 450-7295
Brian Kilpatrick, *Pr*
John Kilpatrick, *Mgr*
EMP: 2 **EST:** 2001
SALES (est): 196.08K **Privately Held**
Web: www.jbjcustomwoodworking.com
SIC: 2431 Millwork

(G-12071)
MONROVLLE BOX PLLET WD PDTS LL
Also Called: Freedom Lumber Company
20009 Monroeville Rd (46773-9589)
P.O. Box 505 (46773-0505)
PHONE.................................260 623-3128
Eric Kissinger, *Pr*
Donald Witte, *CEO*
EMP: 24 **EST:** 1953

SQ FT: 44,000
SALES (est): 2.38MM **Privately Held**
Web: www.packerjack.com
SIC: 2448 2441 Pallets, wood; Shipping cases, wood: nailed or lock corner

(G-12072)
PRECAST SPECIALTIES INC
111 Utility Dr (46773-9315)
P.O. Box 452 (46773-0452)
PHONE.................................260 623-6131
EMP: 16 **EST:** 1995
SQ FT: 12,000
SALES (est): 1MM **Privately Held**
Web: www.precastspec.com
SIC: 3271 3272 Architectural concrete: block, split, fluted, screen, etc.; Concrete products, nec

(G-12073)
RL STRAHM WOODWORKING INC
18609 Paulding Rd (46773-9793)
PHONE.................................260 623-3228
EMP: 4 **EST:** 2019
SALES (est): 114.6K **Privately Held**
SIC: 2431 Millwork

(G-12074)
S&K SHEET METAL LLC
107 Webster St (46773-1007)
PHONE.................................260 623-3398
EMP: 6 **EST:** 2017
SALES (est): 1.01MM **Privately Held**
Web: www.skmetalfab.com
SIC: 3441 Fabricated structural metal

(G-12075)
STENSLAND ENGINES INC
4933 Morgan Rd (46773-9729)
PHONE.................................260 623-6859
David Stensland, *Prin*
EMP: 3 **EST:** 2005
SALES (est): 240.57K **Privately Held**
SIC: 3519 Internal combustion engines, nec

Monrovia
Morgan County

(G-12076)
AIR-TECH INDUSTRIAL DESIGN
580 W Main St (46157-9547)
PHONE.................................317 797-1804
William R Nelson, *Pr*
EMP: 3 **EST:** 2016
SALES (est): 190.42K **Privately Held**
Web: www.a-tid.com
SIC: 3564 Air purification equipment

(G-12077)
GRAMPAS CEDAR WORKS LLC
8456 N Baltimore Rd (46157-9027)
PHONE.................................317 372-0816
Walter D Osborne, *Prin*
EMP: 5 **EST:** 2018
SALES (est): 72.37K **Privately Held**
SIC: 2431 Millwork

(G-12078)
M JONES CONSULTING LLC
Also Called: Radiant Energy Distribution
208 E Main St (46157-1004)
P.O. Box 466 (46157-0466)
PHONE.................................317 353-3823
Mark Jones, *Managing Member*
EMP: 2 **EST:** 2008
SALES (est): 141.47K **Privately Held**
Web: www.radiantenergydistribution.com

SIC: 3585 Heating and air conditioning combination units

(G-12079)
PRO TECH AUTOMATION INC
8236 N Hall Rd (46157-9253)
PHONE.................................317 201-3875
David A Foxx, *Pr*
EMP: 7 **EST:** 1994
SALES (est): 544.04K **Privately Held**
Web: www.pro-techautomation.com
SIC: 3496 Conveyor belts

Monterey
Pulaski County

(G-12080)
K & B TRAILER SALES & MFG INC
93 E 800 N (46960-9116)
PHONE.................................574 946-4382
Keith Bailey, *Pr*
Connie S Bailey, *VP*
EMP: 2 **EST:** 1988
SALES (est): 263.37K **Privately Held**
SIC: 3523 7692 Trailers and wagons, farm; Welding repair

Montezuma
Parke County

(G-12081)
BIG INCH FABRICATORS CNSTR INC
6127 W Us Highway 36 (47862)
P.O. Box 99 (47862)
PHONE.................................765 245-9353
Douglas Mccord, *Pr*
George Brinkley, *
Dustin Brinkley, *
Tracey Mccord, *Prin*
EMP: 65 **EST:** 1998
SQ FT: 45,000
SALES (est): 8.66MM **Privately Held**
Web: www.biginch.net
SIC: 3441 Fabricated structural metal

(G-12082)
NEWLINS WLDG & TANK MAINT LLC
5360 U S Hwy 36 E (47862-8018)
P.O. Box 439 (47862-0439)
PHONE.................................765 245-2741
Jerry Newlin, *Owner*
EMP: 3 **EST:** 1986
SALES (est): 369.25K **Privately Held**
Web: www.newlinstankparts.com
SIC: 7699 7692 Aircraft and heavy equipment repair services; Welding repair

(G-12083)
SUPERIOR FOREST PRODUCTS LLC
Also Called: Superior Hardwoods
6429 W 100 N (47862-8011)
PHONE.................................765 245-2895
Jeffrey Meyer, *Pr*
EMP: 10 **EST:** 2017
SALES (est): 268.69K **Privately Held**
Web: www.superiorhardwood.com
SIC: 2426 2421 Hardwood dimension and flooring mills; Lumber: rough, sawed, or planed

(G-12084)
TIMBERLAND RESOURCES INC
Also Called: Superior Hardwoods
6429 W 100 N (47862-8011)
PHONE.................................765 245-2634
Jack T Shannon Junior, *Pr*
James Garrard, *VP*
EMP: 1 **EST:** 1999

SALES (est): 905.19K
SALES (corp-wide): 50.79MM **Privately Held**
Web: www.superiorhardwood.com
SIC: 2421 Sawmills and planing mills, general
PA: J.T. Shannon Lumber Company, Inc.
  2200 Cole Rd
  Horn Lake MS 38637
  662 393-3765

Montgomery
Daviess County

(G-12085)
APEXX ENTERPRISES LLC
Also Called: Apexx Engineering
6654 E Us Highway 50 (47558-5316)
PHONE.................................812 486-2443
Shad Truelove, *Pt*
EMP: 15 **EST:** 2013
SQ FT: 8,070
SALES (est): 2.84MM **Privately Held**
Web: www.apexxinc.com
SIC: 3089 3479 3053 2821 Plastics and fiberglass tanks; Painting, coating, and hot dipping; Packing, metallic; Polystyrene resins

(G-12086)
BARBS HOMEMADE NOODLES
787 S 700 E (47558-5562)
PHONE.................................812 486-3762
Frank Grayber, *Pt*
EMP: 2 **EST:** 1993
SALES (est): 91.65K **Privately Held**
SIC: 2098 Noodles (e.g. egg, plain, and water), dry

(G-12087)
BIO HARNESS SHOP
5913 E 350 N (47558-5297)
PHONE.................................812 486-2919
Graber Wilmer, *Owner*
EMP: 1 **EST:** 1988
SALES (est): 47.63K **Privately Held**
SIC: 3199 7699 5941 Harness or harness parts; Harness repair shop; Saddlery and equestrian equipment

(G-12088)
CEDAR WOODWORKING
Also Called: Knapp Engraving
7932 E 625 N (47558-5085)
PHONE.................................812 486-2765
William Knapp, *Owner*
Darvin Knapp, *Owner*
EMP: 3 **EST:** 2008
SALES (est): 104.9K **Privately Held**
SIC: 2434 2759 Wood kitchen cabinets; Engraving, nec

(G-12089)
COBLENTZ CABINET LLC
8876 E 800 N (47558-5107)
PHONE.................................812 687-7525
Paul Coblentz, *Prin*
EMP: 2 **EST:** 2007
SALES (est): 236.05K **Privately Held**
SIC: 2434 Wood kitchen cabinets

(G-12090)
COUNTRYSIDE PRINTING LLC
7243 E 300 N (47558-5626)
PHONE.................................812 486-2454
Virgil Raber, *Prin*
EMP: 6 **EST:** 2015
SALES (est): 229.8K **Privately Held**
SIC: 2759 Screen printing

Montgomery - Daviess County (G-12091)

(G-12091)
COUNTRYSIDE SAWMILL
8753 E 450 N (47558-5197)
PHONE..................812 486-2991
Glenn Knepp, *Prin*
EMP: 3 EST: 2010
SALES (est): 216.87K **Privately Held**
SIC: 2421 Sawmills and planing mills, general

(G-12092)
CUSTOM CABINETS & FURN LLC
4578 N 875 E (47558-5196)
PHONE..................812 486-2503
EMP: 11 EST: 2013
SALES (est): 498.83K **Privately Held**
Web: www.customcabinetsllc.com
SIC: 5712 2434 Cabinet work, custom; Wood kitchen cabinets

(G-12093)
CUSTOM TABLES & CABINETS
Also Called: Piece Vallet Cabinets
5127 E 300 N (47558-5714)
PHONE..................812 486-3831
EMP: 2 EST: 2008
SALES (est): 149.11K **Privately Held**
SIC: 2434 Wood kitchen cabinets

(G-12094)
D & E CABINETS
8835 E 650 N (47558-5143)
PHONE..................812 486-2961
Elmer Wagler, *Owner*
EMP: 4 EST: 2014
SALES (est): 59K **Privately Held**
Web: www.spturboost.com
SIC: 2434 Wood kitchen cabinets

(G-12095)
DELBERT KEMP
3540 N 700 E (47558)
PHONE..................812 486-3325
EMP: 12 EST: 2004
SALES (est): 554.21K **Privately Held**
Web: www.kempcabinets.com
SIC: 1751 2521 Cabinet building and installation; Cabinets, office: wood

(G-12096)
DUTCH CRAFT WOODWORK LLC
4876 N 775 E (47558-5178)
PHONE..................812 486-3675
Elisha Sterling, *Owner*
EMP: 1 EST: 2007
SALES (est): 111.63K **Privately Held**
SIC: 2431 Millwork

(G-12097)
E M WOODWORKING
6000 N 450 E (47558-5044)
PHONE..................812 486-2696
Mervin Knepp, *Prin*
EMP: 9 EST: 2005
SALES (est): 218.01K **Privately Held**
SIC: 2431 Millwork

(G-12098)
G & R WOODWORKING LLC
7747 N 775 E (47558-5099)
PHONE..................812 687-7701
EMP: 8 EST: 2005
SALES (est): 729.72K **Privately Held**
SIC: 2431 Millwork

(G-12099)
GRABER THERMOLOC WINDOWS LLC
9058 E 500 N (47558-5171)
PHONE..................812 486-3273
Delbert K Graber, *Pt*
Ben Graber, *Pt*
Mark Graber, *Pt*
EMP: 3 EST: 1990
SALES (est): 366.85K **Privately Held**
Web: www.graberthermolocwindows.com
SIC: 3442 Window and door frames

(G-12100)
GRABER WOODWORKS INC
5155 N 900 E (47558-5166)
PHONE..................812 486-2861
EMP: 9 EST: 1993
SQ FT: 3,400
SALES (est): 554.25K **Privately Held**
SIC: 2511 2434 5211 Wood household furniture; Wood kitchen cabinets; Cabinets, kitchen

(G-12101)
GREEN FAST CURE LLC
5461 E 300 N (47558-5749)
PHONE..................812 486-2510
Mervin R Knepp, *Prin*
EMP: 6 EST: 2016
SALES (est): 117.4K **Privately Held**
Web: www.greenfastcure.com
SIC: 3567 Industrial furnaces and ovens

(G-12102)
HARDWOOD DOOR MFG LLC
5084 N 575 E (47558-5052)
PHONE..................812 486-3313
Dallas Wagler, *Managing Member*
EMP: 8 EST: 1997
SALES (est): 840.33K **Privately Held**
Web: www.wynnepartners.com
SIC: 2434 Wood kitchen cabinets

(G-12103)
JJS CONCRETE CONSTRUCTION LLC
9149 E 800 N (47558-5109)
PHONE..................812 636-0173
Janet Wagler, *Managing Member*
EMP: 48 EST: 2009
SALES (est): 4.6MM **Privately Held**
Web: www.jjsconcrete.com
SIC: 3273 3272 5211 Ready-mixed concrete; Concrete products, precast, nec; Masonry materials and supplies

(G-12104)
K & K INDUSTRIES INC
8518 E 550 N (47558-5073)
PHONE..................812 486-3281
Jerry Stoll, *VP*
Bonnita Knepp, *
▼ EMP: 100 EST: 1972
SQ FT: 25,000
SALES (est): 9.98MM **Privately Held**
Web: www.kktruss.com
SIC: 2439 Trusses, wooden roof

(G-12105)
KENNETH RABER
Also Called: K & M Woodworking
2436 N 750 E (47558-5647)
PHONE..................812 486-3102
Kenneth Raber, *Owner*
EMP: 1 EST: 2000
SALES (est): 46.65K **Privately Held**
SIC: 5947 2499 Gifts and novelties; Decorative wood and woodwork

(G-12106)
KNEPPS LOGGING BANDMILLING
5220 N 650 E (47558-5279)
PHONE..................812 486-7721
EMP: 3 EST: 2010
SALES (est): 220.7K **Privately Held**
SIC: 2411 Logging camps and contractors

(G-12107)
KNEPPS WOODWORKING
6161 E 350 N (47558-5295)
PHONE..................812 486-3546
Jay Knepp, *Owner*
EMP: 1 EST: 2002
SALES (est): 142.42K **Privately Held**
SIC: 2499 Decorative wood and woodwork

(G-12108)
L & D CUSTOM WOODWORKING LLC
3610 N 900 E (47558-5205)
PHONE..................812 486-2958
Leroy Wittmar, *Owner*
EMP: 5 EST: 2005
SALES (est): 478.16K **Privately Held**
SIC: 2499 Decorative wood and woodwork

(G-12109)
LARRY GRABER CABINETS
9407 E 500 N (47558-5167)
PHONE..................812 486-2713
Ernest Smith, *Owner*
Larry Graber, *Owner*
EMP: 2 EST: 1989
SALES (est): 132.94K **Privately Held**
SIC: 2517 Home entertainment unit cabinets, wood

(G-12110)
LC SCREEN PRINTING LLC
7654 N 650 E (47558-5258)
PHONE..................812 687-7476
Gary Graber, *Prin*
EMP: 5 EST: 2018
SALES (est): 101.92K **Privately Held**
SIC: 2752 Commercial printing, lithographic

(G-12111)
M & H WOODWORKING LLC
3591 N 775 E (47558-5220)
PHONE..................812 486-2570
EMP: 3 EST: 2003
SALES (est): 244.99K **Privately Held**
SIC: 1751 2499 Cabinet and finish carpentry; Decorative wood and woodwork

(G-12112)
MARNER DOOR MANUFACTURING LLC
4254 N 525 E (47558-5025)
PHONE..................812 486-3128
Lester Marner, *Managing Member*
EMP: 19 EST: 1990
SQ FT: 200
SALES (est): 1.67MM **Privately Held**
SIC: 3442 Metal doors, sash, and trim

(G-12113)
MCCRACKEN CURVE DISTILLERY LLC ◆
5663 E Old Us Highway 50 (47558-5526)
PHONE..................812 486-3651
Jeff Kavanaugh, *Mgr*
EMP: 4 EST: 2023
SALES (est): 75.6K **Privately Held**
SIC: 2085 Distilled and blended liquors

(G-12114)
MERVIN KNEPPS MOLDING
6349 N 900 E (47558-5146)
PHONE..................812 486-2971
EMP: 4 EST: 1993
SQ FT: 5,000
SALES (est): 366.13K **Privately Held**
Web: www.kneppmolding.com
SIC: 2431 Moldings, wood: unfinished and prefinished

(G-12115)
MIDWEST EARTHWORKS LLC
Also Called: Midwest Machine & Design
973 S 800 E (47558-5346)
PHONE..................812 486-2443
Shad Truelove, *Managing Member*
EMP: 4 EST: 2011
SALES (est): 243.78K **Privately Held**
SIC: 3599 Machine and other job shop work

(G-12116)
MONTGOMERY WELDING INC
6216 E Us Highway 50 (47558-5695)
PHONE..................812 486-3710
Jacob Gingich, *Pr*
EMP: 2 EST: 1985
SALES (est): 237.7K **Privately Held**
SIC: 7692 Welding repair

(G-12117)
PAUL KNEPP SAWMILL INC
Also Called: Paul Knepp Saw Mill
3589 N 900 E (47558-5206)
PHONE..................812 486-3773
Martha Knepp, *Pr*
EMP: 4 EST: 1972
SALES (est): 328.71K **Privately Held**
SIC: 2421 Sawmills and planing mills, general

(G-12118)
PEACE VALLEY CABINETS INC
5127 E 300 N (47558-5714)
PHONE..................812 486-3831
Kevin Wittmer, *Prin*
EMP: 7 EST: 2011
SALES (est): 288.17K **Privately Held**
SIC: 2434 Wood kitchen cabinets

(G-12119)
PRAIRIE CREEK PRTG & BK STR
Also Called: Prairie Creek Book Store
9309 E 800 N (47558-5110)
PHONE..................812 636-7243
Amos Graver, *Owner*
EMP: 4 EST: 1996
SALES (est): 226.56K **Privately Held**
SIC: 2752 5942 Offset printing; Book stores

(G-12120)
RABER BUGGY SHOP LLC
7209 E 300 N (47558-5626)
PHONE..................812 486-3789
Victor Raber, *Owner*
EMP: 6 EST: 1975
SQ FT: 2,000
SALES (est): 632.88K **Privately Held**
SIC: 7692 3496 Welding repair; Cages, wire

(G-12121)
RABER WHEEL WORKS LLC
7226 E 300 N (47558-5626)
PHONE..................812 486-2786
Paul Raber, *Owner*
EMP: 8 EST: 1985
SALES (est): 717.79K **Privately Held**
Web: www.montgomeryinhorsecarriagestand.com
SIC: 2499 Spokes, wood

(G-12122)
SHEPHERDS LOFT
8008 E 625 N (47558-5084)
PHONE..................812 486-2304
EMP: 4 EST: 2013
SALES (est): 86.35K **Privately Held**

GEOGRAPHIC SECTION
Monticello - White County (G-12150)

SIC: 3944 Craft and hobby kits and sets

(G-12123)
SOUTHERN INDIANA COLLAR CO
Also Called: Southern Indiana Collar Mfg Co
1692 N 725 E (47558-5653)
PHONE..........................812 486-3714
Marlon Ray Raber, *Pt*
Ken Raber, *Pt*
EMP: 3 EST: 1982
SQ FT: 150
SALES (est): 150K Privately Held
SIC: 5941 3199 Saddlery and equestrian equipment; Harness or harness parts

(G-12124)
STARLIGHT PRINTING
3792 N 525 E (47558-5024)
PHONE..........................812 486-3905
EMP: 3 EST: 2017
SALES (est): 83.91K Privately Held
SIC: 2752 Commercial printing, lithographic

(G-12125)
SWARTZENTRUBER SAWMILL LLC
5912 N 900 E (47558-5739)
PHONE..........................812 486-3350
Randy Swartzentrube, *Owner*
EMP: 3 EST: 2006
SALES (est): 219.28K Privately Held
SIC: 2421 Sawmills and planing mills, general

(G-12126)
TRUCUSTOM CABINETS LLC ✪
5161 N 900 E (47558)
PHONE..........................812 486-2861
EMP: 5 EST: 2022
SALES (est): 75.19K Privately Held
Web: www.trucustomcabinets.com
SIC: 2434 Wood kitchen cabinets

(G-12127)
W & J SAWMILL LLC
9533 E 600 N (47558-5152)
PHONE..........................812 486-2719
Jonas Knepp, *Pr*
EMP: 3 EST: 2002
SALES (est): 202.95K Privately Held
SIC: 2421 Sawmills and planing mills, general

(G-12128)
W & W PALLET CO LLC
7799 E 300 N (47558-5632)
PHONE..........................812 486-3548
Vernon Wagler, *Owner*
EMP: 7 EST: 2015
SALES (est): 153.43K Privately Held
SIC: 2448 Pallets, wood

(G-12129)
WAGLER CUSTOM CABINETS LLC
8152 N 200 N (47558-5639)
PHONE..........................812 486-2878
EMP: 6 EST: 2009
SALES (est): 252.09K Privately Held
Web: waglers-custom-cabinets.business.site
SIC: 2434 Wood kitchen cabinets

(G-12130)
WITTMER WOODWORKING LLC
4637 E 200 N (47558-5013)
PHONE..........................812 486-3115
Joseph Witwicke, *Managing Member*
Harold Wittmer, *Managing Member*
EMP: 8 EST: 2011
SALES (est): 493.08K Privately Held

SIC: 2431 Woodwork, interior and ornamental, nec

(G-12131)
YODERS CABINETS
5207 N 775 E (47558-5240)
PHONE..........................812 486-3826
Wayne Yoder, *Prin*
EMP: 5 EST: 2010
SALES (est): 160.85K Privately Held
SIC: 2434 Wood kitchen cabinets

Monticello
White County

(G-12132)
ADKEV INC
1207 N 6th St (47960-1542)
PHONE..........................574 583-4420
EMP: 17
Web: www.adkev.com
SIC: 3089 Molding primary plastics
PA: Adkev, Inc.
664 S Iroquois St
Goodland IN 47948

(G-12133)
AFFORDABLE SCREEN PRINTING EMB
8262 N Kiger Dr (47960-7102)
PHONE..........................574 278-7885
Tina Frybort, *Owner*
EMP: 2 EST: 2006
SALES (est): 137.46K Privately Held
SIC: 2752 Commercial printing, lithographic

(G-12134)
ALLEN MONUMENT CO
Also Called: Allen Monument Co
706 N Main St Ste H (47960-1889)
PHONE..........................574 240-1880
EMP: 1
SALES (corp-wide): 878.9K Privately Held
Web: www.allenmonuments.com
SIC: 3272 3281 5999 Monuments and grave markers, except terrazzo; Monument or burial stone, cut and shaped; Monuments and tombstones
PA: Allen Monument Company
212 Hamilton St
Crawfordsville IN 47933
765 362-8886

(G-12135)
ANTIQUE STOVE INFORMATION
Also Called: Autonomy House Publications
421 N Main St (47960-1932)
PHONE..........................574 583-6465
Clifford Boram, *Owner*
EMP: 1 EST: 1982
SALES (est): 59.9K Privately Held
SIC: 5099 1411 7641 Antiques; Verde' antique, dimension-quarrying; Antique furniture repair and restoration

(G-12136)
BALL CORPORATION
1104 N 6th St (47960-1555)
PHONE..........................574 583-9418
EMP: 13
SALES (corp-wide): 14.03B Publicly Held
Web: www.ball.com
SIC: 3411 Metal cans
PA: Ball Corporation
9200 W 108th Cir
Westminster CO 80021
303 469-3131

(G-12137)
BALL METAL BEVERAGE CONT CORP
Also Called: Ball Metal Beverage Cont Div
501 N 6th St (47960-1840)
PHONE..........................574 583-9418
Ross Rittvreg, *Brnch Mgr*
EMP: 153
SALES (corp-wide): 14.03B Publicly Held
Web: www.ball.com
SIC: 3411 Can lids and ends, metal
HQ: Ball Metal Beverage Container Corp.
9300 W 108th Cir
Westminster CO 80021

(G-12138)
BLASTED WORKS
214 N Main St (47960-2131)
PHONE..........................574 583-3211
Trina Jo Clerget, *Pt*
Stephen A Clerget, *Pt*
EMP: 3 EST: 1985
SQ FT: 4,500
SALES (est): 244.39K Privately Held
Web: www.theblastedworks.com
SIC: 2752 7374 2789 7699 Offset printing; Computer graphics service; Trade binding services; Photographic and optical goods equipment repair services

(G-12139)
BOAT WORX OF MONTICELLO
624 S Main St (47960-2447)
PHONE..........................574 297-7961
EMP: 4 EST: 2018
SALES (est): 61.39K Privately Held
SIC: 7692 Welding repair

(G-12140)
BULLY GRAPHICS AND SIGNS
6242 E 700 N (47960-7288)
PHONE..........................574 870-0783
Jim Roller, *Prin*
EMP: 5 EST: 2017
SALES (est): 64.54K Privately Held
Web: www.rtsigroup.com
SIC: 3993 Signs and advertising specialties

(G-12141)
CARTER SEPTIC TANK INC
1720 N Buckeye St (47960-1301)
PHONE..........................574 583-5796
Max K Van Meter, *Pr*
Margaret E Van Meter, *Sec*
EMP: 5 EST: 1953
SALES (est): 429.24K Privately Held
Web: www.davistaxandaccounting.com
SIC: 3272 Septic tanks, concrete

(G-12142)
CARTERS CONCRETE BLOCK INC
1846 N Francis St (47960-1334)
PHONE..........................574 583-7811
Bill Sermon, *Mgr*
EMP: 2
SALES (corp-wide): 2.46MM Privately Held
SIC: 3271 Blocks, concrete or cinder: standard
PA: Carter's Concrete Block Inc
2200 Lafontain St
Fort Wayne IN 46802
574 722-2644

(G-12143)
COVERITE-CUSTOM COVERS
Also Called: Coverite
8593 N State Road 39 (47960-7216)
P.O. Box 4 (47925-0004)
PHONE..........................574 278-7152

Donna Mccormick, *Owner*
EMP: 2 EST: 1996
SALES (est): 173.38K Privately Held
Web: www.coverite4covers.com
SIC: 2394 Canvas and related products

(G-12144)
D & S BOAT LIFTS
4285 E Chalmers Rd (47960-7633)
PHONE..........................574 583-8972
EMP: 4 EST: 2018
SALES (est): 60.08K Privately Held
SIC: 3536 Boat lifts

(G-12145)
DON ANDERSON
Also Called: Liberty Signs
10739 N 650 E (47960-7125)
PHONE..........................574 278-7243
EMP: 2 EST: 1989
SALES (est): 70.48K Privately Held
SIC: 3993 Signs and advertising specialties

(G-12146)
DONALDSON COMPANY INC
Also Called: Donaldson Co
303 N 6th St (47960-1859)
PHONE..........................952 887-3131
Dave Page, *Brnch Mgr*
EMP: 8
SALES (corp-wide): 3.43B Publicly Held
Web: www.donaldson.com
SIC: 3564 Blowers and fans
PA: Donaldson Company, Inc.
1400 W 94th St
Minneapolis MN 55431
952 887-3131

(G-12147)
DONNA MCCORMICK
8593 N State Road 39 (47960-7216)
PHONE..........................574 278-3152
EMP: 4 EST: 2016
SALES (est): 49.54K Privately Held
Web: www.coverite4covers.com
SIC: 2394 Canvas and related products

(G-12148)
EMERSON INDUSTRIAL AUTOMATION
705 N 6th St (47960-1711)
PHONE..........................574 583-9171
EMP: 6 EST: 2017
SALES (est): 216.85K Privately Held
SIC: 3562 Ball and roller bearings

(G-12149)
EVANGELINE ORCHARD & WINERY
10737 N 800 E (47960-7585)
PHONE..........................574 278-6301
Lenn Gapinski, *Owner*
EMP: 2 EST: 2011
SALES (est): 94.53K Privately Held
Web: www.communionsupplycompany.com
SIC: 2084 Wines

(G-12150)
FRATCO INC (PA)
Also Called: Fratco
105 W Broadway St (47960)
P.O. Box 368 (47946)
PHONE..........................800 854-7120
▲ EMP: 65 EST: 1923
SALES (est): 11.1MM
SALES (corp-wide): 11.1MM Privately Held
Web: www.fratco.com
SIC: 3084 Plastics pipe

Monticello - White County (G-12151) GEOGRAPHIC SECTION

(G-12151)
GIRTZ INDUSTRIES INC
Also Called: Girtz Engineering
5262 N East Shafer Dr (47960)
PHONE..................................844 464-4789
David Girtz, *CEO*
David A Girtz, *
Elizabeth Girtz, *Corporate Secretary**
▲ **EMP:** 135 **EST:** 1960
SQ FT: 50,000
SALES (est): 21.11MM **Privately Held**
Web: www.girtzindustries.com
SIC: 3444 Sheet metal specialties, not stamped

(G-12152)
HALSEN BROTHERS SHTMTL INC
Also Called: Honeywell Authorized Dealer
300 Tioga Rd (47960-2459)
PHONE..................................574 583-3358
Ronald Hansen, *Pr*
Ron Halsen, *Pr*
Randy Halsen, *VP*
EMP: 2 **EST:** 1972
SQ FT: 2,000
SALES (est): 251.19K **Privately Held**
Web: www.honeywell.com
SIC: 3444 1711 Sheet metalwork; Warm air heating and air conditioning contractor

(G-12153)
HORIZON FARMS LLC
6942 E 350 N (47960-7382)
PHONE..................................765 427-3685
EMP: 2 **EST:** 2019
SALES (est): 201.38K **Privately Held**
SIC: 2075 Soybean oil mills

(G-12154)
JACOBS MFG LLC
806 N 1st St (47960-1722)
PHONE..................................574 583-3883
EMP: 3 **EST:** 2007
SALES (est): 490.69K **Privately Held**
SIC: 3523 Farm machinery and equipment

(G-12155)
JORDAN MANUFACTURING CO INC (PA)
1200 S 6th St (47960-8200)
PHONE..................................800 328-6522
David N Jordan, *Pr*
Nancy Jordan, *
◆ **EMP:** 169 **EST:** 1986
SQ FT: 180,000
SALES (est): 95.1MM
SALES (corp-wide): 95.1MM **Privately Held**
Web: www.jordanmanufacturing.com
SIC: 2392 5021 Cushions and pillows; Outdoor and lawn furniture, nec

(G-12156)
LIBERTY ARMS INC
6942 E 350 N (47960-7382)
PHONE..................................574 583-5630
EMP: 7 **EST:** 2010
SALES (est): 429K **Privately Held**
Web: www.libertyarmsinc.com
SIC: 3489 Ordnance and accessories, nec

(G-12157)
MCGILL MANUFACTURING CO INC
705 N 6th St (47960-1799)
PHONE..................................219 465-2200
Tony Pajk, *Pr*
◆ **EMP:** 510 **EST:** 1905
SQ FT: 200,000
SALES (est): 42.98MM
SALES (corp-wide): 6.25B **Publicly Held**
SIC: 3562 Ball and roller bearings
HQ: Regal Beloit America, Inc.
111 W Michigan St
Milwaukee WI 53203
608 364-8800

(G-12158)
MONTICELLO SIGNS & SCRN
728 N Main St (47960-1712)
PHONE..................................815 848-4111
EMP: 4 **EST:** 2018
SALES (est): 67.77K **Privately Held**
Web: www.monticelloin.gov
SIC: 3993 Signs and advertising specialties

(G-12159)
MONTICELLO VAULT BURIAL CO
2304 N 750 E (47960-8738)
PHONE..................................574 583-3206
EMP: 2 **EST:** 1986
SALES (est): 185.34K **Privately Held**
SIC: 3272 Burial vaults, concrete or precast terrazzo

(G-12160)
MSCA LLC
303 N 6th St (47960-1859)
PHONE..................................574 583-6220
Patrick Yoder, *Prin*
▲ **EMP:** 10 **EST:** 2005
SALES (est): 184.47K **Privately Held**
SIC: 3089 Plastics products, nec

(G-12161)
NEWS REMINDER
114 S Main St (47960-2328)
P.O. Box 409 (47960-0409)
PHONE..................................574 583-5121
Don Herd, *Pr*
EMP: 5 **EST:** 2008
SALES (est): 76.26K **Privately Held**
Web: www.newsbug.info
SIC: 2711 Newspapers, publishing and printing

(G-12162)
OUTDOOR ROOMSCAPES INC
11965 W 800 N (47960-8058)
PHONE..................................574 965-2009
Michelle Schwindler, *Pr*
EMP: 2 **EST:** 2009
SALES (est): 100.77K **Privately Held**
Web: www.outdoorroomscapes.com
SIC: 2499 Kitchen, bathroom, and household ware: wood

(G-12163)
OWENS MACHINE & WELDING
1110 N 6th St (47960-1555)
PHONE..................................574 583-9566
Rudy Owens, *Owner*
EMP: 5 **EST:** 1976
SQ FT: 8,100
SALES (est): 376.6K **Privately Held**
SIC: 7692 3444 Welding repair; Sheet metalwork

(G-12164)
PATRIOT PORCELAIN LLC
114 Constitution Plz (47960-2113)
P.O. Box 290 (47960-0290)
PHONE..................................574 583-5128
EMP: 2 **EST:** 2011
SALES (est): 248.53K **Privately Held**
SIC: 3261 Vitreous plumbing fixtures

(G-12165)
PIMMLER HOLDINGS INC (PA)
3137 S Freeman Rd (47960-7793)
P.O. Box 705 (47960-0705)
PHONE..................................574 583-8090
Thomas Pimmler, *Prin*
▲ **EMP:** 3 **EST:** 1995
SALES (est): 323.61K **Privately Held**
SIC: 3495 Wire springs

(G-12166)
POLYMER SCIENCE INC (PA)
Also Called: PSI
2577 S Freeman Rd (47960-7831)
PHONE..................................574 583-3751
Fred E Ennis, *Pr*
▲ **EMP:** 1 **EST:** 1998
SQ FT: 28,000
SALES (est): 5MM
SALES (corp-wide): 5MM **Privately Held**
Web: www.polymerscience.com
SIC: 3081 Unsupported plastics film and sheet

(G-12167)
REGAL BELOIT AMERICA INC
Also Called: Rollway Bearing
705 N 6th St (47960-1711)
PHONE..................................219 465-2200
Allen Davis, *Mgr*
EMP: 38
SALES (corp-wide): 6.25B **Publicly Held**
SIC: 3562 Ball and roller bearings
HQ: Regal Beloit America, Inc.
111 W Michigan St
Milwaukee WI 53203
608 364-8800

(G-12168)
REGAL REXNORD CORPORATION
705 N 6th St (47960-1711)
PHONE..................................574 583-9171
Glenn Fischer, *Brnch Mgr*
EMP: 41
SALES (corp-wide): 6.25B **Publicly Held**
Web: www.regalrexnord.com
SIC: 3644 3621 Electric conduits and fittings; Motors, electric
PA: Regal Rexnord Corporation
111 W Michigan St
Milwaukee WI 53203
608 364-8800

(G-12169)
RGR ENGINES
3540 E 425 N (47960-7069)
PHONE..................................630 488-7966
EMP: 6 **EST:** 2015
SALES (est): 275.1K **Privately Held**
Web: www.rgrengines.com
SIC: 3714 Motor vehicle parts and accessories

(G-12170)
SPRING MONTICELLO CORPORATION
3137 S Freeman Rd (47960)
P.O. Box 705 (47960)
PHONE..................................574 583-8090
EMP: 80 **EST:** 1970
SALES (est): 13.18MM **Privately Held**
Web: www.monticellospring.com
SIC: 3495 Wire springs

(G-12171)
T & G GAMES INC
4900 N Boxman Pl (47960-7322)
PHONE..................................574 297-5455
EMP: 2 **EST:** 1987
SALES (est): 83K **Privately Held**
SIC: 3944 Games, toys, and children's vehicles

(G-12172)
T & L SHARPENING INC
2663 S Freeman Rd (47960-7843)
P.O. Box 338 (47960-0338)
PHONE..................................574 583-3868
Thomas E All, *Pr*
EMP: 15 **EST:** 1978
SQ FT: 7,000
SALES (est): 390.2K **Privately Held**
Web: www.cutting-tools.com
SIC: 7699 3545 Professional instrument repair services; Files, machine tool

(G-12173)
TRICIAS EMBROIDERY
4789 Shenandoah Ct (47960-7783)
PHONE..................................574 583-4371
Tricia L Mendel, *Owner*
Tricia Mendeo, *Owner*
EMP: 1 **EST:** 2005
SALES (est): 56.32K **Privately Held**
SIC: 2395 Embroidery products, except Schiffli machine

(G-12174)
TWIN LAKES CANVAS INC
1103 N 6th St (47960-1547)
PHONE..................................574 583-2000
Roger Mitchell, *Pr*
EMP: 4 **EST:** 1973
SQ FT: 5,000
SALES (est): 239.09K **Privately Held**
Web: www.twinlakescanvas.net
SIC: 2394 Awnings, fabric: made from purchased materials

(G-12175)
UNIQUE GRAPHIC DESIGNS INC
Also Called: Embroidery Designs
1279 N State Road 39 (47960-7286)
PHONE..................................574 583-7119
Denise Hood, *Owner*
EMP: 5 **EST:** 1996
SQ FT: 1,100
SALES (est): 480.85K **Privately Held**
Web: www.uniquegraphicsinc.com
SIC: 2395 2759 Embroidery products, except Schiffli machine; Screen printing

(G-12176)
WHYTE HORSE WINERY LLC
1510 S Airport Rd (47960-2701)
PHONE..................................574 583-2345
Abbey Franks, *Mgr*
EMP: 3 **EST:** 2005
SALES (est): 192.19K **Privately Held**
Web: www.whytehorsewinery.com
SIC: 2084 Wines

Montpelier
Blackford County

(G-12177)
BRC RUBBER & PLASTICS INC
623 W Monroe St (47359-1240)
PHONE..................................765 728-8510
Jerry Odom, *Mgr*
EMP: 18
SALES (corp-wide): 95.9MM **Privately Held**
Web: www.brcrp.com
SIC: 3061 2822 Mechanical rubber goods; Synthetic rubber
PA: Brc Rubber & Plastics, Inc.
1029a W State Blvd
Fort Wayne IN 46808
260 693-2171

(G-12178)
I MI ERIE STONE
5067 E Cummins Rd (47359-9653)
PHONE.................................765 728-5335
Earl Brinker, *CFO*
EMP: 6 **EST:** 2013
SALES (est): 84.88K **Privately Held**
SIC: 3273 Ready-mixed concrete

(G-12179)
IRVING MATERIALS INC
5067 E Cummins Rd (47359-9653)
PHONE.................................765 728-5335
Joe Langel, *Brnch Mgr*
EMP: 9
SALES (corp-wide): 814.09MM **Privately Held**
Web: www.irvmat.com
SIC: 3273 Ready-mixed concrete
PA: Irving Materials, Inc.
8032 N State Road 9
Greenfield IN 46140
317 326-3101

(G-12180)
MONTPELIER AG LLC
240 W Windsor St (47359-1152)
PHONE.................................765 728-2222
EMP: 1 **EST:** 2010
SALES (est): 110K **Privately Held**
Web: www.montpelieragway.com
SIC: 5191 2068 Seeds: field, garden, and flower; Seeds: dried, dehydrated, salted or roasted

(G-12181)
SMITH CONSULTING INC
850 W Huntington St (47359-1294)
P.O. Box 159 (47359-0159)
PHONE.................................765 728-5980
Terry Smith, *Pr*
EMP: 32 **EST:** 1970
SQ FT: 52,000
SALES (est): 4.18MM **Privately Held**
Web: www.smithconsultinginc.net
SIC: 2653 8742 Boxes, solid fiber: made from purchased materials; Quality assurance consultant

(G-12182)
STANLEY ENGNERED FASTENING LLC
Stanley Engineered Fastening
7345 N 400 E (47359-9646)
PHONE.................................765 728-2433
Mark Grey, *Mgr*
EMP: 120
SALES (corp-wide): 15.78B **Publicly Held**
Web: www.stanleyengineeredfastening.com
SIC: 3541 3452 5085 Machine tools, metal cutting type; Bolts, nuts, rivets, and washers; Fasteners, industrial: nuts, bolts, screws, etc.
HQ: Stanley Engineered Fastening Llc
4 Shelter Rock Ln
Danbury CT 06810
800 783-6427

(G-12183)
T-MACK MACHINERY LLC
418 W Oil St (47359-1243)
P.O. Box 72 (47359-0072)
PHONE.................................765 728-8655
EMP: 5 **EST:** 1992
SALES (est): 246.65K **Privately Held**
SIC: 3599 Machine and other job shop work

Mooreland
Henry County

(G-12184)
DAVID MURRAY
Also Called: 911 Led Lights
6645 E County Road 600 N (47360-9704)
PHONE.................................765 766-5229
David Murray, *Owner*
EMP: 1 **EST:** 2016
SALES (est): 67.86K **Privately Held**
SIC: 3647 Vehicular lighting equipment

(G-12185)
KAREMAR PRODUCTIONS
6789 E State Road 36 (47360-9529)
PHONE.................................765 766-5117
Marlin Evans, *Owner*
EMP: 2 **EST:** 1989
SALES (est): 178.02K **Privately Held**
Web: www.karemar.productions
SIC: 2759 7336 Visiting cards (including business): printing, nsk; Commercial art and graphic design

Moores Hill
Dearborn County

(G-12186)
APPALACHIAN LOG STRUCTURES
Also Called: Heritage Log Homes
10994 Chesterville Rd (47032-9258)
PHONE.................................812 744-5711
Anita Dyer, *Owner*
EMP: 2 **EST:** 1995
SALES (est): 174.79K **Privately Held**
Web: www.applog.com
SIC: 2452 Log cabins, prefabricated, wood

(G-12187)
KEMPER TOOL INC
11804 Long Branch Rd (47032-9684)
PHONE.................................812 744-8633
Dan Kemper, *Pr*
EMP: 1 **EST:** 1998
SQ FT: 600
SALES (est): 127.45K **Privately Held**
SIC: 3089 Injection molded finished plastics products, nec

(G-12188)
TEAMAIR MRO LTD
12978 Josephs Field Ln (47032-9499)
PHONE.................................812 584-3733
EMP: 4 **EST:** 2010
SALES (est): 73.61K **Privately Held**
SIC: 3724 Aircraft engines and engine parts

(G-12189)
YORK & SONS WELDING LLC
1437 N County Line Rd (47032-9602)
PHONE.................................812 577-6352
Cody York, *Prin*
EMP: 4 **EST:** 2019
SALES (est): 91.09K **Privately Held**
SIC: 7692 Welding repair

Mooresville
Morgan County

(G-12190)
ADVANCE AERO INC
135 E Harrison St (46158-1626)
PHONE.................................317 513-6071
Todd N Wilson, *Pr*
EMP: 25 **EST:** 2007
SQ FT: 5,000
SALES (est): 2.58MM **Privately Held**
Web: www.advanceaeroinc.com
SIC: 3441 Fabricated structural metal

(G-12191)
AFFINIS GROUP LLC (PA)
1050 Indianapolis Rd (46158)
P.O. Box 236 (46158)
PHONE.................................317 831-3830
EMP: 2 **EST:** 2001
SALES (est): 2.04MM
SALES (corp-wide): 2.04MM **Privately Held**
Web: www.affinis.biz
SIC: 2656 3089 Sanitary food containers; Plastics kitchenware, tableware, and houseware

(G-12192)
ALTERNATIVE MACHINING INC
29 S Franklin St (46158-1620)
PHONE.................................317 830-8109
Michael Bridges, *Admn*
EMP: 5 **EST:** 2008
SALES (est): 95.78K **Privately Held**
SIC: 3599 Machine shop, jobbing and repair

(G-12193)
AMBASSADOR STEEL CORPORATION
Also Called: AMBASSADOR STEEL CORPORATION
149 Sycamore Ln (46158-7923)
PHONE.................................317 834-3434
Tony Gaskins, *Mgr*
EMP: 19
SALES (corp-wide): 34.71B **Publicly Held**
Web: www.harrisrebar.com
SIC: 5051 3449 3441 Steel; Miscellaneous metalwork; Fabricated structural metal
HQ: Nucor Rebar Fabrication Services Central Corp.
1340 S Grandstaff Dr
Auburn IN 46706
260 925-5440

(G-12194)
ARCOSA LW HPB LLC
Also Called: Arcosa Lightweight
6618 N Tidewater Rd (46158-7046)
PHONE.................................317 831-0710
EMP: 23
SALES (corp-wide): 2.31B **Publicly Held**
Web: www.arcosa.com
SIC: 3295 Minerals, ground or treated
HQ: Arcosa Lw Hpb, Llc
500 N Akard St
Dallas TX 75201
214 631-4420

(G-12195)
BKB CUSTOM CABINETRY LLC
5055 Oakridge Dr (46158-7444)
PHONE.................................317 439-9427
Kathleen Shea, *Bd of Dir*
EMP: 4 **EST:** 2010
SALES (est): 77.95K **Privately Held**
SIC: 2434 Wood kitchen cabinets

(G-12196)
BROWNS SIMPLY PRINTINGS
126 S Jefferson St (46158-1654)
PHONE.................................317 490-7493
Joshua A Brown, *Owner*
EMP: 5 **EST:** 2015
SALES (est): 92.3K **Privately Held**
SIC: 2752 Commercial printing, lithographic

(G-12197)
CAPITAL ADHESIVES & PACKG CORP
1260 S Old State Road 67 (46158-8243)
PHONE.................................317 834-5415
Roger Wathen, *Pr*
Mark Angermeier, *VP*
Natalie Wathen, *Sec*
Elaine Angermeier, *Treas*
EMP: 12 **EST:** 1987
SQ FT: 15,000
SALES (est): 3.36MM **Privately Held**
Web: www.capitaladhesives.com
SIC: 2891 5085 5084 Adhesives; Adhesives, tape and plasters; Industrial machinery and equipment

(G-12198)
CAPITAL CITY TRANSIT LLC
5657 E State Road 144 (46158-6065)
PHONE.................................317 813-5800
Andrew Bunten, *CEO*
Buck Retmier, *CEO*
Cathy Retmier, *Pr*
Sherry Byram, *Mgr*
EMP: 8 **EST:** 2002
SALES (est): 990.07K **Privately Held**
Web: www.cctcustoms.com
SIC: 3711 Buses, all types, assembly of

(G-12199)
CARTER LEE BUILDING COMPONENT
Also Called: A Pro-Build Company
9028 N Old State Road 67 (46158-6366)
PHONE.................................317 834-5380
David Carter, *CEO*
Dale Kukowski, *
EMP: 24 **EST:** 2001
SQ FT: 400,000
SALES (est): 893.09K **Privately Held**
SIC: 2439 Trusses, wooden roof

(G-12200)
COUGAR BAG EB LLC
3310 Hancel Cir (46158-8205)
PHONE.................................317 831-9720
Keith Simmons, *
EMP: 26 **EST:** 1993
SQ FT: 7,000
SALES (est): 4.99MM **Privately Held**
SIC: 2673 Plastic bags: made from purchased materials

(G-12201)
DEFELICE ENGINEERING INC
7451 N Ridgeway Ln (46158-6687)
PHONE.................................317 834-2832
Brian V Defelice, *Pr*
Joann Hendriyx, *Sec*
EMP: 2 **EST:** 1983
SQ FT: 5,400
SALES (est): 259.32K **Privately Held**
Web: www.defeliceenginc.com
SIC: 3544 Special dies and tools

(G-12202)
DIAMONDBACK METALCRAFTS INC
Also Called: Manufacturing
980 Westbrook Dr (46158-1031)
PHONE.................................317 363-7760
Kevin Loechel, *Pr*
EMP: 3 **EST:** 2010
SALES (est): 107.6K **Privately Held**
SIC: 3999 Manufacturing industries, nec

(G-12203)
DIRECT PRINTING CO
106 David Ln (46158)
PHONE.................................317 831-1047

Mooresville - Morgan County (G-12204) — GEOGRAPHIC SECTION

Sherry Andarron, *Owner*
EMP: 1 **EST:** 2008
SALES (est): 110.03K **Privately Held**
SIC: 2759 Commercial printing, nec

(G-12204)
EQUIPMENT TECHNOLOGIES INC (PA)
Also Called: Et Sprayers
2201 Hancel Pkwy (46158-8297)
PHONE.................................800 861-2142
◆ **EMP:** 24 **EST:** 2000
SQ FT: 20,000
SALES (est): 19.01MM **Privately Held**
Web: www.etsprayers.com
SIC: 3523 Sprayers and spraying machines, agricultural

(G-12205)
ET AG CENTER LLC
2201 Hancel Pkwy (46158-8297)
PHONE.................................317 834-4500
EMP: 16 **EST:** 2011
SALES (est): 1.69MM **Privately Held**
Web: www.spraysmarter.com
SIC: 3523 Farm machinery and equipment

(G-12206)
ET WORKS INC (HQ)
Also Called: Equipment Technologies
2201 Hancel Pkwy (46158-8297)
PHONE.................................317 834-4500
Matthew Hayes, *Pr*
EMP: 14 **EST:** 2005
SALES (est): 11.01MM
SALES (corp-wide): 31.16K **Privately Held**
Web: www.etsprayers.com
SIC: 3523 Sprayers and spraying machines, agricultural
PA: Exel
  30 Rue Du 1er Mai
  Seclin
  952035205

(G-12207)
FENESTRATION PRODUCTS LLC
Also Called: Linel Signature
101 Linel Dr (46158-8254)
PHONE.................................317 831-5314
EMP: 80
SIC: 3444 3479 Sheet metalwork; Painting of metal products

(G-12208)
FLOSOURCE INC
1405 Hancel Pkwy (46158-8299)
PHONE.................................800 752-5959
Amy Macowan, *Pr*
Kean Macowan, *VP*
Matt Macowan, *Sec*
EMP: 22 **EST:** 2004
SALES (est): 7.05MM **Privately Held**
Web: www.flosource.com
SIC: 3491 3625 5074 Industrial valves; Actuators, industrial; Steam fittings

(G-12209)
HIMES CASTING REPAIR
171 Center Dr (46158-8337)
PHONE.................................317 831-2571
Robert Himes Junior, *Prin*
EMP: 1 **EST:** 2003
SALES (est): 48.69K **Privately Held**
SIC: 7692 Cracked casting repair

(G-12210)
HOLLYS CSTM CANVAS & UPHL LLC
5564 E Orchard Rd (46158-6305)
PHONE.................................317 550-6818
Holly Speelman, *Prin*
EMP: 4 **EST:** 2019
SALES (est): 196.22K **Privately Held**
Web: www.hollysmarineupholstery.com
SIC: 2211 Canvas

(G-12211)
HOPKINS GRAVEL SAND & CONCRETE
540 State Road 267 (46158-8949)
P.O. Box 636 (46158-0636)
PHONE.................................317 831-2704
Jeremy Hopkins, *Pr*
Jeremy Hopkins Junior, *VP*
EMP: 8 **EST:** 1966
SQ FT: 500
SALES (est): 730K **Privately Held**
Web: www.hopkinsgravel.com
SIC: 1442 3273 Gravel mining; Ready-mixed concrete

(G-12212)
HYDRAULIC PRESS BRICK COMPANY
6618 N Tidewater Rd (46158-7046)
P.O. Box 130 (46111-0130)
PHONE.................................317 290-1140
Ira Smith, *Brnch Mgr*
EMP: 105
SALES (corp-wide): 573.33MM **Privately Held**
Web: www.arcosalightweight.com
SIC: 3295 1442 Minerals, ground or treated; Construction sand and gravel
HQ: Hydraulic Press Brick Company Inc
  3600 Woodview Trce # 300
  Indianapolis IN 46268
  317 290-1140

(G-12213)
INDY ASSET BROKERS CORPORATION
Also Called: Commercial Trucks
11762 N Smokey Row Rd (46158-6398)
PHONE.................................317 502-2749
Brian B Blackburn, *Pr*
EMP: 1 **EST:** 2005
SALES (est): 89.98K **Privately Held**
SIC: 3715 Truck trailers

(G-12214)
INDY PRODUCTS COMPANY
1225 Indianapolis Rd (46158-1161)
PHONE.................................317 831-1114
John A Spees, *Pr*
Mike Mellinger, *VP*
Max Orr, *VP*
Barbara Spees, *Treas*
EMP: 1 **EST:** 1976
SQ FT: 5,000
SALES (est): 130.16K **Privately Held**
Web: www.indyproducts.com
SIC: 3944 Craft and hobby kits and sets

(G-12215)
INSIDE SYSTEMS
1053 E Jessup Way (46158-7259)
PHONE.................................317 831-3772
John Littlejohn, *Owner*
John Bradley, *Pt*
EMP: 2 **EST:** 1976
SALES (est): 173.12K **Privately Held**
Web: www.insidesystems.com
SIC: 3089 Plastics processing

(G-12216)
IRVING MATERIALS INC
Also Called: I M I
501 N Samuel Moore Pkwy (46158-1418)
PHONE.................................317 831-0224
EMP: 10
SALES (corp-wide): 814.09MM **Privately Held**
Web: www.irvmat.com
SIC: 3273 Ready-mixed concrete
PA: Irving Materials, Inc.
  8032 N State Road 9
  Greenfield IN 46140
  317 326-3101

(G-12217)
JACOBS MACHINE & TOOL CO INC
Also Called: Jmt
315 E Washington St (46158-1462)
P.O. Box 2 (46158-0002)
PHONE.................................317 831-2917
Janet Jacobs, *Pr*
Michael Jacobs, *Sec*
EMP: 18 **EST:** 1967
SQ FT: 13,800
SALES (est): 408.69K **Privately Held**
Web: www.jacobsmachinetool.com
SIC: 3544 Special dies and tools

(G-12218)
JOHNSON & JOHNSON INCORPORATED
9440 S State Road 39 (46158-0017)
PHONE.................................317 539-8420
EMP: 10 **EST:** 2011
SALES (est): 208.38K **Privately Held**
SIC: 3273 Ready-mixed concrete

(G-12219)
MAINLINE CONVEYOR SYSTEMS INC
3301 Hancel Cir (46158-8205)
P.O. Box 24 (46158-0024)
PHONE.................................317 831-2795
Roger D Brown, *Pr*
EMP: 10 **EST:** 1991
SALES (est): 1.94MM **Privately Held**
Web: www.mainlineconveyor.com
SIC: 3535 5084 Conveyors and conveying equipment; Industrial machinery and equipment

(G-12220)
MD HOLDINGS LLC
Also Called: Saniserv
451 E County Line Rd (46158-1811)
P.O. Box 1089 (46158-5089)
PHONE.................................317 831-7030
▲ **EMP:** 4 **EST:** 1998
SQ FT: 75,000
SALES (est): 2.04MM
SALES (corp-wide): 2.04MM **Privately Held**
Web: www.saniserv.com
SIC: 3556 3589 5046 Ice cream manufacturing machinery; Commercial cooking and foodwarming equipment; Restaurant equipment and supplies, nec
PA: Affinis Group Llc
  1050 Indianapolis Rd
  Mooresville IN 46158
  317 831-3830

(G-12221)
MESTEK INC
Linel
101 Linel Dr (46158-8254)
PHONE.................................317 831-5314
Rebecca Morris, *Contrlr*
EMP: 106
SALES (corp-wide): 689.94MM **Privately Held**
Web: www.mestek.com
SIC: 3444 3479 Sheet metalwork; Painting of metal products
PA: Mestek, Inc.
  260 N Elm St
  Westfield MA 01085
  413 568-9571

(G-12222)
MIDWEST OFFICE SOLUTIONS LLC
5825 E County Road 800 S (46158)
PHONE.................................262 658-2679
Cindy Renee Chevallier, *Managing Member*
EMP: 5 **EST:** 2019
SALES (est): 116.55K **Privately Held**
SIC: 3577 Printers, computer

(G-12223)
MOLEX LLC
1500 Hancel Pkwy (46158-8296)
PHONE.................................317 834-5600
Gene Hill, *Mgr*
EMP: 11
SALES (corp-wide): 64.37B **Privately Held**
Web: www.molex.com
SIC: 3669 3678 Emergency alarms; Electronic connectors
HQ: Molex, Llc
  2222 Wellington Ct
  Lisle IL 60532
  630 969-4550

(G-12224)
MOORESVILLE TIRE & SERVICE CTR
Also Called: Mooresville Goodyear Tire
432 N Monroe St (46158-1581)
PHONE.................................317 831-1215
Tom Duh, *CEO*
EMP: 6 **EST:** 1990
SALES (est): 692.08K **Privately Held**
Web: www.mooresvilleautoandtire.com
SIC: 7538 7534 5531 General automotive repair shops; Tire repair shop; Automotive tires

(G-12225)
MOORESVILLE WELDING INC
220 E Washington St (46158-1459)
PHONE.................................317 831-2265
Jeff Allen, *Pr*
EMP: 7 **EST:** 1939
SQ FT: 14,000
SALES (est): 956.59K **Privately Held**
Web: www.mooresvillewelding.com
SIC: 3713 3536 7692 3537 Truck beds; Hoists; Automotive welding; Industrial trucks and tractors

(G-12226)
MOTORAMA AUTO CTR INC (PA)
Also Called: Motorama Kart Parts
10509 N Old State Road 67 (46158-6362)
PHONE.................................317 831-0036
William L Mclaughlin, *CEO*
EMP: 5 **EST:** 1987
SQ FT: 25,000
SALES (est): 2.02MM **Privately Held**
SIC: 5521 3714 Automobiles, used cars only; Motor vehicle parts and accessories

(G-12227)
MT OLIVE MANUFACTURING LLC
Also Called: Mt. Olive Manufacturing, Inc.
3304 Hancel Cir (46158-8205)
PHONE.................................317 834-8525
Steven Paul Langley, *Pr*
Lisa Langley, *
▲ **EMP:** 90 **EST:** 1990
SQ FT: 48,000
SALES (est): 9.82MM
SALES (corp-wide): 198.24MM **Privately Held**
Web: www.creativefoam.com
SIC: 2891 Sealing wax
HQ: Bremen Corporation
  405 Industrial Dr
  Bremen IN 46506

Morgantown - Morgan County (G-12252)

(G-12228)
NICE-PAK PRODUCTS INC
1 Nice Pak Rd (46158-1398)
PHONE.............................845 365-1700
Rusty Ables, *Brnch Mgr*
EMP: 550
SALES (corp-wide): 674.94MM **Privately Held**
Web: www.nicepak.com
SIC: 2621 2392 Towels, tissues and napkins; paper and stock; Household furnishings, nec
PA: Nice-Pak Products, Inc.
2 Nice Pak Park
Orangeburg NY 10962
845 365-1700

(G-12229)
NUCOR HARRIS REBAR MIDWEST LLC
149 Sycamore Ln (46158-7923)
PHONE.............................317 831-2456
EMP: 18
SALES (corp-wide): 13.49MM **Privately Held**
Web: www.harrisrebar.com
SIC: 3312 3291 Coal gas, derived from chemical recovery coke ovens; Abrasive metal and steel products
PA: Nucor Harris Rebar Midwest Llc
1342 S Grandstaff Dr
Auburn IN 46706
260 925-5440

(G-12230)
OLIVER MACHINE AND TOOL CORP
110 Industrial Dr (46158)
P.O. Box 1454 (46151-0454)
PHONE.............................765 349-2271
Robert Green, *Pr*
Eric Strohmeyer, *Sec*
Kerry Weaver, *VP*
EMP: 10 **EST:** 1991
SQ FT: 3,000
SALES (est): 1.04MM **Privately Held**
Web: www.olivermachineandtool.com
SIC: 3599 Machine shop, jobbing and repair

(G-12231)
OMEGA CO
12494 N Woodlawn Dr (46158-6178)
PHONE.............................317 831-4471
Michael A Kemp, *Pr*
EMP: 5 **EST:** 2004
SALES (est): 224.82K **Privately Held**
SIC: 3999 Manufacturing industries, nec

(G-12232)
OVERTON & SONS TL & DIE CO INC (PA)
Also Called: Overton Industries
1250 S Old State Road 67 (46158)
P.O. Box 69 (46158)
PHONE.............................317 831-4542
Steve Overton, *CEO*
Ron E Overton, *
Rick Overton, *
Elnora Overton, *Stockholder**
EMP: 35 **EST:** 1968
SALES (est): 22.22MM
SALES (corp-wide): 22.22MM **Privately Held**
Web: www.overtonind.com
SIC: 3544 7692 3545 Special dies and tools; Welding repair; Machine tool accessories

(G-12233)
PACMOORE PROCESS TECH LLC
Also Called: 110495 - Pacmoore Process Tech
100 Pacmoore Pkwy (46158-6195)
P.O. Box 1299 (46325-1299)
PHONE.............................317 831-2666
Gary Vandelaarschot, *Pr*
EMP: 5 **EST:** 2004
SALES (est): 1.53MM **Privately Held**
Web: www.pacmoore.com
SIC: 3556 Food products machinery
HQ: Glanbia Nutritionals, Inc.
227 W Monroe St Ste 5100
Chicago IL 60606

(G-12234)
PACMOORE PRODUCTS INC
PACMOORE PRODUCTS, INC.
100 Pacmoore Pkwy (46158-6195)
P.O. Box 397 (46158-0397)
PHONE.............................317 831-2666
William Moore, *Brnch Mgr*
EMP: 30
SALES (corp-wide): 179.67MM **Privately Held**
Web: www.pacmoore.com
SIC: 2046 Starch, nsk
HQ: Msi Express
1844 Summer St
Hammond IN 46320

(G-12235)
PINK SIGNS LLC
502 State Road 267 Mooresville (46158)
PHONE.............................317 509-8805
EMP: 4 **EST:** 2011
SALES (est): 122.84K **Privately Held**
SIC: 3993 Signs and advertising specialties

(G-12236)
PRECISION POWDER COAT LLC
141 E South St Ste E (46158)
PHONE.............................317 483-3670
EMP: 4 **EST:** 2019
SALES (est): 75.53K **Privately Held**
SIC: 3479 Coating of metals and formed products

(G-12237)
PROTO ENGINEERING LLC
319 Harlan Dr (46158-1359)
PHONE.............................800 522-6752
Rhonda Egler, *VP*
EMP: 2 **EST:** 2008
SALES (est): 262.39K **Privately Held**
Web: www.proto-engineering.com
SIC: 3672 Printed circuit boards

(G-12238)
RECONSERVE OF INDIANA INC
3315 Hancel Cir (46158-8205)
PHONE.............................812 299-2191
Gary Adams, *Genl Mgr*
EMP: 1 **EST:** 2013
SALES (est): 4.41MM
SALES (corp-wide): 203.79MM **Privately Held**
Web: www.reconserve.com
SIC: 2048 Prepared feeds, nec
PA: Reconserve, Inc.
2811 Wilshire Blvd # 410
Santa Monica CA 90403
310 458-1574

(G-12239)
ROBERT J MATT
Also Called: Tackle Service Center
246 E Washington St (46158-1459)
PHONE.............................317 831-2400
Robert J Matt, *Owner*
EMP: 4 **EST:** 1973
SQ FT: 4,000
SALES (est): 150K **Privately Held**
Web: www.tackleservicecenter.com
SIC: 7699 5941 5091 3949 Fishing equipment repair; Bait and tackle; Fishing tackle; Sporting and athletic goods, nec

(G-12240)
S EDWARDS INC
Also Called: Ace Tool & Engineering Co
292 W Harrison St (46158-1633)
P.O. Box 326 (46158-0326)
PHONE.............................317 831-0261
Stephen A Edwards, *Pr*
Cheryl Edwards, *Owner*
EMP: 6 **EST:** 1941
SQ FT: 10,000
SALES (est): 467.86K **Privately Held**
SIC: 3599 Machine shop, jobbing and repair

(G-12241)
SANISERV
451 E County Line Rd (46158-1811)
P.O. Box 1089 (46158-5089)
PHONE.............................317 831-7030
Robert Mcafee, *CEO*
EMP: 8 **EST:** 2013
SALES (est): 355.53K **Privately Held**
Web: www.affinis.biz
SIC: 2024 Dairy based frozen desserts

(G-12242)
SIGN FOR IT LLC
68 W Main St (46158-1660)
PHONE.............................317 834-4636
EMP: 2 **EST:** 2004
SALES (est): 182.75K **Privately Held**
Web: www.signforit.net
SIC: 3993 Signs and advertising specialties

(G-12243)
SONNY SCAFFOLDS INC (PA)
319 Harlan Dr (46158-1359)
P.O. Box 747 (46158-0747)
PHONE.............................317 831-3900
Charlotte Cosgrove, *Pr*
Richard Blake, *VP*
EMP: 14 **EST:** 1986
SQ FT: 7,200
SALES (est): 2.46MM
SALES (corp-wide): 2.46MM **Privately Held**
Web: www.sonnyscaffolds.com
SIC: 3446 Scaffolds, mobile or stationary: metal

(G-12244)
STRYKER CORPORATION
Also Called: Stryker Cdc2
2496 Westpoint Blvd (46158-7340)
PHONE.............................832 509-9988
Kevin A Lobo, *Ch Bd*
EMP: 1
SALES (corp-wide): 20.5B **Publicly Held**
Web: www.stryker.com
SIC: 3841 Surgical and medical instruments
PA: Stryker Corporation
1941 Stryker Way
Portage MI 49002
269 385-2600

(G-12245)
STS PACKAGING ✪
2630 Westpoint Blvd (46158-7341)
PHONE.............................317 210-0305
EMP: 6 **EST:** 2024
SALES (est): 283.27K **Privately Held**
SIC: 2621 Paper mills

(G-12246)
SUN POLYMERS INTERNATIONAL INC (HQ)
100 Sun Polymers Dr (46158)
P.O. Box 249 (46158)
PHONE.............................317 834-6410
Chang Pei Kuo, *Pr*
Lily Hsiao, *Treas*
Hsiao Hui Li, *Sec*
EMP: 10 **EST:** 1997
SALES (est): 5.2MM **Privately Held**
Web: www.sunpolymers.com
SIC: 2821 Polyethylene resins
PA: Chan Sieh Enterprises Co., Ltd.
3f, 90, Nanking E. Rd., Sec. 2,
Taipei City TAP 10409

(G-12247)
TOA (USA) LLC
2000 Pleiades Dr (46158-7144)
PHONE.............................317 834-0522
Kazuo Murai, *CEO*
Kuniaki Hasegawa, *Pr*
▲ **EMP:** 292 **EST:** 2000
SQ FT: 440,000
SALES (est): 103.28MM **Privately Held**
Web: www.toa-usa.com
SIC: 3714 Air brakes, motor vehicle

(G-12248)
TOP LOCK CORPORATION
319 Harlan Dr (46158-1359)
PHONE.............................317 831-2000
EMP: 6 **EST:** 2007
SALES (est): 122.6K **Privately Held**
Web: www.toplockcorp.com
SIC: 3429 1799 Locks or lock sets; Scaffolding

(G-12249)
VEMME KART USA LLC
6163 E Neitzel Rd (46158-6478)
PHONE.............................317 407-7172
EMP: 5 **EST:** 2018
SALES (est): 98.83K **Privately Held**
Web: www.vemmekart.com
SIC: 3999 Manufacturing industries, nec

(G-12250)
WOOD WIZ INC
6 W Main St (46158-1660)
PHONE.............................317 834-9079
John Trischer, *Pr*
EMP: 1 **EST:** 1997
SALES (est): 125.8K **Privately Held**
SIC: 2431 1751 Millwork; Cabinet building and installation

Morgantown
Morgan County

(G-12251)
ALL 4U PRINTING LLC
Also Called: Sunpress South
6710 W 425 S (46160-8235)
PHONE.............................317 845-2955
Misty Slentz, *Pr*
EMP: 2 **EST:** 1983
SALES (est): 181.7K **Privately Held**
SIC: 2752 Offset printing

(G-12252)
ALL-PRO PUMP & REPAIR INC
7907 W 500 S (46160-9667)
PHONE.............................317 738-4203
Patrick Beach, *Pr*
EMP: 3 **EST:** 1994
SALES (est): 319.56K **Privately Held**
SIC: 3561 Pumps and pumping equipment

Morgantown - Morgan County (G-12253)

(G-12253)
AMERICAN DOOR CONTROLS INC
51 W State Road 45 (46160-8928)
PHONE..................812 988-4853
Martha Jessup, CEO
Frank Jessup, Pr
EMP: 2 EST: 1984
SQ FT: 800
SALES (est): 152.47K Privately Held
Web: www.amerdoor.com
SIC: 3699 Door opening and closing devices, electrical

(G-12254)
CENTURION ARMS LLC
8985 N Carmel Ridge Rd (46160-9482)
PHONE..................619 994-5756
EMP: 12 EST: 2013
SALES (est): 487.07K Privately Held
Web: www.centurionarms.com
SIC: 5941 3949 Firearms; Hunting equipment

(G-12255)
CIRCLE S INDUSTRIES LLC
1780 S Hickey Rd (46160-9357)
PHONE..................317 727-6752
Jacob T Starks, Owner
EMP: 1 EST: 2013
SALES (est): 79.54K Privately Held
SIC: 3999 Manufacturing industries, nec

(G-12256)
CJ LOGGING LLC
2336 S Conservation Club Rd (46160-9370)
PHONE..................812 360-0163
EMP: 2 EST: 2014
SALES (est): 95.76K Privately Held
SIC: 2411 Logging

(G-12257)
CSN INDUSTRIES INC
1797 S Conservation Club Rd (46160-9363)
PHONE..................317 697-6549
Carolyn Neff, Pr
EMP: 5 EST: 2012
SALES (est): 108.15K Privately Held
SIC: 3999 Manufacturing industries, nec

(G-12258)
INDIAN CREEK OUTDOOR POWER LLC
250 W Mulberry St (46160-9716)
PHONE..................812 597-3055
EMP: 2 EST: 2015
SALES (est): 57.66K Privately Held
SIC: 7538 7694 5088 Engine repair; Motor repair services; Golf carts

(G-12259)
KMLS LLC
Also Called: Sunpress South
6710 W 425 S (46160-8235)
PHONE..................317 845-2955
Ken Lane, Managing Member
EMP: 1 EST: 2013
SALES (est): 112.99K Privately Held
SIC: 2759 Commercial printing, nec

(G-12260)
LEISTNER AQUATIC SERVICES INC
7657 N State Road 135 (46160-8989)
PHONE..................317 535-6099
Keith Leistner, Pr
EMP: 5 EST: 1996
SALES (est): 666.89K Privately Held
Web: www.sprayboats.com
SIC: 1629 7389 7999 3589 Pond construction; Water softener service; Fishing lakes and piers, operation; Sewage and water treatment equipment

(G-12261)
NJ LOGGING LLC
1766 W Three Story Hill Rd (46160-9257)
PHONE..................812 597-0782
Nina Law, Owner
EMP: 3 EST: 2009
SALES (est): 212.77K Privately Held
SIC: 2411 Logging camps and contractors

(G-12262)
PARSONS WELDING SERVICE
9655 N Haasetown Rd (46160-9464)
PHONE..................812 597-4914
Duane Parsons, Prin
EMP: 1 EST: 2010
SALES (est): 42.18K Privately Held
SIC: 7692 Welding repair

(G-12263)
SHADY OAKS LOGGING LLC
7705 Gartner Dr (46160-8905)
PHONE..................317 902-9741
Christina A Buccos, Prin
EMP: 7 EST: 2013
SALES (est): 71.2K Privately Held
SIC: 2411 Logging camps and contractors

(G-12264)
SPEEDY STITCH EMBROIDERY
550 S State Road 135 (46160-8596)
PHONE..................812 597-4654
Nina Smith, Owner
EMP: 1 EST: 2010
SALES (est): 54.84K Privately Held
Web: www.speedystitch.com
SIC: 2395 Embroidery products, except Schiffli machine

(G-12265)
STRITTO SIGN ART COMPANY
6639 Allender Trce (46160-9079)
PHONE..................317 356-2126
Joseph Allio, Pr
EMP: 4 EST: 1945
SALES (est): 341.33K Privately Held
SIC: 3993 Signs, not made in custom sign painting shops

(G-12266)
WYATT SURVIVAL SUPPLY LLC
1750 S Conservation Club Rd (46160-9363)
PHONE..................765 318-2872
Cynthia A Wyatt, Managing Member
EMP: 1 EST: 2013
SALES (est): 73.29K Privately Held
Web: www.wyattsurvivalsupplyllc.com
SIC: 3949 5099 5091 7389 Archery equipment, general; Lifesaving and survival equipment (non-medical); Camping equipment and supplies; Business services, nec

Morocco
Newton County

(G-12267)
ACTION COOLING TOWERS INC
2649 S 500 W (47963-8048)
P.O. Box 480 (47963-0480)
PHONE..................219 285-2660
EMP: 5 EST: 1996
SALES (est): 375.24K Privately Held
SIC: 2499 Cooling towers, wood or wood and sheet metal combination

(G-12268)
L YOUNG COMPANY INC (PA)
2673 W State Road 114 (47963-8153)
P.O. Box 629 (47963-0629)
PHONE..................219 285-8107
EMP: 1 EST: 1992
SALES (est): 197.81K Privately Held
SIC: 3599 Machine shop, jobbing and repair

(G-12269)
ROAD ALERT SYSTEMS LLC
Also Called: Trot
112 E State St (47963-7500)
P.O. Box 501 (47963-0501)
PHONE..................219 669-1206
Luis G Reis, Prin
Victor Reis, Prin
George F Williams, Prin
Sondra Banister, Prin
EMP: 1 EST: 2019
SALES (est): 122.67K Privately Held
Web: www.roadalertsystems.com
SIC: 7389 3531 9532 7359 Flagging service (traffic control); Construction machinery; Urban and community development; Work zone traffic equipment (flags, cones, barrels, etc.)

(G-12270)
SOUTHLAKE MACHINE CORP
112 N Polk St (47963-8297)
P.O. Box 487 (47963-0487)
PHONE..................219 285-6150
Rex Clark, Pr
EMP: 7 EST: 1974
SQ FT: 5,000
SALES (est): 589.74K Privately Held
Web: www.southlakemachine.com
SIC: 3547 7699 Steel rolling machinery; Industrial equipment services

Morristown
Shelby County

(G-12271)
APEX ELECTRIC & SIGN INC (PA)
500 N Range Line Rd (46161-9641)
P.O. Box 130 (46154-0130)
PHONE..................317 326-1325
Greg Heuer, Prin
EMP: 1 EST: 2010
SALES (est): 488.25K
SALES (corp-wide): 488.25K Privately Held
Web: www.apexelectricandsign.com
SIC: 3993 Signs and advertising specialties

(G-12272)
CALDWELLS INC
10911 N 600 E (46161-9438)
P.O. Box 272 (46161-0272)
PHONE..................765 740-4300
Jordan Caldwell, Pr
Jj Crafton, *
EMP: 30 EST: 2021
SALES (est): 2.88MM Privately Held
Web: www.caldwells-inc.com
SIC: 3537 Trucks, tractors, loaders, carriers, and similar equipment

(G-12273)
CGS SERVICES INC
Also Called: Caldwell Gravel Sales Tm
2920 E Us Highway 52 (46161-9649)
PHONE..................765 763-6258
Paul Cadwell, CEO
Paul Caldwell, CEO
Dana Caldwell, Pr
Wanda Caldwell, Sec
EMP: 3 EST: 1968
SQ FT: 1,700
SALES (est): 901.67K
SALES (corp-wide): 20.43B Publicly Held
Web: www.cgsservices.com
SIC: 1442 4953 Gravel mining; Sanitary landfill operation
HQ: Advanced Disposal Services, Inc.
90 Fort Wade Rd Ste 200
Ponte Vedra FL 32081
904 737-7900

(G-12274)
CRANEWERKS INC
511 N Range Line Rd (46161-9641)
PHONE..................765 663-2909
Mark Thomas, Pr
EMP: 58 EST: 1997
SQ FT: 7,500
SALES (est): 9.43MM Privately Held
Web: www.cranewerks.com
SIC: 3536 Hoists

(G-12275)
DOTY GRAPHICS
9038 N State Road 9 (46161-9762)
P.O. Box 310 (46161-0310)
PHONE..................765 763-7178
John Doty, Pt
Dale Doty, Pt
EMP: 2 EST: 2003
SALES (est): 126.55K Privately Held
SIC: 3993 Signs and advertising specialties

(G-12276)
FOR THE LOVE OF WORDS LLC
625 E Freeport Rd (46161-9763)
PHONE..................317 550-8805
Ruth A Dean, Prin
EMP: 3 EST: 2018
SALES (est): 99.48K Privately Held
Web: www.fortheloveofwordsllc.com
SIC: 2741 Miscellaneous publishing

(G-12277)
FREUDENBERG-NOK GENERAL PARTNR
General Industries Division
487 W Main St (46161-9745)
P.O. Box 245 (46161-0245)
PHONE..................765 763-7246
Stacy Flora, Mgr
EMP: 150
SQ FT: 45,000
SALES (corp-wide): 12.23B Privately Held
Web: www.freudenberg.com
SIC: 3053 3965 3714 3643 Gaskets, all materials; Fasteners, buttons, needles, and pins; Motor vehicle parts and accessories; Current-carrying wiring services
HQ: Freudenberg-Nok General Partnership
47774 W Anchor Ct
Plymouth MI 48170
734 451-0020

(G-12278)
KBI INC
2618 E Us Highway 52 (46161-9802)
PHONE..................765 763-6114
Kenneth Klosterman, Ch Bd
Bob Jung, *
EMP: 100 EST: 1978
SQ FT: 25,000
SALES (est): 511.97K
SALES (corp-wide): 190.57MM Privately Held
SIC: 2051 Buns, bread type: fresh or frozen
PA: Klosterman Baking Co., Llc

GEOGRAPHIC SECTION

Mount Vernon - Posey County (G-12301)

4760 Paddock Rd
Cincinnati OH 45229
513 242-1004

(G-12279)
LOCAVORE PRODUCTIONS LLC
Also Called: Hoosier Locavore
6559 E 1200 N (46161-9753)
PHONE.....................317 371-2970
EMP: 1 EST: 2016
SALES (est): 47.92K Privately Held
SIC: 2721 Periodicals, publishing only

(G-12280)
PARK 100 FOODS INC
Also Called: Kettle Processed Foods
205 Central Pkwy (46161-9647)
P.O. Box 448 (46161-0448)
PHONE.....................765 763-6064
Will Copass, Owner
EMP: 36
SALES (corp-wide): 105.14MM Privately Held
Web: www.park100foods.com
SIC: 3999 Barber and beauty shop equipment
PA: Park 100 Foods Inc
  326 E Adams St
  Tipton IN 46072
  765 675-3480

(G-12281)
TMK MANUFACTURING LLC
307 E Fletcher St (46161-4630)
PHONE.....................765 763-6754
Charles W Kile, Prin
EMP: 5 EST: 2016
SALES (est): 39.69K Privately Held
SIC: 3999 Manufacturing industries, nec

(G-12282)
WOODS OF AMBER
632 S Washington St (46161-9771)
PHONE.....................765 763-6926
Ronald Zellar, Owner
EMP: 2 EST: 2001
SALES (est): 73.42K Privately Held
SIC: 2499 Carved and turned wood

Mount Pleasant
Perry County

(G-12283)
CASH LOGGING LLC
20198 N State Road 66 (47520-5100)
PHONE.....................812 843-5335
James Cash, Owner
EMP: 3 EST: 2003
SALES (est): 159.02K Privately Held
SIC: 2411 Logging camps and contractors

Mount Summit
Henry County

(G-12284)
AMERICAN STEEL CARPORTS INC
404 W Main St (47361)
PHONE.....................419 737-1331
Primo Castillo, Managing Member
EMP: 1
SALES (corp-wide): 20.62MM Privately Held
Web: www.americansteelinc.com
SIC: 5511 3448 New and used car dealers; Prefabricated metal buildings and components
PA: American Steel Carports, Inc.
  457 N Broadway St
  Joshua TX 76058
  866 471-8761

(G-12285)
KAIROS SPECIALTY METALS CORP
404 W Main St (47361)
PHONE.....................765 836-5540
John Deradoorian, Pr
EMP: 35 EST: 2017
SALES (est): 3.9MM Privately Held
Web: www.kairosspecialtymetals.com
SIC: 3444 Sheet metalwork

Mount Vernon
Posey County

(G-12286)
ADM MILLING CO
Also Called: ADM
614 W 2nd St (47620-1706)
PHONE.....................812 838-4445
Kim Banks, Brnch Mgr
EMP: 10
SALES (corp-wide): 93.94B Publicly Held
Web: www.adm.com
SIC: 2041 Grain mills (except rice)
HQ: Adm Milling Co.
  4666 E Faries Pkwy
  Decatur IL 62526
  913 491-9400

(G-12287)
ASTRAZENECA PHARMACEUTICALS LP
6400 William Keck Byp (47620-6929)
PHONE.....................240 252-0125
Bill Tucker, Brnch Mgr
EMP: 8
SALES (corp-wide): 45.81B Privately Held
Web: www.astrazeneca.com
SIC: 2834 Pharmaceutical preparations
HQ: Astrazeneca Pharmaceuticals Lp
  1800 Concord Pike
  Wilmington DE 19850

(G-12288)
ASTRAZENECA PHARMACEUTICALS LP
4601 Highway 62 E (47620-9682)
PHONE.....................812 429-5000
EMP: 40
SALES (corp-wide): 45.81B Privately Held
Web: www.astrazeneca.com
SIC: 2834 Pharmaceutical preparations
HQ: Astrazeneca Pharmaceuticals Lp
  1800 Concord Pike
  Wilmington DE 19850

(G-12289)
ATI INC (DH)
103 Brown St (47620-1425)
P.O. Box 686 (47620-0686)
PHONE.....................812 431-5409
Duane Tiede, Pr
Kenneth Juncker, Ch Bd
David L Juncker, Sec
C Anthony Juncker, Prin
Steve Hannam, Prin
◆ EMP: 9 EST: 1997
SQ FT: 36,000
SALES (est): 4.93MM Privately Held
Web: www.ati-tracks.com
SIC: 3545 3061 3829 Cutting tools for machine tools; Automotive rubber goods (mechanical); Meteorologic tracking systems
HQ: Cnh Industrial America Llc
  711 Jorie Blvd
  Oak Brook IL 60523
  630 887-2233

(G-12290)
ATI INC
204a Main St (47620-1840)
P.O. Box 686 (47620-0686)
PHONE.....................812 520-5409
EMP: 1
Web: www.ati-tracks.com
SIC: 3061 3545 Automotive rubber goods (mechanical); Cutting tools for machine tools
HQ: Ati, Inc.
  103 Brown St
  Mount Vernon IN 47620
  812 431-5409

(G-12291)
AVENTINE RENEWABLE ENERGY
Also Called: Aventine Renewable Fuels
7201 Port Rd (47620-8524)
PHONE.....................812 838-9598
Mike Murray, Engr
EMP: 2 EST: 2006
SALES (est): 269.62K Privately Held
SIC: 2869 Ethanolamines

(G-12292)
BEYOND MONOGRAMS LLC
525 Locust St (47620-1932)
P.O. Box 741 (47620-0741)
PHONE.....................812 746-2624
EMP: 3 EST: 2015
SALES (est): 50.8K Privately Held
SIC: 2395 Embroidery and art needlework

(G-12293)
BRISTOL-MYERS SQUIBB COMPANY
Also Called: Bristol-Myers Squibb
6400 William Keck Byp (47620)
PHONE.....................812 307-2000
Phil Campbell, Dir
EMP: 130
SALES (corp-wide): 45.01B Publicly Held
Web: www.bms.com
SIC: 2834 Pharmaceutical preparations
PA: Bristol-Myers Squibb Company
  Route 206/Prvince Line Rd
  Princeton NJ 08540
  609 252-4621

(G-12294)
BWXT NCLEAR OPRTIONS GROUP INC
1400 Old Highway 69 S (47620-8749)
PHONE.....................812 838-1200
Michael Keene, Pr
EMP: 151
Web: www.bwxt.com
SIC: 3462 Nuclear power plant forgings, ferrous
HQ: Bwxt Nuclear Operations Group, Inc.
  2016 Mount Athos Rd
  Lynchburg VA 24504

(G-12295)
COUNTRYMARK REF LOGISTICS LLC
Also Called: Countrymark Cooperative
1200 Refinery Rd (47620-9265)
PHONE.....................812 838-4341
Matthew Smorch, CEO
Kent Lambert Hoffman, *
Nina J Zike, *
EMP: 425 EST: 2001
SALES (est): 122.74MM
SALES (corp-wide): 532.74MM Privately Held
SIC: 2911 1382 1311 Petroleum refining; Aerial geophysical exploration, oil and gas; Crude petroleum and natural gas production

PA: Countrymark Cooperative Holding Corporation
  225 S East St Ste 144
  Indianapolis IN 46202
  800 808-3170

(G-12296)
COZY COTTAGE LLC
1808 Greenbrier Ct (47620-9294)
P.O. Box 552 (47620-0552)
PHONE.....................812 838-6891
Susan B Marshall, Prin
EMP: 5 EST: 2016
SALES (est): 59.89K Privately Held
SIC: 2395 Embroidery and art needlework

(G-12297)
GOTTMAN ELECTRIC COMPANY INC
3350 Old Highway 62 (47620-6924)
P.O. Box 752 (47620-0752)
PHONE.....................812 838-0037
Terry Gottman, Pr
Herschel E Gottman, Ex VP
EMP: 6 EST: 1979
SQ FT: 6,000
SALES (est): 600K Privately Held
Web: www.gottco.co
SIC: 1731 7694 General electrical contractor; Electric motor repair

(G-12298)
GREEN PLAINS GRAIN COMPANY LLC
Also Called: Green Plains Mount Vernon
8999 W Franklin Rd (47620-9179)
PHONE.....................812 985-7480
Dan Labhart, Mgr
EMP: 20
SALES (corp-wide): 3.3B Publicly Held
Web: www.gpreinc.com
SIC: 2869 Ethyl alcohol, ethanol
HQ: Green Plains Grain Company Llc
  401 Railroad Ave
  Saint Edward NE 68660
  402 884-8700

(G-12299)
GREEN PLAINS INC
8999 W Franklin Rd (47620-9179)
PHONE.....................812 985-7480
Dan Labhart, Brnch Mgr
EMP: 50
SALES (corp-wide): 3.3B Publicly Held
Web: www.gpreinc.com
SIC: 2869 Ethyl alcohol, ethanol
PA: Green Plains Inc.
  1811 Aksarben Dr
  Omaha NE 68106
  402 884-8700

(G-12300)
INFINITY MOLDING & ASSEMBLY INC
5520 Industrial Rd (47620-7200)
PHONE.....................812 838-0370
EMP: 85 EST: 1982
SALES (est): 9.67MM Privately Held
Web: www.infinity-mai.com
SIC: 3089 Injection molded finished plastics products, nec

(G-12301)
INFINITY PLASTICS GROUP LTD
5520 Industrial Rd (47620-7200)
PHONE.....................812 838-0370
EMP: 10 EST: 2019
SALES (est): 154.49K Privately Held
Web: www.infinity-mai.com
SIC: 3089 Injection molding of plastics

Mount Vernon - Posey County (G-12302)

GEOGRAPHIC SECTION

(G-12302)
INOTIV INC
10424 Middle Mount Vernon Rd
(47620-9627)
PHONE..................812 985-5900
Jacqueline M Lemke, *CEO*
EMP: 1
SALES (corp-wide): 572.42MM **Publicly Held**
Web: www.basinc.com
SIC: 8731 3841 Medical research, commercial; Surgical and medical instruments
PA: Inotiv, Inc.
2701 Kent Ave
West Lafayette IN 47906
765 463-4527

(G-12303)
J & J WELDING INC
1114 W 4th St (47620-1688)
P.O. Box 579 (47620-0579)
PHONE..................812 838-4391
Dorothy Smith, *CEO*
Bryan Smith, *VP*
Timothy Smith, *VP*
Darren Saltzman, *Stockholder*
▲ **EMP:** 20 **EST:** 1944
SQ FT: 11,250
SALES (est): 2.05MM **Privately Held**
Web: www.jjwelding.com
SIC: 7692 3443 3599 3471 Welding repair; Fabricated plate work (boiler shop); Machine shop, jobbing and repair; Plating and polishing

(G-12304)
JAMPLAST INC
7451 Highway 62 E (47620-9131)
P.O. Box 504 (47620-0504)
PHONE..................812 838-8562
◆ **EMP:** 13 **EST:** 1994
SALES (est): 1.07MM **Privately Held**
Web: www.jamplast.com
SIC: 2821 Thermoplastic materials

(G-12305)
K S OIL CORP
8681 Waterford Dr (47620-9502)
PHONE..................812 453-3026
Larry Schmitt, *Pr*
Melody Schmitt, *Sec*
Georgia Nattles, *Sec*
Mildred Kohlmeyer, *VP*
EMP: 9 **EST:** 1972
SALES (est): 783.61K **Privately Held**
SIC: 1311 1389 Crude petroleum production; Pumping of oil and gas wells

(G-12306)
MAC INDUSTRIAL HOLDINGS LLC
901 E 3rd St (47620-2109)
PHONE..................812 838-1832
EMP: 15
SALES (est): 1.08MM **Privately Held**
Web: www.macindustrialservices.net
SIC: 3569 Blast cleaning equipment, dustless

(G-12307)
MATHESON TRI-GAS INC
1101 Holler Rd (47620)
PHONE..................812 838-5518
Mike Curtis, *Mgr*
EMP: 7
Web: www.mathesongas.com
SIC: 5084 2813 Welding machinery and equipment; Nitrogen
HQ: Matheson Tri-Gas, Inc.
3 Mountainview Rd Ste 3 # 3
Warren NJ 07059
908 991-9200

(G-12308)
MEAD JOHNSON & COMPANY LLC
Also Called: Mead Johnson Nutritionals
62 West State Rd (47620)
PHONE..................812 429-5000
Philena Mead, *Brnch Mgr*
EMP: 4
SALES (corp-wide): 18.21B **Privately Held**
Web: www.meadjohnson.com
SIC: 2834 Pharmaceutical preparations
HQ: Mead Johnson & Company, Llc
2400 W Lloyd Pkwy
Evansville IN 47721
812 429-5000

(G-12309)
MICHROCHEM LLC
Also Called: Mac Industrial Services
901 E 3rd St (47620-2109)
PHONE..................812 838-1832
Michael Andrews, *Mng Pt*
EMP: 6 **EST:** 2004
SALES (est): 513.87K **Privately Held**
Web: www.macindustrialservices.net
SIC: 3589 High pressure cleaning equipment

(G-12310)
MT VERNON COAL TRANSFER CO
Alliance Resource Partners
3300 Bluff Rd (47620-8528)
P.O. Box 742 (47620-0742)
PHONE..................812 838-5531
V F Mayer, *Brnch Mgr*
EMP: 21
SIC: 1221 Bituminous coal and lignite-surface mining
HQ: Mt Vernon Coal Transfer Co (Inc)
1717 S Boulder Ave
Tulsa OK 74119
918 295-7600

(G-12311)
MT VERNON TRANSFER TRML LLC
3300 Bluff Rd (47620-8528)
PHONE..................812 838-5531
Joseph W Craft Iii, *Pr*
EMP: 9 **EST:** 2017
SALES (est): 2.47MM **Publicly Held**
Web: www.evwr.com
SIC: 1221 1241 Coal preparation plant, bituminous or lignite; Coal mining services
HQ: Alliance Resource Partners Lp
1717 S Boulder Ave Ste 400
Tulsa OK 74119
918 295-7600

(G-12312)
MULZER CRUSHED STONE INC
10700 Highway 69 S (47620-7038)
PHONE..................812 838-3472
Kenny Mulder, *Pr*
EMP: 5
SALES (corp-wide): 34.95B **Privately Held**
Web: www.mulzer.com
SIC: 1422 Crushed and broken limestone
HQ: Mulzer Crushed Stone Inc
534 Mozart St
Tell City IN 47586
812 547-7921

(G-12313)
OASIS PUMPS MFG CO
3001 Curtis Rd (47620-8903)
PHONE..................812 783-2146
Timothy Schaefer, *Owner*
EMP: 1 **EST:** 2002
SALES (est): 142.9K **Privately Held**
Web: www.oasispumps.com
SIC: 3561 Pumps, oil well and field

(G-12314)
PENGUIN PETES
1809 Westridge Dr (47620-9488)
PHONE..................812 838-9670
EMP: 1 **EST:** 1996
SALES (est): 77.42K **Privately Held**
SIC: 2024 Ice cream and frozen deserts

(G-12315)
PRINTCRAFTERS INC
304 W 4th St (47620-1822)
P.O. Box 487 (47620-0487)
PHONE..................812 838-4106
Harriette Alley, *Pr*
EMP: 5 **EST:** 1978
SQ FT: 2,200
SALES (est): 404.41K **Privately Held**
Web: www.printcrafters.com
SIC: 2752 2759 Offset printing; Letterpress printing

(G-12316)
PROFESSIONAL SOFTWARE CORP
109 E 2nd St (47620-1817)
P.O. Box 716 (47620-0716)
PHONE..................812 781-1422
Mark Holly, *Owner*
EMP: 1 **EST:** 1992
SALES (est): 72.07K **Privately Held**
Web: www.supportmastersoftware.com
SIC: 7372 Prepackaged software

(G-12317)
ROBERT C KUEBER
Also Called: Kueber Cabinet Shop
20 Highway 62 W (47620-8185)
PHONE..................812 838-5813
Robert C Kueber, *Owner*
EMP: 1 **EST:** 1954
SALES (est): 140.17K **Privately Held**
SIC: 1521 2434 General remodeling, single-family houses; Wood kitchen cabinets

(G-12318)
RUSSELLS EXCVTG SPTIC TNKS INC
Also Called: Russell's Septic Tank Service
6800 Leonard Rd S (47620-8123)
P.O. Box 512 (47620-0512)
PHONE..................812 838-2471
John Russell, *Pr*
Jeffrey Russell, *VP*
Ruth Russell, *Sec*
EMP: 14 **EST:** 1971
SALES (est): 2.29MM **Privately Held**
Web: www.russell-excavating.com
SIC: 1794 1711 3272 Excavation and grading, building construction; Septic system construction; Septic tanks, concrete

(G-12319)
SABIC INNOVATIVE PLAS US LLC
2101 Hwy 69 S (47620)
PHONE..................812 831-4054
EMP: 259
Web: www.sabic.com
SIC: 2821 3087 3081 Plastics materials and resins; Custom compound purchased resins; Unsupported plastics film and sheet
HQ: Sabic Innovative Plastics Us Llc
2500 Ctywest Blvd Ste 100
Houston TX 77042

(G-12320)
SABIC INNVTIVE PLAS MT VRNON L
Also Called: Sabic Innovative Plastics
1 Lexan Ln (47620)
PHONE..................812 838-4385
Michael L Walsh, *
◆ **EMP:** 1342 **EST:** 2000
SALES (est): 417.52MM **Privately Held**

Web: ff.sabic.eu
SIC: 2821 3087 3081 Plastics materials and resins; Custom compound purchased resins; Unsupported plastics film and sheet
HQ: Sabic Innovative Plastics Us Llc
2500 Ctywest Blvd Ste 100
Houston TX 77042

(G-12321)
SCHENK AND SONS TREE SVC INC
11018 Altheide Rd (47620-9684)
PHONE..................812 985-3954
Steve Schenk, *Owner*
EMP: 2 **EST:** 1997
SALES (est): 118.15K **Privately Held**
SIC: 0783 7692 Ornamental shrub and tree services; Welding repair

(G-12322)
SOUTHERN IN DISTILLERY
Also Called: Dusty Barn Distillery
6861 Carson School Rd (47620-8427)
PHONE..................812 454-0135
EMP: 3 **EST:** 2018
SALES (est): 78.55K **Privately Held**
SIC: 2085 Distilled and blended liquors

(G-12323)
STANDARD INDUSTRIES INC
Also Called: GAF Materials
901 Givens Rd (47620-8200)
PHONE..................812 838-4861
John Washuta, *Brnch Mgr*
EMP: 1
SALES (corp-wide): 6.35B **Privately Held**
Web: www.gaf.com
SIC: 2493 Insulation and roofing material, reconstituted wood
HQ: Standard Building Solutions Inc.
1 Campus Dr
Parsippany NJ 07054

(G-12324)
TRON MECHANICAL INCORPORATED
Also Called: TMI Contractors
331 W 2nd St (47620)
P.O. Box 691 (47620)
PHONE..................812 838-4715
Phillip R Wells, *Pr*
EMP: 120 **EST:** 1979
SQ FT: 45,000
SALES (est): 24.87MM
SALES (corp-wide): 550.89MM **Privately Held**
Web: www.tmicontractors.com
SIC: 1711 3441 Process piping contractor; Fabricated structural metal
PA: Enerfab, Llc
4430 Chickering Ave
Cincinnati OH 45232
513 641-0500

(G-12325)
UNITED MINERALS AND PRPTS INC
Also Called: Cimbar Performance Mineral
2700 Bluff Rd (47620-8521)
PHONE..................812 838-5236
Paul Householder, *Mgr*
EMP: 1
SALES (corp-wide): 86.16MM **Privately Held**
Web: www.cimbar.com
SIC: 3295 2851 2822 2816 Minerals, ground or treated; Paints and allied products; Synthetic rubber; Inorganic pigments
PA: United Minerals And Properties, Inc.
49 Jackson Lake Rd Ste O
Chatsworth GA 30705
770 387-0319

▲ = Import ▼ = Export
◆ = Import/Export

GEOGRAPHIC SECTION

Muncie - Delaware County (G-12350)

(G-12326)
VALERO RENEWABLE FUELS CO LLC
7201 Port Rd (47620-8524)
PHONE.................812 833-3900
Travis Defrief, *Brnch Mgr*
EMP: 1
SALES (corp-wide): 144.77B **Publicly Held**
Web: www.valero.com
SIC: **2869** Ethyl alcohol, ethanol
HQ: Valero Renewable Fuels Company, Llc
1 Valero Way
San Antonio TX 78249

(G-12327)
WESTECH BUILDING PRODUCTS INC
7451 Highway 62 E (47620-9131)
PHONE.................812 985-3628
◆ EMP: 29
SIC: **3275** Gypsum products

(G-12328)
ZELLER ELEVATOR CO
8875 Meinschein Rd (47620-9709)
PHONE.................812 985-5888
L M Zeller, *Owner*
EMP: 8 EST: 1967
SALES (est): 575.72K **Privately Held**
SIC: **1796 3534** Elevator installation and conversion; Elevators and moving stairways

Mulberry
Clinton County

(G-12329)
CYC LURES
7929 W County Road 550 N (46058-9772)
PHONE.................574 702-1237
EMP: 4 EST: 2016
SALES (est): 52.74K **Privately Held**
SIC: **3949** Snowshoes

(G-12330)
PUBLISHERS SOVEREIGN GRACE
307 S Glick St (46058-2229)
P.O. Box 491 (46058-0491)
PHONE.................765 296-5538
Charles V Turner, *Prin*
EMP: 4 EST: 2011
SALES (est): 178.22K **Privately Held**
Web: www.sgpbooks.com
SIC: **2741** Miscellaneous publishing

Muncie
Delaware County

(G-12331)
1 STOP SIGNS
900 E Streeter Ave (47303-2152)
PHONE.................765 748-2902
Skip Smith, *Owner*
EMP: 4 EST: 2014
SALES (est): 284.2K **Privately Held**
Web: www.1stopsigns.com
SIC: **3993** Signs and advertising specialties

(G-12332)
A-1 GRAPHICS INC
2500 W 7th St (47302-1692)
PHONE.................765 289-1851
Mike Green, *Pr*
EMP: 7 EST: 1964
SQ FT: 6,900
SALES (est): 894.88K **Privately Held**
Web: www.a-1graphics.com
SIC: **2791 2752 2675** Photocomposition, for the printing trade; Offset printing; Die-cut paper and board

(G-12333)
AAA GALVANIZING - JOLIET INC
Also Called: Azz Galvanizing - Muncie
2415 S Walnut St (47302-4143)
PHONE.................765 289-3427
Mike Kern, *Manager*
EMP: 49
SALES (corp-wide): 1.54B **Publicly Held**
SIC: **3479** Hot dip coating of metals or formed products
HQ: Aaa Galvanizing - Joliet, Inc.
625 Mills Rd
Joliet IL 60433

(G-12334)
ACADEMY OF MDEL ARONAUTICS INC
Also Called: A M A
5161 E Memorial Dr (47302-9252)
PHONE.................765 287-1256
Bob Brown, *Pr*
Gary Fitch, *
EMP: 54 EST: 1936
SQ FT: 25,000
SALES (est): 8.75MM **Privately Held**
Web: www.modelaircraft.org
SIC: **8699 2741** Personal interest organization; Miscellaneous publishing

(G-12335)
ACE SIGN SYSTEMS INC
3621 W Royerton Rd (47304-9101)
PHONE.................765 288-1000
Bob Jones, *Pr*
Russel Jones, *Sec*
EMP: 8 EST: 1995
SQ FT: 12,000
SALES (est): 550K **Privately Held**
Web: www.acesign.com
SIC: **3993** Signs, not made in custom sign painting shops

(G-12336)
ADVANCED SIGN & GRAPHICS INC
3000 S Walnut St (47302-5076)
PHONE.................765 284-8360
Dave Flannery, *Pr*
Gary Mader, *VP*
EMP: 13 EST: 1993
SALES (est): 976.9K **Privately Held**
Web: www.advancedsigns.com
SIC: **3993** Neon signs

(G-12337)
ALL STEEL CARPORTS INC
2200 N Granville Ave (47303)
PHONE.................765 284-0694
Ignaclo Chavez, *Pr*
▲ EMP: 8 EST: 2001
SALES (est): 1.98MM **Privately Held**
Web: www.allsteelcarports.com
SIC: **3448** Buildings, portable: prefabricated metal

(G-12338)
ALL STEEL CRPRTS BUILDINGS LLC
2200 N Granville Ave (47303-2165)
PHONE.................765 284-0694
Ignaclo Chavez, *Pr*
▲ EMP: 9 EST: 2010
SALES (est): 160.07K **Privately Held**
SIC: **3448** Carports, prefabricated metal

(G-12339)
ALLIED ENTERPRISES LLC
3228 W Kilgore Ave (47304-4908)
P.O. Box 267 (47308-0267)
PHONE.................765 288-8849
David Woolley, *CEO*
◆ EMP: 30 EST: 1983
SQ FT: 28,000
SALES (est): 5.13MM
SALES (corp-wide): 4.18MM **Privately Held**
Web: www.alliedenterprises.net
SIC: **3714 5013 5088 5084** Motor vehicle transmissions, drive assemblies, and parts; Automotive supplies and parts; Marine propulsion machinery and equipment; Engines and transportation equipment
PA: Concentric Ab
Stockholm 102 4
854504950

(G-12340)
ALM SERVICES INC
2100 N Granville Ave (47303-2153)
P.O. Box 2505 (47307-0505)
PHONE.................765 288-6624
Robert E Kersey, *Pr*
Patrick D Hellman, *Sec*
Martha E Kersey, *Sec*
EMP: 3 EST: 1895
SQ FT: 4,800
SALES (est): 491.8K **Privately Held**
Web: www.almservices.construction
SIC: **3524** Lawn and garden equipment

(G-12341)
AMERICAN MOBILE SOUND IND LLC
Also Called: AMS Pro Sound and Lightingame
2418 W 7th St (47302-1600)
P.O. Box 842 (47308-0842)
PHONE.................765 288-1500
Slade S Member, *Pr*
EMP: 6 EST: 2001
SALES (est): 487.31K **Privately Held**
Web: www.amsindiana.com
SIC: **3651** Amplifiers: radio, public address, or musical instrument

(G-12342)
ANNETTE BALFOUR
2201 E Memorial Dr Rear (47302-4673)
PHONE.................765 286-1910
Annette Balfour, *Owner*
EMP: 2 EST: 1997
SALES (est): 75K **Privately Held**
SIC: **7692** Welding repair

(G-12343)
ARC EDM INCORPORATED
1800 W Mt Pleasant Blvd (47302-9559)
PHONE.................765 284-3820
EMP: 7 EST: 2016
SALES (est): 114.99K **Privately Held**
Web: www.cuttingedgewire.com
SIC: **3599** Machine shop, jobbing and repair

(G-12344)
ARDAGH GLASS INC
Also Called: Verallia Henrico Co
1509 S Macedonia Ave (47302-3664)
P.O. Box 50487 (46250-0487)
PHONE.................610 341-7885
EMP: 1
SALES (corp-wide): 2.67MM **Privately Held**
Web: www.ardaghgroup.com
SIC: **3221 3411** Bottles for packing, bottling, and canning: glass; Metal cans
HQ: Ardagh Glass Inc
10194 Crsspint Blvd Ste 4
Indianapolis IN 46256

(G-12345)
ARROWHEAD PLASTIC ENGRG INC (PA)
Also Called: Arrowhead Composites
2909 S Hoyt Ave (47302-3935)
P.O. Box 75 (47338-0075)
PHONE.................765 286-0533
Thomas W Kishel, *Pr*
Faith Adair, *
EMP: 24 EST: 1972
SQ FT: 35,000
SALES (est): 10.53MM
SALES (corp-wide): 10.53MM **Privately Held**
Web: www.arrowheadinc.com
SIC: **3089** Injection molding of plastics

(G-12346)
ARTISAN TOOL & DIE INC
3805 W State Road 28 (47303-8902)
PHONE.................765 288-6653
H Doug Mansfield, *Pr*
EMP: 25 EST: 1980
SQ FT: 15,000
SALES (est): 858.84K **Privately Held**
Web: www.artisantoolanddie.com
SIC: **3544** Special dies and tools

(G-12347)
AUTOMATED LOGIC CORPORATION
Also Called: Automated Logic - Indiana
117 N High St (47305-1613)
PHONE.................765 286-1993
EMP: 10
SALES (corp-wide): 22.1B **Publicly Held**
Web: www.automatedlogic.com
SIC: **3822** Temperature controls, automatic
HQ: Automated Logic Corporation
1150 Roberts Blvd
Kennesaw GA 30144
770 429-3000

(G-12348)
B&B TOOL AND MOLDING CO INC
624 S Jefferson St (47305-2440)
P.O. Box 2404 (47307-0404)
EMP: 21 EST: 2010
SQ FT: 45,000
SALES (est): 714.32K **Privately Held**
Web: www.bbtool.net
SIC: **3089 3544 3599** Injection molding of plastics; Forms (molds), for foundry and plastics working machinery; Electrical discharge machining (EDM)

(G-12349)
BALL STATE UNIVERSITY
Also Called: Ball State Daily News
276 Park Journalism Bldg (47306-0001)
PHONE.................765 285-8218
Joy Coleman, *Mgr*
EMP: 5
SALES (corp-wide): 155.63MM **Privately Held**
Web: www.ballstatedailynews.com
SIC: **2711 8221** Newspapers; University
PA: Ball State University
2000 W University Ave
Muncie IN 47306
765 289-1241

(G-12350)
BECKETT BRONZE COMPANY INC (PA)
401 W 23rd St (47302-5083)
P.O. Box 2425 (47307-0425)
PHONE.................765 282-2261
Susan Herro, *Pr*
Stephen Dixon, *
EMP: 25 EST: 1913

Muncie - Delaware County (G-12351)

SQ FT: 22,000
SALES (est): 4.19MM
SALES (corp-wide): 4.19MM **Privately Held**
Web: www.beckettbronze.com
SIC: **3451** 3366 Screw machine products; Copper foundries

(G-12351)
BECKETT BRONZE COMPANY INC
106 E 20th St (47302-5003)
P.O. Box 2425 (47307-0425)
PHONE.....................................765 282-2261
Kay Dixon, *Brnch Mgr*
EMP: 22
SALES (corp-wide): 4.19MM **Privately Held**
Web: www.beckettbronze.com
SIC: **3366** Bushings and bearings, bronze (nonmachined)
PA: Beckett Bronze Company, Inc.
    401 W 23rd St
    Muncie IN 47302
    765 282-2261

(G-12352)
BEREAN BUILDERS PUBLISHING INC
3001 W Woodbridge Dr (47304-1074)
PHONE.....................................765 287-5157
John Nichols, *Pr*
EMP: 1 EST: 2013
SALES (est): 179.34K **Privately Held**
Web: www.bereanbuilders.com
SIC: **2741** Miscellaneous publishing

(G-12353)
BETTER GUTTER SYSTEMS
1435 S Kinney Ave (47302-3139)
PHONE.....................................765 282-2724
EMP: 2
SALES (est): 83.2K **Privately Held**
SIC: **3544** Special dies, tools, jigs, and fixtures

(G-12354)
BLAIR INDUSTRIES LLC
1900 W Mt Pleasant Blvd Ste A (47302-9566)
PHONE.....................................765 215-2735
Lucas Blair, *Prin*
EMP: 1 EST: 2017
SALES (est): 139.23K **Privately Held**
SIC: **3084** Plastics pipe

(G-12355)
BOOMERS
2627 S Walnut St (47302-5063)
PHONE.....................................765 741-4031
EMP: 4 EST: 2016
SALES (est): 86.78K **Privately Held**
SIC: **2899** Chemical preparations, nec

(G-12356)
BRAND SHEET METAL WORKS INC
Also Called: Brand Restaurant Equipment
907 S Burlington Dr (47302-2899)
PHONE.....................................765 284-5594
Michael B Brand, *Pr*
Kathy Brand, *Sec*
Alex M Brand, *VP*
EMP: 7 EST: 1946
SQ FT: 12,500
SALES (est): 585.24K **Privately Held**
SIC: **3444** 5046 7692 3351 Sheet metal specialties, not stamped; Commercial cooking and food service equipment; Welding repair; Copper rolling and drawing

(G-12357)
BRILLIANT BLONDES LLC
Also Called: Auntie Anne's
3501 N Granville Ave Ste 3 (47303)
PHONE.....................................765 288-8077
Kermit Willer, *Brnch Mgr*
EMP: 12
SALES (corp-wide): 220.24K **Privately Held**
Web: www.auntieannes.com
SIC: **5461** 2052 Pretzels; Pretzels
PA: Brilliant Blondes, Llc
    1718 Noble Kinsmen Pl
    Fort Wayne IN

(G-12358)
C & J PLATING & GRINDING LLC
411 E 3rd St (47302-2415)
PHONE.....................................765 288-8728
EMP: 4 EST: 2009
SALES (est): 256.73K **Privately Held**
Web: www.cj-plating.com
SIC: **1446** 3471 Grinding sand mining; Plating and polishing

(G-12359)
C4 POLYMERS INC
1407 S Meeker Ave (47302-3827)
PHONE.....................................440 543-3866
EMP: 1
Web: www.c4poly.com
SIC: **2821** Plastics materials and resins
PA: C4 Polymers, Inc.
    33 River St Ste 8
    Chagrin Falls OH 44022

(G-12360)
CAFFEINERY LLC
401 S Walnut St (47305-2459)
PHONE.....................................765 896-9123
Franklin Reber, *CEO*
EMP: 7 EST: 2013
SALES (est): 275.63K **Privately Held**
Web: www.thecaffeinery.com
SIC: **5812** 2095 Coffee shop; Coffee roasting (except by wholesale grocers)

(G-12361)
CALUMET PARALOGICS LLC
Also Called: Paralogics
301 S Butterfield Rd (47303-4317)
PHONE.....................................765 587-4618
EMP: 16
SALES (est): 1.4MM
SALES (corp-wide): 4.18B **Publicly Held**
Web: www.calumet.com
SIC: **2911** 2999 Mineral waxes, natural; Waxes, petroleum: not produced in petroleum refineries
HQ: Calumet Specialty Products Partners Lp
    1060 N Cptol Ave Ste 6-40
    Indianapolis IN 46204

(G-12362)
CALUMET REFINING LLC
301 S Butterfield Rd (47303-4317)
PHONE.....................................765 587-4618
EMP: 1
SALES (corp-wide): 4.18B **Publicly Held**
Web: www.calumet.com
SIC: **2911** Petroleum refining
HQ: Calumet Refining, Llc
    2780 Wtrfront Pkwy E Dr S
    Indianapolis IN 46214

(G-12363)
CAMTOOL INC
Also Called: Camtool
3690 S Hoyt Ave (47302)
PHONE.....................................765 286-9725
EMP: 6 EST: 1995
SQ FT: 10,000
SALES (est): 583.46K **Privately Held**
Web: www.camtoolinc.com
SIC: **3599** Machine shop, jobbing and repair

(G-12364)
CANPACK US LLC
2451 W Fuson Rd (47302-9430)
PHONE.....................................272 226-7225
EMP: 3945
SALES (corp-wide): 554.4MM **Privately Held**
Web: www.canpack.com
SIC: **3411** Metal cans
HQ: Canpack Us Llc
    1400 E Lackawanna Ave
    Olyphant PA 18447
    272 226-7225

(G-12365)
CAROL BURT
605 E County Road 700 N (47303)
PHONE.....................................765 282-5383
Carol Burt, *Owner*
EMP: 1 EST: 1979
SALES (est): 44.89K **Privately Held**
SIC: **0119** 0211 3269 Cash grains, nec; Beef cattle feedlots; Cookware: stoneware, coarse earthenware, and pottery

(G-12366)
CLEAN KUTZ LLC ◆
2851 N Oakwood Ave (47304)
PHONE.....................................765 808-3232
Christopher Kirtz, *CEO*
EMP: 1 EST: 2024
SALES (est): 63.4K **Privately Held**
SIC: **3999** Hair clippers for human use, hand and electric

(G-12367)
CLEARLINE OPERATIONS LLC
3301 W Mt Pleasant Blvd (47302-9103)
PHONE.....................................765 381-8361
Justin Clauson, *Mgr*
EMP: 6 EST: 2021
SALES (est): 520.2K **Privately Held**
SIC: **3069** Reclaimed rubber (reworked by manufacturing processes)

(G-12368)
COMPLETE PROPERTY CARE LLC
806 W Jackson St (47305-1551)
P.O. Box 2443 (47307-0443)
PHONE.....................................765 288-0890
Daniel Norton, *Managing Member*
EMP: 8 EST: 2006
SQ FT: 600
SALES (est): 847.51K **Privately Held**
Web: www.completepropertycarellc.com
SIC: **7349** 1389 6519 6531 Building maintenance services, nec; Construction, repair, and dismantling services; Real property lessors, nec; Real estate brokers and agents

(G-12369)
CONCANNONS PASTRY SHOP
4801 N Baker Ln (47304)
PHONE.....................................765 288-8551
J Michael Concannon, *Owner*
EMP: 10 EST: 1959
SALES (est): 245.21K **Privately Held**
Web: www.concannonsbakery.com
SIC: **5461** 2051 Cakes; Bread, cake, and related products

(G-12370)
CS KERN INC
3401 S Hamilton Ave (47302-9115)
PHONE.....................................765 289-8600
C Steven Kern, *Pr*
Bart Dawson, *
EMP: 34 EST: 1987
SQ FT: 5,500
SALES (est): 4.6MM **Privately Held**
Web: www.cskern.com
SIC: **2759** 7336 Commercial printing, nec; Commercial art and graphic design

(G-12371)
CUTTING EDGE WIRE EDM INC
1800 W Mt Pleasant Blvd (47302-9559)
PHONE.....................................765 284-3820
EMP: 3 EST: 1994
SQ FT: 2,000
SALES (est): 276.27K **Privately Held**
Web: www.cuttingedgewire.com
SIC: **3544** Special dies and tools

(G-12372)
DARGO INDUSTRIES
4121 W Pickell St (47303-9344)
PHONE.....................................765 716-9272
Lucas Dargo, *Pr*
EMP: 4 EST: 2015
SALES (est): 39.69K **Privately Held**
SIC: **3999** Manufacturing industries, nec

(G-12373)
DAVID GONZALES
Also Called: Montezuma Jewelry
701 E Mcgalliard Rd (47303-2020)
PHONE.....................................765 284-6960
David Gonzales, *Owner*
EMP: 3 EST: 1977
SQ FT: 900
SALES (est): 234.31K **Privately Held**
Web: www.montezumajewelers.com
SIC: **3911** 5944 Jewelry, precious metal; Jewelry, precious stones and precious metals

(G-12374)
DD DANNAR LLC
4620 W Bethel Ave Ste 1 (47304-5506)
PHONE.....................................765 216-7191
Matt Kantz, *Ofcr*
EMP: 15 EST: 2013
SQ FT: 25,000
SALES (est): 2.55MM **Privately Held**
Web: dannar.us.com
SIC: **3691** Alkaline cell storage batteries

(G-12375)
DEANS PLACE
4203 E Jackson St (47303-4423)
PHONE.....................................765 282-5712
Arnold Dodd, *Owner*
EMP: 1 EST: 1996
SALES (est): 153.35K **Privately Held**
Web: www.deansplaceautorepair.com
SIC: **7549** 7539 3585 Inspection and diagnostic service, automotive; Electrical services; Air conditioning, motor vehicle

(G-12376)
DEBBIES HANDMADE SOAP
1140 E County Road 500 S (47302-8709)
PHONE.....................................765 747-5090
Debbie Acree, *Prin*
EMP: 6 EST: 2010
SALES (est): 171.84K **Privately Held**
SIC: **2079** Olive oil

GEOGRAPHIC SECTION

Muncie - Delaware County (G-12402)

(G-12377)
DELAWARE COUNTY HOME BLDRS INC
Also Called: Delaware County Mobile Homes
2411 N Dr Martin Luther King Jr Blvd (47303-5188)
PHONE.................................765 289-6328
Annette Steen, *Prin*
Kevin D Steen, *Pr*
Jone A Steen, *Sec*
Annette Steen, *CEO*
EMP: 2 **EST:** 1982
SQ FT: 1,000
SALES (est): 250K **Privately Held**
SIC: 2452 5271 Modular homes, prefabricated, wood; Mobile home dealers

(G-12378)
DELAWARE DYNAMICS LLC
700 S Mulberry St (47302-2356)
PHONE.................................765 284-3335
▲ **EMP:** 120 **EST:** 2010
SALES (est): 23.83MM **Privately Held**
Web: www.delawaredynamics.com
SIC: 3544 Special dies, tools, jigs, and fixtures

(G-12379)
DELAWARE EMPLOYEES ABENEF
700 S Mulberry St (47302-2356)
PHONE.................................765 284-1565
Robert A Haas, *Owner*
EMP: 1 **EST:** 2001
SALES (est): 68.6K **Privately Held**
Web: co.delaware.in.us
SIC: 3711 Automobile assembly, including specialty automobiles

(G-12380)
DELAWARE MACHINERY & TOOL COMPANY INC
700 S Mulberry St (47302-2356)
P.O. Box 2665 (47307-0665)
PHONE.................................765 284-3335
▲ **EMP:** 175
SIC: 3544 Special dies, tools, jigs, and fixtures

(G-12381)
DELBERT M DAWSON AND SON INC
Also Called: Dawson Sheet Metal
1405 W Kilgore Ave (47305-2134)
PHONE.................................765 284-9711
Leon Van Ulzen, *Pr*
Albert Oliver, *VP*
EMP: 8 **EST:** 1926
SQ FT: 7,000
SALES (est): 722.47K **Privately Held**
SIC: 3441 3444 3599 Fabricated structural metal; Sheet metalwork; Machine shop, jobbing and repair

(G-12382)
DIAMOND PLASTICS CORPORATION
4100 Niles Rd (47302-9544)
P.O. Box 2447 (47307-0447)
PHONE.................................765 287-9234
EMP: 53
SALES (corp-wide): 115.04MM **Privately Held**
Web: www.dpcpipe.com
SIC: 3084 Plastics pipe
PA: Diamond Plastics Corporation
1212 Johnstown Rd
Grand Island NE 68803
765 287-9234

(G-12383)
DIAMOND WELDING
4401 S Delaware Dr (47302-9400)
P.O. Box 2608 (47307-0608)
PHONE.................................765 741-2760
Bob Nottingham, *Owner*
EMP: 1 **EST:** 2010
SALES (est): 48.98K **Privately Held**
Web: www.luick.com
SIC: 7692 Welding repair

(G-12384)
DIRECT CONTROL SYSTEMS INC
8409 W Greenview Dr (47304-9394)
P.O. Box 267 (47342-0267)
PHONE.................................765 282-7474
Randy Sayre, *Pr*
EMP: 8 **EST:** 1988
SQ FT: 5,000
SALES (est): 669.93K **Privately Held**
SIC: 3625 8711 3613 Electric controls and control accessories, industrial; Electrical or electronic engineering; Switchgear and switchboard apparatus

(G-12385)
DIVINE ESSENTIALS LLC
2815 N Oakwood Ave (47304-2254)
PHONE.................................765 400-8609
Latosha Wilson, *CEO*
EMP: 1 **EST:** 2019
SALES (est): 30.77K **Privately Held**
SIC: 7231 5087 2844 3999 Beauty shops; Beauty salon and barber shop equipment and supplies; Hair preparations, including shampoos; Hair curlers, designed for beauty parlors

(G-12386)
DRIESSEN WATER INC
Also Called: Culligan
1509 N Wheeling Ave (47303-2880)
PHONE.................................765 529-4905
James Ewing, *Mgr*
EMP: 6
SALES (corp-wide): 50.72MM **Privately Held**
Web: www.culliganiswater.com
SIC: 5999 7389 2899 Water purification equipment; Water softener service; Water treating compounds
PA: Driessen Water, Inc.
110 W Fremont St
Owatonna MN 55060
507 200-0820

(G-12387)
DRIVE PROCESS SERVICES INC
6017 W Hellis Dr (47304-3453)
PHONE.................................765 741-9717
Susan Posocco, *Pr*
Raymond Posocco, *VP*
EMP: 2 **EST:** 1994
SALES (est): 149.02K **Privately Held**
SIC: 3511 Turbines and turbine generator sets

(G-12388)
EAGLE CNC MACHINING INC
801 W Riggin Rd (47303-6417)
PHONE.................................765 289-2816
Greg Phillips, *Pr*
Nadine Phillips, *VP*
Gerald Phillips Junior, *Sec*
EMP: 16 **EST:** 1990
SQ FT: 4,800
SALES (est): 593.31K **Privately Held**
SIC: 3599 Machine and other job shop work

(G-12389)
ECLIPSE INC (HQ)
201 E 18th St (47302-4124)
◆ **EMP:** 64 **EST:** 1908
SALES (est): 106.77MM **Publicly Held**
Web: process.honeywell.com
SIC: 3564 3433 3822 3823 Blowing fans: industrial or commercial; Gas-oil burners, combination; Gas burner, automatic controls; Temperature instruments: industrial process type
PA: Honeywell International Inc.
855 S Mint St
Charlotte NC 28202

(G-12390)
ELEGANT NEEDLEWORKS INC
7500 N Janna Dr (47303-9766)
PHONE.................................765 284-9427
Masha Bawden, *Pr*
Linda Beurkhardt, *Sec*
EMP: 2 **EST:** 1993
SALES (est): 119.84K **Privately Held**
SIC: 2284 Needle and handicraft thread

(G-12391)
ELEMENTAL S A PROTECTION
509 N Forest Ave (47304-3816)
PHONE.................................765 717-7325
Chadwick L Menning, *Admn*
EMP: 4 **EST:** 2014
SALES (est): 45.36K **Privately Held**
SIC: 2819 Industrial inorganic chemicals, nec

(G-12392)
FDS NORTHWOOD LLC
420 S Ohio Ave (47302-2650)
PHONE.................................765 289-2481
David Stanley, *Prin*
EMP: 4 **EST:** 2015
SALES (est): 62.77K **Privately Held**
SIC: 2499 Wood products, nec

(G-12393)
FEMYER DRAPERY SHOP
4409 W Burton Dr (47304-3538)
PHONE.................................765 282-3398
Allen Femyer, *Owner*
EMP: 2 **EST:** 1967
SALES (est): 82.57K **Privately Held**
SIC: 2391 Curtains and draperies

(G-12394)
FERRELLOK LIFESCIENCES LLC
3905 N Linden St (47304-1530)
PHONE.................................765 716-0056
EMP: 4 **EST:** 2009
SALES (est): 72.22K **Privately Held**
Web: www.ferrellok.com
SIC: 3841 Surgical and medical instruments

(G-12395)
FICKLE PEACH INC
117 E Charles St (47305-2413)
PHONE.................................765 282-5211
Brion Fickle, *Owner*
EMP: 4 **EST:** 2005
SALES (est): 253.67K **Privately Held**
Web: www.munciebeer.com
SIC: 2599 Bar, restaurant and cafeteria furniture

(G-12396)
FLEMING AND SONS HOME IMPRV
621 N Mulberry St (47305-1437)
PHONE.................................765 717-6690
Joseph Fleming, *Owner*
EMP: 6 **EST:** 2018
SALES (est): 200K **Privately Held**
Web: www.flemingandsonshomeimprovement.com
SIC: 1389 Construction, repair, and dismantling services

(G-12397)
FRANKLIN STAMPING INDS INC
105 W Fuson Rd (47303-8601)
P.O. Box 2898 (47307-0898)
PHONE.................................765 282-5138
Vicki Franklin, *Pr*
Sharon Franklin, *VP*
Walter Franklin, *Stockholder*
EMP: 13 **EST:** 1981
SQ FT: 40,000
SALES (est): 1.83MM **Privately Held**
Web: www.franklinstamping.com
SIC: 3469 3544 Stamping metal for the trade; Special dies and tools

(G-12398)
FULLY PROMOTED MUNCIE
Also Called: Fully Promoted
2201 N Granville Ave (47303-2151)
PHONE.................................765 281-8870
EMP: 6 **EST:** 2018
SALES (est): 63.45K **Privately Held**
Web: www.fullypromoted.com
SIC: 2395 Embroidery and art needlework

(G-12399)
GENERAL CNSTR & CONSULTING LLC
2200 N Dr Martin Luther King Jr Blvd (47303-5144)
PHONE.................................812 340-5673
EMP: 2
SALES (est): 75.7K **Privately Held**
SIC: 1389 Construction, repair, and dismantling services

(G-12400)
GERDAU AMERISTEEL US INC
Also Called: Gerdau Ameristeel Texas
1810 S Macedonia Ave (47302-3669)
P.O. Box 2747 (46304-5847)
PHONE.................................765 286-5454
Mike Barrett, *Mgr*
EMP: 29
SALES (corp-wide): 1.56B **Privately Held**
Web: gerdau.com
SIC: 3312 Iron and steel products, hot-rolled
HQ: Gerdau Ameristeel Us Inc.
4221 W Boy Scout Blvd Ste
Tampa FL 33607
813 286-8383

(G-12401)
GIBSON NEHEMIAH GROUP INC
Also Called: LLC
801 N Mulberry St (47305-1441)
PHONE.................................317 643-3838
Gregory Dupree-gibson, *CEO*
EMP: 10 **EST:** 2018
SALES (est): 228.5K **Privately Held**
SIC: 2741 8742 Internet publishing and broadcasting; Administrative services consultant

(G-12402)
GKN AEROSPACE MUNCIE INC
Also Called: Sermatech-Aeroforge
3901 S Delaware Dr (47302-9549)
PHONE.................................765 747-7147
Kevin Cummins, *CEO*
EMP: 40 **EST:** 1988
SALES (est): 11.95MM
SALES (corp-wide): 4.18B **Privately Held**
Web: www.gknaerospace.com
SIC: 3356 Titanium
HQ: Gkn Limited
11th Floor, The Colmore Building
Birmingham W MIDLANDS B4 6A
121 210-9800

Muncie - Delaware County (G-12403)

(G-12403)
GODFREY & WING INC
3416 S Hoyt Ave (47302)
PHONE.................................765 284-5050
Alexander Alford, *CEO*
EMP: 12
SALES (corp-wide): 19.38MM **Privately Held**
Web: www.godfreywing.com
SIC: 3398 Metal burning
PA: Godfrey & Wing Inc.
220 Campus Dr
Aurora OH 44202
330 562-1440

(G-12404)
GOLD SEALE WOODWORKING
4100 W Robinwood Dr (47304-2835)
PHONE.................................765 744-4159
Phil Seale, *Owner*
EMP: 1 EST: 2004
SALES (est): 73.45K **Privately Held**
SIC: 2431 Millwork

(G-12405)
GRAPHICS UNLIMITED
500 S Celia Ave # B (47303-4616)
PHONE.................................765 288-6816
EMP: 2 EST: 1970
SQ FT: 1,000
SALES (est): 163K **Privately Held**
Web: www.unlimitedgraphics.com
SIC: 2752 Offset printing

(G-12406)
GREAT STATES CORP
2100 N Granville Ave (47303-2153)
P.O. Box 2505 (47307-0505)
PHONE.................................765 288-6624
EMP: 5 EST: 2019
SALES (est): 192.85K **Privately Held**
Web: www.greatstatescorp.com
SIC: 3524 Lawn and garden equipment

(G-12407)
H & H COMMERCIAL HEAT TREATING
2200 E 8th St (47302-3701)
P.O. Box 948 (47308-0948)
PHONE.................................765 288-3618
Arthur D Hensley, *Pr*
Tony Hensley, *VP*
Mary Hensley, *Sec*
Brandon Hensley, *VP*
EMP: 4 EST: 1940
SQ FT: 6,000
SALES (est): 378.97K **Privately Held**
Web: www.wgefcu.org
SIC: 3398 Annealing of metal

(G-12408)
HALAL PROCESSING SOLUTIONS
2100 E Willard St (47302-3737)
P.O. Box 271965 (77277-1965)
PHONE.................................832 385-2394
Bilal Aquil, *CFO*
Thomas Johnson, *
Firas Al-ibrahim, *Prin*
EMP: 35 EST: 2013
SQ FT: 50,000
SALES (est): 2.19MM **Privately Held**
SIC: 2013 Sausages and other prepared meats

(G-12409)
HAWKINS INC
4601 S Delaware Dr (47302-9177)
PHONE.................................765 288-8930
Keith Uccello, *Brnch Mgr*
EMP: 7
SALES (corp-wide): 919.16MM **Publicly Held**
Web: www.hawkinsinc.com
SIC: 3312 Chemicals and other products derived from coking
PA: Hawkins, Inc.
2381 Rosegate
Roseville MN 55113
612 331-6910

(G-12410)
HAWKINS DARRYAL
Also Called: Hawkins Industrial Resource Co
1001 E 18th St (47302-4324)
P.O. Box 2631 (47307-0631)
PHONE.................................765 282-6021
Darryal Hawkins, *Prin*
Darryal Hawkins, *Owner*
EMP: 3 EST: 1983
SQ FT: 20,000
SALES (est): 300.94K **Privately Held**
SIC: 5084 3069 Industrial machinery and equipment; Molded rubber products

(G-12411)
HAYLEX MANUFACTURING LLC
Also Called: Luick Quality Gage & Tool
4401 S Delaware Dr (47302)
P.O. Box 2608 (47307)
PHONE.................................765 288-1818
Jeannie Flanagan, *Managing Member*
Chris Flanagan, *Pr*
EMP: 22 EST: 2011
SQ FT: 62,000
SALES (est): 839.21K **Privately Held**
SIC: 3599 Machine shop, jobbing and repair

(G-12412)
HC FARMS
1010 E County Road 700 N (47303-9463)
PHONE.................................765 289-9909
EMP: 4 EST: 2011
SALES (est): 194.15K **Privately Held**
SIC: 3523 Driers (farm): grain, hay, and seed

(G-12413)
HENKEL US OPERATIONS CORP
3416 S Hoyt Ave (47302-2081)
PHONE.................................765 284-5050
EMP: 140
SALES (corp-wide): 23.39B **Privately Held**
Web: www.henkel.com
SIC: 3479 Coating of metals with plastic or resins
HQ: Henkel Us Operations Corporation
1 Henkel Way
Rocky Hill CT 06067
860 571-5100

(G-12414)
HENMAN ENGINEERING AND MACHINE INC
3301 W Mt Pleasant Blvd (47302-9103)
P.O. Box 2633 (47307-0633)
PHONE.................................765 288-8098
▲ EMP: 62
SIC: 3714 Transmission housings or parts, motor vehicle

(G-12415)
HIATT ENTERPRISES INC (PA)
Also Called: Hiatt Printing
1716 N Wheeling Ave Ste 1 (47303-1673)
PHONE.................................765 289-7756
Chris Hiatt, *Pr*
David G Hiatt, *VP*
EMP: 13 EST: 1974
SQ FT: 3,000
SALES (est): 883.18K
SALES (corp-wide): 883.18K **Privately Held**
Web: www.hiattprinting.com
SIC: 7334 2759 7389 2791 Photocopying and duplicating services; Card printing and engraving, except greeting; Printing broker; Typesetting

(G-12416)
HIATT ENTERPRISES INC
Also Called: Hiatt Printing
506 N Mckinley Ave (47303-3543)
PHONE.................................765 289-2700
Chris Savage, *Mgr*
EMP: 7
SALES (corp-wide): 883.18K **Privately Held**
Web: www.hiattprinting.com
SIC: 7334 2791 2789 2759 Photocopying and duplicating services; Typesetting; Bookbinding and related work; Commercial printing, nec
PA: Hiatt Enterprises, Inc.
1716 N Wheeling Ave Ste 1
Muncie IN 47303
765 289-7756

(G-12417)
HITACHI ASTEMO INDIANA INC
Also Called: Kim Plant 2
4400 N Superior Dr (47303-6436)
PHONE.................................765 213-4915
Dan Fugate, *Brnch Mgr*
EMP: 140
Web: www.hitachi-automotive.us
SIC: 3585 Air conditioning, motor vehicle
HQ: Hitachi Astemo Indiana, Inc.
400 W New Rd
Greenfield IN 46140
317 462-3015

(G-12418)
HITE WELDING & CHASSIS
1715 E 18th St (47302-4517)
PHONE.................................765 741-0046
Charles Hite, *Owner*
EMP: 2 EST: 2005
SALES (est): 70K **Privately Held**
SIC: 7692 Welding repair

(G-12419)
HONEYWELL INTERNATIONAL INC
Also Called: Honeywell
201 E 18th St (47302-4124)
PHONE.................................765 284-3300
Richard Clasby, *Genl Mgr*
EMP: 36
Web: www.honeywell.com
SIC: 3724 Aircraft engines and engine parts
PA: Honeywell International Inc.
855 S Mint St
Charlotte NC 28202

(G-12420)
HOOSIER HORSE REVIEW LLC
7301 S County Road 400 W (47302-9770)
P.O. Box 493 (47334-0493)
PHONE.................................765 212-1320
EMP: 5 EST: 1972
SALES (est): 254.86K **Privately Held**
SIC: 2759 Publication printing

(G-12421)
HORIZON ATOMTN FABRICATION LLC
3620 S Hoyt Ave (47302-4900)
PHONE.................................765 896-9491
EMP: 2 EST: 2016
SALES (est): 237.87K **Privately Held**
Web: www.horizonaf.com
SIC: 3599 1796 Machine shop, jobbing and repair; Millwright

(G-12422)
HOTRICITY LLC
3008 E Tanner Dr (47302-7556)
PHONE.................................765 212-0411
EMP: 5 EST: 2021
SALES (est): 20K **Privately Held**
SIC: 3161 Clothing and apparel carrying cases

(G-12423)
IMA INOX MARKET AMERICA LLC
4401 S Cowan Rd (47302-9569)
PHONE.................................765 896-4411
Emilio Padoan, *Managing Member*
EMP: 20 EST: 2020
SALES (est): 7.24MM **Privately Held**
Web: www.inoxmarketamerica.com
SIC: 3312 Stainless steel

(G-12424)
INDIANA BRIDGE INC
Also Called: Indiana Bridge
1810 S Macedonia Ave (47302-3669)
P.O. Box 2686 (47307-0686)
PHONE.................................765 288-1985
Chunilal H Gala, *Pr*
Gary R Broad, *
Ken Crismore, *
EMP: 56 EST: 1987
SALES (est): 9.99MM **Privately Held**
Web: www.munciechamber.org
SIC: 3441 Fabricated structural metal

(G-12425)
INDIANA NEWSPAPERS LLC
Muncie Star Press
220 S Walnut St (47305-2861)
P.O. Box 2408 (47307-0408)
PHONE.................................765 213-5700
Emith Smelser, *Mgr*
EMP: 80
SALES (corp-wide): 2.66B **Publicly Held**
Web: www.indystar.com
SIC: 2711 Newspapers, publishing and printing
HQ: Indiana Newspapers Llc
130 S Meridian St
Indianapolis IN 46225
317 444-4000

(G-12426)
IRVING MATERIALS INC
4304 E County Road 350 N (47303-9142)
PHONE.................................765 836-4007
Fritz Ford, *Brnch Mgr*
EMP: 6
SALES (corp-wide): 814.09MM **Privately Held**
Web: www.irvmat.com
SIC: 3273 Ready-mixed concrete
PA: Irving Materials, Inc.
8032 N State Road 9
Greenfield IN 46140
317 326-3101

(G-12427)
IRVING MATERIALS INC
4312 E County Road 350 N (47303-9142)
PHONE.................................765 288-5566
Rock Shideler, *Mgr*
EMP: 8
SALES (corp-wide): 814.09MM **Privately Held**
Web: www.irvmat.com
SIC: 3273 Ready-mixed concrete
PA: Irving Materials, Inc.
8032 N State Road 9
Greenfield IN 46140
317 326-3101

GEOGRAPHIC SECTION

Muncie - Delaware County (G-12452)

(G-12428)
IRVING MATERIALS INC
Also Called: I M I
4304 E County Road 350 N (47303-9142)
PHONE.................................765 288-0288
Lawrence Robinson, *Mgr*
EMP: 5
SALES (corp-wide): 814.09MM **Privately Held**
Web: www.irvmat.com
SIC: 3273 5032 Ready-mixed concrete; Aggregate
PA: Irving Materials, Inc.
  8032 N State Road 9
  Greenfield IN 46140
  317 326-3101

(G-12429)
ISHKADIDDLE PUBLISHING LLC
2405 N Moors St (47304-2458)
PHONE.................................765 744-8588
EMP: 4 **EST:** 2016
SALES (est): 65.96K **Privately Held**
SIC: 2741 Miscellaneous publishing

(G-12430)
J P WHITT INC
Also Called: Budget Blinds
827 S Tillotson Ave (47304-4500)
PHONE.................................765 759-0521
Jeff Whittern, *Pr*
EMP: 2 **EST:** 1999
SALES (est): 249.59K **Privately Held**
Web: www.budgetblinds.com
SIC: 5719 2591 Window furnishings; Window blinds

(G-12431)
JEREMY PARKER
Also Called: Squeeze Play
3501 N Granville Ave Ste 95 (47303)
PHONE.................................765 284-5414
Jeremy Parker, *Owner*
EMP: 3
SIC: 2759 Screen printing
PA: Jeremy Parker
  194 W 600 N
  Alexandria IN 46001

(G-12432)
KEIHIN AIRCON NORTH AMERICA
4400 N Superior Dr (47303-6436)
PHONE.................................765 213-4915
Hiroshi Seikai, *Prin*
Robert Riddle, *
▲ **EMP:** 175 **EST:** 2000
SALES (est): 40.7MM **Privately Held**
Web: www.keihin-na.com
SIC: 3714 Air conditioner parts, motor vehicle
HQ: Hitachi Astemo Indiana, Inc.
  400 W New Rd
  Greenfield IN 46140
  317 462-3015

(G-12433)
KENDON CORPORATION
3904 S Hoyt Ave (47302-8805)
P.O. Box 2343 (47307-0343)
PHONE.................................765 282-1515
EMP: 25
SIC: 3544 Industrial molds

(G-12434)
KEPPLER STEEL AND FABRICATING
1401 S Macedonia Ave (47302-3662)
P.O. Box 668 (47308-0668)
PHONE.................................765 289-1529
Jack Keppler Junior, *Pr*
Dan Keppler, *VP*
EMP: 10 **EST:** 1961
SQ FT: 20,000
SALES (est): 2.02MM **Privately Held**
SIC: 3441 Fabricated structural metal

(G-12435)
KIRBY RISK CORPORATION
Store 10
1619 S Walnut St (47302-3268)
PHONE.................................765 254-5460
Gary A Latta, *Brnch Mgr*
EMP: 13
SALES (corp-wide): 501.02MM **Privately Held**
Web: www.kirbyrisk.com
SIC: 5063 7694 Electrical supplies, nec; Rebuilding motors, except automotive
PA: Kirby Risk Corporation
  1815 Sagamore Pkwy N
  Lafayette IN 47904
  765 448-4567

(G-12436)
LABEL TECH INC
2601 S Walnut St (47302-5063)
P.O. Box 2666 (47307-0666)
PHONE.................................765 747-1234
Kirk Mcshurley, *Pr*
Jay Mcshurley, *Stockholder*
EMP: 20 **EST:** 1995
SQ FT: 15,000
SALES (est): 2.1MM **Privately Held**
Web: www.labeltechin.com
SIC: 2759 5112 2761 2672 Labels and seals: printing, nsk; Stationery and office supplies; Manifold business forms; Paper; coated and laminated, nec

(G-12437)
LAKEMASTER INC
2407 S Walnut St (47302-4143)
P.O. Box 2462 (47307-0462)
PHONE.................................765 288-3718
Wayne C Willitzer, *Pr*
Carol Willitzer, *VP*
EMP: 13 **EST:** 1980
SQ FT: 7,000
SALES (est): 544.55K **Privately Held**
Web: www.lakemasterinc.com
SIC: 3448 3441 3354 2531 Prefabricated metal buildings and components; Fabricated structural metal; Aluminum extruded products; Public building and related furniture

(G-12438)
LARRY FLOWERS WHOLESALE
Also Called: Paper Products
2948 S Chippewa Ln (47302-5596)
PHONE.................................765 747-5156
Larry Flowers, *Owner*
EMP: 5 **EST:** 1991
SALES (est): 326.65K **Privately Held**
SIC: 2679 5992 Paper products, converted, nec; Flowers, fresh

(G-12439)
LEHI PROSTHETICS DNTL LAB INC
1501 W Jackson St (47303-4943)
PHONE.................................765 288-4613
Lee W Hicks, *Pr*
EMP: 3 **EST:** 1958
SQ FT: 3,400
SALES (est): 229.01K **Privately Held**
SIC: 3843 Dental equipment and supplies

(G-12440)
LIFT-A-LOFT MANUFACTURING INC
9501 S Center Rd (47302-9443)
P.O. Box 2645 (47307-0645)
PHONE.................................317 288-3691
Todd E Hunt, *Pr*
Jacquelyn S Duggan, *CFO*
EMP: 3 **EST:** 1961
SQ FT: 110,000
SALES (est): 655.86K
SALES (corp-wide): 15.18MM **Privately Held**
Web: www.liftaloft.com
SIC: 3537 Lift trucks, industrial: fork, platform, straddle, etc.
PA: Lal Acquisition , Inc.
  9501 S Center Rd
  Muncie IN 47302
  765 288-3691

(G-12441)
LOWERYS HOME MADE CANDIES INC
Also Called: Lowery's Candies
6255 W Kilgore Ave (47304-4731)
PHONE.................................765 288-7300
Michael Brown, *Pr*
Vicky Brown Good, *Sec*
Sharon Brown Crecelius, *VP*
Donald H Brown, *CEO*
Charles Good, *Pr*
EMP: 8 **EST:** 1940
SALES (est): 230.93K **Privately Held**
Web: www.loweryscandies.com
SIC: 5441 2064 2066 Candy; Candy and other confectionery products; Chocolate and cocoa products

(G-12442)
MACHINE KEYS INC
3809 N Chadam Ln Apt 1b (47304-5250)
PHONE.................................765 228-4208
▲ **EMP:** 6 **EST:** 2007
SALES (est): 246.07K **Privately Held**
Web: www.machine-keys.com
SIC: 3452 Machine keys

(G-12443)
MAGNA POWERTRAIN AMERICA INC
Also Called: Mpt Muncie East
1400 W Fuson Rd (47302-8684)
P.O. Box 2778 (47307-0778)
PHONE.................................765 587-1300
EMP: 40
SALES (corp-wide): 42.8B **Privately Held**
Web: www.magna.com
SIC: 3714 Motor vehicle parts and accessories
HQ: Magna Powertrain Of America, Inc.
  1870 Technology Dr
  Troy MI 48083

(G-12444)
MAGNA POWERTRAIN AMERICA INC
Mpt Muncie
4701 S Cowan Rd (47302-9560)
P.O. Box 2950 (47307-0950)
PHONE.................................765 587-1300
Dan Mills, *Brnch Mgr*
EMP: 150
SALES (corp-wide): 42.8B **Privately Held**
Web: www.magna.com
SIC: 3714 Motor vehicle parts and accessories
HQ: Magna Powertrain Of America, Inc.
  1870 Technology Dr
  Troy MI 48083

(G-12445)
MAGNA-TECH MANUFACTURING CORPORATION
3416 S Hoyt Ave (47302-2081)
PHONE.................................765 284-5050
▲ **EMP:** 105
Web: www.magnatechmfg.com
SIC: 3479 Coating of metals with plastic or resins

(G-12446)
MAILROOM LLC
1305 N Granville Ave (47303-3018)
PHONE.................................765 254-0000
Shawn Phillips, *Prin*
EMP: 4 **EST:** 2008
SALES (est): 437.73K **Privately Held**
Web: www.importantlocalbusinesses.com
SIC: 3444 Mail (post office) collection or storage boxes, sheet metal

(G-12447)
MARY KITE LLC
4300 W University Ave (47304-3658)
PHONE.................................765 749-1133
Mary E Kite, *Owner*
EMP: 4 **EST:** 2018
SALES (est): 41.02K **Privately Held**
SIC: 3944 Kites

(G-12448)
MATRIX TECHNOLOGIES INC
Also Called: Delaware Machinery
700 S Mulberry St (47302-2356)
PHONE.................................765 284-3335
Robert A Haas, *CEO*
EMP: 6 **EST:** 1988
SQ FT: 8,000
SALES (est): 998.83K **Privately Held**
Web: www.delawaredynamics.com
SIC: 3829 Measuring and controlling devices, nec

(G-12449)
MAXON CORPORATION (HQ)
Also Called: Maxon, A Honeywell Company
201 E 18th St (47302-4199)
P.O. Box 2068 (47307-0068)
PHONE.................................765 284-3304
◆ **EMP:** 220 **EST:** 1916
SALES (est): 87.27MM **Publicly Held**
Web: process.honeywell.com
SIC: 3494 3433 Plumbing and heating valves ; Gas burners, industrial
PA: Honeywell International Inc.
  855 S Mint St
  Charlotte NC 28202

(G-12450)
MCINTIRE CONCRETE
4701 W County Road 1000 N (47303-9601)
PHONE.................................765 759-7111
Richard Mcintire, *Pr*
Brad Mcintire, *VP*
▲ **EMP:** 10 **EST:** 1997
SQ FT: 8,000
SALES (est): 618.44K **Privately Held**
SIC: 5211 3273 Concrete and cinder block; Ready-mixed concrete

(G-12451)
MERRYWOOD GROUP LLC
3709 W Woodstock Ln (47302-9422)
PHONE.................................765 729-5927
Diana Jeffers, *Prin*
EMP: 5 **EST:** 2014
SALES (est): 114.56K **Privately Held**
SIC: 3999 Candles

(G-12452)
MID-CITY PLATING CO INC
921 E Charles St (47305-2697)
P.O. Box 6 (47308-0006)
PHONE.................................765 289-2374
Anton Muzzarelli, *Pr*

Muncie - Delaware County (G-12453)   GEOGRAPHIC SECTION

Helen Muzzarelli, *
Marsha Muzzarelli, *
Rodney Muzzarelli, *
EMP: 22 **EST:** 1966
SQ FT: 70,000
SALES (est): 757.58K **Privately Held**
Web: www.mcplating.com
SIC: 3471 Electroplating of metals or formed products

(G-12453)
MID-WEST METAL PRODUCTS CO INC
3500 S Hoyt Ave (47302-6419)
PHONE.................................765 741-3140
Ted Baker, *Brnch Mgr*
EMP: 47
SALES (corp-wide): 29.04MM **Privately Held**
Web: www.midwestmetal.com
SIC: 3315 3599 Wire, steel: insulated or armored; Machine shop, jobbing and repair
PA: Mid-West Metal Products Company, Inc.
    3142 S Cowan Rd
    Muncie IN 47302
    888 741-1044

(G-12454)
MID-WEST METAL PRODUCTS CO INC (PA)
Also Called: Mid-West Homes For Pets
3142 S Cowan Rd (47302-9106)
P.O. Box 1031 (47308-1031)
PHONE.................................888 741-1044
Steven Smith, *CEO*
Steven M Smith, *CEO*
Chad S Smith, *CFO*
John W Smith Iii, *Sec*
◆ **EMP:** 25 **EST:** 1921
SQ FT: 120,000
SALES (est): 29.04MM
SALES (corp-wide): 29.04MM **Privately Held**
Web: www.midwestmetal.com
SIC: 3441 3291 Fabricated structural metal; Abrasive metal and steel products

(G-12455)
MIDWEST MAT COMPANY
2204 N Dr Martin Luther King Jr Blvd (47303-5144)
PHONE.................................765 286-0831
Charles Tucker, *Pr*
EMP: 1 **EST:** 1988
SQ FT: 15,000
SALES (est): 243.6K **Privately Held**
SIC: 5013 3069 5014 Automotive supplies and parts; Mats or matting, rubber, nec; Truck tires and tubes

(G-12456)
MIDWESTERN STRUCTURES LLC
9500 N Wheeling Ave (47304-9151)
PHONE.................................574 835-9733
EMP: 2
SALES (est): 92.67K **Privately Held**
SIC: 3448 7389 Prefabricated metal buildings and components; Business Activities at Non-Commercial Site

(G-12457)
MITTLER SUPPLY INC
810 S Liberty St (47302-2319)
PHONE.................................765 289-6341
Tom Mittler, *Ch*
EMP: 4 **EST:** 2017
SALES (est): 60.08K **Privately Held**
SIC: 3531 Construction machinery

(G-12458)
MONEY TREE SOFTWARE LTD
115 S Walnut St (47305-2811)
P.O. Box 637 (97370-0637)
PHONE.................................541 754-3701
Mark Snodgrass, *Pr*
Michael Vitkauskas, *Ch*
EMP: 25 **EST:** 1981
SALES (est): 585.36K **Privately Held**
Web: www.moneytree.com
SIC: 7372 5045 5734 7371 Business oriented computer software; Computer software; Software, business and non-game ; Computer software development and applications

(G-12459)
MPT MUNCIE LLC
4701 S Cowan Rd (47302-9560)
PHONE.................................765 587-1300
Jake Hirsch, *Pr*
Thomas More, *
▲ **EMP:** 35 **EST:** 2004
SALES (est): 9.22MM
SALES (corp-wide): 42.8B **Privately Held**
Web: www.magna.com
SIC: 3714 Motor vehicle engines and parts
HQ: Magna Powertrain Usa, Inc.
    1870 Technology Dr
    Troy MI 48083
    248 597-7811

(G-12460)
MUNCIE CABINET DISCOUNTERS
4205 N Wheeling Ave (47304-1202)
PHONE.................................765 216-7367
Greg Rawson, *Pr*
EMP: 2 **EST:** 2011
SALES (est): 158.95K **Privately Held**
SIC: 2434 Wood kitchen cabinets

(G-12461)
MUNCIE CASTING CORP
1406 E 18th St (47302-4511)
P.O. Box 2328 (47307-0328)
PHONE.................................765 288-2611
Wayne Vest, *Pr*
EMP: 45 **EST:** 1972
SQ FT: 53,000
SALES (est): 5.36MM **Privately Held**
Web: www.munciecasting.com
SIC: 3543 3365 3544 3322 Industrial patterns ; Aluminum and aluminum-based alloy castings; Special dies, tools, jigs, and fixtures; Malleable iron foundries

(G-12462)
MUNCIE METAL SPINNING INC
Also Called: Spunlite
1100 E 20th St (47302-5399)
PHONE.................................765 288-1937
Donald Ulrich, *Pr*
Paul Ulrich, *Sec*
William Ulrich, *Treas*
EMP: 10 **EST:** 1944
SQ FT: 55,000
SALES (est): 991.08K **Privately Held**
Web: www.munciemetalspinning.com
SIC: 3469 3446 Spinning metal for the trade; Ornamental metalwork

(G-12463)
MUNCIE NOVELTY COMPANY INC
Also Called: Indiana Ticket Company
9610 N State Road 67 (47303-9123)
P.O. Box 823 (47308-0823)
PHONE.................................765 288-8301
David Broyles, *Pr*
James Broyles, *
Robert Broyles, *
Joseph Broyles, *
EMP: 100 **EST:** 1936
SQ FT: 35,000
SALES (est): 22.7MM **Privately Held**
Web: www.muncienovelty.com
SIC: 2791 2759 2752 Typesetting; Schedule, ticket, and tag printing and engraving; Commercial printing, lithographic

(G-12464)
MUNCIE POWER PRODUCTS INC (HQ)
201 E Jackson St Ste 500 (47305-2838)
P.O. Box 548 (47308-0548)
PHONE.................................765 284-7721
Andrea Zanellotti, *Pr*
◆ **EMP:** 47 **EST:** 1935
SQ FT: 71,000
SALES (est): 100.71MM **Privately Held**
Web: www.munciepower.com
SIC: 3714 5013 Motor vehicle parts and accessories; Motor vehicle supplies and new parts
PA: Interpump Group Spa
    Via Enrico Fermi 25
    Sant'ilario D'enza RE 42049

(G-12465)
MUNCIE POWER PRODUCTS INC
342 N Pershing Dr (47305-1933)
PHONE.................................785 284-7721
EMP: 4
Web: www.munciepower.com
SIC: 3714 Motor vehicle parts and accessories
HQ: Muncie Power Products, Inc.
    201 E Jackson St Ste 500
    Muncie IN 47305
    765 284-7721

(G-12466)
MUNCIE SAND & GRAVEL INC
Also Called: Schick Sand & Gravel
4210 E Mcgalliard Rd (47303-9172)
PHONE.................................765 282-6422
William Hood, *Pr*
Robert A Shick, *Mgr*
EMP: 4 **EST:** 1976
SALES (est): 438.34K **Privately Held**
SIC: 1442 Construction sand and gravel

(G-12467)
NASG INDIANA LLC
Also Called: North American Stamping Group
3401 W 8th St (47302)
PHONE.................................765 381-4310
EMP: 39 **EST:** 2010
SALES (est): 9.32MM **Privately Held**
Web: www.nasg.net
SIC: 3465 Automotive stampings

(G-12468)
NATIONAL HANDICAPPED WORKSHOP
5900 W Kilgore Ave (47304-4724)
PHONE.................................765 287-8331
Jake Guinn, *VP*
Cheryl Guinn, *
Dean Guinn, *
EMP: 10 **EST:** 1996
SALES (est): 203.2K **Privately Held**
SIC: 7389 2842 2841 5063 Telemarketing services; Polishes and sanitation goods; Soap and other detergents; Light bulbs and related supplies

(G-12469)
NINA GAIL DIAMONDS LLC
Also Called: N.G.D. Global
2013 S Lazy Creek Dr (47302)
PHONE.................................765 591-0477
Thomas Myers, *CEO*
Thomas Andrew Myers, *CEO*
EMP: 1 **EST:** 2010
SALES (est): 62.35K **Privately Held**
SIC: 5094 1499 1481 Diamonds (gems); Miscellaneous nonmetallic minerals, except fuels; Nonmetallic mineral services

(G-12470)
OSC HOLDINGS LLC
1150 W Kilgore Ave (47305-1588)
PHONE.................................765 751-7000
Wilbur R Davis, *Pr*
Donald J Engel, *Sec*
David L Hahn, *Treas*
Ronald K Fauquher, *Sr VP*
EMP: 4 **EST:** 2003
SALES (est): 433.06K **Privately Held**
Web: www.finvi.com
SIC: 5045 7372 Computer peripheral equipment; Prepackaged software

(G-12471)
OUTFITTER
Also Called: Outfitter
2704 N Walnut St (47303-1959)
PHONE.................................765 289-6456
EMP: 2 **EST:** 1993
SALES (est): 177.98K **Privately Held**
Web: www.outfitter289.com
SIC: 2759 2395 Screen printing; Embroidery and art needlework

(G-12472)
PARALOGICS LLC
301 S Butterfield Rd (47303-4317)
PHONE.................................765 587-4618
EMP: 27 **EST:** 2012
SALES (est): 6.63MM
SALES (corp-wide): 4.18B **Publicly Held**
Web: www.paralogicsolutions.com
SIC: 2911 2999 Mineral waxes, natural; Waxes, petroleum: not produced in petroleum refineries
HQ: Calumet Specialty Products Partners Lp
    1060 N Cptol Ave Ste 6-40
    Indianapolis IN 46204

(G-12473)
PENGAD/WEST INC
Also Called: Pengad/Indy
1106 E Seymour St Ste A (47302-2592)
P.O. Box 1776 (47308-1776)
PHONE.................................765 286-3000
James D Funkhouser, *Brnch Mgr*
EMP: 36
SALES (corp-wide): 22.42MM **Privately Held**
Web: www.pengad.com
SIC: 2759 2796 2761 2752 Commercial printing, nec; Platemaking services; Manifold business forms; Commercial printing, lithographic
PA: Pengad/West, Inc.
    55 Oak St
    Bayonne NJ 07002
    201 436-5625

(G-12474)
PETER AUSTIN CO
900 W 1st St (47305-2214)
P.O. Box 1147 (47308-1147)
PHONE.................................765 288-6397
Peter Austin, *Pt*
Adam Austin, *Pt*
EMP: 2 **EST:** 1902
SQ FT: 4,000
SALES (est): 132.94K **Privately Held**
Web: www.amko-world.com

SIC: 7694 7629 5085 Electric motor repair; Tool repair, electric; Tools, nec

(G-12475)
PHILLIPS PATTERN & CASTING INC
(PA)
1001 W Riggin Rd (47303-6419)
PHONE.................................765 288-2319
Greg Phillips, *Pr*
Nadine E Phillips, *VP*
EMP: 15 **EST:** 1947
SALES (est): 7.59MM
SALES (corp-wide): 7.59MM **Privately Held**
Web: www.phillipspatterns.com
SIC: 3365 3366 Aluminum and aluminum-based alloy castings; Castings (except die), nec, brass

(G-12476)
PPG INDUSTRIES INC
2701 N Wheeling Ave (47303-1647)
PHONE.................................765 282-0316
EMP: 2
SALES (corp-wide): 17.65B **Publicly Held**
Web: www.ppg.com
SIC: 2851 Paints and allied products
PA: Ppg Industries, Inc.
1 Ppg Pl
Pittsburgh PA 15272
412 434-3131

(G-12477)
PREMIER LABEL COMPANY INC
1205 E Washington St (47305-2051)
PHONE.................................765 289-5000
Mark Ratliff, *Pr*
Lowell Pequignot, *Stockholder*
Susan Haynes, *VP*
EMP: 10 **EST:** 1981
SQ FT: 6,000
SALES (est): 948.19K **Privately Held**
Web: www.premierlabel.com
SIC: 2752 Offset printing

(G-12478)
PRETTY XQUISITE HAIR LLC
3813 N Chadam Ln Apt 1a (47304-5251)
PHONE.................................765 760-6948
EMP: 1 **EST:** 2021
SALES (est): 20K **Privately Held**
SIC: 3999 Hair and hair-based products

(G-12479)
PROGRESS RAIL LOCOMOTIVE INC
3500 S Cowan Rd (47302-9555)
PHONE.................................765 281-2685
EMP: 12
SALES (corp-wide): 67.06B **Publicly Held**
SIC: 3743 Railroad equipment
HQ: Progress Rail Locomotive Inc.
9301 W 55th St
La Grange IL 60525
800 255-5355

(G-12480)
PROGRESS RAIL MFG CORP
3500 S Cowan Rd (47302)
PHONE.................................765 281-2685
EMP: 104 **EST:** 2010
SALES (est): 34.39MM
SALES (corp-wide): 67.06B **Publicly Held**
SIC: 4789 3312 7389 Railroad maintenance and repair services; Structural and rail mill products; Metal cutting services
HQ: Progress Rail Services Corporation
1600 Progress Dr
Albertville AL 35950
800 476-8769

(G-12481)
QUAKER OATS COMPANY
Also Called: Quaker Oats
3300 S Hoyt Ave (47302-6416)
PHONE.................................765 288-1503
EMP: 33
SALES (corp-wide): 86.39B **Publicly Held**
SIC: 2099 Food preparations, nec
HQ: The Quaker Oats Company
433 W Van Buren St Ste 3n
Chicago IL 60607
312 821-1000

(G-12482)
QUALITY PALLET
1000 E Seymour St (47302-2564)
PHONE.................................765 212-2215
EMP: 4 **EST:** 2018
SALES (est): 138.03K **Privately Held**
SIC: 2448 Pallets, wood

(G-12483)
RAMAR INDUSTRIES INC
6200 N Wheeling Ave (47304-9117)
PHONE.................................765 288-7319
Raymond E Weeks, *Pr*
Mark Wiley, *Sec*
EMP: 2 **EST:** 1985
SALES (est): 176.85K **Privately Held**
Web: www.ramar.net
SIC: 3531 Backhoes

(G-12484)
RAMIFICATIONS LLC
11559 S County Road 300 W (47302-9468)
PHONE.................................765 729-5484
EMP: 1 **EST:** 2007
SALES (est): 75.7K **Privately Held**
SIC: 2499 7389 Decorative wood and woodwork; Engraving service

(G-12485)
REBER MACHINE & TOOL CO INC
1112 S Liberty St (47302-3141)
P.O. Box 2403 (47307-0403)
PHONE.................................765 288-0297
Neil Reber, *Pr*
Terry Reber, *
EMP: 40 **EST:** 1942
SQ FT: 60,000
SALES (est): 4.59MM **Privately Held**
Web: www.rebermachine.com
SIC: 3544 3599 Jigs and fixtures; Machine and other job shop work

(G-12486)
REEDS PLASTIC TOPS INC
2150 E Memorial Dr (47302-4670)
PHONE.................................765 282-1471
Ronald F Reed, *Pr*
Lisa Reed, *Sec*
EMP: 7 **EST:** 1962
SQ FT: 45,000
SALES (est): 462.9K **Privately Held**
Web: www.reedscountertops.com
SIC: 2541 5031 3442 Counter and sink tops; Molding, all materials; Metal doors, sash, and trim

(G-12487)
REGAL INC
Also Called: Regal Marketing
305 N Gray St (47303-4415)
PHONE.................................765 284-5722
Steve Nale, *Pr*
Richard Lee, *Sec*
EMP: 2 **EST:** 1991
SQ FT: 1,200
SALES (est): 195.89K **Privately Held**
SIC: 2389 5999 Men's miscellaneous accessories; Trophies and plaques

(G-12488)
RELIANCE MACHINE COMPANY INC
(PA)
4605 S Walnut St (47302-8532)
PHONE.................................765 284-0151
Richard Cardemon, *CEO*
Christopher Cardemon, *
Jammie Lynn Minniear, *
EMP: 60 **EST:** 1983
SQ FT: 80,000
SALES (est): 5.39MM
SALES (corp-wide): 5.39MM **Privately Held**
Web: www.reliancemachinecompany.com
SIC: 3599 Machine shop, jobbing and repair

(G-12489)
RELIANCE MANUFACTURING LLC
4605 S Walnut St (47302-8532)
PHONE.................................765 284-0151
EMP: 1 **EST:** 2009
SQ FT: 80,000
SALES (est): 218.05K **Privately Held**
Web: www.reliancemanufacturing.com
SIC: 3544 Special dies, tools, jigs, and fixtures

(G-12490)
ROCHESTER METAL PRODUCTS CORP
2100 N Granville Ave (47303-2153)
PHONE.................................765 288-6624
Robert E Kersey, *Brnch Mgr*
EMP: 30
SALES (corp-wide): 35.67MM **Privately Held**
Web: www.rochestermetals.com
SIC: 3524 Lawnmowers, residential: hand or power
PA: Rochester Metal Products Corp.
616 Indiana Ave
Rochester IN 46975
574 223-3164

(G-12491)
SEA SALT & CINNAMON LLC
228 N Monroe St (47305-1924)
PHONE.................................727 481-4024
Amanda Reninger, *Pr*
EMP: 12 **EST:** 2016
SALES (est): 287.21K **Privately Held**
Web: www.seasaltandcinnamon.com
SIC: 2051 2099 Bakery: wholesale or wholesale/retail combined; Food preparations, nec

(G-12492)
SIGN PROS
3509 W County Road 400 N (47304-9040)
PHONE.................................765 289-2177
Rick Brinson, *Prin*
EMP: 2 **EST:** 2013
SALES (est): 160.25K **Privately Held**
SIC: 3993 Signs and advertising specialties

(G-12493)
SINFLEX PAPER CO INC
301 S Butterfield Rd (47303-4317)
PHONE.................................765 789-6688
Matthew Burton, *Pr*
EMP: 30 **EST:** 1985
SQ FT: 55,000
SALES (est): 4MM **Privately Held**
Web: www.sinflexpaper.com

SIC: 2679 2653 Corrugated paper: made from purchased material; Sheets, corrugated: made from purchased materials

(G-12494)
SP HOLDINGS INC
Also Called: Smart Products
3401 N Commerce Dr (47303-1509)
PHONE.................................765 284-9545
Ken Hess, *Pr*
EMP: 10 **EST:** 2003
SQ FT: 1,300
SALES (est): 2.45MM **Privately Held**
Web: www.palletrecyclingequipment.com
SIC: 3553 Bandsaws, woodworking

(G-12495)
SPARTECH LLC
Also Called: Muncie Manufacturing Plant
1401 E Memorial Dr (47302-4402)
PHONE.................................765 281-5100
Greg Bauer, *Mgr*
EMP: 88
SALES (corp-wide): 344.31MM **Privately Held**
Web: www.spartech.com
SIC: 2821 2671 Plastics materials and resins; Plastic film, coated or laminated for packaging
PA: Spartech Llc
11650 Lkeside Crossing Ct
Saint Louis MO 63146
314 569-7400

(G-12496)
SPENCER PRINTING INC
4404 S Madison St (47302-5669)
P.O. Box 1701 (47308-1701)
PHONE.................................765 288-6111
Gary Watson, *Pr*
Richard Mikels, *Treas*
EMP: 8 **EST:** 1987
SQ FT: 3,000
SALES (est): 837.38K **Privately Held**
Web: www.spencerprinting.com
SIC: 2752 Offset printing

(G-12497)
STEVEN BLOCK
7805 N Tanglewood Ln (47304-9105)
PHONE.................................765 749-5394
Steven Block, *Prin*
EMP: 4 **EST:** 2011
SALES (est): 211.09K **Privately Held**
SIC: 2431 Millwork

(G-12498)
TAURUS TECH & ENGRG LLC
4401 S Delaware Dr (47302-9400)
PHONE.................................765 282-2090
James Mcdonald, *Pr*
EMP: 28 **EST:** 1972
SALES (est): 4.11MM **Privately Held**
Web: www.taurustool.com
SIC: 3599 3544 Machine shop, jobbing and repair; Jigs and fixtures

(G-12499)
TAURUS TOOL & ENGINEERING INC
4401 S Delaware Dr (47302-9400)
PHONE.................................765 282-2090
James Mcdonald, *CEO*
EMP: 1 **EST:** 1972
SALES (est): 100.73K **Privately Held**
SIC: 3599 Industrial machinery, nec

(G-12500)
TEE TRUDYS RAINBOW PALAC
701 E 8th St (47302-3428)
PHONE.................................765 273-7571

Muncie - Delaware County (G-12501)

Andrea Edwards, *Prin*
EMP: 5 **EST:** 2019
SALES (est): 100.95K **Privately Held**
SIC: 2759 Screen printing

(G-12501)
TEES AND BLUES LLC
3715 N Bennington Ct Apt F (47303-5921)
PHONE....................765 808-4081
Edward Fuse, *Owner*
EMP: 4 **EST:** 2018
SALES (est): 83.61K **Privately Held**
SIC: 2759 Screen printing

(G-12502)
TISHLER INDUSTRIES INC (PA)
Also Called: Ameristeel
1810 S Macedonia Ave (47302-3669)
PHONE....................765 286-5454
Ravi Talwar, *Pr*
Eleanor C Talwar, *Sec*
EMP: 22 **EST:** 1990
SQ FT: 8,000
SALES (est): 5.66MM **Privately Held**
Web: www.tishlerindustries.com
SIC: 3443 Fabricated plate work (boiler shop)

(G-12503)
TITLE TEN MANUFACTURING LLC
Also Called: Warrior Rack
401 W Willard St (47302-3152)
PHONE....................765 388-2482
Robert Moore, *CEO*
EMP: 2 **EST:** 2016
SALES (est): 113.8K **Privately Held**
Web: www.warriorrack.com
SIC: 2542 Racks, merchandise display or storage: except wood

(G-12504)
TODAYS SIGNS AND GRAPHICS
1804 N Wheeling Ave Ste 1 (47303-1699)
PHONE....................765 288-4771
Jim Hathaway, *Owner*
Greg Hathaway, *Genl Mgr*
EMP: 4 **EST:** 1998
SALES (est): 146.97K **Privately Held**
SIC: 3993 Signs and advertising specialties

(G-12505)
TOMKEN PLASTIC TECH INC
4601 N Superior Dr (47303-6430)
PHONE....................765 284-2472
Bill Szekesy, *Pr*
▼ **EMP:** 48 **EST:** 1960
SQ FT: 56,100
SALES (est): 9.13MM **Privately Held**
Web: www.tomkenplastics.com
SIC: 3089 Injection molding of plastics

(G-12506)
TONNE WINERY INCORPORATED
101 W Royerton Rd (47303-9382)
PHONE....................765 896-9821
Kathy Simmons, *Prin*
EMP: 4 **EST:** 2009
SALES (est): 317.6K **Privately Held**
Web: www.tonnewinery.com
SIC: 2084 Wines

(G-12507)
TOOL ROOM SERVICE
1403 S Liberty St (47302-3147)
PHONE....................765 287-0062
EMP: 7 **EST:** 2016
SALES (est): 218.49K **Privately Held**
Web: www.toolroomservice.com
SIC: 3599 Machine shop, jobbing and repair

(G-12508)
TRI STATE OPTICAL INC
Also Called: Cunningham Optical One
1608 W Mcgalliard Rd (47304-2205)
PHONE....................765 289-4475
TOLL FREE: 800
Paula Schull, *Mgr*
EMP: 62
SALES (corp-wide): 4.64MM **Privately Held**
Web: www.cunninghamopticalone.com
SIC: 5995 3851 Opticians; Ophthalmic goods
PA: Tri State Optical Inc
5233 Coldwater Rd
Fort Wayne IN 46825
260 482-1555

(G-12509)
UNITED HOME SUPPLY INC
Also Called: Kitchen & Baths By Untd HM Sup
3600 N Everbrook Ln Ste C (47304-6371)
PHONE....................765 288-2737
Gary L West, *Pr*
EMP: 6 **EST:** 1961
SQ FT: 18,000
SALES (est): 484.07K **Privately Held**
Web: www.agreatkitchen.com
SIC: 2599 5211 Cabinets, factory; Bathroom fixtures, equipment and supplies

(G-12510)
UNLIMITED VENDING LLC
3504 W Moore Rd (47304-5944)
PHONE....................765 288-5952
Efrain Miranda, *Owner*
EMP: 6 **EST:** 2014
SALES (est): 77.88K **Privately Held**
SIC: 3581 5046 Automatic vending machines; Vending machines, coin-operated

(G-12511)
UTZ QUALITY FOODS LLC
4600 N Superior Dr (47303-6429)
PHONE....................717 982-3066
EMP: 1
SALES (corp-wide): 732.3MM **Privately Held**
Web: www.utzsnacks.com
SIC: 2099 Food preparations, nec
PA: Utz Quality Foods, Llc
900 High St
Hanover PA 17331
800 367-7629

(G-12512)
VERSATILE METAL WORKS LLC
1403 S Liberty St (47302-3147)
P.O. Box 2487 (47307-0487)
PHONE....................765 754-7470
EMP: 12 **EST:** 2010
SQ FT: 18,000
SALES (est): 2.02MM **Privately Held**
Web: www.versatilemetalworks.com
SIC: 3541 3542 3443 Machine tools, metal cutting type; Machine tools, metal forming type; Metal parts

(G-12513)
WALBURN SERVICES INC
Also Called: Walburn Kitchens
109 S Claypool Rd (47303-5130)
PHONE....................765 289-3383
William T Walburn, *Pr*
Barbara Walburn, *Sec*
William L Walburn, *VP*
▲ **EMP:** 3 **EST:** 1961
SQ FT: 5,000
SALES (est): 245.47K **Privately Held**
SIC: 2434 Wood kitchen cabinets

(G-12514)
WALLYS LOCKSHOP
606 W 11th St (47302-3129)
PHONE....................765 748-2282
Walter Beall, *Owner*
EMP: 6 **EST:** 2008
SALES (est): 132.97K **Privately Held**
SIC: 3429 Locks or lock sets

(G-12515)
WATERFIELD AUTOMOTIVE MCH SP
Also Called: Waterfield Automotive
3600 S Meeker Ave (47302-9094)
PHONE....................765 288-6262
Stan Waters, *Pt*
Laura Waters, *Pt*
EMP: 2 **EST:** 1985
SQ FT: 3,500
SALES (est): 209.92K **Privately Held**
Web: automotive-machine-shops.cmac.ws
SIC: 3599 7539 Machine shop, jobbing and repair; Machine shop, automotive

(G-12516)
WATERJET FABRICATING LLC
1725 W Kilgore Ave (47304-4924)
PHONE....................765 288-4575
EMP: 5 **EST:** 2008
SALES (est): 475.65K **Privately Held**
SIC: 3599 Machine shop, jobbing and repair

(G-12517)
WEARLY MONUMENTS INC (PA)
Also Called: Wearly Monuments
4000 W Kilgore Ave (47304-4814)
PHONE....................765 284-9796
Brian Whittaker, *Pr*
▲ **EMP:** 17 **EST:** 1899
SQ FT: 10,000
SALES (est): 2.15MM
SALES (corp-wide): 2.15MM **Privately Held**
Web: www.wearlymonuments.com
SIC: 5999 3281 Monuments, finished to custom order; Cut stone and stone products

(G-12518)
WELDORS INC
2702 S Monroe St (47302-5219)
PHONE....................765 289-9074
Samuel Norris, *Pr*
Jana Norris, *Sec*
EMP: 3 **EST:** 1976
SQ FT: 3,000
SALES (est): 171.66K **Privately Held**
SIC: 7692 Welding repair

(G-12519)
WHISLER CUSTOM LEATHER CO
1108 E Royerton Rd (47303-9440)
PHONE....................765 212-8932
Connie Whisler, *Prin*
EMP: 5 **EST:** 2012
SALES (est): 126.33K **Privately Held**
SIC: 3199 Leather goods, nec

(G-12520)
WILHOITE MONUMENTS INC
4710 S Madison St (47302-5681)
PHONE....................765 286-7423
James Wilhoite, *Pr*
Patricia Wilhoite, *Sec*
▲ **EMP:** 5 **EST:** 1920
SQ FT: 3,700
SALES (est): 482.23K **Privately Held**
Web: www.wilhoitemonuments.net
SIC: 5999 3366 Monuments, finished to custom order; Bronze foundry, nec

(G-12521)
WILSONS HEARING AID CENTER LLC
3716 N Wheeling Ave (47304-1766)
PHONE....................765 747-4131
Chuck Wilson, *Owner*
EMP: 5 **EST:** 1986
SQ FT: 2,600
SALES (est): 497.84K **Privately Held**
Web: www.wilsonshearing.com
SIC: 3842 5999 Hearing aids; Hearing aids

(G-12522)
WINE N VINE
1524 E Mcgalliard Rd (47303-2210)
PHONE....................765 282-3300
Jeffrey Johnson, *Owner*
EMP: 2 **EST:** 2005
SALES (est): 151.11K **Privately Held**
Web: www.wine-n-vine.com
SIC: 2084 5921 Wine cellars, bonded: engaged in blending wines; Wine

(G-12523)
WITT INDUSTRIES INC
Muncie Division
2415 S Walnut St (47302-4143)
P.O. Box 2368 (47307-0368)
PHONE....................765 289-3427
Joe Wendel, *Mgr*
EMP: 27
Web: www.witt.com
SIC: 3479 3547 Hot dip coating of metals or formed products; Galvanizing lines (rolling mill equipment)
HQ: Witt Industries, Inc.
4600 N Masn Montgomery Rd
Mason OH 45040
513 871-5700

Munster
Lake County

(G-12524)
411 NEWSPAPER
1130 Camellia Dr (46321-3619)
PHONE....................219 922-8846
Jackie Harris, *Prin*
EMP: 9 **EST:** 2007
SALES (est): 203.91K **Privately Held**
Web: www.gary411news.com
SIC: 2711 Commercial printing and newspaper publishing combined

(G-12525)
A & M RUBBER STAMPS INC
424 Hickory Ln (46321-2322)
PHONE....................219 836-0892
Gail Reno, *Prin*
EMP: 2 **EST:** 2001
SALES (est): 122.06K **Privately Held**
SIC: 3953 Embossing seals and hand stamps

(G-12526)
A M MANUFACTURING CO INC
9200 Calumet Ave Ste Nw07 (46321-0047)
PHONE....................219 472-7272
Mark Vandrunen, *Pr*
Claudia Kunis, *
Holly Rentner, *
▼ **EMP:** 32 **EST:** 1953
SQ FT: 25,000
SALES (est): 4.24MM **Privately Held**
Web: www.ammfg.com
SIC: 3556 Bakery machinery

GEOGRAPHIC SECTION

Munster - Lake County (G-12553)

(G-12527)
ACCURATE PUBLISHING CO
8445 Manor Ave Apt 301 (46321-2288)
PHONE.....................219 836-1397
Doctor Irma Langston, *Owner*
EMP: 2 **EST:** 2005
SALES (est): 84K **Privately Held**
SIC: 2741 Miscellaneous publishing

(G-12528)
AM MANUFACTURING COMPANY IND
9200 Calumet Ave Ste Nw7 (46321-0047)
PHONE.....................800 342-6744
Claudia Kunis, *Prin*
EMP: 13 **EST:** 2014
SALES (est): 589.35K **Privately Held**
Web: www.ammfg.com
SIC: 3999 Barber and beauty shop equipment

(G-12529)
AMERICAN MACHINE WORKS INC
570 Progress Ave (46321-5804)
PHONE.....................219 924-3574
Joseph M Yerga, *Pr*
Pam Yerga, *Sec*
EMP: 4 **EST:** 1999
SQ FT: 4,400
SALES (est): 479.89K **Privately Held**
Web: www.americanmachineworksinc.com
SIC: 3599 Machine shop, jobbing and repair

(G-12530)
AMERICAN PRINTING
8208 Calumet Ave (46321-1704)
PHONE.....................219 836-5600
John Yerga, *Owner*
EMP: 6 **EST:** 2015
SALES (est): 176.14K **Privately Held**
Web: www.americanprintingandadvertising.com
SIC: 2752 Offset printing

(G-12531)
AUTOMTION CTRL PANL SLTONS INC
514 Jenna Dr (46321-4233)
PHONE.....................219 961-8308
Ritesh Parikh, *Pr*
EMP: 10 **EST:** 2011
SALES (est): 824.52K **Privately Held**
Web: www.acpsinfo.com
SIC: 3699 Electrical equipment and supplies, nec

(G-12532)
BASIC ELEMENTS LLC
1305 Macarthur Blvd (46321-3107)
PHONE.....................219 838-1325
EMP: 4 **EST:** 2015
SALES (est): 100.42K **Privately Held**
SIC: 2819 Industrial inorganic chemicals, nec

(G-12533)
C & J K INDUSTRIES INC
230 Timrick Dr (46321-2139)
PHONE.....................219 746-5760
Loydd A Hayes, *Pr*
EMP: 2 **EST:** 2012
SALES (est): 124.16K **Privately Held**
SIC: 3999 Manufacturing industries, nec

(G-12534)
CARELOGIQ CORP
10326 Sandy Ln (46321-4333)
PHONE.....................219 682-0327
Sanjeev Rastogi, *Pr*
EMP: 1 **EST:** 2016
SALES (est): 39.65K **Privately Held**
SIC: 7372 8748 8742 Business oriented computer software; Business consulting, nec; Hospital and health services consultant

(G-12535)
CARL BUDDIG COMPANY
215 45th St (46321-2848)
PHONE.....................708 210-3130
Robert Buddig, *CEO*
EMP: 17 **EST:** 2016
SALES (est): 478.82K **Privately Held**
Web: www.buddig.com
SIC: 2099 Ready-to-eat meals, salads, and sandwiches

(G-12536)
CONTACT PRODUCTS INC
Also Called: Everett Charles Technologies
8736 Schreiber Dr (46321-2640)
PHONE.....................219 838-1911
David Vanloan, *Pr*
EMP: 9 **EST:** 1995
SALES (est): 241.81K **Privately Held**
SIC: 3825 Test equipment for electronic and electric measurement

(G-12537)
DAILY RENTAL
8327 Oakwood Ave (46321-1912)
PHONE.....................773 881-7762
Aisha Daily, *CEO*
EMP: 1 **EST:** 2007
SALES (est): 89.69K **Privately Held**
SIC: 2711 6531 Newspapers, publishing and printing; Rental agent, real estate

(G-12538)
DEEDGRABBERCOM INC
9812 Twin Creek Blvd (46321-4123)
P.O. Box 3348 (46321-0348)
PHONE.....................219 712-9722
Richard Dawson, *Pr*
EMP: 1 **EST:** 2008
SALES (est): 338.34K **Privately Held**
Web: www.deedgrabber.com
SIC: 6799 6726 7372 2741 Real estate investors, except property operators; Investors syndicates; Business oriented computer software; Technical manuals: publishing only, not printed on site

(G-12539)
HETTY INCORPORATED (PA)
Also Called: Miss Print
8244 Calumet Ave (46321-1704)
PHONE.....................219 836-2517
Rick Baltensberger, *Owner*
EMP: 6 **EST:** 1979
SALES (est): 925.39K
SALES (corp-wide): 925.39K **Privately Held**
Web: www.missprintindiana.com
SIC: 2752 7336 2791 2789 Offset printing; Graphic arts and related design; Typesetting ; Bookbinding and related work

(G-12540)
HONEYWELL INTERNATIONAL INC
Also Called: Honeywell
9200 Calumet Ave Ste N510 (46321-2862)
PHONE.....................219 836-3803
Stan Laker, *Mgr*
EMP: 2
Web: www.honeywell.com
SIC: 3724 1629 Aircraft engines and engine parts; Industrial plant construction
PA: Honeywell International Inc.
855 S Mint St
Charlotte NC 28202

(G-12541)
IDENTITY LOGIX LLC
Also Called: Identitylogix
10048 Wellington Ter (46321-4371)
PHONE.....................219 379-5560
Gus Kremmidas, *Prin*
EMP: 8 **EST:** 2008
SALES (est): 477.56K **Privately Held**
SIC: 7372 Business oriented computer software

(G-12542)
IM IMPRESSED
9540 Fran Lin Pkwy (46321-3921)
PHONE.....................219 838-7959
EMP: 4 **EST:** 1989
SALES (est): 202K **Privately Held**
Web: www.tridentwinery.com
SIC: 2759 Screen printing

(G-12543)
INTELLIGENT SOFTWARE INC
9609 Cypress Ave (46321-3417)
PHONE.....................219 923-6166
Paul Gordon, *Pr*
Curtis Blaine, *VP*
EMP: 5 **EST:** 1983
SALES (est): 459.74K **Privately Held**
Web: www.mathtutor.com
SIC: 7372 5734 Application computer software; Software, business and non-game

(G-12544)
INTERNATIONAL INFUSION LP
8618 Jefferson Ave (46321-2421)
PHONE.....................708 710-9200
Jeffrey A Stephens, *Pr*
EMP: 6 **EST:** 2014
SALES (est): 223.86K **Privately Held**
Web: www.internationalinfusion.com
SIC: 2834 Pharmaceutical preparations

(G-12545)
KATIES CANDY LLC
8126 Van Buren Ave (46321-1638)
PHONE.....................800 558-9898
Jean Fager, *Managing Member*
EMP: 4 **EST:** 2020
SALES (est): 78.74K **Privately Held**
SIC: 2064 Candy and other confectionery products

(G-12546)
LARGUS SPEEDY PRINT CORP
Also Called: Largus Printing
732 45th St (46321)
P.O. Box 3232 (46321)
PHONE.....................219 922-8414
Thomas Largus, *Pr*
Carol Largus, *Prin*
EMP: 20 **EST:** 1977
SALES (est): 2.32MM **Privately Held**
Web: www.largusprinting.com
SIC: 2752 2791 2789 2759 Offset printing; Typesetting; Bookbinding and related work; Commercial printing, nec

(G-12547)
LEE ENTERPRISES INC TIMES
Also Called: Times, The
601 45th St (46321-2875)
PHONE.....................219 933-3200
William Howard, *Pr*
EMP: 22 **EST:** 1911
SALES (est): 4.55MM
SALES (corp-wide): 691.14MM **Publicly Held**
Web: www.nwitimes.com
SIC: 2711 Newspapers, publishing and printing
PA: Lee Enterprises, Incorporated
4600 E 53rd St
Davenport IA 52807
563 383-2100

(G-12548)
LITHOGRPHIC COMMUNICATIONS LLC
9701 Indiana Pkwy (46321-4003)
PHONE.....................219 924-9779
Robert Evans, *
EMP: 50 **EST:** 1988
SQ FT: 28,000
SALES (est): 9.37MM **Privately Held**
Web: www.litho-com.com
SIC: 2752 Offset printing

(G-12549)
MIDWEST PEDIATRIC CRDIOLGY PC
Also Called: Midwest Pediatric Cardiology
800 Macarthur Blvd Ste 3 (46321-2917)
PHONE.....................219 836-1355
EMP: 95
Web: www.advocatehealth.com
SIC: 2834 Drugs acting on the cardiovascular system, except diagnostic
PA: Midwest Pediatric Cardiology, Pc
4440 W 95th St
Oak Lawn IL 60453

(G-12550)
MORGANBLAIR LOGISTICS LLC ✪
8330 Columbia Ave (46321-1807)
PHONE.....................219 249-2689
Andrea Johnson, *Managing Member*
EMP: 1 **EST:** 2023
SALES (est): 69.27K **Privately Held**
SIC: 3575 7389 Computer terminals, monitors and components; Business Activities at Non-Commercial Site

(G-12551)
MOTION & CONTROL ENTPS LLC
Also Called: Primet Fluid Power
616 Progress Ave (46321-2872)
PHONE.....................219 844-4224
Daniel Lafontaine, *Brnch Mgr*
EMP: 10
Web: www.mceautomation.com
SIC: 5084 7699 3629 Hydraulic systems equipment and supplies; Hydraulic equipment repair; Electronic generation equipment
HQ: Motion & Control Enterprises Llc
100 Williams Dr
Zelienople PA 16063
724 452-6000

(G-12552)
NIX & COMPANY LLC
417 Mayfair Ct (46321-9178)
PHONE.....................219 595-5541
Tracy L Clark, *Prin*
EMP: 5 **EST:** 2019
SALES (est): 99.3K **Privately Held**
SIC: 7692 Welding repair

(G-12553)
NWITIMESCOM
601 45th St (46321-2875)
PHONE.....................219 933-3200
Deb Anselm, *Genl Mgr*
Dominic Crews, *Dir*
EMP: 37 **EST:** 2007
SALES (est): 1.16MM **Privately Held**
Web: www.nwitimes.com
SIC: 2711 Newspapers, publishing and printing

Munster - Lake County (G-12554)

(G-12554)
OHARAS SPORTS INC
1844 45th St (46321-3916)
PHONE...............................219 836-5554
William O'hara, *Owner*
EMP: 8 **EST:** 1978
SALES (est): 648.11K **Privately Held**
Web: www.oharassportsinc.com
SIC: 5941 5699 2261 Football equipment; Uniforms; Screen printing of cotton broadwoven fabrics

(G-12555)
ORTHOTIC PROSTHETIC SPECIALIST
625 Ridge Rd Ste D (46321-1695)
PHONE...............................219 836-8668
Joseph C Rooker, *Prin*
EMP: 2 **EST:** 2004
SALES (est): 498.85K **Privately Held**
Web: www.ops-indiana.com
SIC: 3842 Limbs, artificial

(G-12556)
P-AMERICAS LLC
Also Called: Pepsico
9300 Calumet Ave (46321-2810)
PHONE...............................219 836-1800
TOLL FREE: 800
Winston Wright, *Brnch Mgr*
EMP: 200
SQ FT: 40,000
SALES (corp-wide): 86.39B **Publicly Held**
Web: www.pepsico.com
SIC: 2086 Carbonated soft drinks, bottled and canned
HQ: P-Americas Llc
1 Pepsi Way
Somers NY 10589
336 896-5740

(G-12557)
PEPSI BEVERAGES COMPANY
Also Called: Pepsico
9300 Calumet Ave (46321-2810)
PHONE...............................219 836-1800
Mark Jaske, *Mgr*
EMP: 35
SALES (corp-wide): 86.39B **Publicly Held**
Web: www.pepsico.com
SIC: 2086 Carbonated soft drinks, bottled and canned
HQ: Pepsi Beverages Company
110 S Byhalia Rd
Collierville TN 38017
901 853-5736

(G-12558)
PINDER INSTRUMENTS COMPANY INC
Also Called: Pinder Industries
9751 Indiana Pkwy Ste A (46321-4061)
P.O. Box 4099 (46324-0099)
PHONE...............................219 924-7070
Walter Tokarz, *CEO*
William Tokarz, *
EMP: 9 **EST:** 1953
SQ FT: 14,500
SALES (est): 362.39K **Privately Held**
Web: www.pinderindustries.com
SIC: 3679 3822 3613 3672 Harness assemblies, for electronic use: wire or cable; Temperature controls, automatic; Panel and distribution boards and other related apparatus; Wiring boards

(G-12559)
POM BY ARI LLC
612 Broadmoor Ave (46321-1202)
PHONE...............................312 978-1668
Ebonie L Bledsoe, *CEO*
EMP: 1 **EST:** 2018
SALES (est): 200K **Privately Held**
Web: www.pombyari.com
SIC: 2844 Cosmetic preparations

(G-12560)
RADAR ASSOCIATES CORPORATION
1117 Melbrook Dr (46321-3007)
PHONE...............................219 838-8030
Barbara J Hannigan, *Pr*
Glenn Hannigan, *Treas*
EMP: 2 **EST:** 1986
SALES (est): 152.91K **Privately Held**
Web: www.policeelectronics.com
SIC: 3812 Radar systems and equipment

(G-12561)
ROCKWELL AUTOMATION INC
225 45th St (46321)
PHONE...............................219 924-3002
John Van Fossen, *Mgr*
EMP: 51
Web: www.rockwellautomation.com
SIC: 3625 Control equipment, electric
PA: Rockwell Automation, Inc.
1201 S 2nd St
Milwaukee WI 53204

(G-12562)
ROYAL BRUSH MANUFACTURING INC (PA)
Also Called: Royal & Langnickel Brush Mfg
515 45th St (46321)
PHONE...............................219 660-4170
George Michael Dovellos, *Pr*
Bill Dovellos, *
Gus Dovellos, *
William Dovellos, *
◆ **EMP:** 10 **EST:** 1950
SQ FT: 38,000
SALES (est): 9.31MM
SALES (corp-wide): 9.31MM **Privately Held**
Web: www.royalbrush.com
SIC: 3991 Brushes, except paint and varnish

(G-12563)
SECURITY INTEGRATED CORP
Also Called: Hobart Cleaners
109 Leicester Rd (46321-9113)
PHONE...............................219 942-9666
Syed Aftab, *Pr*
EMP: 1 **EST:** 2008
SALES (est): 237.41K **Privately Held**
SIC: 3582 Commercial laundry equipment

(G-12564)
SPRIGATI LLC
8250 Baring Ave (46321-1409)
PHONE...............................219 484-9455
Ryan Lamb, *Prin*
EMP: 2 **EST:** 2015
SALES (est): 78.02K **Privately Held**
Web: www.sprigati.com
SIC: 2033 Spaghetti and other pasta sauce: packaged in cans, jars, etc

(G-12565)
STAR CASE MANUFACTURING CO LLC
648 Superior Ave (46321-4035)
PHONE...............................219 922-4440
Darren Eason, *Pr*
◆ **EMP:** 50 **EST:** 1975
SQ FT: 25,000
SALES (est): 4.81MM **Privately Held**
Web: www.starcase.com

SIC: 2449 3469 Wood containers, nec; Electronic enclosures, stamped or pressed metal

(G-12566)
T-A WIND DOWN INC
9200 Calumet Ave Ste N1 (46321-2885)
PHONE...............................708 839-1400
▲ **EMP:** 250
SIC: 3089 3469 Injection molded finished plastics products, nec; Metal stampings, nec

(G-12567)
TEAM SPIRIT
10429 Columbia Ave (46321-4017)
PHONE...............................219 924-6272
Kathleen Hulse, *Owner*
EMP: 3 **EST:** 1985
SALES (est): 153.9K **Privately Held**
SIC: 2399 Military insignia, textile

(G-12568)
TEC AIR INC
9200 Calumet Ave Ste Nw1 (46321-0048)
PHONE...............................219 301-7084
EMP: 18 **EST:** 2019
SALES (est): 289.4K **Privately Held**
Web: www.tecairinc.com
SIC: 3089 Injection molding of plastics

(G-12569)
TEC-AIR LLC
9200 Calumet Ave Ste Nw01 (46321-0048)
PHONE...............................219 301-7084
Nagesh Palakurthi, *CEO*
Robert J Mcmurtry, *Pr*
Nancy Pearson, *
EMP: 100 **EST:** 2018
SQ FT: 130,000
SALES (est): 12.31MM **Privately Held**
Web: www.tecairllc.com
SIC: 3089 3469 Injection molded finished plastics products, nec; Metal stampings, nec
HQ: Angstrom Usa Llc
26980 Trolley Indus Dr
Taylor MI 48180
313 295-0100

(G-12570)
THEGOOSECOMPANY LLC
8547 Monroe Ave (46321-2307)
PHONE...............................708 280-7512
EMP: 1
SALES (est): 41.07K **Privately Held**
SIC: 1389 7389 Construction, repair, and dismantling services; Business services, nec

(G-12571)
THREE FLOYDS DISTILLING CO LLC
9750 Indiana Pkwy (46321-4004)
PHONE...............................219 922-3565
Nicholas Floyd, *Managing Member*
EMP: 15 **EST:** 2014
SALES (est): 581.45K **Privately Held**
Web: www.3floyds.com
SIC: 2085 Distilled and blended liquors

(G-12572)
TWISTED MTAL FBRCTION SVCS INC
1331 Azalea Dr (46321-3707)
PHONE...............................219 923-8045
Thomas Montella, *Prin*
EMP: 5 **EST:** 2017
SALES (est): 106.07K **Privately Held**
SIC: 3499 Fabricated metal products, nec

(G-12573)
VELKO HINGE INC
9325 Kennedy Ct (46321-2817)
PHONE...............................219 924-6363
Alina Jansen, *Pr*
EMP: 27 **EST:** 1969
SQ FT: 34,500
SALES (est): 2.67MM **Privately Held**
Web: www.velko.com
SIC: 3429 Hardware, nec

Nabb
Clark County

(G-12574)
GINAS ESSENTIALS
7705 Carrol Rd (47147-9639)
PHONE...............................812 406-3276
Martin Baird, *Prin*
EMP: 4 **EST:** 2016
SALES (est): 56.44K **Privately Held**
Web: ginas-essentials-goat-milk-soaps.business.site
SIC: 2841 Soap and other detergents

Napoleon
Ripley County

(G-12575)
NAPOLEON LUMBER CO
Us Hwy 421 S (47034)
P.O. Box 88 (47034)
PHONE...............................812 852-4545
Neal M Dean, *Pr*
EMP: 3 **EST:** 1918
SQ FT: 1,500
SALES (est): 239.39K **Privately Held**
Web: www.napoleonstatebank.com
SIC: 2452 6519 Log cabins, prefabricated, wood; Farm land leasing

(G-12576)
WAGNER TRUSS MANUFACTURING INC
9410 N Us 421 (47034)
P.O. Box 121 (47034-0121)
PHONE...............................812 852-2206
Joe Wagner, *Pr*
Janet Wagner, *Sec*
EMP: 24 **EST:** 1993
SQ FT: 15,000
SALES (est): 662.59K **Privately Held**
Web: www.wagnertruss.com
SIC: 2439 Trusses, wooden roof

Nappanee
Elkhart County

(G-12577)
AG PROCESSING A COOPERATIVE
Also Called: Supersweet Farm Service
302 S Main St (46550-2528)
PHONE...............................574 773-4138
Bobby Gluck, *Mgr*
EMP: 8
SALES (corp-wide): 902.55MM **Privately Held**
Web: www.agp.com
SIC: 2075 5191 Soybean oil, cake or meal; Animal feeds
PA: Ag Processing Inc A Cooperative
12700 W Dodge Rd
Omaha NE 68154
402 496-7809

(G-12578)
ALPINE ENTERPRISES
12844 N 700 W (46550-9707)

GEOGRAPHIC SECTION
Nappanee - Elkhart County (G-12602)

P.O. Box 409 (46550-0409)
PHONE....................................574 773-5475
Kenneth Mullet, Genl Mgr
EMP: 5 EST: 2005
SALES (est): 372.59K **Privately Held**
SIC: 2499 Decorative wood and woodwork

(G-12579)
ALUMINUM TRAILER COMPANY (HQ)
Also Called: Atc Trailers
751 N Tomahawk Trl (46550-9070)
P.O. Box 396 (46550-0396)
PHONE....................................574 773-2440
Robert Paden, Pr
Jeffrey Shenk, VP
Pete Gingerich, CFO
EMP: 169 EST: 1999
SQ FT: 25,000
SALES (est): 53.3MM **Privately Held**
Web: www.atctrailers.com
SIC: 3799 3537 5599 Trailers and trailer equipment; Industrial trucks and tractors; Utility trailers
PA: Atc Trailers Holdings, Inc.
751 North Tomahawk Trl
Nappanee IN 46550

(G-12580)
ARCHER-DANIELS-MIDLAND COMPANY
Also Called: ADM
252 S Jackson St (46550-2113)
PHONE....................................574 773-4138
EMP: 4
SALES (corp-wide): 93.94B **Publicly Held**
Web: www.adm.com
SIC: 2041 Flour and other grain mill products
PA: Archer-Daniels-Midland Company
77 W Wacker Dr Ste 4600
Chicago IL 60601
312 634-8100

(G-12581)
ASCOT ENTERPRISES INC
Also Called: Ascot Plant 10
1901 Cheyenne St (46550-9463)
PHONE....................................574 773-7751
EMP: 33
SALES (corp-wide): 41.85MM **Privately Held**
Web: www.ascotent.com
SIC: 2391 2591 Curtains, window: made from purchased materials; Window shades
PA: Ascot Enterprises Inc
503 S Main St
Nappanee IN 46550
877 773-7751

(G-12582)
ASCOT ENTERPRISES INC (PA)
Also Called: Imperial Fabrics
503 S Main St (46550-2531)
P.O. Box 165 (46550-0165)
PHONE....................................877 773-7751
Howard Yoder, CEO
Kenneth J Manning, *
Alan Sands, *
▲ EMP: 25 EST: 1976
SQ FT: 12,000
SALES (est): 41.85MM
SALES (corp-wide): 41.85MM **Privately Held**
Web: www.ascotent.com
SIC: 2391 2591 2392 Curtains, window: made from purchased materials; Window shades; Bedspreads and bed sets: made from purchased materials

(G-12583)
BARKMAN CUSTOM WOODWORKING
30235 Us Highway 6 (46550-9469)
PHONE....................................574 773-9212
Sam Barkman, Prin
Sam Barkman, Pr
Gerald Barkman, Pr
EMP: 13 EST: 1975
SQ FT: 4,500
SALES (est): 420.96K **Privately Held**
SIC: 2431 Moldings, wood: unfinished and prefinished

(G-12584)
BEER AND SLABAUGH INC
23965 Us Highway 6 (46550-3396)
PHONE....................................574 773-3413
Rodney Beer, Pr
Tracey Beer, *
Barney Beer, *
EMP: 25 EST: 1958
SQ FT: 6,000
SALES (est): 963.27K **Privately Held**
Web: www.beerandslabaugh.com
SIC: 1794 1623 1622 1442 Excavation and grading, building construction; Sewer line construction; Bridge construction; Construction sand and gravel

(G-12585)
BORKHOLDER CORPORATION (PA)
Also Called: Borkholder Building Supply
786 Us Highway 6 (46550-9526)
P.O. Box 32 (46550-0032)
PHONE....................................574 773-4083
Freeman D Borkholder, Pr
Dwayne Borkholder, *
Carl Bals, *
Brandon Myers, *
EMP: 50 EST: 1982
SQ FT: 25,000
SALES (est): 20.22MM
SALES (corp-wide): 20.22MM **Privately Held**
Web: www.borkholderbuildings.com
SIC: 5031 2511 Building materials, interior; Wood bedroom furniture

(G-12586)
BORKHOLDER LAVON
Also Called: Lb Woodworking
492 Us Highway 6 (46550-9523)
PHONE....................................574 773-3714
Lavon Borkholder, Owner
EMP: 2 EST: 1993
SALES (est): 115.98K **Privately Held**
Web: www.borkholderbuildings.com
SIC: 2431 Woodwork, interior and ornamental, nec

(G-12587)
CAMBRIDGE MOLDING INC
1574 Us Highway 6 (46550-9534)
PHONE....................................574 546-4311
EMP: 5
SALES (est): 93K **Privately Held**
SIC: 3089 Molding primary plastics

(G-12588)
CHASE MANUFACTURING LLC (PA)
506 S Oakland Ave (46550-2327)
PHONE....................................574 546-4776
Zachary Nickell, Managing Member
EMP: 140 EST: 2008
SALES (est): 38.71MM **Privately Held**
Web: www.chasemfg.com
SIC: 2431 Millwork

(G-12589)
CHUPPVILLE CARVING
11726 N 1000 W (46550-8749)
PHONE....................................574 354-7642
Henry Chupp, Owner
EMP: 1 EST: 1988
SALES (est): 65.45K **Privately Held**
SIC: 2426 2511 Carvings, furniture: wood; Wood household furniture

(G-12590)
COMMERCIAL STRUCTURES CORP (PA)
655 N Tomahawk Trl (46550-9362)
PHONE....................................574 773-7931
David H Johnson, Pr
Eric Johnson, *
Jack Lawrence, *
EMP: 35 EST: 1973
SQ FT: 40,000
SALES (est): 4.93MM
SALES (corp-wide): 4.93MM **Privately Held**
Web: www.comstruc.com
SIC: 2451 Mobile buildings: for commercial use

(G-12591)
COUNTRY CRAFTSMAN WDWKG LLC
8563 W 1100 N (46550-8628)
PHONE....................................574 773-4911
Gene L Miller, Prin
EMP: 4 EST: 2012
SALES (est): 209.93K **Privately Held**
Web: www.wooddesignrv.com
SIC: 2431 Millwork

(G-12592)
CRAFTECH BUILDING SYSTEMS INC
Also Called: Heckaman Homes
2676 E Market St (46550-9397)
P.O. Box 229 (46550-0229)
PHONE....................................574 773-4167
John Mahnken, CEO
Marlene Myers, *
Dale Klein, *
Steve Burkins, *
EMP: 27 EST: 1969
SQ FT: 180,000
SALES (est): 5.26MM **Privately Held**
Web: www.heckamanhomes.com
SIC: 2452 Modular homes, prefabricated, wood

(G-12593)
DB POLISHING
6445 W 1350 N (46550-9709)
PHONE....................................574 518-2443
Katy Berger, Off Mgr
EMP: 5 EST: 2013
SALES (est): 208.58K **Privately Held**
Web: www.db-polishing.com
SIC: 3471 Polishing, metals or formed products

(G-12594)
DH MACHINE INC
352 N Tomahawk Trl (46550)
PHONE....................................574 773-9211
Delbert W Helmuth, Pr
Levi Helmuth, *
Karl E Miller, *
▲ EMP: 90 EST: 1998
SQ FT: 69,000
SALES (est): 8.78MM **Privately Held**
Web: www.dhmachinecorp.com
SIC: 3441 Fabricated structural metal for ships

(G-12595)
DIPT LLC ✪
Also Called: Dipt
110 S Main St (46550-1917)
PHONE....................................574 354-8471
T Graverson, Managing Member
EMP: 1 EST: 2023
SALES (est): 65.51K **Privately Held**
SIC: 7372 Prepackaged software

(G-12596)
FARWALL TSG LLC
Also Called: Sullivan Group
302 Dal Mar Way (46550-9202)
PHONE....................................574 773-2108
EMP: 18 EST: 2016
SALES (est): 1.18MM **Privately Held**
Web: www.sullivangroupusa.com
SIC: 2339 2323 7389 Women's and misses' outerwear, nec; Men's and boy's neckwear; Advertising, promotional, and trade show services

(G-12597)
FM HOLDINGS LLC
Also Called: Cross-Cut Wood Shop, The
2051 Cheyenne St Ste 1 (46550-9055)
PHONE....................................574 773-2814
EMP: 6 EST: 2019
SALES (est): 700.29K **Privately Held**
SIC: 2436 Panels, softwood plywood

(G-12598)
GEHL INDUSTRIES INC
9547 W 1050 N (46550-8623)
PHONE....................................574 773-7663
Rohman Lehman, Pr
Deborah Lehman, VP
EMP: 10 EST: 1985
SALES (est): 887.51K **Privately Held**
Web: www.gehlindustries.com
SIC: 2521 Cabinets, office: wood

(G-12599)
GEM INDUSTRIES INC
1400 Northwood Dr (46550-1112)
PHONE....................................574 773-4513
Ernie Germann, Pr
EMP: 2 EST: 2000
SALES (est): 88.22K **Privately Held**
SIC: 3999 Candles

(G-12600)
GRAVELTON MACHINE SHOP INC
23965 Us Highway 6 (46550-9106)
PHONE....................................574 773-3413
Harlan D Beer, Pr
EMP: 4 EST: 1946
SALES (est): 391.21K **Privately Held**
SIC: 7699 7692 Industrial machinery and equipment repair; Welding repair

(G-12601)
GRRREAT CREATIONS
Also Called: G C I
597 Shawnee St (46550-9052)
P.O. Box 231 (46550-0231)
PHONE....................................574 773-5331
Devon Eby, Managing Member
Jim Reed, *
EMP: 24 EST: 1987
SQ FT: 6,000
SALES (est): 1.99MM **Privately Held**
Web: www.gciclamps.com
SIC: 3429 Clamps, metal

(G-12602)
GULF STREAM COACH INC
Also Called: Gulf Stream Coach Plant 59
2404 E Market St (46550-9457)

Nappanee - Elkhart County (G-12603)

PHONE..................................574 773-7761
EMP: 1064
SALES (corp-wide): 90.62MM **Privately Held**
Web: www.gulfstreamcoach.com
SIC: 3716 Motor homes
PA: Gulf Stream Coach, Inc.
503 S Oakland Ave
Nappanee IN 46550
574 773-7761

(G-12603)
GULF STREAM COACH INC (PA)
Also Called: Yellowstone Rv
503 S Oakland Ave (46550-2328)
P.O. Box 1005 (46550-0905)
PHONE..................................574 773-7761
Dan Shea, *Pr*
James F Shea Junior, *Ch Bd*
Brian Shea, *
Kenneth C Brinker, *
Phil Savari, *
◆ EMP: 125 EST: 1983
SQ FT: 500,000
SALES (est): 90.62MM
SALES (corp-wide): 90.62MM **Privately Held**
Web: www.gulfstreamcoach.com
SIC: 3792 3714 2451 3716 Travel trailers and campers; Motor vehicle parts and accessories; Mobile homes; Recreational van conversion (self-propelled), factory basis

(G-12604)
HB INTERNATIONAL LLC
Also Called: Challenger Door Plant 58
501 S Oakland Ave (46550-2328)
PHONE..................................574 773-8200
EMP: 8
SALES (corp-wide): 3.78B **Publicly Held**
Web: corporate.lippert.com
SIC: 3442 Shutters, door or window: metal
HQ: Hb International, Llc
1205 E Lincoln St
Nappanee IN 46550
574 773-0470

(G-12605)
HB INTERNATIONAL LLC (DH)
1205 E Lincoln St (46550-2240)
PHONE..................................574 773-0470
EMP: 85 EST: 2008
SALES (est): 25.43MM
SALES (corp-wide): 3.78B **Publicly Held**
Web: corporate.lippert.com
SIC: 3442 Shutters, door or window: metal
HQ: Lippert Components, Inc.
3501 County Rd 6 E
Elkhart IN 46514
574 535-1125

(G-12606)
HB INTERNATIONAL LLC
Also Called: Challenger Design
24785 Us Highway 6 (46550-9404)
PHONE..................................574 773-8200
Rich Moore, *Prin*
EMP: 8
SALES (corp-wide): 3.78B **Publicly Held**
Web: corporate.lippert.com
SIC: 2599 Cabinets, factory
HQ: Hb International, Llc
1205 E Lincoln St
Nappanee IN 46550
574 773-0470

(G-12607)
HEARTLAND METAL LLC
5481 W 1350 N (46550-9710)
PHONE..................................574 773-0509
EMP: 1 EST: 2008
SALES (est): 146.34K **Privately Held**
Web: www.heartlandmetalllc.com
SIC: 1542 3444 Nonresidential construction, nec; Metal roofing and roof drainage equipment

(G-12608)
HEPTON WELDING LLC
9352 W Hepton Rd (46550-8702)
PHONE..................................800 570-4238
David Mast, *Managing Member*
EMP: 6 EST: 1982
SQ FT: 7,000
SALES (est): 438.22K **Privately Held**
SIC: 7692 Welding repair

(G-12609)
HERBS G&W INC
10517 W 1100 N (46550-8770)
PHONE..................................574 646-2134
Gerald D Miller, *Pr*
Wanda Miller, *VP*
EMP: 2 EST: 1995
SALES (est): 228.4K **Privately Held**
Web: www.gwherbs.com
SIC: 2833 5499 Vitamins, natural or synthetic: bulk, uncompounded; Spices and herbs

(G-12610)
HILLTOP METAL FABRICATING LLC
71024 County Road 13 (46550-9126)
PHONE..................................574 773-4975
EMP: 7 EST: 2005
SALES (est): 513.07K **Privately Held**
SIC: 3446 Gratings, tread: fabricated metal

(G-12611)
HILLTOP SPECIALTIES LLC
71024 County Road 13 (46550-9126)
PHONE..................................574 773-4975
Mel Lehman, *Mgr*
EMP: 9 EST: 2003
SALES (est): 410.8K **Privately Held**
SIC: 3291 Steel wool

(G-12612)
HOCHSTETLER WELDING LLC
7262 W 1350 N (46550-9782)
PHONE..................................574 773-0600
Brian E Hochstetler, *Prin*
EMP: 5 EST: 2008
SALES (est): 288.13K **Privately Held**
SIC: 7692 Welding repair

(G-12613)
HOOSIER POWDER COATING LLC
9583 W 1350 N (46550-8790)
PHONE..................................574 253-7737
James Faroh, *Prin*
EMP: 8 EST: 2016
SALES (est): 555.97K **Privately Held**
Web: www.hoosiercoatings.com
SIC: 3479 Coating of metals and formed products

(G-12614)
INTECH TRAILERS INC
29286 County Road 52 (46550-9470)
P.O. Box 486 (46550-0486)
PHONE..................................574 221-8231
▼ EMP: 56 EST: 2010
SALES (est): 23.53MM **Privately Held**
Web: www.intech.com
SIC: 5599 3799 Utility trailers; Trailers and trailer equipment

(G-12615)
JOHNS BUTCHER SHOP INC
158 N Main St (46550-1938)
PHONE..................................574 773-4632
Marlin Miller, *CEO*
Miller Russell, *Owner*
Nancy Miller, *Prin*
EMP: 14 EST: 1941
SQ FT: 4,000
SALES (est): 1.44MM **Privately Held**
Web: www.johnsbutchershop.com
SIC: 2011 5421 Meat packing plants; Meat markets, including freezer provisioners

(G-12616)
K2 PLASTICS INC
26400 County Road 50 (46550-9426)
PHONE..................................574 773-2243
Brian L Williams, *Prin*
EMP: 1 EST: 2011
SALES (est): 71K **Privately Held**
Web: www.k2-plastics.com
SIC: 3089 Injection molding of plastics

(G-12617)
KAY INDUSTRIES INC (PA)
Also Called: Kay Industries
207 E Market St (46550-2119)
P.O. Box 1323 (46624-1323)
PHONE..................................574 236-6220
Lawrence Katz, *Pr*
Aaron Katz, *Ch*
Greg Schroff, *Genl Mgr*
EMP: 5 EST: 1972
SALES (est): 1.5MM
SALES (corp-wide): 1.5MM **Privately Held**
Web: www.kayind.com
SIC: 3612 Transformers, except electric

(G-12618)
KOUNTRY WOOD PRODUCTS LLC (PA)
352 Shawnee St (46550-9061)
PHONE..................................574 773-5673
Ola Yoder, *Managing Member*
Perry Miller, *
Greg Shank, *
Virgil Yoder, *
EMP: 210 EST: 1998
SQ FT: 270,000
SALES (est): 48.42MM
SALES (corp-wide): 48.42MM **Privately Held**
Web: www.kountrywood.com
SIC: 2434 5211 5031 Wood kitchen cabinets ; Cabinets, kitchen; Kitchen cabinets

(G-12619)
L & L WOODWORKING LLC
13614 N 700 W (46550-9722)
PHONE..................................574 535-4613
EMP: 3 EST: 1975
SQ FT: 2,592
SALES (est): 225.25K **Privately Held**
SIC: 2431 Interior and ornamental woodwork and trim

(G-12620)
LEGACY WOOD CREATIONS LLC
24675 County Road 54 (46550-9433)
PHONE..................................574 773-4405
Andrew Miller, *Prin*
EMP: 6 EST: 2012
SALES (est): 308.8K **Privately Held**
Web: www.legacywoodcabinets.com
SIC: 2431 Millwork

(G-12621)
MARTINS BUGGY SHOP
24070 County Road 46 (46550-9331)
PHONE..................................574 831-3699
Leroy M Martin, *Owner*
EMP: 2 EST: 1960
SALES (est): 118.01K **Privately Held**
SIC: 3799 Carriages, horse drawn

(G-12622)
MIDWEST MACHINING LLC
10485 W 1350 N (46550-8782)
PHONE..................................212 696-7322
Carl Schwartz, *Pr*
EMP: 6 EST: 2011
SALES (est): 83.72K **Privately Held**
SIC: 3599 Machine shop, jobbing and repair

(G-12623)
MILLER CABINS AND BARNS LLC
30695 County Road 150 (46550-9476)
PHONE..................................574 773-7661
EMP: 4 EST: 2008
SALES (est): 257.54K **Privately Held**
Web: www.tidyteams.com
SIC: 2431 Millwork

(G-12624)
MILLER HARDWOODS LLC
8760 W 1350 N (46550-8788)
PHONE..................................574 773-9371
EMP: 2 EST: 1975
SALES (est): 241.73K **Privately Held**
SIC: 2421 Sawmills and planing mills, general

(G-12625)
MILLER MACHINE SHOP INC LLC
10780 W 1100 N (46550-8769)
PHONE..................................574 646-2900
EMP: 6 EST: 2008
SALES (est): 81.49K **Privately Held**
SIC: 3599 Machine shop, jobbing and repair

(G-12626)
MILLER MFG CORP
901 E Lincoln St (46550-2145)
P.O. Box 72 (46550-0072)
PHONE..................................574 773-4136
Ronald Hestad, *Pr*
Daniel Poston, *
EMP: 35 EST: 1952
SQ FT: 52,000
SALES (est): 4.92MM **Privately Held**
Web: www.millermfgcorp.com
SIC: 3499 3714 3469 3444 Metal ladders; Motor vehicle wheels and parts; Metal stampings, nec; Sheet metalwork

(G-12627)
MULLET CUSTOM INTERIOR LLC
106 3b Rd (46550-9558)
PHONE..................................574 773-9442
Ben J Mullet, *Managing Member*
Julie Hochstetler, *Managing Member*
EMP: 14 EST: 1996
SALES (est): 1.18MM **Privately Held**
Web: www.mulletcustominteriorllc.com
SIC: 2431 Moldings, wood: unfinished and prefinished

(G-12628)
MULLETS FENCING AND SUPPLIES
Also Called: Northern Indiana Axle Co
7749 W 1000 N (46550-8636)
P.O. Box 335 (46550-0335)
PHONE..................................574 646-3300
Kenneth A Mullet, *Owner*
▲ EMP: 1 EST: 1986
SQ FT: 5,000
SALES (est): 360.91K **Privately Held**
SIC: 1799 3714 Fence construction; Axles, motor vehicle

GEOGRAPHIC SECTION

Nappanee - Elkhart County (G-12656)

(G-12629)
MULLETS WELDING LLC
12848 N 700 W (46550-9707)
PHONE.................... 574 773-0189
EMP: 4 EST: 2019
SALES (est): 166.54K Privately Held
Web: www.mulletswelding.com
SIC: 7692 Welding repair

(G-12630)
NC COATINGS LLC
30338 County Road 56 (46550-9105)
PHONE.................... 574 213-4754
EMP: 6 EST: 2017
SALES (est): 69.98K Privately Held
SIC: 3479 Metal coating and allied services

(G-12631)
NEWMAR CORPORATION (HQ)
355 Delaware St (46550)
P.O. Box 30 (46550)
PHONE.................... 574 773-7791
Richard Parks, Ch Bd
Casey Tubman, *
Pamela Culp, *
EMP: 1 EST: 1968
SQ FT: 600,000
SALES (est): 241.55MM
SALES (corp-wide): 3.49B Publicly Held
Web: www.newmarcorp.com
SIC: 3716 3792 Motor homes; Travel trailers and campers
PA: Winnebago Industries, Inc.
13200 Pioneer Trl
Eden Prairie MN 55347
952 829-8600

(G-12632)
NEXGEN GROUP INC
Also Called: Gen-Y Hitch
3400 W Market St (46550)
PHONE.................... 574 218-6363
Danny Miller, Pr
EMP: 1 EST: 2018
SALES (est): 1MM Privately Held
Web: www.genyhitch.com
SIC: 5599 3799 Utility trailers; Towing bars and systems

(G-12633)
NORTHERN INDIANA AXLE LLC
1780 W Market St (46550-9046)
PHONE.................... 574 773-3039
EMP: 16 EST: 2010
SALES (est): 1.98MM Privately Held
SIC: 3312 Blast furnaces and steel mills

(G-12634)
OMNIMAX INTERNATIONAL LLC
Amerimax Building Products
2341 E Market St (46550-9306)
PHONE.................... 574 773-7981
Mitchell B Lewis, CEO
EMP: 37
Web: www.omnimax.com
SIC: 3444 Sheet metalwork
HQ: Omnimax International, Llc
30 Technlogy Pkwy S Ste 4
Peachtree Corners GA 30092
770 449-7066

(G-12635)
PD SOLUTIONS INC
504 S Oakland Ave (46550-2327)
P.O. Box 112 (46550-0112)
PHONE.................... 800 289-8787
Rick Jones, Pr
EMP: 5 EST: 2017
SALES (est): 116.03K Privately Held
SIC: 7372 Prepackaged software

(G-12636)
PERFECT TWIST PRETZELS LLC
401 E Market St (46550-2154)
PHONE.................... 574 248-1715
EMP: 6 EST: 2018
SALES (est): 322.98K Privately Held
Web: www.perfecttwistpretzels.com
SIC: 2052 Pretzels

(G-12637)
PWI
7930 W 1000 N (46550-8795)
PHONE.................... 574 646-2015
Ryan Miller, CEO
Kyle Miller, *
EMP: 62 EST: 1979
SALES (est): 5.01MM Privately Held
Web: www.pwiworks.com
SIC: 3536 3999 Cranes, overhead traveling; Manufacturing industries, nec

(G-12638)
PWI CORP
7930 W 1000 N (46550)
PHONE.................... 574 646-2015
Ryan Miller, CEO
Paul H Miller, *
Dean Grass, *
EMP: 24 EST: 1979
SALES (est): 2.33MM Privately Held
Web: www.pwiworks.com
SIC: 7699 3441 Farm machinery repair; Fabricated structural metal

(G-12639)
QUALITY HARDWOOD SALES LLC
493 Shawnee St (46550-9064)
PHONE.................... 574 773-2505
▲ EMP: 84
SIC: 2499 2431 2452 Decorative wood and woodwork; Moldings and baseboards, ornamental and trim; Panels and sections, prefabricated, wood

(G-12640)
R & R CUSTOM WOODWORKING INC
30480 County Road 52 (46550-9472)
PHONE.................... 574 773-5436
Raymond J Yoder, Pr
EMP: 9 EST: 1991
SALES (est): 364.71K Privately Held
SIC: 2434 2426 2499 Wood kitchen cabinets; Furniture stock and parts, hardwood; Decorative wood and woodwork

(G-12641)
RIGHT ANGLE STL & FABRICATION
401 E Lincoln St (46550)
P.O. Box 559 (46573)
PHONE.................... 574 773-7148
Carl Cook, Pr
Carol Cook, *
EMP: 50 EST: 2001
SALES (est): 4.51MM Privately Held
Web: www.rightanglesteel.com
SIC: 3449 Bars, concrete reinforcing; fabricated steel

(G-12642)
RUSTIC CREATIONS LLC
71703 County Road 9 (46550-9442)
PHONE.................... 574 349-8156
EMP: 3 EST: 2017
SALES (est): 53.8K Privately Held
SIC: 2431 Millwork

(G-12643)
S & H CABINETS
70932 County Road 3 (46550-8976)
PHONE.................... 574 773-7465
Warren S Hochstetler, Owner
EMP: 4 EST: 2017
SALES (est): 164.02K Privately Held
SIC: 2434 Wood kitchen cabinets

(G-12644)
SAWS WOODWORKING LLC
72990 County Road 101 (46550-9574)
PHONE.................... 574 773-4216
EMP: 1 EST: 2008
SALES (est): 129.97K Privately Held
SIC: 2431 Millwork

(G-12645)
SLABAUGH MEAT PROCESSING LLC
72700 County Road 101 (46550-9444)
PHONE.................... 574 773-0381
Mark Slabaugh, Prin
EMP: 6 EST: 2010
SALES (est): 117.46K Privately Held
SIC: 2011 Meat packing plants

(G-12646)
STRESCO MACHINE INC
2365 Beech Rd (46550-9515)
PHONE.................... 574 773-7334
Ross Yoder, Pr
Julie Yoder, Sec
EMP: 6 EST: 1987
SQ FT: 3,240
SALES (est): 492.4K Privately Held
SIC: 3599 Machine shop, jobbing and repair

(G-12647)
SUPERIOR SOURCE WOODWORKS LLC
2881 E County Line Rd (46550-9556)
PHONE.................... 574 773-4841
Lyndon J Yoder, Owner
EMP: 6 EST: 2017
SALES (est): 76.68K Privately Held
SIC: 2431 Millwork

(G-12648)
TECK MACHINE LLC
70793 County Road 11 (46550-9418)
PHONE.................... 574 773-7004
EMP: 6 EST: 2018
SALES (est): 250.63K Privately Held
SIC: 7692 Welding repair

(G-12649)
UFP NAPPANEE LLC
Also Called: Quality Hardwood Sales
493 Shawnee St (46550-9064)
PHONE.................... 574 773-2505
EMP: 84 EST: 2017
SALES (est): 9.77MM
SALES (corp-wide): 9.63B Publicly Held
Web: www.qhsales.com
SIC: 2499 2431 2452 Decorative wood and woodwork; Moldings and baseboards, ornamental and trim; Panels and sections, prefabricated, wood
PA: Ufp Industries, Inc.
2801 E Beltline Ave Ne
Grand Rapids MI 49525
616 364-6161

(G-12650)
UFP STRUCTURAL PACKAGING LLC
493 Shawnee St (46550-9064)
PHONE.................... 574 773-2505
EMP: 1
SALES (corp-wide): 7.22B Publicly Held
SIC: 2448 Pallets, wood

HQ: Ufp Structural Packaging, Llc
5840 Wi-60
Hartford WI 53027
262 673-6090

(G-12651)
US ROD MANUFACTURING LLC
502 S Oakland Ave (46550-2327)
PHONE.................... 574 227-1288
EMP: 5
SALES (corp-wide): 508.71MM Privately Held
Web: www.lufkin.com
SIC: 3317 Tubes, seamless steel
HQ: Us Rod Manufacturing, Llc
13212 N Macarthur Blvd
Oklahoma City OK 73142
405 838-1544

(G-12652)
WILLIAMSBURG FURNITURE INC (HQ)
2096 Cheyenne St (46550-9464)
PHONE.................... 800 582-8183
L G Feiler Iii, Pr
▲ EMP: 67 EST: 1992
SQ FT: 45,000
SALES (est): 20.28MM
SALES (corp-wide): 3.47B Publicly Held
Web: www.wbfusa.com
SIC: 2512 2515 Upholstered household furniture; Mattresses and foundations
PA: Patrick Industries, Inc.
107 W Franklin St
Elkhart IN 46516
574 294-7511

(G-12653)
WILLIAMSBURG MARINE LLC
2096 Cheyenne St (46550-9464)
PHONE.................... 574 658-3409
EMP: 116 EST: 2019
SALES (est): 13.98MM
SALES (corp-wide): 3.47B Publicly Held
Web: www.wbfusa.com
SIC: 3275 Plaster and plasterboard, gypsum
PA: Patrick Industries, Inc.
107 W Franklin St
Elkhart IN 46516
574 294-7511

(G-12654)
WILLIE LEHMAN
Also Called: Lehmans Slid Surfc Fabrication
24793 County Road 52 (46550-9115)
PHONE.................... 574 935-2809
Willie Lehman, Owner
EMP: 1 EST: 1998
SALES (est): 50K Privately Held
SIC: 3449 Miscellaneous metalwork

(G-12655)
WYATT FARM CENTER INC
Also Called: Mz Ventur Partners
26545 County Road 52 (46550-8911)
PHONE.................... 574 354-2998
Mark Zeltwanger, CEO
Mark Zeltwanger, Pr
EMP: 5 EST: 1979
SALES (est): 921.35K Privately Held
SIC: 7353 3532 5032 Heavy construction equipment rental; Mining machinery; Aggregate

(G-12656)
YODER KITCHEN CORP (PA)
501 S Main St (46550-2531)
PHONE.................... 574 773-3197
Shawn Yoder, Owner
Shawn Yoder, Pr
Stephanie Yoder, *

Nappanee - Elkhart County (G-12657)

EMP: 25 EST: 1953
SQ FT: 13,000
SALES (est): 4.23MM
SALES (corp-wide): 4.23MM **Privately Held**
Web: www.yoderkitchens.com
SIC: 2434 Vanities, bathroom: wood

(G-12657)
YODERS WOODWORKING LLC
13941 N 700 W (46550-9783)
PHONE.....................574 773-0699
John Yoder Iii, *Owner*
EMP: 1 EST: 2013
SALES (est): 61K **Privately Held**
Web: www.yoderswoodworkingin.com
SIC: 2431 Millwork

Nashville
Brown County

(G-12658)
A WILD HARE LLC
44 N Van Buren St (47448-7029)
PHONE.....................812 988-9453
EMP: 13 EST: 2012
SALES (est): 532.35K **Privately Held**
Web: www.thewildolive.com
SIC: 2079 Olive oil

(G-12659)
AIM MEDIA INDIANA OPER LLC
Brown County Democrat
147 E Main St (47448-7008)
PHONE.....................812 988-2221
Sara Clifford, *Brnch Mgr*
EMP: 5
SALES (corp-wide): 26.88MM **Privately Held**
Web: www.aimmediaindiana.com
SIC: 2711 Commercial printing and newspaper publishing combined
PA: Aim Media Indiana Operating, Llc
2980 N National Rd # A
Columbus IN 47201
812 372-7811

(G-12660)
ANGLERS MANUFACTURING
217 Salt Creek Rd (47448-8694)
PHONE.....................812 988-8040
Mark Settles, *Prin*
EMP: 5 EST: 2007
SALES (est): 83.9K **Privately Held**
SIC: 3999 Manufacturing industries, nec

(G-12661)
AVIONICS MOUNTS INC
4510 State Road 46 E (47448-8673)
PHONE.....................812 988-2949
Archie Johnson, *Pr*
EMP: 4 EST: 1956
SALES (est): 453.41K **Privately Held**
Web: www.avionicsmounts.com
SIC: 3444 Sheet metalwork

(G-12662)
BEAR WALLOW DISTILLERY
4484 Old State Road 46 (47448-8128)
PHONE.....................812 657-4923
EMP: 4 EST: 2015
SALES (est): 101.65K **Privately Held**
Web: www.bearwallowdistillery.com
SIC: 2085 Distilled and blended liquors

(G-12663)
BRIAN NEWTON
Also Called: Broomcorn Johnny's
58 E Main St Ste 4 # 483 (47448-7092)
PHONE.....................812 200-3149
Brian Newton, *Owner*
EMP: 1 EST: 2012
SALES (est): 53.58K **Privately Held**
Web: www.broomcornjohnnys.com
SIC: 3991 Brooms

(G-12664)
BROCKWOOD FARM
7867 Axsom Branch Rd (47448-9592)
PHONE.....................812 837-9607
Harry Hopkins, *Owner*
EMP: 2 EST: 1995
SALES (est): 249.55K **Privately Held**
Web: www.brockwoodfarm.com
SIC: 3589 6531 Sewer cleaning equipment, power; Real estate agents and managers

(G-12665)
BROWN COUNTY KETTLE CORN LLC
245 Van Buren St (47448-7038)
P.O. Box 283 (47402-0283)
PHONE.....................812 558-4536
Andrew W Tilton, *Prin*
EMP: 4 EST: 2020
SALES (est): 63.4K **Privately Held**
Web: www.browncountykettlecorn.com
SIC: 2096 Popcorn, already popped (except candy covered)

(G-12666)
BROWN COUNTY WINE COMPANY INC (PA)
4520 State Road 46 E (47448-8673)
PHONE.....................812 988-6144
David Schrodt, *Pr*
Cynthia Schrodt, *Sec*
EMP: 2 EST: 1985
SALES (est): 402.63K
SALES (corp-wide): 402.63K **Privately Held**
Web: www.browncountywinery.com
SIC: 2084 5921 Wines; Wine

(G-12667)
CEDAR CREEK WINERY
36 E Franklin St (47448-7004)
PHONE.....................812 988-1111
EMP: 2 EST: 2013
SALES (est): 147.06K **Privately Held**
Web: www.drinkatthecreek.com
SIC: 5921 2084 Wine; Wines

(G-12668)
COLUMBUS SIGNS
3770 Reed Hollow Rd (47448-9000)
PHONE.....................812 376-7877
Mark Smith, *Owner*
EMP: 2 EST: 1976
SALES (est): 183.53K **Privately Held**
Web: www.columbus.in.us
SIC: 3993 7629 Neon signs; Electrical repair shops

(G-12669)
CRYSTAL SOURCE
Also Called: Wishful Thinking
150 S Old School Way (47448-7033)
P.O. Box 573 (47448-0573)
PHONE.....................812 988-7009
EMP: 4 EST: 1988
SQ FT: 1,240
SALES (est): 289.7K **Privately Held**
Web: www.wishfulthinking-in.com
SIC: 5944 3911 5947 5999 Jewelry, precious stones and precious metals; Jewelry, precious metal; Gifts and novelties; Rubber stamps

(G-12670)
HARD TRUTH DISTILLING CO LLC
Also Called: Hard Truth Hills
418 Old State Road 46 (47448-8375)
PHONE.....................812 720-4840
EMP: 99 EST: 2018
SALES (est): 6.96MM **Privately Held**
Web: www.hardtruth.com
SIC: 2085 Distilled and blended liquors

(G-12671)
HELMSBURG SAWMILL INC
Also Called: Pool Enterprises
2230 State Road 45 (47448-8401)
P.O. Box 3 (47435-0003)
PHONE.....................812 988-6161
Bill Pool, *Pr*
Susan Pool, *Sec*
Kevin S Pool, *VP*
EMP: 20 EST: 1973
SALES (est): 372.38K **Privately Held**
Web: www.helmsburgsawmill.com
SIC: 2421 2426 Lumber: rough, sawed, or planed; Hardwood dimension and flooring mills

(G-12672)
JWB GROUP LLC
Also Called: Brown County Forest Products
357 Brown Hill Rd (47448-8304)
PHONE.....................812 371-7344
John Booe, *CEO*
EMP: 5 EST: 2012
SALES (est): 468.53K **Privately Held**
SIC: 2421 Sawmills and planing mills, general

(G-12673)
KNIGHTS WOODWORKING LLC
3991 State Road 46 W (47448-8632)
PHONE.....................812 988-2106
EMP: 5 EST: 1984
SALES (est): 494.33K **Privately Held**
SIC: 2449 Rectangular boxes and crates, wood

(G-12674)
LE AIR CO INC
1313 Timber Crest Rd (47448-8523)
PHONE.....................812 988-1313
Gary Napier, *Pr*
Bruce Trumbauer, *VP*
Vicki Napier, *Sec*
EMP: 4 EST: 1966
SALES (est): 289.43K **Privately Held**
SIC: 3446 Brasswork, ornamental: structural

(G-12675)
MERCANTILE STORE (PA)
Also Called: Mercantile 1
44 N Van Buren St (47448-7029)
P.O. Box 335 (47448-0335)
PHONE.....................812 988-6939
Clenna Perkins, *Owner*
EMP: 2 EST: 1979
SQ FT: 1,000
SALES (est): 267.97K
SALES (corp-wide): 267.97K **Privately Held**
SIC: 5947 5699 2396 Gift shop; Sports apparel; Stamping fabric articles

(G-12676)
MOONSHINE LEATHER COMPANY INC
38 S Van Buren St (47448-7036)
P.O. Box 1652 (47448-1652)
PHONE.....................812 988-1326
EMP: 4 EST: 1992
SALES (est): 229.22K **Privately Held**
Web: www.moonshineleather.com
SIC: 3199 Equestrian related leather articles

(G-12677)
NASHVILLE TASTING ROOM
26 Honeysuckle Ln (47448-7017)
PHONE.....................812 720-7080
EMP: 3 EST: 2018
SALES (est): 74.47K **Privately Held**
Web: www.saltcreekwinery.com
SIC: 2084 Wines

(G-12678)
PGS LLC (PA)
Also Called: Trilogy Gallery
120 E Main St (47448-7008)
P.O. Box 1097 (47448-1097)
PHONE.....................812 988-4030
Grant Stuart, *Owner*
EMP: 13 EST: 1991
SQ FT: 2,800
SALES (est): 988.42K
SALES (corp-wide): 988.42K **Privately Held**
SIC: 5947 5999 2392 Gift shop; Christmas lights and decorations; Household furnishings, nec

(G-12679)
ROBERT CODY JACOBS
1635 Lucas Hollow Rd (47448-8586)
PHONE.....................812 606-5195
Robert Cody Jacobs, *Owner*
EMP: 1 EST: 2014
SALES (est): 53.91K **Privately Held**
SIC: 2411 Logging

(G-12680)
SINGING PINES PROJECTS INC
Also Called: Our Brown County
2499 State Road 45 (47448-8408)
P.O. Box 157 (47435-0157)
PHONE.....................812 988-8807
EMP: 1 EST: 1995
SALES (est): 229.77K **Privately Held**
Web: www.ourbrowncounty.com
SIC: 2759 Magazines: printing, nsk

(G-12681)
TWISTED WICK CANDLE CO
102 S Van Buren St (47448-7037)
P.O. Box 1249 (47448-1249)
PHONE.....................317 490-4789
EMP: 2 EST: 2007
SALES (est): 103.38K **Privately Held**
Web: www.twistedwick.com
SIC: 3999 Candles

(G-12682)
TYCO WELDING
6473 State Road 46 E (47448-8939)
PHONE.....................812 988-8770
EMP: 2 EST: 1997
SALES (est): 60.22K **Privately Held**
SIC: 7692 Welding repair

(G-12683)
WILKERSON LOGGING INC
4263 Hoover Rd (47448-8549)
PHONE.....................812 988-4960
EMP: 4 EST: 1992
SALES (est): 282.32K **Privately Held**
SIC: 2411 Logging camps and contractors

(G-12684)
WILKERSON SAWMILL
5400 Hoover Rd (47448-8544)
PHONE.....................812 988-7436
Dale Wilkerson, *Pt*
Norman Wilkerson, *Pt*

Kenneth Wilkerson, *Pt*
Robert Wilkerson, *Pt*
Terren Wilkerson, *Pt*
EMP: 7 EST: 1950
SALES (est): 495.46K **Privately Held**
SIC: 2421 Sawmills and planing mills, general

New Albany
Floyd County

(G-12685)
ACCUPRINT OF KENTUCKIANA INC
4101 Reas Ln (47150-2230)
PHONE.................................812 944-8603
Brian Branham, *Pr*
Leslie Reesor, *VP Sls*
EMP: 8 EST: 1997
SALES (est): 853.64K **Privately Held**
Web: www.accuprintink.com
SIC: 2752 Offset printing

(G-12686)
ADVANCE FABRICATORS INC
980 Progress Blvd (47150-2297)
PHONE.................................812 944-6941
Gary Ragsdale, *Pr*
Kimberly Ragsdale, *
EMP: 28 EST: 1976
SQ FT: 15,000
SALES (est): 4.79MM **Privately Held**
Web: www.advancefabricators.com
SIC: 3441 3535 Fabricated structural metal; Conveyors and conveying equipment

(G-12687)
ALLTERRAIN PAVING & CNSTR LLC
Also Called: APC Paving
2235 Corydon Pike (47150-6119)
P.O. Box 1248 (47151-1248)
PHONE.................................502 265-4731
John F Neace, *Managing Member*
EMP: 20 EST: 2015
SQ FT: 6,000
SALES (est): 4.86MM **Privately Held**
Web: www.apc-construct.com
SIC: 2951 Asphalt paving mixtures and blocks

(G-12688)
AMERICAN MACHINE & FABG CO INC
1223 E 8th St (47150-3245)
PHONE.................................812 944-4136
Norbert Andres, *Pr*
EMP: 8 EST: 1991
SQ FT: 4,000
SALES (est): 357.68K **Privately Held**
SIC: 7699 3441 7692 3444 Industrial machinery and equipment repair; Fabricated structural metal; Welding repair; Sheet metalwork

(G-12689)
ANNE PFEIFFER HOLDINGS INC
Also Called: Cimtech
325 Park East Blvd (47150)
PHONE.................................812 948-1422
Jesika Young, *CEO*
Anne Pfeiffer, *
EMP: 32 EST: 1975
SALES (est): 4.82MM **Privately Held**
Web: www.cimtechmachine.com
SIC: 3599 Machine shop, jobbing and repair

(G-12690)
AQUA UTILITY SERVICES LLC
1829 E Spring St Ste 106 (47150-1686)
PHONE.................................812 284-9243
EMP: 8 EST: 2003
SALES (est): 1.38MM **Privately Held**
Web: www.ausllc.com
SIC: 4953 2842 Sewage treatment facility; Disinfectants, household or industrial plant

(G-12691)
ARCHIBALD BROTHERS INTL INC
Also Called: Archibald Frozen Desserts
209 Quality Ave Ste 1 (47150-7256)
PHONE.................................812 941-8267
▲ **EMP: 9 EST:** 1992
SQ FT: 3,000
SALES (est): 951.36K **Privately Held**
SIC: 2024 Ices, flavored (frozen dessert)

(G-12692)
ASEMPAC INC
5300 Foundation Blvd (47150-9321)
PHONE.................................812 945-6303
Gary Parks, *Pr*
John R Slavsky Junior, *Pr*
James M Greer, *Sec*
▲ **EMP: 25 EST:** 1977
SQ FT: 18,000
SALES (est): 973.84K **Privately Held**
SIC: 7389 3479 7336 3993 Packaging and labeling services; Engraving jewelry, silverware, or metal; Silk screen design; Signs and advertising specialties

(G-12693)
ASPIRE INDUSTRIES
5329 Foundation Blvd (47150-9321)
PHONE.................................812 542-1561
Todd Dome, *Pr*
Virginia Morman, *Prin*
EMP: 11 EST: 2005
SALES (est): 239.69K **Privately Held**
Web: www.aerosolindia.in
SIC: 3999 Atomizers, toiletry

(G-12694)
B&W PACKAGING MFG LLC
4140 Capital Dr (47150-2283)
PHONE.................................812 280-9578
Mark Wasdovich, *
EMP: 42 EST: 2013
SQ FT: 100,000
SALES (est): 4.85MM **Privately Held**
Web: www.bandwpack.com
SIC: 2653 3086 Corrugated and solid fiber boxes; Packaging and shipping materials, foamed plastics

(G-12695)
BARE BONES CUSTOM WELDING
245 Merrywood Ln (47150-6167)
PHONE.................................502 773-2338
EMP: 4 EST: 2017
SALES (est): 28.27K **Privately Held**
SIC: 7692 Welding repair

(G-12696)
BARE METAL INC
4160 Capital Dr (47150)
PHONE.................................812 948-1313
Robert Burton, *Pr*
Debra Burton, *VP*
▲ **EMP: 19 EST:** 1982
SQ FT: 28,000
SALES (est): 2.37MM **Privately Held**
Web: www.baremetalinc.com
SIC: 3471 1799 Plating and polishing; Paint and wallpaper stripping

(G-12697)
BEACH ACQUISITION CO LLC
999 Progress Blvd (47150-2258)
PHONE.................................812 945-2688
EMP: 434
SALES (corp-wide): 484.4MM **Privately Held**
Web: www.nyxinc.com
SIC: 3089 Injection molding of plastics
HQ: Beach Acquisition Co. Llc
3900 Green Valley Rd
New Albany IN 47150
812 945-2688

(G-12698)
BEACH ACQUISITION CO LLC (HQ)
Also Called: Nyx New Albany
3900 Green Valley Rd (47150-4266)
P.O. Box 227 (47151-0227)
PHONE.................................812 945-2688
▲ **EMP: 266 EST:** 1972
SALES (est): 107.57MM
SALES (corp-wide): 484.4MM **Privately Held**
Web: www.nyxinc.com
SIC: 3089 3544 Injection molding of plastics; Special dies, tools, jigs, and fixtures
PA: Nyx, Llc
14909 N Beck Rd
Plymouth MI 48170
734 261-4324

(G-12699)
BERT R HUNCILMAN & SON INC
115 Security Pkwy (47150-9366)
P.O. Box 1027 (47151-1027)
PHONE.................................812 945-3544
EMP: 150 EST: 1963
SALES (est): 9.01MM **Privately Held**
Web: www.huncilman.com
SIC: 3444 Sheet metalwork

(G-12700)
BETHLEHEM PACKG DIE CUTNG INC
802 E 8th St (47150-3264)
PHONE.................................812 282-8740
John C Denney, *Pr*
Vicky L Denney, *Pr*
EMP: 25 EST: 1992
SQ FT: 35,000
SALES (est): 2.54MM **Privately Held**
Web: www.bethpac.com
SIC: 2675 5199 Cardboard cut-outs, panels, and foundations: die-cut; Packaging materials

(G-12701)
BIODOT OF INDIANA INC
3081 Autumn Hill Trl (47150-9468)
P.O. Box 2663 (47131-2663)
PHONE.................................812 945-0915
Susan Wagner, *Pr*
EMP: 1 EST: 2004
SALES (est): 122.85K **Privately Held**
Web: www.biodots.net
SIC: 3829 Measuring and controlling devices, nec

(G-12702)
BLACKBIRD
1636 Slate Run Rd (47150-6266)
PHONE.................................812 944-0799
EMP: 3 EST: 2020
SALES (est): 260.56K **Privately Held**
Web: www.blackbirdco.com
SIC: 5063 3648 3643 Electrical apparatus and equipment; Lighting equipment, nec; Current-carrying wiring services

(G-12703)
BLUE GRASS CHEMICAL SPC LLC (PA)
895 Industrial Blvd (47150-2252)
PHONE.................................812 948-1115
Anthony S Manna, *Ch*
Mark S Corr, *Pr*
▲ **EMP: 11 EST:** 1969
SQ FT: 31,500
SALES (est): 2.68MM
SALES (corp-wide): 2.68MM **Privately Held**
Web: www.bluegrasschemical.com
SIC: 2899 3555 2869 Metal treating compounds; Printing trades machinery; Industrial organic chemicals, nec

(G-12704)
BOTTOM SIGN LLC
4239 Earnings Way (47150-7204)
PHONE.................................812 949-7446
EMP: 7 EST: 2020
SALES (est): 243.69K **Privately Held**
Web: www.bsigngroup.com
SIC: 3993 Signs and advertising specialties

(G-12705)
BRILL STUFF LLC
122 Spickert Knob Rd (47150-4240)
PHONE.................................502 889-9705
EMP: 1 EST: 2021
SALES (est): 30K **Privately Held**
Web: www.brillstuff.com
SIC: 2741 Internet publishing and broadcasting

(G-12706)
BRUCE FOX INC (PA)
1909 Mcdonald Ln (47150-2498)
PHONE.................................812 945-3511
John R Slavsky, *Ch Bd*
James M Greer, *Pr*
John R Slavsky Iii, *VP*
David H Morrison, *
Dave Miller, *
▲ **EMP: 129 EST:** 1937
SQ FT: 50,000
SALES (est): 12.57MM
SALES (corp-wide): 12.57MM **Privately Held**
Web: www.brucefox.com
SIC: 3914 5094 Trophies, nsk; Trophies

(G-12707)
BRYANT INDUSTRIES INC
Also Called: Industrial Machine & Tool
201b E 18th St (47150-1601)
P.O. Box 1593 (47151-1593)
PHONE.................................812 944-6010
Lonnie Bryant, *Pr*
Jerry Bryant, *Treas*
EMP: 10 EST: 1992
SQ FT: 10,000
SALES (est): 961.76K **Privately Held**
Web: www.industrialmachineandtool.com
SIC: 3599 3544 Machine shop, jobbing and repair; Special dies, tools, jigs, and fixtures

(G-12708)
CABINETS BY RICK INC
1630 Grant Line Rd (47150-3929)
P.O. Box 113 (47124-0113)
PHONE.................................812 945-2220
Richard L Henson Junior, *Pr*
Patricia A Henson, *Sec*
EMP: 4 EST: 1985
SQ FT: 9,600
SALES (est): 336.2K **Privately Held**
Web: www.cabinetsbyrick.com
SIC: 2434 Wood kitchen cabinets

(G-12709)
CARTON CRAFT CORPORATION
2549 Charlestown Rd Ste 1 (47150-2576)
PHONE.................................812 949-4393
▲ **EMP:** 60

New Albany - Floyd County (G-12710)

SIC: 2653 Boxes, solid fiber: made from purchased materials

(G-12710)
CENVEO WORLDWIDE LIMITED
Also Called: Discount Labels
4115 Profit Ct (47150-7225)
PHONE..................................800 995-9500
Kim Ralston, *Brnch Mgr*
EMP: 65
SALES (corp-wide): 1.04B **Privately Held**
Web: www.discountlabels.com
SIC: 2677 2752 2759 Envelopes; Commercial printing, lithographic; Labels and seals: printing, nsk
HQ: Cenveo Worldwide Limited
200 Frst Stamford Pl Fl 2
Stamford CT 06902
203 595-3000

(G-12711)
CHEF HYMIE INC
Also Called: Chef Hymie Grande
13 Wynn Gate Ct (47150-6529)
PHONE..................................201 218-4378
EMP: 1 EST: 2003
SALES (est): 60K **Privately Held**
SIC: 2099 7389 Sauces: dry mixes; Business Activities at Non-Commercial Site

(G-12712)
CHESTER POOL SYSTEMS INC
5311 Foundation Blvd (47150-9321)
PHONE..................................812 949-7333
Robert D Uhl, *Pr*
Greg Carnforth, *
John W Uhl, *
EMP: 50 EST: 1988
SQ FT: 44,000
SALES (est): 8.86MM **Privately Held**
Web: www.chesterpools.com
SIC: 3949 1799 Swimming pools, except plastic; Swimming pool construction

(G-12713)
CINQ LLC
Also Called: Cinq5
802 E 8th St (47150-3264)
PHONE..................................405 361-0097
Stephen Brady, *CEO*
EMP: 8 EST: 2018
SALES (est): 150K **Privately Held**
Web: www.cinq5llc.com
SIC: 3578 7629 5961 Calculating and accounting equipment; Circuit board repair; Computer equipment and electronics, mail order

(G-12714)
CLARK FOODS INC (PA)
Also Called: American Beverage Marketers
810 Progress Blvd (47150-2257)
P.O. Box 347 (47151-0347)
PHONE..................................812 949-3075
George Wagner Iii, *Pr*
Thomas B Clark, *Sec*
Bill Hinkebein, *VP*
Charles E Wagner, *VP*
William A Hinkebein, *VP*
◆ EMP: 40 EST: 1946
SQ FT: 110,000
SALES (est): 49.23MM
SALES (corp-wide): 49.23MM **Privately Held**
Web: www.abmcocktails.com
SIC: 5149 2086 Soft drinks; Bottled and canned soft drinks

(G-12715)
COFFEYS CUSTOM UPHOLSTERY
610 Silver St (47150-1739)
PHONE..................................812 948-8611
Jim Coffey, *Pt*
Gary Coffey, *Pt*
Mark Anthony Coffey, *Pt*
EMP: 4 EST: 1964
SQ FT: 8,700
SALES (est): 211.32K **Privately Held**
SIC: 7641 5712 2512 Reupholstery; Furniture stores; Upholstered household furniture

(G-12716)
CONFORMA CLAD INC
501 Park East Blvd (47150-7252)
PHONE..................................812 948-2118
▲ EMP: 62 EST: 1996
SALES (est): 9.59MM
SALES (corp-wide): 2.05B **Publicly Held**
Web: www.kennametal.com
SIC: 3479 Coating of metals and formed products
PA: Kennametal Inc.
525 Wlliam Penn Pl Ste 33
Pittsburgh PA 15219
412 248-8000

(G-12717)
CUSTOM PLYWOOD INC (PA)
Also Called: CPI Aircraft Interiors
301 Quality Ave (47150-7264)
PHONE..................................812 944-7300
Roger Ledbetter, *Pr*
Pamela Ledbetter, *Sec*
Doug Durham, *Genl Mgr*
Pat Hecker, *Contrlr*
EMP: 50 EST: 1991
SQ FT: 80,000
SALES (est): 8.86MM **Privately Held**
Web: www.cpiplywood.com
SIC: 2435 Hardwood plywood, prefinished

(G-12718)
CYCLONE ADG LLC
166 Mills Ln (47150-6601)
PHONE..................................520 403-2927
Scott Rollefstad, *Engr*
John Waszczak, *Prin*
Arthur De Leon, *Prin*
Mathew Culbertson, *Prin*
EMP: 2 EST: 2012
SALES (est): 110.62K **Privately Held**
SIC: 3812 Aircraft/aerospace flight instruments and guidance systems

(G-12719)
DIMENSION PLYWOOD INC
Also Called: Architectural Plywood
415 Industrial Blvd (47150-2244)
PHONE..................................812 944-6491
Paul Horstman, *Pr*
EMP: 8 EST: 1977
SALES (est): 1.74MM **Privately Held**
Web: www.dimensionhardwoods.com
SIC: 2435 5031 Plywood, hardwood or hardwood faced; Veneer

(G-12720)
DISCOUNT LABELS LLC
Also Called: Labels Unlimited
4115 Profit Ct (47150-7207)
P.O. Box 709 (47151-0709)
PHONE..................................812 945-2617
▲ EMP: 1318
Web: www.discountlabels.com
SIC: 2679 3069 5199 Labels, paper: made from purchased material; Stationer's rubber sundries; Advertising specialties

(G-12721)
DISTILLERY 64 LLC
800 E 8th St Ste 107 (47150-3264)
PHONE..................................502 536-7485
Brett Schlagel, *Pr*
EMP: 3 EST: 2018
SALES (est): 51.9K **Privately Held**
Web: www.distillery64.com
SIC: 2085 Distilled and blended liquors

(G-12722)
E M CUMMINGS VENEERS INC
601 E 4th St (47150-3312)
P.O. Box 49 (47151-0049)
PHONE..................................812 944-2269
Edward J Zoeller, *Pr*
EMP: 20 EST: 1936
SQ FT: 35,000
SALES (est): 1.69MM **Privately Held**
Web: www.emcveneer.com
SIC: 2435 Veneer stock, hardwood

(G-12723)
EAVK LEGACY INC (PA)
6000 Grant Line Rd (47150-9622)
PHONE..................................812 246-4461
Mike Ludden, *Pr*
Kyle Ludden, *VP*
Gregory Bickel, *VP Sls*
Robert Burgan, *VP*
C O Cross, *Sec*
EMP: 20 EST: 1935
SQ FT: 69,500
SALES (est): 9.24MM
SALES (corp-wide): 9.24MM **Privately Held**
Web: www.leebp.com
SIC: 3272 5211 Concrete products, precast, nec; Brick

(G-12724)
ELECTROMECHANICAL RES LABS
Also Called: Erl
2560 Charlestown Rd (47150)
P.O. Box 1026 (47151)
PHONE..................................812 948-8484
Stephen Wilkins, *Pr*
EMP: 50 EST: 1970
SQ FT: 35,000
SALES (est): 9.55MM **Privately Held**
Web: www.erlinc.com
SIC: 3625 Marine and navy auxiliary controls

(G-12725)
ENCOURAGE PUBLISHING LLC
Also Called: Encourage Books
1116 Creekview Cir (47150)
PHONE..................................812 987-6148
Leslie Turner, *Owner*
EMP: 1 EST: 2014
SALES (est): 119.02K **Privately Held**
Web: www.encouragepublishing.com
SIC: 2741 8748 8999 7338 Miscellaneous publishing; Publishing consultant; Writing for publication; Formal writing services

(G-12726)
ESAREY HARDWOOD CREATIONS LLC
534 Hoffman Dr (47150-7600)
PHONE..................................419 610-6486
Joseph Esarey, *Prin*
EMP: 5 EST: 2015
SALES (est): 50.24K **Privately Held**
Web: www.esareyhardwoodcreations.com
SIC: 2499 Wood products, nec

(G-12727)
FAITH FORGOTTEN FIREARMS LLC
1812 Corydon Pike (47150)
PHONE..................................614 940-9145
EMP: 7 EST: 2017
SALES (est): 404.26K **Privately Held**
Web: www.faithforgotten.com
SIC: 3751 Motorcycles and related parts

(G-12728)
FALLS CITIES PRINTING INC
323 Vincennes St (47150-1622)
PHONE..................................812 949-9051
Phillip M Alles, *Pr*
EMP: 10 EST: 1989
SQ FT: 16,000
SALES (est): 924.43K **Privately Held**
Web: www.fallscities.com
SIC: 2752 2761 Offset printing; Manifold business forms

(G-12729)
FIRE KING INTERNATIONAL LLC (PA)
900 Park Pl (47150)
P.O. Box 559 (47150)
PHONE..................................812 822-5574
Jim Poteet, *CEO*
Gary Weisman, *
William Wolf, *
Ed Carpenter, *
Michael Lynch, *
◆ EMP: 41 EST: 1986
SQ FT: 30,000
SALES (est): 49.4MM
SALES (corp-wide): 49.4MM **Privately Held**
Web: www.fireking.com
SIC: 5044 2522 3499 Vaults and safes; Filing boxes, cabinets, and cases: except wood; Safes and vaults, metal

(G-12730)
FKI SECURITY GROUP LLC
Also Called: Fire King Security Group
101 Security Pkwy (47150-9366)
P.O. Box 559 (47151-0559)
PHONE..................................812 948-8400
◆ EMP: 467
Web: www.fireking.com
SIC: 3429 5044 3499 2522 Locks or lock sets; Vaults and safes; Safes and vaults, metal; Filing boxes, cabinets, and cases: except wood

(G-12731)
FLOYD COUNTY BREWING CO LLC
129 W Main St (47150-5958)
PHONE..................................502 724-3202
Brian Hampton, *Admn*
EMP: 10 EST: 2015
SALES (est): 345.62K **Privately Held**
Web: www.floydcountybrewing.com
SIC: 2082 Malt beverages

(G-12732)
FOAM FABRICATORS INC
Also Called: Foam Fabricators
950 Progress Blvd (47150-2296)
PHONE..................................812 948-1696
James Hughes, *Mgr*
EMP: 1
SQ FT: 30,000
Web: www.foamfabricatorsinc.com
SIC: 2821 3086 Polystyrene resins; Plastics foam products
HQ: Foam Fabricators, Inc.
8722 E San Albrto Dr Ste
Scottsdale AZ 85258

GEOGRAPHIC SECTION

New Albany - Floyd County (G-12759)

(G-12733)
FOUR DAUGHTERS LLC
3000 Overlook Trce (47150-5269)
PHONE..................805 868-7456
Blair Richardson, *Prin*
EMP: 6 **EST:** 2018
SALES (est): 125.13K **Privately Held**
Web: www.4daughters.net
SIC: 2431 Millwork

(G-12734)
FRANK H MONROE HEATING & COOLG
Also Called: Honeywell Authorized Dealer
595 Industrial Blvd (47150-2246)
PHONE..................812 945-2566
Frank H Monroe, *Ch Bd*
Steve Laduke, *Pr*
Carla Johnson, *Sec*
James Crosier, *VP*
EMP: 23 **EST:** 1953
SQ FT: 16,000
SALES (est): 974.1K **Privately Held**
Web: www.frankhmonroe.com
SIC: 1711 3444 Warm air heating and air conditioning contractor; Sheet metalwork

(G-12735)
FUTURE MOLD INC
100 Galvin Way (47150-1500)
PHONE..................812 941-8661
Christopher Poff, *Pr*
Jerry Mehling, *VP*
Marlin Andres, *Stockholder*
EMP: 17 **EST:** 1997
SQ FT: 7,500
SALES (est): 2.46MM **Privately Held**
Web: www.futuremold.com
SIC: 3544 3089 8711 Forms (molds), for foundry and plastics working machinery; Injection molding of plastics; Engineering services

(G-12736)
GEORGES CUSTOM WOOD WKG INC
614 Maple Ln (47150-5245)
PHONE..................812 944-3344
George Kreilein, *Pr*
EMP: 3 **EST:** 1981
SALES (est): 235.46K **Privately Held**
SIC: 2511 Lawn furniture: wood

(G-12737)
GLOBE INDUSTRIES LLC
20 W 7th St (47150)
PHONE..................812 301-2600
Marlin Andres, *Mgr*
EMP: 9 **EST:** 2014
SALES (est): 623.76K **Privately Held**
SIC: 3498 Fabricated pipe and fittings

(G-12738)
GLOBE LLC
20 W 7th St (47150-5912)
PHONE..................812 949-2001
Marlin Andres, *CEO*
Marlin Andres, *Managing Member*
Brian Kruer, *
EMP: 160 **EST:** 2016
SALES (est): 52.98MM **Privately Held**
Web: www.globefab.com
SIC: 3498 Fabricated pipe and fittings

(G-12739)
GLOBE MECHANICAL INC
20 W 7th St (47150-5912)
PHONE..................812 949-2001
Marlin Andres, *Pr*
Bryan Kruer, *
Deanna Beville, *

EMP: 99 **EST:** 1985
SQ FT: 40,000
SALES (est): 55.48MM **Privately Held**
Web: www.globefab.com
SIC: 3498 Tube fabricating (contract bending and shaping)

(G-12740)
HARTFORD HEAT TREATMENT
37 W 5th St (47150-5910)
PHONE..................812 725-8272
Mike Simmons, *VP Opers*
EMP: 6 **EST:** 2013
SALES (est): 192.97K **Privately Held**
SIC: 3398 Metal heat treating

(G-12741)
HIM GENTLEMANS BOUTIQUE
314 Pearl St (47150-3418)
PHONE..................812 924-7441
EMP: 5 **EST:** 2017
SALES (est): 182.13K **Privately Held**
Web: www.shophimandher.com
SIC: 2389 2321 3143 Men's miscellaneous accessories; Men's and boys' dress shirts; Dress shoes, men's

(G-12742)
HUBCAPS GALORE INC
311 W Main St (47150-5923)
PHONE..................812 944-5200
EMP: 1 **EST:** 1996
SALES (est): 121.96K **Privately Held**
SIC: 2396 Automotive and apparel trimmings

(G-12743)
IMAGE VAULT LLC
101 Security Pkwy (47150-9366)
PHONE..................812 948-8400
Jim Poteet, *CEO*
Michael Lynch, *CFO*
EMP: 9 **EST:** 1997
SALES (est): 2.46MM **Privately Held**
Web: www.image-vault.com
SIC: 7371 3699 3651 Computer software systems analysis and design, custom; Electrical equipment and supplies, nec; Household audio and video equipment

(G-12744)
IMI SOUTH LLC
Also Called: Irving Materials
1732 Lincoln Ave (47150-3959)
PHONE..................812 945-6605
Mike Harman, *Brnch Mgr*
EMP: 46
SALES (corp-wide): 814.09MM **Privately Held**
Web: www.irvmat.com
SIC: 3273 Ready-mixed concrete
HQ: Imi South, Llc
  1440 Selinda Ave
  Louisville KY 40213
  502 456-6930

(G-12745)
IMPRESSIVE PRINTING
515 E Daisy Ln (47150-4446)
PHONE..................812 913-1101
Ketra Taylor, *Prin*
EMP: 5 **EST:** 2014
SALES (est): 116.55K **Privately Held**
SIC: 2752 Offset printing

(G-12746)
INDCO INC
4040 Earnings Way (47150-2275)
PHONE..................812 945-4383
Mark Hennis, *Pr*
Kris Wilberding, *VP*

▼ **EMP:** 8 **EST:** 1975
SQ FT: 11,000
SALES (est): 2.19MM **Privately Held**
Web: www.indco.com
SIC: 3559 5084 3586 3531 Paint making machinery; Industrial machinery and equipment; Measuring and dispensing pumps; Construction machinery

(G-12747)
INDUSTRIAL PHYSICS INC
100 Quality Ave (47150-2272)
PHONE..................812 981-3133
EMP: 11 **EST:** 2014
SALES (est): 511.42K **Privately Held**
SIC: 3823 Industrial process measurement equipment

(G-12748)
INSCOPE MEDICAL SOLUTIONS INC
110 E Market St (47150-3410)
P.O. Box 726 (47131-0726)
PHONE..................502 882-0183
Margaret Galloway, *CEO*
Adam Casson, *COO*
EMP: 2 **EST:** 2016
SALES (est): 175.72K **Privately Held**
Web: www.inscopemedical.com
SIC: 3841 Surgical and medical instruments

(G-12749)
INTEGRITY SIGN SOLUTIONS INC
4302 Security Pkwy (47150-9374)
PHONE..................502 233-8755
Melissa Hobbs, *Pr*
Michael Hobbs, *VP*
EMP: 5 **EST:** 2010
SQ FT: 25,000
SALES (est): 1.32MM **Privately Held**
Web: app.integritysign.com
SIC: 5199 3993 Advertising specialties; Signs and advertising specialties

(G-12750)
J & J PALLET CORP (PA)
2234 E Market St (47150-1508)
P.O. Box 583 (47151-0583)
PHONE..................812 944-8670
John C Jones, *Pr*
Susan Jackson, *
EMP: 25 **EST:** 1972
SQ FT: 13,000
SALES (est): 8.49MM
SALES (corp-wide): 8.49MM **Privately Held**
Web: www.jjpallet.com
SIC: 2448 7699 Pallets, wood; Pallet repair

(G-12751)
JACKSON TECHNOLOGIES LLC
3007 Charlestown Xing Ste B200 (47150-8313)
PHONE..................812 258-9939
Brian Jackson, *Prin*
EMP: 7 **EST:** 2016
SALES (est): 194.2K **Privately Held**
Web: www.jacksontechconsult.com
SIC: 3861 Photographic equipment and supplies

(G-12752)
JANS SEWING THINGS
201 Hausfeldt Ln (47150-2214)
PHONE..................812 945-8113
EMP: 1 **EST:** 1992
SALES (est): 49K **Privately Held**
SIC: 2391 Curtains and draperies

(G-12753)
JASON SWORD LLC
1405 Valley View Rd (47150-5434)
PHONE..................502 550-4183
Jason Sword, *Owner*
EMP: 5 **EST:** 2018
SALES (est): 72.1K **Privately Held**
SIC: 3421 Cutlery

(G-12754)
JNJ BLUE ENTERPRISE LLC (PA)
3012 Charlestown Xing (47150-9380)
PHONE..................502 593-8464
Myung Kee Kim, *Admn*
EMP: 5 **EST:** 2016
SALES (est): 152.21K
SALES (corp-wide): 152.21K **Privately Held**
SIC: 2834 Pharmaceutical preparations

(G-12755)
JONES POPCORN INC
Also Called: Clark's Snacks
125 Quality Ave (47150-2287)
P.O. Box 48 (47151-0048)
PHONE..................812 941-8810
Ryan Jones, *Pr*
James Jones, *
Linda Jones, *
EMP: 85 **EST:** 1992
SQ FT: 80,000
SALES (est): 9.41MM **Privately Held**
Web: www.clarksnacks.com
SIC: 2099 Popcorn, packaged: except already popped

(G-12756)
K & I HARD CHROME INC
1900 E Main St (47150-5798)
PHONE..................812 948-1166
Robert A Eckerle, *Pr*
EMP: 35 **EST:** 1974
SQ FT: 32,000
SALES (est): 2.49MM **Privately Held**
Web: ki-hard-chrome.wisebuyingmall.com
SIC: 3471 Electroplating of metals or formed products

(G-12757)
KEEN SCREEN
120 Edgemont Dr (47150-4207)
PHONE..................812 989-8885
EMP: 3 **EST:** 2017
SALES (est): 148.99K **Privately Held**
Web: www.keenscreen.com
SIC: 2759 Screen printing

(G-12758)
KEEN SCREEN
3314 Grant Line Rd (47150-6411)
PHONE..................812 945-5336
Jacob Boger, *Prin*
EMP: 5 **EST:** 2011
SALES (est): 81.77K **Privately Held**
SIC: 2759 Screen printing

(G-12759)
KENNAMETAL INC
Also Called: Kennametal Consora Clad
501 Park East Blvd (47150-7252)
PHONE..................812 948-2118
Johnny Martin, *Brnch Mgr*
EMP: 53
SALES (corp-wide): 2.05B **Publicly Held**
Web: www.kennametal.com
SIC: 3545 Cutting tools for machine tools
PA: Kennametal Inc.
  525 Wlliam Penn Pl Ste 33
  Pittsburgh PA 15219

New Albany - Floyd County (G-12760) — GEOGRAPHIC SECTION

412 248-8000

(G-12760)
KINGS-QLITY RSTRTION SVCS LLC
1818 E Market St (47150-1657)
PHONE..................812 944-4347
EMP: 13 **EST:** 2008
SALES (est): 2.43MM **Privately Held**
Web: www.kingsqualityrestoration.com
SIC: 1522 2842 7217 Residential construction, nec; Specialty cleaning; Carpet and upholstery cleaning

(G-12761)
KONECRANES INC
Also Called: Louisville Division
900 Progress Blvd (47150-2259)
PHONE..................812 941-1250
EMP: 33
Web: www.konecranes.com
SIC: 3536 Hoists, cranes, and monorails
HQ: Konecranes, Inc.
   4401 Gateway Blvd
   Springfield OH 45502

(G-12762)
LAGNAIPPE LLC
Also Called: PIP Printing
802 E 8th St (47150-3264)
PHONE..................812 288-9291
EMP: 7 **EST:** 2003
SALES (est): 707.85K **Privately Held**
Web: www.bethpac.com
SIC: 2752 Offset printing

(G-12763)
LAUYANS HOLDINGS INC
Also Called: W.M. Kelley Co. Inc.
620 Durgee Rd (47150-8816)
P.O. Box 37326 (40233-7326)
EMP: 25 **EST:** 1986
SALES (est): 5.33MM
SALES (corp-wide): 24.66MM **Privately Held**
Web: www.wmkelley.com
SIC: 3535 Conveyors and conveying equipment
PA: W M Kelley Co Inc
   620 Durgee Rd
   New Albany IN 47150
   812 945-3529

(G-12764)
LITHOCRAFT INC
1502 Beeler St (47150-3199)
PHONE..................812 948-1608
EMP: 40
Web: www.lithocraftinc.com
SIC: 2752 Commercial printing, lithographic

(G-12765)
LOUISVILLE VENEER CORP
301 E Elm St (47150-3430)
PHONE..................502 500-7176
Marc Quirici, *CEO*
Giuseppe Quirici, *Pr*
Marc Quirici, *Contrlr*
Richard Witt, *Contrlr*
▼ **EMP:** 6 **EST:** 1996
SQ FT: 45,000
SALES (est): 649.84K **Privately Held**
Web: www.superiorveneer.com
SIC: 2435 Veneer stock, hardwood

(G-12766)
LOZIER MACHINERY INCORPORATED
695 Industrial Blvd (47150-2248)
PHONE..................812 945-2558
Eric R Lozier, *Pr*
EMP: 8 **EST:** 2002
SALES (est): 930.09K **Privately Held**
Web: www.loziermachinery.com
SIC: 3553 Woodworking machinery

(G-12767)
LSI WALLCOVERING INC (PA)
Also Called: LSI Wallcovering
2073 Mcdonald Ave (47150-3759)
PHONE..................502 458-1502
Philip J Tarullo, *Pr*
Greg Bowling, *
Edward Ernest, *
▲ **EMP:** 95 **EST:** 1978
SQ FT: 4,800
SALES (est): 24.34MM
SALES (corp-wide): 24.34MM **Privately Held**
Web: www.versawallcovering.com
SIC: 2851 3999 Vinyl coatings, strippable; Feathers and feather products

(G-12768)
LUME DEODORANT
5102 Barack Obama Way (47150-4444)
PHONE..................623 227-8724
EMP: 4 **EST:** 2020
SALES (est): 176.24K **Privately Held**
Web: www.lumedeodorant.com
SIC: 2844 Perfumes, cosmetics and other toilet preparations

(G-12769)
M & M TABLETOPS LLC
4218 Payne Koehler Rd (47150-9521)
PHONE..................502 396-9236
Shawn Mitchell, *Owner*
EMP: 4 **EST:** 2018
SALES (est): 175.55K **Privately Held**
Web: www.mmtabletops.com
SIC: 2431 Millwork

(G-12770)
MANITOWOC BEVERAGE EQP INC (DH)
Also Called: Flomatic International
645 Park East Blvd Ste 5 (47150-7272)
PHONE..................812 246-7000
Michael J Kachmer, *Pr*
Terry Growcock, *
Tim Wood, *
T G Musial, *
C J Laurino, *
▲ **EMP:** 160 **EST:** 1902
SALES (est): 30.9MM
SALES (corp-wide): 4.8B **Privately Held**
Web: www.multiplexbeverage.com
SIC: 3585 Ice making machinery
HQ: Welbilt, Inc.
   2227 Welbilt Blvd
   Trinity FL 34655
   727 375-7010

(G-12771)
MANITOWOC BEVERAGE SYSTEMS INC (DH)
Also Called: M B S
645 Park East Blvd Ste 5 (47150-7272)
PHONE..................800 367-4233
Terry D Growcock, *Pr*
John Barber, *
Errol D Flynn, *
Glenn E Tellock, *
Robert R Friedl, *
◆ **EMP:** 198 **EST:** 1998
SALES (est): 92.51MM
SALES (corp-wide): 4.8B **Privately Held**
Web: www.multiplexbeverage.com
SIC: 3585 Soda fountain and beverage dispensing equipment and parts
HQ: Welbilt, Inc.
   2227 Welbilt Blvd
   Trinity FL 34655
   727 375-7010

(G-12772)
MARTIN INDUSTRIES
4235 Earnings Way (47150-7204)
PHONE..................502 553-6599
Nancy Martin, *Prin*
EMP: 6 **EST:** 2009
SALES (est): 198.41K **Privately Held**
SIC: 3999 Manufacturing industries, nec

(G-12773)
MEDISHIELD
1598 Rector Ln (47150-1934)
PHONE..................502 939-9903
EMP: 4 **EST:** 2018
SALES (est): 191.69K **Privately Held**
Web: www.medishieldinc.com
SIC: 3845 Electromedical equipment

(G-12774)
MEILINK SAFE COMPANY
101 Security Pkwy (47150-9366)
P.O. Box 559 (47151-0559)
PHONE..................812 941-0024
Van G Carlisle, *Pr*
Douglas J Voet, *
EMP: 83 **EST:** 1994
SALES (est): 1.5MM
SALES (corp-wide): 49.4MM **Privately Held**
SIC: 3499 5044 2522 5021 Safes and vaults, metal; Vaults and safes; Filing boxes, cabinets, and cases: except wood; Filing units
PA: Fk Safety And Security, L.L.C
   900 Park Pl
   New Albany IN 47150
   812 822-5574

(G-12775)
METAL DYNAMICS LTD
30 E 10th St (47150-5837)
PHONE..................812 949-7998
▲ **EMP:** 20 **EST:** 1995
SQ FT: 75,000
SALES (est): 2.22MM **Privately Held**
Web: www.metaldynamicsltd.com
SIC: 2542 3441 3444 Cabinets: show, display, or storage: except wood; Fabricated structural metal; Sheet metalwork

(G-12776)
METALITE CORPORATION
1815 Troy St (47150-5775)
PHONE..................812 944-6600
Marvin Friedman, *Pr*
Wane Friedman, *
EMP: 23 **EST:** 1973
SQ FT: 200,000
SALES (est): 479.94K **Privately Held**
Web: www.metalite.net
SIC: 3645 3646 3648 Residential lighting fixtures; Commercial lighting fixtures; Reflectors, for lighting equipment: metal

(G-12777)
MEYER ICE CREAM LLC
209 Quality Ave Ste 3 (47150-7256)
PHONE..................812 941-8267
Corey Merz, *Pr*
EMP: 5 **EST:** 2015
SALES (est): 468.64K **Privately Held**
Web: www.meyericecream.com
SIC: 2024 Ice cream and frozen deserts

(G-12778)
MIDWEST METAL WORKS INC
921 Progress Blvd (47150)
PHONE..................812 981-0810
Bob Klein, *CEO*
▲ **EMP:** 15 **EST:** 2005
SALES (est): 2.62MM **Privately Held**
Web: www.midwestmetalworksinc.com
SIC: 3444 Sheet metalwork

(G-12779)
MIDWEST SEED COATING LLC
2020 E Main St (47150-1668)
P.O. Box 967 (47150-0967)
PHONE..................812 949-7459
Kent L Johnson, *Genl Mgr*
EMP: 6 **EST:** 2017
SALES (est): 235.46K **Privately Held**
Web: www.summitseedcoatings.com
SIC: 3999 Seeds, coated or treated, from purchased seeds

(G-12780)
MIDWEST-TEK INC
4345 Security Pkwy (47150-9374)
PHONE..................812 981-3551
Stephen R Wallace, *Pr*
Sheila Wallace, *VP*
EMP: 17 **EST:** 2013
SALES (est): 1.15MM **Privately Held**
Web: www.midwest-tekinc.com
SIC: 3089 Injection molding of plastics

(G-12781)
MITCHELL VENEERS INC
4250 Earnings Way (47150-7203)
PHONE..................812 941-9663
Stephen Mitchell, *Pr*
▼ **EMP:** 4 **EST:** 1990
SALES (est): 448.51K **Privately Held**
Web: www.mitchellveneer.net
SIC: 2435 5031 Veneer stock, hardwood; Lumber: rough, dressed, and finished

(G-12782)
MP GLOBAL PRODUCTS LLC
890 Central Ct (47150-2270)
PHONE..................866 751-3765
EMP: 27
SALES (corp-wide): 20.55MM **Privately Held**
Web: www.mpglobalproducts.com
SIC: 2299 Padding and wadding, textile
PA: Mp Global Products, Llc
   2500 Old Hadar Rd
   Norfolk NE 68701
   402 379-9695

(G-12783)
MULTIPLEX COMPANY INC (DH)
645 Park East Blvd Ste 5 (47150-7272)
PHONE..................812 246-7000
Terry Growcock, *CEO*
J Walter Kisling Iii, *Pr*
Ray Uetrecht, *CFO*
◆ **EMP:** 61 **EST:** 1906
SALES (est): 9.54MM
SALES (corp-wide): 4.8B **Privately Held**
Web: www.multiplexbeverage.com
SIC: 3585 Cold drink dispensing equipment (not coin-operated)
HQ: Welbilt, Inc.
   2227 Welbilt Blvd
   Trinity FL 34655
   727 375-7010

(G-12784)
NEXGEN MOLD & TOOL INC
4300 Security Pkwy (47150-9374)
P.O. Box 6747 (47151-6747)

▲ = Import ▼ = Export
◆ = Import/Export

GEOGRAPHIC SECTION

New Albany - Floyd County (G-12809)

PHONE.............................812 945-3375
John Lukes, Pr
Nichole Lukes, *
Kevin Rose, *
▼ EMP: 40 EST: 2008
SQ FT: 26,000
SALES (est): 8.45MM Privately Held
Web: www.nexgenmoldandtool.com
SIC: 3089 3544 Injection molded finished plastics products, nec; Special dies, tools, jigs, and fixtures

(G-12785)
NVSD LLC
2235 Corydon Pike (47150-6119)
PHONE.............................502 561-0007
Darren Pavey, Genl Mgr
EMP: 6 EST: 2015
SALES (est): 116K Privately Held
SIC: 3543 Foundry patternmaking

(G-12786)
NYX LLC
3900 Green Valley Rd (47150-4266)
PHONE.............................734 838-3570
EMP: 1000
SALES (corp-wide): 484.4MM Privately Held
Web: www.nyxinc.com
SIC: 2671 3714 3565 Paper; coated and laminated packaging; Motor vehicle parts and accessories; Packaging machinery
PA: Nyx, Llc
    14909 N Beck Rd
    Plymouth MI 48170
    734 261-4324

(G-12787)
OHIO VALLEY CREATIVE ENRGY INC
626 Albany St (47150-5004)
PHONE.............................502 468-9787
EMP: 3 EST: 2010
SALES (est): 91.24K Privately Held
Web: www.ohiovalleycreativenergy.org
SIC: 3269 Pottery products, nec

(G-12788)
OHIO VALLEY DOOR CORP
2143 Willow St (47150-1520)
P.O. Box 84 (47151-0084)
PHONE.............................812 945-5285
Gerald F Brewer Senior, Ch Bd
Gerald F Brewer Junior, Pr
Angela Taylor, Sec
EMP: 22 EST: 1972
SQ FT: 40,000
SALES (est): 4.17MM Privately Held
Web: www.ohiovalleydoor.com
SIC: 2431 Doors, wood

(G-12789)
OLD CAPITAL PRINTING LLC
3314 Grant Line Rd Ste 3 (47150-6411)
P.O. Box 75 (47114-0075)
PHONE.............................812 946-9444
Elizabeth Mayne, Admn
EMP: 5 EST: 2014
SALES (est): 60.44K Privately Held
Web: old-capital-printing-llc.business.site
SIC: 2752 Offset printing

(G-12790)
PADGETT INC
901 E 4th St (47150-3328)
P.O. Box 1375 (47151-1375)
PHONE.............................812 945-2391
TOLL FREE: 800
James R Padgett, Pr
Robert J Padgett, *
Laura L Bierman, *
Beverly Padgett, *
EMP: 160 EST: 1962
SQ FT: 98,000
SALES (est): 22.38MM Privately Held
Web: www.padgett-inc.com
SIC: 7349 1796 1791 3444 Building maintenance, except repairs; Machine moving and rigging; Structural steel erection; Sheet metalwork

(G-12791)
PATRICK WELDING LLC
1820 Rita Dr (47150-6925)
PHONE.............................812 557-7299
Christopher Patrick, Prin
EMP: 4 EST: 2017
SALES (est): 50.56K Privately Held
Web: patrick-welding-llc.business.site
SIC: 7692 Welding repair

(G-12792)
PAYNE-SPARKMANM MANUFACTURING
2571 Roanoke Ave (47150-3724)
PHONE.............................812 944-4893
Steve Payne, Pr
Ron Sparkman, Stockholder
▲ EMP: 15 EST: 1978
SQ FT: 2,000
SALES (est): 2.42MM Privately Held
Web: www.paynesparkman.com
SIC: 3674 Solid state electronic devices, nec

(G-12793)
PHASE THREE ELECTRIC INC
2115 E Market St (47150-1593)
PHONE.............................812 945-9922
Harold Carey, Pr
Richard Haley, Treas
EMP: 6 EST: 1989
SQ FT: 8,400
SALES (est): 703.53K Privately Held
Web: www.phaseiiielectric.com
SIC: 7694 5063 5999 Electric motor repair; Motors, electric; Motors, electric

(G-12794)
PHOTO SPECIALTIES
232 Maevi Dr (47150-4527)
PHONE.............................812 944-5111
EMP: 2 EST: 1992
SALES (est): 84K Privately Held
SIC: 2759 Screen printing

(G-12795)
PILLSBURY COMPANY LLC
Also Called: Pillsbury
707 Pillsbury Ln (47150-2239)
PHONE.............................812 944-8411
David Woolley, Mgr
EMP: 97
SALES (corp-wide): 19.86B Publicly Held
Web: www.pillsbury.com
SIC: 2041 Flour mills, cereal (except rice)
HQ: The Pillsbury Company Llc
    1 General Mills Blvd
    Minneapolis MN 55426

(G-12796)
POLY GROUP LLC
Also Called: Nouvex
3000 Technology Ave Ste 2221 (47150)
PHONE.............................812 590-4750
EMP: 6 EST: 2010
SALES (est): 701.61K Privately Held
Web: www.polygroupllc.net
SIC: 2835 Microbiology and virology diagnostic products

(G-12797)
PPG INDUSTRIES INC
Also Called: PPG 4313
3314 Grant Line Rd Ste 1 (47150-6411)
PHONE.............................812 944-4164
Jeff Branham, Mgr
EMP: 4
SALES (corp-wide): 17.65B Publicly Held
Web: www.ppgpaints.com
SIC: 2851 Paints and allied products
PA: Ppg Industries, Inc.
    1 Ppg Pl
    Pittsburgh PA 15272
    412 434-3131

(G-12798)
PRINTING ALL STARS
802 E 8th St (47150-3264)
PHONE.............................812 288-9291
EMP: 7 EST: 2014
SALES (est): 234.13K Privately Held
Web: www.printingallstars.com
SIC: 2752 Offset printing

(G-12799)
PROTERIAL CABLE AMERICA INC
Automotive Products Division
5300 Grant Line Rd (47150-9335)
PHONE.............................812 945-9011
Juan Carlos Chequer, Brnch Mgr
EMP: 442
Web: hca.hitachi-cable.com
SIC: 3643 Power line cable
HQ: Proterial Cable America, Inc.
    2 Manhattanville Rd # 301
    Purchase NY 10577
    914 694-9200

(G-12800)
PTG SILICONES INC
827 Progress Blvd (47150-2256)
PHONE.............................812 948-8719
Brendan Cahill, Pr
Amy S Cahill, CEO
Brendan J Cahill, Pr
Jon Marshall, Genl Mgr
Alex Haas, Genl Mgr
EMP: 18 EST: 2007
SQ FT: 5,100
SALES (est): 4.91MM Privately Held
Web: www.ptgsilicones.com
SIC: 2822 3089 Silicone rubbers; Injection molding of plastics

(G-12801)
QUIKSET BOLLARD COMPANY
2234 E Market St (47150-1508)
P.O. Box 583 (47151-0583)
PHONE.............................502 648-6734
Tony Perkins, Genl Mgr
EMP: 6 EST: 2010
SALES (est): 175.56K Privately Held
Web: www.jjpallet.com
SIC: 2097 Manufactured ice

(G-12802)
RAIL PROTECTION PLUS LLC
3913 Horne Ave (47150-9779)
PHONE.............................812 399-1084
Edmund J Holt, Prin
EMP: 3 EST: 1998
SALES (est): 210.49K Privately Held
SIC: 3715 Semitrailers for truck tractors

(G-12803)
RAUCH INC (PA)
Also Called: RAUCH INDUSTRIES
845 Park Pl (47150)
PHONE.............................812 945-4063
Bettye R Dunham, CEO
Danny Mcpheron, CFO
▲ EMP: 24 EST: 1953
SQ FT: 45,000
SALES (est): 10.77MM
SALES (corp-wide): 10.77MM Privately Held
Web: www.rauchinc.org
SIC: 8331 7389 3599 Job training services; Packaging and labeling services; Machine shop, jobbing and repair

(G-12804)
REDRUM INCORPORATED
225 Conner St (47150-4615)
PHONE.............................859 489-1516
Alexandra Rumsey, Prin
EMP: 5 EST: 2019
SALES (est): 100.03K Privately Held
Web: www.palemoontattoo.com
SIC: 2752 Commercial printing, lithographic

(G-12805)
RFI MFG CO
2505 Glenwood Ct (47150-1589)
PHONE.............................812 207-6939
David A Kerr, Prin
EMP: 1 EST: 2007
SALES (est): 90.93K Privately Held
SIC: 3999 Manufacturing industries, nec

(G-12806)
RITE WAY INDUSTRIES INC
4201 Reas Ln (47150-2232)
PHONE.............................812 206-8665
Deborah Embry, Pr
EMP: 30 EST: 1985
SQ FT: 21,000
SALES (est): 4.34MM Privately Held
Web: www.ritewayindustries.com
SIC: 3545 Cutting tools for machine tools

(G-12807)
ROGER HARPER SIGNS
617 Indiana Ave (47150-1722)
PHONE.............................812 945-1581
Roger Harper, S
EMP: 5 EST: 1991
SALES (est): 72.97K Privately Held
SIC: 3993 Signs and advertising specialties

(G-12808)
RONALDO DESIGNER JEWELRY INC (PA)
Also Called: Ronaldo
115 E Spring St Ste 102 (47150-3436)
P.O. Box 1604 (47151-1604)
PHONE.............................812 972-7220
Ronnie E Needham, Pr
Linda Needham, *
Michael J Scheser, *
D Kevin Ryan, *
Martha J Biesel, *
EMP: 11 EST: 2008
SQ FT: 3,744
SALES (est): 4.85MM
SALES (corp-wide): 4.85MM Privately Held
Web: www.ronaldojewelry.com
SIC: 5944 5094 3911 Jewelry, precious stones and precious metals; Jewelry; Jewelry, precious metal

(G-12809)
ROYAL COUTURE TREATS BTQ LTD
216 Pearl St (47150-3416)
PHONE.............................812 914-9057
EMP: 3
SALES (est): 136.08K Privately Held
Web: www.royalcouturetreats.com

New Albany - Floyd County (G-12810)

SIC: 2051 Cakes, bakery: except frozen

(G-12810)
SAFEGUARD NURSERY PRODUCTS LLC
100 Galvin Way (47150-1500)
PHONE..................................502 648-7922
EMP: 4 EST: 2016
SALES (est): 560.14K Privately Held
Web: www.treesupports.com
SIC: 3999 Manufacturing industries, nec

(G-12811)
SAFETYNET LLC
2241 State St (47150-4948)
PHONE..................................502 609-3339
EMP: 4 EST: 2016
SALES (est): 224.62K Privately Held
Web: www.cprsafetynet.com
SIC: 2834 Pharmaceutical preparations

(G-12812)
SAMTEC INC (PA)
Also Called: Samtec USA
520 Park East Blvd (47150)
P.O. Box 1147 (47151)
PHONE..................................812 944-6733
▲ EMP: 800 EST: 1975
SALES (est): 178.24MM
SALES (corp-wide): 178.24MM Privately Held
Web: www.samtec.com
SIC: 3679 Electronic circuits

(G-12813)
SIGN GYPSIES LOUISVILLE LLC
Also Called: Sign Gypsies
1009 Silver St (47150)
PHONE..................................281 743-2137
Heather Cloyd, Owner
EMP: 4 EST: 2017
SALES (est): 46.08K Privately Held
Web: www.signgypsies.com
SIC: 3993 Signs and advertising specialties

(G-12814)
SIGN LIGHTING
1663 Kenwood Ave (47150-6201)
PHONE..................................502 664-6655
EMP: 3 EST: 2017
SALES (est): 54.46K Privately Held
SIC: 3993 Signs and advertising specialties

(G-12815)
SIGNS OF TIMES LLC
714 Mount Tabor Rd (47150-2213)
PHONE..................................812 981-3000
EMP: 4 EST: 1993
SALES (est): 346.74K Privately Held
Web: www.signsthatimpact.com
SIC: 3993 Signs and advertising specialties

(G-12816)
SPAWN MATE INC
Also Called: Spawn Mate
2049 Indiana Ave (47150-3748)
P.O. Box 1144 (47151-1144)
PHONE..................................812 948-2174
Cathy Gahagen, Brnch Mgr
EMP: 4
SALES (corp-wide): 10.28MM Privately Held
Web: www.amycel.com
SIC: 2873 Fertilizers: natural (organic), except compost
PA: Spawn Mate, Inc.
553 Mission Vineyard Rd
San Juan Bautista CA 95045
831 763-5300

(G-12817)
SPECTRUM MGT HOLDG CO LLC
1608 Vance Ave (47150-3961)
PHONE..................................812 941-6899
EMP: 6
SALES (corp-wide): 54.61B Publicly Held
Web: www.spectrum.com
SIC: 2759 Commercial printing, nec
HQ: Spectrum Management Holding Company, Llc
400 Atlantic St
Stamford CT 06901
203 905-7801

(G-12818)
STEMWOOD CORP
2710 Grant Line Rd (47150-4051)
P.O. Box 1347 (47151-1347)
PHONE..................................812 945-6646
David E Wunderlin, Pr
EMP: 25 EST: 1989
SQ FT: 180,000
SALES (est): 2.1MM Privately Held
Web: www.stemwood.com
SIC: 2435 2421 2426 Veneer stock, hardwood; Lumber: rough, sawed, or planed; Hardwood dimension and flooring mills

(G-12819)
SUPERIOR VENEER & PLYWOOD LLC
1819 Dewey St (47150-5767)
PHONE..................................812 941-8850
EMP: 2 EST: 2003
SQ FT: 7,200
SALES (est): 234.92K Privately Held
Web: www.superiorveneer.com
SIC: 2435 Hardwood veneer and plywood

(G-12820)
SWEETJOY COMPANY LLC
1809 Depauw Ave (47150-2747)
PHONE..................................502 821-0511
EMP: 4 EST: 2020
SALES (est): 92.36K Privately Held
Web: www.sweetjoyco.com
SIC: 3999 Candles

(G-12821)
TECHNIDYNE CORPORATION (PA)
100 Quality Ave (47150)
PHONE..................................812 948-2884
Stephen Jerome Popson, Ch Bd
Michael T Popson, *
Helen Popson, *
Theresa Popson, Stockholder*
EMP: 42 EST: 1974
SALES (est): 9.88MM
SALES (corp-wide): 9.88MM Privately Held
Web: www.industrialphysics.com
SIC: 3823 Process control instruments

(G-12822)
VELAZQUEZ WLDG SOLUTIONS LLC
1515 Ekin Ave (47150-3126)
PHONE..................................812 391-9892
Josette Velazquez, Prin
EMP: 4 EST: 2016
SALES (est): 35.3K Privately Held
SIC: 7692 Welding repair

(G-12823)
VENEER CURRY SALES LLC
1014 E 6th St (47150-3359)
PHONE..................................812 945-6623
Michael A Gray, Prin
EMP: 10 EST: 2011
SALES (est): 909.99K Privately Held

SIC: 2435 Hardwood veneer and plywood

(G-12824)
W AY-FM MEDIA GROUP INC
3211 Grant Line Rd Ste 1 (47150-0003)
P.O. Box 1043 (47151-1043)
PHONE..................................812 945-1043
Matthew Hahn, Genl Mgr
EMP: 6 EST: 2008
SALES (est): 355.19K Privately Held
SIC: 7313 3663 Radio advertising representative; Radio receiver networks

(G-12825)
W M KELLEY CO INC (PA)
620 Durgee Rd (47150-8816)
PHONE..................................812 945-3529
Michael Kelley, Pr
Michael A Kelley, *
Frederick J Kelley, *
EMP: 100 EST: 1968
SQ FT: 90,000
SALES (est): 24.66MM
SALES (corp-wide): 24.66MM Privately Held
Web: www.wmkelley.com
SIC: 3535 5084 Conveyors and conveying equipment; Industrial machinery and equipment

(G-12826)
W-M LUMBER AND WOOD PDTS INC
1801 E Main St (47150-5782)
PHONE..................................812 944-6711
Robert W Marshall Junior, Pr
Robert W Marshall Senior, Pr
Robert Marshall Junior, Sec
Lydia Hess, VP
EMP: 19 EST: 1971
SQ FT: 30,000
SALES (est): 1.15MM Privately Held
Web: www.palletsandmore.com
SIC: 2448 Pallets, wood

(G-12827)
WALLACE LEGACY 1 INC
4345 Security Pkwy (47150-9374)
PHONE..................................812 944-9368
Sheila Wallace, Pr
Stephen R Wallace, *
EMP: 25 EST: 1990
SQ FT: 34,000
SALES (est): 4.92MM Privately Held
Web: www.sandjprecision.com
SIC: 3599 Machine shop, jobbing and repair

(G-12828)
WALLACE LEGACY 2 LLC
4345 Security Pkwy (47150-9374)
PHONE..................................812 944-9368
Steve Wallace, Pr
EMP: 13 EST: 1997
SQ FT: 34,000
SALES (est): 264.77K Privately Held
Web: www.filtrationtech.com
SIC: 3599 Machine shop, jobbing and repair

(G-12829)
WILSON INDUSTRIES
1602 Crestview Dr (47150-5504)
PHONE..................................313 330-0643
Frances Bedan, Prin
EMP: 7 EST: 2018
SALES (est): 239.92K Privately Held
Web: www.wilsonindustriesinc.com
SIC: 3999 Manufacturing industries, nec

(G-12830)
WOODLAND STANDARD INC
Also Called: Restonic

901 Park Pl (47150-2260)
P.O. Box 968 (47151-0968)
PHONE..................................812 945-4122
◆ EMP: 105 EST: 1958
SALES (est): 8.67MM Privately Held
SIC: 2515 Mattresses, containing felt, foam rubber, urethane, etc.

(G-12831)
WORKFLOW SOLUTIONS LLC
Also Called: One Source Labs
3211 Grant Line Rd Ste 2 (47150-2175)
PHONE..................................502 627-0257
EMP: 2 EST: 2012
SALES (est): 174.22K Privately Held
SIC: 2899 8099 7381 5199 Drug testing kits, blood and urine; Physical examination and testing services; Fingerprint service; First aid supplies

(G-12832)
YOUNG CIMTECH LLC
325 Park East Blvd (47150-7257)
PHONE..................................812 948-1472
Jesika Young, CEO
EMP: 40 EST: 2018
SQ FT: 23,000
SALES (est): 4.98MM
SALES (corp-wide): 4.98MM Privately Held
Web: www.cimtechmachine.com
SIC: 3599 Machine shop, jobbing and repair
PA: Young Holding Company Llc
1919 Fisher St
Munster IN

(G-12833)
YOUNG MACHINE COMPANY INC
904 Industrial Blvd (47150-2255)
PHONE..................................812 944-5807
Larry Young, Pr
Larry E Young, Pr
Jeremy Young, VP
EMP: 9 EST: 1964
SQ FT: 10,000
SALES (est): 852.34K Privately Held
Web: www.youngmachine.net
SIC: 3599 Machine shop, jobbing and repair

New Carlisle
St. Joseph County

(G-12834)
AXIS MOLD INC
53450 Tamarack Rd (46552-9757)
PHONE..................................574 292-8904
Cole Boniface, Pr
EMP: 2 EST: 2001
SALES (est): 144.47K Privately Held
Web: www.axismoldworks.com
SIC: 3544 Industrial molds

(G-12835)
CLEVELAND-CLIFFS INC
30755 Edison Rd (46552-9728)
PHONE..................................574 654-1000
EMP: 78
SALES (corp-wide): 22B Publicly Held
Web: www.clevelandcliffs.com
SIC: 3312 Blast furnaces and steel mills
PA: Cleveland-Cliffs Inc.
200 Public Sq Ste 3300
Cleveland OH 44114
216 694-5700

(G-12836)
CLEVELAND-CLIFFS KOTE INC (DH)
30755 Edison Rd (46552-9728)
PHONE..................................574 654-1000

John Brett, *CEO*
Keith Howell, *
Marc Jesk, *
Paul Liebensn, *
Laurent Koenig, *
▲ **EMP:** 208 **EST:** 1989
SQ FT: 300,000
SALES (est): 86.78MM
SALES (corp-wide): 22B **Publicly Held**
Web: www.clevelandcliffs.com
SIC: 3471 3479 Electrolizing steel; Galvanizing of iron, steel, or end-formed products
HQ: Cleveland-Cliffs Steel Llc
1 S Dearborn St Fl 19
Chicago IL 60603
312 346-0300

(G-12837)
CLEVELAND-CLIFFS KOTE LP
30755 Edison Rd (46552-9728)
PHONE.................................574 654-1000
John Middle, *Pt*
EMP: 500 **EST:** 2002
SALES (est): 43.18MM
SALES (corp-wide): 22B **Publicly Held**
Web: www.cleveland-cliffs.com
SIC: 2499 Cooling towers, wood or wood and sheet metal combination
PA: Cleveland-Cliffs Inc.
200 Public Sq Ste 3300
Cleveland OH 44114
216 694-5700

(G-12838)
CLEVELND-CLFFS NEW CRLSLE I LP
Also Called: Cleveland-Cliffs Tek L.P.
30755 Edison Rd (46552)
PHONE.................................574 654-1000
Gary V Asperen, *Pt*
▲ **EMP:** 250 **EST:** 2002
SQ FT: 600,000
SALES (est): 49.49MM
SALES (corp-wide): 22B **Publicly Held**
Web: www.clevelandcliffs.com
SIC: 3312 Blast furnaces and steel mills
HQ: Cleveland-Cliffs Steel Llc
1 S Dearborn St Fl 19
Chicago IL 60603
312 346-0300

(G-12839)
EDCOAT LIMITED PARTNERSHIP
30350 Edison Rd (46552-9728)
PHONE.................................574 654-9105
EMP: 40 **EST:** 1995
SQ FT: 260,000
SALES (est): 3.93MM **Privately Held**
Web: www.edcoat.com
SIC: 3479 5051 Painting of metal products; Metals service centers and offices

(G-12840)
FIVE STAR SHEETS LLC
54370 Smilax Rd (46552-9751)
PHONE.................................574 654-8058
EMP: 100 **EST:** 1996
SQ FT: 100,000
SALES (est): 23.86MM **Privately Held**
Web: www.fivestarsheets.com
SIC: 2653 Boxes, corrugated: made from purchased materials

(G-12841)
JP TRUCKING INC
54340 Smilax Rd (46552-9751)
PHONE.................................574 654-7555
James Warrick, *Pr*
EMP: 15 **EST:** 2021
SALES (est): 587.52K **Privately Held**

SIC: 3799 Transportation equipment, nec

(G-12842)
MILES SYSTEMS MFG INC
7385 N Walker Rd (46552-9328)
PHONE.................................574 988-0067
Douglas R Miles, *Pr*
EMP: 10 **EST:** 2016
SALES (est): 492.07K **Privately Held**
Web: www.milessystems.com
SIC: 2511 Kitchen and dining room furniture

(G-12843)
OMNISOURCE LLC
54450 Smilax Rd (46552-9751)
PHONE.................................574 654-7561
EMP: 4
Web: www.omnisource.com
SIC: 5093 3462 3399 Ferrous metal scrap and waste; Iron and steel forgings; Metal powders, pastes, and flakes
HQ: Omnisource, Llc
7575 W Jefferson Blvd
Fort Wayne IN 46804
260 422-5541

(G-12844)
ROBERT BOSCH LLC
Also Called: Bosch Braking System
32104 State Road 2 (46552-9605)
PHONE.................................574 654-4000
EMP: 2
SALES (corp-wide): 230.19MM **Privately Held**
Web: www.bosch.us
SIC: 3714 Motor vehicle parts and accessories
HQ: Robert Bosch Llc
38000 Hills Tech Dr
Farmington Hills MI 48331
248 876-1000

(G-12845)
ROBERT BOSCH LLC
Also Called: Bosch Auto Proving Ground
32104 State Road 2 (46552-9605)
PHONE.................................574 654-4000
Robert G Schmidt, *Prin*
EMP: 4
SALES (corp-wide): 230.19MM **Privately Held**
Web: www.bosch.us
SIC: 3714 Motor vehicle parts and accessories
HQ: Robert Bosch Llc
38000 Hills Tech Dr
Farmington Hills MI 48331
248 876-1000

(G-12846)
SUPERIOR MACHINE INCORPORATED
33721 Early Rd (46552-8233)
PHONE.................................574 654-8243
EMP: 2 **EST:** 1994
SALES (est): 488.93K **Privately Held**
Web: www.superiormachineusa.com
SIC: 3599 Machine shop, jobbing and repair

(G-12847)
TEJAS TUBULAR PRODUCTS INC
31140 Edison Rd (46552-9729)
PHONE.................................574 249-0623
EMP: 131
Web: www.tejastubular.com
SIC: 3317 Steel pipe and tubes
PA: Tejas Tubular Products, Inc.
8526 Green River Dr
Houston TX 77028

(G-12848)
UNIFRAX I LLC
54401 Smilax Rd (46552-9751)
PHONE.................................574 654-7100
Tom J Lord, *Manager*
EMP: 150
Web: www.unifrax.com
SIC: 3299 3296 Ceramic fiber; Mineral wool
HQ: Unifrax I Llc
600 Rverwalk Pkwy Ste 120
Tonawanda NY 14150

New Castle
Henry County

(G-12849)
AMERICAN KEEPER CORPORATION
3300 S Commerce Dr (47362-8706)
PHONE.................................765 521-2080
Hideki Sugiyama, *Pr*
David Alexander, *
▲ **EMP:** 32 **EST:** 2001
SQ FT: 60,000
SALES (est): 6.99MM **Privately Held**
SIC: 2396 Screen printing on fabric articles
PA: Keeper Co., Ltd.
2-4-36, Tsujidokandai
Fujisawa KNG 251-0

(G-12850)
ATI FLAT RLLED PDTS HLDNGS LLC
Also Called: ATI Flat Rolled Products
516 W State Road 38 (47362-9786)
P.O. Box 309 (47362-0309)
PHONE.................................765 529-9570
Greg Counts, *Mgr*
EMP: 10
Web: www.atimaterials.com
SIC: 3312 3471 3398 3316 Stainless steel; Plating and polishing; Metal heat treating; Cold finishing of steel shapes
HQ: Ati Flat Rolled Products Holdings, Llc
1000 Six Ppg Pl
Pittsburgh PA

(G-12851)
BARNS UNLIMITED LLC
3434 S County Road 950 E (47362-9538)
PHONE.................................765 489-6282
Amos Ash, *Owner*
EMP: 1 **EST:** 1998
SALES (est): 119.97K **Privately Held**
SIC: 2542 Cabinets: show, display, or storage: except wood

(G-12852)
BRAUN COMPANIES LLC
7813 E State Road 38 (47362-9344)
PHONE.................................765 332-2084
EMP: 23 **EST:** 1994
SALES (est): 2.18MM **Privately Held**
SIC: 3713 Truck bodies and parts

(G-12853)
BRYANT PRINTING LLC
2601 Broad St (47362-3402)
PHONE.................................765 521-3379
Susanne Mccutchen, *Owner*
EMP: 4 **EST:** 1980
SQ FT: 800
SALES (est): 248.19K **Privately Held**
SIC: 2752 5943 Offset printing; Office forms and supplies

(G-12854)
BUSTERS CEMENT PRODUCTS INC (PA)
3450 S Spiceland Rd (47362-9686)
PHONE.................................765 529-0287

Frank J Hayes, *Pr*
Randall Hayes, *Sec*
Steven Hayes, *VP*
EMP: 9 **EST:** 1956
SQ FT: 1,000
SALES (est): 939.61K
SALES (corp-wide): 939.61K **Privately Held**
Web: www.bigbwaste.com
SIC: 3273 3241 Ready-mixed concrete; Cement, hydraulic

(G-12855)
C & C PALLETS AND LUMBER LLC
1611 S County Road 275 W (47362-9716)
PHONE.................................765 524-3214
Casey Polk, *Managing Member*
EMP: 4 **EST:** 2014
SALES (est): 330.22K **Privately Held**
SIC: 2448 5211 4212 Pallets, wood; Lumber products; Local trucking, without storage

(G-12856)
COURIER-TIMES INC
Also Called: New Castle Courier Times
201 S 14th St (47362-3328)
P.O. Box 369 (47362-0369)
PHONE.................................765 529-1111
David Paxton, *Ch Bd*
David Mathis, *
▲ **EMP:** 56 **EST:** 1841
SQ FT: 17,000
SALES (est): 2.44MM
SALES (corp-wide): 147.64MM **Privately Held**
Web: www.thecouriertimes.com
SIC: 2711 2791 2759 Newspapers, publishing and printing; Typesetting; Commercial printing, nec
PA: Paxton Media Group, Llc
100 Television Ln
Paducah KY 42003
270 575-8630

(G-12857)
CROSSFIRE PRESS CORPORATION
980 W Fair Oaks Rd (47362-9612)
PHONE.................................765 987-7164
Bill Craig, *Owner*
EMP: 5 **EST:** 2015
SALES (est): 51.03K **Privately Held**
SIC: 2741 Miscellaneous publishing

(G-12858)
CROWN EQUIPMENT CORPORATION
Also Called: Crown Lift Trucks
1817 I Ave (47362-2611)
PHONE.................................765 520-2077
Lu Ann, *Brnch Mgr*
EMP: 42
SALES (corp-wide): 7.12B **Privately Held**
Web: www.crown.com
SIC: 3537 Lift trucks, industrial: fork, platform, straddle, etc.
PA: Crown Equipment Corporation
44 S Washington St
New Bremen OH 45869
419 629-2311

(G-12859)
EDUTRONICS
3707 S Memorial Dr (47362-1133)
PHONE.................................765 529-6751
Steven Benson, *Owner*
EMP: 1 **EST:** 1979
SALES (est): 61K **Privately Held**
SIC: 7371 7373 7372 Custom computer programming services; Computer systems analysis and design; Prepackaged software

New Castle - Henry County (G-12860)   GEOGRAPHIC SECTION

(G-12860)
ELLERBROCK WELDING LLC
277 N Hillsboro Rd (47362-9571)
PHONE..................................559 978-2651
EMP: 1 EST: 2021
SALES (est): 54.3K Privately Held
SIC: 7692 1791 7389 Welding repair; Structural steel erection; Business Activities at Non-Commercial Site

(G-12861)
FERGYS CABINETS
2506 Grand Ave (47362-5301)
PHONE..................................765 529-0116
Darrell Ferguson, *Owner*
EMP: 2 EST: 1986
SALES (est): 79.62K Privately Held
SIC: 2434 5211 Wood kitchen cabinets; Cabinets, kitchen

(G-12862)
FOAM RUBBER LLC
Also Called: Foam Rubber Products
2600 Troy Ave (47362-5300)
P.O. Box 525 (47362-0525)
PHONE..................................765 521-2000
Norman Smith, *Pr*
Martin Gonzalez, *Operations Officer*
Terry Warrum, *CFO*
Don Cotleur Gm Tulsa Ok, *Prin*
▲ EMP: 225 EST: 1958
SALES (est): 22.85MM Privately Held
Web: www.hsmsolutions.com
SIC: 3086 5199 Insulation or cushioning material, foamed plastics; Foams and rubber

(G-12863)
FOUR STAR SCREEN PRINTING LLC
1379 N Cadiz Pike (47362-9742)
PHONE..................................765 533-3006
Julia Miller, *Owner*
EMP: 2 EST: 2011
SALES (est): 125.55K Privately Held
SIC: 2752 Commercial printing, lithographic

(G-12864)
GARY M BROWN
Also Called: Enifiy
719 Vine St (47362)
PHONE..................................765 831-2536
EMP: 1 EST: 2012
SALES (est): 95.78K Privately Held
SIC: 7699 7371 8243 5961 Professional instrument repair services; Custom computer programming services; Software training, computer; Computer equipment and electronics, mail order

(G-12865)
GREDE LLC
Also Called: New Castle Foundry
2700 Plum St (47362-3045)
PHONE..................................765 521-8000
Jeff Hipple, *Brnch Mgr*
EMP: 200
SALES (corp-wide): 686.19MM Privately Held
Web: www.grede.com
SIC: 3321 3714 3322 Gray and ductile iron foundries; Motor vehicle parts and accessories; Malleable iron foundries
HQ: Grede Llc
  20750 Civic Center Dr # 100
  Southfield MI 48076

(G-12866)
HD WILLIAMS CO
201 W County Rd 100 S (47362-9769)
PHONE..................................812 372-6476
Dennis Tibbetts, *Pr*
◆ EMP: 6 EST: 1990
SALES (est): 447.57K Privately Held
Web: www.gethdw.com
SIC: 3469 Metal stampings, nec

(G-12867)
HIBBING INTERNATIONAL FRICTION
2001 Troy Ave (47362-5365)
PHONE..................................765 529-7001
James L Taylor Junior, *Pr*
EMP: 10 EST: 1989
SQ FT: 21,000
SALES (est): 872.35K Privately Held
SIC: 3499 5013 Friction material, made from powdered metal; Automotive brakes

(G-12868)
HOOSIER WELDING
1726 S County Road 125 W (47362-8946)
PHONE..................................765 521-4539
Jody Castle, *Pr*
Karen Castle, *Sec*
EMP: 3 EST: 2000
SALES (est): 174.12K Privately Held
SIC: 7692 Welding repair

(G-12869)
INDEPENDENT PLASTIC INC
3060 S Commerce Dr (47362)
PHONE..................................765 521-2251
Duane Flatter, *Mgr*
EMP: 3
SALES (corp-wide): 3.76MM Privately Held
Web: www.independentplastic.com
SIC: 5169 3089 Synthetic resins, rubber, and plastic materials; Plastics processing
PA: Independent Plastic, Inc.
  6611 Petropark Dr
  Houston TX 77041
  713 329-9955

(G-12870)
INTERNTIONAL PIPE CONS SLS LLC
900 New York Ave (47362-4423)
P.O. Box 366 (47362-0366)
PHONE..................................765 388-2222
Tamara Blevins, *Managing Member*
EMP: 10 EST: 2010
SALES (est): 900.78K Privately Held
Web: www.internationalpipeconsultants.com
SIC: 3312 7389 Pipes and tubes; Business services, nec

(G-12871)
KVK US TECHNOLOGIES INC
1016 S 25th St (47362-5367)
PHONE..................................765 529-1100
Chad Mcclung, *Pr*
EMP: 2 EST: 2007
SQ FT: 26,000
SALES (est): 992.76K Privately Held
Web: www.kvkustech.net
SIC: 2821 Plastics materials and resins

(G-12872)
MAGNA MACHINE & TOOL CO INC
3722 N Messick Rd (47362-9315)
PHONE..................................765 766-5388
Eugene Weaver, *Pr*
Michael Broyles, *
EMP: 45 EST: 1975
SQ FT: 26,000
SALES (est): 9.16MM Privately Held
Web: www.magnamachine.com
SIC: 3599 Machine shop, jobbing and repair

(G-12873)
MARGISON GRAPHICS LLC
Also Called: Margison Sign Company
1813 S Memorial Dr (47362-1217)
PHONE..................................765 529-8250
▼ EMP: 3 EST: 2008
SQ FT: 5,500
SALES (est): 233.87K Privately Held
Web: www.margisongraphics.com
SIC: 3993 Signs, not made in custom sign painting shops

(G-12874)
MD/LF INCORPORATED
Also Called: Organi Gro
187 S Denny Dr (47362-9138)
P.O. Box 64 (47362-0064)
PHONE..................................765 575-8130
Dave Denison, *Pr*
EMP: 6 EST: 2007
SQ FT: 2,000
SALES (est): 569.35K Privately Held
SIC: 2875 Fertilizers, mixing only

(G-12875)
NEW CASTLE SAW MILL
2910 Outer Dr (47362-2068)
PHONE..................................765 529-6635
Ronald Gross, *Pr*
EMP: 7 EST: 1945
SALES (est): 451.85K Privately Held
SIC: 2421 5211 Sawmills and planing mills, general; Lumber products

(G-12876)
NEW CASTLE STAINLESS PLATE LLC
549 W State Road 38 (47362-9786)
P.O. Box 370 (47362-0370)
PHONE..................................765 529-0120
Kevin Keeley, *Managing Member*
◆ EMP: 82 EST: 1983
SQ FT: 372,000
SALES (est): 100MM Privately Held
Web: www.ncestainlessplate.com
SIC: 3312 5051 Stainless steel; Steel

(G-12877)
NORTHEDGE STEEL LLC
900 New York Ave (47362-4423)
PHONE..................................336 594-0171
EMP: 9
SALES (corp-wide): 565.32K Privately Held
Web: www.northedgesteel.us
SIC: 3312 Blast furnaces and steel mills
PA: Northedge Steel Llc
  350 Forum Pkwy
  Rural Hall NC 27045
  765 591-8080

(G-12878)
OLSON RACE CARS
129 N 26th St (47362-3430)
PHONE..................................765 529-6933
Herb Olson, *Owner*
EMP: 2 EST: 2000
SALES (est): 138.55K Privately Held
Web: www.olsonracecars.com
SIC: 3711 5531 Automobile assembly, including specialty automobiles; Speed shops, including race car supplies

(G-12879)
PROFESSIONAL DESIGN LLC
1220 Church St (47362-4636)
PHONE..................................765 529-1590
EMP: 5 EST: 2016
SALES (est): 233.29K Privately Held
Web: www.professionaldesignllc.com

SIC: 2752 Commercial printing, lithographic

(G-12880)
QUALITY FABRICATION IND INC
3174 S Commerce Dr (47362-8743)
P.O. Box 1110 (47362-7110)
PHONE..................................765 529-9776
EMP: 19 EST: 1993
SALES (est): 962.33K Privately Held
SIC: 3441 Fabricated structural metal

(G-12881)
R&S SIGN DESIGN
Also Called: Visual Values
3963 S State Road 103 (47362-8701)
PHONE..................................765 520-5594
EMP: 3 EST: 1996
SALES (est): 114.18K Privately Held
SIC: 3993 Signs and advertising specialties

(G-12882)
ROYAL MACHINING & REPAIR LLC
1524 Grand Ave Ste B (47362)
PHONE..................................765 529-3545
Dave Garvin, *Prin*
EMP: 2 EST: 2005
SALES (est): 235.82K Privately Held
Web: www.royalmachiningandrepair.com
SIC: 3599 Machine shop, jobbing and repair

(G-12883)
TREK POOLS LLC
5142 W State Road 38 (47362-8925)
PHONE..................................317 896-0493
EMP: 6 EST: 2018
SALES (est): 328.41K Privately Held
Web: www.trekpools.com
SIC: 5999 3441 Swimming pools, hot tubs, and sauna equipment and supplies; Fabricated structural metal

(G-12884)
TS TECH INDIANA LLC
Also Called: TS Tech
3800 Brooks Dr (47362-8758)
PHONE..................................765 465-4294
▲ EMP: 3 EST: 2007
SALES (est): 5.85MM Privately Held
Web: www.tstech.com
SIC: 2531 Seats, automobile
HQ: Ts Tech Americas, Inc.
  8458 E Broad St
  Reynoldsburg OH 43068
  614 575-4100

(G-12885)
WESTERN PRODUCTS INDIANA INC
387 W State Road 38 (47362-9786)
P.O. Box 545 (47362-0545)
PHONE..................................765 529-6230
Roger K Crowe, *Pr*
Charles Nelson, *VP*
EMP: 15 EST: 1929
SQ FT: 46,225
SALES (est): 2.23MM Privately Held
Web: www.westernproductsinc.com
SIC: 3452 3429 Bolts, nuts, rivets, and washers; Hardware, nec

(G-12886)
WIMMER MFG INC
201 County Rd 100 S (47362-9769)
P.O. Box 43 (47362-0043)
PHONE..................................765 465-9846
Kyle York, *Mgr*
EMP: 8 EST: 2004
SALES (est): 393K Privately Held
SIC: 3999 Manufacturing industries, nec

GEOGRAPHIC SECTION

New Harmony
Posey County

(G-12887)
MAGNUM EXPLORATION INC
4301 Romaine Rd (47631-9512)
PHONE................812 673-4914
Joseph Wildeman, *Pr*
EMP: 1 **EST:** 1984
SALES (est): 104.42K **Privately Held**
SIC: 1382 Oil and gas exploration services

(G-12888)
POSEY COUNTY NEWS
801 North St (47631-7817)
P.O. Box 397 (47631-0397)
PHONE................812 682-3950
Donna Kohlmeyer, *Prin*
EMP: 5 **EST:** 2005
SALES (est): 88.32K **Privately Held**
Web: www.poseycountynews.com
SIC: 2711 Job printing and newspaper publishing combined

New Haven
Allen County

(G-12889)
ACCUTEMP PRODUCTS INC (PA)
Also Called: Accutemp
11919 John Adams Dr (46774-7401)
P.O. Box 10090 (46850-0090)
PHONE................260 493-0415
Scott Swogger, *Pr*
Dean Stanley, *
Doug Myers, *
Dave Ogram, *
John Pennington, *
EMP: 75 **EST:** 1993
SQ FT: 3,000
SALES (est): 11.01MM **Privately Held**
Web: www.accutemp.net
SIC: 3589 Commercial cooking and foodwarming equipment

(G-12890)
ACCUTEMP PRODUCTS INC
12004 Lincoln Hwy E (46774-9378)
P.O. Box 10090 (46850-0090)
PHONE................260 493-6831
Kevin Gold, *Brnch Mgr*
EMP: 1
Web: www.accutemp.net
SIC: 3999 Barber and beauty shop equipment
PA: Accutemp Products, Inc.
11919 John Adams Dr
New Haven IN 46774

(G-12891)
ALMET INC
300 Hartzell Rd (46774-1123)
P.O. Box 346 (46774-0346)
PHONE................260 493-1556
James R Greim, *Pr*
Thomas A Bada, *VP*
Gregory H Lynch, *VP*
Joyce Nahrwold, *Treas*
EMP: 63 **EST:** 1969
SQ FT: 100,000
SALES (est): 24.7MM **Privately Held**
Web: www.almetinc.com
SIC: 3441 Building components, structural steel

(G-12892)
AMOS D GRABER & SONS
5229 Bruick Rd (46774-9760)
PHONE................260 749-0526
Amos D Graber, *Sr Pt*
EMP: 10 **EST:** 1965
SALES (est): 387.95K **Privately Held**
SIC: 7699 7692 5661 Blacksmith shop; Welding repair; Shoe stores

(G-12893)
ARCHER-DANIELS-MIDLAND COMPANY
Also Called: ADM Grain Co
356 Hartzell Rd (46774-1122)
PHONE................260 749-0022
EMP: 2
SALES (corp-wide): 93.94B **Publicly Held**
Web: www.adm.com
SIC: 2074 2046 Cottonseed oil mills; Wet corn milling
PA: Archer-Daniels-Midland Company
77 W Wacker Dr Ste 4600
Chicago IL 60601
312 634-8100

(G-12894)
BOE KNOWS MOLD
488 Courtney Dr (46774-2626)
PHONE................260 760-7136
Robert Mcdowell, *Owner*
EMP: 7 **EST:** 2010
SALES (est): 69.44K **Privately Held**
Web: www.honeywell.com
SIC: 3544 Industrial molds

(G-12895)
BST ENTERPRISES INC
1900 Summit St (46774-9583)
P.O. Box 305 (46774-0305)
PHONE................260 493-4313
Barry K Stroh, *Pr*
Sharon Stroh, *Sec*
EMP: 6 **EST:** 1975
SQ FT: 14,000
SALES (est): 462.5K **Privately Held**
SIC: 3544 3599 Special dies and tools; Machine shop, jobbing and repair

(G-12896)
C-MAR WELDING
16808 Notestine Rd (46774-9747)
PHONE................260 410-8104
David Lengacher, *Prin*
EMP: 5 **EST:** 2019
SALES (est): 177.11K **Privately Held**
SIC: 7692 Welding repair

(G-12897)
CABLECRAFT MOTION CONTROLS LLC (HQ)
2110 Summit St (46774-9524)
PHONE................260 749-5105
▲ **EMP:** 113 **EST:** 2010
SALES (est): 97.18MM
SALES (corp-wide): 115.4MM **Privately Held**
Web: www.cablecraft.com
SIC: 3315 3568 Steel wire and related products; Power transmission equipment, nec
PA: Torque 2020 Cma Acquisition Llc
10896 Industrial Pkwy Nw
Bolivar OH 44612
330 874-2900

(G-12898)
CHALLENGE TOOL & MFG INC
Also Called: Ctm
11725 Lincoln Hwy E (46774-9386)
P.O. Box 306 (46774-0306)
PHONE................260 749-9558
Larry Redmon, *Pr*
Gary Collins, *
Martha Jenkins, *
EMP: 68 **EST:** 1968
SQ FT: 100,000
SALES (est): 9.27MM **Privately Held**
Web: www.ctm-inc.com
SIC: 3599 Machine shop, jobbing and repair

(G-12899)
CONTINENTAL DIAMOND TOOL CORP (PA)
10511 Rose Ave (46774-0020)
P.O. Box 126 (46774-0126)
PHONE................260 493-1294
Nicholas P Viggiano, *Pr*
Raymond P Viggiano, *
EMP: 18 **EST:** 1973
SQ FT: 20,000
SALES (est): 8.54MM
SALES (corp-wide): 8.54MM **Privately Held**
Web: www.cdtusa.net
SIC: 3541 Saws, power (metalworking machinery)

(G-12900)
CSC-INDIANA LLC
2190 Summit St (46774-9524)
PHONE................708 625-3255
▲ **EMP:** 50 **EST:** 2001
SQ FT: 250,000
SALES (est): 10.2MM
SALES (corp-wide): 61.85MM **Privately Held**
Web: www.corrugatedsuppliescompany.com
SIC: 2653 Boxes, corrugated: made from purchased materials
PA: Corrugated Supplies Company, Llc
5043 W 67th St
Bedford Park IL 60638
708 458-5525

(G-12901)
CSD GROUP LLC ✪
3003 Ryan Rd (46774-9347)
PHONE................260 918-3500
Doug Hood, *Managing Member*
EMP: 1 **EST:** 2022
SALES (est): 253.49K **Privately Held**
Web: www.csdus.com
SIC: 3651 Audio electronic systems

(G-12902)
EZ CUT TOOL LLC
110 Rose Ave (46774-1129)
PHONE................260 748-0732
EMP: 4 **EST:** 2008
SALES (est): 494.29K **Privately Held**
Web: www.ezcuttool.com
SIC: 3599 Machine shop, jobbing and repair

(G-12903)
GANAL CORPORATION
Also Called: New Haven Bakery
915 Lincoln Hwy E (46774-1424)
PHONE................260 749-2161
George Branning, *Pr*
Nancy Branning, *Sec*
EMP: 8 **EST:** 1978
SQ FT: 1,600
SALES (est): 490.25K **Privately Held**
SIC: 5461 2051 Bread; Bread, cake, and related products

(G-12904)
GIROD TRUSS LLC
17007 Doty Rd (46774-9726)
PHONE................260 442-8240
Arlen R Girod, *Managing Member*
EMP: 7 **EST:** 2018
SALES (est): 909.45K **Privately Held**
SIC: 2439 Trusses, wooden roof

(G-12905)
GLAZE TOOL AND ENGINEERING INC
1610 Summit St (46774-1522)
P.O. Box 267 (46774-0267)
PHONE................260 493-4557
E William Glaze, *Pr*
Barbara J Glaze, *
E William Glaze Junior, *VP*
EMP: 30 **EST:** 1974
SQ FT: 18,000
SALES (est): 4.72MM **Privately Held**
Web: www.glazetool.com
SIC: 3544 3569 3549 Industrial molds; Assembly machines, non-metalworking; Metalworking machinery, nec

(G-12906)
HUPP & ASSOCIATES INC
Also Called: Hupp Aerospace Defense
1690 Summit St Ste B (46774-1659)
PHONE................260 748-8282
Ron Root, *Pr*
Thomas Walsh, *
Noel Hupp, *
Kyle Rumschlag, *
EMP: 38 **EST:** 1980
SQ FT: 10,000
SALES (est): 20.04MM **Privately Held**
Web: www.huppaerospace.com
SIC: 3728 Aircraft parts and equipment, nec

(G-12907)
JCR AUTOMATION INC
1426 Ryan Rd (46774-9635)
PHONE................260 749-6606
Rick Johnson, *Pr*
Carlo Renninger, *VP*
Jeff Hartman, *Sec*
EMP: 12 **EST:** 2009
SQ FT: 12,000
SALES (est): 2.02MM **Privately Held**
Web: www.jcrautomation.com
SIC: 3549 Assembly machines, including robotic

(G-12908)
KILLER CAMAROS CUSTOM CAMARO
Also Called: Killer Car Customs
4762 Zelt Cv 1/2 (46774-3143)
PHONE................260 255-2425
EMP: 3 **EST:** 2011
SALES (est): 158.64K **Privately Held**
SIC: 3714 Instrument board assemblies, motor vehicle

(G-12909)
KWIK LOK CORPORATION
1222 Ryan Rd (46774-9350)
P.O. Box 96 (46774-0096)
PHONE................260 493-1220
Jerry H Paxton, *Pr*
◆ **EMP:** 36 **EST:** 1960
SQ FT: 20,000
SALES (est): 2.17MM **Privately Held**
Web: www.kwiklok.com
SIC: 3565 Packaging machinery
HQ: Kwik Lok Corporation
2712 S 16th Ave
Union Gap WA 98903
509 248-4770

New Haven - Allen County (G-12910)

(G-12910)
MORTON SALT INC
7024 Parrot Rd (46774)
PHONE..................................219 477-0061
EMP: 77
SALES (corp-wide): 1.22B Privately Held
Web: www.mortonsalt.com
SIC: 2899 Salt
HQ: Morton Salt, Inc.
444 W Lake St Ste 3000
Chicago IL 60606

(G-12911)
NEW HAVEN TROPHIES & SHIRTS
710 Broadway St (46774-1602)
PHONE..................................260 749-0269
William Snyder, Pr
EMP: 5 EST: 1976
SQ FT: 8,000
SALES (est): 385.82K Privately Held
Web: nht.comcastbiz.net
SIC: 2759 5999 Screen printing; Trophies and plaques

(G-12912)
NORMAN STEIN & ASSOCIATES
9520 Paulding Rd (46774-9693)
PHONE..................................260 749-5468
Norman Stein, Pr
Beverly Stein, VP
EMP: 7 EST: 1984
SQ FT: 7,200
SALES (est): 283.3K Privately Held
SIC: 5088 3443 Tanks and tank components; Tanks, standard or custom fabricated: metal plate

(G-12913)
PETER FRANKLIN JEWELERS INC (PA)
507 Broadway St (46774-1403)
PHONE..................................260 749-4315
Peter Franklin Ball, Pr
EMP: 5 EST: 1988
SQ FT: 800
SALES (est): 2.28MM
SALES (corp-wide): 2.28MM Privately Held
Web: www.peterfranklin.com
SIC: 3911 5944 Jewelry, precious metal; Jewelry, precious stones and precious metals

(G-12914)
PETERS ENTERPRISES
Also Called: Peters Equipment
217 State Road 930 W (46774-2147)
PHONE..................................260 493-6435
Ron Peters, Owner
EMP: 3 EST: 1979
SALES (est): 182.19K Privately Held
SIC: 3524 Lawn and garden tractors and equipment

(G-12915)
S & S OPTICAL CO INC
416 Ann St (46774-1278)
PHONE..................................260 749-9614
Richard Stein, Pr
Arno Stein, Treas
Suzanne Stein, Sec
EMP: 16 EST: 1965
SQ FT: 14,000
SALES (est): 2.04MM Privately Held
Web: www.ssoptical.net
SIC: 3229 3827 Pressed and blown glass, nec; Optical instruments and lenses

(G-12916)
S & W SWING SETS
17007 Doty Rd (46774-9726)
PHONE..................................260 414-6200
Sam Schmucker, Pt
William Graver, Pt
EMP: 2 EST: 1989
SALES (est): 100K Privately Held
Web: www.thebbqst.com
SIC: 3949 5945 Playground equipment; Hobby, toy, and game shops

(G-12917)
SAMUEL WAHLI
Also Called: Aleph Bet Document Centre
13539 Old 24 E (46774-9006)
PHONE..................................260 749-2288
Samuel Wahli, Owner
EMP: 1 EST: 2007
SALES (est): 180.12K Privately Held
Web: www.wildoxpress.com
SIC: 2752 Offset printing

(G-12918)
SCHMUCKER WOODWORKING LLC
13131 Ehle Rd (46774-9753)
PHONE..................................260 413-9784
Matthew Schmucker, Managing Member
EMP: 4 EST: 2014
SALES (est): 310.72K Privately Held
SIC: 2431 Millwork

(G-12919)
SDI LAFARGA LLC
Also Called: La Farga
1640 Ryan Rd (46774-9240)
PHONE..................................260 748-6565
▲ EMP: 56 EST: 2010
SALES (est): 24.12MM Privately Held
Web: www.copperworks.com
SIC: 3351 Copper and copper alloy sheet, strip, plate, and products

(G-12920)
ST JOE GROUP INC
Also Called: Custom Sound Designs
3003 Ryan Rd (46774-9347)
PHONE..................................260 918-3500
Doug Hood, Pr
EMP: 20 EST: 1995
SQ FT: 1,500
SALES (est): 4.17MM Privately Held
Web: www.csdus.com
SIC: 3651 5099 Audio electronic systems; Video and audio equipment

(G-12921)
SUPERIOR ALUMINUM ALLOYS LLC
Also Called: Superior Aluminum
14214 Edgerton Rd (46774-9636)
PHONE..................................260 749-7599
Denny Luma, Prin
Russell Rinn, Prin
Denny Luma, Prin
▼ EMP: 123 EST: 1997
SQ FT: 180,000
SALES (est): 46.55MM Publicly Held
Web: www.saalloys.com
SIC: 3341 5051 Aluminum smelting and refining (secondary); Aluminum bars, rods, ingots, sheets, pipes, plates, etc.
HQ: Omnisource, Llc
7575 W Jefferson Blvd
Fort Wayne IN 46804
260 422-5541

(G-12922)
TRAVIS INDUSTRIES INC
2000 Summit St (46774-9670)
PHONE..................................260 479-7807
Brendon Travis, Pr
EMP: 5 EST: 2014
SALES (est): 479.61K Privately Held
Web: www.travisindustries.com
SIC: 3999 Manufacturing industries, nec

(G-12923)
TRINITY CSTM BUILT PALLETS LLC
12802 Irving Rd (46774-9489)
PHONE..................................260 466-4625
Mitchel Thompson, Admn
EMP: 5 EST: 2015
SALES (est): 96.42K Privately Held
SIC: 2448 Pallets, wood

(G-12924)
U B MACHINE INC
1615 Lincoln Hwy E (46774-1569)
P.O. Box 673 (46774-0673)
PHONE..................................260 493-3381
Greg Urbine, Pr
EMP: 14 EST: 1981
SQ FT: 1,300
SALES (est): 447.46K Privately Held
Web: www.ubmachine.com
SIC: 3711 5531 3714 Chassis, motor vehicle; Auto and home supply stores; Motor vehicle parts and accessories

(G-12925)
WOOD CREAT BY DELAGRANGE INC
15818 Darling Rd (46774-9743)
PHONE..................................260 657-5525
Mark Delagrange, Owner
EMP: 1 EST: 1981
SALES (est): 98.94K Privately Held
Web: www.delagranges.com
SIC: 2434 Wood kitchen cabinets

New Market
Montgomery County

(G-12926)
JOE WOODROW
Also Called: New Market Welding
107 W Main St (47965-5004)
P.O. Box 312 (47965-0312)
PHONE..................................765 866-0436
Joe Woodrow, Owner
EMP: 4 EST: 2009
SALES (est): 85.7K Privately Held
Web: www.newmarketwelding.com
SIC: 7692 Welding repair

(G-12927)
MONUMENTAL STONE WORKS INC
105 S 3rd St (47965-5018)
P.O. Box 112 (47965-0112)
PHONE..................................765 866-0658
Friederich Rademacher, Pr
EMP: 11 EST: 2002
SQ FT: 5,000
SALES (est): 1.15MM Privately Held
Web: www.monumentalstoneworks.com
SIC: 3272 5032 Cast stone, concrete; Concrete building products

New Palestine
Hancock County

(G-12928)
AMGI LLC
2345 S Briarwood Dr (46163-9220)
PHONE..................................317 447-1524
Marlon Gill, Pr
EMP: 1 EST: 2019
SALES (est): 217.5K Privately Held
SIC: 5032 5031 5063 3589 Sewer pipe, clay; Building materials, exterior; Electrical supplies, nec; Water treatment equipment, industrial

(G-12929)
AN SQUARED LLC
1375 S 700 W (46163-9785)
PHONE..................................317 517-7139
EMP: 5 EST: 2018
SALES (est): 78.89K Privately Held
Web: www.ansquaredwoodworking.com
SIC: 2431 Millwork

(G-12930)
ANASAZI INSTRUMENTS INC
23 S Westside Dr # A (46163-1113)
PHONE..................................317 861-7657
Craig H Bradley, Pr
Bill Beardon, VP
Diane O'brian, Sec
Christopher Tully, VP
EMP: 12 EST: 1995
SQ FT: 8,000
SALES (est): 2.08MM Privately Held
Web: www.aiinmr.com
SIC: 3826 Spectrometers

(G-12931)
ARK MODEL AND STAMPINGS INC
5894 W 600 S (46163-9687)
PHONE..................................317 549-3394
Charles Kevin Walsh, Pr
Kelley Fidler, Sec
EMP: 15 EST: 1983
SALES (est): 1.14MM Privately Held
SIC: 3469 3544 Stamping metal for the trade; Special dies and tools

(G-12932)
AXE HEAD THREADS LLC
2320 S Richman Way (46163)
PHONE..................................317 607-6330
James Wolsiffer, Owner
EMP: 5 EST: 2017
SALES (est): 79.07K Privately Held
Web: www.axeheadthreads.com
SIC: 2759 Screen printing

(G-12933)
BRAND PRTG & PHOTO-LITHO CO (PA)
Also Called: Brand Quick Printing
4793 W Meadow Lake Dr (46163)
P.O. Box 324 (46082)
PHONE..................................317 921-4095
Kyle Brand, Pr
EMP: 5 EST: 1950
SALES (est): 972.32K
SALES (corp-wide): 972.32K Privately Held
SIC: 2893 2752 5112 2791 Letterpress or offset ink; Lithographing on metal; Business forms; Typesetting

(G-12934)
BRANDYWINE CREEK VNYRDS WNERY
8437 W 1200 N (46163-9300)
PHONE..................................317 403-5669
Jennifer Baker, Prin
EMP: 6 EST: 2014
SALES (est): 165.2K Privately Held
SIC: 2084 Wines

(G-12935)
CARTER CABINET COMPANY INC
5928 W 600 S (46163-9500)
PHONE..................................317 985-5782
Tom Carter, Prin

EMP: 2 EST: 2010
SALES (est): 131.22K **Privately Held**
Web: www.cartercabinets.com
SIC: 2434 Wood kitchen cabinets

(G-12936)
DREAM SYSTEMS LLC
Also Called: Dream Systems
7316 W Beyers Ct (46163-9294)
PHONE...............................715 241-8332
Seth Ferrin, *Pr*
Nicki Ferrin, *CFO*
EMP: 11 EST: 2000
SALES (est): 956.68K **Privately Held**
Web: www.dreamsystemsinc.com
SIC: 3651 Audio electronic systems

(G-12937)
HEIDENREICH WOODWORKING INC
4175 S Kelly Dr (46163-9060)
PHONE...............................317 861-9331
Robert Heidenreich, *Prin*
EMP: 2 EST: 2004
SALES (est): 155.31K **Privately Held**
SIC: 2431 Millwork

(G-12938)
INFORMA BUSINESS MEDIA INC
Also Called: American Trucker
4639 W Stonehaven Ln (46163-8657)
P.O. Box 603 (46206-0603)
PHONE...............................317 233-1310
Ellen Rowlett, *Mgr*
EMP: 1
SALES (corp-wide): 3.98B **Privately Held**
Web: www.informa.com
SIC: 2721 Magazines: publishing only, not printed on site
HQ: Informa Business Media, Inc.
   605 3rd Ave Fl 22
   New York NY 10158
   212 204-4200

(G-12939)
INTEGRITY MACHINE SYSTEMS INC
22 S Westside Dr (46163-1113)
PHONE...............................317 897-3338
Tom East, *Prin*
EMP: 25 EST: 2006
SALES (est): 939.65K **Privately Held**
Web: www.ims-indy.com
SIC: 3599 Machine shop, jobbing and repair

(G-12940)
IRONWORKS ENGINEERING LLC
3683 W 1100 N (46163-9422)
PHONE...............................317 296-9359
George Boyd, *Pr*
EMP: 1 EST: 2014
SALES (est): 20K **Privately Held**
SIC: 8711 3441 Mechanical engineering; Fabricated structural metal

(G-12941)
NP AWARDS LLC
Also Called: New Palestine Awards
5188 W Windmill Way (46163-9099)
PHONE...............................317 861-0825
EMP: 2 EST: 2010
SALES (est): 9.56K **Privately Held**
Web: www.npawards.com
SIC: 2499 Trophy bases, wood

(G-12942)
PLASTIC PIPE TECHNOLOGIES LLC
2907 S Wollenweber Rd (46163-9793)
PHONE...............................317 674-5944
Allen Stratton, *Prin*
EMP: 8 EST: 2019
SALES (est): 441.05K **Privately Held**
Web: www.hdpetraining.com
SIC: 3084 Plastics pipe

(G-12943)
PROPRINT FORMS LLC
2603 S Hillview Dr (46163-8788)
PHONE...............................317 861-8701
Malinda E Smith, *Owner*
EMP: 1 EST: 2002
SALES (est): 147.38K **Privately Held**
Web: www.proprintforms.com
SIC: 2752 Offset printing

(G-12944)
URBAN RUSTIC FARMHOUSE LLC
3114 S 500 W (46163-9711)
PHONE...............................317 238-0945
EMP: 1 EST: 2017
SALES (est): 78.58K **Privately Held**
SIC: 3999 7389 Manufacturing industries, nec; Business Activities at Non-Commercial Site

(G-12945)
WOOD SHAPES UNLIMITED INC
20 S Westside Dr Ste D (46163-1118)
PHONE...............................317 861-1775
Brad Hasecuster, *Pr*
Scott Fulkerson, *VP*
EMP: 4 EST: 1993
SALES (est): 308.89K **Privately Held**
Web: www.woodshapesunlimited.com
SIC: 2434 Wood kitchen cabinets

New Paris
Elkhart County

(G-12946)
ATR TIRE AND REPAIR LLC
21925 County Road 50 (46553-9799)
PHONE...............................574 349-4462
EMP: 5 EST: 2018
SALES (est): 221.77K **Privately Held**
Web: atr-repair-llc.business.site
SIC: 7534 Tire repair shop

(G-12947)
BEAMS OF GRACE PRESS
68080 County Road 23 (46553-9707)
PHONE...............................574 238-1644
EMP: 6 EST: 2005
SALES (est): 98.63K **Privately Held**
Web: www.beamsofgracepress.com
SIC: 2741 Miscellaneous publishing

(G-12948)
BETTER WAY PARTNERS LLC
Also Called: Better Way Products
70891 County Road 23 (46553-9771)
PHONE...............................574 831-3340
Roger Korenstra, *Managing Member*
Bruce Korenstra, *
Tom Ellis, *Prin*
EMP: 420 EST: 1983
SQ FT: 71,000
SALES (est): 42.1MM
SALES (corp-wide): 3.47B **Publicly Held**
Web: www.dockbox.com
SIC: 3089 Laminating of plastics
PA: Patrick Industries, Inc.
   107 W Franklin St
   Elkhart IN 46516
   574 294-7511

(G-12949)
CUTTING EDGE MACHINE & TL INC
19149 County Road 146 (46553-9100)
P.O. Box 128 (46553-0128)
PHONE...............................866 514-1620
EMP: 70 EST: 1990
SQ FT: 40,000
SALES (est): 7.96MM **Privately Held**
Web: www.cemti.com
SIC: 3599 3559 Machine shop, jobbing and repair; Plastics working machinery

(G-12950)
DENNIS POLK & ASSOCIATES INC
Also Called: Polk, Dennis Equipment
4916 N Sr 15 (46553)
P.O. Box 326 (46538-0326)
PHONE...............................574 831-3555
Dennis Polk, *Pr*
Pam Polk, *Sec*
▲ EMP: 8 EST: 1980
SALES (est): 1.01MM **Privately Held**
Web: www.fleastuff.net
SIC: 5083 2721 Agricultural machinery and equipment; Magazines: publishing only, not printed on site

(G-12951)
ELKHART COUNTY GRAVEL INC (PA)
19242 Us Highway 6 (46553-9763)
PHONE...............................574 831-2815
Barney C Beer, *Pr*
Rodney D Beer, *VP*
Tracey Beer, *Sec*
EMP: 10 EST: 1971
SQ FT: 1,500
SALES (est): 4.21MM
SALES (corp-wide): 4.21MM **Privately Held**
Web: www.elkhartcountygravel.com
SIC: 1442 Sand mining

(G-12952)
EXCHANGE PUBLISHING CORP
Also Called: Farmers Exchange
19401 Industrial Dr (46553-9714)
P.O. Box 45 (46553-0045)
PHONE...............................574 831-2138
Matt Yeater, *Prin*
Steve Yeater, *Pr*
EMP: 14 EST: 1926
SQ FT: 11,500
SALES (est): 991.12K **Privately Held**
Web: www.farmers-exchange.net
SIC: 2711 Job printing and newspaper publishing combined

(G-12953)
FOAMITURE
19240 Tarman Rd (46553-9117)
P.O. Box 26 (46553-0026)
PHONE...............................574 831-4775
Robert Steury, *Prin*
EMP: 2 EST: 2007
SALES (est): 107.6K **Privately Held**
Web: www.veadaoem.com
SIC: 3999 Barber and beauty shop equipment

(G-12954)
FRONT PORCH SUGARHOUSE
69515 County Road 21 (46553-9204)
PHONE...............................574 831-5753
Michael Ramer, *Mng Pt*
EMP: 10 EST: 2020
SALES (est): 283.41K **Privately Held**
SIC: 2099 Maple syrup

(G-12955)
FRYS DIGISTITCH
19061 Oak St (46553-9716)
PHONE...............................574 831-6854
Patti Fry, *Owner*
EMP: 1 EST: 2000
SALES (est): 50K **Privately Held**
SIC: 2395 Embroidery and art needlework

(G-12956)
HI-POINT MACHINE AND TOOL INC
19519 Industrial Dr # 2 (46553-9636)
P.O. Box 9 (46553-0009)
PHONE...............................574 831-5361
Don Muhlnickel Junior, *Pr*
EMP: 3 EST: 1985
SQ FT: 6,000
SALES (est): 262.89K **Privately Held**
SIC: 3599 Machine shop, jobbing and repair

(G-12957)
HIGHBALL FABRICATORS LLC
68563 County Road 17 (46553-9790)
PHONE...............................574 831-6647
Timothy Frey, *Managing Member*
EMP: 2 EST: 2019
SALES (est): 251.31K **Privately Held**
Web: www.highballfab.com
SIC: 3441 7699 7692 Fabricated structural metal; Metal reshaping and replating services; Welding repair

(G-12958)
HOOSIER WOOD CREATIONS INC
19881 County Road 146 (46553-9657)
P.O. Box 831 (46527-0831)
PHONE...............................574 831-6330
Mark Eash, *Pr*
Willard Shetler, *Sec*
Harry Hostetler, *Stockholder*
EMP: 14 EST: 1995
SQ FT: 8,000
SALES (est): 541.79K **Privately Held**
SIC: 2511 Wood household furniture

(G-12959)
HOOVER WELL DRILLING INC
20477 County Road 46 (46553-9609)
P.O. Box 187 (46553-0187)
PHONE...............................574 831-4901
William Hoover, *Pr*
EMP: 9 EST: 1984
SALES (est): 988.52K **Privately Held**
Web: www.hooverwelldrillinginc.com
SIC: 1381 1781 Drilling oil and gas wells; Water well drilling

(G-12960)
INDEPENDENT PROTECTION CO
Also Called: Turtle Top
67895 Industrial Dr (46553-9634)
PHONE...............................574 831-5680
Phil Tom, *Brnch Mgr*
EMP: 192
SALES (corp-wide): 42.61MM **Privately Held**
Web: ipclp.com
SIC: 3643 3792 3713 3711 Lightning protection equipment; Travel trailers and campers; Truck and bus bodies; Motor vehicles and car bodies
PA: Independent Protection Co., Inc
   1607 S Main St
   Goshen IN 46526
   574 533-4116

(G-12961)
ITERA LLC
19260 County Road 46 Ste 3 (46553-9660)
P.O. Box 110 (46553-0110)
PHONE...............................574 538-3838
Bostjan Jevsek, *Managing Member*
EMP: 5 EST: 2015
SQ FT: 10,000
SALES (est): 442.15K **Privately Held**
Web: www.iteraspace.com
SIC: 2452 Modular homes, prefabricated, wood

New Paris - Elkhart County (G-12962)   **GEOGRAPHIC SECTION**

(G-12962)
JW WOODWORKING INC
72057 County Road 17 (46553-9659)
PHONE.................................574 831-3033
Jim Wise, *Pr*
David Wise, *Stockholder*
EMP: 4 EST: 1985
SQ FT: 10,000
SALES (est): 375.99K **Privately Held**
Web: www.jwwoodworkinginc.com
SIC: **2431** 2521 2541 2511 Staircases and stairs, wood; Desks, office: wood; Store and office display cases and fixtures; Kitchen and dining room furniture

(G-12963)
KOUNTRY KRAFT WOOD PDTS LLC
68604 County Road 15 (46553-9786)
PHONE.................................574 831-6736
EMP: 5 EST: 1994
SALES (est): 267.71K **Privately Held**
SIC: **2511** Wood household furniture

(G-12964)
KREUTER MANUFACTURING CO INC (PA)
Also Called: KMC Controls
19476 Industrial Dr (46553-9714)
PHONE.................................574 831-4626
Jon Hilberg, *Pr*
▲ **EMP: 5 EST:** 1977
SQ FT: 77,000
SALES (est): 48.49MM
SALES (corp-wide): 48.49MM **Privately Held**
Web: www.kmccontrols.com
SIC: **3625** Control equipment, electric

(G-12965)
MICHAEL RAMER
Also Called: Front Porch Sugarhouse
69515 County Road 21 (46553-9204)
PHONE.................................574 538-8010
Michael Ramer, *Owner*
EMP: 4 EST: 2018
SALES (est): 62.38K **Privately Held**
SIC: **2099** Maple syrup

(G-12966)
MIKE GROSS
68080 County Road 23 (46553-9707)
PHONE.................................574 529-2201
Mike Gross, *Prin*
EMP: 6 EST: 2016
SALES (est): 89.89K **Privately Held**
SIC: **2411** Logging

(G-12967)
ROTATIONAL MOLDING TECH INC
Also Called: Romotech
67742 County Road 23 Ste 1 (46553-9186)
PHONE.................................574 831-6450
Dave Smith, *Pr*
Marian Mantel, *
EMP: 60 EST: 2003
SQ FT: 3,335,000
SALES (est): 7.76MM **Privately Held**
Web: www.romotek.com
SIC: **3089** Injection molding of plastics

(G-12968)
SMOKER CRAFT INC (PA)
68143 Clunette St (46553-3700)
P.O. Box 65 (46553-0065)
PHONE.................................574 831-2103
Douglas Smoker, *Pr*
Byron Smoker, *
R Joe Blackburn, *
Blackburn Joe, *
▼ **EMP: 475 EST:** 1869

SQ FT: 500,000
SALES (est): 85.48MM
SALES (corp-wide): 85.48MM **Privately Held**
Web: www.smokercraft.com
SIC: **3732** 5551 3731 Motorized boat, building and repairing; Boat dealers; Ferryboats, building and repairing

(G-12969)
STEVE MITCHELL
Also Called: Precision Tool
69420 County Road 27 (46553-9739)
PHONE.................................574 831-4848
Steve Mitchell, *Owner*
EMP: 7 EST: 1995
SQ FT: 4,000
SALES (est): 502.98K **Privately Held**
SIC: **3452** 3599 Bolts, metal; Machine shop, jobbing and repair

(G-12970)
SYLVAN MARINE INC (PA)
68143 Clunette St (46553-3700)
P.O. Box 65 (46553-0065)
PHONE.................................574 831-2950
Doug Smoker, *Pr*
▼ **EMP: 400 EST:** 1998
SALES (est): 24.67MM
SALES (corp-wide): 24.67MM **Privately Held**
Web: www.sylvanmarine.com
SIC: **3732** Boatbuilding and repairing

(G-12971)
T S MANUFACTURING
68563 County Road 17 (46553-9790)
PHONE.................................574 831-6647
Lenius Martin, *Prin*
EMP: 2 EST: 2008
SALES (est): 101.93K **Privately Held**
SIC: **3999** Manufacturing industries, nec

(G-12972)
ULTRA MFG LLC
68120 County Road 17 (46553-9790)
PHONE.................................574 354-2564
EMP: 4 EST: 2016
SALES (est): 86.94K **Privately Held**
SIC: **3999** Manufacturing industries, nec

(G-12973)
VEADA INDUSTRIES INC
19240 Tarman Rd (46553)
P.O. Box 26 (46553)
PHONE.................................574 831-4775
Robert W Steury, *Pr*
Douglas V Steury, *Pr*
▲ **EMP: 540 EST:** 1968
SQ FT: 100,000
SALES (est): 48.09MM
SALES (corp-wide): 3.78B **Publicly Held**
Web: www.veadaoem.com
SIC: **2531** 3732 2392 2394 Vehicle furniture; Boatbuilding and repairing; Household furnishings, nec; Tents: made from purchased materials
HQ: Lippert Components, Inc.
    3501 County Rd 6 E
    Elkhart IN 46514
    574 535-1125

(G-12974)
WORLD MISSIONARY PRESS INC
19168 County Road 146 (46553-9225)
P.O. Box 120 (46553-0120)
PHONE.................................574 831-2111
Harold Mack, *Pr*
Vicky Benson, *
Marie Mack, *
Tim Yoder, *

Wes Culver, *
▼ **EMP: 50 EST:** 1961
SQ FT: 30,344
SALES (est): 3.47MM **Privately Held**
Web: www.wmpress.org
SIC: **2731** 8699 Books, publishing and printing; Charitable organization

(G-12975)
YODERS CUSTOM SERVICE
Also Called: Yoder's Lockworks
18638 County Road 46 (46553-9105)
PHONE.................................574 831-4717
Weldon Yoder, *Owner*
EMP: 2 EST: 1981
SALES (est): 177.65K **Privately Held**
SIC: **3873** Watches, clocks, watchcases, and parts

New Point
Decatur County

(G-12976)
NEW POINT PRODUCTS INC
Also Called: New Point Products Martguild
8563 E State Rte 46 (47263)
P.O. Box 92 (47263-0092)
PHONE.................................812 663-6311
Paul F Laugle, *Pr*
Cathy Laugle, *Sec*
EMP: 9 EST: 1968
SQ FT: 6,000
SALES (est): 706.27K **Privately Held**
Web: www.newpointproducts.com
SIC: **3543** 3544 3369 3366 Industrial patterns; Special dies, tools, jigs, and fixtures; Nonferrous foundries, nec; Copper foundries

---

New Richmond
Montgomery County

(G-12977)
CONSTANT VOLTAGE WELDING INC
3231 W 1100 N (47967-8009)
PHONE.................................765 339-7914
Travis Pulley, *Owner*
EMP: 5 EST: 2016
SALES (est): 67.78K **Privately Held**
SIC: **7692** Welding repair

(G-12978)
DAVRON FABRICATING
3873 W 750 N (47967-8018)
PHONE.................................765 339-7303
Ron Grana, *Pt*
Dave Green, *Pt*
EMP: 2 EST: 1997
SALES (est): 93.62K **Privately Held**
SIC: **7692** Welding repair

New Ross
Montgomery County

(G-12979)
J JONES MACHINE LLC
8876 E 400 S (47968)
PHONE.................................765 366-8258
Justin Jones, *Managing Member*
EMP: 2 EST: 2018
SALES (est): 255.34K **Privately Held**
SIC: **3312** Blast furnaces and steel mills

(G-12980)
JJ MACHINE
8834 E 400 S (47968-8046)

PHONE.................................765 723-1511
Nancy Jones, *Owner*
EMP: 4 EST: 1988
SQ FT: 12,000
SALES (est): 496.96K **Privately Held**
Web: www.jjonesmachinellc.com
SIC: **3599** 3544 Machine shop, jobbing and repair; Special dies and tools

(G-12981)
WRIGHTS WOODWORKING
8862 E 500 S (47968-8037)
PHONE.................................765 723-1546
Joseph Wright, *Owner*
EMP: 5 EST: 2013
SALES (est): 71.22K **Privately Held**
SIC: **2431** Millwork

New Salisbury
Harrison County

(G-12982)
AJS GYROS TO GO
441 Rocky Meadow Rd Ne (47161-8108)
PHONE.................................812 951-1715
Alison Hanover, *Prin*
EMP: 7 EST: 2010
SALES (est): 108.92K **Privately Held**
Web: ajsgyrostogo.sqwiz.com
SIC: **2024** Ice cream, bulk

(G-12983)
BENZ
1920 Flatwood Rd Ne (47161-9058)
PHONE.................................812 364-1273
R Scott Benz, *Admn*
EMP: 5 EST: 2010
SALES (est): 93.15K **Privately Held**
Web: www.benztooling.com
SIC: **3599** Machine shop, jobbing and repair

(G-12984)
ECO WATER OF SOUTHERN INDIANA
Also Called: Ecowater
7685 Highway 135 Ne (47161-7723)
P.O. Box 3585 (81402-3585)
PHONE.................................812 734-1407
Wayne Whalen, *Pt*
Teresa Boyd, *Pt*
Dennis Chandler, *Pt*
Deborah Halter-chandler, *Pt*
EMP: 5 EST: 2005
SALES (est): 351.06K **Privately Held**
SIC: **3589** Water treatment equipment, industrial

(G-12985)
LAFF WORX LLC
2475 E Whiskey Run Rd Ne (47161-9338)
PHONE.................................812 267-0430
EMP: 1 EST: 2011
SALES (est): 49.39K **Privately Held**
Web: www.laffworx.com
SIC: **2711** Newspapers, publishing and printing

(G-12986)
PURPLE VERTIGO CANDLES LLC
1145 Old State Road 64 Ne (47161-8204)
PHONE.................................502 807-6619
Laura Hardesty, *CEO*
EMP: 5 EST: 2018
SALES (est): 74.47K **Privately Held**
SIC: **3999** Candles

New Whiteland
Johnson County

(G-12987)
PREDATOR PERCUSSION LLC
1174 Dark Star Ct (46184-9239)
PHONE.....................317 919-7659
EMP: 3 EST: 2017
SALES (est): 58.51K Privately Held
SIC: 3999 Manufacturing industries, nec

Newberry
Greene County

(G-12988)
DARLING INGREDIENTS INC
7358 S Griffin Rd (47449-7044)
PHONE.....................812 659-3399
EMP: 6
SALES (corp-wide): 6.79B Publicly Held
Web: www.darlingii.com
SIC: 2077 Animal and marine fats and oils
PA: Darling Ingredients Inc.
   5601 N Macarthur Blvd
   Irving TX 75038
   972 717-0300

(G-12989)
GRIFFIN INDUSTRIES LLC
7358 S Griffin Rd (47449-7044)
P.O. Box 112 (47449-0112)
PHONE.....................812 659-3399
James Davis, Genl Mgr
EMP: 69
SALES (corp-wide): 6.79B Publicly Held
Web: www.griffinind.com
SIC: 2077 2048 Animal and marine fats and oils; Prepared feeds, nec
HQ: Griffin Industries Llc
   4221 Alexandria Pike
   Cold Spring KY 41076
   859 781-2010

(G-12990)
OCELLA INC
Also Called: Ocella Tech
7970 S Energy Dr (47449-7128)
PHONE.....................845 842-8185
Rajan Kumar, CEO
Carlos Munoz, COO
EMP: 9 EST: 2017
SALES (est): 125K Privately Held
Web: www.ateios.com
SIC: 3691 3692 5063 5999 Batteries, rechargeable; Primary batteries, dry and wet; Batteries; Batteries, non-automotive

Newburgh
Warrick County

(G-12991)
ACADEMY ENERGY GROUP LLC (PA)
Also Called: AEG
106 State St Ste C (47630-1200)
PHONE.....................312 931-7443
EMP: 3 EST: 2011
SALES (est): 4.88MM Privately Held
Web: www.academyenergygroup.com
SIC: 3699 5063 Electrical equipment and supplies, nec; Electrical apparatus and equipment

(G-12992)
ALCOA CORPORATION
Alcoa Warrick Operations
4400 W State Route 66 (47630-9140)
P.O. Box 10 (47629-0010)
PHONE.....................812 853-6111
EMP: 26
SALES (corp-wide): 10.55B Publicly Held
Web: www.alcoa.com
SIC: 3334 Primary aluminum
PA: Alcoa Corporation
   201 Isabella St Ste 500
   Pittsburgh PA 15212
   412 315-2900

(G-12993)
ALCOA CORPORATION
Alcoa Power Plant
4700 Darlington Rd (47630-9708)
PHONE.....................812 842-3350
Kous Kleinfeld, Mgr
EMP: 37
SALES (corp-wide): 10.55B Publicly Held
Web: www.alcoa.com
SIC: 3334 Primary aluminum
PA: Alcoa Corporation
   201 Isabella St Ste 500
   Pittsburgh PA 15212
   412 315-2900

(G-12994)
ALCOA POWER GENERATING INC
4700 Darlington Rd (47630-9708)
PHONE.....................812 842-3350
EMP: 9
SALES (corp-wide): 10.55B Publicly Held
Web: www.alcoa.com
SIC: 3334 Primary aluminum
HQ: Alcoa Power Generating Inc.
   201 Isabella St
   Pittsburgh PA 15212
   412 553-4545

(G-12995)
CABINETS & COUNTERS INC
7387 Savannah Dr (47630-1811)
PHONE.....................812 858-3300
Jim Johnston, Pr
Jacqueline Johnston, VP
▲ EMP: 20 EST: 1988
SQ FT: 6,000
SALES (est): 2.44MM Privately Held
Web: www.cabinetscounters.com
SIC: 2541 2542 2821 Table or counter tops, plastic laminated; Cabinets: show, display, or storage: except wood; Plastics materials and resins

(G-12996)
CARDINAL SIGN SERVICE
5268 Epworth Rd (47630-8765)
PHONE.....................812 499-0311
EMP: 5 EST: 2018
SALES (est): 46.08K Privately Held
Web: www.cardinalsignservice.com
SIC: 3993 Signs and advertising specialties

(G-12997)
CHEMTEC LLC
5309 Ellington Ct (47630-3170)
P.O. Box 310 (47629-0310)
PHONE.....................812 499-8408
EMP: 10 EST: 2017
SALES (est): 520.93K Privately Held
Web: www.chemtecllc.com
SIC: 2899 Chemical preparations, nec

(G-12998)
CINDON INC
Also Called: American Hydraulic Hoses
8400 Golden Dr (47630-2589)
PHONE.....................812 853-5450
Celinda Sisco, Pr
EMP: 10 EST: 1999
SALES (est): 977.58K Privately Held
Web: www.americanhoseandhydraulics.com
SIC: 7699 3492 Construction equipment repair; Hose and tube fittings and assemblies, hydraulic/pneumatic

(G-12999)
CUSTOM SIGN & ENGINEERI
5344 Vann Rd (47630-8481)
PHONE.....................812 401-1550
Scott Elpers, Owner
EMP: 20 EST: 2002
SALES (est): 2.49MM Privately Held
Web: www.customsign.bz
SIC: 3993 Electric signs

(G-13000)
DK EARLEN SIGNS LLC
2699 Anvil Ct (47630-9331)
PHONE.....................812 490-8423
Jamie Brazina, Prin
EMP: 1 EST: 2009
SALES (est): 64.14K Privately Held
SIC: 3993 Signs and advertising specialties

(G-13001)
FAST GRAFIX
5942 Jeffrey Ln (47630-8832)
PHONE.....................812 305-3464
Jamie Dumanski, Owner
EMP: 1 EST: 2003
SALES (est): 84.6K Privately Held
Web: www.fastgrafix.com
SIC: 3993 Signs and advertising specialties

(G-13002)
GREEN LEAFS LLC
2100 Lakes Edge Dr (47630-8000)
P.O. Box 553 (47629-0553)
PHONE.....................812 483-6383
Mohammed Allaw, Prin
EMP: 2 EST: 2020
SALES (est): 63.4K Privately Held
SIC: 2023 Dietary supplements, dairy and non-dairy based

(G-13003)
HELIVIN LLC
7532 Peachwood Dr Ste 307 (47630)
PHONE.....................800 680-7281
Navpreet Singh, Pr
EMP: 1 EST: 2016
SALES (est): 50.95K Privately Held
Web: www.helivin.com
SIC: 2023 Dietary supplements, dairy and non-dairy based

(G-13004)
HOWMET AEROSPACE INC
HOWMET AEROSPACE INC
State Highway 66 (47630)
P.O. Box 10 (47629-0010)
PHONE.....................812 853-6111
Mel Lager, Mgr
EMP: 408
SALES (corp-wide): 6.64B Publicly Held
Web: www.howmet.com
SIC: 3334 3353 Primary aluminum; Aluminum sheet, plate, and foil
PA: Howmet Aerospace Inc.
   201 Isabella St Ste 200
   Pittsburgh PA 15212
   412 553-1950

(G-13005)
HOWMET AEROSPACE INC
Also Called: HOWMET AEROSPACE INC
2792 Laura Lynn Ln (47630-8919)
PHONE.....................412 553-4545
Drew N Harvey, Mgr
EMP: 385
SALES (corp-wide): 6.64B Publicly Held
Web: www.howmet.com
SIC: 3334 3353 1099 Primary aluminum; Aluminum sheet and strip; Bauxite mining
PA: Howmet Aerospace Inc.
   201 Isabella St Ste 200
   Pittsburgh PA 15212
   412 553-1950

(G-13006)
HURST ENTERPRISE
7866 Owens Dr (47630-2625)
P.O. Box 5 (47629-0005)
PHONE.....................812 853-0901
Bill Hurst, Prin
EMP: 6 EST: 2008
SALES (est): 78.21K Privately Held
SIC: 3999 Manufacturing industries, nec

(G-13007)
INDIANA TEAM YEARBOOK
6999 Cottage Ln (47630-9637)
PHONE.....................812 858-7113
Cameron Bardwell, Prin
EMP: 1 EST: 2004
SALES (est): 78.22K Privately Held
SIC: 2731 Book publishing

(G-13008)
INTERNATIONAL FOOD TECH INC
8499 Spencer Dr (47630-8952)
P.O. Box 503 (47629-0503)
PHONE.....................812 853-9432
Joseph Greif, Pr
EMP: 2 EST: 1989
SQ FT: 5,000
SALES (est): 224.27K Privately Held
SIC: 2023 Condensed, concentrated, and evaporated milk products

(G-13009)
INTERRACHEM LLC
Also Called: Interrachem, LLC
5722 Prospect Dr (47630)
P.O. Box 727 (47629)
PHONE.....................812 858-3147
EMP: 21 EST: 2012
SALES (est): 2.79MM Privately Held
Web: www.interrachem.com
SIC: 2899 Chemical preparations, nec

(G-13010)
JOHN R BOWEN & ASSOCIATES
Also Called: John Bowen
7777 Ashwood Ct (47630-9547)
PHONE.....................812 544-2267
John R Bowen, Owner
EMP: 1 EST: 1994
SALES (est): 69.67K Privately Held
Web: www.jrbowen.com
SIC: 8748 2759 Business consulting, nec; Commercial printing, nec

(G-13011)
KAISER ALUMINUM WARRICK LLC
4000 W State Route 66 (47630)
PHONE.....................412 315-2900
Benjamin Kahrs, Managing Member
EMP: 1200 EST: 2016
SALES (est): 351.32MM
SALES (corp-wide): 3.09B Publicly Held
Web: www.kaiseraluminum.com
SIC: 3355 Aluminum rolling and drawing, nec
PA: Kaiser Aluminum Corporation
   1550 W Mcewen Dr Ste 500
   Franklin TN 37067
   629 252-7040

Newburgh - Warrick County (G-13012)

(G-13012)
LOZANO WLDG & FABRICATION LLC
7120 Savannah Dr (47630-2183)
PHONE..................................812 629-2000
Cesar Lozano-capistran, Pr
EMP: 6 EST: 2019
SALES (est): 130.21K Privately Held
SIC: 7692 Welding repair

(G-13013)
MIDWEST CUSTOM CHEMICALS INC
5722 Prospect Dr (47630-8306)
P.O. Box 727 (47629-0727)
PHONE..................................812 858-3147
FAX: 812 858-3160
EMP: 4 EST: 1991
SALES (est): 445.49K Privately Held
SIC: 2899 Chemical preparations, nec

(G-13014)
MTCR SITE SERVICES LLC
6033 Vann Rd (47630-9676)
PHONE..................................812 598-6516
EMP: 8 EST: 2015
SALES (est): 792.45K Privately Held
Web: www.mtcrsiteservices.com
SIC: 3823 Fluidic devices, circuits, and systems for process control

(G-13015)
PAYNE GEORGE A PETROLEUM ENGR
5844 Sharon Rd (47630-9537)
P.O. Box 743 (47629-0743)
PHONE..................................812 853-3813
George A Payne, Owner
EMP: 2 EST: 1978
SALES (est): 163.57K Privately Held
SIC: 1311 1389 Crude petroleum production; Oil consultants

(G-13016)
PBTT INC
Also Called: Pbtt
5622 Vann Rd (47630)
PHONE..................................810 965-3675
Alexander Derderian, CEO
Alexander Derderian, Pr
Shawna Stilwell, *
EMP: 30 EST: 2013
SALES (est): 3.28MM Privately Held
Web: www.pbttcorp.com
SIC: 3812 3542 Defense systems and equipment; High energy rate metal forming machines

(G-13017)
POWER SYSTEMS INNOVATIONS INC
3247 Commerce Dr (47630-8334)
P.O. Box 254 (47629-0254)
PHONE..................................812 480-4380
Chris Kruckenberg, Pr
Alan Wolfinger, VP
▲ EMP: 7 EST: 2008
SALES (est): 889.76K Privately Held
Web: www.powersystemsinnovations.com
SIC: 3679 Electronic components, nec

(G-13018)
RALPH RANSOM VENEERS
Also Called: Ralph Ransom Logging
6599 Heathervale Ct (47630-9696)
PHONE..................................812 858-9956
EMP: 5 EST: 1991
SALES (est): 264.43K Privately Held
SIC: 2411 Logging

(G-13019)
SCHNUCK MARKETS INC
Also Called: Schnucks
8301 Bell Oaks Dr (47630-2586)
PHONE..................................812 853-9505
Scott Berry, Mgr
EMP: 124
SALES (corp-wide): 2.1B Privately Held
Web: www.schnucks.com
SIC: 5411 5812 5912 5992 Supermarkets, chain; Eating places; Drug stores and proprietary stores; Florists
PA: Schnuck Markets, Inc.
     11420 Lackland Rd
     Saint Louis MO 63146
     314 994-9900

(G-13020)
SEILER & SONS
5922 Seiler Rd (47630-8217)
PHONE..................................812 858-9598
Linda Seiler, Owner
EMP: 5 EST: 1996
SALES (est): 249.03K Privately Held
SIC: 3441 Fabricated structural metal

(G-13021)
SIGNS BY DESIGN LLC
4133 Merchant Dr Ste 5 (47630-2530)
PHONE..................................812 853-7784
EMP: 8 EST: 1993
SQ FT: 3,000
SALES (est): 468.31K Privately Held
Web: www.490sign.com
SIC: 3993 Signs, not made in custom sign painting shops

(G-13022)
SLEDGEHAMMER PRINTING CORP
4956 State Route 261 (47630-3801)
PHONE..................................812 629-2160
EMP: 6 EST: 2018
SALES (est): 222.74K Privately Held
Web: www.sledgehammerprinting.com
SIC: 2759 Screen printing

(G-13023)
STRATEGIC SOLUTIONS INC
4133 Merchant Dr Ste 6 (47630-2530)
PHONE..................................812 853-8525
Kelly Culiver, Prin
EMP: 1 EST: 2004
SALES (est): 143.86K Privately Held
Web: www.the-messenger.net
SIC: 3993 Signs and advertising specialties

(G-13024)
SUNBURST STAINED GLASS CO INC
20 W Jennings St (47630-1212)
PHONE..................................812 853-0460
Sue J Morrison, Pr
Harry Thompson, VP
Mildred Thompson, Sec
EMP: 8 EST: 1977
SQ FT: 4,200
SALES (est): 716.14K Privately Held
SIC: 3231 7699 Stained glass: made from purchased glass; Door and window repair

(G-13025)
TREY EXPLORATION INC
2699 State Route 261 (47630)
P.O. Box 906 (47629-0906)
PHONE..................................812 858-3146
Howard Nevins, Pr
EMP: 4 EST: 1987
SQ FT: 1,200
SALES (est): 482.57K Privately Held
Web: www.treyexploration.com
SIC: 1382 1311 Oil and gas exploration services; Crude petroleum production

(G-13026)
TROPHY CASE LLC
Also Called: Abby Grace's Gifts
5388 Epworth Rd (47630-8724)
PHONE..................................812 853-5087
EMP: 1 EST: 2013
SALES (est): 81.14K Privately Held
Web: thetrophycase.business.site
SIC: 3479 3499 Etching and engraving; Novelties and giftware, including trophies

(G-13027)
VIBRONICS INC
10744 State Route 662 W (47630-8830)
P.O. Box 5488 (47716-5488)
PHONE..................................812 853-2300
John E Wiegand, Pr
EMP: 8 EST: 1988
SQ FT: 3,500
SALES (est): 875.23K Privately Held
Web: www.vibronics.com
SIC: 3829 Measuring and controlling devices, nec

(G-13028)
WARRICK NEWCO LLC
Also Called: Alcoa Newco
4400 W State Route 66 (47630-9100)
PHONE..................................812 853-6111
Heather Hudak Managing, Prin
EMP: 700 EST: 2020
SALES (est): 90.2MM
SALES (corp-wide): 10.55B Publicly Held
SIC: 3399 Metal powders, pastes, and flakes
PA: Alcoa Corporation
     201 Isabella St Ste 500
     Pittsburgh PA 15212
     412 315-2900

(G-13029)
WEATHERFORD ENGINEERED
P.O. Box 727 (47629-0727)
PHONE..................................812 858-3147
EMP: 4 EST: 2012
SALES (est): 142.52K Privately Held
Web: www.weatherford.com
SIC: 1389 Oil field services, nec

(G-13030)
WYNN JONES MINING TOOLS L L C
7022 Jenner Rd (47630-8176)
PHONE..................................812 858-5394
Kenneth Wynn, Pr
EMP: 1 EST: 1992
SALES (est): 87.44K Privately Held
SIC: 3546 Drills and drilling tools

Newport
Vermillion County

(G-13031)
NEWPORT PALLET INC
1888 S State Rd 63 (47966)
P.O. Box 279 (47966-0279)
PHONE..................................217 497-8220
Adam Winland, Pr
EMP: 7 EST: 2010
SALES (est): 192.95K Privately Held
Web: www.newportpallet.com
SIC: 2448 Pallets, wood

Noblesville
Hamilton County

(G-13032)
1ST DEFENSE
6613 Crossbridge Dr (46062-7361)
PHONE..................................317 292-3123
Zachary Bush, Admn
EMP: 5 EST: 2013
SALES (est): 80.48K Privately Held
SIC: 3812 Defense systems and equipment

(G-13033)
ABRASIVE WATERJET INDIANA LLC
15513 Stony Creek Way (46060)
P.O. Box 144 (46061)
PHONE..................................317 773-1631
Kyle Cosand, Pr
Kyle Cosand, Managing Member
EMP: 9 EST: 2008
SALES (est): 817.78K Privately Held
Web: www.waterjetindiana.com
SIC: 3599 Machine shop, jobbing and repair

(G-13034)
ALEX VIROK DBA INTEC
6281 Saw Mill Dr (46062-6560)
PHONE..................................317 770-7559
Alex Virok, Prin
EMP: 1 EST: 2007
SALES (est): 89.93K Privately Held
SIC: 3089 Molding primary plastics

(G-13035)
AMERICAN DREAM NUT BUTTER
12033 Logan Hunter Trl (46060-9104)
PHONE..................................317 326-9363
EMP: 1 EST: 2016
SALES (est): 66.56K Privately Held
SIC: 2021 Creamery butter

(G-13036)
AMERICAN FEEDING SYSTEMS INC
15425 Endeavor Dr (46060-4921)
PHONE..................................317 773-5517
Robert Camp, Pr
▲ EMP: 22 EST: 1982
SQ FT: 16,000
SALES (est): 3.85MM Privately Held
Web: www.americanfeeding.com
SIC: 3559 Vibratory parts handling equipment

(G-13037)
B & L LIGHTING AND SIGN INC
21570 Anchor Bay Dr (46062-6791)
PHONE..................................317 984-4206
Bryan Durr, Prin
EMP: 1 EST: 2014
SALES (est): 79.46K Privately Held
SIC: 3993 Signs and advertising specialties

(G-13038)
BANDGAP SEMICONDUCTOR LLC
Also Called: Bandgap Semiconductor
176 W Logan St Ste 231 (46060-1437)
PHONE..................................317 652-3250
Stephen Barlow, Engr
Bryan Barlow, COO
EMP: 3 EST: 2013
SQ FT: 800
SALES (est): 174.59K Privately Held
SIC: 3674 Semiconductors and related devices

(G-13039)
BARLEY ISLAND BREWING CO
5855 E 211th St Ste 32 (46062-6876)

Noblesville - Hamilton County (G-13064)

PHONE....................317 770-5280
Jeff Eaton, *Owner*
EMP: 8 **EST:** 1999
SALES (est): 347.34K **Privately Held**
Web: www.barleyisland.com
SIC: 2082 5812 5181 Beer (alcoholic beverage); Eating places; Beer and ale

(G-13040)
BATTERIES PLUS
2640 Conner St (46060)
PHONE....................317 219-0007
Jay Norvell, *Prin*
EMP: 7 **EST:** 2009
SALES (est): 131.4K **Privately Held**
Web: www.batteriesplus.com
SIC: 5531 5063 3691 Batteries, automotive and truck; Batteries; Storage batteries

(G-13041)
BAVETTES MEAT COMPANY LLC
10794 Standish Pl (46060-8253)
PHONE....................312 590-7141
EMP: 2 **EST:** 2020
SALES (est): 62.38K **Privately Held**
SIC: 2051 Bakery: wholesale or wholesale/retail combined

(G-13042)
BEAVER GRAVEL CORPORATION
Also Called: Beaver Materials
16101 River Rd (46062-9567)
PHONE....................317 773-0679
Allyn Beaver, *Pr*
Gary Beaver, *
John B Shank, *
EMP: 60 **EST:** 1953
SQ FT: 2,100
SALES (est): 8.48MM **Privately Held**
Web: www.beavergravel.com
SIC: 1442 3273 3272 Gravel mining; Ready-mixed concrete; Concrete products, nec

(G-13043)
BEAVER PRODUCTS INC
16101 River Rd (46062-9567)
PHONE....................317 773-0679
R Gary Beaver, *VP*
Allyn Beaver, *Sec*
EMP: 10 **EST:** 1972
SQ FT: 2,100
SALES (est): 1MM **Privately Held**
SIC: 3272 Concrete products, precast, nec

(G-13044)
BOICE MANUFACTURING INC
Also Called: Warner Bodies
1699 S 8th St (46060-3705)
P.O. Box 2076 (46061-2076)
PHONE....................317 773-2100
EMP: 85
SIC: 3713 3469 Truck bodies (motor vehicles); Boxes: tool, lunch, mail, etc.: stamped metal

(G-13045)
BORGWARNER PDS (INDIANA) INC (HQ)
Also Called: Borgwarner Power Drive System
13975 Borgwarner Dr (46060)
PHONE....................765 778-6696
Ronald Hundzinski, *Pr*
Thomas Mcgill, *Treas*
John Gasparovic, *Sec*
Al Vandenbergh, *CFO*
Victor Polen, *COO*
EMP: 124 **EST:** 2014
SALES (est): 1.41B
SALES (corp-wide): 14.2B **Publicly Held**
Web: www.borgwarner.com
SIC: 3694 3714 Battery charging alternators and generators; Motor vehicle engines and parts
PA: Borgwarner Inc.
3850 Hamlin Rd
Auburn Hills MI 48326
248 754-9200

(G-13046)
BRANDWISE LLC
16170 Sundew Dr (46062-7051)
PHONE....................317 574-0066
Andrew Nisenshal, *Admn*
EMP: 5 **EST:** 2016
SALES (est): 226.16K **Privately Held**
Web: www.brandwisepromo.com
SIC: 2759 Screen printing

(G-13047)
BRAZING PREFORMS LLC
15402 Stony Creek Way (46060-4383)
PHONE....................317 705-6455
Kevin Brandenburg, *Mgr*
EMP: 6 **EST:** 1999
SALES (est): 220.28K **Privately Held**
SIC: 7692 Brazing

(G-13048)
BRIDGESTONE RET OPERATIONS LLC
Also Called: Firestone
249 N 10th St (46060-2160)
PHONE....................317 773-2761
Tom Harvey, *Mgr*
EMP: 4
Web: www.bridgestoneamericas.com
SIC: 5531 7534 7538 7539 Automotive tires; Tire retreading and repair shops; General automotive repair shops; Brake services
HQ: Bridgestone Retail Operations, Llc
200 4th Ave S Ste 100
Nashville TN 37201
630 259-9000

(G-13049)
BTC LAPMASTER LLC
Also Called: Bates Technologies, LLC
14560 Bergen Blvd (46060-5204)
PHONE....................317 841-2400
Ted L Bates, *CEO*
Daryll Day, *
Brian Nelson, *
▲ **EMP:** 56 **EST:** 1985
SQ FT: 25,000
SALES (est): 9.51MM **Privately Held**
Web: www.pss-atd.com
SIC: 3545 Wheel turning equipment, diamond point or other
HQ: Lapmaster International, Llc
501 W Algonquin Rd
Mount Prospect IL 60056
224 659-7101

(G-13050)
BURCO MOLDING INC
Also Called: Burco
15015 Herriman Blvd (46060-4253)
PHONE....................317 773-5699
Clovis E Burrow, *Pr*
Randy E Burrow, *
EMP: 58 **EST:** 1970
SQ FT: 34,000
SALES (est): 9.65MM **Privately Held**
Web: www.burco-molding.com
SIC: 3089 3544 Injection molded finished plastics products, nec; Special dies, tools, jigs, and fixtures

(G-13051)
BUTTERFIELD FOODS LLC
Also Called: Butterfield Foods
635 Westfield Rd (46060-1323)
PHONE....................317 776-4775
Frank Violi, *Owner*
D G Elmore, *
EMP: 120 **EST:** 1981
SQ FT: 54,000
SALES (est): 17.42MM **Privately Held**
Web: www.butterfield-foods.com
SIC: 2038 2099 2824 Soups, frozen; Sandwiches, assembled and packaged: for wholesale market; Protein fibers

(G-13052)
C & G SALSA COMPANY LLC
5282 E 156th St (46062-6827)
P.O. Box 6085 (46038-6085)
PHONE....................317 569-9099
Charles Ferguson, *Managing Member*
EMP: 2 **EST:** 2001
SALES (est): 207.9K **Privately Held**
SIC: 2099 Pasta, uncooked: packaged with other ingredients

(G-13053)
CABINET EXPRESSIONS
15503 Outside Trl (46060-8063)
PHONE....................317 366-7669
EMP: 4 **EST:** 2007
SALES (est): 39.67K **Privately Held**
Web: www.cabinetexpressions.com
SIC: 2434 Wood kitchen cabinets

(G-13054)
CANVAS VINYL CREATIONS INC
20230 Hague Rd 189 (46062-9540)
PHONE....................317 371-4227
Richard Worland, *Owner*
EMP: 1 **EST:** 2010
SALES (est): 77.8K **Privately Held**
Web: www.canvasvinylcreations.com
SIC: 2394 Canvas and related products

(G-13055)
CARROLL DISTRG & CNSTR SUP INC
20935 Cicero Rd. (Sr 19) (46060)
PHONE....................317 984-2400
Dan Carroll, *Brnch Mgr*
EMP: 4
SALES (corp-wide): 99.42MM **Privately Held**
Web: www.carrollsupply.com
SIC: 5082 3444 Contractor's materials; Concrete forms, sheet metal
PA: Carroll Distributing & Construction Supply, Inc.
207 W 2nd St Ste 3
Ottumwa IA 52501
641 455-5545

(G-13056)
CHADS SIGNS INSTALLATIONS INC (PA)
Also Called: Csi Signs
555 Park 32 West Dr (46062-9452)
P.O. Box 210 (46074-0210)
PHONE....................317 867-2737
Chad Huff, *Pr*
Steven R Lloyd, *Prin*
EMP: 8 **EST:** 2004
SALES (est): 941.45K
SALES (corp-wide): 941.45K **Privately Held**
Web: www.csi-signs.com
SIC: 3993 Electric signs

(G-13057)
CHAMPIONS IMAGE
19122 Timothy Ln (46060-6759)
PHONE....................317 501-3617
Elizabeth Ann Noll, *Owner*
EMP: 1 **EST:** 2006
SALES (est): 45.35K **Privately Held**
SIC: 2395 Pleating and stitching

(G-13058)
CHEMTREX LLC
6315 Edenshall Ln (46062-4633)
PHONE....................317 508-4223
Darrin T Hugill, *Owner*
EMP: 3 **EST:** 2014
SALES (est): 221.84K **Privately Held**
SIC: 3677 Filtration devices, electronic

(G-13059)
CIBUS FRESH LLC
15510 Stony Creek Way (46060-4385)
PHONE....................317 674-8379
Kurt E Layer, *Pr*
EMP: 15 **EST:** 2017
SQ FT: 11,000
SALES (est): 2.27MM
SALES (corp-wide): 3.63B **Privately Held**
Web: www.cibusfresh.com
SIC: 2099 Food preparations, nec
HQ: Indianapolis Fruit Company, Llc
4501 Massachusetts Ave
Indianapolis IN 46218
317 546-2425

(G-13060)
CIRCLE CITY LIGHTING INC
21570 Anchor Bay Dr (46062-6791)
PHONE....................317 439-0824
Bryan Durr, *Ofcr*
EMP: 5 **EST:** 2015
SALES (est): 119.55K **Privately Held**
Web: www.circlecitylighting.com
SIC: 3648 Lighting equipment, nec

(G-13061)
CJS STOP N GO
5855 E 211th St Ste 34 (46062-6876)
PHONE....................317 877-0681
Chris Matchik, *Prin*
Chris Matchik, *Owner*
EMP: 2 **EST:** 2012
SALES (est): 207.35K **Privately Held**
SIC: 2911 Petroleum refining

(G-13062)
CONTROLLED AUTOMATION INC
15421 Stony Creek Way Ste A (46060-4330)
PHONE....................317 770-3870
Dean A Graham, *Pr*
Rhenda G Graham, *Sec*
EMP: 16 **EST:** 1990
SQ FT: 4,200
SALES (est): 2.4MM **Privately Held**
Web: www.controlledautomationinc.com
SIC: 3613 Control panels, electric

(G-13063)
COUDEN WOODWORKS INC
23808 Couden Rd (46060-9784)
PHONE....................317 370-0835
Mark Sterner, *Owner*
EMP: 6 **EST:** 2004
SALES (est): 137.07K **Privately Held**
Web: www.iwoodwork.net
SIC: 2431 Millwork

(G-13064)
COUNTRY MOON WINERY LLC
Also Called: Country Moon Winery

Noblesville - Hamilton County (G-13065)

16222 Prairie Baptist Rd (46060-9350)
PHONE..................................317 773-7942
Brian Harger, *Managing Member*
EMP: 2 **EST:** 2010
SALES (est): 115.36K **Privately Held**
Web: www.countrymoonwinery.com
SIC: 2084 7299 Wines; Facility rental and party planning services

(G-13065)
CREATIVE LDSCP & COMPOST CO
Also Called: Creative Ldscpg & Compost Co
18377 Deshane Ave (46060-8825)
PHONE..................................317 776-2909
Teri Haas, *Pr*
John Haas, *VP*
EMP: 3 **EST:** 1974
SQ FT: 12,500
SALES (est): 377.77K **Privately Held**
Web: www.clcorganics.com
SIC: 4953 2875 0782 0181 Nonhazardous waste disposal sites; Compost; Landscape contractors; Shrubberies, grown in field nurseries

(G-13066)
CURTIS HONEYCUTT LLC
957 Hannibal St (46060-2746)
PHONE..................................317 645-7540
Curtis Honeycutt, *Owner*
EMP: 5 **EST:** 2017
SALES (est): 92.36K **Privately Held**
Web: www.curtishoneycutt.com
SIC: 2741 Miscellaneous publishing

(G-13067)
D & D MOULDINGS & MILLWORK LLC
15509 Stony Creek Way (46060-4386)
PHONE..................................317 770-5500
Michael L Dilk, *Pr*
Michael L Dilk, *Pr*
Daniel S De Lay, *
EMP: 43 **EST:** 1990
SQ FT: 15,000
SALES (est): 4.99MM **Privately Held**
Web: www.ddmouldings.com
SIC: 2431 Doors, wood

(G-13068)
DCA CUSTOM ARROWS LLC
5861 Daw St (46062-5504)
PHONE..................................317 627-0909
Kyle Davidson, *Prin*
EMP: 5 **EST:** 2019
SALES (est): 121.44K **Privately Held**
Web: www.dcacustomarrows.com
SIC: 3949 Sporting and athletic goods, nec

(G-13069)
DEAR ATHLETES INC
Also Called: Dear Athletes Foundation The
5561 Village Winds Dr Apt D (46062-6441)
PHONE..................................615 682-3332
Cristin Dent, *Pr*
EMP: 4 **EST:** 2020
SALES (est): 141.72K **Privately Held**
SIC: 6732 5699 7999 3999 Educational trust management; Sports apparel; Sports instruction, schools and camps; Education aids, devices and supplies

(G-13070)
DIAMOND HOOSIER
518 Sunset Dr (46060-1223)
PHONE..................................317 773-1411
Dave Jellison, *Owner*
EMP: 3 **EST:** 1991
SALES (est): 127.31K **Privately Held**

SIC: 2721 7941 Periodicals; Sports promotion

(G-13071)
DICKEY CONSUMER PRODUCTS INC
Also Called: DMD Pharmaceuticals
15268 Stony Creek Way Ste 100 (46060-4392)
P.O. Box 1055 (46061-1055)
PHONE..................................317 773-8330
David Dickey, *CEO*
Dawn Dickey, *Ex VP*
David Riddle, *CFO*
EMP: 14 **EST:** 1994
SQ FT: 15,000
SALES (est): 2.37MM **Privately Held**
Web: www.dmdpharm.com
SIC: 2834 Pharmaceutical preparations

(G-13072)
DIRECTED PHOTONICS INC
7178 Oakbay Dr (46062-9760)
PHONE..................................317 877-3142
Robert Marusa, *Pr*
EMP: 6 **EST:** 2010
SALES (est): 475.91K **Privately Held**
Web: www.dpilasers.com
SIC: 3699 Laser systems and equipment

(G-13073)
DISCOUNT COPY SERVICES INC
Also Called: Discount Copier Service
100 Mensa Dr (46062-9250)
PHONE..................................317 773-8783
EMP: 6 **EST:** 1996
SQ FT: 4,000
SALES (est): 580.15K **Privately Held**
Web: www.discount-copies.com
SIC: 2752 Offset printing

(G-13074)
DREW IT YOURSELF WOOD WORKING
12605 Cold Stream Rd (46060-4760)
PHONE..................................317 250-6548
Elizabeth Facsko, *Prin*
EMP: 5 **EST:** 2017
SALES (est): 64.88K **Privately Held**
SIC: 2431 Millwork

(G-13075)
FAST TRACK TECHNOLOGIES LLC
Also Called: Duratech
18882 Mallery Rd (46060-6739)
PHONE..................................317 229-6080
EMP: 10 **EST:** 2010
SALES (est): 899.59K **Privately Held**
Web: www.theeasystrap.com
SIC: 3821 Laboratory apparatus and furniture

(G-13076)
FEEDING CONCEPTS INC
15235 Herriman Blvd (46060-4230)
PHONE..................................317 773-2040
John Graham Ii, *Pr*
EMP: 15 **EST:** 1990
SQ FT: 15,900
SALES (est): 2.47MM **Privately Held**
Web: www.feedingconcepts.com
SIC: 3559 Vibratory parts handling equipment

(G-13077)
FIELD RUBBER PRODUCTS INC
3211 Conner St (46060-2411)
PHONE..................................317 773-3787
John M Field, *Pr*
Michael Field, *Pr*
EMP: 12 **EST:** 1955

SQ FT: 30,000
SALES (est): 2.14MM **Privately Held**
Web: www.fieldrubber.com
SIC: 3069 Molded rubber products

(G-13078)
FILSON EARTHWORK COMPANY
21785 Riverwood Ave (46062-9560)
P.O. Box 538 (46061-0538)
PHONE..................................317 774-3180
Greg Filson, *Pr*
EMP: 14 **EST:** 2004
SALES (est): 1.93MM **Privately Held**
SIC: 1389 Excavating slush pits and cellars

(G-13079)
FLANNIGAN PRESS LLC
10422 Magenta Dr (46060-8398)
PHONE..................................317 776-4914
Jeanna Janes, *Pr*
EMP: 4 **EST:** 2016
SALES (est): 59.85K **Privately Held**
SIC: 2741 Miscellaneous publishing

(G-13080)
FOUNDRY SERVICES INC
10482 Winghaven Dr (46060-4464)
PHONE..................................317 955-8112
EMP: 25 **EST:** 1994
SQ FT: 70,000
SALES (est): 256.22K **Privately Held**
Web: www.foundryservice.com
SIC: 3366 Castings (except die), nsk

(G-13081)
FREW PROCESS GROUP LLC
605 Sheridan Rd Ste 100 (46060-1333)
PHONE..................................317 565-5000
EMP: 6 **EST:** 2012
SALES (est): 889.32K **Privately Held**
Web: www.fpg.co
SIC: 3823 5074 3491 Magnetic flow meters, industrial process type; Heating equipment (hydronic); Industrial valves

(G-13082)
GARED HOLDINGS LLC
Also Called: Gared Sports
9200 E 146th St Ste A (46060-4362)
PHONE..................................317 774-9840
Dimitrios Koukoulomatis, *CEO*
Mary Witte, *
◆ **EMP:** 110 **EST:** 1925
SQ FT: 3,500
SALES (est): 43.55MM **Privately Held**
Web: www.garedsports.com
SIC: 3949 Sporting and athletic goods, nec

(G-13083)
GASCO LLC
Also Called: Gasco
15305 Stony Creek Way (46060-4382)
PHONE..................................317 565-5000
Mike Smith, *Managing Member*
EMP: 2 **EST:** 2012
SALES (est): 241.02K **Privately Held**
SIC: 3612 Generator voltage regulators

(G-13084)
GEM-ROSE CORPORATION
597 Christian Ave (46060-3722)
P.O. Box 644 (46061-0644)
PHONE..................................317 773-6400
Roger Brown, *Pr*
Tammy Brown, *VP*
EMP: 5 **EST:** 1982
SQ FT: 15,000
SALES (est): 473.65K **Privately Held**
SIC: 3441 Fabricated structural metal

(G-13085)
GENERAL AUTOMATION COMPANY
9520 E 206th St (46060-1081)
PHONE..................................317 849-7483
Gabriel Effing, *Pr*
EMP: 10 **EST:** 1983
SALES (est): 2.02MM **Privately Held**
Web: www.appliedintelligencecorp.com
SIC: 3625 8742 Relays and industrial controls; Automation and robotics consultant

(G-13086)
GLASSWING PRESS LLC
18046 Forreston Oak Dr (46062-7525)
PHONE..................................937 554-1784
Wendi S Williams, *Prin*
EMP: 4 **EST:** 2019
SALES (est): 82.39K **Privately Held**
Web: www.glasswingpress.com
SIC: 2741 Miscellaneous publishing

(G-13087)
GLOW DR LLC ◐
16751 Clover Rd (46060-3646)
PHONE..................................317 622-6735
EMP: 1 **EST:** 2022
SALES (est): 39.69K **Privately Held**
SIC: 3999 Fingernails, artificial

(G-13088)
GREEN ILLUMINATING SYSTEMS INC
10330 Pleasant St Ste 600 (46060-3957)
P.O. Box 932 (46061-0932)
PHONE..................................317 869-7430
Thomas Treinen, *Pr*
EMP: 3 **EST:** 2009
SALES (est): 279.62K **Privately Held**
Web: www.hpledlighting.com
SIC: 3646 Commercial lighting fixtures

(G-13089)
GREENCYCLE INC
2695 Cicero Rd (46060-1026)
PHONE..................................317 773-3350
Greg Hart, *Brnch Mgr*
EMP: 2
Web: www.greencycle.com
SIC: 2875 4953 5261 Compost; Sanitary landfill operation; Lawn and garden supplies
PA: Greencycle, Inc
400 Central Ave Ste 115
Northfield IL 60093

(G-13090)
H M C SCREEN PRINTING INC
954 Conner St (46060-2621)
PHONE..................................317 773-8532
Mary Worline, *Pr*
Jamie Worline, *VP*
EMP: 20 **EST:** 1981
SQ FT: 3,000
SALES (est): 384.42K **Privately Held**
Web: www.hmcscreenprinting.com
SIC: 2759 Screen printing

(G-13091)
HAGER INDUSTRIES INC
230 Riverwood Dr (46062-8841)
PHONE..................................317 219-6622
Myles Hager, *Prin*
EMP: 7 **EST:** 2008
SALES (est): 238.04K **Privately Held**
Web: www.hagerindustries.com
SIC: 3999 Manufacturing industries, nec

(G-13092)
HAMILTON COUNTY BUSINESS MAG
1095 Mulberry St (46060-2830)
P.O. Box 502 (46061-0502)
PHONE..................................317 774-7747

GEOGRAPHIC SECTION

Noblesville - Hamilton County (G-13118)

Mike Corbett, *Owner*
EMP: 1 EST: 2008
SALES (est): 115.35K **Privately Held**
Web: www.hamiltoncountybusiness.com
SIC: **2721** 2741 7999 Magazines: publishing only, not printed on site; Maps: publishing only, not printed on site; Exposition operation

(G-13093)
HAYDEN CORP
6192 Stonehenge Blvd (46062-5206)
PHONE..................................317 501-5660
Mark C Hagerty, *Pr*
EMP: 2 EST: 2009
SALES (est): 131.26K **Privately Held**
SIC: **3599** Machine shop, jobbing and repair

(G-13094)
HELMER SCIENTIFIC LLC
Also Called: Helmer Scientific
14400 Bergen Blvd (46060-3307)
PHONE..................................317 773-9073
David Helmer, *Ch*
David Helmer, *Ch*
EMP: 170 EST: 1983
SQ FT: 32,000
SALES (est): 67.83MM **Privately Held**
Web: www.helmerinc.com
SIC: **3841** 3821 Blood transfusion equipment; Autoclaves, laboratory
HQ: Trane Technologies Company Llc
  800-E Beaty St
  Davidson NC 28036
  704 655-4000

(G-13095)
HOLGIN TECHNOLOGIES LLC
15335 Endeavor Dr Ste 100 (46060-4943)
PHONE..................................317 774-5181
Alan Mcmullen, *Managing Member*
EMP: 10 EST: 2016
SALES (est): 496.63K **Privately Held**
Web: www.holgin.net
SIC: **3841** Surgical and medical instruments

(G-13096)
HOME SNACK FOODS LLC
Also Called: Home Foods
16591 Meadow Wood Dr (46062-6715)
PHONE..................................317 764-6644
Jeffrey P Young, *Pr*
William Mcginniss, *Ch*
EMP: 7 EST: 2014
SALES (est): 496.5K **Privately Held**
SIC: **2043** Granola and muesli, except bars and clusters

(G-13097)
HUNTER INDUSTRIES
5477 Cottage Grove Ln (46062-6098)
PHONE..................................630 200-7581
EMP: 6 EST: 2018
SALES (est): 54.57K **Privately Held**
Web: www.hunterindustries.com
SIC: **3523** Farm machinery and equipment

(G-13098)
HUVER MANUFACTURING TECH LLC
Also Called: Hu/Man Tech
10210 Carmine Dr (46060-8379)
PHONE..................................317 460-8605
EMP: 3 EST: 2009
SALES (est): 139.37K **Privately Held**
Web: www.huvermfgtech.com
SIC: **3499** Fabricated metal products, nec

(G-13099)
ICON BEAUTY SUPPLY INC
14350 Mundy Dr Ste 800-268 (46060-7223)
PHONE..................................317 209-6550
Camilla Kimbrough, *CEO*
EMP: 2 EST: 2010
SALES (est): 120K **Privately Held**
Web: www.theiconbeautysupply.com
SIC: **2844** Hair preparations, including shampoos

(G-13100)
IDI FABRICATION INC (PA)
14444 Herriman Blvd (46060)
PHONE..................................317 776-6577
▲ EMP: 89 EST: 2010
SQ FT: 55,000
SALES (est): 22.87MM **Privately Held**
Web: www.idifabrication.com
SIC: **3567** Induction and dielectric heating equipment

(G-13101)
IN DUCTILE LLC
Also Called: Indiana Ductile
1600 S 8th St (46060-3739)
PHONE..................................317 776-8000
EMP: 19 EST: 2000
SQ FT: 225,000
SALES (est): 815.66K **Privately Held**
Web: www.idcastings.com
SIC: **3321** Ductile iron castings

(G-13102)
INDIANA MOBILE WELDING LLC
245 Riverwood Dr (46062-8841)
PHONE..................................317 771-8900
EMP: 2 EST: 2020
SALES (est): 48.8K **Privately Held**
Web: indianamobilewelding.business.site
SIC: **7692** 7699 1542 0761 Welding repair; Industrial machinery and equipment repair; Agricultural building contractors; Farm labor contractors

(G-13103)
INDUSTRIAL DIELECTRICS INC
Also Called: IDI Composites International
407 S 7th St (46060)
P.O. Box 357 (46061)
PHONE..................................317 773-1766
♦ EMP: 282 EST: 2009
SQ FT: 100,000
SALES (est): 83.45MM
SALES (corp-wide): 203.83MM **Privately Held**
Web: www.idicomposites.com
SIC: **2821** Molding compounds, plastics
PA: Industrial Dielectrics Holdings, Inc.
  15389 North Pointe Blvd
  Noblesville IN 46060
  317 773-1766

(G-13104)
INDUSTRIAL DLCTRICS HLDNGS INC (PA)
Also Called: IDI
15389 North Pointe Blvd (46060)
P.O. Box 357 (46061)
PHONE..................................317 773-1766
Thomas K Merrell, *Pr*
John D Merrell, *VP*
Terrence M Doll, *Sec*
♦ EMP: 8 EST: 1966
SQ FT: 15,000
SALES (est): 203.83MM
SALES (corp-wide): 203.83MM **Privately Held**
Web: www.idicomposites.com
SIC: **2821** Plastics materials and resins

(G-13105)
INDY POWDER COATINGS LLC
10482 Winghaven Dr (46060-4464)
PHONE..................................317 236-7177
Harold Aubert, *Mgr*
EMP: 8 EST: 2002
SQ FT: 65,000
SALES (est): 379.89K **Privately Held**
Web: www.indy-powdercoating.com
SIC: **3479** Coating of metals and formed products

(G-13106)
INFOLOGIX INC
14670 Cumberland Rd (46060-8708)
P.O. Box 7000 (06050-7000)
PHONE..................................260 485-7380
▲ EMP: 168
SIC: **7372** Prepackaged software

(G-13107)
INTEGRITY HEARING (PA)
5628 Merritt Cir (46062-2202)
PHONE..................................317 882-9151
EMP: 1 EST: 2013
SALES (est): 225.24K
SALES (corp-wide): 225.24K **Privately Held**
SIC: **5999** 3842 Hearing aids; Hearing aids

(G-13108)
IRVING MATERIALS INC
Also Called: I M I
17050 River Rd (46062-9566)
PHONE..................................317 770-1745
Prent Alfod, *Mgr*
EMP: 10
SALES (corp-wide): 814.09MM **Privately Held**
Web: www.irvmat.com
SIC: **3273** Ready-mixed concrete
PA: Irving Materials, Inc.
  8032 N State Road 9
  Greenfield IN 46140
  317 326-3101

(G-13109)
IRVING MATERIALS INC
Also Called: I M I
12798 State Road 38 E (46060-8806)
PHONE..................................317 773-3640
Tim Burke, *Brnch Mgr*
EMP: 6
SALES (corp-wide): 814.09MM **Privately Held**
Web: www.irvmat.com
SIC: **3273** Ready-mixed concrete
PA: Irving Materials, Inc.
  8032 N State Road 9
  Greenfield IN 46140
  317 326-3101

(G-13110)
J JACOBY INC (PA)
Also Called: Stone Surface Solutions
285 Westchester Blvd (46062-7497)
PHONE..................................317 877-9275
M R Jacoby, *Pr*
Shirley Jacoby, *Sec*
EMP: 1 EST: 1996
SALES (est): 413.31K
SALES (corp-wide): 413.31K **Privately Held**
SIC: **2542** Counters or counter display cases, except wood

(G-13111)
JAMES WAFFORD
Also Called: Logan Street Signs and Banners
1720 S 10th St (46060-3835)
PHONE..................................317 773-7200
James Wafford, *Owner*
EMP: 3 EST: 1991
SQ FT: 800
SALES (est): 311.68K **Privately Held**
Web: www.loganstreetsigns.com
SIC: **2759** 3993 Visiting cards (including business): printing, nsk; Signs and advertising specialties

(G-13112)
JDS INTERNATIONAL INC
15321 Herriman Blvd (46060-4214)
PHONE..................................317 753-4427
EMP: 12 EST: 2008
SALES (est): 1.28MM **Privately Held**
Web: www.jdsinternational.biz
SIC: **3724** 3728 3795 Aircraft engines and engine parts; Aircraft parts and equipment, nec; Tanks and tank components

(G-13113)
JENMAR ENTERPRISES LLC
19268 Chicory Ct (46060-7594)
PHONE..................................219 306-3149
EMP: 4 EST: 2015
SALES (est): 29.47K **Privately Held**
SIC: **3532** Mining machinery

(G-13114)
JOSH ROWLAND
6221 Strathaven Rd (46062-4629)
PHONE..................................574 596-6754
EMP: 5 EST: 2017
SALES (est): 103.91K **Privately Held**
Web: rowland.whirldemo.com
SIC: **2752** Offset printing

(G-13115)
JUST INSTALL LLC
20962 Hinkle Rd (46062-9745)
PHONE..................................317 607-3911
Casey Weaver, *Owner*
EMP: 1 EST: 2007
SALES (est): 137.68K **Privately Held**
Web: www.just-install.com
SIC: **2752** 2399 Commercial printing, lithographic; Banners, pennants, and flags

(G-13116)
KD DIDS QUILTING
8184 Sedge Grass Rd (46060-6149)
PHONE..................................317 460-0646
Kathy Dye, *Prin*
EMP: 1 EST: 2010
SALES (est): 54.52K **Privately Held**
Web: www.kddids.com
SIC: **2395** Quilting and quilting supplies

(G-13117)
KELBY J WALDRIP
18826 Fairfield Blvd (46060-1596)
PHONE..................................812 824-2492
Kelby J Waldrip, *Prin*
EMP: 8 EST: 2008
SALES (est): 214.25K **Privately Held**
SIC: **2011** Meat packing plants

(G-13118)
KELLEY GLOBAL BRANDS LLC
Also Called: Klh Audio
632 Longford Way (46062-8574)
PHONE..................................833 554-8326
David Kelley, *Pr*
John Kerns, *VP Fin*
EMP: 8 EST: 2017
SQ FT: 4,376
SALES (est): 1.11MM **Privately Held**
Web: www.klhaudio.com

(PA)=Parent Co (HQ)=Headquarters
✪ = New Business established in last 2 years

Noblesville - Hamilton County (G-13119)

SIC: 3651 Speaker systems

(G-13119)
KEN-BAR TOOL & ENGINEERING INC
101 Minnow Ln (46060)
PHONE..................765 284-4408
Clemens Burger, *Pr*
EMP: 27 EST: 1957
SALES (est): 4.81MM **Privately Held**
Web: www.kenbarinc.com
SIC: 3545 3544 3549 Gauges (machine tool accessories); Special dies and tools; Assembly machines, including robotic

(G-13120)
KING SYSTEMS CORPORATION
Also Called: Ambu
15011 Herriman Blvd (46060-4253)
PHONE..................317 776-6823
Steve Davis, *CEO*
◆ EMP: 465 EST: 1977
SQ FT: 100,000
SALES (est): 96.39MM
SALES (corp-wide): 437.86K **Privately Held**
Web: www.ambu.com
SIC: 3841 Anesthesia apparatus
HQ: Ambu Inc.
    6721 Columbia Gateway Dr # 200
    Columbia MD 21046
    410 768-6464

(G-13121)
KINNEY DANCEWEAR
14753 Hazel Dell Xing Ste 600
(46062-7032)
PHONE..................317 581-1800
Jeff Kinney, *Brnch Mgr*
EMP: 2
SALES (corp-wide): 210.8K **Privately Held**
Web: www.kinneydancewear.com
SIC: 2389 5661 Men's miscellaneous accessories; Shoe stores
PA: Kinney Dancewear
    1850 S Hurstbrn Pkwy # 117
    Louisville KY 40220
    502 499-6262

(G-13122)
KIRBY MACHINE COMPANY LLC
1709 Cherry St (46060-3029)
PHONE..................317 773-6700
EMP: 20 EST: 2002
SALES (est): 3.18MM **Privately Held**
Web: www.kmcmold.com
SIC: 3544 Special dies and tools

(G-13123)
KISTNER ENTERPRISES INC
Also Called: PIP Printing
623 Westfield Rd (46060-1323)
PHONE..................317 773-7733
Tony Kistner, *Pr*
EMP: 2 EST: 1973
SQ FT: 1,400
SALES (est): 133.7K **Privately Held**
Web: www.pip.com
SIC: 2752 2791 2789 Offset printing; Typesetting; Bookbinding and related work

(G-13124)
KITTERMAN MACHINE CO INC
87 S 8th St (46060-2605)
P.O. Box 277 (46061-0277)
PHONE..................317 773-2383
Randy Burrow, *Pr*
EMP: 8 EST: 1951
SQ FT: 5,280
SALES (est): 933.71K **Privately Held**
Web: www.kittermanmachine.com

SIC: 3544 3599 Industrial molds; Machine and other job shop work

(G-13125)
LADYBUGZ BOOKSTORE LLC
14350 Mundy Dr (46060-7223)
PHONE..................469 459-1780
Rosanne Moss, *Managing Member*
EMP: 1 EST: 2017
SALES (est): 41.25K **Privately Held**
SIC: 7379 2299 5611 5963 Online services technology consultants; Hemp yarn, thread, roving, and textiles; Clothing, male: everyday, except suits and sportswear; Clothing sales, house-to-house

(G-13126)
LAND ENTERPRISES
7116 Summer Oak Dr (46062-7488)
PHONE..................317 774-9475
Gerald Beland, *Owner*
EMP: 2 EST: 2004
SALES (est): 95.35K **Privately Held**
SIC: 3523 Farm machinery and equipment

(G-13127)
LASER AGENT
15402 Stony Creek Way (46060-4383)
PHONE..................317 570-0448
Tony Kokjohn, *Prin*
EMP: 8 EST: 2017
SALES (est): 763.69K **Privately Held**
Web: www.thelaseragent.com
SIC: 3845 Laser systems and equipment, medical

(G-13128)
LIMITLESS WOODWORKING LLC
21218 Cyntheanne Rd (46060-9788)
PHONE..................317 702-1763
Chad Thomas, *Managing Member*
EMP: 9 EST: 2015
SALES (est): 469.3K **Privately Held**
Web: www.limitlesswoodworking.com
SIC: 2431 Millwork

(G-13129)
MA-RI-AL CORP
Also Called: Beaver Readi-Mix
16101 River Rd (46062-9567)
PHONE..................317 773-0679
Allyn Beaver, *Pr*
Gary Beaver, *
EMP: 42 EST: 1959
SQ FT: 3,500
SALES (est): 917.04K **Privately Held**
SIC: 3273 Ready-mixed concrete

(G-13130)
MARIETTA MARTIN MATERIALS INC
Also Called: Noblesville Sand & Gravel
15215 River Rd (46062-9572)
PHONE..................317 776-4460
EMP: 12
Web: www.martinmarietta.com
SIC: 1442 1422 1411 Construction sand and gravel; Crushed and broken limestone; Dimension stone
PA: Martin Marietta Materials Inc
    4123 Parklake Ave
    Raleigh NC 27612

(G-13131)
MARK LAMASTER
Also Called: Lamaster Radiation Consulting
16271 E 191st St (46060-9295)
P.O. Box 135 (46051-0135)
PHONE..................765 534-4185
Mark Lamaster, *Owner*
EMP: 2 EST: 1985

SALES (est): 245.86K **Privately Held**
SIC: 3674 Radiation sensors

(G-13132)
MCI SCREWDRIVER SYSTEMS INC
Also Called: Verizon Business
14800 Herriman Blvd (46060-4313)
P.O. Box 927 (46061-0927)
PHONE..................317 776-1970
S Neal Graham, *Pr*
EMP: 10 EST: 1993
SQ FT: 16,000
SALES (est): 917.16K **Privately Held**
Web: www.mciscrewdriver.com
SIC: 3599 Machine shop, jobbing and repair

(G-13133)
METAL POWDER PRODUCTS CO LLP
14670 Cumberland Rd (46060-8708)
PHONE..................317 805-3764
Dennis Mckeen, *CEO*
EMP: 19 EST: 1998
SALES (est): 813.31K **Privately Held**
Web: www.mppinnovation.com
SIC: 3492 Hose and tube fittings and assemblies, hydraulic/pneumatic

(G-13134)
METAL POWDER PRODUCTS LLC (PA)
Also Called: Mpp
14670 Cumberland Rd (46060-8708)
PHONE..................317 805-3764
▲ EMP: 15 EST: 1946
SALES (est): 154.49MM
SALES (corp-wide): 154.49MM **Privately Held**
Web: www.mppinnovation.com
SIC: 3399 Aluminum atomized powder

(G-13135)
METHENY ENTERPRISES INC
Also Called: Test Publications
145 Stony Creek Overlook (46060-5427)
PHONE..................317 692-9900
Nick J Metheny, *Acctg Mgr*
EMP: 5 EST: 2016
SALES (est): 67.01K **Privately Held**
SIC: 2741 Miscellaneous publishing

(G-13136)
METRO PLASTICS TECH INC
Also Called: Metro Plastics Technologies
17145 Metro Park Ct (46060-4051)
P.O. Box 1208 (46061-1208)
PHONE..................317 776-0860
Lindsey R Hahn, *Pr*
Alice L Hahn, *VP*
▲ EMP: 80 EST: 1975
SQ FT: 50,000
SALES (est): 19.09MM **Privately Held**
Web: www.metroplastics.com
SIC: 3089 Injection molding of plastics

(G-13137)
MEYER FOODS INC
18247 Pennington Rd (46060-8237)
PHONE..................317 773-6594
Jeffery L Meyer, *Prin*
EMP: 9 EST: 2010
SALES (est): 246.54K **Privately Held**
SIC: 2099 Food preparations, nec

(G-13138)
MG IMPRESSIONS LLC
15320 Herriman Blvd (46060-4207)
PHONE..................317 219-5118
EMP: 7 EST: 2013
SALES (est): 206.65K **Privately Held**
SIC: 2759 Screen printing

(G-13139)
MICROCHIP TECHNOLOGY INC
9779 E 146th St Ste 130 (46060-5037)
PHONE..................317 773-8323
Mike Pennington, *Mgr*
EMP: 6
SALES (corp-wide): 7.63B **Publicly Held**
Web: www.microchip.com
SIC: 3674 Semiconductors and related devices
PA: Microchip Technology Inc
    2355 W Chandler Blvd
    Chandler AZ 85224
    480 792-7200

(G-13140)
MPP HOLDINGS INC
14670 Cumberland Rd (46060-8708)
PHONE..................317 805-3764
Marilyn L Fink, *Pr*
EMP: 9 EST: 1980
SALES (est): 237.15K **Privately Held**
SIC: 8742 3448 Business management consultant; Prefabricated metal components

(G-13141)
NEXXT SPINE LLC
14425 Bergen Blvd Ste B (46060-3422)
PHONE..................317 436-7801
EMP: 12 EST: 2009
SALES (est): 4.22MM **Privately Held**
Web: www.nexxtspine.com
SIC: 3841 Fixation appliances, internal

(G-13142)
NOBLE INDUSTRIES INC
17575 Presley Dr (46060-2477)
PHONE..................317 773-1926
William Parker, *CEO*
Gregory Parker, *
Dee Mckinney, *Sec*
EMP: 50 EST: 1970
SQ FT: 70,000
SALES (est): 9.2MM **Privately Held**
Web: www.nobleindustries.com
SIC: 3444 Sheet metal specialties, not stamped

(G-13143)
NOBLE WIRE PRODUCTS INC
P.O. Box 578 (46061-0578)
PHONE..................317 773-1926
Kathleen Wire, *Prin*
EMP: 6 EST: 2011
SALES (est): 237.96K **Privately Held**
Web: www.madsenwire.com
SIC: 3444 Sheet metalwork

(G-13144)
NOBLESVILLE PACK & SHIP
199 N 9th St (46060-2212)
PHONE..................317 776-6306
Abralin Dean, *Prin*
EMP: 2 EST: 2015
SALES (est): 157.58K **Privately Held**
Web: www.noblesvillepackandship.com
SIC: 7389 2621 Mailbox rental and related service; Specialty or chemically treated papers

(G-13145)
NST CAMPBELLSBURG LLC
14670 Cumberland Rd (46060-8708)
PHONE..................812 755-4501
Dax Whitehouse, *CEO*
David Dudding, *CFO*
EMP: 3 EST: 1995
SALES (est): 896.6K
SALES (corp-wide): 154.49MM **Privately Held**

GEOGRAPHIC SECTION

Noblesville - Hamilton County (G-13173)

SIC: 3499 Friction material, made from powdered metal
HQ: Nst Technologies Mim Llc
14670 Cumberland Rd
Noblesville IN 46060
812 248-9273

(G-13146)
NST TECHNOLOGIES MIM LLC (HQ)
Also Called: Mpp
14670 Cumberland Rd (46060-8708)
PHONE..................812 248-9273
Dax Whitehouse, *CEO*
Ric Wrye, *
▲ EMP: 30 EST: 2001
SQ FT: 8,000
SALES (est): 124.23MM
SALES (corp-wide): 154.49MM **Privately Held**
Web: www.mppinnovation.com
SIC: 3339 Antimony refining (primary)
PA: Metal Powder Products, Llc
14670 Cumberland Rd
Noblesville IN 46060
317 805-3764

(G-13147)
OCTOBERS FIRM LABEL LLC
57 Lions Creek Ct S (46062-8615)
PHONE..................317 778-1447
EMP: 2
SALES (est): 88.38K **Privately Held**
SIC: 3651 7389 Music distribution apparatus; Business Activities at Non-Commercial Site

(G-13148)
ORBITAL INSTALLATION TECH LLC
9750 E 150th St Ste 1200 (46060-5583)
PHONE..................317 774-3668
Denise Roberts, *CEO*
EMP: 2 EST: 2013
SALES (est): 974.32K **Privately Held**
Web: www.orbitalinstalls.com
SIC: 3663 Global positioning systems (GPS) equipment

(G-13149)
P F APPLE LLC
19541 Heather Ln (46060-1162)
PHONE..................317 773-8683
Paula Fenn, *Prin*
EMP: 2 EST: 2009
SALES (est): 106.53K **Privately Held**
SIC: 3571 Electronic computers

(G-13150)
PARKER-HANNIFIN CORPORATION
Also Called: Parker Seal Service Ctr
14425 Bergen Blvd Ste C (46060-3422)
PHONE..................317 776-7600
T J Kohinke, *Mgr*
EMP: 8
SALES (corp-wide): 19.93B **Publicly Held**
Web: www.parker.com
SIC: 3594 Fluid power pumps and motors
PA: Parker-Hannifin Corporation
6035 Parkland Blvd
Cleveland OH 44124
216 896-3000

(G-13151)
PARTLOW FARMS LLC
15486 Herriman Blvd (46060-4215)
PHONE..................317 919-8064
EMP: 5 EST: 2020
SALES (est): 235.43K **Privately Held**
SIC: 2087 Flavoring extracts and syrups, nec

(G-13152)
PATEL BALLISTICS CORPORATION
7024 Bladstone Rd (46062-4196)
PHONE..................847 284-0086
EMP: 5 EST: 2019
SALES (est): 70.31K **Privately Held**
SIC: 3949 Sporting and athletic goods, nec

(G-13153)
PAXXAL INC
14425 Bergen Blvd Ste A (46060-3422)
PHONE..................317 296-7724
Ezzeldin El Massry, *Pr*
Abdulmajed Jalali, *Pr*
Richard N San Martin, *COO*
▲ EMP: 9 EST: 2011
SQ FT: 20,000
SALES (est): 2.19MM **Privately Held**
Web: www.paxxal.com
SIC: 3089 Pallets, plastics

(G-13154)
PEACE WATER WINERY LLC
22400 Cammack Rd (46062-8585)
PHONE..................317 810-1330
Scott Burton, *Managing Member*
EMP: 1 EST: 2014
SALES (est): 221.77K **Privately Held**
Web: www.peacewaterwinery.com
SIC: 2084 Wines

(G-13155)
PICKLED PEDALER
5713 Mahogany Dr (46062-1200)
PHONE..................317 877-0624
Nicole Eliason, *Owner*
EMP: 5 EST: 2013
SALES (est): 156.38K **Privately Held**
Web: www.thepickledpedaler.com
SIC: 2035 Pickled fruits and vegetables

(G-13156)
POOLS OF FUN INC
14765 Hazel Dell Xing (46062-7027)
PHONE..................317 843-0337
EMP: 36
SALES (corp-wide): 10.62MM **Privately Held**
Web: www.poolsoffun.com
SIC: 5261 2842 1799 Retail nurseries and garden stores; Polishes and sanitation goods; Antenna installation
PA: Pools Of Fun, Inc.
3891 Clarks Creek Rd A
Plainfield IN 46168
317 839-3311

(G-13157)
PRECISION SURFACING SOLUTIONS ✪
Also Called: Abrasive & Tooling Division
14560 Bergen Blvd Ste 800 (46060-5206)
PHONE..................317 841-2400
EMP: 6 EST: 2024
SALES (est): 78.58K **Privately Held**
SIC: 3545 Machine tool accessories

(G-13158)
PRESS A BUTTON LLC
15478 Harmon Pl (46060-2148)
PHONE..................630 400-1704
Nathan A Press, *Owner*
EMP: 5 EST: 2016
SALES (est): 237.16K **Privately Held**
SIC: 2741 Miscellaneous publishing

(G-13159)
PRO WAKE WATERSPORTS INDIANAP
9175 E 146th St (46060-4310)
PHONE..................801 691-2153
EMP: 5 EST: 2018
SALES (est): 242.9K **Privately Held**
SIC: 3732 Boatbuilding and repairing

(G-13160)
PRODUCTIVITY RESOURCES INC
325 Pickwick Ct (46062-9071)
P.O. Box 15 (46082-0015)
PHONE..................317 245-4040
Gayle Robinson, *Pr*
EMP: 5 EST: 2002
SALES (est): 670.93K **Privately Held**
Web: www.productivityresources.com
SIC: 3469 Capacitor or condenser cans and cases, stamped metal

(G-13161)
PUNKISH PRESS LLC
18762 Long Walk Ln (46060-1013)
PHONE..................812 626-1028
Mindy Schipp, *Prin*
EMP: 4 EST: 2016
SALES (est): 63.97K **Privately Held**
SIC: 2741 Miscellaneous publishing

(G-13162)
PUREWAL PUBLISHING LLC
176 W Logan St (46060-1437)
PHONE..................317 703-6899
Suzanne Purewall, *Prin*
EMP: 1 EST: 2010
SALES (est): 58.84K **Privately Held**
SIC: 2741 Miscellaneous publishing

(G-13163)
QBANK LLC
2117 Dakota Dr (46062-9075)
PHONE..................317 354-5764
Jane Snyder, *Prin*
EMP: 9 EST: 2016
SALES (est): 125.31K **Privately Held**
SIC: 7372 Business oriented computer software

(G-13164)
RAIN SONG FARMS LLC
Also Called: Rain Song Winery
19539 Pilgrim Rd (46060-9440)
PHONE..................317 640-4534
EMP: 2 EST: 2010
SQ FT: 3,000
SALES (est): 83.77K **Privately Held**
SIC: 2084 Wine cellars, bonded: engaged in blending wines

(G-13165)
REALIZE INC
15515 Endeavor Dr (46060-4922)
PHONE..................317 915-0295
Todd Reese, *Pr*
EMP: 13 EST: 1999
SQ FT: 2,400
SALES (est): 2.49MM **Privately Held**
Web: www.realizeinc.com
SIC: 3999 Models, general, except toy

(G-13166)
REVOLVER LLC
13904 Town Center Blvd Ste 800 (46060-4003)
PHONE..................317 418-1824
EMP: 3 EST: 2008
SALES (est): 151.29K **Privately Held**
Web: www.revolvertactical.com
SIC: 2389 Apparel and accessories, nec

(G-13167)
RF MANUFACTURING INC
1780 S 10th St (46060-3835)
PHONE..................317 773-8610
Jeff Query, *Pr*
EMP: 9 EST: 2011
SALES (est): 1.16MM **Privately Held**
Web: www.rfmanufacturing.net
SIC: 3441 3599 7389 Fabricated structural metal; Machine shop, jobbing and repair; Business services, nec

(G-13168)
ROWLAND PRINTING CO INC
Also Called: Image Builders/Rowland Prtg
199 N 9th St (46060-2212)
P.O. Box 69 (46061-0069)
PHONE..................317 773-1829
Dane Rowland, *Pr*
Ted Rowland, *Ex Dir*
EMP: 16 EST: 1967
SALES (est): 2.3MM **Privately Held**
Web: www.rowlandprinting.com
SIC: 2752 2791 7311 2789 Offset printing; Typesetting, computer controlled; Advertising agencies; Bookbinding and related work

(G-13169)
RTP ENTERPRISE INC
15158 Proud Truth Dr (46060-5629)
PHONE..................317 258-3213
Tiffany Anderson, *Owner*
EMP: 9 EST: 2015
SALES (est): 37.24K **Privately Held**
Web: www.rtpcompany.com
SIC: 2821 Plastics materials and resins

(G-13170)
S & Y TRUCKING LLC
15499 Border Dr (46060-4779)
PHONE..................317 642-6222
EMP: 2 EST: 2021
SALES (est): 70K **Privately Held**
SIC: 3537 Trucks: freight, baggage, etc.: industrial, except mining

(G-13171)
SAM MOURON EQUIPMENT CO INC
15535 Stony Creek Way (46060-4386)
PHONE..................317 776-1799
Kerry Creek, *Pr*
Mark Adams, *VP*
EMP: 15 EST: 1953
SQ FT: 23,000
SALES (est): 2.29MM **Privately Held**
Web: www.sammouron.com
SIC: 3444 Sheet metal specialties, not stamped

(G-13172)
SCHWARTZS TRAILER SALES INC
117 Cicero Rd (46060-1402)
PHONE..................317 773-2608
Glen Schwartz, *Pr*
Patricia Schwartz, *Sec*
EMP: 6 EST: 1979
SQ FT: 3,000
SALES (est): 665.23K **Privately Held**
Web: www.schwartztrailer.com
SIC: 3715 5599 Truck trailers; Utility trailers

(G-13173)
SCREENBROIDERY LLC
15255 Endeavor Dr Ste 200 (46060-4911)
PHONE..................317 546-1900
EMP: 20 EST: 2019
SALES (est): 1.08MM **Privately Held**
Web: screenbroidery.business.site
SIC: 2752 Commercial printing, lithographic

(PA)=Parent Co (HQ)=Headquarters
✪ = New Business established in last 2 years

Noblesville - Hamilton County (G-13174)

(G-13174)
SHAWN FERGUSON ◊
Also Called: Boogie Bonez Bbq
12160 E 216th St (46060-6714)
PHONE..................................269 300-7090
Shawn Ferguson, *Owner*
EMP: 1 **EST:** 2023
SALES (est): 65.62K **Privately Held**
SIC: 2099 Sauce, gravy, dressing, and dip mixes

(G-13175)
SIMPLE SIGN SOLUTIONS INC
9985 Waterside Dr (46060-5649)
PHONE..................................317 272-5224
EMP: 2 **EST:** 2012
SALES (est): 166.74K **Privately Held**
SIC: 3993 Signs and advertising specialties

(G-13176)
SMC CORPORATION OF AMERICA (HQ)
Also Called: SMC
10100 Smc Blvd (46060)
P.O. Box 1880 (46060)
PHONE..................................317 899-4440
Yoshiki Takada, *Pr*
Kevin L Hammett, *
Brent Poe, *
Julie Dheehr, *
Stephen Conners, *
▲ **EMP:** 350 **EST:** 1977
SQ FT: 241,300
SALES (est): 492.34MM **Privately Held**
Web: www.smcusa.com
SIC: 3625 3492 3491 3559 Actuators, industrial; Control valves, fluid power: hydraulic and pneumatic; Pressure valves and regulators, industrial; Automotive related machinery
PA: Smc Corporation
4-14-1, Sotokanda
Chiyoda-Ku TKY 101-0

(G-13177)
SOUTHFIELD CORPORATION
15215 River Rd (46060)
PHONE..................................317 773-5340
Tod True, *Mgr*
EMP: 24
SALES (corp-wide): 99.17MM **Privately Held**
Web: www.brickworkssupply.com
SIC: 3273 Ready-mixed concrete
PA: Southfield Corporation
8995 W 95th St
Palos Hills IL 60465
708 344-1000

(G-13178)
SPECIFICATION PRODUCTS INC
1718 Pleasant St (46060-3620)
PHONE..................................888 881-1726
Joseph Shetterley, *CEO*
EMP: 8 **EST:** 2015
SALES (est): 2.29MM **Privately Held**
Web: www.e5nanosilica.com
SIC: 3272 Concrete structural support and building material

(G-13179)
SPECTRUM BRANDS INC
20975 Creek Rd (46060-9383)
PHONE..................................317 773-6367
Shanah Tran, *Brnch Mgr*
EMP: 25
SALES (corp-wide): 2.92B **Publicly Held**
Web: www.spectrumbrands.com
SIC: 3231 3499 3229 3564 Aquariums and reflectors, glass; Aquarium accessories, metal; Pressed and blown glass, nec; Blowers and fans
HQ: Spectrum Brands, Inc.
3001 Deming Way
Middleton WI 53562
608 275-3340

(G-13180)
STRAWTOWN POTTERY & ANTQ INC
12738 Strawtown Ave (46060-6971)
PHONE..................................317 984-5080
Matt Garrison, *Pr*
Diane Garrison, *VP*
EMP: 2 **EST:** 1983
SALES (est): 136.44K **Privately Held**
SIC: 3269 5023 5719 5932 Art and ornamental ware, pottery; Pottery; Pottery; Antiques

(G-13181)
THERAMETRIC TECHNOLOGIES INC (PA)
9880 Douglas Floyd Pkwy (46060-7900)
PHONE..................................317 565-8065
EMP: 17 **EST:** 1996
SQ FT: 2,100
SALES (est): 3.35MM **Privately Held**
Web: www.therametric.com
SIC: 3829 Measuring and controlling devices, nec

(G-13182)
TODD ENTERPRISE INC ◊
6220 Edenshall Ln (46062-4643)
PHONE..................................317 209-6610
Todd Orion, *CEO*
EMP: 10 **EST:** 2022
SALES (est): 413.11K **Privately Held**
SIC: 3651 7389 Recording machines, except dictation and telephone answering; Business Activities at Non-Commercial Site

(G-13183)
TRG WIND
210 Amhurst Cir (46062-9009)
PHONE..................................507 829-6695
EMP: 5 **EST:** 2019
SALES (est): 179.78K **Privately Held**
Web: www.muehlhan.com
SIC: 3599 Industrial machinery, nec

(G-13184)
TRI-GEN INC
16565 River Rd (46062-9566)
P.O. Box 190 (46038-0190)
PHONE..................................317 849-5612
EMP: 26 **EST:** 1967
SALES (est): 7.02MM **Privately Held**
Web: www.generaldrilling.com
SIC: 1481 Nonmetallic mineral services

(G-13185)
TRIUNITY LLC
Also Called: Shear Line Golf
15209 Herriman Blvd (46060-4230)
PHONE..................................317 703-1147
George Doran Senior, *Pr*
EMP: 3 **EST:** 1981
SQ FT: 2,300
SALES (est): 240.82K **Privately Held**
SIC: 3949 Golf equipment

(G-13186)
TUFF SHED INC
15274 Herriman Blvd (46060-4224)
PHONE..................................317 774-2981
Don Mcswain, *Mgr*
EMP: 19

SALES (corp-wide): 347.42MM **Privately Held**
Web: www.tuffshed.com
SIC: 2452 Prefabricated wood buildings
PA: Tuff Shed, Inc.
1777 S Harrison St # 600
Denver CO 80210
303 753-8833

(G-13187)
ULLOM WOODWORKS
18891 Stockton Dr (46062-8102)
PHONE..................................217 369-5769
Christine Ullom, *Prin*
EMP: 6 **EST:** 2017
SALES (est): 139.43K **Privately Held**
SIC: 2431 Millwork

(G-13188)
ULTIMATE WLDG FABRICATION LLC
17625 River Rd (46062-8499)
PHONE..................................317 379-2676
EMP: 4 **EST:** 2016
SALES (est): 56.71K **Privately Held**
SIC: 7692 Welding repair

(G-13189)
UNITED PARCEL SERVICE INC
Also Called: UPS
14350 Mundy Dr Ste 800 (46060-7229)
PHONE..................................317 776-9494
Jane Weaver, *Owner*
EMP: 4
SALES (corp-wide): 90.96B **Publicly Held**
Web: locations.theupsstore.com
SIC: 4215 2752 2789 Package delivery, vehicular; Commercial printing, lithographic; Binding only: books, pamphlets, magazines, etc.
PA: United Parcel Service, Inc.
55 Glenlake Pkwy Ne
Atlanta GA 30328
404 828-6000

(G-13190)
UNIVERSAL BLOWER PAC INC
440 Park 32 W Dr (46062-9213)
PHONE..................................317 773-7256
Ray Fiechter, *Pr*
Fiechter Carol, *Sec*
EMP: 21 **EST:** 1979
SQ FT: 15,000
SALES (est): 4.11MM **Privately Held**
Web: www.universalblowerpac.com
SIC: 3564 Blowing fans: industrial or commercial

(G-13191)
V LUXURIES LLC
16751 Clover Rd (46060-3646)
P.O. Box 1071 (46061-1071)
PHONE..................................877 308-5988
Marcella Ruffin, *Managing Member*
EMP: 1 **EST:** 2020
SALES (est): 83.51K **Privately Held**
Web: www.vluxuries.com
SIC: 2676 Feminine hygiene paper products

(G-13192)
VERDURE SCIENCES INC
17150 Metro Park Ct (46060-4051)
PHONE..................................317 776-3600
EMP: 25 **EST:** 2018
SALES (est): 4.16MM **Privately Held**
Web: www.vs-corp.com
SIC: 2834 Extracts of botanicals: powdered, pilular, solid, or fluid

(G-13193)
VIBROMATIC COMPANY INC (PA)
1301 S 6th St (46060-3712)
P.O. Box 1358 (46061-1358)
PHONE..................................317 773-3885
Terry Hawkins, *Dir*
Brad Graham, *
Cecilia Pearson, *
EMP: 34 **EST:** 1956
SQ FT: 35,000
SALES (est): 4.88MM
SALES (corp-wide): 4.88MM **Privately Held**
Web: www.vibromatic.net
SIC: 3559 3444 3829 Vibratory parts handling equipment; Hoppers, sheet metal; Measuring and controlling devices, nec

(G-13194)
WHIMSICALS INC
1606 Chestnut Ct (46062-9703)
PHONE..................................317 773-6130
Terry Degenkolb, *Pr*
Jackie Conaway, *VP*
Bill Conaway, *Treas*
Tom Degenkolb, *Sec*
EMP: 1 **EST:** 1997
SALES (est): 80K **Privately Held**
Web: www.whimsicalquilts.com
SIC: 7389 2741 7336 Design services; Patterns, paper: publishing and printing; Graphic arts and related design

(G-13195)
WILD GRAIN WOODWORKS LLC
17159 Linda Way (46062-7128)
PHONE..................................317 626-3939
William Long, *Owner*
EMP: 4 **EST:** 2017
SALES (est): 54.13K **Privately Held**
SIC: 2431 Millwork

(G-13196)
WILLEMIN MACODEL
15250 Endeavor Dr (46060-4919)
PHONE..................................317 219-6113
Jim Davis, *Pr*
EMP: 7 **EST:** 2014
SALES (est): 246.88K **Privately Held**
Web: www.willemin-macodel.com
SIC: 3545 Machine tool attachments and accessories

(G-13197)
YANEY MKTG GRAPHIC DESIGN LLC
Also Called: Buttermilk Ridge Publishing
136 S 9th St Ste 18 (46060-2600)
PHONE..................................317 776-0676
Kevin Yaney, *Pt*
EMP: 1 **EST:** 2001
SALES (est): 168.25K **Privately Held**
Web: www.yaney.net
SIC: 7311 2731 Advertising consultant; Book publishing

(G-13198)
YINROOT LLC
12174 E 141st St (46060-4903)
PHONE..................................317 379-9529
Joelle Samples, *Owner*
EMP: 3 **EST:** 2015
SALES (est): 106.75K **Privately Held**
Web: www.yinroot.com
SIC: 2834 Pharmaceutical preparations

(G-13199)
ZERGNET
17279 Bluestone Dr (46062-7183)
PHONE..................................317 201-0889
Brandon Caudill, *Prin*

GEOGRAPHIC SECTION

North Liberty - St. Joseph County (G-13224)

EMP: 7 **EST:** 2018
SALES (est): 118.5K **Privately Held**
Web: www.zergnet.com
SIC: 2711 Newspapers, publishing and printing

(G-13200)
ZIEHL-ABEGG INC
802 Mulberry St Ste Gb-07 (46060-3410)
PHONE..................................317 219-3014
Dave Neal, *Brnch Mgr*
EMP: 1
SALES (corp-wide): 688.71MM **Privately Held**
Web: www.ziehl-abegg.com
SIC: 3694 Engine electrical equipment
HQ: Ziehl-Abegg, Inc.
719 N Regional Rd
Greensboro NC 27419
336 834-9339

(G-13201)
ZR TACTICAL SOLUTIONS LLC
Also Called: Zrts
15223 Herriman Blvd Ste 4 (46060-4218)
PHONE..................................317 721-9787
Adam Hooker, *Genl Mgr*
EMP: 11 **EST:** 2010
SALES (est): 743.88K **Privately Held**
Web: www.zrtacticalsolutions.com
SIC: 3489 Guns or gun parts, over 30 mm.

Norman
Jackson County

(G-13202)
BALDWIN LOGGING INC
11763 State Road 58 E (47264-8631)
PHONE..................................812 834-1040
EMP: 7 **EST:** 2009
SALES (est): 164.65K **Privately Held**
SIC: 2411 Logging

(G-13203)
JUSTIN BLACKWELL
Also Called: Blackwell Limestone
7071 State Road 446 (47264-8685)
P.O. Box 209 (47436-0209)
PHONE..................................812 834-6350
Justin Blackwell, *Owner*
EMP: 16 **EST:** 1999
SALES (est): 1.7MM **Privately Held**
Web: www.blimestoneproducts.com
SIC: 3281 Limestone, cut and shaped

(G-13204)
S&S MACHINERY REPAIR LLC
12807 W Us Highway 50 (47264-9766)
P.O. Box 3 (47264-0003)
PHONE..................................812 521-2368
Beth Singer, *Prin*
EMP: 4 **EST:** 2011
SALES (est): 455.98K **Privately Held**
Web: www.ssmachinerepair.com
SIC: 3541 Machine tool replacement & repair parts, metal cutting types

North Judson
Starke County

(G-13205)
A & S LOGGING INC
2340 E 800 S (46366-8465)
PHONE..................................574 896-3136
EMP: 7 **EST:** 2008
SALES (est): 191.09K **Privately Held**
SIC: 2411 Logging

(G-13206)
AMERICAN OAK PRESERVING CO INC (PA)
Also Called: Starburst Sales
601 Mulberry St (46366-1044)
P.O. Box 187 (46366-0187)
PHONE..................................574 896-2171
Charles K Vorm, *Pr*
James Long, *
Erika Johnston, *
Kirsten Martin, *
◆ **EMP:** 45 **EST:** 1915
SQ FT: 100,000
SALES (est): 9.94MM
SALES (corp-wide): 9.94MM **Privately Held**
Web: www.americanoak.net
SIC: 3999 Foliage, artificial and preserved

(G-13207)
C E KERSTING & SONS
6800 S 300 W (46366-8338)
P.O. Box 296 (46366-0296)
PHONE..................................574 896-2766
Charles Kersting Junior, *Pt*
Melvin Kersting, *Pt*
EMP: 3 **EST:** 1936
SQ FT: 10,000
SALES (est): 219.9K **Privately Held**
SIC: 2448 2441 Pallets, wood; Nailed wood boxes and shook

(G-13208)
CALLISONS INC
Also Called: I P Callison & Sons
7675 S 100 W (46366-8447)
PHONE..................................574 896-5074
Greg Allender, *Mgr*
EMP: 3
SALES (corp-wide): 28.25MM **Privately Held**
Web: www.callisons.com
SIC: 2087 Extracts, flavoring
PA: Callisons, Inc.
2400 Callison Rd Ne
Lacey WA 98516
360 412-3340

(G-13209)
CHESTER INC
Also Called: A B I Dept
6020 S 500 W (46366-8874)
PHONE..................................574 896-5600
Larry Holt, *Brnch Mgr*
EMP: 14
SALES (corp-wide): 20.45MM **Privately Held**
Web: www.chesters.com
SIC: 5083 2096 Agricultural machinery and equipment; Potato chips and similar snacks
PA: Chester Inc
555 Eastport Centre Dr A
Valparaiso IN 46383
219 465-7555

(G-13210)
COMMON COLLABS LLC
508 Lane St (46366-1228)
PHONE..................................574 249-9182
Freddy Lopez, *Managing Member*
EMP: 1
SALES (corp-wide): 4.99MM **Privately Held**
Web: www.commoncollabs.com
SIC: 2087 Flavoring extracts and syrups, nec
PA: Common Collabs, Llc
1820 E Walnut Ave
Fullerton CA 92831
714 519-3245

(G-13211)
EVELYN DOLLAHAN
Also Called: 4d Manufacturing
520 E 625 S (46366-8486)
PHONE..................................574 896-2971
Evelyn Dollahan, *Owner*
EMP: 4 **EST:** 1965
SALES (est): 387.27K **Privately Held**
SIC: 3523 Cattle feeding, handling, and watering equipment

(G-13212)
FINGERHUT BAKERY INC (PA)
119 Lane St (46366-1219)
PHONE..................................574 896-5937
Keith Fingerhut, *Pr*
EMP: 12 **EST:** 1946
SALES (est): 903.99K
SALES (corp-wide): 903.99K **Privately Held**
Web: www.bakerygifts.com
SIC: 5461 2052 2051 Cakes; Cookies and crackers; Bread, cake, and related products

(G-13213)
OUTSTNDING TRDSHOW EXHBT SVCS
Also Called: Outstanding Tradeshow Exhibit
5235 W State Road 10 Ste 1 (46366)
PHONE..................................888 735-4348
Nancy M Wellman, *Pr*
EMP: 12 **EST:** 2016
SALES (est): 499.8K **Privately Held**
Web: www.otesinc.com
SIC: 7389 2542 Advertising, promotional, and trade show services; Fixtures: display, office, or store: except wood

(G-13214)
STUDIO PRINTERS
310 Franklin St (46366-1004)
PHONE..................................574 772-0900
Mike Reimbold, *Prin*
Michael C Reimbold, *Pr*
EMP: 7 **EST:** 1945
SALES (est): 411.01K **Privately Held**
Web: www.studioprinters.com
SIC: 2759 Commercial printing, nec

North Liberty
St. Joseph County

(G-13215)
C&C ELECTRIC MOTORS LLC
1011 Industrial Pkwy (46554-9246)
PHONE..................................574 656-3898
Mike R Walorski, *Owner*
EMP: 5 **EST:** 2020
SALES (est): 444.63K **Privately Held**
SIC: 7694 Electric motor repair

(G-13216)
DETROIT HOLDINGS LLC ✪
24803 Stanton Rd (46554-9463)
PHONE..................................202 309-9681
EMP: 2 **EST:** 2022
SALES (est): 86.08K **Privately Held**
SIC: 3799 8748 Transportation equipment, nec; Business consulting, nec

(G-13217)
HYDRO EXTRUSION USA LLC
400 S Main St (46554-9639)
PHONE..................................888 935-5757
Henry Boots, *Brnch Mgr*
EMP: 267
Web: www.hydro.com
SIC: 3354 3471 3444 Rods, extruded, aluminum; Plating and polishing; Sheet metalwork
HQ: Hydro Extrusion Usa, Llc
6250 N River Rd Ste 5000
Rosemont IL 60018

(G-13218)
LONGHORN SAND AND GRAVEL LLC
30430 Osborne Rd (46554)
PHONE..................................574 532-2788
EMP: 3
SALES (est): 228.88K **Privately Held**
SIC: 1442 Construction sand and gravel

(G-13219)
PAUL APPLEGATE
27884 Quinn Rd (46554-9653)
PHONE..................................574 656-8664
Paul Applegate, *Prin*
EMP: 4 **EST:** 2017
SALES (est): 192.22K **Privately Held**
Web: www.paulapplegate.com
SIC: 2741 Miscellaneous publishing

(G-13220)
R D LANEY FAMILY HONEY COMPANY
25725 New Rd (46554-9379)
PHONE..................................574 656-8701
Dave Laney, *Ch*
Linda Laney, *VP*
Kay Laney, *Prin*
EMP: 6 **EST:** 1978
SALES (est): 479.45K **Privately Held**
Web: www.laneyhoney.com
SIC: 2099 5149 Honey, strained and bottled; Honey

(G-13221)
RAPID RULE CO INC
69159 Pine Rd (46554-9397)
PHONE..................................574 784-2273
Douglas Seely Iii, *Pr*
EMP: 2 **EST:** 1959
SALES (est): 156.48K **Privately Held**
Web: www.rapidrule.com
SIC: 3423 Rules or rulers, metal

(G-13222)
RUSTIC FISHER CREATIONS LLC ✪
67679 Sycamore Rd (46554-9793)
PHONE..................................574 279-5754
Elizabeth Fisher, *Pr*
EMP: 1 **EST:** 2022
SALES (est): 69.27K **Privately Held**
SIC: 2339 7389 Women's and misses' accessories; Business Activities at Non-Commercial Site

(G-13223)
SHOEMAKER WELDING COMPANY
65508 State Road 23 (46554-9404)
PHONE..................................574 656-4412
Alan Shoemaker, *Owner*
EMP: 3 **EST:** 1945
SQ FT: 3,000
SALES (est): 352.78K **Privately Held**
Web: www.shoemakerwelding.com
SIC: 3561 7692 Pumps and pumping equipment; Welding repair

(G-13224)
SINGLE SOURCE MEDICAL LLC
791 Industrial Pkwy (46554-9239)
PHONE..................................574 656-3400
EMP: 25 **EST:** 2021
SALES (est): 1.2MM **Privately Held**
Web: www.singlesourceinc.us

SIC: 3841 Surgical and medical instruments

(G-13225)
SINGLETON MACHINE INC
791 Industrial Pkwy (46554-9239)
PHONE..................574 656-3400
Greg Singleton, *Pr*
Tom Moore, *VP*
EMP: 28 EST: 2001
SQ FT: 8,600
SALES (est): 2.01MM **Privately Held**
Web: www.singlesourceinc.us
SIC: 3599 Machine shop, jobbing and repair

(G-13226)
UNIQUE TOOLING INC
101 S Maple Ave (46554)
P.O. Box 533 (46554-0533)
PHONE..................574 656-3585
EMP: 6 EST: 2007
SALES (est): 946.07K **Privately Held**
SIC: 3545 Cutting tools for machine tools

(G-13227)
WOODS UNLIMITED INC
67850 Sycamore Rd (46554-9214)
PHONE..................574 656-3382
Dean Shoue, *Pr*
John Shoue, *VP*
Ester Shoue, *Sec*
Janet Shoue, *Treas*
EMP: 5 EST: 1982
SALES (est): 332.13K **Privately Held**
Web: www.ohc.net
SIC: 2499 2541 Kitchen, bathroom, and household ware: wood; Cabinets, except refrigerated: show, display, etc.: wood

North Manchester
Wabash County

(G-13228)
AIR FIXTURES INC
1108 N Sycamore St (46962-1151)
P.O. Box 147 (46962-0147)
PHONE..................260 982-2169
Leon L Bazzoni, *Pr*
M B Bazzoni, *VP*
EMP: 10
SQ FT: 3,000
SALES (est): 983.45K **Privately Held**
Web: www.air-fixtures.com
SIC: 3563 3494 Air and gas compressors including vacuum pumps; Valves and pipe fittings, nec

(G-13229)
BKB MANUFACTURING INC
607 S Wabash Rd (46962-8148)
P.O. Box 326 (46962-0326)
PHONE..................260 982-8524
Josh Beery, *Manager*
EMP: 3 EST: 1995
SALES (est): 229.96K **Privately Held**
Web: www.manchestertoolanddie.com
SIC: 3563 Air and gas compressors

(G-13230)
CAM METAL FABRICATION LLC
911 W Main St (46962-1912)
PHONE..................260 982-6280
▲ EMP: 8 EST: 2008
SALES (est): 648.24K **Privately Held**
Web: www.cammetalfab.com
SIC: 3441 Fabricated structural metal

(G-13231)
CUSTOM MAGNETICS INC (PA)
Also Called: James Electronics Div.
801 W Main St (46962-1452)
PHONE..................260 982-8508
Kirti Shah, *Pr*
▲ EMP: 50 EST: 1974
SQ FT: 18,000
SALES (est): 9.29MM
SALES (corp-wide): 9.29MM **Privately Held**
Web: www.custommag.com
SIC: 3612 3613 3677 3621 Specialty transformers; Switchboard apparatus, except instruments; Electronic coils and transformers; Motors and generators

(G-13232)
DALE FLORA
Also Called: D&J Printing
5249 E 1250 N (46962-8494)
PHONE..................260 982-7233
Dale Flora, *Owner*
EMP: 1 EST: 1999
SALES (est): 51.95K **Privately Held**
SIC: 2759 Commercial printing, nec

(G-13233)
EFTEN INC
906 W Hanley Rd (46962)
PHONE..................260 982-1544
EMP: 4 EST: 2018
SALES (est): 39.69K **Privately Held**
SIC: 3999 2631 Manufacturing industries, nec; Paperboard mills

(G-13234)
HF GROUP LLC
Heckman Bindery
1010 N Sycamore St (46962-1252)
P.O. Box 89 (46962-0089)
PHONE..................260 982-2107
Jim Heckman, *Brnch Mgr*
EMP: 410
Web: www.hfgroup.com
SIC: 2789 Bookbinding and related work
PA: Hf Group, Llc
400 Arora Cmmons Cir Unit
Aurora OH 44202

(G-13235)
INTERTECH PRODUCTS INC (HQ)
906 W Hanley Rd (46962-9705)
PHONE..................260 982-1544
EMP: 99 EST: 1997
SALES (est): 24.67MM
SALES (corp-wide): 47.13MM **Privately Held**
Web: www.ojiintertech.com
SIC: 2396 3544 Automotive and apparel trimmings; Extrusion dies
PA: Intertech Holdings, Inc.
12233 Waterside Ct
Fort Wayne IN 46814
260 982-1544

(G-13236)
JOHNSON ENGRAVING & TROPHIES
1302 Beckley St (46962-2115)
P.O. Box 205 (46962-0205)
PHONE..................260 982-7868
Jerry Johnson, *Owner*
EMP: 2 EST: 1991
SALES (est): 71.55K **Privately Held**
SIC: 3993 5999 3479 Signs and advertising specialties; Trophies and plaques; Etching on metals

(G-13237)
KEITH MILLER
701 N Mill St (46962-1241)
PHONE..................260 982-6858
Keith Miller, *Owner*
EMP: 1 EST: 2013
SALES (est): 60.65K **Privately Held**
SIC: 3639 Major kitchen appliances, except refrigerators and stoves

(G-13238)
MANCHESTER NORTH NEWS JOURNAL
Also Called: News Journal
1306 State Road 114 W (46962-1944)
P.O. Box 744 (47960-0744)
PHONE..................260 982-6383
Mike Rees, *Pr*
Tim Mclaughlin, *Managing Editor*
EMP: 4 EST: 1966
SALES (est): 251.6K **Privately Held**
Web: www.nmpaper.com
SIC: 2711 Commercial printing and newspaper publishing combined

(G-13239)
MANCHESTER TOOL & DIE INC
601 S Wabash Rd (46962)
P.O. Box 326 (46962)
PHONE..................260 982-8524
Barry Blocher, *Pr*
EMP: 95 EST: 1981
SQ FT: 65,000
SALES (est): 9.28MM **Privately Held**
Web: www.manchestertoolanddie.com
SIC: 3599 Machine shop, jobbing and repair

(G-13240)
MANCHESTER WELD AND FAB LLC
612 W 4th St (46962-1423)
PHONE..................260 578-5215
Bruce Mcguire Junior, *Admn*
EMP: 6 EST: 2013
SALES (est): 76.6K **Privately Held**
SIC: 3599 Machine shop, jobbing and repair

(G-13241)
MAPLE LEAF INC
11241 N 400 W (46962-8944)
PHONE..................260 982-8655
EMP: 1
SALES (corp-wide): 218.89MM **Privately Held**
Web: www.mapleleaffarms.com
SIC: 0259 2015 Duck farm; Poultry slaughtering and processing
PA: Maple Leaf, Inc.
101 E Church St
Leesburg IN 46538
574 453-4455

(G-13242)
MIDWEST POULTRY SERVICES LP (PA)
Also Called: MPS Egg Farms
800 Wabash Rd (46962-8968)
P.O. Box 307 (46539-0307)
PHONE..................574 353-7651
Robert Krouse, *Pt*
▲ EMP: 16 EST: 1993
SQ FT: 20,000
SALES (est): 80.41MM
SALES (corp-wide): 80.41MM **Privately Held**
Web: www.straussfeedmill.com
SIC: 2015 Egg processing

(G-13243)
MIDWEST POULTRY SERVICES LP
Also Called: Automated Egg Producers
500 Strauss Provimi Rd (46962-1376)
PHONE..................260 982-8122
Robert Wiley, *Mgr*
EMP: 92
SALES (corp-wide): 80.41MM **Privately Held**
Web: www.straussfeedmill.com
SIC: 2015 Egg processing
PA: Midwest Poultry Services, L.P.
800 Wabash Rd
North Manchester IN 46962
574 353-7651

(G-13244)
NICHOLAS PRECISION WORKS LLC
1101 Taylor St (46962-8183)
P.O. Box 150 (46962-0150)
PHONE..................260 306-3426
EMP: 7 EST: 2014
SQ FT: 10,000
SALES (est): 562.65K
SALES (corp-wide): 45.79MM **Privately Held**
Web: www.arch-medical.com
SIC: 3599 Machine shop, jobbing and repair
PA: Arch Medical Solutions Corp.
25040 Easy St
Warren MI 48089
603 760-1554

(G-13245)
NOVAE CORP
Also Called: NOVAE CORP.
11870 N 650 E (46962-8152)
PHONE..................260 982-7075
Chris Storie, *Prin*
EMP: 10
Web: www.novaecorp.com
SIC: 3524 Lawn and garden equipment
PA: Novae Llc
1 Novae Pkwy
Markle IN 46770

(G-13246)
P & J SECTIONAL HOUSING
14385 N 200 E (46962-8619)
PHONE..................260 982-7231
Jeff Walters, *Pt*
EMP: 2 EST: 2004
SALES (est): 113.98K **Privately Held**
SIC: 1389 Construction, repair, and dismantling services

(G-13247)
POET BRFNING - N MNCHESTER LLC
Also Called: Poet Bprcessing - N Manchester
868 E 800 N (46962-8957)
P.O. Box 369 (46962-0369)
PHONE..................260 774-3532
Steve Pittman, *Genl Mgr*
EMP: 3 EST: 2008
SALES (est): 2.19MM **Privately Held**
Web: www.poet.com
SIC: 2869 Ethyl alcohol, ethanol
PA: Poet, Llc
4615 N Lewis Ave
Sioux Falls SD 57104

(G-13248)
ROTAM TOOLING CORPORATION (PA)
11606 N State Road 15 (46962-8688)
PHONE..................260 982-8318
Henry Becker, *Pr*
Gail Becker, *Treas*
EMP: 6 EST: 1976
SQ FT: 20,000
SALES (est): 1.77MM
SALES (corp-wide): 1.77MM **Privately Held**

SIC: 3599 3544 3469 Machine shop, jobbing and repair; Special dies, tools, jigs, and fixtures; Metal stampings, nec

(G-13249)
SCHULER PRECISION TOOL LLC
Also Called: Schuler Precision Tool
6177 W State Road 114 (46962-8600)
PHONE..................260 982-2704
Ned Schuler, *Pr*
EMP: 9 **EST:** 1985
SALES (est): 829.39K **Privately Held**
SIC: 7389 7692 3441 Grinding, precision: commercial or industrial; Welding repair; Fabricated structural metal

(G-13250)
SNEP SIGN CO
14767 N State Road 13 (46962-8665)
PHONE..................260 982-6016
Larry Snep, *Owner*
EMP: 1 **EST:** 1967
SQ FT: 2,500
SALES (est): 90.84K **Privately Held**
SIC: 3993 Signs and advertising specialties

(G-13251)
STRAUSS VEAL FEEDS INC (PA)
600 Strauss Provimi Rd (46962)
P.O. Box 149 (46962)
PHONE..................260 982-8611
Donald Strauss, *Ch*
David Grant, *
▲ **EMP:** 30 **EST:** 1984
SQ FT: 30,000
SALES (est): 24.65MM
SALES (corp-wide): 24.65MM **Privately Held**
Web: www.straussfeedmill.com
SIC: 2048 Livestock feeds

(G-13252)
TOTAL TOTE INC
Also Called: Rotam Tooling
11606 N State Road 15 (46962-8688)
PHONE..................260 982-8318
Henry Becker, *Pr*
EMP: 7 **EST:** 1987
SQ FT: 4,000
SALES (est): 875.1K
SALES (corp-wide): 1.77MM **Privately Held**
Web: www.total-tote.com
SIC: 3599 Custom machinery
PA: Rotam Tooling Corporation
  11606 N State Road 15
  North Manchester IN 46962
  260 982-8318

(G-13253)
TRACHSELS EMBROIDERY
905 N Market St (46962-1146)
PHONE..................260 982-2376
Jean Trachsel, *Owner*
EMP: 1 **EST:** 1991
SALES (est): 41.02K **Privately Held**
SIC: 2395 Embroidery products, except Schiffli machine

North Salem
Hendricks County

(G-13254)
I M S I RENTAL SVCS & REPAIR
Also Called: I M S I
13118 N County Road 900 E (46165-9600)
PHONE..................765 522-1223
Jim Ditworth, *Owner*
EMP: 1 **EST:** 1987

SQ FT: 4,800
SALES (est): 70.18K **Privately Held**
Web: www.rsrwelding.com
SIC: 7692 Welding repair

North Vernon
Jennings County

(G-13255)
AJE SUSPENSION INC
6235 N County Road 275 W (47265-7220)
PHONE..................812 346-7356
Anthony Jones, *Pr*
EMP: 11
SALES (est): 614.53K **Privately Held**
SIC: 3711 7389 Chassis, motor vehicle; Business services, nec

(G-13256)
ATMOSPHERE ANNEALING LLC
Also Called: Aalberts Surface Technologies
1300 Indtl Dr (47265)
P.O. Box 1049 (47265-5049)
PHONE..................812 346-1275
William Baxter, *Mgr*
EMP: 30
SALES (corp-wide): 63.78MM **Privately Held**
Web: www.aalberts-ht.us
SIC: 3398 Annealing of metal
HQ: Atmosphere Annealing, Llc
  209 W Mount Hope Ave # 2
  Lansing MI 48910
  517 485-5090

(G-13257)
CHIYODA MONTROW DIE MFG INC
640 Ertel Ln (47265-4909)
PHONE..................812 767-1885
Mike Montgomery, *Pr*
▲ **EMP:** 3 **EST:** 2005
SALES (est): 254.5K **Privately Held**
SIC: 3544 Special dies and tools

(G-13258)
COLLINS MACHINING LLC
4600 W Sunset Blvd (47265)
PHONE..................812 528-5396
EMP: 1 **EST:** 2015
SALES (est): 51.72K **Privately Held**
SIC: 3599 Machine shop, jobbing and repair

(G-13259)
CONCEPT TOOL & ENGINEERING INC
508 5th St (47265-1229)
P.O. Box 1108 (47265-5108)
PHONE..................812 352-0055
Tim Rickly, *Pr*
Linda Rickly, *Sec*
EMP: 6 **EST:** 2001
SQ FT: 8,500
SALES (est): 626.57K **Privately Held**
Web: www.concept-tool.com
SIC: 3089 Injection molding of plastics

(G-13260)
COWCO INC
3780 S State Highway 7 (47265-7995)
PHONE..................812 346-8993
Michael Biehle, *Pr*
Edward Biehle, *Sec*
Joe Biehle, *Mgr*
▲ **EMP:** 3 **EST:** 1995
SALES (est): 460.61K **Privately Held**
Web: www.cowcoinc.com
SIC: 3523 Farm machinery and equipment

(G-13261)
CSR SUSPENSION LLC
485 S County Road 575 W (47265-6662)
PHONE..................812 346-8620
EMP: 5 **EST:** 2012
SALES (est): 223.09K **Privately Held**
Web: www.csrsuspension.com
SIC: 3714 Motor vehicle parts and accessories

(G-13262)
CULLMAN CASTING CORPORATION
3750 N County Road 75 W (47265-6004)
P.O. Box 894 (47265-0894)
PHONE..................256 735-0900
Yoshihiko Ota, *Pr*
EMP: 1
Web: www.cullmancasting.com
SIC: 3596 Weighing machines and apparatus
HQ: Cullman Casting Corporation
  251 County Road 490
  Cullman AL 35055

(G-13263)
DANIEL SHADE
Also Called: Catalpa Valley
2400 S County Road 550 W (47265-6912)
PHONE..................812 346-6285
EMP: 1 **EST:** 1994
SALES (est): 46.11K **Privately Held**
SIC: 3479 Coating of metals and formed products

(G-13264)
DAVE OMARA PAVING INC (PA)
1100 E O And M Ave (47265-1319)
P.O. Box 423 (47265-0423)
PHONE..................812 346-1214
Nancy O'mara, *Pr*
Amy Hill, *Sec*
Dave O'mara, *Stockholder*
Rob O'mara, *Stockholder*
Dan O'mara, *Stockholder*
EMP: 2 **EST:** 1975
SQ FT: 100
SALES (est): 1.02MM
SALES (corp-wide): 1.02MM **Privately Held**
SIC: 2951 2952 Asphalt paving mixtures and blocks; Asphalt felts and coatings

(G-13265)
DAVID CAMP
Also Called: Express Printing & Copies
101 Hoosier St (47265-1102)
P.O. Box 879 (47265-0879)
PHONE..................812 346-6255
◆ **EMP:** 1 **EST:** 1996
SQ FT: 11,520
SALES (est): 53.42K **Privately Held**
Web: www.expressprintcopy.com
SIC: 2759 7334 4822 Commercial printing, nec; Photocopying and duplicating services ; Facsimile transmission services

(G-13266)
DECATUR MOLD TOOL AND ENGRG
3330 N State Highway 7 (47265)
P.O. Box 387 (47265)
PHONE..................812 346-5188
Rhonda Lustenberger, *Pr*
Richard L Apsley, *
Larry Waltz, *
Rachel Apsley, *
Charles Weber, *
▲ **EMP:** 125 **EST:** 1966
SQ FT: 87,000
SALES (est): 28MM **Privately Held**
Web: www.decaturmold.com

SIC: 3089 3599 7699 Injection molded finished plastics products, nec; Electrical discharge machining (EDM); Industrial machinery and equipment repair

(G-13267)
DECATUR PLASTIC PRODUCTS INC
655 Montrow Pkwy (47265-4908)
PHONE..................812 352-6050
Junior Fields, *Brnch Mgr*
EMP: 75
Web: www.decaturplastics.com
SIC: 3089 Injection molding of plastics
PA: Decatur Plastic Products, Inc.
  3250 N State Highway 7
  North Vernon IN 47265

(G-13268)
DECATUR PLASTIC PRODUCTS INC (PA)
Also Called: Dpp
3250 N State Highway 7 (47265-7490)
P.O. Box 1079 (47265-5079)
PHONE..................812 346-5159
Robert Riley, *CEO*
Gary Riley Junior, *Supply Chain Vice President*
Gary Riley Senior, *COO*
▲ **EMP:** 140 **EST:** 1990
SQ FT: 75,730
SALES (est): 48.59MM **Privately Held**
Web: www.decaturplastics.com
SIC: 3089 Injection molding of plastics

(G-13269)
ERLER INDUSTRIES INC (PA)
418 Stockwell St (47265-1464)
PHONE..................812 346-4421
J Mark Erler, *Pr*
Linda Erler, *
EMP: 99 **EST:** 1988
SQ FT: 200,000
SALES (est): 8.83MM
SALES (corp-wide): 8.83MM **Privately Held**
Web: www.erler.com
SIC: 3479 Coating of metals and formed products

(G-13270)
FIZZ WIZZ
851 N State St (47265-7472)
P.O. Box 493 (47265-0493)
PHONE..................812 718-9045
Mia Daviner, *Prin*
EMP: 6 **EST:** 2013
SALES (est): 91.38K **Privately Held**
SIC: 2096 Potato chips and similar snacks

(G-13271)
FRESH PRINTZ INCORPORATED
61 Norris Ave (47265-1720)
PHONE..................812 352-6400
Aaron Bales, *Pr*
EMP: 12 **EST:** 2012
SALES (est): 299.06K **Privately Held**
Web: www.freshprintzink.com
SIC: 2759 Screen printing

(G-13272)
GERDAU MCSTEEL ATMSPHERE ANNLI
1300 Industrial Dr (47265-4883)
P.O. Box 1049 (47265-5049)
PHONE..................812 346-1275
William Baxter, *Mgr*
EMP: 28
SALES (corp-wide): 1.56B **Privately Held**
SIC: 3398 Tempering of metal

North Vernon - Jennings County (G-13273)   GEOGRAPHIC SECTION

HQ: Gerdau Macsteel Atmosphere
Annealing
209 W Mount Hope Ave # 1
Lansing MI 48910
517 782-0415

(G-13273)
GSW PRESS AUTOMATION INC
Also Called: Gsw Press
5100 N State Highway 7 (47265-7368)
PHONE.................................419 733-5230
Andreas Fischer, CEO
▲ EMP: 1 EST: 1999
SQ FT: 7,500
SALES (est): 58.39K **Privately Held**
Web: www.gswpress.com
SIC: 3542 3549 3547 Presses: hydraulic and pneumatic, mechanical and manual; Metalworking machinery, nec; Rolling mill machinery

(G-13274)
GT INDUSTRIES INC
Also Called: Gt Industries
3765 N State Highway 3 (47265-5541)
PHONE.................................734 241-7242
Kevin Trares, COO
EMP: 30 EST: 2016
SQ FT: 45,000
SALES (est): 4.83MM **Privately Held**
Web: www.jenningsedc.com
SIC: 3465 Automotive stampings
PA: Midway Products Group, Inc.
1 Lyman E Hoyt Dr
Monroe MI 48161

(G-13275)
HARPOON LURE CO DBA FORMING T
1080 N County Road 700 W (47265-7871)
PHONE.................................812 371-3550
Lonnie D Lynch, Prin
EMP: 1 EST: 2007
SALES (est): 95.11K **Privately Held**
SIC: 3949 Lures, fishing: artificial

(G-13276)
HEIDELBERG MTLS MDWEST AGG INC
610 S County Road 250 E (47265-7602)
PHONE.................................812 346-6100
EMP: 1
SALES (corp-wide): 23.02B **Privately Held**
SIC: 1422 Limestones, ground
HQ: Heidelberg Materials Midwest Agg, Inc.
300 E John Carpenter Fwy
Irving TX

(G-13277)
HILEX POLY CO LLC
1001 2nd St (47265)
PHONE.................................812 346-1066
EMP: 248
SALES (corp-wide): 32.64B **Publicly Held**
Web: www.novolex.com
SIC: 2673 2674 Plastic bags: made from purchased materials; Paper bags: made from purchased materials
HQ: Hilex Poly Co. Llc
3436 Tringdon Way Ste 100
Charlotte NC 28277
800 845-6051

(G-13278)
HOOSIER INDUSTRIAL ELECTRIC
1003 Rodgers Park Dr (47265-6428)
P.O. Box 656 (47265-0656)
PHONE.................................812 346-2232
Stephen Blackburn, Pr
Donald Chaille, VP

Stephen Blackburn Junior, Prin
Laurie Blackburn, Prin
EMP: 15 EST: 1984
SQ FT: 15,000
SALES (est): 2.38MM **Privately Held**
Web: www.hie-inc.com
SIC: 1731 5063 7694 General electrical contractor; Motors, electric; Electric motor repair

(G-13279)
IMAGINATION GRAPHICS
3855a N State Highway 3 (47265-4849)
PHONE.................................812 352-8288
Chris Biddinger, Prin
Chris Biddinger, Owner
EMP: 1 EST: 1999
SALES (est): 93.83K **Privately Held**
Web: www.imaginesignco.com
SIC: 3993 Signs, not made in custom sign painting shops

(G-13280)
INDIANA SOUTHERN MILLWORK INC (PA)
Also Called: Jonesville Desk
819 Buckeye St (47265-1623)
PHONE.................................812 346-6129
Jerry R Lowman, Pr
EMP: 25 EST: 1982
SQ FT: 32,000
SALES (est): 1.46MM
SALES (corp-wide): 1.46MM **Privately Held**
SIC: 2431 2541 2521 Millwork; Wood partitions and fixtures; Wood office filing cabinets and bookcases

(G-13281)
INDIANA SOUTHERN MOLD CORP
2945 N State Highway 3 (47265-9252)
P.O. Box 119 (47265-0119)
PHONE.................................812 346-2622
Angela J Grindstaff, Pr
Daisy Rees, Off Mgr
▲ EMP: 21 EST: 1983
SQ FT: 14,000
SALES (est): 2.25MM **Privately Held**
Web: www.soindmoldcorp.com
SIC: 3089 Injection molding of plastics

(G-13282)
INJECTION MOLD INC
134 E O And M Ave (47265-1125)
P.O. Box 443 (47265-0443)
PHONE.................................812 346-7002
Delbert A Vawter, Pr
EMP: 12 EST: 1979
SQ FT: 8,300
SALES (est): 1.78MM **Privately Held**
Web: www.decaturmold.com
SIC: 3544 Industrial molds

(G-13283)
LAYMAN FABRICATION INC
895 W County Road 350 N (47265-9277)
PHONE.................................812 767-2823
Betty Layman, Prin
EMP: 5 EST: 2009
SALES (est): 811.69K **Privately Held**
Web: www.laymanfabricationinc.com
SIC: 3599 Machine shop, jobbing and repair

(G-13284)
LEGACY TRAILER RENTALS LLC
5565 S Base Rd (47265-7728)
PHONE.................................812 873-5218
Jerry Hale, Managing Member
EMP: 2 EST: 2020
SALES (est): 92.67K **Privately Held**
Web: www.legacytrailerrentals.com

SIC: 3799 7389 Trailers and trailer equipment; Business services, nec

(G-13285)
MARTINREA INDUSTRIES INC
Also Called: North Vernon Division
505 Industrial Dr (47265-4887)
P.O. Box 927 (47265-0927)
PHONE.................................812 346-5750
Matt Horak, Brnch Mgr
EMP: 225
SALES (corp-wide): 3.89B **Privately Held**
Web: www.martinrea.com
SIC: 3317 3714 Steel pipe and tubes; Motor vehicle parts and accessories
HQ: Martinrea Industries, Inc.
10501 Mi State Road 52
Manchester MI 48158
734 428-2400

(G-13286)
MASCHINO INDUSTRIES INC
1405 S County Road 750 W (47265-6964)
P.O. Box 1 (47245-0001)
PHONE.................................812 346-3083
EMP: 5 EST: 1994
SQ FT: 6,000
SALES (est): 423.57K **Privately Held**
SIC: 3599 Machine shop, jobbing and repair

(G-13287)
METALDYNE SNTERFORGED PDTS LLC (DH)
Also Called: Metaldyne North Vernon
3100 N State Highway 3 (47265-7289)
PHONE.................................812 346-1566
Dave Pempest, Managing Member
◆ EMP: 8 EST: 2009
SALES (est): 83.11MM
SALES (corp-wide): 6.08B **Publicly Held**
SIC: 3714 Motor vehicle parts and accessories
HQ: Metaldyne, Llc
1 Dauch Dr
Detroit MI 48211

(G-13288)
MONTROW GROUP
950 W Jfk Dr (47265-6427)
PHONE.................................812 352-7356
EMP: 7 EST: 2019
SALES (est): 325.1K **Privately Held**
SIC: 3423 Hand and edge tools, nec

(G-13289)
NORTH VERNON INDUSTRY (HQ)
3750 N County Road 75 W (47265-6004)
P.O. Box 894 (47265-0894)
PHONE.................................812 346-8772
▲ EMP: 261 EST: 1995
SQ FT: 160,000
SALES (est): 49.8MM **Privately Held**
Web: www.nvic-cwt.com
SIC: 3321 Gray and ductile iron foundries
PA: Toyota Industries Corporation
2-1, Toyodacho
Kariya AIC 448-0

(G-13290)
ONSPOT OF NORTH AMERICA INC (HQ)
1075 Rodgers Park Dr (47265-6428)
P.O. Box 1077 (47265-5077)
PHONE.................................203 377-0777
Patrick D Freyer, Pr
EMP: 4 EST: 1988
SQ FT: 2,500
SALES (est): 9.54MM
SALES (corp-wide): 545.93MM **Privately Held**

Web: www.onspot.com
SIC: 3496 5072 Tire chains; Chains
PA: Vbg Group Ab (Publ)
Kungsgatan 57
TrollhAttan 461 3
521277700

(G-13291)
PATRIOT PACKAGING LLC
1002 Rodgers Park Dr (47265-6428)
P.O. Box 131 (47265-0131)
PHONE.................................812 346-0700
EMP: 20 EST: 2013
SALES (est): 2.5MM **Privately Held**
Web: www.patriotpkg.com
SIC: 2631 Container, packaging, and boxboard

(G-13292)
POOLGUARD/PBM INDUSTRIES INC
Also Called: Poolguard
1150 W Jfk Dr (47265)
P.O. Box 658 (47265-0658)
PHONE.................................812 346-2648
Merle Stoner, Pr
Dick Apsley, VP
Ben Stone, Sec
▲ EMP: 15 EST: 1985
SALES (est): 1.21MM **Privately Held**
Web: www.poolguard.com
SIC: 3699 1731 Security devices; Electrical work

(G-13293)
PROCOAT PRODUCTS LLC
604 W Montrow Industrial Pkwy (47265)
P.O. Box 657 (47265-0657)
PHONE.................................812 352-6083
James Messer, Pr
EMP: 7 EST: 2014
SALES (est): 511.13K **Privately Held**
SIC: 3999 Manufacturing industries, nec

(G-13294)
R & M TOOL ENGINEERING INC
3355 N 4th St (47265-5534)
P.O. Box 156 (47265-0156)
PHONE.................................812 352-0240
Mark Williams, Pr
EMP: 11 EST: 2003
SQ FT: 9,600
SALES (est): 1.9MM **Privately Held**
Web: www.rmteinc.com
SIC: 3544 Special dies and tools

(G-13295)
SIT CAN HAPPEN LLC
130 N County Road 400 W (47265-7459)
P.O. Box 44 (47265-0044)
PHONE.................................812 346-4188
EMP: 2 EST: 2007
SALES (est): 98.59K **Privately Held**
Web: www.sitcanhappen.com
SIC: 3399 Primary metal products

(G-13296)
STAPLES PIPE & MUFFLER
523 Hoosier St (47265-1214)
PHONE.................................812 346-2474
Joe Staples, Brnch Mgr
EMP: 1
SALES (corp-wide): 248.37K **Privately Held**
Web: staples-pipe-muffler.edan.io
SIC: 3714 Mufflers (exhaust), motor vehicle
PA: Staples Pipe & Muffler
1365 S County Road 650 E
Butlerville IN 47223
812 522-3569

GEOGRAPHIC SECTION

Notre Dame - St. Joseph County (G-13318)

(G-13297)
STRATEGIC SOURCING LLC
3320 N State Highway 7 (47265-7491)
P.O. Box 1027 (47265-5027)
PHONE..................812 346-6904
Xianghua Jian, *Mng Pt*
Richard Apsley, *Mng Pt*
Thomas Bryant, *Mng Pt*
EMP: 8 **EST:** 2004
SALES (est): 403.96K **Privately Held**
SIC: 3544 Special dies, tools, jigs, and fixtures

(G-13298)
TARGET METAL BLANKING INC
1 Steel Way (47265-1243)
PHONE..................812 346-1700
Michael Simone, *Pr*
EMP: 33
SALES (corp-wide): 252.03MM **Privately Held**
Web: www.targetmetalblanking.com
SIC: 3469 3443 Porcelain enameled products and utensils; Fabricated plate work (boiler shop)
HQ: Target Metal Blanking Inc.
36211 S Huron Rd
New Boston MI 48164
734 753-3410

(G-13299)
TEMPEST TOOL & MACHINE INC
7235 W Us Highway 50 (47265-7574)
PHONE..................812 346-6464
William D Tempest, *Pr*
Dixie L Tempest, *Sec*
EMP: 21 **EST:** 1979
SQ FT: 13,750
SALES (est): 2.07MM **Privately Held**
Web: www.tempesttool.com
SIC: 3544 Special dies and tools

(G-13300)
WEBSTER WEST INC
Also Called: Webster West Packaging
1050 Rodgers Park Dr (47265-6428)
P.O. Box 888 (47265-0888)
PHONE..................812 346-5666
William C Akers Ii, *Pr*
James F Akers, *
EMP: 40 **EST:** 1993
SQ FT: 124,000
SALES (est): 8.92MM **Privately Held**
Web: www.akers-pkg.com
SIC: 2653 Boxes, corrugated: made from purchased materials

(G-13301)
WINDSTREAM TECHNOLOGIES INC (PA)
819 Buckeye St (47265-1623)
PHONE..................812 953-1481
Dan Bates, *Pr*
Daniel C Harris, *Ex VP*
Chris Galazzi, *VP*
Claudio Chami, *VP*
William Thorpe, *CFO*
◆ **EMP:** 11 **EST:** 2008
SALES (est): 6.02MM
SALES (corp-wide): 6.02MM **Privately Held**
Web: www.windstream-inc.com
SIC: 3511 Turbines and turbine generator set units, complete

North Webster
Kosciusko County

(G-13302)
B THYSTRUP US CORPORATION
Also Called: Adventureglass
201 E Epworth Forest Rd (46555-9651)
P.O. Box 467 (46555-0467)
PHONE..................574 834-2554
Dan Thystrup, *Pr*
Bo Thystrup, *VP*
EMP: 5 **EST:** 1952
SALES (est): 956.28K **Privately Held**
Web: www.adventureglass.com
SIC: 5091 3229 Boats, canoes, watercrafts, and equipment; Glass fiber products

(G-13303)
CHEMATICS INC
Also Called: Chem-Elec
4519 Highway 13 S (46555)
P.O. Box 293 (46555-0293)
PHONE..................574 834-2406
William Woenker, *CEO*
Agnes Woenker, *Sec*
EMP: 14 **EST:** 1988
SQ FT: 10,000
SALES (est): 2.19MM **Privately Held**
Web: www.chematics.com
SIC: 2835 Blood derivative diagnostic agents

(G-13304)
DEGOOD DMENSIONAL CONCEPTS INC
7815 N State Road 13 (46555-9609)
PHONE..................574 834-5437
Scott Degood, *Pr*
Mary Degood, *VP*
EMP: 19 **EST:** 1997
SQ FT: 5,000
SALES (est): 695.36K **Privately Held**
Web: www.degooddc.com
SIC: 3599 Machine shop, jobbing and repair

(G-13305)
GROUP DEKKO INC
8701 E Backwater Rd (46555-9534)
P.O. Box 337 (46555-0337)
PHONE..................574 834-2818
EMP: 23
SALES (corp-wide): 4.41B **Publicly Held**
Web: www.dekko.com
SIC: 3694 Ignition systems, high frequency
HQ: Group Dekko, Inc.
7310 Innovation Blvd # 104
Fort Wayne IN 46818

(G-13306)
INDIANA DIMENSIONAL PDTS LLC
Also Called: Idp
7224 N State Road 13 (46555-9602)
P.O. Box 271 (46555-0271)
PHONE..................574 834-7681
Ernie Strichland Junior, *Pr*
Ernie Strichland Senior, *Pr*
Tonya Blanchard, *
Philip Faccenda, *
EMP: 24 **EST:** 1987
SQ FT: 325,000
SALES (est): 2.12MM **Privately Held**
Web: www.indianadimensional.com
SIC: 3993 3161 7336 Advertising novelties; Sample cases; Graphic arts and related design

(G-13307)
J C MFG INC (PA)
7248 N State Road 13 (46555-9602)
P.O. Box 340 (46555-0340)
PHONE..................574 834-2881
Kim M Cripe, *Pr*
Joe Sparks, *
EMP: 39 **EST:** 1977
SQ FT: 1,500
SALES (est): 4.84MM
SALES (corp-wide): 4.84MM **Privately Held**
SIC: 3732 Pontoons, except aircraft and inflatable

(G-13308)
JRZ INDUSTRIES INC
133 S East St (46555)
P.O. Box 515 (46555-0515)
PHONE..................574 834-4543
Murray Rhodes, *Pr*
Joan Rhodes, *Sec*
EMP: 3 **EST:** 1983
SALES (est): 228.58K **Privately Held**
SIC: 3714 Motor vehicle parts and accessories

(G-13309)
LASER GRAPHX INC
7196 N State Road 13 (46555-9701)
PHONE..................574 834-4443
William Hackleman, *Pr*
Kris Hackleman, *Sec*
EMP: 4 **EST:** 1991
SALES (est): 342.14K **Privately Held**
Web: www.lasergraphx.net
SIC: 3479 Engraving jewelry, silverware, or metal

(G-13310)
NORTH WEBSTER CONSTRUCTION INC
Also Called: Pacemaker Buildings
7240 N State Road 13 (46555-9602)
P.O. Box 259 (46555-0259)
PHONE..................574 834-4448
TOLL FREE: 888
Wayne O Schrock, *Pr*
Carl Schrock, *
Jack Brunetto, *
EMP: 21 **EST:** 1975
SQ FT: 2,000
SALES (est): 1MM **Privately Held**
Web: www.pacemakerbuildings.com
SIC: 1542 2439 Commercial and office building, new construction; Trusses, wooden roof

(G-13311)
OPPORTUNITIES INC
6122 N 675 E (46555-9216)
PHONE..................574 518-0606
Theodore Shoemaker, *Owner*
EMP: 6 **EST:** 2010
SALES (est): 105.56K **Privately Held**
SIC: 2842 Specialty cleaning

(G-13312)
PAULUS PLASTIC CO INC
304 E George St (46555-1306)
P.O. Box 223 (46555-0223)
PHONE..................574 834-7663
Cecil H Paulus, *Pr*
Doris Paulus, *Ofcr*
EMP: 5 **EST:** 1957
SQ FT: 7,000
SALES (est): 746.79K **Privately Held**
Web: www.paulusplastic.com
SIC: 5082 7542 3494 Construction and mining machinery; Carwash, self-service; Well adapters

(G-13313)
PRECISION WIRE SUPPLY LLC
Also Called: Precision Wire Service
7493 E 800 N (46555-9607)
PHONE..................574 834-7545
Jodi Mikesell, *Pr*
Jody Stoffel, *
Greg Snavely, *
EMP: 35 **EST:** 1985
SQ FT: 2,500
SALES (est): 3.69MM **Privately Held**
SIC: 3679 Harness assemblies, for electronic use: wire or cable

(G-13314)
WEBSTER CUSTOM CANVAS INC
Also Called: Webster Custom Canvas
221 N Main St (46555-1310)
P.O. Box 250 (46555-0250)
PHONE..................574 834-4497
EMP: 2 **EST:** 1988
SQ FT: 11,000
SALES (est): 246.5K **Privately Held**
SIC: 2394 5551 1761 Awnings, fabric: made from purchased materials; Boat dealers; Roofing contractor

Notre Dame
St. Joseph County

(G-13315)
AVE MARIA PRESS INC
Also Called: Spiritual Book Associates
1865 Moreau Dr (46556)
P.O. Box 428 (46556)
PHONE..................574 287-2831
Karey Circosta, *CEO*
Thomas J O'hara, *Pr*
Mark E Witbeck, *Dir*
Anthony V Szakaly, *Ch*
Robert Hamma, *Sec*
▼ **EMP:** 58 **EST:** 1865
SQ FT: 51,000
SALES (est): 3.63MM **Privately Held**
Web: www.avemariapress.com
SIC: 2731 2752 Books, publishing and printing; Offset printing

(G-13316)
STRATEGIC TANKS INCORPORATED
P.O. Box 568 (46556-0568)
PHONE..................574 807-2403
Michael A Stockrahm, *Pr*
EMP: 5 **EST:** 2013
SALES (est): 456.01K **Privately Held**
Web: www.strategictanks.com
SIC: 1389 Oil field services, nec

(G-13317)
UNIVERSITY NOTRE DAME DU LAC
Also Called: Observer, The
024 S Dinnina Hall (46556)
P.O. Box 779 (46556-0779)
PHONE..................574 631-7471
Chris Hine, *Prin*
EMP: 15
SALES (corp-wide): 1.64B **Privately Held**
Web: www.ndsmcobserver.com
SIC: 2711 8221 Newspapers, publishing and printing; University
PA: University Of Notre Dame Du Lac
805 Grace Hall
Notre Dame IN 46556
574 631-6401

(G-13318)
UNIVERSITY NOTRE DAME DU LAC
Also Called: Notre Dame Press
310 Flanner Hall Fl 3 (46556-4637)

Oakford - Howard County (G-13319)

GEOGRAPHIC SECTION

PHONE.................574 631-6346
Barbara Hanrahan, Dir
EMP: 26
SALES (corp-wide): 1.64B Privately Held
Web: undpress.nd.edu
SIC: 2711 2721 2731 8221 Newspapers; Periodicals; Book publishing; University
PA: University Of Notre Dame Du Lac
805 Grace Hall
Notre Dame IN 46556
574 631-6401

Oakford
Howard County

(G-13319)
HEWITT TOOL & DIE INC
Also Called: Hewitt Molding
1138 E 400 S (46965-9997)
P.O. Box 47 (46965-0047)
PHONE.................765 453-3889
EMP: 75 EST: 1966
SALES (est): 8MM Privately Held
Web: www.hewittmolding.com
SIC: 3089 3544 Molding primary plastics; Special dies, tools, jigs, and fixtures

Oakland City
Gibson County

(G-13320)
BRIDON-AMERICAN CORPORATION
Also Called: Bridon American Oakland
11698 E 200 S (47660-7627)
PHONE.................812 749-3115
Phil Young, Mgr
EMP: 92
SALES (corp-wide): 530.91MM Privately Held
Web: www.bridon.com
SIC: 3496 Woven wire products, nec
HQ: Bridon-American Corporation
280 New Commerce Blvd
Hanover Township PA 18706
570 822-3349

(G-13321)
MORGAN EXCAVATING
5268 S 875 E (47660-8531)
PHONE.................812 385-6036
EMP: 3 EST: 1978
SALES (est): 248.78K Privately Held
Web: www.rockndirt.us
SIC: 1542 1389 Nonresidential construction, nec; Oil field services, nec

(G-13322)
SCHAEFER YARD CARE LDSCPG LLC
Also Called: Schaefer Farms & Excavating
4280 S State Road 57 (47660-7641)
PHONE.................812 215-6424
Ryan W Schaefer, Prin
Dylan Russell, Prin
EMP: 3 EST: 2021
SALES (est): 138.93K Privately Held
SIC: 3531 Construction machinery

(G-13323)
SHAMROCK ENGINEERING INC
1020 W Morton St (47660-7617)
PHONE.................812 867-0009
David Dunn, Pr
Laura-lee M Dunn, VP
EMP: 32 EST: 1998
SQ FT: 10,000
SALES (est): 4.4MM Privately Held
Web: www.shamrockeng.com

SIC: 3569 Assembly machines, non-metalworking

(G-13324)
TRIAD MINING INC
1216 E County Road 900 S (47660-9055)
PHONE.................812 328-2117
Ronnie Thompson, CEO
EMP: 9 EST: 2011
SALES (est): 915.02K Privately Held
SIC: 1241 Coal mining services

Oaktown
Knox County

(G-13325)
BLACK PANTHER MINING LLC
12661 N Agri Care Rd (47561-8086)
PHONE.................812 745-2920
Donald R Blankenberger, Managing Member
EMP: 2 EST: 2006
SALES (est): 953.63K Privately Held
Web: www.blackpantherminingllc.com
SIC: 1241 Coal mining services

(G-13326)
CUSTOM TIRE CUTTING INC
8258 E Freelandville Rd (47561-8277)
PHONE.................812 745-9140
Robert Parks, Pr
EMP: 3 EST: 1975
SALES (est): 200K Privately Held
Web: www.customtirecutting.com
SIC: 7534 0115 0116 0111 Tire retreading and repair shops; Corn; Soybeans; Wheat

(G-13327)
GREEN FOREST SAWMILL LLC
407 W Main St (47561-5406)
PHONE.................812 745-3335
Paige Nicol, Owner
EMP: 11 EST: 2013
SALES (est): 873.43K Privately Held
SIC: 2421 Sawmills and planing mills, general

(G-13328)
PETAL PUSHERS
2276 E Cardinal Rd (47561-8352)
PHONE.................812 396-9383
Susie Cardinal, Prin
EMP: 5 EST: 2018
SALES (est): 85.25K Privately Held
Web: www.petalpushersj.com
SIC: 3545 Pushers

(G-13329)
SUNRISE COAL LLC
6331 E Freelandville Rd (47561-8203)
PHONE.................812 745-2002
EMP: 13
SALES (corp-wide): 634.48MM Publicly Held
Web: www.halladorenergy.com
SIC: 1222 Bituminous coal-underground mining
HQ: Sunrise Coal, Llc
1183 E Canvasback Dr
Terre Haute IN 47802
812 299-2800

Odon
Daviess County

(G-13330)
ANTLER CREEK WOODWORKING LLC
9100 N 1025 E (47562-5174)
PHONE.................812 636-0188
Willis Graber, Prin
EMP: 7 EST: 2016
SALES (est): 41.52K Privately Held
SIC: 2499 Wood products, nec

(G-13331)
BERRY GLOBAL INC
10485 E 1250 N (47562-5321)
PHONE.................812 558-3510
EMP: 25
Web: www.berryglobal.com
SIC: 3089 Plastics containers, except foam
HQ: Berry Global, Inc.
101 Oakley St
Evansville IN 47710

(G-13332)
CEDAR CREEK WOODWORKING LLC
8374 N 650 E (47562-5118)
PHONE.................812 687-7556
Kenneth Knepp, Owner
EMP: 6 EST: 2017
SALES (est): 228.13K Privately Held
SIC: 2431 Millwork

(G-13333)
COUNTRY VIEW FURN MFG & UPHL
8659 N 1000 E (47562-5634)
PHONE.................812 636-5024
Viola Graber, Mng Pt
Henry Graber, Pt
Viola Graber, Pt
EMP: 5 EST: 2003
SQ FT: 3,200
SALES (est): 471.23K Privately Held
Web: www.countryviewupholsteredfurniture.com
SIC: 2511 2512 Wood household furniture; Upholstered household furniture

(G-13334)
COUNTRY WOODWORKING LLC
7650 N 1000 N (47562-5034)
PHONE.................812 636-6004
EMP: 3 EST: 2007
SALES (est): 204.4K Privately Held
SIC: 2431 Millwork

(G-13335)
FLYNN & SONS SAND & GRAVEL LLC
11971 N Us Highway 231 (47562-5402)
PHONE.................812 636-4400
Jeanna W Flynn, Prin
EMP: 2 EST: 2012
SALES (est): 118.34K Privately Held
SIC: 1442 Construction sand and gravel

(G-13336)
GRABER
Also Called: Water Front Rabbitry
6608 E 1000 N (47562-5074)
PHONE.................812 636-7699
Sheila Graber, Owner
EMP: 2 EST: 2011
SALES (est): 84.22K Privately Held
Web: www.grabergranite.com

SIC: 2015 7389 Rabbit, processed: frozen; Business Activities at Non-Commercial Site

(G-13337)
GRABER MANUFACTURING
Also Called: Graber Manufacturing & Repair
Ct Rd 1050 N (47562)
PHONE.................812 636-7725
Lester Graber, Pt
Mark Graber, Pt
Samuel Graber, Pt
Eli Wagler, Pt
EMP: 4 EST: 1974
SALES (est): 410.11K Privately Held
Web: www.graberscarts.com
SIC: 3524 3714 3799 Carts or wagons for lawn and garden; Axles, motor vehicle; Carriages, horse drawn

(G-13338)
GRABER STEEL & FAB LLC
8528 N 900 E (47562-5194)
PHONE.................812 636-8418
Nick M Graber, Owner
EMP: 40 EST: 1972
SQ FT: 22,000
SALES (est): 4.3MM Privately Held
Web: www.nickgraber.com
SIC: 3441 Fabricated structural metal

(G-13339)
GRABERS KOUNTRY KORNER LLC
8902 N 900 E (47562-5186)
PHONE.................812 636-4399
EMP: 19 EST: 1991
SQ FT: 25,000
SALES (est): 559.6K Privately Held
Web: www.donut-hill.com
SIC: 2051 5149 5461 Cakes, pies, and pastries; Groceries and related products, nec; Retail bakeries

(G-13340)
GRABERS PORTABLE BAND MILL
10722 N 1000 E (47562-5223)
PHONE.................812 636-4158
Steve Graber, Prin
EMP: 9 EST: 2008
SALES (est): 600K Privately Held
SIC: 2421 Sawmills and planing mills, general

(G-13341)
JIM GRABER LOGGING LLC
10514 N 1000 E (47562-5222)
PHONE.................812 636-7000
Jim Graber, Mgr
EMP: 6 EST: 2011
SALES (est): 434.08K Privately Held
SIC: 2411 Logging

(G-13342)
JOHN G WAGLER
9639 N 1150 E (47562-5379)
PHONE.................812 709-1681
John G Wagler, Prin
EMP: 6 EST: 2011
SALES (est): 105.07K Privately Held
SIC: 2431 Millwork

(G-13343)
MAST WOODWORKING
9922 E 1000 N (47562-5218)
PHONE.................812 636-7938
Mervin Mast, Prin
EMP: 6 EST: 2011
SALES (est): 129.39K Privately Held
SIC: 2431 Millwork

GEOGRAPHIC SECTION

(G-13344)
MYERS ENTERPRISES INC
Also Called: Odon Journal
102 W Main St (47562-1306)
P.O. Box 307 (47562-0307)
PHONE..................................812 636-7350
John L Meyers, *Pr*
Sue Ann Myers, *VP*
EMP: 4 EST: 1964
SQ FT: 1,000
SALES (est): 245.51K **Privately Held**
SIC: 2711 Newspapers, publishing and printing

(G-13345)
N & R WOODWORKING LLC
10546 N 700 E (47562-5022)
PHONE..................................812 787-0644
Norman Wagler, *Prin*
EMP: 5 EST: 2009
SALES (est): 140.52K **Privately Held**
SIC: 2431 Millwork

(G-13346)
NORMAN WAGLER
Also Called: Wagler Carriages & Wagons
Rd 700 E Rr1 33a (47562)
PHONE..................................812 636-8015
Norman Wagler, *Owner*
EMP: 1 EST: 1990
SALES (est): 91.22K **Privately Held**
SIC: 3523 3799 Trailers and wagons, farm; Carriages, horse drawn

(G-13347)
ODON SAWMILL INC
Also Called: Odon Saw Mill
304 S Gum St (47562)
PHONE..................................812 636-7314
Amos Swartzentruber, *Pr*
Lena Swartzentruber, *VP*
EMP: 20 EST: 1954
SQ FT: 4,000
SALES (est): 706.38K **Privately Held**
SIC: 2421 2431 2426 2411 Lumber: rough, sawed, or planed; Millwork; Hardwood dimension and flooring mills; Logging

(G-13348)
ROLLIN MINI BARNS LLC
6950 E 800 N (47562-5133)
PHONE..................................812 687-7581
Ron Stoll, *Prin*
EMP: 9 EST: 2003
SALES (est): 1.04MM **Privately Held**
Web: www.rollinminibarns.com
SIC: 3448 Buildings, portable: prefabricated metal

(G-13349)
SCHROCK
11981 N 1000 E (47562-5483)
PHONE..................................812 636-7842
Dewayne R Schrock, *Prin*
Dewayne R Schrock, *Owner*
EMP: 1 EST: 2005
SALES (est): 140.52K **Privately Held**
Web: www.schrock.com
SIC: 2434 Wood kitchen cabinets

(G-13350)
SHILOH CUSTOM WOODWORKS
9394 E 1000 N (47562-5221)
PHONE..................................812 636-0100
EMP: 4 EST: 2013
SALES (est): 93.05K **Privately Held**
SIC: 2431 Millwork

(G-13351)
SMITH EXCAVATING
10122 E 1400 N (47562)
PHONE..................................812 636-0054
John Smith, *Prin*
EMP: 3 EST: 2006
SALES (est): 116.5K **Privately Held**
SIC: 3531 Construction machinery

(G-13352)
SOUTHERN INDIANA WDWKG LLC
Also Called: Green City Cabinets
9798 E 1200 N (47562-5455)
PHONE..................................812 636-0127
Paul Graber, *Managing Member*
EMP: 2 EST: 2005
SALES (est): 237.3K **Privately Held**
Web: www.greencitycabinets.com
SIC: 2434 Wood kitchen cabinets

(G-13353)
STOLLS WOODWORKING LLC
8779 N 1025 E (47562-4812)
PHONE..................................812 486-5117
John Stoll Junior, *Prin*
EMP: 8 EST: 2010
SALES (est): 493.38K **Privately Held**
Web: www.stollswoodworking.com
SIC: 2431 Millwork

(G-13354)
VALOR DEFENSE SOLUTIONS INC
15484 N 1350 E (47562-5519)
PHONE..................................812 617-0362
Doctor Sue Davis, *CEO*
Sue Davis, *Prin*
Brent Waltz, *Prin*
Jennifer Wagler, *Prin*
EMP: 14 EST: 2018
SALES (est): 1.77MM **Privately Held**
Web: www.valordefensesolutions.com
SIC: 3812 Defense systems and equipment

(G-13355)
VERNON GREYBER
Also Called: Southern Indiana Vinyl Window
9808 E 1100 N (47562-5230)
PHONE..................................812 636-7880
Vernon Greyber, *Owner*
EMP: 4 EST: 1994
SALES (est): 153.09K **Privately Held**
SIC: 3231 Doors, glass: made from purchased glass

(G-13356)
WAGLER COMPETITION PDTS LLC
9612 N 675 E (47562-5073)
PHONE..................................812 486-9360
Jeremy Wagler, *Prin*
EMP: 19 EST: 2011
SALES (est): 3.87MM **Privately Held**
Web: www.waglercompetition.com
SIC: 3714 Motor vehicle parts and accessories

(G-13357)
WAGLERS CUSTOM WD TURNINGS LLC
8593 N 775 E (47562-5141)
PHONE..................................812 687-7758
Marvin Wagler, *Owner*
EMP: 7 EST: 2007
SALES (est): 82.37K **Privately Held**
SIC: 2499 Decorative wood and woodwork

(G-13358)
WOODRUFF AUTOMOTIVE LLC
10298 N 700 E (47562-5025)
PHONE..................................812 636-4908
Larry Woodruff, *Owner*
EMP: 1 EST: 1985
SALES (est): 126.05K **Privately Held**
SIC: 7538 3599 Engine rebuilding: automotive; Machine shop, jobbing and repair

Oldenburg
Franklin County

(G-13359)
VILLAGE WORKSHOP INC
3047 Washington St (47036-9743)
P.O. Box 151 (47036-0151)
PHONE..................................812 933-1527
Brian Rennekamp, *Pr*
EMP: 2 EST: 2006
SALES (est): 233.68K **Privately Held**
Web: www.villageworkshopinc.com
SIC: 2434 Wood kitchen cabinets

Oolitic
Lawrence County

(G-13360)
VICTOR OOLITIC STONE COMPANY
Also Called: Indiana Limestone Company
301 Main St (47451-3026)
P.O. Box 27 (47451-0027)
PHONE..................................812 275-3341
EMP: 130
SIC: 1411 3281 Limestone, dimension-quarrying; Cut stone and stone products

Orestes
Madison County

(G-13361)
RICHARD BUTTERFIELD
Also Called: Dick's Sign Shop
23 N Superior (46063)
P.O. Box 69 (46063-0069)
PHONE..................................765 754-3129
Richard Butterfield, *Owner*
EMP: 1 EST: 1952
SALES (est): 66.09K **Privately Held**
Web: www.butterfieldspeaks.com
SIC: 3993 Signs and advertising specialties

Orland
Steuben County

(G-13362)
COMMERCIAL PALLET RECYCL INC (PA)
5235 N State Road 327 (46776-9574)
PHONE..................................260 829-1021
Melinda Squier, *Pr*
EMP: 10 EST: 2011
SALES (est): 951.21K
SALES (corp-wide): 951.21K **Privately Held**
Web: www.commercialpalletinc.com
SIC: 2448 5031 Pallets, wood; Pallets, wood

(G-13363)
CPG - OHIO LLC
9880 W Maple St (46776-5442)
PHONE..................................260 829-6721
Benzion Kaufman, *Admn*
EMP: 15
SALES (corp-wide): 57.46MM **Privately Held**
Web: www.conpackgroup.com
SIC: 2671 2673 Plastic film, coated or laminated for packaging; Plastic bags: made from purchased materials
HQ: Cpg - Ohio Llc
470 Northland Blvd
Cincinnati OH 45240
513 825-4800

(G-13364)
CRYSTAL VALLEY FARMS LLC (PA)
Also Called: Miller Meat Poultry
9622 W 350 N (46776-5468)
P.O. Box 239 (46776-0239)
PHONE..................................260 829-6550
EMP: 60 EST: 2007
SALES (est): 88.77MM **Privately Held**
Web: www.millerpoultry.com
SIC: 2015 Poultry slaughtering and processing

(G-13365)
FISHERMAN S LURECRAFT SHOP INC
10195 W State Road 120 (46776-9630)
PHONE..................................260 829-1274
Kim Straley, *Pr*
EMP: 11 EST: 2005
SALES (est): 480.42K **Privately Held**
Web: www.lurecraft.com
SIC: 3949 5199 Fishing tackle, general; Bait, fishing

(G-13366)
KAIN TOOL INC
9775 W Maple St (46776-5420)
P.O. Box 258 (46776-0258)
PHONE..................................260 829-6569
Rod Kain, *Pr*
Melody Kain, *VP*
Ryan L Kain, *VP*
EMP: 2 EST: 1991
SALES (est): 433.75K **Privately Held**
Web: www.kaintool.com
SIC: 3544 Jigs and fixtures

(G-13367)
KEMCO INTERNATIONAL INC
9915 W Maple St (46776-5467)
P.O. Box 467 (46776-0467)
PHONE..................................260 829-1263
EMP: 14 EST: 1994
SQ FT: 13,000
SALES (est): 1.22MM **Privately Held**
Web: www.kemcoinc.biz
SIC: 2899 Chemical preparations, nec

(G-13368)
MADSEN WIRE LLC
101 Madsen St (46776-5417)
PHONE..................................260 829-6561
EMP: 14 EST: 2005
SALES (est): 2.61MM **Privately Held**
Web: www.madsenwire.com
SIC: 3496 Miscellaneous fabricated wire products

(G-13369)
NOBLE WIRE PRODUCTS INC
101 Madsen St (46776-5417)
P.O. Box 578 (46061-0578)
PHONE..................................317 773-1926
Gregory Parker, *Pr*
EMP: 1 EST: 2012
SALES (est): 443.63K **Privately Held**
Web: www.madsenwire.com
SIC: 3496 Miscellaneous fabricated wire products

Orland - Steuben County (G-13370)

GEOGRAPHIC SECTION

(G-13370)
PINE MANOR INC (HQ)
Also Called: Miller Poultry
9622 W 350 N (46776-5468)
P.O. Box 239 (46776-0239)
PHONE.....................800 532-4186
Galen Miller, *Pr*
Ursula Miller, *
John Sauder, *
Karen Brenneman, *
Kevin Diehl, *
▲ **EMP:** 450 **EST:** 1959
SALES (est): 65.3MM **Privately Held**
Web: www.pinemanorfarms.com
SIC: 2048 2015 0254 Poultry feeds; Poultry slaughtering and processing; Chicken hatchery
PA: Crystal Valley Farms, Llc
9622 W 350 N
Orland IN 46776

(G-13371)
QUALITY CONVERTERS INC
Also Called: Q C I
9675 W Maple St (46776-5419)
P.O. Box 308 (46776-0308)
PHONE.....................260 829-6541
Cova Feltner, *Pr*
EMP: 22 **EST:** 1983
SQ FT: 31,800
SALES (est): 903.38K **Privately Held**
Web: www.qualityconvertersinc.com
SIC: 2396 3714 3429 Automotive trimmings, fabric; Motor vehicle parts and accessories; Hardware, nec

(G-13372)
RD SMITH MANUFACTURING INC
5990 N State Road 327 (46776-5436)
P.O. Box 191 (46776-0191)
PHONE.....................260 829-6709
Roger Smith, *Pr*
EMP: 4 **EST:** 1987
SQ FT: 6,000
SALES (est): 475.37K **Privately Held**
Web: www.rdsmithmfg.com
SIC: 3451 Screw machine products

(G-13373)
UCOM INC
9725 W Maple St (46776-5420)
P.O. Box 254 (46776-0254)
PHONE.....................260 829-1294
EMP: 10 **EST:** 1994
SQ FT: 12,500
SALES (est): 2.09MM **Privately Held**
Web: www.ucominc.com
SIC: 3643 Electric connectors

(G-13374)
UNIVERSAL PACKG SYSTEMS INC
Also Called: Paklab
9880 W Naples St (46776)
PHONE.....................260 829-6721
Tammy Detro, *Brnch Mgr*
EMP: 158
SALES (corp-wide): 379.38MM **Privately Held**
Web: www.paklab.com
SIC: 2844 3565 7389 2671 Cosmetic preparations; Bottling machinery: filling, capping, labeling; Packaging and labeling services; Plastic film, coated or laminated for packaging
PA: Universal Packaging Systems, Inc.
14570 Monte Vista Ave
Chino CA 91710
909 517-2442

Orleans
Orange County

(G-13375)
COLEMAN SAWMILL SUPPLY
260 S 6th St (47452-9764)
P.O. Box 201 (47452-0201)
PHONE.....................812 865-4001
EMP: 5 **EST:** 1988
SALES (est): 461.7K **Privately Held**
Web: www.colemansawmillsupply.com
SIC: 2421 Lumber: rough, sawed, or planed

(G-13376)
DANIEL HUDELSON
Also Called: Hudelson Machine & Sharpening
27 W Quarry Rd (47452-9281)
PHONE.....................812 865-3951
EMP: 7 **EST:** 1993
SQ FT: 8,500
SALES (est): 581.46K **Privately Held**
SIC: 3599 Machine shop, jobbing and repair

(G-13377)
LANA HUDELSON
Also Called: Hudelson Fabrication
27 W Quarry Rd (47452-9281)
PHONE.....................812 865-3951
EMP: 4 **EST:** 2010
SALES (est): 242.24K **Privately Held**
SIC: 2431 3312 Brackets, wood; Sheet or strip, steel, hot-rolled

(G-13378)
ORANGE CNTY WLDG & FABRICATION
6063 N County Road 200 E (47452-9174)
PHONE.....................812 653-5754
Heath Grissom, *Owner*
Mike Sampson, *Mgr*
Grissom Heath, *Owner*
EMP: 5 **EST:** 2011
SALES (est): 444.87K **Privately Held**
SIC: 3499 Fabricated metal products, nec

(G-13379)
ORANGE COUNTY PROCESSING
5028 N State Road 37 (47452-9025)
PHONE.....................812 865-2028
Marvin Hammack, *Mgr*
EMP: 10 **EST:** 1945
SALES (est): 645.77K **Privately Held**
SIC: 2011 Meat packing plants

(G-13380)
PROFAB CUSTOM METAL WORKS INC
7040 N State Road 337 (47452-9175)
P.O. Box 300 (47452-0300)
PHONE.....................812 865-3999
James Shelby, *Pr*
EMP: 7 **EST:** 2007
SALES (est): 500.53K **Privately Held**
SIC: 3441 Fabricated structural metal

(G-13381)
PROGRESS EXAMINER
233 S 2nd St (47452-1601)
P.O. Box 225 (47452-0225)
PHONE.....................812 865-3242
John F Noblitt, *Owner*
EMP: 4 **EST:** 1879
SALES (est): 196.51K **Privately Held**
SIC: 2711 Newspapers, publishing and printing

(G-13382)
ROSES SQUARE DANCE ACC
448 E Liberty Rd (47452-1516)
PHONE.....................812 865-2821
Rose Warren, *Pt*
Ralph Warren, *Pt*
EMP: 2 **EST:** 1987
SQ FT: 950
SALES (est): 121.21K **Privately Held**
SIC: 5699 2341 Square dance apparel; Women's and children's undergarments

(G-13383)
WILLIAMS WELD SERVICE LLC
3824 E County Road 625 N (47452-9673)
PHONE.....................812 865-3298
EMP: 1 **EST:** 2002
SALES (est): 191.64K **Privately Held**
Web: www.williamsweldservice.com
SIC: 7692 Welding repair

Osceola
St. Joseph County

(G-13384)
BUY BULK DISPLAYS LLC
1610 3rd St (46561-2054)
PHONE.....................574 222-4378
EMP: 2 **EST:** 2013
SQ FT: 10,000
SALES (est): 140.7K **Privately Held**
Web: www.buybulkdisplays.com
SIC: 3993 Signs and advertising specialties

(G-13385)
CALI NAIL
Also Called: Cali Nail Salon
941 Lincolnway W (46561-2014)
PHONE.....................574 674-4126
Thong Nguyen, *Owner*
EMP: 5 **EST:** 1998
SALES (est): 216.86K **Privately Held**
Web: www.calinailsgurnee.com
SIC: 3999 7231 Fingernails, artificial; Manicurist, pedicurist

(G-13386)
CHAPMAN ENVIRONMENTAL CONTROLS
10463 Pleasant Valley Ct (46561-9336)
P.O. Box 288 (46561-0288)
PHONE.....................574 674-8706
Frank Chapman, *Pr*
Penny Chapman, *Sec*
EMP: 2 **EST:** 1978
SALES (est): 108.94K **Privately Held**
SIC: 7389 3829 Air pollution measuring service; Measuring and controlling devices, nec

(G-13387)
CONRAD MACHINE CO INC
55858 Season Ct (46561-9141)
PHONE.....................574 259-1190
EMP: 2
SALES (est): 268.16K **Privately Held**
SIC: 3599 Machine shop, jobbing and repair

(G-13388)
CUSTOM DESIGN LAMINATES INC
Also Called: Focal Point Cabinetry
10055 Mckinley Hwy (46561-9751)
PHONE.....................574 674-9174
Ralph R Erbe, *Pr*
Vance Erbe, *Sec*
EMP: 16 **EST:** 1978
SQ FT: 18,000
SALES (est): 918.37K **Privately Held**
Web: www.fpcabinetry.com
SIC: 1799 2541 2434 Counter top installation; Table or counter tops, plastic laminated; Wood kitchen cabinets

(G-13389)
DIDDLEBUG PUBLISHING LLC
520 Garfield St (46561-3508)
PHONE.....................574 612-2389
Bruce M Tassell, *Owner*
EMP: 4 **EST:** 2018
SALES (est): 81.72K **Privately Held**
SIC: 2741 Miscellaneous publishing

(G-13390)
ELKHART ELECTRONICS
59425 Apple Rd (46561-9393)
PHONE.....................574 679-4627
Peter Ostapchuk, *Owner*
EMP: 1 **EST:** 1975
SALES (est): 105.47K **Privately Held**
SIC: 3625 Electric controls and control accessories, industrial

(G-13391)
EXPERIMENTAL NYLON PRODUCTS
1610 3rd St (46561-2054)
P.O. Box 266 (46561-0266)
PHONE.....................574 674-8747
FAX: 574 674-5707
EMP: 40 **EST:** 1960
SQ FT: 15,000
SALES (est): 5.38MM **Privately Held**
Web: www.enp-casino-products.com
SIC: 3089 3083 Injection molding of plastics; Laminated plastics plate and sheet

(G-13392)
FLAGS INTERNATIONAL INC
10845 Mckinley Hwy (46561-9199)
PHONE.....................574 674-5125
William O'keefe, *Pr*
EMP: 5 **EST:** 2016
SQ FT: 4,000
SALES (est): 486.01K **Privately Held**
Web: www.flagsinternationalshop.com
SIC: 5999 2399 Flags; Emblems, badges, and insignia

(G-13393)
HOMES & LIFESTYLES MAGAZINE
11859 Lincolnway (46561-1927)
P.O. Box 307 (46561-0307)
PHONE.....................574 674-6639
Fred Bradley, *Pr*
Cheryl Bradley, *
EMP: 16 **EST:** 1979
SQ FT: 6,000
SALES (est): 290.82K **Privately Held**
Web: www.easyhomesearch.com
SIC: 2721 Trade journals: publishing only, not printed on site

(G-13394)
HORIZON PLASTICS & ENGINEERING
Also Called: Horizon Plastics
1243 3rd St (46561-2053)
P.O. Box 57 (46561-0057)
PHONE.....................574 674-5443
Michael Johnson, *Pr*
Charles Books, *Sec*
EMP: 24 **EST:** 1983
SQ FT: 21,400
SALES (est): 2.07MM
SALES (corp-wide): 1.41B **Privately Held**
SIC: 3089 3599 Injection molding of plastics; Machine shop, jobbing and repair
PA: Dexko Global Inc.
39555 Orchrd Hl Pl Ste 52
Novi MI 48375
248 533-0029

GEOGRAPHIC SECTION

Ossian - Wells County (G-13421)

(G-13395)
JPE CONSULTING LLP
10451 Dunn Rd (46561-9033)
P.O. Box 282 (46561-0282)
PHONE..................................574 675-9552
David Parker, *Pt*
Dan Elek, *Pt*
EMP: 2 **EST:** 1997
SALES (est): 150K **Privately Held**
SIC: 7372 7371 Prepackaged software; Custom computer programming services

(G-13396)
KIDSTAR SAFETY
54846 Beech Rd (46561-9442)
PHONE..................................800 785-6015
EMP: 5 **EST:** 2008
SALES (est): 124.93K **Privately Held**
Web: www.kidstarsafety.com
SIC: 3999 Manufacturing industries, nec

(G-13397)
LEHUE MACHINE AND TOOL
55981 Wynnewood Dr (46561-9517)
PHONE..................................574 329-5456
EMP: 4 **EST:** 2015
SALES (est): 239.76K **Privately Held**
SIC: 3544 Special dies and tools

(G-13398)
MIDWEST PLASTICS COMPANY INC (PA)
401 Lincolnway W (46561-2637)
PHONE..................................574 674-0161
Michael Malloy, *Prin*
EMP: 2 **EST:** 2010
SALES (est): 461.57K
SALES (corp-wide): 461.57K **Privately Held**
SIC: 3089 Injection molding of plastics

(G-13399)
MNT DELIVERY COMPANY
72 Sunnycrest Dr (46561-9578)
PHONE..................................574 518-6250
Montgomery Stroup, *Managing Member*
EMP: 1 **EST:** 2014
SALES (est): 116.46K **Privately Held**
SIC: 4212 7699 1381 1711 Delivery service, vehicular; Septic tank cleaning service; Drilling water intake wells; Septic system construction

(G-13400)
PARAGON PRINTING CENTER INC
11194 River Oaks Ln W (46561-9116)
PHONE..................................574 533-5835
Nyal Weaver, *Pr*
EMP: 4 **EST:** 2003
SALES (est): 297.18K **Privately Held**
Web: www.paragonprintingcenter.com
SIC: 2752 Offset printing

(G-13401)
R B TOOL & MACHINERY CO
Also Called: Hollingsworth & Associates
10120 Glenwood Ave (46561-9446)
PHONE..................................574 679-0082
EMP: 6 **EST:** 1989
SALES (est): 489.02K **Privately Held**
SIC: 5084 3561 3545 Industrial machine parts; Pumps and pumping equipment; Machine tool accessories

(G-13402)
SIGNS ETC
10170 Glenwood Ave (46561-9447)
PHONE..................................574 674-9671
Linda Buell, *Owner*
EMP: 1 **EST:** 2003

SALES (est): 50.68K **Privately Held**
Web: www.signs-etc.net
SIC: 3993 Signs and advertising specialties

(G-13403)
TIBBS ENTERPRISES LLC
508 Cloudmont Dr (46561-8423)
PHONE..................................574 360-9552
Jennifer Tibbs, *Managing Member*
EMP: 1 **EST:** 2019
SALES (est): 41.52K **Privately Held**
SIC: 3911 Jewelry apparel

(G-13404)
US SIGNCRAFTERS INC
Also Called: U. S. Signcrafters
216 Lincolnway E (46561-2769)
PHONE..................................574 674-5055
Scott D Franko, *Pr*
Scott Franko, *Pr*
James G Kyle, *CEO*
EMP: 17 **EST:** 1984
SQ FT: 7,500
SALES (est): 2.43MM **Privately Held**
Web: www.ussigncrafters.com
SIC: 3993 1799 Electric signs; Sign installation and maintenance

(G-13405)
VALLEY SHARPENING INC
102 Osceola Ave (46561-2208)
P.O. Box 125 (46561-0125)
PHONE..................................574 674-9077
Kenneth Harlacher, *Pr*
Margaret Harlacher, *Treas*
EMP: 4 **EST:** 1984
SQ FT: 15,000
SALES (est): 266.94K **Privately Held**
SIC: 7699 3425 Knife, saw and tool sharpening and repair; Saws, hand: metalworking or woodworking

(G-13406)
VERTICAL POWER CO
10254 Jefferson Rd (46561-9552)
PHONE..................................574 276-8094
EMP: 6 **EST:** 2011
SALES (est): 217.36K **Privately Held**
Web: www.jumphighertoday.org
SIC: 3841 Muscle exercise apparatus, ophthalmic

Osgood
Ripley County

(G-13407)
DOUBLE E ENTERPRISE INC
205 Western Ave (47037-1054)
PHONE..................................812 689-0671
Michael Effing, *Pr*
EMP: 2 **EST:** 2001
SQ FT: 11,000
SALES (est): 452.74K **Privately Held**
Web: www.doubleeenterpriseinc.com
SIC: 3449 Miscellaneous metalwork

(G-13408)
GARY SIMONS
Also Called: Simon S Pit Stop
3018 W County Road 700 N (47037-8924)
P.O. Box 57 (47037-0057)
PHONE..................................812 852-4316
Gary Simon, *Owner*
EMP: 1 **EST:** 1975
SALES (est): 48.21K **Privately Held**
SIC: 7692 Welding repair

(G-13409)
GERALD S ZINS
910 E County Road 875 N (47037-8857)
PHONE..................................812 623-4980
Gerald S Zins, *Prin*
EMP: 6 **EST:** 2010
SALES (est): 117.05K **Privately Held**
SIC: 3713 7389 Dump truck bodies; Business Activities at Non-Commercial Site

(G-13410)
HICKS FARMS
3871 W County Road 1050 N (47037-9213)
PHONE..................................812 852-4055
EMP: 4 **EST:** 2010
SALES (est): 342.21K **Privately Held**
SIC: 3523 Driers (farm): grain, hay, and seed

(G-13411)
LASER MARKING TECHNOLOGIES
873 W County Road 600 N (47037-8649)
PHONE..................................812 852-7999
Preston Davis, *Pr*
EMP: 5 **EST:** 1996
SALES (est): 276.12K **Privately Held**
Web: www.lasermarking.com
SIC: 7389 2759 Engraving service; Laser printing

(G-13412)
LAUGHERY VALLEY AG CO-OP INC (PA)
Also Called: Laughery Valley AG Co-Op
336 N Buckeye St (47037)
P.O. Box 177 (47037)
PHONE..................................812 689-4401
Richard L Miller, *CEO*
EMP: 8 **EST:** 1928
SQ FT: 4,000
SALES (est): 9.8MM
SALES (corp-wide): 9.8MM **Privately Held**
Web: www.laugheryvalleyag.com
SIC: 5172 5153 2875 2048 Petroleum products, nec; Grains; Fertilizers, mixing only; Prepared feeds, nec

(G-13413)
NATURAL PHARMACEUTICAL MFG LLC
117 S Walnut St (47037-1236)
PHONE..................................812 689-3309
Mike Grubb, *Managing Member*
EMP: 10 **EST:** 2012
SALES (est): 496.12K **Privately Held**
SIC: 3999 Manufacturing industries, nec

(G-13414)
NPM HOLDINGS INC
117 S Walnut St (47037-1236)
PHONE..................................812 689-3309
Hugh Helikson, *CEO*
Martha Helikson, *VP*
EMP: 9 **EST:** 1993
SQ FT: 5,000
SALES (est): 963.86K **Privately Held**
SIC: 2834 Pharmaceutical preparations

(G-13415)
SCHMALTZ READY MIX CONCRETE (PA)
Also Called: Laughery Gravel Co
705 Tanglewood Rd (47037-9013)
P.O. Box 159 (47037-0159)
PHONE..................................812 689-5140
William L Schmaltz, *Owner*
EMP: 5 **EST:** 1958
SALES (est): 1.11MM
SALES (corp-wide): 1.11MM **Privately Held**

SIC: 1442 3273 Sand mining; Ready-mixed concrete

(G-13416)
SIMON AND SONS
5802 N Us Highway 421 (47037-8901)
PHONE..................................812 852-3636
Jim Simon, *Owner*
EMP: 2 **EST:** 2006
SALES (est): 124.33K **Privately Held**
SIC: 3011 Tire and inner tube materials and related products

(G-13417)
SUMMERS METALS & MORE
315 Wilson St (47037-1248)
PHONE..................................812 689-7088
Scott Summers, *Owner*
EMP: 5 **EST:** 2010
SALES (est): 206.13K **Privately Held**
Web: www.summersmetals.com
SIC: 7692 Welding repair

(G-13418)
THOMAS & SKINNER INC
525 Western Ave (47037)
PHONE..................................812 689-4811
EMP: 172
SALES (corp-wide): 38.67MM **Privately Held**
Web: www.thomas-skinner.com
SIC: 3264 Porcelain electrical supplies
PA: Thomas & Skinner Inc
1120 E 23rd St
Indianapolis IN 46205
317 923-2501

Ossian
Wells County

(G-13419)
BERNE APPAREL COMPANY (PA)
Also Called: Berne
2501 E 850 N (46777-9365)
P.O. Box 530 (46777-0530)
PHONE..................................260 622-1500
Ronald W Nussbaum, *Ch*
Richard E Honig, *
▲ **EMP:** 30 **EST:** 1915
SALES (est): 47.91MM
SALES (corp-wide): 47.91MM **Privately Held**
Web: www.bernedirect.com
SIC: 2326 2329 2339 2325 Work apparel, except uniforms; Hunting coats and vests, men's; Women's and misses' outerwear, nec ; Men's and boy's trousers and slacks

(G-13420)
BUSKIRK ENGINEERING INC
Also Called: Buskirk Engineering
7224 E 900 N (46777-9217)
PHONE..................................260 622-5550
James Isaac Wheeler Iv, *Pr*
Stacy Somers, *VP*
EMP: 14 **EST:** 2006
SQ FT: 17,000
SALES (est): 2.92MM **Privately Held**
Web: www.buskirkeng.com
SIC: 5084 3823 Industrial machinery and equipment; Process control instruments

(G-13421)
COTTONWOOD CORP (PA)
Also Called: Cottonwood Farm
1412 Evergreen Ct (46777-9090)
PHONE..................................260 820-0415
Tim Ringger, *Pr*
Dale Gerber, *Sec*

Ossian - Wells County (G-13422)

EMP: 1 EST: 1975
SALES (est): 254.04K **Privately Held**
SIC: 2013 Prepared pork products, from purchased pork

(G-13422)
D & T TOOL SPECIAL MACHINE
8405 N 675 E (46777-9206)
PHONE..................................260 597-7216
Dennis Nahrwold, *Owner*
Maxine Nahrwold, *Sec*
EMP: 1 EST: 1979
SALES (est): 93.27K **Privately Held**
SIC: 3443 Metal parts

(G-13423)
EDWIN RAHN
Also Called: Rahn Printing
706 Millside Ct (46777-9243)
PHONE..................................260 622-7178
Edwin Rahn, *Owner*
EMP: 1 EST: 1976
SALES (est): 68.96K **Privately Held**
SIC: 7389 2741 Printers' services: folding, collating, etc.; Business service newsletters: publishing and printing

(G-13424)
GINGERBREAD HOUSE PUBLICATIONS
11216 N 500 E (46777-9728)
PHONE..................................260 622-4868
Avis Hulvey, *Owner*
EMP: 3 EST: 1983
SALES (est): 124.99K **Privately Held**
SIC: 2731 2741 Book publishing; Newsletter publishing

(G-13425)
HAVEN MANUFACTURING IND LLC
6935 N State Road 1 (46777-9650)
P.O. Box 551 (46703-0551)
PHONE..................................260 622-4150
Leonard Feddema, *Pr*
Jack Feddema, *Sec*
EMP: 15 EST: 2011
SALES (est): 3.28MM **Privately Held**
Web: www.cadrex.com
SIC: 3545 3469 Cutting tools for machine tools; Machine parts, stamped or pressed metal

(G-13426)
HEYERLY BROTHERS INC
Also Called: Heyerly Bakery
107 N Jefferson St (46777-1103)
P.O. Box 391 (46777-0391)
PHONE..................................260 622-4196
Ronald Heyerly, *Pr*
Stanley Heyerly, *Sec*
Lynn Heyerly, *Treas*
Galen Heyerly, *VP*
EMP: 11 EST: 1929
SQ FT: 3,000
SALES (est): 491.53K **Privately Held**
SIC: 5461 2052 2051 Retail bakeries; Cookies and crackers; Bread, cake, and related products

(G-13427)
J R P MACHINE PRODUCTS LLP
420 Carol Ann Ln (46777-9100)
PHONE..................................260 622-4746
John R Perkins Junior, *Mng Pt*
John R Perkins Junior, *Genl Pt*
Mark W Perkins, *Pt*
EMP: 7 EST: 1967
SALES (est): 501.13K **Privately Held**
Web: www.jrpmachine.com

SIC: 3599 Machine shop, jobbing and repair

(G-13428)
MELCHING MACHINE INC
1630 Baker Dr (46777-9391)
PHONE..................................260 622-4315
Ted E Melching, *Pr*
EMP: 35 EST: 1937
SQ FT: 24,000
SALES (est): 3.84MM **Privately Held**
Web: www.melching.com
SIC: 3599 3544 7692 Machine shop, jobbing and repair; Special dies, tools, jigs, and fixtures; Welding repair

(G-13429)
NORTH AMERICA FRAC SAND INC (PA)
215 N Jefferson St (46777-9700)
P.O. Box 591 (46777-0591)
PHONE..................................260 490-9990
Abdiel Castrellon Williams, *CEO*
Joe Kistler, *Interim Chief Financial Officer*
EMP: 8 EST: 2007
SALES (est): 2.46MM
SALES (corp-wide): 2.46MM **Privately Held**
SIC: 1442 Sand mining

(G-13430)
PARKWAY INDUSTRIAL ENTPS LLC
Also Called: Rethceif Packaging
420 Industrial Pkwy (46777-9121)
PHONE..................................260 622-7200
Timothy Fiechter, *Pr*
Jeremy Collins, *VP*
EMP: 14 EST: 2005
SQ FT: 20,000
SALES (est): 3.65MM **Privately Held**
Web: www.rethceif.com
SIC: 3565 Packaging machinery

(G-13431)
ROEMBKE MFG & DESIGN INC
425 Industrial Pkwy (46777-9121)
PHONE..................................260 307-1198
EMP: 10
SALES (corp-wide): 8.75MM **Privately Held**
Web: www.roembke.com
SIC: 3544 Special dies, tools, jigs, and fixtures
PA: Roembke Mfg & Design Inc
1580 Baker Dr
Ossian IN 46777
260 622-4135

(G-13432)
ROEMBKE MFG & DESIGN INC (PA)
Also Called: Roembke
1580 Baker Dr (46777-9391)
PHONE..................................260 622-4135
John Roembke, *CEO*
Greg Roembke, *
Troy Smith, *
Jim Berry, *
Dave Jaskie, *
EMP: 30 EST: 1976
SQ FT: 62,500
SALES (est): 8.75MM
SALES (corp-wide): 8.75MM **Privately Held**
Web: www.roembke.com
SIC: 3069 3544 Hard rubber and molded rubber products; Special dies, tools, jigs, and fixtures

(G-13433)
ROEMBKE MFG & DESIGN INC
Also Called: Custom Precision Components
1580 Baker Dr (46777-9391)
PHONE..................................260 622-4030
EMP: 10
SALES (corp-wide): 8.75MM **Privately Held**
Web: www.roembke.com
SIC: 3069 7692 Hard rubber and molded rubber products; Welding repair
PA: Roembke Mfg & Design Inc
1580 Baker Dr
Ossian IN 46777
260 622-4135

(G-13434)
SEW CREATIVE
401 Ingle Dr (46777-9323)
PHONE..................................260 622-6263
Sally Bracke, *Owner*
EMP: 1 EST: 1997
SALES (est): 32K **Privately Held**
Web: www.sewcreativeonline.com
SIC: 2395 Embroidery products, except Schiffli machine

(G-13435)
SUCCESS HOLDING GROUP CORP USA
6461 N 100 E (46777)
PHONE..................................260 490-9990
Steve Andrew Chen, *Pr*
EMP: 3 EST: 2014
SALES (est): 482.84K **Privately Held**
SIC: 3861 7384 Motion picture film; Home movies, developing and processing

(G-13436)
SUCCESS HOLDING GROUP INTL INC
215 N Jefferson St (46777-9700)
PHONE..................................260 450-1982
Chris Hong, *CEO*
Steve Andrew Chen, *Ch Bd*
Brian Kistler, *Pr*
Y Tristan Kuo, *CFO*
EMP: 7 EST: 2012
SALES (est): 88.16K **Privately Held**
Web: www.successholdinggroupcorpusa.com
SIC: 8331 2086 Job training and related services; Bottled and canned soft drinks

(G-13437)
SURE-FLO SEAMLESS GUTTERS INC
9192 N 750 E (46777-9216)
PHONE..................................260 622-4372
Stanley Worthman, *Owner*
EMP: 3 EST: 1977
SALES (est): 216.04K **Privately Held**
Web: www.seamlessgutter.net
SIC: 1761 3444 Gutter and downspout contractor; Gutters, sheet metal

(G-13438)
THE AKRON EQUIPMENT COMPANY
Also Called: Hower Tool Division
6935 N State Road 1 (46777-9650)
PHONE..................................260 622-4150
EMP: 48
Web: www.howertool.com
SIC: 3545 3469 Cutting tools for machine tools; Machine parts, stamped or pressed metal

(G-13439)
THERMTRON MFG INC
1625 Baker Dr (46777-9391)
PHONE..................................260 622-6000
Mike Gerber, *Prin*
EMP: 6 EST: 2005
SALES (est): 117K **Privately Held**
Web: www.trustedmfg.com

SIC: 3999 Manufacturing industries, nec

(G-13440)
TI AUTOMOTIVE
6879 N State Road 1 (46777)
PHONE..................................260 622-7372
Keith Bayless, *Prin*
▲ EMP: 2 EST: 2010
SALES (est): 249.08K **Privately Held**
Web: aftermarket.tiautomotive.com
SIC: 3714 Motor vehicle parts and accessories

(G-13441)
TI GROUP AUTO SYSTEMS LLC
Also Called: Ossian Plant
1200 Baker Dr (46777-9106)
PHONE..................................260 622-7900
Harold Clinger, *Brnch Mgr*
EMP: 252
SALES (corp-wide): 3.82B **Privately Held**
Web: www.tifluidsystems.com
SIC: 3714 Motor vehicle parts and accessories
HQ: Ti Group Automotive Systems, Llc
2020 Taylor Rd
Auburn Hills MI 48326
248 296-8000

(G-13442)
TOMS PRINTING SERVICE
P.O. Box 185 (46777-0185)
PHONE..................................260 438-3721
EMP: 1 EST: 2009
SALES (est): 67.72K **Privately Held**
SIC: 2759 Business forms: printing, nsk

(G-13443)
TRUSTED SOLUTIONS GROUP INC
1625 Baker Dr (46777-9391)
P.O. Box 341 (46777-0341)
PHONE..................................260 622-6000
EMP: 65 EST: 1994
SALES (est): 9.29MM **Privately Held**
Web: www.trustedmfg.com
SIC: 3325 Steel foundries, nec

(G-13444)
ZIMMER HOLDINGS LLC
Also Called: Zimmer Custom Made Packaging
2687 E 500 N (46777-9652)
EMP: 1 EST: 2001
SALES (est): 201.75K **Privately Held**
SIC: 2671 Waxed paper: made from purchased material

Otis
Laporte County

(G-13445)
SCOTT BERNTH
Also Called: Scott's Custom Cabinets
509 E 1100 N (46391-9443)
PHONE..................................219 926-4836
Scott Bernth, *Owner*
EMP: 1 EST: 2000
SALES (est): 63.06K **Privately Held**
SIC: 2434 Wood kitchen cabinets

Otisco
Clark County

(G-13446)
ARCHITCTRAL OPNING CNSLTING LL
15212 Gum Corner Rd (47163-9764)
PHONE..................................502 836-5545

Christina Lee Hooker, *Pr*
Russ Hooker, *VP*
EMP: 9 **EST:** 2014
SALES (est): 561.93K **Privately Held**
SIC: 3442 Metal doors, sash, and trim

(G-13447)
CONCRETE LADY INC (PA)
4910 Highway 3 (47163-9402)
PHONE....................812 256-2765
Peggy Woods, *Pr*
Carl Woods, *VP*
James Woods, *Dir*
EMP: 21 **EST:** 1973
SQ FT: 4,000
SALES (est): 2.45MM
SALES (corp-wide): 2.45MM **Privately Held**
Web: www.theconcretelady.com
SIC: 3272 5947 Concrete products, precast, nec; Gift shop

(G-13448)
CUSTOM CYCLE OF INDIANA
4914 Highway 3 (47163-9402)
PHONE....................812 256-9089
Richard Lockhart, *Owner*
EMP: 1 **EST:** 1987
SALES (est): 89.71K **Privately Held**
SIC: 3751 Motorcycle accessories

(G-13449)
MO MONEY MOLD CO INC
4818 Highway 3 (47163-9619)
PHONE....................812 256-2681
Jimmy Woods, *Owner*
EMP: 1 **EST:** 1986
SALES (est): 105.81K **Privately Held**
Web: www.momoneymolds.com
SIC: 3544 Industrial molds

Otterbein
Benton County

(G-13450)
BEST ELECTRIC MOTOR SERVICE
Also Called: Best Electric
11430 E Us Hwy 52 (47970)
P.O. Box 547 (47970-0547)
PHONE....................765 583-2408
Jeff Best, *Pt*
Doug Best, *Pt*
EMP: 4 **EST:** 1985
SQ FT: 5,000
SALES (est): 276.08K **Privately Held**
SIC: 7694 7231 Electric motor repair; Unisex hair salons

(G-13451)
HAAN CRAFTS LLC
506 E 2nd St (47970)
PHONE....................765 583-4496
▲ **EMP:** 16 **EST:** 1977
SQ FT: 25,000
SALES (est): 585.59K
SALES (corp-wide): 775.69MM **Privately Held**
Web: www.haancrafts.com
SIC: 3944 Craft and hobby kits and sets
HQ: Nasco Healthcare Inc.
 16 Simulaids Dr
 Saugerties NY 12477
 920 563-2446

(G-13452)
HELENA AGRI-ENTERPRISES LLC
502 W Oxford St (47970-8581)
PHONE....................765 583-4458
EMP: 1

Web: www.helenaagri.com
SIC: 5191 2819 Chemicals, agricultural; Chemicals, high purity: refined from technical grade
HQ: Helena Agri-Enterprises, Llc
 225 Schilling Blvd
 Collierville TN 38017
 901 761-0050

(G-13453)
KERKHOFF ASSOCIATES INC (PA)
Also Called: K A Components
21 W Oxford St (47970-8576)
P.O. Box 578 (47970-0578)
PHONE....................765 583-4491
Timothy C Kerkhoff, *Pr*
Michael Kerkhoff, *Treas*
Julia Kerkhoff, *Sec*
EMP: 20 **EST:** 1953
SQ FT: 2,400
SALES (est): 5.49MM
SALES (corp-wide): 5.49MM **Privately Held**
Web: www.kacomponents.com
SIC: 2439 2431 Trusses, except roof: laminated lumber; Panel work, wood

(G-13454)
KNK BATTERY LLC
9117 E State Road 26 (47970-8062)
PHONE....................765 426-2016
Shawn A Klemme, *Prin*
EMP: 3 **EST:** 2008
SALES (est): 218.1K **Privately Held**
SIC: 3691 Storage batteries

(G-13455)
SIGNS SUCCESS
107 E Us Highway 52 (47970-8082)
PHONE....................765 427-1437
Monica Hartlet, *Prin*
EMP: 5 **EST:** 2016
SALES (est): 46.08K **Privately Held**
SIC: 3993 Signs and advertising specialties

Otwell
Pike County

(G-13456)
AMBROTOS LLC
8640 E County Road 200 N (47564-8903)
PHONE....................413 887-1058
EMP: 3 **EST:** 2020
SALES (est): 62.38K **Privately Held**
SIC: 2087 5499 Beverage bases, concentrates, syrups, powders and mixes; Coffee

(G-13457)
PATTERSON PRODUCTS LLC
8446 W Himsel Rd (47564-9617)
PHONE....................812 309-3614
EMP: 5 **EST:** 2015
SALES (est): 230.93K **Privately Held**
Web: www.pattersonproductsllc.com
SIC: 3999 Atomizers, toiletry

(G-13458)
TURN & BURN WELDING INC ✪
Also Called: Turn & Burn Welding
3668 N State Road 257 (47564-8719)
PHONE....................812 766-0641
Wayne Turner, *Pr*
EMP: 1 **EST:** 2023
SALES (est): 44.57K **Privately Held**
SIC: 7692 7389 Welding repair; Business services, nec

Owensburg
Greene County

(G-13459)
BRAY LOGGING
6399 E State Road 58 (47453-8259)
PHONE....................812 863-7947
Christopher W Bray, *Prin*
EMP: 6 **EST:** 2010
SALES (est): 230.05K **Privately Held**
SIC: 2411 Logging camps and contractors

(G-13460)
CARR LOGGING
9322 E State Road 58 (47453-8273)
PHONE....................812 863-7585
Carl Carr, *Prin*
EMP: 3 **EST:** 2010
SALES (est): 183.46K **Privately Held**
SIC: 2411 Logging camps and contractors

(G-13461)
D & M SYSTEMS INC
6516 S Thomas Ct (47453-8288)
PHONE....................812 327-2384
Millard Reeves, *Pr*
Tyler Reeves, *VP*
Toby Reeves, *Sec*
EMP: 5 **EST:** 2008
SQ FT: 261,360
SALES (est): 492.88K **Privately Held**
SIC: 1791 3441 Structural steel erection; Fabricated structural metal

(G-13462)
DANCING CRANE PUBLISHING LLC
9591 E Mineral-Koleen Rd (47453-8242)
PHONE....................812 675-2362
Rebecca Crane, *Prin*
EMP: 5 **EST:** 2016
SALES (est): 41.35K **Privately Held**
SIC: 2741 Miscellaneous publishing

(G-13463)
MICHAEL FILLEY (PA) ✪
Also Called: Wild Spirit Coffee Company
10736 E Main St (47453-8215)
PHONE....................956 443-6364
Michael Filley, *Owner*
EMP: 6 **EST:** 2023
SALES (est): 65.62K
SALES (corp-wide): 65.62K **Privately Held**
SIC: 2095 7389 Roasted coffee; Business Activities at Non-Commercial Site

Owensville
Gibson County

(G-13464)
ABSOLUTE CUSTOM MACHINE LLC
5954 S 1075 W (47665-8915)
PHONE....................812 724-2284
Erin Smith, *Prin*
EMP: 6 **EST:** 2016
SALES (est): 98.61K **Privately Held**
SIC: 3599 Machine shop, jobbing and repair

(G-13465)
ANCHOR INDUSTRIES
9248 W 280 S (47665-8933)
PHONE....................812 664-0772
Faye Masterson, *Prin*
EMP: 6 **EST:** 2017
SALES (est): 80.69K **Privately Held**
Web: www.anchorinc.com
SIC: 3999 Manufacturing industries, nec

(G-13466)
DRAVA UNDERWATER LLC
509 N 2nd St Ste B (47665-8787)
PHONE....................812 622-0432
EMP: 3
SALES (est): 136.08K **Privately Held**
SIC: 3949 7389 Sporting and athletic goods, nec; Business Activities at Non-Commercial Site

(G-13467)
GIBSON COUNTY COAL LLC
3455 S 700 W (47665-9180)
PHONE....................812 385-1816
EMP: 290 **EST:** 1999
SALES (est): 46.28MM **Publicly Held**
Web: www.gibsoncounty-in.gov
SIC: 1241 1221 Coal mining services; Bituminous coal surface mining
HQ: Alliance Coal, Llc
 1717 S Boulder Ave # 400
 Tulsa OK 74119
 918 295-7600

(G-13468)
GIBSON COUNTY MEATS LLC
9208 W State Road 165 (47665-8750)
PHONE....................812 724-2333
Brian Rexing, *Pr*
EMP: 10 **EST:** 2021
SALES (est): 348.28K **Privately Held**
Web: www.gogibson.org
SIC: 0751 2011 Slaughtering: custom livestock services; Beef products, from beef slaughtered on site

(G-13469)
KENNY DEWIG MEATS SAUSAGE INC
Also Called: Dewig Deer Processing
9208 W State Road 165 (47665-8750)
PHONE....................812 724-2333
Kenny Dewig, *Pr*
Tamara Dewig, *VP*
EMP: 4 **EST:** 1999
SALES (est): 336K **Privately Held**
Web: www.kennydewigmeats.com
SIC: 2011 Meat packing plants

(G-13470)
LARRY SHORTS WELDING
9956 W 450 S (47665-8968)
PHONE....................812 664-4910
EMP: 3 **EST:** 2017
SALES (est): 40.45K **Privately Held**
SIC: 7692 Welding repair

(G-13471)
RANDALL K DIKE ✪
Also Called: Midwest Municipal Supply
5038 S State Road 65 (47665-9299)
PHONE....................812 664-4942
Randall K Dike, *Owner*
EMP: 3 **EST:** 2023
SALES (est): 54.05K **Privately Held**
Web: www.midwestmunicipalsupply.com
SIC: 3498 3443 1629 3491 Fabricated pipe and fittings; Pipe, standpipe, and culverts; Drainage system construction; Water works valves

(G-13472)
RHODES TOOL & MACHINE INC
7864 W State Road 165 (47665-8739)
PHONE....................812 729-7134
EMP: 1 **EST:** 1980
SALES (est): 40K **Privately Held**
SIC: 3599 Machine shop, jobbing and repair

Owensville - Gibson County (G-13473)   GEOGRAPHIC SECTION

(G-13473)
SUPERIOR AG RESOURCES COOP INC
504 S 2nd St (47665)
P.O. Box 247 (47665-0247)
PHONE..................812 724-4455
Wayne Scott, Mgr
EMP: 8
SALES (corp-wide): 78.77MM Privately Held
Web: www.superiorag.com
SIC: 5191 2879 2875 0721 Fertilizer and fertilizer materials; Agricultural chemicals, nec; Fertilizers, mixing only; Crop planting and protection
PA: Superior Ag Resources Cooperative, Inc.
901 N Main St
Huntingburg IN 47542
812 683-2809

Oxford
Benton County

(G-13474)
DRUG PLASTICS AND GLASS CO INC
5 Bottle Dr (47971-8675)
PHONE..................765 385-0035
Darrin Bowman, Mgr
EMP: 38
SALES (corp-wide): 91.9MM Privately Held
Web: www.drugplastics.com
SIC: 3089 Plastics containers, except foam
PA: Drug Plastics And Glass Company, Inc.
1 Bottle Dr
Boyertown PA 19512
610 367-5000

(G-13475)
LANDEC AG INC (HQ)
Also Called: Fielders Choice Direct
201 N Michigan St (47971-8505)
PHONE..................765 385-1000
EMP: 11 EST: 1995
SALES (est): 9.78MM
SALES (corp-wide): 128.26MM Publicly Held
Web: www.landecag.com
SIC: 2879 5153 Agricultural chemicals, nec; Corn
PA: Lifecore Biomedical, Inc.
3515 Lyman Blvd
Chaska MN 55318
952 368-4300

(G-13476)
PLAY 2 WIN SCREENPRINTING LLC
8975 E 200 S (47971-8705)
PHONE..................765 426-0679
Robert Troy Watt, Prin
EMP: 2 EST: 2008
SALES (est): 146.42K Privately Held
SIC: 2759 Screen printing

(G-13477)
RES TECHNICA LLC
3776 S 875 E (47971-8627)
P.O. Box 2665 (47996-2665)
PHONE..................765 366-5089
William P Kealey, Admn
Chad Coats, Proj Mgr
EMP: 1 EST: 2016
SALES (est): 71.92K Privately Held
SIC: 3629 Power conversion units, a.c. to d.c.: static-electric

Palmyra
Harrison County

(G-13478)
BLUE RIVER FARM SUPPLY INC
14485 Greene St Ne (47164-8860)
PHONE..................812 364-6675
John Gammon, Pr
John Gammon Junior, Pr
EMP: 3 EST: 1989
SQ FT: 7,000
SALES (est): 601.46K Privately Held
Web: www.blueriverfarmsupply.com
SIC: 5211 5191 2048 Lumber products; Farm supplies; Prepared feeds, nec

(G-13479)
DAVE BROWN CUSTOMS LLC
11138 S Locust Creek Dr (47164-6983)
PHONE..................812 727-5560
David Brown, CEO
EMP: 1 EST: 2016
SALES (est): 78.09K Privately Held
SIC: 7699 3484 3949 Gun services; Guns (firearms) or gun parts, 30 mm. and below; Shooting equipment and supplies, general

(G-13480)
FOOD SERVICE DISTRIBUTORS INC
14820 N Martin Mathis Rd Ne (47164-8326)
PHONE..................812 267-4846
Darrell Graham, CEO
EMP: 1 EST: 1985
SQ FT: 1,600
SALES (est): 280.61K Privately Held
SIC: 2013 5411 Canned meats (except baby food), from purchased meat; Grocery stores

(G-13481)
KEVIN CHUMBLEY ENTERPRISES
3637 E Wetzel Rd (47164-6980)
PHONE..................502 548-2544
Kevin Chumbley, Prin
EMP: 6 EST: 2014
SALES (est): 215.17K Privately Held
SIC: 7692 Welding repair

(G-13482)
KIESLER MACHINE INC
Also Called: Kmi
13700 Chrissy Ln Ne (47164-8768)
P.O. Box 357 (47164-0357)
PHONE..................812 364-6610
Garry Kiesler, Pr
Betty Keisler, Sec
EMP: 7 EST: 1984
SQ FT: 7,200
SALES (est): 718.29K Privately Held
Web: www.kieslermachine.com
SIC: 3599 Machine shop, jobbing and repair

(G-13483)
OCONNORWOODWORKING
3059 W May Dr (47164-6781)
PHONE..................812 364-1022
EMP: 4 EST: 2017
SALES (est): 58.5K Privately Held
Web: www.ocwwvb.com
SIC: 2431 Millwork

(G-13484)
PREFERRED POPCORN LLC
3055 W Bradford Rd Ne (47164-7935)
PHONE..................308 850-6631
EMP: 1
SALES (corp-wide): 20.11MM Privately Held
Web: www.preferredpopcorn.com
SIC: 2099 Popcorn, packaged: except already popped
PA: Preferred Popcorn, L.L.C.
1132 9th Rd
Chapman NE 68827
308 986-2526

(G-13485)
QBC CATERING LLC
2124 E County Line Rd S (47164-6966)
PHONE..................812 364-4293
EMP: 2 EST: 2010
SALES (est): 76.15K Privately Held
SIC: 2099 Food preparations, nec

(G-13486)
SX4
3363 E Wetzel Rd (47164-6978)
PHONE..................812 967-2502
Steven Robbins, Prin
EMP: 2 EST: 2008
SALES (est): 74.97K Privately Held
Web: www.sx4club.com
SIC: 3799 All terrain vehicles (ATV)

Paoli
Orange County

(G-13487)
ANDIS LOGGING INC
76 W County Road 550 S (47454-9416)
PHONE..................812 723-2357
▼ EMP: 15 EST: 1967
SALES (est): 906.41K Privately Held
SIC: 2411 Logging camps and contractors

(G-13488)
BENHAM SAWMILL LLC
150 W County Road 250 N (47454-9122)
P.O. Box 305 (47454-0305)
PHONE..................812 723-2644
Ronald Benham, Admn
EMP: 2 EST: 2013
SALES (est): 132.91K Privately Held
SIC: 2421 Sawmills and planing mills, general

(G-13489)
BEST CHAIRS INCORPORATED
1700 W Willowcreek Rd (47454-9023)
PHONE..................812 367-1761
Steven M Wahl, Brnch Mgr
EMP: 53
SALES (corp-wide): 225MM Privately Held
Web: www.besthf.com
SIC: 2512 5712 Chairs: upholstered on wood frames; Furniture stores
PA: Best Chairs Incorporated
1 Best Dr
Ferdinand IN 47532
812 367-1761

(G-13490)
CABINETMAKER INC
Also Called: Cabinetmaker, The
1714 E Owl Hollow Rd (47454-9085)
PHONE..................812 723-3461
Mary Barnard, Pr
Dale Barnard, VP
EMP: 2 EST: 1980
SALES (est): 122.68K Privately Held
Web: www.the-cabinetmaker.com
SIC: 2434 2511 2426 8331 Wood kitchen cabinets; Wood household furniture; Hardwood dimension and flooring mills; Skill training center

(G-13491)
CALCAR QUARRIES INCORPORATED
731 Ne Main St (47454-9237)
P.O. Box 287 (47454-0287)
PHONE..................812 723-2109
Jerry Meadows, Pr
Maxine Riester, Sec
Mary Meadows, VP
EMP: 10 EST: 1934
SQ FT: 1,000
SALES (est): 753.88K Privately Held
Web: www.cavequarries.com
SIC: 1422 2951 3274 Limestones, ground; Asphalt and asphaltic paving mixtures (not from refineries); Lime

(G-13492)
CAVE QUARRIES INC
1156 N County Road 425 W (47454-9002)
PHONE..................812 936-7743
EMP: 12
SALES (corp-wide): 5.48MM Privately Held
Web: www.cavequarries.com
SIC: 1422 Crushed and broken limestone
PA: Cave Quarries Inc
1503 S Meridian Rd
Jasper IN
812 634-7115

(G-13493)
ELLIOTT MFG & FABRICATION
2302 W Coffee Dr N (47454-8816)
PHONE..................812 865-0516
EMP: 1 EST: 2016
SALES (est): 138.98K Privately Held
SIC: 3449 Bars, concrete reinforcing: fabricated steel

(G-13494)
FLETCHER HEATING & COOLING
2049 W County Road 500 N (47454-9629)
P.O. Box 49 (47454-0049)
PHONE..................812 865-2984
Bill Fletcher, Owner
EMP: 3 EST: 1994
SALES (est): 185.77K Privately Held
SIC: 1711 3585 Heating and air conditioning contractors; Heating and air conditioning combination units

(G-13495)
G AND P ENTERPRISES IND INC
Also Called: Internal Honing Service
782 N Greenbriar Dr (47454-9667)
P.O. Box 111 (47454-0111)
PHONE..................812 723-3837
Jordan Beck, Prin
EMP: 9 EST: 1971
SQ FT: 8,500
SALES (est): 1.82MM Privately Held
Web: www.internalhoning.com
SIC: 5051 3471 3599 Tubing, metal; Chromium plating of metals or formed products; Machine shop, jobbing and repair

(G-13496)
HARMON HRMON UYSUGI OPTMTRISTS (PA)
488 W Hospital Rd Ste 1 (47454-8808)
PHONE..................812 723-4752
Eric Harmon, Owner
EMP: 10 EST: 1978
SALES (est): 398.21K Privately Held
SIC: 8042 3851 Specialized optometrists; Lenses, ophthalmic

Pekin - Washington County (G-13521)

(G-13497)
HOKE WELD
1194 E County Road 450 S (47454-9374)
PHONE................812 569-0587
William Hoke, *Prin*
EMP: 6 EST: 2007
SALES (est): 122.78K **Privately Held**
SIC: 7692 Welding repair

(G-13498)
JASPER SEATING COMPANY INC
Also Called: Jasper Group
1352 W Hospital Rd (47454-9215)
PHONE................812 723-1323
Chris Edwards, *Mgr*
EMP: 169
SALES (corp-wide): 198.33MM **Privately Held**
Web: jaspergroup.us.com
SIC: 2521 2522 Wood office furniture; Office furniture, except wood
PA: Jasper Seating Company Inc
225 Clay St
Jasper IN 47546
812 482-3204

(G-13499)
LINER PRODUCTS LLC
1468 W Hospital Rd (47454-9215)
PHONE................812 723-0244
EMP: 15 EST: 1999
SALES (est): 5.73MM **Publicly Held**
Web: www.linerproducts.com
SIC: 3084 Plastics pipe
HQ: Reynolds Construction, Llc
6225 N County Road 75 E
Orleans IN 47452
877 770-0127

(G-13500)
STANDS PHOTOGRAPHY
792 S Ridgecrest Ln (47454-9257)
PHONE................812 723-3922
Don Stands, *Owner*
EMP: 2 EST: 1989
SALES (est): 73.18K **Privately Held**
SIC: 7221 2759 Photographer, still or video; Invitations: printing, nsk

Paragon
Morgan County

(G-13501)
J W JONES COMPANY LLC
Also Called: Rock Equipment
2468 S State Road 67 (46166-9502)
P.O. Box 64 (46166-0064)
PHONE................765 537-2279
John W Jones, *Managing Member*
Scott Kimmerly, *
◆ EMP: 50 EST: 1967
SALES (est): 5.03MM **Privately Held**
Web: www.jwjonescompany.com
SIC: 3532 Rock crushing machinery, stationary

(G-13502)
JONES TRUCKING INC
2468 S State Road 67 (46166-9502)
P.O. Box 64 (46166-0064)
PHONE................765 537-2279
EMP: 8 EST: 1986
SALES (est): 773.86K **Privately Held**
SIC: 3532 Mining machinery

Paris Crossing
Jennings County

(G-13503)
NIGHTKRAWLER KUSTOMS LLC
1690 W State Highway 250 (47270-9405)
PHONE................812 599-0251
Jeremy Laufer, *Owner*
EMP: 1 EST: 2010
SQ FT: 3,000
SALES (est): 114.39K **Privately Held**
SIC: 3441 Fabricated structural metal

(G-13504)
PRECISION ENTERPRISES LLC
9775 S County Road 550 W (47270-9527)
PHONE................812 873-6391
Les H Covey, *Prin*
EMP: 6 EST: 2006
SALES (est): 78.29K **Privately Held**
Web: www.precision-enterprises.com
SIC: 3599 Machine shop, jobbing and repair

Parker City
Randolph County

(G-13505)
PHELPS MACHINE INC
150 South Fulton St (47368-5801)
P.O. Box 34 (47368-0034)
PHONE................765 468-6791
Mick Phelps, *Pr*
Joe Phelps, *VP*
Jan Phelps, *Sec*
Jill Phelps, *Treas*
EMP: 4 EST: 1955
SQ FT: 4,800
SALES (est): 400K **Privately Held**
SIC: 3599 Machine shop, jobbing and repair

(G-13506)
SIGNATURE SIGNS
10610 W State Road 32 (47368-9308)
PHONE................765 717-9851
Jessica Traun, *Owner*
EMP: 1 EST: 2015
SALES (est): 61.64K **Privately Held**
Web: www.signaturesignco.com
SIC: 3993 Signs, not made in custom sign painting shops

Patoka
Gibson County

(G-13507)
DENNIS K MARVELL
3700 W 250 N (47666-9249)
PHONE................812 779-5107
Dennis Marvel, *Prin*
EMP: 5 EST: 2011
SALES (est): 69.42K **Privately Held**
SIC: 2411 Logging camps and contractors

(G-13508)
H & H MANUFACTURING INC
499 N 150 W (47666)
P.O. Box 12 (47666-0012)
PHONE................812 664-3582
James Holzmeyer, *Pr*
Rick Hensley, *VP*
EMP: 5 EST: 2016
SQ FT: 2,600
SALES (est): 512.61K **Privately Held**
Web: www.hhmanufacturing.com
SIC: 3462 Pump and compressor forgings, ferrous

(G-13509)
MARVELL LOGGING COMPANY LLC
3700 W 250 N (47666-9249)
PHONE................812 779-5107
De Is Marvell, *Mgr*
EMP: 5 EST: 2018
SALES (est): 116.31K **Privately Held**
SIC: 2411 Logging camps and contractors

Patriot
Switzerland County

(G-13510)
HILLTOP BASIC RESOURCES INC
Also Called: Patriot Plant
14208 State Road 156 (47038-9836)
P.O. Box 157 (47038-0157)
PHONE................812 594-2293
Roger Thayer, *Mgr*
EMP: 9
SALES (corp-wide): 59.62MM **Privately Held**
Web: www.hilltopcompanies.com
SIC: 3273 Ready-mixed concrete
PA: Hilltop Basic Resources, Inc.
50 E Rvrcnter Blvd Ste 10
Covington KY 41011
513 651-5000

(G-13511)
SWITZERLAND HILLS INC
Also Called: Swiss Caps
19091 State Road 250 (47038-9254)
PHONE................812 594-2810
Anthony Gregory, *Pr*
Christie Gregory, *
EMP: 35 EST: 1975
SQ FT: 4,600
SALES (est): 2.5MM **Privately Held**
Web: switzerland.openfos.com
SIC: 3792 5013 Pickup covers, canopies or caps; Truck parts and accessories

Pekin
Washington County

(G-13512)
BREWERS CONTG & WDWRK LLC
Also Called: Remodel Construction
4901 S Eastern School Rd (47165-8009)
PHONE................812 620-8961
Benjamin Brewer, *CEO*
EMP: 1 EST: 2019
SALES (est): 54.13K **Privately Held**
SIC: 2431 Millwork

(G-13513)
CENTURY GRAVE & VAULT SERVICE
2807 S Franklin School Rd (47165-8198)
PHONE................812 967-2110
Carl Hudgens, *Owner*
EMP: 6 EST: 2000
SALES (est): 88.16K **Privately Held**
SIC: 3272 Burial vaults, concrete or precast terrazzo

(G-13514)
CUSTOMER 1ST LLC (PA)
Also Called: Customer 1st Safes & Services
8899 E Daily Rd Lot 51 (47165-8964)
P.O. Box 290 (47106-0290)
PHONE................877 768-9970
Jack Hurst, *CEO*
Deb Gonika, *COO*
▲ EMP: 4 EST: 2007
SALES (est): 449.61K
SALES (corp-wide): 449.61K **Privately Held**
Web: www.customer1stsafes.com
SIC: 3499 7699 Safes and vaults, metal; Locksmith shop

(G-13515)
DALREN ENTERPRISES LLC
3180 S Pixley Knob Rd (47165-9326)
PHONE................502 396-0346
EMP: 4 EST: 2012
SALES (est): 101.18K **Privately Held**
SIC: 3482 Small arms ammunition

(G-13516)
GLOBE INDUSTRIAL LLC
242 S Voyles Rd (47165-7829)
PHONE................812 301-2600
EMP: 10 EST: 2013
SALES (est): 970.56K **Privately Held**
Web: www.globemechanical.com
SIC: 3498 Fabricated pipe and fittings

(G-13517)
INDIANA ORDNANCE WORKS INC (PA)
11020 E Fitzpatrick Ln (47165-8437)
PHONE................812 256-4478
Darwin B Harting, *Pr*
Robert Reed, *Ex VP*
Robert Curts, *Ex VP*
David Hackel, *Treas*
EMP: 4 EST: 1998
SQ FT: 61,000
SALES (est): 2.23MM
SALES (corp-wide): 2.23MM **Privately Held**
Web: www.iowinc.com
SIC: 3489 Ordnance and accessories, nec

(G-13518)
MARK MIDDLETON
5691 S Olive Branch Rd (47165-8241)
PHONE................812 967-2853
Mark Middleton, *Owner*
EMP: 3 EST: 1991
SALES (est): 254.4K **Privately Held**
Web: www.markmiddletonrealestate.com
SIC: 2421 Sawmills and planing mills, general

(G-13519)
MILLERS WLDG & MECH SVCS INC
9556 Voyles Rd (47165-9618)
PHONE................812 923-3359
Mark Miller, *Pr*
EMP: 2 EST: 1975
SALES (est): 246.86K **Privately Held**
SIC: 3599 7692 Custom machinery; Welding repair

(G-13520)
MOULD-RITE INC
5885 E Old Pekin Rd (47165-7187)
P.O. Box 339 (47165-0339)
PHONE................812 967-3200
David Robertson, *Pr*
Cherry Robertson, *Genl Mgr*
▲ EMP: 8 EST: 1986
SQ FT: 16,000
SALES (est): 432.23K **Privately Held**
Web: www.mouldrite.com
SIC: 2426 Dimension, hardwood

(G-13521)
PREMIUM MOLD TOOL
4225 S Hickory Grove Rd (47165-8313)
PHONE................812 967-3187
Brian Stidham, *Owner*
EMP: 1 EST: 1997
SALES (est): 76.51K **Privately Held**

SIC: 3544 Special dies and tools

(G-13522)
SCRAPBOOK NOOK
205 W State Road 60 (47165-7978)
PHONE..................................812 967-3306
EMP: 5 EST: 2007
SALES (est): 193.28K Privately Held
Web: www.scrapbooknook.net
SIC: 2782 Scrapbooks

(G-13523)
WORLEY LUMBER COMPANY INC
5803 E Hurst Rd (47165-7107)
P.O. Box 219 (47165-0219)
PHONE..................................812 967-3521
Rick Lanham, Pr
Debrorah Lanham, Sec
EMP: 25 EST: 1972
SQ FT: 15,000
SALES (est): 1.59MM Privately Held
SIC: 2421 Lumber: rough, sawed, or planed

Pendleton
Madison County

(G-13524)
AIM MEDIA INDIANA OPER LLC
Times Post, The
104 W High St (46064-1102)
P.O. Box 9 (46064-0009)
PHONE..................................765 778-2324
John Senger, Brnch Mgr
EMP: 2
SALES (corp-wide): 26.88MM Privately Held
Web: www.aimmediaindiana.com
SIC: 2711 Commercial printing and newspaper publishing combined
PA: Aim Media Indiana Operating, Llc
2980 N National Rd # A
Columbus IN 47201
812 372-7811

(G-13525)
BECO INC
Also Called: Beco
6642 S State Road 67 (46064-9081)
PHONE..................................765 778-3426
David Baker, Pr
EMP: 1 EST: 1959
SALES (est): 172.09K Privately Held
Web: www.becoinc.biz
SIC: 3799 Recreational vehicles

(G-13526)
BLACK SWAN VAPORS LLC
118 W State St (46064-1034)
PHONE..................................317 645-5210
William Eric Cecil, Managing Member
EMP: 6 EST: 2014
SALES (est): 494.11K Privately Held
Web: www.blackswanvapors.com
SIC: 5194 2131 5993 Smokeless tobacco; Chewing tobacco; Cigar store

(G-13527)
BORGWARNER REMAN HOLDINGS LLC
600 Corporation Dr (46064-8610)
PHONE..................................800 372-5131
Harold Sperlich, Ch Bd
Thomas Snyder, Pr
Susan Goldy, VP
Dave Stoll, CFO
EMP: 1500 EST: 1995
SALES (est): 70.18MM
SALES (corp-wide): 14.2B Publicly Held

SIC: 3714 3694 Motor vehicle engines and parts; Battery charging alternators and generators
HQ: Old Remco Holdings, L.L.C.
600 Corporation Dr
Pendleton IN 46064

(G-13528)
CAD/CAM TECHNOLOGIES INC
178 S Heritage Way (46064-8599)
P.O. Box 320 (46064-0320)
PHONE..................................765 778-2020
Randall Maynard, Pr
EMP: 6 EST: 1996
SQ FT: 1,500
SALES (est): 472.74K Privately Held
Web: www.cad-camtech.com
SIC: 7372 8243 Prepackaged software; Software training, computer

(G-13529)
DAWGHOUSE GRUB PUB LLC
104 W State St (46064-1034)
PHONE..................................765 778-2727
EMP: 6 EST: 2010
SALES (est): 103.95K Privately Held
SIC: 3421 Table and food cutlery, including butchers'

(G-13530)
DOWNEYS WELDING REPAIR
105 Bess Blvd (46064-8804)
PHONE..................................765 778-4727
Larry E Downey, Prin
EMP: 1 EST: 2003
SALES (est): 111.59K Privately Held
SIC: 7692 Welding repair

(G-13531)
ENGINERED REFR SHAPES SVCS LLC (PA)
Also Called: Erss
3370 W 1000 S (46064-9523)
P.O. Box 341 (46064-0341)
PHONE..................................765 778-8040
EMP: 2 EST: 2006
SQ FT: 17,500
SALES (est): 1.8MM Privately Held
Web: www.engineeredrss.com
SIC: 3823 8711 Refractometers, industrial process type; Engineering services

(G-13532)
FLYOVER ENTERPRISES INC
1068 Chipmunk Ln (46064-9166)
PHONE..................................317 417-1747
John Perkins, Pr
Brad Holtz, VP
Bryan Dixon, VP
EMP: 3 EST: 2009
SALES (est): 313.83K Privately Held
Web: www.flyoverpremiersales.com
SIC: 3272 Building materials, except block or brick: concrete

(G-13533)
FOX MANUFACTURING LLC
Also Called: Glas-Master
12910 Bristow Ln (46064-6411)
PHONE..................................317 430-1493
Todd Fox, Pr
EMP: 1 EST: 2019
SALES (est): 42.92K Privately Held
SIC: 3999 Manufacturing industries, nec

(G-13534)
GO PRINT LLC
1260 W 700 S (46064-9118)
PHONE..................................765 778-1711
EMP: 7 EST: 2007

SALES (est): 219.25K Privately Held
SIC: 2752 Offset printing

(G-13535)
GOODRICK TIMBER
3102 Market St (46064-9027)
PHONE..................................765 778-7442
Steven Goodrick, Owner
EMP: 1 EST: 1979
SALES (est): 78.42K Privately Held
SIC: 2411 Logging camps and contractors

(G-13536)
HOMETOWN EMBROIDERY LLC
176 Oxford Ave (46064-8722)
PHONE..................................765 778-7533
Linda O'neill, Owner
EMP: 1 EST: 2014
SALES (est): 44.96K Privately Held
Web: www.hometownemb.com
SIC: 2395 Embroidery products, except Schiffli machine

(G-13537)
INNOVATIVE SIGNS LLC
9571 W Quarter Moon Dr (46064-9463)
PHONE..................................317 747-4454
EMP: 3 EST: 2016
SALES (est): 65.57K Privately Held
Web: www.innovativesignsllc.com
SIC: 3993 Signs and advertising specialties

(G-13538)
JKL SOFTWARE DEVELOPMENT LLC
210 E Water St (46064-1047)
PHONE..................................765 778-3032
Kenneth U Lau D.d.s., Prin
EMP: 2 EST: 2003
SALES (est): 122.69K Privately Held
Web: www.jklsoftware.com
SIC: 7372 Business oriented computer software

(G-13539)
KENT MACHINE INC
8677 S State Road 9 (46064-9569)
PHONE..................................765 778-7777
Zane Kennedy, Pr
Harold Kennedy, Treas
Sandra Kennedy, Sec
EMP: 34 EST: 1980
SQ FT: 17,000
SALES (est): 10.01MM Privately Held
Web: www.kentmachine.com
SIC: 3544 Special dies and tools

(G-13540)
LARRY CONOVER
Also Called: Woodbox & Bin
227 N East St (46064-1005)
PHONE..................................317 787-4020
EMP: 1 EST: 1996
SALES (est): 61.45K Privately Held
SIC: 2499 Decorative wood and woodwork

(G-13541)
MADISON COUNTY CABINETS INC
Also Called: McC
9592 W 650 S (46064-9737)
PHONE..................................765 778-4646
Russell Bowman, Pr
Daniel Bowman, VP
Larry Boone, Sec
EMP: 18 EST: 1973
SQ FT: 17,000
SALES (est): 2.47MM Privately Held
Web: www.madisoncountycabinets.com
SIC: 2434 Wood kitchen cabinets

(G-13542)
MAGNEQUENCH INC (DH)
237 S Pendleton Ave Ste C (46064-1187)
PHONE..................................765 778-7809
Constantine Karayanno, Pr
Hong Zhang, *
Archibald Cox Junior, Pr
Shannon Song, Senior Vice President Strategic Planning*
Gary Riley, *
▲ EMP: 30 EST: 1999
SALES (est): 107.73MM
SALES (corp-wide): 640.3MM Privately Held
Web: www.mqitechnology.com
SIC: 3499 Magnets, permanent: metallic
HQ: Neo Performance Materials Ulc
1740-121 King St W
Toronto ON M5H 3
416 367-8588

(G-13543)
MEGANS WASH AND FOLD LLC
108 Shamrock Cir Apt 26 (46064-8565)
PHONE..................................317 903-5253
EMP: 2 EST: 2021
SALES (est): 88.38K Privately Held
SIC: 3633 7389 Laundry dryers, household or coin-operated; Business services, nec

(G-13544)
MODERN AG SOLUTIONS LLC
738 N Pendleton Ave (46064-8977)
PHONE..................................765 221-1011
EMP: 4 EST: 2013
SALES (est): 150.67K Privately Held
SIC: 0762 3523 Farm management services; Farm machinery and equipment

(G-13545)
MVP DUMPSTERS INC
8093 S 600 W (46064-8779)
PHONE..................................317 502-3155
Robert J Davis, Prin
EMP: 8 EST: 2016
SALES (est): 262.5K Privately Held
SIC: 3443 Dumpsters, garbage

(G-13546)
NEWCO METALS INC (PA)
7268 S State Road 13 (46064-9565)
PHONE..................................317 485-7721
Chris Rasmussen, Pr
Kipp Barber, *
Steve Craver, *
EMP: 29 EST: 1986
SQ FT: 5,000
SALES (est): 9.93MM
SALES (corp-wide): 9.93MM Privately Held
Web: www.newcometals.com
SIC: 5093 5051 3341 Nonferrous metals scrap; Metals service centers and offices; Secondary nonferrous metals

(G-13547)
NYXPERIMENTAL LLC
634 N Pendleton Ave (46064-8976)
PHONE..................................914 506-0266
Frank T Magaletti, Prin
EMP: 6 EST: 2016
SALES (est): 50.48K Privately Held
Web: www.nyxperimental.com
SIC: 3089 Injection molding of plastics

(G-13548)
OLD REMCO HOLDINGS LLC (DH)
600 Corporation Dr (46064-8610)
PHONE..................................765 778-6499
John J Pittas, Pr

Mark R Mcfeely, *Sr VP*
Shawn J Pallagi, *Chief Human Resources Officer**
Michael L Gravelle, *Corporate Secretary**
Barbara J Bitzer, *Global Controller**
◆ **EMP:** 250 **EST:** 1993
SALES (est): 221.28MM
SALES (corp-wide): 14.2B **Publicly Held**
SIC: 3694 3714 Battery charging alternators and generators; Motor vehicle engines and parts
HQ: New Pds Corp.
  3850 Hamlin Rd
  Auburn Hills MI 48326
  765 778-6816

(G-13549)
OUTFITTERS INC
880 S Pendleton Ave (46064-1354)
P.O. Box 164 (46064-0164)
PHONE.................................765 778-9097
Mary Harvey, *Mgr*
Mary Harvey, *Dir*
EMP: 1 **EST:** 2005
SALES (est): 109.37K **Privately Held**
Web: www.outfittersink.com
SIC: 2759 Letterpress and screen printing

(G-13550)
PAUL E SHAW
Also Called: Letter Pro
521 Taylor St (46064-1146)
PHONE.................................765 778-3383
EMP: 2
SALES (est): 90.24K **Privately Held**
SIC: 3993 Signs, not made in custom sign painting shops

(G-13551)
PENDLETON DOOR COMPANY
8680 S 750 W (46064-9757)
PHONE.................................765 778-4164
David Miller, *Pr*
EMP: 8 **EST:** 1987
SQ FT: 2,400
SALES (est): 591.69K **Privately Held**
SIC: 2431 Doors, wood

(G-13552)
PENDLETON TIMES
Also Called: Lapell Post
6837 S State Road 67 (46064-9312)
P.O. Box 9 (46064-0009)
PHONE.................................765 778-2324
Andy Gruehr, *Owner*
EMP: 7 **EST:** 1989
SALES (est): 384.55K **Privately Held**
Web: www.pendletontimespost.com
SIC: 2711 Newspapers, publishing and printing

(G-13553)
SIGN-AGE INC
178 S Heritage Way (46064-8599)
PHONE.................................765 778-5254
Jeremy Adams, *Pr*
EMP: 3 **EST:** 1999
SALES (est): 207.77K **Privately Held**
Web: www.thesignage.biz
SIC: 3993 Neon signs

(G-13554)
SKI INC
204 Lucky Ln (46064-9189)
PHONE.................................317 401-6222
Edward Yates, *Mgr*
EMP: 4 **EST:** 2009
SALES (est): 113.6K **Privately Held**
Web: www.ski-inc.com
SIC: 3949 Sporting and athletic goods, nec

(G-13555)
SLINGSHOT MEDIA LLC
600 Corporation Dr (46064-8610)
PHONE.................................765 778-6848
Chris Campbell, *Managing Member*
EMP: 4 **EST:** 2015
SALES (est): 122.42K **Privately Held**
SIC: 4899 3993 4813 Communication signal enhancement network services; Signs and advertising specialties; Online service providers

(G-13556)
SO INDUSTRIES LLC
4197 W 950 S (46064-9525)
PHONE.................................765 606-7596
Caleb Hardy, *Prin*
EMP: 5 **EST:** 2017
SALES (est): 55.28K **Privately Held**
SIC: 3999 Manufacturing industries, nec

(G-13557)
THREE LITTLE MONKEYS
129 S Pendleton Ave Stop 3 (46064-1183)
PHONE.................................765 778-9370
Heather Suarez, *Owner*
EMP: 3 **EST:** 2010
SALES (est): 137.65K **Privately Held**
SIC: 2339 Maternity clothing

(G-13558)
TOOL SOURCE INC
9279 S State Road 13 (46064-9791)
PHONE.................................765 778-0777
Jeff Dodd, *Pr*
Chad Hinds, *VP*
EMP: 3 **EST:** 2003
SALES (est): 235.21K **Privately Held**
Web: www.toolsourceinc.com
SIC: 3599 Machine shop, jobbing and repair

(G-13559)
TYLER TRUSS LLC
1810 Fairfield Ln (46064-4500)
PHONE.................................765 221-5050
Glenn Cleland, *CEO*
EMP: 70 **EST:** 2019
SALES (est): 4.84MM **Privately Held**
Web: www.tylertruss.com
SIC: 5211 3999 Lumber and other building materials; Stage hardware and equipment, except lighting

(G-13560)
TYLER TRUSS SYSTEMS INC
1810 Fairfield Ln (46064-4500)
PHONE.................................765 221-5050
Mark Dodd, *Pr*
EMP: 11 **EST:** 2004
SALES (est): 2.35MM **Privately Held**
Web: www.tylertruss.com
SIC: 7929 2439 Entertainment service; Structural wood members, nec

(G-13561)
VISHAY AMERICAS INC
555 S Pendleton Ave (46064-1329)
PHONE.................................765 778-4878
EMP: 2
SALES (corp-wide): 3.4B **Publicly Held**
Web: www.vishay.com
SIC: 3674 Semiconductors and related devices
HQ: Vishay Americas, Inc.
  1 Greenwich Pl
  Shelton CT 06484
  203 452-5648

(G-13562)
WOLFE DIVERSIFIED INDS LLC (PA)
Also Called: Esc Promotions
9408 W Constellation Dr (46064-7511)
PHONE.................................765 683-9374
Chris Lyght, *
Dustin Close, *
Chad Wolfe, *
EMP: 18 **EST:** 2005
SQ FT: 4,000
SALES (est): 2.48MM
SALES (corp-wide): 2.48MM **Privately Held**
Web: www.wolfediversifiedindustries.com
SIC: 7372 Educational computer software

Pennville
Jay County

(G-13563)
DYNO NOBEL INC
Also Called: Wampum Hardware
7860 W 400 N (47369-9488)
P.O. Box 352 (47369-0352)
PHONE.................................260 731-4431
Ron Bunch, *Brnch Mgr*
EMP: 8
Web: www.dynonobel.com
SIC: 2892 1629 Explosives; Blasting contractor, except building demolition
HQ: Dyno Nobel Inc.
  6440 S Millrock Dr Ste 150
  Salt Lake City UT 84121
  801 364-4800

Peru
Miami County

(G-13564)
A&A SCREEN PRINTING
311 W 8th St (46970-1928)
PHONE.................................765 473-8783
Andrew Krisher, *Pt*
Anthony Krisher, *Pt*
EMP: 3 **EST:** 2001
SALES (est): 200.63K **Privately Held**
Web: www.sierratechinc.com
SIC: 2759 Screen printing

(G-13565)
AAR LLC
150 E Washington Ave (46970-1031)
PHONE.................................260 591-0100
EMP: 6 **EST:** 2019
SALES (est): 62.35K **Privately Held**
Web: www.aarcorp.com
SIC: 3728 Aircraft parts and equipment, nec

(G-13566)
ASC INC
Also Called: Fullifillment Center
N Miami Industrial Park (46970)
PHONE.................................765 472-5331
EMP: 22
SALES (corp-wide): 19.8MM **Privately Held**
Web: www.americanstationery.com
SIC: 2678 Stationery products
PA: Asc, Inc.
  100 N Park Ave
  Peru IN 46970
  765 473-4438

(G-13567)
ASC INC (PA)
100 N Park Ave (46970-1702)
P.O. Box 207 (46970-0207)
PHONE.................................765 473-4438
EMP: 200 **EST:** 1919
SALES (est): 19.8MM
SALES (corp-wide): 19.8MM **Privately Held**
Web: www.americanstationery.com
SIC: 2679 5013 Gift wrap, paper: made from purchased material; Motor vehicle supplies and new parts

(G-13568)
BORGWARNER (PDS) PERU INC (DH)
Also Called: Wri
588 W 7th St (46970-1880)
PHONE.................................765 472-2002
Sean Mcgowan, *Pr*
Fred Knechtel, *VP*
Sheila Cannon, *Sec*
▲ **EMP:** 99 **EST:** 1950
SQ FT: 115,000
SALES (est): 16.3MM
SALES (corp-wide): 14.2B **Publicly Held**
Web: www.borgwarner.com
SIC: 3714 Rebuilding engines and transmissions, factory basis
HQ: New Pds Corp.
  3850 Hamlin Rd
  Auburn Hills MI 48326
  765 778-6816

(G-13569)
CAPITAL CUSTOM SIGNS
1251 N Lancer St (46970-3642)
PHONE.................................765 689-7170
Michael Murray, *Owner*
EMP: 2 **EST:** 2005
SALES (est): 131.8K **Privately Held**
Web: www.capitalcustomsigns.com
SIC: 3993 Signs and advertising specialties

(G-13570)
CDB SCREEN PRINTING INC
2131 W Otter Creek Dr (46970-8067)
PHONE.................................765 472-4404
Cliff D Bakehorn, *Pr*
EMP: 6 **EST:** 2002
SALES (est): 383.27K **Privately Held**
Web: www.cdbscreenprinting.com
SIC: 2759 Screen printing

(G-13571)
CHINOOK MOTOR COACH CORP
1482 N Eel River Cemetery Rd (46970-7513)
PHONE.................................574 584-3756
Phil Rizzio, *Pr*
Michael Smith, *Dir*
Philomena Moloney, *Dir*
EMP: 70 **EST:** 2017
SALES (est): 5.75MM **Privately Held**
Web: www.chinookrv.com
SIC: 3711 Bus and other large specialty vehicle assembly

(G-13572)
CITY WINEWORKS
69 N Broadway (46970-2237)
PHONE.................................765 460-5563
EMP: 4 **EST:** 2018
SALES (est): 71.58K **Privately Held**
Web: www.citywineworks.com
SIC: 2082 Malt beverages

(G-13573)
CLIF ALLRED
5090 E 100 S (46970-7148)
PHONE.................................765 244-8082
Clif Allred, *Owner*
EMP: 1
SALES (est): 54.05K **Privately Held**

Peru - Miami County (G-13574) GEOGRAPHIC SECTION

SIC: 3312 7389 Blooms, steel; Business Activities at Non-Commercial Site

(G-13574)
CO-TRONICS INC
2935 W 100 N (46970-7587)
P.O. Box 1037 (46947-0937)
PHONE.....................574 722-3850
Ronald L Sink Junior, Pr
David Williams, VP
Diane Denny, Sec
▲ EMP: 12 EST: 1961
SQ FT: 13,000
SALES (est): 2.38MM Privately Held
Web: www.cotronicsinc.com
SIC: 3089 Injection molding of plastics

(G-13575)
CONFORCE INTERNATIONAL INC
Also Called: Conforce USA
2935 W 100 N (46970)
PHONE.....................765 473-3061
EMP: 2 EST: 2010
SALES (est): 143.84K Privately Held
SIC: 2273 Automobile floor coverings, except rubber or plastic

(G-13576)
CUNNINGHAM TIRE SERVICES INC
452 W 14th St (46970-1558)
P.O. Box 1242 (46970-4242)
PHONE.....................765 473-9200
EMP: 7 EST: 2010
SALES (est): 403.47K Privately Held
SIC: 7534 Tire repair shop

(G-13577)
DAILY PERU TRIBUNE PUBG CO
Also Called: Peru Tribune
11 S Broadway (46970-2231)
P.O. Box 87 (46970-0087)
PHONE.....................765 473-6641
Fred Paxton, Pr
EMP: 14 EST: 1921
SALES (est): 841.4K
SALES (corp-wide): 147.64MM Privately Held
Web: www.plaindealerin.com
SIC: 2711 7371 Newspapers, publishing and printing; Custom computer programming services
PA: Paxton Media Group, Llc
    100 Television Ln
    Paducah KY 42003
    270 575-8630

(G-13578)
DEAN BALDWIN PNTG LTD PARTNR
1395 N Hoosier Blvd (46970-3664)
PHONE.....................765 681-1800
Barbara Baldwin, Pt
EMP: 67
Web: www.deanbaldwinpainting.com
SIC: 3721 3728 Aircraft; Aircraft body assemblies and parts
PA: Dean Baldwin Painting Limited Partnership
    2395 Bulverde Rd Ste 105
    Bulverde TX 78163

(G-13579)
DEER CREEK VILLAGE
2934 S 300 W Trlr 220 (46970-3405)
PHONE.....................574 699-6327
Memo Soto, Prin
EMP: 5 EST: 2018
SALES (est): 81.58K Privately Held
Web: www.deercreekvillagemhc.com
SIC: 2522 Office furniture, except wood

(G-13580)
DORIS DRAPERY BOUTIQUE
68 N Broadway (46970-2238)
PHONE.....................765 472-5850
Doris Eliason-wood, Owner
EMP: 7 EST: 1987
SQ FT: 2,000
SALES (est): 406.86K Privately Held
Web: www.dorisdraperyboutique.com
SIC: 2391 1799 5231 5719 Draperies, plastic and textile: from purchased materials; Drapery track installation; Wallpaper; Venetian blinds

(G-13581)
EBERT MACHINE COMPANY INC
Also Called: Thrift Products Heating Spc
2177 S State Road 19 (46970-7473)
PHONE.....................765 473-3728
Joel Ebert, Pr
Weldon M Ebert, *
EMP: 37 EST: 1940
SQ FT: 21,000
SALES (est): 4.08MM Privately Held
Web: www.ebertmachine.com
SIC: 3451 3639 Screw machine products; Hot water heaters, household

(G-13582)
EVO EXHIBITS LLC
1105 American Pkwy (46970-1369)
PHONE.....................630 520-0710
Kent Jean, Prin
EMP: 5 EST: 2010
SALES (est): 2.67MM Privately Held
Web: www.evoexhibits.com
SIC: 5999 5963 3999 8742 Banners; Direct sales, telemarketing; Preparation of slides and exhibits; Marketing consulting services

(G-13583)
FRED ANDERSON
Also Called: Anderson Machine Tool
4757 N 400 E (46970-8569)
PHONE.....................765 985-2099
Debra Anderson, Owner
EMP: 2 EST: 1995
SALES (est): 82.66K Privately Held
SIC: 3599 3544 Machine shop, jobbing and repair; Special dies, tools, jigs, and fixtures

(G-13584)
HERAEUS ELECTRO-NITE CO LLC
1025 Industrial Pkwy (46970-9590)
PHONE.....................765 473-8275
Jim Myers, Mgr
EMP: 130
SALES (corp-wide): 2.67MM Privately Held
Web: www.heraeus-group.com
SIC: 3823 3674 Temperature measurement instruments, industrial; Semiconductors and related devices
HQ: Heraeus Electro-Nite Co., Llc
    541 S Industrial Dr
    Hartland WI 53029
    215 944-9000

(G-13585)
HOLLANDS DEER PROCESSING LLC
1848 W Lovers Lane Rd (46970-8775)
PHONE.....................765 472-5876
Chris Hollands, Managing Member
EMP: 10 EST: 2004
SALES (est): 626.29K Privately Held
Web: www.hollandsdeerprocessing.com
SIC: 2011 Meat packing plants

(G-13586)
HOOSIER MIRACLE INC (PA)
300 N Park Ave (46970-1701)
PHONE.....................765 473-4438
Michael Bakehorn, Pr
EMP: 1 EST: 2014
SALES (est): 498.86K
SALES (corp-wide): 498.86K Privately Held
Web: www.americanstationery.com
SIC: 2759 2679 Invitations: printing, nsk; Gift wrap, paper: made from purchased material

(G-13587)
INTECH AUTOMATION SYSTEMS CORP
Also Called: I A S
206 N Grant St (46970-1618)
PHONE.....................209 836-8610
EMP: 7
SALES (est): 682.41K Privately Held
SIC: 3829 Thermocouples

(G-13588)
JOLENE D PAVEY
Also Called: Wilhelm AG Lime
4641 S 50 W (46970-7623)
PHONE.....................765 473-6171
Jolene D Pavey, Prin
EMP: 2 EST: 2012
SALES (est): 85.87K Privately Held
SIC: 3274 Lime

(G-13589)
K&T PERFORMANCE ENGRG LLC
Also Called: American Performance Engrg
1975 N Lancer St (46970-3670)
PHONE.....................765 437-0185
Matt Thatcher, Managing Member
EMP: 2 EST: 2002
SQ FT: 6,000
SALES (est): 103.67K Privately Held
Web: www.ktperformance.com
SIC: 8711 3599 Mechanical engineering; Machine shop, jobbing and repair

(G-13590)
LOGAN STAMPINGS INC
1105 American Pkwy (46970-1369)
PHONE.....................574 722-3101
EMP: 2
SALES (corp-wide): 8.79MM Privately Held
Web: www.loganstampings.com
SIC: 3469 Stamping metal for the trade
PA: Logan Stampings, Inc.
    40 E Industrial Blvd
    Logansport IN 46947
    574 722-3101

(G-13591)
LSI FABRICATION
1105 American Pkwy (46970-1369)
P.O. Box 298 (46947-0298)
PHONE.....................574 722-3101
EMP: 5 EST: 2019
SALES (est): 240.18K Privately Held
SIC: 3499 Fabricated metal products, nec

(G-13592)
PERU HARDWOOD PRODUCTS INC
2678 N Mexico Rd (46970-8152)
P.O. Box 171 (46970-0171)
PHONE.....................765 473-4844
Jon D Eisaman, Pr
Joseph Eisaman, Sec
EMP: 10 EST: 1955
SQ FT: 5,000
SALES (est): 243.62K Privately Held
SIC: 2448 Pallets, wood

(G-13593)
PRECISION PULSE LLC
323 W 5th St (46970-1945)
PHONE.....................765 472-6002
Donald Byrum, Prin
EMP: 5 EST: 2019
SALES (est): 234.27K Privately Held
SIC: 7692 Welding repair

(G-13594)
PRECISION STITCH INDIANA INC
404 W Canal St (46970-1878)
PHONE.....................765 473-6734
Phil Van Baalen, Pr
Stephanie Van Baalen, Sec
EMP: 8 EST: 1991
SQ FT: 4,000
SALES (est): 525.14K Privately Held
SIC: 2395 Embroidery products, except Schiffli machine

(G-13595)
PRINTWISE LLC
149 W Canal St (46970-2184)
PHONE.....................765 244-1983
EMP: 1 EST: 2017
SALES (est): 32K Privately Held
Web: www.printwiseperu.com
SIC: 2261 Screen printing of cotton broadwoven fabrics

(G-13596)
PROGRESS RAIL SERVICES CORP
405 Life Rd (46970-1382)
PHONE.....................765 472-2002
Keith Walls, Brnch Mgr
EMP: 59
SALES (corp-wide): 67.06B Publicly Held
Web: www.progressrailstore.com
SIC: 3743 Railroad equipment
HQ: Progress Rail Services Corporation
    1600 Progress Dr
    Albertville AL 35950
    800 476-8769

(G-13597)
RADEL WOOD PRODUCTS INC
1630 W Logansport Rd (46970-3149)
PHONE.....................765 472-2940
Gerald Radel, Pr
Marie Radel, Sec
EMP: 10 EST: 1994
SQ FT: 3,000
SALES (est): 436.65K Privately Held
Web: www.radelwoodproducts.com
SIC: 2434 Vanities, bathroom: wood

(G-13598)
REPROCOMM INC (PA)
Also Called: Modern Graphics
179 N Miami St (46970-2106)
PHONE.....................765 472-5700
James Clary, Pr
David R Sattler, *
Harry Rodkey, *
Ronald L Meyer, *
Terence L Lucterhand, *
EMP: 9 EST: 1963
SQ FT: 6,000
SALES (est): 8.82MM
SALES (corp-wide): 8.82MM Privately Held
Web: www.marketing.com
SIC: 5111 2752 2791 2789 Printing and writing paper; Offset printing; Typesetting; Bookbinding and related work

(G-13599)
RICHARDSON WOODWORKING
6395 S Strawtown Pike (46970-7818)

GEOGRAPHIC SECTION

Petersburg - Pike County (G-13625)

PHONE.................................765 689-8348
Mike Richardson, *Owner*
EMP: 1 **EST:** 2007
SALES (est): 43K **Privately Held**
SIC: 2499 Decorative wood and woodwork

(G-13600)
SMITHFIELD DIRECT LLC
3311 S State Road 19 (46970-7476)
PHONE.................................765 473-3086
Micheal Fritz, *Mgr*
EMP: 122
Web: carando.sfdbrands.com
SIC: 2011 Meat packing plants
HQ: Smithfield Direct, Llc
  4225 Naperville Rd # 600
  Lisle IL 60532

(G-13601)
SNAVELYS MACHINE & MFG CO INC
Also Called: Snavely Machine
1070 Industrial Pkwy (46970-9589)
PHONE.................................765 473-8395
Joseph G Kinney, *Pr*
Jason Amonepott, *
Angela Penix, *
EMP: 140 **EST:** 1964
SQ FT: 172,000
SALES (est): 16.5MM **Privately Held**
Web: www.snavelymachine.com
SIC: 3599 Machine shop, jobbing and repair

(G-13602)
STANDARD FUSEE CORPORATION
Also Called: Orion Safety Products
3157 N 500 W (46970-7559)
PHONE.................................765 472-4375
Debbie Townsend, *Prin*
EMP: 74
SALES (corp-wide): 24.33MM **Privately Held**
Web: www.orionsignals.com
SIC: 2899 5047 3949 3842 Flares, fireworks, and similar preparations; Medical and hospital equipment; Sporting and athletic goods, nec; Surgical appliances and supplies
PA: Standard Fusee Corporation
  28320 Saint Michaels Rd
  Easton MD 21601
  410 822-0318

(G-13603)
STONE QUARY (PA)
Also Called: Rock Hollow Golf Club
350 N 150 W (46970-7589)
P.O. Box 187 (46970-0187)
PHONE.................................765 473-5578
Terry W Smith, *Pr*
Todd Smith, *
Rebecca Smith, *
EMP: 27 **EST:** 1977
SALES (est): 2.25MM
SALES (corp-wide): 2.25MM **Privately Held**
Web: www.rockhollowgolf.com
SIC: 7992 1442 1422 Public golf courses; Sand mining; Crushed and broken limestone

(G-13604)
THRUSH CO INC
340 W 8th St (46970-1929)
P.O. Box 228 (46970-0228)
PHONE.................................765 472-3351
Julius P Marburger, *Pr*
Sara M Marburger, *
▲ **EMP:** 39 **EST:** 1923
SQ FT: 60,000
SALES (est): 8.09MM **Privately Held**
Web: www.thrushco.com

SIC: 3561 3443 Pumps and pumping equipment; Heat exchangers, condensers, and components

(G-13605)
TIP TO TAIL AEROSPACE LLC
1697 W Hoosier Blvd (46970-3600)
PHONE.................................765 437-6556
Andrew Boles, *Prin*
EMP: 5 **EST:** 2017
SALES (est): 116.46K **Privately Held**
Web: www.tiptotailaerospace.com
SIC: 3721 Aircraft

(G-13606)
TRACY K HULLETT
Also Called: Hulletts Backhoe Service
268 W 3rd St (46970-1960)
PHONE.................................765 472-3349
Tracy K Hullett, *Prin*
EMP: 2 **EST:** 2012
SALES (est): 137.68K **Privately Held**
SIC: 3531 Backhoes

(G-13607)
WC REDMON CO INC
Also Called: Redmon
200 Harrison Ave (46970-1155)
P.O. Box 7 (46970-0007)
PHONE.................................765 473-6683
C Peter Redmon, *CEO*
C Peter Redmon, *Pr*
Samuel Redmon, *CFO*
Timothy Jackson, *COO*
◆ **EMP:** 15 **EST:** 1920
SQ FT: 103,000
SALES (est): 2.17MM **Privately Held**
Web: www.redmonusa.com
SIC: 2511 2499 5023 Nursery furniture: wood ; Hampers, laundry; Decorative home furnishings and supplies

(G-13608)
WOODCREST MANUFACTURING INC
150 E Washington Ave (46970-1031)
P.O. Box 848 (46970-0848)
PHONE.................................765 472-4471
◆ **EMP:** 160
Web: www.woodcrestmfg.com
SIC: 2511 Juvenile furniture: wood

Petersburg
Pike County

(G-13609)
D & S ENTERPRISES
132 W Branch St (47567-8911)
PHONE.................................812 354-6108
Don Stephens, *Owner*
EMP: 1 **EST:** 1989
SALES (est): 91.94K **Privately Held**
SIC: 1499 1629 Shell mining; Land clearing contractor

(G-13610)
DUTCHTOWN HOMES INC
6518 N County Road 500 E (47567-8965)
PHONE.................................812 354-2197
Shawn Wilson, *Owner*
EMP: 2 **EST:** 2012
SALES (est): 123.61K **Privately Held**
Web: www.dutchtown-homes.com
SIC: 2451 Mobile homes

(G-13611)
F D MCCRARY OPERATOR INC
4295 W County Road 350 N (47567-8660)
PHONE.................................812 354-6520
Fred Mccary, *Pr*

EMP: 4 **EST:** 2008
SALES (est): 282.56K **Privately Held**
SIC: 3533 7389 Oil and gas field machinery; Business Activities at Non-Commercial Site

(G-13612)
FOUR STAR FABRICATORS INC
810 S Ind Park Dr (47567-8311)
P.O. Box 67 (47567-0067)
PHONE.................................812 354-9995
Kim Walhall, *CEO*
Tom Walthall, *
Larry Dick, *
EMP: 75 **EST:** 1981
SQ FT: 55,000
SALES (est): 8.44MM **Privately Held**
Web: www.fourstarfab.com
SIC: 3441 3443 Building components, structural steel; Fabricated plate work (boiler shop)

(G-13613)
FOUR STAR FIELD SERVICES INC
804 S Industrial Park Dr Ste 10 (47567-8311)
P.O. Box 67 (47567-0067)
PHONE.................................812 354-9995
Jesse Nickson, *Prin*
EMP: 7 **EST:** 2014
SALES (est): 409.37K **Privately Held**
Web: www.fourstarfab.com
SIC: 3315 Welded steel wire fabric

(G-13614)
FRED D MCCRARY
Also Called: McCrary, Fred D Oil Co
4295 W County Road 350 N (47567-8660)
PHONE.................................812 354-6520
Fred D Mccrary, *Owner*
EMP: 5 **EST:** 1961
SALES (est): 559.26K **Privately Held**
SIC: 1311 Crude petroleum production

(G-13615)
J & J OIL WELL SERVICE INC
7558 W County Road 225 N (47567-9059)
PHONE.................................812 354-9007
James Blaze, *Pr*
Rhonda Blaze, *Pr*
EMP: 3 **EST:** 1987
SALES (est): 360K **Privately Held**
SIC: 1311 Crude petroleum and natural gas production

(G-13616)
J A DAVIS
802 E Mccoy St (47567-1840)
PHONE.................................812 354-9129
Jason Davis, *Prin*
EMP: 4 **EST:** 2010
SALES (est): 88.77K **Privately Held**
SIC: 2752 Commercial printing, lithographic

(G-13617)
MICHAEL L JERRELL
Also Called: Mpm
4703 N County Road 175 E (47567-8445)
P.O. Box 432 (47567-0432)
PHONE.................................812 354-9297
Michael L Jerrell, *Owner*
EMP: 1 **EST:** 1978
SALES (est): 80.84K **Privately Held**
SIC: 5731 2732 Radio, television, and electronic stores; Book printing

(G-13618)
MOORE DESIGNS UNLMTD
234 E Harvest Ln (47567-8843)
PHONE.................................812 354-2233
Gertrud Moore, *Owner*

EMP: 1 **EST:** 2002
SALES (est): 48.25K **Privately Held**
SIC: 2395 Embroidery and art needlework

(G-13619)
MULZER CRUSHED STONE INC
204 W Illinois St (47567-8085)
PHONE.................................812 354-9650
EMP: 2 **EST:** 2012
SALES (est): 166K **Privately Held**
Web: www.mulzer.com
SIC: 1422 Crushed and broken limestone

(G-13620)
ONYETT WELDING & MACHINE INC
Also Called: Onyett, A.B. & Sons
409 N 8th St (47567-1121)
PHONE.................................812 582-2999
Jack Onyett, *Pr*
EMP: 2 **EST:** 1935
SALES (est): 171.54K **Privately Held**
SIC: 3523 7692 Farm machinery and equipment; Welding repair

(G-13621)
PIKE COUNTY PUBLISHING CORP (PA)
Also Called: Press Dispatch
820 E Poplar St (47567-1258)
P.O. Box 353 (47567-0353)
PHONE.................................812 354-8500
Frank Heuring, *Pr*
EMP: 8 **EST:** 1898
SQ FT: 2,100
SALES (est): 934.18K
SALES (corp-wide): 934.18K **Privately Held**
Web: www.suncommercial.com
SIC: 2711 Newspapers: publishing only, not printed on site

(G-13622)
PIKE PUBLISHING
407 E Walnut St (47567-1443)
P.O. Box 353 (47567-0353)
PHONE.................................812 354-4701
Eric Gogel, *Prin*
EMP: 6 **EST:** 2015
SALES (est): 106.82K **Privately Held**
Web: www.suncommercial.com
SIC: 2741 Miscellaneous publishing

(G-13623)
RESPONSBLE ENRGY OPRATIONS LLC
625 N 9th St (47567-1166)
PHONE.................................812 354-8776
Roy D Hartstein, *CEO*
EMP: 8 **EST:** 2021
SALES (est): 4.77MM **Privately Held**
SIC: 1311 Natural gas production

(G-13624)
RKDJRT INC
3377 N State Road 57 (47567-8048)
PHONE.................................812 354-8899
EMP: 50
SIC: 3449 Bars, concrete reinforcing: fabricated steel

(G-13625)
SMGF LLC
Also Called: Onyett Fabricators
3377 N State Road 57 (47567-8048)
PHONE.................................812 354-8899
Jessica Elpers, *Mgr*
EMP: 35 **EST:** 2012
SQ FT: 28,000
SALES (est): 3.68MM **Privately Held**

(PA)=Parent Co (HQ)=Headquarters
✪ = New Business established in last 2 years

Petersburg - Pike County (G-13626)

SIC: 3542 3441 Machine tools, metal forming type; Fabricated structural metal

(G-13626)
SOLAR SOURCES UNDERGROUND LLC
Also Called: Bowman E&M
1592 N State Road 61 (47567-8355)
P.O. Box 567 (47567-0567)
PHONE....................812 354-2808
EMP: 140 EST: 1994
SALES (est): 19.34MM Privately Held
SIC: 1222 Bituminous coal-underground mining

(G-13627)
T & E WELDING INC
10 W Locust St (47567-1655)
PHONE....................812 324-0140
Timothy Evans, *Prin*
EMP: 10 EST: 2008
SALES (est): 974.47K Privately Held
SIC: 7692 Welding repair

(G-13628)
WELDING UNLIMITED LLC
2278 E County Road 650 N (47567-8810)
PHONE....................812 582-0777
Kyle Query, *Pr*
EMP: 5 EST: 2013
SALES (est): 115.52K Privately Held
Web: www.prathermetalworks.com
SIC: 7692 Welding repair

Pierceton
Kosciusko County

(G-13629)
ALUDYNE NORTH AMERICA LLC
5 Arnolt Dr (46562-9641)
PHONE....................574 594-9681
Andreas Weller, *CEO*
EMP: 159
SALES (corp-wide): 631.06MM Privately Held
Web: www.aludyne.com
SIC: 3465 Automotive stampings
HQ: Aludyne North America Llc
300 Galleria Ofcntr Ste 5
Southfield MI 48034
248 728-8700

(G-13630)
C4 CUSTOM CREATION LLC
6328 E Old Road 30 (46562-9145)
PHONE....................574 551-3904
EMP: 2 EST: 2019
SALES (est): 55.21K Privately Held
SIC: 3993 Signs and advertising specialties

(G-13631)
FIRST SOURCE MANUFACTURING
6511 E Pierceton Rd (46562-9230)
PHONE....................574 527-7192
EMP: 4 EST: 2019
SALES (est): 39.69K Privately Held
Web: www.firstsource.com
SIC: 3999 Manufacturing industries, nec

(G-13632)
HERMAN TOOL & MACHINE INC
Also Called: Hermans' Christmas Land
2 Arnolt Dr (46562)
P.O. Box 357 (46562)
PHONE....................574 594-5544
James Read Junior, *Pr*
EMP: 10 EST: 1967
SQ FT: 23,500
SALES (est): 836.06K Privately Held

SIC: 3544 3446 5999 7692 Dies, plastics forming; Ornamental metalwork; Christmas lights and decorations; Welding repair

(G-13633)
HOWARD LOGGING
680 N 850 W-92 (46562-9627)
PHONE....................260 327-3862
EMP: 4 EST: 2018
SALES (est): 81.72K Privately Held
SIC: 2411 Logging

(G-13634)
ME FABRICATION LLP
8214 E 200 N (46562-9724)
PHONE....................574 594-2801
Dylan Marshall, *Prin*
EMP: 5 EST: 2016
SALES (est): 39.69K Privately Held
SIC: 3999 Manufacturing industries, nec

(G-13635)
MIDWEST ROLL FORMING & MFG INC
Also Called: Omco
1 Arnolt Dr (46562-9641)
PHONE....................574 594-2100
Gary Schuster, *CEO*
Floyd Trouten, *
Clint Cassese, *
Len Parker, *
EMP: 150 EST: 1989
SQ FT: 92,000
SALES (est): 42.47MM Privately Held
Web: www.omcoform.com
SIC: 3449 Miscellaneous metalwork
HQ: Ohio Moulding Corporation
30396 Lakeland Blvd
Wickliffe OH 44092
440 944-2100

(G-13636)
P2 PRECISION MFG LLC
7815 E 500 S (46562-9774)
PHONE....................260 609-6295
EMP: 3 EST: 2019
SALES (est): 48.02K Privately Held
Web: www.p2precision.com
SIC: 3999 Manufacturing industries, nec

(G-13637)
PARAGON MEDICAL INC
Also Called: Pierceton I&I
22 Pequignot Dr (46562-9088)
PHONE....................574 594-2140
EMP: 224
SALES (corp-wide): 6.6B Publicly Held
Web: www.paragonmedical.com
SIC: 3089 3841 Plastics containers, except foam; Surgical and medical instruments
HQ: Paragon Medical, Inc.
8 Matchett Dr
Pierceton IN 46562

(G-13638)
PARAGON MEDICAL INC (HQ)
Also Called: Pierceton Case & Tray
8 Matchett Dr (46562)
PHONE....................574 594-2140
J Robert Atkinson, *Pr*
▲ EMP: 148 EST: 1991
SQ FT: 50,000
SALES (est): 167.83MM
SALES (corp-wide): 6.6B Publicly Held
Web: www.paragonmedical.com
SIC: 3089 3841 7371 Plastics containers, except foam; Surgical and medical instruments; Computer software development and applications
PA: Ametek, Inc.
1100 Cassatt Rd

Berwyn PA 19312
610 647-2121

(G-13639)
PIERCETON RUBBER PRODUCTS INC
3076 S 900 E (46562-9769)
PHONE....................574 594-3002
John Burnau, *CEO*
Tammy Burneau, *Sec*
EMP: 10 EST: 1998
SQ FT: 30,000
SALES (est): 979.85K Privately Held
Web: www.dynacushion.com
SIC: 3069 Mats or matting, rubber, nec

(G-13640)
S P X CORP
5 Arnolt Dr (46562-9641)
PHONE....................574 594-9681
Rob Hollacher, *Pr*
EMP: 8 EST: 1999
SALES (est): 245.54K Privately Held
SIC: 3364 Nonferrous die-castings except aluminum

(G-13641)
TRI-LAKES CONTAINER CORP
533 S First St (46562)
P.O. Box 155 (46562)
PHONE....................574 594-2217
EMP: 71
Web: www.tri-lakes.com
SIC: 2653 Corrugated boxes, partitions, display items, sheets, and pad

(G-13642)
WARSAW METAL PRODUCTS INC
3589 E 100 S (46562-9095)
PHONE....................574 269-6211
Jeffrey Rose, *Pr*
Ruben Rose, *Treas*
Todd Love, *Sec*
▲ EMP: 15 EST: 1980
SQ FT: 24,800
SALES (est): 2.2MM Privately Held
SIC: 3443 7389 Metal parts; Field warehousing

Pine Village
Warren County

(G-13643)
HOOKER CORNER WINERY LLC
444 W State Road 26 (47975-8057)
PHONE....................765 585-1225
Jae Ann Brier, *Prin*
EMP: 6 EST: 2016
SALES (est): 77.44K Privately Held
Web: www.hookercornerwinery.com
SIC: 2084 Wines

Pittsboro
Hendricks County

(G-13644)
DRAKE ENTERPRISES LLC
6135 E County Road 900 N (46167-9421)
PHONE....................317 460-5991
Kory Drake, *Pr*
EMP: 1 EST: 2015
SALES (est): 98.85K Privately Held
SIC: 8748 8711 7692 Business consulting, nec; Engineering services; Welding repair

(G-13645)
ENVIRI CORPORATION
Also Called: Harsco Pittsboro
8000 N County Road 225 E (46167-9094)
PHONE....................317 983-5353
Dave Sams, *Brnch Mgr*
EMP: 6
SALES (corp-wide): 2.07B Publicly Held
Web: www.enviri.com
SIC: 3999 8732 Preparation of slides and exhibits; Commercial nonphysical research
PA: Enviri Corporation
100-120 N 18th St # 17
Philadelphia PA 19103
267 857-8715

(G-13646)
FREEDOM RACING ENGINES
2400 Commerce Way (46167-9667)
PHONE....................317 858-9937
Allen Robbins, *Mgr*
EMP: 4 EST: 2009
SALES (est): 509.2K Privately Held
Web: www.freedomracingengines.com
SIC: 3519 Internal combustion engines, nec

(G-13647)
FREELANCE SERVICES LLC
6151 Canterbury Ct (46167-9569)
PHONE....................317 727-2669
Howard Beckley, *Managing Member*
EMP: 1 EST: 2014
SALES (est): 38.58K Privately Held
SIC: 3625 Electric controls and control accessories, industrial

(G-13648)
HOMETOWN PRODUCTS
Also Called: Home Cookies
9339 N County Road 150 E (46167-9474)
PHONE....................317 625-2447
Lauri Kirkpatrick, *Owner*
EMP: 1 EST: 2001
SALES (est): 42.68K Privately Held
SIC: 2052 Cookies

(G-13649)
JOHNSON CONTROLS INC
Also Called: Johnson Controls
314 Brixton Woods West Dr (46167-8950)
PHONE....................317 917-5043
EMP: 17
Web: www.johnsoncontrols.com
SIC: 2531 3691 3822 8744 Seats, automobile; Lead acid batteries (storage batteries); Building services monitoring controls, automatic; Facilities support services
HQ: Johnson Controls, Inc.
5757 N Green Bay Ave
Milwaukee WI 53209
866 496-1999

(G-13650)
LACOPA INTERNATIONAL INC
5028 Hill Valley Dr (46167-9122)
PHONE....................317 410-1483
▼ EMP: 6 EST: 1997
SALES (est): 625.8K Privately Held
SIC: 3448 Prefabricated metal buildings and components

(G-13651)
MATHESON TRI-GAS INC
8000 N County Road 225 E (46167-9094)
PHONE....................317 892-5221
Shawn Riehle, *Mgr*
EMP: 6
Web: www.mathesongas.com

Plainfield - Hendricks County (G-13677)

SIC: **5084** 2813 Welding machinery and equipment; Nitrogen
HQ: Matheson Tri-Gas, Inc.
3 Mountainview Rd Ste 3 # 3
Warren NJ 07059
908 991-9200

(G-13652)
NALON POWER DEVELOPMENT LLC
10342 N County Road 471 E (46167-9527)
PHONE..........................317 450-7564
Dennis Nalon, *Prin*
EMP: 6 EST: 2019
SALES (est): 158.71K **Privately Held**
Web: www.npdindy.com
SIC: **3714** Motor vehicle parts and accessories

(G-13653)
QUALITY MCH REPR & ENGRG INC
4406 Quail Creek Trce N (46167-8701)
P.O. Box 39231 (46239-0231)
PHONE..........................317 375-1366
Robert R Laugle, *Pr*
Susan Laugle, *VP*
EMP: 5 EST: 2000
SALES (est): 492.55K **Privately Held**
Web: www.qualitymachinerepair.com
SIC: **3599** Machine shop, jobbing and repair

(G-13654)
STEEL DYNAMICS INC
Also Called: Steel Dynamics Engineered Bar
8000 N County Road 225 E (46167-9094)
PHONE..........................317 892-7000
EMP: 369
Web: www.steeldynamics.com
SIC: **3312** Plate, sheet and strip, except coated products
PA: Steel Dynamics, Inc.
7575 W Jefferson Blvd
Fort Wayne IN 46804

(G-13655)
WARREN POWER ATTACHMENTS
4614 E County Road 1000 N (46167-9441)
PHONE..........................317 892-4737
EMP: 5 EST: 1995
SQ FT: 18,000
SALES (est): 847.23K **Privately Held**
Web: www.totalpatcher.com
SIC: **3315** Welded steel wire fabric

Plainfield
Hendricks County

(G-13656)
AEL/SPAN LLC
Also Called: Delphi Pdts & Svc Solutions
6032 Gateway Dr (46168-7655)
PHONE..........................317 203-4602
EMP: 25
Web: www.aelspan.com
SIC: **3625** 4225 Switches, electronic applications; General warehousing and storage
PA: Ael/Span, Llc
41775 Ecorse Rd Ste 100
Van Buren Twp MI 48111

(G-13657)
AMS PRODUCTION MACHINING INC
800 Andico Rd (46168-9659)
P.O. Box 376 (46168-0376)
PHONE..........................317 838-9273
John Anderson, *Prin*
John Anderson, *Pr*
Larry Bowen, *

Bryan Burdine, *
Robert Hines, *
EMP: 50 EST: 1980
SQ FT: 30,000
SALES (est): 4.87MM **Privately Held**
Web: www.amsmachining.com
SIC: **3599** Machine shop, jobbing and repair

(G-13658)
APOTEX CORP
2516 Airwest Blvd (46168-7701)
PHONE..........................317 839-6550
Jim Roudebush, *Brnch Mgr*
EMP: 25
SALES (corp-wide): 1.15B **Privately Held**
Web: www.apotex.com
SIC: **2836** Biological products, except diagnostic
HQ: Apotex Corp.
2400 N Commerce Pkwy # 400
Weston FL 33326

(G-13659)
B & B ARMS INC
3921 Clarks Creek Rd (46168-1952)
PHONE..........................317 339-4929
EMP: 4 EST: 2016
SALES (est): 52.6K **Privately Held**
Web: www.ffleasy.com
SIC: **3489** Ordnance and accessories, nec

(G-13660)
BECTON DICKINSON AND COMPANY
2350 Reeves Rd (46168-7933)
PHONE..........................317 561-2900
Kara Mckee, *Brnch Mgr*
EMP: 92
SALES (corp-wide): 19.37B **Publicly Held**
Web: www.bd.com
SIC: **3841** Hypodermic needles and syringes
PA: Becton, Dickinson And Company
1 Becton Dr
Franklin Lakes NJ 07417
201 847-6800

(G-13661)
BETTYS DAUGHTER INC
2685 E Main St Ste 108 (46168-2760)
PHONE..........................317 500-1490
Deborah Brown, *Pr*
EMP: 3 EST: 2020
SALES (est): 87.03K **Privately Held**
SIC: **7231** 3999 Beauty shops; Eyelashes, artificial

(G-13662)
BRANGENE LLC
815 Walton Dr (46168-2237)
PHONE..........................317 203-9172
EMP: 2 EST: 2014
SALES (est): 120.32K **Privately Held**
SIC: **7372** 7389 Business oriented computer software; Business services, nec

(G-13663)
BUIS ENTERPRISES INC
Also Called: RPS Printing Services
6987 S County Road 750 E (46168-8679)
PHONE..........................317 839-7394
Thomas Buis, *Pr*
EMP: 8 EST: 1982
SQ FT: 16,000
SALES (est): 210.52K **Privately Held**
SIC: **2752** Offset printing

(G-13664)
CANDLE CHEF LLC
890 Ridgewood Dr Bldg 202-D (46168-2267)

PHONE..........................317 406-3391
Sam Green, *Owner*
EMP: 4 EST: 2018
SALES (est): 39.69K **Privately Held**
Web: www.thecandlechef.com
SIC: **3999** Candles

(G-13665)
CATALYST INC (PA)
Also Called: Catalyst USA
2680 E Main St Ste 324 (46168-2829)
PHONE..........................317 227-3499
Steven T Sudler Senior, *Pr*
EMP: 6 EST: 1994
SALES (est): 2.45MM **Privately Held**
Web: www.catalystusa.com
SIC: **7372** Prepackaged software

(G-13666)
CENTRIFUGE SUPPORT & SUPS LLC
1418 Dallas Dr (46168-2173)
PHONE..........................317 830-6141
Kenneth Sucilla, *Managing Member*
EMP: 2 EST: 2014
SALES (est): 169.62K **Privately Held**
SIC: **3556** Cream separators (food products machinery)

(G-13667)
CERTOR SPORTS LLC (PA)
9400 Bradford Rd (46168-5909)
PHONE..........................800 426-9784
Jim Heidenreich, *CEO*
EMP: 53 EST: 2020
SQ FT: 230,000
SALES (est): 25.77MM
SALES (corp-wide): 25.77MM **Privately Held**
Web: www.certorsports.com
SIC: **3949** Team sports equipment

(G-13668)
CHATEAU THOMAS WINERY INC (PA)
6291 Cambridge Way (46168-7905)
P.O. Box 371 (46763-0371)
PHONE..........................317 837-9463
Doctor Charles Thomas, *Pr*
Jill Thomas, *VP*
EMP: 11 EST: 1983
SALES (est): 2.38MM
SALES (corp-wide): 2.38MM **Privately Held**
Web: www.chateauthomas.com
SIC: **2084** Wines

(G-13669)
CLOUD BLUE
501 Airtech Pkwy (46168-7408)
PHONE..........................714 382-2767
EMP: 4 EST: 2019
SALES (est): 131.9K **Privately Held**
SIC: **7372** Prepackaged software

(G-13670)
COLE ENERGY INCORPORATED
660 Andico Rd (46168-9601)
PHONE..........................317 839-9688
Phillip Cole, *Pr*
Betty Cole, *Sec*
EMP: 1 EST: 1983
SQ FT: 6,000
SALES (est): 152.09K **Privately Held**
SIC: **6531** 3369 Real estate leasing and rentals; Nonferrous foundries, nec

(G-13671)
CORNERSTONE CABINETS
206 S County Rd 300 East (46168)
PHONE..........................317 718-0050
Ron Deckard, *Owner*

EMP: 2 EST: 1987
SALES (est): 78.24K **Privately Held**
Web: www.cornerstone-cabinets.com
SIC: **2434** Wood kitchen cabinets

(G-13672)
CORONADO CASUALS LLC
2680 E Main St Ste 228 (46168-2828)
PHONE..........................615 470-5718
Li Yang, *Managing Member*
EMP: 3 EST: 2017
SALES (est): 189.65K **Privately Held**
Web: www.coronadocasuals.com
SIC: **2392** 7389 Household furnishings, nec; Business services, nec

(G-13673)
COUNTY WEST SPORTS
1702 E Main St (46168-1849)
PHONE..........................317 839-4076
Jeffrey Hazelbaker, *Pt*
Janice Hazelbaker, *Pt*
EMP: 2 EST: 1997
SQ FT: 1,200
SALES (est): 248.01K **Privately Held**
SIC: **5192** 2759 Books, periodicals, and newspapers; Screen printing

(G-13674)
COVIDIEN LP
Respiratory Solutions
2824 Airwest Blvd (46168-7700)
PHONE..........................317 837-8199
Doug Van Epps, *Mgr*
EMP: 230
Web: www.nellcor.com
SIC: **3845** 3999 3714 3841 Electromedical apparatus; Wheelchair lifts; Motor vehicle parts and accessories; Surgical and medical instruments
HQ: Covidien Lp
15 Hampshire St
Mansfield MA 02048
763 514-4000

(G-13675)
CRAWL BEFORE YOU WALK LLC
270 Double Creek Dr (46168-5577)
PHONE..........................219 413-6623
EMP: 1
SALES (est): 37.81K **Privately Held**
SIC: **2741** 7389 Internet publishing and broadcasting; Business services, nec

(G-13676)
CREATIVE INDUSTRIES INC
5280 Oakbrook Dr (46168-7402)
PHONE..........................317 248-1102
Mark Clark, *Pr*
Larry Clark, *Ch Bd*
Mike Clark, *Treas*
Susan Clark Schaecher, *Sec*
EMP: 22 EST: 1969
SALES (est): 2.07MM **Privately Held**
Web: www.cibulletproof.com
SIC: **2542** 3231 Partitions and fixtures, except wood; Strengthened or reinforced glass

(G-13677)
CROWN EQUIPMENT CORPORATION
Also Called: Crown Lift Trucks
2495 E Perry Rd (46168-7620)
PHONE..........................317 875-7233
EMP: 81
SALES (corp-wide): 7.12B **Privately Held**
Web: www.crown.com
SIC: **3537** Lift trucks, industrial: fork, platform, straddle, etc.
PA: Crown Equipment Corporation
44 S Washington St

Plainfield - Hendricks County (G-13678)

New Bremen OH 45869
419 629-2311

(G-13678)
ELI LILLY AND COMPANY
Also Called: Elanco Anmal Hlth A Div Eli Ll
2222 Stanley Rd (46168-8400)
PHONE..................................317 433-3624
Faye Doyle, *Brnch Mgr*
EMP: 25
SALES (corp-wide): 34.12B **Publicly Held**
Web: www.lilly.com
SIC: 2834 Pharmaceutical preparations
PA: Eli Lilly And Company
1 Lilly Corporate Ctr
Indianapolis IN 46285
317 276-2000

(G-13679)
EMJ METALS
2301 Airwest Blvd (46168-7718)
PHONE..................................317 838-8899
EMP: 7 **EST:** 2019
SALES (est): 234.21K **Privately Held**
Web: www.emjmetals.com
SIC: 3291 Abrasive metal and steel products

(G-13680)
FORD MOTOR COMPANY
Also Called: Ford
2675 Reeves Rd (46168-7936)
PHONE..................................901 368-8821
Tom Degiacomois, *Mgr*
EMP: 17
SALES (corp-wide): 176.19B **Publicly Held**
Web: www.ford.com
SIC: 5511 3713 3714 6153 Automobiles, new and used; Truck and bus bodies; Motor vehicle parts and accessories; Financing of dealers by motor vehicle manufacturers organ.
PA: Ford Motor Company
1 American Rd
Dearborn MI 48126
313 322-3000

(G-13681)
FOUR SEASON OIL INC
1237 American Ave (46168-3268)
PHONE..................................317 215-1214
Harjinder Badesha, *Prin*
EMP: 9 **EST:** 2016
SALES (est): 125.1K **Privately Held**
SIC: 1311 Crude petroleum and natural gas

(G-13682)
GAC ENTERPRISES USA LLC
849 Whitaker Rd Ste D (46168-7529)
PHONE..................................317 839-9525
Bill Statham, *Pr*
EMP: 17 **EST:** 2014
SQ FT: 3,500
SALES (est): 470.71K **Privately Held**
SIC: 3714 Motor vehicle parts and accessories

(G-13683)
GEORGE GARDNER
Also Called: Gardner Woodcrafts
256 N Center St (46168-1119)
PHONE..................................317 270-8036
George Gardner, *Owner*
EMP: 1
SALES (est): 59K **Privately Held**
SIC: 2521 Cabinets, office: wood

(G-13684)
HAPPY VALLEY SAND AND GRAV INC

Also Called: Happy Valley Sand & Gravel
4232 E Us Highway 40 (46168-8189)
PHONE..................................317 839-6800
Gordon Potts, *Pr*
Kimberly Potts, *Sec*
EMP: 4 **EST:** 1999
SALES (est): 969.35K **Privately Held**
Web: www.happyvalleysandandgravelinc.com
SIC: 1442 Construction sand and gravel

(G-13685)
HARPERCOLLINS PUBLISHERS LLC
716 Airtech Pkwy (46168-7413)
PHONE..................................317 839-4307
EMP: 1
SALES (corp-wide): 10.09B **Publicly Held**
Web: www.harpercollins.com
SIC: 2731 Books, publishing only
HQ: Harpercollins Publishers L.L.C.
195 Broadway
New York NY 10007
212 207-7000

(G-13686)
HARPERCOLLINS PUBLISHERS LLC
700 Airtech Pkwy (46168)
PHONE..................................317 406-8777
EMP: 1
SALES (corp-wide): 10.09B **Publicly Held**
Web: www.harpercollins.com
SIC: 2731 Books, publishing only
HQ: Harpercollins Publishers L.L.C.
195 Broadway
New York NY 10007
212 207-7000

(G-13687)
HP INC
Also Called: HP
1301 Smith Rd Ste 101 (46168-5749)
PHONE..................................317 334-3400
Keith Hangarage, *Dir*
EMP: 19
SALES (corp-wide): 53.72B **Publicly Held**
Web: www.hp.com
SIC: 3571 Personal computers (microcomputers)
PA: Hp Inc.
1501 Page Mill Rd
Palo Alto CA 94304
650 857-1501

(G-13688)
IDGAS INC
915 Corey Ln (46168-2386)
PHONE..................................317 839-1133
Roy E Reed, *Pr*
EMP: 1 **EST:** 2004
SALES (est): 110K **Privately Held**
SIC: 2515 Mattresses and foundations

(G-13689)
INDILABEL LLC
2198 Reeves Rd Ste 4c (46168-7928)
PHONE..................................317 839-8814
EMP: 10 **EST:** 1994
SQ FT: 20,000
SALES (est): 1.03MM **Privately Held**
Web: www.indilabel.com
SIC: 2759 Labels and seals: printing, nsk

(G-13690)
INFINITY PRODUCTS INC
Also Called: C-Level
2340 E Perry Rd Ste 109 (46168-7437)
PHONE..................................317 272-3435
Linda Scott, *Pr*
Gregg E Scott, *Treas*
EMP: 8 **EST:** 1995
SALES (est): 422.58K **Privately Held**

Web: www.infinityproducts.com
SIC: 3842 Personal safety equipment

(G-13691)
INTEGRITY MARKETING TEAM INC
4067 Cheltonham Ct (46168-9094)
PHONE..................................317 517-0012
Donald Denman, *Pr*
Christopher Denman, *Sls Mgr*
Patti Denman, *Sec*
EMP: 3 **EST:** 2012
SALES (est): 236.89K **Privately Held**
SIC: 6799 3613 Investors, nec; Switchgear and switchgear accessories, nec

(G-13692)
INTEGRITY RTTIONAL MOLDING LLC
Also Called: Integrity
701 N Carr Rd (46168)
PHONE..................................317 837-1101
Bill Delong, *Pr*
Garry Richarson, *VP*
Terry Stemple, *VP*
EMP: 20 **EST:** 2001
SQ FT: 10,000
SALES (est): 4.94MM **Privately Held**
Web: www.integrityrotational.com
SIC: 3089 Injection molding of plastics

(G-13693)
INTER-CNTNNTAL GEAR BRAKE USA
923 Whitaker Rd (46168-7409)
PHONE..................................317 268-0040
EMP: 94
SALES (corp-wide): 3.87MM **Privately Held**
Web: www.icgb.ca
SIC: 3714 Motor vehicle parts and accessories
PA: Inter-Continental Gear & Brake (Usa) Inc.
6431 Reames Rd
Charlotte NC 28216
704 599-3420

(G-13694)
INVACARE CORPORATION
1100 Whitaker Rd (46168-7636)
PHONE..................................317 838-5500
Steve Wilson, *Brnch Mgr*
EMP: 10
SALES (corp-wide): 741.73MM **Privately Held**
Web: global.invacare.com
SIC: 3842 Surgical appliances and supplies
PA: Invacare Corporation
1 Invacare Way
Elyria OH 44035
440 329-6000

(G-13695)
J ENNIS FABRICS INC (USA)
853 Columbia Rd Ste 125 (46168-7560)
PHONE..................................877 953-6647
Eric Olsen, *Pr*
Jim Ennis, *Prin*
Lois Ennis, *Sec*
◆ **EMP:** 6 **EST:** 2000
SQ FT: 40,000
SALES (est): 685.75K **Privately Held**
Web: www.ennisfabrics.com
SIC: 2394 5131 Canvas covers and drop cloths; Piece goods and notions

(G-13696)
JECO PLASTIC PRODUCTS LLC
885 Andico Rd (46168-9659)
P.O. Box 26 (46168-0026)
PHONE..................................317 839-4943
Craig Carson, *CEO*

▼ **EMP:** 34 **EST:** 1979
SQ FT: 37,000
SALES (est): 4.99MM **Privately Held**
Web: www.jecoplastics.com
SIC: 3089 Injection molding of plastics

(G-13697)
LEESON ELECTRIC CORPORATION
9899 Bradford Rd (46168-5905)
PHONE..................................317 821-3700
EMP: 34
SALES (corp-wide): 6.25B **Publicly Held**
Web: www.regalrexnord.com
SIC: 3621 Motors and generators
HQ: Leeson Electric Corporation
1051 Cheyenne Ave
Grafton WI 53024
262 377-8810

(G-13698)
LSC COMMUNICATIONS BOOK LLC
Also Called: Lakeside Book Company
716 Airtech Pkwy (46168-7413)
PHONE..................................317 406-8783
EMP: 1
SALES (corp-wide): 8.23B **Privately Held**
SIC: 2731 Book publishing
HQ: Lsc Communications Book Llc
5550 W 74th St
Indianapolis IN 46268
317 715-2402

(G-13699)
MARATHON ELECTRIC ⚙
9899 Bradford Rd (46168)
PHONE..................................317 837-2523
EMP: 6 **EST:** 2024
SALES (est): 78.58K **Privately Held**
SIC: 3621 Motors and generators

(G-13700)
MATRIX LABEL SYSTEMS INC
4692 S County Road 600 E (46168-8620)
PHONE..................................317 839-1973
Gerald Perrill, *Pr*
Cindy Perrill, *
▲ **EMP:** 46 **EST:** 1989
SALES (est): 4.9MM **Privately Held**
Web: www.matrixlabel.com
SIC: 2759 Labels and seals: printing, nsk

(G-13701)
MAXIM PIPETTE SERVICE INC
4310 Saratoga Pkwy Ste 100 (46168-9207)
P.O. Box 387 (46168-0387)
PHONE..................................877 536-2946
EMP: 5 **EST:** 2011
SALES (est): 466.27K **Privately Held**
Web: www.maximpipetteservice.com
SIC: 3823 Industrial flow and liquid measuring instruments

(G-13702)
MEDTRNIC SOFAMOR DANEK USA INC
Also Called: Medtronic
1620 Hawthorne Dr Ste 400 (46168-2814)
PHONE..................................317 837-8142
EMP: 8
Web: www.medtronic.com
SIC: 3841 Surgical and medical instruments
HQ: Medtronic Sofamor Danek Usa, Inc.
4340 Swinnea Rd
Memphis TN 38118
901 396-3133

(G-13703)
MEDTRONIC
2824 Airwest Blvd (46168)
PHONE..................................317 837-8664

GEOGRAPHIC SECTION
Plainfield - Hendricks County (G-13727)

EMP: 9 **EST:** 2017
SALES (est): 781.13K Privately Held
Web: www.medtronic.com
SIC: 3841 Surgical and medical instruments

(G-13704)
MERCK SHARP & DOHME LLC
2150 Stanley Rd (46168-8490)
PHONE..................908 740-4000
EMP: 7
SALES (corp-wide): 60.12B Publicly Held
Web: www.merck.com
SIC: 2834 Pharmaceutical preparations
HQ: Merck Sharp & Dohme Llc
 126 E Lincoln Ave
 Rahway NJ 07065
 908 740-4000

(G-13705)
MEREDITH HUGHES
Also Called: Dream Fishing/Lure, The
2106 Crown Plaza Blvd (46168-2081)
PHONE..................317 354-6073
Meredith Hughes, Owner
EMP: 1 **EST:** 2020
SALES (est): 47.08K Privately Held
SIC: 3949 Lures, fishing: artificial

(G-13706)
MERITOR INC
849 Whitaker Rd (46168-7529)
PHONE..................317 279-2180
Brian Cavagnini, Brnch Mgr
EMP: 8
SALES (corp-wide): 34.06B Publicly Held
Web: www.meritor.com
SIC: 3714 5013 Motor vehicle parts and accessories; Automotive supplies and parts
HQ: Meritor, Inc.
 2135 W Maple Rd
 Troy MI 48084

(G-13707)
NATURES WAY
6246 E County Road 700 S (46168-9066)
PHONE..................317 839-4566
Timothy A Ratliff, Prin
EMP: 1 **EST:** 2005
SALES (est): 106.04K Privately Held
Web: www.naturesway.net
SIC: 3564 Air purification equipment

(G-13708)
NEXT REFORMATION PUBLISHING CO
4086 Hennessey Dr (46168-9058)
PHONE..................317 650-1364
Jon Nessle, Owner
EMP: 1 **EST:** 2012
SALES (est): 51K Privately Held
SIC: 2741 7389 Miscellaneous publishing; Business Activities at Non-Commercial Site

(G-13709)
NIAGARA BOTTLING LLC
1250 Whitaker Rd (46168-7616)
PHONE..................909 758-5313
EMP: 5
SALES (corp-wide): 120MM Privately Held
Web: www.niagarawater.com
SIC: 2086 Water, natural: packaged in cans, bottles, etc.
PA: Niagara Bottling, Llc
 1440 Bridgegate Dr
 Diamond Bar CA 91765
 909 230-5000

(G-13710)
NICE-PAK PRODUCTS INC
381 Airtech Pkwy (46168-7416)
PHONE..................317 839-0373
Mark Sands, Brnch Mgr
EMP: 45
SALES (corp-wide): 674.94MM Privately Held
Web: www.nicepak.com
SIC: 2621 Sanitary tissue paper
PA: Nice-Pak Products, Inc.
 2 Nice Pak Park
 Orangeburg NY 10962
 845 365-1700

(G-13711)
PEAFIELD PRODUCTS INC
4692 S County Road 600 E (46168-8620)
PHONE..................317 839-8473
Gerald Perrill, Pr
EMP: 10 **EST:** 1985
SALES (est): 934.25K Privately Held
Web: www.matrixlabel.com
SIC: 2672 2893 2796 Labels (unprinted), gummed: made from purchased materials; Printing ink; Platemaking services

(G-13712)
PELI BIOTHERMAL LLC
Also Called: Peli Biothermal Service Center
915 Airtech Pkwy Ste 102 (46168)
PHONE..................763 412-4800
EMP: 1
SALES (corp-wide): 481.68MM Privately Held
SIC: 3826 2834 Differential thermal analysis instruments; Pharmaceutical preparations
HQ: Peli Biothermal Llc
 10050 89th Ave N
 Maple Grove MN 55369
 763 412-4800

(G-13713)
PEPITO MILLER BEV IMPORTS LLC
Also Called: P&M Beverage Imports
4188 Scioto Dr (46168-9092)
PHONE..................317 416-3215
Troy Pepito, CEO
Robert Miller, Prin
EMP: 2 **EST:** 2017
SALES (est): 68.62K Privately Held
SIC: 2084 2082 Wine coolers (beverages); Ale (alcoholic beverage)

(G-13714)
PHINIA DELPHI USA LLC
Also Called: Delphi Powertrain
6032 Gateway Dr (46168-7655)
PHONE..................317 203-4602
Ernie Trapp, Brnch Mgr
EMP: 2
SALES (corp-wide): 3.5B Publicly Held
Web: www.phinia.com
SIC: 3714 Motor vehicle parts and accessories
HQ: Phinia Delphi Usa Llc
 3000 University Dr
 Auburn Hills MI 48326
 248 754-9600

(G-13715)
PLAINFIELD EYE CARE
900 Edwards Dr (46168-5680)
PHONE..................317 839-2368
EMP: 16 **EST:** 2019
SALES (est): 758.25K Privately Held
Web: www.plainfieldeyecare.com
SIC: 8042 3851 Specialized optometrists; Ophthalmic goods

(G-13716)
PLAINFIELD WINERY TSTNG RM
6291 Cambridge Way (46168-7905)
PHONE..................317 837-9463
EMP: 4 **EST:** 2019
SALES (est): 87.66K Privately Held
SIC: 2084 Wines

(G-13717)
PRO DOOR MANUFACTURING LLC
Also Called: Pro Door Mfg
6030 Gateway Dr (46168-7655)
PHONE..................317 839-3050
Jd Stearns, Pr
EMP: 51 **EST:** 2016
SALES (est): 5.01MM
SALES (corp-wide): 280.64MM Privately Held
Web: www.prodoorsystems.com
SIC: 2431 Garage doors, overhead, wood
HQ: Professional Garage Door Systems Inc
 6030 Gateway Dr
 Plainfield IN 46168
 317 839-3050

(G-13718)
Q-EDGE CORPORATION
1301 Smith Rd Ste 101 (46168-5749)
PHONE..................317 203-6800
Mark Chien, Pr
▲ **EMP:** 47 **EST:** 2000
SALES (est): 4.53MM Privately Held
SIC: 3571 Electronic computers

(G-13719)
REGAL BELOIT LOGISTICS LLC
Also Called: Regal Bowait
9899 Bradford Rd (46168-5905)
PHONE..................317 837-1150
▲ **EMP:** 11 **EST:** 2013
SALES (est): 1.04MM Privately Held
SIC: 3621 Electric motor and generator parts

(G-13720)
REGAL REXNORD CORPORATION
9899 Bradford Rd (46168-5905)
PHONE..................317 837-2667
EMP: 10
SALES (corp-wide): 6.25B Publicly Held
Web: www.regalrexnord.com
SIC: 3621 Motors and generators
PA: Regal Rexnord Corporation
 111 W Michigan St
 Milwaukee WI 53203
 608 364-8800

(G-13721)
REGENT AEROSPACE CORPORATION
2501 E Perry Rd (46168-7621)
PHONE..................317 837-4000
Michael Lilley, VP
EMP: 117
Web: www.regentaerospace.com
SIC: 1799 3728 Renovation of aircraft interiors; Aircraft parts and equipment, nec
PA: Regent Aerospace Corporation
 28110 W Harrison Parkway
 Valencia CA 91355

(G-13722)
REXNORD INDUSTRIES LLC
9899 Bradford Rd (46168)
PHONE..................414 643-2559
EMP: 9
SALES (corp-wide): 6.25B Publicly Held
SIC: 3566 3714 3568 3625 Speed changers (power transmission equipment), except auto; Motor vehicle parts and accessories; Chain, power transmission; Electromagnetic clutches or brakes
HQ: Rexnord Industries, Llc
 111 W Michigan St
 Milwaukee WI 53203
 414 643-3000

(G-13723)
ROLLS-ROYCE CORPORATION
Also Called: Kuehne Nagel
3051 Midfield Ct Ste 190 (46168-7590)
PHONE..................317 657-0267
Angela Murphy, Mgr
EMP: 35
SALES (corp-wide): 20.55B Privately Held
Web: www.rolls-royce.com
SIC: 3724 Aircraft engines and engine parts
HQ: Rolls-Royce Corporation
 450 S Meridian St
 Indianapolis IN 46225

(G-13724)
RTEES LLC
7013 Stonecreek Dr (46168-7923)
PHONE..................317 345-7445
Phillip C Anderson, Owner
EMP: 6 **EST:** 2017
SALES (est): 92.55K Privately Held
SIC: 2759 Screen printing

(G-13725)
SAFRAN NCLLES SVCS AMRICAS LLC (HQ)
845 Airtech Pkwy Ste 172 (46168-7452)
PHONE..................317 827-0859
Michael Robinson, Managing Member
EMP: 2 **EST:** 2014
SQ FT: 18,234
SALES (est): 5.43MM
SALES (corp-wide): 781.02MM Privately Held
Web: www.safran-group.com
SIC: 3728 Nacelles, aircraft
PA: Safran
 2 Boulevard Du General Martial Valin
 Paris 75015

(G-13726)
SAINT-GOBAIN ABRASIVES INC
1001 Perry Rd (46168-7639)
PHONE..................317 837-0700
Alan Freidman, Mgr
EMP: 64
SALES (corp-wide): 402.18MM Privately Held
Web: www.saint-gobain-abrasives.com
SIC: 3291 Abrasive products
HQ: Saint-Gobain Abrasives, Inc.
 1 New Bond St
 Worcester MA 01615
 508 795-5000

(G-13727)
SCHUTT SPORTS LLC
9400 Bradford Rd (46168-5909)
PHONE..................217 324-2712
Robert Erb, Managing Member
EMP: 250 **EST:** 2020
SALES (est): 25.77MM
SALES (corp-wide): 25.77MM Privately Held
Web: www.schuttsports.com
SIC: 3949 Football equipment and supplies, general
PA: Certor Sports, Llc
 9400 Bradford Rd
 Plainfield IN 46168
 800 426-9784

Plainfield - Hendricks County (G-13728)

(G-13728)
SCHUTT SPORTS RE LLC
9400 Bradford Rd (46168-5909)
PHONE.................217 324-3978
EMP: 5 EST: 2020
SALES (est): 153.75K **Privately Held**
Web: www.schuttsports.com
SIC: 3949 Sporting and athletic goods, nec

(G-13729)
SMITH TECHNOLOGIES
5832 Oberlies Way (46168-7300)
PHONE.................317 839-6766
John H Smigh, Prin
EMP: 5 EST: 2010
SALES (est): 80.29K **Privately Held**
SIC: 1389 Construction, repair, and dismantling services

(G-13730)
SOUTHWIRE COMPANY LLC
Also Called: Southwire Senator Wire
600 Perry Rd Ste 100 (46168-7454)
PHONE.................317 445-2722
EMP: 28
SALES (corp-wide): 1.7B **Privately Held**
Web: www.southwire.com
SIC: 3357 Nonferrous wiredrawing and insulating
PA: Southwire Company, Llc
One Southwire Dr
Carrollton GA 30119
770 832-4529

(G-13731)
STARKEY LABORATORIES INC
Also Called: Starkey Global Dist Ctr
3810 Plainfield Rd Ste 112 (46168)
PHONE.................952 828-6934
EMP: 11
SALES (corp-wide): 539.53MM **Privately Held**
Web: www.starkey.com
SIC: 5999 5047 3842 Hearing aids; Medical equipment and supplies; Hearing aids
PA: Starkey Laboratories, Inc.
6700 Washington Ave S
Eden Prairie MN 55344
952 941-6401

(G-13732)
STRIDE PROSTHETICS LLC
2498 Perry Crossing Way Ste 210 (46168)
PHONE.................317 520-2652
Nicholas Wheeler, CEO
EMP: 5 EST: 2017
SALES (est): 86.67K **Privately Held**
Web: www.strideprosthetics.com
SIC: 3842 Limbs, artificial

(G-13733)
STUDIO DIGITAL SALSA LLC
7820 Lincoln Trl (46168-9334)
PHONE.................317 439-8994
EMP: 4 EST: 2015
SALES (est): 125.88K **Privately Held**
SIC: 2099 Dips, except cheese and sour cream based

(G-13734)
TECHRYAN INC
2680 E Main St Ste 100 (46168-2827)
PHONE.................317 721-4835
EMP: 6 EST: 2018
SALES (est): 283.72K **Privately Held**
Web: www.techryan.com
SIC: 3861 Photographic equipment and supplies

(G-13735)
THERMAL STRUCTURES INC
2800 Airwest Blvd Ste 100 (46168-7737)
PHONE.................951 736-9911
EMP: 19
Web: www.thermalstructures.com
SIC: 3724 Aircraft engines and engine parts
HQ: Thermal Structures, Inc.
2362 Railroad St
Corona CA 92878
951 736-9911

(G-13736)
TKO ENTERPRISES INC (PA)
Also Called: T.K.O. Graphix
2751 Stafford Rd (46168-2198)
PHONE.................317 271-1398
Thomas Taulman Ii, CEO
Tom Mcclelland, VP
Michael K Smith, VP
Christina Hurley, Sec
Denny Smith, COO
EMP: 99 EST: 1985
SQ FT: 50,000
SALES (est): 20.65MM
SALES (corp-wide): 20.65MM **Privately Held**
Web: www.tkographix.com
SIC: 2759 3993 2752 2396 Commercial printing, nec; Signs and advertising specialties; Commercial printing, lithographic; Automotive and apparel trimmings

(G-13737)
TONIS TOUCH LLC
2448 Meadowlark Way Apt C (46168-3200)
PHONE.................317 992-1280
Antoinette R Johnson, CEO
EMP: 4 EST: 2019
SALES (est): 18K **Privately Held**
SIC: 5961 7231 3999 2844 Electronic shopping; Beauty shops; Hair, dressing of, for the trade; Hair preparations, including shampoos

(G-13738)
TROJAN BATTERY
923 Whitaker Rd (46168-7409)
PHONE.................317 561-5650
EMP: 10 EST: 2020
SALES (est): 480.35K **Privately Held**
Web: www.trojanbatterysales.com
SIC: 3691 Storage batteries

(G-13739)
TRUE ANLYTICS MFG SLUTIONS LLC
2230 Stafford Rd Ste 115 (46168-2790)
PHONE.................317 995-3220
John Murphy, CEO
EMP: 4 EST: 2016
SALES (est): 264.22K **Privately Held**
Web: www.tams.ai
SIC: 7372 7389 Application computer software; Business services, nec

(G-13740)
VICKI WRIGHT AND COMPANY
247 Andrews Boulevard East Dr (46168-7680)
PHONE.................317 372-7136
Vicki Wright, Owner
EMP: 1 EST: 2011
SALES (est): 100K **Privately Held**
SIC: 2836 Culture media

(G-13741)
WABTEC CORPORATION
Also Called: Wabtec Plainfield Dcm
1110 Smith Rd (46168-5837)
PHONE.................317 556-4116
EMP: 1
Web: www.wabteccorp.com
SIC: 3743 Railroad equipment
HQ: Wabtec Corporation
30 Isabella St
Pittsburgh PA 15212

(G-13742)
WHIRLPOOL CORPORATION
Also Called: Whirlpool
2801 Airwest Blvd (46168-7700)
PHONE.................317 837-5300
Barry Parker, Brnch Mgr
EMP: 28
SALES (corp-wide): 19.45B **Publicly Held**
Web: www.whirlpoolcorp.com
SIC: 3633 Laundry dryers, household or coin-operated
PA: Whirlpool Corporation
2000 N M-63
Benton Harbor MI 49022
269 923-5000

(G-13743)
WINFIELD SOLUTIONS LLC
923 Whitaker Rd Ste G (46168)
PHONE.................317 838-3733
EMP: 3
SALES (corp-wide): 2.89B **Privately Held**
Web: www.winfieldunited.com
SIC: 5191 2048 8742 Chemicals, agricultural ; Feed concentrates; Business management consultant
HQ: Winfield Solutions, Llc
4001 Lexington Ave N
Arden Hills MN 55126

(G-13744)
WRG PUBLISHING
912 Walton Dr (46168-2240)
P.O. Box 284 (46168-0284)
PHONE.................317 839-6520
William Gouge, Prin
EMP: 5 EST: 2007
SALES (est): 94.85K **Privately Held**
Web: www.wrg.net
SIC: 2741 Miscellaneous publishing

Plainville
Daviess County

(G-13745)
C AND S MACHINE INC
122 Main St (47568-9604)
P.O. Box 39 (47568-0039)
PHONE.................812 687-7203
Matthew Bellamy, Pr
EMP: 6 EST: 1994
SALES (est): 623.24K **Privately Held**
SIC: 3599 Machine shop, jobbing and repair

(G-13746)
TMGG LLC
Also Called: Tri-Star Glove
714 5th St (47568)
P.O. Box 90 (47568)
PHONE.................812 687-7444
Eric Moll, *
▲ EMP: 30 EST: 2001
SQ FT: 30,000
SALES (est): 2.26MM **Privately Held**
Web: www.tri-starglove.com
SIC: 2381 Fabric dress and work gloves

(G-13747)
WAGLER MINI BARN PRODUCTS LLC
8972 N 550 E (47568-5155)
PHONE.................812 687-7372
EMP: 5 EST: 1991
SALES (est): 486.99K **Privately Held**
Web: www.minibarnproducts.com
SIC: 3448 2452 Prefabricated metal buildings and components; Log cabins, prefabricated, wood

Pleasant Lake
Steuben County

(G-13748)
VINYL CREATOR
4698 S East Riley Sq (46779-9504)
PHONE.................260 475-2012
EMP: 5 EST: 2018
SALES (est): 133.47K **Privately Held**
Web: www.thevinylcreator.com
SIC: 3993 Signs and advertising specialties

Plymouth
Marshall County

(G-13749)
3-D SERVICES
16357 14th Rd (46563)
PHONE.................574 933-4819
Dennis L Manuwal Junior, Prin
EMP: 5 EST: 2018
SALES (est): 62.75K **Privately Held**
Web: www.protolabs.com
SIC: 3089 Injection molding of plastics

(G-13750)
3M COMPANY
Also Called: 3M
2925 Gary Dr (46563-8889)
PHONE.................574 948-8103
EMP: 3
SALES (corp-wide): 32.68B **Publicly Held**
Web: www.3m.com
SIC: 3841 Surgical instruments and apparatus
PA: 3m Company
3m Center
Saint Paul MN 55144
651 733-1110

(G-13751)
AAA GALVANIZING - JOLIET INC
Also Called: Azz Galvanizing Plymouth
2631 Jim Neu Dr (46563-3311)
PHONE.................574 935-4500
Bob Shireman, Manager
EMP: 11
SALES (corp-wide): 1.54B **Publicly Held**
SIC: 3479 Hot dip coating of metals or formed products
HQ: Aaa Galvanizing - Joliet, Inc.
625 Mills Rd
Joliet IL 60433

(G-13752)
AK INDUSTRIES INC
2055 Pidco Dr (46563-1374)
P.O. Box 640 (46563-0640)
PHONE.................574 936-6022
John S Sabo, Pr
Stephen A Sabo Junior, Prin
▲ EMP: 90 EST: 1981
SQ FT: 50,000
SALES (est): 22.35MM **Privately Held**
Web: www.akindustries.com
SIC: 3089 3272 Plastics and fiberglass tanks ; Concrete products, nec

GEOGRAPHIC SECTION

Plymouth - Marshall County (G-13776)

(G-13753)
AKER COMPOSITE SOLUTIONS INC
2900 Gary Dr (46563-8897)
P.O. Box 304 (46563-0304)
PHONE.....................574 935-0908
D Mark Aker, *Prin*
EMP: 5 **EST:** 2008
SALES (est): 499.34K **Privately Held**
Web: www.aerotech-atu.com
SIC: 3089 Plastics products, nec

(G-13754)
ALL POINTS TOOL & MFG CORP
2743 Pioneer Dr (46563-6722)
P.O. Box 687 (46563-0687)
PHONE.....................574 935-3944
Jerry Firoky, *Pt*
Mike Cenetar, *Pt*
Leonard Kuzmicz, *Pt*
Krisha Drue, *Pt*
EMP: 4 **EST:** 2002
SQ FT: 5,000
SALES (est): 401.46K **Privately Held**
Web: www.allpointstool.com
SIC: 3599 Machine shop, jobbing and repair

(G-13755)
AMERICAN CONTAINERS INC (PA)
2526 Western Ave (46563-1050)
PHONE.....................574 936-4068
Leonard Isban, *CEO*
Leonard D Isban, *
Michael Isban, *
Joan Isban, *
Steven Tubbs, *
◆ **EMP:** 60 **EST:** 1965
SQ FT: 70,000
SALES (est): 22.65MM
SALES (corp-wide): 22.65MM **Privately Held**
Web: www.acontainers.com
SIC: 2653 2671 2652 2631 Boxes, corrugated: made from purchased materials ; Paper; coated and laminated packaging; Setup paperboard boxes; Paperboard mills

(G-13756)
AMISH WOODWORKING LLC
8870 State Road 17 (46563-9479)
PHONE.....................574 941-4439
Don Green, *Prin*
EMP: 2 **EST:** 2006
SALES (est): 185.2K **Privately Held**
Web: www.amishwoodworking.com
SIC: 2431 Millwork

(G-13757)
BAY VALLEY FOODS LLC
1430 Western Ave (46563-1030)
P.O. Box 19057 (54307-9057)
PHONE.....................574 935-3097
Tony Lenne, *Mgr*
EMP: 155
SALES (corp-wide): 3.43B **Publicly Held**
Web: www.bayvalleyfoods.com
SIC: 2033 2035 Canned fruits and specialties ; Pickles, sauces, and salad dressings
HQ: Bay Valley Foods, Llc
3200 Riverside Dr Ste A
Green Bay WI 54301
800 558-4700

(G-13758)
BOMARKO INC (PA)
Also Called: Bomarko
1955 N Oak Dr (46563)
P.O. Box 1510 (46563)
PHONE.....................574 936-9901
James D Azzar, *Pr*
John Yeakey, *
◆ **EMP:** 110 **EST:** 1963

SQ FT: 180,000
SALES (est): 25.8MM
SALES (corp-wide): 25.8MM **Privately Held**
Web: www.bomarko.com
SIC: 2671 Waxed paper: made from purchased material

(G-13759)
BOWEN PRINTING INC
200 S Michigan St (46563-2238)
PHONE.....................574 936-3924
David Ruff, *Pr*
Alice Ruff, *Sec*
EMP: 6 **EST:** 1983
SQ FT: 4,800
SALES (est): 826.77K **Privately Held**
Web: www.bowenprintingplymouth.com
SIC: 2752 Offset printing

(G-13760)
BOWMANS TIN SHOP INC
1576 Hoham Dr (46563-6732)
PHONE.....................574 936-3234
Heath Bowman, *Pr*
Hal Bowman, *Pr*
Lori Sechrist, *Off Mgr*
EMP: 3 **EST:** 1959
SALES (est): 482.62K **Privately Held**
Web: www.bowmanstinshop.com
SIC: 3444 1711 Sheet metalwork; Irrigation sprinkler system installation

(G-13761)
BPC MANUFACTURING OPERATION
1755 N Oak Dr (46563-3413)
PHONE.....................574 936-9894
Don Rodda, *Owner*
▲ **EMP:** 5 **EST:** 2008
SALES (est): 227.18K **Privately Held**
SIC: 2821 Plastics materials and resins

(G-13762)
BUFFINGTON ELECTRIC MOTORS
Also Called: Buffington Farm Service
2520 Lake Ave (46563-7845)
PHONE.....................574 935-5453
Michael Buffington, *Pr*
EMP: 2 **EST:** 1975
SALES (est): 170.75K **Privately Held**
SIC: 7694 5083 7699 Rewinding stators; Grain elevators equipment and supplies; Farm machinery repair

(G-13763)
CNHI LLC
Also Called: Pilot News
218 N Michigan St (46563-2135)
P.O. Box 220 (46563-0220)
PHONE.....................574 936-3101
Jerry Bingle, *Mgr*
EMP: 1
SALES (corp-wide): 34.97B **Privately Held**
Web: www.cnhi.com
SIC: 2711 Commercial printing and newspaper publishing combined
HQ: Cnhi, Llc
445 Dexter Ave
Montgomery AL 36104

(G-13764)
COCA COLA BTLG CO KOKOMO IND
Coca-Cola
1701 Pidco Dr (46563-1358)
PHONE.....................574 936-3220
Francis Eloert, *Mgr*
EMP: 20
SALES (corp-wide): 885.15K **Privately Held**
Web: www.cckokomo.com

SIC: 2086 Bottled and canned soft drinks
PA: Coca Cola Bottling Co Kokomo Ind Inc
2305 N Davis Rd
Kokomo IN 46901
765 457-4421

(G-13765)
COMPOSITE TECH ASSEMBLIES LLC
Also Called: Oasis Lifestyle
904 Markley Dr (46563-3201)
P.O. Box 82 (46563-0082)
PHONE.....................574 948-0004
Mark Naylor, *Pr*
Andrew Aker, *
EMP: 30 **EST:** 2013
SALES (est): 2.16MM **Privately Held**
SIC: 3088 Shower stalls, fiberglass and plastics

(G-13766)
COUNTERTOP SHOPPE INC
505 W Jefferson St (46563-1647)
PHONE.....................574 936-1423
EMP: 6 **EST:** 2019
SALES (est): 203.19K **Privately Held**
Web: www.ctopshoppe.com
SIC: 2434 Wood kitchen cabinets

(G-13767)
CROWDREVIEWSCOM LLC
1913 N Michigan St Ste F # 218 (46563-1015)
PHONE.....................239 227-2428
EMP: 7 **EST:** 2016
SALES (est): 153.62K **Privately Held**
Web: www.crowdreviews.com
SIC: 2741 Guides: publishing only, not printed on site

(G-13768)
CULVER TOOL & ENGINEERING INC
Also Called: Cte Solutions
1901 Walter Glaub Dr (46563-1387)
P.O. Box 970 (46563-0970)
PHONE.....................574 935-9611
Wade Berger, *Pr*
David Winrotte, *
William Mc Queen, *
Mark Morris, *
EMP: 55 **EST:** 1955
SQ FT: 12,800
SALES (est): 9.28MM **Privately Held**
Web: www.spitrexorthopedics.com
SIC: 7389 3599 Metal cutting services; Machine shop, jobbing and repair

(G-13769)
DANNY WEBB PLUMBING
Also Called: Webb, Danny Plumbing & Heating
18391 6th Rd (46563-8835)
PHONE.....................574 936-2746
EMP: 2 **EST:** 1970
SALES (est): 104.97K **Privately Held**
SIC: 1711 2842 Plumbing contractors; Cleaning or polishing preparations, nec

(G-13770)
DARLING INGREDIENTS INC
Also Called: Plymouth Transfer Station
12091 Plymouth Goshen Trl (46563-7924)
PHONE.....................913 321-9328
Adam Roth, *Brnch Mgr*
EMP: 20
SALES (corp-wide): 6.79B **Publicly Held**
Web: www.darlingii.com
SIC: 2077 Animal and marine fats and oils
PA: Darling Ingredients Inc.
5601 N Macarthur Blvd
Irving TX 75038

972 717-0300

(G-13771)
DOHRN TRANSFER COMPANY
Also Called: DOHRN TRANSFER COMPANY
14555 Lincoln Hwy (46563-8809)
PHONE.....................574 941-4484
Garry Dohrn, *Owner*
EMP: 42
SALES (corp-wide): 95.98MM **Privately Held**
Web: www.dohrn.com
SIC: 3537 Trucks: freight, baggage, etc.: industrial, except mining
PA: Dohrn Enterprises, Inc.
625 3rd Ave
Rock Island IL 61201
309 794-0723

(G-13772)
DURA-VENT CORP
1435 N Michigan St Ste 3 (46563-1100)
PHONE.....................574 936-2432
Gary J Scott, *Pr*
EMP: 12 **EST:** 2005
SALES (est): 365.42K **Privately Held**
Web: www.hitechduravent.com
SIC: 3052 Rubber and plastics hose and beltings

(G-13773)
DUTCH WAFFLE COMPANY LLC
16834 Mill Pond Trl (46563-8112)
PHONE.....................574 312-4578
Bianca Letens, *Pr*
Bianca Letens Van Der Gaag, *Pr*
EMP: 10 **EST:** 2019
SALES (est): 415.25K **Privately Held**
Web: www.dutchwafflecompany.us
SIC: 2051 Bakery: wholesale or wholesale/retail combined

(G-13774)
FARM INNOVATORS INC
2255 Walter Glaub Dr (46563)
P.O. Box 546 (46563)
PHONE.....................574 936-5096
Benjamin T Clark Senior, *Ch Bd*
Benjamin T Clark Junior, *Pr*
Diane M Clark, *
▲ **EMP:** 25 **EST:** 1967
SQ FT: 38,000
SALES (est): 3.93MM **Privately Held**
Web: www.farminnovators.com
SIC: 3567 3523 Electrical furnaces, ovens, & heating devices, exc.induction; Farm machinery and equipment

(G-13775)
FERENTINO TIRE USA INC
400 Lake Ave (46563-2446)
PHONE.....................574 316-6116
Frederick A Harker, *Admn*
EMP: 3 **EST:** 2020
SALES (est): 256.55K **Privately Held**
Web: www.ferentinoindustrial.com
SIC: 5531 3011 Automotive tires; Tires, semi-pneumatic

(G-13776)
FLEXIBLE TECHNOLOGIES INC
HI Tech Duravent
1435 N Michigan St Ste 3 (46563-1100)
PHONE.....................574 936-2432
EMP: 5
SALES (corp-wide): 3.83B **Privately Held**
Web: www.flexibletechnologies.com
SIC: 3052 Rubber hose
HQ: Flexible Technologies, Inc.
528 Carwellyn Rd
Abbeville SC 29620
864 366-5441

Plymouth - Marshall County (G-13777)

(G-13777)
FOIL LAMINATING INC
1000 Pidco Dr (46563-1367)
EMP: 30 **EST:** 1989
SALES (est): 4.26MM **Privately Held**
SIC: 3497 3081 Foil, laminated to paper or other materials; Plastics film and sheet

(G-13778)
GALAXY CONTAINER LLC
1001 Pidco Dr (46563-1368)
PHONE....................574 936-6300
EMP: 6 **EST:** 2003
SALES (est): 441.29K **Privately Held**
Web: www.packpros.net
SIC: 2653 Boxes, corrugated: made from purchased materials

(G-13779)
GFI INNOVATIONS LLC
Also Called: Gfi Innovations
2940 Miller Dr (46563-8083)
PHONE....................847 263-9000
Jeff Baron, *Managing Member*
EMP: 9 **EST:** 2001
SALES (est): 1.65MM **Privately Held**
Web: www.gfiis.com
SIC: 3586 Measuring and dispensing pumps

(G-13780)
GLENMARK INDUSTRIES INC
Also Called: GMI Group
1100 Pidco Dr (46563-1347)
P.O. Box 4098 (30091-4098)
PHONE....................574 936-5788
▲ **EMP:** 130
SIC: 2657 Food containers, folding: made from purchased material

(G-13781)
HARRINGTON NOODLES INC
2915 Commerce St (46563-8991)
P.O. Box 93 (46506-0093)
PHONE....................574 546-3861
Crystal Garza, *Pr*
Francisco Garza, *Pr*
Crystal Garza, *VP*
EMP: 5 **EST:** 1963
SALES (est): 471.21K **Privately Held**
Web: www.harringtonnoodles.com
SIC: 2098 Noodles (e.g. egg, plain, and water), dry

(G-13782)
HONEYWELL INTERNATIONAL INC
Also Called: Honeywell
504 E Garro St (46563-2234)
PHONE....................574 935-0200
Shawn Grobe, *Brnch Mgr*
EMP: 2
Web: www.honeywell.com
SIC: 3724 Aircraft engines and engine parts
PA: Honeywell International Inc.
855 S Mint St
Charlotte NC 28202

(G-13783)
INDIANA METAL STAMPING CO
500 W Harrison St (46563-1324)
PHONE....................574 936-2964
Daniel Altman, *Pr*
EMP: 7 **EST:** 2004
SALES (est): 102.92K **Privately Held**
Web: www.metalstamper.net
SIC: 3469 Stamping metal for the trade

(G-13784)
INDIANA TOOL & MFG CO INC
Also Called: Itamco Company
6100 Michigan Rd (46563)
P.O. Box 399 (46563)
PHONE....................574 936-2112
Gary L Neidig, *CEO*
◆ **EMP:** 138 **EST:** 1955
SQ FT: 80,000
SALES (est): 15.07MM **Privately Held**
Web: www.itamco.com
SIC: 3462 3545 Gear and chain forgings; Machine tool attachments and accessories

(G-13785)
INDUSTRIAL TRANSMISSION EQP
Also Called: I T Equipment
2033 Western Ave (46563-1041)
P.O. Box 340 (46563-0340)
PHONE....................574 936-3028
Dale R Poisel, *Pr*
Paula Poisel, *
▲ **EMP:** 48 **EST:** 1961
SQ FT: 35,000
SALES (est): 7.55MM **Privately Held**
Web: www.itequipment.com
SIC: 3535 5084 3537 3443 Conveyors and conveying equipment; Materials handling machinery; Industrial trucks and tractors; Fabricated plate work (boiler shop)

(G-13786)
INTERSTATE FORESTRY INC
Also Called: Interstate Forestry
10200 W County Line Rd (46563-9418)
PHONE....................574 936-1284
Gary Messer, *Prin*
Bill Carpenter, *Owner*
EMP: 5 **EST:** 1998
SALES (est): 504.12K **Privately Held**
Web: www.interstateforestryinc.com
SIC: 2421 Lumber: rough, sawed, or planed

(G-13787)
IRECO METALS INC
1433 Western Ave (46563-1029)
PHONE....................574 936-2146
John Oliver Junior, *Prin*
EMP: 2 **EST:** 2010
SALES (est): 121.2K **Privately Held**
SIC: 2892 Explosives

(G-13788)
IRVING MATERIALS INC
10988 11th Rd (46563-9037)
PHONE....................574 936-2975
EMP: 5
SALES (corp-wide): 814.09MM **Privately Held**
Web: www.irvmat.com
SIC: 3273 Ready-mixed concrete
PA: Irving Materials, Inc.
8032 N State Road 9
Greenfield IN 46140
317 326-3101

(G-13789)
JOHNS PORTABLE SIIOP WELD
10476 Muckshaw Rd (46563-8557)
PHONE....................574 936-1702
John Cavender, *Owner*
EMP: 5 **EST:** 2017
SALES (est): 25.09K **Privately Held**
Web: www.blackmoonenterprises.com
SIC: 7692 Welding repair

(G-13790)
JOHNS WELDING AND FABRICATION
1203 N Michigan St (46563-1115)
PHONE....................574 936-1702
John Cavinder, *Prin*
EMP: 2 **EST:** 2007
SALES (est): 148.35K **Privately Held**
SIC: 1799 7692 Welding on site; Welding repair

(G-13791)
LASALLE BRISTOL CORPORATION
B P C Manufacturing
1755 N Oak Dr (46563-3413)
PHONE....................574 936-9894
Don Rodda, *Mgr*
EMP: 18
SQ FT: 57,000
SALES (corp-wide): 3.47B **Publicly Held**
Web: www.lasallebristol.com
SIC: 5023 3432 Floor coverings; Faucets and spigots, metal and plastic
HQ: Lasalle Bristol Corporation
601 County Road 17
Elkhart IN 46516
574 295-8400

(G-13792)
LEAR CORPORATION
2000 Walter Glaub Dr (46563-1386)
PHONE....................574 935-3818
EMP: 79
SALES (corp-wide): 23.47B **Publicly Held**
Web: www.lear.com
SIC: 3714 Motor vehicle parts and accessories
PA: Lear Corporation
21557 Telegraph Rd
Southfield MI 48033
248 447-1500

(G-13793)
LOVES TRAVEL STOPS
2952 Gary Dr (46563-8897)
PHONE....................574 935-4103
EMP: 18
SALES (corp-wide): 8.21B **Privately Held**
Web: www.loves.com
SIC: 7534 7349 Rebuilding and retreading tires; Lighting maintenance service
PA: Love's Travel Stops & Country Stores, Inc.
10601 N Pennsylvania Ave
Oklahoma City OK 73120
405 302-6500

(G-13794)
LYONDLLLBSELL ADVNCED PLYMERS I
1301 Flora St (46563-1344)
PHONE....................574 935-5131
Karen Ray, *Brnch Mgr*
EMP: 22
SQ FT: 25,000
Web: www.lyondellbasell.com
SIC: 2851 2816 Lacquers, varnishes, enamels, and other coatings; Inorganic pigments
HQ: Lyondellbasell Advanced Polymers Inc.
1221 Mckinney St Ste 300
Houston TX 77010
713 309-7200

(G-13795)
MAAX INC
Also Called: Maax Aker Plastics
1001 N Oak Dr (46563-3416)
P.O. Box 484 (46563-0484)
PHONE....................574 936-3838
Christopher Perron, *Prin*
EMP: 30
SALES (corp-wide): 582.45MM **Privately Held**
Web: www.maax.com
SIC: 3088 3431 Tubs (bath, shower, and laundry), plastics; Metal sanitary ware
HQ: Maax Bath Inc
160 Boul Saint-Joseph
Lachine QC H8S 2
877 438-6229

(G-13796)
MARTINS LIME SERVICE INC
2551 Michigan Rd (46563-9529)
P.O. Box 154 (46537-0154)
PHONE....................574 784-2270
Gary W Martin, *Pr*
EMP: 1 **EST:** 1980
SALES (est): 117.92K **Privately Held**
SIC: 3299 5211 Sand lime products; Sand and gravel

(G-13797)
MILLENIUM SHEET METAL INC
6730 W County Line Rd (46563-8843)
PHONE....................574 935-9101
John Drews, *Pr*
EMP: 10 **EST:** 1986
SQ FT: 14,900
SALES (est): 261.64K **Privately Held**
SIC: 1711 3444 Ventilation and duct work contractor; Sheet metalwork

(G-13798)
MO SIGNS LLC
1842 W Jefferson St (46563-8020)
PHONE....................574 780-4075
EMP: 6 **EST:** 2011
SALES (est): 344.72K **Privately Held**
SIC: 3993 Signs and advertising specialties

(G-13799)
OASIS LIFESTYLE LLC
Also Called: Oasis Bath
1400 Pidco Dr (46563-1353)
P.O. Box 82 (46563-0082)
PHONE....................574 948-0004
Mark Naylor, *Pr*
Andrew Aker, *VP*
EMP: 16 **EST:** 2007
SALES (est): 4.73MM **Privately Held**
Web: www.oasisbath.com
SIC: 5719 3088 3842 Bath accessories; Shower stalls, fiberglass and plastics; Whirlpool baths, hydrotherapy equipment

(G-13800)
PACTIV LLC
1411 Pidco Dr (46563-1352)
PHONE....................574 936-7065
Dennis Hughes, *Mgr*
EMP: 27
SQ FT: 30,000
Web: www.pactivevergreen.com
SIC: 3069 3081 2821 2671 Foam rubber; Unsupported plastics film and sheet; Plastics materials and resins; Paper; coated and laminated packaging
HQ: Pactiv Llc
1900 W Field Ct
Lake Forest IL 60045
847 482-2000

(G-13801)
PLYMOUTH FOUNDRY INC
523 W Harrison St (46563-1388)
P.O. Box 537 (46563-0537)
PHONE....................574 936-2106
Sam C Schlosser, *Pr*
William F Schlosser, *
James D Bopp, *
EMP: 36 **EST:** 1931
SQ FT: 60,000
SALES (est): 4.82MM **Privately Held**
Web: www.plymouthfoundry.com
SIC: 3321 3599 3322 Gray iron castings, nec; Machine shop, jobbing and repair; Malleable iron foundries

GEOGRAPHIC SECTION

Plymouth - Marshall County (G-13825)

(G-13802)
PLYMOUTH MOLDING GROUP LLC
2925 Commerce St (46563-8991)
PHONE..................574 933-4189
EMP: 10 **EST:** 2013
SALES (est): 1.45MM **Privately Held**
Web: www.plymouthmoldinggroup.com
SIC: 3089 Injection molding of plastics

(G-13803)
PLYMOUTH PALLET COMPANY INC
1145 Markley Dr (46563-3206)
PHONE..................574 935-5553
Vicki Sturgell, *Pr*
Donna Zimmerman, *Pr*
Tom Zimmerman, *VP*
EMP: 11 **EST:** 2003
SALES (est): 1.04MM **Privately Held**
Web: www.plymouthpalletanddrum.co.uk
SIC: 2448 Pallets, wood

(G-13804)
PLYMOUTH PDTS ACQUISITION INC
1800 Jim Neu Dr Ste 7 (46563-3306)
PHONE..................574 936-4757
Don Wisniewski, *Pr*
▲ **EMP:** 6 **EST:** 1959
SQ FT: 10,000
SALES (est): 789.4K **Privately Held**
Web: www.plymouthproducts.com
SIC: 3291 Abrasive products

(G-13805)
PONTIAC ENGRAVING
900 W Garro St (46563)
PHONE..................630 834-4424
Bruce Solyom, *Owner*
EMP: 3 **EST:** 1975
SALES (est): 149.85K **Privately Held**
SIC: 2796 3545 3544 3452 Engraving on copper, steel, wood, or rubber; printing plates; Machine tool accessories; Special dies, tools, jigs, and fixtures; Bolts, nuts, rivets, and washers

(G-13806)
PREGIS LLC
1411 Pidco Dr (46563-1352)
PHONE..................574 936-7065
Ron Duerksen, *Brnch Mgr*
EMP: 5
SALES (corp-wide): 1.28MM **Privately Held**
Web: www.pregis.com
SIC: 5199 3086 Packaging materials; Packaging and shipping materials, foamed plastics
HQ: Pregis Llc
2345 Waukegan Rd Ste 120
Bannockburn IL 60015

(G-13807)
PRETZELS INC
Also Called: PRETZELS INC
2910 Commerce St (46563-8991)
PHONE..................574 941-2201
EMP: 27
SALES (corp-wide): 121.47MM **Privately Held**
Web: www.pretzels-inc.com
SIC: 5461 2099 Pretzels; Food preparations, nec
PA: Pretzels, Llc
123 Harvest Rd
Bluffton IN 46714
800 456-4838

(G-13808)
RBC BEARINGS INCORPORATED
2912 Gary Dr (46563-8897)
PHONE..................574 935-3027
Michael J Hartnett, *Brnch Mgr*
EMP: 1
SALES (corp-wide): 1.56B **Publicly Held**
Web: www.rbcbearings.com
SIC: 3562 3312 Ball and roller bearings; Blast furnaces and steel mills
PA: Rbc Bearings Incorporated
1 Tribiology Ctr
Oxford CT 06478
203 267-7001

(G-13809)
RBC PRCSION PDTS - PLYMUTH INC (DH)
2928 Gary Dr (46563-8897)
PHONE..................574 935-3027
John Toner, *Pr*
Daniel A Bergeron, *
Thomas J Williams, *
Thomas C Crainer, *
Richard J Edwards, *
◆ **EMP:** 60 **EST:** 2004
SQ FT: 32,000
SALES (est): 20.13MM
SALES (corp-wide): 1.56B **Publicly Held**
Web: www.rbcbearings.com
SIC: 3562 3312 Ball and roller bearings; Blast furnaces and steel mills
HQ: Roller Bearing Company Of America, Inc.
102 Willenbrock Rd
Oxford CT 06478
203 267-7001

(G-13810)
READY PAC FOODS INC
Also Called: Tanimura & Antle
2050 N Oak Dr (46563-3407)
PHONE..................574 935-9800
Dan Correll, *Mgr*
EMP: 164
SALES (corp-wide): 2.67MM **Privately Held**
Web: www.readypac.com
SIC: 2099 5148 Salads, fresh or refrigerated; Vegetables, fresh
HQ: Ready Pac Foods, Inc.
4401 Foxdale St
Irwindale CA 91706
626 856-8686

(G-13811)
RIDGE IRON LLC
1911 Western Ave (46563-1039)
PHONE..................646 450-0092
Carson Garner, *Managing Member*
EMP: 6 **EST:** 2017
SALES (est): 242.03K **Privately Held**
Web: www.ridgeiron.com
SIC: 3999 5051 5999 Manufacturing industries, nec; Structural shapes, iron or steel; Miscellaneous retail stores, nec

(G-13812)
RONALD HOLLOWAY
Also Called: Holloway Electric Motor Svc
420 Klinger St (46563-1241)
PHONE..................574 223-6825
Ronald Holloway, *Owner*
EMP: 4 **EST:** 1961
SALES (est): 173.77K **Privately Held**
SIC: 7694 Electric motor repair

(G-13813)
SHILOH SUSIEBELL LLC
304 Webster Ave (46563-2749)
PHONE..................574 936-8412
Shiloh Fonseca, *Prin*
EMP: 6 **EST:** 2016
SALES (est): 100.88K **Privately Held**
Web: www.durashiloh.com
SIC: 3465 Automotive stampings

(G-13814)
STONE QUARY
Also Called: Aggregate Service
10988 11th Rd (46563-9037)
PHONE..................574 936-2975
Sue Drake, *Mgr*
EMP: 7
SQ FT: 800
SALES (corp-wide): 2.25MM **Privately Held**
Web: www.rockhollowgolf.com
SIC: 1442 Construction sand and gravel
PA: The Stone Quary
350 N 150 W
Peru IN 46970
765 473-5578

(G-13815)
SUPERB HORTICULTURE LLC
2811 Us Highway 31 (46563-9196)
PHONE..................800 567-8264
▲ **EMP:** 16 **EST:** 2001
SALES (est): 1.97MM **Privately Held**
Web: www.superbhorticulture.com
SIC: 3523 Farm machinery and equipment

(G-13816)
THERMO CUBE INCORPORATED
2255 Walter Glaub Dr (46563-3435)
P.O. Box 452 (46563-0452)
PHONE..................574 936-5096
Benjamin T Clark Junior, *Pr*
EMP: 8 **EST:** 1999
SALES (est): 156.82K **Privately Held**
Web: www.thermocube.com
SIC: 3699 Electrical equipment and supplies, nec

(G-13817)
TITUS INC
9887 6b Rd (46563-8913)
PHONE..................574 936-3345
Thomas Read, *Pr*
EMP: 13 **EST:** 1992
SQ FT: 17,400
SALES (est): 854.17K **Privately Held**
Web: www.titusmfg.com
SIC: 7692 3599 3541 3446 Welding repair; Custom machinery; Machine tools, metal cutting type; Architectural metalwork

(G-13818)
TITUS MFG LLC
7991 Lilac Rd (46563-9502)
PHONE..................574 286-1928
EMP: 5 **EST:** 2018
SALES (est): 125.25K **Privately Held**
Web: www.titusmfg.com
SIC: 3999 Manufacturing industries, nec

(G-13819)
TNT FABRICATING LLC
9841 Sunnyside Dr (46563-8695)
PHONE..................574 540-2465
EMP: 5 **EST:** 2018
SALES (est): 158.5K **Privately Held**
Web: www.tntfabricating.com
SIC: 7692 Welding repair

(G-13820)
TOWN & COUNTRY PRESS INC
1920 Jim Neu Dr (46563-1396)
P.O. Box 417 (46563-0417)
PHONE..................574 936-9505
Philip Martin, *Pr*
Sherrie Martin, *Sec*
Benjamin Martin, *Prin*
Philip Martin Junior, *VP*
EMP: 12 **EST:** 1972
SQ FT: 10,000
SALES (est): 490.8K **Privately Held**
SIC: 2752 2759 2791 Offset printing; Letterpress printing; Typesetting

(G-13821)
TRADING POST
523 E Jefferson St (46563-1829)
PHONE..................574 935-5460
Diana Harrell, *Owner*
EMP: 8 **EST:** 2007
SALES (est): 99.56K **Privately Held**
SIC: 2711 Newspapers

(G-13822)
U S GRANULES CORPORATION (PA)
1433 Western Ave (46563-1098)
P.O. Box 130 (46563-0130)
PHONE..................574 936-2146
John J Oliver, *Pr*
Joyce Klingerman, *Sec*
▲ **EMP:** 32 **EST:** 1963
SALES (est): 9.76MM
SALES (corp-wide): 9.76MM **Privately Held**
Web: www.usgranules.com
SIC: 3399 Metal powders, pastes, and flakes

(G-13823)
VALMONT TELECOMMUNICATIONS INC (HQ)
Also Called: Valmont Structures
1545 Pidco Dr (46563)
P.O. Box 128 (46563)
PHONE..................574 936-7221
Myron C Noble, *Pr*
R Andrew Massey, *Sec*
Mark C Jaksich, *CFO*
◆ **EMP:** 13 **EST:** 1996
SQ FT: 230,000
SALES (est): 94.57MM
SALES (corp-wide): 4.17B **Publicly Held**
Web: www.valmontstructures.com
SIC: 3441 3365 3369 Tower sections, radio and television transmission; Aluminum and aluminum-based alloy castings; White metal castings (lead, tin, antimony), except die
PA: Valmont Industries, Inc.
15000 Valmont Plz
Omaha NE 68154
402 963-1000

(G-13824)
VALMONT TELECOMMUNICATIONS INC
Also Called: Valmont Site Pro 1
2400 Walter Glaub Dr (46563-3434)
PHONE..................877 467-4763
Myron C Noble, *Ch Bd*
EMP: 18
SALES (corp-wide): 4.17B **Publicly Held**
Web: www.valmontstructures.com
SIC: 3441 3365 3369 Tower sections, radio and television transmission; Aluminum and aluminum-based alloy castings; White metal castings (lead, tin, antimony), except die
HQ: Valmont Telecommunications, Inc.
1545 Pidco Dr
Plymouth IN 46563
574 936-7221

(G-13825)
VIKING PAPER COMPANY
Also Called: Viking Paper
1001 Pidco Dr (46563-1368)
PHONE..................574 936-6300
EMP: 50

(PA)=Parent Co (HQ)=Headquarters
✪ = New Business established in last 2 years

Plymouth - Marshall County (G-13826)

SALES (corp-wide): 21.28MM **Privately Held**
Web: www.packpros.net
SIC: 5113 2631 Bags, paper and disposable plastic; Paperboard mills
PA: Viking Paper Company
5148 Stickney Ave
Toledo OH 43612
419 729-4951

(G-13826)
WDMI INC
2341 W Jefferson St (46563-8023)
PHONE..................574 936-2136
TOLL FREE: 888
EMP: 95
SIC: 3273 7359 Ready-mixed concrete; Tool rental

(G-13827)
WESTROCK COMPANY
1000 Pidco Dr (46563-1367)
PHONE..................219 229-0981
EMP: 7
SALES (corp-wide): 20.31B **Privately Held**
Web: www.westrock.com
SIC: 2653 Boxes, corrugated: made from purchased materials
PA: Westrock Company
1000 Abernathy Rd
Atlanta GA 30328
770 448-2193

(G-13828)
WESTROCK CP LLC
1100 Pidco Dr (46563-1347)
PHONE..................574 936-2118
Owen Glock, *Brnch Mgr*
EMP: 5
SALES (corp-wide): 20.31B **Privately Held**
Web: www.westrock.com
SIC: 4225 2674 2672 2671 General warehousing and storage; Bags: uncoated paper and multiwall; Paper; coated and laminated, nec; Paper; coated and laminated packaging
HQ: Westrock Cp, Llc
1000 Abernathy Rd Ste 125
Atlanta GA 30328

(G-13829)
WESTROCK RKT LLC
1810 Pidco Dr (46563-1361)
PHONE..................574 936-2118
Owen Glock, *Brnch Mgr*
EMP: 6
SALES (corp-wide): 20.31B **Privately Held**
Web: www.westrock.com
SIC: 2653 Boxes, corrugated: made from purchased materials
HQ: Westrock Rkt, Llc
1000 Abernathy Rd Ste 125
Atlanta GA 30328
770 448-2193

(G-13830)
WIERS FLEET PARTNERS INC (PA)
2111 Jim Neu Dr (46563-3302)
PHONE..................574 936-4076
EMP: 10 EST: 1982
SQ FT: 80,000
SALES (est): 5.87MM **Privately Held**
Web: www.wiers.com
SIC: 3713 Truck bodies (motor vehicles)

(G-13831)
WINONA BUILDING PRODUCTS LLC
506 North St (46563-1022)
P.O. Box 170 (46524-0170)
PHONE..................574 822-0100
Jamie Visker, *CEO*
Jamie Veisker, *Prin*
Craig Effenberger, *Pr*
Brian Bailey, *Pr*
EMP: 10 EST: 2016
SALES (est): 2.02MM **Privately Held**
Web: www.winonabp.com
SIC: 3644 Insulators and insulation materials, electrical

(G-13832)
WITT GALVANIZING
2631 Jim Neu Dr (46563-3311)
PHONE..................574 935-4500
R Harris, *Prin*
EMP: 8 EST: 2007
SALES (est): 298.87K **Privately Held**
SIC: 3479 Galvanizing of iron, steel, or end-formed products

(G-13833)
WITT INDUSTRIES INC
2631 Jim Neu Dr (46563-3311)
PHONE..................574 935-4500
Philip Burner, *Mgr*
EMP: 27
Web: www.witt.com
SIC: 3479 Galvanizing of iron, steel, or end-formed products
HQ: Witt Industries, Inc.
4600 N Masn Montgomery Rd
Mason OH 45040
513 871-5700

(G-13834)
WORLD GRAFFIX LLC
14717 Lincoln Hwy (46563-8017)
PHONE..................574 936-1927
EMP: 5 EST: 2000
SALES (est): 233.94K **Privately Held**
Web: www.worldgraffix.com
SIC: 7336 3993 Graphic arts and related design; Signs and advertising specialties

(G-13835)
ZENTIS NORTH AMERICA LLC
2050 N Oak Dr (46563-3407)
PHONE..................574 941-1100
Norbert Weichele, *Brnch Mgr*
EMP: 300
SALES (corp-wide): 738.23MM **Privately Held**
Web: www.zentis.de
SIC: 2033 Canned fruits and specialties
HQ: Zentis North America, Llc
1741 Tomlinson Rd
Philadelphia PA 19116
267 623-8000

(G-13836)
ZENTIS NORTH AMERICA HOLDG LLC
Also Called: Zentis
2050 N Oak Dr (46563-3407)
PHONE..................574 941-1100
Norbert Weichele, *CEO*
▲ EMP: 190 EST: 2006
SALES (est): 42.37MM
SALES (corp-wide): 738.23MM **Privately Held**
Web: www.zentis.de
SIC: 2033 2034 2037 Canned fruits and specialties; Dried and dehydrated fruits; Frozen fruits and vegetables
PA: Zentis Fruchtwelt Gmbh & Co. Kg
Julicher Str. 177
Aachen NW 52070
24147600

Poland
Owen County

(G-13837)
RON GLASSCOCK
Also Called: Signs of Times
3282 N County Road 700 E (47868-8217)
PHONE..................812 986-2342
Ron Glasscock, *Owner*
EMP: 2 EST: 1988
SALES (est): 78K **Privately Held**
SIC: 7336 3993 Creative services to advertisers, except writers; Signs and advertising specialties

(G-13838)
TOM WEST FARMS
Also Called: Tom West Repair
8235 E State Road 42 (47868-8220)
PHONE..................812 986-2162
Tom West, *Owner*
EMP: 1 EST: 1992
SALES (est): 66.72K **Privately Held**
SIC: 0115 0116 0211 3541 Corn; Soybeans; Beef cattle feedlots; Machine tool replacement & repair parts, metal cutting types

Poneto
Wells County

(G-13839)
ANDERSEN CORPORATION
219 W State Road 218 (46781-5430)
P.O. Box 116 (46781-0116)
PHONE..................260 694-6861
William Wolf, *Prin*
EMP: 5
SALES (corp-wide): 1.78B **Privately Held**
Web: www.andersenwindows.com
SIC: 2431 Windows, wood
PA: Andersen Corporation
100 4th Ave N
Bayport MN 55003
651 264-5150

(G-13840)
COUNTRY CABINETS LLC
3900 W State Road 218 (46731-9747)
PHONE..................260 694-6777
Ted Habegger, *Owner*
EMP: 6 EST: 1981
SALES (est): 421.31K **Privately Held**
SIC: 2434 2511 Wood kitchen cabinets; Wood household furniture

(G-13841)
HOOSIER ENGINEERING CO INC
7726 S Meridian Rd (46781-9510)
PHONE..................260 694-6887
Steve Studebaker, *Pr*
EMP: 2 EST: 1997
SALES (est): 208.47K **Privately Held**
Web: www.hoosierengineering.com
SIC: 3325 Steel foundries, nec

Portage
Porter County

(G-13842)
A PLUS DATACOMM
3282 Roswell Dr (46368-5154)
PHONE..................219 472-1644
Jose G Martinez, *Prin*
EMP: 2 EST: 2009
SALES (est): 190.07K **Privately Held**
SIC: 3669 Communications equipment, nec

(G-13843)
ANITA COLE ◊
Also Called: Ramco
3071 Dutch Mill St (46368)
PHONE..................907 479-2245
Anita Cole, *Owner*
EMP: 5 EST: 2022
SALES (est): 65.19K **Privately Held**
SIC: 2999 Petroleum and coal products, nec

(G-13844)
AQUESTIVE THERAPEUTICS INC
6465 Ameriplex Dr (46368-1389)
PHONE..................219 762-4143
EMP: 46
Web: www.aquestive.com
SIC: 2834 Pharmaceutical preparations
PA: Aquestive Therapeutics, Inc.
30 Technology Dr Ste 2a
Warren NJ 07059

(G-13845)
AQUESTIVE THERAPEUTICS INC
6560 Melton Rd (46368-1234)
PHONE..................219 762-3165
Joseph Crusco, *Brnch Mgr*
EMP: 46
Web: www.aquestive.com
SIC: 2834 Pharmaceutical preparations
PA: Aquestive Therapeutics, Inc.
30 Technology Dr Ste 2a
Warren NJ 07059

(G-13846)
AUDIO FLOW LLC
2121 Yule St (46368-1792)
PHONE..................219 230-6330
Jocqueline Protho, *Managing Member*
EMP: 1 EST: 2018
SALES (est): 32.71K **Privately Held**
Web: www.theaudioflow.com
SIC: 5735 3861 Audio tapes, prerecorded; Sound recording and reproducing equipment, motion picture

(G-13847)
B NUTTY LLC
6370 Ameriplex Dr Ste 102 (46368-1798)
PHONE..................844 426-8889
EMP: 80 EST: 2014
SALES (est): 5.25MM **Privately Held**
Web: www.bnutty.com
SIC: 2038 Frozen specialties, nec

(G-13848)
BADGER DAYLIGHTING CORP
5597 Old Porter Rd Ste D (46368-6209)
PHONE..................219 762-9177
EMP: 6 EST: 2015
SALES (est): 142.9K **Privately Held**
Web: www.badgerinc.com
SIC: 3648 Lighting equipment, nec

(G-13849)
BETA STEEL CORP
6500 S Boundary Rd (46368-1334)
PHONE..................219 787-0001
John Goodwin, *Prin*
EMP: 5 EST: 2016
SALES (est): 426.1K **Privately Held**
Web: www.betasteelcorp.com
SIC: 3312 Beehive coke oven products

(G-13850)
BUSINESS CONNECTION LLC
Also Called: Minuteman Press
2708 Willowcreek Rd (46368-3516)
PHONE..................219 762-5660

GEOGRAPHIC SECTION

Portage - Porter County (G-13872)

EMP: 7 **EST:** 2012
SALES (est): 297.13K **Privately Held**
Web: chanhassen-mn.minutemanpress.com
SIC: 2752 Commercial printing, lithographic

(G-13851)
BUSINESS HEALTH
5715 Independence Ave (46368-3311)
PHONE 219 762-7105
Steve Padilla, *Owner*
EMP: 2 **EST:** 1995
SALES (est): 105.22K **Privately Held**
Web: www.businesshealth.com.au
SIC: 2899 Drug testing kits, blood and urine

(G-13852)
CALUMITE COMPANY LLC
1605 Adler Cir Ste I (46368-6414)
PHONE 219 787-8667
Mark Abraham, *Managing Member*
EMP: 7 **EST:** 2002
SALES (est): 2.33MM
SALES (corp-wide): 513.22MM **Privately Held**
Web: www.calumitellc.com
SIC: 5099 3211 Containers: glass, metal or plastic; Sheet glass
PA: Edw. C. Levy Co.
9300 Dix
Dearborn MI 48120
313 429-2200

(G-13853)
CAMACO LLC
6515 Ameriplex Dr Ste B (46368-7755)
PHONE 248 657-0246
Jesus Tome, *Genl Mgr*
EMP: 3 **EST:** 2018
SQ FT: 142,000
SALES (est): 1.08MM
SALES (corp-wide): 494.73MM **Privately Held**
Web: www.camacollc.com
SIC: 3714 Motor vehicle body components and frame
HQ: Camaco, Llc
37000 W Twlve Mile Rd Ste
Farmington Hills MI 48331
248 442-8100

(G-13854)
CENTRAL STEEL AND WIRE CO LLC
Also Called: Central Steel Coil Processing
501 George Nelson Dr (46368)
PHONE 219 787-5000
Kent Pukes, *Brnch Mgr*
EMP: 1
Web: www.centralsteel.com
SIC: 5051 3694 Steel; Engine electrical equipment
HQ: Central Steel And Wire Company, Llc
23301 S Central Ave
University Park IL 60484
773 471-3800

(G-13855)
CHROME DEPOSIT CORPORATION (HQ)
6640 Melton Rd (46368-1279)
PHONE 219 763-1571
Philip Court, *Pr*
Ken Langfitt, *
G R Conley, *
Lisa Woelk, *
EMP: 45 **EST:** 1982
SQ FT: 50,000
SALES (est): 26.78MM
SALES (corp-wide): 18.05B **Publicly Held**
Web: www.chromedeposit.com
SIC: 3471 Chromium plating of metals or formed products
PA: United States Steel Corp
600 Grant St
Pittsburgh PA 15219
412 433-1121

(G-13856)
CLANCYS OF PORTAGE
2542 Portage Mall (46368-3006)
PHONE 219 764-4995
Michelle Clancy, *Pr*
EMP: 25 **EST:** 2002
SALES (est): 186.87K **Privately Held**
SIC: 5812 5182 2599 American restaurant; Liquor; Bar, restaurant and cafeteria furniture

(G-13857)
CROWN ELEC SVCS & AUTOMTN INC (DH)
Also Called: Crown E.S.A.
5960 Southport Rd (46368-6407)
PHONE 972 929-4700
Thomas B Adams, *Pr*
Bradly Hendrickson, *
William English, *
Thomas B Adams, *Sec*
EMP: 97 **EST:** 1992
SQ FT: 33,191
SALES (est): 21.81MM **Privately Held**
Web: crown-electrical-services-automation-inc-in-portage-in.cityfos.com
SIC: 8711 3823 3594 Electrical or electronic engineering; Process control instruments; Fluid power pumps and motors
HQ: Glenmount Global Solutions, Llc
8614 Jacquemin Dr
West Chester OH 45069
219 762-0700

(G-13858)
D & E AUTO ELECTRIC INC
5665 Old Porter Rd (46368-1137)
PHONE 219 763-3892
Edward Carda, *Pr*
Carol Carda, *VP*
Janice Carda, *Sec*
EMP: 10 **EST:** 1980
SQ FT: 3,200
SALES (est): 848.14K **Privately Held**
Web: d-e-auto-electric.business.site
SIC: 3621 3714 3694 3625 Starters, for motors; Drive shafts, motor vehicle; Alternators, automotive; Relays and industrial controls

(G-13859)
DOUGLAS DUMPSTER AND SVCS LLC
6212 Us Highway 6 Unit 294 (46368-5057)
PHONE 630 460-8727
EMP: 1
SALES (est): 69.27K **Privately Held**
SIC: 3443 Dumpsters, garbage

(G-13860)
DUNES INVESTMENT INC
6672 Melton Rd (46368)
PHONE 219 764-4270
William Stockwell, *Pr*
Ron Hough, *Sec*
EMP: 18 **EST:** 1992
SQ FT: 12,000
SALES (est): 2.33MM **Privately Held**
Web: www.skimcut.com
SIC: 3599 7692 3541 Machine shop, jobbing and repair; Welding repair; Machine tools, metal cutting type

(G-13861)
ENTERTAINMENT EXPRESS
3460 Anthony Dr (46368-8004)
P.O. Box 934 (46368-0934)
PHONE 219 763-3610
TOLL FREE: 800
Kerry Kapica, *Owner*
EMP: 3 **EST:** 1988
SALES (est): 65.18K **Privately Held**
Web: www.entertainmentexpressdjs.com
SIC: 5947 7929 2759 Gifts and novelties; Disc jockey service; Invitation and stationery printing and engraving

(G-13862)
EXPRESS PRINTING & COPYING
Also Called: X-Press Printing
2554 Portage Mall (46368-3006)
PHONE 219 762-3508
David Capron Senior, *Pr*
EMP: 6 **EST:** 1983
SQ FT: 3,000
SALES (est): 507.63K **Privately Held**
Web: www.xpressportage.com
SIC: 2752 Offset printing

(G-13863)
FERALLOY CORPORATION
6755 Waterway Dr (46368-1383)
P.O. Box 1349 (62040-1349)
PHONE 219 787-9698
John Hirt, *Brnch Mgr*
EMP: 60
SALES (corp-wide): 14.81B **Publicly Held**
Web: www.feralloy.com
SIC: 5051 3316 Iron or steel flat products; Cold finishing of steel shapes
HQ: Feralloy Corporation
8600 W Bryn Mawr Ave 800n
Chicago IL 60631
503 286-8869

(G-13864)
FINALMILE-LOGISTICS LLC ✪
3125 Yukon St (46368-4597)
PHONE 773 259-0727
EMP: 1 **EST:** 2022
SALES (est): 60.08K **Privately Held**
SIC: 3537 7389 Trucks, tractors, loaders, carriers, and similar equipment; Business Activities at Non-Commercial Site

(G-13865)
FIRST CREATIVE INGREDIENTS INC
Also Called: Fci Flavors
6625 Daniel Burnham Dr Ste D (46368-1698)
PHONE 219 764-0202
EMP: 4
SALES (corp-wide): 295.88K **Privately Held**
SIC: 2087 Flavoring extracts and syrups, nec
PA: First Creative Ingredients, Inc.
1208 N Swift Rd
Addison IL 60101
630 373-1707

(G-13866)
FIVE STAR HYDRAULICS INC
1210 Crisman Rd (46368-1231)
PHONE 219 762-1619
Timothy Bowgren, *Pr*
▲ **EMP:** 31 **EST:** 1977
SQ FT: 2,400
SALES (est): 2.16MM **Privately Held**
Web: www.fivestarhydraulics.com
SIC: 7699 3593 Hydraulic equipment repair; Fluid power cylinders and actuators

(G-13867)
FLOWSERVE CORPORATION
Also Called: Flowserve
6675 Daniel Burnham Dr Ste F (46368-1794)
PHONE 219 763-1000
Scott Ton, *Brnch Mgr*
EMP: 9
SALES (corp-wide): 4.32B **Publicly Held**
Web: www.flowserve.com
SIC: 3561 Pumps and pumping equipment
PA: Flowserve Corporation
5215 N Ocnnor Blvd Ste 70
Irving TX 75039
972 443-6500

(G-13868)
GI PROPERTIES INC (PA)
Also Called: Correct Construction
6610 Melton Rd (46368-1236)
PHONE 219 763-1177
Paul K Graegin, *Pr*
EMP: 5 **EST:** 1977
SALES (est): 47.52MM
SALES (corp-wide): 47.52MM **Privately Held**
Web: www.gipropertiesgroup.com
SIC: 1623 3441 7353 Pipeline construction, nsk; Fabricated structural metal; Heavy construction equipment rental

(G-13869)
GLOBAL STONE PORTAGE LLC
6600 Us Highway 12 (46368-1276)
PHONE 219 787-9190
Richard Powers, *Mgr*
EMP: 10 **EST:** 2007
SALES (est): 207.97K **Privately Held**
SIC: 1422 5211 Crushed and broken limestone; Lime and plaster

(G-13870)
GONZALES ENTERPRISES INC
2681 Teresa St (46368-3641)
PHONE 219 841-1756
Christopher Gonzales, *Prin*
EMP: 9 **EST:** 2014
SALES (est): 205.08K **Privately Held**
SIC: 3732 Boatbuilding and repairing

(G-13871)
GOODYEAR TIRE & RUBBER COMPANY
Also Called: Goodyear
6791 Melton Rd (46368-1246)
PHONE 219 762-0651
Jason Klein, *Brnch Mgr*
EMP: 4
SALES (corp-wide): 20.07B **Publicly Held**
Web: www.goodyear.com
SIC: 5531 3011 Automotive tires; Inner tubes, all types
PA: The Goodyear Tire & Rubber Company
200 Innovation Way
Akron OH 44316
330 796-2121

(G-13872)
GREAT LAKES GRANITE LLC
Also Called: Crop and Drop Granite Surfaces
6050 Eagle Ave (46368)
PHONE 708 474-8800
Connie Grashel, *Managing Member*
EMP: 1 **EST:** 2002
SALES (est): 264.64K **Privately Held**
Web: www.greatlakesgm.com
SIC: 1411 5032 Granite dimension stone; Granite building stone

GEOGRAPHIC SECTION

(G-13873)
HALYARD CORPORATION
6610 Shepherd Ave (46368)
PHONE..................................219 515-2820
Stevan Michael Desancic, *CEO*
EMP: 50 **EST:** 2018
SALES (est): 4.64MM **Privately Held**
Web: www.halyardcorporation.com
SIC: 1796 3423 1389 7699 Millwright; Ironworkers' hand tools; Construction, repair, and dismantling services; Construction equipment repair

(G-13874)
HAMILTON CANVAS INC
2305 Hamstrom Rd Ste F (46368-2274)
PHONE..................................219 763-1686
Rhonda Hamilton, *Owner*
EMP: 6 **EST:** 2006
SALES (est): 79.33K **Privately Held**
Web: www.hamiltoncanvas.com
SIC: 2211 Canvas

(G-13875)
HANDYPRO OF NORTHWEST INDIANA
6212 Us Highway 6 Ste 225 (46368-5057)
PHONE..................................219 707-8240
EMP: 3 **EST:** 2018
SALES (est): 68.28K **Privately Held**
Web: www.handypro.com
SIC: 3732 Boatbuilding and repairing

(G-13876)
HOOSIER DADDY CUSTOM TEES
5364 Central Ave (46368-2812)
PHONE..................................218 308-3544
Amanda White, *Prin*
EMP: 5 **EST:** 2019
SALES (est): 95.07K **Privately Held**
Web: www.importantlocalbusinesses.com
SIC: 2759 Screen printing

(G-13877)
INSANA TEES
2808 Woodward St (46368-3325)
PHONE..................................219 801-5104
EMP: 5 **EST:** 2019
SALES (est): 242.69K **Privately Held**
SIC: 2759 Screen printing

(G-13878)
IONPCS LLC
2867 Carmel St (46368-3119)
PHONE..................................219 510-2073
EMP: 4 **EST:** 2010
SALES (est): 178.66K **Privately Held**
Web: www.ionpcs.net
SIC: 3861 Photographic equipment and supplies

(G-13879)
J V CRANE & ENGINEERING INC
3084 Edgewood St (46368)
P.O. Box 543 (46342)
PHONE..................................219 942-8566
Philip Victor, *Pr*
Wayne Sabin, *Sec*
EMP: 23 **EST:** 1978
SALES (est): 2.28MM **Privately Held**
Web: www.jvcrane.com
SIC: 3536 1731 Cranes, overhead traveling; General electrical contractor

(G-13880)
KONRADY PLASTICS INC
1780 Coppes Ct (46368-1283)
PHONE..................................219 763-7001
TOLL FREE: 800
EMP: 25 **EST:** 1981
SALES (est): 3.74MM **Privately Held**
Web: www.konradyplastics.com
SIC: 3089 Plastics hardware and building products

(G-13881)
LANCES DRVSHAFT COMPONENTS INC
2076 Dombey Rd (46368-1441)
PHONE..................................219 762-2531
TOLL FREE: 800
Lance Morris, *Pr*
EMP: 3 **EST:** 1994
SQ FT: 1,600
SALES (est): 300K **Privately Held**
Web: www.lancesdriveshaft.com
SIC: 7539 3714 Automotive repair shops, nec; Drive shafts, motor vehicle

(G-13882)
LOCC INDUSTRIES LLC
23 Beach Ln (46368-1056)
PHONE..................................219 575-2727
Daniel Coates, *Prin*
EMP: 4 **EST:** 2019
SALES (est): 107.06K **Privately Held**
SIC: 3999 Manufacturing industries, nec

(G-13883)
LYNN BROS ELECTRIC INC
5685 Old Porter Rd (46368-1137)
PHONE..................................219 762-6386
Eric Lynn, *Prin*
EMP: 9 **EST:** 2011
SALES (est): 249.21K **Privately Held**
Web: www.ampselectric.com
SIC: 3699 1731 Electrical equipment and supplies, nec; Electrical work

(G-13884)
MACTECH INC
5589 Old Porter Rd (46368-1135)
PHONE..................................219 734-6503
EMP: 6 **EST:** 2019
SALES (est): 81.49K **Privately Held**
Web: www.mac-tech.com
SIC: 3599 Industrial machinery, nec

(G-13885)
MCP USA INC
Also Called: MCP Performance Plastic
6750 Daniel Burnham Dr Ste E (46368)
PHONE..................................219 734-6598
Eyal Tenenbaume, *CEO*
EMP: 1 **EST:** 2017
SALES (est): 1.59MM **Privately Held**
Web: www.mcpusainc.com
SIC: 3089 Trays, plastics
HQ: M.C.P. Performance Plastic Ltd
   Kibbutz
   Hamaapil 38857

(G-13886)
MELANIE BREWERY COMPANY INC
146 Shore Dr (46368-7748)
PHONE..................................219 762-9652
Melanie Julie Sever, *Prin*
EMP: 6 **EST:** 2001
SALES (est): 50.35K **Privately Held**
SIC: 2082 5813 Beer (alcoholic beverage); Drinking places

(G-13887)
MINTEQ INTERNATIONAL INC
Also Called: MINTEQ INTERNATIONAL INC.
1789 Schiller St (46368-1226)
PHONE..................................219 771-9693
Tim Connors, *Prin*
EMP: 10
SQ FT: 20,000
Web: www.mineralstech.com
SIC: 3312 Blast furnaces and steel mills
HQ: Minteq International Inc.
   35 Highland Ave
   Bethlehem PA 18017

(G-13888)
MINTEQ SHAPES AND SERVICES INC (HQ)
1789 Schiller St (46368-1226)
PHONE..................................219 762-4863
Carl Laib, *Pr*
▲ **EMP:** 59 **EST:** 1985
SQ FT: 3,000
SALES (est): 879.1K **Publicly Held**
SIC: 3297 Nonclay refractories
PA: Minerals Technologies Inc.
   622 3rd Ave
   New York NY 10017

(G-13889)
MISSISSIPPI LIME COMPANY
570 E Boundary Rd (46368-1127)
PHONE..................................800 437-5463
EMP: 1
SALES (corp-wide): 559.81MM **Privately Held**
Web: www.mississippilime.com
SIC: 3274 Quicklime
HQ: Mississippi Lime Company
   3870 S Lndbrgh Blvd Ste 2
   Saint Louis MO 63127
   314 543-6300

(G-13890)
MONOSOL LLC
Also Called: Monosol
1701 County Line Rd (46368-1595)
PHONE..................................219 762-3165
EMP: 4
Web: www.monosol.com
SIC: 2821 Plastics materials and resins
HQ: Monosol, Llc
   707 E 80th Pl Ste 301
   Merrillville IN 46410
   219 762-3165

(G-13891)
MONOSOL LLC
1500 Louis Sullivan Dr (46368-6435)
PHONE..................................219 763-7589
Tim Boyle, *Mgr*
EMP: 5
Web: www.monosol.com
SIC: 2671 3565 Plastic film, coated or laminated for packaging; Packaging machinery
HQ: Monosol, Llc
   707 E 80th Pl Ste 301
   Merrillville IN 46410
   219 762-3165

(G-13892)
MOOSEIN INDUSTRIES LLC
1256 Camelot Mnr (46368-5336)
PHONE..................................219 406-7306
EMP: 6 **EST:** 2012
SALES (est): 350.56K **Privately Held**
SIC: 3999 Manufacturing industries, nec

(G-13893)
MORTAR NET USA LTD
6575 Daniel Burnham Dr Ste G (46368-6416)
PHONE..................................800 664-6638
Gary Johnson, *Pr*
Tom Sourlis, *Ch*
▲ **EMP:** 7 **EST:** 1992
SALES (est): 800.76K **Privately Held**
Web: www.mortarnet.com
SIC: 3531 Catch basin cleaners

(G-13894)
MSI EXPRESS INC
Also Called: Co-Packaging
6515 Ameriplex Dr (46368-7610)
PHONE..................................219 871-9882
Daniel Lodics, *Brnch Mgr*
EMP: 26
SALES (corp-wide): 179.67MM **Privately Held**
Web: www.msiexpress.com
SIC: 2671 Paper; coated and laminated packaging
PA: Msi Express, Inc.
   5900 Carlson Ave
   Portage IN 46368
   219 762-4855

(G-13895)
NEIGHBORHOOD FLOORS & MORE LLC
5822 Us Highway 6 Ste A (46368-4807)
PHONE..................................219 510-5737
Brian Mallams, *Managing Member*
EMP: 1 **EST:** 2014
SQ FT: 2,800
SALES (est): 239.48K **Privately Held**
SIC: 5713 3999 Floor covering stores; Carpet tackles

(G-13896)
NEO INDUSTRIES LLC
1775 Willowcreek Rd (46368-1324)
PHONE..................................219 762-6075
EMP: 7
Web: www.neodelivers.com
SIC: 3471 Plating and polishing
HQ: Neo Industries, Llc
   1400 E Angela Blvd
   South Bend IN 46617
   574 217-4078

(G-13897)
NEO INDUSTRIES (INDIANA) INC
1775 Willowcreek Rd (46368-1324)
PHONE..................................219 762-6075
▲ **EMP:** 58 **EST:** 1991
SALES (est): 2.38MM **Privately Held**
SIC: 3471 Plating of metals or formed products
HQ: Neo Industries, Llc
   1400 E Angela Blvd
   South Bend IN 46617
   574 217-4078

(G-13898)
NETEGRITY INC
5787 Us Highway 6 (46368-4853)
PHONE..................................219 763-6400
EMP: 10
SALES (corp-wide): 35.82B **Publicly Held**
SIC: 3674 Semiconductors and related devices
HQ: Netegrity, Inc
   100 Baylis Rd Ste 250
   Melville NY 11747
   631 342-6000

(G-13899)
NLMK INDIANA LLC
Also Called: Nlmk
6500 S Boundary Rd (46368)
PHONE..................................219 787-8200
Robert Miller, *Pr*
Alexander Tseitline, *
Corinn Grossetti, *
Joseph Gazarkiewicz, *
▲ **EMP:** 380 **EST:** 1989
SQ FT: 600,000
SALES (est): 119.87MM **Privately Held**

Web: us.nlmk.com
SIC: 3312 Iron and steel products, hot-rolled
PA: Nlmk, Pao
2 Pl. Metallurgov
Lipetsk 39804

(G-13900)
NORTHERN TRANS & DIFFERENTIAL
6641 Melton Rd (46368-1884)
PHONE..................219 764-4009
Kevin Westerman, Owner
EMP: 2 EST: 1995
SQ FT: 3,300
SALES (est): 240.32K Privately Held
SIC: 3714 7537 Differentials and parts, motor vehicle; Automotiv e transmission repair shops

(G-13901)
OZINGA BROS INC
Also Called: Ozinga Ready Mix
1575 Adler Cir Ste B (46368-6408)
PHONE..................219 949-9800
Donald Rapley, Pr
EMP: 177
SQ FT: 15,000
SALES (corp-wide): 552.21MM Privately Held
Web: www.ozinga.com
SIC: 3273 Ready-mixed concrete
PA: Ozinga Bros., Inc.
19001 Old Lagrange Rd # 3
Mokena IL 60448
708 326-4200

(G-13902)
P R F
6737 Central Ave Ste D (46368-3273)
PHONE..................219 477-8660
Gerald Sampson, Owner
EMP: 2 EST: 2010
SALES (est): 124.92K Privately Held
SIC: 3799 Trailers and trailer equipment

(G-13903)
PHOENIX SERVICES LLC
Also Called: PHOENIX SERVICES, LLC
1190 E Loop Dr (46368-1168)
PHONE..................219 787-0019
Paul Overton, Brnch Mgr
EMP: 30
SALES (corp-wide): 84.08MM Privately Held
Web: www.phoenixglobal.com
SIC: 3399 Iron ore recovery from open hearth slag
PA: Phoenix Services, L.L.C.
100 W Matsonford Rd # 520
Wayne PA 19087
610 347-0444

(G-13904)
POLYMER LOGISTICS INC
6750 Daniel Burnham Dr (46368-1870)
PHONE..................219 706-5985
Craig Didion, Genl Mgr
EMP: 64
SALES (corp-wide): 217.91MM Privately Held
Web: www.toscaltd.com
SIC: 3089 5085 5162 Pallets, plastics; Boxes, crates, etc., other than paper; Plastics materials and basic shapes
HQ: Polymer Logistics, Inc.
1175 Peachtree St Ne # 1900
Atlanta GA 30261

(G-13905)
PORTAGE CUSTOM WEAR LLC
2294 Swanson Rd (46368-1505)
PHONE..................219 841-9070
Brandon Starr, Admn
EMP: 7 EST: 2014
SALES (est): 248.35K Privately Held
Web: www.portagecustomwear.com
SIC: 2759 Screen printing

(G-13906)
PRECOAT METALS
Also Called: PRECOAT METALS
6144 Us Highway 12 (46368-1871)
PHONE..................219 763-1504
Jeff Hoffmeister, Mgr
EMP: 10
SALES (corp-wide): 1.54B Publicly Held
Web: www.azz.com
SIC: 3724 2891 2851 3479 Aircraft engines and engine parts; Adhesives and sealants; Paints and allied products; Aluminum coating of metal products
HQ: Precoat Metals Corp.
635 Mryvlle Cntre Dr Ste
Saint Louis MO 63141

(G-13907)
PYRO INDUSTRIAL SERVICES INC
6610 Shepherd Ave (46368-6400)
PHONE..................219 787-5700
John L Carlson, CEO
Raymond W Mcmillan, Pr
James R Harting, *
Margaret K Warnke, *
EMP: 50 EST: 1975
SQ FT: 12,000
SALES (est): 824.08K Privately Held
Web: www.pyroindustrial.com
SIC: 1741 5085 3297 Refractory or acid brick masonry; Refractory material; Nonclay refractories

(G-13908)
RAEMARIE ESSENTIALS LLC
5481 Sand Ave (46368-1836)
PHONE..................219 248-5482
Sheree Edwards, Managing Member
EMP: 1 EST: 2021
SALES (est): 55.37K Privately Held
Web: www.raemarieessentials.com
SIC: 2844 Perfumes, cosmetics and other toilet preparations

(G-13909)
RATNER STEEL SUPPLY CO
655 George Nelson Dr (46368-1271)
PHONE..................219 787-6700
EMP: 5
SALES (corp-wide): 44.52MM Privately Held
Web: www.ratnersteel.com
SIC: 3312 Stainless steel
PA: Ratner Steel Supply Co.
2500 W County Rd B Ste 1a
Roseville MN 55113
651 631-8515

(G-13910)
REBECCA L HAMANN & ASSOCIATES
Also Called: Reg Prof Reporter
5069 Stagecoach Rd (46368-1123)
PHONE..................219 763-1233
Rebecca L Hamann, Owner
EMP: 1 EST: 1976
SALES (est): 108.03K Privately Held
SIC: 7334 2711 Photocopying and duplicating services; Newspapers, publishing and printing

(G-13911)
SEA QUEST LURES INC
2141 Whippoorwill St (46368-1681)
PHONE..................219 762-4362
Richard Holm, Prin
EMP: 2 EST: 2010
SALES (est): 102.64K Privately Held
Web: www.seaquestlures.com
SIC: 3949 Sporting and athletic goods, nec

(G-13912)
SEDONA INC
3195 Willowcreek Rd (46368-4446)
PHONE..................219 764-9675
Sharon Garbertt, Brnch Mgr
EMP: 88
Web: www.sedonatek.com
SIC: 7372 Business oriented computer software
HQ: Sedona, Inc.
612 Valley View Dr
Moline IL 61265

(G-13913)
SHEUNG T CHENG
5833 Pinstrip Ave (46368-8725)
PHONE..................646 220-2195
Sheung T Cheng, Owner
EMP: 1 EST: 2008
SALES (est): 58.09K Privately Held
SIC: 2899 Water treating compounds

(G-13914)
SIEMENS INDUSTRY INC
Also Called: Siemens Industrial Services
6625 Daniel Burnham Dr (46368-1698)
PHONE..................219 763-7927
EMP: 62
SALES (corp-wide): 96.96B Privately Held
SIC: 3613 3823 3625 3621 Switchgear and switchgear accessories, nec; Process control instruments; Relays and industrial controls; Motors and generators
HQ: Siemens Industry, Inc.
1000 Deerfield Pkwy
Buffalo Grove IL 30005
847 215-1000

(G-13915)
SIGNIFIED SIGNS INC
P.O. Box 300 (46308-0300)
PHONE..................219 712-7385
Karin Kegebein, Prin
EMP: 2 EST: 2003
SALES (est): 85.75K Privately Held
SIC: 3993 Signs and advertising specialties

(G-13916)
STEEL TECHNOLOGIES LLC
5830 Southport Rd (46368-1289)
PHONE..................502 245-2110
Bill Horvath, Mgr
EMP: 180
SQ FT: 60,000
Web: www.steeltechnologies.com
SIC: 3316 3398 3312 Cold finishing of steel shapes; Metal heat treating; Blast furnaces and steel mills
HQ: Steel Technologies Llc
700 N Hurstbourne Pkwy # 400
Louisville KY 40222
502 245-2110

(G-13917)
UNITED STATES STEEL CORP
Midwest Plant
6300 Us Highway 12 (46368-1267)
P.O. Box 220 (46368-0220)
PHONE..................219 762-3131
John Guidan, Brnch Mgr
EMP: 1
SALES (corp-wide): 18.05B Publicly Held
Web: www.ussteel.com
SIC: 3312 3471 3316 Sheet or strip, steel, hot-rolled; Plating and polishing; Cold finishing of steel shapes
PA: United States Steel Corp
600 Grant St
Pittsburgh PA 15219
412 433-1121

(G-13918)
USW LU 6103-07
1919 Willowcreek Rd (46368-1514)
PHONE..................219 762-4433
EMP: 6 EST: 2010
SALES (est): 653.18K Privately Held
SIC: 3441 Fabricated structural metal

(G-13919)
WESTROCK CP LLC
5900 Carlson Ave (46368-1309)
PHONE..................219 762-4855
Les Crouch, Mgr
EMP: 1
SALES (corp-wide): 20.31B Privately Held
Web: www.westrock.com
SIC: 2653 Boxes, corrugated: made from purchased materials
HQ: Westrock Cp, Llc
1000 Abernathy Rd Ste 125
Atlanta GA 30328

(G-13920)
YONGLI AMERICA LLC
6625 Daniel Burnham Dr Ste A (46368-1698)
PHONE..................219 763-7920
Richard Garrity, Pr
EMP: 5 EST: 2015
SQ FT: 18,000
SALES (est): 525.05K Privately Held
SIC: 3496 Conveyor belts

Porter
Porter County

(G-13921)
ANTIQUE CANDLE WORKS LLC
913 Waverly Rd (46304-1458)
PHONE..................765 586-6013
EMP: 1 EST: 2014
SALES (est): 64.57K Privately Held
Web: www.antiquecandleco.com
SIC: 3999 Candles

(G-13922)
CUSTOM FITZ LLC
10 Wagner Rd (46304-1748)
PHONE..................219 405-0896
EMP: 6 EST: 2013
SALES (est): 100.71K Privately Held
SIC: 3999 Manufacturing industries, nec

(G-13923)
CUSTOM TS & TROPHIES
30 E Burwell Dr (46304)
PHONE..................219 926-4174
Joe Mullet, Pt
Laurie Mullet, Pt
EMP: 2 EST: 1985
SALES (est): 95.02K Privately Held
SIC: 3479 7336 Engraving jewelry, silverware, or metal; Silk screen design

(G-13924)
DMC DISTRIBUTION LLC
172 S 19th St (46304-1906)
PHONE..................219 926-6401
EMP: 4 EST: 2015
SALES (est): 118.06K Privately Held

Porter - Porter County (G-13925) GEOGRAPHIC SECTION

SIC: 8748 3999 5961 4832 Educational consultant; Education aids, devices and supplies; Educational supplies and equipment, mail order; Educational

(G-13925)
WORTHINGTON STEEL COMPANY
100 Worthington Dr (46304-8812)
PHONE..................................219 929-4000
Mike Pagniano, *Mgr*
EMP: 1
SALES (corp-wide): 545.03MM **Privately Held**
Web: www.worthingtonsteel.com
SIC: 3316 3471 3312 Cold finishing of steel shapes; Plating and polishing; Blast furnace and related products
PA: The Worthington Steel Company
100 W Old Wlson Bridge Rd
Worthington OH 43085
800 944-2255

Portland
Jay County

(G-13926)
ACCELERATED CURING INC
304 E 100 N (47371-7646)
P.O. Box 1286 (47371-3286)
PHONE..................................260 726-3202
Robert Mc Cabe, *Pr*
EMP: 10 **EST:** 1993
SQ FT: 30,000
SALES (est): 881.78K **Privately Held**
Web: www.acceleratedcuring.com
SIC: 3089 Plastics processing

(G-13927)
ALLEGHENY LUDLUM CORP
250 E Lafayette St (47371-1099)
PHONE..................................412 394-2800
Preston Costa, *Prin*
EMP: 10 **EST:** 2016
SALES (est): 250.61K **Privately Held**
SIC: 3312 Blast furnaces and steel mills

(G-13928)
B & B POWDER COATING
6353 S Us Highway 27 (47371-8955)
PHONE..................................260 726-4290
Robert Dewitt, *Owner*
Brenda Dewitt, *VP*
EMP: 2 **EST:** 2003
SALES (est): 187.75K **Privately Held**
Web: www.bbpowdercoating.com
SIC: 3479 Coating of metals and formed products

(G-13929)
B&W ENVIRONMENTAL
1423 E State Road 26 (47371-9637)
PHONE..................................260 766-4135
EMP: 5 **EST:** 2019
SALES (est): 137.5K **Privately Held**
Web: www.babcock.com
SIC: 3511 Turbines and turbine generator sets

(G-13930)
CENTRAL COCA-COLA BTLG CO INC
Also Called: Coca-Cola
1617 N Meridian St (47371-9301)
PHONE..................................260 726-7126
EMP: 33
SALES (corp-wide): 45.75B **Publicly Held**
Web: www.coca-cola.com
SIC: 2086 8741 Bottled and canned soft drinks; Management services

HQ: Central Coca-Cola Bottling Company, Inc.
555 Taxter Rd Ste 550
Elmsford NY 10523
914 789-1100

(G-13931)
COCA-COLA BOTTLING CO PORTLAND
Also Called: Coca-Cola
1617 N Meridian St (47371-9301)
PHONE..................................260 729-6124
Marvin J Herb, *Pr*
EMP: 26 **EST:** 1921
SQ FT: 92,000
SALES (est): 1.5MM **Privately Held**
Web: www.coca-cola.com
SIC: 2086 Bottled and canned soft drinks

(G-13932)
COLLEGIATE PRIDE INC
Also Called: THE FALCON MINT
807 N Meridian St (47371-1126)
PHONE..................................260 726-7818
John Goodrich, *Pr*
EMP: 7 **EST:** 1992
SALES (est): 510K **Privately Held**
Web: www.falconmint.com
SIC: 3911 5944 Jewelry, precious metal; Jewelry stores

(G-13933)
COMMERCIAL ELECTRIC CO INC
Also Called: Pennville Custom Cabinetry
600 E Votaw St (47371-1610)
P.O. Box 1266 (47371-3266)
PHONE..................................260 726-9357
Mark S Goldman, *Ch*
Doris Goldman, *
EMP: 25 **EST:** 1921
SQ FT: 50,000
SALES (est): 2.35MM **Privately Held**
Web: www.pennvillecabinetry.com
SIC: 2434 2511 Wood kitchen cabinets; Wood household furniture
PA: Commercial Electric Co Inc
2296 S Brookview Dr
Portland IN 47371

(G-13934)
COOL CAYENNE
601 N Meridian St (47371-1122)
PHONE..................................260 376-0977
EMP: 4 **EST:** 2018
SALES (est): 97.35K **Privately Held**
SIC: 2759 Screen printing

(G-13935)
CUSTOM INK WRITERS
5451 E 400 S (47371-8129)
PHONE..................................260 202-9350
Anthony Campofiore, *Prin*
EMP: 5 **EST:** 2017
SALES (est): 46.74K **Privately Held**
SIC: 2759 Screen printing

(G-13936)
D J INVESTMENTS INC
Also Called: Hearing Aid Outlet
111 W North St Ste C (47371-1153)
PHONE..................................260 726-7346
Dan Ahrens, *Brnch Mgr*
EMP: 2
SALES (corp-wide): 574.23K **Privately Held**
Web: www.sonushearing.com
SIC: 7349 3842 Building maintenance, except repairs; Hearing aids
PA: D J Investments Inc
0660 E 200 S
Hartford City IN 47348

765 348-4381

(G-13937)
DONALD H & SUSAN K MINCH
2825 W 400 N (47371-8448)
PHONE..................................260 726-9486
Susan Minch, *Owner*
EMP: 2 **EST:** 1986
SALES (est): 47.64K **Privately Held**
SIC: 3269 Art and ornamental ware, pottery

(G-13938)
ERNST ENTERPRISES INC
1125 W Water St (47371-1759)
PHONE..................................260 726-8282
John Ernst, *Brnch Mgr*
EMP: 3
SALES (corp-wide): 240.08MM **Privately Held**
Web: www.ernstconcrete.com
SIC: 3273 Ready-mixed concrete
PA: Ernst Enterprises, Inc.
3361 Successful Way
Dayton OH 45414
937 233-5555

(G-13939)
FCC (INDIANA) LLC
555 Industrial Dr (47371-9399)
PHONE..................................260 726-8023
Yoshitaka Saito, *Pr*
▲ **EMP:** 742 **EST:** 1988
SQ FT: 357,000
SALES (est): 313.88MM **Privately Held**
Web: www.fcc-na.com
SIC: 3714 Clutches, motor vehicle
PA: F.C.C.Co., Ltd.
7000-36, Hosoechonakagawa,
Hamana-Ku
Hamamatsu SZO 431-1

(G-13940)
FCC (NORTH AMERICA) INC (HQ)
555 Industrial Dr (47371-9399)
PHONE..................................260 726-8023
Satoshi Makaya, *Pr*
EMP: 47 **EST:** 2002
SALES (est): 10.65MM **Privately Held**
Web: www.fcc-na.com
SIC: 3714 Transmissions, motor vehicle
PA: F.C.C.Co., Ltd.
7000-36, Hosoechonakagawa,
Hamana-Ku
Hamamatsu SZO 431-1

(G-13941)
FISHER PACKING COMPANY
300 W Walnut St (47371-1810)
PHONE..................................260 726-7355
John Fisher, *Pr*
Janice Fisher, *
EMP: 25 **EST:** 1945
SQ FT: 8,000
SALES (est): 1.98MM **Privately Held**
Web: www.fishermeats.com
SIC: 5421 5147 0751 2013 Meat markets, including freezer provisioners; Meats, fresh; Slaughtering: custom livestock services; Sausages and other prepared meats

(G-13942)
FLAMESPRAY MACHINE SERVICE
237 E Votaw St (47371-1418)
PHONE..................................260 726-6236
Jack Batt, *Pr*
Kristie Batt, *VP*
EMP: 4 **EST:** 1991
SALES (est): 219.73K **Privately Held**
Web: www.flamespraymachineandfab.com

SIC: 7699 3599 Industrial machinery and equipment repair; Machine shop, jobbing and repair

(G-13943)
FREDS CUSTOM FURNITURE
2612 S Blaine Pike (47371-8742)
PHONE..................................260 726-2519
Fred Dehoff, *Owner*
EMP: 1 **EST:** 2009
SALES (est): 80.47K **Privately Held**
SIC: 2599 Factory furniture and fixtures

(G-13944)
FULLENKAMP MACHINE & MFG INC
Also Called: Fullenkamp Machine
1507 N Meridian St (47371-9000)
P.O. Box 525 (47371-0525)
PHONE..................................260 726-8345
Richard E Fullenkamp, *Pr*
EMP: 16 **EST:** 1954
SQ FT: 20,000
SALES (est): 2.43MM **Privately Held**
Web: www.fullenkampmachine.com
SIC: 3599 7692 Machine shop, jobbing and repair; Welding repair

(G-13945)
FUSONWEAVER PUBLISHING LLC
931 W Walnut St (47371-1730)
PHONE..................................260 251-3946
EMP: 4 **EST:** 2019
SALES (est): 66.05K **Privately Held**
SIC: 2741 Miscellaneous publishing

(G-13946)
GOODYEAR TIRE CENTER
Also Called: Goodyear
210 S Meridian St (47371-2115)
PHONE..................................260 726-9321
Tom Godfry, *Owner*
EMP: 5 **EST:** 1991
SALES (est): 434.63K **Privately Held**
Web: www.goodyear.com
SIC: 5531 7534 Automotive tires; Tire repair shop

(G-13947)
GRAPHIC PRINTING CO INC (PA)
Also Called: Commercial Review, The
309 W Main St (47371-1803)
P.O. Box 1049 (47371-3149)
PHONE..................................260 726-8141
John C Ronald, *Pr*
Stephen Ronald, *Stockholder**
EMP: 27 **EST:** 1946
SQ FT: 20,000
SALES (est): 2.38MM
SALES (corp-wide): 2.38MM **Privately Held**
Web: www.thecr.com
SIC: 2711 Commercial printing and newspaper publishing combined

(G-13948)
GREAZY PICKLE LLC
211 W Main St (47371-2124)
P.O. Box 128 (47371-0128)
PHONE..................................260 726-9200
Chris Grieshop, *Owner*
EMP: 7 **EST:** 2007
SALES (est): 205.19K **Privately Held**
Web: greazy-pickle.edan.io
SIC: 2599 Bar, restaurant and cafeteria furniture

(G-13949)
GREG MOSER ENGINEERING INC
Also Called: Moser Engineering
102 Performance Dr (47371-9012)

PHONE..................260 726-6689
Greg Moser, Pr
EMP: 46 **EST:** 1985
SQ FT: 50,000
SALES (est): 9.53MM **Privately Held**
Web: www.moserengineering.com
SIC: 7539 3714 3444 Machine shop, automotive; Motor vehicle parts and accessories; Sheet metalwork

(G-13950)
GREG WHITENACK
1338 W 100 N (47371-8069)
PHONE..................260 726-7321
Greg Whitenack, Owner
EMP: 1 **EST:** 2000
SALES (est): 96.7K **Privately Held**
SIC: 3523 Driers (farm): grain, hay, and seed

(G-13951)
J & P CUSTOM PLATING INC
807 N Meridian St (47371-1126)
PHONE..................260 726-9696
John B Goodrich, Pr
EMP: 6 **EST:** 1971
SQ FT: 2,400
SALES (est): 490.86K **Privately Held**
Web: www.jpcustomplating.com
SIC: 3471 5531 Plating of metals or formed products; Auto and home supply stores

(G-13952)
JOYCE/DAYTON CORP
Also Called: Portland Division
1621 N Meridian St (47371-9301)
PHONE..................260 726-9361
Gary Fulton, Mgr
EMP: 48
SALES (corp-wide): 4.41B **Publicly Held**
Web: www.joycedayton.com
SIC: 3569 3537 3462 Jack screws; Industrial trucks and tractors; Iron and steel forgings
HQ: Joyce/Dayton Corp.
 3300 S Dixie Dr Ste 101
 Dayton OH 45439
 937 294-6261

(G-13953)
JRDS INDUSTRIES
1700 N Meridian St (47371-9303)
PHONE..................260 729-5037
Ken Fredericksen, Prin
EMP: 6 **EST:** 2015
SALES (est): 81.23K **Privately Held**
Web: www.jrds.org
SIC: 3999 Manufacturing industries, nec

(G-13954)
KABLE TOOL & ENGINEERING
530 E 300 N (47371-7917)
PHONE..................260 726-9670
Jason Kable, Owner
EMP: 2 **EST:** 1996
SALES (est): 179.77K **Privately Held**
SIC: 3469 Machine parts, stamped or pressed metal

(G-13955)
LPI PAVING & EXCAVATING (PA)
1401 W Votaw St (47371-9501)
PHONE..................260 726-9564
Bill Davis, Pr
EMP: 6 **EST:** 1975
SQ FT: 6,000
SALES (est): 1.75MM
SALES (corp-wide): 1.75MM **Privately Held**
SIC: 1794 4212 1442 Excavation work; Dump truck haulage; Gravel mining

(G-13956)
MARV KAHLIG & SONS INC
3229 S 500 E (47371-7182)
PHONE..................260 335-2212
Marvin Kahlig, Pr
Jayne Kahlig, Sec
EMP: 4 **EST:** 1998
SALES (est): 248.86K **Privately Held**
SIC: 3259 Clay sewer and drainage pipe and tile

(G-13957)
MOTHERSON SUMI SYSTEMS LIMITED
700 Industrial Dr (47371-1156)
PHONE..................260 726-6501
James Kennedy, Mgr
EMP: 700
Web: www.motherson.com
SIC: 3714 3694 Automotive wiring harness sets; Engine electrical equipment
PA: Samvardhana Motherson International Limited
 Corporate Tower, 11th Floor,
 Noida UP 20130

(G-13958)
MSSL WIRING SYSTEM INC (HQ)
700 Industrial Dr (47371)
PHONE..................330 856-3366
Jitender Mahajan, Pr
▲ **EMP:** 52 **EST:** 2014
SQ FT: 24,570
SALES (est): 51.1MM **Privately Held**
SIC: 3679 Harness assemblies, for electronic use: wire or cable
PA: Samvardhana Motherson International Limited
 Corporate Tower, 11th Floor,
 Noida UP 20130

(G-13959)
PERFORMANCE TOOL INC
103 Performance Dr (47371-9012)
PHONE..................260 726-6572
Lon R Racster, Pr
EMP: 18 **EST:** 2006
SALES (est): 2.13MM **Privately Held**
Web: www.performancetoolinc.com
SIC: 3449 Miscellaneous metalwork

(G-13960)
PIONEER TRANSPORT LLC
1617 N Meridian St (47371-9301)
PHONE..................260 726-4840
Mary Lou, Managing Member
EMP: 25
SALES (est): 1MM **Privately Held**
SIC: 3537 Trucks, tractors, loaders, carriers, and similar equipment

(G-13961)
POET BOREFINING - PORTLAND LLC
Also Called: Poet Brfining- Portland 18200
1542 S 200 W (47371)
PHONE..................260 726-2681
Matt Tomano, Genl Mgr
EMP: 5 **EST:** 2005
SALES (est): 2.92MM **Privately Held**
Web: www.poet.com
SIC: 2869 Ethyl alcohol, ethanol
PA: Poet, Llc
 4615 N Lewis Ave
 Sioux Falls SD 57104

(G-13962)
PORTLAND TIRE & SERVICE INC
210 S Meridian St (47371-2115)
PHONE..................260 726-9321
William Gentis, Pr

Tom Godfrey, VP
Ann Dunwiddie, Sec
EMP: 5 **EST:** 1969
SALES (est): 600K **Privately Held**
Web: www.portlandgoodyear.com
SIC: 5531 7534 5014 Automotive tires; Tire repair shop; Tires and tubes

(G-13963)
PREMIER FORGE GROUP LLC (PA)
250 E Lafayette St (47371-1099)
PHONE..................800 727-8121
Bill Kerfin, Managing Member
EMP: 70 **EST:** 2019
SALES (est): 34.87MM
SALES (corp-wide): 34.87MM **Privately Held**
Web: www.premierforge.com
SIC: 3312 Forgings, iron and steel

(G-13964)
PRIORITY PLASTICS INC (PA)
500 Industrial Dr (47371-9399)
PHONE..................260 726-7000
Andrew Srenco, CEO
Scott Dowrey, *
Tom Wood, *
David Kunkle, *
◆ **EMP:** 44 **EST:** 2008
SALES (est): 28.96MM
SALES (corp-wide): 28.96MM **Privately Held**
Web: www.priorityplastics.com
SIC: 3089 Injection molding of plastics

(G-13965)
QUALTECH TOOL & ENGRG INC
103 Performance Dr (47371-9012)
PHONE..................260 726-6572
EMP: 10 **EST:** 1994
SQ FT: 22,000
SALES (est): 195.54K **Privately Held**
SIC: 3312 3545 3544 Tool and die steel and alloys; Machine tool accessories; Special dies, tools, jigs, and fixtures

(G-13966)
RED GOLD INC
957 W 200 S (47371-8338)
PHONE..................260 726-8140
Doug Harris, Asst Sec
EMP: 2
SALES (corp-wide): 451.21MM **Privately Held**
Web: www.redgoldfoods.com
SIC: 2033 4783 Tomato products, packaged in cans, jars, etc.; Containerization of goods for shipping
PA: Red Gold, Inc.
 1520 S 22nd St
 Elwood IN 46036
 765 557-5500

(G-13967)
SONOCO PRTECTIVE SOLUTIONS INC
1619 N Meridian St (47371-9301)
PHONE..................260 726-9333
EMP: 49
SALES (corp-wide): 6.78B **Publicly Held**
Web: www.sonoco.com
SIC: 3086 Plastics foam products
HQ: Sonoco Protective Solutions, Inc.
 3930 N Ventura Dr
 Arlington Heights IL 60004
 847 398-0110

(G-13968)
TDY INDUSTRIES LLC
Portland Forge
250 E Lafayette St (47371-1099)

P.O. Box 905 (47371-0905)
PHONE..................260 726-8121
Joday Auker, Acctnt
EMP: 300
SQ FT: 200,000
SIC: 3463 3462 Nonferrous forgings; Iron and steel forgings
HQ: Tdy Industries, Llc
 1000 Six Ppg Pl
 Pittsburgh PA 15222
 412 394-2800

(G-13969)
THANATOS MANUFACTURING LLC
4263 W 200 S (47371-7291)
PHONE..................260 251-8498
Madison Valentine, Admn
EMP: 5 **EST:** 2016
SALES (est): 53.34K **Privately Held**
SIC: 3999 Manufacturing industries, nec

(G-13970)
TIPSY GLASS LLC
1756 W State Road 67 (47371-8504)
PHONE..................260 251-0021
Audrey Muhlenkamp, Prin
EMP: 5 **EST:** 2016
SALES (est): 83.03K **Privately Held**
Web: www.tipsyglasswinery.com
SIC: 2084 Wines

(G-13971)
TIRE CENTER OF PORTLAND INC
Also Called: Tire Center
421 N Meridian St (47371-1907)
PHONE..................260 726-8947
Mike Wangler, Pr
EMP: 9 **EST:** 1969
SQ FT: 2,000
SALES (est): 782.34K **Privately Held**
SIC: 5531 7534 Automotive tires; Tire repair shop

(G-13972)
TNT CONSTRUCTION
114 Jack Imel Ave (47371-3038)
PHONE..................260 726-2643
Eric Trobridge, Owner
EMP: 8 **EST:** 1997
SALES (est): 422.22K **Privately Held**
SIC: 2452 Prefabricated wood buildings

(G-13973)
TYSON FOODS INC
1355 W Tyson Rd (47371)
PHONE..................260 726-3118
EMP: 5
SALES (corp-wide): 52.88B **Publicly Held**
Web: www.tyson.com
SIC: 2015 2032 2096 2048 Chicken slaughtering and processing; Ethnic foods, canned, jarred, etc.; Potato chips and similar snacks; Feeds from meat and from meat and vegetable meals
PA: Tyson Foods, Inc.
 2200 W Don Tyson Pkwy
 Springdale AR 72762
 479 290-4000

(G-13974)
TYSON MEXICAN ORIGINAL INC
1355 W Tyson Rd (47371-7997)
PHONE..................260 726-3118
EMP: 73
SALES (corp-wide): 52.88B **Publicly Held**
Web: www.tysonfoods.com
SIC: 2032 2096 2051 Mexican foods, nec: packaged in cans, jars, etc.; Potato chips and similar snacks; Bread, cake, and related products
HQ: Tyson Mexican Original, Inc.

2200 W Don Tyson Pkwy
Springdale AR 72762
479 290-6111

(G-13975)
WALNUT CREEK FABRICATION INC
4891 S 475 E (47371-7775)
PHONE..................................765 749-1226
Kent Kahlig, Prin
EMP: 6 **EST:** 2016
SALES (est): 244.8K **Privately Held**
SIC: 3999 Manufacturing industries, nec

Poseyville
Posey County

(G-13976)
AGRI-POWER INC
Also Called: Hr Agri-Power
10100 Highway 165 (47633-9404)
PHONE..................................812 874-3316
EMP: 15
Web: www.hragripower.com
SIC: 3523 Farm machinery and equipment
PA: Agri-Power, Inc.
4900 Eagle Way
Hopkinsville KY 42241

(G-13977)
HOEHN PLASTICS INC
11481 W 925 S (47633)
P.O. Box 248 (47633)
PHONE..................................812 874-3646
Jason Hoehn, Pr
Melissa Higgins, *
EMP: 68 **EST:** 1997
SQ FT: 60,000
SALES (est): 9.02MM **Privately Held**
Web: www.hoehnplastics.com
SIC: 2821 Plastics materials and resins

(G-13978)
INFINITY DRONES LLC
5700 High School Rd (47633-8861)
PHONE..................................812 457-7140
EMP: 4 **EST:** 2017
SALES (est): 113.72K **Privately Held**
SIC: 3721 Motorized aircraft

(G-13979)
INTEGRATED POWER SERVICES LLC
6751 Frontage Rd (47633-8846)
PHONE..................................812 665-4400
Jeff Moffett, Managing Member
EMP: 14 **EST:** 2007
SALES (est): 191.09K **Privately Held**
Web: www.ips.us
SIC: 7694 Electric motor repair

(G-13980)
PC IMPRINTS LLC
10521 Emge Rd (47633-8764)
PHONE..................................812 622-0855
EMP: 4 **EST:** 2018
SALES (est): 72.18K **Privately Held**
SIC: 2752 Commercial printing, lithographic

Princeton
Gibson County

(G-13981)
ALTEK INC
1603 E Broadway St (47670-3110)
P.O. Box 262 (47670-0262)
PHONE..................................812 385-2561
Karl Koch, Pr
EMP: 8 **EST:** 1963
SQ FT: 5,400
SALES (est): 2.47MM **Privately Held**
Web: www.altek.us
SIC: 7694 5063 7699 Electric motor repair; Motors, electric; Pumps and pumping equipment repair

(G-13982)
BEMR LLC
Also Called: RPM Tool
333 S 2nd Ave (47670-1067)
P.O. Box 610 (47670-0610)
PHONE..................................812 385-8509
Matthew Robbins, Managing Member
EMP: 3 **EST:** 2004
SQ FT: 7,000
SALES (est): 302.55K **Privately Held**
Web: www.rpmtool.com
SIC: 3599 Machine shop, jobbing and repair

(G-13983)
BERRY GLOBAL INC
889 W Gach Rd (47670-9240)
PHONE..................................812 386-1525
EMP: 7
Web: www.berryglobal.com
SIC: 3089 3081 Bottle caps, molded plastics; Unsupported plastics film and sheet
HQ: Berry Global, Inc.
101 Oakley St
Evansville IN 47710

(G-13984)
BERRY GLOBAL GROUP INC
889 W Gach Rd (47670-9240)
PHONE..................................812 868-7429
EMP: 10
SALES (corp-wide): 6.49B **Publicly Held**
SIC: 3089 Plastics containers, except foam
PA: Berry Global Group, Inc.
101 Oakley St
Evansville IN 47710
812 424-2904

(G-13985)
BPREX CLOSURES LLC
Also Called: Rexam
889 W Gach Rd (47670-9240)
PHONE..................................812 386-1525
Bob Fella, Brnch Mgr
EMP: 98
Web: www.berryglobal.com
SIC: 3089 2671 Bowl covers, plastics; Paper; coated and laminated packaging
HQ: Bprex Closures, Llc
101 Oakley St
Evansville IN 47710
812 424-2904

(G-13986)
BURT PRODUCTS INC
315 S West St (47670-2155)
PHONE..................................812 386-6890
Roger P Mizeur, Pr
Jane E Mizeur, Sec
EMP: 5 **EST:** 1980
SQ FT: 6,600
SALES (est): 436.65K **Privately Held**
SIC: 3621 3613 Motors, electric; Switches, electric power except snap, push button, etc.

(G-13987)
CARL A NIX WELDING SERVICE INC
Nix Mtals Heritg Machining Div
4827 W State Road 64 (47670)
PHONE..................................812 386-6281
EMP: 15
SALES (corp-wide): 19.78MM **Privately Held**

Web: www.nixcompanies.com
SIC: 3599 Custom machinery
PA: Carl A. Nix Welding Service, Inc.
129 W Fletchall St
Poseyville IN
812 874-2422

(G-13988)
CROOKED STIC BOWS LLC
214 E Emerson St (47670-1804)
PHONE..................................812 677-2715
Mike Miller, Prin
EMP: 5 **EST:** 2014
SALES (est): 47.08K **Privately Held**
SIC: 3949 Sporting and athletic goods, nec

(G-13989)
DIVERSITY - VUTEQ LLC
825 E 350 S (47670-9222)
PHONE..................................812 761-0210
Chris Spence, Managing Member
Kazumasa Watanabe, *
Taro Fukuda, *
▲ **EMP:** 153 **EST:** 2009
SALES (est): 11.34MM **Privately Held**
Web: www.diversityvuteq.com
SIC: 3089 Automotive parts, plastic

(G-13990)
EBP AND ASSOCIATES INC
115 S Hall St (47670)
PHONE..................................812 386-7062
EMP: 4 **EST:** 2020
SALES (est): 39.69K **Privately Held**
SIC: 3999 Manufacturing industries, nec

(G-13991)
ELECTROCRAFT INC
901 S 1st St (47670-2369)
PHONE..................................812 385-3013
EMP: 75
Web: www.hansen-motor.com
SIC: 3625 3621 Relays and industrial controls; Electric motor and generator parts
HQ: Electrocraft, Inc.
2 Marin Way Ste 3
Stratham NH 03885

(G-13992)
ENGLER MACHINE & TOOL INC
1106 W 150 S (47670-9305)
PHONE..................................812 386-6254
Tim Engler, Pr
Tammy Engler, Sec
EMP: 10 **EST:** 1980
SQ FT: 10,000
SALES (est): 1.62MM **Privately Held**
Web: www.englermachine.com
SIC: 5531 3519 Auto and truck equipment and parts; Engines, diesel and semi-diesel or dual-fuel

(G-13993)
ENOVAPREMIER LLC
858 E 350 S (47670-9222)
PHONE..................................812 385-0576
Jim Schum, Brnch Mgr
EMP: 46
Web: www.enovapremier.com
SIC: 3089 3714 3011 Automotive parts, plastic; Motor vehicle parts and accessories; Motorcycle tires, pneumatic
PA: Enovapremier Llc
1630 Lyndon Frms Ct Ste 1
Louisville KY 40223

(G-13994)
FIRST PLACE TROPHIES
1595 E State Road 64 (47670-8827)
PHONE..................................812 385-3279

TOLL FREE: 800
Phyllis Ernst, Owner
EMP: 3 **EST:** 1983
SQ FT: 1,000
SALES (est): 180.32K **Privately Held**
Web: www.firstplacetrophies.com
SIC: 5999 3993 Trophies and plaques; Signs and advertising specialties

(G-13995)
GLITTERED PIG LLC
107 S Spring St (47670-2049)
PHONE..................................812 779-6154
Jacinda Thompson, Prin
EMP: 6 **EST:** 2017
SALES (est): 75.96K **Privately Held**
Web: www.shoptheglitteredpig.com
SIC: 2759 Screen printing

(G-13996)
GOAD MACHINE WORKS INC
3746 E 50 N (47670-8908)
PHONE..................................812 385-8985
EMP: 1 **EST:** 1986
SALES (est): 98.63K **Privately Held**
SIC: 3599 Machine shop, jobbing and repair

(G-13997)
HANSEN CORPORATION
901 S 1st St (47670-2369)
PHONE..................................812 385-3000
John Arico, Sec
◆ **EMP:** 300 **EST:** 1977
SQ FT: 135,000
SALES (est): 42.03MM **Privately Held**
Web: www.hansen-motor.com
SIC: 3621 3873 3566 Motors, electric; Watches, clocks, watchcases, and parts; Speed changers, drives, and gears
HQ: Electrocraft, Inc.
2 Marin Way Ste 3
Stratham NH 03885

(G-13998)
HIGHWAY MACHINE CO INC
Also Called: H M C
3010 S Old Us Highway 41 (47670-9206)
PHONE..................................812 385-3639
Robert J Smith Iii, Pr
Cynthia D Smith, *
◆ **EMP:** 45 **EST:** 1921
SQ FT: 25,000
SALES (est): 9.9MM **Privately Held**
Web: www.hmcgears.com
SIC: 3599 Machine shop, jobbing and repair

(G-13999)
HUGHES WELDING AND FABRICATION
906 Virgil Blvd (47670-2314)
PHONE..................................812 385-2770
Michael Hughes, Pr
EMP: 1 **EST:** 1986
SALES (est): 60.05K **Privately Held**
SIC: 7692 5051 Welding repair; Forms, concrete construction (steel)

(G-14000)
IN STITCHES CUSTOM EMBROIDERY
129 E Broadway St (47670-9998)
PHONE..................................812 385-2877
EMP: 5 **EST:** 2017
SALES (est): 45.41K **Privately Held**
Web: institchesembllc.squarespace.com
SIC: 2395 Embroidery and art needlework

(G-14001)
IN TEX SIGNS AND GRAPHICS
533 N Main St (47670-1405)
P.O. Box 167 (47670-0167)

PHONE.....................812 385-2471
Connie Elliot, *Owner*
EMP: 1 **EST:** 1997
SALES (est): 85.89K **Privately Held**
SIC: 3993 Signs and advertising specialties

(G-14002)
J R AND D EXPLORATION INC
1938 W Brumfield Ave (47670-1033)
PHONE.....................812 677-2895
James Sutter, *Owner*
EMP: 1 **EST:** 2013
SALES (est): 70.01K **Privately Held**
SIC: 1382 Oil and gas exploration services

(G-14003)
MAKE YOUR MARK - CUSTOM EMB
106 N 1st Ave (47670-1002)
PHONE.....................812 664-0026
Jessica Schenk, *Prin*
EMP: 1 **EST:** 2013
SALES (est): 79.92K **Privately Held**
SIC: 2395 Embroidery and art needlework

(G-14004)
MEUTH CONSTRUCTION SUPPLY INC
Also Called: Meuth Concrete
200 Tennessee St (47670-3016)
PHONE.....................270 826-8554
Roger Meuth, *Brnch Mgr*
EMP: 1
SALES (corp-wide): 9.81MM **Privately Held**
Web: www.meuthconcrete.com
SIC: 3273 Ready-mixed concrete
PA: Meuth Construction Supply, Inc.
   703 8th St
   Henderson KY 42420
   270 827-8063

(G-14005)
MID-STATES RUBBER PRODUCTS INC
1232 S Race St (47670-3034)
P.O. Box 370 (47670-0370)
PHONE.....................812 385-3473
▲ **EMP:** 300 **EST:** 1944
SALES (est): 23.23MM **Privately Held**
Web: www.mid-states.com
SIC: 3061 Mechanical rubber goods

(G-14006)
MIDNITE GRAFIX
3437 S 125 E (47670-9214)
PHONE.....................812 386-9430
Lori Barrell, *Owner*
EMP: 3 **EST:** 1999
SALES (est): 110.3K **Privately Held**
SIC: 2759 Screen printing

(G-14007)
NIDEC MOTOR CORPORATION
Also Called: Hurst Manufacturing Division
1551 E Broadway St (47670-3137)
PHONE.....................812 385-2564
Greg Davis, *Brnch Mgr*
EMP: 85
Web: acim.nidec.com
SIC: 3625 3594 Motor controls, electric; Fluid power pumps and motors
HQ: Nidec Motor Corporation
   8050 W Florissant Ave
   Saint Louis MO 63136

(G-14008)
NO LIMITS JUST PSSBILITIES LLC ✪
1509 Cottonwood Dr (47670-3321)
PHONE.....................930 465-1218
Jordan Simmons, *Managing Member*
EMP: 2 **EST:** 2022
SALES (est): 92.67K **Privately Held**
Web: www.nolimitsjustpossibilities.com
SIC: 3944 7389 Craft and hobby kits and sets; Business services, nec

(G-14009)
PAPER CHASE
503 W State St (47670-1345)
PHONE.....................812 385-4757
Cindy Flaningam, *Owner*
EMP: 1 **EST:** 2004
SALES (est): 89.51K **Privately Held**
Web: www.paperchase47670.com
SIC: 2741 2759 4822 7334 Miscellaneous publishing; Commercial printing, nec; Facsimile transmission services; Photocopying and duplicating services

(G-14010)
PRINCETON PUBLISHING INC
Also Called: Princeton Daily Clarion
100 N Gibson St (47670-1855)
P.O. Box 30 (47670-0030)
PHONE.....................812 385-2525
Gary Blackburn, *Pr*
William Brehm, *VP*
Mona J Brehm, *Sec*
EMP: 1 **EST:** 1846
SQ FT: 10,000
SALES (est): 929.62K
SALES (corp-wide): 106.45MM **Privately Held**
Web: www.pdclarion.com
SIC: 2711 2752 2731 Commercial printing and newspaper publishing combined; Commercial printing, lithographic; Book publishing
PA: Brehm Communications, Inc.
   16644 W Bernardo Dr # 300
   San Diego CA 92127
   858 451-6200

(G-14011)
SIGNS BY SUSIE
4288 S Old State Road 65 (47670)
PHONE.....................812 385-2739
Mark Iven, *Pt*
Susie Iven, *Pt*
EMP: 2 **EST:** 2001
SALES (est): 174.78K **Privately Held**
Web: www.signsbysusie.net
SIC: 3993 Signs and advertising specialties

(G-14012)
SOUTHLAND CONTAINER CORP
Also Called: Milagro Packaging
Rr 1 Box 174 (47670)
PHONE.....................812 385-0774
Dave Kaat, *Owner*
EMP: 235
SALES (corp-wide): 371.15MM **Privately Held**
Web: www.southlandcontainer.com
SIC: 2653 Boxes, corrugated: made from purchased materials
PA: Southland Container Corporation
   60 Fairview Church Rd
   Spartanburg SC 29303
   864 578-0085

(G-14013)
TBIN LLC
Also Called: Toyota Boshoku Indiana
1698 S 100 W (47670-9351)
PHONE.....................812 491-9100
EMP: 2 **EST:** 2007
SALES (est): 223.12K **Privately Held**
Web: www.tbprinceton.com
SIC: 3999 Barber and beauty shop equipment

(G-14014)
TOYOTA BOSHOKU INDIANA LLC
Also Called: Tisa
1698 S 100 W (47670-9351)
PHONE.....................812 491-9100
Brian Malinao, *Pr*
▲ **EMP:** 575 **EST:** 2000
SQ FT: 200,000
SALES (est): 79.91MM **Privately Held**
Web: www.tbprinceton.com
SIC: 2531 Seats, automobile
HQ: Toyota Boshoku America, Inc.
   1360 Dolwick Dr Ste 125
   Erlanger KY 41018
   859 817-4000

(G-14015)
TOYOTA MOTOR MFG IND INC (HQ)
Also Called: Tmmi
4000 S Tulip Tree Dr (47670-2300)
PHONE.....................812 387-2266
Seizo Okamoto, *Ch Bd*
Leah Curry, *
Tsutomu Kobayashi, *
◆ **EMP:** 90 **EST:** 1996
SALES (est): 658.62MM **Privately Held**
Web: www.toyotamanufacturing.com
SIC: 3711 Automobile assembly, including specialty automobiles
PA: Toyota Motor Corporation
   1, Toyotacho
   Toyota AIC 471-0

(G-14016)
TOYOTA MOTOR MFG IND INC
Also Called: Tmmi
528 W Poplar Ave (47670-2360)
PHONE.....................812 385-5153
EMP: 1403
Web: www.toyota.com
SIC: 3711 Automobile assembly, including specialty automobiles
HQ: Toyota Motor Manufacturing, Indiana, Inc.
   4000 S Tulip Tree Dr
   Princeton IN 47670
   812 387-2266

(G-14017)
TRI STATE MONUMENT COMPANY
425 N Main St (47670-1515)
PHONE.....................812 386-7303
EMP: 3 **EST:** 1994
SALES (est): 266.34K **Privately Held**
Web: www.tristatememorialcompany.com
SIC: 3272 Monuments and grave markers, except terrazzo

(G-14018)
VUTEQ USA INC
400 W 550 S (47670-9292)
PHONE.....................502 863-6322
EMP: 302
Web: www.vutequsa.com
SIC: 3231 3714 Windshields, glass: made from purchased glass; Sun roofs, motor vehicle
HQ: Vuteq Usa, Inc.
   100 Carley Dr
   Georgetown KY 40324
   502 863-6322

(G-14019)
VUTEQ USA INC
819 E 350 S (47670-9222)
PHONE.....................812 385-2584
Shuji Mapsuyama, *Brnch Mgr*
EMP: 5
Web: www.vutequsa.com
SIC: 3711 Automobile assembly, including specialty automobiles
HQ: Vuteq Usa, Inc.
   100 Carley Dr
   Georgetown KY 40324
   502 863-6322

(G-14020)
WALKER FAMILY ENTERPRISES LLC
1607 W Broadway St (47670-1090)
PHONE.....................812 385-2945
EMP: 5
SALES (est): 257.35K **Privately Held**
SIC: 3842 Walkers

Quincy
Owen County

(G-14021)
HOOSIER MARINE
10151 N Us Highway 231 (47456-8551)
PHONE.....................812 879-5549
EMP: 2 **EST:** 2007
SALES (est): 89.9K **Privately Held**
SIC: 3732 Boatbuilding and repairing

(G-14022)
PROMINENT PROMOTIONAL PDTS LLC
Also Called: Athena Branding Solutions
10550 Millgrove Rd (47456-8558)
PHONE.....................317 376-5772
Olivia Crossett, *Managing Member*
EMP: 1 **EST:** 2019
SALES (est): 55.25K **Privately Held**
SIC: 3999 Candles

Ramsey
Harrison County

(G-14023)
ALVIN J NIX
2820 Fairdale Rd Nw (47166-8408)
PHONE.....................812 347-2510
Alvin J Nix, *Prin*
EMP: 5 **EST:** 1999
SALES (est): 91.47K **Privately Held**
SIC: 3715 Truck trailers

(G-14024)
CAMM MACHINE AND WELDING LLC
10035 Buffalo Trace Rd Nw (47166-8956)
P.O. Box 102 (47166-0102)
PHONE.....................812 347-2040
Adam Camm, *Owner*
EMP: 1 **EST:** 2002
SALES (est): 141.04K **Privately Held**
SIC: 7692 Welding repair

(G-14025)
KELLUM IMPRINTS INC
Also Called: Kellum Imprints & Trophies
1675 Highway 64 Nw (47166-8546)
PHONE.....................812 347-2546
Annissa J Reas, *Pr*
Annissa Reas, *Pr*
Joseph Kellum, *VP*
Ann Kellum, *Sec*
EMP: 3 **EST:** 1991
SALES (est): 242.83K **Privately Held**
Web: www.kellumimprints.com
SIC: 2395 Embroidery products, except Schiffli machine

(G-14026)
RAMSEY POPCORN CO INC
5645 Clover Valley Rd Nw (47166-8252)
PHONE..................................812 347-2441
Wilfred E Sieg Junior, *Pr*
Daniel R Sieg, *
Eric Sieg, *
◆ **EMP:** 35 **EST:** 1946
SQ FT: 30,000
SALES (est): 9.71MM **Privately Held**
Web: www.ramseypopcorn.com
SIC: 2099 5145 Popcorn, packaged: except already popped; Popcorn and supplies

(G-14027)
TYSON CHICKEN INC
Also Called: Tyson
495 Highway 64 Nw (47166-8534)
PHONE..................................812 347-2452
Jay Wall, *Mgr*
EMP: 922
SALES (corp-wide): 52.88B **Publicly Held**
Web: www.tysonfoods.com
SIC: 2015 Poultry slaughtering and processing
HQ: Tyson Chicken, Inc.
    2200 Don Tyson Pkwy
    Springdale AR 72762
    479 290-4000

Redkey
Jay County

(G-14028)
FAB SOLUTIONS LLC
10135 W 800 S (47373-9236)
PHONE..................................765 744-2671
EMP: 6 **EST:** 2011
SQ FT: 4,000
SALES (est): 494.06K **Privately Held**
SIC: 3496 Miscellaneous fabricated wire products

(G-14029)
R N A INDUSTRIES CORP
251 E Sheridan St (47373-9279)
P.O. Box 61 (47373-0061)
PHONE..................................765 288-4413
EMP: 4 **EST:** 2017
SALES (est): 100.7K **Privately Held**
SIC: 3999 Manufacturing industries, nec

Reelsville
Putnam County

(G-14030)
C C COOK AND SON LBR CO INC
6236 W Us Highway 40 (46171-8809)
PHONE..................................765 672-4235
Richard R Cook, *Pr*
Charles H Cook, *
EMP: 40 **EST:** 1941
SQ FT: 40,000
SALES (est): 2.8MM **Privately Held**
Web: www.cooklumber.com
SIC: 2448 2421 Pallets, wood; Kiln drying of lumber

(G-14031)
FABSHOP
8732 W County Road 1075 S (46171-8875)
PHONE..................................317 549-1681
Nevil Algie, *Owner*
EMP: 2 **EST:** 1997
SALES (est): 89.08K **Privately Held**
SIC: 3498 Tube fabricating (contract bending and shaping)

Remington
Jasper County

(G-14032)
AGRICON LLC ✪
3823 W 1800 S (47977-8831)
PHONE..................................219 261-2157
EMP: 17 **EST:** 2023
SALES (est): 1.08MM **Privately Held**
SIC: 3448 Prefabricated metal buildings and components

(G-14033)
AMERICAN FIBERTECH CORPORATION (PA)
Also Called: Fibertech
4 N New York St (47977-8000)
P.O. Box 220 (47977-0220)
PHONE..................................219 261-3586
Robin R Meister, *Pr*
Jay A Wiegand, *
EMP: 74 **EST:** 1986
SQ FT: 36,160
SALES (est): 49.88MM
SALES (corp-wide): 49.88MM **Privately Held**
Web: www.ind-pallet-corp.com
SIC: 2448 Pallets, wood

(G-14034)
DUPONT DE NEMOURS INC
Also Called: Solae
600 Harrington St (47977-8881)
PHONE..................................219 261-2124
Dale Perman, *Brnch Mgr*
◆ **EMP:** 3
SALES (corp-wide): 2.93B **Publicly Held**
Web: www.dupont.com
SIC: 2075 Soybean oil mills
PA: Dupont De Nemours, Inc.
    974 Centre Rd Bldg 730
    Wilmington DE 19805
    302 295-5783

(G-14035)
INTEPLAST GROUP CORPORATION
3505 W Us Highway 24 (47977)
PHONE..................................219 220-2528
John Young, *Mgr*
EMP: 9
Web: www.inteplast.com
SIC: 2673 Bags: plastic, laminated, and coated
PA: Inteplast Group Corporation
    9 Peach Tree Hill Rd
    Livingston NJ 07039

(G-14036)
IONI 2 INC
18325 S 580 W (47977-8601)
P.O. Box 67 (47977-0067)
PHONE..................................219 261-2115
EMP: 156
SIC: 3462 Iron and steel forgings

(G-14037)
IRVING MATERIALS INC
318 W South St (47977-8626)
P.O. Box 328 (47977-0328)
PHONE..................................219 261-2441
Jerry Cyr, *Brnch Mgr*
EMP: 5
SQ FT: 750
SALES (corp-wide): 814.09MM **Privately Held**
Web: www.irvmat.com
SIC: 3273 Ready-mixed concrete
PA: Irving Materials, Inc.
    8032 N State Road 9
    Greenfield IN 46140
    317 326-3101

(G-14038)
SOLAE LLC
413 N Cressy Ave (47977-8830)
PHONE..................................800 325-7108
EMP: 91
SALES (corp-wide): 11.48B **Publicly Held**
SIC: 2075 2076 Soybean oil mills; Vegetable oil mills, nec
HQ: Solae, Llc
    4300 Duncan Ave
    Saint Louis MO 63110
    314 659-3000

(G-14039)
SOLAE LLC (PA)
310 N Cressy Ave (47977-8836)
P.O. Box 127 (47977-0127)
PHONE..................................219 986-6119
Larry Ewen, *Managing Member*
EMP: 12
SALES (est): 1.07MM
SALES (corp-wide): 1.07MM **Privately Held**
SIC: 3999 Manufacturing industries, nec

Rensselaer
Jasper County

(G-14040)
AIRODAPT LLC
809 E Stewart Dr (47978-3218)
PHONE..................................559 331-0156
Frank Airoso, *Managing Member*
Jolyne Airoso, *Managing Member*
EMP: 2 **EST:** 2014
SALES (est): 67.67K **Privately Held**
Web: www.airodapt.com
SIC: 3423 7389 Carpenters' hand tools, except saws: levels, chisels, etc.; Business services, nec

(G-14041)
AMERICAN MELT BLOWN FILTRATION
1030 E Elm St (47978-2364)
PHONE..................................219 866-3500
Fred Geyer, *Pr*
Scott Lucero, *
Stephanie Geyer, *
◆ **EMP:** 33 **EST:** 2011
SQ FT: 50,000
SALES (est): 9.15MM **Privately Held**
Web: www.americanmeltblown.com
SIC: 2621 3589 5075 Milk filter disks; Water filters and softeners, household type; Air filters

(G-14042)
AMERICAN VULKAN CORPORATION
317 S Weston St (47978-3151)
PHONE..................................219 866-7751
Charles Mitchelle, *Prin*
EMP: 1
SALES (corp-wide): 1.97MM **Privately Held**
Web: www.vulkan.com
SIC: 3559 Sewing machines and attachments, industrial, nec
HQ: American Vulkan Corporation
    2525 Dundee Rd
    Winter Haven FL 33884
    863 324-2424

(G-14043)
ARCHER-DANIELS-MIDLAND COMPANY
Also Called: ADM
1201 W State Road 114 (47978-7265)
PHONE..................................219 866-2810
EMP: 6
SALES (corp-wide): 93.94B **Publicly Held**
Web: www.adm.com
SIC: 2041 Flour and other grain mill products
PA: Archer-Daniels-Midland Company
    77 W Wacker Dr Ste 4600
    Chicago IL 60601
    312 634-8100

(G-14044)
ARCHER-DANIELS-MIDLAND COMPANY
Also Called: ADM
9179 W State Road 14 (47978-8645)
PHONE..................................219 866-3939
Jeff Henady, *Mgr*
EMP: 8
SALES (corp-wide): 93.94B **Publicly Held**
Web: www.adm.com
SIC: 2041 Flour and other grain mill products
PA: Archer-Daniels-Midland Company
    77 W Wacker Dr Ste 4600
    Chicago IL 60601
    312 634-8100

(G-14045)
B & C MACHINING INC
Also Called: Hi-Tech Hydraulics
320 E Merritt St (47978-2060)
PHONE..................................219 866-7091
Roman Zdonek, *Ch*
Edward Moskalick, *VP*
Jim Leibrand, *Pr*
EMP: 20 **EST:** 1972
SQ FT: 9,800
SALES (est): 2.29MM **Privately Held**
Web: www.importantlocalbusinesses.com
SIC: 3599 7699 Machine shop, jobbing and repair; Hydraulic equipment repair

(G-14046)
CAMPBELL PRINTING COMPANY
125 N Van Rensselaer St (47978-2651)
PHONE..................................219 866-5913
William Campbell, *Pr*
William F Campbell, *Pr*
EMP: 2 **EST:** 1941
SQ FT: 2,200
SALES (est): 187.01K **Privately Held**
Web: www.printing-by-campbell.com
SIC: 2752 2759 Offset printing; Commercial printing, nec

(G-14047)
CHIEF INDUSTRIES INC
Chief Buildings Div
1225 E Maple St (47978-2120)
P.O. Box 158 (47978-0158)
PHONE..................................219 866-4121
John Price, *Brnch Mgr*
EMP: 133
SALES (corp-wide): 331.11MM **Privately Held**
Web: www.chiefind.com
SIC: 3448 3441 3316 Buildings, portable: prefabricated metal; Fabricated structural metal; Cold finishing of steel shapes
PA: Chief Industries, Inc.
    3942 W Old Highway 30
    Grand Island NE 68803
    308 389-7200

(G-14048)
CONAGRA BRANDS INC
Also Called: Golden Valley Microwave Foods
750 E Drexel Pkwy (47978-7294)
PHONE..................................740 387-2722

EMP: 42
SALES (corp-wide): 12.05B **Publicly Held**
Web: www.conagrabrands.com
SIC: 2099 Popcorn, packaged: except already popped
PA: Conagra Brands, Inc.
222 W Mdse Mart Plz Ste 1
Chicago IL 60654
312 549-5000

(G-14049)
CONAGRA BRANDS INC
Also Called: Hunt Wesson Foods
750 E Drexel Pkwy (47978-7294)
PHONE..............................219 866-3020
EMP: 11
SALES (corp-wide): 12.05B **Publicly Held**
Web: www.conagrabrands.com
SIC: 5149 2099 2096 Groceries and related products, nec; Food preparations, nec; Potato chips and similar snacks
PA: Conagra Brands, Inc.
222 W Mdse Mart Plz Ste 1
Chicago IL 60654
312 549-5000

(G-14050)
DAVIS WATER SERVICES INC
Also Called: Davis Water Conditioning
4898 S 1000 W (47978-8835)
PHONE..............................219 394-2270
EMP: 3 **EST:** 1992
SALES (est): 310K **Privately Held**
Web: www.davis-waterconditioning.com
SIC: 3589 Sewage and water treatment equipment

(G-14051)
DEZIGNS BY CINDY ZIESE
5270 W 300 N (47978-7488)
PHONE..............................219 819-8786
Cindy Ziese, *Owner*
EMP: 4 **EST:** 2012
SALES (est): 96.09K **Privately Held**
Web: www.dezignsbycindy.com
SIC: 3993 Advertising artwork

(G-14052)
FILTRATION PARTS INCORPORATED
513 N Melville St (47978-2369)
PHONE..............................704 661-8135
Fred Geyer, *Pr*
Stephanie Geyer, *Treas*
EMP: 10 **EST:** 2016
SALES (est): 1.59MM **Privately Held**
Web: www.filtrationparts.com
SIC: 3089 3082 Fittings for pipe, plastics; Tubes, unsupported plastics

(G-14053)
HENSLEY CUSTOM CABINETRY
3281 E 400 N (47978-7330)
PHONE..............................219 843-5331
Kim Hensley, *Owner*
Robert Hensley, *Owner*
EMP: 3 **EST:** 2006
SALES (est): 148.17K **Privately Held**
SIC: 2521 Cabinets, office: wood

(G-14054)
IROQUOIS BIO-ENERGY CO LLC (HQ)
751 W State Road 114 (47978-7362)
P.O. Box 218 (47978-0218)
PHONE..............................219 866-2928
Roger Boer, *Treas*
Darlene Hopp, *Sec*
EMP: 9 **EST:** 2002
SALES (est): 23.19MM **Privately Held**
Web: www.ibecethanol.com
SIC: 2869 Fuels
PA: Babcock & Brown Biofuels Ibec Holdings Llc
2 Harrison St Fl 6
San Francisco CA 94105

(G-14055)
JASPER EQUIPMENT COMPANY LLC
701 N Melville St (47978-2117)
P.O. Box 256 (47978-0256)
PHONE..............................219 866-0600
David Hornbeck, *Managing Member*
EMP: 3 **EST:** 2005
SALES (est): 327.37K **Privately Held**
Web: www.jasperequipmentcompany.com
SIC: 3441 Fabricated structural metal

(G-14056)
KANKAKEE VALLEY PUBLISHING CO
Also Called: Rensselaer Republican
117 N Van Rensselaer St (47978-2651)
P.O. Box 298 (47978-0298)
PHONE..............................219 866-5111
Larry Perrotto, *Pr*
J Michael Perrotto, *VP*
EMP: 1 **EST:** 1865
SALES (est): 459.36K **Privately Held**
Web: www.newsbug.info
SIC: 2711 2752 Commercial printing and newspaper publishing combined; Commercial printing, lithographic
PA: Community Media Group Inc.
805 S Logan St
West Frankfort IL 62896

(G-14057)
LEGGETT & PLATT INCORPORATED
Also Called: Sealy Components
1132 N Cullen St (47978-2009)
P.O. Box 258 (47978-0258)
PHONE..............................219 866-7181
Ron Morgan, *Mgr*
EMP: 161
SQ FT: 95,000
SALES (corp-wide): 5.15B **Publicly Held**
Web: www.leggett.com
SIC: 2515 Box springs, assembled
PA: Leggett & Platt, Incorporated
1 Leggett Rd
Carthage MO 64836
417 358-8131

(G-14058)
LIBERTY TRAILERS LLC
Also Called: Talbert Manufacturing
1628 W State Road 114 (47978-7266)
PHONE..............................219 866-7141
EMP: 50 **EST:** 2015
SALES (est): 3.71MM **Privately Held**
Web: www.talbertmfg.com
SIC: 3715 Trailer bodies

(G-14059)
LIQUID FILTER HOUSINGS INC
513 N Melville St (47978-2369)
PHONE..............................414 530-8584
Brian Jones, *Pr*
Brad Gechel, *Sec*
EMP: 6 **EST:** 2017
SALES (est): 701.28K **Privately Held**
Web: www.liquidfilterhousings.com
SIC: 3444 Metal housings, enclosures, casings, and other containers

(G-14060)
MORRIS MACHINE & TOOL
828 N Scott St (47978-2158)
PHONE..............................219 866-3018
Russell Morris, *Owner*
EMP: 2 **EST:** 1983
SALES (est): 86.42K **Privately Held**
Web: www.morrismachinetool.com
SIC: 3599 7692 Machine shop, jobbing and repair; Welding repair

(G-14061)
NORTHWEST DEFENSE LLC
335 E 550 N (47978-8578)
PHONE..............................931 257-0421
Craig Schiesser, *Prin*
EMP: 5 **EST:** 2017
SALES (est): 106.9K **Privately Held**
Web: www.nwdefensellc.com
SIC: 3812 Defense systems and equipment

(G-14062)
OUTTADAWAY LLC
503 W Washington St (47978-2714)
PHONE..............................219 866-8885
Ned J Tonner, *Managing Member*
EMP: 2 **EST:** 2015
SALES (est): 119.02K **Privately Held**
SIC: 3496 Miscellaneous fabricated wire products

(G-14063)
PROFORM FINISHING PRODUCTS LLC
Also Called: National Gypsum Company
1325 E Maple St (47978-2116)
PHONE..............................219 866-7570
David Holston, *Mgr*
EMP: 37
SALES (corp-wide): 795.88MM **Privately Held**
Web: www.nationalgypsum.com
SIC: 3275 Building board, gypsum
HQ: Proform Finishing Products, Llc
2001 Rexford Rd
Charlotte NC 28211

(G-14064)
REINFORCEMENTS DESIGN
3195 1/2 W Clark St (47978-8893)
PHONE..............................219 866-8626
EMP: 5 **EST:** 1985
SALES (est): 227.26K **Privately Held**
Web: www.reinforcementsdesign.com
SIC: 7336 3993 Graphic arts and related design; Signs and advertising specialties

(G-14065)
RENSSELAER EAGLE VAULT CORP
Also Called: Rensselaer Septic Tanks
250 N Mckinley Ave (47978-2641)
P.O. Box 70 (47978-0070)
PHONE..............................219 866-5123
TOLL FREE: 800
Eric Jackson, *Pr*
William C Jackson, *Pr*
Eric Jackson, *Sec*
EMP: 5 **EST:** 1955
SQ FT: 2,000
SALES (est): 881.41K **Privately Held**
Web: www.rensselaerseptic.com
SIC: 5087 3272 Concrete burial vaults and boxes; Monuments, concrete

(G-14066)
RENSSELAER PRINT CO
116 N Cullen St (47978-2644)
PHONE..............................219 866-5000
Morris Barlow, *Owner*
EMP: 2 **EST:** 1952
SQ FT: 200
SALES (est): 169.62K **Privately Held**
SIC: 2752 Offset printing

(G-14067)
RITCHIE ELECTRIC MOTOR CO LLC
615 N Mckinley Ave (47978-2262)
PHONE..............................219 866-5185
Truman Ritchie, *Owner*
EMP: 1 **EST:** 2007
SQ FT: 200
SALES (est): 110.71K **Privately Held**
SIC: 7694 3621 Electric motor repair; Electric motor and generator parts

(G-14068)
SIGNS OF SEASONS
2675 W Clark St (47978-8892)
PHONE..............................219 866-4507
Suzanne Gilmore, *Owner*
EMP: 2 **EST:** 1990
SALES (est): 80K **Privately Held**
SIC: 3993 Signs and advertising specialties

(G-14069)
SOUTHERN FUEL LLC
1250 N Mckinley Ave (47978-2068)
PHONE..............................219 689-3552
Derich Schultz, *Admn*
EMP: 7 **EST:** 2013
SALES (est): 147.6K **Privately Held**
SIC: 2869 Fuels

(G-14070)
STARK TRUSS COMPANY INC
1317 N Owen St (47978-7532)
PHONE..............................219 866-2772
EMP: 61
SALES (corp-wide): 99.05MM **Privately Held**
Web: www.starktruss.com
SIC: 2439 Trusses, wooden roof
PA: Stark Truss Company, Inc.
109 Miles Ave Sw
Canton OH 44710
330 478-2100

(G-14071)
TALBERT MANUFACTURING INC (PA)
1628 W State Road 114 (47978-7266)
PHONE..............................800 348-5232
Andy Tanner, *Pr*
Russell N Stern, *✪*
EMP: 185 **EST:** 1957
SQ FT: 100,000
SALES (est): 94.5MM
SALES (corp-wide): 94.5MM **Privately Held**
Web: www.talbertmfg.com
SIC: 3715 5599 Trailer bodies; Utility trailers

Reynolds
White County

(G-14072)
ERP IRON ORE LLC
64 E 100 N (47980-8208)
PHONE..............................574 270-8608
Tom Clarke, *Mgr*
EMP: 1
SALES (corp-wide): 453.23K **Privately Held**
Web: www.naturalbridgeva.com
SIC: 1011 Iron ore beneficiating
PA: Erp Iron Ore, Llc
15 Appledore Ln
Natural Bridge VA
540 458-3753

(G-14073)
GLOBAL HARVEST FOODS LLC
10 E 100 S (47980-8120)
PHONE..............................219 984-6110

Reynolds - White County (G-14074)

EMP: 23
SALES (corp-wide): 104.29MM **Privately Held**
Web: www.ghfoods.com
SIC: 2048 Bird food, prepared
HQ: Global Harvest Foods, Llc
    16000 Christensen Rd # 30
    Tukwila WA 98188

(G-14074)
MONSANTO COMPANY
Also Called: Monsanto
371 N Diener Rd (47980-8010)
PHONE...................574 870-0397
EMP: 6
SALES (corp-wide): 51.78B **Privately Held**
Web: www.monsanto.com
SIC: 2879 Agricultural chemicals, nec
HQ: Monsanto Technology Llc.
    800 N Lindbergh Blvd
    Saint Louis MO 63167
    314 694-1000

(G-14075)
PERFECT PIG INC
332 W 100 N (47980-8051)
PHONE...................219 984-5355
Brian Furrer, *Pt*
EMP: 19 **EST:** 2005
SALES (est): 477.84K **Privately Held**
SIC: 2013 Pigs' feet, cooked and pickled: from purchased meat

(G-14076)
SCOTTS MIRACLE-GRO COMPANY
Also Called: Morning Song Wild Bird Feed
10 E 100 S (47980-8120)
PHONE...................219 984-6110
EMP: 6
SALES (corp-wide): 3.55B **Publicly Held**
Web: www.scottsmiraclegro.com
SIC: 2873 2048 Fertilizers: natural (organic), except compost; Prepared feeds, nec
PA: The Scotts Miracle-Gro Company
    14111 Scottslawn Rd
    Marysville OH 43041
    937 644-0011

(G-14077)
US MOLDERS INC
59 W 100 N (47980-8052)
PHONE...................219 984-5058
Tim Hebble, *Pr*
EMP: 42 **EST:** 2003
SQ FT: 50,000
SALES (est): 7.26MM **Privately Held**
Web: www.usmolders.com
SIC: 3089 Molding primary plastics

Richland
Spencer County

(G-14078)
GOLDMAN MACHINE SERVICES
5233 W County Road 600 N (47634-9315)
PHONE...................812 359-5440
Kenneth Goldman, *Owner*
EMP: 2 **EST:** 1994
SALES (est): 130.23K **Privately Held**
SIC: 3339 Beryllium metal

(G-14079)
IMAGINATION SET IN STONE LLC
5698 W County Road 600 N (47634-9312)
PHONE...................812 660-0031
EMP: 1 **EST:** 2011
SALES (est): 55.6K **Privately Held**
SIC: 3281 Cut stone and stone products

Richmond
Wayne County

(G-14080)
A PLUS SIGN AREA LTG SPCALISTS
920 Progress Dr (47374-8407)
PHONE...................765 966-4857
Eddie Thompson, *Pt*
Jeff Thompson, *Pt*
EMP: 4 **EST:** 1996
SALES (est): 290K **Privately Held**
Web: www.a-plussigns.net
SIC: 3993 Signs and advertising specialties

(G-14081)
A-PLUS SIGNS LLC
920 Progress Dr (47374-8407)
PHONE...................765 966-4857
Jeff Thompson, *Prin*
EMP: 2 **EST:** 2013
SALES (est): 226.65K **Privately Held**
Web: www.a-plussigns.net
SIC: 3993 Signs, not made in custom sign painting shops

(G-14082)
ABBOTT L ABBOTT NUTRITION
4200 W Industries Rd (47374-1385)
PHONE...................765 935-8650
EMP: 7 **EST:** 2019
SALES (est): 542.47K **Privately Held**
SIC: 3999 Manufacturing industries, nec

(G-14083)
ADKINS AMUSEMENTS
903 N D St (47374-3132)
PHONE...................765 939-0285
EMP: 1 **EST:** 1999
SALES (est): 52.47K **Privately Held**
SIC: 3599 Amusement park equipment

(G-14084)
AHAUS TOOL & ENGINEERING INC
Also Called: Ahaus
200 Industrial Pkwy (47374-3704)
P.O. Box 280 (47375-0280)
PHONE...................765 962-3573
Kevin M Ahaus, *Pr*
Fredric A Ahaus, *
Jeffrey S Sheridan, *
▲ **EMP:** 90 **EST:** 1946
SQ FT: 65,000
SALES (est): 19.14MM **Privately Held**
Web: www.ahaus.com
SIC: 3599 3544 Custom machinery; Special dies and tools

(G-14085)
ALCOA CORPORATION
1701 Williamsburg Pike (47374-1492)
PHONE...................765 983-9200
Timothy Jleveque, *Brnch Mgr*
▼ **EMP:** 2
SALES (corp-wide): 10.55B **Publicly Held**
Web: www.alcoa.com
SIC: 3355 Aluminum rolling and drawing, nec
PA: Alcoa Corporation
    201 Isabella St Ste 500
    Pittsburgh PA 15212
    412 315-2900

(G-14086)
ANGIES PRINTING LLC
1751 Sheridan St (47374-1811)
PHONE...................765 966-6237
Randy Sullivan, *Prin*
EMP: 6 **EST:** 2015
SALES (est): 83.91K **Privately Held**
SIC: 2752 Commercial printing, lithographic

(G-14087)
ASAHI TEC AMERICA CORPORATION
1757 Sheridan St (47374-1811)
PHONE...................765 962-8399
Yoshihiko Okaeaki, *VP*
EMP: 9 **EST:** 1992
SQ FT: 9,000
SALES (est): 930.86K **Privately Held**
Web: www.asahitecamerica.com
SIC: 2759 Screen printing

(G-14088)
AUGUSTIN PRTG & DESIGN SVCS (PA)
Also Called: Prinit Press
211 Nw 7th St (47374-4051)
PHONE...................765 966-7130
TOLL FREE: 800
Mike Gibbs, *Owner*
EMP: 5 **EST:** 1972
SQ FT: 1,800
SALES (est): 489.33K
SALES (corp-wide): 489.33K **Privately Held**
Web: www.infinitprint.com
SIC: 2752 2732 Offset printing; Books, printing only

(G-14089)
B&F PLASTICS INC
540 N 8th St (47374-2304)
PHONE...................765 962-6125
Bruce Upchurch, *Pr*
Bob Cramer, *
Chris Smith, *
Veronica Decker, *
▼ **EMP:** 53 **EST:** 2010
SQ FT: 20,000
SALES (est): 15.33MM **Privately Held**
Web: www.bfplastics.com
SIC: 2821 Plastics materials and resins

(G-14090)
BARRETT PAVING MATERIALS INC
5834 Inke Rd (47374-9618)
PHONE...................765 935-3060
Claude Seibel, *Mgr*
EMP: 1
SQ FT: 2,000
SALES (corp-wide): 105.44MM **Privately Held**
Web: www.barrettpaving.com
SIC: 1422 5032 1611 Crushed and broken limestone; Stone, crushed or broken; Surfacing and paving
HQ: Barrett Paving Materials Inc.
    8590 Bilstein Blvd
    Hamilton OH 45015
    973 533-1001

(G-14091)
BELDEN INC
Mohawk
2200 Us Highway 27 S (47374-7437)
PHONE...................978 537-9961
EMP: 2
SALES (corp-wide): 2.51B **Publicly Held**
Web: www.belden.com
SIC: 1731 3357 Fiber optic cable installation; Fiber optic cable (insulated)
PA: Belden Inc.
    1 N Brentwood Blvd Fl 15
    Saint Louis MO 63105
    314 854-8000

(G-14092)
BELDEN INC
West Penn Wire
2200 Us Highway 27 S (47374-7437)
P.O. Box 762 (15301-0762)
PHONE...................724 222-7060
EMP: 181
SALES (corp-wide): 2.51B **Publicly Held**
Web: www.belden.com
SIC: 3357 3315 2851 Nonferrous wiredrawing and insulating; Steel wire and related products; Paints and allied products
PA: Belden Inc.
    1 N Brentwood Blvd Fl 15
    Saint Louis MO 63105
    314 854-8000

(G-14093)
BELDEN INC
2200 Us Highway 27 S (47374-7437)
PHONE...................765 983-5200
EMP: 9
SALES (corp-wide): 2.51B **Publicly Held**
Web: www.belden.com
SIC: 3357 Communication wire
PA: Belden Inc.
    1 N Brentwood Blvd Fl 15
    Saint Louis MO 63105
    314 854-8000

(G-14094)
BELDEN INC
Also Called: Belden Cdt
350 Nw N St (47374-1828)
P.O. Box 1327 (47375-1327)
PHONE...................765 962-7561
Scott Dillon, *Brnch Mgr*
EMP: 700
SALES (corp-wide): 2.51B **Publicly Held**
Web: www.belden.com
SIC: 3357 3496 3315 Building wire and cable, nonferrous; Miscellaneous fabricated wire products; Steel wire and related products
PA: Belden Inc.
    1 N Brentwood Blvd Fl 15
    Saint Louis MO 63105
    314 854-8000

(G-14095)
BELDEN WIRE & CABLE COMPANY LLC (HQ)
Also Called: Belden
2200 Us Highway 27 S (47374)
PHONE...................765 983-5200
◆ **EMP:** 23 **EST:** 1902
SALES (est): 504.31MM
SALES (corp-wide): 2.51B **Publicly Held**
Web: www.belden.com
SIC: 3357 Nonferrous wiredrawing and insulating
PA: Belden Inc.
    1 N Brentwood Blvd Fl 15
    Saint Louis MO 63105
    314 854-8000

(G-14096)
BERRY GLOBAL INC
630 Commerce Rd (47374)
PHONE...................765 966-1414
EMP: 117
Web: www.berryglobal.com
SIC: 3089 3081 Bottle caps, molded plastics; Unsupported plastics film and sheet
HQ: Berry Global, Inc.
    101 Oakley St
    Evansville IN 47710

GEOGRAPHIC SECTION

Richmond - Wayne County (G-14124)

(G-14097)
BILLS PRINTING
1310 Nw 5th St (47374-1840)
PHONE....................................765 962-7674
William A Cole, Owner
EMP: 6 EST: 1981
SALES (est): 328.7K Privately Held
SIC: 2752 Offset printing

(G-14098)
BLACK DOG PRINTING LLC
Also Called: Screen Printing
711 S 9th St (47374-6233)
PHONE....................................812 955-0577
Jon Bottorff, Pr
EMP: 6 EST: 2015
SALES (est): 242.36K Privately Held
Web: www.blackdogprinting.org
SIC: 2759 Screen printing

(G-14099)
BLUE BUFFALO COMPANY LTD
4748 W Industries Rd (47374-1498)
PHONE....................................203 665-3500
EMP: 477
SALES (corp-wide): 19.86B Publicly Held
Web: www.bluebuffalo.com
SIC: 2047 5149 Dog and cat food; Pet foods
HQ: Blue Buffalo Company, Ltd.
11 River Rd Ste 200
Wilton CT 06897
203 762-9751

(G-14100)
BOSTON TOOL COMPANY INC
800 S 9th St (47374-6236)
P.O. Box 1521 (47375-1521)
PHONE....................................765 935-6282
Suzanne A Meier, Pr
Adolph T Meier, VP
Adolf T Meier, Sec
EMP: 16 EST: 1974
SQ FT: 10,000
SALES (est): 363.86K Privately Held
SIC: 3599 Machine shop, jobbing and repair

(G-14101)
BRYANT WELDING & FABRICATION
Also Called: Bryant Trucking
2693 N Round Barn Rd (47374-9740)
PHONE....................................765 935-4281
James Bryant, Owner
Gayle Bryant, Prin
EMP: 1 EST: 1970
SALES (est): 64.18K Privately Held
SIC: 7692 Welding repair

(G-14102)
CABINET FCTORIES OUTL RICHMOND
633 S H St (47374-6137)
P.O. Box 352798 (43635-2798)
PHONE....................................765 966-3875
EMP: 4 EST: 2011
SALES (est): 133.47K Privately Held
Web: www.cabinetoutletofrichmond.com
SIC: 2434 Wood kitchen cabinets

(G-14103)
CHAMPION TARGET
232 Industrial Pkwy (47374-3704)
P.O. Box 1151 (47375-1151)
PHONE....................................765 966-7745
Tim Emmenegger, Pr
EMP: 10 EST: 2010
SALES (est): 438.04K Privately Held
Web: www.championtarget.com
SIC: 3255 Clay refractories

(G-14104)
CINRAM INC
1600 Rich Rd (47374-1435)
PHONE....................................416 298-8190
◆ EMP: 5400
SIC: 3652 3695 Prerecorded records and tapes; Magnetic and optical recording media

(G-14105)
CIVIC SPARK MEDIA LLC ✪
400 N A St Unit 9 (47375-4001)
PHONE....................................765 357-4335
James C Hardie, Pr
EMP: 7 EST: 2022
SALES (est): 232.01K Privately Held
Web: www.civicsparkmedia.com
SIC: 2711 Newspapers

(G-14106)
CLIPPER COUNTRY
1539 S 9th St (47374-6919)
PHONE....................................765 935-2344
EMP: 5 EST: 2019
SALES (est): 88.38K Privately Held
Web: www.conniffsales.com
SIC: 3621 Motors and generators

(G-14107)
CMJ & ASSOCIATES CORPORATION
160 Fort Wayne Ave (47374-3058)
PHONE....................................765 962-1947
Gregory L Dale, Pr
EMP: 8 EST: 2009
SALES (est): 970.72K Privately Held
Web: cmj-corporation.sbcontract.com
SIC: 3496 Miscellaneous fabricated wire products

(G-14108)
COCA-COLA BOTTLING CO
1700 Industries Rd (47374)
PHONE....................................800 688-2053
EMP: 7 EST: 2019
SALES (est): 208.73K Privately Held
Web: www.coca-cola.com
SIC: 2086 Bottled and canned soft drinks

(G-14109)
COLOR-BOX LLC
Also Called: Georgia-Pacific
623 S G St (47374-6134)
PHONE....................................765 966-7588
EMP: 1100
SIC: 2653 Boxes, corrugated: made from purchased materials

(G-14110)
CONTRACT INDUS TOOLING INC (PA)
Also Called: CIT
2351 Production Ct (47374-8408)
PHONE....................................765 966-1134
Kim Wuertemberger, Pr
Mike Catey, *
Michael J Catey, *
▲ EMP: 54 EST: 1987
SQ FT: 118,000
SALES (est): 21.41MM
SALES (corp-wide): 21.41MM Privately Held
Web: www.c-i-t.com
SIC: 3599 Machine shop, jobbing and repair

(G-14111)
COUNTERTOP MANUFACTURING INC
1600 Nw 11th St (47374-1414)
PHONE....................................765 966-4969
Brad Jones, Pr
EMP: 40 EST: 1967
SQ FT: 30,000
SALES (est): 7.63MM Privately Held
SIC: 5031 2541 2499 2434 Kitchen cabinets; Cabinets, except refrigerated: show, display, etc.: wood; Kitchen, bathroom, and household ware: wood; Wood kitchen cabinets

(G-14112)
CUMMINS HOLDING GROUP LLC
3712 National Rd W (47374-4702)
PHONE....................................765 962-6332
EMP: 6 EST: 2007
SALES (est): 152.39K Privately Held
Web: www.cumminselectric.com
SIC: 3714 6719 Motor vehicle parts and accessories; Holding companies, nec

(G-14113)
DAVIS CUSTOM WELDING
3526 Whitewater Rd (47374-9327)
PHONE....................................765 847-2407
Mike Davis, Owner
EMP: 1 EST: 2001
SALES (est): 94.28K Privately Held
SIC: 7692 Welding repair

(G-14114)
DICK BAUMGARTNERS BASKET
707 Beeson Rd (47374-9452)
PHONE....................................765 220-1767
Richard E Baumgartner, Pr
EMP: 32 EST: 1977
SALES (est): 300.11K Privately Held
Web: www.dickbshootingcamp.com
SIC: 7032 3949 Sporting camps; Basketball equipment and supplies, general

(G-14115)
DODSON LOGISTICS LLC ✪
2526 Nw A St (47374-3808)
PHONE....................................937 657-7490
EMP: 1 EST: 2022
SALES (est): 60.08K Privately Held
SIC: 3537 7389 Trucks: freight, baggage, etc.: industrial, except mining; Business Activities at Non-Commercial Site

(G-14116)
DWYER-WILBERT INC
Also Called: Dwyer-Wilbert Monument
1014 National Rd W (47374-5141)
PHONE....................................765 962-3605
William J Dwyer, Pr
EMP: 6 EST: 1904
SQ FT: 6,500
SALES (est): 469.96K Privately Held
Web: www.dwyerfamilymemorials.com
SIC: 3281 5999 Burial vaults, stone; Monuments, finished to custom order

(G-14117)
E C T FRANKLIN CONTROL SYSTEMS
Also Called: Ect
1831 W Main St (47374-3821)
PHONE....................................765 939-2531
EMP: 8 EST: 1995
SALES (est): 968.32K Privately Held
SIC: 3625 Electric controls and control accessories, industrial

(G-14118)
ELDER GROUP INC
4251 W Industries Rd (47374-1385)
PHONE....................................765 966-7676
Alan H Elder, Ch
Gerald H Davis, *
Mark Harrington, *
EMP: 80 EST: 1985
SQ FT: 125,000
SALES (est): 9.25MM Privately Held
SIC: 2655 3995 Reels (fiber), textile: made from purchased material; Casket linings

(G-14119)
ELEVATOR EQUIPMENT CORPORATION
2230 Nw 12th St (47374-1471)
PHONE....................................765 966-7761
Jerry Benjamin, Mgr
EMP: 52
SALES (corp-wide): 24.17MM Privately Held
Web: www.elevatorequipment.com
SIC: 3534 3621 3594 3593 Elevators and moving stairways; Motors and generators; Fluid power pumps and motors; Fluid power cylinders and actuators
PA: Elevator Equipment Corporation
4035 Goodwin Ave
Los Angeles CA 90039
323 245-0147

(G-14120)
ENVIROTECH EXTRUSION INC
4810 Woodside Dr (47374-2634)
PHONE....................................765 966-8068
▲ EMP: 50 EST: 1995
SQ FT: 76,000
SALES (est): 5.45MM Privately Held
Web: www.envirotechext.com
SIC: 3061 2273 Mechanical rubber goods; Carpets and rugs

(G-14121)
FEDERAL CARTRIDGE COMPANY
232 Industrial Pkwy (47374-3704)
PHONE....................................765 966-7745
Tim Emmenedder, Mgr
EMP: 204
SALES (corp-wide): 2.75B Publicly Held
Web: www.federalpremium.com
SIC: 3949 Trap racks (clay targets)
HQ: Federal Cartridge Company
900 Bob Ehlen Dr
Anoka MN 55303
800 379-1732

(G-14122)
FETZER PUBLISHING
327 Hazelwood Ln (47374)
PHONE....................................765 966-9169
Dudley Fetzer, Prin
EMP: 1 EST: 2001
SALES (est): 57.33K Privately Held
Web: www.fetzerpublishing.com
SIC: 2741 Miscellaneous publishing

(G-14123)
FRICKERS INC
3237 Chester Blvd (47374-1014)
PHONE....................................765 965-6655
Jamie Oler, Genl Mgr
Lisa Willis, *
Carie Outon, *
EMP: 9 EST: 1997
SALES (est): 221.45K Privately Held
Web: www.frickers.com
SIC: 3965 5813 5812 Buttons and parts; Drinking places; Eating places

(G-14124)
GANNETT MEDIA CORP
Also Called: Palladium Item, The
1175 North Dr (47374-1627)
P.O. Box 308 (47375-0308)
PHONE....................................765 962-1575
EMP: 1
SALES (corp-wide): 2.66B Publicly Held
Web: www.gannett.com

Richmond - Wayne County (G-14125)

SIC: 2711 Newspapers, publishing and printing
HQ: Gannett Media Corp.
7950 Jones Branch Dr
Mclean VA 22102
703 854-6000

(G-14125)
GEORGIA DIRECT CARPET INC
Also Called: Georgia Direct Crpt & Cabinets
5200 National Rd E (47374-2670)
P.O. Box 1663 (47375-1663)
PHONE..................................765 966-2548
EMP: 10
Web: www.georgiadirect.biz
SIC: 5023 1752 2273 3253 Carpets; Ceramic floor tile installation; Floor coverings, textile fiber; Ceramic wall and floor tile

(G-14126)
GOOD EARTH PUBLICATIONS INC
815 College Ave (47374-5224)
P.O. Box 2425 (47375-2425)
PHONE..................................540 460-6459
Foreman Patricia, *Prin*
EMP: 4 EST: 2019
SALES (est): 99.83K **Privately Held**
SIC: 2741 Miscellaneous publishing

(G-14127)
GRAFCOR INC
Also Called: Innomark Communications
601 Nw 5th St (47374-2972)
P.O. Box 2239 (47375-2239)
PHONE..................................765 966-7030
William Fair, *Pr*
Gary Boens, *VP*
Paul Molyneaux, *VP*
EMP: 15 EST: 1993
SQ FT: 20,000
SALES (est): 530.98K **Privately Held**
SIC: 2752 Offset printing

(G-14128)
GRASS VALLEY USA LLC
Also Called: Grass Valley
1411 Nw 11th St (47374-1470)
PHONE..................................765 259-1744
Terry Toney, *Prin*
EMP: 7 EST: 2019
SALES (est): 237.31K **Privately Held**
Web: www.grassvalley.com
SIC: 3663 Radio and t.v. communications equipment

(G-14129)
H & P TOOL CO INC
610 S G St (47374-6135)
P.O. Box 486 (47375-0486)
PHONE..................................765 962-4504
George A Peters, *Pr*
Carolyn Peters, *
EMP: 25 EST: 1942
SQ FT: 25,000
SALES (est): 2.75MM **Privately Held**
Web: www.hptoolco.com
SIC: 3545 3544 Tools and accessories for machine tools; Jigs and fixtures

(G-14130)
HAGERSTOWN PLASTICS INC
621 S J St (47374-6139)
PHONE..................................765 939-3849
Debra Wilson, *Pr*
Darrell Rutledge, *Pr*
Leon Pasley Junior, *VP*
EMP: 26 EST: 1973
SQ FT: 3,600
SALES (est): 783.49K **Privately Held**

SIC: 3089 Injection molding of plastics

(G-14131)
HANGER PRSTHTICS ORTHOTICS INC
Also Called: Orpro Prosthetics & Orthotics
4821 Old National Rd E Ste A (47374-2675)
PHONE..................................765 966-5069
Carrie Melton, *Mgr*
EMP: 3
SALES (corp-wide): 1.12B **Privately Held**
Web: corporate.hanger.com
SIC: 3842 5999 Limbs, artificial; Orthopedic and prosthesis applications
HQ: Hanger Prosthetics & Orthotics, Inc.
10910 Domain Dr Ste 300
Austin TX 78758
512 777-3800

(G-14132)
HEARTLAND PET FOOD MFG IND LLC
4748 W Industries Rd (47374-1498)
PHONE..................................765 209-4140
EMP: 11 EST: 2016
SALES (est): 3.26MM **Privately Held**
SIC: 2047 Dog and cat food

(G-14133)
HILLS PET NUTRITION INC
2325 Union Pike (47374-9701)
P.O. Box 2146 (47375-2146)
PHONE..................................765 935-7071
Kathy Zaleha, *Manager*
EMP: 34
SALES (corp-wide): 19.46B **Publicly Held**
Web: www.hillspet.com
SIC: 2047 Dog and cat food
HQ: Hill's Pet Nutrition, Inc.
6180 Sprint Pkwy
Leawood KS 66211
800 255-0449

(G-14134)
HITCHCOCK TOOL LLC
710 Nw 5th St (47374-2241)
PHONE..................................513 276-7345
Jimmy A Hitchcock, *Managing Member*
EMP: 6 EST: 2005
SALES (est): 309.23K **Privately Held**
Web: www.aqmolds.com
SIC: 3465 Moldings or trim, automobile: stamped metal

(G-14135)
HOLLAND COLOURS AMERICAS INC
1501 Progress Dr (47374-1486)
PHONE..................................765 935-0329
Joseph Bauer, *Pr*
Joseph Gleeson, *
Mj Bos, *
▲ EMP: 85 EST: 1985
SQ FT: 60,500
SALES (est): 42.62MM
SALES (corp-wide): 112.12MM **Privately Held**
Web: www.hollandcolors.com
SIC: 2865 Color pigments, organic
HQ: Holland Colours N.V.
Halvemaanweg 1
Apeldoorn GE 7323
553680700

(G-14136)
HOOSIER CONTAINER INC
1001 Indiana Ave (47374-2867)
P.O. Box 546 (47375-0546)
PHONE..................................765 966-2541
William Akers Ii, *Pr*

Michael Akey Junior, *Sec*
James F Akers, *
Grayson Fitzhugh, *Stockholder*
EMP: 35 EST: 1960
SQ FT: 78,000
SALES (est): 2.66MM **Privately Held**
Web: www.akers-pkg.com
SIC: 2653 Boxes, corrugated: made from purchased materials

(G-14137)
HOWA USA INC
1767 Sheridan St (47374-1811)
PHONE..................................765 962-7855
Shin Iwata, *Pr*
EMP: 6 EST: 2018
SALES (est): 63.17K **Privately Held**
SIC: 3999 Manufacturing industries, nec

(G-14138)
IMPERIAL PRODUCTS LLC
Also Called: Homeshield
451 Industrial Pkwy (47374-3709)
PHONE..................................765 966-0322
David Petratis, *Prin*
Kevin P Delaney, *Sec*
Brent L Korb, *CFO*
Jairaj T Chetnani, *Treas*
▲ EMP: 50 EST: 1977
SQ FT: 90,000
SALES (est): 2.02MM **Publicly Held**
SIC: 3442 Window and door frames
PA: Quanex Building Products Corporation
945 Bunker Hl Rd Ste 900
Houston TX 77024

(G-14139)
INFINITPRINT SOLUTIONS INC
217 S 4th St (47374-5405)
PHONE..................................765 962-1507
EMP: 20 EST: 2019
SALES (est): 1.36MM **Privately Held**
Web: www.infinitprint.com
SIC: 2752 Offset printing

(G-14140)
INX INTERNATIONAL INK CO
Also Called: INX INTERNATIONAL INK CO
1056 Industries Rd (47374-9769)
PHONE..................................765 939-6625
Randy Robinson, *Mgr*
EMP: 2
Web: www.inxinternational.com
SIC: 2893 Printing ink
HQ: Inx International Ink Co.
150 N Martingale Rd # 700
Schaumburg IL 60173
630 382-1800

(G-14141)
IU EAST BUSINESS OFFICE
2325 Chester Blvd (47374-1220)
PHONE..................................765 973-8218
Kathryn Cruz-uribe, *Chancellor*
EMP: 46 EST: 2008
SALES (est): 2.29MM **Privately Held**
Web: east.iu.edu
SIC: 2761 Continuous forms, office and business

(G-14142)
J & B SALES & INDUCTION SRVCS
420 S M St (47374-6841)
PHONE..................................765 965-2500
Tom Clements, *Owner*
EMP: 1 EST: 2005
SALES (est): 120.27K **Privately Held**
SIC: 2843 Finishing agents

(G-14143)
J & J WINERY
3415 National Rd W (47374-4416)
PHONE..................................765 969-1188
Melody J Haist, *Prin*
EMP: 4 EST: 2008
SALES (est): 296.81K **Privately Held**
Web: www.jjwinery.com
SIC: 2084 Wines

(G-14144)
J J LITES
4469 Webster Rd (47374-9530)
PHONE..................................765 966-3252
Mike Jenkins, *VP*
EMP: 2 EST: 2002
SALES (est): 125.01K **Privately Held**
SIC: 3647 Automotive lighting fixtures, nec

(G-14145)
J M HUTTON
751 S O St (47374-6851)
PHONE..................................765 935-4817
EMP: 7 EST: 2019
SALES (est): 180.15K **Privately Held**
Web: www.jmhutton.com
SIC: 3469 Stamping metal for the trade

(G-14146)
JAKE EDDIES SIGNS
923 N E St (47374-3137)
PHONE..................................765 962-1892
EMP: 1
SALES (est): 67.88K **Privately Held**
SIC: 3993 Signs and advertising specialties

(G-14147)
JASON HOLDINGS INC (PA)
Also Called: Jason
833 E Michigan St Ste 900 (47374)
PHONE..................................414 277-9300
Brian K Kobylinski, *Ch Bd*
Timm Fields, *
Kevin Kuznicki, *
Chad M Paris, *
Keith A Walz, *
EMP: 160 EST: 2020
SALES (est): 80.67MM
SALES (corp-wide): 80.67MM **Privately Held**
Web: www.osborn.com
SIC: 2297 3625 3469 3844 Nonwoven fabrics; Noise control equipment; Metal stampings, nec; Irradiation equipment, nec

(G-14148)
JASON INCORPORATED
Also Called: Janesville Acoustics
2350 Salisbury Rd N (47374-9726)
PHONE..................................248 455-7919
Dave Cataldi, *Brnch Mgr*
EMP: 7
SALES (corp-wide): 834.99MM **Privately Held**
Web: www.osborn.com
SIC: 3714 Motor vehicle parts and accessories
PA: Jason Incorporated
833 E Michigan St Ste 900
Milwaukee WI 53202

(G-14149)
JASON INCORPORATED
Osborn International
2350 Salisbury Rd N (47374-9726)
PHONE..................................765 965-5333
Doug Pollak, *Brnch Mgr*
EMP: 54
SQ FT: 5,000
SALES (corp-wide): 834.99MM **Privately Held**

GEOGRAPHIC SECTION
Richmond - Wayne County (G-14171)

Web: www.osborn.com
SIC: 3991 3442 Brushes, household or industrial; Metal doors, sash, and trim
PA: Jason Incorporated
833 E Michigan St Ste 900
Milwaukee WI 53202

(G-14150)
JASON INCORPORATED
Assembled Products Group
2350 Salisbury Rd N (47374-9726)
PHONE..................847 215-1948
Steve Carolla, *Brnch Mgr*
EMP: 70
SALES (corp-wide): 834.99MM **Privately Held**
Web: www.osborn.com
SIC: 3469 3699 Metal stampings, nec; Electrical equipment and supplies, nec
PA: Jason Incorporated
833 E Michigan St Ste 900
Milwaukee WI 53202

(G-14151)
JM HUTTON & CO INC
Also Called: JM Hutton & Company
1117 N E St (47374-3249)
P.O. Box 129 (47375-0129)
PHONE..................765 962-3506
Richard N Jeffers, *Pr*
EMP: 20
SALES (corp-wide): 9.68MM **Privately Held**
Web: www.jmhutton.com
SIC: 3995 Burial caskets
PA: J.M. Hutton & Co., Inc.
1501 S 8th St
Richmond IN 47374
765 962-3591

(G-14152)
JM HUTTON & CO INC (PA)
Also Called: J M Hutton & Company
1501 S 8th St (47374-6907)
P.O. Box 129 (47375-0129)
PHONE..................765 962-3591
Mark Jeffers, *Pr*
◆ **EMP:** 80 **EST:** 1968
SQ FT: 170,000
SALES (est): 9.68MM
SALES (corp-wide): 9.68MM **Privately Held**
Web: www.jmhutton.com
SIC: 3995 3469 Burial caskets; Metal stampings, nec

(G-14153)
JOHNS MANVILLE CORPORATION
814 Richmond Ave (47374-2896)
P.O. Box 428 (47375-0428)
PHONE..................765 973-5200
Emerson Bungard, *Brnch Mgr*
EMP: 81
SALES (corp-wide): 364.48B **Publicly Held**
Web: www.jm.com
SIC: 3296 Fiberglass insulation
HQ: Johns Manville Corporation
717 17th St
Denver CO 80202
303 978-2000

(G-14154)
KOENIG EQUIPMENT INC
3421 State Road 38 (47374-9735)
PHONE..................765 962-7330
EMP: 5
SALES (corp-wide): 47.28MM **Privately Held**
Web: www.koenigequipment.com

SIC: 5999 3523 Farm equipment and supplies; Farm machinery and equipment
PA: Koenig Equipment, Inc.
15213 State Route 274
Botkins OH 45306
937 693-5000

(G-14155)
LAND OLAKES INC
Also Called: Land O'Lakes
505 N 4th St (47374-2358)
PHONE..................765 962-9561
EMP: 26
SALES (corp-wide): 2.89B **Privately Held**
Web: www.landolakes-ingredients.com
SIC: 2048 Prepared feeds, nec
PA: Land O'lakes, Inc.
4001 Lexington Ave N
Arden Hills MN 55112
651 375-2222

(G-14156)
LANDIS PLASTICS
630 Commerce Rd (47374-2600)
PHONE..................765 966-1414
Gary Greene, *Prin*
EMP: 6 **EST:** 2018
SALES (est): 103.91K **Privately Held**
SIC: 3089 Plastics products, nec

(G-14157)
MACALLISTER MACHINERY CO INC
Also Called: Caterpillar Authorized Dealer
4791 Old National Rd E (47374-2674)
PHONE..................765 966-0759
EMP: 17
SALES (corp-wide): 658.13MM **Privately Held**
Web: www.macallister.com
SIC: 7359 3541 5084 5082 Equipment rental and leasing, nec; Machine tools, metal cutting type; Machine tools and accessories; Construction and mining machinery
PA: Macallister Machinery Co Inc
6300 Southeastern Ave
Indianapolis IN 46203
317 545-2151

(G-14158)
MAGAWS OF BOSTON
Also Called: Magaws of Boston The
5774 State Road 227 S (47374-9424)
PHONE..................765 935-6170
William Magaw, *Prin*
William Magaw, *Owner*
EMP: 2 **EST:** 2009
SALES (est): 57.1K **Privately Held**
SIC: 8999 7389 3299 Sculptor's studio; Business Activities at Non-Commercial Site; Architectural sculptures: gypsum, clay, papier mache, etc.

(G-14159)
MARTIN EKWLOR PHRMCUTICALS INC
Also Called: Vesco
2800 Se Pwy (47374-5857)
P.O. Box 565 (47375-0565)
PHONE..................765 962-4410
Ike Martin Ekwealor, *Pr*
Susan Ekwealor, *VP*
EMP: 15 **EST:** 1990
SQ FT: 5,000
SALES (est): 2.16MM **Privately Held**
SIC: 2834 5122 Pharmaceutical preparations; Pharmaceuticals

(G-14160)
MASTERBRAND CABINETS LLC
1340 Rose City Blvd (47374-9581)
P.O. Box 1567 (47375-1567)
PHONE..................765 966-3940
Dan Colley, *Brnch Mgr*
EMP: 13
SALES (corp-wide): 2.73B **Publicly Held**
Web: www.masterbrand.com
SIC: 2434 Wood kitchen cabinets
HQ: Masterbrand Cabinets Llc
3300 Entp Pkwy Ste 300
Beachwood OH 44122
812 482-2527

(G-14161)
MATTHEWS INTERNATIONAL CORP
Matthews Casket Division
620 S J St (47374-6140)
PHONE..................765 966-1576
EMP: 100
SALES (corp-wide): 1.88B **Publicly Held**
Web: www.matw.com
SIC: 3995 Burial caskets
PA: Matthews International Corporation
2 N Shore Ctr
Pittsburgh PA 15212
412 442-8200

(G-14162)
MEDLIN CUSTOM WOODWORKING INC
245 S 3rd St (47374-5401)
P.O. Box 1262 (47375-1262)
PHONE..................765 939-0923
Steeve Medlin, *Pr*
EMP: 10 **EST:** 2005
SALES (est): 502.75K **Privately Held**
SIC: 2431 Millwork

(G-14163)
MENASHA PACKAGING COMPANY LLC
Also Called: Color-Box
1056 Industries Rd (47374-9769)
PHONE..................877 818-2016
EMP: 1
SALES (corp-wide): 1.94B **Privately Held**
Web: www.menasha.com
SIC: 2653 Boxes, corrugated: made from purchased materials
HQ: Menasha Packaging Company, Llc
1645 Bergstrom Rd
Neenah WI 54956
920 751-1000

(G-14164)
MEREDITHS INC
Also Called: Saver Systems
800 S 7th St (47374-6123)
PHONE..................765 966-5084
John Meredith, *Pr*
▲ **EMP:** 25 **EST:** 1978
SQ FT: 30,000
SALES (est): 4.68MM **Privately Held**
Web: www.saversystems.com
SIC: 2899 Waterproofing compounds

(G-14165)
MICHAEL DARGIE
Also Called: Dargie Racing Engines
1700 Nw 11th St (47374-1419)
PHONE..................765 935-2241
Michael Dargie, *Owner*
EMP: 3 **EST:** 1997
SALES (est): 238.42K **Privately Held**
Web: www.dargierepair.com
SIC: 3519 Gasoline engines

(G-14166)
MIGHTY MUFFLER LLC
1440 Nw 5th St (47374-1842)
PHONE..................765 966-6833
Darin Doner, *Owner*

EMP: 2 **EST:** 1991
SALES (est): 195.96K **Privately Held**
Web: www.mightymufflers.com
SIC: 7534 7539 7533 Tire retreading and repair shops; Brake repair, automotive; Muffler shop, sale or repair and installation

(G-14167)
MILSO INDUSTRIES INC
Also Called: Milso Industries
401 Industrial Pkwy (47374-3709)
PHONE..................765 966-8012
Dale Palmer, *Mgr*
EMP: 15
SALES (corp-wide): 1.88B **Publicly Held**
SIC: 5087 3995 Caskets; Burial caskets
HQ: Milso Industries Inc.
534 Union St
Brooklyn NY 11215
718 624-4593

(G-14168)
MOSEY MANUFACTURING CO INC
Machine Tool Innovators Div
534 N 17th St (47374-3333)
PHONE..................765 983-8870
EMP: 6
SALES (corp-wide): 44.49MM **Privately Held**
Web: www.moseymfg.com
SIC: 3541 Machine tools, metal cutting type
PA: Mosey Manufacturing Co Inc
262 Fort Wayne Ave
Richmond IN 47374
765 983-8800

(G-14169)
MOSEY MANUFACTURING CO INC
Also Called: Elwood Operations
1700 N F St (47374-2563)
PHONE..................765 983-8870
Travis Marsh, *Mgr*
EMP: 131
SALES (corp-wide): 44.49MM **Privately Held**
Web: www.moseymfg.com
SIC: 3541 Machine tools, metal cutting type
PA: Mosey Manufacturing Co Inc
262 Fort Wayne Ave
Richmond IN 47374
765 983-8800

(G-14170)
MOSEY MANUFACTURING CO INC
Also Called: Mosey Manufacturing Plant 7
1700 N F St (47374-2563)
PHONE..................765 983-8889
EMP: 110
SALES (corp-wide): 44.49MM **Privately Held**
Web: www.moseymfg.com
SIC: 3541 3714 3322 Machine tools, metal cutting type; Motor vehicle parts and accessories; Malleable iron foundries
PA: Mosey Manufacturing Co Inc
262 Fort Wayne Ave
Richmond IN 47374
765 983-8800

(G-14171)
MOSEY MANUFACTURING CO INC
Also Called: Mosey Plant II
1700 N F St (47374-2563)
PHONE..................765 983-8870
Ken Mackey, *Mgr*
EMP: 176
SALES (corp-wide): 44.49MM **Privately Held**
Web: www.moseymfg.com

Richmond - Wayne County (G-14172)

SIC: 3541 3714 Machine tools, metal cutting type; Motor vehicle transmissions, drive assemblies, and parts
PA: Mosey Manufacturing Co Inc
262 Fort Wayne Ave
Richmond IN 47374
765 983-8800

(G-14172)
MOSEY MANUFACTURING CO INC (PA)
262 Fort Wayne Ave (47374-2392)
PHONE.................................765 983-8800
George N Mosey, *Pr*
Stephen A Mosey, *
Dan Kindley, *
Kenneth L Mackey, *
EMP: 27 **EST:** 1946
SQ FT: 40,000
SALES (est): 44.49MM
SALES (corp-wide): 44.49MM **Privately Held**
Web: www.moseymfg.com
SIC: 3599 Machine shop, jobbing and repair

(G-14173)
MVCTC ✪
240 E Farlow Rd (47374-7700)
PHONE.................................765 969-8921
Nikolai Catey, *Owner*
EMP: 3 **EST:** 2023
SALES (est): 99.14K **Privately Held**
SIC: 3571 7389 Electronic computers; Business Activities at Non-Commercial Site

(G-14174)
NEW HOLLAND RICHMOND INC
3100 W Industries Rd (47374-1391)
P.O. Box 249 (47330-0249)
PHONE.................................765 962-7724
Jessie Straeter, *CEO*
Melinda Straeter, *Sec*
EMP: 11 **EST:** 2013
SALES (est): 1.6MM **Privately Held**
Web: www.newhollandrochester.com
SIC: 3523 Farm machinery and equipment

(G-14175)
NIXON TOOL COMPANY INC
301 N 3rd St (47374-3005)
P.O. Box 1505 (47375-1505)
PHONE.................................765 966-6608
Scott Nixon, *Pr*
EMP: 30 **EST:** 1952
SQ FT: 15,000
SALES (est): 2.76MM **Privately Held**
Web: www.nixontool.com
SIC: 3599 3544 3545 Machine shop, jobbing and repair; Jigs and fixtures; Gauges (machine tool accessories)

(G-14176)
OERLIKON BALZERS COATING USA
1580 Progress Dr (47374-1485)
PHONE.................................765 935-7424
Scott Murray, *Genl Mgr*
Norman B Lawton, *Pr*
Bradley L Lawton, *Ex VP*
Jeffrey L Lawton, *VP*
Boyd E Moilanen, *Sec*
EMP: 51 **EST:** 1989
SALES (est): 1.73MM
SALES (corp-wide): 101.14MM **Privately Held**
Web: www.oerlikon.com
SIC: 3479 Coating of metals and formed products
PA: Star Cutter Co.
23461 Industrial Park Dr
Farmington Hills MI 48335
248 474-8200

(G-14177)
OPTICAL DISC SOLUTIONS INC
1767 Sheridan St (47374-1811)
P.O. Box 1769 (47375-1769)
PHONE.................................765 935-7574
EMP: 50
Web: www.opticaldiscsolutions.com
SIC: 3652 Prerecorded records and tapes

(G-14178)
OSBORN LLC (HQ)
Also Called: Matchless
2350 N Salisbury Rd (47374-9726)
PHONE.................................414 277-9300
Kevin Kuznicki, *Managing Member*
EMP: 81 **EST:** 2018
SALES (est): 45.99MM
SALES (corp-wide): 834.99MM **Privately Held**
Web: www.osborn.com
SIC: 2842 Cleaning or polishing preparations, nec
PA: Jason Incorporated
833 E Michigan St Ste 900
Milwaukee WI 53202

(G-14179)
PARAGON CASKET INC
1751 S 8th St (47374-6886)
PHONE.................................888 855-3601
◆ **EMP:** 55 **EST:** 2007
SQ FT: 48,000
SALES (est): 7.44MM **Privately Held**
Web: www.paragoncasketinc.com
SIC: 5087 3995 Caskets; Burial caskets

(G-14180)
PAUST INC (PA)
Also Called: Paust Printers
14 N 10th St (47374-3142)
P.O. Box 1326 (47375-1326)
PHONE.................................765 962-1507
Kenneth E Paust, *Pr*
Linda Paust, *VP*
EMP: 14 **EST:** 1945
SQ FT: 14,500
SALES (est): 2.48MM
SALES (corp-wide): 2.48MM **Privately Held**
Web: www.paust.com
SIC: 5199 2752 Advertising specialties; Offset printing

(G-14181)
PEACOCK PLASTICS INC
4124 High St (47374-4500)
PHONE.................................765 935-9178
Larry L Sandifar Senior, *Prin*
EMP: 7 **EST:** 2016
SALES (est): 54.61K **Privately Held**
Web: peacock-plastics-llc.ueniweb.com
SIC: 3089 Injection molding of plastics

(G-14182)
PETERSON SANKO CORP
505 Industrial Pkwy (47374-7941)
PHONE.................................765 966-9656
Lisa Wolf, *Supervisor*
EMP: 6 **EST:** 2010
SALES (est): 181.57K **Privately Held**
SIC: 3714 Motor vehicle parts and accessories

(G-14183)
PONTONE INDUSTRIES LLC
401 Industrial Pkwy (47374-3709)
PHONE.................................765 966-8012
◆ **EMP:** 130
SALES (est): 8.87MM **Privately Held**
SIC: 3995 Burial caskets

(G-14184)
PRIMEX CLOR CMPNDING ADDTVES C
1235 N F St (47374-2448)
PHONE.................................800 222-5116
EMP: 25
SALES (corp-wide): 2.03B **Privately Held**
Web: www.primexplastics.com
SIC: 2821 Plastics materials and resins
HQ: Primex Color, Compounding & Additives Corporation
61 River Dr
Garfield NJ 07026
973 777-8999

(G-14185)
PRIMEX DESIGN FABRICATION CORP
400 Industrial Pkwy (47374-3727)
PHONE.................................765 935-2990
Mike Cramer, *Pr*
▼ **EMP:** 90 **EST:** 1984
SALES (est): 9.14MM
SALES (corp-wide): 2.03B **Privately Held**
Web: www.primexplastics.com
SIC: 3089 Injection molding of plastics
HQ: Primex Plastics Corporation
1235 N F St
Richmond IN 47374
765 966-7774

(G-14186)
PRIMEX PLASTICS CORPORATION (HQ)
Also Called: Primex
1235 N F St (47374)
PHONE.................................765 966-7774
Mike Cramer, *Pr*
Gus Finet, *
Rob Wells, *
Tim Schultz, *
Blaise Sarcone, *
◆ **EMP:** 500 **EST:** 1965
SQ FT: 1,000,000
SALES (est): 435.53MM
SALES (corp-wide): 2.03B **Privately Held**
Web: www.primexplastics.com
SIC: 3081 2821 Plastics film and sheet; Thermoplastic materials
PA: Icc Industries Inc.
725 5th Ave
New York NY 10022
212 521-1700

(G-14187)
PRODUCTIVITY FABRICATORS INC
2332 Flatley Rd (47374-1334)
PHONE.................................765 966-2896
Jon R Odom, *Pr*
Connie Odom, *VP*
EMP: 10 **EST:** 1994
SQ FT: 40,000
SALES (est): 2.2MM **Privately Held**
Web: www.cyberprofab.com
SIC: 3441 Building components, structural steel

(G-14188)
PROPAGANDA MOTORCYCLES INC
1304 Rose City Blvd (47374-9581)
PHONE.................................765 997-8787
Robert Ray Johnson Junior Incorp, *Prin*
EMP: 6 **EST:** 2020
SALES (est): 59.56K **Privately Held**
Web: www.propagandamotorcycles.com
SIC: 3732 Boatbuilding and repairing

(G-14189)
PTC ALLIANCE CORPORATION
1480 Nw 11th St (47374-1469)
PHONE.................................765 259-3334
Peter Whiting, *CEO*
Cary Hart, *Pr*
Tom Crowley, *CFO*
EMP: 16 **EST:** 2014
SALES (est): 1.91MM **Privately Held**
Web: www.ptcalliance.com
SIC: 3317 Steel pipe and tubes

(G-14190)
PTC TUBULAR PRODUCTS LLC (HQ)
1480 Nw 11th St (47374-1469)
PHONE.................................765 259-3334
EMP: 66 **EST:** 2006
SALES (est): 25.58MM **Privately Held**
Web: www.ptcalliance.com
SIC: 3317 Steel pipe and tubes
PA: Ptc Group Holdings Corp.
6051 Wallace Road Ext # 20
Wexford PA 15090

(G-14191)
PURINA ANIMAL NUTRITION LLC
1700 Industries Rd (47374-1375)
PHONE.................................765 373-9377
EMP: 1
SALES (corp-wide): 2.89B **Privately Held**
Web: www.purinamills.com
SIC: 2048 Prepared feeds, nec
HQ: Purina Animal Nutrition Llc
100 Danforth Dr
Gray Summit MO 63039

(G-14192)
PURINA ANIMAL NUTRITION LLC
505 N 4th St (47374-2358)
PHONE.................................765 962-9561
EMP: 1
SALES (corp-wide): 2.89B **Privately Held**
Web: www.purinamills.com
SIC: 2048 Prepared feeds, nec
HQ: Purina Animal Nutrition Llc
100 Danforth Dr
Gray Summit MO 63039

(G-14193)
PURINA ANIMAL NUTRITION LLC
415 N 6th & Neff St (47374)
PHONE.................................765 962-9561
Heath Stinson, *Brnch Mgr*
EMP: 11
SALES (corp-wide): 2.89B **Privately Held**
Web: www.purinamills.com
SIC: 2048 Prepared feeds, nec
HQ: Purina Animal Nutrition Llc
100 Danforth Dr
Gray Summit MO 63039

(G-14194)
QUANEX HOMESHIELD LLC
451 Industrial Pkwy (47374-3709)
PHONE.................................765 966-0322
EMP: 32
Web: www.quanex.com
SIC: 3442 Window and door frames
HQ: Quanex Homeshield, Llc
311 W Coleman St
Rice Lake WI 54868
715 234-9061

(G-14195)
RECYCLING CENTER INC
630 S M St (47374-6842)
P.O. Box 2038 (47375-2038)
PHONE.................................765 966-8295
TOLL FREE: 800
Jack Edelman, *Pr*
Debra Edelman, *
EMP: 100 **EST:** 1974
SQ FT: 25,000
SALES (est): 8.65MM **Privately Held**

Web: www.recyclingcenterinc.com
SIC: 5093 4953 3341 3231 Ferrous metal scrap and waste; Refuse collection and disposal services; Secondary nonferrous metals; Products of purchased glass

(G-14196)
REEVES MANUFACTURING INC
1214 Sheridan St (47374-2125)
PHONE..................765 935-3875
Dennis Frame, Pr
Deborah Reeves, Sec
EMP: 7 EST: 1980
SQ FT: 15,000
SALES (est): 827.67K Privately Held
Web: www.reevesdecon.com
SIC: 3441 5051 3469 Fabricated structural metal; Iron and steel (ferrous) products; Metal stampings, nec

(G-14197)
RICHMOND BAKING CO
520 N 6th St (47374-2353)
P.O. Box 698 (47375-0698)
PHONE..................765 962-8535
William Quigg, CEO
William M Quigg, *
James Robert Quigg Iii, Treas
Robert A Ramsey, *
Felicia S Quigg, *
EMP: 135 EST: 1902
SQ FT: 180,000
SALES (est): 36.35MM Privately Held
Web: www.richmondbaking.com
SIC: 2052 Cookies

(G-14198)
RICHMOND BAKING GEORGIA INC
520 N 6th St (47374-2353)
P.O. Box 698 (47375-0698)
PHONE..................765 962-8535
EMP: 8 EST: 2016
SALES (est): 398.63K Privately Held
Web: www.richmondbaking.com
SIC: 2052 Cookies and crackers

(G-14199)
RICHMOND CASTING COMPANY
1775 Rich Rd (47374-1479)
P.O. Box 1247 (47375-1247)
PHONE..................765 935-4090
Gill Mcbride, Pr
EMP: 35 EST: 1974
SQ FT: 28,000
SALES (est): 4.82MM Privately Held
Web: www.richmondcasting.com
SIC: 3321 Gray iron castings, nec

(G-14200)
ROMARK INDUSTRIES INC
1751 S 8th St (47374-6897)
P.O. Box 1423 (47375-1423)
PHONE..................765 966-6211
Danny Sullivan, Pr
Patricia Sullivan, *
EMP: 9 EST: 1984
SQ FT: 50,000
SALES (est): 438.82K Privately Held
SIC: 3995 7261 Burial caskets; Funeral service and crematories

(G-14201)
SCANPOWER LLC
Also Called: Fbapower
822 E Main St (47374-4331)
PHONE..................765 277-2308
Chris Green, Pt
EMP: 7 EST: 2010
SALES (est): 491.75K Privately Held

SIC: 4813 2741 Online service providers; Internet publishing and broadcasting

(G-14202)
SCHAFFNER MANUFACTURING CO
2350 Salisbury Rd N (47374-9726)
PHONE..................601 366-9902
Carl Brooks, Brnch Mgr
EMP: 10
SALES (corp-wide): 834.99MM Privately Held
SIC: 3291 Abrasive products
HQ: Schaffner Manufacturing Co., Inc
21 Herron Ave
Pittsburgh PA 15202
412 761-9902

(G-14203)
SERENDIPITY SANCTUARY
532 N 19th St (47374-3428)
P.O. Box 81 (47370-0081)
PHONE..................765 541-2364
Jolie Campbell, Owner
EMP: 1 EST: 2015
SALES (est): 28.37K Privately Held
SIC: 7299 2841 2844 5999 Massage parlor; Soap and other detergents; Lotions, shaving ; Toilet preparations

(G-14204)
SHELL PIPE LINE CORPORATION
Also Called: Shell
1221 S 9th St (47374-6970)
PHONE..................765 962-1329
Mack Kotta, Owner
EMP: 2
SALES (corp-wide): 316.62B Privately Held
SIC: 2911 Gas, refinery
HQ: Shell Pipe Line Corporation
2 Shell Plz Ste 1160
Houston TX 77002

(G-14205)
SILGAN WHITE CAP LLC
Silgan Closures
1701 Williamsburg Pike (47374-1492)
P.O. Box 488 (47375-0488)
PHONE..................765 983-9200
EMP: 337
Web: www.silgancls.com
SIC: 3411 Metal cans
HQ: Silgan White Cap Llc
1140 31st St
Downers Grove IL 60515
630 515-8383

(G-14206)
SOUTHEAST WOOD TREATING INC
Also Called: SOUTHEAST WOOD TREATING, INC.
5353 S D St (47374-7943)
PHONE..................765 962-4077
EMP: 126
SALES (corp-wide): 48.36MM Privately Held
Web: www.southeastforestproducts.com
SIC: 2491 Wood preserving
PA: Southeast Forest Products Treated, Ltd.
3077 Carter Hill Rd
Montgomery AL 36111
321 631-1003

(G-14207)
ST HENRY TILE CO INC
1000 N F St (47374-2325)
PHONE..................765 966-7771
Michael Homan, Brnch Mgr
EMP: 4
SALES (corp-wide): 24.3MM Privately Held

Web: www.sthenrytileco.com
SIC: 3271 Blocks, concrete or cinder: standard
PA: The St Henry Tile Co Inc
281 W Washington St
Saint Henry OH 45883
419 678-4841

(G-14208)
STAMP WORKS
121 S 5th St (47374-4222)
PHONE..................765 962-5201
Richard Williams, Owner
Richard Williams, Pr
EMP: 3 EST: 1990
SALES (est): 50K Privately Held
Web: www.stampworks.net
SIC: 3953 Embossing seals and hand stamps

(G-14209)
STOLLE TOOL INCORPORATED
4693 Webster Rd (47374-9529)
PHONE..................765 935-5185
Ronald E Stolle, Pr
Carol Sue Stolle, VP
EMP: 10 EST: 1983
SQ FT: 6,300
SALES (est): 964.98K Privately Held
Web: www.stolletool.com
SIC: 3544 7692 Special dies and tools; Welding repair

(G-14210)
TBK AMERICA INC
3700 W Industries Rd (47374)
PHONE..................765 962-0147
Keisuke Shinozaki, Pr
◆ EMP: 35 EST: 2002
SQ FT: 60,000
SALES (est): 10.18MM Privately Held
Web: www.tbk-jp.com
SIC: 3561 Pumps and pumping equipment
PA: Tbk Co., Ltd.
4-21-1, Minaminaruse
Machida TKY 194-0

(G-14211)
TEAM GEAR PRINTING LLC
3451 Dorothy Ln (47374-6747)
PHONE..................765 935-4748
Mark A Mendenhall, Brnch Mgr
EMP: 1
SALES (corp-wide): 479.02K Privately Held
SIC: 2752 Commercial printing, lithographic
PA: Team Gear Printing Llc
4714 National Rd E
Richmond IN 47374
765 977-2995

(G-14212)
TEAM GEAR PRINTING LLC (PA)
4714 National Rd E (47374-3736)
PHONE..................765 977-2995
Mark A Mendenhall, Admn
EMP: 3 EST: 2010
SALES (est): 479.02K
SALES (corp-wide): 479.02K Privately Held
SIC: 2752 Commercial printing, lithographic

(G-14213)
TEGELER WELDING SERVICES LLC
6143 Druley Rd (47374-9435)
PHONE..................765 409-6446
Amanda Tegeler, Prin
EMP: 4 EST: 2019
SALES (est): 27.6K Privately Held
SIC: 7692 Welding repair

(G-14214)
TERESA L POWELL CPA
321 Sw 1st St (47374-5303)
PHONE..................765 962-1862
Myron Powell, Owner
EMP: 6 EST: 2015
SALES (est): 255.47K Privately Held
Web: www.terrypowellcpa.com
SIC: 3599 Industrial machinery, nec

(G-14215)
TERRI LOGAN STUDIOS
2101 Reeveston Rd (47374-5752)
PHONE..................765 966-7876
Terri Logan, Owner
EMP: 5 EST: 2004
SALES (est): 223.76K Privately Held
Web: www.a1moversofsaukprairie.com
SIC: 3911 Jewelry, precious metal

(G-14216)
TGC AUTO CARE PRODUCTS INC
421 S 33rd St (47374-6722)
PHONE..................765 962-7725
Terry Christ, Pr
Marthea J Christ, Pr
EMP: 5 EST: 1988
SQ FT: 6,000
SALES (est): 289.38K Privately Held
SIC: 2842 5169 Degreasing solvent; Specialty cleaning and sanitation preparations

(G-14217)
THINKSHORTCUT PUBLISHING LLC
2695 Inke Rd (47374-9360)
PHONE..................765 935-1127
EMP: 5 EST: 2010
SALES (est): 98.68K Privately Held
Web: www.thinkshortcut.com
SIC: 2741 Miscellaneous publishing

(G-14218)
THOUSAND ONE INC
Also Called: Signgrafx & Engraving
1001 Se St (47374-6317)
P.O. Box 1502 (47375-1502)
PHONE..................765 962-3636
Peggy North, Pr
Rollie North, VP
EMP: 6 EST: 1983
SALES (est): 495.62K Privately Held
Web: www.tricountyawards.com
SIC: 3993 Signs and advertising specialties

(G-14219)
TIEDEMANN-BEVS INDUSTRIES LLC
Also Called: Tiedmann and Sons
4225 W Industries Rd (47374-1385)
PHONE..................765 962-4914
Andrew Lawrence, Pr
Lisa Baker, *
Pam Soper, *
Peter Galletly, *
◆ EMP: 44 EST: 1975
SQ FT: 65,000
SALES (est): 19.58MM Privately Held
Web: www.tbevs.com
SIC: 5131 3995 Piece goods and other fabrics; Casket linings
PA: Strength Capital Partners, L.L.C.
102 Pierce St
Birmingham MI 48009

(G-14220)
TRANSCENDIA INC
Also Called: Transilwrap
300 Industrial Pkwy (47374-3706)
PHONE..................765 935-1520
Keith Badgeley, Brnch Mgr

Richmond - Wayne County (G-14221)

EMP: 150
SALES (corp-wide): 290.26MM **Privately Held**
Web: www.transcendia.com
SIC: 3081 2891 2851 Polyvinyl film and sheet; Adhesives and sealants; Paints and allied products
PA: Transcendia, Inc.
9201 W Belmont Ave
Franklin Park IL 60131
847 678-1800

(G-14221)
TURNER PAVING COMPANY
1458 Nw 5th St (47374-1842)
PHONE...................................765 962-4408
Bary Barker, *Owner*
Gary Barker, *Mgr*
EMP: 2 **EST:** 1978
SALES (est): 167K **Privately Held**
SIC: 3531 Pavers

(G-14222)
VANDOR CORPORATION (PA)
4251 W Industries Rd (47374-1385)
PHONE...................................765 966-7676
EMP: 66 **EST:** 1990
SALES (est): 25.75MM
SALES (corp-wide): 25.75MM **Privately Held**
Web: www.vandorcorp.com
SIC: 2655 Fiber cans, drums, and similar products

(G-14223)
VANDOR CORPORATION
Also Called: C.J. Boots Casket Company
4251 W Industries Rd (47374-1385)
PHONE...................................765 683-9760
EMP: 35
SALES (corp-wide): 25.75MM **Privately Held**
Web: www.vandorcorp.com
SIC: 3995 5087 Burial caskets; Caskets
PA: Vandor Corporation
4251 W Industries Rd
Richmond IN 47374
765 966-7676

(G-14224)
WAYNE MACHINE MFRS INC
1747 S 5th St (47374-6823)
P.O. Box 427 (47375-0427)
PHONE...................................765 962-0459
Jeffrey Baker Senior, *Pr*
EMP: 6 **EST:** 1997
SQ FT: 5,000
SALES (est): 788.37K **Privately Held**
Web: www.wayne-machine.com
SIC: 3599 Machine shop, jobbing and repair

(G-14225)
WEBER WOODWORKING
148 S 21st St (47374-5732)
PHONE...................................765 967-3665
EMP: 1 **EST:** 2010
SALES (est): 92.54K **Privately Held**
SIC: 2431 Millwork

(G-14226)
WESTERN-CULLEN-HAYES INC
120 N 3rd St (47374-3002)
P.O. Box 756 (47375-0756)
PHONE...................................765 962-0526
Kevin Hertel, *Genl Mgr*
EMP: 10
SALES (corp-wide): 15.45MM **Privately Held**
Web: www.wch.com

SIC: 5084 3743 3312 Safety equipment; Railroad equipment; Blast furnaces and steel mills
PA: Western-Cullen-Hayes, Inc.
2700 W 36th Pl
Chicago IL 60632
773 254-9600

(G-14227)
WINANDY GREENHOUSE COMPANY
2211 Peacock Rd (47374-3835)
PHONE...................................765 935-2111
Mike Winandy, *Pr*
Michael Doherty, *
Elizabeth Doherty, *
EMP: 30 **EST:** 1921
SQ FT: 3,000
SALES (est): 4.98MM **Privately Held**
Web: www.winandygreenhouse.com
SIC: 3448 3231 Greenhouses, prefabricated metal; Products of purchased glass

(G-14228)
WOOD BLOCK PRESS INC
330 S 28th St (47374-5815)
PHONE...................................405 742-7308
James Barbre, *Ex Dir*
EMP: 1 **EST:** 2018
SALES (est): 59.8K **Privately Held**
Web: www.woodblockpress.org
SIC: 2741 Miscellaneous publishing

(G-14229)
XENNOVATE MEDICAL LLC (PA)
1080 University Blvd (47374-1256)
PHONE...................................765 939-2037
EMP: 3 **EST:** 2004
SALES (est): 735.31K
SALES (corp-wide): 735.31K **Privately Held**
Web: www.xennovate.com
SIC: 2891 5047 Adhesives; Medical laboratory equipment

(G-14230)
YAMAGUCHI MFG USA INC
1771 Sheridan St (47374-1811)
PHONE...................................765 973-9130
Kenzo Yamaguchi, *Pr*
Yasuyuki Imai, *Sec*
Taizo Yamaguchi, *Dir*
EMP: 3 **EST:** 2003
SALES (est): 609.45K **Privately Held**
Web: www.yamaguchi-mfgusa.com
SIC: 3545 Precision tools, machinists'
PA: Yamagichi Manufacturing,Co.,Ltd.
292-69, Ashitaka
Numazu SZO 410-0

(G-14231)
YORK GROUP INC
Also Called: York Technology
1620 Rich Rd (47374-1435)
PHONE...................................765 966-0077
EMP: 61
SALES (corp-wide): 1.88B **Publicly Held**
SIC: 3089 Injection molded finished plastics products, nec
HQ: The York Group Inc
2 N Shore Ctr
Pittsburgh PA 15212
412 995-1600

(G-14232)
YORK GROUP INC
Ambedco Stamping
620 S J St (47374-6140)
PHONE...................................765 966-1576
Scott Wright, *Mgr*
EMP: 114
SQ FT: 80,000

SALES (corp-wide): 1.88B **Publicly Held**
SIC: 3469 3995 Stamping metal for the trade; Burial caskets
HQ: The York Group Inc
2 N Shore Ctr
Pittsburgh PA 15212
412 995-1600

Ridgeville
Randolph County

(G-14233)
CARDEMON INC
Also Called: Car-TEC
108 W 2nd St (47380-1328)
PHONE...................................765 857-1000
Chris Cardemon, *Pr*
Jammie Minniear, *Treas*
EMP: 10 **EST:** 1984
SQ FT: 30,000
SALES (est): 241.12K **Privately Held**
Web: www.cardemon.com
SIC: 3599 Machine shop, jobbing and repair

(G-14234)
JOHN S COTTER
1858 E 700 N (47380-9027)
PHONE...................................765 584-2521
EMP: 1 **EST:** 2002
SALES (est): 95.53K **Privately Held**
Web: www.johncotter.net
SIC: 3537 Trucks: freight, baggage, etc.: industrial, except mining

(G-14235)
KNIT KNOT CROCHET
503 N George St (47380-1009)
PHONE...................................765 730-9416
Coretta Harbold, *Prin*
EMP: 4 **EST:** 2017
SALES (est): 47.16K **Privately Held**
SIC: 2399 Hand woven and crocheted products

(G-14236)
NEWPARK RESOURCES INC
205 S Walnut St (47380-1331)
PHONE...................................765 546-9473
EMP: 1
SALES (corp-wide): 749.6MM **Publicly Held**
Web: www.newpark.com
SIC: 1389 Oil field services, nec
PA: Newpark Resources Inc.
9320 Lkeside Blvd Ste 100
The Woodlands TX 77381
281 362-6800

(G-14237)
RELIANCE MACHINE COMPANY INC
Also Called: Cartec Company
108 W 2nd St (47380-1328)
PHONE...................................765 857-1000
Joe Baker, *Manager*
EMP: 2
SALES (corp-wide): 5.39MM **Privately Held**
Web: www.reliancemachinecompany.com
SIC: 3599 Machine shop, jobbing and repair
PA: Reliance Machine Company Inc
4605 S Walnut St
Muncie IN 47302
765 284-0151

(G-14238)
UTILITY ACCESS SOLUTIONS INC
205 S Walnut St (47380-1331)
PHONE...................................765 744-6528

Joe Goodhew, *Pr*
EMP: 3 **EST:** 2016
SALES (est): 788.82K
SALES (corp-wide): 749.6MM **Publicly Held**
SIC: 1611 1442 General contractor, highway and street construction; Construction sand mining
HQ: Newpark Mats & Integrated Services Llc
9320 Lkeside Blvd Ste 100
The Woodlands TX 77381
281 362-6800

Riley
Vigo County

(G-14239)
MAPLE-HUNTER DECALS
8075 St Rd 46 (47871)
P.O. Box 805 (47871-0805)
PHONE...................................812 894-9759
John Hunter, *Owner*
EMP: 2 **EST:** 2000
SALES (est): 45K **Privately Held**
Web: www.maplehunterdecalsindiana.com
SIC: 2759 Decals: printing, nsk

Rising Sun
Ohio County

(G-14240)
ADVANCED MBILITY SOLUTIONS LLC
4669 Cass Union Rd (47040-9690)
PHONE...................................812 438-2338
Kim F Wagner, *Managing Member*
EMP: 10 **EST:** 2005
SALES (est): 253.54K **Privately Held**
SIC: 8011 3841 Medical centers; Medical instruments and equipment, blood and bone work

(G-14241)
DELPHOS HERALD OF INDIANA INC
Also Called: Ohio County News, The
235 Main St (47040-1224)
P.O. Box 128 (47040-0128)
PHONE...................................812 438-2011
EMP: 112
SALES (corp-wide): 23.87MM **Privately Held**
Web: www.registerpublications.com
SIC: 2711 Newspapers, publishing and printing
HQ: The Delphos Herald Of Indiana Inc
126 W High St
Lawrenceburg IN 47025
812 537-0063

(G-14242)
EVERYTHING UNDER SUN LLC
Also Called: Everything Under The Sun
3379 Nelson Rd (47040-9214)
PHONE...................................812 438-3397
Jessica Hall, *Pr*
EMP: 1 **EST:** 2005
SALES (est): 122.55K **Privately Held**
Web: everythingunderthesun.espwebsite.com
SIC: 2759 Promotional printing

(G-14243)
IOK TECHNOLOGY LLC
Also Called: Iok Tech
3293 Salem Ridge Rd (47040-9437)
P.O. Box 147 (47040-0147)

PHONE..................................812 308-1366
EMP: 8 EST: 2009
SQ FT: 10,000
SALES (est): 870K **Privately Held**
Web: www.ioktech.com
SIC: 3599 Machine shop, jobbing and repair

(G-14244)
OMI INDUSTRIES INC
Also Called: OMI Industries
1300 Barbour Way (47040-8334)
PHONE..................................812 438-9218
Jim Elwood, *Mgr*
EMP: 5
Web: www.omi-industries.com
SIC: 3822 5169 Environmental controls; Aromatic chemicals
PA: Omi Industries, Inc.
220 N Smith St Ste 315
Palatine IL 60067

(G-14245)
REES HARPS INC
Also Called: Harps On Main
222 Main St (47040-1225)
PHONE..................................812 438-3032
William Rees, *CEO*
Pamela Rees, *VP*
Garen Rees, *Genl Mgr*
▲ EMP: 12 EST: 1976
SALES (est): 997.98K **Privately Held**
Web: www.harpsicle.us
SIC: 3931 5736 5099 Harps and parts; Musical instrument stores; Musical instruments

(G-14246)
TRI STATE MOLD
7255 State Route 56 W (47040-9285)
PHONE..................................859 240-7643
Geoff Briceno, *Owner*
EMP: 2 EST: 2006
SALES (est): 83.93K **Privately Held**
SIC: 3544 Industrial molds

Roachdale
Putnam County

(G-14247)
HOMELIFE FOREVER INC
Also Called: Special Tees
1197 E State Road 236 (46172-9534)
PHONE..................................765 307-0416
Lane Butler, *Pr*
Kim Winings, *Sec*
EMP: 1 EST: 2017
SALES (est): 76.51K **Privately Held**
SIC: 2396 Fabric printing and stamping

(G-14248)
NO-SAIL SPLASH GUARD CO INC
Also Called: Adcomm Bindery
10254 N Us Highway 231 (46172-9190)
PHONE..................................765 522-2100
Charles E Phillips, *Pr*
EMP: 7 EST: 1973
SALES (est): 656.53K **Privately Held**
SIC: 3069 2782 3993 Rubber automotive products; Looseleaf binders and devices; Signs and advertising specialties

(G-14249)
VALESCO MANUFACTURING INC (PA)
9875 N County Road 600 E (46172-9133)
PHONE..................................765 522-2740
George Robertson, *Pr*
Craig Robertson, *Contrlr*
EMP: 2 EST: 2007

SQ FT: 2,000
SALES (est): 658.85K
SALES (corp-wide): 658.85K **Privately Held**
Web: www.silo-matic.com
SIC: 3523 Weeding machines, agricultural

Roann
Wabash County

(G-14250)
COUNTRY EMBROIDERY
4795 W 800 N (46974-9565)
PHONE..................................765 833-9002
Loralyn Dyson, *Owner*
EMP: 1 EST: 1999
SALES (est): 42.57K **Privately Held**
SIC: 2395 Embroidery products, except Schiffli machine

(G-14251)
M&M DYSON FARMS INC
6651 N 400 W (46974-9524)
PHONE..................................765 833-2202
Mark Dyson, *VP*
Mike Dyson, *Pr*
EMP: 2 EST: 1980
SALES (est): 226.22K **Privately Held**
SIC: 3635 Household vacuum cleaners

(G-14252)
MANCHESTER INC
6973 E 975 N (46974)
PHONE..................................260 982-2202
Cynthia J Hall, *Pr*
EMP: 9 EST: 2010
SALES (est): 939.46K **Privately Held**
Web: www.manchestermillwrights.com
SIC: 3441 3535 1796 Fabricated structural metal; Conveyors and conveying equipment; Millwright

(G-14253)
RICK HOLLINGSHEAD
Also Called: Pallets R US
7076 W 900 N (46974-9785)
PHONE..................................765 833-2846
Rick Hollingshead, *Owner*
EMP: 1 EST: 2007
SALES (est): 93.69K **Privately Held**
SIC: 2448 5031 Pallets, wood; Pallets, wood

(G-14254)
SIDERS & SON GRAVEL
225 N Washington St (46974-9727)
P.O. Box 297 (46974-0297)
PHONE..................................574 893-4110
Richard Siders, *Owner*
EMP: 1 EST: 1946
SALES (est): 91K **Privately Held**
SIC: 1442 Gravel and pebble mining

Roanoke
Huntington County

(G-14255)
ABR ENTERPRISES LLC
11027 Barrymore Run (46783-8914)
PHONE..................................808 352-4658
Amie Arizmendi, *Managing Member*
EMP: 1 EST: 2019
SALES (est): 43.56K **Privately Held**
SIC: 2869 Industrial organic chemicals, nec

(G-14256)
ALL-TERRAIN CONVERSIONS LLC
13534 Lafayette Center Rd (46783-9602)

PHONE..................................260 758-2525
EMP: 2 EST: 2012
SALES (est): 581.23K **Privately Held**
Web: www.atcmobility.com
SIC: 3441 Fabricated structural metal

(G-14257)
ANDROID INDUSTRIES LLC
Also Called: Android Industries Fort Wayne
12808 Stonebridge Rd # 110 (46783-9336)
PHONE..................................260 672-0112
Dennis Donnay, *Manager*
EMP: 47
SALES (corp-wide): 474.49MM **Privately Held**
Web: www.android-ind.com
SIC: 3711 Automobile assembly, including specialty automobiles
PA: Android Industries, L.L.C.
2155 Executive Hills Blvd
Auburn Hills MI 48326
248 454-0500

(G-14258)
ARCANE WONDERS
384 S Main St (46783-1006)
PHONE..................................469 964-9050
EMP: 4 EST: 2017
SALES (est): 61.05K **Privately Held**
Web: www.arcanewonders.com
SIC: 2741 Miscellaneous publishing

(G-14259)
AUTO TRUCK GROUP LLC
14014 Hitzfield Ct (46783-0109)
PHONE..................................260 493-1800
J S Holman, *Dir*
EMP: 1
SALES (corp-wide): 2.54B **Privately Held**
Web: www.holman.com
SIC: 3599 7692 3444 Machine shop, jobbing and repair; Welding repair; Casings, sheet metal
HQ: Auto Truck Group, Llc
1420 Brewster Creek Blvd
Bartlett IL 60103
630 860-5600

(G-14260)
BEHNING INC
Also Called: Craftsman Lithograph
287 N Main St (46783-1001)
P.O. Box 370 (46783-0370)
PHONE..................................260 672-2663
Barbara Behning, *Pr*
Gertrude Behning, *Sec*
Arthur Behning, *Treas*
EMP: 4 EST: 1963
SQ FT: 1,900
SALES (est): 314.54K **Privately Held**
SIC: 2759 2771 Stationery: printing, nsk; Greeting cards

(G-14261)
BRONZE BOW SOFTWARE INC
7717 Aboite Rd (46783-9649)
PHONE..................................260 672-9516
EMP: 3 EST: 1990
SALES (est): 237.03K **Privately Held**
Web: www.bronzebow.com
SIC: 7372 Application computer software

(G-14262)
EARTH ESSENTIALS LLC
11012 Barrymore Run (46783-8914)
PHONE..................................260 479-0115
Anjanette M Schweier, *Prin*
EMP: 4 EST: 2019
SALES (est): 94.92K **Privately Held**
Web: www.basicearthessentials.com

SIC: 2844 Perfumes, cosmetics and other toilet preparations

(G-14263)
EX-CUT TECHNOLOGY LLC
Also Called: Intri-Cut Tool
5130 E 900 N (46783-9705)
P.O. Box 710 (46783-0710)
PHONE..................................260 672-9602
EMP: 10 EST: 1992
SQ FT: 3,500
SALES (est): 907.99K **Privately Held**
Web: www.intri-cut.com
SIC: 3544 3599 Special dies and tools; Electrical discharge machining (EDM)

(G-14264)
FITCH ENTERPRISES INC
7477 E State Road 114 92 (46783-9211)
PHONE..................................260 672-8462
James Shuff, *Pr*
EMP: 4 EST: 1982
SALES (est): 453.92K **Privately Held**
Web: www.roanokewoodworking.com
SIC: 5211 2499 Cabinets, kitchen; Kitchen, bathroom, and household ware: wood

(G-14265)
FLYINNEEDLE EMBROIDERY INC
3132 E 900 N (46783-8880)
PHONE..................................260 672-0742
Caren Snyder, *Prin*
EMP: 1 EST: 2011
SALES (est): 69.24K **Privately Held**
Web: www.flyinneedle.com
SIC: 2395 Embroidery products, except Schiffli machine

(G-14266)
FOGWELL TECHNOLOGIES INC
10525 W Yoder Rd (46783-9613)
PHONE..................................260 410-1898
Adam Fogwell, *Owner*
EMP: 3 EST: 2010
SALES (est): 446.55K **Privately Held**
SIC: 3465 Automotive stampings

(G-14267)
GENERAL MOTORS LLC
Also Called: General Motors
12808 Stonebridge Rd (46783-9336)
PHONE..................................260 673-2048
Steven Andreen, *Brnch Mgr*
EMP: 10
Web: www.gm.com
SIC: 3714 Motor vehicle parts and accessories
HQ: General Motors Llc
300 Rnaissance Ctr Ste L1
Detroit MI 48243

(G-14268)
GENERAL MOTORS LLC
Also Called: General Motors
12200 Lafayette Center Rd (46783-9628)
PHONE..................................260 672-1224
Cathy Clegg, *COO*
EMP: 442
Web: www.gm.com
SIC: 5511 3713 Automobiles, new and used; Truck and bus bodies
HQ: General Motors Llc
300 Rnaissance Ctr Ste L1
Detroit MI 48243

(G-14269)
GILPIN CUSTOM WOODWORKING LLC
10611 Coopers Hawk Trce (46783-8750)
PHONE..................................260 413-6618

Roanoke - Huntington County (G-14270)

Trevor J Gilpin, *Owner*
EMP: 6 **EST:** 2017
SALES (est): 72.87K **Privately Held**
SIC: 2431 Millwork

(G-14270)
INTELLIQUOTE
13548 Zubrick Rd (46783-8300)
PHONE.................530 669-6840
Janice Seal, *Asst Sec*
EMP: 7 **EST:** 2019
SALES (est): 106.85K **Privately Held**
Web: www.intelliquote.com
SIC: 3911 Jewelry, precious metal

(G-14271)
JAMES DAVID INC
Also Called: Winco Printing & Gift Shop
11323 Nightingale Cv (46783-8798)
PHONE.................260 744-0579
James E Tolbert, *Pr*
Marilyn Tolbert, *Sec*
EMP: 2 **EST:** 1975
SQ FT: 3,125
SALES (est): 140.6K **Privately Held**
SIC: 2752 Offset printing

(G-14272)
VERA BRADLEY INC (PA)
12420 Stonebridge Rd (46783)
PHONE.................877 708-8372
Jacqueline Ardrey, *Pr*
Robert J Hall, *
Michael Schwindle, *CAO*
Mark C Dely, *CLO*
Alison Hiatt, *CMO*
EMP: 285 **EST:** 1982
SQ FT: 188,000
SALES (est): 470.79MM
SALES (corp-wide): 470.79MM **Publicly Held**
Web: www.verabradley.com
SIC: 3171 3111 2392 2844 Women's handbags and purses; Accessory products, leather; Household furnishings, nec; Perfumes, cosmetics and other toilet preparations

(G-14273)
VERA BRADLEY INTERNATIONAL LLC (HQ)
12420 Stonebridge Rd (46783-9300)
PHONE.................260 482-4673
Richard Baum, *Dir*
EMP: 8 **EST:** 2006
SALES (est): 2.9MM
SALES (corp-wide): 470.79MM **Publicly Held**
Web: www.verabradley.com
SIC: 3171 5632 Women's handbags and purses; Women's accessory and specialty stores
PA: Vera Bradley, Inc.
12420 Stonebridge Rd
Roanoke IN 46783
877 708-8372

Rochester
Fulton County

(G-14274)
AD-VANCE MAGNETICS INC
625 Monroe St (46975-1426)
P.O. Box 69 (46975-0069)
PHONE.................574 223-3158
Richard D Vance, *Pr*
Kay Nixon, *
EMP: 38 **EST:** 1971
SQ FT: 32,000
SALES (est): 4.89MM **Privately Held**
Web: www.advancemag.com
SIC: 3499 3444 3341 7389 Magnetic shields, metal; Sheet metalwork; Secondary nonferrous metals; Metal cutting services

(G-14275)
ADVANCED MECHATRONIC TECH LLC
Also Called: Amt
4756 S Wabash Rd (46975-7193)
PHONE.................920 918-0209
John William Radtke, *Prin*
EMP: 5 **EST:** 2017
SALES (est): 245.44K **Privately Held**
Web: www.amtsite.com
SIC: 3625 Relays and industrial controls

(G-14276)
ANDERSON CREATIONS INC
Also Called: Country Folk Works
371 E 450 N (46975-8350)
P.O. Box 48 (46975-0048)
PHONE.................574 223-8932
Doug Anderson, *Pr*
Angie Anderson, *Sec*
EMP: 6 **EST:** 1988
SALES (est): 337.81K **Privately Held**
Web: www.countryfolkwurks.com
SIC: 2392 Household furnishings, nec

(G-14277)
AQSEPTENCE GROUP INC
Also Called: AQSEPTENCE GROUP, INC.
4079 N Old Us Highway 31 (46975-8319)
PHONE.................574 208-5866
EMP: 7
SALES (corp-wide): 355.83K **Privately Held**
Web: www.aqseptence.com
SIC: 2821 Polyvinyl chloride resins, PVC
HQ: Johnson Screens, Inc.
1950 Old Hwy 8 Nw
New Brighton MN 55112
651 636-3900

(G-14278)
AQSEPTENCE GROUP INC
Also Called: Air Vac Sewer Systems
4217 N Old Us Highway 31 (46975-8321)
PHONE.................574 223-3980
Mark Jones, *Brnch Mgr*
EMP: 75
SALES (corp-wide): 355.83K **Privately Held**
Web: www.airvac.com
SIC: 3589 Sewage and water treatment equipment
HQ: Johnson Screens, Inc.
1950 Old Hwy 8 Nw
New Brighton MN 55112
651 636-3900

(G-14279)
BILFINGER AIRVAC WATER TECHNOLOGIES INC
Also Called: Airvac
4217 N Old Us 31 (46975)
P.O. Box 528 (46975-0528)
PHONE.................574 223-3980
▲ **EMP:** 65
SIC: 3492 Fluid power valves and hose fittings

(G-14280)
BRYANT LIFT TRAILER
2917 Barrett Rd (46975-8949)
PHONE.................574 721-2255
Brady Bryant, *CEO*
EMP: 3 **EST:** 2017
SALES (est): 66.08K **Privately Held**
Web: www.lifttrailer.com
SIC: 3536 Hoists, cranes, and monorails

(G-14281)
BTQ MANUFACTURING INC (DH)
Also Called: Topps Safety Apparel, Inc.
2516 E State Road 14 (46975-9604)
P.O. Box 750 (46975-0750)
PHONE.................574 223-4311
EMP: 30 **EST:** 1938
SALES (est): 23.16MM
SALES (corp-wide): 1.79B **Publicly Held**
Web: www.pinnacletextile.com
SIC: 2326 Men's and boy's work clothing
HQ: B T Q Limited
Wathen Street
Bristol BS16
117 956-3101

(G-14282)
CAMCAR LLC
4366 N Old Us Highway 31 (46975-8322)
PHONE.................574 223-3131
▲ **EMP:** 120
SIC: 3452 5072 Bolts, nuts, rivets, and washers; Bolts, nuts, and screws
HQ: Camcar Llc
6125 18 Mile Rd
Sterling Heights MI 48314
586 254-3900

(G-14283)
CONTEGO INTERNATIONAL INC (PA)
1013 Arthur St (46975-2449)
P.O. Box 49 (46975-0049)
PHONE.................574 223-5989
Dan French, *COO*
Todd Beehler, *CEO*
John M Schwartz, *Dir*
◆ **EMP:** 3 **EST:** 2001
SQ FT: 2,000
SALES (est): 7.5MM
SALES (corp-wide): 7.5MM **Privately Held**
Web: www.contegointernational.com
SIC: 2851 Paints and allied products

(G-14284)
CORY PMP LLC
401 E 4th St (46975)
P.O. Box 97 (46975)
PHONE.................574 223-3177
John Cory, *CEO*
EMP: 20 **EST:** 2006
SQ FT: 100,000
SALES (est): 2.42MM **Privately Held**
Web: www.prairiemills.com
SIC: 2041 Grain mills (except rice)

(G-14285)
CULVERS PORT SIDE MARINA
1409 Wentzel St (46975-7661)
PHONE.................574 223-5090
Glenn Bailey, *Pr*
EMP: 9 **EST:** 2008
SALES (est): 189.5K **Privately Held**
SIC: 5551 4493 4491 3732 Motor boat dealers; Marinas; Docks, incl. buildings and facilities: operation and maint.; Boatbuilding and repairing

(G-14286)
DELTA TOOL MANUFACTURING INC
1090 W 325 S (46975-7572)
P.O. Box 241 (46975-0241)
PHONE.................574 223-4863
Dan Hartman, *Pr*
Steve Whistler, *VP*
◆ **EMP:** 6 **EST:** 1983
SQ FT: 30,000
SALES (est): 492.63K **Privately Held**
SIC: 3449 3544 Miscellaneous metalwork; Special dies and tools

(G-14287)
DU-MAR WELDING LLC
2858 E 650 N (46975-7461)
PHONE.................574 223-9889
EMP: 4 **EST:** 1990
SALES (est): 331.57K **Privately Held**
SIC: 7692 Welding repair

(G-14288)
ENYART SIGNS
Also Called: Enyart Signs of All Kinds
2155 N Old Us Highway 31 (46975-7280)
PHONE.................574 223-8254
Gina Enyart, *Owner*
EMP: 1 **EST:** 1981
SALES (est): 25K **Privately Held**
SIC: 3993 Signs and advertising specialties

(G-14289)
FARMER AUTOMATIC AMERICA INC
5571 S State Road 25 (46975-8052)
PHONE.................574 857-3116
EMP: 4
SALES (corp-wide): 2.44MM **Privately Held**
Web: www.farmerautomatic.com
SIC: 2875 Compost
PA: Farmer Automatic Of America, Inc.
9333 Us Highway 301 S
Statesboro GA 30458
912 681-2763

(G-14290)
FBSA LLC (PA)
Also Called: Freedman Mobility Seating
7346 W 400 N (46975-8723)
PHONE.................800 443-4540
EMP: 8 **EST:** 1998
SQ FT: 117,000
SALES (est): 11.55MM
SALES (corp-wide): 11.55MM **Privately Held**
Web: www.braunseating.com
SIC: 2531 Vehicle furniture

(G-14291)
FLENAR MANUFACTURING LLC
2906 Ft Wayne Rd (46975-8616)
PHONE.................574 893-4070
Brian Flenar, *Prin*
Matthew Flenar, *Prin*
EMP: 2 **EST:** 2014
SALES (est): 150.41K **Privately Held**
Web: www.flenarmanufacturing.com
SIC: 3599 Machine shop, jobbing and repair

(G-14292)
FULTON INDUSTRIES INC
Also Called: Rochester Plant
2903 Ft Wayne Rd 25 (46975-8616)
P.O. Box 487 (46975-0487)
PHONE.................574 223-4387
Rob Razzano, *Mgr*
EMP: 207
SALES (corp-wide): 19.9MM **Privately Held**
Web: www.fultonindustries.com
SIC: 3599 Machine shop, jobbing and repair
PA: Fulton Industries, Inc.
51565 Bittersweet Rd B
Granger IN 46530
574 968-3222

(G-14293)
HARDESTY PRINTING CO INC (PA)
1218 N State Road 25 (46975-7551)

P.O. Box 624 (46975-0624)
PHONE..........................574 223-4553
Francis D Hardesty, Pr
Bill Hardesty, VP
Randall Hardesty, VP
William Hardesty, VP
Alice Hardesty, Sec
EMP: 13 **EST:** 1924
SALES (est): 2.4MM
SALES (corp-wide): 2.4MM **Privately Held**
Web: www.hardestyprinting.com
SIC: 2752 2791 2789 Offset printing; Typesetting; Bookbinding and related work

(G-14294)
HASSENPLUG & SON SAND & GRAVEL
1515 W 450 N (46975-8353)
PHONE..........................574 223-5230
Charles Hassenplug, Owner
EMP: 3 **EST:** 1965
SALES (est): 90.55K **Privately Held**
SIC: 1442 Construction sand and gravel

(G-14295)
HEARTLAND FILLED MACHINE LLC
5176 State Road 110 (46975-9052)
PHONE..........................574 223-6931
EMP: 5 **EST:** 2007
SALES (est): 440.79K **Privately Held**
SIC: 3569 7699 Filters; Industrial machinery and equipment repair

(G-14296)
HOFFMAN QUALITY GRAPHICS
2096 Sycamore Dr (46975-8180)
P.O. Box 821 (46975-0821)
PHONE..........................574 223-5738
Art Hoffman, Owner
EMP: 2 **EST:** 1995
SALES (est): 159.89K **Privately Held**
SIC: 2752 Commercial printing, lithographic

(G-14297)
INNOVATIVE COMPOSITES LTD
5408 State St Ste 25 (46975-8806)
PHONE..........................574 857-2224
EMP: 11 **EST:** 1993
SQ FT: 10,000
SALES (est): 296.15K **Privately Held**
Web: www.innovativecomposites.com
SIC: 2821 Plastics materials and resins

(G-14298)
JOBSITE TRAILER CORPORATION
Also Called: Jobsite Mobile Offices
1393 N Lucas St (46975-1156)
P.O. Box 288 (46975-0288)
PHONE..........................574 224-4000
James B Guthrie, CEO
EMP: 26 **EST:** 1971
SQ FT: 40,000
SALES (est): 895.13K **Privately Held**
Web: www.jobsitemobileoffices.com
SIC: 2451 2452 3448 Mobile buildings: for commercial use; Prefabricated buildings, wood; Prefabricated metal buildings and components

(G-14299)
KUERT CONCRETE INC
Also Called: Rochester Concrete Plant
1101 W 13th St (46975-2509)
PHONE..........................574 223-2414
Kent Ganshorn, Brnch Mgr
EMP: 5
SALES (corp-wide): 13.04MM **Privately Held**
Web: www.kuert.com

SIC: 3273 Ready-mixed concrete
PA: Kuert Concrete Inc
5909 Nimtz Pkwy
South Bend IN 46628
574 232-9911

(G-14300)
LAU HOLDINGS LLC
510 N State Road 25 (46975-9776)
PHONE..........................574 223-3181
Scott Marquardt, Mgr
EMP: 100
SALES (corp-wide): 184.04MM **Privately Held**
Web: www.lauparts.com
SIC: 3564 3714 Ventilating fans: industrial or commercial; Motor vehicle parts and accessories
HQ: Lau Holdings, Llc
16900 S Waterloo Rd
Cleveland OH 44110
216 486-4000

(G-14301)
LAWRENCE SHIRKS
Also Called: Shirks Wood Products
4920 State Road 110 (46975-7001)
PHONE..........................574 223-5118
Lawrence Shirks, Owner
EMP: 3 **EST:** 1996
SALES (est): 250.3K **Privately Held**
SIC: 2541 Wood partitions and fixtures

(G-14302)
LRT PRECISION INC
1703 Jefferson St (46975-2617)
PHONE..........................574 223-2578
Christine Ford, Pr
EMP: 6 **EST:** 2020
SALES (est): 78.25K **Privately Held**
Web: www.lrtprecision.com
SIC: 3599 Machine shop, jobbing and repair

(G-14303)
LYNTECH ENGINEERING INC
2516 E State Road 14 (46975-9604)
P.O. Box 58 (46975-0058)
PHONE..........................574 224-2300
Jason Hudkins, Pr
Amanda Hudkins, VP
EMP: 6 **EST:** 2002
SALES (est): 1.02MM **Privately Held**
Web: www.lyntechengineering.com
SIC: 3559 8711 Automotive related machinery; Machine tool design

(G-14304)
MACHINED CASTINGS SPC LLC
290 Blacketor Dr (46975-9090)
PHONE..........................574 223-5694
EMP: 10 **EST:** 1998
SQ FT: 6,000
SALES (est): 1.75MM **Privately Held**
Web: www.machinedcastingsspecialties.com
SIC: 3599 Machine shop, jobbing and repair

(G-14305)
MARSHALL ELECTRIC CORPORATION (PA)
425 N State Road 25 (46975)
P.O. Box 909 (46975)
PHONE..........................574 223-4367
John C Marrs, Pr
Amy S Floor, Treas
◆ **EMP:** 15 **EST:** 1974
SQ FT: 45,000
SALES (est): 9.93MM
SALES (corp-wide): 9.93MM **Privately Held**
Web: www.marshall-electric.com

SIC: 3677 Baluns

(G-14306)
MCGREWS WELL DRILLING INC
7413 S 125 W (46975-7554)
PHONE..........................574 857-3875
Robert Mcgrews, Pr
Keith Mcgrews, VP
Mellie Mcgrews, Sec
EMP: 5 **EST:** 1907
SALES (est): 478.81K **Privately Held**
Web: www.mcgrewswelldrilling.com
SIC: 1381 1781 5251 Service well drilling; Water well drilling; Pumps and pumping equipment

(G-14307)
MIDWEST SHEET METAL INC
2467 E 200 N (46975-7428)
P.O. Box 66 (46975-0066)
PHONE..........................574 223-3332
Ted R Richard Senior, Pr
EMP: 3 **EST:** 1989
SQ FT: 5,200
SALES (est): 279.55K **Privately Held**
SIC: 1711 3444 Warm air heating and air conditioning contractor; Sheet metalwork

(G-14308)
MODERN MATERIALS INC
435 N State Road 25 (46975-9700)
PHONE..........................574 223-4509
Brian Goodman, Pr
▲ **EMP:** 23 **EST:** 1975
SQ FT: 87,000
SALES (est): 1.83MM **Privately Held**
Web: www.modernmaterials.net
SIC: 3479 Coating of metals and formed products

(G-14309)
MODULAR BUILDERS INC
2756 Ft Wayne Rd (46975-8613)
P.O. Box 496 (46787-0496)
PHONE..........................574 223-4934
Randal Fletcher, Pr
Jasper Dulin, VP
Simon Dragan, Treas
EMP: 1 **EST:** 1999
SQ FT: 30,000
SALES (est): 2.55MM **Privately Held**
Web: www.whitleyman.com
SIC: 2452 2451 Prefabricated wood buildings; Mobile homes, industrial or commercial use
PA: Whitley Manufacturing Co., Inc.
201 W First St
South Whitley IN 46787

(G-14310)
OLYMPIC FIBERGLASS INDUSTRIES
1235 E 4th St (46975-9104)
P.O. Box 920 (46975-0920)
PHONE..........................574 223-3101
William A Adams, Pr
Ardith Adams, *
EMP: 14 **EST:** 1967
SQ FT: 100,000
SALES (est): 441K **Privately Held**
SIC: 3089 3799 3431 Toilets, portable chemical: plastics; Trailers and trailer equipment; Metal sanitary ware

(G-14311)
PINNACLE TEXTILE INDS LLC
2516 E State Road 14 (46975-9604)
PHONE..........................574 223-4311
Patrick Methven, Pr
EMP: 80
SALES (corp-wide): 20.32MM **Privately Held**

Web: www.pinnacletextile.com
SIC: 2326 Men's and boy's work clothing
PA: Pinnacle Textile Industries Llc
440 Drew Ct
King Of Prussia PA 19406
800 901-4784

(G-14312)
QLEVER COMPANY LLC
3363 E 550 S Ste 590 (46975-8207)
PHONE..........................765 490-4694
EMP: 4 **EST:** 2014
SALES (est): 50.02K **Privately Held**
SIC: 7372 Prepackaged software

(G-14313)
QUALITY FORKLIFT REPAIR LLC
4662 E State Road 14 (46975-8459)
PHONE..........................574 702-5733
EMP: 5 **EST:** 2020
SALES (est): 47.61K **Privately Held**
Web: www.qfr-lift.com
SIC: 7694 Motor repair services

(G-14314)
RAMCO BUILDER AND SUPPLY LLC
Also Called: Ramco Supply
4572 N Old Us Highway 31 (46975-7387)
PHONE..........................574 223-7802
EMP: 28 **EST:** 1998
SQ FT: 12,000
SALES (est): 5.13MM **Privately Held**
Web: www.ramcosupply.com
SIC: 5211 3444 Lumber products; Metal roofing and roof drainage equipment

(G-14315)
RAPID VIEW LLC
Also Called: Schnabeltier
491 Apache Dr (46975-8019)
PHONE..........................574 224-3373
Rex Robison, Managing Member
Matt Sutton, Managing Member
Kris Robison, Managing Member
Kori Pugh, Opers Mgr
EMP: 5 **EST:** 2014
SALES (est): 500K **Privately Held**
Web: www.schnabeltier.com
SIC: 5149 2082 3556 5451 Dairy products, dried or canned; Beer (alcoholic beverage); Pasteurizing equipment, dairy machinery; Dairy products stores

(G-14316)
ROCHESTER CEMENT PRODUCTS INC
2184 Sweetgum Rd (46975-7585)
PHONE..........................574 223-3917
TOLL FREE: 877
Thomas Grosvenor, Pr
EMP: 6 **EST:** 1954
SALES (est): 675.06K **Privately Held**
SIC: 3272 5084 Septic tanks, concrete; Industrial machinery and equipment

(G-14317)
ROCHESTER HOMES INC (PA)
1345 N Lucas St (46975-1156)
P.O. Box 587 (46975-0587)
PHONE..........................574 223-4321
Kenny Anderson, Pr
Julie Anderson, *
EMP: 102 **EST:** 1972
SQ FT: 137,000
SALES (est): 10.5MM
SALES (corp-wide): 10.5MM **Privately Held**
Web: www.rochesterhomesinc.com

Rochester - Fulton County (G-14318)

SIC: 2452 2451 Modular homes, prefabricated, wood; Mobile homes, personal or private use

(G-14318)
ROCHESTER MANUFACTURING LLC
2903 Ft Wayne Rd (46975-8616)
PHONE..................574 224-2044
EMP: 9 EST: 2016
SALES (est): 517.46K
SALES (corp-wide): 6.08B **Publicly Held**
SIC: 3714 Motor vehicle parts and accessories
HQ: American Axle & Manufacturing, Inc.
  One Dauch Dr
  Detroit MI 48211

(G-14319)
ROCHESTER METAL PRODUCTS CORP (PA)
616 Indiana Ave (46975-1418)
P.O. Box 488 (46975-0488)
PHONE..................574 223-3164
Brad Hinkle, Pr
Greg Loving, *
Patrick D Hellman, *
EMP: 340 EST: 1937
SQ FT: 200,000
SALES (est): 35.67MM
SALES (corp-wide): 35.67MM **Privately Held**
Web: www.rochestermetals.com
SIC: 3321 Gray iron castings, nec

(G-14320)
ROCHESTER RTTIONAL MOLDING INC
Also Called: R R M
1952 E Lucas St (46975-8602)
P.O. Box 205 (46975-0205)
PHONE..................574 223-8844
Marilyn Wade, Pr
Wayne Allen Wade, VP
Cara Shambarger, Sec
▼ EMP: 17 EST: 1988
SQ FT: 16,000
SALES (est): 2.19MM **Privately Held**
Web: www.rrmplastics.com
SIC: 3089 Injection molding of plastics

(G-14321)
RONALD CHILEEN FURNITURE
9369 Ohio St (46975-9775)
PHONE..................574 542-4505
Ronald Chileen, Owner
EMP: 4 EST: 1968
SALES (est): 125.88K **Privately Held**
SIC: 2434 5712 Wood kitchen cabinets; Cabinet work, custom

(G-14322)
RUSKIN
510 N State Road 25 (46975-9776)
PHONE..................574 223-3181
EMP: 10 EST: 2012
SALES (est): 183.72K **Privately Held**
Web: www.ruskin.com
SIC: 3822 Environmental controls

(G-14323)
SCRAPWOOD SAWMILL
3488 S Wabash Rd (46975-7159)
PHONE..................574 223-2725
Dan M Peters, Owner
EMP: 2 EST: 2005
SALES (est): 72.84K **Privately Held**
SIC: 2421 Custom sawmill

(G-14324)
SHOPPING GUIDE NEWS INC
617 Main St (46975-1319)
P.O. Box 229 (46975-0229)
PHONE..................574 223-5417
Barb Foster, Pr
Steve Foster, VP
EMP: 12 EST: 2000
SALES (est): 93.52K **Privately Held**
Web: www.shoppingguidenews.com
SIC: 2711 Newspapers, publishing and printing

(G-14325)
SIGNS & DESIGNS BY LEWIS
2220 W 2nd St (46975-1010)
PHONE..................574 223-9403
Chad Lewis, Owner
EMP: 1 EST: 2008
SALES (est): 101.5K **Privately Held**
Web: www.signsbylewis.com
SIC: 3993 Signs and advertising specialties

(G-14326)
SMITH MACHINE AND TOOL
3392 Wabash Ave (46975)
PHONE..................574 223-2318
Richard Smith, Owner
EMP: 6 EST: 1987
SQ FT: 8,000
SALES (est): 428.67K **Privately Held**
SIC: 3544 Dies, plastics forming

(G-14327)
TEAM PRIDE ATHLETIC AP CORP
2196 Sweetgum Rd (46975-7585)
PHONE..................574 224-8326
Michael Barnett, Pr
Allen Farghing, VP
EMP: 5 EST: 2000
SQ FT: 2,000
SALES (est): 1.88MM **Privately Held**
Web: www.teamprideathletics.com
SIC: 2759 Screen printing

(G-14328)
TICZKUS ELECTRONIC AND MFG
8100 W Olson Rd (46975-8813)
PHONE..................574 542-2325
EMP: 2 EST: 1994
SALES (est): 157.29K **Privately Held**
SIC: 3825 Engine electrical test equipment

(G-14329)
TOPP INDUSTRIES INCORPORATED
420 N State Road 25 (46975-9700)
PHONE..................574 223-3681
Kevin Birchmeyer, Pr
David Birchmeier, *
Timothy Merkel, Prin
Judy Terry, Prin
Randy Utter, Prin
EMP: 90 EST: 1989
SQ FT: 37,000
SALES (est): 20.85MM **Privately Held**
Web: www.toppindustries.com
SIC: 3089 Injection molding of plastics

(G-14330)
TRUCK STYLIN UNLIMITED
Also Called: Truck Stylin & Collision
2123 Southway 31 (46975-8195)
PHONE..................574 223-8800
Richard Smith, Owner
▲ EMP: 10 EST: 2005
SALES (est): 221.36K **Privately Held**
Web: www.truckstylinandcollision.com
SIC: 3479 5531 Painting, coating, and hot dipping; Truck equipment and parts

(G-14331)
VAN DUYNE BLOCK AND GRAVEL
2602 S 500 E (46975-8423)
PHONE..................574 223-6656
Robert Macy, Pr
Carol Sue Macy, Treas
EMP: 3 EST: 1946
SQ FT: 8,000
SALES (est): 252.21K **Privately Held**
SIC: 3271 1442 4212 Blocks, concrete or cinder: standard; Gravel mining; Dump truck haulage

(G-14332)
VICKERY TAPE & LABEL CO INC
Also Called: JI Vincent Enterprises
3107 Barrett Rd (46975)
PHONE..................765 472-1974
Jim Vicent, Pr
Michael Gable, VP
EMP: 10 EST: 1947
SALES (est): 731.75K **Privately Held**
Web: www.vickerytape.com
SIC: 2759 Labels and seals: printing, nsk

(G-14333)
WILSON FERTILIZER & GRAIN INC (PA)
1827 E Lucas St (46975-7793)
P.O. Box 545 (46975-0545)
PHONE..................574 223-3175
Terry Moore, Pr
EMP: 4 EST: 1933
SQ FT: 5,000
SALES (est): 1.57MM
SALES (corp-wide): 1.57MM **Privately Held**
Web: www.wilsonfertgrain.com
SIC: 5191 5153 2875 2874 Animal feeds; Grains; Fertilizers, mixing only; Phosphatic fertilizers

(G-14334)
WINNING EDGE OF ROCHESTER INC
Also Called: Winning Edge
221 Rouch Place Dr (46975-8013)
PHONE..................574 223-6090
Bradly Good, Pr
EMP: 13 EST: 1987
SQ FT: 8,800
SALES (est): 434.64K **Privately Held**
Web: www.thewinningedgeathletics.com
SIC: 2396 5999 5941 5699 Screen printing on fabric articles; Trophies and plaques; Sporting goods and bicycle shops; Uniforms

Rockport
Spencer County

(G-14335)
AIRGAS USA LLC
6500 N Us Highway 231 (47635-9061)
P.O. Box 425 (47635-0425)
PHONE..................812 362-7593
Matt Gronseth, Brnch Mgr
EMP: 6
SALES (corp-wide): 114.13MM **Privately Held**
Web: www.airgas.com
SIC: 5169 5084 5085 2813 Industrial gases; Welding machinery and equipment; Welding supplies; Industrial gases
HQ: Airgas Usa, Llc
  259 N Radnor Chester Rd
  Radnor PA 19087
  216 642-6600

(G-14336)
ALIG LLC
6500 N Us Highway 231 (47635-9061)
P.O. Box 425 (47635-0425)
PHONE..................812 362-7593
Matt Gronseth, Genl Mgr
EMP: 2
SALES (corp-wide): 114.13MM **Privately Held**
SIC: 2819 2813 Hydrogen sulfide; Oxygen, compressed or liquefied
HQ: Alig Llc
  2700 Post Oak Blvd Fl 18
  Houston TX 77056
  212 626-4936

(G-14337)
BECKER ELEC
6500 N Us Highway 231 (47635-9061)
PHONE..................812 362-9000
Dennis Boyd, Mgr
EMP: 2 EST: 2007
SALES (est): 226.62K **Privately Held**
SIC: 3699 Electrical equipment and supplies, nec

(G-14338)
CLEVELAND-CLIFFS STEEL CORP
Also Called: Rockport Works
6500 N Us Highway 231 (47635-9061)
PHONE..................812 362-6000
Eric Petersen, Brnch Mgr
EMP: 110
SALES (corp-wide): 22B **Publicly Held**
Web: www.clevelandcliffs.com
SIC: 3312 Stainless steel
HQ: Cleveland-Cliffs Steel Corporation
  200 Public Sq Ste 3300
  Cleveland OH 44114

(G-14339)
DAWSON MACHINE SHOP INC
614 N State Road 161 (47635-8831)
PHONE..................812 649-4777
Chris Dawson, Pr
Lori Dawson, Sec
EMP: 21 EST: 1998
SQ FT: 4,000
SALES (est): 1.12MM **Privately Held**
SIC: 3599 Machine shop, jobbing and repair

(G-14340)
FISCHER FLEET WASH LLC
204 S Lincoln Ave (47635-1336)
PHONE..................812 661-9947
EMP: 1
SALES (est): 69.27K **Privately Held**
SIC: 3799 7389 Transportation equipment, nec; Business Activities at Non-Commercial Site

(G-14341)
FREEDOM INDUSTRIAL WELDING LLC
709 N 7th St (47635-1104)
PHONE..................812 686-9802
Christopher Schulte, Prin
Charles Smith, Managing Member
EMP: 8 EST: 2018
SALES (est): 447.51K **Privately Held**
Web: www.freedomindustrialllc.com
SIC: 7692 Welding repair

(G-14342)
HOOPLE COUNTRY KITCHENS INC
714 N 5th St (47635-1103)
PHONE..................812 649-2351
David N Caskey, Pr
Denise A Caskey, VP
Katherine Caskey, Sec

Franklin E Caskey, *Treas*
EMP: 14 **EST:** 1950
SQ FT: 22,500
SALES (est): 496.54K **Privately Held**
Web: www.hooplecountrykitchens.com
SIC: 2099 Salads, fresh or refrigerated

(G-14343)
JOHNSON CONTROLS INC
Also Called: Johnson Controls
6500 N Us Highway 231 (47635-9061)
PHONE.................812 362-6901
Gary Cooper, *Mgr*
EMP: 16
Web: www.johnsoncontrols.com
SIC: 2531 Seats, automobile
HQ: Johnson Controls, Inc.
   5757 N Green Bay Ave
   Milwaukee WI 53209
   866 496-1999

(G-14344)
M G INDUSTRIES
6500 N Us Highway 231 (47635-9061)
P.O. Box 425 (47635-0425)
PHONE.................812 362-7593
Matt Gronseth, *Prin*
EMP: 1 **EST:** 2010
SALES (est): 63.73K **Privately Held**
SIC: 3999 Manufacturing industries, nec

(G-14345)
MIDWEST GRAPHIX LLC
1540 S County Road 100 W Ste D
(47635-8643)
PHONE.................812 649-2522
Joshua Allen, *Prin*
EMP: 8 **EST:** 2011
SALES (est): 218.77K **Privately Held**
Web: www.slade.company
SIC: 3993 Signs and advertising specialties

(G-14346)
NEWS PUBLISHING COMPANY LLC
Also Called: Spencer Cnty Journal-Democrat
541 Main St (47635-1429)
P.O. Box 309 (47586-0309)
PHONE.................812 649-4440
Angela Geralds, *Mgr*
EMP: 2
Web: www.duboiscountyherald.com
SIC: 2711 2791 Newspapers: publishing only, not printed on site; Typesetting
HQ: News Publishing Company, Llc
   542 7th St
   Tell City IN 47586
   502 633-4334

(G-14347)
PEPPERS RIDGE LLC
4304 N County Road 200 W (47635-9104)
PHONE.................812 499-3743
EMP: 4 **EST:** 2009
SALES (est): 64.61K **Privately Held**
Web: www.peppersridge.com
SIC: 2084 Wines

(G-14348)
ROCKPORT ROLL SHOP LLC
6500 N Us Highway 231 (47635-9061)
P.O. Box 102 (47635-0102)
PHONE.................812 362-6419
EMP: 26 **EST:** 1997
SQ FT: 86,000
SALES (est): 8.23MM **Privately Held**
Web: www.rockportrollshop.com
SIC: 3355 Aluminum rolling and drawing, nec

Rockville
Parke County

(G-14349)
A PLUS METALS LLC ✪
4353 E 250 N (47872-8252)
PHONE.................915 341-0650
Aaron A Peachey, *Managing Member*
EMP: 5 **EST:** 2023
SALES (est): 62.01K **Privately Held**
SIC: 3441 Fabricated structural metal

(G-14350)
CITY WELDING & FABRICATION
255 N Dormeyer Ave (47872-8107)
P.O. Box 69 (47872-0069)
PHONE.................765 569-5403
Andy Willhite, *Owner*
EMP: 9 **EST:** 1953
SQ FT: 10,000
SALES (est): 961.85K **Privately Held**
Web: www.citywelding.net
SIC: 1799 7692 3523 3444 Welding on site; Welding repair; Farm machinery and equipment; Sheet metalwork

(G-14351)
DOUBLE D
Also Called: Lee's Double D Tire & Muffler
214 E Ohio St (47872-1829)
PHONE.................765 569-6822
Dave Lee, *Owner*
EMP: 2 **EST:** 1983
SQ FT: 4,800
SALES (est): 214.56K **Privately Held**
SIC: 5531 7534 Automotive tires; Tire repair shop

(G-14352)
JUDSON HARNESS & SADDLERY
4889 E 350 N (47872-8152)
PHONE.................765 569-0918
Chris Herschberger, *Owner*
EMP: 3 **EST:** 1998
SQ FT: 3,850
SALES (est): 214.39K **Privately Held**
SIC: 3199 5191 5941 Saddles or parts; Saddlery; Saddlery and equestrian equipment

(G-14353)
PARKE COUNTY AGGREGATES LLC
5081 N State Road 59 (47872-8239)
P.O. Box 399 (47862-0399)
PHONE.................765 245-2344
EMP: 5 **EST:** 2007
SALES (est): 543.32K **Privately Held**
SIC: 5032 3444 1629 Brick, stone, and related material; Culverts, sheet metal; Drainage system construction

(G-14354)
SCOTT PET PRODUCTS INC (PA)
Also Called: T. E. Scott
1543 N Us Highway 41 (47872-7146)
P.O. Box 168 (47872-0168)
PHONE.................765 569-4636
Hal Harlan, *CEO*
James Stormer, *
Paul Hayden, *
Courtney Hostetler, *
◆ **EMP:** 110 **EST:** 1975
SQ FT: 140,000
SALES (est): 62.37MM
SALES (corp-wide): 62.37MM **Privately Held**
Web: www.nutrichomps.com

SIC: 5199 3199 5999 Pet supplies; Dog furnishings: collars, leashes, muzzles, etc.: leather; Pet supplies

(G-14355)
SCOTT PET PRODUCTS INC
840 N Us Highway 41 (47872-7090)
PHONE.................765 569-4636
EMP: 1
SALES (corp-wide): 62.37MM **Privately Held**
Web: www.scottpet.com
SIC: 2047 Dog food
PA: Scott Pet Products, Inc.
   1543 N Us Highway 41
   Rockville IN 47872
   765 569-4636

(G-14356)
STOLTZFUS CUSTOM WELDING LLC
5044 N Judson Rd (47872-8204)
PHONE.................765 569-2362
EMP: 4 **EST:** 2013
SALES (est): 25.09K **Privately Held**
SIC: 7692 Welding repair

(G-14357)
SUCCESS EXPRESS
1501 S Catlin Rd (47872-7302)
PHONE.................317 750-1747
EMP: 4 **EST:** 2018
SALES (est): 161.67K **Privately Held**
Web: www.successexpresscoaching.com
SIC: 2752 Commercial printing, lithographic

(G-14358)
TINCHERS CREATIVE WOODWORKS
11206 E Ferndale Rd (47872-7930)
PHONE.................765 344-0062
Guy Tincher, *Owner*
EMP: 2 **EST:** 1999
SALES (est): 110.9K **Privately Held**
SIC: 2431 Woodwork, interior and ornamental, nec

(G-14359)
TORCH NEWSPAPERS INC
Also Called: Parke County Sentinel
125 W High St (47872-1735)
P.O. Box 187 (47872-0187)
PHONE.................765 569-2033
Mary Jo Harney, *Pr*
Robert Nash, *VP*
Mary Joan Harney, *Sec*
EMP: 8 **EST:** 1970
SQ FT: 2,400
SALES (est): 742.8K **Privately Held**
Web: www.parkecountysentinel.com
SIC: 2711 Newspapers, publishing and printing

(G-14360)
WALNUT ACRES SAWMILL LLC
757 E 200 S (47872-7041)
PHONE.................765 344-0027
EMP: 11 **EST:** 2009
SALES (est): 517.72K **Privately Held**
SIC: 2421 Sawmills and planing mills, general

Rolling Prairie
Laporte County

(G-14361)
FAST MANUFACTURING LLC
3956 E 800 N (46371-8877)
PHONE.................219 778-8238
Catherine R Foreman, *Pr*

EMP: 4 **EST:** 2009
SALES (est): 303.58K **Privately Held**
Web: www.inscerco.com
SIC: 3999 Manufacturing industries, nec

(G-14362)
FRONTIER ELECTRIC INC
3074 N 350 E (46371-9568)
PHONE.................219 778-2553
EMP: 2
SALES (est): 269.68K **Privately Held**
SIC: 3699 Electrical equipment and supplies, nec

(G-14363)
GRIMM MOLD & DIE CO INC
200 S Depot St (46371-7010)
P.O. Box 218 (46371-0218)
PHONE.................219 778-4211
Timothy Grimm, *Pr*
Sheila Grimm, *VP*
EMP: 12 **EST:** 1965
SQ FT: 10,000
SALES (est): 765.14K **Privately Held**
SIC: 3599 3544 3545 Crankshafts and camshafts, machining; Dies, plastics forming; Machine tool accessories

(G-14364)
HARTLAND PRODUCTS INC
Also Called: Ken Co Hartland
5022 E Oak Knoll Rd (46371)
P.O. Box 519 (46371-0519)
PHONE.................219 778-9034
Kenneth Coates, *Pr*
EMP: 10 **EST:** 2003
SALES (est): 375.73K **Privately Held**
SIC: 3089 Injection molded finished plastics products, nec

(G-14365)
J AND G ENTERPRISES
5556 E 300 N (46371-9431)
PHONE.................219 778-4319
Gilbert Bradburn, *Owner*
Janet Bradburn, *Owner*
EMP: 2 **EST:** 1973
SALES (est): 98.89K **Privately Held**
SIC: 2434 Wood kitchen cabinets

(G-14366)
K & M WELD FAB
3381 N 300 E (46371-9518)
PHONE.................219 362-3736
Morrow Lyle, *Owner*
EMP: 4 **EST:** 2015
SALES (est): 39.97K **Privately Held**
SIC: 7692 Welding repair

(G-14367)
OTECH CORPORATION
Also Called: Otech
4744 E Oak Knoll Rd (46371)
P.O. Box 116 (46371-0116)
PHONE.................219 778-8001
Jason Page, *CEO*
Ted Irvine, *
Harold Sullivan, *
Kristine Conley, *
▼ **EMP:** 122 **EST:** 2006
SQ FT: 66,000
SALES (est): 53.81MM **Privately Held**
Web: www.otechcompounds.com
SIC: 2821 Plastics materials and resins

(G-14368)
PRAIRIE SUN VINEYARD LLC
3131 N 700 E (46371-9423)
PHONE.................219 741-5918
Edward H Keiley, *Owner*

Rolling Prairie - Laporte County (G-14369)

EMP: 5 EST: 2017
SALES (est): 88.81K **Privately Held**
SIC: 2084 Wines

(G-14369)
PRINT2PROMO GROUP INC
7592 E 400 N (46371-9486)
PHONE.....................219 778-4649
Barbara S Van Wynsberghe, *Owner*
EMP: 7 EST: 2012
SALES (est): 141.32K **Privately Held**
SIC: 2752 Commercial printing, lithographic

(G-14370)
PYRAMID EQUIPMENT
Also Called: PYRAMID EQUIPMENT
8 S Depot St (46371-7028)
P.O. Box 127 (46371-0127)
PHONE.....................219 778-4253
EMP: 4
SALES (corp-wide): 2.17MM **Privately Held**
Web: www.pyramidequipmentinc.com
SIC: 7692 Welding repair
PA: Pyramid Equipment, Inc.
  211 S Prairie St
  Rolling Prairie IN 46371
  219 778-2591

(G-14371)
PYRAMID EQUIPMENT INC (PA)
211 S Prairie St (46371-7012)
P.O. Box 127 (46371-0127)
PHONE.....................219 778-2591
TOLL FREE: 800
David E Surma, *Pr*
Sandra L Surma, *Sec*
EMP: 10 EST: 1985
SQ FT: 60,000
SALES (est): 2.17MM
SALES (corp-wide): 2.17MM **Privately Held**
Web: www.pyramidequipmentinc.com
SIC: 7692 7538 5084 5531 Welding repair; Engine repair; Industrial machinery and equipment; Trailer hitches, automotive

(G-14372)
WAX CONNECTIONS INC
3628 E Us Highway 20 (46371-9561)
PHONE.....................219 778-2325
Debora K Yergler, *Pr*
EMP: 5 EST: 1993
SALES (est): 399.78K **Privately Held**
Web: www.waxconnections.com
SIC: 3567 Industrial furnaces and ovens

Rome City
Noble County

(G-14373)
AGGREATE SYSTEMS (PA)
102 Industry Bnd (46784-1031)
PHONE.....................260 854-4711
Dick Siebert, *Genl Mgr*
Dick Siebert, *Genl Mgr*
EMP: 12 EST: 2000
SALES (est): 2.4MM
SALES (corp-wide): 2.4MM **Privately Held**
Web: www.aggsystems.net
SIC: 3535 Conveyors and conveying equipment

(G-14374)
AGGREATE SYSTEMS
106 Industry Bnd (46784-1031)
P.O. Box 235 (46784-0235)
PHONE.....................260 854-4711
EMP: 2

SALES (corp-wide): 2.4MM **Privately Held**
Web: www.aggsystems.net
SIC: 3441 Building components, structural steel
PA: Aggreate Systems
  102 Industry Bnd
  Rome City IN 46784
  260 854-4711

(G-14375)
FRUITION INDUSTRIES LLC
105 Warmer Dr (46784-9326)
P.O. Box 416 (46784-0416)
PHONE.....................260 854-2325
EMP: 12 EST: 2010
SALES (est): 1.98MM **Privately Held**
SIC: 3679 Harness assemblies, for electronic use: wire or cable

(G-14376)
GROUP DEKKO INC
105 Warmer Dr (46784-9326)
P.O. Box 640 (46784-0640)
PHONE.....................260 854-4783
Gary Sanders, *Mgr*
EMP: 50
SALES (corp-wide): 4.41B **Publicly Held**
Web: www.dekko.com
SIC: 3679 Harness assemblies, for electronic use: wire or cable
HQ: Group Dekko, Inc.
  7310 Innovation Blvd # 104
  Fort Wayne IN 46818

(G-14377)
ROME CY AREA YOUTH CTR BASBAL
705 Kelly Street Ext (46784-9686)
PHONE.....................260 854-4599
Steven Herendeen, *Commsnr*
EMP: 2 EST: 2003
SALES (est): 64.22K **Privately Held**
SIC: 3949 Baseball equipment and supplies, general

(G-14378)
WEST LAKES MARINE INC (PA)
Also Called: West Lakes Boat Mart
85 E Holiday Pt (46784-9748)
PHONE.....................260 854-2525
Richard Reynolds, *Pr*
William Reynolds, *VP*
Mary L Reynolds, *Asst Tr*
EMP: 10 EST: 1963
SQ FT: 800
SALES (est): 2.37MM
SALES (corp-wide): 2.37MM **Privately Held**
Web: www.westlakesmarine.com
SIC: 5551 5541 4493 3732 Motor boat dealers; Marine service station; Marinas; Boatbuilding and repairing

Romney
Tippecanoe County

(G-14379)
ANDERSONS FERTILIZER SERVICE
527 W 1150 S (47981-9646)
P.O. Box 4 (47981-0004)
PHONE.....................765 538-3285
Richard D Anderson, *Pr*
Beth Miller, *VP*
EMP: 5 EST: 1963
SQ FT: 2,000
SALES (est): 3.23MM **Privately Held**
SIC: 5191 2875 Fertilizer and fertilizer materials; Fertilizers, mixing only

Rosedale
Parke County

(G-14380)
JOE WADE CUSTOMS
324 N Main St (47874-9613)
PHONE.....................765 548-0333
EMP: 6 EST: 2007
SALES (est): 88.73K **Privately Held**
SIC: 3714 Propane conversion equipment, motor vehicle

(G-14381)
KT CAKES
13699 N Rock Run Church Rd (47874-8002)
PHONE.....................812 442-6047
Carla Duis, *Owner*
EMP: 2 EST: 2000
SALES (est): 89.06K **Privately Held**
Web: theweddingscoop.wordpress.com
SIC: 2051 Bakery: wholesale or wholesale/retail combined

(G-14382)
SHADE TREE PRESS
8945 S Coxville Rd (47874-7007)
PHONE.....................765 548-2421
Mike Lunsford, *Prin*
EMP: 1 EST: 2010
SALES (est): 74.07K **Privately Held**
SIC: 2741 Miscellaneous publishing

(G-14383)
SUMMERLOT ENGINEERED PDTS INC
Also Called: S E P
11655 N U S 41 Rosedale (47874)
P.O. Box 5216 (47805-0216)
PHONE.....................812 466-7266
Raymond L Summerlot, *CEO*
Adam Summerlot, *Pr*
Debbie Summerlot, *Sec*
EMP: 18 EST: 1970
SQ FT: 23,000
SALES (est): 4.26MM **Privately Held**
Web: www.summerlot.com
SIC: 3535 5051 7692 3531 Bulk handling conveyor systems; Steel; Welding repair; Construction machinery

(G-14384)
T & T HYDRAULICS INC
7443 S 625 W (47874-7089)
PHONE.....................765 548-2355
Rick Trout, *Pr*
James Trout, *VP*
EMP: 3 EST: 1991
SQ FT: 4,000
SALES (est): 218.36K **Privately Held**
Web: www.tthyd.com
SIC: 7699 3569 Hydraulic equipment repair; Filters

(G-14385)
TAGHLEEF INDUSTRIES INC
Also Called: Aet Films
3600 E Head Ave (47874-9124)
P.O. Box 5038 (47805-0038)
PHONE.....................302 326-5500
John White, *Mgr*
EMP: 603
Web: www.ti-films.com
SIC: 3081 3089 2671 Polypropylene film and sheet; Plastics processing; Paper; coated and laminated packaging
HQ: Taghleef Industries Inc.
  800 Prdes Crssing Ste 200
  Newark DE 19713
  302 326-5500

Rossville
Clinton County

(G-14386)
B & L CUSTOM CABINETS INC
7427 N County Road 300 W (46065-7304)
PHONE.....................765 379-2471
Jesse L Longnecker, *Pr*
Jay E Brubaker, *Sec*
Suzanne Longnecker, *Stockholder*
Julie Brubaker, *Stockholder*
Todd Longnecker, *Stockholder*
EMP: 9 EST: 1976
SQ FT: 10,000
SALES (est): 600.18K **Privately Held**
SIC: 2434 Wood kitchen cabinets

(G-14387)
MAUREEN SHARP
153 N Gaddis St (46065-9435)
PHONE.....................765 379-3644
Maureen Sharp, *Prin*
EMP: 2 EST: 2003
SALES (est): 78.83K **Privately Held**
SIC: 2789 Bookbinding and related work

(G-14388)
TYSON FRESH MEATS INC
Also Called: I B P Hog Buying Station
6870 S Us Highway 421 (46065-9132)
PHONE.....................765 379-3102
EMP: 1
SALES (corp-wide): 52.88B **Publicly Held**
Web: www.tysonfreshmeats.com
SIC: 2011 Meat packing plants
HQ: Tyson Fresh Meats, Inc.
  2200 W Don Tyson Pkwy
  Springdale AR 72765
  479 290-4000

Royal Center
Cass County

(G-14389)
CAMPBELLS WELDING & MACHINE
202 E Day St (46978-9019)
P.O. Box 477 (46978-0477)
PHONE.....................574 643-6705
Dale Campbell, *Owner*
EMP: 2 EST: 1985
SALES (est): 70.74K **Privately Held**
SIC: 7692 Welding repair

(G-14390)
COUNTRY VALLEY CANDLES
9813 W County Road 900 N (46978-9006)
PHONE.....................574 702-1302
Cody Brandt, *Prin*
EMP: 4 EST: 2016
SALES (est): 39.69K **Privately Held**
Web: www.countryvalleycandles.com
SIC: 3999 Candles

(G-14391)
INDIAN TRAIL WINES LLC
7540 N County Road 350 W (46978-8987)
PHONE.....................574 889-2509
Megan Mcdonald, *Pr*
EMP: 3 EST: 2009
SALES (est): 209.6K **Privately Held**
Web: www.indiantrailwines.com
SIC: 2084 Wines

(G-14392)
ROYAL CENTER LOCKER PLANT INC
104 S Chicago St (46978-7029)
P.O. Box 250 (46978-0250)

GEOGRAPHIC SECTION
Rushville - Rush County (G-14417)

PHONE..............................574 643-3275
Steve Layer, *Pr*
EMP: 9 **EST:** 1971
SQ FT: 20,000
SALES (est): 494.43K **Privately Held**
SIC: 0751 5421 2013 2011 Slaughtering: custom livestock services; Meat and fish markets; Sausages and other prepared meats; Meat packing plants

(G-14393)
SRAE CONSTRUCTION LLC
2754 N County Road 825 W (46978-9103)
PHONE..............................219 216-1902
Gina M Hominger, *Managing Member*
EMP: 2 **EST:** 2020
SALES (est): 50K **Privately Held**
SIC: 1389 Construction, repair, and dismantling services

(G-14394)
WHALLON MACHINERY INC
205 N. Chicago Street (Us Hwy 35) (46978-2101)
P.O. Box 429 (46978-0429)
PHONE..............................574 643-9561
Leslie Smith, *Pr*
Leslie G Smith, *
Michael K Wallon, *
Sara Layman, *Stockholder**
Sarah Miller, *
EMP: 50 **EST:** 1973
SQ FT: 40,000
SALES (est): 9.34MM **Privately Held**
Web: www.whallon.com
SIC: 3565 Bottling and canning machinery

Rushville
Rush County

(G-14395)
AMOS WELDING LLC
2117 E 700 N (46173-7590)
PHONE..............................765 561-2359
EMP: 5 **EST:** 2017
SALES (est): 180.29K **Privately Held**
Web: amos-welding.myshopify.com
SIC: 7692 Welding repair

(G-14396)
CHIEF METAL WORKS INC
1705 W Us Highway 52 (46173-8790)
PHONE..............................765 932-2134
Brad Pike, *Pr*
Shannon Phillips, *Sec*
EMP: 2 **EST:** 1985
SALES (est): 264.67K **Privately Held**
Web: www.pikessandblasting.com
SIC: 3471 7692 3479 5599 Sand blasting of metal parts; Welding repair; Painting of metal products; Utility trailers

(G-14397)
COPELAND LP
616 Conrad Harcourt Way (46173-1166)
PHONE..............................765 932-2956
EMP: 17
SALES (corp-wide): 4.71B **Privately Held**
Web: www.copeland.com
SIC: 3823 Process control instruments
PA: Copeland Lp
  1675 W Campbell Rd
  Sidney OH 45365
  937 498-3011

(G-14398)
COPELAND LP
500 Conrad Harcourt Way (46173-1164)
PHONE..............................765 932-1902
Tom Zoskie, *Mgr*
EMP: 220
SALES (corp-wide): 4.71B **Privately Held**
Web: www.copeland.com
SIC: 3823 Process control instruments
PA: Copeland Lp
  1675 W Campbell Rd
  Sidney OH 45365
  937 498-3011

(G-14399)
DIVINE HERITAGE BARNS LLC
4849 E Us Highway 52 (46173)
PHONE..............................812 709-0066
Evan Divine, *Prin*
EMP: 5 **EST:** 2016
SALES (est): 92.72K **Privately Held**
Web: www.divineheritagebarns.com
SIC: 2431 Millwork

(G-14400)
FIELDS OUTDOOR ADVENTURES LLP
126 S Perkins St (46173-1933)
PHONE..............................765 932-3964
Mark Fields, *Mgr*
EMP: 4 **EST:** 2010
SALES (est): 306.04K **Privately Held**
Web: www.fieldsusa.com
SIC: 3949 Sporting and athletic goods, nec

(G-14401)
INTAT PRECISION INC
2148 N State Road 3 (46173-9302)
P.O. Box 488 (46173-0488)
PHONE..............................765 932-5323
Donald Carson, *Pr*
▲ **EMP:** 400 **EST:** 1988
SQ FT: 400,000
SALES (est): 80.24MM **Privately Held**
Web: www.intat.com
SIC: 3321 Ductile iron castings
PA: Aisin Takaoka Co.,Ltd.
  1, Tenno, Takaokashinmachi
  Toyota AIC 473-0

(G-14402)
JLB INDUSTRIAL LLC
5066 S The Farm Rd (46173-7369)
PHONE..............................765 561-1751
Jade Brumfield, *Prin*
EMP: 9 **EST:** 2011
SALES (est): 382.64K **Privately Held**
Web: www.jlbindustrial.com
SIC: 3443 3585 Boiler shop products: boilers, smokestacks, steel tanks; Refrigeration and heating equipment

(G-14403)
KEITH ISON
Also Called: Vinyl Therm of Indiana
615 Conrad Harcourt Way (46173-1167)
PHONE..............................765 938-1460
EMP: 4 **EST:** 1993
SQ FT: 3,600
SALES (est): 315.3K **Privately Held**
SIC: 2431 Windows and window parts and trim, wood

(G-14404)
L&S SANITATION SERVICE
270 S 100 W (46173-7776)
PHONE..............................765 932-5410
Tracy Stanley, *Owner*
EMP: 6 **EST:** 1945
SALES (est): 257.19K **Privately Held**
SIC: 2842 Drain pipe solvents or cleaners

(G-14405)
LEE MACHINE INC
505 E 11th St (46173-1316)
PHONE..............................765 932-3100
Jeff Lee, *Prin*
EMP: 10 **EST:** 2001
SALES (est): 288.78K **Privately Held**
SIC: 3599 Machine shop, jobbing and repair

(G-14406)
MILLS RIVER PUBLISHING COMPANY
611 N Harrison St (46173-1528)
P.O. Box 411 (46173-0411)
PHONE..............................765 561-3445
Brian Rodgers, *Owner*
EMP: 1 **EST:** 2012
SALES (est): 75.26K **Privately Held**
Web: www.millsriverpublishing.com
SIC: 2741 Miscellaneous publishing

(G-14407)
PRT INC
Also Called: Prevention Response Technology
700 W 5th St (46173-1557)
PHONE..............................765 938-3333
Daniel Gehlhausen, *Pr*
Kyle Gehlhausen, *VP*
Caroline Gehlhausen, *Sec*
EMP: 5 **EST:** 1991
SALES (est): 494.64K **Privately Held**
SIC: 2899 Fire retardant chemicals

(G-14408)
QUALITY PALLET RECYCLING LLC
3964 W 700 S (46173-9262)
PHONE..............................317 840-5990
EMP: 1 **EST:** 2006
SALES (est): 124.44K **Privately Held**
SIC: 2448 Pallets, wood

(G-14409)
REFRIGERATION DESIGN IND LLC
319 E 350 S (46173-7257)
P.O. Box 85 (46173-0085)
PHONE..............................317 498-3435
EMP: 1 **EST:** 2008
SALES (est): 159.46K **Privately Held**
Web: www.coolingdesign.com
SIC: 3585 5078 Refrigeration and heating equipment; Commercial refrigeration equipment

(G-14410)
ROBERT S FROMAN
3395 N Henderson Rd (46173-7266)
PHONE..............................765 565-6819
EMP: 6 **EST:** 2007
SALES (est): 189.51K **Privately Held**
SIC: 1381 Drilling oil and gas wells

(G-14411)
SCHELL & KAMPETER INC
2530 N State Road 3 (46173)
PHONE..............................765 570-4262
Michael Kampeter, *CEO*
EMP: 14
SALES (corp-wide): 113.89MM **Privately Held**
Web: www.diamondpet.com
SIC: 2047 Dog and cat food
PA: Schell & Kampeter, Inc.
  103 N Olive St
  Meta MO 65058
  573 229-4203

(G-14412)
SHELBY GRAVEL INC
Also Called: Shelby Gravel
982 S Flatrock River Rd (46173-7349)
PHONE..............................765 932-3292
Aaron Hale, *Mgr*
EMP: 3
SALES (corp-wide): 74.83MM **Privately Held**
Web: www.shelbymaterials.com
SIC: 3273 Ready-mixed concrete
PA: Shelby Gravel, Inc
  157 E Rampart St
  Shelbyville IN 46176
  317 398-4485

(G-14413)
STARKEY WELDING INC
Also Called: Star Weld
709 W 1st St (46173-1708)
PHONE..............................765 932-2005
Tim Starkey, *Pr*
Jane Starkey, *Sec*
EMP: 6 **EST:** 1986
SALES (est): 500.25K **Privately Held**
Web: www.starweldindustrial.com
SIC: 7692 Welding repair

(G-14414)
T K M TRIPLE K MACHINING
Also Called: Ryobi
6972 S 200 W (46173-7388)
PHONE..............................765 629-2805
Doug Herbert, *Owner*
EMP: 1 **EST:** 2008
SALES (est): 70.65K **Privately Held**
SIC: 3599 Machine shop, jobbing and repair

(G-14415)
TRANE US INC
Also Called: Trane
1300 N Benjamin St (46173-1173)
P.O. Box 219 (46173-0219)
PHONE..............................765 932-7200
Greg Harcourt, *Brnch Mgr*
EMP: 100
Web: www.trane.com
SIC: 3585 Refrigeration and heating equipment
HQ: Trane U.S. Inc.
  800-E Beaty St
  Davidson NC 28036
  704 655-4000

(G-14416)
WASHMUTH CABINET COMPANY
507 N Morgan St (46173-1538)
PHONE..............................765 932-2701
Tim Washmuth, *Owner*
EMP: 1 **EST:** 1960
SQ FT: 2,500
SALES (est): 125.53K **Privately Held**
SIC: 2541 2434 Sink tops, plastic laminated; Wood kitchen cabinets

(G-14417)
YER BRANDS INC
Also Called: Soy-Yer Dough
1350 N Commerce Dr Ste B (46173-2117)
PHONE..............................239 307-2925
Sawyer Sparks, *CEO*
Stefan Muehlbauer, *Pr*
EMP: 2 **EST:** 2020
SALES (est): 64.65K **Privately Held**
SIC: 3952 Modeling clay
PA: Sustainable Projects Group Inc.
  225 Banyan Blvd Ste 220
  Naples FL 34102
  239 228-7981

Russellville
Putnam County

(G-14418)
ALBERTSON SEED SALES
3868 W County Road 1200 S (46175-9603)
PHONE..................765 267-0680
Jeff Albertson, *Prin*
EMP: 5 EST: 2017
SALES (est): 189.7K **Privately Held**
SIC: 2074 Cottonseed oil mills

(G-14419)
ST CLAIR GROUP INC
Also Called: Metal Forming Industries
7903 W County Road 1325 N (46175-5500)
PHONE..................765 435-3091
Diane Fordice, *Manager*
EMP: 75
SQ FT: 16,000
SALES (corp-wide): 8.83MM **Privately Held**
Web: www.metalformingindustries.com
SIC: 3599 Machine shop, jobbing and repair
PA: St. Clair Group Inc.
    101 W Main St
    Lebanon IN 46052
    317 339-6149

Russiaville
Howard County

(G-14420)
B&M MILLWRIGHT INC
2719 S 1280 W (46979-9766)
PHONE..................765 883-8177
EMP: 2 EST: 1995
SALES (est): 244.5K **Privately Held**
SIC: 7692 Welding repair

(G-14421)
BRAD BUGHER
Also Called: Bugher Fabricating
360 W Main St (46979-9100)
PHONE..................765 883-8112
Brad Bugher, *Owner*
EMP: 1 EST: 2000
SALES (est): 81.71K **Privately Held**
SIC: 3441 Fabricated structural metal

(G-14422)
HOLLINGSWORTH SAWMILL INC
Also Called: Hollingsworth Lumber
6810 W 400 S (46979)
PHONE..................765 883-5836
Hollingsworth Darin, *Pr*
Joel Hollingsworth, *VP*
Kaleb Hollingsworth, *VP*
Hollingsworth Joel, *Sec*
EMP: 17 EST: 1983
SQ FT: 50,000
SALES (est): 5.32MM **Privately Held**
Web: www.hollingsworthlumber.com
SIC: 2421 5211 5031 Custom sawmill; Lumber products; Lumber: rough, dressed, and finished

(G-14423)
IRON MEN INDUSTRIES INC
6086 W 250 S (46979-9506)
PHONE..................574 596-2251
Chris Thayer, *Treas*
EMP: 6 EST: 2017
SALES (est): 103.42K **Privately Held**
SIC: 3999 Manufacturing industries, nec

(G-14424)
MARTIN MARIETTA MATERIALS INC
Also Called: Kokomo Sand
3891 S 500 W (46979-9491)
PHONE..................765 883-8172
Marty Rainford, *Brnch Mgr*
EMP: 10
Web: www.martinmarietta.com
SIC: 3273 Ready-mixed concrete
PA: Martin Marietta Materials Inc
    4123 Parklake Ave
    Raleigh NC 27612

(G-14425)
RICHARD MYERS MLLWRGHT
2719 S 1280 W (46979-9766)
PHONE..................765 883-8177
Richard Myers, *Owner*
EMP: 5 EST: 2017
SALES (est): 96.52K **Privately Held**
SIC: 7692 Welding repair

Saint Anthony
Dubois County

(G-14426)
BCH IMAGE USA INC ◆
Also Called: Tri-Plastics
4582 S Cross St (47575)
PHONE..................812 326-1025
EMP: 6 EST: 2022
SALES (est): 321.73K **Privately Held**
SIC: 3086 Insulation or cushioning material, foamed plastics

(G-14427)
ERNIES WELDING SHOP LLC
Also Called: Ernie's Welding Shop
3854 E 450 S (47575-9743)
PHONE..................812 326-2600
Martha J Wehr, *Owner*
EMP: 4 EST: 1972
SQ FT: 4,800
SALES (est): 363.9K **Privately Held**
SIC: 7692 Automotive welding

(G-14428)
FISCHER FRMS NATURAL FOODS LLC
4630 S Cross St (47575-9640)
PHONE..................812 481-1411
EMP: 4 EST: 2006
SALES (est): 92.16K **Privately Held**
SIC: 5159 2011 Farm animals; Beef products, from beef slaughtered on site

(G-14429)
INTERNATIONAL PAPER COMPANY
Also Called: International Paper
3565 E 550 S St Rt 6 (47575)
P.O. Box 37 (47575-0037)
PHONE..................812 326-2125
EMP: 7
SALES (corp-wide): 18.92B **Publicly Held**
Web: www.internationalpaper.com
SIC: 2653 Boxes, corrugated: made from purchased materials
PA: International Paper Company
    6400 Poplar Ave
    Memphis TN 38197
    901 419-7000

(G-14430)
P & R FARMS LLC
5195 E State Road 64 (47575-9613)
PHONE..................812 326-2010
Patrick Lueken, *Managing Member*
EMP: 7 EST: 1983
SALES (est): 217.58K **Privately Held**
SIC: 2015 0252 5154 Egg processing; Chicken eggs; Cattle

(G-14431)
RANDYS TOOLING & WDWKG LLC
6017 S 500e (47575-9778)
PHONE..................812 326-2204
EMP: 1 EST: 2004
SALES (est): 94.23K **Privately Held**
SIC: 2431 Millwork

(G-14432)
U B KLEM FURNITURE CO INC
3861 E Schnellville Rd (47575-9633)
PHONE..................812 326-2236
Urban J Klem Junior, *Pr*
U B Klem, *
Kathy Klem, *
Kathleen F Klem, *
▲ EMP: 95 EST: 1973
SQ FT: 110,000
SALES (est): 9.84MM **Privately Held**
Web: www.ubklem.com
SIC: 2511 Wood household furniture

Saint Croix
Perry County

(G-14433)
BEAR HOLLOW WOOD CARVERS LLC
25895 Old State Road 37 (47576)
PHONE..................812 843-5549
EMP: 4 EST: 2010
SALES (est): 140K **Privately Held**
SIC: 2411 Logging camps and contractors

(G-14434)
HILL CONSTRUCTION CO LLC
11266 Ohio Rd (47576-9042)
PHONE..................812 843-3279
Randy Hill, *Prin*
EMP: 1 EST: 2005
SALES (est): 87.86K **Privately Held**
SIC: 3448 Garages, portable: prefabricated metal

(G-14435)
PHIL ETIENNES TIMBER HARVEST
Also Called: Phil Etienne Timber
25993 Saint Croix Rd (47576-9081)
PHONE..................812 843-5132
Phil Etienne, *Pr*
Jo Ann Etienne, *
EMP: 45 EST: 1983
SALES (est): 4.67MM **Privately Held**
Web: www.bearhollowindiana.com
SIC: 2421 2426 Lumber: rough, sawed, or planed; Hardwood dimension and flooring mills

Saint Joe
Dekalb County

(G-14436)
BAKER METALWORKS
5843 County Road 59 (46785-9778)
PHONE..................260 572-9353
EMP: 6 EST: 2016
SALES (est): 133.73K **Privately Held**
Web: www.bakermw.com
SIC: 3441 Fabricated structural metal

(G-14437)
CABINETS UNLIMITED INC
5471 County Road 51 (46785-9766)
PHONE..................260 925-5555
Chet Beam, *Pr*
EMP: 3 EST: 1980
SALES (est): 232K **Privately Held**
Web: www.cabinets-unlimited.net
SIC: 2434 Wood kitchen cabinets

(G-14438)
HOLMAN LUMBER LLC
6878 County Road 62 (46785-9717)
PHONE..................260 337-0338
Carlyle Holman, *Managing Member*
EMP: 3 EST: 2007
SALES (est): 775.75K **Privately Held**
Web: www.ecovantagewood.com
SIC: 5031 2499 Lumber, plywood, and millwork; Fencing, docks, and other outdoor wood structural products

(G-14439)
LIGHT HOUSE WOODWORKING DBA
5553 County Road 79a (46785-9736)
PHONE..................260 704-0589
Durwin Miller, *Prin*
EMP: 2 EST: 2010
SALES (est): 183.36K **Privately Held**
SIC: 2431 Millwork

(G-14440)
NUCOR CORPORATION
Also Called: Vulcraft Division
6610 County Road 60a (46785-9601)
PHONE..................260 337-1800
Shannon Phillips, *Brnch Mgr*
EMP: 100
SALES (corp-wide): 34.71B **Publicly Held**
Web: www.nucor.com
SIC: 3312 Blast furnaces and steel mills
PA: Nucor Corporation
    1915 Rexford Rd
    Charlotte NC 28211
    704 366-7000

(G-14441)
NUCOR CORPORATION
Also Called: Nucor Fastener
6730 County Road 60 (46785-9741)
P.O. Box 6100 (46785-6100)
PHONE..................260 337-1606
Tom Miller, *Genl Mgr*
EMP: 103
SQ FT: 320,000
SALES (corp-wide): 34.71B **Publicly Held**
Web: www.nucor-fastener.com
SIC: 3312 Blast furnaces and steel mills
PA: Nucor Corporation
    1915 Rexford Rd
    Charlotte NC 28211
    704 366-7000

(G-14442)
NUCOR CORPORATION
County Road 60 (46785)
PHONE..................260 337-1808
Lee Batesole, *Brnch Mgr*
EMP: 4
SALES (corp-wide): 34.71B **Publicly Held**
Web: www.vulcraftfcu.com
SIC: 3312 Blast furnaces and steel mills
PA: Nucor Corporation
    1915 Rexford Rd
    Charlotte NC 28211
    704 366-7000

(G-14443)
SECHLERS PICKLES INC (PA)
Also Called: Sechler's Fine Pickles
5686 State Rd 1 (46785)
P.O. Box 152 (46785-0152)
PHONE..................260 337-5461
Max Troyer, *Pr*
▲ EMP: 24 EST: 1921

SQ FT: 58,000
SALES (est): 4.44MM
SALES (corp-wide): 4.44MM Privately Held
Web: www.sechlerspickles.com
SIC: 2035 Pickles, vinegar

(G-14444)
TRIPLE M LEATHER LLC
6454 County Road 71 (46785-9722)
PHONE..................260 238-5850
Nicole Shull, Prin
EMP: 5 EST: 2016
SALES (est): 64.18K Privately Held
SIC: 3199 Leather goods, nec

Saint John
Lake County

(G-14445)
85TH & PINE LLC
14259 Fortress Ct (46373-9804)
PHONE..................219 781-1327
Catherine Wadas, Prin
EMP: 4 EST: 2018
SALES (est): 68.27K Privately Held
SIC: 2399 Hand woven and crocheted products

(G-14446)
CABINETS UNLIMITED CORPORATION
10067 Raven Wood Dr (46373-9045)
PHONE..................219 558-2210
Dan Schild, CEO
EMP: 3 EST: 1999
SQ FT: 2,500
SALES (est): 243.5K Privately Held
Web: www.cabinetsunlimitedcorp.com
SIC: 2434 Wood kitchen cabinets

(G-14447)
CITYBYAPP INC
9440 W 103rd Pl (46373-7026)
PHONE..................844 843-4376
Jerome Mark Mikulich, CEO
EMP: 9 EST: 2014
SALES (est): 120.77K Privately Held
Web: www.citybyapp.com
SIC: 7372 Prepackaged software

(G-14448)
COMPUMARK INDUSTRIES INC
9853 Northcote Ave (46373-9529)
P.O. Box 430 (46373-0430)
PHONE..................219 365-0508
John Beatrice, Pr
EMP: 5 EST: 1996
SALES (est): 402.99K Privately Held
Web: www.compumark-ind.com
SIC: 7373 7378 7372 Computer systems analysis and design; Computer maintenance and repair; Utility computer software

(G-14449)
DIGITAL HELIUM LLC
9301 W 94th Pl (46373-8717)
P.O. Box 423 (46373-0423)
PHONE..................219 365-4038
Matthew B Hanson, Owner
EMP: 3 EST: 2011
SALES (est): 196.82K Privately Held
SIC: 2813 Helium

(G-14450)
GALLAGHER ENVIRONMENTAL INC
Also Called: Cartridge World Chicago
9111 Hibiscus Dr (46373-8428)
PHONE..................773 791-4670
Jeff Dicks, Pr
EMP: 1 EST: 2005
SALES (est): 96.78K Privately Held
SIC: 3955 Print cartridges for laser and other computer printers

(G-14451)
GARDNER DENVER INC
9495 Keilman St Ste 2b (46373-9295)
PHONE..................219 558-0354
EMP: 40
SALES (corp-wide): 1.94B Publicly Held
SIC: 3561 Industrial pumps and parts
HQ: Gardner Denver, Inc.
   222 E Erie St Ste 500
   Milwaukee WI 28036

(G-14452)
HENNESSY SHEET METAL
9791 Rambling Rose Ln (46373-9037)
PHONE..................219 365-7058
EMP: 4 EST: 2018
SALES (est): 237.34K Privately Held
SIC: 3444 Sheet metalwork

(G-14453)
ILLIANA SIGNS
11525 Upper Peninsula Ln (46373-7805)
PHONE..................708 862-9164
EMP: 4 EST: 1990
SQ FT: 1,600
SALES (est): 247.19K Privately Held
Web: www.illianasign.com
SIC: 3993 Signs and advertising specialties

(G-14454)
KLOMP CONSTRUCTION COMPANY
9160 W 106th Ave (46373-7400)
PHONE..................219 308-8372
Crystal Klomp, CEO
EMP: 1 EST: 2013
SALES (est): 181.29K Privately Held
Web: www.klompdesignbuild.com
SIC: 1521 1542 1751 2521 New construction, single-family houses; Custom builders, non-residential; Cabinet and finish carpentry; Wood office furniture

(G-14455)
PERFORMANCE MINERALS CORP (PA)
Also Called: PMC
10220 Wicker Ave Ste 3 (46373-8400)
PHONE..................219 365-8356
Stephen Gleason, Pr
▲ EMP: 8 EST: 1992
SQ FT: 35,000
SALES (est): 4.34MM Privately Held
Web: www.performancemineralscorp.com
SIC: 3295 Minerals, ground or otherwise treated

(G-14456)
PERM INDUSTRIES INC
Also Called: Perm Machine & Tool Co
9660 Industrial Dr (46373-9475)
P.O. Box 660 (46373-0660)
PHONE..................219 365-5000
Lee J Milazzo, Pr
◆ EMP: 25 EST: 1970
SQ FT: 25,000
SALES (est): 2.39MM Privately Held
Web: www.permmachine.com
SIC: 3544 Special dies and tools

(G-14457)
R & B FINE PRINTING INC
9720 Industrial Dr (46373-8881)
PHONE..................219 365-9490
Ronald M Foltman Junior, Pr
EMP: 4 EST: 1987
SQ FT: 3,000
SALES (est): 490.3K Privately Held
Web: www.rbfineprinting.com
SIC: 2752 Offset printing

(G-14458)
SM INDUSTRIES LLC
13701 Limerick Dr (46373-9676)
PHONE..................219 613-5295
Patrick M Fagen, Admn
EMP: 6 EST: 2015
SALES (est): 153.88K Privately Held
SIC: 3999 Manufacturing industries, nec

(G-14459)
TRIPLE JS TRANSPORT LLC
5534 Saint Joe Rd (46373-8012)
PHONE..................708 513-8389
Rickey Turley, Pr
Rickey Turley, Managing Member
EMP: 1 EST: 2021
SALES (est): 75.6K Privately Held
SIC: 2759 Screen printing

Saint Meinrad
Spencer County

(G-14460)
AUTOMATED ROUTING INC
16920 N State Road 545 (47577)
PHONE..................812 357-2429
Barry Schaefer, Pr
Scott Schaefer, *
David Schaeffer, *
EMP: 135 EST: 1993
SQ FT: 119,000
SALES (est): 20.34MM Privately Held
Web: www.automatedrouting.com
SIC: 2499 Decorative wood and woodwork

(G-14461)
KLEM SIGNS & RESTYLING LLC
15875 N State Road 545 (47577-9641)
PHONE..................812 357-2222
EMP: 3 EST: 2019
SALES (est): 246.32K Privately Held
Web: app.tintwiz.com
SIC: 3993 Signs and advertising specialties

(G-14462)
KLEMS GRAPHIC DESIGNS
15875 N State Road 545 (47577-9641)
PHONE..................812 357-2222
EMP: 1 EST: 2011
SALES (est): 54.72K Privately Held
SIC: 3993 Signs and advertising specialties

(G-14463)
MONKEY HOLLOW
11534 E County Road 1740 N (47577-9794)
PHONE..................812 998-2112
EMP: 4 EST: 2018
SALES (est): 71.15K Privately Held
Web: www.monkeyhollowwinery.com
SIC: 2084 Wines

(G-14464)
ST MEINRAD ARCHABBEY (PA)
Also Called: Carenotes
200 Hill Dr (47577-1301)
PHONE..................812 357-6611
Rt Rev Justin Duvall, Pr
Kurt Stasiak, *
◆ EMP: 55 EST: 1854
SQ FT: 720,000
SALES (est): 24.79MM
SALES (corp-wide): 24.79MM Privately Held
Web: www.saintmeinrad.org
SIC: 8221 2731 Theological seminary; Book publishing

Saint Paul
Decatur County

(G-14465)
KITCHEN QUEEN LLC
58 W County Rd 650 N (47272)
PHONE..................812 662-8399
Duane Miller, Managing Member
EMP: 4 EST: 2005
SALES (est): 210.85K Privately Held
Web: www.kitchenqueenstoves.com
SIC: 3444 Flues and pipes, stove or furnace: sheet metal

(G-14466)
KNEPPS CUSTOM WELDING
7586 N County Road 450 W (47272-9780)
PHONE..................765 525-5130
Don Knepp, Owner
EMP: 2 EST: 2005
SALES (est): 51.81K Privately Held
SIC: 7692 Welding repair

(G-14467)
MYERS FRZ FOODS PROVISIONERS
Also Called: Myers
405 W Dorsey St (47272-9569)
P.O. Box 12 (47272-0012)
PHONE..................765 525-6304
Robert A Myers, CEO
Anthony Myers, Pr
Mary Myers, VP
Mike Myers, Sec
EMP: 8 EST: 1957
SQ FT: 13,000
SALES (est): 1.51MM Privately Held
Web: www.myersfrozenfood.com
SIC: 5142 2011 Meat, frozen: packaged; Cured meats, from meat slaughtered on site

(G-14468)
NOBLE WOODWORKS
8988 S 475 E (47272-9509)
PHONE..................765 525-4226
Les Morgan, Owner
EMP: 2 EST: 2005
SALES (est): 120.79K Privately Held
Web: www.noblewoodwork.com
SIC: 2431 Millwork

(G-14469)
SIGN MASTERS
207 S Taylor St (47272-9619)
PHONE..................765 525-7446
TOLL FREE: 800
EMP: 2 EST: 1995
SQ FT: 2,400
SALES (est): 163.29K Privately Held
SIC: 3993 Signs, not made in custom sign painting shops

Salem
Washington County

(G-14470)
ALLSPORTS
210 N Main St (47167-2031)
PHONE..................812 883-3561
Robert Wall, Prin
EMP: 7 EST: 2005
SALES (est): 60.05K Privately Held

Salem - Washington County (G-14471) — GEOGRAPHIC SECTION

Web: www.allsportscafe.net
SIC: 2759 Screen printing

(G-14471)
AMERICAN STAVE COMPANY LLC
Also Called: Blue River Wood Products
5170 W State Road 56 (47167-8441)
PHONE.................812 883-9374
EMP: 1 EST: 2005
SALES (est): 495.54K Privately Held
Web: www.independentstavecompany.com
SIC: 2421 Sawmills and planing mills, general

(G-14472)
AMERICAN WEDGE COMPANY
215 N Tarr Ave (47167-9202)
P.O. Box 275 (47167-0275)
PHONE.................812 883-1086
EMP: 4 EST: 1992
SALES (est): 318.83K Privately Held
SIC: 2499 Handles, wood

(G-14473)
BAIRD HOME CORPORATION
Also Called: Baird Homes of Distinction
1401 W Mulberry St (47167-9452)
PHONE.................812 883-1141
TOLL FREE: 800
Charles Rickard, Brnch Mgr
EMP: 6
SALES (corp-wide): 18.96MM Privately Held
Web: www.bairdhomes.com
SIC: 2392 Household furnishings, nec
PA: Baird Home Corporation
  3495 Us Highway 441
  Fruitland Park FL 34731
  352 787-2500

(G-14474)
BEASLEY WELDING
310 S Canton South Boston Rd (47167-7836)
PHONE.................812 883-2573
Robert Beasley, Prin
EMP: 1 EST: 2008
SALES (est): 47K Privately Held
SIC: 7692 Welding repair

(G-14475)
BEAZER EAST INC
1510 W Market St (47167-9206)
P.O. Box 489 (47167-0489)
PHONE.................812 883-2191
Ken Howell, Superintnt
EMP: 1
SALES (corp-wide): 23.02B Privately Held
SIC: 3281 Cut stone and stone products
HQ: Beazer East, Inc.
  600 River Ave Ste 200
  Pittsburgh PA 15212
  412 428-9407

(G-14476)
CREATIVE METAL WORKS WROUGHT
1901 E State Road 56 (47167-9610)
PHONE.................812 883-2008
EMP: 1 EST: 2009
SALES (est): 127.81K Privately Held
Web: www.creativemetalworks.biz
SIC: 3446 Architectural metalwork

(G-14477)
DENNYS WOODCRAFT INC
5498 E State Road 56 (47167-7058)
PHONE.................812 883-0770
Dennis Bontrager, Owner
EMP: 4 EST: 1987
SALES (est): 301.27K Privately Held
Web: www.dennyswoodcraft.com
SIC: 2434 Wood kitchen cabinets

(G-14478)
GEORGE VOYLES SAWMILL INC
Also Called: George Voyles Logging
4887 W Apple Ln (47167-8244)
PHONE.................812 472-3968
George Voyles, Pr
Wilma Voyles, City Treasurer
EMP: 7 EST: 1988
SQ FT: 2,000
SALES (est): 230.86K Privately Held
SIC: 2411 2426 2421 Logging camps and contractors; Hardwood dimension and flooring mills; Sawmills and planing mills, general

(G-14479)
GKN SINTER METALS LLC
198 S Imperial Dr (47167-6604)
P.O. Box 312 (47167-0312)
PHONE.................812 883-3381
Mark Goss, Brnch Mgr
EMP: 240
SQ FT: 225,000
SALES (corp-wide): 4.18B Privately Held
Web: www.gknpm.com
SIC: 3499 3714 Friction material, made from powdered metal; Motor vehicle parts and accessories
HQ: Gkn Sinter Metals, Llc
  1670 Opdyke Ct
  Auburn Hills MI 48326
  248 883-4500

(G-14480)
HILLCREST PALLET INCORPORATED
5445 W Kansas Church Rd (47167-8237)
PHONE.................812 883-3636
Nelson Garber, Pt
Jesse Garber, Pt
Ella Mae Garber, Pt
EMP: 5 EST: 1989
SALES (est): 469.37K Privately Held
SIC: 2448 Pallets, wood

(G-14481)
HUGHES TIRE SERVICE INC
209 S Water St (47167-1398)
PHONE.................812 883-4981
Dale I Huff, Pr
Bob Huff, VP
Mary Huff, Sec
EMP: 10 EST: 1920
SQ FT: 8,500
SALES (est): 1.25MM Privately Held
Web: www.hughestire.com
SIC: 5531 5014 7534 Automotive tires; Automobile tires and tubes; Tire recapping

(G-14482)
HUNTERS RIDGE WINERY LLC
9945 E Garrison Hollow Rd (47167-6160)
PHONE.................812 967-9463
Gregory Paul Ratliff, Pr
EMP: 6 EST: 2015
SALES (est): 89.62K Privately Held
Web: www.huntersridgewinery.com
SIC: 2084 Wines

(G-14483)
HUSQVRNA CNSMR OTDR PROD NA
Also Called: Peerless Gear
1555 S Jackson St (47167-9189)
PHONE.................812 883-3575
Peter Klas, Mgr
EMP: 180
SALES (corp-wide): 2.23B Privately Held
SIC: 3524 Lawn and garden equipment
HQ: Husqvarna Consumer Outdoor Products N.A., Inc.
  9335 Hrris Crners Pkwy St
  Charlotte NC 28269

(G-14484)
INDIANA HEAT TRANSFER CORPORATION
500 West Harrison Street (47167)
PHONE.................574 936-3171
EMP: 213
Web: www.ihtc.net
SIC: 3714 Radiators and radiator shells and cores, motor vehicle

(G-14485)
INTERNATIONAL WOOD INC
300 W Hackberry St (47167-1753)
PHONE.................812 883-5778
◆ EMP: 25 EST: 1992
SALES (est): 953.85K Privately Held
Web: www.internationalwoodinc.com
SIC: 2421 Lumber: rough, sawed, or planed

(G-14486)
JEANS EXTRUSIONS INC
201 Jeans Dr (47167-9200)
P.O. Box 307 (47167-0307)
PHONE.................812 883-2581
Burl Jean, Pr
Carmelita Jean, *
Vince Lewandowski, *
EMP: 155 EST: 1982
SQ FT: 60,000
SALES (est): 9.66MM Privately Held
Web: www.jeans-extrusions.com
SIC: 3053 Gaskets, all materials

(G-14487)
LEADER PUBLISHING CO OF SALEM
Also Called: Salem Leader, The
117 E Walnut St 119 (47167-2044)
PHONE.................812 883-3281
Nancy Grossman, Pr
Carolyn Grossman, *
Schuyler Grossman, *
EMP: 25 EST: 1827
SQ FT: 4,500
SALES (est): 1.05MM Privately Held
Web: www.salemleader.com
SIC: 2711 2752 2791 2759 Newspapers, publishing and printing; Offset printing; Typesetting; Commercial printing, nec

(G-14488)
MADE-RITE MANUFACTURING INC
3967 E Sullivan Ln (47167-7724)
PHONE.................812 967-2652
EMP: 7 EST: 1982
SQ FT: 100
SALES (est): 806.29K Privately Held
Web: www.maderitemfg.com
SIC: 3449 1799 Miscellaneous metalwork; Welding on site

(G-14489)
MARKETING AND RETAIL SALES
Also Called: Salem Fast Printing Service
1318 S Jackson St (47167-9167)
P.O. Box 532 (47167-0532)
PHONE.................812 883-1813
Donna Spurgeon, Pr
Mark Spurgeon, VP
EMP: 4 EST: 1979
SQ FT: 2,400
SALES (est): 300K Privately Held
SIC: 5943 2752 5044 5699 Office forms and supplies; Commercial printing, lithographic; Office equipment; Sports apparel

(G-14490)
MATTOX MACHINE & WELDING INC
504 Cox Ferry Rd (47167-9414)
PHONE.................812 883-6460
Jerry Mattox, Pr
EMP: 1 EST: 1977
SQ FT: 7,200
SALES (est): 100K Privately Held
SIC: 7692 Welding repair

(G-14491)
MICHAEL L BAKER
8779 E New Philadelphia Rd (47167-6217)
PHONE.................812 967-2160
Michael L Baker, Owner
EMP: 5 EST: 2001
SALES (est): 316.35K Privately Held
SIC: 2411 Logging

(G-14492)
MIDWEST TIRE & SERVICE LLC
3381 N Griffin Ct (47167-9081)
PHONE.................502 377-3722
EMP: 5
SALES (est): 200.06K Privately Held
SIC: 7389 7534 Business Activities at Non-Commercial Site; Tire repair shop

(G-14493)
MILLERS MINI-BARNS LLC
6073 S West Washington School Rd (47167-6761)
PHONE.................812 883-8072
Milan Miller, Managing Member
EMP: 4 EST: 1998
SALES (est): 395.3K Privately Held
Web: www.millersminibarns.com
SIC: 3448 Prefabricated metal buildings and components

(G-14494)
MILLERS SAW MILL
76 E Miller Sawmill Rd (47167-7946)
PHONE.................812 883-5246
Cecil O Miller, Owner
EMP: 3 EST: 1958
SALES (est): 156.47K Privately Held
SIC: 2421 Sawmills and planing mills, general

(G-14495)
P3 GRAPHIX LLC
4225 E Quaker Rd (47167-7046)
PHONE.................812 641-1294
Eric Bryant, Prin
EMP: 4 EST: 2018
SALES (est): 84.45K Privately Held
Web: www.p3graphix.com
SIC: 3993 Signs and advertising specialties

(G-14496)
PAYNTER MACHINE WORKS INC
1302 E Hackberry St (47167-9604)
PHONE.................812 883-2808
William Paynter, Pr
Janet Paynter, Sec
EMP: 6 EST: 1946
SQ FT: 7,200
SALES (est): 496.75K Privately Held
Web: www.wcegp.org
SIC: 3599 Machine shop, jobbing and repair

(G-14497)
PEERLESS GEAR LLC
1555 S Jackson St (47167-9189)
PHONE.................812 883-7900

▲ = Import ▼ = Export
◆ = Import/Export

GEOGRAPHIC SECTION

EMP: 4 **EST:** 2018
SALES (est): 889.67K **Privately Held**
Web: www.peerlessgear.com
SIC: 8748 3714 Business consulting, nec; Axles, motor vehicle

(G-14498)
SILVERTHORN HANDYMAN SVCS LLC
3395 W State Road 60 (47167)
PHONE..................812 896-4201
EMP: 1
SALES (est): 64.69K **Privately Held**
SIC: 1389 7389 Construction, repair, and dismantling services; Business Activities at Non-Commercial Site

(G-14499)
SOUTHERN INDIANA SAWMILL LLC
3325 N Highland Rd (47167-8993)
PHONE..................502 664-5723
Michael Beck, *Prin*
EMP: 6 **EST:** 2015
SALES (est): 234.61K **Privately Held**
Web: www.southernindianasawmill.com
SIC: 2499 Wood products, nec

(G-14500)
STEEL BOX CO LLC
521 S Tristin Ct (47167-7689)
PHONE..................812 620-7043
Thomas Bass, *Prin*
EMP: 5 **EST:** 2019
SALES (est): 59.28K **Privately Held**
Web: www.steelboxco.com
SIC: 3999 Manufacturing industries, nec

(G-14501)
STINGEL ENTERPRISES INC
Also Called: Amtek Wholesale Signs
1002 Webb St (47167-9714)
PHONE..................812 883-0054
John Stingel, *Pr*
Sharon Stingel, *VP*
EMP: 17 **EST:** 1991
SQ FT: 4,000
SALES (est): 2.44MM **Privately Held**
Web: www.amteksigns.com
SIC: 3993 Signs and advertising specialties

(G-14502)
TECUMSEH PRODUCTS COMPANY LLC
Also Called: Tecumseh Peerless Gear Mch Div
1555 S Jackson St (47167-9189)
PHONE..................812 883-3575
Doug Sanders, *Mgr*
EMP: 9
SQ FT: 165,000
Web: www.tecumseh.com
SIC: 7537 3592 3568 3566 Automotive transmission repair shops; Carburetors; Power transmission equipment, nec; Speed changers, drives, and gears
HQ: Tecumseh Products Company Llc
  5683 Hines Dr
  Ann Arbor MI 48108
  734 585-9500

(G-14503)
TERREL AUTOMOTIVE MACHINE INC
707 S Main St (47167-1037)
PHONE..................812 883-3859
Mark Hoke, *Pr*
Jennifer Hoke, *Sec*
EMP: 3 **EST:** 1963
SQ FT: 9,600
SALES (est): 251.49K **Privately Held**

SIC: 3599 Machine shop, jobbing and repair

(G-14504)
TURTLEFISH CLOTHING CO LLC
3010 S Middle Fork Ln (47167-5948)
PHONE..................812 896-2805
EMP: 2 **EST:** 2013
SALES (est): 107.95K **Privately Held**
Web: www.turtlefishclothing.com
SIC: 2759 Screen printing

San Pierre
Starke County

(G-14505)
M A STUDIO INC
Also Called: Memorial Arts Studio
3153 S 900 W (46374-9587)
PHONE..................574 275-2200
Michael Anthony, *Pr*
EMP: 1
SALES (corp-wide): 238.47K **Privately Held**
SIC: 2396 Veils and veiling: bridal, funeral, etc.
PA: M A Studio Inc.
  605 Front St
  Welaka FL 32193
  574 275-2200

Sandford
Vigo County

(G-14506)
JAG METAL SPINNING INC
1022 Crawford St (47885)
PHONE..................812 533-5501
Glen F Price, *Pr*
EMP: 7 **EST:** 2003
SALES (est): 553.77K **Privately Held**
Web: www.jagmetalspinning.com
SIC: 3469 Spinning metal for the trade

Santa Claus
Spencer County

(G-14507)
CURTIS-MARUYASU AMERICA INC
48 S Buffaloville Rd (47579-8536)
PHONE..................812 544-2021
EMP: 346
Web: www.curtismaruyasu.com
SIC: 3714 Motor vehicle parts and accessories
HQ: Curtis-Maruyasu America, Inc.
  665 Metts Dr
  Lebanon KY 40033
  270 692-2109

(G-14508)
MADDOX INDUSTRIAL CONTG LLC
1377 W Ruby Winkler (47579-3200)
PHONE..................812 544-2156
EMP: 20 **EST:** 2013
SQ FT: 6,500
SALES (est): 1.47MM **Privately Held**
SIC: 1799 1541 3531 8742 Athletic and recreation facilities construction; Industrial buildings and warehouses; Construction machinery; Construction project management consultant

Saratoga
Randolph County

(G-14509)
TOWN OF SARATOGA
Also Called: Saratoga
107 N Barber St (47382)
P.O. Box 28 (47382-0028)
PHONE..................765 584-1576
EMP: 5 **EST:** 2010
SALES (est): 113.49K **Privately Held**
Web: www.saratogatodaynewspaper.com
SIC: 2711 Newspapers, publishing and printing

Schererville
Lake County

(G-14510)
103 COLLECTION LLC
7402 Nature View Dr (46375-3111)
P.O. Box 574 (46375-0574)
PHONE..................800 896-2945
Melinda Herron, *Owner*
EMP: 2 **EST:** 2015
SALES (est): 98.66K **Privately Held**
Web: www.103collection.com
SIC: 2844 7389 Shaving preparations; Business Activities at Non-Commercial Site

(G-14511)
141 TRUCKING LLC
3141 Amber Way (46375-4352)
PHONE..................312 581-5121
EMP: 1 **EST:** 2021
SALES (est): 60.08K **Privately Held**
SIC: 3537 Trucks: freight, baggage, etc.: industrial, except mining

(G-14512)
ACTEGA NORTH AMERICA INC
650 W 67th Pl (46375-1357)
PHONE..................800 426-4657
EMP: 2
SALES (corp-wide): 4.22B **Privately Held**
Web: www.actega.com
SIC: 2893 Printing ink
HQ: Actega North America, Inc.
  1450 Taylors Ln A
  Cinnaminson NJ 08077
  856 829-6300

(G-14513)
ALSIP PALLET COMPANY INC
1154 Thiel Dr (46375-3087)
PHONE..................219 322-3288
Frank Jagiella, *Prin*
EMP: 6 **EST:** 2010
SALES (est): 114.25K **Privately Held**
SIC: 2448 Pallets, wood

(G-14514)
AUTOMATION & CONTROL SVCS INC
2440 Ontario St (46375)
PHONE..................219 558-2060
EMP: 12 **EST:** 1994
SQ FT: 10,500
SALES (est): 2.48MM **Privately Held**
Web: www.plcexperts.com
SIC: 3625 Control equipment, electric

(G-14515)
BEACON HOUSE
7203 Starling Dr (46375-4441)
PHONE..................219 756-2131
Salina Mohit, *Pt*
A Mohit, *Pt*

EMP: 2 **EST:** 1996
SALES (est): 75.37K **Privately Held**
SIC: 2731 Books, publishing and printing

(G-14516)
BOFREBO INDUSTRIES INC
Also Called: Endustra Filter Manufacturers
1145 Birch Dr (46375-1334)
PHONE..................219 322-1550
Robert E Geyer, *Pr*
Martha O Geyer, *
▼ **EMP:** 49 **EST:** 1968
SQ FT: 43,500
SALES (est): 4.36MM **Privately Held**
Web: www.endustrafilters.com
SIC: 3569 Filters, general line: industrial

(G-14517)
BRENCO LLC (PA)
Also Called: Brenco Exotic Woods
526 Turnberry Dr (46375-2928)
PHONE..................219 844-9570
◆ **EMP:** 2 **EST:** 2002
SALES (est): 515.55K
SALES (corp-wide): 515.55K **Privately Held**
Web: www.brencollc.com
SIC: 2439 5023 Timbers, structural: laminated lumber; Wood flooring

(G-14518)
CABINETS INC
1220 Birch Dr (46375-1336)
PHONE..................219 322-3900
Wayne Micka, *Owner*
EMP: 3 **EST:** 2010
SALES (est): 248.88K **Privately Held**
Web: www.cabinets.com
SIC: 2434 Wood kitchen cabinets

(G-14519)
ECKART AMERICA CORPORATION
Also Called: Metalure Pigments Facility
650 W 67th Pl Ste 200 (46375-1357)
PHONE..................219 864-4861
EMP: 2
SALES (corp-wide): 4.22B **Privately Held**
Web: www.eckart.net
SIC: 2672 Adhesive papers, labels, or tapes: from purchased material
HQ: Eckart America Corporation
  830 E Erie St
  Painesville OH 44077
  440 954-7600

(G-14520)
EDER BROS LLC
1243 Primrose Ln (46375)
PHONE..................219 718-3335
EMP: 5 **EST:** 2015
SALES (est): 114.3K **Privately Held**
SIC: 2082 Beer (alcoholic beverage)

(G-14521)
FERGUSON ENTERPRISES LLC
Also Called: Ferguson Waterworks
574 Kennedy Ave (46375-1237)
PHONE..................219 440-5254
EMP: 6
SALES (corp-wide): 29.73B **Privately Held**
Web: www.ferguson.com
SIC: 5074 3432 Plumbing fittings and supplies; Plumbing fixture fittings and trim
HQ: Ferguson Enterprises, Llc
  751 Lakefront Commons
  Newport News VA 23606
  757 874-7795

Schererville - Lake County (G-14522)

(G-14522)
FURNACE SOLUTIONS INCORPORATED
Also Called: FSI
5314 Gull Dr (46375-4452)
PHONE..................219 738-2516
Jerry Last, VP
Diana Last, Pr
EMP: 1 EST: 2015
SALES (est): 78.89K Privately Held
Web: www.furnacesolutionsinc.com
SIC: 3559 Foundry, smelting, refining, and similar machinery

(G-14523)
HOFFMASTER ELECTRIC INC
1635 Hartley Dr (46375-2281)
PHONE..................219 616-1313
David Hoffmaster, Pr
EMP: 2 EST: 2015
SQ FT: 1,500
SALES (est): 182.79K Privately Held
SIC: 3612 3613 3644 Power and distribution transformers; Fuses and fuse equipment; Electric outlet, switch, and fuse boxes

(G-14524)
INDUSTRIAL STEEL AND SUP CORP
645 65th St Ste 5 (46375-1365)
PHONE..................219 865-0500
Leonard W Cox, Pr
EMP: 5 EST: 1993
SQ FT: 4,000
SALES (est): 894.8K Privately Held
Web: www.issco.us
SIC: 3441 Fabricated structural metal

(G-14525)
JOHNSON SALES CORP
1145 Birch Dr (46375-1334)
PHONE..................219 322-9558
Robert E Geyer, Pr
EMP: 6 EST: 2007
SALES (est): 91.44K Privately Held
SIC: 3822 Appliance controls,except air-conditioning and refrigeration

(G-14526)
KATHY ZUCCARELLI
1314 Eagle Ridge Dr (46375-1360)
PHONE..................219 865-4095
EMP: 2 EST: 2010
SALES (est): 132.89K Privately Held
Web: www.dentistschererville.com
SIC: 3843 Enamels, dentists'

(G-14527)
KENNEDY METAL PRODUCTS INC
1050 Kennedy Ave (46375-1308)
PHONE..................219 322-9388
Brian De St Jean, Pr
EMP: 15 EST: 2010
SALES (est): 2.29MM Privately Held
Web: www.kennedymetalproducts.com
SIC: 3441 Fabricated structural metal

(G-14528)
LEONS FABRICATION INC
8850 Parrish Ave (46375-2437)
PHONE..................219 365-5272
Timothy Grzych, Pr
Timothy Gryzch, Pr
Cynthia Van Volkenburgh, VP
EMP: 10 EST: 1948
SQ FT: 13,000
SALES (est): 518.98K Privately Held
Web: www.leonsfabrication.com
SIC: 7692 3446 3444 3443 Welding repair; Architectural metalwork; Sheet metalwork; Fabricated plate work (boiler shop)

(G-14529)
LIBERATION
5308 Gull Dr (46375-4452)
PHONE..................219 736-7329
Richard Howard Iii, Prin
EMP: 7 EST: 2010
SALES (est): 82.73K Privately Held
SIC: 3312 Blast furnaces and steel mills

(G-14530)
LINE-X OF SCHERERVILLE INC
Also Called: Line-X
2041 Us Highway 41 (46375-2801)
PHONE..................219 865-1000
William Sonichsen, Prin
EMP: 10 EST: 2016
SALES (est): 493.65K Privately Held
Web: www.linex.com
SIC: 2821 5531 Plastics materials and resins ; Truck equipment and parts

(G-14531)
LOCOLI INC (PA)
Also Called: St John Sports
1650 Us Highway 41 Ste E (46375-1773)
P.O. Box 370 (46373-0370)
PHONE..................219 515-6900
John Collet, Pr
Carol Collet, Sec
EMP: 20 EST: 1985
SQ FT: 12,000
SALES (est): 1.85MM
SALES (corp-wide): 1.85MM Privately Held
Web: www.stjohnsports.net
SIC: 5699 5136 5137 2396 Sports apparel; Sportswear, men's and boys'; Sportswear, women's and children's; Screen printing on fabric articles

(G-14532)
LOVETT ENTERTAINMENT LLC
1825 Lakeview Ct (46375)
PHONE..................773 208-9608
EMP: 5 EST: 2021
SALES (est): 171.12K Privately Held
SIC: 2782 7389 Record albums; Business Activities at Non-Commercial Site

(G-14533)
MASON CORPORATION
1049 Us Highway 41 (46375-1303)
P.O. Box 38 (46375-0038)
PHONE..................219 865-8040
Todd Hofer, Pr
◆ EMP: 39 EST: 1950
SQ FT: 70,000
SALES (est): 8.9MM Privately Held
Web: www.tinchemical.com
SIC: 2819 Tin (stannic/stannous) compounds or salts, inorganic

(G-14534)
MIDWEST AUTO REPAIR INC
Also Called: Midwest Tire & Auto Repair
1901 Lincolnwood Rd (46375-1886)
PHONE..................219 322-0364
William R Jarvis, Pr
John Jarvis, Sec
EMP: 15 EST: 1982
SQ FT: 12,000
SALES (est): 941.26K Privately Held
Web: www.midwesttire.com
SIC: 5014 7539 5531 7538 Tires and tubes; Automotive repair shops, nec; Automotive tires; General automotive repair shops

(G-14535)
MIDWEST PIPECOATING INC
925 Kennedy Ave (46375-1325)
PHONE..................219 322-4564
Joel Chermak, Mgr
EMP: 100
SQ FT: 27,000
SALES (corp-wide): 62.5MM Privately Held
Web: www.midwestpiperebar.com
SIC: 1799 2851 Coating, caulking, and weather, water, and fireproofing; Paints and allied products
HQ: Midwest Pipecoating, Inc.
  7865 Jefferson Hwy
  Maple Grove MN 55369
  763 425-4167

(G-14536)
NECTOR MACHINE & FABRICATING
595 Kennedy Ave (46375-1236)
PHONE..................219 322-6878
John Rakoczy, Pr
Jean Rakoczy, VP
EMP: 6 EST: 1985
SQ FT: 14,000
SALES (est): 794.06K Privately Held
SIC: 3599 3499 7692 3444 Machine shop, jobbing and repair; Machine bases, metal; Welding repair; Sheet metalwork

(G-14537)
OGDEN WELDING SYSTEMS INC
372 Division St (46375-1223)
PHONE..................219 322-5252
Jeffrey W Darnell, Pr
Gordon L Verbeek, *
Rose Mary Wellman, *
◆ EMP: 40 EST: 1963
SQ FT: 50,000
SALES (est): 9.73MM Privately Held
Web: www.ogdenwelding.com
SIC: 5084 3699 3548 3537 Industrial machinery and equipment; Electrical welding equipment; Welding apparatus; Industrial trucks and tractors

(G-14538)
OIL TECHNOLOGY INC
1112 Us Highway 41 # 208 (46375-1361)
PHONE..................219 322-2724
Gerald Piper, Prin
Gerald Piper, Pr
Jerry Harber, Sec
Nick Rovai Sales, Mktg Mgr
Randall L Holland, Opers Mgr
EMP: 23 EST: 1982
SALES (est): 2.24MM Privately Held
Web: www.oiltechnologysolutions.com
SIC: 2992 Re-refining lubricating oils and greases, nec

(G-14539)
PROGRESS GROUP INC
918 Kennedy Ave (46375-1326)
PHONE..................219 322-3700
Steven M Desancic, Pr
EMP: 60 EST: 1973
SQ FT: 59,200
SALES (est): 9.6MM Privately Held
Web: www.theprogressgroupinc.com
SIC: 7699 3599 5251 Pumps and pumping equipment repair; Machine shop, jobbing and repair; Pumps and pumping equipment

(G-14540)
QUALITY PRINTING OF NW IND
Also Called: Minuteman Press
2315 Us Highway 41 (46375-2809)
PHONE..................219 322-6677
Stephen Watson, Pr
Terry Watson, VP
EMP: 5 EST: 1985
SALES (est): 484.6K Privately Held
Web: www.minutemanpress.com
SIC: 2752 2791 2789 2759 Commercial printing, lithographic; Typesetting; Bookbinding and related work; Commercial printing, nec

(G-14541)
QUINTEL INC
628 Gatlin Rd (46375)
P.O. Box 1214 (46384)
PHONE..................219 322-3399
EMP: 20 EST: 1995
SQ FT: 12,000
SALES (est): 4.81MM Privately Held
Web: www.quintel-inc.com
SIC: 3443 Fabricated plate work (boiler shop)

(G-14542)
RENO LLC
7350 Jeffrey St (46375-3500)
PHONE..................708 846-7821
Beth Reno, Prin
EMP: 7 EST: 2016
SALES (est): 102.74K Privately Held
Web: www.rgj.com
SIC: 2711 Newspapers, publishing and printing

(G-14543)
SALABELL PUBLISHING LLC
320 King Henry Dr (46375-1812)
PHONE..................219 865-6906
Lisa Groszek, Managing Member
EMP: 1 EST: 2011
SALES (est): 72.07K Privately Held
SIC: 2741 Miscellaneous publishing

(G-14544)
SIMCHA AI INC ✪
326 W Us Highway 30 (46375)
PHONE..................415 702-5919
Aaron Rau, CEO
EMP: 1 EST: 2024
SALES (est): 53.04K Privately Held
SIC: 7372 Business oriented computer software

(G-14545)
SITESUCCESS INC
521 Saint Andrews Dr (46375-2951)
PHONE..................219 808-4076
Kristen Watson, Prin
EMP: 6 EST: 2008
SALES (est): 116.38K Privately Held
SIC: 2741 Miscellaneous publishing

(G-14546)
THERMAL PRODUCT SOLUTIONS
1470 Mackinaw Pl (46375-1289)
PHONE..................708 758-6530
Charles Lazzara, Mgr
EMP: 6 EST: 2018
SALES (est): 93.68K Privately Held
Web: www.thermalproductsolutions.com
SIC: 3567 Industrial furnaces and ovens

(G-14547)
WHOLEAF ALOE DISTRIBUTORS
46 Oak Ct (46375-1011)
PHONE..................219 322-7217
Russell Crist, Owner
EMP: 6 EST: 1984
SALES (est): 233.84K Privately Held
SIC: 2844 Face creams or lotions

(G-14548)
ZELS
7889 W Lincoln Hwy (46375)
PHONE..................219 864-1011
Don Jeonake, Pt

EMP: 7 **EST:** 2001
SALES (est): 151.7K **Privately Held**
Web: www.zelsroastbeef.com
SIC: 2013 5812 Roast beef, from purchased meat; Eating places

Schneider
Lake County

(G-14549)
EJ BOGNAR INCORPORATED
Also Called: Carb-Rite
23810 Highland St (46376-9757)
P.O. Box 175 (46376-0175)
PHONE.............................412 344-9900
Gene Cox, *Mgr*
EMP: 6
SALES (corp-wide): 6.25MM **Privately Held**
Web: www.ejbognar.com
SIC: 2819 3297 Industrial inorganic chemicals, nec; Nonclay refractories
PA: E.J. Bognar Incorporated
733 Washington Rd Fl 5
Pittsburgh PA 15228
412 344-9900

Scipio
Jennings County

(G-14550)
PEN IT PUBLICATIONS LLC
5110 W County Road 400 N (47273-9577)
PHONE.............................812 392-2658
Debra Stanton, *Prin*
EMP: 1 **EST:** 2013
SALES (est): 60.62K **Privately Held**
Web: www.penitpublications.com
SIC: 2741 Miscellaneous publishing

(G-14551)
SOVERN MACHINING & WELDING
4540 W County Road 740 N (47273-9558)
PHONE.............................812 392-2532
Randall Sovern, *Owner*
EMP: 1 **EST:** 2004
SALES (est): 64.06K **Privately Held**
SIC: 3599 7692 Crankshafts and camshafts, machining; Welding repair

Scottsburg
Scott County

(G-14552)
AMERICAN PLASTIC MOLDING CORP
Also Called: A P M
965 S Elm St (47170)
PHONE.............................813 752-7000
James Allen Myers, *CEO*
Lily Marie Coomer, *
▲ **EMP:** 110 **EST:** 1971
SQ FT: 65,000
SALES (est): 23MM **Privately Held**
Web: www.apmc.com
SIC: 3089 Injection molding of plastics

(G-14553)
DONNA DALTON
Also Called: Techbrokers/Techchic
5319 N Mount Rd (47170-5263)
P.O. Box 562 (47131-0562)
PHONE.............................812 358-6116
Donna Dalton, *Owner*
EMP: 1 **EST:** 2006
SALES (est): 60.94K **Privately Held**
SIC: 7372 Prepackaged software

(G-14554)
ENGINRED PLSTIC COMPONENTS INC
640 N Wilson Rd (47170-7727)
PHONE.............................812 752-6742
EMP: 20
Web: www.epcmfg.com
SIC: 3089 Injection molding of plastics
PA: Engineered Plastic Components, Inc.
4500 Westown Pkwy Ste 277
West Des Moines IA 50266

(G-14555)
EPC-COLUMBIA INC
640 N Wilson Rd (47170-7727)
PHONE.............................812 752-6742
Reza Kargarzadeh, *Brnch Mgr*
EMP: 1
Web: www.epcmfg.com
SIC: 3089 Injection molding of plastics
HQ: Epc-Columbia, Inc.
4000 Waco Rd
Columbia MO 65202
205 702-4166

(G-14556)
GENESIS PLASTICS AND ENGINEERING LLC
Also Called: Viking Plastics
640 N Wilson Rd (47170-7727)
P.O. Box 228 (47170-0228)
PHONE.............................812 752-6742
▲ **EMP:** 110
SIC: 3089 Injection molding of plastics

(G-14557)
GENPAK LLC
845 S Elm St (47170-2172)
PHONE.............................812 752-3111
Rich Rosenberg, *Mgr*
EMP: 1
Web: www.genpak.com
SIC: 3089 2656 Plastics containers, except foam; Sanitary food containers
HQ: Genpak Llc
10601 Westlake Dr
Charlotte NC 28273
800 626-6695

(G-14558)
GREG SAMPLES
5043 N Elk Creek Rd (47170-5472)
PHONE.............................812 595-3033
Greg Samples, *Prin*
EMP: 5 **EST:** 2013
SALES (est): 100.24K **Privately Held**
Web: www.gregsamples.com
SIC: 2741 Miscellaneous publishing

(G-14559)
HS MACHINE WELDING
733 W Bellevue Ave (47170-6734)
PHONE.............................812 752-2825
EMP: 2 **EST:** 1995
SALES (est): 70K **Privately Held**
SIC: 3599 Machine shop, jobbing and repair

(G-14560)
ILPEA INDUSTRIES INC
Also Called: Holm Industries Warehouses
1320 S Main St (47170-6666)
PHONE.............................812 414-2728
EMP: 4
Web: www.ilpeaindustries.com
SIC: 3089 Injection molding of plastics
HQ: Ilpea Industries, Inc.
745 S Gardner St
Scottsburg IN 47170
812 752-2526

(G-14561)
ILPEA INDUSTRIES INC
Jarrow Products Division
745 S Gardner St (47170-2178)
PHONE.............................812 752-2526
Charles Cruz, *Mgr*
EMP: 61
Web: www.ilpeaindustries.com
SIC: 3053 3069 3585 3442 Gaskets, all materials; Weather strip, sponge rubber; Refrigeration and heating equipment; Metal doors, sash, and trim
HQ: Ilpea Industries, Inc.
745 S Gardner St
Scottsburg IN 47170
812 752-2526

(G-14562)
ILPEA INDUSTRIES INC (HQ)
Also Called: Holm Industries
745 S Gardner St (47170)
P.O. Box 450 (47170)
PHONE.............................812 752-2526
Wayne Heverly, *Pr*
Gary L Barrigar, *
Ken Chenoweth, *
▲ **EMP:** 66 **EST:** 1989
SALES (est): 174.43MM **Privately Held**
Web: www.ilpeaindustries.com
SIC: 3053 3089 Gaskets, all materials; Window frames and sash, plastics
PA: Ilpea Parent Inc.
745 S Gardner St
Scottsburg IN 47170

(G-14563)
INDIANAPOLIS WOOD PRODUCTS
1273 S Gardner St (47170)
P.O. Box 185 (47170)
PHONE.............................812 752-6944
Heinrich Ostertag, *Pr*
Siegfried Ostertag, *VP*
▼ **EMP:** 6 **EST:** 1982
SQ FT: 1,100
SALES (est): 505.97K **Privately Held**
SIC: 2421 Sawmills and planing mills, general

(G-14564)
INSON TOOL & MACHINE INC
833 S Gardner St (47170-2179)
P.O. Box 673 (47170-0673)
PHONE.............................812 752-3754
David Ingalls, *Pr*
EMP: 5 **EST:** 1997
SALES (est): 480.33K **Privately Held**
SIC: 3544 Special dies and tools

(G-14565)
IRVING MATERIALS INC
784 N Wilson Rd (47170-7728)
PHONE.............................812 883-4242
Bryan Gross, *Brnch Mgr*
EMP: 3
SALES (corp-wide): 814.09MM **Privately Held**
Web: www.irvmat.com
SIC: 3273 Ready-mixed concrete
PA: Irving Materials, Inc.
8032 N State Road 9
Greenfield IN 46140
317 326-3101

(G-14566)
JOURNAL & CHRONICLE INC
Also Called: J & C Printing Co
39 E Wardell St (47170-1831)
PHONE.............................812 752-5060
Pam Noble, *Pr*
EMP: 4 **EST:** 1978
SALES (est): 248.61K **Privately Held**

SIC: 5943 2759 2791 2789 Office forms and supplies; Commercial printing, nec; Typesetting; Bookbinding and related work

(G-14567)
KELLY BIXLER LOGGING
4769 S Underwood Rd (47170-6330)
PHONE.............................812 752-6636
Kelly Bixler, *Owner*
EMP: 1 **EST:** 1996
SALES (est): 90.74K **Privately Held**
SIC: 2411 Logging camps and contractors

(G-14568)
KING INVESTMENTS INC
Also Called: Proseries Products
505 E Mcclain Ave (47170-1752)
PHONE.............................812 752-6000
Bill Sellers, *Pr*
EMP: 7 **EST:** 1966
SQ FT: 9,100
SALES (est): 110.96K **Privately Held**
Web: www.kingmachine.com
SIC: 7389 3599 Design, commercial and industrial; Custom machinery

(G-14569)
KRISTOPHER COX ✪
Also Called: Reality Gaming
101 N 5th St Apt 16 (47170-1766)
PHONE.............................502 930-9162
Kristopher Cox, *Owner*
EMP: 2 **EST:** 2022
SALES (est): 85.99K **Privately Held**
SIC: 3575 Computer terminals

(G-14570)
MAJESTY ENTERPRISES INC
Also Called: Majesty Express
2068 S Jimtown Ln (47170-8025)
P.O. Box 833 (47170-0833)
PHONE.............................812 752-6446
Girdley Comes, *Pr*
EMP: 8 **EST:** 2005
SALES (est): 602.39K **Privately Held**
SIC: 2391 7363 Curtains and draperies; Truck driver services

(G-14571)
MERRILL MANUFACTURING INC
1052 S Bond St (47170-6745)
PHONE.............................812 752-6688
Jeff Merrill, *Pr*
EMP: 10 **EST:** 1978
SQ FT: 27,000
SALES (est): 620.02K **Privately Held**
Web: www.thewaterbedfactory.com
SIC: 2511 Waterbed frames; wood

(G-14572)
MULTI-COLOR CORPORATION
Also Called: Altivity Packaging
2281 S Us Highway 31 (47170-6754)
PHONE.............................513 396-5600
Terry Skiba, *Brnch Mgr*
EMP: 176
SALES (corp-wide): 14.54B **Privately Held**
Web: www.mcclabel.com
SIC: 2759 Labels and seals: printing, nsk
HQ: Multi-Color Corporation
4053 Clough Woods Dr
Batavia OH 45103
513 381-1480

(G-14573)
MULTI-COLOR CORPORATION
Turfway
2281 S Us Highway 31 (47170-6754)
PHONE.............................812 752-0586
Tom Vogt, *Mgr*

Scottsburg - Scott County (G-14574) GEOGRAPHIC SECTION

EMP: 30
SQ FT: 1,500
SALES (corp-wide): 14.54B **Privately Held**
Web: www.mcclabel.com
SIC: 2759 2796 2754 Labels and seals: printing, nsk; Platemaking services; Commercial printing, gravure
HQ: Multi-Color Corporation
4053 Clough Woods Dr
Batavia OH 45103
513 381-1480

(G-14574)
NEW HOPE SERVICES INC
Also Called: Kids Place
1642 W Mcclain Ave Ste 1 (47170-1171)
PHONE................................812 752-4892
Ashley Wells, *Dir*
EMP: 90
SALES (corp-wide): 8.94MM **Privately Held**
Web: www.newhopeservices.org
SIC: 2396 8322 8331 3993 Automotive and apparel trimmings; Child related social services; Sheltered workshop; Signs and advertising specialties
PA: New Hope Services, Inc.
725 Wall St
Jeffersonville IN 47130
812 288-8248

(G-14575)
REAMS CONCRETE
32 W Leota Rd (47170-7100)
PHONE................................812 752-3746
Arnold D Reams, *Owner*
EMP: 1 **EST:** 1984
SQ FT: 3,200
SALES (est): 109.5K **Privately Held**
SIC: 3272 5999 Concrete products, precast, nec; Concrete products, pre-cast

(G-14576)
RICHEYS MOLD AND TOOL INC
101 E Owen St (47170-1517)
PHONE................................812 752-1059
Chris Richey, *Prin*
EMP: 2 **EST:** 2001
SALES (est): 171.98K **Privately Held**
SIC: 3544 Special dies and tools

(G-14577)
SAMTEC INC
861 S Lake Rd S (47170-6837)
PHONE................................812 517-6081
EMP: 2
SALES (corp-wide): 178.24MM **Privately Held**
Web: www.samtec.com
SIC: 3699 Electrical equipment and supplies, nec
PA: Samtec Inc
520 Park E Blvd
New Albany IN 47150
812 944-6733

(G-14578)
SCOTTSBURG STONEWARE LLC
445 S Whippoorwill Ln (47170-6817)
PHONE................................812 752-6353
Kay Jackson, *Prin*
EMP: 1 **EST:** 2006
SALES (est): 47.45K **Privately Held**
SIC: 3269 Stoneware pottery products

(G-14579)
SOUTHERN MOLD AND TOOL INC
915 S Elm St (47170-2173)
P.O. Box 160 (47170-0160)
PHONE................................812 752-3333
James Allen Myers, *CEO*

EMP: 7 **EST:** 1980
SQ FT: 5,000
SALES (est): 899.72K **Privately Held**
Web: southernmoldandtool.wordpress.com
SIC: 3544 Forms (molds), for foundry and plastics working machinery

(G-14580)
SPANKYS PAINTBALL
2799 E State Road 356 (47170-6207)
PHONE................................812 752-7375
Jeffrey Case, *Prin*
EMP: 5 **EST:** 2010
SALES (est): 122.7K **Privately Held**
SIC: 3523 Farm machinery and equipment

(G-14581)
SPENCER LOGGING
5297 N State Road 39 (47170-5171)
PHONE................................812 595-0987
Joe Spencer, *Owner*
EMP: 2 **EST:** 2000
SALES (est): 100.34K **Privately Held**
SIC: 2411 Logging camps and contractors

(G-14582)
TOTAL CONCEPTS DESIGN INC
1054 S Taylor Mill Rd (47170-6908)
P.O. Box 6 (47170-0006)
PHONE................................812 752-6534
Charles E Mayer, *Pr*
Arthur G Mayer, *
Crystal D Mayer, *
EMP: 80 **EST:** 1989
SQ FT: 40,000
SALES (est): 9.29MM **Privately Held**
Web: www.totalconceptsofdesign.com
SIC: 3086 7692 3444 Packaging and shipping materials, foamed plastics; Welding repair; Sheet metalwork

(G-14583)
VPI ACQUISITION LLC
Also Called: Viking Plastics Indiana
640 N Wilson Rd (47170-7727)
PHONE................................812 752-6742
EMP: 110
Web: www.vikingplastics.com
SIC: 3089 Injection molding of plastics
PA: Vpi Acquisition, Llc
1 Viking St
Corry PA 16407

(G-14584)
WAKELAM JOHN
Also Called: Wakelam Lumber Company
160 E State Road 356 (47170-6624)
PHONE................................812 752-5243
John Wakelam, *Owner*
EMP: 8 **EST:** 1965
SQ FT: 20,000
SALES (est): 639.26K **Privately Held**
SIC: 2421 Sawmills and planing mills, general

Seelyville
Vigo County

(G-14585)
HEARTHSIDE FOOD SOLUTIONS LLC
Also Called: Kellog
9445 Us Hwy 40 (47878)
PHONE................................812 877-1588
Tim Mcgee, *VP*
EMP: 1
Web: www.hearthsidefoods.com

SIC: 2043 Cereal breakfast foods
PA: Hearthside Food Solutions, Llc
333 Finley Road Ste 800
Downers Grove IL 60515

Sellersburg
Clark County

(G-14586)
A LITTLE UNIQUE EMBROIDER
12106 Columbus Mann Rd (47172-9743)
PHONE................................812 246-0592
Linda Little, *Owner*
EMP: 1 **EST:** 2000
SALES (est): 50.25K **Privately Held**
SIC: 2395 Embroidery products, except Schiffli machine

(G-14587)
AXIS MACHINE TOOL INC
1229 Bringham Dr (47172-2028)
PHONE................................812 246-2600
Paul Harstrom, *Genl Mgr*
EMP: 1 **EST:** 2013
SALES (est): 126.69K **Privately Held**
Web: www.axismachineandtool.com
SIC: 3599 Machine shop, jobbing and repair

(G-14588)
BSBW CULTURED MARBLE INC
860 S Penn Ave (47172-1627)
P.O. Box 166 (47172-0166)
PHONE................................812 246-5619
Dewey Daniel, *Pr*
Teresa Goospree, *Sec*
EMP: 10 **EST:** 2005
SALES (est): 427.73K **Privately Held**
SIC: 3281 Cut stone and stone products

(G-14589)
CABINET BARN INC
105 Adkins Ct (47172-1452)
P.O. Box 164 (47172-0164)
PHONE................................812 246-5237
James Larry Gilbert, *Pt*
Gene Stinson, *Pt*
EMP: 4 **EST:** 1970
SQ FT: 5,000
SALES (est): 292.32K **Privately Held**
Web: www.cabinetbarn.com
SIC: 2434 Wood kitchen cabinets

(G-14590)
CENTURY INDUSTRIES LLC
299 Prather Ln (47172-1739)
P.O. Box C (47172-0403)
PHONE................................812 246-3371
EMP: 48 **EST:** 1978
SALES (est): 7.11MM **Privately Held**
Web: www.centuryindustries.com
SIC: 3448 3537 3441 2531 Buildings, portable: prefabricated metal; Industrial trucks and tractors; Fabricated structural metal; Public building and related furniture

(G-14591)
CHAMPION WOOD PRODUCTS INC
840 S Penn Ave Ste A (47172-1671)
PHONE................................812 282-9460
Andrew B Thurstone, *Pr*
Barbara A Lamb, *VP*
EMP: 9 **EST:** 1969
SQ FT: 20,000
SALES (est): 1.24MM **Privately Held**
SIC: 2499 2431 2426 Decorative wood and woodwork; Moldings, wood: unfinished and prefinished; Hardwood dimension and flooring mills

(G-14592)
ERNST ENTERPRISES INC
4710 Utica Sellersburg Rd (47172-9325)
PHONE................................812 284-5205
Scott Elliott, *Brnch Mgr*
EMP: 8
SALES (corp-wide): 240.08MM **Privately Held**
Web: www.ernstconcrete.com
SIC: 3273 Ready-mixed concrete
PA: Ernst Enterprises, Inc.
3361 Successful Way
Dayton OH 45414
937 233-5555

(G-14593)
FABCREATION
7412 Highway 31 E (47172-1944)
PHONE................................812 246-6222
Douglas Pixley, *Owner*
EMP: 2 **EST:** 2008
SALES (est): 59.93K **Privately Held**
SIC: 7699 8999 7692 Blacksmith shop; Artist ; Welding repair

(G-14594)
HAAS CABINET CO INC (PA)
625 W Utica St (47172-1163)
P.O. Box 104 (47172-0104)
PHONE................................812 246-4431
Don C Haas, *Ch*
Jeffrey Todd Haas, *
Bryant L Haas, *
Phillip Flora, *
Thomas K Coats, *
▲ **EMP:** 180 **EST:** 1939
SQ FT: 140,000
SALES (est): 25.43MM
SALES (corp-wide): 25.43MM **Privately Held**
Web: www.haascabinet.com
SIC: 4213 4225 2511 2434 Contract haulers; General warehousing; Wood household furniture; Vanities, bathroom: wood

(G-14595)
HANDSON (HQ)
4700 Utica Sellersburg Rd (47172-9325)
PHONE................................812 246-4481
Robert Liter, *Pr*
John G Liter, *VP*
Susan Neill, *Sec*
Mary Hillibrand, *Treas*
EMP: 15 **EST:** 1974
SQ FT: 1,000
SALES (est): 10.78MM
SALES (corp-wide): 16.33MM **Privately Held**
SIC: 1422 1442 Crushed and broken limestone; Construction sand and gravel
PA: Liter's, Inc.
5918 Haunz Ln
Louisville KY 40241
502 241-7637

(G-14596)
HANSON AGGREGATES WRP INC
301 Highway 31 (47172-1300)
PHONE................................502 244-7550
Doti Ryan, *Mgr*
EMP: 37
SALES (corp-wide): 23.02B **Privately Held**
SIC: 3273 1422 3271 5032 Ready-mixed concrete; Crushed and broken limestone; Concrete block and brick; Brick, stone, and related material
HQ: Hanson Aggregates Wrp, Inc.
1333 Campus Pkwy
Wall Township NJ 07753

GEOGRAPHIC SECTION

Seymour - Jackson County (G-14624)

(G-14597)
HEIDELBERG MTLS MDWEST AGG INC
5417 State Rd 403 (47172)
PHONE..................812 246-1942
Jd Owsley, *Mgr*
EMP: 1
SALES (corp-wide): 23.02B **Privately Held**
SIC: 1422 Crushed and broken limestone
HQ: Heidelberg Materials Midwest Agg, Inc.
300 E John Carpenter Fwy
Irving TX

(G-14598)
HEIDELBERG MTLS STHWEST AGG LL
Also Called: HEIDELBERG MATERIALS SOUTHWEST AGG LLC
4700 Utica Sellersburg Rd (47172-9325)
PHONE..................812 246-4481
Steve Woods, *Brnch Mgr*
EMP: 1
SALES (corp-wide): 23.02B **Privately Held**
Web: www.heidelbergmaterials.us
SIC: 3273 Ready-mixed concrete
HQ: Hanson Aggregates Llc
8505 Freport Pkwy Ste 500
Irving TX 75063
469 417-1200

(G-14599)
HEIDELBERG MTLS US CEM LLC
Hwy 31 (47172)
PHONE..................812 246-5472
Paul Stewart, *Brnch Mgr*
EMP: 24
SALES (corp-wide): 23.02B **Privately Held**
Web: www.heidelbergmaterials.us
SIC: 3273 Ready-mixed concrete
HQ: Heidelberg Materials Us Cement Llc
300 E John Carpenter Fwy
Irving TX 75062
877 534-4442

(G-14600)
HIGH CALIBER CABINETRY LLC
7617 Old State Road 60 Ste 1 (47172-1836)
PHONE..................812 246-5550
EMP: 4 EST: 2012
SALES (est): 365.5K **Privately Held**
Web: www.highcalibercabinetry.com
SIC: 2434 Wood kitchen cabinets

(G-14601)
INDEPENDENT PALLET LLC
3001 Progress Way (47172-2022)
PHONE..................502 356-2757
EMP: 6 EST: 2014
SALES (est): 434.98K **Privately Held**
SIC: 2448 Pallets, wood

(G-14602)
INTERACTIVE SURFACE TECH LLC
1511 Avco Blvd (47172-1875)
PHONE..................812 246-0900
EMP: 3 EST: 2009
SALES (est): 145.73K **Privately Held**
SIC: 2671 Plastic film, coated or laminated for packaging

(G-14603)
JKNK VENTURES INC
Also Called: Pro Laminators
1511 Avco Blvd (47172-1875)
P.O. Box 274 (47172-0274)
PHONE..................812 246-0900
Karen Haywood, *Pr*
Jack Haywood, *Sec*
EMP: 25 EST: 1984
SQ FT: 12,000
SALES (est): 906.55K **Privately Held**
Web: www.prolaminators.com
SIC: 7389 2672 Laminating service; Paper; coated and laminated, nec

(G-14604)
LIGHTUPTOYSCOM LLC (PA)
8512 Commerce Park Dr (47172-1353)
PHONE..................812 246-1916
Christopher Kelly, *CEO*
Joshua Kelly, *
Renata Kelly, *
EMP: 41 EST: 2005
SQ FT: 10,000
SALES (est): 4.88MM **Privately Held**
Web: www.lightuptoys.com
SIC: 3944 Electronic games and toys

(G-14605)
MARTIN INDUSTRIES LLC
P.O. Box 174 (47172-0174)
PHONE..................502 553-6599
Nancy Martin, *Prin*
EMP: 5 EST: 2011
SALES (est): 175.2K **Privately Held**
SIC: 3999 Manufacturing industries, nec

(G-14606)
METAL SALES MANUFACTURING CORP
7800 Highway 60 (47172-1859)
PHONE..................812 246-1866
Craig Mackin, *Prin*
EMP: 23
SALES (corp-wide): 347.39MM **Privately Held**
Web: metalsales.us.com
SIC: 3444 Sheet metalwork
HQ: Metal Sales Manufacturing Corporation
545 S 3rd St Ste 200
Louisville KY 40202
502 855-4300

(G-14607)
MICRO BUSINESSWARE INC
8508 Starview Ct (47172-9065)
PHONE..................502 424-6613
William Dobis, *Pr*
EMP: 1 EST: 2001
SALES (est): 86.05K **Privately Held**
SIC: 7372 7389 Prepackaged software; Business Activities at Non-Commercial Site

(G-14608)
OAKLEY INDUSTRIES LLC
Also Called: Axis Machine and Tool
1229 Bringham Dr Ste B (47172-2028)
PHONE..................812 246-2600
Paul Harstrom, *Genl Mgr*
Matt Oakley, *Pr*
EMP: 4 EST: 2015
SALES (est): 245.39K **Privately Held**
SIC: 3599 Custom machinery

(G-14609)
OWINGS PATTERNS INC
3011 Progress Way (47172-2022)
PHONE..................812 944-5577
Robert Owings, *Pr*
EMP: 15 EST: 1975
SQ FT: 6,000
SALES (est): 2.53MM **Privately Held**
Web: www.owingspatterns.com
SIC: 3543 Industrial patterns

(G-14610)
PHOTONIC LLC
611 Beau Vista Pl (47172-1103)
PHONE..................502 930-9544
EMP: 4 EST: 2020
SALES (est): 154.19K **Privately Held**
Web: www.photonicsinc.com
SIC: 3652 Prerecorded records and tapes

(G-14611)
RCATE PLBG MECH LTD LBLTY CO
7907 Hillside Dr (47172-8925)
PHONE..................812 613-0386
Frederick Cate, *Prin*
EMP: 9 EST: 2016
SALES (est): 408.93K **Privately Held**
SIC: 1711 3432 Plumbing contractors; Faucets and spigots, metal and plastic

(G-14612)
RICHARDS SCALE COMPANY INC
820 S Penn Ave (47172-1627)
P.O. Box 417 (47172-0417)
PHONE..................812 246-3354
Thomas E Best, *Pr*
Dick Lachapell, *Prin*
▲ EMP: 5 EST: 1946
SQ FT: 5,000
SALES (est): 700K **Privately Held**
Web: www.scalepro.com
SIC: 3596 Industrial scales

(G-14613)
SELLERSBURG METALS & WLDG CO
1000 Service Dr (47172-1459)
P.O. Box 414 (47172-0414)
PHONE..................812 248-0811
William Niemann, *Pr*
William Nieman, *Pr*
Karisa Harbin, *Sec*
EMP: 10 EST: 1999
SQ FT: 6,000
SALES (est): 1.49MM **Privately Held**
SIC: 3441 Fabricated structural metal

(G-14614)
SIGNET CABINETRY INC
1400 Service Dr (47172-1461)
PHONE..................812 248-0612
Stephen Brown, *Pr*
EMP: 4 EST: 2005
SALES (est): 355.9K **Privately Held**
Web: www.signetcabinetry.com
SIC: 2434 Wood kitchen cabinets

(G-14615)
SIGNET MILLWORK LLC
1400 Service Dr (47172-1461)
PHONE..................812 248-0612
Steve Brown, *Managing Member*
EMP: 30 EST: 2013
SQ FT: 32,000
SALES (est): 2.28MM **Privately Held**
Web: www.signetmillwork.com
SIC: 2599 Cabinets, factory

(G-14616)
SIGNS TO GO
7904 Old State Road 60 (47172-1842)
PHONE..................502 533-0090
EMP: 3 EST: 2016
SALES (est): 46.08K **Privately Held**
SIC: 3993 Signs and advertising specialties

(G-14617)
SUPERIOR PRINT INC
840 S Indiana Ave (47172-1614)
P.O. Box 401 (47172-0401)
PHONE..................812 246-6311
Dennis Amos, *Pr*
Mark Stewart, *
Charles Stewart, *
EMP: 30 EST: 1988
SQ FT: 7,000
SALES (est): 4.49MM
SALES (corp-wide): 18.17MM **Privately Held**
Web: www.superiorp.com
SIC: 2752 Offset printing
PA: Stewart Graphics, Inc.
1419 Fabricon Blvd
Jeffersonville IN 47130
812 283-0455

(G-14618)
THOMAS HIMEBAUGH
3502 Fairview Knob Rd (47172-9225)
PHONE..................812 246-0197
Thomas Himebaugh, *Owner*
EMP: 1 EST: 2009
SALES (est): 62.59K **Privately Held**
SIC: 3312 Stainless steel

(G-14619)
UNIVERSAL AIR PRODUCTS LLC (PA)
7235 Novas Lndg (47172-1790)
PHONE..................502 451-1825
EMP: 2 EST: 2000
SALES (est): 480.8K **Privately Held**
Web: www.uniairproducts.com
SIC: 3564 Purification and dust collection equipment

Selma
Delaware County

(G-14620)
C M TEC
11200 E State Road 32 (47383-9548)
PHONE..................765 284-3888
Chris Pickering, *Mgr*
EMP: 8 EST: 2014
SALES (est): 180.32K **Privately Held**
Web: www.cm-tec.com
SIC: 3599 Machine shop, jobbing and repair

(G-14621)
CAST METALS TECHNOLOGY
11200 E State Road 32 (47383-9548)
PHONE..................765 284-3888
EMP: 10 EST: 2008
SALES (est): 160.53K **Privately Held**
Web: www.cm-tec.com
SIC: 3599 Machine shop, jobbing and repair

(G-14622)
LEROY R SOLLARS
305 1 2 Rd N (47383)
PHONE..................765 284-9417
Leroy R Sollars, *Prin*
EMP: 6 EST: 2010
SALES (est): 77.71K **Privately Held**
SIC: 3572 Tape storage units, computer

(G-14623)
WELCH WINERY LLC
8600 E Windsor Rd (47383-9667)
PHONE..................707 327-8038
Jack Welch, *Prin*
EMP: 5 EST: 2016
SALES (est): 56.97K **Privately Held**
Web: www.welchwinery.com
SIC: 2084 Wines

Seymour
Jackson County

(G-14624)
ACME FIREARMS MFG LLC
800 E Tipton St (47274-3524)

Seymour - Jackson County (G-14625) — GEOGRAPHIC SECTION

PHONE..................812 522-4008
Joe Hardesty, *Prin*
EMP: 6 **EST:** 2012
SALES (est): 70.88K **Privately Held**
Web: www.acmesportsinc.com
SIC: 3999 Manufacturing industries, nec

(G-14625)
ACME SPORTS INC
800 E Tipton St (47274-3524)
P.O. Box 462 (47274-0462)
PHONE..................812 522-4008
Steve Hardesty, *Owner*
Steve Hardesty, *VP*
Joe Hardesty, *Pr*
EMP: 2 **EST:** 1987
SALES (est): 463.59K **Privately Held**
Web: www.acmesportsinc.com
SIC: 3484 Guns (firearms) or gun parts, 30 mm. and below

(G-14626)
AIM MEDIA INDIANA OPER LLC
Tribune, The
100 Saint Louis Ave (47274-2304)
P.O. Box 447 (47274-0447)
PHONE..................812 522-4871
Melissa Bane, *Brnch Mgr*
EMP: 12
SALES (corp-wide): 26.88MM **Privately Held**
Web: www.aimmediaindiana.com
SIC: 2711 Commercial printing and newspaper publishing combined
PA: Aim Media Indiana Operating, Llc
2980 N National Rd # A
Columbus IN 47201
812 372-7811

(G-14627)
AISIN USA MFG INC
1700 E 4th Street Rd (47274-4309)
PHONE..................812 523-1969
Tsukasa Ito, *Pr*
Dennis Putman, *
Takashi Tanaka, *
▲ **EMP:** 750 **EST:** 1987
SQ FT: 276,000
SALES (est): 228.87MM **Privately Held**
Web: www.aisinusa.com
SIC: 3714 Motor vehicle engines and parts
HQ: Aisin Holdings Of America, Inc.
1665 E 4th St
Seymour IN 47274
812 524-8144

(G-14628)
ALTERRA PLASTICS LLC
2213 Killion Ave (47274-4305)
PHONE..................812 271-1890
Saquib Toor, *Managing Member*
◆ **EMP:** 12 **EST:** 2016
SQ FT: 100,000
SALES (est): 2.51MM **Privately Held**
Web: www.alterraholdings.com
SIC: 2821 Molding compounds, plastics

(G-14629)
AMERICAN EX TRVL RLTED SVCS IN
Also Called: American Express
709 A Ave E (47274-3234)
PHONE..................812 523-0106
EMP: 5
SALES (corp-wide): 67.36B **Publicly Held**
Web: consumer-travel.americanexpress.com
SIC: 4724 7331 2752 Travel agencies; Direct mail advertising services; Commercial printing, lithographic
HQ: American Express Travel Related Services Company, Inc.
200 Vesey St
New York NY 10285
212 640-2000

(G-14630)
B & H ELECTRIC AND SUPPLY INC (PA)
Also Called: B & H
740 C Ave E (47274-3249)
P.O. Box 1005 (47274-1005)
PHONE..................812 522-5607
Greg Hunt, *Pr*
EMP: 23 **EST:** 1995
SALES (est): 7.81MM **Privately Held**
Web: www.bh-electric.com
SIC: 3621 5063 7699 Motors, electric; Motors, electric; Industrial equipment services

(G-14631)
BARRY STUCKWISCH
Also Called: Barry Stuckwisch Mowing
1330 N State Road 11 (47274-8454)
PHONE..................812 525-1052
Barry Stuckwisch, *Owner*
EMP: 4
SALES (est): 150.87K **Privately Held**
SIC: 3523 Grounds mowing equipment

(G-14632)
BETTER BLACC WALL STREETZ LLC
Also Called: G2 House of Styles
6248 Knollview Way # 816 (47274-5527)
PHONE..................812 927-0712
EMP: 10 **EST:** 2019
SIC: 6719 1541 2086 5699 Investment holding companies, except banks; Food products manufacturing or packing plant construction; Fruit drinks (less than 100% juice): packaged in cans, etc.; Designers, apparel

(G-14633)
BLACKERBY & ASSOCIATES
444 Persimmon Dr (47274-8674)
PHONE..................812 216-2370
Jerry Blackerby, *Owner*
EMP: 2 **EST:** 2005
SALES (est): 93.96K **Privately Held**
SIC: 3544 Special dies, tools, jigs, and fixtures

(G-14634)
BLEYS PROSTHETICS & ORTHOTICS
50 Hancock St (47274-4406)
PHONE..................812 704-3894
EMP: 2 **EST:** 2010
SALES (est): 90.86K **Privately Held**
SIC: 3842 Surgical appliances and supplies

(G-14635)
C & T ENGINEERING INC
322 Thompson Rd (47274-3363)
EMP: 12 **EST:** 1976
SQ FT: 6,700
SALES (est): 2.44MM **Privately Held**
Web: www.ctengineeringinc.com
SIC: 3544 7699 Forms (molds), for foundry and plastics working machinery; Plastics products repair

(G-14636)
CALCEAN LLC
Also Called: Calcean
2213 Killion Ave (47274-4305)
PHONE..................812 672-4995
EMP: 7 **EST:** 2015
SALES (est): 122.52K **Privately Held**
Web: www.calcean.com
SIC: 5052 3295 6211 Nonmetallic minerals and concentrate; Minerals, ground or otherwise treated; Mineral leasing dealers

(G-14637)
CEREPLAST INC
2213 Killion Ave (47274-4305)
P.O. Box 6771 (47151-6771)
PHONE..................310 615-1900
▲ **EMP:** 16
Web: www.cereplast.com
SIC: 2821 Plastics materials and resins

(G-14638)
CHATEAU DE PIQUE INC (PA)
101 N Poplar St (47274)
P.O. Box 101nplar (47274)
PHONE..................812 522-9296
Gregory D Pardieck, *CEO*
Ralph Pardeck, *Pr*
Gregg Pardeck, *VP*
EMP: 2 **EST:** 2007
SALES (est): 438.08K
SALES (corp-wide): 438.08K **Privately Held**
Web: www.chateaudepique.com
SIC: 2084 Wines

(G-14639)
COMPETITION TL & ENGRG II INC
2600 Montgomery Dr (47274-8338)
PHONE..................812 524-1991
Richard Findley, *Pr*
Jessie Wyatt, *Sec*
EMP: 6 **EST:** 1999
SQ FT: 9,000
SALES (est): 795.2K **Privately Held**
SIC: 3544 Special dies and tools

(G-14640)
COUNTRY WELDING
233 Western Pkwy (47274-2235)
PHONE..................812 358-4402
Glenn Benter, *Owner*
EMP: 1 **EST:** 1995
SALES (est): 70K **Privately Held**
SIC: 7692 Welding repair

(G-14641)
CRANE HILL MACHINE INC
Also Called: Royalty
2476 E Us Highway 50 (47274-8697)
PHONE..................812 358-3534
Marshall Royalty, *Pr*
EMP: 25 **EST:** 1989
SQ FT: 37,000
SALES (est): 2.24MM **Privately Held**
Web: www.cranehillmachine.com
SIC: 3599 Machine shop, jobbing and repair

(G-14642)
CREATIVE CONCEPTS CABINETRY
335 W Brown St (47274-3118)
PHONE..................812 522-0204
EMP: 5 **EST:** 2015
SALES (est): 240.02K **Privately Held**
Web: www.creativeconceptscabinetry.com
SIC: 2434 Wood kitchen cabinets

(G-14643)
CUMMINS ENGINE COMPANY INC
800 E 3rd St (47274-3906)
PHONE..................812 522-9366
EMP: 20 **EST:** 1989
SALES (est): 1.33MM **Privately Held**
SIC: 3714 Motor vehicle parts and accessories

(G-14644)
CUMMINS INC
845 A Ave E (47274-3236)
PHONE..................812 524-6381
◆ **EMP:** 5
SALES (corp-wide): 34.06B **Publicly Held**
Web: www.cummins.com
SIC: 3714 Motor vehicle parts and accessories
PA: Cummins Inc.
500 Jackson St
Columbus IN 47201
812 377-5000

(G-14645)
CUMMINS INC
800 E 3rd St (47274-3906)
PHONE..................812 522-9366
Darren Wallman, *Mgr*
EMP: 53
SALES (corp-wide): 34.06B **Publicly Held**
Web: www.cummins.com
SIC: 3519 3621 3511 Engines, diesel and semi-diesel or dual-fuel; Motors and generators; Turbines and turbine generator sets
PA: Cummins Inc.
500 Jackson St
Columbus IN 47201
812 377-5000

(G-14646)
DEER COUNTRY EQUIPMENT LLC
Also Called: John Deere Authorized Dealer
1250 W 2nd St (47274-2764)
P.O. Box 549 (47274-0549)
PHONE..................812 522-1922
Thomas C Bryant, *Pr*
Richard L Apsley, *
EMP: 25 **EST:** 1946
SQ FT: 23,000
SALES (est): 996.83K **Privately Held**
Web: www.deercountryequipment.com
SIC: 5083 7699 5261 3524 Agricultural machinery and equipment; Agricultural equipment repair services; Lawn and garden equipment; Lawn and garden equipment

(G-14647)
DICKSONS INC
Also Called: Dicksons Inspirational Gifts
709 B Ave E (47274-3244)
P.O. Box 368 (47274-0368)
PHONE..................812 522-1308
Thomas E Templeton, *Ch Bd*
James M Potts, *
Tomas W Thomas, *
◆ **EMP:** 200 **EST:** 1944
SQ FT: 220,000
SALES (est): 24.46MM
SALES (corp-wide): 183.42MM **Privately Held**
Web: www.dicksonsgifts.com
SIC: 3961 5049 Rosaries and small religious articles, except precious metal; Religious supplies
PA: Templeton Coal Company, Inc.
701 Wabash Ave Ste 501
Terre Haute IN 47807
812 232-7037

(G-14648)
DISCOUNT BOOTS & TACK
1931 N Ewing St (47274-1128)
PHONE..................812 522-9770
Matt Main, *Owner*
EMP: 1 **EST:** 1994
SQ FT: 2,880
SALES (est): 111.78K **Privately Held**

SIC: 3199 5661 Boots, horse; Men's boots

(G-14649)
DOUGLAS K GRESHAM
1540 N County Road 900 W (47274-9479)
PHONE..............................812 445-3174
Douglas K Gresham, *Owner*
EMP: 7 EST: 2007
SALES (est): 142.19K **Privately Held**
SIC: 2033 Barbecue sauce: packaged in cans, jars, etc.

(G-14650)
EXCEL MANUFACTURING INC
1705 E 4th Street Rd (47274-4310)
PHONE..............................812 523-6764
Delbert Kilgas, *Pr*
Brent Kilgas, *
▲ EMP: 80 EST: 1995
SQ FT: 60,000
SALES (est): 21.87MM **Privately Held**
Web: www.excelmanufacturinginc.com
SIC: 3369 3599 Nonferrous foundries, nec; Machine shop, jobbing and repair

(G-14651)
EXCEL TOOL INC
2020 1st Ave (47274-3396)
PHONE..............................812 522-6880
Richard L Elmore, *Pr*
Jay Elmore, *
Craig Elmore, *
EMP: 25 EST: 1967
SQ FT: 55,000
SALES (est): 972.89K **Privately Held**
Web: www.exceleti.com
SIC: 3544 3599 Dies and die holders for metal cutting, forming, die casting; Machine shop, jobbing and repair

(G-14652)
EXTREME FINISHES LLC
105 S Obrien St (47274)
PHONE..............................812 524-2442
Robert Pritchett, *Owner*
EMP: 8
SALES (corp-wide): 42.66K **Privately Held**
Web: www.extremefinishesllc.com
SIC: 3479 Coating of metals and formed products
PA: Extreme Finishes Llc
7572 S County Road 420 W
Greensburg IN 47240
765 717-1519

(G-14653)
FINDLEY FOSTER CORP
14 S County Road 1250 E (47274-9553)
PHONE..............................812 524-7279
Eileen Foster, *Pr*
EMP: 9 EST: 1938
SQ FT: 60,000
SALES (est): 803.82K **Privately Held**
SIC: 2448 2441 Pallets, wood; Nailed wood boxes and shook

(G-14654)
FLOWERS BKG CO BARDSTOWN LLC
1531 W Tipton St (47274-2205)
PHONE..............................502 350-4700
Billy Donaldson, *Mgr*
EMP: 1
SALES (corp-wide): 5.09B **Publicly Held**
Web: www.flowersfoods.com
SIC: 2051 Bread, all types (white, wheat, rye, etc); fresh or frozen
HQ: Flowers Baking Co. Of Bardstown, Llc
1755 Parkway Dr
Bardstown KY 40004
502 350-4700

(G-14655)
HAWKINS MACHINE & TOOL INC
2166 N County Road 900 E (47274-9290)
PHONE..............................812 522-5529
EMP: 2 EST: 1996
SALES (est): 178.46K **Privately Held**
SIC: 3599 Machine shop, jobbing and repair

(G-14656)
HICKMAN WILLIAMS & COMPANY
2083 Upper Heiskell Ct (47274-9618)
PHONE..............................812 522-6293
EMP: 2
SALES (corp-wide): 50.64MM **Privately Held**
Web: www.hicwilco.com
SIC: 3624 Carbon and graphite products
PA: Hickman, Williams & Company
250 E 5th St Ste 300
Cincinnati OH 45202
513 621-1946

(G-14657)
HIGH VALUE METAL INC
101 Blish St (47274-1701)
PHONE..............................812 522-6468
Fred Maschino, *Pr*
Phylis Maschino, *Sec*
EMP: 2 EST: 1998
SALES (est): 148.19K **Privately Held**
SIC: 3441 Fabricated structural metal

(G-14658)
J TEES
9389 N County Road 100 E (47274-9573)
PHONE..............................812 524-9292
EMP: 2 EST: 2007
SALES (est): 71.7K **Privately Held**
Web: www.jteesapparel.com
SIC: 2759 Screen printing

(G-14659)
JACKSON-JENNINGS LLC
103 Community Dr (47274-1955)
P.O. Box 304 (47274-0304)
PHONE..............................812 522-4911
Robert Marley, *Prin*
EMP: 4 EST: 2007
SALES (est): 932.82K **Privately Held**
SIC: 1321 Liquefied petroleum gases (natural) production

(G-14660)
KENNEY ORTHOPEDICS SEYMOUR LLC (HQ)
629 E Tipton St (47274-3519)
PHONE..............................812 271-1627
John M Kenney, *Managing Member*
EMP: 2 EST: 2014
SALES (est): 1.9MM
SALES (corp-wide): 23.4MM **Privately Held**
Web: www.kenneyorthopedics.com
SIC: 3842 Surgical appliances and supplies
PA: Kenney Ortho Group, Inc.
208 Normandy Ct
Nicholasville KY 40356
859 241-1015

(G-14661)
KEURIG DR PEPPER INC
Also Called: RC Canada Dry Bottling Company
1450 Schleter Rd (47274-3361)
PHONE..............................812 522-3823
EMP: 5
Web: www.keurigdrpepper.com
SIC: 2086 Soft drinks: packaged in cans, bottles, etc.
PA: Keurig Dr Pepper Inc.
53 South Ave
Burlington MA 01803

(G-14662)
KING INDUSTRIAL CORPORATION
Also Called: Kinco
105 S Obrien St (47274-2437)
P.O. Box 372 (47274-0372)
PHONE..............................812 522-3261
Mark King, *CEO*
EMP: 17 EST: 1951
SQ FT: 30,000
SALES (est): 473.89K **Privately Held**
Web: www.kingind.com
SIC: 3544 Special dies and tools

(G-14663)
KREMERS URBAN PHRMCUTICALS INC (HQ)
Also Called: Lannett Company, Inc
1101 C Ave W (47274)
▲ EMP: 99 EST: 1930
SQ FT: 263,855
SALES (est): 97.42MM
SALES (corp-wide): 340.58MM **Privately Held**
Web: www.lannett.com
SIC: 2834 Tablets, pharmaceutical
PA: Lannett Company, Inc.
1150 Northbrook Dr # 155
Trevose PA 19053
215 333-9000

(G-14664)
LINDE INC
Also Called: Praxair
1625 Bateman Dr (47274-1833)
PHONE..............................812 524-0173
Dan Dufficy, *Brnch Mgr*
EMP: 1
Web: www.lindeus.com
SIC: 2813 Industrial gases
HQ: Linde Inc.
10 Riverview Dr
Danbury CT 06810
203 837-2000

(G-14665)
LLOYD & MONA SULIVAN
Also Called: Stitch N Time
2169 N County Road 400 E (47274-8613)
PHONE..............................812 522-9191
EMP: 2 EST: 1992
SALES (est): 64.42K **Privately Held**
SIC: 2395 Embroidery and art needlework

(G-14666)
LOGGING
10680 W Seymour Rd (47274-9003)
PHONE..............................812 216-3544
Brittney Anderson, *Prin*
EMP: 7 EST: 2015
SALES (est): 188.64K **Privately Held**
SIC: 2411 Logging

(G-14667)
MAK STEEL SERVICES LLC
1191 King Ave (47274-1822)
PHONE..............................812 525-8879
Andrew Jay Crouse, *Managing Member*
EMP: 4 EST: 2020
SALES (est): 589.55K **Privately Held**
Web: www.maksteelservices.com
SIC: 3441 Fabricated structural metal

(G-14668)
MIDWEST SIGN COMPANY INC
819 N Obrien St (47274-1857)
PHONE..............................317 931-9535
Mark Booher, *Prin*
EMP: 2 EST: 2010
SALES (est): 74.55K **Privately Held**
SIC: 3993 Signs and advertising specialties

(G-14669)
NIPPON STEEL PIPE AMERICA INC (DH)
1515 E 4th Street Rd (47274-4301)
PHONE..............................812 523-0842
Toru Nishikado, *Pr*
Yoshiharu Shibanuma, *
Ken Nagai, *
Yasutaka Nakano, *
▲ EMP: 325 EST: 1988
SQ FT: 358,536
SALES (est): 71.64MM **Privately Held**
Web: www.nipponsteelpipeamerica.com
SIC: 3312 Tubes, steel and iron
HQ: Nittetsu Yosetsu Kokan Management K.K.
2-6-1, Marunouchi
Chiyoda-Ku TKY 100-0

(G-14670)
P-AMERICAS LLC
Also Called: Pepsico
1811 1st Ave (47274-3316)
PHONE..............................812 522-3421
Thomas Levine, *Mgr*
EMP: 1
SALES (corp-wide): 86.39B **Publicly Held**
Web: www.pepsico.com
SIC: 2086 5149 4226 Carbonated soft drinks, bottled and canned; Groceries and related products, nec; Special warehousing and storage, nec
HQ: P-Americas Llc
1 Pepsi Way
Somers NY 10589
336 896-5740

(G-14671)
PACKAGING CORPORATION AMERICA
Also Called: Seymour Division
2200 D Ave E (47274-3259)
PHONE..............................812 522-3100
EMP: 5
SALES (corp-wide): 8.48B **Publicly Held**
Web: www.packagingcorp.com
SIC: 2653 3412 Boxes, corrugated: made from purchased materials; Metal barrels, drums, and pails
PA: Packaging Corporation Of America
1 N Field Ct
Lake Forest IL 60045
847 482-3000

(G-14672)
PACKAGING CORPORATION AMERICA
Also Called: PCA
2209 Killion Ave (47274-4305)
PHONE..............................812 522-3100
Jim Patton, *Genl Mgr*
EMP: 1
SALES (corp-wide): 8.48B **Publicly Held**
Web: www.packagingcorp.com
SIC: 2653 Boxes, corrugated: made from purchased materials
PA: Packaging Corporation Of America
1 N Field Ct
Lake Forest IL 60045
847 482-3000

(G-14673)
PD SUB LLC
Also Called: Jlm Pharmatech
2223 Killion Ave (47274-4305)
PHONE..............................812 524-0534
Jeff Dorries, *CFO*

Seymour - Jackson County (G-14674)

EMP: 50 EST: 2011
SALES (est): 10.21MM
SALES (corp-wide): 16.08MM **Privately Held**
Web: www.jlmpharmatech.com
SIC: 2834 Pharmaceutical preparations
PA: Pd International Holdings, Llc
13161 Lakefront Dr
Earth City MO 63045
314 968-2376

(G-14674)
PHOENIX CUSTOM KITCHENS INC
Also Called: Buffington Custom Kitchens
6600 N Us Highway 31 (47274-8511)
PHONE....................812 523-1890
Ron Buffington, Pr
EMP: 4 EST: 1985
SQ FT: 6,000
SALES (est): 300K **Privately Held**
SIC: 2434 Wood kitchen cabinets

(G-14675)
POLLEY TECH LLC
333 S State Road 11 (47274-7659)
PHONE....................812 524-0688
Ricardo Montero, Prin
EMP: 1 EST: 2008
SALES (est): 80.29K **Privately Held**
Web: www.polleytech.com
SIC: 3449 7389 Miscellaneous metalwork; Business Activities at Non-Commercial Site

(G-14676)
PRAIRIE GOLD RUSH
17390 S State Road 58 (47274-8321)
PHONE....................812 342-3608
EMP: 2 EST: 2008
SALES (est): 66.34K **Privately Held**
Web: www.prairiegoldrush.com
SIC: 2721 Periodicals, publishing only

(G-14677)
PREMIER AG CO-OP INC (PA)
Also Called: Premier AG
811 W 2nd St (47274-2711)
P.O. Box 304 (47274-0304)
PHONE....................812 522-4911
Harold Cooper, CEO
James Geis, Pr
Bruce Morris, Mgr
Bill Metz, Sec
Dennis Stewart, VP
EMP: 20 EST: 1923
SQ FT: 5,000
SALES (est): 117.74MM
SALES (corp-wide): 117.74MM **Privately Held**
Web: www.premierag.com
SIC: 5153 5191 5172 5411 Grain elevators; Farm supplies; Petroleum brokers; Convenience stores

(G-14678)
PREMIER FROZEN DESSERTS
8090 E County Road 100 S (47274-9238)
PHONE....................812 580-8866
EMP: 5 EST: 2012
SALES (est): 80.99K **Privately Held**
SIC: 2024 Ice cream and frozen desserts

(G-14679)
R R DONNELLEY & SONS COMPANY
709 A Ave E (47274-3234)
PHONE....................812 523-1800
Mark A Angelson, CEO
EMP: 11
SALES (corp-wide): 15B **Privately Held**
Web: www.rrd.com
SIC: 2759 Commercial printing, nec
HQ: R. R. Donnelley & Sons Company
35 W Wacker Dr
Chicago IL 60601
312 326-8000

(G-14680)
RBS TEES CO
1102 Gaiser Dr (47274-3642)
PHONE....................812 522-8675
Randy Brown, Owner
EMP: 2 EST: 1981
SALES (est): 63.21K **Privately Held**
SIC: 2396 Screen printing on fabric articles

(G-14681)
RESOURCEMFG
105 W 2nd St Ste 102 (47274-2174)
PHONE....................812 523-2100
EMP: 9 EST: 2017
SALES (est): 97.14K **Privately Held**
Web: www.resourcemfg.com
SIC: 3999 Manufacturing industries, nec

(G-14682)
ROYALTY INVESTMENTS LLC
Also Called: Cranehill Mch & Fabrication
2476 E Us Highway 50 (47274-8697)
PHONE....................812 358-3534
David W Burgess, *
Erin Royalty, *
EMP: 35 EST: 1989
SQ FT: 70,000
SALES (est): 2.25MM **Privately Held**
SIC: 3599 Machine shop, jobbing and repair

(G-14683)
S & S DIESEL MOTORSPORT LLC
1471 W Tipton St (47274-2203)
PHONE....................812 216-3639
Luke Langellier, Managing Member
EMP: 1 EST: 2012
SALES (est): 505.45K **Privately Held**
Web: www.ssdiesel.com
SIC: 5084 7539 3519 Engines and parts, diesel; Fuel system repair, motor vehicle; Diesel, semi-diesel, or duel-fuel engines, including marine

(G-14684)
SCHNEIDERS WOOD SHOP INC
5910 N Us Highway 31 (47274-8514)
PHONE....................812 522-4621
Irving R Schneider Junior, Pr
Gary Schneider, Sec
EMP: 3 EST: 1962
SALES (est): 215.81K **Privately Held**
SIC: 2448 Pallets, wood

(G-14685)
SCHWARZ PARTNERS PACKAGING LLC
Royal Group, The
2245 Killion Ave (47274-4308)
P.O. Box 208 (47274-0208)
PHONE....................812 523-6600
EMP: 1
SALES (corp-wide): 573.33MM **Privately Held**
Web: theroyalgroup.wpengine.com
SIC: 2653 Boxes, corrugated: made from purchased materials
HQ: Schwarz Partners Packaging, Llc
10 W Carmel Dr Ste 300 In
Carmel IN 46032
317 290-1140

(G-14686)
SCHWARZ PHARMA
1101 C Ave W (47274-3342)
P.O. Box 328 (47274-0328)
PHONE....................812 523-3457
Carol Rorig, Admn
EMP: 17 EST: 2017
SALES (est): 1.15MM **Privately Held**
SIC: 2834 Pharmaceutical preparations

(G-14687)
SCRUGGS CONSTRUCTION INC
Also Called: Concrete Construction
110 S Chestnut St (47274)
PHONE....................812 528-8178
EMP: 28 EST: 2017
SALES (est): 2.59MM **Privately Held**
Web: www.scrugssconstructioninc.com
SIC: 1611 1771 1741 3272 Concrete construction: roads, highways, sidewalks, etc.; Concrete work; Retaining wall construction; Slabs, crossing: concrete

(G-14688)
SEXTON ADVERTISING LLC
Also Called: Sexton & Associates
312 W 2nd St (47274-2148)
P.O. Box 642 (47274-0642)
PHONE....................812 522-4059
Melinda Sexton, Managing Member
EMP: 4 EST: 1997
SALES (est): 230.38K **Privately Held**
Web: www.sextonadv.com
SIC: 3993 7336 7311 8742 Signs and advertising specialties; Commercial art and graphic design; Advertising consultant; Marketing consulting services

(G-14689)
SEYMOUR MANUFACTURING CO INC (HQ)
500 N Broadway St (47274-1793)
P.O. Box 248 (47274-0248)
PHONE....................812 522-2900
Bill Henthorn, CEO
Berl Grant, *
Richard V Redmond, *
Roger Hackman, *
Steven Fletcher, *
▲ EMP: 110 EST: 1872
SQ FT: 210,000
SALES (est): 26.73MM **Privately Held**
Web: www.seymourmfg.com
SIC: 3423 3429 Garden and farm tools, including shovels; Fireplace equipment, hardware: andirons, grates, screens
PA: Seymour Midwest Llc
2666 S Country Club Rd
Warsaw IN 46580

(G-14690)
SEYMOUR PRCISION MACHINING INC
1733 1st Ave (47274-3383)
PHONE....................812 524-1813
Keith Staley, Pr
Troy Gohimer, VP
Jenny Staley, Sec
Marsha Gohimer, Treas
EMP: 7 EST: 1996
SQ FT: 3,600
SALES (est): 501.07K **Privately Held**
Web: www.jacksoncochamber.com
SIC: 3599 Machine shop, jobbing and repair

(G-14691)
SEYMOUR TRBUNE A CAL LTD PRTNR
Also Called: Tribune, The
100 Saint Louis Ave (47274-2304)
P.O. Box 447 (47274-0447)
PHONE....................812 522-4871
Richard Davis, Prin
R D Threshie Junior, Genl Pt
EMP: 13 EST: 1997
SQ FT: 6,500
SALES (est): 358.4K **Privately Held**
Web: www.tribtown.com
SIC: 2711 Newspapers, publishing and printing

(G-14692)
SILGAN PLASTICS LLC
Also Called: Silgan
3779 N County Road 850 E (47274-9048)
PHONE....................812 522-0900
Jim Burns, Mgr
EMP: 248
SQ FT: 450,000
Web: www.silganplastics.com
SIC: 3089 Plastics containers, except foam
HQ: Silgan Plastics Llc
14515 N Oter 40 Rd Ste 21
Chesterfield MO 63017
800 274-5426

(G-14693)
SILGAN PLASTICS LLC
Also Called: Silgan
S O Brien St (47274)
PHONE....................812 522-0900
Thomas Hendricks, Pr
EMP: 10
Web: www.silganplastics.com
SIC: 3089 3085 Plastics containers, except foam; Plastics bottles
HQ: Silgan Plastics Llc
14515 N Oter 40 Rd Ste 21
Chesterfield MO 63017
800 274-5426

(G-14694)
SPACEGUARD INC
Also Called: Spaceguard Products
711 S Commerce Dr (47274-4023)
PHONE....................812 523-3044
Edward Murphy, Pr
Edward Murphy, Ch
Hauris Lewis, *
▼ EMP: 66 EST: 1995
SQ FT: 55,000
SALES (est): 13.36MM **Privately Held**
Web: www.spaceguardproducts.com
SIC: 3496 Mesh, made from purchased wire

(G-14695)
SPRAY INC
Also Called: Spray Sand and Gravel
6492 E State Road 258 (47274-9655)
P.O. Box 1139 (47265-5139)
PHONE....................812 346-3197
Daniel Omara, Prin
EMP: 11 EST: 2006
SALES (est): 772.66K **Privately Held**
SIC: 1442 Construction sand and gravel

(G-14696)
SPRAY SAND & GRAVEL INC
6492 E State Road 258 (47274-9655)
P.O. Box 1104 (47274-3704)
PHONE....................812 522-5417
EMP: 7
SALES (corp-wide): 1MM **Privately Held**
SIC: 1442 Construction sand and gravel
PA: Spray Sand & Gravel, Inc
1635 Murray Hill Dr
Seymour IN 47274
812 523-8081

(G-14697)
SPRAY SAND & GRAVEL INC (PA)
1635 Murray Hill Dr (47274-4806)
PHONE....................812 523-8081
John R Schleibaum, Pr
Peggy Schleibaum, Sec
EMP: 4
SALES (est): 1MM

SALES (corp-wide): 1MM Privately Held
SIC: 1442 Gravel mining

(G-14698)
STOGDILL SPORTS
1244 Hickory Hill Rd (47274-2620)
PHONE..................812 524-7081
Howard Stodgill, *Owner*
EMP: 2 EST: 2000
SALES (est): 60K Privately Held
SIC: 2395 Embroidery products, except Schiffli machine

(G-14699)
THORMAX ENTERPRISES LLC
101 W Laurel St (47274)
P.O. Box 683 (47274)
PHONE..................812 530-7744
Chad Whittymore, *Managing Member*
EMP: 1 EST: 2015
SALES (est): 488.02K Privately Held
Web: www.thormaxenterprises.com
SIC: 3317 3498 4225 Steel pipe and tubes; Fabricated pipe and fittings; Miniwarehouse, warehousing

(G-14700)
VALEO LTG SYSTEMS N AMER LLC
1231 A Ave N (47274-3364)
PHONE..................812 523-5200
Francoise Colpron, *Pr*
Stephane Prince, *
Thomas Miller, *
David Arnould, *
▲ EMP: 1000 EST: 1997
SALES (est): 161.95MM
SALES (corp-wide): 2.67MM Privately Held
SIC: 3641 3714 Electric lamps; Motor vehicle parts and accessories
HQ: Valeo North America, Inc.
150 Stephenson Hwy
Troy MI 48083

(G-14701)
VALEO NORTH AMERICA INC
Also Called: Valeo Lighting Systems N Amer
2010 2nd Ave (47274-3214)
PHONE..................812 524-5198
Allen Traylor, *Brnch Mgr*
EMP: 800
SQ FT: 5,000
SALES (corp-wide): 2.67MM Privately Held
SIC: 3647 Clearance lamps and reflectors, motor vehicle
HQ: Valeo North America, Inc.
150 Stephenson Hwy
Troy MI 48083

(G-14702)
VALEO NORTH AMERICA INC
Also Called: Valeo
1231 A Ave N (47274)
PHONE..................248 619-8300
Bertrand Larrere, *Mgr*
EMP: 252
SALES (corp-wide): 2.67MM Privately Held
Web: www.valeo.com
SIC: 3714 Motor vehicle parts and accessories
HQ: Valeo North America, Inc.
150 Stephenson Hwy
Troy MI 48083

(G-14703)
WARNOCK WELDING & FABG LLC
4484 E State Road 258 (47274-8952)
PHONE..................812 498-5408
Jill Warnock, *Prin*
EMP: 1
SALES (est): 47K Privately Held
SIC: 3548 3496 7389 Electric welding equipment; Gas welding rods; Business Activities at Non-Commercial Site

(G-14704)
WH INTERNATIONAL CASTING LLC
Also Called: WH International Casting, LLC
181 Burkart Blvd (47274-1814)
PHONE..................562 521-0727
Brent Craig, *Mgr*
EMP: 2
Web: www.whcast.com
SIC: 3321 Gray and ductile iron foundries
HQ: Wh International Llc
9210 Charles Smith Ave
Rancho Cucamonga CA 91730
562 521-0727

(G-14705)
WICHMAN WOODWORKING INC
8305 N County Road 300 E (47274-9112)
PHONE..................812 522-8450
Dale Wichman, *Pr*
EMP: 2 EST: 1983
SALES (est): 132.45K Privately Held
SIC: 2431 Millwork

(G-14706)
WONNING CABINETS
5875 E County Road 875 N (47274-9143)
PHONE..................812 522-1608
Bill Wonning, *Owner*
EMP: 1 EST: 1981
SALES (est): 67.31K Privately Held
SIC: 2434 Wood kitchen cabinets

(G-14707)
WRIGHT IMPLEMENT I LLC
1250 W 2nd St (47274-2764)
PHONE..................812 522-1922
EMP: 2
SALES (corp-wide): 16.91MM Privately Held
Web: www.wrightimp.com
SIC: 5083 7699 5261 3524 Agricultural machinery and equipment; Agricultural equipment repair services; Lawn and garden equipment; Lawn and garden equipment
PA: Wright Implement I, Llc
3225 Carter Rd
Owensboro KY 42301
270 683-3606

Sharpsville
Tipton County

(G-14708)
A A A MUDJACKERS INC
5925 W 300 N (46068-9472)
PHONE..................317 574-1990
David Mc Donald, *Prin*
EMP: 2 EST: 2005
SALES (est): 234.59K Privately Held
Web: www.aaamudjackers.com
SIC: 1389 1771 Mud service, oil field drilling; Concrete work

(G-14709)
CLAYHILL WIND & SOLAR LLC
3660 W 500 S (46068-9406)
PHONE..................765 437-2395
EMP: 2 EST: 2010
SALES (est): 246.59K Privately Held
Web: www.clayhill-wind-solar.com
SIC: 3511 Turbines and turbine generator sets

(G-14710)
FUNCTIONAL DEVICES LLC
101 Commerce Dr (46068-9412)
P.O. Box 437 (46068-0437)
PHONE..................765 883-5538
Mark Fernandes, *Pr*
Kenneth W Rittmann, *Ch Bd*
▲ EMP: 20 EST: 1969
SQ FT: 50,000
SALES (est): 9.72MM Privately Held
Web: www.functionaldevices.com
SIC: 3625 3643 3823 Relays, for electronic use; Current-carrying wiring services; Process control instruments

(G-14711)
PFEIFFER WELDING & FABRICATION
10373 W 650 N (46068-8921)
PHONE..................765 434-1983
Michael Pfeiffer, *Prin*
EMP: 5 EST: 2017
SALES (est): 43.55K Privately Held
SIC: 7692 Welding repair

(G-14712)
REBEL DEVIL CUSTOMS LLP
4819 N 900 W (46068-9265)
PHONE..................303 921-7131
Michael C Johnson, *Owner*
▲ EMP: 4 EST: 2012
SALES (est): 216.58K Privately Held
Web: rebeldevilcustoms.squarespace.com
SIC: 3711 Motor vehicles and car bodies

(G-14713)
TIPTON ELECTRIC MOTOR SERVICES
113 S Washington St (46068-9298)
PHONE..................765 963-3380
Matthew Braught, *Prin*
EMP: 1 EST: 2005
SALES (est): 65.48K Privately Held
Web: www.tiptonengineering.com
SIC: 7694 Electric motor repair

(G-14714)
TIPTON ENGRG ELC MTR SVCS INC
159 W Vine St (46068-8927)
P.O. Box 76 (46068-0076)
PHONE..................765 963-3380
Matt Braught, *Pr*
Jennifer Braught, *VP*
▲ EMP: 4 EST: 2002
SQ FT: 7,500
SALES (est): 463.47K Privately Held
Web: www.tiptonengineering.com
SIC: 7694 5063 7371 Electric motor repair; Motors, electric; Computer software systems analysis and design, custom

(G-14715)
WAHS CANDLE STUDIO
111 Wood Dr (46068-8939)
PHONE..................734 846-5654
Dah-metrie Shaw, *Prin*
EMP: 4 EST: 2019
SALES (est): 79.52K Privately Held
Web: www.wahs.co
SIC: 3999 Candles

Shelburn
Sullivan County

(G-14716)
ADVANCED MFG SOLUTIONS LLC
227 E County Road 500 N (47879-8263)
PHONE..................812 691-2030
Jeff Scales, *Prin*
EMP: 4 EST: 2017
SALES (est): 74.37K Privately Held
SIC: 3999 Manufacturing industries, nec

(G-14717)
BOSE KNIFE WORKS
Also Called: Professional Custom Knife
7252 N County Road 300 E (47879-8083)
PHONE..................812 397-5114
James Bose, *Owner*
EMP: 1 EST: 1989
SALES (est): 76.87K Privately Held
Web: www.boseknives.com
SIC: 3421 Knife blades and blanks

(G-14718)
NASH SHEET METAL CO
4295 E County Road 800 N (47879-8061)
PHONE..................812 397-5306
Patrick L Nash, *Owner*
EMP: 3 EST: 1972
SALES (est): 217.74K Privately Held
SIC: 3444 Ducts, sheet metal

(G-14719)
P DS MONOGRAMMING
1712 E County Road 650 N (47879-8001)
PHONE..................812 894-2363
EMP: 2 EST: 1990
SALES (est): 48.34K Privately Held
SIC: 2395 Embroidery and art needlework

(G-14720)
ROYSTER CLARK CLOSED
2745 W State Road 48 (47879-8320)
PHONE..................812 397-2617
Scamah Orm, *Prin*
EMP: 6 EST: 2010
SALES (est): 101.85K Privately Held
SIC: 1479 Chemical and fertilizer mining

(G-14721)
SIGNALING SOLUTION INC
Also Called: Tssi
6274 N County Road 25 E (47879-8260)
P.O. Box 168 (21158-0168)
PHONE..................812 533-1345
William Ataras, *Pr*
Colleen Ataras, *Sec*
EMP: 5 EST: 2004
SALES (est): 390.57K Privately Held
Web: www.signalingsolution.com
SIC: 3679 Electronic components, nec

(G-14722)
SKY THUNDER LLC
6521 N Us Highway 41 (47879-8346)
PHONE..................812 397-0102
Michael Kimberling, *Managing Member*
▲ EMP: 40 EST: 2007
SQ FT: 12,000
SALES (est): 4.71MM Privately Held
Web: www.skythunderfireworks.com
SIC: 2899 Flares, fireworks, and similar preparations

(G-14723)
VW CO
6521 N Us Highway 41 (47879-8346)
PHONE..................812 397-0102
Michael Kimberling, *Asstg*
EMP: 2 EST: 2005
SALES (est): 223.41K Privately Held
Web: www.vw.com
SIC: 2899 Fireworks

(G-14724)
WHOLESALE DRAINAGE SUPPLY INC
8300 N Us Highway 41 (47879-8219)

PHONE..................................812 397-5100
Joe Frey, Pr
EMP: 6 **EST:** 2006
SALES (est): 985.43K **Privately Held**
Web: www.wholesaledrainage.com
SIC: 3272 Concrete products used to facilitate drainage

(G-14725)
WRIGHTS TIMBER PRODUCTS
201 S Hymera Church St (47879-8107)
PHONE..................................812 383-7138
EMP: 5 **EST:** 1960
SALES (est): 259.98K **Privately Held**
SIC: 2411 Wood chips, produced in the field

Shelby
Lake County

(G-14726)
HUNTERS MACHINING SERVICES LLC
1305 W 231st Ave (46377)
PHONE..................................219 405-7638
Matt Mader, Prin
EMP: 1 **EST:** 2008
SALES (est): 236.51K **Privately Held**
SIC: 3599 Machine shop, jobbing and repair

(G-14727)
PROEDGE INC
23326 Shelby Rd (46377)
P.O. Box 201 (46377-0201)
PHONE..................................219 552-9550
◆ **EMP:** 25 **EST:** 1995
SQ FT: 45,000
SALES (est): 663.75K **Privately Held**
Web: www.proedgefilms.com
SIC: 4225 2754 General warehousing and storage; Commercial printing, gravure

(G-14728)
SQUARE 1 DESIGNS & SIGNS
23316 Shelby Rd (46377)
P.O. Box 163 (46377-0163)
PHONE..................................219 552-0079
Kathy Shelbourne, Pt
Grant Everman, Pt
EMP: 3 **EST:** 2004
SALES (est): 133.33K **Privately Held**
SIC: 3993 Electric signs

Shelbyville
Shelby County

(G-14729)
A & H ENTERPRISES LLC
Also Called: Office Hub
60 E Washington St (46176-1351)
PHONE..................................317 398-3070
Shannon Huber, Managing Member
EMP: 8 **EST:** 2000
SALES (est): 950.43K **Privately Held**
Web: www.officehubonline.com
SIC: 5943 2754 7349 5712 Office forms and supplies; Business form and card printing, gravure; Building maintenance services, nec; Office furniture

(G-14730)
ASA ABOVE REST
702 E Washington St (46176-1747)
PHONE..................................317 392-2144
EMP: 3 **EST:** 2017
SALES (est): 226.19K **Privately Held**
Web: www.asaabovetherest.com

SIC: 3993 Signs and advertising specialties

(G-14731)
ATMOSPHERE DYNAMICS CORP
1107 Saint Joseph St (46176-3241)
PHONE..................................317 392-6262
John M Coffin, Pr
EMP: 3 **EST:** 1986
SQ FT: 7,000
SALES (est): 393.44K **Privately Held**
Web: www.atmospheredynamics.com
SIC: 2899 Chemical preparations, nec

(G-14732)
BANKS MACHINE & ENGRG LLC
Also Called: Capital Industries
1677 W 400 N (46176)
PHONE..................................317 642-4980
Joseph P Mckinley, Pr
Steve Halfaker, *
Kent Colclazier, *
▼ **EMP:** 60 **EST:** 1999
SQ FT: 68,000
SALES (est): 16.71MM **Privately Held**
Web: www.capitalindustries.com
SIC: 3443 3599 3535 3569 Fabricated plate work (boiler shop); Machine and other job shop work; Conveyors and conveying equipment; Robots, assembly line: industrial and commercial

(G-14733)
BARRINGTON PACKAGING SYSTEMS I
19 W South St (46176-2021)
PHONE..................................847 382-8066
EMP: 8 **EST:** 2014
SALES (est): 144.33K **Privately Held**
Web: www.bpsusa.com
SIC: 2631 Container, packaging, and boxboard

(G-14734)
BASS FARMS LLC
5522 S 75 W (46176-9661)
PHONE..................................317 401-4700
EMP: 1 **EST:** 2011
SALES (est): 51.95K **Privately Held**
Web: www.bassfarms.com
SIC: 2841 7389 Soap: granulated, liquid, cake, flaked, or chip; Business Activities at Non-Commercial Site

(G-14735)
BDC ENTERPRISE LLC
1628 S Miller St (46176-2951)
PHONE..................................317 395-6740
EMP: 2 **EST:** 2019
SALES (est): 100K **Privately Held**
SIC: 2821 Plastics materials and resins

(G-14736)
BLUE RIVER PRINTING INC
55 E Washington St (46176-1350)
P.O. Box 211 (46176-0211)
PHONE..................................317 392-3676
Bryan K Gaffney, Pr
EMP: 6 **EST:** 2001
SALES (est): 521.63K **Privately Held**
Web: www.blueriverprinting.com
SIC: 7334 2759 Photocopying and duplicating services; Commercial printing, nec

(G-14737)
BLUE RIVER STAMPING INC
600 Northridge Dr (46176-8929)
PHONE..................................317 395-5600
Shimana Matsuiosi, Pr
Hiriama Minoru, *

Mitsutake Yanakita, *
Gounami Kacuhiko, *
EMP: 80 **EST:** 1997
SALES (est): 1.81MM **Privately Held**
SIC: 3465 Automotive stampings
HQ: Pk U.S.A., Inc.
600 W Northridge Dr
Shelbyville IN 46176
317 395-5500

(G-14738)
BOBCAT ARMAMENT AND MFG LLC
1640 E State Road 44 Ste A (46176-4030)
PHONE..................................317 699-6127
EMP: 2 **EST:** 2014
SALES (est): 188.9K **Privately Held**
Web: www.bobcatarmament.com
SIC: 5941 3483 3559 Ammunition; Ammunition loading and assembling plant; Ammunition and explosives, loading machinery

(G-14739)
BOBCAT STEEL LLC
1640 E State Road 44 (46176-4029)
PHONE..................................317 699-6127
Kimball Bowden, Prin
EMP: 2 **EST:** 2010
SALES (est): 245.35K **Privately Held**
Web: www.bobcatarmament.com
SIC: 5051 3949 Steel; Target shooting equipment

(G-14740)
BRAZEWAY LLC
1109 Lincoln St (46176-2349)
P.O. Box 436 (46176-0436)
PHONE..................................317 392-2533
Dave Skrzypchak, Brnch Mgr
EMP: 550
SALES (corp-wide): 104.29MM **Privately Held**
Web: www.brazeway.com
SIC: 3354 3444 Aluminum extruded products; Sheet metalwork
PA: Brazeway, Llc
2711 E Maumee St
Adrian MI 49221
517 265-2121

(G-14741)
BREWER MACHINE & MFG INC
1501 Miller Ave (46176-3136)
P.O. Box 985 (46176-3985)
PHONE..................................317 398-3505
Darren Brewer, Pr
Randy Moorhead, *
Vicky Isley, *
EMP: 30 **EST:** 1985
SQ FT: 54,000
SALES (est): 4.54MM **Privately Held**
Web: www.brewermachine.com
SIC: 3599 3842 Machine shop, jobbing and repair; Welders' hoods

(G-14742)
BRUNING ENTERPRISES INC
7718 N State Road 9 (46176-9426)
PHONE..................................317 835-7591
Joseph Bruning, Brnch Mgr
EMP: 9
SALES (corp-wide): 5.32MM **Privately Held**
Web: www.exxon.com
SIC: 3523 Farm machinery and equipment
PA: Bruning Enterprises, Inc.
5603 Finch Farm Rd
Trinity NC 27370
336 476-8200

(G-14743)
CABINET BARN 2COM
1648 E State Road 44 (46176-1844)
PHONE..................................317 421-1750
Wayne Campbell, Owner
EMP: 1 **EST:** 2006
SALES (est): 174.25K **Privately Held**
Web: www.cabinetbarn2.com
SIC: 2434 Wood kitchen cabinets

(G-14744)
CENTRAL COCA-COLA BTLG CO INC
Also Called: Coca-Cola
405 N Harrison St (46176-1303)
PHONE..................................800 241-2653
EMP: 24
SALES (corp-wide): 45.75B **Publicly Held**
Web: www.coca-cola.com
SIC: 2086 8741 Bottled and canned soft drinks; Management services
HQ: Central Coca-Cola Bottling Company, Inc.
555 Taxter Rd Ste 550
Elmsford NY 10523
914 789-1100

(G-14745)
CIRCUITS REPAIR LLC
212 Francis St (46176-1724)
PHONE..................................317 512-1026
EMP: 1 **EST:** 2002
SALES (est): 248.15K **Privately Held**
Web: www.circuitsrepair.com
SIC: 3679 Electronic circuits

(G-14746)
CNC MACHINE INC
1380 N 450 W (46176-9019)
PHONE..................................317 835-4575
Charley Crum, Pr
Becky Crum, Sec
EMP: 5 **EST:** 1982
SQ FT: 5,200
SALES (est): 453.4K **Privately Held**
Web: www.cncmachineinc.net
SIC: 3599 Machine shop, jobbing and repair

(G-14747)
CORVETTE AEROSPACE LLC
130 Rampart St (46176-9404)
PHONE..................................317 512-4616
James Beggs, Pr
Larry Lux, Admn
EMP: 2 **EST:** 2020
SALES (est): 82.7K **Privately Held**
SIC: 3812 Aircraft/aerospace flight instruments and guidance systems

(G-14748)
CUSTOM COATINGS
2446 N Michigan Rd (46176-9726)
P.O. Box 192 (46176-0192)
PHONE..................................317 392-7908
Dennis Metz, Mgr
EMP: 4 **EST:** 2008
SALES (est): 268.9K **Privately Held**
Web: www.customcoatings.co
SIC: 3479 Coating of metals and formed products

(G-14749)
CUSTOM MACHINING INC (PA)
1204 Hale Rd (46176-2371)
P.O. Box 192 (46176-0192)
PHONE..................................317 392-2328
Darrell Mollenkopf, Pr
Patricia Mollenkopf, *
EMP: 25 **EST:** 1938
SALES (est): 4.35MM
SALES (corp-wide): 4.35MM **Privately Held**

GEOGRAPHIC SECTION
Shelbyville - Shelby County (G-14772)

Web: www.custommachininginc.com
SIC: 3541 3554 Grinding machines, metalworking; Coating and finishing machinery, paper

(G-14750)
D & B CABINET SALES INC
660 E Jackson St (46176-1709)
P.O. Box 252 (46176-0252)
PHONE..................317 392-2870
Byron Devoe, *Pr*
Michael De Voe, *VP*
Elaine De Voe, *Bookkpr*
Helen De Voe, *Sec*
EMP: 7 **EST:** 1961
SQ FT: 20,000
SALES (est): 498.44K **Privately Held**
Web: www.dbcabinetsales.com
SIC: 2434 Wood kitchen cabinets

(G-14751)
DENNIS COOPER
1024 Autumn Trce (46176-9500)
PHONE..................847 970-2667
Dennis Cooper, *Prin*
EMP: 5 **EST:** 2010
SALES (est): 92.12K **Privately Held**
Web: www.dennis-cooper.net
SIC: 2741 Miscellaneous publishing

(G-14752)
DRILLING & TRENCHING SUP INC
Also Called: Drilling World
860 Elston Dr (46176-1823)
PHONE..................317 825-0919
Karen Arnett, *Brnch Mgr*
EMP: 6
SALES (corp-wide): 9.31MM **Privately Held**
Web: www.drillingworld.com
SIC: 3545 Drilling machine attachments and accessories
PA: Drilling & Trenching Supply, Incorporated
1458 Mariani Ct
Tracy CA 95376
510 895-1650

(G-14753)
DUNHAM RUBBER BELTING CORP
1689 N Michigan Rd (46176-9386)
PHONE..................317 604-5313
EMP: 7 **EST:** 2017
SALES (est): 184.99K **Privately Held**
Web: www.dunhamrubber.com
SIC: 3052 Rubber belting

(G-14754)
ENBI GLOBAL INC (PA)
Also Called: Enbi
1703 Mccall Dr (46176)
PHONE..................317 395-7324
Christopher Miller, *Pr*
EMP: 10 **EST:** 2014
SALES (est): 15.42MM
SALES (corp-wide): 15.42MM **Privately Held**
Web: www.enbigroup.com
SIC: 3547 Finishing equipment, rolling mill

(G-14755)
ENBI INDIANA INC (PA)
1703 Mccall Dr (46176-9783)
PHONE..................317 398-3267
Ulysses Wong, *Pr*
Robert Sallmann, *
▲ **EMP:** 125 **EST:** 1992
SQ FT: 50,000
SALES (est): 41.35MM
SALES (corp-wide): 41.35MM **Privately Held**

Web: www.enbigroup.com
SIC: 3069 Printers' rolls and blankets: rubber or rubberized fabric

(G-14756)
FREUDENBERG-NOK GENERAL PARTNR
Rubber Products Division
1700 Miller Ave (46176-3114)
P.O. Box 38 (46176-0038)
PHONE..................317 421-3400
Jon Dolan, *Mgr*
EMP: 215
SALES (corp-wide): 12.23B **Privately Held**
Web: www.freudenberg.com
SIC: 3053 5085 3714 Oil seals, rubber; Gaskets; Motor vehicle parts and accessories
HQ: Freudenberg-Nok General Partnership
47774 W Anchor Ct
Plymouth MI 48170
734 451-0020

(G-14757)
FREUDENBERG-NOK GENERAL PARTNR
Also Called: Freudenberg-Nok Sealing Tech
877 Miller Ave Ste B (46176-2309)
PHONE..................734 354-5504
Joe Diale, *Brnch Mgr*
EMP: 104
SALES (corp-wide): 12.23B **Privately Held**
Web: www.freudenberg.com
SIC: 2821 3714 3053 3061 Plastics materials and resins; Motor vehicle parts and accessories; Gaskets; packing and sealing devices; Mechanical rubber goods
HQ: Freudenberg-Nok General Partnership
47774 W Anchor Ct
Plymouth MI 48170
734 451-0020

(G-14758)
G D COX INC
Also Called: Sports Locker Room
105 S Harrison St (46176-1343)
PHONE..................317 398-0035
Diana Cox, *VP*
EMP: 5 **EST:** 1991
SQ FT: 3,500
SALES (est): 491.2K **Privately Held**
SIC: 2759 7389 Screen printing; Embroidery advertising

(G-14759)
HICKORY FURNITURE DESIGNS INC
403 S Noble St (46176-2166)
PHONE..................765 642-0700
Brad Mcqueen, *Pr*
Myrta Mcqueen, *Sec*
EMP: 9 **EST:** 2002
SALES (est): 526.9K **Privately Held**
Web: www.hickoryfurnituredesigns.com
SIC: 2511 Wood household furniture

(G-14760)
INDIANA PRECISION FORGE LLC
Also Called: I P F
302 Northbrook Dr (46176-9305)
PHONE..................317 421-0102
Matsuo Yoshida, *Pr*
Takashi Iwaguchi, *VP*
Norihito Kuntani, *VP*
Rodney Anspaugh, *VP*
▲ **EMP:** 48 **EST:** 1996
SQ FT: 85,000
SALES (est): 16.01MM **Privately Held**
Web: www.ipfllc.com
SIC: 3714 Motor vehicle brake systems and parts
HQ: Nippon Steel Precision Forge, Inc.

1, Nittocho
Handa AIC 475-0

(G-14761)
INDIANA SERVICE PROS LLC
839 Shelbys Crst (46176-8782)
PHONE..................317 658-4673
James Joseph, *CEO*
EMP: 5 **EST:** 2018
SALES (est): 93.81K **Privately Held**
SIC: 1389 Construction, repair, and dismantling services

(G-14762)
INSTALLED BUILDING PDTS LLC
Also Called: B C I
886 W Mausoleum Rd (46176-9719)
PHONE..................317 398-3216
Ted Pike, *Mgr*
EMP: 6
SQ FT: 6,600
SALES (corp-wide): 2.78B **Publicly Held**
Web: www.installedbuildingproducts.com
SIC: 1742 3357 Insulation, buildings; Nonferrous wiredrawing and insulating
HQ: Installed Building Products Llc
495 S High St Ste 150
Columbus OH 43215
614 221-3399

(G-14763)
J & L TOOL & MACHINE INC
1441 Miller Ave (46176-3134)
P.O. Box 367 (46176-0367)
PHONE..................317 398-6281
Kathy Callahan, *Pr*
Robert Landwerlen, *VP*
EMP: 14 **EST:** 1968
SQ FT: 22,000
SALES (est): 1.88MM **Privately Held**
Web: www.jltool.com
SIC: 3599 Machine shop, jobbing and repair

(G-14764)
J BORINSTEIN INC
5936 N Brandywine Rd (46176-8853)
PHONE..................317 252-0875
John Borinstein, *CEO*
EMP: 1 **EST:** 2001
SALES (est): 130.74K **Privately Held**
SIC: 2514 Medicine cabinets and vanities: metal

(G-14765)
JEFFERSON HOMEBUILDERS INC
Also Called: Culpeper Wood Preservers
701 W Mausoleum Rd (46176-9720)
P.O. Box 260 (46176-0260)
PHONE..................317 398-3125
Jim Poweoo, *Brnch Mgr*
EMP: 1
SALES (corp-wide): 100.43MM **Privately Held**
Web: www.culpeperwood.com
SIC: 2491 2861 Structural lumber and timber, treated wood; Gum and wood chemicals
PA: Jefferson Homebuilders, Inc.
501 N Main St
Culpeper VA 22701
540 825-5898

(G-14766)
K-TEC CORP
850 Elston Dr (46176-1898)
PHONE..................317 398-6684
EMP: 1
SALES (est): 69.79K **Privately Held**
SIC: 3334 Primary aluminum

(G-14767)
KASCO MFG CO INC
170 W 600 N (46176-9737)
PHONE..................317 398-7973
P Phil Kaster, *Pr*
Freda P Kaster, *
Danette Kaster, *
EMP: 27 **EST:** 1965
SQ FT: 16,000
SALES (est): 2.14MM **Privately Held**
Web: www.kascomfg.com
SIC: 3523 Planting, haying, harvesting, and processing machinery

(G-14768)
KIRBY RISK CORPORATION
Also Called: Arco Electric Products
2325 E Michigan Rd (46176-1896)
PHONE..................317 398-9713
Hal Pike, *Mgr*
EMP: 96
SALES (corp-wide): 501.02MM **Privately Held**
Web: www.kirbyrisk.com
SIC: 3675 5063 Electronic capacitors; Electrical fittings and construction materials
PA: Kirby Risk Corporation
1815 Sagamore Pkwy N
Lafayette IN 47904
765 448-4567

(G-14769)
KN PLATECH AMERICA CORPORATION
1755 Mccall Dr (46176-9783)
PHONE..................317 392-7707
Hiroyuki Kayashita, *Pr*
Hiroaki Koga, *
Takayuki Masuda, *
▲ **EMP:** 70 **EST:** 2010
SALES (est): 9.77MM **Privately Held**
Web: www.knplatech.com
SIC: 3089 Blow molded finished plastics products, nec

(G-14770)
KNAUF INSULATION INC (HQ)
1 Knauf Dr (46176-8626)
PHONE..................317 398-4434
Matt Parrish, *Pr*
Christopher Griffin, *
Bill Matthias, *
◆ **EMP:** 150 **EST:** 1978
SALES (est): 611.66MM
SALES (corp-wide): 16B **Privately Held**
Web: www.knaufnorthamerica.com
SIC: 3296 Fiberglass insulation
PA: Gebr. Knauf Kg
Am Bahnhof 7
Iphofen BY 97346
9323310

(G-14771)
LACAP CONTAINER CORP
521 One Half E Hendricks St (46176)
P.O. Box 482 (46176-0482)
PHONE..................317 835-4282
Jerry L Caplinger, *Pr*
Roy Knopp, *VP*
Joy Caplinger, *Sec*
EMP: 6 **EST:** 1971
SQ FT: 11,500
SALES (est): 492.84K **Privately Held**
Web: www.lacapcontainer.com
SIC: 2653 Boxes, corrugated: made from purchased materials

(G-14772)
LEES READY-MIX & TRUCKING (PA)
Also Called: Lee's Ready Mix
701 Hodell St Ste 101 (46176)

Shelbyville - Shelby County (G-14773)

GEOGRAPHIC SECTION

EMP: 50 **EST:** 1971
SALES (est): 7.41MM
SALES (corp-wide): 7.41MM **Privately Held**
SIC: 3273 4212 Ready-mixed concrete; Local trucking, without storage

(G-14773)
MAKUTA INC
2155 Intelliplex Dr (46176-8538)
PHONE..................317 642-0001
Stuart P Kaplan, *Pr*
Elmer Kaplan, *Ch Bd*
EMP: 17 **EST:** 1993
SQ FT: 11,000
SALES (est): 2.49MM **Privately Held**
Web: www.makuta.com
SIC: 3089 3714 3544 2821 Injection molding of plastics; Motor vehicle parts and accessories; Special dies, tools, jigs, and fixtures; Plastics materials and resins

(G-14774)
MARK CONCRETE PRODUCTS INC
1126 Miller Ave (46176-2358)
PHONE..................317 398-8616
James Ross, *Pr*
Sharon Ross, *Sec*
EMP: 8 **EST:** 1955
SQ FT: 20,000
SALES (est): 593.93K **Privately Held**
Web: www.markconcreteproducts.com
SIC: 3272 5999 4225 Burial vaults, concrete or precast terrazzo; Monuments, finished to custom order; Warehousing, self storage

(G-14775)
MBCI INC
1780 Mccall Dr (46176-9783)
PHONE..................317 835-2201
Jess Brooks, *Brnch Mgr*
EMP: 137
SALES (corp-wide): 5.58B **Privately Held**
Web: www.mbci.com
SIC: 3448 Prefabricated metal buildings and components
HQ: Mbci, Inc.
  14031 W Hardy Rd
  Houston TX 77060
  281 337-1143

(G-14776)
MBCIINDY
1780 Mccall Dr (46176-9783)
PHONE..................317 398-4400
EMP: 10 **EST:** 2010
SALES (est): 100.49K **Privately Held**
Web: www.mbci.com
SIC: 3444 Sheet metalwork

(G-14777)
METL-SPAN LLC
1717 Mccall Dr (46176-9783)
PHONE..................317 398-1100
EMP: 23 **EST:** 2011
SALES (est): 3.18MM **Privately Held**
Web: www.metlspan.com
SIC: 3444 Sheet metalwork

(G-14778)
MIDWEST GARAGE DOORS LLC
839 Shelbys Crst (46176-8782)
PHONE..................317 739-2534
James Joseph, *Managing Member*
EMP: 2
SALES (est): 74.03K **Privately Held**
SIC: 1389 Construction, repair, and dismantling services

(G-14779)
NAI PRINT SOLUTIONS
168 W Hendricks St (46176-2004)
PHONE..................317 392-1207
EMP: 3 **EST:** 2017
SALES (est): 96.1K **Privately Held**
SIC: 2752 Offset printing

(G-14780)
NEXT PRODUCTS LLC
2201 E Michigan Rd (46176-1821)
P.O. Box 310 (46176-0310)
PHONE..................317 392-4701
◆ **EMP:** 6 **EST:** 2004
SALES (est): 159.45K **Privately Held**
SIC: 3993 Signs and advertising specialties

(G-14781)
OLD HICKORY FURNITURE COMPANY INC (PA)
Also Called: Old Hickory Furniture
403 S Noble St (46176-2166)
PHONE..................317 398-3151
EMP: 68 **EST:** 1899
SALES (est): 8.82MM
SALES (corp-wide): 8.82MM **Privately Held**
Web: www.oldhickory.com
SIC: 2511 2521 Wood household furniture; Wood office furniture

(G-14782)
PIERCY MACHINE CO INC
945 W 300 S (46176-9604)
P.O. Box 5001 (46140-5001)
PHONE..................317 398-9296
EMP: 4 **EST:** 1984
SALES (est): 335.07K **Privately Held**
Web: www.piercymachine.net
SIC: 3599 3544 Machine shop, jobbing and repair; Special dies, tools, jigs, and fixtures

(G-14783)
PILKINGTON NORTH AMERICA INC
Also Called: Shelbyville Plant
300 Northridge Dr (46176-8954)
PHONE..................317 392-7000
Dan Robinson, *Mgr*
EMP: 89
Web: www.pilkington.com
SIC: 3211 3231 Flat glass; Products of purchased glass
HQ: Pilkington North America, Inc.
  811 Madison Ave
  Toledo OH 43604
  419 247-3731

(G-14784)
PK USA INC (HQ)
600 Northridge Dr (46176)
PHONE..................317 395-5500
Kazuhiko Onami, *Pr*
Mori Toki, *
Satoshi Moritoki, *
Masakazu Nakayama, *
◆ **EMP:** 325 **EST:** 1988
SQ FT: 240,000
SALES (est): 126.4MM **Privately Held**
Web: www.pkusa.com
SIC: 3465 3089 3714 3429 Body parts, automobile: stamped metal; Injection molding of plastics; Motor vehicle engines and parts; Furniture, builders' and other household hardware
PA: Press Kogyo Co.,Ltd.
  1-1-1, Shiohama, Kawasaki-Ku
  Kawasaki KNG 210-0

(G-14785)
PLASTIC MOLDINGS COMPANY LLC
Also Called: PMC
1451 Miller Ave (46176-3134)
PHONE..................317 392-4139
Jed Morris, *Mgr*
EMP: 72
SALES (corp-wide): 24.78MM **Privately Held**
Web: www.pmcsmartsolutions.com
SIC: 3089 Injection molding of plastics
PA: Plastic Moldings Company, Llc.
  9825 Kenwood Rd Ste 302
  Blue Ash OH 45242
  513 921-5040

(G-14786)
POET BRFNING - SHELBYVILLE LLC
Also Called: Poet Bprocessing - Shelbyville
2373 W 300 N (46176-9728)
PHONE..................317 699-4199
EMP: 1 **EST:** 2018
SALES (est): 1.37MM **Privately Held**
Web: www.poet.com
SIC: 2869 Ethyl alcohol, ethanol
PA: Poet, Llc
  4615 N Lewis Ave
  Sioux Falls SD 57104

(G-14787)
PRECIOUS TECHNOLOGY GROUP LLC (PA)
Also Called: Wellman Furnaces
1111 W Mckay Rd (46176-3205)
P.O. Box 722 (46176-0722)
PHONE..................317 398-4411
EMP: 19 **EST:** 2003
SALES (est): 2.71MM
SALES (corp-wide): 2.71MM **Privately Held**
Web: www.wellmanfurnaces.com
SIC: 3567 Industrial furnaces and ovens

(G-14788)
PRINT IT WEAR IT INC
679 Brent Woods Dr (46176-9572)
PHONE..................317 946-1456
Michelle L Robbins, *Owner*
EMP: 4 **EST:** 2016
SALES (est): 66.16K **Privately Held**
Web: www.printitwearitink.com
SIC: 2752 Commercial printing, lithographic

(G-14789)
PUDDERS LLC
18 Public Sq (46176-1349)
PHONE..................317 402-3507
Alicia Phares, *Prin*
EMP: 6 **EST:** 2019
SALES (est): 103.91K **Privately Held**
SIC: 2711 Newspapers, publishing and printing

(G-14790)
RADIUS AEROSPACE INC
850 Elston Dr (46176-1823)
PHONE..................317 392-5000
Jim Mason, *Brnch Mgr*
EMP: 1
SALES (corp-wide): 666.39MM **Privately Held**
Web: www.radiusaerospace.com
SIC: 3728 3444 Aircraft parts and equipment, nec; Sheet metalwork
HQ: Radius Aerospace, Inc.
  153 Extrusion Pl
  Hot Springs AR 71901
  501 321-9325

(G-14791)
RISCO PRODUCTS INC
1344 N Michigan Rd (46176-9754)
PHONE..................317 392-6150
Scott Luie, *Pr*
Rich Clark, *VP*
▲ **EMP:** 2 **EST:** 2006
SALES (est): 386.98K **Privately Held**
Web: www.riscousa.com
SIC: 3499 Safe deposit boxes or chests, metal

(G-14792)
ROB NOLLEY INC
Also Called: Tubesock, Inc.
30 E Washington St Ste 400 (46176-1371)
P.O. Box 26 (46176-0026)
PHONE..................317 825-5211
Robert Nolley, *Pr*
EMP: 12 **EST:** 2010
SALES (est): 996.49K **Privately Held**
Web: www.tubesock.net
SIC: 7372 7373 7374 7376 Prepackaged software; Computer integrated systems design; Data processing and preparation; Computer facilities management

(G-14793)
RYOBI DIE CASTING (USA) INC
525 Industrial Park Dr (46176-8899)
PHONE..................317 398-3398
EMP: 1
Web: www.ryobidiecasting.com
SIC: 3714 Transmission housings or parts, motor vehicle
HQ: Ryobi Die Casting (Usa), Inc.
  800 W Mausoleum Rd
  Shelbyville IN 46176
  317 398-3398

(G-14794)
RYOBI DIE CASTING (USA) INC (HQ)
Also Called: Ryobi
800 W Mausoleum Rd (46176-9719)
PHONE..................317 398-3398
Takashi Yokoyama, *CEO*
Thomas L Johnson, *Pr*
Hideki Tanyfuji, *VP*
Ryan S Willhelm, *Pr*
▲ **EMP:** 593 **EST:** 1985
SQ FT: 582,509
SALES (est): 199.62MM **Privately Held**
Web: www.ryobidiecasting.com
SIC: 3714 3444 3365 3363 Transmission housings or parts, motor vehicle; Sheet metalwork; Aluminum foundries; Aluminum die-castings
PA: Ryobi Limited
  762, Mesakicho
  Fuchu HIR 726-0

(G-14795)
SELCO ENGINEERING INC
1677 W 400 N (46176-8586)
EMP: 15 **EST:** 1995
SQ FT: 18,000
SALES (est): 626.9K **Privately Held**
Web: www.selcoeng.com
SIC: 8711 3599 Industrial engineers; Custom machinery

(G-14796)
SHELBY CUSTOM CABINETS INC
3081 S Miller St (46176-9206)
PHONE..................317 398-0344
Charles D Yanzer, *Owner*
EMP: 1 **EST:** 2005
SALES (est): 107.24K **Privately Held**
SIC: 2434 Wood kitchen cabinets

GEOGRAPHIC SECTION

Sheridan - Hamilton County (G-14820)

(G-14797)
SHELBY GRAVEL INC (PA)
Also Called: Shelby Materials
157 E Rampart St (46176-9499)
P.O. Box 242 (46176-0242)
PHONE..................317 398-4485
Philip E Haehl, Pr
Richard H Haehl, *
Greg Wertz, *
EMP: 30 EST: 1951
SQ FT: 5,000
SALES (est): 74.83MM
SALES (corp-wide): 74.83MM Privately Held
Web: www.shelbymaterials.com
SIC: 3273 1442 Ready-mixed concrete; Common sand mining

(G-14798)
SHELBYVILLE NEWSPAPERS INC
Also Called: Extra, The
123 E Washington St (46176-1463)
PHONE..................317 398-6631
Paul Mahoney, Pr
EMP: 23 EST: 1947
SQ FT: 10,000
SALES (est): 856.72K Privately Held
Web: www.shelbynews.com
SIC: 2711 2752 Commercial printing and newspaper publishing combined; Offset printing

(G-14799)
SIGNS MORE
628 Highpointe Blvd (46176-2200)
PHONE..................317 392-9184
Holly Simpson, Owner
EMP: 4 EST: 2010
SALES (est): 15.86K Privately Held
Web: www.signsnmore.us
SIC: 3993 Signs, not made in custom sign painting shops

(G-14800)
SQUARE 1 DSIGN MANUFACTURE INC
Also Called: Square 1 Design
1 Clark Rd (46176)
P.O. Box 998 (46131)
PHONE..................866 647-7771
Sean Hubbard, CEO
EMP: 13 EST: 2013
SQ FT: 1,800
SALES (est): 1.06MM Privately Held
SIC: 3531 3599 5082 5084 Construction machinery; Custom machinery; Construction and mining machinery; Sawmill machinery and equipment

(G-14801)
STAGE DOOR GRAPHICS
207 S Harrison St (46176-2159)
P.O. Box 277 (46176-0277)
PHONE..................317 398-9011
Richard Delaney, Owner
EMP: 5 EST: 1978
SQ FT: 1,600
SALES (est): 246.3K Privately Held
SIC: 2752 2759 Offset printing; Commercial printing, nec

(G-14802)
T&S MIDWEST BEVERAGE LLC
3428 N Brandywine Rd (46176-9730)
PHONE..................317 690-1705
Anthony Thie, Pr
EMP: 5 EST: 2014
SALES (est): 253.08K Privately Held
SIC: 3585 Beer dispensing equipment

(G-14803)
TAYLOR COMMUNICATIONS INC
1750 Miller Ave (46176-3114)
PHONE..................317 392-3235
Greg Schofield, Mgr
EMP: 38
SALES (corp-wide): 3.81B Privately Held
Web: www.taylor.com
SIC: 2759 2761 Business forms: printing, nsk; Manifold business forms
HQ: Taylor Communications, Inc.
1725 Roe Crest Dr
North Mankato MN 56003
866 541-0937

(G-14804)
TEN CATE ENBI INC (INDIANA)
1703 Mccall Dr (46176-9783)
PHONE..................317 398-3267
Daniel Brady, General Vice President
J Lee Mc Neeley, *
EMP: 120
SQ FT: 55,000
SALES (est): 25.33MM Privately Held
Web: www.enbigroup.com
SIC: 3069 3312 Molded rubber products; Blast furnaces and steel mills
PA: Platinum Equity, Llc
360 N Crescent Dr Bldg S
Beverly Hills CA 90210

(G-14805)
THERMO - TRANSFER INC
1601 Miller Ave (46176-3138)
PHONE..................317 398-3503
Narendra P Jhala, Pr
Sondra Jhala, VP
EMP: 12 EST: 1989
SQ FT: 17,000
SALES (est): 1.91MM Privately Held
Web: www.thermotransferinc.com
SIC: 3567 Fuel-fired furnaces and ovens

(G-14806)
TIPPECANOE PRESS INC
230 N Knightstown Rd (46176-8906)
P.O. Box 690 (46176-0690)
PHONE..................317 392-1207
Gregory Wickizer, Pr
EMP: 6 EST: 1924
SQ FT: 27,000
SALES (est): 153.83K Privately Held
Web: www.perfectdomain.com
SIC: 2752 5943 2759 2789 Offset printing; Office forms and supplies; Letterpress printing; Bookbinding and related work

(G-14807)
TORAY RESIN COMPANY (DH)
821 W Mausoleum Rd (46176-9719)
PHONE..................317 398-7833
Dennis D Godwin, Pr
▲ EMP: 60 EST: 1990
SQ FT: 5,800
SALES (est): 55.84MM Privately Held
Web: www.toray.us
SIC: 2821 Plastics materials and resins
HQ: Toray Holding (U.S.A.), Inc.
461 5th Ave Fl 9
New York NY 10017
212 697-8150

(G-14808)
TRIUMPH CONTROLS LLC
1960 N Michigan Rd (46176-9384)
PHONE..................317 421-8760
Dave Tiles, Brnch Mgr
EMP: 13
SIC: 3728 Aircraft parts and equipment, nec
HQ: Triumph Controls, Llc
205 Church Rd
North Wales PA 19454

(G-14809)
TRIUMPH THERMAL SYSTEMS LLC
1960 N Michigan Rd (46176-9384)
PHONE..................419 273-1192
David Rasor, Brnch Mgr
EMP: 3
Web: www.triumph-thermal.com
SIC: 3728 Aircraft parts and equipment, nec
HQ: Triumph Thermal Systems, Llc
200 Railroad St
Forest OH 45843
419 273-2511

(G-14810)
V I P TOOLING INC
739 E Franklin St (46176-1608)
PHONE..................317 398-0753
Paul R Nolting, Pr
EMP: 27 EST: 1971
SQ FT: 50,000
SALES (est): 1.03MM Privately Held
Web: www.viptooling.com
SIC: 3599 Machine shop, jobbing and repair

(G-14811)
V-T INDUSTRIES INC
1406 Meridian St (46176-2936)
P.O. Box 490 (51025-0490)
PHONE..................712 368-4381
EMP: 1
SALES (corp-wide): 434.93MM Privately Held
Web: www.vtindustries.com
SIC: 2434 Wood kitchen cabinets
PA: V-T Industries Inc.
1000 Industrial Park Rd
Holstein IA 51025
712 368-4381

(G-14812)
VERNON SHARP
Also Called: Sharp's Woodshop
2202 W Mckay Rd (46176-9069)
PHONE..................317 398-0631
Vernon Sharp, Owner
EMP: 4 EST: 1965
SQ FT: 3,000
SALES (est): 244.09K Privately Held
Web: www.shelbycountybuilders.com
SIC: 2499 Decorative wood and woodwork

(G-14813)
W A P LLC
Also Called: Pure Flow Airdog
705 W Mausoleum Rd (46176-9720)
PHONE..................317 421-3180
Clifford Strachman, Ex Dir
EMP: 40 EST: 2003
SQ FT: 30,000
SALES (est): 7.93MM
SALES (corp-wide): 18.92MM Privately Held
Web: www.pureflowairdog.com
SIC: 3519 Parts and accessories, internal combustion engines
PA: Shares Inc
1611 S Miller St
Shelbyville IN 46176
317 398-8218

(G-14814)
WAP INC
Also Called: Diesel Rx Products
705 W Mausoleum Rd (46176-9720)
P.O. Box 441014 (46244-1014)
PHONE..................877 421-3187
David E Duba, Pr
EMP: 14 EST: 1995
SALES (est): 1.22MM Privately Held
Web: www.pureflowairdog.com
SIC: 3519 Parts and accessories, internal combustion engines

(G-14815)
WHEELER CORPORATION (PA)
841 Elston Dr (46176-1817)
P.O. Box 283 (46176-0283)
PHONE..................317 398-7500
EMP: 14 EST: 1954
SALES (est): 2.45MM
SALES (corp-wide): 2.45MM Privately Held
Web: www.wheelerblock.com
SIC: 3271 Blocks, concrete or cinder: standard

(G-14816)
YUSHIRO MANUFACTURING AMER INC
Also Called: Yuma
783 W Mausoleum Rd (46176)
P.O. Box 217 (46176)
PHONE..................317 398-9862
Takuya Ishikawa, Pr
Dwane L Rice, *
Charles Parks, *
Marshall Swazay, *
John Bruckmann, *
▲ EMP: 38 EST: 1986
SQ FT: 54,800
SALES (est): 16.76MM Privately Held
Web: www.yushirousa.com
SIC: 2992 2899 2842 2841 Rust arresting compounds, animal or vegetable oil base; Chemical preparations, nec; Polishes and sanitation goods; Soap and other detergents
PA: Yushiro Chemical Industry Co., Ltd.
2-34-16, Chidori
Ota-Ku TKY 146-0

Sheridan
Hamilton County

(G-14817)
BIDDLE PRECISION COMPONENTS INC
Also Called: E M C
701 S Mn St (46069)
PHONE..................317 758-4451
▲ EMP: 200
SIC: 3451 Screw machine products

(G-14818)
BURLINGTON GRAIN & PROD CO LLC
210 S Main St (46069-1142)
PHONE..................866 767-2627
EMP: 3 EST: 2021
SALES (est): 250K Privately Held
SIC: 2099 Popcorn, packaged: except already popped

(G-14819)
CARDWELL SIGNS LLC
112 Arrowhead St (46069-9241)
PHONE..................414 698-3992
Harley Cardwell, Prin
EMP: 5 EST: 2018
SALES (est): 50.69K Privately Held
Web: www.cardwellsigns.com
SIC: 3993 Signs and advertising specialties

(G-14820)
CRAWFORD WATER CARE
22902 Mulebarn Rd (46069-9134)
PHONE..................317 758-6017
John Crawford, Owner
EMP: 1 EST: 2001

Sheridan - Hamilton County (G-14821)

SALES (est): 51.38K **Privately Held**
SIC: **7389** 3589 Water softener service; Sewage and water treatment equipment

(G-14821)
DAJAC INC
805 Wesco Pkwy (46069-0020)
PHONE.................................317 608-0500
EMP: 7 EST: 2000
SALES (est): 793.78K **Privately Held**
Web: www.dajac.com
SIC: **3647** 7389 Headlights (fixtures), vehicular; Business Activities at Non-Commercial Site

(G-14822)
EMC PRECISION MACHINING II LLC
701 S Main St (46069-1340)
PHONE.................................317 758-4451
EMP: 81
SALES (corp-wide): 5.05MM **Privately Held**
Web: www.emcprecision.com
SIC: **3451** Screw machine products
PA: Emc Precision Machining Ii, Llc
145 Northrup St
Elyria OH 44035
440 365-4171

(G-14823)
HUNT CLUB DISTILLERY
3774 W State Road 47 (46069-9133)
PHONE.................................317 441-7194
EMP: 4 EST: 2018
SALES (est): 62.38K **Privately Held**
Web: www.huntclubdistillery.com
SIC: **2085** Distilled and blended liquors

(G-14824)
JBS UNITED INC
322 S Main St (46069-1113)
PHONE.................................317 758-2609
EMP: 18 EST: 2011
SALES (est): 303.86K **Privately Held**
Web: www.unitedanh.com
SIC: **2048** Prepared feeds, nec

(G-14825)
MAD MEDIA LLC ◆
501 E 6th St (46069)
PHONE.................................317 210-5609
Mathew Deleskiewicz, *Managing Member*
EMP: 6 EST: 2024
SALES (est): 262.96K **Privately Held**
SIC: **2731** Book publishing

(G-14826)
R T TIRE & AUTO-LEBANON
24518 Jerkwater Rd (46069-9613)
PHONE.................................317 443-6025
EMP: 4 EST: 2018
SALES (est): 40.34K **Privately Held**
SIC: **7534** Tire retreading and repair shops

(G-14827)
ROCKWELL DIVERSIFIED WOODWORKS
26715 Dunbar Rd (46069-9316)
PHONE.................................317 758-4797
EMP: 4 EST: 2007
SALES (est): 142.98K **Privately Held**
Web: www.rdwoodworks.com
SIC: **2431** Millwork

(G-14828)
SHERIDAN MANUFACTURING CO INC
508 S Main St (46069-1337)
PHONE.................................317 758-6000
Jim Newby, *Pr*
Larry Newby, *Sec*
EMP: 4 EST: 1976
SQ FT: 3,000
SALES (est): 487.62K **Privately Held**
Web: www.sheridanmfg.com
SIC: **3599** Machine shop, jobbing and repair

(G-14829)
SOBER SCIENTIFIC LLC (PA)
17739 Joliet Rd (46069-9118)
PHONE.................................765 465-9803
Ethan Pennington, *Owner*
Ethan Pennington, *Pr*
EMP: 1 EST: 2021
SALES (est): 131.72K
SALES (corp-wide): 131.72K **Privately Held**
Web: www.soberscientific.com
SIC: **5047** 8071 2899 Medical and hospital equipment; Testing laboratories; Drug testing kits, blood and urine

(G-14830)
UNITED ANIMAL HEALTH INC (PA)
Also Called: United Animal Health
322 S Main St (46069)
P.O. Box 108 (46069)
PHONE.................................317 758-4495
Douglas M Webel, *CEO*
John Swisher, *
Ellen Crab, *Vice Chairman**
John M Corbett, *
▼ EMP: 52 EST: 1956
SQ FT: 5,000
SALES (est): 145.88MM
SALES (corp-wide): 145.88MM **Privately Held**
Web: www.jbsunited.com
SIC: **2048** 5153 0213 Livestock feeds; Grains; Hog feedlot

(G-14831)
UNITED-AH II LLC
322 S Main St (46069-1113)
PHONE.................................317 758-4495
EMP: 10 EST: 2004
SALES (est): 960.23K **Privately Held**
Web: www.unitedanh.com
SIC: **2834** Pharmaceutical preparations

(G-14832)
WALLACE GRAIN COMPANY INC
604 S Main St (46069-1339)
P.O. Box 109 (46069-0109)
PHONE.................................317 758-4434
Craig Wallace, *Pr*
Chris Wallace, *VP*
EMP: 14 EST: 1935
SQ FT: 37,000
SALES (est): 2.33MM **Privately Held**
Web: www.wallacegrainco.com
SIC: **5191** 5153 2048 2041 Feed; Grains; Prepared feeds, nec; Flour and other grain mill products

Shipshewana
Lagrange County

(G-14833)
ALL RVS MANUFACTURING INC
1055 N 625 W (46565-8564)
PHONE.................................574 538-1559
Merle Schmucker, *CEO*
Kalynn Schmucker, *Sec*
EMP: 2 EST: 2012
SALES (est): 248.78K **Privately Held**
SIC: **3999** Atomizers, toiletry

(G-14834)
AMERICAN RELIANCE INDS CO
860 N Tuscany Dr (46565)
P.O. Box 246 (46565)
PHONE.................................260 768-4704
Curt L Riegsecker, *Pr*
John Jantzi, *Pr*
Larry J Chupp, *VP*
EMP: 20 EST: 2001
SQ FT: 10,000
SALES (est): 4.94MM **Privately Held**
Web: www.legacysleepers.com
SIC: **3711** Motor vehicles and car bodies

(G-14835)
AMISH COUNTRY DAIRY LLC
1360 N 850 W (46565-9125)
PHONE.................................574 323-1701
John Kuhns, *Managing Member*
EMP: 8 EST: 2017
SALES (est): 348.11K **Privately Held**
SIC: **2023** 7389 Dried and powdered milk and milk products; Business Activities at Non-Commercial Site

(G-14836)
ARTISTIC COATINGS LLC
5654 N State Road 5 (46565)
PHONE.................................260 463-5253
EMP: 10 EST: 2019
SALES (est): 741.57K **Privately Held**
SIC: **3479** Metal coating and allied services

(G-14837)
AURORA SERVICES INC
7155 N 675 W (46565-9743)
P.O. Box 744 (46565-0744)
PHONE.................................260 463-4901
Daniel Byler, *Pr*
Dawn Byler, *VP*
EMP: 3 EST: 2001
SALES (est): 152.78K **Privately Held**
SIC: **2711** Newspapers

(G-14838)
B HONEY & CANDLES
2260 N 1000 W (46565-9011)
PHONE.................................574 642-1145
EMP: 4 EST: 2013
SALES (est): 75.67K **Privately Held**
SIC: **3999** Candles

(G-14839)
BEECHYS MOLDING PLUS LLC
1365 N 500 W (46565-9708)
PHONE.................................260 768-7030
EMP: 6 EST: 2009
SALES (est): 311.6K **Privately Held**
SIC: **3089** Injection molding of plastics

(G-14840)
CANVAS SHOP LLC
850 Taylor Dr (46565-8536)
PHONE.................................260 768-7755
Mike Unternahrer, *Owner*
EMP: 3 EST: 1996
SQ FT: 6,000
SALES (est): 208.17K **Privately Held**
Web: www.shipshecanvas.com
SIC: **2394** Awnings, fabric: made from purchased materials

(G-14841)
CRESTVIEW WOODWORKING LLC
6825 W 450 N (46565-9714)
PHONE.................................260 768-4707
Duane Miller, *Prin*
EMP: 2 EST: 2010
SALES (est): 105.11K **Privately Held**
SIC: **2431** Millwork

(G-14842)
D L MILLER WOODWORKING
5345 N 400 W (46565-8525)
PHONE.................................260 562-9329
D L Miller, *Prin*
EMP: 5 EST: 2008
SALES (est): 290.88K **Privately Held**
Web: www.dlmiller.net
SIC: **2434** Wood kitchen cabinets

(G-14843)
DAVIS HEZAKIH CORP
Also Called: Davis Hotel
255 E Main St (46565-1301)
PHONE.................................260 768-7300
Alvin Miller, *Pr*
Elsie Miller, *VP*
EMP: 10 EST: 1982
SQ FT: 5,600
SALES (est): 390.41K **Privately Held**
SIC: **3499** Fire- or burglary-resistive products

(G-14844)
DUTCHMAID WOODWORKING LLC
2320 N 700 W (46565-9405)
PHONE.................................260 768-7442
Perry Yutzy, *Owner*
EMP: 1 EST: 2005
SALES (est): 141.98K **Privately Held**
Web: www.dutchmaidwoodworking.com
SIC: **2431** Millwork

(G-14845)
FAIRVIEW WOODWORKING
8655 W 100 S (46565-9472)
PHONE.................................260 768-3255
Leroy Bontrager, *Prin*
EMP: 5 EST: 2008
SALES (est): 116.61K **Privately Held**
Web: www.fairviewwoodworking.com
SIC: **2431** Millwork

(G-14846)
FORKS RV INC
11280 W Us Highway 20 (46565-9633)
PHONE.................................574 825-7467
EMP: 60
SIC: **3792** 7539 Travel trailers and campers; Trailer repair

(G-14847)
G & B DIRECTIONAL BORING LLC
2620 N 850 W (46565-9767)
PHONE.................................574 538-8132
Enos L Gingerich, *Admn*
EMP: 14 EST: 2015
SALES (est): 2.3MM **Privately Held**
SIC: **1381** Directional drilling oil and gas wells

(G-14848)
GOLD STAR PRINTING LLC
2075 N 735 W (46565-9403)
PHONE.................................260 768-7920
Ferman Miller, *Managing Member*
EMP: 3 EST: 2006
SALES (est): 259.69K **Privately Held**
Web: www.goldstarprintingllc.com
SIC: **2752** 7389 Offset printing; Business services, nec

(G-14849)
HELMUTHS WOODWORKING LLC
61095 E County Line Rd (46565-9302)
PHONE.................................574 825-0073
Richard Helmuth, *Prin*
EMP: 1 EST: 2015
SALES (est): 58K **Privately Held**
SIC: **2431** Millwork

GEOGRAPHIC SECTION
Shipshewana - Lagrange County (G-14877)

(G-14850)
HIGHLAND RIDGE RV INC
Also Called: Open Range Rv
3195 N State Road 5 (46565-9313)
P.O. Box 460 (46540-0460)
PHONE..................260 768-7771
Randall Graber, *Pr*
Chris Good, *
Derald Bontrager, *
Wilbur Bontrager, *
EMP: 330 **EST:** 2014
SALES (est): 89.84MM
SALES (corp-wide): 11.12B **Publicly Held**
Web: www.highlandridgerv.com
SIC: 5561 3799 3792 Campers (pickup coaches) for mounting on trucks; Recreational vehicles; Camping trailers and chassis
HQ: Jayco, Inc.
903 South Main St
Middlebury IN 46540
574 825-5861

(G-14851)
HILLTOP MACHINE SHOP LLC
10515 W Us Highway 20 (46565-9814)
PHONE..................260 768-9196
EMP: 6 **EST:** 2007
SALES (est): 489.2K **Privately Held**
Web: www.importantlocalbusinesses.com
SIC: 3599 Machine shop, jobbing and repair

(G-14852)
INDIANA CUSTOM TRUCKS LLC
Also Called: Ict
1095 N 925 W (46565-8618)
P.O. Box 210 (46761-0210)
PHONE..................260 463-3244
Michael Baxley, *Managing Member*
EMP: 40 **EST:** 1990
SALES (est): 4.98MM **Privately Held**
Web: www.trucksleeper.com
SIC: 3713 3714 7532 3429 Truck cabs, for motor vehicles; Motor vehicle parts and accessories; Top and body repair and paint shops; Clamps, metal

(G-14853)
INTEGRITY WOODCRAFTING
4285 N 500 W (46565-9712)
PHONE..................260 562-2067
EMP: 4 **EST:** 2018
SALES (est): 131.74K **Privately Held**
Web: www.indianawoodcrafters.com
SIC: 2431 Millwork

(G-14854)
INTERSTATE TRUSS LLC
4875 N 675 W (46565-9774)
PHONE..................260 463-6124
Andrew Lambright, *Managing Member*
EMP: 5 **EST:** 2012
SALES (est): 360.85K **Privately Held**
SIC: 2439 Trusses, wooden roof

(G-14855)
JC REFRIGERATION LLC
6495 W 200 N (46565-8982)
PHONE..................260 768-4067
▼ **EMP:** 3 **EST:** 1991
SALES (est): 251.03K **Privately Held**
Web: www.jc-refrigeration.com
SIC: 7623 3632 Refrigerator repair service; Household refrigerators and freezers

(G-14856)
KZRV LP
985 N 900 W (46565)
PHONE..................260 768-4016
Daryl E Zook, *Genl Pt*
Trista Nunemaker, *Pt*
Tonja Zook Nicholas, *Pt*
◆ **EMP:** 300 **EST:** 1972
SQ FT: 414,225
SALES (est): 27.96MM
SALES (corp-wide): 11.12B **Publicly Held**
Web: www.kz-rv.com
SIC: 3792 Trailer coaches, automobile
PA: Thor Industries, Inc.
601 E Beardsley Ave
Elkhart IN 46514
574 970-7460

(G-14857)
L & C WELDING LLC
11705 W 300 S (46565-8631)
PHONE..................260 593-3410
Larry Miller, *Admn*
EMP: 2 **EST:** 2009
SALES (est): 98.13K **Privately Held**
SIC: 7692 Welding repair

(G-14858)
L & N WOODWORKING LLC
2240 N 925 W (46565-9135)
PHONE..................260 768-7008
Leroy Cambright, *Prin*
EMP: 7 **EST:** 2008
SALES (est): 262.55K **Privately Held**
SIC: 2431 Millwork

(G-14859)
L & R MARINE LLC
8755 W 250 N (46565-9526)
PHONE..................260 768-8094
EMP: 1 **EST:** 2001
SALES (est): 128.25K **Privately Held**
Web: www.landrmarine.com
SIC: 2077 Animal and marine fats and oils

(G-14860)
LAGWANA PRINTING INC
2465 N 850 W (46565-8645)
P.O. Box 70 (46565-0070)
PHONE..................260 463-4901
EMP: 9
SALES (corp-wide): 5.91MM **Privately Held**
Web: www.lagwana.com
SIC: 2752 Offset printing
PA: Lagwana Printing, Inc.
4425 W Us Highway 20 # 3
Lagrange IN 46761
260 463-4901

(G-14861)
LAKEPARK INDUSTRIES IND INC
750 E Middlebury St (46565-8801)
P.O. Box 729 (46565-0729)
EMP: 98 **EST:** 1988
SQ FT: 198,000
SALES (est): 21.78MM **Privately Held**
Web: www.midwayproducts.com
SIC: 3465 3714 3469 Automotive stampings; Motor vehicle parts and accessories; Metal stampings, nec
PA: Midway Products Group, Inc.
1 Lyman E Hoyt Dr
Monroe MI 48161

(G-14862)
LAMB WOODWORKING LLC
5510 W 200 N (46565-9226)
PHONE..................260 768-7992
Lavern Beechy, *Owner*
EMP: 4 **EST:** 2005
SALES (est): 288.54K **Privately Held**
Web: www.viztechfurniture.com
SIC: 2431 Millwork

(G-14863)
LAMBRIGHT COUNTRY CHIMES LLC
8340 W Us Highway 20 Unit 3 (46565)
PHONE..................260 768-9138
Orley Lambright, *Managing Member*
EMP: 3 **EST:** 2008
SALES (est): 208.29K **Privately Held**
SIC: 3999 Wind chimes

(G-14864)
LEGENDARY DESIGNS INC
2685 N 850 W (46565-9767)
P.O. Box 70 (46565-0070)
PHONE..................260 768-9170
Leon Yoder, *Pr*
EMP: 4 **EST:** 1996
SALES (est): 245.6K **Privately Held**
Web: www.lagwana.com
SIC: 3993 Signs, not made in custom sign painting shops

(G-14865)
LIVIN LITE CORP
Also Called: Livin' Lite Rv
985 N 900 W (46565-9139)
PHONE..................574 862-2228
Scott Tuttle, *Pr*
EMP: 23 **EST:** 2001
SQ FT: 32,000
SALES (est): 2.05MM **Privately Held**
Web: www.livinlite.com
SIC: 3792 Travel trailers and campers

(G-14866)
MASTER PIECE KRAFTS LLC
4875 N 675 W (46565-9774)
PHONE..................260 768-4330
Adam Yoder, *Owner*
EMP: 3 **EST:** 2004
SALES (est): 204.56K **Privately Held**
SIC: 1751 2499 Cabinet building and installation; Decorative wood and woodwork

(G-14867)
MILLER CARRIAGE COMPANY LLC
3035 N 850 W (46565-8942)
PHONE..................260 768-4553
John Miller, *Owner*
EMP: 6 **EST:** 1971
SQ FT: 9,600
SALES (est): 462.36K **Privately Held**
Web: www.millercarriage.com
SIC: 3799 Horse trailers, except fifth-wheel type

(G-14868)
MILLER STEEL FABRICATORS
3235 N 675 W (46565-8604)
PHONE..................260 768-7321
Raymond M Miller, *Owner*
Marlene M Miller, *Owner*
EMP: 2 **EST:** 2007
SALES (est): 194.31K **Privately Held**
SIC: 3441 Fabricated structural metal

(G-14869)
MILLERS CUSTOM CABINETS
8170 W State Road 120 (46565-8928)
PHONE..................260 768-7830
Homer Miller, *Prin*
EMP: 2 **EST:** 2008
SALES (est): 100K **Privately Held**
Web: www.millerscustomcabinetry.com
SIC: 2434 Wood kitchen cabinets

(G-14870)
MK MFG LLC
8895 W 250 N (46565-9618)
PHONE..................260 768-4678
Michael Yoder, *Pr*
EMP: 4 **EST:** 2017
SALES (est): 80.69K **Privately Held**
SIC: 3999 Manufacturing industries, nec

(G-14871)
MUDD-OX INC
8525 W 750 N (46565-9294)
PHONE..................260 768-7221
EMP: 10 **EST:** 2007
SQ FT: 2,050
SALES (est): 871.52K **Privately Held**
Web: www.muddox.net
SIC: 3799 Recreational vehicles

(G-14872)
OPEN RANGE RV COMPANY
3195 N State Road 5 (46565-9313)
PHONE..................260 768-7771
EMP: 30
Web: www.highlandridgerv.com
SIC: 3799 Recreational vehicles

(G-14873)
ORLA BONTRATER
Also Called: Country Meadow Wood Products
1310 S 900 W (46565-9460)
PHONE..................260 768-7553
Orla Bontrater, *Owner*
EMP: 5 **EST:** 2021
SALES (est): 170.94K **Privately Held**
SIC: 2411 Wooden logs

(G-14874)
OXBO INTERNATIONAL CORPORATION
10605 W 750 N (46565-9585)
PHONE..................260 768-3217
Jerry Yoder, *Mgr*
EMP: 4
Web: www.oxbo.com
SIC: 3523 Farm machinery and equipment
HQ: Oxbo International Corporation
7275 Batavia Byron Rd
Byron NY 14422
585 548-2665

(G-14875)
PALLET SUBS LLC
5345 W 200 N (46565-9228)
PHONE..................260 768-4021
Howe Wallace, *Pr*
EMP: 63 **EST:** 1974
SALES (est): 6.71MM
SALES (corp-wide): 7.22B **Publicly Held**
SIC: 2448 Pallets, wood
PA: Ufp Industries, Inc.
2801 E Beltline Ave Ne
Grand Rapids MI 49525
616 364-6161

(G-14876)
PALLETONE INC
5345 W 200 N (46565-9228)
PHONE..................260 768-4021
EMP: 1
SALES (corp-wide): 7.22B **Publicly Held**
Web: www.palletone.com
SIC: 2448 Pallets, wood
HQ: Palletone, Inc.
6001 Foxtrot Ave
Bartow FL 33830
866 336-6032

(G-14877)
PALLETONE OF INDIANA INC
5345 W 200 N (46565-9228)
PHONE..................260 768-4021
EMP: 70 **EST:** 1971
SALES (est): 18.23MM
SALES (corp-wide): 9.63B **Publicly Held**

(PA)=Parent Co (HQ)=Headquarters
✪ = New Business established in last 2 years

Shipshewana - Lagrange County (G-14878)

GEOGRAPHIC SECTION

SIC: 2448 2426 Pallets, wood; Lumber, hardwood dimension
HQ: Palletone, Inc.
6001 Foxtrot Ave
Bartow FL 33830
866 336-6032

(G-14878)
PERRY MILLER
Also Called: Countryroad Carriage
2195 N 675 W (46565-9417)
PHONE.....................260 894-1133
Perry Miller, Owner
EMP: 1 EST: 2009
SQ FT: 10,000
SALES (est): 78.87K Privately Held
SIC: 3799 Carriages, horse drawn

(G-14879)
PETER STONE COMPANY
805 E North Village Dr (46565-8651)
P.O. Box 88 (46565-0088)
PHONE.....................260 768-9150
Peter Stone, Pr
Charles Matthews, *
▲ EMP: 9 EST: 1996
SALES (est): 484.65K Privately Held
Web: www.stonehorses.com
SIC: 3944 7371 Hobby horses; Computer software development and applications

(G-14880)
QUALITY FENCE LTD
6450 W 275 N (46565-9103)
PHONE.....................260 768-4986
Mervin Yoder, Pr
Edna Yoder, VP
EMP: 3 EST: 1985
SALES (est): 250.39K Privately Held
Web: www.qualityfence.com
SIC: 1799 2499 2448 Fence construction; Fencing, wood; Pallets, wood

(G-14881)
RED WAGON
255 N Harrison St Ste 206 (46565)
P.O. Box 5 (46565-0005)
PHONE.....................260 768-3090
Heidi Stolppsus, Owner
EMP: 2 EST: 2007
SALES (est): 56K Privately Held
Web: www.davismercantile.com
SIC: 3942 3944 5092 Dolls and stuffed toys; Games, toys, and children's vehicles; Toys and hobby goods and supplies

(G-14882)
RH YODER ENTERPRISES LLC
2375 S 1100 W (46565-8641)
PHONE.....................574 825-6183
Richard D Yoder, Prin
EMP: 3 EST: 2007
SALES (est): 246.5K Privately Held
Web: www.rhyoder.com
SIC: 2431 Millwork

(G-14883)
RIDLEY USA INC
Also Called: Hubbard Feeds
135 Main St (46565)
P.O. Box 156 (46565-0156)
PHONE.....................260 768-4103
Jim Long, Brnch Mgr
EMP: 12
SALES (corp-wide): 1.49B Privately Held
Web: www.hubbardfeeds.com
SIC: 2048 Livestock feeds
HQ: Ridley Usa Inc.
111 W Cherry St Ste 500
Mankato MN 56001
507 388-9400

(G-14884)
RODEX MACHINING
7400 W 650 N (46565-9244)
PHONE.....................260 768-4844
Eli Mast, Owner
EMP: 2 EST: 1988
SALES (est): 81.56K Privately Held
SIC: 3599 Machine shop, jobbing and repair

(G-14885)
SCHERGERS KTTLE JAMS JELLIES -
120 N Morton St (46565-1700)
PHONE.....................800 447-6475
EMP: 4 EST: 2015
SALES (est): 116.39K Privately Held
Web: www.shipshewanajams.com
SIC: 2033 Jams, jellies, and preserves, packaged in cans, jars, etc.

(G-14886)
SHIPSHE WELDING
8435 W Us Highway 20 (46565-9177)
PHONE.....................260 768-7267
EMP: 8 EST: 2008
SALES (est): 290K Privately Held
Web: www.shipshetrailers.com
SIC: 7692 Welding repair

(G-14887)
SHIPSHEWANA BREAD BOX CORP
Also Called: Bread Box Bake Shop
140 One Half N Morton St (46565)
P.O. Box 775 (46565-0775)
PHONE.....................260 768-4629
David Scherger, Pr
Margaret Scherger, VP
EMP: 9 EST: 1987
SALES (est): 220.77K Privately Held
Web: www.shipshewanabakery.com
SIC: 5461 2052 2051 Bread; Cookies and crackers; Bread, cake, and related products

(G-14888)
SHIPSHEWANA WOODWORKS LLC
7720 W 200 N (46565-9209)
PHONE.....................260 768-7034
EMP: 4 EST: 2017
SALES (est): 54.13K Privately Held
Web: www.shipshewanawoodworks.com
SIC: 2431 Millwork

(G-14889)
SLABACH LOGGING LLC
7615 W 200 N (46565-9210)
PHONE.....................260 768-4644
Melvin Slabach, Prin
EMP: 6 EST: 2012
SALES (est): 108.82K Privately Held
Web: www.slabachlogging.com
SIC: 2411 Logging camps and contractors

(G-14890)
SLABAUGH STORAGE BARNS INC
9550 W 375 N (46565-9600)
P.O. Box 216 (46565-0216)
PHONE.....................260 768-7989
EMP: 2 EST: 1994
SALES (est): 224.36K Privately Held
Web: www.customstoragebarns.com
SIC: 3448 Prefabricated metal buildings and components

(G-14891)
STATE LINE WOODWORKING
6520 N 675 W (46565-8559)
PHONE.....................260 768-4577
Steven Miller, Owner
EMP: 2 EST: 2005
SALES (est): 112.8K Privately Held
SIC: 2431 Millwork

(G-14892)
STATELINE WOODTURNINGS LLC
7005 W 650 N (46565-9778)
PHONE.....................260 768-4507
EMP: 2 EST: 2001
SQ FT: 6,000
SALES (est): 211.56K Privately Held
Web: www.statelinewoodturnings.com
SIC: 2426 Hardwood dimension and flooring mills

(G-14893)
STONEY ACRES WOODWORKING LLC
2685 S 1000 W (46565-8617)
PHONE.....................260 768-4367
EMP: 12 EST: 2004
SALES (est): 417.35K Privately Held
SIC: 2431 Millwork

(G-14894)
STREAMSIDE WOODSHOP LLC
2275 N 925 W (46565-9135)
PHONE.....................260 768-7887
EMP: 2 EST: 2004
SALES (est): 143.56K Privately Held
SIC: 2511 Wood bedroom furniture

(G-14895)
VALLEY LINE WOOD PRODUCTS LLC
2935 N 500 W (46565-9235)
PHONE.....................260 768-7807
▲ EMP: 8 EST: 1998
SALES (est): 705.72K Privately Held
Web: www.etchwood.com
SIC: 2514 Household furniture: upholstered on metal frames

(G-14896)
WELLSPRING COMPONENTS LLC
1085 N 850 W (46565-9123)
PHONE.....................260 768-7336
EMP: 8 EST: 1945
SQ FT: 12,000
SALES (est): 1.02MM Privately Held
Web: www.wellspringsolar.com
SIC: 3714 3493 3799 Motor vehicle parts and accessories; Steel springs, except wire ; Carriages, horse drawn

(G-14897)
WEST POINT WOODWORKING LLC
6565 W 200 N (46565-9222)
PHONE.....................260 768-4750
EMP: 8 EST: 2001
SALES (est): 487K Privately Held
SIC: 2431 Millwork

(G-14898)
WINGARDS SA
3670 N State Road 5 (46565-9008)
PHONE.....................260 768-4656
EMP: 4 EST: 2016
SALES (est): 177.56K Privately Held
Web: www.wingardssales.com
SIC: 2679 Converted paper products, nec

(G-14899)
WINGARDS SALES LLC
3715 N State Road 5 (46565-9007)
PHONE.....................260 768-7961
EMP: 4 EST: 1987
SQ FT: 5,000
SALES (est): 478.13K Privately Held
Web: www.wingardssales.com
SIC: 3365 2511 Aluminum and aluminum-based alloy castings; Wood lawn and garden furniture

(G-14900)
YODERS MEATS INC
Also Called: Yoder's Meat Shop
435 S Van Buren St (46565-9176)
PHONE.....................260 768-4715
Robert Yoder, Pr
Perry A Yoder, VP
Rosanna R Yoder, Sec
EMP: 9 EST: 1955
SALES (est): 881.67K Privately Held
Web: www.yodersmeatandcheese.com
SIC: 0751 5812 5421 2013 Slaughtering: custom livestock services; Restaurant, family: independent; Meat markets, including freezer provisioners; Sausages and other prepared meats

(G-14901)
YODERS WOOD SHOP LLC
1675 N 675 W (46565-9108)
PHONE.....................260 768-3246
EMP: 1 EST: 2003
SALES (est): 87.98K Privately Held
SIC: 2511 Wood household furniture

Shirley
Henry County

(G-14902)
TECH CASTINGS LLC
1102 South St (47384-1227)
P.O. Box 332 (47384-0332)
PHONE.....................765 535-4100
Jeff Lantz, Pr
EMP: 23 EST: 2011
SQ FT: 25,000
SALES (est): 1.19MM Privately Held
Web: www.techcastings.com
SIC: 3599 Machine shop, jobbing and repair

Shoals
Martin County

(G-14903)
B & D ELECTRIC INC
8633 Us Highway 50 (47581-7848)
PHONE.....................812 254-2122
Tony D Blessinger, Pr
Greg P Hauser, VP
Jackie Daily, Sec
EMP: 17 EST: 1961
SALES (est): 2.16MM Privately Held
Web: www.bdelectricinc.com
SIC: 1731 7694 General electrical contractor ; Electric motor repair

(G-14904)
BOONDOCKS LOGGING LLC
12471 Sanders Ln (47581-7485)
PHONE.....................812 247-3363
James Carpenter, Owner
EMP: 7 EST: 2017
SALES (est): 240.43K Privately Held
SIC: 2411 Logging camps and contractors

(G-14905)
DIVINE MACHINE
9999 Eagles Nest Ln (47581-7563)
PHONE.....................812 388-6323
Dale Divine, Owner
EMP: 1 EST: 1987
SALES (est): 135.56K Privately Held
Web: www.divinemachinetattoo.com
SIC: 3449 Miscellaneous metalwork

GEOGRAPHIC SECTION

South Bend - St. Joseph County (G-14930)

(G-14906)
DIVINE MACHINE LLC
17246 N Sr 450 (47581)
Rural Route 17246 450 (47581)
PHONE..................812 709-5246
EMP: 1 EST: 2019
SALES (est): 51.72K Privately Held
SIC: 3599 7389 Machine shop, jobbing and repair; Business Activities at Non-Commercial Site

(G-14907)
GOLD BOND BUILDING PDTS LLC
9720 Us Highway 50 (47581-7260)
PHONE..................812 247-2424
EMP: 2
SALES (corp-wide): 96.43MM Privately Held
Web: www.goldbondbuilding.com
SIC: 2621 Paper mills
HQ: Gold Bond Building Products, Llc
2001 Rexford Rd
Charlotte NC 28211
704 365-7300

(G-14908)
GYPSUM EXPRESS LTD
9720 Us Highway 50 (47581-7260)
PHONE..................812 247-2648
Tim Strahley, Brnch Mgr
EMP: 2
SALES (corp-wide): 88.98MM Privately Held
Web: www.gypsumexpress.com
SIC: 3537 Trucks: freight, baggage, etc.: industrial, except mining
PA: Gypsum Express Ltd.
8280 Sixty Rd
Baldwinsville NY 13027
315 638-2201

(G-14909)
OLD PATHS TRACT SOCIETY INC
Also Called: OLD PATHS TRACT SOCIETY
11298 Old Paths Ln (47581)
PHONE..................812 247-2560
Kenneth Montgomery, Pr
Stanley Montgomery, VP
Jerald Montgomery, Sec
EMP: 8 EST: 1937
SQ FT: 12,800
SALES (est): 700.17K Privately Held
Web: www.holinessmovement.org
SIC: 8661 2731 Nonchurch religious organizations; Pamphlets: publishing and printing

(G-14910)
PROFORM FINISHING PRODUCTS LLC
Also Called: National Gypsum Co
9720 Us Highway 50 (47581-7260)
PHONE..................812 247-2424
Charles Newell, Brnch Mgr
EMP: 52
SALES (corp-wide): 795.88MM Privately Held
Web: www.nationalgypsum.com
SIC: 3275 Wallboard, gypsum
HQ: Proform Finishing Products, Llc
2001 Rexford Rd
Charlotte NC 28211

(G-14911)
SHOALS NEWS
311 High St (47581-5502)
P.O. Box 240 (47581-0240)
PHONE..................812 247-2828
Stephen Deckard, Owner
EMP: 2 EST: 1888
SQ FT: 1,875
SALES (est): 167.09K Privately Held
Web: www.theshoalsnews.com
SIC: 2711 Newspapers: publishing only, not printed on site

(G-14912)
TEDROWS WOOD PRODUCTS INC
7910 Coal Hollow Rd (47581-7334)
P.O. Box 561 (47581-0561)
PHONE..................812 247-2260
Mark Tedrow, VP
Brian Tedrow, Treas
Bob Tedrow, Sec
EMP: 10 EST: 1979
SQ FT: 7,500
SALES (est): 874.67K Privately Held
SIC: 2426 Furniture dimension stock, hardwood

(G-14913)
UNITED STATES GYPSUM COMPANY
8754 E State Road 450 (47581-7552)
P.O. Box 1377 (47581-1377)
PHONE..................812 388-6866
Pat Mcfarland, Prin
EMP: 29
SALES (corp-wide): 16B Privately Held
Web: www.usg.com
SIC: 3275 Gypsum products
HQ: United States Gypsum Company
550 W Adams St
Chicago IL 60661
312 606-4000

(G-14914)
UNITED STATES GYPSUM COMPANY
12802 Deep Cut Lake Rd (47581-7746)
P.O. Box 1377 (47581-1377)
PHONE..................812 247-2101
Pat Vogef, Mgr
EMP: 117
SALES (corp-wide): 16B Privately Held
Web: www.usg.com
SIC: 3275 Gypsum products
HQ: United States Gypsum Company
550 W Adams St
Chicago IL 60661
312 606-4000

(G-14915)
WHITE RIVER OUTFITTERS LLC
314 Main St (47581-5507)
P.O. Box 812 (47581-0812)
PHONE..................812 787-0921
Cody Roush, Prin
EMP: 4 EST: 2011
SALES (est): 202.07K Privately Held
Web: www.whiteriveroutfittersonline.com
SIC: 3949 Sporting and athletic goods, nec

Sidney
Kosciusko County

(G-14916)
INNOVATIVE METALWORKS LLC
106 S Main St (46562-8910)
PHONE..................260 839-0295
Justin Dobeurn, Owner
EMP: 2 EST: 2009
SALES (est): 177.96K Privately Held
SIC: 7692 Welding repair

Silver Lake
Kosciusko County

(G-14917)
BENT INDUSTRIAL SERVICES LLC
9730 S State Road 15 (46982-9132)
PHONE..................260 352-0106
Benjamin Philip Kemper, Pr
EMP: 8 EST: 2013
SALES (est): 491.4K Privately Held
SIC: 3441 Fabricated structural metal

(G-14918)
CHUCK SHANE GRAVEL LLC
7930 W State Road 114 (46982-9603)
P.O. Box 615 (46910-0615)
PHONE..................574 893-4110
EMP: 4 EST: 2018
SALES (est): 124.47K Privately Held
SIC: 1442 Construction sand and gravel

(G-14919)
COUNTRY WELDING LLC
11706 S 600 W (46982-9243)
PHONE..................260 352-2938
EMP: 2 EST: 1990
SALES (est): 205.49K Privately Held
SIC: 7692 Welding repair

(G-14920)
PAR-KAN COMPANY LLC
2915 W 900 S (46982-9300)
P.O. Box 8 (43515-0008)
PHONE..................260 352-2141
Steve Parker, CEO
David Caldwell, *
Kenneth Moudy, *
Rick Burton, *
◆ EMP: 100 EST: 1990
SQ FT: 220,000
SALES (est): 8.27MM Privately Held
Web: www.par-kan.com
SIC: 3537 3523 3443 Stands, ground servicing aircraft; Trailers and wagons, farm ; Dumpsters, garbage

(G-14921)
ROH CUSTOM CABINETRY LLC
6784 W State Road 114 Lot 21 (46982-9609)
PHONE..................260 802-1158
Ryan Harshman, Prin
EMP: 5 EST: 2017
SALES (est): 84.76K Privately Held
SIC: 2434 Wood kitchen cabinets

(G-14922)
SPEEDWAY SAND & GRAVEL INC
2896 S 1600 E (46982-8511)
PHONE..................574 893-7355
Bob Roth, Prin
EMP: 2 EST: 2012
SALES (est): 111.36K Privately Held
Web: www.speedwaycp.com
SIC: 1442 Construction sand and gravel

(G-14923)
SPLENDOR BOATS LLC
9526 S State Road 15 (46982-9131)
PHONE..................260 352-2835
EMP: 19 EST: 1964
SQ FT: 52,400
SALES (est): 2.46MM Privately Held
Web: www.splendorboats.com
SIC: 3089 3732 3714 5551 Plastics processing; Boats, fiberglass: building and repairing; Motor vehicle parts and accessories; Boat dealers

Sims
Grant County

(G-14924)
PIPE CREEK JR
6377 W 600 S (46986-9773)
PHONE..................765 922-7991
Ron Lewis, Prin
EMP: 7 EST: 2008
SALES (est): 170.96K Privately Held
SIC: 1429 Crushed and broken stone, nec

Solsberry
Greene County

(G-14925)
FLYNN WELDING & INSPECTION LLC
Also Called: Welding Insptn Cnslting Trning
9405 N Newark Rd (47459-7193)
PHONE..................812 327-7437
Bennie Flynn, Prin
EMP: 1 EST: 2007
SQ FT: 720
SALES (est): 69.21K Privately Held
Web: www.hangtimewakewear.com
SIC: 7692 8734 Welding repair; Testing laboratories

(G-14926)
KIRBY TOOL AND DIE INC
2716 N Pierce Dr (47459-6037)
PHONE..................812 369-7779
EMP: 2 EST: 2011
SALES (est): 120.98K Privately Held
SIC: 3441 Fabricated structural metal

South Bend
St. Joseph County

(G-14927)
3BTECH INC
Also Called: 3b Tech Computers
3431 William Richardson Dr Ste B (46628-9477)
PHONE..................574 233-0508
Jianqing Zhu, Pr
Johnny Zhu, CEO
▲ EMP: 20 EST: 2000
SQ FT: 58,000
SALES (est): 4.89MM Privately Held
Web: www.perfectdomain.com
SIC: 5734 3571 Computer and software stores; Electronic computers

(G-14928)
A J KAY CO
4604 S Burnett Dr (46614-3822)
PHONE..................224 475-0370
Paul Kiscellus, Pr
John Kiscellus, VP
EMP: 11 EST: 1963
SALES (est): 478.27K Privately Held
Web: www.ajkayco.com
SIC: 3493 3496 3495 3452 Cold formed springs; Miscellaneous fabricated wire products; Wire springs; Bolts, nuts, rivets, and washers

(G-14929)
A&J CONSTRUCTION HM RMDLG LLC ✪
1251 N Eddy St (46617-1479)
PHONE..................574 514-5127
EMP: 1 EST: 2022
SALES (est): 158.63K Privately Held
Web: ajconstructionco.business.site
SIC: 1389 Construction, repair, and dismantling services

(G-14930)
A-1 DOOR SPECIALTIES INC
630 E Bronson St Ste 1 (46601-3231)
PHONE..................260 749-1635

South Bend - St. Joseph County (G-14931)

Shawn Rafferty, *Mgr*
EMP: 2
SALES (corp-wide): 1.72MM **Privately Held**
Web: www.a-1door.com
SIC: 1751 5211 3429 Garage door, installation or erection; Door and window products; Door locks, bolts, and checks
PA: A-1 Door Specialties Inc
2216 Wayne Haven St Ste A
Fort Wayne IN 46803
260 749-1635

(G-14931)
AAA TOOL AND DIE COMPANY INC (PA)
25101 Cleveland Rd (46628-9734)
PHONE.............................574 246-1222
John Shirrell, *Pr*
Susanne Shirrell, *Sec*
EMP: 17 **EST:** 1961
SQ FT: 20,000
SALES (est): 1.66MM
SALES (corp-wide): 1.66MM **Privately Held**
SIC: 3544 Special dies and tools

(G-14932)
ABBOTT INDUSTRIAL SEWING LLC
1044 Eclipse Pl (46628-1955)
PHONE.............................574 383-1588
Tim Abbott, *Managing Member*
EMP: 1 **EST:** 2018
SALES (est): 69.5K **Privately Held**
SIC: 2337 2321 Women's and misses' suits and coats; Men's and boy's furnishings

(G-14933)
ABRO INDUSTRIES INC (PA)
Also Called: Abro
3580 Blackthorn Ct (46628)
P.O. Box 1174 (46624)
PHONE.............................574 232-8289
Peter F Baranay, *CEO*
Nancy N Baranay, *Sec*
William Mansfield, *Dir*
◆ **EMP:** 24 **EST:** 1977
SQ FT: 14,000
SALES (est): 23.07MM
SALES (corp-wide): 23.07MM **Privately Held**
Web: www.abro.com
SIC: 5085 5099 5013 3563 Adhesives, tape and plasters; Fire extinguishers; Motor vehicle supplies and new parts; Air and gas compressors

(G-14934)
ABTREX INDUSTRIES INC (PA)
59640 Market St (46614-4021)
PHONE.............................734 728-0550
▲ **EMP:** 16 **EST:** 1968
SALES (est): 18.42MM
SALES (corp-wide): 18.42MM **Privately Held**
Web: www.abtrex.com
SIC: 3443 3088 3081 2891 Tanks, standard or custom fabricated: metal plate; Plastics plumbing fixtures; Unsupported plastics film and sheet; Adhesives and sealants

(G-14935)
ACTION MACHINE INC
1847 Prairie Ave (46613-1444)
PHONE.............................574 287-9650
Roger Klinedinst, *Pr*
Terry Munger, *VP*
Tim Klinedinst, *Prin*
Todd Klinedinst, *Prin*
▲ **EMP:** 16 **EST:** 1947
SQ FT: 12,000

SALES (est): 2.44MM **Privately Held**
Web: www.actionmachineinc.com
SIC: 3599 5013 3714 Machine shop, jobbing and repair; Automotive supplies and parts; Motor vehicle parts and accessories

(G-14936)
ADVANTAGE MANUFACTURING INC
1385 N Bendix Dr (46628-2855)
PHONE.............................773 626-2200
Andrew Radziwonski, *Pr*
Chris Halat, *Mgr*
▲ **EMP:** 15 **EST:** 2000
SALES (est): 587.47K **Privately Held**
Web: www.advantagemfg.biz
SIC: 3442 Window and door frames

(G-14937)
AGALITE SEATTLE
1126 S Lafayette Blvd (46601-3328)
PHONE.............................800 269-8343
EMP: 45
SALES (corp-wide): 459.48K **Privately Held**
Web: www.agalite.com
SIC: 2392 Shower curtains: made from purchased materials
PA: Agalite Seattle
17830 W Valley Hwy
Tukwila WA 98188
425 656-2626

(G-14938)
ALPHA BAKING CO INC
Also Called: Kreamo Bakers
1133 S Main St (46601)
PHONE.............................574 234-0188
Larry K Mitchell, *Mgr*
EMP: 1
SALES (corp-wide): 323.59MM **Privately Held**
Web: www.alphabaking.com
SIC: 2051 4225 Bakery: wholesale or wholesale/retail combined; General warehousing and storage
PA: Alpha Baking Co., Inc.
5001 W Polk St
Chicago IL 60639
773 261-6000

(G-14939)
ALTA EQUIPMENT HOLDINGS INC
3502 W Mcgill St (46628-4351)
PHONE.............................269 578-3182
EMP: 2
SALES (corp-wide): 1.88B **Publicly Held**
Web: www.altg.com
SIC: 3537 Industrial trucks and tractors
HQ: Alta Equipment Holdings, Inc.
13211 Merriman Rd
Livonia MI 48150

(G-14940)
AM GENERAL HOLDINGS LLC
105 N Niles Ave (46617)
P.O. Box 7025 (46634)
PHONE.............................574 237-6222
Charles M Hall, *Pr*
Paul J Cafiero, *VP*
Daniel J Dell'orto, *Ex VP*
Thomas R Douglas, *Sr VP*
EMP: 1021 **EST:** 2004
SALES (est): 196.78MM
SALES (corp-wide): 3.44B **Privately Held**
Web: www.amgeneral.com
SIC: 3714 3711 8711 Motor vehicle parts and accessories; Military motor vehicle assembly; Engineering services
PA: Kps Capital Partners, Lp
1 Vanderbilt Ave Fl 52
New York NY 10017

212 338-5100

(G-14941)
AM GENERAL LLC
711 W Chippewa Ave (46614-3711)
PHONE.............................574 258-6699
James Bryant, *Manager*
EMP: 1
SQ FT: 185,000
SALES (corp-wide): 3.44B **Privately Held**
Web: www.amgeneral.com
SIC: 3711 3714 Military motor vehicle assembly; Motor vehicle parts and accessories
HQ: Am General Llc
105 N Niles Ave
South Bend IN 46617
574 237-6222

(G-14942)
AM GENERAL LLC (HQ)
Also Called: AM General
105 N Niles Ave (46617)
P.O. Box 7025 (46634)
PHONE.............................574 237-6222
◆ **EMP:** 80 **EST:** 1991
SALES (est): 161.92MM
SALES (corp-wide): 3.44B **Privately Held**
Web: www.amgeneral.com
SIC: 3711 3714 8711 Military motor vehicle assembly; Motor vehicle parts and accessories; Engineering services
PA: Kps Capital Partners, Lp
1 Vanderbilt Ave Fl 52
New York NY 10017
212 338-5100

(G-14943)
AMERICAN BOTTLING COMPANY
4610 S Burnett Dr (46614-3822)
PHONE.............................574 291-9000
Bob Shannon, *Mgr*
EMP: 87
SQ FT: 6,000
Web: www.keurigdrpepper.com
SIC: 5149 2086 Soft drinks; Bottled and canned soft drinks
HQ: The American Bottling Company
6425 Hall Of Fame Ln
Frisco TX 75034

(G-14944)
AMERICAN SIGN DESIGN
1702 Lincoln Way W (46628-2618)
PHONE.............................574 287-4387
Angela Temple, *Owner*
EMP: 6 **EST:** 2016
SALES (est): 50.69K **Privately Held**
SIC: 3993 Signs and advertising specialties

(G-14945)
ANGELS WINGS EXPEDITED
1246 Echo Dr (46614-2142)
PHONE.............................574 339-3038
Asher Ray, *Pr*
EMP: 10 **EST:** 2015
SALES (est): 579.69K **Privately Held**
SIC: 3715 Truck trailers

(G-14946)
ANITA LORRAIN LLC
52303 Emmons Rd Ste 20 (46637-4288)
PHONE.............................574 621-0531
Anita Wright, *CEO*
EMP: 1 **EST:** 2017
SALES (est): 85.01K **Privately Held**
SIC: 5621 2331 Women's clothing stores; Women's and misses' blouses and shirts

(G-14947)
APOLLO PRECISION MACHINING INC
4085 Ralph Jones Dr (46628-9465)
PHONE.............................574 271-1197
Joe Mankowski, *Pr*
EMP: 20 **EST:** 1985
SQ FT: 20,000
SALES (est): 1.96MM **Privately Held**
Web: www.apollopm.com
SIC: 3599 Machine shop, jobbing and repair

(G-14948)
APOLLO PRTG & GRAPHICS CTR INC
731 S Michigan St (46601-3101)
PHONE.............................574 287-3707
Gus Koucouthakis Junior, *Pr*
Janet Koucouthakis, *VP*
EMP: 20 **EST:** 1982
SQ FT: 12,000
SALES (est): 2.48MM **Privately Held**
Web: www.apolloprinting.com
SIC: 2759 Letterpress printing

(G-14949)
AROUND CAMPUS LLC
319 Lamonte Ter (46616-1316)
PHONE.............................574 360-6571
Patricia A Kepschull, *Prin*
EMP: 2 **EST:** 2010
SALES (est): 160.52K **Privately Held**
Web: www.aroundthecampusllc.com
SIC: 3648 Decorative area lighting fixtures

(G-14950)
ASTAR INC
645 Wilber St (46628-2358)
P.O. Box 3566 (46619-0566)
PHONE.............................574 234-2137
EMP: 6 **EST:** 2019
SALES (est): 241.32K **Privately Held**
Web: www.astarinc.net
SIC: 3089 Injection molding of plastics

(G-14951)
AUNALYTICS INC (PA)
460 Stull St Ste 100 (46601-3311)
PHONE.............................574 307-9230
Nitesh Chawla, *Pr*
Tracy D Graham, *CFO*
Dave Cieslak, *COO*
EMP: 52 **EST:** 2011
SALES (est): 20.76MM
SALES (corp-wide): 20.76MM **Privately Held**
Web: www.aunalytics.com
SIC: 7371 7372 7374 8748 Computer software systems analysis and design, custom; Business oriented computer software; Data processing and preparation; Business consulting, nec

(G-14952)
AUTO EXTRAS INC
1002 S Lafayette Blvd (46601-3313)
PHONE.............................574 855-2370
James Cretacci, *Prin*
EMP: 9 **EST:** 2010
SALES (est): 240.73K **Privately Held**
Web: www.autoextrasinc.com
SIC: 3465 Body parts, automobile: stamped metal

(G-14953)
AUTOSEM INC
1701 S Main St (46613-2211)
PHONE.............................574 288-8866
Terri Califano, *Pr*
▲ **EMP:** 32 **EST:** 1992

GEOGRAPHIC SECTION
South Bend - St. Joseph County (G-14978)

SQ FT: 30,000
SALES (est): 653.9K **Privately Held**
Web: www.autosem.com
SIC: 3679 3674 Electronic circuits; Semiconductors and related devices

(G-14954)
BAMAR PLASTICS INC
1702 Robinson St (46613-3490)
PHONE.....................574 234-4066
Barry A Lee, *Pr*
James Mcvay, *General Vice President*
EMP: 30 EST: 1978
SQ FT: 35,000
SALES (est): 4.52MM **Privately Held**
Web: www.bamarplastics.com
SIC: 3089 Injection molding of plastics

(G-14955)
BANTAM INC
1822 S Bend Ave (46637-5636)
PHONE.....................574 387-3890
EMP: 8 EST: 2020
SALES (est): 350.33K **Privately Held**
SIC: 2092 Fresh or frozen packaged fish

(G-14956)
BARRY SEAT COVER & AUTO GL CO
1924 S Michigan St (46613-2398)
PHONE.....................574 288-4603
Greg Barth, *Pr*
Gary Barth, *VP*
EMP: 11 EST: 1945
SALES (est): 425.42K **Privately Held**
Web: www.barryseat.com
SIC: 7532 7536 7538 3714 Upholstery and trim shop, automotive; Automotive glass replacement shops; General automotive repair shops; Motor vehicle parts and accessories

(G-14957)
BERTRAND PRODUCTS INC
2323 Foundation Dr (46628)
P.O. Box 3786 (46619)
PHONE.....................574 234-4181
B J Bonin, *Pr*
Deborah Bonin, *
EMP: 30 EST: 1953
SQ FT: 44,000
SALES (est): 5.3MM **Privately Held**
Web: www.bertrandproducts.com
SIC: 3599 Machine and other job shop work

(G-14958)
BEST ONE TIRE & SVC S BEND INC
4411 Quality Dr (46628-9732)
PHONE.....................574 246-4021
Jeremy Pollyea, *Pr*
Paul Zurcher, *Prin*
EMP: 3 EST: 2009
SALES (est): 895.06K **Privately Held**
Web: www.bestonesb.com
SIC: 5531 7534 Automotive tires; Tire retreading and repair shops

(G-14959)
BLUDOT INC
4335 Meghan Beeler Ct (46628-8416)
PHONE.....................574 277-2306
Patrick Turley, *Pr*
Andrew Caine, *VP Fin*
✪ EMP: 6 EST: 1975
SQ FT: 17,900
SALES (est): 988.68K **Privately Held**
Web: www.bludotinc.com
SIC: 3714 3568 Motor vehicle brake systems and parts; Power transmission equipment, nec

(G-14960)
BMK INVESTMENTS INC
Also Called: Bmk Printing
3615 W Mcgill St (46628-4370)
P.O. Box 1510 (46563-5510)
PHONE.....................574 282-2538
James A Azzar, *Pr*
Michael Azzar, *Treas*
EMP: 4 EST: 1988
SQ FT: 20,000
SALES (est): 406.04K
SALES (corp-wide): 25.8MM **Privately Held**
SIC: 2621 Wrapping and packaging papers
PA: Bomarko, Inc.
 1955 N Oak Dr
 Plymouth IN 46563
 574 936-9901

(G-14961)
BRANCH EXPRESS TRUCKING LLC
1149 Wilber St (46628-2638)
PHONE.....................574 807-2212
EMP: 5 EST: 2021
SALES (est): 202.26K **Privately Held**
SIC: 3731 Commercial cargo ships, building and repairing

(G-14962)
BRITER PRODUCTS INC
1901 N Bendix Dr (46628-1603)
PHONE.....................574 386-8167
Babulal Lalwani, *CEO*
Avanti Lalwani, *Sr VP*
EMP: 5 EST: 2016
SALES (est): 435.05K **Privately Held**
Web: www.briterproducts.com
SIC: 3499 Metal ladders

(G-14963)
BWT LLC
802 Fellows St (46601-3121)
PHONE.....................574 232-3338
EMP: 14
Web: www.bwtlogistics.com
SIC: 3398 Metal heat treating
HQ: Bwt Llc
 201 Brkfeld Pkwy Ste 102
 Greenville SC 29607

(G-14964)
C E M PRINTING & SPECIALITIES
50750 Marie Ct (46637-2317)
PHONE.....................269 684-6898
Edward Mollis, *Pr*
Charles Mollis, *VP*
EMP: 2 EST: 2004
SALES (est): 127.29K **Privately Held**
Web: www.cemspecialties.com
SIC: 7389 2759 Printing broker; Commercial printing, nec

(G-14965)
C M GRINDING INCORPORATED
55643 Fairview Ave (46628-1199)
PHONE.....................574 234-6812
Calvis Mayfield, *Pr*
Adrienne Mayfield, *Sec*
EMP: 10 EST: 1983
SQ FT: 6,500
SALES (est): 910.99K **Privately Held**
Web: www.cmgrinding.com
SIC: 3599 Machine shop, jobbing and repair

(G-14966)
CARDBOARD APOTHECARY
60215 Emerald Dr (46614-5203)
PHONE.....................574 309-3007
Errol Pal, *Prin*
EMP: 6 EST: 2018
SALES (est): 90.74K **Privately Held**
SIC: 2631 Cardboard

(G-14967)
CARLETON INC (PA)
Also Called: Financial Publishing Div
1251 N Eddy St Ste 202 (46617-1478)
P.O. Box 570 (46624-0570)
PHONE.....................574 855-3180
Patrick Ruszkowski, *Pr*
Suzanne Ruszkowski, *
EMP: 27 EST: 1968
SQ FT: 15,000
SALES (est): 4.22MM **Privately Held**
Web: www.carletoninc.com
SIC: 7372 Business oriented computer software

(G-14968)
CBIZZE LLC
1709 Pulaski St (46613-1408)
P.O. Box 1011 (85311-1011)
PHONE.....................623 204-9782
Claudine Huddleston, *Prin*
EMP: 1 EST: 2020
SALES (est): 69.95K **Privately Held**
SIC: 5999 1389 1799 5039 Miscellaneous retail stores, nec; Construction, repair, and dismantling services; Construction site cleanup; Air ducts, sheet metal

(G-14969)
CENTRAL COCA-COLA BTLG CO INC
Also Called: Coca-Cola
1400 W Ireland Rd (46614)
PHONE.....................574 291-1511
TOLL FREE: 800
EMP: 40
SALES (corp-wide): 45.75B **Publicly Held**
Web: www.coca-cola.com
SIC: 2086 Bottled and canned soft drinks
HQ: Central Coca-Cola Bottling Company, Inc.
 555 Taxter Rd Ste 550
 Elmsford NY 10523
 914 789-1100

(G-14970)
CENTRAL STATES FABRICATING
3015 N Kenmore St (46628-4307)
PHONE.....................574 288-5607
Michael Cocanower, *Pr*
Clyde Cocanower, *VP*
Ellen Cocanower, *Sec*
EMP: 14 EST: 1972
SQ FT: 18,000
SALES (est): 1.91MM **Privately Held**
Web: www.centralstatesfab.com
SIC: 3441 3599 Fabricated structural metal; Machine shop, jobbing and repair

(G-14971)
CHASE PLASTIC SERVICES INC
5245 Dylan Dr (46628-6501)
PHONE.....................574 239-4090
EMP: 7
Web: www.chaseplastics.com
SIC: 2821 Plastics materials and resins
PA: Chase Plastic Services, Inc.
 6467 Waldon Center Dr # 200
 Clarkston MI 48346

(G-14972)
CHRIST PACKING SYSTEMS CORP
316 S Eddy St (46617-3202)
PHONE.....................574 243-9110
EMP: 3 EST: 1987
SALES (est): 402.25K **Privately Held**
Web: www.christ-ps.com
SIC: 3565 Packaging machinery

(G-14973)
CITY SOUTH BEND BUILDING CORP
Also Called: Central Services Print Shop
1045 W Sample St (46619-3827)
PHONE.....................574 235-9977
EMP: 5 EST: 2011
SALES (est): 990.54K **Privately Held**
Web: www.southbendin.gov
SIC: 2752 Commercial printing, lithographic

(G-14974)
CLAEYS CANDY INC
5229 Nimtz Pkwy (46628)
P.O. Box 1535 (46634-1535)
PHONE.....................574 287-1818
Gregg Claeys, *Pr*
Brian Machalleck, *VP*
Donald H Claeys, *VP*
Michael Machalleck, *Sec*
EMP: 19 EST: 1919
SQ FT: 40,000
SALES (est): 3.85MM **Privately Held**
Web: www.claeyscandy.com
SIC: 2064 2066 Candy and other confectionery products; Chocolate

(G-14975)
CLAYMORE TOOLS INC
5501 Abshire Dr (46614-6009)
PHONE.....................574 255-6483
David Adamson, *Pr*
Isobel Adamson, *Treas*
Ray Lada, *Sec*
EMP: 9 EST: 1980
SALES (est): 740K **Privately Held**
SIC: 3544 3541 3546 3545 Special dies and tools; Machine tools, metal cutting: exotic (explosive, etc.); Power-driven handtools; Machine tool accessories

(G-14976)
CLEAN-SEAL INC
20900 Ireland Rd (46614-3823)
P.O. Box 2919 (46680-2919)
PHONE.....................574 299-1888
Ronald Moore, *Pr*
Chris Moore, *
Bill Dawson, *
Apryl Turczynski, *
EMP: 48 EST: 1978
SQ FT: 90,000
SALES (est): 9.41MM **Privately Held**
Web: www.cleanseal.com
SIC: 3052 5085 Hose, pneumatic: rubber or rubberized fabric, nec; Gaskets and seals

(G-14977)
CLP TOWNE INC
Also Called: Towne Air Freight
24805 Us Highway 20 (46628-5911)
PHONE.....................574 233-3183
Ed Murphy, *Mgr*
EMP: 8
SALES (corp-wide): 1.37B **Publicly Held**
SIC: 3537 Trucks: freight, baggage, etc.: industrial, except mining
HQ: Clp Towne Inc.
 24805 Us Highway 20
 South Bend IN 46628
 574 233-3183

(G-14978)
COCA-COLA ENTERPRISES
Also Called: Coca-Cola
1700 W Ireland Rd (46614-3933)
PHONE.....................574 291-1511
EMP: 8 EST: 2019
SALES (est): 466.52K **Privately Held**
Web: www.coca-colacompany.com
SIC: 2086 Bottled and canned soft drinks

South Bend - St. Joseph County (G-14979)

GEOGRAPHIC SECTION

(G-14979)
COLLIERS GLASSBLOCK INC
Also Called: Collier's Glass Block Windows
824 Park Ave (46616-1338)
PHONE.....................574 288-8682
Casey Collier, *Pr*
Susann Collier, *Sec*
EMP: 3 **EST:** 1986
SALES (est): 208.04K **Privately Held**
Web: www.colliersglassblock.com
SIC: 3229 Blocks and bricks, glass

(G-14980)
COMAN PUBLISHING COMPANY
54377 30th St (46635-2002)
PHONE.....................574 255-9800
EMP: 5 **EST:** 2018
SALES (est): 91.29K **Privately Held**
Web: www.comanpub.com
SIC: 2741 Miscellaneous publishing

(G-14981)
CONRAD SB LLC
2025 S William St (46613-2140)
PHONE.....................574 213-3743
EMP: 1 **EST:** 2019
SALES (est): 60K **Privately Held**
SIC: 3519 Parts and accessories, internal combustion engines

(G-14982)
CONTAINER SERVICE CORP
2811 Viridian Dr (46628-4360)
PHONE.....................574 232-7474
Michael D Harrison, *Pr*
Deborah Harrison, *
EMP: 68 **EST:** 1966
SQ FT: 100,000
SALES (est): 7.61MM **Privately Held**
Web: www.containerservicecorp.com
SIC: 2653 Boxes, corrugated: made from purchased materials

(G-14983)
CONTINENTAL CARBONIC PDTS INC
4075 Ralph Jones Dr (46628-9465)
PHONE.....................574 273-2800
EMP: 2
Web: www.continentalcarbonic.com
SIC: 2813 5169 Dry ice, carbon dioxide (solid); Dry ice
HQ: Continental Carbonic Products, Inc.
3985 E Harrison Ave
Decatur IL 62526
217 428-2068

(G-14984)
CPR MACHINING LLC
4520 S Burnett Dr (46614-3820)
PHONE.....................574 299-0222
Thomas Cleveland, *Pt*
EMP: 23 **EST:** 2019
SALES (est): 1.2MM **Privately Held**
SIC: 3545 3599 3541 Precision tools, machinists'; Machine shop, jobbing and repair; Lathes, metal cutting and polishing

(G-14985)
CROSSROADS SOLAR ENTPS LLC
251 E Sample St Ste 100 (46601-3446)
PHONE.....................607 759-1058
Patrick Regan, *Pr*
EMP: 10 **EST:** 2019
SALES (est): 882.4K **Privately Held**
Web: www.crossroads-solar.com
SIC: 3433 Solar heaters and collectors

(G-14986)
CSPINE INC
3501 Miller Dr (46634)
PHONE.....................574 936-7893
Charles Schnekenburger, *Pr*
Troy Walters, *VP*
EMP: 5 **EST:** 2005
SQ FT: 4,200
SALES (est): 654.35K
SALES (corp-wide): 5.81MM **Privately Held**
SIC: 3841 Surgical and medical instruments
PA: Wishbone Medical, Inc.
100 Capital Dr
Warsaw IN 46582
574 306-4006

(G-14987)
CUBED LABORATORIES LLC
1162 E Lasalle Ave (46617-3322)
PHONE.....................866 935-6165
Bruce Brock, *Managing Member*
Leslie T Ivie, *Pt*
EMP: 5 **EST:** 2008
SALES (est): 372.76K **Privately Held**
SIC: 3826 Analytical instruments

(G-14988)
CUPPRINT LLC
635 S Lafayette Blvd Ste Aa (46601)
P.O. Box 181 (46556-0181)
PHONE.....................574 323-5250
EMP: 11 **EST:** 2015
SALES (est): 843.48K
SALES (corp-wide): 4.53B **Privately Held**
Web: us.cupprint.com
SIC: 2741 Business service newsletters: publishing and printing
PA: Huhtamaki Oyj
Revontulenkuja 1
Espoo 02100
106867000

(G-14989)
CURTIS PRODUCTS INC
722 Carroll St (46601-3111)
PHONE.....................574 289-4891
EMP: 155
SALES (corp-wide): 22.54MM **Privately Held**
Web: www.curtisproducts.com
SIC: 3498 Fabricated pipe and fittings
PA: Curtis Products Inc
401 N Bendix Dr
South Bend IN 46628
574 289-4891

(G-14990)
CURTIS PRODUCTS INC (PA)
401 N Bendix Dr (46628-1744)
PHONE.....................574 289-4891
John Heckaman, *Admn*
David Fheckaman, *
John R Heckaman, *
Andrew Heckaman, *
EMP: 45 **EST:** 1959
SQ FT: 180,000
SALES (est): 22.54MM
SALES (corp-wide): 22.54MM **Privately Held**
Web: www.curtisproducts.com
SIC: 3498 Tube fabricating (contract bending and shaping)

(G-14991)
CUSTOM HONING INC
24840 Us Highway 20 (46628-5912)
PHONE.....................574 233-2846
Stephen P Keller, *Pr*
EMP: 9 **EST:** 1987
SQ FT: 23,000
SALES (est): 977.68K **Privately Held**
Web: www.customhoning.com

SIC: 3599 Machine shop, jobbing and repair

(G-14992)
CUSTOM MACHINE MFR LLC
4111 Technology Dr (46628-9751)
PHONE.....................574 251-0292
◆ **EMP:** 42 **EST:** 1999
SQ FT: 35,000
SALES (est): 4.71MM **Privately Held**
Web: www.machinemotion.com
SIC: 3599 Machine shop, jobbing and repair

(G-14993)
CUSTOM MCH MOTIONEERING INC
4111 Technology Dr (46628-9751)
PHONE.....................574 251-0292
Steve Johnson, *Pr*
Shawn Lewis, *
EMP: 32 **EST:** 2009
SALES (est): 2.71MM **Privately Held**
Web: www.cmmbuilt.com
SIC: 3599 Custom machinery

(G-14994)
CUSTOM MILLWORK & DISPLAY INC
2102 W Washington St Ste 1 (46628-2001)
PHONE.....................574 289-4000
Jerrel Mead, *Pr*
Joe Welker, *VP*
David Welker, *Treas*
Kelle Welker, *Sec*
EMP: 10 **EST:** 2005
SALES (est): 455.65K **Privately Held**
Web: www.custommillworkdisplay.net
SIC: 2431 Millwork

(G-14995)
DALES GOODYEAR TIRE & SERVICE
Also Called: Dale's Auto Service
50942 Indiana State Route 933 (46637-2056)
PHONE.....................574 272-3779
Dale Lowery, *Owner*
EMP: 4 **EST:** 1989
SALES (est): 370.78K **Privately Held**
SIC: 5531 7534 Automotive tires; Tire repair shop

(G-14996)
DELUXE DETAIL LLC
1509 Berkshire Dr (46614-6021)
PHONE.....................574 292-8968
Randy Stephen Moore, *Prin*
EMP: 7 **EST:** 2019
SALES (est): 246.59K **Privately Held**
Web: www.deluxedetailllc.com
SIC: 2782 Blankbooks and looseleaf binders

(G-14997)
DERBY INC
Also Called: Derby Industries
24350 State Road 23 (46614-9696)
PHONE.....................574 233-4500
David M Karafa, *CEO*
Andrew S Karafa, *
Andrew J Karafa, *
Kenneth Chrzan, *
▲ **EMP:** 65 **EST:** 1975
SQ FT: 42,000
SALES (est): 9.05MM **Privately Held**
Web: www.derbyindustries.com
SIC: 2515 3161 Mattresses, innerspring or box spring; Cases, carrying, nec

(G-14998)
DESI TECHNOLOGIES INC ✪
54608 Twyckenham Dr (46637-5526)
PHONE.....................802 488-0954
Liam Redmond, *CEO*
EMP: 3 **EST:** 2022

SALES (est): 62.01K **Privately Held**
SIC: 7372 Prepackaged software

(G-14999)
DIENEN INC (PA)
17530 Dugdale Dr (46635-1583)
PHONE.....................574 233-3352
Bernie Veldman, *CEO*
EMP: 206 **EST:** 2011
SALES (est): 25.64MM
SALES (corp-wide): 25.64MM **Privately Held**
Web: www.surestep.net
SIC: 3842 Surgical appliances and supplies

(G-15000)
DIVA THIS DIVA THAT INC
1251 N Eddy St (46617-1479)
PHONE.....................219 533-0077
Stephanie Edwards, *Pr*
EMP: 5 **EST:** 1998
SALES (est): 250K **Privately Held**
Web: www.divathisdivathat.com
SIC: 2741 Music, book: publishing only, not printed on site

(G-15001)
DKL TOOL & MANUFACTURING LLC
25855 Northwood Dr (46619-9559)
PHONE.....................574 289-2291
David Lauver, *Owner*
EMP: 1 **EST:** 1976
SALES (est): 98K **Privately Held**
SIC: 5251 3599 Tools; Machine shop, jobbing and repair

(G-15002)
DLICOUS DSSERTS BY DEEDEE LLC
411 S Taylor St (46601-2741)
PHONE.....................317 515-1858
EMP: 1
SALES (est): 39.59K **Privately Held**
SIC: 2051 Cakes, bakery: except frozen

(G-15003)
DOCKSIDE
1835 Lincoln Way E (46613-3422)
PHONE.....................574 400-0848
Jason Gobokowiecze, *Pr*
EMP: 6 **EST:** 2015
SALES (est): 136.49K **Privately Held**
Web: www.docksidenightclub.com
SIC: 2082 Malt beverages

(G-15004)
DOMS FROYO LLC
560 W Ireland Rd Ste 1 (46614-3804)
PHONE.....................574 855-1120
Dominic Don Archuleta, *Managing Member*
EMP: 16 **EST:** 2021
SALES (est): 859.75K **Privately Held**
SIC: 2024 Ice cream and frozen deserts

(G-15005)
DR PEPPER SNAPPLE GROUP
Also Called: Dr Pepper
4610 S Burnett Dr (46614-3822)
PHONE.....................574 291-9000
Bob Shannon, *Mgr*
EMP: 6 **EST:** 2018
SALES (est): 213.81K **Privately Held**
Web: www.keurigdrpepper.com
SIC: 2086 Soft drinks: packaged in cans, bottles, etc.

(G-15006)
DURAMOLD CASTINGS INC
Also Called: Duramold
1901 N Bendix Dr (46628-1603)
P.O. Box 424 (46546-0424)

GEOGRAPHIC SECTION — South Bend - St. Joseph County (G-15031)

PHONE..................574 251-1111
Bob A Lalwani, *Pr*
K B Lalwani, *
▲ EMP: 25 EST: 1945
SQ FT: 8,800
SALES (est): 2.34MM **Privately Held**
Web: www.duramoldinc.com
SIC: 3366 Copper foundries

(G-15007)
DWYER INSTRUMENTS INC
Also Called: Dwyer Instruments Inc
1440 Ignition Dr (46601-2900)
PHONE..................574 234-6853
EMP: 1
SALES (corp-wide): 653.43MM **Privately Held**
Web: intl.dwyer-inst.com
SIC: 3823 Process control instruments
HQ: Dwyer Instruments, Llc
102 Indiana Hwy 212
Michigan City IN 46360
219 879-8868

(G-15008)
DWYER INSTRUMENTS INC
Also Called: DWYER INSTRUMENTS INC
6850 Enterprise Dr (46628-8474)
PHONE..................219 879-8868
EMP: 4
SALES (corp-wide): 653.43MM **Privately Held**
Web: intl.dwyer-inst.com
SIC: 3823 Process control instruments
HQ: Dwyer Instruments, Llc
102 Indiana Hwy 212
Michigan City IN 46360
219 879-8868

(G-15009)
EATON CORPORATION
2930 Foundation Dr (46628-4337)
PHONE..................574 283-5004
Bill Armstrong, *Brnch Mgr*
EMP: 46
Web: www.dix-eaton.com
SIC: 3625 Motor controls and accessories
HQ: Eaton Corporation
1000 Eaton Blvd
Cleveland OH 44122
440 523-5000

(G-15010)
ECO OWL PRESS LLC ✪
626 Portage Ave (46616-1355)
PHONE..................574 703-3941
Cassidy Rain Fowler, *CEO*
EMP: 4 EST: 2022
SALES (est): 78.75K **Privately Held**
Web: www.ecoowlpress.com
SIC: 2741 Miscellaneous publishing

(G-15011)
ED STUMP ASSEMBLY INC
Also Called: E S A I
60856 Us 31 S (46614-5190)
PHONE..................574 291-0058
Edward Stump, *Pr*
Sherry Stump, *Sec*
EMP: 2 EST: 1962
SQ FT: 1,500
SALES (est): 126.67K **Privately Held**
SIC: 3911 Jewelry, precious metal

(G-15012)
EM BLACK OXIDE
3702 W Sample St Ste 4052 (46619-2963)
PHONE..................574 233-4933
Kaginielg Tenddrenda, *Owner*
EMP: 2 EST: 2005
SALES (est): 157.14K **Privately Held**
SIC: 3471 Finishing, metals or formed products

(G-15013)
EMINENCE HLTH CARE STFFING AGC
2015 W Western Ave Ste 201 (46619)
PHONE..................866 350-6400
Heidi Brown, *CEO*
EMP: 2 EST: 2018
SALES (est): 145.64K **Privately Held**
SIC: 7389 8099 7361 8734 Notary publics; Health and allied services, nec; Employment agencies; Testing laboratories

(G-15014)
ENDEAVOR MACHINED PRODUCTS INC
1705 N Bendix Dr (46628-1601)
PHONE..................574 232-1940
James Duszynski, *Pr*
Terry Sulich, *VP*
Martin Mitchell, *VP*
EMP: 6 EST: 2009
SALES (est): 741.92K **Privately Held**
Web: www.winndeavor.com
SIC: 3599 Machine shop, jobbing and repair

(G-15015)
ENGEL MANUFACTURING CO INC
Also Called: Engel Manufacturing
411 W Indiana Ave (46613-2017)
PHONE..................574 232-3800
Stephen J Engel, *Pr*
EMP: 30 EST: 1985
SQ FT: 1,500
SALES (est): 1.73MM **Privately Held**
Web: www.engelmfg.com
SIC: 3599 3369 3365 Machine shop, jobbing and repair; Aerospace castings, nonferrous: except aluminum; Aerospace castings, aluminum

(G-15016)
ENVIRONMENTAL TECHNOLOGY INC
Also Called: Environment Tech of Fort Wayne
1850 N Sheridan St (46628-1525)
PHONE..................574 233-1202
Thad M Jones, *Pr*
EMP: 26 EST: 1969
SQ FT: 35,000
SALES (est): 4.81MM **Privately Held**
Web: www.networketi.com
SIC: 3823 3674 3625 3577 Temperature measurement instruments, industrial; Semiconductors and related devices; Relays and industrial controls; Computer peripheral equipment, nec

(G-15017)
ENYART ELECTRIC MOTOR REPR INC
1313 Prairie Ave (46613-1603)
PHONE..................574 288-4731
Rich Siri, *Pr*
Kith Walorsai, *VP*
EMP: 8 EST: 1965
SQ FT: 3,500
SALES (est): 963.57K **Privately Held**
Web: www.enyartelectric.com
SIC: 7694 5063 Electric motor repair; Motors, electric

(G-15018)
ESTHER REID
Also Called: Che's Da'zines and Printz
2121 Inglewood Pl (46616-2022)
P.O. Box 314 (63074-0314)
PHONE..................314 504-6659
Esther Reid, *Owner*
EMP: 5 EST: 2021
SALES (est): 156.91K **Privately Held**
SIC: 2759 Commercial printing, nec

(G-15019)
EVS LTD
24500 Research Dr (46628-5638)
P.O. Box 1363 (46624-1363)
PHONE..................574 233-5707
EMP: 15 EST: 1993
SQ FT: 6,000
SALES (est): 2.08MM **Privately Held**
Web: www.evsltd.com
SIC: 3944 Child restraint seats, automotive

(G-15020)
EXAKTIME INNOVATIONS INC
310 W South St Ste 200 (46601-2733)
PHONE..................818 222-1836
EMP: 13
SALES (corp-wide): 9.47MM **Privately Held**
Web: www.exaktime.com
SIC: 3579 Time clocks and time recording devices
PA: Exaktime Innovations, Inc.
27001 Agoura Rd Ste 280
Calabasas CA 91301
877 435-6411

(G-15021)
EXCLUSIVE FIT TRUCKING LLC
53429 Ba J Er Ln (46635-1474)
PHONE..................708 872-7593
Russell C Buckner, *CEO*
EMP: 5 EST: 2020
SALES (est): 468.2K **Privately Held**
SIC: 3537 Trucks, tractors, loaders, carriers, and similar equipment

(G-15022)
EXPRESS PRESS INDIANA INC
Also Called: Express Press 4
3505 W Mcgill St (46628-4352)
PHONE..................219 874-2223
Janet Beck, *Brnch Mgr*
EMP: 4
SALES (corp-wide): 2.29MM **Privately Held**
Web: www.express-press.com
SIC: 2752 Offset printing
PA: Express Press Of Indiana Incorporated
325 N Dixie Way
South Bend IN 46637
574 277-3355

(G-15023)
EXPRESS PRESS INDIANA INC (PA)
325 N Dixie Way (46637-3311)
PHONE..................574 277-3355
Brian Clauser, *Pr*
Mike Schaefer, *
Dave Kytta, *
EMP: 30 EST: 1977
SALES (est): 2.29MM
SALES (corp-wide): 2.29MM **Privately Held**
Web: www.express-press.com
SIC: 2752 2796 2791 2789 Offset printing; Platemaking services; Typesetting; Bookbinding and related work

(G-15024)
EXXON MOBIL CORPORATION
Also Called: Exxon
3323 Prairie Ave (46614-4312)
PHONE..................574 217-7630
EMP: 5
SALES (corp-wide): 344.58B **Publicly Held**
Web: corporate.exxonmobil.com
SIC: 2911 Petroleum refining
PA: Exxon Mobil Corporation
22777 Sprngwoods Vlg Pkwy
Spring TX 77389
972 940-6000

(G-15025)
F S G INC
222 E Walter St (46614-2641)
PHONE..................574 291-5998
Wayne Farrington, *Pr*
EMP: 3 EST: 1984
SQ FT: 3,400
SALES (est): 326.19K **Privately Held**
SIC: 3599 Machine shop, jobbing and repair

(G-15026)
FAST SIGNS
Also Called: Fastsigns
2411 Mishawaka Ave (46615-2144)
PHONE..................574 254-0545
Tom Sloma, *Owner*
EMP: 5 EST: 1999
SALES (est): 250.69K **Privately Held**
Web: www.fastsigns.com
SIC: 3993 Signs and advertising specialties

(G-15027)
FAULKENS FLOORCOVER
2045 N Meade St (46628-3154)
PHONE..................574 300-4260
EMP: 10 EST: 2010
SALES (est): 269.4K **Privately Held**
SIC: 5713 5031 2273 5023 Floor covering stores; Building materials, interior; Floor coverings, textile fiber; Floor coverings

(G-15028)
FCS INDUSTRIES INCORPORATED
4300 Quality Dr (46628-9665)
PHONE..................574 288-5150
EMP: 1 EST: 2011
SALES (est): 69.16K **Privately Held**
SIC: 3999 Manufacturing industries, nec

(G-15029)
FDC GRAPHICS FILMS INC (PA)
3820 William Richardson Dr (46628-9795)
PHONE..................800 634-7523
Judith A Eck, *Prin*
George Marsh, *
Tammie Nelson, *
▲ EMP: 21 EST: 1988
SQ FT: 45,000
SALES (est): 22.85MM **Privately Held**
Web: www.fdcfilms.com
SIC: 2824 Vinyl fibers

(G-15030)
FEDERAL PROCESS CORP
6851 Enterprise Dr (46628-8402)
PHONE..................574 288-0607
EMP: 6 EST: 2019
SALES (est): 118.64K **Privately Held**
SIC: 2891 Adhesives and sealants

(G-15031)
FEDERAL-MOGUL POWERTRAIN LLC
Also Called: Federal Mogul
3605 Cleveland Rd (46628-9779)
PHONE..................574 271-5954
Mark Tripsa, *Mgr*
EMP: 460
SALES (corp-wide): 18.04B **Privately Held**
Web: www.tenneco.com
SIC: 3053 3592 Gaskets and sealing devices; Pistons and piston rings
HQ: Federal-Mogul Powertrain Llc
15701 Technology Dr

South Bend - St. Joseph County (G-15032)

Northville MI 48168

(G-15032)
FEDERAL-MOGUL POWERTRAIN LLC
Also Called: Tenneco
5435 Dylan Dr Ste 200 (46628-7002)
PHONE....................574 272-5900
Randall Heideman, *Brnch Mgr*
EMP: 1
SALES (corp-wide): 18.04B **Privately Held**
Web: www.tenneco.com
SIC: 3462 3559 3694 3812 Automotive and internal combustion engine forgings; Degreasing machines, automotive and industrial; Automotive electrical equipment, nec; Acceleration indicators and systems components, aerospace
HQ: Federal-Mogul Powertrain Llc
15701 Technology Dr
Northville MI 48168

(G-15033)
FERGUSON EQUIPMENT INC
Also Called: Manufacturing
25170 Edison Rd (46628-5615)
PHONE....................574 234-4303
Timothy Burdue, *Pr*
Melvin Burdue, *Pr*
Sherri Burdue, *VP*
Evelyn Ferguson, *Sec*
EMP: 6 **EST:** 1965
SQ FT: 10,000
SALES (est): 696.88K **Privately Held**
Web: ferguson-equipment-inc.business.site
SIC: 3493 3542 5531 3599 Steel springs, except wire; Machine tools, metal forming type; Automotive parts; Machine and other job shop work

(G-15034)
FISERV MRTG SERVICING SYSTEMS (HQ)
Also Called: Mortgageserv
3575 Moreau Ct # 2 (46628-4401)
PHONE....................574 282-3300
Tom Glamin, *Pr*
Joan Sinnessy, *
EMP: 200 **EST:** 1972
SQ FT: 34,000
SALES (est): 7.02MM
SALES (corp-wide): 19.09B **Publicly Held**
SIC: 7374 7375 7372 8744 Data processing service; On-line data base information retrieval; Business oriented computer software; Facilities support services
PA: Fiserv, Inc.
600 N Vel R Phillips Ave
Milwaukee WI 53203
262 879-5000

(G-15035)
FISHING ABILITIES INC
22770 Adams Rd (46628-9221)
PHONE....................574 273-0842
Daniel Badur, *Prin*
EMP: 2 **EST:** 2010
SALES (est): 96.89K **Privately Held**
Web: www.fishingabilities.com
SIC: 3949 Sporting and athletic goods, nec

(G-15036)
FLORA RACING
3319 W Sample St (46619-3050)
PHONE....................574 233-0642
Jeff Flora, *Owner*
EMP: 2 **EST:** 1994
SALES (est): 164.45K **Privately Held**
Web: www.floraracing.com

SIC: 3714 Motor vehicle body components and frame

(G-15037)
FLOWERS BAKING CO OHIO LLC
1133 S Main St (46601-3337)
PHONE....................502 350-4700
Jamie Wilson, *Mgr*
EMP: 1
SALES (corp-wide): 5.09B **Publicly Held**
SIC: 2051 Bread, all types (white, wheat, rye, etc); fresh or frozen
HQ: Flowers Baking Co. Of Ohio, Llc
325 W Alexis Rd Ste 1
Toledo OH 43612
419 269-9202

(G-15038)
FRANK W MARTINEZ
54555 Pine Rd (46628-5628)
PHONE....................574 232-6081
Frank W Martinez, *Owner*
EMP: 2 **EST:** 2002
SALES (est): 210.2K **Privately Held**
SIC: 3599 Machine shop, jobbing and repair

(G-15039)
FRANKS MACHINE SHOP TOOL & DIE
24133 State Road 2 (46619-5517)
PHONE....................574 288-6899
Frank Szocs, *Owner*
EMP: 3 **EST:** 2000
SALES (est): 196.15K **Privately Held**
Web: www.franksmachininginc.com
SIC: 3599 Machine shop, jobbing and repair

(G-15040)
FYBERDYNE LABORATORIES
19644 Gilmer St (46614-5606)
P.O. Box 10115 (46680-0115)
PHONE....................574 291-9438
Edward Anders, *Owner*
EMP: 1 **EST:** 1988
SALES (est): 51.98K **Privately Held**
SIC: 3069 Reclaimed rubber (reworked by manufacturing processes)

(G-15041)
GENERAL MCH & SAW CO OF IND
Also Called: General Machine & Saw Co Ind
3636 Gagnon St (46628-4365)
PHONE....................574 232-6077
Joseph Murphy, *Pr*
EMP: 15 **EST:** 1995
SALES (est): 954.8K **Privately Held**
Web: www.gmsaw.com
SIC: 3441 Fabricated structural metal

(G-15042)
GENERAL SHEET METAL WORKS INC (PA)
Also Called: General Stamping & Metalworks
25101 Cleveland Rd (46628-9734)
PHONE....................574 288-0611
John Axelberg, *Pr*
John Ryal, *
Taylor Lewis Axelburg, *
EMP: 27 **EST:** 1922
SQ FT: 80,000
SALES (est): 23.85MM
SALES (corp-wide): 23.85MM **Privately Held**
Web: www.gsmwinc.com
SIC: 7692 3469 3444 1799 Welding repair; Metal stampings, nec; Sheet metalwork; Welding on site

(G-15043)
GENERAL TRANSMISSION PDTS LLC
105 N Niles Ave (46617-2705)
P.O. Box 7025 (46634-7025)
PHONE....................574 284-2917
EMP: 1 **EST:** 2008
SALES (est): 2.66MM
SALES (corp-wide): 3.44B **Privately Held**
Web: www.amgeneral.com
SIC: 3612 Transmission and distribution voltage regulators
HQ: Am General Llc
105 N Niles Ave
South Bend IN 46617
574 237-6222

(G-15044)
GLOBAL PARTS NETWORK LLC
5102 Dylan Dr (46628-6503)
PHONE....................574 855-5000
Susan Joyce, *Brnch Mgr*
EMP: 1
Web: www.globalpartsnetwork.com
SIC: 3799 5084 Trailers and trailer equipment; Engines and transportation equipment
HQ: Global Parts Network, Llc
760 Myrtle Dr Ste F
Crystal Lake IL 60014

(G-15045)
GOENGINEER INC
Also Called: Goengineer, Inc.
1251 N Eddy St Ste 200 (46617-1478)
PHONE....................800 276-6486
EMP: 1
SALES (corp-wide): 220.47MM **Privately Held**
Web: www.goengineer.com
SIC: 7372 Prepackaged software
PA: Goengineer, Llc
739 E Fort Union Blvd
Midvale UT 84047
801 359-6100

(G-15046)
GRACE STEEL LLC
2920 W Sample St (46619-3232)
PHONE....................574 387-4612
David Andre, *Managing Member*
EMP: 12 **EST:** 2018
SQ FT: 75,000
SALES (est): 2.46MM
SALES (corp-wide): 2.46MM **Privately Held**
SIC: 3291 Abrasive metal and steel products
PA: Grace Steel Corporation
21601 Durham Way
Bristol IN 46507
574 218-6600

(G-15047)
GRAEF CUSTOM HOMES LLC
52792 Red Fox Trl (46628-9252)
PHONE....................574 807-5859
Eric Graef, *Owner*
EMP: 6 **EST:** 2018
SALES (est): 204.22K **Privately Held**
Web: www.graefcustomhomes.com
SIC: 2431 Millwork

(G-15048)
GRAND MASTER LLC
1619 Miami St (46613-2849)
PHONE....................574 288-8273
Christopher Szajko, *Prin*
EMP: 9 **EST:** 2005
SALES (est): 143.92K **Privately Held**
Web: www.grandmasterstudios.com
SIC: 3663 Studio equipment, radio and television broadcasting

(G-15049)
GRYPHON PRINT STUDIO LLC
3702 W Sample St (46619-2947)
PHONE....................574 514-1644
Steven Estes, *Prin*
EMP: 5 **EST:** 2015
SALES (est): 159.99K **Privately Held**
SIC: 2752 Commercial printing, lithographic

(G-15050)
GTA CONTAINERS INC
3300 W Sample St Ste 1200 (46619-3078)
PHONE....................574 288-3459
Yatish Joshi, *Pr*
EMP: 9 **EST:** 1988
SALES (est): 140.43K **Privately Held**
Web: www.gtacontainers.com
SIC: 3069 Fabricated rubber products, nec

(G-15051)
GTA CONTAINERS INC
Also Called: GTA CONTAINERS, INC.
445 N Sheridan St (46619-1415)
PHONE....................574 288-3459
Yatish Joshi, *Brnch Mgr*
EMP: 2
SALES (corp-wide): 22.46MM **Privately Held**
Web: www.gtacontainers.com
SIC: 3069 Fuel tanks, collapsible: rubberized fabric
PA: Gta Containers, Llc
4201 Linden Ave
South Bend IN 46619
574 288-3459

(G-15052)
GTA CONTAINERS INC
Also Called: Gta Drums
4201 Linden Ave (46619-1744)
PHONE....................574 288-3459
EMP: 34
SALES (corp-wide): 22.46MM **Privately Held**
Web: www.gtacontainers.com
SIC: 3069 Fuel tanks, collapsible: rubberized fabric
PA: Gta Containers, Llc
4201 Linden Ave
South Bend IN 46619
574 288-3459

(G-15053)
GTA CONTAINERS LLC
4201 Linden Ave (46619-1744)
PHONE....................574 288-3459
Yatish Joshi, *Mgr*
EMP: 34
SALES (corp-wide): 22.46MM **Privately Held**
Web: www.gtacontainers.com
SIC: 3069 Fuel tanks, collapsible: rubberized fabric
PA: Gta Containers, Llc
4201 Linden Ave
South Bend IN 46619
574 288-3459

(G-15054)
GTA CONTAINERS LLC (PA)
4201 Linden Ave (46619)
PHONE....................574 288-3459
Michael Fernander, *Pr*
Glenda Lamont, *
Glenda G Lamont, *
Simon Addicott, *
▲ **EMP:** 40 **EST:** 1988
SQ FT: 200,000
SALES (est): 22.46MM
SALES (corp-wide): 22.46MM **Privately Held**

GEOGRAPHIC SECTION

South Bend - St. Joseph County (G-15080)

Web: www.gtacontainers.com
SIC: 3069 2394 3443 5113 Fuel tanks, collapsible: rubberized fabric; Tarpaulins, fabric: made from purchased materials; Industrial vessels, tanks, and containers; Boxes and containers

(G-15055)
GTA DRUM INC
1410 Napier St (46601-2639)
PHONE..................574 288-3459
Yatish J Joshi, Pr
EMP: 4 EST: 2005
SALES (est): 496.88K Privately Held
SIC: 3069 Fuel tanks, collapsible: rubberized fabric

(G-15056)
H D ECCEL LLC
19221 Cleveland Rd (46637-3503)
PHONE..................574 386-2115
EMP: 2
SALES (est): 92.67K Privately Held
SIC: 3537 7389 Trucks, tractors, loaders, carriers, and similar equipment; Business services, nec

(G-15057)
HACKETT & HACKETT LLC
1234 N Eddy St Apt 454 (46617-1475)
PHONE..................574 370-7191
EMP: 1
SALES (est): 110K Privately Held
Web: www.daykahackett.com
SIC: 2653 Boxes, corrugated: made from purchased materials

(G-15058)
HARBOR METALS LLC
Also Called: Bluewater Thermal Solutions
802 Fellows St (46601-3121)
P.O. Box 713733 (45271-3733)
PHONE..................574 232-3338
EMP: 50 EST: 1950
SALES (est): 5.1MM Privately Held
SIC: 3398 Metal heat treating
HQ: Bwt Llc
201 Brkfeld Pkwy Ste 102
Greenville SC 29607

(G-15059)
HATCH PRINTS
901 N Saint Peter St (46617-1542)
PHONE..................312 952-1908
Katrina Harrington, Prin
EMP: 5 EST: 2015
SALES (est): 58.79K Privately Held
SIC: 2752 Commercial printing, lithographic

(G-15060)
HAYES DESIGN COMPANY LLC
1247 Mishawaka Ave (46615-1127)
PHONE..................574 236-5615
EMP: 20 EST: 2016
SALES (est): 906.64K Privately Held
Web: www.hayesdco.com
SIC: 3993 Signs and advertising specialties

(G-15061)
HD CAR DETAILING
50880 Indiana State Route 933 Ste 2 (46637-2095)
PHONE..................574 298-3975
Heidi Juhasz, Managing Member
EMP: 2
SALES (est): 92.67K Privately Held
SIC: 2631 Automobile board

(G-15062)
HEADCO INDUSTRIES INC
Also Called: Bearing Headquarters Co
1625 Commerce Dr (46628-1502)
PHONE..................574 288-4471
Bill Jones, Mgr
EMP: 7
SALES (corp-wide): 162MM Privately Held
Web: www.bearingheadquarters.com
SIC: 5085 5084 3599 Bearings; Hydraulic systems equipment and supplies; Machine shop, jobbing and repair
PA: Headco Industries, Inc.
2601 Parkes Dr
Broadview IL 60155
708 681-4400

(G-15063)
HEARSIGHT INC ✪
410 Howard St (46617-1524)
PHONE..................208 819-8659
Riley Ellingsen, Prin
EMP: 1 EST: 2022
SALES (est): 74.32K Privately Held
SIC: 7372 Prepackaged software

(G-15064)
HEARSIGHT LLC
410 Howard St (46617-1524)
PHONE..................208 819-8659
Riley Ellingsen, Prin
EMP: 3 EST: 2017
SALES (est): 62.01K Privately Held
Web: www.hearsight.net
SIC: 7372 Prepackaged software

(G-15065)
HOERBIGER SERVICE
2834 Southridge Dr (46614-1540)
PHONE..................574 855-4112
EMP: 12 EST: 2018
SALES (est): 47.95K Privately Held
Web: www.hoerbiger.com
SIC: 3491 Industrial valves

(G-15066)
HONEYWELL INTERNATIONAL INC
Also Called: Honeywell
717 N Bendix Dr (46628-1800)
PHONE..................574 231-3322
Vicki Cooper, Mgr
EMP: 2
Web: www.honeywell.com
SIC: 3724 Aircraft engines and engine parts
PA: Honeywell International Inc.
855 S Mint St
Charlotte NC 28202

(G-15067)
HONEYWELL INTERNATIONAL INC
Also Called: Honeywell
3520 Westmoor St (46628-1373)
PHONE..................574 231-3000
Mary Beth Mcgarvey, Pr
EMP: 700
Web: www.honeywell.com
SIC: 3724 Aircraft engines and engine parts
PA: Honeywell International Inc.
855 S Mint St
Charlotte NC 28202

(G-15068)
HONEYWELL INTERNATIONAL INC
Also Called: Honeywell
3520 Westmoor St (46628-1373)
P.O. Box 10 (46624)
PHONE..................574 231-2000
Gretchen Nieb, Brnch Mgr
EMP: 4

Web: www.honeywell.com
SIC: 3728 3494 Aircraft parts and equipment, nec; Valves and pipe fittings, nec
PA: Honeywell International Inc.
855 S Mint St
Charlotte NC 28202

(G-15069)
HOOSIER MOLDED PRODUCTS INC
3603 Progress Dr (46628-1634)
PHONE..................574 235-7900
EMP: 85 EST: 1973
SALES (est): 9.55MM Privately Held
Web: www.hoosiermp.com
SIC: 3089 Injection molding of plastics

(G-15070)
HOOSIER SPRING CO INC
4604 S Burnett Dr (46614-3822)
PHONE..................574 291-7550
Gregory M Suth, Pr
Robert Suth, *
Robert J Canter, *
▼ EMP: 108 EST: 1954
SQ FT: 36,000
SALES (est): 13.95MM Privately Held
Web: www.hoosierspring.com
SIC: 3495 Precision springs

(G-15071)
HOOSIER TANK AND MFG LLC
1710 N Sheridan St (46628-1523)
PHONE..................574 232-8368
Thomas R Kinnucan Junior, Pr
William R Welsch Junior, VP
EMP: 90 EST: 1991
SQ FT: 80,000
SALES (est): 19.16MM Privately Held
Web: www.hoosiertank.com
SIC: 3443 3469 Tanks, standard or custom fabricated: metal plate; Metal stampings, nec

(G-15072)
HOT SHOT MULTIMEDIA ENTPS LLC
Also Called: Hot Shot USA
1610 Hilltop Dr (46614-1515)
PHONE..................317 537-7527
Jeffrey Weber Junior, Ex Dir
EMP: 3 EST: 2011
SALES (est): 110K Privately Held
SIC: 8999 7372 Personal services; Prepackaged software

(G-15073)
HOWSE OV DRMRS LLC
1251 N Eddy St (46617-1479)
PHONE..................574 366-2406
EMP: 1
SALES (est): 69.27K Privately Held
SIC: 3161 Clothing and apparel carrying cases

(G-15074)
IES SUBSIDIARY HOLDINGS INC
1125 S Walnut St (46619-4303)
PHONE..................330 830-3500
John Senese, Mgr
EMP: 1
Web: www.iesci.net
SIC: 3264 7694 3621 Magnets, permanent: ceramic or ferrite; Armature rewinding shops ; Motors and generators
HQ: Ies Subsidiary Holdings, Inc
5433 Westheimer Rd # 500
Houston TX 77056
713 860-1500

(G-15075)
IMAGINEERING ENTERPRISES INC
Also Called: Imagineering Finishing Tech
3722 Foundation Ct (46628-4361)
PHONE..................574 287-0642
F James Hammer, Pr
EMP: 20
SQ FT: 56,000
SALES (corp-wide): 19.58MM Privately Held
Web: www.iftworldwide.com
SIC: 3479 8711 Coating of metals and formed products; Engineering services
PA: Imagineering Enterprises Inc
1302 W Sample St
South Bend IN 46619
574 287-2941

(G-15076)
IMAGINEERING ENTERPRISES INC (PA)
Also Called: Imagineering Finishing Tech
1302 W Sample St (46619)
PHONE..................574 287-2941
F James Hammer, Pr
Michelle M Hammer, *
Joseph Rowan, *
Mathew Huff, *
▲ EMP: 90 EST: 1959
SQ FT: 33,000
SALES (est): 19.58MM
SALES (corp-wide): 19.58MM Privately Held
Web: www.iftworldwide.com
SIC: 3479 8711 Coating of metals and formed products; Engineering services

(G-15077)
INDIANA INTEGRATED CIRCUITS IN
1400 E Angela Blvd (46617-1364)
PHONE..................574 217-4612
Jason Kulick, Prin
EMP: 6 EST: 2010
SALES (est): 240.28K Privately Held
Web: www.indianaic.com
SIC: 3679 Electronic circuits

(G-15078)
INDIANA INTGRATED CIRCUITS LLC
Also Called: Iic
1400 E Angela Blvd Unit 107 (46617-1364)
PHONE..................574 217-4612
EMP: 2 EST: 2009
SALES (est): 214.96K Privately Held
Web: www.indianaic.com
SIC: 3674 Semiconductors and related devices

(G-15079)
INDIANA WHISKEY CO
1115 W Sample St (46619-3829)
PHONE..................574 339-1737
Charles Florance, Pr
Braden Weldy, Ofcr
EMP: 3 EST: 2013
SQ FT: 4,500
SALES (est): 254.49K Privately Held
Web: www.inwhiskey.com
SIC: 2085 Distilled and blended liquors

(G-15080)
INDUSTRIAL METAL-FAB INC
2806 W Sample St (46619-3299)
PHONE..................574 288-8368
Mark E Beaudway, Pr
Monte C Beaudway, *
▲ EMP: 30 EST: 1964
SQ FT: 65,000
SALES (est): 4.92MM Privately Held
Web: www.imfonline.com

SIC: 3443 3599 3441 Fabricated plate work (boiler shop); Machine shop, jobbing and repair; Fabricated structural metal

(G-15081)
INOVATEUS SOLAR LLC
19890 State Line Rd (46637-1553)
PHONE..................................574 485-1400
Tj Kanczuzewski, Pr
Timothy Sutherland, *
Mike Pound, CRO*
Lindsey Foley, *
▼ EMP: 36 EST: 2008
SALES (est): 10.22MM Privately Held
Web: www.inovateus.com
SIC: 5211 3433 Solar heating equipment; Solar heaters and collectors

(G-15082)
INTEGRA-TEC MACHINING LLC
3702 W Sample St Ste 4045 (46619-2976)
P.O. Box 282 (46552-0282)
PHONE..................................574 289-2629
EMP: 4 EST: 2003
SALES (est): 431.38K Privately Held
Web: www.integratecmachining.com
SIC: 3599 Machine shop, jobbing and repair

(G-15083)
INTERNATIONAL BAKERS SERVICE
1902 N Sheridan St (46628-1592)
PHONE..................................574 287-7111
William Busse Junior, Pr
Thomas E Coomes, *
EMP: 29 EST: 1946
SQ FT: 25,000
SALES (est): 4.09MM Privately Held
Web: www.internationalbakers.com
SIC: 2087 Flavoring extracts and syrups, nec

(G-15084)
INTERNATIONAL BRAKE INDS INC
4300 Quality Dr (46628-9665)
PHONE..................................419 905-7468
Char Silver, Prin
EMP: 63
SALES (corp-wide): 8.28B Privately Held
Web: www.internationalbrakeindustries.com
SIC: 3713 3714 Truck and bus bodies; Motor vehicle brake systems and parts
HQ: International Brake Industries, Inc.
1840 Mccullough St
Lima OH 45801

(G-15085)
INTERNATIONAL FUSE LLC
2206 Mishawaka Ave (46615-2141)
PHONE..................................574 340-4042
Aaron White, Prin
EMP: 8 EST: 2018
SALES (est): 515.83K Privately Held
Web: www.internationalfuse.net
SIC: 3679 Electronic components, nec

(G-15086)
INTIMUSIC LLC
56601 Sonora Ave (46619-4707)
PHONE..................................574 210-4562
EMP: 1 EST: 2013
SALES (est): 62.52K Privately Held
SIC: 2741 7389 Music book and sheet music publishing; Business Activities at Non-Commercial Site

(G-15087)
IP CORPORATION
Also Called: Molding Products Division
1545 S Olive St (46619-4295)
PHONE..................................574 234-1105
Troy Wade, Genl Mgr
EMP: 40
SALES (corp-wide): 608.16MM Privately Held
Web: www.interplastic.com
SIC: 2821 Plastics materials and resins
PA: Ip Corporation
1225 Willow Lake Blvd
Saint Paul MN 55110
651 481-6860

(G-15088)
IRONCRAFT CO INC
Also Called: A1 Iron & Aluminum Co
50655 Indiana State Route 933 (46637-2053)
PHONE..................................574 272-0866
Bruce L Calvert, Pr
Beatrice Calvert, Sec
EMP: 5 EST: 1945
SALES (est): 462.43K Privately Held
SIC: 3446 Fences or posts, ornamental iron or steel

(G-15089)
JAMES MCBRYDE
Also Called: Performance Organics
1251 N Eddy St (46617-1479)
PHONE..................................206 504-4689
James Mcbryde, Owner
EMP: 1 EST: 2020
SALES (est): 98K Privately Held
SIC: 2834 Vitamin, nutrient, and hematinic preparations for human use

(G-15090)
JAMES MORRIS
Also Called: J J Powerwashing
1042 N Elmer St (46628-2532)
PHONE..................................574 387-2615
James Morris, Owner
EMP: 1 EST: 2020
SALES (est): 47.5K Privately Held
SIC: 3589 Car washing machinery

(G-15091)
JBL SIGNALS AND LIGHTING LLC
4316 Technology Dr (46628-9752)
PHONE..................................574 855-2251
EMP: 6 EST: 2021
SALES (est): 253.68K Privately Held
Web: www.jblsignalsandlighting.com
SIC: 3993 Signs and advertising specialties

(G-15092)
JKP PRINTING INC
1701 Linden Ave (46628-2346)
PHONE..................................574 246-1650
Evelyn O'neal, Pr
Janice Kimbrough, Pr
EMP: 3 EST: 1988
SQ FT: 900
SALES (est): 195.43K Privately Held
SIC: 2752 Offset printing

(G-15093)
JMS ENGINEERED PLASTICS INC
1705 Commerce Dr (46628-1564)
PHONE..................................574 277-3228
EMP: 1
Web: www.jmsep.com
SIC: 3089 8711 Automotive parts, plastic; Building construction consultant
PA: Jms Engineered Plastics, Inc.
52275 State Rd 933 N
South Bend IN 46637

(G-15094)
JMS ENGINEERED PLASTICS INC (PA)
52275 Indiana State Route 933 (46637)
P.O. Box 1557 (46634)
PHONE..................................574 277-3228
David M Martinez, CEO
EMP: 74 EST: 2008
SALES (est): 9.83MM Privately Held
Web: www.jmsep.com
SIC: 3089 8711 Automotive parts, plastic; Building construction consultant

(G-15095)
JMS MOLD & ENGINEERING CO INC
50941 Indiana State Route 933 (46637-2057)
P.O. Box 927 (46624-0927)
PHONE..................................574 272-0198
Ronald Scope, Pr
EMP: 12 EST: 1967
SALES (est): 260.4K Privately Held
Web: www.jmsep.com
SIC: 3089 Injection molding of plastics

(G-15096)
JOSEPH NORTHERN
2621 Prast Blvd (46628-1827)
PHONE..................................574 309-5508
Joseph Northern, Owner
EMP: 2 EST: 2020
SALES (est): 65.42K Privately Held
SIC: 2499 Signboards, wood

(G-15097)
JOURNEYMAN TOOL & MOLD INC
23755 Kern Rd (46614-9763)
PHONE..................................574 237-1880
Michael Meyer, Pr
Tammi Meyer, VP
EMP: 5 EST: 1989
SALES (est): 384.67K Privately Held
Web: www.jtool.com
SIC: 3544 Industrial molds

(G-15098)
KEN KOWALSKI
Also Called: Ken's Cycle Service
26237 Swallow Ct (46619-4530)
PHONE..................................574 633-4427
Ken Kowalski, Owner
EMP: 1 EST: 1972
SALES (est): 112.5K Privately Held
SIC: 7699 3599 Motorcycle repair service; Machine shop, jobbing and repair

(G-15099)
KENNEDY EXPRESSLINE INC
2933 Council Oak Dr (46628-3435)
PHONE..................................574 272-9072
EMP: 1
SALES (est): 56.34K Privately Held
SIC: 2741 Miscellaneous publishing

(G-15100)
KILL-N-EM INC
Also Called: Carother's Printing Company
2118 Franklin St (46613-2120)
PHONE..................................574 233-6655
Thomas E Podemski, Prin
Carol Podemski, Prin
EMP: 5 EST: 1966
SQ FT: 4,800
SALES (est): 493.74K Privately Held
Web: www.carotherspriting.com
SIC: 2752 Offset printing

(G-15101)
KIYAM TRANSPORT LLC
1251 N Eddy St Ste 200 (46617-1478)
PHONE..................................502 551-6245
EMP: 1 EST: 2017
SALES (est): 77.21K Privately Held

SIC: 3537 Trucks, tractors, loaders, carriers, and similar equipment

(G-15102)
KNOTTED STRANDS CROCHET
733 Roland Ct (46601-3461)
PHONE..................................574 232-9127
Carla Herron, Owner
EMP: 4 EST: 2017
SALES (est): 55.36K Privately Held
SIC: 2399 Hand woven and crocheted products

(G-15103)
KOKOKU WIRE INDUSTRIES CORP
406 Manitou Pl (46616-1325)
PHONE..................................574 287-5610
Kevin Hughes, Pr
EMP: 21 EST: 1987
SQ FT: 200,000
SALES (est): 1.06MM Privately Held
SIC: 3315 Wire, steel: insulated or armored

(G-15104)
KOONTZ-WAGNER CUSTOM CONTROLS HOLDINGS LLC
Also Called: Koontz-Wagner Electric
3801 Voorde Dr Ste B (46628-1643)
PHONE..................................574 387-5802
▲ EMP: 85
SIC: 3448 Prefabricated metal buildings and components

(G-15105)
KRAFTY BRAVO LLC ◊
1251 N Eddy St Ste 200 (46617-1478)
PHONE..................................317 366-3485
EMP: 5 EST: 2022
SALES (est): 125K Privately Held
SIC: 2759 Letterpress and screen printing

(G-15106)
KRISTINE WILLOUGHBY
Also Called: K Willoughby Consulting
23700 Marquette Blvd Lot 5 (46628-5074)
PHONE..................................574 850-5145
Kristine Willoughby, Pr
EMP: 1
SALES (est): 35.17K Privately Held
SIC: 7379 7372 Online services technology consultants; Operating systems computer software

(G-15107)
KROGER CO
Also Called: Kroger
1217 E Ireland Rd (46614-3497)
PHONE..................................574 291-0740
Alf Pesce, Mgr
EMP: 1
SALES (corp-wide): 150.04B Publicly Held
Web: www.kroger.com
SIC: 5411 5912 5992 5812 Supermarkets, chain; Drug stores; Florists; Eating places
PA: The Kroger Co
1014 Vine St
Cincinnati OH 45202
513 762-4000

(G-15108)
KSM LOGISTICS LLC
2009 N Brookfield St (46628-3357)
PHONE..................................574 318-2040
EMP: 2 EST: 2021
SALES (est): 95.58K Privately Held
SIC: 3537 Trucks: freight, baggage, etc.: industrial, except mining

GEOGRAPHIC SECTION
South Bend - St. Joseph County (G-15134)

(G-15109)
KUERT CONCRETE INC (PA)
Also Called: Kuert Concrete
5909 Nimtz Pkwy (46628)
PHONE..................574 232-9911
Steve Fidler, *Pr*
Tim Miller, *
Ron Erickson, *
EMP: 45 EST: 1927
SALES (est): 13.04MM
SALES (corp-wide): 13.04MM **Privately Held**
Web: www.kuert.com
SIC: 3273 5032 Ready-mixed concrete; Concrete building products

(G-15110)
KUHARIC ENTERPRISES
57890 Crumstown Hwy (46619-9646)
PHONE..................574 288-9410
John Kuharic, *Pt*
Christine Kuharic, *Pt*
EMP: 2
SALES (est): 167.87K **Privately Held**
SIC: 0191 4151 0711 3443 General farms, primarily crop; School buses; Lime spreading services; Culverts, metal plate

(G-15111)
KULZER LLC
4315 S Lafayette Blvd (46614-2517)
PHONE..................574 299-5466
Christopher Holden, *Managing Member*
Kira Geiss, *
▲ EMP: 350 EST: 1985
SQ FT: 70,000
SALES (est): 66.09MM **Privately Held**
Web: www.kulzerus.com
SIC: 3843 Dental equipment and supplies
PA: Mitsui Chemicals, Inc.
  2-2-1, Yaesu
  Chuo-Ku TKY 104-0

(G-15112)
KW CUSTOM CONTROLS LLC
4755 Ameritech Dr (46628-9120)
PHONE..................312 343-3920
William Harlan, *Managing Member*
Stephen Vivian, *Managing Member*
EMP: 40 EST: 2018
SALES (est): 9.36MM **Privately Held**
Web: www.kwcustomcontrols.com
SIC: 3448 Prefabricated metal buildings and components

(G-15113)
KW MAINTENANCE SERVICES LLC
Also Called: Koontz-Wagner Maintenance Svcs
3801 Voorde Dr Ste B (46628-1643)
PHONE..................574 232-2051
EMP: 42 EST: 2013
SALES (est): 4.91MM
SALES (corp-wide): 44.23MM **Privately Held**
Web: www.koontzwagnerservices.com
SIC: 7694 Electric motor repair
PA: Kw Services, Llc
  3801 Voorde Dr Ste B
  South Bend IN 46628
  574 232-2051

(G-15114)
LAMINAT LLC
1404 Honan Dr (46614-2176)
PHONE..................574 233-1534
Edward J Jordanich, *Prin*
EMP: 4 EST: 2016
SALES (est): 92.36K **Privately Held**
SIC: 3714 Motor vehicle parts and accessories

(G-15115)
LANEY SOFTWARE CO
17144 Moonlite Dr (46614-9115)
PHONE..................260 312-0759
Michael Laney, *Prin*
EMP: 2 EST: 2004
SALES (est): 167.9K **Privately Held**
SIC: 7372 Prepackaged software

(G-15116)
LANGUAGE COMPANY SOUTH BEND
2002 Mishawaka Ave (46615)
PHONE..................574 287-3622
EMP: 5 EST: 2020
SALES (est): 88.38K **Privately Held**
Web: www.tlc.edu
SIC: 3699 Electrical equipment and supplies, nec

(G-15117)
LASALLES LANDING VINEYARD LLC
51739 Lilac Rd (46628-9782)
PHONE..................574 277-2711
David Sabato, *Prin*
EMP: 2 EST: 2010
SALES (est): 248.37K **Privately Held**
SIC: 2084 Wines

(G-15118)
LASER WELDER COMPANY
1507 S Olive St (46619)
PHONE..................816 807-6971
EMP: 1
SALES (est): 75.6K **Privately Held**
SIC: 3548 Welding apparatus

(G-15119)
LAYMON INDUSTRIES LLC
51878 Westwood Forest Dr (46628-9245)
PHONE..................574 277-4536
EMP: 1 EST: 2013
SALES (est): 57.29K **Privately Held**
SIC: 3999 Candles

(G-15120)
LEA LLC
635 S Lafayette Blvd Bldg 113 (46601)
PHONE..................574 216-1622
Blake Augsburger, *CEO*
EMP: 15 EST: 2018
SALES (est): 1.76MM **Privately Held**
Web: www.leaprofessional.com
SIC: 3651 Audio electronic systems

(G-15121)
LEBERMUTH COMPANY INC (PA)
Also Called: American Home Fragrance
4004 Technology Dr (46628-9745)
P.O. Box 4103 (46634-4103)
PHONE..................574 259-7000
Robert Brown, *Pr*
Alan Brown, *
◆ EMP: 57 EST: 1979
SQ FT: 100,000
SALES (est): 20.62MM
SALES (corp-wide): 20.62MM **Privately Held**
Web: www.lebermuth.com
SIC: 2899 5149 5169 Incense; Organic and diet food; Essential oils

(G-15122)
LECO CORPORATION
Also Called: Flight Dept
4100 Lathrop St (46628-6103)
PHONE..................574 288-9017
Phil Rollins, *Brnch Mgr*
EMP: 3
SALES (corp-wide): 137.69MM **Privately Held**
Web: www.leco.com
SIC: 3821 4493 3826 3825 Laboratory apparatus, except heating and measuring; Boat yards, storage and incidental repair; Analytical instruments; Instruments to measure electricity
PA: Leco Corporation
  3000 Lakeview Ave
  Saint Joseph MI 49085
  269 983-5531

(G-15123)
LEGGITS LLC
1931 Malvern Way (46614-1640)
PHONE..................269 447-3500
Deonta Durell Sims, *CEO*
EMP: 3 EST: 2020
SALES (est): 60.48K **Privately Held**
SIC: 3537 Trucks: freight, baggage, etc.: industrial, except mining

(G-15124)
LESEA INC
3801 Voorde Dr (46628-1643)
PHONE..................574 344-8215
EMP: 6 EST: 2019
SALES (est): 157.99K **Privately Held**
Web: www.whmetv46.com
SIC: 3677 Electronic coils and transformers

(G-15125)
LIPPERT COMPONENTS INC
1280 S Olive St (46619-4208)
PHONE..................574 312-6654
EMP: 10
SALES (corp-wide): 3.78B **Publicly Held**
Web: www.lci1.com
SIC: 3711 Chassis, motor vehicle
HQ: Lippert Components, Inc.
  3501 County Rd 6 E
  Elkhart IN 46514
  574 535-1125

(G-15126)
LJT TEXAS LLC (DH)
Also Called: Lock Joint Tube Texas
515 W Ireland Rd (46614-3805)
PHONE..................800 257-6859
David L Lerman, *CEO*
Gerald Lerman, *Managing Member*
Ted Lerman, *Pr*
Michael Lerman, *VP*
EMP: 51 EST: 2004
SALES (est): 24.58MM **Privately Held**
SIC: 3317 Tubes, wrought: welded or lock joint
HQ: Lock Joint Tube Llc
  515 W Ireland Rd
  South Bend IN 46614

(G-15127)
LOCK JOINT TUBE LLC (DH)
Also Called: L J T
515 W Ireland Rd (46614)
PHONE..................574 299-5326
Gerald Lerman, *
Ted Lerman, *
▲ EMP: 200 EST: 1991
SQ FT: 295,000
SALES (est): 85.76MM **Privately Held**
Web: www.lockjointtube.com
SIC: 3317 Welded pipe and tubes
HQ: Steel Warehouse Company Llc
  2722 W Tucker Dr
  South Bend IN 46624
  574 236-5100

(G-15128)
LOGISTICK INC
19880 State Line Rd (46637)
PHONE..................800 758-5840
Ashley Brickley, *Pr*
EMP: 9 EST: 1992
SQ FT: 8,000
SALES (est): 2.49MM **Privately Held**
Web: www.logistick.com
SIC: 3799 2679 Trailers and trailer equipment; Pallet spacers, fiber: made from purchased material

(G-15129)
LORI HICKS
Also Called: Ladifrog's Clerical Services
310 Barbie St (46614-2611)
PHONE..................574 291-6341
Lori Hicks, *Owner*
EMP: 1 EST: 2004
SALES (est): 36K **Privately Held**
SIC: 7331 2741 Mailing service; Art copy: publishing and printing

(G-15130)
LUBRICATION DEVICES
Also Called: Lubrication Devices Mfg
719 W North Shore Dr (46617-1017)
PHONE..................574 234-4674
P Matz, *Owner*
EMP: 2 EST: 1953
SALES (est): 102.54K **Privately Held**
SIC: 3569 Lubricating equipment

(G-15131)
LUDWICK GRAPHICS INC (PA)
1312 Honan Dr (46614-2174)
P.O. Box 3572 (46619-0572)
PHONE..................574 233-2165
Robert B Ludwick, *Pr*
James Ludwick, *VP*
Ann Farkas, *Sec*
EMP: 8 EST: 1920
SQ FT: 18,000
SALES (est): 747.75K
SALES (corp-wide): 747.75K **Privately Held**
Web: www.ludwickgraphics.com
SIC: 2752 2796 2791 2789 Offset printing; Platemaking services; Typesetting; Bookbinding and related work

(G-15132)
MACHINING SOLUTIONS
942 S 27th St (46615-1724)
PHONE..................574 292-3227
Jason Szabo, *Owner*
EMP: 2 EST: 2009
SALES (est): 80.15K **Privately Held**
SIC: 3552 Textile machinery

(G-15133)
MACK TOOL & ENGINEERING INC
2820 Viridian Dr (46628-4359)
PHONE..................574 233-8424
Melvin W Hartz, *CEO*
Paul Hartz, *
Sondra Hartz, *
EMP: 50 EST: 1988
SQ FT: 27,000
SALES (est): 7.78MM **Privately Held**
Web: www.macktool.com
SIC: 3728 Aircraft parts and equipment, nec

(G-15134)
MAET LLC
242 1234 N Eddy St (46617)
PHONE..................574 220-7668
EMP: 3
SALES (est): 71.13K **Privately Held**
SIC: 7372 Application computer software

South Bend - St. Joseph County (G-15135)

GEOGRAPHIC SECTION

(G-15135)
MAGNETS R US INC
63300 State Road 331 (46614-9498)
PHONE.....................574 633-0061
Larry Frank, *Pr*
▲ **EMP:** 2 **EST:** 1989
SALES (est): 222.59K **Privately Held**
SIC: 3499 Magnets, permanent: metallic

(G-15136)
MAHOGANY SCENTS
53154 Bracken Fern Dr (46637-4583)
PHONE.....................574 271-1364
John Beard, *Owner*
EMP: 5 **EST:** 2015
SALES (est): 75.82K **Privately Held**
SIC: 2844 Perfumes, cosmetics and other toilet preparations

(G-15137)
MAITLAND ENGINEERING INC
2713 Foundation Dr (46628-4334)
PHONE.....................574 287-0155
EMP: 46 **EST:** 1996
SQ FT: 15,000
SALES (est): 5.08MM **Privately Held**
Web: www.maitlandengineering.com
SIC: 3842 3599 Implants, surgical; Machine shop, jobbing and repair

(G-15138)
MANUFACTURING TECHNOLOGY INC (PA)
Also Called: MTI
1702 W Washington St (46628-2061)
P.O. Box 3059 (46619-0059)
PHONE.....................574 230-0258
Robert C Adams Ii, *Pr*
Daniel C Adams, *
Jennifer Borsodi, *
Doug Wait, *
Guy Harper, *
◆ **EMP:** 140 **EST:** 1926
SQ FT: 65,000
SALES (est): 49.88MM
SALES (corp-wide): 49.88MM **Privately Held**
Web: www.mtiwelding.com
SIC: 3548 7692 Welding apparatus; Welding repair

(G-15139)
MASTER METAL MACHINING INC
Also Called: Master Metal Engineering
4520 S Burnett Dr (46614-3820)
PHONE.....................574 299-0222
Brian Pyszka, *Pr*
Thomas Cleveland, *
EMP: 30 **EST:** 1977
SQ FT: 25,000
SALES (est): 4.7MM **Privately Held**
SIC: 3599 Machine shop, jobbing and repair

(G-15140)
MASTERBILT INCORPORATED
3801 Voorde Dr (46628-1643)
P.O. Box 3715 (46619-0715)
PHONE.....................574 287-6567
Robert Michalk, *Pr*
Lawrence Kowalewski, *VP*
▲ **EMP:** 19 **EST:** 1955
SQ FT: 9,900
SALES (est): 2.73MM **Privately Held**
Web: www.masterbilt-inc.com
SIC: 3599 Machine shop, jobbing and repair

(G-15141)
MAUTZ PAINT FACTORY
1201 S Main St (46601-3339)
PHONE.....................574 289-2497
Sherwin Williams, *Mgr*
EMP: 4 **EST:** 2002
SALES (est): 223.91K **Privately Held**
SIC: 2851 5198 Paints and allied products; Paints

(G-15142)
MCCAFFERY SIGN DESIGNS
Also Called: Sign Designs
1310 S Main St Ste 2 (46601-3358)
PHONE.....................574 232-9991
James Mccaffery, *Pr*
EMP: 4 **EST:** 1990
SALES (est): 250.67K **Privately Held**
Web: www.signdesignsinc.com
SIC: 3993 Signs and advertising specialties

(G-15143)
MCCORMICK & COMPANY INC
2741 Foundation Dr (46628-4334)
PHONE.....................410 527-6189
Lawrence Kurzius, *Ch*
EMP: 2
SALES (corp-wide): 6.66B **Publicly Held**
Web: www.mccormickcorporation.com
SIC: 2099 Spices, including grinding
PA: Mccormick & Company Incorporated
24 Schilling Rd Ste 1
Hunt Valley MD 21031
410 771-7301

(G-15144)
MCCORMICK & COMPANY INC
3425 Lathrop St (46628-4393)
PHONE.....................574 234-8101
Mike Calhoun, *Brnch Mgr*
EMP: 101
SQ FT: 50,000
SALES (corp-wide): 6.66B **Publicly Held**
Web: www.mccormickcorporation.com
SIC: 2099 Spices, including grinding
PA: Mccormick & Company Incorporated
24 Schilling Rd Ste 1
Hunt Valley MD 21031
410 771-7301

(G-15145)
MCGOWAN WIRE SPECIALTIES INC
600 United Dr (46601-2808)
PHONE.....................574 232-7110
Kevin Mcgowan, *Pr*
Peggy Mcgowan, *Sec*
EMP: 1 **EST:** 1989
SALES (est): 173.74K **Privately Held**
Web: www.mcgowanwire.com
SIC: 3493 3315 Torsion bar springs; Wire and fabricated wire products

(G-15146)
MCM MANUFACTURING
1902 S Main St (46613-2306)
PHONE.....................574 339-6994
EMP: 6 **EST:** 2019
SALES (est): 77.04K **Privately Held**
Web: www.mcmmanufacturing.com
SIC: 3523 Farm machinery and equipment

(G-15147)
MELANINWISDOMGARMENT
2509 Sampson St (46614-1619)
PHONE.....................574 315-3081
Shanetta Savado, *Owner*
EMP: 6 **EST:** 2020
SALES (est): 236.56K **Privately Held**
SIC: 3161 Clothing and apparel carrying cases

(G-15148)
MESSER LLC
3809 W Calvert St (46613-1020)
PHONE.....................574 234-4887
Tom Sulvinsky, *Brnch Mgr*
EMP: 9
SALES (corp-wide): 1.63B **Privately Held**
Web: www.messeramericas.com
SIC: 5169 2813 Industrial gases; Industrial gases
HQ: Messer Llc
200 Smrst Corp Blvd # 7000
Bridgewater NJ 08807
800 755-9277

(G-15149)
MICHIANA PALLET RECYCLE INC
55022 Pear Rd (46628-4509)
PHONE.....................574 232-8566
Jim Knapp, *Pr*
EMP: 5 **EST:** 1990
SQ FT: 15,000
SALES (est): 429.77K **Privately Held**
Web: www.michianapalletrecycle.com
SIC: 2448 Pallets, wood

(G-15150)
MICROSCREEN LLC
1106 High St (46601-3705)
PHONE.....................574 232-4358
EMP: 23 **EST:** 1999
SALES (est): 3.68MM **Privately Held**
Web: www.microscreenllc.com
SIC: 3674 Semiconductors and related devices

(G-15151)
MILESTONE CONTRACTORS N INC
Also Called: MILESTONE CONTRACTORS NORTH, INC.
24358 State Road 23 (46614-9593)
PHONE.....................219 924-5900
Kevin Kelly, *Brnch Mgr*
EMP: 1
SALES (corp-wide): 894.43MM **Privately Held**
Web: www.walshkelly.com
SIC: 2951 1611 1771 Asphalt and asphaltic paving mixtures (not from refineries); Surfacing and paving; Concrete work
HQ: Milestone Contractors North, Llc
1700 E Main St
Griffith IN 46319
219 924-5900

(G-15152)
MITO-CRAFT INC
Also Called: Graphie-Tees
505 S Logan St (46615-2419)
PHONE.....................574 287-4555
Lynn A Rodriquez, *Pr*
John Rodriquez, *Sec*
Andrea Kaiser, *VP*
EMP: 8 **EST:** 1957
SQ FT: 6,000
SALES (est): 969.31K **Privately Held**
Web: www.graphietees.com
SIC: 2759 2752 2672 2396 Screen printing; Commercial printing, lithographic; Paper; coated and laminated, nec; Automotive and apparel trimmings

(G-15153)
MOBILITY VENTURES LLC
Also Called: Mv-1
105 N Niles Ave (46617-2705)
PHONE.....................734 367-3714
William Gibson, *VP*
EMP: 1 **EST:** 2013
SALES (est): 4.02MM
SALES (corp-wide): 3.44B **Privately Held**
Web: www.amgeneral.com
SIC: 3713 3714 8711 Specialty motor vehicle bodies; Motor vehicle parts and accessories; Engineering services
HQ: Am General Llc
105 N Niles Ave
South Bend IN 46617
574 237-6222

(G-15154)
MOSSBERG & COMPANY INC
4100 Technology Dr (46628-9772)
PHONE.....................574 236-1094
EMP: 14
SALES (corp-wide): 32.28MM **Privately Held**
Web: www.mossbergco.com
SIC: 2752 Offset printing
PA: Mossberg & Company Inc
301 E Sample St
South Bend IN 46601
574 289-9253

(G-15155)
MOSSBERG & COMPANY INC (PA)
Also Called: Mossbev
301 E Sample St (46601-3547)
PHONE.....................574 289-9253
TOLL FREE: 800
James W Hillman, *Pr*
William Knight, *
Anne S Hillman, *
EMP: 98 **EST:** 1930
SQ FT: 80,000
SALES (est): 32.28MM
SALES (corp-wide): 32.28MM **Privately Held**
Web: www.mossbergco
SIC: 2752 2759 Offset printing; Letterpress printing

(G-15156)
MOSSBERG CO
301 E Sample St (46601-3547)
P.O. Box 210 (46624-0210)
PHONE.....................574 850-6285
EMP: 10 **EST:** 2019
SALES (est): 260.96K **Privately Held**
Web: www.mossbergco.com
SIC: 2752 Offset printing

(G-15157)
MYERS INDUSTRIES INC
3300 N Kenmore St (46628-4314)
PHONE.....................866 429-5200
EMP: 12
SALES (corp-wide): 813.07MM **Publicly Held**
Web: www.myersindustries.com
SIC: 3944 Games, toys, and children's vehicles
PA: Myers Industries, Inc.
1293 S Main St
Akron OH 44301
330 253-5592

(G-15158)
NAMACLE LLC
17911 Turners Dr (46635-1529)
PHONE.....................574 320-1436
EMP: 2 **EST:** 2009
SALES (est): 150.46K **Privately Held**
Web: www.bruzerlesslethal.com
SIC: 3484 Guns (firearms) or gun parts, 30 mm. and below

(G-15159)
NATIONAL CONSOLIDATED CORP
Also Called: Natcon
25855 State Road 2 (46619-4736)
PHONE.....................574 289-7885
James Kilbourne, *Pr*

GEOGRAPHIC SECTION

South Bend - St. Joseph County (G-15184)

Carol Kilbourne, *Sec*
EMP: 12 **EST:** 1974
SQ FT: 11,800
SALES (est): 2.07MM **Privately Held**
Web: www.natconusa.com
SIC: 5084 3451 Hydraulic systems equipment and supplies; Screw machine products

(G-15160)
NELLO CAPITAL INC (PA)
Also Called: Nello
105 E Jefferson Blvd Ste 525 (46601-1922)
PHONE..................................574 288-3632
Daniel Ianello, *Pr*
Robert Rumpler, *VP*
Kevin Brisson, *CFO*
EMP: 4 **EST:** 2002
SQ FT: 10,000
SALES (est): 23.27MM
SALES (corp-wide): 23.27MM **Privately Held**
Web: www.nelloinc.com
SIC: 3663 Airborne radio communications equipment

(G-15161)
NELLO INC (HQ)
Also Called: Nello Corporation
1201 S Sheridan St (46619-2941)
P.O. Box 1960 (46634-1960)
PHONE..................................574 288-3632
Dan Ianello, *Pr*
Bob Rumpler, *VP*
Kevin Brisson, *CFO*
◆ **EMP:** 12 **EST:** 2001
SQ FT: 95,000
SALES (est): 23.27MM
SALES (corp-wide): 23.27MM **Privately Held**
Web: www.nelloinc.com
SIC: 3441 Fabricated structural metal
PA: Nello Capital, Inc.
   105 E Jefferson Blvd # 52
   South Bend IN 46601
   574 288-3632

(G-15162)
NEO INDUSTRIES LLC (HQ)
1400 E Angela Blvd (46617-1364)
PHONE..................................574 217-4078
Michael Quig, *Pr*
EMP: 37 **EST:** 1998
SALES (est): 19.55MM **Privately Held**
Web: www.neodelivers.com
SIC: 3471 Plating of metals or formed products
PA: The Heico Companies L L C
   70 W Madison Ste 5600
   Chicago IL 60602

(G-15163)
NERP LLC
58016 Crumstown Hwy (46619-9646)
PHONE..................................574 303-6377
EMP: 2 **EST:** 2006
SALES (est): 213.82K **Privately Held**
SIC: 3714 Motor vehicle brake systems and parts

(G-15164)
NEW CARBON COMPANY LLC
Also Called: Ncd Sbcp
24355 Edison Rd (46628-4949)
PHONE..................................574 247-2270
Beth Morganti, *Mgr*
EMP: 1
SALES (corp-wide): 25.28MM **Privately Held**
Web: www.goldenmalted.com
SIC: 2041 Flour and other grain mill products
HQ: New Carbon Company, Llc
   50 Applied Bank Blvd
   Glen Mills PA 19342
   574 247-2270

(G-15165)
NEW ENERGY CORP
3201 W Calvert St (46613-1010)
P.O. Box 2289 (46680-2289)
PHONE..................................574 233-3116
EMP: 136
Web: www.newenergycorp.com
SIC: 2869 Ethyl alcohol, ethanol

(G-15166)
NEW NELLO OPERATING CO LLC
1201 S Sheridan St (46619-2941)
PHONE..................................574 288-3632
Dan Ianello, *Pr*
EMP: 125 **EST:** 2017
SQ FT: 160,000
SALES (est): 9.15MM **Privately Held**
Web: www.nelloinc.com
SIC: 3441 Fabricated structural metal

(G-15167)
NEXT LEVEL CANDLES LLC ✪
521 Cottage Grove Ave (46616)
PHONE..................................574 347-1030
EMP: 2 **EST:** 2024
SALES (est): 92.67K **Privately Held**
SIC: 3999 7389 Candles; Business Activities at Non-Commercial Site

(G-15168)
NORI METALS
1420 S Walnut St (46619-4310)
PHONE..................................574 213-4344
EMP: 5 **EST:** 2017
SALES (est): 148.92K **Privately Held**
SIC: 3724 Aircraft engines and engine parts

(G-15169)
NORRES NORTH AMERICA INC
701 W Chippewa Ave Ste 200 (46614-3704)
PHONE..................................855 667-7370
Burkhard Mollen, *CEO*
EMP: 25 **EST:** 2013
SALES (est): 3.64MM **Privately Held**
Web: www.norres.com
SIC: 3312 Pipes and tubes

(G-15170)
NORTH AMERICAN SIGNS INC (PA)
Also Called: Site Enhancement Services
3601 Lathrop St (46628-6108)
P.O. Box 30 (46624-0030)
PHONE..................................574 234-5252
John Yarger, *Pr*
Noel H Yarger, *
G Tom Yarger, *
EMP: 80 **EST:** 1934
SQ FT: 51,000
SALES (est): 20.53MM
SALES (corp-wide): 20.53MM **Privately Held**
Web: www.northamericansigns.com
SIC: 3993 Electric signs

(G-15171)
NORTHERN BRACE COMPANY INC (PA)
Also Called: Northern Brace Nthrn Prsthtics
610 N Michigan St Ste 104 (46601-1078)
PHONE..................................574 233-4221
Timothy S West, *Pr*
EMP: 1 **EST:** 1974
SALES (est): 365.12K
SALES (corp-wide): 365.12K **Privately Held**
Web: www.northernbraceco.com
SIC: 3842 5999 Orthopedic appliances; Orthopedic and prosthesis applications

(G-15172)
NORTHERN ELECTRIC COMPANY INC
116 N Hill St (46617-2794)
PHONE..................................574 289-7791
EMP: 30 **EST:** 1946
SALES (est): 5.55MM **Privately Held**
Web: www.northernelectricco.com
SIC: 7694 5999 Electric motor repair; Motors, electric

(G-15173)
NORTHERN INDIANA ORDNANCE CO
Also Called: M & K Services
60161 Mayflower Rd (46614-9320)
PHONE..................................574 289-5938
John B Mumford, *Pr*
James T Mumford, *VP*
Rosanne Kroen, *Sec*
EMP: 4 **EST:** 1979
SQ FT: 700
SALES (est): 400K **Privately Held**
SIC: 8742 8734 3482 5932 Industry specialist consultants; Testing laboratories; Small arms ammunition; Antiques

(G-15174)
NORTHERN PROSTHETICS INC
610 N Michigan St Ste 104 (46601-1078)
PHONE..................................574 233-2459
Kelly L West, *Pr*
Timothy West, *VP*
EMP: 2 **EST:** 1985
SALES (est): 150.18K **Privately Held**
Web: www.northernbraceco.com
SIC: 3842 5999 Prosthetic appliances; Artificial limbs

(G-15175)
NUKEMED INC
Also Called: Spectronrx
17490 Dugdale Dr (46635-1572)
PHONE..................................574 271-2800
John Zehner, *CEO*
Kelli Lightfoot, *Prin*
EMP: 32 **EST:** 2004
SALES (est): 2.61MM **Privately Held**
SIC: 2834 Pharmaceutical preparations

(G-15176)
ODYSSIAN TECHNOLOGY LLC
511 E Colfax Ave (46617-2715)
PHONE..................................574 257-7555
EMP: 6 **EST:** 2001
SQ FT: 6,100
SALES (est): 512.91K **Privately Held**
Web: www.odyssian.com
SIC: 8711 6794 8734 3643 Engineering services; Patent owners and lessors; Testing laboratories; Current-carrying wiring services

(G-15177)
OMICRON BIOCHEMICALS INC
115 S Hill St (46617-2701)
PHONE..................................574 287-6910
Anthony S Serianni, *Pr*
▼ **EMP:** 21 **EST:** 1982
SALES (est): 2.66MM **Privately Held**
Web: www.omicronbio.com
SIC: 2819 2869 Chemicals, reagent grade: refined from technical grade; Industrial organic chemicals, nec

(G-15178)
ONE SOURCE FABRICATION LLC
325 S Lafayette Blvd (46601-2201)
PHONE..................................574 259-6011
David Rafinski, *Managing Member*
Kenneth K Jones, *Managing Member*
Eric W Seigel, *Managing Member*
Kim Perry, *Contrlr*
EMP: 5 **EST:** 2019
SALES (est): 386.85K **Privately Held**
Web: www.onesourcefab.com
SIC: 3281 Table tops, marble

(G-15179)
ONSYTE MOBILE LABS LLC
1251 N Eddy St Ste 200 (46617-1479)
PHONE..................................800 570-6844
EMP: 1
SALES (est): 69.27K **Privately Held**
SIC: 2899 Drug testing kits, blood and urine

(G-15180)
OREO EFFECT LLC
1233 Woodfield Ave (46615-3803)
PHONE..................................574 404-4800
Ariel E Words, *CEO*
EMP: 1 **EST:** 2021
SALES (est): 65.74K **Privately Held**
SIC: 3999 Candles

(G-15181)
ORTHOS INC
100 E Wayne St Ste 410 (46601-2349)
PHONE..................................574 406-8145
Ryan Callahan, *Pr*
EMP: 30 **EST:** 2020
SALES (est): 1.12MM **Privately Held**
Web: www.orthosinc.com
SIC: 3845 Medical cleaning equipment, ultrasonic

(G-15182)
OUTSOURCE TECHNOLOGIES INC
1832 N Kenmore St (46628-1610)
PHONE..................................574 233-1303
Sylvester Klusczinski, *Pr*
Susan Klusczinski, *Sec*
▲ **EMP:** 12 **EST:** 1975
SQ FT: 12,000
SALES (est): 915.6K **Privately Held**
Web: www.o-t-i.com
SIC: 3089 3499 Plastics hardware and building products; Metal household articles

(G-15183)
OVERGAARDS ARTCRAFT PRINTERS
Also Called: Artcraft Printers
2213 S Michigan St (46613-2321)
PHONE..................................574 234-8464
Thomas Overgaard, *Pr*
EMP: 2 **EST:** 1930
SQ FT: 3,000
SALES (est): 489.57K **Privately Held**
Web: www.artcraft-printers.com
SIC: 2752 2759 2791 2789 Offset printing; Letterpress printing; Typesetting; Bookbinding and related work

(G-15184)
OZINGA - CONCRETE
715 W Ireland Rd (46614-3809)
PHONE..................................574 291-7100
EMP: 8 **EST:** 2018
SALES (est): 99.63K **Privately Held**
Web: www.ozinga.com
SIC: 3273 Ready-mixed concrete

(PA)=Parent Co (HQ)=Headquarters
✪ = New Business established in last 2 years

South Bend - St. Joseph County (G-15185)   GEOGRAPHIC SECTION

(G-15185)
PANGAEA INDUSTRIES LLC
3702 W Sample St Ste 4060 # 4060 (46619-2974)
P.O. Box 176 (46563-0176)
PHONE.................574 850-5841
EMP: 9 EST: 2009
SALES (est): 228.86K **Privately Held**
Web: www.pangaeaind.com
SIC: 3999 Manufacturing industries, nec

(G-15186)
PART SOLUTIONS LLC
52167 Farmington Sqr (46624)
P.O. Box 1545 (46384-1545)
PHONE.................219 477-5101
Jeff Derubbo, *Managing Member*
EMP: 1 EST: 2001
SALES (est): 197.8K **Privately Held**
Web: www.partsolutionsllc.com
SIC: 3421 2389 7389 Knife blades and blanks; Garter belts; Business services, nec

(G-15187)
PATHFINDER COMMUNICATIONS CORP
Also Called: Fastsigns
2409 Mishawaka Ave (46615-2144)
PHONE.................574 266-5115
EMP: 5
SALES (corp-wide): 24.04MM **Privately Held**
Web: www.fastsigns.com
SIC: 3993 Signs and advertising specialties
PA: Pathfinder Communications Corporation
    421 S 2nd St Ste 100
    Elkhart IN 46516
    574 295-2500

(G-15188)
PEERLESS MACHINERY INC
4406 Technology Dr (46628-9700)
PHONE.................574 210-5990
Gannon Clark, *Pr*
Ron Nitowski, *VP*
EMP: 2 EST: 2010
SALES (est): 140.14K **Privately Held**
Web: www.peerless-machinery.com
SIC: 7699 3541 Industrial machinery and equipment repair; Machine tools, metal cutting type

(G-15189)
PENS BY MAISIE INC
309 E Pokagon St (46617-1225)
PHONE.................574 287-6178
Michael Jenuwine, *Prin*
EMP: 5 EST: 2015
SALES (est): 80.37K **Privately Held**
SIC: 2395 Embroidery and art needlework

(G-15190)
PEPSICO BEVERAGE SALES LLC
5435 Dylan Dr Ste 100 (46628)
PHONE.................574 314-6001
EMP: 108
SALES (corp-wide): 86.39B **Publicly Held**
Web: www.pepsico.com
SIC: 2086 Carbonated soft drinks, bottled and canned
HQ: Pepsico Beverage Sales, Llc
    700 Anderson Hill Rd
    Purchase NY 10577
    914 767-6000

(G-15191)
PERFECTION MOLD & TOOL INC
22255 Barking Deer Run (46628-6700)
PHONE.................574 292-0824
Patrick Moon, *Pr*
EMP: 6 EST: 1998
SALES (est): 472.81K **Privately Held**
SIC: 3544 Special dies and tools

(G-15192)
PERFORMNCE SFTWR SOLUTIONS INC
Also Called: Pssi
6561 Lonewolf Dr Ste 200 (46628-8465)
P.O. Box 447 (46373-0447)
PHONE.................574 239-2444
Lawrence Lukasik, *Prin*
EMP: 6 EST: 2017
SALES (est): 199.76K **Privately Held**
Web: www.pssiusa.com
SIC: 7372 Prepackaged software

(G-15193)
PERKINELMER HLTH SCIENCES INC
2633 Foundation Dr (46628-4332)
PHONE.................800 385-1555
Joel Goldberg, *Pr*
David Francisco, *Dir*
Drew Adams, *VP*
EMP: 1 EST: 2018
SALES (est): 64.33K **Privately Held**
SIC: 3826 Analytical instruments

(G-15194)
PFIZER INC
Also Called: Pfizer
6879 Enterprise Dr Ste 500 (46628)
PHONE.................574 232-9927
Leon Bertschy, *Mgr*
EMP: 4
SALES (corp-wide): 58.5B **Publicly Held**
Web: www.pfizer.com
SIC: 2834 Pharmaceutical preparations
PA: Pfizer Inc.
    66 Hudson Blvd E
    New York NY 10001
    212 733-2323

(G-15195)
PILKINGTON NORTH AMERICA INC
3725 Cleveland Rd Ste 100 (46628-8469)
PHONE.................574 273-5457
Joe Fraschetti, *Mgr*
EMP: 5
Web: www.pilkington.com
SIC: 3211 Flat glass
HQ: Pilkington North America, Inc.
    811 Madison Ave
    Toledo OH 43604
    419 247-3731

(G-15196)
PIONEER METAL FINISHING LLC
2424 Foundation Dr (46628-4327)
PHONE.................574 287-7239
Robert Pyle, *Pr*
EMP: 70
SALES (corp-wide): 172.31MM **Privately Held**
Web: www.pioneermetal.com
SIC: 3471 Electroplating of metals or formed products
PA: Pioneer Metal Finishing, Llc
    480 Pilgrim Way Ste 1400
    Green Bay WI 54304
    877 721-1100

(G-15197)
PLASTIC MOLDING MFG INC
5102 Dylan Dr (46628-6503)
PHONE.................574 234-9036
Richard Mckenney, *Pr*
EMP: 22
Web: www.plasticmoldingmfg.com
SIC: 3089 Injection molding of plastics
PA: Plastic Molding Mfg, Inc.
    34 Tower St
    Hudson MA 01749

(G-15198)
PMG INCORPORATED
5534 Colonial Ln (46614-6212)
PHONE.................574 291-3805
Chris Cummings, *Pr*
Joe Sorocco, *Pt*
EMP: 2 EST: 1994
SALES (est): 93.65K **Privately Held**
SIC: 3678 Electronic connectors

(G-15199)
POINT MACHINE PRODUCTS INC
621 S Scott St (46601-2823)
PHONE.................574 289-2429
Donald V Lamont, *Pr*
Glenda Lamont, *Sec*
EMP: 5 EST: 1980
SQ FT: 3,600
SALES (est): 379.31K **Privately Held**
SIC: 3451 Screw machine products

(G-15200)
PORTER CASE INC
3718 W Western Ave (46619-2839)
PHONE.................219 289-2616
Gary Pond, *Pr*
▲ EMP: 6 EST: 1990
SQ FT: 6,000
SALES (est): 59.81K **Privately Held**
Web: www.portercase.com
SIC: 3161 Clothing and apparel carrying cases

(G-15201)
PRECISION MILLWORK & PLAS INC
Also Called: Precision Mill Work & Plastics
3311 William Richardson Dr (46628-9747)
PHONE.................574 243-8720
Larry Shoemaker, *Pr*
Diane Shoemaker, *Sec*
EMP: 36 EST: 1990
SQ FT: 20,000
SALES (est): 986.72K **Privately Held**
SIC: 2542 2541 Fixtures, store: except wood ; Store fixtures, wood

(G-15202)
PREMIER BANDAGE 3 INC
4411 Quality Dr (46628-9732)
PHONE.................574 257-0248
Richard E Elliott, *Pr*
Paul Zurcher, *VP*
Tom Gyuriak, *VP*
Darwin Meier, *Sec*
EMP: 11 EST: 1989
SALES (est): 218.11K **Privately Held**
SIC: 7534 Rebuilding and retreading tires

(G-15203)
PREMIUM CORPORATION
1019 Royal Vineyards (46637-4860)
PHONE.................219 258-0141
Terry Hawkins-caldwell, *Pr*
EMP: 48 EST: 2021
SALES (est): 2.41MM **Privately Held**
SIC: 3571 7389 Electronic computers; Business Activities at Non-Commercial Site

(G-15204)
PRESS GANEY HOLDINGS INC
1739 Winston Dr (46635-2033)
PHONE.................574 387-4764
Melvin Hall, *Brnch Mgr*
EMP: 1
SALES (corp-wide): 258.39MM **Privately Held**
Web: www.pressganey.com
SIC: 2741 Miscellaneous publishing
PA: Press Ganey Holdings, Inc.
    404 Columbia Pl
    South Bend IN 46601
    781 295-5000

(G-15205)
PRINT MANAGEMENT SOLUTIONS INC
1833 Hass Dr (46635-2043)
PHONE.................574 234-7269
Thomas Gorski, *Prin*
EMP: 5 EST: 2005
SALES (est): 216.2K **Privately Held**
SIC: 2752 Offset printing

(G-15206)
PRO-TOTE SYSTEMS INC
Also Called: D&A Transportation
1705 S Olive St (46613-1120)
P.O. Box 3966 (46619-0966)
PHONE.................574 287-6006
Lori K Gesto, *Pr*
EMP: 11 EST: 2004
SQ FT: 15,000
SALES (est): 1.03MM **Privately Held**
Web: www.protote.com
SIC: 3531 Automobile wrecker hoists

(G-15207)
PROFORMA PRINT PROMO GROUP
3702 W Sample St (46619-2947)
PHONE.................574 931-2941
EMP: 5 EST: 2017
SALES (est): 236.62K **Privately Held**
Web: www.proforma-promotions.com
SIC: 2752 Commercial printing, lithographic

(G-15208)
PSI MOLDED PLASTICS IND INC
Also Called: PSI Molded Plastics
3615 Voorde Dr (46628-1644)
PHONE.................574 288-2100
Daniel Millf, *Pr*
Dug Pobb, *
Christopher J Lee, *
Steve Schmidt, *
◆ EMP: 502 EST: 1999
SQ FT: 100,000
SALES (est): 22.03MM
SALES (corp-wide): 21.94MM **Privately Held**
Web: www.psimp.com
SIC: 3089 Injection molding of plastics
PA: Psi Molded Plastics, Inc.
    4900 Hwy 501
    Myrtle Beach SC 29579
    843 347-4218

(G-15209)
PUZZLES PLUS LLC
1837 Thornhill Dr (46614-3571)
PHONE.................574 204-2054
Andrew Rector, *Owner*
EMP: 5 EST: 2017
SALES (est): 45.13K **Privately Held**
Web: www.puzzles-plus.com
SIC: 3944 Puzzles

(G-15210)
QUALITY FIRE PROTECTION
5320 S Main St (46614-5285)
PHONE.................269 683-0285
Rick Kidwell, *Owner*
EMP: 1 EST: 1981
SALES (est): 65.81K **Privately Held**
SIC: 2899 5999 Fire extinguisher charges; Fire extinguishers

GEOGRAPHIC SECTION
South Bend - St. Joseph County (G-15235)

(G-15211)
QUALITY MOLDED PRODUCTS INC
Also Called: SPI Industries
19850 State Line Rd (46637-1545)
PHONE.................574 272-3733
James Doster, *Pr*
John W Doster I, *CEO*
Susan M Doster, *Sec*
Kristen D Manz, *Dir*
John W Doster Ii, *Dir*
▲ **EMP:** 55 **EST:** 1988
SQ FT: 44,000
SALES (est): 8.03MM **Privately Held**
Web: www.moldedparts.com
SIC: 3089 Injection molding of plastics

(G-15212)
R 2 DIAGNOSTICS INC
1801 Commerce Dr (46628-1562)
PHONE.................574 288-4377
EMP: 6 **EST:** 1993
SALES (est): 527.24K **Privately Held**
Web: www.r2diagnostics.com
SIC: 3841 2835 Diagnostic apparatus, medical; Diagnostic substances

(G-15213)
R K C INSTRUMENT
4245 Meghan Beeler Ct (46628-8418)
PHONE.................574 273-6099
Teru Hochi, *Pr*
EMP: 10 **EST:** 2001
SALES (est): 825.01K **Privately Held**
Web: www.rkcinst.co.jp
SIC: 3825 Instruments to measure electricity

(G-15214)
R M MFG HOUSING SVC
1001 S Mayflower Rd L (46619-3923)
PHONE.................574 288-5207
M P Fletcher, *Prin*
EMP: 4 **EST:** 2008
SALES (est): 87.95K **Privately Held**
SIC: 3999 Manufacturing industries, nec

(G-15215)
RAB WOOD PRODUCTS
1507 S Olive St Ste B (46619)
PHONE.................574 206-5001
Robert A Bloss, *Owner*
EMP: 1 **EST:** 1995
SALES (est): 85.28K **Privately Held**
SIC: 2499 Applicators, wood

(G-15216)
RAIN NETWORK LLC
23232 Amber Valley Dr (46628-4099)
PHONE.................909 900-7776
Marco Antonio Magallon, *Pr*
EMP: 1 **EST:** 2014
SALES (est): 37.02K **Privately Held**
SIC: 7372 Application computer software

(G-15217)
REDDINGTON DESIGN INC
4221 Ralph Jones Ct (46628-9794)
PHONE.................574 272-0790
Randal Redding, *Pr*
Renee Hums, *VP*
▲ **EMP:** 6 **EST:** 1992
SQ FT: 1,800
SALES (est): 435.81K **Privately Held**
Web: www.reddingtondesign.com
SIC: 3993 Signs and advertising specialties

(G-15218)
RHONDAS TASTY TREATS LLC
706 S 29th St (46615-2238)
PHONE.................574 315-4011
EMP: 1 **EST:** 2020
SALES (est): 39.59K **Privately Held**
SIC: 2051 Cakes, bakery: except frozen

(G-15219)
RIETH-RILEY CNSTR CO INC
25200 State Road 23 (46614-9501)
PHONE.................574 288-8321
John Yadon, *Mgr*
EMP: 14
SALES (corp-wide): 174.41MM **Privately Held**
Web: www.rieth-riley.com
SIC: 1771 2951 Concrete work; Asphalt paving mixtures and blocks
PA: Rieth-Riley Construction Co., Inc.
3626 Elkhart Rd
Goshen IN 46526
574 875-5183

(G-15220)
RINK PRINTING COMPANY
Also Called: Rink Riverside Printing
814 S Main St (46601-3008)
PHONE.................574 232-7935
Michael S Rink, *Pr*
Joseph Castenand, *
Cynthia Rink, *
EMP: 30 **EST:** 1958
SQ FT: 55,000
SALES (est): 4.86MM **Privately Held**
Web: www.rinkprinting.com
SIC: 2752 2759 2791 2789 Offset printing; Letterpress printing; Typesetting; Bookbinding and related work

(G-15221)
RIOS INVESTMENT SERVICES LLC
✪
20266 Richard Ave (46637-2943)
PHONE.................574 514-3999
Mario Ellis, *Pr*
EMP: 3 **EST:** 2022
SALES (est): 80.13K **Privately Held**
SIC: 6799 8742 3799 Investors, nec; Transportation consultant; Trailers and trailer equipment

(G-15222)
RIVER BEND HOSE SPECIALTY INC
Also Called: River Bend Hose Specialty
1111 S Main St (46601-3398)
PHONE.................574 233-1133
EMP: 37 **EST:** 1981
SALES (est): 16.33MM **Privately Held**
Web: www.riverbendhose.com
SIC: 5085 3492 Industrial supplies; Hose and tube fittings and assemblies, hydraulic/pneumatic

(G-15223)
RJV INVESTMENTS INC
2411 Foundation Dr (46628)
PHONE.................574 234-1063
Richard Verwilst, *Pr*
EMP: 47 **EST:** 1962
SQ FT: 26,500
SALES (est): 4.67MM **Privately Held**
Web: www.attco.com
SIC: 3728 3769 3812 Aircraft parts and equipment, nec; Space vehicle equipment, nec; Missile guidance systems and equipment

(G-15224)
ROUND 2 LLC
4073 Meghan Beeler Ct (46628-8410)
PHONE.................574 243-3000
▲ **EMP:** 28 **EST:** 2005
SQ FT: 10,000
SALES (est): 4.62MM **Privately Held**
Web: www.round2corp.com

SIC: 3944 Toy trains, airplanes, and automobiles

(G-15225)
ROWAN INDUSTRIES LLC
52555 Kenilworth Rd (46637-3016)
PHONE.................574 302-1203
Martin A Couch, *Pr*
EMP: 3 **EST:** 2015
SALES (est): 52.66K **Privately Held**
SIC: 3999 Manufacturing industries, nec

(G-15226)
ROYAL ADHESIVES & SEALANTS LLC (HQ)
Also Called: Royal Elastomers
2001 W Washington St (46628-2032)
PHONE.................574 246-5000
Ted Clark, *Pr*
Steven Zens, *Marketing*
Randy Greenlee, *
Gary Stenke, *
◆ **EMP:** 100 **EST:** 2001
SALES (est): 700.5MM
SALES (corp-wide): 3.51B **Publicly Held**
Web: www.hbfuller.com
SIC: 2891 7389 8711 Adhesives and sealants; Packaging and labeling services; Building construction consultant
PA: H.B. Fuller Company
1200 Willow Lake Blvd
Saint Paul MN 55110
651 236-5900

(G-15227)
ROYAL HOLDINGS INC (HQ)
2001 W Washington St (46628-2032)
PHONE.................574 246-5000
Ted Clark, *CEO*
Gary Stenke, *
Steve Zens, *
Randy Greenlee, *
EMP: 107 **EST:** 2001
SALES (est): 98.93MM
SALES (corp-wide): 594.99MM **Privately Held**
Web: www.hbfuller.com
SIC: 2891 Adhesives
PA: Arsenal Capital Partners Lp
277 Park Ave
New York NY 10172
212 771-1717

(G-15228)
RPM MACHINERY LLC
3953 Ralph Jones Dr (46628-9792)
PHONE.................574 271-0800
Jay Courtney, *Mgr*
EMP: 9
SALES (corp-wide): 19.04MM **Privately Held**
Web: www.rpmmachinery.com
SIC: 5531 3599 Truck equipment and parts; Machine shop, jobbing and repair
PA: Rpm Machinery, Llc
3911 Limestone Dr
Fort Wayne IN 46809
260 747-1561

(G-15229)
RUBBER SHOP INC
Also Called: Royal Rubber Company
500 W Chippewa Ave (46614-3708)
P.O. Box 2375 (46680-2375)
PHONE.................574 291-6440
Victor M Grabovez, *Pr*
Claire Grabovez, *VP*
EMP: 5 **EST:** 1946
SQ FT: 30,000
SALES (est): 803.13K **Privately Held**
Web: www.royalrubber.com

SIC: 3061 3053 3052 3011 Mechanical rubber goods; Gaskets; packing and sealing devices; Rubber and plastics hose and beltings; Tires and inner tubes

(G-15230)
SAMPCO INC
Also Called: Sampco of Indiana
915 W Ireland Rd (46614-3842)
PHONE.................413 442-4043
Dennis Boo, *Mgr*
EMP: 4
Web: www.sampco.com
SIC: 2599 7389 3993 2952 Boards: planning, display, notice; Design, commercial and industrial; Signs and advertising specialties; Asphalt felts and coatings
PA: Sampco, Inc.
56 Downing Pkwy
Pittsfield MA 01201

(G-15231)
SAN MAR
54555 Pine Rd (46628-5628)
PHONE.................574 286-6884
EMP: 22 **EST:** 2011
SALES (est): 95.09K **Privately Held**
SIC: 3599 Industrial machinery, nec

(G-15232)
SANDERS PULSED POWER LLC
1400 E Angela Blvd Ste 310 (46617-1364)
PHONE.................630 313-2378
Howard Sanders, *CEO*
EMP: 1 **EST:** 2017
SALES (est): 145.76K **Privately Held**
Web: www.sanderspulsedpower.com
SIC: 3674 Semiconductors and related devices

(G-15233)
SANMAR TOOL & MANUFACTURING
54555 Pine Rd (46628-5628)
PHONE.................574 232-6081
Frank Martinez, *Pr*
Sandy Martinez, *VP*
EMP: 4 **EST:** 1986
SALES (est): 462.22K **Privately Held**
SIC: 3544 0752 Special dies, tools, jigs, and fixtures; Boarding services, kennels

(G-15234)
SCHAFER INDUSTRIES INC (PA)
Also Called: Schafer Gear Works-South Bend
4701 Nimtz Pkwy (46628)
PHONE.................574 234-4116
Bipin Doshi, *Pr*
Stan Blenke, *
Linda Doshi, *
Glenn Duncan, *
▲ **EMP:** 100 **EST:** 2000
SQ FT: 100,000
SALES (est): 40.18MM
SALES (corp-wide): 40.18MM **Privately Held**
Web: www.schaferindustries.com
SIC: 3499 3462 Fire- or burglary-resistive products; Gears, forged steel

(G-15235)
SCHURZ COMMUNICATIONS INC
225 W Colfax Ave (46626-1000)
PHONE.................574 235-6496
David Ray, *Mgr*
EMP: 28
SALES (corp-wide): 3.28B **Publicly Held**
Web: www.schurz.com
SIC: 2711 Commercial printing and newspaper publishing combined
HQ: Schurz Communications, Inc.

South Bend - St. Joseph County (G-15236)

1301 E Douglas Rd Ste 200
Mishawaka IN 46545
574 247-7237

(G-15236)
SEAFLO MARINE & RV N AMER LLC
Also Called: Seaflo
3602 W Sample St (46619-2923)
PHONE.................................844 473-2356
Christopher Kapsaskis, *
EMP: 30 **EST:** 2015
SALES (est): 3.85MM **Privately Held**
Web: www.seaflousa.com
SIC: 5083 3799 Agricultural machinery and equipment; Recreational vehicles

(G-15237)
SEGURA PUBLISHING COMPANY
1045 W Washington St (46601-1434)
PHONE.................................574 631-3143
Joseph Segura, Pr
EMP: 3 **EST:** 1981
SALES (est): 229.24K **Privately Held**
Web: www.segura.com
SIC: 2796 Etching on copper, steel, wood, or rubber: printing plates

(G-15238)
SENGO LLC
Also Called: Sengo Products
219 David St (46637-3413)
PHONE.................................574 383-9833
EMP: 1 **EST:** 2015
SALES (est): 106K **Privately Held**
SIC: 2819 7389 Elements; Business Activities at Non-Commercial Site

(G-15239)
SHAKOUR INDUSTRIES INC
Also Called: South Bend Metal Products Co
1319 Wayne St N (46615-1037)
P.O. Box 3065 (46619-0065)
PHONE.................................574 289-0100
Gabriel R Shakour, Pr
Michelle Shakour, Sec
EMP: 6 **EST:** 1953
SALES (est): 506.61K **Privately Held**
Web: www.sbendmetalproducts.com
SIC: 3469 3544 2759 2796 Stamping metal for the trade; Industrial molds; Laser printing ; Engraving platemaking services

(G-15240)
SHELF IT RIGHT LLC
2015 W Western Ave Ste 333 (46619-3544)
PHONE.................................574 368-6881
EMP: 2
SALES (est): 92.67K **Privately Held**
SIC: 3799 Transportation equipment, nec

(G-15241)
SHIDLER ASSOCIATES
6851 Enterprise Dr (46628-8402)
PHONE.................................574 232-7357
Peter Shidler, Owner
EMP: 1 **EST:** 1991
SALES (est): 75.38K **Privately Held**
SIC: 3088 Plastics plumbing fixtures

(G-15242)
SIERRA MACHINE
26378 Lakeview Dr (46619-4588)
PHONE.................................574 232-5694
Jerry Coon, Prin
EMP: 7 **EST:** 2005
SALES (est): 140K **Privately Held**
SIC: 3451 Screw machine products

(G-15243)
SIGN CREATIONS LLC
55234 Holmes Rd (46628-4912)
PHONE.................................574 855-1246
Timothy Grontkowski, Prin
EMP: 3 **EST:** 2007
SALES (est): 188.59K **Privately Held**
SIC: 3993 Signs and advertising specialties

(G-15244)
SIGN DEALS DELIVERED INC
19355 Sundale Dr (46614-5846)
PHONE.................................574 276-7404
Anjie Brenda, Prin
EMP: 4 **EST:** 2010
SALES (est): 136.36K **Privately Held**
Web: www.signdealsdelivered.com
SIC: 3993 Signs and advertising specialties

(G-15245)
SIMEOC LLC
18125 Chipstead Dr (46637-4424)
PHONE.................................240 210-5685
Cynthia Nikolai, Managing Member
Gregory Madey, Managing Member
EMP: 2 **EST:** 2016
SALES (est): 43.62K **Privately Held**
SIC: 7372 Application computer software

(G-15246)
SLATILE ROOFING AND SHTMTL CO
1703 S Ironwood Dr Ste A (46613-3499)
PHONE.................................574 233-7485
Gerald E Longerot, Pr
Ann C Longerot, *
EMP: 30 **EST:** 1924
SQ FT: 27,000
SALES (est): 4.32MM **Privately Held**
Web: www.slatileroofing.com
SIC: 1761 3444 1741 Roofing contractor; Sheet metalwork; Tuckpointing or restoration

(G-15247)
SLEEP EASY TECHNOLOGY INC
1400 E Angela Blvd Unit 147 (46617-1364)
PHONE.................................208 241-3264
Aaron Esplin, CEO
Anthony Esplin, CEO
EMP: 2 **EST:** 2021
SALES (est): 62.18K **Privately Held**
Web: www.oxyllowsystem.com
SIC: 2392 Cushions and pillows

(G-15248)
SMOR CASES INC
4622 S Burnett Dr (46614-3822)
PHONE.................................574 291-0346
James Watts, Pr
EMP: 28 **EST:** 1987
SQ FT: 15,000
SALES (est): 1.45MM **Privately Held**
SIC: 3161 Cases, carrying, nec

(G-15249)
SOMASCHINI NORTH AMERICA LLC
4601 Nimtz Pkwy (46628)
P.O. Box 1371 (46624-1371)
PHONE.................................574 968-0273
▲ **EMP:** 23 **EST:** 2010
SALES (est): 4.94MM **Privately Held**
Web: www.somaschini.com
SIC: 3714 5085 Gears, motor vehicle; Gears
HQ: Somaschini Spa
Via Nazionale 37
Trescore Balneario BG 24069

(G-15250)
SOUTH BEND BREW WERKS LLC
321 S Main St Ste 105 (46601-2232)
PHONE.................................801 209-2987
EMP: 3 **EST:** 2012
SALES (est): 231.07K **Privately Held**
Web: www.southbendbrewwerks.com
SIC: 2082 Beer (alcoholic beverage)

(G-15251)
SOUTH BEND CHOCOLATE CO INC (PA)
3300 W Sample St Ste 110 (46619-3077)
P.O. Box 4104 (46634-4104)
PHONE.................................574 233-2577
▲ **EMP:** 12 **EST:** 1994
SQ FT: 50,000
SALES (est): 11.09MM **Privately Held**
Web: www.sbchocolate.com
SIC: 5812 2066 5441 Cafe; Chocolate; Candy

(G-15252)
SOUTH BEND ETHANOL LLC
3201 W Calvert St (46613-1010)
PHONE.................................574 703-3360
Major Rhodes, Managing Member
EMP: 65 **EST:** 2013
SALES (est): 48.4MM
SALES (corp-wide): 67.3MM **Privately Held**
Web: www.southbendethanol.com
SIC: 1311 Natural gas production
PA: Verbio North America, Llc
9 W Broad St Ste 400
Stamford CT 06902
866 306-4777

(G-15253)
SOUTH BEND FORM TOOL CO INC
408 W Indiana Ave (46613-2093)
PHONE.................................574 289-2441
Herb Eggers, Pr
Lori Eggers, *
Amy Cavazos, *
EMP: 23 **EST:** 1950
SQ FT: 15,600
SALES (est): 2.4MM **Privately Held**
Web: www.sbform.com
SIC: 3544 Dies and die holders for metal cutting, forming, die casting

(G-15254)
SOUTH BEND HEAT TREAT INC
1331 Northside Blvd (46615-3922)
PHONE.................................574 288-4794
EMP: 6 **EST:** 2007
SALES (est): 23.75K **Privately Held**
SIC: 3398 Metal heat treating

(G-15255)
SOUTH BEND KOLLEL INC
3016 Caroline St (46614-2202)
PHONE.................................574 299-8263
EMP: 5
SALES (est): 139.71K **Privately Held**
Web: www.hocsouthbend.com
SIC: 3498 Tube fabricating (contract bending and shaping)

(G-15256)
SOUTH BEND SMOKE TIME INC
Also Called: South Bend Smoke Time
1841 S Bend Ave (46637-5637)
PHONE.................................574 318-4837
Janpal Singh, Prin
EMP: 15 **EST:** 2016
SALES (est): 563.58K **Privately Held**
SIC: 2111 Cigarettes

(G-15257)
SOUTH BEND TRIBUNE CORP (DH)
225 W Colfax Ave (46626-1001)
PHONE.................................574 235-6161
David C Ray, Pr
Kimberly D Wilson, *
Steven Funk, *
Mark Hocker, *
Cheryl J Morey, *
EMP: 500 **EST:** 1873
SQ FT: 80,000
SALES (est): 75.06MM
SALES (corp-wide): 3.28B **Publicly Held**
Web: www.southbendtribune.com
SIC: 2711 Commercial printing and newspaper publishing combined
HQ: Schurz Communications, Inc.
1301 E Douglas Rd Ste 200
Mishawaka IN 46545
574 247-7237

(G-15258)
SOUTH BEND WOODWORKS LLC
707 S Scott St (46601-2825)
P.O. Box 11523 (46634-0523)
PHONE.................................574 232-8875
Michael Lindurg, Managing Member
EMP: 15 **EST:** 2012
SALES (est): 1.56MM **Privately Held**
Web: www.southbendwoodworks.com
SIC: 2431 Millwork

(G-15259)
SOWN FURNISHINGS LLC
1808 Coachmans Trl (46637-4904)
PHONE.................................574 327-9029
EMP: 1 **EST:** 2021
SALES (est): 24K **Privately Held**
SIC: 3553 Furniture makers machinery, woodworking

(G-15260)
SPECIALTY PRODUCTS & POLYMERS
50869 Hawthorne Meadow Dr (46628-1863)
PHONE.................................269 684-5931
Rick Ray, CEO
EMP: 8 **EST:** 2009
SALES (est): 93.6K **Privately Held**
Web: www.specialtyproductspolymers.com
SIC: 3069 Molded rubber products

(G-15261)
SPECTRON MRC LLC
17490 Dugdale Dr (46635-1572)
PHONE.................................574 271-2800
Robert Galloway, Managing Member
Gregg Hiatt, Managing Member
EMP: 1 **EST:** 2002
SALES (est): 278.17K **Privately Held**
Web: www.spectronmrc.com
SIC: 3089 Thermoformed finished plastics products, nec

(G-15262)
SPYDER CONTROLS INC
1251 N Eddy St Ste 200 (46617-1478)
PHONE.................................866 919-9092
EMP: 5
SALES (est): 151.99K
SALES (corp-wide): 1.08MM **Privately Held**
SIC: 3519 3822 3625 Internal combustion engines, nec; Environmental controls; Relays and industrial controls
PA: Spyder Controls Corp
10-7102 52 St
Lacombe AB T4L 1
866 919-9092

GEOGRAPHIC SECTION

South Bend - St. Joseph County (G-15287)

(G-15263)
SS ELEVATIONS LLC
1143 E Ireland Rd Ste 1073 (46614-3446)
PHONE.....................................574 310-5442
EMP: 1
SALES (est): 41.07K **Privately Held**
SIC: **1389** Construction, repair, and dismantling services

(G-15264)
SSD CONTROL TECHNOLOGY INC
1801 S Main St (46613-2221)
PHONE.....................................574 289-5942
Steve Estes, *Pr*
Dave Konieczny, *
Lowell Tully, *
EMP: 32 EST: 1992
SQ FT: 23,500
SALES (est): 3.78MM **Privately Held**
Web: www.ssdcontrol.com
SIC: **3599** 5084 1799 Custom machinery; Machine tools and accessories; Welding on site

(G-15265)
ST AUGUSTINES PRESS INC (PA)
17917 Killington Way (46614-9773)
P.O. Box 2285 (46680-2285)
PHONE.....................................574 291-3500
Bruce Fingerhut, *Pr*
A J Fred Freddoso, *Treas*
Laila Fingerhut, *Bd of Dir*
EMP: 1 EST: 1996
SALES (est): 245.77K
SALES (corp-wide): 245.77K **Privately Held**
Web: www.staugustine.net
SIC: **2731** Books, publishing only

(G-15266)
STAMPEDE ENTERPRISES INC
24545 State Road 23 (46614-9388)
PHONE.....................................574 232-5997
Ernest Zeller, *Pr*
Daniel Fuchs, *
Richard Zeller, *
Steven Zeller, *
EMP: 70 EST: 1968
SQ FT: 100,000
SALES (est): 9.2MM **Privately Held**
Web: www.armorcontract.com
SIC: **3469** Stamping metal for the trade

(G-15267)
STAR NOVA US LLC (PA)
3702 W Sample St (46619-2947)
PHONE.....................................269 830-5802
Patrick L Magliozzo, *Pr*
Bin Ren, *Pr*
Patrick Magliozzi, *Proj Mgr*
EMP: 5 EST: 2017
SALES (est): 1.21MM
SALES (corp-wide): 1.21MM **Privately Held**
SIC: **2542** Racks, merchandise display or storage: except wood

(G-15268)
STEEL STORAGE INC
1408 Elwood Ave Ste A (46628-2757)
PHONE.....................................574 282-2618
Frank Prusinski, *Pr*
EMP: 11 EST: 1987
SQ FT: 25,000
SALES (est): 412.08K **Privately Held**
SIC: **3443** 5051 Metal parts; Steel

(G-15269)
STREET DREAMS PRODUCTION INC
1218 W Washington St (46601-1431)
PHONE.....................................574 440-9136
Charles Taylor, *Prin*
EMP: 1 EST: 2012
SALES (est): 47.93K **Privately Held**
SIC: **4789** 2741 Transportation services, nec ; Internet publishing and broadcasting

(G-15270)
STRESCORE INC
24445 State Road 23 (46614-9540)
P.O. Box 270 (46624-0270)
PHONE.....................................574 233-1117
Ralph M Hass, *Pr*
John S Reihl, *
▲ EMP: 50 EST: 1969
SQ FT: 2,000
SALES (est): 4.36MM **Privately Held**
Web: www.strescore.com
SIC: **3272** Prestressed concrete products

(G-15271)
STUMP HOME SPECIALTIES MFG INC
2220 S Main St (46613-2316)
PHONE.....................................574 291-0050
Arthur Stump, *Pr*
Louise Stump, *Sec*
EMP: 3 EST: 1959
SQ FT: 15,000
SALES (est): 190K **Privately Held**
Web: www.comfee.com
SIC: **2511** Wood household furniture

(G-15272)
SUGARPASTE
Also Called: Crystal Colors
2211 S Michigan St (46613-2321)
PHONE.....................................574 276-8703
Elizabeth Parvu, *Owner*
EMP: 2 EST: 2005
SALES (est): 110.24K **Privately Held**
Web: www.sugarpaste.com
SIC: **2087** Food colorings

(G-15273)
SUPPLIERIQ LLC
Also Called: Supplieriq
1007 Chapin St (46601-2830)
PHONE.....................................574 323-0707
Piyas Bandyopadhyay, *Pr*
EMP: 1 EST: 2015
SALES (est): 47.98K **Privately Held**
Web: www.supplieriq.us
SIC: **7372** 7375 8742 Business oriented computer software; Data base information retrieval; Materials mgmt. (purchasing, handling, inventory) consultant

(G-15274)
SURESTEP LLC
17530 Dugdale Dr (46635-1583)
PHONE.....................................574 233-3352
EMP: 111 EST: 2008
SALES (est): 13.33MM
SALES (corp-wide): 25.64MM **Privately Held**
Web: www.surestep.net
SIC: **3842** Surgical appliances and supplies
PA: Dienen, Inc.
   17530 Dugdale Dr
   South Bend IN 46635
   574 233-3352

(G-15275)
SUZUKI GARPHYTTAN CORP
Also Called: Garphyttan Wire
4404 Nimtz Pkwy (46628-4317)
PHONE.....................................574 232-8800
Kirk Manning, *Pr*
▲ EMP: 72 EST: 1997
SQ FT: 120,000
SALES (est): 27.71MM **Privately Held**
Web: www.suzuki-garphyttan.com
SIC: **3495** Precision springs
HQ: Suzuki Garphyttan Ab
   Bruksvagen 3
   Garphyttan 719 4
   19295100

(G-15276)
SYSCON INTERNATIONAL INC
Also Called: Syscon-Plantstar
1108 High St (46601-3796)
PHONE.....................................574 232-3900
Townsend Thomas, *Pr*
Magaret Thomas, *
EMP: 200 EST: 1968
SQ FT: 125,000
SALES (est): 13.12MM **Privately Held**
Web: www.syscon-intl.com
SIC: **3823** Analyzers, industrial process type

(G-15277)
SYSTEMS & SERVICES OF MICHIANA (PA)
Also Called: Express Press
3505 W Mcgill St (46628-4352)
PHONE.....................................574 273-1111
Brian Clauser, *Pr*
Norman L Wiggers, *Pr*
Sandra Clauser, *Sec*
EMP: 4 EST: 1977
SALES (est): 2.24MM
SALES (corp-wide): 2.24MM **Privately Held**
Web: www.express-press.com
SIC: **5112** 2752 Office supplies, nec; Offset printing

(G-15278)
SYSTEMS & SERVICES OF MICHIANA
Also Called: Systems and Services
325 N Dixie Way Ste 300 (46637-3311)
PHONE.....................................574 277-3355
Mark D Schaffer, *Brnch Mgr*
EMP: 5
SALES (corp-wide): 2.24MM **Privately Held**
Web: www.express-press.com
SIC: **5112** 2752 Office supplies, nec; Offset printing
PA: Systems & Services Of Michiana Inc
   3505 W Mcgill St
   South Bend IN 46628
   574 273-1111

(G-15279)
TAYCO BRACE INC
205 W Western Ave # 101 (46601-2213)
PHONE.....................................574 850-7910
Gavin Ferlic, *Prin*
EMP: 34 EST: 2017
SALES (est): 2MM **Privately Held**
Web: www.taycobrace.com
SIC: **5047** 3841 Medical equipment and supplies; Bone plates and screws

(G-15280)
TDC LOGGING LLC
24890 Edison Rd (46628-4974)
PHONE.....................................574 289-4243
Rose Calhoun, *Prin*
EMP: 2 EST: 2007
SALES (est): 100.78K **Privately Held**
SIC: **2411** Logging camps and contractors

(G-15281)
TESSELLATED INC
1400 E Angela Blvd (46617-1364)
PHONE.....................................304 277-8896
Kevin Craig, *CEO*
EMP: 1 EST: 2021
SALES (est): 49.15K **Privately Held**
Web: www.tessellatedinc.com
SIC: **3081** Polyethylene film

(G-15282)
TIMKEN COMPANY
Also Called: Timken Furnaces Agency
3010 Mishawaka Ave (46615-2348)
PHONE.....................................574 287-1566
John S Campbell, *Brnch Mgr*
EMP: 3
SALES (corp-wide): 4.77B **Publicly Held**
Web: www.timken.com
SIC: **3562** Ball and roller bearings
PA: The Timken Company
   4500 Mount Pleasant St Nw
   North Canton OH 44720
   234 262-3000

(G-15283)
TIRE RACK INC (HQ)
Also Called: Tire Rack, The
7101 Vorden Pkwy (46628)
PHONE.....................................888 541-1777
Michael Joines, *Pr*
Thomas Veldman, *
◆ EMP: 400 EST: 1973
SQ FT: 530,000
SALES (est): 512.43MM
SALES (corp-wide): 3.69B **Privately Held**
Web: www.tirerack.com
SIC: **5014** 3714 Automobile tires and tubes; Motor vehicle wheels and parts
PA: The Reinalt-Thomas Corporation
   20225 N Scottsdale Rd
   Scottsdale AZ 85255
   480 606-6000

(G-15284)
TK FINISHING LLC
3702 W Sample St Ste 4045 (46619-2976)
PHONE.....................................574 233-1617
Margaret Tenderenda, *Prin*
EMP: 3 EST: 2007
SALES (est): 245.71K **Privately Held**
Web: www.tkfinishing.com
SIC: **3471** Finishing, metals or formed products

(G-15285)
TOYO SEIKO NORTH AMERICA INC
3585 Moreau Ct (46628-4320)
PHONE.....................................574 288-2000
Yoshihiro Watanzabe, *CEO*
EMP: 6 EST: 2014
SALES (est): 502.97K **Privately Held**
Web: www.toyoseiko-na.com
SIC: **3398** Shot peening (treating steel to reduce fatigue)

(G-15286)
TRANE US INC
Also Called: Trane
3725 Cleveland Rd Ste 300 (46628-8470)
PHONE.....................................574 282-4880
Dave Sommer, *Brnch Mgr*
EMP: 7
Web: www.trane.com
SIC: **3585** Refrigeration and heating equipment
HQ: Trane U.S. Inc.
   800-E Beaty St
   Davidson NC 28036
   704 655-4000

(G-15287)
TRANSCEND ORTHTICS PRSTHTICS L (HQ)
17530 Dugdale Dr (46635-1583)

(PA)=Parent Co (HQ)=Headquarters
✪ = New Business established in last 2 years

2024 Harris Indiana Industrial Directory

South Bend - St. Joseph County (G-15288) — GEOGRAPHIC SECTION

PHONE..................574 233-3352
Bernie Veldman, *CEO*
Pam Veldman, *VP*
Jeff Laderer, *CFO*
EMP: 14 **EST:** 2000
SQ FT: 9,000
SALES (est): 12.31MM
SALES (corp-wide): 25.64MM **Privately Held**
Web: www.hangerclinic.com
SIC: 3842 Surgical appliances and supplies
PA: Dienen, Inc.
17530 Dugdale Dr
South Bend IN 46635
574 233-3352

(G-15288)
TRANSFORMATION INDUSTRIES LLC
615 Cushing St (46616-1117)
PHONE..................574 457-9320
Kory Lantz, *Prin*
EMP: 5 **EST:** 2014
SALES (est): 142.9K **Privately Held**
SIC: 3999 Manufacturing industries, nec

(G-15289)
TRC MFG INC
17460 Fleetwood Ln (46635-1365)
PHONE..................574 262-9299
Martin L Borton, *Ch Bd*
Jim Hite, *Pr*
EMP: 8 **EST:** 2013
SQ FT: 40,000
SALES (est): 137.86K **Privately Held**
Web: www.trcmfg.com
SIC: 3799 Recreational vehicles

(G-15290)
TRI-PAC INC
3333 N Kenmore St (46628-4313)
PHONE..................574 855-2197
EMP: 142
SALES (est): 11.39MM **Privately Held**
SIC: 2844 2834 3841 Perfumes, cosmetics and other toilet preparations; Proprietary drug products; Surgical and medical instruments

(G-15291)
TRI-PAC INC
3333 N Kenmore St (46628-4313)
PHONE..................574 855-2197
Vikram Shah, *CEO*
Paras Shah, *
Prasham Shah, *
EMP: 145 **EST:** 2009
SQ FT: 65,000
SALES (est): 126.21MM **Privately Held**
Web: www.tri-pac.us
SIC: 2834 3841 7389 2813 Proprietary drug products; Ophthalmic instruments and apparatus; Filling pressure containers; Aerosols

(G-15292)
TRIANGLE MACHINE INC
3702 W Sample St Ste 1125 (46619-2977)
PHONE..................574 246-0165
EMP: 7 **EST:** 1996
SQ FT: 1,800
SALES (est): 666.18K **Privately Held**
SIC: 3599 Machine shop, jobbing and repair

(G-15293)
TRIBEJEWELS LLC
424 S Michigan St (46624-1601)
PHONE..................574 298-7162
EMP: 1
SALES (est): 69.27K **Privately Held**
SIC: 3961 Jewelry apparel, non-precious metals

(G-15294)
TRION COATINGS LLC
1400 E Angela Blvd # 331 (46617-1364)
PHONE..................312 342-2004
Doug Morrison, *Pr*
EMP: 4 **EST:** 2015
SALES (est): 429.31K **Privately Held**
Web: www.trioncoatings.com
SIC: 3479 Coating of metals and formed products

(G-15295)
ULTRAMONTANE ASSOCIATES INC
Also Called: Culture Wars
206 Marquette Ave (46617-1111)
PHONE..................574 289-9786
Michael Jones, *Pr*
E Michael Jones, *Pr*
Marc Brammer, *VP*
Ruth Jones, *Sec*
EMP: 4 **EST:** 1981
SALES (est): 234.78K **Privately Held**
Web: www.culturewars.com
SIC: 2721 Magazines: publishing only, not printed on site

(G-15296)
UNITED COATINGS TECH INC
1011 S Main St (46601-3335)
PHONE..................574 287-4774
Mark Huffer, *Pr*
▲ **EMP:** 10 **EST:** 2005
SQ FT: 36,000
SALES (est): 1.63MM **Privately Held**
Web: www.unitedcoatingstechnologies.com
SIC: 2851 Paints and paint additives

(G-15297)
US NANO LLC
1400 E Angela Blvd Unit 125 (46617-1368)
PHONE..................941 360-2161
EMP: 3 **EST:** 2020
SALES (est): 60.48K **Privately Held**
Web: www.usnanollc.com
SIC: 3674 Semiconductors and related devices

(G-15298)
US TRUCK TRAILER SERVICE
1311 S Olive St (46619-4209)
PHONE..................574 232-2014
EMP: 5 **EST:** 2020
SALES (est): 291.08K **Privately Held**
Web: www.ustrucktrailer.com
SIC: 3715 Truck trailers

(G-15299)
VALAD MCHNING CNTRLESS GRNDING
Also Called: Kaley Centerless Grinding
2825 S Main St (46614-1021)
PHONE..................574 291-5541
Michael Boyle, *Pr*
EMP: 2 **EST:** 1955
SQ FT: 3,000
SALES (est): 188.98K **Privately Held**
SIC: 3599 Machine shop, jobbing and repair

(G-15300)
VALUE PRODUCTION INC
2629 Foundation Dr (46628-4332)
PHONE..................574 246-1913
Nevin Siqueira, *Pr*
Steven Hartz, *
EMP: 25 **EST:** 2000
SQ FT: 15,000
SALES (est): 935.92K **Privately Held**
Web: www.valuetooleng.com
SIC: 3728 3812 Aircraft parts and equipment, nec; Defense systems and equipment

(G-15301)
VALUE TOOL & ENGINEERING INC (PA)
2629 Foundation Dr (46628-4332)
PHONE..................574 246-1913
Steven Hartz, *Pr*
EMP: 52 **EST:** 1998
SQ FT: 30,000
SALES (est): 10.09MM
SALES (corp-wide): 10.09MM **Privately Held**
Web: www.valuetooleng.com
SIC: 3599 Machine shop, jobbing and repair

(G-15302)
VIOLET SKY LLC
1211 Mishawaka Ave (46615-1127)
PHONE..................574 850-5070
EMP: 1 **EST:** 2014
SALES (est): 68.2K **Privately Held**
SIC: 2066 Cacao bean processing

(G-15303)
W J HAGERTY & SONS LTD INC
3801 Linden Ave (46619)
P.O. Box 1496 (46624)
PHONE..................574 288-4991
Debra Hagerty, *
Shelley Meszaros, *
◆ **EMP:** 45 **EST:** 1895
SQ FT: 57,000
SALES (est): 9.02MM **Privately Held**
Web: www.hagertyusa.com
SIC: 2842 Cleaning or polishing preparations, nec

(G-15304)
WATCON INC (PA)
2215 S Main St (46613-2315)
PHONE..................574 287-3397
George A Resnik Junior, *Pr*
Timothy Henthorn, *VP*
Thomas Resnik, *VP*
EMP: 9 **EST:** 1947
SQ FT: 16,000
SALES (est): 2.34MM
SALES (corp-wide): 2.34MM **Privately Held**
Web: www.watcon-inc.com
SIC: 2899 3589 7389 Water treating compounds; Water treatment equipment, industrial; Inspection and testing services

(G-15305)
WHEEL HORSE SALES & SERVICE
51465 Indiana State Route 933 (46637-1617)
PHONE..................574 272-4242
James Bernath, *Pr*
EMP: 7 **EST:** 1978
SALES (est): 138.17K **Privately Held**
SIC: 3524 Lawn and garden equipment

(G-15306)
WILD CHILD ORGANICS LLC
1143 E Ireland Rd (46614)
PHONE..................574 213-5204
Aquila Lee, *CEO*
EMP: 5
SALES (corp-wide): 320.64K **Privately Held**
SIC: 2844 Hair preparations, including shampoos
PA: Wild Child Organics Llc
18890 Cleveland Rd
South Bend IN 46637
574 520-0440

(G-15307)
WILLIAMSBURG FURNITURE INC
3300 W Sample St (46619-3079)
PHONE..................574 387-5691
Alejeandra Garcia, *Pr*
EMP: 49
SALES (corp-wide): 3.47B **Publicly Held**
Web: www.wbfusa.com
SIC: 2512 2515 Upholstered household furniture; Mattresses and foundations
HQ: Williamsburg Furniture, Inc.
2096 Cheyenne St
Nappanee IN 46550

(G-15308)
WOOD SIGN PRODUCTS
56956 Oak Rd (46619-2236)
PHONE..................574 234-1218
EMP: 1 **EST:** 1982
SALES (est): 58K **Privately Held**
SIC: 2499 Applicators, wood

(G-15309)
WOODS ENTERPRISES
26795 State Road 2 (46619-9795)
PHONE..................574 232-7449
Carl Woods, *Owner*
EMP: 2 **EST:** 1976
SALES (est): 107.02K **Privately Held**
SIC: 0811 2431 2395 2396 Tree farm; Interior and ornamental woodwork and trim; Embroidery and art needlework; Screen printing on fabric articles

(G-15310)
XYLEM VUE INC (HQ)
3725 Foundation Ct Ste E (46628)
PHONE..................574 855-1012
Patrick Decker, *Pr*
EMP: 54 **EST:** 2020
SALES (est): 17.96MM **Publicly Held**
SIC: 3561 Pumps and pumping equipment
PA: Xylem Inc.
301 Water St Se Ste 200
Washington DC 20003

(G-15311)
YODER SOFTWARE INC
1121 N Notre Dame Ave (46617-1342)
PHONE..................574 302-6232
John Yoder, *Pr*
Michael Seelinger, *VP*
EMP: 2 **EST:** 1990
SALES (est): 72.9K **Privately Held**
Web: www.yodersoftware.com
SIC: 7372 Prepackaged software

(G-15312)
ZENDIGO BOUTIQUE LLC
1143 E Ireland Rd (46614-3446)
PHONE..................574 314-8328
Kenya James, *CEO*
EMP: 1 **EST:** 2021
SALES (est): 25K **Privately Held**
SIC: 7991 5632 2339 5399 Physical fitness facilities; Dancewear; Women's and misses' accessories; Miscellaneous general merchandise

(G-15313)
ZOETIS
6879 Enterprise Dr Ste 500 (46628)
PHONE..................574 232-9927
EMP: 6 **EST:** 2018
SALES (est): 233.24K **Privately Held**
Web: www.zoetis.com
SIC: 2834 Pharmaceutical preparations

South Milford
Lagrange County

(G-15314)
WIBLE LUMBER INC
Also Called: Wible U-Pick Hardwoods
7155 S State Rte 3 (46786)
P.O. Box 7 (46786-0007)
PHONE.................................260 351-2441
David Wible, *Pr*
Dennis Nowels, *
EMP: 35 EST: 1951
SQ FT: 40,000
SALES (est): 4.8MM **Privately Held**
Web: www.wiblelumber.com
SIC: 2431 2435 5031 Millwork; Hardwood veneer and plywood; Lumber, plywood, and millwork

South Whitley
Whitley County

(G-15315)
AEROMOTIVE TECH INC
4835 W 800 S (46787-9710)
PHONE.................................260 723-5646
Linda L Long, *Prin*
EMP: 3 EST: 2005
SALES (est): 243.74K **Privately Held**
SIC: 3714 Motor vehicle parts and accessories

(G-15316)
AG PLUS INC (PA)
401 N Main St (46787-1250)
P.O. Box 306 (46787-0306)
PHONE.................................260 723-5141
Kent Hoffman, *Ch*
Jeff Mize, *
Dan Bacon, *
Stanley Studebaker, *
EMP: 24 EST: 1912
SQ FT: 5,000
SALES (est): 51.74MM
SALES (corp-wide): 51.74MM **Privately Held**
Web: www.agplusinc.com
SIC: 5191 2041 5153 Fertilizer and fertilizer materials; Flour and other grain mill products; Grain elevators

(G-15317)
ECOJACKS LLC
Also Called: Lumber WD Furn Mg Sell WD Flrg
503 E Broad St (46787-1017)
PHONE.................................574 306-0414
Brian Mack, *Managing Member*
EMP: 3 EST: 2011
SALES (est): 215.22K **Privately Held**
Web: www.ecojacks.com
SIC: 2426 2431 2521 2511 Lumber, hardwood dimension; Floor baseboards, wood; Wood office furniture; Wood household furniture

(G-15318)
FOX PRODUCTS CORPORATION
6110 S State Road 5 (46787-9770)
P.O. Box 347 (46787-0347)
PHONE.................................260 723-4888
Alan H Fox, *Pr*
Pamela M Fox, *Sec*
Dale Anthony Starkey, *Prin*
▲ EMP: 130 EST: 1949
SQ FT: 50,000
SALES (est): 8.24MM **Privately Held**
Web: www.foxproducts.com
SIC: 3931 5736 Bassoons; Musical instrument stores

(G-15319)
JOHNSON BROS S WHITLEY SIGN CO
Also Called: Johnson Brothers Sign Co.
304 N Calhoun St (46787-1344)
P.O. Box 345 (46787-0345)
PHONE.................................260 723-5161
Hal Howard, *Pr*
Tim Grant, *VP*
Bill Howard, *Pr*
Les Cripe, *Sec*
EMP: 13 EST: 1929
SQ FT: 10,000
SALES (est): 283.67K **Privately Held**
Web: www.johnsonbros-sign.com
SIC: 3993 7629 Electric signs; Electrical repair shops

(G-15320)
KILGORE MANUFACTURING CO
602 Hathaway Dr (46787-1234)
PHONE.................................260 723-5523
EMP: 7 EST: 2014
SALES (est): 60.04K **Privately Held**
Web: www.kilgoremfg.com
SIC: 3599 Machine shop, jobbing and repair

(G-15321)
KUCKUCK TRANSPORT LLC
2165 S 625 W (46787-9651)
PHONE.................................260 609-0316
EMP: 8 EST: 2005
SALES (est): 503.17K **Privately Held**
SIC: 3715 Truck trailers

(G-15322)
NUTRITIONAL RESEARCH ASSOC (PA)
Also Called: Whitley Feeds Div
407 E Broad St (46787-1001)
P.O. Box 354 (46787-0354)
PHONE.................................260 723-4931
Barbar Pook, *Pr*
EMP: 10 EST: 1934
SQ FT: 6,000
SALES (est): 1.52MM
SALES (corp-wide): 1.52MM **Privately Held**
SIC: 5191 2833 2834 2077 Animal feeds; Vegetable oils, medicinal grade: refined or concentrated; Pharmaceutical preparations; Animal and marine fats and oils

(G-15323)
SHODAS TEES & GIFTS
403 S Main St (46787-1442)
PHONE.................................260 418-8448
Rosemary Shoda, *Prin*
EMP: 5 EST: 2017
SALES (est): 67.26K **Privately Held**
SIC: 2759 Screen printing

(G-15324)
SOLID ROCK GBC
213 Reed St (46787-1265)
PHONE.................................260 723-4806
Tonya Swenson, *Prin*
EMP: 4 EST: 2017
SALES (est): 90.74K **Privately Held**
Web: www.solidrockgbc.org
SIC: 2653 Corrugated and solid fiber boxes

(G-15325)
SOUTH WHTLEY TRBUNE PRCTON NEW
113 S State St (46787-1390)
PHONE.................................260 723-4771
EMP: 4 EST: 1970
SALES (est): 196.33K **Privately Held**
Web: www.southwhitley.org
SIC: 2711 Newspapers, publishing and printing

(G-15326)
SQUIRREL DADDY INC
405 W Buffalo St (46787-1208)
PHONE.................................260 723-4946
◆ EMP: 4 EST: 2010
SALES (est): 350.4K **Privately Held**
Web: www.squirreldaddy.com
SIC: 3553 Woodworking machinery

(G-15327)
STEMS & STITCHES
6711 W 200 S (46787-9674)
PHONE.................................260 503-4955
EMP: 4 EST: 2013
SALES (est): 52.75K **Privately Held**
SIC: 2395 Embroidery and art needlework

(G-15328)
STEVE REIFF INC (PA)
Also Called: Farmland Lumber
5650 W 800 S (46787-9764)
P.O. Box 531 (46787-0531)
PHONE.................................260 723-4360
Steven Reiff, *Pr*
Doris Reiff, *
Doug Reiff, *
Stan Reiff, *
EMP: 48 EST: 1971
SQ FT: 9,300
SALES (est): 5.72MM
SALES (corp-wide): 5.72MM **Privately Held**
Web: www.stevereiff.com
SIC: 3471 7532 3479 Sand blasting of metal parts; Truck painting and lettering; Painting of metal products

(G-15329)
STUMP PRINTING CO
111 E Broad St (46787-1335)
PHONE.................................260 723-5171
EMP: 11 EST: 2019
SALES (est): 443.88K **Privately Held**
SIC: 2752 Commercial printing, lithographic

(G-15330)
SYNERGY FEEDS LLC
401 N Main St (46787-1250)
P.O. Box 306 (46787-0306)
PHONE.................................260 723-5141
EMP: 20 EST: 2009
SALES (est): 3.27MM **Privately Held**
Web: www.agplusinc.com
SIC: 2048 5191 Bone meal, prepared as animal feed; Animal feeds

(G-15331)
WHITLEY EVERGREEN INC (HQ)
201 W First St (46787-1256)
P.O. Box 496 (46787-0496)
PHONE.................................260 723-5131
Simon Dragan, *Pr*
Barry Gossett, *
Randall Holler, *General Vice President*
Mike Ransbottom, *
Bob Jones, *
EMP: 14 EST: 1943
SQ FT: 75,000
SALES (est): 25.05MM **Privately Held**
Web: www.whitleyman.com
SIC: 2451 Mobile buildings: for commercial use
PA: Whitley Manufacturing Co., Inc.
201 W First St
South Whitley IN 46787

(G-15332)
WISH FACTORY INC
Also Called: Thread Bear Publishing
509 S Main St (46787-1444)
PHONE.................................260 745-2550
Jana Shellman, *Pr*
EMP: 19 EST: 1995
SALES (est): 898.99K **Privately Held**
SIC: 2731 3652 Books, publishing only; Prerecorded records and tapes

Speedway
Marion County

(G-15333)
BLUE PRINT UNIVERSITY INC
5326 W 16th St (46224-6403)
PHONE.................................317 446-8715
Antonio Lisenbee, *Pr*
EMP: 3 EST: 2020
SALES (est): 185.42K **Privately Held**
SIC: 2752 Commercial printing, lithographic

(G-15334)
DALLARA LLC
Also Called: Dallara Indycar Factory
1201 Main St (46224-6533)
PHONE.................................317 388-5400
Stefano Deponti, *CEO*
Andrea Pontremoli, *CEO*
EMP: 13 EST: 2010
SALES (est): 4.95MM
SALES (corp-wide): 187.23MM **Privately Held**
Web: www.indycarfactory.com
SIC: 3714 Motor vehicle parts and accessories
HQ: Dallara Usa Holding, Inc.
1201 Main St Ste B
Speedway IN 46224
317 388-5400

(G-15335)
DALLARA RESEARCH CENTER LLC
1201 Main St Ste B (46224-6533)
PHONE.................................317 388-5416
Stefano Deponti, *CEO*
EMP: 3 EST: 2014
SALES (est): 493.39K
SALES (corp-wide): 187.23MM **Privately Held**
Web: www.dallara.it
SIC: 7372 Prepackaged software
HQ: Dallara Usa Holding, Inc.
1201 Main St Ste B
Speedway IN 46224
317 388-5400

(G-15336)
DAREDEVIL BREWING COMPANY LLC
Also Called: Daredevil Brewing Co
1151 Main St (46224-6976)
PHONE.................................765 602-1067
EMP: 7 EST: 2011
SALES (est): 505.49K **Privately Held**
Web: www.daredevilbeer.com
SIC: 5813 2082 Bars and lounges; Beer (alcoholic beverage)

(G-15337)
OMR NORTH AMERICA INC
4755 W Gilman St (46224-6981)
PHONE.................................317 510-9700
Marco Bonometti, *Pr*
EMP: 59 EST: 2015
SALES (est): 8.94MM
SALES (corp-wide): 603.81MM **Privately Held**

Spencer - Owen County (G-15338) — GEOGRAPHIC SECTION

Web: www.omrautomotive.com
SIC: 3465 Body parts, automobile: stamped metal
PA: Omr Holding Spa
Via Vittor Pisani 16
Milano MI 20124
030213501

Spencer
Owen County

(G-15338)
ACCENT LIMESTONE & CARVING INC
2255 Wood Dr (47460-6853)
PHONE..................................812 829-5663
Michael Donham, Owner
EMP: 2 EST: 2007
SALES (est): 228.7K Privately Held
Web: www.accentlimestone.com
SIC: 3281 Cut stone and stone products

(G-15339)
BABBS SUPERMARKET INC
Also Called: Babbs Super-Value
459 W Morgan St (47460-1221)
P.O. Box 620 (47460-0620)
PHONE..................................812 829-2231
Robert W Babbs, Pr
EMP: 29 EST: 1928
SQ FT: 22,000
SALES (est): 2.02MM Privately Held
Web: www.babbssupermarket.com
SIC: 5411 2051 Grocery stores, independent; Bread, cake, and related products

(G-15340)
BOSTON SCIENTIFIC CORPORATION
780 Brookside Dr (47460-1021)
PHONE..................................812 829-4877
Dale Jackson, Brnch Mgr
EMP: 1000
SALES (corp-wide): 12.68B Publicly Held
Web: www.bostonscientific.com
SIC: 3841 Surgical and medical instruments
PA: Boston Scientific Corporation
300 Boston Scientific Way
Marlborough MA 01752
508 683-4000

(G-15341)
CHECKERED RACING & CHROME LLC
2221 N St Rd (47260)
PHONE..................................812 275-2875
Eddie Pierce, Managing Member
EMP: 10 EST: 2013
SQ FT: 8,000
SALES (est): 921.12K Privately Held
Web: www.checkeredracing.com
SIC: 3711 Chassis, motor vehicle

(G-15342)
COOK CAPITAL EQUIPMENT LLC
1100 W Morgan St (47460-9426)
PHONE..................................800 457-4500
Walter Ryan, Mgr
EMP: 10 EST: 2018
SALES (est): 585.54K Privately Held
SIC: 3841 Surgical and medical instruments

(G-15343)
COOK INCORPORATED
Also Called: Cook Urological
1100 W Morgan St (47460-9426)
PHONE..................................812 829-4891
Nate Myers, Genl Mgr
EMP: 1
SALES (corp-wide): 1.61B Privately Held
Web: www.cookmedical.com
SIC: 3841 Surgical and medical instruments
HQ: Cook Incorporated
750 Daniels Way
Bloomington IN 47404
812 339-2235

(G-15344)
CRESCENDO INC
Also Called: Winner's Circle
56 E Jefferson St (47460-1705)
PHONE..................................812 829-4759
Marilyn Keith, Pr
Joe Keith, Sec
EMP: 3 EST: 1976
SQ FT: 5,500
SALES (est): 375.68K Privately Held
SIC: 5091 5941 2791 2752 Sporting and recreation goods; Sporting goods and bicycle shops; Typesetting; Commercial printing, lithographic

(G-15345)
EVANS ADHESIVE CORPORATION
7140 State Highway 246 (47460-6412)
PHONE..................................812 859-4245
Carla Mccracken, Prin
EMP: 6 EST: 2017
SALES (est): 123.28K Privately Held
Web: www.evansadhesive.com
SIC: 2891 Adhesives

(G-15346)
FENDER 4 STAR MEATS PROCESSING
Also Called: Fender 4 Star Meat Processing
1494 Rocky Hill Rd (47460-5598)
PHONE..................................812 829-3240
Lewis Fender, Pr
Steve Fender, Sec
Janice Fender, Treas
EMP: 7 EST: 1981
SQ FT: 5,000
SALES (est): 511.38K Privately Held
Web: www.fender4star.com
SIC: 2011 Meat packing plants

(G-15347)
FRANKLINS MERCANTILE
7115 Kimberly Ln (47460-5872)
PHONE..................................812 876-0426
Kathleen Franklins, Owner
EMP: 3 EST: 2012
SALES (est): 180.06K Privately Held
SIC: 5411 2038 Grocery stores; Pizza, frozen

(G-15348)
HENRY HOLSTERS LLC
224 State Highway 43 (47460-6725)
PHONE..................................812 369-2266
EMP: 10 EST: 2008
SALES (est): 584.34K Privately Held
Web: www.henryholsters.com
SIC: 2821 Plastics materials and resins

(G-15349)
HOLLOWHEART INDUSTRIES LLC
5916 N Us Highway 231 (47460)
PHONE..................................812 737-4002
Danica Richmond, Mgr
EMP: 4 EST: 2021
SALES (est): 64.19K Privately Held
SIC: 3999 Manufacturing industries, nec

(G-15350)
INDIANA CAST STONE COMPANY
4288 Freedom Rd (47460-9004)
PHONE..................................317 847-5429
Jim Grubaugh, Pr
EMP: 10 EST: 2021
SALES (est): 989.42K Privately Held
Web: www.indianacaststone.com
SIC: 3363 Aluminum die-castings

(G-15351)
INNOVTIVE SURGICAL DESIGNS INC
Also Called: Isd Precision
3206 Hardscrabble Rd (47460-5091)
PHONE..................................812 369-4252
Cherie Anderson, Admn
Mark Bartosh, CEO
EMP: 15 EST: 2006
SALES (est): 1.13MM Privately Held
Web: www.innovativesurgicaldesigns.com
SIC: 3841 Surgical and medical instruments

(G-15352)
IONIC CUT STONE INCORPORATED
1201 Kelley Farm Dr (47460-7046)
P.O. Box 409 (47460-0409)
PHONE..................................812 829-3416
EMP: 9 EST: 1993
SALES (est): 1.28MM Privately Held
Web: www.ioniccutstone.com
SIC: 5032 3281 Limestone; Limestone, cut and shaped

(G-15353)
IRVING MATERIALS INC
Also Called: I M I
947 W State Highway 46 (47460-6749)
PHONE..................................812 829-9445
Randy Lawrence, Mgr
EMP: 1
SALES (corp-wide): 814.09MM Privately Held
Web: www.irvmat.com
SIC: 3273 Ready-mixed concrete
PA: Irving Materials, Inc.
8032 N State Road 9
Greenfield IN 46140
317 326-3101

(G-15354)
MADER MILL INC
3720 State Highway 43 (47460-5925)
PHONE..................................812 876-9754
Scott Mader, Prin
EMP: 8 EST: 2019
SALES (est): 277.71K Privately Held
Web: www.madermill.com
SIC: 2448 Pallets, wood

(G-15355)
MARK PARMENTER
Also Called: White Rver Fndry/Creative Arts
358 S East St (47460-1814)
PHONE..................................812 829-6583
▲ EMP: 5 EST: 1988
SALES (est): 318.87K Privately Held
Web: www.ceoevanssecurity.com
SIC: 3366 Bronze foundry, nec

(G-15356)
OWEN VALLEY WINERY LLC
491 Timber Ridge Rd (47460-5980)
PHONE..................................812 828-0883
EMP: 2 EST: 2007
SALES (est): 167.11K Privately Held
Web: www.owenvalleywinery.com
SIC: 2084 Wines

(G-15357)
PRESTON LEADERBRAND
491 Timber Ridge Rd (47460-5980)
PHONE..................................812 828-0883
Preston Leaderbrand, Owner
EMP: 13 EST: 2017
SALES (est): 392.28K Privately Held
SIC: 2084 Wines

(G-15358)
QUALITY SURFACES INC
2087 Franklin Rd (47460-5038)
PHONE..................................812 876-5838
Monte Job, Pr
Sky Job, VP
EMP: 24 EST: 1993
SALES (est): 2.33MM Privately Held
Web: www.qualitysurfaces.com
SIC: 2541 3281 1799 Counter and sink tops; Cut stone and stone products; Counter top installation

(G-15359)
R E CASEBEER & SONS INC
661 W Market St (47460-1131)
P.O. Box 130 (47460-0130)
PHONE..................................812 829-3284
R Keith Casebeer, Pr
Kevin B Casebeer, Sec
Robert Casebeer, VP
EMP: 8 EST: 1952
SALES (est): 660.23K Privately Held
SIC: 2421 6552 2426 2411 Sawmills and planing mills, general; Land subdividers and developers, commercial; Hardwood dimension and flooring mills; Logging

(G-15360)
RAYS LOGGING LLC
746 Cuba Rd (47460-5447)
PHONE..................................812 935-5307
Phillip Ray, Prin
EMP: 6 EST: 2019
SALES (est): 199.15K Privately Held
SIC: 2411 Logging

(G-15361)
RICES QUALITY FARM MEATS INC
1294 Freeman Rd (47460-7427)
PHONE..................................812 829-4562
TOLL FREE: 800
Timothy Rice, Pr
James R Rice, Sec
Mary J Rice, Sec
EMP: 6 EST: 1970
SALES (est): 348.7K Privately Held
Web: www.ricequalityfarmmeats.com
SIC: 5421 5147 0751 2011 Meat markets, including freezer provisioners; Meats, cured or smoked; Slaughtering: custom livestock services; Meat by-products, from meat slaughtered on site

(G-15362)
SPENCER EVENING WORLD (PA)
Also Called: Evening World
114 E Franklin St (47460)
P.O. Box 226 (47460)
PHONE..................................812 829-2255
John Gillaspy, Pr
Thomas B Gillaspy, *
Philip L Gillaspy, *
EMP: 60 EST: 1927
SQ FT: 13,400
SALES (est): 4.98MM
SALES (corp-wide): 4.98MM Privately Held
Web: www.spencereveningworld.com
SIC: 2752 2711 2791 Offset printing; Commercial printing and newspaper publishing combined; Typesetting

(G-15363)
STEPHEN G MORROW INC
Also Called: Steve's Automotive Center
2632 Schooling Rd (47460-5155)
P.O. Box 352 (47460-0352)
PHONE..................................812 876-7837

GEOGRAPHIC SECTION

Springville - Lawrence County (G-15387)

Stephen Morrow, Pr
EMP: 5 EST: 1983
SALES (est): 437.43K Privately Held
SIC: 3714 Transmissions, motor vehicle

(G-15364)
VANCE PRODUCTS INCORPORATED
Also Called: Cook Urological
1100 W Morgan St (47460-9426)
PHONE..........................812 829-4891
Pete Yonkman, Pr
Fredrick Roemer, *
John R Kamstra, *
Steve Ferguson, *
EMP: 109 EST: 1977
SQ FT: 45,000
SALES (est): 19.34MM
SALES (corp-wide): 1.61B Privately Held
Web: www.cookmedical.com
SIC: 3841 Catheters
PA: Cook Group Incorporated
750 Daniels Way
Bloomington IN 47404
812 339-2235

(G-15365)
WORLD ARTS INC
156 E Franklin St (47460-1818)
P.O. Box 597 (47460-0597)
PHONE..........................812 829-2255
John Gillaspy, Pr
Shelly Keasling, *
Philip Gillaspy, *
▼ EMP: 60 EST: 1993
SALES (est): 8.88MM Privately Held
Web: www.waprinting.com
SIC: 2752 Offset printing

Spencerville
Allen County

(G-15366)
AGRI - TRADERS & REPAIR LLC
16702 Campbell Rd (46788-9641)
PHONE..........................260 238-4225
Lorn Lengagher, Managing Member
▲ EMP: 5 EST: 2006
SALES (est): 345.96K Privately Held
SIC: 3715 Trailer bodies

(G-15367)
AGRITRADERS MFG INC
16702 Campbell Rd (46788-9641)
PHONE..........................260 238-4225
Robert Pfister, Pr
EMP: 8 EST: 1985
SALES (est): 800K Privately Held
SIC: 3715 Truck trailers

(G-15368)
CAMPBELL ROAD SAWMILL LP
17127 Campbell Rd (46788-9641)
PHONE..........................260 238-4252
John R Graber, Owner
EMP: 10 EST: 1970
SALES (est): 1.02MM Privately Held
SIC: 2421 Sawmills and planing mills, general

(G-15369)
DEEP THREE INC
Also Called: Stealth Furniture
17607 Rupert Rd (46788-9660)
PHONE..........................260 705-2283
Lee Hershberger, Pr
Michelle Hershberger, VP
EMP: 8 EST: 2013
SALES (est): 295.82K Privately Held

SIC: 3089 7389 Plastics products, nec; Business Activities at Non-Commercial Site

(G-15370)
GRABER LUMBER LP
17528 Cuba Rd (46788-9629)
PHONE..........................260 238-4124
Neil Graber, Pt
Neil Graber, Genl Pt
Jason Graber, Pt
EMP: 23 EST: 2001
SALES (est): 2.48MM Privately Held
SIC: 2411 7389 Logging camps and contractors; Business Activities at Non-Commercial Site

(G-15371)
HULL PRECISION MACHINING INC
6974 State Road 1 (46788-9431)
P.O. Box 113 (46788-0113)
PHONE..........................260 238-4372
Clarence Hull, Pr
Jetteree W Hull, Sec
EMP: 5 EST: 1981
SALES (est): 332.06K Privately Held
SIC: 3599 Machine shop, jobbing and repair

(G-15372)
KRAFFT GRAVEL INC (PA)
6031 County Road 68 (46788-9409)
PHONE..........................260 238-4653
Gerald Krafft, Pr
Jennie Krafft, VP
Beverly Krafft, Sec
EMP: 1 EST: 1926
SALES (est): 551.05K
SALES (corp-wide): 551.05K Privately Held
SIC: 1442 4212 Construction sand mining; Local trucking, without storage

(G-15373)
RHINEHART DEVELOPMENT CORP
Also Called: Calf-Teria
5345 County Road 68 (46788-9719)
PHONE..........................260 238-4442
Phillip R Rhinehart, Pr
EMP: 20 EST: 1945
SQ FT: 30,000
SALES (est): 3.32MM Privately Held
Web: www.rhinehartdevelopment.com
SIC: 3469 3523 Stamping metal for the trade; Barn, silo, poultry, dairy, and livestock machinery

(G-15374)
RHINEHART FINISHING LLC
5345 County Road 68 (46788-9719)
PHONE..........................260 238-4442
Phillip Rhinehart, Managing Member
EMP: 75 EST: 2000
SQ FT: 85,000
SALES (est): 8.04MM Privately Held
Web: www.rhinehartfinishing.com
SIC: 3471 Finishing, metals or formed products

(G-15375)
TIMBER LINE CRATING LP
17501 Campbell Rd (46788-9640)
PHONE..........................260 238-3075
John Schwartz, Pt
EMP: 8 EST: 2002
SALES (est): 278.25K Privately Held
SIC: 2449 Berry crates, wood wirebound

Spiceland
Henry County

(G-15376)
AMERICAN BOTTLING COMPANY
6083 State Rd (47385)
PHONE..........................765 987-7800
Ed Cole, Mgr
EMP: 64
Web: www.keurigdrpepper.com
SIC: 2086 Soft drinks: packaged in cans, bottles, etc.
HQ: The American Bottling Company
6425 Hall Of Fame Ln
Frisco TX 75034

(G-15377)
DRAPER INC (PA)
411 S Pearl St (47385-9637)
P.O. Box 425 (47385-0425)
PHONE..........................765 987-7999
Chris Broome, Pr
Michael D Broome, *
Gary Knowles, *
Christopher M Broome, *
◆ EMP: 447 EST: 1902
SQ FT: 462,000
SALES (est): 100.39MM
SALES (corp-wide): 100.39MM Privately Held
Web: www.draperinc.com
SIC: 3861 Film, sensitized motion picture, X-ray, still camera, etc.

(G-15378)
MR FUEL
140 Holwager Dr (47385-9639)
PHONE..........................317 531-0891
EMP: 4 EST: 2013
SALES (est): 131.7K Privately Held
SIC: 2869 Fuels

(G-15379)
SPICELAND WOOD PRODUCTS INC
Also Called: Spiceland Wood Products
609 S Pearl St (47385-9766)
P.O. Box 406 (47385-0406)
PHONE..........................765 987-8156
Rob Davis, Owner
EMP: 16 EST: 1981
SQ FT: 19,000
SALES (est): 1.45MM Privately Held
Web: www.spicelandwood.com
SIC: 2434 Wood kitchen cabinets

Springport
Henry County

(G-15380)
IRVING MATERIALS INC
Also Called: I M I
1078 E Luray Rd (47386-9715)
PHONE..........................765 755-3447
Kevin Gibson, Brnch Mgr
EMP: 5
SALES (corp-wide): 814.09MM Privately Held
Web: www.irvmat.com
SIC: 3273 Ready-mixed concrete
PA: Irving Materials, Inc.
8032 N State Road 9
Greenfield IN 46140
317 326-3101

(G-15381)
MFD EXPRESS INC
8463 N County Road 200 W (47386-9757)
PHONE..........................765 717-3539

Matthew Chapman, Pr
EMP: 9 EST: 2017
SALES (est): 72K Privately Held
SIC: 3999 Manufacturing industries, nec

Springville
Lawrence County

(G-15382)
BENS QUARRY LLC
303 E Ingram Rd (47462-9416)
PHONE..........................812 824-3730
EMP: 2 EST: 2011
SALES (est): 233K Privately Held
Web: www.grasslandwetlands.com
SIC: 1422 Crushed and broken limestone

(G-15383)
CLARKS CNC LLC
1718 S Jackson Pike (47462-6262)
PHONE..........................812 508-1773
Monty Clark, Owner
EMP: 4 EST: 2016
SALES (est): 233.68K Privately Held
Web: www.clarkscnc.com
SIC: 3545 Measuring tools and machines, machinists' metalworking type

(G-15384)
D & M TOOL CORPORATION (HQ)
699 Washboard Rd (47462-5180)
PHONE..........................812 279-8882
John Lucas, CEO
Bill Gilbert, *
Ansel Deckard Junior, Ch
Bill Maddox, *
EMP: 25 EST: 1970
SQ FT: 28,000
SALES (est): 9.99MM
SALES (corp-wide): 22.09MM Privately Held
Web: www.spcmfg.com
SIC: 3544 Special dies and tools
PA: Specialty Manufacturers, Inc.
2410 Executive Dr Ste 201
Indianapolis IN
317 241-1111

(G-15385)
EMBREE MACHINE INC
1435 Greer Ln (47462-5046)
PHONE..........................812 275-5729
Patrick Embree Ii, Pr
EMP: 5 EST: 2004
SQ FT: 1,100
SALES (est): 485.31K Privately Held
Web: www.embreemachineinc.com
SIC: 3599 Machine shop, jobbing and repair

(G-15386)
INGRAM ROAD QUARRY LLC
303 E Ingram Rd (47462-9416)
PHONE..........................812 824-3730
EMP: 5 EST: 2021
SALES (est): 540.78K Privately Held
SIC: 1442 Construction sand and gravel

(G-15387)
INTEGRITY DEFENSE SERVICES INC
1463 S State Road 45 (47462-6343)
PHONE..........................812 675-4913
David W Burkett, CEO
Kristin R Schnarr, COO
Richard N Speer Junior, CFO
EMP: 21 EST: 2017
SQ FT: 40,640
SALES (est): 4.92MM Privately Held
Web: www.integritydefenseservices.us

Springville - Lawrence County (G-15388)

SIC: 3812 3441 Defense systems and equipment; Fabricated structural metal

(G-15388)
LEER CUSTOM MACHINE LLC
301 Pinewood Ln (47462)
PHONE..................................317 385-2443
Ethan Leer, CEO
EMP: 2 EST: 2016
SALES (est): 359.3K Privately Held
SIC: 3599 Machine and other job shop work

(G-15389)
MQP MACHINING LLC
6581 State Road 54 W (47462-5143)
P.O. Box 148 (47462-0148)
PHONE..................................812 278-8374
Kent Miller, Managing Member
EMP: 3 EST: 2005
SALES (est): 98.64K Privately Held
Web: www.mqpmachining.com
SIC: 3599 Machine shop, jobbing and repair

(G-15390)
PLASTICS RESEARCH AND DEV INC
Also Called: Prd
747 Washboard Rd (47462-5181)
PHONE..................................812 279-8885
John Lucas, CEO
John Passanisi, *
▲ EMP: 29 EST: 1989
SALES (est): 9.99MM
SALES (corp-wide): 22.09MM Privately Held
Web: www.prd-inc.com
SIC: 3544 3089 Special dies, tools, jigs, and fixtures; Injection molded finished plastics products, nec
HQ: D & M Tool Corporation
   699 Washboard Rd
   Springville IN 47462
   812 279-8882

(G-15391)
ROBERT L YOUNG
Also Called: Circle Y Farms
4436 S Young Dr (47462-6414)
PHONE..................................812 863-4475
Robert L Young, Owner
EMP: 4 EST: 1975
SALES (est): 261.58K Privately Held
SIC: 0211 2411 Beef cattle feedlots; Logging

(G-15392)
ROGERS GROUP INC
Also Called: Sieboldt Quarry
938 Sieboldt Quarry Rd (47462-5353)
PHONE..................................812 275-7860
EMP: 14
SALES (corp-wide): 1.05B Privately Held
Web: www.rogersgroupincint.com
SIC: 1442 Gravel mining
PA: Rogers Group, Inc.
   421 Great Cir Rd
   Nashville TN 37228
   615 242-0585

Stanford
Monroe County

(G-15393)
BLINDS PLUS LLC
P.O. Box 70 (47463-0070)
PHONE..................................812 825-1932
EMP: 4 EST: 2008
SALES (est): 142.55K Privately Held
SIC: 2211 Draperies and drapery fabrics, cotton

Star City
Pulaski County

(G-15394)
ALAN DAILY
7300 S 600 E (46985-9075)
PHONE..................................574 595-6253
Alan Daily, Owner
EMP: 2 EST: 1999
SALES (est): 126.09K Privately Held
SIC: 2711 Newspapers, publishing and printing

(G-15395)
ASTELLAS PHARMA US INC
6946 E 450 S (46985-9059)
PHONE..................................574 595-7569
EMP: 1
Web: www.astellas.com
SIC: 2834 Pharmaceutical preparations
HQ: Astellas Pharma Us, Inc.
   2375 Waterview Dr
   Northbrook IL 60062

(G-15396)
BONNELL GRAIN HANDLING INC
3191 E 800 S (46985-8898)
PHONE..................................574 595-7827
Tyler Hanson, Pr
Ryan Nethercutt, VP
EMP: 21 EST: 1977
SALES (est): 2.97MM Privately Held
Web: www.bonnellgrain.com
SIC: 5083 7699 3523 Agricultural machinery and equipment; Agricultural equipment repair services; Farm machinery and equipment

(G-15397)
ROUDEBUSH CO INC
583 S State Rd 119 (46985)
P.O. Box 348 (46985-0348)
PHONE..................................574 595-7115
Scott Roudebush, Pr
Clara Roudebush, Sec
▲ EMP: 3 EST: 1981
SQ FT: 3,000
SALES (est): 256.37K Privately Held
Web: www.roudebushco.com
SIC: 2511 5712 5961 2499 Wood household furniture; Furniture stores; Furniture and furnishings, mail order; Decorative wood and woodwork

Stendal
Pike County

(G-15398)
CLARIDGES WOOD SHOP
9424 S County Road 400 E (47585-8955)
PHONE..................................812 536-2569
EMP: 1 EST: 1988
SALES (est): 51.18K Privately Held
Web: www.claridgewoodshop.com
SIC: 7641 1751 2499 Furniture repair and maintenance; Cabinet and finish carpentry; Decorative wood and woodwork

Stockwell
Tippecanoe County

(G-15399)
COCHRAN CUSTOM WOODWORKING LLC
9036 Vine St (47983)
P.O. Box 98 (47983-0098)
PHONE..................................765 523-3220
EMP: 5 EST: 2014
SALES (est): 263.37K Privately Held
Web: www.cochrancustom.com
SIC: 2434 Wood kitchen cabinets

Straughn
Henry County

(G-15400)
WHITES WELDING & MACHINING LLC
1591 E County Road 600 S (47387-9752)
PHONE..................................765 987-7984
Thomas White, Pr
EMP: 3 EST: 1969
SQ FT: 3,500
SALES (est): 191.17K Privately Held
SIC: 7692 5083 Welding repair; Farm equipment parts and supplies

Stroh
Lagrange County

(G-15401)
HAYWARD & SAMS LLP
Also Called: Stroh Fixit Shop
4250 E 1175 S (46789)
P.O. Box 190 (46789-0190)
PHONE..................................260 351-4166
Mark Hayward, Mng Pr
David Sams, Pt
EMP: 5 EST: 2000
SALES (est): 392.28K Privately Held
Web: www.strohfixit.com
SIC: 7699 1711 3561 Lawn mower repair shop; Heating and air conditioning contractors; Pumps, domestic: water or sump

Sullivan
Sullivan County

(G-15402)
ALLOMATIC PRODUCTS COMPANY (DH)
609 E Chaney St (47882-7452)
P.O. Box 267 (47882-0267)
PHONE..................................800 686-4729
David Coolidge, Pr
Curtis T Short, VP
Martha Slopsema, VP
John Shell, Treas
Barbara Anderson, Sec
▲ EMP: 1 EST: 1988
SQ FT: 170,000
SALES (est): 8.52MM
SALES (corp-wide): 49.09MM Privately Held
Web: www.allomatic.com
SIC: 3714 Motor vehicle transmissions, drive assemblies, and parts
HQ: Raybestos Powertrain, Llc
   711 Tech Dr
   Crawfordsville IN 47933

(G-15403)
BUTLERS GENERAL REPAIR
1259 W State Road 154 (47882-7117)
PHONE..................................812 268-5631
Bill Butler, Owner
EMP: 1 EST: 1995
SALES (est): 108.97K Privately Held
SIC: 7692 3569 Welding repair; Filters

(G-15404)
DANKO FARM SUPPLY & FEED INC
755 W Washington St (47882-7183)
PHONE..................................812 870-7413
Jason L Danko, Pr
Michelle S Danko, VP
EMP: 2 EST: 2016
SALES (est): 165.75K Privately Held
SIC: 3523 2048 Farm machinery and equipment; Feed concentrates

(G-15405)
DODD SAWMILLS INCORPORATED
85 E County Road 450 N (47882-7542)
PHONE..................................812 268-4811
Louis Glascock, Pr
Donna Glascock, *
EMP: 14 EST: 1937
SQ FT: 50,000
SALES (est): 222.03K Privately Held
Web: www.doddsawmill.com
SIC: 2448 Pallets, wood

(G-15406)
GEARBOX GROUP INC
609 E Chaney St (47882-7452)
PHONE..................................812 268-0322
EMP: 9 EST: 2010
SALES (est): 177.66K Privately Held
SIC: 3711 5084 Motor vehicles and car bodies; Industrial machinery and equipment

(G-15407)
GRAYSVILLE MFG INC
4391 N County Road 875 W (47882-7141)
PHONE..................................812 382-4616
Scott W Snyder, Prin
EMP: 7 EST: 2016
SALES (est): 233.49K Privately Held
SIC: 3999 Manufacturing industries, nec

(G-15408)
J JARRETT ENGINEERING INC
603 S County Road 450 E (47882-7710)
PHONE..................................812 268-3338
Jeffrey L Jarrett, Pr
Jack Jarrett, VP
Jo Jarrett, Sec
EMP: 7 EST: 1984
SALES (est): 340K Privately Held
SIC: 2791 Typesetting

(G-15409)
JTLEDM LLC
2816 N County Rd 800 W (47882-7248)
PHONE..................................317 292-2548
James T Lentz, Owner
EMP: 7 EST: 2013
SALES (est): 248.28K Privately Held
Web: www.jtledm.com
SIC: 3599 Machine shop, jobbing and repair

(G-15410)
KELK PUBLISHING LLC
249 W Washington St (47882-1433)
P.O. Box 130 (47882-0130)
PHONE..................................812 268-6356
Gillian Kelk, Pr
EMP: 6 EST: 2014
SALES (est): 204.34K Privately Held
Web: www.sullivan-times.com
SIC: 2741 Miscellaneous publishing

(G-15411)
KENS TOOL & DESIGN
2437 N Section St (47882-7522)
PHONE..................................812 268-6653
Ken Plummer, Owner
▲ EMP: 10 EST: 1962
SALES (est): 505.41K Privately Held

SIC: 3599 Machine shop, jobbing and repair

(G-15412)
LILY GROUP INC
103 N Court St (47882-1214)
PHONE.................................812 268-5459
EMP: 3
Web: www.lilygroup.com
SIC: 1241 Coal mining services

(G-15413)
MCCAMMON ENGINEERING CORP
1863 W County Road 500 S (47882-7772)
PHONE.................................812 356-4455
Brent Mc Cammon, *Pr*
EMP: 5 EST: 1985
SQ FT: 7,200
SALES (est): 494.45K Privately Held
Web: www.mccammonengineering.com
SIC: 3069 3087 Molded rubber products; Custom compound purchased resins

(G-15414)
MEIER WINERY & VINYARD LLC
4251 N State Road 63 (47882-7581)
PHONE.................................812 382-4220
Pamela A Meier, *Admn*
EMP: 6 EST: 2016
SALES (est): 198.74K Privately Held
Web: www.meierwineryandvinyard.com
SIC: 2084 Wines

(G-15415)
NORTH AMERICAN LATEX CORP
49 Industrial Park Dr (47882-7521)
PHONE.................................812 268-6608
Kevin Beard, *Pr*
Nelson Ellis, *
J Bradley Stewart, *
Kevin Beard, *VP*
Bruce R Wolfe, *
EMP: 62 EST: 1987
SQ FT: 60,000
SALES (est): 4.78MM Privately Held
Web: www.northamericanlatex.net
SIC: 3069 Medical and laboratory rubber sundries and related products

(G-15416)
PIERCE OIL CO INC
Also Called: Sullivan Daily Times
115 W Jackson St (47882-1505)
P.O. Box 447 (47882-0447)
PHONE.................................812 268-6356
Nancy P Gettinger, *Pr*
Sarah J Geitz, *Sec*
Tom P Gettinger, *VP*
EMP: 11 EST: 1905
SQ FT: 5,800
SALES (est): 219.13K Privately Held
Web: www.sullivan-times.com
SIC: 2711 2791 2759 Commercial printing and newspaper publishing combined; Typesetting; Commercial printing, nec

(G-15417)
PULSE ENERGY
3137 N Old 41 (47882-9233)
PHONE.................................812 268-6700
Bryan Anderson, *Prin*
EMP: 2 EST: 2007
SALES (est): 99.89K Privately Held
SIC: 1389 Oil consultants

(G-15418)
RAYBESTOS POWERTRAIN LLC
609 E Chaney St (47882-7452)
PHONE.................................812 268-0322
Susan Conkright, *Brnch Mgr*
EMP: 1

SALES (corp-wide): 49.09MM Privately Held
Web: www.raybestospowertrain.com
SIC: 3714 Motor vehicle parts and accessories
HQ: Raybestos Powertrain, Llc
711 Tech Dr
Crawfordsville IN 47933

(G-15419)
RAYBESTOS POWERTRAIN LLC
110 Industrial Park Dr (47882-7520)
P.O. Box 227 (47882-0227)
PHONE.................................812 268-0322
EMP: 5
SALES (corp-wide): 49.09MM Privately Held
Web: www.raybestospowertrain.com
SIC: 3714 Motor vehicle parts and accessories
HQ: Raybestos Powertrain, Llc
711 Tech Dr
Crawfordsville IN 47933

(G-15420)
RAYBESTOS POWERTRAIN LLC
Also Called: Raybestos
312 S St Clair St (47882-7497)
PHONE.................................812 268-1211
David Coolidge, *Brnch Mgr*
EMP: 18
SALES (corp-wide): 49.09MM Privately Held
Web: www.raybestospowertrain.com
SIC: 3714 Motor vehicle engines and parts
HQ: Raybestos Powertrain, Llc
711 Tech Dr
Crawfordsville IN 47933

(G-15421)
SALESMAN SAWMILL INC
3396 N County Road 550 W (47882-7577)
PHONE.................................812 382-9154
James Salesman, *Pr*
EMP: 7 EST: 1970
SALES (est): 672.8K Privately Held
SIC: 2421 Sawmills and planing mills, general

(G-15422)
SANDERS & CROSLEY LLC
662 E Leach St (47882-7399)
PHONE.................................812 268-4472
Gavin P Crosley, *Prin*
EMP: 5 EST: 2008
SALES (est): 91.69K Privately Held
Web: www.hrconstructionservicesinc.com
SIC: 1446 Industrial sand

(G-15423)
SULLIVAN IMI
939 S Section St (47882-7834)
PHONE.................................812 268-3306
EMP: 6 EST: 2012
SALES (est): 198.5K Privately Held
SIC: 3273 Ready-mixed concrete

(G-15424)
VALLEY TILE CORPORATION
2437 N Section St (47882-7522)
PHONE.................................812 268-3328
Kenn Plummer, *Pr*
Dan Plummer, *VP*
Dennis Long, *VP*
Jeff Long, *Sec*
EMP: 4 EST: 1998
SQ FT: 36,000
SALES (est): 391.67K Privately Held
SIC: 3069 Tile, rubber

(G-15425)
VHGI HOLDINGS INC
103 N Court St (47882-1214)
EMP: 7 EST: 2010
SALES (est): 821.02K Privately Held
SIC: 1081 1311 Exploration, metal mining; Crude petroleum and natural gas

Summitville
Madison County

(G-15426)
NUT HOUSE WOODWORKS LLC
247 E 1550 N (46070-9355)
PHONE.................................317 345-7177
EMP: 1
SALES (est): 65.99K Privately Held
SIC: 2434 7389 Wood kitchen cabinets; Business Activities at Non-Commercial Site

(G-15427)
PANNELL & SON WELDING INC
207 N Summit St (46070-9325)
PHONE.................................765 948-3606
Mark Pannell, *Pr*
EMP: 5 EST: 1984
SALES (est): 414.4K Privately Held
SIC: 3545 7692 Machine tool accessories; Welding repair

(G-15428)
PRAISEWORTHY PRESS LLC
151 W Indiana St (46070-9762)
PHONE.................................765 536-2077
EMP: 3 EST: 2003
SALES (est): 230K Privately Held
SIC: 2741 Miscellaneous publishing

(G-15429)
R & R ENGINEERING CO INC
Also Called: U-Bolts Engineering
801 S Main St (46070-8900)
P.O. Box 428 (46070-0428)
PHONE.................................765 536-2331
Ralph Amos, *Pr*
Scott Amos, *
Janet Amos, *
▲ EMP: 46 EST: 1969
SQ FT: 300,000
SALES (est): 9.74MM Privately Held
Web: www.randrengineering.com
SIC: 3452 3496 Bolts, metal; Miscellaneous fabricated wire products

(G-15430)
ROBERT ATKINS (PA)
Also Called: A&M Tool & Die
303 E North Main St (46070-9318)
P.O. Box 445 (46070-0445)
PHONE.................................765 536-4164
Robert Atkins, *Owner*
EMP: 3 EST: 1990
SQ FT: 5,000
SALES (est): 305.56K Privately Held
SIC: 3544 3465 Special dies and tools; Automotive stampings

(G-15431)
ROOKIES UNLIMITED INC
103 South Mn (46070)
P.O. Box 96 (46070-0096)
PHONE.................................765 536-2726
Steve Horn, *Pr*
EMP: 6 EST: 2008
SQ FT: 9,000
SALES (est): 528.52K Privately Held
Web: www.rookiesink.com

SIC: 3993 7389 2759 5941 Signs and advertising specialties; Embroidery advertising; Screen printing; Specialty sport supplies, nec

(G-15432)
SPIRITBUILDING PUBLISHING
15591 N State Road 9 (46070-9622)
PHONE.................................765 623-2238
Ivan Benson, *Prin*
EMP: 7 EST: 2010
SALES (est): 111.12K Privately Held
Web: www.spiritbuilding.com
SIC: 2741 Miscellaneous publishing

(G-15433)
TCS CABINETS
557 E 1450 N (46070-9390)
PHONE.................................765 208-5350
Scott Rowland, *Prin*
EMP: 1 EST: 2010
SALES (est): 238.04K Privately Held
SIC: 2434 Wood kitchen cabinets

(G-15434)
TH CUSTOM PRINTING
871 E 1550 N (46070-8917)
PHONE.................................765 251-3986
Todd Harris, *Pr*
EMP: 1 EST: 2004
SALES (est): 14.84K Privately Held
SIC: 2752 Commercial printing, lithographic

Sunman
Ripley County

(G-15435)
DAVID L HUBER
Also Called: Quality Tooling
12218 N Schneider Rd (47041-7728)
PHONE.................................812 623-4772
David L Huber, *Owner*
EMP: 1 EST: 1995
SALES (est): 131.49K Privately Held
SIC: 3599 Machine shop, jobbing and repair

(G-15436)
E G AMMERMAN JR
825 N Meridian St (47041-8048)
PHONE.................................812 623-3504
E G Ammerman Junior, *Owner*
EMP: 1 EST: 2004
SALES (est): 130.33K Privately Held
SIC: 3444 Culverts, sheet metal

(G-15437)
ENDLESS CREATIONS
224 Nieman St (47041-2503)
PHONE.................................812 623-0190
Carol Schmiet, *Owner*
EMP: 1 EST: 2002
SALES (est): 74.92K Privately Held
SIC: 3479 Etching and engraving

(G-15438)
GOODS ON TARGET SPORTING INC
Also Called: On Target
14224 N Rosfeld Rd (47041-9382)
PHONE.................................812 623-2300
Leon Kersey, *Pr*
Rebecca Kersey, *Sec*
EMP: 6 EST: 1990
SALES (est): 630.52K Privately Held
Web: www.ontargetpolaris.com
SIC: 3799 5941 5611 All terrain vehicles (ATV); Sporting goods and bicycle shops; Clothing, sportswear, men's and boys'

(G-15439)
HOOKER DEER DRAG CO LLC
27499 Lawrenceville Rd (47041-9683)
PHONE................................812 623-2706
EMP: 2 **EST:** 2011
SALES (est): 88.15K **Privately Held**
SIC: 3949 Sporting and athletic goods, nec

(G-15440)
LAKER WINERY LLC
13654 Tangman Rd (47041-9484)
PHONE................................812 934-4633
Gregory Keith Laker, *Pr*
EMP: 4 **EST:** 2016
SALES (est): 62.38K **Privately Held**
SIC: 2084 Wines

(G-15441)
M S & J QUALITY SCREW MCH PDTS
8925 E County Road 1000 N (47041-8065)
PHONE................................812 623-3002
EMP: 13 **EST:** 1994
SALES (est): 1.36MM **Privately Held**
Web: www.msandj.com
SIC: 3599 Machine shop, jobbing and repair

(G-15442)
OCCASIONS GROUP INC
957 N Meridian St (47041-7771)
P.O. Box 188 (47041-0188)
PHONE................................812 623-2225
Darryl Mills, *Genl Mgr*
Gregory Jackson, *Sec*
Kenny Schuman, *Prin*
Waverly Jutzi, *Prin*
Kyle Brock, *Prin*
EMP: 20 **EST:** 2006
SALES (est): 4.46MM
SALES (corp-wide): 3.81B **Privately Held**
SIC: 2759 Commercial printing, nec
HQ: The Occasions Group Inc
1750 Tower Blvd
North Mankato MN 56003

(G-15443)
ROBERTS C WLDG TRCK HVY EQUIP
8448 E County Road 1100 N (47041-8072)
PHONE................................812 623-1525
Carl Roberts, *Owner*
EMP: 1 **EST:** 1994
SALES (est): 66.44K **Privately Held**
SIC: 7692 Welding repair

(G-15444)
SAMCO INC
19992 N Manchester Rd (47041-8766)
PHONE................................812 926-4282
EMP: 3
Web: www.samcoinc.us
SIC: 3589 5084 Water purification equipment, household type; Pollution control equipment, air (environmental)
PA: Samco Inc
5599 Kugler Mill Rd
Cincinnati OH

(G-15445)
SELECT GOURMET POPCORN
9632 N County Road 800 E (47041-7711)
PHONE................................812 212-2202
Eric Riehle, *Owner*
EMP: 2 **EST:** 2010
SALES (est): 105.9K **Privately Held**
Web: www.selectpopcorn.com
SIC: 2099 Popcorn, packaged: except already popped

(G-15446)
SUNMAN ENGINEERING INC
131 W Washington St (47041-7706)
P.O. Box 397 (47041-0397)
PHONE................................812 623-4072
Michael Thomas, *Pr*
EMP: 4 **EST:** 1943
SQ FT: 1,500
SALES (est): 456.96K **Privately Held**
Web: www.sunmantechnology.com
SIC: 3599 Machine shop, jobbing and repair

(G-15447)
TRIMBLE COMBUSTION SYSTEMS INC
215 Nieman St Ste 2 (47041-8931)
P.O. Box 191 (47041-0191)
PHONE................................812 623-4545
Patrick W Trimble, *Pr*
Lori A Trimble, *VP*
EMP: 5 **EST:** 2000
SQ FT: 2,500
SALES (est): 1.05MM **Privately Held**
Web: www.trimblecombustion.com
SIC: 3433 Gas burners, industrial

(G-15448)
WIRE-TEK INC
234 Industrial Dr (47041-7790)
PHONE................................812 623-8300
Greg Hauck, *Pr*
EMP: 8 **EST:** 1970
SQ FT: 30,000
SALES (est): 955.49K **Privately Held**
SIC: 3496 Miscellaneous fabricated wire products

(G-15449)
WOLFE ENGINEERED PLASTICS LLC
215 Nieman St (47041-8931)
P.O. Box 518 (47041-0518)
PHONE................................812 623-8403
▲ **EMP:** 3 **EST:** 2004
SQ FT: 4,500
SALES (est): 447.5K **Privately Held**
SIC: 5031 3952 Composite board products, woodboard; Boards, drawing, artists'

Swayzee
Grant County

(G-15450)
HIGH NOTE PUBLISHING
571 S 1400 E34 (46986-9732)
P.O. Box 455 (46986-0455)
PHONE................................765 313-1699
Jeremey Johnson, *Prin*
EMP: 5 **EST:** 2011
SALES (est): 101.73K **Privately Held**
SIC: 2741 Miscellaneous publishing

(G-15451)
IRVING MATERIALS INC
Also Called: Calcium Products
6455 W 600 S (46986-9773)
PHONE................................765 922-7931
Kelvin Holcom, *Mgr*
EMP: 9
SALES (corp-wide): 814.09MM **Privately Held**
Web: www.irvmat.com
SIC: 3273 Ready-mixed concrete
PA: Irving Materials, Inc.
8032 N State Road 9
Greenfield IN 46140
317 326-3101

(G-15452)
IRVING MATERIALS INC
I M I
6377 W 600 S (46986-9773)
PHONE................................765 922-7991
Ray Rich, *Brnch Mgr*
EMP: 10
SALES (corp-wide): 814.09MM **Privately Held**
Web: www.irvmat.com
SIC: 3273 Ready-mixed concrete
PA: Irving Materials, Inc.
8032 N State Road 9
Greenfield IN 46140
317 326-3101

Sweetser
Grant County

(G-15453)
ALL THINGS CUSTOM LLC
102 S Main St (46987)
P.O. Box 578 (46987-0578)
PHONE................................765 618-5332
Debra Freeman, *Managing Member*
Kiley Freeman, *Managing Member*
EMP: 4 **EST:** 2014
SALES (est): 233.76K **Privately Held**
Web: www.allthings-custom.com
SIC: 2261 5699 Screen printing of cotton broadwoven fabrics; T-shirts, custom printed

Syracuse
Kosciusko County

(G-15454)
ALUMINUM INSIGHTS LLC
104 E Innovation Blvd (46567)
PHONE................................574 534-5547
Jeffery Miller, *Managing Member*
Steve Brenneman, *
Niles Graber Alvarez, *
Valerio Presezzi, *
EMP: 45 **EST:** 2020
SALES (est): 5.44MM **Privately Held**
Web: www.aluminuminsights.com
SIC: 3354 Aluminum extruded products

(G-15455)
BAR-WAL PRODUCTS
6537 E Waco Dr (46567-9440)
PHONE................................574 457-5311
Ray Grumme, *Prin*
EMP: 6 **EST:** 2009
SALES (est): 62.74K **Privately Held**
SIC: 3451 Screw machine products

(G-15456)
BAYVIEW ESTATES
400 S Harkless Dr (46567-2011)
PHONE................................574 457-4136
Larry Nelson, *Owner*
Lyn Tolson, *Prin*
EMP: 2 **EST:** 2010
SALES (est): 106.81K **Privately Held**
Web: www.frcommunity.com
SIC: 2451 Mobile homes

(G-15457)
BOAT WORKS
6348 E Trusdell Ave (46567-9406)
PHONE................................574 457-4034
Shawn Senter, *Owner*
EMP: 6 **EST:** 2016
SALES (est): 94.61K **Privately Held**
Web: www.wawaseeboatworks.com
SIC: 3732 Boatbuilding and repairing

(G-15458)
BRITTANY BUSHONG
Also Called: Rich Beauty
808 S Huntington St (46567-1810)
PHONE................................574 457-4970
Brittany Bushong, *Owner*
EMP: 1 **EST:** 2020
SALES (est): 39.69K **Privately Held**
SIC: 3999 Hair, dressing of, for the trade

(G-15459)
COLBIN TOOL COMPANY INC
1021 N Indiana Ave (46567-1016)
PHONE................................574 457-3183
Don Strouse, *Pr*
Dave Blanchard, *
Sally Strouse, *
Richard Williamson, *Stockholder**
EMP: 26 **EST:** 1963
SQ FT: 18,500
SALES (est): 1.81MM **Privately Held**
Web: www.colbintool.com
SIC: 3446 3714 3469 Railings, prefabricated metal; Motor vehicle parts and accessories; Metal stampings, nec

(G-15460)
CUSTOM SHEDS PLUS LLC
13836 County Road 48 (46567-9215)
PHONE................................260 215-3988
EMP: 3 **EST:** 2021
SALES (est): 79.72K **Privately Held**
SIC: 2452 Prefabricated wood buildings

(G-15461)
GROSS & SONS LUMBER AND VENEER
8516 E 1250 N (46567-8298)
PHONE................................574 457-5214
Charles Gross, *Owner*
EMP: 2 **EST:** 1933
SALES (est): 99.5K **Privately Held**
SIC: 2421 5211 Sawmills and planing mills, general; Lumber products

(G-15462)
HELMUTH QUALITY POWER SYSTEM
100 S Huntington St (46567-1515)
PHONE................................574 457-2002
Helmuth Howard, *Prin*
EMP: 6 **EST:** 2015
SALES (est): 141.77K **Privately Held**
SIC: 3569 Generators: steam, liquid oxygen, or nitrogen

(G-15463)
HIGHWATER MARINE LLC
Godfrey Marine Syracuse
300 E Chicago St (46567-1624)
PHONE................................574 457-2082
Ted Hegge, *Mgr*
EMP: 30
Web: www.rinkerboats.com
SIC: 3732 Boatbuilding and repairing
PA: Highwater Marine Llc
4500 Middlebury St
Elkhart IN 46516

(G-15464)
JM WOODWORKING LLC
12198 N Syracuse Webster Rd (46567-9138)
PHONE................................574 354-7093
James Slabaugh, *Prin*
EMP: 6 **EST:** 2015
SALES (est): 112.86K **Privately Held**
SIC: 2431 Millwork

(G-15465)
JP INCORPORATED - INDIANA
Also Called: Jasper Plastics Solutions
501 W Railroad Ave (46567-1568)
PHONE................................574 457-2062
Roger Korenstra, *CEO*

Sam Korenstra, *
EMP: 300 **EST:** 1968
SQ FT: 163,000
SALES (est): 23.3MM **Privately Held**
Web: www.jasperplastics.info
SIC: 2821 Plastics materials and resins

(G-15466)
KOCH FOODS
4823 E 1200 N (46567-8279)
PHONE...............................574 457-4384
Julie Nordin, *Mgr*
EMP: 3 **EST:** 2006
SALES (est): 148.42K **Privately Held**
Web: www.kochfoods.com
SIC: 2015 Poultry slaughtering and processing

(G-15467)
LAKE TOOL & DIE INC
1009 W Brooklyn St (46567-1494)
P.O. Box 190 (46555-0190)
PHONE...............................574 457-8274
Gloria Herman, *Pr*
Greg Herman, *Prin*
EMP: 5 **EST:** 1996
SALES (est): 498.4K **Privately Held**
SIC: 3544 Special dies and tools

(G-15468)
MESUMES INCORPORATED
Also Called: Motivated Entrepreneur, The
1204 N Algonquin Dr (46567-2101)
PHONE...............................574 529-3444
Thomas Taylor, *Pr*
EMP: 1 **EST:** 2014
SALES (est): 37.47K **Privately Held**
SIC: 7372 Business oriented computer software

(G-15469)
NATIONAL PRODUCTS INC
201 E Medusa St (46567-1337)
PHONE...............................574 457-4565
Everardo Ganz, *Pr*
Dale R Ganz, *Sec*
EMP: 23 **EST:** 1981
SQ FT: 6,240
SALES (est): 1.82MM **Privately Held**
Web: www.omeganationalproducts.com
SIC: 5031 2421 Plywood; Custom sawmill

(G-15470)
PARKER-HANNIFIN CORPORATION
Engineered Seals Division
501 S Sycamore St (46567-1529)
PHONE...............................574 528-9400
Doug Van Lue, *Brnch Mgr*
EMP: 200
SALES (corp-wide): 19.93B **Publicly Held**
Web: www.parker.com
SIC: 3061 3594 Mechanical rubber goods; Fluid power pumps and motors
PA: Parker-Hannifin Corporation
  6035 Parkland Blvd
  Cleveland OH 44124
  216 896-3000

(G-15471)
PARKER-HANNIFIN CORPORATION
Also Called: Integrated Sealing Systems Div
501 S Sycamore St (46567-1529)
P.O. Box 29 (46767-0029)
PHONE...............................260 894-7125
Jason Brown, *Brnch Mgr*
EMP: 41
SALES (corp-wide): 19.93B **Publicly Held**
Web: www.parker.com

SIC: 3714 3568 3053 Transmission housings or parts, motor vehicle; Power transmission equipment, nec; Gaskets; packing and sealing devices
PA: Parker-Hannifin Corporation
  6035 Parkland Blvd
  Cleveland OH 44124
  216 896-3000

(G-15472)
PASOU FOODS INC
1103 S Huntington St (46567-1935)
PHONE...............................574 457-4092
John Pangani, *Pr*
EMP: 6 **EST:** 1987
SQ FT: 2,000
SALES (est): 467.72K **Privately Held**
SIC: 2038 Snacks, incl. onion rings, cheese sticks, etc.

(G-15473)
POLY-WOOD LLC
925a Polywood Way (46567)
PHONE...............................877 457-3284
EMP: 1
SALES (corp-wide): 594.99MM **Privately Held**
Web: www.polywood.com
SIC: 2514 3821 Metal household furniture; Laboratory apparatus and furniture
HQ: Poly-Wood, Llc
  1000 Polywood Way
  Syracuse IN 46567

(G-15474)
POLY-WOOD LLC (HQ)
1000 Polywood Way (46567)
PHONE...............................574 457-3284
Doug Rassi, *Pr*
◆ **EMP:** 100 **EST:** 1990
SQ FT: 166,422
SALES (est): 93.77MM
SALES (corp-wide): 594.99MM **Privately Held**
Web: www.polywood.com
SIC: 2514 3821 Metal household furniture; Laboratory apparatus and furniture
PA: Arsenal Capital Partners Lp
  277 Park Ave
  New York NY 10172
  212 771-1717

(G-15475)
PRO WAKE WATERSPORTS SYRACUSE
1309 S Harkless Dr (46567-1915)
PHONE...............................801 691-2153
EMP: 6 **EST:** 2018
SALES (est): 217.18K **Privately Held**
Web: www.prowakewatersports.com
SIC: 3732 Boatbuilding and repairing

(G-15476)
RODESWOOD LLC
14852 County Road 50 (46567-9299)
PHONE...............................574 457-4496
Enos Rodes, *Managing Member*
EMP: 2 **EST:** 1990
SALES (est): 204.08K **Privately Held**
SIC: 2511 2431 2451 1751 Wood household furniture; Moldings and baseboards, ornamental and trim; Mobile homes, industrial or commercial use; Carpentry work

(G-15477)
ROGERS ELECTRO-MATICS INC
405 W Chicago St (46567-1506)
P.O. Box 186 (46567-0186)
PHONE...............................574 457-2305
Robert W Haller, *Pr*

EMP: 15 **EST:** 1947
SQ FT: 7,500
SALES (est): 2.49MM **Privately Held**
Web: www.rogerselectromatics.com
SIC: 3625 Relays and industrial controls

(G-15478)
SPECIALTY COMPOUNDS LLC
501 W Railroad Ave (46567-1568)
PHONE...............................574 529-0872
Jessica Losee, *CEO*
EMP: 4 **EST:** 2021
SALES (est): 244.51K **Privately Held**
SIC: 3999

(G-15479)
SPIDER TIE
501 W Railroad Ave (46567-1568)
PHONE...............................574 596-3073
EMP: 7 **EST:** 2017
SALES (est): 307.31K **Privately Held**
Web: www.spidertiesystem.com
SIC: 3272 Concrete products, nec

(G-15480)
STEVES PALLETS INC
12661 N Pleasant Grove Rd (46567-9708)
PHONE...............................574 457-3620
Steven R Sturgill, *Pr*
EMP: 8 **EST:** 2001
SALES (est): 319.13K **Privately Held**
SIC: 2448 Pallets, wood

(G-15481)
SWISS PERFECTION LLC
100 S Huntington St (46567-1515)
PHONE...............................574 457-4457
Roy Schwartz, *Pr*
EMP: 10 **EST:** 1982
SQ FT: 15,000
SALES (est): 2.06MM **Privately Held**
Web: www.swissperfection.com
SIC: 3523 Barn, silo, poultry, dairy, and livestock machinery

(G-15482)
SYRACUSE GLASS INC
1107 S Huntington St Ste D (46567-1979)
PHONE...............................574 457-5516
Pat Eakins, *Pr*
Valerie Eakins, *Sec*
EMP: 3 **EST:** 1992
SQ FT: 2,900
SALES (est): 335.17K **Privately Held**
Web: www.syracusein.com
SIC: 1793 3442 Glass and glazing work; Metal doors, sash, and trim

(G-15483)
T-N-T PERFORMANCE MCH SP LLC
210 E Maple Grove St (46567-1705)
PHONE...............................574 457-5056
Timothy Bowling, *Prin*
EMP: 5 **EST:** 2015
SALES (est): 180.67K **Privately Held**
SIC: 3599 Machine shop, jobbing and repair

(G-15484)
THADDEUS LUXURY HBAGS & HM ACC
101 E Main St (46567-1176)
PHONE...............................907 301-1373
EMP: 4 **EST:** 2017
SALES (est): 46.58K **Privately Held**
SIC: 2299 Jute and flax textile products

(G-15485)
THOMAS STRICKLER
Also Called: Tesco
6749 E Cornelius Rd (46567-9769)

PHONE...............................574 457-2473
Thomas Strickler, *Owner*
EMP: 3 **EST:** 1982
SALES (est): 108.48K **Privately Held**
SIC: 3999 Manufacturing industries, nec

(G-15486)
THOMSON INDUSTRIES INC
1209 Shore Ln (46567-2160)
PHONE...............................574 529-2496
Thomas Hodgson, *Prin*
EMP: 6 **EST:** 2004
SALES (est): 108.36K **Privately Held**
SIC: 3999 Manufacturing industries, nec

(G-15487)
TRANTER GRAPHICS INC
Also Called: 500 Line
8094 N State Road 13 (46567-7206)
P.O. Box 338 (46567-0338)
PHONE...............................574 834-2626
Tammy C Tranter, *Pr*
C Patrick Tranter, *
M Jennelle Dohan, *
Jenelle Tranter, *
EMP: 95 **EST:** 1980
SQ FT: 52,000
SALES (est): 9.09MM **Privately Held**
Web: www.trantergraphics.com
SIC: 2759 7336 Flexographic printing; Silk screen design

(G-15488)
TRAVEL LITE INC
107 E Innovation Blvd (46567)
PHONE...............................574 831-3000
Larry Johns, *Pr*
Dustin Johns, *
▼ **EMP:** 23 **EST:** 1998
SALES (est): 6.18MM **Privately Held**
Web: www.travelliterv.com
SIC: 3715 Truck trailers

(G-15489)
VANDELAY PROPERTIES LLC
101 E Main St Ste A101 (46567-1195)
PHONE...............................574 529-4795
EMP: 5 **EST:** 2014
SALES (est): 50.58K **Privately Held**
SIC: 3999 Manufacturing industries, nec

(G-15490)
WAWASEE ALUMINUM WORKS INC
Also Called: Polar Kraft Boats
206 S Front St (46567-1520)
P.O. Box 336 (46567-0336)
PHONE...............................574 457-2082
Andy Cripe, *Pr*
Susan Cripe, *
EMP: 42 **EST:** 2016
SALES (est): 4.62MM **Privately Held**
SIC: 3732 Motorized boat, building and repairing

(G-15491)
WAYSEEKER LLC
9521 N Koher Rd E (46567-8331)
PHONE...............................574 529-0199
Karl Keiper, *Admn*
EMP: 2 **EST:** 2011
SALES (est): 98.83K **Privately Held**
SIC: 2732 Books, printing only

(G-15492)
WERZALIT OF AMERICA INC
Also Called: Werzalit
501 W Railroad Ave (46567-1568)
PHONE...............................814 362-3881
◆ **EMP:** 51

Syracuse - Kosciusko County (G-15493) GEOGRAPHIC SECTION

SIC: 2426 3995 2511 2421 Furniture stock and parts, hardwood; Burial caskets; Wood household furniture; Sawmills and planing mills, general

(G-15493)
WILLIAM D DARR
5416 E 950 N (46567-7616)
PHONE.................................574 518-0453
Will Darr, *Owner*
EMP: 6 EST: 2004
SALES (est): 153.88K **Privately Held**
SIC: 3699 Electrical equipment and supplies, nec

Taswell
Crawford County

(G-15494)
AS LOGGING LLC
1760 N Belcher Rd (47175-7015)
PHONE.................................812 613-0577
Abram Smith, *Admn*
EMP: 6 EST: 2015
SALES (est): 69.56K **Privately Held**
SIC: 2411 Logging camps and contractors

(G-15495)
REDS CUSTOM DESIGN LLC
3910 W State Road 64 (47175-7645)
PHONE.................................812 698-0763
EMP: 1 EST: 2019
SALES (est): 92.93K **Privately Held**
Web: www.redscustomdesign.com
SIC: 3715 Truck trailers

Tell City
Perry County

(G-15496)
ARC ANGLE WELDING/FABRICATION
535 10th St Apt 8 (47586-2279)
PHONE.................................812 619-1731
Marc Schroy, *CEO*
EMP: 16 EST: 2017
SALES (est): 795.51K **Privately Held**
SIC: 3541 7692 Plasma process metal cutting machines; Welding repair

(G-15497)
ATTC MANUFACTURING INC
Also Called: Attc
10455 State Road 37 (47586-8322)
PHONE.................................812 547-5060
Hideaki Ando, *Pr*
Mack Sawada, *
Takashi Kondo, *
Yoshiharu Higuchi, *
▲ EMP: 281 EST: 2000
SQ FT: 160,000
SALES (est): 53.89MM **Privately Held**
Web: www.attcmfg.com
SIC: 3714 Motor vehicle parts and accessories
PA: Aisin Takaoka Co.,Ltd.
     1, Tenno, Takaokashinmachi
     Toyota AIC 473-0

(G-15498)
CHARLES E WATTS
Also Called: Catholic Church School Market
42 Zurich Way (47586-2032)
PHONE.................................812 547-8516
Charles E Watts, *Owner*
EMP: 2 EST: 1977
SALES (est): 161.47K **Privately Held**
SIC: 7311 2752 Advertising agencies; Post cards, picture: lithographed

(G-15499)
DEER CREEK CUSTOM LLC
11833 Deer Creek Rd (47586-8843)
PHONE.................................812 719-5902
EMP: 5 EST: 2018
SALES (est): 231.57K **Privately Held**
SIC: 3441 Fabricated structural metal

(G-15500)
DONS AUTOMOTIVE AND MCH INC
1047 6th St (47586-2323)
PHONE.................................812 547-6292
Donald Froehlich, *Owner*
EMP: 4 EST: 1984
SALES (est): 485.15K **Privately Held**
SIC: 7538 3599 Engine rebuilding: automotive; Machine shop, jobbing and repair

(G-15501)
ETTENSOHN & COMPANY LLC
Also Called: Ettensohn & Company
9018 State Road 237 (47586-8569)
PHONE.................................812 547-5491
EMP: 8 EST: 1996
SQ FT: 17,000
SALES (est): 969.05K **Privately Held**
Web: ettensohnconstruction.aiwaycent.com
SIC: 1521 2431 1751 New construction, single-family houses; Millwork; Cabinet and finish carpentry

(G-15502)
FINE GUYS INC
Also Called: Logos
1002 Tell St (47586-2140)
PHONE.................................812 547-8630
Zac Heartz, *Managing Member*
EMP: 4 EST: 2003
SALES (est): 360.8K **Privately Held**
Web: www.logostc.com
SIC: 3993 Signs and advertising specialties

(G-15503)
FIREHOUSE PRINTING LLC
Also Called: Fedex Office Print & Ship Ctr
711 Humboldt St (47586-2265)
PHONE.................................812 547-3109
Christopher Cail, *Admn*
EMP: 6 EST: 2013
SALES (est): 229.49K **Privately Held**
SIC: 2752 Commercial printing, lithographic

(G-15504)
FRETINA CORPORATION
2001 Main St (47586-1388)
P.O. Box 39 (47586-0039)
PHONE.................................812 547-6471
Jonathan Smith, *Pr*
Tina Smith, *VP*
Lahna Fisher, *Treas*
EMP: 10 EST: 1975
SALES (est): 497.53K **Privately Held**
SIC: 8741 1241 Management services; Coal mining services

(G-15505)
INDUSTRIAL MACHINE
1645 Main St (47586-1361)
P.O. Box 532 (47586-0532)
PHONE.................................812 547-5656
Bill Burnette, *Owner*
EMP: 6 EST: 1982
SALES (est): 291.27K **Privately Held**
SIC: 3599 Machine shop, jobbing and repair

(G-15506)
L L WELDING
806 22nd St (47586-2509)
PHONE.................................812 499-2961
Larry Little, *Owner*
EMP: 1 EST: 2003
SALES (est): 40.56K **Privately Held**
SIC: 7692 Welding repair

(G-15507)
LASHER LUMBER INC
15147 State Road 145 (47586-8525)
PHONE.................................812 836-2618
David Lasher, *Owner*
EMP: 7 EST: 1975
SALES (est): 628.79K **Privately Held**
SIC: 2421 Sawmills and planing mills, general

(G-15508)
LITTLE CABIN EMBROIDERY
9225 Sunset Rd (47586-8431)
PHONE.................................812 719-3888
EMP: 4 EST: 2012
SALES (est): 48.26K **Privately Held**
SIC: 2395 Embroidery and art needlework

(G-15509)
LULUS PROM AND BRIDAL LLC
1408 Main St (47586-1404)
PHONE.................................812 772-2013
EMP: 4 EST: 2013
SALES (est): 120K **Privately Held**
Web: www.luluspromandbridal.com
SIC: 2335 7389 Wedding gowns and dresses; Decoration service for special events

(G-15510)
MCFALL FAMILY MEATS LLC
1414 20th St (47586-2812)
PHONE.................................812 547-6546
Ron Mcfall, *Owner*
EMP: 8 EST: 1998
SALES (est): 158.09K **Privately Held**
SIC: 2011 Meat packing plants

(G-15511)
MICHAEL DEOM PROFESSIONAL
9394 Abner Rd (47586-9021)
PHONE.................................812 836-2206
Michael Deom, *Prin*
EMP: 5 EST: 2005
SALES (est): 73.44K **Privately Held**
SIC: 2411 Logging camps and contractors

(G-15512)
MULZER CRUSHED STONE INC
Also Called: Stone Sand & Concrete Sales
3rd Lafayette St (47586)
P.O. Box 249 (47586-0249)
PHONE.................................812 547-3467
Edward Hagedorn, *Mgr*
EMP: 48
SALES (corp-wide): 34.95B **Privately Held**
Web: www.mulzer.com
SIC: 5032 3273 Stone, crushed or broken; Ready-mixed concrete
HQ: Mulzer Crushed Stone Inc
     534 Mozart St
     Tell City IN 47586
     812 547-7921

(G-15513)
MULZER CRUSHED STONE INC (DH)
Also Called: Tell City Concrete Supply
534 Mozart St (47586-2446)
P.O. Box 744207 (30374-4207)
PHONE.................................812 547-7921
Kenneth Mulzer Junior, *Pr*
Timothy Mulzer, *Sec*
EMP: 20 EST: 1939
SQ FT: 3,600
SALES (est): 388.62MM
SALES (corp-wide): 34.95B **Privately Held**
Web: www.mulzer.com
SIC: 1422 3273 5191 5085 Crushed and broken limestone; Ready-mixed concrete; Limestone, agricultural; Industrial supplies
HQ: Crh Americas, Inc.
     900 Ashwood Pkwy Ste 600
     Atlanta GA 30338
     770 804-3363

(G-15514)
NEON ATTRACTIONS INCORPORATED
535 10th St (47586-2277)
PHONE.................................812 843-5881
Larry Fleming, *Pr*
EMP: 1 EST: 2004
SALES (est): 75.62K **Privately Held**
SIC: 3993 Neon signs

(G-15515)
NEWS PUBLISHING COMPANY LLC (DH)
Also Called: News Publishing
542 7th St (47586-2256)
PHONE.................................502 633-4334
Michael Abernathey, *Pr*
Louis F Ryan, *Sec*
Gary D Miller, *Sec*
EMP: 2 EST: 1904
SQ FT: 5,600
SALES (est): 401.07K **Privately Held**
Web: www.duboiscountyherald.com
SIC: 2711 Newspapers, publishing and printing
HQ: Landmark Community Newspapers, Llc
     601 Taylorsville Rd
     Shelbyville KY 40065
     502 633-4334

(G-15516)
RUDYS FOOD & FUEL LLC
740 9th St (47586-1711)
PHONE.................................812 547-2530
EMP: 2 EST: 2007
SALES (est): 320.43K **Privately Held**
SIC: 2869 Fuels

(G-15517)
SISK RIFLES MANUFACTURING LLC
914 S Boundary Way (47586-2275)
PHONE.................................812 686-8067
Charles Sisk, *Managing Member*
EMP: 1 EST: 2020
SALES (est): 84K **Privately Held**
SIC: 5091 3484 3489 Firearms, sporting; Small arms; Ordnance and accessories, nec

(G-15518)
WAUPACA FOUNDRY INC
9856 W State Road 66 (47586)
PHONE.................................812 547-0700
Gary Gigante, *Pr*
EMP: 1810
SALES (corp-wide): 403.14MM **Privately Held**
Web: www.waupacafoundry.com
SIC: 3321 Gray iron castings, nec
PA: Waupaca Foundry, Inc.
     1955 Brunner Dr
     Waupaca WI 54981
     715 258-6611

(G-15519)
WEBB WHEEL PRODUCTS INC
9840 W State Road 66 (47586)
PHONE.................................812 548-0477

GEOGRAPHIC SECTION

Kent Finkbiner, *Brnch Mgr*
EMP: 177
SALES (corp-wide): 364.48B **Publicly Held**
Web: www.webbwheel.com
SIC: 3714 Motor vehicle parts and accessories
HQ: Webb Wheel Products, Inc.
2310 Industrial Dr Sw
Cullman AL 35055
256 739-6660

(G-15520)
WGS GLOBAL SERVICES LC
840 5th St (47586-2424)
PHONE..................812 548-4446
EMP: 333
Web: www.wgsglobalservices.com
SIC: 3711 Automobile assembly, including specialty automobiles
PA: Wgs Global Services, L.C.
6350 Taylor Dr
Flint MI 48507

(G-15521)
WGS GLOBAL SERVICES LC
9856 W State Road 66 (47586-8581)
PHONE..................810 239-4947
EMP: 2
Web: www.wgsglobalservices.com
SIC: 3599 Machine shop, jobbing and repair
PA: Wgs Global Services, L.C.
6350 Taylor Dr
Flint MI 48507

Templeton
Benton County

(G-15522)
TABERTS MACHINE SHOP
5833 E Old Us Highway 52 (47986-4700)
PHONE..................765 464-9181
EMP: 4 **EST:** 2019
SALES (est): 80.39K **Privately Held**
SIC: 3599 Machine shop, jobbing and repair

Tennyson
Warrick County

(G-15523)
DON DETZER LLC
12859 N County Road 125 W (47637-9437)
PHONE..................812 362-7599
Don Detzer, *Prin*
EMP: 4 **EST:** 2009
SALES (est): 214.35K **Privately Held**
SIC: 3569 Filters

(G-15524)
PIGEON SWITCH POTTERY
1896 Pigeon Switch (47637)
P.O. Box 196 (47637-0196)
PHONE..................812 567-4124
Penny Williams, *Owner*
EMP: 2 **EST:** 2000
SALES (est): 68.53K **Privately Held**
SIC: 3269 Pottery products, nec

(G-15525)
TRIPLE H TOOL CO
7677 Folsomville Rd (47637-7257)
PHONE..................812 567-4600
Donald Hunt, *Owner*
EMP: 2 **EST:** 1980
SQ FT: 1,200
SALES (est): 154.83K **Privately Held**
SIC: 3544 Industrial molds

(G-15526)
YOUR FACE OUR PLACE PRINT SHOP
3877 State Road 161 N (47637-9003)
PHONE..................812 567-4510
John Maltby, *Pt*
Karen Maltby, *Pt*
EMP: 2 **EST:** 1997
SALES (est): 128.97K **Privately Held**
SIC: 2752 Offset printing

Terre Haute
Vigo County

(G-15527)
A H EMERY COMPANY
Also Called: Emery Winslow Scale Co.
1355 Aberdeen St (47804-4202)
PHONE..................812 466-5265
William Fischer, *Brnch Mgr*
EMP: 2
SALES (corp-wide): 9.91MM **Privately Held**
Web: www.emerywinslow.com
SIC: 3596 Industrial scales
PA: The A H Emery Company
73 Cogwheel Ln
Seymour CT 06483
203 881-9333

(G-15528)
A P MACHINE & TOOL CO INC
1301 Elm St (47807-2194)
PHONE..................812 232-4939
Andre G Ponsot, *Pr*
Antionette Ponsot, *VP*
EMP: 10 **EST:** 1966
SQ FT: 11,000
SALES (est): 862.46K **Privately Held**
Web: www.apmachineandtool.com
SIC: 3599 Machine shop, jobbing and repair

(G-15529)
A-R-T PRINTING
1309 N 19th St (47807-1341)
P.O. Box 3571 (47803-0571)
PHONE..................812 235-8600
Timothy Adams, *Owner*
EMP: 1 **EST:** 1997
SALES (est): 70.39K **Privately Held**
Web: www.art.com
SIC: 2752 Offset printing

(G-15530)
ACE SIGN COMPANY INC
1140 3rd Ave (47807-1544)
PHONE..................812 232-4206
Jeffrey Bose, *Pr*
EMP: 8 **EST:** 2010
SALES (est): 864.92K **Privately Held**
Web: www.acesignawning.com
SIC: 3993 Signs and advertising specialties

(G-15531)
ADVANCED ORTHOPRO INC
3185 S 3rd Pl (47802-3785)
PHONE..................812 478-3656
Mike Mansoori, *Brnch Mgr*
EMP: 1
SALES (corp-wide): 1.12B **Privately Held**
Web: www.hangerclinic.com
SIC: 5999 3842 Artificial limbs; Limbs, artificial
HQ: Advanced Orthopro, Inc.
1820 N Illinois St
Indianapolis IN 46202
317 924-4444

(G-15532)
ADVANCED WUND LIMB CARE CTR IN
303 S 14th St (47807-4019)
PHONE..................812 232-0957
John Trench, *Prin*
EMP: 8 **EST:** 1992
SALES (est): 213.02K **Privately Held**
SIC: 3842 Limbs, artificial

(G-15533)
ADVICS MANUFACTURING IND LLC
Also Called: ABI
10550 James Adams St (47802-9294)
PHONE..................812 298-1617
Ryoichi Koizumi, *Managing Member*
Atsushi Takenaga, *
Kazuza Tsukamoto, *
Tetsuya Saida, *
▲ **EMP:** 400 **EST:** 2001
SQ FT: 150,000
SALES (est): 84.52MM **Privately Held**
Web: www.advics-na.com
SIC: 3714 Air brakes, motor vehicle
HQ: Advics North America, Inc.
1650 Kingsview Dr
Lebanon OH 45036
513 696-5450

(G-15534)
AERO INNOVATIONS LLC
7750 State Road 42 (47803-7728)
PHONE..................812 233-0384
EMP: 4 **EST:** 2015
SALES (est): 54.82K **Privately Held**
Web: www.aeroinnovationsllc.com
SIC: 3728 Aircraft parts and equipment, nec

(G-15535)
AIR PRODUCTS AND CHEMICALS INC
Also Called: Air Products
5901 N 13th St (47805-1695)
PHONE..................812 466-6492
Jack Askren, *Brnch Mgr*
EMP: 1
SALES (corp-wide): 12.6B **Publicly Held**
Web: www.airproducts.com
SIC: 2813 5169 Nitrogen; Oxygen
PA: Air Products And Chemicals, Inc.
1940 Air Products Blvd
Allentown PA 18106
610 481-4911

(G-15536)
AIRFX USA LLC
501 S Airport Street (47803)
PHONE..................812 917-5573
Jeff Stark, *Pr*
EMP: 21
SALES (corp-wide): 1.01MM **Privately Held**
Web: www.airfxusa.com
SIC: 3714 Motor vehicle parts and accessories
PA: Airfx Usa Llc
1484 E County Road 600 N
Brazil IN 47834
812 878-8135

(G-15537)
ALL AMERICAN TENT & AWNING INC
Also Called: Ace Sign & Awning
1140 3rd Ave (47807-1544)
PHONE..................812 232-4206
Russell Ferrell, *Pr*
Jeffrey Bose, *VP*
EMP: 20 **EST:** 2003
SQ FT: 7,000
SALES (est): 483.15K **Privately Held**
Web: www.acesignawning.com
SIC: 3993 3444 7359 Electric signs; Awnings and canopies; Tent and tarpaulin rental

(G-15538)
ALL STATE MANUFACTURING CO INC
Also Called: Allstate Mfg
4024 2nd Pkwy (47804-4243)
PHONE..................812 466-2276
Peggy Thomas, *Mgr*
Rudy Stakeman, *CEO*
EMP: 10 **EST:** 1961
SQ FT: 90,000
SALES (est): 1.63MM **Privately Held**
Web: www.allstatemfg.com
SIC: 2522 Cabinets, office: except wood

(G-15539)
ALUMINA PRODUCTS INCORPORATED
1400 N 14th St (47807)
PHONE..................727 934-9781
Mike Rourke, *Pr*
▲ **EMP:** 2 **EST:** 1996
SALES (est): 208.41K **Privately Held**
Web: www.aluminaproducts.com
SIC: 3354 Aluminum extruded products

(G-15540)
ALWAYS SUN TANNING CENTER (PA)
1420 N 25th St (47803-1065)
PHONE..................812 238-2786
Cathy Sweat, *Owner*
EMP: 5 **EST:** 1996
SALES (est): 436.69K
SALES (corp-wide): 436.69K **Privately Held**
Web: www.alwayssuntan.com
SIC: 3648 7299 Sun tanning equipment, incl. tanning beds; Tanning salon

(G-15541)
AMATSIGROUP INC (DH)
2458 N Chamberlain St (47805-9757)
PHONE..................617 576-2005
Jean Pierre Arnaud, *CEO*
Marie Landel, *Corporate Secretary*
EMP: 2 **EST:** 2006
SQ FT: 10,000
SALES (est): 347K
SALES (corp-wide): 336.21K **Privately Held**
SIC: 2834 Pharmaceutical preparations
HQ: Eurofins Amatsigroup Sas
Za Espeche
Fontenilles 31470
562147314

(G-15542)
AMCOR FLEXIBLES NORTH AMER INC
Bemis North America
1350 N Fruitridge Ave (47804-1716)
P.O. Box 905 (47808-0905)
PHONE..................812 466-2213
Neal Ganly, *Brnch Mgr*
EMP: 305
SALES (corp-wide): 14.69B **Privately Held**
Web: www.amcor.com
SIC: 3081 Polyethylene film
HQ: Amcor Flexibles North America, Inc.
2200 Badger Ave
Oshkosh WI 54904
920 727-4100

(G-15543)
AMPACET CORPORATION
Also Called: Ampacet Research & Development

Terre Haute - Vigo County (G-15544) GEOGRAPHIC SECTION

3801 N Fruitridge Ave (47804-1771)
P.O. Box 5086 (47805-0086)
PHONE..................812 466-9828
Prakash Patel, Mgr
EMP: 27
SALES (corp-wide): 455.35MM Privately Held
Web: www.ampacet.com
SIC: 8733 8731 2851 Research institute; Commercial physical research; Paints and allied products
PA: Ampacet Corporation
 660 White Plins Rd Ste 36
 Tarrytown NY 10591
 914 631-6600

(G-15544)
AMPACET CORPORATION
3701 N Fruitridge Ave (47804-4263)
PHONE..................812 466-5231
George Hiland, Brnch Mgr
EMP: 98
SALES (corp-wide): 455.35MM Privately Held
Web: www.ampacet.com
SIC: 2821 2851 5169 2865 Plastics materials and resins; Paints and allied products; Synthetic resins, rubber, and plastic materials; Color pigments, organic
PA: Ampacet Corporation
 660 White Plins Rd Ste 36
 Tarrytown NY 10591
 914 631-6600

(G-15545)
ARBOR PRESERVATIVE SYSTEMS LLC
2901 Ohio Blvd (47803-2248)
PHONE..................812 232-2316
Stella Jones, Mgr
EMP: 15 EST: 2011
SALES (est): 385.22K Privately Held
SIC: 3743 Railroad equipment

(G-15546)
ASSOCIATED LABEL INC
8402 E Davis Ave (47805-9739)
P.O. Box 339 (47878-0339)
PHONE..................812 877-3682
Brian Grayless, Pr
Darrell Bland, VP
Brent Grayless, Treas
EMP: 4 EST: 1988
SQ FT: 3,500
SALES (est): 448.48K Privately Held
SIC: 2679 Labels, paper: made from purchased material

(G-15547)
B S R INC
Also Called: Graham Feed Company
2612 Prairieton Rd (47802-1947)
PHONE..................812 235-4444
Richard Smith, Pr
EMP: 1
SQ FT: 10,000
SIC: 2048 Prepared feeds, nec
PA: B S R Inc
 200 W Voorhees St
 Terre Haute IN 47802

(G-15548)
B S R INC
Also Called: Graham Feed Company
3130 S State Road 63 (47802-8704)
PHONE..................812 235-4444
Richard B Smith, Pr
EMP: 1

SIC: 2048 5191 5169 5999 Prepared feeds, nec; Animal feeds; Chemicals and allied products, nec; Farm equipment and supplies
PA: B S R Inc
 200 W Voorhees St
 Terre Haute IN 47802

(G-15549)
B S R INC (PA)
Also Called: Graham Feed Company
200 W Voorhees St (47802-2967)
PHONE..................812 235-4444
EMP: 23 EST: 1935
SALES (est): 6.1MM Privately Held
SIC: 2048 5191 5999 5169 Prepared feeds, nec; Animal feeds; Farm equipment and supplies; Chemicals and allied products, nec

(G-15550)
BANE-WELKER EQUIPMENT LLC
Also Called: Kubota Authorized Dealer
300 W Margaret Dr (47802-3789)
PHONE..................812 234-2627
Joseph Minnis, Brnch Mgr
EMP: 17
SALES (corp-wide): 44.85MM Privately Held
Web: www.bane-welker.com
SIC: 3524 5083 Grass catchers, lawn mower; Farm and garden machinery
PA: Bane-Welker Equipment, Llc
 33 E 700 S
 Ladoga IN 47954
 765 866-0494

(G-15551)
BENCHMARK INC
Also Called: Benchmark Fabricated Steel
4149 4th Pkwy (47804-4262)
PHONE..................812 238-0659
Edward T Hazledine, Pr
Dale Arnett, VP
Joseph E Harazin, CFO
EMP: 18 EST: 1971
SQ FT: 24,000
SALES (est): 2.48MM Privately Held
Web: www.benchmarksteel.com
SIC: 3441 Building components, structural steel

(G-15552)
BIBLES FOR BLIND VSLLY HNDCPPE
3228 E Rose Hill Ave (47805-1228)
PHONE..................812 466-3134
Keith Reedy, Owner
EMP: 9 EST: 1983
SALES (est): 125.15K Privately Held
Web: www.biblesfortheblind.org
SIC: 2731 5942 Book publishing; Books, religious

(G-15553)
BIG PICTURE DATA IMAGING LLC
608 N 13th St (47807-2114)
PHONE..................812 235-0202
EMP: 3 EST: 2005
SQ FT: 1,100
SALES (est): 461.77K Privately Held
Web: www.bigpiconline.com
SIC: 2759 7379 7374 Screen printing; Data processing consultant; Computer graphics service

(G-15554)
BRIDGESTONE RET OPERATIONS LLC
Also Called: Firestone
940 Wabash Ave (47807-3230)
PHONE..................812 232-9478

Steven Daugherty, Mgr
EMP: 6
Web: www.bridgestoneamericas.com
SIC: 5531 7534 Automotive tires; Rebuilding and retreading tires
HQ: Bridgestone Retail Operations, Llc
 200 4th Ave S Ste 100
 Nashville TN 37201
 630 259-9000

(G-15555)
CARD CALENDER PUBLISHING LLC
200 Arcadia (47803-1704)
PHONE..................812 234-5999
EMP: 4 EST: 2007
SALES (est): 148.22K Privately Held
Web: www.cardcalendarllc.com
SIC: 2741 Miscellaneous publishing

(G-15556)
CARDIS NAILS
1458 S 7th St Unit 2 (47802-1234)
PHONE..................812 264-9906
Cardelia Moore, CEO
EMP: 1 EST: 2021
SALES (est): 8K Privately Held
SIC: 3999 Fingernails, artificial

(G-15557)
CENTER FOR DIAGNOSTIC IMAGING
4313 S 7th St (47802-4365)
PHONE..................812 234-0555
Adrian Lauer, Pr
EMP: 18 EST: 1994
SALES (est): 1.02MM Privately Held
Web: www.rayusradiology.com
SIC: 8071 3829 X-ray laboratory, including dental; Medical diagnostic systems, nuclear

(G-15558)
CENTRAL BRACE & LIMB CO INC
500 E Springhill Dr Ste G (47802-4439)
PHONE..................812 232-2145
Jan Gunnett, Mgr
EMP: 2
SALES (corp-wide): 2.38MM Privately Held
Web: www.centralbraceandlimb.com
SIC: 3842 5999 Braces, orthopedic; Orthopedic and prosthesis applications
PA: Central Brace & Limb Co., Inc.
 1901 N Capitol Ave
 Indianapolis IN 46202
 317 925-4296

(G-15559)
CERTAINTEED LLC
1001 W Industrial Dr (47802-7506)
PHONE..................812 645-0400
Jeff Heffner, Brnch Mgr
EMP: 5
SALES (corp-wide): 402.18MM Privately Held
Web: www.certainteed.com
SIC: 3255 Fire clay blocks, bricks, tile, or special shapes
HQ: Certainteed Llc
 20 Moores Rd
 Malvern PA 19355
 610 893-5000

(G-15560)
CH MANUFACTURING
4411 S Trudys Pl (47802-4478)
PHONE..................812 234-4600
EMP: 1 EST: 1983
SALES (est): 56.73K Privately Held
SIC: 3961 Costume jewelry

(G-15561)
CHAPPELLE CANVAS AND UPHL
3655 E Grant Ave (47805-9573)
PHONE..................765 505-3925
Marsha Chappelle, Prin
EMP: 4 EST: 2019
SALES (est): 46.58K Privately Held
Web: chappelle-canvas-and-upholstery.business.site
SIC: 2211 Canvas

(G-15562)
CHEETAH BUILDING PRODUCTS
4600 N 13th St (47805-1602)
PHONE..................812 466-1234
H Baton, Owner
EMP: 6 EST: 2017
SALES (est): 91.37K Privately Held
SIC: 3272 Concrete products, nec

(G-15563)
CLABBER GIRL CORPORATION
900 Wabash Ave (47807-3208)
P.O. Box 150 (47808-0150)
PHONE..................812 232-9446
Gary L Morri, Pr
◆ EMP: 100 EST: 2001
SALES (est): 10.17MM
SALES (corp-wide): 2.06B Publicly Held
Web: www.clabbergirl.com
SIC: 2099 2046 2045 Baking powder; Corn starch; Prepared flour mixes and doughs
PA: B&G Foods, Inc.
 4 Gatehall Dr
 Parsippany NJ 07054
 973 401-6500

(G-15564)
CLEAR VIEW CSTM WNDOWS DORS IN
9630 E Us Highway 40 (47803-9224)
PHONE..................812 877-1000
Kelly Mcginty, Pr
EMP: 5 EST: 1995
SQ FT: 1,010
SALES (est): 526.32K Privately Held
Web: www.clearviewcustomwindows.com
SIC: 2431 Window frames, wood

(G-15565)
COLONIAL BAKING CO INC
660 N 1st St (47807-1916)
PHONE..................812 232-4466
Glen Brock, Mgr
EMP: 2 EST: 2011
SALES (est): 73.2K Privately Held
SIC: 2051 Bread, cake, and related products

(G-15566)
COMPUTER SOLUTIONS SYSTEMS INC
Also Called: Cs Technology
19 S 6th St Ste 900 (47807-3534)
PHONE..................812 235-9008
Nicholas Mahurin, Pr
EMP: 10 EST: 1989
SQ FT: 8,500
SALES (est): 444.75K Privately Held
Web: www.cstechnologycenter.com
SIC: 3571 5734 7376 Electronic computers; Modems, monitors, terminals, and disk drives; computers, Computer facilities management

(G-15567)
CONTINENTAL WELDING SUP CORP
1317 Poplar St (47807-4569)
P.O. Box 2610 (47802-0610)

GEOGRAPHIC SECTION
Terre Haute - Vigo County (G-15593)

PHONE.................................812 232-2488
Vicki L Swofford, *Pr*
John Huster, *VP Opers*
Pat Moore, *VP Sls*
EMP: 5 **EST:** 1982
SALES (est): 414.62K **Privately Held**
Web: www.continentalweld.com
SIC: 7692 Welding repair

(G-15568)
CORLENS INC
129 Lakeshore (47803-1400)
PHONE.................................843 822-6174
Tim Tenne, *CEO*
EMP: 3
SALES (est): 136.08K **Privately Held**
SIC: 3827 7389 Optical instruments and lenses; Business Activities at Non-Commercial Site

(G-15569)
COUNTRY CABIN LLC
5125 S Us Highway 41 (47802-4789)
PHONE.................................812 232-4635
EMP: 4 **EST:** 2010
SALES (est): 354.12K **Privately Held**
Web: www.countrycabingifts.com
SIC: 5023 3944 Decorating supplies; Craft and hobby kits and sets

(G-15570)
CROSSROADS DOOR & HARDWARE INC
1301 Eagle St (47807-2731)
PHONE.................................812 234-9751
Michael Jones, *Pr*
Joseph Harazin, *CFO*
EMP: 7 **EST:** 2001
SQ FT: 14,000
SALES (est): 999.4K **Privately Held**
Web: www.crossroadsdoor.com
SIC: 3442 3429 Metal doors, sash, and trim; Hardware, nec

(G-15571)
CULTOR FOOD SCIENCE
100 Pfizer Dr (47802-8019)
PHONE.................................812 299-6700
Lloyd Driggers, *Prin*
EMP: 5 **EST:** 2000
SALES (est): 184.94K **Privately Held**
SIC: 2099 Food preparations, nec

(G-15572)
D D SIGNS INC
1720 N 1st St (47804-4058)
PHONE.................................812 243-0084
EMP: 3 **EST:** 2019
SALES (est): 46.08K **Privately Held**
SIC: 3993 Signs and advertising specialties

(G-15573)
D&D AUTOMATION INC
1207 E Dallas Dr (47802-8682)
PHONE.................................812 299-1045
EMP: 9 **EST:** 1989
SQ FT: 8,500
SALES (est): 1.31MM **Privately Held**
Web: www.ddautomation.com
SIC: 3599 3544 7699 Machine shop, jobbing and repair; Forms (molds), for foundry and plastics working machinery; Industrial machinery and equipment repair

(G-15574)
DALEX FBRICATION MACHINING INC
Also Called: Dalex
925 N Fruitridge Ave Ste 3 (47803-1124)
P.O. Box 3013 (47803-0013)
PHONE.................................812 232-7081
EMP: 15 **EST:** 1995
SQ FT: 33,000
SALES (est): 1.51MM **Privately Held**
Web: www.dalexfabrication.com
SIC: 3441 Fabricated structural metal

(G-15575)
DANISCO USA INC
11 W Litesse Dr (47802-8036)
PHONE.................................812 299-6700
EMP: 66
SALES (corp-wide): 11.48B **Publicly Held**
Web: www.iff.com
SIC: 2099 Food preparations, nec
HQ: Danisco Usa Inc.
  4 New Century Pkwy
  New Century KS 66031
  913 764-8100

(G-15576)
DANISCO USA INC
Also Called: Danisco USA
33 W Litesse Dr (47802-8036)
P.O. Box 8266 (47808)
PHONE.................................812 299-6700
Lloyd Driggers, *Mgr*
EMP: 66
SALES (corp-wide): 11.48B **Publicly Held**
Web: www.iff.com
SIC: 2869 Industrial organic chemicals, nec
HQ: Danisco Usa Inc.
  4 New Century Pkwy
  New Century KS 66031
  913 764-8100

(G-15577)
DATA LABEL INC (PA)
1000 Spruce St (47807-2195)
PHONE.................................800 457-0676
Jeff Tyree, *Pr*
Jackie Krantz, *
▼ **EMP:** 150 **EST:** 1980
SQ FT: 78,675
SALES (est): 22.94MM
SALES (corp-wide): 22.94MM **Privately Held**
Web: www.data-label.com
SIC: 2759 Labels and seals: printing, nsk

(G-15578)
DEDE TOOL & MACHINE INC
799 W Springhill Dr (47802-8760)
P.O. Box 10126 (47801-0126)
PHONE.................................812 232-7365
Daniel Farmer, *Pr*
EMP: 8 **EST:** 1998
SQ FT: 8,000
SALES (est): 797.68K **Privately Held**
Web: www.dedetool.com
SIC: 3599 Machine shop, jobbing and repair

(G-15579)
DRONE WORKS LLC
933 S 5th St Apt 3 (47807-5026)
PHONE.................................812 917-4691
Christopher Garner, *Prin*
EMP: 9 **EST:** 2016
SALES (est): 265.38K **Privately Held**
Web: www.drone-works.com
SIC: 3721 Motorized aircraft

(G-15580)
EAST 40 SPORTS APPAREL INC
215 Deming Ln (47803-2082)
PHONE.................................812 877-3695
Patricia Gard, *Pr*
James Gard, *Treas*
EMP: 3 **EST:** 1985
SQ FT: 3,000
SALES (est): 188.05K **Privately Held**
SIC: 7336 5941 2396 Silk screen design; Sporting goods and bicycle shops; Automotive and apparel trimmings

(G-15581)
EBC LLC
1075 Crawford St (47807-4907)
PHONE.................................812 234-4111
John Nugent, *Managing Member*
◆ **EMP:** 40 **EST:** 1986
SQ FT: 150,000
SALES (est): 978.16K **Privately Held**
SIC: 3441 Fabricated structural metal

(G-15582)
ECONOTEC INC
4677 E Mclean Dr (47802-8512)
PHONE.................................812 299-1642
Robert G Mood, *Pr*
EMP: 1 **EST:** 2005
SALES (est): 40K **Privately Held**
Web: www.econotecinc.com
SIC: 3431 Bathroom fixtures, including sinks

(G-15583)
EIDP INC
Also Called: Dupont Nutrition & Health
11 W Litesse Dr (47802-8036)
PHONE.................................812 299-6700
Gary Reid, *Brnch Mgr*
EMP: 3
SALES (corp-wide): 17.23B **Publicly Held**
Web: www.dupont.com
SIC: 2819 Industrial inorganic chemicals, nec
HQ: Eidp, Inc.
  9330 Zionsville Rd
  Indianapolis IN 46268
  833 267-8382

(G-15584)
ELANCO US INC
1445 S 1st St (47802-1910)
PHONE.................................812 242-5999
EMP: 3
SALES (corp-wide): 4.42B **Publicly Held**
Web: www.elanco.com
SIC: 2048 Prepared feeds, nec
HQ: Elanco Us Inc.
  2500 Innovation Way N
  Greenfield IN 46140

(G-15585)
ELI LILLY AND COMPANY
1445 S 1st St (47802-1910)
PHONE.................................812 242-5900
David Shore, *Brnch Mgr*
EMP: 5
SALES (corp-wide): 34.12B **Publicly Held**
Web: www.lilly.com
SIC: 2834 Pharmaceutical preparations
PA: Eli Lilly And Company
  1 Lilly Corporate Ctr
  Indianapolis IN 46285
  317 276-2000

(G-15586)
ENJET AERO TERRE HAUTE LLC
501 S Airport St (47803-9705)
PHONE.................................913 717-7390
EMP: 80 **EST:** 2017
SQ FT: 88,000
SALES (est): 10.07MM
SALES (corp-wide): 78.96MM **Privately Held**
Web: www.enjetaero.com
SIC: 3724 Aircraft engines and engine parts
PA: Enjet Aero, Llc
  9401 Indian Creek Pkwy
  Overland Park KS 66210
  913 717-7396

(G-15587)
ENMAC INC
13200 S Us Highway 41 (47802-9139)
P.O. Box 141 (47866-0141)
PHONE.................................812 298-8711
Curtis Dodine, *Owner*
EMP: 7 **EST:** 2008
SALES (est): 167.25K **Privately Held**
SIC: 3421 Table and food cutlery, including butchers'

(G-15588)
FITESA INDIANA LLC
1069 Crawford St (47807-4907)
PHONE.................................812 466-0202
EMP: 1
SIC: 3081 Unsupported plastics film and sheet
HQ: Fitesa Indiana Llc
  840 Se Main St
  Simpsonville SC 29681

(G-15589)
FITESA INDIANA LLC
3400-A Fort Harrison Rd (47804-1711)
PHONE.................................812 466-0266
EMP: 294
Web: www.fitesa.com
SIC: 3081 Unsupported plastics film and sheet
HQ: Fitesa Indiana Llc
  840 Se Main St
  Simpsonville SC 29681

(G-15590)
FORSYTH BROTHERS CON PDTS INC (PA)
4500 N Fruitridge St (47805-2360)
P.O. Box 5183 (47805-0183)
PHONE.................................812 466-4080
Jeffrey A Bell, *Pr*
Lydia Dalton, *Sec*
EMP: 6 **EST:** 1907
SQ FT: 13,200
SALES (est): 969.84K
SALES (corp-wide): 969.84K **Privately Held**
Web: www.forsyth-puttmann.com
SIC: 3272 5074 Burial vaults, concrete or precast terrazzo; Plumbing fittings and supplies

(G-15591)
FORSYTH PUTTMANN LLC
4500 N Fruitridge St (47805-2360)
P.O. Box 5183 (47805-0183)
PHONE.................................812 466-2925
EMP: 7 **EST:** 2018
SALES (est): 709.88K **Privately Held**
Web: www.forsyth-puttmann.com
SIC: 3272 Burial vaults, concrete or precast terrazzo

(G-15592)
FROGS LEAP
100 N Fruitridge Ave Ste 2 (47803-1326)
PHONE.................................812 235-5759
Ruth Brady, *Owner*
EMP: 1 **EST:** 2005
SALES (est): 71.87K **Privately Held**
Web: www.frogsleap.com
SIC: 2084 Wines

(G-15593)
FUTUREX INDUSTRIES INC
10000 S Carlisle St (47802-8693)
PHONE.................................812 299-5708
Brandon Vest, *Mgr*
EMP: 34
SALES (corp-wide): 48.34MM **Privately Held**

Terre Haute - Vigo County (G-15594)

Web: www.futurexind.com
SIC: 3081 2865 Plastics film and sheet; Styrene
PA: Futurex Industries, Inc.
70 N Main St
Bloomingdale IN 47832
765 498-3900

(G-15594)
GARTLAND FOUNDRY COMPANY INC
330 Grant St (47802-3063)
P.O. Box 2008 (47802-0008)
PHONE..................812 232-0226
Bill Grimes, *Pr*
David Grimes, *Prin*
Steve Cass, *Prin*
Don Powell, *
Mark Nelson, *
▲ EMP: 110 EST: 1902
SQ FT: 100,000
SALES (est): 24.61MM **Privately Held**
Web: www.gartlandfoundry.com
SIC: 3321 Gray iron castings, nec

(G-15595)
GDT TERRE HAUTE MFG
4955 N 13th St Bldg 12 (47805-1607)
PHONE..................812 460-7706
EMP: 5 EST: 2020
SALES (est): 173.69K **Privately Held**
Web: www.terrehauteedc.com
SIC: 3999 Manufacturing industries, nec

(G-15596)
GEON PERFORMANCE SOLUTIONS LLC
3915 1st Pkwy (47804-4234)
PHONE..................812 466-5116
EMP: 7
SALES (corp-wide): 2.67MM **Privately Held**
Web: www.geon.com
SIC: 2821 3087 Thermoplastic materials; Custom compound purchased resins
HQ: Geon Performance Solutions, Llc
25777 Detroit Rd Ste 202
Westlake OH 44145
800 438-4366

(G-15597)
GIBSON INNOVATIONS LLC
2017 N 26th St (47804-3710)
P.O. Box 2112 (47802-0112)
PHONE..................317 561-0932
EMP: 1 EST: 2017
SALES (est): 137.64K **Privately Held**
Web: www.gibsoninnovationsllc.com
SIC: 2621 7336 Printing paper; Commercial art and graphic design

(G-15598)
GIRLS
6860 E Manor Dr (47802-9020)
PHONE..................812 299-1382
Gari Kenworthy, *Owner*
▼ EMP: 1 EST: 2003
SALES (est): 102.93K **Privately Held**
SIC: 2621 1721 Wallpaper (hanging paper); Wallcovering contractors

(G-15599)
GLAS-COL LLC
711 Hulman St (47802-1629)
PHONE..................812 235-6167
EMP: 44 EST: 2002
SALES (est): 11.43MM
SALES (corp-wide): 183.42MM **Privately Held**
Web: www.glascol.com

SIC: 3281 Cut stone and stone products
PA: Templeton Coal Company, Inc.
701 Wabash Ave Ste 501
Terre Haute IN 47807
812 232-7037

(G-15600)
GOETZ PRINTING
Also Called: Goetz Printing & Copy Center
415 Barton Ave (47803-2138)
PHONE..................812 243-2086
John Mullican, *Owner*
EMP: 7 EST: 1955
SQ FT: 10,000
SALES (est): 271.86K **Privately Held**
Web: www.goetzprinting.com
SIC: 2752 2791 2789 Offset printing; Typesetting; Bookbinding and related work

(G-15601)
GRAPHIC FX INC
1130 Walnut St (47807-3823)
PHONE..................812 234-0000
Chad Mckay, *Pr*
EMP: 24 EST: 1995
SQ FT: 9,000
SALES (est): 991.26K **Privately Held**
Web: www.graphicfx.com
SIC: 2759 5699 7389 3949 Promotional printing; Customized clothing and apparel; Advertising, promotional, and trade show services; Team sports equipment

(G-15602)
GREAT DANE LLC
Also Called: Great Dane Trailers
4955 N 13th St (47805-1607)
PHONE..................812 460-7706
EMP: 1
SALES (corp-wide): 1.98B **Publicly Held**
Web: www.greatdane.com
SIC: 3715 Truck trailers
HQ: Great Dane Llc
222 N La Salle St Ste 920
Chicago IL 60601

(G-15603)
HALLADOR ENERGY COMPANY (PA)
Also Called: HALLADOR
1183 E Canvasback Dr (47802)
PHONE..................812 299-2800
Brent K Bilsland, *Ch Bd*
Marjorie Hargrave, *CFO*
EMP: 50 EST: 1949
SALES (est): 634.48MM
SALES (corp-wide): 634.48MM **Publicly Held**
Web: www.halladorenergy.com
SIC: 1241 1311 1382 Coal mining services; Crude petroleum and natural gas production ; Oil and gas exploration services

(G-15604)
HAPCO REBUILDERS INC
129 N 2nd St (47807-2908)
PHONE..................812 232-2550
William J Groth, *Pr*
EMP: 2
SALES (est): 120K **Privately Held**
SIC: 3714 Camshafts, motor vehicle

(G-15605)
HONEY CREEK MACHINE INC
1537 W Harlan Dr (47802-9771)
PHONE..................812 299-5255
Danny Kerr, *Managing Member*
EMP: 20 EST: 1970
SQ FT: 28,500
SALES (est): 2.24MM **Privately Held**
SIC: 3559 Plastics working machinery

(G-15606)
HOOSIER FIBERGLASS INDUSTRIES
2011 S 3rd St (47802-3042)
P.O. Box 9625 (47808-9625)
PHONE..................812 232-5027
Lyndon Tucker, *Pr*
EMP: 19 EST: 1958
SQ FT: 60,000
SALES (est): 374.42K **Privately Held**
Web: www.heartlandfootwearinc.com
SIC: 3089 3081 Thermoformed finished plastics products, nec; Unsupported plastics film and sheet

(G-15607)
HORNER INDUSTRIAL SERVICES INC
3601 Scherer Rd (47804-4265)
PHONE..................812 466-5281
Phil Horner, *Prin*
EMP: 4
SALES (corp-wide): 55.43MM **Privately Held**
Web: www.hornerindustrial.com
SIC: 3625 7694 7699 7629 Electric controls and control accessories, industrial; Electric motor repair; Pumps and pumping equipment repair; Electrical equipment repair, high voltage
PA: Horner Industrial Services, Inc.
1521 E Washington St
Indianapolis IN 46201
317 639-4261

(G-15608)
HULMAN & COMPANY
4780 E Margaret Dr (47803-9303)
PHONE..................812 232-9446
EMP: 1
SALES (corp-wide): 42.81MM **Privately Held**
Web: www.clabbergirl.com
SIC: 2099 Baking powder
PA: Hulman & Company
900 Wabash Ave
Terre Haute IN 47807
812 232-9446

(G-15609)
HULMAN & COMPANY (PA)
Also Called: Clabber Girl
900 Wabash Ave (47807-3208)
P.O. Box 150 (47808-0150)
PHONE..................812 232-9446
Mary H George, *Ch Bd*
Jeffery G Belskus, *
Jeffrey G Belskus, *
Gary Morris, *
Gretchen E Snelling, *
▼ EMP: 120 EST: 1916
SQ FT: 200,000
SALES (est): 42.81MM
SALES (corp-wide): 42.81MM **Privately Held**
Web: www.clabbergirl.com
SIC: 2099 Baking powder

(G-15610)
HUX OIL CORP
5451 Riley Rd (47802-8875)
P.O. Box 1027 (47871-1027)
PHONE..................812 894-2096
Cynthia S Martin, *Pr*
Alice K Prothero, *Sec*
EMP: 6 EST: 1987
SQ FT: 2,500
SALES (est): 914.67K **Privately Held**
Web: www.huxoil.net
SIC: 1311 Crude petroleum production

(G-15611)
HYDRITE CHEMICAL CO
2250 S 13th St (47802-3145)
PHONE..................812 232-5411
Val Kizik, *Brnch Mgr*
EMP: 96
SALES (corp-wide): 424.27MM **Privately Held**
Web: www.hydrite.com
SIC: 2819 5169 2899 Industrial inorganic chemicals, nec; Chemicals and allied products, nec; Chemical preparations, nec
PA: Hydrite Chemical Co.
17385 Golf Parkway
Brookfield WI 53045
262 792-1450

(G-15612)
I2R
711 Hulman St (47802-1629)
P.O. Box 2128 (47802-0128)
PHONE..................812 235-6167
Steve Sterrett, *Prin*
EMP: 6 EST: 2010
SALES (est): 87.61K **Privately Held**
Web: www.glascol.com
SIC: 3821 Laboratory apparatus and furniture

(G-15613)
ILLIANA RAILCAR SERVICES LLC
5110 N 15th St (47805-1639)
P.O. Box 5117 (47805-0117)
PHONE..................812 264-4687
Heath Cottom, *Prin*
EMP: 1 EST: 2010
SALES (est): 205.48K **Privately Held**
SIC: 3743 Railroad equipment

(G-15614)
IMPRINT IT ALL
1419 S 25th St (47803-2927)
PHONE..................812 234-0024
Paul Williams, *Owner*
EMP: 3 EST: 2009
SALES (est): 181.7K **Privately Held**
SIC: 2759 Screen printing

(G-15615)
INDEV GAUGING SYSTEMS INC
5350 N 13th St (47805-1615)
P.O. Box 3667 (43016-0338)
PHONE..................815 282-4463
Jim Wickert, *Mgr*
▲ EMP: 21 EST: 1999
SALES (est): 409.11K **Privately Held**
Web: www.advanzgauge.com
SIC: 3823 Draft gauges, industrial process type
PA: Jasch Industries Limited
502, Block C, Ndm-2, Netaji Subhash Place,
New Delhi DL 11003

(G-15616)
INDIANA COAL MINING INSTITUTE
322 S 6th St (47807-4217)
P.O. Box 9456 (47808-9456)
PHONE..................812 232-5011
EMP: 1 EST: 2000
SALES (est): 65.16K **Privately Held**
SIC: 1241 Coal mining exploration and test boring

(G-15617)
INDIANA SCALE COMPANY INC
1607 Maple Ave (47804-3234)
PHONE..................812 232-0893
Fred Herrmann, *Pr*
▲ EMP: 14 EST: 1990
SQ FT: 35,000

GEOGRAPHIC SECTION
Terre Haute - Vigo County (G-15642)

SALES (est): 2.36MM **Privately Held**
Web: www.inscale-incell.com
SIC: **3596** 5046 8741 Industrial scales; Scales, except laboratory; Management services

(G-15618)
INTERNATIONAL LABEL MFG LLC
1925 S 13th St (47802-2411)
P.O. Box 6129 (47802-6129)
PHONE.................................812 235-5071
EMP: 13 EST: 1994
SQ FT: 40,000
SALES (est): 1.22MM **Privately Held**
Web: www.internationallabelmfg.com
SIC: **2752** 2759 2761 Offset printing; Labels and seals: printing, nsk; Manifold business forms

(G-15619)
INTERNATIONAL PAPER COMPANY
Also Called: International Paper
320 S 25th St Ste 2 (47803-2232)
PHONE.................................800 643-7244
Doug Roberts, *Brnch Mgr*
EMP: 74
SALES (corp-wide): 18.92B **Publicly Held**
Web: www.internationalpaper.com
SIC: **2672** 2611 2653 2656 Paper; coated and laminated, nec; Pulp mills; Boxes, corrugated: made from purchased materials ; Food containers (liquid tight), including milk cartons
PA: International Paper Company
 6400 Poplar Ave
 Memphis TN 38197
 901 419-7000

(G-15620)
JAG METAL
1633 Harding Ave (47802-1038)
PHONE.................................812 235-7200
Glen Price, *Pr*
EMP: 6 EST: 2018
SALES (est): 177K **Privately Held**
Web: www.jagmetalspinninginc.com
SIC: **3469** Spinning metal for the trade

(G-15621)
JBS NEW THIRD PUBLISHING LLC
2 Fairhurst Ct (47802-4905)
PHONE.................................812 262-8595
EMP: 3 EST: 2017
SALES (est): 97.8K **Privately Held**
SIC: **2741** Miscellaneous publishing

(G-15622)
JONES & SONS INC
Also Called: JONES & SONS, INC.
3527 Erie Canal Rd (47802-9115)
PHONE.................................812 299-2287
Kurt Jones, *Mgr*
EMP: 24
SALES (corp-wide): 18.09MM **Privately Held**
Web: www.jonesandsons.com
SIC: **3273** 5083 3272 1711 Ready-mixed concrete; Landscaping equipment; Concrete products, precast, nec; Septic system construction
PA: Jones And Sons, Inc.
 1262 S State Road 57
 Washington IN 47501
 812 254-4731

(G-15623)
JONES FBRICATION MACHINING INC
5600 N Us Highway 41 (47805-9523)
PHONE.................................812 466-2337
Ronald Miller, *Pr*
Bryan Kaufman, *

EMP: 15 EST: 2004
SALES (est): 1.15MM **Privately Held**
Web: www.jonesfabmachine.com
SIC: **3599** Machine shop, jobbing and repair

(G-15624)
KBSHIMMER BATH AND BODY INC
2820 S State Road 63 (47802-8798)
PHONE.................................317 979-2307
Jason Rose, *Pr*
Christina Rose, *VP*
EMP: 2 EST: 2013
SALES (est): 188.29K **Privately Held**
Web: www.kbshimmer.com
SIC: **2844** Cosmetic preparations

(G-15625)
KOSTYO WOODWORKING INC
3399 Fort Harrison Rd (47804-1758)
PHONE.................................812 466-7350
Steve Kostyo, *Pr*
EMP: 5 EST: 1986
SQ FT: 6,000
SALES (est): 754.49K
SALES (corp-wide): 754.49K **Privately Held**
Web: www.kostyowoodworking.com
SIC: **2431** 1799 1751 Millwork; Counter top installation; Cabinet and finish carpentry
PA: Specialty Bottlers Inc
 2155 N 13th St # 57
 Terre Haute IN

(G-15626)
KROCS BUTCHER SHOP LLC
3000 Kussner St (47802-2864)
PHONE.................................812 208-8116
EMP: 6 EST: 2015
SALES (est): 327.32K **Privately Held**
SIC: **3421** Table and food cutlery, including butchers'

(G-15627)
LAMARVIS INDUSTRIES LLC
1457 S 13th 1/2 St (47802-1430)
P.O. Box 3672 (47803-0672)
PHONE.................................317 797-0483
EMP: 3 EST: 2015
SALES (est): 92.81K **Privately Held**
SIC: **3999** Manufacturing industries, nec

(G-15628)
LAMI-CRAFTS INC
2806 S 7th St (47802-3888)
PHONE.................................812 232-3012
Michael Burk, *Pr*
EMP: 5 EST: 1963
SQ FT: 5,000
SALES (est): 355.01K **Privately Held**
Web: www.lami-craft.com
SIC: **2434** 2541 Wood kitchen cabinets; Counter and sink tops

(G-15629)
LARRY H POOLE
Also Called: Gear Up Awards
7826 E Rose Hill Ave (47805-9703)
PHONE.................................812 466-9345
EMP: 2 EST: 1996
SALES (est): 77.01K **Privately Held**
SIC: **3479** 5999 Engraving jewelry, silverware, or metal; Trophies and plaques

(G-15630)
LAUNDRY ON US LLC
2333 S Fruitridge Ave (47803-3514)
PHONE.................................812 567-3653
Matt Mershon, *CEO*
EMP: 1 EST: 2018
SALES (est): 27.18K **Privately Held**

Web: www.foundrylink.com
SIC: **7215** 3582 3633 Laundry, coin-operated ; Washing machines, laundry: commercial, incl. coin-operated; Laundry dryers, household or coin-operated

(G-15631)
LAWRENCO STEEL INC
4000 E Evans Ave (47805-9548)
PHONE.................................812 466-7115
Scott A Lawrence, *Pr*
EMP: 7 EST: 1979
SQ FT: 20,000
SALES (est): 960.55K **Privately Held**
Web: www.lawrenco.com
SIC: **3441** Fabricated structural metal

(G-15632)
LENEX STEEL COMPANY
2325 S 6th St (47802-3018)
PHONE.................................317 818-1622
EMP: 26
SALES (corp-wide): 24.63MM **Privately Held**
Web: www.lenexsteel.com
SIC: **5051** 3444 Steel; Sheet metalwork
PA: Lenex Steel Company
 450 E 96th St Ste 100
 Indianapolis IN 46240
 317 818-1622

(G-15633)
LSC COMMUNICATIONS INC
200 Hulman St (47802-1042)
PHONE.................................812 234-1585
Greg Ruddell, *Brnch Mgr*
EMP: 6
SALES (corp-wide): 8.23B **Privately Held**
Web: www.lsccom.com
SIC: **2732** Book printing
HQ: Lsc Communications, Inc.
 4101 Winfield Rd
 Warrenville IL 60555
 844 572-5720

(G-15634)
MACHINE TOOL SERVICE INC
117 Elm St (47807)
PHONE.................................812 232-1912
Samuel G Hoar, *Pr*
Forrest Jim Perry, *Pr*
Samuel Hoar, *VP*
Bruce Hines, *Sec*
EMP: 14 EST: 1965
SQ FT: 20,000
SALES (est): 1.29MM **Privately Held**
Web: www.machinetoolservice.com
SIC: **3599** 5084 Machine shop, jobbing and repair; Industrial machinery and equipment

(G-15635)
MAHER SUPPLY INC
Also Called: Maher Cnstr Roofg & Siding
910 N 10th St (47807-1525)
PHONE.................................812 234-7699
Thomas R Maher, *Pr*
Marcia Maher, *
EMP: 7 EST: 1969
SQ FT: 60,000
SALES (est): 356.87K **Privately Held**
SIC: **5211** 1761 3442 1521 Lumber and other building materials; Roofing contractor; Storm doors or windows, metal; General remodeling, single-family houses

(G-15636)
MARY DUNCAN
Also Called: Embroidery Express
601 W Honey Creek Dr (47802-2218)
PHONE.................................812 238-3637
EMP: 8 EST: 1994

SQ FT: 4,000
SALES (est): 447.09K **Privately Held**
SIC: **2395** Embroidery products, except Schiffli machine

(G-15637)
MASCHINO WOODWORKS LLC
739 N Forest Dr (47803-4216)
PHONE.................................812 230-7428
Craig Maschino, *Prin*
EMP: 5 EST: 2010
SALES (est): 97.24K **Privately Held**
SIC: **2431** Millwork

(G-15638)
MASTER MACHINE INC
600 E Voorhees St (47802-3072)
PHONE.................................812 232-6583
Randy Flowers, *Pr*
EMP: 1 EST: 1998
SQ FT: 2,000
SALES (est): 232.46K **Privately Held**
Web: www.mastermach.com
SIC: **3599** Machine shop, jobbing and repair

(G-15639)
MCCORD TIRE SERVICE INC
Also Called: Mc Cord Tire & Auto Service
3503 S Us Highway 41 (47802-4101)
PHONE.................................812 235-8016
Chris Elliott, *Pr*
Joanna Elliott, *Sec*
Ross Fischer, *VP*
EMP: 10 EST: 1983
SQ FT: 10,000
SALES (est): 1.63MM **Privately Held**
Web: www.mccordtireandautoservice.com
SIC: **5531** 7534 5014 Automotive tires; Tire repair shop; Automobile tires and tubes

(G-15640)
MED-PHARM PHARMACY
2723 S 7th St Ste M (47802-3558)
PHONE.................................812 232-2086
Eli Kabous, *Owner*
EMP: 1 EST: 2007
SALES (est): 91.34K **Privately Held**
Web: www.medpharm.net
SIC: **2834** Pharmaceutical preparations

(G-15641)
MENARD INC
Also Called: Midwest Manufacturing
4600 N 13th St (47805-1602)
PHONE.................................812 466-1234
EMP: 167
SALES (corp-wide): 1.7B **Privately Held**
Web: www.menards.com
SIC: **2499** 2421 3444 3271 Fencing, wood; Building and structural materials, wood; Roof deck, sheet metal; Blocks, concrete: landscape or retaining wall
PA: Menard, Inc.
 5101 Menard Dr
 Eau Claire WI 54703
 715 876-2000

(G-15642)
MERIDIAN BRICK LLC
5601 E Price Dr (47802-8527)
PHONE.................................812 894-2454
EMP: 25
SALES (corp-wide): 5.17B **Privately Held**
Web: www.meridianbrick.com
SIC: **3251** Brick and structural clay tile
HQ: Meridian Brick Llc
 3015 Bristol Hwy
 Johnson City TN 37601
 770 645-4500

Terre Haute - Vigo County (G-15643) **GEOGRAPHIC SECTION**

(G-15643)
MERVIS INDUSTRIES INC
Also Called: Goodman & Wolfe
830 S 13th St (47807-4915)
PHONE............................812 232-1251
Tom Haley, *Brnch Mgr*
EMP: 6
SALES (corp-wide): 99.07MM **Privately Held**
Web: www.mervis.com
SIC: 5093 3341 4953 Metal scrap and waste materials; Secondary nonferrous metals; Recycling, waste materials
PA: Mervis Industries, Inc.
   3295 E Main St Ste C
   Danville IL 61834
   217 442-5300

(G-15644)
MIAMI GARDENS MILLWORK
11437 E Us Highway 40 (47803-9536)
PHONE............................812 208-4541
Marty Hansen, *Prin*
EMP: 6 **EST:** 2016
SALES (est): 79.44K **Privately Held**
Web: www.miamigardensmillwork.com
SIC: 2431 Millwork

(G-15645)
MIDWEST PRINTING
1925 S 13th St (47802-2411)
P.O. Box 6125 (47802-6125)
PHONE............................812 238-1641
Cecilia Meyers, *Pr*
EMP: 2 **EST:** 2008
SALES (est): 243.88K **Privately Held**
Web: www.midwestprinting.net
SIC: 2752 Offset printing

(G-15646)
MIKRO FURNITURE
Also Called: Welcome Friends
7975 E Chandler Ave (47803-7700)
PHONE............................812 877-9550
Michael D Roe, *Owner*
EMP: 2 **EST:** 1975
SALES (est): 110.88K **Privately Held**
SIC: 2426 Hardwood dimension and flooring mills

(G-15647)
MODERN WLDG & BOILER WORKS INC
3500 Plum St (47803-1133)
P.O. Box 3106 (47803-0106)
PHONE............................812 232-5039
Terry Sanders, *Pr*
Chris Sanders, *VP*
EMP: 2 **EST:** 1946
SQ FT: 52,000
SALES (est): 164.31K **Privately Held**
SIC: 7692 Welding repair

(G-15648)
MOORE-LANGEN PRINTING COMPANY INC
200 Hulman St (47802-1042)
PHONE............................812 234-1585
EMP: 90
SIC: 2752 Offset printing

(G-15649)
N E W INTERSTATE CONCRETE INC
2223 E Margaret Dr (47802-3338)
PHONE............................812 234-5983
N Cameron White, *Pr*
Preston White, *VP*
Pam White, *Sec*
EMP: 10 **EST:** 1985
SQ FT: 9,500
SALES (est): 1.01MM **Privately Held**
Web: www.newinterstateconcrete.com
SIC: 3273 Ready-mixed concrete

(G-15650)
NEOTERIC INCORPORATED
Also Called: Neoteric Hovercraft
1649 Tippecanoe St (47807)
PHONE............................812 234-1120
Christopher Fitzgerald, *Pr*
Barbara R Johnson, *Sec*
▲ **EMP:** 11 **EST:** 1976
SQ FT: 10,000
SALES (est): 1.74MM **Privately Held**
Web: www.neoterichovercraft.com
SIC: 3732 Boatbuilding and repairing

(G-15651)
NEWSPAPER HOLDING INC
Also Called: Tribune Star
222 S 7th St (47807-3601)
P.O. Box 149 (47808)
PHONE............................812 231-4200
Jeremiah Turner, *Prin*
EMP: 1
SALES (corp-wide): 34.97B **Privately Held**
Web: www.tribstar.com
SIC: 2711 Newspapers, publishing and printing
HQ: Newspaper Holding, Inc.
   425 Locust St
   Johnstown PA 15901
   814 532-5102

(G-15652)
NOVELIS CORPORATION
5901 N 13th St (47805-1695)
P.O. Box 1607 (47808-1607)
PHONE............................812 462-2287
Chris Koszewski, *Mgr*
EMP: 250
Web: www.novelis.com
SIC: 3353 3444 5051 Aluminum sheet and strip; Sheet metalwork; Aluminum bars, rods, ingots, sheets, pipes, plates, etc.
HQ: Novelis Corporation
   One Phpps Plz 3550 Pchtre
   Atlanta GA 30326
   404 760-4000

(G-15653)
NRK INC
924 Lafayette Ave (47804-2930)
PHONE............................812 232-1800
Randy Keyes, *Pr*
Amy K Land, *
EMP: 45 **EST:** 1993
SALES (est): 4.85MM **Privately Held**
Web: www.nrkinc.com
SIC: 1731 3699 General electrical contractor ; Security control equipment and systems

(G-15654)
NUMERICAL CONCEPTS INC
4040 1st Pkwy (47804-4298)
PHONE............................812 466-5261
Nancy S Jones, *CEO*
Nancy S Jones, *Pr*
Nancy Seidel Jones, *Sec*
EMP: 30 **EST:** 1973
SQ FT: 76,000
SALES (est): 4.82MM **Privately Held**
Web: www.numericalconcepts.com
SIC: 3555 3599 Printing trades machinery; Machine shop, jobbing and repair

(G-15655)
OHIO TRANSMISSION CORPORATION
Also Called: Otp Industrial Solutions
1502 Lafayette Ave (47804-2504)
PHONE............................812 466-2734
Rod Garing, *Brnch Mgr*
EMP: 8
SALES (corp-wide): 1.04B **Privately Held**
Web: www.otcindustrial.com
SIC: 7629 3561 3536 Electrical repair shops; Pumps and pumping equipment; Hoists, cranes, and monorails
PA: Ohio Transmission Llc
   1900 Jetway Blvd
   Columbus OH 43219
   614 342-6247

(G-15656)
P & M FABRICATION
2820 S Center St (47802-3842)
PHONE............................812 232-7640
Melvin Ennen, *Owner*
EMP: 4 **EST:** 2015
SALES (est): 58.29K **Privately Held**
SIC: 3999 Manufacturing industries, nec

(G-15657)
PARTY CASK
Also Called: Party Cask Southeast
1652 S 25th St (47803-3623)
PHONE............................812 234-3008
Don Thompson, *Owner*
EMP: 2 **EST:** 1987
SALES (est): 85.12K **Privately Held**
SIC: 5921 2086 Wine; Bottled and canned soft drinks

(G-15658)
PATRIOT LABEL INC
9192 E Hwy 40 (47803-9656)
PHONE............................812 877-1611
Jack Kirchner, *Pr*
EMP: 4 **EST:** 2005
SALES (est): 363.54K **Privately Held**
SIC: 2679 Labels, paper: made from purchased material

(G-15659)
PEACE LOVE CUPCAKES
3833 N 25th St (47805-2936)
PHONE............................812 239-1591
Rhonda Noe, *Prin*
EMP: 4 **EST:** 2011
SALES (est): 62.52K **Privately Held**
SIC: 2051 Bread, cake, and related products

(G-15660)
PFIZER INC
Also Called: Pfizer
411 E Dallas Dr (47802-8035)
PHONE............................212 733-2323
Ed Grey, *Mgr*
EMP: 55
SALES (corp-wide): 58.5B **Publicly Held**
Web: www.pfizer.com
SIC: 2833 2834 2865 8731 Medicinals and botanicals; Pharmaceutical preparations; Biological stains; Commercial physical research
PA: Pfizer Inc.
   66 Hudson Blvd E
   New York NY 10001
   212 733-2323

(G-15661)
PHOENIX COLOR CORP
Also Called: M L X Graphics
200 Hulman St (47802-1042)
PHONE............................812 238-1551
Brian Brough, *Mgr*
EMP: 10
SQ FT: 2,900
SALES (corp-wide): 8.23B **Privately Held**
Web: www.phoenixcolor.com
SIC: 2752 Offset printing
HQ: Phoenix Color Llc
   18249 Phoenix Dr
   Hagerstown MD 21742
   301 733-0018

(G-15662)
PHOENIX COLOR CORP
Also Called: Phoenix Color
200 Hulman St (47802-1042)
PHONE............................812 234-1585
EMP: 90
SALES (corp-wide): 8.23B **Privately Held**
Web: www.phoenixcolor.com
SIC: 2752 Offset printing
HQ: Phoenix Color Llc
   18249 Phoenix Dr
   Hagerstown MD 21742
   301 733-0018

(G-15663)
PLM HOLDINGS INC
3956 S State Road 63 (47802-8747)
P.O. Box 10038 (47801-0038)
PHONE............................812 232-0624
Percy L Mossbarger, *Pr*
William N Mossbarger, *
EMP: 24 **EST:** 1973
SQ FT: 8,000
SALES (est): 1.94MM
SALES (corp-wide): 9.27MM **Privately Held**
Web: www.maleyandwertz.com
SIC: 2421 Sawmills and planing mills, general
PA: Maley & Wertz, Inc.
   900 E Columbia St
   Evansville IN 47711
   812 425-3358

(G-15664)
PPG ARCHITECTURAL FINISHES INC
Porter Paints
1700 Wabash Ave (47807-3323)
PHONE............................812 232-0672
Chris Hook, *Mgr*
EMP: 3
SALES (corp-wide): 17.65B **Publicly Held**
Web: www.ppgpmc.com
SIC: 2851 Paints and allied products
HQ: Ppg Architectural Finishes, Inc.
   1 Ppg Pl
   Pittsburgh PA 15272
   412 434-3131

(G-15665)
PPG INDUSTRIES INC
Also Called: PPG 4378
1700 Wabash Ave (47807-3323)
PHONE............................812 232-0672
Lisa Dashiell, *Brnch Mgr*
EMP: 4
SALES (corp-wide): 17.65B **Publicly Held**
Web: www.ppg.com
SIC: 2851 Paints and allied products
PA: Ppg Industries, Inc.
   1 Ppg Pl
   Pittsburgh PA 15272
   412 434-3131

(G-15666)
PRAIRIE GROUP
Also Called: Perry Material Sales
5222 E Margaret Dr (47803-9319)
PHONE............................812 877-9886
Tom Plant, *Mgr*
EMP: 10 **EST:** 1950
SALES (est): 212.24K **Privately Held**
SIC: 3273 5211 Ready-mixed concrete; Brick

GEOGRAPHIC SECTION
Terre Haute - Vigo County (G-15692)

(G-15667)
PRAIRIETON PRINTING
3878 W Newton Dr (47802-8952)
PHONE.................................812 299-9611
Mike Brewer, *Owner*
EMP: 1 **EST:** 1993
SALES (est): 86.44K **Privately Held**
Web: www.midwestprinting.net
SIC: 2752 Offset printing

(G-15668)
PRECISION LABEL INCORPORATED
8890 E Davis Ave (47805-7964)
P.O. Box 397 (47878-0397)
PHONE.................................812 877-3811
Randy Bland, *Pr*
Darrell Bland, *VP*
EMP: 17 **EST:** 1986
SQ FT: 6,000
SALES (est): 855.72K **Privately Held**
Web: www.precisionlabelinc.com
SIC: 2672 2759 Labels (unprinted), gummed: made from purchased materials; Commercial printing, nec

(G-15669)
PRESSTIME GRAPHICS INC
1016 Poplar St (47807-3820)
PHONE.................................812 234-3815
EMP: 10 **EST:** 1989
SQ FT: 14,800
SALES (est): 955.66K **Privately Held**
Web: www.presstime.com
SIC: 2752 7331 2791 2789 Offset printing; Direct mail advertising services; Typesetting ; Bookbinding and related work

(G-15670)
PRINT IT PLUS INC
2151 Lafayette Ave Ste 101 (47805-2910)
PHONE.................................812 466-7446
Lisa Wilson, *Pr*
EMP: 3 **EST:** 2021
SALES (est): 238.04K **Privately Held**
Web: www.print-it-plus.com
SIC: 2752 Offset printing

(G-15671)
PRINT PLUS EXPRESS INC
7623 N 42nd St (47805-9562)
PHONE.................................812 466-6150
Gerald Badeaux, *CEO*
EMP: 4 **EST:** 2017
SALES (est): 59.23K **Privately Held**
Web: www.white-emerson.com
SIC: 3993 Signs and advertising specialties

(G-15672)
PRODUCTION MACHINING COMPANY
4850 N 13th St (47805-1600)
PHONE.................................812 466-2885
Thomas J Haverkamp, *Pr*
EMP: 7 **EST:** 1968
SQ FT: 10,000
SALES (est): 506.51K **Privately Held**
Web: www.productionmachining.com
SIC: 3599 Machine shop, jobbing and repair

(G-15673)
QUICK PANIC RELEASE LLC
2216 Dutch Ln (47802-2754)
PHONE.................................812 841-5733
Jeff Bensinger, *Managing Member*
EMP: 2 **EST:** 2011
SALES (est): 87.11K **Privately Held**
Web: www.quickpanicrelease.com
SIC: 3699 Security devices

(G-15674)
RACO INDUSTRIES LLC
1607 Maple Ave (47804-3234)
PHONE.................................812 232-3676
EMP: 7 **EST:** 2017
SALES (est): 85.99K **Privately Held**
SIC: 3596 Scales and balances, except laboratory

(G-15675)
RANKIN PUMP AND SUPPLY CO INC
130 N 11th St (47807-2796)
PHONE.................................812 238-2535
Thomas G Rankin Junior, *Pr*
EMP: 8 **EST:** 1974
SQ FT: 6,000
SALES (est): 894.21K **Privately Held**
Web: www.rankinecowater.com
SIC: 3561 5084 5051 5085 Pumps and pumping equipment; Pumps and pumping equipment, nec; Cable, wire; Industrial fittings

(G-15676)
RECOGNITION PLUS
25 S 6th St (47807-3510)
PHONE.................................812 232-2372
Jim Pendergast, *Pr*
EMP: 6 **EST:** 1944
SQ FT: 12,000
SALES (est): 337.78K **Privately Held**
Web: www.recognitionplus.net
SIC: 5999 3993 Trophies and plaques; Signs and advertising specialties

(G-15677)
REFRESHMENT SERVICES INC
Pepsico
3875 4th Pkwy (47804-4256)
PHONE.................................812 466-0602
Gloria Chambers, *Mgr*
EMP: 73
SALES (corp-wide): 50.8MM **Privately Held**
Web: www.refreshmentservicespepsi.com
SIC: 2086 Carbonated soft drinks, bottled and canned
PA: Refreshment Services, Inc.
1121 Locust St
Quincy IL 62301
217 223-8600

(G-15678)
REHABLTTION INST INDNPOLIS INC
Also Called: Prosthetic Solutions Indiana
3501 S 3rd Pl (47802-4140)
PHONE.................................888 456-7440
James Goff Junior, *Brnch Mgr*
EMP: 1
Web: www.prosindiana.com
SIC: 3842 Limbs, artificial
PA: Rehabilitation Institute Of Indianapolis, Inc.
2437 N Meridian St
Indianapolis IN 46208

(G-15679)
RESOURCEMFG
2501 Ohio Blvd (47803-2211)
PHONE.................................812 231-8500
EMP: 8 **EST:** 2017
SALES (est): 39.69K **Privately Held**
Web: www.resourcemfg.com
SIC: 3999 Manufacturing industries, nec

(G-15680)
REVOLUTION MATERIALS (IN) LLC (DH)
300 N Fruitridge Ave (47803-1330)
PHONE.................................812 234-2724
Shaun Whitley, *Managing Member*
EMP: 56 **EST:** 2021
SALES (est): 48.57MM
SALES (corp-wide): 802.51MM **Privately Held**
SIC: 3089 4225 Plastics containers, except foam; General warehousing and storage
HQ: Revolution Sustainable Solutions Llc
8801 Frazier St
Little Rock AR 72206
833 806-0356

(G-15681)
REYNOLDS & CO INC
1916 S 25th St (47802-2799)
PHONE.................................812 232-5313
Gerald S Reynolds, *Pr*
Kevin Collenbaugh, *
Jean Reynolds, *
EMP: 21 **EST:** 1946
SQ FT: 17,000
SALES (est): 2.27MM **Privately Held**
Web: www.reynoldsandco.com
SIC: 3599 7699 Custom machinery; Industrial machinery and equipment repair

(G-15682)
REYNOLDS NORTH
1025 N Fruitridge Ave (47804-1770)
PHONE.................................812 235-5313
Gerry Reynolds, *Prin*
EMP: 2 **EST:** 2008
SALES (est): 102.09K **Privately Held**
Web: www.reynoldsandco.com
SIC: 3599 Machine shop, jobbing and repair

(G-15683)
RK MACHINE INC
Also Called: A-1 Machine
3170 N 25th St (47804-1610)
PHONE.................................812 466-0550
Ronald C Miller Junior, *Pr*
EMP: 19 **EST:** 1989
SQ FT: 15,000
SALES (est): 2.47MM **Privately Held**
SIC: 3599 Machine shop, jobbing and repair

(G-15684)
ROSE HL LAWN CARE LDSCPG SNOW
920 N 25th St (47803-1069)
P.O. Box 14124 (47803-8124)
PHONE.................................812 230-0024
EMP: 8 **EST:** 2007
SALES (est): 451.7K **Privately Held**
Web: www.vistaprint.com
SIC: 0782 0781 3271 1741 Lawn care services; Landscape services; Blocks, concrete: landscape or retaining wall; Unit paver installation

(G-15685)
S & G EXCAVATING INC (PA)
545 E Margaret Dr (47802-3795)
PHONE.................................812 234-4848
Kenneth E Steiner Junior, *Pr*
Jack D Steiner, *
EMP: 15 **EST:** 1956
SQ FT: 2,000
SALES (est): 9.82MM
SALES (corp-wide): 9.82MM **Privately Held**
Web: www.sandgexcavating.net
SIC: 1429 1442 1794 Trap rock, crushed and broken-quarrying; Construction sand and gravel; Excavation work

(G-15686)
S & T FULFILLMENT LLC
351 S Airport St (47803-9705)
P.O. Box 2244 (47802-0244)
PHONE.................................812 466-4900
▲ **EMP:** 21 **EST:** 2007
SALES (est): 486.7K **Privately Held**
Web: www.stfulfillment.com
SIC: 3953 Marking devices

(G-15687)
SATURN PETCARE INC
1400 E Polymer Dr (47802-9202)
PHONE.................................812 263-5646
Andy Volkl, *COO*
EMP: 1
SALES (corp-wide): 125MM **Privately Held**
SIC: 2047 Dog and cat food
PA: Saturn Petcare Inc
170 Beaverbrook Rd
Lincoln Park NJ 07035
973 628-7330

(G-15688)
SATURN PETCARE INC
100 E Saturn Petcare Dr (47802)
PHONE.................................812 872-5646
Andy Volkl, *Mgr*
EMP: 209
SALES (corp-wide): 125MM **Privately Held**
SIC: 2047 Dog and cat food
PA: Saturn Petcare Inc
170 Beaverbrook Rd
Lincoln Park NJ 07035
973 628-7330

(G-15689)
SATURN PETCARE INC
93 E Dallas Dr (47802)
PHONE.................................812 872-5646
EMP: 1
SALES (corp-wide): 125MM **Privately Held**
Web: www.saturnpetcare.us
SIC: 2047 Cat food
PA: Saturn Petcare Inc
170 Beaverbrook Rd
Lincoln Park NJ 07035
973 628-7330

(G-15690)
SHADOW SCREEN PRINTING
1521 Maple Ave (47804-3132)
PHONE.................................812 234-3104
EMP: 1 **EST:** 1990
SQ FT: 1,200
SALES (est): 89.54K **Privately Held**
SIC: 2752 2759 Commercial printing, lithographic; Screen printing

(G-15691)
SHENANGO LLC
1200 College Ave (47801-1496)
PHONE.................................812 235-2058
EMP: 14 **EST:** 2004
SQ FT: 12,000
SALES (est): 2.45MM **Privately Held**
Web: www.shenango.com
SIC: 3325 Alloy steel castings, except investment

(G-15692)
SHERWOOD-TEMPLETON INC
Also Called: Sherwood-Templeton Coal Co Inc
701 Wabash Ave Ste 501 (47807-3219)
PHONE.................................812 232-7037
Thomas E Templeton, *Pr*

Terre Haute - Vigo County (G-15693) — GEOGRAPHIC SECTION

Tomas W Thomas, *Sec*
Andrew Myers, *OF LANDS & MINING*
David J Wulf, *Admn Execs*
Thomas W Higgins, *Dir*
EMP: 7 **EST:** 1929
SQ FT: 4,000
SALES (est): 1.02MM
SALES (corp-wide): 183.42MM **Privately Held**
Web: www.templetoncoal.com
SIC: 3567 Heating units and devices, industrial: electric
PA: Templeton Coal Company, Inc.
701 Wabash Ave Ste 501
Terre Haute IN 47807
812 232-7037

(G-15693)
SIGN STOP LLC ◆
1515 S 3rd St (47802)
PHONE..........................812 460-0119
Ali Anvari, *CEO*
EMP: 6 **EST:** 2023
SALES (est): 75.6K **Privately Held**
SIC: 3993 Signs and advertising specialties

(G-15694)
SIGNCENTER INC
333 N Fruitridge Ave (47803-1329)
PHONE..........................812 232-4994
John B Criss, *Pr*
Helene C Steppe, *Sec*
EMP: 5 **EST:** 1974
SQ FT: 8,300
SALES (est): 439.84K **Privately Held**
Web: www.thsigncenter.com
SIC: 3993 1799 Electric signs; Sign installation and maintenance

(G-15695)
SIMMA SOFTWARE INC
5940 S Ernest St (47802-8114)
PHONE..........................812 418-0526
Thomas Simma Junior, *Pr*
EMP: 2 **EST:** 2005
SALES (est): 235.2K **Privately Held**
Web: www.simmasoftware.com
SIC: 7372 Business oriented computer software

(G-15696)
SIMPLE TO ELEGANT LLC
1601 S 3rd St (47802-1013)
P.O. Box 3693 (47803-0693)
PHONE..........................812 234-8700
Jeanette Winchester, *Owner*
EMP: 6 **EST:** 1999
SALES (est): 442.59K **Privately Held**
Web: www.simpletoelegant.org
SIC: 2335 7299 Wedding gowns and dresses ; Miscellaneous personal service

(G-15697)
SINGLE INC
96 Woodbine (47803-1750)
PHONE..........................812 877-2220
EMP: 4 **EST:** 2016
SALES (est): 128.09K **Privately Held**
Web: www.singleink.com
SIC: 2759 Screen printing

(G-15698)
SMITHS AROSPC COMPONENTS HAUTE
333 S 3rd St (47807-3410)
PHONE..........................812 235-5210
James Donohue, *Manager*
EMP: 3 **EST:** 2008
SALES (est): 221K **Privately Held**
SIC: 3724 Aircraft engines and engine parts

(G-15699)
SMITHS SMALL ENGINES INC
Also Called: Smith's Small Engines
1515 N 25th St (47803-1076)
PHONE..........................812 232-1318
James Smith, *Owner*
EMP: 4 **EST:** 1974
SQ FT: 6,000
SALES (est): 384.3K **Privately Held**
Web: smithssmallengines.stihldealer.net
SIC: 3599 7699 3469 Machine shop, jobbing and repair; Engine repair and replacement, non-automotive; Metal stampings, nec

(G-15700)
SOAPY SOAP CO
2001 N Hunt St (47805-8002)
PHONE..........................812 269-8812
EMP: 10 **EST:** 2018
SALES (est): 470.12K **Privately Held**
Web: www.soapysoapcompany.com
SIC: 2841 Soap and other detergents

(G-15701)
SOAPY SOAP COMPANY
2001 N Hunt St (47805-8002)
PHONE..........................812 269-8812
Mohammed Mahdi, *CEO*
Mohammed Mahdi, *Dir*
Anthony Duncan, *Dir*
EMP: 4 **EST:** 2012
SALES (est): 464.24K **Privately Held**
Web: www.soapysoapcompany.com
SIC: 2841 2844 Soap: granulated, liquid, cake, flaked, or chip; Shampoos, rinses, conditioners: hair

(G-15702)
SOILMAX INC
Also Called: Soil-Max
1201 S 1st St (47802-1907)
PHONE..........................888 764-5629
Al Myers, *Pr*
▼ **EMP:** 34 **EST:** 1997
SALES (est): 5.35MM **Privately Held**
Web: www.soilmax.com
SIC: 3523 Plows, agricultural: disc, moldboard, chisel, listers, etc.
PA: Ag Leader Technology, Inc.
2202 S Riverside Dr
Ames IA 50010

(G-15703)
SONY CORPORATION OF AMERICA
1800 N Fruitridge Ave (47804-1780)
PHONE..........................812 462-8726
EMP: 11
Web: www.sonydadc.com
SIC: 3695 Magnetic and optical recording media
HQ: Sony Corporation Of America
25 Madison Ave Fl 27
New York NY 10010

(G-15704)
SONY DADC US INC
3181 N Fruitridge Ave (47804-1700)
PHONE..........................812 462-8116
James M Frische, *Pr*
EMP: 13
Web: www.sonydadc.com
SIC: 3695 Optical disks and tape, blank
HQ: Sony Dadc Us Inc.
1800 N Fruitridge Ave
Terre Haute IN 47804
812 462-8100

(G-15705)
SONY DADC US INC
1600 N Fruitridge Ave (47804-1792)
PHONE..........................812 462-8784
EMP: 13
Web: www.sonydadc.com
SIC: 3695 Optical disks and tape, blank
HQ: Sony Dadc Us Inc.
1800 N Fruitridge Ave
Terre Haute IN 47804
812 462-8100

(G-15706)
SONY DADC US INC (DH)
Also Called: Sony Dadc
1800 N Fruitridge Ave (47804)
P.O. Box 3710 (47803)
PHONE..........................812 462-8100
David Rubenstein, *Pr*
Wallace R Page, *
Warren Maccaroni, *
Michael Frey, *
▲ **EMP:** 1100 **EST:** 1983
SQ FT: 250,000
SALES (est): 276.37MM **Privately Held**
Web: www.sonydadc.com
SIC: 3695 3652 3651 3577 Optical disks and tape, blank; Compact laser discs, prerecorded; Household audio and video equipment; Computer peripheral equipment, nec
HQ: Sony Corporation Of America
25 Madison Ave Fl 27
New York NY 10010

(G-15707)
SPARKLE POOLS INC
2225 N 25th St (47804-3698)
PHONE..........................812 232-1292
Thomas Sedltzeck, *Pr*
Marti Trimble, *Sec*
EMP: 17 **EST:** 1966
SQ FT: 4,500
SALES (est): 496.77K **Privately Held**
Web: www.mysparklepools.com
SIC: 1799 3949 5091 5999 Swimming pool construction; Swimming pools, plastic; Swimming pools, equipment and supplies; Swimming pool chemicals, equipment, and supplies

(G-15708)
SPECIALTY BLANKS INC
500 S 9th St (47807)
PHONE..........................812 232-8775
EMP: 4 **EST:** 2020
SALES (est): 36.24K **Privately Held**
SIC: 8711 3465 3354 Engineering services; Automotive stampings; Aluminum extruded products

(G-15709)
SPECIALTY RIM SUPPLY INC
1033 Crawford St (47807-4907)
P.O. Box 2238 (47802-0238)
PHONE..........................812 234-3002
Jeff Blaylock, *Prin*
EMP: 1
Web: www.specialtyrim.com
SIC: 3465 Automotive stampings
PA: Specialty Rim Supply, Inc.
500 S 9th St
Terre Haute IN 47807

(G-15710)
SPECIALTY RIM SUPPLY INC (PA)
500 S 9th St (47807-4420)
PHONE..........................812 234-3002
Kevin Bishop, *Pr*
Richard Cuvelier, *CEO*
▼ **EMP:** 4 **EST:** 1991
SALES (est): 1.86MM **Privately Held**
Web: www.specialtyrim.com
SIC: 3714 Motor vehicle parts and accessories

(G-15711)
SPECILTY BLNKS INC AN IND CORP
Also Called: Specialty Rim Supply
1033 Crawford St (47807-4907)
P.O. Box 3480 (47803-0480)
PHONE..........................812 234-3002
John Mooche, *VP*
John Mooche, *S&M/VP*
Jack Fenoglio, *TECHNICAL**
EMP: 181 **EST:** 1987
SALES (est): 10.02MM **Privately Held**
SIC: 3469 3398 3599 Metal stampings, nec; Metal heat treating; Machine shop, jobbing and repair

(G-15712)
SPECTRUM INDUSTRY
500 8th Ave (47804-4072)
P.O. Box 4323 (47804-0323)
PHONE..........................812 231-8355
Mary Clark, *Prin*
EMP: 8 **EST:** 2008
SALES (est): 146.63K **Privately Held**
SIC: 3825 Spectrum analyzers

(G-15713)
SPENCE/BANKS HOLDINGS INC (PA)
Also Called: Automated Fuels
700 N 1st St (47807-1923)
P.O. Box 2009 (47802-0009)
PHONE..........................812 235-8123
James D Owen, *Pr*
EMP: 14 **EST:** 1979
SQ FT: 3,800
SALES (est): 2.26MM
SALES (corp-wide): 2.26MM **Privately Held**
Web: www.spencebanks.com
SIC: 2992 5172 5983 Lubricating oils; Petroleum products, nec; Fuel oil dealers

(G-15714)
SQUARE DONUTS INC
935 Wabash Ave (47807-3229)
PHONE..........................812 232-6463
Richard A Comer, *Pr*
Patricia Comer, *Sec*
Richard A Comer, *Resident Agent*
EMP: 6 **EST:** 1954
SALES (est): 666.66K **Privately Held**
Web: www.squaredonuts.com
SIC: 2051 5461 Doughnuts, except frozen; Doughnuts

(G-15715)
STARK PRECISION MACHINE LLC
1205 E Dallas Dr (47802-8682)
PHONE..........................812 239-5291
Craig Kraft, *Prin*
Don Brown, *VP*
EMP: 2
SALES (est): 81.49K **Privately Held**
SIC: 3599 Industrial machinery, nec

(G-15716)
STEEL DYNAMICS HEARTLAND LLC
455 W Industrial Dr (47802-9266)
PHONE..........................812 299-8866
Mark D Millett, *Pr*
Jerry Richardson, *
Roberto Bohrer, *
▲ **EMP:** 200 **EST:** 2001
SQ FT: 800,000
SALES (est): 51.91MM **Publicly Held**
Web: www.steeldynamics.com

GEOGRAPHIC SECTION — Terre Haute - Vigo County (G-15739)

SIC: 3316 3312 Cold-rolled strip or wire; Galvanized pipes, plates, sheets, etc.: iron and steel
PA: Steel Dynamics, Inc.
7575 W Jefferson Blvd
Fort Wayne IN 46804

(G-15717) SUN CHEMICAL CORPORATION
Also Called: Sun Chemical
1350 N Fruitridge Ave (47804-1716)
PHONE..................812 235-8031
Al Dean, *Mgr*
EMP: 2
Web: www.sunchemical.com
SIC: 2893 Printing ink
HQ: Sun Chemical Corporation
35 Waterview Blvd
Parsippany NJ 07054
973 404-6000

(G-15718) SUNRISE COAL LLC (HQ)
1183 E Canvasback Dr (47802-5304)
PHONE..................812 299-2800
Brent K Bilsland, *Pr*
Lawrence D Martin, *Pr*
EMP: 4 EST: 2002
SQ FT: 1,500
SALES (est): 106.83MM
SALES (corp-wide): 361.99MM **Publicly Held**
Web: www.halladorenergy.com
SIC: 1221 Bituminous coal and lignite- surface mining
PA: Hallador Energy Company
1183 E Canvasback Dr
Terre Haute IN 47802
812 299-2800

(G-15719) SWAGERLE SCREEN PRINTING
Also Called: Swag's Screen Prtg Sportswear
2950 S 7th St (47802-3840)
PHONE..................812 232-6947
Mike Swagerle, *Owner*
EMP: 1 EST: 1978
SALES (est): 93.36K **Privately Held**
Web: www.swagstees.com
SIC: 2759 2752 Screen printing; Commercial printing, lithographic

(G-15720) SYCAMORE COAL INC
Also Called: Vectren Fuels, Inc.
1183 E Canvasback Dr (47802-5304)
PHONE..................812 491-4000
Carl Chapman, *Pr*
EMP: 1 EST: 1996
SALES (est): 1.24MM
SALES (corp-wide): 634.48MM **Publicly Held**
SIC: 1241 Coal mining services
HQ: Sunrise Coal, Llc
1183 E Canvasback Dr
Terre Haute IN 47802
812 299-2800

(G-15721) T SHIRT 1 INC
2319 N 25th St (47804-2106)
P.O. Box 3841 (47803-0841)
PHONE..................812 232-5046
Lynn Zimmerman, *Dir*
EMP: 9 EST: 2001
SALES (est): 458.63K **Privately Held**
Web: www.tshirt1.com
SIC: 2759 Screen printing

(G-15722) TAGHLEEF INDUSTRIES INC
425 N Brown Ave (47803-1240)
PHONE..................812 460-5657
EMP: 1
Web: www.ti-films.com
SIC: 3081 Unsupported plastics film and sheet
HQ: Taghleef Industries Inc.
800 Prdes Crssing Ste 200
Newark DE 19713
302 326-5500

(G-15723) TANGENT RAIL PRODUCTS INC
2901 Ohio Blvd Ste 252 (47803-2248)
PHONE..................412 325-0202
Celeste Frazee, *Brnch Mgr*
EMP: 36
SALES (corp-wide): 2.42B **Privately Held**
SIC: 2491 3743 Wood preserving; Railroad equipment
HQ: Tangent Rail Products, Inc.
101 W Station Square Dr # 600
Pittsburgh PA 15219
412 325-0202

(G-15724) TECHNICOTE INC
3200 N 25th St (47804-1602)
PHONE..................812 466-9844
Tim Mundy, *Mgr*
EMP: 41
SALES (corp-wide): 47.02MM **Privately Held**
Web: www.technicote.com
SIC: 2891 2851 Adhesives; Paints and allied products
PA: Technicote, Inc.
222 Mound Ave
Miamisburg OH 45342
800 358-4448

(G-15725) TEMPLETON COAL COMPANY INC (PA)
Also Called: Glas-Col Div
701 Wabash Ave Ste 501 (47807-3293)
P.O. Box 2128 (47802-0128)
PHONE..................812 232-7037
Thomas E Templeton, *CEO*
Tomas Thomas, *Sec*
Scott B Anshutz, *Dir*
EMP: 8 EST: 1920
SQ FT: 4,000
SALES (est): 183.42MM
SALES (corp-wide): 183.42MM **Privately Held**
Web: www.templetoncoal.com
SIC: 5074 3567 3961 5049 Plumbing fittings and supplies; Heating units and devices, industrial: electric; Rosaries and small religious articles, except precious metal; Religious supplies

(G-15726) TEMPLETON COAL COMPANY INC
Glas-Col Apparatus Division
711 Hulman St (47802-1629)
P.O. Box 2128 (47802-0128)
PHONE..................812 232-7037
Steve Sterredt, *Managing Member*
EMP: 141
SQ FT: 44,000
SALES (corp-wide): 183.42MM **Privately Held**
Web: www.templetoncoal.com
SIC: 3585 3826 3821 3531 Heating equipment, complete; Analytical instruments; Laboratory apparatus and furniture; Construction machinery

PA: Templeton Coal Company, Inc.
701 Wabash Ave Ste 501
Terre Haute IN 47807
812 232-7037

(G-15727) TERRE HUTE WLBERT BRIAL VLT IN
509 E Preston St (47802-3576)
PHONE..................812 235-0339
Timothy A Puttmann, *Pr*
▲ EMP: 12 EST: 1957
SQ FT: 13,800
SALES (est): 1.92MM **Privately Held**
Web: www.thwilbert.com
SIC: 3272 3281 Burial vaults, concrete or precast terrazzo; Monuments, cut stone (not finishing or lettering only)

(G-15728) TERREMAX FARMS LLC (PA)
3260 Red Barn Rd (47805-7973)
PHONE..................812 242-0276
Dennis Bell, *Managing Member*
EMP: 1 EST: 2012
SALES (est): 617.28K
SALES (corp-wide): 617.28K **Privately Held**
Web: www.terremax.com
SIC: 2873 0711 Fertilizers: natural (organic), except compost; Soil preparation services

(G-15729) TERRY HAUTE PROPANE PLANT
6625 E Margaret Dr (47803-7727)
PHONE..................812 877-3406
Mike Stroud, *Mgr*
EMP: 1 EST: 2002
SALES (est): 67K **Privately Held**
SIC: 1321 Natural gas liquids production

(G-15730) THIS & THAT PRODUCTS
3784 Hotel St (47802-8893)
PHONE..................812 299-2688
Bob Dillion, *Owner*
EMP: 2 EST: 1979
SALES (est): 77K **Privately Held**
SIC: 2499 Woodenware, kitchen and household

(G-15731) TINAS CERAMICS & THINGS
1001 N 3rd St (47807-1829)
PHONE..................812 917-4190
EMP: 4 EST: 2014
SALES (est): 56.81K **Privately Held**
SIC: 3269 Pottery products, nec

(G-15732) TJ HAASE WINERY LTD LBLTY CO
8249 Hannah Ave (47805-8903)
PHONE..................765 505-1382
EMP: 2 EST: 2013
SALES (est): 120.88K **Privately Held**
Web: www.tjhaasewinery.com
SIC: 2084 Wines

(G-15733) TODDS HYDRLCS RPR & STL FBRCT
3904 4th Pkwy (47804-4257)
P.O. Box 3369 (47803-0369)
PHONE..................812 466-3457
Dennis Givens, *Pr*
EMP: 1 EST: 1991
SQ FT: 8,000
SALES (est): 214.09K **Privately Held**
SIC: 7699 5051 3999 1799 Agricultural equipment repair services; Rope, wire (not insulated); Wheelchair lifts; Welding on site

(G-15734) TREDEGAR CORPORATION
Tredegar Film Products Div
3400 Fort Harrison Rd (47804-1799)
P.O. Box 1072 (47808-1072)
PHONE..................812 466-0266
Bill Bendick, *Mgr*
EMP: 80
Web: www.tredegar.com
SIC: 3354 3089 3081 Aluminum extruded products; Plastics processing; Polyethylene film
PA: Tredegar Corporation
1100 Boulders Pkwy
North Chesterfield VA 23225

(G-15735) TRH SOFTWARE INC
1503 7th Ave (47807-1217)
PHONE..................812 264-2428
Terry R Higgins, *Prin*
EMP: 2 EST: 2008
SALES (est): 97.96K **Privately Held**
Web: www.trh-software.com
SIC: 7372 Prepackaged software

(G-15736) TRI AEROSPACE LLC
1055 S Hunt St (47803-9702)
PHONE..................812 872-2400
R Laurence Cross, *Genl Mgr*
Rodney Goodrich, *
EMP: 37 EST: 1985
SQ FT: 27,000
SALES (est): 4.96MM **Privately Held**
Web: www.triaerospace.com
SIC: 3724 3728 3714 3511 Air scoops, aircraft; Aircraft body and wing assemblies and parts; Motor vehicle engines and parts; Turbines and turbine generator set units, complete

(G-15737) TURBINES INC
7303 Maynard Wheeler Ln (47803-9561)
PHONE..................812 877-2587
James M Mills, *Pr*
Peggy Mills, *Sec*
EMP: 20 EST: 1980
SQ FT: 13,200
SALES (est): 995.24K **Privately Held**
Web: www.turbinesinc.com
SIC: 4581 5088 3724 Aircraft cleaning and janitorial service; Transportation equipment and supplies; Aircraft engines and engine parts

(G-15738) UNISON ENGINE COMPONENTS INC
Also Called: Unison Engine Components
333 S 3rd St (47807-3410)
PHONE..................904 739-4000
EMP: 180 EST: 1952
SALES (est): 35.57MM
SALES (corp-wide): 67.95B **Publicly Held**
Web: www.unisonec.com
SIC: 3724 3443 3519 3441 Aircraft engines and engine parts; Missile silos and components, metal plate; Internal combustion engines, nec; Fabricated structural metal
HQ: Ge Aviation Systems Llc
1 Neumann Way
Cincinnati OH 45215
937 898-9600

(G-15739) VCO INC
Also Called: Logo Connxtion
1210 Wabash Ave (47807-3312)
PHONE..................812 235-3540

Terre Haute - Vigo County (G-15740)

TOLL FREE: 877
Doug Lemond, *Pr*
Angie Lemond, *VP*
EMP: 6 **EST:** 1981
SALES (est): 534.31K **Privately Held**
Web: www.logoconnxtion.com
SIC: 2395 Embroidery products, except Schiffli machine

(G-15740)
VIGO MACHINE SHOP INC
3920 Locust St (47803-1337)
PHONE.................................812 235-8393
Gary Michl, *Pr*
Gary P Michl, *
Pat Michl, *
EMP: 25 **EST:** 2005
SQ FT: 24,000
SALES (est): 2.4MM **Privately Held**
Web: www.vigomachine.net
SIC: 3599 Machine shop, jobbing and repair

(G-15741)
VOGES MACHINE
Also Called: Voges Machine Shop
4876 W Kennett Dr (47802-9823)
PHONE.................................812 299-1546
David Voges, *Owner*
EMP: 3 **EST:** 1955
SALES (est): 168.16K **Privately Held**
SIC: 3599 Machine shop, jobbing and repair

(G-15742)
VOGES RESTORATION AND WDWKG
5696 W Cantrell Dr (47802-9440)
PHONE.................................812 299-1546
David Voges, *Owner*
EMP: 4 **EST:** 2001
SALES (est): 167.85K **Privately Held**
SIC: 2499 3449 Applicators, wood; Miscellaneous metalwork

(G-15743)
WABASH VALLEY MOTOR & MCH INC
3909 N Fruitridge Ave (47805-2350)
P.O. Box 5221 (47805-0221)
PHONE.................................812 466-7400
Lee Shippley, *Pr*
Jim Everhart, *Sec*
EMP: 6 **EST:** 1984
SQ FT: 10,000
SALES (est): 2.3MM **Privately Held**
Web: www.wabashvalleymotor.com
SIC: 5063 7694 Motors, electric; Electric motor repair

(G-15744)
WABASH VALLEY PACKAGING CORP
1303 E Industrial Dr (47802)
PHONE.................................812 299-7181
EMP: 10 **EST:** 1999
SALES (est): 2.13MM **Privately Held**
Web: www.wabashvalleypkg.com
SIC: 2653 Boxes, corrugated: made from purchased materials

(G-15745)
WESTFIELD STEEL INC
3345 Fort Harrison Rd (47804-1758)
PHONE.................................812 466-3500
EMP: 5
SALES (corp-wide): 86.07MM **Privately Held**
Web: www.westfieldsteel.com
SIC: 5051 3441 Steel; Fabricated structural metal
PA: Westfield Steel Inc
530 W State Road 32
Westfield IN 46074
317 896-5587

(G-15746)
WHEELS IN SKY
1026 Monterey Ave (47803-2767)
PHONE.................................812 249-8233
Mike Wheeler, *Prin*
EMP: 7 **EST:** 2004
SALES (est): 139.66K **Privately Held**
Web: www.wheelsinthesky.com
SIC: 3312 Wheels

(G-15747)
WINSLOW SCALE COMPANY
1355 Aberdeen St (47804-4202)
PHONE.................................812 466-5265
Walter Young, *CEO*
William K Fischer, *Pr*
EMP: 24 **EST:** 1896
SALES (est): 2.07MM
SALES (corp-wide): 9.91MM **Privately Held**
Web: www.emerywinslow.com
SIC: 3596 Industrial scales
PA: The A H Emery Company
73 Cogwheel Ln
Seymour CT 06483
203 881-9333

(G-15748)
WOODBURN GRAPHICS INC
25 S 6th St (47807-3510)
P.O. Box 9299 (47808-9299)
PHONE.................................812 232-0323
Marilyn Pendergast, *Pr*
James Pendergast, *
Curt Pendergast, *
EMP: 19 **EST:** 1902
SQ FT: 62,000
SALES (est): 775.04K **Privately Held**
Web: www.woodburngraphics.com
SIC: 2752 2791 2789 2761 Offset printing; Typesetting; Bookbinding and related work; Manifold business forms

(G-15749)
X-TREME LAZER TAG
844 W Johnson Dr (47802-4189)
PHONE.................................812 238-8412
Gerry Modesitt, *Owner*
EMP: 7 **EST:** 2008
SALES (est): 730.86K **Privately Held**
Web: www.xtremelazertag.com
SIC: 3699 Laser systems and equipment

Thorntown
Boone County

(G-15750)
BENAKOVICH BUILDERS
Also Called: Construction
10725 W State Road 47 (46071-9043)
PHONE.................................219 204-2777
EMP: 2 **EST:** 2011
SALES (est): 152.61K **Privately Held**
Web: www.benakovichbuilders.com
SIC: 1521 1751 3429 New construction, single-family houses; Carpentry work; Furniture, builders' and other household hardware

(G-15751)
HERITAGE AGGREGATES LLC
6990 N 875 W (46071-8957)
PHONE.................................765 436-7665
Robert J Simpson, *Ch Bd*
EMP: 2
SALES (corp-wide): 4.06MM **Privately Held**
Web: www.usagg.com
SIC: 1422 Limestones, ground
PA: Heritage Aggregates, Llc
5400 W 86th St
Indianapolis IN 46268
317 872-6010

(G-15752)
J & J WOODCRAFTERS
2416 N State Road 75 (46071-9235)
PHONE.................................765 436-2466
John Dieterline, *Owner*
EMP: 3 **EST:** 1986
SALES (est): 200K **Privately Held**
Web: www.jjfinewood.com
SIC: 2517 2434 Home entertainment unit cabinets, wood; Wood kitchen cabinets

(G-15753)
MIDWEST EQUIPMENT MFG INC
5225 Serum Plant Rd (46071-9266)
PHONE.................................765 436-2496
Dan Kallevig, *Pr*
EMP: 18 **EST:** 2017
SALES (est): 1.32MM **Privately Held**
Web: www.trac-vac.com
SIC: 3524 Lawn and garden equipment

(G-15754)
PERDUE FARMS INC
Also Called: Perdue Farms
4586 N Us Highway 52 (46071-9287)
PHONE.................................765 436-7990
Michael Maroney, *Mgr*
EMP: 172
SALES (corp-wide): 1.24B **Privately Held**
Web: www.perdue.com
SIC: 2015 Chicken slaughtering and processing
PA: Perdue Farms Incorporated
31149 Old Ocean City Rd
Salisbury MD 21804
800 473-7383

(G-15755)
SKY HIGH SIGN SERVICE
6716 N 1075 W (46071-9090)
PHONE.................................765 436-7012
Thomas Crow, *Owner*
EMP: 1 **EST:** 1980
SALES (est): 96.23K **Privately Held**
SIC: 3993 Signs and advertising specialties

(G-15756)
STALCOP LLC (PA)
Also Called: Stalcop Cold US
1217 W Main St (46071-8986)
PHONE.................................765 436-7926
Ron St Clair, *Pt*
Ron St Clair, *Pt*
Dave Riddle, *CFO*
▲ **EMP:** 48 **EST:** 1994
SQ FT: 60,000
SALES (est): 10.83MM
SALES (corp-wide): 10.83MM **Privately Held**
Web: www.stalcop.com
SIC: 3444 3366 3354 3316 Sheet metalwork; Copper foundries; Aluminum extruded products; Cold finishing of steel shapes

(G-15757)
U S AGGREGATES INC
6990 N 875 W (46071-8957)
PHONE.................................765 436-7665
EMP: 8
SALES (corp-wide): 894.43MM **Privately Held**
Web: www.usagg.com
SIC: 1422 Crushed and broken limestone
HQ: U S Aggregates Inc
5400 W 86th St
Indianapolis IN 46268
317 872-6010

Tippecanoe
Marshall County

(G-15758)
A J COIL INC
20015 Apple Rd (46570-9763)
PHONE.................................574 353-7174
Rachel Banghart, *Pr*
Russell Rex Yazel, *VP*
Margaret Yazel, *Prin*
EMP: 5 **EST:** 1978
SALES (est): 437.77K **Privately Held**
Web: www.medt.com
SIC: 3495 Wire springs

(G-15759)
GEN ENTERPRISES
Also Called: Singles Ministry, The
3500 18b Rd (46570-9799)
PHONE.................................574 498-6777
EMP: 2 **EST:** 1998
SALES (est): 162.74K **Privately Held**
SIC: 2673 2759 Bags: plastic, laminated, and coated; Publication printing

(G-15760)
HENSLEY FABRICATING & EQP CO
Also Called: Hensley Hydra-Haulers
17624 State Road 331 (46570-9750)
PHONE.................................574 498-6514
Paul Hensley, *Ch Bd*
Gregory L Hensley, *
Beatrice Hensley, *
Pam Pennington, *Stockholder*
Paula Poisel, *Stockholder*
▼ **EMP:** 40 **EST:** 1963
SQ FT: 37,000
SALES (est): 5.65MM **Privately Held**
Web: www.hensleyfab.com
SIC: 3443 Tanks, standard or custom fabricated: metal plate

(G-15761)
LEE E NORRIS CNSTR & GRN CO (PA)
Also Called: B.N.W. Industries
7930 N 700 E (46570-9613)
PHONE.................................574 353-7855
Dan Norris, *Pr*
Aaron Norris, *Sec*
▲ **EMP:** 1 **EST:** 1965
SQ FT: 32,000
SALES (est): 2.16MM
SALES (corp-wide): 2.16MM **Privately Held**
Web: www.beltomatic.com
SIC: 3523 Driers (farm): grain, hay, and seed

(G-15762)
NORRIS THERMAL TECH INC
7930 N 700 E (46570-9613)
PHONE.................................574 353-7855
W Woelfer, *Mgr*
◆ **EMP:** 2 **EST:** 2013
SALES (est): 447.41K **Privately Held**
Web: www.norristhermal.com
SIC: 3556 Food products machinery

GEOGRAPHIC SECTION

Tipton - Tipton County (G-15788)

Tipton
Tipton County

(G-15763)
ACRA-LINE PRODUCTS INC
641 Cleveland St (46072-1132)
PHONE..................................765 675-8841
Jim Overholt, *General TECHNICAL*
EMP: 11 **EST:** 1985
SALES (est): 292.8K **Privately Held**
Web: www.acraline.com
SIC: 3443 Fabricated plate work (boiler shop)

(G-15764)
APPLE GROUP INC
122 N East St (46072-1740)
PHONE..................................765 675-4777
Judith Burton, *Pr*
Ed Burton, *Sec*
EMP: 20 **EST:** 1993
SQ FT: 15,000
SALES (est): 2.47MM **Privately Held**
Web: www.applegroup.com
SIC: 2396 2395 5199 Fabric printing and stamping; Embroidery and art needlework; Advertising specialties

(G-15765)
ASHLEYS ELEMENTS LLC
588 S 100 E (46072-8809)
PHONE..................................765 480-2168
EMP: 3 **EST:** 2019
SALES (est): 78.48K **Privately Held**
SIC: 2819 Elements

(G-15766)
ATKISSON ENTERPRISES INC
Also Called: Progress Tool & Die Shop
632 Mill St (46072-1052)
P.O. Box 28 (46072-0028)
PHONE..................................765 675-7593
Michael Atkisson, *Pr*
Jaime Atkisson, *Sec*
EMP: 10 **EST:** 1967
SQ FT: 25,000
SALES (est): 506.3K **Privately Held**
Web: www.progresstoolanddie.com
SIC: 3544 3469 Special dies and tools; Metal stampings, nec

(G-15767)
BML GRAPHICS LLC
4484 S State Road 19 (46072-9352)
PHONE..................................317 984-5500
EMP: 10 **EST:** 2017
SALES (est): 358.36K **Privately Held**
Web: www.hsgsigns.com
SIC: 3993 Signs and advertising specialties

(G-15768)
BOTTCHER AMERICA CORPORATION
717 Industrial Dr (46072-1071)
PHONE..................................765 675-4449
Jeff Hoover, *Mgr*
EMP: 5
SALES (corp-wide): 254.88MM **Privately Held**
Web: www.bottcher.com
SIC: 5084 2796 Printing trades machinery, equipment, and supplies; Platemaking services
HQ: Bottcher America Corporation
    4600 Mercedes Dr
    Belcamp MD 21017
    410 273-7000

(G-15769)
BRETT TISHNER
Also Called: Bat Signs & Graphics
213 Armstrong St (46072-1418)
PHONE..................................765 675-2180
Brett Tishner, *Owner*
EMP: 1 **EST:** 1997
SQ FT: 1,500
SALES (est): 185K **Privately Held**
Web: bat-signs-graphics.hub.biz
SIC: 3993 Signs and advertising specialties

(G-15770)
DC COATERS INC
550 Industrial Dr (46072-8463)
PHONE..................................765 675-6006
Dennis Cook, *Pr*
Stephen Gill, *Ex VP*
Linda Cook, *VP*
Max Mc Neal, *Sec*
EMP: 72 **EST:** 1993
SALES (est): 5.04MM **Privately Held**
Web: www.dccoaters.net
SIC: 3479 1721 Coating of metals and formed products; Painting and paper hanging

(G-15771)
ED HENRY & SON
3340 S 400 W (46072-8974)
PHONE..................................765 675-7235
Edward Henry, *Owner*
EMP: 1 **EST:** 1948
SALES (est): 107.43K **Privately Held**
SIC: 3274 Agricultural lime

(G-15772)
ELWOOD PUBLISHING COMPANY INC
Also Called: Alexandria Tribune, The
116 S Main St Ste A (46072-1864)
P.O. Box 248 (46072-0248)
PHONE..................................765 675-2115
EMP: 5
SALES (corp-wide): 8.23MM **Privately Held**
Web: www.elwoodpublishing.com
SIC: 2711 Newspapers, publishing and printing
HQ: Elwood Publishing Company Incorporated
    317 S Anderson St
    Elwood IN 46036
    765 552-3355

(G-15773)
FLAIR EXCHANGE LLC
5266 E 100 S (46072-8710)
PHONE..................................765 210-4604
Sarah Marie Barber, *Prin*
EMP: 7 **EST:** 2017
SALES (est): 53.34K **Privately Held**
Web: www.theflairexchange.com
SIC: 2721 Magazines: publishing only, not printed on site

(G-15774)
FRANCO CORPORATION
600 Industrial Dr (46072-8429)
PHONE..................................765 675-6691
Thomas H Hammonds, *Pr*
EMP: 3 **EST:** 1980
SQ FT: 10,000
SALES (est): 409.71K **Privately Held**
Web: www.francosteel.com
SIC: 2891 Sealing compounds, synthetic rubber or plastic

(G-15775)
INTEGRITY EDM LLC
641 Cleveland St (46072-1132)
PHONE..................................317 333-7630
Kevin Davis, *Managing Member*
Dave Langenkamp, *Genl Mgr*
EMP: 1 **EST:** 2002
SQ FT: 2,500
SALES (est): 4.14MM **Privately Held**
Web: www.integrityedm.com
SIC: 3599 Machine shop, jobbing and repair

(G-15776)
INTERNATIONAL PAPER COMPANY
Also Called: International Paper
815 Industrial Dr (46072-1067)
PHONE..................................765 675-6732
Gary Schmidt, *Genl Mgr*
EMP: 8
SALES (corp-wide): 18.92B **Publicly Held**
Web: www.internationalpaper.com
SIC: 2621 Paper mills
PA: International Paper Company
    6400 Poplar Ave
    Memphis TN 38197
    901 419-7000

(G-15777)
IRVING MATERIALS INC
Also Called: I M I
929 E Jefferson St (46072-9497)
PHONE..................................765 675-6327
EMP: 4
SALES (corp-wide): 814.09MM **Privately Held**
Web: www.irvmat.com
SIC: 3273 Ready-mixed concrete
PA: Irving Materials, Inc.
    8032 N State Road 9
    Greenfield IN 46140
    317 326-3101

(G-15778)
KENNETH E ZIEGLER
2899 E 150 S (46072-8721)
PHONE..................................765 675-2222
Kenneth E Ziegler, *Owner*
EMP: 1 **EST:** 2011
SALES (est): 93.96K **Privately Held**
SIC: 3537 Industrial trucks and tractors

(G-15779)
LEX TOOLING LLC
604 Berryman Pike (46072-8596)
PHONE..................................765 675-6301
James Tucker, *Managing Member*
EMP: 3 **EST:** 1998
SQ FT: 2,400
SALES (est): 240.23K **Privately Held**
Web: www.lextooling.com
SIC: 3544 Special dies and tools

(G-15780)
LIFE SENTENCES PUBLISHING LLC
434 Kentucky Ave (46072-1237)
PHONE..................................765 437-0149
EMP: 3 **EST:** 2018
SALES (est): 71.85K **Privately Held**
Web: www.lifesentencespublishing.com
SIC: 2741 Miscellaneous publishing

(G-15781)
M U HOLDINGS INC
Also Called: Marble Uniques
815 W Jefferson St Bldg 4 (46072-1860)
PHONE..................................317 596-9786
Janusz J Jaworski, *Pr*
▲ **EMP:** 23 **EST:** 2005
SALES (est): 1.09MM **Privately Held**
SIC: 1411 Granite dimension stone

(G-15782)
MANIER WLDG & FABRICATION LLC
859 Market Rd (46072-8413)
PHONE..................................765 675-6078
Mark Manier, *Owner*
EMP: 3 **EST:** 1997
SQ FT: 8,400
SALES (est): 248.16K **Privately Held**
SIC: 7692 Welding repair

(G-15783)
MCCORMACK PRTG IMPRESSIONS INC
618 Oak St (46072-1142)
PHONE..................................765 675-9556
EMP: 7 **EST:** 1975
SQ FT: 6,500
SALES (est): 513.23K **Privately Held**
Web: www.mccormackprinting.com
SIC: 2752 Offset printing

(G-15784)
MCCREARY CONCRETE PRODUCTS INC
875 Industrial Dr (46072)
P.O. Box A (46072)
PHONE..................................765 932-3058
Chris Elbrecht, *Pr*
Mike Shumaker, *
EMP: 25 **EST:** 1945
SQ FT: 5,000
SALES (est): 2.35MM **Privately Held**
Web: www.mccrearyconcrete.com
SIC: 3272 Concrete products, precast, nec

(G-15785)
OGRE HOLDINGS INC
641 Cleveland St (46072)
PHONE..................................765 675-8841
Harry Moyer Stackhouse, *CFO*
EMP: 11 **EST:** 1979
SALES (est): 243.89K **Privately Held**
SIC: 3599 Industrial machinery, nec

(G-15786)
PARK 100 FOODS INC (PA)
326 E Adams St (46072-2001)
PHONE..................................765 675-3480
Jim Washburn, *Ch*
Gary Meade, *
David Alves, *
Thom Bondus, *
▲ **EMP:** 80 **EST:** 1975
SQ FT: 45,000
SALES (est): 105.14MM
SALES (corp-wide): 105.14MM **Privately Held**
Web: www.park100foods.com
SIC: 2013 2032 2035 Frozen meats, from purchased meat; Soups, except seafood: packaged in cans, jars, etc.; Pickles, sauces, and salad dressings

(G-15787)
PRO SIGNS & GRAPHICS
704 W Jefferson St (46072-1822)
PHONE..................................765 675-7446
Ginny Billings, *Mgr*
EMP: 1 **EST:** 2006
SALES (est): 76.97K **Privately Held**
SIC: 3993 Signs and advertising specialties

(G-15788)
QUALITY STEEL TREATING CO INC
641 Cleveland St (46072-1132)
PHONE..................................317 357-8691
Lloyd R Mattson Junior, *Pr*
Kevin Mattson, *

Tipton - Tipton County (G-15789) GEOGRAPHIC SECTION

Sonja Mattson, *
EMP: 32 **EST:** 1949
SALES (est): 993.68K **Privately Held**
Web: www.qualitysteeltreating.com
SIC: 3398 Brazing (hardening) of metal

(G-15789)
RENEWED PERFORMANCE COMPANY
1095 Development Dr (46072-1070)
P.O. Box 196 (46072-0196)
PHONE................................765 675-7586
Christopher A Palabrica, *Pr*
Elfie R Palabrica, *Stockholder*
EMP: 10 **EST:** 2013
SQ FT: 24,000
SALES (est): 952.96K **Privately Held**
Web: www.rpiusa.net
SIC: 3711 Fire department vehicles (motor vehicles), assembly of

(G-15790)
SMITH WELDING
3170 S 110 W (46072-8911)
PHONE................................765 438-4173
Debbie Smith, *Prin*
EMP: 5 **EST:** 2017
SALES (est): 62.87K **Privately Held**
SIC: 7692 Welding repair

(G-15791)
STEEL PARTS CORPORATION
801 Berryman Pike (46072-8492)
P.O. Box 700 (46072-0700)
PHONE................................765 675-2191
Doctor James E Ashton, *Ch Bd*
Doctor James E Ashton, *Ch*
John Riggle, *VP*
Howard Sinclair, *
Mike Smith, *
EMP: 713 **EST:** 2000
SQ FT: 235,000
SALES (est): 5.58MM
SALES (corp-wide): 315.22MM **Privately Held**
SIC: 3465 3594 3568 3469 Automotive stampings; Fluid power pumps and motors; Power transmission equipment, nec; Metal stampings, nec
PA: Resilience Capital Partners Llc
25101 Chgrin Blvd Ste 350
Cleveland OH 44122
216 292-0200

(G-15792)
STEEL PARTS MANUFACTURING INC (HQ)
801 Berryman Pike (46072-8492)
P.O. Box 700 (46072-0700)
PHONE................................765 675-2191
Robert W Potokar, *Pr*
Kevin W Bliss, *CFO*
John F Riggle, *VP Engg*
David A Systermann, *Dir Opers*
Todd W Norwood, *S&M/Dir*
EMP: 140 **EST:** 2006
SALES (est): 25.38MM **Privately Held**
Web: www.steelparts.com
SIC: 3714 Transmissions, motor vehicle
PA: Monomoy Capital Partners, L.P.
600 3rd Ave Fl 27
New York NY 10016

(G-15793)
TEMPLE-INLAND INC
815 Industrial Dr (46072-1067)
PHONE................................765 675-6732
EMP: 7 **EST:** 2014
SALES (est): 65.95K **Privately Held**
SIC: 8661 2653 Temples; Corrugated and solid fiber boxes

(G-15794)
TIPTON TRIBUNE
116 S Main St Ste A (46072-1864)
P.O. Box 85 (46036-0085)
PHONE................................765 675-2115
Jenny Lamoreaux, *Prin*
EMP: 1 **EST:** 2010
SALES (est): 73.27K **Privately Held**
Web: www.elwoodpublishing.com
SIC: 2711 Commercial printing and newspaper publishing combined

---

Topeka
Lagrange County

(G-15795)
ASCOT ENTERPRISES INC
129 Roy St (46571)
PHONE................................260 593-3733
Cory Manning, *Mgr*
EMP: 73
SALES (corp-wide): 41.85MM **Privately Held**
Web: www.ascotent.com
SIC: 2391 Curtains and draperies
PA: Ascot Enterprises Inc
503 S Main St
Nappanee IN 46550
877 773-7751

(G-15796)
CLEARSPRING MANUFACTURING LLC
4225 W 350 S (46571-9527)
PHONE................................260 593-2086
Daniel Beechy Junior, *Managing Member*
EMP: 13 **EST:** 2003
SALES (est): 848.73K **Privately Held**
SIC: 2431 7389 Door sashes, wood; Business Activities at Non-Commercial Site

(G-15797)
CONNECTION LLC
128 S Main St (46571-9305)
P.O. Box 603 (46571-0603)
PHONE................................260 593-3999
Doretta Yoter, *Managing Member*
EMP: 3 **EST:** 2003
SALES (est): 184.8K **Privately Held**
SIC: 2721 Magazines: publishing only, not printed on site

(G-15798)
COOPER-STANDARD AUTOMOTIVE INC
Also Called: Cooper
324 Morrow St (46571-9076)
PHONE................................260 593-2156
Ruby Crider, *Brnch Mgr*
EMP: 22
SALES (corp-wide): 2.82B **Publicly Held**
Web: www.cooperstandard.com
SIC: 3443 Heat exchangers, condensers, and components
HQ: Cooper-Standard Automotive Inc.
40300 Traditions Dr
Northville MI 48168
248 596-5900

(G-15799)
D & E WORKSHOP
9680 W 700 S (46571-9134)
PHONE................................260 593-0195
EMP: 7 **EST:** 1994
SALES (est): 402.63K **Privately Held**
SIC: 2511 Rockers, except upholstered: wood

(G-15800)
D A HOCHSTETLER & SONS LLP
4165 S 500 W (46571-9546)
PHONE................................574 642-1144
Albert L Hochstetler, *Prin*
Daniel A Hochstetler, *Prin*
Ivan J Hochstetler, *Prin*
EMP: 18 **EST:** 1950
SQ FT: 10,000
SALES (est): 1.16MM **Privately Held**
SIC: 3544 3523 3441 3594 Special dies and tools; Farm machinery and equipment; Fabricated structural metal; Fluid power pumps and motors

(G-15801)
DALAM WELDING LLC
7665 S 200 W (46571-9622)
PHONE................................260 593-0167
EMP: 1 **EST:** 2008
SALES (est): 82.58K **Privately Held**
SIC: 7692 Welding repair

(G-15802)
DNH WOODWORKING
4885 S 900 W (46571-9140)
PHONE................................260 593-0439
EMP: 3 **EST:** 2018
SALES (est): 54.13K **Privately Held**
SIC: 2431 Millwork

(G-15803)
DOUBLE E WOODWORKING LLC
9880 W 700 S (46571-9132)
PHONE................................260 593-0522
Ernie Bontrager, *Prin*
EMP: 1 **EST:** 2005
SALES (est): 99.79K **Privately Held**
SIC: 2431 Millwork

(G-15804)
DS CORP
Also Called: Rossroads Rv
1115 W Lake St (46571-9787)
P.O. Box 2000 (46527-2000)
PHONE................................260 593-3850
▲ **EMP:** 87 **EST:** 1997
SQ FT: 33,000
SALES (est): 3.57MM
SALES (corp-wide): 11.12B **Publicly Held**
Web: www.crossroadsrv.com
SIC: 3716 3792 Motor homes; Travel trailers and campers
PA: Thor Industries, Inc.
601 E Beardsley Ave
Elkhart IN 46514
574 970-7460

(G-15805)
FOREST RIVER CHEROKEE INC
402 Lehman Ave (46571-9456)
PHONE................................260 593-2566
John Quake, *Mgr*
EMP: 2 **EST:** 2005
SALES (est): 188.95K **Privately Held**
Web: www.forestriverinc.com
SIC: 3792 Travel trailers and campers

(G-15806)
FOUR WOODS LAMINATING INC (PA)
7550 W 500 S (46571-9444)
PHONE................................260 593-2246
Glen Yoder, *Pr*
Wayne Miller, *
Glen Riegsecker, *
EMP: 33 **EST:** 1985
SALES (est): 2.53MM **Privately Held**
Web: www.kabriproducts.com

SIC: 1751 3714 2431 Cabinet building and installation; Motor vehicle parts and accessories; Millwork

(G-15807)
GL CUSTOM WELDING LLC
5760 S State Road 5 (46571-9724)
PHONE................................260 593-0253
Eugene Yoder, *Owner*
EMP: 5 **EST:** 2014
SALES (est): 84.06K **Privately Held**
Web: www.weldingtopeka.com
SIC: 7692 Welding repair

(G-15808)
HOCHSTETLER WOODWORKING LLC
3085 S 600 W (46571-9542)
PHONE................................260 593-3255
Alvin W Hochstetler, *Admn*
EMP: 1 **EST:** 2013
SALES (est): 142.96K **Privately Held**
Web: www.hochstetlerwoodworkingtopeka.com
SIC: 2431 Millwork

(G-15809)
HONEYVILLE METAL INC
Also Called: Hmi Machinery
4200 S 900 W (46571-9142)
PHONE................................800 593-8377
TOLL FREE: 800
Ora Hochstetler, *Ch*
Mark Hochstetler, *
Ivan Birky, *
Melvin Gingerich, *
Matthew Beachy, *
EMP: 67 **EST:** 1951
SQ FT: 137,000
SALES (est): 9.06MM **Privately Held**
Web: www.honeyvillemetal.com
SIC: 3523 3564 Farm machinery and equipment; Dust or fume collecting equipment, industrial

(G-15810)
HOOSIER BUGGY SHOP
5345 W 600 S (46571-9551)
PHONE................................260 593-2192
Maynard Hochstetler, *Owner*
EMP: 4 **EST:** 1960
SALES (est): 196.13K **Privately Held**
SIC: 3799 7699 Carriages, horse drawn; Horse drawn vehicle repair

(G-15811)
LAMBRIGHT WOODWORKING LLC
7785 W 300 S (46571-9752)
PHONE................................260 593-2721
Cletus Lambright, *Genl Mgr*
EMP: 15 **EST:** 1978
SQ FT: 12,900
SALES (est): 472.95K **Privately Held**
SIC: 2434 2511 5712 2431 Wood kitchen cabinets; Wood household furniture; Furniture stores; Doors and door parts and trim, wood

(G-15812)
NEW STYLE OF CROSSROADS LLC
9585 W 700 S (46571-9130)
PHONE................................260 593-3800
Leroy Yoeler, *Owner*
EMP: 11 **EST:** 2005
SQ FT: 8,600
SALES (est): 475.15K **Privately Held**
SIC: 2431 Moldings, wood: unfinished and prefinished

(G-15813)
NISHIKAWA COOPER LLC (DH)
Also Called: Nisco
324 Morrow St (46571-9076)
PHONE................................260 593-2156
Futoshi Higashida, *Pr*
Michael Talaga, *
▲ **EMP:** 452 **EST:** 1987
SQ FT: 250,000
SALES (est): 205.86MM **Privately Held**
Web: www.niscoseals.com
SIC: 3069   Weather strip, sponge rubber
HQ: Nishikawa Of America Inc
 324 Morrow St
 Topeka IN 46571

(G-15814)
NISHIKAWA OF AMERICA INC (HQ)
324 Morrow St (46571-9076)
PHONE................................260 593-2156
Bunji Yamamoti, *Pr*
Bill Burga, *VP*
▲ **EMP:** 6 **EST:** 1989
SALES (est): 205.86MM **Privately Held**
Web: www.niscoseals.com
SIC: 3069   Weather strip, sponge rubber
PA: Nishikawa Rubber Co.,Ltd.
 2-2-8, Misasamachi, Nishi-Ku
 Hiroshima HIR 733-0

(G-15815)
PERFORMANCE COATINGS SPC LLC
7030 W 665 S (46571-9745)
PHONE................................574 606-8153
Amie Ernsberger, *Admn*
EMP: 7 **EST:** 2012
SALES (est): 105.14K **Privately Held**
Web: www.hmcperformancecoatings.com
SIC: 3479   Coating of metals and formed products

(G-15816)
ROYAL DESIGN CUSTOM KITCHENS &
9685 W 300 S (46571-9794)
PHONE................................260 593-0508
EMP: 5 **EST:** 2016
SALES (est): 140.76K **Privately Held**
Web: www.importantlocalbusinesses.com
SIC: 2434   Wood kitchen cabinets

(G-15817)
S & H METAL PRODUCTS INC
122 Redman Dr (46571-9786)
P.O. Box 35 (46571-0035)
PHONE................................260 593-2565
Freeman J Helmuth, *Pr*
Tina M Helmuth, *Sec*
EMP: 26 **EST:** 1972
SQ FT: 31,000
SALES (est): 4.66MM **Privately Held**
Web: www.shmetalproducts.com
SIC: 3714 3444   Motor vehicle body components and frame; Ducts, sheet metal

(G-15818)
SCHWAN PRODUCTS LLC
9560 W 700 S (46571-9467)
PHONE................................260 350-4764
EMP: 8 **EST:** 2021
SALES (est): 452.45K **Privately Held**
SIC: 2431   Millwork

(G-15819)
SNAX IN PAX INC
204 Hawpatch Dr (46571-9472)
PHONE................................260 593-3066
Bill Huggins, *Pr*
Ruby Huggins, *Sec*
EMP: 23 **EST:** 1993
SQ FT: 30,000
SALES (est): 5.49MM **Privately Held**
Web: www.snaxinpax.com
SIC: 5145 2038   Snack foods; Snacks, incl. onion rings, cheese sticks, etc.

(G-15820)
SUN RISE METAL SHOP
3070 W 350 S (46571-8946)
PHONE................................260 463-4026
Enos A Kuhns, *Owner*
EMP: 3 **EST:** 1958
SQ FT: 3,120
SALES (est): 244.82K **Privately Held**
SIC: 3523 5231 5074 5191   Cattle feeding, handling, and watering equipment; Paint; Plumbing and hydronic heating supplies; Farm supplies

(G-15821)
TOWER ADVERTISING PRODUCTS INC (PA)
Also Called: Tower Ribbons
1015 W Lake St (46571-9611)
P.O. Box 540 (46571-0540)
PHONE................................260 593-2103
C Craig Miller, *Pr*
Mary Sue Miller, *
▲ **EMP:** 80 **EST:** 1955
SQ FT: 40,000
SALES (est): 9.81MM
SALES (corp-wide): 9.81MM **Privately Held**
Web: www.toweradv.com
SIC: 2241 5094 3993   Ribbons, nec; Trophies ; Signs and advertising specialties

(G-15822)
VERNE LAMBRIGHT
Also Called: Lambright Aluminum
1390 S 700 W (46571-9744)
PHONE................................260 593-0250
Verne Lambright, *Owner*
EMP: 1 **EST:** 1998
SALES (est): 90.9K **Privately Held**
SIC: 3999   Wind chimes

(G-15823)
YODER FIBERGLASS LLC
9755 W 600 S (46571-9185)
PHONE................................260 593-0234
Lester Yoder, *Prin*
EMP: 1 **EST:** 2013
SALES (est): 127.23K **Privately Held**
Web: www.goodmenproject.com
SIC: 3732   Boats, fiberglass: building and repairing

(G-15824)
YODERS & SONS REPAIR SHOP
6035 W 800 S (46571-9563)
PHONE................................260 593-2727
Perry Yoder, *Owner*
EMP: 2 **EST:** 1975
SALES (est): 152.44K **Privately Held**
SIC: 7692   Welding repair

Trafalgar
Johnson County

(G-15825)
ANTHONY WISE
5655 S 50 W (46181-9797)
PHONE................................317 933-2458
Anthony Wise, *Owner*
EMP: 1 **EST:** 1998
SALES (est): 63.12K **Privately Held**
SIC: 3531   Automobile wrecker hoists

(G-15826)
BESSE VENEERS INC
718 E Park St (46181-8745)
PHONE................................906 428-3113
John Besse, *Pr*
EMP: 24 **EST:** 1994
SALES (est): 1.38MM **Privately Held**
SIC: 2435   Hardwood veneer and plywood

(G-15827)
GLUE-LAM ERECTORS INC
723 E Park St (46181-8745)
P.O. Box 10 (46181-0010)
PHONE................................317 878-9717
Rory Wray, *CEO*
Rory Wray, *Pr*
Kyle Heminger, *Sec*
Val Heminger, *VP*
EMP: 10 **EST:** 2005
SALES (est): 2.07MM **Privately Held**
Web: www.glue-lamerectorsinc.com
SIC: 2439   Structural wood members, nec

(G-15828)
HOOSIER BULLETS LLC
Also Called: Hoosier Bullets & Training
6620 S 200 W (46181-9095)
PHONE................................317 694-1257
Allen J Hopson Iv, *Managing Member*
EMP: 5 **EST:** 2021
SALES (est): 64.33K **Privately Held**
SIC: 3482   Small arms ammunition

(G-15829)
INDIANA ARCHITECTURAL PLYWOOD (PA)
750 E Park St (46181-8745)
P.O. Box 39 (46181-0039)
PHONE................................317 878-4822
Horst Michaelis, *CEO*
James A Moreland, *
Frank Michaelis, *
Helga Michaelis, *
▲ **EMP:** 39 **EST:** 1983
SQ FT: 55,000
SALES (est): 7.05MM
SALES (corp-wide): 7.05MM **Privately Held**
Web: www.iaplywood.com
SIC: 2435 2431 3429 2511   Plywood, hardwood or hardwood faced; Doors and door parts and trim, wood; Hardware, nec; Wood household furniture

(G-15830)
JDS PUGHS CABINETS INC
Also Called: Pugh's Cabinets
4195 W Pitcher Dr (46181-8897)
PHONE................................317 835-2910
Joseph Pugh, *Pr*
Dan Pugh, *VP*
Ron Pugh, *CFO*
EMP: 8 **EST:** 1970
SALES (est): 249.49K **Privately Held**
SIC: 2511 2434   Bookcases, household: wood ; Vanities, bathroom: wood

(G-15831)
RING-CO LLC
8402 S 250 W (46181-9260)
PHONE................................317 641-7050
Patricia Ringer, *Mgr*
EMP: 4 **EST:** 2014
SALES (est): 302.84K **Privately Held**
Web: www.ring-co.com
SIC: 3711   Truck and tractor truck assembly

(G-15832)
RING-CO MOBILE LLC
8402 S 250 W (46181-9260)
PHONE................................317 641-7050
EMP: 6 **EST:** 2016
SALES (est): 358.58K **Privately Held**
Web: www.ring-co.com
SIC: 3799 3842   All terrain vehicles (ATV); Wheelchairs

(G-15833)
SIGNATURE FORMULATIONS LLC
3 Trafalgar Sq (46181-9515)
PHONE................................317 878-4086
EMP: 8 **EST:** 2007
SALES (est): 607.16K **Privately Held**
Web: shop.signatureformulations.com
SIC: 2844   Hair preparations, including shampoos

(G-15834)
YARD SIGNS
6840 S 300 W (46181-8986)
PHONE................................317 736-7446
EMP: 4 **EST:** 2018
SALES (est): 245.91K **Privately Held**
Web: www.736sign.com
SIC: 3993   Signs and advertising specialties

Trail Creek
Laporte County

(G-15835)
BLOCKSOM & CO
Also Called: Paratex Products
110 Menke Rd (46360-6530)
PHONE................................219 878-4458
Andrew Swan, *Pr*
EMP: 9
SALES (corp-wide): 56.59MM **Privately Held**
Web: www.blocksom.com
SIC: 2299 3564   Batting, wadding, padding and fillings; Blowers and fans
PA: Blocksom & Co.
 110 Menke Rd
 Trail Creek IN 46360
 219 878-4455

(G-15836)
BLOCKSOM & CO (PA)
110 Menke Rd (46360-6530)
PHONE................................219 878-4455
Greg Wilkerson, *Pr*
Douglas Smith, *Ch*
Dean Sassman, *Vice Chairman*
▲ **EMP:** 15 **EST:** 1919
SALES (est): 56.59MM
SALES (corp-wide): 56.59MM **Privately Held**
Web: www.blocksom.com
SIC: 3564   Filters, air: furnaces, air conditioning equipment, etc.

(G-15837)
FIBER BOND OPERATING LLC
110 Menke Rd (46360-6596)
PHONE................................219 879-4541
Greg Wilkerson, *Pr*
Douglas Smith, *Ch*
Matt Demke, *CFO*
EMP: 140 **EST:** 2019
SQ FT: 200,000
SALES (est): 49.29MM
SALES (corp-wide): 56.59MM **Privately Held**
Web: www.fiberbond.net
SIC: 2297   Bonded-fiber fabrics, except felt
HQ: Lofted Products Llc

Trail Creek - Laporte County (G-15838)

GEOGRAPHIC SECTION

12770 Merit Dr Ste 800
Dallas TX

(G-15838)
GAIUS JULIUS CRASSUS INC
Also Called: Fiber Bond
110 Menke Rd (46360-6530)
PHONE.....................219 879-4541
Barre Seid, *Ch Bd*
Daniel Dobbins, *Pr*
John Marienau, *Pr*
◆ **EMP:** 8 **EST:** 1952
SQ FT: 200,000
SALES (est): 2.2MM **Privately Held**
Web: www.fiberbond.net
SIC: 2297 Nonwoven fabrics

(G-15839)
SENTINEL ALARM INC
2815 E Michigan Blvd (46360-5398)
PHONE.....................219 874-6051
Ken Stokes, *Pr*
EMP: 6 **EST:** 1977
SQ FT: 10,000
SALES (est): 499.43K **Privately Held**
Web: www.sentinelalarmcompany.net
SIC: 1731 3669 Fire detection and burglar alarm systems specialization; Burglar alarm apparatus, electric

(G-15840)
SWEET KEEPSAKES
319 Black Oak Dr (46360-6458)
PHONE.....................219 872-8467
EMP: 1 **EST:** 1999
SALES (est): 57.78K **Privately Held**
SIC: 3993 5947 Advertising artwork; Gift, novelty, and souvenir shop

(G-15841)
T R BULGER INC
3123 E Michigan Blvd (46360-6523)
PHONE.....................219 879-8525
Thomas R Bulger, *Pr*
EMP: 9 **EST:** 1987
SQ FT: 5,600
SALES (est): 993.53K **Privately Held**
Web: www.trbulger.com
SIC: 1711 8711 3444 Heating and air conditioning contractors; Heating and ventilation engineering; Furnace casings, sheet metal

(G-15842)
TRAIL CREEK LEATHER
315 Johnson Rd (46360-6429)
PHONE.....................219 874-6702
Raymond M Chapala, *Owner*
EMP: 2 **EST:** 2018
SALES (est): 48.29K **Privately Held**
Web: www.trailcreekleather.com
SIC: 3111 Leather tanning and finishing

Troy
Spencer County

(G-15843)
TROY MEGGITT INC (HQ)
Also Called: Meggitt Control Systems
3 Industrial Dr (47588)
P.O. Box 40 (47588)
PHONE.....................812 547-7071
Stephen Young, *CEO*
EMP: 95 **EST:** 1987
SQ FT: 125,000
SALES (est): 140.22MM
SALES (corp-wide): 19.93B **Publicly Held**

SIC: 3443 3433 7699 5088 Heat exchangers, condensers, and components; Heating equipment, except electric; Aircraft flight instrument repair; Aircraft engines and engine parts
PA: Parker-Hannifin Corporation
6035 Parkland Blvd
Cleveland OH 44124
216 896-3000

Twelve Mile
Cass County

(G-15844)
FIELD CONSTRUCTION
5222 E County Road 650 N (46988-9530)
PHONE.....................574 664-2010
John Field, *Owner*
EMP: 8 **EST:** 1990
SALES (est): 453.03K **Privately Held**
SIC: 1389 Construction, repair, and dismantling services

Underwood
Scott County

(G-15845)
MC CUSTOM CABINETS INC
2157 W Salem Rd (47177-6713)
PHONE.....................502 641-1528
Michael B Allgood, *Pr*
Clara Allgood, *Sec*
EMP: 2 **EST:** 2010
SALES (est): 157.41K **Privately Held**
SIC: 2434 Wood kitchen cabinets

Union City
Randolph County

(G-15846)
A 2 Z UNIVERSAL SOLUTIONS
1350 W State Road 28 (47390-9490)
PHONE.....................317 496-7435
Will Dunlap Iv, *Owner*
EMP: 1 **EST:** 2017
SALES (est): 76.51K **Privately Held**
Web: www.a2zuniversalsolutions.com
SIC: 7349 2842 7549 Janitorial service, contract basis; Automobile polish; Automotive maintenance services

(G-15847)
AMERICAN PRESS SERVICES ✪
935 W Pearl St (47390-1200)
PHONE.....................937 338-3000
EMP: 1 **EST:** 2023
SALES (est): 99.5K **Privately Held**
SIC: 3542 Presses: forming, stamping, punching, sizing (machine tools)

(G-15848)
APPLEGATE LIVESTOCK EQP INC (DH)
Also Called: Applegate
902 S State Road 32 (47390-9153)
P.O. Box 10 (42528-0010)
PHONE.....................765 964-3715
Gary Anderson, *Pr*
Paul Franzmann, *
Duane Brim, *
Steve Sommerfeld, *
▲ **EMP:** 65 **EST:** 2008
SQ FT: 131,500
SALES (est): 27.05MM **Privately Held**

SIC: 3523 3317 Barn, silo, poultry, dairy, and livestock machinery; Welded pipe and tubes
HQ: Tarter Gate Company, Llc
10739 S Us 127
Dunnville KY 42528
800 733-4283

(G-15849)
B & M STEEL & WELDING INC
Also Called: B&M Steel Fabrication
1251 S Jackson Pike (47390-8316)
P.O. Box 405 (47390-0405)
PHONE.....................765 964-5868
Richard Rader, *Pr*
EMP: 8 **EST:** 1974
SQ FT: 6,000
SALES (est): 959.28K **Privately Held**
Web: www.bandmsteel.com
SIC: 3441 Fabricated structural metal

(G-15850)
CARDINAL ETHANOL LLC (PA)
1554 N 600 E (47390)
PHONE.....................765 964-3137
Jeffrey L Painter, *Pr*
Robert J Davis, *Ch Bd*
Thomas E Chalfant, *V Ch Bd*
William Dartt, *CFO*
Thomas C Chronister, *Sec*
EMP: 63 **EST:** 2005
SALES (est): 502.73MM **Publicly Held**
Web: www.cardinalethanol.com
SIC: 2869 2085 Ethyl alcohol, ethanol; Distiller's dried grains and solubles, and alcohol

(G-15851)
CROSS ROAD PRECISION TOOL INC
7747 E 800 S (47390-9349)
PHONE.....................260 335-2772
John H Fennig, *Pr*
EMP: 1 **EST:** 2001
SALES (est): 229.25K **Privately Held**
Web: www.crossroadpt.com
SIC: 3599 Machine shop, jobbing and repair

(G-15852)
ECO VEHICLE SYSTEMS LLC
1274 S State Road 32 (47390-9130)
PHONE.....................765 964-6009
EMP: 20 **EST:** 2012
SALES (est): 2.42MM **Privately Held**
Web: www.ecovehiclesystems.com
SIC: 3714 Motor vehicle parts and accessories

(G-15853)
FRANK MILLER LUMBER CO INC (PA)
Also Called: Frank Miller
1690 Frank Miller Rd (47390-8446)
PHONE.....................800 345-2643
Steven P James, *Pr*
Joann Johnson, *
Martha M Mathias, *
Tina M Root, *
Robert A Miller, *
▼ **EMP:** 150 **EST:** 1903
SQ FT: 2,000
SALES (est): 24.73MM
SALES (corp-wide): 24.73MM **Privately Held**
Web: www.frankmiller.com
SIC: 2426 2421 Hardwood dimension and flooring mills; Custom sawmill

(G-15854)
GARVER MANUFACTURING INC
224 N Columbia St Rear (47390-1432)
P.O. Box 306 (47390-0306)
PHONE.....................765 964-5828

Michael Read, *Pr*
Fredrick Read, *VP*
Alberta Read, *Sec*
EMP: 3 **EST:** 1915
SQ FT: 10,000
SALES (est): 343.46K **Privately Held**
Web: www.garvermfg.com
SIC: 3523 Farm machinery and equipment

(G-15855)
HUB CITY STL & FABRICATION LLC
4487 S Arba Pike (47390-8528)
PHONE.....................260 760-0370
EMP: 3 **EST:** 2008
SALES (est): 241.44K **Privately Held**
SIC: 3444 Sheet metalwork

(G-15856)
NICKS AUTOMOTIVE INC
2741 N 700 E (47390-9131)
P.O. Box 403 (47390-0403)
PHONE.....................765 964-6843
Nick Mcowen, *Pr*
Nick Mc Eowen, *Pr*
EMP: 10 **EST:** 1979
SQ FT: 5,000
SALES (est): 824.75K **Privately Held**
Web: www.nicksautoinc.com
SIC: 7532 5531 3312 Body shop, automotive ; Truck equipment and parts; Blast furnaces and steel mills

(G-15857)
ONCITE LLC
6741 E 500 S (47390-8532)
PHONE.....................765 874-1500
Mark Kniesly, *Brnch Mgr*
EMP: 41
SALES (corp-wide): 469.94K **Privately Held**
SIC: 3312 Blast furnaces and steel mills
PA: Oncite Llc
7073 E 700 S
Lynn IN

(G-15858)
PEPCON CONCRETE INC
1567 Frank Miller Rd (47390-8999)
PHONE.....................765 964-6572
Larry Grimes, *Manager*
EMP: 9 **EST:** 2008
SALES (est): 200.99K **Privately Held**
Web: www.poeppelmanmaterials.com
SIC: 3273 Ready-mixed concrete

(G-15859)
REIT PRICE CO
532 W Chestnut St (47390-1308)
PHONE.....................765 964-3252
Thomas W Kerns, *Prin*
EMP: 6 **EST:** 2012
SALES (est): 56.02K **Privately Held**
Web: www.reitprice.com
SIC: 2392 Household furnishings, nec

(G-15860)
REIT-PRICE MFG CO INCORPORATED
522 W Chestnut St (47390-1308)
PHONE.....................765 964-3252
Roger L Stewart, *Pr*
EMP: 5 **EST:** 1900
SQ FT: 10,000
SALES (est): 333.1K **Privately Held**
Web: www.reitprice.com
SIC: 2392 3991 Mops, floor and dust; Brooms and brushes

GEOGRAPHIC SECTION

(G-15861)
UNIFLEX RELAY SYSTEMS LLC
526 W Division St (47390-1007)
PHONE..................................765 232-4675
Linda D Wilcox, *Ex Dir*
EMP: 5 **EST:** 2011
SALES (est): 246.82K **Privately Held**
SIC: 3931 Musical instruments

(G-15862)
UNION CITY COATINGS LLC
301 S Jackson Pike Ste C (47390-8903)
PHONE..................................765 717-3919
EMP: 3
SALES (est): 136.08K **Privately Held**
SIC: 3999 Manufacturing industries, nec

Union Mills
Laporte County

(G-15863)
AUTOMATED PROC EQP SVCS LLC
952 W 1150 S (46382-9742)
PHONE..................................219 206-2517
Shawn Pepple, *Managing Member*
EMP: 6 **EST:** 2019
SALES (est): 499.01K **Privately Held**
Web: www.apesfillingsystems.com
SIC: 3569 Liquid automation machinery and equipment

(G-15864)
FLYING PIG WOODWORKS LLC
5076 W Madura Rd (46382-9774)
PHONE..................................219 242-5557
EMP: 5 **EST:** 2013
SALES (est): 59.54K **Privately Held**
Web: www.flyingpigwoodworks.com
SIC: 2431 Millwork

(G-15865)
HOT STAMPING & PRINTING
Also Called: D&D Manufacturing
6601 W 900 S (46382-9623)
PHONE..................................219 767-2429
John Doll Junior, *Owner*
EMP: 3 **EST:** 1992
SQ FT: 3,000
SALES (est): 246.89K **Privately Held**
Web: www.ddguitarpicks.com
SIC: 3089 Novelties, plastics

(G-15866)
MONSANTO COMPANY
Also Called: Monsanto
10201 S 700 W (46382-9523)
PHONE..................................219 733-2938
EMP: 6
SALES (corp-wide): 51.78B **Privately Held**
Web: www.monsanto.com
SIC: 2879 Agricultural chemicals, nec
HQ: Monsanto Technology Llc.
    800 N Lindbergh Blvd
    Saint Louis MO 63167
    314 694-1000

(G-15867)
ROESLER FINE ART SERVICES
11888 S Hunsley Rd (46382-9509)
PHONE..................................219 797-4955
EMP: 1 **EST:** 1986
SALES (est): 51.9K **Privately Held**
SIC: 3993 Signs and advertising specialties

(G-15868)
THERMO-CYCLER INDUSTRIES INC (PA)
111 E Hamilton St (46382-9702)
P.O. Box 22 (46382-0022)
PHONE..................................219 767-2990
Gregory Kelver, *Pr*
EMP: 8 **EST:** 1984
SALES (est): 2.18M
SALES (corp-wide): 2.18MM **Privately Held**
Web: www.thermocycler.com
SIC: 5075 3564 Warm air heating equipment and supplies; Ventilating fans: industrial or commercial

(G-15869)
WELSHCO LLC
Also Called: Welshco
3637 W 900 S (46382-9601)
PHONE..................................219 767-2786
Matt Welsh, *Pr*
EMP: 3 **EST:** 1980
SALES (est): 454K **Privately Held**
SIC: 7692 Welding repair

Uniondale
Wells County

(G-15870)
PREMIER SIGNS LLC
726 W Us Highway 224 (46791-9709)
PHONE..................................888 518-2498
EMP: 6 **EST:** 2018
SALES (est): 403.82K **Privately Held**
Web: www.premiersigns.com
SIC: 3993 Signs and advertising specialties

(G-15871)
PREMIERE SIGNS LLC
888 W Railroad St (46791-9775)
PHONE..................................260 543-2612
EMP: 4 **EST:** 2018
SALES (est): 161.7K **Privately Held**
Web: www.premieresigns.com
SIC: 3993 Signs and advertising specialties

(G-15872)
R P IMEL
Also Called: Imel Machining Co
1501 W Us Highway 224 (46791-9705)
PHONE..................................260 543-2465
EMP: 1 **EST:** 1965
SALES (est): 59.99K **Privately Held**
SIC: 3541 3469 3463 Machine tools, metal cutting type; Metal stampings, nec; Nonferrous forgings

(G-15873)
TGM MANUFACTURING INC
Also Called: Gilberts Machine
5980 N 400 W (46791-9736)
PHONE..................................260 758-3055
Terry Gilbert, *Pr*
Todd Gehring, *VP*
▲ **EMP:** 10 **EST:** 1975
SQ FT: 4,000
SALES (est): 702.82K **Privately Held**
SIC: 3599 Machine shop, jobbing and repair

Unionville
Monroe County

(G-15874)
EMBROIDERY CONCEPTS
4689 Point Idalawn Dr (47468-9565)
PHONE..................................812 988-6499
William Weber, *Owner*
EMP: 1 **EST:** 2003
SALES (est): 38.49K **Privately Held**
SIC: 2395 Embroidery and art needlework

Universal
Vermillion County

(G-15875)
HOG SLAT INCORPORATED
Also Called: Parking Bumper Company
18506 S Rangeline Rd (47884)
P.O. Box 181 (47884-0181)
PHONE..................................765 828-0828
April Kenkins, *Mgr*
EMP: 52
SALES (corp-wide): 538.94MM **Privately Held**
Web: www.hogslat.com
SIC: 3523 3272 Hog feeding, handling, and watering equipment; Concrete products, nec
PA: Hog Slat, Incorporated
    206 Fayetteville St
    Newton Grove NC 28366
    800 949-4647

Upland
Grant County

(G-15876)
AVIS INDUSTRIAL CORPORATION (PA)
1909 S Main St (46989)
P.O. Box 548 (46989)
PHONE..................................765 998-8100
Greg King, *Pr*
Michelle W Patishall, *
Angela M Darlington, *
▲ **EMP:** 25 **EST:** 1983
SQ FT: 23,000
SALES (est): 474.53MM
SALES (corp-wide): 474.53MM **Privately Held**
Web: www.avisindustrial.com
SIC: 3429 3462 3312 3531 Locks or lock sets ; Iron and steel forgings; Tubes, steel and iron; Construction machinery

(G-15877)
HAPPY BUDDAH
62 E Berry Ave (46989-9144)
PHONE..................................765 998-3008
EMP: 6 **EST:** 2009
SALES (est): 78.25K **Privately Held**
SIC: 3421 Table and food cutlery, including butchers'

(G-15878)
HORSE N AROUND ANIMAL & TACK
7288 S 825 E (46989-9718)
P.O. Box 525 (46989-0525)
PHONE..................................765 618-2032
Tim Rumler, *Owner*
EMP: 2 **EST:** 2001
SALES (est): 50.38K **Privately Held**
SIC: 3111 Bridle leather

(G-15879)
NATES BEEF JERKY
9642 E 811 S (46989-9724)
PHONE..................................765 348-6569
Nate Maurer, *Prin*
EMP: 6 **EST:** 2018
SALES (est): 62.38K **Privately Held**
SIC: 2013 Snack sticks, including jerky: from purchased meat

(G-15880)
PIERCE COMPANY INC (HQ)
35 North 8th St (46989)
P.O. Box 548 (46989-0548)
PHONE..................................765 998-8100
Leland E Boren, *Pr*
Angela M Taylor, *
Tracee L Pennington, *
▲ **EMP:** 61 **EST:** 1985
SQ FT: 185,000
SALES (est): 2.44MM
SALES (corp-wide): 474.53MM **Privately Held**
Web: www.piercechurch.org
SIC: 3714 Fuel pipes, motor vehicle
PA: Avis Industrial Corporation
    1909 S Main St
    Upland IN 46989
    765 998-8100

(G-15881)
ROSS MACHINING
8855 E 500 S (46989-9463)
PHONE..................................765 998-2400
Ross Malonek, *Owner*
EMP: 2 **EST:** 2007
SALES (est): 106.28K **Privately Held**
SIC: 3599 Machine shop, jobbing and repair

(G-15882)
UPLAND PRINT AND STITCH
230 N Main St (46989-9180)
PHONE..................................765 506-7011
Upland Print Stitch, *CEO*
Andrew Preston, *Prin*
EMP: 1 **EST:** 2008
SALES (est): 96.74K **Privately Held**
Web: www.uplandprintandstitch.com
SIC: 2759 Screen printing

(G-15883)
UPLAND PRINT STITCH
40 E Berry Ave (46989-9144)
PHONE..................................765 506-7011
EMP: 3 **EST:** 2020
SALES (est): 59.02K **Privately Held**
Web: www.uplandprintandstitch.com
SIC: 2759 Screen printing

(G-15884)
UPLAND TIRE & SERVICE CTR INC
148 S Main St (46989-9250)
P.O. Box 598 (46989-0598)
PHONE..................................765 998-0871
EMP: 7 **EST:** 1996
SQ FT: 10,000
SALES (est): 973.19K **Privately Held**
Web: www.bestonetire.com
SIC: 5531 7534 7513 7538 Automotive tires; Tire repair shop; Truck rental and leasing, no drivers; General automotive repair shops

Urbana
Wabash County

(G-15885)
CYCLONE MANUFACTURING CO INC
151 N Washington St (46990-9539)
P.O. Box 67 (46990-0067)
PHONE..................................260 774-3311
Daniel E Speicher Iii, *Pr*
EMP: 15 **EST:** 1868
SQ FT: 40,000
SALES (est): 2.44MM **Privately Held**
Web: cyclone.us.com
SIC: 3444 Sheet metal specialties, not stamped

(G-15886)
KALENBORN ABRESIST CORPORATION (HQ)
5541 N State Road 13 (46990-9548)

Urbana - Wabash County (G-15887)

P.O. Box 38 (46990-0038)
PHONE..........................800 348-0717
Craig Frendewey, *Pr*
Troy Ray, *
▲ EMP: 37 EST: 1977
SQ FT: 30,000
SALES (est): 9.46MM
SALES (corp-wide): 55.13MM **Privately Held**
Web: www.kalenborn.us
SIC: 3444 3317 Pipe, sheet metal; Steel pipe and tubes
PA: Kalenborn International Gmbh & Co.Kg
Asbacher Str. 50
VettelschoB RP 53560
2645180

(G-15887)
RACK HUB LLC
3276 N 500 E (46990-9312)
PHONE..........................260 571-7028
EMP: 3 EST: 2018
SALES (est): 46.43K **Privately Held**
Web: www.rack-hub.com
SIC: 2789 Display mounting

Valparaiso
Porter County

(G-15888)
A & JS BELTS INC
215 Sauk Trl (46385-7931)
PHONE..........................219 628-0074
John Barbossa, *Prin*
▲ EMP: 5 EST: 2013
SALES (est): 245.99K **Privately Held**
Web: www.ajsbelts.com
SIC: 3949 Sporting and athletic goods, nec

(G-15889)
A TO Z SIGN SHOP
55 Us Highway 30 Bldg B (46383)
PHONE..........................219 462-7489
Jack Adams, *Pt*
Ted Zoumis, *Pt*
EMP: 2 EST: 1997
SALES (est): 97.17K **Privately Held**
SIC: 3993 Signs and advertising specialties

(G-15890)
ABSOGRAPH SIGN CO
125 Windridge Rd (46385-6045)
PHONE..........................630 940-4093
Melissa West, *Prin*
EMP: 4 EST: 2008
SALES (est): 161.94K **Privately Held**
Web: www.absograph.com
SIC: 3993 Signs and advertising specialties

(G-15891)
ACCURATE HEARING AID SVCS LLC
2150 Smoke Rd (46385-9001)
PHONE..........................219 464-1937
EMP: 2
SALES (corp-wide): 397.89K **Privately Held**
Web: www.accuratehearingaidservices.com
SIC: 3842 Hearing aids
PA: Accurate Hearing Aid Services Llc
551 E 4th St
Hobart IN 46342
219 942-8881

(G-15892)
ADVANCED PROTECTIVE TECH LLC (PA)
Also Called: Kbs Coatings
310 N 400 E (46383-9704)
PHONE..........................888 531-4527
Jim Krolak, *VP*
Jim Krolak, *1st VP* JIM KROLAK
EMP: 4 EST: 2005
SALES (est): 1.24MM **Privately Held**
Web: www.kbs-coatings.com
SIC: 2851 Paints and paint additives

(G-15893)
AERO MACHINE LLC
1251 Transport Dr Ste A (46383-8476)
PHONE..........................219 548-0490
Tom Jaeger, *Pr*
Don Freeman, *
EMP: 32 EST: 2003
SQ FT: 35,000
SALES (est): 4.68MM **Privately Held**
Web: www.aeromachine.com
SIC: 3599 Machine shop, jobbing and repair

(G-15894)
AFTERMATH CIDERY AND WINERY
454 Greenwich St (46383-6532)
PHONE..........................219 299-8463
EMP: 5 EST: 2016
SALES (est): 83.03K **Privately Held**
Web: www.aftermathcidery.com
SIC: 2084 Wines

(G-15895)
AGRATI - PARK FOREST LLC
4001 Redbow Dr (46383-5963)
PHONE..........................219 531-2202
EMP: 72
SALES (corp-wide): 798.77MM **Privately Held**
Web: www.agrati.com
SIC: 3452 Bolts, metal
HQ: Agrati - Park Forest, Llc
24000 S Western Ave
Park Forest IL 60466
708 228-5193

(G-15896)
AM STABILIZERS CORPORATION
Also Called: AM Stabilizers
705 Silhavy Rd (46383-4463)
PHONE..........................219 844-3980
Benjamin Labovitz, *Pr*
▲ EMP: 1 EST: 2012
SALES (est): 4.3MM **Privately Held**
Web: www.amstabilizers.com
SIC: 2821 Polyvinyl chloride resins, PVC
HQ: Amfine Chemical Corporation
777 Perrace Ave Ste 602b
Hasbrouck Heights NJ 07604

(G-15897)
AMA DESIGN PRINT
389 E Us Highway 30 (46383-9554)
PHONE..........................219 462-8683
EMP: 6 EST: 2019
SALES (est): 224.82K **Privately Held**
Web: www.printama.com
SIC: 2752 Offset printing

(G-15898)
AMERICAN DIRECT SALES LLC
711 Garfield Ave (46383-5412)
PHONE..........................877 462-2621
Jeff Svhilik, *CEO*
Tim O'neil, *VP*
EMP: 70 EST: 2011
SQ FT: 50,000
SALES (est): 4.57MM **Privately Held**
Web: www.americandirectsales.com
SIC: 2759 Publication printing

(G-15899)
AMERICAN FIRE COMPANY
2603 Oakwood Dr (46383-2223)
P.O. Box 1264 (46384-1264)
PHONE..........................219 840-0630
Michael Brettin, *Prin*
EMP: 4 EST: 2011
SALES (est): 285.52K **Privately Held**
Web: www.americanfirecompany.net
SIC: 5063 1731 7382 3669 Fire alarm systems; Fire detection and burglar alarm systems specialization; Fire alarm maintenance and monitoring; Fire alarm apparatus, electric

(G-15900)
AOC LLC
2552 Industrial Dr (46383-9507)
PHONE..........................219 465-4384
EMP: 90
Web: www.aocresins.com
SIC: 2851 2821 Paints and allied products; Plastics materials and resins
PA: Aoc, Llc
955 Hwy 57
Collierville TN 38017

(G-15901)
APPLE--DAY CSTM HNDCRFTED PDTS
2005 Worthington Dr (46383-3931)
PHONE..........................219 841-6602
EMP: 2
SALES (est): 85.99K **Privately Held**
SIC: 3571 Personal computers (microcomputers)

(G-15902)
ARCELORMITTAL
506 Rainier Ct (46385-8716)
PHONE..........................219 787-7432
EMP: 87 EST: 2018
SALES (est): 430.33K **Privately Held**
SIC: 3312 Blast furnaces and steel mills

(G-15903)
ARCH CHEMICALS INC
2852 Raystone Dr (46383)
PHONE..........................219 464-3949
EMP: 4 EST: 2020
SALES (est): 201.66K **Privately Held**
SIC: 2899 Chemical preparations, nec

(G-15904)
ARCH WOOD PROTECTION INC
Also Called: Arxada
2852 Raystone Dr (46383-0616)
PHONE..........................219 464-3949
Lauri Findling, *Mgr*
EMP: 1
SQ FT: 11,250
SALES (corp-wide): 2.67MM **Privately Held**
Web: www.wolmanizedwood.com
SIC: 2819 2899 2861 Industrial inorganic chemicals, nec; Chemical preparations, nec ; Gum and wood chemicals
HQ: Arch Wood Protection, Inc.
1200 Bluegrass Lakes Pkwy
Alpharetta GA 30004

(G-15905)
ARTEMIS INTL SOLUTIONS CORP
2600 Roosevelt Rd Ste 200-6 (46383-0970)
PHONE..........................708 665-3155
Amy Rouse-ho, *Brnch Mgr*
EMP: 25
Web: www.aurea.com
SIC: 7372 Prepackaged software

HQ: Artemis International Solutions Corporation
401 Congress Ave Ste 2650
Austin TX 78701
512 201-8222

(G-15906)
AWARDS AMERICA INC
397 E Us Highway 30 (46383-9554)
P.O. Box 2013 (46384-2013)
PHONE..........................219 462-7903
Donna North, *Pr*
EMP: 15 EST: 1950
SQ FT: 12,000
SALES (est): 1.04MM **Privately Held**
Web: www.awards-america.com
SIC: 3999 5999 Plaques, picture, laminated; Trophies and plaques

(G-15907)
BABCOCK
67 Sanctuary Dr (46385-7148)
PHONE..........................219 462-8851
Mark Babcock, *Prin*
EMP: 6 EST: 2010
SALES (est): 101.83K **Privately Held**
Web: www.babcock.com
SIC: 3511 Turbines and turbine generator sets

(G-15908)
BACH TECH INC
67 S 500 W (46385-9036)
PHONE..........................219 531-7424
Jeff Reidenbach, *Pr*
EMP: 2 EST: 1996
SQ FT: 2,672
SALES (est): 171.18K **Privately Held**
SIC: 3579 Mailing, letter handling, and addressing machines

(G-15909)
BARNETT INDUSTRIAL INC
3012 Grand Trunk Rd (46383-9145)
PHONE..........................219 814-7500
Robert Edward Barnett, *Pr*
EMP: 10 EST: 2008
SQ FT: 8,500
SALES (est): 763.81K **Privately Held**
SIC: 3499 Machine bases, metal

(G-15910)
BATH & BODY WORKS LLC
2410 Laporte Ave Ste 140 (46383-6969)
PHONE..........................219 531-2146
Meridith Bradford, *Mgr*
EMP: 11
SALES (corp-wide): 7.43B **Publicly Held**
Web: www.bathandbodyworks.com
SIC: 5999 2844 Perfumes and colognes; Perfumes, cosmetics and other toilet preparations
HQ: Bath & Body Works, Llc
7 Limited Pkwy E
Reynoldsburg OH 43068

(G-15911)
BATH GALLERY SHOWROOM
709 Morthland Dr (46383-6409)
PHONE..........................219 531-2150
Jack Hodurek, *Pr*
EMP: 2 EST: 2005
SALES (est): 93.66K **Privately Held**
Web: www.thebathgallery.com
SIC: 3432 5074 Plumbing fixture fittings and trim; Plumbing fittings and supplies

(G-15912)
BAXTER DESIGN & ADVERTISING
656 Franklin St (46383-6427)

GEOGRAPHIC SECTION
Valparaiso - Porter County (G-15937)

PHONE..................................219 464-9237
Sue Baxter, *Owner*
EMP: 2 EST: 1979
SALES (est): 130.84K **Privately Held**
Web: www.panoramanow.com
SIC: 7311 2721 Advertising consultant; Periodicals

(G-15913)
BEULAH INC
808 N 360 W (46385)
P.O. Box 1516 (46384)
PHONE..................................219 309-5635
Chrisitna Nevill, *Prin*
Sheila Nevill, *Pr*
David Nevill, *VP*
EMP: 8 EST: 1994
SALES (est): 846.54K **Privately Held**
Web: www.beulahinc.com
SIC: 3542 Machine tools, metal forming type

(G-15914)
BIONIC PROSTHETICS AND ORTHO
1101 Glendale Blvd (46383-3767)
PHONE..................................219 791-9200
Felix Martinez, *Brnch Mgr*
EMP: 1
Web: www.bionicpo.com
SIC: 3842 Surgical appliances and supplies
PA: Bionic Prosthetics And Orthotics
    Group Llc
    8695 Connecticut St Ste E
    Merrillville IN 46410

(G-15915)
BIRD PUBLISHING COMPANY
1600 Edgewater Beach Rd (46383-1185)
PHONE..................................219 462-6330
EMP: 2 EST: 1985
SALES (est): 67.27K **Privately Held**
SIC: 2731 7812 Book publishing; Video tape production

(G-15916)
BLYTHES SPORT SHOP INC
2810 Calumet Ave (46383-2606)
PHONE..................................219 476-0026
Michael Blythe, *VP*
EMP: 25
SQ FT: 11,000
SALES (corp-wide): 3.97MM **Privately Held**
Web: www.blythesgungear.com
SIC: 5941 2396 Firearms; Automotive and apparel trimmings
PA: Blythes Sport Shop Inc
    138 N Broad St
    Griffith IN 46319
    219 924-4403

(G-15917)
BOARDWORKS INC
369 E Us Highway 30 (46383-9554)
PHONE..................................219 464-8111
Robert P Klett, *Pr*
EMP: 3 EST: 1981
SALES (est): 287.86K **Privately Held**
Web: www.boardworksinc.com
SIC: 2541 2519 Table or counter tops, plastic laminated; Fiberglass furniture, household: padded or plain

(G-15918)
BOB PRESCOTT
Also Called: Signs By Tomorrow
101 W 78th Pl (46385-9076)
PHONE..................................219 736-7804
Bob Prescott, *Owner*
EMP: 4 EST: 2005
SALES (est): 249.69K **Privately Held**
Web: www.signsbytomorrow.com
SIC: 3993 Signs and advertising specialties

(G-15919)
BOLTTECH-MANNINGS INC
1403 Boca Lago Dr (46383-4419)
PHONE..................................219 682-5864
Alan Huchel, *Owner*
EMP: 8 EST: 2016
SALES (est): 81.01K **Privately Held**
Web: www.bolttechmannings.com
SIC: 3452 Bolts, nuts, rivets, and washers

(G-15920)
BOY-CONN PRINTERS INCORPORATED
803 Glendale Blvd (46383)
P.O. Box 1083 (46384-1083)
PHONE..................................219 462-2665
Gary Connors, *Pr*
Susan Connors, *VP*
EMP: 4 EST: 1963
SQ FT: 3,500
SALES (est): 344.28K **Privately Held**
Web: www.boyconn.com
SIC: 2752 Offset printing

(G-15921)
BROWNS DAIRY INC (PA)
Also Called: Valpo Velvet Shoppe
57 Monroe St (46383-5535)
PHONE..................................219 464-4141
Mike Brown, *Pr*
Mark Brown, *VP*
Sue Cain, *Sec*
Elizabeth Brown, *Treas*
EMP: 14 EST: 1947
SQ FT: 10,000
SALES (est): 1.19MM
SALES (corp-wide): 1.19MM **Privately Held**
Web: www.valpovelvet.com
SIC: 2024 5812 Ice cream, bulk; Ice cream stands or dairy bars

(G-15922)
BRYAN JANKY
453 Andover Dr (46385-1300)
PHONE..................................708 921-7676
Bryan Janky, *Prin*
EMP: 4 EST: 2010
SALES (est): 71.88K **Privately Held**
Web: www.bryanjankyart.com
SIC: 2752 Commercial printing, lithographic

(G-15923)
BWAY CORPORATION
4002 Montdale Park Dr (46383-0606)
PHONE..................................219 462-8915
Ronald Brockway, *Brnch Mgr*
EMP: 1
Web: www.bwaycorp.com
SIC: 3411 3499 Metal cans; Ammunition boxes, metal
HQ: Bway Corporation
    1515 W 22nd St Ste 1100
    Oak Brook IL 60523

(G-15924)
C MILLIGAN INVESTMENTS LLC
1208 Pine Creek Rd (46383-7203)
PHONE..................................219 241-5811
Carolyn A Milligan, *Managing Member*
EMP: 5 EST: 2008
SALES (est): 209.43K **Privately Held**
Web: www.cmilligainvestments.com
SIC: 1311 Oil shale mining

(G-15925)
CASE WEINKAUFF
671 E 100 S (46383-9516)
PHONE..................................219 733-9484
Case Weinkauff, *Prin*
EMP: 2 EST: 2005
SALES (est): 245.33K **Privately Held**
SIC: 3523 Farm machinery and equipment

(G-15926)
CHICAGO AUTOMATED LABELING INC
44 N 450 E (46383-9310)
PHONE..................................219 531-0646
EMP: 9 EST: 1995
SQ FT: 5,200
SALES (est): 742.53K **Privately Held**
Web: www.chicagoautolabel.com
SIC: 3565 Packaging machinery

(G-15927)
CHRISTY REFRACTORIES CO LLC
Also Called: Christy Minerals
402 Wall St (46383-2562)
PHONE..................................219 464-2856
Robert Harkel, *Prin*
EMP: 5
SALES (est): 245.49K **Privately Held**
SIC: 1459 Nonclay refractory minerals

(G-15928)
CITY OF VALPARAISO
Also Called: Valparaiso Fire Fighters
2065 Cumberland Dr (46383)
PHONE..................................219 462-5291
EMP: 8
Web: www.valparaisoutilities.org
SIC: 9224 3711 Fire department, not including volunteer; Ambulances (motor vehicles), assembly of
PA: City Of Valparaiso
    166 Lincolnway
    Valparaiso IN 46383
    219 462-1161

(G-15929)
COUNTERFITTERS INC
359 Franklin St Ste C (46383-5432)
PHONE..................................219 531-0848
Darrell Mech, *Pr*
EMP: 2 EST: 1996
SALES (est): 242.57K **Privately Held**
SIC: 5211 2434 Cabinets, kitchen; Wood kitchen cabinets

(G-15930)
CRISMAN SAND COMPANY INC
736 N 400 E (46383-9721)
P.O. Box 2196 (46384-2196)
PHONE..................................219 462-3114
Glenda Snyder, *Pr*
John Magurean, *Sec*
Craig Vincent, *Pr*
Eric Hein, *Mgr*
EMP: 5 EST: 1924
SALES (est): 492.79K **Privately Held**
SIC: 1442 Sand mining

(G-15931)
CSM INDUSTRIES LLC
472 Ridgeland Ave (46385-4163)
PHONE..................................219 465-2009
Shauna Moench, *Prin*
EMP: 1 EST: 2013
SALES (est): 73.45K **Privately Held**
SIC: 3999 Manufacturing industries, nec

(G-15932)
CUSTOM MACHINING SERVICES INC
318 N 400 E (46383-9704)
PHONE..................................219 462-6128
EMP: 1
SALES (corp-wide): 45.02B **Privately Held**
Web: www.customcrimp.com
SIC: 3599 7692 Machine shop, jobbing and repair; Welding repair
HQ: Custom Machining Services Inc
    326 N 400 E
    Valparaiso IN 46383
    219 462-6128

(G-15933)
CUSTOM MACHINING SERVICES INC (HQ)
Also Called: Custom Crimp
326 N 400 E (46383-9704)
PHONE..................................219 462-6128
Jack L Thompson, *Pr*
Joe Intagliata, *VP*
Mary Ann Thompson, *Sec*
◆ EMP: 45 EST: 1931
SQ FT: 28,000
SALES (est): 13.87MM
SALES (corp-wide): 45.02B **Privately Held**
Web: www.customcrimp.com
SIC: 3599 7692 Machine shop, jobbing and repair; Welding repair
PA: Continental Ag
    Continental-Plaza 1
    Hannover NI 30175
    51193801

(G-15934)
CUSTOM QLTING PLLOW CSHION SVC
102 Harmel Dr (46383-5928)
PHONE..................................219 464-7316
Curt Bielski, *Owner*
EMP: 5 EST: 1986
SALES (est): 239.21K **Privately Held**
SIC: 2211 5949 Draperies and drapery fabrics, cotton; Sewing, needlework, and piece goods

(G-15935)
D-J PRINTING SPECIALISTS INC
Also Called: American Speedy Printing
2600 Roosevelt Rd Ste 200-4 (46383-0970)
PHONE..................................219 465-1164
Phyllis Grutz, *Pr*
EMP: 3 EST: 1988
SQ FT: 1,728
SALES (est): 250K **Privately Held**
Web: www.americanspeedy.com
SIC: 2752 Offset printing

(G-15936)
DYNATECT MANUFACTURING INC
Gortrac Division
386 E State Road 2 (46383-9701)
PHONE..................................219 462-0822
Keith Powell, *Brnch Mgr*
EMP: 40
SQ FT: 12,600
SALES (corp-wide): 2.8B **Privately Held**
Web: www.dynatect.com
SIC: 3999 Barber and beauty shop equipment
HQ: Dynatect Manufacturing, Inc.
    2300 S Calhoun Rd
    New Berlin WI 53151
    262 786-1500

(G-15937)
DYNATECT MANUFACTURING INC
386 E State Road 2 (46383-9701)
PHONE..................................219 465-1898
EMP: 13 EST: 2014
SALES (est): 2.9MM **Privately Held**
Web: www.dynatect.com
SIC: 3999 Barber and beauty shop equipment

Valparaiso - Porter County (G-15938)   GEOGRAPHIC SECTION

(G-15938)
EIDP INC
Also Called: Dupont
218 N 250 W (46385-9242)
PHONE..................................219 462-4587
Paul Landgrete, *Mgr*
EMP: 1
SALES (corp-wide): 17.23B **Publicly Held**
Web: www.dupont.com
SIC: 2819 Industrial inorganic chemicals, nec
HQ: Eidp, Inc.
  9330 Zionsville Rd
  Indianapolis IN 46268
  833 267-8382

(G-15939)
EL POPULAR SAUSAGE FACTORY LLC
Also Called: El Popular
1251 Transport Dr Ste C (46383-8476)
P.O. Box 2237 (46384-2237)
PHONE..................................219 476-7040
Edward Garza, *Managing Member*
Pete Peuquet, *Pr*
Drew Peuquet, *VP*
Kevin Mcguffey, *Treas*
EMP: 7 **EST:** 2005
SQ FT: 9,000
SALES (est): 773.87K **Privately Held**
Web: www.elpopular.com
SIC: 2013 Sausages and other prepared meats

(G-15940)
ELEGAN GRAPHICS
5905 Murvihill Rd (46383-8376)
PHONE..................................219 462-9921
Chuck Williams, *Prin*
EMP: 2 **EST:** 2005
SALES (est): 154.68K **Privately Held**
Web: www.elegan.com
SIC: 2759 Screen printing

(G-15941)
ELEGAN SPORTSWEAR INC
Also Called: Elegan Customwear
212 Lincolnway (46383-5691)
PHONE..................................219 464-8416
EMP: 23 **EST:** 1982
SQ FT: 12,000
SALES (est): 827.73K **Privately Held**
Web: www.elegan.com
SIC: 2395 2396 Embroidery products, except Schiffli machine; Screen printing on fabric articles

(G-15942)
ELITE CRETE SYSTEMS INC (PA)
1151 Transport Dr (46383-8491)
PHONE..................................219 465-7671
Ken Freestone, *Pr*
Kathy Paxton, *CFO*
◆ **EMP:** 11 **EST:** 1999
SQ FT: 125,000
SALES (est): 9.8MM
SALES (corp-wide): 9.8MM **Privately Held**
Web: www.elitecrete.com
SIC: 2295 Resin or plastic coated fabrics

(G-15943)
EMBROIDME
2254 Morthland Dr (46385-5372)
PHONE..................................219 465-1400
Tony Miccllche, *Prin*
EMP: 2 **EST:** 2007
SALES (est): 74.42K **Privately Held**
Web: www.embroidme-valparaiso.com

SIC: 5949 5947 5942 2759 Sewing, needlework, and piece goods; Gift, novelty, and souvenir shop; Book stores; Screen printing

(G-15944)
EMERSON ELECTRIC CO
Also Called: Emerson
2300 Evans Ave (46383-4054)
PHONE..................................219 465-2411
EMP: 5
SALES (corp-wide): 15.16B **Publicly Held**
Web: www.emerson.com
SIC: 3823 Process control instruments
PA: Emerson Electric Co.
  8000 W Florissant Ave
  Saint Louis MO 63136
  314 553-2000

(G-15945)
EXCEL MACHINE TECHNOLOGIES INC
405 Elm St (46383-3620)
PHONE..................................219 548-0708
David L Defries, *Pr*
Kathleen Defries, *VP*
EMP: 23 **EST:** 1997
SQ FT: 120,000
SALES (est): 509.86K **Privately Held**
Web: www.emtcnc.com
SIC: 3599 Machine shop, jobbing and repair

(G-15946)
FAIRWAY LASER SYSTEMS INC
950 Transport Dr (46383-8434)
PHONE..................................219 462-6892
Dan Molchan, *Pr*
EMP: 4 **EST:** 1998
SQ FT: 1,600
SALES (est): 499.32K **Privately Held**
Web: www.fairwaylaser.com
SIC: 3699 Laser systems and equipment

(G-15947)
FASHION FLOORING AND LTG INC
Also Called: Fashion Flooring and Lighting
2510 Beech St (46383-4097)
EMP: 7 **EST:** 2005
SQ FT: 12,700
SALES (est): 1.33MM **Privately Held**
Web: www.fashionflooringllc.com
SIC: 5713 3645 Carpets; Residential lighting fixtures

(G-15948)
FASTENER EQUIPMENT CORPORATION
3604 Meadowlark Dr (46383-2275)
PHONE..................................708 957-5100
Le Roy Loudermilk, *Pr*
▲ **EMP:** 6 **EST:** 1975
SALES (est): 842.04K **Privately Held**
Web: www.fastenerequipmentcorp.com
SIC: 5084 3545 Machine tools and accessories; Machine tool attachments and accessories

(G-15949)
FEHRING F N & SON PRINTERS
Also Called: Fehring Printers
450 N 325 E (46383-8312)
PHONE..................................219 933-0439
Frank N Fehring, *Owner*
EMP: 3 **EST:** 1937
SALES (est): 234.74K **Privately Held**
Web: www.fehringprinters.com
SIC: 2752 2759 Offset printing; Letterpress printing

(G-15950)
FOUR CORNERS WINERY LLC
294 E 600 N (46383-9710)
PHONE..................................219 730-5311
EMP: 6 **EST:** 2011
SALES (est): 398.18K **Privately Held**
Web: www.fourcornerswinery.com
SIC: 2084 Wines

(G-15951)
FROZEN GARDEN LLC
315 E 316 N Ste C (46383-8467)
PHONE..................................219 286-3578
EMP: 10 **EST:** 2015
SALES (est): 906.18K **Privately Held**
Web: www.thefrozengarden.com
SIC: 2037 Frozen fruits and vegetables

(G-15952)
G N U INC
2252 Industrial Dr (46383-9511)
PHONE..................................219 464-7813
Tom Woods, *Brnch Mgr*
EMP: 235
Web: www.ugn.com
SIC: 3714 Motor vehicle parts and accessories
HQ: U.G.N., Inc.
  2650 Wrrnville Rd Ste 300
  Downers Grove IL 60515
  773 437-2400

(G-15953)
GARY ELECTRIC MOTOR SERVICE CO
393 E Us Highway 30 (46383-9554)
P.O. Box 1938 (46384-1938)
PHONE..................................219 884-6555
Randal Massena, *Pr*
Frank Kantroski, *VP*
EMP: 12 **EST:** 1989
SQ FT: 35,000
SALES (est): 945.37K **Privately Held**
Web: www.electricmotorrepairvalparaiso.com
SIC: 7694 Electric motor repair

(G-15954)
GAST SIGN CO
499 W Us Highway 30 (46385-5551)
PHONE..................................219 759-4336
Joseph Gast, *Owner*
EMP: 3 **EST:** 1966
SALES (est): 203.31K **Privately Held**
SIC: 3993 Signs and advertising specialties

(G-15955)
GIANT PAW PRINTS INC
549 N 300 E (46383-8345)
PHONE..................................219 241-9299
EMP: 4 **EST:** 2016
SALES (est): 86.41K **Privately Held**
Web: www.giantpawprints.com
SIC: 2752 Commercial printing, lithographic

(G-15956)
GKD TOOLS LLC
1152 West St (46385-6219)
PHONE..................................219 309-7758
EMP: 6 **EST:** 2016
SALES (est): 171.92K **Privately Held**
SIC: 3599 Industrial machinery, nec

(G-15957)
GLOBAL ENERGY RESOURCES LLC
Also Called: Ger
5206 Garden Gtwy (46383-1002)
PHONE..................................219 712-2556
EMP: 3 **EST:** 2008
SQ FT: 4,000

SALES (est): 463.61K **Privately Held**
Web: www.gergreen.com
SIC: 2869 Industrial organic chemicals, nec

(G-15958)
GOATEE SHIRT PRINTING LLC
1039 N 200 W (46385-8517)
PHONE..................................219 916-2443
Megan Sexton, *Prin*
EMP: 5 **EST:** 2016
SALES (est): 58.44K **Privately Held**
SIC: 2752 Commercial printing, lithographic

(G-15959)
HARDWOODS BY BILL LLC
2902 Kickbush Dr (46385-7104)
PHONE..................................219 465-5346
William Stocky, *Prin*
EMP: 5 **EST:** 2014
SALES (est): 94.53K **Privately Held**
SIC: 2499 Wood products, nec

(G-15960)
HAVEN CAPITAL LLC
5 Washington St (46383-4768)
PHONE..................................219 802-5044
David Montagueo, *Managing Member*
EMP: 6 **EST:** 2019
SALES (est): 493.74K **Privately Held**
Web: www.havencapitalllc.com
SIC: 1389 6411 Construction, repair, and dismantling services; Pension and retirement plan consultants

(G-15961)
HEAT WAGONS INC
Also Called: Wood Kovers
342 N Co Rd 400 E (46383)
PHONE..................................219 464-8818
John Walsh, *Pr*
Marcus Smith, *VP*
John Barney, *Sec*
▲ **EMP:** 10 **EST:** 1981
SQ FT: 24,000
SALES (est): 1.6MM **Privately Held**
Web: www.heatwagon.com
SIC: 3433 3567 7359 Space heaters, except electric; Industrial furnaces and ovens; Equipment rental and leasing, nec

(G-15962)
HOME MOUNTAIN PUBLISHING CO INC
Also Called: Home Mountain Printing
3602 Enterprise Ave (46383-8318)
PHONE..................................219 462-6601
EMP: 38
Web: www.homemountain.com
SIC: 2752 2789 2791 Offset printing; Bookbinding and related work; Typesetting

(G-15963)
HOME RUN LLC
Also Called: Hoosier Bat Company
312 N 325 E Ste B (46383-6965)
P.O. Box 432 (46384-0432)
PHONE..................................219 531-1006
Dave Cook, *Managing Member*
EMP: 4 **EST:** 1991
SQ FT: 6,000
SALES (est): 242.7K **Privately Held**
Web: www.hoosierbat.com
SIC: 3949 Baseball equipment and supplies, general

(G-15964)
HOOSIER BAT COMPANY
1556 W Lincolnway Ste 2 (46385-0303)
PHONE..................................219 531-1006
EMP: 3 **EST:** 2020

GEOGRAPHIC SECTION
Valparaiso - Porter County (G-15992)

SALES (est): 86.73K **Privately Held**
Web: www.hoosierbat.com
SIC: **3949** Sporting and athletic goods, nec

(G-15965)
HOOSIER FIRE EQUIPMENT INC (PA)
4009 Montdale Park Dr (46383-0607)
PHONE..................................219 462-1707
Nick Swartz, *Pr*
Cindy Swartz, *Sec*
EMP: 10 **EST:** 1957
SQ FT: 15,500
SALES (est): 10.51MM
SALES (corp-wide): 10.51MM **Privately Held**
Web: www.hoosierfire.com
SIC: **5087 3561 5084 5063** Firefighting equipment; Pumps and pumping equipment ; Industrial machinery and equipment; Electrical apparatus and equipment

(G-15966)
I E M C
Also Called: Industrial Elec Maint Co
1150 Lincolnway Ste 1 (46385-5800)
PHONE..................................219 464-2890
Bryant Mitol, *Owner*
EMP: 3 **EST:** 1979
SQ FT: 1,000
SALES (est): 186.35K **Privately Held**
SIC: **7629 3663** Electrical equipment repair services; Radio and t.v. communications equipment

(G-15967)
IDEAL SIGN CORP
507 N 325 W (46385-8717)
P.O. Box 1302 (46384-1302)
PHONE..................................219 406-2092
Jamie Bartok, *Prin*
EMP: 2 **EST:** 2010
SALES (est): 142.73K **Privately Held**
SIC: **3993** Signs and advertising specialties

(G-15968)
IFOK INC
447 E Us Highway 6 (46383-9746)
PHONE..................................219 477-5107
David Ales, *Prin*
EMP: 13 **EST:** 2019
SALES (est): 136.23K **Privately Held**
Web: www.ifok.de
SIC: **3714** Motor vehicle parts and accessories

(G-15969)
ILLIANA ELECTRICAL SVCS LLC
501 Garfield Ave (46383-5027)
PHONE..................................219 276-1743
EMP: 5 **EST:** 2018
SALES (est): 27.52K **Privately Held**
Web: www.illianaelectrical.com
SIC: **7694** Electric motor repair

(G-15970)
ILLIANA INDUS ELC MTR SVCS INC
393 E Us Highway 30 (46383-9554)
PHONE..................................219 286-3654
Frank Kantroski, *Pr*
Avery R Massena, *VP*
EMP: 18 **EST:** 2000
SQ FT: 35,000
SALES (est): 1.87MM **Privately Held**
Web: www.illianaindustrial.com
SIC: **7694** Electric motor repair

(G-15971)
INDIANA GROCERY GROUP LLC
Also Called: Central Bakery
555 Coolwood Dr (46385-6173)
PHONE..................................219 462-5147
EMP: 43
SALES (corp-wide): 384.88MM **Privately Held**
Web: www.strackandvantil.com
SIC: **2051** Bakery: wholesale or wholesale/retail combined
PA: Indiana Grocery Group, Llc
2244 W 45th St
Highland IN 46322
219 924-7588

(G-15972)
INDIANA POLYMERS INC
333 W 806 N Valparaiso (46385)
P.O. Box 710 (46368)
PHONE..................................219 762-9550
Richard D Pyle, *Pr*
Nicole F Pyle, *VP*
EMP: 7 **EST:** 1989
SQ FT: 2,400
SALES (est): 1.38MM **Privately Held**
Web: www.indianapolymers.com
SIC: **2821** Plastics materials and resins

(G-15973)
INDUSTRIAL AND COML CONTG INC
3206 Cascade Dr (46383-9132)
PHONE..................................219 405-8599
Gene Lane, *Pr*
EMP: 10 **EST:** 1989
SALES (est): 526.3K **Privately Held**
SIC: **2097** Manufactured ice

(G-15974)
INK DAWGZ LLC
380 S 100 W (46385-9660)
PHONE..................................219 781-6972
Theodore A Ames, *Prin*
EMP: 2 **EST:** 2019
SALES (est): 162.23K **Privately Held**
Web: www.inkdawgz.com
SIC: **2396 2759 2261 2262** Screen printing on fabric articles; Screen printing; Screen printing of cotton broadwoven fabrics; Screen printing: manmade fiber and silk broadwoven fabrics

(G-15975)
INNOVATED MACHINE SERVICE INC
514 E 400 S (46383-7839)
PHONE..................................219 462-4467
Rich Payne, *Prin*
EMP: 3 **EST:** 2007
SALES (est): 244.99K **Privately Held**
Web: www.innovatedmachine.com
SIC: **3599** Machine shop, jobbing and repair

(G-15976)
INNOVATIVE RESCUE SYSTEMS LLC (PA)
Also Called: Amkus Rescue Systems
4201 Montdale Dr (46383)
PHONE..................................219 548-1028
Kyle Smith, *Pr*
Neal Wilhelm, *CFO*
EMP: 8 **EST:** 2016
SALES (est): 11.99MM
SALES (corp-wide): 11.99MM **Privately Held**
Web: www.amkus.com
SIC: **3546** Power-driven handtools

(G-15977)
IRA WILLIAM SCOTT
Also Called: Xetex Bottling Group
407 Center St (46385-4504)
PHONE..................................219 241-5674
Ira William Scott, *Owner*
Ira W Scott, *Owner*
EMP: 1 **EST:** 2004
SQ FT: 1,200
SALES (est): 6.17K **Privately Held**
SIC: **2086** Bottled and canned soft drinks

(G-15978)
J AND N ENTERPRISES INC
Also Called: Sensit Technologies
851 Transport Dr (46383-8432)
PHONE..................................219 465-2700
◆ **EMP:** 3 **EST:** 1979
SALES (est): 840.47K **Privately Held**
Web: www.gasleaksensors.com
SIC: **3829** Gas detectors

(G-15979)
J V C MACHINING
766 N 500 E (46383-9733)
PHONE..................................219 462-0363
John V Cortez, *Prin*
EMP: 2 **EST:** 2004
SQ FT: 3,096
SALES (est): 118.83K **Privately Held**
SIC: **3599** Machine shop, jobbing and repair

(G-15980)
JANICE CABINETRY LLC
1066 Farrell St (46385-4522)
PHONE..................................219 741-8120
Daniel Jones, *Prin*
EMP: 5 **EST:** 2018
SALES (est): 196.76K **Privately Held**
SIC: **2434** Wood kitchen cabinets

(G-15981)
JEMARKEL HEALTH-TECH LLC
2701 Beech St Ste R (46383-6001)
PHONE..................................219 548-5881
▲ **EMP:** 5 **EST:** 2003
SALES (est): 68.79K **Privately Held**
Web: risingsunkarate.itgo.com
SIC: **3841** Muscle exercise apparatus, ophthalmic

(G-15982)
JPC TRUCKING LLC
2106 Morthland Dr (46383-5914)
PHONE..................................219 207-2300
EMP: 1
SALES (est): 60.08K **Privately Held**
SIC: **3537** Trucks: freight, baggage, etc.: industrial, except mining

(G-15983)
KAT TALES EMBROIDERY
3503 Sunset Dr (46383-1827)
PHONE..................................219 299-2693
Kathleen Haworth, *Prin*
EMP: 1 **EST:** 2010
SALES (est): 72.9K **Privately Held**
SIC: **2395** Embroidery and art needlework

(G-15984)
KEENVILLE & COMPANY LLC ✪
1703 Vale Park Rd (46383-2726)
PHONE..................................219 916-6737
EMP: 1 **EST:** 2022
SALES (est): 69.27K **Privately Held**
Web: www.keenville.com
SIC: **3999 7389** Manufacturing industries, nec; Business Activities at Non-Commercial Site

(G-15985)
KELLER LOGGING LLC
210 W 375 S (46385-9623)
P.O. Box 9 (46384-0009)
PHONE..................................219 309-0379
Ben Keller, *Pr*
EMP: 5 **EST:** 2017
SALES (est): 199.15K **Privately Held**
Web: www.indianalogging.com
SIC: **2411** Logging

(G-15986)
KELLER MACHINE & WELDING INC
5705 Murvihill Rd (46383-6313)
P.O. Box 168 (46384-0168)
PHONE..................................219 464-4915
Daniel S Keller, *Pr*
Daniel Keller, *
EMP: 23 **EST:** 2000
SQ FT: 1,200
SALES (est): 835.36K **Privately Held**
Web: www.kellermachineandwelding.com
SIC: **3441 3599** Fabricated structural metal; Custom machinery

(G-15987)
KMSD INC
5705 Murvihill Rd (46383-6313)
P.O. Box 168 (46384-0168)
PHONE..................................219 808-7159
Gerri Davis-parker, *Prin*
EMP: 17 **EST:** 2020
SALES (est): 1.21MM **Privately Held**
Web: www.kellermachineweld.com
SIC: **3499** Fabricated metal products, nec

(G-15988)
KOBALTEC LLC
1450 Clark Rd (46385-7169)
PHONE..................................219 462-1483
Matthew Berg, *CEO*
Brittany Taroli, *CFO*
▲ **EMP:** 5 **EST:** 2014
SQ FT: 10,000
SALES (est): 265.81K **Privately Held**
SIC: **3492** Hose and tube fittings and assemblies, hydraulic/pneumatic

(G-15989)
KOEHLER
1905 Whitney Ave (46383-3065)
PHONE..................................219 462-4128
Henry Koehler, *Pr*
EMP: 5 **EST:** 2005
SALES (est): 62.33K **Privately Held**
SIC: **3953** Marking devices

(G-15990)
LAKE CABLE OF INDIANA LLC
2700 Evans Ave (46383-4440)
PHONE..................................847 238-3000
Emile Tohme, *Pr*
EMP: 103 **EST:** 2003
SQ FT: 126,000
SALES (est): 10.69MM **Privately Held**
Web: www.lakecable.com
SIC: **3496** Miscellaneous fabricated wire products

(G-15991)
LANDGREBE MANUFACTURING INC
208 N 250 W (46385-9242)
PHONE..................................219 462-9587
George Landgrebe, *Pr*
Beth Landgrebe, *VP*
EMP: 3 **EST:** 1968
SQ FT: 8,500
SALES (est): 304.1K **Privately Held**
Web: www.towtrailer.com
SIC: **3537 3799** Dollies (hand or power trucks), industrial,except mining; Towing bars and systems

(G-15992)
LAPIS SERVICES INC
1101 Cumberland Xing (46383-2356)
PHONE..................................219 464-9131

Valparaiso - Porter County (G-15993)

GEOGRAPHIC SECTION

Jere Brigg, *Pr*
Mary Kwiatkowski, *CFO*
EMP: 3 **EST:** 2005
SALES (est): 461.96K **Privately Held**
Web: www.lapisinc.com
SIC: 3444 Sheet metalwork

(G-15993)
LASER SYSTEMS
104 Billings St Ste A (46383-3601)
PHONE..................................219 465-1155
Drew Watson, *Pr*
EMP: 3 **EST:** 1990
SALES (est): 242.16K **Privately Held**
SIC: 3861 Toners, prepared photographic (not made in chemical plants)

(G-15994)
LEE PUBLICATIONS INC
Also Called: Howard Pblctions Vidette Times
1111 Glendale Blvd (46383-3724)
PHONE..................................219 462-5151
Don Asher, *Brnch Mgr*
EMP:
SALES (corp-wide): 691.14MM **Publicly Held**
Web: www.lee.net
SIC: 2711 Newspapers, publishing and printing
HQ: Lee Publications, Inc.
 4600 E 53rd St
 Davenport IA 52807
 563 383-2100

(G-15995)
LEGACY VULCAN LLC
Also Called: Ralston Yard
651 Axe Ave (46383-6479)
PHONE..................................219 462-5832
Nan Ralston, *Pr*
EMP: 5
Web: www.vulcanmaterials.com
SIC: 3272 Concrete products, nec
HQ: Legacy Vulcan, Llc
 1200 Urban Center Dr
 Birmingham AL 35242
 205 298-3000

(G-15996)
LEGACY VULCAN LLC
Also Called: Whitcomb Yard
4105 Montdale Park Dr (46383-0608)
PHONE..................................219 465-3066
Gary Whitcomb, *Mgr*
EMP: 4
Web: www.vulcanmaterials.com
SIC: 3273 Ready-mixed concrete
HQ: Legacy Vulcan, Llc
 1200 Urban Center Dr
 Birmingham AL 35242
 205 298-3000

(G-15997)
LESLIE NUSS
Also Called: Little Leaf Records
3161 Heavilin Rd (46385-9062)
PHONE..................................219 462-3499
Leslie Nuss, *Owner*
EMP: 1 **EST:** 1994
SALES (est): 73.39K **Privately Held**
Web: www.leslienuss.com
SIC: 2325 Jeans: men's, youths', and boys'

(G-15998)
LITKO AEROSYSTEMS INC
Also Called: Litko Game Accessories
2006 Warbler Dr (46383-4274)
PHONE..................................219 462-9295
Kenneth Litko, *CEO*
Kenneth R Litko, *Pr*
▼ **EMP:** 7 **EST:** 2002
SALES (est): 502.48K **Privately Held**
Web: www.litko.net
SIC: 3944 5092 Games, toys, and children's vehicles; Toys and games

(G-15999)
MACHINE ELEMENTS INC
244 Crabapple Ln (46383-9778)
PHONE..................................219 508-3968
Edward M Vavrek, *Prin*
EMP: 5 **EST:** 2009
SALES (est): 214.53K **Privately Held**
Web: www.machineelements.com
SIC: 2819 Elements

(G-16000)
MAURICES SGNTURE CHSECAKES LLC ◆
889 Thoreau Trl (46383-7145)
PHONE..................................708 879-0031
EMP: 2 **EST:** 2022
SALES (est): 92.67K **Privately Held**
SIC: 2051 7389 Bakery: wholesale or wholesale/retail combined; Business Activities at Non-Commercial Site

(G-16001)
MECHANICAL PARTS & SVCS INC
304 Burlington Beach Rd (46383-1939)
P.O. Box 4030 (46082-4030)
PHONE..................................219 670-1986
David E Baldea, *Pr*
Nancy J Baldea, *Sec*
▲ **EMP:** 3 **EST:** 1994
SALES (est): 224.04K **Privately Held**
SIC: 3824 Mechanical counters

(G-16002)
MIDWEST ELECTRICAL SALES
Also Called: MIDWEST ELECTRICAL SALES
961 Sheffield Dr (46385-2851)
PHONE..................................708 821-7490
Mike Overlay, *Brnch Mgr*
EMP: 1
SIC: 3699 7389 Electrical equipment and supplies, nec; Business services, nec
PA: Midwest Electrical Sales Inc
 3026
 Barrington IL 60011

(G-16003)
MINKS & BEYOND LLC ◆
2106 Morthland Dr (46383-5914)
PHONE..................................219 402-7011
EMP: 1 **EST:** 2022
SALES (est): 39.69K **Privately Held**
SIC: 3999 Hair and hair-based products

(G-16004)
MJE INDUSTRIES INC
460 Lincolnway Unit 343 (46384-3151)
PHONE..................................219 299-3535
EMP: 4 **EST:** 2017
SALES (est): 74.87K **Privately Held**
SIC: 3999 Manufacturing industries, nec

(G-16005)
MR COPYRITE
308 Lincolnway (46385-5609)
PHONE..................................219 462-1108
Diane Price, *Owner*
EMP: 3 **EST:** 1974
SALES (est): 196.41K **Privately Held**
Web: www.mrcopyrite.com
SIC: 2752 Offset printing

(G-16006)
MURPHY MILL SERVICES LLC
154 Curtis Dr (46383-9111)
PHONE..................................219 246-9290
Charles Murphy, *Managing Member*
EMP: 3 **EST:** 2013
SALES (est): 500K **Privately Held**
Web: www.murphymillsevices.com
SIC: 3441 7389 Fabricated structural metal; Business services, nec

(G-16007)
NANCY FERBER
Also Called: Top Notch Embroidery
143 Woodland Hickory Ct (46385-9264)
PHONE..................................219 548-3645
Nancy Ferber, *Owner*
EMP: 1 **EST:** 1994
SALES (est): 35.99K **Privately Held**
SIC: 2395 Embroidery and art needlework

(G-16008)
NARROW GATE PUBLISHING LLC
113 Shorewood Dr (46385-8067)
PHONE..................................219 464-8579
Monica J Kerr, *Owner*
EMP: 5 **EST:** 2015
SALES (est): 69.68K **Privately Held**
SIC: 2741 Miscellaneous publishing

(G-16009)
NATIONAL EQUIPMENT INC
Also Called: Enduring Graphics
358 Harrison Blvd (46383-3414)
PHONE..................................219 462-1205
Wayne Cobb, *Pr*
Edward Cobb, *VP*
EMP: 7 **EST:** 1956
SALES (est): 683.11K **Privately Held**
Web: www.crispyaz.com
SIC: 3523 5083 Farm machinery and equipment; Agricultural machinery and equipment

(G-16010)
NELSEN STEEL
1501 Boca Lago Dr (46383-3901)
PHONE..................................708 308-6749
Mark Stymiest, *Prin*
EMP: 10 **EST:** 2018
SALES (est): 103.77K **Privately Held**
Web: www.nelsensteel.com
SIC: 3312 Blast furnaces and steel mills

(G-16011)
NEW ELEMENTS LLC
212 Morthland Dr (46383-6221)
PHONE..................................219 465-1389
Justine Goodwin, *Admn*
EMP: 5 **EST:** 2016
SALES (est): 202.02K **Privately Held**
SIC: 2819 Industrial inorganic chemicals, nec

(G-16012)
NGH RETAIL LLC
315 E 316 N Ste A (46383-8467)
PHONE..................................219 476-0772
Mark A Laursen, *Managing Member*
▲ **EMP:** 3 **EST:** 2009
SALES (est): 177.35K **Privately Held**
Web: www.nghretail.com
SIC: 5999 3724 Engines and parts, air-cooled; Aircraft engines and engine parts

(G-16013)
NGH RETAIL LLC
301 W 550 N (46385-8715)
PHONE..................................219 476-0772
Mark Laursen, *Pr*
▲ **EMP:** 5 **EST:** 2003
SALES (est): 489.32K **Privately Held**
Web: www.nghretail.com
SIC: 3433 Heating equipment, except electric

(G-16014)
NOODLE SHOP CO - COLORADO INC
71 Silhavy Rd Ste 101 (46383-4493)
PHONE..................................219 548-0921
EMP: 4 **EST:** 2009
SALES (est): 136.05K **Privately Held**
SIC: 2098 Noodles (e.g. egg, plain, and water), dry

(G-16015)
NORTH AMERICA PACKAGING CORP
Also Called: Southcorp Packaging North Amer
4002 Montdale Park Dr (46383-0606)
PHONE..................................219 462-8915
Jeff Nicolee, *Brnch Mgr*
EMP: 1
SIC: 3089 Pails, plastics
HQ: North America Packaging Corp
 1515 W 22nd St Ste 550
 Oak Brook IL 60523
 630 203-4100

(G-16016)
NORTH STAR STONE INC
312 N 325 E (46383-6964)
PHONE..................................219 464-7272
Mary C Andrews, *Pr*
Chris Andrews, *
EMP: 16 **EST:** 2003
SALES (est): 2.39MM **Privately Held**
Web: www.ourstonehome.com
SIC: 3271 Architectural concrete: block, split, fluted, screen, etc.

(G-16017)
OLYMPUS MANUFACTURING SYSTEMS
4703 N Calumet Ave (46383-1611)
PHONE..................................219 465-1520
EMP: 5 **EST:** 1994
SQ FT: 1,200
SALES (est): 496.89K **Privately Held**
Web: www.valparaisohottub.com
SIC: 3542 Machine tools, metal forming type

(G-16018)
OMNITECH SYSTEMS INC
450 Campbell St Ste 2 (46385-6299)
PHONE..................................219 531-5532
EMP: 40 **EST:** 1994
SQ FT: 10,000
SALES (est): 4.17MM **Privately Held**
Web: www.omnitechsystems.com
SIC: 3841 Surgical and medical instruments

(G-16019)
ONLYDRAMS LLC
814 N 400 E (46383-9748)
PHONE..................................219 707-6025
EMP: 1
SALES (est): 64.36K **Privately Held**
SIC: 7372 Prepackaged software

(G-16020)
OWENS CORNING SALES LLC
Also Called: Owens Corning
2552 Industrial Dr (46383-9507)
PHONE..................................219 465-4324
Craig Gule, *Mgr*
EMP: 2
SIC: 3296 Fiberglass insulation
HQ: Owens Corning Sales, Llc
 1 Owens Corning Pkwy
 Toledo OH 43659
 419 248-8000

(G-16021)
PAILTON INC
2901 Bertholet Blvd (46383-7938)
PHONE..................................219 476-0085

GEOGRAPHIC SECTION

Valparaiso - Porter County (G-16048)

John Nollett, *Pr*
Robert S Kilhefner, *VP Sls*
▲ **EMP:** 2 **EST:** 1999
SQ FT: 10,000
SALES (est): 825.16K
SALES (corp-wide): 24.08MM **Privately Held**
Web: www.pailton.com
SIC: 3714 Motor vehicle parts and accessories
PA: Pailton Engineering Limited
  Phoenix House
  Coventry W MIDLANDS CV6 4
  247 668-0445

(G-16022)
PAULA ROSENBAUM
Also Called: Soy Creamy
2752 Hearthstone Dr (46383-7815)
PHONE...........................319 484-2941
Paula Rosenbaum, *Owner*
EMP: 1 **EST:** 2010
SALES (est): 56.78K **Privately Held**
SIC: 3999 5999 Candles; Candle shops

(G-16023)
PERFECTION BAKERIES INC
Also Called: Aunt Millies Bakeries
2650 Barley Rd (46383-8038)
PHONE...........................219 789-4816
EMP: 1
SALES (corp-wide): 486.65MM **Privately Held**
Web: www.auntmillies.com
SIC: 2051 Bread, cake, and related products
PA: Perfection Bakeries, Inc.
  6230 Bluffton Rd
  Fort Wayne IN 46809
  260 424-8245

(G-16024)
PERMA LUBRICATION
2503 Chicago St Ste A (46383-5863)
PHONE...........................219 531-9155
Garland Bridgewater, *Pr*
EMP: 6 **EST:** 1989
SALES (est): 531.06K **Privately Held**
Web: www.permausa.com
SIC: 3569 Lubricating equipment

(G-16025)
PERMA-GREEN SUPREME INC
5609 Murvihill Rd (46383-6315)
PHONE...........................219 548-3801
Thomas F Jessen, *Pr*
Thomas Jessen, *
EMP: 25 **EST:** 1980
SQ FT: 30,000
SALES (est): 4.79MM **Privately Held**
Web: www.permagreen.com
SIC: 3523 Farm machinery and equipment

(G-16026)
PHOENIX SERVICES LLC
280 Scotscraig Dr (46385-8006)
P.O. Box 3190 (46312-8190)
PHONE...........................219 399-7808
Tony Cunningham, *Mgr*
EMP: 88 **EST:** 2017
SALES (est): 9.19MM **Privately Held**
Web: www.phoenixglobal.com
SIC: 3312 Blast furnaces and steel mills

(G-16027)
POWDER PROCESSING & TECH LLC
5103 Evans Ave (46383-8387)
PHONE...........................219 462-4141
John J Kaziow, *Managing Member*
Errol Menke, *
▲ **EMP:** 42 **EST:** 2002
SALES (est): 9.93MM **Privately Held**
Web: www.pptechnology.com
SIC: 3399 Powder, metal

(G-16028)
POWDERTECH CORP
5103 Evans Ave (46383-8387)
PHONE...........................219 462-4141
Ken Bartelt, *Pr*
Masao Ogawa, *
Toshio Honjo, *
James Jorgensen, *
Alan Zurawski, *
◆ **EMP:** 52 **EST:** 1988
SQ FT: 200,000
SALES (est): 1.27MM **Privately Held**
Web: www.pptechnology.com
SIC: 3399 Iron, powdered
PA: Powdertech Co., Ltd.
  217, Toyofuta
  Kashiwa CHI 277-0

(G-16029)
POWERWELD INC (PA)
2501 Beech St (46383-5217)
PHONE...........................219 462-8700
Tallon Macdonald, *Pr*
Michael Argue, *Prin*
▲ **EMP:** 4 **EST:** 2010
SALES (est): 824.46K
SALES (corp-wide): 824.46K **Privately Held**
Web: www.powerweldinc.com
SIC: 7692 Welding repair

(G-16030)
PRATT (JET CORR) INC
Also Called: Pratt Industries USA
3155 S State Road 49 (46383-7831)
PHONE...........................219 548-9191
Robert Young, *Genl Mgr*
EMP: 300
Web: www.prattindustries.com
SIC: 2653 Boxes, corrugated: made from purchased materials
HQ: Pratt (Jet Corr), Inc.
  1800 Sarasot Bus Pkwy Ne B
  Conyers GA 30013
  770 929-1300

(G-16031)
PRATT PAPER (IN) LLC
3050 Anthony Pratt Dr (46383-0032)
PHONE...........................219 477-1040
Jay Henessey, *Genl Mgr*
EMP: 1
Web: www.prattindustries.com
SIC: 2621 Paper mills
HQ: Pratt Paper (In), Llc
  1800 Sarasot Bus Pkwy Ne C
  Conyers GA 30013
  770 918-5678

(G-16032)
Q AIR INC
4008 Murvihill Rd. (46383)
PHONE...........................219 476-7048
Steve Qualizza, *Pr*
EMP: 2 **EST:** 2002
SALES (est): 212.51K **Privately Held**
Web: www.q-air.com
SIC: 3728 Aircraft parts and equipment, nec

(G-16033)
QUALITY TOOL & MACHINE CO
393 S State Road 49 (46383-7858)
PHONE...........................219 464-2411
Robert Malackowski, *Owner*
EMP: 4 **EST:** 1967
SQ FT: 5,000
SALES (est): 239.35K **Privately Held**
SIC: 3599 Machine shop, jobbing and repair

(G-16034)
R F EXPRESS CORP
2601 Vale Park Rd (46383-2737)
PHONE...........................219 510-5193
Zlata Krcma, *Pr*
Jan Krcma, *VP*
◆ **EMP:** 2 **EST:** 1988
SALES (est): 236.49K **Privately Held**
SIC: 3826 Gas testing apparatus

(G-16035)
REGAL BELOIT AMERICA INC
Also Called: McGill Manufacturing Company
2300 Evans Ave (46383-4054)
PHONE...........................219 465-2200
Jim Johnson, *Brnch Mgr*
EMP: 23
SALES (corp-wide): 6.25B **Publicly Held**
SIC: 3562 Ball and roller bearings
HQ: Regal Beloit America, Inc.
  111 W Michigan St
  Milwaukee WI 53203
  608 364-8800

(G-16036)
REGIONAL DEVELOPMENT COMPANY
1757 Thornapple Cir (46385-6164)
PHONE...........................219 476-0504
Tony Rodriguez, *Pr*
EMP: 1 **EST:** 2004
SALES (est): 606.46K **Privately Held**
Web: www.rdc504.org
SIC: 1222 Bituminous coal-underground mining

(G-16037)
RELIABLE INDUS SLS & SVC LLC
1707 Whittier Park Dr (46383-4037)
PHONE...........................219 929-8295
EMP: 4 **EST:** 2017
SALES (est): 70.58K **Privately Held**
Web: www.illianaindustrial.com
SIC: 7694 Electric motor repair

(G-16038)
RESPRIN INC
53 Jefferson St (46383-4761)
PHONE...........................219 996-5864
Rhys G Mussman, *Pr*
Margaret A Williford, *Prin*
EMP: 9 **EST:** 2007
SALES (est): 220.92K **Privately Held**
Web: www.resprin.com
SIC: 2833 Medicinals and botanicals

(G-16039)
RICH HALSTEAD
302 Morgan Blvd (46383-4853)
PHONE...........................219 462-8888
EMP: 2
SALES (est): 62.38K **Privately Held**
SIC: 2095 Roasted coffee

(G-16040)
ROBERT W SHEFFER
4411 Evans Ave (46383-8407)
PHONE...........................219 464-2095
Robert Sheffer, *Prin*
EMP: 9 **EST:** 2007
SALES (est): 143.9K **Privately Held**
SIC: 2499 Decorative wood and woodwork

(G-16041)
RUNNING VINES WINERY
15 Washington St (46383-4750)
PHONE...........................219 617-2429
EMP: 4 **EST:** 2019

SALES (est): 157.04K **Privately Held**
Web: www.runningvines.com
SIC: 2084 Wines

(G-16042)
SALT CREEK HARVEST LLC
Also Called: Salt Creek Harvest
314 W 700 N (46385-8403)
PHONE...........................708 927-5569
Noel Pol, *Pt*
Patricia Melanie Beauchamp, *Prin*
EMP: 2 **EST:** 2012
SALES (est): 145.08K **Privately Held**
SIC: 2426 5193 0252 Lumber, hardwood dimension; Flowers and nursery stock; Chicken eggs

(G-16043)
SEISMIC VISION LLC
967 Misty Glen Dr (46385-8870)
PHONE...........................219 548-8704
EMP: 2 **EST:** 2013
SALES (est): 83.2K **Privately Held**
SIC: 1382 Seismograph surveys

(G-16044)
SELLERS DENTAL LAB
378 E 400 N (46383-9708)
PHONE...........................219 465-8719
Robert Sellers, *Owner*
EMP: 1 **EST:** 1981
SALES (est): 76.67K **Privately Held**
SIC: 3843 8072 Dental equipment and supplies; Dental laboratories

(G-16045)
SENSIT TECHNOLOGIES LLC (HQ)
851 Transport Dr (46383-8432)
PHONE...........................219 465-2700
J Scott Kleppe, *Pr*
Steven Fullenkamp, *CFO*
Christine Murry, *Sec*
EMP: 16 **EST:** 2014
SQ FT: 28,000
SALES (est): 10.75MM
SALES (corp-wide): 2.58B **Privately Held**
Web: www.gasleaksensors.com
SIC: 3829 Measuring and controlling devices, nec
PA: Halma Public Limited Company
  Misbourne Court
  Amersham BUCKS HP7 0
  149 472-1111

(G-16046)
SEPARATION TECHNOLOGIES INC
463 E Us Highway 30 Ste 4 (46383-9586)
PHONE...........................219 548-5814
Deborah J Lamb, *Pr*
EMP: 2 **EST:** 1989
SQ FT: 2,000
SALES (est): 266.74K **Privately Held**
Web: www.separationtechnologies.com
SIC: 3677 5084 Filtration devices, electronic; Chemical process equipment

(G-16047)
SHARON S CHEESECAKES
2214 Dixon Dr (46383-3121)
PHONE...........................219 477-5773
EMP: 8 **EST:** 2008
SALES (est): 223.44K **Privately Held**
SIC: 2591 Window blinds

(G-16048)
SHINABARGAR CUSTOM STAIRS
176 Goodview Dr (46385-9611)
PHONE...........................219 462-1735
Gene Shinabargar, *Owner*
EMP: 3 **EST:** 2000

SALES (est): 215.51K **Privately Held**
SIC: 2431 Staircases and stairs, wood

(G-16049)
SHOREMET LLC
3601 Enterprise Ave (46383-8318)
PHONE..................................219 390-3336
Danny Mislenkov, *Pr*
Dana Cassidy, *VP*
EMP: 18 **EST:** 2010
SALES (est): 6.58MM **Privately Held**
Web: www.shoremet.com
SIC: 2819 Industrial inorganic chemicals, nec

(G-16050)
SIGN WRITE SIGNS LLC
1451 Joliet Rd (46385-5407)
PHONE..................................219 477-3840
EMP: 6 **EST:** 1983
SQ FT: 5,600
SALES (est): 376.56K **Privately Held**
SIC: 3993 1799 Electric signs; Sign installation and maintenance

(G-16051)
SIGNWORKS
2003 Calumet Ave (46383-2705)
PHONE..................................219 462-5353
EMP: 2 **EST:** 1986
SALES (est): 181.41K **Privately Held**
Web: www.signworksvalpo.com
SIC: 3993 Signs, not made in custom sign painting shops

(G-16052)
SIMPLY AMAZING
2801 Evans Ave (46383-6940)
PHONE..................................219 464-9621
EMP: 6 **EST:** 2017
SALES (est): 108.47K **Privately Held**
Web: www.dogoodies.org
SIC: 2064 Candy and other confectionery products

(G-16053)
SISTER PINES SIGNS)
875 Thoreau Trl (46383-7145)
PHONE..................................219 242-1824
Katie Rizer, *Prin*
EMP: 4 **EST:** 2018
SALES (est): 46.08K **Privately Held**
SIC: 3993 Signs and advertising specialties

(G-16054)
SMITH READY MIX INC (PA)
251 Lincolnway (46383-5525)
P.O. Box 489 (46384-0489)
PHONE..................................219 462-3191
Douglas Smith, *Pr*
David P Smith, *Sec*
Byron Smith Iii, *Treas*
Paul Manoski, *VP*
EMP: 15 **EST:** 1949
SQ FT: 11,000
SALES (est): 27.6MM
SALES (corp-wide): 27.6MM **Privately Held**
Web: www.smithreadymix.com
SIC: 3273 Ready-mixed concrete

(G-16055)
SPECIALTY FOOD GROUP LLC
463 E Us Highway 30 (46383-9585)
PHONE..................................219 531-2142
Bill Karris, *Brnch Mgr*
EMP: 68
SALES (corp-wide): 83.25MM **Privately Held**
Web: www.specialtyfoodsgroup.online

SIC: 2096 Corn chips and other corn-based snacks
HQ: Specialty Food Group, L.L.C.
14400 Nw 112th Ave
Hialeah FL 33018

(G-16056)
STAR TRACKS COMMAND
3705 Chimney Hill Dr (46383-0513)
PHONE..................................574 596-5331
EMP: 6 **EST:** 2011
SALES (est): 150K **Privately Held**
Web: www.startrackscommand.com
SIC: 3663 Mobile communication equipment

(G-16057)
STEELCO INDUSTRIAL LUBRICANTS
358 Ruge St (46385-6266)
P.O. Box 136 (46384-0136)
PHONE..................................219 462-0333
Donald Lee, *Pr*
C A Max, *VP*
EMP: 3 **EST:** 1991
SQ FT: 1,000
SALES (est): 467.78K **Privately Held**
Web: www.steelcolubricants.com
SIC: 2911 5085 Greases, lubricating; Industrial supplies

(G-16058)
STEELE ROOFING CO LLC
349-1 W 100 S (46385-9105)
PHONE..................................219 243-1563
EMP: 1
SALES (est): 60.62K **Privately Held**
SIC: 7389 1442 Business Activities at Non-Commercial Site; Construction sand and gravel

(G-16059)
STRADELLA STRING INSTRS INC
120 Sylvan Dr (46385-6075)
PHONE..................................219 464-3390
Larry Allen, *Pr*
EMP: 1 **EST:** 1997
SALES (est): 57.77K **Privately Held**
Web: www.stradellabooks.com
SIC: 3931 Guitars and parts, electric and nonelectric

(G-16060)
SUN COSMETICS LLC
4901 Evans Ave (46383-8383)
PHONE..................................219 531-5359
EMP: 54 **EST:** 2018
SALES (est): 7.87MM **Privately Held**
SIC: 2893 Printing ink
HQ: Sun Chemical Corporation
35 Waterview Blvd
Parsippany NJ 07054
973 404-6000

(G-16061)
SUNOCS LLC
5907 Murvihill Rd (46383-8376)
PHONE..................................219 286-7081
Rachel Sun, *Managing Member*
EMP: 3 **EST:** 2009
SALES (est): 452.03K **Privately Held**
Web: www.sunocs.com
SIC: 2899 Chemical preparations, nec

(G-16062)
SUPREME SIGNS INC
265 Springhill Dr (46385-8888)
PHONE..................................219 384-0198
Raymond Wlodarski, *Prin*
EMP: 3 **EST:** 2008
SALES (est): 246.96K **Privately Held**

SIC: 3993 Signs and advertising specialties

(G-16063)
TASK FORCE TIPS INC
Also Called: Production Dynamics
3701 Innovation Way (46383-8395)
PHONE..................................219 462-6161
Bob Allen, *Mgr*
EMP: 10
SALES (corp-wide): 99.81MM **Privately Held**
Web: www.tft.com
SIC: 3429 3599 Nozzles, fire fighting; Machine shop, jobbing and repair
PA: Task Force Tips Llc
3701 Innovation Way
Valparaiso IN 46383
219 462-6161

(G-16064)
TASK FORCE TIPS LLC (PA)
3701 Innovation Way (46383-8395)
PHONE..................................219 462-6161
Stewart G Mcmillan, *Pr*
Julie Behnke, *
Rod Carringer, *
Martin Sonnenberg, *
◆ **EMP:** 195 **EST:** 1971
SQ FT: 175,000
SALES (est): 99.81MM
SALES (corp-wide): 99.81MM **Privately Held**
Web: www.tft.com
SIC: 3429 3569 Nozzles, fire fighting; Firefighting and related equipment

(G-16065)
THOMAS R CLARK
Also Called: Industrial Chemical & Envmt Co
1812 Beech St (46383-5310)
PHONE..................................219 508-7412
EMP: 1 **EST:** 2011
SALES (est): 66.56K **Privately Held**
SIC: 2819 Industrial inorganic chemicals, nec

(G-16066)
THORGREN TOOL & MOLDING CO
912 Roosevelt Rd (46383-4346)
PHONE..................................219 462-1801
EMP: 8 **EST:** 2018
SALES (est): 127.38K **Privately Held**
Web: www.thorgren.com
SIC: 3089 Injection molding of plastics

(G-16067)
THORGREN TOOL & MOLDING CO
1100 Evans Ave (46383-3717)
PHONE..................................219 462-1801
Robert G Thorgren Junior, *Pr*
Tyler Thorgren, *Prin*
◆ **EMP:** 96 **EST:** 1943
SQ FT: 100,000
SALES (est): 21.55MM **Privately Held**
Web: www.thorgren.com
SIC: 3089 3544 2221 Injection molding of plastics; Special dies, tools, jigs, and fixtures; Broadwoven fabric mills, manmade

(G-16068)
TIMES 10 ASSOCIATES LLC
Also Called: Greaseco
1101 Cumberland Xing Ste 252 (46383-2356)
PHONE..................................800 773-6432
Garry Adams, *Managing Member*
EMP: 4 **EST:** 2013
SALES (est): 500K **Privately Held**
Web: www.times-10.com
SIC: 2911 Greases, lubricating

(G-16069)
TOP DESIGN CNC INC
41 N 400 E (46383-0618)
PHONE..................................219 662-2915
Michael Pavlo, *Pr*
Chris Pavlo, *VP*
EMP: 5 **EST:** 1992
SQ FT: 1,500
SALES (est): 455.73K **Privately Held**
SIC: 2599 3131 Cabinets, factory; Counters

(G-16070)
UFS CORPORATION
330 N 400 E (46383-9704)
PHONE..................................219 464-2027
H Frederick Hess Iii, *Pr*
Julia F Hess, *Sec*
▲ **EMP:** 11 **EST:** 1977
SQ FT: 6,000
SALES (est): 2.59MM **Privately Held**
Web: www.ufsc.com
SIC: 3559 Paint making machinery

(G-16071)
UNION ELECTRIC STEEL CORP
3702 Montdale Dr (46383)
P.O. Box 29 (46384-0029)
PHONE..................................219 464-1031
Barry Kahot, *Mgr*
EMP: 1
SALES (corp-wide): 422.34MM **Publicly Held**
Web: www.uniones.com
SIC: 3325 3462 3312 Rolling mill rolls, cast steel; Iron and steel forgings; Blast furnaces and steel mills
HQ: Union Electric Steel Corporation
726 Bell Ave Ste 101
Carnegie PA 15106
412 429-7655

(G-16072)
UNITED MACHINE CORPORATION
753 Axe Ave (46383-6477)
PHONE..................................219 548-8050
EMP: 24 **EST:** 1995
SQ FT: 30,000
SALES (est): 361.01K **Privately Held**
Web: www.unitedmachinecorp.com
SIC: 3599 3542 7629 Machine shop, jobbing and repair; Machine tools, metal forming type; Electrical repair shops

(G-16073)
USKERT WELDING
211 N 750 W (46385-9255)
PHONE..................................219 759-2794
Thomas Uskert, *Prin*
EMP: 1 **EST:** 2008
SALES (est): 41.52K **Privately Held**
SIC: 7692 Welding repair

(G-16074)
VALPARAISO II LLC
2710 Laporte Ave (46383-6975)
PHONE..................................219 464-0431
Bill Oeding, *Prin*
EMP: 1 **EST:** 2006
SALES (est): 80.3K **Privately Held**
SIC: 3421 Table and food cutlery, including butchers'

(G-16075)
VEOLIA WTS USA INC
Also Called: Betzdearborn Division
109 Fairview Ave (46383-6362)
PHONE..................................219 746-4060
Wanda Moroz, *Brnch Mgr*
EMP: 1
Web: www.watertechnologies.com

GEOGRAPHIC SECTION

Versailles - Ripley County (G-16102)

SIC: 2899 Sizes
HQ: Veolia Wts Usa, Inc.
3600 Horizon Blvd
Trevose PA 19053
866 439-2837

(G-16076)
VINTAGE BAKED MODERN LLC
601 Lincolnway Ste 1e (46383-5410)
PHONE..................................219 252-9820
Apryl S Niksch, CEO
EMP: 4 EST: 2020
SALES (est): 79.93K **Privately Held**
Web: www.vintagebakedmodern.com
SIC: 2045 Prepared flour mixes and doughs

(G-16077)
VITAL SIGNS LLC
4411 Evans Ave Ste D (46383-8411)
PHONE..................................219 548-1605
Steve Jacobs, Owner
EMP: 3 EST: 1993
SALES (est): 198.87K **Privately Held**
Web: www.vitalsignsin.com
SIC: 3993 Signs, not made in custom sign painting shops

(G-16078)
WARD ELECTRIC LLC
1858 Hayes Leonard Rd (46385-6012)
PHONE..................................219 462-8780
Mark Ward, Owner
EMP: 1 EST: 1990
SALES (est): 97.24K **Privately Held**
Web: www.wardelectriccompany.com
SIC: 3634 Electric housewares and fans

(G-16079)
WATERAX CORPORATION
Also Called: Waterax
3701 Innovation Way (46383-9327)
PHONE..................................360 574-1818
▲ EMP: 4 EST: 2010
SALES (est): 951.22K **Privately Held**
Web: www.waterax.com
SIC: 3561 Pumps and pumping equipment

(G-16080)
WEGENER STEEL AND FABRICATING
906 Evans Ave (46383-3797)
PHONE..................................219 462-3911
Ed Cobb, Pr
EMP: 9 EST: 1944
SQ FT: 21,000
SALES (est): 2.37MM **Privately Held**
Web: www.wegenersteel.com
SIC: 5051 3324 Steel; Steel investment foundries

(G-16081)
WILLIAM H SADLIER INC
4405 Blair Ln (46383-9166)
PHONE..................................219 465-0453
Mike Collins, Prin
EMP: 2 EST: 2010
SALES (est): 60.58K **Privately Held**
Web: www.sadlier.com
SIC: 2731 Books, publishing only

(G-16082)
X-L BOX INC
1035 N State Road 149 (46385-8518)
PHONE..................................219 763-3736
James G Kyle, Pr
Christopher Peres, *
EMP: 16 EST: 1991
SQ FT: 12,000
SALES (est): 415.58K **Privately Held**

SIC: 2448 7699 Pallets, wood; Pallet repair

(G-16083)
ZIMMER BIOMET HIBBARD LLC
3209 Cascade Dr Ste H (46383)
PHONE..................................800 352-2982
EMP: 8 EST: 2019
SALES (est): 147.67K **Privately Held**
Web: www.zimmerbiomet.com
SIC: 3842 Orthopedic appliances

Van Buren
Grant County

(G-16084)
DADS CUSTOM INTERCOOLER TANKS
4473 N 700 E (46991-9712)
PHONE..................................765 243-9070
Donny Dailey, Owner
EMP: 6 EST: 2015
SALES (est): 71.89K **Privately Held**
Web: www.dadscustomintercoolertank.com
SIC: 3443 Fabricated plate work (boiler shop)

(G-16085)
HUNTINGTON TOOL & DIE INC
9742 E 700 N (46991-9738)
PHONE..................................260 356-5940
Mark L Thompson, Pr
Jane Spears, Mgr
EMP: 10 EST: 1965
SALES (est): 842.52K **Privately Held**
SIC: 3544 Special dies and tools

(G-16086)
MODERN MACHINE & TOOL INC
106 W Main St (46991-7013)
P.O. Box 318 (46991-0318)
PHONE..................................765 934-3110
Darroll Korporal, Pr
EMP: 9 EST: 1999
SALES (est): 1.43MM **Privately Held**
Web: www.modernmachinevb.com
SIC: 3599 Machine shop, jobbing and repair

Veedersburg
Fountain County

(G-16087)
GOINGS PROPERTIES LLC
450 E Division Rd (47987-8312)
PHONE..................................765 294-2380
Jerry D Goings, Prin
EMP: 3 EST: 2005
SALES (est): 194.26K **Privately Held**
Web: www.donovanconstructionllc.com
SIC: 2434 Wood kitchen cabinets

(G-16088)
GOLDSTAR TRUSS LLC
2302 S Us Highway 41 (47987-8024)
PHONE..................................765 366-2679
EMP: 8 EST: 2019
SALES (est): 718.98K **Privately Held**
Web: www.goldstartruss.com
SIC: 2439 Trusses, wooden roof

(G-16089)
PAYTONS BARBECUE INC
119 E Washington St (47987-1551)
P.O. Box 97 (47993-0097)
PHONE..................................765 294-2716
Marylin Payton, Owner
EMP: 7 EST: 1953
SQ FT: 4,000

SALES (est): 801.88K **Privately Held**
Web: www.paytonsbbq.com
SIC: 2013 2099 Prepared pork products, from purchased pork; Food preparations, nec

(G-16090)
ROBERT WARRICK
Also Called: Twin W Enterprise
100 N Eagle St (47987-8201)
PHONE..................................765 294-4335
Robert Warrick, Owner
EMP: 1 EST: 2001
SALES (est): 56.49K **Privately Held**
SIC: 7692 Welding repair

(G-16091)
STERLING SALES AND ENGRG INC
324 S Sterling Ave (47987-8210)
P.O. Box 164 (47987-0164)
PHONE..................................765 376-0454
Robert Gross, Pr
Scott Bratcher, Treas
Kathleen Gross, Sec
EMP: 2 EST: 1999
SALES (est): 415.32K **Privately Held**
Web: www.sterlingsalesinc.com
SIC: 5051 3366 Foundry products; Brass foundry, nec

(G-16092)
WRIB MANUFACTURING INC
110 E Jackson St (47987-1520)
P.O. Box 246 (47987-0246)
PHONE..................................765 294-2841
Joshua Rubin, Pr
Jeff Rubin, Sec
EMP: 3 EST: 1977
SALES (est): 458.83K **Privately Held**
Web: www.wribmfg.com
SIC: 3559 7692 3441 3325 Foundry machinery and equipment; Welding repair; Fabricated structural metal; Steel foundries, nec

Velpen
Pike County

(G-16093)
JTEX CNSTR & CONSULTING LLC
9841 E County Road 850 S (47590-8856)
PHONE..................................812 486-9123
Amanda John, Adm/Asst
EMP: 1 EST: 2015
SALES (est): 50.76K **Privately Held**
SIC: 8742 7389 1389 Management consulting services; Business Activities at Non-Commercial Site; Construction, repair, and dismantling services

(G-16094)
LOUANNA STILWELL
6451 S County Road 1075 E (47590-8847)
PHONE..................................812 631-0647
EMP: 3 EST: 2010
SALES (est): 138.51K **Privately Held**
SIC: 2411 Logging

(G-16095)
WRAITH ARMS RESOLUTIONS LLC
9602 E 475s (47590-9626)
PHONE..................................812 380-1208
Jesse Smith, CEO
EMP: 3 EST: 2017
SALES (est): 210.53K **Privately Held**
SIC: 3484 Guns (firearms) or gun parts, 30 mm. and below

Vernon
Jennings County

(G-16096)
INDIANA SPIKE & RAIL CO LLC
39 N Pike St (47282-9700)
PHONE..................................812 352-7349
Jaime Deen, Pr
EMP: 6 EST: 2017
SALES (est): 90.89K **Privately Held**
SIC: 3312 Rails, rerolled or renewed

(G-16097)
LONE STAR TOOL & DIE WELD
432 4th St (47282)
PHONE..................................812 346-9681
John Raymer, Owner
John Raymer, Prin
EMP: 7 EST: 2006
SALES (est): 166.86K **Privately Held**
SIC: 3544 Special dies and tools

(G-16098)
QUALITY MOLD AND ENGRG INC
230 N State Highways 3 & 7 (47282)
P.O. Box 202 (47282-0202)
PHONE..................................812 346-6577
EMP: 7 EST: 1995
SQ FT: 3,000
SALES (est): 490.76K **Privately Held**
Web: www.quality-molds.com
SIC: 3544 Special dies and tools

Versailles
Ripley County

(G-16099)
ELGIN FASTENER GROUP LLC
1415 S Benham Rd (47042-8411)
PHONE..................................812 689-8917
EMP: 1
SALES (corp-wide): 406.38MM **Privately Held**
Web: www.mwcomponents.com
SIC: 3399 3452 Metal fasteners; Bolts, metal
HQ: Elgin Fastener Group, Llc
288 Holbrook Dr
Wheeling IL 60090

(G-16100)
HEIDELBERG MTLS MDWEST AGG INC
606 W County Road 300 S (47042-9152)
PHONE..................................812 689-5017
Neal Allen, Mgr
EMP: 1
SALES (corp-wide): 23.02B **Privately Held**
Web: www.heidelbergmaterials.us
SIC: 3273 Ready-mixed concrete
HQ: Heidelberg Materials Midwest Agg, Inc.
300 E John Carpenter Fwy
Irving TX

(G-16101)
IRON TIMBERS LLC
342 Harvest Ct (47042-9087)
PHONE..................................812 614-0467
Dustin Payne, Managing Member
EMP: 5 EST: 2017
SALES (est): 129.48K **Privately Held**
Web: www.irontimbers.com
SIC: 2431 Millwork

(G-16102)
MIRRUS CORPORATION INC
225 N Us Highway 421 (47042-9014)
P.O. Box 175 (47042-0175)

Versailles - Ripley County (G-16103)

PHONE..........................812 689-1411
Russell Stenger, *Pr*
EMP: 15 **EST:** 1999
SQ FT: 10,000
SALES (est): 2.26MM **Privately Held**
Web: www.mirruscorp.com
SIC: 5013 3711 Automotive engines and engine parts; Automobile assembly, including specialty automobiles

(G-16103)
RIPLEY PUBLISHING CO INC
Also Called: Osgood Journal
115 S Washington St (47042-8016)
P.O. Box 158 (47042-0158)
PHONE..........................812 689-6364
Linda Chandler, *Pr*
Gene Demaree, *Pr*
Dorothy Craig, *Sec*
Linda Chandler, *Publisher*
Jo Jean Demaree, *VP*
EMP: 10 **EST:** 1902
SALES (est): 466.18K **Privately Held**
Web: www.ripleynews.com
SIC: 2711 Newspapers: publishing only, not printed on site

(G-16104)
T & M PRECISION INC (PA)
Also Called: Gutman, Anthony & Mary
1861 S Us Highway 421 (47042-8302)
PHONE..........................812 689-5769
Anthony Gutman, *Owner*
EMP: 2 **EST:** 1991
SALES (est): 475.43K **Privately Held**
Web: www.tandmprecision.com
SIC: 3599 Custom machinery

(G-16105)
T & M PRECISION INC
1861 S Us Highway 421 (47042-8302)
PHONE..........................513 253-2274
Mary Gutman, *Brnch Mgr*
EMP: 3
Web: www.tandmprecision.com
SIC: 3599 Machine shop, jobbing and repair
PA: T & M Precision, Inc.
  1861 S Us Highway 421
  Versailles IN 47042

Vevay
Switzerland County

(G-16106)
BESI MANUFACTURING INC
503 Vineyard St (47043-1050)
PHONE..........................812 427-4114
Gary Pavy, *Mgr*
EMP: 4
SALES (corp-wide): 9.74MM **Privately Held**
Web: www.besi-inc.com
SIC: 3711 Buses, all types, assembly of
PA: Besi Manufacturing Inc
  9087 Sutton Pl
  West Chester OH 45011
  513 874-0232

(G-16107)
COUNTRYMARK LOG HOMES INC
5112 Parks Ridge Rd (47043-8703)
PHONE..........................866 468-3301
Thomas E Demaree, *Pr*
EMP: 5 **EST:** 2017
SALES (est): 209.83K **Privately Held**
Web: www.countrymarkloghomes.com
SIC: 2452 Log cabins, prefabricated, wood

(G-16108)
CROSS COUNTRY HARDWOOD LLC
Also Called: Hardwood Flooring
10071 Bill Peelman Rd (47043-2659)
PHONE..........................812 571-4226
Nathan E Miller, *Pr*
Betty Miller, *VP*
EMP: 12 **EST:** 2013
SQ FT: 2,200
SALES (est): 1.05MM **Privately Held**
SIC: 2426 Flooring, hardwood

(G-16109)
FERRY STREET WOODWORKS
319 Ferry St (47043-1103)
PHONE..........................812 427-9663
EMP: 2 **EST:** 2011
SALES (est): 175.9K **Privately Held**
SIC: 2431 Millwork

(G-16110)
HERITAGE LOG HOMES
10648 Stevens Rd (47043-2809)
PHONE..........................812 427-2591
Tony Fisher, *Prin*
EMP: 5 **EST:** 2006
SALES (est): 200.24K **Privately Held**
SIC: 2452 Log cabins, prefabricated, wood

(G-16111)
RIDGE WINERY INC
227 Parks Ridge Rd (47043-8701)
PHONE..........................812 427-3380
Mary Jane Demaree, *Pr*
Tom Demaree, *Sec*
EMP: 2 **EST:** 1989
SALES (est): 146.25K **Privately Held**
Web: www.theridgewinery.com
SIC: 2084 Wines

(G-16112)
SPIRAL-FAB INC
14679 Upper Tinker Rd (47043-9346)
PHONE..........................812 427-3006
EMP: 5
Web: www.spiral-fab.com
SIC: 3444 Sheet metalwork

(G-16113)
SWISS ALPS PRINTING INC
Also Called: Swiss Alps Printing & Off Sups
108 W Pike St (47043-1132)
P.O. Box 13 (47043-0013)
PHONE..........................812 427-3844
Tonya Krall, *Pr*
EMP: 3 **EST:** 1972
SQ FT: 2,000
SALES (est): 328.62K **Privately Held**
Web: www.swissalpsprinting.com
SIC: 2752 Offset printing

(G-16114)
VEVAY NEWSPAPERS INC
111 W Market St (47043-1159)
P.O. Box 157 (47043-0157)
PHONE..........................812 427-2311
Jane W Jacobs, *Pr*
Don R Wallis Senior, *Sec*
EMP: 6 **EST:** 1959
SALES (est): 374.56K **Privately Held**
Web: www.vevaynewspapers.com
SIC: 2711 Newspapers, publishing and printing

Vincennes
Knox County

(G-16115)
BIRDEYE INC
Also Called: Waggway Tool
483 N Mount Zion Rd (47591-9683)
PHONE..........................812 886-0598
Craig Waggoner, *Pr*
Jamie Waggoner, *Sec*
EMP: 10 **EST:** 1997
SALES (est): 971.23K **Privately Held**
Web: www.birdeye.com
SIC: 3531 Construction machinery

(G-16116)
C & S SOLUTIONS LLC
2064 N Old Highway 41 (47591-8926)
P.O. Box 33 (47591-0033)
PHONE..........................812 895-0048
Steven E Howder, *Prin*
EMP: 5 **EST:** 2004
SALES (est): 427.95K **Privately Held**
Web: www.cssolutions.biz
SIC: 7372 Prepackaged software

(G-16117)
CELESTIAL CANDLE
138 E 17th St (47591-4300)
PHONE..........................812 886-4819
D M Sprinkle, *Prin*
EMP: 5 **EST:** 2001
SALES (est): 211.68K **Privately Held**
SIC: 3999 Candles

(G-16118)
DANIEL STEFFY
3572 N Bruceville Rd (47591-9029)
PHONE..........................812 726-4769
EMP: 3 **EST:** 1960
SALES (est): 119.3K **Privately Held**
SIC: 2411 0115 0116 0111 Logging camps and contractors; Corn; Soybeans; Wheat

(G-16119)
ENERGY DRILLING LLC
1290 N State Road 67 (47591-8011)
PHONE..........................618 943-5314
Donald E Jones Junior, *Managing Member*
EMP: 4 **EST:** 2011
SALES (est): 296.18K **Privately Held**
Web: www.energydrilling.com
SIC: 1381 Drilling oil and gas wells

(G-16120)
EWING PRINTING COMPANY INC
516 Vigo St (47591-1145)
P.O. Box 537 (47591-0537)
PHONE..........................812 882-2415
Jim Zeigler, *Pr*
Jerry Zeigler, *VP*
EMP: 19 **EST:** 1961
SALES (est): 913.11K **Privately Held**
Web: www.ewingprinting.com
SIC: 2752 2796 2791 2789 Offset printing; Platemaking services; Typesetting; Bookbinding and related work

(G-16121)
EXCELL USA INC
1065 E Beckes Ln (47591-8029)
PHONE..........................812 895-1687
John Davis, *CEO*
Mokoto Yamaguchi, *
Motohiro Abe, *
Tatsuya Nakagawa, *
Gota Nakagawa, *Prin*
◆ **EMP:** 100 **EST:** 1998
SQ FT: 40,000
SALES (est): 23.16MM **Privately Held**
SIC: 3069 Floor coverings, rubber
PA: Excell Corporation
  2-10-2, Kyobashi
  Chuo-Ku TKY 104-0

(G-16122)
EXPRESS PRESS INC
Also Called: Express Signs
2129 Washington Ave (47591-4947)
PHONE..........................812 882-3278
Brian Phillips, *Pr*
EMP: 7 **EST:** 1988
SQ FT: 2,200
SALES (est): 602K **Privately Held**
Web: www.express-press.com
SIC: 2752 7334 Offset printing; Photocopying and duplicating services

(G-16123)
EXPRESS SIGN & NEON LLC
119 S 15th St (47591-5421)
PHONE..........................812 882-0104
Brian Phillips, *Owner*
EMP: 5 **EST:** 2007
SALES (est): 417.57K **Privately Held**
Web: www.expresssignandneon.com
SIC: 3993 Neon signs

(G-16124)
EYC DRONES LLC
1834 S Old Us 41 Ste 1 (47591-6129)
PHONE..........................812 890-9068
EMP: 4
SALES (est): 78.58K **Privately Held**
SIC: 3728 Aircraft parts and equipment, nec

(G-16125)
FORD SAWMILLS INC
2019 E Old Terre Haute Rd (47591-6825)
PHONE..........................812 324-2134
David Ford, *Pr*
Emily Ridgley, *
John Ford, *
EMP: 18 **EST:** 1969
SQ FT: 64,000
SALES (est): 394.1K **Privately Held**
Web: www.fordsawmills.com
SIC: 2448 2426 Pallets, wood; Hardwood dimension and flooring mills

(G-16126)
FRANKLIN WELL SERVICE LLC
400 Main St (47591-2020)
P.O. Box 237 (47591-0237)
PHONE..........................877 943-4680
Mark A Jones, *Asst Sec*
Roger Meier, *Genl Mgr*
EMP: 16 **EST:** 1994
SALES (est): 4.98MM **Privately Held**
Web: www.franklinwell.com
SIC: 1389 Oil field services, nec

(G-16127)
FUTABA INDIANA AMERICA CORP
3320 S Keller Rd (47591-7630)
PHONE..........................812 895-4700
Hiroharu Murahashi, *Pr*
Masumi Ishikawa, *
Hiroshi Ishikawa, *
Shingo Tsuchiya, *
T Sanmiya, *
▲ **EMP:** 500 **EST:** 2001
SQ FT: 400,000
SALES (est): 96.57MM **Privately Held**
Web: www.futabaindiana.com
SIC: 3089 3465 2396 Automotive parts, plastic; Body parts, automobile: stamped metal; Automotive and apparel trimmings
HQ: Fic America Corp.
  485 E Lies Rd

GEOGRAPHIC SECTION

Vincennes - Knox County (G-16150)

Carol Stream IL 60188

(G-16128)
HICKORY CORNER CUSTOM WLDG LLC
5041 S Hickory Corner Rd (47591-8805)
PHONE..................812 890-2926
Justin Downey, Prin
EMP: 1 EST: 2010
SALES (est): 56.36K Privately Held
SIC: 7692 Welding repair

(G-16129)
HOOSIER FAMILY LIVING LLC
P.O. Box 131 (47591-0131)
PHONE..................812 396-7880
Laneal Evans, Publisher
EMP: 7 EST: 2007
SQ FT: 1,500
SALES (est): 243.58K Privately Held
SIC: 3999 Advertising display products

(G-16130)
HURRICANE DITCHER COMPANY INC
2425 S Cathlinette Rd (47591-5572)
PHONE..................812 886-9663
John L Snyder, Pr
Paul M Snyder, Sec
Virgina Snyder, VP
EMP: 15 EST: 1984
SQ FT: 14,450
SALES (est): 2.39MM Privately Held
Web: www.hurricane-ditcher.com
SIC: 3531 3523 Entrenching machines; Farm machinery and equipment

(G-16131)
INDIANA NEWSPAPERS LLC
Also Called: Vincennes Sun-Commercial
702 Main St (47591-2910)
P.O. Box 396 (47591-0396)
PHONE..................812 886-9955
Michael E Quayle, Brnch Mgr
EMP: 80
SALES (corp-wide): 2.66B Publicly Held
Web: www.indystar.com
SIC: 2711 2791 2752 Newspapers, publishing and printing; Typesetting; Commercial printing, lithographic
HQ: Indiana Newspapers Llc
130 S Meridian St
Indianapolis IN 46225
317 444-4000

(G-16132)
JACQMAIN MACHINE & WELDING
1070 N Mcclure Rd (47591-9252)
PHONE..................812 726-4409
Andrew Jacqmain, Owner
EMP: 1 EST: 1997
SALES (est): 87.37K Privately Held
SIC: 3599 Machine shop, jobbing and repair

(G-16133)
JAY C FOOD 84
1400 Washington Ave (47591-2256)
PHONE..................812 886-9311
Jess Hendershot, Mgr
EMP: 7 EST: 2010
SALES (est): 123.1K Privately Held
SIC: 2051 Cakes, bakery: except frozen

(G-16134)
JFS MILLING INC
3672 S Keller Rd (47591-7620)
P.O. Box 1400 (47591-7400)
PHONE..................812 683-4200
Ted J Seger, Brnch Mgr
EMP: 2

SALES (corp-wide): 2.46MM Privately Held
Web: www.farbestfoods.com
SIC: 5144 2015 Poultry and poultry products ; Poultry slaughtering and processing
PA: Jfs Milling, Inc.
5570 E Kalb Zehr Rd
Dubois IN 47527
812 678-2402

(G-16135)
JONES & SONS INC
Also Called: JONES & SONS, INC.
784 S 6th Street Rd (47591-9246)
P.O. Box 671 (47591-0671)
PHONE..................812 882-2957
Aaron Alrnes, Brnch Mgr
EMP: 33
SALES (corp-wide): 18.09MM Privately Held
Web: www.jonesandsons.com
SIC: 3273 5032 3446 3272 Ready-mixed concrete; Stone, crushed or broken; Architectural metalwork; Concrete products, nec
PA: Jones And Sons, Inc.
1262 S State Road 57
Washington IN 47501
812 254-4731

(G-16136)
KNOX CNTY ASSN FOR RMRKBLE CTZ (PA)
Also Called: KCARC
2525 N 6th St (47591-2405)
PHONE..................812 886-4312
Michael R Carney, Pr
EMP: 100 EST: 1972
SALES (est): 19.96MM
SALES (corp-wide): 19.96MM Privately Held
Web: www.knoxcountyarc.com
SIC: 8322 2448 2441 Association for the handicapped; Skids, wood and metal combination; Ammunition boxes, wood

(G-16137)
LEWIS BROTHERS BAKERIES INC
Also Called: Lewis Bakeries
2792 S Old Decker Rd (47591-7603)
PHONE..................812 886-6533
Carl Finfrock, Genl Mgr
EMP: 175
SQ FT: 4,000
SALES (corp-wide): 9.76MM Privately Held
Web: www.lewisbakeries.net
SIC: 5149 2053 2051 Bakery products; Frozen bakery products, except bread; Bread, cake, and related products
PA: Lewis Brothers Bakeries Inc
500 N Fulton Ave
Evansville IN 47710
812 425-4642

(G-16138)
M & D DRAPERIES
2022 Jackson Dr (47591-5921)
PHONE..................812 886-4608
Ruth Bard, Prin
EMP: 3 EST: 2003
SALES (est): 107.62K Privately Held
SIC: 2391 Curtains and draperies

(G-16139)
MIDWEST FAST STRUCTURES LLC
2341 S Old Decker Rd (47591-6122)
PHONE..................812 886-3060
Rex Alton, Pr
EMP: 2 EST: 2009
SQ FT: 36,000

SALES (est): 177.51K Privately Held
SIC: 2452 Prefabricated wood buildings

(G-16140)
MILLER MACHINE AND WELDING LLC
2610 S Old Decker Rd (47591-7604)
PHONE..................812 882-7566
Rick Miller, Owner
EMP: 6 EST: 1965
SQ FT: 10,000
SALES (est): 494.04K Privately Held
Web: www.millermw.com
SIC: 7692 3599 Welding repair; Machine shop, jobbing and repair

(G-16141)
OPTIVIZ MEDIA LLC
1420 Wheeler St (47591-4348)
PHONE..................812 681-1711
Matthew Ramsey, Pr
EMP: 1 EST: 2021
SALES (est): 55.05K Privately Held
SIC: 4899 2759 5199 3861 Communication services, nec; Advertising literature: printing, nsk; Calendars; Printing frames, photographic

(G-16142)
PACKAGING CORPORATION AMERICA
Pca/Vincennes 390
408 E Saint Clair St (47591-2364)
P.O. Box 786 (47591-0786)
PHONE..................812 882-7631
Bob Muffat, Mgr
EMP: 117
SALES (corp-wide): 8.48B Publicly Held
Web: www.packagingcorp.com
SIC: 2653 Boxes, corrugated: made from purchased materials
PA: Packaging Corporation Of America
1 N Field Ct
Lake Forest IL 60045
847 482-3000

(G-16143)
PERDUE FARMS INC
Also Called: Perdue Farms
500 Perdue Rd (47591-9373)
PHONE..................812 886-0593
John Snyder, Mgr
EMP: 86
SALES (corp-wide): 1.24B Privately Held
Web: www.perdue.com
SIC: 2015 Poultry slaughtering and processing
PA: Perdue Farms Incorporated
31149 Old Ocean City Rd
Salisbury MD 21804
800 473-7383

(G-16144)
PIONEER OIL COMPANY INC
Also Called: Don Jones Oil Company
400 Main St (47591-2020)
P.O. Box 237 (47591-0237)
PHONE..................812 494-2800
Donald E Jones Junior, Pr
Debra L Jones, Sec
Mark Jones, VP
Brent Jones, VP
Jenna Sibert, VP
EMP: 16 EST: 1972
SQ FT: 15,600
SALES (est): 2.47MM Privately Held
Web: www.pioneeroil.net
SIC: 1382 Oil and gas exploration services

(G-16145)
PIONEER OILFIELD SERVICES LLC
1290 N State Road 67 (47591-8011)
P.O. Box 237 (47591-0237)
PHONE..................812 882-0999
Donald E Jones Junior, Pr
Mark Jones, *
Brent Jones, *
EMP: 15 EST: 2005
SALES (est): 1.76MM Privately Held
Web: www.pioneeroilfieldservices.org
SIC: 1389 Oil field services, nec

(G-16146)
PPG ARCHITECTURAL FINISHES INC
Also Called: Porter Paints
417 Main St (47591-2006)
PHONE..................812 882-0440
Bill Swain, Mgr
EMP: 3
SALES (corp-wide): 17.65B Publicly Held
Web: www.ppgpaints.com
SIC: 2851 Paints and allied products
HQ: Ppg Architectural Finishes, Inc.
1 Ppg Pl
Pittsburgh PA 15272
412 434-3131

(G-16147)
PPG INDUSTRIES INC
Also Called: PPG 4379
417 Main St (47591-2006)
PHONE..................812 882-0440
Bill Swain, Brnch Mgr
EMP: 4
SALES (corp-wide): 17.65B Publicly Held
Web: www.ppgpaints.com
SIC: 2851 Paints and allied products
PA: Ppg Industries, Inc.
1 Ppg Pl
Pittsburgh PA 15272
412 434-3131

(G-16148)
PRECISION SPRAY LLC
2474 N Palomino Dr (47591-8929)
PHONE..................812 830-8443
Codey Mccoy, Prin
EMP: 5 EST: 2018
SALES (est): 82.22K Privately Held
Web: www.spray.com
SIC: 3499 Fabricated metal products, nec

(G-16149)
REX ALTON & COMPANIES INC
Also Called: Rex Alton Trucking
2341 S Old Decker Rd (47591-6122)
PHONE..................812 882-8519
Rex Alton, Pr
Rita Alton, Sec
EMP: 19 EST: 1927
SQ FT: 32,000
SALES (est): 890.81K Privately Held
Web: www.rexaltoncompanies.com
SIC: 1771 1442 4212 1721 Concrete work; Construction sand and gravel; Local trucking, without storage; Industrial painting

(G-16150)
ROGERS GROUP INC
Also Called: Knox City Sand & Gravel
1200 S 6th St (47591-9382)
P.O. Box 943 (47591-0943)
PHONE..................812 882-3640
Maurice Holscher, Pr
EMP: 24
SALES (corp-wide): 1.05B Privately Held
Web: www.rogersgroupincint.com

Vincennes - Knox County (G-16151)

SIC: 2951 1771 3274 2875 Asphalt and asphaltic paving mixtures (not from refineries); Blacktop (asphalt) work; Lime; Fertilizers, mixing only
PA: Rogers Group, Inc.
421 Great Cir Rd
Nashville TN 37228
615 242-0585

(G-16151)
SCALES AND MORE
Also Called: Ritecount
1098 E Beckes Ln (47591-8029)
PHONE..................................812 886-4245
Kim Barmes, Owner
▲ EMP: 1 EST: 2005
SALES (est): 18.78K Privately Held
Web: www.usbalance.com
SIC: 3578 Coin counters

(G-16152)
SCHOTT GEMTRON CORPORATION
Schott Hometech North America
2000 Chestnut St (47591-1760)
P.O. Box 317 (47591-0317)
PHONE..................................812 882-2680
Dale Biehl, Mgr
EMP: 500
SQ FT: 275,000
SALES (corp-wide): 482.27MM Privately Held
Web: www.sswtechnologies.com
SIC: 3231 Tempered glass: made from purchased glass
HQ: Schott Gemtron Corporation
615 Highway 68
Sweetwater TN 37874
423 337-3522

(G-16153)
SHAAL JOHN
503 Grouseland Dr (47591-5134)
PHONE..................................812 882-2396
John Shall, Owner
EMP: 1 EST: 1998
SALES (est): 60.89K Privately Held
SIC: 1241 Mine preparation services

(G-16154)
SHIRT PRINT AVE
2038 Washington Ave (47591-4949)
PHONE..................................812 882-9610
David Ray, Owner
EMP: 1 EST: 1992
SALES (est): 146.08K Privately Held
Web: www.shirtprintavenue.com
SIC: 2752 2211 Commercial printing, lithographic; Print cloths, cotton

(G-16155)
SLICERS
2715 Washington Ave (47591-3657)
PHONE..................................812 255-0655
Mark E Melton, Prin
EMP: 2 EST: 2012
SALES (est): 95.39K Privately Held
SIC: 3799 Recreational vehicles

(G-16156)
SUNRISE ENERGY LLC
1290 N State Road 67 (47591)
P.O. Box 237 (47591)
PHONE..................................812 886-9990
Don Jones, Owner
Donald Jones, Pr
EMP: 5 EST: 2010
SALES (est): 452.4K Privately Held
Web: www.sunrise-energy.net
SIC: 1389 Oil and gas wells: building, repairing and dismantling

(G-16157)
TABCO BUSINESS FORMS INC
638 Broadway St (47591-2028)
PHONE..................................812 882-2836
Brad Pilyeu, Pr
Kris K, VP
EMP: 4 EST: 1959
SQ FT: 7,000
SALES (est): 485.47K
SALES (corp-wide): 9.13MM Privately Held
SIC: 2752 2791 2789 2759 Offset printing; Typesetting; Bookbinding and related work; Commercial printing, nec
PA: Tabco Business Forms, Inc.
1100 S State Road 46
Terre Haute IN 47803
812 232-4660

(G-16158)
TAYLOR GARY
3561 E Crystal Valley Dr (47591-6183)
PHONE..................................812 895-0715
Taylor Gary, Prin
EMP: 1 EST: 2010
SALES (est): 57.47K Privately Held
SIC: 2273 Carpets and rugs

(G-16159)
TRI STATE PRINTING & EMBROIDER
24 N 1st St (47591-1211)
PHONE..................................812 316-0094
Burdetta Scott, Pr
EMP: 4 EST: 2014
SALES (est): 247.59K Privately Held
Web: www.tri-spe.com
SIC: 2759 Screen printing

(G-16160)
VINCENNES WELDING CO INC
923 N 13th St (47591-4721)
PHONE..................................812 882-9682
Bruce Cooper, Pr
EMP: 14 EST: 1912
SQ FT: 5,000
SALES (est): 968.22K Privately Held
SIC: 7692 3599 3441 Welding repair; Machine shop, jobbing and repair; Fabricated structural metal

(G-16161)
WABASH HERITAGE MFG LLC
2525 N 6th St (47591-2405)
PHONE..................................812 886-0147
EMP: 1 EST: 2007
SALES (est): 121.22K Privately Held
Web: www.wabashheritage.com
SIC: 2448 Wood pallets and skids

(G-16162)
WABASH STEEL LLC
2007 Oliphant Dr (47591-1763)
P.O. Box 117 (47591-0117)
PHONE..................................317 818-1622
EMP: 5 EST: 2006
SQ FT: 220,000
SALES (est): 2.07MM
SALES (corp-wide): 24.63MM Privately Held
Web: www.wabashsteel.biz
SIC: 3441 Bridge sections, prefabricated, highway
PA: Lenex Steel Company
450 E 96th St Ste 100
Indianapolis IN 46240
317 818-1622

(G-16163)
WABASH VALLEY PUBLISHING LLC
611 N 7th St (47591-3101)
P.O. Box 131 (47591-0131)
PHONE..................................812 494-2152
Mary Daniel-evans, Admn
EMP: 5 EST: 2016
SALES (est): 76.22K Privately Held
SIC: 2711 Newspapers

(G-16164)
WAG-WAY TOOL INCORPORATED
483 N Mount Zion Rd (47591-9683)
PHONE..................................812 886-0598
Craig Waggoner, Pr
EMP: 10 EST: 1988
SQ FT: 18,000
SALES (est): 1.33MM Privately Held
Web: www.wagway.com
SIC: 3531 Buckets, excavating: clamshell, concrete, dragline, etc.

(G-16165)
WARREN HOMES INC
Also Called: Gallery of Kitchens
2807 Adams Meyer Ln (47591-3600)
PHONE..................................812 882-1059
Douglas Warren, Pr
Brent Kehl, Sec
EMP: 4 EST: 1978
SALES (est): 385.44K Privately Held
SIC: 2514 Kitchen cabinets: metal

(G-16166)
WILBERT SEXTON CORPORATION
426 S 15th St (47591-5409)
PHONE..................................812 882-3555
Jay Foreman, Mgr
EMP: 4
SALES (corp-wide): 2.46MM Privately Held
Web: www.sextonwilbertconcrete.com
SIC: 3272 Burial vaults, concrete or precast terrazzo
PA: Wilbert Sexton Corporation
1908 W Allen St
Bloomington IN 47403
812 336-6469

(G-16167)
WININGERS MANUFACTURING LLC
1117 Ritterskamp Ave (47591-4925)
PHONE..................................812 887-6129
EMP: 1
SALES (est): 69.27K Privately Held
Web: www.winingersmanufacturing.com
SIC: 3489 Guns or gun parts, over 30 mm.

(G-16168)
WITHERSPOON FARMS INC
2263 E Shawnee Dr (47591-1979)
PHONE..................................812 882-5272
Ellen Bardole, Pr
EMP: 4 EST: 1978
SALES (est): 329.55K Privately Held
SIC: 3523 Driers (farm): grain, hay, and seed

(G-16169)
WOODCRAFT MANUFACTURING CO
810 S 17th St (47591-4325)
PHONE..................................812 882-2354
EMP: 7 EST: 2018
SALES (est): 44.81K Privately Held
Web: www.woodcraftmanufacturing.com
SIC: 2499 Wood products, nec

Wabash
Wabash County

(G-16170)
10X ENGINEERED MATERIALS LLC
1162 Manchester Ave (46992-1637)
PHONE..................................260 209-1207
Stephen Ricci, CEO
Steven Edris, Prin
Jacob Vaillancourt, Prin
Carrie Gillenwater, Prin
EMP: 14 EST: 2018
SALES (est): 2.43MM Privately Held
Web: www.10xem.com
SIC: 3291 Abrasive products

(G-16171)
12154 HOLDING CORP
3837 Mill St (46992-7838)
PHONE..................................260 563-8371
EMP: 175 EST: 2015
SQ FT: 175,000
SALES (est): 34.53MM
SALES (corp-wide): 272.96MM Privately Held
Web: www.wabashcastings.com
SIC: 3365 Aluminum foundries
PA: Callidus Capital Corporation
4620-181 Bay St
Toronto ON M5J 2
416 945-3016

(G-16172)
AJ MASONRY & SON LLC
65 Noble St (46992-1830)
PHONE..................................260 569-0082
David Judy, Prin
EMP: 6 EST: 2019
SALES (est): 62.38K Privately Held
SIC: 2024 Yogurt desserts, frozen

(G-16173)
AL-FE HEAT TREATING LLC
Also Called: Aalberts Surface Technologies
200 Wedcor Ave (46992-4200)
PHONE..................................260 563-8321
Dan Andersen, Mgr
EMP: 19
SALES (corp-wide): 63.78MM Privately Held
Web: www.aalberts-ht.us
SIC: 3398 Metal heat treating
HQ: Al-Fe Heat Treating, Llc
209 W Mount Hope Ave
Lansing MI 48910
517 485-5090

(G-16174)
B WALTER & COMPANY INC
655 Factory St (46992-3213)
P.O. Box 278 (46992-0278)
PHONE..................................260 563-2181
Arthur Jasen, CEO
Thomas Frank, CFO
▲ EMP: 20 EST: 1887
SQ FT: 80,474
SALES (est): 1.98MM Privately Held
Web: www.bwalter.com
SIC: 3469 3452 Stamping metal for the trade ; Bolts, nuts, rivets, and washers

(G-16175)
BUEHRER INDUSTRIES LLC
655 Factory St (46992-3213)
PHONE..................................260 563-2181
EMP: 9 EST: 2019
SALES (est): 612.09K Privately Held
SIC: 3999 Manufacturing industries, nec

(G-16176)
BULLDOG BATTERY CORPORATION (PA)
Also Called: Precision Battery Fabrication
98 E Canal St (46992-3104)
P.O. Box 766 (46992-0766)
PHONE..................................260 563-0551
Norman L Benjamin, Pr

Wabash - Wabash County (G-16202)

June L Dawkins, *
John Dawkins, *
Thomas Wagner, *
Regina M Thompson, *
◆ EMP: 66 EST: 1977
SQ FT: 120,000
SALES (est): 17.95MM
SALES (corp-wide): 17.95MM **Privately Held**
Web: www.bulldog-battery.com
SIC: 3691 Storage batteries

(G-16177)
CARVER INC
1569 Morris St (46992-3538)
P.O. Box 298 (46992-0298)
PHONE..................................260 563-7577
Billy Carver, Pr
EMP: 1 EST: 2001
SALES (est): 299.76K **Privately Held**
Web: www.carverpress.com
SIC: 5084 3542 Hydraulic systems equipment and supplies; Presses: hydraulic and pneumatic, mechanical and manual

(G-16178)
COLLEEN COBLE INCORPORATED
53 Highland Dr (46992-2123)
PHONE..................................260 563-2028
David Coble, VP
EMP: 6 EST: 2017
SALES (est): 151.13K **Privately Held**
Web: www.colleencoble.com
SIC: 2741 Miscellaneous publishing

(G-16179)
CUSTOM CARTON INC
3758 W Old 24 (46992-7779)
P.O. Box 727 (46992-0727)
PHONE..................................260 563-7411
Margret Marquardt, Pr
Allan Marquardt, Sec
EMP: 10 EST: 1966
SQ FT: 23,000
SALES (est): 2.16MM **Privately Held**
Web: www.customcartonsinc.com
SIC: 2657 7389 Folding paperboard boxes; Packaging and labeling services

(G-16180)
DENNEYCREATIVE
56 W Market St Ste 6 (46992-3242)
PHONE..................................260 494-0862
Melissa Denney, Prin
EMP: 3 EST: 2013
SALES (est): 61.41K **Privately Held**
Web: www.denneycreative.com
SIC: 2759 Screen printing

(G-16181)
DIE-NAMIC CERAMICS LLC ✪
948 Manchester Ave (46992-1640)
PHONE..................................260 563-7573
EMP: 4 EST: 2022
SALES (est): 62.9K **Privately Held**
Web: www.die-namicceramic.com
SIC: 3599 Machine shop, jobbing and repair

(G-16182)
DS PRODUCTS INC
Also Called: Global Precision Parts
202 Wedcor Ave (46992)
PHONE..................................260 563-9030
Todd Kriegel, Pr
David Kriegel, Ch
Yolanada Von Lehmden, Contrlr
▲ EMP: 50 EST: 2000
SQ FT: 48,000
SALES (est): 6.77MM **Privately Held**
Web: www.ds-products.com

SIC: 3451 Screw machine products
PA: Kriegel Holding Company, Inc.
7600 Us Rte 127
Van Wert OH 45891

(G-16183)
ESCALADE INC
251 Wedcor Ave (46992-4201)
PHONE..................................260 569-7233
C W Reed, Pr
Terry Frandsen, Sec
EMP: 23 EST: 1987
SALES (est): 174.07K **Privately Held**
Web: www.escaladeinc.com
SIC: 3949 5091 Sporting and athletic goods, nec; Sporting and recreation goods

(G-16184)
F J RETTIG & SONS INC
Also Called: Rettigs Industrial Supply
485 W Canal St (46992-3221)
PHONE..................................260 563-6603
J L Gillespie, Pr
Jay L Gillespie, Pr
Don M Gillespie, VP
EMP: 7 EST: 1888
SQ FT: 8,000
SALES (est): 894.21K **Privately Held**
Web: www.rettigs.com
SIC: 3351 Copper pipe

(G-16185)
FAIRMONT DOOR CORP
209 S Huntington St (46992-3118)
PHONE..................................260 563-6307
Douglas Chopson, Prin
EMP: 1 EST: 2010
SALES (est): 91.9K **Privately Held**
SIC: 2431 Door frames, wood

(G-16186)
FLIGHT1 AVIATION TECH INC
1677 King St (46992-3910)
PHONE..................................404 504-7010
EMP: 3 EST: 2003
SQ FT: 400
SALES (est): 263.93K **Privately Held**
Web: www.flight1tech.com
SIC: 4813 7372 Online service providers; Prepackaged software

(G-16187)
FOAM X-PRESS LLC
675 E 250 S (46992-8928)
PHONE..................................260 563-5767
Don Holmes, Prin
EMP: 5 EST: 2009
SALES (est): 218.95K **Privately Held**
SIC: 3715 Truck trailers

(G-16188)
FRED S CARVER INC (DH)
Also Called: Carver
1569 Morris St (46992-3538)
P.O. Box 298 (46992-0298)
PHONE..................................260 563-7577
James E Holbrook, Pr
Beth Gillespie, VP
Michael P Santoni, VP
Jeffery A Deplanty, Sec
▲ EMP: 6 EST: 1977
SALES (est): 1.07MM **Privately Held**
Web: www.carverpress.com
SIC: 3542 Presses: hydraulic and pneumatic, mechanical and manual
HQ: Sterling, Inc.
2900 S 160th St
New Berlin WI 53151
414 354-0970

(G-16189)
GENTRY WELL & PUMP SERVICE LLC
8939 S 100 W (46992-9151)
PHONE..................................260 563-1907
EMP: 1 EST: 2011
SALES (est): 134.79K **Privately Held**
SIC: 1781 1381 1629 1623 Water well drilling; Service well drilling; Trenching contractor; Water, sewer, and utility lines

(G-16190)
HARVEY INDUSTRIES LLC
Also Called: Harvey Industries
3837 Mill St (46992-7838)
PHONE..................................260 563-8371
▲ EMP: 350
Web: www.harvey-industries.com
SIC: 3463 3365 Aluminum forgings; Aluminum foundries

(G-16191)
HAYNES HONEY LLC
1269 E 500 S (46992-7962)
PHONE..................................260 563-6397
Shirley Haynes, Owner
EMP: 5 EST: 2014
SALES (est): 91.34K **Privately Held**
SIC: 3999 Beekeepers' supplies

(G-16192)
HIPSHER TOOL & DIE INC
1593 S State Road 115 (46992-8380)
PHONE..................................260 563-4143
Jerry Hipsher, VP
Julie Hook Dahl, Sec
EMP: 16 EST: 1946
SQ FT: 39,000
SALES (est): 2.19MM **Privately Held**
Web: www.hipshertool.com
SIC: 3544 Special dies and tools

(G-16193)
HOOSIER JIFFY PRINT
675 Stitt St (46992-2211)
PHONE..................................260 563-8715
Rob Wilson, Pr
EMP: 4 EST: 1976
SQ FT: 4,000
SALES (est): 401.33K **Privately Held**
Web: www.hoosierjiffyprint.com
SIC: 2759 2752 Letterpress printing; Offset printing

(G-16194)
HOT OFF PRESS
832 Manchester Ave (46992-1422)
PHONE..................................260 591-8331
Lisa Ulrey, Admn
EMP: 5 EST: 2014
SALES (est): 55.03K **Privately Held**
SIC: 2741 Miscellaneous publishing

(G-16195)
M & M CONVERTING INC
3758 W Old 24 (46992-7779)
PHONE..................................260 563-7411
Alan L Marquardt, Pr
EMP: 4 EST: 2007
SALES (est): 180.51K **Privately Held**
SIC: 3999 Pads, permanent waving

(G-16196)
M F Y DESIGNS INC
1051 N State Road 15 (46992-8631)
PHONE..................................260 563-6662
EMP: 3 EST: 1996
SALES (est): 234.53K **Privately Held**
Web: www.mfydesigns.com

SIC: 3993 Signs and advertising specialties

(G-16197)
MAFCOTE WABASH PAPER COATING
301 Wedcor Ave (46992-4202)
PHONE..................................260 563-4181
Daryl Evans, VP
EMP: 10 EST: 2015
SALES (est): 239.8K **Privately Held**
Web: www.mafcote.com
SIC: 2621 Paper mills

(G-16198)
MARTIN YALE INDUSTRIES LLC
251 Wedcor Ave (46992-4201)
PHONE..................................260 563-0641
Greg German, Pr
◆ EMP: 129 EST: 1941
SQ FT: 140,000
SALES (est): 23.03MM
SALES (corp-wide): 23.03MM **Privately Held**
Web: www.martinyale.com
SIC: 3579 Paper cutters, trimmers, and punches
PA: Lv2 Equity Partners, Llc
2013 W Wackerly St # 200
Midland MI 48640
989 631-2687

(G-16199)
MCKILLIP MACHINERY INC
697 W 50 N (46992-9141)
PHONE..................................260 330-2842
Brent E Mckillip, Prin
EMP: 1 EST: 2018
SALES (est): 172.71K **Privately Held**
SIC: 3523 Farm machinery and equipment

(G-16200)
METAL SOURCE LLC
1733 S Wabash St (46992-4119)
P.O. Box 238 (46992-0238)
PHONE..................................260 563-8833
Benjamin Gebhart, Pr
Chris Lochner, *
Marcus Olson, *
◆ EMP: 50 EST: 1998
SQ FT: 9,000
SALES (est): 10.43MM
SALES (corp-wide): 17.02MM **Privately Held**
Web: www.metalsourcellc.com
SIC: 3356 Zinc and zinc alloy bars, plates, sheets, etc.
PA: Gebhart Holdings, Inc.
231 W Canal St
Wabash IN 46992
260 563-8833

(G-16201)
MIDWEST EYE SERVICES LLC
Also Called: Bridgeview Eye Partners
835 N Cass St (46992)
P.O. Box 509 (46992)
PHONE..................................833 592-7434
Bruce L Trump, CEO
EMP: 29 EST: 2021
SALES (est): 2.01MM **Privately Held**
SIC: 3841 Eye examining instruments and apparatus

(G-16202)
MIDWESTERN PALLET SERVICE INC
Also Called: MPS
3632 W Old 24 (46992-8408)
PHONE..................................260 563-1526
EMP: 4 EST: 1986
SQ FT: 3,200
SALES (est): 487.11K **Privately Held**

Wabash - Wabash County (G-16203)

SIC: 2448 Pallets, wood

(G-16203)
MILLINER PRINTING COMPANY INC
425 S Wabash St (46992-3325)
P.O. Box 282 (46992-0282)
PHONE..............................260 563-5717
TOLL FREE: 800
Tim Eslava, *Pr*
EMP: 5 EST: 1950
SQ FT: 4,500
SALES (est): 412.12K **Privately Held**
Web: www.millinerprintingcompany.com
SIC: 2752 Offset printing

(G-16204)
MORTON BUILDINGS INC
1873 S State Road 115 (46992)
P.O. Box 564 (46992-0564)
PHONE..............................260 563-2118
David Mc Vicker, *Mgr*
EMP: 10
SALES (corp-wide): 213.04MM **Privately Held**
Web: www.mortonbuildings.com
SIC: 5039 3448 2452 Prefabricated structures; Prefabricated metal buildings and components; Prefabricated wood buildings
PA: Morton Buildings, Inc.
    252 W Adams St
    Morton IL 61550
    800 447-7436

(G-16205)
MOSIERS TARPS LLC
4021 S State Road 15 (46992-9014)
PHONE..............................260 563-3332
Jeffrey Mosier, *Owner*
EMP: 7 EST: 1949
SQ FT: 5,000
SALES (est): 458.09K **Privately Held**
Web: www.mosierstarps.com
SIC: 2394 7532 Tarpaulins, fabric: made from purchased materials; Tops (canvas or plastic), installation or repair: automotive

(G-16206)
OLYMPIA BUSINESS SYSTEMS INC
Also Called: Intimus International NA
251 Wedcor Ave (46992-4201)
P.O. Box 357 (46992-0357)
PHONE..............................800 225-5644
Javier Ortiz De Zarate, *CEO*
EMP: 10 EST: 1998
SALES (est): 3.16MM
SALES (corp-wide): 263.57MM **Publicly Held**
Web: www.intimus.com
SIC: 3589 Shredders, industrial and commercial
HQ: Wedcor Holdings, Inc.
    251 Wedcor Ave
    Wabash IN 46992
    260 563-0641

(G-16207)
OWENS CORNING SALES LLC
Also Called: Owens Corning Sales Therm
3711 Mill St (46992-7778)
PHONE..............................260 563-2111
EMP: 6
SIC: 3296 Fiberglass insulation
HQ: Owens Corning Sales, Llc
    1 Owens Corning Pkwy
    Toledo OH 43659
    419 248-8000

(G-16208)
PAPER OF WABASH COUNTY INC
Also Called: The Paper
606 N State Road 13 (46992-7735)
P.O. Box 744 (47960-0744)
PHONE..............................260 563-8326
Wayne Rees, *Pr*
Mike Rees, *
Mona Rees, *
Julie Freegan, *
EMP: 14 EST: 1977
SQ FT: 5,000
SALES (est): 895.81K **Privately Held**
Web: www.thepaperofwabash.com
SIC: 2711 Commercial printing and newspaper publishing combined

(G-16209)
PAPERWORKS INDUSTRIES INC
455 Factory St (46992-3212)
P.O. Box 217 (46992-0217)
PHONE..............................260 569-3352
EMP: 123
Web: www.onepaperworks.com
SIC: 2631 Paperboard mills
PA: Paperworks Industries, Inc.
    1300 Virginia Dr Ste 220
    Fort Washington PA 19034

(G-16210)
PAPERWORKS INDUSTRIES INC
Also Called: Smurfit Stone Container
455 Factory St (46992-3212)
P.O. Box 217 (46992-0217)
PHONE..............................260 563-3102
Richard Townley, *Genl Mgr*
EMP: 225
Web: www.onepaperworks.com
SIC: 2653 Boxes, corrugated: made from purchased materials
PA: Paperworks Industries, Inc.
    1300 Virginia Dr Ste 220
    Fort Washington PA 19034

(G-16211)
PAPERWORKS WABASH INC
455 Factory St (46992-3212)
PHONE..............................260 569-3303
Kevin Kwilinski, *Pr*
C Anderson Bolton, *CEO*
Scott Gomez, *VP*
EMP: 23 EST: 2008
SALES (est): 303.67K **Privately Held**
Web: www.onepaperworks.com
SIC: 2631 Paperboard mills

(G-16212)
PETTIT PRINTING INC
789 S Carroll St (46992-3210)
P.O. Box 704 (46992-0704)
PHONE..............................260 563-2346
Gregory Pettit, *Pr*
Gabriele Pettit, *VP*
EMP: 6 EST: 1946
SQ FT: 2,600
SALES (est): 443.89K **Privately Held**
Web: www.pettitprinting.com
SIC: 2752 Offset printing

(G-16213)
PRECIOUS GEMS METALS
112 W Market St (46992)
PHONE..............................260 563-4780
EMP: 4 EST: 2020
SALES (est): 309.83K **Privately Held**
Web: www.preciousgemsandmetals.com
SIC: 3339 Precious metals

(G-16214)
REAL ALLOY RECYCLING LLC
305 Dimension Ave (46992-4131)
P.O. Box 747 (46992-0747)
PHONE..............................260 563-2409
EMP: 1
SALES (corp-wide): 112.7MM **Publicly Held**
Web: www.realalloy.com
SIC: 3341 Aluminum smelting and refining (secondary)
HQ: Real Alloy Recycling, Llc
    3700 Park E Dr Ste 300
    Beachwood OH 44122
    216 755-8900

(G-16215)
SHERMS MARINE INC
8662 S 400 W (46992-9291)
PHONE..............................260 563-8051
Sherman Truss, *Owner*
EMP: 10 EST: 2015
SALES (est): 687.27K **Privately Held**
Web: www.shermsmarine.com
SIC: 5551 3732 Motor boat dealers; Non-motorized boat, building and repairing

(G-16216)
TAS WELDING AND GRN SVCS LLC
5459 W Old 24 (46992-8358)
PHONE..............................765 210-4274
Tim Sparks, *Pr*
EMP: 7 EST: 2010
SALES (est): 248.06K **Privately Held**
Web: www.tasweldinggrainservices.com
SIC: 7692 Welding repair

(G-16217)
THE FORD METER BOX COMPANY INC (PA)
775 Manchester Ave (46992)
P.O. Box 443 (46992)
PHONE..............................260 563-3171
◆ EMP: 234 EST: 1900
SALES (est): 12.47MM
SALES (corp-wide): 12.47MM **Privately Held**
Web: www.fordmeterbox.com
SIC: 3494 Valves and pipe fittings, nec

(G-16218)
TRU-CUT MACHINE & TOOL INC
Also Called: Statzer C Mark
556 E Baumbauer Rd Lot 41 (46992-9306)
PHONE..............................260 569-1802
EMP: 3 EST: 1994
SQ FT: 55,000
SALES (est): 248.92K **Privately Held**
SIC: 3542 Machine tools, metal forming type

(G-16219)
UNITED TOOL COMPANY INC
838 Lafontaine Ave (46992-4107)
P.O. Box 242 (46992-0242)
PHONE..............................260 563-3143
Michael R Bechtol, *Pr*
Troy Poland, *VP*
Debra Bechtol, *Sec*
Deborah Bechtol, *Sec*
EMP: 14 EST: 1966
SQ FT: 12,000
SALES (est): 1.42MM **Privately Held**
Web: www.unitedtoolcompany.com
SIC: 3599 7692 Machine shop, jobbing and repair; Welding repair

(G-16220)
WABASH CASTINGS LLC
3837 Mill St (46992-7838)
PHONE..............................260 563-8371
Robert Hollacher, *Managing Member*
EMP: 15 EST: 2021
SALES (est): 932.04K **Privately Held**
Web: www.wabashcastings.com
SIC: 3365 Aluminum foundries

(G-16221)
WABASH PLAIN DEALER CO LLC
123 W Canal St (46992-3042)
P.O. Box 379 (46992-0379)
PHONE..............................260 563-2131
J Fred Paxton, *Pr*
EMP: 26 EST: 1859
SQ FT: 15,000
SALES (est): 436.02K
SALES (corp-wide): 147.64MM **Privately Held**
Web: www.wabashplaindealer.com
SIC: 2711 2752 Commercial printing and newspaper publishing combined; Commercial printing, lithographic
PA: Paxton Media Group, Llc
    100 Television Ln
    Paducah KY 42003
    270 575-8630

(G-16222)
WABASH VALLEY TOOL & ENGRG
1253 S State Road 115 (46992-9241)
PHONE..............................260 563-7690
Laureen D Deeter, *Pr*
EMP: 2 EST: 1969
SQ FT: 1,200
SALES (est): 234.12K **Privately Held**
SIC: 3544 Special dies and tools

(G-16223)
WABASH WELDING SERVICES INC (PA)
150 Smith St (46992-3322)
P.O. Box 241 (46992-0241)
PHONE..............................260 563-2363
Amber Price, *Pr*
Thomas C Ehret, *Pr*
Teresa Ehret, *VP*
EMP: 5 EST: 1975
SQ FT: 15,000
SALES (est): 887.24K
SALES (corp-wide): 887.24K **Privately Held**
Web: www.wabashwelding.com
SIC: 1796 3441 Millwright; Fabricated structural metal

(G-16224)
WEST PLAINS DISTRIBUTION LLC
Also Called: Kentner Creek
1600 S Olive St (46992)
PHONE..............................260 563-9500
EMP: 11 EST: 2015
SALES (est): 260.7K **Privately Held**
Web: www.westplainsmining.com
SIC: 1442 Gravel mining

(G-16225)
WEST PLAINS MINING LLC
6601 W Old 24 (46992-1421)
P.O. Box 584 (46992-0584)
PHONE..............................260 563-9500
William A Woodward, *Managing Member*
EMP: 40 EST: 2003
SALES (est): 7.01MM **Privately Held**
Web: www.wp-mining.com
SIC: 1422 Limestones, ground

Wadesville
Posey County

(G-16226)
AZTEC PRINTING INC (PA)
9800 Highway 66 (47638-9011)
PHONE..................812 422-1462
Joyce Gumbrell, *Pr*
EMP: 4 **EST:** 1962
SQ FT: 2,500
SALES (est): 492.66K
SALES (corp-wide): 492.66K **Privately Held**
Web: www.aztecprintonline.com
SIC: 2752 Offset printing

(G-16227)
MSK MOLD INC
2591 Juanita Ave (47638)
PHONE..................812 985-5457
Scott Allen Pate, *Pr*
Lisa Pate, *VP*
EMP: 4 **EST:** 1995
SALES (est): 379.5K **Privately Held**
SIC: 3544 Special dies and tools

(G-16228)
PARKER EXPLORATION & PRODUCTIO
2940 Donner Rd (47638-9057)
PHONE..................812 673-4017
Delwin Parker, *Prin*
EMP: 2 **EST:** 2001
SALES (est): 210.07K **Privately Held**
SIC: 3824 Production counters

(G-16229)
REXING-GOEDDE ELECTRIC SERVICE
13100 St Wendel Rd (47638)
PHONE..................812 963-5725
Jerry Goedde, *Owner*
EMP: 1
SALES (corp-wide): 327.52K **Privately Held**
SIC: 3559 Parking facility equipment and supplies
PA: Rexing-Goedde Electric Service Inc
  13100 Saint Wendel Rd
  Evansville IN 47720
  812 963-5725

(G-16230)
SCHMITT MTLWRKS FBRCATIONS LLC
9121 Damm Rd (47638-9004)
PHONE..................812 510-3677
EMP: 2 **EST:** 2021
SALES (est): 54.36K **Privately Held**
Web: www.schmittmetalworks.com
SIC: 3499 Fabricated metal products, nec

Wakarusa
Elkhart County

(G-16231)
DWYER INSTRUMENTS INC
Also Called: DWYER INSTRUMENTS INC
55 Ward St (46573-9588)
PHONE..................574 862-2590
Doug Sowder, *Brnch Mgr*
EMP: 6
SQ FT: 1,800
SALES (corp-wide): 653.43MM **Privately Held**
Web: intl.dwyer-inst.com

SIC: 3823 Process control instruments
HQ: Dwyer Instruments, Llc
  102 Indiana Hwy 212
  Michigan City IN 46360
  219 879-8868

(G-16232)
EAGLE MOLD & TOOL
1011 E Waterford St (46573-9304)
PHONE..................574 862-1966
Mark Bemlier, *Owner*
EMP: 1 **EST:** 2002
SALES (est): 221.99K **Privately Held**
SIC: 3544 3089 Industrial molds; Molding primary plastics

(G-16233)
FREIGHTLINER CSTM CHASSIS CORP
66540 State Road 19 (46573-9597)
PHONE..................260 517-9678
EMP: 128
SALES (corp-wide): 60.75B **Privately Held**
Web: www.freightlinerchassis.com
SIC: 3711 Truck tractors for highway use, assembly of
HQ: Freightliner Custom Chassis Corporation
  552 Hyatt St
  Gaffney SC 29341

(G-16234)
HAHN ENTERPRISES INC
Also Called: Weldy Enterprises
911 E Waterford St (46573-9560)
PHONE..................574 862-4491
TOLL FREE: 800
Don Hahn, *Pr*
Darren Hahn, *VP*
Linda Hahn, *Sec*
EMP: 9 **EST:** 1971
SQ FT: 15,000
SALES (est): 1.62MM **Privately Held**
Web: www.weldyenterprises.com
SIC: 5083 3523 Farm and garden machinery ; Farm machinery and equipment

(G-16235)
J & R WELDING
29823 County Road 40 (46573-9547)
PHONE..................574 862-1590
Joas Schmucker, *Owner*
EMP: 6 **EST:** 2012
SALES (est): 163.75K **Privately Held**
SIC: 7692 Welding repair

(G-16236)
KAEB SALES INC
27481 County Road 40 (46573-9709)
PHONE..................574 862-2777
Craig Coon, *Mgr*
EMP: 6
SALES (corp-wide): 11.38MM **Privately Held**
Web: www.kaebsales.com
SIC: 3556 Dairy and milk machinery
PA: Kaeb Sales, Inc.
  484 N State Route 49
  Cissna Park IL 60924
  815 457-2649

(G-16237)
KEYSTONE RV COMPANY
Also Called: Keystone Plant 35
608 Nelsons Pkwy (46573-9674)
PHONE..................574 535-2100
EMP: 167
SALES (corp-wide): 11.12B **Publicly Held**
Web: www.keystonerv.com

SIC: 3792 Travel trailer chassis
HQ: Keystone Rv Company
  2642 Hackberry Dr
  Goshen IN 46526

(G-16238)
LUE MANUFACTURING CORPORATION
27667 County Road 40 (46573-9709)
PHONE..................574 862-4249
Steven R Gongwer, *Pr*
EMP: 10 **EST:** 1970
SQ FT: 15,000
SALES (est): 497.23K **Privately Held**
Web: www.luemfg.com
SIC: 2434 Wood kitchen cabinets

(G-16239)
LYCRO PRODUCTS CO INC
66557 State Road 19 (46573-9799)
P.O. Box 571 (46573-0571)
PHONE..................574 862-4981
Gregory Schoen, *Pr*
EMP: 45 **EST:** 1970
SQ FT: 55,000
SALES (est): 4.16MM **Privately Held**
Web: www.lycroproducts.com
SIC: 3599 Machine shop, jobbing and repair

(G-16240)
MARTIN WELDING SHOP
27585 County Road 40 (46573-9709)
PHONE..................574 862-2578
Mervin Martin, *Owner*
EMP: 2 **EST:** 1964
SALES (est): 115.1K **Privately Held**
SIC: 7692 Welding repair

(G-16241)
MERVIN M BURKHOLDER
26253 County Road 42 (46573-9673)
PHONE..................574 862-4144
Mervin M Burkholder, *Prin*
EMP: 5 **EST:** 2004
SALES (est): 238.29K **Privately Held**
SIC: 7692 Welding repair

(G-16242)
PERFORMANCE TECHNOLOGY INC
65251 State Road 19 (46573-9310)
P.O. Box 461 (46573-0461)
PHONE..................574 862-2116
Neil Hannewyk, *VP*
James Mikel, *Pr*
Tina Mikel, *Sec*
M Sherman Drew, *Treas*
Tina Mikel Sect, *Mgr*
EMP: 9 **EST:** 1983
SQ FT: 7,850
SALES (est): 997.45K **Privately Held**
SIC: 3714 7538 Motor vehicle engines and parts; Engine rebuilding: automotive

(G-16243)
PRIME TIME MANUFACTURING
66149 State Road 19 (46573-9327)
P.O. Box 3030 (46515-3030)
PHONE..................574 862-3001
EMP: 2 **EST:** 2012
SALES (est): 223.74K **Privately Held**
Web: www.primetimerv.com
SIC: 3999 Manufacturing industries, nec

(G-16244)
PRO IT SOLUTIONS LLC
111 W Waterford St (46573-2008)
P.O. Box 861 (46573-0861)
PHONE..................574 862-0021
Alex J Cook, *Managing Member*
EMP: 11 **EST:** 2010

SALES (est): 977.93K **Privately Held**
Web: www.pro-it-solutions.com
SIC: 7382 7372 Security systems services; Application computer software

(G-16245)
PROVIDENT TOOL & DIE INC
Also Called: Turnomat
66100 State Road 19 (46573-9330)
P.O. Box 214 (46573-0214)
PHONE..................574 862-1233
EMP: 7 **EST:** 1994
SQ FT: 4,000
SALES (est): 528.68K **Privately Held**
Web: www.providenttool.com
SIC: 3599 Machine shop, jobbing and repair

(G-16246)
RAVEN INDUSTRIES INC
Also Called: Agsync
29769 County Road 40 (46573-9546)
PHONE..................877 923-5832
EMP: 3
Web: www.ravenind.com
SIC: 3999 Barber and beauty shop equipment
HQ: Raven Industries, Inc
  205 E 6th St
  Sioux Falls SD 57104
  605 336-2750

(G-16247)
REM INDUSTRIES INC
902 Nelsons Pkwy (46573-9580)
P.O. Box 408 (46573-0408)
PHONE..................574 862-2127
Robert Miller, *Pr*
Jason Miller, *
EMP: 16 **EST:** 1991
SQ FT: 10,000
SALES (est): 1.73MM **Privately Held**
Web: www.rem-ind.com
SIC: 3429 5712 2531 2511 Furniture hardware; Furniture stores; Public building and related furniture; Wood household furniture

(G-16248)
RIGHT ANGLE STL FBRICATION INC
29508 County Road 38 (46573-9705)
P.O. Box 559 (46573-0559)
PHONE..................574 862-2432
Carl E Cook, *Pr*
EMP: 2 **EST:** 2001
SALES (est): 216.36K **Privately Held**
SIC: 3441 Expansion joints (structural shapes), iron or steel

(G-16249)
SCHMIDT CABINETRY & FURN LLC
903 Nelsons Pkwy (46573-9580)
PHONE..................574 862-2200
EMP: 5 **EST:** 1999
SALES (est): 79.73K **Privately Held**
Web: www.schmidtfurniture.com
SIC: 2434 Wood kitchen cabinets

(G-16250)
SCHROCK AGGREGATE COMPANY INC (HQ)
111 Industrial Dr (46573-8513)
PHONE..................574 862-4167
EMP: 1 **EST:** 1995
SALES (est): 24.72MM
SALES (corp-wide): 24.72MM **Privately Held**
SIC: 2951 3272 1442 Paving mixtures; Paving materials, prefabricated concrete; Gravel mining
PA: Schrock Excavating, Inc.
  111 Industrial Dr

Wakarusa - Elkhart County (G-16251)

Wakarusa IN 46573
574 862-4167

(G-16251)
SCHROCK EXCAVATING INC (PA)
111 Industrial Dr (46573-8513)
P.O. Box 473 (46506-0473)
PHONE...................................574 862-4167
David L Schrock, *Pr*
Diana Schrock, *
EMP: 39 **EST:** 1986
SQ FT: 26,000
SALES (est): 24.72MM
SALES (corp-wide): 24.72MM **Privately Held**
SIC: 1794 1771 1795 2951 Excavation and grading, building construction; Driveway, parking lot, and blacktop contractors; Demolition, buildings and other structures; Paving mixtures

(G-16252)
SOUTHWEST WELDING LLC
28125 County Road 42 (46573-9323)
PHONE...................................574 862-4453
John D Martin, *Managing Member*
EMP: 3 **EST:** 1985
SALES (est): 565.61K **Privately Held**
Web: www.southwestweldingllc.com
SIC: 7692 1799 Welding repair; Welding on site

(G-16253)
THOR INDUSTRIES INC
Also Called: THOR INDUSTRIES, INC.
505 Ward St (46573-9671)
PHONE...................................574 584-2151
Betty Young, *Brnch Mgr*
EMP: 2
SALES (corp-wide): 11.12B **Publicly Held**
Web: www.thorindustries.com
SIC: 3792 Travel trailers and campers
PA: Thor Industries, Inc.
    601 E Beardsley Ave
    Elkhart IN 46514
    574 970-7460

(G-16254)
THOR INDUSTRIES INC
606 Nelsons Pkwy (46573-9674)
P.O. Box 1486 (46515-1486)
PHONE...................................800 860-5658
Jeff Kime, *Brnch Mgr*
EMP: 3
SALES (corp-wide): 11.12B **Publicly Held**
Web: www.thorindustries.com
SIC: 3792 3716 Travel trailers and campers; Motor homes
PA: Thor Industries, Inc.
    601 E Beardsley Ave
    Elkhart IN 46514
    574 970-7460

(G-16255)
THOR MOTOR COACH INC
510 Ward St (46573-9671)
PHONE...................................800 860-5658
Jeff Kime, *Pr*
EMP: 29
SALES (corp-wide): 11.12B **Publicly Held**
Web: www.thormotorcoach.com
SIC: 3792 3716 Travel trailers and campers; Recreational van conversion (self-propelled), factory basis
HQ: Thor Motor Coach, Inc.
    701 County Rd 15 Ste 100
    Elkhart IN 46516

(G-16256)
WAKARUSA AG LLC
905 Nelsons Pkwy (46573)
PHONE...................................574 862-1163
Frank Martin, *Admn*
EMP: 10 **EST:** 2014
SALES (est): 2.67MM **Privately Held**
Web: www.wakarusaag.com
SIC: 5083 3531 5012 Tractors, agricultural; Tractors, construction; Truck tractors

---

Waldron
Shelby County

(G-16257)
BENTZ WOODWORKING
6850 S State Road 9 (46182-9758)
PHONE...................................765 525-4946
Shawn Bentz, *Prin*
EMP: 5 **EST:** 2015
SALES (est): 78.53K **Privately Held**
SIC: 2431 Millwork

(G-16258)
HEWITT MANUFACTURING COMPANY
5365 S 600 E (46182-9559)
P.O. Box 262 (46182-0262)
PHONE...................................765 525-9829
Donald G Hewitt, *Owner*
EMP: 10 **EST:** 1976
SQ FT: 6,000
SALES (est): 670.59K **Privately Held**
Web: www.hewittmfg.com
SIC: 3496 Miscellaneous fabricated wire products

(G-16259)
HOOSIER WASHER
4711 S 375 E (46182-9617)
PHONE...................................317 460-8354
Valerie Freeman, *Pt*
EMP: 6 **EST:** 2015
SALES (est): 79.28K **Privately Held**
SIC: 3469 Stamping metal for the trade

(G-16260)
LARRY ATWOOD
Also Called: Atwood Concrete Construction
6597 S 250 E (46182-9736)
PHONE...................................765 525-6851
Larry Atwood, *Owner*
EMP: 3 **EST:** 1987
SALES (est): 424.54K **Privately Held**
SIC: 5032 3444 Concrete and cinder building products; Concrete forms, sheet metal

---

Walkerton
St. Joseph County

(G-16261)
ACCURATE CASTINGS INC
104 Fulmer St (46574)
PHONE...................................224 563-3200
EMP: 23
SALES (corp-wide): 21.81MM **Privately Held**
Web: www.hilerindustries.com
SIC: 3599 Machine shop, jobbing and repair
PA: Accurate Castings Inc
    118 Koomler Dr
    La Porte IN 46350
    219 362-8531

(G-16262)
AFM INDUSTRIES LLC
72960 Poplar Rd (46574-8936)
PHONE...................................574 910-0982
Kyle Anderson, *Brnch Mgr*
EMP: 27
SALES (corp-wide): 591.96K **Privately Held**
SIC: 3999 Barber and beauty shop equipment
PA: Afm Industries Llc
    412 Illinois St
    Walkerton IN

(G-16263)
AMERICAN ROLLER COMPANY LLC
Also Called: Walkerton Plant
201 Industrial Park Dr (46574-1069)
PHONE...................................574 586-3101
Chris Stouffer, *Brnch Mgr*
EMP: 57
SALES (corp-wide): 109.53MM **Privately Held**
Web: www.americanroller.com
SIC: 3069 Rubber rolls and roll coverings
PA: American Roller Company, Llc
    1440 13th Ave
    Union Grove WI 53182
    262 878-8665

(G-16264)
AUSTIN & AUSTIN INC (PA)
Also Called: Ultra Manufacturing
648 Stephens St (46574-1264)
PHONE...................................574 586-2320
Michael Austin, *Prin*
Tammy Austin, *Treas*
EMP: 15 **EST:** 2015
SALES (est): 6.23MM
SALES (corp-wide): 6.23MM **Privately Held**
Web: www.ultramfg1.com
SIC: 3599 Machine shop, jobbing and repair

(G-16265)
CREEKSIDE EMBROIDERY
26181 Stanton Rd (46574-8701)
PHONE...................................574 656-8333
Kathy Holderread, *Owner*
EMP: 2 **EST:** 2008
SALES (est): 126.97K **Privately Held**
SIC: 2395 Embroidery and art needlework

(G-16266)
FREEHOLD GAMES LLC
69080 Sycamore Rd (46574-9744)
PHONE...................................574 656-9031
EMP: 2 **EST:** 2013
SALES (est): 142.85K **Privately Held**
Web: www.freeholdgames.com
SIC: 7372 7389 Home entertainment computer software; Business services, nec

(G-16267)
HOOSIER TRAPS
20112 W 3b Rd (46574-8233)
PHONE...................................574 586-2401
Rudy Adams, *Owner*
EMP: 1 **EST:** 2003
SALES (est): 59.16K **Privately Held**
SIC: 3496 Traps, animal and fish

(G-16268)
M & M CUSTOM EMBROIDERY
3489 S 700 E (46574-8539)
PHONE...................................407 334-5076
Ann Shirley, *Prin*
EMP: 5 **EST:** 2017
SALES (est): 57.01K **Privately Held**
SIC: 2395 Embroidery and art needlework

(G-16269)
MASONITE CORPORATION
105 Industrial Park Dr (46574-1068)
PHONE...................................574 586-3192
Andrew Graham Thayer, *Pr*
EMP: 14 **EST:** 1963
SALES (est): 189.33K **Privately Held**
Web: www.masonite.com
SIC: 2431 Doors, wood

(G-16270)
MASONITE INTERNATIONAL CORP
111 Muskin Dr (46574-1063)
PHONE...................................574 586-3192
Lance Singleton, *Brnch Mgr*
EMP: 40
Web: www.masonite.com
SIC: 2431 Doors, wood
HQ: Masonite International Corporation
    1242 E 5th Ave
    Tampa FL 33605
    813 877-2726

(G-16271)
MODERN DOOR CORPORATION
1300 Virginia St (46574-1073)
PHONE...................................574 586-3117
Garry L Matz, *Pr*
Thomas R Blend, *
▲ **EMP:** 100 **EST:** 1977
SQ FT: 150,000
SALES (est): 22.23MM
SALES (corp-wide): 52.62MM **Privately Held**
SIC: 3442 3444 Garage doors, overhead: metal; Sheet metalwork
PA: Plyco Corporation
    500 Industrial Dr
    Elkhart Lake WI 53020
    920 876-3611

(G-16272)
NORTHERN WOOD PRODUCTS INC
3573 Thorn Rd (46574-8227)
PHONE...................................574 586-3068
Richard Maher, *Pr*
June Maher, *Sec*
EMP: 9 **EST:** 1985
SALES (est): 808.2K **Privately Held**
SIC: 2421 Sawmills and planing mills, general

(G-16273)
OPTA MINERALS (HOLDCO) INC
205 Plymouth Laporte Tr State Hwy 104 (46574)
PHONE...................................574 586-9559
Barnie Rumble, *Mgr*
EMP: 1
Web: www.optagroupllc.com
SIC: 3299 1481 Tile, sand lime; Nonmetallic mineral services
PA: Opta Minerals (Holdco) Inc.
    300 Corporate Pkwy
    Amherst NY 14226

(G-16274)
POLYGON COMPANY
Tenesse St (46574)
P.O. Box 176 (46574-0176)
PHONE...................................574 586-3145
EMP: 55
SALES (corp-wide): 78.63MM **Privately Held**
Web: www.polygoncomposites.com
SIC: 3082 Unsupported plastics profile shapes
PA: Polygon Company
    103 Industrial Park Dr

GEOGRAPHIC SECTION

Walkerton IN 46574
574 586-3145

(G-16275)
POLYGON COMPANY (PA)
103 Industrial Park Dr (46574)
P.O. Box 176 (46574)
PHONE..................................574 586-3145
James Shobert, *CEO*
Timothy Shobert, *
▲ **EMP:** 190 **EST:** 1950
SALES (est): 78.63MM
SALES (corp-wide): 78.63MM **Privately Held**
Web: www.polygoncomposites.com
SIC: 3082 Unsupported plastics profile shapes

(G-16276)
ROSS ENGINEERING & MACHINE INC
70100 Stephens St (46574-1243)
PHONE..................................574 586-7791
Eric Morris, *Prin*
EMP: 21 **EST:** 1985
SQ FT: 6,500
SALES (est): 1.92MM **Privately Held**
Web: www.rosseam.com
SIC: 3544 Special dies and tools

(G-16277)
TRIPLE J MACHINING AND MFG INC
324 Liberty St (46574)
P.O. Box 13 (46574)
PHONE..................................574 586-7500
Sheree Rudecki, *Pr*
Sheree K Rudecki, *Prin*
EMP: 14 **EST:** 2015
SALES (est): 2.26MM **Privately Held**
Web: www.triplejmachining.com
SIC: 3469 1389 3599 Metal stampings, nec; Construction, repair, and dismantling services; Machine and other job shop work

(G-16278)
ULTRA MANUFACTURING INC
648 Stephens St (46574-1264)
P.O. Box 28 (46574-0028)
PHONE..................................574 586-2320
Michael Austin, *Pr*
Tammy Austin, *
EMP: 25 **EST:** 2006
SQ FT: 12,000
SALES (est): 6.23MM
SALES (corp-wide): 6.23MM **Privately Held**
Web: www.ultramfg1.com
SIC: 3469 Machine parts, stamped or pressed metal
PA: Austin & Austin, Inc.
648 Stephens St
Walkerton IN 46574
574 586-2320

(G-16279)
WALKERTON TOOL & DIE INC
106 Industrial Park Dr (46574-1065)
P.O. Box 58 (46574-0058)
PHONE..................................574 586-3162
Scott Rizek, *Pr*
Harold Rizek, *
EMP: 25 **EST:** 1963
SQ FT: 17,000
SALES (est): 1.08MM **Privately Held**
Web: www.walkertoncnc.com
SIC: 2759 3544 3599 3549 Publication printing; Special dies and tools; Machine shop, jobbing and repair; Metalworking machinery, nec

Walton
Cass County

(G-16280)
ADVANCED PROTECTION SYSTEMS
Also Called: Advance Protection System
6257 S County Road 900 E (46994-9439)
P.O. Box 549 (46994-0549)
PHONE..................................574 626-2939
EMP: 1 **EST:** 1982
SALES (est): 89.45K **Privately Held**
SIC: 3669 Emergency alarms

(G-16281)
BRAYDEN SHEDRON ✪
Also Called: Signal 10 Supply
403 N Davis St (46994-9396)
PHONE..................................765 480-7675
Brayden Shedron, *Owner*
EMP: 1 **EST:** 2022
SALES (est): 54.05K **Privately Held**
SIC: 3842 7389 Clothing, fire resistant and protective; Business Activities at Non-Commercial Site

(G-16282)
CONNER SAWMILL INC
Also Called: Conner Saw Mill
300 North St (46994-4177)
P.O. Box 308 (46994-0308)
PHONE..................................574 626-3227
Eldon Conner, *Pr*
Jean Conner, *Sec*
EMP: 15 **EST:** 1964
SQ FT: 7,000
SALES (est): 2.5MM **Privately Held**
Web: www.connersawmill.com
SIC: 2448 2421 2449 Pallets, wood; Custom sawmill; Wood containers, nec

(G-16283)
TERICK SALES
Also Called: Terick Sales & Service
3519 E County Road 800 S (46994-9246)
PHONE..................................574 626-3173
Rick Canfield, *Owner*
Teri Canfield, *Owner*
EMP: 2 **EST:** 1987
SALES (est): 157.09K **Privately Held**
SIC: 3699 Electronic training devices

(G-16284)
WALTON INDUSTRIAL PARK INC
Also Called: Ironmonger Spring Division
7585 S Us Hwy 35 (46994)
P.O. Box 318 (46994-0318)
PHONE..................................574 626-2929
Jo Ellen Ironmonger, *Pr*
Steven Ironmonger, *VP*
Crystal Slldck, *Sec*
EMP: 12 **EST:** 1977
SQ FT: 18,000
SALES (est): 1.18MM **Privately Held**
Web: www.ironmongerspringdiv.com
SIC: 3495 7389 3679 Precision springs; Bicycle assembly service; Harness assemblies, for electronic use: wire or cable

Wanatah
Laporte County

(G-16285)
AMERICA CORN CUTTER
9203 Twin Acres Dr (46390-9415)
PHONE..................................219 733-0885
Carol Bunton-benkie, *Owner*
EMP: 2 **EST:** 2007
SALES (est): 132.1K **Privately Held**

SIC: 3999 Manufacturing industries, nec

(G-16286)
ASL TECHNOLOGIES LLC
10525 W Us Highway 30 Bldg 3d (46390-9412)
PHONE..................................219 733-2777
EMP: 7 **EST:** 2000
SQ FT: 4,500
SALES (est): 830.69K **Privately Held**
Web: www.aslfilter.com
SIC: 3569 Filters

(G-16287)
B PLUS ENTERPRISES INC
122 S Illinois St (46390-9998)
P.O. Box 75 (46390-0075)
PHONE..................................219 733-9404
Phillipe E Boule, *Pr*
EMP: 3 **EST:** 1987
SQ FT: 5,000
SALES (est): 310.82K **Privately Held**
SIC: 3089 Molding primary plastics

(G-16288)
COMMTINEO LLC
Also Called: Comtineo
10525 W Us Highway 30 Bldg 4c (46390-9411)
PHONE..................................219 476-3667
EMP: 10 **EST:** 2014
SQ FT: 9,600
SALES (est): 410.25K **Privately Held**
Web: www.comtineo.com
SIC: 8741 1731 4812 1623 Business management; Electrical work; Radiotelephone communication; Transmitting tower (telecommunication) construction

(G-16289)
CONTINNTAL CRPNTRY CMPNNTS LLC
9702 W Us Highway 30 (46390)
PHONE..................................219 733-0367
Justin Wright, *Managing Member*
EMP: 40 **EST:** 2011
SQ FT: 16,500
SALES (est): 5.15MM
SALES (corp-wide): 101.52MM **Privately Held**
Web: www.continentalcomponents.com
SIC: 1751 2439 2452 Carpentry work; Structural wood members, nec; Prefabricated wood buildings
HQ: Ambassador Supply Llc
2817 E Dupont Rd
Fort Wayne IN 46825
260 487-4000

(G-16290)
INSULATION SPECIALTIES OF AMER
1095 Kabert Dr (46390-9633)
P.O. Box 10 (46390-0010)
PHONE..................................219 733-2502
Monie Parker, *Pr*
Don Sommers, *
Robert Peacock, *
EMP: 20 **EST:** 1976
SQ FT: 30,000
SALES (est): 1.36MM **Privately Held**
Web: www.insulationspecialties.com
SIC: 3297 3296 3264 1742 Nonclay refractories; Mineral wool; Porcelain electrical supplies; Insulation, buildings

(G-16291)
STEINDLER SIGNS & GRAPHIX LLC
105 Koselke St (46390-9577)
P.O. Box 285 (46390-0285)
PHONE..................................219 733-2551

Tom Steindler Junior, *Owner*
EMP: 3 **EST:** 2008
SALES (est): 251.36K **Privately Held**
Web: www.steindlersigns.com
SIC: 3993 Electric signs

(G-16292)
W KENDALL & SONS INC (PA)
10270 W Us Highway 30 (46390-9542)
P.O. Box 9 (46390-0009)
PHONE..................................219 733-2412
Gary Rice, *Pr*
Scott Rice, *Sec*
Wayne Rice, *Stockholder*
EMP: 3 **EST:** 1970
SQ FT: 25,000
SALES (est): 876.07K
SALES (corp-wide): 876.07K **Privately Held**
Web: www.wkendall.com
SIC: 3471 3479 Sand blasting of metal parts; Painting, coating, and hot dipping

Warren
Huntington County

(G-16293)
ALLIANCE GROUP TECH INC
311 9th St (46792-9650)
PHONE..................................260 375-2810
Craig Murphy, *Pr*
EMP: 74 **EST:** 2017
SALES (est): 386.1K **Privately Held**
Web: www.alliancegroup-inc.com
SIC: 3674 3679 3496 Integrated circuits, semiconductor networks, etc.; Harness assemblies, for electronic use: wire or cable ; Cable, uninsulated wire: made from purchased wire
PA: Ag Express Electronics, Inc.
6280 Ne 14th St
Des Moines IA 50313

(G-16294)
COMMODITY BLENDERS LLC
10643 S Hartford City Rd (46792-9624)
PHONE..................................260 375-3202
Chase Leighty, *Managing Member*
EMP: 1 **EST:** 2019
SALES (est): 69.27K **Privately Held**
Web: www.commodityblenders.com
SIC: 2048 Prepared feeds, nec

(G-16295)
DAUGHERTY BOX FACTORY
311 9th St (46792-9650)
PHONE..................................260 375-2810
EMP: 6 **EST:** 2016
SALES (est): 53.65K **Privately Held**
Web: www.daughertyinc.com
SIC: 3999 Manufacturing industries, nec

(G-16296)
DEBRA LINDHORST
Also Called: Type Galley , The
103 N Wayne St (46792-9652)
P.O. Box 608 (46792-0608)
PHONE..................................260 375-3285
Debra Lindhorst, *Owner*
EMP: 1 **EST:** 1996
SALES (est): 86.69K **Privately Held**
SIC: 2791 Typesetting

(G-16297)
ECOLAB INC
2847 E 600 S (46792-9426)
P.O. Box 462 (46792-0462)
PHONE..................................260 375-4710
Chris Lewe, *Mgr*

Warren - Huntington County (G-16298)

EMP: 2
SALES (corp-wide): 15.32B **Publicly Held**
Web: www.ecolab.com
SIC: 2841 Soap and other detergents
PA: Ecolab Inc.
1 Ecolab Pl
Saint Paul MN 55102
800 232-6522

(G-16298)
GEMINI OIL LLC
1323 W 600 S (46792-9747)
PHONE...................260 571-8388
Dennis Wiles, *Managing Member*
EMP: 7 **EST:** 2011
SALES (est): 374.03K **Privately Held**
SIC: 1382 Oil and gas exploration services

(G-16299)
GOLFO DI NAPOLI LLC
7916 S Warren Rd (46792-9278)
PHONE...................260 479-9890
EMP: 60 **EST:** 2018
SALES (est): 4.49MM **Privately Held**
Web: www.golfodinapolidairy.com
SIC: 2022 Processed cheese

(G-16300)
HY-LINE NORTH AMERICA LLC
1029 Mill Site Dr (46792-9605)
PHONE...................260 375-3041
Curt Schmidt, *Mgr*
EMP: 51
SALES (corp-wide): 4.24B **Privately Held**
Web: www.hylinena.com
SIC: 0254 2015 Chicken hatchery; Poultry slaughtering and processing
HQ: Hy-Line North America, Llc
1755 W Lakes Pkwy Ste A
West Des Moines IA 50266
515 225-6030

(G-16301)
MIDWEST WELDING FABRICATION
1138 E 600 S (46792-9497)
PHONE...................260 355-9354
Justin Martin, *Prin*
EMP: 4 **EST:** 2016
SALES (est): 48.69K **Privately Held**
Web: www.midwestweldingin.com
SIC: 7692 Welding repair

(G-16302)
NUPOINTE ENERGY LLC
1323 W 600 S (46792)
PHONE...................765 981-2664
EMP: 10 **EST:** 2017
SALES (est): 2.28MM **Privately Held**
SIC: 1389 1799 Oil and gas wells: building, repairing and dismantling; Construction site cleanup

(G-16303)
ROTO-FAB LLC
587 E 1000 S (46792-9781)
P.O. Box 563 (46792-0563)
PHONE...................260 375-4480
EMP: 5 **EST:** 2019
SALES (est): 198.24K **Privately Held**
Web: www.roto-fab.com
SIC: 3089 Plastics products, nec

(G-16304)
SALAMONIE MILLS INC
525 N Wayne St (46792-9456)
PHONE...................260 375-2200
Kevin Grayer, *Pr*
Don Mcdaniels, *VP*
Wendell Jackson, *Sec*
EMP: 14 **EST:** 1834

SQ FT: 1,200
SALES (est): 2.33MM **Privately Held**
Web: www.salamoniemills.com
SIC: 5191 5153 2041 Feed; Grain elevators; Flour and other grain mill products

(G-16305)
SATURN WHEEL COMPANY INC
507 E 9th St (46792-9269)
P.O. Box 610 (46792-0610)
PHONE...................260 375-4720
Mike Haggerty, *Pr*
Stacy Haggerty, *
Fred Mccracken, *CFO*
Roger Mcclellan, *COO*
EMP: 23 **EST:** 2004
SQ FT: 36,000
SALES (est): 878.61K **Privately Held**
SIC: 3471 Coloring and finishing of aluminum or formed products

Warsaw
Kosciusko County

(G-16306)
3G CONCEPTS LLC
3824 S Industrial Dr (46580-6057)
PHONE...................574 267-6100
EMP: 3 **EST:** 2011
SALES (est): 252.89K **Privately Held**
Web: www.3gconceptsllc.com
SIC: 3559 Automotive related machinery

(G-16307)
AARDVARK GRAPHICS
Also Called: Branded By Jdh
4121 Deer Run N (46582-6908)
PHONE...................574 267-4799
EMP: 2 **EST:** 1994
SALES (est): 21K **Privately Held**
SIC: 2759 Screen printing

(G-16308)
AARONS WELDING LLC
6421 E Mckenna Rd (46582-8037)
PHONE...................574 529-3885
Aaron Harteup, *Pr*
EMP: 1 **EST:** 2009
SALES (est): 49.69K **Privately Held**
SIC: 7692 Welding repair

(G-16309)
ACEYS TROPHIES & AWARDS
222 W Prairie St (46580-4339)
PHONE...................574 267-1426
Chuck Lisenbee, *Owner*
EMP: 2 **EST:** 1995
SALES (est): 99.01K **Privately Held**
SIC: 5999 3479 Trophies and plaques; Etching on metals

(G-16310)
AKZO NOBEL COATINGS INC
1102 Leiter Dr (46580-2475)
PHONE...................574 372-2000
EMP: 40
SALES (corp-wide): 11.6B **Privately Held**
SIC: 2819 2821 Industrial inorganic chemicals, nec; Plastics materials and resins
HQ: Akzo Nobel Coatings Inc.
535 Marriott Dr Ste 500
Nashville TN 37214
440 297-5100

(G-16311)
ALPHA LLC
3000 N Airport Rd (46582-9372)
PHONE...................574 292-1805

EMP: 13 **EST:** 2018
SALES (est): 849.41K **Privately Held**
Web: www.alpha-mfg.com
SIC: 3599 Machine shop, jobbing and repair

(G-16312)
ALPHA LLC
3000 N Airport Rd 7a (46582-9372)
PHONE...................574 646-2304
David Lynn Stackhouse, *Pr*
EMP: 8 **EST:** 2014
SALES (est): 215.66K **Privately Held**
SIC: 3599 Machine shop, jobbing and repair

(G-16313)
APPLIED THERMAL TECH INC
2169 N 100 E (46582-7872)
PHONE...................574 269-7116
Miroslav Bradican, *Pr*
Charles V Zichichi, *VP*
Robert Gunow Junior, *Treas*
EMP: 20 **EST:** 1992
SQ FT: 8,000
SALES (est): 2.69MM **Privately Held**
Web: www.appliedthermaltechnologies.com
SIC: 3398 Metal heat treating

(G-16314)
ARCH MED SLUTIONS - WARSAW LLC ✪
2070 N Cessna Rd (46582-6420)
PHONE...................574 267-2171
Benjamin Garden, *Pr*
EMP: 13 **EST:** 2022
SALES (est): 1.02MM
SALES (corp-wide): 45.79MM **Privately Held**
SIC: 3549 Assembly machines, including robotic
PA: Arch Medical Solutions Corp.
25040 Easy St
Warren MI 48089
603 760-1554

(G-16315)
AVIENT CORPORATION
Also Called: Spartech Plastics
3454 N Detroit St (State Rd 15) (46582-2284)
P.O. Box 958 (46581-0958)
PHONE...................574 267-1100
Julie A Mcalindon, *Mgr*
EMP: 32
Web: www.avient.com
SIC: 2821 Plastics materials and resins
PA: Avient Corporation
33587 Walker Rd
Avon Lake OH 44012

(G-16316)
BABSCO SUPPLY INC
Also Called: Babsco Electric
2361 Shelby Dr (46580-2164)
P.O. Box 1958 (46581-1958)
PHONE...................574 267-8999
Joe Hammond, *Prin*
EMP: 5
SALES (corp-wide): 9.51MM **Privately Held**
Web: www.babsco.com
SIC: 5063 3699 Electrical supplies, nec; Electrical equipment and supplies, nec
PA: Babsco Supply, Inc.
2410 S Main St
Elkhart IN 46517
574 293-0631

(G-16317)
BARTEL PRINTING COMPANY INC
310 Cedar St (46580-3026)
PHONE...................574 267-7421
Penny Bartel, *Pr*
Murray Bartel, *VP*
EMP: 8 **EST:** 1970
SQ FT: 3,000
SALES (est): 948.02K **Privately Held**
Web: www.bartelprinting.com
SIC: 2752 2759 Offset printing; Commercial printing, nec

(G-16318)
BCF PRECISION LLC
930 Executive Dr (46580-8535)
PHONE...................888 556-2264
Thomas Teach, *Managing Member*
EMP: 1 **EST:** 2016
SALES (est): 56.89K **Privately Held**
SIC: 3599 Industrial machinery, nec

(G-16319)
BEACHWOOD LUMBER CO INC
Also Called: Beachwood Manufacturing
7878 W Old Road 30 (46580-8367)
PHONE...................574 858-9325
TOLL FREE: 866
Dan Burns, *Pr*
EMP: 9 **EST:** 1970
SQ FT: 2,000
SALES (est): 336.53K **Privately Held**
SIC: 2439 Trusses, except roof: laminated lumber

(G-16320)
BILTZ SIGNS
5843 E Mckenna Rd (46582-8027)
PHONE...................574 594-2703
Ray Biltz, *Prin*
EMP: 5 **EST:** 2009
SALES (est): 74K **Privately Held**
SIC: 3993 Signs and advertising specialties

(G-16321)
BIOMET
320 Hepler Dr (46580-2566)
PHONE...................574 551-8959
EMP: 11 **EST:** 2019
SALES (est): 361.93K **Privately Held**
Web: www.zimmerbiomet.com
SIC: 3842 Orthopedic appliances

(G-16322)
BIOMET INC
56 E Bell Dr (46582-6924)
PHONE...................574 371-3760
EMP: 11
SALES (corp-wide): 7.39B **Publicly Held**
Web: www.oxfordknee.com
SIC: 3842 Orthopedic appliances
HQ: Biomet, Inc.
345 East Main Str
Warsaw IN 46580
574 267-6639

(G-16323)
BIOMET INC (HQ)
Also Called: Zimmer Biomet
345 E Main St (46580)
P.O. Box 587 (46581)
PHONE...................574 267-6639
Ivan Tornos, *Pr*
Bradley Tandy, *Sr VP*
Adam R Johnson, *Sr VP*
Robin T Barney, *Sr VP*
Tony W Collins, *CAO*
◆ **EMP:** 950 **EST:** 1977
SQ FT: 769,333
SALES (est): 1.01B

Warsaw - Kosciusko County (G-16344)

SALES (corp-wide): 7.39B **Publicly Held**
Web: www.zimmerbiomet.com
SIC: **3842** 3841 3845 Orthopedic appliances; Surgical and medical instruments; Electromedical equipment
PA: Zimmer Biomet Holdings, Inc.
345 E Main St
Warsaw IN 46580
574 267-6131

(G-16324)
BIOMET BIOLOGICS LLC
56 E Bell Dr (46582-6924)
P.O. Box 587 (46581-0587)
PHONE...................574 267-2038
EMP: 25 EST: 2002
SALES (est): 2.38MM
SALES (corp-wide): 7.39B **Publicly Held**
Web: www.zimmerbiomet.com
SIC: **3842** Orthopedic appliances
HQ: Biomet, Inc.
345 East Main Str
Warsaw IN 46580
574 267-6639

(G-16325)
BIOMET EUROPE LTD
56 E Bell Dr (46582-6924)
PHONE...................574 267-2038
EMP: 45 EST: 1984
SALES (est): 953.42K
SALES (corp-wide): 7.39B **Publicly Held**
Web: www.zimmerbiomet.com
SIC: **3842** 3841 3845 Implants, surgical; Medical instruments and equipment, blood and bone work; Electromedical apparatus
HQ: Biomet, Inc.
345 East Main Str
Warsaw IN 46580
574 267-6639

(G-16326)
BIOMET LEASING INC
56 E Bell Dr (46582-6924)
P.O. Box 587 (46581-0587)
PHONE...................574 267-6639
Debra Nielsen, Pr
EMP: 25 EST: 2006
SALES (est): 5.46MM
SALES (corp-wide): 7.39B **Publicly Held**
SIC: **3842** Orthopedic appliances
PA: Zimmer Biomet Holdings, Inc.
345 E Main St
Warsaw IN 46580
574 267-6131

(G-16327)
BIOMET ORTHOPEDICS LLC
56 E Bell Dr (46582-6924)
P.O. Box 587 (46581-0587)
PHONE...................574 267-6639
Jeffrey R Binder, Pr
Jacqueline K Huber, *
Debra Neilson, *
EMP: 49 EST: 1999
SALES (est): 22.69MM
SALES (corp-wide): 7.39B **Publicly Held**
Web: www.zimmerbiomet.com
SIC: **3842** Orthopedic appliances
PA: Zimmer Biomet Holdings, Inc.
345 E Main St
Warsaw IN 46580
574 267-6131

(G-16328)
BIOMET SPORTS MEDICINE LLC
Also Called: Biomet
56 E Bell Dr (46581)
P.O. Box 587 (46581-0587)
PHONE...................574 267-6639
David A Nolan Junior, Pr
Kevin Stone, *
Michael T Hodges, *
Bradley J Tandy, *
EMP: 90 EST: 1990
SQ FT: 36,000
SALES (est): 20.68MM
SALES (corp-wide): 7.39B **Publicly Held**
Web: www.zimmerbiomet.com
SIC: **3842** Orthopedic appliances
HQ: Biomet, Inc.
345 East Main Str
Warsaw IN 46580
574 267-6639

(G-16329)
BIOMET TRAUMA LLC
56 E Bell Dr (46582-6924)
PHONE...................574 267-6639
EMP: 13 EST: 2010
SALES (est): 2.36MM
SALES (corp-wide): 7.39B **Publicly Held**
SIC: **3842** Orthopedic appliances
PA: Zimmer Biomet Holdings, Inc.
345 E Main St
Warsaw IN 46580
574 267-6131

(G-16330)
BIOMET US RECONSTRUCTION LLC
56 E Bell Dr (46582-6924)
PHONE...................800 348-9500
EMP: 10 EST: 2012
SALES (est): 878.77K
SALES (corp-wide): 7.39B **Publicly Held**
SIC: **3842** Orthopedic appliances
PA: Zimmer Biomet Holdings, Inc.
345 E Main St
Warsaw IN 46580
574 267-6131

(G-16331)
BUHRT ENGINEERING & CNSTR
27 E 250 N (46582-6956)
PHONE...................574 267-3720
Dennis R Buhrt, Pr
Janice L Buhrt, *
EMP: 25 EST: 1977
SQ FT: 25,000
SALES (est): 4.92MM **Privately Held**
Web: www.buhrt.com
SIC: **3444** 1791 7699 3537 Sheet metalwork; Iron work, structural; Industrial equipment services; Industrial trucks and tractors

(G-16332)
CARDINAL SERVICES INC INDIANA
Also Called: CCI Big Boy Products
504 N Bay Dr (46580-4627)
PHONE...................574 267-3823
Mark Randall, Brnch Mgr
EMP: 95
SALES (corp-wide): 26.13MM **Privately Held**
Web: www.cardinalservices.org
SIC: **3714** Trailer hitches, motor vehicle
PA: Cardinal Services Inc Of Indiana
504 N Bay Dr
Warsaw IN 46580
574 267-3823

(G-16333)
CARDINAL SERVICES INC INDIANA (PA)
504 N Bay Dr (46580)
PHONE...................574 267-3823
N Jane Greene, Pr
Randy Hall, *
Ray Hunsberger, *
Leanne Ford, *
EMP: 75 EST: 1954
SQ FT: 44,600
SALES (est): 26.13MM
SALES (corp-wide): 26.13MM **Privately Held**
Web: www.cardinalservices.org
SIC: **8331** 8361 4131 3523 Job training services; Rehabilitation center, residential: health care incidental; Intercity and rural bus transportation; Barn, silo, poultry, dairy, and livestock machinery

(G-16334)
CARDINAL SERVICES INC INDIANA
Also Called: CCI Contract Manufacturing
1770 E Smith St (46580-4659)
PHONE...................574 371-1305
Jay Tate, Genl Mgr
EMP: 86
SQ FT: 45,000
SALES (corp-wide): 26.13MM **Privately Held**
Web: www.cardinalservices.org
SIC: **3569** Assembly machines, non-metalworking
PA: Cardinal Services Inc Of Indiana
504 N Bay Dr
Warsaw IN 46580
574 267-3823

(G-16335)
CIRCLE M SPRING INC
930 Executive Dr (46580-8535)
PHONE...................574 267-2883
Thadd Mellott, Pr
Dena Mellott, *
▲ EMP: 35 EST: 1998
SALES (est): 4.03MM **Privately Held**
Web: www.circlemspring.com
SIC: **3841** 3495 Surgical and medical instruments; Wire springs

(G-16336)
CNC CONCEPTS INC
3019 S County Farm Rd (46580-8240)
PHONE...................574 269-2301
Stephen S Kline, Prin
EMP: 2 EST: 2008
SALES (est): 94.35K **Privately Held**
Web: www.cncci.com
SIC: **3599** Machine shop, jobbing and repair

(G-16337)
CONCEPTS IN STONE & TILE INC
118 N Buffalo St (46580-2728)
PHONE...................574 267-4712
EMP: 3 EST: 1986
SALES (est): 337.03K **Privately Held**
Web: www.conceptsinstoneandtile.com
SIC: **3281** 1743 Curbing, granite or stone; Tile installation, ceramic

(G-16338)
CRYSTAL LAKE LLC
6500 W Crystal Lake Rd (46580-8986)
P.O. Box 220 (46502-0220)
PHONE...................574 858-2514
EMP: 74
SQ FT: 56,341
SALES (corp-wide): 5.04MM **Privately Held**
Web: www.crystallakellc.net
SIC: **2015** 2038 Egg processing; Frozen specialties, nec
PA: Crystal Lake Llc
4217 W Old Road 30
Warsaw IN 46580
574 267-3101

(G-16339)
CRYSTAL LAKE LLC (PA)
4217 W Old Road 30 (46580-6842)
P.O. Box 220 (46502-0220)
PHONE...................574 267-3101
EMP: 1 EST: 1967
SQ FT: 10,000
SALES (est): 5.04MM
SALES (corp-wide): 5.04MM **Privately Held**
Web: www.crystallakellc.net
SIC: **2015** Eggs, processed: frozen

(G-16340)
CRYSTAL SHADOWS
1080 W 200 S (46580-7304)
PHONE...................574 269-2722
Gary Eshleman, Owner
EMP: 1 EST: 1998
SALES (est): 49.29K **Privately Held**
SIC: **3231** Cut and engraved glassware: made from purchased glass

(G-16341)
CXR COMPANY INC
2599 N Fox Farm Rd (46580-6536)
P.O. Box 1114 (46581-1114)
PHONE...................574 269-6020
Barbara Calhan, CEO
Cassandra Stewart, Pr
Paula Zeigler, VP
EMP: 10 EST: 1987
SQ FT: 8,000
SALES (est): 480.99K **Privately Held**
Web: www.cxrcompany.com
SIC: **3844** 7699 X-ray apparatus and tubes; X-ray equipment repair

(G-16342)
DA-LITE SCREEN COMPANY LLC
3100 N Detroit St (46582-2288)
P.O. Box 137 (46581-0137)
PHONE...................574 267-8101
Richard E Lundin, Pr
Judith D Loughran, *
Jerry C Young, *
◆ EMP: 415 EST: 1909
SQ FT: 311,300
SALES (est): 78.77MM **Privately Held**
Web: www.legrandav.com
SIC: **3861** Screens, projection
HQ: Legrand Av Inc.
6436 City W Pkwy
Eden Prairie MN 55344
866 977-3901

(G-16343)
DAIRYLAND WOODWORKS LLC
2131 N 700 W (46580-6531)
PHONE...................715 271-2110
EMP: 5 EST: 2003
SALES (est): 468.35K **Privately Held**
Web: dairyland-woodworks-llc.business.site
SIC: **2431** Interior and ornamental woodwork and trim

(G-16344)
DALTON CORP WARSAW MFG FCILTY
Also Called: Warsaw Manufacturing Facility
Lincoln & Jefferson St (46581)
PHONE...................574 267-8111
Stephen Shaffer, Pr
Jacob Yahne, *
EMP: 6 EST: 1910
SALES (est): 509.52K
SALES (corp-wide): 110.99MM **Privately Held**
Web: www.daltoncorporation.com
SIC: **3321** Gray and ductile iron foundries
PA: New Dalton Foundry, Llc
1900 E Jefferson St
Warsaw IN 46580
574 267-8111

Warsaw - Kosciusko County (G-16345)

GEOGRAPHIC SECTION

(G-16345)
DALTON CORPORATION
Also Called: Dalton Foundries
1900 E Jefferson St (46580-3761)
P.O. Box 1388 (46581-1388)
PHONE.................574 267-8111
Joe Derita, *Pr*
EMP: 15
SALES (corp-wide): 110.99MM **Privately Held**
Web: www.daltoncorporation.com
SIC: 7389 3322 3321 Personal service agents, brokers, and bureaus; Malleable iron foundries; Gray and ductile iron foundries
HQ: The Dalton Corporation
1900 E Jefferson St
Warsaw IN 46580
574 267-8111

(G-16346)
DANIEL PUBLICATIONS
2212 E 225 S (46580-6213)
PHONE.................574 269-2825
Daniel Coplen, *Owner*
EMP: 1 **EST:** 1995
SALES (est): 48.86K **Privately Held**
SIC: 2741 Miscellaneous publishing

(G-16347)
DEPUY ORTHOPAEDICS INC (DH)
Also Called: Depuy Synthes
700 Orthopaedic Dr (46582)
PHONE.................574 267-8143
Amy M Ellixson, *VP*
John D Lottier, *VP*
Scott R Ryan, *Sec*
EMP: 21 **EST:** 1895
SALES (est): 45.67MM
SALES (corp-wide): 85.16B **Publicly Held**
SIC: 3842 Surgical appliances and supplies
HQ: Medical Device Business Services, Inc.
700 Orthopaedic Dr
Warsaw IN 46582

(G-16348)
DEPUY PRODUCTS INC (HQ)
700 Orthopaedic Dr (46582-3900)
PHONE.................574 267-8143
Andrew Ekdahl, *Pr*
Peter Batesko Iii, *VP*
Scott R Ryan, *
EMP: 101 **EST:** 2000
SALES (est): 2.07B
SALES (corp-wide): 85.16B **Publicly Held**
Web: www.depuysynthes.com
SIC: 3842 Surgical appliances and supplies
PA: Johnson & Johnson
1 Johnson & Johnson Plz
New Brunswick NJ 08933
732 524-0400

(G-16349)
DEPUY SYNTHES INC (DH)
Also Called: Synthes USA
700 Orthopaedic Dr (46582-3900)
PHONE.................574 267-8143
Michel Orsinger, *CEO*
▲ **EMP:** 109 **EST:** 1996
SQ FT: 15,000
SALES (est): 1.81B
SALES (corp-wide): 85.16B **Publicly Held**
Web: www.jnjmedicaldevices.com
SIC: 3841 Medical instruments and equipment, blood and bone work
HQ: Depuy Products, Inc.
700 Orthopaedic Dr
Warsaw IN 46582
574 267-8143

(G-16350)
DEPUY SYNTHES PRODUCTS INC
700 Orthopaedic Dr (46582-3900)
PHONE.................574 267-8143
EMP: 13
SALES (corp-wide): 85.16B **Publicly Held**
SIC: 3841 Surgical and medical instruments
HQ: Depuy Synthes Products, Inc.
325 Paramount Dr
Raynham MA 02767
508 880-8100

(G-16351)
DEPUY SYNTHES SALES INC
Depuy Synthes Jint Rcnstrction
700 Orthopaedic Dr (46582-3900)
PHONE.................574 267-8143
EMP: 1
SALES (corp-wide): 85.16B **Publicly Held**
SIC: 3842 Surgical appliances and supplies
HQ: Depuy Synthes Sales Inc
325 Paramount Dr
Raynham MA 02767
508 880-8100

(G-16352)
DESIGNS BY KIM
408 E Lynnwood Dr S (46580-7559)
PHONE.................574 268-9904
Kim Overmeyer, *Owner*
EMP: 1 **EST:** 2004
SALES (est): 76.93K **Privately Held**
SIC: 2395 Embroidery products, except Schiffli machine

(G-16353)
DMP INDUSTRIES LLC
1411 E Springhill Rd (46580-1815)
PHONE.................260 413-6701
April Isch, *Owner*
EMP: 5 **EST:** 2017
SALES (est): 99.84K **Privately Held**
SIC: 3999 Manufacturing industries, nec

(G-16354)
ECPCA SAFE-WAY LLC (PA)
Also Called: Safe-Way Door
3814 E Us Highway 30 (46580-6711)
PHONE.................574 267-4861
TOLL FREE: 800
EMP: 65 **EST:** 1974
SALES (est): 9.87MM
SALES (corp-wide): 9.87MM **Privately Held**
Web: www.safewaydoor.com
SIC: 3442 5211 2431 Garage doors, overhead: metal; Garage doors, sale and installation; Garage doors, overhead, wood

(G-16355)
EGG INNOVATIONS LLC (PA)
Also Called: Egg Innovations
4799 W 100 N (46580-8997)
P.O. Box 1275 (46581-1275)
PHONE.................574 267-7545
EMP: 68 **EST:** 1999
SQ FT: 48,000
SALES (est): 23.16MM **Privately Held**
Web: www.egginnovations.com
SIC: 2015 2048 Egg processing; Prepared feeds, nec

(G-16356)
EGGPRESS LLC
4217 W Old Road 30 (46580-6842)
PHONE.................574 267-2847
Ron Truex, *Pr*
EMP: 6 **EST:** 2012
SALES (est): 188.43K **Privately Held**
SIC: 2034 Dried and dehydrated fruits, vegetables and soup mixes

(G-16357)
ELKHART COUNTY GRAVEL INC
2042 W 300 N (46582-8312)
PHONE.................574 831-2815
EMP: 5
SALES (corp-wide): 4.21MM **Privately Held**
Web: www.elkhartcountygravel.com
SIC: 1442 Sand mining
PA: Elkhart County Gravel Inc
19242 Us Highway 6
New Paris IN 46553
574 831-2815

(G-16358)
ELMOS
1900 Plaza Dr (46580-1207)
PHONE.................574 371-2050
Jeryl Leamon, *Mgr*
EMP: 2 **EST:** 2010
SALES (est): 154.32K **Privately Held**
Web: www.lassus.com
SIC: 3578 Automatic teller machines (ATM)

(G-16359)
ELYSIAN COMPANY LLC
110 E Center St (46580-2840)
PHONE.................574 267-2259
Elise Lauren Wright, *Pr*
EMP: 5 **EST:** 2017
SALES (est): 197.3K **Privately Held**
Web: www.elysianco.com
SIC: 2335 Women's, junior's, and misses' dresses

(G-16360)
ENPAK LLC
939 E Pound Dr N (46582-6943)
PHONE.................574 268-7273
Marlene Mulero-betances, *Prin*
Marlene Mulero-betances, *Pr*
Rick Rivera, *VP*
EMP: 4 **EST:** 2011
SALES (est): 454.01K **Privately Held**
Web: www.enpakllc.com
SIC: 7389 3569 8742
; Robots, assembly line: industrial and commercial; Management consulting services

(G-16361)
FANCIL WELDING LLC
Also Called: Fancil Welding Service
721 S Buffalo St (46580-4312)
PHONE.................574 267-8627
Robert Fancil, *Pr*
Jerry Fancil, *VP*
EMP: 3 **EST:** 1986
SALES (est): 213.78K **Privately Held**
SIC: 7692 Welding repair

(G-16362)
FLEXAUST INC (DH)
Also Called: Flexaust
1510 Armstrong Rd (46580)
P.O. Box 4275 (46581)
PHONE.................574 267-7909
◆ **EMP:** 42 **EST:** 1995
SQ FT: 106,000
SALES (est): 88.89MM
SALES (corp-wide): 276.12MM **Privately Held**
Web: www.flexaust.com
SIC: 3052 Rubber and plastics hose and beltings
HQ: Flexaust Company Inc
1200 Prospect St Ste 325
La Jolla CA 92037
619 232-8429

(G-16363)
FLINT GROUP US LLC
Also Called: Flint Ink North America Div
3025 E Old Road 30 (46582-8078)
P.O. Box 287 (46581-0287)
PHONE.................574 269-4603
Kent Blackford, *Mgr*
EMP: 13
SALES (corp-wide): 1.91B **Privately Held**
Web: www.flintgrp.com
SIC: 2893 Printing ink
PA: Flint Group Us Llc
17177 N Laurel Park Dr # 300
Livonia MI 48152
734 781-4600

(G-16364)
FRITO LAY
2162 N Cessna Rd (46582-6401)
PHONE.................574 269-1410
EMP: 6 **EST:** 2017
SALES (est): 142.24K **Privately Held**
SIC: 2096 Potato chips and similar snacks

(G-16365)
FRONTLINE MFG INC
Also Called: Front Line Manufacturing
2466 W 200 N (46580-8320)
PHONE.................574 269-6751
Marty White, *Mgr*
EMP: 50
Web: www.diamondtubshowers.com
SIC: 3088 Plastics plumbing fixtures
PA: Frontline Mfg., Inc.
1445 Polk Dr
Warsaw IN 46582

(G-16366)
FRONTLINE MFG INC (PA)
1445 Polk Dr (46582-8605)
PHONE.................574 453-2902
EMP: 100 **EST:** 1994
SALES (est): 9.49MM **Privately Held**
Web: www.diamondtubshowers.com
SIC: 3088 Shower stalls, fiberglass and plastics

(G-16367)
GAPTOOTH PUBLISHING
403 S Union St (46580-4236)
PHONE.................574 551-6386
Trina Hoy, *Prin*
EMP: 4 **EST:** 2017
SALES (est): 61.53K **Privately Held**
SIC: 2741 Miscellaneous publishing

(G-16368)
GRABER RONALD D YODER &
Also Called: D and R Custom Logging
1515 Fox Farm Rd (46580-2136)
PHONE.................574 268-9512
Ronald Yoder, *Pt*
David Graber, *Pt*
EMP: 2 **EST:** 1995
SALES (est): 156.66K **Privately Held**
SIC: 2411 Logging camps and contractors

(G-16369)
GRACE MANUFACTURING INC
1500 W Center St (46580-2410)
P.O. Box 856 (46581-0856)
PHONE.................574 267-8000
Nancy Hoeppner, *Ch Bd*
Dan Hoeppner, *Pr*
Rhonda Hoeppner, *Sec*
Robert Hoeppner, *Dir*
EMP: 15 **EST:** 1969
SQ FT: 11,200
SALES (est): 1.1MM **Privately Held**
Web: www.grace-mfg.com

SIC: 3499 3429 Metal household articles; Hardware, nec

(G-16370)
GRAYCRAFT SIGNS PLUS INC
3304 Lake City Hwy (46580-3923)
PHONE.....................574 269-3780
Scott Gray, Brnch Mgr
EMP: 3
Web: www.graycraftsigns.com
SIC: 3993 Signs and advertising specialties
PA: Graycraft Signs Plus Inc.
2428 Getz Rd
Fort Wayne IN 46804

(G-16371)
GREATBATCH LTD
Also Called: Greatbatch Medical
265 E Bell Dr Ste A (46582-9301)
PHONE.....................260 755-7484
EMP: 3
SALES (corp-wide): 1.6B Publicly Held
Web: www.integer.net
SIC: 3675 3692 3691 Electronic capacitors; Primary batteries, dry and wet; Storage batteries
HQ: Greatbatch Ltd.
10000 Wehrle Dr
Clarence NY 14031
612 331-6750

(G-16372)
GUARDIAN DEFENSE INC
3765 S Britney Dr (46580-6240)
PHONE.....................574 265-4474
Abraham Heller, Prin
EMP: 5 EST: 2017
SALES (est): 183.37K Privately Held
Web: www.guardiandefenseinc.com
SIC: 3812 Defense systems and equipment

(G-16373)
HAND INDUSTRIES INC
Also Called: Acorn Ridge Highlands
315 S Hand Ave (46580-2596)
PHONE.....................574 267-3525
Terry E Hand, CEO
William F Hand, Ch
John G Hand, Pr
Leon Horn, Sec
EMP: 40 EST: 1956
SQ FT: 19,000
SALES (est): 2.27MM Privately Held
Web: www.handindustries.com
SIC: 3471 3499 0212 Cleaning, polishing, and finishing; Novelties and giftware, including trophies; Beef cattle, except feedlots

(G-16374)
HARDESTY PRINTING CO INC
411 W Market St (46580-2832)
PHONE.....................574 267-7591
EMP: 12
SALES (corp-wide): 2.4MM Privately Held
Web: www.hardestyprinting.com
SIC: 2752 2791 2789 Offset printing; Typesetting; Bookbinding and related work
PA: Hardesty Printing Co Inc
1218 N State Road 25
Rochester IN 46975
574 223-4553

(G-16375)
HUGH K EAGAN
Also Called: Allegra Print & Imaging
201 W Center St (46580-2816)
PHONE.....................574 269-5411
Hugh K Eagan, Owner
EMP: 2 EST: 2010
SALES (est): 248.51K Privately Held
Web: www.allegramarketingprint.com
SIC: 2752 Offset printing

(G-16376)
INDIANA COATED FABRICS INC
Also Called: Icf/Eco
102 Enterprise Dr (46580-1204)
P.O. Box 1017 (46581-1017)
PHONE.....................574 269-1280
Timothy R Foster, Pr
David P Brettell Senior, VP
William J Haldewang, Ch
EMP: 10 EST: 2014
SALES (est): 1.15MM Privately Held
Web: www.indianacoatedfabrics.com
SIC: 2295 Coated fabrics, not rubberized

(G-16377)
INDIANA DISCOUNT TIRE COMPANY
Also Called: Discount Tire
857 N Parker St (46580-6802)
PHONE.....................574 549-6060
EMP: 2
SALES (corp-wide): 3.69B Privately Held
SIC: 7534 5013 Tire retreading and repair shops; Radiators
HQ: Indiana Discount Tire Company Inc
20225 N Scottsdale Rd
Scottsdale AZ 85255

(G-16378)
INDIANA VAC-FORM INC
Also Called: Easterwood
2030 N Boeing Rd (46582-7860)
PHONE.....................574 269-1725
Greg Wood, Pr
Donald Robinson, Pr
Donna Robinson, Sec
▲ EMP: 29 EST: 1977
SQ FT: 45,000
SALES (est): 928.22K Privately Held
Web: www.invacform.com
SIC: 3089 Injection molding of plastics

(G-16379)
INSTRUMENTAL MACHINE & DEV INC
Also Called: IMD
2098 N Pound Dr W (46582-6550)
PHONE.....................574 267-7713
Todd Speicher, Pr
EMP: 70 EST: 1991
SQ FT: 12,000
SALES (est): 8.67MM Privately Held
Web: www.imdortho.com
SIC: 3599 Machine shop, jobbing and repair

(G-16380)
JENCO ENGINEERING INC
27 E 250 N (46582-6956)
PHONE.....................574 267-4608
Dennis Buhrt, Pr
EMP: 2 EST: 1983
SALES (est): 249.76K Privately Held
SIC: 3569 3599 General industrial machinery, nec; Industrial machinery, nec

(G-16381)
JERRY OPPERED
Also Called: Makit
2534 S Country Club Rd (46580-7409)
P.O. Box 102 (46581-0102)
PHONE.....................574 269-5363
Jerry Opperud, Owner
Jerry Oppered, Owner
EMP: 1 EST: 1974
SALES (est): 87.78K Privately Held
SIC: 3089 3229 Planters, plastics; Pressed and blown glass, nec

(G-16382)
KESTERS ELECTRIC MOTOR SVC LLC
1408 Armstrong Rd (46580-2420)
PHONE.....................574 269-2889
Tim Hudson, Managing Member
EMP: 5 EST: 1955
SALES (est): 300.7K Privately Held
Web: www.kesterselectric.com
SIC: 7694 Electric motor repair

(G-16383)
KMC CORPORATION
602 Leiter Dr (46580-2461)
PHONE.....................574 267-7033
Richard L Grover, Pr
EMP: 31 EST: 1990
SQ FT: 50,000
SALES (est): 544.45K Privately Held
SIC: 2512 2515 Upholstered household furniture; Mattresses and bedsprings

(G-16384)
KUERT CONCRETE INC
155 W 600 N (46582-7790)
PHONE.....................574 453-3993
EMP: 9
SALES (corp-wide): 13.04MM Privately Held
Web: www.kuert.com
SIC: 3273 Ready-mixed concrete
PA: Kuert Concrete Inc
5909 Nimtz Pkwy
South Bend IN 46628
574 232-9911

(G-16385)
LAKELAND PIER AND LIFT LLC
1401 N Antler Dr (46582-7397)
P.O. Box 743 (46555-0743)
PHONE.....................574 377-3481
Chris Carman, Managing Member
EMP: 12 EST: 2014
SALES (est): 922.74K Privately Held
Web: www.pierandlift.com
SIC: 3536 7389 Boat lifts; Business Activities at Non-Commercial Site

(G-16386)
LASER PLUS INC
3950 N Blue Heron Dr (46582-7778)
PHONE.....................574 269-1246
Jon Schutz, Owner
EMP: 5 EST: 1986
SALES (est): 351.59K Privately Held
Web: www.laserplus.net
SIC: 3577 Printers, computer

(G-16387)
LEGRAND AV INC
Also Called: Da-Lite
3100 N Detroit St (46582-2288)
PHONE.....................574 267-8101
EMP: 415
Web: www.legrandav.com
SIC: 3861 Screens, projection
HQ: Legrand Av Inc.
6436 City W Pkwy
Eden Prairie MN 55344
866 977-3901

(G-16388)
LSC COMMUNICATIONS US LLC
2801 W Old Road 30 (46580-8783)
P.O. Box 837 (46581-0837)
PHONE.....................574 267-7101
EMP: 1
SALES (corp-wide): 8.23B Privately Held
Web: www.lsccom.com
SIC: 2752 Commercial printing, lithographic
HQ: Lsc Communications Us, Llc
4101 Winfield Rd
Warrenville IL 60555
844 572-5720

(G-16389)
LVB ACQUISITION HOLDING LLC
56 E Bell Dr (46582-6989)
PHONE.....................574 267-6639
EMP: 9279
SIC: 3842 3841 3845 Implants, surgical; Medical instruments and equipment, blood and bone work; Electromedical apparatus

(G-16390)
MARINE MOORING INC
3404 N 600 E (46582-8030)
PHONE.....................574 594-5787
Randall P Pollen, Pr
Donna J Pollen, *
▲ EMP: 40 EST: 1986
SQ FT: 8,000
SALES (est): 4.68MM Privately Held
Web: www.marinemooring.com
SIC: 2394 Canopies, fabric: made from purchased materials

(G-16391)
MARTINEZ CUSTOM WELDING
2063 E Riverside Dr (46582-7959)
PHONE.....................574 377-2251
Hector Martinez, Prin
EMP: 5 EST: 2016
SALES (est): 25.09K Privately Held
SIC: 7692 Welding repair

(G-16392)
MAVRON INC
Also Called: Mavron
152 S Zimmer Rd (46580-2369)
PHONE.....................574 267-3044
Sheal Dirck, Pr
Ronald L Dirck, Ch
Nancy Dirck, Sec
▼ EMP: 14 EST: 1973
SQ FT: 40,000
SALES (est): 2.23MM Privately Held
Web: www.mavron.com
SIC: 3713 Specialty motor vehicle bodies

(G-16393)
MEAGAN INC
Also Called: J & B Pallet
711 S Buffalo St (46580-4312)
P.O. Box 2341 (46515-2341)
PHONE.....................574 267-8626
James Marsillet, Pr
James R Marsillett Senior, Pr
Mary A Marsillett, VP
EMP: 32 EST: 1973
SQ FT: 4,800
SALES (est): 724.22K Privately Held
SIC: 2448 Pallets, wood

(G-16394)
MED-CUT INC
Also Called: Instru-Med
727 N Detroit St (46580-2910)
PHONE.....................574 269-1982
Daniel M Carteaux, Pr
Cathy J Miller, *
H Anthony Miller Junior, Sec
EMP: 55 EST: 1978
SQ FT: 30,000
SALES (est): 7.6MM Privately Held
Web: www.instru-med.com
SIC: 3841 Surgical and medical instruments

Warsaw - Kosciusko County (G-16395)

GEOGRAPHIC SECTION

(G-16395)
MEDICAL DEVICE BUS SVCS INC (HQ)
700 Orthopaedic Dr (46582-3994)
P.O. Box 988 (46581-0988)
PHONE.................574 267-8143
▲ EMP: 1200 EST: 1992
SQ FT: 400,000
SALES (est): 434.12MM
SALES (corp-wide): 85.16B Publicly Held
SIC: 3842 Surgical appliances and supplies
PA: Johnson & Johnson
    1 Johnson & Johnson Plz
    New Brunswick NJ 08933
    732 524-0400

(G-16396)
MEDTRNIC SOFAMOR DANEK USA INC
Also Called: Medtronic
2500 Silveus Xing (46582-8598)
PHONE.................574 267-6826
Dean Zentz, Brnch Mgr
EMP: 5
Web: www.medtronic.com
SIC: 3841 Surgical and medical instruments
HQ: Medtronic Sofamor Danek Usa, Inc.
    4340 Swinnea Rd
    Memphis TN 38118
    901 396-3133

(G-16397)
MEGAN INC
711 S Buffalo St (46580-4312)
PHONE.................574 267-8626
Mary Marsillett, Pr
EMP: 17 EST: 2011
SQ FT: 55,000
SALES (est): 1.61MM Privately Held
SIC: 2448 Skids, wood

(G-16398)
MICROTECH WELDING CORP
265 E Bell Dr (46582-9300)
PHONE.................574 268-5314
Melissa Christman, Mgr
EMP: 1
Web: www.microtechwelding.com
SIC: 7692 Welding repair
PA: Microtech Welding Corp.
    3601 Focus Dr
    Fort Wayne IN 46818

(G-16399)
MUSCULSKELETAL PUBL ANALIS INC
1691 S Meadow Dr (46580-7073)
PHONE.................574 269-4861
William Pietrzak, Prin
EMP: 5 EST: 2015
SALES (est): 51.18K Privately Held
SIC: 2741 Miscellaneous publishing

(G-16400)
NEW DALTON FOUNDRY LLC (PA)
1900 E Jefferson St (46580-3761)
PHONE.................574 267-8111
EMP: 19 EST: 2016
SALES (est): 110.99MM
SALES (corp-wide): 110.99MM Privately Held
Web: www.daltoncorporation.com
SIC: 3321 Gray iron castings, nec

(G-16401)
NGINSTRUMENTS LLC
Also Called: Ng Instruments, Inc.
4643 N State Road 15 (46582)
PHONE.................574 268-2112
Jeff Mccaulley, CEO
Timothy M Nicholas, *
Daisy Nicholas, *
Richard Franco, *
EMP: 78 EST: 1995
SALES (est): 10.21MM Privately Held
Web: www.avalign.com
SIC: 3841 Surgical and medical instruments
PA: Avalign Technologies, Inc.
    10275 W Higgins Rd # 920
    Rosemont IL 60018

(G-16402)
NORTHERN INDIANA TRUSS LLC
2208 N 500 W (46580-6527)
PHONE.................574 858-0505
Jay A Hostetler, Prin
EMP: 22 EST: 2015
SALES (est): 2.96MM Privately Held
Web: www.askthelactationconsultant.com
SIC: 2439 Structural wood members, nec

(G-16403)
OFFICIAL SPORTS INTL INC
4120 Corridor Dr (46582-6998)
PHONE.................574 269-1404
Mary Lou Tobin, Pr
Paul Tobin, VP
▲ EMP: 15 EST: 1984
SQ FT: 5,000
SALES (est): 2.14MM Privately Held
Web: www.officialsports.com
SIC: 3949 2329 2339 5961 Soccer equipment and supplies; Men's and boys' athletic uniforms; Uniforms, athletic: women's, misses', and juniors'; Fitness and sporting goods, mail order

(G-16404)
ORTHOPEDIATRICS CORP (PA)
Also Called: Orthopediatrics
2850 Frontier Dr (46582)
PHONE.................574 268-6379
Mark C Throdahl, CEO
Terry D Schlotterback, Ch Bd
David R Bailey, Pr
Gregory A Odle, Ex VP
Daniel J Gerritzen, VP
EMP: 8 EST: 2006
SQ FT: 22,000
SALES (est): 148.73MM Publicly Held
Web: www.orthopediatrics.com
SIC: 3842 Surgical appliances and supplies

(G-16405)
ORTHOPEDIATRICS US DIST
2850 Frontier Dr (46582-7001)
PHONE.................574 268-6379
Mark Throdahl, Pr
Fred Hite, *
EMP: 28 EST: 2012
SQ FT: 3,000
SALES (est): 1.25MM Publicly Held
Web: www.orthopediatrics.com
SIC: 3842 Surgical appliances and supplies
PA: Orthopediatrics Corp.
    2850 Frontier Dr
    Warsaw IN 46582

(G-16406)
OSBORN MANUFACTURING CORP
960 N Lake St (46580-2528)
P.O. Box 1650 (46581-1650)
PHONE.................574 267-6156
Vivian Kelly, Pr
Jerry Kelly, Product Vice President
Aimee Kintzel, VP
Scott Kelly, General Vice President
EMP: 10 EST: 1997
SQ FT: 22,000
SALES (est): 956.86K Privately Held
Web: www.osbornmfg.com
SIC: 3423 3089 Hand and edge tools, nec; Thermoformed finished plastics products, nec

(G-16407)
OUTDOOR INDUSTRIES
221 S Hand Ave (46580-2515)
PHONE.................574 551-5936
EMP: 4 EST: 2016
SALES (est): 70.89K Privately Held
Web: www.outdoorind.com
SIC: 3999 Manufacturing industries, nec

(G-16408)
PANDORA PRINTING
1831 Rosemont Ave (46580-2344)
PHONE.................574 551-9624
Fernando Malagon, Prin
EMP: 5 EST: 2018
SALES (est): 70.71K Privately Held
SIC: 2752 Commercial printing, lithographic

(G-16409)
PAPERS INC
114 W Market St (46580-2812)
PHONE.................574 269-2932
Margaret Smith, Mgr
EMP: 6
SALES (corp-wide): 20.23MM Privately Held
Web: www.thepapersonline.com
SIC: 2711 Newspapers: publishing only, not printed on site
PA: The Papers Inc
    206 S Main St
    Milford IN 46542
    574 658-4111

(G-16410)
PENDRY COATINGS LLC
1119 Seymour Midwest Dr (46580-1215)
PHONE.................574 268-2956
George Pendry, VP Opers
EMP: 1 EST: 2016
SALES (est): 376.19K Privately Held
SIC: 2851 5169 Coating, air curing; Chemicals and allied products, nec
PA: Seymour Midwest Llc
    2666 S Country Club Rd
    Warsaw IN 46580

(G-16411)
PHTAL AOY INDUSTRIES LLC
810 S Buffalo St Ste D (46580-4710)
PHONE.................260 267-0025
Barnabas Brown, Prin
EMP: 4 EST: 2017
SALES (est): 72.49K Privately Held
SIC: 3999 Manufacturing industries, nec

(G-16412)
PRECISION MEDICAL TECH INC
2059 N Pound Dr W (46582-6546)
PHONE.................574 267-6385
EMP: 35 EST: 1993
SQ FT: 6,000
SALES (est): 7.85MM Privately Held
Web: www.premedtec.com
SIC: 3599 Machine shop, jobbing and repair

(G-16413)
PREMIER CONCEPTS INC
2371 N Rainbow Dr (46582-6718)
PHONE.................574 269-7570
Raymond Doss, Pr
EMP: 5 EST: 2006
SALES (est): 486.91K Privately Held

(G-16414)
R R DONNELLEY & SONS COMPANY
Also Called: Warsaw Mfg Div
2801 W Old Road 30 (46580-8783)
P.O. Box 837 (46581-0837)
PHONE.................574 267-7101
Grant Mcguire, Mgr
EMP: 59
SQ FT: 800,000
SALES (corp-wide): 15B Privately Held
Web: www.rrd.com
SIC: 2759 Commercial printing, nec
HQ: R. R. Donnelley & Sons Company
    35 W Wacker Dr
    Chicago IL 60601
    312 326-8000

(G-16415)
RAYCO STEEL PROCESS INC
207 S Lincoln St (46580-3771)
P.O. Box 1016 (46581-1016)
PHONE.................574 267-7676
Jim Rooney, Pr
Sharon Swartz, Sec
Deb Pilther, Stockholder
EMP: 11 EST: 1940
SQ FT: 10,000
SALES (est): 2.04MM Privately Held
Web: www.raycotools.com
SIC: 3842 3599 Orthopedic appliances; Machine shop, jobbing and repair

(G-16416)
RAYMOND TRUEX
5383 W 400 N (46582-8505)
PHONE.................574 858-2260
Tina Truex, Prin
EMP: 3 EST: 2001
SALES (est): 159.28K Privately Held
SIC: 2395 Embroidery products, except Schiffli machine

(G-16417)
RBK DEVELOPMENT INC
Also Called: Superior Wood Products
1058 W 400 N (46582-7038)
PHONE.................574 267-5879
Gale Schaffer, Pr
Bruce Korenstra, *
EMP: 32 EST: 1989
SQ FT: 35,000
SALES (est): 2.37MM Privately Held
SIC: 2434 2517 2541 2511 Wood kitchen cabinets; Home entertainment unit cabinets, wood; Wood partitions and fixtures; Wood household furniture

(G-16418)
RIEPEN LLC
Also Called: Danco Anodizing
2450 Deelyn Dr (46580-8500)
P.O. Box 2050 (46581-2050)
PHONE.................574 269-5900
Sherri V Scherer, Genl Pt
EMP: 83 EST: 2008
SALES (est): 11.16MM Privately Held
Web: www.danco.net
SIC: 3471 Electroplating of metals or formed products

(G-16419)
RMI HOLDINGS LLC
Also Called: R M I
4130 Corridor Dr (46582-6998)
PHONE.................317 214-7076
Jim Evans, Prin
EMP: 16 EST: 2006
SALES (est): 2.46MM Privately Held

GEOGRAPHIC SECTION
Warsaw - Kosciusko County (G-16443)

Web: www.rmiholdingsllc.com
SIC: 3842 3841 Orthopedic appliances; Surgical and medical instruments

(G-16420)
SAFE-WAY GARAGE DOORS LLC
3814 E Us Hwy 3 (46580)
PHONE.................574 267-4861
EMP: 50 EST: 2015
SALES (est): 6.85MM
SALES (corp-wide): 144.38MM **Privately Held**
Web: www.safewaydoor.com
SIC: 5211 3442 Garage doors, sale and installation; Garage doors, overhead; metal
PA: Capitalworks, Llc
1100 Sprior Ave Fl 17 Ste
Cleveland OH 44122
216 781-3233

(G-16421)
SEMMATERIALS LP
2820 Durbin St (46580-3883)
PHONE.................574 267-5076
Jason Conrad, Brnch Mgr
EMP: 7
SQ FT: 720
Web: www.semgroupcorp.com
SIC: 2951 Asphalt paving mixtures and blocks
HQ: Semmaterials, L.P.
6520 S Yale Ave Ste 700
Tulsa OK 74136

(G-16422)
SEYMOUR MIDWEST LLC
1037 Seymour Midwest Dr Bldg C (46580-1214)
PHONE.................574 267-7875
EMP: 9 EST: 1966
SALES (est): 88.64K **Privately Held**
Web: www.seymourmidwest.com
SIC: 3423 Hand and edge tools, nec

(G-16423)
SEYMOUR MIDWEST LLC (PA)
2666 S Country Club Rd (46580)
P.O. Box 1674 (46581)
PHONE.................574 267-7875
Bill Henthorn, Pr
Daniel E Miller, VP Fin
▲ EMP: 20 EST: 1996
SQ FT: 18,000
SALES (est): 48.15MM **Privately Held**
Web: www.seymourmidwest.com
SIC: 3423 Garden and farm tools, including shovels

(G-16424)
SITES-WORKMAN HOLDINGS INC
Also Called: Lakeland Technology
1195 Polk Dr (46582-8602)
PHONE.................574 267-1503
Rod K Mayer, Pr
Dan Stichter, *
EMP: 25 EST: 1986
SALES (est): 4.03MM **Privately Held**
SIC: 3599 Machine shop, jobbing and repair

(G-16425)
SJG ENTERPRISES INC
Also Called: Graycraft Signs Plus
3304 Lake City Hwy (46580-3923)
PHONE.................574 269-4806
EMP: 4 EST: 1996
SALES (est): 489.06K **Privately Held**
Web: www.graycraftsignswarsaw.com
SIC: 3993 Signs, not made in custom sign painting shops

(G-16426)
SJS COMPONENTS LLC
6778 S State Road 13 (46580-8648)
PHONE.................260 578-0192
Scott Brown, Managing Member
EMP: 3 EST: 2009
SALES (est): 208.5K **Privately Held**
Web: www.sjscomponents.com
SIC: 2541 Wood partitions and fixtures

(G-16427)
SMITH TIRE INC
2335 N Detroit St Ste A (46580-2272)
PHONE.................574 267-8261
Craig A Smith, Owner
▲ EMP: 11 EST: 1956
SQ FT: 10,000
SALES (est): 563.84K **Privately Held**
SIC: 5531 7534 5541 Automotive tires; Tire repair shop; Filling stations, gasoline

(G-16428)
SPARROW GROUP INCORPORATED
911 Hawthorn Dr (46582-5821)
PHONE.................574 968-7335
Holly Bejar, Prin
EMP: 6 EST: 2019
SALES (est): 63.4K **Privately Held**
SIC: 3732 Boatbuilding and repairing

(G-16429)
STOUT LASER ETCH LLC
2345 S Sunrise Cir (46580-7405)
PHONE.................574 376-9296
EMP: 5
SALES (est): 103.91K **Privately Held**
Web: www.stoutlaseretch.com
SIC: 3599 Machine shop, jobbing and repair

(G-16430)
STOUT LASER ETCH LLC
2345 S Sunrise Cir (46580-7405)
PHONE.................574 527-9523
EMP: 5 EST: 2019
SALES (est): 69.98K **Privately Held**
Web: www.stoutlaseretch.com
SIC: 3479 Etching on metals

(G-16431)
STREVEN DISTILLING COMPANY LLC
733 N Detroit St (46580-2910)
PHONE.................574 527-4061
Mitcell Miller, Prin
EMP: 5 EST: 2017
SALES (est): 155.82K **Privately Held**
Web: www.strevendistilling.com
SIC: 2085 Distilled and blended liquors

(G-16432)
SURFACE ENHANCEMENTS INC
Also Called: Warsaw Electropolishing
125 W 250 N (46582-7864)
P.O. Box 1929 (46581-1929)
PHONE.................574 269-1366
Earl H Kline, Owner
Earl H Kline, Prin
Cheri A Kline, Prin
EMP: 10 EST: 1991
SQ FT: 4,000
SALES (est): 794.41K **Privately Held**
Web: www.warsawelectropolishing.com
SIC: 3471 Electroplating of metals or formed products

(G-16433)
SYMMETRY MEDICAL INC (DH)
3724 N State Road 15 (46582-7000)
PHONE.................574 267-8700
▲ EMP: 9 EST: 1996
SQ FT: 15,800
SALES (est): 196.94MM
SALES (corp-wide): 832.81MM **Privately Held**
Web: www.tecomet.com
SIC: 3841 3842 Surgical and medical instruments; Orthopedic appliances
HQ: Tecomet Inc.
115 Eames St
Wilmington MA 01887
978 642-2400

(G-16434)
SYMMETRY MEDICAL INC
486 W 350 N (46582-7744)
PHONE.................574 267-8700
EMP: 237
SALES (corp-wide): 832.81MM **Privately Held**
Web: www.tecomet.com
SIC: 3841 Surgical instruments and apparatus
HQ: Symmetry Medical Inc.
3724 N State Road 15
Warsaw IN 46582

(G-16435)
SYMMETRY MEDICAL MFG INC
Also Called: Jet Engineering
3724 N State Road 15 (46582-7000)
PHONE.................574 371-2284
Bryan Lair, Genl Mgr
▲ EMP: 207 EST: 1995
SQ FT: 42,000
SALES (est): 22.61MM
SALES (corp-wide): 832.81MM **Privately Held**
Web: www.tecomet.com
SIC: 3369 3469 3463 Titanium castings, except die-casting; Metal stampings, nec; Nonferrous forgings
HQ: Symmetry Medical Inc.
3724 N State Road 15
Warsaw IN 46582

(G-16436)
SYMMETRY MEDICAL USA INC
3724 N State Road 15 (46582-7000)
PHONE.................574 267-8700
Brian S Moore, Pr
Fred Hite, Sec
Thomas J Sullivan, CEO
EMP: 5 EST: 2001
SALES (est): 2.47MM
SALES (corp-wide): 832.81MM **Privately Held**
Web: www.tecomet.com
SIC: 3841 Surgical and medical instruments
HQ: Symmetry Medical Inc.
3724 N State Road 15
Warsaw IN 46582

(G-16437)
TEXMO BLANK USA INC
Also Called: Texmo Blank
596 E 200 N (46582)
PHONE.................574 696-9990
Satish Patel, Pr
Milind Ranadive, *
▲ EMP: 60 EST: 1985
SQ FT: 30,000
SALES (est): 9.38MM **Privately Held**
Web: www.medcast-inc.com
SIC: 3324 3823 Commercial investment castings, ferrous; Absorption analyzers: infrared, x-ray, etc.: industrial

(G-16438)
THE DALTON CORPORATION (HQ)
1900 E Jefferson St (46580-3761)
P.O. Box 1388 (46581-1388)
PHONE.................574 267-8111
▼ EMP: 75 EST: 1989
SALES (est): 41.68MM
SALES (corp-wide): 110.99MM **Privately Held**
Web: www.daltoncorporation.com
SIC: 3321 Gray iron castings, nec
PA: New Dalton Foundry, Llc
1900 E Jefferson St
Warsaw IN 46580
574 267-8111

(G-16439)
TORNIER INC
100 Capital Dr Ste 201 (46582-6704)
PHONE.................574 268-0861
EMP: 1
Web: www.wright.com
SIC: 3842 5999 Implants, surgical; Orthopedic and prosthesis applications
PA: Tornier, Inc.
10801 Nesbitt Ave S
Bloomington MN 55437

(G-16440)
UNION TOOL CORP
1144 N Detroit St (46580-2917)
P.O. Box 935 (46581-0935)
PHONE.................574 267-3211
Michael T Simpson, Pr
Chuck T Simpson, *
◆ EMP: 32 EST: 1943
SQ FT: 37,000
SALES (est): 4.64MM **Privately Held**
Web: www.uniontoolcorp.com
SIC: 3599 3559 Custom machinery; Metal finishing equipment for plating, etc.

(G-16441)
VAN EXPLORER COMPANY INC (PA)
Also Called: Explorer Sport Trucks
2749 N Fox Farm Rd (46580-6547)
P.O. Box 4527 (46581-4527)
PHONE.................574 267-7666
Robert Kesler, Ch Bd
Steve Kesler, *
Doris Kesler, *
◆ EMP: 25 EST: 1980
SQ FT: 140,000
SALES (est): 22.94MM
SALES (corp-wide): 22.94MM **Privately Held**
Web: www.explorervan.com
SIC: 3716 Recreational van conversion (self-propelled), factory basis

(G-16442)
WARSAW CHEMICAL COMPANY INC
390 Argonne Rd (46580-3884)
P.O. Box 858 (46581-0858)
PHONE.................574 267-3251
EMP: 85
Web: www.warsawchemical.com
SIC: 5169 2842 2891 2841 Industrial chemicals; Cleaning or polishing preparations, nec; Adhesives and sealants; Soap and other detergents

(G-16443)
WARSAW COIL CO INC
1809 W Winona Ave (46580-2351)
P.O. Box 1057 (46581-1057)
PHONE.................574 267-6041
Thomas Joyner, Pr
Bradley C Joyner, *
Diane Doran, *
▲ EMP: 100 EST: 1954
SQ FT: 55,000
SALES (est): 17.37MM **Privately Held**
Web: www.warsawcoil.com

Warsaw - Kosciusko County (G-16444)

SIC: 3677 Electronic coils and transformers

(G-16444)
WARSAW CUSTOM CABINET (PA)
1697 W 350 S (46580-8201)
PHONE..................574 267-5794
Paul F Mundinger, *Owner*
EMP: 2 EST: 1966
SQ FT: 3,500
SALES (est): 178.84K
SALES (corp-wide): 178.84K **Privately Held**
Web: www.warsawcustomcabinets.com
SIC: 2434 Vanities, bathroom: wood

(G-16445)
WARSAW CUT GLASS COMPANY INC
505 S Detroit St (46580-4406)
P.O. Box 1322 (46581-1322)
PHONE..................574 267-6581
Randolph Kirkendall, *Pr*
Linda Kirkendall, *VP*
EMP: 8 EST: 1911
SQ FT: 4,000
SALES (est): 502.05K **Privately Held**
Web: www.warsawcutglass.net
SIC: 3231 5719 Cut and engraved glassware: made from purchased glass; Glassware

(G-16446)
WARSAW FOUNDRY COMPANY INC
1212 N Detroit St (46580-2919)
P.O. Box 227 (46581-0227)
PHONE..................574 267-8772
John W Petro, *Pr*
John W Petro, *Senior President*
Mike Petro, *
John Petro, *
EMP: 60 EST: 1923
SALES (est): 4.16MM **Privately Held**
Web: www.warsawfoundry.com
SIC: 3321 1446 2431 Gray iron castings, nec ; Molding sand mining; Moldings, wood: unfinished and prefinished

(G-16447)
WARSAW ORTHOPEDIC INC
Also Called: Sofamor/Danek Group Mfg Div
2500 Silveus Xing (46582-8598)
PHONE..................901 396-3133
Gene Sponseller, *Pr*
William Reynolds, *
Richard Duerr, *
J Mark Merrill, *
EMP: 82 EST: 1951
SQ FT: 80,000
SALES (est): 977.32K **Privately Held**
SIC: 3842 Implants, surgical
HQ: Medtronic Sofamor Danek Usa, Inc.
4340 Swinnea Rd
Memphis TN 38118
901 396-3133

(G-16448)
WHIMET INC
2100 N Detroit St (46580-2210)
PHONE..................574 267-8062
Murvel D Whitehead, *Pr*
◆ EMP: 70 EST: 1969
SALES (est): 8.95MM **Privately Held**
Web: www.whimetinc.com
SIC: 3471 Electroplating of metals or formed products

(G-16449)
WHITE MACHINE INC
1903 White Industrial Dr (46580-2370)
PHONE..................574 267-5895
John White, *Pr*
EMP: 3 EST: 1961
SQ FT: 2,000
SALES (est): 251.2K **Privately Held**
Web: white-machine-inc.business.site
SIC: 3599 Machine shop, jobbing and repair

(G-16450)
WHITMAN PUBLISHING
302 E Winona Ave (46580-4438)
PHONE..................574 267-3941
Wendell Whitman, *Owner*
EMP: 1 EST: 2010
SALES (est): 62.15K **Privately Held**
SIC: 2741 Miscellaneous publishing

(G-16451)
WILDMAN BUSINESS GROUP LLC (PA)
Also Called: Wildman Corporate Apparel
800 S Buffalo St (46580)
PHONE..................866 369-1552
TOLL FREE: 800
Brent Wildman, *Pr*
Josh Wildman, *CEO*
Steve Bryant, *COO*
EMP: 1 EST: 1952
SQ FT: 55,000
SALES (est): 9.1MM
SALES (corp-wide): 9.1MM **Privately Held**
Web: www.wildmanbg.com
SIC: 7218 7213 5087 5199 Industrial uniform supply; Linen supply, non-clothing; Janitors' supplies; First aid supplies

(G-16452)
WILEY YOUNG & ASSOCIATES
Also Called: Zimmer Medwest
121 W Market St Ste B (46580-2866)
PHONE..................574 269-7006
Fred J Rowland, *Prin*
EMP: 8 EST: 2007
SALES (est): 979.38K **Privately Held**
SIC: 3842 Orthopedic appliances

(G-16453)
WINONA PVD COATINGS LLC
1180 Polk Dr (46582-8602)
P.O. Box 1856 (46581-1856)
PHONE..................574 269-3255
Jamie T Visker, *Managing Member*
◆ EMP: 45 EST: 2006
SQ FT: 68,000
SALES (est): 8.92MM **Privately Held**
Web: www.winonapvd.com
SIC: 3479 Coating of metals and formed products

(G-16454)
WISHBONE MEDICAL INC (PA)
100 Capital Dr (46582)
PHONE..................574 306-4006
Mark Figgie, *Interim Chief Executive Officer*
Mary Wetzel, *Pr*
Dawn Nielsen, *CFO*
Kevin Blue, *CRO*
Chip Davenport, *Contrlr*
EMP: 7 EST: 2016
SALES (est): 5.81MM
SALES (corp-wide): 5.81MM **Privately Held**
Web: www.wishbonemedical.com
SIC: 3842 Surgical appliances and supplies

(G-16455)
WJH INVESTMENTS INC
102 Enterprise Dr (46580-1204)
P.O. Box 1017 (46581-1017)
▲ EMP: 1 EST: 1966
SQ FT: 150,000
SALES (est): 482.51K **Privately Held**
Web: www.indianacoatedfabrics.com
SIC: 2295 Chemically coated and treated fabrics

(G-16456)
WORTH TAX AND FINANCIAL SVC
Also Called: Jackson Hewitt Tax Service
3201 E Center Street Ext (46582-3907)
P.O. Box 725 (46590-0725)
PHONE..................574 267-4687
Beverly Worth, *Owner*
EMP: 5 EST: 1973
SQ FT: 5,700
SALES (est): 234.61K **Privately Held**
Web: www.worthfinancial.com
SIC: 7291 8299 2731 6282 Tax return preparation services; Educational services; Books, publishing only; Investment advice

(G-16457)
XYZ MACHINING INC
5141 W 100 S (46580-8962)
PHONE..................574 269-5541
Steve Kline, *Pr*
Tim Norman, *Pr*
EMP: 2 EST: 1998
SALES (est): 198.13K **Privately Held**
Web: www.xyzmachining.com
SIC: 3599 Machine shop, jobbing and repair

(G-16458)
ZIMMER INC
56 E Bell Dr (46582-6924)
PHONE..................574 267-2038
EMP: 1
SALES (corp-wide): 7.39B **Publicly Held**
Web: www.zimmerbiomet.com
SIC: 3842 Orthopedic appliances
HQ: Zimmer, Inc.
1800 W Center St
Warsaw IN 46580
800 348-9500

(G-16459)
ZIMMER INC
Also Called: Zimmer Biomet
2094 N Boeing Rd (46582-7860)
PHONE..................800 348-9500
EMP: 3
SALES (corp-wide): 7.39B **Publicly Held**
Web: www.zimmerbiomet.com
SIC: 3842 Orthopedic appliances
HQ: Zimmer, Inc.
1800 W Center St
Warsaw IN 46580
800 348-9500

(G-16460)
ZIMMER INC
Also Called: Zimmer Biomet
1800 W Center St (46580-2304)
P.O. Box 708 (46581-0708)
PHONE..................574 267-6131
Raymond Elloit, *Brnch Mgr*
EMP: 5
SALES (corp-wide): 7.39B **Publicly Held**
Web: www.zimmerbiomet.com
SIC: 3842 Orthopedic appliances
HQ: Zimmer, Inc.
1800 W Center St
Warsaw IN 46580
800 348-9500

(G-16461)
ZIMMER INC
1777 W Center St (46580-2303)
PHONE..................574 267-6131
EMP: 5
SALES (corp-wide): 7.39B **Publicly Held**
Web: www.zimmerbiomet.com
SIC: 3842 Orthopedic appliances
HQ: Zimmer, Inc.
1800 W Center St
Warsaw IN 46580
800 348-9500

(G-16462)
ZIMMER INC
Also Called: Zimmer Biomet
1535 W Center St Bldg 19 (46580-2411)
PHONE..................574 527-7297
EMP: 6
SALES (corp-wide): 7.39B **Publicly Held**
Web: www.zimmerbiomet.com
SIC: 3842 Orthopedic appliances
HQ: Zimmer, Inc.
1800 W Center St
Warsaw IN 46580
800 348-9500

(G-16463)
ZIMMER INC
1113 W Lake St (46580-2532)
PHONE..................574 371-1557
EMP: 10
SALES (corp-wide): 7.39B **Publicly Held**
Web: www.zimmerbiomet.com
SIC: 3842 Orthopedic appliances
HQ: Zimmer, Inc.
1800 W Center St
Warsaw IN 46580
800 348-9500

(G-16464)
ZIMMER INC (HQ)
Also Called: Zimmer Biomet
1800 W Center St (46580)
P.O. Box 708 (46581)
PHONE..................800 348-9500
David C Dvorak, *Pr*
James T Crines, *
◆ EMP: 500 EST: 1927
SQ FT: 108,000
SALES (est): 713.07MM
SALES (corp-wide): 7.39B **Publicly Held**
Web: www.zimmerbiomet.com
SIC: 3842 Orthopedic appliances
PA: Zimmer Biomet Holdings, Inc.
345 E Main St
Warsaw IN 46580
574 267-6131

(G-16465)
ZIMMER BIOMET HIBBARD
3550 E Us Highway 30 (46580-6720)
PHONE..................574 267-0670
EMP: 11 EST: 2017
SALES (est): 122.31K **Privately Held**
Web: www.zimmerbiomet.com
SIC: 3842 Orthopedic appliances

(G-16466)
ZIMMER BIOMET HOLDINGS INC (PA)
Also Called: Zimmer Biomet
345 E Main St (46580)
PHONE..................574 267-6131
Ivan Tornos, *CEO*
Suketu Upadhyay, *Ex VP*
Rachel Ellingson, *CSO*
Lori Winkler, *Chief Human Resources Officer*
Chad Phipps, *Sr VP*
EMP: 1842 EST: 1927
SALES (est): 7.39B
SALES (corp-wide): 7.39B **Publicly Held**
Web: www.zimmerbiomet.com
SIC: 3842 Orthopedic appliances

(G-16467)
ZIMMER BMET CONNECTED HLTH LLC

GEOGRAPHIC SECTION
Washington - Daviess County (G-16490)

345 E Main St (46580-2746)
PHONE..................800 613-6131
EMP: 50 EST: 2016
SALES (est): 8.44MM
SALES (corp-wide): 7.39B **Publicly Held**
Web: www.zimmerbiomet.com
SIC: 3842 Orthopedic appliances
PA: Zimmer Biomet Holdings, Inc.
345 E Main St
Warsaw IN 46580
574 267-6131

(G-16468)
ZIMMER PRODUCTION INC
Also Called: Zimmer Biomet
56 E Bell Dr Bldg A (46582-6989)
PHONE..................574 267-6131
EMP: 1
SALES (corp-wide): 7.39B **Publicly Held**
Web: www.zimmerbiomet.com
SIC: 3842 Orthopedic appliances
HQ: Zimmer Production, Inc.
345 E Main St
Warsaw IN 46580
574 267-6131

(G-16469)
ZIMMER PRODUCTION INC (HQ)
345 E Main St (46580)
PHONE..................574 267-6131
Keneth R Coonce, *Pr*
James T Crines, *VP*
EMP: 1 EST: 2003
SALES (est): 4.29MM
SALES (corp-wide): 7.39B **Publicly Held**
Web: www.zimmerbiomet.com
SIC: 3842 Orthopedic appliances
PA: Zimmer Biomet Holdings, Inc.
345 E Main St
Warsaw IN 46580
574 267-6131

(G-16470)
ZIMMER SPINE INC
1800 W Center St Bldg 5 (46580-2304)
PHONE..................800 655-2614
Daniel Florin, *Sr VP*
EMP: 21 EST: 1998
SALES (est): 506.6K **Privately Held**
Web: www.zimmerbiomet.com
SIC: 3842 Orthopedic appliances

(G-16471)
ZIMMER US INC
Also Called: Zimmer Biomet
1800 W Center St (46580-2304)
P.O. Box 708 (46581-0708)
PHONE..................574 267-6131
Jeffery Mccaulley, *Pr*
David C Dvorak, *
James T Crines, *
Joseph A Cucolo, *
EMP: 233 EST: 2002
SALES (est): 22.27MM
SALES (corp-wide): 7.39B **Publicly Held**
Web: www.zimmerbiomet.com
SIC: 3842 Orthopedic appliances
PA: Zimmer Biomet Holdings, Inc.
345 E Main St
Warsaw IN 46580
574 267-6131

Washington
Daviess County

(G-16472)
ATLATL GROUP LLC
Also Called: Axiom Yachts
1987 Troy Rd (47501-8215)
PHONE..................602 233-2628
Aaron Browning, *Managing Member*
Robert Gutierrez, *
Andrew Marshall, *
EMP: 42 EST: 2017
SALES (est): 5.43MM **Privately Held**
Web: www.bravadayachts.com
SIC: 3732 Yachts, building and repairing

(G-16473)
BELT TECH INDUSTRIAL INC (PA)
1996 S 300 W (47501)
P.O. Box 620 (47501)
PHONE..................812 258-5959
▲ EMP: 50 EST: 1992
SQ FT: 13,000
SALES (est): 20.92MM **Privately Held**
Web: www.belttech1.com
SIC: 3535 Conveyors and conveying equipment

(G-16474)
CORNELIUS MANUFACTURING INC
1912 E Us Hwy 50 (47501)
PHONE..................812 636-4319
Gerald A Frette, *Pr*
David R Frette, *
EMP: 60 EST: 1983
SQ FT: 90,000
SALES (est): 7.05MM **Privately Held**
Web: www.cornpro.com
SIC: 3523 Trailers and wagons, farm

(G-16475)
DAVIESS COUNTY TIRE & SUP INC
879 S State Road 57 (47501-4373)
P.O. Box 289 (47501-0289)
PHONE..................812 254-1035
EMP: 1 EST: 2010
SALES (est): 514.91K
SALES (corp-wide): 8.49MM **Privately Held**
Web: www.duboiscountytire.com
SIC: 7534 5531 Tire retreading and repair shops; Auto and home supply stores
PA: Dubois County Tire And Supply Inc
2124 Newton St
Jasper IN 47546
812 482-2020

(G-16476)
DAVIESS COUNTY TIRE INC
879 S State Road 57 (47501-4373)
P.O. Box 289 (47501-0289)
PHONE..................812 254-1035
John Grannan, *Pr*
EMP: 5 EST: 1996
SALES (est): 186.2K **Privately Held**
Web: www.duboiscountytire.com
SIC: 7534 5531 Tire repair shop; Automotive tires

(G-16477)
DIGITAL SOLUTIONS
402 S State Road 57 (47501-4027)
PHONE..................812 257-0333
Dan Leigh, *Prin*
EMP: 6 EST: 2011
SALES (est): 95.78K **Privately Held**
SIC: 3663 Space satellite communications equipment

(G-16478)
DOUGLAS P TERRELL
Also Called: D Terrell & Company
1289 S State Road 57 (47501-4367)
PHONE..................812 254-1976
Doug Terrell, *Owner*
EMP: 2 EST: 1998
SALES (est): 200K **Privately Held**
SIC: 2759 Commercial printing, nec

(G-16479)
FRESH START INC
113 N Industrial Park Rd (47501-7747)
PHONE..................812 254-3398
EMP: 12 EST: 1985
SALES (est): 514.48K **Privately Held**
Web: www.freshstarttrainingcenter.org
SIC: 8361 2511 8322 8661 Residential care; Wood lawn and garden furniture; Alcoholism counseling, nontreatment; Miscellaneous denomination church

(G-16480)
GEBERTS CLEANING SERVICE
216 Apraw Rd (47501-1006)
PHONE..................812 254-4658
Lyle Gebert, *Owner*
EMP: 1 EST: 1998
SALES (est): 56.74K **Privately Held**
SIC: 2842 Specialty cleaning

(G-16481)
GRAIN PROCESSING CORPORATION
1443 S 300 W (47501-7410)
PHONE..................812 257-0480
Brad Quigley, *Mgr*
EMP: 21
SALES (corp-wide): 515.77MM **Privately Held**
Web: www.grainprocessing.com
SIC: 2869 2085 2046 Grain alcohol, industrial ; Grain alcohol for beverage purposes; Corn starch
HQ: Grain Processing Corporation
1600 Oregon St
Muscatine IA 52761
563 264-4265

(G-16482)
GREEN STREAK PULLING INC
1312 E 200 N (47501-7669)
PHONE..................812 254-6858
Steve Boyd, *Pr*
EMP: 2 EST: 2010
SALES (est): 149.75K **Privately Held**
SIC: 3537 Tractors, used in plants, docks,terminals, etc.: industrial

(G-16483)
GWALTNEY DRILLING INC
101 Se 3rd St (47501-3208)
P.O. Box 520 (47501-0520)
PHONE..................812 254-5085
Michael Crouch, *Pr*
Michael V Crouch, *Pr*
Dave Osman, *VP*
EMP: 1 EST: 1950
SQ FT: 3,000
SALES (est): 15.75MM
SALES (corp-wide): 15.75MM **Privately Held**
SIC: 1381 Drilling oil and gas wells
HQ: Natural Gas Processors Inc
107 Se 3rd St
Washington IN
812 254-5087

(G-16484)
HOOSIER READY MIX LLC
Also Called: Hoosier Ready Mix
1115 S 300 W (47501-8217)
PHONE..................812 254-7625
Stacy Culver, *Managing Member*
Joseph Knepp, *Prin*
EMP: 10 EST: 2015
SALES (est): 1.18MM **Privately Held**
SIC: 3273 Ready-mixed concrete

(G-16485)
HUSKEY PARTS COMPANY LLC
615 W Hefron St (47501-1567)
PHONE..................812 899-0950
EMP: 5 EST: 2017
SALES (est): 468.08K **Privately Held**
Web: www.huskeyparts.com
SIC: 3799 Golf carts, powered

(G-16486)
IRVING MATERIALS INC
Also Called: I M I
611 W Main St (47501-2510)
PHONE..................812 254-0820
Brad Wagler, *Brnch Mgr*
EMP: 3
SALES (corp-wide): 814.09MM **Privately Held**
Web: www.irvmat.com
SIC: 3273 5032 Ready-mixed concrete; Concrete building products
PA: Irving Materials, Inc.
8032 N State Road 9
Greenfield IN 46140
317 326-3101

(G-16487)
JEFFS FARM SVC
1328 N 300 W (47501-9259)
PHONE..................812 254-1980
Jeff Hart, *Owner*
EMP: 3 EST: 2020
SALES (est): 89.06K **Privately Held**
SIC: 3523 Farm machinery and equipment

(G-16488)
JOHNNY LONG
Also Called: Johnny's Savory Sauces
1360 S 125 E (47501-8052)
PHONE..................812 698-2516
Johnny Long, *Owner*
EMP: 2 EST: 2020
SALES (est): 10K **Privately Held**
Web: www.indyhomenow.com
SIC: 2099 Sauce, gravy, dressing, and dip mixes

(G-16489)
JONES AND SONS INC (PA)
1262 S State Road 57 (47501-4366)
P.O. Box 2357 (47501-0997)
PHONE..................812 254-4731
Darrell Jones, *Pr*
Marsha Jones-bauer, *Sec*
Bert Marcus Jones, *
Mike Healy, *
EMP: 35 EST: 1963
SQ FT: 10,000
SALES (est): 18.09MM
SALES (corp-wide): 18.09MM **Privately Held**
Web: www.jonesandsons.com
SIC: 3273 3271 Ready-mixed concrete; Blocks, concrete or cinder: standard

(G-16490)
JONES ENGINEERING INC
897 W 150 S (47501-7371)
PHONE..................812 254-6456
Sam Jones, *Pr*
Jeff Jones, *VP*
Madonna Jones, *Sec*
EMP: 3 EST: 1967
SQ FT: 7,000
SALES (est): 324.18K **Privately Held**
Web: www.jonesenginc.com
SIC: 3621 Motors and generators

Washington - Daviess County (G-16491)

GEOGRAPHIC SECTION

(G-16491)
LEVEL SET CABINET WORKS LLC
2835 E 250 S (47501-7955)
PHONE..................................812 787-0830
Christie King, *Owner*
EMP: 5 **EST:** 2018
SALES (est): 39.65K **Privately Held**
SIC: 2434 Wood kitchen cabinets

(G-16492)
M & M WOODWORKING
4192 E 350 N (47501-7654)
PHONE..................................812 486-2418
Martin Knepp, *Prin*
EMP: 1 **EST:** 2003
SALES (est): 134.02K **Privately Held**
SIC: 2431 Woodwork, interior and ornamental, nec

(G-16493)
M&C TECH INDIANA CORPORATION
1928 Technology Dr (47501-1769)
PHONE..................................812 674-2122
Summer Morgan, *Prs Mgr*
EMP: 36 **EST:** 2018
SALES (est): 2.79MM **Privately Held**
Web: www.mctechin.com
SIC: 3533 Oil and gas field machinery

(G-16494)
NASCO INDUSTRIES INC
3 Ne 21st St (47501-3111)
P.O. Box 427 (47501-0427)
PHONE..................................812 254-7393
Todd N Smith, *Pr*
Neil A Smith, *
Janet Smith, *
John Richardson, *
▲ **EMP:** 120 **EST:** 1979
SQ FT: 56,000
SALES (est): 22.55MM **Privately Held**
Web: www.nascoinc.com
SIC: 2385 Waterproof outerwear

(G-16495)
NEW END ZONE SPORTING GOODS
3089 E. National Hwy (47501)
PHONE..................................812 254-1895
Donald Kelso, *Sec*
EMP: 4 **EST:** 2011
SQ FT: 4,000
SALES (est): 364.45K **Privately Held**
Web: www.newendzone.com
SIC: 2759 Screen printing

(G-16496)
NEWSPAPER HOLDING INC
Also Called: Washington Times Herald
102 E Van Trees St (47501-2943)
P.O. Box 471 (47501-0471)
PHONE..................................812 254-0480
Ron Smith, *Mgr*
EMP: 1
SALES (corp-wide): 34.97B **Privately Held**
Web: www.tribdem.com
SIC: 2711 Newspapers, publishing and printing
HQ: Newspaper Holding, Inc.
425 Locust St
Johnstown PA 15901
814 532-5102

(G-16497)
OLON INDUSTRIES INC (US)
2510 E National Hwy (47501-9597)
P.O. Box 669 (47501-0669)
PHONE..................................812 254-0427
EMP: 7
SALES (corp-wide): 38.47MM **Privately Held**
Web: www.olon.ca
SIC: 3429 2431 2426 Furniture hardware; Millwork; Hardwood dimension and flooring mills
HQ: Olon Industries Inc. (Us)
411 Union St
Geneva IL 60134
630 232-4705

(G-16498)
P J J T DISTRIBUTORS INC
501 N Meridian St (47501-2013)
P.O. Box 633 (47501-0633)
PHONE..................................812 254-2218
Mary Lynne Portee, *Pr*
Lynne Portee, *Sec*
EMP: 5 **EST:** 1983
SALES (est): 98.78K **Privately Held**
Web: www.pjjtdistributors.com
SIC: 2721 8748 Magazines: publishing only, not printed on site; Publishing consultant

(G-16499)
P3 POLYMERS LLC
110 E Main St (47501-2908)
PHONE..................................812 674-2051
Daniel Jones, *Mgr*
EMP: 2 **EST:** 2013
SALES (est): 195.97K **Privately Held**
Web: www.rockhardscp.com
SIC: 3272 5999 Paving materials, prefabricated concrete; Concrete products, pre-cast

(G-16500)
PEABODY MIDWEST MINING LLC
Also Called: Standard Coal Lab
1281 S 300 W (47501-8207)
PHONE..................................812 254-7714
Melody Cockerham, *Mgr*
EMP: 3
SALES (corp-wide): 4.95B **Publicly Held**
SIC: 1221 Bituminous coal surface mining
HQ: Peabody Midwest Mining, Llc
566 Dickeyville Rd
Lynnville IN 47619

(G-16501)
PERDUE FARMS INC
Also Called: Oak Tree Experimental Farm
100 W 400 N (47501)
PHONE..................................757 787-5210
Bruce Roberts, *Brnch Mgr*
EMP: 21
SALES (corp-wide): 1.24B **Privately Held**
Web: www.perdue.com
SIC: 2015 Poultry slaughtering and processing
PA: Perdue Farms Incorporated
31149 Old Ocean City Rd
Salisbury MD 21804
800 473-7383

(G-16502)
PERDUE FARMS INC
Also Called: Perdue Farms
65 S 200 W (47501-3482)
P.O. Box 539 (47501-0539)
PHONE..................................812 254-8500
Tom Schaffer, *Mgr*
EMP: 1461
SALES (corp-wide): 1.24B **Privately Held**
Web: www.perdue.com
SIC: 2015 Poultry slaughtering and processing
PA: Perdue Farms Incorporated
31149 Old Ocean City Rd
Salisbury MD 21804
800 473-7383

(G-16503)
PERDUE FARMS INC
Also Called: Washington Prcoessing Plant
65 S 200 W (47501-3482)
PHONE..................................812 254-8515
Bruce Roberts, *Brnch Mgr*
EMP: 129
SALES (corp-wide): 1.24B **Privately Held**
Web: www.perdue.com
SIC: 2015 Poultry sausage, luncheon meats, and other poultry products
PA: Perdue Farms Incorporated
31149 Old Ocean City Rd
Salisbury MD 21804
800 473-7383

(G-16504)
PORTEE PUBLISHING LLC
501 N Meridian St (47501-2013)
P.O. Box 633 (47501-0633)
PHONE..................................812 259-5446
L Portee, *Pr*
EMP: 6 **EST:** 2015
SALES (est): 200.12K **Privately Held**
SIC: 2741 Miscellaneous publishing

(G-16505)
PRECIBALL USA
219 E Main St Ste 4x (47501-2990)
PHONE..................................812 257-5555
EMP: 2 **EST:** 2010
SALES (est): 58.32K **Privately Held**
SIC: 3999 Bristles, dressing of

(G-16506)
RAPAR INC
705 W National Hwy (47501-3330)
PHONE..................................812 254-9886
Mellisa Williams, *Owner*
EMP: 5 **EST:** 2008
SALES (est): 182.38K **Privately Held**
SIC: 2599 7389 Bar, restaurant and cafeteria furniture; Business Activities at Non-Commercial Site

(G-16507)
RIVERSIDE PETROLEUM IND LLC
2873 N State Road 57 (47501-7577)
PHONE..................................812 639-0859
EMP: 4
SALES (corp-wide): 2.33MM **Privately Held**
Web: www.riversideenergygroup.com
SIC: 1382 Oil and gas exploration services
PA: Riverside Petroleum Indiana, Llc
2829 Tech Frest Blvd Ste
Spring TX 77381
713 589-8810

(G-16508)
RUSTY SHELDEN DUWANE
Also Called: Shelden Welding & Fabrication
209 Se 2nd St (47501-3514)
PHONE..................................812 890-5780
Rusty D Shelden, *Owner*
EMP: 4 **EST:** 2007
SALES (est): 87.71K **Privately Held**
SIC: 7692 Welding repair

(G-16509)
SOUTHERN INDIANA CHEMICAL INC (PA)
Also Called: Pete's Peaches
358 E 900 N (47501-7256)
PHONE..................................812 687-7118
Pete Slowik, *Pr*
EMP: 3 **EST:** 1992
SALES (est): 603.25K
SALES (corp-wide): 603.25K **Privately Held**
SIC: 0175 2879 Peach orchard; Agricultural chemicals, nec

(G-16510)
TROY STUART
Also Called: Source Hospitality Mfg Group
1 Fountain View Est Bldg 2 (47501-9590)
PHONE..................................812 887-0403
Troy D Stuart, *Owner*
EMP: 5 **EST:** 2013
SALES (est): 211.92K **Privately Held**
SIC: 2599 Hotel furniture

(G-16511)
TYSON FRESH MEATS INC
Also Called: I B P
Rr 3 (47501)
PHONE..................................812 486-2800
Robert Peterson, *Brnch Mgr*
EMP: 1
SALES (corp-wide): 52.88B **Publicly Held**
Web: www.tysonfreshmeats.com
SIC: 2011 Meat packing plants
HQ: Tyson Fresh Meats, Inc.
2200 W Don Tyson Pkwy
Springdale AR 72765
479 290-4000

(G-16512)
WALLYS CONSTRUCTION
1279 South 3t (47501)
PHONE..................................812 254-4154
Wallace Knapp, *Prin*
EMP: 5 **EST:** 2006
SALES (est): 232.66K **Privately Held**
SIC: 1389 Construction, repair, and dismantling services

(G-16513)
WILLIAMS BROS HLTH CARE PHRM I (PA)
10 Williams Brothers Dr (47501-4535)
P.O. Box 271 (47501-0271)
PHONE..................................812 254-2497
Charles C Williams, *Pr*
Jeffrey W Williams, *
Mark Williams, *
EMP: 110 **EST:** 1990
SALES (est): 88.5MM
SALES (corp-wide): 88.5MM **Privately Held**
Web: www.williamsbrospharmacy.com
SIC: 5912 7352 5999 5169 Drug stores; Medical equipment rental; Telephone and communication equipment; Oxygen

Waterloo
Dekalb County

(G-16514)
ARES DIVISION LLC
345 Cobblers Way (46793-9489)
PHONE..................................260 349-9803
EMP: 1 **EST:** 2013
SALES (est): 168.1K **Privately Held**
Web: www.aresdivision.com
SIC: 3533 3724 3714 Oil field machinery and equipment; Turbines, aircraft type; Motor vehicle parts and accessories

(G-16515)
BOWMAN & BOWMAN FARMS INC
4678 County Road 22 (46793-9744)
PHONE..................................260 837-4171
Kevin Bowman, *Pr*
EMP: 3 **EST:** 1983
SALES (est): 243.94K **Privately Held**
SIC: 3523 Driers (farm): grain, hay, and seed

(G-16516)
CHARLESTON METAL PRODUCTS INC
Also Called: H & N Machine Division of
350 Grant St (46793-9442)
P.O. Box 213 (47383-0213)
PHONE..................................260 837-8211
Jeff Dragoo, *Mgr*
EMP: 19
SALES (corp-wide): 17.54MM **Privately Held**
Web: www.charlestonmetal.com
SIC: 3599 3541 3451 Machine shop, jobbing and repair; Machine tools, metal cutting type ; Screw machine products
PA: Charleston Metal Products Inc
350 Grant St
Waterloo IN 46793
260 837-8211

(G-16517)
CHARLESTON METAL PRODUCTS INC (PA)
350 Grant St (46793-9442)
PHONE..................................260 837-8211
George William Tucker Senior, *Pr*
George William Tucker Senior, *Prin*
G William Tucker Senior, *CEO*
Darlene Tucker, *
▼ **EMP:** 75 **EST:** 1946
SQ FT: 124,000
SALES (est): 17.54MM
SALES (corp-wide): 17.54MM **Privately Held**
Web: www.charlestonmetal.com
SIC: 3451 Screw machine products

(G-16518)
COUNTRY STONE
Also Called: Wilhelm Gravel
2280 County Road 27 (46793-9413)
P.O. Box 151 (61264-0151)
PHONE..................................260 837-7134
Chris Albright, *Genl Mgr*
Ron Bjustrom, *Pr*
▲ **EMP:** 12 **EST:** 1989
SQ FT: 340
SALES (est): 304.09K **Privately Held**
SIC: 1442 Common sand mining

(G-16519)
ELSIE MANUFACTURING COMPANY
600 W Maple St (46793-9547)
P.O. Box 97 (46793-0097)
PHONE..................................260 837-8841
Sandra Shipe, *Sec*
Brian Ruegsegger, *Pr*
EMP: 9 **EST:** 1947
SQ FT: 5,000
SALES (est): 916.73K **Privately Held**
Web: www.elsiemfg.com
SIC: 3443 3452 Fabricated plate work (boiler shop); Bolts, nuts, rivets, and washers

(G-16520)
GARRY MERTZ
Also Called: Mertz Custom Trailer Mfg
702 County Road 39 (46793-9779)
PHONE..................................260 837-6451
Garry Mertz, *Owner*
Gary Mertz, *Owner*
EMP: 1 **EST:** 1984
SQ FT: 1,300
SALES (est): 100K **Privately Held**
Web: www.mertztrailer.com
SIC: 3799 Trailers and trailer equipment

(G-16521)
HEARTLAND CASTINGS INC
675 E Union St (46793)
P.O. Box 37 (46793-0037)
PHONE..................................260 837-8311
Jordan Pfister, *Pr*
EMP: 20 **EST:** 2015
SQ FT: 36,000
SALES (est): 2.37MM **Privately Held**
Web: www.heartlandcastings.com
SIC: 3363 3364 Aluminum die-castings; Zinc and zinc-base alloy die-castings

(G-16522)
KCMA & SERVICES LLC
1954 County Road 43 (46793-9708)
PHONE..................................260 645-0885
EMP: 2 **EST:** 2012
SALES (est): 223.48K **Privately Held**
SIC: 2099 3625 8299 Maple syrup; Motor controls and accessories; Educational services

(G-16523)
LOCKWOOD WELDING INCORPORATED
2450 County Road 32 (46793-9423)
PHONE..................................260 925-2086
Ken Lockwood, *Pr*
EMP: 5 **EST:** 1988
SALES (est): 490.93K **Privately Held**
Web: www.lockwoodwelding.com
SIC: 7692 Welding repair

(G-16524)
MERRITT SAND AND GRAVEL INC (PA)
2007 County Road 39 (46793-9788)
PHONE..................................260 665-2513
John E Merritt, *Pr*
Stuart Wilson, *Treas*
EMP: 10 **EST:** 1992
SQ FT: 2,300
SALES (est): 1.05MM **Privately Held**
SIC: 5211 1442 Sand and gravel; Sand mining

(G-16525)
NUCOR CORPORATION
305 Industrial Pkwy (46793)
PHONE..................................260 837-7891
Leon Topalian, *Brnch Mgr*
EMP: 10
SALES (corp-wide): 34.71B **Publicly Held**
Web: www.nucor.com
SIC: 3312 Blast furnaces and steel mills
PA: Nucor Corporation
1915 Rexford Rd
Charlotte NC 28211
704 366-7000

(G-16526)
NUCOR CORPORATION
Also Called: Nucor Building Systems
250 Industrial Pkwy (46793-9438)
PHONE..................................260 837-7891
Johanna Threm, *Genl Mgr*
EMP: 25
SALES (corp-wide): 34.71B **Publicly Held**
Web: www.nucor.com
SIC: 3312 Blast furnaces and steel mills
PA: Nucor Corporation
1915 Rexford Rd
Charlotte NC 28211
704 366-7000

(G-16527)
NUCOR CORPORATION
Nucor Building Systems
250 Industrial Pkwy (46793-9438)
PHONE..................................260 837-7891
Bob Lowe, *Mgr*
EMP: 100

SALES (corp-wide): 34.71B **Publicly Held**
Web: www.nucor.com
SIC: 3312 Blast furnaces and steel mills
PA: Nucor Corporation
1915 Rexford Rd
Charlotte NC 28211
704 366-7000

(G-16528)
R P WAKEFIELD COMPANY INC
600 W Maple St (46793)
P.O. Box 97 (46793)
PHONE..................................260 837-8841
Brian Ruegsegger, *Pr*
Robert Simon, *
Sandra Rhoads, *
EMP: 25 **EST:** 1953
SQ FT: 60,000
SALES (est): 2.45MM **Privately Held**
Web: www.rpwakefield.com
SIC: 2431 Mantels, wood

(G-16529)
RDD PROPERTIES INC
300 E Railroad St (46793-9359)
P.O. Box 788 (46793-0788)
PHONE..................................317 870-1940
Dan Dickerhoof, *Pr*
Darrin Dickerhoof, *
▲ **EMP:** 50 **EST:** 1963
SQ FT: 75,000
SALES (est): 1.46MM **Privately Held**
Web: www.indianaubolts.com
SIC: 3462 3429 3452 3444 Automotive forgings, ferrous: crankshaft, engine, axle, etc.; Metal fasteners; Bolts, nuts, rivets, and washers; Sheet metalwork

(G-16530)
RICHARD SQUIER PALLETS INC
2522 Us Highway 6 (46793-9414)
P.O. Box 668 (46793-0668)
PHONE..................................260 281-2434
Richard Squier Junior, *Pr*
EMP: 19 **EST:** 1955
SQ FT: 40,000
SALES (est): 934.97K **Privately Held**
SIC: 2448 Pallets, wood

(G-16531)
STAR TECHNOLOGY INC
200 Executive Dr (46793-9448)
PHONE..................................260 837-7833
Joe Zimmermanm, *Pr*
Donn R Starkey, *Pr*
◆ **EMP:** 23 **EST:** 1989
SQ FT: 13,000
SALES (est): 6.53MM **Privately Held**
Web: www.star-technology.com
SIC: 2821 Epoxy resins

(G-16532)
TRITON ENERGY LLC
205 Industrial Pkwy (46793-9438)
EMP: 4 **EST:** 2007
SALES (est): 419.13K **Privately Held**
SIC: 2911 Diesel fuels

(G-16533)
WHOLISTIC GARDENS
4840 County Road 4 (46793-9770)
PHONE..................................260 573-1088
EMP: 2 **EST:** 2013
SQ FT: 1,280
SALES (est): 274.22K **Privately Held**
SIC: 2023 Dietary supplements, dairy and non-dairy based

(G-16534)
WILHELM GRAVEL CO INC
Also Called: Country Stones and The Gravel
2280 County Road 27 (46793-9413)
P.O. Box 151 (61264-0151)
PHONE..................................260 837-6511
Ron Bjustrom, *Pr*
EMP: 26 **EST:** 1936
SQ FT: 2,500
SALES (est): 707.19K **Privately Held**
SIC: 1442 Gravel mining

Waveland
Montgomery County

(G-16535)
JOSEPH FISHER
6492 E 850 N (47989-7514)
PHONE..................................765 435-7231
Joseph Fisher, *Owner*
EMP: 2 **EST:** 2004
SALES (est): 116.9K **Privately Held**
SIC: 2221 Comforters and quilts, manmade fiber and silk

Wawaka
Noble County

(G-16536)
B & J SPECIALTY INC (PA)
7919 N 100 E (46794-9734)
PHONE..................................260 761-5011
John Wicker, *Pr*
▲ **EMP:** 66 **EST:** 1975
SQ FT: 29,000
SALES (est): 9.7MM **Privately Held**
Web: www.bjspecialtyinc.com
SIC: 3544 Special dies and tools

(G-16537)
BASELINE TOOL COMPANY
8458 N Baseline Rd (46794-9736)
PHONE..................................260 761-4932
Clayton Morr, *Pr*
Carolyn Morr, *Sec*
EMP: 10 **EST:** 1987
SQ FT: 11,840
SALES (est): 967.58K **Privately Held**
Web: www.baselinetool.com
SIC: 3543 7629 Foundry patternmaking; Electrical repair shops

(G-16538)
BERKEY MACHINE CORPORATION
7037a N Triplett St (46794-9799)
PHONE..................................260 761-4002
Dennis Berkey, *Pr*
Doug Allen, *Pr*
Amy Allen, *Sec*
EMP: 5 **EST:** 1976
SQ FT: 5,000
SALES (est): 406.94K **Privately Held**
Web: www.plastechmd.com
SIC: 3544 3545 Special dies and tools; Machine tool accessories

(G-16539)
FRICK SERVICES INC (PA)
3154 W Depot St (46794)
PHONE..................................260 761-3311
Dan Frick, *Ex VP*
Louise R Frick, *
▲ **EMP:** 30 **EST:** 1920
SQ FT: 3,000
SALES (est): 23.84MM
SALES (corp-wide): 23.84MM **Privately Held**
Web: www.frickservices.com

SIC: 5191 5153 5261 4221 Fertilizer and fertilizer materials; Grains; Fertilizer; Farm product warehousing and storage

(G-16540)
METALCRAFT INC
3330 W Us Highway 6 (46794-9750)
P.O. Box 57 (46794-0057)
PHONE....................260 761-3001
John Muholland, Pr
Tim Gage, VP
EMP: 10 EST: 1985
SQ FT: 18,000
SALES (est): 1.83MM Privately Held
Web: www.metalcft.com
SIC: 3444 Sheet metalwork

Waynetown
Montgomery County

(G-16541)
JEWELRY IN CANDLES
6188 W Division Rd (47990-8161)
PHONE....................765 401-6228
Michele Enlow, Prin
EMP: 5 EST: 2016
SALES (est): 39.69K Privately Held
Web: www.jewelrycandles.com
SIC: 3999 Candles

West Baden Springs
Orange County

(G-16542)
MARK A MORIN LOGGING INC
757 N Walnut St (47469-7722)
P.O. Box 127 (47469-0127)
PHONE....................812 327-4917
Mark A Morin, Pr
EMP: 8 EST: 2014
SALES (est): 174.42K Privately Held
SIC: 2411 Logging

West College Corner
Union County

(G-16543)
RONS GENERAL REPAIR
403 Ramsey St (47003-1205)
PHONE....................765 732-3805
George Clinton, Owner
EMP: 3 EST: 2001
SALES (est): 93.24K Privately Held
SIC: 7692 Welding repair

(G-16544)
UC INK LLC
6549 S Kirker Rd (47003-9366)
PHONE....................765 220-5502
EMP: 2 EST: 2009
SALES (est): 81.21K Privately Held
SIC: 2261 Screen printing of cotton broadwoven fabrics

West Harrison
Dearborn County

(G-16545)
CDS LLC
99 Mill St (47060-1000)
PHONE....................812 637-0900
Mark Rob, Managing Member
EMP: 6 EST: 2019
SALES (est): 251.52K Privately Held

SIC: 3694 Automotive electrical equipment, nec

(G-16546)
H NAGEL & SON CO (PA)
Also Called: Brighton Mills
707 Harrison Brookville Rd Unit 220 (47060-9677)
PHONE....................513 665-4550
Edward Nagel, Pr
Michael Norris, VP
EMP: 10 EST: 1860
SQ FT: 46,000
SALES (est): 4.51MM
SALES (corp-wide): 4.51MM Privately Held
Web: www.brightonmills.com
SIC: 2041 Flour: blended, prepared, or self-rising

(G-16547)
HARRISON SAND AND GRAVEL CO
4215 Harrison Brookville Rd (47060)
PHONE....................812 656-8149
Donnie Gauck, Mgr
EMP: 8
SALES (corp-wide): 1.84MM Privately Held
SIC: 1442 Construction sand and gravel
PA: Harrison Sand And Gravel Co
992 S County Road 800 E
Greensburg IN 47240
812 663-2021

(G-16548)
HOGAN STAMPING LLC
305 Maple St (47060-1016)
PHONE....................812 656-8222
Robert Howeler, Managing Member
EMP: 6 EST: 2001
SALES (est): 229.53K Privately Held
SIC: 3353 Aluminum sheet, plate, and foil

(G-16549)
M-TECH MACHINE PRODUCTS LLC
27755 Daugherty Ln Ste A (47060-9600)
PHONE....................812 637-3500
Michael Hamonds, Owner
EMP: 4 EST: 1990
SQ FT: 2,200
SALES (est): 384.12K Privately Held
SIC: 3599 Machine shop, jobbing and repair

(G-16550)
NORTHBEND PATTERN WORKS INC
28080 Ziegler Blvd (47060)
P.O. Box 160 (45030-0160)
PHONE....................812 637-3000
Dale L Ziegler, Pr
Nancy Ziegler, *
EMP: 28 EST: 1973
SQ FT: 35,000
SALES (est): 2.47MM Privately Held
SIC: 3543 Industrial patterns

(G-16551)
SIEMER MILLING COMPANY
707 Harrison Brookville Rd (47060-9677)
PHONE....................513 814-9216
Joseph Siemer, Pr
EMP: 11 EST: 2015
SALES (est): 1.32MM Privately Held
Web: www.siemermilling.com
SIC: 2041 Grain mills (except rice)

(G-16552)
TOP OF HILL PERFORMANCE LLC
28730 Chappelow Hill Rd (47060-8751)
PHONE....................812 637-3693
EMP: 1 EST: 2003

SALES (est): 151.84K Privately Held
SIC: 3625 Electric controls and control accessories, industrial

West Lafayette
Tippecanoe County

(G-16553)
34 LIVES PBC
Also Called: Renovera, Pbc.
1281 Win Hentschel Blvd Ste 2574 (47906)
PHONE....................303 550-9989
Christopher Jaynes, CEO
Kathleen St Jean, CCO
Henri Leuvenink, CSO
EMP: 6 EST: 2020
SALES (est): 316.36K Privately Held
SIC: 3841 8621 Surgical and medical instruments; Health association

(G-16554)
A-1 SCREENPRINTING LLC
Also Called: Underground Printing
314 W State St (47906-3539)
PHONE....................765 588-3851
EMP: 2
Web: www.undergroundshirts.com
SIC: 2759 Screen printing
PA: A-1 Screenprinting, Llc
1476 Seaver Way
Ypsilanti MI 48197

(G-16555)
ACCUPS LLC
1050 Roxboro St (47906-7228)
PHONE....................765 586-5021
EMP: 1 EST: 2014
SALES (est): 118.33K Privately Held
Web: www.webintravel-japan.com
SIC: 3577 Input/output equipment, computer

(G-16556)
ADDIVANT USA LLC
1435 Win Hentschel Blvd Ste 115 (47906-4147)
PHONE....................765 497-6020
EMP: 5 EST: 2013
SALES (est): 91.85K Privately Held
SIC: 2821 Plastics materials and resins

(G-16557)
ADRANOS ENERGETICS LLC
137 Prophet Dr (47906-1235)
PHONE....................208 539-2439
Brandon Terry, Engr
EMP: 3 EST: 2015
SALES (est): 515.79K Privately Held
SIC: 3764 Space propulsion units and parts

(G-16558)
ADVANCED DIGITAL IMAGING
1231 Cumberland Ave Ste A (47906-1358)
PHONE....................765 491-9434
Scot Benham, Owner
EMP: 1 EST: 2000
SALES (est): 77.05K Privately Held
SIC: 2759 Commercial printing, nec

(G-16559)
AKINA INC
Also Called: Akina
3495 Kent Ave Ste M200 (47906-4181)
PHONE....................765 464-0501
Kinam Park, Pr
John Garner, Mgr
Marietta Smith, Acctg Mgr
Sarah Skidmore, Research & Development
EMP: 10 EST: 2001
SQ FT: 5,000

SALES (est): 1.84MM Privately Held
Web: www.akinainc.com
SIC: 2834 Pharmaceutical preparations

(G-16560)
AMPLIFIED SCIENCES LLC
3000 Kent Ave (47906-1185)
PHONE....................317 490-0511
Vincent Davisson, Admn
EMP: 2 EST: 2016
SALES (est): 251.01K Privately Held
Web: www.amplifiedsciences.com
SIC: 3841 Diagnostic apparatus, medical

(G-16561)
ANAEROBIC INNOVATIONS LLC
2221 Huron Rd (47906-1921)
PHONE....................765 491-1174
Leila Nyberg, CEO
EMP: 1 EST: 2013
SALES (est): 66.38K Privately Held
SIC: 3589 8748 Water treatment equipment, industrial; Environmental consultant

(G-16562)
ANALYSWIFT LLC
444 Jennings St (47906-1146)
PHONE....................801 599-5879
EMP: 2 EST: 2011
SALES (est): 144.97K Privately Held
Web: www.analyswift.com
SIC: 7372 Publisher's computer software

(G-16563)
ANIMATED DYNAMICS INC
1281 Win Hentschel Blvd (47906-4335)
PHONE....................765 418-5359
David D Nolte, Prin
John Turek, Prin
EMP: 2 EST: 2011
SALES (est): 171.97K Privately Held
Web: www.anidyn.com
SIC: 3826 Analytical instruments

(G-16564)
AZLAND INC
345 Burnetts Rd Ste 300 (47906-9761)
PHONE....................765 429-6200
Brian Vorst, Pr
Darryl Hatke, VP
EMP: 4 EST: 2009
SALES (est): 362.58K Privately Held
SIC: 3523 Farm machinery and equipment

(G-16565)
BIOKORF LLC
1008 Ravinia Rd (47906-2327)
PHONE....................765 727-0782
EMP: 2 EST: 2013
SALES (est): 104.63K Privately Held
Web: www.biokorf.com
SIC: 2834 2899 8731 Tablets, pharmaceutical; Gelatin: edible, technical, photographic, or pharmaceutical; Medical research, commercial

(G-16566)
BIOSCIENCE VACCINES INC
1425 Innovation Pl (47906-1000)
PHONE....................765 464-5890
EMP: 6 EST: 2010
SALES (est): 416.71K Privately Held
Web: www.biosciencevaccines.com
SIC: 2836 Biological products, except diagnostic

(G-16567)
BOILERS INC
Also Called: Gold & Black Illustrated
2605 Yeager Rd (47906-1337)

GEOGRAPHIC SECTION
West Lafayette - Tippecanoe County (G-16596)

PHONE..................765 742-5855
Allen Karpick, *Pr*
Bart Burrell, *Sec*
EMP: 7 EST: 1990
SALES (est): 500K **Privately Held**
Web: www.goldandblackdigital.com
SIC: 2721 Periodicals

(G-16568)
BOOTMAKERS LLC
2550 Kent Ave Ste 2 (47906-1576)
PHONE..................765 412-7243
Vidhya Iyer, *CEO*
EMP: 3 EST: 2014
SALES (est): 247.16K **Privately Held**
Web: www.bootmakers.us
SIC: 5139 3131 Boots; Footwear cut stock

(G-16569)
CONTANGO INC
1281 Win Hentschel Blvd Ste 1300 (47906-4335)
PHONE..................765 418-0756
Ben Brame, *CEO*
EMP: 1
SALES (est): 65.51K **Privately Held**
SIC: 7372 Business oriented computer software

(G-16570)
COVERT DEFENSES LLC
1195 S Sharon Chapel Rd (47906-4300)
PHONE..................919 749-9717
Hany Abdel-khalik, *Prin*
EMP: 1 EST: 2018
SALES (est): 49.15K **Privately Held**
SIC: 3812 Defense systems and equipment

(G-16571)
COX JOHN
Also Called: Spaulding Products and Mfg Co
140 Tamiami Ct (47906-1205)
P.O. Box 2612 (47996-2612)
PHONE..................765 463-6396
John Cox, *Owner*
EMP: 2 EST: 1987
SALES (est): 50K **Privately Held**
SIC: 3559 2653 Automotive maintenance equipment; Display items, corrugated: made from purchased materials

(G-16572)
CREATECH/REHDER DEVELOPMENT CO
2139 Klondike Rd (47906-5124)
PHONE..................765 252-0257
Tom Houck, *Owner*
EMP: 1 EST: 2017
SQ FT: 1,200
SALES (est): 63.35K **Privately Held**
Web: www.rehder-dev.com
SIC: 3825 Digital test equipment, electronic and electrical circuits

(G-16573)
CREATIVE CONSTRUCTION PUBG INC
2720 S River Rd (47906-4347)
PHONE..................765 743-9704
EMP: 2 EST: 1995
SALES (est): 217.05K **Privately Held**
Web: www.creativeconstruction.com
SIC: 2721 Trade journals: publishing only, not printed on site

(G-16574)
CURIA INDIANA LLC
Also Called: Ssci
3065 Kent Ave (47906-1076)
PHONE..................765 463-0112
William S Marth, *Pr*
EMP: 90 EST: 2011
SQ FT: 48,800
SALES (est): 19.31MM
SALES (corp-wide): 927.92MM **Privately Held**
Web: www.ssci-inc.com
SIC: 2834 Pharmaceutical preparations
HQ: Curia Global, Inc.
24 Corporate Cir
Albany NY 12203

(G-16575)
DAYTON-PHOENIX GROUP INC
4750 Swisher Rd (47906-9782)
PHONE..................765 742-4410
EMP: 57
Web: www.dayton-phoenix.com
SIC: 3621 Motors and generators
PA: Dayton-Phoenix Group, Inc.
1619 Kuntz Rd
Dayton OH 45404

(G-16576)
DIOR PUBLISHING
606 Hillcrest Rd (47906-2350)
PHONE..................765 471-2249
Kathie Dior, *Owner*
EMP: 1 EST: 2001
SALES (est): 57.6K **Privately Held**
Web: www.thetwisteddoors.com
SIC: 2741 Miscellaneous publishing

(G-16577)
DOW AGROSCIENCE
1281 Win Hentschel Blvd (47906-4335)
PHONE..................765 743-0015
EMP: 2 EST: 2010
SALES (est): 203.69K **Privately Held**
SIC: 2879 Agricultural chemicals, nec

(G-16578)
DOW AGROSCIENCES
3400 Kent Ave Ste 100 (47906-1581)
PHONE..................765 775-2918
EMP: 8 EST: 2018
SALES (est): 143.42K **Privately Held**
Web: www.corteva.com
SIC: 2879 Agricultural chemicals, nec

(G-16579)
EFIL PHARMACEUTICALS CORP
3706 Litchfield Pl (47906-8738)
PHONE..................765 491-7247
Kee-hong Kim, *CEO*
EMP: 2
SALES (est): 225.27K **Privately Held**
SIC: 2833 Medicinal chemicals

(G-16580)
FENWICK PHARMA LLC
5315 Shootingstar Ln (47906-8713)
PHONE..................765 412-1889
Daniel T Smith, *Prin*
EMP: 2 EST: 2010
SALES (est): 143.08K **Privately Held**
SIC: 2834 Pharmaceutical preparations

(G-16581)
FWDNXT LLC
923 Windsor Dr (47906-2044)
PHONE..................203 645-0736
Eugenio Culurciello, *Pr*
EMP: 1 EST: 2016
SALES (est): 47.99K **Privately Held**
SIC: 7372 Application computer software

(G-16582)
GH LLC
3000 Kent Ave (47906-1184)
PHONE..................765 775-3776
EMP: 1
SALES (corp-wide): 66.91K **Privately Held**
SIC: 2731 Book publishing
PA: Gh Llc
7923 Sedgewick Pl
Fort Wayne IN 46835
260 496-1005

(G-16583)
GH PRODUCTS INC
3917 Sunnycroft Pl (47906-8817)
PHONE..................619 208-4823
Eli Weinstein, *Prin*
EMP: 5 EST: 2009
SALES (est): 361.53K **Privately Held**
SIC: 3663 Radio and t.v. communications equipment

(G-16584)
GLCC LAUREL LLC
1 Geddes Way (47906-5394)
PHONE..................765 497-6100
EMP: 1 EST: 2004
SALES (est): 14.86MM
SALES (corp-wide): 8.55B **Privately Held**
SIC: 2819 Bromine, elemental
HQ: Lanxess Corporation
111 Ridc Park West Dr
Pittsburgh PA 15275
412 809-1000

(G-16585)
GOLDSTONE JEWELRY INC
3617 Montclair St (47906-8607)
PHONE..................765 742-1975
EMP: 2 EST: 1994
SALES (est): 231.32K **Privately Held**
Web: www.goldstonejewelry.com
SIC: 5944 3911 7631 Jewelry, precious stones and precious metals; Jewelry, precious metal; Jewelry repair services

(G-16586)
GOODAR & HARRIS LLC
4433 N Candlewick Ln (47906-7121)
PHONE..................312 465-3899
Jeanelle Goodar, *Managing Member*
EMP: 1 EST: 2020
SALES (est): 47.23K **Privately Held**
SIC: 2899 Gelatin capsules

(G-16587)
GREEN TECH AMERICA INC
606 Riley Ln (47906-2370)
PHONE..................765 588-3834
Nancy W Y Ho, *Pr*
EMP: 1 EST: 2006
SALES (est): 242.94K **Privately Held**
Web: www.greentechamerica.com
SIC: 2869 Industrial organic chemicals, nec

(G-16588)
GRIFFIN ANALYTICAL TECHNOLOGIES LLC
3000 Kent Ave Ste E1 (47906-1075)
PHONE..................765 775-1701
EMP: 43
Web: www.griffinanalytical.com
SIC: 3826 Analytical instruments

(G-16589)
GROWING CHILD INC
1325 Palmer Dr (47906-1804)
P.O. Box 2505 (47996-2505)
PHONE..................765 463-1696
Dennis Dunn, *Pr*
EMP: 2 EST: 2005
SALES (est): 134.9K **Privately Held**
Web: www.growingchild.com

SIC: 2711 2741 Newspapers, publishing and printing; Newsletter publishing

(G-16590)
HASSER ENTERPRISES INC
8023 Us Highway 52 W (47906-9457)
PHONE..................765 583-1444
Melvin Hasser, *Pr*
Linda Hasser, *Sec*
EMP: 3 EST: 1995
SQ FT: 11,000
SALES (est): 250.59K **Privately Held**
SIC: 3469 Stamping metal for the trade

(G-16591)
HAZON LEARNING LLC
1281 Win Hentschel Blvd Rm 2935 (47906-4335)
PHONE..................765 490-6321
EMP: 1 EST: 2013
SALES (est): 46.23K **Privately Held**
SIC: 7372 Educational computer software

(G-16592)
HENDRICKSON ENGINEERING LLC
3080 Hamilton St (47906-1157)
PHONE..................765 404-9132
L Vernon Hendrickson Iii, *Admn*
EMP: 7 EST: 2015
SALES (est): 72.08K **Privately Held**
SIC: 3714 Motor vehicle parts and accessories

(G-16593)
I NOODLES
111 N Chauncey Ave (47906-3003)
PHONE..................765 447-2288
EMP: 4 EST: 2018
SALES (est): 90.56K **Privately Held**
Web: www.noodles.com
SIC: 2098 Noodles (e.g. egg, plain, and water), dry

(G-16594)
IMAGINESTICS LLC
1801 Kalberer Rd Ste A100 (47906)
PHONE..................765 464-1700
EMP: 4 EST: 2020
SALES (est): 56.54K **Privately Held**
Web: www.vizseek.com
SIC: 7372 7371 3579 Prepackaged software; Custom computer programming services; Office machines, nec

(G-16595)
INDIANA MANUFACTURING INST
1105 Challenger Ave (47906-1168)
PHONE..................765 494-4935
EMP: 6 EST: 2016
SALES (est): 156.2K **Privately Held**
SIC: 3999 Barber and beauty shop equipment

(G-16596)
IRVING MATERIALS INC
Also Called: I M I
301 Ahlers Dr (47906-5992)
PHONE..................765 743-3806
Bob Johnson, *Brnch Mgr*
EMP: 6
SQ FT: 3,000
SALES (corp-wide): 814.09MM **Privately Held**
Web: www.irvmat.com
SIC: 3273 Ready-mixed concrete
PA: Irving Materials, Inc.
8032 N State Road 9
Greenfield IN 46140
317 326-3101

West Lafayette - Tippecanoe County (G-16597)

GEOGRAPHIC SECTION

(G-16597)
JUA TECHNOLOGIES INTL INC
1281 Win Hentschel Blvd Ste 1300 (47906)
PHONE.................................765 204-5533
Klein Ileleji, *CEO*
EMP: 1 EST: 2016
SALES (est): 198.17K **Privately Held**
Web: www.juatechnology.com
SIC: 3556 Dehydrating equipment, food processing

(G-16598)
KDP LLC
1301 Palmer Dr (47906-1852)
PHONE.................................630 362-7346
EMP: 4 EST: 2021
SALES (est): 84.77K **Privately Held**
SIC: 7372 Prepackaged software

(G-16599)
LACTOR LLC
3221 Covington St (47906-1189)
PHONE.................................765 496-6838
Jeffrey Brewer, *Prin*
Azza Ahmed, *Prin*
Elisha Hollandbeck, *Adm/Asst*
EMP: 2
SALES (est): 56.54K **Privately Held**
SIC: 7372 Application computer software

(G-16600)
LAFAYETTE MARKETING INC
Also Called: Tree Pro
3180 W 250 N (47906-5143)
PHONE.................................765 474-5374
Tom Mills, *Pr*
David Mills Stckhlder, *Prin*
Donna Mills, *Sec*
▲ EMP: 15 EST: 1980
SQ FT: 36,000
SALES (est): 835.22K **Privately Held**
Web: www.treepro.com
SIC: 3524 Lawn and garden tractors and equipment

(G-16601)
LAFAYETTE VENETIAN BLIND INC (PA)
Also Called: Lafayette Interior Fashions
3000 Klondike Rd (47906-5210)
P.O. Box 2838 (47996-2838)
PHONE.................................765 464-2500
Joseph N Morgan, *Pr*
Dennis Morgan, *
Toni Morgan, *Stockholder*
Pam Bastable Stlhldr, *Prin*
◆ EMP: 850 EST: 1950
SQ FT: 300,000
SALES (est): 91.88MM
SALES (corp-wide): 91.88MM **Privately Held**
Web: www.lafvb.com
SIC: 2591 2391 Window blinds; Draperies, plastic and textile: from purchased materials

(G-16602)
LODOS THERANOSTICS LLC
132 Vigo Ct (47906-1171)
PHONE.................................765 427-2492
You-yeon Won, *CEO*
Younjae Kim, *CFO*
EMP: 2 EST: 2015
SALES (est): 125.47K **Privately Held**
SIC: 2834 Solutions, pharmaceutical

(G-16603)
M4 SCIENCES LLC
4840 Us Highway 231 N (47906)
PHONE.................................765 479-6215
James B Mann, *CEO*
Brian Gootee, *COO*
EMP: 5 EST: 2005
SALES (est): 470K **Privately Held**
Web: www.m4sciences.com
SIC: 3545 Machine tool accessories

(G-16604)
M4 SCIENCES CORPORATION
4840 Us Highway 231 N (47906)
PHONE.................................765 479-6215
James Mann, *CEO*
Brian Gootee, *COO*
EMP: 2 EST: 2006
SALES (est): 200.32K **Privately Held**
Web: www.m4sciences.com
SIC: 3545 Machine tool accessories

(G-16605)
MIDWEST DESIGN HYDRAULIC
4807 Homewood Dr (47906-5632)
PHONE.................................765 714-3016
EMP: 1 EST: 2018
SALES (est): 65.69K **Privately Held**
SIC: 7389 3052 5085 3494 Design services; Rubber and plastics hose and beltings; Industrial supplies; Valves and pipe fittings, nec

(G-16606)
MIDWEST TRANSIT AUTHORITY LLC
4410 Crossbow Ct (47906-7116)
PHONE.................................765 414-5097
EMP: 1 EST: 2021
SALES (est): 60.08K **Privately Held**
Web: www.midwesttransit.com
SIC: 3537 Trucks: freight, baggage, etc.: industrial, except mining

(G-16607)
MIFTEK CORPORATION
Also Called: Miftek
1231 Cumberland Ave Ste H (47906-1358)
PHONE.................................765 491-3848
Joseph Robinson, *Pr*
Masanobu Yamamoto, *VP*
EMP: 2 EST: 2013
SALES (est): 251.08K **Privately Held**
Web: www.miftek.com
SIC: 3841 Diagnostic apparatus, medical

(G-16608)
MIX ON SITE
2252 Us Highway 52 W (47906-5571)
PHONE.................................765 607-2140
EMP: 4 EST: 2018
SALES (est): 59.12K **Privately Held**
SIC: 3273 Ready-mixed concrete

(G-16609)
MOBILE ENERLYTICS LLC
1281 Win Hentschel Blvd Ste 1707 (47906-4358)
PHONE.................................765 464-6909
Yu Charlie Hu, *Prin*
EMP: 2 EST: 2014
SALES (est): 131.68K **Privately Held**
Web: www.mobileenerlytics.com
SIC: 7372 Application computer software

(G-16610)
MOBILE LIMB & BRACE INC
2041 Klondike Rd (47906-5122)
P.O. Box 1437 (34786-1437)
PHONE.................................765 463-4100
Greg Decamp, *Pr*
Darci Decamp, *VP*
EMP: 3 EST: 1994
SQ FT: 1,800
SALES (est): 266.34K **Privately Held**
Web: www.mobilelimbandbrace.com
SIC: 3842 Limbs, artificial

(G-16611)
MOHAWK GROUP LLC
2550 Yeager Rd Apt 2-1 (47906-4015)
PHONE.................................765 250-5458
Robert Braddy, *Owner*
EMP: 6 EST: 2015
SALES (est): 99.37K **Privately Held**
SIC: 2273 Carpets and rugs

(G-16612)
NATUREGENIC INC (PA)
1281 Win Hentschel Blvd Ste 1573 (47906-4331)
PHONE.................................765 807-5525
Miyoung Kim, *CEO*
Jihon Choe, *Treas*
EMP: 1 EST: 2014
SALES (est): 587.18K
SALES (corp-wide): 587.18K **Privately Held**
Web: www.naturegenic.com
SIC: 2834 8731 Proprietary drug products; Agricultural research

(G-16613)
NEXT OFFSET SOLUTIONS INC
203 Gardenia Dr (47906-9067)
PHONE.................................773 844-1784
Jeffrey Rhoads, *CEO*
Janine Rhoads, *Pr*
Ibrahim Emre Gunduz, *VP*
EMP: 7 EST: 2017
SALES (est): 272.59K **Privately Held**
Web: www.nextoffset.com
SIC: 2752 Offset printing

(G-16614)
NORTHEAST QUALITY SERVICES LLC
719 Bexley Rd (47906-2307)
PHONE.................................860 632-7242
▲ EMP: 50 EST: 1980
SALES (est): 5.7MM **Privately Held**
Web: www.northeastquality.com
SIC: 3599 Machine shop, jobbing and repair

(G-16615)
NUTRAMAIZE LLC
Also Called: Nutramaize
1281 Win Hentschel Blvd Unit 046 (47906-4360)
PHONE.................................765 273-8274
Evan Rocheford, *Managing Member*
EMP: 2 EST: 2015
SALES (est): 139.44K **Privately Held**
Web: www.nutramaize.com
SIC: 2041 Corn meal

(G-16616)
PAPER STREET PRESS
1841 King Eider Dr (47906-6508)
PHONE.................................765 894-0027
EMP: 3 EST: 2015
SALES (est): 81.89K **Privately Held**
Web: www.bakpakdurden.com
SIC: 2741 Miscellaneous publishing

(G-16617)
PARSOLEX GMP CENTER INC
Also Called: Parsolex
3000 Kent Ave Ste 1510 (47906-1169)
PHONE.................................765 464-8414
Michael Chao, *Ch*
Alfonso Chang, *Pr*
EMP: 18 EST: 2004
SALES (est): 4.53MM **Privately Held**
Web: www.parsolexinc.com
SIC: 2834 Pharmaceutical preparations

(G-16618)
PETAL SOLUTIONS LLC
5164 Flowermound Dr (47906-9051)
PHONE.................................765 404-7747
EMP: 1 EST: 2017
SALES (est): 54.57K **Privately Held**
Web: www.petal-solutions.com
SIC: 3511 3823 Turbines and turbine generator sets; Thermocouples, industrial process type

(G-16619)
PHARMAPRINTER INC
1201 Cumberland Ave Ste 105 (47906-1359)
P.O. Box 3938 (47996-3938)
PHONE.................................765 543-1520
Arun Giridhar, *CEO*
EMP: 1 EST: 2016
SALES (est): 55.01K **Privately Held**
SIC: 2759 Commercial printing, nec

(G-16620)
PHYTOPTION LLC
3316 Morgan St (47906-1280)
PHONE.................................765 490-7738
EMP: 2 EST: 2011
SALES (est): 183.55K **Privately Held**
Web: www.phytoption.com
SIC: 2834 Pharmaceutical preparations

(G-16621)
PUCL BINDLEY BIOSCIENCE CTR
1203 W State St (47907-2057)
PHONE.................................765 496-3975
Vincent Jo Davisson, *Prin*
EMP: 8 EST: 2005
SALES (est): 169.7K **Privately Held**
SIC: 2836 Biological products, except diagnostic

(G-16622)
PURDUE STUDENT PUBG FOUNDATION
Also Called: PURDUE EXPONENT, THE
460 Northwestern Ave (47906-2966)
P.O. Box 2506 (47996-2506)
PHONE.................................765 743-1111
Patrick Kuhnle, *Publisher*
EMP: 55 EST: 1889
SQ FT: 22,500
SALES (est): 364.9K **Privately Held**
Web: www.purdueexponent.org
SIC: 2711 Commercial printing and newspaper publishing combined

(G-16623)
PURSPEC TECHNOLOGIES INC
Also Called: Purspec Technologies
1281 Win Hentschel Blvd (47906-4335)
PHONE.................................765 532-2208
Zheng Ouyang, *CEO*
EMP: 1 EST: 2015
SALES (est): 243.7K **Privately Held**
Web: www.purspec.co
SIC: 3826 3845 7389 Analytical instruments; Electromedical equipment; Business Activities at Non-Commercial Site

(G-16624)
R DREW & CO INC
Also Called: Clay Critters
4866 N 9th Street Rd (47906-9762)
PHONE.................................765 420-7232
Rebecca Bollinger, *Pr*
▼ EMP: 8 EST: 1980
SQ FT: 1,500
SALES (est): 451.38K **Privately Held**

GEOGRAPHIC SECTION

West Lebanon - Warren County (G-16649)

Web: www.claycritters.com
SIC: 3269 4724 Figures: pottery, china, earthenware, and stoneware; Travel agencies

(G-16625)
ROADWORKS MAUFACTURING
2482 Klondike Rd (47906-5129)
PHONE..................................765 742-7200
Susan Linson C.p.a., *Prin*
EMP: 7 **EST:** 2019
SALES (est): 252.44K **Privately Held**
Web: www.roadworksmfg.com
SIC: 3647 Vehicular lighting equipment

(G-16626)
ROLLS-ROYCE CORPORATION
1801 Newman Rd Ste 1700 (47906-4526)
PHONE..................................317 230-8515
Hal Raines, *Brnch Mgr*
EMP: 41
SALES (corp-wide): 20.55B **Privately Held**
Web: www.rolls-roycemotorcars.com
SIC: 5511 3443 3462 3731 New and used car dealers; Industrial vessels, tanks, and containers; Nuclear power plant forgings, ferrous; Submarines, building and repairing
HQ: Rolls-Royce Corporation
450 S Meridian St
Indianapolis IN 46225

(G-16627)
SAAB AERONAUTICS INDIANA LLC
2099 Hypersonic Pkwy (47906-4541)
PHONE..................................315 445-5009
EMP: 30 **EST:** 2017
SALES (est): 6.5MM
SALES (corp-wide): 2.78B **Privately Held**
SIC: 3728 Aircraft parts and equipment, nec
PA: Saab Ab
Broderna Ugglas Gata
Linkoping 581 8
13180000

(G-16628)
SKYEPACK LLC
3000 Kent Ave (47906-1184)
PHONE..................................765 323-8568
Eric Davis, *Ch Bd*
EMP: 1 **EST:** 2012
SQ FT: 161
SALES (est): 210.67K **Privately Held**
Web: www.skyepack.com
SIC: 7372 Educational computer software

(G-16629)
SMITH SOUND
2340 Sagamore Pkwy W Lot 4 (47906-7517)
P.O. Box 115 (47970-0215)
PHONE..................................765 464-2961
EMP: 1 **EST:** 1986
SQ FT: 3,500
SALES (est): 84.54K **Privately Held**
Web: www.smithsound.net
SIC: 3861 Sound recording and reproducing equipment, motion picture

(G-16630)
SPEAK ABILITIES LLP
221 W Wood St Apt 6 (47906)
PHONE..................................303 827-8269
Dave Moore, *Pt*
EMP: 2
SALES (est): 83.76K **Privately Held**
SIC: 7389 7372 Business Activities at Non-Commercial Site; Educational computer software

(G-16631)
SPIRROW THERAPEUTICS LLC
132 Vigo Ct (47906-1171)
PHONE..................................317 750-8879
EMP: 3 **EST:** 2018
SALES (est): 30.77K **Privately Held**
Web: www.spirrowtherapeutics.com
SIC: 2834 Pharmaceutical preparations

(G-16632)
SWIFT FUELS LLC
1435 Win Hentschel Blvd Ste 205 (47906-4152)
PHONE..................................765 464-8336
Rob Broin, *Ch*
Chris Dacosta, *CEO*
Joel Dykstra, *CFO*
Jon Ziulkowski, *VP*
Don Bower, *VP*
◆ **EMP:** 9 **EST:** 2012
SALES (est): 3.09MM **Privately Held**
Web: www.swiftfuels.com
SIC: 2869 5172 Fuels; Fuel oil

(G-16633)
TELEDYNE FLIR LLC
3495 Kent Ave Ste Q100 (47906)
PHONE..................................412 423-2100
Keith Lejeune, *CEO*
EMP: 25
SALES (corp-wide): 5.64B **Publicly Held**
Web: www.flir.com
SIC: 3826 Infrared analytical instruments
HQ: Teledyne Flir, Llc
27700 Sw Parkway Ave
Wilsonville OR 97070
503 498-3547

(G-16634)
TELEDYNE FLIR DEFENSE INC
Also Called: Flir Systems
3495 Kent Ave Ste V100 (47906-4189)
PHONE..................................765 775-1701
Dennis Barket, *Genl Mgr*
EMP: 50
SALES (corp-wide): 5.64B **Publicly Held**
Web: www.flir.com
SIC: 3826 Analytical instruments
HQ: Teledyne Flir Defense, Inc.
1024 S Innovation Dr
Stillwater OK 74074

(G-16635)
TELEDYNE FLIR DETECTION INC
Also Called: Flir Detection
3495 Kent Ave Ste V100 (47906-4189)
PHONE..................................765 775-1701
EMP: 43
SALES (corp-wide): 5.64B **Publicly Held**
Web: www.flir.com
SIC: 3826 Analytical instruments
HQ: Teledyne Flir Defense, Inc.
1024 S Innovation Dr
Stillwater OK 74074

(G-16636)
TERAGRAPHICS INK LLC
204 E Pine Ave (47906-4881)
PHONE..................................765 430-2863
Raul Renz, *Admn*
EMP: 9 **EST:** 2013
SALES (est): 439.41K **Privately Held**
Web: www.teragraphicsink.com
SIC: 2711 Commercial printing and newspaper publishing combined

(G-16637)
THERMPHYSCAL PRPTS RES LAB INC
Also Called: Tprl

3080 Kent Ave (47906-1075)
PHONE..................................765 463-1581
Thomas Goerz, *Pr*
Robert Larsen, *VP*
EMP: 4 **EST:** 1976
SQ FT: 10,500
SALES (est): 474.52K **Privately Held**
Web: www.tprl.com
SIC: 8734 3823 Product testing laboratory, safety or performance; Process control instruments

(G-16638)
TOKUMEI LLC
4955 State Road 43 N (47906)
P.O. Box 1683 (47902)
PHONE..................................765 772-0073
Ayrianna C Lain, *Managing Member*
EMP: 3 **EST:** 2020
SALES (est): 83.89K **Privately Held**
Web: www.tokumei-llc.com
SIC: 5092 5961 5734 3944 Video games; Toys and games (including dolls and models), mail order; Software, computer games; Electronic games and toys

(G-16639)
TRIGNETRA INC
1032 Onyx St (47906-7231)
PHONE..................................765 637-8447
Mithuna Thottethodi, *CEO*
EMP: 1
SALES (est): 57.14K **Privately Held**
SIC: 3679 Electronic circuits

(G-16640)
TRIPLE XXX ROOT BEER CORP
20 N Salisbury St (47906-3027)
PHONE..................................765 743-5373
EMP: 8 **EST:** 2008
SALES (est): 155.81K **Privately Held**
Web: www.triplexxxfamilyrestaurant.com
SIC: 2082 Malt beverage products

(G-16641)
ULTIMATE SPORTS INC
Also Called: USI
820 Hillcrest Rd (47906-2354)
PHONE..................................765 423-2984
Kevin Metheny, *Pr*
Pamela Metheny, *VP*
EMP: 2 **EST:** 1987
SQ FT: 30,000
SALES (est): 504.41K **Privately Held**
Web: www.usi-skis.com
SIC: 3714 Motor vehicle parts and accessories

(G-16642)
VIPER USA INC
Also Called: Excenart
345 Burnetts Rd (47906)
PHONE..................................765 742-4200
Beth Vorst, *CEO*
Brian Vorst, *
Darryl Hatke, *General Vice President*
EMP: 57 **EST:** 2001
SQ FT: 70,000
SALES (est): 9.6MM **Privately Held**
Web: www.proaxisinc.com
SIC: 3444 3312 Sheet metalwork; Structural shapes and pilings, steel

(G-16643)
WABASH VALLEY CABINET COMPANY
3218 N 775 W (47906-9460)
PHONE..................................765 337-2859
Josh Gipson, *Prin*
EMP: 5 **EST:** 2017
SALES (est): 84.18K **Privately Held**

Web: www.wabashvalleycabinet.com
SIC: 2434 Wood kitchen cabinets

(G-16644)
WABASH VLY WOODWORKERS CLB INC
2738 Westminster Ct (47906-1418)
PHONE..................................317 538-2956
William H Reese, *Prin*
EMP: 5 **EST:** 2019
SALES (est): 109.42K **Privately Held**
Web: www.wvww.net
SIC: 2431 Millwork

(G-16645)
WASU INC
Also Called: Aardvark Furniture
4418 Lake Villa Dr (47906-5433)
PHONE..................................765 448-4450
Carl R Mullen, *Pr*
Michelle Mullen, *VP*
Willard Casey, *Sec*
EMP: 3 **EST:** 1979
SALES (est): 264.74K **Privately Held**
SIC: 5999 2395 Infant furnishings and equipment; Embroidery and art needlework

(G-16646)
WELL INK
360 Brown St (47906-3243)
PHONE..................................765 743-3413
EMP: 7 **EST:** 2007
SALES (est): 107.91K **Privately Held**
Web: www.theinkwellusa.com
SIC: 2752 Offset printing

West Lebanon
Warren County

(G-16647)
DYNA-FAB CORPORATION
3893 S State Road 263 (47991-8005)
PHONE..................................765 893-4423
John Rew, *VP*
EMP: 21 **EST:** 1976
SQ FT: 30,000
SALES (est): 852.24K **Privately Held**
Web: www.dyna-fab.org
SIC: 3531 3444 3443 Backhoes, tractors, cranes, plows, and similar equipment; Sheet metalwork; Fabricated plate work (boiler shop)

(G-16648)
GILLUM MACHINE & TOOL INC
3365 W State Road 28 (47991-8077)
PHONE..................................765 893-4426
Jack P Gillum, *Pr*
Dan Gillum, *VP*
Mary I Gillum, *Treas*
Debby Beckett, *Sec*
EMP: 14 **EST:** 1978
SQ FT: 7,500
SALES (est): 465.51K **Privately Held**
SIC: 3599 7692 3544 Machine shop, jobbing and repair; Welding repair; Special dies, tools, jigs, and fixtures

(G-16649)
TRU-FLEX LLC (HQ)
Also Called: Custom-Flex
2391 S State Road 263 (47991-8132)
P.O. Box 247 (47991-0247)
PHONE..................................765 893-4403
▲ **EMP:** 120 **EST:** 2011
SALES (est): 46.92MM **Privately Held**
Web: www.tru-flex.com

(PA)=Parent Co (HQ)=Headquarters
✪ = New Business established in last 2 years

West Lebanon - Warren County (G-16650)

SIC: 3714 3499 Motor vehicle parts and accessories; Fire- or burglary-resistive products
PA: Nelson Global Products, Inc.
1560 Williams Dr
Stoughton WI 53589

(G-16650)
TRU-FLEX REAL ESTATE HOLDINGS LLC
2391 S State Rd Ste 263 (47991)
P.O. Box 247 (47991-0247)
PHONE..................................765 893-4403
▲ EMP: 100
SIC: 3599 3714 3498 3429 Hose, flexible metallic; Motor vehicle parts and accessories; Fabricated pipe and fittings; Hardware, nec

West Terre Haute
Vigo County

(G-16651)
DEER RIDGEWOOD CRAFT LLC
5330 Yuma Rd (47885-8523)
PHONE..................................812 535-3744
Wade Biggs, Managing Member
EMP: 4 EST: 2010
SALES (est): 229.56K Privately Held
Web: www.deerridgewoodcraft.com
SIC: 7641 2499 Antique furniture repair and restoration; Trophy bases, wood

(G-16652)
MARION TOOL & DIE INC (PA)
Also Called: Marion Manufacturing
1126 W National Ave (47885-1336)
PHONE..................................812 533-9800
▲ EMP: 69 EST: 1996
SQ FT: 20,000
SALES (est): 21.14MM Privately Held
Web: www.mariontool.com
SIC: 3599 Machine shop, jobbing and repair

(G-16653)
QUALITY COUNCIL INDIANA INC
Also Called: Qci
602 W Paris Ave (47885-1124)
P.O. Box 360 (47885-0360)
PHONE..................................812 533-4215
Bill Wortman, Pr
Diana Magnetti, Admn
EMP: 8 EST: 1986
SALES (est): 973K Privately Held
Web: www.qualitycouncil.com
SIC: 7372 Publisher's computer software

(G-16654)
SG SOLUTIONS LLC
444 W Sandford Ave (47885-8200)
PHONE..................................812 535-6000
Steven Chichester, Managing Member
Rick Koons, *
◆ EMP: 28 EST: 2004
SALES (est): 3.76MM Privately Held
SIC: 1311 Coal gasification

(G-16655)
SYCAMORE WINERY LLC
1320 Durkees Ferry Rd (47885-9626)
PHONE..................................812 243-0565
EMP: 2 EST: 2015
SALES (est): 214.68K Privately Held
Web: www.thesycamorewinery.com
SIC: 2084 Wines

(G-16656)
WABASH RIVER ENERGY LLC
444 W Sandford Ave (47885-8200)
PHONE..................................812 535-6067
Harry H Graves, Mgr
EMP: 60 EST: 1993
SALES (est): 3.02MM Privately Held
SIC: 1311 Coal gasification

(G-16657)
WABASH VALLEY RESOURCES LLC
444 W Sandford Ave (47885-8200)
PHONE..................................929 400-5230
Nalin Gupta, Managing Member
EMP: 1 EST: 2016
SALES (est): 3.94MM Privately Held
Web: www.wvresc.com
SIC: 1311 Coal gasification

(G-16658)
WEST VIGO MACHINE SHOP INC
339 N 4th St (47885-1042)
P.O. Box 84 (47885-0084)
PHONE..................................812 533-1961
G Pat Michl, Pr
EMP: 14 EST: 1982
SQ FT: 17,000
SALES (est): 1.3MM Privately Held
SIC: 3599 7692 Machine shop, jobbing and repair; Welding repair

Westfield
Hamilton County

(G-16659)
1205 DISTILLERY
120 Camilla Ct (46074-9863)
PHONE..................................317 804-5675
EMP: 4 EST: 2020
SALES (est): 62.38K Privately Held
Web: www.1205distillery.com
SIC: 2085 Distilled and blended liquors

(G-16660)
1GLOBALDS LLC
16750 Glen Way (46062-6837)
PHONE..................................765 413-2211
Kim Arbuckle, Pr
EMP: 15 EST: 2013
SALES (est): 495.45K Privately Held
SIC: 3993 7389 Signs and advertising specialties; Business Activities at Non-Commercial Site

(G-16661)
ABSOLUTE STONE POLSG REPR LLC
Also Called: Granite and Marble
3801 Crest Point Dr (46062-6541)
PHONE..................................317 709-9539
EMP: 2 EST: 2010
SALES (est): 140.06K Privately Held
SIC: 3281 Cut stone and stone products

(G-16662)
ACORN WOODWORKS
16116 Ditch Rd (46074-9639)
P.O. Box 468 (46074-0468)
PHONE..................................317 867-4377
David R Sochar, Owner
EMP: 5 EST: 1998
SALES (est): 400.38K Privately Held
Web: www.acornwoodworks.com
SIC: 2431 Millwork

(G-16663)
AIRBOTX LLC
Also Called: Hydroxyl Rentals
16525 Southpark Dr (46074)
PHONE..................................317 981-1811
EMP: 7 EST: 2020
SALES (est): 571.67K Privately Held
Web: www.airbotx.com
SIC: 5999 3564 7359 Air purification equipment; Air purification equipment; Equipment rental and leasing, nec

(G-16664)
AMERICAN VETERAN GROUP LLC
17020 Emerald Green Cir (46074-9155)
PHONE..................................317 600-4749
Jennifer Reinking, Mgr
EMP: 2 EST: 2013
SALES (est): 70.66K Privately Held
SIC: 2759 3841 3842 5084 Commercial printing, nec; Surgical and medical instruments; Surgical appliances and supplies; Industrial machinery and equipment

(G-16665)
APTIV SERVICES US LLC
Advanced Sfety User Exprnce As
17001 Oak Ridge Rd (46074-7907)
PHONE..................................765 867-4435
Jason Shahan, Mgr
EMP: 749
SALES (corp-wide): 20.05B Privately Held
Web: www.aptiv.com
SIC: 3714 Instrument board assemblies, motor vehicle
HQ: Aptiv Services Us, Llc
5725 Innovation Dr
Troy MI 48098

(G-16666)
AUTOMATIC POOL COVERS INC
17397 Oak Ridge Rd Ste 100 (46074-7832)
PHONE..................................317 579-2000
Michael J Shebek, Pr
Katherine Shebek, *
▲ EMP: 35 EST: 1979
SQ FT: 30,000
SALES (est): 10.17MM Privately Held
Web: www.automaticpoolcovers.com
SIC: 5999 3561 5091 Swimming pool chemicals, equipment, and supplies; Pumps and pumping equipment; Swimming pools, equipment and supplies

(G-16667)
BALL SYSTEMS INC
Also Called: Ball Systems Technologies
16469 Southpark Dr (46074-8435)
PHONE..................................317 804-2330
Patrick Turley, Pr
Andrew Caine, *
EMP: 27 EST: 1966
SQ FT: 8,500
SALES (est): 9.27MM Privately Held
Web: www.ballsystems.com
SIC: 3825 3612 Test equipment for electronic and electrical circuits; Transformers, except electric

(G-16668)
BASTIAN SOLUTIONS LLC
Also Called: Bastian Sltons Advnced Mfg Ctr
1821 Bastian Ct (46074-3200)
PHONE..................................317 575-9992
EMP: 17
Web: www.bastiansolutions.com
SIC: 3535 Belt conveyor systems, general industrial use
HQ: Bastian Solutions, Llc
10585 N Meridian St # 300
Carmel IN 46290
317 575-9992

(G-16669)
BDX I LLC
17219 Foundation Pkwy (46074-9805)
PHONE..................................317 741-5173
EMP: 10 EST: 2019
SALES (est): 757.44K Privately Held
SIC: 3999

(G-16670)
BECOMING PRESS LLC
18847 Goldwater Rd (46062-9358)
PHONE..................................317 823-9983
Ashley Ferris, Genl Mgr
EMP: 2 EST: 2011
SALES (est): 85.28K Privately Held
SIC: 2741 Miscellaneous publishing

(G-16671)
BREATH OF LIFE HOME MEDICAL EQUIPMENT AND RESPIRATORY SYSTEMS INC
Also Called: Breath of Life
430 Alpha Dr Ste 100 (46074-7001)
PHONE..................................317 896-3048
EMP: 12
SIC: 5047 3845 Medical and hospital equipment; Respiratory analysis equipment, electromedical

(G-16672)
CBDM INC
14655 N Gray Rd (46062-9274)
PHONE..................................317 218-3786
William Baker, Pr
EMP: 9 EST: 2010
SALES (est): 225.45K Privately Held
SIC: 3999

(G-16673)
CENTURA SOLID SURFACING INC
3525 W State Road 32 (46074-9363)
PHONE..................................317 867-5555
EMP: 13 EST: 1989
SQ FT: 100,000
SALES (est): 250.56K Privately Held
Web: www.centurasolidsurface.com
SIC: 1799 3281 Counter top installation; Cut stone and stone products

(G-16674)
CENTURY MARBLE CO INC
3525 W State Road 32 (46074-9363)
PHONE..................................317 867-5555
Ronald Maurer, Pr
Jean Maurer, *
Benjamin A Maurer, *
EMP: 40 EST: 1975
SQ FT: 100,000
SALES (est): 4.05MM Privately Held
Web: centurymarble.openfos.com
SIC: 3281 Furniture, cut stone

(G-16675)
CHATTERUP LLC
16272 Dandborn Dr (46074-8408)
PHONE..................................317 213-6283
Nathan Marquardt, Prin
EMP: 3 EST: 2014
SALES (est): 59.14K Privately Held
Web: www.gochatterup.com
SIC: 3652 Prerecorded records and tapes

(G-16676)
CLASSIC KITCHEN AND GRAN LLC
17408 Tiller Ct Ste 300 (46074-8511)
PHONE..................................317 575-8883
Greg Milanowski, Pr
EMP: 4 EST: 2007
SALES (est): 358.14K Privately Held
Web: www.classickitchenandgranite.com

GEOGRAPHIC SECTION

Westfield - Hamilton County (G-16703)

SIC: 5712 3281 Furniture stores; Granite, cut and shaped

(G-16677)
COGNEX CORPORATION
804 Allen Ct (46074-9323)
PHONE.................317 867-5079
EMP: 24
SALES (corp-wide): 837.55MM **Publicly Held**
Web: www.cognex.com
SIC: 3823 Process control instruments
PA: Cognex Corporation
1 Vision Dr
Natick MA 01760
508 650-3000

(G-16678)
COVER CARE LLC
Also Called: Automtic Pool Cver Prfssionals
17397 Oak Ridge Rd Ste 100 (46074-7832)
PHONE.................513 297-4094
Curtis J Greene, *Acctg Mgr*
EMP: 66 EST: 2014
SALES (est): 960.85K **Privately Held**
Web: www.covercare.com
SIC: 3949 Swimming pools, plastic

(G-16679)
CREATIVE MCHINING CONCEPTS INC
Also Called: Creative Machining Concept
17018 Westfield Park Rd (46074-9303)
PHONE.................317 896-9250
John Bailey, *Pr*
John A Huser Junior, *VP*
EMP: 6 EST: 1995
SQ FT: 10,500
SALES (est): 693.44K **Privately Held**
Web: www.creativemachiningconcepts.com
SIC: 3599 Machine shop, jobbing and repair

(G-16680)
CRETACEOUS CURES
15541 Wildflower Ln (46074-9780)
PHONE.................317 379-7744
Scott Babbitt, *Pr*
Stafford Babbitt, *VP*
Paul Babbitt, *VP*
Brittany Babbitt, *VP*
EMP: 4 EST: 2015
SALES (est): 248.02K **Privately Held**
Web: www.cretaceouscures.com
SIC: 2834 Drugs affecting parasitic and infective diseases

(G-16681)
CURTIS DYNA-FOG
525 Park St (46074-9409)
PHONE.................317 896-2561
EMP: 12 EST: 2019
SALES (est): 523.01K **Privately Held**
Web: www.dynafog.com
SIC: 3499 Fabricated metal products, nec

(G-16682)
CUSTOM CAST STONE INC
734 E 169th St (46074-7902)
PHONE.................317 896-1700
James Kent Grubaugh, *Pr*
Bruce R Lyon, *
EMP: 53 EST: 1993
SQ FT: 20,000
SALES (est): 9.63MM **Privately Held**
Web: www.customcaststone.com
SIC: 3272 Cast stone, concrete

(G-16683)
DAMALAK PRINTING INC
Also Called: Cave & Co. Printing
104 W Main St (46074-9480)
PHONE.................317 896-5337
Laurie L Damalak, *Pr*
Troy A Damalak, *VP*
EMP: 5 EST: 2007
SALES (est): 476.51K **Privately Held**
SIC: 2752 Offset printing

(G-16684)
DAVIS TOOL & MACHINE LLC
19224 Eagletown Rd (46074-9228)
PHONE.................317 896-9278
Steven Davis, *Pr*
Mary Ann Davis, *Sec*
EMP: 15 EST: 1989
SQ FT: 12,000
SALES (est): 1.96MM **Privately Held**
SIC: 3599 7692 Custom machinery; Welding repair

(G-16685)
DESHAZO LLC
1022 Kendall Ct Ste 2 (46074-9558)
PHONE.................317 867-7677
EMP: 1
SALES (corp-wide): 117.33MM **Privately Held**
Web: www.deshazo.com
SIC: 3536 Hoists, cranes, and monorails
PA: Deshazo, Llc
200 Kilsby Cir
Bessemer AL 35022
205 664-2006

(G-16686)
DOTTED LIME RESALE LLC
4232 Zachary Ln (46062-0005)
PHONE.................317 908-3905
Elena Vaughner, *Prin*
EMP: 2 EST: 2011
SALES (est): 182.89K **Privately Held**
SIC: 3274 Lime

(G-16687)
DURAMARK TECHNOLOGIES INC (PA)
Also Called: Duramark
16450 Southpark Dr (46074-8396)
PHONE.................317 867-5700
Bill Bussick, *Managing Member*
Brandon Mills, *VP*
EMP: 59 EST: 2007
SQ FT: 18,000
SALES (est): 8.62MM **Privately Held**
Web: www.duramarktechnologies.com
SIC: 2752 Decals, lithographed

(G-16688)
ETI FAB INC
17055 Oak Ridge Rd (46074-7907)
PHONE.................574 233-1202
Benny Crawford, *CEO*
Benjamin Crawford, *CEO*
EMP: 3 EST: 2018
SALES (est): 509.48K **Privately Held**
Web: www.eti-fab.com
SIC: 3441 Fabricated structural metal

(G-16689)
EVECXIA THERAPEUTICS INC
20267 Chatham Creek Dr (46074-4310)
P.O. Box 13169 (27709-3169)
PHONE.................919 597-8762
John Kaiser, *Interim Chairman of the Board*
Jacob Jacobsen, *VP*
EMP: 3 EST: 2013
SQ FT: 100
SALES (est): 204.61K **Privately Held**
Web: www.evecxia.com
SIC: 2834 Pharmaceutical preparations

(G-16690)
EZ SERVICES LLC
4106 Dunedin Ct (46062-7384)
PHONE.................317 965-3013
Jesus Esteves, *Prin*
EMP: 8 EST: 2019
SALES (est): 214.3K **Privately Held**
SIC: 3444 Sheet metalwork

(G-16691)
GLOBAL PACKAGING LLC
16707 Southpark Dr (46074-8078)
PHONE.................317 896-2089
EMP: 30 EST: 2006
SALES (est): 4.75MM **Privately Held**
Web: www.globalpack.us
SIC: 2099 Chili pepper or powder

(G-16692)
GLOBAL USA INC
Also Called: Z-Athletic
17401 Tiller Ct Ste A (46074-8967)
PHONE.................317 219-5647
Jian Zhao, *Pr*
◆ EMP: 4 EST: 1993
SALES (est): 370.4K **Privately Held**
SIC: 3949 Sporting and athletic goods, nec

(G-16693)
GREEN APPLE ACTIVE LLC (PA)
17304 Tilbury Way (46074-2239)
PHONE.................910 585-1151
Michelle Petrowski, *Pr*
EMP: 5 EST: 2018
SALES (est): 315.55K
SALES (corp-wide): 315.55K **Privately Held**
Web: www.greenappleactive.com
SIC: 3571 Electronic computers

(G-16694)
GRINDS MANUFACTURING LLC
17065 Oak Ridge Rd (46074-7907)
PHONE.................510 763-1088
EMP: 17 EST: 2019
SALES (est): 934.35K **Privately Held**
Web: www.getgrinds.com
SIC: 2095 Roasted coffee

(G-16695)
GS SALES INC
2802 Pyrenean Pl (46074-5411)
PHONE.................317 595-6750
George Southard, *Owner*
EMP: 2 EST: 1991
SALES (est): 156.95K **Privately Held**
Web: www.gssales.com
SIC: 3861 8743 Diazotype (whiteprint) reproduction machines and equipment; Sales promotion

(G-16696)
HARTSOCK INDUSTRIAL SALES INC
480 Enterprise Dr (46074-8868)
P.O. Box 408 (46074-0408)
PHONE.................317 858-8250
Andrew Hartsock, *Pr*
EMP: 3 EST: 1989
SALES (est): 479.49K **Privately Held**
Web: www.hartsockindustrial.com
SIC: 3829 3679 3674 Thermometers and temperature sensors; Transducers, electrical; Infrared sensors, solid state

(G-16697)
HIDDEN ELECTRICAL LLC
15287 Decl Dr (46074)
PHONE.................317 628-4233
EMP: 3 EST: 2017
SALES (est): 39.69K **Privately Held**
SIC: 3999 Manufacturing industries, nec

(G-16698)
HUSTON SIGNS LLC
E 181st St (46074)
PHONE.................317 804-9009
Corky Huston, *Pr*
EMP: 20 EST: 2019
SALES (est): 965.18K **Privately Held**
Web: www.hustonsigns.com
SIC: 3993 Signs and advertising specialties

(G-16699)
INDIANA MILLS & MANUFACTURING (PA)
Also Called: Immi
18881 Immi Way (46074-3001)
PHONE.................317 896-9531
Larry Gray, *CEO*
James R Anthony, *
Beverly S Anthony, *
Scott Caudill, *
Norm Gould, *
◆ EMP: 500 EST: 1961
SQ FT: 250,000
SALES (est): 241.71MM
SALES (corp-wide): 241.71MM **Privately Held**
Web: www.imminet.com
SIC: 3714 Motor vehicle parts and accessories

(G-16700)
INFRARED LAB SYSTEMS LLC
17408 Tiller Ct Ste 1900 (46074-8521)
PHONE.................317 896-1565
Craig L Denney, *Owner*
EMP: 8 EST: 2011
SALES (est): 496.04K **Privately Held**
Web: www.irlabsystems.com
SIC: 3826 Analytical instruments

(G-16701)
INNOVATIVE CORP
Also Called: Innovative Home Offices
17401 Tiller Ct Ste H (46074-8967)
PHONE.................317 804-5977
Christopher Radseck, *Pr*
John Lustig, *VP*
EMP: 25 EST: 1984
SQ FT: 14,000
SALES (est): 2.54MM **Privately Held**
Web: www.inncorp.com
SIC: 3089 2517 2434 5211 Organizers for closets, drawers, etc.: plastics; Wood television and radio cabinets; Wood kitchen cabinets; Closets, interiors and accessories

(G-16702)
JB GRAPHICS INC
250 W Tansey Xing (46074)
PHONE.................317 819-0008
Jane Berry, *Pr*
EMP: 2 EST: 1989
SALES (est): 240.63K **Privately Held**
Web: www.jbgraphicsinc.com
SIC: 2759 Commercial printing, nec

(G-16703)
KAN JAM LLC
17401 Tiller Ct Ste A (46074-8967)
P.O. Box 864 (14068-0864)
PHONE.................317 804-9129
EMP: 2 EST: 2006

Westfield - Hamilton County (G-16704)

SALES (est): 489.38K
SALES (corp-wide): 7.86MM **Privately Held**
Web: www.kanjam.com
SIC: 3944 Darts and dart games
PA: Ws Tailgating, Llc
 20 Commerce Blvd Ste E
 Succasunna NJ 07876
 317 804-9160

(G-16704)
KINETECH LLC
Also Called: Kinetech NM
16840 Joliet Rd (46074)
PHONE.............................317 441-1924
Jeremy Armstrong, *Admn*
EMP: 8 EST: 2011
SALES (est): 248.1K **Privately Held**
Web: www.kinetechllc.com
SIC: 3714 Motor vehicle parts and accessories

(G-16705)
KINTAIL INC
Also Called: Renobi
17399 Dovehouse Ln (46074-6206)
PHONE.............................317 993-8220
Camille Mackenzie, *CEO*
Carson Mackenzie, *Prin*
EMP: 2 EST: 2020
SALES (est): 57.88K **Privately Held**
SIC: 7372 Prepackaged software

(G-16706)
KP HOLDINGS LLC
2000 E 196th St (46074-3801)
PHONE.............................317 867-0234
John Ball, *Pr*
Gregory Griffin, *SLS**
Mike Bance, *
EMP: 430 EST: 1999
SQ FT: 110,000
SALES (est): 36.57MM **Privately Held**
SIC: 3714 Motor vehicle parts and accessories

(G-16707)
KPH ENGINEERED SYSTEMS INC
Also Called: Pl Porter
2000 E 196th St (46074-3801)
PHONE.............................317 867-0234
◆ EMP: 400
SIC: 3714 Motor vehicle parts and accessories

(G-16708)
LOGO USA CORPORATION (PA)
320 Parkway Cir (46074-9306)
PHONE.............................317 867-8518
George Sanburn, *Pr*
Kim Sanburn, *Sec*
Angie Sanburn, *VP*
EMP: 15 EST: 1989
SQ FT: 10,000
SALES (est): 2.04MM **Privately Held**
Web: www.mylogoshop.com
SIC: 2759 Screen printing

(G-16709)
MAGNETIC CONCEPTS CORPORATION
17005 Westfield Park Rd Ste 100 (46074-8429)
PHONE.............................317 580-4021
James P Covert, *Pr*
EMP: 19 EST: 1987
SALES (est): 1.64MM **Privately Held**
Web: www.magneticconcepts.com
SIC: 2599 Boards: planning, display, notice

(G-16710)
MAXIM INTEGRATED PRODUCTS INC
Also Called: MAXIM INTEGRATED PRODUCTS, INC.
16848 Southpark Dr (46074-8131)
PHONE.............................252 227-7202
EMP: 7
SALES (corp-wide): 12.31B **Publicly Held**
Web: www.analog.com
SIC: 3674 Microcircuits, integrated (semiconductor)
HQ: Maxim Integrated Products, Llc
 160 Rio Robles
 San Jose CA 95134
 408 601-1000

(G-16711)
MELAY LLC ✪
1624 S Waterleaf Dr Apt 203 (46074-7979)
PHONE.............................614 726-0565
Melissa Yildiz, *Managing Member*
EMP: 1 EST: 2022
SALES (est): 49.15K **Privately Held**
SIC: 3142 House slippers

(G-16712)
MOTION ENGINEERING COMPANY INC
Also Called: M E C
17338 Westfield Park Rd Ste 4 (46074)
P.O. Box 427 (46074-0427)
PHONE.............................317 804-7990
Ronald D Jones, *Pr*
Judy K Jones, *VP*
EMP: 5 EST: 1986
SQ FT: 2,000
SALES (est): 833.62K **Privately Held**
Web: www.highspeedimaging.com
SIC: 5065 7359 7812 3827 Video equipment, electronic; Equipment rental and leasing, nec; Motion picture and video production; Magnifying instruments, nec, optical

(G-16713)
OFF THE PALLET LLC
3276 E State Road 32 (46074)
PHONE.............................317 674-2711
Jane Ann Jacobson, *Pr*
EMP: 4 EST: 2019
SALES (est): 111.07K **Privately Held**
SIC: 2448 Pallets, wood

(G-16714)
OLD REV LLC (PA)
16855 Southpark Dr Ste 100 (46074)
PHONE.............................317 580-2420
Jim Hamelink, *Managing Member*
EMP: 4 EST: 1999
SALES (est): 96.3M **Privately Held**
SIC: 3089 3399 3363 3497 Injection molding of plastics; Aluminum atomized powder; Aluminum die-castings; Metal foil and leaf

(G-16715)
OLYMPUS MANAGEMENT LLC
17062 Olympus Ct (46062-6964)
PHONE.............................317 412-7977
EMP: 1 EST: 2011
SALES (est): 153.52K **Privately Held**
SIC: 2879 7389 Pesticides, agricultural or household; Business Activities at Non-Commercial Site

(G-16716)
OSRAM INC
310 E Main St (46074-9493)
PHONE.............................317 847-6268
EMP: 5 EST: 2019
SALES (est): 243.13K **Privately Held**
Web: www.osram.us
SIC: 2834 Pharmaceutical preparations

(G-16717)
PICKETTS PLACE INC
17041 Westfield Park Rd (46074-9373)
PHONE.............................317 763-1168
Dan Pickett, *Pr*
Jason Pickett, *VP*
EMP: 2 EST: 1990
SQ FT: 800
SALES (est): 405.93K **Privately Held**
SIC: 3491 3561 3545 Industrial valves; Industrial pumps and parts; Measuring tools and machines, machinists' metalworking type

(G-16718)
PORTER SYSTEMS INC (DH)
Also Called: Porter Engineered Systems
2000 E 196th St (46074-3801)
PHONE.............................519 737-1678
Yudi Zorzi, *Pr*
▲ EMP: 16 EST: 2014
SALES (est): 8.48MM
SALES (corp-wide): 365.51MM **Privately Held**
SIC: 3441 Expansion joints (structural shapes), iron or steel
HQ: Pangeo Corporation
 3000 Temple Dr
 Windsor ON N8W 5
 519 737-1678

(G-16719)
PPG INDUSTRIES INC
Also Called: PPG 4371
3132 E State Road 32 (46074-8730)
PHONE.............................317 867-5934
Steve Taylor, *Mgr*
EMP: 4
SALES (corp-wide): 17.65B **Publicly Held**
Web: www.ppgpaints.com
SIC: 2851 Paints and allied products
PA: Ppg Industries, Inc.
 1 Ppg Pl
 Pittsburgh PA 15272
 412 434-3131

(G-16720)
R J HANLON COMPANY INC
345 E 175th St (46074-8959)
PHONE.............................317 867-0028
Robert Hanlon, *Brnch Mgr*
EMP: 1
SALES (corp-wide): 5.11MM **Privately Held**
Web: www.rjhanlon.com
SIC: 2394 Cloth, drop (fabric): made from purchased materials
PA: R J Hanlon Company Inc
 17408 Tiller Ct Ste 600
 Westfield IN 46074
 317 867-2900

(G-16721)
R J HANLON COMPANY INC (PA)
17408 Tiller Ct Ste 600 (46074-8517)
PHONE.............................317 867-2900
Robert J Hanlon, *Pr*
Kathleen C Hanlon, *
Anthony Parisi, *
EMP: 49 EST: 1976
SQ FT: 8,000
SALES (est): 5.11MM
SALES (corp-wide): 5.11MM **Privately Held**
Web: www.rjhanlon.com
SIC: 2394 Cloth, drop (fabric): made from purchased materials

(G-16722)
RELATIONAL INTELLIGENCE LLC
14948 Annabel Ct (46074-2219)
PHONE.............................317 669-8900
Tim A Gardner, *Prin*
EMP: 5 EST: 2008
SALES (est): 97.59K **Privately Held**
Web: www.timagardner.com
SIC: 7372 Prepackaged software

(G-16723)
ROBERT ENGLE
Also Called: Engle Enterprises
4243 Bullfinch Way (46062-6116)
PHONE.............................317 522-7761
Robert Engle, *Owner*
EMP: 2 EST: 2020
SALES (est): 86.08K **Privately Held**
SIC: 3732 Boatbuilding and repairing

(G-16724)
ROBINSON INDUSTRIES INC
Also Called: Frakes Industrial Sales & Svc
17111 Westfield Park Rd (46074-9537)
PHONE.............................317 867-3214
Richard J Robinson, *Pr*
Carolyn A Robinson, *Sec*
Craig Cook, *Contrlr*
EMP: 24 EST: 1985
SALES (est): 705.44K **Privately Held**
Web: www.robinsonind.com
SIC: 7694 5084 5063 5251 Electric motor repair; Industrial machinery and equipment; Electrical apparatus and equipment; Hardware stores

(G-16725)
SCREEN PRINTING SUPER STORE
17408 Tiller Ct Ste 100 (46074-8510)
PHONE.............................317 804-9904
Bubba Thomas, *Mgr*
EMP: 2 EST: 2011
SALES (est): 76.38K **Privately Held**
SIC: 2759 Screen printing

(G-16726)
SHELBY GRAVEL INC
17701 Spring Mill Rd (46074-9232)
PHONE.............................317 804-8100
EMP: 10
SALES (corp-wide): 74.83MM **Privately Held**
Web: www.shelbymaterials.com
SIC: 5211 3273 Cement; Ready-mixed concrete
PA: Shelby Gravel, Inc
 157 E Rampart St
 Shelbyville IN 46176
 317 398-4485

(G-16727)
SHELF TAG SUPPLY CORPORATION
611 3rd Ave Sw (46074-8429)
PHONE.............................317 580-4030
Dixie A Covert, *Pr*
EMP: 9 EST: 1993
SALES (est): 928.94K **Privately Held**
Web: www.shelftagsupply.com
SIC: 2679 Tags and labels, paper

(G-16728)
SILICIS TECHNOLOGIES INC
17225 Westfield Park Rd (46074-9537)
PHONE.............................317 896-5044
Michael Stigler, *CEO*
EMP: 35 EST: 2008
SQ FT: 36,000
SALES (est): 4.78MM **Privately Held**
Web: www.silicis.com

GEOGRAPHIC SECTION
Westport - Decatur County (G-16754)

SIC: 3812 8731 3721 Aircraft/aerospace flight instruments and guidance systems; Electronic research; Nonmotorized and lighter-than-air aircraft

(G-16729)
STANDARD LOCKNUT LLC
1045 E 169th St (46074-9630)
P.O. Box 780 (46074-0780)
PHONE...................................317 399-2230
Ollie Martins, *Pr*
Ed Wetzel, *
Richard Goddard, *
▲ **EMP:** 155 **EST:** 1941
SQ FT: 125,000
SALES (est): 20MM **Privately Held**
Web: www.miether.com
SIC: 3562 3451 3541 3452 Roller bearings and parts; Screw machine products; Machine tools, metal cutting type; Bolts, nuts, rivets, and washers

(G-16730)
SUN POWER TECHNOLOGIES LLC
17406 Tiller Ct Ste 900 (46074-8987)
PHONE...................................317 399-8113
EMP: 2 **EST:** 2005
SQ FT: 1,200
SALES (est): 248.76K **Privately Held**
Web: www.sunpowertech.com
SIC: 3699 Electrical equipment and supplies, nec

(G-16731)
SYNERMED INTERNATIONAL INC
17408 Tiller Ct Ste 1900 (46074-8521)
PHONE...................................317 896-1565
Jerry Denney, *Pr*
EMP: 6 **EST:** 2003
SALES (est): 931.35K **Privately Held**
Web: www.synermedinc.com
SIC: 2835 In vitro diagnostics

(G-16732)
THACH LLC
14939 Maggie Ct (46074-9057)
PHONE...................................317 373-3734
EMP: 2 **EST:** 2020
SALES (est): 83.91K **Privately Held**
SIC: 2752 Playing cards, lithographed

(G-16733)
UN SEEN PRESS CO
Also Called: Un Seen Tesh
17272 Futch Way (46074-8801)
PHONE...................................317 867-5594
Nicole Kobrowsky, *CEO*
Michael Kabrowsky, *CFO*
EMP: 3 **EST:** 2004
SALES (est): 151.52K **Privately Held**
Web: www.unseenpress.com
SIC: 2741 Miscellaneous publishing

(G-16734)
UNIFORM HOOD LACE INC
18881 Immi Way Ste B (46074-3001)
PHONE...................................317 896-9555
James R Anthony, *Pr*
Anthony M Schelonka, *CFO*
EMP: 6 **EST:** 1915
SQ FT: 6,100
SALES (est): 490.54K **Privately Held**
Web: www.imminet.com
SIC: 3053 Packing materials

(G-16735)
UPPER LEVEL NETWORKS INC
16545 Southpark Dr (46074-8347)
PHONE...................................317 863-0955
Gregory S Paton, *Pr*
EMP: 9 **EST:** 2009
SALES (est): 107.82K **Privately Held**
Web: www.ulnets.com
SIC: 3131 Footwear cut stock

(G-16736)
URBAN VINES LLC
120 E 161st St (46074-7610)
PHONE...................................317 763-0678
Noah Herron, *Prin*
EMP: 9
SALES (est): 916.82K **Privately Held**
Web: www.urban-vines.com
SIC: 2084 Wines

(G-16737)
VOEGE PRECISION MCH PDTS LLC
Also Called: Voege Precision Machine Pdts
17808 Commerce Dr (46074-9089)
PHONE...................................317 867-4699
John Voege, *Managing Member*
EMP: 6 **EST:** 1999
SQ FT: 6,000
SALES (est): 890.83K **Privately Held**
SIC: 3599 Machine shop, jobbing and repair

(G-16738)
WEAS ENGINEERING INC
17297 Oak Ridge Rd (46074-7907)
P.O. Box 550 (46074-0550)
PHONE...................................317 867-4477
W Andrew Weas Senior, *Pr*
Hannelore Weas, *Sec*
EMP: 15 **EST:** 1980
SALES (est): 3.55MM **Privately Held**
Web: www.weasengineering.com
SIC: 2899 Water treating compounds

(G-16739)
WESTFIELD DONUTS
212 E Main St (46074-9347)
P.O. Box 649 (46074-0649)
PHONE...................................317 896-5856
James Hicks, *Owner*
EMP: 2 **EST:** 1991
SALES (est): 75.73K **Privately Held**
Web: www.quackdaddydonuts.com
SIC: 5461 2051 Doughnuts; Doughnuts, except frozen

(G-16740)
WHOLESALE HRDWOOD INTRIORS INC
Also Called: W H I
17715 Commerce Dr Ste 300 (46074-8972)
PHONE...................................317 867-3660
Keith Bell, *Brnch Mgr*
EMP: 16
SALES (corp-wide): 9.17MM **Privately Held**
Web: www.wholesalehardwoodint.com
SIC: 2861 2435 Hardwood distillates; Plywood, hardwood or hardwood faced
PA: Wholesale Hardwood Interiors, Inc.
1030 Campbellsville Byp
Campbellsville KY 42718
270 789-1323

(G-16741)
WRIGHT HORIZON ENTERPRISES LLC ✪
Also Called: Wright Woodworks
9 English Grn (46074)
PHONE...................................317 779-8182
EMP: 1 **EST:** 2023
SALES (est): 66.3K **Privately Held**
SIC: 2431 2499 6719 Interior and ornamental woodwork and trim; Decorative wood and woodwork; Personal holding companies, except banks

Westpoint
Tippecanoe County

(G-16742)
APL WELDING & FABRICATION LLC
7436 Turner Rd (47992-9286)
PHONE...................................765 572-1088
Paul Crouse, *Prin*
EMP: 1 **EST:** 2014
SALES (est): 74.85K **Privately Held**
SIC: 7692 Welding repair

(G-16743)
ARBORAMERICA INC
7852 W 200 S (47992-9362)
PHONE...................................765 572-1212
Javier Arregui, *CEO*
EMP: 13 **EST:** 2001
SALES (est): 507.55K **Privately Held**
Web: www.arboramerica.com
SIC: 0783 0851 2411 Ornamental shrub and tree services; Forestry services; Logging

(G-16744)
FREED MACHINING AND TOOL INC
6033 W 800 S (47992-9262)
PHONE...................................765 538-3019
Micheal Freed, *Pr*
Holly Freed, *VP*
EMP: 3 **EST:** 1997
SALES (est): 293.04K **Privately Held**
SIC: 3599 Machine shop, jobbing and repair

(G-16745)
INNOVATIVE EQUIPMENT INC
Also Called: Its
9227 W 600 S (47992-9247)
PHONE...................................765 572-2367
Chris Sims, *Pr*
EMP: 4 **EST:** 2004
SALES (est): 305.52K **Privately Held**
SIC: 3799 Transportation equipment, nec

(G-16746)
MILLER EXPRESS INC
7724 S 700 W (47992-9215)
PHONE...................................765 572-2303
Bern Miller, *CEO*
Joan Miller, *Sec*
EMP: 3 **EST:** 2001
SALES (est): 139.58K **Privately Held**
SIC: 2741 Miscellaneous publishing

(G-16747)
ROOF MASTERS PLUS LLC
7800 W 650 S (47992-9327)
PHONE...................................765 572-1321
Mike Freeman, *Owner*
EMP: 2 **EST:** 2013
SALES (est): 219.31K **Privately Held**
Web: www.roofmasters-plus.com
SIC: 1761 3444 Roofing contractor; Metal roofing and roof drainage equipment

Westport
Decatur County

(G-16748)
AMCOR PHRM PACKG USA LLC
1108 N State Road 3 (47283-9513)
PHONE...................................812 591-2332
Chuck Bendixen, *Mgr*
EMP: 53
SALES (corp-wide): 14.69B **Privately Held**
SIC: 3221 Vials, glass
HQ: Amcor Pharmaceutical Packaging Usa, Llc
625 Sharp St N
Millville NJ 08332
856 327-1540

(G-16749)
NIPRO PHRMPCKGING AMRICAS CORP
1108 N State Road 3 (47283-9513)
PHONE...................................812 591-2332
EMP: 72
Web: www.nipro-group.com
SIC: 3221 Vials, glass
HQ: Nipro Pharmapackaging Americas Corp.
1200 N 10th St
Millville NJ 08332

(G-16750)
PRIORITY DETAILING
3484 W Laytons Dr (47283-5506)
P.O. Box 280 (47283-0280)
PHONE...................................812 591-0299
Steven Kearney, *Owner*
EMP: 1 **EST:** 1989
SALES (est): 69.73K **Privately Held**
Web: www.prioritydetailing.com
SIC: 7389 1099 Drafting service, except temporary help; Metal ores, nec

(G-16751)
SARDINIA MACHINE INCORPORATED
12337 S State Road 3 (47283-9353)
PHONE...................................812 591-2091
Ron Pyles, *Pt*
Fritz Reichel, *Genl Pt*
EMP: 6 **EST:** 1981
SQ FT: 9,000
SALES (est): 491.08K **Privately Held**
SIC: 3599 Machine shop, jobbing and repair

(G-16752)
STAY PUT DOGGY LLC
401 E Paul St (47283-9789)
PHONE...................................812 591-8232
Earl Asher, *Prin*
EMP: 6 **EST:** 2008
SALES (est): 163.93K **Privately Held**
Web: www.stayputdoggy.com
SIC: 3089 Fences, gates, and accessories: plastics

(G-16753)
WILLOWS AND MORE
8094 W County Road 1270 S (47283-9273)
PHONE...................................812 560-1088
Suzy Tomlinson, *Owner*
EMP: 5 **EST:** 2015
SALES (est): 50K **Privately Held**
Web: www.willowsandmore.com
SIC: 2499 5023 5999 Decorative wood and woodwork; Decorating supplies; Alarm and safety equipment stores

(G-16754)
WINCHESTER STEEL
10622 S County Road 100 W (47283-9770)
PHONE...................................812 591-2071
Roberta Cruser, *Owner*
Roberta Cruser, *Prin*
Phillip Cruser, *Prin*
EMP: 2 **EST:** 2006
SALES (est): 100.41K **Privately Held**
SIC: 3324 Steel investment foundries

(PA)=Parent Co (HQ)=Headquarters
✪ = New Business established in last 2 years

Westville
Laporte County

(G-16755)
AHERN ELECTRIC INC
11527 W 50 N (46391-9515)
PHONE..................................219 874-3508
Brian Ahern, *Owner*
EMP: 1 **EST:** 2002
SALES (est): 87.84K **Privately Held**
SIC: 3542 Machine tools, metal forming type

(G-16756)
BOBILYN PRINTING
615 E 900 N (46391-9415)
PHONE..................................219 926-7087
EMP: 4 **EST:** 2019
SALES (est): 93.04K **Privately Held**
Web: www.bobilynprinting.com
SIC: 2752 Offset printing

(G-16757)
BUCHANAN IRON WORKS INC
103 Greenway St (46391-8502)
P.O. Box 823 (46391-0823)
PHONE..................................219 785-4480
Kim Buchanan, *Pr*
Jan Buchanan, *VP*
EMP: 5 **EST:** 1976
SQ FT: 8,000
SALES (est): 485K **Privately Held**
SIC: 3441 7692 Fabricated structural metal; Welding repair

(G-16758)
G G B INC
7512 S 800 W (46391-9734)
PHONE..................................219 733-2897
Greg Bekavac, *Pr*
EMP: 3 **EST:** 1994
SALES (est): 264.78K **Privately Held**
SIC: 3568 Power transmission equipment, nec

(G-16759)
GET DOWN GET ARUND PRCOUS MTLS
9954 W Us Highway 6 (46391-8301)
PHONE..................................219 243-2105
Frank Wroblewski, *Prin*
EMP: 7 **EST:** 2017
SALES (est): 180.93K **Privately Held**
SIC: 3339 Precious metals

(G-16760)
GIANT PAW PRINTS RESCUE
857 Main St (46391-9501)
PHONE..................................219 241-9299
Curt Riggen, *Brnch Mgr*
EMP: 3 **EST:** 2019
SALES (est): 75.08K **Privately Held**
Web: www.giantpawprints.com
SIC: 2752 Commercial printing, lithographic

(G-16761)
HEADS FIRST
Also Called: Heads 1st
7 Plain St (46391-8400)
P.O. Box 112 (46391-0112)
PHONE..................................219 785-4100
James Mcmahon, *Mgr*
EMP: 4 **EST:** 2004
SALES (est): 381.64K **Privately Held**
Web: www.heads1st.com
SIC: 3714 7699 Motor vehicle engines and parts; Professional instrument repair services

(G-16762)
HUNTS MAINTENANCE INC
107 Greenway St (46391-8500)
P.O. Box 50 (46391-0050)
PHONE..................................219 785-2333
Paul Shafer, *Prin*
EMP: 6 **EST:** 2015
SALES (est): 350.05K **Privately Held**
Web: www.huntsmaintenance.com
SIC: 4953 3443 1794 Rubbish collection and disposal; Dumpsters, garbage; Excavation work

(G-16763)
LEGACY SIGN GROUP LLC
7933 W Us Highway 6 (46391-9731)
PHONE..................................219 728-5102
Shaun Obrien, *CEO*
EMP: 28 **EST:** 2019
SALES (est): 3MM **Privately Held**
Web: www.legacysigngroup.com
SIC: 3993 Signs and advertising specialties

(G-16764)
NORTHWEST FARM FERTILIZERS
4725 S Us Highway 421 (46391-9678)
PHONE..................................219 785-2331
Kevin Hannon, *Mgr*
EMP: 7 **EST:** 1928
SALES (est): 828.12K **Privately Held**
SIC: 5153 5191 2875 Grain elevators; Farm supplies; Fertilizers, mixing only

(G-16765)
WAR - LLC- WESTVILLE PRTG
Also Called: Slater Publishing Co
361 W Main St (46391-9356)
P.O. Box 617 (46391-0617)
PHONE..................................219 785-2821
Robert Warth, *Pr*
Carol Warth, *Sec*
Scott Warth, *VP*
EMP: 6 **EST:** 1929
SQ FT: 9,500
SALES (est): 462.32K **Privately Held**
SIC: 2759 2791 2789 2752 Screen printing; Typesetting; Bookbinding and related work; Commercial printing, lithographic

Wheatfield
Jasper County

(G-16766)
GEORGIA-PACIFIC LLC
Also Called: Georgia-Pacific
604 Na Sandifer Rd (46392)
P.O. Box 159 (46392-0159)
PHONE..................................219 776-0069
Curt Riggen, *Brnch Mgr*
EMP: 5
SALES (corp-wide): 64.37B **Privately Held**
Web: www.gp.com
SIC: 2679 Corrugated paper: made from purchased material
HQ: Georgia-Pacific Llc
133 Peachtree St Nw
Atlanta GA 30303
404 652-4000

(G-16767)
GEORGIA-PACIFIC LLC
Also Called: Georgia-Pacific
484 E 1400 N (46392-8817)
PHONE..................................219 956-3100
Mark Harris, *Mgr*
EMP: 58
SALES (corp-wide): 64.37B **Privately Held**
Web: www.gp.com
SIC: 2431 3275 Millwork; Gypsum products
HQ: Georgia-Pacific Llc
133 Peachtree St Nw
Atlanta GA 30303
404 652-4000

(G-16768)
IN-PRINT
886 E 900 N (46392-8229)
PHONE..................................219 956-3001
EMP: 4 **EST:** 2017
SALES (est): 164.39K **Privately Held**
Web: www.inprintin.com
SIC: 2752 Offset printing

(G-16769)
JP CUSTOM CABINETRY INC
13467 Whippoorwill Ln (46392-7439)
PHONE..................................219 956-3587
EMP: 2 **EST:** 2009
SALES (est): 83.77K **Privately Held**
Web: www.skiplaw.com
SIC: 2434 Wood kitchen cabinets

(G-16770)
OZINGA BROS INC
Also Called: Ozinga Ready Mix
11607 N State Road 49 (46392-8217)
PHONE..................................219 956-3418
Daryl Sculley, *Mgr*
EMP: 23
SALES (corp-wide): 552.21MM **Privately Held**
Web: www.ozinga.com
SIC: 3273 Ready-mixed concrete
PA: Ozinga Bros., Inc.
19001 Old Lagrange Rd # 3
Mokena IL 60448
708 326-4200

(G-16771)
PETERSON MFG LLC
2848 W 1700 N (46392-8810)
PHONE..................................574 876-1427
Stephen M Peterson, *Managing Member*
EMP: 1 **EST:** 2006
SALES (est): 114.62K **Privately Held**
SIC: 3523 7389 Farm machinery and equipment; Business Activities at Non-Commercial Site

(G-16772)
R D-N-P DRILLING INC
3759 W 900 N (46392-9717)
PHONE..................................219 956-3481
Karen Eger, *Pr*
Paul Eger, *VP*
Vicki Eger, *Sec*
EMP: 9 **EST:** 2001
SALES (est): 857.83K **Privately Held**
SIC: 1241 Test boring, anthracite mining

(G-16773)
TEFFT BRIDGE AND IRON LLC
Also Called: Tbi
12632 N 400 E (46392-9239)
P.O. Box 277 (46392-0277)
PHONE..................................219 828-4011
EMP: 40
Web: www.tbiron.com
SIC: 3441 Fabricated structural metal

Wheatland
Knox County

(G-16774)
CYPRESS SPRINGS ENTPS INC
11536 E Lucky Point Rd (47597-8231)
PHONE..................................812 743-8888
EMP: 5 **EST:** 2008
SALES (est): 892.95K **Privately Held**
Web: www.cypressspringsent.com
SIC: 3761 3769 3812 Guided missiles and space vehicles; Guided missile and space vehicle parts and aux. equip., R&D; Defense systems and equipment

(G-16775)
JIM MCCARTER LOGGING
2752 S Enley Rd (47597-8188)
PHONE..................................812 321-5661
Jim Mccarter, *Owner*
EMP: 1 **EST:** 2000
SALES (est): 100K **Privately Held**
SIC: 2411 Logging

Whiteland
Johnson County

(G-16776)
A & M INNOVATIONS LLC
37 Erins Ct (46184-9670)
PHONE..................................317 306-6118
Anita Hill, *Admn*
EMP: 5 **EST:** 2015
SALES (est): 91.47K **Privately Held**
Web: www.aminnovationsllc.com
SIC: 2759 Screen printing

(G-16777)
CAD & MACHINING SERVICES INC
Also Called: CMS
518 Williamson St (46184-1672)
PHONE..................................317 535-1067
John Meyer, *Pr*
EMP: 19 **EST:** 1993
SQ FT: 7,500
SALES (est): 598.13K **Privately Held**
SIC: 3599 Machine shop, jobbing and repair

(G-16778)
CELLOFOAM NORTH AMERICA INC
Also Called: Indiana Division
150 Crossroads Dr (46184-9778)
PHONE..................................317 535-9008
Mark Slade, *Mgr*
EMP: 54
SALES (corp-wide): 143.46MM **Privately Held**
Web: www.cellofoam.com
SIC: 2821 3086 Polystyrene resins; Plastics foam products
PA: Cellofoam North America Inc.
1977 Weaver Ct
Conyers GA 30013
770 929-3688

(G-16779)
CHILDRENS OUTREACH
26 Erins Ct (46184-9670)
PHONE..................................317 535-7014
Elaine Cole, *Owner*
EMP: 2 **EST:** 1994
SALES (est): 71K **Privately Held**
SIC: 2731 Book publishing

(G-16780)
CRYSTAL GRAPHICS INC
530 E Main St (46184-1517)
PHONE..................................317 535-9202
Richard Ashbrook, *Pr*
Crystal Ashbrook, *VP*
EMP: 6 **EST:** 1990
SQ FT: 2,500
SALES (est): 485.13K **Privately Held**
Web: www.crystalgraphics.us
SIC: 2752 Offset printing

GEOGRAPHIC SECTION
Whitestown - Boone County (G-16807)

(G-16781)
CTSI
Also Called: Axis Fiber Solutions
4671 N Graham Rd (46184)
PHONE...................317 868-8087
Kevin Kissick, *Pr*
EMP: 35 **EST:** 2017
SALES (est): 3.22MM **Privately Held**
Web: www.ctsinet.com
SIC: 3546 Drills and drilling tools

(G-16782)
CUMMINS INC
5635 N Graham Rd (46184)
PHONE...................317 751-4567
EMP: 6
SALES (corp-wide): 34.06B **Publicly Held**
Web: www.cummins.com
SIC: 3519 3694 3621 Internal combustion engines, nec; Engine electrical equipment; Generator sets: gasoline, diesel, or dual-fuel
PA: Cummins Inc.
 500 Jackson St
 Columbus IN 47201
 812 377-5000

(G-16783)
EDS CRANE SERVICE
660 Parkway St (46184-1458)
PHONE...................317 535-7385
Edmund Williams, *Owner*
EMP: 1 **EST:** 1962
SALES (est): 43.19K **Privately Held**
SIC: 7692 1799 Welding repair; Welding on site

(G-16784)
ELEMENT ARMAMENT
51 N Us Highway 31 (46184-1545)
PHONE...................317 530-9013
David Hill, *Prin*
EMP: 6 **EST:** 2018
SALES (est): 402.26K **Privately Held**
Web: www.elementarmament.com
SIC: 2819 Elements

(G-16785)
ELIBA COLLECTIONS LLC
512 Genisis Dr (46184-9106)
PHONE...................646 675-6196
EMP: 1 **EST:** 2014
SALES (est): 114.11K **Privately Held**
Web: www.elibacollections.com
SIC: 2321 2339 5699 Men's and boy's furnishings; Women's and misses' outerwear, nec; Customized clothing and apparel

(G-16786)
ETCHED IN STONE ENGRV & EMB
459 E Main St (46184-1515)
PHONE...................317 535-8160
Scott Ferrell, *Owner*
EMP: 1 **EST:** 1997
SALES (est): 60.5K **Privately Held**
Web: www.etchedinstoneinc.com
SIC: 7389 2395 Engraving service; Embroidery and art needlework

(G-16787)
GRAHAMS WRECKER SERVICE INC
Also Called: Generations Collision Services
300 White St (46184-9557)
PHONE...................317 736-4355
Mark E Graham, *Pr*
Carole Graham, *VP*
EMP: 6 **EST:** 1964
SALES (est): 555.31K **Privately Held**
Web: www.grahamswreckerservice.com

SIC: 3713 7549 Automobile wrecker truck bodies; Towing service, automotive

(G-16788)
HUBBARD INC
6774 N Us Highway 31 (46184-9552)
PHONE...................317 535-1926
Phillip Hubbard Junior, *Pr*
EMP: 2 **EST:** 2000
SALES (est): 232.33K **Privately Held**
Web: www.hubbinc.com
SIC: 1731 3536 General electrical contractor; Hoists, cranes, and monorails

(G-16789)
INGREDION INCORPORATED
319 Warrior Trl (46184-8013)
PHONE...................800 713-0208
EMP: 11
SALES (corp-wide): 8.16B **Publicly Held**
Web: www.ingredion.com
SIC: 2046 Corn and other vegetable starches
PA: Ingredion Incorporated
 5 Westbrook Corporate Ctr
 Westchester IL 60154
 708 551-2600

(G-16790)
IRVING MATERIALS INC
Also Called: I M I
600 Tracy Rd (46184-9698)
PHONE...................317 535-7566
EMP: 9
SALES (corp-wide): 814.09MM **Privately Held**
Web: www.irvmat.com
SIC: 3273 Ready-mixed concrete
PA: Irving Materials, Inc.
 8032 N State Road 9
 Greenfield IN 46140
 317 326-3101

(G-16791)
LITTLE ENGINEERING LLC
6406 N 75 W (46184-9532)
PHONE...................317 517-3323
EMP: 1 **EST:** 2015
SALES (est): 70.27K **Privately Held**
SIC: 3544 Die sets for metal stamping (presses)

(G-16792)
MAYES POWDER COATING LLC
49 N Railroad St (46184)
PHONE...................317 403-6549
Larry Mayes Mayes Ii, *Pr*
EMP: 6 **EST:** 2018
SALES (est): 274.51K **Privately Held**
Web: www.mayespowdercoating.com
SIC: 3479 Coating of metals and formed products

(G-16793)
PRINTWORKS INC
655 Tracy Rd (46184-9698)
PHONE...................317 535-1250
Jeff Helton, *Pr*
Nancy Helton, *Sec*
EMP: 7 **EST:** 1989
SQ FT: 5,500
SALES (est): 598.63K **Privately Held**
Web: www.printworksindy.com
SIC: 2752 Offset printing

(G-16794)
RYAN PIERCY
Also Called: Piercy Sports
3180 E 600 N (46184-9436)
PHONE...................317 796-2253
Ryan Piercy, *Owner*

EMP: 4 **EST:** 2019
SALES (est): 52.65K **Privately Held**
Web: www.piercysports.com
SIC: 3949 Sporting and athletic goods, nec

(G-16795)
SANDPAPER STUDIO LLC
6403 N 300 E (46184-9725)
PHONE...................317 435-7479
Torrey Dawley, *Prin*
EMP: 8 **EST:** 2008
SALES (est): 217.83K **Privately Held**
Web: www.sandpaperstudio.com
SIC: 3291 Sandpaper

(G-16796)
SIGN SOLUTIONS INC
121 Crossroads Dr (46184-9778)
PHONE...................317 535-5757
EMP: 12 **EST:** 1994
SQ FT: 4,000
SALES (est): 750K **Privately Held**
Web: www.signsolution.com
SIC: 3993 Signs and advertising specialties

(G-16797)
SOLID SURFACE CRAFTSMEN INC
100 Crossroads Dr Ste D (46184-9782)
PHONE...................317 535-2333
Randy Davis, *Pr*
EMP: 4 **EST:** 1988
SQ FT: 4,600
SALES (est): 487.87K **Privately Held**
Web: www.solidsurfaceofsouthside.com
SIC: 2542 2821 2541 Counters or counter display cases, except wood; Plastics materials and resins; Wood partitions and fixtures

(G-16798)
TOWN PLANNER
410 N Us Highway 31 Ste 3 (46184-1481)
PHONE...................317 888-6750
John Martin, *Owner*
EMP: 3 **EST:** 2018
SALES (est): 40.67K **Privately Held**
Web: www.townplanner.com
SIC: 2741 Miscellaneous publishing

(G-16799)
WALLS LAWN & GARDEN INC
Also Called: Wall's Enterprises
201 N Us Highway 31 (46184-1461)
P.O. Box 235 (46184-0235)
PHONE...................317 535-9059
Gregg Wall, *Pr*
Wayne Wall, *VP*
Jerie Wall, *VP*
Aubrey Wall, *VP*
EMP: 8 **EST:** 1976
SQ FT: 4,000
SALES (est): 527.73K **Privately Held**
Web: www.wallenterprises.net
SIC: 0782 3999 Lawn and garden services; Grinding and pulverizing of materials, nec

Whitestown
Boone County

(G-16800)
ASI LIMITED
4485 S Perry Worth Rd (46075-8804)
◆ **EMP:** 200 **EST:** 1989
SQ FT: 180,000
SALES (est): 9MM **Privately Held**
Web: www.asilimited.com
SIC: 1793 3441 Glass and glazing work; Fabricated structural metal

(G-16801)
BEL-MAR PRODUCTS CORPORATION
5 E Pierce St (46075-9380)
PHONE...................317 769-3262
Quinton Elrod, *Pr*
Mary Lou Elrod, *Sec*
Steve Elrod, *VP*
EMP: 8 **EST:** 1945
SQ FT: 10,000
SALES (est): 656.71K **Privately Held**
SIC: 3724 3599 3545 7692 Aircraft engines and engine parts; Machine shop, jobbing and repair; Tools and accessories for machine tools; Welding repair

(G-16802)
CANATURE WATERGROUP USA INC (HQ)
Also Called: Independent Water Tech
6353 Commerce Dr Ste 300 (46075-0318)
PHONE...................877 771-6789
▲ **EMP:** 4 **EST:** 1986
SALES (est): 4.33MM
SALES (corp-wide): 2.69MM **Privately Held**
Web: www.watergroup.com
SIC: 3589 Sewage and water treatment equipment
PA: Canature Watergroup Canada Inc
 855 Park St Unit 1
 Regina SK S4N 6
 306 790-4423

(G-16803)
CEMEX MATERIALS LLC
4360 Whitelick Dr (46075-9376)
PHONE...................317 769-5801
Rob Davoren, *Brnch Mgr*
EMP: 56
SIC: 3273 Ready-mixed concrete
HQ: Cemex Materials Llc
 1720 Cntrpark Dr E Ste 10
 West Palm Beach FL 33401
 561 833-5555

(G-16804)
COUNTY MATERIALS CORP
6142 S Indianapolis Rd (46075-9526)
PHONE...................317 769-5503
Bud Wirey Mechanical, *Tech*
EMP: 9 **EST:** 2020
SALES (est): 182.66K **Privately Held**
Web: www.countymaterials.com
SIC: 3273 Ready-mixed concrete

(G-16805)
FF - TOP OF PIE LLC
5000 Anson Blvd (46075-4549)
PHONE...................317 876-1951
EMP: 12
SALES (est): 516.97K **Privately Held**
SIC: 2022 Cheese; natural and processed

(G-16806)
FORTERRA CONCRETE INDS INC
4360 Whitelick Dr (46075-9376)
PHONE...................859 254-4242
William Delay, *Mgr*
EMP: 22
SIC: 3272 Concrete products, nec
HQ: Forterra Concrete Industries, Inc.
 4108 Dakota Ave
 Nashville TN 37209
 615 889-0700

(G-16807)
FROET GROUP LLC
7529 E State Road 32 (46075)
PHONE...................317 414-2538

Whitestown - Boone County (G-16808) — GEOGRAPHIC SECTION

Jeff Tomlinson, *Pr*
EMP: 19 **EST:** 2017
SALES (est): 1.42MM **Privately Held**
SIC: 2051 8742 Bakery: wholesale or wholesale/retail combined; Management consulting services

(G-16808)
GREENCYCLE OF INDIANA INC
Also Called: Greencycle
4227 S Perry Worth Rd (46075-9398)
PHONE..............................317 769-5668
Mike Braher, *Genl Mgr*
EMP: 4
Web: www.greencycle.com
SIC: 2499 Mulch or sawdust products, wood
HQ: Greencycle Of Indiana, Inc.
400 Central Ave Ste 115
Northfield IL 60093

(G-16809)
HYDRO CONDUIT OF TEXAS LP
Also Called: Whitestown - Precast
4360 Whitelick Dr (46075-9376)
PHONE..............................317 769-2261
Wayne Terhune, *Mgr*
EMP: 1
Web: www.rinkerpipe.com
SIC: 3272 Concrete products, nec
HQ: Hydro Conduit Of Texas, Lp
19500 State Highway 249 # 5
Houston TX 77070

(G-16810)
INDIANA INDUSTRIAL SVCS LLC (PA)
Also Called: Texas Industrial Services
5294 Performance Way (46075-8812)
PHONE..............................317 769-6099
▼ **EMP:** 80 **EST:** 2002
SQ FT: 23,000
SALES (est): 15.53MM
SALES (corp-wide): 15.53MM **Privately Held**
Web: www.indianaindustrial.com
SIC: 7692 1796 Welding repair; Machinery installation

(G-16811)
MIDWEST METAL SOLUTIONS INC
6145 S Indianapolis Rd (46075-9526)
PHONE..............................317 769-6489
John Davis, *CEO*
Eric Shabi, *VP*
EMP: 6 **EST:** 2019
SALES (est): 913.89K **Privately Held**
Web: www.midwestmetalfabandrolling.com
SIC: 3443 Fabricated plate work (boiler shop)

(G-16812)
MONSANTO WHITESTOWN SEED
5224 Performance Way (46075-8812)
PHONE..............................317 692-9485
EMP: 4 **EST:** 2018
SALES (est): 155.06K **Privately Held**
SIC: 2879 Agricultural chemicals, nec

(G-16813)
PEPSICO
3124 Perry Blvd (46075)
PHONE..............................317 334-0153
EMP: 24 **EST:** 2012
SALES (est): 2.14MM **Privately Held**
Web: www.pepsico.com
SIC: 2086 Carbonated soft drinks, bottled and canned

(G-16814)
PITNEY BOWES INC
Also Called: Pitney Bowes
5490 Industrial Ct (46075-8811)
PHONE..............................317 769-8300
Gary Mcguire, *Brnch Mgr*
EMP: 7
SALES (corp-wide): 3.27B **Publicly Held**
Web: www.pitneybowes.com
SIC: 3579 Canceling machinery, post office
PA: Pitney Bowes Inc.
3001 Summer St
Stamford CT 06926
203 356-5000

(G-16815)
POLYMER TECHNOLOGY SYSTEMS INC (HQ)
Also Called: Pts Diagnostics
4600 Anson Blvd (46075)
PHONE..............................317 870-5610
Robert Huffstodt, *Pr*
William Benedict, *General Vice President*
Stephen Riendeau, *VP*
Schuyler Buck, *VP*
Keith Moskowitz, *
▲ **EMP:** 87 **EST:** 1992
SALES (est): 26.59MM **Privately Held**
Web: www.ptsdiagnostics.com
SIC: 3841 Diagnostic apparatus, medical
PA: Sannuo Biological Sensor Co., Ltd.
No.265, Guyuan Road, High-Tech Industrial Development Zone
Changsha HN 41020

(G-16816)
PRECAST SOLUTIONS INC
Also Called: Cgm
6145 S Indianapolis Rd (46075-9526)
PHONE..............................317 545-6557
John R Davis Iii, *CEO*
EMP: 15 **EST:** 1989
SQ FT: 10,000
SALES (est): 2.3MM **Privately Held**
Web: www.precastsolutions-inc.com
SIC: 3275 3273 Gypsum products; Ready-mixed concrete

(G-16817)
PREMIER PAVING
3384 Preakness St (46075-7562)
PHONE..............................302 396-8851
Dorothy Miller, *Owner*
EMP: 4 **EST:** 2019
SALES (est): 120.51K **Privately Held**
SIC: 2951 Creosoted wood paving blocks

(G-16818)
R W MACHINE INCORPORATED
3463 S 500 E (46075-9555)
PHONE..............................317 769-6798
EMP: 2 **EST:** 1995
SALES (est): 137.55K **Privately Held**
SIC: 3511 Steam engines

(G-16819)
ROCKWELL AUTOMATION INC
4255 S 500 E (46075-9822)
PHONE..............................765 481-0766
EMP: 5
Web: www.rockwellautomation.com
SIC: 3625 Relays and industrial controls
PA: Rockwell Automation, Inc.
1201 S 2nd St
Milwaukee WI 53204

(G-16820)
SCHAFER POWDER COATING INC
5450 Industrial Ct (46075-8808)
PHONE..............................317 228-9987
Mark P Schafer, *Pr*
EMP: 30 **EST:** 1997
SALES (est): 3.52MM **Privately Held**
Web: www.schaferpowdercoating.com
SIC: 3479 Coating of metals and formed products

(G-16821)
SHEPHERD & DAVID LLC
1640 N Us 421 (46075-4217)
PHONE..............................317 769-4751
Colleen David, *Pt*
Elanie Akermann, *Pt*
EMP: 5 **EST:** 1997
SALES (est): 191.49K **Privately Held**
SIC: 2741 Miscellaneous publishing

(G-16822)
SOFTWARE SALES INCORPORATED
3370 S 450 E (46075-9707)
PHONE..............................317 258-7442
Brad Schweibold, *Prin*
EMP: 2 **EST:** 2010
SALES (est): 159.42K **Privately Held**
SIC: 7372 Prepackaged software

(G-16823)
TANK CONSTRUCTION & SERVICE CO
Also Called: Tmr Group
6145 S Indianapolis Rd (46075-9526)
PHONE..............................317 509-6294
Thomas Riddle, *Pr*
EMP: 10 **EST:** 1968
SALES (est): 276.9K **Privately Held**
SIC: 7699 1791 1731 3443 Tank repair; Storage tanks, metal: erection; Electrical work; Fabricated plate work (boiler shop)

(G-16824)
TELAMON CORPORATION
4656 Anson Blvd (46075-4489)
PHONE..............................317 818-6888
EMP: 1
SQ FT: 110,000
SALES (corp-wide): 674.34MM **Privately Held**
Web: www.telamon.com
SIC: 3663 Antennas, transmitting and communications
PA: Telamon Corporation
1000 E 116th St
Carmel IN 46032
317 818-6888

(G-16825)
TFI INC
Also Called: Tf Fulfillment
4257 S 500 E (46075-9822)
PHONE..............................317 290-1333
▲ **EMP:** 33 **EST:** 2001
SQ FT: 22,000
SALES (est): 9.86MM **Privately Held**
Web: www.tfpublishing.com
SIC: 4225 2752 5199 General warehousing; Calendar and card printing, lithographic; Calendars

(G-16826)
THEDAILYGRIND LLC
607 S Main St (46075)
PHONE..............................317 531-1276
Bradley Claretto, *Managing Member*
EMP: 5 **EST:** 2017
SALES (est): 73.55K **Privately Held**
SIC: 2095 Roasted coffee

(G-16827)
TRILOGY TECHNOLOGIES LLC
5583 Wafer Ash Dr (46075-4468)
P.O. Box 31 (46075-0031)
PHONE..............................317 769-0215
Sasa Katic, *Prin*
EMP: 3 **EST:** 2016
SALES (est): 97.77K **Privately Held**
SIC: 7372 Prepackaged software

(G-16828)
ULTIMATE EXHIBITS
3499 Firethorn Dr (46075-9771)
PHONE..............................317 353-7374
EMP: 4 **EST:** 2019
SALES (est): 92.53K **Privately Held**
Web: www.ultimateexhibits.com
SIC: 3993 Signs and advertising specialties

(G-16829)
WSG MANUFACTURING LLC
4485 Perry Worth Rd (46075-8804)
PHONE..............................765 934-2101
Brian Hamilton, *Admn*
EMP: 9 **EST:** 2014
SALES (est): 423.47K **Privately Held**
SIC: 2064 Popcorn balls or other treated popcorn products

Whiting
Lake County

(G-16830)
ALMOST FAMOUS PRINTING
1309 119th St (46394-1625)
PHONE..............................219 793-6388
Keely Schalk, *Prin*
EMP: 2 **EST:** 2007
SALES (est): 117.88K **Privately Held**
SIC: 2759 Screen printing

(G-16831)
ANALYTICALAB INC (PA)
1404 119th St Ste A (46394-1734)
PHONE..............................219 473-9777
Mary Lordsburg, *Pr*
Joy Stevens, *Sec*
EMP: 4 **EST:** 1999
SALES (est): 300K
SALES (corp-wide): 300K **Privately Held**
SIC: 3823 Analyzers, industrial process type

(G-16832)
BAKER PETROLITE LLC
2831 Indian Airforce Blvd (46394)
PHONE..............................219 473-5329
EMP: 8
SALES (corp-wide): 25.51B **Publicly Held**
Web: bakerhughesdirect.lookchem.com
SIC: 1389 Oil field services, nec
HQ: Baker Petrolite Llc
12645 W Airport Blvd
Sugar Land TX 77478
281 276-5400

(G-16833)
CALUMET ARSENAL LLC
1517 Fischrupp Ave 2nd Fl (46394-2030)
PHONE..............................219 256-9885
EMP: 1 **EST:** 2020
SALES (est): 46.61K **Privately Held**
SIC: 3484 Guns (firearms) or gun parts, 30 mm. and below

(G-16834)
DX HAMMOND OPCO LLC (PA)
100-500 Indianapolis Blvd (46394)
PHONE..............................219 501-0905
Peter Feldman, *CEO*
Chris Fraudnberger, *CFO*
EMP: 3 **EST:** 2018
SALES (est): 151K
SALES (corp-wide): 151K **Privately Held**
SIC: 7374 3357 Data processing service; Fiber optic cable (insulated)

GEOGRAPHIC SECTION

(G-16835)
EASTLAKE METALS LLC
2230 Indianapolis Blvd (46394-1956)
P.O. Box 454 (46394-0454)
PHONE.................................219 655-5526
Alexander Gross, *Managing Member*
EMP: 15 **EST:** 2017
SALES (est): 2.5MM **Privately Held**
Web: www.eastlakemetals.com
SIC: 3444 Sheet metalwork

(G-16836)
NEW TIME INC ✪
1464 Indianapolis Blvd (46394-1133)
PHONE.................................219 655-5041
Karen D Rothe, *Prin*
EMP: 8 **EST:** 2022
SALES (est): 60.98K **Privately Held**
Web: www.nwitimes.com
SIC: 2711 Newspapers, publishing and printing

(G-16837)
OXBOW CARBON & MINERALS
2815 Indianapolis Blvd (46394-2197)
PHONE.................................219 473-0359
Lonnie Griffith, *Mgr*
Lonnie Griffith, *Prin*
EMP: 3 **EST:** 2002
SALES (est): 239.76K **Privately Held**
Web: www.oxbow.com
SIC: 2911 Petroleum refining

(G-16838)
REGION SIGNS INC
1345 119th St (46394-1627)
PHONE.................................219 473-1616
Carolyn Sarvanidin, *CEO*
EMP: 10 **EST:** 2003
SALES (est): 937.72K **Privately Held**
Web: www.regionsigns.com
SIC: 3993 5099 Signs, not made in custom sign painting shops; Safety equipment and supplies

(G-16839)
UNION TANK CAR CO
2815 Indianapolis Blvd (46394-2197)
PHONE.................................219 880-5248
EMP: 9 **EST:** 2018
SALES (est): 469.53K **Privately Held**
Web: www.utlx.com
SIC: 3743 Railroad equipment

(G-16840)
WHITING CLEAN ENERGY INC
2155 Standard Ave (46394-2201)
PHONE.................................219 473-0653
Cameron Eveland, *Genl Mgr*
Erika Harding, *
Richard Moroney, *
Steven Bray, *
Dale Bell, *
EMP: 28 **EST:** 2001
SALES (est): 5.24MM
SALES (corp-wide): 171.22B **Privately Held**
SIC: 3612 Transformers, except electric
HQ: Bp Alternative Energy North America Inc.
700 Louisiana St Ste 3300
Houston TX 77002

(G-16841)
WHITING METALS LLC
2230 Indianapolis Blvd (46394-1956)
P.O. Box 482 (46394-0482)
PHONE.................................219 659-6955
Alexander Gross, *Managing Member*
EMP: 8 **EST:** 2009

SALES (est): 988.32K **Privately Held**
SIC: 3339 Primary nonferrous metals, nec

Wilkinson
Hancock County

(G-16842)
DB&H WELDING AND FABRICATION
8296 N Main Cross St (46186-9618)
PHONE.................................765 617-8474
EMP: 5 **EST:** 2015
SALES (est): 39.07K **Privately Held**
Web: www.dbandhwelding.com
SIC: 7692 Welding repair

(G-16843)
MAINS ENTERPRISES INC
9762 N Nashville Rd (46186-9729)
PHONE.................................765 425-0162
Bill Mains, *Pr*
Brandon Blackwell, *VP*
EMP: 2 **EST:** 2002
SALES (est): 162.91K **Privately Held**
SIC: 3479 7389 Engraving jewelry, silverware, or metal; Engraving service

(G-16844)
RAIL SCALE INC
5303 N 800 E (46186-9765)
PHONE.................................317 339-6486
EMP: 6 **EST:** 2011
SALES (est): 76.94K **Privately Held**
Web: www.railscale.com
SIC: 3825 Instruments to measure electricity

Williamsport
Warren County

(G-16845)
ACCUBURN WILLIAMSPORT INC
304 W Washington St (47993-1078)
P.O. Box 35 (47993-0035)
PHONE.................................765 762-1100
EMP: 14 **EST:** 1996
SQ FT: 37,000
SALES (est): 2.2MM **Privately Held**
Web: www.accuburninc.com
SIC: 3441 Fabricated structural metal for bridges

(G-16846)
CRYOGENIC SUPPORT SYSTEMS INC
Also Called: Kaniewski & Odle Trckg & Repr
1903 W State Road 63 (47993-8063)
PHONE.................................765 764-4961
Dave Kaniewski, *Pr*
EMP: 2 **EST:** 1974
SQ FT: 7,200
SALES (est): 174.96K **Privately Held**
SIC: 3441 Fabricated structural metal

(G-16847)
D H GRAVEL COMPANY
7794 S State Road 263 (47993-8271)
PHONE.................................765 893-4914
James Salts, *Prin*
EMP: 3 **EST:** 2008
SALES (est): 180.19K **Privately Held**
SIC: 1442 Construction sand and gravel

(G-16848)
HOSE TECHNOLOGY INC
2520 E Us Hwy 41 (47993)
P.O. Box 206 (47993-0206)
PHONE.................................765 762-5501
Trajan Trajanovski, *Pr*

Gene Mcgowen, *Pr*
Gloria J Mcgowen, *Sec*
EMP: 20 **EST:** 1982
SALES (est): 4.6MM **Privately Held**
Web: www.hosetec.com
SIC: 3599 Hose, flexible metallic
HQ: Kuriyama Of America, Inc.
150 N Mrtngale Rd Ste 900
Schaumburg IL 60173
847 755-0360

(G-16849)
INDIANA PRECISION PLASTICS INC
701 State Road 28 E (47993-1071)
PHONE.................................765 762-2452
Tony Sciotto, *Ch Bd*
Samuel Lombard, *Pr*
Pattsy Johnson, *Treas*
EMP: 22 **EST:** 1988
SQ FT: 20,000
SALES (est): 994.6K **Privately Held**
Web: www.ipplastics.com
SIC: 3089 Injection molding of plastics

(G-16850)
KURI TEC MANUFACTURING INC
2600 E Us Hwy 41 (47993)
P.O. Box 220 (47993-0220)
PHONE.................................765 764-6000
Trajan Trajanovski, *Pr*
Fred Bobzien, *Treas*
EMP: 22 **EST:** 1999
SALES (est): 4.99MM **Privately Held**
Web: www.kuriyama.com
SIC: 3084 Plastics pipe
HQ: Kuriyama Of America, Inc.
150 N Mrtngale Rd Ste 900
Schaumburg IL 60173
847 755-0360

(G-16851)
LINCO GROUP LLC
2310 W Division Rd (47993-8439)
PHONE.................................765 418-5567
EMP: 5 **EST:** 2013
SALES (est): 109.6K **Privately Held**
Web: www.lincofood.com
SIC: 3556 Food products machinery

(G-16852)
PRAIRIES EDGE MACHINING INC
4920 W Division Rd (47993-8408)
PHONE.................................765 986-2222
EMP: 3 **EST:** 1997
SALES (est): 347.1K **Privately Held**
Web: www.inkworkx.com
SIC: 3599 Machine shop, jobbing and repair

(G-16853)
ROGERS GROUP INC
Also Called: Interstate Gravel
3255 W 650 S (47993-8212)
PHONE.................................765 893-4463
Sandy Williams, *Brnch Mgr*
EMP: 24
SQ FT: 1,500
SALES (corp-wide): 1.05B **Privately Held**
Web: www.rogersgroupincint.com
SIC: 5032 1442 Gravel; Construction sand and gravel
PA: Rogers Group, Inc.
421 Great Cir Rd
Nashville TN 37228
615 242-0585

(G-16854)
TMF CENTER INC
105 Slauter Ln (47993-1088)
PHONE.................................765 762-3800
Lloyd Gowen, *Mgr*
EMP: 20

SALES (corp-wide): 24.03MM **Privately Held**
Web: www.tmfcenter.com
SIC: 3531 Construction machinery attachments
PA: Tmf Center, Inc.
300 W Washington St
Williamsport IN 47993
765 762-1000

(G-16855)
TMF CENTER INC (PA)
300 W Washington St (47993-1078)
PHONE.................................765 762-1000
Andy Van Meter, *Pr*
Lloyd Mcgowen, *CFO*
Lori Van Meter, *
EMP: 180 **EST:** 1979
SQ FT: 250,000
SALES (est): 24.03MM
SALES (corp-wide): 24.03MM **Privately Held**
Web: www.tmfcenter.com
SIC: 3531 Construction machinery attachments

Winamac
Pulaski County

(G-16856)
BRAUN CORPORATION
627 W 11th St (46996-1245)
P.O. Box 310 (46996-0310)
PHONE.................................574 946-7413
Frank Smith, *Mgr*
EMP: 83
SALES (corp-wide): 6.86B **Privately Held**
Web: www.braunability.com
SIC: 3534 3842 Elevators and moving stairways; Surgical appliances and supplies
HQ: The Braun Corporation
631 W 11th St
Winamac IN 46996
574 946-6153

(G-16857)
BRAUN CORPORATION (DH)
Also Called: Braunability
631 W 11th St (46996-1245)
P.O. Box 310 (46996-0310)
PHONE.................................574 946-6153
Nick Gutwein, *Pr*
Nick Gutwein, *CEO*
Brad Johnston, *
Thomas Eastman, *
▼ **EMP:** 500 **EST:** 1965
SQ FT: 500,000
SALES (est): 117.38MM
SALES (corp-wide): 6.86B **Privately Held**
Web: www.braunability.com
SIC: 3999 Wheelchair lifts
HQ: Patricia Industries Ab
Arsenalsgatan 8c
Stockholm

(G-16858)
BRAUN MOTOR WORKS INC (PA)
Also Called: Legend Valley Products
144 S 100 W (46996-7711)
P.O. Box 7 (46996-0007)
PHONE.................................574 205-0102
Ralph Braun, *CEO*
▲ **EMP:** 7 **EST:** 1986
SALES (est): 2.67MM
SALES (corp-wide): 2.67MM **Privately Held**
SIC: 5084 3713 Compaction equipment; Truck and bus bodies

Winamac - Pulaski County (G-16859)

(G-16859)
CHESAPEAKE RECYCLING INC
1600 S Us Highway 35 (46996-7403)
PHONE..................574 946-6602
Rob Howe, *Pr*
Rob Hal, *Pr*
Scott Roudebush, *VP*
David Rosenau, *Treas*
EMP: 26 EST: 2002
SQ FT: 54,000
SALES (est): 1.24MM **Privately Held**
SIC: **2611** Pulp mills, mechanical and recycling processing

(G-16860)
GALBREATH LLC (DH)
480 E 150 S (46996-7768)
P.O. Box 220 (46996-0220)
PHONE..................219 946-6631
Larry Harvey, *
◆ EMP: 48 EST: 1947
SQ FT: 250,000
SALES (est): 42.41MM **Privately Held**
Web: www.galbreathproducts.com
SIC: **3443** 3523 Industrial vessels, tanks, and containers; Planting, haying, harvesting, and processing machinery
HQ: Wastequip, Llc
6525 Carnegie Blvd # 300
Charlotte NC 28211

(G-16861)
GALFAB LLC (DH)
612 W 11th St (46996-1211)
PHONE..................574 946-7767
Jerome Samson, *CEO*
EMP: 15 EST: 1991
SALES (est): 24.28MM **Privately Held**
Web: www.galfab.com
SIC: **3537** 3443 3536 3531 Industrial trucks and tractors; Dumpsters, garbage; Hoists, cranes, and monorails; Construction machinery
HQ: Hiab Ab
Hyllie Vattenparksgata 12c
Malmo 215 3
84453800

(G-16862)
HB GUTTERS LLC
2444 E 100 N (46996-8600)
PHONE..................765 414-5698
EMP: 4 EST: 2018
SALES (est): 137.47K **Privately Held**
SIC: **3444** 1761 Gutters, sheet metal; Gutter and downspout contractor

(G-16863)
HEALEY CUSTOM CABINETRY LLC
802 N Us Highway 35 (46996-8000)
P.O. Box 99 (46996-0099)
PHONE..................574 946-4000
Belinda Healey, *Prin*
EMP: 4 EST: 2014
SALES (est): 237.09K **Privately Held**
Web: www.healeycustomcabinetry.com
SIC: **2434** Wood kitchen cabinets

(G-16864)
IRVING MATERIALS INC
1132 S Us Highway 35 (46996-7746)
P.O. Box 458 (46996-0458)
PHONE..................574 946-3754
George Scheffer, *Mgr*
EMP: 10
SALES (corp-wide): 814.09MM **Privately Held**
Web: www.irvmat.com
SIC: **3273** Ready-mixed concrete
PA: Irving Materials, Inc.
8032 N State Road 9
Greenfield IN 46140
317 326-3101

(G-16865)
KNOTS & SPOTS INC
5341 N Us Highway 35 (46996-8046)
PHONE..................574 946-6000
Jacqueline Podell, *Off Mgr*
EMP: 5 EST: 2014
SALES (est): 104.16K **Privately Held**
SIC: **2752** Commercial printing, lithographic

(G-16866)
MANDALA SCREEN PRINTING INC
950 E 250 N (46996-8512)
PHONE..................574 946-6290
Greg Hildebrandt, *Pr*
EMP: 2 EST: 1976
SALES (est): 187.5K **Privately Held**
SIC: **2759** Screen printing

(G-16867)
METAL FAB ENGINEERING INC
9341 S State Road 39 (46996-7726)
PHONE..................574 278-7150
Travis Mcdowell, *Pr*
EMP: 35 EST: 1950
SQ FT: 22,000
SALES (est): 4.35MM **Privately Held**
Web: www.metalfabengineering.com
SIC: **3499** 3465 3469 7699 Novelties and specialties, metal; Body parts, automobile: stamped metal; Stamping metal for the trade; Agricultural equipment repair services

(G-16868)
NCS WELDING INC
827 E 25 S (46996-8712)
PHONE..................574 946-7485
Mike Maddox, *Owner*
EMP: 1 EST: 2000
SALES (est): 37.06K **Privately Held**
SIC: **7692** Welding repair

(G-16869)
PENTAIR
9449 S 550 W (46996-8463)
PHONE..................574 278-7161
EMP: 9 EST: 2018
SALES (est): 239.27K **Privately Held**
Web: www.pentair.com
SIC: **3491** Industrial valves

(G-16870)
PITCHER ENTERPRISES LLC
524 N Plymouth Rd (46996-1125)
PHONE..................574 242-1113
Patrick C Pitcher, *CEO*
EMP: 1 EST: 2021
SALES (est): 143.24K **Privately Held**
SIC: **3993** Signs and advertising specialties

(G-16871)
PLYMOUTH TUBE COMPANY
Also Called: Winamac Cold Draw
572 W State Road 14 (46996-8873)
P.O. Box 278 (46996-0278)
PHONE..................574 946-6191
Kyle Kroening, *Mgr*
EMP: 83
SALES (corp-wide): 188.14MM **Privately Held**
Web: www.plymouth.com
SIC: **3317** 3354 3498 3341 Steel pipe and tubes; Aluminum extruded products; Fabricated pipe and fittings; Secondary nonferrous metals
PA: Plymouth Tube Company
29w 150 Warrenville Rd
Warrenville IL 60555
630 393-3550

(G-16872)
PULASKI COUNTY PRESS INC
114 W Main St (46996-1208)
P.O. Box 19 (46996-0019)
PHONE..................574 946-6628
John Haley, *Pr*
Elizabeth Haley, *Sec*
Carolyn Haley-majors, *Treas*
EMP: 9 EST: 1976
SQ FT: 7,000
SALES (est): 777.07K **Privately Held**
Web: www.pulaskijournal.com
SIC: **2711** 2752 Newspapers: publishing only, not printed on site; Offset printing

(G-16873)
R & D MACHINE SHOP INC
935 N Us Highway 35 (46996-8001)
PHONE..................574 946-6109
EMP: 2 EST: 1994
SALES (est): 128.46K **Privately Held**
SIC: **3599** Machine shop, jobbing and repair

(G-16874)
S & S PRECAST INC
840 W 25 S (46996)
P.O. Box 138 (46996-0138)
PHONE..................574 946-4123
Clara Schmicker, *Pr*
Susan Shinn, *Sec*
EMP: 23 EST: 1993
SQ FT: 7,500
SALES (est): 885.62K **Privately Held**
SIC: **3272** Concrete products, precast, nec

(G-16875)
SAWDUST FARMS WOODWORKING LLC
6518 W 300 S (46996-8899)
PHONE..................574 946-3399
Matt Heigl, *Prin*
EMP: 5 EST: 2016
SALES (est): 61.96K **Privately Held**
SIC: **2431** Millwork

(G-16876)
STANDARD INDUSTRIAL SUPPLY INC
100 Michigan (46996)
P.O. Box 10 (46996)
PHONE..................574 946-6661
Bryce Brumm, *Pr*
Lori Brumm, *
Rob Howe, *
Paul Miller, *
Jeremy Tucker, *
EMP: 48 EST: 2004
SALES (est): 4.96MM **Privately Held**
Web: www.standardinc.net
SIC: **3714** Motor vehicle parts and accessories

(G-16877)
STANDARD INTGRTED SLUTIONS INC
100 Michigan (46996-1272)
PHONE..................574 946-6661
Bryce J Brumm, *Pr*
EMP: 10 EST: 2011
SALES (est): 499.39K **Privately Held**
SIC: **3714** Motor vehicle parts and accessories

(G-16878)
TWO GUYS MECHANICAL CONTRS INC
461 E Rosser Rd (46996-8928)
P.O. Box 48 (46996-0048)
PHONE..................574 946-7671
Scott Fagner, *Pr*
EMP: 32 EST: 1987
SALES (est): 3.02MM **Privately Held**
Web: www.2guysmci.com
SIC: **1796** 1711 1799 7692 Millwright; Mechanical contractor; Welding on site; Welding repair

(G-16879)
VITA PLUS CORP
3836 N 215 E (46996-8693)
PHONE..................574 595-0901
EMP: 5 EST: 2018
SALES (est): 88.22K **Privately Held**
SIC: **2048** Prepared feeds, nec

(G-16880)
WASTEQUIP MANUFACTURING CO LLC
480 E 150 S (46996-7768)
PHONE..................574 946-6631
Robert Rasmussen, *Brnch Mgr*
▲ EMP: 58
Web: www.wastequip.com
SIC: **3549** Metalworking machinery, nec
HQ: Wastequip Manufacturing Company Llc
6525 Carnegie Blvd # 300
Charlotte NC 28211

Winchester
Randolph County

(G-16881)
ANCHOR GLASS CONTAINER CORP
603 E North St (47394-1717)
PHONE..................765 584-6101
Gary Jarrett, *Brnch Mgr*
EMP: 58
Web: www.anchorglass.com
SIC: **3221** 3229 Packers' ware (containers), glass; Pressed and blown glass, nec
PA: Anchor Glass Container Corporation
3001 N Rocky Point Dr E # 300
Tampa FL 33607

(G-16882)
APEX AG SOLUTIONS LLC
130 S 100 E (47394)
PHONE..................765 305-1930
Torey W Hunt, *Managing Member*
EMP: 14 EST: 2013
SALES (est): 1.14MM **Privately Held**
Web: www.apexag.net
SIC: **8711** 1389 Engineering services; Construction, repair, and dismantling services

(G-16883)
CAST METALS TECHNOLOGY INC
1036 N Old Highway 27 (47394-8571)
PHONE..................765 584-6501
EMP: 4
Web: www.cm-tec.com
SIC: **3599** Machine shop, jobbing and repair
PA: Cast Metals Technology, Inc.
550 Liberty Rd
Delaware OH 43015

(G-16884)
CCM INDUSTRIES INC
610 N 100 E (47394-8302)
PHONE..................765 545-0597
Kevin Cook, *Prin*
EMP: 7 EST: 2012
SALES (est): 101.81K **Privately Held**
SIC: **3999** Manufacturing industries, nec

GEOGRAPHIC SECTION

Winona Lake - Kosciusko County (G-16908)

(G-16885)
CM TECH (PA)
1036 N Old Highway 27 (47394-8571)
P.O. Box 69 (47394-0069)
PHONE.................................765 584-6501
Russell Symmes, *CEO*
EMP: 8 **EST:** 2018
SALES (est): 498.06K
SALES (corp-wide): 498.06K **Privately Held**
Web: www.cm-tec.com
SIC: 3325 Steel foundries, nec

(G-16886)
ERNST ENTERPRISES INC
1041 N Old Highway 27 (47394-8571)
PHONE.................................765 584-5700
James A Ernest, *Brnch Mgr*
EMP: 3
SALES (corp-wide): 240.08MM **Privately Held**
Web: www.ernstconcrete.com
SIC: 3273 Ready-mixed concrete
PA: Ernst Enterprises, Inc.
3361 Successful Way
Dayton OH 45414
937 233-5555

(G-16887)
FUTURE SIGNS SALES & SERVICE
709 S Main St (47394-2147)
P.O. Box 211 (47394-0211)
PHONE.................................765 749-5180
Dan Mcknight, *Prin*
EMP: 6 **EST:** 2009
SALES (est): 93.83K **Privately Held**
SIC: 3993 Signs, not made in custom sign painting shops

(G-16888)
GOLIATH AG LLC
2230 E State Road 32 (47394-8792)
PHONE.................................765 305-1141
EMP: 10 **EST:** 2020
SALES (est): 1MM **Privately Held**
Web: www.goliathag.com
SIC: 3523 7359 Farm machinery and equipment; Stores and yards equipment rental

(G-16889)
HARTFORD CITY NEWS TIMES
Also Called: News-Times
123 W Franklin St (47394-1861)
PHONE.................................765 348-0110
Larry Perrotto, *Pr*
Roy Trahan Li, *Prin*
EMP: 10 **EST:** 1914
SALES (est): 243.24K **Privately Held**
Web: www.hartfordcitynewstimes.com
SIC: 2711 2752 Newspapers, publishing and printing; Offset printing

(G-16890)
HYDROJET SIGNS
Also Called: Hydrojet Signs and Fabricating
707 N Co Rd 400 E (47394)
PHONE.................................765 584-2125
Leslie Isenberger, *Owner*
EMP: 9 **EST:** 2016
SALES (est): 238.19K **Privately Held**
Web: www.hydrojetsigns.com
SIC: 3993 Signs and advertising specialties

(G-16891)
INDIANA MARUJUN LLC
Also Called: I M L
200 Inks Dr (47394-9454)
PHONE.................................765 584-7339
Ryoji Takagi, *Pr*
Atsushi Watanabe, *
John Pleiman, *
Yasuharu Masuda, *
Masaki Akiho, *
▲ **EMP:** 53 **EST:** 1999
SQ FT: 182,500
SALES (est): 10.17MM **Privately Held**
Web: www.indianamarujun.com
SIC: 3714 Motor vehicle parts and accessories

(G-16892)
JABRA SIGNS & GRAPHICS
406 S Brown St (47394-2203)
PHONE.................................765 584-7100
Richard Sanders, *Owner*
EMP: 5 **EST:** 2006
SALES (est): 64.69K **Privately Held**
SIC: 3993 Signs and advertising specialties

(G-16893)
KMC ENTERPRISES INC
1094 N Old Highway 27 (47394-8571)
P.O. Box 186 (47394-0186)
PHONE.................................765 584-1533
Keith Covert, *Pr*
Jim Covert, *Treas*
EMP: 6 **EST:** 1986
SALES (est): 824.84K **Privately Held**
SIC: 3469 Machine parts, stamped or pressed metal

(G-16894)
MAUL TECHNOLOGY CO
300 W Martin St (47394-1012)
P.O. Box 310 (47394-0310)
PHONE.................................765 584-2101
Steven J Smith, *Pr*
Beverly Edwards, *CFO*
EMP: 15 **EST:** 1991
SQ FT: 40,000
SALES (est): 682.41K
SALES (corp-wide): 6.55B **Privately Held**
Web: www.maultechnology.com
SIC: 3229 Pressed and blown glass, nec
HQ: Vhc Ltd.
300 W Martin St
Winchester IN 47394
765 584-2101

(G-16895)
NEWS-GAZETTE
123 W Franklin St (47394-1862)
P.O. Box 429 (47394-0429)
PHONE.................................765 584-4501
Larry Perrato, *Pr*
Ricky Williams, *VP*
EMP: 10 **EST:** 1934
SALES (est): 468.05K **Privately Held**
Web: www.winchesternewsgazette.com
SIC: 2711 Job printing and newspaper publishing combined

(G-16896)
OMEGA ENTERPRISES INC
732 W Washington St (47394)
P.O. Box 514 (47394)
PHONE.................................765 584-1990
Jim Jarrett, *Pr*
Mary Jarrett, *Sec*
EMP: 23 **EST:** 1992
SALES (est): 2.08MM **Privately Held**
Web: www.omegaenterprises.net
SIC: 3544 Industrial molds

(G-16897)
PALLET BUILDER INC (PA)
112 Inks Dr (47394-8283)
PHONE.................................765 584-1441
Gene Goodnight, *Pr*
EMP: 9 **EST:** 1982
SQ FT: 8,500
SALES (est): 1.1MM **Privately Held**
Web: www.thepalletbuilders.com
SIC: 2448 Pallets, wood

(G-16898)
PAUL NUNEZ ROAD SERVICE
Also Called: Nunez Farm & Road Svc
2711 E 500 N (47394-8674)
PHONE.................................765 584-1628
Paul Nunez, *Owner*
EMP: 1 **EST:** 1980
SALES (est): 88.17K **Privately Held**
Web: nunez-farm-road-service.business.site
SIC: 7534 Tire repair shop

(G-16899)
SHED CRAFT CREATIONS LLC
1204 S Huntsville Rd (47394-8558)
PHONE.................................765 993-1161
Benuel Beiler, *Managing Member*
EMP: 8 **EST:** 2019
SALES (est): 490.34K **Privately Held**
SIC: 2542 Partitions and fixtures, except wood

(G-16900)
THORNBURY SOFTWARE
205 W Franklin St (47394-1842)
PHONE.................................765 546-8640
Robert Thornbury, *Prin*
EMP: 3 **EST:** 2011
SALES (est): 88.73K **Privately Held**
Web: www.thornburysoftware.com
SIC: 7372 Prepackaged software

(G-16901)
TOA WINCHESTER LLC
200 Inks Dr (47394-9454)
PHONE.................................765 584-7639
Mikio Yoshida, *Pr*
Shinichi Iizuka, *
EMP: 300 **EST:** 2016
SQ FT: 450,000
SALES (est): 32.71MM **Privately Held**
Web: www.toawinchester.com
SIC: 3465 Automotive stampings

(G-16902)
VHC LTD (HQ)
Also Called: Maul Technology
300 W Martin St (47394-1012)
P.O. Box 310 (47394-0310)
PHONE.................................765 584-2101
James Pike, *Ch Bd*
Steven J Smith, *
Beverly Edwards, *
▲ **EMP:** 33 **EST:** 1952
SQ FT: 120,000
SALES (est): 7.2MM
SALES (corp-wide): 6.55B **Privately Held**
Web: www.maultechnology.com
SIC: 3559 Glass making machinery: blowing, molding, forming, etc.
PA: Cerberus Capital Management, L.P.
875 3rd Ave
New York NY 10022
212 891-2100

Windfall
Tipton County

(G-16903)
BAYER GREAT LAKES PROD CO LLC
Also Called: Monsanto
908 N Independence St (46076-9213)
P.O. Box 367 (46076-0367)
PHONE.................................317 945-7121
Donn Cummings, *Brnch Mgr*
EMP: 25
SALES (corp-wide): 3.12MM **Privately Held**
Web: www.monsanto.com
SIC: 2879 Agricultural chemicals, nec
PA: Bayer Great Lakes Production Co., Llc
67760 Us Highway 131 S
Constantine MI

(G-16904)
CHEGAR MANUFACTURING COMPANY
951 N Independence St (46076-9213)
P.O. Box 338 (46076-0338)
PHONE.................................765 945-7444
Mark Mcclelland, *Pr*
EMP: 22 **EST:** 1973
SQ FT: 10,000
SALES (est): 879.82K **Privately Held**
SIC: 3443 Fabricated plate work (boiler shop)

(G-16905)
HIGH PERFORMANCE ALLOYS INC (PA)
Also Called: Hpalloy
1985 E 500 N (46076-9467)
P.O. Box 40 (46072-0040)
PHONE.................................765 945-8230
◆ **EMP:** 22 **EST:** 1984
SALES (est): 28.18MM
SALES (corp-wide): 28.18MM **Privately Held**
Web: www.hpalloy.com
SIC: 5051 3463 Metals service centers and offices; Flange, valve or pipe fitting forgings, nonferrous

Wingate
Montgomery County

(G-16906)
DEE SCENTS LLC
110 E South St (47994-8060)
PHONE.................................765 275-2242
EMP: 4 **EST:** 2012
SALES (est): 56.38K **Privately Held**
SIC: 2844 Perfumes, cosmetics and other toilet preparations

Winona Lake
Kosciusko County

(G-16907)
ABC INDUSTRIES INC (PA)
Also Called: ABC
301 Kings Hwy (46590-1132)
P.O. Box 77 (46581-0077)
PHONE.................................800 426-0921
Steven Fleagle, *Pr*
William R Linnemeier, *
▲ **EMP:** 65 **EST:** 1926
SQ FT: 85,000
SALES (est): 23.71MM
SALES (corp-wide): 23.71MM **Privately Held**
Web: www.abc-industries.net
SIC: 1711 3089 5199 Ventilation and duct work contractor; Reinforcing mesh, plastics; Packaging materials

(G-16908)
AGILENT TECHNOLOGIES
1000 Park Ave (46590-1052)
P.O. Box 313 (46590-0313)
PHONE.................................617 694-7692
EMP: 6 **EST:** 2018
SALES (est): 45.42K **Privately Held**

Winona Lake - Kosciusko County (G-16909)

Web: www.agilent.com
SIC: 3825 Instruments to measure electricity

(G-16909)
BRETHREN IN CHRST MDIA MNSTRIE
Also Called: Evangel Press
1104 Kings Hwy (46590-1333)
P.O. Box 544 (46590-0544)
PHONE.................574 267-7400
Kenneth Herman, *Mgr*
EMP: 1
SALES (corp-wide): 2.31MM **Privately Held**
Web: www.evangelpublishing.com
SIC: 2741 Miscellaneous publishing
PA: Brethren In Christ Media Ministries, Inc.
431 Grantham Rd
Mechanicsburg PA 17055
574 773-3164

(G-16910)
DEPUY INC
2809 William Dr (46590-2025)
PHONE.................574 372-7010
EMP: 5 EST: 2011
SALES (est): 72.03K **Privately Held**
SIC: 3842 Surgical appliances and supplies

(G-16911)
JRS POLISHING LLC
1446 E 225 S (46590-2041)
PHONE.................574 306-2351
Barry Ousley, *Prin*
EMP: 6 EST: 2017
SALES (est): 92.82K **Privately Held**
SIC: 3471 Plating of metals or formed products

(G-16912)
LAKE HOUSE
720 E Canal St (46590-1070)
PHONE.................574 265-6945
Jake England, *Prin*
EMP: 4 EST: 2010
SALES (est): 350.2K **Privately Held**
Web: www.lakehousesurf.com
SIC: 3949 Surfboards

(G-16913)
OLD GUY WOODCRAFTERS LLC
1312 Freedom Pkwy (46590-5794)
PHONE.................574 527-9044
Philip W Barkey, *Pr*
EMP: 5 EST: 2011
SALES (est): 129.95K **Privately Held**
SIC: 2511 Wood household furniture

(G-16914)
PICKSLAYS WOODWORKING
1313 Wooster Rd (46590-5721)
PHONE.................530 388-8697
EMP: 3 EST: 2015
SALES (est): 82.32K **Privately Held**
Web: www.pickslayswoodworking.com
SIC: 2431 Millwork

(G-16915)
RAINMAKER POLYMERS LLC (PA)
2986 E Prestwick Rd (46590-8911)
PHONE.................574 268-0010
John Urschalitz, *Pr*
Lee Luckasevic, *VP*
EMP: 1 EST: 2006
SALES (est): 896.3K **Privately Held**
Web: www.rainmakerpolymers.com
SIC: 2821 Plastics materials and resins

(G-16916)
WARSAW CUSTOM CABINET
904 Chestnut Ave (46590-1316)
PHONE.................574 267-5794
Timothy P Mundinger, *Brnch Mgr*
EMP: 1
SALES (corp-wide): 178.84K **Privately Held**
Web: www.warsawcustomcabinets.com
SIC: 2434 Wood kitchen cabinets
PA: Warsaw Custom Cabinet
1697 W 350 S
Warsaw IN 46580
574 267-5794

(G-16917)
WATERMELON WORLD PUBLISHING
Also Called: Mk List
307 Administration Blvd (46590-1006)
PHONE.................574 267-2505
Andrew Kerr, *Owner*
EMP: 1 EST: 1997
SALES (est): 37.13K **Privately Held**
SIC: 2731 Book clubs: publishing only, not printed on site

(G-16918)
WHITMAN PUBLICATIONS INC
401 Kings Hwy (46590-1133)
PHONE.................574 268-2062
Wendall Whitman, *Pr*
Julie Kline, *Sec*
EMP: 3 EST: 1991
SALES (est): 142.25K **Privately Held**
SIC: 2731 Book publishing

(G-16919)
WORKROOM INC
204 13th St (46590-1311)
PHONE.................574 269-6624
Rhonda Raber, *Pr*
EMP: 2 EST: 1997
SALES (est): 100.27K **Privately Held**
SIC: 2399 Fabricated textile products, nec

Winslow
Pike County

(G-16920)
METAL HEAD WELDING
211 N Main St (47598-5423)
PHONE.................812 582-4234
Tffani Kline, *Prin*
EMP: 3 EST: 2017
SALES (est): 25.09K **Privately Held**
Web: www.metalheadwelding.com
SIC: 7692 Welding repair

(G-16921)
MILLS CUSTOM POWDER COATING
1444 E County Road 475 S (47598-8487)
PHONE.................812 766-0308
Jason Mills, *Prin*
EMP: 6 EST: 2013
SALES (est): 160.1K **Privately Held**
Web: www.millscustompowdercoating.com
SIC: 3479 Coating of metals and formed products

(G-16922)
SISSON STEEL INC
739 S State Road 61 (47598-8453)
PHONE.................812 354-8701
Jim Gaskins, *Pr*
Cindy Gaskins, *Sec*
Stephanie Gaskins-mcguire, *Prin*
Greg Mullins, *Prin*
Emily J Mullins, *Treas*

EMP: 17 EST: 1983
SQ FT: 16,000
SALES (est): 2.16MM **Privately Held**
Web: www.sissonsteel.com
SIC: 3441 3446 3444 3443 Building components, structural steel; Architectural metalwork; Sheet metalwork; Fabricated plate work (boiler shop)

(G-16923)
SSM LOGISTICS LLC
6242 E State Road 56 (47598-8433)
PHONE.................812 354-4509
Brian Simpson, *Managing Member*
EMP: 1 EST: 2019
SALES (est): 50K **Privately Held**
SIC: 3537 Trucks: freight, baggage, etc.: industrial, except mining

(G-16924)
STELLA-JONES CORPORATION
3818 S County Road 50 E (47598-8866)
PHONE.................812 789-5331
EMP: 20
SALES (corp-wide): 2.42B **Privately Held**
Web: www.stella-jones.com
SIC: 2491 Railroad cross bridges and switch ties, treated wood
HQ: Stella-Jones Corporation
1000 Cliffmine Rd Ste 500
Pittsburgh PA 15275

(G-16925)
TANGENT RAIL PRODUCTS INC
3818 S County Road 50 E (47598-8866)
PHONE.................812 789-5331
Steve Basham, *Brnch Mgr*
EMP: 39
SALES (corp-wide): 2.42B **Privately Held**
SIC: 2421 Outdoor wood structural products
HQ: Tangent Rail Products, Inc.
101 W Station Square Dr # 600
Pittsburgh PA 15219
412 325-0202

(G-16926)
WILLIAM R ARVIN
Also Called: Arvin's Creative Woodworking
699 S County Road 700 E (47598-8519)
PHONE.................812 486-5255
William R Arvin, *Owner*
EMP: 2 EST: 2001
SALES (est): 117.3K **Privately Held**
SIC: 2434 Wood kitchen cabinets

Wolcott
White County

(G-16927)
CIVES CORPORATION
Also Called: Cives Steel Company
337 N 700 W (47995-8204)
P.O. Box 98 (47995-0098)
PHONE.................219 279-4000
EMP: 120
SALES (corp-wide): 340.87MM **Privately Held**
Web: www.vikingcives.com
SIC: 3441 Building components, structural steel
PA: Cives Corporation
3700 Mansell Rd Ste 500
Alpharetta GA 30022
770 993-4424

(G-16928)
DWYER INSTRUMENTS INC
Also Called: DWYER INSTRUMENTS INC
204 E Sherry Ln (47995-8329)

P.O. Box 404 (47995-0404)
PHONE.................219 279-2031
Jeff Nelson, *Brnch Mgr*
EMP: 7
SALES (corp-wide): 653.43MM **Privately Held**
Web: intl.dwyer-inst.com
SIC: 3823 Pressure measurement instruments, industrial
HQ: Dwyer Instruments, Llc
102 Indiana Hwy 212
Michigan City IN 46360
219 879-8868

(G-16929)
EGGLIFE FOODS INC
911 N 1200 W (47995-8330)
PHONE.................219 261-5500
David Kroll, *CEO*
EMP: 135 EST: 2017
SALES (est): 16.15MM **Privately Held**
Web: www.egglifefoods.com
SIC: 2015 Egg processing

(G-16930)
EMOND ELDON
Also Called: Emond's Drainage Service
3522 N 900 W (47995-8242)
PHONE.................219 279-2442
Eldon Emond, *Owner*
EMP: 1 EST: 1973
SALES (est): 66.67K **Privately Held**
SIC: 3491 Water works valves

(G-16931)
INDIANA RIBBON INC
106 N 2nd St (47995-8326)
P.O. Box 355 (47995-0355)
PHONE.................219 279-2112
Joseph Hickman, *Pr*
David Hickman, *
Jane Johnson, *
▲ EMP: 50 EST: 1952
SQ FT: 150,000
SALES (est): 4.8MM **Privately Held**
Web: www.giftwrapgifts.com
SIC: 2655 2241 5949 2631 Spools, fiber: made from purchased material; Ribbons, nec; Notions, including trim; Paperboard mills

(G-16932)
LIFE ESSENTIALS INC
Also Called: Life Essentials
5364 S Us Highway 231 (47995-8032)
PHONE.................765 423-4192
Hubert Vonholten, *Prin*
EMP: 16 EST: 1999
SALES (est): 1.76MM **Privately Held**
Web: www.lifelyfts.com
SIC: 3999 Wheelchair lifts

(G-16933)
LIVING PRAIRIE EQUIPMENT LLC
2768 N 1000 W (47995-8253)
PHONE.................765 479-0759
Jason Federer, *Managing Member*
EMP: 1 EST: 2018
SALES (est): 54.57K **Privately Held**
SIC: 3523 Farm machinery and equipment

(G-16934)
MILLER CUSTOM METALS LLC
1530 N 800 W (47995-8201)
PHONE.................219 279-2671
EMP: 1 EST: 2004
SALES (est): 175.05K **Privately Held**
Web: www.millercustommetals.com
SIC: 7692 Welding repair

GEOGRAPHIC SECTION

Worthington - Greene County (G-16959)

(G-16935)
SWEETENER SUPPLY CORPORATION
11048 Mac Park Dr (47995-8136)
PHONE....................708 588-8400
EMP: 6
Web: www.sweetenersupply.com
SIC: 2099 Food preparations, nec
PA: Sweetener Supply Corporation
9501 W Southview Ave
Brookfield IL 60513

Wolcottville
Lagrange County

(G-16936)
CLEARSPRING WELDING
1497 W 550 S (46795-9734)
PHONE....................260 463-8754
Mervin C Miller, *Owner*
EMP: 1 **EST:** 2002
SALES (est): 56.18K **Privately Held**
SIC: 7692 Welding repair

(G-16937)
HEADLANDS LTD
Also Called: Herrero Printing Co
9125 E 480 S (46795-8713)
PHONE....................260 426-9884
Diana J Hensch, *Pr*
EMP: 2 **EST:** 1971
SQ FT: 3,500
SALES (est): 212.54K **Privately Held**
SIC: 2759 Labels and seals: printing, nsk

(G-16938)
HEARTLAND TABLE PADS LLC
401 N Main St (46795-9209)
PHONE....................888 487-2377
Zoran Unger, *Managing Member*
EMP: 6 **EST:** 2016
SALES (est): 502.48K **Privately Held**
Web: www.heartlandtablepads.com
SIC: 3292 Table pads and padding, asbestos

(G-16939)
JACOBS ADVERTISING INC
6170 S 520 E (46795-9436)
PHONE....................260 854-2054
Phillip Jacobs, *Pr*
EMP: 1 **EST:** 1984
SALES (est): 96.69K **Privately Held**
Web: www.jacobsadvertisinginc.com
SIC: 3993 Signs, not made in custom sign painting shops

(G-16940)
L & W WOODWORKING LLC
4635 S 200 W (46795-9508)
PHONE....................260 463-8938
Lester A Beechy, *Prin*
EMP: 9 **EST:** 2001
SALES (est): 372.68K **Privately Held**
SIC: 2431 Millwork

(G-16941)
MATRIX MANUFACTURING INC
4935 S 300 E (46795-9240)
PHONE....................260 854-4659
George Tetzloff, *Pr*
Rob Hanselman, *VP*
EMP: 8 **EST:** 1986
SQ FT: 15,000
SALES (est): 895.05K **Privately Held**
SIC: 3444 3544 Sheet metal specialties, not stamped; Special dies and tools

(G-16942)
SCHWARTZ WOODWORKING LLC
7240 S 075 W # B (46795-9500)
PHONE....................260 854-9457
EMP: 5 **EST:** 2008
SALES (est): 190K **Privately Held**
SIC: 2431 Millwork

(G-16943)
VINO OF INDIANA LLC
305 S Main St (46795-9633)
PHONE....................260 710-7464
▲ **EMP:** 17 **EST:** 2013
SALES (est): 1.62MM **Privately Held**
Web: www.vinoindiana.com
SIC: 2084 Wines, brandy, and brandy spirits

(G-16944)
VINYL CREATOR
11889 N Angling Rd 57 - 57 (46795-9618)
PHONE....................260 318-5133
EMP: 4 **EST:** 2015
SALES (est): 57.71K **Privately Held**
Web: www.thevinylcreator.com
SIC: 2759 Commercial printing, nec

(G-16945)
WOODSIDE WOODWORKS LLC
4795 S 200 W (46795-9508)
PHONE....................260 499-3220
Lavern Bontrager, *Owner*
EMP: 8 **EST:** 2010
SALES (est): 331.97K **Privately Held**
SIC: 2431 Millwork

Woodburn
Allen County

(G-16946)
BF GOODRICH TIRE MANUFACTURING
18906 Old 24 (46797-9048)
P.O. Box 277 (46797-0277)
PHONE....................260 493-8100
EMP: 3 **EST:** 2006
SALES (est): 429.69K **Privately Held**
Web: www.goodyear.com
SIC: 5531 3999 Automotive tires; Atomizers, toiletry

(G-16947)
CUMMINS INC
Also Called: Cummins
20329 Notestine Rd (46797-9791)
PHONE....................260 657-1436
Daniel L Cummins, *Brnch Mgr*
EMP: 3
SALES (corp-wide): 34.06B **Publicly Held**
Web: www.cummins.com
SIC: 3714 Motor vehicle parts and accessories
PA: Cummins Inc.
500 Jackson St
Columbus IN 47201
812 377-5000

(G-16948)
HEIDELBERG MTLS MDWEST AGG INC
22821 Dawkins Rd (46797-9520)
P.O. Box 32 (45879-0032)
PHONE....................260 632-1410
Bruce Rowley, *Mgr*
EMP: 7
SALES (corp-wide): 23.02B **Privately Held**
SIC: 1422 5032 Limestones, ground; Limestone
HQ: Heidelberg Materials Midwest Agg, Inc.
300 E John Carpenter Fwy
Irving TX

(G-16949)
HEIDELBERG MTLS MDWEST AGG INC
17831 Us Highway 24 (46797-9048)
PHONE....................260 632-4252
Bruce Rowley, *Brnch Mgr*
EMP: 8
SALES (corp-wide): 23.02B **Privately Held**
SIC: 2951 Asphalt paving mixtures and blocks
HQ: Heidelberg Materials Midwest Agg, Inc.
300 E John Carpenter Fwy
Irving TX

(G-16950)
KENN FELD GROUP LLC (PA)
4724 N State Road 101 (46797-9690)
P.O. Box 487 (46797-0487)
PHONE....................260 632-4242
Ralph Thieme, *Prin*
EMP: 7 **EST:** 2009
SALES (est): 2.08MM
SALES (corp-wide): 2.08MM **Privately Held**
Web: www.trulandequip.com
SIC: 3531 Excavators: cable, clamshell, crane, derrick, dragline, etc.

(G-16951)
MICHELIN NORTH AMERICA INC
Also Called: BF Goodrich
18906 Us Highway 24 (46797-9048)
P.O. Box 277 (46797-0277)
PHONE....................260 493-8100
Bill Elks, *Brnch Mgr*
EMP: 1335
SALES (corp-wide): 1.05B **Privately Held**
Web: www.michelinman.com
SIC: 3011 Tires and inner tubes
HQ: Michelin North America, Inc.
1 Parkway S
Greenville SC 29615
864 458-5000

(G-16952)
MIDWEST TILE AND CONCRETE PDTS
Also Called: Midwest Tile & Concrete Pdts
4309 Webster Rd (46797-9571)
PHONE....................260 749-5173
Linda Ohlwine, *Mgr*
EMP: 2
SALES (corp-wide): 9.54MM **Privately Held**
Web: www.midwesttile.net
SIC: 3272 Concrete products, nec
PA: Midwest Tile And Concrete Products Inc
4309 Webster Rd
Woodburn IN 46797
260 749-5173

(G-16953)
MIDWEST TILE AND CONCRETE PDTS (PA)
4309 Webster Rd (46797-9571)
PHONE....................260 749-5173
Terry Hamlin, *Pr*
Joseph Schaeffer, *Sec*
EMP: 2 **EST:** 1962
SQ FT: 7,000
SALES (est): 9.54MM
SALES (corp-wide): 9.54MM **Privately Held**
Web: www.midwesttile.net
SIC: 3272 5032 Septic tanks, concrete; Sewer pipe, clay

(G-16954)
MJS CONCRETE
19427 Notestine Rd (46797-9672)
PHONE....................260 341-5640
Steve Schmucker, *Prin*
EMP: 6 **EST:** 2018
SALES (est): 103.44K **Privately Held**
SIC: 3272 Concrete products, nec

(G-16955)
NONEMAN MACHINE CORP
4517 Bull Rapids Rd (46797-9014)
P.O. Box 31 (46797-0031)
PHONE....................260 632-5311
Lowell Noneman, *Pr*
EMP: 1 **EST:** 1973
SQ FT: 5,900
SALES (est): 106.48K **Privately Held**
SIC: 3599 Machine shop, jobbing and repair

(G-16956)
WATTRE INC
9301 Roberts Rd (46797-9758)
PHONE....................260 657-3701
Curtis Graber, *Pr*
Julia Graber, *Sec*
EMP: 5 **EST:** 2002
SALES (est): 492.33K **Privately Held**
Web: www.wattre.com
SIC: 3679 Electronic loads and power supplies

(G-16957)
WOODBURN DIAMOND DIE INC (PA)
23012 Tile Mill Rd (46797)
P.O. Box 155 (46797)
PHONE....................260 632-4217
Farver Rex C, *Pr*
Jane E Farver, *
Chris Farver, *
Michelle Rumpz, *
▲ **EMP:** 30 **EST:** 1958
SQ FT: 21,000
SALES (est): 4.96MM
SALES (corp-wide): 4.96MM **Privately Held**
Web: www.woodburndd.com
SIC: 3544 3915 3291 Diamond dies, metalworking; Jewelers' materials and lapidary work; Abrasive products

Worthington
Greene County

(G-16958)
CORN FLOUR PRODUCERS LLC
7383 N 100 W (47471-6310)
P.O. Box 128 (47471-0128)
PHONE....................812 875-3113
EMP: 48
SIC: 2041 Corn flour

(G-16959)
DMP LLC
2868 W 325 N (47471-5149)
PHONE....................812 699-0086
Dia Serach, *Admn*
Mike Gallagher Sales, *Marketing*
Dia Serach, *CEO*
EMP: 2 **EST:** 2016
SALES (est): 166.14K **Privately Held**
SIC: 1541 3949 2819 Food products manufacturing or packing plant construction ; Team sports equipment; Inorganic metal compounds or salts, nec

Worthington - Greene County (G-16960)

(G-16960)
HILLCREST ENTERPRISES LLC (PA)
11267 Coal City Arney Rd (47471-6212)
PHONE..................812 875-2500
EMP: 1 EST: 2008
SQ FT: 1,500
SALES (est): 844.32K **Privately Held**
Web: www.hillcrest-enterprises.com
SIC: 2426 Flooring, hardwood

(G-16961)
INDIANA GREEN BURIAL LLC
219 Terre Haute Rd (47471-2006)
PHONE..................812 961-1960
Nathan Butler, *Prin*
EMP: 5 EST: 2013
SALES (est): 386.88K **Privately Held**
Web: www.indianagreenburials.com
SIC: 3272 Burial vaults, concrete or precast terrazzo

(G-16962)
OWEN COUNTY PALLET LLC
9611 Stahl Rd (47471)
PHONE..................812 384-6568
Joseph Hochstetler, *Managing Member*
EMP: 6 EST: 2007
SALES (est): 349.4K **Privately Held**
SIC: 2448 7389 Pallets, wood; Business Activities at Non-Commercial Site

Wyatt
St. Joseph County

(G-16963)
BADLANDS PICK UP VAN ACC SALV
Also Called: Badlands Accessories Salvage
66521 State Rd 331 (46595)
PHONE..................574 633-2156
EMP: 2 EST: 1995
SALES (est): 196.58K **Privately Held**
SIC: 3711 Trucks, pickup, assembly of

Yoder
Allen County

(G-16964)
ALRO STEEL CORPORATION
2912 Pleasant Center Rd (46798-9742)
PHONE..................260 749-9661
TOLL FREE: 800
Jack Bigham, *Mgr*
EMP: 23
SALES (corp-wide): 3.04B **Privately Held**
Web: www.alro.com
SIC: 5051 3312 Steel; Blast furnaces and steel mills
PA: Alro Steel Corporation
    3100 E High St
    Jackson MI 49203
    517 787-5500

(G-16965)
DEDICATED SOFTWARE
Also Called: Affordable Computer Repair
6018 Hamilton Rd (46798-9787)
PHONE..................260 341-4166
Don Huguenard, *Owner*
EMP: 2 EST: 1983
SALES (est): 100.83K **Privately Held**
SIC: 7372 Prepackaged software

(G-16966)
LIPPERT COMPONENTS INC
2909 Pleasant Center Rd (46798-9742)
PHONE..................260 234-4303
EMP: 10
SALES (corp-wide): 3.78B **Publicly Held**
Web: corporate.lippert.com
SIC: 3711 3469 3444 3714 Chassis, motor vehicle; Stamping metal for the trade; Metal roofing and roof drainage equipment; Motor vehicle parts and accessories
HQ: Lippert Components, Inc.
    3501 County Rd 6 E
    Elkhart IN 46514
    574 535-1125

Yorktown
Delaware County

(G-16967)
651 EMERGENCY LIGHTING
1801 S Lindell Dr (47396-1099)
PHONE..................765 748-6664
Derek Rains, *Owner*
EMP: 1 EST: 2021
SALES (est): 54.05K **Privately Held**
SIC: 3559 7389 Automotive maintenance equipment; Business Activities at Non-Commercial Site

(G-16968)
AUL BROTHERS TOOL & DIE INC
101 S Buckingham Rd (47396)
PHONE..................765 759-5124
Gregory Filkovski, *Pr*
EMP: 14 EST: 1942
SALES (est): 1.95MM **Privately Held**
SIC: 3469 3544 Stamping metal for the trade; Special dies, tools, jigs, and fixtures
PA: Mursix Corporation
    2401 N Executive Park Dr
    Yorktown IN 47396

(G-16969)
AUL IN THE FAMILY TOOL AND DIE
Also Called: Aftco Manufacturing
9801 W Jackson St (47396-9657)
PHONE..................765 759-5161
Staci Corle, *Ch Bd*
Adrian Aul, *Ch Bd*
Mark Aul, *Pr*
EMP: 4 EST: 1964
SQ FT: 5,000
SALES (est): 369.92K **Privately Held**
SIC: 3544 Special dies and tools

(G-16970)
AUTUMN MAKERS MOBILE HM SUBDV
2800 S Andrews Rd (47396-9107)
PHONE..................765 759-7878
John Hough, *Admn*
EMP: 1 EST: 1986
SALES (est): 84.7K **Privately Held**
SIC: 2451 Mobile homes

(G-16971)
BBS CELEBRATION CENTER
1019 S Yorkchester Dr (47396-9396)
PHONE..................765 730-6575
Barbara Baker, *Owner*
EMP: 2 EST: 2005
SALES (est): 129.65K **Privately Held**
SIC: 3999 5199 5947 Manufacturing industries, nec; Gifts and novelties; Gifts and novelties

(G-16972)
DANA SAC USA INC (DH)
Also Called: Dana
14141 W Brevini Dr Ste 10 (47396-9137)
PHONE..................765 759-2300
▲ EMP: 14 EST: 1977
SALES (est): 9.54MM **Publicly Held**
Web: www.breviniusa.com
SIC: 3566 Reduction gears and gear units for turbines, except auto
HQ: Dana Motion Systems Italia Srl
    Via Luciano Brevini 1/A
    Reggio Nell'emilia RE 42124
    05229281

(G-16973)
DYNAMIC TOOL MACHINE
4750 S County Road 500 W (47396-9138)
PHONE..................765 730-0167
Troy Dugger, *Owner*
EMP: 1 EST: 2003
SALES (est): 109.25K **Privately Held**
SIC: 3544 Special dies and tools

(G-16974)
HOLLOWAY VINYL SIGNS GRAP
4100 S Native Ct (47396-9124)
PHONE..................765 717-1581
William Holloway, *Prin*
EMP: 5 EST: 2009
SALES (est): 177.71K **Privately Held**
Web: www.stickwithholloway.com
SIC: 3993 Signs and advertising specialties

(G-16975)
LIQUIVINYL LLC
7405 W Augusta Blvd (47396-9353)
PHONE..................765 283-6265
EMP: 7 EST: 2018
SALES (est): 516.57K **Privately Held**
Web: www.liquivinyl.com
SIC: 3714 Motor vehicle parts and accessories

(G-16976)
MIASA AUTOMOTIVE LLC
2101 S West St (47396)
PHONE..................765 751-9967
▲ EMP: 22 EST: 2006
SALES (est): 3.24MM **Privately Held**
Web: www.miasa.com
SIC: 3714 Power transmission equipment, motor vehicle

(G-16977)
MURSIX CORPORATION (PA)
Also Called: Mursix
2401 N Executive Park Dr (47396)
P.O. Box 591 (47308)
PHONE..................765 282-2221
Todd Murray, *CEO*
Jeff Frost, *Pr*
Bradley A Murray, *Dir*
▲ EMP: 200 EST: 1990
SQ FT: 85,000
SALES (est): 47.64MM **Privately Held**
Web: www.mursix.com
SIC: 3469 3679 Stamping metal for the trade; Harness assemblies, for electronic use: wire or cable

(G-16978)
NEON AMENITIES INCORPORATED ◆
4060 S County Road 550 W (47396-9509)
PHONE..................765 759-9133
EMP: 6 EST: 2022
SALES (est): 286.8K **Privately Held**
SIC: 2813 Neon

(G-16979)
NORTHEDGE STEEL LLC
13901 W Jackson St (47396)
PHONE..................765 444-6021
EMP: 9
SALES (corp-wide): 565.32K **Privately Held**
Web: www.northedgesteel.us
SIC: 3448 Prefabricated metal buildings and components
PA: Northedge Steel Llc
    350 Forum Pkwy
    Rural Hall NC 27045
    765 591-8080

(G-16980)
PINNACLE MAILING PRODUCTS
7701 W Kilgore Ave Ste 5 (47396-9275)
PHONE..................765 405-1194
Kim Laffoon, *Pt*
EMP: 10 EST: 2010
SALES (est): 1.5MM **Privately Held**
Web: www.pinnaclemailing.net
SIC: 5044 3579 5021 Office equipment; Mailing, letter handling, and addressing machines; Lockers

(G-16981)
PIVOT MANUFACTURING INC
2401 N Executive Park Dr Ste 1000 (47396-9806)
PHONE..................317 371-3560
Susan Carlock, *Prin*
EMP: 1 EST: 2020
SALES (est): 41.52K **Privately Held**
Web: www.pivotmanufacturing.com
SIC: 3599 Machine shop, jobbing and repair

(G-16982)
PRINTING CREATIONS INC
2410 S Vine St (47396-1516)
P.O. Box 3 (47396-0003)
PHONE..................765 759-9679
Carolyn A Grieves, *Pr*
Michael Grieves, *VP*
EMP: 3 EST: 1983
SQ FT: 2,600
SALES (est): 254.6K **Privately Held**
Web: www.munciechamber.org
SIC: 2752 7311 8743 Offset printing; Advertising agencies; Public relations services

(G-16983)
TFX PLATING COMPANY LLC
2401 N Executive Park Dr (47396-9806)
P.O. Box 591 (47308-0591)
PHONE..................765 289-2436
Todd Murray, *Managing Member*
EMP: 8 EST: 1964
SQ FT: 10,000
SALES (est): 898.09K **Privately Held**
SIC: 3471 Electroplating of metals or formed products

(G-16984)
TYSOFT LLC
2211 S Walnut St (47396-1230)
PHONE..................765 405-0098
Ty E Hudson Ii, *Pr*
EMP: 4 EST: 2017
SALES (est): 113.21K **Privately Held**
Web: www.tysoft.me
SIC: 7372 7371 Prepackaged software; Computer software development

Young America
Cass County

(G-16985)
SANDRA HENRY
Also Called: Precision Design
1475 Denmark St (46998-3114)
PHONE..................574 699-7867
Sandra Henry, *Owner*
Kristin Shellman, *Mgr*

GEOGRAPHIC SECTION
Zionsville - Boone County (G-17013)

EMP: 1 EST: 2009
SALES (est): 89.8K Privately Held
Web: www.precisiondesignin.com
SIC: 3699 Electrical equipment and supplies, nec

Zanesville
Allen County

(G-16986)
LENGERICH MEATS INC
3095 Van Horn (46799-9027)
PHONE..................260 638-4123
Jim Strephen, Pr
Richard Keiffer, Treas
William Stephan, Prin
EMP: 14 EST: 1950
SALES (est): 481.18K Privately Held
Web: www.lengerichmeats.com
SIC: 2011 0751 5421 Meat packing plants; Slaughtering: custom livestock services; Meat and fish markets

Zionsville
Boone County

(G-16987)
120 WATER AUDIT INC
250 S Elm St (46077)
P.O. Box 604 (46077)
PHONE..................888 317-1510
Megan Glover, CEO
Patrick Moore, Prin
EMP: 88 EST: 2016
SQ FT: 350
SALES (est): 18MM Privately Held
Web: www.120water.com
SIC: 7372 Prepackaged software

(G-16988)
A J SCHNELL WOOD WORKS LLC
9894 Equestrian Way (46077-7602)
PHONE..................317 370-8890
Andrew Schnell, Owner
EMP: 5 EST: 2017
SALES (est): 59.54K Privately Held
Web: www.ajschnellwoodworks.com
SIC: 2431 Millwork

(G-16989)
AMERICAN ACADEMY OF SPORTS
9264 Greenthread Ln (46077-8144)
P.O. Box 431 (46077-0431)
PHONE..................877 732-5009
Mark S Decarlo, Ex Dir
EMP: 7 EST: 1973
SALES (est): 89.24K Privately Held
Web: www.sportspt.org
SIC: 8621 7372 Medical field-related associations; Application computer software

(G-16990)
AMERICAN CABINET REFACING INC
10650 Bennett Pkwy Ste 300 (46077-7851)
PHONE..................317 875-7453
Jay Powell, Pr
EMP: 6 EST: 1994
SALES (est): 383.45K Privately Held
Web: www.refaceamerica.net
SIC: 2434 Wood kitchen cabinets

(G-16991)
AMERICAN LABEL PRODUCTS INC
4949 W 106th St (46077-8717)
P.O. Box 488 (46077-0488)
PHONE..................317 873-9850
Michelle Misterka, Pr
EMP: 3 EST: 2003
SQ FT: 3,000
SALES (est): 394.98K Privately Held
Web: www.americanlabelproducts.com
SIC: 2759 Labels and seals: printing, nsk

(G-16992)
AMERICAN SPCIALTY BUS INTL LLC
5701 S 800 E (46077-9021)
PHONE..................317 271-5000
Scott Genung, Pr
Mark Genung, CEO
EMP: 3 EST: 2008
SALES (est): 170K Privately Held
Web: www.magnumpc.com
SIC: 3993 5045 Advertising novelties; Computers, peripherals, and software

(G-16993)
ARTISANZ FABRICATION & MACHINE
130 Scranton Ct (46077-1040)
P.O. Box 435 (46077-0435)
PHONE..................317 956-2384
EMP: 5 EST: 2015
SALES (est): 208.75K Privately Held
SIC: 3441 Fabricated structural metal

(G-16994)
B HAPPY PEANUT BUTTER LLC
10830 Bennett Pkwy Ste F (46077)
PHONE..................317 733-3831
Jonathan Weed, Managing Member
EMP: 2 EST: 2013
SALES (est): 187.17K Privately Held
Web: www.bhappypeanutbutter.com
SIC: 2099 Peanut butter

(G-16995)
BALD SPOT RACING LLC
Also Called: Bald Spot Sports
4629 Northwestern Dr (46077-9248)
PHONE..................317 402-7188
Travis Cobb, Managing Member
EMP: 6 EST: 2002
SALES (est): 594.16K Privately Held
Web: baldspotsports.blogspot.com
SIC: 2531 Seats, automobile

(G-16996)
BENTZ TRANSPORT PRODUCTS INC
3943 Weston Pointe Dr (46077-8584)
PHONE..................260 622-9100
Keith Bentz, Pr
EMP: 10 EST: 1993
SQ FT: 45,000
SALES (est): 685K Privately Held
SIC: 3713 3714 Truck bodies and parts; Motor vehicle parts and accessories

(G-16997)
CELESTIAL DESIGNS LLC
Also Called: Celestial Designs
80 N First St (46077-1544)
PHONE..................317 733-3110
EMP: 2 EST: 1996
SALES (est): 120K Privately Held
Web: www.villagecustomembroidery.com
SIC: 7389 5699 5199 5162 Sewing contractor; Customized clothing and apparel; Advertising specialties; Plastics materials, nec

(G-16998)
CLEAR SOFTWARE INC
112 N Ninth St (46077-1275)
PHONE..................317 732-8831
Jonathan Gilman, CEO
Bob Boehnlein, CRO
EMP: 5 EST: 2015
SALES (est): 1.37MM
SALES (corp-wide): 245.12B Publicly Held
Web: www.clearsoftware.com
SIC: 7372 Business oriented computer software
PA: Microsoft Corporation
1 Microsoft Way
Redmond WA 98052
425 882-8080

(G-16999)
CURTIS LIFE RESEARCH LLC
7000 Hull Rd (46077-9361)
PHONE..................317 873-4519
EMP: 5 EST: 2014
SALES (est): 488.5K Privately Held
Web: www.curtisliferesearch.com
SIC: 3699 Electronic training devices

(G-17000)
DART CONTROLS LLC
5000 W 106th St (46077-9233)
P.O. Box 10 (46077-0010)
PHONE..................317 873-5211
EMP: 40 EST: 1963
SALES (est): 4.98MM Privately Held
Web: www.dartcontrols.com
SIC: 3625 Relays and industrial controls

(G-17001)
DEBRA COLLINS
480 Benderfield Dr (46077-1175)
PHONE..................317 873-1977
Debra Collins, Prin
EMP: 1 EST: 2010
SALES (est): 58.51K Privately Held
SIC: 2741 Miscellaneous publishing

(G-17002)
DEGLER MKTG & MAILING SVCS
8930 Cooper Rd (46077-8493)
PHONE..................317 873-5550
Ward Degler, Owner
Jeanne Degler, Pt
EMP: 7 EST: 1970
SALES (est): 100.89K Privately Held
SIC: 7331 7311 2741 Direct mail advertising services; Advertising agencies; Catalogs: publishing and printing

(G-17003)
DOODLES AND DREAMS PUBG LLC
795 Bloor Ln (46077-1104)
PHONE..................317 796-6059
Lorinda Hockema, Prin
EMP: 5 EST: 2017
SALES (est): 71.39K Privately Held
SIC: 2741 Miscellaneous publishing

(G-17004)
ELEVATE WELLNESS CORPORATION ✪
480 W Poplar St (46077)
PHONE..................317 370-9852
Jon Gilman, Pr
EMP: 3 EST: 2024
SALES (est): 128.77K Privately Held
SIC: 7372 Prepackaged software

(G-17005)
ELLIOTT SMITH INTERIORS LLC
7650 W 96th St (46077-8422)
PHONE..................317 966-5101
EMP: 4 EST: 2017
SALES (est): 46.08K Privately Held
SIC: 3993 Signs and advertising specialties

(G-17006)
FANIM INDUSTRIES INC
Also Called: Fanimation
10983 Bennett Pkwy (46077-9187)
PHONE..................888 567-2055
Dwayne C Isaacs, Pr
EMP: 10 EST: 2008
SALES (est): 229.41K Privately Held
SIC: 2395 Decorative and novelty stitching: for the trade

(G-17007)
FANIMATION INC
Also Called: Wind Deco
10983 Bennett Pkwy (46077-9187)
PHONE..................317 733-4113
Tom Frampton, CEO
Rachel Frampton, *
Nathan Frampton, *
Ed Frampton, *
▲ EMP: 45 EST: 1984
SQ FT: 16,000
SALES (est): 8.96MM Privately Held
Web: www.fanimation.com
SIC: 3634 Ceiling fans

(G-17008)
FINLEY CREEK VINEYARDS LLC
795 S Us 421 (46077-4216)
PHONE..................317 769-5483
EMP: 4 EST: 2017
SALES (est): 68.62K Privately Held
Web: www.finleycreekvineyard.com
SIC: 2084 Wines

(G-17009)
GALLEYWARE COMPANY INC
10505 Bennett Pkwy Ste 200 (46077)
PHONE..................302 996-9480
Kris Nonnenmacher, Pr
Melinda Nonnenmacher, Sec
◆ EMP: 3 EST: 1991
SALES (est): 452.97K Privately Held
Web: www.galleyware.com
SIC: 3089 Dishes, plastics, except foam

(G-17010)
GAMEFACE INC
1555 W Oak St Ste 100 (46077-1959)
P.O. Box 342 (46077-0342)
PHONE..................317 363-8855
Stacy Smallwood, Pr
Richard Calkins, VP Sls
▲ EMP: 4 EST: 2007
SQ FT: 1,200
SALES (est): 395.06K Privately Held
SIC: 3949 Sporting and athletic goods, nec

(G-17011)
GCI SLINGERS LLC
5005 W 106th St (46077-9228)
PHONE..................317 873-8686
EMP: 14 EST: 2016
SALES (est): 6.41MM Privately Held
Web: www.gravelconveyors.com
SIC: 1442 Construction sand and gravel

(G-17012)
GENERAL OPTICS LLC
11955 Eaglerun Way (46077-4618)
PHONE..................765 637-5578
Houxun Miao, Pr
EMP: 1 EST: 2017
SALES (est): 83.77K Privately Held
Web: www.geneoptics.com
SIC: 3827 Optical instruments and lenses

(G-17013)
GENIPHYS INC
Also Called: Geniphys

Zionsville - Boone County (G-17014) — GEOGRAPHIC SECTION

10307 Oak Ridge Dr (46077-8313)
PHONE..................................317 973-0523
EMP: 1 EST: 2014
SALES (est): 68.63K **Privately Held**
Web: www.geniphys.com
SIC: 2836 7389 Biological products, except diagnostic; Business services, nec

(G-17014)
GRAVEL CONVEYORS INC (PA)
5005 W 106th St (46077-9228)
PHONE..................................317 873-8686
Michael Pettijohn, *Pr*
Ronald Pettijohn, *Sec*
Joe A Pettijohn, *VP*
EMP: 15 EST: 1989
SALES (est): 4.52MM **Privately Held**
Web: www.gravelconveyors.com
SIC: 3535 4212 3713 3594 Conveyors and conveying equipment; Dump truck haulage; Truck and bus bodies; Fluid power pumps and motors

(G-17015)
GVS FILTER TECHNOLOGY INC
4522 Winterspring Cres (46077-9276)
PHONE..................................317 442-3925
Hugh Chilton, *Prin*
EMP: 2 EST: 2010
SALES (est): 211.3K **Privately Held**
Web: www.gvs.com
SIC: 3569 Filters

(G-17016)
HOPWOOD CELLARS WINERY LLC
12 E Cedar St (46077-1501)
PHONE..................................317 873-4099
Ron Hopwood, *Prin*
EMP: 9 EST: 2012
SQ FT: 1,890
SALES (est): 957.82K **Privately Held**
Web: www.hopwoodcellars.com
SIC: 2084 Wines

(G-17017)
IMEL JOHN
Also Called: U-Haul
4901 W 106th St (46077-8717)
PHONE..................................317 873-8764
John Imel, *Owner*
EMP: 1 EST: 2001
SALES (est): 69.18K **Privately Held**
Web: offline.uhaul.com
SIC: 1389 7519 7513 Haulage, oil field; Trailer rental; Truck rental and leasing, no drivers

(G-17018)
INDY COMPOSITE WORKS INC
4960 Markham Way Apt 532 (46077-7432)
PHONE..................................317 280-9766
Greg Strydesky, *Pr*
EMP: 20 EST: 2004
SALES (est): 893.56K **Privately Held**
Web: www.indycompositeworks.com
SIC: 2824 Organic fibers, noncellulosic

(G-17019)
INDY MEDICAL SUPPLIES LLC
650 S 800 E (46077-9716)
PHONE..................................866 744-9013
Harry Coleman, *Pr*
Bonita Webster, *CEO*
EMP: 5 EST: 2007
SALES (est): 459.2K **Privately Held**
Web: www.indymedicalsupplies.com
SIC: 5047 2836 Medical equipment and supplies; Veterinary biological products

(G-17020)
INDYS PRO GRAPHIX INC
11275 E 300 S (46077-9438)
P.O. Box 175 (46075-0175)
PHONE..................................317 769-3205
Mark A Robinson, *Pr*
EMP: 24 EST: 2001
SALES (est): 581.62K **Privately Held**
Web: www.indysprographix.com
SIC: 3993 Signs and advertising specialties

(G-17021)
INSIGHTFUL APPS LLC ◆
1357 James Ct (46077-1247)
PHONE..................................812 361-1057
EMP: 1 EST: 2023
SALES (est): 74.32K **Privately Held**
SIC: 7372 Prepackaged software

(G-17022)
JENSEN PUBLICATIONS INC
7333 Fox Hollow Rdg (46077-8206)
PHONE..................................317 514-8864
Chris Jensen, *Prin*
EMP: 5 EST: 2011
SALES (est): 222.98K **Privately Held**
SIC: 2741 Miscellaneous publishing

(G-17023)
JERRY L FUELLING
8470 E 300 S (46077-8696)
PHONE..................................317 709-6978
Jerry L Fuelling, *Prin*
EMP: 5 EST: 2014
SALES (est): 222.4K **Privately Held**
SIC: 2869 Fuels

(G-17024)
JEZROC METALWORKS LLC
205 S 1100 E (46077-8505)
PHONE..................................317 417-1132
Matt Quanrud, *Owner*
EMP: 4 EST: 2010
SALES (est): 476.5K **Privately Held**
Web: www.jezrocmetalworks.com
SIC: 3441 Fabricated structural metal

(G-17025)
JOHNSON SAFE COMPANY LLC
8750 E 200 S (46077-8796)
PHONE..................................317 876-7233
Jeffrey D Johnson, *Owner*
EMP: 4 EST: 1940
SQ FT: 3,000
SALES (est): 291.53K **Privately Held**
Web: www.johnsonsafes.net
SIC: 5999 3499 Vaults and safes; Safes and vaults, metal

(G-17026)
JULIAN COFFEE ROASTERS INC
Also Called: Julian Coffee Roasters
10830 Bennett Pkwy Ste N (46077-1188)
PHONE..................................317 247-4208
Ken Julian, *Pr*
EMP: 1 EST: 2004
SALES (est): 254.99K **Privately Held**
Web: www.juliancoffee.com
SIC: 5411 2095 Grocery stores; Coffee roasting (except by wholesale grocers)

(G-17027)
KIDS WORLD PRODUCTIONS INC
11551 Willow Bend Dr (46077-7717)
PHONE..................................317 674-6090
Don M Newman, *Pr*
Stacy Johnson, *VP*
Troy Holder, *Sec*
▲ EMP: 4 EST: 2008
SALES (est): 232.34K **Privately Held**
SIC: 2731 5999 Book publishing; Toiletries, cosmetics, and perfumes

(G-17028)
KING TUT INC
4720 Pebblepointe Pass (46077-8950)
P.O. Box 314 (46077-0314)
PHONE..................................317 938-9907
Amardeep Singh, *Prin*
EMP: 5 EST: 2015
SALES (est): 90.91K **Privately Held**
SIC: 2711 Newspapers

(G-17029)
LAMINIQUE INC
105 Bennington Dr (46077)
PHONE..................................765 482-4222
Keith Hammer, *Pr*
Robert Brown, *VP*
EMP: 10 EST: 1981
SALES (est): 419.77K **Privately Held**
Web: www.laminique.com
SIC: 2519 2541 2434 Fiberglass and plastic furniture; Wood partitions and fixtures; Wood kitchen cabinets

(G-17030)
LLC 2 HOLDINGS LIMITED LLC
Also Called: Ultra Infiltrant
1868 Corniche Dr (46077-8700)
PHONE..................................317 319-9825
EMP: 3 EST: 2005
SALES (est): 243.2K **Privately Held**
Web: www.ultra-infiltrant.com
SIC: 3399 7389 Powder, metal; Business services, nec

(G-17031)
MARTECK INC
10505 Bennett Pkwy Ste 200 (46077-7853)
PHONE..................................800 569-9849
Robert Copeland, *CEO*
EMP: 20 EST: 2001
SALES (est): 4.04MM **Privately Held**
Web: www.marteckinc.com
SIC: 3577 Bar code (magnetic ink) printers

(G-17032)
MGTC INC (DH)
Also Called: Kimber Creek Ltd
11541 Trail Ridge Pl (46077-9726)
PHONE..................................317 873-8697
Thomas J Wilson, *Pr*
Emily S Wilson, *
Robert D Wilson, *
Theresa Mason, *
▲ EMP: 51 EST: 1988
SQ FT: 25,000
SALES (est): 19.05MM **Privately Held**
Web: www.motionwear.com
SIC: 2339 Sportswear, women's
HQ: Fila U.S.A., Inc.
    1 W Pennsylvania Ave
    Towson MD 21204
    410 773-3000

(G-17033)
MID WEST DIGITAL EXPRESS INC
Also Called: Corporate Printing
10815 Deandra Dr (46077-9253)
PHONE..................................317 733-1214
Joseph Matly, *Pr*
EMP: 16 EST: 1991
SQ FT: 8,000
SALES (est): 868.38K **Privately Held**
SIC: 2752 7336 Offset printing; Graphic arts and related design

(G-17034)
MW AIRCRAFT INC
9730 Soaring Hawk Cir (46077-9789)
PHONE..................................317 873-4627
Dennis L Wagner, *Pr*
EMP: 1 EST: 1986
SALES (est): 109.22K **Privately Held**
SIC: 3721 Aircraft

(G-17035)
N K HURST CO INC
10505 Bennett Pkwy Ste 100 (46077-7852)
PHONE..................................317 634-6425
EMP: 32 EST: 1938
SALES (est): 4.33MM **Privately Held**
Web: www.nkhurst.com
SIC: 2034 Dried and dehydrated fruits, vegetables and soup mixes

(G-17036)
NAPTOWN ETCHING INC
7313 Mayflower Park Dr (46077-7903)
PHONE..................................317 733-8776
Tony Hughes, *Owner*
EMP: 7 EST: 2015
SALES (est): 190.43K **Privately Held**
Web: www.naptownetching.com
SIC: 3229 Pressed and blown glass, nec

(G-17037)
NITTO INC
Also Called: Nistem
10505 Bennett Pkwy Ste 300 (46077-7853)
PHONE..................................317 879-2840
Mak Sakuraeda, *Mgr*
EMP: 2
Web: www.nitto.com
SIC: 3053 5085 Gaskets; packing and sealing devices; Gaskets and seals
HQ: Nitto, Inc.
    400 Frank W Burr Blvd # 66
    Teaneck NJ 07666
    732 901-7905

(G-17038)
NPP PACKAGING GRAPHICS
610 White Oak Ct (46077-9049)
PHONE..................................317 522-2010
Dave Norton, *VP*
EMP: 4 EST: 2015
SALES (est): 173.91K **Privately Held**
SIC: 2759 Commercial printing, nec

(G-17039)
P413 CORPORATION (PA)
Also Called: UPS Store 6991
7163 Whitestown Pkwy (46077-7626)
PHONE..................................317 769-0679
Donald Barrett, *Pr*
EMP: 2 EST: 2017
SQ FT: 1,580
SALES (est): 436.56K
SALES (corp-wide): 436.56K **Privately Held**
Web: locations.theupsstore.com
SIC: 7389 2759 Mailbox rental and related service; Commercial printing, nec

(G-17040)
PFM AUTOMOTIVE MANAGEMENT INC
4902 W 106th St (46077-8717)
PHONE..................................317 733-3977
John S Neely, *Pr*
John Neely, *Pr*
EMP: 8 EST: 2017
SALES (est): 817.64K **Privately Held**
Web: www.greatwater360autocare.com

Zionsville - Boone County (G-17065)

SIC: **5013** 7534 7538 Motor vehicle supplies and new parts; Tire retreading and repair shops; General automotive repair shops

(G-17041)
PIENIADZE INC
Also Called: Game Face Brands
1555 W Oak St Ste 100 (46077-1959)
P.O. Box 342 (46077-0342)
PHONE..................888 226-6241
Stacy Smallwood, *Pr*
EMP: 3 **EST:** 2013
SQ FT: 1,200
SALES (est): 241.22K **Privately Held**
SIC: **2844** 3949 Perfumes, cosmetics and other toilet preparations; Arrows, archery

(G-17042)
PIPER FLYERS II INC
230 Woodstock Ct (46077-1060)
PHONE..................317 858-9538
Jason B Greeson, *CEO*
Jason B Greeson, *Pr*
Elizabeth A Greeson, *
EMP: 46 **EST:** 2017
SQ FT: 34,000
SALES (est): 4.64MM **Privately Held**
Web: www.imh.com
SIC: **3599** Custom machinery

(G-17043)
POSTERS 2 PRINTS LLC
9389 Timberwolf Ln (46077-8322)
PHONE..................317 769-3784
Michael Slate, *Prin*
EMP: 2 **EST:** 2009
SALES (est): 85.99K **Privately Held**
SIC: **2752** Commercial printing, lithographic

(G-17044)
PRESS BRAKE SAFETY LLC
1938 S 925 E (46077-9542)
PHONE..................317 413-7593
Jason Boyer, *Prin*
EMP: 5 **EST:** 2016
SALES (est): 197.12K **Privately Held**
Web: www.pressbrakesafety.com
SIC: **3542** Press brakes

(G-17045)
RE WILSON LLC
235 Wakefield Way (46077-1963)
PHONE..................317 730-4846
Robert Wilson, *Prin*
EMP: 5 **EST:** 2010
SALES (est): 112.4K **Privately Held**
SIC: **2711** Commercial printing and newspaper publishing combined

(G-17046)
REMCO PRODUCTS CORPORATION
Also Called: Poly Pro Tools
4735 W 106th St (46077-8761)
PHONE..................317 876-9856
Carsten Pedersen, *Pr*
Mike Garrison, *
Lois R Garrison, *
David L Garrison, *
▲ **EMP:** 58 **EST:** 1985
SQ FT: 27,000
SALES (est): 8.84MM **Privately Held**
Web: www.remcoproducts.com
SIC: **3089** Plastics containers, except foam

(G-17047)
ROBERT COPELAND
Also Called: Marteck of California
10505 Bennett Pkwy Ste 200 (46077-7852)
PHONE..................951 245-0041
Robert Copeland, *Owner*
EMP: 5 **EST:** 2018
SALES (est): 212.51K **Privately Held**
SIC: **2759** Labels and seals: printing, nsk

(G-17048)
ROLLS-ROYCE CORPORATION
11747 Shadowwood Ct (46077-7807)
PHONE..................317 230-2736
EMP: 25
SALES (corp-wide): 20.55B **Privately Held**
Web: www.rolls-roycemotorcars.com
SIC: **3724** Aircraft engines and engine parts
HQ: Rolls-Royce Corporation
450 S Meridian St
Indianapolis IN 46225

(G-17049)
SHARP WRAPS LLC
2114 Williams Glen Blvd (46077-1180)
PHONE..................317 989-8447
EMP: 4 **EST:** 2016
SALES (est): 133.56K **Privately Held**
SIC: **3713** Specialty motor vehicle bodies

(G-17050)
SHELBURNE ENGRAVING
8888 W 96th St (46077-8701)
PHONE..................317 873-6257
Brian Shelburne, *Owner*
EMP: 1 **EST:** 1992
SALES (est): 41.6K **Privately Held**
SIC: **2499** Engraved wood products

(G-17051)
SOMER INC
Also Called: Somer Dental Laboratories
11707 N Michigan Rd (46077-9325)
P.O. Box 250 (46077-0250)
PHONE..................317 873-1111
Larry Sowinski, *Pr*
Keith Spencer, *Sec*
EMP: 32 **EST:** 1982
SQ FT: 14,700
SALES (est): 2.32MM **Privately Held**
Web: www.somer.com
SIC: **8072** 8021 3843 3842 Crown and bridge production; Offices and clinics of dentists; Dental equipment and supplies; Surgical appliances and supplies

(G-17052)
SPORTSMANIA SALES INC
260 S First St Ste 4 (46077-1602)
PHONE..................317 873-5501
Bob Rogers, *Pr*
Sandra Rogers, *Sec*
EMP: 4 **EST:** 1986
SQ FT: 1,400
SALES (est): 253.27K **Privately Held**
Web: www.insurancesettlements.com
SIC: **2395** 5699 Emblems, embroidered; T-shirts, custom printed

(G-17053)
STEALTH ENERGY GROUP LLC
6807 Wellington Cir (46077-8035)
PHONE..................316 260-0064
EMP: 6 **EST:** 2016
SALES (est): 261.6K **Privately Held**
Web: www.stealthenergygroup.com
SIC: **1389** Oil field services, nec

(G-17054)
STENIDY INDUSTRIES INC
10305 Cottonwood Ct (46077-8388)
PHONE..................317 873-5343
Stephen L Kessel, *Pr*
Elaine Kessel, *Sec*
Stephen Kessel, *Prin*
EMP: 2 **EST:** 1997
SQ FT: 1,500
SALES (est): 243.96K **Privately Held**
Web: www.stenidy.com
SIC: **2821** Molding compounds, plastics

(G-17055)
SUPERIOR PLASTICS LLC
9502 E 100 S (46077-9840)
PHONE..................317 698-6422
Cathy Espey, *Pr*
Cathy Espey, *Pr*
EMP: 2 **EST:** 2011
SQ FT: 10,000
SALES (est): 200.12K **Privately Held**
SIC: **3089** Injection molding of plastics

(G-17056)
TEN POINT TRIM CORP
4750 Nw Plaza West Dr (46077-9181)
PHONE..................317 875-5424
Thomas J Sampsell, *Pr*
Shelly S Williams, *
Thomas L Mcnulty, *VP*
EMP: 40 **EST:** 1949
SQ FT: 70,000
SALES (est): 7.66MM **Privately Held**
Web: www.tenpointtrim.com
SIC: **3444** 3449 3316 Forming machine work, sheet metal; Miscellaneous metalwork ; Cold finishing of steel shapes

(G-17057)
TINTS & PRINTS BY TIERNEY LLC
4211 Honeysuckle Ln (46077-8536)
PHONE..................317 769-5895
Tierney Williams, *Owner*
EMP: 2 **EST:** 2011
SALES (est): 73.78K **Privately Held**
SIC: **2752** Commercial printing, lithographic

(G-17058)
TISSUE SOURCE LLC
7163 Whitestown Pkwy Box 221 (46077-7626)
PHONE..................765 746-6679
EMP: 3 **EST:** 2007
SALES (est): 1.1MM **Privately Held**
Web: www.tissue-source.com
SIC: **2836** Biological products, except diagnostic

(G-17059)
UHS USA INC
10715 Andrade Dr (46077)
PHONE..................833 459-9403
Lee Markham, *Pr*
Michael Bowyer, *VP*
EMP: 2 **EST:** 2017
SALES (est): 89.05K **Privately Held**
SIC: **2522** Office desks and tables, except wood

(G-17060)
VILLAGE CUSTOM EMBROIDERY INC
80 N First St (46077-1544)
PHONE..................317 733-3110
Karen P Maier, *Pr*
EMP: 3 **EST:** 2003
SALES (est): 230.49K **Privately Held**
Web: www.villagecustomembroidery.com
SIC: **2395** Embroidery and art needlework

(G-17061)
VIVA TIA MARIA LLC
Also Called: Viva Tia Maria
4738 Northwestern Dr (46077-9225)
PHONE..................317 509-2650
Adam Gonzalez, *Managing Member*
EMP: 25 **EST:** 2020
SALES (est): 2.5MM **Privately Held**
Web: www.vivatiamaria.com
SIC: **2032** 2099 2656 Spanish foods: packaged in cans, jars, etc.; Sauce, gravy, dressing, and dip mixes; Frozen food and ice cream containers

(G-17062)
WOODGRAIN CONSTRUCTION INC
3380 S 875 E (46077-9527)
PHONE..................317 873-5608
Tom Harvard, *Pr*
Scott Staser, *VP*
EMP: 8 **EST:** 1992
SALES (est): 811K **Privately Held**
Web: www.woodgrain.com
SIC: **2431** Millwork

(G-17063)
ZIONSVILLE CUSTOM CABINETS LLC
10830 Bennett Pkwy Ste E (46077-1188)
PHONE..................317 339-0380
EMP: 5 **EST:** 2017
SALES (est): 237.63K **Privately Held**
Web: www.zionsvillecustomcabinets.com
SIC: **2434** Wood kitchen cabinets

(G-17064)
ZIONSVILLE TOWING INC
4901 W 106th St (46077-8717)
PHONE..................317 873-4550
John Imel, *Pr*
Steve Imel, *Pr*
EMP: 5 **EST:** 1963
SQ FT: 5,000
SALES (est): 391.48K **Privately Held**
Web: www.zionsville-in.gov
SIC: **7699** 7549 5261 7692 Lawn mower repair shop; Towing service, automotive; Retail nurseries and garden stores; Welding repair

(G-17065)
ZOGMAN ENTERPRISES INC
Also Called: Good Impressions Printing
170 W Hawthorne St (46077-1617)
PHONE..................317 873-6809
Charles Herzog, *Pr*
Dennis Disman, *VP*
EMP: 3 **EST:** 2015
SALES (est): 309.79K **Privately Held**
Web: www.zionsvilleprintingpros.com
SIC: **2752** Offset printing

SIC INDEX

Standard Industrial Classification Alphabetical Index

SIC NO PRODUCT

A

3291 Abrasive products
8721 Accounting, auditing, and bookkeeping
2891 Adhesives and sealants
7322 Adjustment and collection services
7311 Advertising agencies
7319 Advertising, nec
2879 Agricultural chemicals, nec
3563 Air and gas compressors
3721 Aircraft
3724 Aircraft engines and engine parts
3728 Aircraft parts and equipment, nec
4581 Airports, flying fields, and services
2812 Alkalies and chlorine
3363 Aluminum die-castings
3354 Aluminum extruded products
3365 Aluminum foundries
3355 Aluminum rolling and drawing, nec
3353 Aluminum sheet, plate, and foil
3483 Ammunition, except for small arms, nec
7999 Amusement and recreation, nec
3826 Analytical instruments
2077 Animal and marine fats and oils
0279 Animal specialties, nec
0752 Animal specialty services
2389 Apparel and accessories, nec
3446 Architectural metalwork
8712 Architectural services
7694 Armature rewinding shops
3292 Asbestos products
2952 Asphalt felts and coatings
2951 Asphalt paving mixtures and blocks
5531 Auto and home supply stores
7533 Auto exhaust system repair shops
3581 Automatic vending machines
5012 Automobiles and other motor vehicles
2396 Automotive and apparel trimmings
5599 Automotive dealers, nec
7536 Automotive glass replacement shops
7539 Automotive repair shops, nec
7549 Automotive services, nec
3465 Automotive stampings
7537 Automotive transmission repair shops

B

2673 Bags: plastic, laminated, and coated
2674 Bags: uncoated paper and multiwall
3562 Ball and roller bearings
7241 Barber shops
7231 Beauty shops
0211 Beef cattle feedlots
0212 Beef cattle, except feedlots
5181 Beer and ale
0171 Berry crops
2836 Biological products, except diagnostic
1221 Bituminous coal and lignite-surface mining
1222 Bituminous coal-underground mining
2782 Blankbooks and looseleaf binders
3312 Blast furnaces and steel mills
3564 Blowers and fans
5551 Boat dealers
3732 Boatbuilding and repairing
3452 Bolts, nuts, rivets, and washers
2732 Book printing
2731 Book publishing
5942 Book stores
2789 Bookbinding and related work
5192 Books, periodicals, and newspapers
2086 Bottled and canned soft drinks
2051 Bread, cake, and related products
3251 Brick and structural clay tile
5032 Brick, stone, and related material
1622 Bridge, tunnel, and elevated highway
2211 Broadwoven fabric mills, cotton
2221 Broadwoven fabric mills, manmade
2231 Broadwoven fabric mills, wool

3991 Brooms and brushes
7349 Building maintenance services, nec
3995 Burial caskets
8611 Business associations
8748 Business consulting, nec
7389 Business services, nec

C

4841 Cable and other pay television services
3578 Calculating and accounting equipment
5946 Camera and photographic supply stores
2064 Candy and other confectionery products
5441 Candy, nut, and confectionery stores
2091 Canned and cured fish and seafoods
2033 Canned fruits and specialties
2032 Canned specialties
2394 Canvas and related products
3624 Carbon and graphite products
2895 Carbon black
3955 Carbon paper and inked ribbons
3592 Carburetors, pistons, rings, valves
1751 Carpentry work
7217 Carpet and upholstery cleaning
2273 Carpets and rugs
7542 Carwashes
0119 Cash grains, nec
5961 Catalog and mail-order houses
2823 Cellulosic manmade fibers
3241 Cement, hydraulic
6553 Cemetery subdividers and developers
3253 Ceramic wall and floor tile
2043 Cereal breakfast foods
2022 Cheese; natural and processed
1479 Chemical and fertilizer mining
2899 Chemical preparations, nec
5169 Chemicals and allied products, nec
2131 Chewing and smoking tobacco
0252 Chicken eggs
5641 Children's and infants' wear stores
2066 Chocolate and cocoa products
2111 Cigarettes
8641 Civic and social associations
1459 Clay and related minerals, nec
3255 Clay refractories
5052 Coal and other minerals and ores
1241 Coal mining services
2295 Coated fabrics, not rubberized
7993 Coin-operated amusement devices
7215 Coin-operated laundries and cleaning
3316 Cold finishing of steel shapes
8221 Colleges and universities
7336 Commercial art and graphic design
5046 Commercial equipment, nec
3582 Commercial laundry equipment
3646 Commercial lighting fixtures
8732 Commercial nonphysical research
7335 Commercial photography
8731 Commercial physical research
2754 Commercial printing, gravure
2752 Commercial printing, lithographic
2759 Commercial printing, nec
6221 Commodity contracts brokers, dealers
4899 Communication services, nec
3669 Communications equipment, nec
5734 Computer and software stores
7376 Computer facilities management
7373 Computer integrated systems design
7378 Computer maintenance and repair
3577 Computer peripheral equipment, nec
7379 Computer related services, nec
3572 Computer storage devices
3575 Computer terminals
5045 Computers, peripherals, and software
3271 Concrete block and brick
3272 Concrete products, nec
1771 Concrete work

5145 Confectionery
5082 Construction and mining machinery
3531 Construction machinery
5039 Construction materials, nec
1442 Construction sand and gravel
2679 Converted paper products, nec
3535 Conveyors and conveying equipment
2052 Cookies and crackers
3366 Copper foundries
3351 Copper rolling and drawing
2298 Cordage and twine
0115 Corn
2653 Corrugated and solid fiber boxes
3961 Costume jewelry
2074 Cottonseed oil mills
4215 Courier services, except by air
2021 Creamery butter
0721 Crop planting and protection
0723 Crop preparation services for market
3466 Crowns and closures
1311 Crude petroleum and natural gas
1422 Crushed and broken limestone
1429 Crushed and broken stone, nec
3643 Current-carrying wiring devices
2391 Curtains and draperies
3087 Custom compound purchased resins
7371 Custom computer programming services
3281 Cut stone and stone products
3421 Cutlery
2865 Cyclic crudes and intermediates

D

0241 Dairy farms
5451 Dairy products stores
5143 Dairy products, except dried or canned
7911 Dance studios, schools, and halls
7374 Data processing and preparation
8243 Data processing schools
0175 Deciduous tree fruits
2034 Dehydrated fruits, vegetables, soups
3843 Dental equipment and supplies
8072 Dental laboratories
7381 Detective and armored car services
2835 Diagnostic substances
2675 Die-cut paper and board
1411 Dimension stone
7331 Direct mail advertising services
5963 Direct selling establishments
7342 Disinfecting and pest control services
2085 Distilled and blended liquors
2047 Dog and cat food
3942 Dolls and stuffed toys
5714 Drapery and upholstery stores
2591 Drapery hardware and blinds and shades
1381 Drilling oil and gas wells
5813 Drinking places
5912 Drug stores and proprietary stores
5122 Drugs, proprietaries, and sundries
2023 Dry, condensed, evaporated products
7216 Drycleaning plants, except rugs
5099 Durable goods, nec
6514 Dwelling operators, except apartments

E

5812 Eating places
2079 Edible fats and oils
4931 Electric and other services combined
3634 Electric housewares and fans
3641 Electric lamps
4911 Electric services
5063 Electrical apparatus and equipment
5064 Electrical appliances, television and radio
3699 Electrical equipment and supplies, nec
3629 Electrical industrial apparatus
7629 Electrical repair shops
1731 Electrical work

SIC INDEX

SIC NO	PRODUCT
3845	Electromedical equipment
3671	Electron tubes
3675	Electronic capacitors
3677	Electronic coils and transformers
3679	Electronic components, nec
3571	Electronic computers
3678	Electronic connectors
5065	Electronic parts and equipment, nec
3676	Electronic resistors
8211	Elementary and secondary schools
3534	Elevators and moving stairways
7361	Employment agencies
3694	Engine electrical equipment
8711	Engineering services
7929	Entertainers and entertainment groups
2677	Envelopes
3822	Environmental controls
7359	Equipment rental and leasing, nec
1794	Excavation work
2892	Explosives

F

SIC NO	PRODUCT
2381	Fabric dress and work gloves
3499	Fabricated metal products, nec
3498	Fabricated pipe and fittings
3443	Fabricated plate work (boiler shop)
3069	Fabricated rubber products, nec
3441	Fabricated structural metal
2399	Fabricated textile products, nec
8744	Facilities support services
5651	Family clothing stores
5083	Farm and garden machinery
0761	Farm labor contractors
3523	Farm machinery and equipment
0762	Farm management services
4221	Farm product warehousing and storage
5191	Farm supplies
5159	Farm-product raw materials, nec
3965	Fasteners, buttons, needles, and pins
2875	Fertilizers, mixing only
2655	Fiber cans, drums, and similar products
0139	Field crops, except cash grain
2261	Finishing plants, cotton
2262	Finishing plants, manmade
2269	Finishing plants, nec
9224	Fire protection
5146	Fish and seafoods
3211	Flat glass
2087	Flavoring extracts and syrups, nec
5713	Floor covering stores
1752	Floor laying and floor work, nec
5992	Florists
2041	Flour and other grain mill products
5193	Flowers and florists supplies
3824	Fluid meters and counting devices
2026	Fluid milk
3593	Fluid power cylinders and actuators
3594	Fluid power pumps and motors
3492	Fluid power valves and hose fittings
2657	Folding paperboard boxes
0182	Food crops grown under cover
2099	Food preparations, nec
3556	Food products machinery
5139	Footwear
3131	Footwear cut stock
3149	Footwear, except rubber, nec
0851	Forestry services
4731	Freight transportation arrangement
5148	Fresh fruits and vegetables
2092	Fresh or frozen packaged fish
2053	Frozen bakery products, except bread
2037	Frozen fruits and vegetables
2038	Frozen specialties, nec
5989	Fuel dealers, nec
5983	Fuel oil dealers
6099	Functions related to depository banking
7261	Funeral service and crematories
5021	Furniture
2599	Furniture and fixtures, nec
5712	Furniture stores

G

SIC NO	PRODUCT
3944	Games, toys, and children's vehicles
4925	Gas production and/or distribution
3053	Gaskets; packing and sealing devices
5541	Gasoline service stations
7538	General automotive repair shops
0291	General farms, primarily animals
0191	General farms, primarily crop
3569	General industrial machinery,
4225	General warehousing and storage
5947	Gift, novelty, and souvenir shop
2361	Girl's and children's dresses, blouses
2369	Girl's and children's outerwear, nec
1793	Glass and glazing work
3221	Glass containers
5153	Grain and field beans
3321	Gray and ductile iron foundries
2771	Greeting cards
5149	Groceries and related products, nec
5141	Groceries, general line
5411	Grocery stores
3761	Guided missiles and space vehicles
2861	Gum and wood chemicals
3275	Gypsum products

H

SIC NO	PRODUCT
3423	Hand and edge tools, nec
3996	Hard surface floor coverings, nec
5072	Hardware
5251	Hardware stores
3429	Hardware, nec
2426	Hardwood dimension and flooring mills
2435	Hardwood veneer and plywood
2353	Hats, caps, and millinery
8099	Health and allied services, nec
3433	Heating equipment, except electric
7353	Heavy construction equipment rental
1629	Heavy construction, nec
7363	Help supply services
1611	Highway and street construction
5945	Hobby, toy, and game shops
0213	Hogs
3536	Hoists, cranes, and monorails
6719	Holding companies, nec
8082	Home health care services
5023	Homefurnishings
2252	Hosiery, nec
7011	Hotels and motels
3142	House slippers
5722	Household appliance stores
3639	Household appliances, nec
3651	Household audio and video equipment
3631	Household cooking equipment
2392	Household furnishings, nec
2519	Household furniture, nec
3633	Household laundry equipment
3632	Household refrigerators and freezers
3635	Household vacuum cleaners

I

SIC NO	PRODUCT
2024	Ice cream and frozen deserts
8322	Individual and family services
5113	Industrial and personal service paper
1541	Industrial buildings and warehouses
3567	Industrial furnaces and ovens
2813	Industrial gases
2819	Industrial inorganic chemicals, nec
7218	Industrial launderers
5084	Industrial machinery and equipment
3599	Industrial machinery, nec
2869	Industrial organic chemicals, nec
3543	Industrial patterns
1446	Industrial sand
5085	Industrial supplies
3537	Industrial trucks and tractors
3491	Industrial valves
7375	Information retrieval services
2816	Inorganic pigments
4785	Inspection and fixed facilities
1796	Installing building equipment
3825	Instruments to measure electricity
6411	Insurance agents, brokers, and service
6399	Insurance carriers, nec
4131	Intercity and rural bus transportation
3519	Internal combustion engines, nec
6282	Investment advice
6726	Investment offices, nec
6799	Investors, nec
3462	Iron and steel forgings
1011	Iron ores

J

SIC NO	PRODUCT
3915	Jewelers' materials and lapidary work
5094	Jewelry and precious stones
5944	Jewelry stores
3911	Jewelry, precious metal
8331	Job training and related services

K

SIC NO	PRODUCT
1455	Kaolin and ball clay
2253	Knit outerwear mills
2254	Knit underwear mills

L

SIC NO	PRODUCT
8631	Labor organizations
3821	Laboratory apparatus and furniture
3083	Laminated plastics plate and sheet
0781	Landscape counseling and planning
7219	Laundry and garment services, nec
3524	Lawn and garden equipment
0782	Lawn and garden services
3952	Lead pencils and art goods
2386	Leather and sheep-lined clothing
3151	Leather gloves and mittens
3199	Leather goods, nec
3111	Leather tanning and finishing
8111	Legal services
9121	Legislative bodies
8231	Libraries
3648	Lighting equipment, nec
3274	Lime
7213	Linen supply
5984	Liquefied petroleum gas dealers
5921	Liquor stores
5154	Livestock
0751	Livestock services, except veterinary
6163	Loan brokers
4214	Local trucking with storage
4212	Local trucking, without storage
2411	Logging
2992	Lubricating oils and greases
3161	Luggage
5211	Lumber and other building materials
5031	Lumber, plywood, and millwork

M

SIC NO	PRODUCT
2098	Macaroni and spaghetti
3545	Machine tool accessories
3541	Machine tools, metal cutting type
3542	Machine tools, metal forming type
3695	Magnetic and optical recording media
3322	Malleable iron foundries
2083	Malt
2082	Malt beverages
8742	Management consulting services
6722	Management investment, open-ended
8741	Management services
2761	Manifold business forms
2097	Manufactured ice
3999	Manufacturing industries, nec
4493	Marinas
4491	Marine cargo handling
3953	Marking devices
1741	Masonry and other stonework
2515	Mattresses and bedsprings
3829	Measuring and controlling devices, nec
3586	Measuring and dispensing pumps
5421	Meat and fish markets
2011	Meat packing plants
5147	Meats and meat products
3061	Mechanical rubber goods
5047	Medical and hospital equipment
7352	Medical equipment rental
8071	Medical laboratories
2833	Medicinals and botanicals

2024 Harris Indiana Industrial Directory

SIC INDEX

SIC NO	PRODUCT
8699	Membership organizations, nec
7997	Membership sports and recreation clubs
5136	Men's and boy's clothing
2329	Men's and boy's clothing, nec
2321	Men's and boy's furnishings
2323	Men's and boy's neckwear
2311	Men's and boy's suits and coats
2325	Men's and boy's trousers and slacks
2322	Men's and boy's underwear and nightwear
2326	Men's and boy's work clothing
5611	Men's and boys' clothing stores
3143	Men's footwear, except athletic
5962	Merchandising machine operators
3412	Metal barrels, drums, and pails
3411	Metal cans
3479	Metal coating and allied services
3442	Metal doors, sash, and trim
3497	Metal foil and leaf
3398	Metal heat treating
2514	Metal household furniture
1081	Metal mining services
1099	Metal ores, nec
3431	Metal sanitary ware
3469	Metal stampings, nec
5051	Metals service centers and offices
3549	Metalworking machinery, nec
2431	Millwork
3296	Mineral wool
3295	Minerals, ground or treated
3532	Mining machinery
5699	Miscellaneous apparel and accessories
3496	Miscellaneous fabricated wire products
5499	Miscellaneous food stores
5399	Miscellaneous general merchandise
5719	Miscellaneous homefurnishings
0919	Miscellaneous marine products
3449	Miscellaneous metalwork
1499	Miscellaneous nonmetallic mining
7299	Miscellaneous personal services
2741	Miscellaneous publishing
5999	Miscellaneous retail stores, nec
5271	Mobile home dealers
6515	Mobile home site operators
2451	Mobile homes
7822	Motion picture and tape distribution
7812	Motion picture and video production
3716	Motor homes
3714	Motor vehicle parts and accessories
5015	Motor vehicle parts, used
5013	Motor vehicle supplies and new parts
3711	Motor vehicles and car bodies
5571	Motorcycle dealers
3751	Motorcycles, bicycles, and parts
3621	Motors and generators
8412	Museums and art galleries
5736	Musical instrument stores
3931	Musical instruments

N

SIC NO	PRODUCT
2441	Nailed wood boxes and shook
2241	Narrow fabric mills
9711	National security
4924	Natural gas distribution
1321	Natural gas liquids
4922	Natural gas transmission
5511	New and used car dealers
2711	Newspapers
2873	Nitrogenous fertilizers
3297	Nonclay refractories
8733	Noncommercial research organizations
3644	Noncurrent-carrying wiring devices
5199	Nondurable goods, nec
3364	Nonferrous die-castings except aluminum
3463	Nonferrous forgings
3369	Nonferrous foundries, nec
3356	Nonferrous rolling and drawing, nec
3357	Nonferrous wiredrawing and insulating
3299	Nonmetallic mineral products,
1481	Nonmetallic mineral services
6512	Nonresidential building operators
1542	Nonresidential construction, nec
2297	Nonwoven fabrics

O

SIC NO	PRODUCT
5044	Office equipment
2522	Office furniture, except wood
3579	Office machines, nec
8021	Offices and clinics of dentists
8011	Offices and clinics of medical doctors
8042	Offices and clinics of optometrists
8049	Offices of health practitioner
1382	Oil and gas exploration services
3533	Oil and gas field machinery
1389	Oil and gas field services, nec
3851	Ophthalmic goods
5048	Ophthalmic goods
5995	Optical goods stores
3827	Optical instruments and lenses
3489	Ordnance and accessories, nec
2824	Organic fibers, noncellulosic
0181	Ornamental nursery products
0783	Ornamental shrub and tree services
7312	Outdoor advertising services

P

SIC NO	PRODUCT
5142	Packaged frozen goods
3565	Packaging machinery
4783	Packing and crating
5231	Paint, glass, and wallpaper stores
1721	Painting and paper hanging
2851	Paints and allied products
5198	Paints, varnishes, and supplies
3554	Paper industries machinery
2621	Paper mills
2671	Paper; coated and laminated packaging
2672	Paper; coated and laminated, nec
2631	Paperboard mills
2542	Partitions and fixtures, except wood
7515	Passenger car leasing
7514	Passenger car rental
6794	Patent owners and lessors
3951	Pens and mechanical pencils
2721	Periodicals
6141	Personal credit institutions
3172	Personal leather goods, nec
2999	Petroleum and coal products, nec
5171	Petroleum bulk stations and terminals
5172	Petroleum products, nec
2911	Petroleum refining
2834	Pharmaceutical preparations
2874	Phosphatic fertilizers
7334	Photocopying and duplicating services
7384	Photofinish laboratories
3861	Photographic equipment and supplies
5043	Photographic equipment and supplies
7221	Photographic studios, portrait
7991	Physical fitness facilities
2035	Pickles, sauces, and salad dressings
5131	Piece goods and notions
1742	Plastering, drywall, and insulation
3085	Plastics bottles
3086	Plastics foam products
5162	Plastics materials and basic shapes
2821	Plastics materials and resins
3084	Plastics pipe
3088	Plastics plumbing fixtures
3089	Plastics products, nec
2796	Platemaking services
3471	Plating and polishing
2395	Pleating and stitching
5074	Plumbing and hydronic heating supplies
3432	Plumbing fixture fittings and trim
1711	Plumbing, heating, air-conditioning
2842	Polishes and sanitation goods
3264	Porcelain electrical supplies
2096	Potato chips and similar snacks
3269	Pottery products, nec
0259	Poultry and eggs, nec
5144	Poultry and poultry products
0254	Poultry hatcheries
2015	Poultry slaughtering and processing
3568	Power transmission equipment, nec
3546	Power-driven handtools
3448	Prefabricated metal buildings
2452	Prefabricated wood buildings
7372	Prepackaged software
2048	Prepared feeds, nec
2045	Prepared flour mixes and doughs
3652	Prerecorded records and tapes
3229	Pressed and blown glass, nec
3334	Primary aluminum
3692	Primary batteries, dry and wet
3331	Primary copper
3399	Primary metal products
3339	Primary nonferrous metals, nec
3672	Printed circuit boards
5111	Printing and writing paper
2893	Printing ink
3555	Printing trades machinery
3823	Process control instruments
3231	Products of purchased glass
5049	Professional equipment, nec
8621	Professional organizations
2531	Public building and related furniture
7992	Public golf courses
8743	Public relations services
2611	Pulp mills
3561	Pumps and pumping equipment

R

SIC NO	PRODUCT
7948	Racing, including track operation
3663	Radio and t.v. communications equipment
4832	Radio broadcasting stations
5731	Radio, television, and electronic stores
7313	Radio, television, publisher representatives
4812	Radiotelephone communication
3743	Railroad equipment
4011	Railroads, line-haul operating
3273	Ready-mixed concrete
6531	Real estate agents and managers
6519	Real property lessors, nec
2493	Reconstituted wood products
5735	Record and prerecorded tape stores
5561	Recreational vehicle dealers
4222	Refrigerated warehousing and storage
3585	Refrigeration and heating equipment
5078	Refrigeration equipment and supplies
7623	Refrigeration service and repair
4953	Refuse systems
3625	Relays and industrial controls
8661	Religious organizations
4741	Rental of railroad cars
7699	Repair services, nec
8361	Residential care
1522	Residential construction, nec
3645	Residential lighting fixtures
5461	Retail bakeries
5261	Retail nurseries and garden stores
7641	Reupholstery and furniture repair
2095	Roasted coffee
2384	Robes and dressing gowns
3547	Rolling mill machinery
5033	Roofing, siding, and insulation
1761	Roofing, siding, and sheetmetal work
3021	Rubber and plastics footwear
3052	Rubber and plastics hose and beltings

S

SIC NO	PRODUCT
2068	Salted and roasted nuts and seeds
2656	Sanitary food containers
2676	Sanitary paper products
4959	Sanitary services, nec
2013	Sausages and other prepared meats
3425	Saw blades and handsaws
2421	Sawmills and planing mills, general
3596	Scales and balances, except laboratory
2397	Schiffli machine embroideries
4151	School buses
8299	Schools and educational services
5093	Scrap and waste materials
3451	Screw machine products
3812	Search and navigation equipment
3341	Secondary nonferrous metals
7338	Secretarial and court reporting
6231	Security and commodity exchanges
6211	Security brokers and dealers
7382	Security systems services

SIC INDEX

SIC NO	PRODUCT
3674	Semiconductors and related devices
5087	Service establishment equipment
3589	Service industry machinery, nec
7819	Services allied to motion pictures
8999	Services, nec
2652	Setup paperboard boxes
5949	Sewing, needlework, and piece goods
3444	Sheet metalwork
3731	Shipbuilding and repairing
5661	Shoe stores
6153	Short-term business credit
3993	Signs and advertising specialties
3914	Silverware and plated ware
1521	Single-family housing construction
3484	Small arms
3482	Small arms ammunition
2841	Soap and other detergents
2436	Softwood veneer and plywood
0711	Soil preparation services
2075	Soybean oil mills
0116	Soybeans
3764	Space propulsion units and parts
3769	Space vehicle equipment, nec
3544	Special dies, tools, jigs, and fixtures
3559	Special industry machinery, nec
2429	Special product sawmills, nec
1799	Special trade contractors, nec
4226	Special warehousing and storage, nec
3566	Speed changers, drives, and gears
3949	Sporting and athletic goods, nec
5091	Sporting and recreation goods
7032	Sporting and recreational camps
5941	Sporting goods and bicycle shops
7941	Sports clubs, managers, and promoters
5112	Stationery and office supplies
2678	Stationery products
5943	Stationery stores
4961	Steam and air-conditioning supply
3325	Steel foundries, nec
3324	Steel investment foundries
3317	Steel pipe and tubes
3493	Steel springs, except wire
3315	Steel wire and related products
3691	Storage batteries
3259	Structural clay products, nec
1791	Structural steel erection
2439	Structural wood members, nec
6552	Subdividers and developers, nec
2843	Surface active agents
3841	Surgical and medical instruments
3842	Surgical appliances and supplies
8713	Surveying services
3613	Switchgear and switchboard apparatus
2822	Synthetic rubber

T

SIC NO	PRODUCT
3795	Tanks and tank components
7291	Tax return preparation services
4822	Telegraph and other communications
3661	Telephone and telegraph apparatus
4813	Telephone communication, except radio
4833	Television broadcasting stations
1743	Terrazzo, tile, marble, mosaic work
8734	Testing laboratories
2393	Textile bags
2299	Textile goods, nec
3552	Textile machinery
7922	Theatrical producers and services
2284	Thread mills
2282	Throwing and winding mills
0811	Timber tracts
2296	Tire cord and fabrics
7534	Tire retreading and repair shops
3011	Tires and inner tubes
5014	Tires and tubes
5194	Tobacco and tobacco products
5993	Tobacco stores and stands
2844	Toilet preparations
7532	Top and body repair and paint shops
4492	Towing and tugboat service
5092	Toys and hobby goods and supplies
3612	Transformers, except electric
5088	Transportation equipment and supplies
3799	Transportation equipment, nec
4789	Transportation services, nec
4724	Travel agencies
3792	Travel trailers and campers
3713	Truck and bus bodies
7513	Truck rental and leasing, without drivers
3715	Truck trailers
4231	Trucking terminal facilities
4213	Trucking, except local
6732	Trusts: educational, religious, etc.
3511	Turbines and turbine generator sets
2791	Typesetting

U

SIC NO	PRODUCT
3081	Unsupported plastics film and sheet
3082	Unsupported plastics profile shapes
2512	Upholstered household furniture
9532	Urban and community development
5521	Used car dealers
5932	Used merchandise stores
7519	Utility trailer rental

V

SIC NO	PRODUCT
3494	Valves and pipe fittings, nec
5331	Variety stores
2076	Vegetable oil mills, nec
0161	Vegetables and melons
3647	Vehicular lighting equipment
0742	Veterinary services, specialties
7841	Video tape rental
3261	Vitreous plumbing fixtures
8249	Vocational schools, nec

W

SIC NO	PRODUCT
5075	Warm air heating and air conditioning
7631	Watch, clock, and jewelry repair
3873	Watches, clocks, watchcases, and parts
4449	Water transportation of freight
1781	Water well drilling
1623	Water, sewer, and utility lines
2385	Waterproof outerwear
3548	Welding apparatus
7692	Welding repair
2046	Wet corn milling
0111	Wheat
5182	Wine and distilled beverages
2084	Wines, brandy, and brandy spirits
3495	Wire springs
5632	Women's accessory and specialty stores
5137	Women's and children's clothing
2341	Women's and children's underwear
2331	Women's and misses' blouses and shirts
2339	Women's and misses' outerwear, nec
2337	Women's and misses' suits and coats
5621	Women's clothing stores
3144	Women's footwear, except athletic
3171	Women's handbags and purses
2335	Women's, junior's, and misses' dresses
2449	Wood containers, nec
2511	Wood household furniture
2434	Wood kitchen cabinets
2521	Wood office furniture
2448	Wood pallets and skids
2541	Wood partitions and fixtures
2491	Wood preserving
2499	Wood products, nec
2517	Wood television and radio cabinets
3553	Woodworking machinery
1795	Wrecking and demolition work

X

SIC NO	PRODUCT
3844	X-ray apparatus and tubes

Y

SIC NO	PRODUCT
2281	Yarn spinning mills

SIC INDEX

Standard Industrial Classification Numerical Index

SIC NO	PRODUCT

01 agricultural production - crops
0111 Wheat
0115 Corn
0116 Soybeans
0119 Cash grains, nec
0139 Field crops, except cash grain
0161 Vegetables and melons
0171 Berry crops
0175 Deciduous tree fruits
0181 Ornamental nursery products
0182 Food crops grown under cover
0191 General farms, primarily crop

02 agricultural production - livestock and animal specialties
0211 Beef cattle feedlots
0212 Beef cattle, except feedlots
0213 Hogs
0241 Dairy farms
0252 Chicken eggs
0254 Poultry hatcheries
0259 Poultry and eggs, nec
0279 Animal specialties, nec
0291 General farms, primarily animals

07 agricultural services
0711 Soil preparation services
0721 Crop planting and protection
0723 Crop preparation services for market
0742 Veterinary services, specialties
0751 Livestock services, except veterinary
0752 Animal specialty services
0761 Farm labor contractors
0762 Farm management services
0781 Landscape counseling and planning
0782 Lawn and garden services
0783 Ornamental shrub and tree services

08 forestry
0811 Timber tracts
0851 Forestry services

09 fishing, hunting and trapping
0919 Miscellaneous marine products

10 metal mining
1011 Iron ores
1081 Metal mining services
1099 Metal ores, nec

12 coal mining
1221 Bituminous coal and lignite-surface mining
1222 Bituminous coal-underground mining
1241 Coal mining services

13 oil and gas extraction
1311 Crude petroleum and natural gas
1321 Natural gas liquids
1381 Drilling oil and gas wells
1382 Oil and gas exploration services
1389 Oil and gas field services, nec

14 mining and quarrying of nonmetallic minerals, except fuels
1411 Dimension stone
1422 Crushed and broken limestone
1429 Crushed and broken stone, nec
1442 Construction sand and gravel
1446 Industrial sand
1455 Kaolin and ball clay
1459 Clay and related minerals, nec
1479 Chemical and fertilizer mining
1481 Nonmetallic mineral services
1499 Miscellaneous nonmetallic mining

15 construction - general contractors & operative builders
1521 Single-family housing construction
1522 Residential construction, nec
1541 Industrial buildings and warehouses
1542 Nonresidential construction, nec

16 heamy construction, except building construction, contractor
1611 Highway and street construction
1622 Bridge, tunnel, and elevated highway
1623 Water, sewer, and utility lines
1629 Heavy construction, nec

17 construction - special trade contractors
1711 Plumbing, heating, air-conditioning
1721 Painting and paper hanging
1731 Electrical work
1741 Masonry and other stonework
1742 Plastering, drywall, and insulation
1743 Terrazzo, tile, marble, mosaic work
1751 Carpentry work
1752 Floor laying and floor work, nec
1761 Roofing, siding, and sheetmetal work
1771 Concrete work
1781 Water well drilling
1791 Structural steel erection
1793 Glass and glazing work
1794 Excavation work
1795 Wrecking and demolition work
1796 Installing building equipment
1799 Special trade contractors, nec

20 food and kindred products
2011 Meat packing plants
2013 Sausages and other prepared meats
2015 Poultry slaughtering and processing
2021 Creamery butter
2022 Cheese; natural and processed
2023 Dry, condensed, evaporated products
2024 Ice cream and frozen deserts
2026 Fluid milk
2032 Canned specialties
2033 Canned fruits and specialties
2034 Dehydrated fruits, vegetables, soups
2035 Pickles, sauces, and salad dressings
2037 Frozen fruits and vegetables
2038 Frozen specialties, nec
2041 Flour and other grain mill products
2043 Cereal breakfast foods
2045 Prepared flour mixes and doughs
2046 Wet corn milling
2047 Dog and cat food
2048 Prepared feeds, nec
2051 Bread, cake, and related products
2052 Cookies and crackers
2053 Frozen bakery products, except bread
2064 Candy and other confectionery products
2066 Chocolate and cocoa products
2068 Salted and roasted nuts and seeds
2074 Cottonseed oil mills
2075 Soybean oil mills
2076 Vegetable oil mills, nec
2077 Animal and marine fats and oils
2079 Edible fats and oils
2082 Malt beverages
2083 Malt
2084 Wines, brandy, and brandy spirits
2085 Distilled and blended liquors
2086 Bottled and canned soft drinks
2087 Flavoring extracts and syrups, nec
2091 Canned and cured fish and seafoods
2092 Fresh or frozen packaged fish
2095 Roasted coffee
2096 Potato chips and similar snacks
2097 Manufactured ice
2098 Macaroni and spaghetti
2099 Food preparations, nec

21 tobacco products
2111 Cigarettes
2131 Chewing and smoking tobacco

22 textile mill products
2211 Broadwoven fabric mills, cotton
2221 Broadwoven fabric mills, manmade
2231 Broadwoven fabric mills, wool
2241 Narrow fabric mills
2252 Hosiery, nec
2253 Knit outerwear mills
2254 Knit underwear mills
2261 Finishing plants, cotton
2262 Finishing plants, manmade
2269 Finishing plants, nec
2273 Carpets and rugs
2281 Yarn spinning mills
2282 Throwing and winding mills
2284 Thread mills
2295 Coated fabrics, not rubberized
2296 Tire cord and fabrics
2297 Nonwoven fabrics
2298 Cordage and twine
2299 Textile goods, nec

23 apparel, finished products from fabrics & similar materials
2311 Men's and boy's suits and coats
2321 Men's and boy's furnishings
2322 Men's and boy's underwear and nightwear
2323 Men's and boy's neckwear
2325 Men's and boy's trousers and slacks
2326 Men's and boy's work clothing
2329 Men's and boy's clothing, nec
2331 Women's and misses' blouses and shirts
2335 Women's, junior's, and misses' dresses
2337 Women's and misses' suits and coats
2339 Women's and misses' outerwear, nec
2341 Women's and children's underwear
2353 Hats, caps, and millinery
2361 Girl's and children's dresses, blouses
2369 Girl's and children's outerwear, nec
2381 Fabric dress and work gloves
2384 Robes and dressing gowns
2385 Waterproof outerwear
2386 Leather and sheep-lined clothing
2389 Apparel and accessories, nec
2391 Curtains and draperies
2392 Household furnishings, nec
2393 Textile bags
2394 Canvas and related products
2395 Pleating and stitching
2396 Automotive and apparel trimmings
2397 Schiffli machine embroideries
2399 Fabricated textile products, nec

24 lumber and wood products, except furniture
2411 Logging
2421 Sawmills and planing mills, general
2426 Hardwood dimension and flooring mills
2429 Special product sawmills, nec
2431 Millwork
2434 Wood kitchen cabinets
2435 Hardwood veneer and plywood
2436 Softwood veneer and plywood
2439 Structural wood members, nec
2441 Nailed wood boxes and shook
2448 Wood pallets and skids
2449 Wood containers, nec
2451 Mobile homes
2452 Prefabricated wood buildings

SIC INDEX

SIC NO	PRODUCT
2491	Wood preserving
2493	Reconstituted wood products
2499	Wood products, nec

25 furniture and fixtures

2511	Wood household furniture
2512	Upholstered household furniture
2514	Metal household furniture
2515	Mattresses and bedsprings
2517	Wood television and radio cabinets
2519	Household furniture, nec
2521	Wood office furniture
2522	Office furniture, except wood
2531	Public building and related furniture
2541	Wood partitions and fixtures
2542	Partitions and fixtures, except wood
2591	Drapery hardware and blinds and shades
2599	Furniture and fixtures, nec

26 paper and allied products

2611	Pulp mills
2621	Paper mills
2631	Paperboard mills
2652	Setup paperboard boxes
2653	Corrugated and solid fiber boxes
2655	Fiber cans, drums, and similar products
2656	Sanitary food containers
2657	Folding paperboard boxes
2671	Paper; coated and laminated packaging
2672	Paper; coated and laminated, nec
2673	Bags: plastic, laminated, and coated
2674	Bags: uncoated paper and multiwall
2675	Die-cut paper and board
2676	Sanitary paper products
2677	Envelopes
2678	Stationery products
2679	Converted paper products, nec

27 printing, publishing and allied industries

2711	Newspapers
2721	Periodicals
2731	Book publishing
2732	Book printing
2741	Miscellaneous publishing
2752	Commercial printing, lithographic
2754	Commercial printing, gravure
2759	Commercial printing, nec
2761	Manifold business forms
2771	Greeting cards
2782	Blankbooks and looseleaf binders
2789	Bookbinding and related work
2791	Typesetting
2796	Platemaking services

28 chemicals and allied products

2812	Alkalies and chlorine
2813	Industrial gases
2816	Inorganic pigments
2819	Industrial inorganic chemicals, nec
2821	Plastics materials and resins
2822	Synthetic rubber
2823	Cellulosic manmade fibers
2824	Organic fibers, noncellulosic
2833	Medicinals and botanicals
2834	Pharmaceutical preparations
2835	Diagnostic substances
2836	Biological products, except diagnostic
2841	Soap and other detergents
2842	Polishes and sanitation goods
2843	Surface active agents
2844	Toilet preparations
2851	Paints and allied products
2861	Gum and wood chemicals
2865	Cyclic crudes and intermediates
2869	Industrial organic chemicals, nec
2873	Nitrogenous fertilizers
2874	Phosphatic fertilizers
2875	Fertilizers, mixing only
2879	Agricultural chemicals, nec
2891	Adhesives and sealants
2892	Explosives
2893	Printing ink
2895	Carbon black
2899	Chemical preparations, nec

29 petroleum refining and related industries

2911	Petroleum refining
2951	Asphalt paving mixtures and blocks
2952	Asphalt felts and coatings
2992	Lubricating oils and greases
2999	Petroleum and coal products, nec

30 rubber and miscellaneous plastic products

3011	Tires and inner tubes
3021	Rubber and plastics footwear
3052	Rubber and plastics hose and beltings
3053	Gaskets; packing and sealing devices
3061	Mechanical rubber goods
3069	Fabricated rubber products, nec
3081	Unsupported plastics film and sheet
3082	Unsupported plastics profile shapes
3083	Laminated plastics plate and sheet
3084	Plastics pipe
3085	Plastics bottles
3086	Plastics foam products
3087	Custom compound purchased resins
3088	Plastics plumbing fixtures
3089	Plastics products, nec

31 leather and leather products

3111	Leather tanning and finishing
3131	Footwear cut stock
3142	House slippers
3143	Men's footwear, except athletic
3144	Women's footwear, except athletic
3149	Footwear, except rubber, nec
3151	Leather gloves and mittens
3161	Luggage
3171	Women's handbags and purses
3172	Personal leather goods, nec
3199	Leather goods, nec

32 stone, clay, glass, and concrete products

3211	Flat glass
3221	Glass containers
3229	Pressed and blown glass, nec
3231	Products of purchased glass
3241	Cement, hydraulic
3251	Brick and structural clay tile
3253	Ceramic wall and floor tile
3255	Clay refractories
3259	Structural clay products, nec
3261	Vitreous plumbing fixtures
3264	Porcelain electrical supplies
3269	Pottery products, nec
3271	Concrete block and brick
3272	Concrete products, nec
3273	Ready-mixed concrete
3274	Lime
3275	Gypsum products
3281	Cut stone and stone products
3291	Abrasive products
3292	Asbestos products
3295	Minerals, ground or treated
3296	Mineral wool
3297	Nonclay refractories
3299	Nonmetallic mineral products,

33 primary metal industries

3312	Blast furnaces and steel mills
3315	Steel wire and related products
3316	Cold finishing of steel shapes
3317	Steel pipe and tubes
3321	Gray and ductile iron foundries
3322	Malleable iron foundries
3324	Steel investment foundries
3325	Steel foundries, nec
3331	Primary copper
3334	Primary aluminum
3339	Primary nonferrous metals, nec
3341	Secondary nonferrous metals
3351	Copper rolling and drawing
3353	Aluminum sheet, plate, and foil
3354	Aluminum extruded products
3355	Aluminum rolling and drawing, nec
3356	Nonferrous rolling and drawing, nec
3357	Nonferrous wiredrawing and insulating
3363	Aluminum die-castings
3364	Nonferrous die-castings except aluminum
3365	Aluminum foundries
3366	Copper foundries
3369	Nonferrous foundries, nec
3398	Metal heat treating
3399	Primary metal products

34 fabricated metal products

3411	Metal cans
3412	Metal barrels, drums, and pails
3421	Cutlery
3423	Hand and edge tools, nec
3425	Saw blades and handsaws
3429	Hardware, nec
3431	Metal sanitary ware
3432	Plumbing fixture fittings and trim
3433	Heating equipment, except electric
3441	Fabricated structural metal
3442	Metal doors, sash, and trim
3443	Fabricated plate work (boiler shop)
3444	Sheet metalwork
3446	Architectural metalwork
3448	Prefabricated metal buildings
3449	Miscellaneous metalwork
3451	Screw machine products
3452	Bolts, nuts, rivets, and washers
3462	Iron and steel forgings
3463	Nonferrous forgings
3465	Automotive stampings
3466	Crowns and closures
3469	Metal stampings, nec
3471	Plating and polishing
3479	Metal coating and allied services
3482	Small arms ammunition
3483	Ammunition, except for small arms, nec
3484	Small arms
3489	Ordnance and accessories, nec
3491	Industrial valves
3492	Fluid power valves and hose fittings
3493	Steel springs, except wire
3494	Valves and pipe fittings, nec
3495	Wire springs
3496	Miscellaneous fabricated wire products
3497	Metal foil and leaf
3498	Fabricated pipe and fittings
3499	Fabricated metal products, nec

35 industrial and commercial machinery and computer equipment

3511	Turbines and turbine generator sets
3519	Internal combustion engines, nec
3523	Farm machinery and equipment
3524	Lawn and garden equipment
3531	Construction machinery
3532	Mining machinery
3533	Oil and gas field machinery
3534	Elevators and moving stairways
3535	Conveyors and conveying equipment
3536	Hoists, cranes, and monorails
3537	Industrial trucks and tractors
3541	Machine tools, metal cutting type
3542	Machine tools, metal forming type
3543	Industrial patterns
3544	Special dies, tools, jigs, and fixtures
3545	Machine tool accessories
3546	Power-driven handtools
3547	Rolling mill machinery
3548	Welding apparatus
3549	Metalworking machinery, nec
3552	Textile machinery
3553	Woodworking machinery
3554	Paper industries machinery
3555	Printing trades machinery
3556	Food products machinery
3559	Special industry machinery, nec
3561	Pumps and pumping equipment
3562	Ball and roller bearings
3563	Air and gas compressors

SIC INDEX

SIC NO	PRODUCT
3564	Blowers and fans
3565	Packaging machinery
3566	Speed changers, drives, and gears
3567	Industrial furnaces and ovens
3568	Power transmission equipment, nec
3569	General industrial machinery,
3571	Electronic computers
3572	Computer storage devices
3575	Computer terminals
3577	Computer peripheral equipment, nec
3578	Calculating and accounting equipment
3579	Office machines, nec
3581	Automatic vending machines
3582	Commercial laundry equipment
3585	Refrigeration and heating equipment
3586	Measuring and dispensing pumps
3589	Service industry machinery, nec
3592	Carburetors, pistons, rings, valves
3593	Fluid power cylinders and actuators
3594	Fluid power pumps and motors
3596	Scales and balances, except laboratory
3599	Industrial machinery, nec

36 electronic & other electrical equipment & components

SIC NO	PRODUCT
3612	Transformers, except electric
3613	Switchgear and switchboard apparatus
3621	Motors and generators
3624	Carbon and graphite products
3625	Relays and industrial controls
3629	Electrical industrial apparatus
3631	Household cooking equipment
3632	Household refrigerators and freezers
3633	Household laundry equipment
3634	Electric housewares and fans
3635	Household vacuum cleaners
3639	Household appliances, nec
3641	Electric lamps
3643	Current-carrying wiring devices
3644	Noncurrent-carrying wiring devices
3645	Residential lighting fixtures
3646	Commercial lighting fixtures
3647	Vehicular lighting equipment
3648	Lighting equipment, nec
3651	Household audio and video equipment
3652	Prerecorded records and tapes
3661	Telephone and telegraph apparatus
3663	Radio and t.v. communications equipment
3669	Communications equipment, nec
3671	Electron tubes
3672	Printed circuit boards
3674	Semiconductors and related devices
3675	Electronic capacitors
3676	Electronic resistors
3677	Electronic coils and transformers
3678	Electronic connectors
3679	Electronic components, nec
3691	Storage batteries
3692	Primary batteries, dry and wet
3694	Engine electrical equipment
3695	Magnetic and optical recording media
3699	Electrical equipment and supplies, nec

37 transportation equipment

SIC NO	PRODUCT
3711	Motor vehicles and car bodies
3713	Truck and bus bodies
3714	Motor vehicle parts and accessories
3715	Truck trailers
3716	Motor homes
3721	Aircraft
3724	Aircraft engines and engine parts
3728	Aircraft parts and equipment, nec
3731	Shipbuilding and repairing
3732	Boatbuilding and repairing
3743	Railroad equipment
3751	Motorcycles, bicycles, and parts
3761	Guided missiles and space vehicles
3764	Space propulsion units and parts
3769	Space vehicle equipment, nec
3792	Travel trailers and campers
3795	Tanks and tank components
3799	Transportation equipment, nec

38 measuring, photographic, medical, & optical goods, & clocks

SIC NO	PRODUCT
3812	Search and navigation equipment
3821	Laboratory apparatus and furniture
3822	Environmental controls
3823	Process control instruments
3824	Fluid meters and counting devices
3825	Instruments to measure electricity
3826	Analytical instruments
3827	Optical instruments and lenses
3829	Measuring and controlling devices, nec
3841	Surgical and medical instruments
3842	Surgical appliances and supplies
3843	Dental equipment and supplies
3844	X-ray apparatus and tubes
3845	Electromedical equipment
3851	Ophthalmic goods
3861	Photographic equipment and supplies
3873	Watches, clocks, watchcases, and parts

39 miscellaneous manufacturing industries

SIC NO	PRODUCT
3911	Jewelry, precious metal
3914	Silverware and plated ware
3915	Jewelers' materials and lapidary work
3931	Musical instruments
3942	Dolls and stuffed toys
3944	Games, toys, and children's vehicles
3949	Sporting and athletic goods, nec
3951	Pens and mechanical pencils
3952	Lead pencils and art goods
3953	Marking devices
3955	Carbon paper and inked ribbons
3961	Costume jewelry
3965	Fasteners, buttons, needles, and pins
3991	Brooms and brushes
3993	Signs and advertising specialties
3995	Burial caskets
3996	Hard surface floor coverings, nec
3999	Manufacturing industries, nec

40 railroad transportation

SIC NO	PRODUCT
4011	Railroads, line-haul operating

41 local & suburban transit & interurban highway transportation

SIC NO	PRODUCT
4131	Intercity and rural bus transportation
4151	School buses

42 motor freight transportation

SIC NO	PRODUCT
4212	Local trucking, without storage
4213	Trucking, except local
4214	Local trucking with storage
4215	Courier services, except by air
4221	Farm product warehousing and storage
4222	Refrigerated warehousing and storage
4225	General warehousing and storage
4226	Special warehousing and storage, nec
4231	Trucking terminal facilities

44 water transportation

SIC NO	PRODUCT
4449	Water transportation of freight
4491	Marine cargo handling
4492	Towing and tugboat service
4493	Marinas

45 transportation by air

SIC NO	PRODUCT
4581	Airports, flying fields, and services

47 transportation services

SIC NO	PRODUCT
4724	Travel agencies
4731	Freight transportation arrangement
4741	Rental of railroad cars
4783	Packing and crating
4785	Inspection and fixed facilities
4789	Transportation services, nec

48 communications

SIC NO	PRODUCT
4812	Radiotelephone communication
4813	Telephone communication, except radio
4822	Telegraph and other communications
4832	Radio broadcasting stations
4833	Television broadcasting stations
4841	Cable and other pay television services
4899	Communication services, nec

49 electric, gas and sanitary services

SIC NO	PRODUCT
4911	Electric services
4922	Natural gas transmission
4924	Natural gas distribution
4925	Gas production and/or distribution
4931	Electric and other services combined
4953	Refuse systems
4959	Sanitary services, nec
4961	Steam and air-conditioning supply

50 wholesale trade - durable goods

SIC NO	PRODUCT
5012	Automobiles and other motor vehicles
5013	Motor vehicle supplies and new parts
5014	Tires and tubes
5015	Motor vehicle parts, used
5021	Furniture
5023	Homefurnishings
5031	Lumber, plywood, and millwork
5032	Brick, stone, and related material
5033	Roofing, siding, and insulation
5039	Construction materials, nec
5043	Photographic equipment and supplies
5044	Office equipment
5045	Computers, peripherals, and software
5046	Commercial equipment, nec
5047	Medical and hospital equipment
5048	Ophthalmic goods
5049	Professional equipment, nec
5051	Metals service centers and offices
5052	Coal and other minerals and ores
5063	Electrical apparatus and equipment
5064	Electrical appliances, television and radio
5065	Electronic parts and equipment, nec
5072	Hardware
5074	Plumbing and hydronic heating supplies
5075	Warm air heating and air conditioning
5078	Refrigeration equipment and supplies
5082	Construction and mining machinery
5083	Farm and garden machinery
5084	Industrial machinery and equipment
5085	Industrial supplies
5087	Service establishment equipment
5088	Transportation equipment and supplies
5091	Sporting and recreation goods
5092	Toys and hobby goods and supplies
5093	Scrap and waste materials
5094	Jewelry and precious stones
5099	Durable goods, nec

51 wholesale trade - nondurable goods

SIC NO	PRODUCT
5111	Printing and writing paper
5112	Stationery and office supplies
5113	Industrial and personal service paper
5122	Drugs, proprietaries, and sundries
5131	Piece goods and notions
5136	Men's and boy's clothing
5137	Women's and children's clothing
5139	Footwear
5141	Groceries, general line
5142	Packaged frozen goods
5143	Dairy products, except dried or canned
5144	Poultry and poultry products
5145	Confectionery
5146	Fish and seafoods
5147	Meats and meat products
5148	Fresh fruits and vegetables
5149	Groceries and related products, nec
5153	Grain and field beans
5154	Livestock
5159	Farm-product raw materials, nec
5162	Plastics materials and basic shapes
5169	Chemicals and allied products, nec
5171	Petroleum bulk stations and terminals
5172	Petroleum products, nec
5181	Beer and ale
5182	Wine and distilled beverages
5191	Farm supplies
5192	Books, periodicals, and newspapers
5193	Flowers and florists supplies

SIC INDEX

SIC NO	PRODUCT

5194 Tobacco and tobacco products
5198 Paints, varnishes, and supplies
5199 Nondurable goods, nec

52 building materials, hardware, garden supplies & mobile homes
5211 Lumber and other building materials
5231 Paint, glass, and wallpaper stores
5251 Hardware stores
5261 Retail nurseries and garden stores
5271 Mobile home dealers

53 general merchandise stores
5331 Variety stores
5399 Miscellaneous general merchandise

54 food stores
5411 Grocery stores
5421 Meat and fish markets
5441 Candy, nut, and confectionery stores
5451 Dairy products stores
5461 Retail bakeries
5499 Miscellaneous food stores

55 automotive dealers and gasoline service stations
5511 New and used car dealers
5521 Used car dealers
5531 Auto and home supply stores
5541 Gasoline service stations
5551 Boat dealers
5561 Recreational vehicle dealers
5571 Motorcycle dealers
5599 Automotive dealers, nec

56 apparel and accessory stores
5611 Men's and boys' clothing stores
5621 Women's clothing stores
5632 Women's accessory and specialty stores
5641 Children's and infants' wear stores
5651 Family clothing stores
5661 Shoe stores
5699 Miscellaneous apparel and accessories

57 home furniture, furnishings and equipment stores
5712 Furniture stores
5713 Floor covering stores
5714 Drapery and upholstery stores
5719 Miscellaneous homefurnishings
5722 Household appliance stores
5731 Radio, television, and electronic stores
5734 Computer and software stores
5735 Record and prerecorded tape stores
5736 Musical instrument stores

58 eating and drinking places
5812 Eating places
5813 Drinking places

59 miscellaneous retail
5912 Drug stores and proprietary stores
5921 Liquor stores
5932 Used merchandise stores
5941 Sporting goods and bicycle shops
5942 Book stores
5943 Stationery stores
5944 Jewelry stores
5945 Hobby, toy, and game shops
5946 Camera and photographic supply stores
5947 Gift, novelty, and souvenir shop
5949 Sewing, needlework, and piece goods
5961 Catalog and mail-order houses
5962 Merchandising machine operators
5963 Direct selling establishments
5983 Fuel oil dealers
5984 Liquefied petroleum gas dealers
5989 Fuel dealers, nec
5992 Florists
5993 Tobacco stores and stands
5995 Optical goods stores
5999 Miscellaneous retail stores, nec

60 depository institutions

6099 Functions related to depository banking

61 nondepository credit institutions
6141 Personal credit institutions
6153 Short-term business credit
6163 Loan brokers

62 security & commodity brokers, dealers, exchanges & services
6211 Security brokers and dealers
6221 Commodity contracts brokers, dealers
6231 Security and commodity exchanges
6282 Investment advice

63 insurance carriers
6399 Insurance carriers, nec

64 insurance agents, brokers and service
6411 Insurance agents, brokers, and service

65 real estate
6512 Nonresidential building operators
6514 Dwelling operators, except apartments
6515 Mobile home site operators
6519 Real property lessors, nec
6531 Real estate agents and managers
6552 Subdividers and developers, nec
6553 Cemetery subdividers and developers

67 holding and other investment offices
6719 Holding companies, nec
6722 Management investment, open-ended
6726 Investment offices, nec
6732 Trusts: educational, religious, etc.
6794 Patent owners and lessors
6799 Investors, nec

70 hotels, rooming houses, camps, and other lodging places
7011 Hotels and motels
7032 Sporting and recreational camps

72 personal services
7213 Linen supply
7215 Coin-operated laundries and cleaning
7216 Drycleaning plants, except rugs
7217 Carpet and upholstery cleaning
7218 Industrial launderers
7219 Laundry and garment services, nec
7221 Photographic studios, portrait
7231 Beauty shops
7241 Barber shops
7261 Funeral service and crematories
7291 Tax return preparation services
7299 Miscellaneous personal services

73 business services
7311 Advertising agencies
7312 Outdoor advertising services
7313 Radio, television, publisher representatives
7319 Advertising, nec
7322 Adjustment and collection services
7331 Direct mail advertising services
7334 Photocopying and duplicating services
7335 Commercial photography
7336 Commercial art and graphic design
7338 Secretarial and court reporting
7342 Disinfecting and pest control services
7349 Building maintenance services, nec
7352 Medical equipment rental
7353 Heavy construction equipment rental
7359 Equipment rental and leasing, nec
7361 Employment agencies
7363 Help supply services
7371 Custom computer programming services
7372 Prepackaged software
7373 Computer integrated systems design
7374 Data processing and preparation
7375 Information retrieval services
7376 Computer facilities management
7378 Computer maintenance and repair
7379 Computer related services, nec

7381 Detective and armored car services
7382 Security systems services
7384 Photofinish laboratories
7389 Business services, nec

75 automotive repair, services and parking
7513 Truck rental and leasing, without drivers
7514 Passenger car rental
7515 Passenger car leasing
7519 Utility trailer rental
7532 Top and body repair and paint shops
7533 Auto exhaust system repair shops
7534 Tire retreading and repair shops
7536 Automotive glass replacement shops
7537 Automotive transmission repair shops
7538 General automotive repair shops
7539 Automotive repair shops, nec
7542 Carwashes
7549 Automotive services, nec

76 miscellaneous repair services
7623 Refrigeration service and repair
7629 Electrical repair shops
7631 Watch, clock, and jewelry repair
7641 Reupholstery and furniture repair
7692 Welding repair
7694 Armature rewinding shops
7699 Repair services, nec

78 motion pictures
7812 Motion picture and video production
7819 Services allied to motion pictures
7822 Motion picture and tape distribution
7841 Video tape rental

79 amusement and recreation services
7911 Dance studios, schools, and halls
7922 Theatrical producers and services
7929 Entertainers and entertainment groups
7941 Sports clubs, managers, and promoters
7948 Racing, including track operation
7991 Physical fitness facilities
7992 Public golf courses
7993 Coin-operated amusement devices
7997 Membership sports and recreation clubs
7999 Amusement and recreation, nec

80 health services
8011 Offices and clinics of medical doctors
8021 Offices and clinics of dentists
8042 Offices and clinics of optometrists
8049 Offices of health practitioner
8071 Medical laboratories
8072 Dental laboratories
8082 Home health care services
8099 Health and allied services, nec

81 legal services
8111 Legal services

82 educational services
8211 Elementary and secondary schools
8221 Colleges and universities
8231 Libraries
8243 Data processing schools
8249 Vocational schools, nec
8299 Schools and educational services

83 social services
8322 Individual and family services
8331 Job training and related services
8361 Residential care

84 museums, art galleries and botanical and zoological gardens
8412 Museums and art galleries

86 membership organizations
8611 Business associations
8621 Professional organizations
8631 Labor organizations
8641 Civic and social associations

SIC INDEX

SIC NO	PRODUCT
8661	Religious organizations
8699	Membership organizations, nec

87 engineering, accounting, research, and management services

8711	Engineering services
8712	Architectural services
8713	Surveying services
8721	Accounting, auditing, and bookkeeping
8731	Commercial physical research
8732	Commercial nonphysical research
8733	Noncommercial research organizations
8734	Testing laboratories
8741	Management services
8742	Management consulting services
8743	Public relations services
8744	Facilities support services
8748	Business consulting, nec

89 services, not elsewhere classified

8999	Services, nec

91 executive, legislative & general government, except finance

9121	Legislative bodies

92 justice, public order and safety

9224	Fire protection

95 administration of environmental quality and housing programs

9532	Urban and community development

97 national security and international affairs

9711	National security

SIC SECTION

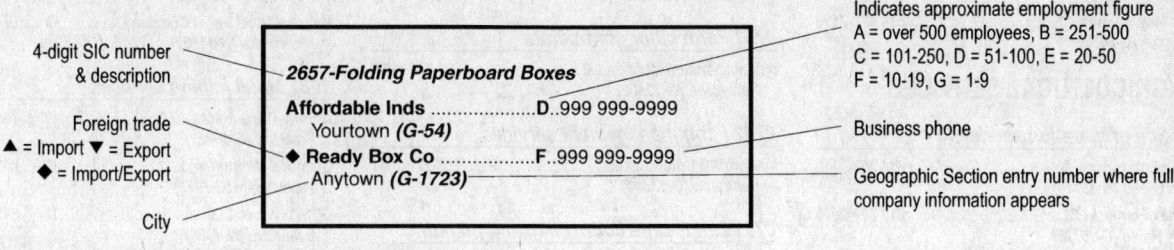

- 4-digit SIC number & description
- Foreign trade ▲ = Import ▼ = Export ◆ = Import/Export
- City
- Indicates approximate employment figure A = over 500 employees, B = 251-500 C = 101-250, D = 51-100, E = 20-50 F = 10-19, G = 1-9
- Business phone
- Geographic Section entry number where full company information appears

See footnotes for symbols and codes identification.
- The SIC codes in this section are from the latest Standard Industrial Classification manual published by the U.S. Government's Office of Management and Budget. For more information regarding SICs, see the Explanatory Notes.
- Companies may be listed under multiple classifications.

01 AGRICULTURAL PRODUCTION - CROPS

0111 Wheat
Custom Tire Cutting Inc...........................G.....812 745-9140
  Oaktown *(G-13326)*
Daniel Steffy...G.....812 726-4769
  Vincennes *(G-16118)*
Eckstein Welding & Fabrication.............G.....812 934-2059
  Batesville *(G-586)*
William Donson......................................G.....765 628-3236
  Kokomo *(G-10358)*

0115 Corn
Custom Tire Cutting Inc...........................G.....812 745-9140
  Oaktown *(G-13326)*
Daniel Steffy...G.....812 726-4769
  Vincennes *(G-16118)*
Flinn Frms Bdford Feed Seed In............G.....812 279-4136
  Bedford *(G-636)*
Jolliff Diesel Service LLC.......................G.....812 692-5725
  Elnora *(G-3815)*
Tom West Farms....................................G.....812 986-2162
  Poland *(G-13838)*
William Donson......................................G.....765 628-3236
  Kokomo *(G-10358)*

0116 Soybeans
Custom Tire Cutting Inc...........................G.....812 745-9140
  Oaktown *(G-13326)*
Daniel Steffy...G.....812 726-4769
  Vincennes *(G-16118)*
Flinn Frms Bdford Feed Seed In............G.....812 279-4136
  Bedford *(G-636)*
Tom West Farms....................................G.....812 986-2162
  Poland *(G-13838)*

0119 Cash grains, nec
Carol Burt...G.....765 282-5383
  Muncie *(G-12365)*

0139 Field crops, except cash grain
Powers Hardwoods................................G.....260 665-5498
  Angola *(G-286)*

0161 Vegetables and melons
▲ Huber Orchards Inc...........................D.....812 923-9463
  Borden *(G-1110)*
Sappers Market and Greenhouses........G.....219 942-4995
  Hobart *(G-7206)*

0171 Berry crops
Adrian Orchards Inc..............................G.....317 784-0550
  Indianapolis *(G-7434)*

0175 Deciduous tree fruits
Adrian Orchards Inc..............................G.....317 784-0550
  Indianapolis *(G-7434)*
▲ Huber Orchards Inc...........................D.....812 923-9463
  Borden *(G-1110)*
Southern Indiana Chemical Inc.............G.....812 687-7118
  Washington *(G-16509)*

0181 Ornamental nursery products
Creative Ldscp & Compost Co..............G.....317 776-2909
  Noblesville *(G-13065)*
Sappers Market and Greenhouses........G.....219 942-4995
  Hobart *(G-7206)*

0182 Food crops grown under cover
Roka Urban Ag LLC..............................G.....317 513-8828
  Indianapolis *(G-9322)*

0191 General farms, primarily crop
Conder Water Services.........................G.....812 825-9883
  Bloomington *(G-835)*
Kuharic Enterprises...............................G.....574 288-9410
  South Bend *(G-15110)*
Milroy Canning Company......................G.....765 629-2221
  Milroy *(G-11827)*
▲ Schwartz Manufacturing Inc..............G.....260 589-3865
  Berne *(G-725)*
This Old Farm Inc..................................E.....765 324-2161
  Colfax *(G-2113)*

02 AGRICULTURAL PRODUCTION - LIVESTOCK AND ANIMAL SPECIALTIES

0211 Beef cattle feedlots
Becks Bird Feeders...............................G.....765 874-1496
  Markleville *(G-11367)*
Carol Burt...G.....765 282-5383
  Muncie *(G-12365)*
Powers Hardwoods................................G.....260 665-5498
  Angola *(G-286)*
Robert L Young......................................G.....812 863-4475
  Springville *(G-15391)*
Tom West Farms....................................G.....812 986-2162
  Poland *(G-13838)*

0212 Beef cattle, except feedlots
Daniel Steffy...G.....812 726-4769
  Vincennes *(G-16118)*
Eckstein Welding & Fabrication.............G.....812 934-2059
  Batesville *(G-586)*
Hand Industries Inc...............................E.....574 267-3525
  Warsaw *(G-16373)*

0213 Hogs
Eckstein Welding & Fabrication.............G.....812 934-2059
  Batesville *(G-586)*
▼ United Animal Health Inc..................D.....317 758-4495
  Sheridan *(G-14830)*

0241 Dairy farms
Kuehnert Dairy Inc.................................G.....260 489-3766
  Fort Wayne *(G-5164)*

0252 Chicken eggs
P & R Farms Llc....................................G.....812 326-2010
  Saint Anthony *(G-14430)*
Salt Creek Harvest LLC........................G.....708 927-5569
  Valparaiso *(G-16042)*

0254 Poultry hatcheries
Hy-Line North America LLC..................D.....260 375-3041
  Warren *(G-16300)*
Pine Manor Inc.......................................G.....574 533-4186
  Goshen *(G-6238)*
▲ Pine Manor Inc..................................B.....800 532-4186
  Orland *(G-13370)*

0259 Poultry and eggs, nec
Maple Leaf Inc.......................................G.....260 982-8655
  North Manchester *(G-13241)*
◆ Maple Leaf Inc..................................B.....574 453-4455
  Leesburg *(G-10958)*
◆ Maple Leaf Farms Inc......................A.....574 453-4500
  Milford *(G-11798)*

0279 Animal specialties, nec
Elizabeth A Taylor..................................G.....815 353-4798
  Freedom *(G-5799)*
Envigo Rms Inc......................................G.....317 806-6080
  Greenfield *(G-6500)*
Envigo Rms Inc......................................G.....317 806-6060
  Greenfield *(G-6501)*
▲ Envigo Rms Inc................................C.....317 806-6080
  Indianapolis *(G-8125)*

0291 General farms, primarily animals

02 AGRICULTURAL PRODUCTION - LIVESTOCK AND ANIMAL SPECIALTIES

Harris Farms Inc.................................... G..... 765 468-6264
  Modoc (G-12052)
Steven Ray Hughes............................. G..... 574 491-2128
  Claypool (G-2058)

07 AGRICULTURAL SERVICES

0711 Soil preparation services

Kuharic Enterprises............................. G..... 574 288-9410
  South Bend (G-15110)
Terremax Farms LLC........................... G..... 812 242-0276
  Terre Haute (G-15728)
V Global Holdings LLC......................... E..... 317 247-8141
  Indianapolis (G-9695)

0721 Crop planting and protection

Corteva Inc... G..... 765 586-4077
  Indianapolis (G-7882)
Corteva Inc... A..... 833 267-8382
  Indianapolis (G-7883)
◆ Corteva Agriscience LLC.................. A..... 317 337-3000
  Indianapolis (G-7884)
◆ Mycogen Corporation...................... F..... 317 337-3000
  Indianapolis (G-8977)
Superior AG Resources Coop Inc........ G..... 812 724-4455
  Owensville (G-13473)

0723 Crop preparation services for market

Keystone Cooperative Inc.................. G..... 765 489-4141
  Hagerstown (G-6838)
Langeland Farms Inc........................... G..... 812 663-9546
  Greensburg (G-6614)

0742 Veterinary services, specialties

Elanco Animal Health Inc.................... A..... 877 352-6261
  Greenfield (G-6493)
Elanco International Inc..................... D..... 877 352-6261
  Greenfield (G-6494)

0751 Livestock services, except veterinary

Butcher Block Inc............................... G..... 219 696-9111
  Lowell (G-11157)
Fisher Packing Company..................... E..... 260 726-7355
  Portland (G-13941)
Gibson County Meats LLC................... F..... 812 724-2333
  Owensville (G-13468)
Lengerich Meats Inc........................... F..... 260 638-4123
  Zanesville (G-16986)
Millers Locker Plant........................... G..... 765 234-2381
  Crawfordsville (G-2591)
Pates Slaughtering & Proc.................. G..... 812 866-4710
  Hanover (G-7045)
Rices Quality Farm Meats Inc............ G..... 812 829-4562
  Spencer (G-15361)
Royal Center Locker Plant Inc............ G..... 574 643-3275
  Royal Center (G-14392)
Wilsons Locker & Proc Plant............... G..... 812 358-2632
  Bedford (G-683)
Yoders Meats Inc............................... G..... 260 768-4715
  Shipshewana (G-14700)

0752 Animal specialty services

Cozy Cat Inc...................................... G..... 765 463-1254
  Lafayette (G-10559)
Elizabeth A Taylor.............................. G..... 815 353-4798
  Freedom (G-5799)
Furtrieve LLC..................................... G..... 317 325-8010
  Fishers (G-4529)
Good Poppi LLC................................. G..... 812 319-1660
  Evansville (G-4093)
International English Inc.................... G..... 260 868-2670
  Butler (G-1467)

Sanmar Tool & Manufacturing............. G..... 574 232-6081
  South Bend (G-15233)

0761 Farm labor contractors

Indiana Mobile Welding LLC............... G..... 317 771-8900
  Noblesville (G-13102)

0762 Farm management services

Modern AG Solutions LLC................... G..... 765 221-1011
  Pendleton (G-13544)

0781 Landscape counseling and planning

Rose HI Lawn Care Ldscpg Snow......... G..... 812 230-0024
  Terre Haute (G-15684)

0782 Lawn and garden services

All-Phase Construction Co LLC........... G..... 317 345-7057
  Fishers (G-4461)
Creative Ldscp & Compost Co............ G..... 317 776-2909
  Noblesville (G-13065)
D A Merriman Inc................................ G..... 260 636-3464
  Albion (G-22)
Festive Lights LLC............................. G..... 317 998-0627
  Indianapolis (G-8181)
Huehls Salcoating Lawncare LLC........ G..... 317 782-4069
  Indianapolis (G-8433)
◆ Knox Fertilizer Company Inc........... C..... 574 772-6275
  Knox (G-10213)
Professional Grade Svcs LLC............. G..... 317 688-8898
  Indianapolis (G-9222)
Rose HI Lawn Care Ldscpg Snow......... G..... 812 230-0024
  Terre Haute (G-15684)
Walls Lawn & Garden Inc.................... G..... 317 535-9059
  Whiteland (G-16799)

0783 Ornamental shrub and tree services

Arboramerica Inc................................ F..... 765 572-1212
  Westpoint (G-16743)
Owens Property Solutions LLC............ G..... 708 374-2626
  Gary (G-5992)
Schenk and Sons Tree Svc Inc............ G..... 812 985-3954
  Mount Vernon (G-12321)

08 FORESTRY

0811 Timber tracts

Woods Enterprises............................. G..... 574 232-7449
  South Bend (G-15309)

0851 Forestry services

Arboramerica Inc................................ F..... 765 572-1212
  Westpoint (G-16743)
PFC Farm Services Inc....................... G..... 260 235-0817
  Fremont (G-5831)

09 FISHING, HUNTING AND TRAPPING

0919 Miscellaneous marine products

Paf Construction LLC.......................... E..... 812 496-4669
  Columbus (G-2371)

10 METAL MINING

1011 Iron ores

◆ Arcelormittal Holdings LLC.............. D..... 219 399-1200
  East Chicago (G-2990)
Clevelnd-Clffs Mnorca Mine Inc.......... B..... 219 787-2002
  Chesterton (G-1915)
◆ Clevelnd-Clffs Mnorca Mine Inc...... G..... 219 399-1200
  East Chicago (G-3001)

Erp Iron Ore LLC................................ G..... 574 270-8608
  Reynolds (G-14072)
National Steel Pellet Company............ G..... 574 273-7000
  Mishawaka (G-11963)

1081 Metal mining services

A-Rose Consultants LLC..................... F..... 765 650-8700
  Frankfort (G-5648)
Diamond Mining Lead.......................... G..... 317 340-7760
  Indianapolis (G-7970)
GES Services LLC.............................. G..... 812 270-3090
  Evansville (G-4090)
Hydro Vac Services LLC..................... E..... 317 345-2120
  Indianapolis (G-8443)
James F Reilly 3 Ent.......................... G..... 574 277-8267
  Mishawaka (G-11916)
P M I LLC... G..... 812 374-3856
  Edinburgh (G-3094)
Postle Aluminum Company LLC........... E..... 574 389-0800
  Elkhart (G-3611)
Richard M Judd................................... G..... 916 704-3364
  Bloomington (G-955)
Turner Mining Group LLC.................... C..... 812 277-9077
  Bloomington (G-1001)
Vhgi Holdings Inc............................... G
  Sullivan (G-15425)

1099 Metal ores, nec

Howmet Aerospace Inc....................... B..... 412 553-4545
  Newburgh (G-13005)
Priority Detailing............................... G..... 812 591-0299
  Westport (G-16750)
Reelement Technologies Corp............. G..... 317 855-9926
  Fishers (G-4594)

12 COAL MINING

1221 Bituminous coal and lignite-surface mining

American Resources Corporation......... C..... 317 855-9926
  Fishers (G-4463)
ANR Pipeline Company........................ G..... 260 463-3342
  Lagrange (G-10728)
Gibson County Coal LLC..................... B..... 812 385-1816
  Owensville (G-13467)
Hickman Williams & Company.............. G..... 219 379-5199
  La Porte (G-10419)
Mt Vernon Coal Transfer Co............... E..... 812 838-5531
  Mount Vernon (G-12310)
Mt Vernon Transfer Trml LLC.............. G..... 812 838-5531
  Mount Vernon (G-12311)
Peabody Bear Run Mining LLC............. C..... 314 342-7676
  Carlisle (G-1542)
Peabody Midwest Mining LLC.............. B..... 812 782-3209
  Francisco (G-5646)
Peabody Midwest Mining LLC.............. G..... 812 254-7714
  Washington (G-16500)
Peabody Midwest Mining LLC.............. E..... 812 297-7661
  Lynnville (G-11192)
Phoenix Natural Resources Inc........... G..... 636 537-0283
  Jasper (G-9903)
Rogers Group Inc............................... D..... 812 332-6341
  Bloomington (G-960)
Sandy Little Coal Company Inc............ G..... 812 529-8216
  Evanston (G-3854)
Sunrise Coal LLC............................... G..... 812 299-2800
  Terre Haute (G-15718)
Vigo Coal Operating Co Inc................ C..... 812 759-8446
  Evansville (G-4374)

1222 Bituminous coal-underground mining

SIC SECTION
13 OIL AND GAS EXTRACTION

Peabody Midwest Mining LLC............. E 812 297-7661
   Lynnville *(G-11192)*

Regional Development Company........... G 219 476-0504
   Valparaiso *(G-16036)*

Solar Sources Underground LLC........... C 812 354-2808
   Petersburg *(G-13626)*

Sunrise Coal LLC............................ F 812 745-2002
   Oaktown *(G-13329)*

1241 Coal mining services

Al Perry Enterprises Inc..................... G 812 867-7727
   Evansville *(G-3879)*

B B Mining Inc................................ G 812 845-2717
   Cynthiana *(G-2785)*

Black Panther Mining LLC................. G 812 745-2920
   Oaktown *(G-13325)*

Eagle River Coal LLC........................ G 618 252-0490
   Evansville *(G-4024)*

▲ English Resources Inc..................... G 812 423-6716
   Evansville *(G-4038)*

ERC Mining Indiana Corp.................... G 812 665-9780
   Jasonville *(G-9823)*

Fretina Corporation........................... F 812 547-6471
   Tell City *(G-15504)*

Gibson County Coal LLC..................... B 812 385-1816
   Owensville *(G-13467)*

Hallador Energy Company.................. E 812 299-2800
   Terre Haute *(G-15603)*

Indiana Coal Mining Institute............... G 812 232-5011
   Terre Haute *(G-15616)*

K Q Servicing LLC............................ G 812 486-9244
   Loogootee *(G-11140)*

Lily Group Inc................................. G 812 268-5459
   Sullivan *(G-15412)*

Mt Vernon Transfer Trml LLC............... G 812 838-5531
   Mount Vernon *(G-12311)*

Peabody Energy Corporation................ G 314 342-3400
   Lynnville *(G-11191)*

Peabody Midwest Mining LLC............. E 812 297-7661
   Lynnville *(G-11192)*

Pittman Mine Service LLC................... G 812 847-2340
   Linton *(G-11042)*

R D-N-P Drilling Inc.......................... G 219 956-3481
   Wheatfield *(G-16772)*

Rogers Group Inc............................ C 812 333-6324
   Bloomington *(G-959)*

Shaal John..................................... G 812 882-2396
   Vincennes *(G-16153)*

Stone Coal Services LLC.................... G 812 455-8215
   Elberfeld *(G-3119)*

Sycamore Coal Inc........................... G 812 491-4000
   Terre Haute *(G-15720)*

Triad Mining Inc.............................. G 812 328-2117
   Oakland City *(G-13324)*

Vectren LLC................................... G 812 424-6411
   Evansville *(G-4369)*

Vectren LLC................................... A 812 491-4000
   Evansville *(G-4368)*

13 OIL AND GAS EXTRACTION

1311 Crude petroleum and natural gas

Ah Medora Lfg LLC.......................... G 346 440-1416
   Medora *(G-11460)*

ANR Pipeline Company...................... G 260 463-3342
   Lagrange *(G-10728)*

B N Oil LLC.................................... G 859 816-2244
   Lawrenceburg *(G-10830)*

Barger Engineering Inc...................... G 812 476-3077
   Evansville *(G-3909)*

Briggs Exploration Prod Co LLC............ G 812 249-0564
   Evansville *(G-3953)*

C Milligan Investments LLC................. G 219 241-5811
   Valparaiso *(G-15924)*

Carlton West Oil Company LLC............ G 812 375-9689
   Columbus *(G-2234)*

Common Sense Producing LLC............ G 317 622-1682
   Greenfield *(G-6482)*

Countrymark Ref Logistics LLC............ B 812 838-4341
   Mount Vernon *(G-12295)*

Four Season Oil Inc........................... G 317 215-1214
   Plainfield *(G-13681)*

Fred D McCrary.............................. G 812 354-6520
   Petersburg *(G-13614)*

Gallagher Drilling Inc........................ F 812 477-6746
   Evansville *(G-4083)*

Green Cow Power LLC...................... G 219 984-5915
   Goshen *(G-6154)*

Hallador Energy Company.................. E 812 299-2800
   Terre Haute *(G-15603)*

Hux Oil Corp.................................. G 812 894-2096
   Terre Haute *(G-15610)*

Imperial Petroleum Inc....................... E 812 867-1433
   Darmstadt *(G-2836)*

Indy High Btu LLC........................... G 317 749-0732
   Indianapolis *(G-8528)*

J & J Oil Well Service Inc................... G 812 354-9007
   Petersburg *(G-13615)*

K S Oil Corp................................... G 812 453-3026
   Mount Vernon *(G-12305)*

Lassus Bros Oil Inc........................... F 260 625-4003
   Fort Wayne *(G-5175)*

Mannon L Walters Inc....................... F 812 867-5946
   Evansville *(G-4187)*

Meridian Resources LLC..................... G 812 463-2281
   Carmel *(G-1697)*

Mittler Supply Inc............................ G 317 290-0121
   Indianapolis *(G-8937)*

Moore Engineering & Prod Co.............. F 812 479-1051
   Evansville *(G-4211)*

Nichols Operating LLC....................... G 812 753-3600
   Fort Branch *(G-4706)*

Paul E Potts................................... G 812 354-3241
   Hazleton *(G-7095)*

Payne George A Petroleum Engr........... G 812 853-3813
   Newburgh *(G-13015)*

Pulse Energy Systems LLC.................. G 618 392-5502
   Evansville *(G-4264)*

Responsble Enrgy Oprations LLC.......... G 812 354-8776
   Petersburg *(G-13623)*

Robinson Engineering & Oil Co............. F 812 477-1575
   Evansville *(G-4291)*

Sater Enterprises.............................. G 812 477-1529
   Evansville *(G-4297)*

◆ Sg Solutions LLC........................... E 812 535-6000
   West Terre Haute *(G-16654)*

South Bend Ethanol LLC..................... D 574 703-3360
   South Bend *(G-15252)*

Trey Exploration Inc......................... G 812 858-3146
   Newburgh *(G-13025)*

Universal Operating Inc...................... G 812 477-1584
   Evansville *(G-4363)*

Vhgi Holdings Inc............................. G
   Sullivan *(G-15425)*

Victor R Gallagher............................ G 812 425-8256
   Evansville *(G-4373)*

Wabash River Energy LLC.................. D 812 535-6067
   West Terre Haute *(G-16656)*

Wabash Valley Resources LLC............. G 929 400-5230
   West Terre Haute *(G-16657)*

1321 Natural gas liquids

Citizens By-Products Coal Co............... F 317 927-4738
   Indianapolis *(G-7811)*

Daylight Engineering Inc..................... G 812 983-2518
   Elberfeld *(G-3111)*

Jackson-Jennings LLC....................... G 812 522-4911
   Seymour *(G-14659)*

Nicholas Bryant............................... G 765 366-0108
   Hillsboro *(G-7161)*

Rdb Environmental LLC..................... G 708 362-3618
   Francesville *(G-5644)*

Terry Haute Propane Plant.................. G 812 877-3406
   Terre Haute *(G-15729)*

Trade & Industrial Supply Inc............... G 812 537-1300
   Batesville *(G-609)*

1381 Drilling oil and gas wells

Amazing Well Drill Pump Plbg.............. G 317 384-9132
   Indianapolis *(G-7495)*

Basin Energy Inc.............................. G 812 983-2519
   Evansville *(G-3912)*

Blue Moon Oil Company LLC............... G 317 892-2499
   Brownsburg *(G-1351)*

C N J Well Drilling........................... F 317 892-2100
   Indianapolis *(G-7709)*

Elmers Service LLC.......................... G 260 463-8287
   Howe *(G-7234)*

Energy Drilling LLC.......................... G 618 943-5314
   Vincennes *(G-16119)*

Energy Inc..................................... G 765 948-3504
   Alexandria *(G-51)*

G & B Directional Boring LLC............... F 574 538-8132
   Shipshewana *(G-14847)*

Gallagher Drilling Inc........................ F 812 477-6746
   Evansville *(G-4083)*

Gentry Well & Pump Service LLC.......... G 260 563-1907
   Wabash *(G-16189)*

Gwaltney Drilling Inc........................ G 812 254-5085
   Washington *(G-16483)*

Hamilton Bros Inc............................ F 317 241-2571
   Indianapolis *(G-8353)*

Hoover Well Drilling Inc..................... G 574 831-4901
   New Paris *(G-12959)*

Indiana Drilling Company Inc............... G 812 477-1575
   Evansville *(G-4119)*

McGrews Well Drilling Inc.................. G 574 857-3875
   Rochester *(G-14306)*

Michael R Harris.............................. G 812 425-9411
   Evansville *(G-4201)*

Midwest Energy Partners LLC.............. G 317 600-3235
   Indianapolis *(G-8909)*

Mnt Delivery Company...................... G 574 518-6250
   Osceola *(G-13399)*

Remmler Well Drilling LLC................. G 812 663-8178
   Greensburg *(G-6627)*

Robert S Froman.............................. G 765 565-6819
   Rushville *(G-14410)*

Sr Petroleum Inc.............................. G 574 383-5879
   Granger *(G-6382)*

Tru Bore Company........................... G 317 442-6766
   Brownsburg *(G-1410)*

Universal Operating Inc...................... G 812 477-1584
   Evansville *(G-4363)*

US Oilfield Company LLC................... F 888 584-7565
   Carmel *(G-1796)*

Western Kentucky Drilling................... G 812 457-5639
   Evansville *(G-4382)*

1382 Oil and gas exploration services

Barger Engineering Inc...................... G 812 476-3077
   Evansville *(G-3909)*

Black and Gold Energy LLC................ G 812 618-6744
   Evansville *(G-3933)*

Black Gold Ventures Ind LLC............... G 260 820-0771
   Bluffton *(G-1029)*

13 OIL AND GAS EXTRACTION

Carlisle Mine... G 812 398-2200
   Carlisle *(G-1540)*

Core Minerals Operating Co Inc.................. G 812 759-6950
   Evansville *(G-3983)*

Countrymark Ref Logistics LLC.................. B 812 838-4341
   Mount Vernon *(G-12295)*

Covey Rise Minerals LLC........................... G 812 897-2356
   Boonville *(G-1086)*

Domco LLC... G 317 902-4404
   Carmel *(G-1609)*

Enviropeel USA... G 317 631-9100
   Indianapolis *(G-8126)*

Freeport Minerals Corporation.................... G 260 421-5400
   Fort Wayne *(G-5010)*

Gemini Oil LLC... G 260 571-8388
   Warren *(G-16298)*

Hallador Energy Company.......................... E 812 299-2800
   Terre Haute *(G-15603)*

Hjr Oil Inc... G 317 849-4503
   Fishers *(G-4539)*

Imperial Petroleum Inc............................... E 812 867-1433
   Darmstadt *(G-2836)*

J R and D Exploration Inc........................... G 812 677-2895
   Princeton *(G-14002)*

Legacy Resources Co LP............................ G 317 328-5660
   Indianapolis *(G-8734)*

Magnum Exploration Inc............................. G 812 673-4914
   New Harmony *(G-12887)*

Mannon Oil LLC.. F 812 867-5946
   Evansville *(G-4188)*

Michael R Harris.. G 812 425-9411
   Evansville *(G-4201)*

Pioneer Oil Company Inc........................... G 812 494-2800
   Vincennes *(G-16144)*

Plymouth Oil and Gas Inc........................... G 574 875-4808
   Goshen *(G-6241)*

Richard M Judd.. G 916 704-3364
   Bloomington *(G-955)*

Riverside Petroleum Ind LLC...................... G 812 639-0859
   Washington *(G-16507)*

Seismic Vision LLC................................... G 219 548-8704
   Valparaiso *(G-16043)*

Sun Energy Services LLC........................... G 765 251-1526
   Marion *(G-11339)*

Trey Exploration Inc.................................. G 812 858-3146
   Newburgh *(G-13025)*

United Minerals Inc................................... G 812 683-5024
   Huntingburg *(G-7294)*

Wellspring Water Services LLC................... G 337 962-5767
   Carmel *(G-1803)*

1389 Oil and gas field services, nec

3rd Rock Energy Services LLC.................. G 314 750-2722
   Fishers *(G-4456)*

A A A Mudjackers Inc............................... G 317 574-1990
   Sharpsville *(G-14708)*

A&J Construction HM Rmdlg LLC............... G 574 514-5127
   South Bend *(G-14929)*

A&J Development Group LLC..................... G 317 767-1182
   Indianapolis *(G-7404)*

AB&b Services LLC................................... G 317 405-7219
   Carmel *(G-1547)*

Abstrakt Group LLC.................................. G 800 200-8994
   Indianapolis *(G-7418)*

Advanced Community Enhancement.......... G 513 615-6730
   Guilford *(G-6826)*

Alexander Thompson................................ G 218 577-7627
   Hammond *(G-6870)*

All Around Construction LLC..................... G 219 902-0742
   Merrillville *(G-11481)*

All-Phase Construction Co LLC.................. G 317 345-7057
   Fishers *(G-4461)*

Anderson Shykia...................................... G 773 304-6852
   Gary *(G-5894)*

Apex AG Solutions LLC............................ F 765 305-1930
   Winchester *(G-16882)*

B & N Rentals LLC................................... G 219 850-3304
   Chesterton *(G-1906)*

Baker Petrolite LLC.................................. G 219 473-5329
   Whiting *(G-16832)*

Beecher Hairston Hairston LLC.................. G 317 714-6703
   Indianapolis *(G-7609)*

Bigg Dawg Construction LLC..................... G 317 506-1436
   Indianapolis *(G-7624)*

Bst Corp.. G 812 925-7911
   Boonville *(G-1083)*

Cbizze LLC... G 623 204-9782
   South Bend *(G-14968)*

Cbrk LLC.. G 317 601-8546
   Indianapolis *(G-7764)*

Centre Township....................................... E 765 482-1729
   Lebanon *(G-10883)*

Cheri-Theree Inc....................................... G 812 529-8132
   Lamar *(G-10795)*

Clean Lines Painting LLC........................... G 708 200-2210
   Michigan City *(G-11588)*

Complete Property Care LLC..................... G 765 288-0890
   Muncie *(G-12368)*

Core Laboratories LP................................ G 260 312-0455
   Fort Wayne *(G-4876)*

Countryside Property LLC.......................... G 800 711-5926
   Evansville *(G-3986)*

Covey Rise Minerals LLC........................... G 812 897-2356
   Boonville *(G-1086)*

Csa Racking LLC...................................... G 414 241-3585
   Hammond *(G-6908)*

Dayson Geological Consulting.................... G 812 868-0957
   Evansville *(G-4008)*

Diamond J Construction LLC..................... G 260 433-5571
   Huntertown *(G-7253)*

Diane Vander Vliet.................................... G 574 389-9360
   Elkhart *(G-3296)*

E Z Choice... G 219 852-4281
   Hammond *(G-6917)*

Elevated Cnstr Group LLC......................... G 708 731-7232
   Hammond *(G-6924)*

Elite Construction Northwest..................... F 888 811-0212
   Merrillville *(G-11512)*

Empire Contractors Inc............................. D 812 424-3865
   Evansville *(G-4035)*

Field Construction.................................... G 574 664-2010
   Twelve Mile *(G-15844)*

Filson Earthwork Company........................ F 317 774-3180
   Noblesville *(G-13078)*

Five Dmensions Restoration LLC............... G 347 490-8904
   Indianapolis *(G-8198)*

Fleming and Sons Home Imprv.................. G 765 717-6690
   Muncie *(G-12396)*

Franklin Well Service LLC......................... F 877 943-4680
   Vincennes *(G-16126)*

Gabriel V Fulkerson.................................. G 502 727-0038
   Lanesville *(G-10797)*

Gallagher Drilling Inc................................. F 812 477-6746
   Evansville *(G-4083)*

Gas City B & K Inc................................... G 765 674-9651
   Gas City *(G-6037)*

General Cnstr & Consulting LLC................. G 812 340-5673
   Muncie *(G-12399)*

Get Right Home Solutions LLC.................. G 574 374-2001
   Goshen *(G-6148)*

Gockel Inc.. G 574 402-0220
   Goshen *(G-6151)*

Grider & Co Construction LLC................... G 310 986-7533
   Indianapolis *(G-8329)*

Guardian Enterprises LLC.......................... G 317 416-8926
   Indianapolis *(G-8340)*

Halyard Corporation.................................. E 219 515-2820
   Portage *(G-13873)*

Haven Capital LLC................................... G 219 802-5044
   Valparaiso *(G-15960)*

Helvie and Sons Inc.................................. G 765 674-1372
   Marion *(G-11292)*

Imel John... G 317 873-8764
   Zionsville *(G-17017)*

Imperial Petroleum Inc............................... E 812 867-1433
   Darmstadt *(G-2836)*

Indiana Home Pro LLC.............................. G 812 968-4822
   Corydon *(G-2501)*

Indiana Petroleum Contractors.................. G 812 477-1575
   Evansville *(G-4120)*

Indiana Service Pros LLC.......................... G 317 658-4673
   Shelbyville *(G-14761)*

Jay Costas Companies Inc....................... G 219 663-4364
   Crown Point *(G-2700)*

Jdh Logistics LLC..................................... G 573 529-2005
   Fort Branch *(G-4705)*

JE Mnnix Well Srvcing Mini E.................... G 765 855-5464
   Centerville *(G-1850)*

Jjs Enterprise LLC.................................... G 812 736-0062
   Corydon *(G-2502)*

Jtex Cnstr & Consulting LLC..................... G 812 486-9123
   Velpen *(G-16093)*

JTI Inc... G 317 797-9698
   Indianapolis *(G-8647)*

Jtm Home & Building................................ G 219 690-1445
   Lowell *(G-11165)*

K S Oil Corp... G 812 453-3026
   Mount Vernon *(G-12305)*

K&D&s Trucking and Reality LLC............... G 847 791-6848
   Hammond *(G-6964)*

Kite Greyhound LLC................................. G 317 577-5600
   Indianapolis *(G-8690)*

Kreative Concepts LLC............................. G 260 579-0922
   Fort Wayne *(G-5160)*

Lamonicos Cnstr & Maint LLC................... G 219 951-8554
   Gary *(G-5977)*

Lewis Property Solutions LLC.................... G 574 361-0168
   Bristol *(G-1271)*

Lucas Oil Pro Plling Prmotions................... G 812 246-3350
   Charlestown *(G-1881)*

M2i LLC... G 765 618-2162
   Marion *(G-11311)*

Majestic Creations LLC............................. G 317 258-2794
   Indianapolis *(G-8815)*

Man Child Property Dev LLC..................... G 317 205-4109
   Indianapolis *(G-8824)*

Mast Services Lafayette LLC..................... G 765 464-6940
   Lafayette *(G-10643)*

Max of All Trades LLC............................. G 317 703-4242
   Kokomo *(G-10305)*

Michael Holland.. G 317 538-1776
   Indianapolis *(G-8897)*

Midwest Garage Doors LLC....................... G 317 739-2534
   Shelbyville *(G-14778)*

Minnix J E Well Servicing......................... G 765 855-5464
   Centerville *(G-1852)*

Morgan Excavating................................... G 812 385-6036
   Oakland City *(G-13321)*

Mp Constructions LLC.............................. G 888 520-7005
   Indianapolis *(G-8963)*

Nelson Salomon Cruz Ramos LLC............. G 765 863-2885
   Kokomo *(G-10316)*

Newpark Resources Inc............................ G 765 546-9473
   Ridgeville *(G-14236)*

Noble Project Services LLC....................... G 219 484-9669
   Hobart *(G-7202)*

SIC SECTION
14 MINING AND QUARRYING OF NONMETALLIC MINERALS, EXCEPT FUELS

Northwest Ind Backflow Testers............ G 219 663-8390
  Crown Point *(G-2726)*

Nupointe Energy LLC.................................. F 765 981-2664
  Warren *(G-16302)*

Oilfield Research Inc................................... G 812 424-2907
  Evansville *(G-4226)*

On Call McGraw LLC................................. G 317 938-8777
  Indianapolis *(G-9051)*

On The Ball Rmdlg & Repr LLP................ G 812 910-9408
  Bicknell *(G-736)*

Onsite Construction Services.................... E 312 723-8060
  Chesterton *(G-1951)*

Owens Property Solutions LLC................. G 708 374-2626
  Gary *(G-5992)*

P & J Sectional Housing............................. G 260 982-7421
  North Manchester *(G-13246)*

Pappas Construction LLC.......................... G 219 314-7068
  Hobart *(G-7203)*

Payne George A Petroleum Engr.............. G 812 853-3813
  Newburgh *(G-13015)*

Penn-Mar Capital LLC................................ G 463 239-2632
  Indianapolis *(G-9115)*

Phoenix Infiniti LLC.................................... G 260 443-2782
  Fort Wayne *(G-5213)*

Pinnacle Oil Trading LLC........................... E 317 875-9465
  Indianapolis *(G-9147)*

Pioneer Oilfield Services LLC................... F 812 882-0999
  Vincennes *(G-16145)*

Presidential Bath & Fix LLC....................... G 812 259-9817
  Evansville *(G-4257)*

Project Field Solutions Inc........................ G 317 590-7678
  Fishers *(G-4584)*

Pulse Energy... G 812 268-6700
  Sullivan *(G-15417)*

Quest Energy Inc.. F 317 318-5737
  Fishers *(G-4589)*

Quick To Fix LLC.. G 812 660-2044
  Bedford *(G-662)*

Rackcollections LLC................................... G 317 779-4302
  Indianapolis *(G-9259)*

Radon Environmental Inc......................... G 317 843-0804
  Elkhart *(G-3637)*

Rai LLC.. G 765 227-0111
  Indianapolis *(G-9263)*

Rakk LLC... G 812 271-4300
  Austin *(G-470)*

RC Enterprise LLC..................................... G 317 935-5628
  Carmel *(G-1735)*

RC Property Preservation LLC.................. G 765 660-3808
  Marion *(G-11334)*

Rs Used Oil Services Inc........................... F 866 778-7336
  Carmel *(G-1748)*

Rt Smart Solutions LLC............................. F 317 435-2200
  Indianapolis *(G-9345)*

S M Smith LLC - S Stngel Mnged.............. G 219 802-6064
  Gary *(G-6007)*

Santos Herrera.. F 260 849-3454
  Berne *(G-724)*

Saybolt.. G 812 944-5001
  Clarksville *(G-2033)*

Saybolt LP... G 812 282-7242
  Clarksville *(G-2034)*

Short 9th LLC... G 270 313-5665
  Indianapolis *(G-9422)*

Silverthorn Handyman Svcs LLC............. G 812 896-4201
  Salem *(G-14498)*

Simmons Equipment Sales Inc................. F 260 625-3308
  Columbia City *(G-2197)*

Smith Technologies................................... G 317 839-6766
  Plainfield *(G-13729)*

Srae Construction LLC............................. G 219 216-1902
  Royal Center *(G-14393)*

Ss Elevations LLC...................................... G 574 310-5442
  South Bend *(G-15263)*

Stealth Energy Group LLC........................ G 316 260-0064
  Zionsville *(G-17053)*

Strategic Tanks Incorporated.................... G 574 807-2403
  Notre Dame *(G-13316)*

Study Studsters LLC.................................. G 574 635-1018
  Elkhart *(G-3702)*

Suncoke Lake Terminal LLC..................... F 630 824-1963
  East Chicago *(G-3043)*

Sunrise Energy LLC................................... G 812 886-9990
  Vincennes *(G-16156)*

T&T Elite Construction LLC...................... G 317 657-8898
  Indianapolis *(G-9545)*

Team Handy LLC.. G 812 962-3630
  Evansville *(G-4340)*

Thegoosecompany LLC............................. G 708 280-7512
  Munster *(G-12570)*

Thomas Taylor.. G 317 557-3287
  Indianapolis *(G-9595)*

Tj Constructions LLC................................. G 470 406-2804
  Indianapolis *(G-9611)*

Tradebe Environmental Svcs LLC........... E 800 388-7242
  Merrillville *(G-11568)*

Tradebe GP... A 800 388-7242
  East Chicago *(G-3045)*

Tradebe Industrial Svcs LLC.................... D 800 388-7242
  East Chicago *(G-3046)*

Trevares D Smith....................................... G 765 603-0468
  Marion *(G-11343)*

Tri-State Guttertopper Inc........................ G 812 455-1460
  Evansville *(G-4350)*

Triple J Machining and Mfg Inc................ F 574 586-7500
  Walkerton *(G-16277)*

United Oil Corp... G 260 489-3511
  Fort Wayne *(G-5521)*

Uprizing LLC... G 317 500-9359
  Indianapolis *(G-9685)*

US Oilfield Company LLC.......................... F 888 584-7565
  Carmel *(G-1796)*

Us Premier Business LLC......................... G 540 822-0329
  Crown Point *(G-2769)*

Valley Scale Company LLC....................... F 812 282-5269
  Clarksville *(G-2041)*

Vectren Power Supply............................... G 812 491-4310
  Evansville *(G-4370)*

Veterans Promise Cnstr LLC.................... G 317 501-4570
  Indianapolis *(G-9715)*

Vlc Services LLC.. F 260 459-9501
  Fort Wayne *(G-5535)*

Wallys Construction................................... G 812 254-4154
  Washington *(G-16512)*

Weatherford Engineered........................... G 812 858-3147
  Newburgh *(G-13029)*

Well Spring Automation LLC.................... G 317 324-1119
  Carmel *(G-1802)*

Whatever It Tkes HM Imprvs LLC............ G 317 494-9568
  Camby *(G-1516)*

Williams Prprty Prsrvation LLC................ G 219 336-3047
  La Porte *(G-10499)*

14 MINING AND QUARRYING OF NONMETALLIC MINERALS, EXCEPT FUELS

1411 Dimension stone

Antique Stove Information......................... G 574 583-6465
  Monticello *(G-12135)*

B G Hoadley Quarries Inc......................... E 812 332-1447
  Bloomington *(G-790)*

Demotte Decorative Stone Inc.................. G 219 987-5461
  Demotte *(G-2915)*

Garrity Stone Inc.. G 317 546-0893
  Indianapolis *(G-8263)*

Great Lakes Granite LLC........................... G 708 474-8800
  Portage *(G-13872)*

Heritage Ldscp Sup Group Inc................. E 317 849-9100
  Indianapolis *(G-8389)*

Independent Limestone Co LLC............... E 812 824-4951
  Bloomington *(G-887)*

Indiana Lmstone Acqisition LLC............... D 812 275-5556
  Bedford *(G-645)*

▲ Indiana Lmstone Acqisition LLC........... E 812 275-3341
  Bloomington *(G-888)*

Indiana Quarriers & Carvers..................... F 812 935-8383
  Bedford *(G-646)*

▼ Indiana Stone Works.............................. G 812 279-0448
  Bedford *(G-648)*

▲ M U Holdings Inc.................................... E 317 596-9786
  Tipton *(G-15781)*

Marietta Martin Materials Inc.................... F 317 776-4460
  Noblesville *(G-13130)*

Reed Quarries Inc...................................... F 812 332-2771
  Bloomington *(G-954)*

Rush County Stone Co Inc....................... G 765 629-2211
  Milroy *(G-11830)*

Tremain Ceramic Tile & Flr Cvg............... E 317 542-1491
  Indianapolis *(G-9633)*

Victor Oolitic Stone Company................... C 812 275-3341
  Oolitic *(G-13360)*

1422 Crushed and broken limestone

3d Stone Inc.. E 812 824-5805
  Bloomington *(G-766)*

Aggrock Quarries Inc................................. G 812 246-2582
  Charlestown *(G-1870)*

Barrett Paving Materials Inc..................... G 765 935-3060
  Richmond *(G-14090)*

Bedford Limestone Suppliers.................... G 812 279-9120
  Bedford *(G-623)*

Bens Quarry LLC.. G 812 824-3730
  Springville *(G-15382)*

Big Creek LLC.. F 812 876-0835
  Gosport *(G-6283)*

Brummett Enterprises LLC....................... G 812 325-6993
  Bloomington *(G-817)*

Calcar Quarries Incorporated................... F 812 723-2109
  Paoli *(G-13491)*

Carmeuse Lime Inc................................... D 219 949-1450
  Gary *(G-5912)*

Cave Quarries Inc...................................... F 812 936-7743
  Paoli *(G-13492)*

Francesville Vulcan Materials.................... G 219 567-9155
  Francesville *(G-5640)*

Global Stone Portage LLC......................... F 219 787-9190
  Portage *(G-13869)*

Handson.. F 812 246-4481
  Sellersburg *(G-14595)*

Hanson Aggregates Wrp Inc..................... E 502 244-7550
  Sellersburg *(G-14596)*

Harris Stone Service Inc.......................... F 765 522-6241
  Bainbridge *(G-563)*

Heidelberg Mtls Mdwest Agg Inc............. G 765 653-7205
  Cloverdale *(G-2086)*

Heidelberg Mtls Mdwest Agg Inc............. F 765 653-1956
  Greencastle *(G-6411)*

Heidelberg Mtls Mdwest Agg Inc............. G 812 889-2120
  Lexington *(G-10977)*

Heidelberg Mtls Mdwest Agg Inc............. G 812 346-6100
  North Vernon *(G-13276)*

Heidelberg Mtls Mdwest Agg Inc............. G 812 246-1942
  Sellersburg *(G-14597)*

14 MINING AND QUARRYING OF NONMETALLIC MINERALS, EXCEPT FUELS — SIC SECTION

Heidelberg Mtls Mdwest Agg Inc............ G ... 260 632-1410
  Woodburn *(G-16948)*
Heidelberg Mtls Sthast Agg LLC............. E ... 317 788-4086
  Indianapolis *(G-8380)*
Heritage Aggregates LLC......................... G ... 317 434-4600
  Indianapolis *(G-8386)*
Heritage Aggregates LLC......................... G ... 765 436-7665
  Thorntown *(G-15751)*
Heritage Aggregates LLC......................... G ... 317 872-6010
  Indianapolis *(G-8387)*
Iowa Limestone Company....................... F ... 317 981-7919
  Cloverdale *(G-2087)*
Kellers Limestone Service Inc................. G ... 219 326-1688
  La Porte *(G-10432)*
LLC Ward Stone...................................... E ... 812 587-0272
  Flat Rock *(G-4654)*
Marietta Martin Materials Inc................... G ... 317 789-4020
  Indianapolis *(G-8834)*
Marietta Martin Materials Inc................... F ... 765 459-3194
  Kokomo *(G-10304)*
Marietta Martin Materials Inc................... G ... 317 831-7391
  Martinsville *(G-11411)*
Marietta Martin Materials Inc................... F ... 317 776-4460
  Noblesville *(G-13130)*
Martin Marietta Materials Inc.................... G ... 317 846-8540
  Carmel *(G-1692)*
Martin Marietta Materials Inc.................... F ... 317 573-4460
  Carmel *(G-1693)*
Martin Marietta Materials Inc.................... F ... 317 846-5942
  Carmel *(G-1694)*
Martin Marietta Materials Inc.................... G ... 317 244-4460
  Indianapolis *(G-8841)*
Meshberger Brothers Stone..................... D ... 260 334-5311
  Bluffton *(G-1041)*
Mulzer Crushed Stone Inc........................ E ... 812 256-3346
  Charlestown *(G-1886)*
Mulzer Crushed Stone Inc........................ G ... 812 937-2442
  Dale *(G-2791)*
Mulzer Crushed Stone Inc........................ E ... 812 365-2145
  English *(G-3844)*
Mulzer Crushed Stone Inc........................ E ... 844 480-6803
  Evansville *(G-4216)*
Mulzer Crushed Stone Inc........................ E ... 812 739-4777
  Leavenworth *(G-10871)*
Mulzer Crushed Stone Inc........................ E ... 812 732-1002
  Mauckport *(G-11440)*
Mulzer Crushed Stone Inc........................ G ... 812 838-3472
  Mount Vernon *(G-12312)*
Mulzer Crushed Stone Inc........................ G ... 812 354-9650
  Petersburg *(G-13619)*
Mulzer Crushed Stone Inc........................ E ... 812 547-7921
  Tell City *(G-15513)*
Nalc LLC... G ... 502 548-9590
  Cloverdale *(G-2091)*
New Point Stone Co Inc............................ E ... 812 852-4225
  Batesville *(G-598)*
New Point Stone Co Inc............................ G ... 765 698-2227
  Laurel *(G-10825)*
▲ New Point Stone Co Inc....................... F ... 812 663-2021
  Greensburg *(G-6622)*
Paul H Rohe Company Inc....................... E ... 812 926-1471
  Aurora *(G-451)*
Robertson Crushed Stone Inc.................. E ... 812 633-4881
  Milltown *(G-11820)*
Rock Creek Stone LLC............................ D ... 260 694-6880
  Bluffton *(G-1052)*
Rogers Group Inc.................................... D ... 812 333-8560
  Bloomington *(G-961)*
Rogers Group Inc.................................... D ... 219 474-5125
  Kentland *(G-10163)*
Seminole Stone Inc.................................. F ... 812 634-7115
  Jasper *(G-9909)*

Stone Quary... E ... 765 473-5578
  Peru *(G-13603)*
Stone-Street Quarries Inc......................... F ... 260 639-6511
  Hoagland *(G-7171)*
U S Aggregates Inc.................................. E ... 765 564-2282
  Delphi *(G-2910)*
U S Aggregates Inc.................................. G ... 765 436-7665
  Thorntown *(G-15757)*
West Plains Mining LLC........................... E ... 260 563-9500
  Wabash *(G-16225)*

1429 Crushed and broken stone, nec

Heidelberg Mtls Sthast Agg LLC............. E ... 317 788-4086
  Indianapolis *(G-8380)*
Pipe Creek Jr... G ... 765 922-7991
  Sims *(G-14924)*
S & G Excavating Inc............................... F ... 812 234-4848
  Terre Haute *(G-15685)*

1442 Construction sand and gravel

Asphalt Materials Inc................................ G ... 317 875-4670
  Indianapolis *(G-7553)*
Asphalt Materials Inc................................ B ... 317 872-6010
  Indianapolis *(G-7552)*
Beaver Gravel Corporation....................... D ... 317 773-0679
  Noblesville *(G-13042)*
Beer and Slabaugh Inc............................. E ... 574 773-3413
  Nappanee *(G-12584)*
Brookfield Sand & Gravel Inc................... E ... 317 835-2235
  Fairland *(G-4398)*
Cgs Services Inc..................................... G ... 765 763-6258
  Morristown *(G-12273)*
Chuck Shane Gravel LLC........................ G ... 574 893-4110
  Silver Lake *(G-14918)*
Cimentos N Votorantim Amer Inc............ E ... 812 384-9463
  Bloomfield *(G-744)*
▲ Country Stone..................................... F ... 260 837-7134
  Waterloo *(G-16518)*
Crisman Sand Company Inc.................... G ... 219 462-3114
  Valparaiso *(G-15930)*
D H Gravel Company............................... G ... 765 893-4914
  Williamsport *(G-16847)*
D Robertson Gravel Co Inc...................... F ... 765 832-2768
  Clinton *(G-2065)*
Elkhart County Gravel Inc........................ G ... 574 831-2815
  Warsaw *(G-16357)*
Elkhart County Gravel Inc........................ F ... 574 831-2815
  New Paris *(G-12951)*
Engineering Aggregates Corp.................. G ... 765 249-3073
  Michigantown *(G-11690)*
Flynn & Sons Sand & Gravel LLC............ G ... 812 636-4400
  Odon *(G-13335)*
GCI Slingers LLC.................................... F ... 317 873-8686
  Zionsville *(G-17011)*
Gibson County Sand & Grav Inc.............. G ... 812 851-5800
  Haubstadt *(G-7085)*
Gravel Doctor Indianapolis LLC............... G ... 317 399-4585
  Indianapolis *(G-8313)*
Greenfield Gravel Inc............................... G ... 317 326-4003
  Greenfield *(G-6506)*
Greensboro Sand & Gravel LLC.............. G ... 765 624-9342
  Knightstown *(G-10195)*
Handson... F ... 812 246-4481
  Sellersburg *(G-14595)*
Happy Valley Sand and Grav Inc.............. G ... 317 839-6800
  Plainfield *(G-13684)*
Harrison Hauling Inc................................ G ... 574 862-3196
  Goshen *(G-6162)*
Harrison Sand and Gravel Co.................. G ... 812 656-8149
  West Harrison *(G-16547)*
Harrison Sand and Gravel Co.................. G ... 812 663-2021
  Greensburg *(G-6600)*

Hassenplug & Son Sand & Gravel........... G ... 574 223-5230
  Rochester *(G-14294)*
Heidelberg Mtls Sthast Agg LLC............. E ... 317 788-4086
  Indianapolis *(G-8380)*
Henschen Sand and Gravel..................... G ... 260 367-2636
  Howe *(G-7236)*
Holcim (us) Inc.. G ... 219 378-1193
  East Chicago *(G-3017)*
Hopkins Gravel Sand & Concrete............ G ... 317 831-2704
  Mooresville *(G-12211)*
Hydraulic Press Brick Company.............. C ... 317 290-1140
  Mooresville *(G-12212)*
Illiana Remedial Action Inc...................... G ... 219 844-4862
  Hammond *(G-6954)*
Indiana Gravel LLC.................................. G ... 574 538-7152
  Goshen *(G-6173)*
Ingram Road Quarry LLC......................... G ... 812 824-3730
  Springville *(G-15386)*
Irving Materials Inc.................................. F ... 765 778-4760
  Anderson *(G-136)*
Irving Materials Inc.................................. F ... 765 922-7285
  Kokomo *(G-10291)*
Krafft Gravel Inc...................................... G ... 260 238-4653
  Spencerville *(G-15372)*
Lafontaine Gravel Inc.............................. G ... 765 981-4849
  La Fontaine *(G-10369)*
Lake County Sand & Gravel LLC............. G ... 219 988-4540
  Merrillville *(G-11528)*
Lees Ready-Mix & Trucking Inc............... F ... 812 372-1800
  Columbus *(G-2339)*
Longhorn Sand and Gravel LLC............... G ... 574 532-2788
  North Liberty *(G-13218)*
LPI Paving & Excavating......................... G ... 260 726-9564
  Portland *(G-13955)*
Marietta Martin Materials Inc................... G ... 317 831-7391
  Martinsville *(G-11411)*
Marietta Martin Materials Inc................... F ... 317 776-4460
  Noblesville *(G-13130)*
Merritt Sand and Gravel Inc..................... F ... 260 665-2513
  Waterloo *(G-16524)*
Michele L Gravel..................................... G ... 317 889-0521
  Indianapolis *(G-8899)*
Mulzer Crushed Stone Inc........................ E ... 844 480-6803
  Evansville *(G-4216)*
Muncie Sand & Gravel Inc....................... G ... 765 282-6422
  Muncie *(G-12466)*
North America Frac Sand Inc.................. G ... 260 490-9990
  Ossian *(G-13429)*
Nugent Sand Company............................ G ... 812 372-7508
  Columbus *(G-2363)*
Old Dutch Sand Co Inc............................ G ... 219 938-7020
  Gary *(G-5988)*
Paddack Brothers Inc.............................. G ... 765 659-4777
  Frankfort *(G-5689)*
Paul H Rohe Company Inc....................... E ... 812 926-1471
  Aurora *(G-451)*
Pebble Natursutten LLC.......................... G ... 866 228-1473
  Greenfield *(G-6536)*
Phend and Brown Inc.............................. E ... 574 658-4166
  Milford *(G-11802)*
Quikrete Companies LLC........................ E ... 317 251-2281
  Indianapolis *(G-9252)*
Rex Alton & Companies Inc.................... F ... 812 882-8519
  Vincennes *(G-16149)*
Rogers Group Inc.................................... C ... 812 333-6324
  Bloomington *(G-959)*
Rogers Group Inc.................................... G ... 765 342-6898
  Martinsville *(G-11424)*
Rogers Group Inc.................................... D ... 812 849-3530
  Mitchell *(G-12047)*
Rogers Group Inc.................................... F ... 812 275-7860
  Springville *(G-15392)*

15 CONSTRUCTION - GENERAL CONTRACTORS & OPERATIVE BUILDERS

Rogers Group Inc .... E 812 882-3640
  Vincennes *(G-16150)*

Rogers Group Inc .... E 765 893-4463
  Williamsport *(G-16853)*

Roskovenski Sand & Gravel Inc .... G 765 832-6748
  Clinton *(G-2076)*

S & G Excavating Inc .... F 812 234-4848
  Terre Haute *(G-15685)*

Schmaltz Ready Mix Concrete .... G 812 689-5140
  Osgood *(G-13415)*

Schrock Aggregate Company Inc .... G 574 862-4167
  Wakarusa *(G-16250)*

Schrock Excavating Inc .... E 574 862-4167
  Wakarusa *(G-16251)*

Shelby Gravel Inc .... F 812 526-2731
  Edinburgh *(G-3104)*

Shelby Gravel Inc .... F 317 738-3445
  Franklin *(G-5776)*

Shelby Gravel Inc .... E 317 398-4485
  Shelbyville *(G-14797)*

Siders & Son Gravel .... G 574 893-4110
  Roann *(G-14254)*

Southfield Corporation .... E 812 824-1355
  Bloomington *(G-978)*

Southfield Corporation .... G 317 846-6060
  Carmel *(G-1767)*

Speedway Sand & Gravel Inc .... G 574 893-7355
  Silver Lake *(G-14922)*

Spray Inc .... F 812 346-3197
  Seymour *(G-14695)*

Spray Sand & Gravel Inc .... G 812 522-5417
  Seymour *(G-14696)*

Spray Sand & Gravel Inc .... G 812 523-8081
  Seymour *(G-14697)*

Stafford Gravel Inc .... F 260 868-2503
  Butler *(G-1479)*

Steele Roofing Co LLC .... G 219 243-1563
  Valparaiso *(G-16058)*

Stone Quary .... G 574 936-2975
  Plymouth *(G-13814)*

Stone Quary .... E 765 473-5578
  Peru *(G-13603)*

Todd L Wise .... G 260 799-4828
  Albion *(G-46)*

U S Aggregates Inc .... E 765 564-2282
  Delphi *(G-2910)*

Utility Access Solutions Inc .... G 765 744-6528
  Ridgeville *(G-14238)*

Van Duyne Block and Gravel .... G 574 223-6656
  Rochester *(G-14331)*

Wallace Construction Inc .... F 317 422-5356
  Martinsville *(G-11434)*

Wells Trckg A Div Wlls Assoc I .... G 317 250-2616
  Indianapolis *(G-9750)*

West Plains Distribution LLC .... F 260 563-9500
  Wabash *(G-16224)*

White Sand & Gravel Inc .... G 317 882-7791
  Indianapolis *(G-9759)*

Wilhelm Gravel Co Inc .... E 260 837-6511
  Waterloo *(G-16534)*

1446 Industrial sand

C & J Plating & Grinding LLC .... G 765 288-8728
  Muncie *(G-12358)*

Sanders & Crosley LLC .... G 812 268-4472
  Sullivan *(G-15422)*

Warsaw Foundry Company Inc .... D 574 267-8772
  Warsaw *(G-16446)*

1455 Kaolin and ball clay

Covia Holdings Corporation .... G 812 683-2179
  Huntingburg *(G-7275)*

1459 Clay and related minerals, nec

Christy Refractories Co Llc .... G 219 464-2856
  Valparaiso *(G-15927)*

1479 Chemical and fertilizer mining

Royster Clark Closed .... G 812 397-2617
  Shelburn *(G-14720)*

Wild Boar Mine .... G 812 922-1015
  Lynnville *(G-11193)*

1481 Nonmetallic mineral services

243 Quarry .... G 765 653-4100
  Cloverdale *(G-2081)*

Detroit Salt Company LC .... G 313 841-5144
  Indianapolis *(G-7967)*

Fort Wayne Diamond Pdts Inc .... G 260 747-1681
  Fort Wayne *(G-4991)*

McCullugh Archlogical Svcs LLC .... G 260 402-3462
  Indianapolis *(G-8863)*

Nina Gail Diamonds LLC .... G 765 591-0477
  Muncie *(G-12469)*

Opta Minerals (holdco) Inc .... G 574 586-9559
  Walkerton *(G-16273)*

Tri-Gen Inc .... E 317 849-5612
  Noblesville *(G-13184)*

1499 Miscellaneous nonmetallic mining

Classic Rock Face Block Inc .... G 260 704-3113
  Fort Wayne *(G-4856)*

D & S Enterprises .... G 812 354-6108
  Petersburg *(G-13609)*

Hanson Agrigoods Midwest Inc .... G 317 635-9048
  Cloverdale *(G-2085)*

Nina Gail Diamonds LLC .... G 765 591-0477
  Muncie *(G-12469)*

15 CONSTRUCTION - GENERAL CONTRACTORS & OPERATIVE BUILDERS

1521 Single-family housing construction

ALE Enterprises Inc .... G 317 856-2981
  Indianapolis *(G-7467)*

◆ All American Group Inc .... E 574 262-0123
  Elkhart *(G-3160)*

American Adventures Inc .... G 574 875-6850
  Elkhart *(G-3170)*

Assured General Contg LLC .... G 260 740-4744
  Fort Wayne *(G-4776)*

Bee Window Incorporated .... C 317 283-8522
  Fishers *(G-4473)*

Benakovich Builders .... G 219 204-2777
  Thorntown *(G-15750)*

Bigg Dawg Construction LLC .... G 317 506-1436
  Indianapolis *(G-7624)*

Clean Lines Painting LLC .... G 708 200-2210
  Michigan City *(G-11588)*

Concord Realstate Corp .... F 765 423-5555
  Lafayette *(G-10554)*

E & L Construction Inc .... G 765 525-7081
  Manilla *(G-11260)*

Ettensohn & Company LLC .... G 812 547-5491
  Tell City *(G-15501)*

Expedition Log Homes .... G 219 663-5555
  Crown Point *(G-2683)*

H & H Home Improvement Inc .... G 812 288-8700
  Clarksville *(G-2017)*

Hudec Construction Company .... E 219 922-9811
  Griffith *(G-6807)*

JB Bond Construction LLC .... G 219 628-4606
  Chesterton *(G-1939)*

Klomp Construction Company .... G 219 308-8372
  Saint John *(G-14454)*

Landmark Home & Land Company ..... G 219 874-4065
  Michigan City *(G-11630)*

Leroy E Doty Cabinet Shop .... G 219 663-1139
  Crown Point *(G-2717)*

Maher Supply Inc .... G 812 234-7699
  Terre Haute *(G-15635)*

Miller Brothers Builders Inc .... E 574 533-8602
  Goshen *(G-6222)*

Powerclean Inc .... E 260 483-1375
  Fort Wayne *(G-5329)*

Rackcollections LLC .... G 317 779-4302
  Indianapolis *(G-9259)*

Robert C Kueber .... G 812 838-5813
  Mount Vernon *(G-12317)*

1522 Residential construction, nec

Alexander Thompson .... G 218 577-7627
  Hammond *(G-6870)*

Kings-Qlity Rstrtion Svcs LLC .... F 812 944-4347
  New Albany *(G-12760)*

Miller Brothers Builders Inc .... E 574 533-8602
  Goshen *(G-6222)*

1541 Industrial buildings and warehouses

3c Coman Ltd .... G 317 650-5156
  Fortville *(G-5585)*

All-Phase Construction Co LLC .... G 317 345-7057
  Fishers *(G-4461)*

Better Blacc Wall Streetz LLC .... F 812 927-0712
  Seymour *(G-14632)*

Clean Lines Painting LLC .... G 708 200-2210
  Michigan City *(G-11588)*

Csa Racking LLC .... G 414 241-3585
  Hammond *(G-6908)*

Dmp LLC .... G 812 699-0086
  Worthington *(G-16959)*

Egenolf Contg & Rigging II Inc .... F 317 787-5301
  Indianapolis *(G-8059)*

Empire Contractors Inc .... D 812 424-3865
  Evansville *(G-4035)*

◆ Hale Industries Inc .... F 317 577-0337
  Fortville *(G-5598)*

Hgmc Supply Inc .... F 317 351-9500
  Indianapolis *(G-8394)*

Maddox Industrial Contg LLC .... E 812 544-2156
  Santa Claus *(G-14508)*

Milani Custom Homes LLC .... G 219 455-5804
  Merrillville *(G-11538)*

Miles Farm Supply LLC .... D 812 359-4463
  Boonville *(G-1090)*

Rakk LLC .... G 812 271-4300
  Austin *(G-470)*

Reed Contracting Company .... E 765 452-2638
  Kokomo *(G-10326)*

Sterling Industrial LLC .... C 812 423-7832
  Evansville *(G-4333)*

▼ Trifab & Construction Inc .... G 219 845-1300
  Hammond *(G-7024)*

Trivett Contracting Inc .... E 317 539-5150
  Clayton *(G-2062)*

1542 Nonresidential construction, nec

ALE Enterprises Inc .... G 317 856-2981
  Indianapolis *(G-7467)*

Bc Countertops Inc .... E 317 637-4427
  Indianapolis *(G-7600)*

Burns Construction Inc .... E 574 382-2315
  Macy *(G-11195)*

15 CONSTRUCTION - GENERAL CONTRACTORS & OPERATIVE BUILDERS

Classic Buildings Inc .... E 812 944-5821
Clarksville *(G-2013)*

Cozy Cat Inc .... G 765 463-1254
Lafayette *(G-10559)*

DC Construction Services Inc .... E 317 577-0276
Indianapolis *(G-7958)*

Heartland Metal LLC .... G 574 773-0509
Nappanee *(G-12607)*

Indiana Mobile Welding LLC .... G 317 771-8900
Noblesville *(G-13102)*

Indy Hoods LLC .... F 317 731-7170
Indianapolis *(G-8529)*

J G Bowers Inc .... E 765 677-1000
Marion *(G-11297)*

K Q Servicing LLC .... G 812 486-9244
Loogootee *(G-11140)*

Kammerer Inc .... D 260 349-9098
Kendallville *(G-10124)*

Klomp Construction Company .... G 219 308-8372
Saint John *(G-14454)*

Lowes Pellets and Grain Inc .... E 812 663-7863
Greensburg *(G-6615)*

Marshall Companies Indiana .... G 317 769-2666
Lebanon *(G-10913)*

Max of All Trades LLC .... G 317 703-4242
Kokomo *(G-10305)*

Milani Custom Homes LLC .... G 219 455-5804
Merrillville *(G-11538)*

Miller Brothers Builders Inc .... E 574 533-8602
Goshen *(G-6222)*

Morgan Excavating .... G 812 385-6036
Oakland City *(G-13321)*

North Webster Construction Inc .... E 574 834-4448
North Webster *(G-13310)*

Over Top Roofing and Rmdlg LLC .... G 513 704-5422
Lawrenceburg *(G-10851)*

Reed Contracting Company .... E 765 452-2638
Kokomo *(G-10326)*

T Organization Inc .... E 463 204-5118
Greenwood *(G-6771)*

Tri-Esco Inc .... F 765 446-7937
Colburn *(G-2112)*

Wise Energy LLC .... G 317 475-0305
Indianapolis *(G-9776)*

16 HEAMY CONSTRUCTION, EXCEPT BUILDING CONSTRUCTION, CONTRACTOR

1611 Highway and street construction

All American Ex Solutions LLC .... E 317 789-3070
Indianapolis *(G-7472)*

Barrett Paving Materials Inc .... G 765 935-3060
Richmond *(G-14090)*

Bi-State Asphalt .... G 765 832-5000
Clinton *(G-2064)*

C & R Cnstr & Consulting LLC .... G 812 738-4493
Corydon *(G-2489)*

E & B Paving Inc .... E 765 674-5848
Marion *(G-11284)*

E & B Paving Inc .... E 765 643-5358
Anderson *(G-112)*

Globe Asphalt Paving Co Inc .... E 317 568-4344
Indianapolis *(G-8293)*

Huehls Salcoating Lawncare LLC .... G 317 782-4069
Indianapolis *(G-8433)*

Irving Materials Inc .... F 765 922-7285
Kokomo *(G-10291)*

Lewis Sealing & Cleaning .... G 317 783-1424
Indianapolis *(G-8742)*

Milestone Contractors LP .... D 812 579-5248
Columbus *(G-2356)*

Milestone Contractors LP .... D 765 772-7500
Lafayette *(G-10650)*

Milestone Contractors N Inc .... G 219 924-5900
South Bend *(G-15151)*

Niblock Excavating Inc .... G 260 248-2100
Columbia City *(G-2174)*

Niblock Excavating Inc .... D 574 848-4437
Bristol *(G-1281)*

Paving Plus Company .... G 317 784-1857
Indianapolis *(G-9105)*

Phend and Brown Inc .... E 574 658-4166
Milford *(G-11802)*

Rieth-Riley Cnstr Co Inc .... E 574 875-5183
Gary *(G-6005)*

Rogers Group Inc .... F 812 333-8550
Bloomington *(G-962)*

Scotts Grant County Asp Inc .... G 765 664-2754
Marion *(G-11337)*

Scruggs Construction Inc .... G 812 528-8178
Seymour *(G-14687)*

Sssi Inc .... F 219 880-0818
Gary *(G-6015)*

Triangle Asphalt Paving Corp .... E 765 482-5701
Lebanon *(G-10947)*

Uprizing LLC .... G 317 500-9359
Indianapolis *(G-9685)*

Utility Access Solutions Inc .... G 765 744-6528
Ridgeville *(G-14238)*

Vans Industrial Inc .... E 219 931-4881
Hammond *(G-7028)*

Wallace Construction Inc .... F 317 422-5356
Martinsville *(G-11434)*

1622 Bridge, tunnel, and elevated highway

Beer and Slabaugh Inc .... E 574 773-3413
Nappanee *(G-12584)*

C & R Cnstr & Consulting LLC .... G 812 738-4493
Corydon *(G-2489)*

Milestone Contractors LP .... D 812 579-5248
Columbus *(G-2356)*

1623 Water, sewer, and utility lines

Avid Operations Inc .... G 260 220-2001
Fort Wayne *(G-4784)*

Beer and Slabaugh Inc .... E 574 773-3413
Nappanee *(G-12584)*

Benson Tower LLC .... G 270 577-7598
Evansville *(G-3914)*

Commtineo LLC .... F 219 476-3667
Wanatah *(G-16288)*

Gentry Well & Pump Service LLC .... G 260 563-1907
Wabash *(G-16189)*

GI Properties Inc .... G 219 763-1177
Portage *(G-13868)*

Hd Mechanical Inc .... F 219 924-6050
Griffith *(G-6806)*

LGS Plumbing Inc .... E 219 663-2177
Crown Point *(G-2718)*

Milestone Contractors LP .... D 812 579-5248
Columbus *(G-2356)*

Mnt Delivery Company .... G 574 518-6250
Osceola *(G-13399)*

Niblock Excavating Inc .... D 574 848-4437
Bristol *(G-1281)*

Phend and Brown Inc .... E 574 658-4166
Milford *(G-11802)*

Swager Communications Inc .... E 260 495-2515
Fremont *(G-5837)*

Vectren LLC .... A 812 491-4000
Evansville *(G-4368)*

Watershipblue LLC .... G 317 910-8585
Indianapolis *(G-9741)*

1629 Heavy construction, nec

Astbury Water Technology Inc .... D 317 328-7153
Indianapolis *(G-7556)*

D & S Enterprises .... G 812 354-6108
Petersburg *(G-13609)*

Dyno Nobel Inc .... G 260 731-4431
Pennville *(G-13563)*

Gentry Well & Pump Service LLC .... G 260 563-1907
Wabash *(G-16189)*

Hampton Equipment LLC .... G 260 740-8704
Fort Wayne *(G-5049)*

Honeywell International Inc .... G 219 836-3803
Munster *(G-12540)*

Lakemaster Inc .... F 765 288-3718
Muncie *(G-12437)*

Leistner Aquatic Services Inc .... G 317 535-6099
Morgantown *(G-12260)*

Paf Construction LLC .... E 812 496-4669
Columbus *(G-2371)*

Parke County Aggregates LLC .... G 765 245-2344
Rockville *(G-14353)*

Paving Plus Company .... G 317 784-1857
Indianapolis *(G-9105)*

PFC Farm Services Inc .... G 260 235-0817
Fremont *(G-5831)*

Pond Doctors Inc .... G 812 744-5258
Aurora *(G-453)*

Randall K Dike .... G 812 664-4942
Owensville *(G-13471)*

Sanco Industries Inc .... G 260 467-1791
Fort Wayne *(G-5397)*

Sanco Industries Inc .... E 260 426-6281
Fort Wayne *(G-5398)*

Sdf Engineering LLC .... G 317 674-2643
Carmel *(G-1755)*

Thatcher Engineering Corp .... D 219 949-2084
Gary *(G-6018)*

17 CONSTRUCTION - SPECIAL TRADE CONTRACTORS

1711 Plumbing, heating, air-conditioning

A & A Prcsion Htg Colg Rfrgn L .... G 812 401-1711
Evansville *(G-3859)*

▲ ABC Industries Inc .... D 800 426-0921
Winona Lake *(G-16907)*

All Pro Property Services LLC .... G 317 721-1227
Indianapolis *(G-7474)*

Bowmans Tin Shop Inc .... G 574 936-3234
Plymouth *(G-13760)*

Brackett Heating & AC Inc .... E 812 476-1138
Evansville *(G-3949)*

Brouillette Htg Coolg Plbg LLC .... G 765 884-0176
Fowler *(G-5622)*

C & K United Shtmtl & Mech .... E 812 423-5090
Evansville *(G-3958)*

Clarios LLC .... B 317 638-7611
Indianapolis *(G-7816)*

◆ Cor-A-Vent Inc .... F 574 255-1910
Mishawaka *(G-11866)*

Danny Webb Plumbing .... G 574 936-2746
Plymouth *(G-13769)*

Eaton Septic Tank Company .... G 765 396-3275
Eaton *(G-3060)*

Economy Electric Htg & Coolg .... G 219 923-4441
Highland *(G-7134)*

Evansville Sheet Metal Works Inc .... D 812 423-7871
Evansville *(G-4057)*

17 CONSTRUCTION - SPECIAL TRADE CONTRACTORS

Expert Electrical Services LLC .... G 765 664-6642
  Marion *(G-11285)*

Fletcher Heating & Cooling .... G 812 865-2984
  Paoli *(G-13494)*

Frank H Monroe Heating & Coolg .... E 812 945-2566
  New Albany *(G-12734)*

Gentry Well & Pump Service LLC .... G 260 563-1907
  Wabash *(G-16189)*

▲ Geo-Flo Corporation .... F 812 275-8513
  Bedford *(G-639)*

Griffen Plmbng-Heating-Cooling .... E 574 295-2440
  Elkhart *(G-3392)*

Griffin Clark LLC .... G 765 491-9059
  Bloomington *(G-871)*

Halsen Brothers Shtmtl Inc .... G 574 583-3358
  Monticello *(G-12152)*

Hayward & Sams LLP .... G 260 351-4166
  Stroh *(G-15401)*

▲ Hightec Solar Inc .... F 219 814-4279
  Michigan City *(G-11624)*

Huntingburg Machine Works Inc .... F 812 683-3531
  Huntingburg *(G-7282)*

Hydro Fire Protection Inc .... E 317 780-6980
  Indianapolis *(G-8442)*

In Cloudbrst Lawn Sprnklr Svcs .... F 260 492-8400
  Fort Wayne *(G-5097)*

Jack Frost LLC .... E 812 477-7244
  Evansville *(G-4136)*

JO Mory Inc .... F 260 897-3541
  Avilla *(G-479)*

JO Mory Inc .... G 260 347-3753
  Kendallville *(G-10121)*

Johnson Cntrls Fire Prtction L .... G 317 826-2130
  Indianapolis *(G-8633)*

Jones & Sons Inc .... E 812 299-2287
  Terre Haute *(G-15622)*

Knox Inc .... F 260 665-6617
  Angola *(G-269)*

Midwest Sheet Metal Inc .... G 574 223-3332
  Rochester *(G-14307)*

Millenium Sheet Metal Inc .... F 574 935-9101
  Plymouth *(G-13797)*

Mnt Delivery Company .... G 574 518-6250
  Osceola *(G-13399)*

Paniccia Heating & Cooling Inc .... G 219 872-2198
  Michigan City *(G-11650)*

Rcate Plbg Mech Ltd Lblty Co .... G 812 613-0386
  Sellersburg *(G-14611)*

◆ Reflectix Inc .... D 765 533-4332
  Markleville *(G-11370)*

Rex Byers Htg & Coolg Systems .... F 765 459-8858
  Kokomo *(G-10328)*

Rpg Energy Group Inc .... F 317 614-0054
  Indianapolis *(G-9342)*

Russells Excvtg Sptic Tnks Inc .... F 812 838-2471
  Mount Vernon *(G-12318)*

Schmidt Contracting Inc .... E 812 482-3923
  Jasper *(G-9908)*

Shank Brothers Inc .... F 260 744-4802
  Fort Wayne *(G-5411)*

Slate Mechanical Inc .... F 765 452-9611
  Kokomo *(G-10335)*

Sprinkguard LLC .... F 877 274-7976
  Mishawaka *(G-12006)*

Sterling Industrial LLC .... C 812 479-5447
  Evansville *(G-4334)*

Superior Distribution .... G 317 308-5525
  Indianapolis *(G-9528)*

T R Bulger Inc .... G 219 879-8525
  Trail Creek *(G-15841)*

Temptek Inc .... G 317 887-6352
  Greenwood *(G-6773)*

Tri-State Mechanical Inc .... F 260 471-0345
  Fort Wayne *(G-5506)*

Tron Mechanical Incorporated .... C 812 838-4715
  Mount Vernon *(G-12324)*

Two Guys Mechanical Contrs Inc .... E 574 946-7671
  Winamac *(G-16878)*

US Metals Inc .... G 219 802-8465
  Hammond *(G-7027)*

Vans Industrial Inc .... E 219 931-4881
  Hammond *(G-7028)*

Vincent Aliano Elc & Hvac Inc .... G 812 332-3332
  Bloomington *(G-1007)*

Washburn Heating & AC .... G 574 825-7697
  Middlebury *(G-11757)*

1721 Painting and paper hanging

Clean Lines Painting LLC .... G 708 200-2210
  Michigan City *(G-11588)*

◆ Creative Liquid Coatings Inc .... B 260 349-1862
  Kendallville *(G-10105)*

Csi Manufacturing Inc .... F 574 825-7891
  Middlebury *(G-11708)*

DC Coaters Inc .... D 765 675-6006
  Tipton *(G-15770)*

Deco Coatings Inc .... E 317 889-9290
  Indianapolis *(G-7960)*

Dr Restorations Inc .... G 317 646-7150
  Clermont *(G-2063)*

▼ Girls .... G 812 299-1382
  Terre Haute *(G-15598)*

Helming Bros Inc .... G 812 634-9797
  Jasper *(G-9842)*

Northern Ind Indus Catings LLC .... G 574 893-4621
  Akron *(G-6)*

Quality Pnt Prstned Fnshes Inc .... G 574 294-6944
  Elkhart *(G-3633)*

Rex Alton & Companies Inc .... F 812 882-8519
  Vincennes *(G-16149)*

Saran LP C
  Indianapolis *(G-9373)*

Van Zandt Enterprises Inc .... F 812 423-3511
  Evansville *(G-4366)*

1731 Electrical work

American Fire Company .... G 219 840-0630
  Valparaiso *(G-15899)*

Automation Control Service .... G 812 472-3292
  Hardinsburg *(G-7047)*

Avid Operations Inc .... G 260 220-2001
  Fort Wayne *(G-4784)*

B & D Electric Inc .... F 812 254-2122
  Shoals *(G-14903)*

Belden Inc .... G 978 537-9961
  Richmond *(G-14091)*

Boone County Electric Inc .... G 765 482-1430
  Lebanon *(G-10880)*

Cambridge Enterprise Inc .... G 765 544-3402
  Merrillville *(G-11496)*

Commtineo LLC .... G 219 476-3667
  Wanatah *(G-16288)*

Complete Controls Inc .... G 260 489-0852
  Fort Wayne *(G-4868)*

Corrquest Automation Inc .... G 812 596-0049
  Crandall *(G-2536)*

Current Electric Inc .... F 219 872-7736
  Michigan City *(G-11591)*

Custom Controls & Engrg Inc .... G 812 663-0755
  Greensburg *(G-6587)*

Cybernaut Industria LLC .... G 317 664-5316
  Indianapolis *(G-7939)*

Electric Plus .... F 812 336-4992
  Bloomington *(G-860)*

Electric Plus Inc .... D 317 718-0100
  Avon *(G-516)*

Electronic Services LLC .... E 765 457-3894
  Kokomo *(G-10262)*

Erosion & Cnstr Solutions Inc .... E 219 885-9676
  Merrillville *(G-11514)*

Expert Electrical Services LLC .... G 765 664-6642
  Marion *(G-11285)*

Gottman Electric Company Inc .... G 812 838-0037
  Mount Vernon *(G-12297)*

Hoosier Industrial Electric .... F 812 346-2232
  North Vernon *(G-13278)*

Hubbard Inc .... G 317 535-1926
  Whiteland *(G-16788)*

J V Crane & Engineering Inc .... E 219 942-8566
  Portage *(G-13879)*

JO Mory Inc .... G 260 347-3753
  Kendallville *(G-10121)*

Johnson Cntrls Fire Prtction L .... G 317 826-2130
  Indianapolis *(G-8633)*

Joseph Matthew Biaso .... G 812 277-6871
  Mitchell *(G-12041)*

Lancon Electric Inc .... G 260 897-3285
  Laotto *(G-10809)*

Liberty Automation LLC .... G 574 524-0436
  Albion *(G-31)*

Link Electrical Service .... G 812 288-8184
  Jeffersonville *(G-10013)*

Loud Clear Communications LLC .... G 260 433-9479
  Auburn *(G-403)*

Lynn Bros Electric Inc .... G 219 762-6386
  Portage *(G-13883)*

Nrk Inc .... E 812 232-1800
  Terre Haute *(G-15653)*

Ohio Valley Electric .... G 812 532-5288
  Lawrenceburg *(G-10848)*

Phil & Son Inc .... G 219 663-5757
  Crown Point *(G-2730)*

▲ Poolguard/Pbm Industries Inc .... F 812 346-2648
  North Vernon *(G-13292)*

Quantum Technologies LLC .... G 765 426-0156
  Elizabethtown *(G-3132)*

Rex Byers Htg & Coolg Systems .... F 765 459-8858
  Kokomo *(G-10328)*

Sentinel Alarm Inc .... G 219 874-6051
  Trail Creek *(G-15839)*

Signdoc Identity LLC .... G 317 247-9670
  Indianapolis *(G-9435)*

Tank Construction & Service Co .... F 317 509-6294
  Whitestown *(G-16823)*

▲ Trilithic Inc .... C 317 895-3600
  Indianapolis *(G-9641)*

Vidicom Corporation .... G 219 923-7475
  Hammond *(G-7029)*

Watershipblue LLC .... G 317 910-8585
  Indianapolis *(G-9741)*

1741 Masonry and other stonework

Accent Limestone & Carving Inc .... G 812 876-7040
  Bloomington *(G-772)*

Charles Coons .... G 765 362-6509
  Crawfordsville *(G-2552)*

Empire Contractors Inc .... D 812 424-3865
  Evansville *(G-4035)*

Oesterling Chimney Sweep Inc .... G 812 372-3512
  Columbus *(G-2364)*

Pyro Industrial Services Inc .... E 219 787-5700
  Portage *(G-13907)*

Rose Hl Lawn Care Ldscpg Snow .... G 812 230-0024
  Terre Haute *(G-15684)*

Scruggs Construction Inc .... E 812 528-8178
  Seymour *(G-14687)*

17 CONSTRUCTION - SPECIAL TRADE CONTRACTORS

Slatile Roofing and Shtmtl Co............... E 574 233-7485
South Bend *(G-15246)*

Thatcher Engineering Corp................... D 219 949-2084
Gary *(G-6018)*

Tremain Ceramic Tile & Flr Cvg........... E 317 542-1491
Indianapolis *(G-9633)*

1742 Plastering, drywall, and insulation

All-Phase Construction Co LLC............ G 317 345-7057
Fishers *(G-4461)*

Clean Lines Painting LLC...................... G 708 200-2210
Michigan City *(G-11588)*

Dr Restorations Inc................................ G 317 646-7150
Clermont *(G-2063)*

Fit Tight Covers Company Inc............. E 812 492-3370
Evansville *(G-4072)*

Gribbins Specialty Group Inc............... G 812 422-3340
Evansville *(G-4099)*

Installed Building Pdts LLC.................. G 317 398-3216
Shelbyville *(G-14762)*

Insulation Specialties of Amer............. E 219 733-2502
Wanatah *(G-16290)*

Milani Custom Homes LLC.................. G 219 455-5804
Merrillville *(G-11538)*

Proline Spray Foam Inc........................ G 317 981-2158
Indianapolis *(G-9229)*

PSC Industries Inc................................ G 317 547-5439
Indianapolis *(G-9237)*

1743 Terrazzo, tile, marble, mosaic work

Concepts In Stone & Tile Inc............... G 574 267-4712
Warsaw *(G-16337)*

Max of All Trades LLC......................... G 317 703-4242
Kokomo *(G-10305)*

◆ Santarossa Mosaic Tile Co Inc.......... C 317 632-9494
Indianapolis *(G-9371)*

Stone Artisans Ltd................................ G 847 219-7862
Indianapolis *(G-9513)*

Tremain Ceramic Tile & Flr Cvg........... E 317 542-1491
Indianapolis *(G-9633)*

1751 Carpentry work

A-1 Door Specialties Inc...................... G 260 749-1635
South Bend *(G-14930)*

Academy Inc.. G 574 293-7113
Elkhart *(G-3147)*

Benakovich Builders............................. G 219 204-2777
Thorntown *(G-15750)*

Bleacherpro LLC.................................... G 813 394-5316
Fort Wayne *(G-4806)*

Claridges Wood Shop........................... G 812 536-2569
Stendal *(G-15398)*

Concord Realstate Corp....................... F 765 423-5555
Lafayette *(G-10554)*

Continntal Crpntry Cmpnnts LLC......... E 219 733-0367
Wanatah *(G-16289)*

Country Corner Woodworks LLC......... G 574 825-6782
Middlebury *(G-11706)*

Country Mill Cabinet Co Inc................. F 260 693-9289
Laotto *(G-10804)*

Delbert Kemp.. F 812 486-3325
Montgomery *(G-12095)*

Douglas Dye and Associates Inc......... G 317 844-1709
Carmel *(G-1611)*

Dutch Country Woodworking Inc......... G 260 499-4847
Lagrange *(G-10734)*

E & E Garage Doors LLC..................... G 317 575-9677
Carmel *(G-1615)*

Empire Contractors Inc........................ D 812 424-3865
Evansville *(G-4035)*

Ettensohn & Company LLC................. G 812 547-5491
Tell City *(G-15501)*

Four Woods Laminating Inc................. E 260 593-2246
Topeka *(G-15806)*

Freedom Valley Cabinets..................... G 717 606-2811
Freedom *(G-5800)*

Gary E Ellsworth................................... G 260 639-3078
Hoagland *(G-7168)*

H & H Home Improvement Inc............ G 812 288-8700
Clarksville *(G-2017)*

Huntington Exteriors Inc....................... F 260 356-1621
Huntington *(G-7322)*

Innovative Corp..................................... E 317 804-5977
Westfield *(G-16701)*

Klomp Construction Company............. G 219 308-8372
Saint John *(G-14454)*

Kostyo Woodworking Inc..................... G 812 466-7350
Terre Haute *(G-15625)*

M & H Woodworking LLC.................... G 812 486-2570
Montgomery *(G-12111)*

Marquise Enterprises Ltd..................... G 317 578-3400
Indianapolis *(G-8840)*

Master Piece Krafts LLC...................... G 260 768-4330
Shipshewana *(G-14866)*

▲ Mhp Holdings Inc............................. C 574 825-9524
Middlebury *(G-11736)*

Rodeswood LLC.................................... G 574 457-4496
Syracuse *(G-15476)*

Wood Wiz Inc.. G 317 834-9079
Mooresville *(G-12250)*

1752 Floor laying and floor work, nec

Coronado Stone Inc.............................. E 812 284-2845
Jeffersonville *(G-9962)*

Doris Drapery Boutique....................... G 765 472-5850
Peru *(G-13580)*

Eds Wood Craft..................................... G 812 768-6617
Haubstadt *(G-7084)*

Georgia Direct Carpet Inc.................... F 765 966-2548
Richmond *(G-14125)*

Jeff Hury Hrdwood Flors Pntg S......... G 812 204-8650
Evansville *(G-4141)*

Milani Custom Homes LLC.................. G 219 455-5804
Merrillville *(G-11538)*

◆ Santarossa Mosaic Tile Co Inc.......... C 317 632-9494
Indianapolis *(G-9371)*

1761 Roofing, siding, and sheetmetal work

Arrow Metals Inc................................... E 765 825-4443
Connersville *(G-2426)*

Assured General Contg LLC............... G 260 740-4744
Fort Wayne *(G-4776)*

B & L Shtmtl Rofg A Tcta Amer......... E 812 332-4309
Bloomington *(G-789)*

Bright Sheet Metal Company Inc........ D 317 783-3181
Indianapolis *(G-7683)*

Bright Sheet Metal Company Inc........ D 317 291-7600
Indianapolis *(G-7684)*

C & K United Shtmtl & Mech.............. E 812 423-5090
Evansville *(G-3958)*

Clover Sheet Metal Company.............. F 574 293-5912
Elkhart *(G-3255)*

H & H Home Improvement Inc............ G 812 288-8700
Clarksville *(G-2017)*

HB Gutters LLC..................................... G 765 414-5698
Winamac *(G-16862)*

Helming Bros Inc.................................. G 812 634-9797
Jasper *(G-9842)*

Hinshaw Roofing & Sheet Metal Co Inc. E 765 659-3311
Frankfort *(G-5674)*

Huntington Exteriors Inc....................... F 260 356-1621
Huntington *(G-7322)*

Icon Metal Forming LLC...................... B 812 738-5900
Corydon *(G-2499)*

J Coffey Metal Masters Inc.................. D 317 780-1864
Indianapolis *(G-8604)*

JO Mory Inc... F 260 897-3541
Avilla *(G-479)*

Maher Supply Inc.................................. G 812 234-7699
Terre Haute *(G-15635)*

Osterholt Construction Inc................... G 260 672-3493
Huntington *(G-7348)*

Over Top Roofing and Rmdlg LLC...... G 513 704-5422
Lawrenceburg *(G-10851)*

Pb Metal Works..................................... G 765 489-1311
Hagerstown *(G-6841)*

River Valley Sheet Metal Inc............... F 574 259-2538
Mishawaka *(G-11988)*

Roof Masters Plus LLC........................ G 765 572-1321
Westpoint *(G-16747)*

Schmidt Contracting Inc....................... E 812 482-3923
Jasper *(G-9908)*

Seib Machine & Tool Co Inc................ G 812 453-6174
Evansville *(G-4304)*

Slatile Roofing and Shtmtl Co............. E 574 233-7485
South Bend *(G-15246)*

Sure-Flo Seamless Gutters Inc........... G 260 622-4372
Ossian *(G-13437)*

SW Watkins Limited............................. D 260 484-4844
Fort Wayne *(G-5462)*

Tri-State Guttertopper Inc.................... G 812 455-1460
Evansville *(G-4350)*

United Coatings Mfg Co....................... G 317 845-8830
Indianapolis *(G-9679)*

V M Integrated...................................... F 877 296-0621
Indianapolis *(G-9696)*

Vidimos Inc.. D 219 397-2728
East Chicago *(G-3054)*

Webster Custom Canvas Inc............... G 574 834-4497
North Webster *(G-13314)*

1771 Concrete work

A A A Mudjackers Inc.......................... G 317 574-1990
Sharpsville *(G-14708)*

All American Ex Solutions LLC........... E 317 789-3070
Indianapolis *(G-7472)*

C & R Cnstr & Consulting LLC............ G 812 738-4493
Corydon *(G-2489)*

E & B Paving Inc................................... E 765 674-5848
Marion *(G-11284)*

Empire Contractors Inc........................ D 812 424-3865
Evansville *(G-4035)*

Jeff Hury Hrdwood Flors Pntg S......... G 812 204-8650
Evansville *(G-4141)*

Lewis Jerry Cnstr & Excvtg................. G 765 653-2800
Greencastle *(G-6418)*

Milestone Contractors LP.................... D 812 579-5248
Columbus *(G-2356)*

Milestone Contractors N Inc............... G 219 924-5900
South Bend *(G-15151)*

Niblock Excavating Inc......................... G 260 248-2100
Columbia City *(G-2174)*

Niblock Excavating Inc......................... D 574 848-4437
Bristol *(G-1281)*

Rex Alton & Companies Inc................ F 812 882-8519
Vincennes *(G-16149)*

Rieth-Riley Cnstr Co Inc...................... F 574 288-8321
South Bend *(G-15219)*

Rogers Group Inc................................. E 812 882-3640
Vincennes *(G-16150)*

◆ Santarossa Mosaic Tile Co Inc.......... C 317 632-9494
Indianapolis *(G-9371)*

Schrock Excavating Inc....................... E 574 862-4167
Wakarusa *(G-16251)*

Scruggs Construction Inc.................... E 812 528-8178
Seymour *(G-14687)*

17 CONSTRUCTION - SPECIAL TRADE CONTRACTORS

Tri-Esco Inc .... F 765 446-7937
 Colburn *(G-2112)*

Vans TV & Appliance Inc .... F 260 927-8267
 Auburn *(G-433)*

1781 Water well drilling

▲ Bonar Inc .... G 260 636-7430
 Albion *(G-19)*

Dilden Brothers Inc .... E 765 742-1717
 Lafayette *(G-10571)*

Gentry Well & Pump Service LLC .... G 260 563-1907
 Wabash *(G-16189)*

Helvie and Sons Inc .... G 765 674-1372
 Marion *(G-11292)*

Hoover Well Drilling Inc .... G 574 831-4901
 New Paris *(G-12959)*

McGrews Well Drilling Inc .... G 574 857-3875
 Rochester *(G-14306)*

Remmler Well Drilling LLC .... G 812 663-8178
 Greensburg *(G-6627)*

Rose-Wall Mfg Inc .... G 317 894-4497
 Greenfield *(G-6544)*

1791 Structural steel erection

Arrow Metals Inc .... E 765 825-4443
 Connersville *(G-2426)*

Buhrt Engineering & Cnstr .... E 574 267-3720
 Warsaw *(G-16331)*

D & M Systems Inc .... G 812 327-2384
 Owensburg *(G-13461)*

Ellerbrock Welding LLC .... G 559 978-2651
 New Castle *(G-12860)*

Harpring Steel Inc .... G 812 256-6326
 Charlestown *(G-1878)*

Hgmc Supply Inc .... F 317 351-9500
 Indianapolis *(G-8394)*

Hmt LLC .... G 219 736-9901
 Merrillville *(G-11522)*

Padgett Inc .... C 812 945-2391
 New Albany *(G-12790)*

Precision Surveillance Corp .... E 219 397-4295
 East Chicago *(G-3035)*

Reese Forge Orna Ironwork .... G 219 775-1039
 Lake Village *(G-10782)*

Tank Construction & Service Co ... F 317 509-6294
 Whitestown *(G-16823)*

Tj Maintenance LLC .... G 219 776-8427
 Lake Village *(G-10784)*

Triple J Ironworks Inc .... G 765 544-9152
 Carthage *(G-1819)*

1793 Glass and glazing work

◆ Asi Limited C
 Whitestown *(G-16800)*

Botti Stdio Archtctral Arts In .... E 847 869-5933
 La Porte *(G-10391)*

Hartford TEC Glass Co Inc .... E 765 348-1282
 Hartford City *(G-7068)*

Helming Bros Inc .... G 812 634-9797
 Jasper *(G-9842)*

◆ Horizon Terra Incorporated .... D 812 280-0000
 Jeffersonville *(G-9999)*

Kaleidoscope Inc .... G 765 423-1951
 Lafayette *(G-10618)*

Lazzaro Companies Inc .... E 219 980-0860
 Merrillville *(G-11529)*

Moss L Glass Co Inc .... G 765 642-4946
 Indianapolis *(G-8957)*

Syracuse Glass Inc .... G 574 457-5516
 Syracuse *(G-15482)*

1794 Excavation work

Beer and Slabaugh Inc .... E 574 773-3413
 Nappanee *(G-12584)*

C & R Cnstr & Consulting LLC ...... G 812 738-4493
 Corydon *(G-2489)*

Durcholz Excvtg & Cnstr Co Inc ... G 812 634-1764
 Huntingburg *(G-7278)*

E & B Paving Inc .... E 765 643-5358
 Anderson *(G-112)*

Globe Asphalt Paving Co Inc .... E 317 568-4344
 Indianapolis *(G-8293)*

Hunts Maintenance Inc .... G 219 785-2333
 Westville *(G-16762)*

Kellers Limestone Service Inc ...... G 219 326-1688
 La Porte *(G-10432)*

Lewis Jerry Cnstr & Excvtg .... G 765 653-2800
 Greencastle *(G-6418)*

LPI Paving & Excavating .... G 260 726-9564
 Portland *(G-13955)*

Niblock Excavating Inc .... G 260 248-2100
 Columbia City *(G-2174)*

Niblock Excavating Inc .... D 574 848-4437
 Bristol *(G-1281)*

Paf Construction LLC .... E 812 496-4669
 Columbus *(G-2371)*

Phend and Brown Inc .... G 574 658-4166
 Milford *(G-11802)*

Rogers Group Inc .... C 812 333-6324
 Bloomington *(G-959)*

Russells Excvtg Sptic Tnks Inc ..... F 812 838-2471
 Mount Vernon *(G-12318)*

S & G Excavating Inc .... F 812 234-4848
 Terre Haute *(G-15685)*

Schrock Excavating Inc .... E 574 862-4167
 Wakarusa *(G-16251)*

Scruggs Construction Inc .... E 812 528-8178
 Seymour *(G-14687)*

Seiler Excavating Inc .... G 260 925-0507
 Auburn *(G-422)*

Teague Concrete Backhoe .... G 765 674-4692
 Jonesboro *(G-10081)*

Thatcher Engineering Corp .... D 219 949-2084
 Gary *(G-6018)*

Tri-Esco Inc .... F 765 446-7937
 Colburn *(G-2112)*

1795 Wrecking and demolition work

A & T Cnstr & Excvtg Inc .... G 219 314-2439
 Cedar Lake *(G-1826)*

C & R Cnstr & Consulting LLC ...... G 812 738-4493
 Corydon *(G-2489)*

Onsite Construction Services .... E 312 723-8060
 Chesterton *(G-1951)*

Schrock Excavating Inc .... E 574 862-4167
 Wakarusa *(G-16251)*

Uprizing LLC .... G 317 500-9359
 Indianapolis *(G-9685)*

1796 Installing building equipment

Centurion Industries Inc .... D 260 357-6665
 Garrett *(G-5855)*

▲ Daifuku Intrlgistics Amer Corp .... D 219 777-2220
 Hobart *(G-7186)*

Discount Power Equipment .... G 765 642-0040
 Anderson *(G-104)*

Egenolf Contg & Rigging II Inc ..... F 317 787-5301
 Indianapolis *(G-8059)*

Egenolf Machine Inc .... F 317 787-5301
 Indianapolis *(G-8061)*

Electro Corp .... F 219 393-5571
 Kingsbury *(G-10177)*

Engineered Conveyors Inc .... F 765 459-4545
 Kokomo *(G-10263)*

Halyard Corporation .... E 219 515-2820
 Portage *(G-13873)*

Horizon Atomtn Fabrication LLC .. G 765 896-9491
 Muncie *(G-12421)*

▼ Indiana Industrial Svcs LLC .... D 317 769-6099
 Whitestown *(G-16810)*

Manchester Inc .... G 260 982-2202
 Roann *(G-14252)*

Mid-State Automation Inc .... G 765 795-5500
 Cloverdale *(G-2089)*

Millwright Riggers Inc (mri) .... E 765 673-4000
 Marion *(G-11319)*

Padgett Inc .... C 812 945-2391
 New Albany *(G-12790)*

Precision Surveillance Corp .... E 219 397-4295
 East Chicago *(G-3035)*

RPC Machinery Inc .... G 765 458-5655
 Liberty *(G-10998)*

Tk Elevator Corporation .... D 317 595-1125
 Indianapolis *(G-9612)*

Triple J Ironworks Inc .... G 765 544-9152
 Carthage *(G-1819)*

Trivett Contracting Inc .... E 317 539-5150
 Clayton *(G-2062)*

Two Guys Mechanical Contrs Inc .. E 574 946-7671
 Winamac *(G-16878)*

V-Tech Engineering Inc .... F 260 824-4322
 Bluffton *(G-1067)*

Wabash Welding Services Inc ...... G 260 563-2363
 Wabash *(G-16223)*

Zeller Elevator Co .... G 812 985-5888
 Mount Vernon *(G-12328)*

1799 Special trade contractors, nec

3c Coman Ltd .... G 317 650-5156
 Fortville *(G-5585)*

▼ Abda Incorporated .... G 317 273-8343
 Indianapolis *(G-7416)*

Accu-Built Tooling and Weld .... G 574 825-7878
 Goshen *(G-6087)*

All About Organizing .... G 513 238-8157
 Lawrenceburg *(G-10827)*

All American Ex Solutions LLC ..... E 317 789-3070
 Indianapolis *(G-7472)*

Alveys Sign Co Inc .... E 812 867-2567
 Evansville *(G-3883)*

Anderson Fab Llc .... G 317 534-7306
 Martinsville *(G-11381)*

Assured General Contg LLC .... G 260 740-4744
 Fort Wayne *(G-4776)*

Aynes Upholstery LLC .... G 812 829-1321
 Freedom *(G-5798)*

▲ Bare Metal Inc .... F 812 948-1313
 New Albany *(G-12696)*

Benson Tower LLC .... G 270 577-7598
 Evansville *(G-3914)*

Best Weld Inc .... G 765 641-7720
 Anderson *(G-83)*

Bishop Lifting Products Inc .... G 260 478-4700
 Fort Wayne *(G-4805)*

Bleacherpro LLC .... G 813 394-5316
 Fort Wayne *(G-4806)*

Broadway Auto Glass LLC .... F 219 884-5277
 Merrillville *(G-11493)*

Carmel Engineering Inc .... F 765 279-8955
 Kirklin *(G-10187)*

Carmichael Welding Inc .... G 812 825-5156
 Bloomfield *(G-742)*

Cbizze LLC .... G 623 204-9782
 South Bend *(G-14968)*

CD & Ws Bordner Entps Inc .... G 765 268-2120
 Cutler *(G-2783)*

17 CONSTRUCTION - SPECIAL TRADE CONTRACTORS

Centura Solid Surfacing Inc .... F 317 867-5555
  Westfield *(G-16673)*
Cerline Ceramic Corp .... G 765 649-7222
  Anderson *(G-92)*
Chester Pool Systems Inc .... E 812 949-7333
  New Albany *(G-12712)*
Christie Machine Works Co Inc .... G 317 638-8840
  Indianapolis *(G-7801)*
City Welding & Fabrication .... G 765 569-5403
  Rockville *(G-14350)*
Complete Property Care LLC .... G 765 288-0890
  Muncie *(G-12368)*
Conover Custom Fabrication Inc .... F 317 784-1904
  Indianapolis *(G-7853)*
Csa Racking LLC .... G 414 241-3585
  Hammond *(G-6908)*
Custom Blacksmith Shop .... G 765 292-2745
  Atlanta *(G-341)*
Custom Design Laminates Inc .... F 574 674-9174
  Osceola *(G-13388)*
Davern Machine Shop .... G 765 505-1051
  Dana *(G-2804)*
Dexter Chassis Group Inc .... D 574 266-7356
  Elkhart *(G-3294)*
Doris Drapery Boutique .... G 765 472-5850
  Peru *(G-13580)*
Dr Restorations Inc .... G 317 646-7150
  Clermont *(G-2063)*
E & R Fabricating Inc .... G 812 275-0388
  Bedford *(G-634)*
Eds Crane Service .... G 317 535-7385
  Whiteland *(G-16783)*
Elliott-Williams Company Inc .... E 317 453-2295
  Indianapolis *(G-8097)*
Fencescapes LLC .... F 317 210-3912
  Avon *(G-519)*
Freda Inc .... F 260 665-8431
  Angola *(G-253)*
General Sheet Metal Works Inc .... E 574 288-0611
  South Bend *(G-15042)*
Helming Bros Inc .... G 812 634-9797
  Jasper *(G-9842)*
Hunter Venetian Blind Co .... G 812 471-1100
  Evansville *(G-4113)*
Hutchison Signs & Elec Co Inc .... E 317 894-8787
  Indianapolis *(G-8439)*
Indiana Mobile Welding LLC .... G 317 771-8900
  Noblesville *(G-13102)*
Indy Aerospace Inc .... G 817 521-6508
  Indianapolis *(G-8522)*
J & J Repair .... G 574 831-3075
  Goshen *(G-6178)*
Johnny Graber Woodworking .... G 260 466-4957
  Grabill *(G-6305)*
Johns Welding and Fabrication .... G 574 936-1702
  Plymouth *(G-13790)*
Jomar Machining & Fabg Inc .... E 574 825-9837
  Middlebury *(G-11728)*
Just For Granite LLC .... G 317 842-8255
  Indianapolis *(G-8649)*
JW Signs Inc .... G 260 747-5168
  Fort Wayne *(G-5140)*
K & K Fence Inc .... E 317 359-5425
  Indianapolis *(G-8652)*
K C Cmponents Wldg Fabrication .... G 317 539-6067
  Greencastle *(G-6416)*
K2 Industrial Services Inc .... F 219 933-1100
  Highland *(G-7141)*
Kelco Steel Fabrication Inc .... G 317 248-9229
  Indianapolis *(G-8667)*
Kostyo Woodworking Inc .... G 812 466-7350
  Terre Haute *(G-15625)*

Landmark Home & Land Company .... G 219 874-4065
  Michigan City *(G-11630)*
Lesh Advertising Inc .... G 574 859-2141
  Camden *(G-1521)*
M & J Shelton Enterprises Inc .... G 260 745-1616
  Fort Wayne *(G-5194)*
Maddox Industrial Contg LLC .... E 812 544-2156
  Santa Claus *(G-14508)*
Made-Rite Manufacturing Inc .... G 812 967-2652
  Salem *(G-14488)*
McL Window Coverings Inc .... F 317 577-2670
  Fishers *(G-4563)*
Mid-State Truck Equipment Inc .... E 317 849-4903
  Fishers *(G-4566)*
Midwest Pipecoating Inc .... D 219 322-4564
  Schererville *(G-14535)*
Mobile Power Washing LLC .... F 219 863-0066
  Bloomington *(G-922)*
Mofab Inc .... G 765 649-5577
  Anderson *(G-157)*
▲ Moores Welding Service Inc .... G 260 627-2177
  Leo *(G-10969)*
▲ Mullets Fencing and Supplies .... G 574 646-3300
  Nappanee *(G-12628)*
Nupointe Energy LLC .... F 765 981-2664
  Warren *(G-16302)*
Onsite Construction Services .... E 312 723-8060
  Chesterton *(G-1951)*
Organized Living Inc .... C 812 334-8839
  Bloomington *(G-938)*
Paving Plus Company .... G 317 784-1857
  Indianapolis *(G-9105)*
Pool Shop .... G 812 446-0026
  Brazil *(G-1162)*
Pools of Fun Inc .... E 317 843-0337
  Noblesville *(G-13156)*
Powerclean Inc .... E 260 483-1375
  Fort Wayne *(G-5329)*
Premiere Signs Co Inc .... G 574 533-8585
  Goshen *(G-6242)*
Pyramid Equipment Inc .... F 219 778-2591
  Rolling Prairie *(G-14371)*
Quality Fence Ltd .... G 260 768-4986
  Shipshewana *(G-14880)*
Quality Surfaces Inc .... E 812 876-5838
  Spencer *(G-15358)*
R & M Welding & Fabricating Sp .... G 812 295-9130
  Loogootee *(G-11148)*
Radon Environmental Inc .... G 317 843-0804
  Elkhart *(G-3637)*
Red Earth LLC .... G 260 338-1439
  Fort Wayne *(G-5373)*
Reed Contracting Company .... E 765 452-2638
  Kokomo *(G-10326)*
Regent Aerospace Corporation .... C 317 837-4000
  Plainfield *(G-13721)*
Rex Alton & Companies Inc .... F 812 882-8519
  Vincennes *(G-16149)*
▲ S C Pryor Inc .... F 317 352-1281
  Indianapolis *(G-9354)*
Safeguard Solutions LLC .... G 317 519-0255
  Greenfield *(G-6548)*
Saran LP C
  Indianapolis *(G-9373)*
Shade By Design Inc .... G 317 602-3513
  Indianapolis *(G-9410)*
Sign Group Inc .... G 317 875-6969
  Indianapolis *(G-9430)*
Sign Write Signs LLC .... G 219 477-3840
  Valparaiso *(G-16050)*
Signcenter Inc .... G 812 232-4994
  Terre Haute *(G-15694)*

Signdoc Identity LLC .... G 317 247-9670
  Indianapolis *(G-9435)*
Signrite .... G 812 320-5245
  Bloomington *(G-972)*
Signs AP & Awards On Time LLC .... G 219 661-4488
  Crown Point *(G-2752)*
Smart Manufacturing Inc .... G 765 482-7481
  Lebanon *(G-10943)*
Southwest Welding LLC .... G 574 862-4453
  Wakarusa *(G-16252)*
Sparkle Pools Inc .... F 812 232-1292
  Terre Haute *(G-15707)*
Speedcraft Prototypes .... G 765 644-6449
  Anderson *(G-198)*
SSd Control Technology Inc .... E 574 289-5942
  South Bend *(G-15264)*
Sun Control Center LLC .... F 260 490-9902
  Fort Wayne *(G-5456)*
Tank Construction & Service Co .... F 317 509-6294
  Whitestown *(G-16823)*
Thursday Pools LLC .... G 317 973-0200
  Fortville *(G-5607)*
Todds Hydrlcs RPR & Stl Fbrct .... G 812 466-3457
  Terre Haute *(G-15733)*
Top Lock Corporation .... G 317 831-2000
  Mooresville *(G-12248)*
Trivett Contracting Inc .... E 317 539-5150
  Clayton *(G-2062)*
Two Guys Mechanical Contrs Inc .... E 574 946-7671
  Winamac *(G-16878)*
US Signcrafters Inc .... F 574 674-5055
  Osceola *(G-13404)*
Van Zandt Enterprises Inc .... F 812 423-3511
  Evansville *(G-4366)*
Wallar Additions Inc .... G 574 262-1989
  Elkhart *(G-3778)*
Whitehead Signs Inc .... F 317 632-1800
  Indianapolis *(G-9760)*
Wilson Burial Vault Inc .... G 260 356-5722
  Huntington *(G-7380)*
Zimmer Welding LLC .... G 317 632-5212
  Indianapolis *(G-9812)*

20 FOOD AND KINDRED PRODUCTS

2011 Meat packing plants

4 Bar M Inc .... G 765 653-7119
  Gosport *(G-6281)*
Bains Packing and Rfrgn .... F 260 244-5209
  Columbia City *(G-2122)*
Berne Locker Storage .... G 260 589-2806
  Berne *(G-705)*
Beutler Meat Processing Co .... G 765 742-7285
  Lafayette *(G-10536)*
Blackpoint Distribution Co LLC .... E 260 414-9096
  Leo *(G-10964)*
Brook Locker Plant .... G 219 275-2611
  Brook *(G-1303)*
Butcher Block Inc .... G 219 696-9111
  Lowell *(G-11157)*
Cannelburg Proc Plant LLC .... G 812 486-3223
  Cannelburg *(G-1529)*
Cargill Incorporated .... B 402 533-4227
  Hammond *(G-6895)*
Dewig Bros Packing Co Inc .... E 812 768-6208
  Haubstadt *(G-7083)*
Drews Deer Processing .... G 812 279-6246
  Mitchell *(G-12038)*
El Popular Inc .... F 219 397-3728
  East Chicago *(G-3005)*

SIC SECTION
20 FOOD AND KINDRED PRODUCTS

Emge Foods LLC.................................. D 317 894-7777
  Greenfield (G-6496)
Fender 4 Star Meats Processing........... G 812 829-3240
  Spencer (G-15346)
Ferdinand Processing Inc..................... G 812 367-2073
  Ferdinand (G-4432)
Fischer Frms Natural Foods LLC........... G 812 481-1411
  Saint Anthony (G-14428)
Gibson County Meats LLC..................... F 812 724-2333
  Owensville (G-13468)
Griffin Industries LLC............................. D 812 379-9528
  Columbus (G-2315)
H P Schmitt Packing Co Inc................... G 260 724-3146
  Decatur (G-2861)
Hobart Locker & Meat Pkg Co................ G 219 942-5952
  Crown Point (G-2693)
Hollands Deer Processing LLC.............. F 765 472-5876
  Peru (G-13585)
Hrr Enterprises Inc................................ E 219 362-9050
  La Porte (G-10425)
◆ Indiana Packers Corporation............... A 765 564-3680
  Delphi (G-2899)
Johns Butcher Shop Inc......................... F 574 773-4632
  Nappanee (G-12615)
K W Deer Processing............................. G 812 824-2492
  Bloomington (G-898)
Kelby J Waldrip..................................... G 812 824-2492
  Noblesville (G-13117)
Kenny Dewig Meats Sausage Inc........... G 812 724-2333
  Owensville (G-13469)
Lengacher Meats LLC........................... G 260 627-8060
  Grabill (G-6309)
Lengerich Meats Inc............................. F 260 638-4123
  Zanesville (G-16986)
▲ Manley Meats Inc............................... F 260 592-7313
  Decatur (G-2871)
▲ Mariah Foods Corp............................. C 812 378-3366
  Columbus (G-2348)
Mariah Retail Store................................ G 812 372-8712
  Columbus (G-2349)
McFall Family Meats LLC...................... G 812 547-6546
  Tell City (G-15510)
▼ Meats By Linz Inc............................... E 708 862-0830
  Hammond (G-6979)
Merkley & Sons Inc............................... E 812 482-7020
  Jasper (G-9890)
Milan Food Bank.................................. G 812 654-3682
  Milan (G-11781)
Monon Meat Packing Company............. G 219 253-6363
  Monon (G-12057)
Moody Meats.. G 317 272-4533
  Avon (G-538)
Myers Frz Foods Provisioners............... G 765 525-6304
  Saint Paul (G-14467)
Old Hoosier Meats................................. G 574 825-2940
  Middlebury (G-11743)
ONu Acres LLC..................................... G 765 565-1355
  Carthage (G-1816)
Orange County Processing..................... F 812 865-2028
  Orleans (G-13379)
P&Y Farm Fresh Market LLC................. G 812 767-1902
  Butlerville (G-1487)
Parretts Meat Proc & Catrg Inc............... F 574 967-3711
  Flora (G-4663)
Pates Slaughtering & Proc..................... G 812 866-4710
  Hanover (G-7045)
Peer Foods Group Inc........................... G 317 894-7777
  Greenfield (G-6537)
Peer Foods Group Inc........................... G 317 735-4283
  Indianapolis (G-9111)
Plumrose Usa Inc.................................. C 574 295-8190
  Elkhart (G-3607)

Rices Quality Farm Meats Inc................ G 812 829-4562
  Spencer (G-15361)
Rihm Inc.. G 765 478-3426
  Cambridge City (G-1502)
Royal Center Locker Plant Inc............... G 574 643-3275
  Royal Center (G-14392)
Ruwaldt Packing Company Inc.............. F 219 942-2911
  Hobart (G-7204)
Sander Processing Incorporated........... F 812 481-0044
  Celestine (G-1843)
Slabaugh Meat Processing LLC............. G 574 773-0381
  Nappanee (G-12645)
Smithfield Direct LLC........................... D 812 867-6644
  Evansville (G-4322)
Smithfield Direct LLC........................... C 765 473-3086
  Peru (G-13600)
Smithfield Foods Inc............................. F 812 446-2328
  Brazil (G-1165)
Smithfield Foods Inc............................. E 317 891-1888
  Greenfield (G-6554)
Smithland Butchering Co Inc................ G 317 729-5398
  Elizabethtown (G-3133)
Tyson Foods... C 317 791-8430
  Indianapolis (G-9669)
Tyson Foods Inc................................... G 260 726-3118
  Portland (G-13973)
Tyson Fresh Meats Inc.......................... G 765 339-4512
  Linden (G-11033)
Tyson Fresh Meats Inc.......................... C 574 753-6121
  Logansport (G-11114)
Tyson Fresh Meats Inc.......................... G 574 753-6134
  Logansport (G-11115)
Tyson Fresh Meats Inc.......................... G 765 379-3102
  Rossville (G-14388)
Tyson Fresh Meats Inc.......................... G 812 486-2800
  Washington (G-16511)
Uselman Packing Co............................ G 765 832-2112
  Clinton (G-2080)
W & W Locker...................................... G 260 344-3400
  Andrews (G-222)
Wallace Processing LLC....................... G 765 397-3363
  Hillsboro (G-7162)
Wilsons Locker & Proc Plant................. G 812 358-2632
  Bedford (G-683)
Yoders Meats Inc.................................. G 260 768-4715
  Shipshewana (G-14900)

2013 Sausages and other prepared meats

▲ Big B Distributors Inc......................... F 812 425-5235
  Evansville (G-3930)
Butcher Block Inc................................. G 219 696-9111
  Lowell (G-11157)
Conagra Brands Inc............................. G 402 240-5000
  Indianapolis (G-7848)
Cosmos Superior Foods LLC................ E 317 975-2747
  Indianapolis (G-7886)
Cottonwood Corp.................................. G 260 820-0415
  Ossian (G-13421)
El Popular Sausage Factory LLC........... G 219 476-7040
  Valparaiso (G-15939)
Farm Boy Meats of Evansville............... G 812 425-5231
  Evansville (G-4064)
Fisher Packing Company...................... E 260 726-7355
  Portland (G-13941)
Food Service Distributors Inc............... G 812 267-4846
  Palmyra (G-13480)
Grabill Country Meat 1 Inc.................... F 260 627-3691
  Grabill (G-6300)
Grandpas Beef Jerky LLC.................... G 317 258-3209
  Fishers (G-4534)
Halal Processing Solutions................... E 832 385-2394
  Muncie (G-12408)

Hillshire Brands Company.................... G 260 456-4802
  Fort Wayne (G-5067)
Hinsdale Farms Ltd............................. G 574 848-0344
  Bristol (G-1266)
◆ Indiana Packers Corporation............... A 765 564-3680
  Delphi (G-2899)
▲ Manley Meats Inc............................... F 260 592-7313
  Decatur (G-2871)
▼ Meats By Linz Inc............................... E 708 862-0830
  Hammond (G-6979)
Merkley & Sons Inc............................... E 812 482-7020
  Jasper (G-9890)
Millers Locker Plant............................. G 765 234-2381
  Crawfordsville (G-2591)
Monogram Comfort Foods LLC............. D 574 848-0344
  Bristol (G-1277)
Monogram Food Solutions LLC............. G 574 848-0344
  Bristol (G-1278)
▲ Monogram Frozen Foods LLC............ C 574 848-0344
  Bristol (G-1279)
Nates Beef Jerky.................................. G 765 348-6569
  Upland (G-15879)
Park 100 Foods Inc.............................. E 317 549-4545
  Indianapolis (G-9093)
▲ Park 100 Foods Inc............................ D 765 675-3480
  Tipton (G-15786)
Parretts Meat Proc & Catrg Inc............. F 574 967-3711
  Flora (G-4663)
Pates Slaughtering & Proc................... G 812 866-4710
  Hanover (G-7045)
Paytons Barbecue Inc.......................... G 765 294-2716
  Veedersburg (G-16089)
Peer Foods Group Inc.......................... G 773 927-1440
  Columbus (G-2374)
Peer Foods Group Inc.......................... G 812 703-2081
  Edinburgh (G-3096)
Perfect Pig Inc..................................... F 219 984-5355
  Reynolds (G-14075)
Red Beard Beef Jerky.......................... G 574 596-7054
  Elkhart (G-3645)
Rihm Inc.. G 765 478-3426
  Cambridge City (G-1502)
Royal Center Locker Plant Inc............. G 574 643-3275
  Royal Center (G-14392)
Rubicon Foods LLC.............................. F 317 826-8793
  Indianapolis (G-9347)
Ruwaldt Packing Company Inc............. F 219 942-2911
  Hobart (G-7204)
Saint Adrian Meats Sausage LLC.......... G 317 403-3305
  Lebanon (G-10938)
Sander Processing Incorporated.......... F 812 481-0044
  Celestine (G-1843)
This Old Farm Inc................................ E 765 324-2161
  Colfax (G-2113)
Wilsons Locker & Proc Plant................ G 812 358-2632
  Bedford (G-683)
Yoders Meats Inc................................. G 260 768-4715
  Shipshewana (G-14900)
Zels... G 219 864-1011
  Schererville (G-14548)

2015 Poultry slaughtering and processing

Cargill Incorporated............................. B 402 533-4227
  Hammond (G-6895)
Crystal Lake LLC................................. D 574 858-2514
  Warsaw (G-16338)
Crystal Lake LLC................................. G 574 267-3101
  Warsaw (G-16339)
Crystal Valley Farms LLC..................... D 260 829-6550
  Orland (G-13364)
▼ Culver Duck Farms Inc....................... C 574 825-9537
  Middlebury (G-11709)

Employee Codes: A=Over 500 employees, B=251-500
C=101-250, D=51-100, E=20-50, F=10-19, G=1-9

20 FOOD AND KINDRED PRODUCTS

▲ Dutch Country Organics LLC .... E 574 536-7403
  Middlebury *(G-11713)*
Egg Innovations LLC .... D 574 267-7545
  Warsaw *(G-16355)*
Egglife Foods Inc .... C 219 261-5500
  Wolcott *(G-16929)*
Farbest Farms Inc .... F 812 481-1034
  Huntingburg *(G-7279)*
Farbest Foods Inc .... A 812 683-4200
  Jasper *(G-9837)*
Farbest Foods Intl Inc 812 683-4200
  Huntingburg *(G-7280)*
Graber .... G 812 636-7699
  Odon *(G-13336)*
Hy-Line North America LLC .... D 260 375-3041
  Warren *(G-16300)*
Jfs Milling Inc 812 683-4200
  Vincennes *(G-16134)*
Koch Foods .... G 574 457-4384
  Syracuse *(G-15466)*
Lambrights Inc .... G 260 463-2178
  Lagrange *(G-10750)*
Maple Leaf Inc .... G 260 982-8655
  North Manchester *(G-13241)*
◆ Maple Leaf Co .... B 574 453-4455
  Leesburg *(G-10958)*
Maple Leaf Farms Inc .... C 574 658-4121
  Milford *(G-11799)*
◆ Maple Leaf Farms Inc .... A 574 453-4500
  Milford *(G-11798)*
Midwest Poultry Services LP .... D 260 982-8122
  North Manchester *(G-13243)*
▲ Midwest Poultry Services LP .... F 574 353-7651
  North Manchester *(G-13242)*
P & R Farms Llc .... G 812 326-2010
  Saint Anthony *(G-14430)*
Perdue Farms Inc .... G 765 325-2997
  Lebanon *(G-10931)*
Perdue Farms Inc .... G 765 436-7990
  Thorntown *(G-15754)*
Perdue Farms Inc .... D 812 886-0593
  Vincennes *(G-16143)*
Perdue Farms Inc .... E 757 787-5210
  Washington *(G-16501)*
Perdue Farms Inc .... A 812 254-8500
  Washington *(G-16502)*
Perdue Farms Inc .... C 812 254-8515
  Washington *(G-16503)*
▲ Pine Manor Inc .... B 800 532-4186
  Orland *(G-13370)*
Tyson Chicken Inc .... A 812 347-2452
  Ramsey *(G-14027)*
Tyson Foods Inc .... E 812 738-3219
  Corydon *(G-2520)*
Tyson Foods Inc .... G 260 726-3118
  Portland *(G-13973)*
Tyson Sales and Dist Inc .... C 479 290-7776
  Indianapolis *(G-9670)*

2021 Creamery butter

American Dream Nut Butter .... G 317 326-9363
  Noblesville *(G-13035)*
Chillers Microcreamery LLC .... F 812 987-1298
  Floyds Knobs *(G-4671)*
Dillman Farm Incorporated .... G 812 825-5525
  Bloomington *(G-857)*
Tulip Tree Creamery LLC .... F 317 331-5469
  Indianapolis *(G-9660)*

2022 Cheese; natural and processed

Ff - Top of Pie LLC .... F 317 876-1951
  Whitestown *(G-16805)*

Golfo Di Napoli LLC .... D 260 479-9890
  Warren *(G-16299)*
▲ Huber Orchards Inc .... D 812 923-9463
  Borden *(G-1110)*
Kroger Limited Partnership II .... G 765 364-5200
  Crawfordsville *(G-2583)*
Kroger Limited Partnership II .... G 317 229-7600
  Indianapolis *(G-8703)*
Kuehnert Dairy Inc .... G 260 489-3766
  Fort Wayne *(G-5164)*
Middlebury Cheese Company LLC .... F 574 825-9511
  Middlebury *(G-11737)*
Steckler Grassfed LLC .... G 812 683-3098
  Dale *(G-2793)*
Tulip Tree Creamery LLC .... F 317 331-5469
  Indianapolis *(G-9660)*

2023 Dry, condensed, evaporated products

Aibmr Life Sciences Inc .... G 812 822-1400
  Bloomington *(G-776)*
Alani Nutrition LLC .... G 502 509-4922
  Jeffersonville *(G-9927)*
Amish Country Dairy LLC .... G 574 323-1701
  Shipshewana *(G-14835)*
Baird Ice Cream Co .... G 812 283-3345
  Clarksville *(G-2008)*
Capricorn Foods LLC .... G 219 670-1872
  Hammond *(G-6853)*
Denver Marketing Co LLC .... G 866 692-2326
  Indianapolis *(G-7964)*
Drshopecom LLC .... G 800 255-1510
  Indianapolis *(G-8012)*
Garden of Remedies Inc .... G 463 241-5991
  Camby *(G-1510)*
Green Leafs LLC .... G 812 483-6383
  Newburgh *(G-13002)*
Helivin LLC .... G 800 680-7281
  Newburgh *(G-13003)*
Herbs Rebel Inc 812 762-4400
  Bloomfield *(G-748)*
International Food Tech Inc .... G 812 853-9432
  Newburgh *(G-13008)*
Poland Chapel Historical Soc .... G 213 977-2280
  Centerpoint *(G-1846)*
Previnex LLC .... G 877 212-0310
  Carmel *(G-1729)*
Rose Sharon All Naturals LLC .... G 317 500-4725
  Indianapolis *(G-9334)*
Wellsource Nutraceuticals LLC .... G 219 213-6173
  Crown Point *(G-2773)*
Wholistic Gardens .... G 260 573-1088
  Waterloo *(G-16533)*

2024 Ice cream and frozen deserts

Aj Masonry & Son LLC .... G 260 569-0082
  Wabash *(G-16172)*
AJS Gyros To Go .... G 812 951-1715
  New Salisbury *(G-12982)*
▲ Archibald Brothers Intl Inc .... G 812 941-8267
  New Albany *(G-12691)*
Big Cone Inc .... G 812 424-1416
  Evansville *(G-3931)*
Brics .... F 317 257-5757
  Indianapolis *(G-7680)*
Browns Dairy Inc .... F 219 464-4141
  Valparaiso *(G-15921)*
Buckner Inc .... E 317 570-0533
  Indianapolis *(G-7699)*
Cloverleaf Farms Dairy .... G 219 938-5140
  Gary *(G-5919)*
Doms Froyo LLC .... F 574 855-1120
  South Bend *(G-15004)*

Dreyers Grand Ice Cream Inc .... B 260 483-3102
  Fort Wayne *(G-4928)*
Glovers Ice Cream Inc .... G 765 654-6712
  Frankfort *(G-5671)*
Ice Cream On Wheels Inc .... G 800 884-9793
  Griffith *(G-6808)*
Ice Cream Specialties Inc .... D 765 474-2989
  Lafayette *(G-10603)*
Ice Cream Specialties Inc .... F 219 980-0800
  Merrillville *(G-11523)*
Indiana Masonry LLC .... G 317 937-4275
  Indianapolis *(G-8482)*
La Michoacana .... G 574 293-9799
  Elkhart *(G-3463)*
Meyer Ice Cream LLC .... G 812 941-8267
  New Albany *(G-12777)*
Mishawaka Frozen Custard .... G 574 255-8000
  Mishawaka *(G-11956)*
Moo-Over LLC .... G 260 224-2108
  Columbia City *(G-2172)*
Penguin Enterprises LLC .... E 812 333-0475
  Bloomington *(G-944)*
Penguin Petes .... G 812 838-9670
  Mount Vernon *(G-12314)*
Premier Frozen Desserts .... G 812 580-8866
  Seymour *(G-14678)*
Saniserv .... G 317 831-7030
  Mooresville *(G-12241)*
Sweet Moon Macaron LLC .... G 219 484-9851
  Griffith *(G-6817)*
Teejays Sweet Tooth LLC .... G 219 208-5229
  Indianapolis *(G-9572)*
U Want Icecream LLC .... G 317 577-4057
  Fishers *(G-4619)*

2026 Fluid milk

Heritage Distributing Company .... G 317 413-6514
  Columbus *(G-2316)*
HM Lowry Enterprises LLC .... G 765 524-8435
  Cambridge City *(G-1495)*
Instantwhip-Indianapolis Inc .... F 317 899-1533
  Indianapolis *(G-8563)*
Jacobs & Brichford LLC .... G 765 692-0056
  Connersville *(G-2447)*
Royal Food Products Inc .... D 317 782-2660
  Indianapolis *(G-9340)*
William Donson .... G 765 628-3236
  Kokomo *(G-10358)*
Yogurtz .... G 317 853-6600
  Carmel *(G-1811)*

2032 Canned specialties

Dieng Group LLC .... G 317 699-1909
  Indianapolis *(G-7973)*
Eden Foods Inc .... E 765 396-3344
  Eaton *(G-3061)*
Frito-Lay North America Inc .... B 765 659-1831
  Frankfort *(G-5669)*
H & H Partnership Inc .... G 765 513-4739
  Kokomo *(G-10274)*
◆ Mead Johnson & Company LLC ...... C 812 429-5000
  Evansville *(G-4193)*
▲ Morgan Foods Inc .... A 812 794-1170
  Austin *(G-467)*
Park 100 Foods Inc .... E 317 549-4545
  Indianapolis *(G-9093)*
▲ Park 100 Foods Inc .... D 765 675-3480
  Tipton *(G-15786)*
Tyson Foods Inc .... G 260 726-3118
  Portland *(G-13973)*
Tyson Mexican Original Inc .... D 260 726-3118
  Portland *(G-13974)*

SIC SECTION
20 FOOD AND KINDRED PRODUCTS

Vitamins Inc.. E 219 879-7356
  Michigan City *(G-11686)*

Viva Tia Maria LLC.. E 317 509-2650
  Zionsville *(G-17061)*

2033 Canned fruits and specialties

Bay Valley Foods LLC.................................. C 574 935-3097
  Plymouth *(G-13757)*

Blackpoint Distribution Co LLC.................... E 260 414-9096
  Leo *(G-10964)*

▲ Caj Food Products Inc............................. G 888 524-6882
  Fishers *(G-4481)*

Dillman Farm Incorporated.......................... G 812 825-5525
  Bloomington *(G-857)*

Douglas K Gresham..................................... G 812 445-3174
  Seymour *(G-14649)*

Dutch Kettle LLC... F 574 546-4033
  Bremen *(G-1188)*

Eden Foods Inc... E 765 396-3344
  Eaton *(G-3061)*

Greenleaf Foods Spc Inc.............................. D 317 554-4322
  Indianapolis *(G-8319)*

Holic LLC.. E 765 444-8115
  Middletown *(G-11770)*

Kens Foods Inc... D 765 505-7900
  Lebanon *(G-10908)*

Kraft Heinz Foods Company........................ D 260 347-1300
  Kendallville *(G-10131)*

Lakeside Foods... G 219 924-4860
  Highland *(G-7142)*

Millers Mill... G 574 825-2010
  Middlebury *(G-11738)*

Milroy Canning Company.............................. G 765 629-2221
  Milroy *(G-11827)*

Rays Juice Company.................................... G 219 809-7400
  Michigan City *(G-11656)*

Red Gold Inc... G 765 557-5500
  Elwood *(G-3834)*

Red Gold Inc... G 765 557-5500
  Elwood *(G-3835)*

Red Gold Inc... C 765 552-3386
  Elwood *(G-3836)*

Red Gold Inc... C 260 368-9017
  Geneva *(G-6050)*

Red Gold Inc... C 765 557-5500
  Geneva *(G-6051)*

Red Gold Inc... G 260 726-8140
  Portland *(G-13966)*

◆ Red Gold Inc.. C 765 557-5500
  Elwood *(G-3837)*

Schergers Kttle Jams Jellies -..................... G 800 447-6475
  Shipshewana *(G-14885)*

Smoked Q LLC.. G 260 494-5029
  Fort Wayne *(G-5423)*

Sprigati LLC... G 219 484-9455
  Munster *(G-12564)*

Youth JAM LLC.. G 765 644-6375
  Anderson *(G-220)*

Zentis North America LLC............................ B 574 941-1100
  Plymouth *(G-13835)*

▲ Zentis North America Holdg LLC............. C 574 941-1100
  Plymouth *(G-13836)*

2034 Dehydrated fruits, vegetables, soups

Arneys Freeze-Dried Treats LLC................. G 812 801-1386
  Fort Wayne *(G-4772)*

▲ Bella Food Sales LLC.............................. G 574 229-8803
  Mishawaka *(G-11849)*

Doehler Dry Ingrdent Sltons LL................... F 574 797-0364
  Mishawaka *(G-11884)*

Eggpress LLC.. G 574 267-2847
  Warsaw *(G-16356)*

Mayasaris LLC.. G 812 593-2881
  Greensburg *(G-6617)*

Mayasaris LLC.. G 812 222-6292
  Greensburg *(G-6616)*

N K Hurst Co Inc... E 317 634-6425
  Zionsville *(G-17035)*

Williams West & Witts Pdts Co.................... G 219 879-8236
  Michigan City *(G-11687)*

▲ Zentis North America Holdg LLC............. C 574 941-1100
  Plymouth *(G-13836)*

2035 Pickles, sauces, and salad dressings

Assalys House Garlic LLC............................ G 219 310-5934
  Hebron *(G-7097)*

Bay Valley Foods LLC.................................. C 574 935-3097
  Plymouth *(G-13757)*

▲ Big B Distributors Inc............................... F 812 425-5235
  Evansville *(G-3930)*

Christina Ann Clark....................................... G 317 778-7832
  Indianapolis *(G-7802)*

El Popular Inc.. F 219 397-3728
  East Chicago *(G-3005)*

Fritz Distribution LLC.................................... G 463 207-8210
  Indianapolis *(G-8234)*

Grafton Peek Incorporated........................... F 317 557-8377
  Greenwood *(G-6709)*

Grandma Irma Sauces Corp........................ G 773 688-9029
  Merrillville *(G-11519)*

Hair of Ferret... G 219 663-1599
  Crown Point *(G-2691)*

Holic LLC.. E 765 444-8115
  Middletown *(G-11770)*

Joey Chestnut Foods LLC............................ G 317 602-4830
  Indianapolis *(G-8629)*

Kaiser Pickles LLC.. G 812 954-5115
  Aurora *(G-446)*

▲ Kolossos Inc... G 312 952-6991
  Long Beach *(G-11122)*

Lava Lips... G 317 965-6629
  Indianapolis *(G-8728)*

Masters Hand Bbq LLC................................ G 260 247-5807
  Fort Wayne *(G-5205)*

Mild To Wild Pepper & Herb Co................... G 317 736-8300
  Greenwood *(G-6741)*

Park 100 Foods Inc....................................... E 317 549-4545
  Indianapolis *(G-9093)*

▲ Park 100 Foods Inc.................................. D 765 675-3480
  Tipton *(G-15786)*

Pickle Bites LLC.. G 773 780-7559
  Hammond *(G-6992)*

Pickled Pedaler... G 317 877-0624
  Noblesville *(G-13155)*

Reckitt Benckiser LLC.................................. E 812 429-5000
  Evansville *(G-4276)*

Red Gold Inc... C 260 368-9017
  Geneva *(G-6050)*

Red Gold Inc... C 765 557-5500
  Geneva *(G-6051)*

◆ Red Gold Inc.. C 765 557-5500
  Elwood *(G-3837)*

Richards Restaurant Inc............................... F 260 997-6823
  Bryant *(G-1436)*

Rickles Pickles LLC...................................... G 260 495-9024
  Fremont *(G-5834)*

Royal Food Products Inc.............................. F 317 782-2660
  Indianapolis *(G-9340)*

▲ Sechlers Pickles Inc................................. E 260 337-5461
  Saint Joe *(G-14443)*

Van Schouwen Farms LLC........................... G 219 696-0877
  Hebron *(G-7107)*

2037 Frozen fruits and vegetables

▲ Caj Food Products Inc............................. G 888 524-6882
  Fishers *(G-4481)*

Frozen Garden LLC...................................... F 219 286-3578
  Valparaiso *(G-15951)*

Hawaiian Smoothie LLC................................ G 317 881-7290
  Fishers *(G-4537)*

Pepsico Inc.. G 317 830-4011
  Indianapolis *(G-9119)*

▲ Zentis North America Holdg LLC............. C 574 941-1100
  Plymouth *(G-13836)*

2038 Frozen specialties, nec

B Nutty LLC... D 844 426-8889
  Portage *(G-13847)*

Butterfield Foods LLC................................... C 317 776-4775
  Noblesville *(G-13051)*

Canary Brothers LLC.................................... G 317 954-1225
  Indianapolis *(G-7730)*

Canary Brothers LLC.................................... G 317 954-1225
  Indianapolis *(G-7731)*

Conagra Brands Inc...................................... C 402 240-5000
  Indianapolis *(G-7848)*

Crystal Lake LLC... D 574 858-2514
  Warsaw *(G-16338)*

Cygnus Home Service LLC.......................... D 317 882-6624
  Danville *(G-2810)*

Franklins Mercantile...................................... G 812 876-0426
  Spencer *(G-15347)*

Grabill Country Meat 1 Inc........................... F 260 627-3691
  Grabill *(G-6300)*

Pasou Foods Inc... G 574 457-4092
  Syracuse *(G-15472)*

Snax In Pax Inc... E 260 593-3066
  Topeka *(G-15819)*

Zerocarb LLC... G 812 214-1084
  Evansville *(G-4392)*

2041 Flour and other grain mill products

ADM Milling Co.. G 317 783-3321
  Beech Grove *(G-685)*

ADM Milling Co.. F 812 838-4445
  Mount Vernon *(G-12286)*

AG Plus Inc.. G 260 623-6121
  Monroeville *(G-12066)*

AG Plus Inc.. E 260 723-5141
  South Whitley *(G-15316)*

▼ Agricor Inc... D 765 662-0606
  Marion *(G-11269)*

Archer-Daniels-Midland Company................ G 317 783-3321
  Beech Grove *(G-686)*

Archer-Daniels-Midland Company................ E 260 824-0079
  Bluffton *(G-1025)*

Archer-Daniels-Midland Company................ G 765 362-2965
  Crawfordsville *(G-2545)*

Archer-Daniels-Midland Company................ G 765 299-1672
  Fowler *(G-5618)*

Archer-Daniels-Midland Company................ G 574 773-4138
  Nappanee *(G-12580)*

Archer-Daniels-Midland Company................ G 219 866-2810
  Rensselaer *(G-14043)*

Archer-Daniels-Midland Company................ G 219 866-3939
  Rensselaer *(G-14044)*

Azteca Milling LP.. G 812 867-3190
  Evansville *(G-3905)*

Big Brick House Bakery LLP........................ G 260 563-1071
  Fort Wayne *(G-4799)*

Cargill Incorporated...................................... B 574 353-7621
  Mentone *(G-11471)*

Cargill Dry Corn Ingrdents Inc..................... E 317 632-1481
  Indianapolis *(G-7744)*

Clunette Elevator Co Inc.............................. F 574 858-2281
  Leesburg *(G-10952)*

20 FOOD AND KINDRED PRODUCTS

Corn Flour Producers Llc .... E 812 875-3113
  Worthington *(G-16958)*
Cory Pmp LLC .... E 574 223-3177
  Rochester *(G-14284)*
Crust N More Inc .... F 317 890-7878
  Indianapolis *(G-7915)*
Dillman Farm Incorporated .... G 812 825-5525
  Bloomington *(G-857)*
H Nagel & Son Co .... F 513 665-4550
  West Harrison *(G-16546)*
Kerry Inc .... C 812 464-9151
  Evansville *(G-4151)*
Laughery Valley AG Co-Op Inc .... G 812 689-4401
  Osgood *(G-13412)*
▲ Martinsville Milling Co Inc .... G 317 253-2581
  Indianapolis *(G-8844)*
New Carbon Company LLC .... G 574 247-2270
  South Bend *(G-15164)*
Nutramaize LLC .... G 765 273-8274
  West Lafayette *(G-16615)*
PHM Brands LLC .... E 219 879-7356
  Michigan City *(G-11651)*
Pillsbury Company LLC .... D 812 944-8411
  New Albany *(G-12795)*
Roy Umbarger and Sons Inc .... F 317 422-5195
  Franklin *(G-5775)*
Salamonie Mills Inc .... F 260 375-2200
  Warren *(G-16304)*
Siemer Milling Company .... F 513 814-9216
  West Harrison *(G-16551)*
Tribine Industries LLC .... G 316 282-8011
  Logansport *(G-11112)*
Vitamins Inc .... E 219 879-7356
  Michigan City *(G-11686)*
Wallace Grain Company Inc .... F 317 758-4434
  Sheridan *(G-14832)*

2043 Cereal breakfast foods

BEEFREE INC .... G 317 402-1019
  Cicero *(G-1994)*
General Mills Inc .... G 317 509-3709
  Fishers *(G-4530)*
Hearthside Food Solutions LLC .... G 812 877-1588
  Seelyville *(G-14585)*
Home Snack Foods LLC .... G 317 764-6644
  Noblesville *(G-13096)*
Loutsa Inc .... G 317 273-0123
  Indianapolis *(G-8784)*
Pepsico Inc .... G 317 830-4011
  Indianapolis *(G-9119)*
Victory Crunch Granola Snacks .... G 219 613-3594
  Merrillville *(G-11571)*

2045 Prepared flour mixes and doughs

◆ Clabber Girl Corporation .... D 812 232-9446
  Terre Haute *(G-15563)*
Harlan Bakeries LLC .... C 317 272-3600
  Indianapolis *(G-8361)*
▲ Harlan Bakeries LLC .... G 317 272-3600
  Avon *(G-523)*
▲ Harlan Bakeries-Avon LLC .... B 317 272-3600
  Avon *(G-524)*
John F Semrau .... G 765 337-8831
  Medaryville *(G-11459)*
JW Packaging LLC .... G 317 414-9038
  Converse *(G-2477)*
Loaded Dough Cookie Co LLC .... G 765 969-6513
  Centerville *(G-1851)*
M&C Wndrink Rverside Farms Inc ... G 928 897-0061
  Lowell *(G-11170)*
New Carbon Company LLC .... G 574 247-2270
  Indianapolis *(G-9002)*

Vintage Baked Modern LLC .... G 219 252-9820
  Valparaiso *(G-16076)*

2046 Wet corn milling

Archer-Daniels-Midland Company .... G 765 299-1672
  Fowler *(G-5618)*
Archer-Daniels-Midland Company .... G 260 749-0022
  New Haven *(G-12893)*
Cargill Incorporated .... B 402 533-4227
  Hammond *(G-6895)*
◆ Clabber Girl Corporation .... D 812 232-9446
  Terre Haute *(G-15563)*
Colorcon Inc .... D 317 545-6211
  Indianapolis *(G-7837)*
Enjoy Life Natural Brands LLC .... G 844 624-7162
  Jeffersonville *(G-9978)*
Grain Processing Corporation .... E 812 257-0480
  Washington *(G-16481)*
Ingredion Incorporated .... D 317 635-4455
  Indianapolis *(G-8545)*
Ingredion Incorporated .... B 317 295-4122
  Indianapolis *(G-8546)*
Ingredion Incorporated .... F 800 713-0208
  Whiteland *(G-16789)*
Pacmoore Products Inc .... E 317 831-2666
  Mooresville *(G-12234)*
Primary Pdts Ingrdnts Amrcas L ...... D 765 448-7123
  Lafayette *(G-10670)*
Primary Pdts Ingrdnts Amrcas L ...... B 765 474-5474
  Lafayette *(G-10671)*

2047 Dog and cat food

Albrecht Incorporated .... G 260 422-9440
  Fort Wayne *(G-4736)*
Bhj Usa LLC .... G 574 722-3933
  Logansport *(G-11062)*
Blue Buffalo Company Ltd .... B 203 665-3500
  Richmond *(G-14099)*
▲ Canines Choice Inc .... G 765 662-2633
  Marion *(G-11276)*
◆ Eagle Pet Products Inc .... D 574 259-7834
  Mishawaka *(G-11888)*
Good Poppi LLC .... G 812 319-1660
  Evansville *(G-4093)*
Heartland Pet Food Mfg Ind LLC ..... F 765 209-4140
  Richmond *(G-14132)*
Hills Pet Nutrition Inc .... E 765 935-7071
  Richmond *(G-14133)*
Macor .... G 574 255-2658
  Mishawaka *(G-11935)*
◆ Midwestern Pet Foods Inc .... F 812 867-7466
  Evansville *(G-4205)*
Nick-Em Builders LLC .... F 574 992-8313
  Logansport *(G-11099)*
Nick-Em Builders LLC .... E 574 516-1060
  Logansport *(G-11100)*
Nutritional Research Assoc .... F 260 723-4931
  South Whitley *(G-15322)*
Phillips Feed Service Inc .... E 610 250-2099
  Indianapolis *(G-9137)*
Purina Mills LLC .... D 812 424-5501
  Evansville *(G-4266)*
Purina Mills LLC .... E 574 658-4137
  Milford *(G-11805)*
Saturn Petcare Inc .... G 812 263-5646
  Terre Haute *(G-15687)*
Saturn Petcare Inc .... G 812 872-5646
  Terre Haute *(G-15688)*
Saturn Petcare Inc .... G 812 872-5646
  Terre Haute *(G-15689)*
Schell & Kampeter Inc .... F 765 570-4262
  Rushville *(G-14411)*

Scott Pet Products Inc .... D 765 569-4702
  Hillsdale *(G-7164)*
Scott Pet Products Inc .... G 765 569-4636
  Rockville *(G-14355)*
Underdog Diner LLP .... G 812 598-2970
  Evansville *(G-4359)*
Wellness Pet LLC .... E 574 259-7834
  Mishawaka *(G-12026)*

2048 Prepared feeds, nec

Alliance Feed LLC .... G 260 244-6100
  Columbia City *(G-2119)*
Audubon Workshop .... G 812 537-3583
  Greendale *(G-6438)*
Avari Reef Labs LLC .... G 317 201-9615
  Anderson *(G-80)*
B S R Inc .... G 812 235-4444
  Terre Haute *(G-15547)*
B S R Inc .... G 812 235-4444
  Terre Haute *(G-15548)*
B S R Inc .... E 812 235-4444
  Terre Haute *(G-15549)*
Back To Eden Herbs Corp .... G 317 455-1033
  Camby *(G-1507)*
Belstra Milling Co Inc .... G 219 766-2284
  Kouts *(G-10361)*
▲ Belstra Milling Co Inc .... E 219 987-4343
  Demotte *(G-2911)*
Birds Nest Inc .... G 574 247-0201
  Granger *(G-6337)*
Blue River Farm Supply Inc .... G 812 364-6675
  Palmyra *(G-13478)*
Bristow Milling Co LLC .... G 812 843-5176
  Bristow *(G-1299)*
Bundy Bros and Sons Inc .... F 812 966-2551
  Medora *(G-11462)*
C D C P Inc .... E 219 766-2284
  Kouts *(G-10362)*
Cargill Incorporated .... G 765 665-3326
  Dana *(G-2803)*
Cargill Incorporated .... B 402 533-4227
  Hammond *(G-6895)*
Cargill Incorporated .... G 574 353-7623
  Mentone *(G-11470)*
Cargill Incorporated .... G 574 353-7621
  Mentone *(G-11471)*
Cargill Dry Corn Ingrdents Inc .... E 317 632-1481
  Indianapolis *(G-7744)*
Commodity Blenders LLC .... G 260 375-3202
  Warren *(G-16294)*
Danko Farm Supply & Feed Inc .... G 812 870-7413
  Sullivan *(G-15404)*
Egg Innovations LLC .... D 574 267-7545
  Warsaw *(G-16355)*
Egg Innvtons Organic Feeds LLC .... G 800 337-1951
  Gary *(G-5927)*
Elanco US Inc .... G 812 242-5999
  Terre Haute *(G-15584)*
Envigo Rms Inc .... G 317 806-6080
  Greenfield *(G-6500)*
Envigo Rms Inc .... G 317 806-6060
  Greenfield *(G-6501)*
▲ Envigo Rms Inc .... C 317 806-6080
  Indianapolis *(G-8125)*
Flinn Frms Bdford Feed Seed In ...... G 812 279-4136
  Bedford *(G-636)*
▲ Frick Services Inc .... E 260 761-3311
  Wawaka *(G-16539)*
Gem Elevator Inc .... G 317 894-7722
  Greenfield *(G-6505)*
Global Harvest Foods LLC .... E 219 984-6110
  Reynolds *(G-14073)*

SIC SECTION
20 FOOD AND KINDRED PRODUCTS

Griffin Industries LLC .... D 812 379-9528
   Columbus *(G-2315)*

Griffin Industries LLC .... D 812 659-3399
   Newberry *(G-12989)*

Gro-Tec Inc .... F 765 853-1246
   Modoc *(G-12051)*

HMS Zoo Diets Inc .... G 260 824-5157
   Bluffton *(G-1037)*

Hog Slat Incorporated .... D 574 967-4145
   Camden *(G-1520)*

Hoosier Processing LLC .... F 260 422-9440
   Fort Wayne *(G-5080)*

Hunter Nutrition Inc .... F 765 563-1003
   Brookston *(G-1311)*

Innovative Concepts Group Inc .... G 317 408-0292
   Indianapolis *(G-8554)*

Jbs United Inc .... F 317 758-2609
   Sheridan *(G-14824)*

Kent Nutrition Group Inc .... F 574 722-5368
   Logansport *(G-11087)*

Keystone Cooperative Inc .... G 765 489-4141
   Hagerstown *(G-6838)*

Klabunde LLC .... G 765 635-1101
   Fortville *(G-5601)*

Lambrights Inc .... G 260 463-2178
   Lagrange *(G-10750)*

Land OLakes Inc .... F 574 967-3064
   Flora *(G-4660)*

Land OLakes Inc .... E 765 962-9561
   Richmond *(G-14155)*

Laughery Valley AG Co-Op Inc .... G 812 689-4401
   Osgood *(G-13412)*

Lowes Pellets and Grain Inc .... E 812 663-7863
   Greensburg *(G-6615)*

Mainstreet Marketing Entps LLC .... G 765 482-6815
   Lebanon *(G-10912)*

Mark Hackman .... G 812 522-8257
   Brownstown *(G-1425)*

▼ Matam Corp .... G 317 264-9908
   Indianapolis *(G-8851)*

▲ Micronutrients USA LLC .... D 317 486-5880
   Indianapolis *(G-8903)*

◆ Midwestern Pet Foods Inc .... F 812 867-7466
   Evansville *(G-4205)*

Mitchell Marketing Group Inc .... G 317 816-7010
   Carmel *(G-1700)*

Nutritional Research Assoc .... F 260 723-4931
   South Whitley *(G-15322)*

Pine Manor Inc .... G 574 533-4186
   Goshen *(G-6238)*

▲ Pine Manor Inc .... B 800 532-4186
   Orland *(G-13370)*

Platinum Feeds and Supply LLC .... G 812 593-7232
   Greensburg *(G-6623)*

Purina Animal Nutrition LLC .... G 812 424-5501
   Evansville *(G-4265)*

Purina Animal Nutrition LLC .... G 765 659-4791
   Frankfort *(G-5692)*

Purina Animal Nutrition LLC .... G 574 658-4137
   Milford *(G-11804)*

Purina Animal Nutrition LLC .... G 765 373-9377
   Richmond *(G-14191)*

Purina Animal Nutrition LLC .... G 765 962-9561
   Richmond *(G-14192)*

Purina Animal Nutrition LLC .... F 765 962-9561
   Richmond *(G-14193)*

Reconserve of Indiana Inc .... G 812 299-2191
   Mooresville *(G-12238)*

Regal Mills Odon .... G 812 295-2299
   Loogootee *(G-11149)*

Ridley USA Inc .... F 260 768-4103
   Shipshewana *(G-14883)*

Sappers Market and Greenhouses .... G 219 942-4995
   Hobart *(G-7206)*

Scotts Miracle-Gro Company .... G 219 984-6110
   Reynolds *(G-14076)*

Shaklee Authorized Distributor .... G 260 471-8232
   Fort Wayne *(G-5410)*

▲ Strauss Veal Feeds Inc .... E 260 982-8611
   North Manchester *(G-13251)*

Super Blend Inc .... G 260 463-7486
   Lagrange *(G-10766)*

Synergy Feeds LLC .... E 260 723-5141
   South Whitley *(G-15330)*

Trouw Nutrition Usa LLC .... D 618 654-2070
   Indianapolis *(G-9648)*

Tyson Foods Inc .... G 260 726-3118
   Portland *(G-13973)*

▼ United Animal Health Inc .... D 317 758-4495
   Sheridan *(G-14830)*

United Feeds .... G 317 627-5637
   Carmel *(G-1794)*

United Pet Foods Inc .... F 574 674-5981
   Elkhart *(G-3758)*

Vita Plus Corp .... G 574 595-0901
   Winamac *(G-16879)*

Wallace Grain Company Inc .... F 317 758-4434
   Sheridan *(G-14832)*

Wanafeed Corporation .... G 317 862-4032
   Indianapolis *(G-9736)*

Wilson Fertilizer & Grain Inc .... G 574 223-3175
   Rochester *(G-14333)*

Winfield Solutions LLC .... G 317 838-3733
   Plainfield *(G-13743)*

2051 Bread, cake, and related products

A Pinch of Sweetness LLC .... G 765 838-2358
   Lafayette *(G-10513)*

Alexson LLC .... G 219 210-3642
   Michigan City *(G-11576)*

Almiras Bakery .... F 219 844-4334
   Hammond *(G-6872)*

Alpha Baking Co Inc .... C 219 324-7440
   La Porte *(G-10381)*

Alpha Baking Co Inc .... G 574 234-0188
   South Bend *(G-14938)*

Always Fresh Baked Goods Inc .... E 317 319-4747
   Martinsville *(G-11380)*

B&B Goodiez .... G 765 338-6833
   Connersville *(G-2427)*

Babbs Supermarket Inc .... E 812 829-2231
   Spencer *(G-15339)*

Baked With Billie LLC .... G 317 517-1575
   Indianapolis *(G-7591)*

Bavettes Meat Company LLC .... G 312 590-7141
   Noblesville *(G-13041)*

Bea MA Bkes Spclty Dsserts LLC .... G 219 302-6716
   Merrillville *(G-11487)*

Bimbo Bakeries Usa Inc .... G 317 570-1741
   Indianapolis *(G-7627)*

Black Rose Pastries LLC .... G 773 708-3650
   Gary *(G-5901)*

Blue Dolphin Ffy LLC .... G 773 255-3591
   Hammond *(G-6887)*

Borman Distributing Inc .... G 219 713-8523
   Crown Point *(G-2661)*

C Is For Cookie LLP .... G 574 538-9841
   Goshen *(G-6108)*

C Johnson Group LLC .... G 219 512-0619
   Indianapolis *(G-7708)*

Cassie Cakes LLC .... G 219 308-3320
   Hammond *(G-6896)*

Colonial Baking Co Inc .... G 812 232-4466
   Terre Haute *(G-15565)*

Concannons Pastry Shop .... F 765 288-8551
   Muncie *(G-12369)*

Cookie Please .... G 317 879-6589
   Indianapolis *(G-7867)*

Cornerstone Bread Co .... G 317 897-9671
   Indianapolis *(G-7877)*

▲ Craftmark Bakery LLC .... G 317 548-3929
   Indianapolis *(G-7898)*

Dawn Food Products Inc .... C 800 333-3296
   Crown Point *(G-2674)*

Dlicous Dsserts By Deedee LLC .... G 317 515-1858
   South Bend *(G-15002)*

Donut Bank Inc .... E 812 426-0011
   Evansville *(G-4019)*

Dutch Waffle Company LLC .... F 574 312-4578
   Plymouth *(G-13773)*

Eat Da Cake LLC .... G 765 479-4985
   Merrillville *(G-11510)*

Enjoy Life Natural Brands LLC .... G 844 624-7162
   Jeffersonville *(G-9978)*

Ernestine Foods Inc .... G 219 274-0188
   Crown Point *(G-2681)*

Fingerhut Bakery Inc .... F 574 896-5937
   North Judson *(G-13212)*

Flowers Baking Co Ohio LLC .... G 502 350-4700
   Hobart *(G-7188)*

Flowers Baking Co Ohio LLC .... G 502 350-4700
   Marion *(G-11286)*

Flowers Baking Co Ohio LLC .... G 502 350-4700
   South Bend *(G-15037)*

Flowers Bkg Co Bardstown LLC .... G 502 350-4700
   Seymour *(G-14654)*

Fountain Acres Foods .... G 765 847-1897
   Fountain City *(G-5611)*

Froet Group LLC .... F 317 414-2538
   Whitestown *(G-16807)*

Ganal Corporation .... G 260 749-2161
   New Haven *(G-12903)*

Grabers Kountry Korner LLC .... F 812 636-4399
   Odon *(G-13339)*

Gutierrez Mexican Bky Mkt Inc .... G 574 534-9979
   Goshen *(G-6158)*

Harlan Bakeries LLC .... C 317 272-3600
   Indianapolis *(G-8361)*

▲ Harlan Bakeries LLC .... G 317 272-3600
   Avon *(G-523)*

▲ Harlan Bakeries-Avon LLC .... B 317 272-3600
   Avon *(G-524)*

Hartford Bakery Inc .... D 812 425-4642
   Evansville *(G-4104)*

Hearthside Food Solutions LLC .... B 219 878-1522
   Michigan City *(G-11622)*

Heyerly Brothers Inc .... F 260 622-4196
   Ossian *(G-13426)*

Holsum of Fort Wayne Inc .... A 219 362-4561
   La Porte *(G-10421)*

Holsum of Fort Wayne Inc .... C 260 456-2130
   Fort Wayne *(G-5071)*

Houchens Industries Inc .... F 812 467-7255
   Evansville *(G-4111)*

Indiana Baking Co .... F 260 483-5997
   Fort Wayne *(G-5098)*

Indiana Grocery Group LLC .... E 219 462-5147
   Valparaiso *(G-15971)*

Jay C Food 84 .... G 812 886-9311
   Vincennes *(G-16133)*

Kbi Inc .... D 765 763-6114
   Morristown *(G-12278)*

Klosterman Baking Co .... F 317 359-5545
   Indianapolis *(G-8696)*

Kroger Co .... G 574 294-6092
   Elkhart *(G-3460)*

Employee Codes: A=Over 500 employees, B=251-500
C=101-250, D=51-100, E=20-50, F=10-19, G=1-9

20 FOOD AND KINDRED PRODUCTS

Kroger Co .... G 574 291-0740
  South Bend *(G-15107)*

Kt Cakes .... G 812 442-6047
  Rosedale *(G-14381)*

Lakeshore Foods Corp .... D 219 362-8513
  La Porte *(G-10444)*

Lewis Brothers Bakeries Inc .... C 812 886-6533
  Vincennes *(G-16137)*

▲ Lewis Brothers Bakeries Inc .... C 812 425-4642
  Evansville *(G-4166)*

Loves Enterprise LLC .... G 219 307-9191
  Gary *(G-5978)*

Maurices Sgnture Chsecakes LLC .... G 708 879-0031
  Valparaiso *(G-16000)*

May Suu Mon LLC .... G 786 556-8295
  Fort Wayne *(G-5209)*

Mel-Rhon Inc .... G 574 546-4559
  Bremen *(G-1205)*

Michael Greene .... G 317 753-7226
  Ladoga *(G-10508)*

Miller Distributions Inc .... F 574 533-1940
  Goshen *(G-6224)*

Moores Pie Shop Inc .... G 765 457-2428
  Kokomo *(G-10314)*

Namsou Lims LLC .... G 347 641-5886
  Indianapolis *(G-8981)*

Nanas Cakes and Sweets LLC .... G 317 694-4271
  Indianapolis *(G-8982)*

Neeta Sweet Cupcakes n Minis ...... G 574 286-7032
  Granger *(G-6366)*

New Horizons Baking Co LLC .... C 260 495-7055
  Fremont *(G-5828)*

Ohana Donuts and Ice Cream LLC .. G 317 288-0922
  Fishers *(G-4570)*

On-Time LLC .... G 708 890-0230
  Hammond *(G-6989)*

Organic Bread of Heaven LLC .... F 219 883-5126
  Gary *(G-5991)*

Pasteleria Gresil LLC .... G 317 299-8801
  Indianapolis *(G-9096)*

Peace Love Cupcakes .... G 812 239-1591
  Terre Haute *(G-15659)*

Perfection Bakeries Inc .... G 219 789-4816
  Valparaiso *(G-16023)*

▼ Perfection Bakeries Inc .... C 260 424-8245
  Fort Wayne *(G-5306)*

Rhondas Tasty Treats LLC .... G 574 315-4011
  South Bend *(G-15218)*

Richards Bakery .... F 260 424-4012
  Fort Wayne *(G-5383)*

Royal Couture Treats Btq Ltd .... G 812 914-9057
  New Albany *(G-12809)*

Schnuck Markets Inc .... C 812 853-9505
  Newburgh *(G-13019)*

Sea Salt & Cinnamon LLC .... F 727 481-4024
  Muncie *(G-12491)*

Shipshewana Bread Box Corp .... G 260 768-4629
  Shipshewana *(G-14887)*

Sib Inc .... F 812 331-6029
  Bloomington *(G-969)*

Sound Mind Treats .... G 317 809-5832
  Indianapolis *(G-9461)*

Square Donuts Inc .... G 812 232-6463
  Terre Haute *(G-15714)*

Sweet Obsssons Bake Shoppe LLC .. G 260 273-2145
  Bluffton *(G-1060)*

Sweet Tooth LLC .... G 317 986-3764
  Indianapolis *(G-9538)*

Tasty Treats Bakery LLC .... G 317 622-8829
  Indianapolis *(G-9556)*

Tyson Mexican Original Inc .... D 260 726-3118
  Portland *(G-13974)*

United Pies of Elkhart Inc .... G 574 294-3419
  Elkhart *(G-3759)*

Vanilla Bean Inc .... G 260 415-4652
  Fort Wayne *(G-5528)*

Wb Frozen Us LLC .... A 317 858-9000
  Greenwood *(G-6779)*

Westfield Donuts .... G 317 896-5856
  Westfield *(G-16739)*

Weston Foods US Holdings LLC .... A 317 858-9000
  Brownsburg *(G-1413)*

2052 Cookies and crackers

Almiras Bakery .... F 219 844-4334
  Hammond *(G-6872)*

Blondies Cookies Inc .... F 765 628-3978
  Greentown *(G-6645)*

Bloomington Cookies LLC .... D 812 668-7779
  Bloomington *(G-811)*

Brilliant Blondes LLC .... F 765 288-8077
  Muncie *(G-12357)*

Chestnut Land Company .... G 574 271-8740
  Mishawaka *(G-11860)*

Clif Bar & Company .... D 510 596-6451
  Indianapolis *(G-7822)*

Darlington Cookie Company .... G 800 754-2202
  Indianapolis *(G-7952)*

Debra M Lewis .... G 219 937-4240
  Hammond *(G-6912)*

▼ Ellison Bakery LLC .... C 800 711-8091
  Fort Wayne *(G-4946)*

Fingerhut Bakery Inc .... F 574 896-5937
  North Judson *(G-13212)*

Grace Island Spcalty Foods Inc ..... G 260 357-3336
  Garrett *(G-5863)*

Hartzells Homemade Ice Cream ..... G 812 332-3502
  Bloomington *(G-875)*

Hearthside Food Solutions LLC ..... B 219 878-1522
  Michigan City *(G-11622)*

Heaven Sent Gurmet Cookies Inc ... G 219 980-1066
  Gary *(G-5948)*

Heyerly Brothers Inc .... F 260 622-4196
  Ossian *(G-13426)*

Hometown Products .... G 317 625-2447
  Pittsboro *(G-13648)*

Houchens Industries Inc .... F 812 467-7255
  Evansville *(G-4111)*

Lance Snyder .... G 717 632-4477
  Indianapolis *(G-8720)*

Mike-Sells West Virginia Inc .... G 317 241-7422
  Indianapolis *(G-8917)*

Perfect Twist Pretzels LLC .... G 574 248-1715
  Nappanee *(G-12636)*

▼ Pretzels LLC .... C 800 456-4838
  Bluffton *(G-1049)*

Richmond Baking Co .... C 765 962-8535
  Richmond *(G-14197)*

Richmond Baking Georgia Inc .... G 765 962-8535
  Richmond *(G-14198)*

Schnuck Markets Inc .... C 812 853-9505
  Newburgh *(G-13019)*

Shipshewana Bread Box Corp .... G 260 768-4629
  Shipshewana *(G-14887)*

Snyders-Lance Inc .... G 317 270-7599
  Fishers *(G-4605)*

Snyders-Lance Inc .... G 317 858-2209
  Indianapolis *(G-9456)*

Snyders-Lance Inc .... G 812 285-0939
  Jeffersonville *(G-10055)*

Somethin Sweet Llc .... G 317 804-4894
  Indianapolis *(G-9460)*

Sugar Daddys Sweet Shop .... G 812 824-2253
  Bloomington *(G-982)*

Victorian House Scones LLC .... G 765 586-6295
  Lafayette *(G-10712)*

Weston Foods US Holdings LLC .... A 317 858-9000
  Brownsburg *(G-1413)*

2053 Frozen bakery products, except bread

Alpha Baking Co Inc .... C 219 324-7440
  La Porte *(G-10381)*

La Braid Inc .... G 219 754-2501
  La Crosse *(G-10366)*

Lewis Brothers Bakeries Inc .... C 812 886-6533
  Vincennes *(G-16137)*

Moms Pound Cakes LLC .... G 773 220-3822
  Merrillville *(G-11544)*

Moores Pie Shop Inc .... G 765 457-2428
  Kokomo *(G-10314)*

Phoenix Press Inc .... D 765 644-3959
  Anderson *(G-178)*

Sue & Kims Pies LLC .... G 219 779-2140
  Merrillville *(G-11562)*

United Pies of Elkhart Inc .... G 574 294-3419
  Elkhart *(G-3759)*

2064 Candy and other confectionery products

Abbotts Candy and Gifts Inc .... E 765 489-4442
  Hagerstown *(G-6832)*

Albanese Conf Group Inc .... E 219 947-3070
  Merrillville *(G-11479)*

◆ Albanese Conf Group Inc .... D 219 947-3070
  Merrillville *(G-11480)*

▲ American Licorice Company ...... E 219 324-1400
  La Porte *(G-10382)*

Candied Cakes .... G 800 261-0823
  Indianapolis *(G-7732)*

Candy Com .... G 317 939-0102
  Brownsburg *(G-1357)*

Catalent Wellness Indiana LLC ...... F 812 537-5203
  Greendale *(G-6443)*

◆ CK Products LLC .... D 260 484-2517
  Fort Wayne *(G-4850)*

Claeys Candy Inc .... F 574 287-1818
  South Bend *(G-14974)*

Copper Kttle Fudge Popcorn LLC ... G 260 417-1036
  Fort Wayne *(G-4873)*

David M Pszonka .... G 219 988-2235
  Hebron *(G-7098)*

▲ Debrand Inc .... D 260 969-8333
  Fort Wayne *(G-4909)*

Donaldsons Chocolates Inc .... G 765 482-3334
  Lebanon *(G-10891)*

Gary Poppins LLC .... E 866 354-1300
  Knox *(G-10209)*

Katies Candy LLC .... G 800 558-9898
  Munster *(G-12545)*

Lowerys Home Made Candies Inc .. G 765 288-7300
  Muncie *(G-12441)*

Marengo Candy Barn Inc .... G 812 365-2141
  Marengo *(G-11264)*

Old World Fudge & Cds Dogs LLC . G 260 610-2249
  Columbia City *(G-2177)*

Olympia Candy Kitchen LLC .... G 574 533-5040
  Goshen *(G-6230)*

Poptique Popcorn LLC .... G 260 244-3745
  Columbia City *(G-2182)*

Schimpffs Confectionery LLC .... F 812 283-8367
  Jeffersonville *(G-10052)*

Simply Amazing .... G 219 464-9621
  Valparaiso *(G-16052)*

Stephen Libs Candy Company Inc .. F 812 473-0048
  Evansville *(G-4331)*

SIC SECTION 20 FOOD AND KINDRED PRODUCTS

Sweet Properties LLC .... G 812 283-8367
  Jeffersonville *(G-10062)*
Ugo Bars LLC .... G 812 322-3499
  Bloomington *(G-1003)*
Wsg Manufacturing LLC .... G 765 934-2101
  Whitestown *(G-16829)*

2066 Chocolate and cocoa products

Abbotts Candy and Gifts Inc .... E 765 489-4442
  Hagerstown *(G-6832)*
Claeys Candy Inc .... F 574 287-1818
  South Bend *(G-14974)*
▲ Debrand Inc .... D 260 969-8333
  Fort Wayne *(G-4909)*
◆ Deco Chem Inc .... F 574 255-2366
  Mishawaka *(G-11883)*
Donaldsons Chocolates Inc .... G 765 482-3334
  Lebanon *(G-10891)*
El Popular Inc .... F 219 397-3728
  East Chicago *(G-3005)*
LLC Tipton Mills .... G
  Columbus *(G-2345)*
Lowerys Home Made Candies Inc .... G 765 288-7300
  Muncie *(G-12441)*
Olympia Candy Kitchen LLC .... G 574 533-5040
  Goshen *(G-6230)*
▲ South Bend Chocolate Co Inc .... F 574 233-2577
  South Bend *(G-15251)*
Stephen Libs Candy Company Inc .... F 812 473-0048
  Evansville *(G-4331)*
Sweet Things Inc .... F 317 872-8720
  Carmel *(G-1774)*
True Essence Foods Inc .... F 317 430-3156
  Indianapolis *(G-9651)*
Violet Sky LLC .... G 574 850-5070
  South Bend *(G-15302)*

2068 Salted and roasted nuts and seeds

Lgin LLC .... G 260 562-2233
  Howe *(G-7238)*
Montpelier AG LLC .... G 765 728-2222
  Montpelier *(G-12180)*
Stephen Libs Candy Company Inc .... F 812 473-0048
  Evansville *(G-4331)*

2074 Cottonseed oil mills

Albertson Seed Sales .... G 765 267-0680
  Russellville *(G-14418)*
Archer-Daniels-Midland Company .... G 765 299-1672
  Fowler *(G-5618)*
Archer-Daniels-Midland Company .... G 260 749-0022
  New Haven *(G-12893)*

2075 Soybean oil mills

AG Processing A Cooperative .... G 574 773-4138
  Nappanee *(G-12577)*
Archer-Daniels-Midland Company .... G 765 299-1672
  Fowler *(G-5618)*
Bunge North America East LLC .... D 260 724-2101
  Decatur *(G-2849)*
Cargill Incorporated .... B 402 533-4227
  Hammond *(G-6895)*
◆ Dupont De Nemours Inc .... G 219 261-2124
  Remington *(G-14034)*
Horizon Farms LLC .... G 765 427-3685
  Monticello *(G-12153)*
◆ Solae .... G 260 724-2101
  Decatur *(G-2884)*
Solae LLC .... D 800 325-7108
  Remington *(G-14038)*

2076 Vegetable oil mills, nec

Catchrs LLC .... G 310 902-9723
  Indianapolis *(G-7759)*
▲ Innoleo LLC .... G 561 994-8905
  Indianapolis *(G-8551)*
Matthew Schlachter .... G 812 686-5486
  Bristow *(G-1300)*
Skinny & Co Inc .... E 888 865-4278
  Indianapolis *(G-9445)*
Solae LLC .... D 800 325-7108
  Remington *(G-14038)*

2077 Animal and marine fats and oils

Bunge North America East LLC .... D 260 724-2101
  Decatur *(G-2849)*
Darling Ingredients Inc .... G 317 708-3070
  Columbus *(G-2279)*
Darling Ingredients Inc .... E 317 784-4486
  Indianapolis *(G-7951)*
Darling Ingredients Inc .... G 812 659-3399
  Newberry *(G-12988)*
Darling Ingredients Inc .... E 913 321-9328
  Plymouth *(G-13770)*
Geo Pfaus Sons Company Inc .... E 800 732-8645
  Jeffersonville *(G-9992)*
Griffin Industries LLC .... F 812 379-9528
  Columbus *(G-2315)*
Griffin Industries LLC .... D 812 659-3399
  Newberry *(G-12989)*
Hrr Enterprises Inc .... E 219 362-9050
  La Porte *(G-10425)*
L & R Marine LLC .... G 260 768-8094
  Shipshewana *(G-14859)*
Nutritional Research Assoc .... F 260 723-4931
  South Whitley *(G-15322)*
Standard Fertilizer Company .... F 812 663-8391
  Greensburg *(G-6632)*
Sustainable Sourcing LLC .... E 765 505-2338
  Clinton *(G-2078)*
USA Bassin LLC .... F 812 276-8043
  Bedford *(G-680)*

2079 Edible fats and oils

A Wild Hare LLC .... F 812 988-9453
  Nashville *(G-12658)*
Blackpoint Distribution Co LLC .... E 260 414-9096
  Leo *(G-10964)*
Bunge North America East LLC .... D 260 724-2101
  Decatur *(G-2849)*
Debbies Handmade Soap .... G 765 747-5090
  Muncie *(G-12376)*
Heartland Harvest Proc LLC .... G 260 228-0736
  Hartford City *(G-7069)*
Heartland Harvest Proc LLC .... G 260 228-0736
  Gas City *(G-6038)*
Northern Indiana Oil LLC .... F 317 966-0288
  Indianapolis *(G-9022)*

2082 Malt beverages

Ash & Elm Cider Company LLC .... G 317 600-3164
  Indianapolis *(G-7550)*
Barley Island Brewing Co .... G 317 770-5280
  Noblesville *(G-13039)*
Beach House Beverages LLC .... G 260 969-1064
  Fort Wayne *(G-4789)*
Best Beers LLC .... E 812 332-1234
  Bloomington *(G-803)*
▲ Black Acre Brewing Company LLC ... G 317 207-6266
  Indianapolis *(G-7637)*
▲ Calumet Breweries Inc .... E 219 845-2242
  Hammond *(G-6891)*
Centerpoint Brewing Co LLC .... F 317 602-8386
  Indianapolis *(G-7768)*

Chapmans Cider Company LLC .... G 260 444-1194
  Angola *(G-239)*
Charles Wnngs DBA Dassault AVI .... G 928 276-4983
  Indianapolis *(G-7786)*
City Wineworks .... G 765 460-5563
  Peru *(G-13572)*
Crankshaft Brewing Co .... G 317 939-0138
  Brownsburg *(G-1361)*
Daredevil Brewing Company LLC .... G 765 602-1067
  Speedway *(G-15336)*
Dockside .... G 574 400-0848
  South Bend *(G-15003)*
Drinkgp LLC .... G 317 410-4748
  Indianapolis *(G-8009)*
Eder Bros LLC .... G 219 718-3335
  Schererville *(G-14520)*
Ekos Manufacturing LLC .... G 847 630-9717
  Indianapolis *(G-8068)*
Floyd County Brewing Co LLC .... F 502 724-3202
  New Albany *(G-12731)*
Indiana City Brewing LLC .... F 317 643-1103
  Carmel *(G-1666)*
Jaszy Drinks LLC .... G 219 742-5013
  Gary *(G-5969)*
Laotto Brewing LLC .... G 260 897-3152
  Avilla *(G-486)*
Lennies Inc .... E 812 323-2112
  Bloomington *(G-910)*
Lost Hollow Beer Co LLC .... G 317 796-9516
  Greencastle *(G-6420)*
Melanie Brewery Company Inc .... G 219 762-9652
  Portage *(G-13886)*
Michigan City Brewing Co Inc .... G 219 879-4677
  Michigan City *(G-11637)*
Mishawaka Brewing Company .... G 574 256-9993
  Granger *(G-6362)*
Monarch Distributing LLC .... A 800 382-9851
  Indianapolis *(G-8947)*
Myfin Inc .... F 812 287-8579
  Bloomington *(G-928)*
Oaken Barrel Brewing Co Inc .... E 317 887-2287
  Greenwood *(G-6748)*
Pepito Miller Bev Imports LLC .... G 317 416-3215
  Plainfield *(G-13713)*
Proximo Distillers LLC .... D 201 204-1718
  Lawrenceburg *(G-10855)*
Rapid View LLC .... G 574 224-3373
  Rochester *(G-14315)*
Round Town Brewery LLC .... G 317 657-6397
  Indianapolis *(G-9337)*
South Bend Brew Werks LLC .... G 801 209-2987
  South Bend *(G-15250)*
Sugar Creek Hops LLC .... G 317 319-1164
  Carmel *(G-1772)*
▲ Sun King Brewing Company LLC ..... D 317 602-3702
  Indianapolis *(G-9525)*
Tavistock Restaurants LLC .... G 317 488-1230
  Indianapolis *(G-9557)*
▲ Terrance A Smith Distributing .... E 765 644-3396
  Anderson *(G-205)*
Triple Xxx Root Beer Corp .... G 765 743-5373
  West Lafayette *(G-16640)*
Turonis Forget-Me-Not Inc .... F 812 477-7500
  Evansville *(G-4356)*
Upland Brewing Company Inc .... F 812 330-7421
  Bloomington *(G-1005)*
Wasser Brewing Company LLC .... F 765 653-3240
  Greencastle *(G-6435)*

2083 Malt

Archer-Daniels-Midland Company .... G 765 299-1672
  Fowler *(G-5618)*

20 FOOD AND KINDRED PRODUCTS

2084 Wines, brandy, and brandy spirits

Aftermath Cidery and Winery................... G 219 299-8463
Valparaiso *(G-15894)*

Ambrosia Orchard Inc........................... G 260 639-4101
Hoagland *(G-7165)*

Ancient Cellars................................... G 503 437-4827
Indianapolis *(G-7515)*

At The Barn Winery............................ G 513 310-8810
Lawrenceburg *(G-10829)*

B and C Enterprises............................ G 260 691-2171
Albion *(G-18)*

Bacchus Winery Golf Vinyrd LLC........... G 574 732-4663
Logansport *(G-11059)*

Bacchus Winery LLC........................... G 574 722-1416
Logansport *(G-11060)*

Belgian Horse Winery LLC.................... G 765 779-3002
Middletown *(G-11767)*

Best Vineyards LLC............................. G 812 969-9463
Elizabeth *(G-3124)*

▲ Blue Heron Vineyards LLC................. G 812 619-6045
Cannelton *(G-1533)*

Bonaccorsi Wine Company LLC........... G 310 777-3704
Carmel *(G-1570)*

Brandywine Creek................................ G 317 868-0563
Indianapolis *(G-7672)*

Brandywine Creek Vnyrds Wnery........... G 317 403-5669
New Palestine *(G-12934)*

Briali Vineyards LLC............................. G 260 316-5156
Fremont *(G-5812)*

Brown County Wine Company Inc.......... G 812 988-6144
Nashville *(G-12666)*

Butler Vineyards................................... G 219 929-1400
Chesterton *(G-1907)*

Butler Vineyards................................... G 812 332-6660
Bloomington *(G-819)*

Carousel Winery.................................. G 812 849-1005
Mitchell *(G-12035)*

Cedar Creek Winery............................ G 765 342-9000
Martinsville *(G-11385)*

Cedar Creek Winery............................ G 812 988-1411
Nashville *(G-12667)*

Chateau De Pique Inc.......................... G 812 522-9296
Seymour *(G-14638)*

Chateau Thomas Winery Inc................. F 317 837-9463
Plainfield *(G-13668)*

Cherry Hill Vineyard LLC...................... G 317 846-5170
Carmel *(G-1586)*

Copia Vineyards and Winery LLC.......... G 805 835-6094
Indianapolis *(G-7870)*

Country Hritg Wnery Vinyrd Inc............. F 260 637-2980
Laotto *(G-10803)*

Country Moon Winery LLC.................... G 317 773-7942
Noblesville *(G-13064)*

Cupkas Bee Good Meadery LLC.......... G 260 927-3837
Auburn *(G-381)*

Cupkas Bee Good Meadery LLC.......... G 260 927-3837
Auburn *(G-382)*

Daniels Vineyard LLC........................... F 317 894-6860
Greenfield *(G-6487)*

Dulcius Vineyards LLC......................... G 260 602-9259
Columbia City *(G-2140)*

Dune Ridge Winery LLC....................... G 219 548-4605
Chesterton *(G-1921)*

Durm Vineyard Inc.............................. G 317 862-9463
Indianapolis *(G-8021)*

Easley Enterprises Inc.......................... G 317 636-4516
Indianapolis *(G-8036)*

Ertel Cellars Winery Inc........................ G 812 933-1500
Batesville *(G-588)*

Evangeline Orchard & Winery................ G 574 278-6301
Monticello *(G-12149)*

Family Vineyard LLC............................ G 812 322-1720
Indianapolis *(G-8165)*

Finley Creek Vineyards LLC.................. G 317 769-5483
Zionsville *(G-17008)*

First Miracle LLC................................. G 812 472-3527
Fredericksburg *(G-5793)*

Four Corners Winery LLC..................... G 219 730-5311
Valparaiso *(G-15950)*

Frogs Leap... G 812 235-5759
Terre Haute *(G-15592)*

Fruit Hills Winery Orchrd LLC................ G 574 848-9463
Bristol *(G-1262)*

Graybull Organic Wines Inc................... G 317 797-2186
Indianapolis *(G-8316)*

Harmony Winery.................................. G 317 585-9463
Knightstown *(G-10196)*

Heagy Vineyards LLC.......................... G 317 752-4484
Carmel *(G-1652)*

Home - Little Creek Winery................... G 812 319-3951
Evansville *(G-4107)*

Hooker Corner Winery LLC................... G 765 585-1225
Pine Village *(G-13643)*

Hopwood Cellars Winery LLC................ G 317 873-4099
Zionsville *(G-17016)*

Hotel Tango Whiskey Inc...................... E 317 653-1806
Indianapolis *(G-8422)*

▲ Huber Orchards Inc......................... D 812 923-9463
Borden *(G-1110)*

Huckleberry Winery............................. G 317 850-4445
Bargersville *(G-568)*

Hunters Ridge Winery LLC................... G 812 967-9463
Salem *(G-14482)*

Indian Trail Wines LLC......................... G 574 889-2509
Royal Center *(G-14391)*

Indiana Artisan Inc.............................. G 317 607-8715
Carmel *(G-1665)*

▲ Indiana Whl Wine & Lq Co Inc............ G 317 667-0231
Indianapolis *(G-8501)*

J & J Winery....................................... G 765 969-1188
Richmond *(G-14143)*

James Lake Vineyard Inc...................... G 260 495-9463
Fremont *(G-5824)*

John King... G 317 801-3080
Indianapolis *(G-8630)*

Laker Winery LLC................................ G 812 934-4633
Sunman *(G-15440)*

Lane Byler Inc.................................... G 260 920-4377
Auburn *(G-402)*

Lane Legacy Vineyard.......................... G 937 902-7738
Brookville *(G-1328)*

Lanthier Winery LLC............................ G 502 663-2399
Madison *(G-11234)*

Lanthier Winery & Restaurant................ G 812 273-2409
Madison *(G-11235)*

Las Arribes LLC.................................. E 317 892-9463
Bloomington *(G-907)*

Lasalles Landing Vineyard LLC.............. G 574 277-2711
South Bend *(G-15117)*

Manic Meadery................................... G 219 614-1846
Crown Point *(G-2722)*

Meier Winery & Vinyard LLC................. G 812 382-4220
Sullivan *(G-15414)*

Monkey Hollow................................... G 812 998-2112
Saint Meinrad *(G-14463)*

Mystique Winery and Vinyrd LLC........... G 812 922-5612
Lynnville *(G-11190)*

Nashville Tasting Room........................ G 812 720-7080
Nashville *(G-12677)*

New Day Meadery LLC........................ G 317 602-7030
Indianapolis *(G-9004)*

Nob Hill Vineyards LLC........................ G 260 402-6070
Fremont *(G-5829)*

Oak Hill Winery LLC............................ G 765 395-3632
Converse *(G-2479)*

▲ Oliver Wine Company Inc.................. D 812 876-5800
Bloomington *(G-935)*

Owen Valley Winery LLC...................... G 812 828-0883
Spencer *(G-15356)*

Pacheco Winery Ltd Lblty Co................ F 812 799-0683
Columbus *(G-2369)*

Peace Water Winery LLC..................... G 317 810-1330
Noblesville *(G-13154)*

Pepito Miller Bev Imports LLC............... G 317 416-3215
Plainfield *(G-13713)*

Peppers Ridge LLC............................. G 812 499-3743
Rockport *(G-14347)*

Pfeiffer Winery & Vineyard Inc............... G 812 952-2650
Corydon *(G-2511)*

Plainfield Winery Tstng Rm................... G 317 837-9463
Plainfield *(G-13716)*

Poco A Poco LLC................................ G 317 443-5753
Leo *(G-10971)*

Prairie Sun Vineyard LLC..................... G 219 741-5918
Rolling Prairie *(G-14368)*

Preston Leaderbrand............................ F 812 828-0883
Spencer *(G-15357)*

Proud Spirits Inc.................................. G 301 775-0386
Carmel *(G-1731)*

Prp Wine International.......................... F 317 288-0005
Indianapolis *(G-9234)*

Rain Song Farms LLC......................... G 317 640-4534
Noblesville *(G-13164)*

Red Gate Farms Inc............................ G 812 277-9750
Bedford *(G-667)*

Rick Black Associates LLC................... G 765 838-3498
Lafayette *(G-10680)*

Ridge Winery Inc................................. G 812 427-3380
Vevay *(G-16111)*

Running Vines Winery.......................... G 219 617-2429
Valparaiso *(G-16041)*

S L Thomas Family Winery Inc.............. G 812 273-3755
Madison *(G-11250)*

Schmitt Bennett.................................. G 812 459-8523
Haubstadt *(G-7089)*

Scout Mountain Farm - Hideaway.......... G 812 738-7196
Corydon *(G-2515)*

Shady Creek Vineyard LLC................... G 219 874-9463
Michigan City *(G-11666)*

Simmons Winery & Farm Mkt Inc.......... G 812 546-0091
Columbus *(G-2393)*

Stoney Creek Winery LLC.................... G 574 642-4454
Millersburg *(G-11819)*

Sugar Creek Vinyrd Winery Inc.............. G 317 844-3785
Carmel *(G-1773)*

Sycamore Winery LLC......................... G 812 243-0565
West Terre Haute *(G-16655)*

Tilted Compass Winery LLC.................. G 812 691-1766
Clay City *(G-2047)*

Tippy Creek Winery LLC...................... G 574 253-1862
Leesburg *(G-10962)*

Tipsy Glass LLC.................................. G 260 251-0021
Portland *(G-13970)*

Tj Haase Winery Ltd Lblty Co................ G 765 505-1382
Terre Haute *(G-15732)*

Tonne Winery Incorporated................... G 765 896-9821
Muncie *(G-12506)*

Twe Wholesale Inc.............................. G 317 450-5409
Carmel *(G-1791)*

Twin Willows LLC................................ G 812 497-0254
Freetown *(G-5805)*

Two Ees Winery.................................. F 260 672-2000
Huntington *(G-7375)*

Urban Vines LLC................................. G 317 763-0678
Westfield *(G-16736)*

SIC SECTION
20 FOOD AND KINDRED PRODUCTS

Vineyard Fishery Products LLC .... G 317 902-0753
Indianapolis *(G-9721)*

▲ **Vino of Indiana LLC** .... F 260 710-7464
Wolcottville *(G-16943)*

Welch Winery LLC .... G 707 327-8038
Selma *(G-14623)*

Whyte Horse Winery LLC .... G 574 583-2345
Monticello *(G-12176)*

Wine and Canvas Dev LLC .... G 317 914-2806
Columbus *(G-2420)*

Wine N Vine .... G 765 282-3300
Muncie *(G-12522)*

Winzerwald Winery LLC .... G 812 357-7000
Bristow *(G-1302)*

Zeising Winery .... G 812 518-0607
Huntingburg *(G-7295)*

2085 Distilled and blended liquors

12-05 Distillery LLC .... G 317 402-4818
Indianapolis *(G-7383)*

1205 Distillery .... G 317 804-5675
Westfield *(G-16659)*

18th Street Distillery LLC .... F 219 803-0820
Hammond *(G-6865)*

8th Day Distillery LLC .... G 317 690-2202
Indianapolis *(G-7394)*

Bear Wallow Distillery .... G 812 657-4923
Nashville *(G-12662)*

Bemis Distillers LLC .... G 317 619-0711
Greenwood *(G-6675)*

Blue Marble Cocktails Inc .... E 888 400-3090
Indianapolis *(G-7645)*

Cardinal Ethanol LLC .... D 765 964-3137
Union City *(G-15850)*

▲ **Cardinal Spirits LLC** .... E 812 202-6789
Bloomington *(G-820)*

Distillery 64 LLC .... G 502 536-7485
New Albany *(G-12721)*

Easley Enterprises Inc .... G 317 636-4516
Indianapolis *(G-8036)*

Edwin Coe LLC .... G 260 438-7678
Churubusco *(G-1984)*

Fuzzys Spirits LLC .... G 317 489-6572
Indianapolis *(G-8249)*

Grain Processing Corporation .... E 812 257-0480
Washington *(G-16481)*

Hard Truth Distilling Co LLC .... D 812 720-4840
Nashville *(G-12670)*

Hotel Tango Whiskey Inc .... E 317 653-1806
Indianapolis *(G-8422)*

Hunt Club Distillery .... G 317 441-7194
Sheridan *(G-14823)*

Indiana Natural Infusions LLC .... G 847 754-9277
Lowell *(G-11163)*

Indiana Whiskey Co .... G 574 339-1737
South Bend *(G-15079)*

McCracken Curve Distillery LLC .... G 812 486-3651
Montgomery *(G-12113)*

Mgpi Processing Inc .... F 812 532-4100
Greendale *(G-6448)*

Oakley Brothers Distillery .... G 765 274-5590
Anderson *(G-171)*

Old Fort Distillery Inc .... G 260 705-5128
Grabill *(G-6317)*

Repeal 1205 LLC .... G 317 402-4818
Indianapolis *(G-9292)*

Royal Inc .... F 812 424-4925
Evansville *(G-4295)*

Southern In Distillery .... G 812 454-0135
Mount Vernon *(G-12322)*

Streven Distilling Company LLC .... G 574 527-4061
Warsaw *(G-16431)*

Three Floyds Distilling Co LLC .... F 219 922-3565
Munster *(G-12571)*

Three Rivers Distilling Co LLC .... E 260 745-9355
Fort Wayne *(G-5483)*

Turkey Run Distillery LLC .... G 765 505-2044
Bloomingdale *(G-762)*

West Fork Whiskey Co .... G 812 583-9797
Indianapolis *(G-9751)*

2086 Bottled and canned soft drinks

American Bottling Company .... D 260 484-4177
Fort Wayne *(G-4752)*

American Bottling Company .... C 317 875-4900
Indianapolis *(G-7500)*

American Bottling Company .... D 574 291-9000
South Bend *(G-14943)*

American Bottling Company .... D 765 987-7800
Spiceland *(G-15376)*

Better Blacc Wall Streetz LLC .... F 812 927-0712
Seymour *(G-14632)*

Blended LLC .... G 317 268-8005
Danville *(G-2808)*

Bollygood Inc .... G 317 215-5616
Indianapolis *(G-7658)*

▼ **Capitol Source Network** .... G 260 248-9747
Columbia City *(G-2129)*

Central Coca-Cola Btlg Co Inc .... D 765 642-9951
Anderson *(G-91)*

Central Coca-Cola Btlg Co Inc .... E 800 241-2653
Bloomington *(G-828)*

Central Coca-Cola Btlg Co Inc .... D 260 478-2978
Fort Wayne *(G-4840)*

Central Coca-Cola Btlg Co Inc .... E 800 241-2653
Indianapolis *(G-7770)*

Central Coca-Cola Btlg Co Inc .... D 317 398-0129
Indianapolis *(G-7771)*

Central Coca-Cola Btlg Co Inc .... E 317 243-3771
Indianapolis *(G-7772)*

Central Coca-Cola Btlg Co Inc .... G 812 482-7475
Jasper *(G-9827)*

Central Coca-Cola Btlg Co Inc .... E 260 726-7126
Portland *(G-13930)*

Central Coca-Cola Btlg Co Inc .... E 800 241-2653
Shelbyville *(G-14744)*

Central Coca-Cola Btlg Co Inc .... E 574 291-1511
South Bend *(G-14969)*

Circle City Sonorans LLC .... G 317 395-3693
Indianapolis *(G-7807)*

◆ **Clark Foods Inc** .... E 812 949-3075
New Albany *(G-12714)*

Coca Cola Bottling Company I .... E 812 376-3381
Columbus *(G-2240)*

Coca Cola Btlg Co Kokomo Ind .... E 574 936-3220
Plymouth *(G-13764)*

▲ **Coca Cola Btlg Co Kokomo Ind** .... D 765 457-4421
Kokomo *(G-10248)*

Coca-Cola Bottling Co .... E 812 332-4434
Bloomington *(G-831)*

Coca-Cola Bottling Co .... G 800 688-2053
Richmond *(G-14108)*

Coca-Cola Bottling Co Portland .... E 260 729-6124
Portland *(G-13931)*

Coca-Cola Consolidated Inc .... C 812 228-3200
Evansville *(G-3974)*

Coca-Cola Enterprises .... G 574 291-1511
South Bend *(G-14978)*

Dads Root Beer Company LLC .... G 812 482-5352
Jasper *(G-9830)*

Dr Pepper Bottling Co .... G 765 647-3576
Brookville *(G-1319)*

Dr Pepper Snapple Group .... G 574 291-9000
South Bend *(G-15005)*

Dr Pepper Snapple Group I .... G 260 484-4177
Fort Wayne *(G-4927)*

Gamer Energy LLC .... G 317 660-9262
Carmel *(G-1639)*

Indianapolis Gatorade .... G 317 821-6400
Indianapolis *(G-8505)*

Interactions Incorporated .... D 574 722-6207
Logansport *(G-11083)*

Ira William Scott .... G 219 241-5674
Valparaiso *(G-15977)*

Keurig Dr Pepper Inc .... G 812 522-3823
Seymour *(G-14661)*

Liquid Ninja Energy LLC .... F 812 746-2830
Evansville *(G-4171)*

Niagara Bottling LLC .... G 909 230-5000
Jeffersonville *(G-10025)*

Niagara Bottling LLC .... G 909 758-5313
Plainfield *(G-13709)*

Northeast Bottling Co .... G 260 343-0208
Kendallville *(G-10139)*

P-Americas LLC .... G 812 794-4455
Austin *(G-468)*

P-Americas LLC .... G 812 332-1200
Bloomington *(G-940)*

P-Americas LLC .... G 765 647-3576
Brookville *(G-1332)*

P-Americas LLC .... G 765 289-0270
Indianapolis *(G-9081)*

P-Americas LLC .... C 219 836-1800
Munster *(G-12556)*

P-Americas LLC .... G 812 522-3421
Seymour *(G-14670)*

Party Cask .... G 812 234-3008
Terre Haute *(G-15657)*

PD Kangaroo Inc .... G 317 417-7143
Indianapolis *(G-9109)*

Pepsi 3449 .... F 317 760-7335
Indianapolis *(G-9117)*

Pepsi Beverages Company .... E 260 428-9156
Fort Wayne *(G-5301)*

Pepsi Beverages Company .... E 219 836-1800
Munster *(G-12557)*

Pepsi Bottling Ventures LLC .... E 765 659-7313
Frankfort *(G-5690)*

Pepsi-Cola .... G 812 634-1844
Jasper *(G-9902)*

Pepsi-Cola Metro Btlg Co Inc .... F 812 332-1200
Bloomington *(G-945)*

Pepsico .... G 260 750-9106
Fort Wayne *(G-5302)*

▲ **Pepsico** .... C 317 821-6400
Indianapolis *(G-9118)*

Pepsico .... G 317 334-0153
Whitestown *(G-16813)*

Pepsico Inc .... E 260 579-3461
Fort Wayne *(G-5303)*

Pepsico Inc .... G 317 830-4011
Indianapolis *(G-9119)*

Pepsico Inc .... G 765 345-7668
Knightstown *(G-10201)*

Pepsico Beverage Sales LLC .... C 574 314-6001
South Bend *(G-15190)*

Qtg Pepsi Co Larry Davi .... G 317 830-4020
Indianapolis *(G-9244)*

Quaker Oats Company .... C 317 821-6442
Indianapolis *(G-9245)*

RC Transportation LLC .... D 812 424-7978
Evansville *(G-4274)*

Refresco Beverages US Inc .... F 812 537-7300
Greendale *(G-6455)*

Refreshment Services Inc .... D 812 466-0602
Terre Haute *(G-15677)*

20 FOOD AND KINDRED PRODUCTS

Rolling Hills Springs LLC .... G 844 454-6866
  Linton *(G-11044)*
Royal Crown Bottling Corp .... C 812 424-7978
  Evansville *(G-4294)*
Snapple Beverage Corp .... G 812 424-7978
  Evansville *(G-4323)*
Success Holding Group Intl Inc .... G 260 450-1982
  Ossian *(G-13436)*
Swanel Inc .... E 219 932-7676
  Hammond *(G-7017)*
▲ Vin Elite Imports Inc .... G 317 264-9250
  Indianapolis *(G-9720)*
Wp Beverages LLC .... F 574 722-6207
  Logansport *(G-11120)*

2087 Flavoring extracts and syrups, nec

Ambrotos LLC .... G 413 887-1058
  Otwell *(G-13456)*
Callisons Inc .... G 574 896-5074
  North Judson *(G-13208)*
Central Coca-Cola Btlg Co Inc .... E 317 243-3771
  Indianapolis *(G-7772)*
Common Collabs LLC .... G 574 249-9182
  North Judson *(G-13210)*
▲ Dairychem Laboratories Inc .... E 317 849-8400
  Fishers *(G-4501)*
DWG Global Services LLC .... G 469 605-0567
  Avon *(G-514)*
First Creative Ingredients Inc .... G 219 764-0202
  Portage *(G-13865)*
International Bakers Service .... E 574 287-7111
  South Bend *(G-15083)*
Mbv-Midwest LLC .... G 800 400-3090
  Indianapolis *(G-8859)*
Moseley Laboratories Inc .... F 317 866-8460
  Greenfield *(G-6533)*
Partlow Farms LLC .... G 317 919-8064
  Noblesville *(G-13151)*
Pepsico Inc .... G 317 830-4011
  Indianapolis *(G-9119)*
Savor Flavor LLC .... G 812 667-1030
  Dillsboro *(G-2952)*
Sugarpaste .... G 574 276-8703
  South Bend *(G-15272)*
▼ Tc Heartland LLC .... A 317 566-9750
  Carmel *(G-1776)*
Vitamins Inc .... E 219 879-7356
  Michigan City *(G-11686)*
Wild Flavors Inc .... G 859 991-5229
  Indianapolis *(G-9765)*
William Leman Co .... E 574 546-2371
  Bremen *(G-1230)*

2091 Canned and cured fish and seafoods

Midwest Caviar LLC .... G 812 338-3610
  English *(G-3843)*
Tropical Delights LLC .... G 317 261-1001
  Indianapolis *(G-9647)*

2092 Fresh or frozen packaged fish

Bantam Inc .... G 574 387-3890
  South Bend *(G-14955)*
Collins Caviar Company .... G 269 231-5100
  Michigan City *(G-11590)*
H & H Partnership Inc .... G 765 513-4739
  Kokomo *(G-10274)*
Ohio Valley Caviar .... G 812 338-4367
  English *(G-3845)*

2095 Roasted coffee

Allen Street Roasters LLC .... G 815 955-7472
  La Porte *(G-10380)*

Caffeinery LLC .... G 765 896-9123
  Muncie *(G-12360)*
Copper Moon Coffee LLC .... D 317 541-9000
  Lafayette *(G-10555)*
Devil Doc Coffee .... G 317 417-8486
  Avon *(G-512)*
Dry Heat Coffee LLC .... G 760 422-9865
  Indianapolis *(G-8013)*
Grinds Manufacturing LLC .... F 510 763-1088
  Westfield *(G-16694)*
Harvest Cafe Coffee & Tea LLC .... G 317 585-9162
  Indianapolis *(G-8369)*
Hoosier Roaster Llc .... G 574 257-1415
  Mishawaka *(G-11909)*
Julian Coffee Roasters Inc .... G 317 247-4208
  Zionsville *(G-17026)*
Michael Filley .... G 956 443-6364
  Owensburg *(G-13463)*
Rich Halstead .... G 219 462-8888
  Valparaiso *(G-16039)*
Roast Haus Coffee LLC .... G 224 544-9550
  Crown Point *(G-2746)*
Seraphim Coffee .... G 765 409-1942
  Lafayette *(G-10690)*
Smalltown Coffee Co LLC .... F 816 288-0687
  Crown Point *(G-2759)*
Suncoast Coffee Inc .... E 317 251-3198
  Indianapolis *(G-9526)*
Thedailygrind LLC .... G 317 531-1276
  Whitestown *(G-16826)*
Utopian Coffee Company LLC .... G 888 558-8674
  Fort Wayne *(G-5525)*
Wildcat Java LLC .... G 765 438-3682
  Burlington *(G-1447)*

2096 Potato chips and similar snacks

Broad Ripple Chip Co LLC .... G 317 590-7687
  Indianapolis *(G-7687)*
Brown County Kettle Corn LLC .... G 812 558-4536
  Nashville *(G-12665)*
Chester Inc .... F 574 896-5600
  North Judson *(G-13209)*
Conagra Brands Inc .... F 219 866-3020
  Rensselaer *(G-14049)*
Fizz Wizz .... G 812 718-9045
  North Vernon *(G-13270)*
Frito Lay .... G 574 269-1410
  Warsaw *(G-16364)*
Frito-Lay North America Inc .... E 765 659-4517
  Frankfort *(G-5668)*
Frito-Lay North America Inc .... B 765 659-1831
  Frankfort *(G-5669)*
Gary Poppins LLC .... E 866 354-1300
  Knox *(G-10209)*
Grace Island Spcalty Foods Inc .... G 260 357-3336
  Garrett *(G-5863)*
Inventure Foods Inc .... E 260 824-2800
  Bluffton *(G-1038)*
▲ Magic Company .... E 260 747-1502
  Fort Wayne *(G-5199)*
Mike-Sells West Virginia Inc .... G 317 241-7422
  Indianapolis *(G-8917)*
◆ Olde York Potato Chips Inc .... E
  Fort Wayne *(G-5284)*
Pepsico Inc .... G 317 830-4011
  Indianapolis *(G-9119)*
Poore Brothers - Bluffton LLC .... C 260 824-2800
  Bluffton *(G-1048)*
◆ Popcorn Weaver Mfg LLC .... C 765 934-2101
  Indianapolis *(G-9162)*
Specialty Food Group LLC .... D 219 531-2142
  Valparaiso *(G-16055)*

Super-Pufft Snacks Usa Inc .... G 850 295-9891
  Bluffton *(G-1059)*
Tyson Foods Inc .... G 260 726-3118
  Portland *(G-13973)*
Tyson Mexican Original Inc .... D 260 726-3118
  Portland *(G-13974)*
Utz Quality Foods LLC .... G 717 443-7230
  Bluffton *(G-1066)*
Utz Quality Foods LLC .... G 812 430-5751
  Georgetown *(G-6076)*
Utz Quality Foods LLC .... G 717 443-7230
  Indianapolis *(G-9693)*

2097 Manufactured ice

Airgas Inc .... G 317 632-7106
  Indianapolis *(G-7463)*
Arctic Glacier USA Inc .... F 800 562-1990
  Bedford *(G-620)*
Arctic Ice Express Inc .... F 812 333-0423
  Bloomington *(G-783)*
Bryant Ice Co Inc .... G 765 459-4543
  Kokomo *(G-10242)*
Celebration Ice LLC .... F 812 634-9801
  Jasper *(G-9826)*
Home City Ice Company .... F 765 762-6096
  Attica *(G-352)*
Home City Ice Company .... G 317 926-2451
  Indianapolis *(G-8404)*
Home City Ice Company .... F 317 926-2451
  Indianapolis *(G-8405)*
Industrial and Coml Contg Inc .... F 219 405-8599
  Valparaiso *(G-15973)*
Quikset Bollard Company .... G 502 648-6734
  New Albany *(G-12801)*
United States Cold Storage Inc .... E 765 482-2653
  Lebanon *(G-10949)*

2098 Macaroni and spaghetti

Barbs Homemade Noodles .... G 812 486-3762
  Montgomery *(G-12086)*
Essenhaus Inc .... B 574 825-6790
  Middlebury *(G-11715)*
Harrington Noodles Inc .... G 574 546-3861
  Plymouth *(G-13781)*
I Noodles .... G 765 447-2288
  West Lafayette *(G-16593)*
Noodle Shop Co - Colorado Inc .... G 219 548-0921
  Valparaiso *(G-16014)*

2099 Food preparations, nec

5 Knight LLC .... G 219 680-6661
  Anderson *(G-69)*
A Taste of Court Valjean LLC .... G 812 802-8584
  Evansville *(G-3861)*
Adrian Orchards Inc .... G 317 784-0550
  Indianapolis *(G-7434)*
Ameriqual Group LLC .... F 812 867-1444
  Evansville *(G-3887)*
◆ Ameriqual Group LLC .... A 812 867-1444
  Evansville *(G-3888)*
Amish Country Popcorn Inc .... E 260 589-8513
  Berne *(G-703)*
Anns Boba Tea LLC .... G 317 681-3143
  Indianapolis *(G-7520)*
Archer-Daniels-Midland Company ...... E 765 654-4411
  Frankfort *(G-5649)*
B Happy Peanut Butter LLC .... G 317 733-3831
  Zionsville *(G-16994)*
Best Boy Products LLC .... G 317 442-9735
  Indianapolis *(G-7615)*
Big Brick House Bakery LLP .... G 260 563-1071
  Fort Wayne *(G-4799)*

20 FOOD AND KINDRED PRODUCTS

Big Bruhs Seasoning LLP .... G 502 751-5516
Clarksville *(G-2009)*

Burlington Grain & Prod Co LLC .... G 866 767-2627
Sheridan *(G-14818)*

Butterfield Foods LLC .... C 317 776-4775
Noblesville *(G-13051)*

C & G Salsa Company LLC .... G 317 569-9099
Noblesville *(G-13052)*

California Sugars LLC .... F 219 886-9151
Gary *(G-5909)*

Carl Buddig Company .... F 708 210-3130
Munster *(G-12535)*

Cater To You Catering LLC .... G 219 301-1091
Hobart *(G-7179)*

Cavity Factory LLC .... G 317 937-5385
Indianapolis *(G-7761)*

Cbfc LLC .... G 317 677-1577
Indianapolis *(G-7763)*

Ceadogs LLC-S .... G 219 779-1352
Gary *(G-5914)*

Chef Hymie Inc .... G 201 218-4378
New Albany *(G-12711)*

Chicken and Salsa Inc .... G 812 480-6580
Evansville *(G-3971)*

Cibus Fresh LLC .... F 317 674-8379
Noblesville *(G-13059)*

Ciderleaf Tea Company Inc .... G 812 375-1937
Columbus *(G-2236)*

◆ Clabber Girl Corporation .... D 812 232-9446
Terre Haute *(G-15563)*

Combined Technologies Inc .... G 847 968-4855
Bristol *(G-1254)*

Conagra Brands Inc .... D 765 563-3182
Brookston *(G-1310)*

Conagra Brands Inc .... D 317 329-3700
Indianapolis *(G-7847)*

Conagra Brands Inc .... C 402 240-5000
Indianapolis *(G-7848)*

Conagra Brands Inc .... E 740 387-2722
Rensselaer *(G-14048)*

Conagra Brands Inc .... F 219 866-3020
Rensselaer *(G-14049)*

Conagra Dairy Foods Company .... A 317 329-3700
Indianapolis *(G-7849)*

Corner Sto LLC .... G 219 798-2822
Indianapolis *(G-7876)*

Cultor Food Science .... G 812 299-6700
Terre Haute *(G-15571)*

Danisco USA Inc .... D 812 299-6700
Terre Haute *(G-15575)*

Dem Guys LLC .... G 708 552-3056
Greenwood *(G-6684)*

Deonta Walker .... G 317 970-3586
Indianapolis *(G-7965)*

Dragonwood LLC .... G 765 947-0097
Kempton *(G-10086)*

Dugdale Beef Company Inc .... E 317 291-9660
Indianapolis *(G-8019)*

Eiseles Honey LLC .... G 317 896-5830
Indianapolis *(G-8066)*

El Popular Inc .... F 219 397-3728
East Chicago *(G-3005)*

Ethels Kitchen LLC .... G 317 441-2712
Indianapolis *(G-8139)*

Flavor Imperium LLC .... G 765 499-0854
Indianapolis *(G-8200)*

Foods Alive Inc .... F 260 488-4497
Angola *(G-252)*

▲ Freeze Dried Partners LLC .... G 800 783-1326
Fishers *(G-4526)*

Fresh Fenix LLC .... G 260 385-2584
Fort Wayne *(G-5012)*

Fresh Fenix LLC .... G 260 385-2584
Fort Wayne *(G-5011)*

Frito-Lay North America Inc .... E 765 659-4517
Frankfort *(G-5668)*

Frito-Lay North America Inc .... B 765 659-1831
Frankfort *(G-5669)*

Front Porch Sugarhouse .... F 574 831-5753
New Paris *(G-12954)*

G and G Peppers LLC .... E 765 358-4519
Gaston *(G-6045)*

Gem City Junction LLC .... G 765 659-6733
Frankfort *(G-5670)*

Gleaners Food Bank of Ind Inc .... D 317 925-0191
Indianapolis *(G-8284)*

Global Packaging LLC .... E 317 896-2089
Westfield *(G-16691)*

Grabill Canning Company LLC .... G 815 692-6036
Grabill *(G-6299)*

Graveyardgarlic LLC .... G 502 523-8148
Indianapolis *(G-8315)*

Harris Sugar Bush LLC .... G 765 653-5108
Greencastle *(G-6407)*

Harvey Hinklemeyers .... G 765 452-1942
Kokomo *(G-10276)*

Hoople Country Kitchens Inc .... F 812 649-2351
Rockport *(G-14342)*

Hulman & Company .... G 812 232-9446
Terre Haute *(G-15608)*

▼ Hulman & Company .... G 812 232-9446
Terre Haute *(G-15609)*

Imma Jerk LLC .... G 219 885-8613
Gary *(G-5958)*

Jeff Snyder .... G 260 349-0405
Kendallville *(G-10120)*

Johnny Long .... G 812 698-2516
Washington *(G-16488)*

Jones Popcorn Inc .... D 812 941-8810
New Albany *(G-12755)*

Kalustyan Corporation .... F 908 688-6111
Hobart *(G-7195)*

Kcma & Services LLC .... G 260 645-0885
Waterloo *(G-16522)*

Kerry Inc .... F 812 464-9151
Evansville *(G-4150)*

Kerry Inc .... C 812 464-9151
Evansville *(G-4151)*

Langeland Farms Inc .... G 812 663-9546
Greensburg *(G-6614)*

Life Spice and Ingredients LLC .... E 708 301-0447
Lowell *(G-11168)*

LLC Black Jewell .... E 800 948-2302
Columbus *(G-2344)*

Lm Sugarbush LLC .... G 812 967-4491
Borden *(G-1115)*

▲ Magic Company .... E 260 747-1502
Fort Wayne *(G-5199)*

McCormick & Company Inc .... G 410 527-6189
South Bend *(G-15143)*

McCormick & Company Inc .... C 574 234-8101
South Bend *(G-15144)*

◆ Mead Johnson & Company LLC ...... G 812 429-5000
Evansville *(G-4193)*

Meyer Foods Inc .... G 317 773-6594
Noblesville *(G-13137)*

MI Tierra .... G 812 376-0668
Columbus *(G-2353)*

Michael Ramer .... G 574 538-8010
New Paris *(G-12965)*

Mike-Sells West Virginia Inc .... G 317 241-7422
Indianapolis *(G-8917)*

Millers Mill .... G 574 825-2010
Middlebury *(G-11738)*

Mishawaka Food Pantry Inc .... G 574 220-6213
Mishawaka *(G-11955)*

Myfoodmixer LLC .... G 219 229-7036
Michigan City *(G-11644)*

Nates LLC .... G 765 400-4613
Anderson *(G-166)*

Natural Answers .... G 219 922-3663
Highland *(G-7147)*

◆ O-M Distributors Inc .... E 219 853-1900
Hammond *(G-6988)*

Ole Mexican Foods Inc .... G 574 359-7262
Indianapolis *(G-9045)*

Open Kitchen LLC .... G 317 974-9966
Indianapolis *(G-9063)*

Pacific Beach Peanut BTR LLC .... G 858 522-9297
Indianapolis *(G-9082)*

Passions Fruitopia LLC .... G 800 515-1891
Highland *(G-7151)*

Paytons Barbecue Inc .... G 765 294-2716
Veedersburg *(G-16089)*

Pb & J Factory LLC .... G 317 504-4714
Indianapolis *(G-9107)*

Peanut Butter Ministries Inc .... G 260 627-0777
Leo *(G-10970)*

Pgp International Inc .... E 812 867-5129
Evansville *(G-4237)*

Pgp International Inc .... E 812 449-0650
Evansville *(G-4238)*

Poore Brothers - Bluffton LLC .... C 260 824-2800
Bluffton *(G-1048)*

Preferred Popcorn LLC .... G 308 850-6631
Palmyra *(G-13484)*

▼ Pretzels LLC .... C 800 456-4838
Bluffton *(G-1049)*

Pretzels Inc .... E 574 941-2201
Plymouth *(G-13807)*

Qbc Catering LLC .... G 812 364-4293
Palmyra *(G-13485)*

Quaker Oats Company .... E 765 288-1503
Muncie *(G-12481)*

R D Laney Family Honey Company ...... G 574 656-8701
North Liberty *(G-13220)*

◆ Ramsey Popcorn Co Inc .... E 812 347-2441
Ramsey *(G-14026)*

Ready Pac Foods Inc .... C 574 935-9800
Plymouth *(G-13810)*

Reeves Feed & Grain LLC .... G 812 453-3313
Griffin *(G-6784)*

Reidco Inc .... E 812 358-3000
Brownstown *(G-1426)*

Revival LLC .... G 812 345-4317
Indianapolis *(G-9296)*

Roka Urban Ag LLC .... G 317 513-8828
Indianapolis *(G-9322)*

Sdgs Rubs & Spices LLC .... G 773 531-5497
Hammond *(G-7005)*

Sea Salt & Cinnamon LLC .... F 727 481-4024
Muncie *(G-12491)*

Select Gourmet Popcorn .... G 812 212-2202
Sunman *(G-15445)*

Shawn Ferguson .... G 269 300-7090
Noblesville *(G-13174)*

Silas Beachler .... G 260 578-1625
Claypool *(G-2057)*

Simply Good Foods Usa Inc .... G 317 622-4154
Greenfield *(G-6552)*

Skjodt-Barrett Foods Inc .... E 765 482-6856
Lebanon *(G-10942)*

Smoked Bros LLC .... G 360 440-6948
Georgetown *(G-6075)*

Studio Digital Salsa LLC .... G 317 439-8994
Plainfield *(G-13733)*

Employee Codes: A=Over 500 employees, B=251-500
C=101-250, D=51-100, E=20-50, F=10-19, G=1-9

2024 Harris Indiana
Industrial Directory

20 FOOD AND KINDRED PRODUCTS

Sweetener Supply Corporation .... G 708 588-8400
  Wolcott (G-16935)
Tc Heartland LLC .... G 317 876-7121
  Indianapolis (G-9560)
That Beverage Company LLC .... G 260 413-9660
  Fort Wayne (G-5479)
Thyme In Kitchen LLC .... G 812 624-0344
  Evansville (G-4345)
Tipton Mills Foods LLC .... D 812 372-0900
  Columbus (G-2402)
Tordilleria Del Valle .... G 765 654-9590
  Frankfort (G-5699)
Treehugger Maple Syrup LLC .... G 765 698-3728
  Laurel (G-10826)
Utz Quality Foods LLC .... G 717 982-3066
  Muncie (G-12511)
Viva Tia Maria LLC .... E 317 509-2650
  Zionsville (G-17061)
Vivolac Cultures Corporation .... E 317 866-9528
  Greenfield (G-6569)
Weavers Dtch Cntry Ssnings LLC .... G 260 768-7550
  Lagrange (G-10769)
Williams West & Witts Pdts Co .... G 219 879-8235
  Michigan City (G-11687)

21 TOBACCO PRODUCTS

2111 Cigarettes

Big Red Liquors Inc .... G 812 339-9552
  Bloomington (G-806)
Liggett Group LLC .... G 812 479-7635
  Evansville (G-4167)
Smoker Friendly .... G 812 556-0244
  Jasper (G-9912)
South Bend Smoke Time Inc .... F 574 318-4837
  South Bend (G-15256)

2131 Chewing and smoking tobacco

Black Swan Vapors LLC .... G 317 645-5210
  Pendleton (G-13526)
La Porte Smokes and Beverages .... G 219 575-7754
  La Porte (G-10441)

22 TEXTILE MILL PRODUCTS

2211 Broadwoven fabric mills, cotton

American Binders LLC .... G 260 827-7799
  Avilla (G-472)
Anippe .... G 317 979-1110
  Fishers (G-4465)
Aon(all or Nothing) LLC .... G 219 405-0163
  Indianapolis (G-7524)
APS Kreative Kustomz LLC .... G 317 384-1267
  Indianapolis (G-7536)
Blinds Plus LLC .... G 812 825-1932
  Stanford (G-15393)
Canvas & Conversation LLC .... G 812 425-5960
  Evansville (G-3960)
Chappelle Canvas and Uphl .... G 765 505-3925
  Terre Haute (G-15561)
Coopers Canvas .... G 317 292-2165
  Indianapolis (G-7869)
Covers of Indiana Inc .... G 317 244-0291
  Indianapolis (G-7891)
Creations In Canvas Vinyl .... G 317 984-5712
  Cicero (G-1995)
Creative Mnds Work Pblctns LL .... G 317 759-1002
  Indianapolis (G-7901)
Custom Qlting Pllow Cshion Svc .... G 219 464-7316
  Valparaiso (G-15934)
Cynthia Bergstrand .... G 574 277-6160
  Granger (G-6342)

Denim and Honey .... G 812 222-2009
  Greensburg (G-6591)
Dimo Multiservices LLC .... F 463 256-0561
  Avon (G-513)
East Cast Erosion Holdings LLC .... G 812 867-4873
  Evansville (G-4026)
Enduring Endeavors LLC .... G 260 410-1025
  Fort Wayne (G-4951)
Hamilton Canvas Inc .... G 219 763-1686
  Portage (G-13874)
Hollys Cstm Canvas & Uphl LLC .... G 317 550-6818
  Mooresville (G-12210)
Kcc Inc .... G 317 632-5258
  Indianapolis (G-8665)
Larrys Marine Canvas .... G 252 725-2902
  Bedford (G-655)
Lazzerini Corporation .... F 574 206-4769
  Elkhart (G-3474)
Lee Reed Holdings LLC .... G 219 255-0555
  Hammond (G-6970)
Midwest Sandbags LLC .... G 847 366-6555
  Elkhart (G-3541)
Millers Custom Care Candes .... G 574 658-4976
  Milford (G-11800)
Moore Shirts LLC .... G 317 350-4342
  Fort Wayne (G-5241)
▲ Mpr Corporation .... E 574 848-5100
  Bristol (G-1280)
Nays Custom Canvas .... G 317 523-4279
  Lebanon (G-10925)
Ninas Scrub Boutique LLC .... G 833 445-1955
  Anderson (G-169)
ONu Acres LLC .... G 765 565-1355
  Carthage (G-1816)
Panel Solutions Inc .... G 574 295-0222
  Elkhart (G-3581)
Perfect Seating .... G 317 564-8173
  Carmel (G-1716)
Perfect World Denim LLC .... G 260 449-9099
  Fort Wayne (G-5305)
▲ Pyro Shield Inc .... F 219 661-8600
  Crown Point (G-2739)
Salon Canvas LLC .... G 574 703-7018
  Granger (G-6375)
Sassy Scrubz LLC .... G 463 224-5693
  Indianapolis (G-9376)
Savage Yet Civilized LLC .... G 855 560-9223
  Merrillville (G-11556)
Shirt Print Ave .... G 812 882-9610
  Vincennes (G-16154)
Spobric LLC .... G 302 249-1045
  Indianapolis (G-9479)
Uinspire LLC .... G 574 575-6949
  Elkhart (G-3756)
Unjust LLC .... G 317 443-2584
  Fishers (G-4622)
Wine & Canvas South Bend LLC .... G 574 807-1562
  Elkhart (G-3786)
Wine and Canvas .... G 574 514-9942
  Elkhart (G-3787)
Wine and Canvas Dev LLC .... G 812 345-1019
  Bloomington (G-1013)
Wine and Canvas Dev LLC .... G 765 278-0432
  Indianapolis (G-9772)
Wine and Canvas Dev LLC .... G 317 345-1567
  Indianapolis (G-9773)
Wnc of Dayton LLC .... G 937 999-8868
  Indianapolis (G-9780)
Word 4 Word LLC .... G 317 601-3995
  Indianapolis (G-9787)
Zig-Zag Crnr Qilts Baskets LLC .... G 317 326-3915
  Greenfield (G-6573)

SIC SECTION

2221 Broadwoven fabric mills, manmade

Altec Engineering Inc .... E 574 293-1965
  Elkhart (G-3167)
Custom Sewing Service .... G 812 428-7015
  Evansville (G-4004)
Goldshield Fiber Glass Inc .... C 260 728-2476
  Decatur (G-2859)
Hard Surface Fabrications Inc .... G 574 259-4843
  Mishawaka (G-11905)
Joseph Fisher .... G 765 435-7231
  Waveland (G-16535)
Kabert Industries Inc .... D 765 874-2335
  Lynn (G-11184)
McL Window Coverings Inc .... F 317 577-2670
  Fishers (G-4563)
Raine Inc .... F 765 622-7687
  Anderson (G-182)
Sampson Fiberglass Inc .... E 574 255-4356
  Mishawaka (G-11990)
Satin & Stems .... G 765 318-2211
  Indianapolis (G-9378)
Services Everyone Needs Today .... G 260 368-9262
  Geneva (G-6052)
Structural Composites Ind Inc .... D 260 894-4083
  Ligonier (G-11024)
◆ Thorgren Tool & Molding Co .... D 219 462-1801
  Valparaiso (G-16067)
Word 4 Word LLC .... G 317 601-3995
  Indianapolis (G-9787)

2231 Broadwoven fabric mills, wool

Blumenau Alpacas .... G 219 713-6171
  Lowell (G-11156)
Bw Wholesale LLC .... G 775 856-3522
  Greenwood (G-6678)
Duneland Alpacas Ltd .... G 219 877-4417
  Michigan City (G-11602)
Kds Industries LLC .... G 574 333-2720
  Elkhart (G-3448)
RB Concepts .... G 317 735-2172
  Bloomington (G-952)
Spobric LLC .... G 302 249-1045
  Indianapolis (G-9479)

2241 Narrow fabric mills

▲ Indiana Ribbon Inc .... E 219 279-2112
  Wolcott (G-16931)
Masson Inc .... F 317 632-8021
  Indianapolis (G-8848)
Permawick Company Inc .... F 812 376-0703
  Columbus (G-2376)
▲ Tower Advertising Products Inc .... D 260 593-2103
  Topeka (G-15821)
▲ Web Industries Fort Wayne Inc .... E 260 432-0027
  Fort Wayne (G-5559)

2252 Hosiery, nec

Aeromind LLC .... G 800 905-2157
  Indianapolis (G-7453)
For Bare Feet LLC .... G 812 322-9317
  Martinsville (G-11393)
J J P Enterprise .... G 219 947-3154
  Hobart (G-7194)
Just Standout LLC .... G 317 531-6956
  Indianapolis (G-8651)
Standout Socks .... G 317 531-6950
  Indianapolis (G-9494)
Warm Socks Inc .... G 309 868-3398
  Indianapolis (G-9737)

2253 Knit outerwear mills

22 TEXTILE MILL PRODUCTS

All Things Kingdom LLC .... G 312 200-4569
  Highland *(G-7120)*
Dyer Signwerks Inc .... G 219 322-7722
  Dyer *(G-2971)*
Mammoth Hats Inc .... F 812 849-2772
  Mitchell *(G-12044)*
Professional Gifting Inc .... F 800 350-1796
  Indianapolis *(G-9221)*

2254 Knit underwear mills

Dontstoptillyougetenough LLC .... G 812 250-8262
  Evansville *(G-4018)*

2261 Finishing plants, cotton

323ink LLC .... G 812 282-3620
  Jeffersonville *(G-9920)*
A D I Screen Printing .... G 765 457-8580
  Kokomo *(G-10231)*
Action Embroidery Inc .... G 850 626-1796
  Charlestown *(G-1869)*
All Things Custom LLC .... G 765 618-5332
  Sweetser *(G-15453)*
Bens Creative Ventures LLC .... G 574 279-1057
  Fort Wayne *(G-4795)*
▲ Concept Prints Inc .... F 317 290-1222
  Indianapolis *(G-7851)*
Graphic22 Inc .... G 219 921-5409
  Chesterton *(G-1930)*
ID Graphics Incorporated .... G 765 649-9988
  Anderson *(G-133)*
Ink Dawgz LLC .... G 219 781-6972
  Valparaiso *(G-15974)*
OHaras Sports Inc .... G 219 836-5554
  Munster *(G-12554)*
Pretty Chique LLC .... G 317 922-5899
  Indianapolis *(G-9194)*
Printwise LLC .... G 765 244-1983
  Peru *(G-13595)*
Tony London Co Inc .... G 812 373-0748
  Columbus *(G-2403)*
UC Ink LLC .... G 765 220-5502
  West College Corner *(G-16544)*

2262 Finishing plants, manmade

Abercrombie Textiles I LLC .... G 574 848-5100
  Bristol *(G-1240)*
▲ Classic Products Corp .... E 260 484-2695
  Fort Wayne *(G-4855)*
Graphic22 Inc .... G 219 921-5409
  Chesterton *(G-1930)*
Ink Dawgz LLC .... G 219 781-6972
  Valparaiso *(G-15974)*
▲ Main Event Mdsg Group LLC .... F 317 570-8900
  Indianapolis *(G-8812)*
Spectrum Marketing .... G 765 643-5566
  Anderson *(G-197)*

2269 Finishing plants, nec

Graphic22 Inc .... G 219 921-5409
  Chesterton *(G-1930)*
Masson Inc .... F 317 632-8021
  Indianapolis *(G-8848)*
Melissa Lambino .... G 317 506-5274
  Indianapolis *(G-8874)*
Tt2 LLC .... G 260 438-4575
  Fort Wayne *(G-5511)*

2273 Carpets and rugs

Advanced Services LLC .... F 317 780-6909
  Indianapolis *(G-7441)*
All Day Carpet Binding LLC .... G 219 851-8071
  Lafayette *(G-10518)*

Bock Engineering Company Inc .... G 574 522-3191
  Elkhart *(G-3229)*
Conforce International Inc .... G 765 473-3061
  Peru *(G-13575)*
▲ Envirotech Extrusion Inc .... E 765 966-8068
  Richmond *(G-14120)*
Faulkens Floorcover .... F 574 300-4260
  South Bend *(G-15027)*
Georgia Direct Carpet Inc .... F 765 966-2548
  Richmond *(G-14125)*
Indiana Rug Company .... G 574 252-4653
  Mishawaka *(G-11911)*
▲ Jpc LLC .... F 574 293-8030
  Elkhart *(G-3437)*
Manta Rugs .... G 765 869-5940
  Boswell *(G-1118)*
Mat Matrs of Indiana Inc .... G 260 624-2882
  Angola *(G-274)*
Mohawk Group LLC .... G 765 250-5458
  West Lafayette *(G-16611)*
Mountville Mats .... G 574 753-8858
  Logansport *(G-11094)*
Recreation Insites LLC .... G 317 578-0588
  Fishers *(G-4592)*
Rtw Enterprises Inc .... E 574 294-3275
  Elkhart *(G-3654)*
Taylor Gary .... G 812 895-0715
  Vincennes *(G-16158)*
Tekmodo Oz Holdings LLC .... G 574 970-5800
  Elkhart *(G-3721)*
Todd K Hockemeyer Inc .... G 260 639-3591
  Fort Wayne *(G-5492)*
Too Tuft LLC .... G 317 719-2182
  Indianapolis *(G-9618)*

2281 Yarn spinning mills

Elizabeth A Taylor .... G 815 353-4798
  Freedom *(G-5799)*
Regal Manufacturing Company .... G 765 334-8118
  Cambridge City *(G-1501)*

2282 Throwing and winding mills

BP Wind Energy North Amer Inc .... G 765 884-1000
  Fowler *(G-5621)*
Elmotec-Statolmat .... G 260 758-8300
  Markle *(G-11355)*

2284 Thread mills

Elegant Needleworks Inc .... G 765 284-9427
  Muncie *(G-12390)*
Profit Over Romance LLC .... G 219 900-3592
  Gary *(G-5997)*
Three Moons Fiberworks LLC .... G 219 841-5387
  Chesterton *(G-1960)*

2295 Coated fabrics, not rubberized

Abercrombie Textiles I LLC .... G 574 848-5100
  Bristol *(G-1240)*
C M I Enterprises Inc .... D 305 685-9651
  Elkhart *(G-3244)*
CP Polymer Solutions LLC .... G 812 426-1350
  Evansville *(G-3989)*
D K Enterprises LLC .... G 260 356-9011
  Huntington *(G-7307)*
◆ Elite Crete Systems Inc .... F 219 465-7671
  Valparaiso *(G-15942)*
Ferrill-Fisher Incorporated .... G 812 935-9000
  Bloomington *(G-865)*
Indiana Coated Fabrics Inc .... F 574 269-1280
  Warsaw *(G-16376)*
Innovations Amplified LLC .... G 317 339-4685
  Indianapolis *(G-8552)*

ISI of Indiana Inc .... G 317 241-2999
  Indianapolis *(G-8595)*
Mid Mountain Materials Inc .... F 812 550-5867
  Evansville *(G-4203)*
▲ Mpr Corporation .... E 574 848-5100
  Bristol *(G-1280)*
Patrick Industries Inc .... G 574 255-9692
  Mishawaka *(G-11970)*
▲ Sirmax North America Inc .... D 765 639-0300
  Anderson *(G-194)*
▲ Wjh Investments Inc .... G
  Warsaw *(G-16455)*

2296 Tire cord and fabrics

▲ Muhlen Sohn Inc .... F 765 640-9674
  Anderson *(G-163)*

2297 Nonwoven fabrics

Carver Non-Woven Indiana LLC .... G 260 627-0033
  Fremont *(G-5814)*
Carver Non-Woven Tech LLC .... C 260 627-0033
  Fremont *(G-5815)*
Fiber Bond Operating LLC .... C 219 879-4541
  Trail Creek *(G-15837)*
◆ Gaius Julius Crassus Inc .... G 219 879-4541
  Trail Creek *(G-15838)*
Jason Holdings Inc .... G 414 277-9300
  Richmond *(G-14147)*
Midwest Nonwovens Indiana LLC .... E 317 241-8956
  Indianapolis *(G-8912)*
Twe Nonwovens Us Inc .... E 260 747-0990
  Fort Wayne *(G-5517)*

2298 Cordage and twine

▲ Hessville Cable & Sling Co .... E 773 768-8181
  Gary *(G-5951)*
Kentuckiana Wire Rope & Supply .... F 812 282-3667
  Jeffersonville *(G-10005)*

2299 Textile goods, nec

3w Enterprises LLC .... G 847 366-6555
  Elkhart *(G-3137)*
Backwoods Vynl Werks LLC .... G 765 607-1292
  Lafayette *(G-10534)*
Blocksom & Co .... G 219 878-4458
  Trail Creek *(G-15835)*
Blush Salon Boutique .... F 317 523-1635
  Fishers *(G-4475)*
East Heat Wood Pellets LLC .... G 317 638-4840
  Indianapolis *(G-8037)*
Elizabeth A Taylor .... G 815 353-4798
  Freedom *(G-5799)*
Foremost Flexible Fabricating .... F 812 663-4756
  Greensburg *(G-6594)*
Harold Mailand .... G 317 266-8398
  Indianapolis *(G-8364)*
Ladybugz Bookstore LLC .... G 469 459-1780
  Noblesville *(G-13125)*
Midwest Sandbags LLC .... G 847 366-6555
  Elkhart *(G-3541)*
Mp Global Products LLC .... E 866 751-3765
  New Albany *(G-12782)*
Ruby Enterprises Inc .... G 765 649-2060
  Anderson *(G-186)*
Thaddeus Luxury Hbags & HM ACC ...... G 907 301-1373
  Syracuse *(G-15484)*
Tippmann Products LLC .... G 260 438-7946
  Fort Wayne *(G-5487)*
True You Naturally Inc .... G 317 518-2268
  Fishers *(G-4617)*
◆ Wolf Corporation .... E 260 749-9393
  Fort Wayne *(G-5574)*

23 APPAREL, FINISHED PRODUCTS FROM FABRICS & SIMILAR MATERIALS

2311 Men's and boy's suits and coats

▲ Ashley Worldwide Inc........................ G..... 574 259-2481
 Granger *(G-6332)*
Formal Affairs Tuxedo Shop.................. G..... 574 875-6654
 Elkhart *(G-3357)*
Hearts Rmned Lifestyle Cir LLC............ G..... 800 807-0485
 Gary *(G-5947)*
▲ Impact Racing Inc............................... D..... 317 852-3067
 Indianapolis *(G-8468)*
Kevin Koch... G..... 574 971-8094
 Goshen *(G-6187)*
Legacy Enterprises Inc........................... G..... 219 484-9483
 Merrillville *(G-11531)*
Raine Inc.. F..... 765 622-7687
 Anderson *(G-182)*
Sugar Tree Incorporated......................... G..... 260 417-3362
 Fort Wayne *(G-5450)*
United Seams Apparel Cnstr LLC.......... G..... 773 397-3831
 Hammond *(G-7026)*

2321 Men's and boy's furnishings

Abbott Industrial Sewing LLC................. G..... 574 383-1588
 South Bend *(G-14932)*
Eliba Collections LLC.............................. G..... 646 675-6196
 Whiteland *(G-16785)*
European Concepts LLC......................... G..... 888 797-9005
 Fort Wayne *(G-4966)*
Him Gentlemans Boutique..................... G..... 812 924-7441
 New Albany *(G-12741)*
Hoogies Sports House Inc..................... G..... 574 533-9875
 Goshen *(G-6165)*

2322 Men's and boy's underwear and nightwear

Krazy Klothes Ltd.................................... G..... 317 687-8310
 Indianapolis *(G-8702)*

2323 Men's and boy's neckwear

Farwall Tsg LLC...................................... F..... 574 773-2108
 Nappanee *(G-12596)*
Impulse of Jasper Inc............................. G..... 812 481-2880
 Jasper *(G-9844)*
Provisa International Inc........................ G..... 812 207-9137
 Charlestown *(G-1892)*
Sugar and Bruno Inc.............................. F..... 317 991-4422
 Indianapolis *(G-9520)*
Sycamore Enterprises Inc...................... G..... 812 477-2266
 Evansville *(G-4339)*

2325 Men's and boy's trousers and slacks

▲ Berne Apparel Company..................... E..... 260 622-1500
 Ossian *(G-13419)*
Leslie Nuss.. G..... 219 462-3499
 Valparaiso *(G-15997)*

2326 Men's and boy's work clothing

▲ Berne Apparel Company..................... E..... 260 622-1500
 Ossian *(G-13419)*
Browmi By Misha LLC............................ G..... 317 801-3911
 Indianapolis *(G-7689)*
Btq Manufacturing Inc............................ E..... 574 223-4311
 Rochester *(G-14281)*
Clinical Scrubs LLC................................. G..... 317 607-3991
 Indianapolis *(G-7823)*
Creative Mnds Work Pblctons LL........... G..... 317 759-1002
 Indianapolis *(G-7901)*
Dance Sophisticates Inc......................... E..... 317 634-7728
 Indianapolis *(G-7948)*
Gohn Bros Manufacturing Co................ G..... 574 825-2400
 Middlebury *(G-11718)*
J B Hinchman Inc................................... G..... 317 359-1808
 Indianapolis *(G-8602)*
Nitas Scrubs Zone LLC........................... G..... 317 204-6576
 Indianapolis *(G-9012)*
Pinnacle Textile Inds LLC....................... D..... 574 223-4311
 Rochester *(G-14311)*
Steel Grip Inc.. G..... 765 397-3344
 Kingman *(G-10174)*
▲ Twin Hill Acquisition Co Inc................ E..... 888 206-0699
 Jeffersonville *(G-10067)*
Working Pitbull Kennell........................... G..... 708 762-9725
 East Chicago *(G-3058)*

2329 Men's and boy's clothing, nec

Adidas North America Inc...................... G..... 219 878-5822
 Michigan City *(G-11575)*
▲ Berne Apparel Company..................... E..... 260 622-1500
 Ossian *(G-13419)*
Designs 4 U Inc...................................... G..... 765 793-3026
 Covington *(G-2528)*
Fanatics Lids College LLC..................... E..... 888 814-4287
 Indianapolis *(G-8166)*
Fashion City... G..... 260 744-6753
 Fort Wayne *(G-4975)*
Heart Struggle LLC................................. G..... 812 480-2580
 Fort Wayne *(G-5054)*
Hush Clothing 317 LLC.......................... G..... 317 935-2184
 Indianapolis *(G-8438)*
Igotkickz LLC... G..... 812 893-7674
 Evansville *(G-4115)*
◆ Indiana Knitwear Corporation.............. E..... 317 462-4413
 Greenfield *(G-6513)*
Lgndz Customs LLC................................ G..... 765 293-9303
 Marion *(G-11308)*
▲ Official Sports Intl Inc........................... F..... 574 269-1404
 Warsaw *(G-16403)*
Paris Black Fashion LLC......................... G..... 317 529-7119
 Greencastle *(G-6423)*
Red Storm Athletics Inc.......................... G..... 765 464-3336
 Lafayette *(G-10678)*
Sports Licensed Division........................ A..... 317 895-7000
 Indianapolis *(G-9481)*
Torrid LLC... F..... 219 769-1192
 Merrillville *(G-11567)*

2331 Women's and misses' blouses and shirts

Anita Lorrain LLC.................................... G..... 574 621-0531
 South Bend *(G-14946)*
August Gill Apparel LLC......................... G..... 317 342-2800
 Fort Wayne *(G-4779)*
Luxe Fashion Palace LLC...................... G..... 317 379-1372
 Indianapolis *(G-8799)*
Working Pitbull Kennell........................... G..... 708 762-9725
 East Chicago *(G-3058)*

2335 Women's, junior's, and misses' dresses

Elysian Company LLC............................. G..... 574 267-2259
 Warsaw *(G-16359)*
House of Delrenee LLC.......................... G..... 219 670-1153
 Indianapolis *(G-8427)*
Kitwana Kouture LLC.............................. G..... 812 589-7135
 Evansville *(G-4155)*
Kurvy Kurves Kouture LLC..................... F..... 812 340-6090
 Bloomington *(G-904)*
Lj Motive LLC... F..... 219 588-5480
 Hobart *(G-7200)*
Lulus Prom and Bridal LLC.................... G..... 812 772-2013
 Tell City *(G-15509)*
Simple To Elegant LLC........................... G..... 812 234-8700
 Terre Haute *(G-15696)*
Sugar Tree Incorporated......................... G..... 260 417-3362
 Fort Wayne *(G-5450)*

2337 Women's and misses' suits and coats

Abbott Industrial Sewing LLC................. G..... 574 383-1588
 South Bend *(G-14932)*
Classy Stitches....................................... G..... 317 856-3261
 Indianapolis *(G-7821)*
Legacy Enterprises Inc........................... G..... 219 484-9483
 Merrillville *(G-11531)*

2339 Women's and misses' outerwear, nec

▲ Berne Apparel Company..................... E..... 260 622-1500
 Ossian *(G-13419)*
Best Friends Inc...................................... G..... 765 985-3872
 Denver *(G-2934)*
Catherine J Bergren................................ G..... 219 225-2819
 Gary *(G-5913)*
CM Reed LLC.. G..... 517 546-4100
 Greendale *(G-6444)*
Dance Sophisticates Inc......................... E..... 317 634-7728
 Indianapolis *(G-7948)*
Designs 4 U Inc...................................... G..... 765 793-3026
 Covington *(G-2528)*
Eliba Collections LLC.............................. G..... 646 675-6196
 Whiteland *(G-16785)*
Fanatics Lids College LLC..................... E..... 888 814-4287
 Indianapolis *(G-8166)*
Farwall Tsg LLC...................................... F..... 574 773-2108
 Nappanee *(G-12596)*
Grnwman LLC.. G..... 219 359-9237
 Chesterton *(G-1933)*
Hidinghilda LLC....................................... G..... 260 760-7093
 Kendallville *(G-10118)*
Hoogies Sports House Inc..................... G..... 574 533-9875
 Goshen *(G-6165)*
Legends Maingate LLC........................... F..... 317 243-2000
 Indianapolis *(G-8735)*
▲ Maingate LLC... D
 Indianapolis *(G-8814)*
Mgtc Inc... D..... 317 780-0609
 Indianapolis *(G-8896)*
▲ Mgtc Inc... D..... 317 873-8697
 Zionsville *(G-17032)*
▲ Official Sports Intl Inc........................... F..... 574 269-1404
 Warsaw *(G-16403)*
Reloaded Activewear LLC...................... G..... 317 652-7394
 Indianapolis *(G-9289)*
Rustic Fisher Creations LLC.................. G..... 574 279-5754
 North Liberty *(G-13222)*
Scrubs2therescue LLC........................... G..... 317 748-7677
 Indianapolis *(G-9397)*
Sports Licensed Division........................ A..... 317 895-7000
 Indianapolis *(G-9481)*
Still Safety Products LLC....................... G..... 855 249-0009
 Evanston *(G-3855)*
Sycamore Enterprises Inc...................... G..... 812 477-2266
 Evansville *(G-4339)*
Three Little Monkeys.............................. G..... 765 778-9370
 Pendleton *(G-13557)*
True Royalty Boutique LLC.................... F..... 260 706-5121
 Fort Wayne *(G-5510)*
Truu Confidence LLC.............................. G..... 317 795-0042
 Indianapolis *(G-9653)*
Zendigo Boutique LLC............................ G..... 574 314-8328
 South Bend *(G-15312)*

23 APPAREL, FINISHED PRODUCTS FROM FABRICS & SIMILAR MATERIALS

2341 Women's and children's underwear

Krazy Klothes Ltd........................... G 317 687-8410
  Indianapolis *(G-8702)*

Roses Square Dance Acc................ G 812 865-2821
  Orleans *(G-13382)*

Vanity Fair Brands LP.................... E 219 861-0205
  Michigan City *(G-11685)*

2353 Hats, caps, and millinery

League of Fancy Hats LLC.............. G 260 355-7115
  Huntington *(G-7336)*

Mammoth Hats Inc.......................... F 812 849-2772
  Mitchell *(G-12044)*

2361 Girl's and children's dresses, blouses

Shop Lulu Bean LLC........................ G 219 525-5336
  Merrillville *(G-11559)*

2369 Girl's and children's outerwear, nec

◆ Indiana Knitwear Corporation........ E 317 462-4413
  Greenfield *(G-6513)*

Lubber Dubbers.............................. G 812 475-1725
  Evansville *(G-4176)*

2381 Fabric dress and work gloves

Dappered Man LLC.......................... G 317 520-1194
  Brownsburg *(G-1363)*

Setser Fabricating LLC.................... G 812 546-2169
  Columbus *(G-2390)*

Steel Grip Inc................................... G 765 397-3344
  Kingman *(G-10174)*

▲ Tmgg LLC..................................... E 812 687-7444
  Plainville *(G-13746)*

2384 Robes and dressing gowns

Wells Robe Sales & Rental............. G 317 542-9062
  Indianapolis *(G-9749)*

2385 Waterproof outerwear

Mad Dasher Inc............................... E 260 747-0545
  Fort Wayne *(G-5198)*

▲ Nasco Industries Inc..................... C 812 254-7393
  Washington *(G-16494)*

2386 Leather and sheep-lined clothing

Clinton Harness Shop LLC.............. G 574 533-9797
  Goshen *(G-6113)*

Fox Uniform Inc............................... G 317 350-2684
  Brownsburg *(G-1368)*

Hilltop Leather................................. G 317 508-3404
  Martinsville *(G-11401)*

Martin Uniforms LLC....................... G 317 408-9186
  Indianapolis *(G-8843)*

2389 Apparel and accessories, nec

80of80 Group LLC........................... G 812 814-1167
  Indianapolis *(G-7393)*

All Things Jchari LLC...................... G 260 414-4065
  Fort Wayne *(G-4740)*

Benjamin Carrier............................. G 337 366-2603
  Jeffersonville *(G-9940)*

Brittany Hornsby.............................. G 219 789-0984
  Hammond *(G-6888)*

Cfn 260 LLC..................................... G 260 241-5678
  Fort Wayne *(G-4842)*

Costumes By Design....................... G 812 334-2029
  Bloomington *(G-849)*

Dance Sophisticates Inc................. E 317 634-7728
  Indianapolis *(G-7948)*

Death Studios................................... G 219 362-4321
  La Porte *(G-10400)*

Designs 4 U Inc............................... G 765 793-3026
  Covington *(G-2528)*

Dream Beauty Lab........................... G 773 571-1817
  Marion *(G-11283)*

Fall Creek Corporation.................... G 765 482-1861
  Lebanon *(G-10893)*

▼ Ghost Forge L T D........................ G 765 362-8654
  Crawfordsville *(G-2570)*

Golden Pride Hair Company LLC... G 812 777-9604
  Indianapolis *(G-8298)*

Haus Love Inc.................................. G 317 601-6521
  Indianapolis *(G-8370)*

Higgins Dyan................................... G 812 876-0754
  Ellettsville *(G-3809)*

Him Gentlemans Boutique............... G 812 924-7441
  New Albany *(G-12741)*

Hometown Shirts & Graphix LLC.... G 765 564-3066
  Delphi *(G-2898)*

Igetpaid LLC.................................... G 708 916-2967
  Gary *(G-5957)*

Jackie Collection LLC...................... G 219 678-8176
  Gary *(G-5966)*

Kinney Dancewear........................... G 317 581-1800
  Noblesville *(G-13121)*

Laced Cake LLC............................... G 317 520-6235
  Indianapolis *(G-8711)*

Lululemon.. G 574 271-3260
  Mishawaka *(G-11933)*

Marie Collective LLC....................... G 317 683-0408
  Indianapolis *(G-8832)*

Marked LLC...................................... G 317 777-3625
  Indianapolis *(G-8837)*

Modele LLC...................................... G 219 300-6929
  Highland *(G-7146)*

Moose Lodge.................................... G 219 362-2446
  La Porte *(G-10455)*

Nebo Ridge Enterprises LLC........... G 317 471-1089
  Carmel *(G-1703)*

No Fan Clothing LLC........................ G 312 371-7648
  Fishers *(G-4569)*

Part Solutions LLC........................... G 219 477-5101
  South Bend *(G-15186)*

Patchwork Costumes LLC............... G 317 750-6162
  Indianapolis *(G-9097)*

Pdb II Inc.. G 219 865-1888
  Dyer *(G-2980)*

Pearison Inc..................................... D 812 963-8890
  Cynthiana *(G-2788)*

Precise Title Inc............................... G 219 987-2286
  Demotte *(G-2926)*

Princess Palayse.............................. G 317 937-9394
  Indianapolis *(G-9198)*

Regal Inc.. G 765 284-5722
  Muncie *(G-12487)*

Revolver LLC.................................... G 317 418-1824
  Noblesville *(G-13166)*

Rittenhouse Square......................... G 260 824-4200
  Bluffton *(G-1051)*

▲ Rivars Inc..................................... E 765 789-6119
  Indianapolis *(G-9309)*

Scramboosay LLC............................ F 317 654-0595
  Indianapolis *(G-9395)*

Seraphim Lux LLC............................ G 872 201-8273
  Merrillville *(G-11557)*

Shop Lulu Bean LLC........................ G 219 525-5336
  Merrillville *(G-11559)*

Unjust LLC....................................... G 317 443-2584
  Fishers *(G-4622)*

Vxa Apparel..................................... G 219 259-6279
  Indianapolis *(G-9732)*

Yalel Unbland LLC........................... G 404 232-9139
  Indianapolis *(G-9799)*

2391 Curtains and draperies

Artisan Interiors Inc......................... D 574 825-9494
  Middlebury *(G-11699)*

Ascot Enterprises Inc...................... D 877 773-7751
  Elkhart *(G-3195)*

Ascot Enterprises Inc...................... G 574 658-3000
  Milford *(G-11786)*

Ascot Enterprises Inc...................... E 574 773-7751
  Nappanee *(G-12581)*

Ascot Enterprises Inc...................... D 260 593-3733
  Topeka *(G-15795)*

▲ Ascot Enterprises Inc................... E 877 773-7751
  Nappanee *(G-12582)*

Custom Draperies of Indiana.......... G 219 924-2500
  Hammond *(G-6909)*

Designers Touch.............................. G 812 944-2267
  Floyds Knobs *(G-4676)*

Dixie Lee Drapery Co Inc................ G 317 783-9869
  Indianapolis *(G-7989)*

Doris Drapery Boutique.................. G 765 472-5850
  Peru *(G-13580)*

Femyer Drapery Shop...................... G 765 282-3398
  Muncie *(G-12393)*

Industrial Sewing Machine Co........ G 812 425-2255
  Evansville *(G-4124)*

Jans Sewing Things......................... G 812 945-8113
  New Albany *(G-12752)*

K M Davis Inc................................... G 765 426-9227
  Lafayette *(G-10617)*

Katherine Mackey............................ G 765 825-0634
  Connersville *(G-2448)*

◆ Lafayette Venetian Blind Inc....... A 765 464-2500
  West Lafayette *(G-16601)*

M & D Draperies.............................. G 812 886-4608
  Vincennes *(G-16138)*

Majestic Draperies Inc.................... G 574 257-8465
  Elkhart *(G-3510)*

Majesty Enterprises Inc.................. G 812 752-6446
  Scottsburg *(G-14570)*

Merin Interiors Indianapolis............ G 317 251-6603
  Indianapolis *(G-8877)*

Northwest Interiors Inc................... F 574 294-2326
  Elkhart *(G-3575)*

Ping Custom Drapery Workroom.... G 317 984-3251
  Cicero *(G-1999)*

Quality Drapery Corporation.......... G 765 481-2370
  Lebanon *(G-10936)*

Schroer Drapery............................... G 812 523-3633
  Brownstown *(G-1427)*

Silk Mountain Creations Inc........... G 317 815-1660
  Carmel *(G-1761)*

Touch of Class Interiors.................. G 765 452-5879
  Kokomo *(G-10351)*

Work Room....................................... G 765 268-2634
  Bringhurst *(G-1238)*

2392 Household furnishings, nec

Agalite Seattle.................................. E 800 269-8343
  South Bend *(G-14937)*

Anderson Creations Inc.................. G 574 223-8932
  Rochester *(G-14276)*

Arden Companies LLC..................... D 260 747-1657
  Fort Wayne *(G-4770)*

Artisan Interiors Inc......................... D 574 825-9494
  Middlebury *(G-11699)*

▲ Ascot Enterprises Inc................... E 877 773-7751
  Nappanee *(G-12582)*

Bags By Brenda............................... G 765 779-4287
  Markleville *(G-11366)*

Baird Home Corporation................. G 812 883-1141
  Salem *(G-14473)*

23 APPAREL, FINISHED PRODUCTS FROM FABRICS & SIMILAR MATERIALS

Barrett Manufacturing Inc................... G 812 753-5808
Fort Branch *(G-4702)*

▲ Berger Table Pads Inc .... E 317 631-2577
Indianapolis *(G-7614)*

Bleu Rooster Designs........................ G 317 845-0899
Fishers *(G-4474)*

Capeable Sensory Products LLC....... G 260 387-5939
Fort Wayne *(G-4832)*

Coronado Casuals LLC...................... G 615 470-5718
Plainfield *(G-13672)*

Evansville Assn For The Blind............ C 812 422-1181
Evansville *(G-4047)*

▲ Inhabit Inc..................................... G 317 636-1699
Indianapolis *(G-8548)*

◆ Jordan Manufacturing Co Inc.......... C 800 328-6522
Monticello *(G-12155)*

K M Davis Inc................................... G 765 426-9227
Lafayette *(G-10617)*

Katherine Mackey............................. G 765 825-0634
Connersville *(G-2448)*

Keter North America Inc................... D 765 298-6800
Anderson *(G-141)*

Nice-Pak Products Inc...................... A 845 365-1700
Mooresville *(G-12228)*

Pgs LLC.. F 812 988-4030
Nashville *(G-12678)*

▲ Pontoonstuff Inc............................ G 574 970-0003
Elkhart *(G-3609)*

Reit Price Co.................................... G 765 964-3252
Union City *(G-15859)*

Reit-Price Mfg Co Incorporated......... G 765 964-3252
Union City *(G-15860)*

Rhyne & Associates Inc.................... F 317 786-4459
Indianapolis *(G-9299)*

SLEEP EASY TECHNOLOGY INC........ G 208 241-3264
South Bend *(G-15247)*

▲ Veada Industries Inc...................... A 574 831-4775
New Paris *(G-12973)*

Vera Bradley Inc.............................. B 877 708-8372
Roanoke *(G-14272)*

2393 Textile bags

B&C Distributor Inc........................... G 609 293-3257
Indianapolis *(G-7585)*

Raine Inc.. F 765 622-7687
Anderson *(G-182)*

Websters Protective Cases Inc........... G 219 263-3039
Chesterton *(G-1967)*

2394 Canvas and related products

AK Supply Inc................................... G 317 895-0410
Indianapolis *(G-7465)*

American Colors Clothing.................. G 812 822-0476
Bloomington *(G-778)*

◆ Anchor Industries Inc.................... D 812 867-2421
Evansville *(G-3891)*

Angola Canvas Co............................. F 260 665-9913
Angola *(G-227)*

Awning Partners Mfg Group LLC........ E 317 644-3793
Indianapolis *(G-7579)*

Blessing Enterprises Inc.................... F 219 736-9800
Merrillville *(G-11491)*

Canvas Shop LLC.............................. G 260 768-7755
Shipshewana *(G-14840)*

Canvas Vinyl Creations Inc................ G 317 371-4227
Noblesville *(G-13054)*

Cool Planet LLC................................ G 317 927-9000
Indianapolis *(G-7868)*

Coverite-Custom Covers.................... G 574 278-7152
Monticello *(G-12143)*

Dometic Corporation......................... B 260 463-7657
Elkhart *(G-3301)*

Donna McCormick.............................. G 574 278-3152
Monticello *(G-12147)*

Doyle Pitner..................................... G 574 699-6046
Galveston *(G-5852)*

▲ Gosport Manufacturing Co Inc........ E 800 457-4406
Gosport *(G-6284)*

▲ Gta Containers LLC....................... E 574 288-3459
South Bend *(G-15054)*

◆ J Ennis Fabrics Inc (usa)................ G 877 953-6647
Plainfield *(G-13695)*

Lafayette Tents & Events LLC........... E 765 742-4277
Lafayette *(G-10630)*

Larrys Canvas Cleaning..................... G 260 463-2220
Lagrange *(G-10751)*

Laudeman Place Inc.......................... F 574 546-4404
Bremen *(G-1203)*

Lc Covers LLC................................... G 260 463-2220
Lagrange *(G-10752)*

Lomont Holdings Co Inc.................... E 800 545-9023
Angola *(G-273)*

▲ Marine Mooring Inc........................ E 574 594-5787
Warsaw *(G-16390)*

Marion Tent & Awning Co................. G 765 664-7722
Marion *(G-11317)*

▼ Meese Inc...................................... F 800 829-4535
Madison *(G-11241)*

Mkmclain Inc.................................... G 260 478-1636
Fort Wayne *(G-5235)*

Montgomery Tent & Awning Co......... F 317 357-9759
Indianapolis *(G-8951)*

Mosiers Tarps LLC............................ G 260 563-3332
Wabash *(G-16205)*

Nose and Mustache LLC.................... G 260 758-8800
Markle *(G-11360)*

R J Hanlon Company Inc................... G 317 867-0028
Westfield *(G-16720)*

R J Hanlon Company Inc................... E 317 867-2900
Westfield *(G-16721)*

Shade By Design Inc........................ G 317 602-3513
Indianapolis *(G-9410)*

T K Sales & Service.......................... G 219 962-8982
Gary *(G-6017)*

◆ Transhield Inc................................ G 574 266-4118
Elkhart *(G-3744)*

▲ Tumacs LLC................................... E 574 264-5000
Elkhart *(G-3753)*

Twin Lakes Canvas Inc..................... G 574 583-2000
Monticello *(G-12174)*

▲ Veada Industries Inc...................... A 574 831-4775
New Paris *(G-12973)*

Webster Custom Canvas Inc.............. G 574 834-4497
North Webster *(G-13314)*

Wickey Canvas Outdoor Cooking....... G 260 223-8890
Berne *(G-731)*

Wild Hair Canvas Shop..................... G 812 290-1086
Aurora *(G-460)*

2395 Pleating and stitching

A D I Screen Printing....................... G 765 457-8580
Kokomo *(G-10231)*

A Great Stitch.................................. G 317 698-3743
Angola *(G-223)*

A Little Unique Embroider................. G 812 246-0592
Sellersburg *(G-14586)*

▲ A-1 Awards Inc............................. F 317 546-9000
Indianapolis *(G-7406)*

ABC Embroidery Inc.......................... G 260 636-7311
Albion *(G-16)*

Abracadabra Graphics....................... G 812 336-1971
Bloomington *(G-771)*

Advantage Embroidery Inc................ G 765 471-0188
Bringhurst *(G-1234)*

After Hours Embroidery..................... G 812 926-9355
Aurora *(G-436)*

Alpha Loop Inc.................................. G 317 710-0076
Martinsville *(G-11379)*

Apparel Plus Inc............................... G 812 951-2111
Georgetown *(G-6054)*

Apple Group Inc............................... E 765 675-4777
Tipton *(G-15764)*

Arizona Sport Shirts Inc.................... E 317 481-2160
Indianapolis *(G-7544)*

Aunt Lindas Embroidery.................... G 574 256-0508
Mishawaka *(G-11844)*

Avon Sports Apparel Corp................. G 317 887-2673
Greenwood *(G-6674)*

Baron Embroidery Corp..................... G 260 484-8700
Auburn *(G-368)*

Barrett Manufacturing Inc................. G 812 753-5808
Fort Branch *(G-4702)*

Bears Den EMB & More LLC.............. G 260 724-4070
Decatur *(G-2846)*

Beyond Monograms LLC.................... G 812 746-2624
Mount Vernon *(G-12292)*

Bloomington Stitchery LLC................ G 208 371-9598
Bloomington *(G-813)*

Branding Stitch LLC.......................... G 765 468-8463
Farmland *(G-4423)*

▲ Burston Marketing Inc................... F 574 262-4005
Elkhart *(G-3238)*

Caa Inc... G 574 537-0933
Goshen *(G-6109)*

Celestial Designs LLC....................... G 317 733-3110
Zionsville *(G-16997)*

Champions Image.............................. G 317 501-3617
Noblesville *(G-13057)*

Charles Coons................................... G 765 362-6509
Crawfordsville *(G-2552)*

Cindys Embroidery............................ G 574 551-4521
Akron *(G-3)*

Cindys In Stitches Inc....................... G 317 841-1408
Fishers *(G-4488)*

▲ Classic Products Corp.................... E 260 484-2695
Fort Wayne *(G-4855)*

CLC Embroidery LLC......................... G 219 395-9600
Chesterton *(G-1912)*

Coachs Connection Inc...................... G 260 356-0400
Huntington *(G-7306)*

▲ Concept Prints Inc......................... F 317 290-1222
Indianapolis *(G-7851)*

Connies Satin Stitch Inc.................... G 219 942-1887
Hobart *(G-7183)*

Corporate Shirts Direct Inc................ G 317 474-6033
Franklin *(G-5722)*

Country Embroidery.......................... G 765 833-9002
Roann *(G-14250)*

Country Stitches Embroidery............. G 219 324-7625
La Porte *(G-10396)*

Covington and Martin LLC................. G 812 946-3846
Jeffersonville *(G-9963)*

Cowpokes Inc................................... E 765 642-3911
Anderson *(G-99)*

Cozy Cottage LLC............................. G 812 838-6891
Mount Vernon *(G-12296)*

Creekside Embroidery....................... G 574 656-8333
Walkerton *(G-16265)*

Crescendo Inc................................... G 812 829-4759
Spencer *(G-15344)*

Custom Embroideries LLC.................. G 708 257-0415
Merrillville *(G-11501)*

Custom Embroidery........................... G 317 459-6603
Fishers *(G-4499)*

Custom Imprint Corporation............... F 800 378-3397
Merrillville *(G-11502)*

23 APPAREL, FINISHED PRODUCTS FROM FABRICS & SIMILAR MATERIALS

Custom Stitcher .... G 219 306-7784
   Lowell *(G-11159)*

D & J Custom Embroidery .... G 219 874-9061
   Michigan City *(G-11594)*

Dave Turner .... G 765 674-3360
   Gas City *(G-6035)*

Designs By Kim .... G 574 268-9904
   Warsaw *(G-16352)*

Digistitch .... G 574 538-3960
   Goshen *(G-6121)*

▲ Dkm Embroidery Inc .... G 260 471-4070
   Fort Wayne *(G-4920)*

Dmb Embroidery LLC .... G 812 592-3301
   Edinburgh *(G-3079)*

Drike Inc .... F 574 259-8822
   Mishawaka *(G-11885)*

Dugout .... G 765 642-8528
   Anderson *(G-111)*

Elegan Sportswear Inc .... E 219 464-8416
   Valparaiso *(G-15941)*

Embroidered Planet .... G 812 599-7951
   Madison *(G-11217)*

Embroidery By Jackie .... G 765 438-6240
   Forest *(G-4700)*

Embroidery Concepts .... G 812 988-6499
   Unionville *(G-15874)*

Embroidery Design Inc .... G 260 625-5538
   Fort Wayne *(G-4949)*

Embroidery N Beyond .... G 540 903-4861
   Avon *(G-518)*

Embroidery Plus Inc .... G 317 243-3445
   Indianapolis *(G-8100)*

Embroidery Sew Into It LLC .... G 317 734-3891
   Indianapolis *(G-8101)*

Embroidery Solutions LLC .... G 812 923-9152
   Greenville *(G-6651)*

Embroidery Unlimited .... G 812 265-4575
   Madison *(G-11218)*

Enhanced Embroidery .... G 812 448-8452
   Brazil *(G-1141)*

Esii - Embroidery Sew Into It .... G 317 734-3891
   Indianapolis *(G-8132)*

Etched In Stone Engrv & EMB .... G 317 535-8160
   Whiteland *(G-16786)*

Eyb Promotions .... G 812 376-3212
   Columbus *(G-2300)*

Fanim Industries Inc .... F 888 567-2055
   Zionsville *(G-17006)*

Favor It Promotions Inc .... F 317 733-1112
   Carmel *(G-1634)*

First Impressions Embroidery .... G 574 276-0750
   Bremen *(G-1191)*

Flyinneedle Embroidery Inc .... G 260 672-0742
   Roanoke *(G-14265)*

Freckles Grphics Lafayette Inc .... F 765 448-4692
   Lafayette *(G-10581)*

Frys Digistitch .... G 574 831-6854
   New Paris *(G-12955)*

Fully Promoted .... G 317 884-9290
   Greenwood *(G-6706)*

Fully Promoted Muncie .... G 765 281-8870
   Muncie *(G-12398)*

Gettelfinger Holdings LLC .... G 812 923-9065
   Floyds Knobs *(G-4679)*

Giraffe-X Graphics Inc .... G 317 546-4944
   Indianapolis *(G-8282)*

Golden Thread LLC .... G 765 557-7801
   Elwood *(G-3825)*

Graphic22 Inc .... G 219 921-5409
   Chesterton *(G-1930)*

Handstitched Memories .... G 765 430-4346
   Lafayette *(G-10594)*

Hometown Embroidery LLC .... G 765 778-7533
   Pendleton *(G-13536)*

Hometown Shirts & Graphix LLC .... G 765 564-3066
   Delphi *(G-2898)*

Hoop-It Embroidery .... G 260 224-6577
   Huntington *(G-7320)*

ID Graphics Incorporated .... G 765 649-9988
   Anderson *(G-133)*

Imperial Designs .... G 765 985-2712
   Denver *(G-2935)*

Imperial Trophy & Awards Co .... G 260 432-8161
   Fort Wayne *(G-5096)*

In Stitches Inc .... G 574 294-2121
   Elkhart *(G-3420)*

In Stitches Custom Embroidery .... G 812 385-2877
   Princeton *(G-14000)*

In Stitchz & Signz LLC .... G 574 892-5956
   Argos *(G-323)*

Indy W EMB Silk Screening LLC .... G 317 634-4906
   Indianapolis *(G-8536)*

J&P Custom Designs Inc .... G 317 253-2198
   Indianapolis *(G-8611)*

Janets Embroidery .... G 219 261-2812
   Goodland *(G-6082)*

Jasper EMB & Screen Prtg .... G 812 482-4787
   Jasper *(G-9852)*

Jer-Maur Corporation .... G 812 384-8290
   Bloomfield *(G-750)*

Just Monograms LLC .... G 812 827-3693
   Jasper *(G-9862)*

Kat Tales Embroidery .... G 219 299-2693
   Valparaiso *(G-15983)*

Kd Dids Quilting .... G 317 460-0646
   Noblesville *(G-13116)*

Kellum Imprints Inc .... G 812 347-2546
   Ramsey *(G-14025)*

Kerham Inc .... E 260 483-5444
   Fort Wayne *(G-5146)*

Kevin Koch .... G 574 971-8094
   Goshen *(G-6187)*

King of Mountain Kom EMB LLC .... G 812 799-0611
   Columbus *(G-2335)*

Lake Effect Embroidery .... G 219 785-4551
   La Porte *(G-10443)*

Lakeside Embroidery .... G 260 691-3289
   Columbia City *(G-2165)*

Lavender Patch Fabr Quilts LLC .... G 574 848-0011
   Bristol *(G-1270)*

Legends Maingate LLC .... F 317 243-2000
   Indianapolis *(G-8735)*

Little Cabin Embroidery .... G 812 719-3888
   Tell City *(G-15508)*

Lloyd & Mona Sulivan .... G 812 522-9191
   Seymour *(G-14665)*

Locoli Inc .... E 219 515-6900
   Schererville *(G-14531)*

Logo Boys Inc .... G 574 256-6844
   Mishawaka *(G-11932)*

Love To Stitch LLC .... G 812 342-8565
   Columbus *(G-2346)*

M & M Custom Embroidery .... G 407 334-5076
   Walkerton *(G-16268)*

M and M Embroidery .... G 317 504-2235
   Indianapolis *(G-8804)*

▲ Maingate LLC .... D
   Indianapolis *(G-8814)*

Make Your Mark - Custom EMB .... G 812 664-0026
   Princeton *(G-14003)*

Mary Duncan .... G 812 238-3637
   Terre Haute *(G-15636)*

McBeth Designs Inc .... G 317 848-7313
   Carmel *(G-1696)*

Mjs Apparel EMB Screenprinting .... G 260 357-0199
   Garrett *(G-5870)*

Monogrammed Mrs LLC .... G 317 605-8471
   Indianapolis *(G-8949)*

Moore Designs Unlmtd .... G 812 354-2233
   Petersburg *(G-13618)*

Nancy Ferber .... G 219 548-3645
   Valparaiso *(G-16007)*

Nathaniel Bowman .... G 765 365-2358
   Crawfordsville *(G-2592)*

National Athc Sportswear Inc .... F 260 436-2248
   Fort Wayne *(G-5255)*

Needles Contract EMB Inc .... G 812 491-9636
   Evansville *(G-4219)*

Next Phase Graphics .... G 260 627-6259
   Huntertown *(G-7259)*

Nsignia Screen Printing .... G 260 420-0500
   Fort Wayne *(G-5278)*

Outfitter .... G 765 289-6456
   Muncie *(G-12471)*

P DS Monogramming .... G 812 894-2363
   Shelburn *(G-14719)*

P Js Custom Embroidering LLC .... G 219 787-9161
   Chesterton *(G-1953)*

Paige Marschall .... G 574 277-1631
   Granger *(G-6368)*

Park Embroidery Designs LLC .... G 317 780-1515
   Indianapolis *(G-9094)*

Pens By Maisie Inc .... G 574 287-6178
   South Bend *(G-15189)*

Perdue Printed Products Inc .... G 260 456-7575
   Fort Wayne *(G-5304)*

Picture It Inc .... F 260 463-7373
   Lagrange *(G-10758)*

Picture This & Stitch That .... G 219 797-4006
   Hanna *(G-7038)*

Precision Stitch Indiana Inc .... G 765 473-6734
   Peru *(G-13594)*

Profit Finders Incorporated .... F 317 251-7792
   Indianapolis *(G-9223)*

Progressive Design Apparel Inc .... E 317 293-5888
   Indianapolis *(G-9225)*

Quilt Bug .... G 812 926-3092
   Aurora *(G-454)*

Quilters Garden .... G 812 539-4939
   Lawrenceburg *(G-10856)*

Ram Graphics Inc .... F 765 724-7783
   Alexandria *(G-58)*

Raymond Truex .... G 574 858-2260
   Warsaw *(G-16416)*

Red Stitch Creative LLC .... G 202 255-8940
   Carmel *(G-1736)*

Robert Burkhart .... G 219 448-0365
   Alexandria *(G-62)*

Safety Vehicle Emblem Inc .... F 317 885-7565
   Indianapolis *(G-9364)*

Screens .... G 812 472-3274
   Fredericksburg *(G-5796)*

Select Embroidery/Top It Off .... F 812 337-8049
   Bloomington *(G-968)*

Sentimental Stitches .... G 317 694-1244
   Indianapolis *(G-9403)*

Sew Beautiful Embroidry .... G 812 793-2245
   Crothersville *(G-2646)*

Sew Creative .... G 260 622-6263
   Ossian *(G-13434)*

Sharon K Utter .... G 765 349-8991
   Martinsville *(G-11427)*

Shilling Sales Inc .... E 260 426-2626
   Fort Wayne *(G-5413)*

Spectrum Marketing .... G 765 643-5566
   Anderson *(G-197)*

Employee Codes: A=Over 500 employees, B=251-500
C=101-250, D=51-100, E=20-50, F=10-19, G=1-9

23 APPAREL, FINISHED PRODUCTS FROM FABRICS & SIMILAR MATERIALS

Speedy Stitch Embroidery...................... G 812 597-4654
  Morgantown (G-12264)
Sportsmania Sales Inc............................ G 317 873-5501
  Zionsville (G-17052)
Stems & Stitches..................................... G 260 503-4955
  South Whitley (G-15327)
Stitch Glitch.. G 765 274-1435
  Anderson (G-201)
Stitchery Garden LLC.............................. G 765 450-4695
  Kokomo (G-10343)
◆ Stoffel Seals Corporation.................... E 845 353-3800
  Angola (G-296)
Stogdill Sports.. G 812 524-7081
  Seymour (G-14698)
Strong Stitches....................................... G 260 450-1456
  Laotto (G-10810)
Tatianas Embroidery............................... G 574 875-1654
  Elkhart (G-3715)
Team Image.. G 317 477-0027
  Greenfield (G-6562)
Topstitch Inc... F
  Elkhart (G-3739)
Trachsels Embroidery............................. G 260 982-2376
  North Manchester (G-13253)
Tricias Embroidery................................. G 574 583-4371
  Monticello (G-12173)
Twisted Stitcher..................................... G 765 330-1083
  Hartford City (G-7080)
Unique Graphic Designs Inc................... G 574 583-7119
  Monticello (G-12175)
Vco Inc.. G 812 235-3540
  Terre Haute (G-15739)
Vickers Graphics Inc............................... G 765 868-4646
  Kokomo (G-10354)
Village Custom Embroidery Inc.............. G 317 733-3110
  Zionsville (G-17060)
Wanda Harrington.................................. G 765 642-1628
  Anderson (G-215)
Wasu Inc... G 765 448-4450
  West Lafayette (G-16645)
Whiteman Embroidery........................... G 574 342-3697
  Bourbon (G-1130)
Wildman Business Group LLC................ G 866 369-1552
  Warsaw (G-16451)
Winning Edge of Rochester Inc.............. F 574 223-6090
  Rochester (G-14334)
Winters Assoc Prmtnal Pdts Inc............. F 812 330-7000
  Bloomington (G-1015)
Woods Enterprises................................. G 574 232-7449
  South Bend (G-15309)
Zig-Zag Crnr Qilts Baskets LLC.............. G 317 326-3115
  Greenfield (G-6573)

2396 Automotive and apparel trimmings

▲ A-1 Awards Inc.................................. F 317 546-9000
  Indianapolis (G-7406)
▲ American Keeper Corporation........... E 765 521-2080
  New Castle (G-12849)
Anew Company Inc................................ F 574 293-9088
  Elkhart (G-3184)
Apple Group Inc..................................... E 765 675-4777
  Tipton (G-15764)
Arizona Sport Shirts Inc......................... E 317 481-2160
  Indianapolis (G-7544)
▲ Asempac Inc...................................... E 812 945-6303
  New Albany (G-12692)
Athletic Edge Inc.................................... F 260 489-6613
  Fort Wayne (G-4778)
▲ Berry Plastics Ik LLC........................ C 641 648-5047
  Evansville (G-3925)
Blythes Sport Shop Inc........................... E 219 476-0026
  Valparaiso (G-15916)

▲ Burston Marketing Inc....................... F 574 262-4005
  Elkhart (G-3238)
Charles Coons.. G 765 362-6509
  Crawfordsville (G-2552)
Coachs Connection Inc.......................... G 260 356-0400
  Huntington (G-7306)
Codybro LLC... G 765 827-5441
  Connersville (G-2432)
Crescendo Inc... G 812 829-4759
  Spencer (G-15344)
Cross Printwear Inc................................ G 317 293-1776
  Indianapolis (G-7906)
Custom Imprint Corporation.................. F 800 378-3397
  Merrillville (G-11502)
Dance World Bazaar Corporation.......... G 812 663-7679
  Greensburg (G-6589)
Dave Turner... G 765 674-3360
  Gas City (G-6035)
Diverse Sales Solutions LLC................. G 317 514-2403
  Indianapolis (G-7981)
Dse Inc.. E 812 376-0310
  Columbus (G-2291)
East 40 Sports Apparel Inc.................... G 812 877-3695
  Terre Haute (G-15580)
EDS Teez LLC... G 224 518-3388
  Hammond (G-6921)
Elegan Sportswear Inc........................... E 219 464-8416
  Valparaiso (G-15941)
F Robert Gardner Co Inc........................ G 317 634-2333
  Indianapolis (G-8161)
Fiedeke Vinyl Coverings Inc.................. F 574 534-3408
  Goshen (G-6135)
Flag & Banner Company Inc.................. F 317 299-4880
  Indianapolis (G-8199)
▲ Futaba Indiana America Corp............ B 812 895-4700
  Vincennes (G-16127)
Game Plan Graphics LLC....................... G 812 663-3238
  Greensburg (G-6596)
Geckos.. G 765 762-0822
  Attica (G-349)
Graphix Unlimited Inc............................ E 574 546-3770
  Bremen (G-1193)
Greensburg Printing Co Inc................... G 812 663-8265
  Greensburg (G-6598)
Greenwood Models Inc.......................... G 317 859-2988
  Greenwood (G-6710)
H3r Garage LLC...................................... G 317 519-1368
  Indianapolis (G-8349)
Homelife Forever Inc............................. G 765 307-0416
  Roachdale (G-14247)
Hometown Shirts & Graphix LLC........... G 765 564-3066
  Delphi (G-2898)
Hubcaps Galore Inc................................ G 812 944-5200
  New Albany (G-12742)
Imperial Trophy & Awards Co................ G 260 432-8161
  Fort Wayne (G-5096)
In Case of Emergency Press.................. G 812 650-3352
  Bloomington (G-886)
▲ Indiana Ribbon Inc............................ E 219 279-2112
  Wolcott (G-16931)
Indianapolis Container Company.......... G 317 580-5000
  Indianapolis (G-8503)
Ink Dawgz LLC....................................... G 219 781-6972
  Valparaiso (G-15974)
▲ Innovtive Cating Solutions Inc.......... E 317 879-2222
  Indianapolis (G-8559)
Intertech Products Inc........................... D 260 982-1544
  North Manchester (G-13235)
Jasper EMB & Screen Prtg..................... G 812 482-4787
  Jasper (G-9852)
Jer-Maur Corporation............................ G 812 384-8290
  Bloomfield (G-750)

Kennyleeholmescom.............................. G 574 612-2526
  Elkhart (G-3451)
Kerham Inc.. E 260 483-5444
  Fort Wayne (G-5146)
▼ Kewanna Screen Printing Inc............ G 574 653-2683
  Kewanna (G-10167)
Lady Q LLC-S.. G 219 304-8404
  Indianapolis (G-8712)
Legends Maingate LLC.......................... F 317 243-2000
  Indianapolis (G-8735)
Locoli Inc.. E 219 515-6900
  Schererville (G-14531)
Lomont Holdings Co Inc........................ E 800 545-9023
  Angola (G-273)
M A Studio Inc.. G 574 275-2200
  San Pierre (G-14505)
▲ Maingate LLC..................................... D
  Indianapolis (G-8814)
Masco Corporation of Indiana............... E 317 848-1812
  Indianapolis (G-8847)
Mercantile Store..................................... G 812 988-6939
  Nashville (G-12675)
Mito-Craft Inc... G 574 287-4555
  South Bend (G-15152)
Modern Muscle Car Factory Inc............. G 574 329-6390
  Elkhart (G-3549)
New Hope Services Inc.......................... D 812 752-4892
  Scottsburg (G-14574)
New Hope Services Inc.......................... E 812 288-8248
  Jeffersonville (G-10022)
◆ Prentice Products Inc........................ E 260 747-3195
  Fort Wayne (G-5347)
Progressive Design Apparel Inc............ E 317 293-5888
  Indianapolis (G-9225)
Quality Converters Inc........................... E 260 829-6541
  Orland (G-13371)
Ram Graphics Inc................................... F 765 724-7783
  Alexandria (G-58)
Rbs Tees Co... G 812 522-8675
  Seymour (G-14680)
Robert Burkhart..................................... G 219 448-0365
  Alexandria (G-62)
Safety Vehicle Emblem Inc.................... F 317 885-7565
  Indianapolis (G-9364)
Select Embroidery/Top It Off................. F 812 337-8049
  Bloomington (G-968)
Sir Graphics Inc...................................... G 574 272-9330
  Granger (G-6379)
Specialty Shoppe.................................... G 574 772-7873
  Knox (G-10225)
Spectrum Marketing............................... G 765 643-5566
  Anderson (G-197)
▲ Spi-Binding Company Inc.................. F 765 794-4992
  Darlington (G-2834)
Sport Form Inc....................................... G 260 589-2200
  Berne (G-727)
Sportscenter Inc..................................... G 260 436-6198
  Fort Wayne (G-5432)
Star Quality Awards Inc......................... G 812 273-1740
  Madison (G-11252)
Stines Printing Inc.................................. G 260 356-5994
  Huntington (G-7371)
Sycamore Enterprises Inc...................... G 812 477-2266
  Evansville (G-4339)
Titan Graphics LLC................................. G 317 496-2188
  Mccordsville (G-11457)
Tko Enterprises Inc................................ D 317 271-1398
  Plainfield (G-13736)
Trams Design LLC.................................. G 574 206-3232
  Elkhart (G-3742)
Travis Britton... G 317 762-6018
  Indianapolis (G-9632)

▲ Wagner Zip-Change Inc............... E 708 681-4100
  Fort Wayne (G-5540)
Winning Edge of Rochester Inc........... F 574 223-6090
  Rochester (G-14334)
Winters Assoc Prmtnal Pdts Inc........... F 812 330-7000
  Bloomington (G-1015)
Woods Enterprises............... G 574 232-7449
  South Bend (G-15309)

2397 Schiffli machine embroideries

Dhgraphix and Apparel Co LLC........... G 317 908-2634
  Greenwood (G-6685)
Lee Reed Holdings LLC............... G 219 255-0555
  Hammond (G-6970)
Twisted Kilts Tees & Such Inc........... G 317 413-8900
  Indianapolis (G-9665)

2399 Fabricated textile products, nec

85th & Pine LLC............... G 219 781-1327
  Saint John (G-14445)
Art Ovation............... G 317 769-4301
  Brownsburg (G-1348)
Building Indiana............... G 219 226-0300
  Crown Point (G-2663)
▲ Carcapsule USA Inc............... F 219 945-9493
  Hobart (G-7178)
Classy Stitches............... G 317 856-3261
  Indianapolis (G-7821)
Country Sewing............... G 260 347-9733
  Kendallville (G-10103)
Eastern Banner Supply Corp........... G 812 448-2222
  Brazil (G-1140)
◆ Fabri-Tech Inc............... G 317 849-7755
  Mccordsville (G-11447)
Flags International Inc............... G 574 674-5125
  Osceola (G-13392)
Foremost Flexible Fabricating............ F 812 663-4756
  Greensburg (G-6594)
Gerardot Performance Pdts Inc........... G 260 623-3048
  Monroeville (G-12069)
Indiana Fabric Solutions Inc............ E 812 279-0255
  Bedford (G-644)
Just Install LLC............... G 317 607-3911
  Noblesville (G-13115)
Knit Knot Crochet............... G 765 730-9416
  Ridgeville (G-14235)
Knotted Strands Crochet............ G 574 232-9127
  South Bend (G-15102)
Lakestreet Enterprises LLC............ G 260 768-7991
  Lagrange (G-10749)
Mint City Sewing & Tack LLC........... G 574 546-2230
  Bremen (G-1206)
Summit Seating Inc............... F 574 264-9636
  Elkhart (G-3706)
T K T Inc............... G 574 825-5233
  Middlebury (G-11753)
Team Spirit............... G 219 924-6272
  Munster (G-12567)
Upanaway LLC............... G 866 218-7143
  Greenfield (G-6568)
Wiseguys Seating & Accessry Co........... G 574 294-6030
  Elkhart (G-3788)
Wolf Technical Engineering LLC........... G 800 783-9653
  Indianapolis (G-9781)
Workroom Inc............... G 574 269-6624
  Winona Lake (G-16919)

24 LUMBER AND WOOD PRODUCTS, EXCEPT FURNITURE

2411 Logging

A & S Logging Inc............... G 574 896-3136
  North Judson (G-13205)
▼ Andis Logging Inc............... F 812 723-2357
  Paoli (G-13487)
Anthony D Etienne Logging............... G 812 843-5872
  Magnet (G-11258)
Arboramerica Inc............... F 765 572-1212
  Westpoint (G-16743)
Artys Logging Inc............... G 812 969-3124
  Elizabeth (G-3123)
AS Logging LLC............... G 812 613-0577
  Taswell (G-15494)
Baldwin Logging Inc............... G 812 834-1040
  Norman (G-13202)
Bear Hollow Wood Carvers LLC........... G 812 843-5549
  Saint Croix (G-14433)
Billy R Ransom............... G 812 897-5921
  Boonville (G-1082)
Blackwood Solutions LLC............... D 812 676-8770
  Bloomington (G-809)
Blue River Timber LLC............... G 812 291-0411
  Evansville (G-3935)
Boondocks Logging LLC............... G 812 247-3363
  Shoals (G-14904)
Bray Logging............... G 812 863-7947
  Owensburg (G-13459)
Brocks Incorporated............... G 765 721-3068
  Bainbridge (G-559)
Burton Lumber Co Inc............... F 812 866-4438
  Lexington (G-10975)
Calhoun Logging Corporation............ G 260 839-0268
  Claypool (G-2051)
Campbell Logging LLC............... G 812 972-6280
  Birdseye (G-738)
Cannon Timber LLC............... G 219 754-1088
  La Crosse (G-10364)
Carr Logging............... G 812 863-7585
  Owensburg (G-13460)
Cash Logging LLC............... G 812 843-5335
  Mount Pleasant (G-12283)
Charles Kolb Logging............... G 765 458-7766
  Liberty (G-10985)
Charles Kolb Sons Logging............ G 765 647-4309
  Brookville (G-1317)
Christman Logging............... G 502 525-2649
  Madison (G-11208)
CJ Logging LLC............... G 812 360-0163
  Morgantown (G-12256)
Coffman Dallas Log & Excvtg........... G 812 738-1528
  Corydon (G-2493)
Coffman Logging............... G 812 732-4857
  Corydon (G-2494)
Coleman Logging............... G 765 458-7219
  Liberty (G-10986)
Cory Williamson............... G 812 242-0400
  Clay City (G-2042)
Crone Logging LLC............... G 765 346-0025
  Martinsville (G-11386)
D Timber Inc............... G 219 374-8085
  Crown Point (G-2672)
Daniel Steffy............... G 812 726-4769
  Vincennes (G-16118)
Delmar Knepp Logging............... G 812 486-2565
  Loogootee (G-11131)
Dennis Etiennes Logging Inc........... G 812 843-4518
  Cannelton (G-1535)
Dennis K Marvell............... G 812 779-5107
  Patoka (G-13507)
Dwight Smith Logging............... G 812 834-5546
  Heltonville (G-7110)
Ferree Logging LLC............... G 812 786-1676
  Corydon (G-2496)

Gabhart Logging LLC............... G 812 365-2425
  Marengo (G-11263)
George Voyles Sawmill Inc........... G 812 472-3968
  Salem (G-14478)
Goodrick Timber............... G 765 778-7442
  Pendleton (G-13535)
Gordon D Browning............... G 765 458-7792
  Liberty (G-10988)
Graber Lumber LP............... E 260 238-4124
  Spencerville (G-15370)
Graber Ronald D Yoder &............... G 574 268-9512
  Warsaw (G-16368)
Greg Abplanalp Logging LLC........... G 812 873-8463
  Butlerville (G-1483)
Hartman Logging............... G 765 653-3889
  Greencastle (G-6408)
Hearthglow Inc............... G 260 839-3205
  Claypool (G-2053)
Howard Logging............... G 260 327-3862
  Pierceton (G-13633)
IMI Southwest Inc............... F 260 432-3973
  Fort Wayne (G-5095)
J Robert Switzer............... G 765 474-1307
  Lafayette (G-10612)
Jim Graber Logging LLC............... G 812 636-7000
  Odon (G-13341)
Jim McCarter Logging............... G 812 321-5661
  Wheatland (G-16775)
Jim Rhodes Logging............... G 812 739-4221
  English (G-3841)
John Collier Logging Inc............... G 317 539-9663
  Fillmore (G-4454)
Joseph M Schmidt............... G 260 223-3498
  Decatur (G-2865)
Keith Bixler............... G 812 866-1637
  Lexington (G-10978)
Keller Logging LLC............... G 219 309-0379
  Valparaiso (G-15985)
Kelly Bixler Logging............... G 812 752-6636
  Scottsburg (G-14567)
Kelsie Pierce............... G 812 279-1335
  Bedford (G-651)
Kinser Timber Products Inc........... G 812 876-4775
  Gosport (G-6285)
Knepp Logging LLC............... G 812 486-3741
  Loogootee (G-11142)
Knepps Logging Bandmilling............ G 812 486-7721
  Montgomery (G-12106)
Loggers Incorporated............... E 812 939-2797
  Clay City (G-2045)
Logging............... G 812 216-3544
  Seymour (G-14666)
Louanna Stilwell............... G 812 631-0647
  Velpen (G-16094)
Mark A Morin Logging Inc............ G 812 327-4917
  West Baden Springs (G-16542)
Marvell Logging Company LLC........... G 812 779-5107
  Patoka (G-13509)
Michael Deom Professional............ G 812 836-2206
  Tell City (G-15511)
Michael L Baker............... G 812 967-2160
  Salem (G-14491)
Michael L Reynolds............... G 812 528-7844
  Medora (G-11463)
Michael Skaggs............... G 812 732-8809
  Mauckport (G-11438)
Midwest Logging & Veneer............... G 765 342-2774
  Martinsville (G-11414)
Mike Fisher Logging............... G 812 357-2169
  Ferdinand (G-4444)
Mike Gross............... G 574 529-2201
  New Paris (G-12966)

24 LUMBER AND WOOD PRODUCTS, EXCEPT FURNITURE

Mitchell L Kline .... G 812 449-6518
Evanston *(G-3853)*

NJ Logging LLC .... G 812 597-0782
Morgantown *(G-12261)*

Odon Sawmill Inc .... E 812 636-7314
Odon *(G-13347)*

Ohio River Veneer LLC .... F 812 824-7928
Bloomington *(G-933)*

Orla Bontrater .... G 260 768-7553
Shipshewana *(G-14873)*

Peacock Logging Inc .... G 812 794-3579
Austin *(G-469)*

PFC Farm Services Inc .... G 260 235-0817
Fremont *(G-5831)*

Pingleton Logging Inc .... G 765 653-2878
Greencastle *(G-6425)*

Pingleton Sawmill Inc .... E 765 653-2878
Greencastle *(G-6426)*

R E Casebeer & Sons Inc .... G 812 829-3284
Spencer *(G-15359)*

Ralph Ransom Veneers .... G 812 858-9956
Newburgh *(G-13018)*

Rays Logging LLC .... G 812 935-5307
Spencer *(G-15360)*

Robert Cody Jacobs .... G 812 606-5195
Nashville *(G-12679)*

Robert L Young .... G 812 863-4475
Springville *(G-15391)*

Rodney Sloan Logging Inc .... G 812 934-5321
Batesville *(G-605)*

Ronald Lee Allen .... G 812 644-7649
Loogootee *(G-11150)*

Ronald Wright Logging LLC .... G 812 338-2665
English *(G-3847)*

Russell Beeman Logging Inc .... G 765 387-0064
Anderson *(G-188)*

Shady Oaks Logging LLC .... G 317 902-9741
Morgantown *(G-12263)*

Slabach Logging LLC .... G 260 768-4644
Shipshewana *(G-14889)*

Spencer Logging .... G 812 595-0987
Scottsburg *(G-14581)*

Tdc Logging LLC .... G 574 289-4243
South Bend *(G-15280)*

Tri-State Forest Products Inc .... F 317 328-1850
Indianapolis *(G-9637)*

Universal Frest Pdts Ind Ltd P .... E 574 273-6326
Granger *(G-6388)*

Walton Logging .... G 812 365-9635
Marengo *(G-11267)*

Waninger Knneth Sons Log Tmber ...... G 812 357-5200
Fulda *(G-5850)*

Weaver Logging Incorporated .... G 260 589-9985
Berne *(G-730)*

White Oak Land & Timber LLC .... G 812 482-5102
Jasper *(G-9917)*

Wilkerson Logging Inc .... G 812 988-4960
Nashville *(G-12683)*

William Browning .... G 765 647-6397
Brookville *(G-1342)*

Williams Bros Logging LLC .... G 270 547-0266
Mauckport *(G-11442)*

Wrights Timber Products .... G 812 383-7138
Shelburn *(G-14725)*

2421 Sawmills and planing mills, general

A&R Sawmill LLC .... G 765 238-8829
Greens Fork *(G-6574)*

Adkins Sawmill Inc .... G 812 849-4036
Mitchell *(G-12029)*

American Fibertech Corporation .... D 812 849-6095
Mitchell *(G-12031)*

American Stave Company LLC .... G 812 883-9374
Salem *(G-14471)*

Arbor Industries Inc .... E 574 825-2375
Middlebury *(G-11698)*

Architura Corporation .... G 317 348-1000
Indianapolis *(G-7541)*

B & B Sawmill Inc .... G 812 834-5072
Bedford *(G-621)*

Baxter Lumber LLC .... F 812 873-6868
Deputy *(G-2940)*

Benham Sawmill LLC .... G 812 723-2644
Paoli *(G-13488)*

Bent Tree Custom Sawing LLC .... G 260 693-9781
Churubusco *(G-1972)*

Better Built Barns Inc .... G 812 477-2001
Evansville *(G-3929)*

Buchan Logging Inc .... F 260 749-4697
Decatur *(G-2848)*

Burton Lumber Co Inc .... F 812 866-4438
Lexington *(G-10975)*

Byler Sawmill .... G 812 577-5761
Bennington *(G-702)*

C & L Lumber Inc .... G 812 536-2171
Huntingburg *(G-7272)*

C A Lakey Family Saw Mill Inc .... G 765 378-7528
Daleville *(G-2796)*

C C Cook and Son Lbr Co Inc .... E 765 672-4235
Reelsville *(G-14030)*

Campbell Road Sawmill LP .... F 260 238-4252
Spencerville *(G-15368)*

Cedar Creek Sawmill LLC .... E 260 627-3985
Grabill *(G-6291)*

Chisholm Lumber & Supply Co .... E 317 547-3535
Indianapolis *(G-7799)*

Classic Manufacturing Co LLC .... E 765 344-1619
Brazil *(G-1138)*

Coleman Sawmill Supply .... G 812 865-4001
Orleans *(G-13375)*

Conner Sawmill Inc .... F 574 626-3227
Walton *(G-16282)*

Coomer & Sons Sawmill Inc .... D 765 659-2846
Frankfort *(G-5655)*

Countryside Sawmill .... G 812 486-2991
Montgomery *(G-12091)*

Crone Lumber Co Inc .... E 765 342-1160
Martinsville *(G-11387)*

Darlage Sawmill .... G 812 358-3574
Brownstown *(G-1422)*

Deer Run Sawmill LLC .... G 812 732-4608
Mauckport *(G-11437)*

Dehart Pallet & Lumber Co .... F 812 794-2974
Austin *(G-464)*

Dg Timber Inc .... G 812 295-9876
Loogootee *(G-11132)*

Dla Construction .... G 404 992-0805
Crown Point *(G-2677)*

Eastern Red Cedar Products LLC .... G 812 365-2495
Marengo *(G-11262)*

Eichers Sawmill .... G 260 624-5882
Hamilton *(G-6853)*

Fiber By-Products Corp .... G
Goshen *(G-6134)*

Flodder Sawmill LLC .... G 765 628-0280
Greentown *(G-6646)*

Forest Products Group Inc .... F 765 659-1807
Frankfort *(G-5665)*

Forest Products Mfg Co .... E 812 482-5625
Jasper *(G-9838)*

▼ Frank Miller Lumber Co Inc .... C 800 345-2643
Union City *(G-15853)*

George Voyles Sawmill Inc .... G 812 472-3968
Salem *(G-14478)*

Grabers Portable Band Mill .... G 812 636-4158
Odon *(G-13340)*

Great Lakes Forest Pdts Inc .... C 574 389-9663
Elkhart *(G-3389)*

Green Forest Sawmill LLC .... F 812 745-3335
Oaktown *(G-13327)*

Gross & Sons Lumber and Veneer ...... G 574 457-5214
Syracuse *(G-15461)*

Helmsburg Sawmill Inc .... E 812 988-6161
Nashville *(G-12671)*

Herberts Sawmill Inc .... F 812 663-9347
Greensburg *(G-6601)*

Hites Hardwood Lumber Corp .... F 574 278-7783
Buffalo *(G-1438)*

Hollingsworth Sawmill Inc .... F 765 883-5836
Russiaville *(G-14422)*

◆ Holmes & Company LLC .... E 260 244-6149
Columbia City *(G-2151)*

Homestead Properties Inc .... F 812 866-4415
Deputy *(G-2941)*

Hope Hardwoods Inc .... F 812 546-4427
Hope *(G-7226)*

Indiana Wood Products Inc .... D 574 825-2129
Middlebury *(G-11724)*

▼ Indianapolis Wood Products .... G 812 752-6944
Scottsburg *(G-14563)*

◆ International Wood Inc .... E 812 883-5778
Salem *(G-14485)*

Interstate Forestry Inc .... G 574 936-1284
Plymouth *(G-13786)*

J M McCormick .... G 317 874-4444
Indianapolis *(G-8607)*

Jackson Brothers Lumber Co .... F 812 847-7812
Linton *(G-11036)*

Jwb Group LLC .... G 812 371-7344
Nashville *(G-12672)*

Kinser Timber Products Inc .... G 812 876-4775
Gosport *(G-6285)*

Koetter Woodworking .... G 812 923-8875
Borden *(G-1112)*

Lakeland Pallets Inc .... G 574 674-5906
Elkhart *(G-3467)*

Landmark Wood Products Inc .... F 812 338-2641
English *(G-3842)*

Lasher Lumber Inc .... G 812 836-2618
Tell City *(G-15507)*

Laughery Sawmill .... G 812 432-5649
Dillsboro *(G-2949)*

Ledgerwood & Sons Sawmill LLC .... G 812 939-8212
Coal City *(G-2100)*

Loggers Incorporated .... E 812 939-2797
Clay City *(G-2045)*

▼ Maley & Wertz Inc .... E 812 425-3358
Evansville *(G-4186)*

Mark Middleton .... G 812 967-2853
Pekin *(G-13518)*

Menard Inc .... C 812 466-1234
Terre Haute *(G-15641)*

Miller Hardwoods LLC .... G 574 773-9371
Nappanee *(G-12624)*

Millers Saw Mill .... G 812 883-5246
Salem *(G-14494)*

Millwork Specialties Co Inc .... G 219 362-2960
La Porte *(G-10453)*

Mobili Fiver Usa Corp .... G 219 900-3751
Indianapolis *(G-8942)*

Modular Green Systems LLC .... G 260 547-4121
Craigville *(G-2535)*

National Products Inc .... E 574 457-4565
Syracuse *(G-15469)*

New Castle Saw Mill .... G 765 529-6635
New Castle *(G-12875)*

SIC SECTION
24 LUMBER AND WOOD PRODUCTS, EXCEPT FURNITURE

◆ Norstam Veneers Inc .... D 812 732-4391
   Mauckport *(G-11441)*

North Central Ind Shavings LLC .... G 765 395-3875
   Converse *(G-2478)*

Northern Wood Products Inc .... G 574 586-3068
   Walkerton *(G-16272)*

Odon Sawmill Inc .... E 812 636-7314
   Odon *(G-13347)*

Oldenburg Pallet Inc .... G 812 933-0568
   Batesville *(G-599)*

ONeal Wood Products Inc .... G 765 342-2709
   Martinsville *(G-11420)*

Paul Knepp Sawmill Inc .... G 812 486-3773
   Montgomery *(G-12117)*

Phil Etiennes Timber Harvest .... E 812 843-5132
   Saint Croix *(G-14435)*

Pike Lumber Company Inc .... E 574 893-4511
   Carbon *(G-1538)*

◆ Pike Lumber Company Inc .... C 574 893-4511
   Akron *(G-7)*

Pingleton Sawmill Inc .... E 765 653-2878
   Greencastle *(G-6426)*

PLM Holdings Inc .... E 812 232-0624
   Terre Haute *(G-15663)*

Quality Hardwood Products Inc .... F 260 982-2043
   Claypool *(G-2056)*

R Booe & Son Hardwoods Inc .... E 812 835-2663
   Centerpoint *(G-1847)*

R E Casebeer & Sons Inc .... G 812 829-3284
   Spencer *(G-15359)*

Randall Lowe Sons Sawmill LLC .... F 812 936-2254
   French Lick *(G-5848)*

Rodney Sloan Logging Inc .... G 812 934-5321
   Batesville *(G-605)*

Ronald Wright Logging LLC .... G 812 338-2665
   English *(G-3847)*

Salesman Sawmill Inc .... G 812 382-9154
   Sullivan *(G-15421)*

Sawmill Pride LLC .... G 317 442-2958
   Coatesville *(G-2109)*

Scrapwood Sawmill .... G 574 223-2725
   Rochester *(G-14323)*

Shouse Sawmill Inc .... F 812 743-2017
   Monroe City *(G-12065)*

Southern Indiana Hardwoods Inc .... E 812 326-2053
   Huntingburg *(G-7291)*

Spohn Associates Inc .... G 317 921-2445
   Indianapolis *(G-9480)*

Stemwood Corp .... E 812 945-6646
   New Albany *(G-12818)*

Stillions Saw Mill .... G 812 824-6542
   Bloomington *(G-979)*

Superior Forest Products LLC .... F 765 245-2895
   Montezuma *(G-12083)*

Swartzentruber Sawmill LLC .... G 812 486-3350
   Montgomery *(G-12125)*

Tangent Rail Products Inc .... E 812 789-5331
   Winslow *(G-16925)*

Terry L Ray .... G 765 342-3180
   Martinsville *(G-11430)*

Timberland Resources Inc .... G 765 245-2634
   Montezuma *(G-12084)*

Tree City Saw Mill .... G 812 663-6363
   Greensburg *(G-6636)*

Tri State Timber LLC .... G 812 327-8161
   Bloomington *(G-993)*

Ufp Granger LLC .... F 574 277-7670
   Granger *(G-6387)*

Universal Frest Pdts Ind Ltd P .... E 574 273-6326
   Granger *(G-6388)*

W & J Sawmill Llc .... G 812 486-2719
   Montgomery *(G-12127)*

Wakelam John .... G 812 752-5243
   Scottsburg *(G-14584)*

Walnut Acres Sawmill LLC .... F 765 344-0027
   Rockville *(G-14360)*

Werner Sawmill Inc .... E 812 482-7565
   Jasper *(G-9916)*

◆ Werzalit of America Inc .... D 814 362-3881
   Syracuse *(G-15492)*

Wilkerson Sawmill .... G 812 988-7436
   Nashville *(G-12684)*

Wood-Mizer LLC .... E 317 271-1542
   Indianapolis *(G-9783)*

▲ Woodparts International Corp .... F 574 293-0566
   Elkhart *(G-3791)*

Worley Lumber Company Inc .... E 812 967-3521
   Pekin *(G-13523)*

2426 Hardwood dimension and flooring mills

A New Covenant Woodwork LLC ...... G 812 737-2929
   Laconia *(G-10504)*

Als Woodcraft Inc .... F 812 967-4458
   Borden *(G-1105)*

Brown Ridge Studio .... G 812 335-0643
   Bloomington *(G-816)*

Burton Lumber Co Inc .... F 812 866-4438
   Lexington *(G-10975)*

Cabinetmaker Inc .... G 812 723-3461
   Paoli *(G-13490)*

Champion Wood Products Inc .... G 812 282-9460
   Sellersburg *(G-14591)*

Chisholm Lumber & Supply Co .... E 317 547-3535
   Indianapolis *(G-7799)*

Chuppville Carving .... G 574 354-7642
   Nappanee *(G-12589)*

Coopers Wood Heat Supply LLC ...... G 765 918-1039
   Crawfordsville *(G-2555)*

Cross Country Hardwood LLC .... F 812 571-4226
   Vevay *(G-16108)*

Dehart Pallet & Lumber Co .... F 812 794-2974
   Austin *(G-464)*

Digital Carvings LLC .... G 812 269-6123
   Ellettsville *(G-3807)*

Dutch Made Inc .... G 260 657-3331
   Harlan *(G-7054)*

Ecojacks LLC .... G 574 306-0414
   South Whitley *(G-15317)*

Ford Sawmills Inc .... F 812 324-2134
   Vincennes *(G-16125)*

Forest Products Group Inc .... F 765 659-1807
   Frankfort *(G-5665)*

Forest Products Mfg Co .... E 812 482-5625
   Jasper *(G-9838)*

▼ Frank Miller Lumber Co Inc .... C 800 345-2643
   Union City *(G-15853)*

George Voyles Sawmill Inc .... G 812 472-3968
   Salem *(G-14478)*

Graber Furniture .... G 812 295-4939
   Loogootee *(G-11136)*

Helmsburg Sawmill Inc .... E 812 988-6161
   Nashville *(G-12671)*

Herberts Sawmill Inc .... F 812 663-9347
   Greensburg *(G-6601)*

Heritage Hardwoods KY Inc .... D 812 288-5855
   Jeffersonville *(G-9994)*

Hillcrest Enterprises LLC .... G 812 875-2500
   Worthington *(G-16960)*

Homestead Properties Inc .... F 812 866-4415
   Deputy *(G-2941)*

Indiana Wood Products Inc .... D 574 825-2129
   Middlebury *(G-11724)*

Jackson Brothers Lumber Co .... F 812 847-7812
   Linton *(G-11036)*

James A Andrew Inc .... G 765 269-9807
   Lafayette *(G-10614)*

Jeff Hury Hrdwood Flors Pntg S .... G 812 204-8650
   Evansville *(G-4141)*

Knies Sawmill Inc .... G 812 683-3402
   Huntingburg *(G-7285)*

Love Upholstery LLC .... G 812 639-3789
   Jasper *(G-9883)*

Mikro Furniture .... G 812 877-9550
   Terre Haute *(G-15646)*

▲ Mould-Rite Inc .... G 812 967-3200
   Pekin *(G-13520)*

◆ Norstam Veneers Inc .... D 812 732-4391
   Mauckport *(G-11441)*

Odon Sawmill Inc .... E 812 636-7314
   Odon *(G-13347)*

Olon Industries Inc (us) .... G 812 256-6400
   Jeffersonville *(G-10030)*

Olon Industries Inc (us) .... G 812 254-0427
   Washington *(G-16497)*

Palletone of Indiana Inc .... D 260 768-4021
   Shipshewana *(G-14877)*

Phil Etiennes Timber Harvest .... E 812 843-5132
   Saint Croix *(G-14435)*

Pike Lumber Company Inc .... E 574 893-4511
   Carbon *(G-1538)*

Pingleton Sawmill Inc .... G 765 653-2878
   Greencastle *(G-6426)*

Prized Possession .... G 317 842-1498
   Indianapolis *(G-9214)*

Quality Hardwood Products Inc .... F 260 982-2043
   Claypool *(G-2056)*

R & R Custom Woodworking Inc ...... G 574 773-5436
   Nappanee *(G-12640)*

R E Casebeer & Sons Inc .... G 812 829-3284
   Spencer *(G-15359)*

Randall Lowe Sons Sawmill LLC .... F 812 936-2254
   French Lick *(G-5848)*

Rogers Group Inc .... C 812 333-6324
   Bloomington *(G-959)*

Rwh Woodworking LLC .... G 317 714-5179
   Greenfield *(G-6547)*

Salt Creek Harvest LLC .... G 708 927-5569
   Valparaiso *(G-16042)*

◆ Santarossa Mosaic Tile Co Inc .... C 317 632-9494
   Indianapolis *(G-9371)*

Stateline Woodturnings LLC .... G 260 768-4507
   Shipshewana *(G-14892)*

Stemwood Corp .... E 812 945-6646
   New Albany *(G-12818)*

Superior Forest Products LLC .... F 765 245-2895
   Montezuma *(G-12083)*

Swartzndrber Hrdwood Creat LLC .... G 574 534-2502
   Goshen *(G-6266)*

Tedrows Wood Products Inc .... F 812 247-2260
   Shoals *(G-14912)*

Universal Frest Pdts Ind Ltd P .... E 574 273-6326
   Granger *(G-6388)*

US Lbm Operating Co 3009 LLC ...... G 812 464-2428
   Evansville *(G-4364)*

Weberdings Carving Shop Inc .... F 812 934-3710
   Batesville *(G-610)*

Werner Sawmill Inc .... E 812 482-7565
   Jasper *(G-9916)*

◆ Werzalit of America Inc .... D 814 362-3881
   Syracuse *(G-15492)*

2429 Special product sawmills, nec

Premier AG Co-Op Inc .... E 812 522-4911
   Seymour *(G-14677)*

◆ Western Excelsior Corporation .... E 970 533-7412
   Evansville *(G-4381)*

24 LUMBER AND WOOD PRODUCTS, EXCEPT FURNITURE   SIC SECTION

2431 Millwork

A & M Woodworking .... G 574 642-4555
  Millersburg *(G-11810)*
A AMP R Woodworking .... G 574 849-1477
  Goshen *(G-6084)*
A J Schnell Wood Works LLC .... G 317 370-8890
  Zionsville *(G-16988)*
A&J Woodworking LLC .... G 574 642-4551
  Goshen *(G-6085)*
Aaron Dickinson .... G 317 503-0922
  Greenfield *(G-6457)*
Acorn Woodworks .... G 317 867-4377
  Westfield *(G-16662)*
Alberding Woodworking Inc .... F 260 728-9526
  Decatur *(G-2841)*
◆ Alexandria Mw LLC .... G 219 324-9541
  La Porte *(G-10379)*
AMC Acquisition Corporation .... D 215 572-0738
  Elkhart *(G-3169)*
American Heritage Shutters LLC .... G 317 598-6908
  Indianapolis *(G-7504)*
American Millwork LLC .... G 574 295-4158
  Elkhart *(G-3174)*
Amish Woodworking LLC .... G 574 941-4439
  Plymouth *(G-13756)*
An Squared LLC .... G 317 517-7139
  New Palestine *(G-12929)*
Andersen Corporation .... G 260 694-6861
  Poneto *(G-13839)*
Antreasian Design Inc .... F 317 546-3234
  Indianapolis *(G-7523)*
Arnold Family Woodworks .... G 765 246-6593
  Fillmore *(G-4452)*
Assured General Contg LLC .... G 260 740-4744
  Fort Wayne *(G-4776)*
Auto Wood Restoration .... G 219 797-3775
  Hanna *(G-7036)*
B Nickell Woodworking LLC .... G 574 333-2863
  Elkhart *(G-3212)*
B T Door .... G 574 534-1726
  Goshen *(G-6094)*
B&M Wood Inc .... G 574 535-0024
  Goshen *(G-6095)*
Barkman Custom Woodworking .... F 574 773-9212
  Nappanee *(G-12583)*
Bawling Acres Woodworking LLC .... G 260 768-3214
  Middlebury *(G-11702)*
Bc Countertops Inc .... E 317 637-4427
  Indianapolis *(G-7600)*
Bear Hollow Wood Carvers .... G 812 936-3030
  French Lick *(G-5844)*
Beeline Woodworking .... G 260 894-3806
  Ligonier *(G-11005)*
Bentz Woodworking .... G 765 525-4946
  Waldron *(G-16257)*
Bittersweet LLC .... G 317 254-0677
  Indianapolis *(G-7632)*
Bloomers Woodworking Inc .... G 317 502-9360
  Indianapolis *(G-7643)*
Borkholder Lavon .... G 574 773-3714
  Nappanee *(G-12586)*
Borkholder Wood Products Inc .... G 574 546-2613
  Bremen *(G-1176)*
Botti Stdio Archtctral Arts In .... E 847 869-5933
  La Porte *(G-10391)*
Bowtie Woodworks LLC .... G 765 667-1934
  Indianapolis *(G-7666)*
Branik Inc .... G 260 467-1808
  Fort Wayne *(G-4814)*
Bratco Inc .... G 812 536-4071
  Holland *(G-7214)*

Brewers Contg & Wdwrk LLC .... G 812 620-8961
  Pekin *(G-13512)*
Browns Woodworking Limited .... G 260 693-2868
  Churubusco *(G-1975)*
Bryan Snyder Inc .... G 574 238-4481
  Goshen *(G-6102)*
Burkes Garden Wood Pdts LLC .... E 765 344-1724
  Brazil *(G-1137)*
Burks Door & Sash Inc .... E 317 844-2484
  Carmel *(G-1576)*
By-Pass Paint Shop Inc .... F 574 264-5334
  Elkhart *(G-3240)*
Byler Family Wood Working .... G 574 825-3339
  Goshen *(G-6107)*
C&M Woodworking LLC .... G 260 403-4555
  Leo *(G-10965)*
Cac Wallpanels LLC .... G 260 437-4003
  Harlan *(G-7051)*
Cana Inc .... G 574 266-6566
  Elkhart *(G-3246)*
Carriage House Woodworking .... G 765 352-8514
  Martinsville *(G-11383)*
Cash & Carry Lumber Co Inc .... E 765 378-7575
  Daleville *(G-2797)*
Catholic Woodworker .... G 317 413-4276
  Carmel *(G-1583)*
Cedar Creek Woodworking LLC .... G 812 687-7556
  Odon *(G-13332)*
Centerline Woodworking .... G 260 768-4116
  Lagrange *(G-10731)*
Central Indiana Woodworkers .... G 317 407-9228
  Indianapolis *(G-7773)*
Champion Wood Products Inc .... G 812 282-9460
  Sellersburg *(G-14591)*
Chase Manufacturing LLC .... C 574 546-4776
  Nappanee *(G-12588)*
Chisholm Lumber & Supply Co .... E 317 547-3535
  Indianapolis *(G-7799)*
Chris Schwartz .... G 260 615-9574
  Grabill *(G-6292)*
Circle City Woodworking .... G 765 637-6687
  Indianapolis *(G-7808)*
Ckh Two Inc .... E 317 841-7800
  Fishers *(G-4489)*
Clark Millworks .... G 260 665-1270
  Angola *(G-240)*
Clear View Cstm Wndows Dors In .... G 812 877-1000
  Terre Haute *(G-15564)*
Clearspring Manufacturing LLC .... F 260 593-2086
  Topeka *(G-15796)*
Clinton Custom Wood Turning .... G 574 535-0543
  Goshen *(G-6112)*
Cns Custom Woodworks Inc .... G 812 350-2431
  Columbus *(G-2239)*
Cois Coillte Woodworking LLC .... G 812 340-3718
  Bloomington *(G-832)*
Comptons Woodworking LLC .... G 765 712-0568
  Cloverdale *(G-2084)*
Concord Realstate Corp .... F 765 423-5555
  Lafayette *(G-10554)*
Cornerstone Mill Work .... G 260 357-0754
  Garrett *(G-5856)*
Cornerstone Moulding Inc .... E 574 546-4249
  Bremen *(G-1182)*
Couden Woodworks Inc .... G 317 370-0835
  Noblesville *(G-13063)*
Country Craftsman Wdwkg LLC .... G 574 773-4911
  Nappanee *(G-12591)*
Country Woodworking LLC .... G 812 636-6004
  Odon *(G-13334)*
Cox Interior Inc .... G 317 896-2227
  Indianapolis *(G-7892)*

Creative Wood Designs Inc .... E 260 894-4533
  Ligonier *(G-11010)*
Crestview Woodworking LLC .... G 260 768-4707
  Shipshewana *(G-14841)*
Cumberland Millwork & Supply .... G 260 471-6936
  Fort Wayne *(G-4892)*
Custom Door Manufacturing .... G 812 636-3667
  Loogootee *(G-11130)*
Custom Draperies of Indiana .... G 219 924-2500
  Hammond *(G-6909)*
Custom Interior Dynamics LLC .... F 317 632-0477
  Indianapolis *(G-7930)*
Custom Millwork & Display Inc .... F 574 289-4000
  South Bend *(G-14994)*
Custom Wood Creations LLC .... G 765 860-1983
  Kokomo *(G-10254)*
Custom Woodworking .... G 812 339-6601
  Bloomington *(G-851)*
Custom Woodworking .... G 812 422-6786
  Evansville *(G-4005)*
D & D Mouldings & Millwork LLC .... E 317 770-5500
  Noblesville *(G-13067)*
Dairyland Woodworks LLC .... G 715 271-2110
  Warsaw *(G-16343)*
Dan Barnett Woodworking LLC .... G 765 724-7828
  Alexandria *(G-49)*
Dickinson Woodworking LLC .... G 317 519-5254
  Greenfield *(G-6490)*
Diverse Woodworking LLC .... G 812 366-3000
  Georgetown *(G-6058)*
Divine Heritage Barns LLC .... G 812 709-0066
  Rushville *(G-14399)*
Dnh Woodworking .... G 260 593-0439
  Topeka *(G-15802)*
Dobbins Interior Woodworks .... G 812 221-0058
  Dillsboro *(G-2945)*
Doors & Drawers Inc .... F 574 533-3509
  Goshen *(G-6125)*
Double E Woodworking LLC .... G 260 593-0522
  Topeka *(G-15803)*
Double J Woodworking .... G 812 290-8877
  Lawrenceburg *(G-10834)*
Double L Woodworking LLC .... F 260 768-3155
  Goshen *(G-6126)*
Dr Restorations Inc .... G 317 646-7150
  Clermont *(G-2063)*
Drew It Yourself Wood Working .... G 317 250-6548
  Noblesville *(G-13074)*
Dutch Craft Woodwork LLC .... G 812 486-3675
  Montgomery *(G-12096)*
Dutch Made Inc .... G 260 657-3331
  Harlan *(G-7054)*
Dutchcraft Corporation .... G 260 463-8366
  Lagrange *(G-10735)*
Dutchmaid Woodworking LLC .... G 260 768-7442
  Shipshewana *(G-14844)*
E M Woodworking .... G 812 486-2696
  Montgomery *(G-12097)*
Eckhart Woodworking Inc .... E 260 692-6218
  Monroe *(G-12060)*
Ecojacks LLC .... G 574 306-0414
  South Whitley *(G-15317)*
Ecpca Safe-Way LLC .... D 574 267-4861
  Warsaw *(G-16354)*
Ed Lloyd Co .... G 812 342-2505
  Columbus *(G-2294)*
Englehardt Custom Wdwkg LLC .... G 812 425-9282
  Evansville *(G-4037)*
Ettensohn & Company LLC .... G 812 547-5491
  Tell City *(G-15501)*
Expert Woodworks .... G 219 345-2705
  Lake Village *(G-10780)*

SIC SECTION
24 LUMBER AND WOOD PRODUCTS, EXCEPT FURNITURE

Company	Code	Phone
Fairmont Door Corp	G	260 563-6307
Wabash (G-16185)		
Fairview Woodworking	G	260 768-3255
Shipshewana (G-14845)		
Faske Wood Moulding Inc	F	812 923-5601
Borden (G-1108)		
Ferry Street Woodworks	G	812 427-9663
Vevay (G-16109)		
Fine Woodworks	G	765 346-2630
Martinsville (G-11392)		
First Age Woodworking LLC	G	765 667-1847
Indianapolis (G-8191)		
Fischer Woodcraft Incorporated	G	317 627-6035
Beech Grove (G-689)		
Fitzpatrick Sons Woodworks LLC	G	219 987-2223
Demotte (G-2916)		
Flp Woodworks	G	260 424-3904
Fort Wayne (G-4987)		
Flying Pig Woodworks LLC	G	219 242-5557
Union Mills (G-15864)		
Forest Products Group Inc	F	765 659-1807
Frankfort (G-5665)		
Four Daughters LLC	G	805 868-7456
New Albany (G-12733)		
Four Woods Laminating Inc	E	260 593-2246
Topeka (G-15806)		
Franklin Garage Ltd	G	260 442-2439
Fort Wayne (G-5008)		
From Woods	G	765 468-7387
Farmland (G-4425)		
Frontier Woodworks	G	260 463-2049
Lagrange (G-10739)		
G & R Woodworking LLC	G	812 687-7701
Montgomery (G-12098)		
G & S Rural Woodworking	G	765 348-7781
Hartford City (G-7065)		
Gary E Ellsworth	G	260 639-3078
Hoagland (G-7168)		
Garyrae Inc	F	574 255-7141
Mishawaka (G-11898)		
Gauger Woodworking Plus	G	812 421-8223
Evansville (G-4085)		
Genesis Products LLC	C	574 266-8293
Elkhart (G-3373)		
Genesis Products LLC	E	877 266-8292
Elkhart (G-3375)		
Genesis Products LLC	B	574 533-5089
Goshen (G-6145)		
▲ Genesis Products LLC	C	877 266-8292
Goshen (G-6146)		
Georgia-Pacific LLC	D	219 956-3100
Wheatfield (G-16767)		
Gilpin Custom Woodworking LLC	G	260 413-6618
Roanoke (G-14269)		
Gold Seale Woodworking	G	765 744-4159
Muncie (G-12404)		
Goosecreek Woodworking LLC	G	317 557-9189
Carthage (G-1814)		
Graef Custom Homes LLC	G	574 807-5859
South Bend (G-15047)		
Grampas Cedar Works LLC	G	317 372-0816
Monrovia (G-12077)		
Grundy Woodworks	G	765 337-4596
Crawfordsville (G-2572)		
Gutter One Supply	F	317 872-1257
Indianapolis (G-8344)		
Guys Wood N Things	G	812 689-0433
Holton (G-7216)		
Hd Woodworking	G	260 310-9427
Fort Wayne (G-5053)		
Heidenreich Woodworking Inc	G	317 861-9331
New Palestine (G-12937)		
Helmuths Woodworking LLC	G	574 825-0073
Shipshewana (G-14849)		
Hickory Valley Woodworking LLC	G	812 486-2857
Loogootee (G-11138)		
Hochstetler Woodworking LLC	G	260 593-3255
Topeka (G-15808)		
Hoosier Custom Woodworking	G	574 642-3764
Millersburg (G-11814)		
Hoosier Interior Doors Inc	G	574 534-3072
Goshen (G-6169)		
Hoosier Reclaimed Timber	G	812 322-3912
Bloomington (G-881)		
Hoosier Wood Works	G	812 325-9823
Bloomington (G-884)		
◆ House of Fara Incorporated	D	219 362-8544
La Porte (G-10422)		
Hudec Construction Company	E	219 922-9811
Griffith (G-6807)		
▲ Indiana Architectural Plywood	E	317 878-4822
Trafalgar (G-15829)		
▲ Indiana Dimension Inc	D	574 739-2319
Logansport (G-11082)		
Indiana Lumber Inc	G	812 837-9493
Bloomington (G-889)		
Indiana Southern Millwork Inc	E	812 346-6129
North Vernon (G-13280)		
Indianapolis Woodworking	G	317 345-4180
Fishers (G-4546)		
Integrity Woodcrafting	G	260 562-2067
Shipshewana (G-14853)		
Interior Fixs & Mllwk Co Inc	G	812 446-0933
Knightsville (G-10202)		
International Wood Inc	F	260 248-1491
Albion (G-29)		
Iron Timbers LLC	G	812 614-0467
Versailles (G-16101)		
▲ Irvine Shade & Door Inc	D	574 522-1446
Elkhart (G-3430)		
J T Woodworking LLC	G	513 543-1130
Lawrenceburg (G-10842)		
Jackson Brothers Lumber Co	F	812 847-7812
Linton (G-11036)		
Jacksons Woodworks LLC	G	765 623-0638
Elwood (G-3827)		
James G Henager	G	812 795-2230
Elberfeld (G-3115)		
Jays Woodworking Direct LLC	G	219 345-3335
Lake Village (G-10781)		
Jbj Custom Woodworking Inc	G	260 450-7295
Monroeville (G-12070)		
Jeff Goodnight	G	765 779-4867
Middletown (G-11771)		
Jeff Hurst Custom Wdwkg Inc	G	812 367-1430
Ferdinand (G-4437)		
JI Woodworking LLC	G	317 910-2976
Carmel (G-1678)		
JM Woodworking Enterprise LLC	G	574 773-0444
Milford (G-11795)		
JM Woodworking LLC	G	574 354-7093
Syracuse (G-15464)		
John G Wagler	G	812 709-1681
Odon (G-13342)		
John Gebhart Woodworkings	G	765 492-3898
Cayuga (G-1823)		
Jri Woodworks	G	812 401-1234
Evansville (G-4145)		
Jrs Wood Shop	G	765 498-2663
Kingman (G-10172)		
JW Woodworking Inc	G	574 831-3033
New Paris (G-12962)		
Kaizen Woodworks	G	714 350-6281
Granger (G-6356)		
Keith Ison	G	765 938-1460
Rushville (G-14403)		
Kentucky Wood Floors LLC	G	812 256-2164
Borden (G-1111)		
Kerkhoff Associates Inc	E	765 583-4491
Otterbein (G-13453)		
Kleeman Cabinetry	G	812 926-0428
Aurora (G-447)		
▲ Knapke & Sons Inc	E	260 639-0112
Hoagland (G-7169)		
Knothole Woodworks LLC	G	317 600-8151
Kirklin (G-10191)		
◆ Koetter Woodworking Inc	B	812 923-8875
Borden (G-1113)		
Kostyo Woodworking Inc	G	812 466-7350
Terre Haute (G-15625)		
Kraigs Custom Woodworking	G	574 904-7501
Mishawaka (G-11924)		
Kuntry Lumber and Farm Sup Ltd	F	260 463-3242
Lagrange (G-10746)		
L & L Woodworking LLC	G	574 535-4613
Nappanee (G-12619)		
L & N Woodworking LLC	G	260 768-7008
Shipshewana (G-14858)		
L & W Woodworking LLC	G	260 463-8938
Wolcottville (G-16940)		
LA Woodworking LLC	G	574 825-5580
Middlebury (G-11731)		
Lakeview Woodworking	G	574 642-1335
Goshen (G-6196)		
LAMB Woodworking LLC	G	260 768-7992
Shipshewana (G-14862)		
Lambert Wood Works LLC	G	812 952-4204
Lanesville (G-10801)		
Lambright Woodworking LLC	F	260 593-2721
Topeka (G-15811)		
Lana Hudelson	G	812 865-3951
Orleans (G-13377)		
▲ Larry Robertson Associates	F	812 537-4090
Indianapolis (G-8723)		
Learning Cedar Woodworking	G	574 862-1864
Elkhart (G-3482)		
Legacy Wood Creations LLC	G	574 773-4405
Nappanee (G-12620)		
Licar America LLC	E	812 256-6400
Jeffersonville (G-10012)		
Light House Woodworking DBA	G	260 704-0589
Saint Joe (G-14439)		
Ligonier Woodworking	G	260 894-9969
Ligonier (G-11019)		
Limitless Woodworking LLC	G	317 702-1763
Noblesville (G-13128)		
Limon Woodworking LLC	G	317 362-9179
Indianapolis (G-8757)		
Lions Pride Customs LLC	G	765 490-8296
Lafayette (G-10637)		
Lockerbie Square Cab Co Inc	G	317 635-1134
Indianapolis (G-8775)		
Loggers Incorporated	E	812 939-2797
Clay City (G-2045)		
Louisiana-Pacific Corporation	D	574 825-5845
Middlebury (G-11735)		
Lucky Man Wdwkg Hndyman Svcs L	G	810 247-3099
Fishers (G-4559)		
M & D Woodworking	G	260 450-0484
Grabill (G-6312)		
M & M Tabletops LLC	G	502 396-9236
New Albany (G-12769)		
M & M Woodworking	G	812 486-2418
Washington (G-16492)		
Madison Millwork Inc	G	765 649-7883
Anderson (G-150)		

Employee Codes: A=Over 500 employees, B=251-500
C=101-250, D=51-100, E=20-50, F=10-19, G=1-9

24 LUMBER AND WOOD PRODUCTS, EXCEPT FURNITURE

Makers Hand Woodworking.................. G..... 317 797-8776
    Albany *(G-13)*

Marc Woodworking Inc................ D..... 317 635-9663
    Indianapolis *(G-8827)*

Mark Foster........................ G..... 574 965-4558
    Delphi *(G-2902)*

Marquise Enterprises Ltd................... G..... 317 578-3400
    Indianapolis *(G-8840)*

Martell & Co....................... G..... 317 752-2847
    Greenwood *(G-6733)*

Marvelous Woodworking LLC............... G..... 317 679-5890
    Lebanon *(G-10914)*

Maschino Woodworks LLC............... G..... 812 230-7428
    Terre Haute *(G-15637)*

Masonite Corporation................... F..... 574 586-3192
    Walkerton *(G-16269)*

Masonite International Corp............... E..... 574 586-3192
    Walkerton *(G-16270)*

Mast Woodworking..................... G..... 812 636-7938
    Odon *(G-13343)*

Mata Custom Woodworking............... G..... 812 987-2676
    Jeffersonville *(G-10018)*

Mdl Woodworking LLC.................. G..... 260 242-1824
    Fort Wayne *(G-5213)*

Meadowlark Wdwkg Cabinetry LLC........... G..... 765 541-3660
    Connersville *(G-2456)*

Medlin Custom Woodworking Inc............ F..... 765 939-0923
    Richmond *(G-14162)*

Mervin Knepps Molding.................. G..... 812 486-2971
    Montgomery *(G-12114)*

▲ Mhp Holdings Inc................. C..... 574 825-9524
    Middlebury *(G-11736)*

Miami Gardens Millwork.................. G..... 812 208-4541
    Terre Haute *(G-15644)*

Mikes Creative Woodworks LLC............ G..... 502 649-3665
    Charlestown *(G-1884)*

Mill Creek Lumber Co................... G..... 765 347-8546
    Hartford City *(G-7072)*

Miller Cabins and Barns LLC.............. G..... 574 773-7661
    Nappanee *(G-12623)*

Miller Door & Trim Inc.................. G..... 574 533-8141
    Goshen *(G-6225)*

Millrose Custom Woodworking............. G..... 812 699-5101
    Bloomfield *(G-754)*

Mishawaka Door LLC................... G..... 574 259-2822
    Mishawaka *(G-11954)*

Mo-Wood Products Inc.................. G..... 812 482-5625
    Jasper *(G-9892)*

Molargik Woodworking Inc............... G..... 260 357-6625
    Garrett *(G-5871)*

Mountjoy Wooding..................... G..... 317 897-6792
    Indianapolis *(G-8961)*

Mullet Custom Interior LLC............... F..... 574 773-9442
    Nappanee *(G-12627)*

Mustard Seed Woodworking LLC........... G..... 765 336-4423
    Lebanon *(G-10922)*

N & R Woodworking Llc................. G..... 812 787-0644
    Odon *(G-13345)*

New Style of Crossroads LLC.............. F..... 260 593-3800
    Topeka *(G-15812)*

Newtons Legacy Wdwkg Engrv LLC......... G..... 812 322-3360
    Bloomington *(G-930)*

Nhi-Jrj Corp........................ C..... 574 293-9690
    Elkhart *(G-3569)*

Noble Woodworks..................... G..... 765 525-4226
    Saint Paul *(G-14468)*

Northeast Woodworking................. G..... 260 665-1986
    Angola *(G-278)*

Nov Oak Woodworking................. G..... 812 422-1973
    Evansville *(G-4222)*

Nuevopoly LLC...................... G..... 317 260-0026
    Indianapolis *(G-9033)*

Oconnorwoodworking.................. G..... 812 364-1022
    Palmyra *(G-13483)*

Odon Sawmill Inc..................... E..... 812 636-7314
    Odon *(G-13347)*

Ohio Valley Door Corp.................. E..... 812 945-5285
    New Albany *(G-12788)*

Olon Industries Inc (us)................. G..... 812 254-0427
    Washington *(G-16497)*

Omega National Products LLC............ C..... 574 295-5353
    Elkhart *(G-3579)*

Owen Woodworking................... G..... 317 331-6936
    Danville *(G-2822)*

Patrick Industries Inc.................. G..... 574 293-1521
    Elkhart *(G-3597)*

Pax Custom Woodworking LLC............ G..... 805 300-3720
    Indianapolis *(G-9106)*

Pendleton Door Company................ G..... 765 778-4164
    Pendleton *(G-13551)*

Philip Konrad & Sons Inc................ F..... 574 772-3966
    Knox *(G-10219)*

Phoenix Woodworking Co LLC............ G..... 317 340-0726
    Carmel *(G-1717)*

Pickslays Woodworking................. G..... 530 388-8697
    Winona Lake *(G-16914)*

Powell Woodworking LLC................ G..... 812 279-5029
    Bedford *(G-660)*

Power Plant Service Inc................. E..... 260 432-6716
    Fort Wayne *(G-5328)*

Pro Door Manufacturing LLC............. D..... 317 839-3050
    Plainfield *(G-13717)*

▼ Pro-Form Plastics Inc................ E..... 812 522-4433
    Crothersville *(G-2644)*

Prospect Distribution Inc................ E..... 317 359-9551
    Indianapolis *(G-9231)*

PTG Inc........................... G..... 317 892-4625
    Brownsburg *(G-1396)*

▲ Quality Hardwood Sales LLC........... D..... 574 773-2505
    Nappanee *(G-12639)*

R P Wakefield Company Inc.............. E..... 260 837-8841
    Waterloo *(G-16528)*

Raad Custom Woodworking LLC........... G..... 765 432-1385
    Kokomo *(G-10325)*

Randys Tooling & Wdwkg LLC............ G..... 812 326-2204
    Saint Anthony *(G-14431)*

Real Wood Works.................... G..... 812 277-1462
    Bedford *(G-665)*

Redlin Custom Woodworking LLC.......... G..... 317 578-1852
    Fishers *(G-4593)*

Regenbogen Woodworks LLC............ G..... 317 902-8221
    Indianapolis *(G-9282)*

RH Yoder Enterprises LLC............... G..... 574 825-6183
    Shipshewana *(G-14882)*

Riddle Ridge Woodworks................ G..... 812 596-4503
    English *(G-3846)*

Rl Strahm Woodworking Inc.............. G..... 260 623-3228
    Monroeville *(G-12073)*

Ro-Vic Wood Products Inc............... F..... 812 283-9199
    Jeffersonville *(G-10049)*

▲ Robert Weed Plywood Corp............ B..... 574 848-7631
    Bristol *(G-1288)*

Rockwell Diversified Woodworks........... G..... 317 758-4797
    Sheridan *(G-14827)*

Rodeswood LLC..................... G..... 574 457-4496
    Syracuse *(G-15476)*

Rogers Group Inc.................... C..... 812 333-6324
    Bloomington *(G-959)*

Rst Custom Woodworking LL............. G..... 317 602-2490
    Indianapolis *(G-9344)*

Rustic Creations LLC.................. G..... 574 349-8156
    Nappanee *(G-12642)*

Sandwabi Woodworking LLC............. G..... 765 891-0774
    Lebanon *(G-10939)*

Sawdust Farms Woodworking LLC......... G..... 574 946-3399
    Winamac *(G-16875)*

SAWs Woodworking LLC................ G..... 574 773-4216
    Nappanee *(G-12644)*

▼ Schertz Craftsmen Inc................ C..... 877 472-2782
    Grabill *(G-6324)*

Schindler Woodwork................... G..... 513 314-5943
    Cedar Grove *(G-1824)*

Schlabach Hardwoods LLC............... G..... 574 642-1157
    Goshen *(G-6251)*

Schmucker Woodworking LLC............ G..... 260 413-9784
    New Haven *(G-12918)*

Schuhler Woodworking LLC.............. G..... 317 626-0452
    Danville *(G-2826)*

Schwan Products LLC.................. G..... 260 350-4764
    Topeka *(G-15818)*

Schwartz Woodworking................. G..... 260 593-3193
    Millersburg *(G-11817)*

Schwartz Woodworking LLC.............. G..... 260 854-9457
    Wolcottville *(G-16942)*

Scp Building Products LLC............... G..... 574 772-2955
    Knox *(G-10223)*

Sego Woodworking................... G..... 317 431-9087
    Indianapolis *(G-9399)*

Shamrock Cabinets Inc................. E..... 812 482-7969
    Jasper *(G-9911)*

Shiloh Custom Woodworks............... G..... 812 636-0100
    Odon *(G-13350)*

Shinabargar Custom Stairs............... G..... 219 462-1735
    Valparaiso *(G-16048)*

Shipshewana Woodworks LLC............ G..... 260 768-7034
    Shipshewana *(G-14888)*

Sorg Millwork....................... G..... 260 639-3223
    Fort Wayne *(G-5427)*

South Bend Woodworks LLC............. F..... 574 232-8875
    South Bend *(G-15258)*

Specialized Wood Products Inc............ E..... 574 522-6376
    Elkhart *(G-3691)*

Spectrum Finishing LLC................. G..... 260 463-7300
    Lagrange *(G-10762)*

State Line Woodworking................ G..... 260 768-4577
    Shipshewana *(G-14891)*

Steven Block....................... G..... 765 749-5394
    Muncie *(G-12497)*

Steves Woodworking LLC................ G..... 317 507-4194
    Martinsville *(G-11428)*

Stolls Woodworking LLC................. G..... 812 486-5117
    Odon *(G-13353)*

Stoney Acres Woodworking LLC........... F..... 260 768-4367
    Shipshewana *(G-14893)*

Studabker Spclty Woodworks LLC.......... G..... 260 273-1326
    Bluffton *(G-1058)*

Sunrise Wood Products LLC.............. G..... 260 463-4822
    Lagrange *(G-10765)*

Superior Source Woodworks LLC.......... G..... 574 773-4841
    Nappanee *(G-12647)*

Swanson Woodworking................. G..... 765 585-0328
    Attica *(G-354)*

Swiss Woodworking LLC................ G..... 260 849-9669
    Berne *(G-729)*

Tall Oaks Woodworking................. G..... 708 275-5723
    Cedar Lake *(G-1839)*

Tartan Properties LLC.................. G..... 317 714-7337
    Indianapolis *(G-9554)*

TE Custom Woodwork LLC.............. G..... 317 910-6906
    Indianapolis *(G-9564)*

Tim Weberding Woodworking LLC......... G..... 865 430-8811
    Batesville *(G-608)*

Timber Arts LLC..................... G..... 765 522-4121
    Bainbridge *(G-564)*

Tinchers Creative Woodworks............. G..... 765 344-0062
    Rockville *(G-14358)*

SIC SECTION
24 LUMBER AND WOOD PRODUCTS, EXCEPT FURNITURE

Trim-A-Door Corporation .... G 317 769-8746
    Elwood *(G-3839)*

▲ Trim-A-Door Corporation .... E 574 254-0300
    Mishawaka *(G-12016)*

Trinity Woodworking .... G 513 535-1964
    Lawrenceburg *(G-10864)*

▲ Tru-Cut Inc .... E 765 683-9920
    Anderson *(G-209)*

Ubelhor Construction Inc .... F 812 357-2220
    Bristow *(G-1301)*

Ufp Nappanee LLC .... D 574 773-2505
    Nappanee *(G-12649)*

Ullom Woodworks .... G 765 610-3188
    Anderson *(G-211)*

Ullom Woodworks .... G 217 369-5769
    Noblesville *(G-13187)*

Uniquely Divine Yonis LLC .... G 317 918-9112
    Indianapolis *(G-9678)*

Universal Door Carrier Inc .... G 317 241-3447
    Indianapolis *(G-9682)*

Universal Frest Pdts Ind Ltd P .... E 574 273-6326
    Granger *(G-6388)*

US Lbm Operating Co 3009 LLC .... G 812 464-2428
    Evansville *(G-4364)*

Verns Woodworking .... G 574 773-7930
    Bremen *(G-1228)*

Vk Studios .... G 317 224-6867
    Fishers *(G-4653)*

W & M Woodworking .... G 260 854-3126
    Lagrange *(G-10768)*

Wabash Vly Woodworkers CLB Inc .... G 317 538-2956
    West Lafayette *(G-16644)*

Wagler Woodworking .... G 812 486-6357
    Loogootee *(G-11154)*

Walnut Lane Woodworking .... G 574 633-2114
    Bremen *(G-1229)*

Warburton Wood Works LLC .... G 317 318-9113
    Greenfield *(G-6570)*

Warsaw Foundry Company Inc .... D 574 267-8772
    Warsaw *(G-16446)*

Weaver Woodworking .... G 260 565-3647
    Bluffton *(G-1069)*

Weber Woodworking .... G 765 967-3665
    Richmond *(G-14225)*

Weberdings Carving Shop Inc .... F 812 934-3710
    Batesville *(G-610)*

Werner Custom Woodworking .... G 812 852-0029
    Batesville *(G-611)*

West Point Woodworking LLC .... G 260 768-4750
    Shipshewana *(G-14897)*

Whites Woodworks .... G 765 341-6678
    Martinsville *(G-11435)*

Wible Lumber Inc .... E 260 351-2441
    South Milford *(G-15314)*

Wichman Woodworking Inc .... G 812 522-8450
    Seymour *(G-14705)*

Wild Grain Woodworks LLC .... G 317 626-3939
    Noblesville *(G-13195)*

Wildwood Millwork LLC .... G 574 535-9104
    Goshen *(G-6277)*

Wittmer Woodworking LLC .... G 812 486-3115
    Montgomery *(G-12130)*

Wood Creations Inc .... G 574 522-7765
    Elkhart *(G-3789)*

Wood Spc By Fehrenbacher Inc .... E 812 963-9414
    Evansville *(G-4389)*

Wood Wiz Inc .... G 317 834-9079
    Mooresville *(G-12250)*

◆ Wood-Mizer Holdings Inc .... C 317 271-1542
    Indianapolis *(G-9784)*

Woodgrain Construction Inc .... G 317 873-5608
    Zionsville *(G-17062)*

Woodland Ridge Woodworking LLC .... G 812 821-8032
    Ellettsville *(G-3812)*

Woods Enterprises .... G 574 232-7449
    South Bend *(G-15309)*

Woodside Woodworks LLC .... G 260 499-3220
    Wolcottville *(G-16945)*

Woodworking .... G 574 825-5858
    Middlebury *(G-11761)*

Woodwright Door & Trim Inc .... G 574 522-1667
    Elkhart *(G-3792)*

Wright Horizon Enterprises LLC .... G 317 779-8182
    Westfield *(G-16741)*

Wrights Woodworking .... G 765 723-1546
    New Ross *(G-12981)*

Yankee Made Woodworks LLC .... G 513 607-3152
    Bath *(G-612)*

Yoder Woodworking .... G 574 825-0402
    Middlebury *(G-11762)*

Yoders Woodworking LLC .... G 574 773-0699
    Nappanee *(G-12657)*

2434 Wood kitchen cabinets

Academy Inc .... G 574 293-7113
    Elkhart *(G-3147)*

Acme Cabinet Corporation .... G 219 924-1800
    Griffith *(G-6785)*

Acpi Wood Products LLC .... D 574 842-2066
    Culver *(G-2777)*

Advanced Cabinet Systems Inc .... D 765 677-8000
    Marion *(G-11268)*

All About Organizing .... G 513 238-8157
    Lawrenceburg *(G-10827)*

American Cabinet Refacing Inc .... G 317 875-7453
    Zionsville *(G-16990)*

American Woodmark Corporation .... B 765 677-1690
    Gas City *(G-6031)*

Americas Cabinet Co Ind Inc .... F 317 788-9533
    Greenfield *(G-6461)*

Anderson Amish Cabinets LLC .... G 317 575-9277
    Carmel *(G-1560)*

▲ Aristocrat Inc .... G 812 634-0460
    Jasper *(G-9824)*

Aristoline Cabinets Inc .... E 260 482-9719
    Fort Wayne *(G-4771)*

B & L Custom Cabinets Inc .... G 765 379-2471
    Rossville *(G-14386)*

Barker Kitchen & Bath Cabinets .... G 812 493-4693
    Hanover *(G-7039)*

Beattys Custom Woods .... G 574 722-2752
    Logansport *(G-11061)*

Beebe Cabinet Co Inc .... F 574 293-3580
    Elkhart *(G-3222)*

Best Custom Cabinet Refacing .... G 260 459-1448
    Columbia City *(G-2123)*

Bkb Custom Cabinetry LLC .... G 317 439-9427
    Mooresville *(G-12195)*

Boger Cabinetry & Design Inc .... G 317 588-6954
    Fishers *(G-4476)*

Brandenberger Door Mfg .... G 260 657-1494
    Grabill *(G-6289)*

Bremtown Fine Cstm Cbnetry Inc .... D 574 546-2781
    Bremen *(G-1179)*

Brookwood Cabinet Company Inc .... F 260 749-5012
    Fort Wayne *(G-4819)*

Burns Cabinets and Disp Inc .... G 260 897-2219
    Avilla *(G-473)*

C & J Cabinets .... G 574 255-5812
    Mishawaka *(G-11856)*

C & R Woodworks .... G 317 422-9603
    Martinsville *(G-11382)*

Cabinet and Stone Expo .... G 317 879-1688
    Indianapolis *(G-7712)*

▲ Cabinet and Stone Expo LLC .... G 317 879-1688
    Indianapolis *(G-7713)*

Cabinet Barn 2com .... G 317 421-1750
    Shelbyville *(G-14743)*

Cabinet Barn Inc .... G 812 246-5237
    Sellersburg *(G-14589)*

Cabinet Crafters Corp .... G 765 724-7074
    Alexandria *(G-47)*

Cabinet Expressions .... G 317 366-7669
    Noblesville *(G-13053)*

Cabinet Fctories Outl Richmond .... G 765 966-3875
    Richmond *(G-14102)*

Cabinetmaker Inc .... G 812 723-3461
    Paoli *(G-13490)*

Cabinetry Green LLC .... G 317 842-1550
    Fishers *(G-4480)*

Cabinetry Ideas Inc .... G 317 722-1300
    Indianapolis *(G-7714)*

Cabinetry Solutions LLC .... G 574 326-3699
    Elkhart *(G-3245)*

Cabinets By Rick Inc .... G 812 945-2220
    New Albany *(G-12708)*

Cabinets Inc .... G 219 322-3900
    Schererville *(G-14518)*

Cabinets Plus By Ptrick Geer I .... F 765 642-0329
    Anderson *(G-87)*

Cabinets To Go LLC .... G 317 486-0888
    Indianapolis *(G-7715)*

Cabinets Unlimited Corporation .... G 219 558-2210
    Saint John *(G-14446)*

Cabinets Unlimited Inc .... G 260 925-5555
    Saint Joe *(G-14437)*

Carriage House Woodworking Inc .... G 317 406-3042
    Coatesville *(G-2104)*

Carter Cabinet Company Inc .... G 317 985-5782
    New Palestine *(G-12935)*

Cedar Woodworking .... G 812 486-2765
    Montgomery *(G-12088)*

Claires Cabinet Refinishing .... G 317 495-5406
    Indianapolis *(G-7815)*

Classic Cabinets LLC .... G 317 507-3775
    Carmel *(G-1589)*

Coblentz Cabinet LLC .... G 812 687-7525
    Montgomery *(G-12089)*

Cochran Custom Woodworking LLC .... G 765 523-3220
    Stockwell *(G-15399)*

Columbus Cabinetry LLC .... G 812 447-1005
    Columbus *(G-2241)*

Columbus Cstm Cbinets Furn LLC .... G 812 379-9411
    Columbus *(G-2242)*

Commercial Electric Co Inc .... E 260 726-9357
    Portland *(G-13933)*

Concept Cabinet Shop .... G 765 653-1080
    Greencastle *(G-6398)*

Concepts Cabinet Shop Inc .... G 317 272-7430
    Avon *(G-511)*

Corbetts Custom Cabinetry LLC .... G 812 670-6211
    Jeffersonville *(G-9961)*

Corner Cabinet .... G 317 859-6336
    Greenwood *(G-6682)*

Cornerstone Cabinets .... G 317 718-0050
    Plainfield *(G-13671)*

Corsi Cabinet Company Inc .... D 317 786-1434
    Indianapolis *(G-7881)*

Counter Design Co Inc .... E 812 477-1243
    Evansville *(G-3985)*

Counterfitters Inc .... G 219 531-0848
    Valparaiso *(G-15929)*

Countertop Connections Inc .... G 317 822-9858
    Franklin *(G-5723)*

Countertop Manufacturing Inc .... E 765 966-4969
    Richmond *(G-14111)*

Employee Codes: A=Over 500 employees, B=251-500
C=101-250, D=51-100, E=20-50, F=10-19, G=1-9

2024 Harris Indiana Industrial Directory

24 LUMBER AND WOOD PRODUCTS, EXCEPT FURNITURE

Countertop Shoppe Inc .... G 574 936-1423
  Plymouth *(G-13766)*
Country Cabinets LLC .... G 260 694-6777
  Poneto *(G-13840)*
Country Craft Cabinets LLC .... G 574 596-8624
  Bristol *(G-1255)*
Country View Cabinets LLC .... G 574 825-3150
  Goshen *(G-6116)*
Countryside Cabinetry LLC .... G 765 597-2391
  Marshall *(G-11371)*
County Line Cabinetry LLC .... G 574 642-1202
  Middlebury *(G-11707)*
Creative Cabinets .... G 574 264-9041
  Elkhart *(G-3270)*
Creative Concepts Cabinetry .... G 812 522-0204
  Seymour *(G-14642)*
Cregg Custom Cabinets .... G 812 342-3605
  Columbus *(G-2249)*
Crickys Country Cabinets LLC .... G 812 486-3705
  Loogootee *(G-11129)*
Crossrads Cntrtops Cbnetry LLC .... G 317 908-9254
  Indianapolis *(G-7909)*
Custom Cabinets & Furn LLC .... F 812 486-2503
  Montgomery *(G-12092)*
Custom Design Laminates Inc .... F 574 674-9174
  Osceola *(G-13388)*
Custom Tables & Cabinets .... G 812 486-3831
  Montgomery *(G-12093)*
D & B Cabinet Sales Inc .... G 317 392-2870
  Shelbyville *(G-14750)*
D & E Cabinets .... G 812 486-2961
  Montgomery *(G-12094)*
D L Miller Woodworking .... G 260 562-9329
  Shipshewana *(G-14842)*
Daugherty Cabinets .... G 574 272-9205
  Granger *(G-6343)*
Davis Cabinet and Flooring LLC .... G 765 530-8170
  Hagerstown *(G-6836)*
Dennys Woodcraft Inc .... G 812 883-0770
  Salem *(G-14477)*
Distinctive Kitchen & Bath Inc .... G 317 882-7100
  Greenwood *(G-6687)*
Doors & Drawers Inc .... F 574 533-3509
  Goshen *(G-6125)*
Double T Manufacturing Corp .... F 574 262-1340
  Elkhart *(G-3302)*
Douglas Dye and Associates Inc .... G 317 844-1709
  Carmel *(G-1611)*
DS Woods Custom Cabinets .... G 260 692-6565
  Decatur *(G-2853)*
Dutch Made Inc .... G 260 657-3331
  Harlan *(G-7054)*
Dutch Made Inc .... C 260 657-3311
  Grabill *(G-6294)*
E & S Wood Creations LLC .... F 260 768-3033
  Lagrange *(G-10736)*
Eds Wood Craft .... G 812 768-6617
  Haubstadt *(G-7084)*
Elko Inc .... F 812 473-8400
  Evansville *(G-4030)*
Evia Custom Cabinets LLC .... G 317 987-5504
  Carmel *(G-1630)*
Faes Cabinet LLC .... G 567 259-8571
  Fort Wayne *(G-4972)*
▲ Fehrenbacher Cabinets Inc .... E 812 963-3377
  Evansville *(G-4066)*
Fergys Cabinets .... G 765 529-0116
  New Castle *(G-12861)*
Finish Alternatives .... G 317 440-2899
  Indianapolis *(G-8189)*
Genrich Custom Cabinetry Mllwk .... F 317 351-0991
  Indianapolis *(G-8277)*

Gentrys Cabinet Inc .... G 765 643-6611
  Anderson *(G-120)*
Goings Properties LLC .... G 765 294-2380
  Veedersburg *(G-16087)*
Graber Cabinetry LLC .... E 260 627-2243
  Grabill *(G-6297)*
Graber Furniture .... G 812 295-4939
  Loogootee *(G-11136)*
Graber Woodworks Inc .... G 812 486-2861
  Montgomery *(G-12100)*
▲ Granitech .... G 574 674-6988
  Elkhart *(G-3386)*
▲ H-C Liquidating Corp .... A 574 535-9300
  Goshen *(G-6159)*
▲ Haas Cabinet Co Inc .... C 812 246-4431
  Sellersburg *(G-14594)*
Hardwood Door Mfg LLC .... G 812 486-3313
  Montgomery *(G-12102)*
Harlan Cabinets Inc .... F 260 657-5154
  Harlan *(G-7056)*
Healey Custom Cabinetry LLC .... G 574 946-4000
  Winamac *(G-16863)*
Herb Rahman & Sons Inc .... G 812 367-2513
  Ferdinand *(G-4435)*
High Caliber Cabinetry LLC .... G 812 246-5550
  Sellersburg *(G-14600)*
Homemark Cabinetry LLC .... E 678 234-4519
  Connersville *(G-2440)*
Hoosier House Furnishings LLC .... G 574 975-0357
  Goshen *(G-6166)*
Houck Industries Inc .... F 812 663-5675
  Greensburg *(G-6606)*
Hurst Custom Cabinets Inc .... G 812 683-3378
  Huntingburg *(G-7283)*
Independent Cabinets .... G 502 594-6026
  Memphis *(G-11465)*
Innovative Corp .... E 317 804-5977
  Westfield *(G-16701)*
Interior Fixs & Mllwk Co Inc .... G 812 446-0933
  Knightsville *(G-10202)*
J & J Woodcrafters .... G 765 436-2466
  Thorntown *(G-15752)*
J and G Enterprises .... G 219 778-4319
  Rolling Prairie *(G-14365)*
J G Cabinet & Counter Inc .... G 260 723-4275
  Larwill *(G-10820)*
J Miller Cabinet Company Inc .... G 260 691-2032
  Columbia City *(G-2158)*
James G Henager .... G 812 795-2230
  Elberfeld *(G-3115)*
Janice Cabinetry LLC .... G 219 741-8120
  Valparaiso *(G-15980)*
Jds Pughs Cabinets Inc .... G 317 835-2910
  Trafalgar *(G-15830)*
Jerry Hillenburg Co .... G 317 422-8884
  Martinsville *(G-11409)*
Johnny Graber Woodworking .... G 260 466-4957
  Grabill *(G-6305)*
JP Custom Cabinetry Inc .... G 219 956-3587
  Wheatfield *(G-16769)*
Jrs Custom Cabinets Co .... E 219 696-7205
  Lowell *(G-11164)*
K & K Cabinets & Supply .... G 317 852-4808
  Brownsburg *(G-1379)*
Ka Crown Point Inc .... F 219 595-5276
  Crown Point *(G-2707)*
Kelwood Designs LLC .... G 574 862-2472
  Goshen *(G-6184)*
Key Millwork Inc .... G 260 426-6501
  Fort Wayne *(G-5147)*
Kitchen Kompact Inc .... C 812 282-6681
  Jeffersonville *(G-10011)*

Kitchens By Gregory Ltd .... G 219 769-1551
  Merrillville *(G-11527)*
Kline Cabinet Makers LLC .... F 317 326-3049
  Maxwell *(G-11444)*
Klomp Construction Company .... G 219 308-8372
  Saint John *(G-14454)*
Kountry Wood Products LLC .... C 574 773-5673
  Nappanee *(G-12618)*
Kramer Furn & Cab Makers Inc .... E 812 526-2711
  Edinburgh *(G-3089)*
Lakeside Woodworking .... G 812 687-7901
  Freedom *(G-5802)*
Lambright Woodworking LLC .... F 260 593-2721
  Topeka *(G-15811)*
Lami-Crafts Inc .... G 812 232-3012
  Terre Haute *(G-15628)*
Laminique Inc .... F 765 482-4222
  Zionsville *(G-17029)*
Leroy E Doty Cabinet Shop .... G 219 663-1139
  Crown Point *(G-2717)*
Level Set Cabinet Works LLC .... G 812 787-0830
  Washington *(G-16491)*
Lockerbie Square Cab Co Inc .... G 317 635-1134
  Indianapolis *(G-8775)*
Lue Manufacturing Corporation .... F 574 862-4249
  Wakarusa *(G-16238)*
Madison Cabinets Inc .... G 260 639-3915
  Hoagland *(G-7170)*
Madison County Cabinets Inc .... F 765 778-4646
  Pendleton *(G-13541)*
Marcotte Cabinets .... G 574 520-1342
  Granger *(G-6359)*
Martinson Cabinet Shop .... G 219 926-1566
  Chesterton *(G-1947)*
Masterbrand Inc .... B 812 482-2527
  Jasper *(G-9887)*
Masterbrand Cabinets LLC .... F 812 482-2527
  Celestine *(G-1842)*
Masterbrand Cabinets LLC .... G 812 367-1104
  Ferdinand *(G-4442)*
Masterbrand Cabinets LLC .... E 812 367-1104
  Ferdinand *(G-4443)*
Masterbrand Cabinets LLC .... G 574 535-9300
  Goshen *(G-6216)*
Masterbrand Cabinets LLC .... D 812 482-2527
  Huntingburg *(G-7287)*
Masterbrand Cabinets LLC .... D 812 482-2513
  Jasper *(G-9888)*
Masterbrand Cabinets LLC .... F 765 966-3940
  Richmond *(G-14160)*
Masterbrand US Holdings Corp .... C 812 482-2527
  Jasper *(G-9889)*
Mc Custom Cabinets Inc .... G 502 641-1528
  Underwood *(G-15845)*
Medallion Cabinetry .... F 574 842-2066
  Culver *(G-2781)*
Meyer Custom Woodworking Inc .... G 812 695-2021
  Dubois *(G-2954)*
Micka Cabinets .... G 219 838-5450
  Highland *(G-7144)*
Mid Continent Cabinetry .... G 866 527-0141
  Jasper *(G-9891)*
Midwest Country Cabinets .... G 812 486-8580
  Loogootee *(G-11146)*
Milestone Cabinetry .... F 219 947-0600
  Merrillville *(G-11539)*
Miller Cabinetry & Furn LLC .... G 260 657-5052
  Grabill *(G-6315)*
Miller Maid Cabinets Inc .... G 317 780-8280
  Indianapolis *(G-8922)*
Millers Custom Cabinets .... G 260 768-7830
  Shipshewana *(G-14869)*

SIC SECTION
24 LUMBER AND WOOD PRODUCTS, EXCEPT FURNITURE

Mouron & Company Inc .... F 317 243-7955
Indianapolis *(G-8962)*

Muncie Cabinet Discounters .... G 765 216-7367
Muncie *(G-12460)*

Myers Cabinet Company .... G 765 342-7781
Martinsville *(G-11418)*

New Image Cabinet Coating .... G 812 228-4666
Floyds Knobs *(G-4686)*

Nka Cabinet Designs LLC .... G 765 490-4661
Lafayette *(G-10659)*

Norcraft Companies Inc .... D 800 297-0661
Jasper *(G-9896)*

◆ Norcraft Companies LP .... B 812 482-2527
Jasper *(G-9897)*

Nut House Woodworks LLC .... G 317 345-7177
Summitville *(G-15426)*

Oehlers Woods .... G 317 848-2698
Carmel *(G-1710)*

◆ Omega Cabinets Ltd .... A 319 235-5700
Jasper *(G-9900)*

Orchard Lane Cabinets .... G 574 825-7568
Goshen *(G-6232)*

Orr Cabinet Co .... G 260 636-7757
Albion *(G-39)*

Oxford Cabinet Company LLC .... G 765 223-2101
Liberty *(G-10995)*

Patrick Industries Inc .... G 574 293-1521
Elkhart *(G-3589)*

Paynes Fine Cabrinetry .... G 765 589-9176
Lafayette *(G-10665)*

Peace Valley Cabinets Inc .... G 812 486-3831
Montgomery *(G-12118)*

Philip Konrad & Sons Inc .... F 574 772-3966
Knox *(G-10219)*

Phoenix Custom Kitchens Inc .... G 812 523-1890
Seymour *(G-14674)*

Ponderosa Cabinet Company LLC .... G 260 349-2509
Kendallville *(G-10143)*

Pumpkin Patch Market Inc .... G 574 825-3312
Middlebury *(G-11747)*

R & R Custom Woodworking Inc .... G 574 773-5436
Nappanee *(G-12640)*

Rabb and Howe Cabinet Top Co .... F 317 926-6442
Indianapolis *(G-9258)*

Radel Wood Products Inc .... F 765 472-2940
Peru *(G-13597)*

Rbk Development Inc .... E 574 267-5879
Warsaw *(G-16417)*

Rentown Cabinets LLC .... G 574 546-2569
Bremen *(G-1218)*

Richeson Contracting Inc .... E 317 889-5995
Indianapolis *(G-9304)*

Rmg Cabinetry Inc .... G 219 712-6129
Hammond *(G-6999)*

Robert C Kueber .... G 812 838-5813
Mount Vernon *(G-12317)*

Rogers Cabinetry .... G 574 664-9931
Logansport *(G-11105)*

ROH Custom Cabinetry LLC .... G 260 802-1158
Silver Lake *(G-14921)*

Ronald Chileen Furniture .... G 574 542-4505
Rochester *(G-14321)*

Roomworks LLC .... G 317 846-2090
Carmel *(G-1745)*

Royal Design Custom Kitchens & .... G 260 593-0508
Topeka *(G-15816)*

Rush County Wood Products .... G 765 629-0603
Milroy *(G-11831)*

S & H Cabinets .... G 574 773-7465
Nappanee *(G-12643)*

Saco Industries Inc .... B 219 690-9900
Lowell *(G-11178)*

▼ Schertz Craftsmen Inc .... C 877 472-2782
Grabill *(G-6324)*

Schmidt Cabinetry & Furn LLC .... G 574 862-2200
Wakarusa *(G-16249)*

Schrock .... G 812 636-7842
Odon *(G-13349)*

Scott Bernth .... G 219 926-4836
Otis *(G-13445)*

Shamrock Cabinets Inc .... E 812 482-7969
Jasper *(G-9911)*

Shelby Custom Cabinets Inc .... G 317 398-0344
Shelbyville *(G-14796)*

Signet Cabinetry Inc .... G 812 248-0612
Sellersburg *(G-14614)*

Sims Cabinet Co Inc .... E 317 634-1747
Danville *(G-2828)*

Smith Custom Cabinets .... G 812 342-4797
Columbus *(G-2394)*

Southern Indiana Wdwkg LLC .... G 812 636-0127
Odon *(G-13352)*

Spiceland Wood Products Inc .... F 765 987-8156
Spiceland *(G-15379)*

Strohbeck Cabinet Install .... G 812 923-5013
Floyds Knobs *(G-4694)*

Superior Laminating Inc .... G 574 361-7266
Goshen *(G-6261)*

Talent Cabinet LLC .... G 317 733-2149
Carmel *(G-1775)*

TCS Cabinets .... G 765 208-5350
Summitville *(G-15433)*

Tracaron Designs Inc .... G 317 839-9006
Avon *(G-554)*

Trillium Cabinet Company Inc .... G 317 471-8870
Indianapolis *(G-9642)*

Trucustom Cabinets LLC .... G 812 486-2861
Montgomery *(G-12126)*

V-T Industries Inc .... G 712 368-4381
Shelbyville *(G-14811)*

Vans Cabinet Shop Inc .... G 574 658-9625
Milford *(G-11808)*

Versatile Cab Solid Surfc Inc .... G 574 753-2359
Logansport *(G-11118)*

Village Workshop Inc .... G 812 933-1527
Oldenburg *(G-13359)*

Wabash Valley Cabinet Company .... G 765 337-2859
West Lafayette *(G-16643)*

Wagler Custom Cabinets LLC .... G 812 486-2878
Montgomery *(G-12129)*

▲ Walburn Services Inc .... G 765 289-3383
Muncie *(G-12513)*

▲ Walters Cabinet Shop .... G 765 452-9634
Kokomo *(G-10355)*

Warsaw Custom Cabinet .... G 574 267-5794
Winona Lake *(G-16916)*

Warsaw Custom Cabinet .... G 574 267-5794
Warsaw *(G-16444)*

Washmuth Cabinet Company .... G 765 932-2701
Rushville *(G-14416)*

William R Arvin .... G 812 486-5255
Winslow *(G-16926)*

Wiseman Custom Cabinets Inc .... G 812 678-3601
Dubois *(G-2955)*

Wonning Cabinets .... G 812 522-1608
Seymour *(G-14706)*

Wood Creat By Delagrange Inc .... G 260 657-5525
New Haven *(G-12925)*

Wood Shapes Unlimited Inc .... G 317 861-1775
New Palestine *(G-12945)*

Wood Shoppe .... G 260 758-3453
Huntington *(G-7381)*

Woods Cabinets .... G 812 279-6494
Bedford *(G-684)*

Yoder Kitchen Corp .... E 574 773-3197
Nappanee *(G-12656)*

Yoders Cabinets .... G 812 486-3826
Montgomery *(G-12131)*

Zinn Kitchens Inc .... E 574 967-4179
Bringhurst *(G-1239)*

Zionsville Custom Cabinets LLC .... G 317 339-0380
Zionsville *(G-17063)*

2435 Hardwood veneer and plywood

◆ Amos-Hill Associates Inc .... C 812 526-2671
Edinburgh *(G-3067)*

Besse Veneers Inc .... E 906 428-3113
Trafalgar *(G-15826)*

Chisholm Lumber & Supply Co .... E 317 547-3535
Indianapolis *(G-7799)*

Custom Plywood Inc .... E 812 944-7300
New Albany *(G-12717)*

D & M Sales LLC .... G 574 825-9024
Middlebury *(G-11710)*

◆ Danzer Services Inc .... G 812 526-2601
Edinburgh *(G-3074)*

Danzer Veneer Americas Inc .... F 812 526-6789
Edinburgh *(G-3075)*

Dimension Plywood Inc .... G 812 944-6491
New Albany *(G-12719)*

E M Cummings Veneers Inc .... E 812 944-2269
New Albany *(G-12722)*

▲ Flexible Materials Inc .... D 812 280-7000
Jeffersonville *(G-9984)*

▲ Form Wood Industries Inc .... E 812 284-3676
Jeffersonville *(G-9986)*

Grizzly Ridge Hardwoods LLC .... G 574 546-3600
Bremen *(G-1194)*

▲ Heitink Veneers Incorporated .... E 812 336-6436
Bloomington *(G-876)*

Heritage Hardwoods KY Inc .... D 812 288-5855
Jeffersonville *(G-9994)*

Heritage Unlimited LLC .... G 574 538-8021
Goshen *(G-6164)*

Hoehn Hardwoods .... G 812 968-3242
Corydon *(G-2498)*

▲ Indiana Architectural Plywood .... E 317 878-4822
Trafalgar *(G-15829)*

◆ Indiana Veneers Corp .... D 317 926-2458
Indianapolis *(G-8499)*

J Pinto Wood and Veneer Corp .... G 317 389-0440
Indianapolis *(G-8608)*

Jasper Veneer Inc .... F 812 482-4245
Jasper *(G-9859)*

Kimball Furniture Group LLC .... B 812 482-8401
Jasper *(G-9871)*

Land of Indiana Inc .... F 812 788-1560
Bedford *(G-654)*

▼ Louisville Veneer Corp .... G 502 500-7176
New Albany *(G-12765)*

Marwood Sales Co .... G 812 288-8344
Jeffersonville *(G-10017)*

▼ Miller Veneers Inc .... C 317 638-2326
Indianapolis *(G-8923)*

▼ Mitchell Veneers Inc .... G 812 941-9663
New Albany *(G-12781)*

◆ Norstam Veneers Inc .... D 812 732-4391
Mauckport *(G-11441)*

Patrick Industries Inc .... D 574 294-8828
Elkhart *(G-3592)*

Patrick Industries Inc .... D 574 522-7710
Elkhart *(G-3598)*

▲ Patrick Industries Inc .... B 574 294-7511
Elkhart *(G-3593)*

◆ Pleasant Hill Veneer Corp .... G 812 725-8924
Jeffersonville *(G-10039)*

24 LUMBER AND WOOD PRODUCTS, EXCEPT FURNITURE

Powers Hardwoods .... G 260 665-5498
  Angola *(G-286)*

▲ Robert Weed Plywood Corp .... B 574 848-7631
  Bristol *(G-1288)*

Sexton Plywood & Veneer Co .... G 812 454-0488
  Evansville *(G-4308)*

Sims-Lohman Inc .... G 317 467-0710
  Greenfield *(G-6553)*

Stemwood Corp .... E 812 945-6646
  New Albany *(G-12818)*

Superior Veneer & Plywood LLC .... G 812 941-8850
  New Albany *(G-12819)*

Universal Frest Pdts Ind Ltd P .... E 574 273-6326
  Granger *(G-6388)*

Veneer Curry Sales LLC .... F 812 945-6623
  New Albany *(G-12823)*

Wholesale Hrdwood Intriors Inc .... F 317 867-3660
  Westfield *(G-16740)*

Wible Lumber Inc .... E 260 351-2441
  South Milford *(G-15314)*

2436 Softwood veneer and plywood

Douglas Dye and Associates Inc .... G 317 844-1709
  Carmel *(G-1611)*

FM Holdings LLC .... G 574 773-2814
  Nappanee *(G-12597)*

▲ HI Tech Veneer LLC .... E 812 284-9775
  Jeffersonville *(G-9995)*

▲ JDC Veneers Inc .... D 812 284-9775
  Jeffersonville *(G-10003)*

Kimball Furniture Group LLC .... B 812 482-8401
  Jasper *(G-9871)*

◆ Pleasant Hill Veneer Corp .... G 812 725-8924
  Jeffersonville *(G-10039)*

2439 Structural wood members, nec

Beachwood Lumber Co Inc .... G 574 858-9325
  Warsaw *(G-16319)*

◆ Brenco LLC .... G 219 844-9570
  Schererville *(G-14517)*

Carter Lee Building Component .... E 317 834-5380
  Mooresville *(G-12199)*

Carter-Lee Building Components .... E 317 639-5431
  Indianapolis *(G-7752)*

Classic Truss WD Cmponents Inc .... E 812 944-5821
  Clarksville *(G-2014)*

Composite Designs Inc .... F 574 453-2902
  Leesburg *(G-10953)*

Continntal Crpntrny Cmpnnts LLC .... E 219 733-0367
  Wanatah *(G-16289)*

Daviess County Metal Sales .... D 812 486-4299
  Cannelburg *(G-1530)*

Georgetown Truss Company Inc .... E 812 951-2647
  Georgetown *(G-6061)*

Ghk Truss LLC .... E 812 282-6600
  Clarksville *(G-2016)*

Girod Truss LLC .... G 260 442-8240
  New Haven *(G-12904)*

Glue-Lam Erectors Inc .... F 317 878-9717
  Trafalgar *(G-15827)*

Goldstar Truss LLC .... G 765 366-2679
  Veedersburg *(G-16088)*

Interstate Truss LLC .... G 260 463-6124
  Shipshewana *(G-14854)*

James G Henager .... G 812 795-2230
  Elberfeld *(G-3115)*

▼ K & K Industries Inc .... D 812 486-3281
  Montgomery *(G-12104)*

Kerkhoff Associates Inc .... E 765 583-4491
  Otterbein *(G-13453)*

Martin Truss Mfg LLC .... G 574 862-4457
  Elkhart *(G-3517)*

North Webster Construction Inc .... E 574 834-4448
  North Webster *(G-13310)*

Northern Indiana Truss LLC .... E 574 858-0505
  Warsaw *(G-16402)*

Osterholt Construction Inc .... G 260 672-3493
  Huntington *(G-7348)*

Protec Panel & Truss Mfg LLC .... D 574 281-9080
  Bremen *(G-1215)*

Stark Truss Company Inc .... D 219 866-2772
  Rensselaer *(G-14070)*

Superior Truss & Panel Inc .... E 708 339-1200
  Gary *(G-6016)*

Truss Systems Inc .... F 812 897-3064
  Boonville *(G-1100)*

Trusslink .... G 219 362-3968
  La Porte *(G-10496)*

Tyler Truss Systems Inc .... F 765 221-5050
  Pendleton *(G-13560)*

Ufp Granger LLC .... E 574 277-7670
  Granger *(G-6387)*

US Lbm Operating Co 3009 LLC .... G 812 464-2428
  Evansville *(G-4364)*

Wagner Truss Manufacturing Inc .... G 812 852-2206
  Napoleon *(G-12576)*

White Water Truss Llc .... G 765 489-6261
  Hagerstown *(G-6847)*

2441 Nailed wood boxes and shook

A S M Inc .... G 260 724-8220
  Decatur *(G-2839)*

American Fibertech Corporation .... D 219 261-3586
  Lafayette *(G-10521)*

Ash-Lin Inc .... F 317 861-1540
  Fountaintown *(G-5613)*

C & C Mailbox Products .... G 765 358-4880
  Gaston *(G-6044)*

C E Kersting & Sons .... G 574 896-2766
  North Judson *(G-13207)*

Findley Foster Corp .... G 812 524-7279
  Seymour *(G-14653)*

Hoosier Box and Skid Inc .... G 574 256-2111
  Mishawaka *(G-11908)*

Indiana Wood Products Inc .... D 574 825-2129
  Middlebury *(G-11724)*

▼ Industrial Woodkraft Inc .... E 812 897-4893
  Boonville *(G-1087)*

JR Grber Sons Fmly Ltd Prtnr .... G 260 657-1071
  Grabill *(G-6307)*

Knox Cnty Assn For Rmrkble Ctz .... D 812 886-4312
  Vincennes *(G-16136)*

Leclere Manufacturing Inc .... G 812 683-5627
  Jasper *(G-9882)*

Meyer Custom Woodworking Inc .... G 812 695-2021
  Dubois *(G-2954)*

Millers Wood Specialties Inc .... E 765 478-3248
  Cambridge City *(G-1499)*

Monrovlle Box Pllet WD Pdts LL .... E 260 623-3128
  Monroeville *(G-12071)*

Whitakerr Dalemon .... G 812 738-2396
  Corydon *(G-2522)*

2448 Wood pallets and skids

421 Pallet & Crate .... G 765 249-5088
  Frankfort *(G-5647)*

A One Pallet Inc .... G 859 282-6137
  Greendale *(G-6436)*

A Pallet Company .... G 317 687-9020
  Indianapolis *(G-7401)*

A S M Inc .... G 260 724-8220
  Decatur *(G-2839)*

A-1 Pallet Co Inc Clarksville .... E 812 288-6339
  Clarksville *(G-2005)*

A-1 Pallet Co of Clarksville .... G 812 288-6339
  Clarksville *(G-2006)*

A1 Pallet Liquidators .... G 765 356-4020
  Anderson *(G-70)*

A1 Pallets Inc .... G 812 425-0381
  Evansville *(G-3862)*

Alsip Pallet Company Inc .... G 219 322-3288
  Schererville *(G-14513)*

American Fibertech Corporation .... D 219 261-3586
  Lafayette *(G-10521)*

American Fibertech Corporation .... D 219 261-3586
  Remington *(G-14033)*

American Pallet & Recycl Inc .... G 219 322-4391
  Dyer *(G-2966)*

Anthony Wyne Rhbittion Ctr For .... D 260 744-6145
  Fort Wayne *(G-4762)*

Artistic Composite Pallets LLC .... E 317 960-5813
  Carmel *(G-1565)*

Ash-Lin Inc .... F 317 861-1540
  Fountaintown *(G-5613)*

Axtrom Inds Pallet Div LLC .... G 812 859-4873
  Freedom *(G-5797)*

Billy D Snider .... G 765 795-6426
  Cloverdale *(G-2083)*

Bristol Pallet .... G 574 862-1862
  Goshen *(G-6100)*

Buckeye Diamond Logistics Inc .... G 317 524-9304
  Indianapolis *(G-7698)*

Buckingham Pallets Inc .... G 317 846-8601
  Carmel *(G-1574)*

Burton Lumber Co Inc .... F 812 866-4438
  Lexington *(G-10975)*

C & C Pallets and Lumber LLC .... G 765 524-3214
  New Castle *(G-12855)*

C C Cook and Son Lbr Co Inc .... E 765 672-4235
  Reelsville *(G-14030)*

C E Kersting & Sons .... G 574 896-2766
  North Judson *(G-13207)*

Calumet Pallet Company Inc .... D 219 932-4550
  Michigan City *(G-11584)*

Chep (usa) Inc .... G 317 780-0700
  Indianapolis *(G-7795)*

Columbus Pallet Corp .... G 812 372-7272
  Columbus *(G-2246)*

Commercial Pallet Recycl Inc .... G 260 668-6208
  Hudson *(G-7245)*

Commercial Pallet Recycl Inc .... F 260 829-1021
  Orland *(G-13362)*

Conner Sawmill Inc .... F 574 626-3227
  Walton *(G-16282)*

Coomer & Sons Sawmill Inc .... D 765 659-2846
  Frankfort *(G-5655)*

Corey Kerst .... G 765 585-3026
  Attica *(G-346)*

Corr-Wood Manufacturing Inc .... G 812 867-0700
  Evansville *(G-3984)*

Custom Pallet Recycl Trnsp LLC .... G 317 903-4447
  Indianapolis *(G-7934)*

Danwood Industries .... G 219 369-1484
  La Porte *(G-10399)*

Dehart Pallet & Lumber Co .... F 812 794-2974
  Austin *(G-464)*

Dodd Sawmills Incorporated .... F 812 268-4811
  Sullivan *(G-15405)*

Duro Inc .... G 574 293-6860
  Elkhart *(G-3305)*

Duro Recycling Inc .... F 574 522-2572
  Elkhart *(G-3306)*

Ernest A Cooper .... F 812 284-0436
  Jeffersonville *(G-9980)*

Evansville Pallets .... G 812 550-0199
  Evansville *(G-4056)*

SIC SECTION
24 LUMBER AND WOOD PRODUCTS, EXCEPT FURNITURE

Fca LLC .... G 765 448-1775
   Lafayette *(G-10578)*

Findley Foster Corp .... G 812 524-7279
   Seymour *(G-14653)*

Ford Sawmills Inc .... F 812 324-2134
   Vincennes *(G-16125)*

Fowler Ridge IV Wind Farm LLC ...... G 765 884-1029
   Fowler *(G-5624)*

Gonzalez Pallets .... G 317 644-1242
   Indianapolis *(G-8303)*

Graber Box Pllet Fmly Ltd Prtn .... E 260 657-5657
   Grabill *(G-6296)*

Green Stream Company .... C 574 293-1949
   Elkhart *(G-3391)*

Greene County Pallets Inc .... F 812 384-8362
   Bloomfield *(G-746)*

H & A Products Inc .... G 574 226-0079
   Elkhart *(G-3394)*

H & M Bay Inc .... F 410 463-5430
   Fort Wayne *(G-5046)*

H H Pallet .... G 765 505-1682
   Crawfordsville *(G-2575)*

H H Pallet .... G 765 323-3117
   Crawfordsville *(G-2576)*

Hagemier Products .... G 812 526-0377
   Franklin *(G-5737)*

Henry Street LLC .... D 317 788-7225
   Franklin *(G-5738)*

Hillcrest Pallet Incorporated .... G 812 883-3636
   Salem *(G-14480)*

Hoosier Box and Skid Inc .... G 574 256-2111
   Mishawaka *(G-11908)*

Hoosier Pallet Inc .... G 765 629-2899
   Milroy *(G-11825)*

Independent Pallet LLC .... G 502 356-2757
   Sellersburg *(G-14601)*

Indiana Pallet Company .... E 219 398-4223
   East Chicago *(G-3022)*

Indiana Wood Products Inc .... D 574 825-2129
   Middlebury *(G-11724)*

Industrial Lumber Products Inc .... G 219 324-7697
   La Porte *(G-10427)*

Industrial Woodkraft Inc .... G 812 827-6544
   Jasper *(G-9846)*

▼ Industrial Woodkraft Inc .... E 812 897-4893
   Boonville *(G-1087)*

J & J Pallet Corp .... D 812 288-4487
   Clarksville *(G-2020)*

J & J Pallet Corp .... E 812 944-8670
   New Albany *(G-12750)*

Jennings County Pallets Inc .... E 812 458-6288
   Butlerville *(G-1484)*

Jennings County Pallets Inc .... E 812 458-6288
   Butlerville *(G-1485)*

Jodo Investments Inc .... E 765 651-0200
   Marion *(G-11301)*

JR Grber Sons Fmly Ltd Prtnr .... G 260 657-1071
   Grabill *(G-6307)*

K & S Pallet Inc .... E 260 422-1264
   Fort Wayne *(G-5141)*

Kamps Inc .... E 317 634-8360
   Indianapolis *(G-8659)*

Kentuckiana Wood Products Inc .... E 812 288-7989
   Jeffersonville *(G-10006)*

Knox Cnty Assn For Rmrkble Ctz ...... D 812 886-4312
   Vincennes *(G-16136)*

Leclere Manufacturing Inc .... G 812 683-5627
   Jasper *(G-9882)*

Lovett Pallet Recycling LLC .... G 317 638-4840
   Indianapolis *(G-8787)*

Mader Mill Inc .... G 812 876-9754
   Spencer *(G-15354)*

Matco Pallets .... G 260 223-0585
   Decatur *(G-2872)*

Meagan Inc .... E 574 267-8626
   Warsaw *(G-16393)*

Megan Inc .... F 574 267-8626
   Warsaw *(G-16397)*

Michiana Pallet Recycle Inc .... G 574 232-8566
   South Bend *(G-15149)*

Midwestern Pallet Service Inc .... G 260 563-1526
   Wabash *(G-16202)*

Millwood Box & Pallet .... G 765 628-7330
   Kokomo *(G-10310)*

Milroy Pallet Inc .... G 765 629-2919
   Milroy *(G-11828)*

Monrovlle Box Pllet WD Pdts LL .... E 260 623-3128
   Monroeville *(G-12071)*

Muro Pallets Corporation .... G 219 803-0500
   Hammond *(G-6985)*

Myers Wood Products .... G 765 597-2147
   Bloomingdale *(G-761)*

Neumayr Lumber Co Inc .... F 765 764-4148
   Attica *(G-353)*

Newport Pallet Inc .... G 217 497-8220
   Newport *(G-13031)*

Newport Pallet Inc .... E 765 505-9463
   Hillsdale *(G-7163)*

North Central Pallets Inc .... E 574 892-6142
   Argos *(G-325)*

Off The Pallet LLC .... G 317 674-2711
   Westfield *(G-16713)*

Oldenburg Pallet Inc .... G 812 933-0568
   Batesville *(G-599)*

Owen County Pallet LLC .... G 812 384-6568
   Worthington *(G-16962)*

Pallet Builder Inc .... G 765 948-3345
   Fairmount *(G-4412)*

Pallet Builder Inc .... G 765 584-1441
   Winchester *(G-16897)*

Pallet Depot .... G 317 897-1774
   Indianapolis *(G-9088)*

Pallet Recyclers LLC .... G 812 402-0095
   Evansville *(G-4232)*

Pallet Subs LLC .... D 260 768-4021
   Shipshewana *(G-14875)*

Palletone Inc .... G 260 768-4021
   Shipshewana *(G-14876)*

Palletone of Indiana Inc .... D 260 768-4021
   Shipshewana *(G-14877)*

Perfect Pallets Inc .... F 888 553-5559
   Indianapolis *(G-9123)*

Peru Hardwood Products Inc .... F 765 473-4844
   Peru *(G-13592)*

Plymouth Pallet Company Inc .... F 574 935-5553
   Plymouth *(G-13803)*

Powell Systems Inc .... E 765 884-0980
   Fowler *(G-5630)*

Powell Systems Inc .... G 765 884-0613
   Fowler *(G-5631)*

Premier Lumber Company Inc .... G 219 801-6018
   Chesterton *(G-1954)*

Pro Pallet LLC .... G 219 292-3389
   Gary *(G-5996)*

Professional Pallets LLC .... F 859 393-4328
   Greendale *(G-6454)*

Quality Fence Ltd .... G 260 768-4986
   Shipshewana *(G-14880)*

Quality Pallet .... G 765 348-4840
   Hartford City *(G-7075)*

Quality Pallet .... G 765 212-2215
   Muncie *(G-12482)*

Quality Pallet Recycling LLC .... G 317 840-5990
   Rushville *(G-14408)*

Quality Pallets Inc .... G 812 873-6818
   Commiskey *(G-2421)*

R & E Pallet Inc .... G 219 873-9671
   Michigan City *(G-11655)*

Rhino Shipping Solutions LLC .... G 317 721-9476
   Fishers *(G-4649)*

Richard Squier Pallets Inc .... F 260 281-2434
   Waterloo *(G-16530)*

Rick Hollingshead .... G 765 833-2846
   Roann *(G-14253)*

Rs Pallet Inc .... G 574 596-8777
   Bristol *(G-1289)*

Satco Inc .... D 317 856-0301
   Indianapolis *(G-9377)*

Schneiders Wood Shop Inc .... G 812 522-4621
   Seymour *(G-14684)*

Schwartzville Pallet .... G 260 244-4144
   Columbia City *(G-2196)*

Servants Inc .... D 812 634-2201
   Jasper *(G-9910)*

Sonlite Pallet Services Inc .... G 219 798-5003
   Merrillville *(G-11561)*

Sparkman Pallet & Lumber Inc .... G 812 873-6052
   Commiskey *(G-2422)*

Steves Pallets .... G 260 856-2047
   Cromwell *(G-2633)*

Steves Pallets Inc .... G 574 457-3620
   Syracuse *(G-15480)*

Tc Pallets & Peddler Sweet LLC .... G 812 283-1090
   Jeffersonville *(G-10063)*

Total Quality Pallets Inc .... G 317 822-9888
   Indianapolis *(G-9624)*

Trinity Cstm Built Pallets LLC .... G 260 466-4625
   New Haven *(G-12923)*

Ufp Granger LLC .... E 574 277-7670
   Granger *(G-6387)*

Ufp Structural Packaging LLC .... G 574 773-2505
   Nappanee *(G-12650)*

Vision IV Inc .... E 812 423-0119
   Evansville *(G-4376)*

W & W Pallet Co LLC .... G 812 486-3548
   Montgomery *(G-12128)*

W-M Lumber and Wood Pdts Inc ...... F 812 944-6711
   New Albany *(G-12826)*

Wabash Heritage Mfg LLC .... G 812 886-0147
   Vincennes *(G-16161)*

Whitakerr Dalemon .... G 812 738-2396
   Corydon *(G-2522)*

Williams Quality Pallets Inc .... G 770 265-1030
   Huntertown *(G-7269)*

Wood Pile Pallet Company LLC .... F 317 750-9272
   Marion *(G-11351)*

X-L Box Inc .... F 219 763-3736
   Valparaiso *(G-16082)*

2449 Wood containers, nec

A S M Inc .... G 260 724-8220
   Decatur *(G-2839)*

A-1 Pallet Co of Clarksville .... G 812 288-6339
   Clarksville *(G-2006)*

American Fibertech Corporation .... D 219 261-3586
   Lafayette *(G-10521)*

Anthony Wyne Rhblttion Ctr For .... D 260 744-6145
   Fort Wayne *(G-4762)*

Bryan Ward .... G 812 696-5126
   Farmersburg *(G-4417)*

Case Indy Products Inc .... G 317 677-0200
   Indianapolis *(G-7753)*

▲ CH Ellis Co Inc .... E 317 636-3351
   Indianapolis *(G-7782)*

Conner Sawmill Inc .... F 574 626-3227
   Walton *(G-16282)*

Employee Codes: A=Over 500 employees, B=251-500
C=101-250, D=51-100, E=20-50, F=10-19, G=1-9

24 LUMBER AND WOOD PRODUCTS, EXCEPT FURNITURE

Corr-Wood Manufacturing Inc .... G 812 867-0700
  Evansville *(G-3984)*
Gordon Lumber Company .... G 219 924-0500
  Griffith *(G-6804)*
▼ Industrial Woodkraft Inc .... E 812 897-4893
  Boonville *(G-1087)*
JR Graber & Sons LLC .... G 260 657-1071
  Grabill *(G-6306)*
Knights Woodworking LLC .... G 812 988-2106
  Nashville *(G-12673)*
Marys Gift Baskets LLC .... G 502 819-3022
  Georgetown *(G-6069)*
Southern Indiana Hardwoods Inc .... E 812 326-2053
  Huntingburg *(G-7291)*
◆ Star Case Manufacturing Co LLC .... E 219 922-4440
  Munster *(G-12565)*
Timber Line Crating LP .... G 260 238-3075
  Spencerville *(G-15375)*
W & M Enterprises Inc .... F 812 537-4656
  Lawrenceburg *(G-10865)*
Zehrhaus Inc .... G 260 486-3198
  Fort Wayne *(G-5583)*

2451 Mobile homes

Accent Complex Inc .... G 574 522-2368
  Elkhart *(G-3148)*
Autumn Makers Mobile HM Subdv .... G 765 759-7878
  Yorktown *(G-16970)*
Bayview Estates .... G 574 457-4136
  Syracuse *(G-15456)*
Beck Industries LP .... D 574 294-5621
  Elkhart *(G-3221)*
Bilbees Service and Supply Inc .... G 317 895-8288
  Indianapolis *(G-7625)*
Commercial Structures Corp .... G 574 773-7931
  Goshen *(G-6115)*
Commercial Structures Corp .... E 574 773-7931
  Nappanee *(G-12590)*
Dutchtown Homes Inc .... G 812 354-2197
  Petersburg *(G-13610)*
Fr Chinook LLC .... G 317 356-1666
  Indianapolis *(G-8219)*
◆ Gulf Stream Coach Inc .... C 574 773-7761
  Nappanee *(G-12603)*
Heritage Financial Group Inc .... E 574 522-8000
  Elkhart *(G-3404)*
Home Phone Inc .... G 812 941-8551
  Jeffersonville *(G-9997)*
Jobsite Trailer Corporation .... E 574 224-4000
  Rochester *(G-14298)*
Kropf Industries Inc .... E 574 533-2171
  Goshen *(G-6192)*
Lcf Enterprises LLC .... G 260 483-3248
  Fort Wayne *(G-5179)*
Mark-Line Industries LLC .... C 574 825-5851
  Bristol *(G-1273)*
Modular Builders Inc .... G 574 223-4934
  Rochester *(G-14309)*
Rev Recreation Group Inc .... D 260 724-4217
  Decatur *(G-2879)*
Rochester Homes Inc .... C 574 223-4321
  Rochester *(G-14317)*
Rodeswood LLC .... G 574 457-4496
  Syracuse *(G-15476)*
Schult Homes Corp .... F 574 825-5880
  Middlebury *(G-11750)*
Skyline Corporation .... C 574 294-2463
  Elkhart *(G-3682)*
Skyline Homes Inc .... E 574 294-6521
  Elkhart *(G-3683)*
Softexpert Usa LLC .... G 260 925-7674
  Auburn *(G-424)*
Thermo Bond Buildings LLC .... D 574 295-1214
  Elkhart *(G-3726)*
Thornes Homes Inc .... G 812 275-4656
  Bedford *(G-678)*
Trophy Homes Inc .... E 574 264-4911
  Elkhart *(G-3748)*
Whitley Evergreen Inc .... F 260 723-5131
  South Whitley *(G-15331)*
Willow Creek Crossing Inc .... G 219 809-8952
  La Porte *(G-10500)*
Woodland Park Inc .... E 574 825-2104
  Middlebury *(G-11760)*
▲ Zieman Manufacturing Comp .... C 574 535-1125
  Goshen *(G-6279)*

2452 Prefabricated wood buildings

(ebs Cmpstes Engnred Bnded Str .... F 574 266-3471
  Elkhart *(G-3136)*
Affordable Luxury Homes Inc .... D 260 758-2141
  Markle *(G-11353)*
All American Group Inc .... G 574 262-0123
  Elkhart *(G-3161)*
◆ All American Group Inc .... E 574 262-0123
  Elkhart *(G-3160)*
All American Homes LLC .... E 574 266-3044
  Elkhart *(G-3162)*
All American Homes Indiana LLC .... G 260 724-9171
  Decatur *(G-2843)*
Appalachian Log Structures .... G 812 744-5711
  Moores Hill *(G-12186)*
Burns Construction Inc .... E 574 382-2315
  Macy *(G-11195)*
Classic Buildings Inc .... E 812 944-5821
  Clarksville *(G-2013)*
Colluci Construction-Log Homes .... G 812 843-5607
  English *(G-3840)*
Commodore Homes LLC .... A 574 533-7100
  Elkhart *(G-3258)*
Continntal Crpntry Cmpnnts LLC .... E 219 733-0367
  Wanatah *(G-16289)*
Country Charm .... G 765 572-2588
  Attica *(G-347)*
Countrymark Log Homes Inc .... G 866 468-3301
  Vevay *(G-16107)*
Craftech Building Systems Inc .... E 574 773-4167
  Nappanee *(G-12592)*
Custom Built Barns Inc .... G 765 457-9037
  Kokomo *(G-10253)*
Custom Sheds Plus LLC .... G 260 215-3988
  Syracuse *(G-15460)*
Delaware County Home Bldrs Inc .... G 765 289-6328
  Muncie *(G-12377)*
E & L Construction Inc .... G 765 525-7081
  Manilla *(G-11260)*
Expedition Log Homes .... G 219 663-5555
  Crown Point *(G-2683)*
Heritage Log Homes .... G 812 427-2591
  Vevay *(G-16110)*
Homestead Barns LLC .... E 740 624-0997
  Greencastle *(G-6413)*
Homette Corporation .... G 574 294-6521
  Elkhart *(G-3410)*
Indiana Operations LLC .... E 812 847-8924
  Linton *(G-11035)*
Itera LLC .... G 574 538-3838
  New Paris *(G-12961)*
Jobsite Trailer Corporation .... E 574 224-4000
  Rochester *(G-14298)*
Lakeside Manor .... E 219 362-3956
  La Porte *(G-10445)*
Landmark Home & Land Company ...... G 219 874-4065
  Michigan City *(G-11630)*

Lauer Log Homes Inc .... G 260 486-7010
  Fort Wayne *(G-5176)*
Lawrenceburg Mini Barns .... G 513 290-5794
  Lawrenceburg *(G-10844)*
Light House Center Inc .... F 765 448-4502
  Lafayette *(G-10636)*
Mbsi Holdings LLC .... G 574 295-1214
  Elkhart *(G-3520)*
Midwest Fast Structures LLC .... G 812 886-3060
  Vincennes *(G-16139)*
Miller Brothers Builders Inc .... E 574 533-8602
  Goshen *(G-6222)*
Milroy Spindle Shop .... G 765 629-2176
  Milroy *(G-11829)*
Mobile/Modular Express II LLC .... G 574 295-1214
  Elkhart *(G-3548)*
Modular Builders Inc .... G 574 223-4934
  Rochester *(G-14309)*
Morton Buildings Inc .... F 260 563-2118
  Wabash *(G-16204)*
Mosier Pallet & Lumber Co .... G 812 366-4817
  Corydon *(G-2506)*
Napoleon Lumber Co .... G 812 852-4545
  Napoleon *(G-12575)*
Omega National Products LLC .... C 574 295-5353
  Elkhart *(G-3579)*
Permabase Building Pdts LLC .... G 765 828-0898
  Clinton *(G-2075)*
▲ Quality Hardwood Sales LLC .... D 574 773-2505
  Nappanee *(G-12639)*
Rochester Homes Inc .... C 574 223-4321
  Rochester *(G-14317)*
RPI Components Inc .... G 574 536-2283
  Elkhart *(G-3653)*
Schroeder Log Home Supply Inc .... G 574 825-1054
  Middlebury *(G-11749)*
Sidney & Janice Bond .... G 812 366-8160
  Floyds Knobs *(G-4693)*
Skyline Champion Corporation .... G 574 294-6521
  Elkhart *(G-3681)*
The Commodore Corporation .... E 574 533-7100
  Elkhart *(G-3724)*
TNT Construction .... G 260 726-2643
  Portland *(G-13972)*
Tomahawk Log & County Homes .... G 260 833-6429
  Angola *(G-301)*
Travis C and Jan B Page .... G 812 398-5507
  Carlisle *(G-1544)*
Tuff Shed Inc .... G 317 481-8388
  Indianapolis *(G-9659)*
Tuff Shed Inc .... F 317 774-2981
  Noblesville *(G-13186)*
Ufp Nappanee LLC .... D 574 773-2505
  Nappanee *(G-12649)*
Wagler Mini Barn Products LLC .... G 812 687-7372
  Plainville *(G-13747)*
Woodland Manufacturing & Sup .... F 317 271-2266
  Avon *(G-557)*

2491 Wood preserving

Birch Wood .... G 260 432-0011
  Fort Wayne *(G-4803)*
▲ FTC Liquidation Inc .... F 574 295-6700
  Elkhart *(G-3359)*
Hampels Woodland Products .... G 574 293-2124
  Elkhart *(G-3397)*
Jefferson Homebuilders Inc .... G 317 398-3125
  Shelbyville *(G-14765)*
Kustom Kilns LLC .... G 317 512-5813
  Columbus *(G-2337)*
Preserving Past .... G 574 835-0833
  Elkhart *(G-3618)*

SIC SECTION
24 LUMBER AND WOOD PRODUCTS, EXCEPT FURNITURE

▲ Primix Corporation .... G 574 858-0069
   Atwood *(G-357)*

Pumpkin Patch Market Inc .... G 574 825-3312
   Middlebury *(G-11747)*

Rookstools Pier Shop Inc .... E 574 453-4771
   Leesburg *(G-10960)*

Southeast Wood Treating Inc .... C 765 962-4077
   Richmond *(G-14206)*

Steinkamp Warehouses Inc .... E 812 683-3860
   Huntingburg *(G-7292)*

Stella-Jones Corporation .... E 812 789-5331
   Winslow *(G-16924)*

Tangent Rail Products Inc .... E 412 325-0202
   Terre Haute *(G-15723)*

Universal Frest Pdts Ind Ltd P .... E 574 273-6326
   Granger *(G-6388)*

2493 Reconstituted wood products

GAF .... G 219 872-1111
   Michigan City *(G-11616)*

Good Earth Compost LLC .... G 812 824-7928
   Bloomington *(G-868)*

Kay Company Inc .... E 765 659-3388
   Frankfort *(G-5677)*

Michiana Column & Truss LLC .... G 574 862-2828
   Goshen *(G-6220)*

Patrick Industries Inc .... D 574 294-8828
   Elkhart *(G-3592)*

Patrick Industries Inc .... G 574 294-5758
   Elkhart *(G-3596)*

▲ Patrick Industries Inc .... B 574 294-7511
   Elkhart *(G-3593)*

Proline Spray Foam Inc .... G 317 981-2158
   Indianapolis *(G-9229)*

Standard Industries Inc .... G 219 872-1111
   Michigan City *(G-11672)*

Standard Industries Inc .... G 812 838-4861
   Mount Vernon *(G-12323)*

Structural Composites LLC .... E 574 294-7511
   Elkhart *(G-3701)*

2499 Wood products, nec

A S M Inc .... G 260 724-8220
   Decatur *(G-2839)*

Action Cooling Towers Inc .... G 219 285-2660
   Morocco *(G-12267)*

Alpine Enterprises .... G 574 773-5475
   Nappanee *(G-12578)*

American Adventures Inc .... G 574 875-6850
   Elkhart *(G-3170)*

American Wedge Company .... G 812 883-1086
   Salem *(G-14472)*

Anndys Paradise LLC .... G 317 258-7531
   Indianapolis *(G-7519)*

Antler Creek Woodworking LLC .... G 812 636-0188
   Odon *(G-13330)*

Automated Routing Inc .... C 812 357-2429
   Saint Meinrad *(G-14460)*

Bello Custom Woodcrafts .... G 574 314-5973
   Mishawaka *(G-11850)*

Buckaroos Inc .... G 317 899-9100
   Indianapolis *(G-7696)*

Bushwood Ventures Htc LLC .... G 317 523-0991
   Fishers *(G-4640)*

Ccd Northwoods LLC .... G 219 690-1868
   Lowell *(G-11158)*

Champion Wood Products Inc .... G 812 282-9460
   Sellersburg *(G-14591)*

Claridges Wood Shop .... G 812 536-2569
   Stendal *(G-15398)*

Cleveland-Cliffs Kote LP .... B 574 654-1000
   New Carlisle *(G-12837)*

Clm Pallet Recycling Inc .... G 317 485-4080
   Fortville *(G-5589)*

Corr-Wood Manufacturing Inc .... G 812 867-0700
   Evansville *(G-3984)*

Countertop Manufacturing Inc .... E 765 966-4969
   Richmond *(G-14111)*

County Line Woodworking .... G 574 935-7107
   Bremen *(G-1183)*

Custom Woodwork Design LLC .... G 317 254-1358
   Indianapolis *(G-7936)*

Daed Toolworks .... G 317 861-7419
   Greenfield *(G-6486)*

Deer Ridgewood Craft LLC .... G 812 535-3744
   West Terre Haute *(G-16651)*

Deonta Walker .... G 317 970-3586
   Indianapolis *(G-7965)*

Detweilers Cabinet Shop .... G 765 629-2698
   Milroy *(G-11823)*

Dutch Country Woodworking Inc .... G 260 499-4847
   Lagrange *(G-10734)*

Dynamic Designs Scottys .... G 219 809-7268
   Michigan City *(G-11605)*

Earth First Kentuckiana Inc .... F 812 923-1227
   Charlestown *(G-1875)*

Editions Ltd Gllery Fine Art I .... G 317 466-9940
   Indianapolis *(G-8055)*

Engineered Dock Systems Inc .... G 317 803-2443
   Indianapolis *(G-8120)*

Esarey Hardwood Creations LLC .... G 419 610-6486
   New Albany *(G-12726)*

FDS Northwood LLC .... G 765 289-2481
   Muncie *(G-12392)*

Fitch Enterprises Inc .... G 260 672-8462
   Roanoke *(G-14264)*

G & J .... G 765 457-9889
   Kokomo *(G-10268)*

Gessner Woodworking .... G 812 389-2594
   Celestine *(G-1841)*

Gibbs Susie Framing & Art .... G 765 428-2434
   Lafayette *(G-10589)*

Gowdy Woodworks .... G 574 293-4399
   Elkhart *(G-3385)*

Grace Henderson .... G 765 661-9063
   Marion *(G-11289)*

Greencycle of Indiana Inc .... G 317 780-8175
   Indianapolis *(G-8318)*

Greencycle of Indiana Inc .... G 317 769-5668
   Whitestown *(G-16808)*

Greenwood Ladies Auxiliary 252 .... G 317 788-8458
   Indianapolis *(G-8325)*

H J J Inc .... G 219 362-4421
   La Porte *(G-10414)*

Harder Woods .... G 402 572-0433
   Goshen *(G-6161)*

Hardwoods By Bill LLC .... G 219 465-5346
   Valparaiso *(G-15959)*

Hartley J Company Inc .... G 812 376-9708
   Hartsville *(G-7082)*

◆ Herff Jones LLC .... C 317 297-3741
   Indianapolis *(G-8383)*

Heritage Custom Products .... G 812 425-8639
   Evansville *(G-4105)*

Hilltop Wood Working .... G 270 604-1962
   Madison *(G-11225)*

Holman Lumber LLC .... G 260 337-0338
   Saint Joe *(G-14438)*

Indiwoodworks Company .... G 317 283-6931
   Indianapolis *(G-8515)*

J M Woodworking Co Inc .... G 260 627-8362
   Grabill *(G-6304)*

J R Newby .... G 765 664-3501
   Marion *(G-11298)*

Jolar Enterprises .... G 574 875-8369
   Elkhart *(G-3435)*

Jorh Frame & Moulding Co Inc .... G 708 747-3440
   Crown Point *(G-2705)*

Joseph Northern .... G 574 309-5508
   South Bend *(G-15096)*

Ken Duikhoff .... G 765 668-8697
   Marion *(G-11303)*

Kenneth Raber .... G 812 486-3102
   Montgomery *(G-12105)*

Kinzie Mill Work .... G 765 564-4355
   Delphi *(G-2901)*

Knepps Woodworking .... G 812 486-3546
   Montgomery *(G-12107)*

▲ Knorr Brake Truck Systems Co .... G 260 356-9720
   Huntington *(G-7334)*

Koetter Woodworking .... F 812 923-8875
   Borden *(G-1112)*

L & D Custom Woodworking LLC .... G 812 486-2958
   Montgomery *(G-12108)*

Larry Conover .... G 317 787-4020
   Pendleton *(G-13540)*

Lillsun Manufacturing Co Inc .... G 260 356-6514
   Huntington *(G-7337)*

Little Bird Picture Framing .... G 812 437-0285
   Evansville *(G-4172)*

Love Handle LLC .... G 317 384-1102
   Indianapolis *(G-8785)*

M & H Woodworking LLC .... G 812 486-2570
   Montgomery *(G-12111)*

Mark Dekonindk .... G 260 357-5443
   Avilla *(G-488)*

Master Piece Krafts LLC .... G 260 768-4330
   Shipshewana *(G-14866)*

Menard Inc .... C 812 466-1234
   Terre Haute *(G-15641)*

Miller Creations .... G 574 903-9961
   Goshen *(G-6223)*

Millers Woodnthings Inc .... F 574 825-2996
   Middlebury *(G-11740)*

Mj Finishing LLC .... G 574 646-2080
   Bremen *(G-1207)*

MJB Wood Group LLC .... G 574 295-5228
   Elkhart *(G-3547)*

Moores Country Wood Crafting .... F 317 984-3326
   Arcadia *(G-315)*

Mullis Custom Framing LLC .... G 317 627-4024
   Coatesville *(G-2108)*

Nhi-Jrj Corp .... C 574 293-9690
   Elkhart *(G-3569)*

NP Awards LLC .... G 317 861-0825
   New Palestine *(G-12941)*

Omega National Products LLC .... C 574 295-5353
   Elkhart *(G-3579)*

Ostler Enterprises Inc .... G 765 656-1275
   Frankfort *(G-5688)*

Outdoor Roomscapes Inc .... G 574 965-2009
   Monticello *(G-12162)*

Parke County Wood You Like .... G 317 575-9530
   Carmel *(G-1715)*

Patrick Industries Inc .... G 574 294-5758
   Elkhart *(G-3596)*

Pfortune Art & Design Inc .... G 317 872-4123
   Indianapolis *(G-9133)*

Pgc Mulch LLC .... G 812 455-0700
   Evansville *(G-4236)*

Pioneer Cane & Handle Co .... G 812 859-4415
   Clay City *(G-2046)*

Pumpkin Patch Market Inc .... G 574 825-3312
   Middlebury *(G-11747)*

Quality Fence Ltd .... G 260 768-4986
   Shipshewana *(G-14880)*

Employee Codes: A=Over 500 employees, B=251-500
C=101-250, D=51-100, E=20-50, F=10-19, G=1-9

24 LUMBER AND WOOD PRODUCTS, EXCEPT FURNITURE

▲ Quality Hardwood Sales LLC............ D 574 773-2505
  Nappanee *(G-12639)*
R & R Custom Woodworking Inc........... G 574 773-5436
  Nappanee *(G-12640)*
Rab Wood Products............................... G 574 206-5001
  South Bend *(G-15215)*
Raber Wheel Works LLC....................... G 812 486-2786
  Montgomery *(G-12121)*
Ramifications LLC................................. G 765 729-5484
  Muncie *(G-12484)*
Richardson Woodworking....................... G 765 689-8348
  Peru *(G-13599)*
Riegsecker Woodworks Inc................... G 574 642-3504
  Goshen *(G-6247)*
Robert W Sheffer.................................... G 219 464-2095
  Valparaiso *(G-16040)*
Rookstools Pier Shop Inc..................... E 574 453-4771
  Leesburg *(G-10960)*
Rosies Holistic Lifestyle LLC................ G 812 682-1212
  Evansville *(G-4293)*
▲ Roudebush Co Inc............................. G 574 595-7115
  Star City *(G-15397)*
Rpf Inc... G 317 727-6386
  Boggstown *(G-1076)*
Schmuckers Wood Shop....................... G 260 485-1434
  Fort Wayne *(G-5402)*
Schug Awards LLC................................ G 765 447-0002
  Lafayette *(G-10686)*
Sharon Sperry...................................... G 219 736-0121
  Merrillville *(G-11558)*
Shelburne Engraving............................. G 317 873-6257
  Zionsville *(G-17050)*
Southern Indiana Sawmill LLC.............. G 502 664-5723
  Salem *(G-14499)*
Special Projects Corp........................... G 219 874-7184
  Michigan City *(G-11669)*
Specialized Wood Products Inc............ E 574 522-6376
  Elkhart *(G-3691)*
Stitch N Frame...................................... G 260 478-1301
  Fort Wayne *(G-5443)*
Tanglewood LLC.................................... G 607 621-1189
  Boonville *(G-1099)*
This & That Products............................ G 812 299-2688
  Terre Haute *(G-15730)*
True North Group LLC........................... D 574 247-1866
  Mishawaka *(G-12018)*
Ufp Nappanee LLC................................ D 574 773-2505
  Nappanee *(G-12649)*
Urban Logging Company LLC............... G 317 710-4070
  Indianapolis *(G-9687)*
Valentine Woodworking LLC................. G 574 206-0697
  Elkhart *(G-3765)*
Vernon Sharp.. G 317 398-0631
  Shelbyville *(G-14812)*
Voges Restoration and Wdwkg............. G 812 299-1546
  Terre Haute *(G-15742)*
W & S Woodworking LLC...................... G 812 486-3673
  Loogootee *(G-11153)*
Waglers Custom WD Turnings LLC....... G 812 687-7758
  Odon *(G-13357)*
◆ WC Redmon Co Inc........................... F 765 473-6683
  Peru *(G-13607)*
Weberdings Carving Shop Inc.............. F 812 934-3710
  Batesville *(G-610)*
Williams Woodshop............................... G 574 686-2324
  Camden *(G-1522)*
Willows and More................................... G 812 560-1088
  Westport *(G-16753)*
Wood Parts Inc..................................... F 574 326-3431
  Elkhart *(G-3790)*
Wood Sign Products............................. G 574 234-1218
  South Bend *(G-15308)*

Woodcraft Manufacturing Co................ G 812 882-2354
  Vincennes *(G-16169)*
Woodenware Usa Inc........................... G 574 372-8400
  Etna Green *(G-3852)*
Woodhollow LLC.................................... G 219 384-2802
  Highland *(G-7159)*
Woodland Lbor Rltons Cnslting............ G 219 879-6095
  Michigan City *(G-11688)*
Woods of Amber.................................... G 765 763-6926
  Morristown *(G-12282)*
Woods Unlimited Inc............................. G 574 656-3382
  North Liberty *(G-13227)*
Wright Horizon Enterprises LLC............ G 317 779-8182
  Westfield *(G-16741)*

25 FURNITURE AND FIXTURES

2511 Wood household furniture

A S M Inc.. G 260 724-8220
  Decatur *(G-2839)*
ALE Enterprises Inc.............................. G 317 856-2981
  Indianapolis *(G-7467)*
Als Woodcraft Inc.................................. F 812 967-4458
  Borden *(G-1105)*
Antreasian Design Inc.......................... F 317 546-3234
  Indianapolis *(G-7523)*
Barry A Wilcox...................................... G 260 495-3677
  Fremont *(G-5809)*
Beebe Cabinet Co Inc........................... F 574 293-3580
  Elkhart *(G-3222)*
Best Chairs Incorporated..................... C 812 367-1761
  Cannelton *(G-1532)*
Bills Furniture....................................... G 317 695-8347
  Bloomington *(G-807)*
Borkholder Corporation........................ E 574 773-4083
  Nappanee *(G-12585)*
C & P Woodworking Inc........................ G 260 637-3088
  Auburn *(G-373)*
Cabinetmaker Inc.................................. G 812 723-3461
  Paoli *(G-13490)*
Cherished Woodcraft............................ G 317 502-4451
  Greenfield *(G-6480)*
Chuppville Carving............................... G 574 354-7642
  Nappanee *(G-12589)*
Commercial Electric Co Inc.................. E 260 726-9357
  Portland *(G-13933)*
Country Cabinets LLC.......................... G 260 694-6777
  Poneto *(G-13840)*
Country Lane Woodworking LLC........... G 574 642-0662
  Millersburg *(G-11811)*
Country View Furn Mfg & Uphl.............. G 812 636-5024
  Odon *(G-13333)*
Country Woodshop LLC........................ E 574 642-3681
  Goshen *(G-6117)*
Creative Wood Designs Inc.................. E 260 894-4533
  Ligonier *(G-11010)*
Custom Built Barns Inc......................... G 765 457-9037
  Kokomo *(G-10253)*
▲ Custom Wood Products Inc.............. D 574 522-3300
  Elkhart *(G-3283)*
D & E Workshop.................................... G 260 593-0195
  Topeka *(G-15799)*
Dorel Home Furnishings Inc................. D 812 372-0141
  Columbus *(G-2285)*
◆ Dorel USA Inc................................... D 812 372-0141
  Columbus *(G-2290)*
Douglas Dye and Associates Inc......... G 317 844-1709
  Carmel *(G-1611)*
Dubois Wood Products Inc.................. C 812 683-3613
  Huntingburg *(G-7277)*
Durogreen Outdoor LLC........................ F 574 327-6943
  Elkhart *(G-3307)*

E & S Wood Creations LLC................... F 260 768-3033
  Lagrange *(G-10736)*
Ecojacks Inc... G 574 306-0414
  South Whitley *(G-15317)*
Ed Lloyd Co... G 812 342-2505
  Columbus *(G-2294)*
Efurnituremax LLC................................ G 317 697-9504
  Indianapolis *(G-8058)*
F & N Woodworking LLC....................... G 260 463-8938
  Lagrange *(G-10738)*
▲ Fehrenbacher Cabinets Inc.............. E 812 963-3377
  Evansville *(G-4066)*
Fresh Start Inc..................................... F 812 254-3398
  Washington *(G-16479)*
From Trees To These Inc..................... G 260 592-7397
  Decatur *(G-2856)*
Furniture Distributors Inc.................... F 317 357-8508
  Indianapolis *(G-8243)*
Georges Custom Wood Wkg Inc........... G 812 944-3344
  New Albany *(G-12736)*
Gloria J Burnworth............................... G 765 366-3950
  Attica *(G-350)*
Graber Manufacturing LLC................... F 260 657-3400
  Grabill *(G-6298)*
Graber Woodworks Inc......................... G 812 486-2861
  Montgomery *(G-12100)*
▲ Haas Cabinet Co Inc......................... C 812 246-4431
  Sellersburg *(G-14594)*
Hickory Furniture Designs Inc............. G 765 642-0700
  Shelbyville *(G-14759)*
Hoosier Wood Creations Inc................ F 574 831-6330
  New Paris *(G-12958)*
▲ Indiana Architectural Plywood......... E 317 878-4822
  Trafalgar *(G-15829)*
J Miller Cabinet Company Inc.............. G 260 691-2032
  Columbia City *(G-2158)*
◆ J Squared Inc................................... D 317 866-5638
  Greenfield *(G-6521)*
▲ Jasper Chair Company..................... D 812 482-5239
  Jasper *(G-9848)*
Jds Pughs Cabinets Inc....................... G 317 835-2910
  Trafalgar *(G-15830)*
JW Woodworking Inc............................ G 574 831-3033
  New Paris *(G-12962)*
Kasnak Restorations Inc...................... G 317 852-9770
  Brownsburg *(G-1381)*
Kelco Steel Fabrication Inc.................. G 317 248-9229
  Indianapolis *(G-8667)*
◆ Kimball International Inc.................. C 812 482-1600
  Jasper *(G-9878)*
Kountry Kraft Wood Pdts LLC............... G 574 831-6736
  New Paris *(G-12963)*
Kramer Furn & Cab Makers Inc............ E 812 526-2711
  Edinburgh *(G-3089)*
L R Nisley & Sons................................. G 574 642-1245
  Goshen *(G-6195)*
Lambright Woodworking LLC................ F 260 593-2721
  Topeka *(G-15811)*
Leibering Dimension Inc...................... G 812 367-2971
  Ferdinand *(G-4440)*
Lockerbie Square Cab Co Inc............... G 317 635-1134
  Indianapolis *(G-8775)*
Logic Furniture LLC.............................. B 574 975-0007
  Indianapolis *(G-8777)*
Madison Cabinets Inc........................... G 260 639-3915
  Hoagland *(G-7170)*
Martins Wood Works............................ G 574 862-4080
  Goshen *(G-6215)*
Merrill Manufacturing Inc..................... F 812 752-6688
  Scottsburg *(G-14571)*
▲ Mhp Holdings Inc............................. C 574 825-9524
  Middlebury *(G-11736)*

SIC SECTION
25 FURNITURE AND FIXTURES

Miles Systems Mfg Inc............................ F 574 988-0067
  New Carlisle (G-12842)
Millers Woodnthings Inc......................... F 574 825-2996
  Middlebury (G-11740)
Mission Woodworking Inc....................... E 574 848-5697
  Bristol (G-1274)
Mobel Inc... C 812 367-1214
  Ferdinand (G-4445)
Moores Country Wood Crafting............... F 317 984-3326
  Arcadia (G-315)
▲ Numark Industries Company Ltd......... G 317 718-2502
  Avon (G-543)
Oakleaf Industries Inc............................ G 317 414-2040
  Fishers (G-4645)
Oaklief LLC.. G 765 642-9010
  Anderson (G-172)
Oeding Corporation............................... G 812 367-1271
  Ferdinand (G-4446)
Oehlers Woods..................................... G 317 848-2698
  Carmel (G-1710)
▲ Ofs Brands Holdings Inc.................... D 800 521-5381
  Huntingburg (G-7289)
Old Guy Woodcrafters LLC..................... G 574 527-9044
  Winona Lake (G-16913)
Old Hickory Furniture Company Inc......... D 317 398-3151
  Shelbyville (G-14781)
Patrick Industries Inc............................ G 574 293-1521
  Elkhart (G-3589)
Pinetree Woodcraft LLC......................... G 765 886-1177
  Greens Fork (G-6576)
Rbk Development Inc............................ E 574 267-5879
  Warsaw (G-16417)
REM Industries Inc................................ F 574 862-2127
  Wakarusa (G-16247)
Richcraft Wood Products LLC................. G 812 320-7884
  Bloomington (G-957)
Ro-Vic Wood Products Inc..................... F 812 283-9199
  Jeffersonville (G-10049)
▲ Rock Creek 2019 Inc......................... E 812 933-0388
  Batesville (G-604)
Rodeswood LLC.................................... G 574 457-4496
  Syracuse (G-15476)
▲ Roudebush Co Inc............................. G 574 595-7115
  Star City (G-15397)
Sampler Inc... F 765 663-2233
  Homer (G-7221)
▼ Schertz Craftsmen Inc....................... C 877 472-2782
  Grabill (G-6324)
Shamrock Cabinets Inc.......................... E 812 482-7969
  Jasper (G-9911)
Streamside Woodshop LLC..................... G 260 768-7887
  Shipshewana (G-14894)
Stump Home Specialties Mfg Inc............ G 574 291-0050
  South Bend (G-15271)
Superior Woodcrafts LLC....................... G 260 357-3743
  Garrett (G-5877)
Swartzndrber Hrdwood Creat LLC........... G 574 534-2502
  Goshen (G-6266)
Thomasville Furniture Inds Inc................ G 336 476-2175
  Hammond (G-7020)
Timber Creek Design Co Inc................... G 317 297-5336
  Indianapolis (G-9603)
▲ U B Klem Furniture Co Inc................. D 812 326-2236
  Saint Anthony (G-14432)
▲ Walters Cabinet Shop........................ G 765 452-9634
  Kokomo (G-10355)
◆ WC Redmon Co Inc............................ F 765 473-6683
  Peru (G-13607)
Weberdings Carving Shop Inc................. F 812 934-3710
  Batesville (G-610)
◆ Werzalit of America Inc..................... D 814 362-3881
  Syracuse (G-15492)

Wingards Sales LLC.............................. G 260 768-7961
  Shipshewana (G-14899)
Woodcrafters LLC................................. G 765 469-5103
  Denver (G-2936)
◆ Woodcrest Manufacturing Inc............. C 765 472-4471
  Peru (G-13608)
Yoders Wood Shop LLC......................... G 260 768-3246
  Shipshewana (G-14901)

2512 Upholstered household furniture

Aaron Company Inc............................... F 219 838-0852
  Gary (G-5886)
Best Chairs Incorporated....................... C 812 367-1761
  Cannelton (G-1532)
Best Chairs Incorporated....................... D 812 367-1761
  Paoli (G-13489)
◆ Best Chairs Incorporated................... A 812 367-1761
  Ferdinand (G-4429)
Coffeys Custom Upholstery.................... G 812 948-8611
  New Albany (G-12715)
Country View Furn Mfg & Uphl............... G 812 636-5024
  Odon (G-13333)
▲ Custom Wood Products Inc................ D 574 522-3300
  Elkhart (G-3283)
David Edward Furniture Inc................... G 812 482-1600
  Jasper (G-9831)
Furniture Distributors Inc...................... F 317 357-8508
  Indianapolis (G-8243)
Furniture Sales & Marketing................... G 317 849-1508
  Indianapolis (G-8244)
▼ Home Reserve LLC............................ F 260 969-6939
  Fort Wayne (G-5072)
▲ Indiana Furniture Industries Inc......... G 812 482-5727
  Jasper (G-9845)
▲ Jasper Chair Company...................... D 812 482-5239
  Jasper (G-9848)
◆ Kimball International Inc.................... C 812 482-1600
  Jasper (G-9878)
KMC Corporation.................................. E 574 267-7033
  Warsaw (G-16383)
La-Z-Boy Inc.. G 812 367-0190
  Ferdinand (G-4439)
Love Upholstery LLC............................. G 812 639-3789
  Jasper (G-9883)
Mastercraft Inc..................................... C 260 463-8702
  Lagrange (G-10755)
Red Chair Designs................................ G 317 852-9880
  Brownsburg (G-1397)
▲ Seating Technology Inc..................... D 574 971-4100
  Goshen (G-6253)
Shelby Westside Upholstering................ G 317 631-8911
  Indianapolis (G-9419)
▲ Smith Brothers Berne Inc.................. A 260 589-2131
  Berne (G-726)
Sylvia Kay Hartley................................. G 317 984-3424
  Arcadia (G-318)
Tls By Design LLC................................ E 765 683-1971
  Indianapolis (G-9613)
Transformations By Wieland Inc............. D 800 440-9337
  Fort Wayne (G-5500)
Vans TV & Appliance Inc....................... F 260 927-8267
  Auburn (G-433)
Williamsburg Furniture Inc.................... E 574 387-5691
  South Bend (G-15307)
▲ Williamsburg Furniture Inc................ D 800 582-8183
  Nappanee (G-12652)

2514 Metal household furniture

◆ Austin-Westran LLC........................... E 815 234-2811
  Indianapolis (G-7569)
Benz Custom Metal LLC........................ G 812 365-2613
  Marengo (G-11261)

Best Chairs Incorporated....................... C 812 367-1761
  Cannelton (G-1532)
Bo-Mar Industries Inc........................... E 317 899-1240
  Indianapolis (G-7651)
◆ Dorel USA Inc.................................. D 812 372-0141
  Columbus (G-2290)
Flambeau Inc....................................... G 812 372-4899
  Columbus (G-2310)
J Borinstein Inc.................................... G 317 252-0875
  Shelbyville (G-14764)
Lakemaster Inc..................................... F 765 288-3718
  Muncie (G-12437)
Mastercraft Inc..................................... C 260 463-8702
  Lagrange (G-10755)
Mouron & Company Inc......................... F 317 243-7955
  Indianapolis (G-8962)
Poly-Wood LLC..................................... G 877 457-3284
  Syracuse (G-15473)
◆ Poly-Wood LLC................................. D 574 457-3284
  Syracuse (G-15474)
▲ Seating Technology Inc..................... D 574 971-4100
  Goshen (G-6253)
Sills Custom Works & Fab LLC............... G 219 200-9813
  Knox (G-10224)
▲ Valley Line Wood Products LLC......... G 260 768-7807
  Shipshewana (G-14895)
Warren Homes Inc................................ G 812 882-1059
  Vincennes (G-16165)

2515 Mattresses and bedsprings

Blue Bell Mattress Company LLC............ C 260 749-9393
  Fort Wayne (G-4808)
Bowles Mattress Company Inc................ G 812 288-8614
  Jeffersonville (G-9945)
Crossroads Furniture Co LLC................. F 765 307-2095
  Crawfordsville (G-2558)
▲ Derby Inc... D 574 233-4500
  South Bend (G-14997)
Elkhart Bedding Co Inc......................... F 574 293-6200
  Elkhart (G-3318)
Firesmoke Org..................................... G 317 690-2542
  Indianapolis (G-8190)
Futon Factory Inc................................. F 317 549-8639
  Indianapolis (G-8245)
Helping Hrts Helping Hands Inc............. G 248 980-5090
  Middlebury (G-11720)
Holder Bedding Inc............................... G 765 642-1256
  Anderson (G-128)
Holder Bedding Inc............................... G 765 447-7907
  Lafayette (G-10600)
Idgas Inc... G 317 839-1133
  Plainfield (G-13688)
Kimalco Inc.. G 812 463-3105
  Evansville (G-4153)
KMC Corporation.................................. E 574 267-7033
  Warsaw (G-16383)
Leggett & Platt Incorporated................. C 219 866-7181
  Rensselaer (G-14057)
Leggett & Platt Incorporated................. D 260 347-2600
  Kendallville (G-10133)
Leggett & Platt Incorporated................. E 219 766-2261
  Kouts (G-10363)
Loewenstein Furniture Inc..................... F 800 521-5381
  Huntingburg (G-7286)
Mastercraft Inc..................................... C 260 463-8702
  Lagrange (G-10755)
May and Co Inc.................................... E 317 236-6500
  Greenwood (G-6735)
Seal Tec Inc.. E 812 282-4388
  Jeffersonville (G-10053)
▲ Seating Technology Inc..................... D 574 971-4100
  Goshen (G-6253)

25 FURNITURE AND FIXTURES

Sleepmadecom LLC.............................. E 662 350-0999
  Evansville *(G-4318)*

Tempur Production Usa LLC................ D 859 455-1000
  Crawfordsville *(G-2624)*

Vans TV & Appliance Inc...................... F 260 927-8267
  Auburn *(G-433)*

Williamsburg Furniture Inc.................... E 574 387-5691
  South Bend *(G-15307)*

▲ Williamsburg Furniture Inc................ D 800 582-8183
  Nappanee *(G-12652)*

◆ Wolf Corporation................................ G 260 749-9393
  Fort Wayne *(G-5574)*

◆ Woodland Standard Inc...................... C 812 945-4122
  New Albany *(G-12830)*

2517 Wood television and radio cabinets

Eds Wood Craft..................................... G 812 768-6617
  Haubstadt *(G-7084)*

▲ Fehrenbacher Cabinets Inc................ E 812 963-3377
  Evansville *(G-4066)*

Graber Cabinetry LLC........................... E 260 627-2243
  Grabill *(G-6297)*

Heather Sound Amplification................ G 574 255-6100
  Mishawaka *(G-11906)*

Innovative Corp..................................... E 317 804-5977
  Westfield *(G-16701)*

J & J Woodcrafters............................... G 765 436-2466
  Thorntown *(G-15752)*

◆ Kimball International Inc.................... C 812 482-1600
  Jasper *(G-9878)*

Larry Graber Cabinets........................... G 812 486-2713
  Montgomery *(G-12109)*

Lewis & Lee Presents LLC................... G 219 484-5298
  Hammond *(G-6971)*

M Bryant Denisa.................................... G 317 350-3878
  Indianapolis *(G-8805)*

Madison Cabinets Inc........................... G 260 639-3915
  Hoagland *(G-7170)*

Rbk Development Inc........................... E 574 267-5879
  Warsaw *(G-16417)*

Schuhler Woodworking LLC.................. G 317 626-0452
  Danville *(G-2826)*

Shamrock Cabinets Inc......................... E 812 482-7969
  Jasper *(G-9911)*

▲ Walters Cabinet Shop........................ G 765 452-9634
  Kokomo *(G-10355)*

2519 Household furniture, nec

Beachfront Furniture Inc....................... G 574 875-0817
  Elkhart *(G-3219)*

Boardworks Inc..................................... G 219 464-8111
  Valparaiso *(G-15917)*

Columbus Cstm Cbinets Furn LLC....... G 812 379-9411
  Columbus *(G-2242)*

Ditto Sales Inc...................................... G 812 424-4098
  Evansville *(G-4015)*

Elite Transit LLC................................... G 317 507-2126
  Indianapolis *(G-8095)*

Fibertech Plastics LLC.......................... D 812 983-2642
  Elberfeld *(G-3113)*

Keter North America Inc....................... D 765 298-6800
  Anderson *(G-141)*

◆ Keter Us Inc....................................... C 317 575-4700
  Anderson *(G-142)*

Laminique Inc....................................... F 765 482-4222
  Zionsville *(G-17029)*

Loewenstein Furniture Inc.................... F 800 521-5431
  Huntingburg *(G-7286)*

Midwest Cabinet Solutions Inc............. G 765 664-3938
  Marion *(G-11318)*

Myers Design Inc.................................. G 317 955-2450
  Logansport *(G-11095)*

Philipps Wood Processing.................... G 812 357-2824
  Ferdinand *(G-4447)*

Resin Partners Inc................................ D 765 724-7761
  Alexandria *(G-61)*

Russell E Martin................................... G 574 354-2563
  Akron *(G-8)*

Smiths Woodcraft.................................. G 765 395-8044
  Converse *(G-2480)*

Sprinter Xpress Delivery LLC................ G 317 496-5959
  Indianapolis *(G-9483)*

Useful Home Products LLC.................. G 765 459-0095
  Kokomo *(G-10353)*

Weaver Fine Furn Cabinets Inc............ G 812 342-4833
  Columbus *(G-2416)*

2521 Wood office furniture

ALE Enterprises Inc.............................. G 317 856-2981
  Indianapolis *(G-7467)*

Antreasian Design Inc.......................... F 317 546-3234
  Indianapolis *(G-7523)*

Aynes Upholstery LLC.......................... G 812 829-1321
  Freedom *(G-5798)*

Beebe Cabinet Co Inc........................... F 574 293-3580
  Elkhart *(G-3222)*

Ckh Two Inc.. E 317 841-7800
  Fishers *(G-4489)*

▲ Custom Wood Products Inc.............. D 574 522-3300
  Elkhart *(G-3283)*

David Edward Furniture Inc.................. C 812 482-1600
  Jasper *(G-9831)*

Delbert Kemp.. F 812 486-3325
  Montgomery *(G-12095)*

Double T Manufacturing Corp............... F 574 262-1340
  Elkhart *(G-3302)*

Ecojacks LLC.. G 574 306-0414
  South Whitley *(G-15317)*

Eds Wood Craft..................................... G 812 768-6617
  Haubstadt *(G-7084)*

◆ Environmental Products Inc............... F 219 393-3446
  Kingsbury *(G-10178)*

Fanatics.. G 317 844-5478
  Carmel *(G-1632)*

Gehl Industries Inc................................ F 574 773-7663
  Nappanee *(G-12598)*

George Gardner.................................... G 317 270-8036
  Plainfield *(G-13683)*

Graber Cabinetry LLC........................... E 260 627-2243
  Grabill *(G-6297)*

Hensley Custom Cabinetry................... G 219 843-5331
  Rensselaer *(G-14053)*

▲ Indiana Furniture Industries Inc........ D 812 482-5727
  Jasper *(G-9845)*

Indiana Southern Millwork Inc.............. E 812 346-6129
  North Vernon *(G-13280)*

Inwood Office Furniture Inc.................. D 812 482-6121
  Jasper *(G-9847)*

◆ J Squared Inc.................................... D 317 866-5638
  Greenfield *(G-6521)*

▲ Jasper Chair Company..................... D 812 482-5239
  Jasper *(G-9848)*

Jasper Desk Company Inc................... D 812 482-4132
  Jasper *(G-9849)*

Jasper Seating Company Inc............... C 812 936-9977
  French Lick *(G-5847)*

Jasper Seating Company Inc............... C 812 771-4500
  Jasper *(G-9857)*

Jasper Seating Company Inc............... C 812 723-1323
  Paoli *(G-13498)*

◆ Jasper Seating Company Inc............ C 812 482-3204
  Jasper *(G-9858)*

◆ Jofco Inc.. C 812 482-5154
  Jasper *(G-9861)*

Johnco Corp.. G 317 576-4417
  Indianapolis *(G-8632)*

JW Woodworking Inc............................ G 574 831-3033
  New Paris *(G-12962)*

▲ Kimball Furniture Group LLC............ B 812 482-1600
  Jasper *(G-9872)*

Kimball Hospitality Inc.......................... E 812 482-8090
  Jasper *(G-9875)*

◆ Kimball International Inc.................... C 812 482-1600
  Jasper *(G-9878)*

Klomp Construction Company.............. G 219 308-8372
  Saint John *(G-14454)*

Leroy E Doty Cabinet Shop.................. G 219 663-1139
  Crown Point *(G-2717)*

Millmade Incorporated.......................... G 812 424-7778
  Evansville *(G-4206)*

Mouron & Company Inc....................... F 317 243-7955
  Indianapolis *(G-8962)*

▲ Ofs Brands Holdings Inc................... D 800 521-5381
  Huntingburg *(G-7289)*

Old Hickory Furniture Company Inc..... D 317 398-3151
  Shelbyville *(G-14781)*

Rabb and Howe Cabinet Top Co.......... F 317 926-6442
  Indianapolis *(G-9258)*

Robert M Kolarich................................ G 317 596-9753
  Fishers *(G-4597)*

Shamrock Cabinets Inc......................... E 812 482-7969
  Jasper *(G-9911)*

Steffy Wood Products Inc..................... F 260 665-8016
  Angola *(G-294)*

Swartzndrber Hrdwood Creat LLC....... G 574 534-2502
  Goshen *(G-6266)*

2522 Office furniture, except wood

All State Manufacturing Co Inc............ F 812 466-2276
  Terre Haute *(G-15538)*

Apollo Otdoor Cstm Designs Inc.......... F 317 430-1373
  Indianapolis *(G-7525)*

David Edward Furniture Inc.................. C 812 482-1600
  Jasper *(G-9831)*

Deer Creek Village............................... G 574 699-6327
  Peru *(G-13579)*

Deerwood Group................................... G 219 866-5521
  Monon *(G-12055)*

Edsal Manufacturing Co LLC............... C 773 254-0600
  Gary *(G-5926)*

◆ Environmental Products Inc............... F 219 393-3446
  Kingsbury *(G-10178)*

Evansville Corp Design Inc.................. G 812 426-0911
  Evansville *(G-4050)*

◆ Fire King International LLC............... E 812 822-5574
  New Albany *(G-12729)*

◆ Fki Security Group LLC..................... B 812 948-8400
  New Albany *(G-12730)*

Genesis Products LLC.......................... C 574 262-4054
  Elkhart *(G-3374)*

▲ Global.. G 317 494-6174
  Franklin *(G-5732)*

▲ Jasper Chair Company..................... D 812 482-5239
  Jasper *(G-9848)*

Jasper Seating Company Inc............... C 812 723-1323
  Paoli *(G-13498)*

Kimball Furniture Group LLC................ E 812 482-8517
  Jasper *(G-9873)*

Kimball Furniture Group LLC................ C 812 634-3526
  Jasper *(G-9874)*

▲ Kimball Furniture Group LLC............ B 812 482-1600
  Jasper *(G-9872)*

◆ Kimball Hospitality Inc...................... B 812 482-8090
  Jasper *(G-9876)*

◆ Kimball Inc... A 812 482-1600
  Jasper *(G-9877)*

SIC SECTION

25 FURNITURE AND FIXTURES

Kimball International Inc............................ E 812 937-3284
  Jasper *(G-9879)*
◆ Kimball International Inc............................ C 812 482-1600
  Jasper *(G-9878)*
Kimball International Transit....................... C 812 634-3346
  Jasper *(G-9880)*
▲ Kimball Intl Brands Inc............................... B 812 482-1600
  Jasper *(G-9881)*
Kramer Furn & Cab Makers Inc................. E 812 526-2711
  Edinburgh *(G-3089)*
Lui Plus... G 812 309-9350
  Indianapolis *(G-8795)*
Meilink Safe Company................................. D 812 941-0024
  New Albany *(G-12774)*
▲ Modernfold Inc... C 800 869-9685
  Greenfield *(G-6531)*
▲ Ofs Brands Holdings Inc............................ D 800 521-5381
  Huntingburg *(G-7289)*
P-Kelco Inc... E 260 356-6326
  Huntington *(G-7353)*
Rivers Resources LLC................................. G 317 572-5029
  Indianapolis *(G-9310)*
Sdn Specialty Wallcoverin........................... G 812 736-1806
  Georgetown *(G-6074)*
UHS USA Inc... G 833 459-9403
  Zionsville *(G-17059)*
Unique Global Solutions LLC..................... G 765 779-5030
  Anderson *(G-212)*

2531 Public building and related furniture

Bald Spot Racing LLC................................. G 317 402-7188
  Zionsville *(G-16995)*
Bleacherpro LLC... G 813 394-5316
  Fort Wayne *(G-4806)*
Century Industries LLC................................ E 812 246-3371
  Sellersburg *(G-14590)*
Clarios LLC... E 260 485-9999
  Fort Wayne *(G-4851)*
Clarios LLC... C 260 479-4400
  Fort Wayne *(G-4852)*
Clarios LLC... B 317 638-7611
  Indianapolis *(G-7816)*
County of Steuben.. G 260 833-2401
  Angola *(G-243)*
▲ Custom Wood Products Inc...................... D 574 522-3300
  Elkhart *(G-3283)*
Fbsa LLC.. G 800 443-4540
  Rochester *(G-14290)*
▲ Flair Interiors Inc... D 574 534-2163
  Goshen *(G-6137)*
▲ Indiana Furniture Industries Inc................ D 812 482-5727
  Jasper *(G-9845)*
Inwood Office Furniture Inc......................... D 812 482-6121
  Jasper *(G-9847)*
◆ J Squared Inc.. D 317 866-5638
  Greenfield *(G-6521)*
▲ Jasper Chair Company............................... D 812 482-5239
  Jasper *(G-9848)*
◆ Jasper Seating Company Inc.................... C 812 482-3204
  Jasper *(G-9858)*
Johnson Controls Inc................................... F 219 736-7105
  Crown Point *(G-2704)*
Johnson Controls Inc................................... F 812 868-1374
  Evansville *(G-4144)*
Johnson Controls Inc................................... F 317 917-5043
  Pittsboro *(G-13649)*
Johnson Controls Inc................................... F 812 362-6901
  Rockport *(G-14343)*
Lakemaster Inc.. F 765 288-3718
  Muncie *(G-12437)*
Lear Corporation... B 219 852-0014
  Hammond *(G-6969)*

Lexington LLC... E 574 295-8166
  Elkhart *(G-3487)*
Lippert Components Inc............................. E 574 295-8166
  Elkhart *(G-3494)*
Lippert Components Inc............................. D 574 534-8177
  Goshen *(G-6201)*
Mj Aircraft Inc... F 765 378-7700
  Anderson *(G-156)*
▼ National Rcreation Systems Inc................ F 260 482-6023
  Fort Wayne *(G-5256)*
Nhk Seating of America Inc....................... C 765 605-2443
  Frankfort *(G-5683)*
▲ Nhk Seating of America Inc....................... E 765 659-4781
  Frankfort *(G-5684)*
Norco Industries Inc.................................... C 574 262-3400
  Elkhart *(G-3573)*
Norcraft Holding LLC................................... C 812 482-2527
  Jasper *(G-9898)*
▲ Nvb Playgrounds Inc................................... G 317 826-2777
  Indianapolis *(G-9037)*
▼ Occoutdoors Inc... G 317 862-2584
  Boggstown *(G-1075)*
Pauls Seating Inc.. G 574 522-0630
  Elkhart *(G-3601)*
Preferred Seating Company LLC.............. G 317 782-3323
  Indianapolis *(G-9190)*
Recreation Insites LLC............................... G 317 578-0588
  Fishers *(G-4592)*
Recycle Design Inc...................................... G 765 374-0316
  Anderson *(G-184)*
REM Industries Inc....................................... F 574 862-2127
  Wakarusa *(G-16247)*
Superior Seating Inc.................................... F 574 389-9011
  Elkhart *(G-3709)*
Tfs Inc... G 260 422-5896
  Fort Wayne *(G-5478)*
Tls By Design LLC....................................... E 765 683-1971
  Indianapolis *(G-9613)*
▲ Toyota Boshoku Indiana LLC.................... A 812 491-9100
  Princeton *(G-14014)*
▲ Transportation Tech Inds........................... F 812 962-5000
  Evansville *(G-4347)*
▲ TS Tech Indiana LLC.................................. G 765 465-4294
  New Castle *(G-12884)*
▲ Veada Industries Inc.................................... A 574 831-4775
  New Paris *(G-12973)*
Weberdings Carving Shop Inc................... F 812 934-3710
  Batesville *(G-610)*
▲ Wieland Designs Inc.................................... C 574 533-2168
  Goshen *(G-6276)*
Wolf Technical Engineering LLC............... G 800 783-9653
  Indianapolis *(G-9781)*
Woodcrafters Home Products LLC........... A 812 482-2527
  Jasper *(G-9918)*

2541 Wood partitions and fixtures

▼ American Stonecast Pdts Inc..................... F 574 206-0097
  Elkhart *(G-3176)*
Beebe Cabinet Co Inc................................. F 574 293-3580
  Elkhart *(G-3222)*
Boardworks Inc.. G 219 464-8111
  Valparaiso *(G-15917)*
▲ Cabinets & Counters Inc............................ E 812 858-3300
  Newburgh *(G-12995)*
Carl Fox Cabinets Inc.................................. G 812 342-3020
  Jonesville *(G-10084)*
Countertop Connections Inc...................... G 812 822-9858
  Franklin *(G-5723)*
Countertop Manufacturing Inc................... E 765 966-4969
  Richmond *(G-14111)*
◆ Creative Works Inc...................................... F 317 834-4770
  Indianapolis *(G-7902)*

Custom Design Laminates Inc.................. F 574 674-9174
  Osceola *(G-13388)*
Deem & Loureiro Inc................................... G 770 652-9871
  Indianapolis *(G-7961)*
Double T Manufacturing Corp................... F 574 262-1340
  Elkhart *(G-3302)*
Eash LLC.. F 574 295-4450
  Elkhart *(G-3311)*
Eds Wood Craft... G 812 768-6617
  Haubstadt *(G-7084)*
Elko Inc... G 812 473-8400
  Evansville *(G-4030)*
Euronique Inc.. G 812 983-3337
  Elberfeld *(G-3112)*
▲ Fehrenbacher Cabinets Inc........................ E 812 963-3377
  Evansville *(G-4066)*
Fisher Specialties Inc.................................. G 260 385-8251
  Harlan *(G-7055)*
Freedom Valley Cabinets............................ G 717 606-2811
  Freedom *(G-5800)*
Garyrae Inc.. F 574 255-7141
  Mishawaka *(G-11898)*
Graber Cabinetry LLC.................................. E 260 627-2243
  Grabill *(G-6297)*
H & S Custom Countertops Inc................. G 812 422-6314
  Evansville *(G-4100)*
▲ Hackney Home Furnishings Inc................ C 317 895-4300
  Indianapolis *(G-8352)*
◆ Horizon Terra Incorporated....................... D 812 280-0000
  Jeffersonville *(G-9999)*
Indiana Southern Millwork Inc................... E 812 346-6129
  North Vernon *(G-13280)*
J G Bowers Inc.. E 765 677-1000
  Marion *(G-11297)*
▲ JC Moag Corporation.................................. D 812 284-8400
  Georgetown *(G-6063)*
Jensen Cabinet Inc...................................... E 260 456-2131
  Fort Wayne *(G-5134)*
JW Woodworking Inc................................... G 574 831-3033
  New Paris *(G-12962)*
Kline Cabinet Makers LLC.......................... F 317 326-3049
  Maxwell *(G-11444)*
Lambright Woodworking LLC.................... F 260 593-2721
  Topeka *(G-15811)*
Lami-Crafts Inc.. G 812 232-3012
  Terre Haute *(G-15628)*
Laminated Tops Central Ind Inc................ E 812 824-6299
  Bloomington *(G-906)*
Laminique Inc.. F 765 482-4222
  Zionsville *(G-17029)*
Lawrence Shirks.. G 574 223-5118
  Rochester *(G-14301)*
▲ Mhp Holdings Inc... C 574 825-9524
  Middlebury *(G-11736)*
Mica Shop Inc.. E 574 533-1102
  Goshen *(G-6218)*
Michael Cary Ross....................................... G 765 631-2565
  Martinsville *(G-11413)*
Mishawaka Whse & Distrg LLC................ G 574 259-6011
  Mishawaka *(G-11957)*
Mission Woodworking Inc........................... E 574 848-5697
  Bristol *(G-1274)*
Molargik Woodworking Inc......................... G 260 357-6625
  Garrett *(G-5871)*
Mouron & Company Inc.............................. F 317 243-7955
  Indianapolis *(G-8962)*
Newlett Inc... D 574 294-8899
  Elkhart *(G-3567)*
Nhi-Jrj Corp... C 574 293-9690
  Elkhart *(G-3569)*
Oehlers Woods.. G 317 848-2698
  Carmel *(G-1710)*

Employee Codes: A=Over 500 employees, B=251-500
C=101-250, D=51-100, E=20-50, F=10-19, G=1-9

2024 Harris Indiana
Industrial Directory

25 FURNITURE AND FIXTURES

Our Country Home Entps Inc .... D 260 657-5605
   Grabill *(G-6318)*

▲ Our Country Home Entps Inc .... E 260 657-5605
   Harlan *(G-7058)*

Patrick Industries Inc .... G 574 293-1521
   Elkhart *(G-3589)*

Patrick Industries Inc .... G 574 266-8400
   Elkhart *(G-3595)*

Patrick Industries Inc .... G 574 294-5758
   Elkhart *(G-3596)*

Plastic Top Fabricators Inc .... G 317 786-4367
   Indianapolis *(G-9152)*

Platinum Display Group .... G 317 731-5026
   Indianapolis *(G-9154)*

Precision Millwork & Plas Inc .... E 574 243-8720
   South Bend *(G-15201)*

Premier Mfg Group Inc .... D 203 924-6617
   Fort Wayne *(G-5345)*

Quality Surfaces Inc .... E 812 876-5838
   Spencer *(G-15358)*

Rabb and Howe Cabinet Top Co .... F 317 926-6442
   Indianapolis *(G-9258)*

Rbk Development Inc .... E 574 267-5879
   Warsaw *(G-16417)*

Reeds Plastic Tops Inc .... G 765 282-1471
   Muncie *(G-12486)*

Sims Cabinet Co Inc .... E 317 634-1747
   Danville *(G-2828)*

SJS Components LLC .... G 260 578-0192
   Warsaw *(G-16426)*

Solid Surface Craftsmen Inc .... G 317 535-2333
   Whiteland *(G-16797)*

Tremain Ceramic Tile & Flr Cvg .... E 317 542-1491
   Indianapolis *(G-9633)*

Wagners Plasti Craft Co .... G 260 627-3147
   Fort Wayne *(G-5541)*

▲ Walters Cabinet Shop .... G 765 452-9634
   Kokomo *(G-10355)*

Washmuth Cabinet Company .... G 765 932-2701
   Rushville *(G-14416)*

▼ Wood Technologies LLC .... E 260 627-8858
   Grabill *(G-6326)*

Woods Unlimited Inc .... G 574 656-3382
   North Liberty *(G-13227)*

Yourspace LLC .... G 260 702-9595
   Fort Wayne *(G-5582)*

Zehrhaus Inc .... G 260 486-3198
   Fort Wayne *(G-5583)*

2542 Partitions and fixtures, except wood

▼ A & A Sheet Metal Products .... D 219 326-1288
   La Porte *(G-10371)*

Barns Unlimited LLC .... G 765 489-6282
   New Castle *(G-12851)*

Burns Cabinets and Disp Inc .... G 260 897-2219
   Avilla *(G-473)*

▲ Cabinets & Counters Inc .... E 812 858-3300
   Newburgh *(G-12995)*

Cottom Automated Bus Soluti .... G 317 853-6531
   Carmel *(G-1599)*

Creative Industries Inc .... E 317 248-1102
   Plainfield *(G-13676)*

◆ Deflecto LLC .... B 317 849-9555
   Indianapolis *(G-7962)*

Edsal Manufacturing Co LLC .... C 773 254-0600
   Gary *(G-5926)*

Elkhart Brass Manufacturing Co .... E 800 346-0250
   Elkhart *(G-3321)*

Flambeau Inc .... G 812 372-4899
   Columbus *(G-2310)*

▲ Georg Utz Inc .... E 812 526-2240
   Edinburgh *(G-3085)*

Hitzer Inc .... F 260 589-8536
   Berne *(G-714)*

J Jacoby Inc .... G 317 877-9275
   Noblesville *(G-13110)*

▲ Metal Dynamics Ltd .... E 812 949-7998
   New Albany *(G-12775)*

Michiana Laminated Products .... E 260 562-2871
   Howe *(G-7240)*

▲ Modernfold Inc .... C 800 869-9685
   Greenfield *(G-6531)*

Organized Living Inc .... C 812 334-8839
   Bloomington *(G-938)*

Out of Box Solutions Inc .... G 317 605-8719
   Indianapolis *(G-9076)*

Outstnding Trdshow Exhbt Svcs .... F 888 735-4348
   North Judson *(G-13213)*

Patrick Industries Inc .... G 574 293-1521
   Elkhart *(G-3589)*

Precision Millwork & Plas Inc .... E 574 243-8720
   South Bend *(G-15201)*

Shamrock Cabinets Inc .... E 812 482-7969
   Jasper *(G-9911)*

Shed Craft Creations LLC .... G 765 993-1161
   Winchester *(G-16899)*

Solid Surface Craftsmen Inc .... G 317 535-2333
   Whiteland *(G-16797)*

Star Nova US LLC .... G 269 830-5802
   South Bend *(G-15267)*

Tamwall Inc .... F 317 546-5055
   Indianapolis *(G-9548)*

Title Ten Manufacturing LLC .... G 765 388-2482
   Muncie *(G-12503)*

▲ Tru-Form Steel & Wire Inc .... F 765 348-5001
   Hartford City *(G-7078)*

Walter Ostermeyer .... G 260 705-1960
   Fort Wayne *(G-5543)*

Ynwa Industries Inc .... D 574 295-6641
   Elkhart *(G-3800)*

2591 Drapery hardware and blinds and shades

▼ Abda Incorporated .... G 317 273-8343
   Indianapolis *(G-7416)*

Ascot Enterprises Inc .... E 574 773-7751
   Nappanee *(G-12581)*

▲ Ascot Enterprises Inc .... E 877 773-7751
   Nappanee *(G-12582)*

Best Blinds .... G 260 490-4422
   Fort Wayne *(G-4796)*

Blinds At Home LLC .... G 317 489-8133
   Indianapolis *(G-7641)*

Custom Blind and Shade Company .... G 812 867-9280
   Evansville *(G-4001)*

Custom Blind Co .... G 812 867-9280
   Evansville *(G-4002)*

Custom Draperies of Indiana .... G 219 924-2500
   Hammond *(G-6909)*

Delaney Window Fashions LLC .... G 317 567-7672
   Fishers *(G-4503)*

Essex .... G 317 201-7099
   Indianapolis *(G-8136)*

Hunter Venetian Blind Co .... G 812 471-1100
   Evansville *(G-4113)*

▲ Irvine Shade & Door Inc .... D 574 522-1446
   Elkhart *(G-3430)*

J P Whitt Inc .... G 765 759-0521
   Muncie *(G-12430)*

◆ Lafayette Venetian Blind Inc .... A 765 464-2500
   West Lafayette *(G-16601)*

Merin Interiors Indianapolis .... G 317 251-6603
   Indianapolis *(G-8877)*

Midwest Blind & Shade Co .... G 574 271-0770
   Mishawaka *(G-11947)*

Midwest Shade & Drapery Co .... G 317 849-2131
   Indianapolis *(G-8913)*

Mitchell Fabrics Inc .... E 309 674-8631
   Lafayette *(G-10651)*

Nacjam Interior Blinds Inc .... G 765 449-8035
   Lafayette *(G-10656)*

▲ Oxford House Incorporated .... D 765 884-3265
   Fowler *(G-5629)*

Rva LLC .... G 317 800-9800
   Fishers *(G-4602)*

Sharon S Cheesecakes .... G 219 477-5773
   Valparaiso *(G-16047)*

United Services Inc .... G 812 989-3320
   Jeffersonville *(G-10068)*

United Services Inc .... G 812 989-3320
   Clarksville *(G-2040)*

▲ United Shade LLC .... D 574 262-0954
   Elkhart *(G-3761)*

Vertical Sale .... G 260 438-4299
   Fort Wayne *(G-5531)*

Vertical Vegetation MGT LLC .... F 765 366-4447
   Darlington *(G-2835)*

2599 Furniture and fixtures, nec

American Natural Resources LLC ..... F 219 922-6444
   Griffith *(G-6790)*

▲ Anodyne Medical Device Inc .... D 954 340-0500
   Batesville *(G-578)*

B&B Urban Eats Corporation .... G 317 998-9848
   Indianapolis *(G-7584)*

Bollock Inerprises Inc .... F 765 448-6000
   Lafayette *(G-10541)*

Brick .... G 812 522-8636
   Jonesville *(G-10082)*

Clancys of Portage .... E 219 764-4995
   Portage *(G-13856)*

Country Corner Woodworks LLC ...... G 574 825-6782
   Middlebury *(G-11706)*

Country Mill Cabinet Co Inc .... F 260 693-9289
   Laotto *(G-10804)*

Creative Woodworks LLC .... G 260 450-1742
   Fort Wayne *(G-4887)*

Csr Associates LLC .... G 317 255-2247
   Indianapolis *(G-7918)*

David Fleming .... G 414 202-6586
   Indianapolis *(G-7954)*

Deerwood Group .... G 219 866-5521
   Monon *(G-12055)*

Edsal Manufacturing Co LLC .... C 773 254-0600
   Gary *(G-5926)*

Fickle Peach Inc .... G 765 282-5211
   Muncie *(G-12395)*

Flat Rock .... G 219 852-5262
   Hammond *(G-6931)*

Freds Custom Furniture .... G 260 726-2519
   Portland *(G-13943)*

Glens Pact LLC .... G 317 540-5869
   Indianapolis *(G-8286)*

Greazy Pickle LLC .... G 260 726-9200
   Portland *(G-13948)*

Growlers .... G 219 924-0245
   Highland *(G-7139)*

▲ Hanco Inc .... E
   Carmel *(G-1648)*

HB International LLC .... G 574 773-8200
   Nappanee *(G-12606)*

◆ Hill-Rom Inc .... A 812 934-7777
   Batesville *(G-589)*

▲ Knu LLC .... E 812 367-1761
   Ferdinand *(G-4438)*

26 PAPER AND ALLIED PRODUCTS

Lafayette Furniture .... G 765 446-9777
  Lafayette *(G-10625)*
Lafayette Materials MGT Co Inc .... G 765 447-7400
  Lafayette *(G-10627)*
Limanis Pop Up Concessions LLC .... G 317 966-1507
  Avon *(G-536)*
Magnetic Concepts Corporation .... F 317 580-4021
  Westfield *(G-16709)*
Mamas Soul Rollin LLC .... G 256 479-4171
  Indianapolis *(G-8823)*
Max of All Trades LLC .... G 317 703-4242
  Kokomo *(G-10305)*
Myfin Inc .... F 812 287-8579
  Bloomington *(G-928)*
▲ Ofs Brands Holdings Inc .... D 800 521-5381
  Huntingburg *(G-7289)*
Rabb and Howe Cabinet Top Co .... F 317 926-6442
  Indianapolis *(G-9258)*
Rapar Inc .... G 812 254-9886
  Washington *(G-16506)*
Respect Da Flava LLC .... G 765 243-1629
  Indianapolis *(G-9293)*
Sampco Inc .... G 413 442-4043
  South Bend *(G-15230)*
Signet Millwork LLC .... E 812 248-0612
  Sellersburg *(G-14615)*
Tfs Inc .... G 260 422-5896
  Fort Wayne *(G-5478)*
Tls By Design LLC .... E 765 683-1971
  Indianapolis *(G-9613)*
Top Design Cnc Inc .... G 219 662-2915
  Valparaiso *(G-16069)*
Troy Stuart .... G 812 887-0403
  Washington *(G-16510)*
Twisted Stixx LLC .... G 317 435-5034
  Indianapolis *(G-9666)*
United Cabinet Corporation Nit .... G 812 482-2561
  Jasper *(G-9915)*
United Home Supply Inc .... G 765 288-2737
  Muncie *(G-12509)*

26 PAPER AND ALLIED PRODUCTS

2611 Pulp mills

Chesapeake Recycling Inc .... E 574 946-6602
  Winamac *(G-16859)*
Gpi Midwest LLC .... G 260 925-6060
  Kendallville *(G-10113)*
Integrity Fiber Supply LLC .... E 317 290-1140
  Carmel *(G-1672)*
International Paper Company .... D 800 643-7244
  Terre Haute *(G-15619)*
Jeda Equipment Services Inc .... G 317 842-9377
  Fishers *(G-4550)*
Premier Scrap Processing LLC .... F 317 242-9502
  Indianapolis *(G-9191)*
Recycling Center Inc .... D 765 966-8295
  Richmond *(G-14195)*
Recycling Works LLC .... G 574 293-3751
  Elkhart *(G-3644)*
Waelz Sustainable Products LLC .... E 317 334-7067
  Logansport *(G-11119)*
Welder On Way LLC .... G 260 920-4705
  Ashley *(G-340)*

2621 Paper mills

◆ American Melt Blown Filtration .... E 219 866-3500
  Rensselaer *(G-14041)*
Bmk Investments Inc .... G 574 282-2538
  South Bend *(G-14960)*

Bristol Ventures LLC .... G 765 649-8452
  Anderson *(G-84)*
Cascades Holding US Inc .... B 219 697-2900
  Brook *(G-1304)*
Codybro LLC .... G 765 827-5441
  Connersville *(G-2432)*
Elkhart Bristol Corp .... E 574 264-7600
  Elkhart *(G-3323)*
Encorr Sheets LLC .... G 317 290-1140
  Indianapolis *(G-8113)*
Freddie Powell .... G 574 658-3345
  Lafayette *(G-10582)*
Gibson Innovations LLC .... G 317 561-0932
  Terre Haute *(G-15597)*
▼ Girls .... G 812 299-1382
  Terre Haute *(G-15598)*
Gold Bond Building Pdts LLC .... G 812 247-2424
  Shoals *(G-14907)*
Gov 6 Corp .... G 317 847-4942
  Indianapolis *(G-8310)*
Gypsy Moon Ragdolls Inc .... G 260 589-2852
  Berne *(G-712)*
Huhtamaki Inc .... C 219 972-4264
  Hammond *(G-6950)*
Inland Paper Board & Packaging .... G 317 879-9710
  Indianapolis *(G-8550)*
International Paper Company .... D 260 868-2151
  Butler *(G-1468)*
International Paper Company .... C 260 747-9111
  Fort Wayne *(G-5115)*
International Paper Company .... G 219 844-6509
  Hammond *(G-6959)*
International Paper Company .... G 317 870-0192
  Indianapolis *(G-8578)*
International Paper Company .... F 317 481-4000
  Indianapolis *(G-8579)*
International Paper Company .... F 317 715-9080
  Indianapolis *(G-8580)*
International Paper Company .... E 317 871-6999
  Indianapolis *(G-8581)*
International Paper Company .... D 800 643-7244
  Terre Haute *(G-15619)*
International Paper Company .... G 765 675-6732
  Tipton *(G-15776)*
Jodo Investments Inc .... E 765 651-0200
  Marion *(G-11301)*
Lsc Communications Us LLC .... G 765 362-1300
  Crawfordsville *(G-2587)*
Mafcote Wabash Paper Coating .... F 260 563-4181
  Wabash *(G-16197)*
New-Indy Hartford City LLC .... D 765 348-5440
  Hartford City *(G-7073)*
Nice-Pak Products Inc .... A 845 365-1700
  Mooresville *(G-12228)*
Nice-Pak Products Inc .... E 317 839-0373
  Plainfield *(G-13710)*
Noblesville Pack & Ship .... G 317 776-6306
  Noblesville *(G-13144)*
▲ Panel Solutions Inc .... G 574 389-8494
  Elkhart *(G-3580)*
Pratt Paper (in) LLC .... G 219 477-1040
  Valparaiso *(G-16031)*
▲ Roi Marketing Company Inc .... G 317 644-0797
  Indianapolis *(G-9321)*
Sil Publishing Co LLC .... G 812 989-8871
  Marengo *(G-11265)*
Simco of Southern Indiana .... F 812 890-6225
  Corydon *(G-2516)*
▼ Space Kraft .... F 317 871-6999
  Indianapolis *(G-9466)*
Staltari Enterprises Inc .... G 574 522-1988
  Elkhart *(G-3694)*

STS Packaging .... G 317 210-0305
  Mooresville *(G-12245)*
Supremex Midwest Inc .... G 317 253-4321
  Indianapolis *(G-9532)*
Supremex Midwest LLC .... E 317 253-4321
  Indianapolis *(G-9533)*
Supremex USA Inc .... E 317 253-4321
  Indianapolis *(G-9535)*
Temple Inland .... G 765 362-1074
  Crawfordsville *(G-2623)*
Twinrocker Hand Made Paper Inc .... G 765 563-3119
  Brookston *(G-1314)*
Twisted Jute LLC .... G 317 885-4276
  Indianapolis *(G-9664)*

2631 Paperboard mills

◆ American Containers Inc .... D 574 936-4068
  Plymouth *(G-13755)*
Barrington Packaging Systems I .... G 847 382-8066
  Shelbyville *(G-14733)*
Cardboard Apothecary .... G 574 309-3007
  South Bend *(G-14966)*
◆ Clondalkin Pharma & Healthcare Inc .. A 336 292-4555
  Indianapolis *(G-7824)*
Combined Technologies Inc .... G 847 968-4855
  Bristol *(G-1254)*
Custom Kraft Pack LLC .... F 502 595-8146
  Jeffersonville *(G-9966)*
Eften Inc .... G 260 982-1544
  North Manchester *(G-13233)*
Elite Packaging LLC .... G 502 232-2596
  Jeffersonville *(G-9975)*
Graphic Packaging Holding Co .... G 219 324-6160
  La Porte *(G-10410)*
Guy Cardboard .... G 812 989-4809
  Elizabeth *(G-3127)*
Hd Car Detailing .... G 574 298-3975
  South Bend *(G-15061)*
▲ Indiana Ribbon Inc .... E 219 279-2112
  Wolcott *(G-16931)*
International Paper Company .... G 765 359-0107
  Crawfordsville *(G-2579)*
International Paper Company .... D 800 643-7244
  Terre Haute *(G-15619)*
Jenson Industries Inc .... G 317 871-0122
  Indianapolis *(G-8622)*
Ox Industries Inc .... G 765 396-3317
  Eaton *(G-3064)*
Paperworks Industries Inc .... C 260 569-3352
  Wabash *(G-16209)*
Paperworks Wabash Inc .... E 260 569-3303
  Wabash *(G-16211)*
Patriot Packaging LLC .... E 812 346-0700
  North Vernon *(G-13291)*
PSC Industries Inc .... F 812 425-9071
  Evansville *(G-4263)*
Sonoco Products Company .... D 574 598-2731
  Akron *(G-9)*
Sonoco Products Company .... D 812 526-5511
  Edinburgh *(G-3105)*
Sunbeam Packaging Services LLC .... G 812 867-3551
  Evansville *(G-4337)*
Viking Paper Company .... E 574 936-6300
  Plymouth *(G-13825)*
Westrock Cp LLC .... G 574 936-2118
  Plymouth *(G-13828)*
Westrock Rkt LLC .... E 812 372-8873
  Columbus *(G-2418)*

2652 Setup paperboard boxes

◆ American Containers Inc .... D 574 936-4068
  Plymouth *(G-13755)*

Employee Codes: A=Over 500 employees, B=251-500
C=101-250, D=51-100, E=20-50, F=10-19, G=1-9

26 PAPER AND ALLIED PRODUCTS

Artistic Carton... F 260 925-6060
  Kendallville *(G-10091)*

Colbert Packaging Corporation.............. D 574 295-6605
  Elkhart *(G-3256)*

Jessup Paper Box LLC............................... F 765 588-9137
  Lafayette *(G-10615)*

Pathfinder Services Inc............................. E 260 356-0500
  Huntington *(G-7354)*

2653 Corrugated and solid fiber boxes

◆ American Containers Inc.....................D 574 936-4068
  Plymouth *(G-13755)*

American Corrugated................................. G 812 425-4056
  Evansville *(G-3885)*

Arrow Container LLC................................. D 317 882-6444
  Indianapolis *(G-7548)*

B&H Capital Inc.. B 812 376-9301
  Columbus *(G-2225)*

B&W Packaging Mfg LLC........................... E 812 280-9578
  New Albany *(G-12694)*

Buckeye Corrugated Inc........................... D 317 856-3701
  Indianapolis *(G-7697)*

Capitol City Container Corp..................... E 317 875-0290
  Indianapolis *(G-7735)*

Cardinal Container Corp.......................... E 317 898-2715
  Indianapolis *(G-7739)*

▲ Carton Craft Corporation..................... D 812 949-4393
  New Albany *(G-12709)*

Color-Box LLC... A 765 966-7588
  Richmond *(G-14109)*

Combined Technologies Inc.................... G 847 968-4855
  Bristol *(G-1254)*

Container Service Corp............................ D 574 232-7474
  South Bend *(G-14982)*

Corrugated Concepts LLC........................ G 317 290-1140
  Indianapolis *(G-7880)*

Cox John... G 765 463-6396
  West Lafayette *(G-16571)*

Cps Inc.. F 317 804-2300
  Indianapolis *(G-7895)*

CRA-Wal Inc... D 317 856-3701
  Indianapolis *(G-7896)*

▲ Csc-Indiana LLC..................................... E 708 625-3255
  New Haven *(G-12900)*

Custom Packaging Inc.............................. F 317 876-9559
  Indianapolis *(G-7933)*

Elite Packaging LLC................................... G 502 232-2596
  Jeffersonville *(G-9975)*

Evansville Arc Inc...................................... D 812 471-1633
  Evansville *(G-4046)*

Five Star Sheets LLC................................ D 574 654-8058
  New Carlisle *(G-12840)*

Freedom Corrugated LLC........................ G 317 290-1140
  Indianapolis *(G-8227)*

Galaxy Container LLC................................ G 574 936-6300
  Plymouth *(G-13778)*

Hackett & Hackett LLC.............................. G 574 370-7191
  South Bend *(G-15057)*

Hoosier Container Inc.............................. E 765 966-2541
  Richmond *(G-14136)*

Indiana Box Company................................E 317 462-7743
  Greenfield *(G-6512)*

Indiana Box Company................................E 260 356-9660
  Huntington *(G-7326)*

▲ Indiana Carton Company Inc............. D 574 546-3848
  Bremen *(G-1197)*

Inland Container.. G 317 876-0768
  Indianapolis *(G-8549)*

Innovative Packaging Inc........................ E 260 356-6577
  Huntington *(G-7329)*

Innovative Packaging Assoc Inc............ E 260 356-6577
  Huntington *(G-7330)*

International Paper Company................. G 765 492-3341
  Cayuga *(G-1822)*

International Paper Company................. D 765 364-5342
  Crawfordsville *(G-2580)*

International Paper Company................. D 317 390-3300
  Indianapolis *(G-8582)*

International Paper Company................. G 812 326-2125
  Saint Anthony *(G-14429)*

International Paper Company................. D 800 643-7244
  Terre Haute *(G-15619)*

▲ Jamil Packaging Corporation............. E 574 256-2600
  Mishawaka *(G-11917)*

Jcmz Enterprises Inc............................... E 812 372-0288
  Columbus *(G-2329)*

Kelly Box and Packaging Corp................ G 317 804-7044
  Indianapolis *(G-8668)*

Kelly Box and Packaging Corp................ D 260 432-4570
  Fort Wayne *(G-5145)*

Lacap Container Corp.............................. G 317 835-4282
  Shelbyville *(G-14771)*

Marion Paper Box Company................... F 765 664-6435
  Marion *(G-11314)*

Menasha Packaging Company LLC....... G 877 818-2016
  Richmond *(G-14163)*

▲ Met-Pak Specialties Corp.................... E 260 420-2217
  Fort Wayne *(G-5215)*

◆ Michigan City Paper Box Co................D 219 872-8383
  Michigan City *(G-11638)*

Northern Box Company Inc.................... E 574 264-2161
  Elkhart *(G-3574)*

Northern Indiana Packg Co Inc.............. E 260 356-9660
  Huntington *(G-7345)*

Nova Packaging Group Inc..................... E 765 651-2600
  Marion *(G-11321)*

Orora Packaging Solutions..................... F 317 879-4628
  Indianapolis *(G-9071)*

Packaging Corporation America............ B 812 376-9301
  Columbus *(G-2370)*

Packaging Corporation America............ G 812 526-5919
  Edinburgh *(G-3095)*

Packaging Corporation America............ D 765 674-9781
  Gas City *(G-6039)*

Packaging Corporation America............ G 317 247-0193
  Indianapolis *(G-9084)*

Packaging Corporation America............ G 812 482-4598
  Jasper *(G-9901)*

Packaging Corporation America............ G 812 522-3100
  Seymour *(G-14671)*

Packaging Corporation America............ G 812 522-3100
  Seymour *(G-14672)*

Packaging Corporation America............ C 812 882-7631
  Vincennes *(G-16142)*

Packaging Lgstics Slutions LLC............. G 502 807-8346
  Jeffersonville *(G-10033)*

Paperworks Industries Inc..................... C 260 563-3102
  Wabash *(G-16210)*

PCA Suthern Ind Corrugated LLC.......... E 812 376-9301
  Columbus *(G-2373)*

Pli LLC... E 219 326-1350
  La Porte *(G-10463)*

Powell Systems Inc.................................. G 765 884-0613
  Fowler *(G-5631)*

Pratt (jet Corr) Inc................................... B 219 548-9191
  Valparaiso *(G-16030)*

Royal Box Group LLC............................... C 317 462-7743
  Greenfield *(G-6545)*

Royal Box Group LLC............................... C 765 728-2416
  Huntington *(G-7361)*

Schwarz Partners Packaging LLC......... G 812 523-6600
  Seymour *(G-14685)*

Servants Inc.. D 812 634-2201
  Jasper *(G-9910)*

Sinflex Paper Co Inc................................. E 765 789-6688
  Muncie *(G-12493)*

Sisco Corporation...................................... D 812 422-2090
  Evansville *(G-4316)*

Smith Consulting Inc................................ E 765 728-5980
  Montpelier *(G-12181)*

Solid Rock Gbc... G 260 723-4806
  South Whitley *(G-15324)*

Southland Container Corp....................... C 812 385-0774
  Princeton *(G-14012)*

Temple-Inland Inc...................................... G 765 675-6732
  Tipton *(G-15793)*

Temple-Island... G 901 419-9000
  Indianapolis *(G-9574)*

Tre Paper Company.................................. G 765 649-2536
  Anderson *(G-208)*

Tri-Lakes Container Corp........................ D 574 594-2217
  Pierceton *(G-13641)*

Wabash Valley Packaging Corp............. F 812 299-7181
  Terre Haute *(G-15744)*

Webster West Inc..................................... E 812 346-5666
  North Vernon *(G-13300)*

Welch Packaging Marion LLC................ G 765 651-2600
  Marion *(G-11348)*

Westrock Company................................... G 219 229-0981
  Plymouth *(G-13827)*

Westrock Cp LLC...................................... G 812 372-8873
  Columbus *(G-2417)*

Westrock Cp LLC...................................... E 574 772-5545
  Knox *(G-10228)*

Westrock Cp LLC...................................... G 574 256-0318
  Mishawaka *(G-12027)*

Westrock Cp LLC...................................... G 219 762-4855
  Portage *(G-13919)*

Westrock Mwv LLC.................................. D 317 787-3361
  Indianapolis *(G-9754)*

Westrock Rkt LLC.................................... G 574 936-2118
  Plymouth *(G-13829)*

2655 Fiber cans, drums, and similar products

Charmaran Company LLC....................... F 260 347-3347
  Kendallville *(G-10098)*

Elder Group Inc... D 765 966-7676
  Richmond *(G-14118)*

Great Lakes Lamination Inc................... G 574 389-9663
  Elkhart *(G-3390)*

Great Lakes Lamination Inc................... G 574 389-9663
  Bristol *(G-1265)*

Greif Inc... G 740 657-6606
  Indianapolis *(G-8326)*

▲ Indiana Ribbon Inc................................ E 219 279-2112
  Wolcott *(G-16931)*

Jt Composites LLC.................................... G 317 297-9520
  Indianapolis *(G-8645)*

Mach 1 Paper and Poly Pdts Inc........... F 574 522-4500
  Elkhart *(G-3508)*

Mito Material Solutions Inc.................... G 855 344-6486
  Indianapolis *(G-8936)*

Precision Products Group Inc............... E 260 484-4111
  Fort Wayne *(G-5340)*

Precision Products Group Inc............... G 260 424-3734
  Fort Wayne *(G-5341)*

Star Packaging Company Inc................. G 317 357-3707
  Indianapolis *(G-9498)*

Vandor Corporation.................................. D 765 966-7676
  Richmond *(G-14222)*

2656 Sanitary food containers

Affinis Group LLC...................................... G 317 831-3830
  Mooresville *(G-12191)*

Divine Grace Homecare........................... G 219 290-5911
  Gary *(G-5923)*

SIC SECTION
26 PAPER AND ALLIED PRODUCTS

Genpak LLC.. G 812 752-3111
 Scottsburg (G-14557)

Hoffmaster Group Inc............................... D 855 230-5281
 Fort Wayne (G-5070)

Howe House Ltd Editions Inc................. G 765 742-6831
 Lafayette (G-10602)

International Paper Company................ D 800 643-7244
 Terre Haute (G-15619)

◆ Letica Corporation.................................. A 812 421-3136
 Evansville (G-4165)

Sustainables LLC..................................... G 502 741-4834
 Indianapolis (G-9536)

Viva Tia Maria LLC................................... E 317 509-2650
 Zionsville (G-17061)

Wethington... G 317 594-6000
 Greenfield (G-6571)

2657 Folding paperboard boxes

Americraft Carton Inc.............................. A 812 537-1784
 Lawrenceburg (G-10828)

Colbert Packaging Corporation............. D 574 295-6605
 Elkhart (G-3256)

Combined Technologies Inc................... G 847 968-4855
 Bristol (G-1254)

Custom Carton Inc................................... F 260 563-7411
 Wabash (G-16179)

▲ Glenmark Industries Inc....................... C 574 936-5788
 Plymouth (G-13780)

Tre Paper Company................................. G 765 649-2536
 Anderson (G-208)

Westrock Cp LLC..................................... G 574 936-2118
 Plymouth (G-13828)

2671 Paper; coated and laminated packaging

3M Company.. E 765 348-3200
 Hartford City (G-7060)

Accu-Label Inc.. E 260 482-5223
 Fort Wayne (G-4720)

◆ American Containers Inc...................... D 574 936-4068
 Plymouth (G-13755)

◆ Bomarko Inc... C 574 936-9901
 Plymouth (G-13758)

Bowers Envelope Company Inc............. G 317 253-4321
 Indianapolis (G-7665)

Bprex Closures LLC................................. D 812 386-1525
 Princeton (G-13985)

Cpg - Ohio LLC.. F 260 829-6721
 Orland (G-13363)

Crichlow Industries Inc........................... G 317 925-5178
 Indianapolis (G-7903)

Custom Packaging Inc............................ F 317 876-9559
 Indianapolis (G-7933)

Dynamic Packg Solutions Inc................ C 574 848-1410
 Bristol (G-1257)

Eagle Packaging Inc............................... G 260 281-2333
 Goshen (G-6128)

Elite Packaging LLC................................ G 502 232-2596
 Jeffersonville (G-9975)

Filmtech Inc... G 888 399-7442
 Greensburg (G-6592)

G & T Industries Inc................................ G 812 634-2252
 Jasper (G-9839)

Huhtamaki Inc... C 219 972-4264
 Hammond (G-6950)

▲ Innovative Energy Inc.......................... E 219 696-3639
 Crown Point (G-2697)

Interactive Surface Tech LLC................ G 812 246-0900
 Sellersburg (G-14602)

Label Tech Inc.. E 765 747-1234
 Muncie (G-12436)

Max Katz Bag Company Inc................... D 317 635-9561
 Indianapolis (G-8855)

Monosol LLC... G 219 324-9459
 La Porte (G-10454)

Monosol LLC... G 219 763-7589
 Portage (G-13891)

MSI Express Inc....................................... E 219 871-9882
 Portage (G-13894)

Multi-Wall Packaging Corp..................... D 219 882-0070
 Gary (G-5986)

NP Converters Inc................................... D 812 448-2555
 Brazil (G-1158)

Nyx LLC.. A 734 838-3570
 New Albany (G-12786)

Pactiv LLC.. E 574 936-7065
 Plymouth (G-13800)

Pennplastics LLC..................................... G 574 286-0705
 Mishawaka (G-11973)

PSC Industries Inc................................... F 812 425-9071
 Evansville (G-4263)

Sabert Corporation.................................. G 260 747-3149
 Fort Wayne (G-5395)

Sonoco Products Company.................... D 812 526-5511
 Edinburgh (G-3105)

Spartech LLC... D 765 281-5100
 Muncie (G-12495)

◆ Stoffel Seals Corporation..................... E 845 353-3800
 Angola (G-296)

Supremex Midwest LLC.......................... G 317 898-2000
 Indianapolis (G-9534)

Taghleef Industries Inc........................... A 302 326-5500
 Rosedale (G-14385)

Universal Package LLC........................... F 812 937-3605
 Ferdinand (G-4450)

Universal Packg Systems Inc................ C 260 829-6721
 Orland (G-13374)

Vti Packaging Specialties....................... G 574 277-4119
 Granger (G-6389)

Westrock Cp LLC..................................... G 574 936-2118
 Plymouth (G-13828)

Zimmer Holdings LLC............................. G
 Ossian (G-13444)

▲ Zimmer Paper Products Del LLC....... D 317 263-3420
 Indianapolis (G-9811)

2672 Paper; coated and laminated, nec

3M Company.. E 765 348-3200
 Hartford City (G-7060)

3M Company.. B 317 692-6666
 Indianapolis (G-7388)

◆ Abro Industries Inc............................... E 574 232-8289
 South Bend (G-14933)

Accu-Label Inc.. E 260 482-5223
 Fort Wayne (G-4720)

Adhesive Products Inc........................... G 317 899-0565
 Indianapolis (G-7432)

Avery Dennison Corporation................. C 260 481-4500
 Fort Wayne (G-4783)

Avery Dennison Corporation................. D 317 462-1988
 Greenfield (G-6467)

Avery Dennison Corporation................. D 219 696-7777
 Lowell (G-11155)

Bruno Cb Inc... G 317 619-7467
 Indianapolis (G-7693)

◆ Covalnce Spcialty Coatings LLC....... E 812 424-2904
 Evansville (G-3988)

Daubert Vci Inc... E 574 772-9310
 Knox (G-10204)

Eckart America Corporation.................. G 219 864-4861
 Schererville (G-14519)

F Robert Gardner Co Inc........................ G 317 634-2333
 Indianapolis (G-8161)

Fedex Office & Print Svcs Inc.............. G 317 337-2679
 Indianapolis (G-8177)

Gindor Inc.. G 574 642-4004
 Goshen (G-6149)

Hi-Tech Label Inc..................................... F 765 659-1800
 Frankfort (G-5673)

International Paper Company................ D 800 643-7244
 Terre Haute (G-15619)

Jknk Ventures Inc.................................... E 812 246-0900
 Sellersburg (G-14603)

L & L Press Inc.. F 765 664-3162
 Marion (G-11305)

Label Tech Inc.. E 765 747-1234
 Muncie (G-12436)

Lambel Corporation................................. G 317 849-6828
 Indianapolis (G-8716)

Lamco Finishers Inc................................ E 317 471-1010
 Indianapolis (G-8717)

Mito-Craft Inc... G 574 287-4555
 South Bend (G-15152)

Morgan Adhesives Company LLC........ B 812 342-2004
 Columbus (G-2357)

NP Converters Inc................................... D 812 448-2555
 Brazil (G-1158)

Peafield Products Inc............................. F 317 839-8473
 Plainfield (G-13711)

Precision Label Incorporated................ F 812 877-3811
 Terre Haute (G-15668)

▲ Quality Engineered Pdts Inc............. F 574 294-6943
 Elkhart (G-3630)

R R Donnelley & Sons Company......... B 260 624-2350
 Angola (G-291)

Specialty Adhesive Film Co................... E 812 926-0156
 Aurora (G-455)

Tippecanoe Press Inc.............................. G 317 392-1207
 Shelbyville (G-14806)

Westrock Cp LLC..................................... G 574 936-2118
 Plymouth (G-13828)

▲ Zimmer Paper Products Del LLC....... D 317 263-3420
 Indianapolis (G-9811)

2673 Bags: plastic, laminated, and coated

Bagbarn Co.. F 847 850-2592
 Madison (G-11204)

▼ Berry Global Group Inc........................ A 812 424-2904
 Evansville (G-3921)

Cougar Bag Eb LLC................................. E 317 831-9720
 Mooresville (G-12200)

Cpg - Ohio LLC.. F 260 829-6721
 Orland (G-13363)

D & M Enterprises LLC.......................... F 260 483-4008
 Fort Wayne (G-4901)

Eagle Industries Inc................................ F 812 282-1393
 Jeffersonville (G-9973)

Gen Enterprises....................................... G 574 498-6777
 Tippecanoe (G-15759)

▲ Grrk Holdings Inc................................. E 317 872-0172
 Indianapolis (G-8336)

Hilex Poly Co LLC.................................... C 812 346-1066
 North Vernon (G-13277)

Inteplast Group Corporation................. G 219 220-2528
 Remington (G-14035)

Midwest Sandbags LLC.......................... G 847 366-6555
 Elkhart (G-3541)

Npx One LLC.. D 201 791-7600
 Indianapolis (G-9031)

Printpack Inc... C 812 663-5091
 Greensburg (G-6625)

Putnam Plastics Inc................................ E 765 795-6102
 Cloverdale (G-2094)

Universal Transparent Bag Inc............. G 317 634-6425
 Indianapolis (G-9683)

Witham Machine LLC.............................. G 317 835-2076
 Boggstown (G-1077)

26 PAPER AND ALLIED PRODUCTS

2674 Bags: uncoated paper and multiwall

Hilex Poly Co LLC .... C 812 346-1066
  North Vernon (G-13277)
▼ Lesac Corporation .... E 219 879-3215
  Michigan City (G-11632)
Westrock Cp LLC .... G 574 936-2118
  Plymouth (G-13828)

2675 Die-cut paper and board

A-1 Graphics Inc .... G 765 289-1851
  Muncie (G-12332)
AK Tool and Die Inc .... G 574 286-9010
  Mishawaka (G-11836)
American Steel Rule Die Inc .... G 574 262-3437
  Elkhart (G-3175)
Bethlehem Packg Die Cutng Inc .... E 812 282-8740
  New Albany (G-12700)
Bruce Payne .... G 260 492-2259
  Fort Wayne (G-4820)
C & W Inkd .... F 317 352-1000
  Indianapolis (G-7706)
Graphix Unlimited Inc .... E 574 546-3770
  Bremen (G-1193)
▲ Harcourt Industries Inc .... E 765 629-2625
  Milroy (G-11824)
Millcraft Paper Company .... G 317 240-3500
  Indianapolis (G-8920)
Rink Printing Company .... E 574 232-7935
  South Bend (G-15220)
◆ Ross-Gage Inc .... E 317 283-2323
  Indianapolis (G-9335)
Tre Paper Company .... G 765 649-2536
  Anderson (G-208)
Westrock Rkt LLC .... E 812 372-8873
  Columbus (G-2418)

2676 Sanitary paper products

Bobby Little Creations .... G 219 313-5102
  Crown Point (G-2658)
Diaper Stone Opco LLC .... G 866 221-2145
  Greenfield (G-6489)
Johnson & Johnson .... G 732 524-0400
  Fishers (G-4551)
Luxxeen America Corporation .... F 888 589-9336
  Carmel (G-1687)
Med Pad Incorporated .... G 812 422-6154
  Evansville (G-4195)
V Luxuries LLC .... G 877 308-5988
  Noblesville (G-13191)

2677 Envelopes

Bowers Envelope Company Inc .... G 317 253-4321
  Indianapolis (G-7665)
BSC Vntres Acquisition Sub LLC .... D 260 665-7521
  Angola (G-237)
Cenveo Worldwide Limited .... D 800 995-9500
  New Albany (G-12710)
Double Envelope Corp .... G 260 434-0500
  Fort Wayne (G-4926)
Envelope Service Inc .... E 260 432-6277
  Fort Wayne (G-4952)
Gov 6 Corp .... G 317 847-4942
  Indianapolis (G-8310)
Our Sunday Visitor Apps LLC .... E 800 348-2440
  Huntington (G-7349)
Ray Envelope Company Inc .... E 317 353-6251
  Indianapolis (G-9267)

2678 Stationery products

Altstadt Business Forms Inc .... F 812 425-3393
  Evansville (G-3882)

Asc Inc .... E 765 472-5331
  Peru (G-13566)
Avery Dennison Corporation .... D 219 696-7777
  Lowell (G-11155)
Bowers Envelope Company Inc .... G 317 253-4321
  Indianapolis (G-7665)
Foxxie Planner L L C .... G 260 247-6303
  Fort Wayne (G-5004)
Gov 6 Corp .... G 317 847-4942
  Indianapolis (G-8310)
Judkins Sr Renaldo G .... G 812 944-4251
  Clarksville (G-2022)
Rose & Petal LLC .... G 260 704-5731
  Fort Wayne (G-5389)

2679 Converted paper products, nec

▲ Applied Coating Converting LLC ...... G 260 436-4455
  Fort Wayne (G-4764)
Asc Inc .... C 765 473-4438
  Peru (G-13567)
Associated Label Inc .... G 812 877-3682
  Terre Haute (G-15546)
Avery Dennison Corporation .... D 219 696-7777
  Lowell (G-11155)
B&H Capital Inc .... B 812 376-9301
  Columbus (G-2225)
◆ Discount Labels LLC .... A 812 945-2617
  New Albany (G-12720)
Flutes Inc .... D 844 317-2021
  Indianapolis (G-8209)
Flutes Inc .... D 317 870-6010
  Indianapolis (G-8208)
Georgia-Pacific Corrugated III LLC .... G
  Indianapolis (G-8279)
Georgia-Pacific LLC .... G 219 776-0069
  Wheatfield (G-16766)
Gov 6 Corp .... G 317 847-4942
  Indianapolis (G-8310)
Hi-Tech Label Inc .... F 765 659-1800
  Frankfort (G-5673)
Hoosier Miracle Inc .... G 765 473-4438
  Peru (G-13586)
Hoosier Wallbeds Incorporated .... G 812 747-7154
  Lawrenceburg (G-10840)
Label Tech Inc .... E 765 747-1234
  Muncie (G-12436)
Larry Flowers Wholesale .... G 765 747-5156
  Muncie (G-12438)
Logistick Inc .... G 800 758-5840
  South Bend (G-15128)
Mach 1 Paper and Poly Pdts Inc .... F 574 522-4500
  Elkhart (G-3508)
Manchester Industries Inc VA .... E 765 489-4521
  Hagerstown (G-6839)
Patriot Label Inc .... G 812 877-1611
  Terre Haute (G-15658)
◆ Reflectix Inc .... D 765 533-4332
  Markleville (G-11370)
S R Wood Inc .... E 812 288-9201
  Clarksville (G-2032)
Schwarz Partners LP .... E 317 290-1140
  Carmel (G-1753)
Second Cycle LLC .... G 765 432-8178
  Kokomo (G-10331)
Sheets LLC .... G 317 290-1140
  Carmel (G-1759)
Shelf Tag Supply Corporation .... G 317 580-4030
  Westfield (G-16727)
Sinflex Paper Co Inc .... E 765 789-6688
  Muncie (G-12493)
▲ Ufp LLC .... G 219 697-2900
  Brook (G-1307)

▲ Web Industries Dallas Inc .... D 260 432-0027
  Fort Wayne (G-5558)
Welch Packaging Kentucky LLC .... E 574 295-2460
  Elkhart (G-3781)
Westrock Rkt LLC .... E 812 372-8873
  Columbus (G-2418)
Wingards SA .... G 260 768-4656
  Shipshewana (G-14898)

27 PRINTING, PUBLISHING AND ALLIED INDUSTRIES

2711 Newspapers

411 Newspaper .... G 219 922-8846
  Munster (G-12524)
Aim Media Indiana Oper LLC .... G 812 358-2111
  Brownstown (G-1416)
Aim Media Indiana Oper LLC .... D 812 372-7811
  Columbus (G-2215)
Aim Media Indiana Oper LLC .... E 317 736-7101
  Franklin (G-5704)
Aim Media Indiana Oper LLC .... G 812 736-7101
  Franklin (G-5705)
Aim Media Indiana Oper LLC .... E 317 462-5528
  Greenfield (G-6458)
Aim Media Indiana Oper LLC .... G 317 462-5528
  Greenfield (G-6459)
Aim Media Indiana Oper LLC .... E 317 462-5528
  Greenfield (G-6460)
Aim Media Indiana Oper LLC .... G 812 988-2221
  Nashville (G-12659)
Aim Media Indiana Oper LLC .... G 765 778-2324
  Pendleton (G-13524)
Aim Media Indiana Oper LLC .... F 812 522-4871
  Seymour (G-14626)
Aim Media Indiana Oper LLC .... D 812 372-7811
  Columbus (G-2216)
Alan Daily .... G 574 595-6253
  Star City (G-15394)
All Printing and Publications .... G 260 636-2727
  Albion (G-17)
All Time Low Magazine LLC .... G 317 286-7221
  Indianapolis (G-7477)
Allen C Terhune & Associates .... G 765 948-4164
  Fairmount (G-4407)
American Classifieds .... G 317 782-8111
  Greenwood (G-6667)
American Senior Homecare .... G 317 849-4968
  Indianapolis (G-7507)
Andre Renee Writes Pubg Co LLC ...... G 219 746-4329
  Hammond (G-6879)
Aurora Services Inc .... G 260 463-4901
  Shipshewana (G-14837)
Ball State University .... G 765 285-8218
  Muncie (G-12349)
Benton Review Newspaper .... G 765 884-1902
  Fowler (G-5619)
Bingo Bugle .... G 765 348-2859
  Hartford City (G-7062)
BJ Corporation of Indiana LLC .... G 317 507-6672
  Indianapolis (G-7635)
Carroll Papers Inc .... G 765 564-2222
  Delphi (G-2892)
Carroll Papers Inc .... G 574 967-4135
  Flora (G-4657)
Catholic Moment .... G 765 742-2050
  Lafayette (G-10551)
Catholic Press of Evansville .... G 812 424-5536
  Evansville (G-3966)
Chicago Crusader News Group .... G 219 885-4357
  Gary (G-5917)

SIC SECTION — 27 PRINTING, PUBLISHING AND ALLIED INDUSTRIES

Citiview Publications LLC .... G 502 296-1623
  Floyds Knobs *(G-4672)*
Civic Spark Media LLC .... G 765 357-4335
  Richmond *(G-14105)*
Ckmt Associates Inc .... F 219 924-2820
  Hammond *(G-6902)*
Cliff A Ostermeyer .... G 615 361-7902
  Fort Wayne *(G-4860)*
Cnhi LLC .... G 765 640-4893
  Anderson *(G-95)*
Cnhi LLC .... G 812 944-6481
  Jeffersonville *(G-9955)*
Cnhi LLC .... G 574 936-3101
  Plymouth *(G-13763)*
Colormax Digital Imaging Inc .... F 812 477-3805
  Evansville *(G-3975)*
Community Holdings Indiana Inc .... F 765 622-1212
  Anderson *(G-97)*
Community Holdings Indiana Inc .... G 812 663-3111
  Greensburg *(G-6585)*
Community Holdings Indiana Inc .... G 765 457-4130
  Kokomo *(G-10249)*
Community Holdings Indiana Inc .... G 765 482-4650
  Lebanon *(G-10885)*
Community Holdings Indiana Inc .... G 317 873-6397
  Lebanon *(G-10886)*
Community Holdings Indiana Inc .... G 574 722-5000
  Logansport *(G-11068)*
Community Papers Inc .... G 317 241-7363
  Indianapolis *(G-7841)*
Cornerstone Fllwship Kndllvlle .... G 260 347-0615
  Kendallville *(G-10102)*
Courier Printing Co Allen Cnty .... G 260 627-2728
  Grabill *(G-6293)*
▲ Courier-Times Inc .... D 765 529-1111
  New Castle *(G-12856)*
Criterion Press Inc .... E 317 236-1570
  Indianapolis *(G-7904)*
Crothersville Times .... G 812 793-2188
  Crothersville *(G-2639)*
Daily II Larry .... G 765 884 9355
  Fowler *(G-5623)*
Daily Money Managers Ind LLC .... G 317 797-0012
  Carmel *(G-1604)*
Daily Peru Tribune Pubg Co .... F 765 473-6641
  Peru *(G-13577)*
Daily Rental .... G 773 881-7762
  Munster *(G-12537)*
Decatur Publishing Co Inc .... E 260 724-2121
  Decatur *(G-2851)*
Delphos Herald of Indiana Inc .... C 812 438-2011
  Rising Sun *(G-14241)*
Delphos Herald of Indiana Inc .... E 812 537-0063
  Lawrenceburg *(G-10833)*
Don Taylor .... G 219 662-0597
  Crown Point *(G-2678)*
Dubois County Free Press LLC .... G 812 639-9651
  Huntingburg *(G-7276)*
Dubois-Spncer Cunties Pubg Inc .... F 812 367-2041
  Ferdinand *(G-4430)*
Eastside Vice Cmnty News Mdia .... G 317 356-2222
  Indianapolis *(G-8041)*
Ebony & Co Inc .... G 260 246-4691
  Fort Wayne *(G-4940)*
El Mexicano Inc .... G 260 456-6843
  Fort Wayne *(G-4943)*
Elwood Publishing Company Inc .... G 765 724-4469
  Alexandria *(G-50)*
Elwood Publishing Company Inc .... G 765 675-2115
  Tipton *(G-15772)*
Elwood Publishing Company Inc .... E 765 552-3355
  Elwood *(G-3823)*

Evansville Courier Co .... B 812 464-7500
  Evansville *(G-4051)*
Evansville Thunderbolts .... F 812 435-0872
  Evansville *(G-4058)*
Exchange Publishing Corp .... F 574 831-2138
  New Paris *(G-12952)*
Fairmount News .... G 765 948-4164
  Fairmount *(G-4409)*
Fort Wayne Newspapers Inc .... B 260 461-8444
  Fort Wayne *(G-4999)*
Fountain County Neighbor .... G 765 762-2411
  Attica *(G-348)*
Frankfort Newspaper .... G 859 254-2385
  Frankfort *(G-5666)*
Franklin Township Civic League .... G 317 862-1774
  Indianapolis *(G-8225)*
Fresh News LLC .... G 219 929-5558
  Chesterton *(G-1929)*
Ft Wayne Reader .... G 260 420-8580
  Fort Wayne *(G-5014)*
Gannett Co Inc .... G 765 423-5511
  Lafayette *(G-10584)*
Gannett Media Corp .... C 765 423-5512
  Lafayette *(G-10585)*
Gannett Media Corp .... G 765 962-1575
  Richmond *(G-14124)*
George P Stewart Printing Co .... E 317 924-5143
  Indianapolis *(G-8278)*
Granger Gazette Inc .... G 574 277-2679
  Granger *(G-6350)*
Graphic Printing Co Inc .... E 260 726-8141
  Portland *(G-13947)*
Great Deals Racing .... G 765 288-4608
  Gaston *(G-6046)*
Green Banner Publications Inc .... E 812 967-3176
  Borden *(G-1109)*
Growing Child Inc .... G 765 463-1696
  West Lafayette *(G-16589)*
Harrison Press .... G 513 367-4582
  Lawrenceburg *(G-10839)*
Hartford City News Times .... F 765 348-0110
  Winchester *(G-16889)*
Herald Argus .... G 219 362-2161
  Michigan City *(G-11623)*
Heritage Lake Community Svcs .... G 317 766-4118
  Coatesville *(G-2106)*
Hielo Services LLC .... G 219 973-1952
  Hobart *(G-7189)*
Home News Enterprises LLC .... B 800 876-7811
  Columbus *(G-2318)*
Hoosier Times Inc .... C 812 275-3372
  Bedford *(G-641)*
Hoosier Times Inc .... F 812 332-4401
  Beech Grove *(G-691)*
Hoosier Times Inc .... C 765 342-3311
  Martinsville *(G-11402)*
Hoosier Times Inc .... C 812 331-4270
  Bloomington *(G-882)*
Hoosier Tribune Corp .... G 907 570-8888
  Carmel *(G-1658)*
Horizon Publications Inc .... G 260 244-5153
  Columbia City *(G-2152)*
Huntington County Tab Inc .... G 260 356-1107
  Huntington *(G-7321)*
IBJ Corporation .... D 317 634-6200
  Indianapolis *(G-8448)*
Illinois Agri-News .... G 317 726-5391
  Indianapolis *(G-8460)*
Indiana News Media LLC .... G 812 703-2025
  Columbus *(G-2323)*
Indiana News Media LLC .... G 812 546-4940
  Hope *(G-7228)*

Indiana Newspapers LLC .... D 317 444-3800
  Indianapolis *(G-8486)*
Indiana Newspapers LLC .... D 765 213-5700
  Muncie *(G-12425)*
Indiana Newspapers LLC .... D 812 886-9955
  Vincennes *(G-16131)*
Indiana Newspapers LLC .... A 317 444-4000
  Indianapolis *(G-8487)*
Indianapolis Power .... G 317 834-3871
  Martinsville *(G-11405)*
Indianplis Legislative Insight .... G 317 955-9997
  Indianapolis *(G-8510)*
Info Publishing Impact LLC .... G 317 912-3642
  Fishers *(G-4547)*
Innovative Media Sciences Inc .... G 317 366-4371
  Indianapolis *(G-8556)*
Iu International Svc Ctr .... F 812 855-9086
  Bloomington *(G-893)*
James Smith .... G 260 414-1237
  Fort Wayne *(G-5132)*
Janis Buhl .... G 765 478-5448
  Cambridge City *(G-1497)*
Journal of Teaching Writing .... G 317 274-0092
  Indianapolis *(G-8640)*
Kaiser Press LLC .... G 317 619-7092
  Indianapolis *(G-8655)*
Kankakee Valley Post News .... G 219 987-5111
  Demotte *(G-2920)*
Kankakee Valley Publishing Co .... G 219 866-5111
  Rensselaer *(G-14056)*
Kendallville Mall .... G 260 897-2697
  Avilla *(G-482)*
King Tut Inc .... G 317 938-9907
  Zionsville *(G-17028)*
Kpc Media Group Inc .... F 678 645-0000
  Angola *(G-270)*
Kpc Media Group Inc .... F 260 925-2611
  Auburn *(G-400)*
Kpc Media Group Inc .... G 260 868-5501
  Auburn *(G-401)*
Kpc Media Group Inc .... F 260 426-2640
  Fort Wayne *(G-5158)*
Kpc Media Group Inc .... C 260 347-0400
  Kendallville *(G-10130)*
La Grange Publishing Co Inc .... F 260 463-3243
  Lagrange *(G-10747)*
La Ola Latino Americana .... G 317 822-0345
  Indianapolis *(G-8707)*
La Voz De Indiana Inc .... G 317 636-7970
  Indianapolis *(G-8708)*
La Voz De Indiana Inc .... G 317 423-0957
  Indianapolis *(G-8709)*
Labor News Inc .... F 317 251-1287
  Indianapolis *(G-8710)*
Laff Worx LLC .... G 812 267-0430
  New Salisbury *(G-12985)*
Leader Publishing Co of Salem .... E 812 883-3281
  Salem *(G-14487)*
Lee Enterprises Inc Times .... E 219 933-3200
  Munster *(G-12547)*
Lee Publications Inc .... G 219 462-5151
  Valparaiso *(G-15994)*
Liberty Herald .... G 765 458-5114
  Liberty *(G-10991)*
Life Path Numerology Center .... G 317 638-9752
  Indianapolis *(G-8747)*
Loogootee Tribune Inc .... G 812 295-2500
  Loogootee *(G-11143)*
Macednian Ptrtic Orgnztion of .... G 260 422-5900
  Fort Wayne *(G-5196)*
Madison Courier .... E 812 265-3641
  Madison *(G-11237)*

Employee Codes: A=Over 500 employees, B=251-500
C=101-250, D=51-100, E=20-50, F=10-19, G=1-9

27 PRINTING, PUBLISHING AND ALLIED INDUSTRIES

Manchester North News Journal............ G 260 982-6383
  North Manchester *(G-13238)*
Mayhill Publications Inc........................ E 765 345-5133
  Knightstown *(G-10199)*
Midcountry Media Inc........................... D 765 345-5133
  Knightstown *(G-10200)*
Mittera Group Inc................................. G 812 256-3396
  Charlestown *(G-1885)*
Montgomery & Associates Inc.............. F 219 879-0088
  Michigan City *(G-11641)*
Mooresville Times................................. E 317 831-0280
  Martinsville *(G-11415)*
My Daily Wedding Deals LLC................ G 812 603-6149
  Indianapolis *(G-8975)*
Myers Enterprises Inc........................... G 812 636-7350
  Odon *(G-13344)*
New Time Inc....................................... G 219 655-5041
  Whiting *(G-16836)*
News and Tribune................................. F 812 206-2168
  Jeffersonville *(G-10023)*
▲ News Dispatch.................................. C 219 874-7211
  Michigan City *(G-11645)*
News Examiner Circulation Dept.......... G 765 825-2914
  Connersville *(G-2458)*
News Publishing Company LLC............ G 812 649-4440
  Rockport *(G-14346)*
News Publishing Company LLC............ G 502 633-4334
  Tell City *(G-15515)*
News Publishing Company Inc............. G 260 461-8444
  Fort Wayne *(G-5270)*
News Reminder..................................... G 574 583-5121
  Monticello *(G-12161)*
News-Banner Publications Inc............. E 260 824-0224
  Bluffton *(G-1046)*
News-Gazette.. F 765 584-4501
  Winchester *(G-16895)*
News-Herald Inc................................... G 765 425-8903
  Marion *(G-11320)*
Newsnow Dubois County..................... G 812 827-6131
  Jasper *(G-9895)*
Newspaper Holding Inc........................ G 270 678-5171
  Jeffersonville *(G-10024)*
Newspaper Holding Inc........................ G 812 231-4200
  Terre Haute *(G-15651)*
Newspaper Holding Inc........................ G 812 254-0480
  Washington *(G-16496)*
Northwest Indiana Newsppr Inc........... G 574 722-5000
  Logansport *(G-11101)*
Northwest News & Printing.................. G 260 637-9003
  Fort Wayne *(G-5276)*
Nuvo Inc.. E 317 254-2400
  Indianapolis *(G-9035)*
Nwhoodtales Corp................................ G 708 858-0598
  Highland *(G-7148)*
Nwitimescom.. E 219 933-3200
  Munster *(G-12553)*
OBannon Publishing Company............ E 812 738-4552
  Corydon *(G-2508)*
Odb Inc... G 260 673-0062
  Fort Wayne *(G-5281)*
Paper of Montgomery County.............. G 765 361-8888
  Crawfordsville *(G-2600)*
Paper of Wabash County Inc................ F 260 563-8326
  Wabash *(G-16208)*
Papers Inc... G 574 534-2591
  Goshen *(G-6235)*
Papers Inc... G 574 269-2932
  Warsaw *(G-16409)*
Pathfinder Communications Corp........ E 574 295-2500
  Elkhart *(G-3587)*
Patriot Inc... G 317 462-5172
  Greenfield *(G-6535)*

Paxton Media Group LLC..................... G 765 664-5111
  Marion *(G-11324)*
Pendleton Times................................... G 765 778-2324
  Pendleton *(G-13552)*
Pierce Oil Co Inc................................... F 812 268-6356
  Sullivan *(G-15416)*
Pike County Publishing Corp............... G 812 354-8500
  Petersburg *(G-13621)*
Planet Goshen LLC............................... G 574 830-5797
  Goshen *(G-6239)*
Posey County News.............................. G 812 682-3950
  New Harmony *(G-12888)*
Poultry Press.. G 765 827-0932
  Connersville *(G-2462)*
Prairie Preservation Guild Ltd.............. G 765 884-1902
  Fowler *(G-5632)*
Princeton Publishing Inc...................... G 812 385-2525
  Princeton *(G-14010)*
Printers Group...................................... G 317 835-7720
  Fairland *(G-4401)*
Progress Examiner................................ G 812 865-3242
  Orleans *(G-13381)*
Pudders LLC... G 317 402-3507
  Shelbyville *(G-14789)*
Pulaski County Press Inc..................... G 574 946-6628
  Winamac *(G-16872)*
Purdue Student Pubg Foundation........ D 765 743-1111
  West Lafayette *(G-16622)*
R R Donnelley Inc................................. F 317 614-2508
  Indianapolis *(G-9256)*
RE Wilson LLC...................................... G 317 730-4846
  Zionsville *(G-17045)*
Rebecca L Hamann & Associates......... G 219 763-1233
  Portage *(G-13910)*
Region Communications Inc................ G 219 662-8888
  Crown Point *(G-2743)*
Reno LLC... G 708 846-7821
  Schererville *(G-14542)*
Republic Inc.. E 812 342-8028
  Columbus *(G-2386)*
Republican.. G 317 745-2777
  Danville *(G-2825)*
Richard K Williams............................... G 616 745-9319
  Albion *(G-43)*
Ripley Publishing Co Inc...................... F 812 689-6364
  Versailles *(G-16103)*
Rowland Printing Co Inc....................... F 317 773-1829
  Noblesville *(G-13168)*
Russ Print Shp/Hbron Advrtser............ F 219 996-3142
  Hebron *(G-7106)*
Russ Publishing.................................... F 812 847-4487
  Linton *(G-11045)*
Schurz Communications Inc................ E 574 235-6496
  South Bend *(G-15235)*
Schurz Communications Inc................ F 574 247-7237
  Mishawaka *(G-11992)*
Seymour Trbune A Cal Ltd Prtnr........... F 812 522-4871
  Seymour *(G-14691)*
Shelbyville Newspapers Inc................. G 317 398-6631
  Shelbyville *(G-14798)*
Shoals News.. G 812 247-2828
  Shoals *(G-14911)*
Shopping Guide News Inc.................... F 574 223-5417
  Rochester *(G-14324)*
SLM Mrkting Communications Inc...... G 812 426-7993
  Evansville *(G-4319)*
Sommer Letter Company LLC.............. G 260 414-6686
  Huntertown *(G-7266)*
South Bend Tribune Corp..................... F 574 971-5651
  Goshen *(G-6256)*
South Bend Tribune Corp..................... B 574 235-6161
  South Bend *(G-15257)*

South Gibson Star-Times Inc................ F 812 753-3553
  Fort Branch *(G-4707)*
South Whtley Trbune Prcton New........ G 260 723-4771
  South Whitley *(G-15325)*
Southern Indiana Bus Source.............. G 812 206-6397
  Jeffersonville *(G-10056)*
Southsider.. G 317 781-0023
  Indianapolis *(G-9465)*
Special Ideas Incorporated.................. G 812 834-5691
  Heltonville *(G-7111)*
Spencer Evening World........................ D 812 829-2255
  Spencer *(G-15362)*
Static Media Inc................................... G 212 366-4500
  Fishers *(G-4606)*
Teragraphics Ink LLC............................ G 765 430-2863
  West Lafayette *(G-16636)*
That Print Lady LLC.............................. G 317 339-7411
  Indianapolis *(G-9587)*
The Findlay Publishing Co.................... G 812 222-8000
  Batesville *(G-606)*
The Papers Inc...................................... C 574 658-4111
  Milford *(G-11807)*
Times.. E 765 659-4622
  Frankfort *(G-5698)*
Times Leader Publications LLC............ F 317 300-8782
  Avon *(G-552)*
Tipton Tribune...................................... G 765 675-2115
  Tipton *(G-15794)*
Topics Newspapers Inc........................ F 888 357-7827
  Fishers *(G-4614)*
Torch Newspapers Inc.......................... G 765 569-2033
  Rockville *(G-14359)*
Town of Saratoga.................................. G 765 584-1576
  Saratoga *(G-14509)*
Trading Post... G 574 935-5460
  Plymouth *(G-13821)*
Triple Crown Media LLC....................... G 574 533-2151
  Goshen *(G-6273)*
Trustees Indiana University................. G 812 855-7995
  Bloomington *(G-995)*
Trustees Indiana University................. E 812 855-0763
  Bloomington *(G-996)*
Truth Publishing Company Inc............. G 765 653-5151
  Greencastle *(G-6434)*
▲ Truth Publishing Company Inc......... C 574 294-1661
  Elkhart *(G-3750)*
Twice Daily LLC.................................... G 812 484-5417
  Evansville *(G-4357)*
Twin City Journal Reporter.................. G 765 674-0070
  Gas City *(G-6041)*
University Notre Dame Du Lac............. F 574 631-7471
  Notre Dame *(G-13317)*
University Notre Dame Du Lac............. E 574 631-6346
  Notre Dame *(G-13318)*
USA Today.. G 212 715-2188
  Fishers *(G-4624)*
Vevay Newspapers Inc......................... G 812 427-2311
  Vevay *(G-16114)*
Wabash Plain Dealer Co LLC................ E 260 563-2131
  Wabash *(G-16221)*
Wabash Valley Publishing LLC............. G 812 494-2152
  Vincennes *(G-16163)*
Waynedale News Inc............................ G 260 747-4535
  Fort Wayne *(G-5556)*
Western Wayne News........................... G 765 478-5448
  Cambridge City *(G-1504)*
Whatzup LLC.. G 260 407-3198
  Fort Wayne *(G-5562)*
Whitewater Publications Inc................ F 765 647-4221
  Brookville *(G-1341)*
Wilson Media Group Inc....................... F 765 452-0055
  Kokomo *(G-10359)*

SIC SECTION — 27 PRINTING, PUBLISHING AND ALLIED INDUSTRIES

Wpta Television Inc .... D 217 221-3353
  Fort Wayne *(G-5577)*
Zergnet .... G 317 201-0889
  Noblesville *(G-13199)*

2721 Periodicals

12 Stone Ventures Inc .... G 765 573-4605
  Converse *(G-2476)*
1632 Inc .... G 219 398-4155
  East Chicago *(G-2987)*
American Legion National .... D 317 630-1200
  Indianapolis *(G-7505)*
American School Health Assn .... G 703 506-7675
  Bloomington *(G-779)*
Americas Coml Trnsp RES Co LLC .... F 812 379-2085
  Columbus *(G-2219)*
Ameriforce Media LLC .... G 812 961-9478
  Bloomington *(G-780)*
Athletes Management & Services .... G 317 925-8200
  Indianapolis *(G-7559)*
Baxter Design & Advertising .... G 219 464-9237
  Valparaiso *(G-15912)*
Boilers Inc .... G 765 742-5855
  West Lafayette *(G-16567)*
Brian Bex Report Inc .... G 765 489-5566
  Hagerstown *(G-6834)*
Christian Sound & Song Inc .... G 574 294-2893
  Elkhart *(G-3251)*
Ci Publishing Ecomm LLC .... G 317 679-1866
  Fort Wayne *(G-4847)*
Compucomics .... G 812 876-1480
  Ellettsville *(G-3804)*
Connection LLC .... G 260 593-3999
  Topeka *(G-15797)*
Construction Bus Media LLC .... G 847 359-6493
  Carmel *(G-1593)*
Cr Publications .... G 219 931-6700
  Hammond *(G-6906)*
Creative Construction Pubg Inc .... G 765 743-9704
  West Lafayette *(G-16573)*
▲ Dennis Polk & Associates Inc .... G 574 831-3555
  New Paris *(G-12950)*
Diamond Hoosier .... G 317 773-1411
  Noblesville *(G-13070)*
Dynamic Resource Group Inc .... E 260 589-4000
  Berne *(G-709)*
Eco Partners Inc .... G 317 450-3346
  Carmel *(G-1619)*
Emmis Corporation .... D 317 266-0100
  Indianapolis *(G-8106)*
Emmis Operating Company .... E 317 266-0100
  Indianapolis *(G-8107)*
Emmis Publishing LP .... E 317 266-0100
  Indianapolis *(G-8108)*
Emmis Publishing Corporation .... E 317 266-0100
  Indianapolis *(G-8109)*
Emp of Evansville .... F 812 962-1309
  Evansville *(G-4034)*
Endowment Development Services .... F 317 542-9829
  Indianapolis *(G-8114)*
Flair Exchange LLC .... G 765 210-4604
  Tipton *(G-15773)*
Fort Wayne Newspapers Inc .... B 260 461-8444
  Fort Wayne *(G-4999)*
Galbe Magazine LLC .... G 248 742-5231
  Carmel *(G-1638)*
Greencastle Offset Inc .... G 765 653-4026
  Greencastle *(G-6406)*
Hamilton County Business Mag .... G 317 774-7447
  Noblesville *(G-13092)*
Homes & Lifestyles Magazine .... F 574 674-6639
  Osceola *(G-13393)*

Horizon Publishing Company LLC .... F 219 852-3200
  Hammond *(G-6949)*
How You Perceive Ever .... G 301 579-4973
  Indianapolis *(G-8429)*
Indiana State Medical Assn .... E 317 261-2060
  Indianapolis *(G-8494)*
Indys Infant Center LLC .... G 317 717-3622
  Indianapolis *(G-8539)*
Informa Business Media Inc .... G 317 233-1310
  New Palestine *(G-12938)*
International English Inc .... G 260 868-2670
  Butler *(G-1467)*
Julie Stergen .... G 317 888-6146
  Greenwood *(G-6719)*
Kamrex Inc .... E 317 204-3779
  Avon *(G-530)*
Linear Publishing Corp .... G 317 722-8500
  Indianapolis *(G-8763)*
Linker Media Group Inc .... G 219 230-3777
  Dyer *(G-2977)*
Literature Sales .... G 219 873-3093
  Michigan City *(G-11635)*
Locavore Productions LLC .... G 317 371-2970
  Morristown *(G-12279)*
Lsc Communications Inc .... C 765 364-2247
  Crawfordsville *(G-2586)*
Lsc Communications Us LLC .... G 765 362-1300
  Crawfordsville *(G-2587)*
Magazine Fulfillment Corp .... F 219 874-4245
  Michigan City *(G-11636)*
Market Place Publications .... G 219 769-7733
  Merrillville *(G-11536)*
McPubs Inc .... G 317 539-6461
  Coatesville *(G-2107)*
Michiana Bus Publications Inc .... G 260 497-0433
  Fort Wayne *(G-5220)*
Michiana Executive Journal .... G 574 256-6666
  Mishawaka *(G-11943)*
Midcountry Media Inc .... D 765 345-5133
  Knightstown *(G-10200)*
Muzfeed Inc .... G 815 252-7676
  Fort Wayne *(G-5253)*
Omega One Connect Inc .... G 317 626-3445
  Indianapolis *(G-9048)*
◆ Our Sunday Visitor Inc .... B 260 359-2564
  Huntington *(G-7350)*
P J J T Distributors Inc .... G 812 254-2218
  Washington *(G-16498)*
Pages Editorial Services Inc .... F 765 674-4212
  Marion *(G-11323)*
Pearson Education Inc .... G 765 483-6738
  Lebanon *(G-10929)*
Prairie Gold Rush .... G 812 342-3608
  Seymour *(G-14676)*
Project House .... G 317 691-4237
  Indianapolis *(G-9227)*
Racestar Publications .... G 219 987-2096
  Demotte *(G-2927)*
Relx Inc .... G 317 849-9806
  Fishers *(G-4595)*
Rick Singleton .... F 574 259-5555
  Mishawaka *(G-11986)*
Roann Publishers .... G 574 831-2795
  Goshen *(G-6248)*
Rough Notes Company Inc .... E 317 582-1600
  Carmel *(G-1746)*
Saturday Evening Post Soc Inc .... D 317 634-1100
  Indianapolis *(G-9379)*
Servaas Inc .... G 317 633-2020
  Indianapolis *(G-9405)*
Society For Ethnmusicology Inc .... G 812 855-6672
  Bloomington *(G-977)*

Sophistcted Lving Indianapolis .... F 317 565-4555
  Carmel *(G-1766)*
Stork News Northwest Indiana .... G 219 808-5221
  Hobart *(G-7210)*
Tokumei LLC .... G 765 772-0073
  West Lafayette *(G-16638)*
Towne Post Network Inc .... G 317 288-7101
  Indianapolis *(G-9625)*
Travelhost Mag Indianapolis .... G 317 416-7780
  Carmel *(G-1790)*
Trustees Indiana University .... G 812 855-3439
  Bloomington *(G-997)*
Trustees Indiana University .... G 812 856-4186
  Bloomington *(G-998)*
Ultramontane Associates Inc .... G 574 289-9786
  South Bend *(G-15295)*
University Notre Dame Du Lac .... E 574 631-6346
  Notre Dame *(G-13318)*
USA Travel Magazine .... G 317 834-3683
  Martinsville *(G-11433)*
Whitetail Heartbeat .... G 260 336-1052
  Middlebury *(G-11758)*

2731 Book publishing

A & E Publications LLC .... G 317 795-4308
  Indianapolis *(G-7395)*
A Page Beyond LLC .... G 317 589-8218
  Fishers *(G-4638)*
Abundant Life Publications LLC .... G 219 730-7621
  Gary *(G-5887)*
AM Publishing Inc .... G 317 806-0001
  Fishers *(G-4462)*
Apologia Eductl Ministries Inc .... E 765 608-3280
  Anderson *(G-79)*
▼ Author Solutions LLC .... C 812 339-6000
  Bloomington *(G-786)*
▼ Ave Maria Press Inc .... D 574 287-2831
  Notre Dame *(G-13315)*
Beacon House .... G 219 756-2131
  Schererville *(G-14515)*
Bertelsmann Pubg Group Inc .... G 410 386-7717
  Crawfordsville *(G-2547)*
Bibles For Blind Vslly Hndcppe .... G 812 466-3134
  Terre Haute *(G-15552)*
Bird Publishing Company .... G 219 462-6330
  Valparaiso *(G-15915)*
Bk Royston Publishing LLC .... G 502 802-5385
  Jeffersonville *(G-9943)*
Book of US LLC .... G 331 256-5953
  Crown Point *(G-2660)*
Brendacurtis Recipe Books LLC .... E 574 216-2261
  Indianapolis *(G-7677)*
Bright Corp .... F 765 642-3114
  Griffith *(G-6797)*
Childrens Outreach .... G 317 535-7014
  Whiteland *(G-16779)*
Cr Publications .... G 219 931-6700
  Hammond *(G-6906)*
Creative Blessings Co LLC .... G 219 293-9595
  Indianapolis *(G-7900)*
Distance Learning Systems Ind .... E 888 955-3276
  Greenwood *(G-6686)*
Emmantony Productions .... G 765 649-5967
  Anderson *(G-114)*
Frugal Times .... G 317 326-4165
  Greenfield *(G-6504)*
Get Published Inc .... B 812 334-5279
  Bloomington *(G-867)*
Gh LLC .... G 765 775-3776
  West Lafayette *(G-16582)*
Gingerbread House Publications .... G 260 622-4868
  Ossian *(G-13424)*

27 PRINTING, PUBLISHING AND ALLIED INDUSTRIES

Good Morning Publishing Co................ G 317 782-8381
   Beech Grove *(G-690)*
Hachette Book Group Inc..................... C 765 483-9900
   Lebanon *(G-10894)*
Hackett Publishing Company................ G 317 635-9250
   Indianapolis *(G-8350)*
Hackett Publishing Company................ F 317 635-9250
   Indianapolis *(G-8351)*
Harpercollins Publishers LLC................ G 800 242-7737
   Indianapolis *(G-8365)*
Harpercollins Publishers LLC................ D 219 324-4880
   La Porte *(G-10415)*
Harpercollins Publishers LLC................ G 317 839-4307
   Plainfield *(G-13685)*
Harpercollins Publishers LLC................ G 317 406-8777
   Plainfield *(G-13686)*
Helping Hands....................................... G 219 696-4564
   Lowell *(G-11162)*
Herff Jones LLC................................... E 317 612-3400
   Indianapolis *(G-8384)*
Horizon Publishing Company LLC......... F 219 852-3200
   Hammond *(G-6949)*
Houghton Mifflin Harcourt Co................ C 317 359-5585
   Indianapolis *(G-8425)*
Houghton Mifflin Harcourt Pubg............ D 317 359-5585
   Indianapolis *(G-8426)*
Hpc International Inc............................ F 219 922-4868
   Crown Point *(G-2694)*
Hussleaire LLC....................................... G 312 889-4866
   Gary *(G-5955)*
Indiana Team Yearbook........................ G 812 858-7113
   Newburgh *(G-13007)*
▼ Iuniverse Inc....................................... B 812 330-2909
   Bloomington *(G-894)*
John Wiley & Sons Inc.......................... F 317 572-3000
   Indianapolis *(G-8631)*
Kamrex Inc.. E 317 204-3779
   Avon *(G-530)*
▲ Kids World Productions Inc............... G 317 674-6090
   Zionsville *(G-17027)*
Kmm Creative LLC................................ G 813 764-9294
   Fort Wayne *(G-5152)*
▲ Lakota Language Consortium............ F 888 525-6828
   Bloomington *(G-905)*
Lions Quarter LLC............................... G 219 932-5531
   Hammond *(G-6972)*
Lsc Communications Book LLC........... G 317 715-2406
   Indianapolis *(G-8789)*
Lsc Communications Book LLC........... G 317 715-2406
   Indianapolis *(G-8790)*
Lsc Communications Book LLC........... G 317 406-8783
   Plainfield *(G-13698)*
Lsc Communications Book LLC........... G 317 715-2402
   Indianapolis *(G-8791)*
Mad Media LLC.................................... G 317 210-5609
   Sheridan *(G-14825)*
Main1media LLC.................................... G 317 841-7000
   Indianapolis *(G-8813)*
Mbpc Progressive Consultants............. G 765 301-1864
   Greencastle *(G-6421)*
Naporamic LLC..................................... G 463 249-8265
   Indianapolis *(G-8984)*
National Fdrtion State High SC............ E 317 972-6900
   Indianapolis *(G-8988)*
No-Load Fund Investor Inc.................. G 317 571-1471
   Carmel *(G-1707)*
Old Paths Tract Society Inc................. E 812 247-2560
   Shoals *(G-14909)*
Otis Dynamic Enterprises LLC............. G 860 978-6003
   Fort Wayne *(G-5288)*
Our Sunday Visitor Apps LLC............. E 800 348-2440
   Huntington *(G-7349)*

Palibrio... G 812 671-9757
   Bloomington *(G-941)*
Pearson Education Inc........................ F 317 428-3049
   Indianapolis *(G-9110)*
Penguin Random House LLC............... F 800 733-3000
   Crawfordsville *(G-2601)*
Penguin Random House LLC............... D 765 362-5125
   Crawfordsville *(G-2602)*
Penguin Random House LLC............... G 800 672-7836
   Lebanon *(G-10930)*
Performers Edition LLC........................ G 317 429-1300
   Indianapolis *(G-9125)*
Phillip D Kennedy Publishing............... G 317 872-6366
   Indianapolis *(G-9136)*
Princeton Publishing Inc...................... G 812 385-2525
   Princeton *(G-14010)*
Relaxura LLC... G 317 333-1324
   Indianapolis *(G-9287)*
Sacred Selections................................. G 260 347-3758
   Kendallville *(G-10151)*
▲ Sdi Innovations Inc.......................... C 765 471-8883
   Lafayette *(G-10689)*
Sound System....................................... G 317 407-4092
   Indianapolis *(G-9462)*
St Augustines Press Inc....................... G 574 291-3500
   South Bend *(G-15265)*
◆ St Meinrad Archabbey....................... D 812 357-6611
   Saint Meinrad *(G-14464)*
Studio Indiana....................................... G 812 332-5073
   Bloomington *(G-981)*
Tanguero Inc... G 415 236-2642
   Bloomington *(G-983)*
Three Cups LLC................................... G 317 633-8082
   Indianapolis *(G-9600)*
▲ Tom Doherty Company Inc.............. G 317 352-8200
   Indianapolis *(G-9617)*
Trafford Holdings Ltd............................ C 888 232-4444
   Bloomington *(G-991)*
Trustees Indiana University.................. E 812 855-0763
   Bloomington *(G-996)*
University Notre Dame Du Lac............ E 574 631-6346
   Notre Dame *(G-13318)*
University Publishing Corp................... E 812 339-9033
   Bloomington *(G-1004)*
Vanessa Collins LLC............................. G 219 985-5705
   Floyds Knobs *(G-4697)*
Vdb Creative Publishing LLC............... G 317 441-9204
   Indianapolis *(G-9703)*
Vivid Dragonfly Press LLC.................. G 609 954-1010
   Fort Wayne *(G-5534)*
▼ Voice of God Recordings Inc............ D 812 246-2137
   Jeffersonville *(G-10069)*
Watermelon World Publishing............... G 574 267-2505
   Winona Lake *(G-16917)*
Wesleyan Church Corporation............. E 317 774-7900
   Fishers *(G-4632)*
Whitman Publications Inc.................... G 574 268-2062
   Winona Lake *(G-16918)*
Wiley.. G 317 794-6765
   Fishers *(G-4633)*
William H Sadlier Inc............................ G 219 465-0453
   Valparaiso *(G-16081)*
▲ Winters Publishing............................ G 812 663-4948
   Greensburg *(G-6641)*
Wish Factory Inc.................................. F 260 745-2550
   South Whitley *(G-15332)*
▼ World Missionary Press Inc............... E 574 831-2111
   New Paris *(G-12974)*
Worth Tax and Financial Svc.............. G 574 267-4687
   Warsaw *(G-16456)*
▲ Xlibris Corporation............................. B 812 671-9162
   Bloomington *(G-1017)*

Yaney Mktg Graphic Design LLC......... G 317 776-0676
   Noblesville *(G-13197)*

2732 Book printing

▲ Annies Publishing LLC..................... C 260 589-4000
   Berne *(G-704)*
Augustin Prtg & Design Svcs............... G 765 966-7130
   Richmond *(G-14088)*
Biblical Enterprises LLC....................... G 812 391-0071
   Bloomington *(G-805)*
Burkert-Walton Inc................................ G 812 425-7157
   Evansville *(G-3957)*
▲ C-Point Inc.. C 260 478-9551
   Fort Wayne *(G-4828)*
Codybro LLC... G 765 827-5441
   Connersville *(G-2432)*
Direct Point LLC................................... G 260 705-2279
   Fort Wayne *(G-4917)*
Diversified Bus Systems Inc................ G 317 254-8668
   Indianapolis *(G-7984)*
▲ Franklin Publishing Inc.................... G 800 634-1993
   Greenwood *(G-6705)*
Herff Jones LLC................................... E 317 612-3400
   Indianapolis *(G-8384)*
Kendallville Custom Printing................ F 260 347-9233
   Kendallville *(G-10125)*
Lsc Communications Inc..................... C 765 364-2247
   Crawfordsville *(G-2586)*
Lsc Communications Inc.................... G 812 234-1585
   Terre Haute *(G-15633)*
Lsc Communications Us LLC............. G 765 362-1300
   Crawfordsville *(G-2587)*
Michael L Jerrell................................... G 812 354-9297
   Petersburg *(G-13617)*
Mitchell-Fleming Printing Inc............... F 317 462-5467
   Greenfield *(G-6529)*
Priority Printing LLC............................ G 317 241-4234
   Indianapolis *(G-9213)*
R R Donnelley & Sons Company......... C 765 362-1300
   Crawfordsville *(G-2607)*
▲ Solema USA Inc............................... G 765 361-0806
   Crawfordsville *(G-2616)*
University Publishing Corp................... E 812 339-9033
   Bloomington *(G-1004)*
Wayseeker LLC.................................... G 574 529-0199
   Syracuse *(G-15491)*

2741 Miscellaneous publishing

39 Degrees North LLC......................... F 855 447-3939
   Bloomington *(G-765)*
Abundant Life Publications LLC.......... G 219 730-7621
   Gary *(G-5887)*
Academy of Mdel Aronautics Inc........ D 765 287-1256
   Muncie *(G-12334)*
Accurate Publishing Co........................ G 219 836-1397
   Munster *(G-12527)*
Adamswells Phonebooks LLC............. G 260 622-6046
   Bluffton *(G-1022)*
Agate Workshop.................................... G 812 333-0900
   Bloomington *(G-775)*
Aim Media Indiana Oper LLC.............. D 812 372-7811
   Columbus *(G-2216)*
Air In Motion Publishers LLC............. G 317 850-0149
   Indianapolis *(G-7461)*
Aj Express Broker Service................... G 812 866-1380
   Madison *(G-11197)*
American Classifieds............................ G 317 782-8111
   Greenwood *(G-6667)*
Anthonyjean LLC................................... G 317 513-4981
   Greenwood *(G-6670)*
Arcane Wonders.................................... G 469 964-9050
   Roanoke *(G-14258)*

27 PRINTING, PUBLISHING AND ALLIED INDUSTRIES

Artful Living... G..... 317 764-7232
  Carmel (G-1564)
Artistic Expressions Pubg Inc.................... G..... 317 502-6213
  Gas City (G-6032)
Associated Cnstr Publications................... E..... 317 660-2395
  Indianapolis (G-7554)
Automobile Dealers Assn of Ind................ G..... 317 635-1441
  Indianapolis (G-7576)
Azami Press... G..... 765 242-7988
  Frankfort (G-5651)
Balboa Press.. G..... 812 671-9756
  Bloomington (G-792)
Beams of Grace Press................................ G..... 574 238-1644
  New Paris (G-12947)
Becoming Press LLC................................... G..... 317 823-9983
  Westfield (G-16670)
Berean Builders Publishing Inc................... G..... 765 287-5157
  Muncie (G-12352)
Beunerfarm Publishing Inc......................... G..... 317 514-1505
  Indianapolis (G-7618)
Biblical Publishing Svcs Inc........................ G..... 219 213-2078
  Crown Point (G-2656)
Bizness As Usual Pubg LLC......................... G..... 463 701-6433
  Indianapolis (G-7634)
Bk Royston Publishing LLC......................... G..... 502 802-5385
  Jeffersonville (G-9943)
Blue Sky Life Stories LLC............................ G..... 574 298-1254
  Elkhart (G-3228)
Bradford Press Inc...................................... G..... 574 876-3601
  Mishawaka (G-11853)
Brasilia Press Inc....................................... G..... 574 262-9700
  Elkhart (G-3234)
Breadmansrt Llc... G..... 219 238-9169
  Gary (G-5906)
Brent Devers.. G..... 812 657-3786
  Columbus (G-2229)
Brethren In Chrst Mdia Mnstrie................... G..... 574 267-7400
  Winona Lake (G-16909)
Bright Books... F..... 765 642-3114
  Griffith (G-6797)
Brill Stuff LLC... G..... 502 889-9705
  New Albany (G-12705)
Brooks Publications Inc.............................. G..... 317 756-9830
  Indianapolis (G-7688)
Buddy Eugene Publishing LLC..................... G..... 574 223-6048
  Akron (G-2)
Caine Publishing LLC.................................. G..... 312 215-5253
  Long Beach (G-11121)
Card Calender Publishing Llc..................... G..... 812 234-5999
  Terre Haute (G-15555)
Carden Jennings Publishing....................... G..... 317 490-7080
  Indianapolis (G-7738)
Carl Hugness Publishing............................. G..... 812 273-2472
  Madison (G-11205)
Carol Butler.. G..... 201 292-4364
  Fort Wayne (G-4834)
Carter & Carter Publishing LLC................... G..... 317 882-0748
  Indianapolis (G-7751)
Cat People Press LLC................................. G..... 260 750-8652
  Fort Wayne (G-4838)
Chatter House Press.................................. G..... 317 514-4133
  Indianapolis (G-7789)
Cheyenne Enterprises LLC.......................... G..... 317 253-7795
  Indianapolis (G-7796)
Circles Legacy Publishing LLC.................... G..... 219 322-1278
  Dyer (G-2969)
Civic Press Inc... G..... 219 750-9361
  Merrillville (G-11497)
Clutch Graphics.. G..... 812 244-9673
  Carbon (G-1537)
Coach Monay Publishing LLC...................... G..... 463 256-5096
  Indianapolis (G-7829)

Cola Voce Music Inc................................... G..... 317 466-0624
  Indianapolis (G-7834)
Collective Press Inc.................................... G..... 812 325-1385
  Bloomington (G-833)
Collective Publishing LLC........................... G..... 317 418-0503
  Fishers (G-4492)
Colleen Coble Incorporated........................ G..... 260 563-2028
  Wabash (G-16178)
College Network Inc................................... D..... 800 395-3276
  Indianapolis (G-7835)
Coman Publishing Company....................... G..... 574 255-9800
  South Bend (G-14980)
Companion Publications LLC...................... G..... 317 294-8189
  Indianapolis (G-7842)
Contemporary Books Inc............................. G..... 317 753-5247
  Indianapolis (G-7857)
Counter Column LLC.................................. G..... 815 564-7569
  Lafayette (G-10558)
Couragio Press LLC.................................... G..... 260 471-5603
  Fort Wayne (G-4879)
Cr Publications.. G..... 219 931-6700
  Hammond (G-6907)
Crawl Before You Walk LLC........................ G..... 219 413-6623
  Plainfield (G-13675)
Creative Mnds Work Pblctons LL................ G..... 317 759-1002
  Indianapolis (G-7901)
Criterion Press Inc..................................... E..... 317 236-1570
  Indianapolis (G-7904)
Crossfire Press Corporation....................... G..... 765 987-7164
  New Castle (G-12857)
Crowdreviewscom LLC............................... G..... 239 227-2428
  Plymouth (G-13767)
Crown Point Shopping News...................... G..... 219 663-4212
  Crown Point (G-2671)
Crown Training and Dev Inc....................... F..... 219 947-0845
  Merrillville (G-11500)
Cto Publishing LLC.................................... G..... 765 210-8290
  Kokomo (G-10251)
Cupprint LLC.. F..... 574 323-5250
  South Bend (G-14988)
Current Publishing LLC.............................. E..... 317 489-4444
  Carmel (G-1602)
Curtis Honeycutt LLC................................. G..... 317 645-7540
  Noblesville (G-13066)
D P Woods Unlimited.................................. G..... 765 362-3625
  Crawfordsville (G-2562)
D R G Publishing.. F..... 260 589-4000
  Berne (G-708)
Dancing Crane Publishing LLC................... G..... 812 675-2362
  Owensburg (G-13462)
Daniel Publications................................... G..... 574 269-2825
  Warsaw (G-16346)
Dark Source Records LLC.......................... G..... 616 378-6060
  Indianapolis (G-7950)
Darner Golden Publishing LLC................... G..... 812 675-0897
  Bedford (G-629)
David L Phillips.. G..... 312 937-0299
  Bloomington (G-852)
Debra Collins... G..... 317 873-1977
  Zionsville (G-17001)
Deedgrabbercom Inc.................................. G..... 219 712-9722
  Munster (G-12538)
Degler Mktg & Mailing Svcs....................... G..... 317 873-5550
  Zionsville (G-17002)
Dennis Cooper... G..... 847 970-2667
  Shelbyville (G-14751)
Dialectical Publishing LLC......................... G..... 812 650-1094
  Bloomington (G-854)
Diddlebug Publishing LLC.......................... G..... 574 612-2389
  Osceola (G-13389)
Dior Publishing.. G..... 765 471-2249
  West Lafayette (G-16576)

Diva This Diva That Inc............................... G..... 219 533-0077
  South Bend (G-15000)
Dog Ear Publishing..................................... F..... 317 228-3656
  Indianapolis (G-7995)
Domaindress LLC....................................... G..... 812 430-4856
  Evansville (G-4017)
Doodles and Dreams Pubg LLC.................. G..... 317 796-6059
  Zionsville (G-17003)
Douglas Estes.. G..... 219 718-0911
  Hebron (G-7099)
Dow Theory Forecasts Inc.......................... E..... 219 931-6480
  Hammond (G-6915)
Dream Center Evansville Inc...................... G..... 812 401-5558
  Evansville (G-4020)
Dream Theory Publishing LLC.................... G..... 317 598-0320
  Fishers (G-4505)
DSM Publications...................................... G..... 312 730-7375
  Hammond (G-6916)
Dungan Aerial Service Inc......................... G..... 765 827-1355
  Connersville (G-2437)
East Fork Studio & Press Inc...................... G..... 765 458-6103
  Brownsville (G-1431)
Ebenezer Press LLC................................... G..... 260 482-2864
  Fort Wayne (G-4939)
Eco Owl Press LLC..................................... G..... 574 703-3941
  South Bend (G-15010)
Editarts.. G..... 317 702-1215
  Indianapolis (G-8054)
Edwin Rahn.. G..... 260 622-7178
  Ossian (G-13423)
El Mexicano Inc... G..... 260 456-6843
  Fort Wayne (G-4943)
Emerge Curriculum Pubg LLC..................... G..... 317 523-2687
  Indianapolis (G-8104)
Encourage Publishing LLC......................... G..... 812 987-6148
  New Albany (G-12725)
Endowment Development Services............ F..... 317 542-9829
  Indianapolis (G-8114)
Entourage Yearbooks................................. G..... 317 552-2207
  Indianapolis (G-8124)
Eorigami Publishing LLC............................ G..... 317 842-9659
  Indianapolis (G-8127)
Eskape Press LLC...................................... G..... 765 659-1237
  Frankfort (G-5661)
Etcetera Press.. G..... 317 845-9999
  Fishers (G-4518)
Except As A Child Pubg LLC....................... G..... 317 658-0075
  Indianapolis (G-8150)
Exploding Brain Press................................ G..... 219 393-0796
  Michigan City (G-11608)
Express Motors.. G..... 812 437-9495
  Evansville (G-4063)
Faith Nicole Publications LLC.................... G..... 708 238-3101
  Hammond (G-6925)
Fetzer Publishing....................................... G..... 765 966-9169
  Richmond (G-14122)
Ffd Publishing LLC..................................... G..... 260 423-2119
  Fort Wayne (G-4981)
Fideli Publishing.. G..... 888 343-3542
  Martinsville (G-11391)
Fierce Publishing....................................... G..... 765 251-3262
  Indianapolis (G-8186)
Figg Publishing Inc.................................... G..... 317 797-2022
  Avon (G-520)
Figid Press LLC.. G..... 717 809-0092
  Brownsburg (G-1367)
First Databank Inc..................................... G..... 317 571-7200
  Carmel (G-1636)
Fish Factory.. G..... 219 929-9375
  Chesterton (G-1927)
Flannigan Press LLC................................... G..... 317 776-4914
  Noblesville (G-13079)

27 PRINTING, PUBLISHING AND ALLIED INDUSTRIES — SIC SECTION

Flying Turtle Publishing Inc .... G 219 221-8488
   Hammond *(G-6932)*

Folk Art To Go .... G 317 753-8553
   Indianapolis *(G-8213)*

For The Love of Words LLC .... G 317 550-8805
   Morristown *(G-12276)*

Forro Press Inc .... G 317 576-1797
   Fishers *(G-4525)*

Fostrom Press LLC .... G 812 945-0071
   Floyds Knobs *(G-4678)*

Freedom Intentional LLC .... G 219 576-2699
   Indianapolis *(G-8228)*

Frostbite Press LLC .... G 812 216-1372
   Crothersville *(G-2640)*

Fusonweaver Publishing LLC .... G 260 251-3946
   Portland *(G-13945)*

G & J Publishing LLC .... G 765 914-3378
   Brookville *(G-1321)*

Gaptooth Publishing .... G 574 551-6386
   Warsaw *(G-16367)*

Gaunt Family LLC .... G 812 473-3167
   Evansville *(G-4086)*

Gibson Nehemiah Group Inc .... F 317 643-3838
   Muncie *(G-12401)*

Gingerbread House Publications .... G 260 622-4868
   Ossian *(G-13424)*

Glasswing Press LLC .... G 937 554-1784
   Noblesville *(G-13086)*

Golden Press Studio .... G 765 318-7936
   Franklin *(G-5734)*

Goldenmarc LLC .... G 317 855-1651
   Indianapolis *(G-8301)*

Good Earth Publications Inc .... G 540 460-6459
   Richmond *(G-14126)*

Good News Network LLC .... G 812 219-2376
   Crown Point *(G-2690)*

Gorganite Publishing LLC .... G 812 480-2787
   Fort Wayne *(G-5030)*

Grace To Grow Publications .... G 219 932-0711
   Hammond *(G-6936)*

Grape Arbor Publishing LLC .... G 317 219-9337
   Carmel *(G-1643)*

Graves Media & Pubg Group LLC .... G 317 679-4072
   Indianapolis *(G-8314)*

Greg Samples .... G 812 595-3033
   Scottsburg *(G-14558)*

Growing Child Inc .... G 765 463-1696
   West Lafayette *(G-16589)*

Guide Book Publishing .... G 317 259-0599
   Indianapolis *(G-8341)*

H&H Media LLC .... G 317 213-0480
   Anderson *(G-124)*

Hamilton County Business Mag .... G 317 774-7747
   Noblesville *(G-13092)*

Hammer Marketing .... G 317 841-1567
   Fishers *(G-4536)*

Harry S Watts .... G 219 879-1606
   Michigan City *(G-11621)*

Haymons Publishing LLC .... G 219 484-8510
   Gary *(G-5946)*

Heartland Express LLC .... G 317 422-1438
   Bargersville *(G-567)*

Hedgehog Press LLC .... G 260 387-5237
   Fort Wayne *(G-5060)*

Help4u Publications LLC .... G 219 771-0189
   Chesterton *(G-1936)*

Herff Jones LLC .... E 317 612-3400
   Indianapolis *(G-8384)*

◆ Herff Jones LLC .... C 317 297-3741
   Indianapolis *(G-8383)*

Heron Blue Publications LLC .... G 317 696-0474
   Carmel *(G-1655)*

High Note Publishing .... G 765 313-1699
   Swayzee *(G-15450)*

His Love Kept ME Pubg LLC .... G 408 893-5908
   Indianapolis *(G-8400)*

Home Mag Pub Indianapolis .... G 317 810-1341
   Carmel *(G-1657)*

Home Publishing LLC .... G 317 886-1137
   Indianapolis *(G-8406)*

Homeland Sports LLC .... G 219 962-2315
   Hobart *(G-7190)*

Horizon Management Svcs Inc .... G 219 852-3200
   Hammond *(G-6948)*

Horizon Publishing Company LLC .... F 219 852-3200
   Hammond *(G-6949)*

Hot Heart Press LLC .... G 317 846-6057
   Carmel *(G-1660)*

Hot Off Press .... G 260 591-8331
   Wabash *(G-16194)*

Ihs Campaign For Ind Exprnce .... G 317 234-5232
   Indianapolis *(G-8456)*

In The Am LLC .... G 408 836-8200
   Avon *(G-526)*

Indiana Auto Dealers Assn Svcs .... G 317 635-1441
   Indianapolis *(G-8473)*

Indiana Interactive LLC .... E 317 233-2010
   Indianapolis *(G-8480)*

Indiana Rmnce Writers Amer Inc .... G 317 695-5255
   Fishers *(G-4545)*

Indianapolis Social SEC Off .... G 800 772-1213
   Indianapolis *(G-8509)*

Indianplis Press CLB Fndtion I .... G 317 701-1130
   Indianapolis *(G-8511)*

Ingroup .... G 317 817-9997
   Indianapolis *(G-8547)*

International Code Council Inc .... G 317 879-1677
   Indianapolis *(G-8576)*

Intimusic LLC .... G 574 210-4562
   South Bend *(G-15086)*

Ishkadiddle Publishing LLC .... G 765 744-8588
   Muncie *(G-12429)*

Jbs New Third Publishing LLC .... G 812 262-8595
   Terre Haute *(G-15621)*

Jensen Publications Inc .... G 317 514-8864
   Zionsville *(G-17022)*

JKS Music Publishing LLC .... G 888 461-8703
   Lafayette *(G-10616)*

Jossey-Bass Publishers .... G 877 762-2974
   Indianapolis *(G-8639)*

Keith Smith .... G 317 336-6746
   Mccordsville *(G-11453)*

Kelk Publishing LLC .... G 812 268-6356
   Sullivan *(G-15410)*

Kendallville Publishing Co Inc .... G 260 347-0400
   Kendallville *(G-10127)*

Kennedy Expressline Inc .... G 574 272-9072
   South Bend *(G-15099)*

Ketch Publishing .... G 812 327-0072
   Bloomington *(G-901)*

Kids At Heart Publishing Llc .... F 765 478-5773
   Cambridge City *(G-1498)*

Kiel Media LLC .... G 219 544-2060
   La Crosse *(G-10365)*

Knight Davis Publishing LLC .... G 812 568-9646
   Evansville *(G-4158)*

Know Wonder Publishing LLC .... G 317 506-4611
   Indianapolis *(G-8698)*

Kokomo Press LLC .... G 317 575-9903
   Fort Wayne *(G-5153)*

Laptop Publishing LLC .... G 317 379-5716
   Carmel *(G-1682)*

Lazy Dog Press LLC .... G 510 227-9404
   Lafayette *(G-10635)*

Leader Publishing Co of Salem .... E 812 883-3281
   Salem *(G-14487)*

Lemonwire LLC .... G 317 243-1758
   Indianapolis *(G-8737)*

Letterkenny Press Inc .... G 317 752-4375
   Indianapolis *(G-8741)*

Life Garden Publishing Inc .... G 812 246-2113
   Borden *(G-1114)*

Life Sentences Publishing LLC .... G 765 437-0149
   Tipton *(G-15780)*

Lori Hicks .... G 574 291-6341
   South Bend *(G-15129)*

Lost Legends Publishing LLC .... G 765 606-5342
   Anderson *(G-147)*

Lost Realms Publishing LLC .... G 319 230-3666
   Anderson *(G-148)*

Love2readlove2write Pubg LLC .... G 317 550-9755
   Indianapolis *(G-8786)*

Lynn Beck .... G 765 523-2260
   Clarks Hill *(G-2004)*

MA Publishing Inc .... G 812 217-0925
   Evansville *(G-4182)*

Macs Express Inc .... G 765 865-9700
   Kokomo *(G-10303)*

Martys Desktop Publish .... G 715 520-7682
   Elkhart *(G-3518)*

Mavrick Entrmt Netwrk Inc .... G 317 779-1237
   Brownsburg *(G-1386)*

McMillan Express .... G 260 447-7648
   Fort Wayne *(G-5212)*

Measure Press Inc .... G 812 473-0361
   Evansville *(G-4194)*

Metheny Enterprises Inc .... G 317 692-9900
   Noblesville *(G-13135)*

Mightier Press .... G 260 609-6582
   Fort Wayne *(G-5227)*

Miller Express Inc .... G 765 572-2303
   Westpoint *(G-16746)*

Mills River Publishing Company .... G 765 561-3445
   Rushville *(G-14406)*

Mining Media Inc .... G 317 802-7116
   Indianapolis *(G-8930)*

Mockenhaupt Publishing Inc .... G 315 778-0067
   Fort Wayne *(G-5238)*

Mougeotte Publishing Inc .... G 765 649-3302
   Anderson *(G-162)*

MT Publishing Company Inc .... G 812 468-8022
   Evansville *(G-4214)*

Musculskeletal Publ Analis Inc .... G 574 269-4861
   Warsaw *(G-16399)*

N2 Publishing .... G 812 449-0408
   Evansville *(G-4217)*

Narrow Gate Publishing LLC .... G 219 464-8579
   Valparaiso *(G-16008)*

Natalie Anderson LLC .... G 812 951-3532
   Georgetown *(G-6071)*

Nationwide Publishing Company .... G 260 312-3924
   Fort Wayne *(G-5258)*

Neely Publishing LLC .... G 574 271-7978
   Granger *(G-6365)*

New Century Publishing .... G 317 366-9691
   Indianapolis *(G-9003)*

New Philosopher Prss .... G 812 964-0786
   Bloomington *(G-929)*

New Readers Press .... G 317 514-6515
   Avon *(G-541)*

News-Banner Publications Inc .... E 260 824-0224
   Bluffton *(G-1046)*

Newslink Inc .... G 317 202-0210
   Indianapolis *(G-9007)*

Next Reformation Publishing Co .... G 317 650-1364
   Plainfield *(G-13708)*

27 PRINTING, PUBLISHING AND ALLIED INDUSTRIES

▼ Noel Studio Inc .... F 317 297-1117
   Indianapolis (G-9019)
Norlightspresscom .... G 812 675-8054
   Bedford (G-659)
Novels By Nellotie .... G 812 583-1196
   Mitchell (G-12045)
Paper Chase .... G 812 385-4757
   Princeton (G-14009)
Paper Street Press .... G 765 894-0027
   West Lafayette (G-16616)
Path Bright Publications LLC .... G 888 505-6780
   Indianapolis (G-9098)
Patria Press LLC .... G 317 508-7239
   Fishers (G-4572)
Pattern Inc .... G 317 733-8302
   Indianapolis (G-9102)
Paul Applegate .... G 574 656-8664
   North Liberty (G-13219)
Pbp Publishing LLC .... G 574 707-1010
   Fort Wayne (G-5299)
PCA Publishing Inc .... G 317 658-2055
   Indianapolis (G-9108)
Peas In A Pod Publications LLC .... G 812 923-5365
   Floyds Knobs (G-4687)
Pen & Pink .... G 317 372-6465
   Indianapolis (G-9113)
Pen It Publications LLC .... G 812 392-2658
   Scipio (G-14550)
Pentera Group Inc .... E 317 543-2055
   Indianapolis (G-9116)
Performers Edition LLC .... G 317 429-1300
   Indianapolis (G-9125)
Personal Record Media LLC .... G 317 507-4459
   Fishers (G-4573)
Phoenix Int Publications .... G 317 796-2375
   Lafayette (G-10668)
Phonozoic .... G 812 331-0047
   Bloomington (G-947)
Photoprose Productions Inc .... G 316 371-4634
   Jeffersonville (G-10038)
Pike Publishing .... G 812 354-4701
   Petersburg (G-13622)
Pocket Press LLC .... G 888 237-2110
   Fort Wayne (G-5320)
Polymath Publishing LLC .... G 317 410-5551
   Indianapolis (G-9161)
Porchlight Group Inc .... G 317 804-1166
   Fishers (G-4579)
Portee Publishing LLC .... G 812 259-5446
   Washington (G-16504)
Praiseworthy Press LLC .... G 765 536-2077
   Summitville (G-15428)
Pratt-Kulsrud LLC .... G 317 844-9122
   Carmel (G-1726)
Precisely Write Inc .... G 317 585-7701
   Indianapolis (G-9178)
Press A Button LLC .... G 630 400-1704
   Noblesville (G-13158)
Press A Dent .... G 260 760-1585
   Fort Wayne (G-5348)
Press Ganey Holdings Inc .... G 574 387-4764
   South Bend (G-15204)
Publishers Consulting Corp .... F 219 874-4245
   Michigan City (G-11652)
Publishers Sovereign Grace .... G 765 296-5538
   Mulberry (G-12330)
Punkish Press LLC .... G 812 626-1028
   Noblesville (G-13161)
Pure Creative Publishing LLC .... G 765 860-8999
   Fort Wayne (G-5356)
Purewal Publishing LLC .... G 317 703-6899
   Noblesville (G-13162)

Purple Door Press .... G 219 690-1046
   Lowell (G-11177)
Queen City Press .... G 317 840-1135
   Fishers (G-4588)
Raging Rocket Web Design LLC .... G 219 381-5027
   Crown Point (G-2741)
Really Good Stuff Inc .... G 812 402-8275
   Evansville (G-4275)
Redhead Publishing LLC .... G 317 535-7400
   Franklin (G-5772)
Region Design Co LLC .... G 219 851-1308
   La Porte (G-10471)
Retrieving With Evie .... G 812 455-5292
   Evansville (G-4286)
Rol Publications .... G 812 366-4154
   Greenville (G-6655)
Rosswyvern Press LLC .... G 859 421-0864
   Clarksville (G-2031)
Rough Notes Company Inc .... E 317 582-1600
   Carmel (G-1746)
▲ Round World Products Inc .... G 317 257-7352
   Carmel (G-1747)
Russ Print Shp/Hbron Advrtser .... F 219 996-3142
   Hebron (G-7106)
Rust Publishing In LLC .... G 765 653-5151
   Greencastle (G-6429)
Ryobi Press Parts .... G 800 901-3304
   Carmel (G-1750)
Salabell Publishing LLC .... G 219 865-6906
   Schererville (G-14543)
Sams Technical Publishing LLC .... F 800 428-7267
   Indianapolis (G-9368)
Sandy Island Press .... G 812 360-7288
   Bloomington (G-966)
Scalable Press .... F 510 396-5226
   Indianapolis (G-9383)
Scanpower LLC .... G 765 277-2308
   Richmond (G-14201)
Schatzi Press .... G 317 335-2335
   Fishers (G-4650)
Scher Maihem Publishing Ltd .... G 260 897-2697
   Avilla (G-494)
Scholastic Education .... G 260 437-1485
   Fort Wayne (G-5403)
Scoop LLC .... G 317 713-2141
   Indianapolis (G-9393)
Scurvy Palace Publishing LLC .... G 317 809-4591
   Martinsville (G-11425)
Shade Tree Press .... G 765 548-2421
   Rosedale (G-14382)
SHE Publishing LLC .... G 219 515-8032
   Indianapolis (G-9414)
Shepherd & David LLC .... G 317 769-4751
   Whitestown (G-16821)
Simone-Chrisette Pubg LLC .... G 317 985-9851
   Indianapolis (G-9441)
Sitesuccess Inc .... G 219 808-4076
   Schererville (G-14545)
SL Terrastar Group LLC .... G 317 702-7240
   Indianapolis (G-9447)
Slavica Publishers .... G 812 856-4186
   Bloomington (G-974)
Spiritbuilding Publishing .... G 765 623-2238
   Summitville (G-15432)
Stacy Publishing Inc .... G 812 923-1111
   Greenville (G-6656)
Static Pen Publishing LLC .... G 765 609-0202
   Lafayette (G-10699)
Stonefly Press LLC .... G 812 369-4147
   Bloomington (G-980)
Street Dreams Production Inc .... G 574 440-9136
   South Bend (G-15269)

Synthypnion Press LLC .... G 317 885-8394
   Indianapolis (G-9541)
Tacair Publications .... G 260 429-7975
   Churubusco (G-1990)
▲ Tanglewood Publishing Inc .... G 812 877-9488
   Indianapolis (G-9549)
Taylor & Francis .... G 765 364-1300
   Indianapolis (G-9558)
Teck USA Inc .... G 888 995-1972
   Indianapolis (G-9570)
Tempesta Media LLC .... G 312 371-0555
   Michigan City (G-11677)
Tendre Press LLC .... G 812 606-9563
   Bloomington (G-986)
Testimony Publications LLC .... G 812 602-3031
   Evansville (G-4341)
Thinkshortcut Publishing LLC .... G 765 935-1127
   Richmond (G-14217)
Thomson Reuters Corporation .... F 317 570-9387
   Fishers (G-4612)
Thunder Rolls Express .... G 812 667-5111
   Canaan (G-1528)
Timothy Reed Carry ME Mus Pubg .... G 812 322-7187
   Bloomington (G-989)
Titan Graphics LLC .... G 317 496-2188
   Mccordsville (G-11457)
TM Shadow Publishing LLC .... G 502 794-8435
   Fort Wayne (G-5491)
▲ Tom Doherty Company Inc .... G 317 352-8200
   Indianapolis (G-9617)
Town Planner .... G 317 888-6750
   Whiteland (G-16798)
Trained Thoughts Pubg LLC .... G 773 661-7237
   Hammond (G-7022)
Triangle Publishing .... G 765 677-2544
   Marion (G-11344)
Trinette Clark Agency Corp .... G 317 671-6097
   Indianapolis (G-9643)
True Stories Publishing Co LLC .... G 765 425-8224
   Indianapolis (G-9652)
Trustees Indiana University .... F 812 855-4848
   Bloomington (G-999)
Tucker Publishing Group Inc .... F 812 426-2115
   Evansville (G-4355)
Tuggle Publishing .... G 678 702-2139
   Fort Wayne (G-5513)
TV Excel Inc .... D 323 797-8538
   Fort Wayne (G-5516)
Tylayculture LLC .... G 219 678-8359
   Highland (G-7158)
Un Seen Press Co .... G 317 867-5594
   Westfield (G-16733)
University Publishing Corp .... E 812 339-9033
   Bloomington (G-1004)
Very Vocal Viking .... G 317 919-8903
   Bloomington (G-1006)
Vintage AVI Publications LLC .... E 260 440-3144
   Huntington (G-7379)
Vintage AVI Publications LLC .... G 260 440-3144
   Huntington (G-7378)
Vintage Publishing LLC .... G 812 719-7200
   Evansville (G-4375)
Vivid Internet Publishing .... G 317 858-3882
   Brownsburg (G-1412)
Vk Press LLC .... G 317 400-6883
   Indianapolis (G-9728)
Vocel Inc .... G 858 774-2063
   Fishers (G-4630)
Waite Adel (marlane) .... G 812 939-2252
   Clay City (G-2048)
Warner Press Inc .... F 800 741-7721
   Anderson (G-216)

Employee Codes: A=Over 500 employees, B=251-500
C=101-250, D=51-100, E=20-50, F=10-19, G=1-9

2024 Harris Indiana
Industrial Directory

27 PRINTING, PUBLISHING AND ALLIED INDUSTRIES

Westbow Press... E 866 928-1240
   Bloomington *(G-1009)*

Whimsicals Inc... G 317 773-6130
   Noblesville *(G-13194)*

Whitman Publishing................................... G 574 267-3941
   Warsaw *(G-16450)*

Williams Woods Pubg Svcs LLC.............. G 317 270-0976
   Indianapolis *(G-9769)*

Willowgreen Inc... G 260 490-2222
   Fort Wayne *(G-5570)*

Winspear Publishing LLC.......................... G 812 204-7973
   Bloomington *(G-1014)*

Wood Block Press Inc............................... G 405 742-7308
   Richmond *(G-14228)*

Wordpro Communication Services........... G 847 296-3964
   Indianapolis *(G-9788)*

Worth Publications LLC............................. G 219 808-4001
   Crown Point *(G-2775)*

Wrg Publishing... G 317 839-6520
   Plainfield *(G-13744)*

Write Word.. G 219 987-5254
   Demotte *(G-2933)*

Www Writing Co... G 317 498-4041
   Carthage *(G-1820)*

Zachary T Laffin.. G 317 480-2248
   Greenfield *(G-6572)*

Zana Peabody Publishing LLC................. G 463 210-5111
   Carmel *(G-1812)*

2752 Commercial printing, lithographic

323ink LLC.. G 812 282-3620
   Jeffersonville *(G-9920)*

3stax Printing & EMB LLC........................ G 317 612-7122
   Indianapolis *(G-7389)*

A-1 Graphics Inc.. G 765 289-1851
   Muncie *(G-12332)*

A-R-T Printing.. G 812 235-8600
   Terre Haute *(G-15529)*

AC Printing Inc... G 708 418-9100
   Highland *(G-7118)*

Accent Complex Inc.................................. G 574 522-2368
   Elkhart *(G-3148)*

Acclaim Graphics Inc................................ G 812 424-5035
   Evansville *(G-3866)*

Accu-Label Inc... E 260 482-5223
   Fort Wayne *(G-4720)*

Accuprint of Kentuckiana Inc................... G 812 944-8603
   New Albany *(G-12685)*

Ace Printing.. G 812 275-3412
   Bedford *(G-617)*

Advantage Print Solutions........................ F 812 473-5945
   Evansville *(G-3876)*

Affordable Screen Printing EMB.............. G 574 278-7885
   Monticello *(G-12133)*

AG Apparel and Screen Prtg LLC........... G 260 483-3817
   Fort Wayne *(G-4732)*

AG Printing Specialists LLC..................... G 866 445-6824
   Lafayette *(G-10517)*

Aim Media Indiana Oper LLC................... E 317 736-7101
   Franklin *(G-5704)*

Aim Media Indiana Oper LLC................... E 317 462-5528
   Greenfield *(G-6458)*

Aj Screen Printing LLC............................. G 574 274-4333
   Bremen *(G-1171)*

All 4u Printing LLC.................................... G 317 845-2955
   Morgantown *(G-12251)*

All Printing and Publications.................... G 260 636-2727
   Albion *(G-17)*

Allegra Marketing Print Mail..................... G 317 643-6248
   Indianapolis *(G-7479)*

Allen C Terhune & Associates................. G 765 948-4164
   Fairmount *(G-4407)*

Allison Pymnt Systems LLC DBA............ C 317 808-2400
   Indianapolis *(G-7485)*

Altstadt Business Forms Inc.................... F 812 425-3393
   Evansville *(G-3882)*

AMA Design Print...................................... G 219 462-8683
   Valparaiso *(G-15897)*

American Business Forms I...................... G 317 852-8956
   Brownsburg *(G-1345)*

American Elite Printing LLC..................... G 765 513-0889
   Fishers *(G-4639)*

American Ex Trvl Rlted Svcs In............... G 812 523-0106
   Seymour *(G-14629)*

American Printing....................................... G 219 836-5600
   Munster *(G-12530)*

American Printing & Advg Inc.................. F 219 937-1844
   Hammond *(G-6874)*

American Printing Company.................... G 574 533-5399
   Goshen *(G-6092)*

Anchor Enterprises..................................... G 812 282-7220
   Jeffersonville *(G-9933)*

Angies Printing LLC.................................. G 765 966-6237
   Richmond *(G-14086)*

Apparel Design Group.............................. G 812 339-3355
   Bloomington *(G-781)*

Apple Press Inc.. G 317 253-7752
   Indianapolis *(G-7530)*

AR Shot It LLC... G 317 654-0187
   Indianapolis *(G-7537)*

Augustin Prtg & Design Svcs.................. G 765 966-7130
   Richmond *(G-14088)*

▼ Ave Maria Press Inc............................. D 574 287-2831
   Notre Dame *(G-13315)*

Aztec Printing Inc...................................... G 812 422-1462
   Wadesville *(G-16226)*

B-Hive Printing... G 812 897-3905
   Boonville *(G-1081)*

Bartel Printing Company Inc.................... G 574 267-7421
   Warsaw *(G-16317)*

Baugh Enterprises Inc............................... F 812 334-8189
   Bloomington *(G-796)*

Baxter Printing Incorporated.................... G 219 923-1999
   Griffith *(G-6793)*

Beast Custom Athletic Printing................ G 765 610-6802
   Fairmount *(G-4408)*

Belcher Printing Services......................... G 812 305-1093
   Evansville *(G-3913)*

Bhar Printing Incorporated....................... G 317 899-1020
   Indianapolis *(G-7622)*

Biela Printing... G 219 874-8094
   Michigan City *(G-11581)*

Bills Printing.. G 765 962-7674
   Richmond *(G-14097)*

Bizcard... G 317 436-8649
   Greenfield *(G-6471)*

Blasted Works.. G 574 583-3211
   Monticello *(G-12138)*

Bloomington Letter Shop.......................... G 812 824-6363
   Bloomington *(G-812)*

Blue Creek Trail Map Co.......................... G 765 455-9867
   Kokomo *(G-10239)*

Blue Print Specialties Inc......................... G 765 742-6976
   Lafayette *(G-10539)*

Blue Print University Inc........................... G 317 446-8715
   Speedway *(G-15333)*

Bobilyn Printing.. G 219 926-7087
   Westville *(G-16756)*

Bowen Printing Inc.................................... G 574 936-3924
   Plymouth *(G-13759)*

Boy-Conn Printers Incorporated.............. G 219 462-2665
   Valparaiso *(G-15920)*

Brainstorm Print LLC................................. G 317 466-1600
   Indianapolis *(G-7670)*

Brand Prtg & Photo-Litho Co................... G 317 921-4095
   New Palestine *(G-12933)*

Bredensteiner Imaging Inc...................... G 317 921-1900
   Indianapolis *(G-7674)*

Bright Corp.. F 765 642-3114
   Griffith *(G-6797)*

Brinkman Press Inc................................... G 317 722-0305
   Indianapolis *(G-7686)*

Broadway Press LLC................................ G 765 644-8813
   Anderson *(G-85)*

Browns Simply Printings.......................... G 317 490-7493
   Mooresville *(G-12196)*

Bryan Janky... G 708 921-7676
   Valparaiso *(G-15922)*

Bryant Printing LLC................................... G 765 521-3379
   New Castle *(G-12853)*

Budget Printing Centers Inc.................... G 812 282-8832
   Jeffersonville *(G-9948)*

Buis Enterprises Inc.................................. G 317 839-7394
   Plainfield *(G-13663)*

Burkert-Walton Inc.................................... G 812 425-7157
   Evansville *(G-3957)*

Business Art & Designs Inc..................... G 317 782-9108
   Beech Grove *(G-688)*

Business Connection LLC........................ G 219 762-5660
   Portage *(G-13850)*

C J P Corporation...................................... G 219 924-1685
   Highland *(G-7127)*

C R Graphics.. G 317 881-6192
   Greenwood *(G-6679)*

▲ C-Point Inc.. C 260 478-9551
   Fort Wayne *(G-4828)*

Campbell Printing Company.................... G 219 866-5913
   Rensselaer *(G-14046)*

Cardcarecom.. G 574 315-5294
   Mishawaka *(G-11858)*

Carlton Ventures Inc................................. G 317 637-2590
   Indianapolis *(G-7746)*

Cave Company Printing Inc..................... G 812 863-4333
   Bloomfield *(G-743)*

Cecils Printing & Off Sups Inc................. G 812 683-4416
   Huntingburg *(G-7273)*

Cenveo Worldwide Limited..................... D 800 995-9500
   New Albany *(G-12710)*

Chameleon Lifestyles LLC....................... G 317 468-3246
   Greenfield *(G-6479)*

Charles E Watts... G 812 547-8516
   Tell City *(G-15498)*

Chesterton Printing Co............................. G 219 250-2896
   Chesterton *(G-1910)*

▲ Chromasource Inc............................... C 260 420-3000
   Columbia City *(G-2130)*

Circle Printing LLC.................................... G 812 663-7367
   Greensburg *(G-6584)*

City South Bend Building Corp............... G 574 235-9977
   South Bend *(G-14973)*

CJ Printing.. G 219 924-1685
   Hammond *(G-6900)*

Ckmt Associates Inc................................. F 219 924-2820
   Hammond *(G-6902)*

Classic Graphics Inc................................. F 260 482-3487
   Fort Wayne *(G-4853)*

Classic LLC.. G 260 241-4353
   Fort Wayne *(G-4854)*

◆ Clondalkin Pharma & Healthcare Inc..A 336 292-4555
   Indianapolis *(G-7824)*

Cnhi LLC... G 812 944-6481
   Jeffersonville *(G-9955)*

Coachs Connection Inc........................... G 260 356-0400
   Huntington *(G-7306)*

Colormax Digital Imaging Inc................. F 812 477-3805
   Evansville *(G-3975)*

27 PRINTING, PUBLISHING AND ALLIED INDUSTRIES

Colwell Inc.. C 260 347-1981
  Kendallville *(G-10100)*
▲ Colwell Inc.. C 260 347-1981
  Kendallville *(G-10099)*
Commercial Print Shop Inc........................ G 260 724-3722
  Decatur *(G-2850)*
Community Holdings Indiana Inc............... G 812 663-3111
  Greensburg *(G-6585)*
Community Holdings Indiana Inc............... G 765 482-4650
  Lebanon *(G-10885)*
Community Holdings Indiana Inc............... G 574 722-5000
  Logansport *(G-11068)*
Complete Prtg Solutions Inc...................... G 812 285-9200
  Jeffersonville *(G-9958)*
Consolidated Printing Svcs Inc.................. G 765 468-6033
  Farmland *(G-4424)*
Continuous Care Trnsp LLC...................... G 463 336-0555
  Indianapolis *(G-7859)*
Copies Plus LLC.. G 317 545-5083
  Indianapolis *(G-7871)*
Copy Solutions Inc..................................... G 260 436-2679
  Fort Wayne *(G-4874)*
Copy-Print Shop Inc................................... E 765 447-6868
  Lafayette *(G-10556)*
Copymat Services Inc................................ G 765 743-5995
  Lafayette *(G-10557)*
Cornerstone Business Prtg LLC................ G 574 642-4060
  Middlebury *(G-11705)*
Courier Printing Co Allen Cnty................... G 260 627-2728
  Grabill *(G-6293)*
CPC... G 812 358-5010
  Brownstown *(G-1420)*
Craigs Printing Co...................................... G 812 358-5010
  Brownstown *(G-1421)*
Creative Computer Services..................... G 317 729-5779
  Franklin *(G-5724)*
Creative Concept Ventures Inc................. G 812 282-9442
  Jeffersonville *(G-9964)*
Crescendo Inc.. G 812 829-4759
  Spencer *(G-15344)*
Crossroads Imprints Inc............................ G 765 482-2931
  Lebanon *(G-10887)*
Crown Point Printing LLC.......................... G 219 226-0900
  Crown Point *(G-2670)*
Crystal Graphics Inc.................................. G 317 535-9202
  Whiteland *(G-16780)*
▲ Custom Forms Inc.................................. F 765 463-6162
  Lafayette *(G-10565)*
D & E Printing Company Inc..................... G 317 852-9048
  Brownsburg *(G-1362)*
D & M Printing Inc..................................... G 812 847-4837
  Linton *(G-11034)*
D-J Printing Specialists Inc....................... G 219 465-1164
  Valparaiso *(G-15935)*
Damalak Printing Inc................................. G 317 896-5337
  Westfield *(G-16683)*
Data Mail Incorporated.............................. E 812 424-7835
  Evansville *(G-4007)*
Data Print Initiatives LLC.......................... G 260 489-2665
  Fort Wayne *(G-4905)*
Delp Printing & Mailing Inc....................... G 317 872-9744
  Indianapolis *(G-7963)*
Delphos Herald of Indiana Inc................... E 812 537-0063
  Lawrenceburg *(G-10833)*
Digital Image Editions................................ G 812 876-4770
  Bloomington *(G-856)*
Digital Printing Incorporated..................... G 812 265-2205
  Madison *(G-11214)*
Discount Copy Services Inc...................... G 317 773-8783
  Noblesville *(G-13073)*
Discover Putnam County........................... G 765 653-4026
  Greencastle *(G-6403)*

Diverse Sales Solutions LLC..................... G 317 514-2403
  Indianapolis *(G-7981)*
Diversfied Cmmnctons Group Inc............. F 317 755-3191
  Indianapolis *(G-7983)*
Diversified Bus Systems Inc..................... G 317 254-8668
  Indianapolis *(G-7984)*
Diversity Press LLC................................... G 317 241-4234
  Indianapolis *(G-7986)*
Dla Document Services............................. G 812 854-1465
  Crane *(G-2537)*
Docu-Tech Services Inc............................ G 219 769-7115
  Merrillville *(G-11508)*
Doerr Printing Co....................................... G 317 568-0135
  Indianapolis *(G-7994)*
Dove Printing Services Inc....................... G 317 469-7546
  Indianapolis *(G-7999)*
Dps Printing LLC.. G 260 503-9681
  Columbia City *(G-2139)*
Dragon Printing LLC.................................. G 317 919-9619
  Greenwood *(G-6690)*
Drike Inc... F 574 259-8822
  Mishawaka *(G-11885)*
Drs Graphix Group Inc.............................. G 317 569-1855
  Indianapolis *(G-8011)*
Duley Press Inc.. E 574 259-5203
  Mishawaka *(G-11887)*
Duramark Technologies Inc...................... D 317 867-5700
  Westfield *(G-16687)*
Dynamark Graphics Group Inc................. G 317 569-1855
  Indianapolis *(G-8024)*
Dynamark Graphics Group Inc................. E 317 328-2555
  Indianapolis *(G-8023)*
E D H Inc.. G 219 712-5145
  Lake Station *(G-10772)*
Economy Offset Printers Inc..................... G 574 534-6270
  Goshen *(G-6129)*
Ed Sons Inc... F 317 897-8821
  Indianapolis *(G-8051)*
Eight Ten Twelve LLC................................ G 317 773-8532
  Indianapolis *(G-8065)*
Elite Printing Inc... G 317 781-9701
  Indianapolis *(G-8093)*
Elite Printing Inc... G 317 257-2744
  Indianapolis *(G-8094)*
Em Printing & Embroidery LLC................. G 812 373-0082
  Columbus *(G-2297)*
Envelope Service Inc................................. E 260 432-6277
  Fort Wayne *(G-4952)*
Envision Graphics Inc................................ G 260 925-2266
  Auburn *(G-388)*
▲ EP Graphics Inc..................................... C 877 589-2145
  Berne *(G-710)*
Epi Printers Inc.. D 317 579-4870
  Indianapolis *(G-8129)*
Evansville Bindery Inc............................... G 812 423-2222
  Evansville *(G-4048)*
Evansville Lithograph Co Inc..................... G 812 477-0506
  Evansville *(G-4052)*
Evansvlle Print Specialist Inc.................... G 812 423-5831
  Evansville *(G-4060)*
Ewing Printing Company Inc..................... F 812 882-2415
  Vincennes *(G-16120)*
Excel Business Printing Inc...................... G 317 259-1075
  Indianapolis *(G-8149)*
Excell Color Graphics Inc......................... E 260 482-2720
  Fort Wayne *(G-4967)*
Express Press Inc..................................... G 812 882-3278
  Vincennes *(G-16122)*
Express Press Indiana Inc........................ G 219 874-2223
  South Bend *(G-15022)*
Express Press Indiana Inc........................ E 574 277-3355
  South Bend *(G-15023)*

Express Printing & Copying...................... G 219 762-3508
  Portage *(G-13862)*
F Robert Gardner Co Inc........................... G 317 634-2333
  Indianapolis *(G-8161)*
Falls Cities Printing Inc............................. F 812 949-9051
  New Albany *(G-12728)*
Faris Mailing Inc.. F 317 246-3315
  Indianapolis *(G-8167)*
Fast Print Incorporated............................. G 260 484-5487
  Fort Wayne *(G-4976)*
Faulkenberg Printing Co Inc..................... F 317 638-1359
  Franklin *(G-5730)*
Fedex Office & Print Svcs Inc.................. G 317 974-0378
  Indianapolis *(G-8172)*
Fedex Office & Print Svcs Inc.................. G 317 917-1529
  Indianapolis *(G-8173)*
Fedex Office & Print Svcs Inc.................. G 317 631-6862
  Indianapolis *(G-8178)*
Fedex Office & Print Svcs Inc.................. F 765 449-4950
  Lafayette *(G-10579)*
Fehring F N & Son Printers...................... G 219 933-0439
  Valparaiso *(G-15949)*
Figtree Print LLC....................................... G 978 503-1779
  Evansville *(G-4068)*
Fineline Digital Group Inc......................... E 317 872-4490
  Indianapolis *(G-8187)*
Fineline Graphics Incorporated................ D 317 872-4490
  Indianapolis *(G-8188)*
Firehouse Printing LLC............................. G 812 547-3109
  Tell City *(G-15503)*
First Quality Printing Inc.......................... G 317 506-8633
  Indianapolis *(G-8195)*
First Quality Printing Center..................... G 317 546-5531
  Indianapolis *(G-8196)*
Four Part Inc.. G 219 926-7777
  Chesterton *(G-1928)*
Four Star Printing...................................... G 765 620-9728
  Frankton *(G-5791)*
Four Star Screen Printing LLC................. G 765 533-3006
  New Castle *(G-12863)*
Franklin Barry Gallery............................... G 317 822-8455
  Indianapolis *(G-8224)*
Friends of Third World Inc........................ G 260 422-6821
  Fort Wayne *(G-5013)*
Gannett Media Corp.................................. C 765 423-5512
  Lafayette *(G-10585)*
Garco Graphics... G 219 980-1113
  Gary *(G-5935)*
Garrett Prtg & Graphics Inc...................... G 812 422-6005
  Evansville *(G-4084)*
Gary Printing Inc....................................... G 219 886-1767
  Gary *(G-5938)*
Gen-Twelve Corporation........................... G 260 483-7075
  Fort Wayne *(G-5018)*
Get Printing Inc... G 574 533-6827
  Goshen *(G-6147)*
Giant Paw Prints Inc................................. G 219 241-9299
  Valparaiso *(G-15955)*
Giant Paw Prints Rescue.......................... G 219 241-9299
  Westville *(G-16760)*
Giles Agency Incorporated....................... G 317 842-5546
  Indianapolis *(G-8281)*
Gkb Holdings Inc....................................... E 260 471-7744
  Fort Wayne *(G-5025)*
Go Print LLC.. G 765 778-1111
  Pendleton *(G-13534)*
Goatee Shirt Printing LLC........................ G 219 916-2443
  Valparaiso *(G-15958)*
Goetz Printing... G 812 243-2086
  Terre Haute *(G-15600)*
Gold Star Printing LLC............................. G 260 768-7920
  Shipshewana *(G-14848)*

27 PRINTING, PUBLISHING AND ALLIED INDUSTRIES

Company	Code	Phone
Gospel Echoes Team Association	G	574 533-0211
Goshen (G-6153)		
Grace Amazing Graphics	G	812 737-2841
Laconia (G-10505)		
Gracies Paw Prints	G	317 910-9969
Fishers (G-4532)		
Grafcor Inc	F	765 966-7030
Richmond (G-14127)		
Granger Gazette Inc	G	574 277-2679
Granger (G-6350)		
Graphic Expressions	G	219 663-2085
Merrillville (G-11520)		
Graphic Expressions Inc	G	317 577-9622
Fishers (G-4535)		
Graphic Menus Inc	F	765 396-3003
Eaton (G-3062)		
Graphics Unlimited	G	765 288-6816
Muncie (G-12405)		
Green Banner Publications Inc	E	812 967-3176
Borden (G-1109)		
Greencastle Offset Inc	G	765 653-4026
Greencastle (G-6406)		
Greenline Screen Printing	G	317 572-1155
Indianapolis (G-8321)		
Greensburg Printing Co Inc	G	812 663-8265
Greensburg (G-6598)		
Gryphon Print Studio LLC	G	574 514-1644
South Bend (G-15049)		
Hardesty Printing Co Inc	F	574 267-7591
Warsaw (G-16374)		
Hardesty Printing Co Inc	F	574 223-4553
Rochester (G-14293)		
Hardingpoorman Inc	C	317 876-3355
Indianapolis (G-8359)		
Hardingpoorman Group Inc	G	317 876-3355
Indianapolis (G-8360)		
Harmony Press Inc	E	800 525-3742
Bourbon (G-1122)		
Hartford City News Times	F	765 348-0110
Winchester (G-16889)		
Hatch Prints	G	312 952-1908
South Bend (G-15059)		
Haywood Printing Co	G	812 384-8639
Bloomfield (G-747)		
Haywood Printing Co Inc	E	765 742-4085
Indianapolis (G-8372)		
Heckley Printing Inc	G	260 434-1370
Fort Wayne (G-5058)		
Hennessey Montage Prints	G	317 841-7562
Carmel (G-1654)		
Herff Jones LLC	E	317 612-3400
Indianapolis (G-8384)		
Hetty Incorporated	G	219 933-0833
Hammond (G-6945)		
Hetty Incorporated	G	219 836-2517
Munster (G-12539)		
Hiatt Enterprises Inc	G	765 289-2700
Muncie (G-12416)		
Hiatt Enterprises Inc	F	765 289-7756
Muncie (G-12415)		
Highway Press Inc	G	812 283-6462
Jeffersonville (G-9996)		
Hinen Printing Co	G	260 248-8984
Columbia City (G-2150)		
Hoffman Quality Graphics	G	574 223-5738
Rochester (G-14296)		
Home Mountain Publishing Co Inc	E	219 462-6601
Valparaiso (G-15962)		
Home News Enterprises LLC	B	800 876-7811
Columbus (G-2318)		
Hoosier Jiffy Print	G	260 563-8715
Wabash (G-16193)		
Hoosier Press Inc	G	765 649-3716
Anderson (G-129)		
Hoosier Times Inc	C	812 275-3372
Bedford (G-641)		
Hoosier Times Inc	C	812 331-4270
Bloomington (G-882)		
Horoho Printing Company Inc	G	765 452-8862
Kokomo (G-10282)		
Howard Print Shop LLC	G	765 453-6161
Kokomo (G-10283)		
Huelseman Printing Co	G	765 647-3947
Brookville (G-1324)		
Hugh K Eagan	G	574 269-5411
Warsaw (G-16375)		
Iiiimpressions That Count Inc	G	317 423-0581
Indianapolis (G-8457)		
Impression Printing	G	765 342-6977
Martinsville (G-11403)		
Impressions LLC	G	765 490-2575
Lafayette (G-10604)		
Impressions Printing Inc	G	812 634-2574
Jasper (G-9843)		
Impressive Printing	G	812 913-1101
New Albany (G-12745)		
In-Print	G	219 956-3001
Wheatfield (G-16768)		
Indiana Business People LLC	G	317 455-4040
Indianapolis (G-8474)		
Indiana Newspapers LLC	D	812 886-9955
Vincennes (G-16131)		
Indiana Newspapers LLC	A	317 444-4000
Indianapolis (G-8487)		
Indy Color Printing LLC	G	317 371-8829
Indianapolis (G-8524)		
Infinitprint Solutions Inc	E	765 962-1507
Richmond (G-14139)		
Ink Spot	G	260 482-4492
Fort Wayne (G-5107)		
Ink Spot Tattoo	G	260 244-0025
Columbia City (G-2156)		
Inline Shirt Printing LLC	G	765 647-6356
Brookville (G-1326)		
Innerprint Inc	G	317 509-6511
Fishers (G-4643)		
Innovative Printing Svcs Inc	C	812 443-1007
Brazil (G-1147)		
Instant Warehouse	G	765 342-3430
Martinsville (G-11406)		
Insty-Prints	G	317 788-1504
Indianapolis (G-8564)		
Inter Print At Ions	G	765 404-0887
Brownsburg (G-1376)		
International Label Mfg LLC	F	812 235-5071
Terre Haute (G-15618)		
J & J Printing Co	G	765 642-6642
Anderson (G-137)		
J A Davis	G	812 354-9129
Petersburg (G-13616)		
J4 Printing LLC	G	260 417-5382
Fort Wayne (G-5127)		
Jackson Group Inc	C	317 791-9000
Indianapolis (G-8614)		
Jacob Adams	G	765 564-2314
Delphi (G-2900)		
Jacobs Company LLC	F	317 818-8500
Carmel (G-1676)		
Jam Printing Inc	F	765 649-9292
Anderson (G-138)		
James David Inc	G	260 744-0579
Roanoke (G-14271)		
JC Printing	G	574 721-9000
Logansport (G-11085)		
Jem Printing Inc	G	812 376-9264
Columbus (G-2330)		
Jewett Printing LLC	G	812 232-0087
Farmersburg (G-4419)		
Jewett Publications Inc	F	812 232-0087
Farmersburg (G-4420)		
Jkp Printing Inc	G	574 246-1650
South Bend (G-15092)		
Joans Tshirt Printing LLC	G	812 934-2616
Batesville (G-593)		
Jomark Inc	F	248 478-2600
Angola (G-265)		
Josh Rowland	G	574 596-6754
Noblesville (G-13114)		
Journal & Chronicle Inc	G	812 752-5060
Scottsburg (G-14566)		
JP Ownership Group Inc	D	317 791-1122
Indianapolis (G-8643)		
Just Install LLC	G	317 607-3911
Noblesville (G-13115)		
K Irpcheadstart Program	G	219 345-2011
Demotte (G-2919)		
Kalems Enterprises Inc	G	317 399-1645
Indianapolis (G-8658)		
Kankakee Valley Publishing Co	G	219 866-5111
Rensselaer (G-14056)		
Kasting Printing Service	G	317 881-9411
Indianapolis (G-8662)		
Kc Designs	G	812 876-4020
Bloomington (G-899)		
Keefer Printing Company Inc	E	260 424-4543
Fort Wayne (G-5144)		
Kellmark Corporation	F	574 264-9695
Elkhart (G-3449)		
Kendallville Custom Printing	F	260 347-9233
Kendallville (G-10125)		
Kevin M Walters	G	317 565-9564
Fishers (G-4554)		
Kile Enterprises Inc	F	317 844-6629
Carmel (G-1681)		
Kill-N-Em Inc	G	574 233-6655
South Bend (G-15100)		
Kim Print LLC	G	812 223-5333
Indianapolis (G-8683)		
Kinkos Inc	G	765 449-4950
Lafayette (G-10620)		
Kistner Enterprises Inc	G	317 773-7733
Noblesville (G-13123)		
Knots & Spots Inc	G	574 946-6000
Winamac (G-16865)		
Kozs Quality Printing Inc	G	219 696-6711
Lowell (G-11166)		
Kpc Media Group Inc	F	260 426-2640
Fort Wayne (G-5158)		
Kpc Media Group Inc	C	260 347-0400
Kendallville (G-10130)		
L & L Press Inc	F	765 664-3162
Marion (G-11305)		
L and P Brothers	G	219 313-6946
Hammond (G-6967)		
La Grange Publishing Co Inc	F	260 463-3243
Lagrange (G-10747)		
Lagnaippe LLC	G	812 288-9291
New Albany (G-12762)		
Lagwana Printing Inc	G	260 463-4901
Shipshewana (G-14860)		
Lagwana Printing Inc	G	260 463-4901
Lagrange (G-10748)		
Langley Fine Art Prints	G	219 872-0087
Long Beach (G-11123)		
Largus Speedy Print Corp	E	219 922-8414
Munster (G-12546)		

27 PRINTING, PUBLISHING AND ALLIED INDUSTRIES

Lbw Printing & Dtp................................ G 260 347-9053
  Kendallville (G-10132)
Lc Screen Printing LLC........................ G 812 687-7476
  Montgomery (G-12110)
Leader Publishing Co of Salem............ E 812 883-3281
  Salem (G-14487)
Leed Samples-Fulfillment..................... F 812 867-4340
  Evansville (G-4163)
Legacy Screen Prtg Prmtons LLC......... F 219 262-4000
  Michigan City (G-11631)
Lesha and Wade Printing Svcs............. G 317 738-4992
  Franklin (G-5752)
Light & Ink Corporation........................ G 812 421-1400
  Evansville (G-4168)
Light Printing Co................................... G 815 429-3724
  Brook (G-1305)
Lincoln Printing Corporation................ A 260 424-5200
  Fort Wayne (G-5186)
Link Printing Services LLC.................. G 317 902-6374
  Indianapolis (G-8765)
Link Printing Services LLC.................. G 317 826-9852
  Indianapolis (G-8764)
▲ Litho Press Inc................................. E 317 634-6468
  Indianapolis (G-8771)
Lithocraft Inc.. E 812 948-1608
  New Albany (G-12764)
Lithogrphic Communications LLC........ E 219 924-9779
  Munster (G-12548)
Lithotone Inc.. E 574 294-5521
  Elkhart (G-3497)
Livings Graphics Inc............................ G 574 264-4114
  Elkhart (G-3498)
Longhorn Marketing Group................... G 765 650-4430
  Frankfort (G-5680)
Lsc Communications Us LLC............... G 574 267-7101
  Warsaw (G-16388)
Ludwick Graphics Inc........................... G 574 233-2165
  South Bend (G-15131)
Maco Press Inc..................................... G 317 846-5754
  Carmel (G-1690)
Maco Reprograhics LLC...................... G 812 464-8108
  Evansville (G-4183)
Madison Courier................................... E 812 265-3641
  Madison (G-11237)
Maple Leaf Graphics Inc...................... G 317 410-0321
  Carmel (G-1691)
Maple Leaf Printing Co Inc................... G 574 534-7790
  Goshen (G-6212)
Marketing and Retail Sales.................. G 812 883-1813
  Salem (G-14489)
Marketing Kreativo................................ G 574 370-5410
  Goshen (G-6213)
Masco Corporation of Indiana.............. E 317 848-1812
  Indianapolis (G-8847)
Maury Boyd & Associates Inc............... F 317 849-6110
  Indianapolis (G-8853)
Maximum Business Solutions Inc......... G 219 933-1809
  Hammond (G-6978)
McCormack Prtg Impressions Inc........ G 765 675-9556
  Tipton (G-15783)
McCrory Publishing............................... G 260 485-1812
  Fort Wayne (G-5211)
MD Laird Inc.. G 317 842-6338
  Greenwood (G-6737)
Mecom Ltd Inc..................................... D 317 218-2600
  Indianapolis (G-8868)
▲ Messenger LLC................................ C 260 925-1700
  Auburn (G-405)
Metro Printed Products Inc................... G 317 885-0077
  Greenwood (G-6738)
Metropolitan Printing Svcs LLC............ C 812 332-7279
  Bloomington (G-917)

Mid America Print Council Inc.............. G 765 463-3971
  Lafayette (G-10647)
Mid West Digital Express Inc................ F 317 733-1214
  Zionsville (G-17033)
Midwest Color Printing LLC................. G 812 822-2947
  Bloomington (G-919)
Midwest Empire LLC............................ G 317 786-7446
  Indianapolis (G-8908)
Midwest Graphics Inc.......................... E 317 780-4600
  Indianapolis (G-8910)
Midwest Printing................................... G 812 238-1641
  Terre Haute (G-15645)
Mignone Communications In................ C 260 358-0266
  Huntington (G-7344)
Mik Mocha Prints LLC.......................... G 812 376-8891
  Columbus (G-2355)
Mike Mugler.. G 812 945-4266
  Clarksville (G-2023)
Miles Printing Corporation................... F 317 243-8571
  Indianapolis (G-8919)
Milliner Printing Company Inc.............. G 260 563-5717
  Wabash (G-16203)
Minute Print It Inc................................ G 765 482-9019
  Lebanon (G-10916)
Minuteman Press................................. F 317 209-1677
  Indianapolis (G-8931)
Mitchell-Fleming Printing Inc............... F 317 462-5467
  Greenfield (G-6529)
Mito-Craft Inc....................................... G 574 287-4555
  South Bend (G-15152)
Mla Printing Inc.................................... G 219 398-8888
  Merrillville (G-11540)
Moan Racing Products LLC................. G 317 644-3100
  Greenfield (G-6530)
Moeller Printing Co Inc........................ E 317 353-2224
  Indianapolis (G-8944)
Montgomery & Associates Inc.............. F 219 879-0088
  Michigan City (G-11641)
Mooney Copy Service Inc.................... G 812 423-6626
  Evansville (G-4210)
Moore Services Incorporated............... G 317 571-9800
  Carmel (G-1702)
Moore-Langen Printing Company Inc... D 812 234-1585
  Terre Haute (G-15648)
Morris Printing Company Inc............... G 317 639-5553
  Indianapolis (G-8956)
Mossberg & Company Inc.................... F 574 236-1094
  South Bend (G-15154)
Mossberg & Company Inc.................... D 574 289-9253
  South Bend (G-15155)
Mossberg Co....................................... F 574 850-6285
  South Bend (G-15156)
Movie Poster Print............................... G 812 679-7301
  Columbus (G-2358)
MPS Printing Incorporated................... G 812 273-4446
  Madison (G-11245)
Mr Copy Inc... G 812 334-2679
  Bloomington (G-925)
Mr Copyrite.. G 219 462-1108
  Valparaiso (G-16005)
Multi Packaging Solutions Inc.............. G 317 241-2020
  Indianapolis (G-8971)
Muncie Novelty Company Inc.............. D 765 288-8301
  Muncie (G-12463)
Nai Print Solutions............................... G 317 392-1207
  Shelbyville (G-14779)
Nea LLC... G 574 295-0024
  Elkhart (G-3565)
Nelmar Printing Co............................... G 317 504-7840
  Avon (G-539)
New Image Prtg & Design Inc.............. F 260 969-0410
  Fort Wayne (G-5266)

News-Banner Publications Inc............. E 260 824-0224
  Bluffton (G-1046)
Newsletter Express Ltd........................ G 317 876-8916
  Indianapolis (G-9006)
Next Offset Solutions Inc..................... G 773 844-1784
  West Lafayette (G-16613)
Nicholson and Sons Prtg Inc................ E 812 283-1200
  Jeffersonville (G-10026)
Nielsen Company................................. G 812 889-3493
  Lexington (G-10979)
Novaprints LLC.................................... F 317 577-6682
  Indianapolis (G-9028)
Nussmeier Engraving Company........... E 812 425-1339
  Evansville (G-4224)
Nwi Print & Mail LLC............................ G 219 916-1358
  Dyer (G-2979)
Oce Corporate Printing Div.................. G 260 436-7395
  Fort Wayne (G-5280)
Office Sup of Southern Ind Inc............. G 812 283-5523
  Jeffersonville (G-10027)
Offset House Inc.................................. F 317 849-5155
  Indianapolis (G-9042)
Offset One Inc..................................... F 260 456-8828
  Fort Wayne (G-5282)
Old Capital Printing LLC...................... G 812 946-9444
  New Albany (G-12789)
Ordonez Construccion Svcs LLC......... G 317 771-1213
  Indianapolis (G-9068)
Outfield Prsnlzed Spt Blls Inc.............. G 219 661-8942
  Crown Point (G-2727)
Ovation Communications Inc............... G 812 401-9100
  Evansville (G-4230)
Overgaards Artcraft Printers................ G 574 234-8464
  South Bend (G-15183)
P A Rogers Printing Service................ G 317 823-7627
  Indianapolis (G-9079)
Pack Printing LLC................................ G 317 437-9779
  Indianapolis (G-9083)
Pagels-Kelley Enterprises LLC............. F 219 872-8552
  Long Beach (G-11126)
Pam C Jones Enterprises Inc.............. G 812 294-1862
  Borden (G-1117)
Panda Prints.. G 574 322-1050
  Bristol (G-1282)
Pandora Printing.................................. G 574 551-9624
  Warsaw (G-16408)
Panther Graphics LLC......................... G 317 223-3845
  Indianapolis (G-9089)
Par Digital Imaging Inc........................ G 317 787-3330
  Greenwood (G-6749)
Paragon Printing Center Inc................. G 574 533-5835
  Osceola (G-13400)
Parrot Press Inc................................... E 260 422-6402
  Fort Wayne (G-5298)
Paust Inc.. F 765 962-1507
  Richmond (G-14180)
PC Imprints LLC................................... G 812 622-0855
  Poseyville (G-13980)
Pearson Printing Company................... G 765 664-8769
  Marion (G-11325)
Peerless Printing Corporation.............. G 765 664-8341
  Marion (G-11327)
Pengad/West Inc.................................. E 765 286-3000
  Muncie (G-12473)
Pentzer Printing Inc............................. F 812 372-2896
  Columbus (G-2375)
Perdue Printed Products Inc................ G 260 456-7575
  Fort Wayne (G-5304)
Perfect Impressions Printing................ G 317 923-1756
  Indianapolis (G-9121)
Pettit Printing Inc................................. G 260 563-2346
  Wabash (G-16212)

Employee Codes: A=Over 500 employees, B=251-500
C=101-250, D=51-100, E=20-50, F=10-19, G=1-9

27 PRINTING, PUBLISHING AND ALLIED INDUSTRIES

Phan Gear Prints LLC .... G 260 450-2539
Fort Wayne *(G-5308)*

Phoenix Color Corp. .... F 812 238-1551
Terre Haute *(G-15661)*

Phoenix Color Corp. .... D 812 234-1585
Terre Haute *(G-15662)*

Phoenix Press Inc .... D 765 644-3959
Anderson *(G-178)*

Piccolo Printing .... G 888 901-8648
Evansville *(G-4243)*

Picture Perfect Printing .... G 765 482-4241
Lebanon *(G-10933)*

Pinpoint Printer .... G 812 577-0630
Aurora *(G-452)*

PIP Marketing Signs Print .... G 317 843-5755
Carmel *(G-1719)*

Plastic Cardz LLC .... G 260 431-6380
Fort Wayne *(G-5317)*

Posters 2 Prints LLC .... E 317 414-8972
Indianapolis *(G-9166)*

Posters 2 Prints LLC .... G 800 598-5837
Indianapolis *(G-9165)*

Posters 2 Prints LLC .... G 317 769-3784
Zionsville *(G-17043)*

Prairie Creek Prtg & Bk Str .... G 812 636-7243
Montgomery *(G-12119)*

Prairieton Printing .... G 812 299-9611
Terre Haute *(G-15667)*

Precision Print LLC .... G 765 789-8799
Albany *(G-15)*

Preferred Print .... G 317 371-8829
Indianapolis *(G-9189)*

Premier Label Company Inc .... F 765 289-5000
Muncie *(G-12477)*

Premier Printing .... G 765 459-8339
Kokomo *(G-10323)*

Premier Prints LLC .... G 812 987-1129
Jeffersonville *(G-10040)*

◆ **Prentice Products Inc** .... E 260 747-3195
Fort Wayne *(G-5347)*

Presstime Graphics Inc .... F 812 234-3815
Terre Haute *(G-15669)*

Prestige Printing Inc .... E 812 372-2500
Columbus *(G-2381)*

Primal Prints LLC .... G 260 494-8435
Huntertown *(G-7264)*

Princeton Publishing Inc .... G 812 385-2525
Princeton *(G-14010)*

Print 2 Finish LLC .... G 812 256-5515
Charlestown *(G-1891)*

Print Center Inc .... G 219 874-9683
Long Beach *(G-11128)*

Print Ideas .... G 317 299-8766
Indianapolis *(G-9199)*

Print It Inc .... G 317 774-6848
Indianapolis *(G-9200)*

Print It Plus Inc .... G 812 466-7446
Terre Haute *(G-15670)*

Print It Wear It Inc .... G 317 946-1456
Shelbyville *(G-14788)*

Print Management Solutions Inc .... G 574 234-7269
South Bend *(G-15205)*

Print My Merch LLC .... G 765 269-6772
Mishawaka *(G-11979)*

Print Resources Inc .... D 317 833-7000
Indianapolis *(G-9202)*

Print Sharp Enterprises Inc .... G 317 899-2754
Indianapolis *(G-9203)*

Print Shop Inc .... G 574 264-0023
Elkhart *(G-3620)*

Print Solutions of Indiana .... G 219 988-4186
Crown Point *(G-2736)*

Print Source Corporation .... G 260 824-3911
Bluffton *(G-1050)*

Print2promo Group Inc .... G 219 778-4649
Rolling Prairie *(G-14369)*

Printcraft Press Inc .... G 765 457-2141
Kokomo *(G-10324)*

Printcrafters Inc .... G 812 838-4106
Mount Vernon *(G-12315)*

Printed By Erik Inc .... G 574 295-1203
Elkhart *(G-3621)*

Printing All Stars .... G 812 288-9291
New Albany *(G-12798)*

Printing Center Inc .... G 317 545-8518
Indianapolis *(G-9204)*

Printing Company LLC .... G 812 367-2668
Ferdinand *(G-4448)*

Printing Concepts Inc .... G 317 899-2754
Indianapolis *(G-9205)*

Printing Creations Inc .... G 765 759-9679
Yorktown *(G-16982)*

Printing Impression .... G 812 537-4077
Lawrenceburg *(G-10854)*

Printing In Time Inc .... G 502 807-3545
Elizabeth *(G-3128)*

Printing Partners Inc .... D 317 635-2282
Indianapolis *(G-9206)*

Printing Partners East Inc .... G 317 356-2522
Indianapolis *(G-9207)*

Printing Place Inc .... F 260 665-8444
Angola *(G-289)*

Printing Solutions Inc .... G 812 923-0756
Floyds Knobs *(G-4689)*

Printing Technologies Inc .... E 800 428-3786
Indianapolis *(G-9209)*

Printsource .... G 317 507-6526
Indianapolis *(G-9210)*

Printworks Inc .... G 317 535-1250
Whiteland *(G-16793)*

Priority Press Inc .... G 317 240-0103
Indianapolis *(G-9212)*

Priority Printing LLC .... G 317 241-4234
Indianapolis *(G-9213)*

Pro Prints .... G 812 932-3800
Batesville *(G-600)*

Professional Design LLC .... G 765 529-1590
New Castle *(G-12879)*

Proforma Premier Printing .... G 317 842-9181
Indianapolis *(G-9224)*

Proforma Print Promo Group .... G 574 931-2941
South Bend *(G-15207)*

Progressive Printing Co Inc .... G 765 653-3814
Greencastle *(G-6427)*

Proprint Forms LLC .... G 317 861-8701
New Palestine *(G-12943)*

Publishers Consulting Corp .... F 219 874-4245
Michigan City *(G-11652)*

Pulaski County Press Inc .... G 574 946-6628
Winamac *(G-16872)*

Qgraphics Inc .... G 765 564-2314
Delphi *(G-2906)*

Quad/Graphics Inc .... G 260 748-5300
Fort Wayne *(G-5361)*

Quality Graphics Corp .... G 219 845-7084
Hammond *(G-6994)*

Quality Printing of NW Ind .... G 219 322-6677
Schererville *(G-14540)*

R & B Fine Printing Inc .... G 219 365-9490
Saint John *(G-14457)*

Rainbow Printing LLC .... F 812 275-3372
Bedford *(G-663)*

Randall Corp .... G 812 425-7122
Evansville *(G-4272)*

Rasure Prints LLC .... G 812 454-6222
Evansville *(G-4273)*

Red Line Graphics Incorporated .... E 317 784-3777
Indianapolis *(G-9278)*

Redrum Incorporated .... G 859 489-1516
New Albany *(G-12804)*

Rensselaer Print Co .... G 219 866-5000
Rensselaer *(G-14066)*

Reprocomm Inc .... G 765 423-2578
Lafayette *(G-10679)*

Reprocomm Inc .... G 765 472-5700
Peru *(G-13598)*

Rhr Corporation .... G 317 788-1504
Indianapolis *(G-9298)*

Richards Printery .... G 812 406-0295
Greenville *(G-6654)*

Riden Inc .... G 219 362-5511
La Porte *(G-10473)*

Rightcolors LLC .... G 812 675-8775
Bedford *(G-668)*

Rink Printing Company .... E 574 232-7935
South Bend *(G-15220)*

Riverside Printing Co .... G 812 275-1950
Bedford *(G-669)*

Rj Partners of Indiana Inc C
Indianapolis *(G-9311)*

Rock Hard Stnes Cstm Prtg Rhns .... G 219 613-0112
Merrillville *(G-11554)*

Ronnie Elmore Jr .... G 765 719-1681
Cloverdale *(G-2095)*

Roteck Enterprises Inc .... G 219 322-4132
Dyer *(G-2982)*

Row Printing Inc .... G 317 796-3289
Brownsburg *(G-1399)*

Row Printing Inc .... G 317 441-4301
Brownsburg *(G-1400)*

Rowland Printing Co Inc .... F 317 773-1829
Noblesville *(G-13168)*

◆ **Rrc Corporation** .... F 317 687-8325
Indianapolis *(G-9343)*

Russ Print Shp/Hbron Advrtser .... F 219 996-3142
Hebron *(G-7106)*

Samuel Wahli .... G 260 749-2288
New Haven *(G-12917)*

Schutte Lithography Inc .... F 812 469-3500
Evansville *(G-4300)*

Scott Printing LLC .... G 812 306-7477
Evansville *(G-4301)*

Screenbroidery LLC .... E 317 546-1900
Noblesville *(G-13173)*

Service Graphics Inc .... D 317 471-8246
Indianapolis *(G-9408)*

▲ **Service Printers Inc** .... E 574 266-6710
Elkhart *(G-3669)*

Shackelford Graphics .... G 317 783-3582
Indianapolis *(G-9409)*

Shadow Screen Printing .... G 812 234-3104
Terre Haute *(G-15690)*

Sharon K Utter .... G 765 349-8991
Martinsville *(G-11427)*

Sharp Printing Services Inc .... G 317 842-5159
Fishers *(G-4604)*

Shearer Printing Service Inc .... E 765 457-3274
Kokomo *(G-10334)*

Shelbyville Newspapers Inc .... E 317 398-6631
Shelbyville *(G-14798)*

Shirt Print Ave .... G 812 882-9610
Vincennes *(G-16154)*

Small Town Printers LLC .... G 812 596-1536
Elizabeth *(G-3130)*

Smiling Cross Inc .... G 812 323-9290
Bloomington *(G-976)*

SIC SECTION 27 PRINTING, PUBLISHING AND ALLIED INDUSTRIES

Smith & Butterfield Co Inc .... F 812 422-3261
 Evansville *(G-4320)*

Smith & Butterfield Co Inc .... G 812 422-3261
 Evansville *(G-4321)*

Smith Business Supply Inc .... G 765 654-4442
 Frankfort *(G-5694)*

Smitson Cmmnications Group LLC ...... G 317 876-8916
 Indianapolis *(G-9451)*

Solutions For Print LLC .... G 812 584-2701
 Fountaintown *(G-5616)*

Sound & Graphics .... G 219 963-7293
 Lake Station *(G-10777)*

Specialized Printed Products .... G 260 483-7075
 Fort Wayne *(G-5428)*

Spectrum Print and Mktg LLC .... G 317 908-7471
 Avon *(G-551)*

Speedy-Screen LLC .... G 317 910-0724
 Indianapolis *(G-9478)*

Spencer Evening World .... D 812 829-2255
 Spencer *(G-15362)*

Spencer Printing Inc .... G 765 288-6111
 Muncie *(G-12496)*

St Clair Press .... G 317 612-9100
 Indianapolis *(G-9484)*

Stage Door Graphics .... G 317 398-9011
 Shelbyville *(G-14801)*

Starlight Printing .... G 812 486-3905
 Montgomery *(G-12124)*

State Cleaning Solutions .... G 812 336-4817
 Indianapolis *(G-9500)*

Steve Weaver Art .... G 574 546-3530
 Bremen *(G-1224)*

Stines Printing Inc .... G 260 356-5994
 Huntington *(G-7371)*

Stump Printing Co .... F 260 723-5171
 South Whitley *(G-15329)*

Success Express .... G 317 750-1747
 Rockville *(G-14357)*

Summit LLC .... G 574 287-7468
 Elkhart *(G-3705)*

Summit Business Products Inc .... G 260 244-1820
 Churubusco *(G-1987)*

Superior Print Inc .... E 812 246-6311
 Sellersburg *(G-14617)*

Swagerle Screen Printing .... G 812 232-6947
 Terre Haute *(G-15719)*

Swiss Alps Printing Inc .... G 812 427-3844
 Vevay *(G-16113)*

Systems & Services of Michiana .... G 574 277-3355
 South Bend *(G-15278)*

Systems & Services of Michiana .... G 574 273-1111
 South Bend *(G-15277)*

T and J Printing Supply .... G 317 986-4765
 Indianapolis *(G-9544)*

T N D Printing .... G 260 493-4949
 Fishers *(G-4609)*

T-Flyerz Printing and Prom LLC .... G 260 729-7392
 Bryant *(G-1437)*

Tabco Business Forms Inc .... G 812 882-2836
 Vincennes *(G-16157)*

Target Printing Inc .... G 260 744-6038
 Fort Wayne *(G-5469)*

Tatman Inc .... E 765 825-2164
 Connersville *(G-2472)*

Tdk Graphics Inc .... F 219 663-7799
 Crown Point *(G-2762)*

Team Gear Printing LLC .... G 765 935-4748
 Richmond *(G-14211)*

Team Gear Printing LLC .... G 765 977-2995
 Richmond *(G-14212)*

Tek Print LLC .... G 812 336-2525
 Bedford *(G-677)*

Templeton Myers Inc .... E 317 898-6688
 Indianapolis *(G-9575)*

▲ Tfi Inc .... E 317 290-1333
 Whitestown *(G-16825)*

Th Custom Printing .... G 765 251-3986
 Summitville *(G-15434)*

Thach LLC .... G 317 373-3734
 Westfield *(G-16732)*

The Deaton Family Company .... D 815 726-6234
 Auburn *(G-429)*

The Office Shop Inc .... E 812 934-5611
 Batesville *(G-607)*

This That EMB Screen Prtg LLC .... G 317 541-8548
 Indianapolis *(G-9591)*

Thomas E Slade Inc .... F 812 437-5233
 Evansville *(G-4343)*

Thomas Madison .... G 312 625-9152
 Michigan City *(G-11678)*

Thompson Printing Service Inc .... G 317 783-7448
 Indianapolis *(G-9598)*

Times .... E 765 659-4622
 Frankfort *(G-5698)*

Tints & Prints By Tierney LLC .... G 317 769-5895
 Zionsville *(G-17057)*

Tippecanoe Press Inc .... G 317 392-1207
 Shelbyville *(G-14806)*

Titan Graphics LLC .... G 317 496-2188
 Mccordsville *(G-11457)*

Tko Enterprises Inc .... D 317 271-1398
 Plainfield *(G-13736)*

Tonya Gerhardt .... G 260 434-1370
 Fort Wayne *(G-5493)*

Town & Country Industries Inc .... E 219 712-0893
 Crown Point *(G-2766)*

Town & Country Press Inc .... F 574 936-9505
 Plymouth *(G-13820)*

Triple Crown Media LLC .... G 574 533-2151
 Goshen *(G-6273)*

Truth Publishing Company Inc .... G 765 653-5151
 Greencastle *(G-6434)*

Twin Prints Inc .... G 765 742-8656
 Lafayette *(G-10711)*

Two B Enterprises Inc .... F 260 245-0119
 Fort Wayne *(G-5518)*

United Hero Apparel Printing .... G 812 306-1998
 Evansville *(G-4362)*

United Parcel Service Inc .... G 317 776-9494
 Noblesville *(G-13189)*

University Publishing Corp .... E 812 339-9033
 Bloomington *(G-1004)*

UPS Store 5219 .... G 219 750-9597
 Merrillville *(G-11570)*

V & P Printing .... G 260 495-3741
 Fremont *(G-5838)*

▲ Valley Screen Process Co Inc .... D 574 256-0901
 Mishawaka *(G-12020)*

Vdk Printing LLC .... G 260 602-8212
 Fort Wayne *(G-5529)*

Virtu Fine Art Services Inc .... G 317 822-1800
 Indianapolis *(G-9722)*

▼ Voice of God Recordings Inc .... D 812 246-2137
 Jeffersonville *(G-10069)*

Wabash Plain Dealer Co LLC .... E 260 563-2131
 Wabash *(G-16221)*

WAr - LLC- Westville Prtg .... G 219 785-2821
 Westville *(G-16765)*

Wayne Press Incorporated .... G 260 744-3022
 Fort Wayne *(G-5553)*

Web Printing Connection Inc .... G 260 637-4037
 Fort Wayne *(G-5560)*

Well Ink .... G 765 743-3413
 West Lafayette *(G-16646)*

Whitewater Print Solutions LLC .... G 513 405-3452
 Brookville *(G-1340)*

Whitewater Publications Inc .... F 765 647-4221
 Brookville *(G-1341)*

William E Steiner .... G 317 575-9018
 Carmel *(G-1806)*

Williams Printing Inc .... G 765 468-6033
 Farmland *(G-4427)*

Wilson Printing .... G 317 745-5868
 Danville *(G-2830)*

Wise Business Forms Inc .... D 260 489-1561
 Fort Wayne *(G-5572)*

Wise Printing Inc .... G 317 351-9477
 Indianapolis *(G-9777)*

Woodburn Graphics Inc .... F 812 232-0323
 Terre Haute *(G-15748)*

Woodfield Printing Inc .... G 317 848-2000
 Carmel *(G-1808)*

Woods Printing Company Inc .... F 812 536-2261
 Holland *(G-7215)*

Work Field Collaborative Inc .... G 360 581-9476
 Indianapolis *(G-9789)*

▼ World Arts Inc .... D 812 829-2255
 Spencer *(G-15365)*

Wraco Enterprises Inc .... G 812 339-3987
 Bloomington *(G-1016)*

Writeguard Business Systems .... G 317 849-7292
 Indianapolis *(G-9793)*

Xl Graphics Inc .... F 317 738-3434
 Franklin *(G-5789)*

Your Face Our Place Print Shop .... G 812 567-4510
 Tennyson *(G-15526)*

Zipp Printing LLC .... G 574 256-0059
 Mishawaka *(G-12028)*

Zogman Enterprises Inc .... G 317 873-6809
 Zionsville *(G-17065)*

2754 Commercial printing, gravure

A & H Enterprises LLC .... G 317 398-3070
 Shelbyville *(G-14729)*

Enterprise Marking Pdts Inc .... E 317 867-7600
 Fishers *(G-4516)*

Gary Printing Inc .... G 219 886-1767
 Gary *(G-5938)*

I4 Identity LLC .... G 317 662-0448
 Fishers *(G-4541)*

Inteprintations .... G 765 404-0887
 Indianapolis *(G-8571)*

Magical Moments LLC .... G 463 209-5766
 Greenwood *(G-6731)*

Mid America Coop Education .... G 317 726-6910
 Indianapolis *(G-8906)*

Multi-Color Corporation .... E 812 752-0586
 Scottsburg *(G-14573)*

Nussmeier Engraving Company .... E 812 425-1339
 Evansville *(G-4224)*

OBannon Publishing Company .... E 812 738-4552
 Corydon *(G-2508)*

PostNet Postal & Business Svcs .... G 317 462-7118
 Greenfield *(G-6541)*

♦ Proedge Inc .... E 219 552-9550
 Shelby *(G-14727)*

Scott Culbertson .... G 260 357-6430
 Garrett *(G-5876)*

Stien Designs & Graphics Inc .... G 260 347-9136
 Kendallville *(G-10153)*

Viking Business Ventures Inc .... G 260 489-7787
 Fort Wayne *(G-5532)*

Westwood Paper Company .... G 317 843-1212
 Carmel *(G-1804)*

2759 Commercial printing, nec

Employee Codes: A=Over 500 employees, B=251-500
C=101-250, D=51-100, E=20-50, F=10-19, G=1-9

2024 Harris Indiana
Industrial Directory

27 PRINTING, PUBLISHING AND ALLIED INDUSTRIES — SIC SECTION

18 Threads LLC .... F 260 409-2923
   Fort Wayne *(G-4710)*

1z2z Imprints .... G 303 918-8979
   Bloomington *(G-764)*

47tee LLC .... G 317 373-8070
   Fishers *(G-4457)*

4ink Fullfillment Services .... G 812 738-4465
   Corydon *(G-2483)*

A & M Innovations LLC .... G 317 306-6118
   Whiteland *(G-16776)*

A-1 Screenprinting LLC .... G 812 558-0286
   Bloomington *(G-769)*

A-1 Screenprinting LLC .... G 765 588-3851
   West Lafayette *(G-16554)*

A&A Screen Printing .... G 765 473-8783
   Peru *(G-13564)*

A+ Images Inc .... G 317 405-8955
   Indianapolis *(G-7405)*

A1 Deliveries LLC .... G 317 828-3951
   Indianapolis *(G-7408)*

Aardvark Graphics .... G 574 267-4799
   Warsaw *(G-16307)*

▲ Abr Images Inc .... F 866 342-4764
   Bloomington *(G-770)*

Abracadabra Graphics .... G 812 336-1971
   Bloomington *(G-771)*

Acclaim Graphics Inc .... G 812 424-5035
   Evansville *(G-3866)*

Accu-Label Inc .... E 260 482-5223
   Fort Wayne *(G-4720)*

Adams Smith .... G 219 661-2812
   Crown Point *(G-2648)*

Adlink Promotions .... G 574 271-7003
   Granger *(G-6330)*

Advanced Digital Imaging .... G 765 491-9434
   West Lafayette *(G-16558)*

Advantex Inc .... G 812 339-6479
   Bloomington *(G-774)*

After Hours Embroidery .... G 812 926-9355
   Aurora *(G-436)*

All Gussied Up Embroidery .... G 317 517-1557
   Indianapolis *(G-7473)*

Allsports .... G 812 883-3561
   Salem *(G-14470)*

Almost Famous Printing .... G 219 793-6388
   Whiting *(G-16830)*

Altstadt Business Forms Inc .... F 812 425-3393
   Evansville *(G-3882)*

American Direct Sales LLC .... D 877 462-2621
   Valparaiso *(G-15898)*

American Label Products Inc .... G 317 873-9850
   Zionsville *(G-16991)*

American Printing Indiana LLC .... G 765 825-7600
   Anderson *(G-76)*

American Veteran Group LLC .... G 317 600-4749
   Westfield *(G-16664)*

Anchor Enterprises .... G 812 282-7220
   Jeffersonville *(G-9933)*

Andresen Graphic Processors .... F 317 291-7071
   Brownsburg *(G-1346)*

Anthony Wyne Rhbltton Ctr For .... C 317 972-1000
   Indianapolis *(G-7522)*

Apollo Prtg & Graphics Ctr Inc .... E 574 287-3707
   South Bend *(G-14948)*

Apparel Design Group .... G 812 339-3355
   Bloomington *(G-781)*

As You Wish Custom .... G 502 216-3144
   Jeffersonville *(G-9935)*

Asahi TEC America Corporation .... G 765 962-8399
   Richmond *(G-14087)*

Ascl Printwear LLC .... G 317 507-0548
   Avon *(G-505)*

Axe Head Threads LLC .... G 317 607-6330
   New Palestine *(G-12932)*

B-Hive Printing .... G 812 897-3905
   Boonville *(G-1081)*

Bartel Printing Company Inc .... G 574 267-7421
   Warsaw *(G-16317)*

Bartons Screen Printing .... G 812 422-4303
   Evansville *(G-3910)*

Bartons Teez .... G 812 422-4303
   Evansville *(G-3911)*

Baxter Printing Incorporated .... G 219 923-1999
   Griffith *(G-6793)*

Behning Inc .... G 260 672-2663
   Roanoke *(G-14260)*

Bell Graphics and Design LLC .... G 765 827-5441
   Connersville *(G-2428)*

Bennett Printing .... G 812 966-2917
   Medora *(G-11461)*

Bev Can Printers LLC .... G 219 617-6181
   La Porte *(G-10388)*

Bex Screen Printing Inc .... G 317 791-0375
   Indianapolis *(G-7620)*

Big Picture Data Imaging LLC .... G 812 235-0202
   Terre Haute *(G-15553)*

Bills Industries LLC .... G 765 629-0227
   Milroy *(G-11821)*

Black Dog Printing LLC .... G 812 955-0577
   Richmond *(G-14098)*

Black Hustle Holdings Corp .... G 800 988-7067
   Indianapolis *(G-7638)*

Bloomington Letter Shop .... G 812 824-6363
   Bloomington *(G-812)*

Blue Octopus Printing Company .... F 317 247-1997
   Indianapolis *(G-7646)*

Blue River Printing Inc .... G 317 392-3676
   Shelbyville *(G-14736)*

Blue River Services Inc .... E 812 738-2437
   Corydon *(G-2488)*

Bm Creations Inc .... E 219 922-8935
   Griffith *(G-6796)*

Brand Prtg & Photo-Litho Co .... G 317 921-4095
   New Palestine *(G-12933)*

Brandwise LLC .... G 317 574-0066
   Noblesville *(G-13046)*

Bredensteiner & Associates .... G 317 921-2226
   Indianapolis *(G-7673)*

Brenmeer LLC .... G 260 267-0249
   Fort Wayne *(G-4816)*

Broken Tee LLC .... G 812 559-0741
   Jasper *(G-9825)*

Bruce Payne .... G 260 492-2259
   Fort Wayne *(G-4820)*

BT Management Inc .... G 219 794-9546
   Merrillville *(G-11494)*

Burkert-Walton Inc .... G 812 425-7157
   Evansville *(G-3957)*

Business Forms Designs Inc .... G 317 353-6647
   Indianapolis *(G-7703)*

C E M Printing & Specialities .... G 269 684-6898
   South Bend *(G-14964)*

California Colors Inc .... G 317 435-1351
   Fishers *(G-4482)*

Campbell Printing Company .... G 219 866-5913
   Rensselaer *(G-14046)*

Cause Printing Company .... G 765 573-3330
   Huntington *(G-7305)*

Ccmp Inc .... E 219 922-8935
   Griffith *(G-6799)*

CD Grafix LLC .... G 812 945-4443
   Clarksville *(G-2011)*

Cdb Screen Printing Inc .... G 765 472-4404
   Peru *(G-13570)*

Cecils Printing & Off Sups Inc .... G 812 683-4416
   Huntingburg *(G-7273)*

Cedar Woodworking .... G 812 486-2765
   Montgomery *(G-12088)*

Celestial Designs LLC .... G 317 733-3110
   Zionsville *(G-16997)*

Cenveo Worldwide Limited .... D 800 995-9500
   New Albany *(G-12710)*

Classic Graphics Inc .... F 260 482-3487
   Fort Wayne *(G-4853)*

Clover Printing LLC .... G 260 657-3003
   Harlan *(G-7052)*

Coachs Connection Inc .... G 260 356-0400
   Huntington *(G-7306)*

Coffey Connection LLC .... G 317 300-9639
   Greenwood *(G-6681)*

Colorrush Inc .... G 317 374-3494
   Indianapolis *(G-7838)*

Commercial Print Shop Inc .... G 260 724-3722
   Decatur *(G-2850)*

Consolidated Printing Svcs Inc .... G 765 468-6033
   Farmland *(G-4424)*

Cool Cayenne .... G 260 376-0977
   Portland *(G-13934)*

Cool Cayenne LLC .... G 765 282-0977
   Albany *(G-12)*

Countryside Printing LLC .... G 812 486-2454
   Montgomery *(G-12090)*

County West Sports .... G 317 839-4076
   Plainfield *(G-13673)*

Courier Printing Co Allen Cnty .... G 260 627-2728
   Grabill *(G-6293)*

▲ Courier-Times Inc .... D 765 529-1111
   New Castle *(G-12856)*

Cozy Cat Inc .... G 765 463-1254
   Lafayette *(G-10559)*

Craigs Printing Co .... G 812 358-5010
   Brownstown *(G-1421)*

Criterion Press Inc .... E 317 236-1570
   Indianapolis *(G-7904)*

Cs Kern Inc .... E 765 289-8600
   Muncie *(G-12370)*

Custom Candy Wrappers Company .... G 574 247-0756
   Granger *(G-6340)*

Custom Ink Writers .... G 260 202-9350
   Portland *(G-13935)*

Custom Packaging Inc .... F 317 876-9559
   Indianapolis *(G-7933)*

Custom Prints and Tees LLC .... G 317 891-4550
   Indianapolis *(G-7935)*

D S Custom Tees .... G 219 802-3127
   Gary *(G-5921)*

Daisy Tees LLC .... G 574 259-1933
   Mishawaka *(G-11876)*

Dale Flora .... G 260 982-7233
   North Manchester *(G-13232)*

Dance World Bazaar Corporation .... G 812 663-7679
   Greensburg *(G-6589)*

▼ Data Label Inc .... C 800 457-0676
   Terre Haute *(G-15577)*

◆ David Camp .... G 812 346-6255
   North Vernon *(G-13265)*

David Indus Process Pdts Inc .... G 317 577-0351
   Fishers *(G-4502)*

Dec-O-Art Inc .... E 574 294-6451
   Elkhart *(G-3287)*

Defining Trndstting Cstm Print .... G 260 755-1038
   Fort Wayne *(G-4910)*

Denneycreative .... G 260 494-0862
   Wabash *(G-16180)*

Dimensional Imprinting Inc .... G 260 417-0202
   Milton *(G-11832)*

27 PRINTING, PUBLISHING AND ALLIED INDUSTRIES

Direct Printing Co .... G 317 831-1047
  Mooresville (G-12203)
Dirty Squeegee Screen Prtg LLC .... G 574 358-0003
  Middlebury (G-11712)
Distinct Images Inc .... F 317 613-4413
  Indianapolis (G-7977)
Diversified Bus Systems Inc .... G 317 254-8668
  Indianapolis (G-7984)
Dna Designs LLC .... G 812 329-1310
  Bedford (G-631)
Docutech Document Service .... G 219 690-3038
  Lowell (G-11160)
Doerr Printing Co .... G 317 568-0135
  Indianapolis (G-7994)
Douglas P Terrell .... G 812 254-1976
  Washington (G-16478)
Drike Inc .... F 574 259-8822
  Mishawaka (G-11885)
Dse Inc .... E 812 376-0310
  Columbus (G-2291)
Eastern Engineering Supply Inc .... F 260 426-3119
  Fort Wayne (G-4938)
Ed Sons Inc .... F 317 897-8821
  Indianapolis (G-8051)
El Shaddai Inc .... G 260 359-9080
  Huntington (G-7309)
Elegan Graphics .... G 219 462-9921
  Valparaiso (G-15940)
Elengas Customwear .... G 317 577-1677
  Fishers (G-4510)
Em Global LLC .... G 812 258-9993
  Jeffersonville (G-9976)
Embroidme .... G 219 465-1400
  Valparaiso (G-15943)
Engraving and Stamp Center Inc .... G 812 336-0606
  Bloomington (G-861)
Entertainment Express .... G 219 763-3610
  Portage (G-13861)
Epic Graphics and Printing .... G 219 545-1240
  Gary (G-5930)
Esther Reid .... G 314 504-6659
  South Bend (G-15018)
Evansville Bindery Inc .... G 812 423-2222
  Evansville (G-4048)
Evansvlle Print Specialist Inc .... G 812 423-5831
  Evansville (G-4060)
Everything Under Sun LLC .... G 812 438-3397
  Rising Sun (G-14242)
Ewing Printing Company Inc .... F 812 882-2415
  Vincennes (G-16120)
Excell Color Graphics Inc .... E 260 482-2720
  Fort Wayne (G-4967)
Expressions Custom Tees .... G 317 205-6229
  Indianapolis (G-8158)
Extensive Design LLC .... G 260 267-6752
  Fort Wayne (G-4969)
F Robert Gardner Co Inc .... G 317 634-2333
  Indianapolis (G-8161)
Faith Walkers .... G 219 873-1900
  Michigan City (G-11610)
Faulkenberg Printing Co Inc .... F 317 638-1359
  Franklin (G-5730)
Fedex Office & Print Svcs Inc .... G 317 251-2406
  Indianapolis (G-8179)
Fehring F N & Son Printers .... G 219 933-0439
  Valparaiso (G-15949)
Fired Up Tees LLC .... G 317 412-4113
  Bargersville (G-566)
First Class Printing .... G 317 808-2222
  Indianapolis (G-8192)
Formal Affairs Tuxedo Shop .... G 574 875-6654
  Elkhart (G-3357)

Fort Wayne Newspapers Inc .... B 260 461-8444
  Fort Wayne (G-4999)
Freckles Grphics Lafayette Inc .... F 765 448-4692
  Lafayette (G-10581)
Fresh Printz Incorporated .... F 812 352-6400
  North Vernon (G-13271)
G D Cox Inc .... G 317 398-0035
  Shelbyville (G-14758)
Garco Graphics .... G 219 980-1113
  Gary (G-5935)
Gary Printing Inc .... G 219 886-1767
  Gary (G-5938)
Gen Enterprises .... G 574 498-6777
  Tippecanoe (G-15759)
Gettelfinger Holdings LLC .... G 812 923-9065
  Floyds Knobs (G-4679)
Giraffe-X Graphics Inc .... G 317 546-4944
  Indianapolis (G-8282)
Glittered Pig LLC .... G 812 779-6154
  Princeton (G-13995)
Gogolaks Engraving .... G 219 972-3995
  Hammond (G-6935)
Goldden Corporation .... F 765 423-4366
  Lafayette (G-10591)
Goldleaf Promotional Pdts Inc .... G 317 202-2754
  Indianapolis (G-8302)
▲ Goose Graphics L L C .... G 260 563-4516
  Fort Wayne (G-5029)
Grafac Industries Inc .... G 812 474-0930
  Evansville (G-4094)
Graphic 2000 Forms Labels .... G 260 387-5943
  Fort Wayne (G-5033)
Graphic Fx Inc .... E 812 234-0000
  Terre Haute (G-15601)
Graphic Menus Inc .... F 765 396-3003
  Eaton (G-3062)
Graphic Visions .... G 812 331-7446
  Bloomington (G-869)
Graphic22 Inc .... G 219 921-5409
  Chesterton (G-1930)
Graphics Lab Uv Printing Inc .... F 765 457-5784
  Kokomo (G-10272)
Graphics Unlmted McRpublishing .... G 260 665-3443
  Angola (G-256)
Graphix Unlimited Inc .... E 574 546-3770
  Bremen (G-1193)
Greensburg Printing Co Inc .... G 812 663-8265
  Greensburg (G-6598)
H M C Screen Printing Inc .... E 317 773-8532
  Noblesville (G-13090)
Happy Tees LLC .... G 317 465-0122
  Indianapolis (G-8355)
▲ Harcourt Industries Inc .... E 765 629-2625
  Milroy (G-11824)
Harmony Press Inc .... E 800 525-3742
  Bourbon (G-1122)
Hartley J Company Inc .... G 812 376-9708
  Hartsville (G-7082)
Hat Plug US .... G 574 575-2520
  Elkhart (G-3401)
Haywood Printing Co .... G 812 384-8639
  Bloomfield (G-747)
Haywood Printing Co Inc .... E 765 742-4085
  Indianapolis (G-8372)
Headlands Ltd .... G 260 426-9884
  Wolcottville (G-16937)
Hi-Tech Label Inc .... F 765 659-1800
  Frankfort (G-5673)
Hiatt Enterprises Inc .... G 765 289-2700
  Muncie (G-12416)
Hiatt Enterprises Inc .... F 765 289-7756
  Muncie (G-12415)

Highway Press Inc .... G 812 283-6462
  Jeffersonville (G-9996)
Hinen Printing Co .... G 260 248-8984
  Columbia City (G-2150)
Hoosier Daddy Custom Tees .... G 218 308-3544
  Portage (G-13876)
Hoosier Horse Review LLC .... G 765 212-1320
  Muncie (G-12420)
Hoosier Jiffy Print .... G 260 563-8715
  Wabash (G-16193)
Hoosier Miracle Inc .... G 765 473-4438
  Peru (G-13586)
Hot Cake .... E 317 889-2253
  Indianapolis (G-8419)
Hot Off Press .... G 317 253-5987
  Indianapolis (G-8420)
Ics Inks LLP .... G 317 690-9254
  Indianapolis (G-8452)
IM Impressed .... G 219 838-7959
  Munster (G-12542)
Image Plus Original LLC .... G 800 226-7316
  Indianapolis (G-8463)
Imagination Graphics .... G 812 423-6503
  Evansville (G-4117)
Imprint It All .... G 812 234-0024
  Terre Haute (G-15614)
In Business For Life Inc .... G 317 691-6169
  Carmel (G-1664)
Indilabel LLC .... F 317 839-8814
  Plainfield (G-13689)
Ink Dawgz LLC .... G 219 781-6972
  Valparaiso (G-15974)
Inkworks Studio LLC .... G 812 401-6203
  Evansville (G-4126)
Insana Tees .... G 219 801-5104
  Portage (G-13877)
International Label Mfg LLC .... F 812 235-5071
  Terre Haute (G-15618)
J Tees .... G 812 524-9292
  Seymour (G-14658)
J&J Sprts Screen Prtg Sprit Wr .... G 812 909-2686
  Evansville (G-4135)
J&P Custom Designs Inc .... G 317 253-2198
  Indianapolis (G-8611)
Jac Jmr Inc .... G 219 663-6700
  Crown Point (G-2698)
James Wafford .... G 317 773-7200
  Noblesville (G-13111)
JB Graphics Inc .... G 317 819-0008
  Westfield (G-16702)
Jer-Maur Corporation .... G 812 384-8290
  Bloomfield (G-750)
Jeremy Parker .... G 765 284-5414
  Muncie (G-12431)
John R Bowen & Associates .... G 812 544-2267
  Newburgh (G-13010)
Jomark Inc .... F 248 478-2600
  Angola (G-265)
Jones & Webb Associates Inc .... G 317 236-9755
  Indianapolis (G-8637)
Journal & Chronicle Inc .... G 812 752-5060
  Scottsburg (G-14566)
Jt Printing LLC .... G 317 271-7700
  Avon (G-529)
Karemar Productions .... G 765 766-5117
  Mooreland (G-12185)
Keen Screen .... G 812 989-8885
  New Albany (G-12757)
Keen Screen .... G 812 945-5336
  New Albany (G-12758)
Kendallville Custom Printing .... F 260 347-9233
  Kendallville (G-10125)

Employee Codes: A=Over 500 employees, B=251-500
C=101-250, D=51-100, E=20-50, F=10-19, G=1-9

2024 Harris Indiana
Industrial Directory

27 PRINTING, PUBLISHING AND ALLIED INDUSTRIES

Kennyleeholmescom .... G 574 612-2526
  Elkhart *(G-3451)*
Kessler Concepts Inc .... F 317 630-9901
  Indianapolis *(G-8675)*
▼ Kewanna Screen Printing Inc .... G 574 653-2683
  Kewanna *(G-10167)*
Kingery Group Inc .... G 317 823-9585
  Indianapolis *(G-8687)*
Kirchoff Custom Sports Inc .... G 812 434-0355
  Evansville *(G-4154)*
Kmls LLC .... G 317 845-2955
  Morgantown *(G-12259)*
Knoy Apparel .... G 765 448-1031
  Lafayette *(G-10624)*
Kozs Quality Printing Inc .... G 219 696-6711
  Lowell *(G-11166)*
Krafty Bravo LLC .... G 317 366-3485
  South Bend *(G-15105)*
Kwik Kopy Printing .... G 219 663-7799
  Crown Point *(G-2714)*
L & L Press Inc .... F 765 664-3162
  Marion *(G-11305)*
▲ L R Green Co Inc .... D 317 781-4200
  Indianapolis *(G-8705)*
La Grange Publishing Co Inc .... F 260 463-3243
  Lagrange *(G-10747)*
Label Logic Inc .... E 574 266-6007
  Elkhart *(G-3464)*
Label Tech Inc .... E 765 747-1234
  Muncie *(G-12436)*
Laconia Laser Engraving .... G 812 786-3641
  Laconia *(G-10506)*
Lambel Corporation .... G 317 849-6828
  Indianapolis *(G-8716)*
Lamco Finishers Inc .... E 317 471-1010
  Indianapolis *(G-8717)*
Largus Speedy Print Corp .... E 219 922-8414
  Munster *(G-12546)*
Laser Marking Technologies .... G 812 852-7999
  Osgood *(G-13411)*
Leader Publishing Co of Salem .... E 812 883-3281
  Salem *(G-14487)*
Leap Frogz Ink LLC .... G 317 786-2441
  Greenwood *(G-6728)*
Lee Reed Holdings LLC .... G 219 255-0555
  Hammond *(G-6970)*
Legacy Enterprises Inc .... G 219 484-9483
  Merrillville *(G-11531)*
Legacy Screen Printing Promoti .... G 219 262-4000
  Chesterton *(G-1944)*
▲ Liberty Book & Bb Manufactures .... E 317 633-1450
  Indianapolis *(G-8744)*
Liberty Screen Printing .... G 812 273-4358
  Madison *(G-11236)*
Lightning Printing .... G 765 362-5999
  Crawfordsville *(G-2585)*
Lila J Athletic Wear .... G 502 619-2898
  Floyds Knobs *(G-4685)*
Lincoln Printing Corporation .... A 260 424-5200
  Fort Wayne *(G-5186)*
Logo USA Corporation .... F 317 867-8518
  Westfield *(G-16708)*
Logo Zone Inc .... G 574 753-7569
  Logansport *(G-11091)*
Logos Express Inc .... G 317 272-1200
  Lebanon *(G-10911)*
Logowear LLC .... G 317 462-3376
  Greenfield *(G-6525)*
Louies Companies Inc .... G 765 448-4300
  Lafayette *(G-10639)*
Lsc Communications Us LLC .... G 812 256-3396
  Charlestown *(G-1880)*

M M Printing Plus .... G 574 658-9345
  Milford *(G-11797)*
Macdesign Inc .... G 317 580-9390
  Carmel *(G-1689)*
Maco Press Inc .... G 317 846-5754
  Carmel *(G-1690)*
Mama Fox Tee Company .... G 260 438-4054
  Fort Wayne *(G-5201)*
Mandala Screen Printing Inc .... G 574 946-6290
  Winamac *(G-16866)*
Maple-Hunter Decals .... G 812 894-9759
  Riley *(G-14239)*
Marketing Services Group Inc .... B 317 381-2268
  Indianapolis *(G-8838)*
Masco Corporation of Indiana .... E 317 848-1812
  Indianapolis *(G-8847)*
▲ Matrix Label Systems Inc .... G 317 839-1973
  Plainfield *(G-13700)*
Mexabilly Brothers LLC .... G 765 621-6334
  Anderson *(G-152)*
Mg Impressions LLC .... G 317 219-5118
  Noblesville *(G-13138)*
Midnite Grafix .... G 812 386-9430
  Princeton *(G-14006)*
Minds Eye Graphics Inc .... F 260 724-2050
  Decatur *(G-2874)*
Minuteman Press .... F 317 209-1677
  Indianapolis *(G-8931)*
Mito-Craft Inc .... G 574 287-4555
  South Bend *(G-15152)*
Mooney Copy Service Inc .... G 812 423-6626
  Evansville *(G-4210)*
Moose Lake Products Co Inc .... F 260 432-2768
  Fort Wayne *(G-5242)*
Mossberg & Company Inc .... F 260 755-6283
  Fort Wayne *(G-5246)*
Mossberg & Company Inc .... D 574 289-9253
  South Bend *(G-15155)*
▲ MPS Indianapolis Inc .... C 317 241-2020
  Indianapolis *(G-8966)*
MPS Printing Incorporated .... G 812 273-4446
  Madison *(G-11245)*
Multi Packaging Solutions Inc .... G 317 241-2020
  Indianapolis *(G-8971)*
Multi-Color Corporation .... C 513 396-5600
  Scottsburg *(G-14572)*
Multi-Color Corporation .... E 812 752-0586
  Scottsburg *(G-14573)*
Muncie Novelty Company Inc .... D 765 288-8301
  Muncie *(G-12463)*
New End Zone Sporting Goods .... G 812 254-1895
  Washington *(G-16495)*
New Haven Trophies & Shirts .... G 260 749-0269
  New Haven *(G-12911)*
New Process Graphics LLC .... E 260 489-1700
  Fort Wayne *(G-5268)*
Newton Business Forms .... G 812 256-5399
  Charlestown *(G-1887)*
Next Level Logo Store Inc .... G 219 344-5141
  La Porte *(G-10458)*
Next Phase Graphics .... G 260 627-6259
  Huntertown *(G-7259)*
Nicholas Mendel .... G 574 870-8856
  Delphi *(G-2904)*
Nickprint Inc .... G 317 489-3033
  Carmel *(G-1705)*
Nielsen Enterprises Inc .... G 574 277-3748
  Granger *(G-6367)*
Nite Owl Promotions Inc .... G 812 876-3888
  Ellettsville *(G-3810)*
Npp Packaging Graphics .... G 317 522-2010
  Zionsville *(G-17038)*

Nsignia Screen Printing .... G 260 420-0500
  Fort Wayne *(G-5278)*
Nussmeier Engraving Company .... E 812 425-1339
  Evansville *(G-4224)*
Occasions Group Inc .... E 812 623-2225
  Sunman *(G-15442)*
Offset House Inc .... F 317 849-5155
  Indianapolis *(G-9042)*
Offset One Inc .... F 260 456-8828
  Fort Wayne *(G-5282)*
Ohio Vly Screen Prtrs EMB Engr .... G 812 539-3307
  Lawrenceburg *(G-10850)*
Old Fort Tee Company LLC .... G 248 506-3762
  Fort Wayne *(G-5283)*
◆ Omnisource Marketing Group Inc ..... E 317 575-3300
  Indianapolis *(G-9050)*
Ooshirts Inc .... G 317 246-9083
  Indianapolis *(G-9060)*
Optiviz Media LLC .... G 812 681-1711
  Vincennes *(G-16141)*
Outfitter .... G 765 289-6456
  Muncie *(G-12471)*
Outfitters Inc .... G 765 778-9097
  Pendleton *(G-13549)*
Overgaards Artcraft Printers .... G 574 234-8464
  South Bend *(G-15183)*
P413 Corporation .... G 317 769-0679
  Zionsville *(G-17039)*
Pagels-Kelley Enterprises LLC .... F 219 872-8552
  Long Beach *(G-11126)*
Paper Chase .... G 812 385-4757
  Princeton *(G-14009)*
Parlor City Trophy & AP Inc .... G 260 824-0216
  Bluffton *(G-1047)*
Parrot Press Inc .... E 260 422-6402
  Fort Wayne *(G-5298)*
Pearl Screen Printing .... G 812 429-1686
  Evansville *(G-4235)*
Pengad/West Inc .... E 765 286-3000
  Muncie *(G-12473)*
Pentzer Printing Inc .... F 812 372-2896
  Columbus *(G-2375)*
Perdue Printed Products Inc .... G 260 456-7575
  Fort Wayne *(G-5304)*
Perfect Apparel LLC .... G 317 389-5553
  Indianapolis *(G-9120)*
Perfect Plastic Printing Corp .... G 317 888-9447
  Greenwood *(G-6750)*
Personal Impressions Inc .... G 317 485-4409
  Fortville *(G-5604)*
Phantom Neon LLC .... G 765 362-2221
  Crawfordsville *(G-2604)*
Pharmaprinter Inc .... G 765 543-1520
  West Lafayette *(G-16619)*
Phil Irwin Advertising Inc .... F 317 547-5117
  Indianapolis *(G-9134)*
Phillip Westrick .... G 219 232-8337
  Kentland *(G-10161)*
Phillips Diversified Services .... G 260 248-2975
  Columbia City *(G-2180)*
Photo Screen Service Inc .... G 317 636-7712
  Indianapolis *(G-9140)*
Photo Specialties .... G 812 944-5111
  New Albany *(G-12794)*
Pierce Oil Co Inc .... F 812 268-6356
  Sullivan *(G-15416)*
Planks Printing Service Inc .... G 574 533-1739
  Goshen *(G-6240)*
Plastimatic Arts Corp .... E 574 254-9000
  Mishawaka *(G-11975)*
Play 2 Win Screenprinting LLC .... G 765 426-0679
  Oxford *(G-13476)*

SIC SECTION
27 PRINTING, PUBLISHING AND ALLIED INDUSTRIES

Pontiac Engraving .... G 630 834-4424
  Plymouth *(G-13805)*
Portage Custom Wear LLC .... G 219 841-9070
  Portage *(G-13905)*
Ppi Acquisition LLC .... E 765 674-8627
  Marion *(G-11329)*
Pratt Visual Solutions Company .... E 800 428-7728
  Indianapolis *(G-9176)*
Precision Label Incorporated .... F 812 877-3811
  Terre Haute *(G-15668)*
Premier Print & Svcs Group Inc .... F 574 273-2525
  Granger *(G-6372)*
Premiere Advertising .... G 317 722-2400
  Indianapolis *(G-9193)*
Prentice Products Holdings LLC .... E 260 747-3195
  Fort Wayne *(G-5346)*
◆ Prentice Products Inc .... E 260 747-3195
  Fort Wayne *(G-5347)*
Presstime Graphics Inc .... F 812 234-3815
  Terre Haute *(G-15669)*
Prince Manufacturing Corp .... D 260 357-4484
  Garrett *(G-5874)*
Printcrafters Inc .... G 812 838-4106
  Mount Vernon *(G-12315)*
◆ Printing Inc Louisville KY .... F 800 237-5894
  Jeffersonville *(G-10041)*
Printing Partners Inc .... D 317 635-2282
  Indianapolis *(G-9206)*
Printing Place Inc .... F 260 665-8444
  Angola *(G-289)*
Printing Services Inc .... G 317 300-0363
  Indianapolis *(G-9208)*
Printpack Inc .... C 812 663-5091
  Greensburg *(G-6625)*
Printwerk Graphics & Design .... G 219 322-7722
  Dyer *(G-2981)*
Priority Press Inc .... G 317 848-9695
  Carmel *(G-1730)*
Priority Press Inc .... G 317 240-0103
  Indianapolis *(G-9212)*
Priority Press Inc .... E 317 241-4234
  Indianapolis *(G-9211)*
Pro Link .... G 765 225-1051
  Crawfordsville *(G-2605)*
Progressive Printing Co Inc .... G 765 653-3814
  Greencastle *(G-6427)*
Quality Imagination Corp .... G 317 753-0042
  Indianapolis *(G-9246)*
Quality Printing of NW Ind .... G 219 322-6677
  Schererville *(G-14540)*
R R Donnelley & Sons Company .... F 812 523-1800
  Seymour *(G-14679)*
R R Donnelley & Sons Company .... D 574 267-7101
  Warsaw *(G-16414)*
Rayco Marketing .... G 574 293-8416
  Elkhart *(G-3640)*
Raymond Little Print Shop .... G 317 246-9083
  Indianapolis *(G-9271)*
Reckon With It Tees Stuff LLC .... G 765 585-3610
  Covington *(G-2533)*
Reprocomm Inc .... G 765 472-5700
  Peru *(G-13598)*
Rink Printing Company .... E 574 232-7935
  South Bend *(G-15220)*
Rivera Screenprinting .... G 812 663-0816
  Burney *(G-1448)*
Riverside Printing Co .... G 812 275-1950
  Bedford *(G-669)*
Robert Copeland .... G 951 245-0041
  Zionsville *(G-17047)*
Rock Garden Engraving .... G 765 647-3357
  Brookville *(G-1334)*

Rogers Marketing & Prtg Inc .... G 317 838-7203
  Avon *(G-549)*
Romanart Incorporated .... G 219 736-9150
  Merrillville *(G-11555)*
Rookies Unlimited Inc .... G 765 536-2726
  Summitville *(G-15431)*
Rose True Graphics .... G 812 844-1559
  Loogootee *(G-11151)*
Rowland Printing Co Inc .... F 317 773-1829
  Noblesville *(G-13168)*
Rtees LLC .... G 317 345-7445
  Plainfield *(G-13724)*
Rubenstein LLC .... G 317 946-2752
  Indianapolis *(G-9346)*
Running Around Screen Prtg LLC .... G 260 248-1216
  Columbia City *(G-2194)*
Sampan Group LLC .... G 812 280-6094
  Jeffersonville *(G-10050)*
Sampan Screen Print New Image .... G 812 282-8499
  Jeffersonville *(G-10051)*
Schutte Lithography Inc .... F 812 469-3500
  Evansville *(G-4300)*
Scoop Entertainment Source .... G 317 475-0615
  Indianapolis *(G-9392)*
Screen Printing Super Store .... G 317 804-9904
  Westfield *(G-16725)*
Screenprint Special Tees LLC .... G 317 396-0349
  Indianapolis *(G-9396)*
Screens .... G 812 472-3274
  Fredericksburg *(G-5796)*
▼ Seedline International Inc .... G 765 795-2500
  Greencastle *(G-6430)*
Selby Publishing & Printing .... G 765 453-5417
  Kokomo *(G-10332)*
Service Graphics Inc .... D 317 471-8246
  Indianapolis *(G-9408)*
Shadow Graphix Inc .... G 317 481-9710
  Indianapolis *(G-9411)*
Shadow Screen Printing .... G 812 234-3104
  Terre Haute *(G-15690)*
Shakour Industries Inc .... G 574 289-0100
  South Bend *(G-15239)*
Shodas Tees & Gifts .... G 260 418-8448
  South Whitley *(G-15323)*
Sign Art Quality Advertising .... G 219 763-6122
  Hobart *(G-7207)*
Signs AP & Awards On Time LLC .... G 219 661-4488
  Crown Point *(G-2752)*
Siman Promotions Inc .... G 260 637-5621
  Fort Wayne *(G-5417)*
Simplified Imaging LLC .... G 219 663-5122
  Crown Point *(G-2756)*
Singing Pines Projects Inc .... G 812 988-8807
  Nashville *(G-12680)*
Single Inc .... G 812 877-2220
  Terre Haute *(G-15697)*
Sir Graphics Inc .... G 574 272-9330
  Granger *(G-6379)*
Six Six Sublimation LLC .... G 317 858-5211
  Brownsburg *(G-1403)*
Sledgehammer Printing Corp .... G 812 629-2160
  Newburgh *(G-13022)*
Sonoco Products Company .... D 812 526-5511
  Edinburgh *(G-3105)*
South Bend Screen Process Inc .... G 574 254-9000
  Mishawaka *(G-12003)*
Southwest Grafix and AP Inc .... F 812 425-5104
  Evansville *(G-4325)*
Spark Marketing LLC .... G 219 301-0071
  Dyer *(G-2983)*
Spectrum MGT Holdg Co LLC .... G 812 941-6899
  New Albany *(G-12817)*

Sports Screen Impact .... G 812 926-9355
  Aurora *(G-456)*
Sports Unlimited Printed AP .... G 574 772-4239
  Knox *(G-10226)*
Squeegeepie Merch Co LLC .... G 765 376-6358
  Crawfordsville *(G-2618)*
Stage Door Graphics .... G 317 398-9011
  Shelbyville *(G-14801)*
Standard Label Co Inc .... F 574 522-3548
  Elkhart *(G-3696)*
Standout Creations LLC .... G 765 203-9110
  Anderson *(G-200)*
Stands Photography .... G 812 723-3922
  Paoli *(G-13500)*
Sterling Impressions Inc .... G 317 329-9773
  Indianapolis *(G-9507)*
Steve Weaver Art .... G 574 546-3530
  Bremen *(G-1224)*
Stines Printing Inc .... G 260 356-5994
  Huntington *(G-7371)*
◆ Stoffel Seals Corporation .... E 845 353-3800
  Angola *(G-296)*
Stranco Inc .... F 219 874-5221
  Michigan City *(G-11673)*
Studio Printers .... G 574 772-0900
  North Judson *(G-13214)*
Swagerle Screen Printing .... G 812 232-6947
  Terre Haute *(G-15719)*
T Productions Inc .... G 574 257-8610
  Mishawaka *(G-12012)*
T Shirt 1 Inc .... G 812 232-5046
  Terre Haute *(G-15721)*
Tabco Business Forms Inc .... G 812 882-2836
  Vincennes *(G-16157)*
Table Thyme Designs LLC .... G 317 634-0281
  Indianapolis *(G-9546)*
Tatman Inc .... E 765 825-2164
  Connersville *(G-2472)*
Taulman3d LLC .... G 401 996-8868
  Linton *(G-11047)*
Taylor Communications Inc .... E 317 392-3235
  Shelbyville *(G-14803)*
Team Image LLC .... E 317 477-7468
  Greenfield *(G-6564)*
Team Image LLC .... E 317 468-0802
  Greenfield *(G-6563)*
Team Mantra Wear LLC .... G 260 273-0421
  Bluffton *(G-1061)*
Team Mantra Wear LLC .... G 260 827-0061
  Bluffton *(G-1062)*
Team Pride Athletic AP Corp .... G 574 224-8326
  Rochester *(G-14327)*
TEC Photography .... G 812 332-9847
  Bloomington *(G-985)*
Tee Trudys Rainbow Palac .... G 765 273-7571
  Muncie *(G-12500)*
Teeki Hut Custom Tees Inc .... G 317 205-3589
  Indianapolis *(G-9573)*
Tees and Blues LLC .... G 765 808-4081
  Muncie *(G-12501)*
Teras Sporty Ink .... G 219 369-6276
  La Porte *(G-10488)*
The Deaton Family Company .... D 815 726-6234
  Auburn *(G-429)*
Thomas E Slade Inc .... F 812 437-5233
  Evansville *(G-4343)*
Thoughts Are Things Inc .... G 317 585-8053
  Indianapolis *(G-9599)*
Tims Tees .... G 317 503-5736
  Indianapolis *(G-9607)*
Tippecanoe Press Inc .... G 317 392-1207
  Shelbyville *(G-14806)*

Employee Codes: A=Over 500 employees, B=251-500
C=101-250, D=51-100, E=20-50, F=10-19, G=1-9

27 PRINTING, PUBLISHING AND ALLIED INDUSTRIES

Tko Enterprises Inc.................................. D 317 271-1398
   Plainfield *(G-13736)*

Tma Enterprises Inc................................ G 317 272-0694
   Avon *(G-553)*

TNT Top Notch Tees................................ G 219 775-3812
   Crown Point *(G-2764)*

To A Tee Inc... F 317 757-8842
   Indianapolis *(G-9615)*

Toms Printing Service.............................. G 260 438-3721
   Ossian *(G-13442)*

Top Cat Printing Inc................................. G 812 683-2773
   Huntingburg *(G-7293)*

Topstitch Inc... F
   Elkhart *(G-3739)*

Town & Country Press Inc...................... F 574 936-9505
   Plymouth *(G-13820)*

Tranter Graphics Inc................................ D 574 834-2626
   Syracuse *(G-15487)*

Travis Britton... G 317 762-6018
   Indianapolis *(G-9632)*

Trendsettin Tees LLC.............................. G 219 201-1410
   Indianapolis *(G-9635)*

Tri State Printing & Embroider................ G 812 316-0094
   Vincennes *(G-16159)*

Trident Engraving Inc.............................. G 812 282-2098
   Jeffersonville *(G-10065)*

Trinity Cmmnications Group Inc............. G 260 484-1029
   Fort Wayne *(G-5508)*

Triple Crown Media LLC.......................... G 574 533-2151
   Goshen *(G-6273)*

Triple Js Transport LLC........................... G 708 513-8389
   Saint John *(G-14459)*

Triumphant Jrney MBL Ntary Svc........... G 608 208-5604
   Madison *(G-11254)*

Turtlefish Clothing Co LLC...................... G 812 896-2805
   Salem *(G-14504)*

Unique Graphic Designs Inc................... G 574 583-7119
   Monticello *(G-12175)*

Upland Print and Stitch........................... G 765 506-7011
   Upland *(G-15882)*

Upland Print Stitch.................................. G 765 506-7011
   Upland *(G-15883)*

Useful Products LLC............................... E 877 304-9036
   Goodland *(G-6083)*

V & P Printing.. G 260 495-3741
   Fremont *(G-5838)*

Varsity Sports Inc................................... G 219 987-7200
   Demotte *(G-2931)*

Vickers Graphics Inc............................... G 765 868-4646
   Kokomo *(G-10354)*

Vickery Tape & Label Co Inc................... F 765 472-1974
   Rochester *(G-14332)*

Vinyl Creator... G 260 318-5133
   Wolcottville *(G-16944)*

Vivid Social Group LLC.......................... G 317 447-7319
   Indianapolis *(G-9726)*

W/S Packaging Group Inc...................... G 317 578-4454
   Indianapolis *(G-9734)*

Walkerton Tool & Die Inc........................ E 574 586-3162
   Walkerton *(G-16279)*

WAr - LLC- Westville Prtg....................... G 219 785-2821
   Westville *(G-16765)*

Warren Printing Services LLC................ F 812 738-6508
   Corydon *(G-2521)*

Wayne Press Incorporated..................... G 260 744-3022
   Fort Wayne *(G-5553)*

◆ Werzalit of America Inc........................ D 814 362-3881
   Syracuse *(G-15492)*

White River Press Inc............................. G 317 507-4684
   Anderson *(G-217)*

Whitewater Publications Inc................... F 765 647-4221
   Brookville *(G-1341)*

Wildman Business Group LLC............... G 866 369-1552
   Warsaw *(G-16451)*

Wilson Enterprises Inc........................... G 765 362-1089
   Crawfordsville *(G-2627)*

Wise Business Forms Inc....................... D 260 489-1561
   Fort Wayne *(G-5572)*

Woodburn Graphics Inc.......................... F 812 232-0323
   Terre Haute *(G-15748)*

Woodfield Printing Inc............................ G 317 848-2000
   Carmel *(G-1808)*

Writeguard Business Systems............... G 317 849-7292
   Indianapolis *(G-9793)*

XI Graphics Inc....................................... F 317 738-3434
   Franklin *(G-5789)*

Xoxo Invites.. G 773 744-2504
   Crown Point *(G-2776)*

Xtreme Graphics..................................... G 812 989-6948
   Jeffersonville *(G-10076)*

▲ Zimmer Paper Products Del LLC....... G 317 263-3420
   Indianapolis *(G-9811)*

2761 Manifold business forms

Altstadt Business Forms Inc.................. F 812 425-3393
   Evansville *(G-3882)*

Anchor Enterprises................................. G 812 282-7220
   Jeffersonville *(G-9933)*

Falls Cities Printing Inc.......................... F 812 949-9051
   New Albany *(G-12728)*

Highland Computer Forms Inc................ F 260 665-6268
   Angola *(G-259)*

International Label Mfg LLC................... F 812 235-5071
   Terre Haute *(G-15618)*

Iu East Business Office.......................... E 765 973-8218
   Richmond *(G-14141)*

Kendallville Custom Printing.................. F 260 347-9233
   Kendallville *(G-10125)*

Label Tech Inc.. E 765 747-1234
   Muncie *(G-12436)*

Lincoln Printing Corporation.................. A 260 424-5200
   Fort Wayne *(G-5186)*

NP Converters Inc.................................. D 812 448-2555
   Brazil *(G-1158)*

Pengad/West Inc..................................... E 765 286-3000
   Muncie *(G-12473)*

R R Donnelley & Sons Company............ B 260 624-2350
   Angola *(G-291)*

Stewart Graphics Inc.............................. E 812 283-0455
   Jeffersonville *(G-10060)*

Taylor Communications Inc.................... E 317 392-3235
   Shelbyville *(G-14803)*

Tippecanoe Press Inc............................. G 317 392-1207
   Shelbyville *(G-14806)*

Wise Business Forms Inc....................... D 260 489-1561
   Fort Wayne *(G-5572)*

Woodburn Graphics Inc.......................... F 812 232-0323
   Terre Haute *(G-15748)*

Writeguard Business Systems............... G 317 849-7292
   Indianapolis *(G-9793)*

2771 Greeting cards

Behning Inc... G 260 672-2663
   Roanoke *(G-14260)*

Kellmark Corporation............................. F 574 264-9695
   Elkhart *(G-3449)*

Mejjm Inc... G 317 893-6929
   Indianapolis *(G-8873)*

Nussmeier Engraving Company............. E 812 425-1339
   Evansville *(G-4224)*

2782 Blankbooks and looseleaf binders

Clarke Harland Corp............................... G 812 283-9598
   Jeffersonville *(G-9953)*

Clarke Harland Corp............................... G 812 283-9598
   Jeffersonville *(G-9954)*

Codybro LLC... G 765 827-5441
   Connersville *(G-2432)*

Delux Illumination.................................. G 219 331-9525
   Chesterton *(G-1917)*

Deluxe Detail LLC................................... G 574 292-8968
   South Bend *(G-14996)*

Deluxe Wheel Company.......................... G 219 395-8003
   Chesterton *(G-1918)*

Eckhart & Company Inc.......................... E 317 347-2665
   Indianapolis *(G-8046)*

Futurex Industries Inc............................ E 765 498-8900
   Bloomingdale *(G-759)*

▲ Harcourt Industries Inc..................... E 765 629-2625
   Milroy *(G-11824)*

Hard Hustla Muzik LLC........................... G 812 214-1995
   Evansville *(G-4103)*

Lamco Finishers Inc............................... E 317 471-1010
   Indianapolis *(G-8717)*

Leed Selling Tools Corp......................... C 812 482-7888
   Ireland *(G-9816)*

Leed Selling Tools Corp......................... E 812 867-4340
   Evansville *(G-4164)*

Lovett Entertainment LLC...................... G 773 208-9608
   Schererville *(G-14532)*

Neu Scrapbooking Store LLC................. G 317 781-7970
   Indianapolis *(G-9000)*

No-Sail Splash Guard Co Inc................. G 765 522-2100
   Roachdale *(G-14248)*

Nussmeier Engraving Company............. E 812 425-1339
   Evansville *(G-4224)*

Papercharm Scrpbking Stdio LLC......... G 317 624-2878
   Indianapolis *(G-9090)*

Raine Inc.. F 765 622-7687
   Anderson *(G-182)*

Scrapbook Nook..................................... G 812 967-3306
   Pekin *(G-13522)*

Segundo Deluxe LLC.............................. G 260 414-7820
   Indianapolis *(G-9400)*

▲ Spi-Binding Company Inc................. F 765 794-4992
   Darlington *(G-2834)*

Timelessmusicgroup LLC....................... G 317 721-6671
   Carmel *(G-1786)*

Writeguard Business Systems............... G 317 849-7292
   Indianapolis *(G-9793)*

2789 Bookbinding and related work

▲ A-1 Awards Inc................................... F 317 546-9000
   Indianapolis *(G-7406)*

Acclaim Graphics Inc............................. G 812 424-5035
   Evansville *(G-3866)*

Art Bookbinders of America................... F 312 226-4100
   Hammond *(G-6880)*

Baxter Printing Incorporated................. G 219 923-1999
   Griffith *(G-6793)*

Blasted Works... G 574 583-3211
   Monticello *(G-12138)*

Brand Prtg & Photo-Litho Co................. G 317 921-4095
   New Palestine *(G-12933)*

C & W Inkd.. F 317 352-1000
   Indianapolis *(G-7706)*

C J P Corporation................................... G 219 924-1685
   Highland *(G-7127)*

Cecils Printing & Off Sups Inc............... G 812 683-4416
   Huntingburg *(G-7273)*

Centennial Group Inc............................. F 812 948-2886
   Clarksville *(G-2012)*

Ckmt Associates Inc.............................. F 219 924-2820
   Hammond *(G-6902)*

Classic Graphics Inc.............................. F 260 482-3487
   Fort Wayne *(G-4853)*

27 PRINTING, PUBLISHING AND ALLIED INDUSTRIES

Colophon Book Arts Supply LLC........... G 812 671-0577
  Bloomington *(G-834)*
Consolidated Printing Svcs Inc............ G 765 468-6033
  Farmland *(G-4424)*
Courier Printing Co Allen Cnty............ G 260 627-2728
  Grabill *(G-6293)*
Creative Concept Ventures Inc............. G 812 282-9442
  Jeffersonville *(G-9964)*
Crossrads Rhbilitation Ctr Inc............ C 317 897-7320
  Indianapolis *(G-7910)*
Digital Printing Incorporated............. G 812 265-2205
  Madison *(G-11214)*
Doerr Printing Co......................... G 317 568-0135
  Indianapolis *(G-7994)*
Dynamark Graphics Group Inc............... E 317 328-2555
  Indianapolis *(G-8023)*
Eckhart & Company Inc..................... E 317 347-2665
  Indianapolis *(G-8046)*
Ed Sons Inc............................... F 317 897-8821
  Indianapolis *(G-8051)*
Elkhart Binding Inc....................... G 574 522-5455
  Elkhart *(G-3319)*
Epi Printers Inc.......................... D 317 579-4870
  Indianapolis *(G-8129)*
Evansville Bindery Inc.................... G 812 423-2222
  Evansville *(G-4048)*
Ewing Printing Company Inc................ F 812 882-2415
  Vincennes *(G-16120)*
Express Binding Inc....................... G 317 269-8114
  Carmel *(G-1631)*
Express Press Indiana Inc................. E 574 277-3355
  South Bend *(G-15023)*
Faulkenberg Printing Co Inc............... F 317 638-1359
  Franklin *(G-5730)*
Fedex Office & Print Svcs Inc............. G 317 849-9683
  Indianapolis *(G-8174)*
Fedex Office & Print Svcs Inc............. G 317 885-6480
  Indianapolis *(G-8175)*
Fedex Office & Print Svcs Inc............. G 317 295-1063
  Indianapolis *(G-8176)*
Fedex Office & Print Svcs Inc............. G 317 337-2679
  Indianapolis *(G-8177)*
Fedex Office & Print Svcs Inc............. G 317 631-6862
  Indianapolis *(G-8178)*
Fedex Office & Print Svcs Inc............. G 317 251-2406
  Indianapolis *(G-8179)*
Fedex Office & Print Svcs Inc............. F 765 449-4950
  Lafayette *(G-10579)*
Gateway Builders & Properties............. G 574 295-9944
  Elkhart *(G-3367)*
Goetz Printing............................ G 812 243-2086
  Terre Haute *(G-15600)*
Granger Gazette Inc....................... G 574 277-2679
  Granger *(G-6350)*
Green Banner Publications Inc............. E 812 967-3176
  Borden *(G-1109)*
Greencastle Offset Inc.................... G 765 653-4026
  Greencastle *(G-6406)*
Greensburg Printing Co Inc................ G 812 663-8265
  Greensburg *(G-6598)*
Hardesty Printing Co Inc.................. F 574 267-7591
  Warsaw *(G-16374)*
Hardesty Printing Co Inc.................. F 574 223-4553
  Rochester *(G-14293)*
Hetty Incorporated........................ G 219 933-0833
  Hammond *(G-6945)*
Hetty Incorporated........................ G 219 836-2517
  Munster *(G-12539)*
Hf Group LLC.............................. B 260 982-2107
  North Manchester *(G-13234)*
Hiatt Enterprises Inc..................... G 765 289-2700
  Muncie *(G-12416)*

Hiatt Enterprises Inc..................... F 765 289-7756
  Muncie *(G-12415)*
Hinen Printing Co......................... G 260 248-8984
  Columbia City *(G-2150)*
Home Mountain Publishing Co Inc........... E 219 462-6601
  Valparaiso *(G-15962)*
Howard Print Shop LLC..................... G 765 453-6161
  Kokomo *(G-10283)*
Infobind Systems Inc...................... G 260 248-4989
  Fort Wayne *(G-5106)*
Journal & Chronicle Inc................... G 812 752-5060
  Scottsburg *(G-14566)*
Kendallville Custom Printing.............. F 260 347-9233
  Kendallville *(G-10125)*
Kistner Enterprises Inc................... G 317 773-7733
  Noblesville *(G-13123)*
L & L Press Inc........................... G 765 664-3162
  Marion *(G-11305)*
La Grange Publishing Co Inc............... F 260 463-3243
  Lagrange *(G-10747)*
Lamco Finishers Inc....................... E 317 471-1010
  Indianapolis *(G-8717)*
Largus Speedy Print Corp.................. E 219 922-8414
  Munster *(G-12546)*
Leed Selling Tools Corp................... E 812 867-4340
  Evansville *(G-4164)*
▲ Liberty Book & Bb Manufactures......... E 317 633-1450
  Indianapolis *(G-8744)*
Lincoln Printing Corporation.............. A 260 424-5200
  Fort Wayne *(G-5186)*
Ludwick Graphics Inc...................... G 574 233-2165
  South Bend *(G-15131)*
Masco Corporation of Indiana.............. E 317 848-1812
  Indianapolis *(G-8847)*
Maureen Sharp............................. G 765 379-3644
  Rossville *(G-14387)*
Maury Boyd & Associates Inc............... F 317 849-6110
  Indianapolis *(G-8853)*
Mignone Communications In................. C 260 358-0266
  Huntington *(G-7344)*
Millcraft Paper Company................... G 317 240-3500
  Indianapolis *(G-8920)*
Mitchell-Fleming Printing Inc............. F 317 462-5467
  Greenfield *(G-6529)*
Montgomery & Associates Inc............... F 219 879-0088
  Michigan City *(G-11641)*
National Lib Bindery Co of Ind............ G 317 636-5606
  Indianapolis *(G-8989)*
Offset House Inc.......................... F 317 849-5155
  Indianapolis *(G-9042)*
Offset One Inc............................ F 260 456-8828
  Fort Wayne *(G-5282)*
Overgaards Artcraft Printers.............. G 574 234-8464
  South Bend *(G-15183)*
Parrot Press Inc.......................... E 260 422-6402
  Fort Wayne *(G-5298)*
Phoenix Press Inc......................... D 765 644-3959
  Anderson *(G-178)*
PIP Marketing Signs Print................. G 317 843-5755
  Carmel *(G-1719)*
Presstime Graphics Inc.................... F 812 234-3815
  Terre Haute *(G-15669)*
Printing Place Inc........................ F 260 665-8444
  Angola *(G-289)*
Progressive Printing Co Inc............... G 765 653-3814
  Greencastle *(G-6427)*
Quality Printing of NW Ind................ G 219 322-6677
  Schererville *(G-14540)*
R R Donnelley & Sons Company.............. C 765 362-1300
  Crawfordsville *(G-2607)*
Rack Hub LLC.............................. G 260 571-7028
  Urbana *(G-15887)*

Reprocomm Inc............................. G 765 423-2578
  Lafayette *(G-10679)*
Reprocomm Inc............................. G 765 472-5700
  Peru *(G-13598)*
Rhr Corporation........................... G 317 788-1504
  Indianapolis *(G-9298)*
Riden Inc................................. G 219 362-5511
  La Porte *(G-10473)*
Rink Printing Company..................... E 574 232-7935
  South Bend *(G-15220)*
Rise Inc.................................. D 260 665-9408
  Angola *(G-292)*
Rowland Printing Co Inc................... F 317 773-1829
  Noblesville *(G-13168)*
Schutte Lithography Inc................... F 812 469-3500
  Evansville *(G-4300)*
Service Graphics Inc...................... D 317 471-8246
  Indianapolis *(G-9408)*
▲ Service Printers Inc.................... E 574 266-6710
  Elkhart *(G-3669)*
Specialized Printed Products.............. G 260 483-7075
  Fort Wayne *(G-5428)*
▲ Spi-Binding Company Inc................. F 765 794-4992
  Darlington *(G-2834)*
Stines Printing Inc....................... G 260 356-5994
  Huntington *(G-7371)*
▲ Superior Sample Co Inc.................. E 260 894-3136
  Ligonier *(G-11025)*
Tabco Business Forms Inc.................. G 812 882-2836
  Vincennes *(G-16157)*
Tatman Inc................................ E 765 825-2164
  Connersville *(G-2472)*
The Deaton Family Company................. D 815 726-6234
  Auburn *(G-429)*
Thomas E Slade Inc........................ F 812 437-5233
  Evansville *(G-4343)*
Tippecanoe Press Inc...................... G 317 392-1207
  Shelbyville *(G-14806)*
United Parcel Service Inc................. G 317 776-9494
  Noblesville *(G-13189)*
University Publishing Corp................ E 812 339-9033
  Bloomington *(G-1004)*
▼ Voice of God Recordings Inc............. D 812 246-2137
  Jeffersonville *(G-10069)*
WAr - LLC- Westville Prtg................. G 219 785-2821
  Westville *(G-16765)*
Whitewater Publications Inc............... F 765 647-4221
  Brookville *(G-1341)*
Woodburn Graphics Inc..................... F 812 232-0323
  Terre Haute *(G-15748)*

2791 Typesetting

A-1 Graphics Inc.......................... G 765 289-1851
  Muncie *(G-12332)*
Acclaim Graphics Inc...................... G 812 424-5035
  Evansville *(G-3866)*
Advantage Productions..................... G 219 879-6892
  La Porte *(G-10376)*
Aim Media Indiana Oper LLC................ E 317 462-5528
  Greenfield *(G-6458)*
Annual Reports Inc........................ G 317 736-8838
  Franklin *(G-5709)*
Brand Prtg & Photo-Litho Co............... G 317 921-4095
  New Palestine *(G-12933)*
BSC Vntres Acquisition Sub LLC............ D 260 665-7521
  Angola *(G-237)*
C J P Corporation......................... G 219 924-1685
  Highland *(G-7127)*
Cecils Printing & Off Sups Inc............ G 812 683-4416
  Huntingburg *(G-7273)*
Ckmt Associates Inc....................... F 219 924-2820
  Hammond *(G-6902)*

27 PRINTING, PUBLISHING AND ALLIED INDUSTRIES

Classic Graphics Inc .... F 260 482-3487
  Fort Wayne (G-4853)
Cnhi LLC .... G 812 944-6481
  Jeffersonville (G-9955)
Community Holdings Indiana Inc .... G 812 663-3111
  Greensburg (G-6585)
Community Holdings Indiana Inc .... G 765 482-4650
  Lebanon (G-10885)
Community Papers Inc .... G 317 241-7363
  Indianapolis (G-7841)
Composition LLC .... G 317 979-7214
  Fishers (G-4493)
Consolidated Printing Svcs Inc .... G 765 468-6033
  Farmland (G-4424)
Copyfire Typesetting Inc .... G 317 894-0408
  Indianapolis (G-7873)
Copymat Services Inc .... G 765 743-5995
  Lafayette (G-10557)
Courier Printing Co Allen Cnty .... G 260 627-2728
  Grabill (G-6293)
▲ Courier-Times Inc .... D 765 529-1111
  New Castle (G-12856)
Coy & Associates .... G 317 787-5089
  Indianapolis (G-7893)
Creative Concept Ventures Inc .... G 812 282-9442
  Jeffersonville (G-9964)
Crescendo Inc .... G 812 829-4759
  Spencer (G-15344)
D & M Printing Inc .... G 812 847-4837
  Linton (G-11034)
Debra Lindhorst .... G 260 375-3285
  Warren (G-16296)
Digital Printing Incorporated .... G 812 265-2205
  Madison (G-11214)
Doerr Printing Co .... G 317 568-0135
  Indianapolis (G-7994)
Dynamark Graphics Group Inc .... E 317 328-2555
  Indianapolis (G-8023)
Ed Sons Inc .... F 317 897-8421
  Indianapolis (G-8051)
Evansville Bindery Inc .... G 812 423-2222
  Evansville (G-4048)
Evansville Courier Co .... B 812 464-7500
  Evansville (G-4051)
Ewing Printing Company Inc .... F 812 882-2415
  Vincennes (G-16120)
Excell Color Graphics Inc .... E 260 482-2720
  Fort Wayne (G-4967)
Express Press Indiana Inc .... E 574 277-3355
  South Bend (G-15023)
Fedex Office & Print Svcs Inc .... G 317 849-9683
  Indianapolis (G-8174)
Fedex Office & Print Svcs Inc .... G 317 885-6480
  Indianapolis (G-8175)
Fedex Office & Print Svcs Inc .... G 317 295-1063
  Indianapolis (G-8176)
Fedex Office & Print Svcs Inc .... G 317 337-2679
  Indianapolis (G-8177)
Fedex Office & Print Svcs Inc .... G 317 631-6862
  Indianapolis (G-8178)
Fedex Office & Print Svcs Inc .... G 317 251-2406
  Indianapolis (G-8179)
Fedex Office & Print Svcs Inc .... F 765 449-4950
  Lafayette (G-10579)
Fineline Graphics Incorporated .... D 317 872-4490
  Indianapolis (G-8188)
First Quality Printing Inc .... G 317 506-8633
  Indianapolis (G-8195)
Gary Printing Inc .... G 219 886-1767
  Gary (G-5938)
Gkb Holdings Inc .... E 260 471-7744
  Fort Wayne (G-5025)

Goetz Printing .... G 812 243-2086
  Terre Haute (G-15600)
Granger Gazette Inc .... G 574 277-2679
  Granger (G-6350)
Green Banner Publications Inc .... E 812 967-3176
  Borden (G-1109)
Greensburg Printing Co Inc .... G 812 663-8265
  Greensburg (G-6598)
Hardesty Printing Co Inc .... F 574 267-7591
  Warsaw (G-16374)
Hardesty Printing Co Inc .... F 574 223-4553
  Rochester (G-14293)
Hetty Incorporated .... G 219 933-0833
  Hammond (G-6945)
Hetty Incorporated .... G 219 836-2517
  Munster (G-12539)
Hiatt Enterprises Inc .... G 765 289-2700
  Muncie (G-12416)
Hiatt Enterprises Inc .... F 765 289-7756
  Muncie (G-12415)
Hinen Printing Co .... G 260 248-8984
  Columbia City (G-2150)
Home Mountain Publishing Co Inc ..... E 219 462-6601
  Valparaiso (G-15962)
Hoosier Times Inc .... C 812 331-4270
  Bloomington (G-882)
Howard Print Shop LLC .... G 765 453-6161
  Kokomo (G-10283)
Indiana Newspapers LLC .... D 812 886-9955
  Vincennes (G-16131)
J Jarrett Engineering Inc .... G 812 268-3338
  Sullivan (G-15408)
Jomark Inc .... F 248 478-2600
  Angola (G-265)
Journal & Chronicle Inc .... G 812 752-5060
  Scottsburg (G-14566)
Kendallville Custom Printing .... F 260 347-9233
  Kendallville (G-10125)
Kistner Enterprises Inc .... G 317 773-7733
  Noblesville (G-13123)
Kpc Media Group Inc .... F 260 426-2640
  Fort Wayne (G-5158)
Kpc Media Group Inc .... C 260 347-0400
  Kendallville (G-10130)
L & L Press Inc .... F 765 664-3162
  Marion (G-11305)
La Grange Publishing Co Inc .... F 260 463-3243
  Lagrange (G-10747)
Largus Speedy Print Corp .... E 219 922-8414
  Munster (G-12546)
Leader Publishing Co of Salem .... E 812 883-3281
  Salem (G-14487)
Light Printing Co .... G 815 429-3724
  Brook (G-1305)
Lincoln Printing Corporation .... A 260 424-5200
  Fort Wayne (G-5186)
Ludwick Graphics Inc .... G 574 233-2165
  South Bend (G-15131)
Maury Boyd & Associates Inc .... F 317 849-6110
  Indianapolis (G-8853)
Mignone Communications In .... C 260 358-0266
  Huntington (G-7344)
Minute Print It Inc .... G 765 482-9019
  Lebanon (G-10916)
Muncie Novelty Company Inc .... D 765 288-8301
  Muncie (G-12463)
News Publishing Company LLC .... G 812 649-4440
  Rockport (G-14346)
Nussmeier Engraving Company .... E 812 425-1339
  Evansville (G-4224)
Offset House Inc .... F 317 849-5155
  Indianapolis (G-9042)

Offset One Inc .... F 260 456-8828
  Fort Wayne (G-5282)
Overgaards Artcraft Printers .... G 574 234-8464
  South Bend (G-15183)
Pierce Oil Co Inc .... F 812 268-6356
  Sullivan (G-15416)
PIP Marketing Signs Print .... G 317 843-5755
  Carmel (G-1719)
Presstime Graphics Inc .... F 812 234-3815
  Terre Haute (G-15669)
Printing Place Inc .... F 260 665-8444
  Angola (G-289)
Priority Printing LLC .... G 317 241-4234
  Indianapolis (G-9213)
Progressive Printing Co Inc .... G 765 653-3814
  Greencastle (G-6427)
Publishers Consulting Corp .... F 219 874-4245
  Michigan City (G-11652)
Qgraphics Inc .... G 574 967-3733
  Flora (G-4664)
Quality Printing of NW Ind .... G 219 322-6677
  Schererville (G-14540)
Reprocomm Inc .... G 765 472-5700
  Peru (G-13598)
Rhr Corporation .... G 317 788-1504
  Indianapolis (G-9298)
Rick Whitt .... G 317 873-5507
  Indianapolis (G-9305)
Riden Inc .... G 219 362-5511
  La Porte (G-10473)
Rink Printing Company .... E 574 232-7935
  South Bend (G-15220)
Rowland Printing Co Inc .... G 317 773-1829
  Noblesville (G-13168)
◆ Rrc Corporation .... F 317 687-8325
  Indianapolis (G-9343)
Russ Print Shp/Hbron Advrtser .... F 219 996-3142
  Hebron (G-7106)
▲ Service Printers Inc .... E 574 266-6710
  Elkhart (G-3669)
Specialized Printed Products .... G 260 483-7075
  Fort Wayne (G-5428)
Spencer Evening World .... D 812 829-2255
  Spencer (G-15362)
Stines Printing Inc .... G 260 356-5994
  Huntington (G-7371)
Tabco Business Forms Inc .... G 812 882-2836
  Vincennes (G-16157)
Tatman Inc .... E 765 825-2164
  Connersville (G-2472)
The Deaton Family Company .... D 815 726-6234
  Auburn (G-429)
Thomas E Slade Inc .... F 812 437-5233
  Evansville (G-4343)
Times .... E 765 659-4622
  Frankfort (G-5698)
Town & Country Press Inc .... F 574 936-9505
  Plymouth (G-13820)
Triple Crown Media LLC .... G 574 533-2151
  Goshen (G-6273)
Truth Publishing Company Inc .... G 765 653-5151
  Greencastle (G-6434)
University Publishing Corp .... E 812 339-9033
  Bloomington (G-1004)
Vitruvian Composition LLC .... G 317 447-8383
  Indianapolis (G-9725)
▼ Voice of God Recordings Inc .... D 812 246-2137
  Jeffersonville (G-10069)
WAr - LLC- Westville Prtg .... G 219 785-2821
  Westville (G-16765)
Woodburn Graphics Inc .... F 812 232-0323
  Terre Haute (G-15748)

SIC SECTION

28 CHEMICALS AND ALLIED PRODUCTS

Writeguard Business Systems............... G 317 849-7292
   Indianapolis (G-9793)

XI Graphics Inc............................... F 317 738-3434
   Franklin (G-5789)

Zipp Printing LLC............................... G 574 256-0059
   Mishawaka (G-12028)

2796 Platemaking services

Accucraft Imaging Inc......................... G 219 933-3007
   Hammond (G-6867)

Bottcher America Corporation............... G 765 675-4449
   Tipton (G-15768)

Cecils Printing & Off Sups Inc.............. G 812 683-4416
   Huntingburg (G-7273)

Crichlow Industries Inc........................ G 317 925-5178
   Indianapolis (G-7903)

▲ Cylicron LLC................................. D 812 283-4600
   Jeffersonville (G-9967)

Diverse Sales Solutions LLC................ G 317 514-2403
   Indianapolis (G-7981)

Dynamic Dies Inc............................. E 317 247-4706
   Indianapolis (G-8026)

Evantek Manufacturing Inds LLC........... G 812 437-9100
   Evansville (G-4061)

Ewing Printing Company Inc................ F 812 882-2415
   Vincennes (G-16120)

Excell Color Graphics Inc.................... E 260 482-2720
   Fort Wayne (G-4967)

Express Press Indiana Inc................... E 574 277-3355
   South Bend (G-15023)

Fedex Office & Print Svcs Inc.............. F 765 449-4950
   Lafayette (G-10579)

Finzer Roller Inc............................... G 219 325-8808
   La Porte (G-10408)

Gary Printing Inc............................... G 219 886-1767
   Gary (G-5938)

▲ Grandview Aluminum Products........ F 812 649-2569
   Grandview (G-6328)

Graphik Mechanix Inc........................ G 260 426-7001
   Fort Wayne (G-5035)

Its Personal Laser Engraving.............. G 812 934-6657
   Batesville (G-592)

Ludwick Graphics Inc........................ G 574 233-2165
   South Bend (G-15131)

Maury Boyd & Associates Inc.............. F 317 849-6110
   Indianapolis (G-8853)

Multi-Color Corporation....................... E 812 752-0586
   Scottsburg (G-14573)

Peafield Products Inc......................... F 317 839-8473
   Plainfield (G-13711)

Pengad/West Inc............................. E 765 286-3000
   Muncie (G-12473)

Phasefour LLP................................. G 812 583-7247
   Evansville (G-4239)

Pontiac Engraving............................. G 630 834-4424
   Plymouth (G-13805)

Segura Publishing Company................ G 574 631-3143
   South Bend (G-15237)

Shakour Industries Inc....................... G 574 289-0100
   South Bend (G-15239)

28 CHEMICALS AND ALLIED PRODUCTS

2812 Alkalies and chlorine

Eco Services Operations Corp............. E 219 932-7651
   Hammond (G-6919)

▲ Hf Chlor-Alkali LLC....................... F 317 591-0000
   Indianapolis (G-8391)

Jci Jones Chemicals Inc..................... E 317 787-8382
   Beech Grove (G-694)

▲ Ulrich Chemical Inc........................ E 317 898-8632
   Indianapolis (G-9675)

Warsaw Chemical Company Inc........... D 574 267-3251
   Warsaw (G-16442)

2813 Industrial gases

A G A Gas Inc.................................. G 317 783-2331
   Indianapolis (G-7399)

Air Products and Chemicals Inc........... G 812 466-6492
   Terre Haute (G-15535)

Airgas Inc....................................... G 317 632-7106
   Indianapolis (G-7463)

Airgas Usa LLC................................ G 812 474-0440
   Evansville (G-3878)

Airgas Usa LLC................................ F 260 749-9576
   Fort Wayne (G-4733)

Airgas Usa LLC................................ G 317 248-8072
   Indianapolis (G-7464)

Airgas Usa LLC................................ G 812 362-7593
   Rockport (G-14335)

Alig LLC... G 812 362-7593
   Rockport (G-14336)

Continental Carbonic Pdts Inc.............. G 574 273-2800
   South Bend (G-14983)

Digital Helium LLC............................. G 219 365-4038
   Saint John (G-14449)

Durhat Transportation LLC................... G 463 204-9119
   Greenwood (G-6691)

Ferrellgas LP................................... G 574 936-2725
   Crawfordsville (G-2566)

Indiana Oxygen Company Inc.............. D 317 290-0003
   Indianapolis (G-8488)

Jt Composites LLC............................ G 317 297-9520
   Indianapolis (G-8645)

Linde Gas & Equipment Inc................ G 260 423-4468
   Fort Wayne (G-5187)

Linde Gas & Equipment Inc................ G 574 537-1366
   Goshen (G-6198)

Linde Gas & Equipment Inc................ G 317 782-4661
   Indianapolis (G-8760)

Linde Gas & Equipment Inc................ G 317 481-4550
   Indianapolis (G-8761)

Linde Inc.. G 317 984-7002
   Cicero (G-1998)

Linde Inc.. E 219 391-5100
   East Chicago (G-3027)

Linde Inc.. G 317 881-6825
   Indianapolis (G-8762)

Linde Inc.. G 765 456-1128
   Kokomo (G-10297)

Linde Inc.. F 219 326-7808
   La Porte (G-10446)

Linde Inc.. G 812 524-0173
   Seymour (G-14664)

Matheson Tri-Gas Inc......................... G 812 838-5518
   Mount Vernon (G-12307)

Matheson Tri-Gas Inc......................... G 317 892-5221
   Pittsboro (G-13651)

Messer LLC.................................... E 908 464-8100
   Indianapolis (G-8881)

Messer LLC.................................... D 219 324-0498
   La Porte (G-10450)

Messer LLC.................................... G 574 234-4887
   South Bend (G-15148)

Neon Amenities Incorporated.............. G 765 759-9133
   Yorktown (G-16978)

Petrogas International Corp.................. G 260 484-0859
   Auburn (G-416)

Tri-Pac Inc..................................... C 574 855-2197
   South Bend (G-15291)

Weaver Air Products LLC.................... G 317 848-4420
   Carmel (G-1800)

2816 Inorganic pigments

Altair Nanotechnologies Inc................. A 317 333-7617
   Anderson (G-75)

Icl Specialty Products Inc.................... G 219 933-1560
   Hammond (G-6951)

▲ Kibbechem Inc............................. E 574 266-1234
   Elkhart (G-3454)

Lyondllbsell Advnced Plymers I............ E 574 935-5131
   Plymouth (G-13794)

Sunrise Pigment USA LLC.................. G 773 449-8265
   Camby (G-1515)

United Minerals and Prpts Inc.............. G 812 838-5236
   Mount Vernon (G-12325)

2819 Industrial inorganic chemicals, nec

Addenda LLC................................... F 317 290-5007
   Indianapolis (G-7430)

Airgas Usa LLC................................ G 812 362-7593
   Rockport (G-14335)

Akzo Nobel Coatings Inc..................... E 574 372-2000
   Warsaw (G-16310)

Alig LLC... G 812 362-7593
   Rockport (G-14336)

Arch Wood Protection Inc................... G 219 464-3949
   Valparaiso (G-15904)

Arizona Isotope Science RES.............. G 702 219-1243
   Bunker Hill (G-1440)

Ashleys Elements LLC....................... G 765 480-2168
   Tipton (G-15765)

Astec Corp..................................... G 317 872-7550
   Indianapolis (G-7557)

Basic Elements LLC.......................... G 219 838-1325
   Munster (G-12532)

Benchmark Chemical Corp.................. G 317 875-0051
   Indianapolis (G-7613)

Celanese Corporation........................ G 812 421-8900
   Evansville (G-3967)

Central Indiana Ethanol LLC................ G 765 384-4001
   Carmel (G-1584)

Central Indiana Ethanol LLC................ E 765 384-4001
   Marion (G-11277)

Chemtrade Solutions LLC.................... G 317 917-0319
   Indianapolis (G-7794)

Craft Laboratories Inc......................... E 260 432-9467
   Fort Wayne (G-4882)

▲ Crown Technology Inc.................... E 317 845-0045
   Indianapolis (G-7914)

Dallas Group of America Inc................ B 812 283-6675
   Jeffersonville (G-9968)

▲ Davies-Imperial Coatings Inc........... E 219 933-0877
   Hammond (G-6911)

Dmp LLC.. G 812 699-0086
   Worthington (G-16959)

Dover Chemical Corporation................ G 219 852-0042
   Hammond (G-6914)

Eco Services Operations Corp............. E 219 932-7651
   Hammond (G-6919)

Eidp Inc... G 812 299-6700
   Terre Haute (G-15583)

Eidp Inc... G 219 462-4587
   Valparaiso (G-15938)

EJ Bognar Incorporated...................... G 412 344-9900
   Schneider (G-14549)

Element Armament............................ G 317 530-9013
   Whiteland (G-16784)

Element Armament LLC..................... G 317 442-7924
   Bargersville (G-565)

Element Clumbus.............................. G 812 526-2329
   Columbus (G-2296)

Elemental S A Protection.................... G 765 717-7325
   Muncie (G-12391)

28 CHEMICALS AND ALLIED PRODUCTS

Elements Elearning LLC...............................G..... 317 986-2113
  Indianapolis *(G-8070)*

G&S Research Inc..G..... 317 815-1443
  Carmel *(G-1637)*

Giles Chemical Corporation.......................G..... 812 537-4852
  Greendale *(G-6445)*

Giles Manufacturing Company...................G..... 812 537-4852
  Greendale *(G-6446)*

Gill Carbide Saw & TI Svc LLC...................G..... 317 698-6787
  Martinsville *(G-11397)*

Glcc Laurel LLC..G..... 765 497-6100
  West Lafayette *(G-16584)*

◆ Hammond Group Inc................................F..... 219 931-9360
  Hammond *(G-6938)*

Helena Agri-Enterprises LLC.......................G..... 765 869-5518
  Ambia *(G-66)*

Helena Agri-Enterprises LLC.......................G..... 812 654-3177
  Dillsboro *(G-2946)*

Helena Agri-Enterprises LLC.......................G..... 765 583-4458
  Otterbein *(G-13452)*

Hydrite Chemical Co....................................D..... 812 232-5411
  Terre Haute *(G-15611)*

Icl Specialty Products Inc............................E..... 219 933-1560
  Hammond *(G-6952)*

Indiana Oxide Corporation..........................F..... 812 446-2525
  Brazil *(G-1145)*

Industrial Water MGT Inc............................G..... 317 889-0836
  Indianapolis *(G-8521)*

J 2 Systems and Supply LLC.......................G..... 317 602-3940
  Indianapolis *(G-8601)*

Jci Jones Chemicals Inc..............................E..... 317 787-8382
  Beech Grove *(G-694)*

Kemira Water Solutions Inc........................D..... 219 397-2646
  East Chicago *(G-3024)*

Kennametal Inc...G..... 219 362-1000
  La Porte *(G-10435)*

Kml Inc..G..... 260 897-3723
  Laotto *(G-10808)*

Lightcrafters Nanotech LLC........................G..... 610 844-8341
  Crown Point *(G-2719)*

Machine Elements Inc.................................G..... 219 508-3968
  Valparaiso *(G-15999)*

◆ Mason Corporation...................................E..... 219 865-8040
  Schererville *(G-14533)*

Metals and Additives LLC...........................G..... 812 446-2525
  Brazil *(G-1153)*

Metalworking Lubricants Co.......................C..... 317 269-2444
  Indianapolis *(G-8891)*

Mobex Global US Inc...................................G..... 319 269-3848
  Albion *(G-35)*

New Elements LLC.......................................G..... 219 465-1389
  Valparaiso *(G-16011)*

Nochar Inc...G..... 317 613-3046
  Indianapolis *(G-9018)*

▼ Omicron Biochemicals Inc......................E..... 574 287-6910
  South Bend *(G-15177)*

PQ LLC...D..... 812 288-7186
  Clarksville *(G-2027)*

Pure Elements LLC.......................................G..... 317 503-0411
  Indianapolis *(G-9241)*

Reagent Chemical & RES Inc......................D..... 574 772-7424
  Knox *(G-10220)*

Reagent Chemical & RES Inc......................G..... 574 772-7424
  Knox *(G-10221)*

Remedium Services Group LLC..................F..... 317 660-6868
  Carmel *(G-1741)*

Sengo LLC...G..... 574 383-9833
  South Bend *(G-15238)*

Servaas Manufacturing Corp......................G..... 317 253-0454
  Indianapolis *(G-9407)*

Shell Catalysts & Tech LP...........................C..... 219 874-6211
  Michigan City *(G-11667)*

Shoremet LLC...F..... 219 390-3336
  Valparaiso *(G-16049)*

Silberline Mfg Co Inc...................................E..... 260 728-2111
  Decatur *(G-2883)*

Soulbrain Mi Inc...F..... 248 869-3079
  Kokomo *(G-10336)*

Substrate Treatments & Lubr.....................F..... 574 258-0904
  Mishawaka *(G-12010)*

Surface Elements Inc..................................F..... 574 546-5455
  Bremen *(G-1227)*

Thomas R Clark..G..... 219 508-7412
  Valparaiso *(G-16065)*

Usalco Michigan City Plant LLC..................G..... 219 873-0914
  Michigan City *(G-11682)*

V Global Holdings LLC.................................E..... 317 247-8141
  Indianapolis *(G-9695)*

W R Grace & Co-Conn.................................E..... 219 398-2040
  East Chicago *(G-3055)*

Wayne Chemical Inc....................................E..... 260 432-1120
  Fort Wayne *(G-5551)*

2821 Plastics materials and resins

Addivant USA LLC..G..... 765 497-6020
  West Lafayette *(G-16556)*

Advance Prtective Coatings Inc.................G..... 317 228-0123
  Indianapolis *(G-7435)*

Aearo Technologies LLC..............................C..... 317 692-6666
  Indianapolis *(G-7447)*

Akzo Nobel Coatings Inc.............................E..... 574 372-2000
  Warsaw *(G-16310)*

◆ Alterra Plastics LLC..................................F..... 812 271-1890
  Seymour *(G-14628)*

▲ AM Stabilizers Corporation....................G..... 219 844-3980
  Valparaiso *(G-15896)*

Ameri-Kart Corp..D..... 225 642-7874
  Bristol *(G-1243)*

▲ Ameri-Kart Corp.......................................C..... 574 848-7462
  Bristol *(G-1244)*

Ampacet Corporation..................................D..... 812 466-5231
  Terre Haute *(G-15544)*

Aoc LLC..D..... 219 465-4384
  Valparaiso *(G-15900)*

Apexx Enterprises LLC.................................F..... 812 486-2443
  Montgomery *(G-12085)*

Apr Plastics Inc..F..... 812 258-8888
  Evansville *(G-3895)*

Aqseptence Group Inc................................G..... 574 208-5866
  Rochester *(G-14277)*

Atc Plastics LLC...G..... 317 469-7552
  Indianapolis *(G-7558)*

Avient Corporation......................................E..... 574 267-1100
  Warsaw *(G-16315)*

▼ B&F Plastics Inc.......................................D..... 765 962-6125
  Richmond *(G-14089)*

Bd Medical Development Inc.....................G..... 219 310-8551
  Crown Point *(G-2653)*

Bdc Enterprise LLC......................................G..... 317 395-6740
  Shelbyville *(G-14735)*

Better Way Products....................................G..... 574 546-2868
  Bremen *(G-1175)*

Blehm Plastics...G..... 317 736-4090
  Franklin *(G-5717)*

▲ Bpc Manufacturing Operation...............G..... 574 936-9894
  Plymouth *(G-13761)*

C4 Polymers Inc...G..... 440 543-3866
  Muncie *(G-12359)*

▲ Cabinets & Counters Inc........................E..... 812 858-3300
  Newburgh *(G-12995)*

Cellofoam North America Inc.....................D..... 317 535-9008
  Whiteland *(G-16778)*

▲ Cereplast Inc..F..... 310 615-1900
  Seymour *(G-14637)*

Chase Plastic Services Inc..........................G..... 574 239-4090
  South Bend *(G-14971)*

Chemtrusion Inc..E..... 812 280-2910
  Jeffersonville *(G-9951)*

Complete Packaging Group Inc.................G..... 765 547-1300
  Brookville *(G-1318)*

Covestro LLC..G..... 765 659-4721
  Frankfort *(G-5656)*

▲ Createc Corporation................................B..... 317 566-0022
  Indianapolis *(G-7899)*

▲ Crossroads Sourcing Group Ltd............G..... 847 940-4123
  Carmel *(G-1600)*

Custom Fiber Composites LLC..................G..... 765 376-1360
  Lebanon *(G-10889)*

Double H Plastics Inc..................................F..... 765 664-9090
  Marion *(G-11282)*

Dubois County Liners LLP..........................G..... 812 634-1294
  Jasper *(G-9835)*

▲ Echo Engrg & Prod Sups Inc..................E..... 317 876-8848
  Indianapolis *(G-8045)*

Efficient Plas Solutions Inc........................E..... 574 965-4690
  Delphi *(G-2896)*

◆ Eidp Inc...A..... 833 267-8382
  Indianapolis *(G-8064)*

▲ Encom Polymers LLC..............................E..... 812 421-7700
  Evansville *(G-4036)*

◆ Envalior Engineering Materials Inc.....C..... 800 333-4237
  Evansville *(G-4039)*

Envalior Engineering Mtls Inc...................E..... 812 435-7500
  Evansville *(G-4040)*

Envalior Engineering Mtls Inc...................E..... 812 435-7500
  Evansville *(G-4041)*

Erj Composites LLC.....................................G..... 574 360-3517
  Mishawaka *(G-11895)*

Evoqua Water Technologies LLC...............E..... 317 280-4251
  Indianapolis *(G-8144)*

Fiber Technologies LLC...............................G..... 812 569-4641
  Bloomington *(G-866)*

Foam Fabricators Inc..................................G..... 812 948-1696
  New Albany *(G-12732)*

Foamcraft Inc...E..... 574 534-4343
  Goshen *(G-6139)*

Freudenberg-Nok General Partnr.............C..... 734 354-5504
  Shelbyville *(G-14757)*

Future Foam Inc...E..... 574 294-7694
  Elkhart *(G-3363)*

G & T Industries Inc....................................G..... 812 634-2252
  Jasper *(G-9839)*

◆ Gaska Tape Inc...D..... 574 294-5431
  Elkhart *(G-3366)*

Geon Performance Solutions LLC.............G..... 812 466-5116
  Terre Haute *(G-15596)*

Glass City Inc...G..... 219 887-2100
  Gary *(G-5943)*

Graber Cabinetry LLC..................................E..... 260 627-2243
  Grabill *(G-6297)*

▲ Green Tree Plastics LLC..........................G..... 812 402-4127
  Evansville *(G-4097)*

Henry Holsters LLC......................................F..... 812 369-2266
  Spencer *(G-15348)*

Hoehn Plastics Inc......................................D..... 812 874-3646
  Poseyville *(G-13977)*

Huntsman Intl Trdg Corp............................D..... 812 334-7090
  Bloomington *(G-885)*

Indiana Polymers Inc..................................G..... 219 762-9550
  Valparaiso *(G-15972)*

◆ Industrial Dielectrics Inc........................B..... 317 773-1766
  Noblesville *(G-13103)*

◆ Industrial Dlctrics Hldngs Inc................G..... 317 773-1766
  Noblesville *(G-13104)*

◆ Industrial Plastics Group LLC................E..... 812 831-4053
  Evansville *(G-4123)*

28 CHEMICALS AND ALLIED PRODUCTS

Innovations Amplified LLC .... G 317 339-4685
  Indianapolis (G-8552)
Innovative Composites Ltd .... F 574 857-2224
  Rochester (G-14297)
Integral Technologies Inc .... G 812 550-1770
  Evansville (G-4127)
Ip Corporation .... F 574 259-1505
  Mishawaka (G-11913)
Ip Corporation .... E 574 234-1105
  South Bend (G-15087)
Ip Moulding Inc .... D 574 825-5845
  Middlebury (G-11726)
◆ Jamplast Inc .... F 812 838-8562
  Mount Vernon (G-12304)
Jp Incorporated - Indiana .... B 574 457-2062
  Syracuse (G-15465)
Kvk US Technologies Inc .... G 765 529-1100
  New Castle (G-12871)
Leepoxy Plastics Inc .... G 260 747-7411
  Fort Wayne (G-5180)
Line-X of Schererville Inc .... F 219 865-1000
  Schererville (G-14530)
▼ Lucent Polymers Inc .... D 812 421-2216
  Evansville (G-4177)
LyondllbselI Advnced Plymers I .... E 812 202-1968
  Evansville (G-4179)
Makuta Inc .... F 317 642-0001
  Shelbyville (G-14773)
Martin Holding Company LLC .... E 812 401-9988
  Evansville (G-4190)
Matrix Tool Inc .... F 574 259-3093
  Mishawaka (G-11939)
Meyer Plastics Inc .... F 260 482-4595
  Fort Wayne (G-5219)
Mitsubishi Chemical Advncd Mtr .... C 260 479-4100
  Fort Wayne (G-5233)
Mitsubshi Chem Advnced Mtls In ...... D 260 479-4700
  Fort Wayne (G-5234)
Molded Foam Products Inc .... F 574 848-1500
  Bristol (G-1276)
Monosol LLC .... G 765 485-5400
  Lebanon (G-10918)
Monosol LLC .... G 219 762-3165
  Portage (G-13890)
▲ Monosol LLC .... F 219 762-3165
  Merrillville (G-11546)
▲ Monument Chemical LLC .... D 317 223-2630
  Indianapolis (G-8952)
Naturespire LLC .... G 463 266-0395
  Indianapolis (G-8992)
Nova Polymers Incorporated .... E 812 476-0339
  Evansville (G-4223)
▲ Omni Plastics LLC .... D 812 422-0888
  Evansville (G-4227)
Omni Technologies Inc .... F 812 539-4144
  Greendale (G-6451)
▼ OTech Corporation .... C 219 778-8001
  Rolling Prairie (G-14367)
Pactiv LLC .... E 574 936-7065
  Plymouth (G-13800)
Plastic Recycl Export Ltd LLC .... G 301 758-6885
  Fort Wayne (G-5318)
◆ Plastic Recycling Inc .... E 317 780-6100
  Indianapolis (G-9151)
Polyfusion LLC .... G 260 624-7659
  Angola (G-284)
Polymod Technologies Inc .... F 260 436-1322
  Fort Wayne (G-5325)
Polytek Development Corp .... G 317 494-6420
  Franklin (G-5767)
Precision Colors LLC .... F 260 969-6402
  Fort Wayne (G-5335)

Primex Clor Cmpnding Addtves C ..... E 800 222-5116
  Richmond (G-14184)
◆ Primex Plastics Corporation .... B 765 966-7774
  Richmond (G-14186)
Process Systems & Services .... G 812 427-2331
  Florence (G-4666)
Rainmaker Polymers LLC .... G 574 268-0010
  Winona Lake (G-16915)
▲ Rbc Holding Inc .... F 317 340-3845
  Greenwood (G-6759)
Replas of Texas Inc .... G 812 421-3600
  Evansville (G-4284)
Rtp Enterprise Inc .... G 317 258-3213
  Noblesville (G-13169)
Sabic Innovative Plas US LLC .... D 812 372-0197
  Columbus (G-2388)
Sabic Innovative Plas US LLC .... B 812 831-4054
  Mount Vernon (G-12319)
◆ Sabic Innvtive Plas Mt Vrnon L ...... A 812 838-4385
  Mount Vernon (G-12320)
Shaw Polymers Holdings LLC .... G 219 779-9450
  Crown Point (G-2750)
▲ Silcotec Inc .... F 219 324-4411
  La Porte (G-10482)
Solid Surface Craftsmen Inc .... G 317 535-2333
  Whiteland (G-16797)
Spartech LLC .... D 765 281-5100
  Muncie (G-12495)
◆ Star Technology Inc .... E 260 837-7833
  Waterloo (G-16531)
Stenidy Industries Inc .... G 317 873-5343
  Zionsville (G-17054)
Sun Polymers .... G 219 426-1220
  Fort Wayne (G-5457)
Sun Polymers International Inc .... F 317 834-6910
  Mooresville (G-12246)
▲ Toray Resin Company .... D 317 398-7833
  Shelbyville (G-14807)
Transfoam LLC .... G 631 747-0255
  Indianapolis (G-9630)
Triangle Rubber Co LLC .... E 574 533-3118
  Elkhart (G-3746)
Triangle Rubber Co LLC .... G 574 533-3118
  Goshen (G-6271)
◆ Triangle Rubber Co LLC .... C 574 533-3118
  Goshen (G-6272)
V Global Holdings LLC .... E 317 247-8141
  Indianapolis (G-9695)
Vahala Foam Inc .... D 574 293-1287
  Elkhart (G-3764)

2822 Synthetic rubber

BRC Rubber & Plastics Inc .... F 765 728-8510
  Montpelier (G-12177)
Coleman Cable LLC .... D 765 449-7227
  Lafayette (G-10553)
CT Polymers LLC .... F 574 598-6132
  Bourbon (G-1120)
Exactseal Inc .... G 317 559-2220
  Indianapolis (G-8148)
▲ Gdc Inc .... C 574 533-3128
  Goshen (G-6143)
Green Earth Polymers Inc .... G 812 602-4070
  Evansville (G-4096)
Gumena LLC .... G 574 339-6510
  Mishawaka (G-11903)
Iris Rubber Co Inc .... F 317 984-3561
  Cicero (G-1997)
Parker-Hannifin Corporation .... D 574 533-1111
  Goshen (G-6236)
PTG Silicones Inc .... F 812 948-8719
  New Albany (G-12800)

Sealwrap Systems LLC .... G 317 462-3310
  Greenfield (G-6549)
◆ T & M Rubber Inc .... E 574 533-3173
  Goshen (G-6267)
◆ Triangle Rubber Co LLC .... C 574 533-3118
  Goshen (G-6272)
United Minerals and Prpts Inc .... G 812 838-5236
  Mount Vernon (G-12325)

2823 Cellulosic manmade fibers

Applied Composites Engrg Inc .... E 317 243-4225
  Indianapolis (G-7533)
Huhtamaki Inc .... C 219 972-4264
  Hammond (G-6950)
Huhtamaki Inc .... D 765 677-0395
  Marion (G-11293)
Multi Fiber LLC .... F 260 353-1510
  Bluffton (G-1044)

2824 Organic fibers, noncellulosic

Butterfield Foods LLC .... C 317 776-4775
  Noblesville (G-13051)
Debra Schneider .... G 317 420-9360
  Arcadia (G-312)
◆ Eidp Inc .... A 833 267-8382
  Indianapolis (G-8064)
▲ Fdc Graphics Films Inc .... E 800 634-7523
  South Bend (G-15029)
Indy Composite Works Inc .... E 317 280-9766
  Zionsville (G-17018)
Jackson Seed Service LLC .... G 812 480-6555
  Evansville (G-4137)
Mitsubishi Chemical Advncd Mtr .... C 260 479-4100
  Fort Wayne (G-5233)
Mitsubshi Chem Advnced Mtls In ...... D 260 479-4700
  Fort Wayne (G-5234)
No More Bugs .... G 317 658-6096
  Indianapolis (G-9014)

2833 Medicinals and botanicals

1500 South Tibbs LLC .... C 317 247-8141
  Indianapolis (G-7384)
Acell Inc .... C 765 464-8198
  Lafayette (G-10514)
Animalsinkcom LLC .... G 317 496-8467
  Brownsburg (G-1347)
Boehrnger Mnnheim Phrmctcals C .... F 317 521-2000
  Indianapolis (G-7655)
Cgenetech Inc .... G 317 295-1925
  Indianapolis (G-7781)
Developmental Natural Res .... G 317 543-4886
  Indianapolis (G-7968)
Efil Pharmaceuticals Corp .... G 765 491-7247
  West Lafayette (G-16579)
▲ Green Nursery Inc .... G 812 269-2220
  Bloomington (G-870)
Herbs G&W Inc .... G 574 646-2134
  Nappanee (G-12609)
◆ Indiana Botanic Gardens Inc .... C 219 947-4040
  Hobart (G-7191)
Medtric LLC .... G 765 427-7234
  Lafayette (G-10645)
Nuaxon Bioscience Inc .... G 812 762-4400
  Bloomington (G-931)
Nutritional Research Assoc .... F 260 723-4931
  South Whitley (G-15322)
Pfizer Inc .... D 212 733-2323
  Terre Haute (G-15660)
Resprin Inc .... G 219 996-5864
  Valparaiso (G-16038)
Vitamins Inc .... E 219 879-7356
  Michigan City (G-11686)

Employee Codes: A=Over 500 employees, B=251-500
C=101-250, D=51-100, E=20-50, F=10-19, G=1-9

28 CHEMICALS AND ALLIED PRODUCTS

◆ VSI Acquisition Corp.................................C 317 247-8141
Indianapolis (G-9730)

Wisemed Inc..G 317 644-1169
Indianapolis (G-9778)

2834 Pharmaceutical preparations

Abbott Inc..D 765 647-2523
Brookville (G-1315)

▲ Accra-Pac Inc.......................................D 574 295-0000
Elkhart (G-3151)

Accra-Pac Inc..D 574 295-0000
Elkhart (G-3150)

Acura Pharmaceutical Tech....................G 574 842-3305
Culver (G-2778)

Akina Inc..F 765 464-0501
West Lafayette (G-16559)

Allergan Sales LLC................................F 888 786-6471
Charlestown (G-1871)

Amatsigroup Inc....................................G 617 576-2005
Terre Haute (G-15541)

▲ American Family Pharmacy LLC...........G 317 334-1933
Indianapolis (G-7503)

▲ Applied Laboratories Inc......................E 812 372-2607
Columbus (G-2221)

Aquestive Therapeutics Inc....................E 219 762-4143
Portage (G-13844)

Aquestive Therapeutics Inc....................E 219 762-3165
Portage (G-13845)

Aratana Therapeutics Inc......................D 913 353-1000
Greenfield (G-6466)

Ardena Company...................................G 219 926-1018
Chesterton (G-1903)

Areva Pharmaceuticals Inc....................F 855 853-4760
Georgetown (G-6055)

▲ Artemis International Inc.....................F 260 436-6899
Fort Wayne (G-4774)

Astellas Pharma Us Inc..........................G 574 595-7569
Star City (G-15395)

Astrazeneca Pharmaceuticals LP...........G 240 252-0125
Mount Vernon (G-12287)

Astrazeneca Pharmaceuticals LP...........E 812 429-5000
Mount Vernon (G-12288)

▲ Bamboo US Bidco LLC.........................G 812 355-5289
Bloomington (G-793)

Baxter Intl..G 812 355-4283
Bloomington (G-797)

▲ Baxter Phrm Solutions LLC...................C 812 333-0887
Bloomington (G-798)

Bayer Healthcare LLC............................E 574 262-6136
Elkhart (G-3218)

Bayer Healthcare LLC............................E 574 252-4735
Mishawaka (G-11846)

Bayer Healthcare LLC............................E 574 252-4734
Mishawaka (G-11847)

Biokorf LLC..G 765 727-0782
West Lafayette (G-16565)

Biota Biosciences Inc.............................G 765 702-3744
Cambridge City (G-1491)

Bloom Pharmaceutical............................G 260 615-2633
Fort Wayne (G-4807)

Bristol Myers...F 812 428-1927
Evansville (G-3955)

Bristol-Myers Squibb Company..............F 812 429-5505
Evansville (G-3956)

Bristol-Myers Squibb Company..............G 260 432-2764
Fort Wayne (G-4818)

Bristol-Myers Squibb Company..............C 812 307-2000
Mount Vernon (G-12293)

Brogan Pharmaceuticals LLC.................F 219 644-3693
Crown Point (G-2662)

Bruce A Hodson....................................G 765 212-7757
Attica (G-344)

Bulent Gumusel....................................G 812 803-5912
Bloomington (G-818)

Caicos Solutions LLC............................G 317 314-3776
Indianapolis (G-7716)

Cardinal Health 414 LLC.......................F 317 981-4100
Indianapolis (G-7740)

Catalent Indiana LLC............................G 812 355-6746
Bloomington (G-823)

Catalent Indiana LLC............................B 812 355-6746
Bloomington (G-824)

Catalent Pharma Solutions Inc..............D 812 355-4498
Bloomington (G-825)

Catalent Wellness LLC..........................F 800 344-6225
Greendale (G-6441)

Catalent Wellness Holdings LLC...........D 800 344-6225
Greendale (G-6442)

Century Pharmaceuticals Inc.................E 317 849-4210
Indianapolis (G-7775)

Colorcon Inc..G 317 545-6211
Indianapolis (G-7836)

Colorcon Inc..D 317 545-6211
Indianapolis (G-7837)

Confluence Pharmaceuticals LLC..........G 317 379-7498
Arcadia (G-311)

▲ Corange International.........................G
Indianapolis (G-7874)

Cretaceous Cures..................................G 317 379-7744
Westfield (G-16680)

Crossroads Biologicals LLC..................G 765 239-9113
Lafayette (G-10562)

Crosswind Pharmacy.............................G 812 381-4815
Indianapolis (G-7912)

Curia Indiana LLC.................................D 765 463-0112
West Lafayette (G-16574)

Damor & Co LLC....................................G 317 790-8360
Indianapolis (G-7947)

Dickey Consumer Products Inc.............F 317 773-8330
Noblesville (G-13071)

DSM Enterprises LLC............................G 317 698-3317
Lebanon (G-10892)

◆ Eidp Inc..A 833 267-8382
Indianapolis (G-8064)

Elan Corp PLC.......................................G 317 442-1502
Fishers (G-4509)

Elanco Animal Health Inc......................A 877 352-6261
Greenfield (G-6493)

Elanco International Inc.........................D 877 352-6261
Greenfield (G-6494)

Elanco US Inc..G 765 832-4400
Clinton (G-2066)

◆ Elanco US Inc.....................................C 877 352-6261
Greenfield (G-6495)

Eli Lilly and Company............................G 317 748-1622
Fishers (G-4511)

Eli Lilly and Company............................G 317 276-2000
Indianapolis (G-8072)

Eli Lilly and Company............................G 317 276-7907
Indianapolis (G-8073)

Eli Lilly and Company............................G 317 276-2118
Indianapolis (G-8074)

Eli Lilly and Company............................G 317 276-2000
Indianapolis (G-8075)

Eli Lilly and Company............................G 317 276-2000
Indianapolis (G-8076)

Eli Lilly and Company............................G 317 276-5925
Indianapolis (G-8077)

Eli Lilly and Company............................G 317 276-2000
Indianapolis (G-8078)

Eli Lilly and Company............................F 317 651-7790
Indianapolis (G-8079)

Eli Lilly and Company............................F 317 277-0147
Indianapolis (G-8080)

Eli Lilly and Company............................F 317 276-2000
Indianapolis (G-8081)

Eli Lilly and Company............................F 317 276-2000
Indianapolis (G-8082)

Eli Lilly and Company............................F 317 276-2000
Indianapolis (G-8083)

Eli Lilly and Company............................F 317 276-7907
Indianapolis (G-8084)

Eli Lilly and Company............................E 317 276-2000
Indianapolis (G-8085)

Eli Lilly and Company............................D 317 277-1307
Indianapolis (G-8086)

Eli Lilly and Company............................C 317 276-2000
Indianapolis (G-8087)

Eli Lilly and Company............................C 317 276-2000
Indianapolis (G-8089)

Eli Lilly and Company............................E 317 433-3624
Plainfield (G-13678)

Eli Lilly and Company............................G 812 242-5900
Terre Haute (G-15585)

Eli Lilly and Company............................A 317 276-2000
Indianapolis (G-8088)

Eli Lilly Interamerica Inc.......................F 317 276-2000
Indianapolis (G-8090)

Eli Lilly International Corp....................F 317 276-2000
Indianapolis (G-8091)

Energy Delivery Solutions LLC.............G 502 271-8753
Jeffersonville (G-9977)

Evecxia Therapeutics Inc......................G 919 597-8762
Westfield (G-16689)

Exelead Inc..D 317 612-2900
Indianapolis (G-8154)

Exelead Inc..E 317 347-2800
Indianapolis (G-8153)

F Hoffmann-La Roche Ltd.....................F 317 370-8578
Indianapolis (G-8160)

F Hoffmann-La Roche Ltd.....................G 317 370-8578
Indianapolis (G-8159)

Fenwick Pharma LLC.............................G 765 412-1889
West Lafayette (G-16580)

Fisher Clinical Services Inc..................E 317 277-0337
Indianapolis (G-8197)

Genoa Healthcare LLC..........................G 219 427-1837
Gary (G-5940)

Giles Manufacturing Company..............G 812 537-4852
Greendale (G-6446)

▲ Hawthorne Products Inc....................G 765 768-6585
Dunkirk (G-2962)

Horizon Biotechnologies LLC................G 317 534-2540
Greenwood (G-6712)

Incog Biopharma Services Inc.............F 812 320-4236
Fishers (G-4543)

Indiana Univ Schl Medicine..................F 317 278-6518
Indianapolis (G-8498)

Ingenus LLC..F 317 430-1855
Indianapolis (G-8543)

Inspire LLC..G 317 339-7718
Indianapolis (G-8562)

International Infusion LP.......................G 708 710-9200
Munster (G-12544)

Ips-Integrated Prj Svcs LLC..................G 317 247-1200
Indianapolis (G-8588)

James McBryde.....................................G 206 504-4689
South Bend (G-15089)

Jbs United Inc.......................................G 765 296-4539
Frankfort (G-5676)

Jnj Blue Enterprise LLC........................G 502 593-8464
New Albany (G-12754)

Kindred Biosciences Inc.......................D 650 701-7901
Greenfield (G-6524)

Komodo Pharmaceuticals Inc...............F 317 485-0023
Fortville (G-5602)

SIC SECTION
28 CHEMICALS AND ALLIED PRODUCTS

Kp Pharmaceutical Tech Inc................ E 812 330-8121
  Bloomington (G-903)
▲ Kremers Urban Phrmcuticals Inc....... D
  Seymour (G-14663)
Lake Effect Pharma LLC....................... G 315 694-1111
  Indianapolis (G-8714)
Lexington Pharmaceuticals................... G 317 870-0370
  Indianapolis (G-8743)
Lexington Phrmcticals Labs LLC........... G 317 566-9750
  Carmel (G-1683)
Lgenia Inc... F 317 861-8850
  Fortville (G-5603)
Lilly Research Laboratories................... G 317 276-0127
  Indianapolis (G-8754)
▼ Lilly Usa LLC....................................... C 317 276-2000
  Indianapolis (G-8755)
Lilly Ventures.. G 317 651-3050
  Indianapolis (G-8756)
Lodos Theranostics LLC....................... G 765 427-2492
  West Lafayette (G-16602)
Martin Ekwlor Phrmcuticals Inc............ F 765 962-4410
  Richmond (G-14159)
Mattox and Moore Inc........................... G 317 632-7534
  Indianapolis (G-8852)
MBX Biosciences Inc............................ E 317 659-0200
  Carmel (G-1695)
Mead Johnson & Company LLC........... G 812 429-5000
  Mount Vernon (G-12308)
◆ Mead Johnson & Company LLC........C 812 429-5000
  Evansville (G-4193)
Med-Pharm Pharmacy........................... G 812 232-2086
  Terre Haute (G-15640)
Merck Sharp & Dohme LLC.................. G 908 740-4000
  Plainfield (G-13704)
Merrill Corporation................................ E 574 255-2988
  Mishawaka (G-11942)
Midwest Pediatric Crdiolgy PC.............. D 219 836-1355
  Munster (G-12549)
Millipore Sigma.................................... F 317 453-5490
  Indianapolis (G-8925)
Msd Group LLC.................................... G 260 444-4658
  Fort Wayne (G-5249)
Mvk Pharmaceuticals LLC.................... G 317 374-2178
  Indianapolis (G-8973)
Mwi Veterinary Supply Co.................... G 317 769-7771
  Lebanon (G-10923)
Mwi Veterinary Supply Co.................... G 317 769-7771
  Lebanon (G-10924)
Naturegenic Inc..................................... G 765 807-5525
  West Lafayette (G-16612)
Noah Worcester Derm Society.............. G 317 257-5907
  Indianapolis (G-9015)
Northwind Pharmaceuticals LLC........... G 317 436-8522
  Indianapolis (G-9025)
Northwind Pharmaceuticals LLC........... G 800 722-0772
  Indianapolis (G-9026)
Novartis Corporation............................. G 317 852-3839
  Brownsburg (G-1392)
Novo Nrdisk RES Ctr Indnplis I............. G 541 520-8030
  Indianapolis (G-9029)
Npm Holdings Inc.................................. G 812 689-3309
  Osgood (G-13414)
Nukemed Inc... G 765 437-1631
  Bunker Hill (G-1442)
Nukemed Inc... E 574 271-2800
  South Bend (G-15175)
Nutritional Research Assoc................... F 260 723-4931
  South Whitley (G-15322)
Optum Pharmacy 702 LLC................... D 812 256-8600
  Jeffersonville (G-10031)
Orano Med LLC.................................... G 469 638-0632
  Brownsburg (G-1393)

Osram Inc.. G 317 847-6268
  Westfield (G-16716)
Parsolex Gmp Center Inc..................... F 765 464-8414
  West Lafayette (G-16617)
Pd Sub LLC.. E 812 524-0534
  Seymour (G-14673)
Peli Biothermal LLC............................. G 763 412-4800
  Plainfield (G-13712)
Pfizer Inc.. G 574 232-9927
  South Bend (G-15194)
Pfizer Inc.. D 212 733-2323
  Terre Haute (G-15660)
Pharma Form Finders LLC................... G 317 362-1191
  Fishers (G-4574)
Phytoption LLC.................................... G 765 490-7738
  West Lafayette (G-16620)
Pipe Dream Innovations LLC............... G 503 910-8815
  Marion (G-11328)
Point Biopharma Global Inc................. F 317 543-9957
  Indianapolis (G-9158)
Point Biopharma Inc............................ E 833 544-2637
  Indianapolis (G-9159)
Point Biopharma USA Inc.................... G 317 543-9957
  Indianapolis (G-9160)
R J Smithey LLC.................................. G 317 435-8473
  Greenwood (G-6757)
R2 Pharma LLC................................... G 317 810-6205
  Carmel (G-1733)
Relevo Inc... G 317 644-0099
  Carmel (G-1738)
Reliv.. G 317 507-1548
  Carmel (G-1740)
Robert J Stankovich............................. G 317 844-0886
  Carmel (G-1744)
▲ Roche Diabetes Care Inc.................. D 317 521-2000
  Indianapolis (G-9316)
Roche Diagnostics Corp....................... E 317 521-2000
  Indianapolis (G-9317)
Roche Diagnostics Corporation............ C 317 521-2000
  Indianapolis (G-9318)
Roche Operations Ltd.......................... D 787 285-0170
  Indianapolis (G-9320)
Rph On Call LLC.................................. G 317 622-4800
  Greenfield (G-6546)
Safetynet LLC...................................... G 502 609-3339
  New Albany (G-12811)
Sanofi US Services Inc........................ D 317 228-5750
  Indianapolis (G-9370)
Schwarz Pharma................................... F 812 523-3457
  Seymour (G-14686)
Sepracor Inc... G 317 513-6257
  Fishers (G-4651)
Somersaults LLC................................. G 317 747-7496
  Fishers (G-4652)
Spirrow Therapeutics LLC................... G 317 750-8879
  West Lafayette (G-16631)
Sysgenomics LLC................................ G 574 302-5396
  Granger (G-6384)
Takeda.. F 812 972-0957
  Corydon (G-2517)
Takeda Pharmaceuticals USA Inc......... G 812 738-0452
  Corydon (G-2518)
Telix Pharmaceuticals US Inc.............. D 317 588-9700
  Fishers (G-4611)
Toralgen Inc... G 812 820-3374
  Indianapolis (G-9622)
Treat America Roche Diagnostic.......... G 317 521-1490
  Fishers (G-4616)
Tri-Pac Inc.. C 574 855-2197
  South Bend (G-15290)
Tri-Pac Inc.. C 574 855-2197
  South Bend (G-15291)

United-Ah II LLC................................. F 317 758-4495
  Sheridan (G-14831)
Verdure Sciences Inc........................... E 317 776-3600
  Noblesville (G-13192)
Verista Inc.. A 317 849-0330
  Fishers (G-4628)
Vesta Ingredients Inc........................... G 317 895-9000
  Indianapolis (G-9712)
▲ Vesta Pharmaceuticals Inc............... E 317 895-9000
  Indianapolis (G-9713)
Vitamins Inc... E 219 879-7356
  Michigan City (G-11686)
Windsor Wartcare................................. G 574 266-6555
  Elkhart (G-3785)
Yinroot LLC.. G 317 379-9529
  Noblesville (G-13198)
Zoetis... G 574 232-9927
  South Bend (G-15313)

2835 Diagnostic substances

Cardinal Health 414 LLC...................... F 317 981-4100
  Indianapolis (G-7740)
Chematics Inc....................................... F 574 834-2406
  North Webster (G-13303)
Core Biologic LLC................................ G 888 390-8838
  Fort Wayne (G-4875)
Intervention Diagnostics Inc................. G 317 432-6091
  Indianapolis (G-8584)
Microworks Inc..................................... G 219 661-8620
  Crown Point (G-2724)
Mwi Veterinary Supply Co.................... G 317 769-7771
  Lebanon (G-10924)
Petnet Indiana LLC.............................. E 865 218-2000
  Indianapolis (G-9129)
Poly Group LLC................................... G 812 590-4750
  New Albany (G-12796)
R 2 Diagnostics Inc.............................. G 574 288-4377
  South Bend (G-15212)
◆ Roche Diagnostics Corporation........A 800 428-5076
  Indianapolis (G-9319)
Siemens Hlthcare Dgnostics Inc........... G 574 262-6139
  Elkhart (G-3675)
Stanbio Laboratory LP......................... G 830 249-0772
  Elkhart (G-3695)
Strand Diagnostics LLC....................... G 317 455-2100
  Indianapolis (G-9517)
Synermed International Inc.................. G 317 896-1565
  Westfield (G-16731)
Sysgenomics LLC................................ G 574 302-5396
  Granger (G-6384)

2836 Biological products, except diagnostic

Acro Biomedical Co Ltd....................... G 317 286-6788
  Fishers (G-4460)
Apotex Corp... F 317 334-1314
  Indianapolis (G-7526)
Apotex Corp... E 317 839-6550
  Plainfield (G-13658)
Aratana Therapeutics Inc..................... D 913 353-1000
  Greenfield (G-6466)
Arkley Biotek LLC................................ G 317 331-7580
  Indianapolis (G-7545)
Biosafe Engineering LLC..................... E 317 858-8099
  Indianapolis (G-7629)
Bioscience Vaccines Inc...................... G 765 464-5890
  West Lafayette (G-16566)
Corebiologic LLC................................. G 260 437-0353
  Fort Wayne (G-4878)
Envigo Rms Inc.................................... G 317 806-6080
  Greenfield (G-6500)
▲ Envigo Rms Inc................................. C 317 806-6080
  Indianapolis (G-8125)

28 CHEMICALS AND ALLIED PRODUCTS

Friction-Free LLC.. G..... 317 385-6975
   Indianapolis (G-8233)

Gcam Inc.. G..... 714 738-6462
   Indianapolis (G-8265)

Geniphys Inc.. G..... 317 973-0523
   Zionsville (G-17013)

Harlan Development Company...................... G..... 317 352-1583
   Indianapolis (G-8362)

Immunotek Bio Centers LLC......................... G..... 337 500-1294
   Indianapolis (G-8467)

Immunotek Bio Centers LLC......................... G..... 337 500-1294
   Jeffersonville (G-10002)

Indy Medical Supplies LLC............................ G..... 866 744-9013
   Zionsville (G-17019)

Indycoast Partners LLC................................. G..... 317 454-1050
   Carmel (G-1668)

Mwi Veterinary Supply Co............................. G..... 317 769-7771
   Lebanon (G-10924)

Nelson Global Products Inc.......................... F..... 317 787-5747
   Greenwood (G-6746)

Pucl Bindley Bioscience Ctr......................... G..... 765 496-3975
   West Lafayette (G-16621)

Rimedion Inc.. G..... 415 513-5535
   Indianapolis (G-9308)

Roth Bioscience LLC..................................... G..... 574 533-3351
   Goshen (G-6249)

Stem Point LLC... G..... 352 870-0122
   Franklin (G-5778)

Tissue Source LLC... G..... 765 746-6679
   Zionsville (G-17058)

Vasmo Inc.. F..... 317 549-3722
   Indianapolis (G-9702)

Vicki Wright and Company............................ G..... 317 372-7136
   Plainfield (G-13740)

2841 Soap and other detergents

3rivers Soap Company LLC.......................... G..... 260 418-0241
   Fort Wayne (G-4712)

Bass Farms LLC... G..... 317 401-4700
   Shelbyville (G-14734)

Belcher Tobiah.. G..... 765 513-2211
   Kokomo (G-10238)

Black Lavish Essentials LLC......................... G..... 800 214-8664
   Indianapolis (G-7639)

◆ Brulin & Company Inc................................ D..... 317 923-3211
   Indianapolis (G-7691)

▲ Circle - Prosco Inc................................... E..... 812 339-3653
   Bloomington (G-829)

Craft Laboratories Inc.................................... E..... 260 432-9467
   Fort Wayne (G-4882)

Ecolab Inc.. G..... 317 567-2876
   Fishers (G-4508)

Ecolab Inc.. E..... 260 359-3280
   Huntington (G-7308)

Ecolab Inc.. G..... 260 375-4710
   Warren (G-16297)

Ginas Essentials.. G..... 812 406-3276
   Nabb (G-12574)

Hickory Hill Soap.. G..... 574 825-9853
   Middlebury (G-11721)

▲ Holloway House Inc.................................. E..... 317 485-4272
   Fortville (G-5599)

J 2 Systems and Supply LLC........................ G..... 317 602-3940
   Indianapolis (G-8601)

Kt Soap Products LLC................................... F..... 219 344-5871
   La Porte (G-10437)

Lather Up LLC... G..... 260 638-4978
   Markle (G-11357)

Metalworking Lubricants Co.......................... C..... 317 269-2444
   Indianapolis (G-8891)

Monofoilusa LLC... G..... 317 340-9951
   Elwood (G-3832)

National Handicapped Workshop.................. F..... 765 287-8331
   Muncie (G-12468)

Nkahoots Bdy Bath Butters LLC................... G..... 317 559-2442
   Crawfordsville (G-2595)

Original Brdford Soap Wrks Inc.................... D..... 812 342-6854
   Columbus (G-2366)

Paradigm Industries Inc................................. G..... 317 574-8590
   Carmel (G-1714)

◆ Phoenix Brands LLC.................................. F..... 203 975-0319
   Indianapolis (G-9138)

Serendipity Sanctuary.................................... G..... 765 541-2364
   Richmond (G-14203)

Simply Natural By J LLC................................ G..... 317 464-7299
   Indianapolis (G-9442)

Soapy Soap Co... F..... 812 269-8812
   Terre Haute (G-15700)

Soapy Soap Company.................................... G..... 812 269-8812
   Terre Haute (G-15701)

Tall Cotton Marketing LLC............................. G..... 312 320-5862
   La Porte (G-10486)

Unilever United States Inc............................. A..... 219 659-3200
   Hammond (G-7025)

▲ Vintage Chemical Inc................................ G..... 260 745-7272
   Fort Wayne (G-5533)

Warsaw Chemical Company Inc................... D..... 574 267-3251
   Warsaw (G-16442)

Wayne Concept Mfg Inc................................. G..... 260 482-8615
   Fort Wayne (G-5552)

Willow Way LLC.. G..... 765 886-4642
   Hagerstown (G-6848)

▲ Yushiro Manufacturing Amer Inc.............. E..... 317 398-9862
   Shelbyville (G-14816)

2842 Polishes and sanitation goods

3M Company.. B..... 317 692-6666
   Indianapolis (G-7388)

A 2 Z Universal Solutions.............................. G..... 317 496-7435
   Union City (G-15846)

◆ Abro Industries Inc................................... E..... 574 232-8289
   South Bend (G-14933)

American Hydro Systems Inc........................ F..... 866 357-5063
   Fort Wayne (G-4755)

Andersons Agriculture Group LP.................. F..... 765 564-6135
   Delphi (G-2890)

Aon(all or Nothing) LLC................................. G..... 219 405-0163
   Indianapolis (G-7524)

Aqua Utility Services LLC.............................. G..... 812 284-9243
   New Albany (G-12690)

Arden Companies LLC................................... D..... 260 747-1657
   Fort Wayne (G-4770)

Astec Corp... G..... 317 872-7550
   Indianapolis (G-7557)

Bane-Clene Corp... G..... 317 546-5448
   Indianapolis (G-7594)

Bane-Clene Corp... F..... 317 546-5448
   Indianapolis (G-7595)

◆ Blitz Manufacturing Co Ind...................... D..... 812 284-2548
   Jeffersonville (G-9944)

Blue Ribbon Products Inc.............................. G..... 317 972-7970
   Indianapolis (G-7648)

Blueprint Restoration LLC.............................. G..... 301 730-4727
   Indianapolis (G-7650)

◆ Brulin & Company Inc............................... D..... 317 923-3211
   Indianapolis (G-7691)

Brulin Holding Company Inc......................... E..... 317 923-3211
   Indianapolis (G-7692)

Chem-Dry of Allen County............................. G..... 260 490-2705
   Fort Wayne (G-4844)

Craft Laboratories Inc.................................... E..... 260 432-9467
   Fort Wayne (G-4882)

Custom Bottling & Packg Inc......................... E..... 877 401-7195
   Ashley (G-332)

Danny Webb Plumbing................................... G..... 574 936-2746
   Plymouth (G-13769)

Disaster Masters Inc...................................... G..... 317 385-2216
   Fishers (G-4504)

Dry Inc... E..... 503 977-9204
   Fort Wayne (G-4929)

Ecolab Inc.. E..... 260 359-3280
   Huntington (G-7308)

▼ F B C Inc... E..... 574 848-5288
   Bristol (G-1260)

First Image... G..... 219 791-9900
   Merrillville (G-11517)

Geberts Cleaning Service.............................. G..... 812 254-4658
   Washington (G-16480)

▲ Gillis Company... G..... 574 273-9086
   Granger (G-6349)

Global Ozone Innovations LLC..................... G..... 574 294-5797
   Elkhart (G-3383)

Golden Ventures Inc....................................... E..... 317 872-2705
   Indianapolis (G-8300)

▲ Holloway House Inc.................................. E..... 317 485-4272
   Fortville (G-5599)

Ideal Inc... G..... 765 457-6222
   Kokomo (G-10284)

Iron Out Inc... E..... 800 654-0791
   Fort Wayne (G-5119)

J 2 Systems and Supply LLC........................ G..... 317 602-3940
   Indianapolis (G-8601)

Jzj Services LLC... G..... 574 642-3182
   Goshen (G-6181)

Jzj Services LLC... E..... 812 424-8268
   Evansville (G-4147)

K2 Industrial Services Inc............................. F..... 219 933-1100
   Highland (G-7141)

Kings-Qlity Rstrtion Svcs LLC....................... F..... 812 944-4347
   New Albany (G-12760)

Kleen-Rite Supply Inc.................................... F..... 812 422-7483
   Evansville (G-4156)

L&S Sanitation Service.................................. G..... 765 932-5410
   Rushville (G-14404)

Metalworking Lubricants Co.......................... C..... 317 269-2444
   Indianapolis (G-8891)

Michael Montgomery...................................... G..... 317 478-6080
   Indianapolis (G-8898)

Modrak Products Company Inc.................... F..... 219 838-0308
   Gary (G-5985)

Mold Removers LLC....................................... G..... 317 846-0977
   Indianapolis (G-8946)

Monofoilusa LLC... G..... 317 340-9951
   Elwood (G-3832)

National Handicapped Workshop.................. F..... 765 287-8331
   Muncie (G-12468)

National Products LLC................................... G..... 219 393-5536
   Kingsbury (G-10182)

NCH Corporation... F..... 317 899-3660
   Indianapolis (G-8996)

Online Packaging Incorporated..................... E..... 219 872-0925
   Michigan City (G-11648)

Opportunities Inc.. G..... 574 518-0606
   North Webster (G-13311)

Osborn LLC... D..... 414 277-9300
   Richmond (G-14178)

Parts Cleaning Tech LLC............................... G..... 317 243-4205
   Indianapolis (G-9095)

Pools of Fun Inc... E..... 317 843-0337
   Noblesville (G-13156)

Powerclean Inc.. E..... 260 483-1375
   Fort Wayne (G-5329)

Professionally Polished LLC......................... G..... 219 779-7664
   Crown Point (G-2738)

Reckitt Benckiser LLC.................................... E..... 812 429-5000
   Evansville (G-4276)

SIC SECTION   28 CHEMICALS AND ALLIED PRODUCTS

Reeders Cleaners Inc .... G 812 945-4833
  Clarksville *(G-2030)*
Relevo Labs LLC .... G 317 900-6949
  Carmel *(G-1739)*
Rexford Rand Corp .... E 219 872-5561
  Michigan City *(G-11657)*
Roebic Laboratories Inc .... F 317 578-0135
  Fishers *(G-4598)*
Sand Dcl LLC .... G 260 459-9565
  Fort Wayne *(G-5399)*
Servaas Inc .... G 317 633-2020
  Indianapolis *(G-9405)*
◆ Servaas Laboratories Inc .... E 317 636-7760
  Indianapolis *(G-9406)*
Smart Systems .... G 800 348-0823
  Mishawaka *(G-11997)*
Sorbtech Inc .... G 812 944-9108
  Clarksville *(G-2037)*
Steritech-Usa Inc .... G 260 745-7272
  Fort Wayne *(G-5441)*
Tate Soaps & Surfactants Inc .... G 765 868-4488
  Kokomo *(G-10347)*
Tgc Auto Care Products Inc .... G 765 962-7725
  Richmond *(G-14216)*
◆ W J Hagerty & Sons Ltd Inc .... E 574 288-4991
  South Bend *(G-15303)*
Warsaw Chemical Company Inc .... D 574 267-3251
  Warsaw *(G-16442)*
Wayne Chemical Inc .... E 260 432-1120
  Fort Wayne *(G-5551)*
▲ Yushiro Manufacturing Amer Inc .... E 317 398-9862
  Shelbyville *(G-14816)*

2843 Surface active agents

▼ Classic Chemical Corp .... G 812 934-3289
  Indianapolis *(G-7819)*
Dse Inc .... E 812 376-0310
  Columbus *(G-2291)*
J & B Sales & Induction Srvcs .... G 765 965-2500
  Richmond *(G-14142)*

2844 Toilet preparations

103 Collection LLC .... G 800 896-2945
  Schererville *(G-14510)*
A & AS Beauty Barn LLC .... G 812 589-8559
  Evansville *(G-3860)*
Accra-Pac Inc .... G 574 295-0000
  Elkhart *(G-3149)*
Adjust Your Crown Hair Care Pd .... G 317 970-1144
  Indianapolis *(G-7433)*
Aesthtcally Pleasing Skin Soak .... G 317 551-0156
  Indianapolis *(G-7454)*
All Good Things LLC .... G 812 871-2844
  Madison *(G-11199)*
All Good Things Soaps and .... G 812 801-4700
  Madison *(G-11200)*
All You Naturally LLC .... G 574 215-5425
  Elkhart *(G-3164)*
Ambre Blends .... G 317 257-0202
  Indianapolis *(G-7496)*
Amorlai Organics LLC .... G 219 595-9102
  Highland *(G-7121)*
▲ Annie Oakley Enterprises Inc .... F 260 894-7100
  Ligonier *(G-11004)*
Apg Inc .... D 574 295-0000
  Elkhart *(G-3185)*
Bath & Body Works LLC .... F 317 209-1517
  Avon *(G-506)*
Bath & Body Works LLC .... F 317 468-0834
  Greenfield *(G-6469)*
Bath & Body Works LLC .... F 219 531-2146
  Valparaiso *(G-15910)*

Be Body Butters LLC .... G 317 362-9248
  Indianapolis *(G-7602)*
Blessed Humbled Beginnings LLC ..... G 219 255-3820
  Merrillville *(G-11490)*
Blush Bath Bombs By Amor .... G 219 313-3993
  Crown Point *(G-2657)*
Bodycare Bodega LLC .... G 317 643-3562
  Indianapolis *(G-7653)*
Bunny Beautiful Cosmetics LLC .... G 219 433-1698
  East Chicago *(G-2994)*
Burst of Beauty LLC .... G 708 970-2181
  Gary *(G-5907)*
Burton Debiceious .... G 317 495-0123
  Indianapolis *(G-7702)*
Bush Pilot Beard Balm .... G 574 535-4949
  Goshen *(G-6106)*
Carmel Indiana .... G 317 575-9942
  Carmel *(G-1580)*
Carmichael Solutions LLC .... G 317 356-2883
  Indianapolis *(G-7747)*
Century Pharmaceuticals Inc .... E 317 849-4210
  Indianapolis *(G-7775)*
Chanel J Luxury Collection LLC .... G 470 210-4706
  Indianapolis *(G-7784)*
Classique Hair Style .... G 317 738-2104
  Franklin *(G-5721)*
Cocoaloca Cosmetics LLC .... G 352 246-6629
  Fort Wayne *(G-4864)*
Conopco Inc .... D 219 659-3200
  Hammond *(G-6904)*
Corsica Scents LLC .... G 603 219-1287
  Carmel *(G-1597)*
Damor & Co LLC .... G 317 790-8360
  Indianapolis *(G-7947)*
Darden Corporation Corp .... G 317 376-5724
  Indianapolis *(G-7949)*
Dee Scents LLC .... G 765 275-2242
  Wingate *(G-16906)*
Dentisse Inc .... G 260 444-3046
  Fort Wayne *(G-4915)*
Desirable Scents .... G 317 504-4976
  Lafayette *(G-10570)*
Diamond State Naturals LLC .... G 479 970-4755
  Indianapolis *(G-7971)*
Dianas Beauty Salon .... G 812 699-7904
  Bloomfield *(G-745)*
Divine Essentials LLC .... G 765 400-8609
  Muncie *(G-12385)*
Earth Essentials LLC .... G 260 479-0115
  Roanoke *(G-14262)*
Earthly-Love .... G 708 896-0191
  Hammond *(G-6918)*
Energy Delivery Solutions LLC .... G 502 271-8753
  Jeffersonville *(G-9977)*
Essence In Harmony .... G 317 727-6420
  Indianapolis *(G-8133)*
Essence Scents LLC .... G 317 679-5627
  Indianapolis *(G-8134)*
Gems Quality Extensions LLC .... G 219 501-6320
  East Chicago *(G-3010)*
Get Lathered .... G 317 201-7291
  Indianapolis *(G-8280)*
Honey Pot Development .... G 260 318-0001
  Kendallville *(G-10119)*
Icon Beauty Supply Inc .... G 317 209-6550
  Noblesville *(G-13099)*
Indiana Nanotech LLC .... G 317 385-1578
  Indianapolis *(G-8485)*
Indiana Soap Company .... G 317 448-5295
  Greenfield *(G-6515)*
Jerrels & Company LLC .... G 317 691-6045
  Carmel *(G-1677)*

Kbshimmer Bath and Body Inc .... G 317 979-2307
  Terre Haute *(G-15624)*
Kenra Professional LLC .... F 800 428-8073
  Indianapolis *(G-8673)*
Komun Scents .... G 317 308-0714
  Indianapolis *(G-8701)*
Legacy Enterprises Inc .... G 219 484-9483
  Merrillville *(G-11531)*
Love-Toi LLC .... G 317 537-7635
  Anderson *(G-149)*
Lume Deodorant .... G 623 227-8724
  New Albany *(G-12768)*
Mahogany Scents .... G 574 271-1364
  South Bend *(G-15136)*
Majesty Hair Care System LLC .... G 317 900-6789
  Indianapolis *(G-8818)*
▲ Malibu Wellness Inc .... E 317 624-7560
  Indianapolis *(G-8821)*
Maple Hill Naturals LLC .... G 765 427-9413
  Lafayette *(G-10642)*
▲ Maverick Packaging Inc .... E 574 264-2891
  Elkhart *(G-3519)*
Monarch Elite Naturals LLC .... G 219 201-1816
  Merrillville *(G-11545)*
My Felicity Creations LLC .... G 317 363-3269
  Martinsville *(G-11417)*
Natural Essentials .... G 310 493-6509
  Indianapolis *(G-8990)*
Naturespire LLC .... G 463 266-0395
  Indianapolis *(G-8992)*
North Coast Organics LLC .... G 260 246-0289
  Fort Wayne *(G-5274)*
Nspire LLC .... G 219 301-2446
  Gary *(G-5987)*
Oil Palace Limited .... G 317 679-9187
  Indianapolis *(G-9043)*
Pieniadze Inc .... G 888 226-6241
  Zionsville *(G-17041)*
Plz Corp .... D 317 788-0750
  Indianapolis *(G-9156)*
Pom By ARI LLC .... G 312 978-1668
  Munster *(G-12559)*
Raemarie Essentials LLC .... G 219 248-5482
  Portage *(G-13908)*
Redmaster Fusion LLC .... G 260 273-5819
  Fort Wayne *(G-5374)*
Relevo Inc .... G 317 644-0099
  Carmel *(G-1738)*
Relevo Labs LLC .... G 317 900-6949
  Carmel *(G-1739)*
Rugged Company .... G 317 441-0927
  Anderson *(G-187)*
Sazzys Place LLC .... G 317 414-6332
  Indianapolis *(G-9381)*
Seductive Lifestyle LLC .... G 708 990-0720
  Gary *(G-6008)*
Serendipity Sanctuary .... G 765 541-2364
  Richmond *(G-14203)*
Signature Formulations LLC .... G 317 878-4086
  Trafalgar *(G-15833)*
Simply Saidahs LLC .... G 317 650-4256
  Carmel *(G-1762)*
Sincerely Different LLC .... G 574 292-1727
  Granger *(G-6378)*
Soapy Soap Company .... G 812 269-8812
  Terre Haute *(G-15701)*
Star Nail .... G 765 453-0743
  Kokomo *(G-10338)*
Sweet Scents LLC .... G 219 902-6853
  Evansville *(G-4338)*
Tonis Touch LLC .... G 317 992-1280
  Plainfield *(G-13737)*

28 CHEMICALS AND ALLIED PRODUCTS

Tri-Pac Inc..C.....574 855-2197
South Bend *(G-15290)*

Tri-Pac Inc..C.....574 855-2197
South Bend *(G-15291)*

Universal Packg Systems Inc.....................C.....260 829-6721
Orland *(G-13374)*

Vera Bradley Inc...B.....877 708-8372
Roanoke *(G-14272)*

Well Groomed Mens Care LLC..................G.....317 908-4451
Indianapolis *(G-9747)*

Wholeaf Aloe Distributors...........................G.....219 322-7217
Schererville *(G-14547)*

Wild Child Organics LLC..............................G.....574 213-5204
South Bend *(G-15306)*

With Love Bath Bombs................................G.....317 523-9197
Indianapolis *(G-9779)*

2851 Paints and allied products

3b Photonics LLC..G.....574 702-2620
Logansport *(G-11053)*

▲ Abtrex Industries Inc................................F.....734 728-0550
South Bend *(G-14934)*

Aci Construction Company Inc.................E.....317 549-1833
Indianapolis *(G-7422)*

Advanced Protective Tech LLC..................G.....888 531-4527
Valparaiso *(G-15892)*

Ampacet Corporation..................................E.....812 466-9828
Terre Haute *(G-15543)*

Ampacet Corporation..................................D.....812 466-5231
Terre Haute *(G-15544)*

Aoc LLC..D.....219 465-4384
Valparaiso *(G-15900)*

Baril Coatings Usa LLC...............................E.....260 665-8431
Angola *(G-233)*

Belden Inc..C.....724 222-7060
Richmond *(G-14092)*

Bloomington Con Surfaces Corp..............G.....812 345-0011
Bloomington *(G-810)*

Bondline Adhesives Inc..............................F.....812 423-4651
Evansville *(G-3939)*

Chad Simons...G.....219 405-1620
Chesterton *(G-1909)*

Connersville Paint Mfgco...........................G.....765 825-4111
Connersville *(G-2433)*

Contego International Inc...........................G.....317 580-0665
Carmel *(G-1594)*

◆ Contego International Inc........................G.....574 223-5989
Rochester *(G-14283)*

Cp Inc..E.....765 825-4111
Connersville *(G-2434)*

D & L Industrial Finishes Inc......................G.....765 458-5157
Liberty *(G-10987)*

▲ Davies-Imperial Coatings Inc.................E.....219 933-0877
Hammond *(G-6911)*

Deco Coatings Inc..E.....317 889-9290
Indianapolis *(G-7960)*

Dist Council 91..G.....812 962-9191
Evansville *(G-4014)*

Dse Inc..E.....812 376-0310
Columbus *(G-2291)*

Dynamic Finish Solutions LLC..................G.....574 529-0121
Bremen *(G-1189)*

Freeband Custom Paint LLC......................G.....219 216-2553
Indianapolis *(G-8226)*

Icl Specialty Products Inc..........................G.....219 933-1560
Hammond *(G-6951)*

◆ IVc Industrial Coatings Inc.....................C.....812 442-5080
Brazil *(G-1149)*

Katalyst Corporation...................................G.....317 783-6500
Beech Grove *(G-696)*

Keystone Industrial Flrg LLC.....................G.....317 403-8747
Avon *(G-533)*

▲ LSI Wallcovering Inc................................D.....502 458-1502
New Albany *(G-12767)*

Lyondllbsell Advnced Plymers I................E.....574 935-5131
Plymouth *(G-13794)*

◆ Magnum International Inc.......................E.....708 889-9999
Crown Point *(G-2721)*

▲ Margco International LLC.......................G.....317 568-4274
Indianapolis *(G-8828)*

Masson Inc..F.....317 632-8021
Indianapolis *(G-8848)*

Mautz Paint Factory....................................G.....574 289-2497
South Bend *(G-15141)*

Midwest Pipecoating Inc............................D.....219 322-4564
Schererville *(G-14535)*

▲ Nanochem Technologies LLC................E.....574 970-2436
Elkhart *(G-3563)*

Ncp Coatings Inc...G.....574 255-9678
Mishawaka *(G-11964)*

Pendry Coatings LLC..................................G.....574 268-2956
Warsaw *(G-16410)*

Pinder Polyurethane & Plas Inc................G.....219 397-8248
East Chicago *(G-3034)*

Polytek Development Corp........................G.....317 494-6420
Franklin *(G-5767)*

Powder Blue...F.....918 835-2629
Corydon *(G-2512)*

PPG Architectural Finishes Inc.................G.....317 745-0427
Avon *(G-545)*

PPG Architectural Finishes Inc.................G.....317 575-8011
Carmel *(G-1722)*

PPG Architectural Finishes Inc.................G.....317 575-8011
Carmel *(G-1723)*

PPG Architectural Finishes Inc.................G.....317 471-8250
Carmel *(G-1724)*

PPG Architectural Finishes Inc.................G.....812 473-0339
Evansville *(G-4251)*

PPG Architectural Finishes Inc.................G.....260 436-1854
Fort Wayne *(G-5330)*

PPG Architectural Finishes Inc.................G.....260 436-1854
Fort Wayne *(G-5331)*

PPG Architectural Finishes Inc.................G.....260 373-2373
Fort Wayne *(G-5332)*

PPG Architectural Finishes Inc.................G.....317 634-2547
Indianapolis *(G-9168)*

PPG Architectural Finishes Inc.................G.....317 787-9393
Indianapolis *(G-9169)*

PPG Architectural Finishes Inc.................G.....765 447-9334
Lafayette *(G-10669)*

PPG Architectural Finishes Inc.................G.....812 232-0672
Terre Haute *(G-15664)*

PPG Architectural Finishes Inc.................G.....812 882-0440
Vincennes *(G-16146)*

PPG Holdings Inc...G.....317 663-4590
Indianapolis *(G-9170)*

PPG Industries Inc.......................................G.....317 745-0427
Avon *(G-546)*

PPG Industries Inc.......................................G.....317 870-0345
Carmel *(G-1725)*

PPG Industries Inc.......................................G.....812 948-9253
Clarksville *(G-2026)*

PPG Industries Inc.......................................G.....812 867-6601
Evansville *(G-4252)*

PPG Industries Inc.......................................G.....812 424-4774
Evansville *(G-4253)*

PPG Industries Inc.......................................G.....812 473-0339
Evansville *(G-4254)*

PPG Industries Inc.......................................G.....317 598-9448
Fishers *(G-4581)*

PPG Industries Inc.......................................G.....317 577-2344
Fishers *(G-4582)*

PPG Industries Inc.......................................G.....260 373-2873
Fort Wayne *(G-5333)*

PPG Industries Inc.......................................E.....260 432-6900
Fort Wayne *(G-5334)*

PPG Industries Inc.......................................G.....317 251-9494
Indianapolis *(G-9171)*

PPG Industries Inc.......................................G.....317 267-0511
Indianapolis *(G-9172)*

PPG Industries Inc.......................................G.....317 897-3836
Indianapolis *(G-9173)*

PPG Industries Inc.......................................G.....317 787-9393
Indianapolis *(G-9174)*

PPG Industries Inc.......................................G.....317 546-5714
Indianapolis *(G-9175)*

PPG Industries Inc.......................................G.....765 282-0316
Muncie *(G-12476)*

PPG Industries Inc.......................................G.....812 944-4164
New Albany *(G-12797)*

PPG Industries Inc.......................................G.....812 232-0672
Terre Haute *(G-15665)*

PPG Industries Inc.......................................G.....812 882-0440
Vincennes *(G-16147)*

PPG Industries Inc.......................................G.....317 867-5934
Westfield *(G-16719)*

Precoat Metals..F.....219 763-1504
Portage *(G-13906)*

◆ Protech Powder Coatings Inc................G.....814 456-1243
Liberty *(G-10997)*

Quality Coatings Inc...................................F.....812 925-3314
Chandler *(G-1865)*

▲ Rbc Holding Inc..F.....317 340-3845
Greenwood *(G-6759)*

Red Spot Paint & Varnish Co.....................G.....812 428-9100
Evansville *(G-4278)*

Red Spot Paint & Varnish Co.....................G.....812 428-9100
Evansville *(G-4279)*

Red Spot Paint & Varnish Co.....................G.....812 428-9100
Evansville *(G-4280)*

▲ Red Spot Paint & Varnish Co.................B.....812 428-9100
Evansville *(G-4281)*

Redspot Paint and Varnish Co..................E.....812 428-9100
Evansville *(G-4282)*

Rollie Williams Paint Spot..........................G.....812 827-2488
Jasper *(G-9906)*

Sansher Corporation...................................G.....260 484-2000
Fort Wayne *(G-5400)*

Snow Management Group.........................G.....574 252-5253
Mishawaka *(G-12000)*

Sonoco Products Company.......................D.....812 526-5511
Edinburgh *(G-3105)*

Stoncor Group Inc.......................................G.....260 747-9724
Fort Wayne *(G-5444)*

Technicote Inc..E.....812 466-9844
Terre Haute *(G-15724)*

Tnemec Company Inc.................................G.....317 884-1806
Greenwood *(G-6774)*

Transcendia Inc..C.....765 935-1520
Richmond *(G-14220)*

United Coatings Mfg Co.............................G.....317 845-8830
Indianapolis *(G-9679)*

▲ United Coatings Tech Inc.......................F.....574 287-4774
South Bend *(G-15296)*

United Minerals and Prpts Inc..................G.....812 838-5236
Mount Vernon *(G-12325)*

Van Zandt Enterprises Inc.........................F.....812 423-3511
Evansville *(G-4366)*

Vanex Inc...E.....618 244-1413
Brazil *(G-1169)*

▼ Weatherall Indiana Inc............................F.....812 256-3378
Charlestown *(G-1896)*

Winslow-Browning Inc...............................E.....765 458-5157
Liberty *(G-11000)*

Woodys Paint Spot Ltd...............................G.....574 255-0348
Bremen *(G-1231)*

28 CHEMICALS AND ALLIED PRODUCTS

Worwag Coatings.................................. G 765 746-6037
  Lafayette (G-10719)
Wurth Additive Group Inc .... F 551 269-7695
  Greenwood (G-6782)

2861 Gum and wood chemicals

Arch Wood Protection Inc..................... G 219 464-3949
  Valparaiso (G-15904)
Jefferson Homebuilders Inc.................. G 317 398-3125
  Shelbyville (G-14765)
Pag Holdings Inc .... G 814 446-2525
  Brazil (G-1161)
◆ Pag Holdings LLC............................. G..... 317 290-5006
  Indianapolis (G-9087)
Wholesale Hrdwood Intriors Inc............ F 317 867-3660
  Westfield (G-16740)

2865 Cyclic crudes and intermediates

Ampacet Corporation............................ D 812 466-5231
  Terre Haute (G-15544)
AURORIUM LLC.................................. E 317 247-8141
  Indianapolis (G-7566)
Eco Services Operations Corp.............. E 219 932-7651
  Hammond (G-6919)
◆ Eidp Inc... A 833 267-8382
  Indianapolis (G-8064)
Flint CPS Inks North Amer LLC............ E 317 870-4422
  Indianapolis (G-8204)
Futurex Industries Inc.......................... E 812 299-5708
  Terre Haute (G-15593)
▲ Futurex Industries Inc..................... C 765 498-3900
  Bloomingdale (G-760)
Hammond Group Inc............................ G 219 931-9360
  Hammond (G-6939)
▲ Holland Colours Americas Inc......... D 765 935-0329
  Richmond (G-14135)
Icl Specialty Products Inc.................... G 219 933-1560
  Hammond (G-6951)
▲ Kibbechem Inc................................. E 574 266-1234
  Elkhart (G-3454)
Pfizer Inc... D 212 733-2323
  Terre Haute (G-15660)
Styrene Solutions LLC......................... G 270 317-2427
  Mishawaka (G-12009)
Styrene Solutions LLC......................... G 574 876-4610
  Elkhart (G-3703)
◆ Vertellus Health & Specia................ A 317 247-8141
  Indianapolis (G-9709)

2869 Industrial organic chemicals, nec

Abr Enterprises LLC............................ G 808 352-4658
  Roanoke (G-14255)
ACS Technical Products Inc................ E 219 924-4370
  Griffith (G-6786)
All American Ex Solutions LLC............ E 317 789-3070
  Indianapolis (G-7472)
Alternative Fuel Solutions LLC............. F 260 224-1965
  Huntington (G-7297)
Ambandash... G 260 415-1709
  Fort Wayne (G-4749)
AMP Americas LLC............................. G 312 300-6700
  Fair Oaks (G-4394)
Andersons Clymers Ethanol LLC......... G 574 722-2627
  Logansport (G-11057)
Aurorium Foreign Holdings LLC.......... G 317 247-8141
  Indianapolis (G-7563)
Aurorium Holdings LLC...................... G 317 247-8141
  Indianapolis (G-7564)
Aurorium LLC..................................... G 317 247-8141
  Indianapolis (G-7565)
AURORIUM LLC................................. E 317 247-8141
  Indianapolis (G-7566)

Aurorium Ppc Holdings LLC................ G 317 247-8141
  Indianapolis (G-7567)
Aventine Renewable Energy................ G 812 838-9598
  Mount Vernon (G-12291)
Beckman Coulter Inc........................... D 317 471-8029
  Indianapolis (G-7606)
Bio-Alternative LLC............................. E 765 793-5731
  Covington (G-2527)
Biodyne-Midwest LLC......................... F 888 970-0955
  Fort Wayne (G-4801)
▲ Blue Grass Chemical Spc LLC........ F 812 948-1115
  New Albany (G-12703)
Brown & Brown Fuel............................ G 219 984-5173
  Chalmers (G-1857)
Cardinal Ethanol LLC.......................... D 765 964-3137
  Union City (G-15850)
▼ Classic Chemical Corp.................... G 812 934-3289
  Indianapolis (G-7819)
Coeus Technology Inc......................... G 765 203-2304
  Anderson (G-96)
Danisco USA Inc................................. D 812 299-6700
  Terre Haute (G-15576)
Dover Chemical Corporation............... G 219 852-0042
  Hammond (G-6914)
Eco Services Operations Corp............ E 219 932-7651
  Hammond (G-6919)
Elwood Fuel and Cigs LLC.................. G 317 244-5744
  Indianapolis (G-8098)
Energy Quest Inc................................. G 317 827-9212
  Indianapolis (G-8117)
Enzyme Solutions Inc.......................... G 800 523-1323
  Fort Wayne (G-4955)
◆ Enzyme Solutions Inc..................... F 260 553-9100
  Garrett (G-5861)
Evonik Corporation.............................. A 765 477-4300
  Lafayette (G-10575)
Fuel Vm LLC....................................... G 317 828-6060
  Indianapolis (G-8239)
▲ Gdc Inc... C 574 533-3128
  Goshen (G-6143)
Global Energy Resources LLC............ G 219 712-2556
  Valparaiso (G-15957)
Grain Processing Corporation............. E 812 257-0480
  Washington (G-16481)
Green Plains Grain Company LLC...... E 812 985-7480
  Mount Vernon (G-12298)
Green Plains Inc.................................. E 812 985-7480
  Mount Vernon (G-12299)
Green Tech.. G 260 350-0089
  Lagrange (G-10740)
Green Tech America Inc...................... G 765 588-3834
  West Lafayette (G-16587)
Hoosier Ethanol Energy LLC............... G 260 407-6161
  Fort Wayne (G-5077)
Hoosier Penn Oil Co Inc...................... G 812 284-9433
  Jeffersonville (G-9998)
Hucks Food Fuel.................................. F 812 683-5566
  Huntingburg (G-7281)
International Fuel Systems.................. G 317 345-3302
  Franklin (G-5749)
Iroquois Bio-Energy Co LLC................ G 219 866-2928
  Rensselaer (G-14054)
Jerry L Fuelling................................... G 317 709-6978
  Zionsville (G-17023)
Louis Dreyfus Co AG Inds LLC........... A
  Claypool (G-2055)
Lyondllbsell Advnced Plymers I........... D 219 392-3375
  East Chicago (G-3028)
Lyondllbsell Advnced Plymers I........... D 713 309-7148
  Evansville (G-4180)
Lyondllbsell Advnced Plymers I........... D 812 253-5203
  Evansville (G-4181)

Midwest Bio-Products Inc.................... G 765 793-3426
  Covington (G-2531)
Mirteq Holdings Inc............................. G 260 490-3706
  Fort Wayne (G-5232)
Momentive Performance Mtls Inc........ E 612 499-3902
  Fort Wayne (G-5240)
Momentive Performance Mtls Inc........ B 260 357-2000
  Garrett (G-5872)
Mr Fuel.. G 317 531-0891
  Spiceland (G-15378)
New Energy Corp................................ C 574 233-3116
  South Bend (G-15165)
Ohio Vly Fuel Injction Svc Inc............. G 812 987-5857
  Charlestown (G-1889)
▼ Omicron Biochemicals Inc.............. E 574 287-6910
  South Bend (G-15177)
▲ Org Chem Group LLC..................... D 812 464-4446
  Evansville (G-4228)
Owens Fuel Center.............................. G 260 358-1211
  Huntington (G-7351)
Poet Borefining - Portland LLC........... G 260 726-2681
  Portland (G-13961)
Poet Brfining - Alexandria LLC........... G 765 724-4384
  Alexandria (G-57)
Poet Brfining - Cloverdale LLC........... D 765 795-3235
  Cloverdale (G-2093)
Poet Brfning - N Mnchester LLC........ G 260 774-3532
  North Manchester (G-13247)
Poet Brfining - Shelbyville LLC........... G 317 699-4199
  Shelbyville (G-14786)
Precision Medical Inds Inc.................. G 260 234-3112
  Albion (G-41)
Quality Fuel Solutions.......................... G 574 293-1423
  Elkhart (G-3631)
Racing Fuel Ignite............................... G 765 733-0833
  Marion (G-11333)
Reilly Industries Inc............................. G 317 247-8141
  Indianapolis (G-9284)
Rudys Food & Fuel LLC...................... G 812 547-2530
  Tell City (G-15516)
Ryan Fuelling....................................... G 260 403-6450
  Fort Wayne (G-5392)
Skyway Fuels Inc................................ G 219 575-7624
  La Porte (G-10484)
Southern Fuel LLC.............................. G 219 689-3552
  Rensselaer (G-14069)
◆ Swift Fuels LLC............................... G 765 464-8336
  West Lafayette (G-16632)
Top Fuel Crossfit Inc.......................... G 219 281-7001
  Crown Point (G-2765)
◆ Triangle Rubber Co LLC.................. C 574 533-3118
  Goshen (G-6272)
US Enzyme LLC.................................. G 317 268-4975
  Avon (G-556)
US Silicones LLC................................ G 260 497-0819
  Fort Wayne (G-5522)
US Silicones LLC................................ F 260 480-0171
  Fort Wayne (G-5523)
Valero Renewable Fuels Co LLC........ D 260 846-0011
  Bluffton (G-1068)
Valero Renewable Fuels Co LLC........ G 812 833-3900
  Mount Vernon (G-12326)
◆ VSI Liquidating Inc.......................... G 317 247-8141
  Indianapolis (G-9731)
Williams Distribution LLC.................... G 317 749-0006
  Indianapolis (G-9767)

2873 Nitrogenous fertilizers

Andersons Agriculture Group LP........ G 574 626-2522
  Galveston (G-5851)
Andersons Agriculture Group LP........ G 574 753-4974
  Logansport (G-11056)

Employee Codes: A=Over 500 employees, B=251-500
C=101-250, D=51-100, E=20-50, F=10-19, G=1-9

28 CHEMICALS AND ALLIED PRODUCTS

▲ Hello Nature Usa Inc..................... G..... 765 615-1900
  Anderson (G-126)
Keystone Cooperative Inc................. G..... 765 659-2596
  Frankfort (G-5678)
◆ Knox Fertilizer Company Inc............ C..... 574 772-6275
  Knox (G-10213)
Scotts Miracle-Gro Company.............. G..... 219 984-6110
  Reynolds (G-14076)
Spawn Great Mate Inc...................... G..... 812 948-2174
  New Albany (G-12816)
Terremax Farms LLC........................ G..... 812 242-0276
  Terre Haute (G-15728)

2874 Phosphatic fertilizers

Andersons Agriculture Group LP.......... G..... 574 626-2522
  Galveston (G-5851)
Andersons Agriculture Group LP.......... G..... 574 753-4974
  Logansport (G-11056)
Wilson Fertilizer & Grain Inc............. G..... 574 223-3175
  Rochester (G-14333)

2875 Fertilizers, mixing only

Agbest Cooperative Inc..................... G..... 765 358-3388
  Gaston (G-6043)
Andersons Agriculture Group LP.......... G..... 574 626-2522
  Galveston (G-5851)
Andersons Agriculture Group LP.......... G..... 574 753-4974
  Logansport (G-11056)
Andersons Fertilizer Service............... G..... 765 538-3285
  Romney (G-14379)
Bundy Bros and Sons Inc................... F..... 812 966-2551
  Medora (G-11462)
Clunette Elevator Co Inc................... F..... 574 858-2281
  Leesburg (G-10952)
Creative Ldscp & Compost Co............. G..... 317 776-2909
  Noblesville (G-13065)
Earth Mama Compost........................ G..... 317 759-4589
  Indianapolis (G-8033)
Earthcare LLC................................ G..... 812 455-9258
  Evansville (G-4025)
Elvin L Nuest Sales and Servic............ G..... 219 863-5216
  Francesville (G-5639)
Farmer Automatic America Inc............ G..... 574 857-3116
  Rochester (G-14289)
Greencycle Inc............................... G..... 317 773-3350
  Noblesville (G-13089)
Keystone Cooperative Inc.................. G..... 317 861-5080
  Fountaintown (G-5615)
Keystone Cooperative Inc.................. G..... 765 489-4141
  Hagerstown (G-6838)
Keystone Cooperative Inc.................. G..... 765 249-2233
  Michigantown (G-11691)
◆ Keystone Cooperative Inc............... C..... 800 525-0272
  Indianapolis (G-8680)
Kova Fertilizer Inc........................... E..... 812 663-5081
  Greensburg (G-6613)
Laughery Valley AG Co-Op Inc............ G..... 812 689-4401
  Osgood (G-13412)
Md/Lf Incorporated......................... G..... 765 575-8130
  New Castle (G-12874)
Miles Farm Supply LLC..................... D..... 812 359-4463
  Boonville (G-1090)
Nachurs Alpine Solutions LLC............ G..... 812 738-1333
  Corydon (G-2507)
Northwest Farm Fertilizers................ G..... 219 785-2331
  Westville (G-16764)
Ostler Enterprises Inc...................... G..... 765 656-1275
  Frankfort (G-5688)
Rogers Group Inc........................... E..... 812 882-3640
  Vincennes (G-16150)
Roy Umbarger and Sons Inc............... F..... 317 422-5195
  Franklin (G-5775)

Superior AG Resources Coop Inc......... G..... 812 724-4455
  Owensville (G-13473)
Wilson Fertilizer & Grain Inc............. G..... 574 223-3175
  Rochester (G-14333)

2879 Agricultural chemicals, nec

Agriselect Evansville LLC................... G..... 812 453-2235
  Evansville (G-3877)
Bayer Great Lakes Prod Co LLC........... E..... 317 945-7121
  Windfall (G-16903)
Corteva Inc................................... G..... 765 586-4077
  Indianapolis (G-7882)
Corteva Inc................................... A..... 833 267-8382
  Indianapolis (G-7883)
◆ Corteva Agriscience LLC................ A..... 317 337-3000
  Indianapolis (G-7884)
◆ Dintec Agrichemicals..................... G..... 317 337-7870
  Indianapolis (G-7976)
Dow Agroscience............................ G..... 765 743-0015
  West Lafayette (G-16577)
Dow Agrosciences........................... G..... 765 775-2918
  West Lafayette (G-16578)
Dow Agrosciences LLC...................... G..... 317 846-7873
  Carmel (G-1612)
Dow Agrosciences LLC...................... E..... 317 252-5602
  Indianapolis (G-8000)
Dow Elanco Sciences........................ G..... 317 337-3691
  Indianapolis (G-8002)
Dupont and Tonkel Partners LLC......... G..... 260 444-2264
  Fort Wayne (G-4932)
Dupont Circle III............................. G..... 260 489-9508
  Fort Wayne (G-4933)
Dupont Commons LLC....................... G..... 260 637-3215
  Fort Wayne (G-4934)
◆ Eidp Inc.................................... A..... 833 267-8382
  Indianapolis (G-8064)
Eli Lilly International Corp................. F..... 317 276-2000
  Indianapolis (G-8091)
Helena Agri-Enterprises LLC.............. G..... 574 268-4762
  Huntington (G-7317)
Kep Chem Inc................................ G..... 574 739-0501
  Logansport (G-11088)
Keystone Cooperative Inc.................. G..... 765 489-4141
  Hagerstown (G-6838)
Koch Industries Inc......................... G..... 260 356-7191
  Huntington (G-7335)
Landec Ag Inc................................ F..... 765 385-1000
  Oxford (G-13475)
Monofoilusa LLC............................. G..... 317 340-9951
  Elwood (G-3832)
Monsanto Company.......................... G..... 229 759-0034
  Evansville (G-4209)
Monsanto Company.......................... G..... 323 265-1025
  Lafayette (G-10653)
Monsanto Company.......................... G..... 574 870-0397
  Reynolds (G-14074)
Monsanto Company.......................... G..... 219 733-2938
  Union Mills (G-15866)
Monsanto Whitestown Seed............... G..... 317 692-9485
  Whitestown (G-16812)
◆ Mycogen Corporation..................... F..... 317 337-3000
  Indianapolis (G-8977)
Olympus Management LLC................. G..... 317 412-7977
  Westfield (G-16715)
Prime Source LLC........................... G..... 812 867-8921
  Evansville (G-4258)
Roy Umbarger and Sons Inc............... F..... 317 422-5195
  Franklin (G-5775)
▲ Sepro Corporation........................ E..... 317 580-8282
  Carmel (G-1758)
Southern Indiana Chemical Inc........... G..... 812 687-7118
  Washington (G-16509)

Superior AG Resources Coop Inc......... G..... 812 724-4455
  Owensville (G-13473)
United Turf Alliance LLC................... G..... 770 335-3015
  Fishers (G-4620)
V Global Holdings LLC...................... E..... 317 247-8141
  Indianapolis (G-9695)
Wellington Global LLC...................... G..... 317 590-1755
  Indianapolis (G-9748)

2891 Adhesives and sealants

3M Company.................................. B..... 317 692-6666
  Indianapolis (G-7388)
▲ Abtrex Industries Inc.................... F..... 734 728-0550
  South Bend (G-14934)
Ace Extrusion LLC........................... E..... 812 463-5230
  Evansville (G-3871)
Adhesive Solutions Company LLC........ G..... 260 691-0304
  Columbia City (G-2117)
Aeromind LLC................................ G..... 800 905-2157
  Indianapolis (G-7453)
American Sealants Inc...................... E..... 800 325-7040
  Fort Wayne (G-4757)
Big Dog Adhesives LLC..................... F..... 574 350-2237
  Elkhart (G-3224)
Bondline Adhesives Inc.................... F..... 812 423-4651
  Evansville (G-3939)
Capital Adhesives & Packg Corp......... F..... 317 834-5415
  Mooresville (G-12197)
Cast Products LP............................ G..... 574 255-9619
  Mishawaka (G-11859)
▲ Cast Products LP......................... E..... 574 294-2684
  Elkhart (G-3249)
Chem Tech Inc............................... F..... 574 848-1001
  Bristol (G-1253)
Coleman Cable LLC.......................... D..... 765 449-7227
  Lafayette (G-10553)
Colorimetric Inc.............................. F..... 574 255-9619
  Mishawaka (G-11862)
▼ Covalnce Spcalty Adhesives LLC...... B..... 812 424-2904
  Evansville (G-3987)
Custom Building Products LLC........... C..... 765 656-0234
  Frankfort (G-5659)
▲ Davies-Imperial Coatings Inc.......... E..... 219 933-0877
  Hammond (G-6911)
▲ Dehco Inc.................................. D..... 574 294-2684
  Elkhart (G-3288)
Evans Adhesive Corporation.............. G..... 812 859-4245
  Spencer (G-15345)
Federal Process Corp....................... G..... 574 288-0607
  South Bend (G-15030)
Franco Corporation.......................... G..... 765 675-6691
  Tipton (G-15774)
Freda Inc..................................... F..... 260 665-8431
  Angola (G-253)
▲ Gdc Inc..................................... C..... 574 533-3128
  Goshen (G-6143)
▲ Geocel Holdings Corporation.......... D..... 574 264-0645
  Elkhart (G-3376)
Hco Holding I Corporation................. G..... 317 248-1344
  Indianapolis (G-8373)
▲ Heartland Adhesives Inc................ G..... 219 310-8645
  Crown Point (G-2692)
Howmet Corporation........................ G..... 219 325-4143
  La Porte (G-10424)
▲ Industrial Adhesives Indiana.......... G..... 317 271-2100
  Indianapolis (G-8516)
Iron Out Inc.................................. E..... 800 654-0791
  Fort Wayne (G-5119)
◆ Koch Enterprises Inc.................... G..... 812 465-9800
  Evansville (G-4159)
Laticrete International Inc................ G..... 317 298-8510
  Indianapolis (G-8726)

SIC SECTION
28 CHEMICALS AND ALLIED PRODUCTS

Lomont Holdings Co Inc .... E 800 545-9023
  Angola (G-273)
Lord Corporation .... D 317 259-4161
  Indianapolis (G-8782)
Mito Material Solutions Inc .... G 855 344-6486
  Indianapolis (G-8936)
Morgan Adhesives Company LLC .... B 812 342-2004
  Columbus (G-2357)
▲ Mt Olive Manufacturing LLC .... D 317 834-8525
  Mooresville (G-12227)
Multiseal Inc .... C 812 428-3422
  Evansville (G-4215)
▲ Parr Corp .... F 574 264-9614
  Elkhart (G-3584)
▲ Parr Holdings LLC .... E 423 468-1855
  Elkhart (G-3585)
Parr Technologies LLC .... G 574 264-9614
  Elkhart (G-3586)
Parson Adhesives Inc .... C 812 401-7277
  Evansville (G-4234)
Patrick Industries Inc .... F 574 295-5206
  Elkhart (G-3588)
Patrick Industries Inc .... D 574 294-8828
  Elkhart (G-3592)
▲ Patrick Industries Inc .... B 574 294-7511
  Elkhart (G-3593)
PRC - Desoto International Inc .... E 317 290-1600
  Indianapolis (G-9177)
Precoat Metals .... F 219 763-1504
  Portage (G-13906)
PSC Industries Inc .... G 317 547-5439
  Indianapolis (G-9237)
◆ Royal Adhesives & Sealants LLC .... D 574 246-5000
  South Bend (G-15226)
Royal Holdings Inc .... C 574 246-5000
  South Bend (G-15227)
▲ Saimax Products Inc .... G 248 299-5585
  Evansville (G-4296)
Saran LP C
  Indianapolis (G-9373)
Seal Corp .... G 812 868-0790
  Evansville (G-4302)
▲ SealCorpUSA Inc .... D 866 868-0791
  Evansville (G-4303)
Specialty Adhesive Film Co .... E 812 926-0156
  Aurora (G-455)
Technicote Inc .... E 812 466-9844
  Terre Haute (G-15724)
Transcendia Inc .... C 765 935-1520
  Richmond (G-14220)
Trelleborg Sling Sltions US Inc .... C 260 748-5895
  Fort Wayne (G-5502)
Uniseal Inc .... C 812 425-1361
  Evansville (G-4360)
▲ Uniseal Inc .... C 812 425-1361
  Evansville (G-4361)
Warsaw Chemical Company Inc .... D 574 267-3251
  Warsaw (G-16442)
▼ Weatherall Indiana Inc .... F 812 256-3378
  Charlestown (G-1896)
Xennovate Medical LLC .... G 765 939-2037
  Richmond (G-14229)

2892 Explosives

Austin Powder Company .... G 812 342-1237
  Columbus (G-2222)
Dyno Nobel Inc .... G 260 731-4431
  Pennville (G-13563)
Ireco Metals Inc .... G 574 936-2146
  Plymouth (G-13787)
Nelson Brothers .... G 812 250-7520
  Evansville (G-4220)

2893 Printing ink

Actega North America Inc .... G 800 426-4657
  Schererville (G-14512)
Braden Sutphin Ink Co .... G 317 352-8781
  Indianapolis (G-7669)
Brand Prtg & Photo-Litho Co .... G 317 921-4095
  New Palestine (G-12933)
Budget Inks LLC .... G 877 636-4657
  Angola (G-238)
Enviro Ink .... G 260 748-0636
  Fort Wayne (G-4953)
Flint CPS Inks North Amer LLC .... E 317 870-4422
  Indianapolis (G-8204)
Flint Group US LLC .... F 574 269-4603
  Warsaw (G-16363)
Industrial Organic Inks Inc .... G 219 878-0613
  Chesterton (G-1938)
INX International Ink Co .... G 765 939-6625
  Richmond (G-14140)
INX LLC .... G 219 779-0508
  Gary (G-5965)
Nor-Cote International Inc .... G 800 488-9180
  Crawfordsville (G-2596)
▲ Nor-Cote International Inc .... E 800 488-9180
  Crawfordsville (G-2597)
North American Ink .... G 765 659-6000
  Frankfort (G-5685)
Peafield Products Inc .... F 317 839-8473
  Plainfield (G-13711)
Stamp N Scrap Ink Corp .... G 219 440-7239
  Dyer (G-2984)
Sun Chemical Corporation .... E 972 270-6735
  Frankfort (G-5695)
Sun Chemical Corporation .... E 765 659-6000
  Frankfort (G-5696)
Sun Chemical Corporation .... G 812 235-8031
  Terre Haute (G-15717)
Sun Cosmetics LLC .... D 219 531-5359
  Valparaiso (G-16060)

2895 Carbon black

Dean Co Inc .... G 317 891-2518
  Greenfield (G-6488)

2899 Chemical preparations, nec

Alebro LLC .... F 317 876-9212
  Indianapolis (G-7468)
▲ Amalgamated Incorporated .... G 260 489-2549
  Fort Wayne (G-4747)
Andersons Agriculture Group LP .... G 574 626-2522
  Galveston (G-5851)
Arch Chemicals Inc .... G 219 464-3949
  Valparaiso (G-15903)
Arch Wood Protection Inc .... G 219 464-3949
  Valparaiso (G-15904)
Astbury Water Technology Inc .... G 260 668-8900
  Angola (G-231)
Atmosphere Dynamics Corp .... G 317 392-6262
  Shelbyville (G-14731)
Bada Boom Fireworks LLC .... G 219 472-6700
  Gary (G-5897)
Bangs Laboratories Inc .... F 317 570-7020
  Fishers (G-4470)
Bedlam Beard Company LLC .... G 317 800-9631
  Lizton (G-11048)
Beverly Harris .... G 317 910-0542
  Indianapolis (G-7619)
Biokorf LLC .... G 765 727-0782
  West Lafayette (G-16565)
▲ Blue Grass Chemical Spc LLC .... F 812 948-1115
  New Albany (G-12703)
Boomers .... G 765 741-4031
  Muncie (G-12355)
Bundoo Laboratories LLC .... G 317 978-5574
  Beech Grove (G-687)
Business Health .... G 219 762-7105
  Portage (G-13851)
Chemicals Inc USA .... G 317 334-1000
  Indianapolis (G-7792)
Chemque Inc .... G 800 268-6111
  Indianapolis (G-7793)
Chemtec LLC .... F 812 499-8408
  Newburgh (G-12997)
Consolidated Recycling Co Inc .... D 812 547-7951
  Evansville (G-3981)
Craig Hydraulic Enterprises .... G 812 432-5108
  Dillsboro (G-2944)
▲ Crown Technology Inc .... E 317 845-0045
  Indianapolis (G-7914)
Custom Building Products LLC .... C 765 656-0234
  Frankfort (G-5659)
Dow Chemical Company .... C 317 337-3819
  Indianapolis (G-8001)
Dribot LLC .... G 317 885-6330
  Indianapolis (G-8007)
Driessen Water Inc .... G 765 529-4905
  Muncie (G-12386)
Eco Services Operations Corp .... E 219 932-7651
  Hammond (G-6919)
Eminence Hlth Care Stffing AGC .... G 866 350-6400
  South Bend (G-15013)
Enviri Corporation .... F 219 397-0200
  East Chicago (G-3007)
Es Deicing .... G 260 422-2020
  Fort Wayne (G-4960)
Gabriel Products Inc .... G 502 291-5388
  Jeffersonville (G-9989)
GCI LLC .... G 317 574-4970
  Carmel (G-1640)
Giles Chemical Corporation .... G 812 537-4852
  Greendale (G-6445)
Goodar & Harris LLC .... G 312 465-3899
  West Lafayette (G-16586)
H&G Legacy Co .... G 317 241-9233
  Indianapolis (G-8348)
Heidelberg Mtls US Cem LLC .... C 574 753-5121
  Logansport (G-11076)
Honey & Salt LLC .... G 317 625-1135
  Indianapolis (G-8407)
Hydrite Chemical Co .... D 812 232-5411
  Terre Haute (G-15611)
I N C O M Wholesale Supply .... G 574 722-2442
  Logansport (G-11080)
Ideal Testing and Services LLC .... G 812 431-8500
  Indianapolis (G-8454)
Ifs Coatings .... G 317 471-5122
  Indianapolis (G-8455)
Incense Incense .... G 317 544-9444
  Avon (G-527)
Indiana Chemical LLC .... G 317 912-3800
  Indianapolis (G-8476)
Ink - LLC .... G 317 502-6473
  Franklin (G-5746)
Innovative Chem Resources Inc .... G 317 695-6001
  Indianapolis (G-8553)
Insultech LLC .... F 317 389-5134
  Indianapolis (G-8565)
Interrachem LLC .... E 812 858-3147
  Newburgh (G-13009)
Iron Out Inc .... G 260 483-2519
  Fort Wayne (G-5118)
Iron Out Inc .... E 800 654-0791
  Fort Wayne (G-5119)

Employee Codes: A=Over 500 employees, B=251-500
C=101-250, D=51-100, E=20-50, F=10-19, G=1-9

28 CHEMICALS AND ALLIED PRODUCTS

Jackson Hewitt Tax Service............. F 574 255-2200
  Mishawaka (G-11915)
▲ Johnny Lemas.............................. G 260 833-8850
  Angola (G-264)
Kaze Energy LLC........................... G 502 664-5519
  Georgetown (G-6064)
Kemco International Inc................. F 260 829-1263
  Orland (G-13367)
Kenra Professional LLC.................. F 800 428-8073
  Indianapolis (G-8673)
▲ Kibbechem Inc............................. E 574 266-1234
  Elkhart (G-3454)
Klinge Enameling Company Inc....... E 317 359-8291
  Indianapolis (G-8694)
Le Kem of Indiana Inc................... G 812 932-5536
  Batesville (G-595)
◆ Lebermuth Company Inc...............D 574 259-7000
  South Bend (G-15121)
Magnifiscents................................. G 317 549-3880
  Indianapolis (G-8811)
Majestic Water Company................ G 317 790-2448
  Indianapolis (G-8817)
▲ Merediths Inc............................... E 765 966-5084
  Richmond (G-14164)
Metals and Additives LLC............. G 812 446-2525
  Brazil (G-1153)
▼ Metals and Additives LLC........... F 317 290-5007
  Indianapolis (G-8890)
Metalworking Lubricants Co........... C 317 269-2444
  Indianapolis (G-8891)
Midwest Custom Chemicals Inc...... G 812 858-3147
  Newburgh (G-13013)
Millennial Fireworks........................ G 812 732-5126
  Mauckport (G-11439)
Miller Chemical Tech & MGT Inc.... G 317 560-5437
  Franklin (G-5757)
Morton Salt Inc.............................. D 219 477-0061
  New Haven (G-12910)
Ncp Coatings Inc........................... G 574 255-9678
  Mishawaka (G-11964)
Nochar Inc..................................... G 317 613-3046
  Indianapolis (G-9018)
Onsyte Mobile Labs LLC................ G 800 570-6844
  South Bend (G-15179)
Opta (usa) Inc................................ E 716 446-8888
  Kingsbury (G-10184)
Ploog Engineering Co Inc............... G 219 663-2854
  Crown Point (G-2731)
Polyfusion LLC............................... G 260 624-7659
  Angola (G-285)
Prt Inc... G 765 938-3333
  Rushville (G-14407)
Quaker Chemical Corp................... G 765 668-2441
  Marion (G-11332)
Quality Fire Protection.................... G 269 683-0285
  South Bend (G-15210)
Rayes Rpid Rslts - MBL DRG ALC.. G 317 721-1065
  Indianapolis (G-9270)
Reliable Diagnstc Bus Lab LLC...... G 219 401-3122
  Merrillville (G-11553)
Ricca Chemical Company LLC...... E 812 932-1161
  Batesville (G-603)
Sanco Industries Inc...................... G 260 467-1791
  Fort Wayne (G-5397)
Sanco Industries Inc...................... E 260 426-6281
  Fort Wayne (G-5398)
Sassy Organics Collection LLC...... G 231 942-0751
  Indianapolis (G-9375)
Scp Holdings Inc........................... G 260 925-2588
  Auburn (G-421)
Sheung T Cheng............................ G 646 220-2195
  Portage (G-13913)

▲ Sky Thunder LLC........................ E 812 397-0102
  Shelburn (G-14722)
Sober Scientific LLC....................... G 765 465-9803
  Sheridan (G-14829)
Sol Melanin Beauty LLC................. G 317 354-3977
  Indianapolis (G-9459)
Standard Fusee Corporation........... D 765 472-4375
  Peru (G-13602)
Sunocs LLC................................... C 219 286-7081
  Valparaiso (G-16061)
▲ Superior Indus Solutions Inc........ E 317 781-4400
  Indianapolis (G-9529)
Total Cleaning Solutions LLC......... G 260 471-7761
  Fort Wayne (G-5496)
Tri-Pac Inc.................................... C 574 855-2197
  South Bend (G-15291)
Ulerys Fireworks Inc...................... G 574 722-9119
  Logansport (G-11116)
Universal Services Inc................... G 219 397-4373
  East Chicago (G-3051)
◆ Univertical LLC............................F 260 665-1500
  Angola (G-304)
Veolia Wts Usa Inc........................ G 219 746-4060
  Valparaiso (G-16075)
Vw Co... G 812 397-0102
  Shelburn (G-14723)
◆ Warsaw Black Oxide Inc.............. E 574 491-2975
  Burket (G-1445)
Watcon Inc.................................... G 574 287-3397
  South Bend (G-15304)
Water Sciences Inc........................ G 260 485-4655
  Fort Wayne (G-5548)
Weas Engineering Inc.................... F 317 867-4477
  Westfield (G-16738)
William L Theby............................. G 812 477-6673
  Evansville (G-4386)
Workflow Solutions LLC.................. G 502 627-0257
  New Albany (G-12831)
▲ Yushiro Manufacturing Amer Inc.. E 317 398-9862
  Shelbyville (G-14816)
Zeller LLC..................................... G 317 343-2930
  Indianapolis (G-9809)

29 PETROLEUM REFINING AND RELATED INDUSTRIES

2911 Petroleum refining

Advance Energy LLC...................... G 312 665-0022
  Merrillville (G-11477)
Airgas Inc..................................... G 317 632-7106
  Indianapolis (G-7463)
Apollo America.............................. G 812 284-3300
  Jeffersonville (G-9934)
Calumet Inc................................... E 317 328-5660
  Indianapolis (G-7717)
Calumet Finance Corp................... E 317 328-5660
  Indianapolis (G-7718)
Calumet Gp LLC............................ E 317 328-5660
  Indianapolis (G-7719)
Calumet International Inc............... G 317 328-5660
  Indianapolis (G-7720)
◆ Calumet Karns City Ref LLC........ E 317 328-5660
  Indianapolis (G-7721)
▲ Calumet Missouri LLC................. E 318 795-3800
  Indianapolis (G-7722)
Calumet Operating LLC................. F 317 328-5660
  Indianapolis (G-7723)
Calumet Paralogics LLC................ F 765 587-4618
  Muncie (G-12361)
Calumet Refining LLC.................... G 765 587-4618
  Muncie (G-12362)

◆ Calumet Refining LLC.................. E 317 328-5660
  Indianapolis (G-7724)
Calumet Shreveport Llc................. G 317 328-5660
  Indianapolis (G-7725)
Calumet Shreveport Ref LLC......... F 317 328-5660
  Indianapolis (G-7727)
▼ Calumet Spclty Pdts Prtners LP... C 317 328-5660
  Indianapolis (G-7728)
Cjs Stop N Go............................... G 317 877-0681
  Noblesville (G-13061)
Countrymark Ref Logistics LLC...... B 812 838-4341
  Mount Vernon (G-12295)
Don Hartman Oil Co Inc................. G 765 643-5026
  Anderson (G-106)
Emerald Cast Rnewable Fuel LLC.. G 765 942-5019
  Ladoga (G-10507)
Exxon Mobil Corporation................ G 574 217-7630
  South Bend (G-15024)
Fuel Recovery Service Inc............. G 317 372-3029
  Indianapolis (G-8238)
Heritage-Crystal Clean Inc............. G 317 390-3642
  Indianapolis (G-8390)
HK Petroleum Ltd.......................... G 229 366-1313
  Madison (G-11226)
Hometown Energy LLC.................. G 812 663-3391
  Greensburg (G-6603)
Hoosier Penn Oil Co Inc................. E 317 390-5406
  Indianapolis (G-8411)
Imperial Petroleum Inc................... E 812 867-1433
  Darmstadt (G-2836)
Jpt Enterprises Inc......................... G 260 672-1605
  Fort Wayne (G-5139)
Keil Chemical Corporation.............. E 219 931-2630
  Hammond (G-6966)
Leesburg Stop-N-Go LLC............... G 574 453-3004
  Leesburg (G-10956)
Oxbow Carbon & Minerals.............G 219 473-0359
  Whiting (G-16837)
Paralogics LLC.............................. E 765 587-4618
  Muncie (G-12472)
Petroleum Solutions Inc................. G 574 546-2133
  Bremen (G-1214)
Residual Pays Daily....................... G 260 267-1617
  Fort Wayne (G-5381)
Shell Pipe Line Corporation............ G 765 962-1329
  Richmond (G-14204)
Steelco Industrial Lubricants.......... G 219 462-0333
  Valparaiso (G-16057)
Superior Indus Solutions Inc.......... F 574 264-0161
  Elkhart (G-3708)
Times 10 Associates LLC.............. G 800 773-6432
  Valparaiso (G-16068)
Triton Energy LLC......................... G
  Waterloo (G-16532)
Universal Services Inc................... G 219 397-4373
  East Chicago (G-3051)

2951 Asphalt paving mixtures and blocks

Allterrain Paving & Cnstr LLC........ E 502 265-4731
  New Albany (G-12687)
Armor Coat LLC............................ G 260 210-1307
  Huntington (G-7298)
Asphalt Cutbacks Inc..................... F 219 398-4230
  East Chicago (G-2991)
Asphalt Materials Inc..................... G 317 243-8304
  Indianapolis (G-7551)
Asphalt Materials Inc..................... G 317 875-4670
  Indianapolis (G-7553)
Asphalt Materials Inc..................... B 317 872-6010
  Indianapolis (G-7552)
Bituminous Materials & Sup LP...... G 317 228-8203
  Indianapolis (G-7633)

SIC SECTION
30 RUBBER AND MISCELLANEOUS PLASTIC PRODUCTS

Blaney Sealcoating .... G 219 241-3622
   La Porte *(G-10389)*

C & R Cnstr & Consulting LLC .... G 812 738-4493
   Corydon *(G-2489)*

Calcar Quarries Incorporated .... F 812 723-2109
   Paoli *(G-13491)*

Concrete & Asphalt Recycl Inc .... G 574 237-1928
   Mishawaka *(G-11864)*

Dave OMara Paving Inc .... G 812 346-1214
   North Vernon *(G-13264)*

DC Construction Services Inc .... E 317 577-0276
   Indianapolis *(G-7958)*

E & B Paving Inc .... E 765 674-5848
   Marion *(G-11284)*

E & B Paving Inc .... E 765 643-5358
   Anderson *(G-112)*

Globe Asphalt Paving Co Inc .... E 317 568-4344
   Indianapolis *(G-8293)*

Harding Group LLC .... D 317 536-8364
   Indianapolis *(G-8357)*

Hco Holding I Corporation .... G 317 248-1344
   Indianapolis *(G-8373)*

Heidelberg Mtls Mdwest Agg Inc .... G 260 632-4252
   Woodburn *(G-16949)*

Heritage Asphalt Llc .... G 317 872-6010
   Indianapolis *(G-8388)*

Holcim (us) Inc .... G 219 378-1193
   East Chicago *(G-3017)*

Hotmix Inc .... G 812 663-2020
   Greensburg *(G-6605)*

Hotmix Inc .... G 812 926-1471
   Aurora *(G-445)*

Irving Materials Inc .... D 317 326-3101
   Greenfield *(G-6518)*

Jenstar Asphalt LLC .... F 219 963-6263
   Gary *(G-5970)*

Laketon Refining Corporation .... F 260 982-0703
   Laketon *(G-10787)*

Lewis Sealing & Cleaning .... G 317 783-1424
   Indianapolis *(G-8742)*

Meshberger Brothers Stone .... D 260 334-5311
   Bluffton *(G-1041)*

Milestone Contractors LP .... D 812 579-5248
   Columbus *(G-2356)*

Milestone Contractors LP .... D 765 772-7500
   Lafayette *(G-10650)*

Milestone Contractors N Inc .... G 219 924-5900
   South Bend *(G-15151)*

▲ Monument Chemical LLC .... D 317 223-2630
   Indianapolis *(G-8952)*

Niblock Excavating Inc .... G 260 248-2100
   Columbia City *(G-2174)*

Niblock Excavating Inc .... G 574 848-4437
   Bristol *(G-1281)*

Parsleys Seal Coating Inc .... G 812 876-5450
   Ellettsville *(G-3811)*

Paul H Rohe Company Inc .... E 812 926-1471
   Aurora *(G-451)*

Paving Plus Company .... G 317 784-1857
   Indianapolis *(G-9105)*

Powco Inc .... F 765 334-4210
   Cambridge City *(G-1500)*

Premier Paving .... G 302 396-8851
   Whitestown *(G-16817)*

Rieth-Riley Cnstr Co Inc .... E 574 875-5183
   Gary *(G-6005)*

Rieth-Riley Cnstr Co Inc .... F 574 288-8321
   South Bend *(G-15219)*

Rogers Group Inc .... F 812 333-8550
   Bloomington *(G-962)*

Rogers Group Inc .... G 765 342-6898
   Martinsville *(G-11424)*

Rogers Group Inc .... E 812 882-3640
   Vincennes *(G-16150)*

Schrock Aggregate Company Inc .... G 574 862-4167
   Wakarusa *(G-16250)*

Schrock Excavating Inc .... E 574 862-4167
   Wakarusa *(G-16251)*

Scotts Grant County Asp Inc .... G 765 664-2754
   Marion *(G-11337)*

Semmaterials LP .... G 574 267-5076
   Warsaw *(G-16421)*

Triangle Asphalt Paving Corp .... E 765 482-5701
   Lebanon *(G-10947)*

Valley Asphalt Corporation .... G 812 926-1471
   Aurora *(G-458)*

Wallace Construction Inc .... F 317 422-5356
   Martinsville *(G-11434)*

Walters Development Co LLC .... G 260 747-7531
   Fort Wayne *(G-5544)*

2952 Asphalt felts and coatings

Alphajak LLC .... G 574 800-4810
   Mishawaka *(G-11839)*

Asphalt Cutbacks Inc .... F 219 398-4230
   East Chicago *(G-2991)*

Carlisle Companies Inc .... G 812 334-8793
   Bloomington *(G-821)*

Central States Mfg Inc .... C 219 879-4770
   Michigan City *(G-11586)*

Dave OMara Paving Inc .... G 812 346-1214
   North Vernon *(G-13264)*

Dupouy Enterprises LLC .... G 765 453-1466
   Kokomo *(G-10260)*

Fibrosan Inc .... F 574 612-4736
   Elkhart *(G-3346)*

Green Tek LLC .... F 317 294-1614
   Carmel *(G-1644)*

Hco Holding I Corporation .... G 317 248-1344
   Indianapolis *(G-8373)*

K Tech Specialty Coatings Inc .... F 260 587-3888
   Ashley *(G-333)*

Maple Lane Metals LLC .... F 260 627-0987
   Grabill *(G-6313)*

Polar Seal Inc .... G 260 356-2369
   Huntington *(G-7357)*

Pro-Mark Bldg Solutions LLC .... F 812 798-1178
   Linton *(G-11043)*

Prophalt Sealcoating LLC .... G 502 356-3238
   Henryville *(G-7114)*

R & J Excvtg & Sealcoating LLC .... G 812 799-1849
   Columbus *(G-2385)*

Sampco Inc .... G 413 442-4043
   South Bend *(G-15230)*

Schmidt Contracting Inc .... E 812 482-3923
   Jasper *(G-9908)*

Standard Industries Inc .... G 219 872-1111
   Michigan City *(G-11672)*

Triangle Asphalt Paving Corp .... E 765 482-5701
   Lebanon *(G-10947)*

United Coatings Mfg Co .... G 317 845-8830
   Indianapolis *(G-9679)*

2992 Lubricating oils and greases

▲ D-A Lubricant Company Inc .... E 317 923-5321
   Lebanon *(G-10890)*

Dnd Dust Control Inc .... G 765 362-3774
   Crawfordsville *(G-2563)*

▼ F B C Inc .... E 574 848-5288
   Bristol *(G-1260)*

◆ Idemitsu Lubricants Amer Corp .... D 812 284-3300
   Jeffersonville *(G-10000)*

Illinois Lubricants LLC .... G 260 436-2444
   Fort Wayne *(G-5092)*

J 2 Systems and Supply LLC .... G 317 602-3940
   Indianapolis *(G-8601)*

Keil Chemical Corporation .... E 219 931-2630
   Hammond *(G-6966)*

Klotz Synthetic Lubricants LLC .... F 260 490-0489
   Fort Wayne *(G-5151)*

◆ Lucas Oil Products Inc .... C 951 270-0154
   Indianapolis *(G-8793)*

Metalworking Lubricants Co .... C 317 269-2444
   Indianapolis *(G-8891)*

Michiana Elkhart Inc .... F 574 206-0620
   Elkhart *(G-3531)*

Miller Industrial Fluids LLC .... E 317 634-7300
   Indianapolis *(G-8921)*

Oil Technology Inc .... E 219 322-2724
   Schererville *(G-14538)*

Packaging Group Corp .... F 219 879-2500
   Michigan City *(G-11649)*

Permawick Company Inc .... F 812 376-0703
   Columbus *(G-2376)*

Petrochoice Holdings Inc .... E 317 634-7300
   Indianapolis *(G-9130)*

Petroleum Solutions Inc .... G 574 546-2133
   Bremen *(G-1214)*

Pinnacle Oil Holdings LLC .... F 317 875-9465
   Indianapolis *(G-9144)*

Pinnacle Oil Holdings LLC .... F 317 875-9465
   Indianapolis *(G-9145)*

▲ Pinnacle Oil Inc .... C 317 875-9465
   Indianapolis *(G-9146)*

Pro-Chem-Co Inc .... F 219 962-8554
   Lake Station *(G-10775)*

Spence/Banks Holdings Inc .... F 812 235-8123
   Terre Haute *(G-15713)*

Tj Performance LLC .... G 765 580-0481
   Brownsville *(G-1432)*

▲ Yushiro Manufacturing Amer Inc .... E 317 398-9862
   Shelbyville *(G-14816)*

2999 Petroleum and coal products, nec

Anita Cole .... G 907 479-2245
   Portage *(G-13843)*

Calumet Paralogics LLC .... F 765 587-4618
   Muncie *(G-12361)*

Calumet Shreveport Fuels Llc .... D 317 328-5660
   Indianapolis *(G-7726)*

Calumet Superior LLC .... C 317 328-5660
   Indianapolis *(G-7729)*

Paralogics LLC .... E 765 587-4618
   Muncie *(G-12472)*

30 RUBBER AND MISCELLANEOUS PLASTIC PRODUCTS

3011 Tires and inner tubes

E & D Tire & Repair LLC .... G 812 486-6493
   Loogootee *(G-11134)*

Enovapremier LLC .... E 812 385-0576
   Princeton *(G-13993)*

Ferentino Tire USA Inc .... G 574 316-6116
   Plymouth *(G-13775)*

Goodyear Tire & Rubber Company .... G 219 762-0651
   Portage *(G-13871)*

◆ Hoosier Racing Tire Corp .... G 574 784-3152
   Lakeville *(G-10792)*

◆ Lionshead Specialty Tire & Whe .... F 574 533-6169
   Goshen *(G-6200)*

Michelin North America Inc .... A 260 493-8100
   Woodburn *(G-16951)*

▲ Richards Liquidation Corp .... F 574 807-8588
   Mishawaka *(G-11985)*

30 RUBBER AND MISCELLANEOUS PLASTIC PRODUCTS

Rubber Shop Inc .... G 574 291-6440
  South Bend *(G-15229)*
Sams Tech Tire LLC .... G 219 942-7317
  Hobart *(G-7205)*
Simon and Sons .... G 812 852-3636
  Osgood *(G-13416)*
T K T Inc .... G 574 825-5233
  Middlebury *(G-11753)*

3021 Rubber and plastics footwear

Nike Inc .... G 219 879-1320
  Michigan City *(G-11646)*
Orb LLC .... G 833 946-4672
  Indianapolis *(G-9067)*
Piro Shoes LLC .... F 888 849-0916
  Fishers *(G-4575)*

3052 Rubber and plastics hose and beltings

American Rubber Corp .... G 317 548-8455
  Anderson *(G-77)*
Clean-Seal Inc .... E 574 299-1888
  South Bend *(G-14976)*
CRS-Drs Corporation .... G 260 478-7555
  Fort Wayne *(G-4891)*
Dunham Rubber Belting Corp .... G 317 604-5313
  Shelbyville *(G-14753)*
Dura-Vent Corp .... F 574 936-2432
  Plymouth *(G-13772)*
Exactseal Inc .... G 317 559-2220
  Indianapolis *(G-8148)*
◆ Flexaust Inc .... E 574 267-7909
  Warsaw *(G-16362)*
Flexible Technologies Inc .... G 574 936-2432
  Plymouth *(G-13776)*
▲ General Rbr Plas of Evansville .... E 812 464-5153
  Evansville *(G-4087)*
◆ Kilgore Manufacturing Co Inc .... D 260 248-2002
  Columbia City *(G-2162)*
Midwest Design Hydraulic .... G 765 714-3016
  West Lafayette *(G-16605)*
Mitsubishi Chemical Advncd Mtr .... C 260 479-4100
  Fort Wayne *(G-5233)*
Mitsubshi Chem Advnced Mtls In .... D 260 479-4700
  Fort Wayne *(G-5234)*
Mulhern Belting Inc .... G 201 337-5700
  Michigan City *(G-11643)*
Omega Process Solutions LLC .... E 574 546-5606
  Bremen *(G-1209)*
▼ Omega Products Inc .... E 574 546-5606
  Bremen *(G-1210)*
Radiator Specialty Company .... D 574 546-5606
  Bremen *(G-1216)*
Rubber Shop Inc .... G 574 291-6440
  South Bend *(G-15229)*
S & R Welding Inc .... G 317 710-0360
  Indianapolis *(G-9353)*
Sdbd Incorporated .... G 260 376-1134
  Leo *(G-10972)*
▲ Slb Corporation .... F 574 255-9774
  Mishawaka *(G-11996)*
Sperry & Rice Manufacturi .... C 765 647-4141
  Brookville *(G-1335)*

3053 Gaskets; packing and sealing devices

Aearo Technologies LLC .... C 317 692-6666
  Indianapolis *(G-7447)*
American Elkhart LLC .... F 574 293-0333
  Elkhart *(G-3172)*
American Rubber Corp .... G 317 548-8455
  Anderson *(G-77)*
Anchor Seals Incorporated .... G 412 299-6900
  Gary *(G-5893)*
Apexx Enterprises LLC .... F 812 486-2443
  Montgomery *(G-12085)*
Bellahauss Distributers .... G 260 485-4343
  Fort Wayne *(G-4794)*
▲ Bonar Inc .... G 260 636-7430
  Albion *(G-19)*
BRC Rubber & Plastics Inc .... E 260 827-0871
  Bluffton *(G-1032)*
BRC Rubber & Plastics Inc .... F 260 203-5300
  Churubusco *(G-1974)*
BRC Rubber & Plastics Inc .... E 260 894-4121
  Ligonier *(G-11007)*
▲ BRC Rubber & Plastics Inc .... C 260 693-2171
  Fort Wayne *(G-4815)*
Breiner Company Inc .... F 317 272-2521
  Avon *(G-509)*
▲ Cannon Fabrication Company .... F 765 629-2277
  Milroy *(G-11822)*
Cedar Creek Studios Inc .... G 260 627-7320
  Leo *(G-10966)*
◆ EJ Brooks Company .... D 800 348-4777
  Angola *(G-247)*
Espi Enterprises Inc .... G 219 787-8711
  Chesterton *(G-1923)*
Exactseal Inc .... G 317 559-2220
  Indianapolis *(G-8148)*
Federal-Mogul Powertrain LLC .... B 574 271-5954
  South Bend *(G-15031)*
Fellwocks Automotive .... G 812 867-3658
  Evansville *(G-4067)*
Freudenberg-Nok General Partnr .... C 765 763-7246
  Morristown *(G-12277)*
Freudenberg-Nok General Partnr .... C 317 421-3400
  Shelbyville *(G-14756)*
Freudenberg-Nok General Partnr .... C 734 354-5504
  Shelbyville *(G-14757)*
◆ Gaska Tape Inc .... D 574 294-5431
  Elkhart *(G-3366)*
▲ General Rbr Plas of Evansville .... E 812 464-5153
  Evansville *(G-4087)*
Gindor Inc .... G 574 642-4004
  Goshen *(G-6149)*
Griffith Rbr Mills of Garrett .... C 260 357-0876
  Garrett *(G-5865)*
▲ Hi-Tech Foam Products LLC .... E 317 737-2298
  Indianapolis *(G-8396)*
▲ Hoosier Gasket Corporation .... D 317 545-2000
  Indianapolis *(G-8409)*
Ilpea Industries Inc .... D 812 752-2526
  Scottsburg *(G-14561)*
▲ Ilpea Industries Inc .... D 812 752-2526
  Scottsburg *(G-14562)*
Iris Rubber Co Inc .... F 317 984-3561
  Cicero *(G-1997)*
Jeans Extrusions Inc .... G 812 883-2581
  Salem *(G-14486)*
Knox Enterprises Inc .... G 317 714-3073
  Indianapolis *(G-8699)*
Long Jim Jay Jr .... G 317 446-4409
  Indianapolis *(G-8779)*
Metallic Seals Inc .... G 317 780-0773
  Indianapolis *(G-8889)*
▲ Midwest Gasket Corporation .... E 765 629-2221
  Milroy *(G-11826)*
Nishikawa Cooper LLC .... D 260 593-2156
  Bremen *(G-1208)*
Nitto Inc .... G 317 879-2840
  Zionsville *(G-17037)*
Parker-Hannifin Corporation .... D 574 533-1111
  Goshen *(G-6236)*
Parker-Hannifin Corporation .... E 260 894-7125
  Syracuse *(G-15471)*
Press-Seal Corporation .... G 260 436-0521
  Fort Wayne *(G-5349)*
▼ Press-Seal Corporation .... C 260 436-0521
  Fort Wayne *(G-5350)*
Rits Ltd Brokers Inc .... G 260 348-0786
  Fort Wayne *(G-5385)*
Rubber Shop Inc .... G 574 291-6440
  South Bend *(G-15229)*
▲ Seal Products LLC .... G 260 436-5628
  Fort Wayne *(G-5405)*
Seals & Components Inc .... G 708 895-5222
  La Porte *(G-10478)*
◆ T & M Rubber Inc .... E 574 533-3173
  Goshen *(G-6267)*
Tfco Incorporated .... G 219 324-4166
  La Porte *(G-10492)*
▲ Tfco Incorporated .... G 219 324-4166
  La Porte *(G-10491)*
◆ Triangle Rubber Co LLC .... C 574 533-3118
  Goshen *(G-6272)*
▼ Trifab & Construction Inc .... G 219 845-1300
  Hammond *(G-7024)*
Uniform Hood Lace Inc .... G 317 896-9555
  Westfield *(G-16734)*

3061 Mechanical rubber goods

Ace Extrusion LLC .... F 812 868-8640
  Evansville *(G-3869)*
Ati Inc .... G 812 520-5409
  Mount Vernon *(G-12290)*
◆ Ati Inc .... G 812 431-5409
  Mount Vernon *(G-12289)*
Bawaenterprises LLC .... G 269 228-1258
  Granger *(G-6336)*
Bluffton Rubber .... G 260 824-4501
  Bluffton *(G-1031)*
BRC Rubber & Plastics Inc .... E 260 827-0871
  Bluffton *(G-1032)*
BRC Rubber & Plastics Inc .... F 260 203-5300
  Churubusco *(G-1974)*
BRC Rubber & Plastics Inc .... E 260 894-4121
  Ligonier *(G-11007)*
BRC Rubber & Plastics Inc .... F 765 728-8510
  Montpelier *(G-12177)*
▲ BRC Rubber & Plastics Inc .... C 260 693-2171
  Fort Wayne *(G-4815)*
BRC Rubber Plastics Inc .... G 260 894-7263
  Ligonier *(G-11008)*
Coleman Cable LLC .... D 765 449-7227
  Lafayette *(G-10553)*
Contitech Usa Inc .... B 260 925-0700
  Auburn *(G-378)*
Contitech Usa Inc .... B 260 925-0700
  Auburn *(G-379)*
▲ Envirotech Extrusion Inc .... E 765 966-8068
  Richmond *(G-14120)*
Fellwocks Automotive .... G 812 867-3658
  Evansville *(G-4067)*
Freudenberg-Nok General Partnr .... C 765 763-7246
  Morristown *(G-12277)*
Freudenberg-Nok General Partnr .... C 734 354-5504
  Shelbyville *(G-14757)*
▲ Griffith Rbr Mills of Garrett .... E 260 357-3125
  Garrett *(G-5864)*
Iris Rubber Co Inc .... F 317 984-3561
  Cicero *(G-1997)*
Jasper Rubber Products Inc .... D 812 482-3242
  Jasper *(G-9855)*
▲ Jasper Rubber Products Inc .... B 812 482-3242
  Jasper *(G-9856)*
▲ Mid-States Rubber Products Inc .... B 812 385-3473
  Princeton *(G-14005)*

SIC SECTION
30 RUBBER AND MISCELLANEOUS PLASTIC PRODUCTS

Parker-Hannifin Corporation................ D 574 533-1111
  Goshen *(G-6236)*
Parker-Hannifin Corporation................ C 574 528-9400
  Syracuse *(G-15470)*
▼ Polycraft Products Inc....................... E 812 577-3401
  Greendale *(G-6452)*
Rd Rubber Products Inc........................ G 260 357-3571
  Garrett *(G-5875)*
Rubber Shop Inc.................................... G 574 291-6440
  South Bend *(G-15229)*
◆ T & M Rubber Inc.............................. E 574 533-3173
  Goshen *(G-6267)*
◆ Triangle Rubber Co LLC....................C 574 533-3118
  Goshen *(G-6272)*
Viking Inc... E 260 244-6141
  Columbia City *(G-2211)*
Western Consolidated Tech Inc............ D 260 495-9866
  Fremont *(G-5842)*
Worldcell Extrusions LLC..................... G 574 333-2249
  Elkhart *(G-3794)*

3069 Fabricated rubber products, nec

Acme Masking Company Inc................ E 317 272-6202
  Avon *(G-503)*
American Roller Company LLC........... D 574 586-3101
  Walkerton *(G-16263)*
American Rubber Corp.......................... G 317 548-8455
  Anderson *(G-77)*
Apex Procurement LLC........................ G 574 304-2679
  Claypool *(G-2050)*
BRC Rubber & Plastics Inc.................. E 260 827-0871
  Bluffton *(G-1032)*
Central Rubber & Plastics Inc.............. E 574 534-6411
  Goshen *(G-6110)*
Clearline Operations LLC.................... G 765 381-8361
  Muncie *(G-12367)*
▲ Discount Labels LLC....................... A 812 945-2617
  New Albany *(G-12720)*
Eis Fibercoating Inc............................. E 574 722-5192
  Logansport *(G-11071)*
▲ ENBI INDIANA INC......................... C 317 398-3267
  Shelbyville *(G-14755)*
Engraving and Stamp Center Inc........... G 812 336-0606
  Bloomington *(G-861)*
Exactseal Inc.. G 317 559-2220
  Indianapolis *(G-8148)*
◆ Excell Usa Inc..................................D 812 895-1687
  Vincennes *(G-16121)*
◆ Exemplary Foam Inc........................F 574 295-8888
  Elkhart *(G-3338)*
Field Rubber Products Inc................... F 317 773-3787
  Noblesville *(G-13077)*
Finzer Roller Inc.................................. G 219 325-8808
  La Porte *(G-10409)*
Fluid Handling Technology Inc............ G 317 216-9629
  Indianapolis *(G-8207)*
Foamcraft Inc....................................... E 574 534-4343
  Goshen *(G-6139)*
Fred Schock Company Inc.................... F 765 647-4648
  Brookville *(G-1320)*
Fuel Bladder Distributors Inc................ G 317 852-9156
  Brownsburg *(G-1371)*
Fyberdyne Laboratories........................ G 574 291-9438
  South Bend *(G-15040)*
▲ Gdc Inc.. C 574 533-3128
  Goshen *(G-6143)*
▲ Goodtime Technology Dev Ltd........ G 317 876-3661
  Indianapolis *(G-8306)*
Gorilla Plastic Rbr Group LLC............. F 317 635-9616
  Indianapolis *(G-8307)*
Griffith Rbr Mills of Garrett................. C 260 357-0876
  Garrett *(G-5865)*

Gta Containers Inc............................... G 574 288-3459
  South Bend *(G-15050)*
Gta Containers Inc............................... G 574 288-3459
  South Bend *(G-15051)*
Gta Containers Inc............................... E 574 288-3459
  South Bend *(G-15052)*
Gta Containers LLC............................. E 574 288-3459
  South Bend *(G-15053)*
▲ Gta Containers LLC......................... E 574 288-3459
  South Bend *(G-15054)*
Gta Drum Inc.. E 574 288-3459
  South Bend *(G-15055)*
H A King Co Inc................................... G 260 482-6376
  Fort Wayne *(G-5047)*
Hawkins Darryal................................... G 765 282-6021
  Muncie *(G-12410)*
▲ Hi-Tech Foam Products LLC........... E 317 737-2298
  Indianapolis *(G-8396)*
Ilpea Industries Inc............................... D 812 752-2526
  Scottsburg *(G-14561)*
Indiana Factory Outlet Mar Inc............. G 260 799-4764
  Larwill *(G-10819)*
Indianapolis Industrial Pdts................... G 317 359-3078
  Indianapolis *(G-8506)*
Infinity Performance Inc....................... G 317 479-1017
  Indianapolis *(G-8542)*
Iris Rubber Co Inc................................. F 317 984-3561
  Cicero *(G-1997)*
▲ Jpc LLC.. F 574 293-8030
  Elkhart *(G-3437)*
Klh Holding Corporation....................... E 317 634-3976
  Indianapolis *(G-8693)*
Knox Enterprises Inc............................. G 317 714-3073
  Indianapolis *(G-8699)*
Larry G Byrd.. F 765 458-7285
  Liberty *(G-10990)*
LTI Holdings Inc.................................. G 574 389-1878
  Elkhart *(G-3502)*
McCammon Engineering Corp............. G 812 356-4455
  Sullivan *(G-15413)*
Midwest Mat Company......................... G 765 286-0831
  Muncie *(G-12455)*
Midwest Rubber Sales Inc.................... G 765 468-7105
  Farmland *(G-4426)*
Nishikawa Cooper LLC........................ C 260 593-2156
  Fort Wayne *(G-5271)*
Nishikawa Cooper LLC........................ C 248 978-6953
  Fort Wayne *(G-5272)*
▲ Nishikawa Cooper LLC.................... B 260 593-2156
  Topeka *(G-15813)*
▲ Nishikawa of America Inc............... G 260 593-2156
  Topeka *(G-15814)*
No-Sail Splash Guard Co Inc................ G 765 522-2100
  Roachdale *(G-14248)*
North American Latex Corp.................. D 812 268-6608
  Sullivan *(G-15415)*
Obelisk Re-Play Opco LLC.................. G 866 228-1485
  Greenfield *(G-6534)*
Pactiv LLC.. E 574 936-7065
  Plymouth *(G-13800)*
Phoenix Closures Inc............................. F 765 658-1800
  Greencastle *(G-6424)*
Pierceton Rubber Products Inc.............. F 574 594-3002
  Pierceton *(G-13639)*
Protective Coatings Inc......................... E 260 424-2900
  Fort Wayne *(G-5354)*
Qpoly LLC.. G 574 386-4671
  Elkhart *(G-3628)*
Recreation Insites LLC........................ G 317 578-0588
  Fishers *(G-4592)*
Robco Engineered Rbr Pdts Inc............. F 260 248-2888
  Columbia City *(G-2192)*

Roembke Mfg & Design Inc................ F 260 622-4030
  Ossian *(G-13433)*
Roembke Mfg & Design Inc................ E 260 622-4135
  Ossian *(G-13432)*
Rubber Products Distrs Inc................... F 317 883-6700
  Greenwood *(G-6762)*
▲ Schacht-Pfister Inc.......................... G 260 356-9775
  Huntington *(G-7365)*
Servaas Inc... G 317 633-2020
  Indianapolis *(G-9405)*
Specialty Products & Polymers............ G 269 684-5931
  South Bend *(G-15260)*
Ten Cate Enbi Inc (indiana).................. C 317 398-3267
  Shelbyville *(G-14804)*
Terra Health North America LLC........ G 317 675-9990
  Connersville *(G-2473)*
Valley Tile Corporation........................ E 812 268-3328
  Sullivan *(G-15424)*
◆ Vestil Manufacturing Corp...............C 260 665-7586
  Angola *(G-306)*

3081 Unsupported plastics film and sheet

▲ Abtrex Industries Inc....................... F 734 728-0550
  South Bend *(G-14934)*
Amcor Flexibles North Amer Inc......... B 812 466-2213
  Terre Haute *(G-15542)*
American Renolit Corp La.................... G 856 241-4901
  La Porte *(G-10383)*
◆ American Renolit Corporation.........C 219 324-6886
  La Porte *(G-10384)*
Avery Dennison Corporation................ D 219 696-7777
  Lowell *(G-11155)*
▲ Bcw Diversified Inc......................... E 765 644-2033
  Middletown *(G-11766)*
Berry Global Inc................................... D 812 334-7090
  Bloomington *(G-802)*
Berry Global Inc................................... E 812 867-6671
  Evansville *(G-3919)*
Berry Global Inc................................... B 812 421-3136
  Franklin *(G-5714)*
Berry Global Inc................................... B 812 386-1525
  Princeton *(G-13983)*
Berry Global Inc................................... C 765 966-1414
  Richmond *(G-14096)*
◆ Berry Global Inc.............................. A 812 424-2904
  Evansville *(G-3918)*
▼ Berry Global Group Inc................... A 812 424-2904
  Evansville *(G-3921)*
Custom Covers Inc............................... G 765 481-7800
  Lebanon *(G-10888)*
D & M Enterprises LLC....................... F 260 483-4008
  Fort Wayne *(G-4901)*
Fitesa Indiana LLC............................... E 812 466-0202
  Terre Haute *(G-15588)*
Fitesa Indiana LLC............................... B 812 466-0266
  Terre Haute *(G-15589)*
Foil Laminating Inc............................... E
  Plymouth *(G-13777)*
Futurex Industries Inc........................... E 765 498-8900
  Bloomingdale *(G-759)*
Futurex Industries Inc........................... E 765 597-2221
  Marshall *(G-11373)*
Futurex Industries Inc........................... E 812 299-5708
  Terre Haute *(G-15593)*
▲ Futurex Industries Inc..................... C 765 498-3900
  Bloomingdale *(G-760)*
Hoosier Fiberglass Industries................ F 812 232-5027
  Terre Haute *(G-15606)*
Jack Laurie Coml Floors Inc................. G 317 569-2095
  Indianapolis *(G-8613)*
Mad Dasher Inc.................................... E 260 747-0545
  Fort Wayne *(G-5198)*

30 RUBBER AND MISCELLANEOUS PLASTIC PRODUCTS

▲ Mirwec Film Incorporated .... F 812 331-7194
  Bloomington *(G-920)*
Pactiv LLC .... E 574 936-7065
  Plymouth *(G-13800)*
Pliant LLC .... E 253 872-2253
  Evansville *(G-4246)*
▲ Polymer Science Inc .... G 574 583-3751
  Monticello *(G-12166)*
▲ Polyweave Industries Inc .... E 812 467-0300
  Evansville *(G-4249)*
◆ Primex Plastics Corporation .... B 765 966-7774
  Richmond *(G-14186)*
Printpack Inc .... C 812 663-5091
  Greensburg *(G-6625)*
Sabic Innovative Plas US LLC .... B 812 831-4054
  Mount Vernon *(G-12319)*
◆ Sabic Innvtive Plas Mt Vrnon L .... A 812 838-4385
  Mount Vernon *(G-12320)*
Sonoco Products Company .... D 812 526-5511
  Edinburgh *(G-3105)*
Specialty Adhesive Film Co .... E 812 926-0156
  Aurora *(G-455)*
Taghleef Industries Inc .... A 302 326-5500
  Rosedale *(G-14385)*
Taghleef Industries Inc .... G 812 460-5657
  Terre Haute *(G-15722)*
Tessellated Inc .... G 304 277-8896
  South Bend *(G-15281)*
Transcendia Inc .... C 765 935-1520
  Richmond *(G-14220)*
Tredegar Corporation .... G 574 262-4685
  Elkhart *(G-3745)*
Tredegar Corporation .... D 812 466-0266
  Terre Haute *(G-15734)*

3082 Unsupported plastics profile shapes

▲ 3d Parts Mfg LLC .... G 317 860-6941
  Anderson *(G-68)*
Filtration Parts Incorporated .... F 704 661-8135
  Rensselaer *(G-14052)*
Mitsubishi Chemical Advncd Mtr .... C 260 479-4100
  Fort Wayne *(G-5233)*
Mitsubshi Chem Advnced Mtls In ...... D 260 479-4700
  Fort Wayne *(G-5234)*
Polygon Company .... D 574 586-3145
  Walkerton *(G-16274)*
▲ Polygon Company .... C 574 586-3145
  Walkerton *(G-16275)*
▲ Precision Products Group Inc .... F 317 663-4590
  Indianapolis *(G-9184)*
Prolon Inc .... E 574 522-8900
  Elkhart *(G-3623)*
S H Leggitt Company .... G 574 264-0230
  Elkhart *(G-3656)*
▲ Sabin Corporation .... C 812 323-4500
  Bloomington *(G-965)*
▲ Specialty Mfg Ind Inc .... E 812 256-4633
  Charlestown *(G-1894)*
▲ Stratikore Inc .... G 574 807-0028
  La Porte *(G-10485)*

3083 Laminated plastics plate and sheet

Ameri-Kart Corp .... D 225 642-7874
  Bristol *(G-1243)*
◆ American Art Clay Co Inc .... C 317 244-6871
  Indianapolis *(G-7499)*
Applied Composites Engrg Inc .... E 317 243-4225
  Indianapolis *(G-7533)*
▼ Berry Global Group Inc .... A 812 424-2904
  Evansville *(G-3921)*
Brownsburg Custom Cabinets Inc ...... G 317 271-1887
  Indianapolis *(G-7690)*

Elko Inc .... F 812 473-8400
  Evansville *(G-4030)*
◆ Envalior Engineering Materials Inc .. C 800 333-4237
  Evansville *(G-4039)*
Envalior Engineering Mtls Inc .... G 812 435-7500
  Evansville *(G-4041)*
Experimental Nylon Products .... E 574 674-8747
  Osceola *(G-13391)*
F Robert Gardner Co Inc .... G 317 634-2333
  Indianapolis *(G-8161)*
General Fabricators Inc .... G 317 787-9354
  Indianapolis *(G-8271)*
Hancor Inc .... E 812 443-2080
  Brazil *(G-1144)*
Hartson-Kennedy Cabinet Top Co ...... B 765 668-8144
  Marion *(G-11291)*
Heywood Williams Inc .... G 574 295-8400
  Elkhart *(G-3405)*
◆ Jaeger-Ntek Sling Slutions Inc .... D 219 324-1111
  La Porte *(G-10431)*
Lockerbie Square Cab Co Inc .... G 317 635-1134
  Indianapolis *(G-8775)*
Midwest Cabinet Solutions Inc .... E 765 664-3938
  Marion *(G-11318)*
Miller Waste Mills Inc .... G 507 454-6900
  Indianapolis *(G-8924)*
▲ Omni Plastics LLC .... D 812 422-0888
  Evansville *(G-4227)*
◆ Parkland Plastics Inc .... E 574 825-4336
  Middlebury *(G-11745)*
Patrick Industries Inc .... E 574 825-4336
  Middlebury *(G-11746)*
Plasticraft-Complete Acrylics .... G 765 610-9502
  Anderson *(G-180)*
Positron Corporation .... E 574 295-8777
  Elkhart *(G-3610)*
Sabic Innovative Plas US LLC .... D 812 372-0197
  Columbus *(G-2388)*
▲ Sabin Corporation .... C 812 323-4500
  Bloomington *(G-965)*
Sims Cabinet Co Inc .... E 317 634-1747
  Danville *(G-2828)*
Skips Bumper Repair .... G 773 289-2255
  Gary *(G-6010)*
Sonoco Products Company .... D 812 526-5511
  Edinburgh *(G-3105)*
Thrust Industries Inc .... F 812 437-3643
  Evansville *(G-4344)*
◆ Triangle Rubber Co LLC .... C 574 533-3118
  Goshen *(G-6272)*

3084 Plastics pipe

Ace Extrusion LLC .... E 812 463-5230
  Evansville *(G-3871)*
Advanced Drainage Systems Inc .... G 812 443-2080
  Brazil *(G-1131)*
Advanced Drainage Systems Inc .... G 317 917-7960
  Indianapolis *(G-7438)*
Blair Industries LLC .... G 765 215-2735
  Muncie *(G-12354)*
Corrosion Technologies Inc .... G 317 894-0627
  Greenfield *(G-6484)*
▲ Cresline Plastic Pipe Co Inc .... E 812 428-9300
  Evansville *(G-3994)*
Cresline-Northwest LLC .... F 812 428-9300
  Evansville *(G-3995)*
Cresline-West Inc .... G 812 428-9300
  Evansville *(G-3996)*
Diamond Plastics Corporation .... D 765 287-9234
  Muncie *(G-12382)*
▲ Fratco Inc .... D 800 854-7120
  Monticello *(G-12150)*

Hancor Inc .... E 812 443-2080
  Brazil *(G-1144)*
Kuri TEC Manufacturing Inc .... E 765 764-6000
  Williamsport *(G-16850)*
Liner Products LLC .... F 812 723-0244
  Paoli *(G-13499)*
Plastic Pipe Technologies LLC .... G 317 674-5944
  New Palestine *(G-12942)*
Uniseal Inc .... E 812 425-1361
  Evansville *(G-4360)*
Viking Group Inc .... B 812 256-8500
  Charlestown *(G-1895)*

3085 Plastics bottles

▲ Ahf Industries Inc .... C 812 936-9988
  French Lick *(G-5843)*
Amcor Rigid Packaging Usa LLC .... G 317 736-4313
  Greenwood *(G-6666)*
▼ Berry Global Group Inc .... A 812 424-2904
  Evansville *(G-3921)*
▲ Crown Packaging International Inc ... D 219 738-1000
  Merrillville *(G-11499)*
North America Packaging Corp .... G 317 291-2396
  Indianapolis *(G-9021)*
Plastic Recycl Export Ltd LLC .... G 301 758-6885
  Fort Wayne *(G-5318)*
Polycon Industries Inc .... G 219 738-1000
  Merrillville *(G-11551)*
◆ Setco LLC .... B 812 424-2904
  Evansville *(G-4307)*
Silgan Plastics LLC .... F 812 522-0900
  Seymour *(G-14693)*
▲ Specialty Mfg Ind Inc .... E 812 256-4633
  Charlestown *(G-1894)*

3086 Plastics foam products

Abbp LLC .... G 812 402-2000
  Evansville *(G-3864)*
Ace Extrusion LLC .... E 812 463-5230
  Evansville *(G-3871)*
Aearo Technologies LLC .... C 317 692-6666
  Indianapolis *(G-7447)*
American Whitetail Inc .... F 812 937-7185
  Ferdinand *(G-4428)*
Aqua Lily Products LLC .... G 951 246-9610
  Elkhart *(G-3187)*
B&W Packaging Mfg LLC .... E 812 280-9578
  New Albany *(G-12694)*
Bch Image USA Inc .... G 812 326-1025
  Saint Anthony *(G-14426)*
▲ Bremen Corporation .... B 574 546-4238
  Bremen *(G-1178)*
Cellofoam North America Inc .... D 317 535-9008
  Whiteland *(G-16778)*
▲ Century Foam Inc .... D 574 293-5547
  Elkhart *(G-3250)*
▲ Createc Corporation .... B 317 566-0022
  Indianapolis *(G-7899)*
Creative Foam Corporation .... D 574 546-4238
  Bremen *(G-1184)*
Cryovac LLC .... E 317 876-4100
  Indianapolis *(G-7916)*
Efp LLC .... E 812 602-0019
  Evansville *(G-4029)*
▲ Efp LLC .... D 574 295-4690
  Elkhart *(G-3314)*
Elliott Co of Indianapolis .... F 317 291-1213
  Indianapolis *(G-8096)*
Exemplary Foam South LLC .... F 423 302-0962
  Elkhart *(G-3339)*
Foam Fabricators Inc .... G 812 948-1696
  New Albany *(G-12732)*

SIC SECTION

30 RUBBER AND MISCELLANEOUS PLASTIC PRODUCTS

▲ Foam Rubber LLC .... C 765 521-2000
New Castle *(G-12862)*

Foamcraft Inc .... E 574 293-8569
Elkhart *(G-3352)*

Foamcraft Inc .... E 574 534-4343
Goshen *(G-6139)*

Foamcraft Inc .... E 812 849-3350
Mitchell *(G-12039)*

▲ Foamcraft Inc .... E 317 545-3626
Indianapolis *(G-8212)*

Foamex LP .... E 800 417-4257
Fort Wayne *(G-4990)*

Forefront Foam LLC .... F 574 343-1146
Mishawaka *(G-11897)*

Fxi Inc .... G 260 925-1073
Auburn *(G-392)*

Fxi Inc .... G 260 747-7485
Fort Wayne *(G-5015)*

Fxi Auburn .... E 260 925-1073
Auburn *(G-393)*

G & T Industries Inc .... G 812 634-2252
Jasper *(G-9840)*

◆ Gaska Tape Inc .... D 574 294-5431
Elkhart *(G-3366)*

▲ Gdc Inc .... C 574 533-3128
Goshen *(G-6143)*

▲ Hi-Tech Foam Products LLC .... E 317 737-2298
Indianapolis *(G-8396)*

Innocor Foam Tech - Acp Inc .... G 574 294-7694
Elkhart *(G-3427)*

Innovative Packaging Assoc Inc .... E 260 356-6577
Huntington *(G-7330)*

Jcmz Enterprises Inc .... E 812 372-0288
Columbus *(G-2329)*

Johns Manville Corporation .... C 574 546-4666
Bremen *(G-1200)*

▲ Kibbechem Inc .... E 574 266-1234
Elkhart *(G-3454)*

Knox Enterprises Inc .... G 317 714-3073
Indianapolis *(G-8699)*

Lifoam Industries LLC .... D 410 889-1023
Fishers *(G-4556)*

M & C LLC .... G 812 482-7447
Jasper *(G-9885)*

▼ Molded Foam LLC .... E 574 848-1500
Bristol *(G-1275)*

Mossberg Industries Inc .... D 260 357-5141
Garrett *(G-5873)*

Nobleman Logistics LLC .... G 317 340-7406
Indianapolis *(G-9017)*

Opflex Solutions Inc .... F 800 568-7036
Indianapolis *(G-9064)*

Opflex Technologies LLC .... E 317 731-6123
Indianapolis *(G-9066)*

Opflex Technologies LLC .... F 518 568-7036
Indianapolis *(G-9065)*

Pregis LLC .... G 574 936-7065
Plymouth *(G-13806)*

PSC Industries Inc .... F 812 425-9071
Evansville *(G-4263)*

Residue West Inc .... F 731 587-9596
Evansville *(G-4285)*

Security Paks Intl LLC .... F 317 536-2662
Carmel *(G-1756)*

Sevenoks Inc .... G 800 523-8715
La Porte *(G-10480)*

Sonoco Prtective Solutions Inc .... E 260 726-9333
Portland *(G-13967)*

Total Concepts Design Inc .... D 812 752-6534
Scottsburg *(G-14582)*

Tp/Elm Acquisition Sbusid Inc .... D 260 728-2161
Decatur *(G-2886)*

Useful Products LLC .... E 877 304-9036
Goodland *(G-6083)*

Vahala Foam Inc .... D 574 293-1287
Elkhart *(G-3764)*

◆ Worldwide Foam Ltd .... E 574 968-8268
Elkhart *(G-3796)*

3087 Custom compound purchased resins

Color Master Inc .... D 260 868-2320
Butler *(G-1461)*

Crosspoint Polymer Tech LLC .... E 812 426-1350
Evansville *(G-3997)*

◆ Envalior Engineering Materials Inc .... C 800 333-4237
Evansville *(G-4039)*

Envalior Engineering Mtls Inc .... G 812 435-7500
Evansville *(G-4041)*

▲ Enviroplas LLC .... D 812 868-0808
Evansville *(G-4043)*

Enviroplas LLC .... D 812 868-0808
Evansville *(G-4044)*

Geon Performance Solutions LLC .... G 812 466-5116
Terre Haute *(G-15596)*

Innovations Amplified LLC .... G 317 339-4685
Indianapolis *(G-8552)*

Lush & Luxe Creations LLC .... G 317 561-0574
Indianapolis *(G-8798)*

▲ Matrixx-Qtr Inc .... D 812 429-0901
Evansville *(G-4192)*

McCammon Engineering Corp .... G 812 356-4455
Sullivan *(G-15413)*

Miller Waste Mills Inc .... G 507 454-6900
Indianapolis *(G-8924)*

Mwf LLC .... G 812 936-5303
Bloomington *(G-927)*

Polyram Compounds LLC .... F 812 401-5830
Evansville *(G-4248)*

Polytek Development Corp .... G 317 494-6420
Franklin *(G-5767)*

▲ Rbc Holding Inc .... F 317 340-3845
Greenwood *(G-6759)*

Sabic Innovative Plas US LLC .... B 812 831-4054
Mount Vernon *(G-12319)*

◆ Sabic Innvtive Plas Mt Vrnon L .... A 812 838-4385
Mount Vernon *(G-12320)*

3088 Plastics plumbing fixtures

▲ Abtrex Industries Inc .... F 734 728-0550
South Bend *(G-14934)*

Altec Engineering Inc .... E 574 293-1965
Elkhart *(G-3167)*

Composite Tech Assemblies LLC .... E 574 948-0004
Plymouth *(G-13765)*

Frontline Mfg Inc .... E 574 269-6751
Warsaw *(G-16365)*

Frontline Mfg Inc .... D 574 453-2902
Warsaw *(G-16366)*

Hotel Vanities Intl LLC .... G 317 787-2330
Indianapolis *(G-8423)*

▲ Hotel Vanities Intl LLC .... F 317 787-2330
Indianapolis *(G-8424)*

Maax Inc .... E 574 936-3838
Plymouth *(G-13795)*

◆ Masco Bath Corporation .... A 317 254-5959
Indianapolis *(G-8846)*

Nibco Inc .... C 574 296-1240
Goshen *(G-6227)*

Oasis Lifestyle LLC .... F 574 948-0004
Plymouth *(G-13799)*

▲ Royal Spa Corporation .... D 317 781-0828
Indianapolis *(G-9341)*

Shidler Associates .... G 574 232-7357
South Bend *(G-15241)*

Thursday Pools LLC .... G 317 973-0200
Fortville *(G-5607)*

Ultra/Glas of Lakeville Inc .... F 574 784-8958
Lakeville *(G-10793)*

Upanaway LLC .... G 866 218-7143
Greenfield *(G-6568)*

3089 Plastics products, nec

20/20 Custom Molded Plas LLC .... B 260 565-2020
Bluffton *(G-1020)*

3-D Services .... G 574 933-4819
Plymouth *(G-13749)*

A S V Plastics Inc .... F 574 264-9694
Elkhart *(G-3141)*

▲ ABC Industries Inc .... D 800 426-0921
Winona Lake *(G-16907)*

ABI Plastics LLC .... G 574 294-1700
Elkhart *(G-3145)*

Accelerated Curing Inc .... F 260 726-3202
Portland *(G-13926)*

Accu-Mold LLC .... E 269 323-0388
Mishawaka *(G-11834)*

▲ Ace Mobility Inc .... F 317 241-2444
Indianapolis *(G-7421)*

Adkev Inc .... F 574 583-4420
Monticello *(G-12132)*

▲ Adkev Inc .... D 219 297-4484
Goodland *(G-6078)*

Affinis Group LLC .... G 317 831-3830
Mooresville *(G-12191)*

▲ Aircom Manufacturing Inc .... B 317 545-5383
Indianapolis *(G-7462)*

▲ AK Industries Inc .... D 574 936-6022
Plymouth *(G-13752)*

Aker Composite Solutions Inc .... G 574 935-0908
Plymouth *(G-13753)*

Akka Plastics Inc .... E 812 849-9256
Mitchell *(G-12030)*

Alex Virok DBA Intec .... G 317 770-7559
Noblesville *(G-13034)*

Allen Apr Plastics Repair Inc .... E 260 482-8523
Fort Wayne *(G-4741)*

Allin Plastic Engraving Inc .... G 219 972-2223
Hammond *(G-6871)*

Altec Engineering Inc .... E 574 293-1965
Elkhart *(G-3167)*

Amcor Rigid Packaging Usa LLC .... G 317 736-4313
Franklin *(G-5708)*

▲ Ameri-Kart Corp .... C 574 848-7462
Bristol *(G-1244)*

▲ Ameri-Kart(mi) Corp .... D 269 641-5811
Bristol *(G-1245)*

▲ American Plastic Molding Corp .... C 813 752-7000
Scottsburg *(G-14552)*

American Window and Glass Inc .... C 812 464-9400
Evansville *(G-3886)*

An-Mar Wiring Systems Inc .... F 574 255-5523
Mishawaka *(G-11842)*

Anderson Products .... G 765 794-4242
Darlington *(G-2831)*

Apexx Enterprises LLC .... F 812 486-2443
Montgomery *(G-12085)*

◆ API Indiana Inc .... D 574 293-5574
Elkhart *(G-3186)*

Apr Plastic Fabricating Inc .... E 260 482-8523
Fort Wayne *(G-4768)*

Ar-Tee Enterprises Inc .... G 574 848-5543
Bristol *(G-1246)*

Arran Isle Inc .... E 574 295-4400
Elkhart *(G-3191)*

Arrowhead Plastic Engrg Inc .... F 765 396-9113
Eaton *(G-3059)*

Employee Codes: A=Over 500 employees, B=251-500
C=101-250, D=51-100, E=20-50, F=10-19, G=1-9

30 RUBBER AND MISCELLANEOUS PLASTIC PRODUCTS

Arrowhead Plastic Engrg Inc .... E 765 286-0533
  Muncie *(G-12345)*
▼ Artek Inc .... E 260 484-4222
  Fort Wayne *(G-4773)*
Artistic Composite Pallets LLC .... E 317 960-5813
  Carmel *(G-1565)*
Ashley Industrial Molding Inc .... E 260 349-1982
  Kendallville *(G-10092)*
◆ Ashley Industrial Molding Inc .... D 260 587-9155
  Ashley *(G-330)*
Assmann Corporation America .... E 260 357-3181
  Garrett *(G-5854)*
Astar Inc .... G 574 234-2137
  South Bend *(G-14950)*
Auburn Hardwood Molding .... G 260 925-5959
  Auburn *(G-363)*
Avr Products Inc .... G 574 294-6101
  Bristol *(G-1247)*
▲ B & B Molders LLC .... D 574 259-7838
  Mishawaka *(G-11845)*
B D Custom Manufacturing Inc .... F 574 848-0925
  Bristol *(G-1248)*
B Plus Enterprises Inc .... G 219 733-9404
  Wanatah *(G-16287)*
B&B Tool and Molding Co Inc .... E
  Muncie *(G-12348)*
B&M Plastics Inc .... G 812 422-0888
  Evansville *(G-3906)*
Bamar Plastics Inc .... E 574 234-4066
  South Bend *(G-14954)*
Beach Acquisition Co LLC .... B 812 945-2688
  New Albany *(G-12697)*
▲ Beach Acquisition Co LLC .... B 812 945-2688
  New Albany *(G-12698)*
Bee Window Incorporated .... C 317 283-8522
  Fishers *(G-4473)*
Beechys Molding Plus LLC .... G 260 768-7030
  Shipshewana *(G-14839)*
Bender Mold & Machine Inc .... F 574 255-5176
  Mishawaka *(G-11851)*
Bender Products Inc .... E 574 255-5350
  Mishawaka *(G-11852)*
Berry Film Products Co Inc .... C 812 306-2690
  Evansville *(G-3917)*
Berry Global Inc .... D 812 334-7090
  Bloomington *(G-802)*
Berry Global Inc .... E 812 867-6671
  Evansville *(G-3919)*
Berry Global Inc .... G 812 421-3136
  Franklin *(G-5714)*
Berry Global Inc .... G 260 495-2000
  Fremont *(G-5811)*
Berry Global Inc .... E 812 558-3510
  Odon *(G-13331)*
Berry Global Inc .... G 812 386-1525
  Princeton *(G-13983)*
Berry Global Inc .... C 765 966-1414
  Richmond *(G-14096)*
◆ Berry Global Inc .... A 812 424-2904
  Evansville *(G-3918)*
Berry Global Escrow Corp .... G 812 424-2904
  Evansville *(G-3920)*
Berry Global Group Inc .... F 812 868-7429
  Princeton *(G-13984)*
▼ Berry Global Group Inc .... A 812 424-2904
  Evansville *(G-3921)*
Berry Plas Technical Svcs Inc .... F 812 424-2904
  Evansville *(G-3922)*
Berry Plastics Escrow Corp .... F 812 424-2904
  Evansville *(G-3923)*
Berry Plastics Group Inc .... E 812 424-2904
  Evansville *(G-3924)*

◆ Berry Plastics Ik LLC .... C 641 648-5047
  Evansville *(G-3925)*
Berry Plastics Opco Inc .... G 812 402-2903
  Evansville *(G-3926)*
Berry Plastics Opco Inc .... E 812 424-2904
  Evansville *(G-3927)*
Best Formed Plastics LLC .... E 574 293-6128
  Elkhart *(G-3223)*
Better Way Partners LLC .... B 574 831-3340
  New Paris *(G-12948)*
Bhar Incorporated .... C 260 749-5168
  Fort Wayne *(G-4797)*
Bhaura Inc .... G 260 745-5700
  Fort Wayne *(G-4798)*
Bprex Brazil Holding Inc .... E 812 306-2764
  Evansville *(G-3944)*
▼ Bprex Closure Systems LLC .... F 812 424-2904
  Evansville *(G-3945)*
Bprex Closures LLC .... C 812 867-6671
  Evansville *(G-3947)*
Bprex Closures LLC .... D 812 386-1525
  Princeton *(G-13985)*
Bprex Closures LLC .... E 812 424-2904
  Evansville *(G-3946)*
Bprex Healthcare Packaging Inc .... F 812 424-2904
  Evansville *(G-3948)*
Bremen Composites LLC .... D 574 546-3791
  Bremen *(G-1177)*
▲ Brianza USA Corp .... G 574 855-9520
  Elkhart *(G-3235)*
Buc Construction Supply Inc .... G 574 532-9345
  Lafayette *(G-10547)*
Burco Molding Inc .... D 317 773-5699
  Noblesville *(G-13050)*
▲ Butler-Macdonald Inc .... D 317 872-5115
  Indianapolis *(G-7704)*
▲ Calico Precision Molding LLC .... E 260 484-4500
  Fort Wayne *(G-4829)*
Cambridge Molding Inc .... G 574 546-4311
  Nappanee *(G-12587)*
Caps Inc .... G 773 859-0111
  Hammond *(G-6894)*
Captive Holdings LLC .... D 812 424-2904
  Evansville *(G-3962)*
◆ Captive Plastics LLC .... C 812 424-2904
  Evansville *(G-3963)*
Carrera Manufacturing Inc .... D 260 726-9800
  Bluffton *(G-1033)*
Cedar Creek Studios Inc .... G 260 627-7320
  Leo *(G-10966)*
Cedar Plastics Inc .... F 765 483-3260
  Lebanon *(G-10882)*
▲ Challenge Plastic Products Inc ..... F 812 526-0582
  Edinburgh *(G-3071)*
Clean By Design Inc .... G 260 414-4444
  Fort Wayne *(G-4857)*
Closure Systems Intl Inc .... B 765 364-6300
  Crawfordsville *(G-2554)*
Cluster Packaging LLC .... G 612 803-1056
  Crown Point *(G-2666)*
CMS Technologies Inc .... G 219 395-8272
  Chesterton *(G-1916)*
▲ Co-Tronics Inc .... F 574 722-3850
  Peru *(G-13574)*
Color Master Inc .... D 260 868-2320
  Butler *(G-1461)*
Columbia City Plastics Inc .... F 260 244-0065
  Columbia City *(G-2134)*
▲ Complex Plastics LLC .... G 574 389-9911
  Elkhart *(G-3259)*
Complex Plastics LLC .... G 603 305-3043
  Elkhart *(G-3260)*

Composites Syndicate LLC .... F 260 484-3139
  Fort Wayne *(G-4870)*
Concept Assembly Solutions LLC ..... F 574 855-2534
  Mishawaka *(G-11863)*
Concept Tool & Engineering Inc .... G 812 352-0055
  North Vernon *(G-13259)*
Cor-A-Vent Inc .... F 574 258-6161
  Mishawaka *(G-11865)*
◆ Cor-A-Vent Inc .... F 574 255-1910
  Mishawaka *(G-11866)*
▲ CPI Card Group - Indiana Inc .... C 260 424-4920
  Fort Wayne *(G-4881)*
CPI Holding Corporation .... F 812 424-2904
  Evansville *(G-3990)*
▲ Cpx Inc .... B 219 474-5280
  Kentland *(G-10159)*
Craddock Furniture Corporation .... E 812 425-2691
  Evansville *(G-3991)*
Crane Composites Inc .... G 574 295-9391
  Elkhart *(G-3269)*
Crane Composites Inc .... G 815 467-8600
  Goshen *(G-6118)*
▲ Crawford Industries LLC .... E 800 428-0840
  Crawfordsville *(G-2557)*
Crescent Plastics Inc .... C 812 428-9305
  Evansville *(G-3992)*
Crescnt-CrsIn-Wbash Plas Fndti .... G 812 428-9300
  Evansville *(G-3993)*
Custom Plastics LLC .... E 574 259-2340
  Mishawaka *(G-11874)*
Custom Urethanes Inc .... G 219 924-1644
  Highland *(G-7131)*
▼ D M Sales & Engineering Inc .... E 317 783-5493
  Indianapolis *(G-7944)*
D&W Fine Pack LLC .... D 260 432-3027
  Fort Wayne *(G-4902)*
▲ DA Inc .... E 812 730-2130
  Charlestown *(G-1874)*
▲ Decatur Mold Tool and Engrg .... G 812 346-5188
  North Vernon *(G-13266)*
Decatur Plastic Products Inc .... D 812 352-6050
  North Vernon *(G-13267)*
▲ Decatur Plastic Products Inc .... C 812 346-5159
  North Vernon *(G-13268)*
Deep Three Inc .... G 260 705-2283
  Spencerville *(G-15369)*
◆ Deflecto LLC .... B 317 849-9555
  Indianapolis *(G-7962)*
▲ Dekalb Molded Plastics Company .. D 260 868-2105
  Butler *(G-1462)*
Dexterous Mold and Tool Inc .... E 812 422-8046
  Evansville *(G-4012)*
Diamond Manufacturing Company .... D 219 874-2374
  Michigan City *(G-11600)*
Digger Specialties Inc .... G 574 546-2811
  Bremen *(G-1186)*
▲ Digger Specialties Inc .... D 574 546-5999
  Bremen *(G-1187)*
▲ Diversity - Vuteq LLC .... C 812 761-0210
  Princeton *(G-13989)*
Dlb Custom Extrusions LLC .... F 812 423-6405
  Evansville *(G-4016)*
Dorel Juvenile Group Inc .... G 812 372-0141
  Columbus *(G-2286)*
Drug Plastics and Glass Co Inc .... E 765 385-0035
  Oxford *(G-13474)*
Drug Plastics Closures Inc .... E 812 526-0555
  Edinburgh *(G-3080)*
Dutchland LLC .... G 812 254-5400
  Loogootee *(G-11133)*
Eagle Mold & Tool .... G 574 862-1966
  Wakarusa *(G-16232)*

SIC SECTION
30 RUBBER AND MISCELLANEOUS PLASTIC PRODUCTS

Earthwise Plastics Inc.............................. E 765 673-0308
   Gas City *(G-6036)*

▲ Eckco Plastics Inc................................. G 574 258-5552
   Mishawaka *(G-11889)*

Eclipse Molding Company LLC............... G 812 546-0050
   Hope *(G-7223)*

Eis Fibercoating Inc................................. E 574 722-5192
   Logansport *(G-11071)*

Elkcases Inc.. G 574 295-7700
   Elkhart *(G-3317)*

▲ Elkhart Cases Inc................................. F 574 295-7700
   Elkhart *(G-3324)*

Elkhart Plastics Inc.................................. G 574 370-1079
   Michigan City *(G-11607)*

Enginred Plstic Components Inc............. E 812 752-6742
   Scottsburg *(G-14554)*

Enovapremier LLC.................................... E 812 385-0576
   Princeton *(G-13993)*

Epc-Columbia Inc..................................... G 812 752-6742
   Scottsburg *(G-14555)*

Exhibit A Plastics LLC............................ F 765 386-6702
   Coatesville *(G-2105)*

◆ Exo-S US LLC... C 260 562-4100
   Howe *(G-7235)*

Experimental Nylon Products.................. E 574 674-8747
   Osceola *(G-13391)*

Exton Inc... F 574 533-0447
   Goshen *(G-6132)*

▲ Fairview Fittings & Mfg....................... G 574 206-8884
   Elkhart *(G-3341)*

▲ Fas Plastic Enterprises Inc................ E 812 265-2928
   Hanover *(G-7041)*

Fencescapes LLC..................................... F 317 210-3912
   Avon *(G-519)*

Fiberglas & Plastic Fabg.......................... E 317 549-1779
   Indianapolis *(G-8183)*

Fibergrate Composite............................... G 317 752-2500
   Indianapolis *(G-8184)*

Fibertech Plastics LLC............................. D 812 983-2642
   Elberfeld *(G-3113)*

Filtration Parts Incorporated................... F 704 661-8135
   Rensselaer *(G-14052)*

First Metals & Plastics Inc..................... E 812 379-4400
   Columbus *(G-2307)*

First Metals & Plastics T........................ E 812 379-4400
   Columbus *(G-2308)*

First Place Trophy Inc.............................. G 574 293-6147
   Elkhart *(G-3347)*

Flair Molded Plastics Inc......................... D 812 425-6155
   Evansville *(G-4074)*

Flambeau Inc... G 812 372-4899
   Columbus *(G-2309)*

Flambeau Inc... G 812 372-4899
   Columbus *(G-2310)*

Flexseals Mfg LLC.................................... G 574 293-0333
   Elkhart *(G-3351)*

Flw Plastics Inc.. F 812 546-0050
   Hope *(G-7224)*

Focus Mold and Machine Inc................. G 812 422-9627
   Evansville *(G-4079)*

Form/TEC Plastics Incorporated............. E 765 342-2300
   Martinsville *(G-11395)*

◆ Fort Wayne Plastics Inc....................... C 260 432-2520
   Fort Wayne *(G-5000)*

Frankfort Plastics Inc.............................. F 931 510-0525
   Frankfort *(G-5667)*

Fred Schock Company Inc....................... F 765 647-4648
   Brookville *(G-1320)*

Fred Smith Store Fixtures....................... F 812 347-2363
   Corydon *(G-2497)*

Fred Smith Store Fixtures Inc................ D 812 347-2363
   Depauw *(G-2938)*

▼ Fti Inc... D 812 983-2642
   Elberfeld *(G-3114)*

▲ Full Tank Freedom Inc......................... E 317 485-7887
   Fortville *(G-5596)*

▲ Futaba Indiana America Corp............. B 812 895-4700
   Vincennes *(G-16127)*

Future Form Plastics................................ F 574 293-4004
   Elkhart *(G-3364)*

Future Mold Inc....................................... F 812 941-8661
   New Albany *(G-12735)*

Futurex Industries Inc............................. E 765 498-8900
   Bloomingdale *(G-759)*

◆ Galleyware Company Inc..................... G 302 996-9480
   Zionsville *(G-17009)*

Gdc Inc.. E 574 533-3128
   Elkhart *(G-3368)*

General Fabricators Inc........................... G 317 787-9354
   Indianapolis *(G-8271)*

▲ Genesis Molding Inc............................ D 574 256-9271
   Mishawaka *(G-11899)*

▲ Genesis Plastics and Engi.................. C 812 752-6742
   Scottsburg *(G-14556)*

Genesis Plastics Solutions LLC.............. G 812 283-4435
   Jeffersonville *(G-9990)*

Genpak LLC.. F 812 256-7040
   Jeffersonville *(G-9991)*

Genpak LLC.. G 812 752-3111
   Scottsburg *(G-14557)*

Gieseck+dvrent Epymnts Amer In.......... G 866 484-0611
   Fort Wayne *(G-5024)*

Glass Molders Pottery Pla...................... G 812 398-6222
   Carlisle *(G-1541)*

▲ Global Plastics Inc.............................. D 317 299-2345
   Indianapolis *(G-8290)*

Gmv LLC.. G 765 635-4842
   Carmel *(G-1642)*

Graber Manufacturing LLC..................... D 260 657-3400
   Grabill *(G-6298)*

Grafco Industries Ltd Partnr.................. C 812 424-2904
   Evansville *(G-4095)*

▲ Green Leaf Inc...................................... C 812 877-1546
   Fontanet *(G-4699)*

Green Plus Plastics LLC.......................... G 317 672-2410
   Indianapolis *(G-8317)*

Greystone Logistics Inc.......................... G 812 459-9978
   Evansville *(G-4098)*

▲ Group Dekko Inc................................... D 260 357-3621
   Fort Wayne *(G-5042)*

▲ Grrk Holdings Inc................................. E 317 872-0172
   Indianapolis *(G-8336)*

H & W Molders Inc.................................. G 812 423-9340
   Evansville *(G-4101)*

▲ H A P Industries Inc............................ F 765 948-3385
   Jonesboro *(G-10079)*

H W Molders... G 812 423-3552
   Evansville *(G-4102)*

Hagerstown Plastics Inc......................... E 765 939-3849
   Richmond *(G-14130)*

Hammer Plastics Incorporated............... E 574 255-7230
   Mishawaka *(G-11904)*

Hancor Inc... E 812 443-2080
   Brazil *(G-1144)*

Hart Plastics Inc...................................... E 574 264-7060
   Elkhart *(G-3400)*

Hartland Products Inc............................. F 219 778-9034
   Rolling Prairie *(G-14364)*

Hewitt Tool & Die Inc............................. D 765 453-3889
   Oakford *(G-13319)*

▲ Hightec Solar Inc................................. F 219 814-4279
   Michigan City *(G-11624)*

Hillenbrand Inc.. A 812 931-5000
   Batesville *(G-590)*

Hinseys Pro Paint Inc............................. G 260 407-2000
   Fort Wayne *(G-5068)*

▲ Home Guard Industries Inc................ D 260 627-6060
   Grabill *(G-6302)*

▲ Hoosier Custom Plastics LLC............ E 574 772-2120
   Knox *(G-10210)*

Hoosier Fiberglass Industries................. F 812 232-5027
   Terre Haute *(G-15606)*

Hoosier Molded Products Inc................. D 574 235-7900
   South Bend *(G-15069)*

Hoosier Plastics Inc................................ G 812 232-5027
   Angola *(G-261)*

Hoosier Pride Plastics Inc..................... E 260 497-7080
   Fort Wayne *(G-5079)*

Hopper Development Inc......................... F 574 753-6621
   Logansport *(G-11077)*

Horizon Plastics & Engineering.............. E 574 674-5443
   Osceola *(G-13394)*

Hot Stamping & Printing......................... G 219 767-2429
   Union Mills *(G-15865)*

Ilpea Industries Inc................................. E 812 414-2728
   Scottsburg *(G-14560)*

▲ Ilpea Industries Inc............................. D 812 752-2526
   Scottsburg *(G-14562)*

Imp Holdings LLC..................................... D 260 665-6112
   Angola *(G-263)*

Independent Plastic Inc.......................... G 765 521-2251
   New Castle *(G-12869)*

Indiana Plastics LLC................................ E 574 294-3253
   Elkhart *(G-3422)*

Indiana Precision Plastics Inc................ E 765 762-2452
   Williamsport *(G-16849)*

▲ Indiana Southern Mold Corp............... E 812 346-2622
   North Vernon *(G-13281)*

▲ Indiana Vac-Form Inc.......................... E 574 269-1725
   Warsaw *(G-16378)*

Indianapolis Container Company............ G 317 580-5000
   Indianapolis *(G-8503)*

Indy Parts Inc.. G 317 243-7171
   Indianapolis *(G-8532)*

Infinity Molding & Assembly Inc............ D 812 838-0370
   Mount Vernon *(G-12300)*

Infinity Plastics Group Ltd.................... F 812 838-0370
   Mount Vernon *(G-12301)*

Injection Plastics..................................... G 574 784-2070
   Lapaz *(G-10815)*

Injection Plastics & Mfg Co.................... E 574 784-2070
   Lapaz *(G-10816)*

Innovative Corp.. E 317 804-5977
   Westfield *(G-16701)*

Innovative Mold & Machine Inc.............. G 317 634-1177
   Indianapolis *(G-8557)*

Inside Systems... G 317 831-3772
   Mooresville *(G-12215)*

Integrity Rttional Molding LLC............... E 317 837-1101
   Plainfield *(G-13692)*

Inteplast Building Products.................... F 574 825-5845
   Middlebury *(G-11725)*

Interactive Engineering Inc..................... G 574 272-5851
   Granger *(G-6354)*

▲ Irvine Shade & Door Inc..................... D 574 522-1446
   Elkhart *(G-3430)*

J H J Inc.. E 574 256-6966
   Mishawaka *(G-11914)*

J L Wickey Corp....................................... G 260 627-3109
   Grabill *(G-6303)*

J Plus Products Inc................................. G 317 660-1003
   Carmel *(G-1675)*

◆ Janco Engineered Products LLC......... C 574 255-3169
   Mishawaka *(G-11918)*

JD Engineered Products LLC.................. G 260 316-2907
   Hamilton *(G-6857)*

Employee Codes: A=Over 500 employees, B=251-500
C=101-250, D=51-100, E=20-50, F=10-19, G=1-9

30 RUBBER AND MISCELLANEOUS PLASTIC PRODUCTS

▼ Jeco Plastic Products LLC .... E 317 839-4943
  Plainfield (G-13696)
Jerry Oppered .... G 574 269-5363
  Warsaw (G-16381)
Jet Technologies Inc .... E 574 264-3613
  Elkhart (G-3433)
JMS Engineered Plastics Inc .... G 574 277-3228
  South Bend (G-15093)
JMS Engineered Plastics Inc .... D 574 277-3228
  South Bend (G-15094)
JMS Mold & Engineering Co Inc ..... F 574 272-0198
  South Bend (G-15095)
Jones Machine & Tool Inc .... E 812 364-4588
  Fredericksburg (G-5794)
Jushi USA Fiberglass .... G 574 293-0061
  Elkhart (G-3439)
K C Form Plastics LLC .... G 574 333-2523
  Elkhart (G-3441)
K S Mold Inc .... G 260 357-5141
  Elkhart (G-3444)
K2 Mold LLC .... G 574 293-4613
  Goshen (G-6183)
K2 Plastics Inc .... G 574 773-2243
  Nappanee (G-12616)
Kemper Tool Inc .... G 812 744-8633
  Moores Hill (G-12187)
Kenco Plastics Inc .... F 219 324-6621
  La Porte (G-10433)
Kenco Plastics Inc .... F 219 362-7565
  La Porte (G-10434)
Kendrion (mishawaka) LLC .... E 574 257-2422
  Mishawaka (G-11922)
Kerr Group LLC .... C 812 424-2904
  Evansville (G-4149)
Keusch Glass Inc .... E 812 482-2566
  Jasper (G-9864)
▲ Khorporate Holdings Inc .... C 260 357-3365
  Laotto (G-10807)
▲ Kibbechem Inc .... F 574 266-1234
  Elkhart (G-3454)
Kimball Electronics Inc .... E 317 357-3175
  Indianapolis (G-8685)
Kimball Electronics Inc .... D 317 545-5383
  Indianapolis (G-8686)
▲ Kn Platech America Corporation .... D 317 392-7707
  Shelbyville (G-14769)
Konrady Plastics Inc .... E 219 763-7001
  Portage (G-13880)
Landis Plastics .... G 765 966-1414
  Richmond (G-14156)
◆ Lasalle Bristol Corporation .... C 574 295-8400
  Elkhart (G-3469)
Lawson Design Inc .... G 812 967-2810
  Henryville (G-7113)
Lepark Mold & Tool .... F 574 262-0518
  Elkhart (G-3485)
◆ Letica Corporation .... A 812 421-3136
  Evansville (G-4165)
Life Management Inc .... G 260 747-7408
  Fort Wayne (G-5185)
Lighthouse Industries Inc .... F 772 429-1774
  Michigan City (G-11633)
▲ Lighthouse Industries Inc .... E 219 879-1550
  Michigan City (G-11634)
▲ Lincoln Industries Inc .... E 812 897-0715
  Boonville (G-1088)
Link Engineering LLC .... G 765 457-1166
  Kokomo (G-10298)
▲ Lorentson Manufacturing Co .... E 765 452-4425
  Kokomo (G-10300)
M&M Performance Inc .... G 574 536-6103
  Goshen (G-6208)

Mad Dasher Inc .... E 260 747-0545
  Fort Wayne (G-5198)
Maddox Engineering Inc .... F 812 903-0048
  Greenville (G-6652)
Maks Plastic LLC .... F 574 215-1800
  Mishawaka (G-11936)
Makuta Inc .... F 317 642-0001
  Shelbyville (G-14773)
◆ Manar Inc .... D 812 526-2891
  Edinburgh (G-3092)
▲ Manar Medical Inc .... E 812 526-6734
  Edinburgh (G-3093)
Mar-Kan Marketing Inc .... G 317 228-9335
  Indianapolis (G-8826)
Marco Plastics Inc .... F 812 333-0062
  Bloomington (G-915)
Mary Jonas .... F 317 500-0600
  Indianapolis (G-8845)
Mauser Packaging Solutions .... G 317 297-4638
  Indianapolis (G-8854)
Mayco International LLC .... G 765 348-5780
  Hartford City (G-7070)
MCP Usa Inc .... G 219 734-6598
  Portage (G-13885)
Meer Enterprises Inc .... D 574 522-7527
  Elkhart (G-3526)
▼ Meese Inc .... F 800 829-4535
  Madison (G-11241)
▲ Metro Plastics Tech Inc .... D 317 776-0860
  Noblesville (G-13136)
▲ Meyer Plastics Inc .... D 317 259-4131
  Indianapolis (G-8895)
Mide Products LLC .... G 574 333-5906
  Goshen (G-6221)
Midwest Plastics Company Inc ...... G 574 264-4994
  Elkhart (G-3540)
Midwest Plastics Company Inc ...... G 574 674-0161
  Osceola (G-13398)
Midwest Willys LLC .... G 765 362-2247
  Crawfordsville (G-2590)
Midwest-Tek Inc .... F 812 981-3551
  New Albany (G-12780)
▲ Models LLC .... E 765 676-6700
  Lebanon (G-10917)
Moriroku Technology N Amer Inc ... G 765 221-7576
  Anderson (G-161)
Mossberg Industries Inc .... D 260 357-5141
  Garrett (G-5873)
▲ Msca LLC .... F 574 583-6220
  Monticello (G-12160)
MTA Technology LLC .... F 765 447-2221
  Lafayette (G-10655)
▲ Mytex Polymers US Corp .... E 812 280-2900
  Jeffersonville (G-10021)
Neptune Flotation LLC .... F 317 588-3600
  Carmel (G-1704)
New Market Plastics Inc .... F 317 758-5494
  Crawfordsville (G-2593)
▲ Newell Industrial LLC .... E 260 636-3336
  Albion (G-36)
▼ Nexgen Mold & Tool Inc .... E 812 945-3375
  New Albany (G-12784)
Nibco Inc .... F 812 256-8500
  Charlestown (G-1888)
Nibco Inc .... C 574 296-1240
  Goshen (G-6227)
◆ Nibco Inc .... B 574 295-3000
  Elkhart (G-3570)
Nicosin Extursion Inc .... G 812 442-6751
  Brazil (G-1157)
North America Packaging Corp ..... G 219 462-8915
  Valparaiso (G-16015)

▲ North American Extrusn & Assem .... G 260 636-3336
  Albion (G-37)
Norton Packaging Inc .... E 574 867-6002
  Hamlet (G-6864)
▲ Nyx Fort Wayne LLC .... D 260 484-0595
  Mishawaka (G-11968)
Nyxperimental LLC .... G 765 684-7077
  Middletown (G-11776)
Nyxperimental LLC .... G 914 506-0266
  Pendleton (G-13547)
Odyssey Machine Inc .... G 812 951-1160
  Georgetown (G-6072)
▲ Old Ip Inc .... E 574 294-3253
  Elkhart (G-3578)
Old Plastics Company Inc .... G 812 699-0379
  Linton (G-11041)
Old Rev LLC .... G 317 580-2420
  Westfield (G-16714)
Olympic Fiberglass Industries .... F 574 223-3101
  Rochester (G-14310)
Omni Tech Intrmdate Hldngs LLC ... G 786 201-2094
  Greendale (G-6449)
Omni Technologies Inc .... D 812 537-4102
  Greendale (G-6450)
Osborn Manufacturing Corp .... F 574 267-6156
  Warsaw (G-16406)
▲ Outsource Technologies Inc .... F 574 233-1303
  South Bend (G-15182)
Panolam Industries Inc .... D 574 264-0702
  Elkhart (G-3582)
Paragon Medical Inc .... C 574 594-2140
  Pierceton (G-13637)
▲ Paragon Medical Inc .... C 574 594-2140
  Pierceton (G-13638)
Paramount Plastics Inc .... E 574 264-2143
  Elkhart (G-3583)
Patrick Industries Inc .... D 260 665-6112
  Angola (G-282)
Patrick Industries Inc .... F 574 546-5222
  Bremen (G-1212)
Patrick Industries Inc .... G 574 293-1521
  Elkhart (G-3589)
Patrick Industries Inc .... G 574 294-8828
  Elkhart (G-3594)
Paul Tirotta .... F 574 255-4101
  Mishawaka (G-11972)
▲ Paxxal Inc .... G 317 296-7724
  Noblesville (G-13153)
Peacock Plastics Inc .... G 765 935-9178
  Richmond (G-14181)
Pent Assemblies .... E 260 347-5828
  Kendallville (G-10141)
▲ Pent Plastics Inc .... C 260 897-3775
  Kendallville (G-10142)
▲ Penz Inc .... E 574 255-4736
  Mishawaka (G-11974)
Perfect Manufacturing LLC .... G 317 924-5284
  Indianapolis (G-9122)
Permalatt Products Inc .... G 574 546-6311
  Bremen (G-1213)
▲ Perry Foam Products Inc .... E 765 474-3404
  Lafayette (G-10667)
Petoskey Plastics Inc .... D 765 348-9808
  Hartford City (G-7074)
Phoenix Closures Inc .... F 765 658-1800
  Greencastle (G-6424)
Pioneer Plastics Corporation .... C 574 264-0702
  Elkhart (G-3604)
◆ Pk USA Inc .... B 317 395-5500
  Shelbyville (G-14784)
Placon Corporation .... F 608 278-4920
  Elkhart (G-3606)

30 RUBBER AND MISCELLANEOUS PLASTIC PRODUCTS

Plas-Tech Molding & Design Inc .... E 260 761-3006
  Brimfield *(G-1233)*
Plastic Dynamics Inc .... G 574 272-4576
  Granger *(G-6370)*
Plastic Extrusions Company .... G 812 479-3232
  Evansville *(G-4245)*
Plastic Molding Mfg Inc .... E 574 234-9036
  South Bend *(G-15197)*
Plastic Moldings Company Llc .... D 317 392-4139
  Shelbyville *(G-14785)*
Plastic Processors Inc .... F 260 488-3999
  Hamilton *(G-6860)*
Plastic Project Resource LLC .... G 812 390-9790
  Hope *(G-7231)*
Plastics Family Holdings Inc .... G 317 890-1808
  Indianapolis *(G-9153)*
▲ Plastics Research and Dev Inc .... E 812 279-8885
  Springville *(G-15390)*
Plymouth Molding Group LLC .... F 574 933-4189
  Plymouth *(G-13802)*
▲ Poly HI Solidur Inc .... D 260 479-4100
  Fort Wayne *(G-5324)*
▲ Poly-Seal LLC .... E 812 306-2573
  Evansville *(G-4247)*
Polycon Industries Inc .... C 219 738-1000
  Merrillville *(G-11551)*
Polymer Logistics Inc .... D 219 706-5985
  Portage *(G-13904)*
Poppy Co .... G 317 442-2491
  Brownsburg *(G-1395)*
PRC - Desoto International Inc .... E 317 290-1600
  Indianapolis *(G-9177)*
▲ Precise Tooling Solutions Inc .... E 812 378-0247
  Columbus *(G-2380)*
Precision Plastics Indiana Inc .... C 260 244-6114
  Columbia City *(G-2183)*
Premier Fiberglass Co Inc .... E 574 264-5457
  Elkhart *(G-3617)*
▼ Primex Design Fabrication Corp .... D 765 935-2990
  Richmond *(G-14185)*
◆ Priority Plastics Inc .... E 260 726-7000
  Portland *(G-13964)*
▼ Pro-Form Plastics Inc .... E 812 522-4433
  Crothersville *(G-2644)*
Pro-Form Plastics Inc .... F 812 522-4433
  Columbus *(G-2382)*
Prodigy Mold & Tool Inc .... E 812 753-3029
  Haubstadt *(G-7088)*
Production Partners Inc .... F 574 229-5960
  Mishawaka *(G-11980)*
▲ Production Plastic Molding .... G 317 872-4669
  Indianapolis *(G-9219)*
▲ Progressive Plastics Inc .... F 765 552-2004
  Elwood *(G-3833)*
Prolon Inc .... E 574 522-8900
  Elkhart *(G-3623)*
◆ PSI Molded Plastics Ind Inc .... A 574 288-2100
  South Bend *(G-15208)*
PTG Silicones Inc .... F 812 948-8719
  New Albany *(G-12800)*
Puck Supply & Machine LLC .... F 574 293-3333
  Elkhart *(G-3625)*
Pyramid Plastic Group Inc .... G 260 327-3145
  Larwill *(G-10821)*
Quad 4 Plastics Inc .... E 574 293-8660
  Elkhart *(G-3629)*
▲ Quality Molded Products Inc .... D 574 272-3733
  South Bend *(G-15211)*
▲ Quality Plas Engrg Acqstion Co .... E 574 262-2621
  Elkhart *(G-3632)*
R & R Plastics Inc .... D 219 393-5505
  Kingsbury *(G-10185)*

R & R Technologies LLC .... E 812 526-2655
  Edinburgh *(G-3100)*
R3 Composites Corp .... D 260 627-0033
  Grabill *(G-6321)*
Ram North America Inc .... F 317 984-1971
  Arcadia *(G-316)*
Red Star Contract Mfg Inc .... E 260 327-3145
  Larwill *(G-10822)*
▲ Remco Products Corporation .... D 317 876-9856
  Zionsville *(G-17046)*
Reschcor Inc .... G 574 295-2413
  Elkhart *(G-3647)*
Reschcor Inc .... D 574 295-2413
  Bristol *(G-1285)*
◆ Resin Partners Inc .... C 765 298-6800
  Anderson *(G-185)*
Revere Plastics Systems LLC .... C 812 670-2240
  Jeffersonville *(G-10045)*
Revolution Materials (in) LLC .... D 812 234-2724
  Terre Haute *(G-15680)*
▼ Rfbp Inc .... B
  Evansville *(G-4288)*
Richardson Molding LLC .... G 317 787-9463
  Indianapolis *(G-9303)*
◆ Rieke LLC .... B 260 925-3700
  Auburn *(G-419)*
Rim Molding and Engrg Inc .... F 574 294-1932
  Mishawaka *(G-11987)*
Rite Products Inc .... G 260 627-6465
  Grabill *(G-6322)*
River Valley Plastics Inc .... E 574 262-5221
  Elkhart *(G-3649)*
Rix Products Inc .... G 812 426-1749
  Evansville *(G-4290)*
▼ Rochester Rttional Molding Inc .... F 574 223-8844
  Rochester *(G-14320)*
▲ Roi Marketing Company Inc .... G 317 644-0797
  Indianapolis *(G-9321)*
Rookstools Pier Shop Inc .... E 574 453-4771
  Leesburg *(G-10960)*
Rotational Molding Tech Inc .... D 574 831-6450
  New Paris *(G-12967)*
Roto-Fab LLC .... G 260 375-4480
  Warren *(G-16303)*
▲ Royer Corporation .... D 800 457-8997
  Madison *(G-11249)*
S S & E Enterprises .... G 260 749-0026
  Fort Wayne *(G-5393)*
Sabert Corporation .... E 260 222-0758
  Fort Wayne *(G-5394)*
▲ Sabin Corporation .... C 812 323-4500
  Bloomington *(G-965)*
Sasaki Coating North Amer Inc .... F 317 956-2232
  Indianapolis *(G-9374)*
Seals & Components Inc .... G 708 895-5222
  La Porte *(G-10478)*
Ser North America LLC .... F 765 639-0300
  Anderson *(G-190)*
Shadowhouse Jiu-Jitsu Inc .... G 219 873-4556
  La Porte *(G-10481)*
Silgan Plastics LLC .... D 260 894-7814
  Ligonier *(G-11023)*
Silgan Plastics LLC .... C 812 522-0900
  Seymour *(G-14692)*
Silgan Plastics LLC .... F 812 522-0900
  Seymour *(G-14693)*
Smiths Enterprises Inc .... G 765 378-6267
  Chesterfield *(G-1898)*
Sonoco Teq LLC .... G 260 495-9842
  Fremont *(G-5835)*
Specialty Manufacturers Inc .... G 317 241-1111
  Carmel *(G-1768)*

Spectron MRC LLC .... G 574 271-2800
  South Bend *(G-15261)*
◆ Spencer Industries Inc .... C 812 937-4561
  Dale *(G-2792)*
Splendor Boats LLC .... F 260 352-2835
  Silver Lake *(G-14923)*
▲ Srg Global Trim Inc .... A 812 473-6200
  Evansville *(G-4329)*
Standard Plastic Corporation .... F 260 824-0214
  Bluffton *(G-1056)*
Stay Put Doggy LLC .... G 812 591-8232
  Westport *(G-16752)*
▼ Sterling Berry Corporation .... D 812 424-2904
  Evansville *(G-4332)*
Stien Designs & Graphics Inc .... G 260 347-9136
  Kendallville *(G-10153)*
◆ Stoffel Seals Corporation .... E 845 353-3800
  Angola *(G-296)*
Stryten Energy LLC .... D 812 342-0139
  Columbus *(G-2397)*
Styles Kitchen LLC .... G 765 405-6875
  Lafayette *(G-10701)*
Superior Plastics LLC .... G 317 698-6422
  Zionsville *(G-17055)*
◆ Syndicate Sales Inc .... B 765 457-7277
  Kokomo *(G-10345)*
▲ T-A Wind Down Inc .... C 708 839-1400
  Munster *(G-12566)*
Tactile Engineering Inc .... E 765 233-6620
  Lafayette *(G-10709)*
Taghleef Industries Inc .... A 302 326-5500
  Rosedale *(G-14385)*
▲ Tasus Corporation .... C 812 333-6500
  Bloomington *(G-984)*
TEC Air Inc .... F 219 301-7084
  Munster *(G-12568)*
TEC-Air LLC .... D 219 301-7084
  Munster *(G-12569)*
▲ Tecnoplast Usa LLC .... G 317 769-4929
  Anderson *(G-204)*
Tedco Inc .... G 765 489-5807
  Hagerstown *(G-6845)*
Teg Holdings Inc .... E 574 264-7514
  Elkhart *(G-3719)*
Teijin Automotive Tech Inc .... C 260 627-0890
  Grabill *(G-6325)*
Teijin Automotive Tech Inc .... B 260 355-4011
  Huntington *(G-7373)*
Tekmodo LLC .... F 574 970-5800
  Elkhart *(G-3720)*
Tekmodo Structures LLC .... G 574 970-5800
  Elkhart *(G-3722)*
Templeton Coal Company Inc .... G 812 232-7037
  Terre Haute *(G-15725)*
▲ The Killion Corporation .... D 317 271-4536
  Indianapolis *(G-9589)*
Thorgren Tool & Molding Co .... G 219 462-1801
  Valparaiso *(G-16066)*
◆ Thorgren Tool & Molding Co .... D 219 462-1801
  Valparaiso *(G-16067)*
Thrust Industries Inc .... F 812 437-3643
  Evansville *(G-4344)*
Titus Precision Company .... G 260 244-6114
  Columbia City *(G-2206)*
Tj Maintenance LLC .... G 219 776-8427
  Lake Village *(G-10784)*
▼ Tomken Plastic Tech Inc .... E 765 284-2472
  Muncie *(G-12505)*
Topp Industries Incorporated .... D 574 223-3681
  Rochester *(G-14329)*
◆ TP Remainco In Inc .... B 574 256-1521
  Mishawaka *(G-12015)*

Employee Codes: A=Over 500 employees, B=251-500
C=101-250, D=51-100, E=20-50, F=10-19, G=1-9

30 RUBBER AND MISCELLANEOUS PLASTIC PRODUCTS

Tredegar Corporation..................D..... 812 466-0266
  Terre Haute *(G-15734)*
◆ Trellborg Sling Sltions US Inc...........E..... 260 749-9631
  Fort Wayne *(G-5503)*
Trim-Lok Inc..............................F..... 574 227-1143
  Elkhart *(G-3747)*
Trivalence Technologies LLC...........E..... 800 209-2517
  Evansville *(G-4353)*
Tru-Form Steel & Wire Inc.............F..... 765 348-5001
  Hartford City *(G-7079)*
▲ Tru-Form Steel & Wire Inc...........E..... 765 348-5001
  Hartford City *(G-7078)*
▲ Tulox Plastics Corporation...........F..... 765 664-5155
  Marion *(G-11345)*
Ultima Plastics LLC.......................G..... 812 459-1430
  Evansville *(G-4358)*
US Molders Inc............................E..... 219 984-5058
  Reynolds *(G-14077)*
V N C Inc...................................F..... 219 696-5031
  Lowell *(G-11179)*
Variotech Corp............................G..... 404 566-2935
  Indianapolis *(G-9701)*
Vee Engineering Inc.....................D..... 260 424-6635
  Fort Wayne *(G-5530)*
Vee Engineering Inc.....................G..... 765 778-7895
  Anderson *(G-213)*
Viking Group Inc.........................B..... 812 256-8500
  Charlestown *(G-1895)*
▲ Vixen Composites LLC...............G..... 574 970-1224
  Elkhart *(G-3774)*
Vmw Tooling Group LLC...............G..... 574 293-5090
  Mishawaka *(G-12024)*
▲ Voss Automotive Inc..................D..... 260 373-2277
  Fort Wayne *(G-5536)*
VPI Acquisition LLC......................G..... 812 283-4435
  Jeffersonville *(G-10070)*
VPI Acquisition LLC......................C..... 812 752-6742
  Scottsburg *(G-14583)*
Vytec Inc...................................E..... 574 277-4295
  Granger *(G-6390)*
Wabash Plastics Inc.....................C..... 812 867-2447
  Evansville *(G-4378)*
◆ Wabash Plastics Inc...................G..... 812 428-9300
  Evansville *(G-4377)*
Waste 1.....................................F..... 765 477-9138
  Lafayette *(G-10718)*
West Phrm Svcs AZ Inc................G..... 765 650-2300
  Frankfort *(G-5701)*
Western Consolidated Tech Inc.......D..... 260 495-9866
  Fremont *(G-5842)*
Wunder Company Inc...................F..... 219 962-8573
  Lake Station *(G-10779)*
Yanfeng US Auto Intr Systems I......D..... 260 347-0500
  Kendallville *(G-10156)*
York Group Inc............................D..... 765 966-0077
  Richmond *(G-14231)*
ZF Active Safety & Elec US LLC......D..... 765 429-1984
  Lafayette *(G-10721)*
Zing Polymer Formations LLC.........G..... 317 598-0480
  Fishers *(G-4637)*

31 LEATHER AND LEATHER PRODUCTS

3111 Leather tanning and finishing

Clinton Harness Shop LLC..............G..... 574 533-9797
  Goshen *(G-6113)*
Color Glo....................................G..... 812 926-2639
  Aurora *(G-441)*
Horse N Around Animal & Tack......G..... 765 618-2032
  Upland *(G-15878)*
▲ Liberty Book & Bb Manufactures...E..... 317 633-1450
  Indianapolis *(G-8744)*
Loon Creek Leather LLC................G..... 260 356-0726
  Huntington *(G-7338)*
Midwest Leather LLC....................G..... 435 257-7880
  Grabill *(G-6314)*
Pathfinder Cutting Tech LLC...........F..... 424 342-9723
  Indianapolis *(G-9099)*
Trail Creek Leather.......................G..... 219 874-6702
  Trail Creek *(G-15842)*
Trutex Equestrian LLC...................G..... 812 350-6368
  Edinburgh *(G-3107)*
Vera Bradley Inc...........................B..... 877 708-8372
  Roanoke *(G-14272)*

3131 Footwear cut stock

Airfeet LLC..................................G..... 317 441-1817
  Greenwood *(G-6663)*
Bootmakers LLC...........................G..... 765 412-7243
  West Lafayette *(G-16568)*
Four Quarters RE LLC...................G..... 765 474-2295
  Lafayette *(G-10580)*
Marion Quarters At Fort.................G..... 317 672-4841
  Indianapolis *(G-8835)*
Top Design Cnc Inc.......................G..... 219 662-2915
  Valparaiso *(G-16069)*
Upper Level Networks Inc..............G..... 317 863-0955
  Westfield *(G-16735)*
Upper Level Sports LLC.................G..... 317 681-3754
  Indianapolis *(G-9684)*

3142 House slippers

Melay LLC...................................G..... 614 726-0565
  Westfield *(G-16711)*

3143 Men's footwear, except athletic

Him Gentlemans Boutique.............G..... 812 924-7441
  New Albany *(G-12741)*
Orb LLC......................................G..... 833 946-4672
  Indianapolis *(G-9067)*

3144 Women's footwear, except athletic

Orb LLC......................................G..... 833 946-4672
  Indianapolis *(G-9067)*

3149 Footwear, except rubber, nec

Drillmaster Corp...........................G..... 732 919-3088
  Cynthiana *(G-2787)*
Integrated Orthotic Lab Inc............G..... 317 852-4640
  Brownsburg *(G-1375)*
Onfield Apparel Group LLC............G..... 317 895-7249
  Indianapolis *(G-9055)*

3151 Leather gloves and mittens

5m Poultry LLC............................G..... 812 890-5558
  Carlisle *(G-1539)*

3161 Luggage

4ever Chosen LLC........................G..... 765 431-7548
  Kokomo *(G-10230)*
B Word LLC.................................G..... 317 654-6873
  Indianapolis *(G-7583)*
Bag Corporation...........................G..... 317 699-5523
  Indianapolis *(G-7590)*
Bbliss & Jus Be Zany....................G..... 215 251-9235
  Indianapolis *(G-7599)*
C H Ellis LLC................................G..... 317 636-3451
  Indianapolis *(G-7707)*
▲ CH Ellis Co Inc..........................E..... 317 636-3451
  Indianapolis *(G-7782)*
▲ Cinda B USA LLC......................G..... 260 469-0803
  Fort Wayne *(G-4848)*

SIC SECTION

Death Enn LLC.............................G..... 219 402-4436
  Merrillville *(G-11504)*
▲ Derby Inc..................................D..... 574 233-4500
  South Bend *(G-14997)*
East Coast Treasure Finds LLC......G..... 845 879-8744
  Carmel *(G-1618)*
Elkcases Inc................................G..... 574 295-7700
  Elkhart *(G-3317)*
Frances Monforte.........................G..... 317 875-0880
  Indianapolis *(G-8221)*
Hotricity LLC................................G..... 765 212-0411
  Muncie *(G-12422)*
Howse Ov Drmrs LLC....................G..... 574 366-2406
  South Bend *(G-15073)*
▲ Humes & Berg Mfg Co Inc..........G..... 219 391-5880
  East Chicago *(G-3018)*
Imagine Like God LLC..................G..... 574 575-5023
  Elkhart *(G-3418)*
Indiana Dimensional Pdts LLC........E..... 574 834-7681
  North Webster *(G-13306)*
Intellectual Quality LLC.................G..... 708 979-3127
  Lafayette *(G-10609)*
L M Products Inc..........................E..... 765 643-3802
  Anderson *(G-145)*
Leed Selling Tools Corp.................C..... 812 482-7888
  Ireland *(G-9816)*
Markley Enterprise Inc..................D..... 574 295-4195
  Elkhart *(G-3513)*
Melaninwisdomgarment..................G..... 574 315-3081
  South Bend *(G-15147)*
◆ MTS Products Corp....................E..... 574 295-3142
  Elkhart *(G-3559)*
One-Stop Travel Shop Inc.............G..... 812 339-9496
  Bloomington *(G-937)*
Oxford Industries Inc....................G..... 317 569-0866
  Indianapolis *(G-9077)*
▲ Porter Case Inc.........................G..... 219 289-2616
  South Bend *(G-15200)*
Raine Inc....................................F..... 765 622-7687
  Anderson *(G-182)*
Ramo & Co LLC...........................G..... 219 381-1843
  Gary *(G-5999)*
Rva LLC......................................G..... 317 800-9800
  Fishers *(G-4602)*
Sarah Johnson Nettles..................G..... 317 778-0023
  Indianapolis *(G-9372)*
Smor Cases Inc...........................E..... 574 291-0346
  South Bend *(G-15248)*
▲ Tetrafab Corporation..................F..... 812 258-0000
  Floyds Knobs *(G-4696)*
Word 4 Word LLC........................G..... 317 601-3995
  Indianapolis *(G-9787)*
Zotic Scents LLC..........................G..... 317 766-6501
  Indianapolis *(G-9814)*

3171 Women's handbags and purses

Amanda Elizabeth LLC..................G..... 602 317-9633
  Fort Wayne *(G-4748)*
Arm Kandy LLC............................G..... 317 975-1576
  Indianapolis *(G-7546)*
Aubry Lane LLC...........................G..... 317 644-6372
  Indianapolis *(G-7561)*
CM Reed LLC..............................G..... 517 546-4100
  Greendale *(G-6444)*
Vera Bradley Inc..........................B..... 877 708-8372
  Roanoke *(G-14272)*
Vera Bradley International LLC......G..... 260 482-4673
  Roanoke *(G-14273)*

3172 Personal leather goods, nec

Long Leather Works LLC...............G..... 812 336-5309
  Bloomington *(G-913)*

SIC SECTION

32 STONE, CLAY, GLASS, AND CONCRETE PRODUCTS

Luxetrend LLC................................. G 502 208-9344
Evansville *(G-4178)*

Moses Leathers.............................. G 260 203-8799
Fort Wayne *(G-5245)*

3199 Leather goods, nec

Beams Seatbelts Inc...................... G 574 970-2667
Elkhart *(G-3220)*

Bear Arms Holsters........................ G 260 310-2376
Fort Wayne *(G-4790)*

Bio Harness Shop........................... G 812 486-2919
Montgomery *(G-12087)*

Campbell Pet Company.................. G 812 692-5208
Elnora *(G-3813)*

Daltech Enterprises Inc.................. G 260 527-4590
Fremont *(G-5818)*

David W Imhoff............................... G 574 862-4375
Goshen *(G-6119)*

Discount Boots & Tack.................. G 812 522-9770
Seymour *(G-14648)*

Double T Leather Inc..................... G 765 393-3676
Anderson *(G-108)*

Fast Holster LLC............................ G 317 727-5243
Carmel *(G-1633)*

Judson Harness & Saddlery.......... G 765 569-0918
Rockville *(G-14352)*

L M Products Inc............................ E 765 643-3802
Anderson *(G-145)*

Leather Yoder Company LLC......... G 260 833-4030
Angola *(G-271)*

Moonshine Leather Company Inc... G 812 988-1326
Nashville *(G-12676)*

◆ **Scott Pet Products Inc**................. C 765 569-4636
Rockville *(G-14354)*

Southern Indiana Collar Co............ G 812 486-3714
Montgomery *(G-12123)*

Sue S Sheep Quarters.................... G 765 998-2067
Fairmount *(G-4413)*

Superior Concepts Indus LLC....... F 765 628-2956
Greentown *(G-6649)*

Triple M Leather LLC..................... G 260 238-5850
Saint Joe *(G-14444)*

Whisler Custom Leather Co........... G 765 212-8932
Muncie *(G-12519)*

32 STONE, CLAY, GLASS, AND CONCRETE PRODUCTS

3211 Flat glass

Calumite Company LLC.................. G 219 787-8667
Portage *(G-13852)*

Carlex Glass America LLC............. B 260 925-5656
Auburn *(G-374)*

Carlex Glass America LLC............. B 260 894-7750
Ligonier *(G-11009)*

Chicago Bifold................................ G 708 532-4365
Highland *(G-7129)*

Cloudmaker Studio Inc.................. G 219 879-1724
Michigan City *(G-11589)*

Fox Studios Inc.............................. F 317 253-0135
Indianapolis *(G-8217)*

Indiana Bevel Inc............................ G 317 596-0001
Fishers *(G-4544)*

Indy Glass Center Inc.................... E 317 591-5000
Indianapolis *(G-8527)*

Midwest Fade Control.................... G 219 926-5043
Lafayette *(G-10649)*

Mr Tintz... G 219 844-5500
Hammond *(G-6983)*

Pilkington North America Inc......... G 317 346-0621
Franklin *(G-5766)*

Pilkington North America Inc......... D 317 392-7000
Shelbyville *(G-14783)*

Pilkington North America Inc......... G 574 273-5457
South Bend *(G-15195)*

Spohn Associates Inc.................... G 317 921-2445
Indianapolis *(G-9480)*

Timecpsual Antiq GL Cllctables.... G 317 902-6201
Indianapolis *(G-9605)*

Tint Masters.................................... G 260 704-2676
Fort Wayne *(G-5484)*

Wallar Additions Inc....................... G 574 262-1989
Elkhart *(G-3778)*

3221 Glass containers

Amcor Phrm Packg USA LLC......... D 812 591-2332
Westport *(G-16748)*

Anchor Glass Container Corp........ D 812 537-1655
Greendale *(G-6437)*

Anchor Glass Container Corp........ D 765 584-6101
Winchester *(G-16881)*

Ardagh Glass Inc............................ G 765 768-7891
Dunkirk *(G-2960)*

Ardagh Glass Inc............................ G 765 662-1172
Marion *(G-11270)*

Ardagh Glass Inc............................ G 610 341-7885
Muncie *(G-12344)*

◆ **Ardagh Glass Inc**.......................... B 317 558-1002
Indianapolis *(G-7542)*

Ardagh Glass Packaging Inc.......... G 317 558-1002
Indianapolis *(G-7543)*

Indianapolis Container Company... G 317 580-5000
Indianapolis *(G-8503)*

Nipro Phrmpckging Amricas Corp... D 812 591-2332
Westport *(G-16749)*

3229 Pressed and blown glass, nec

Anchor Glass Container Corp........ D 765 584-6101
Winchester *(G-16881)*

▲ **Apollo Design Technology Inc**..... D 260 497-9191
Fort Wayne *(G-4763)*

B Thystrup US Corporation........... G 574 834-2554
North Webster *(G-13302)*

Cedar Shack.................................... G 219 682-5531
Cedar Lake *(G-1829)*

Colliers Glassblock Inc.................. G 574 288-8682
South Bend *(G-14979)*

Creations In Glass.......................... G 219 326-7941
La Porte *(G-10397)*

Diversified Ophthalmics Inc.......... E 317 780-1677
Indianapolis *(G-7985)*

▲ **Dsh Indiana Inc**........................... G 317 704-8130
Carmel *(G-1613)*

General Signals Inc........................ E 812 474-4256
Evansville *(G-4088)*

Global Composites Inc................... C 574 522-9956
Elkhart *(G-3380)*

HH Rellim Inc.................................. G 812 662-9944
Greensburg *(G-6602)*

Ink Dawgz LLC................................ G 219 781-6972
Valparaiso *(G-15974)*

Inspired Fire GL Stdio Gllery......... G 765 474-1981
Lafayette *(G-10608)*

Jerry Oppered................................. G 574 269-5363
Warsaw *(G-16381)*

Maul Technology Co....................... F 765 584-2101
Winchester *(G-16894)*

Naptown Etching Inc....................... G 317 733-8776
Zionsville *(G-17036)*

▲ **Northern Indiana Manufacturing**.. E 574 342-2105
Bourbon *(G-1125)*

Palmetto Planters LLC.................... G 765 396-4446
Eaton *(G-3065)*

Pjkellynet... G 765 457-5864
Kokomo *(G-10321)*

Pyrotek Incorporated...................... D 260 248-4141
Columbia City *(G-2184)*

S & S Optical Co Inc....................... F 260 749-9614
New Haven *(G-12915)*

Spagheady Inc................................. G 317 499-6184
Indianapolis *(G-9467)*

Spectrum Brands Inc...................... E 317 773-6627
Noblesville *(G-13179)*

Stability America Inc...................... G 574 642-3029
Goshen *(G-6257)*

Starline Mfg LLC............................. G 765 847-1306
Fountain City *(G-5612)*

Talon Products LLC........................ F 574 218-0100
Bristol *(G-1294)*

Toppan Photomasks Inc................. C 765 854-7500
Kokomo *(G-10350)*

V & H Fiberglass Repair................. G 574 772-4920
Knox *(G-10227)*

Zimmerman Art Glass LLC.............. G 812 738-2206
Corydon *(G-2524)*

3231 Products of purchased glass

All Glass LLC................................... G 260 969-1839
Fort Wayne *(G-4739)*

American Window and Glass Inc.... C 812 464-9400
Evansville *(G-3886)*

Anew Company Inc......................... F 574 293-9088
Elkhart *(G-3184)*

Botti Stdio Archtctral Arts In......... E 847 869-5933
La Porte *(G-10391)*

Cardinal Glass Industries Inc......... B 260 495-4105
Fremont *(G-5813)*

Carlex Glass America LLC.............. B 260 925-5656
Auburn *(G-374)*

Cleer Vision Windows Inc.............. E 574 262-0449
Elkhart *(G-3254)*

Crafted Vanity Company................. G 219 293-6063
Gary *(G-5920)*

Creative Industries Inc................... E 317 248-1102
Plainfield *(G-13676)*

Crystal Shadows............................. G 574 269-2722
Warsaw *(G-16340)*

▲ **Cvg Sprague Devices LLC**........... C 614 289-5360
Michigan City *(G-11593)*

▲ **D & W Inc**..................................... D 574 264-9674
Elkhart *(G-3284)*

Fox Studios Inc............................... F 317 253-0135
Indianapolis *(G-8217)*

Gardner Glass Products Inc........... G 317 464-0881
Indianapolis *(G-8260)*

Gardner Mirror Corp....................... G 317 464-0881
Indianapolis *(G-8261)*

Glass Surgeons Inc........................ G 219 374-2500
Cedar Lake *(G-1831)*

Great Panes Glass Co..................... G 260 426-0203
Fort Wayne *(G-5039)*

Greene Woodworking & Glass LLC... G 812 755-4331
Campbellsburg *(G-1523)*

◆ **Grote Industries Inc**..................... A 812 273-2121
Madison *(G-11222)*

Grote Industries LLC...................... A 812 265-8273
Madison *(G-11223)*

Hartford TEC Glass Co Inc............. E 765 348-1282
Hartford City *(G-7068)*

Helming Bros Inc............................ G 812 634-9797
Jasper *(G-9842)*

Indy Glass Center Inc..................... E 317 591-5000
Indianapolis *(G-8527)*

▲ **International Steel Company**....... D 812 425-3311
Evansville *(G-4130)*

Employee Codes: A=Over 500 employees, B=251-500
C=101-250, D=51-100, E=20-50, F=10-19, G=1-9

32 STONE, CLAY, GLASS, AND CONCRETE PRODUCTS

▲ JC Moag Corporation .... D 812 284-8400
   Georgetown *(G-6063)*

Kaleidoscope Inc .... G 765 423-1951
   Lafayette *(G-10618)*

▲ Larry Robertson Associates .... F 812 537-4090
   Indianapolis *(G-8723)*

Lazzaro Companies Inc .... E 219 980-0860
   Merrillville *(G-11529)*

May First Inc .... G 317 330-1000
   Fishers *(G-4562)*

▲ Middletown Enterprises Inc .... E 765 348-3100
   Hartford City *(G-7071)*

Mominee Studios Inc .... G 812 473-1691
   Evansville *(G-4208)*

Moores Country Wood Crafting .... F 317 984-3326
   Arcadia *(G-315)*

Moss L Glass Co Inc .... F 765 642-4946
   Indianapolis *(G-8957)*

Oldcastle Buildingenvelope Inc .... D 317 876-1155
   Indianapolis *(G-9044)*

Omega National Products LLC .... C 574 295-5353
   Elkhart *(G-3579)*

Pilkington North America Inc .... G 317 392-7000
   Shelbyville *(G-14783)*

▲ Ramco Engineering Inc .... G 574 266-1455
   Elkhart *(G-3638)*

Recycling Center Inc .... D 765 966-8295
   Richmond *(G-14195)*

Recycling Works LLC .... F 574 293-3751
   Elkhart *(G-3644)*

Schott Gemtron Corporation .... B 812 882-2680
   Vincennes *(G-16152)*

◆ Sherwood Industries Inc .... E 574 262-2639
   Elkhart *(G-3672)*

Spectrum Brands Inc .... E 317 773-6627
   Noblesville *(G-13179)*

St Regis Inc .... F 317 591-3500
   Indianapolis *(G-9486)*

◆ State Wide Aluminum Inc .... C 574 262-2594
   Elkhart *(G-3699)*

Sunburst Stained Glass Co Inc .... G 812 853-0460
   Newburgh *(G-13024)*

Vernon Greyber .... G 812 636-7880
   Odon *(G-13355)*

Vuteq Usa Inc .... B 502 863-6322
   Princeton *(G-14018)*

Warsaw Cut Glass Company Inc .... G 574 267-6581
   Warsaw *(G-16445)*

Whitaker Glass & Mirror LLC .... G 765 482-1500
   Lebanon *(G-10950)*

Winandy Greenhouse Company .... E 765 935-2111
   Richmond *(G-14227)*

3241 Cement, hydraulic

Busters Cement Products Inc .... G 765 529-0287
   New Castle *(G-12854)*

Buzzi Unicem USA Inc .... E 317 706-3352
   Carmel *(G-1577)*

Buzzi Unicem USA Inc .... G 574 674-8873
   Elkhart *(G-3239)*

Buzzi Unicem USA Inc .... C 765 653-9766
   Greencastle *(G-6393)*

Buzzi Unicem USA Inc .... E 317 780-9860
   Indianapolis *(G-7705)*

D and D Custom Concrete Inc .... G 574 274-6013
   Mishawaka *(G-11875)*

Heidelberg Mtls US Cem LLC .... C 574 753-5121
   Logansport *(G-11076)*

Heidelberg Mtls US Cem LLC .... B 812 849-2191
   Mitchell *(G-12040)*

Holcim (us) Inc .... G 219 378-1193
   East Chicago *(G-3017)*

Irving Materials Inc .... F 765 922-7285
   Kokomo *(G-10291)*

Light House Center Inc .... F 765 448-4502
   Lafayette *(G-10636)*

Lone Star Industries Inc .... G 574 674-8873
   Elkhart *(G-3499)*

Lone Star Industries Inc .... G 260 482-4559
   Fort Wayne *(G-5190)*

Lone Star Industries Inc .... G 765 653-9766
   Greencastle *(G-6419)*

Lone Star Industries Inc .... G 317 780-9860
   Indianapolis *(G-8778)*

▲ Lone Star Industries Inc .... D 317 706-3314
   Carmel *(G-1685)*

River Cement Sales Company .... G 812 285-1003
   Jeffersonville *(G-10048)*

Southfield Corporation .... E 317 846-6060
   Carmel *(G-1767)*

3251 Brick and structural clay tile

▲ Ceramica Inc .... F 317 546-0087
   Indianapolis *(G-7777)*

Heb Development LLC .... E 616 363-3825
   Centerpoint *(G-1845)*

Meridian Brick LLC .... E 812 894-2454
   Terre Haute *(G-15642)*

National Chimney Supply-VT Inc .... E 317 636-0552
   Indianapolis *(G-8986)*

◆ Santarossa Mosaic Tile Co Inc .... C 317 632-9494
   Indianapolis *(G-9371)*

Whimsical Gardens .... G 317 257-4704
   Indianapolis *(G-9758)*

3253 Ceramic wall and floor tile

Georgia Direct Carpet Inc .... F 765 966-2548
   Richmond *(G-14125)*

Universal Export Partnr LLC .... G 219 939-9529
   Gary *(G-6024)*

3255 Clay refractories

Back Alley Creations LLC .... G 219 306-6590
   Dyer *(G-2968)*

Bmi Refractory Services Inc .... G 219 885-2209
   Gary *(G-5903)*

Can-Clay Corp .... E
   Cannelton *(G-1534)*

Certainteed LLC .... G 812 645-0400
   Terre Haute *(G-15559)*

Champion Target .... F 765 966-7745
   Richmond *(G-14103)*

◆ Hale Industries Inc .... F 317 577-0337
   Fortville *(G-5598)*

Harbisonwalker Intl Inc .... G 219 881-4440
   Gary *(G-5945)*

Ht Enterprises Inc .... G 765 794-4174
   Crawfordsville *(G-2578)*

Quikrete Companies LLC .... E 317 251-2281
   Indianapolis *(G-9252)*

R T W Refractory Inc .... F 812 468-4299
   Evansville *(G-4269)*

◆ Refractory Engineers Inc .... E 317 273-2000
   Indianapolis *(G-9281)*

Refractory Specialists LLC .... G 260 969-1099
   Fort Wayne *(G-5376)*

Resco Products Inc .... F 219 844-7830
   Hammond *(G-6997)*

Rhi Magnesita .... G 219 237-2420
   Hammond *(G-6998)*

Superior Radiant Products Inc .... F 800 527-4328
   Fortville *(G-5606)*

Thermal Ceramics Inc .... E 574 296-3500
   Elkhart *(G-3725)*

Wb Refractory Service Inc .... G 317 450-7386
   Indianapolis *(G-9743)*

3259 Structural clay products, nec

Can-Clay Corp .... E
   Cannelton *(G-1534)*

Jag Mobile Solutions Inc .... E 260 562-1045
   Howe *(G-7237)*

Marv Kahlig & Sons Inc .... G 260 335-2212
   Portland *(G-13956)*

Stone Artisans Ltd .... G 317 362-0107
   Indianapolis *(G-9512)*

3261 Vitreous plumbing fixtures

Bootz Manufacturing Co LLC .... C 812 425-4646
   Evansville *(G-3942)*

Coast OEM LLC .... G 765 553-5904
   Kokomo *(G-10247)*

◆ Josam Company .... D 219 872-5531
   Michigan City *(G-11628)*

Leeps Supply Co Inc .... E 219 756-5337
   Merrillville *(G-11530)*

▲ Next Gen Power Holdings LLC .... G 574 971-4490
   Elkhart *(G-3568)*

Patriot Porcelain LLC .... G 574 583-5128
   Monticello *(G-12164)*

3264 Porcelain electrical supplies

Ies Subsidiary Holdings Inc .... G 219 937-0100
   Hammond *(G-6953)*

Ies Subsidiary Holdings Inc .... G 330 830-3500
   South Bend *(G-15074)*

Insulation Specialties of Amer .... E 219 733-2502
   Wanatah *(G-16290)*

Leco Corporation .... G 574 288-9017
   South Bend *(G-15122)*

Thomas & Skinner Inc .... C 812 689-4811
   Osgood *(G-13418)*

3269 Pottery products, nec

Carol Burt .... G 765 282-5383
   Muncie *(G-12365)*

Davis Vachon Artworks .... G 260 489-9160
   Fort Wayne *(G-4907)*

Donald H & Susan K Minch .... G 260 726-9486
   Portland *(G-13937)*

Grateful Heart Enterprises LLC .... G 765 838-2266
   Lafayette *(G-10593)*

Julie Edwards Ceramics .... G 317 681-9523
   Indianapolis *(G-8648)*

Molded Acstcal Pdts Easton Inc .... E 574 968-3124
   Granger *(G-6363)*

Ohio Valley Creative Enrgy Inc .... G 502 468-9787
   New Albany *(G-12787)*

Pigeon Switch Pottery .... G 812 567-4124
   Tennyson *(G-15524)*

▼ R Drew & Co Inc .... G 765 420-7232
   West Lafayette *(G-16624)*

Reiberg Ceramics .... G 317 283-8441
   Indianapolis *(G-9283)*

Schmidt Marken Designs .... G 219 785-4238
   La Porte *(G-10477)*

Scottsburg Stoneware LLC .... G 812 752-6353
   Scottsburg *(G-14578)*

Shafer Stoneware .... G 765 855-2409
   Centerville *(G-1854)*

Sissys Ceramics .... G 951 550-7728
   Elkhart *(G-3679)*

Strawtown Pottery & Antq Inc .... G 317 984-5080
   Noblesville *(G-13180)*

Tinas Ceramics & Things .... G 812 917-4190
   Terre Haute *(G-15731)*

SIC SECTION
32 STONE, CLAY, GLASS, AND CONCRETE PRODUCTS

3271 Concrete block and brick

▲ Brampton Brick Inc .... E 812 397-2190
   Farmersburg *(G-4416)*

Camilles Studio .... G 219 365-5902
   Cedar Lake *(G-1828)*

Carters Concrete Block Inc .... G 574 583-7811
   Monticello *(G-12142)*

Cash Concrete Products Inc .... F 765 653-4007
   Greencastle *(G-6395)*

Crown Brick & Supply Inc .... E 219 663-7880
   Crown Point *(G-2668)*

Devening Block Inc .... E 812 372-4458
   Columbus *(G-2282)*

Dubois Cnty Block & Brick Inc .... F 812 482-6293
   Jasper *(G-9834)*

Engineered Products Inc .... G 219 662-2080
   Crown Point *(G-2680)*

Evansville Block Co Inc .... E 812 422-2864
   Evansville *(G-4049)*

Glen-Gery Corporation .... F 317 784-2505
   Indianapolis *(G-8285)*

Hanson Aggregates Wrp Inc .... E 502 244-7550
   Sellersburg *(G-14596)*

▲ Hessit Works Inc .... G 812 829-6246
   Freedom *(G-5801)*

Holcim (us) Inc .... G 219 378-1193
   East Chicago *(G-3017)*

Hydro Conduit .... G 561 651-7177
   Greenfield *(G-6510)*

Irving Materials Inc .... D 317 326-3101
   Greenfield *(G-6518)*

Jones and Sons Inc .... E 812 254-4731
   Washington *(G-16489)*

Majestic Block & Supply Inc .... G 317 842-6602
   Fishers *(G-4560)*

Menard Inc .... C 812 466-1234
   Terre Haute *(G-15641)*

North Star Stone Inc .... F 219 464-7272
   Valparaiso *(G-16016)*

Precast Specialties Inc .... F 260 623-6131
   Monroeville *(G-12072)*

Rose Hl Lawn Care Ldscpg Snow .... G 812 230-0024
   Terre Haute *(G-15684)*

Shelby Gravel Inc .... F 317 738-3445
   Franklin *(G-5776)*

Slater Concrete Products Inc .... G 260 347-0164
   Kendallville *(G-10152)*

Slon Inc .... E 765 884-1792
   Fowler *(G-5633)*

Southfield Corporation .... E 812 824-1355
   Bloomington *(G-978)*

St Henry Tile Co Inc .... E 260 589-2880
   Berne *(G-728)*

St Henry Tile Co Inc .... G 765 966-7771
   Richmond *(G-14207)*

Stotlar Hill LLC .... F 260 497-0808
   Fort Wayne *(G-5446)*

Van Duyne Block and Gravel .... G 574 223-6656
   Rochester *(G-14331)*

Wheeler Corporation .... F 317 398-7500
   Shelbyville *(G-14815)*

3272 Concrete products, nec

Accucast Industries .... G 219 929-1137
   Chesterton *(G-1900)*

Ace Extrusion LLC .... E 812 436-4840
   Evansville *(G-3870)*

▲ AK Industries Inc .... D 574 936-6022
   Plymouth *(G-13752)*

Akron Concrete Products Inc .... G 574 893-4841
   Akron *(G-1)*

Alberding Woodworking Inc .... F 260 728-9526
   Decatur *(G-2841)*

Allen Monument Co .... G 317 941-7047
   Indianapolis *(G-7480)*

Allen Monument Co .... G 574 240-1880
   Monticello *(G-12134)*

Allen Monument Company .... G 765 362-8886
   Crawfordsville *(G-2544)*

Anderson Memorial Park Inc .... F 765 643-3211
   Anderson *(G-78)*

Arrow Vault Co Inc .... G 765 742-1704
   Lafayette *(G-10527)*

Beaver Gravel Corporation .... D 317 773-0679
   Noblesville *(G-13042)*

Beaver Products Inc .... F 317 773-0679
   Noblesville *(G-13043)*

Beazer East Inc .... G 260 490-9006
   Fort Wayne *(G-4791)*

Bowsman Tank Co .... G 260 244-7129
   Columbia City *(G-2125)*

Brickworks Supply Center LLC .... E 317 786-9208
   Carmel *(G-1573)*

Brim Concrete Inc .... G 765 564-4975
   Delphi *(G-2891)*

Calumet Wilbert Vault Co Inc .... F 219 980-1173
   Gary *(G-5910)*

Carter Septic Tank Inc .... G 574 583-5796
   Monticello *(G-12141)*

Carters LLC .... F 260 432-3568
   Fort Wayne *(G-4835)*

Carters Concrete Block Inc .... E 574 722-2644
   Fort Wayne *(G-4836)*

Cash Concrete Products Inc .... F 765 653-4007
   Greencastle *(G-6395)*

Cast Stone .... G 317 617-1088
   Indianapolis *(G-7756)*

Century Grave & Vault Service .... G 812 967-2110
   Pekin *(G-13513)*

Cheetah Building Products .... G 812 466-1234
   Terre Haute *(G-15562)*

Columbus Vault Co .... G 812 372-3210
   Columbus *(G-2247)*

Combi Institiute Inc .... G 602 269-2288
   Carmel *(G-1592)*

Concrete Lady Inc .... E 812 256-2765
   Otisco *(G-13447)*

Concrete Supply LLC .... E 812 474-6715
   Evansville *(G-3979)*

Coreslab Strctres Indnplis Inc .... D 317 353-2118
   Indianapolis *(G-7875)*

County Materials Corp .... E 317 323-6000
   Maxwell *(G-11443)*

Creed & Dyer Precast Inc .... E 574 784-3361
   Lakeville *(G-10789)*

Crenshaw Paving Incorporated .... G 765 249-2342
   Michigantown *(G-11689)*

Custom Cast Stone Inc .... D 317 896-1700
   Westfield *(G-16682)*

Dyer Vault Company Inc .... E 219 865-2521
   Dyer *(G-2972)*

Dynamic Composites LLC .... G 260 625-8686
   Columbia City *(G-2141)*

Eaton Septic Tank Company .... G 765 396-3275
   Eaton *(G-3060)*

Eavk Legacy Inc .... E 812 246-4461
   New Albany *(G-12723)*

Erie-Haven Inc .... D 260 478-1674
   Fort Wayne *(G-4959)*

Farmer Legacy Inc .... G 574 264-4625
   Elkhart *(G-3343)*

Flyover Enterprises Inc .... G 317 417-1747
   Pendleton *(G-13532)*

Forsyth Brothers Con Pdts Inc .... G 812 466-4080
   Terre Haute *(G-15590)*

Forsyth Puttmann LLC .... G 812 466-2925
   Terre Haute *(G-15591)*

Forterra Concrete Inds Inc .... E 859 254-4242
   Whitestown *(G-16806)*

Grable Burial Vault Svc Inc .... G 574 753-4514
   Logansport *(G-11075)*

Hanson Pipe Precast .... G 219 873-9509
   Michigan City *(G-11619)*

Harris Burial Service Inc .... G 812 939-3605
   Clay City *(G-2043)*

Harris Precast Inc .... G 219 362-2457
   La Porte *(G-10416)*

Harris Precast Inc .... G 219 362-9671
   La Porte *(G-10417)*

▲ Hessit Works Inc .... G 812 829-6246
   Freedom *(G-5801)*

Hi-Tech Concrete Inc .... G 765 477-5550
   Lafayette *(G-10597)*

Hog Slat Incorporated .... D 765 828-0828
   Universal *(G-15875)*

Holcim (us) Inc .... G 219 378-1193
   East Chicago *(G-3017)*

Holman Septic Tank Sls Rdymix I .... F 812 689-1913
   Holton *(G-7271)*

Homeowners Equity & Rlty Corp .... G 219 981-1700
   Gary *(G-5952)*

Horn Pre-Cast Inc .... F 812 372-4458
   Columbus *(G-2320)*

Howard & Sons Cement Pdts Inc .... G 574 293-1906
   Elkhart *(G-3412)*

Hydro Conduit of Texas LP .... G 317 769-2261
   Whitestown *(G-16809)*

ICP Liquidating Company .... D 419 841-3361
   Indianapolis *(G-8451)*

Independent Concrete Pipe Company .... E 317 262-4920
   Indianapolis *(G-8471)*

Indiana Barrier Wall LLC .... G 260 747-5777
   Fort Wayne *(G-5099)*

Indiana Green Burial LLC .... G 812 961-1960
   Worthington *(G-16961)*

Indiana Precast Inc .... E 812 372-7771
   Columbus *(G-2324)*

James Harper .... G 812 267-4251
   Depauw *(G-2939)*

Jjs Concrete Construction LLC .... E 812 636-0173
   Montgomery *(G-12103)*

Johnsons Burial Designs .... G 317 549-2148
   Indianapolis *(G-8636)*

Jones & Sons Inc .... E 812 299-2287
   Terre Haute *(G-15622)*

Jones & Sons Inc .... E 812 882-2957
   Vincennes *(G-16135)*

Lebanon Berg Vault Co Inc .... G 765 482-0302
   Lebanon *(G-10909)*

Legacy Vulcan LLC .... G 219 987-3040
   Demotte *(G-2922)*

Legacy Vulcan LLC .... G 219 462-5832
   Valparaiso *(G-15995)*

Lowell Concrete Products Inc .... E 219 696-3339
   Lowell *(G-11169)*

Mark Concrete Products Inc .... G 317 398-8616
   Shelbyville *(G-14774)*

McCreary Concrete Products Inc .... E 765 932-3058
   Tipton *(G-15784)*

Midwest Tile and Concrete Pdts .... G 260 749-5173
   Woodburn *(G-16952)*

Midwest Tile and Concrete Pdts .... G 260 749-5173
   Woodburn *(G-16953)*

Minnick Services Corp .... E 260 432-5031
   Fort Wayne *(G-5231)*

32 STONE, CLAY, GLASS, AND CONCRETE PRODUCTS

Mjs Concrete .... G 260 341-5640
  Woodburn (G-16954)
Monticello Vault Burial Co .... G 574 583-3206
  Monticello (G-12159)
Monument Lighthouse Chart .... G 317 657-0160
  Indianapolis (G-8953)
Monumental Stone Works Inc .... F 765 866-0658
  New Market (G-12927)
Northfield Block Company .... G 800 424-0190
  Indianapolis (G-9023)
P3 Polymers LLC .... G 812 674-2051
  Washington (G-16499)
Pavers Inc .... G 317 271-0823
  Indianapolis (G-9104)
Plaster Shak .... G 317 881-6518
  Greenwood (G-6752)
Precast Specialties Inc .... F 260 623-6131
  Monroeville (G-12072)
Prestress Services Inc .... C 260 724-7117
  Decatur (G-2877)
Quality Tank Trucks & Eqp Inc .... G 317 635-0000
  Indianapolis (G-9247)
Quality Vault Company .... G 812 336-8127
  Bloomington (G-949)
Quikrete Companies LLC .... E 317 241-8237
  Indianapolis (G-9251)
Quikrete Companies LLC .... E 317 251-2281
  Indianapolis (G-9252)
Ram North America Inc .... F 317 984-1971
  Arcadia (G-316)
Reams Concrete .... G 812 752-3746
  Scottsburg (G-14575)
Rensselaer Eagle Vault Corp .... G 219 866-5123
  Rensselaer (G-14065)
Rochester Cement Products Inc ...... G 574 223-3917
  Rochester (G-14316)
Rogers Group Inc .... G 765 342-6898
  Martinsville (G-11424)
Rosskovenski Concrete & Rdymx .... G 765 832-6103
  Clinton (G-2077)
Russells Excvtg Sptic Tnks Inc .... F 812 838-2471
  Mount Vernon (G-12318)
S & M Precast Inc .... D 812 246-6258
  Henryville (G-7115)
S & S Precast Inc .... E 574 946-4123
  Winamac (G-16874)
◆ S S M Inc .... G 317 357-4552
  Indianapolis (G-9356)
Schrock Aggregate Company Inc ..... G 574 862-4167
  Wakarusa (G-16250)
Scruggs Construction Inc .... E 812 528-8178
  Seymour (G-14687)
Slon Inc .... E 765 884-1792
  Fowler (G-5633)
Southern Indiana Supply Inc .... F 812 482-2267
  Jasper (G-9914)
Specification Products Inc .... G 888 881-1726
  Noblesville (G-13178)
Spider Tie .... G 574 596-3073
  Syracuse (G-15479)
St Regis Culvert Inc .... F 317 353-8065
  Indianapolis (G-9487)
▲ Strescore Inc .... E 574 233-1117
  South Bend (G-15270)
▲ Terre Hute Wlbert Brial Vlt In .... F 812 235-0339
  Terre Haute (G-15727)
Terrys Sewer Service .... G 219 756-5238
  Merrillville (G-11566)
Trenwa Inc .... F 812 427-2217
  Florence (G-4667)
Tri State Monument Company .... G 812 386-7303
  Princeton (G-14017)

Tribute Precast Systems LLC .... G 260 587-9555
  Ashley (G-339)
Van Gard Vault Co Inc .... G 219 980-6233
  Gary (G-6026)
Van Gard Vault Company Inc .... F 219 949-7723
  Gary (G-6027)
Vernon L Goedecke Company Inc ... G 812 421-9633
  Evansville (G-4372)
Wayne Burial Vault Company Inc ..... G 317 357-4656
  Indianapolis (G-9742)
White Cap LP .... E 260 471-7619
  Fort Wayne (G-5565)
Wholesale Drainage Supply Inc .... G 812 397-5100
  Shelburn (G-14724)
▲ Wilbert Burial Vault Co Inc .... E 317 547-1387
  Indianapolis (G-9762)
Wilbert Sexton Corporation .... G 812 372-3210
  Columbus (G-2419)
Wilbert Sexton Corporation .... G 812 882-3555
  Vincennes (G-16166)
Wilbert Sexton Corporation .... G 812 336-6469
  Bloomington (G-1011)
Wilson Burial Vault Inc .... G 260 356-5722
  Huntington (G-7380)

3273 Ready-mixed concrete

A & T Concrete Supply Inc .... E 812 753-4252
  Fort Branch (G-4701)
All-Rite Ready Mix Inc .... F 812 926-0920
  Aurora (G-437)
Armstrongs .... G 219 977-8368
  Gary (G-5896)
Atkins Quarry .... G 972 653-5550
  Jeffersonville (G-9936)
Attica Ready Mixed Concrete .... F 765 762-2424
  Attica (G-343)
Beaver Gravel Corporation .... D 317 773-0679
  Noblesville (G-13042)
Brim Concrete Inc .... G 765 564-4975
  Delphi (G-2891)
Builders Concrete & Supply Co Inc .. C 317 570-6201
  Fishers (G-4478)
Busters Cement Products Inc .... G 765 529-0287
  New Castle (G-12854)
Cash Concrete Products Inc .... G 765 653-4887
  Greencastle (G-6394)
Cash Concrete Products Inc .... F 765 653-4007
  Greencastle (G-6395)
Cemex .... F 317 351-9912
  Indianapolis (G-7766)
Cemex Materials LLC .... C 317 891-7500
  Greenfield (G-6477)
Cemex Materials LLC .... C 317 891-3015
  Indianapolis (G-7767)
Cemex Materials LLC .... D 317 769-5801
  Whitestown (G-16803)
Center Concrete Inc .... G 800 453-4224
  Butler (G-1460)
Central Concrete Supply LLC .... F 812 481-2331
  Jasper (G-9828)
Century Concrete Inc .... G 765 739-6210
  Bainbridge (G-56C)
Concrete Supply LLC .... E 812 474-6715
  Evansville (G-3979)
County Materials Corp .... G 317 769-5503
  Whitestown (G-16804)
Crawford County Concrete .... G 812 739-2707
  Leavenworth (G-10869)
Elkhart County Gravel Inc .... G 574 825-7913
  Middlebury (G-11714)
Environ Corporation .... G 317 774-0541
  Carmel (G-1625)

Erie Haven Inc .... G 260 665-2052
  Angola (G-249)
Erie-Haven Inc .... G 260 478-1674
  Auburn (G-389)
Erie-Haven Inc .... F 260 353-1133
  Bluffton (G-1036)
Erie-Haven Inc .... G 260 483-3865
  Fort Wayne (G-4958)
Erie-Haven Inc .... D 260 478-1674
  Fort Wayne (G-4959)
Ernst Enterprises Inc .... G 260 726-8282
  Portland (G-13938)
Ernst Enterprises Inc .... G 812 284-5205
  Sellersburg (G-14592)
Ernst Enterprises Inc .... G 765 584-5700
  Winchester (G-16886)
Gra-Rock Redi Mix Precast LLC ...... F 765 395-7275
  Amboy (G-67)
Hanson Aggregates Wrp Inc .... E 502 244-7550
  Sellersburg (G-14596)
Harrison Concrete .... G 812 275-6682
  Bedford (G-640)
Heidelberg Mtls Mdwest Agg Inc ..... G 260 747-3105
  Fort Wayne (G-5061)
Heidelberg Mtls Mdwest Agg Inc ..... F 765 653-1956
  Greencastle (G-6411)
Heidelberg Mtls Mdwest Agg Inc ..... G 812 689-5017
  Versailles (G-16100)
Heidelberg Mtls Sthwest Agg LL ...... G 260 665-2626
  Angola (G-257)
Heidelberg Mtls Sthwest Agg LL ...... G 260 747-5011
  Fort Wayne (G-5062)
Heidelberg Mtls Sthwest Agg LL ...... G 812 246-4481
  Sellersburg (G-14598)
Heidelberg Mtls US Cem LLC .... B 812 849-2191
  Mitchell (G-12040)
Heidelberg Mtls US Cem LLC .... E 812 246-5472
  Sellersburg (G-14599)
Hilltop Basic Resources Inc .... G 812 594-2293
  Patriot (G-13510)
Holcim - Mwr Inc .... G 260 665-2052
  Angola (G-260)
Holcim (us) Inc .... G 219 378-1193
  East Chicago (G-3017)
Hollingshead Mixer Company LLC ... D 260 897-4397
  Avilla (G-477)
Holzer Ready Mix LLC .... F 317 306-9327
  Indianapolis (G-8403)
Hoosier Ready Mix LLC .... F 812 254-7625
  Washington (G-16484)
Hopkins Gravel Sand & Concrete .... G 317 831-2704
  Mooresville (G-12211)
I MI Erie Stone .... G 765 728-5335
  Montpelier (G-12178)
Im Indiana Holdings Inc .... G 260 478-1674
  Fort Wayne (G-5093)
IMI Bloomfield .... G 812 384-0045
  Bloomfield (G-749)
IMI Riving Materials Inc .... G 812 753-4201
  Fort Branch (G-4704)
IMI South LLC .... G 812 284-9732
  Clarksville (G-2019)
IMI South LLC .... G 812 738-4173
  Corydon (G-2500)
IMI South LLC .... G 812 273-1428
  Madison (G-11229)
IMI South LLC .... E 812 945-6605
  New Albany (G-12744)
IMI Southwest Inc .... E 812 424-3554
  Evansville (G-4118)
Indiana Im Holdings Inc .... E 260 637-3101
  Fort Wayne (G-5101)

SIC SECTION
32 STONE, CLAY, GLASS, AND CONCRETE PRODUCTS

Interstate Block Corporation .... G 812 273-1742
   Madison *(G-11230)*

Irving Materials Inc .... G 765 644-8819
   Anderson *(G-135)*

Irving Materials Inc .... F 765 778-4760
   Anderson *(G-136)*

Irving Materials Inc .... G 812 275-7450
   Bedford *(G-649)*

Irving Materials Inc .... F 812 333-8530
   Bloomington *(G-892)*

Irving Materials Inc .... F 260 824-3428
   Bluffton *(G-1039)*

Irving Materials Inc .... G 812 443-4661
   Brazil *(G-1148)*

Irving Materials Inc .... G 765 647-6533
   Brookville *(G-1327)*

Irving Materials Inc .... G 765 478-4914
   Cambridge City *(G-1496)*

Irving Materials Inc .... G 765 825-2581
   Connersville *(G-2446)*

Irving Materials Inc .... G 765 362-6904
   Crawfordsville *(G-2581)*

Irving Materials Inc .... G 765 552-5041
   Elwood *(G-3826)*

Irving Materials Inc .... G 812 424-3551
   Evansville *(G-4132)*

Irving Materials Inc .... F 317 326-3101
   Fort Wayne *(G-5120)*

Irving Materials Inc .... F 765 654-5333
   Frankfort *(G-5675)*

Irving Materials Inc .... G 317 888-0157
   Greenwood *(G-6717)*

Irving Materials Inc .... G 812 683-4444
   Huntingburg *(G-7284)*

Irving Materials Inc .... F 260 356-7214
   Huntington *(G-7331)*

Irving Materials Inc .... G 317 843-2944
   Indianapolis *(G-8589)*

Irving Materials Inc .... G 317 872-0152
   Indianapolis *(G-8590)*

Irving Materials Inc .... G 317 783-3381
   Indianapolis *(G-8591)*

Irving Materials Inc .... G 317 243-7391
   Indianapolis *(G-8592)*

Irving Materials Inc .... G 317 899-2187
   Indianapolis *(G-8593)*

Irving Materials Inc .... G 765 452-4044
   Kokomo *(G-10290)*

Irving Materials Inc .... F 765 922-7285
   Kokomo *(G-10291)*

Irving Materials Inc .... G 765 423-2533
   Lafayette *(G-10610)*

Irving Materials Inc .... G 765 482-5620
   Lebanon *(G-10903)*

Irving Materials Inc .... G 574 722-3420
   Logansport *(G-11084)*

Irving Materials Inc .... G 765 674-2271
   Marion *(G-11296)*

Irving Materials Inc .... G 765 342-3369
   Martinsville *(G-11408)*

Irving Materials Inc .... G 765 728-5435
   Montpelier *(G-12179)*

Irving Materials Inc .... F 317 831-0224
   Mooresville *(G-12216)*

Irving Materials Inc .... G 765 836-4007
   Muncie *(G-12426)*

Irving Materials Inc .... G 765 288-5566
   Muncie *(G-12427)*

Irving Materials Inc .... G 765 288-0288
   Muncie *(G-12428)*

Irving Materials Inc .... F 317 770-1745
   Noblesville *(G-13108)*

Irving Materials Inc .... G 317 773-3640
   Noblesville *(G-13109)*

Irving Materials Inc .... G 574 936-2975
   Plymouth *(G-13788)*

Irving Materials Inc .... G 219 261-2441
   Remington *(G-14037)*

Irving Materials Inc .... G 812 883-4242
   Scottsburg *(G-14565)*

Irving Materials Inc .... G 812 829-9445
   Spencer *(G-15353)*

Irving Materials Inc .... G 765 755-3447
   Springport *(G-15380)*

Irving Materials Inc .... G 765 922-7931
   Swayzee *(G-15451)*

Irving Materials Inc .... F 765 922-7991
   Swayzee *(G-15452)*

Irving Materials Inc .... G 765 675-6327
   Tipton *(G-15777)*

Irving Materials Inc .... G 812 254-0820
   Washington *(G-16486)*

Irving Materials Inc .... G 765 743-3806
   West Lafayette *(G-16596)*

Irving Materials Inc .... G 317 535-7566
   Whiteland *(G-16790)*

Irving Materials Inc .... F 574 946-3754
   Winamac *(G-16864)*

Irving Materials Inc .... D 317 326-3101
   Greenfield *(G-6518)*

Irving Materials Inc .... E 260 356-7214
   Huntington *(G-7332)*

J & K Supply Inc .... G 765 448-1188
   Lafayette *(G-10611)*

Jack Mix .... G 812 923-8679
   Floyds Knobs *(G-4682)*

Jjs Concrete Construction LLC .... E 812 636-0173
   Montgomery *(G-12103)*

Johnson & Johnson Incorporated .... F 317 539-8420
   Mooresville *(G-12218)*

Jones & Sons Inc .... E 812 299-2287
   Terre Haute *(G-15622)*

Jones & Sons Inc .... E 812 882-2957
   Vincennes *(G-16135)*

Jones and Sons Inc .... E 812 254-4731
   Washington *(G-16489)*

Kentucky Concrete Indiana LLC .... E 812 282-6671
   Jeffersonville *(G-10008)*

Keystone Concrete Inc .... E 260 693-6437
   Churubusco *(G-1986)*

Kuert Concrete Inc .... F 574 293-0430
   Goshen *(G-6193)*

Kuert Concrete Inc .... G 574 223-2414
   Rochester *(G-14299)*

Kuert Concrete Inc .... G 574 453-3993
   Warsaw *(G-16384)*

Kuert Concrete Inc .... E 574 232-9911
   South Bend *(G-15109)*

Lees Ready-Mix & Trucking .... E
   Shelbyville *(G-14772)*

Lees Ready-Mix & Trucking Inc .... F 812 372-1800
   Columbus *(G-2339)*

Legacy Vulcan LLC .... G 574 293-1536
   Elkhart *(G-3483)*

Legacy Vulcan LLC .... G 219 567-9155
   Francesville *(G-5643)*

Legacy Vulcan LLC .... G 219 696-5467
   Lowell *(G-11167)*

Legacy Vulcan LLC .... G 219 253-6686
   Monon *(G-12056)*

Legacy Vulcan LLC .... G 219 465-3066
   Valparaiso *(G-15996)*

Lewis Jerry Cnstr & Excvtg .... G 765 653-2800
   Greencastle *(G-6418)*

▲ Lone Star Industries Inc .... D 317 706-3314
   Carmel *(G-1685)*

Ma-Ri-Al Corp .... E 317 773-0679
   Noblesville *(G-13129)*

Martin Marietta Materials Inc .... F 765 883-8172
   Russiaville *(G-14424)*

McClure Concrete .... G 765 525-6098
   Flat Rock *(G-4655)*

▲ McIntire Concrete .... F 765 759-7111
   Muncie *(G-12450)*

Mendozas Incorporated .... G 219 791-9034
   Merrillville *(G-11537)*

Mes Legacy Pc Inc .... E 317 769-5503
   Indianapolis *(G-8880)*

Meuth Construction Supply Inc .... G 812 424-8554
   Evansville *(G-4199)*

Meuth Construction Supply Inc .... G 270 826-8554
   Princeton *(G-14004)*

Mix On Site .... G 765 607-2140
   West Lafayette *(G-16608)*

Mulzer Crushed Stone Inc .... E 812 547-3467
   Tell City *(G-15512)*

Mulzer Crushed Stone Inc .... E 812 547-7921
   Tell City *(G-15513)*

N E W Interstate Concrete Inc .... F 812 234-5983
   Terre Haute *(G-15649)*

Ohio Valley Ready Mix Inc .... E 812 282-6671
   Jeffersonville *(G-10028)*

Ozinga - Concrete .... G 574 291-7100
   South Bend *(G-15184)*

Ozinga Bros Inc .... E 574 546-2550
   Bremen *(G-1211)*

Ozinga Bros Inc .... E 219 662-0925
   Crown Point *(G-2728)*

Ozinga Bros Inc .... E 574 971-8239
   Goshen *(G-6233)*

Ozinga Bros Inc .... E 574 642-4455
   Goshen *(G-6234)*

Ozinga Bros Inc .... C 219 949-9800
   Portage *(G-13901)*

Ozinga Bros Inc .... E 219 956-3418
   Wheatfield *(G-16770)*

Ozinga Inc .... G 219 324-2286
   La Porte *(G-10461)*

Ozinga Indiana Rdymx Con Inc .... F 219 949-9800
   Gary *(G-5993)*

Pepcon Concrete Inc .... G 765 964-6572
   Union City *(G-15858)*

Prairie Group .... F 812 877-9886
   Terre Haute *(G-15666)*

Prairie Group Inc .... G 812 824-1355
   Bloomington *(G-948)*

Precast Solutions Inc .... F 317 545-6557
   Whitestown *(G-16816)*

Primed & Ready LLC .... G 317 694-2028
   Indianapolis *(G-9197)*

Prmi 1 Inc .... G 219 474-5022
   Kentland *(G-10162)*

Purdy Concrete Inc .... G 765 477-7687
   Lafayette *(G-10672)*

Purdy Materials Inc .... E 765 474-8993
   Lafayette *(G-10673)*

Quikrete Companies LLC .... E 317 251-2281
   Indianapolis *(G-9252)*

Raver Ready Mix Concrete LLC .... G 812 662-7900
   Batesville *(G-601)*

Ready Set Go Inc .... G 765 564-2847
   Delphi *(G-2907)*

Rosskovenski Concrete & Rdymx .... G 765 832-6103
   Clinton *(G-2077)*

Sagamore Ready-Mix LLC .... G 765 759-8999
   Daleville *(G-2802)*

32 STONE, CLAY, GLASS, AND CONCRETE PRODUCTS

Sagamore Ready-Mix LLC .... G 317 570-6201
  Fishers *(G-4603)*

Schmaltz Ready Mix Concrete .... G 812 689-5140
  Osgood *(G-13415)*

Shelby Gravel Inc .... F 317 738-3445
  Franklin *(G-5776)*

Shelby Gravel Inc .... F 317 784-6678
  Indianapolis *(G-9417)*

Shelby Gravel Inc .... F 317 216-7556
  Indianapolis *(G-9418)*

Shelby Gravel Inc .... G 765 932-3292
  Rushville *(G-14412)*

Shelby Gravel Inc .... F 317 804-8100
  Westfield *(G-16726)*

Shelby Gravel Inc .... E 317 398-4485
  Shelbyville *(G-14797)*

Shoreline East Inc .... G 219 878-9991
  Michigan City *(G-11668)*

Smith Ready Mix Inc .... F 219 462-3191
  Valparaiso *(G-16054)*

Southfield Corporation .... E 812 824-1355
  Bloomington *(G-978)*

Southfield Corporation .... E 317 846-6060
  Carmel *(G-1767)*

Southfield Corporation .... E 317 773-5340
  Noblesville *(G-13177)*

Speedway Redi Mix Inc .... G 260 665-5999
  Angola *(G-293)*

Speedway Redi Mix Inc .... G 260 244-7205
  Columbia City *(G-2201)*

Speedway Redi-Mix Inc .... G 260 356-5600
  Huntington *(G-7370)*

Speedway Redi-Mix Inc .... F 260 496-8877
  Fort Wayne *(G-5430)*

Spurlino Mtls Indianapolis LLC .... G 765 339-4055
  Linden *(G-11032)*

St Henry Tile Co Inc .... E 260 589-2880
  Berne *(G-728)*

Sullivan IMI .... G 812 268-3306
  Sullivan *(G-15423)*

Wdmi Inc .... D 574 936-2136
  Plymouth *(G-13826)*

Zimco Materials Inc .... G 219 883-0870
  Gary *(G-6029)*

3274 Lime

Calcar Quarries Incorporated .... F 812 723-2109
  Paoli *(G-13491)*

Dotted Lime Resale LLC .... G 317 908-3905
  Westfield *(G-16686)*

Ed Henry & Son .... G 765 675-7235
  Tipton *(G-15771)*

Harris Stone Service Inc .... F 765 522-6241
  Bainbridge *(G-563)*

Heidelberg Mtls Mdwest Agg Inc .... G 812 889-2120
  Lexington *(G-10977)*

Jolene D Pavey .... G 765 473-6171
  Peru *(G-13588)*

Mississippi Lime Company .... G 800 437-5463
  Portage *(G-13889)*

Mulzer Crushed Stone Inc .... E 812 365-2145
  English *(G-3844)*

Rogers Group Inc .... D 219 474-5125
  Kentland *(G-10163)*

Rogers Group Inc .... G 765 342-6898
  Martinsville *(G-11424)*

Rogers Group Inc .... D 812 849-3530
  Mitchell *(G-12047)*

Rogers Group Inc .... E 812 882-3640
  Vincennes *(G-16150)*

Rush County Stone Co Inc .... G 765 629-2211
  Milroy *(G-11830)*

3275 Gypsum products

Esco Industries Inc .... F 574 522-4500
  Elkhart *(G-3334)*

Georgia-Pacific LLC .... D 219 956-3100
  Wheatfield *(G-16767)*

Ng Operations LLC .... E 765 828-0898
  Clinton *(G-2073)*

Ng Operations LLC .... D 765 828-0371
  Clinton *(G-2074)*

Patrick Industries Inc .... G 574 294-1975
  Elkhart *(G-3590)*

Patrick Industries Inc .... F 574 295-9660
  Elkhart *(G-3591)*

Patrick Industries Inc .... D 574 294-8828
  Elkhart *(G-3592)*

▲ Patrick Industries Inc .... B 574 294-7511
  Elkhart *(G-3593)*

Precast Solutions Inc .... F 317 545-6557
  Whitestown *(G-16816)*

Proform Finishing Products LLC .... E 219 866-7570
  Rensselaer *(G-14063)*

Proform Finishing Products LLC .... D 812 247-2424
  Shoals *(G-14910)*

Structural Composites LLC .... E 574 294-7511
  Elkhart *(G-3701)*

United States Gypsum Company .... D 219 392-4600
  East Chicago *(G-3049)*

United States Gypsum Company .... E 812 388-6866
  Shoals *(G-14913)*

United States Gypsum Company .... C 812 247-2101
  Shoals *(G-14914)*

◆ Westech Building Products Inc .... E 812 985-3628
  Mount Vernon *(G-12327)*

Williamsburg Marine LLC .... C 574 658-3409
  Nappanee *(G-12653)*

3281 Cut stone and stone products

3d Stone Purchaser Inc .... F 812 824-5805
  Bloomington *(G-767)*

Absolute Stone Polsg Repr LLC .... G 317 709-9539
  Westfield *(G-16661)*

Accent Limestone & Carving Inc .... G 812 876-7040
  Bloomington *(G-772)*

Accent Limestone & Carving Inc .... G 812 829-5663
  Spencer *(G-15338)*

Allen Monument Co .... G 317 941-7047
  Indianapolis *(G-7480)*

Allen Monument Co .... G 574 240-1880
  Monticello *(G-12134)*

Allen Monument Company .... G 765 362-8886
  Crawfordsville *(G-2544)*

American Bronze Craft Inc .... F 501 729-3018
  Indianapolis *(G-7501)*

American Urn Inc .... G 812 379-5555
  Columbus *(G-2218)*

Architectural Stone Sales Inc .... F 812 279-2421
  Bedford *(G-619)*

◆ Aurora Casket Company LLC .... B 800 457-1111
  Aurora *(G-439)*

Beazer East Inc .... G 812 883-2191
  Salem *(G-14475)*

Bedford Stonecrafters Inc .... G 812 275-2646
  Bedford *(G-625)*

Botti Stdio Archtctral Arts In .... E 847 869-5933
  La Porte *(G-10391)*

Bsbw Cultured Marble Inc .... F 812 246-5619
  Sellersburg *(G-14588)*

Bybee Stone Company Inc .... D 812 876-2215
  Ellettsville *(G-3801)*

Centura Solid Surfacing Inc .... F 317 867-5555
  Westfield *(G-16673)*

Century Marble Co Inc .... E 317 867-5555
  Westfield *(G-16674)*

▲ Ceramica Inc .... F 317 546-0087
  Indianapolis *(G-7777)*

Classic Kitchen and Gran LLC .... G 317 575-8883
  Westfield *(G-16676)*

Concepts In Stone & Tile Inc .... G 574 267-4712
  Warsaw *(G-16337)*

Coronado Stone Inc .... E 812 284-2845
  Jeffersonville *(G-9962)*

Covia Holdings Corporation .... G 812 683-2179
  Huntingburg *(G-7275)*

Dwyer-Wilbert Inc .... G 765 962-3605
  Richmond *(G-14116)*

Edw C Levy Co .... G 765 364-9251
  Crawfordsville *(G-2565)*

Evans Limestone Co .... F 812 279-9744
  Bedford *(G-635)*

Flagstone Village LLC .... G 219 989-3265
  Hammond *(G-6930)*

Glas-Col LLC .... E 812 235-6167
  Terre Haute *(G-15599)*

▲ Granitech .... G 574 674-6988
  Elkhart *(G-3386)*

Heidelberg Mtls Mdwest Agg Inc .... G 812 889-2120
  Lexington *(G-10977)*

Heritage Ldscp Sup Group Inc .... E 317 849-9100
  Indianapolis *(G-8389)*

Imagination Set In Stone LLC .... G 812 660-0031
  Richland *(G-14079)*

Indiana Cut Stone Inc .... F 812 275-0264
  Bedford *(G-643)*

Indiana Lmstone Acqisition LLC .... D 812 275-5556
  Bedford *(G-645)*

▲ Indiana Lmstone Acqisition LLC .... E 812 275-3341
  Bloomington *(G-888)*

▼ Indiana Stone Works .... G 812 279-0448
  Bedford *(G-648)*

Ionic Cut Stone Incorporated .... G 812 829-3416
  Spencer *(G-15352)*

John Ley Monument Sales Inc .... G 260 347-7346
  Avilla *(G-480)*

Justin Blackwell .... F 812 834-6350
  Norman *(G-13203)*

Kopelov Cut Stone Inc .... G 812 675-0099
  Bedford *(G-653)*

Liberty Cut Stone Inc .... G 812 935-5515
  Gosport *(G-6287)*

▲ Majestic Marble Imports Inc .... F 317 237-4400
  Indianapolis *(G-8816)*

▲ Marstone Products Ltd .... E 800 466-7465
  Fairland *(G-4400)*

Michael and Sons Incorporated .... F 812 876-4736
  Bloomfield *(G-752)*

New Point Stone Co Inc .... G 765 698-2227
  Laurel *(G-10825)*

Ohio River Trading Co .... G 765 653-4100
  Cloverdale *(G-2092)*

One Source Fabrication LLC .... G 574 259-6011
  South Bend *(G-15178)*

Quality Surfaces Inc .... E 812 276-5838
  Spencer *(G-15358)*

Rush County Stone Co Inc .... G 765 629-2211
  Milroy *(G-11830)*

Slon Inc .... E 765 884-1792
  Fowler *(G-5633)*

Stone Artisans Ltd .... G 317 362-0107
  Indianapolis *(G-9512)*

Stone Artisans Ltd .... G 847 219-7862
  Indianapolis *(G-9513)*

Stone-Street Quarries Inc .... F 260 639-6511
  Hoagland *(G-7171)*

SIC SECTION
32 STONE, CLAY, GLASS, AND CONCRETE PRODUCTS

Superior Canopy Corporation .... E 260 488-4065
  Hamilton *(G-6862)*
▲ Terre Hute Wlbert Brial Vlt In .... F 812 235-0339
  Terre Haute *(G-15727)*
Texacon Cut Stone LLC .... G 812 824-3211
  Bloomington *(G-987)*
Thomas Monuments Inc .... G 317 244-6525
  Indianapolis *(G-9594)*
Tremain Ceramic Tile & Flr Cvg .... E 317 542-1491
  Indianapolis *(G-9633)*
Victor Oolitic Stone Company .... C 812 275-3341
  Oolitic *(G-13360)*
▲ Wearly Monuments Inc .... F 765 284-9796
  Muncie *(G-12517)*
Wilbert Sexton Corporation .... G 812 334-0883
  Bloomington *(G-1010)*

3291 Abrasive products

10x Engineered Materials LLC .... F 260 209-1207
  Wabash *(G-16170)*
11/18 Pro Aluminum LLC .... G 260 204-3577
  Fort Wayne *(G-4709)*
3M Company .... E 765 348-3200
  Hartford City *(G-7060)*
3M Company .... B 317 692-6666
  Indianapolis *(G-7388)*
Advanced Cutting Systems Inc .... E 260 423-3394
  Fort Wayne *(G-4725)*
Andersons Agriculture Group LP .... F 765 564-6135
  Delphi *(G-2890)*
Chance Abrasives .... G 219 871-0977
  Michigan City *(G-11587)*
EMJ Metals .... G 317 838-8899
  Plainfield *(G-13679)*
Enviri Corporation .... F 219 944-6250
  Gary *(G-5928)*
G & S Super Abrasives Inc .... E 260 665-5562
  Angola *(G-254)*
Grace Steel LLC .... F 574 387-4612
  South Bend *(G-15046)*
Grace Steel Corporation .... G 574 218-6600
  Bristol *(G-1264)*
Hilltop Specialties LLC .... G 574 773-4975
  Nappanee *(G-12611)*
Keener Metal Fabricating LLC .... E 765 825-2100
  Connersville *(G-2450)*
◆ Mid-West Metal Products Co Inc .... E 888 741-1044
  Muncie *(G-12454)*
Nicorr LLC .... G 574 342-0700
  Bourbon *(G-1124)*
Nucor Harris Rebar Midwest LLC .... F 317 831-2456
  Mooresville *(G-12229)*
Phoenix Corporation .... F 513 727-4763
  Hammond *(G-6991)*
▲ Plymouth Pdts Acquisition Inc .... G 574 936-4757
  Plymouth *(G-13804)*
Royer Enterprises Inc .... G 260 359-0689
  Huntington *(G-7362)*
Saint-Gobain Abrasives Inc .... D 317 837-0700
  Plainfield *(G-13726)*
Sandpaper Studio LLC .... G 317 435-7479
  Whiteland *(G-16795)*
Sandusky Abrasive Wheel Co .... E 219 879-6601
  Michigan City *(G-11663)*
Schaffner Manufacturing Co .... F 601 366-9902
  Richmond *(G-14202)*
Surface Generation Tech LLC .... G 765 425-2741
  Anderson *(G-203)*
▲ Woodburn Diamond Die Inc .... E 260 632-4217
  Woodburn *(G-16957)*

3292 Asbestos products

Heartland Table Pads LLC .... G 888 487-2377
  Wolcottville *(G-16938)*
Thermal Structures Inc .... F 317 876-7213
  Indianapolis *(G-9590)*

3295 Minerals, ground or treated

◆ American Art Clay Co Inc .... C 317 244-6871
  Indianapolis *(G-7499)*
Arcosa Lw Hpb LLC .... E 317 831-0710
  Mooresville *(G-12194)*
Beemsterboer Slag Corp .... C 219 392-1930
  East Chicago *(G-2992)*
Beemsterboer Slag Corp .... E 773 785-6000
  Hammond *(G-6884)*
Calcean LLC .... G 812 672-4995
  Seymour *(G-14636)*
Covia Holdings Corporation .... G 812 683-2179
  Huntingburg *(G-7275)*
Edw C Levy Co .... G 765 364-9251
  Crawfordsville *(G-2565)*
Enviri Corporation .... F 219 944-6250
  Gary *(G-5928)*
Enviro Group Inc .... G 317 882-9360
  Greenwood *(G-6702)*
Grefco Minerals Inc .... F 765 362-6000
  Crawfordsville *(G-2571)*
Hydraulic Press Brick Company .... C 317 290-1140
  Mooresville *(G-12212)*
Hydraulic Press Brick Company .... E 317 290-1140
  Indianapolis *(G-8441)*
Irving Materials Inc .... F 765 922-7285
  Kokomo *(G-10291)*
Levy Environmental Services Co .... E 260 868-5123
  Butler *(G-1470)*
Levy Environmental Services Co .... E 260 625-4930
  Columbia City *(G-2168)*
Metal Services LLC .... G 219 787-1514
  Burns Harbor *(G-1454)*
Metal Services LLC .... G 219 397-0650
  East Chicago *(G-3029)*
▲ Performance Minerals Corp .... G 219 365-8356
  Saint John *(G-14455)*
Reed Minerals .... G 219 944-6250
  Gary *(G-6001)*
Rogers Group Inc .... D 812 849-3530
  Mitchell *(G-12047)*
South Shore Slag LLC .... E 219 881-6544
  Hammond *(G-7010)*
United Minerals and Prpts Inc .... G 812 838-5236
  Mount Vernon *(G-12325)*
Veolia Wts Usa Inc .... G 219 397-0554
  East Chicago *(G-3053)*

3296 Mineral wool

Aearo Technologies LLC .... C 317 692-6666
  Indianapolis *(G-7447)*
◆ API Indiana Inc .... D 574 293-5574
  Elkhart *(G-3186)*
Global Composites Inc .... G 574 294-7681
  Elkhart *(G-3381)*
Hy-TEC Fiberglass Inc .... G 260 489-6601
  Fort Wayne *(G-5087)*
Insul-Coustic Corporation .... E 260 420-1480
  Fort Wayne *(G-5113)*
Insulation Fabricators Inc .... D 219 845-2008
  Hammond *(G-6956)*
Insulation Specialties of Amer .... E 219 733-2502
  Wanatah *(G-16290)*
Johns Manville Corporation .... D 765 973-5200
  Richmond *(G-14153)*
◆ Knauf Insulation Inc .... C 317 398-4434
  Shelbyville *(G-14770)*

Molded Acstcal Pdts Easton Inc .... E 610 253-7135
  Elkhart *(G-3550)*
Owens Corning Sales LLC .... G 260 665-7318
  Angola *(G-279)*
Owens Corning Sales LLC .... G 765 647-2857
  Brookville *(G-1330)*
Owens Corning Sales LLC .... C 765 647-4131
  Brookville *(G-1331)*
Owens Corning Sales LLC .... G 219 465-4324
  Valparaiso *(G-16020)*
Owens Corning Sales LLC .... G 260 563-2111
  Wabash *(G-16207)*
PSC Industries Inc .... G 317 547-5439
  Indianapolis *(G-9237)*
Unifrax I LLC .... C 574 654-7100
  New Carlisle *(G-12848)*
Usmpc Buyer Inc .... E 260 356-2040
  Huntington *(G-7376)*

3297 Nonclay refractories

Allied Mineral Products Inc .... F 219 923-5875
  Griffith *(G-6789)*
EJ Bognar Incorporated .... G 412 344-9900
  Schneider *(G-14549)*
Indiana Refractories Inc .... E 260 426-3286
  Fort Wayne *(G-5102)*
Insulation Specialties of Amer .... E 219 733-2502
  Wanatah *(G-16290)*
▲ J W Hicks Inc .... E 219 736-2212
  Merrillville *(G-11526)*
▲ JW Hicks Inc .... E 574 772-7755
  Knox *(G-10212)*
Magneco/Metrel Inc .... D 219 885-4190
  Gary *(G-5979)*
Minteq International Inc .... E 219 886-9555
  Gary *(G-5984)*
▲ Minteq Shapes and Services Inc .... D 219 762-4863
  Portage *(G-13888)*
One Eight Seven Incorporated .... E 219 886-2060
  Gary *(G-5989)*
Pyro Industrial Services Inc .... E 219 787-5700
  Portage *(G-13907)*
Refractory Service Corporation .... E 219 853-0885
  Hammond *(G-6996)*
▲ Refractory Service Corporation .... E 219 397-7108
  East Chicago *(G-3038)*
Simko & Sons Inc .... F 219 933-9100
  Hammond *(G-7007)*

3299 Nonmetallic mineral products,

Ceramic Fiber Enterprises Inc .... G 765 362-2179
  Crawfordsville *(G-2551)*
Concrete Monkey Studios LLC .... G 812 630-2339
  Evansville *(G-3978)*
Double E Distributing Co Inc .... G 812 334-2220
  Bloomington *(G-858)*
Image LLC .... G 260 436-6125
  Fort Wayne *(G-5094)*
Indiana PQ Stucco LLC .... G 317 685-0246
  Indianapolis *(G-8489)*
Magaws of Boston .... G 765 935-6170
  Richmond *(G-14158)*
Martins Lime Service Inc .... G 574 784-2270
  Plymouth *(G-13796)*
Nf Friction Composites Inc .... G 574 516-1131
  Logansport *(G-11098)*
Opta Minerals (holdco) Inc .... G 574 586-9559
  Walkerton *(G-16273)*
Plaster Shak .... G 317 881-6518
  Greenwood *(G-6752)*
Silhouette Body Sculpt LLC .... G 219 237-2391
  Highland *(G-7155)*

32 STONE, CLAY, GLASS, AND CONCRETE PRODUCTS

Thermal Ceramics Inc............................. E 574 296-3500
 Elkhart *(G-3725)*
Unifrax I LLC... C 574 654-7100
 New Carlisle *(G-12848)*
Zing Polymer Formations LLC............... G 317 598-0480
 Fishers *(G-4637)*

33 PRIMARY METAL INDUSTRIES

3312 Blast furnaces and steel mills

101 Tool & Die LLC................................ G 260 203-2981
 Fort Wayne *(G-4708)*
▲ 3d Parts Mfg LLC................................ G 317 860-6941
 Anderson *(G-68)*
Advanced Engineering Inc..................... F 260 356-8077
 Huntington *(G-7296)*
Allegheny Ludlum Corp......................... F 412 394-2800
 Portland *(G-13927)*
Allied Tube & Conduit Corp................... F 765 459-8811
 Kokomo *(G-10232)*
Alro Steel Corporation........................... E 260 749-9661
 Yoder *(G-16964)*
Arcelormittal.. D 219 787-7432
 Valparaiso *(G-15902)*
◆ Arcelormittal Holdings LLC.................. D 219 399-1200
 East Chicago *(G-2990)*
Armco.. G 219 981-8864
 Merrillville *(G-11485)*
▲ ATI... F 317 238-3073
 Indianapolis *(G-7560)*
ATI Flat Rlled Pdts Hldngs LLC............. F 765 529-9570
 New Castle *(G-12850)*
▲ Avis Industrial Corporation.................. E 765 998-8100
 Upland *(G-15876)*
Bahr Bros Mfg Inc.................................. E 765 664-6235
 Marion *(G-11274)*
Best Tires & Wheels.............................. F 317 306-3379
 Franklin *(G-5715)*
Beta Steel Corp..................................... G 219 787-0001
 Portage *(G-13849)*
Black Plate Catering.............................. F 317 255-8030
 Indianapolis *(G-7640)*
Brinco Manufacturing Inc....................... G 574 213-1008
 Bristol *(G-1250)*
By The Sword Inc................................. F 877 433-9368
 Huntingburg *(G-7271)*
Calbrite Industries................................. G 219 844-6800
 Hammond *(G-6890)*
Chicago Flame Hardening Co............... E 773 768-3608
 East Chicago *(G-2995)*
Chicago Steel Ltd Partnership............... E 219 949-1111
 Gary *(G-5918)*
Citizens Energy Group.......................... F 317 261-8794
 Indianapolis *(G-7812)*
Classic Industries Inc............................ G 812 421-4006
 Evansville *(G-3972)*
◆ Cleveland-Cliffs Burns Harbor............. A 219 787-2120
 Burns Harbor *(G-1449)*
Cleveland-Cliffs Burns Hbr LLC............ A 219 787-2120
 Burns Harbor *(G-1450)*
Cleveland-Cliffs Inc............................... B 219 787-2120
 Burns Harbor *(G-1451)*
Cleveland-Cliffs Inc............................... D 574 654-1000
 New Carlisle *(G-12835)*
Cleveland-Cliffs Indiana Hbr.................. G 219 399-1200
 East Chicago *(G-2996)*
Cleveland-Cliffs Steel Corp.................... C 812 362-6000
 Rockport *(G-14338)*
Cleveland-Cliffs Steel LLC..................... D 219 787-2120
 Chesterton *(G-1914)*
Cleveland-Cliffs Steel LLC..................... G 219 399-6500
 East Chicago *(G-2997)*

Cleveland-Cliffs Steel LLC..................... G 312 346-0300
 East Chicago *(G-2998)*
Cleveland-Cliffs Steel LLC..................... A 219 399-1000
 East Chicago *(G-2999)*
Cleveland-Cliffs Steel LLC..................... A 219 399-1200
 East Chicago *(G-3000)*
▲ Clevelnd-Clffs New Crlsle I LP............ C 574 654-1000
 New Carlisle *(G-12838)*
Clif Allred.. G 765 244-8082
 Peru *(G-13573)*
CPM Acquisition Corp........................... F 765 362-2600
 Crawfordsville *(G-2556)*
Delaco Kasle Proc Ind LLC................... D 812 280-8800
 Jeffersonville *(G-9969)*
Dietrich Industries Inc........................... C 219 931-6344
 Hammond *(G-6913)*
Elkhart Steel Service Inc....................... E 574 262-2552
 Elkhart *(G-3329)*
EVille Iron Street Rods Ltd.................... G 812 428-3764
 Evansville *(G-4062)*
Extrasurplus LLC................................... G 252 619-8604
 Gary *(G-5931)*
Fratco Inc... G 800 854-7120
 Francesville *(G-5641)*
Gerdau Ameristeel US Inc..................... E 765 286-5454
 Muncie *(G-12400)*
Great Lakes Steel Corporation.............. G 574 273-7000
 Mishawaka *(G-11902)*
Hawkins Inc... G 765 288-8930
 Muncie *(G-12409)*
Haynes International Inc........................ G 765 450-4310
 Kokomo *(G-10279)*
▲ Haynes International Inc..................... A 765 456-6000
 Kokomo *(G-10278)*
Hebron Ventures North America............ G 260 437-7733
 Fort Wayne *(G-5057)*
Heidtman Steel Products Inc................. D 419 691-4646
 Butler *(G-1465)*
Ima Inox Market America LLC............... E 765 896-4411
 Muncie *(G-12423)*
IMS Surface Conditioning...................... G 219 881-0155
 Gary *(G-5959)*
▲ Indiana Arcelormittal Harbor LLC........ A 219 399-1200
 East Chicago *(G-3020)*
▲ Indiana Harbor Coke Company LP...... C 219 397-5769
 East Chicago *(G-3021)*
Indiana Spike & Raii Co LLC................. G 812 352-7349
 Vernon *(G-16096)*
Indiana Steel Fabricating Inc................. F 765 742-1031
 Lafayette *(G-10606)*
Indiana Tool Inc..................................... F 765 825-7117
 Connersville *(G-2444)*
Industrial Steel Cnstr Inc....................... C 219 885-5610
 Gary *(G-5962)*
Ingleside Holdings L P........................... G 574 273-7000
 Mishawaka *(G-11912)*
Insight Equity Holdings LLC.................. B 219 378-1930
 East Chicago *(G-3023)*
International Mill Service Inc.................. G 219 881-0155
 Gary *(G-5963)*
Interntional Pipe Cons Sls LLC.............. F 765 388-2222
 New Castle *(G-12870)*
▲ Iron Dynamics Inc............................... C 260 868-8800
 Butler *(G-1469)*
Isg Burns Harbor Services LLC............. F 219 787-2120
 Burns Harbor *(G-1452)*
J Jones Machine LLC............................ G 765 366-8258
 New Ross *(G-12979)*
Kammerer Inc.. D 260 349-9098
 Kendallville *(G-10124)*
Kanoff Enterprises................................. G 574 575-6787
 Mishawaka *(G-11921)*

Kelco Steel Fabrication Inc.................... G 317 248-9229
 Indianapolis *(G-8667)*
Kretler Tool & Engineering Inc.............. G 260 897-2662
 Avilla *(G-484)*
L B Foster Company............................. G 260 244-2887
 Columbia City *(G-2164)*
Lana Hudelson...................................... G 812 865-3951
 Orleans *(G-13377)*
Leed Thermal Processing Inc............... G 317 637-5102
 Indianapolis *(G-8733)*
Liberation.. G 219 736-7329
 Schererville *(G-14529)*
Mayors Office City of Madison.............. G 812 273-4248
 Madison *(G-11240)*
McCombs and Son Company................ G 765 825-4581
 Connersville *(G-2454)*
▲ Meriwether Tool & Engrg Inc.............. E 260 744-6955
 Fort Wayne *(G-5214)*
Midwest Tube Mills Inc.......................... D 812 265-1553
 Madison *(G-11243)*
Minteq International Inc........................ F 219 771-9093
 Portage *(G-13887)*
Modern Forge Companies LLC............. A 708 388-1806
 Merrillville *(G-11542)*
◆ Nachi America Inc............................... E 877 622-4487
 Greenwood *(G-6743)*
National Caster Acquisition................... G 574 273-7000
 Mishawaka *(G-11958)*
National Casting Corporation................. G 574 273-7000
 Mishawaka *(G-11959)*
National Coating Line Corp................... F 574 273-7000
 Mishawaka *(G-11960)*
National Material LP.............................. C 219 397-5088
 East Chicago *(G-3031)*
National Mtls Procurement Corp........... G 574 273-7000
 Mishawaka *(G-11961)*
National Steel Funding Corp................. G 574 273-7000
 Mishawaka *(G-11962)*
Nelsen Steel.. F 708 308-6749
 Valparaiso *(G-16010)*
Nelson Acquisition LLC......................... E 574 753-6377
 Logansport *(G-11097)*
◆ New Castle Stainless Plate LLC.......... D 765 529-0120
 New Castle *(G-12876)*
Nicks Automotive Inc............................. F 765 964-6843
 Union City *(G-15856)*
▲ Nippon Steel Pipe America Inc........... B 812 523-0842
 Seymour *(G-14669)*
▲ Nlmk Indiana LLC................................ B 219 787-8200
 Portage *(G-13899)*
▼ Nonferrous Products Inc..................... E 317 738-2558
 Franklin *(G-5761)*
Norres North America Inc...................... E 855 667-7370
 South Bend *(G-15169)*
Northedge Steel LLC............................. G 336 594-0171
 New Castle *(G-12877)*
Northern Indiana Axle LLC.................... F 574 773-3039
 Nappanee *(G-12633)*
NS Holdings Corporation....................... G 574 273-7000
 Mishawaka *(G-11966)*
NS Land Company................................ G 574 273-7000
 Mishawaka *(G-11967)*
Ntk Prcsion Axle Corp - Andrso............ F 765 221-7800
 Anderson *(G-170)*
▲ Ntk Precision Axle Corporation........... B 765 656-1000
 Frankfort *(G-5687)*
Nucor Corporation................................. A 765 364-1323
 Crawfordsville *(G-2598)*
Nucor Corporation................................. D 260 337-1800
 Saint Joe *(G-14440)*
Nucor Corporation................................. C 260 337-1606
 Saint Joe *(G-14441)*

SIC SECTION
33 PRIMARY METAL INDUSTRIES

Nucor Corporation................................. G 260 337-1808
  Saint Joe *(G-14442)*
Nucor Corporation................................. F 260 837-7891
  Waterloo *(G-16525)*
Nucor Corporation................................. E 260 837-7891
  Waterloo *(G-16526)*
Nucor Corporation................................. D 260 837-7891
  Waterloo *(G-16527)*
Nucor Harris Rebar Midwest LLC........... F 317 831-2456
  Mooresville *(G-12229)*
Nucor Steel Corp................................... E 765 364-1323
  Crawfordsville *(G-2599)*
Oncite LLC.. E 765 874-1500
  Union City *(G-15857)*
Parker-Hannifin Corporation................. D 260 636-2104
  Albion *(G-40)*
Parker-Hannifin Corporation................. E 260 587-9102
  Ashley *(G-335)*
Phoenix Services LLC.......................... D 219 399-7808
  Valparaiso *(G-16026)*
Pizo Operating Company LLC.............. E 317 243-0811
  Indianapolis *(G-9149)*
Plymouth Tube Company...................... D 574 946-6191
  Winamac *(G-16871)*
Pope Steel... G 317 498-0504
  Greenfield *(G-6540)*
Premier Forge Group LLC................... D 800 727-8121
  Portland *(G-13963)*
Progress Rail Mfg Corp........................ C 765 281-2685
  Muncie *(G-12480)*
Progress Rail Services Corp................ C 219 397-5326
  East Chicago *(G-3037)*
Protherm Supply Inc............................ G 812 492-3386
  Evansville *(G-4262)*
Qualtech Tool & Engrg Inc................... F 260 726-6572
  Portland *(G-13965)*
Ratner Steel Supply Co........................ G 219 787-6700
  Portage *(G-13909)*
Rbc Bearings Incorporated................... G 574 935-3027
  Plymouth *(G-13808)*
◆ Rbc Prcsion Pdts - Plymouth Inc....... D 574 935-3027
  Plymouth *(G-13809)*
▲ Richards Liquidation Corp................. F 574 807-8588
  Mishawaka *(G-11985)*
Robinson Steel Co Inc......................... C 219 398-4600
  East Chicago *(G-3040)*
▲ Ryerson Tull Inc............................... D 219 764-3500
  Burns Harbor *(G-1455)*
Schwartz Wheel Co............................. G 574 546-0101
  Bremen *(G-1219)*
Sssi Inc.. F 219 880-0818
  Gary *(G-6015)*
Steel Avenue Inc.................................. G
  Mishawaka *(G-12008)*
Steel Dynamics Inc.............................. A 260 868-8000
  Butler *(G-1480)*
Steel Dynamics Inc.............................. A 866 740-8700
  Columbia City *(G-2202)*
Steel Dynamics Inc.............................. G 260 969-3500
  Fort Wayne *(G-5437)*
Steel Dynamics Inc.............................. D 812 218-1490
  Jeffersonville *(G-10059)*
Steel Dynamics Inc.............................. B 317 892-7000
  Pittsboro *(G-13654)*
◆ Steel Dynamics Inc........................... B 260 969-3500
  Fort Wayne *(G-5438)*
Steel Dynamics Columbus LLC........... B 260 969-3500
  Fort Wayne *(G-5439)*
▲ STEEL DYNAMICS HEARTLAND.... C 812 299-8866
  Terre Haute *(G-15716)*
Steel Dynamics Sls N Amer Inc........... A 260 868-8000
  Butler *(G-1481)*

Steel Dynamics Sls N Amer Inc........... E 260 969-3500
  Fort Wayne *(G-5440)*
Steel Technologies LLC....................... C 765 362-3110
  Crawfordsville *(G-2619)*
Steel Technologies LLC....................... D 812 663-9704
  Greensburg *(G-6633)*
Steel Technologies LLC....................... C 502 245-2110
  Portage *(G-13916)*
Suncoke Energy Inc............................. G 219 397-0243
  East Chicago *(G-3042)*
Swi.. G 812 342-2409
  Columbus *(G-2400)*
Swva Kentucky LLC............................. F 260 969-3500
  Fort Wayne *(G-5464)*
Teal Lake Iron Mining Company........... G 574 273-7000
  Mishawaka *(G-12013)*
Ten Cate Enbi Inc (indiana).................. G 317 398-3267
  Shelbyville *(G-14804)*
Thomas Himebaugh............................. G 812 246-0197
  Sellersburg *(G-14618)*
Tms International LLC........................ F 219 787-5220
  Burns Harbor *(G-1456)*
Tms International LLC........................ G 219 881-0155
  East Chicago *(G-3044)*
Tms International LLC........................ F 219 881-0155
  Gary *(G-6020)*
Tms International LLC........................ E 219 881-0266
  Gary *(G-6021)*
Tms International LLC........................ F 219 762-2176
  Hammond *(G-7021)*
Trinity Products LLC........................... G 636 639-5244
  East Chicago *(G-3048)*
True Precision Tech Inc....................... G 765 432-2177
  Kokomo *(G-10352)*
▲ Tube Fabrication Inds Inc................ E 574 753-6377
  Logansport *(G-11113)*
Union Electric Steel Corp..................... G 219 464-1031
  Valparaiso *(G-16071)*
United Ccp Inc..................................... E 812 442-7468
  Brazil *(G-1168)*
United States Steel Corp...................... F 219 391-2045
  East Chicago *(G-3050)*
United States Steel Corp...................... G 219 888-2000
  Gary *(G-6023)*
United States Steel Corp...................... G 219 762-3131
  Portage *(G-13917)*
Upg Enterprises LLC........................... D 708 594-9200
  Gary *(G-6025)*
Vicksmetal Armco Associates.............. E 765 659-5555
  Frankfort *(G-5700)*
Viper USA Inc...................................... D 765 742-4200
  West Lafayette *(G-16642)*
Western-Cullen-Hayes Inc................... F 765 962-0526
  Richmond *(G-14226)*
Wheels In Sky..................................... G 812 249-8233
  Terre Haute *(G-15746)*
Windsor Steel Inc................................ F 574 294-1060
  Elkhart *(G-3784)*
Worthington Steel Company................ G 219 929-4000
  Porter *(G-13925)*

3315 Steel wire and related products

▲ 1st Source Products Inc................... F 812 288-7466
  Jeffersonville *(G-9919)*
▲ Accel International........................... F 260 897-9990
  Avilla *(G-471)*
Belden Inc... C 724 222-7060
  Richmond *(G-14092)*
Belden Inc... A 765 962-7561
  Richmond *(G-14094)*
Best Weld Inc..................................... G 765 641-7720
  Anderson *(G-83)*

▲ Cablecraft Motion Controls LLC........ C 260 749-5105
  New Haven *(G-12897)*
◆ D Martin Enterprises Inc.................. F 219 872-8211
  Michigan City *(G-11596)*
EH Baare Corporation......................... G 765 778-7895
  Anderson *(G-113)*
Elektrsola Dr Gerd Schldbach G.......... B 765 477-8000
  Lafayette *(G-10574)*
Essex Frkawa Mgnt Wire USA LLC..... G 260 424-1708
  Columbia City *(G-2144)*
Essex Frkawa Mgnt Wire USA LLC..... F 260 248-5500
  Columbia City *(G-2146)*
Fort Wayne Metals RES Pdts.............. G 260 747-4154
  Fort Wayne *(G-4994)*
Fort Wayne Metals RES Pdts LLC...... G 260 747-4154
  Columbia City *(G-2147)*
Fort Wayne Metals RES Pdts LLC...... G 260 747-4154
  Fort Wayne *(G-4995)*
Fort Wayne Metals RES Pdts LLC...... G 260 747-4154
  Fort Wayne *(G-4997)*
▲ Fort Wayne Metals RES Pdts LLC... A 260 747-4154
  Fort Wayne *(G-4996)*
Four Star Field Services Inc................ G 812 354-9995
  Petersburg *(G-13613)*
Fuzion Products LLC........................... G 317 536-0745
  Indianapolis *(G-8248)*
▲ Group Dekko Inc.............................. D 260 357-3621
  Fort Wayne *(G-5042)*
Hammond Steel Components LLC........ F 630 816-1343
  Hammond *(G-6943)*
Ifc Fence LLC...................................... G 219 977-4000
  Gary *(G-5956)*
Innovative Fabrication LLC.................. D 317 215-5988
  Indianapolis *(G-8555)*
Kingsford Products Inc........................ F 740 862-4450
  Decatur *(G-2866)*
Kokoku Wire Industries Corp................ E 574 287-5610
  South Bend *(G-15103)*
McGowan Wire Specialties Inc............ G 574 232-7110
  South Bend *(G-15145)*
▼ Metal Technologies Auburn LLC....... B 260 527-1410
  Auburn *(G-407)*
Mid-West Metal Products Co Inc......... E 765 741-3140
  Muncie *(G-12453)*
Midwest Bale Ties Inc......................... F 765 364-0113
  Crawfordsville *(G-2589)*
National Material Company LLC.......... E 219 397-5088
  East Chicago *(G-3030)*
Nsci... G 317 820-6526
  Carmel *(G-1709)*
Pwt Group LLC.................................... E 260 490-6477
  Fort Wayne *(G-5357)*
◆ Sanlo Inc.. D 219 879-0241
  Michigan City *(G-11664)*
Suggs Custom Design Solutions......... G 574 549-2174
  Elkhart *(G-3704)*
▲ Tru-Form Steel & Wire Inc............... E 765 348-5001
  Hartford City *(G-7078)*
Truckpro LLC....................................... F 765 482-6525
  Lebanon *(G-10948)*
Tway Company Incorporated............... E 317 636-2591
  Indianapolis *(G-9662)*
Warren Power Attachments................. G 317 892-4737
  Pittsboro *(G-13655)*
Wolfpack Chassis LLC........................ E 260 349-1887
  Kendallville *(G-10155)*

3316 Cold finishing of steel shapes

ATI Flat Rlled Pdts Hldngs LLC........... F 765 529-9570
  New Castle *(G-12850)*
Chicago Cold Rolling LLC................... E 219 787-2021
  Chesterton *(G-1911)*

33 PRIMARY METAL INDUSTRIES

Chief Industries Inc..................................C 219 866-4121
  Rensselaer (G-14047)
Cleveland-Cliffs Steel LLC......................D 219 787-2120
  Chesterton (G-1914)
Dietrich Industries Inc............................C 219 931-6344
  Hammond (G-6913)
Feralloy Corporation...............................D 219 787-9698
  Portage (G-13863)
Friedman Industries Inc..........................E 219 392-3400
  East Chicago (G-3008)
Heidtman Steel Products Inc..................D 419 691-4646
  Butler (G-1465)
Heidtman Steel Products Inc..................E 219 256-7426
  East Chicago (G-3015)
Mill Steel Co..F 765 622-4545
  Anderson (G-154)
New Process Steel LP.............................E 260 868-1445
  Butler (G-1474)
▲ Niagara Lasalle Corporation................D 219 853-6000
  Hammond (G-6986)
Nucor Corporation..................................A 765 364-1323
  Crawfordsville (G-2598)
Plymouth Tube Company.......................D 574 946-6191
  Winamac (G-16871)
Robinson Steel Co Inc............................C 219 398-4600
  East Chicago (G-3040)
▲ Ryerson Tull Inc..................................D 219 764-3500
  Burns Harbor (G-1455)
S&S Steel Services Inc...........................C 765 622-4545
  Anderson (G-189)
Stalcop LLC..E 765 436-7926
  Thorntown (G-15756)
◆ Steel Dynamics Inc.............................B 260 969-3500
  Fort Wayne (G-5438)
▲ STEEL DYNAMICS HEARTLAND........C 812 299-8866
  Terre Haute (G-15716)
Steel Technologies LLC..........................C 765 362-3110
  Crawfordsville (G-2619)
Steel Technologies LLC..........................C 502 245-2110
  Portage (G-13916)
Ten Point Trim Corp...............................E 317 875-5424
  Zionsville (G-17056)
United States Steel Corp........................G 219 762-3131
  Portage (G-13917)
Ward Forging Company Inc....................G 812 923-7463
  Floyds Knobs (G-4698)
Worthington Steel Company..................G 219 929-4000
  Porter (G-13925)

3317 Steel pipe and tubes

37 Pipe & Supply LLC............................G 812 275-5676
  Bedford (G-615)
Allied Tube & Conduit Corp....................F 812 265-9255
  Madison (G-11201)
American Hydroformers Inc....................E 260 428-2660
  Fort Wayne (G-4756)
▲ Applegate Livestock Eqp Inc..............D 765 964-3715
  Union City (G-15848)
Beck Industries LP..................................D 574 294-5621
  Elkhart (G-3221)
◆ Bock Industries Inc.............................E 574 295-8070
  Elkhart (G-3230)
Cal Pipe Manufacturing Inc....................G 219 844-6800
  Hobart (G-7175)
Century Tube LLC..................................C 812 265-9255
  Madison (G-11206)
Clevelnd-Cliffs Tblar Cmpnnts L............C 812 341-3200
  Columbus (G-2237)
Down Range Industries LLC...................G 219 895-0434
  Cedar Lake (G-1830)
Hd Mechanical Inc.................................F 219 924-6050
  Griffith (G-6806)

Illinois Ni Cast LLC.................................F 260 897-3768
  Avilla (G-478)
▼ Indiana Tube Corporation...................B 812 467-7155
  Evansville (G-4121)
Ist Liquidating Inc...................................E 812 358-3894
  Brownstown (G-1424)
▲ Kalenborn Abresist Corporation..........E 800 348-0717
  Urbana (G-15886)
Ljt Texas LLC..D 800 257-6859
  South Bend (G-15126)
▲ Lock Joint Tube LLC...........................C 574 299-5326
  South Bend (G-15127)
Martinrea Industries Inc..........................C 812 346-5750
  North Vernon (G-13285)
Moyers Inc..F 574 264-3119
  Elkhart (G-3557)
Napier & Napier.....................................G 765 580-9116
  Liberty (G-10992)
Nelson Global Products Inc....................C 317 782-9486
  Indianapolis (G-8999)
Nucor Tubular Products..........................E 812 265-7548
  Madison (G-11246)
▲ Paragon Tube Corporation..................E 260 424-1266
  Fort Wayne (G-5295)
Plymouth Tube Company.......................D 574 946-6191
  Winamac (G-16871)
Ptc Alliance Corporation.........................F 765 259-3334
  Richmond (G-14189)
Ptc Tubular Products LLC.......................C 765 259-3334
  Richmond (G-14190)
Rookstools Pier Shop Inc.......................E 574 453-4771
  Leesburg (G-10960)
Specialty Steel Holdco Inc......................A 877 289-2277
  Hammond (G-7013)
Specialty Steel Works Inc.......................G 877 289-2277
  Hammond (G-7014)
Steuben County Welding & Fabg............G 260 665-3001
  Angola (G-295)
Tejas Tubular Products Inc.....................C 574 249-0623
  New Carlisle (G-12847)
Thormax Enterprises LLC.......................G 812 530-7744
  Seymour (G-14699)
Tube Processing Corp............................C 317 782-9486
  Indianapolis (G-9656)
US Rod Manufacturing LLC....................G 574 227-1288
  Nappanee (G-12651)
Utility Pipe Sales Indiana Inc..................G 317 224-2300
  Indianapolis (G-9691)

3321 Gray and ductile iron foundries

37 Pipe & Supply LLC............................G 812 275-5676
  Bedford (G-615)
Accucast Inc...G 317 849-5521
  Fishers (G-4459)
Accurate Castings Inc.............................E 219 393-3122
  La Porte (G-10374)
Atlas Foundry Company Inc...................C 765 662-2525
  Marion (G-11272)
Bahr Bros Mfg Inc..................................E 765 664-6235
  Marion (G-11274)
BCI Solutions Inc....................................C 574 546-2411
  Bremen (G-1174)
▼ Ce Systems Inc..................................E 812 372-8234
  Columbus (G-2235)
▼ Dalton Corp Kndllvlle Mfg Fclt............C 260 637-6047
  Kendallville (G-10108)
Dalton Corp Warsaw Mfg Fcilty..............G 574 267-8111
  Warsaw (G-16344)
Dalton Corporation.................................F 574 267-8111
  Warsaw (G-16345)
Ej Usa Inc...G 765 744-1184
  Indianapolis (G-8067)

▲ Gartland Foundry Company Inc.........C 812 232-0226
  Terre Haute (G-15594)
Grede LLC..C 765 521-8000
  New Castle (G-12865)
In Ductile LLC..F 317 776-8000
  Noblesville (G-13101)
▲ Intat Precision Inc..............................B 765 932-5323
  Rushville (G-14401)
J A Smit Inc..G 812 424-8141
  Evansville (G-4133)
Kitley Company......................................E 317 546-2427
  Indianapolis (G-8691)
La Porte Technologies LLC....................F 219 362-1000
  La Porte (G-10442)
Leons Fabrication Inc.............................F 219 365-5272
  Schererville (G-14528)
Metal Technologies Inc Alabama............D 260 925-4717
  Auburn (G-408)
◆ Metal Technologies Indiana LLC........C 260 925-4717
  Auburn (G-409)
Milwaukee Ductile Iron Inc.....................G 260 925-4717
  Auburn (G-410)
Minneapolis Die Casting LLC.................C 763 536-5500
  Auburn (G-411)
▲ Navistar Cmponent Holdings LLC......A 317 352-4500
  Indianapolis (G-8994)
New Dalton Foundry LLC.......................F 574 267-8111
  Warsaw (G-16400)
▲ North Vernon Industry........................B 812 346-8772
  North Vernon (G-13289)
Plymouth Foundry Inc............................E 574 936-2106
  Plymouth (G-13801)
Precision Gage LLC................................G 260 925-4717
  Auburn (G-417)
Richmond Casting Company..................E 765 935-4090
  Richmond (G-14199)
Rochester Metal Products Corp..............B 574 223-3164
  Rochester (G-14319)
▼ The Dalton Corporation......................D 574 267-8111
  Warsaw (G-16438)
▲ Transportation Tech Inds....................F 812 962-5000
  Evansville (G-4347)
Warsaw Foundry Company Inc..............D 574 267-8772
  Warsaw (G-16446)
Waupaca Foundry Inc............................A 812 547-0700
  Tell City (G-15518)
West Allis Gray Iron................................E 260 925-4717
  Auburn (G-434)
Wh International Casting LLC................G 562 521-0727
  Seymour (G-14704)

3322 Malleable iron foundries

Accurate Castings Inc.............................E 219 393-3122
  La Porte (G-10374)
▼ Ce Systems Inc..................................E 812 372-8234
  Columbus (G-2235)
Dalton Corporation.................................F 574 267-8111
  Warsaw (G-16345)
Ewing Light Metals Co Inc......................E 317 926-4591
  Indianapolis (G-8146)
Grede LLC..C 765 521-8000
  New Castle (G-12865)
Mosey Manufacturing Co Inc..................C 765 983-8889
  Richmond (G-14170)
Muncie Casting Corp..............................E 765 288-2611
  Muncie (G-12461)
Plymouth Foundry Inc............................E 574 936-2106
  Plymouth (G-13801)
Wirco Inc..C 260 897-3768
  Avilla (G-500)

3324 Steel investment foundries

SIC SECTION
33 PRIMARY METAL INDUSTRIES

▲ Aero Metals Inc .... B 219 326-1976
La Porte *(G-10377)*

Howmet Aerospace Inc .... A 219 326-7400
La Porte *(G-10423)*

▲ J & T Marine Specialists Inc .... G 317 890-9444
Indianapolis *(G-8600)*

▲ Texmo Blank USA Inc .... D 574 696-9990
Warsaw *(G-16437)*

Wegener Steel and Fabricating .... G 219 462-3911
Valparaiso *(G-16080)*

Winchester Steel .... G 812 591-2071
Westport *(G-16754)*

3325 Steel foundries, nec

Bahr Bros Mfg Inc .... E 765 664-6235
Marion *(G-11274)*

▲ Ball Brass and Aluminum F .... E 260 925-3515
Auburn *(G-367)*

Cleveland-Cliffs Steel LLC .... D 219 787-2120
Chesterton *(G-1914)*

CM Tech .... G 765 584-6501
Winchester *(G-16885)*

FCA North America Holdings LLC ...... B 765 454-0018
Kokomo *(G-10264)*

Hoosier Engineering Co Inc .... G 260 694-6887
Poneto *(G-13841)*

▲ IBC US Holdings Inc .... G 317 738-2558
Franklin *(G-5743)*

Jec Steel Company .... G 574 326-3829
Goshen *(G-6179)*

Jec Steel Company .... G 574 326-3829
Bristol *(G-1268)*

Shenango LLC .... F 812 235-2058
Terre Haute *(G-15691)*

Southland Metals Inc .... G 574 252-4441
Mishawaka *(G-12004)*

▲ The Harrison Steel Castings Co .... A 765 762-2481
Attica *(G-356)*

Trusted Solutions Group Inc .... D 260 622-6000
Ossian *(G-13443)*

Union Electric Steel Corp .... G 219 464-1031
Valparaiso *(G-16071)*

United States Steel Corp .... F 219 391-2045
East Chicago *(G-3050)*

United States Steel Corp .... G 219 888-2000
Gary *(G-6023)*

West Allis Gray Iron .... E 260 925-4717
Auburn *(G-434)*

Wrib Manufacturing Inc .... G 765 294-2841
Veedersburg *(G-16092)*

3331 Primary copper

◆ Univertical LLC .... F 260 665-1500
Angola *(G-304)*

3334 Primary aluminum

Alcoa Corporation .... E 812 853-6111
Newburgh *(G-12992)*

Alcoa Corporation .... E 812 842-3350
Newburgh *(G-12993)*

Alcoa Power Generating Inc .... G 812 842-3350
Newburgh *(G-12994)*

Closure Systems Intl Hldngs In .... G 765 364-6300
Crawfordsville *(G-2553)*

Closure Systems Intl Inc .... B 765 364-6300
Crawfordsville *(G-2554)*

◆ Closure Systems Intl Inc .... C 317 390-5000
Indianapolis *(G-7825)*

G & L Machine LLP .... G 260 488-2100
Hamilton *(G-6854)*

Howmet Aerospace Inc .... B 812 853-6111
Newburgh *(G-13004)*

Howmet Aerospace Inc .... B 412 553-4545
Newburgh *(G-13005)*

Industrial Sales & Supply Inc .... E 317 240-0560
Indianapolis *(G-8519)*

K-TEC Corp .... G 317 398-6684
Shelbyville *(G-14766)*

Kingsford Products Inc .... F 740 862-4450
Decatur *(G-2866)*

◆ Nanshan Amer Advnced Alum Tech .. C 765 838-8645
Lafayette *(G-10657)*

Scepter Inc .... F 812 735-2600
Bicknell *(G-737)*

3339 Primary nonferrous metals, nec

▲ ABM Advanced Bearing Mtls LLC ..... G 812 663-3401
Greensburg *(G-6578)*

Dallas Group of America Inc .... B 812 283-6675
Jeffersonville *(G-9968)*

Eco-Bat America LLC .... C 317 247-1303
Indianapolis *(G-8048)*

Get Down Get Arund Prcous Mtls ...... G 219 243-2105
Westville *(G-16759)*

Goldman Machine Services .... G 812 359-5440
Richland *(G-14078)*

▲ Nst Technologies Mim LLC .... E 812 248-9273
Noblesville *(G-13146)*

Precious Gems Metals .... G 260 563-4780
Wabash *(G-16213)*

Univertical Holdings Inc .... G 260 665-1500
Angola *(G-303)*

Whiting Metals LLC .... G 219 659-6955
Whiting *(G-16841)*

3341 Secondary nonferrous metals

Ad-Vance Magnetics Inc .... E 574 223-3158
Rochester *(G-14274)*

All Pro Shearing Inc .... F 317 691-1005
Indianapolis *(G-7475)*

▲ Aluminum Conversion Inc .... G 260 856-2180
Cromwell *(G-2629)*

American Scrap Processing Inc .... C 219 398-1444
East Chicago *(G-2989)*

▲ Dz Investments LLC .... E 317 895-4141
Indianapolis *(G-8027)*

Eco-Bat America LLC .... C 317 247-1303
Indianapolis *(G-8048)*

Ecobat Resources Cal Inc .... B 317 247-1303
Indianapolis *(G-8049)*

Haynes International Inc .... F 219 326-8530
La Porte *(G-10418)*

Howmet Aerospace Inc .... A 219 326-7400
La Porte *(G-10423)*

Induction Iron Incorporated .... F 813 969-3300
Evansville *(G-4122)*

▼ J Trockman & Sons Inc .... E 812 425-5271
Evansville *(G-4134)*

Joe W Morgan Inc .... D 812 423-5914
Evansville *(G-4143)*

Kendallville Iron & Metal Inc .... F 260 347-1958
Kendallville *(G-10126)*

◆ Koch Enterprises Inc .... G 812 465-9800
Evansville *(G-4159)*

Mervis Industries Inc .... G 765 454-5800
Kokomo *(G-10306)*

Mervis Industries Inc .... G 812 232-1251
Terre Haute *(G-15643)*

Metal Spinners Inc .... F 260 665-2158
Angola *(G-275)*

◆ Nanshan Amer Advnced Alum Tech .. C 765 838-8645
Lafayette *(G-10657)*

National Material Company LLC .... E 219 397-5088
East Chicago *(G-3030)*

Newco Metals Inc .... G 765 644-6649
Anderson *(G-168)*

Newco Metals Inc .... E 317 485-7721
Pendleton *(G-13546)*

P & H Iron & Supply Inc .... F 219 853-0240
Hammond *(G-6990)*

Plymouth Tube Company .... D 574 946-6191
Winamac *(G-16871)*

Porter County Ir & Met Recycle .... F 219 996-7630
Hebron *(G-7104)*

Real Alloy Recycling LLC .... G 260 563-2409
Wabash *(G-16214)*

Recycling Center Inc .... D 765 966-8295
Richmond *(G-14195)*

Recycling Services Indiana Inc .... E 812 279-8114
Bedford *(G-666)*

Recycling Works LLC .... F 574 293-3751
Elkhart *(G-3644)*

Scepter Inc .... F 812 735-2600
Bicknell *(G-737)*

Special Metals Corporation .... B 574 262-3451
Elkhart *(G-3690)*

▼ Superior Aluminum Alloys LLC .... C 260 749-7599
New Haven *(G-12921)*

Tcb International LLC .... E 502 619-3191
Indianapolis *(G-9561)*

Winski Brothers Inc .... G 765 654-5323
Frankfort *(G-5702)*

3351 Copper rolling and drawing

▲ Alconex Specialty Products .... E 260 744-3446
Fort Wayne *(G-4738)*

Brand Sheet Metal Works Inc .... G 765 284-5594
Muncie *(G-12356)*

Cerro Wire LLC .... D 812 793-2929
Crothersville *(G-2638)*

E M F Corp .... E 260 488-2479
Hamilton *(G-6852)*

Elektrsola Dr Gerd Schldbach G .... B 765 477-8000
Lafayette *(G-10574)*

Essex Frkawa Mgnt Wire USA LLC ..... E 260 461-4000
Fort Wayne *(G-4962)*

F J Rettig & Sons Inc .... G 260 563-6603
Wabash *(G-16184)*

International Wire Group Inc .... E 574 546-4680
Bremen *(G-1198)*

▲ Lake Copper Conductors LLC .... F 847 238-3000
Elkhart *(G-3466)*

▲ Sdi Lafarga LLC .... D 260 748-6565
New Haven *(G-12919)*

Southwire Company LLC .... D 574 546-5115
Bremen *(G-1222)*

Southwire Company LLC .... E 765 449-7227
Lafayette *(G-10693)*

3353 Aluminum sheet, plate, and foil

Applied Logic Electronics LLC .... G 317 633-7300
Indianapolis *(G-7534)*

Arconic US LLC .... G 765 447-1707
Lafayette *(G-10524)*

Arconic US LLC .... A 412 553-2500
Lafayette *(G-10526)*

Arroyo Industries LLC .... G 317 605-4163
Greenwood *(G-6671)*

Garmco (usa) Inc .... G 352 404-8998
Indianapolis *(G-8262)*

Gusa Holdings Inc .... D 317 545-1221
Indianapolis *(G-8343)*

Hogan Stamping LLC .... G 812 656-8222
West Harrison *(G-16548)*

Howmet Aerospace Inc .... G 317 241-9393
Indianapolis *(G-8432)*

33 PRIMARY METAL INDUSTRIES

Howmet Aerospace Inc............................. B 812 853-6111
Newburgh (G-13004)

Howmet Aerospace Inc............................. B 412 553-4545
Newburgh (G-13005)

Jupiter Aluminum Corporation................ D 219 932-3322
Fairland (G-4399)

▲ Jupiter Aluminum Corporation............ C 219 932-3322
Hammond (G-6962)

Lawrence Industries Inc........................... G 260 432-9693
Fort Wayne (G-5177)

New Process Steel LP............................. E 260 868-1445
Butler (G-1474)

Novelis Corporation................................. C 812 462-2287
Terre Haute (G-15652)

Southern Alum Finshg Co Inc................ G 800 357-9016
Indianapolis (G-9464)

Summit Manufacturing Corp.................... E 260 428-2600
Fort Wayne (G-5453)

Taylor Made Enterprises Inc................... G 765 653-8481
Greencastle (G-6433)

V N C Inc.. F 219 696-5031
Lowell (G-11179)

3354 Aluminum extruded products

◆ 80/20 LLC... B 260 248-8030
Columbia City (G-2114)

▲ Alconex Specialty Products................. E 260 744-3446
Fort Wayne (G-4738)

Alexandria Extrsion Mdmrica LL............ G 317 545-1221
Indianapolis (G-7470)

Alliance Aluminum Products Inc............ D 574 848-4300
Bristol (G-1242)

Altec LLC.. D 812 282-8256
Jeffersonville (G-9928)

▲ Alumina Products Incorporated........... G 727 934-9781
Terre Haute (G-15539)

Aluminum Dynamics LLC....................... G 260 969-3500
Fort Wayne (G-4746)

Aluminum Extrusions.............................. G 574 206-0100
Elkhart (G-3168)

Aluminum Insights LLC.......................... E 574 534-5547
Syracuse (G-15454)

Arconic US LLC..................................... A 765 771-3600
Lafayette (G-10525)

Bonnell Aluminum Inc............................. A 815 351-6802
Kentland (G-10157)

Brazeway LLC.. A 317 392-2533
Shelbyville (G-14740)

Gusa Holdings Inc.................................. D 317 545-1221
Indianapolis (G-8343)

Hautau Tube Cutoff Systems LLC.......... F 765 647-1600
Brookville (G-1323)

Hoosier Trim Products LLC.................... G 317 271-4007
Indianapolis (G-8412)

Hydro Extrusion Usa LLC...................... C 765 825-1141
Connersville (G-2442)

Hydro Extrusion Usa LLC...................... C 574 262-2667
Elkhart (G-3415)

Hydro Extrusion Usa LLC...................... G 888 935-5757
North Liberty (G-13217)

Indalex Inc.. G 765 457-1117
Kokomo (G-10286)

▼ Indiana Gratings Inc............................ F 765 342-7191
Martinsville (G-11404)

Indilex Aluminum Solutions.................... G 765 825-1141
Connersville (G-2445)

▲ Jupiter Aluminum Corporation............ C 219 932-3322
Hammond (G-6962)

Lakemaster Inc....................................... F 765 288-3718
Muncie (G-12437)

▲ Matalco Bluffton LLC......................... D 260 353-3100
Bluffton (G-1040)

Napier & Napier...................................... G 765 580-9116
Liberty (G-10992)

Parco Incorporated................................. F 260 451-0810
Fort Wayne (G-5296)

Patrick Industries Inc............................. C 574 534-5300
Goshen (G-6237)

Patrick Industries Inc............................. G 574 255-9692
Mishawaka (G-11971)

Plymouth Tube Company........................ D 574 946-6191
Winamac (G-16871)

Specialty Blanks Inc............................... G 812 232-8775
Terre Haute (G-15708)

▲ Stalcop LLC....................................... E 765 436-7926
Thorntown (G-15756)

Tredegar Corporation.............................. D 812 466-0266
Terre Haute (G-15734)

3355 Aluminum rolling and drawing, nec

A/C Fabricating Corp.............................. E 574 534-1415
Goshen (G-6086)

▼ Alcoa Corporation............................... G 765 983-9200
Richmond (G-14085)

Alconex Specialty Products................... E 260 744-3446
Fort Wayne (G-4737)

▲ Alconex Specialty Products................ E 260 744-3446
Fort Wayne (G-4738)

Arconic US LLC..................................... A 412 553-2500
Lafayette (G-10526)

Elektrsola Dr Gerd Schldbach G............ B 765 477-8000
Lafayette (G-10574)

Gerard... G 219 924-6388
Highland (G-7138)

Highmark Technologies LLC................... E 260 483-0012
Fort Wayne (G-5066)

Kaiser Aluminum Warrick LLC............... A 412 315-2900
Newburgh (G-13011)

L-Source Ltd LLC................................. G 260 459-1971
Fort Wayne (G-5168)

Lionshead Alloys LLC............................ G 574 533-6169
Goshen (G-6199)

Postle Operating LLC............................ D 574 266-7720
Elkhart (G-3612)

▲ Postle Operating LLC........................ D 574 389-0800
Elkhart (G-3613)

Rockport Roll Shop LLC........................ E 812 362-6419
Rockport (G-14348)

Southwire Company LLC....................... D 574 546-5115
Bremen (G-1222)

Spectra Metal Sales Inc........................ G 317 822-8291
Indianapolis (G-9476)

3356 Nonferrous rolling and drawing, nec

Cleveland-Cliffs Steel LLC..................... D 219 787-2120
Chesterton (G-1914)

Dnm Converters & Cores....................... G 502 599-5225
Clarksville (G-2015)

Eco-Bat America LLC............................ C 317 247-1303
Indianapolis (G-8048)

Ed Nickels.. G 219 887-6128
Merrillville (G-11511)

Exeon Processors LLC......................... F 765 674-2266
Jonesboro (G-10078)

GKN Aerospace Muncie Inc.................. E 765 747-7147
Muncie (G-12402)

Hammond Group Inc.............................. G 219 931-9360
Hammond (G-6939)

Hammond Group Inc.............................. E 219 845-0031
Hammond (G-6940)

▲ Hammond Lead Products Llc............ E 219 931-9360
Hammond (G-6941)

Haynes International Inc........................ B 765 457-3790
Kokomo (G-10277)

Haynes International Inc........................ F 219 326-8530
La Porte (G-10418)

▲ Haynes International Inc................... A 765 456-6000
Kokomo (G-10278)

Liteauto Inc.. G 317 813-5045
Indianapolis (G-8769)

◆ Metal Source LLC.............................. E 260 563-8833
Wabash (G-16200)

Metals and Additives LLC..................... G 812 446-2525
Brazil (G-1153)

Murrays Tin Cup.................................... G 260 349-1002
Kendallville (G-10138)

Patricia J Nickels Inc............................ G 502 489-4358
Charlestown (G-1890)

▲ Rdd Properties Inc............................. E 317 870-1940
Waterloo (G-16529)

TI Group Auto Systems LLC.................. D 260 587-6100
Ashley (G-338)

Titanium LLC... G 765 236-6906
Kokomo (G-10349)

Titanium Rails Nutrition LLC................. G 219 940-3704
Hobart (G-7212)

Tube Processing Corp........................... G 317 264-7760
Indianapolis (G-9657)

▲ Tube Processing Corp....................... B 317 787-1321
Indianapolis (G-9658)

▲ Wagner Zip-Change Inc..................... E 708 681-4100
Fort Wayne (G-5540)

3357 Nonferrous wiredrawing and insulating

▲ Accel International............................. F 260 897-9990
Avilla (G-471)

▲ Alconex Specialty Products................ E 260 744-3446
Fort Wayne (G-4738)

◆ Almega/Tru-Flex Inc........................... E 574 546-2113
Bremen (G-1172)

Belden Inc.. C 317 818-6300
Carmel (G-1566)

Belden Inc.. G 978 537-9961
Richmond (G-14091)

Belden Inc.. C 724 222-7060
Richmond (G-14092)

Belden Inc.. G 765 983-5200
Richmond (G-14093)

Belden Inc.. A 765 962-7561
Richmond (G-14094)

◆ Belden Wire & Cable Company LLC... E 765 983-5200
Richmond (G-14095)

Cerro Wire LLC..................................... D 812 793-2929
Crothersville (G-2638)

Dx Hammond Opco LLC....................... G 219 501-0905
Whiting (G-16834)

Elektrsola Dr Gerd Schldbach G............ E 260 421-5400
Fort Wayne (G-4945)

Elektrsola Dr Gerd Schldbach G............ B 765 477-8000
Lafayette (G-10574)

Essex Brownell LLC.............................. B 260 424-1708
Fort Wayne (G-4961)

Essex Frkawa Mgnt Wire USA LLC...... E 260 248-5500
Columbia City (G-2145)

Essex Frkawa Mgnt Wire USA LLC...... F 260 248-5500
Columbia City (G-2146)

Essex Frkawa Mgnt Wire USA LLC...... A 260 461-4000
Fort Wayne (G-4962)

Essex Frkawa Mgnt Wire USA LLC...... A 260 461-4000
Fort Wayne (G-4963)

Essex Frkawa Mgnt Wire USA LLC...... A 260 461-4183
Fort Wayne (G-4964)

Essex Frkawa Mgnt Wire USA LLC...... E 317 738-4365
Franklin (G-5729)

Essex Services Inc................................ B 260 461-4000
Fort Wayne (G-4965)

33 PRIMARY METAL INDUSTRIES

Flex Appeals Family and Frien............... G 219 863-3830
  Demotte (G-2917)
Indy Wiring Services LLC.................... G 317 371-7044
  Brownsburg (G-1374)
Installed Building Pdts LLC.................. G 317 398-3216
  Shelbyville (G-14762)
International Wire Group Inc................ E 574 546-4680
  Bremen (G-1198)
Latch Gard Co Inc............................. G 574 862-2373
  Elkhart (G-3471)
Precision Utilities Group Inc................. D 260 485-8300
  Fort Wayne (G-5342)
Prysmian Cbles Systems USA LLC........... D 317 271-8447
  Indianapolis (G-9235)
Prysmian Cbles Systems USA LLC........... D 317 271-8447
  Indianapolis (G-9236)
Prysmian Cbles Systems USA LLC........... D 765 483-1760
  Lebanon (G-10934)
Prysmian Cbles Systems USA LLC........... C 765 664-2321
  Marion (G-11331)
◆ REA Magnet Wire Company Inc........... D 800 732-9473
  Fort Wayne (G-5370)
▲ Sandin Mfg LLC............................. D 219 872-2253
  Michigan City (G-11662)
◆ Sanlo Inc..................................... D 219 879-0241
  Michigan City (G-11664)
Sigma Wire International LLC................ G 574 295-9660
  Elkhart (G-3677)
Southwire Company LLC..................... D 574 546-5115
  Bremen (G-1222)
Southwire Company LLC..................... E 317 445-2722
  Plainfield (G-13730)
Superior Essex Inc............................ C 260 420-1565
  Fort Wayne (G-5458)
Superior Essex Intl LP........................ C 260 461-4000
  Fort Wayne (G-5459)
▲ Telamon Corporation...................... C 317 818-6888
  Carmel (G-1777)
Telamon Spv LLC............................. G 800 788-6680
  Carmel (G-1780)
W Michael Ssan Wlls Fndtion I.............. G 317 844-6006
  Carmel (G-1798)
Wireamerica Inc............................... G 260 969-1700
  Fort Wayne (G-5571)

3363 Aluminum die-castings

▲ Batesville Products Inc..................... D 513 381-2057
  Lawrenceburg (G-10831)
▲ Enkei America Moldings Inc.............. G 812 373-7000
  Columbus (G-2299)
FCA US LLC................................... C 765 454-1005
  Kokomo (G-10267)
General Aluminum Mfg Company........... C 260 495-2600
  Fremont (G-5822)
General Motors LLC.......................... B 812 279-7321
  Bedford (G-638)
▲ Grandview Aluminum Products........... F 812 649-2569
  Grandview (G-6328)
Heartland Castings Inc....................... E 260 837-8311
  Waterloo (G-16521)
Indiana Cast Stone Company................ F 317 847-5429
  Spencer (G-15350)
Kitchen-Quip Inc.............................. E 260 837-8311
  Kendallville (G-10129)
◆ Koch Enterprises Inc....................... G 812 465-9800
  Evansville (G-4159)
▲ Madison Precision Products Inc........... B 812 273-4702
  Madison (G-11238)
Noblitt International Corp.................... E 812 372-9969
  Columbus (G-2361)
Old Rev LLC................................... G 317 580-2420
  Westfield (G-16714)

▲ Ryobi Die Casting (usa) Inc............... A 317 398-3398
  Shelbyville (G-14794)
▲ SUS Cast Products Inc..................... D 574 753-4111
  Logansport (G-11109)

3364 Nonferrous die-castings except aluminum

Accurate Castings Inc........................ D 219 362-8531
  La Porte (G-10373)
▲ Aero Metals Inc.............................. B 219 326-1976
  La Porte (G-10377)
Heartland Castings Inc....................... E 260 837-8311
  Waterloo (G-16521)
▼ Indiana Gratings Inc........................ F 765 342-7191
  Martinsville (G-11404)
S P X Corp..................................... G 574 594-9681
  Pierceton (G-13640)

3365 Aluminum foundries

12154 Holding Corp........................... C 260 563-8371
  Wabash (G-16171)
▲ Ball Brass and Aluminum F................ E 260 925-3515
  Auburn (G-367)
Batesville Products Inc....................... F 812 926-4230
  Aurora (G-440)
▲ Bud LLC...................................... E 574 534-5300
  Goshen (G-6103)
▼ Ce Systems Inc............................. E 812 372-8234
  Columbus (G-2235)
Cuda II Inc..................................... G 317 514-0885
  Indianapolis (G-7920)
Dillon Pattern Works Inc..................... F 765 642-3549
  Anderson (G-103)
Dualtech Inc................................... E 317 738-9043
  Franklin (G-5727)
Duplicast Metalworks Inc.................... G 317 926-0745
  Indianapolis (G-8020)
Engel Manufacturing Co Inc................. E 574 232-3800
  South Bend (G-15015)
◆ Enkei America Inc.......................... A 812 373-7000
  Columbus (G-2298)
Ewing Light Metals Co Inc................... E 317 926-4591
  Indianapolis (G-8146)
FCA North America Holdings LLC.......... B 765 454-0018
  Kokomo (G-10264)
FCA US LLC................................... C 765 454-1005
  Kokomo (G-10267)
Foley Pattern Company Inc.................. E 260 925-4113
  Auburn (G-391)
General Aluminum Mfg Company........... C 260 495-2600
  Fremont (G-5822)
General Aluminum Mfg Company........... C 260 356-3900
  Huntington (G-7314)
▲ Global... G 317 494-6174
  Franklin (G-5732)
▲ Grandview Aluminum Products........... F 812 649-2569
  Grandview (G-6328)
▲ Harvey Industries LLC..................... B 260 563-8371
  Wabash (G-16190)
▲ Heartland Aluminum Inc................... E 260 375-4652
  Huntington (G-7316)
Innovative Casting Tech Inc.................. F 317 738-5966
  Franklin (G-5748)
Kessington LLC................................ D 574 266-4500
  Elkhart (G-3452)
Linamar Strctures USA Mich Inc............ G 260 636-7030
  Avilla (G-487)
▲ Madison Precision Products Inc........... B 812 273-4702
  Madison (G-11238)
Mahoney Foundries Inc....................... E 260 347-1768
  Kendallville (G-10134)

Midwest Aerospace Casting LLC........... G 708 597-1300
  Crown Point (G-2725)
Minneapolis Die Casting LLC................ C 763 536-5500
  Auburn (G-411)
Mpi Products LLC............................. E 248 237-3007
  Knox (G-10218)
Muncie Casting Corp.......................... E 765 288-2611
  Muncie (G-12461)
New Point Products Inc....................... G 812 663-6311
  New Point (G-12976)
Phillips Pattern & Casting Inc................ F 765 288-2319
  Muncie (G-12475)
▲ Ryobi Die Casting (usa) Inc............... A 317 398-3398
  Shelbyville (G-14794)
▲ SUS Cast Products Inc..................... D 574 753-4111
  Logansport (G-11109)
Valmont Telecommunications Inc........... F 877 467-4763
  Plymouth (G-13824)
◆ Valmont Telecommunications Inc........ F 574 936-7221
  Plymouth (G-13823)
▲ Vice Bros Pattern Sp & Fndry............. G 260 782-2585
  Lagro (G-10770)
Wabash Castings LLC........................ G 260 563-8371
  Wabash (G-16220)
▲ Ward Corporation........................... C 260 426-8700
  Fort Wayne (G-5545)
▲ Ward Pattern & Engineering Inc.......... C 260 426-8700
  Fort Wayne (G-5547)
Wingards Sales LLC.......................... G 260 768-7961
  Shipshewana (G-14899)

3366 Copper foundries

Araymond Mfg Ctr N Amer Inc.............. C 574 722-5168
  Logansport (G-11058)
▲ Ball Brass and Aluminum F................ E 260 925-3515
  Auburn (G-367)
Beckett Bronze Company Inc................ E 765 282-2261
  Muncie (G-12351)
Beckett Bronze Company Inc................ E 765 282-2261
  Muncie (G-12350)
Complete Drives Inc.......................... F 260 489-6033
  Fort Wayne (G-4869)
Crosbie Foundry Company Inc.............. F 574 262-1502
  Elkhart (G-3272)
Cunningham Pattern & Engrg Inc........... F 812 379-9571
  Columbus (G-2276)
▲ Duramold Castings Inc..................... E 574 251-1111
  South Bend (G-15006)
Ewing Light Metals Co Inc................... E 317 926-4591
  Indianapolis (G-8146)
Fog Foundry Frankfort........................ G 765 670-6445
  Frankfort (G-5663)
Foundry Services Inc......................... E 317 955-8112
  Noblesville (G-13080)
▲ Grandview Aluminum Products........... F 812 649-2569
  Grandview (G-6328)
Mahoney Foundries Inc....................... E 260 347-1768
  Kendallville (G-10134)
▲ Mark Parmenter............................. G 812 829-6583
  Spencer (G-15355)
MTI Mexico Machining LLC.................. G 260 925-4717
  Auburn (G-412)
Neenah Foundry Company................... G 317 875-7245
  Indianapolis (G-8998)
New Beginnings Art Foundry................ G 219 326-7059
  La Porte (G-10456)
New Point Products Inc....................... G 812 663-6311
  New Point (G-12976)
Nst Technologies Mim LLC................... C 812 755-4501
  Campbellsburg (G-1526)
Parker-Hannifin Corporation................. D 260 636-2104
  Albion (G-40)

33 PRIMARY METAL INDUSTRIES

Phillips Pattern & Casting Inc .... F 765 288-2319
Muncie *(G-12475)*

▲ Stalcop LLC .... E 765 436-7926
Thorntown *(G-15756)*

Sterling Sales and Engrg Inc .... G 765 376-0454
Veedersburg *(G-16091)*

▲ Wilhoite Monuments Inc .... G 765 286-7423
Muncie *(G-12520)*

Yamaha Motor Corporation USA .... E 317 545-9080
Indianapolis *(G-9800)*

3369 Nonferrous foundries, nec

Accurate Castings Inc .... E 219 393-3122
La Porte *(G-10374)*

Batesville Products Inc .... F 812 926-4230
Aurora *(G-440)*

▲ Batesville Products Inc .... D 513 381-2057
Lawrenceburg *(G-10831)*

Cole Energy Incorporated .... G 317 839-9688
Plainfield *(G-13670)*

Crosbie Foundry Company Inc .... F 574 262-1502
Elkhart *(G-3272)*

Engel Manufacturing Co Inc .... E 574 232-3800
South Bend *(G-15015)*

Ewing Light Metals Co Inc .... E 317 926-4591
Indianapolis *(G-8146)*

▲ Excel Manufacturing Inc .... D 812 523-6764
Seymour *(G-14650)*

▲ General Products Delaware .... B 260 668-1440
Angola *(G-255)*

Howmet Aerospace Inc .... A 219 326-7400
La Porte *(G-10423)*

Kitchen-Quip Inc .... E 260 837-8311
Kendallville *(G-10129)*

Lite Magnesium Products Inc .... G 765 299-3644
Indianapolis *(G-8768)*

New Point Products Inc .... G 812 663-6311
New Point *(G-12976)*

▼ Nonferrous Products Inc .... E 317 738-2558
Franklin *(G-5761)*

▲ Orthodontic Design & Prod Inc .... E 317 346-6655
Franklin *(G-5763)*

▲ Symmetry Medical Mfg Inc .... C 574 371-2284
Warsaw *(G-16435)*

Valmont Telecommunications Inc .... F 877 467-4763
Plymouth *(G-13824)*

◆ Valmont Telecommunications Inc .... F 574 936-7221
Plymouth *(G-13823)*

▲ Ward Corporation .... C 260 426-8700
Fort Wayne *(G-5545)*

3398 Metal heat treating

Al-Fe Heat Treating LLC .... F 260 563-8321
Wabash *(G-16173)*

Albany Metal Treating Inc .... F 765 789-6470
Albany *(G-11)*

Applied Thermal Tech Inc .... E 574 269-7116
Warsaw *(G-16313)*

Araymond Mfg Ctr N Amer Inc .... C 574 722-5168
Logansport *(G-11058)*

ATI Flat Rlled Pdts Hldngs LLC .... F 765 529-9570
New Castle *(G-12850)*

Atmosphere Annealing LLC .... E 812 346-1275
North Vernon *(G-13256)*

▲ B&J Rocket America Inc .... E 574 825-5802
Middlebury *(G-11700)*

Bodycote Testing Group Inc .... G 219 882-4283
Gary *(G-5904)*

Bodycote Thermal Proc Inc .... E 574 295-2491
Elkhart *(G-3231)*

Bodycote Thermal Proc Inc .... E 260 423-1691
Fort Wayne *(G-4811)*

Bodycote Thermal Proc Inc .... E 812 662-0500
Greensburg *(G-6582)*

Bodycote Thermal Proc Inc .... E 317 924-4321
Indianapolis *(G-7654)*

Boyd Machine and Repair Co .... E 260 635-2195
Kimmell *(G-10169)*

Bwt LLC .... F 574 232-3338
South Bend *(G-14963)*

Chicago Flame Hardening Co .... E 773 768-3608
East Chicago *(G-2995)*

Circle City Heat Treating Inc .... F 317 440-9102
Indianapolis *(G-7805)*

D & D Industries Inc .... G 219 844-5600
Hammond *(G-6910)*

Dependable Metal Treating Inc .... F 260 347-5744
Kendallville *(G-10110)*

Electro Seal Corporation .... G 219 926-8606
Chesterton *(G-1922)*

▲ Exotic Metal Treating Inc .... F 317 784-8565
Indianapolis *(G-8156)*

Fremont Coatings Div .... G 260 495-4445
Fremont *(G-5821)*

Gerdau Macsteel Inc .... E 260 356-9520
Huntington *(G-7315)*

Gerdau McSteel Atmsphere Annli .... E 812 346-1275
North Vernon *(G-13272)*

Godfrey & Wing Inc .... F 765 284-5050
Muncie *(G-12403)*

H & H Commercial Heat Treating .... G 765 288-3618
Muncie *(G-12407)*

Harbor Metals LLC .... F 574 232-3338
South Bend *(G-15058)*

Hartford Heat Treatment .... G 812 725-8272
New Albany *(G-12740)*

HTI .... F 574 722-2814
Logansport *(G-11078)*

Indianna .... G 219 947-9533
Hobart *(G-7192)*

Learman Elctrnic Tl Assctesinc .... G 574 293-4641
Elkhart *(G-3480)*

Learman Electronic Tool Assoc .... G 574 226-0420
Elkhart *(G-3481)*

Leed Thermal Processing Inc .... G 317 637-5102
Indianapolis *(G-8733)*

Legacy Heat Treatment LLC .... D 219 237-4500
Griffith *(G-6811)*

McLaughlin Services LLC .... G 260 897-4328
Avilla *(G-489)*

Melting Point Metalworks LLC .... G 317 984-0037
Brownsburg *(G-1387)*

Metal Improvement Company LLC .... G 317 875-6030
Indianapolis *(G-8886)*

Nitrex Inc .... E 317 346-7700
Franklin *(G-5760)*

▲ Northern Indiana Manufacturing .... E 574 342-2105
Bourbon *(G-1125)*

Ooley Products Inc .... E 317 787-9351
Indianapolis *(G-9059)*

Precision Heat Treating Corp .... E 260 749-5125
Fort Wayne *(G-5338)*

Quality Steel Treating Co Inc .... E 317 357-8691
Tipton *(G-15788)*

◆ Rogers Engineering and Mfg Co .... E 765 478-5444
Cambridge City *(G-1503)*

Simpson Alloy Services Inc .... G 812 969-2766
Elizabeth *(G-3129)*

Sinden Racing Service Inc .... F 317 243-7171
Indianapolis *(G-9443)*

South Bend Heat Treat Inc .... G 574 288-4794
South Bend *(G-15254)*

Specilty Blnks Inc An Ind Corp .... C 812 234-3002
Terre Haute *(G-15711)*

Steel Technologies LLC .... C 502 245-2110
Portage *(G-13916)*

Sturm Heat Treating Inc .... F 317 357-2368
Indianapolis *(G-9518)*

Tool Dynamics LLC .... E 812 379-4243
Columbus *(G-2404)*

Toyo Seiko North America Inc .... G 574 288-2000
South Bend *(G-15285)*

Tri-State Metal Inc .... G 219 397-0470
East Chicago *(G-3047)*

Ward Corporation .... F 260 489-2281
Fort Wayne *(G-5546)*

Wesleys Pallets & Heat Treat .... G 812 526-0377
Franklin *(G-5787)*

3399 Primary metal products

A2 Sales LLC .... E 708 924-1200
Gary *(G-5885)*

Algalco LLC .... G 317 361-2787
Indianapolis *(G-7471)*

Creative Powder Coatings LLC .... D 260 489-3580
Fort Wayne *(G-4884)*

Elgin Fastener Group LLC .... G 812 689-8917
Versailles *(G-16099)*

▲ Golden Beam Metals LLC .... G 317 806-2750
Indianapolis *(G-8297)*

Hawk Precision Components Inc .... G 812 755-4501
Campbellsburg *(G-1524)*

Indiana Whitesell Corporation .... B 317 279-3278
Indianapolis *(G-8500)*

Intermetco Processing Inc .... G 812 423-5914
Evansville *(G-4129)*

▲ ITW Gema .... F 317 298-5000
Indianapolis *(G-8598)*

Jbs Powder Coating LLC .... G 812 952-1204
Lanesville *(G-10799)*

Keywest Metal .... G 219 513-8429
Griffith *(G-6810)*

Keywest Metal .... G 219 654-4063
Hobart *(G-7197)*

L M Corporation .... E 574 535-0581
Goshen *(G-6194)*

LLC 2 Holdings Limited LLC .... G 317 319-9825
Zionsville *(G-17030)*

Metal Powder Products LLC .... G 317 214-8120
Indianapolis *(G-8887)*

▲ Metal Powder Products LLC .... F 317 805-3764
Noblesville *(G-13134)*

National Material Company LLC .... E 219 397-5088
East Chicago *(G-3030)*

Nst Technologies Mim LLC .... C 812 755-4501
Campbellsburg *(G-1526)*

Old Rev LLC .... C 317 580-2420
Westfield *(G-16714)*

Omnisource LLC .... G 574 654-7561
New Carlisle *(G-12843)*

◆ Omnisource LLC .... C 260 422-5541
Fort Wayne *(G-5286)*

Phoenix Services LLC .... E 219 787-0019
Portage *(G-13903)*

▲ Powder Processing & Tech LLC .... E 219 462-4141
Valparaiso *(G-16027)*

◆ Powdertech Corp .... D 219 462-4141
Valparaiso *(G-16028)*

Sit Can Happen LLC .... E 812 346-4188
North Vernon *(G-13295)*

Tjr Fabrication LLC .... F 765 384-4455
Marion *(G-11342)*

Trinity Metals LLC .... F 317 358-8265
Indianapolis *(G-9645)*

◆ Trinity Metals LLC .... G 317 358-8265
Indianapolis *(G-9644)*

34 FABRICATED METAL PRODUCTS

▲ U S Granules Corporation............... E 574 936-2146
Plymouth *(G-13822)*

Warrick Newco LLC........................... A 812 853-6111
Newburgh *(G-13028)*

Wendell Denton.................................. G 317 736-8397
Franklin *(G-5786)*

34 FABRICATED METAL PRODUCTS

3411 Metal cans

Ardagh Glass Inc............................... G 610 341-7885
Muncie *(G-12344)*

Armor Products Inc........................... C 502 228-1458
Madison *(G-11202)*

Ball Corporation................................. F 574 583-9418
Monticello *(G-12136)*

Ball Inc.. A 317 736-8236
Franklin *(G-5712)*

Ball Metal Beverage Cont Corp........ C 574 583-9418
Monticello *(G-12137)*

Bway Corporation.............................. G 219 462-8915
Valparaiso *(G-15923)*

Canpack US LLC............................... A 272 226-7225
Muncie *(G-12364)*

Crown Cork & Seal Usa Inc............. C 765 362-3200
Crawfordsville *(G-2560)*

Ican Solutions LLC........................... G 574 355-6500
Logansport *(G-11081)*

Indianapolis Container Company..... G 317 580-5000
Indianapolis *(G-8503)*

Industrial Container Svcs LLC......... F 812 283-7659
Alton *(G-65)*

J&K Generations................................ G 812 508-1094
Bedford *(G-650)*

Norton Packaging Inc....................... E 574 867-6002
Hamlet *(G-6864)*

Powell Systems Inc........................... G 765 884-6013
Fowler *(G-5631)*

R & M Welding & Fabricating Sp..... G 812 295-9130
Loogootee *(G-11148)*

Red Gold LP....................................... E 765 754-8750
Alexandria *(G-59)*

Sangsin Indiana Inc........................... G 765 432-4143
Kokomo *(G-10329)*

Silgan Containers Mfg Corp............. E 219 845-1500
Hammond *(G-7006)*

Silgan Containers Mfg Corp............. E 219 362-7002
La Porte *(G-10483)*

Silgan White Cap LLC...................... C 812 425-6222
Evansville *(G-4314)*

Silgan White Cap LLC...................... B 765 983-9200
Richmond *(G-14205)*

3412 Metal barrels, drums, and pails

Anthony Wyne Rhbltttion Ctr For.... D 260 744-6145
Fort Wayne *(G-4762)*

Armor Products Inc........................... C 502 228-1458
Madison *(G-11202)*

Industrial Container Svcs LLC......... F 812 283-7659
Alton *(G-65)*

North America Packaging Corp....... G 317 291-2396
Indianapolis *(G-9021)*

Nova Packaging Group Inc.............. E 765 651-2600
Marion *(G-11321)*

OBryan Barrel Company Inc............ E 812 479-6741
Evansville *(G-4225)*

Packaging Corporation America..... G 812 522-3100
Seymour *(G-14671)*

Powell Systems Inc........................... G 765 884-0980
Fowler *(G-5630)*

Powell Systems Inc........................... G 765 884-0613
Fowler *(G-5631)*

▲ Tru-Form Steel & Wire Inc............ E 765 348-5001
Hartford City *(G-7078)*

3421 Cutlery

Alan Sword LLC................................. G 812 913-1412
Jeffersonville *(G-9926)*

▲ Allen-Davis Enterprises Inc.......... G 574 303-2173
Mishawaka *(G-11837)*

▲ Andys Global Inc............................ G 317 595-8825
Indianapolis *(G-7518)*

Barrett Custom Knives...................... G 574 533-4297
Goshen *(G-6096)*

Bemcor Inc.. F 219 937-1600
Hammond *(G-6885)*

Bird and Cleaver LLC....................... G 260 579-2799
Fort Wayne *(G-4804)*

Bose Knife Works.............................. G 812 397-5114
Shelburn *(G-14717)*

Certified Clipper Inc.......................... G 317 894-3787
Greenfield *(G-6478)*

Cleaver Enterprises Inc.................... G 260 625-5822
Fort Wayne *(G-4859)*

Custom Creations By Heather......... G 574 302-7525
Mishawaka *(G-11871)*

Dawghouse Grub Pub LLC............... G 765 778-2727
Pendleton *(G-13529)*

Enmac Inc.. G 812 298-8711
Terre Haute *(G-15587)*

Grannys LLC....................................... G 812 969-3058
Elizabeth *(G-3126)*

Happy Buddah.................................... G 765 998-3008
Upland *(G-15877)*

Harry & Izzys Northside LLC........... G 317 915-8045
Indianapolis *(G-8367)*

Hayabusa LLC.................................... G 317 594-1188
Indianapolis *(G-8371)*

His Word Is My Sword LLC.............. G 260 433-9911
Fort Wayne *(G-5069)*

Jason Sword LLC............................... G 502 550-4183
New Albany *(G-12753)*

Kjs Beauty Lounge LLC.................... G 317 426-0621
Indianapolis *(G-8692)*

Krocs Butcher Shop LLC.................. G 812 208-8116
Terre Haute *(G-15626)*

Mister Hicbachi.................................. G 812 339-6288
Bloomington *(G-921)*

Molti Gusti LLC.................................. G 317 660-5692
Carmel *(G-1701)*

Part Solutions LLC............................ G 219 477-5101
South Bend *(G-15186)*

Pates Processing LLC...................... G 812 866-4710
Hanover *(G-7044)*

Pettigrew... G 260 868-2032
Butler *(G-1475)*

Punjab Empire Inc............................. G 765 987-8786
Greenfield *(G-6543)*

Rush Hour Station............................. G 812 323-7874
Bloomington *(G-964)*

◆ Samco Group Inc........................... G 219 872-4413
Michigan City *(G-11660)*

Sushiya-US... G 260 444-4263
Fort Wayne *(G-5461)*

Valparaiso II LLC............................... G 219 464-0431
Valparaiso *(G-16074)*

Vogel Brothers Corporation............. E 812 376-2775
Columbus *(G-2415)*

3423 Hand and edge tools, nec

Airodapt LLC...................................... G 559 331-0156
Rensselaer *(G-14040)*

AK Tool and Die Inc.......................... G 574 286-9010
Mishawaka *(G-11836)*

▲ Atlas Die LLC................................. D 574 295-0050
Elkhart *(G-3200)*

◆ Bloomfield Mfg Co Inc................... E 812 384-4441
Bloomfield *(G-740)*

◆ Brinly-Hardy Company.................. D 812 218-7200
Jeffersonville *(G-9947)*

▲ BT&f LLC.. G 574 272-6128
Granger *(G-6338)*

Bully Products Inc............................. G 574 312-0511
Goshen *(G-6104)*

Carpenter Co Inc............................... E 317 297-2900
Indianapolis *(G-7748)*

Foresee LLC....................................... F 219 226-9663
Crown Point *(G-2687)*

▲ FTC Liquidation Inc...................... F 574 295-6700
Elkhart *(G-3359)*

Halyard Corporation.......................... E 219 515-2820
Portage *(G-13873)*

Ideal Pro Cnc Inc............................... G 260 693-1954
Churubusco *(G-1985)*

Illiana Grinding Machining Inc........ G 219 306-0253
East Chicago *(G-3019)*

Indiana Precision Tooling Inc.......... F 812 667-5141
Dillsboro *(G-2947)*

Indy Side Piece LLC.......................... G 317 426-3927
Indianapolis *(G-8534)*

Indy Stud Welding Inc...................... G 317 416-3617
Indianapolis *(G-8535)*

James W Hager................................... G 765 643-0188
Alexandria *(G-54)*

◆ Josam Company............................. D 219 872-5531
Michigan City *(G-11628)*

Kaiser Tool Company Inc................. E 260 484-3620
Fort Wayne *(G-5142)*

Laidig Inc... E 574 256-0204
Mishawaka *(G-11925)*

Master Manufacturing Company..... E 812 425-1561
Evansville *(G-4191)*

Mid-West Spring Mfg Co.................. D 574 353-1409
Mentone *(G-11474)*

Montrow Group.................................. G 812 352-7356
North Vernon *(G-13288)*

Nestor Sales LLC............................... G 574 295-5535
Elkhart *(G-3566)*

Osborn Manufacturing Corp............ F 574 267-6156
Warsaw *(G-16406)*

Perry Products Inc............................ G 260 316-8816
Angola *(G-283)*

▼ Pro-Form Plastics Inc................... E 812 522-4433
Crothersville *(G-2644)*

Rapid Rule Co Inc.............................. G 574 784-2273
North Liberty *(G-13221)*

Rich Manufacturing Inc.................... G 765 436-2744
Lebanon *(G-10937)*

▲ Seymour Manufacturing Co Inc... C 812 522-2900
Seymour *(G-14689)*

Seymour Midwest LLC...................... G 574 267-7875
Warsaw *(G-16422)*

▲ Seymour Midwest LLC.................. E 574 267-7875
Warsaw *(G-16423)*

Stanley Black & Decker Inc............. D 860 225-5111
Indianapolis *(G-9495)*

Stone Artisans Ltd............................. G 317 362-0107
Indianapolis *(G-9512)*

3425 Saw blades and handsaws

Archer Products Inc.......................... G 317 899-0700
Indianapolis *(G-7540)*

Milwaukee Electric Tool Corp.......... E 800 729-3878
Greenwood *(G-6742)*

34 FABRICATED METAL PRODUCTS

Tsb LLC .... G 812 314-8331
   Edinburgh *(G-3108)*

Valley Sharpening Inc .... G 574 674-9077
   Osceola *(G-13405)*

◆ Wood-Mizer Holdings Inc .... C 317 271-1542
   Indianapolis *(G-9784)*

3429 Hardware, nec

A-1 Door Specialties Inc .... G 260 749-1635
   South Bend *(G-14930)*

Allegion Public Ltd Company .... D 317 810-3700
   Carmel *(G-1554)*

Allegion S&S Holding Co Inc .... B 317 810-3700
   Carmel *(G-1555)*

Allegion US Holding Co Inc .... E 317 810-3700
   Carmel *(G-1556)*

▲ American Flame LLC .... D 260 459-1703
   Fort Wayne *(G-4754)*

Aquabee Coolers LLC .... G 615 947-7962
   Bloomington *(G-782)*

Araymond Mfg Ctr N Amer Inc .... C 574 722-5168
   Logansport *(G-11058)*

Armored Locks Inc .... G 219 798-6502
   Michigan City *(G-11579)*

▲ Avis Industrial Corporation .... E 765 998-8100
   Upland *(G-15876)*

▲ Batesville Products Inc .... D 513 381-2057
   Lawrenceburg *(G-10831)*

Benakovich Builders .... G 219 204-2777
   Thorntown *(G-15750)*

◆ Bloomfield Mfg Co Inc .... E 812 384-4441
   Bloomfield *(G-740)*

▲ Bottom Line Management Inc .... F 812 944-7388
   Clarksville *(G-2010)*

Control Key Plus .... G 317 567-2194
   Indianapolis *(G-7862)*

Crossroads Door & Hardware Inc .... G 812 234-9751
   Terre Haute *(G-15570)*

Dorma .... G 317 468-6742
   Greenfield *(G-6491)*

Dormakaba USA Inc .... A 317 806-4605
   Indianapolis *(G-7997)*

◆ Elkhart Brass Manufacturi .... C 574 295-8330
   Elkhart *(G-3322)*

Elkhart Hinge Co Inc .... F 574 293-2841
   Elkhart *(G-3325)*

Engineered Dock Systems Inc .... G 317 803-2443
   Indianapolis *(G-8120)*

▼ Epco Products Inc .... E 260 747-8888
   Fort Wayne *(G-4956)*

◆ Fabri-Tech Inc .... F 317 849-7755
   Mccordsville *(G-11447)*

Fiedeke Vinyl Coverings Inc .... F 574 534-3408
   Goshen *(G-6135)*

◆ Fki Security Group LLC .... B 812 948-8400
   New Albany *(G-12730)*

◆ G E C O M Corp .... A 812 663-2270
   Greensburg *(G-6595)*

◆ Geneva Manufacturing Inc .... E 260 368-7555
   Fort Wayne *(G-5021)*

Gibson Brothers Welding Inc .... F 765 948-5775
   Fairmount *(G-4410)*

Govparts LLC .... G 260 449-9741
   Fort Wayne *(G-5031)*

Grace Manufacturing Inc .... F 574 267-8000
   Warsaw *(G-16369)*

Grrreat Creations .... E 574 773-5331
   Nappanee *(G-12601)*

▲ Guardian Ind Inc .... E 219 874-5248
   Michigan City *(G-11618)*

Hart Plastics Inc .... E 574 264-7060
   Elkhart *(G-3400)*

High Quality Flasks LLC .... G 765 357-6392
   Lafayette *(G-10598)*

Hingecraft Corporation .... E 574 293-6543
   Elkhart *(G-3407)*

Holland Metal Fab Inc .... F 574 522-1434
   Elkhart *(G-3409)*

Houck Industries Inc .... F 812 663-5675
   Greensburg *(G-6606)*

▲ Indiana Architectural Plywood .... E 317 878-4822
   Trafalgar *(G-15829)*

Indiana Custom Trucks LLC .... E 260 463-3244
   Shipshewana *(G-14852)*

Indy Aerospace Inc .... G 817 521-6508
   Indianapolis *(G-8522)*

J Game Ventures LLC .... G 812 241-7096
   Danville *(G-2814)*

▲ JM Fittings LLC .... E 260 747-9200
   Fort Wayne *(G-5137)*

Key Made Now .... G 317 664-8582
   Indianapolis *(G-8676)*

Keys R US .... G 317 616-0267
   Indianapolis *(G-8679)*

L & S Lumber .... F 765 886-1452
   Greens Fork *(G-6575)*

L & W Engineering Inc .... C 574 825-5351
   Middlebury *(G-11730)*

L E Johnson Products Inc .... G 574 293-5664
   Elkhart *(G-3461)*

◆ L E Johnson Products Inc .... C 574 293-5664
   Elkhart *(G-3462)*

Latch Gard Co Inc .... G 574 862-2373
   Elkhart *(G-3471)*

Maurer Specialty Pools and Con .... G 574 320-2429
   Mishawaka *(G-11940)*

Modern Forge Companies LLC .... A 708 388-1806
   Merrillville *(G-11542)*

▲ Oak Security Group LLC .... F 317 585-9830
   Indianapolis *(G-9040)*

Olon Industries Inc (us) .... G 812 254-0427
   Washington *(G-16497)*

▲ Osr Inc .... F 812 342-7642
   Columbus *(G-2368)*

Parker-Hannifin Corporation .... A 260 748-6000
   Fort Wayne *(G-5297)*

▲ Pk USA Inc .... B 317 395-5500
   Shelbyville *(G-14784)*

Pridgeon & Clay Inc .... G 317 738-4885
   Franklin *(G-5770)*

▲ Qmp Inc .... E 574 262-1575
   Elkhart *(G-3627)*

Quality Converters Inc .... E 260 829-6541
   Orland *(G-13371)*

R & R Regulators Inc .... F 574 522-3500
   Elkhart *(G-3636)*

▲ Rdd Properties Inc .... E 317 870-1940
   Waterloo *(G-16529)*

◆ Reelcraft Industries Inc .... C 855 634-9109
   Columbia City *(G-2188)*

REM Industries Inc .... F 574 862-2127
   Wakarusa *(G-16247)*

Rookstools Pier Shop Inc .... E 574 453-4771
   Leesburg *(G-10960)*

▲ S C Pryor Inc .... F 317 352-1281
   Indianapolis *(G-9354)*

Samaron Corp .... E 574 970-7070
   Elkhart *(G-3661)*

▲ Schlage Lock Company LLC .... B 317 810-3700
   Carmel *(G-1752)*

▲ Seymour Manufacturing Co Inc .... C 812 522-2900
   Seymour *(G-14689)*

▲ Slb Corporation .... F 574 255-9774
   Mishawaka *(G-11996)*

Sparks Belting Company Inc .... G 800 451-4537
   Hammond *(G-7012)*

Sportcrafters Inc .... G 574 243-2453
   Granger *(G-6381)*

Standard Fusee Corporation .... D 765 472-4375
   Peru *(G-13602)*

Steel Parts Corporation .... A 765 675-2191
   Tipton *(G-15791)*

Summer Cottage Inc .... G 317 873-4176
   Indianapolis *(G-9523)*

Sur-Loc Inc .... F 260 495-4065
   Fremont *(G-5836)*

Task Force Tips Inc .... F 219 462-6161
   Valparaiso *(G-16063)*

◆ Task Force Tips LLC .... C 219 462-6161
   Valparaiso *(G-16064)*

Terry Liquidation III Inc .... F 219 362-3557
   La Porte *(G-10490)*

Timberline Industries LLC .... G 812 442-0949
   Brazil *(G-1167)*

▲ Titus Tool Company Inc .... F 206 447-1489
   Columbia City *(G-2207)*

Top Lock Corporation .... G 317 831-2000
   Mooresville *(G-12248)*

▲ Tru-Flex Real Estate Holdings LLC ... D 765 893-4403
   West Lebanon *(G-16650)*

◆ Ultra-Fab Acquisitions Inc .... F 574 294-7571
   Elkhart *(G-3757)*

Velko Hinge Inc .... E 219 924-6363
   Munster *(G-12573)*

Viking Inc .... E 260 244-6141
   Columbia City *(G-2211)*

VMS Products Inc .... G 888 321-4698
   Anderson *(G-214)*

◆ Von Duprin LLC .... A 317 429-2866
   Indianapolis *(G-9729)*

Wallys Lockshop .... G 765 748-2282
   Muncie *(G-12514)*

Ward Industries Inc .... F 574 825-2548
   Middlebury *(G-11756)*

Western Products Indiana Inc .... F 765 529-6230
   New Castle *(G-12885)*

Wood & More LLC .... G 260 350-1537
   Goshen *(G-6278)*

Yoder Woodworking Inc .... Pk 574 546-5100
   Bremen *(G-1232)*

3431 Metal sanitary ware

▲ Alsons Corporation .... D 800 421-0001
   Carmel *(G-1558)*

Bootz Manufacturing Co LLC .... G 812 423-5019
   Evansville *(G-3940)*

Bootz Manufacturing Co LLC .... C 812 425-4646
   Evansville *(G-3942)*

◆ Bootz Manufacturing Co LLC .... E 812 423-5401
   Evansville *(G-3941)*

Charles Stewart .... G 812 801-9694
   Madison *(G-11207)*

Econotec Inc .... G 812 299-1642
   Terre Haute *(G-15582)*

▲ H A P Industries Inc .... G 765 948-3385
   Jonesboro *(G-10079)*

◆ Josam Company .... D 219 872-5531
   Michigan City *(G-11628)*

Maax Inc .... E 574 936-3838
   Plymouth *(G-13795)*

Olympic Fiberglass Industries .... F 574 223-3101
   Rochester *(G-14310)*

Sdg Elkhart LLC .... G 574 294-4646
   Elkhart *(G-3666)*

Shank Brothers Inc .... F 260 744-4802
   Fort Wayne *(G-5411)*

34 FABRICATED METAL PRODUCTS

Stanley Oliver Products LLC.................. G 260 499-3506
  Lagrange (G-10764)
◆ TSF Co Inc.. E 812 985-2630
  Evansville (G-4354)

3432 Plumbing fixture fittings and trim

Ashley F Ward Inc................................... G 574 294-1502
  Elkhart (G-3196)
Ashley F Ward Inc................................... G 219 879-4177
  Michigan City (G-11580)
Barry Company Inc.................................. G 812 333-1850
  Bloomington (G-795)
Bath Gallery Showroom............................ G 219 531-2150
  Valparaiso (G-15911)
Bootz Manufacturing Co LLC................... C 812 425-4646
  Evansville (G-3942)
Buckaroos Inc... G 317 899-9100
  Indianapolis (G-7696)
City Supply Inc....................................... G 574 259-6028
  Mishawaka (G-11861)
Ferguson Enterprises LLC...................... G 219 440-5254
  Schererville (G-14521)
In Cloudbrst Lawn Sprnklr Svcs............. F 260 492-8400
  Fort Wayne (G-5097)
◆ Josam Company.....................................D 219 872-5531
  Michigan City (G-11628)
Kipps Plumbing Inc................................. G 219 661-9320
  Crown Point (G-2710)
Lasalle Bristol Corporation...................... F 574 936-9894
  Plymouth (G-13791)
Lee Supply Corp..................................... F 812 333-4343
  Bloomington (G-909)
LGS Plumbing Inc................................... E 219 663-2177
  Crown Point (G-2718)
Mark Miller.. G 317 626-9441
  Indianapolis (G-8836)
Nibco Inc... C 574 296-1240
  Goshen (G-6227)
Parker-Hannifin Corporation.................... D 260 636-2104
  Albion (G-40)
Rcate Plbg Mech Ltd Lblty Co................. G 812 613-0386
  Sellersburg (G-14611)
Rex Byers Htg & Coolg Systems............ F 765 459-8858
  Kokomo (G-10328)
Schmidt Contracting Inc.......................... E 812 482-3923
  Jasper (G-9908)
Siteone Landscape Supply LLC............. G 219 769-2351
  Merrillville (G-11560)
St Regis Culvert Inc................................ F 317 353-8065
  Indianapolis (G-9487)
Stanley Oliver Products LLC.................. G 260 499-3506
  Lagrange (G-10764)
TMI... G 574 533-4741
  Goshen (G-6270)
US Metals Inc... G 219 802-8465
  Hammond (G-7027)
Willoughby Industries Inc........................ C 317 875-0830
  Indianapolis (G-9770)

3433 Heating equipment, except electric

▲ Canvas Mw LLC..................................... D 630 560-3703
  Michigan City (G-11585)
Carrier Corporation................................. D 317 243-0851
  Indianapolis (G-7749)
Crossroads Solar Entps LLC................... F 607 759-1058
  South Bend (G-14985)
◆ Eclipse Inc...D
  Muncie (G-12389)
Fives N Amercn Combustn Inc................ G 219 662-9600
  Crown Point (G-2685)
Gmp Holdings LLC.................................. G 317 353-6580
  Indianapolis (G-8294)

◆ Hale Industries Inc................................. F 317 577-0337
  Fortville (G-5598)
▲ Heat Wagons Inc.................................... F 219 464-8818
  Valparaiso (G-15961)
Hitzer Inc.. F 260 589-8536
  Berne (G-714)
▼ Inovateus Solar LLC............................... E 574 485-1400
  South Bend (G-15081)
Maxon Corporation.................................. C 765 284-3304
  Muncie (G-12449)
▲ Ngh Retail LLC....................................... F 219 476-0772
  Valparaiso (G-16013)
Oesterling Chimney Sweep Inc............... G 812 372-3512
  Columbus (G-2364)
◆ Our Country Home Entps Inc................. E 260 657-5605
  Harlan (G-7058)
◆ Purolator Pdts A Filtration Co.................C 866 925-2247
  Jeffersonville (G-10043)
Quanex Heat Treat.................................. G 260 356-9520
  Huntington (G-7358)
Schmidt Contracting Inc.......................... E 812 482-3923
  Jasper (G-9908)
Southwark Metal Mfg Co......................... C 317 823-5300
  Mccordsville (G-11456)
Temptek Inc.. G 317 887-6352
  Greenwood (G-6773)
Trimble Combustion Systems Inc............ G 812 623-4545
  Sunman (G-15447)
Troy Meggitt Inc...................................... D 812 547-7071
  Troy (G-15843)
◆ Wayne/Scott Fetzer Company.................D 260 425-9200
  Fort Wayne (G-5555)
Wrib Manufacturing Inc........................... G 765 294-2841
  Veedersburg (G-16092)

3441 Fabricated structural metal

A & A Industries Inc............................... G 812 663-5584
  Greensburg (G-6577)
A & B Fabricating & Maint Inc................. F 574 353-1012
  Mentone (G-11468)
A and R Erectors Incorporated............... G 317 271-3429
  Indianapolis (G-7396)
A Plus Metals LLC.................................. G 915 341-0650
  Rockville (G-14349)
Accuburn Williamsport Inc...................... F 765 762-1100
  Williamsport (G-16845)
Advance Aero Inc................................... G 317 513-6071
  Mooresville (G-12190)
Advance Fabricators Inc......................... E 812 944-6941
  New Albany (G-12686)
Advanced Systems Intgrtion LLC............ G 260 447-5555
  Fort Wayne (G-4728)
Aeromotive Mfg Inc................................. G 765 552-0668
  Elwood (G-3817)
Aggreate Systems.................................. G 260 854-4711
  Rome City (G-14374)
Ajem Welding... G 812 595-3541
  Austin (G-462)
All-Terrain Conversions LLC.................. G 260 758-2525
  Roanoke (G-14256)
Allen Fabricators Inc.............................. F 260 458-0008
  Fort Wayne (G-4742)
▼ Alliance Steel Corporation...................... E 708 924-1200
  Gary (G-5890)
Almet Inc.. D 260 493-1556
  New Haven (G-12891)
Alum-Elec Structures Inc....................... G 260 347-9362
  Kendallville (G-10088)
Aluminum Wldg & Mch Works Inc........... G 219 787-8066
  Chesterton (G-1901)
Ambassador Steel Corporation............... F 317 834-3474
  Mooresville (G-12193)

American Co... G 812 250-9575
  Evansville (G-3884)
American Crane & Millwright................... G 765 452-5000
  Gas City (G-6030)
American Fabricating.............................. G 812 897-0900
  Boonville (G-1080)
American Fabricators Inc....................... E 219 844-4744
  Hammond (G-6873)
American Machine & Fabg Co Inc........... G 812 944-4136
  New Albany (G-12688)
American Stair Corp............................... G 815 886-9600
  Hammond (G-6875)
▲ Amerifab Inc... D 317 231-0100
  Indianapolis (G-7509)
Amrosia Metal Fabrication Inc................ G 812 425-5707
  Evansville (G-3890)
Anthony Wyne Rhbltition Ctr For............. D 260 744-6145
  Fort Wayne (G-4762)
Apar Technological Inc........................... G 812 430-2025
  Evansville (G-3893)
Armor Group..G 574 293-1791
  Elkhart (G-3190)
Armor Products Inc................................ C 502 228-1458
  Madison (G-11202)
Arrow Metals Inc.................................... E 765 825-4443
  Connersville (G-2426)
Artisanz Fabrication & Machine............... G 317 956-2384
  Zionsville (G-16993)
Artisanz Fabrication and Mch................. G 765 859-5118
  Lebanon (G-10876)
◆ Asi Limited..C
  Whitestown (G-16800)
Awol Metal Contorsion LLC.................... G 260 909-0411
  Kendallville (G-10093)
B & M Steel & Welding Inc..................... G 765 964-5868
  Union City (G-15849)
B Stevens Service LLC.......................... G 812 622-2039
  Cynthiana (G-2786)
Baker Metalworks................................... G 260 572-9353
  Saint Joe (G-14436)
Bastins Custom Fabricating LLC............ G 765 987-8385
  Knightstown (G-10193)
Beck Industries LP................................. D 574 294-5621
  Elkhart (G-3221)
Bedford Crane Service LLC................... F 812 275-4411
  Bedford (G-622)
Benchmark Inc.. F 812 238-0659
  Terre Haute (G-15551)
Bent Industrial Services LLC.................. G 260 352-0106
  Silver Lake (G-14917)
Big Inch Fabricators Cnstr Inc................ D 765 245-9353
  Montezuma (G-12081)
Bills Gar & Auto Refinishing................... G 765 296-4978
  Lafayette (G-10537)
Bombtrack Fabrication............................ G 317 286-7711
  Brownsburg (G-1352)
Brad Bugher... G 765 883-8112
  Russiaville (G-14421)
Brahm Corporation................................. G 317 502-3133
  Carmel (G-1572)
Bralin Laser Services Inc....................... E 260 357-6511
  Auburn (G-370)
Buchanan Iron Works Inc....................... G 219 785-4480
  Westville (G-16757)
Buhrt Engineering & Cnstr..................... E 574 267-3720
  Warsaw (G-16331)
Builders Iron Works Inc......................... E 574 254-1553
  Mishawaka (G-11854)
C & C Iron Inc.. E 219 769-2511
  Merrillville (G-11495)
C & P Engineering and Mfg Inc............... F 765 825-4293
  Connersville (G-2430)

34 FABRICATED METAL PRODUCTS

C Fabco/L Inc... F 219 785-4181
　La Porte (G-10392)
C&W Fabrication LLC................................. D 812 282-0488
　Jeffersonville (G-9949)
▲ CAM Metal Fabrication LLC.................... G 260 982-6280
　North Manchester (G-13230)
Central Illinois Steel Company.................. G 219 882-1026
　Gary (G-5915)
Central States Fabricating........................ F 574 288-5607
　South Bend (G-14970)
Central States Mfg Inc............................... C 219 879-4770
　Michigan City (G-11586)
Century Industries LLC.............................. E 812 246-3371
　Sellersburg (G-14590)
Century Steel Fabricating Inc................... F 317 834-1295
　Camby (G-1508)
Chief Industries Inc................................... C 219 866-4121
　Rensselaer (G-14047)
Circle City Rebar LLC................................ F 317 917-8566
　Indianapolis (G-7806)
Cives Corporation..................................... C 219 279-4000
　Wolcott (G-16927)
Coffee Lomont & Moyer Inc..................... F 260 422-7825
　Fort Wayne (G-4865)
Craig Welding and Mfg Inc....................... E 574 353-7912
　Mentone (G-11472)
Crossrads Rhbilitation Ctr Inc.................. C 317 897-7320
　Indianapolis (G-7910)
Crow Welding and Fabrication................. G 317 619-3190
　Indianapolis (G-7913)
Crown Mtal Fbricators Erectors............... G 219 661-8277
　Crown Point (G-2669)
Cryogenic Support Systems Inc.............. F 765 764-4961
　Williamsport (G-16846)
▲ Crystal Industries Inc............................. E 574 264-6166
　Elkhart (G-3276)
D & M Systems Inc.................................... G 812 327-2384
　Owensboro (G-13461)
D A Hochstetler & Sons LLP.................... F 574 642-1144
　Topeka (G-15800)
Dalex Fbrication Machining Inc.............. F 812 232-7081
　Terre Haute (G-15574)
Davenport Mfg Group LLC....................... E 260 495-1818
　Fremont (G-5819)
Deer Creek Custom LLC........................... G 812 719-5902
　Tell City (G-15499)
Deg Corp... F 219 663-7900
　Crown Point (G-2675)
Deister Machine Company Inc................ E 260 422-0354
　Fort Wayne (G-4912)
Delbert M Dawson and Son Inc............... G 765 284-9711
　Muncie (G-12381)
Delphi Body Works.................................. F 765 564-2212
　Delphi (G-2893)
▲ DH Machine Inc...................................... D 574 773-9211
　Nappanee (G-12594)
Diamond Waterjet..................................... G 219 713-1727
　East Chicago (G-3003)
Die-Mensional Metal Stampg Inc........... F 812 265-3946
　Madison (G-11213)
Direct Innovations LLC............................. G 812 343-6085
　Columbus (G-2284)
Dpc Inc.. E 765 564-3752
　Delphi (G-2895)
Drinan Racing Products Inc.................... G 317 486-9710
　Indianapolis (G-8008)
Dynamic Fabrication LLC......................... G 812 305-5576
　Evansville (G-4022)
Dynamic Fabrication LLC......................... G 812 305-5576
　Evansville (G-4023)
Dynamic Industrial Group LLC................ E 574 295-5525
　Elkhart (G-3309)

▼ Dynamic Metals LLC.............................. E 574 262-2497
　Elkhart (G-3310)
E & H Bridge Inc....................................... G 812 279-2308
　Bedford (G-633)
◆ Ebc LLC.. E 812 234-4111
　Terre Haute (G-15581)
Edge Manufacturing Inc........................... E 260 827-0482
　Bluffton (G-1035)
Edgewood Metal Fab LLC........................ G 574 546-5947
　Bremen (G-1190)
Eje Industries LLC.................................... G 574 326-3269
　Elkhart (G-3315)
◆ Electronics Research Inc....................... C 812 925-6000
　Chandler (G-1861)
Elevator Equipment Corporation............. D 765 966-7761
　Richmond (G-14119)
Elixir Industries.. F 574 259-7133
　Mishawaka (G-11892)
Emergency Radio Service LLC................ G 800 377-2929
　Ligonier (G-11011)
Emergency Radio Service LLC................ E 206 894-4145
　Ligonier (G-11012)
Engineered Conveyors Inc....................... G 765 459-4545
　Kokomo (G-10263)
▲ Ernstberger Enterprises Inc.................. D 812 282-0488
　Jeffersonville (G-9981)
Ers Holding Company Inc....................... G 260 894-4145
　Ligonier (G-11013)
Ers Tower LLC.. E 260 894-4145
　Ligonier (G-11014)
Eta Fabrication Inc................................... G 260 897-3711
　Avilla (G-476)
Eti Fab Inc... G 574 233-1202
　Westfield (G-16688)
Evans Metal Products Co Inc.................. F 574 264-2166
　Elkhart (G-3335)
Fab-Tech Industries Inc........................... G 765 478-4191
　Cambridge City (G-1494)
Fabricated Metals Corp........................... G 219 734-6896
　Chesterton (G-1925)
Fabricated Metals Corp........................... G 219 871-0230
　Michigan City (G-11609)
Fabricated Steel Corporation.................. G 317 899-0012
　Indianapolis (G-8162)
Fabtron Corporation................................ G 260 925-5770
　Auburn (G-390)
Farm Fab... G 574 862-4775
　Goshen (G-6133)
Fasttimes Fabrication Cus...................... G 574 858-9222
　Etna Green (G-3848)
Faulkner Fabricating Inc.......................... E 574 342-0022
　Bourbon (G-1121)
First Metals & Plastics Inc...................... E 812 379-4400
　Columbus (G-2307)
Five Star Fab & Erectors LLC................. G 812 614-9558
　Greensburg (G-6593)
Four Star Fabricators Inc........................ D 812 354-9995
　Petersburg (G-13612)
G & H Diversified Mfg LP........................ E 713 849-2111
　Indianapolis (G-8251)
Gannon Mtal Fbrcators Erectors............ G 219 398-0299
　East Chicago (G-3009)
Gary Bridge and Iron Co Inc................... G 219 884-3792
　Gary (G-5936)
Gary Ratcliff... G 765 538-3170
　Lafayette (G-10587)
Garys Welding & Machining LLC............ G 812 279-6780
　Bedford (G-637)
Geiger & Peters Inc.................................. D 317 322-7740
　Indianapolis (G-8266)
Gem-Rose Corporation............................ G 317 773-6400
　Noblesville (G-13084)

General Mch & Saw Co of Ind................. F 574 232-6077
　South Bend (G-15041)
GI Properties Inc...................................... G 219 763-1177
　Portage (G-13868)
Graber Steel & Fab LLC........................... E 812 636-8418
　Odon (G-13338)
Grant County Steel Inc............................ F 765 668-7547
　Marion (G-11290)
Greensgroomer Worldwide Inc............... G 317 388-0695
　Indianapolis (G-8323)
Greensgroomer Worldwide Inc............... G 317 388-0695
　Indianapolis (G-8324)
GTC Machining LLC................................. G 317 541-1400
　Indianapolis (G-8339)
H & R Industrial LLC................................ D 765 868-8408
　Kokomo (G-10275)
Hamilton Iron Works Inc......................... G 574 533-3784
　Goshen (G-6160)
Hammond Group Inc................................ E 219 845-0031
　Hammond (G-6940)
Harpring Steel Inc.................................... G 812 256-6326
　Charlestown (G-1878)
Heidtman Steel Products Inc.................. D 419 691-4646
　Butler (G-1465)
Helgeson Steel Inc................................... F 574 293-5576
　Elkhart (G-3403)
High Value Metal Inc................................ G 812 522-6468
　Seymour (G-14657)
Highball Fabricators LLC......................... G 574 831-6647
　New Paris (G-12957)
Horner Industrial Services Inc................ F 317 634-7165
　Indianapolis (G-8418)
Huntington Sheet Metal Inc.................... F 260 356-9011
　Huntington (G-7324)
Igh Steel Fabrication Inc......................... D 765 482-7534
　Lebanon (G-10901)
Imagine Metals... G 574 971-3902
　Goshen (G-6171)
▲ Imperial Stamping Corporation............. D 574 294-3780
　Elkhart (G-3419)
In-Fab Inc.. G 812 279-8144
　Bedford (G-642)
Indiana Bridge Inc.................................... D 765 288-1985
　Muncie (G-12424)
Indiana Cast Metals Assn Inc................. G 317 974-1830
　Indianapolis (G-8475)
Indiana Custom Fabrication Inc............. G 812 727-8900
　Hope (G-7227)
▼ Indiana Gratings Inc............................... F 765 342-7191
　Martinsville (G-11404)
Indiana Steel & Engrg Inc....................... E 812 275-3363
　Bedford (G-647)
Indiana Steel Fabricating Inc.................. F 765 742-1031
　Lafayette (G-10606)
Indiana Steel Fabricating Inc.................. E 317 247-4545
　Indianapolis (G-8495)
▲ Indianapolis Fabrications LLC.............. F 317 600-3522
　Indianapolis (G-8504)
▲ Industrial Metal-Fab Inc........................ E 574 288-8368
　South Bend (G-15080)
Industrial Steel and Sup Corp................ G 219 865-0500
　Schererville (G-14524)
Industrial Steel Cnstr Inc........................ C 219 885-5610
　Gary (G-5962)
▲ Industrial Transmission Eqp................. E 574 936-3028
　Plymouth (G-13785)
Integrity Defense Services Inc............... E 812 675-4913
　Springville (G-15387)
Interebar Fabricators LLC....................... F 630 701-9204
　Hammond (G-6957)
Interstate Steel Erectors Inc................... F 765 754-7508
　Frankton (G-5792)

SIC SECTION
34 FABRICATED METAL PRODUCTS

Ironworks Engineering LLC................ G 317 296-9359
　New Palestine *(G-12940)*

J & J Boat Works Inc............................ G 812 667-5902
　Madison *(G-11231)*

J A Smit Inc... G 812 424-8141
　Evansville *(G-4133)*

J Coffey Metal Masters Inc.................. D 317 780-1864
　Indianapolis *(G-8604)*

J L Squared Inc..................................... G 317 354-1513
　Indianapolis *(G-8606)*

Jasper Equipment Company LLC........ G 219 866-0600
　Rensselaer *(G-14055)*

Jerico Metal Specialties Inc................. F 812 339-3182
　Bloomington *(G-897)*

Jezroc Metalworks LLC........................ G 317 417-1132
　Zionsville *(G-17024)*

JI 2 Incorporated................................... F 317 783-3340
　Indianapolis *(G-8627)*

JL Walter & Associates Inc.................. D 317 524-3600
　Indianapolis *(G-8628)*

Just For Granite LLC............................ G 317 842-8255
　Indianapolis *(G-8649)*

K-K Tool and Design Inc...................... E 260 758-2940
　Markle *(G-11356)*

Kammerer Dynamics Inc...................... F 260 349-9098
　Kendallville *(G-10122)*

Kammerer Inc.. F 260 347-0389
　Kendallville *(G-10123)*

Keller Machine & Welding Inc............. E 219 464-4915
　Valparaiso *(G-15986)*

Kenley Corporation............................... G 765 825-7150
　Connersville *(G-2452)*

Kennedy Metal Products Inc................ F 219 322-9388
　Schererville *(G-14527)*

Keppler Steel and Fabricating............. F 765 289-1529
　Muncie *(G-12434)*

Kirby Tool and Die Inc.......................... G 812 369-7779
　Solsberry *(G-14926)*

Kokomo Metal Fabricators Inc............ G 765 459-8173
　Kokomo *(G-10292)*

L & W Engineering Inc.......................... C 574 825-5351
　Middlebury *(G-11730)*

Lacay Fabrication and Mfg Inc............ E 574 288-4678
　Elkhart *(G-3465)*

Lakemaster Inc..................................... F 765 288-3718
　Muncie *(G-12437)*

▲ Lawrence Cnty Fabrication Corp..... E 812 849-0124
　Mitchell *(G-12043)*

Lawrenco Steel Inc............................... G 812 466-7115
　Terre Haute *(G-15631)*

Lenex Steel Company........................... G 317 818-1622
　Indianapolis *(G-8738)*

Leons Fabrication Inc........................... F 219 365-5272
　Schererville *(G-14528)*

Lippert Components Inc....................... F 574 537-8900
　Goshen *(G-6203)*

Loughmiller Mch Tl Design Inc............ E 812 295-3903
　Loogootee *(G-11144)*

LSI Metal Fabrication Inc..................... E 574 722-3101
　Logansport *(G-11092)*

Lt Metal Masters Inc............................. F 317 780-1864
　Indianapolis *(G-8792)*

M & S Indus Met Fbricators Inc........... D 260 356-0300
　Huntington *(G-7339)*

◆ M & S Steel Corp.............................. E 260 357-5184
　Garrett *(G-5869)*

M&M Fabrication LLC........................... E 812 692-5511
　Bicknell *(G-735)*

Mak Steel Services LLC....................... G 812 525-8879
　Seymour *(G-14667)*

Manchester Inc...................................... G 260 982-2202
　Roann *(G-14252)*

Marine Builders Inc............................... D 812 283-7932
　Jeffersonville *(G-10016)*

Marion Metal Products Inc.................. F 765 662-8333
　Marion *(G-11313)*

Marion Steel Fabrication Inc............... E 765 664-1478
　Marion *(G-11315)*

Marion Steel Fabrication Inc............... F 765 664-1478
　Marion *(G-11316)*

◆ Marson International LLC................ D 574 295-4222
　Elkhart *(G-3515)*

Massey-Null Inc..................................... E 260 447-7900
　Fort Wayne *(G-5204)*

McCombs Fabrication LLC................... G 765 265-0594
　Connersville *(G-2455)*

Metafab.. G 317 217-1546
　Indianapolis *(G-8883)*

▲ Metal Dynamics Ltd......................... E 812 949-7998
　New Albany *(G-12775)*

Metal Fabricators Plus LLC................. G 317 757-3672
　Indianapolis *(G-8884)*

Metal Masters Inc................................. G 812 421-9162
　Evansville *(G-4198)*

Metal Solutions Inc.............................. F 317 781-6734
　Indianapolis *(G-8888)*

Metal Technologies Inc........................ E 812 384-9800
　Bloomfield *(G-751)*

▲ Metal Technologies Inc................... D 812 384-9800
　Auburn *(G-406)*

▲ Metaltec Inc...................................... G 219 362-9811
　La Porte *(G-10452)*

Mettle Holdings Incorporated.............. E 260 447-3880
　Fort Wayne *(G-5217)*

◆ Mid-West Metal Products Co Inc.... E 888 741-1044
　Muncie *(G-12454)*

Midwest Indus Met Fbrction Inc.......... E 260 356-5262
　Huntington *(G-7342)*

Midwest Industrial Metal...................... G 260 358-0373
　Huntington *(G-7343)*

Miller Mfg Corp..................................... E 574 773-4136
　Nappanee *(G-12626)*

Miller Steel Fabricators....................... E 260 768-7321
　Shipshewana *(G-14868)*

Millmark Enterprises Inc...................... F 574 389-9904
　Elkhart *(G-3544)*

Millwright Riggers Inc (mri)................. E 765 673-4000
　Marion *(G-11319)*

Mirage Computers Inc.......................... G 260 665-5072
　Angola *(G-276)*

Mofab Inc... G 765 649-1288
　Anderson *(G-158)*

Mofab Inc... E 765 649-5577
　Anderson *(G-159)*

Morse Metal Fab Inc............................. F 574 674-6237
　Granger *(G-6364)*

Mr2 Performance LLC.......................... G 765 483-9371
　Lebanon *(G-10921)*

Munster Steel Co Inc............................ E 219 924-5198
　Hammond *(G-6984)*

Murphy Mill Services LLC.................... G 219 246-9290
　Valparaiso *(G-16006)*

◆ Nello Inc.. F 574 288-3632
　South Bend *(G-15161)*

New Millennium Bldg Systems LLC..... C 260 868-6000
　Butler *(G-1473)*

▼ New Millennium Bldg Systems LLC... G 260 969-3500
　Fort Wayne *(G-5267)*

New Nello Operating Co LLC............... C 574 288-3632
　South Bend *(G-15166)*

Nightkrawler Kustoms LLC................. G 812 599-0251
　Paris Crossing *(G-13503)*

Noble County Welding Inc................... F 260 897-4082
　Avilla *(G-490)*

Northwest Alum Fabricators Inc.......... G 219 844-4354
　Hammond *(G-6987)*

Northwest Ind Fabrication LLC........... F 219 613-7461
　Merrillville *(G-11548)*

Nucor Rebar Fabrication S LLC.......... D 260 925-5440
　Auburn *(G-414)*

▲ Ottenweller Co Inc........................... C 260 484-3166
　Fort Wayne *(G-5289)*

P & E Products...................................... G 765 969-2644
　Connersville *(G-2459)*

P H Drew Incorporated......................... E 317 297-5152
　Indianapolis *(G-9080)*

Palladin Services Inc............................ G 317 745-6741
　Danville *(G-2823)*

▲ Penz Inc.. E 574 255-4736
　Mishawaka *(G-11974)*

▲ Porter Systems Inc.......................... F 519 737-1678
　Westfield *(G-16718)*

▲ Poseidon LLC.................................... C 260 422-8767
　Berne *(G-722)*

Precision Fabrication Inc..................... F 260 422-4448
　Fort Wayne *(G-5337)*

Precision Surveillance Corp................ E 219 397-4295
　East Chicago *(G-3035)*

Precision Technologies I LLC.............. F 260 668-7500
　Angola *(G-288)*

Preferred Tank & Tower Inc................. E 270 826-7950
　Evansville *(G-4256)*

Prestress Services Inc......................... C 260 724-7117
　Decatur *(G-2877)*

Priority Steel Indus Contg LLC........... E 937 626-4361
　Greendale *(G-6453)*

◆ Process Development & Fab............ C 812 443-6000
　Brazil *(G-1163)*

Productivity Fabricators Inc................ F 765 966-2896
　Richmond *(G-14187)*

Profab Custom Metal Works Inc......... G 812 865-3999
　Orleans *(G-13380)*

Prokuma Incorporated.......................... F 812 461-1681
　Evansville *(G-4261)*

Pwi Corp... E 574 646-2015
　Nappanee *(G-12638)*

Quality Fabrication Ind Inc.................. F 765 529-9776
　New Castle *(G-12880)*

Quikcut LLC.. E 260 447-3880
　Fort Wayne *(G-5363)*

RAD Fabrication Llc............................. E 317 903-0065
　Indianapolis *(G-9261)*

Reeves Manufacturing Inc................... G 765 935-3875
　Richmond *(G-14196)*

Refax Inc.. C 219 977-0414
　Gary *(G-6002)*

Refax Wear Products Inc..................... F 219 977-0414
　Gary *(G-6003)*

Reiss Orna & Structurall Pdts............. E 317 925-2371
　Indianapolis *(G-9285)*

Rex Alton & Companies Inc................ F 812 882-8519
　Vincennes *(G-16149)*

Rf Manufacturing Inc........................... G 317 773-8610
　Noblesville *(G-13167)*

Right Angle Stl Fbrication Inc............. G 574 862-2432
　Wakarusa *(G-16248)*

◆ Ring-R Inc... E 260 565-3347
　Decatur *(G-2882)*

Robert D Meadows................................ G 812 797-8294
　Bedford *(G-670)*

Ronard Industries Inc........................... F 219 874-4801
　Michigan City *(G-11658)*

S&K Sheet Metal LLC........................... G 260 623-3398
　Monroeville *(G-12074)*

Sabre Integrated Services................... G 317 844-9100
　Indianapolis *(G-9361)*

Employee Codes: A=Over 500 employees, B=251-500
C=101-250, D=51-100, E=20-50, F=10-19, G=1-9

2024 Harris Indiana
Industrial Directory

34 FABRICATED METAL PRODUCTS

San Jo Steel Inc .... F 317 888-6227
  Greenwood (G-6766)
Sanbar of Indiana Inc .... G 317 375-6220
  Indianapolis (G-9369)
Schmidt Contracting Inc .... E 812 482-3923
  Jasper (G-9908)
Schrock Metal Fab LLC .... G 574 825-5653
  Middlebury (G-11748)
Schuckers Orna Ir Works Co .... G 812 422-7057
  Evansville (G-4299)
Schuler Precision Tool LLC .... G 260 982-2704
  North Manchester (G-13249)
Scott Steel Services Inc .... G 219 663-4740
  Crown Point (G-2749)
Seiler & Sons .... G 812 858-9598
  Newburgh (G-13020)
Sellersburg Metals & Wldg Co .... F 812 248-0811
  Sellersburg (G-14613)
Service Steel Framing Inc .... F 260 868-5853
  Butler (G-1476)
Shank Welding Inc .... G 260 897-2068
  Avilla (G-495)
Shape Shifters Inc .... G 812 400-0580
  Bloomfield (G-757)
Sigma Steel Inc .... E 812 275-4489
  Bedford (G-672)
Simko Industrial Fabricators .... E 219 933-9100
  Hammond (G-7008)
Sinden Racing Service Inc .... F 317 243-7171
  Indianapolis (G-9443)
Sisson Steel Inc .... F 812 354-8701
  Winslow (G-16922)
Smartt Innovations Inc .... F 574 266-5432
  Elkhart (G-3685)
Smco Inc .... E 574 295-1482
  Elkhart (G-3686)
Smgf LLC .... E 812 354-8899
  Petersburg (G-13625)
SMS Group Inc .... E 219 880-0256
  Gary (G-6012)
Special Fabrication Services .... G 812 384-5384
  Elnora (G-3816)
Specilty Stnless Stl Fbrction .... G 317 430-3490
  Indianapolis (G-9473)
Specilty Stnless Stl Fbrction .... G 317 337-9800
  Indianapolis (G-9474)
Spreuer & Son Inc .... F 260 463-3513
  Lagrange (G-10763)
Staab Sheet Metal Inc .... G 317 241-2553
  Indianapolis (G-9488)
Stahl Equipment Inc .... F 812 925-3341
  Gentryville (G-6053)
Steel Services Inc .... G 317 783-5255
  Indianapolis (G-9501)
Steel Tank & Fabricating Corp .... E 260 248-8971
  Columbia City (G-2203)
▲ Steeltech Partners LLC .... G 812 849-0124
  Mitchell (G-12049)
Sterling Industrial LLC .... C 812 423-7832
  Evansville (G-4333)
Stone City Ironworks Inc .... E 812 279-3023
  Bedford (G-675)
Structral Cmpnnts Fbrction Inc .... F 765 342-9188
  Martinsville (G-11429)
Structural Iron & Fab Inc .... G 260 758-2273
  Markle (G-11363)
Superior Equipment & Mfg .... G 260 925-0152
  Auburn (G-427)
Superior Layout .... G 812 371-1709
  Columbus (G-2399)
Swager Communications Inc .... E 260 495-2515
  Fremont (G-5837)

Swan Real Estate Mgmt Inc .... G 765 664-1478
  Marion (G-11341)
Tank Construction & Service Co .... F 317 509-6294
  Whitestown (G-16823)
Tefft Bridge and Iron LLC .... E 219 828-4011
  Wheatfield (G-16773)
Thomas Cubit Inc .... G 219 933-0566
  Hammond (G-7019)
Titus Inc .... F 574 936-3345
  Plymouth (G-13817)
Todds Wldg & Stl Fabrication .... G 812 824-2407
  Bloomington (G-990)
Tradeline Fabricating Inc .... E 812 637-1444
  Lawrenceburg (G-10862)
Traylor Industrial LLC .... C 812 428-3708
  Evansville (G-4348)
Trek Pools LLC .... G 317 896-0493
  New Castle (G-12883)
Tri-State Mechanical Inc .... F 260 471-0345
  Fort Wayne (G-5506)
Triton Metal Products Inc .... E 260 488-1800
  Hamilton (G-6863)
Tron Mechanical Incorporated .... C 812 838-4715
  Mount Vernon (G-12324)
Tru-Form Steel & Wire Inc .... F 765 348-5001
  Hartford City (G-7079)
▲ Tru-Form Steel & Wire Inc .... E 765 348-5001
  Hartford City (G-7078)
Trufab Stainless Inc .... F 812 287-8278
  Bloomington (G-994)
Tube Processing Corp .... C 317 782-9486
  Indianapolis (G-9656)
Unison Engine Components Inc .... C 904 739-4000
  Terre Haute (G-15738)
United States Steel Corp .... G 219 888-2000
  Gary (G-6023)
Universal Door Carrier Inc .... G 317 241-3447
  Indianapolis (G-9682)
Usw Lu 6103-07 .... G 219 762-4433
  Portage (G-13918)
Valmont Industries Inc .... D 574 295-6942
  Elkhart (G-3767)
Valmont Telecommunications Inc .... F 877 467-4763
  Plymouth (G-13824)
◆ Valmont Telecommunications Inc ...... F 574 936-7221
  Plymouth (G-13823)
Vandergriff & Associates Inc .... G 812 422-6033
  Evansville (G-4367)
Vans Industrial Inc .... E 219 931-4881
  Hammond (G-7028)
Varied Products Indiana Inc .... E 219 763-2526
  Chesterton (G-1966)
Vertical Steel Maintenance LLC .... G 912 710-0626
  Indianapolis (G-9711)
Veterans Fabrication LLC .... G 317 604-7704
  Fishers (G-4629)
Vidimos Inc .... D 219 397-2728
  East Chicago (G-3054)
Viewrail .... E 574 742-1030
  Goshen (G-6274)
Vincennes Welding Co Inc .... F 812 882-9682
  Vincennes (G-16160)
Wabash Steel LLC .... G 317 818-1622
  Vincennes (G-16162)
Wabash Welding Services Inc .... G 260 563-2363
  Wabash (G-16223)
Waka Manufacturing Inc .... G 574 258-0019
  Mishawaka (G-12025)
Ware Industries Inc .... F 219 378-7100
  East Chicago (G-3056)
Washington and Scoville .... G 317 798-2911
  Indianapolis (G-9738)

Wayne Steel Supply Inc .... E 260 489-6249
  Fort Wayne (G-5554)
Westfield Steel Inc .... G 812 466-3500
  Terre Haute (G-15745)
Westlund Concepts .... F 317 819-0611
  Lapel (G-10818)
Wick - Fab Inc .... E 260 897-3303
  Avilla (G-499)
Willoughby Industries Inc .... C 317 875-0830
  Indianapolis (G-9770)
Wiw Inc .... E 219 663-7900
  Crown Point (G-2774)
Wnt .... G 260 440-0485
  Fort Wayne (G-5573)
Worthington Industries Inc .... E 219 465-6107
  Greensburg (G-6643)
Wrib Manufacturing Inc .... G 765 294-2841
  Veedersburg (G-16092)
Ynwa Industries Inc .... D 574 295-6641
  Elkhart (G-3800)
▲ Zieman Manufacturing Comp .... C 574 535-1125
  Goshen (G-6279)

3442 Metal doors, sash, and trim

▼ A & A Sheet Metal Products .... D 219 326-1288
  La Porte (G-10371)
A Shutter In Time LLC .... G 317 512-6753
  Manilla (G-11259)
▲ Advantage Manufacturing Inc .... F 773 626-2200
  South Bend (G-14936)
All-Weather Products Inc .... G 812 867-6403
  Evansville (G-3880)
American Window and Glass Inc .... C 812 464-9400
  Evansville (G-3886)
Architctral Opning Cnslting LL .... G 502 836-5545
  Otisco (G-13446)
Assa Abloy Door Group LLC .... G 800 826-2617
  Elkhart (G-3197)
Classee Vinyl Windows LLC .... G 574 825-7863
  Middlebury (G-11703)
Cleer Vision Windows Inc .... E 574 262-0449
  Elkhart (G-3254)
Crossroads Door & Hardware Inc .... G 812 234-9751
  Terre Haute (G-15570)
Davis Exteriors Inc .... G 260 786-1600
  Andrews (G-221)
◆ Dexter Axle Company LLC .... D 574 295-7888
  Elkhart (G-3292)
Door Service Supply .... G 317 496-0391
  Greenwood (G-6689)
Ecpca Safe-Way LLC .... D 574 267-4861
  Warsaw (G-16354)
Evansville Metal Products Inc .... D 812 423-5632
  Evansville (G-4054)
Global Building Products LLC .... E 574 296-6868
  Elkhart (G-3379)
Graber Thermoloc Windows LLC .... G 812 486-3273
  Montgomery (G-12099)
HB International LLC .... G 574 773-8200
  Nappanee (G-12604)
HB International LLC .... D 574 773-0470
  Nappanee (G-12605)
Heartland Shutter Company LLC .... G 317 710-3350
  Indianapolis (G-8378)
▲ Home Guard Industries Inc .... D 260 627-6060
  Grabill (G-6302)
◆ House of Fara Incorporated .... D 219 362-8544
  La Porte (G-10422)
Ilpea Industries Inc .... D 812 752-2526
  Scottsburg (G-14561)
▲ Imperial Products LLC .... E 765 966-0322
  Richmond (G-14138)

SIC SECTION
34 FABRICATED METAL PRODUCTS

▲ International Steel Company............ D 812 425-3311
   Evansville *(G-4130)*

Invign LLC.. G 574 971-5498
   Goshen *(G-6176)*

IRD Group Inc..................................... E 812 425-3311
   Evansville *(G-4131)*

Jason Incorporated............................. D 765 965-5333
   Richmond *(G-14149)*

Kinro Manufacturing Inc..................... C 803 385-5171
   Elkhart *(G-3455)*

Kinro Manufacturing Inc..................... E 574 535-1125
   Elkhart *(G-3456)*

▲ Kinro Manufacturing Inc................. E 574 535-1125
   Elkhart *(G-3457)*

Lazzaro Companies Inc...................... E 219 980-0860
   Merrillville *(G-11529)*

LCI Industries..................................... A 574 535-1125
   Elkhart *(G-3476)*

Maher Supply Inc................................ G 812 234-7699
   Terre Haute *(G-15635)*

Marner Door Manufacturing LLC....... F 812 486-3128
   Montgomery *(G-12112)*

Meridian Metalform Inc....................... G 812 422-1524
   Evansville *(G-4196)*

▲ Modern Door Corporation.............. D 574 586-3117
   Walkerton *(G-16271)*

Multiple Resource Solution................ G 317 862-2584
   Indianapolis *(G-8972)*

Mx5 & Associates Inc........................ F 574 226-0733
   Elkhart *(G-3561)*

Patrick Industries Inc......................... F 574 295-5206
   Elkhart *(G-3588)*

Quanex Homeshield LLC.................... E 765 966-0322
   Richmond *(G-14194)*

Reeds Plastic Tops Inc....................... G 765 282-1471
   Muncie *(G-12486)*

Safe-Way Garage Doors LLC.............. E 574 267-4861
   Warsaw *(G-16420)*

Sun Control Center LLC..................... F 260 490-9902
   Fort Wayne *(G-5456)*

Syracuse Glass Inc............................ G 574 457-5516
   Syracuse *(G-15482)*

Therma-Tru Corp................................. F 260 562-1009
   Howe *(G-7243)*

Trim-A-Seal of Indiana Inc................. F 219 883-2180
   Gary *(G-6022)*

Universal Door Carrier Inc................. G 317 241-3447
   Indianapolis *(G-9682)*

▲ Worldwide Door Cmpnnts Ind Inc.. G 219 992-9225
   Lake Village *(G-10785)*

3443 Fabricated plate work (boiler shop)

A & B Fabricating & Maint Inc............ F 574 353-1012
   Mentone *(G-11468)*

▲ Abtrex Industries Inc..................... F 734 728-0550
   South Bend *(G-14934)*

Ace Welding and Machine Inc............ G 812 379-9625
   Columbus *(G-2213)*

Acra-Line Products Inc...................... F 765 675-8841
   Tipton *(G-15763)*

Advantage Engineering Inc................ D 317 887-0729
   Greenwood *(G-6660)*

Aearo Technologies LLC..................... C 317 692-6666
   Indianapolis *(G-7447)*

▼ Alloy Custom Products LLC........... D 765 564-4684
   Lafayette *(G-10520)*

Aluminum Wldg & Mch Works Inc...... G 219 787-8066
   Chesterton *(G-1901)*

Amsted Rail International Inc............. G 800 621-8442
   Hammond *(G-6878)*

Apex Engineered Entps LLC.............. G 317 346-7148
   Franklin *(G-5710)*

Armor Products Inc............................ C 502 228-1458
   Madison *(G-11202)*

Arrow Metals Inc................................. E 765 825-4443
   Connersville *(G-2426)*

◆ Asphalt Equipment Company Inc.... E 260 672-3004
   Fort Wayne *(G-4775)*

Assurance Waste Management LLC.. G 765 341-4431
   Cloverdale *(G-2082)*

Axis Unlimited LLC............................. G 574 370-8923
   Elkhart *(G-3208)*

▼ Banks Machine & Engrg LLC......... D 317 642-4980
   Shelbyville *(G-14732)*

▲ Batesville Products Inc.................. D 513 381-2057
   Lawrenceburg *(G-10831)*

Beck Industries LP............................. D 574 294-5621
   Elkhart *(G-3221)*

Buhrt Engineering & Cnstr.................. E 574 267-3720
   Warsaw *(G-16331)*

Bulk Truck & Transport Service......... G 812 866-2155
   Hanover *(G-7040)*

Caliente LLC....................................... E 260 426-3800
   Fort Wayne *(G-4830)*

Carmel Engineering Inc...................... F 765 279-8955
   Kirklin *(G-10187)*

Chart Lifecycle Inc............................. F 317 535-4315
   Franklin *(G-5719)*

Chegar Manufacturing Company....... E 765 945-7444
   Windfall *(G-16904)*

Codeweld Inc...................................... G 317 784-4140
   Indianapolis *(G-7831)*

Coffee Lomont & Moyer Inc............... F 260 422-7825
   Fort Wayne *(G-4865)*

Contech Engnered Solutions LLC..... G 317 407-4914
   Fishers *(G-4494)*

Contech Engnered Solutions LLC..... F 317 842-7766
   Indianapolis *(G-7856)*

Contech Engnered Solutions LLC..... G 812 849-3933
   Mitchell *(G-12036)*

Contech Engnered Solutions LLC..... G 812 849-3933
   Mitchell *(G-12037)*

Cooper-Standard Automotive Inc....... E 574 546-5938
   Bremen *(G-1181)*

Cooper-Standard Automotive Inc....... E 260 593-2156
   Topeka *(G-15798)*

Ctb Inc.. G 574 658-4191
   Milford *(G-11789)*

◆ Ctb Inc... A 574 658-4191
   Milford *(G-11790)*

CTB Inc Employee Benefit Tr A.......... F 574 658-5132
   Milford *(G-11792)*

◆ CTB International Corp.................. G 574 658-9431
   Milford *(G-11793)*

◆ CTB MN Investment Co Inc........... E 574 658-4191
   Milford *(G-11794)*

D & T Tool Special Machine................ G 260 597-7216
   Ossian *(G-13422)*

Dads Custom Intercooler Tanks........ G 765 243-9070
   Van Buren *(G-16084)*

Dietrich Industries Inc........................ C 219 931-6344
   Hammond *(G-6913)*

Don R Fruchey Inc............................... E 260 493-3626
   Fort Wayne *(G-4923)*

Douglas Dumpster and Svcs LLC..... G 630 460-8727
   Portage *(G-13859)*

Dpc Inc... E 765 564-3752
   Delphi *(G-2895)*

▲ Dragon ESP Ltd.............................. E 574 893-1569
   Akron *(G-4)*

Dx 4 LLC... F 260 749-0632
   Fort Wayne *(G-4935)*

Dyna-Fab Corporation....................... E 765 893-4423
   West Lebanon *(G-16647)*

E-Tank Ltd... F 317 296-0510
   Indianapolis *(G-8030)*

◆ Eclipse Inc......................................D
   Muncie *(G-12389)*

Elsie Manufacturing Company........... G 260 837-8841
   Waterloo *(G-16519)*

Erapsco.. G 386 740-5361
   Columbia City *(G-2142)*

Estes Waste Solutions LLC............... F 812 283-6400
   Jeffersonville *(G-9982)*

Fabstar Inc.. F 765 230-0261
   Cayuga *(G-1821)*

Four Star Fabricators Inc................... D 812 354-9995
   Petersburg *(G-13612)*

◆ Galbreath LLC................................. E 219 946-6631
   Winamac *(G-16860)*

Galfab LLC... F 574 946-7767
   Winamac *(G-16861)*

Gldn Rule Truss & Metal Sales........... G 812 866-1800
   Lexington *(G-10976)*

Goudy Bros Boiler Co Inc................... G 765 459-4416
   Kokomo *(G-10271)*

Grabill Truss Incorporated................. G 260 627-0933
   Grabill *(G-6301)*

Grant County Steel Inc....................... F 765 668-7547
   Marion *(G-11290)*

▲ Gta Containers LLC....................... E 574 288-3459
   South Bend *(G-15054)*

◆ Hale Industries Inc......................... F 317 577-0337
   Fortville *(G-5598)*

Hammond Machine Works Inc........... E 219 933-0479
   Hammond *(G-6942)*

◆ Heat Exchanger Design Inc............E 317 686-9000
   Indianapolis *(G-8379)*

▼ Hensley Fabricating & Eqp Co....... E 574 498-6514
   Tippecanoe *(G-15760)*

Hmt LLC... G 219 736-9901
   Merrillville *(G-11522)*

Hoosier Tank and Mfg LLC................. D 574 232-8368
   South Bend *(G-15071)*

◆ Howden Compressors Inc..............F 610 313-9800
   Connersville *(G-2441)*

Hunts Maintenance Inc...................... G 219 785-2333
   Westville *(G-16762)*

Industrial Container Svcs LLC........... F 812 283-7659
   Alton *(G-65)*

▲ Industrial Metal-Fab Inc................. E 574 288-8368
   South Bend *(G-15080)*

Industrial Steel Cnstr Inc................... C 219 885-5610
   Gary *(G-5962)*

▲ Industrial Transmission Eqp.......... E 574 936-3028
   Plymouth *(G-13785)*

▲ J & J Welding Inc............................ E 812 838-4391
   Mount Vernon *(G-12303)*

J A Smit Inc.. G 812 424-8141
   Evansville *(G-4133)*

Jason Holdings Inc............................. C 414 277-9300
   Richmond *(G-14147)*

Jlb Industrial LLC............................... G 765 561-1751
   Rushville *(G-14402)*

Kammerer Inc...................................... F 260 347-0389
   Kendallville *(G-10123)*

Kelco Steel Fabrication Inc................ G 317 248-9229
   Indianapolis *(G-8667)*

Kelvion Products Inc.......................... C 865 606-6027
   Indianapolis *(G-8669)*

Kennedy Tank & Mfg Co...................... C 317 787-1311
   Indianapolis *(G-8671)*

Kleerblue Solutions............................ G 800 320-2122
   Evansville *(G-4157)*

Kokomo Metal Fabricators Inc........... G 765 459-8173
   Kokomo *(G-10292)*

34 FABRICATED METAL PRODUCTS

Kuharic Enterprises.................................. G 574 288-9410
  South Bend *(G-15110)*
Kumas Dumpster Rentals LLC.............. G 662 422-1508
  Crown Point *(G-2713)*
Lagrange Products Inc........................... C 260 495-3025
  Fremont *(G-5826)*
Lakeview Engineered Pdts Inc................ G 260 432-3479
  Fort Wayne *(G-5172)*
Lemar Industries Corporat..................... F 515 266-7264
  Milford *(G-11796)*
Leons Fabrication Inc............................. F 219 365-5272
  Schererville *(G-14528)*
Lynn Tool Company Inc........................... G 765 874-2471
  Lynn *(G-11185)*
◆ M & S Steel Corp................................. E 260 357-5184
  Garrett *(G-5869)*
M A C Corporation.................................. D 317 545-3341
  Indianapolis *(G-8803)*
Marion Steel Fabrication Inc.................. E 765 664-1478
  Marion *(G-11315)*
Marion Steel Fabrication Inc.................. F 765 664-1478
  Marion *(G-11316)*
▼ Meese Inc... F 800 829-4535
  Madison *(G-11241)*
◆ Metal Technologies Indiana LLC......... C 260 925-4717
  Auburn *(G-409)*
Mettle Holdings Incorporated................ G 260 447-3880
  Fort Wayne *(G-5218)*
Midwest Metal Solutions Inc................. G 317 769-6489
  Whitestown *(G-16811)*
Miller Mfg Corp....................................... E 574 773-4136
  Nappanee *(G-12626)*
Mobile Disposal..................................... G 260 267-6348
  Fort Wayne *(G-5236)*
Moon Fabricating Corp.......................... E 765 459-4194
  Kokomo *(G-10312)*
Mvp Dumpsters Inc................................ G 317 502-3155
  Pendleton *(G-13545)*
Norman Stein & Associates................... G 260 749-5468
  New Haven *(G-12912)*
▲ Ottenweller Co Inc............................. C 260 484-3166
  Fort Wayne *(G-5289)*
Pacvan Inc... G 317 791-2020
  Indianapolis *(G-9086)*
◆ Par-Kan Company LLC....................... D 260 352-2141
  Silver Lake *(G-14920)*
Pb Metal Works....................................... G 765 489-1311
  Hagerstown *(G-6841)*
Penway Inc.. E 812 526-2645
  Edinburgh *(G-3097)*
Phoenix Fbrcators Erectors LLC............ C 317 271-7002
  Avon *(G-544)*
Precision Cryogenic Systems................ F 317 273-2800
  Indianapolis *(G-9182)*
Precision Tank & Equipment Co............ G 260 894-4002
  Ligonier *(G-11022)*
Production Partners Inc......................... F 574 229-5960
  Mishawaka *(G-11980)*
Quick Tanks Inc...................................... G 260 347-3850
  Kendallville *(G-10145)*
Quick Tanks Inc...................................... D 260 347-3850
  Kendallville *(G-10146)*
Quintel Inc.. E 219 322-3399
  Schererville *(G-14541)*
Randall K Dike.. G 812 664-4942
  Owensville *(G-13471)*
Robinson Steel Co Inc............................ C 219 398-4600
  East Chicago *(G-3040)*
◆ Rogers Engineering and Mfg Co........ E 765 478-5444
  Cambridge City *(G-1503)*
Rolls-Royce Corporation........................ E 317 230-2000
  Indianapolis *(G-9325)*

Rolls-Royce Corporation........................ E 317 230-8515
  West Lafayette *(G-16626)*
Rugged Steel Works LLC........................ F 260 444-4241
  Fort Wayne *(G-5390)*
Sabre Manufacturing LLC....................... C 574 772-5380
  Knox *(G-10222)*
Sigma Steel Inc....................................... E 812 275-4489
  Bedford *(G-672)*
Sisson Steel Inc...................................... F 812 354-8701
  Winslow *(G-16922)*
Sleegers Engineered Pdts Inc............... G 317 786-7770
  Indianapolis *(G-9448)*
◆ Small Parts Inc................................... B 574 753-6323
  Logansport *(G-11107)*
SMS Group Inc.. E 219 880-0256
  Gary *(G-6012)*
Spreuer & Son Inc................................... F 260 463-3513
  Lagrange *(G-10763)*
SPX Corporation..................................... D 219 879-6561
  Michigan City *(G-11671)*
SPX Corporation..................................... G 812 849-5647
  Mitchell *(G-12048)*
Stahl Equipment Co................................ F 812 925-3341
  Gentryville *(G-6053)*
Steel Storage Inc.................................... F 574 282-2618
  South Bend *(G-15268)*
Steel Tank & Fabricating Corp............... E 260 248-8971
  Columbia City *(G-2203)*
Sterling Industrial LLC........................... C 812 423-7832
  Evansville *(G-4333)*
Sterling Industrial LLC........................... C 812 479-5447
  Evansville *(G-4334)*
Summit Manufacturing Corp.................. E 260 428-2600
  Fort Wayne *(G-5453)*
Sun Engineering Inc............................... E 219 962-1191
  Lake Station *(G-10778)*
T J B Inc... G 219 293-8030
  Elkhart *(G-3712)*
Tank Construction & Service Co............ F 317 509-6294
  Whitestown *(G-16823)*
Target Metal Blanking Inc...................... E 812 346-1700
  North Vernon *(G-13298)*
Temptek Inc... G 317 887-6352
  Greenwood *(G-6773)*
Thermax Inc.. E 978 844-2528
  Franklin *(G-5782)*
▲ Thrush Co Inc..................................... E 765 472-3351
  Peru *(G-13604)*
Tishler Industries Inc............................. E 317 581-8811
  Indianapolis *(G-9610)*
Tishler Industries Inc............................. E 765 286-5454
  Muncie *(G-12502)*
Tj Maintenance LLC................................ G 219 776-8427
  Lake Village *(G-10784)*
Troy Meggitt Inc...................................... D 812 547-7071
  Troy *(G-15843)*
▲ Turbonetics Holdings Inc................... E 805 581-0333
  Crown Point *(G-2768)*
Unison Engine Components Inc............ C 904 739-4000
  Terre Haute *(G-15738)*
Varied Products Indiana Inc.................. E 219 763-2526
  Chesterton *(G-1966)*
Versatile Metal Works LLC..................... F 765 754-7470
  Muncie *(G-12512)*
▲ Warsaw Metal Products Inc............... F 574 269-6211
  Pierceton *(G-13642)*
Wayne Metals LLC.................................. D 260 758-3121
  Markle *(G-11364)*
◆ Wessels Company.............................. D 317 888-9800
  Greenwood *(G-6780)*
Wrib Manufacturing Inc.......................... G 765 294-2841
  Veedersburg *(G-16092)*

3444 Sheet metalwork

37 Pipe & Supply LLC............................. G 812 275-5676
  Bedford *(G-615)*
3c Coman Ltd.. G 317 650-5156
  Fortville *(G-5585)*
A & B Fabricating & Maint Inc................ F 574 353-1012
  Mentone *(G-11468)*
A Shade Faster Products LLC............... G 574 584-5744
  Elkhart *(G-3142)*
Accuracy Laser Fabrication LLC........... G 812 322-6431
  Bedford *(G-616)*
Ace Welding and Machine Inc............... G 812 379-9625
  Columbus *(G-2213)*
Ad-Vance Magnetics Inc........................ E 574 223-3158
  Rochester *(G-14274)*
Advanced Mtlwrking Prctces LLC......... G 317 337-0441
  Carmel *(G-1552)*
Advantage Manufacturing LLC.............. G 317 237-4289
  Indianapolis *(G-7444)*
Aearo Technologies LLC........................ C 317 692-6666
  Indianapolis *(G-7447)*
All American Tent & Awning Inc............ E 812 232-4206
  Terre Haute *(G-15537)*
Ameri-Kart Corp...................................... D 225 642-7874
  Bristol *(G-1243)*
American Machine & Fabg Co Inc......... G 812 944-4136
  New Albany *(G-12688)*
Antiques At 200 East LLC...................... E 812 933-0863
  Batesville *(G-579)*
Applied Fabricators Inc......................... G 317 284-0685
  Greenfield *(G-6465)*
Applied Metals & Mch Works Inc.......... E 260 424-4834
  Fort Wayne *(G-4766)*
Arion Roofing & Shtmtl Inc.................... G 317 525-1984
  Frankfort *(G-5650)*
Armor Products Inc................................ C 502 228-1458
  Madison *(G-11202)*
Arrow Metals Inc..................................... E 765 825-4443
  Connersville *(G-2426)*
▲ ASC Industries Inc............................ E 574 264-1987
  Elkhart *(G-3194)*
Atco-Gary Metal Tech LLC..................... F 219 885-3232
  Griffith *(G-6791)*
◆ Austin-Westran LLC........................... E 815 234-2811
  Indianapolis *(G-7569)*
Auto Truck Group LLC............................ G 260 356-1610
  Huntington *(G-7299)*
Auto Truck Group LLC............................ G 260 493-1800
  Roanoke *(G-14259)*
Avionics Mounts Inc............................... G 812 988-2949
  Nashville *(G-12661)*
▲ Awningtec Usa Incorporated............ E 812 734-0423
  Corydon *(G-2486)*
▲ B&J Rocket America Inc.................... E 574 825-5802
  Middlebury *(G-11700)*
Ba Romines Sheetmetal Inc.................. E 260 657-5500
  Harlan *(G-7049)*
Bar Processing Corporation.................. F 219 931-0702
  Hammond *(G-6881)*
Bearcat Corp... E 574 533-0448
  Goshen *(G-6098)*
Benthall Bros Inc.................................... E 800 488-5995
  Evansville *(G-3915)*
Berg... G 219 226-4350
  Crown Point *(G-2655)*
Bert R Hunciliman & Son Inc................. C 812 945-3544
  New Albany *(G-12699)*
Blume Metal Sales LLC.......................... G 765 490-0600
  Brookston *(G-1308)*
Bo-Mar Industries Inc............................ G 317 899-1240
  Indianapolis *(G-7651)*

SIC SECTION
34 FABRICATED METAL PRODUCTS

Bonnell Aluminum Inc .... A 815 351-6802
  Kentland (G-10157)
Bowmans Tin Shop Inc .... G 574 936-3234
  Plymouth (G-13760)
Brackett Heating & AC Inc .... E 812 476-1138
  Evansville (G-3949)
Brand Sheet Metal Works Inc .... G 765 284-5594
  Muncie (G-12356)
Brazeway LLC .... A 317 392-2533
  Shelbyville (G-14740)
Bright Sheet Metal Company Inc .... D 317 783-3181
  Indianapolis (G-7683)
Bright Sheet Metal Company Inc .... D 317 291-7600
  Indianapolis (G-7684)
Buckaroos Inc .... G 317 899-9100
  Indianapolis (G-7696)
Buhrt Engineering & Cnstr .... E 574 267-3720
  Warsaw (G-16331)
C & C Mailbox Products .... G 765 358-4880
  Gaston (G-6044)
C & K United Shtmtl & Mech .... E 812 423-5090
  Evansville (G-3958)
C & L Sheet Metal LLC .... G 812 449-9126
  Evansville (G-3959)
C & P Engineering and Mfg Inc .... F 765 825-4293
  Connersville (G-2430)
C&F Fabricating LLC .... G 765 362-5922
  Crawfordsville (G-2550)
Captive-Aire Systems Inc .... G 317 852-3770
  Brownsburg (G-1358)
Captive-Aire Systems Inc .... G 352 467-4439
  Indianapolis (G-7736)
Cardinal Manufacturing Co Inc .... F 317 283-4175
  Indianapolis (G-7741)
Carroll Distrg & Cnstr Sup Inc .... G 317 984-2400
  Noblesville (G-13055)
Cartesian Corp .... E 765 742-0293
  Lafayette (G-10548)
CB Fabrication .... G 765 649-1336
  Anderson (G-90)
Central States Mfg Inc .... C 219 879-4770
  Michigan City (G-11586)
Centurion Industries Inc .... D 260 357-6665
  Garrett (G-5855)
Chappelles Sheet Metal Shop .... G 812 246-2121
  Borden (G-1106)
Charmaran Company LLC .... F 260 347-3347
  Kendallville (G-10098)
Chisholm Lumber & Supply Co .... E 317 547-3535
  Indianapolis (G-7799)
Citadel Architectural Pdts LLC .... E 800 446-8828
  Greenfield (G-6481)
City Welding & Fabrication .... G 765 569-5403
  Rockville (G-14350)
Cline Brothers Welding Inc .... G 812 738-3537
  Corydon (G-2491)
Clover Sheet Metal Company .... F 574 293-5912
  Elkhart (G-3255)
CMa Supply Co Fort Wayne Inc .... E 260 471-9000
  Fort Wayne (G-4862)
Cmg Inc .... G 317 890-1999
  Indianapolis (G-7827)
Coffee Lomont & Moyer Inc .... F 260 422-7825
  Fort Wayne (G-4865)
Columbus Engineering Inc .... E 812 342-1231
  Columbus (G-2243)
Conover Custom Fabrication Inc .... F 317 784-1904
  Indianapolis (G-7853)
Contech Engnered Solutions LLC .... F 812 849-3933
  Mitchell (G-12037)
Continental Industries Inc .... D 574 262-4511
  Elkhart (G-3265)

Cyclone Manufacturing Co Inc .... F 260 774-3311
  Urbana (G-15885)
D & V Precision Sheetmetal .... E 317 462-2601
  Greenfield (G-6485)
D A Hochstetler & Sons LLP .... F 574 642-1144
  Topeka (G-15800)
◆ D Martin Enterprises Inc .... F 219 872-8211
  Michigan City (G-11596)
D-10 Services Inc .... G 317 889-7235
  Greenwood (G-6683)
Davids Inc .... F 812 376-6870
  Columbus (G-2280)
Daviess County Metal Sales .... D 812 486-4299
  Cannelburg (G-1530)
Deister Machine Company Inc .... E 260 422-0354
  Fort Wayne (G-4912)
Delbert M Dawson and Son Inc .... G 765 284-9711
  Muncie (G-12381)
Die-Mensional Metal Stampg Inc .... F 812 265-3946
  Madison (G-11213)
Dietrich Industries Inc .... C 219 931-6344
  Hammond (G-6913)
▲ Ditech Inc .... E 812 526-0850
  Edinburgh (G-3077)
Dpc Inc .... E 765 564-3752
  Delphi (G-2895)
Drinan Racing Products Inc .... G 317 486-9710
  Indianapolis (G-8008)
Dud(e)s N Roses LLC .... G 260 739-9053
  Fort Wayne (G-4930)
Dyna-Fab Corporation .... E 765 893-4423
  West Lebanon (G-16647)
E & R Fabricating Inc .... G 812 275-0388
  Bedford (G-634)
E Fab Inc .... G 317 786-9593
  Indianapolis (G-8029)
E G Ammerman Jr .... G 812 623-3504
  Sunman (G-15436)
Eagle Magnetic Company Inc .... E 317 297-1030
  Indianapolis (G-8032)
Eastlake Metals LLC .... F 219 655-5526
  Whiting (G-16835)
Edwards Steel Inc .... F 317 462-9451
  Greenfield (G-6492)
EH Baare Corporation .... G 765 778-7895
  Anderson (G-113)
Enconco Inc .... E 317 251-1251
  Indianapolis (G-8112)
Erny Sheet Metal Inc .... E 812 482-1044
  Jasper (G-9836)
Estes Design and Mfg Inc .... D 317 899-2203
  Indianapolis (G-8138)
Eta Fabrication Inc .... F 260 897-3711
  Avilla (G-476)
Evansville Sheet Metal Works Inc .... D 812 423-7871
  Evansville (G-4057)
Exact Shtmtl & Skylights Inc .... G 219 670-3520
  Crown Point (G-2682)
Ez Services LLC .... G 317 965-3013
  Westfield (G-16690)
Fenestration Products LLC .... D 317 831-5314
  Mooresville (G-12207)
Flexco Products Inc .... C 574 294-2502
  Elkhart (G-3348)
Floor Works Mfg & Fab .... G 812 394-2311
  Fairbanks (G-4395)
Fort Wayne Fabrication .... G 260 459-8848
  Fort Wayne (G-4992)
Frank H Monroe Heating & Coolg .... E 812 945-2566
  New Albany (G-12734)
Freudenberg-Nok General Partnr .... C 260 894-7183
  Ligonier (G-11015)

G & G Metal Spinners Inc .... E 317 923-3225
  Indianapolis (G-8250)
▲ Gammons Metal & Mfg Co Inc .... E 317 546-7091
  Indianapolis (G-8258)
Gary Metal Mfg LLC .... E 219 885-3232
  Gary (G-5937)
General Crafts Corp .... G 574 533-1936
  Goshen (G-6144)
General Motors LLC .... B 765 668-2000
  Marion (G-11287)
General Sheet Metal Works Inc .... E 574 288-0611
  South Bend (G-15042)
▲ Girtz Industries Inc .... C 844 464-4789
  Monticello (G-12151)
Gleason Corporation .... C 574 533-1141
  Goshen (G-6150)
Goudy Bros Boiler Co Inc .... G 765 459-4416
  Kokomo (G-10271)
Grant County Steel Inc .... F 765 668-7547
  Marion (G-11290)
Greenwood Models Inc .... G 317 859-2988
  Greenwood (G-6710)
Greg Moser Engineering Inc .... E 260 726-6689
  Portland (G-13949)
H & H Home Improvement Inc .... G 812 288-8700
  Clarksville (G-2017)
H & H Metal Products Inc .... F 812 256-0444
  Charlestown (G-1877)
Halsen Brothers Shtmtl Inc .... G 574 583-3358
  Monticello (G-12152)
HB Gutters LLC .... G 765 414-5698
  Winamac (G-16862)
Heartland Metal LLC .... G 574 773-0509
  Nappanee (G-12607)
Heidtman Steel Products Inc .... D 419 691-4646
  Butler (G-1465)
Hennessy Sheet Metal .... G 219 365-7058
  Saint John (G-14452)
Herman Tool & Machine Inc .... F 574 594-5544
  Pierceton (G-13632)
Hinshaw Roofing & Sheet Metal Co Inc . E 765 659-3311
  Frankfort (G-5674)
Hittler Insurance LLC .... G 260 519-1275
  Huntington (G-7319)
Hmi Investments LLC .... G 317 736-9387
  Franklin (G-5739)
Horner Industrial Services Inc .... F 317 634-7165
  Indianapolis (G-8418)
Hub City Stl & Fabrication LLC .... G 260 760-0370
  Union City (G-15855)
Huntington Sheet Metal Inc .... D 260 356-9011
  Huntington (G-7323)
Hy-Flex Corporation .... E 765 571-5125
  Knightstown (G-10198)
Hydro Extrusion Usa LLC .... B 888 935-5757
  North Liberty (G-13217)
Imh Fabrication LLC .... E 317 252-5566
  Indianapolis (G-8465)
Imh Fabrication LLC .... F 317 508-7462
  Indianapolis (G-8466)
▼ Independent Protection Co .... E 574 533-4116
  Goshen (G-6172)
▼ Indiana Gratings Inc .... F 765 342-7191
  Martinsville (G-11404)
Indiana Model Company Inc .... D 317 787-6358
  Indianapolis (G-8484)
Indiana Steel & Engrg Inc .... E 812 275-3363
  Bedford (G-647)
Industrial Steel Cnstr Inc .... C 219 885-5610
  Gary (G-5962)
Indy Hoods LLC .... F 317 731-7170
  Indianapolis (G-8529)

Employee Codes: A=Over 500 employees, B=251-500
C=101-250, D=51-100, E=20-50, F=10-19, G=1-9

34 FABRICATED METAL PRODUCTS

▲ Italmac USA Inc..................................G..... 574 243-0217
Granger *(G-6355)*

J & J Repair..G..... 574 831-3075
Goshen *(G-6178)*

▲ J & J Welding Inc................................E..... 812 838-4391
Mount Vernon *(G-12303)*

J T D Spiral Inc..G..... 260 497-1300
Fort Wayne *(G-5125)*

J-N Sheet Metal Company Inc..............G..... 260 436-7916
Fort Wayne *(G-5126)*

Jack Frost LLC.......................................E..... 812 477-7244
Evansville *(G-4136)*

Jack Howard..G..... 317 788-7643
Indianapolis *(G-8612)*

JO Mory Inc..F..... 260 897-3541
Avilla *(G-479)*

JO Mory Inc..G..... 260 347-3753
Kendallville *(G-10121)*

Johns Archtctral Met Solutions.............F..... 219 440-2116
Crown Point *(G-2703)*

◆ Josam Company.................................D..... 219 872-5531
Michigan City *(G-11628)*

K C Cmponents Wldg Fabrication........G..... 317 539-6067
Greencastle *(G-6416)*

K Diamond Sheet Metal..........................G..... 765 671-9847
Marion *(G-11302)*

K-K Tool and Design Inc.........................E..... 260 758-2940
Markle *(G-11356)*

K&A Sheet Metal LLC..............................G..... 317 300-1518
Indianapolis *(G-8654)*

Kairos Specialty Metals Corp................E..... 765 836-5540
Mount Summit *(G-12285)*

▲ Kalenborn Abresist Corporation.......E..... 800 348-0717
Urbana *(G-15886)*

Kammerer Inc...F..... 260 347-0389
Kendallville *(G-10123)*

Kelco Steel Fabrication Inc....................G..... 317 248-9229
Indianapolis *(G-8667)*

Key Sheet Metal Inc................................G..... 317 546-7151
Indianapolis *(G-8677)*

Kitchen Queen LLC.................................G..... 812 662-8399
Saint Paul *(G-14465)*

Knox Inc..F..... 260 665-6617
Angola *(G-269)*

Koester Metals Inc..................................E..... 260 495-1818
Fremont *(G-5825)*

Kokomo Metal Fabricators Inc...............G..... 765 459-8173
Kokomo *(G-10292)*

Koomler & Sons Inc................................F..... 260 482-7641
Fort Wayne *(G-5155)*

L & W Engineering Inc............................C..... 574 825-5351
Middlebury *(G-11730)*

Lake Air Balance......................................G..... 219 988-2449
Hebron *(G-7101)*

Lapis Services Inc...................................G..... 219 464-9131
Valparaiso *(G-15992)*

Larry Atwood..G..... 765 525-6851
Waldron *(G-16260)*

Lasalle Bristol Corporation....................F..... 574 293-5526
Elkhart *(G-3470)*

Lauck Manufacturing Co Inc..................F..... 317 787-6269
Indianapolis *(G-8727)*

Lazzaro Companies Inc..........................E..... 219 980-0860
Merrillville *(G-11529)*

Lenex Steel Company.............................E..... 317 818-1622
Terre Haute *(G-15632)*

Leons Fabrication Inc.............................G..... 219 365-5272
Schererville *(G-14528)*

Lionshead Precision Metals LLC..........D..... 317 787-6358
Greenwood *(G-6729)*

Lippert Components Inc........................G..... 574 535-1125
Elkhart *(G-3492)*

Lippert Components Inc........................D..... 574 535-1125
Goshen *(G-6202)*

Lippert Components Inc........................G..... 574 536-7803
Goshen *(G-6204)*

Lippert Components Inc........................G..... 574 849-0869
Goshen *(G-6206)*

Lippert Components Inc........................F..... 574 971-4320
Goshen *(G-6207)*

Lippert Components Inc........................G..... 574 312-7445
Middlebury *(G-11734)*

Lippert Components Inc........................E..... 800 551-9149
Mishawaka *(G-11930)*

Lippert Components Inc........................F..... 260 234-4303
Yoder *(G-16966)*

▲ Lippert Components Inc...................B..... 574 535-1125
Elkhart *(G-3493)*

Liquid Filter Housings Inc.....................G..... 414 530-8584
Rensselaer *(G-14059)*

Loyal Mfg Corp...F..... 317 359-3185
Indianapolis *(G-8788)*

Mailroom LLC...G..... 765 254-0000
Muncie *(G-12446)*

◆ Major Tool and Machine Inc..............C..... 317 636-6433
Indianapolis *(G-8820)*

Marion Steel Fabrication Inc.................E..... 765 664-1478
Marion *(G-11315)*

Marion Steel Fabrication Inc.................E..... 765 664-1478
Marion *(G-11316)*

Marion Tent & Awning Co......................G..... 765 664-7722
Marion *(G-11317)*

Maron Products Incorporated...............D..... 574 259-1971
Mishawaka *(G-11938)*

Mary Jonas...F..... 317 500-0600
Indianapolis *(G-8845)*

Matrix Manufacturing Inc......................G..... 260 854-4659
Wolcottville *(G-16941)*

Mbciindy..G..... 317 398-4400
Shelbyville *(G-14776)*

McD Machine Incorporated..................G..... 812 339-1240
Bloomington *(G-916)*

Menard Inc..C..... 812 466-1234
Terre Haute *(G-15641)*

Mestek Inc...C..... 317 831-5314
Mooresville *(G-12221)*

Metal Art Inc..G..... 765 354-4571
Middletown *(G-11774)*

▲ Metal Dynamics Ltd..........................E..... 812 949-7998
New Albany *(G-12775)*

Metal Sales Manufacturing Corp..........E..... 812 246-1866
Sellersburg *(G-14606)*

Metalcraft Inc..F..... 260 761-3001
Wawaka *(G-16540)*

Metl-Span LLC..E..... 317 398-1100
Shelbyville *(G-14777)*

Michael D Metz.......................................G..... 812 526-9606
Columbus *(G-2354)*

Microform Inc..G..... 574 522-9851
Elkhart *(G-3536)*

Micrometl Corporation..........................C..... 317 524-5400
Indianapolis *(G-8902)*

Mid America Powered Vehicles............G..... 812 925-7745
Chandler *(G-1864)*

▲ Midwest Metal Works Inc................F..... 812 981-0810
New Albany *(G-12778)*

Midwest Sheet Metal Inc......................G..... 574 223-3332
Rochester *(G-14307)*

Millenium Sheet Metal Inc....................F..... 574 935-9101
Plymouth *(G-13797)*

Miller Mfg Corp......................................E..... 574 773-4136
Nappanee *(G-12626)*

Mishawaka Sheet Metal LLC...............D..... 574 294-5959
Elkhart *(G-3546)*

▲ Models LLC..E..... 765 676-6700
Lebanon *(G-10917)*

▲ Modern Door Corporation...............D..... 574 586-3117
Walkerton *(G-16271)*

Moore Metal Works & A/C LLC............E..... 812 422-9473
Evansville *(G-4213)*

Mooresville Welding Inc.......................G..... 317 831-2265
Mooresville *(G-12225)*

Morris Sheet Metal Corp.......................D..... 260 497-1300
Fort Wayne *(G-5244)*

Morse Metal Fab Inc..............................F..... 574 674-6237
Granger *(G-6364)*

Mossman Metal Works..........................G..... 765 676-6055
Lebanon *(G-10919)*

Moyers Inc..F..... 574 264-3119
Elkhart *(G-3557)*

Mssh Inc...G..... 812 663-2180
Greensburg *(G-6620)*

Mtm Machining Inc...............................F..... 219 872-8677
Michigan City *(G-11642)*

Napier & Napier.....................................G..... 765 580-9116
Liberty *(G-10992)*

Nash Sheet Metal Co............................G..... 812 397-5306
Shelburn *(G-14718)*

Nector Machine & Fabricating..............G..... 219 322-6878
Schererville *(G-14536)*

New England Sheets LLC.....................E..... 978 487-2500
Indianapolis *(G-9005)*

Noble Industries Inc..............................E..... 317 773-1926
Noblesville *(G-13142)*

Noble Wire Products Inc......................G..... 317 773-1926
Noblesville *(G-13143)*

Novelis Corporation..............................C..... 812 462-2287
Terre Haute *(G-15652)*

Omnimax International LLC................D..... 574 848-7432
Fort Wayne *(G-5285)*

Omnimax International LLC................G..... 574 773-7981
Nappanee *(G-12634)*

Original Tractor Cab Co Inc.................F..... 765 663-2214
Arlington *(G-329)*

▲ Ottenweller Co Inc............................C..... 260 484-3166
Fort Wayne *(G-5289)*

Over Top Roofing and Rmdlg LLC......G..... 513 704-5422
Lawrenceburg *(G-10851)*

Owens Machine & Welding..................G..... 574 583-9566
Monticello *(G-12163)*

P-Kelco Inc..E..... 260 356-1376
Huntington *(G-7352)*

P-Kelco Inc..E..... 260 356-6326
Huntington *(G-7353)*

Padgett Inc..C..... 812 945-2391
New Albany *(G-12790)*

Palmor Products Inc.............................E..... 800 872-2822
Lebanon *(G-10928)*

Paniccia Heating & Cooling Inc..........G..... 219 872-2198
Michigan City *(G-11650)*

Parke County Aggregates LLC...........G..... 765 245-2344
Rockville *(G-14353)*

Patrick Industries Inc..........................D..... 574 294-5959
Elkhart *(G-3600)*

Pinnacle Equipment Company Inc.....F..... 317 259-1180
Indianapolis *(G-9143)*

Powell Systems Inc..............................G..... 765 884-0613
Fowler *(G-5631)*

Poynter Sheet Metal Inc......................B..... 317 893-1193
Greenwood *(G-6753)*

Preferred Shtmtl Fbrcation LLC.........G..... 317 494-6232
Franklin *(G-5769)*

Pro-Fab Sheet Metal Ind Inc...............G
Crown Point *(G-2737)*

PSI Group Inc.......................................G..... 317 297-3211
Indianapolis *(G-9238)*

34 FABRICATED METAL PRODUCTS

◆ Pzm Indiana LLC .... G 317 337-0441
 Carmel *(G-1732)*

Quality Galvanized Pdts Inc .... G 574 848-5151
 Bristol *(G-1283)*

R & M Welding & Fabricating Sp .... G 812 295-9130
 Loogootee *(G-11148)*

R & R Manufacturing .... G 260 244-5621
 Columbia City *(G-2187)*

Radius Aerospace Inc .... G 317 392-5000
 Shelbyville *(G-14790)*

Ramco Builder and Supply LLC .... E 574 223-7802
 Rochester *(G-14314)*

Rance Aluminum Fabrication .... E 574 266-9028
 Elkhart *(G-3639)*

▲ Rdd Properties Inc .... E 317 870-1940
 Waterloo *(G-16529)*

Rite-Way Steel Inc .... F 574 262-3465
 Elkhart *(G-3648)*

River Valley Sheet Metal Inc .... F 574 259-2538
 Mishawaka *(G-11988)*

Robinson Steel Co Inc .... C 219 398-4600
 East Chicago *(G-3040)*

◆ Rogers Engineering and Mfg Co .... E 765 478-5444
 Cambridge City *(G-1503)*

Rohrs Custom Metal .... G 812 689-3764
 Holton *(G-7220)*

Roof Masters Plus LLC .... G 765 572-1321
 Westpoint *(G-16747)*

▲ Ryobi Die Casting (usa) Inc .... A 317 398-3398
 Shelbyville *(G-14794)*

S & H Metal Products Inc .... E 260 593-2565
 Topeka *(G-15817)*

Sam Mouron Equipment Co Inc .... F 317 776-1799
 Noblesville *(G-13171)*

Sanbar of Indiana Inc .... G 317 375-6220
 Indianapolis *(G-9369)*

Schuckers Orna Ir Works Co .... G 812 422-7057
 Evansville *(G-4299)*

Schuster Sheet Metal Inc .... G 574 293-4802
 Elkhart *(G-3665)*

Scotia Corporation .... F 260 479-8800
 Fort Wayne *(G-5404)*

Sheet Metal Models Inc .... F 317 783-1303
 Indianapolis *(G-9415)*

Sheet Metal Services Inc .... F 219 924-1206
 Highland *(G-7154)*

Sheet Mtal Wkrs Lcal 20 Apprnt .... F 317 541-0050
 Indianapolis *(G-9416)*

Sigma Steel Inc .... E 812 275-4489
 Bedford *(G-672)*

Sisson Steel Inc .... F 812 354-8701
 Winslow *(G-16922)*

Slabaugh Metal Fab LLC .... E 574 342-0554
 Bourbon *(G-1128)*

Slate Mechanical Inc .... F 765 452-9611
 Kokomo *(G-10335)*

Slatile Roofing and Shtmtl Co .... E 574 233-7485
 South Bend *(G-15246)*

Southwark Metal Mfg Co .... C 317 823-5300
 Mccordsville *(G-11456)*

Spiral-Fab Inc .... G 812 427-3006
 Vevay *(G-16112)*

Spreuer & Son Inc .... F 260 463-3513
 Lagrange *(G-10763)*

Stadry Enclosure Co .... G 812 284-2244
 Jeffersonville *(G-10058)*

Stahl Equipment Inc .... F 812 925-3341
 Gentryville *(G-6053)*

▲ Stalcop LLC .... E 765 436-7926
 Thorntown *(G-15756)*

◆ State Wide Aluminum Inc .... C 574 262-2594
 Elkhart *(G-3699)*

Steel Tank & Fabricating Corp .... E 260 248-8971
 Columbia City *(G-2203)*

Sterling Industrial LLC .... C 812 423-7832
 Evansville *(G-4333)*

Summit Manufacturing Corp .... E 260 428-2600
 Fort Wayne *(G-5453)*

Superior Canopy Corporation .... E 260 488-4065
 Hamilton *(G-6862)*

Sur-Loc Inc .... F 260 495-4065
 Fremont *(G-5836)*

Sure-Flo Seamless Gutters Inc .... G 260 622-4372
 Ossian *(G-13437)*

SW Watkins Limited .... D 260 484-4844
 Fort Wayne *(G-5462)*

T Organization Inc .... E 463 204-5118
 Greenwood *(G-6771)*

T R Bulger Inc .... G 219 879-8525
 Trail Creek *(G-15841)*

Tarpenning-Lafollette Co Inc .... E 317 780-1500
 Indianapolis *(G-9553)*

Ten Point Trim Corp .... E 317 875-5424
 Zionsville *(G-17056)*

Thomas Cubit Inc .... G 219 933-0566
 Hammond *(G-7019)*

Thomco Inc .... G 317 359-3539
 Indianapolis *(G-9597)*

Tin Man Shtmtl & Roofg LLC .... G 513 276-1716
 Guilford *(G-6830)*

Tomlinson Manufacturing Co .... G 765 719-3700
 Franklin *(G-5783)*

Total Concepts Design Inc .... D 812 752-6534
 Scottsburg *(G-14582)*

Tradeline Fabricating Inc .... E 812 637-1444
 Lawrenceburg *(G-10862)*

Trim-A-Seal of Indiana Inc .... F 219 883-2180
 Gary *(G-6022)*

Triple J Ironworks Inc .... G 765 544-9152
 Carthage *(G-1819)*

Tube Processing Corp .... C 317 782-9486
 Indianapolis *(G-9656)*

Tube Processing Corp .... G 317 264-7760
 Indianapolis *(G-9657)*

▲ Tube Processing Corp .... B 317 787-1321
 Indianapolis *(G-9658)*

▲ Tuttle Aluminum & Bronze Inc .... D 317 842-2420
 Fishers *(G-4618)*

Universal Metalcraft Inc .... E 260 547-4457
 Decatur *(G-2888)*

V N C Inc .... F 219 696-5031
 Lowell *(G-11179)*

Vibromatic Company Inc .... E 317 773-3885
 Noblesville *(G-13193)*

Viper USA Inc .... D 765 742-4200
 West Lafayette *(G-16642)*

Vogler Copperworks LLC .... G 812 630-9010
 Haubstadt *(G-7091)*

Vogler Metalwork & Design Inc .... G 812 615-0042
 Haubstadt *(G-7092)*

W & W Fabricating Inc .... G 765 362-2182
 Crawfordsville *(G-2625)*

▲ Wagner Zip-Change Inc .... E 708 681-4100
 Fort Wayne *(G-5540)*

Wait Industries LLC .... E 574 347-4320
 Elkhart *(G-3776)*

Wiley Metal Fabricating Inc .... G 765 674-9707
 Marion *(G-11349)*

Wiley Metal Fabricating Inc .... G 765 671-7865
 Marion *(G-11350)*

Williams Tool & Machine Corp .... G 765 676-5859
 Jamestown *(G-9821)*

Ynwa Industries Inc .... D 574 295-6641
 Elkhart *(G-3800)*

Zimmer Metal Sales LLC .... G 574 862-1800
 Goshen *(G-6280)*

Zimmer Welding LLC .... G 317 632-5212
 Indianapolis *(G-9812)*

3446 Architectural metalwork

American Stair Corporation Inc .... D 800 872-7824
 Hammond *(G-6876)*

Arrow Metals Inc .... E 765 825-4443
 Connersville *(G-2426)*

B & L Shtmtl Rofg A Tcta Amer .... E 812 332-4309
 Bloomington *(G-789)*

Backyard Company .... G 317 727-0298
 Indianapolis *(G-7588)*

▲ Barnett-Bates Corporation .... F 815 726-5223
 Anderson *(G-82)*

Botti Stdio Archtctral Arts In .... E 847 869-5933
 La Porte *(G-10391)*

Builders Iron Works Inc .... E 574 254-1553
 Mishawaka *(G-11854)*

Capstone Rail LLC .... G 877 242-4252
 Anderson *(G-88)*

Centrum Force Fabrication .... G 574 295-5367
 Goshen *(G-6111)*

Coffee Lomont & Moyer Inc .... F 260 422-7825
 Fort Wayne *(G-4865)*

Colbin Tool Company Inc .... E 574 457-3183
 Syracuse *(G-15459)*

Continental Industries Inc .... D 574 262-4511
 Elkhart *(G-3265)*

Creative Metal Works Wrought .... G 812 883-2008
 Salem *(G-14476)*

Custom Interior Dynamics LLC .... F 317 632-0477
 Indianapolis *(G-7930)*

Davids Inc .... F 812 376-6870
 Columbus *(G-2280)*

Dormakaba USA Inc .... A 317 806-4605
 Indianapolis *(G-7997)*

Dpc Inc .... E 765 564-3752
 Delphi *(G-2895)*

E & H Bridge and Grating Inc .... G 812 277-8343
 Bedford *(G-632)*

Evans Metal Products Co Inc .... F 574 264-2166
 Elkhart *(G-3335)*

F G Metal .... G 260 580-0361
 Fort Wayne *(G-4970)*

F W A Decks & Fencing .... G 219 865-3275
 Dyer *(G-2974)*

Flag & Banner Company Inc .... F 317 299-4880
 Indianapolis *(G-8199)*

Forged Alliance Inc .... F 815 726-5223
 Anderson *(G-118)*

▲ Gammons Metal & Mfg Co Inc .... E 317 546-7091
 Indianapolis *(G-8258)*

General Crafts Corp .... G 574 533-1936
 Goshen *(G-6144)*

▲ Gilpin Inc .... E 260 724-9155
 Decatur *(G-2858)*

Goudy Bros Boiler Co Inc .... G 765 459-4416
 Kokomo *(G-10271)*

Hamilton Iron Works Inc .... G 574 533-3784
 Goshen *(G-6160)*

Hampton Ironworks Inc .... G 219 929-6448
 Chesterton *(G-1934)*

Herman Tool & Machine Inc .... F 574 594-5544
 Pierceton *(G-13632)*

Hgmc Supply Inc .... F 317 351-9500
 Indianapolis *(G-8394)*

Hilltop Metal Fabricating LLC .... G 574 773-4975
 Nappanee *(G-12610)*

▲ Imperial Stamping Corporation .... D 574 294-3780
 Elkhart *(G-3419)*

34 FABRICATED METAL PRODUCTS

Imperial Trophy & Awards Co................ G..... 260 432-8161
  Fort Wayne (G-5096)
▼ Independent Protection Co................ E..... 574 533-4116
  Goshen (G-6172)
▼ Indiana Gratings Inc........................ F..... 765 342-7191
  Martinsville (G-11404)
◆ Iron Baluster LLC............................ G..... 574 975-0288
  Goshen (G-6177)
Ironcraft Co Inc................................ G..... 574 272-0866
  South Bend (G-15088)
J A Smit Inc................................... G..... 812 424-8141
  Evansville (G-4133)
Jones & Sons Inc.............................. E..... 812 882-2957
  Vincennes (G-16135)
K & K Fence Inc................................ E..... 317 359-5425
  Indianapolis (G-8652)
Kawneer Company Inc......................... D..... 317 882-2314
  Greenwood (G-6721)
Le Air Co Inc................................... G..... 812 988-1313
  Nashville (G-12674)
Leons Fabrication Inc.......................... F..... 219 365-5272
  Schererville (G-14528)
Liquidspring LLC................................ G..... 765 474-7816
  Lafayette (G-10638)
Metalfor LLC.................................... G..... 812 212-2248
  Batesville (G-597)
Midwest Minis LLC.............................. G..... 317 500-3294
  Indianapolis (G-8911)
Mofab Inc....................................... G..... 765 649-5577
  Anderson (G-157)
Mofab Inc....................................... E..... 765 649-5577
  Anderson (G-159)
Muncie Metal Spinning Inc..................... F..... 765 288-1937
  Muncie (G-12462)
Open Gate LLC.................................. F..... 765 734-1314
  Anderson (G-174)
Original Tractor Cab Co Inc.................... F..... 765 663-2214
  Arlington (G-329)
Ottenweller Company LLC...................... G..... 260 245-0197
  Fort Wayne (G-5290)
Paragon Manufacturing Inc.................... F..... 260 665-1492
  Angola (G-280)
Power Train Corp Fort Wayne.................. F..... 317 241-9393
  Indianapolis (G-9167)
Projectione LLC................................. G..... 812 480-6006
  Indianapolis (G-9228)
Reese Forge Orna Ironwork.................... F..... 219 775-1039
  Lake Village (G-10782)
Refax Wear Products Inc....................... F..... 219 977-0414
  Gary (G-6003)
Rock Run Industries LLC....................... E..... 574 361-0848
  Millersburg (G-11816)
◆ S S M Inc..................................... G..... 317 357-4552
  Indianapolis (G-9356)
San Jo Steel Inc................................ F..... 317 888-6227
  Greenwood (G-6766)
Schouten Metal Craft Inc....................... G..... 317 546-2639
  Indianapolis (G-9391)
Schuckers Orna Ir Works Co................... G..... 812 422-7057
  Evansville (G-4299)
Sharps Baton Mfg Corp......................... G..... 574 214-9389
  Elkhart (G-3671)
Sigma Steel Inc................................ E..... 812 275-4489
  Bedford (G-672)
Signature Metals Inc........................... G..... 317 335-2207
  Mccordsville (G-11455)
Sisson Steel Inc................................ F..... 812 354-8701
  Winslow (G-16922)
Sonny Scaffolds Inc............................ F..... 317 831-3900
  Mooresville (G-12243)
Sterling Industrial LLC.......................... C..... 812 423-7832
  Evansville (G-4333)

Sugar Creek Fabricators Inc................... G..... 765 361-0891
  Crawfordsville (G-2620)
Titus Inc....................................... F..... 574 936-3345
  Plymouth (G-13817)
▲ Tuttle Aluminum & Bronze Inc.............. D..... 317 842-2420
  Fishers (G-4618)
Upright Iron Works Inc......................... G..... 219 922-1994
  Griffith (G-6821)
Ward Industries Inc............................ F..... 574 825-2548
  Middlebury (G-11756)
Wiw Inc.. E..... 219 663-7900
  Crown Point (G-2774)
Wrought Iron Werks LLC........................ G..... 219 779-7476
  Lake Village (G-10786)

3448 Prefabricated metal buildings

(ebs Cmpstes Engnred Bnded Str............. F..... 574 266-3471
  Elkhart (G-3136)
123carportz.................................... G..... 574 376-0470
  Mishawaka (G-11833)
Agricon LLC..................................... F..... 219 261-2157
  Remington (G-14032)
All American Group Inc......................... G..... 260 724-7391
  Decatur (G-2842)
All Star Manufacturing Inc..................... G..... 574 293-8141
  Culver (G-2779)
▲ All Steel Carports Inc....................... G..... 765 284-0694
  Muncie (G-12337)
▲ All Steel Crprts Buildings LLC.............. G..... 765 284-0694
  Muncie (G-12338)
American Steel Carports Inc................... G..... 419 737-1331
  Mount Summit (G-12284)
◆ Asphalt Equipment Company Inc........... E..... 260 672-3004
  Fort Wayne (G-4775)
B & A Cnstr & Design Inc...................... G..... 812 683-4600
  Huntingburg (G-7270)
Beh IL Corp..................................... G..... 219 886-2710
  Gary (G-5899)
Biologics Modular LLC.......................... G..... 317 626-4093
  Brownsburg (G-1350)
Burns Construction Inc......................... E..... 574 382-2315
  Macy (G-11195)
Carter-Lee Building Components.............. E..... 317 639-5431
  Indianapolis (G-7752)
Central States Mfg Inc......................... C..... 219 879-4770
  Michigan City (G-11586)
Century Industries LLC......................... E..... 812 246-3371
  Sellersburg (G-14590)
Chief Industries Inc............................ C..... 219 866-4121
  Rensselaer (G-14047)
Classic Buildings Inc........................... E..... 812 944-5821
  Clarksville (G-2013)
◆ CTB MN Investment Co Inc................ E..... 574 658-4191
  Milford (G-11794)
Daily Co.. G..... 574 546-5126
  Bremen (G-1185)
Dytec-Nci LLC................................... G..... 317 919-0000
  Fishers (G-4507)
Five Starr Inc.................................. G..... 812 367-1554
  Ferdinand (G-4433)
Full Metal Solutions LLC........................ F..... 812 725-9660
  Jeffersonville (G-9988)
Heartland Industries Inc........................ G..... 317 569-1718
  Carmel (G-1653)
Hill Construction Co LLC........................ G..... 812 843-3279
  Saint Croix (G-14434)
Huntington Exteriors Inc........................ F..... 260 356-1621
  Huntington (G-7322)
Jobsite Trailer Corporation.................... E..... 574 224-4000
  Rochester (G-14298)
▲ Koontz-Wagner Custom Cont.............. D..... 574 387-5802
  South Bend (G-15104)

SIC SECTION

Kw Custom Controls LLC....................... E..... 312 343-3920
  South Bend (G-15112)
▼ Lacopa International Inc.................... G..... 317 410-1483
  Pittsboro (G-13650)
Laidig Inc...................................... E..... 574 256-0204
  Mishawaka (G-11925)
Lakemaster Inc................................ F..... 765 288-3718
  Muncie (G-12437)
Martins Mini Barns LLC......................... G..... 574 238-0045
  Goshen (G-6214)
Maurer Constructors Inc....................... G..... 812 236-5950
  Brazil (G-1152)
Mbci Inc....................................... C..... 317 835-2201
  Shelbyville (G-14775)
McElroy Metal Mill Inc......................... G..... 317 823-6895
  Indianapolis (G-8864)
Midwestern Structures LLC..................... G..... 574 835-9733
  Muncie (G-12456)
Miller Brothers Builders Inc.................... E..... 574 533-8602
  Goshen (G-6222)
Millers Mini-Barns LLC.......................... G..... 812 883-8072
  Salem (G-14493)
Morton Buildings Inc........................... F..... 765 653-9781
  Cloverdale (G-2090)
Morton Buildings Inc........................... F..... 800 447-7436
  Jasper (G-9893)
Morton Buildings Inc........................... F..... 260 563-2118
  Wabash (G-16204)
Mpi Products Holdings LLC..................... G..... 248 237-3007
  Knox (G-10217)
Mpp Holdings Inc............................... G..... 317 805-3764
  Noblesville (G-13140)
Northedge Steel LLC............................ G..... 765 444-6021
  Yorktown (G-16979)
Okos Family Farms LLC.......................... G..... 765 567-2750
  Battle Ground (G-613)
Rollin Mini Barns LLC........................... G..... 812 687-7581
  Odon (G-13348)
RPI Components Inc............................ G..... 574 536-2283
  Elkhart (G-3653)
Sigma Steel Inc................................ E..... 812 275-4489
  Bedford (G-672)
Slabaugh Storage Barns Inc.................... G..... 260 768-7989
  Shipshewana (G-14890)
Sunrooms of Indiana Inc....................... E..... 317 891-3232
  Fishers (G-4608)
▲ T & S Equipment Company.................. D..... 260 665-9521
  Angola (G-297)
Wagler Mini Barn Products LLC................ G..... 812 687-7372
  Plainville (G-13747)
Williams Scotsman Inc......................... E..... 260 749-6611
  Fort Wayne (G-5569)
Williams Scotsman Inc......................... F..... 317 782-2463
  Indianapolis (G-9768)
Winandy Greenhouse Company................ E..... 765 935-2111
  Richmond (G-14227)
Woodland Manufacturing & Sup................ F..... 317 271-2266
  Avon (G-557)
Yoders Quality Barns LLC....................... G..... 260 565-4122
  Bluffton (G-1071)

3449 Miscellaneous metalwork

6 Twenty-Six Inc............................... F..... 260 471-2002
  Fort Wayne (G-4713)
Alexander Screw Products Inc.................. E..... 317 898-5313
  Indianapolis (G-7469)
Aluminum Wldg & Mch Works Inc.............. G..... 219 787-8066
  Chesterton (G-1901)
Ambassador Steel Corporation................ F..... 317 834-3434
  Mooresville (G-12193)
Anderson Fab Llc............................... G..... 317 534-7306
  Martinsville (G-11381)

2024 Harris Indiana Industrial Directory

SIC SECTION
34 FABRICATED METAL PRODUCTS

CMa Steel & Fabrication Inc .... F 260 207-9000
  Fort Wayne (G-4861)

Coffee Lomont & Moyer Inc .... F 260 422-7825
  Fort Wayne (G-4865)

Complex Structures Group LLC .... E 219 947-3939
  Merrillville (G-11498)

◆ Delta Tool Manufacturing Inc .... G 574 223-4863
  Rochester (G-14286)

Divine Machine .... G 812 388-6323
  Shoals (G-14905)

Double E Enterprise Inc .... G 812 689-0671
  Osgood (G-13407)

Elliott Mfg & Fabrication .... G 812 865-0516
  Paoli (G-13493)

Ertl Fabricating Inc .... F 765 393-1376
  Anderson (G-116)

▼ Fabtration LLC .... F 812 989-6730
  Georgetown (G-6060)

General Crafts Corp .... G 574 533-1936
  Goshen (G-6144)

Hoosier Trim Products LLC .... E 317 271-4007
  Indianapolis (G-8412)

Induction Iron Incorporated .... F 813 969-3300
  Evansville (G-4122)

▲ Interntnal Mtl Hdlg Systems In .... F 812 222-4488
  Greensburg (G-6609)

Ironhorse Detailing Inc .... G 812 939-3300
  Clay City (G-2044)

J & F Steel Corporation .... G 219 764-3500
  Burns Harbor (G-1453)

K & S Farm Machine Shop Inc .... F 812 663-8567
  Greensburg (G-6610)

Made-Rite Manufacturing Inc .... G 812 967-2652
  Salem (G-14488)

McD Machine Incorporated .... G 812 339-1240
  Bloomington (G-916)

Metal Spinners Inc .... F 260 665-2158
  Angola (G-275)

Midland Metal Products Co .... D 773 927-5700
  Hammond (G-6981)

Midwest Roll Forming & Mfg Inc .... C 574 594-2100
  Pierceton (G-13635)

Morryde International Inc .... C 574 293-1581
  Elkhart (G-3555)

Performance Tool Inc .... F 260 726-6572
  Portland (G-13959)

Polley Tech LLC .... G 812 524-0688
  Seymour (G-14675)

Qfs Holdings LLC .... G 317 634-2543
  Indianapolis (G-9243)

Rebar Corp of Indiana .... G 260 471-2002
  Fort Wayne (G-5371)

Rfc LLC .... D 812 284-0650
  Jeffersonville (G-10046)

Right Angle Stl & Fabrication .... E 574 773-7148
  Nappanee (G-12641)

Rkdjrt Inc .... E 812 354-8899
  Petersburg (G-13624)

Scheffler Hartmut Romanus .... G 765 855-2917
  Centerville (G-1853)

Sherman Enterprises Inc .... G 260 636-6225
  Albion (G-45)

Sigma Steel Inc .... E 812 275-4489
  Bedford (G-672)

Stolz Structural Inc .... G 812 983-4720
  Elberfeld (G-3118)

Stoutco Inc .... D 574 848-4411
  Bristol (G-1293)

Structral Cmpnnts Fbrction Inc .... F 765 342-9188
  Martinsville (G-11429)

Superior Coatings Inc .... G 574 546-0591
  Bremen (G-1226)

Ten Point Trim Corp .... E 317 875-5424
  Zionsville (G-17056)

Trivett Contracting Inc .... E 317 539-5150
  Clayton (G-2062)

◆ United Roll Forming Corp .... E 574 294-2800
  Elkhart (G-3760)

US Metals Inc .... G 219 398-1350
  East Chicago (G-3052)

Voges Restoration and Wdwkg .... G 812 299-1546
  Terre Haute (G-15742)

Willie Lehman .... G 574 935-2809
  Nappanee (G-12654)

Z Rodz & Customs LLC .... G 574 806-5774
  Knox (G-10229)

3451 Screw machine products

▲ Accurate Mnfctred Pdts Group I .... E 317 472-9000
  Indianapolis (G-7420)

Aegis Sales and Engineering .... F 260 483-4160
  Fort Wayne (G-4731)

Alexander Screw Products Inc .... E 317 898-5313
  Indianapolis (G-7469)

Ashley F Ward Inc .... G 574 294-1502
  Elkhart (G-3196)

Ashley F Ward Inc .... G 219 879-4177
  Michigan City (G-11580)

Auburn Manufacturing Inc .... E 260 925-8651
  Auburn (G-364)

Bar-Wal Products .... G 574 457-5311
  Syracuse (G-15455)

Beckett Bronze Company Inc .... F 765 282-2261
  Muncie (G-12350)

▲ Biddle Precision Components Inc .... C 317 758-4451
  Sheridan (G-14817)

Charleston Metal Products Inc .... F 260 837-8211
  Waterloo (G-16516)

▼ Charleston Metal Products Inc .... D 260 837-8211
  Waterloo (G-16517)

D & S Machine Products Inc .... E 812 926-6250
  Aurora (G-442)

▲ Ds Products Inc .... E 260 563-9030
  Wabash (G-16182)

Dual Machine Corporation .... F 317 921-9850
  Indianapolis (G-8017)

Ebert Machine Company Inc .... E 765 473-3728
  Peru (G-13581)

EMC Precision Machining II LLC .... D 317 758-4451
  Sheridan (G-14822)

▼ Epco Products Inc .... E 260 747-8888
  Fort Wayne (G-4956)

Exactifab .... G 812 420-2723
  Brazil (G-1142)

F & F Screw Machine Products .... E 574 293-0362
  Elkhart (G-3340)

Fitech Inc .... E 513 398-1414
  Michigan City (G-11613)

Gapco Inc .... G 317 787-6440
  Indianapolis (G-8259)

H & E Machined Specialties .... F 260 424-2527
  Fort Wayne (G-5045)

Ham Enterprises Machine Co .... F 765 342-7966
  Martinsville (G-11399)

Jerden Industries Inc .... E 812 332-1762
  Bloomington (G-896)

Jessen Manufacturing Co Inc .... D 574 295-3836
  Elkhart (G-3432)

Jrp Machine Co .... G 317 955-1905
  Indianapolis (G-8644)

Kent Brenneke .... G 260 446-5383
  Harlan (G-7057)

▲ Madison Tool and Die Inc .... D 812 273-2250
  Madison (G-11239)

▲ Mid America Screw Products .... F 574 294-6905
  Elkhart (G-3537)

Mitchel & Scott Machine Co .... F 317 639-5331
  Indianapolis (G-8933)

▲ Mitchel Group Incorporated .... C 317 639-5331
  Indianapolis (G-8934)

National Consolidated Corp .... F 574 289-7885
  South Bend (G-15159)

▲ Northern Indiana Manufacturing .... E 574 342-2105
  Bourbon (G-1125)

Performance Cnc LLC .... G 574 780-4864
  Bourbon (G-1126)

Point Machine Products Inc .... G 574 289-2429
  South Bend (G-15199)

Precision Piece Parts Inc .... D 574 255-3185
  Mishawaka (G-11978)

Prodigy Mold & Tool Inc .... E 812 753-3029
  Haubstadt (G-7088)

▲ RCO-Reed Corporation .... E 317 736-8014
  Franklin (G-5771)

RD Smith Manufacturing Inc .... G 260 829-6709
  Orland (G-13372)

RTC .... G 260 503-9770
  Columbia City (G-2193)

S H Leggitt Company .... G 574 264-0230
  Elkhart (G-3656)

Sierra Machine .... G 574 232-5694
  South Bend (G-15242)

▲ Standard Locknut LLC .... C 317 399-2230
  Westfield (G-16729)

Terry Liquidation III Inc .... F 219 362-3557
  La Porte (G-10490)

Tri Aerospace LLC .... E 812 872-2400
  Terre Haute (G-15736)

Winn Machine Inc .... G 219 324-2978
  La Porte (G-10501)

3452 Bolts, nuts, rivets, and washers

A J Kay Co .... F 224 475-0370
  South Bend (G-14928)

Agrati - Park Forest LLC .... D 219 531-2202
  Valparaiso (G-15895)

Andre Corp .... G 574 293-0207
  Elkhart (G-3183)

Ashley F Ward Inc .... G 219 879-4177
  Michigan City (G-11580)

B K & M Inc .... G 219 924-0184
  Griffith (G-6792)

▲ B Walter & Company Inc .... E 260 563-2181
  Wabash (G-16174)

▲ Blush and Bobby Pins LLC .... G 317 789-5166
  Carmel (G-1568)

▲ Bollhoff Inc .... D 260 347-3903
  Kendallville (G-10097)

Bolttech-Mannings Inc .... G 219 682-5864
  Valparaiso (G-15919)

▲ Camcar LLC .... C 574 223-3131
  Rochester (G-14282)

Cold Heading Co .... E 260 495-7003
  Fremont (G-5816)

Cold Heading Co .... E 260 495-4222
  Fremont (G-5817)

Cold Heading Co .... E 260 587-3231
  Hudson (G-7244)

Elgin Fastener Group LLC .... G 812 689-8917
  Versailles (G-16099)

Elsie Manufacturing Company .... G 260 837-8841
  Waterloo (G-16519)

▲ Fontana Fasteners Inc .... C 765 654-0477
  Frankfort (G-5664)

G4 Tool and Technology Inc .... F 574 970-0844
  Elkhart (G-3365)

Employee Codes: A=Over 500 employees, B=251-500
C=101-250, D=51-100, E=20-50, F=10-19, G=1-9

34 FABRICATED METAL PRODUCTS

▲ Hadady Corporation .... E 219 322-7417
Dyer *(G-2976)*

♦ Hanger Bolt & Stud Co Inc .... F 317 462-4477
Greenfield *(G-6508)*

Herff Jones Co Indiana - Inc .... E 317 297-3740
Indianapolis *(G-8385)*

▲ Hoosier Gasket Corporation .... D 317 545-2000
Indianapolis *(G-8409)*

▲ Imperial Stamping Corporation .... D 574 294-3780
Elkhart *(G-3419)*

▲ Indiana Automotive Fas Inc .... B 317 467-0100
Greenfield *(G-6511)*

Kent Brenneke .... G 260 446-5383
Harlan *(G-7057)*

▲ Machine Keys Inc .... G 765 228-4208
Muncie *(G-12442)*

▲ Mc Coy Bolt Works Inc .... D 260 482-4476
Fort Wayne *(G-5210)*

Mr Pin Shi Peter Lee .... G 574 264-9754
Elkhart *(G-3558)*

Norco Industries Inc .... C 574 262-3400
Elkhart *(G-3573)*

NSK Corporation .... D 765 458-5000
Liberty *(G-10993)*

NSK Precision America Inc .... D 317 738-5000
Franklin *(G-5762)*

Philip Pins .... G 219 769-1059
Merrillville *(G-11550)*

Pin Oak Group LLC .... G 260 637-7778
Fort Wayne *(G-5315)*

Pin Point Av LLC .... G 317 750-3120
Indianapolis *(G-9142)*

Pin-Up Curls LLC .... G 260 241-5871
Fort Wayne *(G-5316)*

Pontiac Engraving .... G 630 834-4424
Plymouth *(G-13805)*

▲ R & R Engineering Co Inc .... E 765 536-2331
Summitville *(G-15429)*

♦ Rdd Properties Inc .... E 317 870-1940
Waterloo *(G-16529)*

Rits Ltd Brokers Inc .... G 260 348-0786
Fort Wayne *(G-5385)*

Rohder Machine & Tool Inc .... E 219 663-3697
Crown Point *(G-2747)*

Rose Engineering Company Inc .... G 317 788-4446
Indianapolis *(G-9333)*

Schafer Power Washing .... G 812 866-1956
Lexington *(G-10981)*

Standard Die Supply of Indiana Inc .... D 317 236-6200
Indianapolis *(G-9493)*

▲ Standard Locknut LLC .... C 317 399-2230
Westfield *(G-16729)*

Stanley Engnered Fastening LLC .... C 765 728-2433
Montpelier *(G-12182)*

Steve Mitchell .... G 574 831-4848
New Paris *(G-12969)*

▲ Sunright America Inc .... C 812 342-3430
Columbus *(G-2398)*

Tek Coat and Spray LLC .... G 260 748-0314
Fort Wayne *(G-5473)*

Tristate Bolt Company .... F 260 357-5541
Garrett *(G-5879)*

Western Products Indiana Inc .... F 765 529-6230
New Castle *(G-12885)*

3462 Iron and steel forgings

▲ Accugear Inc .... C 260 497-6600
Fort Wayne *(G-4721)*

Ashley F Ward Inc .... G 219 879-4177
Michigan City *(G-11580)*

Autoform Tool & Mfg LLC .... C 260 624-2014
Angola *(G-232)*

▲ Avis Industrial Corporation .... E 765 998-8100
Upland *(G-15876)*

Beachy Machine Shop LLC .... G 765 452-9051
Kokomo *(G-10236)*

Bowmans Hoof Trimming .... G 574 522-2838
Elkhart *(G-3233)*

Bwxt Nclear Oprtions Group Inc .... C 812 838-1200
Mount Vernon *(G-12294)*

Custom Blacksmith Shop .... G 765 292-2745
Atlanta *(G-341)*

Deister Concentrator Na LLC .... F 260 747-2700
Fort Wayne *(G-4911)*

Emco Gears Inc .... G 317 243-3836
Indianapolis *(G-8103)*

♦ Fairfield Manufacturing Co Inc .... A 765 772-4000
Lafayette *(G-10576)*

Federal-Mogul Powertrain LLC .... G 574 272-5900
South Bend *(G-15032)*

Flexible Concepts Inc .... D 574 296-0941
Elkhart *(G-3350)*

Fountaintown Forge Inc .... E 317 861-5403
Fountaintown *(G-5614)*

▲ General Products Delaware .... B 260 668-1440
Angola *(G-255)*

H & H Manufacturing Inc .... G 812 664-3582
Patoka *(G-13508)*

Harrell Family LLC .... F 317 770-4550
Indianapolis *(G-8366)*

Horneco Fabrication Inc .... G 260 672-2064
Fort Wayne *(G-5082)*

Impact Forge Group Inc .... C 812 342-5527
Columbus *(G-2321)*

Impact Forge Group Inc .... G 812 342-4437
Columbus *(G-2322)*

♦ Indiana Tool & Mfg Co Inc .... C 574 936-2112
Plymouth *(G-13784)*

Ioni 2 Inc .... C 219 261-2115
Remington *(G-14036)*

Joyce/Dayton Corp .... E 260 726-9361
Portland *(G-13952)*

Kanoff Enterprises .... G 574 575-6787
Mishawaka *(G-11921)*

Mafco & Poseidon Barge .... G 260 589-9000
Berne *(G-718)*

McCallister Industries Inc .... G 317 417-7365
Indianapolis *(G-8861)*

▲ Modern Drop Forge Company LLC ..... B 708 489-4208
Merrillville *(G-11541)*

Modern Forge Indiana LLC .... E 219 945-5945
Merrillville *(G-11543)*

Mtr Machining Concept Inc .... G 260 587-3381
Ashley *(G-334)*

▲ Nagakura Engrg Works Co Inc .... E 812 375-1382
Columbus *(G-2359)*

Nst Technologies Mim LLC .... C 812 755-4501
Campbellsburg *(G-1526)*

Omnisource LLC .... G 574 654-7561
New Carlisle *(G-12843)*

♦ Omnisource LLC .... C 260 422-5541
Fort Wayne *(G-5286)*

▲ Rdd Properties Inc .... E 317 870-1940
Waterloo *(G-16529)*

Rolls-Royce Corporation .... E 317 230-2000
Indianapolis *(G-9325)*

Rolls-Royce Corporation .... E 317 230-8515
West Lafayette *(G-16626)*

▲ Schafer Industries Inc .... D 574 234-4116
South Bend *(G-15234)*

Servaas Inc .... G 317 633-2020
Indianapolis *(G-9405)*

Spectra Prmium Mblity Sltons U .... G 800 628-5442
Greenfield *(G-6558)*

T-H Licensing Inc .... E 765 772-4128
Lafayette *(G-10708)*

Tdy Industries LLC .... B 260 726-8121
Portland *(G-13968)*

Tecumseh Products Company LLC .... G 812 883-3575
Salem *(G-14502)*

Ty Bowells Farrier Service .... G 812 537-3990
Greendale *(G-6456)*

Union Electric Steel Corp .... G 219 464-1031
Valparaiso *(G-16071)*

3463 Nonferrous forgings

Autoform Tool & Mfg LLC .... C 260 624-2014
Angola *(G-232)*

CMI Pgi Holdings LLC .... F 812 377-5000
Columbus *(G-2238)*

Fountaintown Forge Inc .... E 317 861-5403
Fountaintown *(G-5614)*

▲ Harvey Industries LLC .... B 260 563-8371
Wabash *(G-16190)*

♦ High Performance Alloys Inc .... E 765 945-8230
Windfall *(G-16905)*

Impact Forge Group Inc .... G 812 342-4437
Columbus *(G-2322)*

▲ JM Fittings LLC .... E 260 747-9200
Fort Wayne *(G-5137)*

Parker-Hannifin Corporation .... D 260 636-2104
Albion *(G-40)*

R P Imel .... G 260 543-2465
Uniondale *(G-15872)*

▲ Symmetry Medical Mfg Inc .... C 574 371-2284
Warsaw *(G-16435)*

Tdy Industries LLC .... B 260 726-8121
Portland *(G-13968)*

Terrecorp Inc .... F 317 951-8325
Indianapolis *(G-9578)*

3465 Automotive stampings

Afco Performance Group LLC .... F 812 897-0900
Boonville *(G-1079)*

Almco Steel Products Corp .... C 260 824-1118
Bluffton *(G-1023)*

Aludyne North America LLC .... B 260 925-4711
Auburn *(G-361)*

Aludyne North America LLC .... C 574 594-9681
Pierceton *(G-13629)*

Auto Extras Inc .... G 574 855-2370
South Bend *(G-14952)*

Blue River Stamping Inc .... D 317 395-5600
Shelbyville *(G-14737)*

Body Panels Co .... F 812 962-6262
Evansville *(G-3937)*

▲ Fayette Tool and Engineering .... D 765 825-7518
Connersville *(G-2438)*

Fenders Inc .... G 574 293-3717
Elkhart *(G-3344)*

Flex-N-Gate LLC .... G 260 665-8288
Angola *(G-251)*

Fogwell Technologies Inc .... G 260 410-1898
Roanoke *(G-14266)*

Francine Bond Insur Agcy Inc .... G 317 262-2250
Brownsburg *(G-1369)*

Fukai Toyotetsu Indiana Corp .... D 765 676-4800
Jamestown *(G-9817)*

▲ Futaba Indiana America Corp .... B 812 895-4700
Vincennes *(G-16127)*

Grouper Wild LLC .... C 574 534-1499
Goshen *(G-6156)*

Gt Industries Inc .... E 734 241-7242
North Vernon *(G-13274)*

♦ Heritage Products Inc .... C 765 364-9002
Crawfordsville *(G-2577)*

SIC SECTION
34 FABRICATED METAL PRODUCTS

Hitchcock Tool LLC .... G 513 276-7345
Richmond *(G-14134)*

Hudson Industries Inc .... C 260 587-3288
Hudson *(G-7246)*

Jason Holdings Inc .... C 414 277-9300
Richmond *(G-14147)*

Kousei Usa Inc .... G 812 373-7315
Columbus *(G-2336)*

Lakepark Industries Ind Inc .... D
Shipshewana *(G-14861)*

Lcm Realty IV LLC .... G 574 312-6182
Goshen *(G-6197)*

Metal Fab Engineering Inc .... E 574 278-7150
Winamac *(G-16867)*

Mpi Engineered Tech Win LLC .... G 574 772-3850
Knox *(G-10216)*

Multimatic Indiana Inc .... C 260 749-3700
Fort Wayne *(G-5250)*

◆ Multimatic Indiana Inc .... E 260 868-1000
Butler *(G-1472)*

Nasg Indiana LLC .... E 765 381-4310
Muncie *(G-12467)*

Omr North America Inc .... D 317 510-9700
Speedway *(G-15337)*

▲ Oreca North America Inc .... G 317 517-2948
Indianapolis *(G-9069)*

◆ Pk USA Inc .... B 317 395-5500
Shelbyville *(G-14784)*

Pridgeon & Clay Inc .... G 317 738-4885
Franklin *(G-5770)*

Pro-Tech Tool & Stamping Inc .... E 765 258-3613
Frankfort *(G-5691)*

Robert Atkins .... G 765 536-4164
Summitville *(G-15430)*

Sanoh America Inc .... G 419 425-2600
Lafayette *(G-10683)*

Shiloh Susiebell LLC .... G 574 936-8412
Plymouth *(G-13813)*

Specialty Blanks Inc .... G 812 232-8775
Terre Haute *(G-15708)*

Specialty Rim Supply Inc .... G 812 234-3002
Terre Haute *(G-15709)*

▲ Spheros North America Inc .... G 734 218-7350
Elkhart *(G-3693)*

Steel Parts Corporation .... A 765 675-2191
Tipton *(G-15791)*

Techna Fit of Indiana .... G 317 350-2153
Brownsburg *(G-1407)*

TOA Winchester LLC .... B 765 584-7639
Winchester *(G-16901)*

Tower Atmtive Oprtons USA II L .... C 260 920-1500
Auburn *(G-431)*

Tru-Form Metal Products Inc .... F 574 266-8020
Elkhart *(G-3749)*

3466 Crowns and closures

Charmaran Company LLC .... F 260 347-3347
Kendallville *(G-10098)*

Drug Plastics Closures Inc .... E 812 526-0555
Edinburgh *(G-3080)*

◆ Rieke LLC .... B 260 925-3700
Auburn *(G-419)*

3469 Metal stampings, nec

Absolute Custom Coins Inc .... G 812 733-4043
Borden *(G-1102)*

Advanced Metal Fabricators Inc .... F 574 259-1263
Mishawaka *(G-11835)*

▲ Aircom Manufacturing Inc .... B 317 545-5383
Indianapolis *(G-7462)*

Almco Steel Products Corp .... C 260 824-1118
Bluffton *(G-1023)*

Ameri-Tek Manufacturing Inc .... F 574 753-8058
Logansport *(G-11055)*

Araymond Mfg Ctr N Amer Inc .... C 574 722-5168
Logansport *(G-11058)*

Ark Model and Stampings Inc .... F 317 549-3394
New Palestine *(G-12931)*

Atkisson Enterprises Inc .... F 765 675-7593
Tipton *(G-15766)*

Aul Brothers Tool & Die Inc .... F 765 759-5124
Yorktown *(G-16968)*

▲ Austin Tri-Hawk Automotive Inc .... C 812 794-0062
Austin *(G-463)*

▲ B Walter & Company Inc .... E 260 563-2181
Wabash *(G-16174)*

▲ B&J Rocket America Inc .... E 574 825-5802
Middlebury *(G-11700)*

▲ Batesville Tool & Die Inc .... B 812 934-5616
Batesville *(G-584)*

Boice Manufacturing Inc .... D 317 773-2100
Noblesville *(G-13044)*

Btd Manufacturing Inc .... G 812 934-5616
Batesville *(G-585)*

C E R Metal Marking Corp .... G 219 924-9710
Highland *(G-7126)*

▲ Capco LLC .... D 812 375-1700
Columbus *(G-2233)*

CCT Enterprises LLC .... E 260 925-1420
Auburn *(G-375)*

Charmaran Company LLC .... F 260 347-3347
Kendallville *(G-10098)*

Cnc Industries Inc .... E 260 490-5700
Fort Wayne *(G-4863)*

Colbin Tool Company Inc .... E 574 457-3183
Syracuse *(G-15459)*

Computer Technology .... G 812 283-5094
Jeffersonville *(G-9959)*

Countryside Tool .... G 260 357-3839
Garrett *(G-5857)*

Crichlow Industries Inc .... G 317 925-5178
Indianapolis *(G-7903)*

Crossrads Rhbilitation Ctr Inc .... C 317 897-7320
Indianapolis *(G-7910)*

Curtis Tom Tool and Dye .... G 574 293-3832
Elkhart *(G-3282)*

Da-Mar Industries Inc .... F 260 347-1662
Kendallville *(G-10107)*

Diamond Manufacturing Company .... D 219 874-2374
Michigan City *(G-11600)*

Die-Mensional Metal Stampg Inc .... F 812 265-3946
Madison *(G-11213)*

Dietech Corporation .... G 260 724-8946
Decatur *(G-2852)*

Dixie Metal Spinning Corp .... G 317 541-1330
Indianapolis *(G-7990)*

▲ Domar Machine & Tool Inc .... G 574 295-8791
Elkhart *(G-3299)*

Drews Parts LLC .... F 317 800-8713
Anderson *(G-110)*

Dwyer Instruments Inc .... G 219 393-5250
La Porte *(G-10402)*

Eaton Corporation .... C 260 925-3800
Auburn *(G-387)*

Economy Dumpster .... G 317 308-7774
Indianapolis *(G-8050)*

▼ Epco Products Inc .... E 260 747-8888
Fort Wayne *(G-4956)*

Evansville Metal Products Inc .... D 812 423-5632
Evansville *(G-4054)*

▲ Ffesar Inc .... G 812 378-4220
Mccordsville *(G-11448)*

First Metals & Plastics T .... E 812 379-4400
Columbus *(G-2308)*

Flambeau Inc .... G 812 372-4899
Columbus *(G-2310)*

▲ Form Wood Industries Inc .... E 812 284-3676
Jeffersonville *(G-9986)*

Franklin Stamping Inds Inc .... F 765 282-5138
Muncie *(G-12397)*

Galloway Fabricating .... G 574 453-3802
Leesburg *(G-10954)*

▲ Gammons Metal & Mfg Co Inc .... E 317 546-7091
Indianapolis *(G-8258)*

Gbo Corporation .... F 574 825-7670
Middlebury *(G-11717)*

General Devices Co Inc .... E 317 897-7000
Indianapolis *(G-8270)*

General Motors LLC .... B 765 668-2000
Marion *(G-11287)*

General Sheet Metal Works Inc .... E 574 288-0611
South Bend *(G-15042)*

Gentec LLC .... G 260 436-7333
Fort Wayne *(G-5022)*

▲ Group Dekko Inc .... D 260 357-3621
Fort Wayne *(G-5042)*

Gt Stamping Inc .... D 574 533-4108
Goshen *(G-6157)*

Harold Precision Products Inc .... E 765 348-2710
Hartford City *(G-7067)*

Hasser Enterprises Inc .... G 765 583-1444
West Lafayette *(G-16590)*

Haven Manufacturing Ind LLC .... F 260 622-4150
Ossian *(G-13425)*

◆ HD Williams Co .... G 812 372-6476
New Castle *(G-12866)*

High Tech Fabricators Inc .... E 260 744-4467
Fort Wayne *(G-5065)*

▲ Hoosier Stamping LLC .... G 812 426-2778
Chandler *(G-1862)*

▲ Hoosier Stamping & Mfg Corp .... E 812 426-2778
Evansville *(G-4110)*

Hoosier Tank and Mfg LLC .... D 574 232-8368
South Bend *(G-15071)*

Hoosier Trim Products LLC .... E 317 271-4007
Indianapolis *(G-8412)*

Hoosier Washer .... G 317 460-8354
Waldron *(G-16259)*

Humphrey Tool Co Inc .... G 574 753-3853
Logansport *(G-11079)*

Imh Fabrication LLC .... E 317 252-5566
Indianapolis *(G-8465)*

Imh Fabrication LLC .... F 317 508-7462
Indianapolis *(G-8466)*

▲ Imperial Stamping Corporation .... D 574 294-3780
Elkhart *(G-3419)*

Indiana Fine Blanking .... G 574 772-3850
Knox *(G-10211)*

Indiana Metal Stamping Co .... G 574 936-2964
Plymouth *(G-13783)*

▲ Indianapolis Metal Spinning Co .... F 317 273-7440
Indianapolis *(G-8507)*

Irwin Hodson Group Indiana LLC .... G 260 482-8052
Fort Wayne *(G-5121)*

J & K Associates Inc .... G 317 255-3588
Indianapolis *(G-8599)*

J M Hutton .... G 765 935-4817
Richmond *(G-14145)*

Jag Metal .... G 812 235-7200
Terre Haute *(G-15620)*

Jag Metal Spinning Inc .... G 812 533-5501
Sandford *(G-14506)*

Jason Holdings Inc .... C 414 277-9300
Richmond *(G-14147)*

Jason Incorporated .... D 847 215-1948
Richmond *(G-14150)*

Employee Codes: A=Over 500 employees, B=251-500
C=101-250, D=51-100, E=20-50, F=10-19, G=1-9

2024 Harris Indiana
Industrial Directory

34 FABRICATED METAL PRODUCTS

◆ JM Hutton & Co Inc .... D 765 962-3591
Richmond *(G-14152)*

Kable Tool & Engineering .... G 260 726-9670
Portland *(G-13954)*

Kimball Electronics Inc .... D 317 545-5383
Indianapolis *(G-8686)*

Kitchen & Bath Fixtures .... G 574 296-7617
Elkhart *(G-3458)*

KMC Enterprises Inc .... G 765 584-1533
Winchester *(G-16893)*

Koester Metals Inc .... E 260 495-1818
Fremont *(G-5825)*

Krukemeier Machine & Tool Co .... E 317 784-7042
Beech Grove *(G-697)*

▲ L H Carbide Corporation .... D 260 432-5563
Fort Wayne *(G-5165)*

L H Stamping Corporation .... E 260 432-5563
Fort Wayne *(G-5167)*

Lakepark Industries Ind Inc .... D
Shipshewana *(G-14861)*

Lauck Manufacturing Co Inc .... F 317 787-6269
Indianapolis *(G-8727)*

LH Industries Corp .... E 260 432-5563
Fort Wayne *(G-5181)*

Lippert Components Inc .... G 574 535-1125
Elkhart *(G-3492)*

Lippert Components Inc .... D 574 535-1125
Goshen *(G-6202)*

Lippert Components Inc .... G 574 849-0869
Goshen *(G-6206)*

Lippert Components Inc .... F 574 971-4320
Goshen *(G-6207)*

Lippert Components Inc .... E 574 312-7445
Middlebury *(G-11734)*

Lippert Components Inc .... E 800 551-9149
Mishawaka *(G-11930)*

Lippert Components Inc .... F 260 234-4303
Yoder *(G-16966)*

▲ Lippert Components Inc .... B 574 535-1125
Elkhart *(G-3493)*

Logan Stampings Inc .... G 574 722-3101
Peru *(G-13590)*

Logan Stampings Inc .... E 574 722-3101
Logansport *(G-11089)*

▲ Long Item Development Corp .... G 317 780-1077
Indianapolis *(G-8780)*

Lynn Tool Company Inc .... G 765 874-2471
Lynn *(G-11185)*

MA Metal Co Inc .... E 812 526-2666
Edinburgh *(G-3091)*

▼ Mac Machine & Metal Works Inc .... E 765 825-4121
Connersville *(G-2453)*

Mahan Technical Design LLC .... G 765 341-0533
Martinsville *(G-11410)*

Maron Products Incorporated .... D 574 259-1971
Mishawaka *(G-11938)*

Master Manufacturing Company .... E 812 425-1561
Evansville *(G-4191)*

Mc Metalcraft Inc .... G 574 259-8101
Mishawaka *(G-11941)*

Metal Fab Engineering Inc .... E 574 278-7150
Winamac *(G-16867)*

Metal Spinners Inc .... F 260 665-2158
Angola *(G-275)*

Mid-West Spring Mfg Co .... D 574 353-1409
Mentone *(G-11474)*

Midway Products Group Inc .... F 734 241-7242
Hudson *(G-7248)*

Mier Products Inc .... E 765 457-0223
Kokomo *(G-10307)*

Miller Mfg Corp .... E 574 773-4136
Nappanee *(G-12626)*

Mpi Engineered Tech LLC .... B 574 772-3850
Knox *(G-10215)*

Mpi Engineered Tech Win LLC .... G 574 772-3850
Knox *(G-10216)*

Muncie Metal Spinning Inc .... F 765 288-1937
Muncie *(G-12462)*

▼ Mursix Corporation .... C 765 282-2221
Yorktown *(G-16977)*

NA Holding-Lime City LLC .... F 260 212-2294
Fort Wayne *(G-5254)*

P & A Machine Company Inc .... G 317 634-3673
Bargersville *(G-571)*

▼ Pent Plastics Inc .... C 260 897-3775
Kendallville *(G-10142)*

▼ Perfecto Tool & Engineering Co .... E 765 644-2821
Anderson *(G-176)*

Phoenix Stamping Group LLC .... E 404 699-2882
Fort Wayne *(G-5314)*

Precision Stamping Inc .... F 574 522-8987
Elkhart *(G-3616)*

Precision Stmping Slutions LLC .... G 317 501-4436
Fishers *(G-4583)*

Premier Concepts Inc .... F 574 269-7570
Warsaw *(G-16413)*

Productivity Resources Inc .... G 317 245-4040
Noblesville *(G-13160)*

▲ Qmp Inc .... E 574 262-1575
Elkhart *(G-3627)*

Quality Die Set Corp .... E 574 967-4411
Logansport *(G-11104)*

R P Imel .... E 260 543-2465
Uniondale *(G-15872)*

Rbm Manufacturing Inc .... G 765 364-6933
Crawfordsville *(G-2613)*

Reber Enterprises LLC .... G 260 356-6826
Huntington *(G-7360)*

Reeves Manufacturing Inc .... G 765 935-3875
Richmond *(G-14196)*

Rhinehart Development Corp .... E 260 238-4442
Spencerville *(G-15373)*

Rotam Tooling Corporation .... G 260 982-8318
North Manchester *(G-13248)*

Samco Inc .... E 812 279-8131
Bedford *(G-671)*

Sha-Do Corp .... G 574 848-9296
Bristol *(G-1290)*

Shakour Industries Inc .... G 574 289-0100
South Bend *(G-15239)*

Small Parts Inc .... G 574 739-6236
Logansport *(G-11106)*

Smiths Small Engines Inc .... G 812 232-1318
Terre Haute *(G-15699)*

Specilty Blnks Inc An Ind Corp .... C 812 234-3002
Terre Haute *(G-15711)*

Stamina Metal Products Inc .... G 574 534-7410
Goshen *(G-6258)*

Stampede Enterprises Inc .... D 574 232-5997
South Bend *(G-15266)*

◆ Star Case Manufacturing Co LLC .... E 219 922-4440
Munster *(G-12565)*

Steel Parts Corporation .... A 765 675-2191
Tipton *(G-15791)*

▼ Stone City Products Inc .... D 812 275-3373
Bedford *(G-676)*

Swiss Metal Spinning Co .... G 260 692-1401
Monroe *(G-12064)*

▼ Symmetry Medical Mfg Inc .... C 574 371-2284
Warsaw *(G-16435)*

▲ T-A Wind Down Inc .... C 708 839-1400
Munster *(G-12566)*

Target Metal Blanking Inc .... E 812 346-1700
North Vernon *(G-13298)*

TEC-Air LLC .... D 219 301-7084
Munster *(G-12569)*

The Akron Equipment Company .... E 260 622-4150
Ossian *(G-13438)*

Titan Metal Spinning Inc .... G 260 665-1067
Angola *(G-299)*

TLC Metals Inc .... D 317 894-8684
Greenfield *(G-6566)*

Triple J Machining and Mfg Inc .... F 574 586-7500
Walkerton *(G-16277)*

Trivector Manufacturing Inc .... E 260 637-0141
Fort Wayne *(G-5509)*

Tube Processing Corp .... G 317 264-7760
Indianapolis *(G-9657)*

▲ Tube Processing Corp .... B 317 787-1321
Indianapolis *(G-9658)*

Ultra Manufacturing Inc .... E 574 586-2320
Walkerton *(G-16278)*

Valley Tool & Die Stampings .... E 574 722-4566
Logansport *(G-11117)*

Versatile Fabrication LLC .... G 574 293-8504
Elkhart *(G-3769)*

Wayne Manufacturing LLC .... D 260 637-5586
Laotto *(G-10811)*

Webber Manufacturing Company .... E 317 357-8681
Indianapolis *(G-9745)*

Wenzel Acquisition Inc .... G 260 495-9898
Fremont *(G-5839)*

Wenzel Metal Spinning Inc .... D 260 495-9898
Fremont *(G-5840)*

Wenzel Metal Spinning Inc Ind .... F 260 495-9898
Fremont *(G-5841)*

Ynwa Industries Inc .... D 574 295-6641
Elkhart *(G-3800)*

York Group Inc .... C 765 966-1576
Richmond *(G-14232)*

ZF Active Safety & Elec US LLC .... D 765 429-1984
Lafayette *(G-10721)*

▲ Zojila Ltd Liability Company .... G 765 404-3767
Lafayette *(G-10726)*

3471 Plating and polishing

502 Mold Polishing LLC .... G 502 436-0239
Greenville *(G-6650)*

Abrasive Processing & Tech LLC .... G 317 485-5157
Fortville *(G-5587)*

Albany Metal Treating Inc .... F 765 789-6470
Albany *(G-11)*

Allfab LLC .... G 317 359-3539
Indianapolis *(G-7482)*

▼ Alliance Steel Corporation .... E 708 924-1200
Gary *(G-5890)*

Altec LLC .... D 812 282-8256
Jeffersonville *(G-9928)*

Anderson Silver Plating Co .... F 574 294-6447
Elkhart *(G-3182)*

Araymond Mfg Ctr N Amer Inc .... C 574 722-5168
Logansport *(G-11058)*

ATI Flat Rlled Pdts Hldngs LLC .... F 765 529-9570
New Castle *(G-12850)*

B-D Industries Inc .... F 574 295-1420
Elkhart *(G-3214)*

Bar Processing Corporation .... F 219 931-0702
Hammond *(G-6881)*

▲ Bare Metal Inc .... F 812 948-1313
New Albany *(G-12696)*

▲ Batesville Products Inc .... D 513 381-2057
Lawrenceburg *(G-10831)*

Bearcat Anodizing LLC .... G 574 533-0448
Goshen *(G-6097)*

◆ Blitz Manufacturing Co Ind .... D 812 284-2548
Jeffersonville *(G-9944)*

SIC SECTION
34 FABRICATED METAL PRODUCTS

Bonnell Aluminum Inc .... A 815 351-6802
  Kentland (G-10157)
Bonnell Aluminum Elkhart Inc .... C 574 262-4685
  Elkhart (G-3232)
Brunswick Corporation .... D 260 459-8200
  Fort Wayne (G-4821)
Bye Buy Cci Inc .... F 260 925-0623
  Auburn (G-371)
C & J Plating & Grinding LLC .... G 765 288-8728
  Muncie (G-12358)
C & R Plating Corp .... E 586 755-4900
  Columbia City (G-2128)
▲ Ceramica Inc .... F 317 546-0087
  Indianapolis (G-7777)
Chief Metal Works Inc .... G 765 932-2134
  Rushville (G-14396)
Chrome Deposit Corporation .... E 219 763-1571
  Portage (G-13855)
Circle City Heat Treating Inc .... F 317 440-9102
  Indianapolis (G-7805)
▲ Cleveland-Cliffs Kote Inc .... C 574 654-1000
  New Carlisle (G-12836)
Commercial Finishing Corp .... F 317 267-0377
  Indianapolis (G-7840)
Complete Finish Inc .... F 260 587-3588
  Ashley (G-331)
Custom Mtal Fnshng-Indiana LLC .... G 765 489-4089
  Hagerstown (G-6835)
Custom Polish & Chrome .... G 260 665-7448
  Angola (G-244)
Db Polishing .... G 574 518-2443
  Nappanee (G-12593)
Dekalb Metal Finishing Inc .... D 260 925-1820
  Auburn (G-386)
Diamond Manufacturing Company .... D 219 874-2374
  Michigan City (G-11600)
DOT America Inc .... F 260 244-5700
  Columbia City (G-2138)
Doug Wilcox .... G 812 476-1957
  Lynnville (G-11189)
Electro-Spec Inc .... D 317 738-9199
  Franklin (G-5728)
Elkhart Plating Corp .... F 574 294-1800
  Elkhart (G-3327)
Em Black Oxide .... G 574 233-4933
  South Bend (G-15012)
Emi LLC .... E 812 437-9100
  Evansville (G-4033)
Evans Herron .... G 317 492-1384
  Indianapolis (G-8140)
Franke Plating Works Inc .... D 260 422-8477
  Fort Wayne (G-5005)
G and P Enterprises Ind Inc .... G 812 723-3837
  Paoli (G-13495)
Hand Industries Inc .... E 574 267-3525
  Warsaw (G-16373)
Heidtman Steel Products Inc .... D 419 691-4646
  Butler (G-1465)
Huthone LLC .... G 260 248-2384
  Columbia City (G-2153)
Hydro Extrusion Usa LLC .... B 888 935-5757
  North Liberty (G-13217)
Industrial Anodizing Co Inc .... E 317 637-4641
  Indianapolis (G-8517)
Industrial Plating Inc .... D 765 447-5036
  Lafayette (G-10607)
Indy Metal Finishing Co .... E 317 858-5353
  Brownsburg (G-1372)
▲ J & J Welding Inc .... E 812 838-4851
  Mount Vernon (G-12303)
J & L Dimensional Services Inc .... E 219 325-3588
  La Porte (G-10430)

J & P Custom Plating Inc .... G 260 726-9696
  Portland (G-13951)
Jrs Polishing LLC .... G 574 306-2351
  Winona Lake (G-16911)
Just Perfection LLC .... G 347 559-5878
  Indianapolis (G-8650)
K & I Hard Chrome Inc .... E 812 948-1166
  New Albany (G-12756)
Kadet Products Inc .... F 765 552-7341
  Elwood (G-3828)
Klinge Enameling Company Inc .... E 317 359-8291
  Indianapolis (G-8694)
Lambert Metal Finishing Inc .... F 260 493-0529
  Fort Wayne (G-5174)
Linden Machine Shop LLC .... G 765 339-7244
  Linden (G-11031)
McDowell Enterprises Inc .... E 574 293-1042
  Elkhart (G-3521)
Metal Finishing Co Inc .... G 317 546-9004
  Indianapolis (G-8885)
Michiana Metal Finishing Inc .... G 574 206-0666
  Elkhart (G-3534)
Mid-City Plating Co Inc .... E 765 289-2374
  Muncie (G-12452)
Midwest Surface Prep LLC .... G 317 726-1336
  Indianapolis (G-8915)
Mnbkc LLC .... F 317 956-6558
  Indianapolis (G-8939)
Mpp Inc .... E 260 422-5426
  Fort Wayne (G-5248)
Napier & Napier .... G 765 580-9116
  Liberty (G-10992)
National Material LP .... C 219 397-5088
  East Chicago (G-3031)
Neo Industries LLC .... G 219 762-6075
  Portage (G-13896)
Neo Industries LLC .... E 574 217-4078
  South Bend (G-15162)
▲ Neo Industries (Indiana) Inc .... G 219 762-6075
  Portage (G-13897)
P & J Industries Inc .... E 260 894-7143
  Ligonier (G-11021)
Performance Powder Coating .... G 765 438-5224
  Kokomo (G-10320)
Pioneer Metal Finishing LLC .... D 574 287-7239
  South Bend (G-15196)
Poiry Partners LLC .... G 260 436-7070
  Fort Wayne (G-5321)
Poiry Partners LLC .... E 260 424-1030
  Fort Wayne (G-5322)
▲ Poseidon LLC .... C 260 422-8767
  Berne (G-722)
Precision Buffing & Polsg Inc .... G 574 262-3430
  Elkhart (G-3614)
Precision Polishing & Buffing .... G 317 352-0165
  Indianapolis (G-9183)
Professional Metal Refinishing .... G 260 436-2828
  Fort Wayne (G-5353)
Progressive Plating Company .... E 317 923-2413
  Indianapolis (G-9226)
Quick Turn Anodizing LLC .... F 877 716-1150
  Edinburgh (G-3099)
R & S Plating Inc .... G 317 925-2396
  Indianapolis (G-9255)
▲ Rci Hv Inc .... D 724 538-3180
  Chesterton (G-1956)
Reckon Plating Inc .... E 260 744-4339
  Fort Wayne (G-5372)
Rhinehart Finishing LLC .... D 260 238-4442
  Spencerville (G-15374)
Riepen LLC .... D 574 269-5900
  Warsaw (G-16418)

Roll Coater Inc .... G 317 652-1102
  Indianapolis (G-9323)
Saran LP C
  Indianapolis (G-9373)
Saturn Wheel Company Inc .... E 260 375-4720
  Warren (G-16305)
Schaffsteins Truck Clean LLC .... F 812 464-2424
  Evansville (G-4298)
Shaklee Authorized Distributor .... G 260 471-8232
  Fort Wayne (G-5410)
Southern Alum Finshg Co Inc .... G 800 357-9016
  Indianapolis (G-9464)
Southside Plating Works Inc .... G 219 293-5508
  Elkhart (G-3689)
Sterling Industrial LLC .... C 812 423-7832
  Evansville (G-4333)
Steve Reiff Inc .... E 260 723-4360
  South Whitley (G-15328)
◆ Sumco LLC .... D 317 241-7600
  Indianapolis (G-9521)
Sumco Group LLC .... D 317 241-7600
  Indianapolis (G-9522)
▲ Superior Metal Tech LLC .... D 317 897-9850
  Indianapolis (G-9530)
Surface Enhancements Inc .... F 574 269-1366
  Warsaw (G-16432)
Ternet Metal Finishing Inc .... G 260 897-3903
  Avilla (G-496)
Tfx Plating Company Llc .... G 765 289-2436
  Yorktown (G-16983)
Tk Finishing LLC .... G 574 233-1617
  South Bend (G-15284)
▲ Transportation Tech Inds .... F 812 962-5000
  Evansville (G-4347)
Triplex Plating Inc .... E 219 874-3209
  Michigan City (G-11680)
United States Steel Corp .... G 219 762-3131
  Portage (G-13917)
W Kendall & Sons Inc .... G 219 733-2412
  Wanatah (G-16292)
Wayne Black Oxide Inc .... G 260 484-0280
  Fort Wayne (G-5550)
◆ Whimet Inc .... D 574 267-8062
  Warsaw (G-16448)
Whitlocks Pressure Wash .... F 765 825-5868
  Connersville (G-2475)
Worthington Steel Company .... G 219 929-4000
  Porter (G-13925)
Wrr Inc .... E 317 577-1149
  Indianapolis (G-9794)
Yellow Dog Anodizing .... G 574 343-2247
  Elkhart (G-3799)

3479 Metal coating and allied services

AAA Galvanizing - Joliet Inc .... F 260 488-4477
  Hamilton (G-6850)
AAA Galvanizing - Joliet Inc .... E 765 289-3427
  Muncie (G-12333)
AAA Galvanizing - Joliet Inc .... F 574 935-4500
  Plymouth (G-13751)
Aceys Trophies & Awards .... G 574 267-1426
  Warsaw (G-16309)
Allegheny Coatings RE LLC .... F 260 495-4445
  Fremont (G-5807)
Allied Applications LLC .... F 502 817-6478
  Corydon (G-2484)
▲ Alocit USA .... G 317 631-9111
  Indianapolis (G-7492)
▲ Angola Wire Products Inc .... C 260 665-9447
  Angola (G-229)
Apexx Enterprises LLC .... F 812 486-2443
  Montgomery (G-12085)

Employee Codes: A=Over 500 employees, B=251-500
C=101-250, D=51-100, E=20-50, F=10-19, G=1-9

34 FABRICATED METAL PRODUCTS

Applied Metals & Mch Works Inc............ E 260 424-4834
  Fort Wayne *(G-4766)*
Artistic Coatings LLC............................. F 260 463-5253
  Shipshewana *(G-14836)*
▲ Asempac Inc..................................... E 812 945-6303
  New Albany *(G-12692)*
B & B Powder Coating........................... G 260 726-4290
  Portland *(G-13928)*
B-D Industries Inc.................................. F 574 295-1420
  Elkhart *(G-3214)*
Babcocks Coatings LLC......................... G 812 624-2120
  Evansville *(G-3907)*
Beacon Industries Inc........................... E 812 526-0100
  Edinburgh *(G-3068)*
Bi-State Asphalt................................... G 765 832-5000
  Clinton *(G-2064)*
Big Dipper Inc...................................... F 317 272-6202
  Avon *(G-508)*
Blackfoot Powder Coating..................... G 812 531-9315
  Brazil *(G-1134)*
Carmel Trophies Plus LLC.................... G 317 844-3770
  Carmel *(G-1581)*
Carrara Industries Inc.......................... G 765 643-3430
  Anderson *(G-89)*
Chemcoaters LLC................................. E 219 977-1929
  Gary *(G-5916)*
Chief Metal Works Inc.......................... G 765 932-2134
  Rushville *(G-14396)*
▲ Cleveland-Cliffs Kote Inc................... C 574 654-1000
  New Carlisle *(G-12836)*
Commercial Coatings Assoc LLC........... G 812 773-3526
  Evansville *(G-3976)*
Commercial Finishing Corp.................... F 317 267-0377
  Indianapolis *(G-7840)*
▲ Conforma Clad Inc............................ D 812 948-2118
  New Albany *(G-12716)*
Craddock Furniture Corporation............. E 812 425-2691
  Evansville *(G-3991)*
Creative Finishing LLC......................... G 812 591-8111
  Greensburg *(G-6586)*
Creative Liquid Coatings Inc................ G 260 349-1862
  Kendallville *(G-10104)*
◆ Creative Liquid Coatings Inc............ B 260 349-1862
  Kendallville *(G-10105)*
Crichlow Industries Inc.......................... G 317 925-5178
  Indianapolis *(G-7903)*
Crossroads Galvanizing LLC................. F 765 421-6741
  Lafayette *(G-10563)*
Crown Group Co................................... E 260 432-6900
  Fort Wayne *(G-4890)*
Custom Coatings................................... G 317 392-7908
  Shelbyville *(G-14748)*
Custom TS & Trophies........................... G 219 926-4174
  Porter *(G-13923)*
Daniel Shade.. G 812 346-6285
  North Vernon *(G-13263)*
DC Coaters Inc..................................... D 765 675-6006
  Tipton *(G-15770)*
Dearborn Coatings LLC......................... G 513 600-9580
  Lawrenceburg *(G-10832)*
Debamc Inc... F 765 608-2100
  Anderson *(G-100)*
◆ Deloro Stellite Holdings Corporation. A 574 534-2585
  Goshen *(G-6120)*
Diamond Manufacturing Company.......... D 219 874-2374
  Michigan City *(G-11600)*
Dse Inc... E 812 376-0310
  Columbus *(G-2291)*
Durusa LLC... G 574 312-0923
  Granger *(G-6346)*
Edcoat Limited Partnership................... E 574 654-9105
  New Carlisle *(G-12839)*

▼ Electric Coating Tech LLC................... E 219 378-1930
  East Chicago *(G-3006)*
Electro-Coat Technologies..................... F 574 266-7356
  Elkhart *(G-3316)*
Elite Protective Coatings....................... G 317 476-1712
  Greenwood *(G-6693)*
Endless Creations................................. G 812 623-0190
  Sunman *(G-15437)*
Erler Industries Inc.............................. D 812 346-4421
  North Vernon *(G-13269)*
Evansville Metal Products Inc................ D 812 423-5632
  Evansville *(G-4054)*
Excel Finishings LLC............................ G 260 768-7667
  Lagrange *(G-10737)*
Extreme Finishes LLC............................ G 812 524-2442
  Seymour *(G-14652)*
Fasi Coatings LLC................................. G 219 985-0788
  Gary *(G-5932)*
Fenestration Products LLC.................... D 317 831-5314
  Mooresville *(G-12207)*
Fishers Laser Carvers LLC.................... G 317 845-0500
  Fishers *(G-4523)*
Forefront Foam LLC.............................. F 574 343-1146
  Mishawaka *(G-11897)*
Frema Holdings LLC............................ F 317 822-8002
  Indianapolis *(G-8231)*
French International Coatings................ G 574 505-0774
  Akron *(G-5)*
Gale Enameling Co Inc......................... G 317 839-7474
  Indianapolis *(G-8255)*
▲ Gammons Metal & Mfg Co Inc........... E 317 546-7091
  Indianapolis *(G-8258)*
Garrett Products................................... G 260 357-5988
  Garrett *(G-5862)*
▲ Gema USA Inc.................................. G 317 298-5000
  Indianapolis *(G-8267)*
Genesis Products LLC.......................... C 574 266-8293
  Elkhart *(G-3373)*
◆ Group Dekko Inc.............................. D 260 357-3621
  Fort Wayne *(G-5042)*
Henkel US Operations Corp................... C 765 284-5050
  Muncie *(G-12413)*
▲ Holscher Products Inc..................... E 765 884-8021
  Fowler *(G-5625)*
Hoosier Powder Coating LLC................ G 574 253-7737
  Nappanee *(G-12613)*
▲ IBC Coatings Technologies Ltd......... E 317 418-3725
  Lebanon *(G-10898)*
IBC Materials & Tech LLC..................... E 765 481-2900
  Lebanon *(G-10899)*
Ibc-Sputtek Inc.................................... G 765 482-9802
  Lebanon *(G-10900)*
Ideal Coatings LLC................................ F 574 358-0182
  Middlebury *(G-11722)*
Imagineering Enterprises Inc.................. E 317 635-8565
  Indianapolis *(G-8464)*
Imagineering Enterprises Inc.................. E 574 287-0642
  South Bend *(G-15075)*
▲ Imagineering Enterprises Inc............ D 574 287-2941
  South Bend *(G-15076)*
Indiana Galvanizing LLC........................ G 574 822-9102
  Middlebury *(G-11723)*
Indiana Powder Coatings Inc................ E 615 347-2787
  Brazil *(G-1146)*
Indy Powder Coating Inc...................... G 317 244-2231
  Indianapolis *(G-8533)*
Indy Powder Coatings LLC.................... G 317 236-7177
  Noblesville *(G-13105)*
Ink - LLC.. G 317 502-6473
  Franklin *(G-5746)*
Intratek Inc... G 260 484-3877
  Fort Wayne *(G-5116)*

Itsuwa America Inc.............................. F 812 375-0323
  Columbus *(G-2327)*
▲ Itsuwa Usa LLC............................... D 812 375-0323
  Columbus *(G-2328)*
Job Shop Coatings Inc.......................... F 317 462-9714
  Greenfield *(G-6522)*
Johnson Engraving & Trophies.............. G 260 982-7868
  North Manchester *(G-13236)*
Jupiter Aluminum Corporation............... D 219 932-3322
  Fairland *(G-4399)*
▲ Keco Engineered Coatings Inc.......... G 317 356-7279
  Indianapolis *(G-8666)*
◆ Kennametal Stellite LP..................... D 574 534-9532
  Goshen *(G-6186)*
Khamis Fine Jewelers Inc...................... G 317 841-8440
  Indianapolis *(G-8681)*
Klinge Enameling Company Inc............. E 317 359-8291
  Indianapolis *(G-8694)*
Lansing Mtlizing Grinding Inc................ G 219 931-1785
  Hammond *(G-6968)*
Larry H Poole....................................... G 812 466-9345
  Terre Haute *(G-15629)*
Laser Graphx Inc.................................. G 574 834-4443
  North Webster *(G-13309)*
Lein Corporation................................... E 765 674-6950
  Marion *(G-11307)*
◆ Linde Advanced Material Techno...... C 317 240-2500
  Indianapolis *(G-8758)*
Linde Advanced Mtl Tech Inc................. C 317 240-2500
  Indianapolis *(G-8759)*
Line-X.. G 812 491-9475
  Evansville *(G-4170)*
M S Powder Coating.............................. G 260 356-0300
  Huntington *(G-7340)*
▲ Magna-Tech Manufacturing............... C 765 284-5050
  Muncie *(G-12445)*
Mains Enterprises Inc............................ G 765 425-0162
  Wilkinson *(G-16843)*
Make It Black Seal Coating................... G 219 629-6230
  Gary *(G-5980)*
Mayes Powder Coating LLC................... G 317 403-6549
  Whiteland *(G-16792)*
Mays+red Spot Coatings LLC................ G 317 558-2024
  Indianapolis *(G-8858)*
McNeil Coatings Cons Inc...................... G 317 885-1557
  Greenwood *(G-6736)*
Mestek Inc.. C 317 831-5314
  Mooresville *(G-12221)*
Metalized Coatings LLC......................... G 219 851-0683
  La Porte *(G-10451)*
Midwest Custom Finishing Inc.............. F 219 874-0099
  Michigan City *(G-11639)*
Midwest Custom Finishing Inc.............. G 574 258-0099
  Mishawaka *(G-11948)*
Midwest Wheelcoaters LLC................... E 219 874-0099
  Michigan City *(G-11640)*
Mills Custom Powder Coating................ G 812 766-0308
  Winslow *(G-16921)*
▲ Modern Materials Inc....................... E 574 223-4509
  Rochester *(G-14308)*
Momentive Performance Mtls Inc........... B 260 357-2000
  Garrett *(G-5872)*
Natural Coating Systems...................... G 765 642-2464
  Anderson *(G-167)*
NC Coatings LLC................................... G 574 213-4754
  Nappanee *(G-12630)*
New Process Steel LP.......................... E 260 868-1445
  Butler *(G-1474)*
▲ New Star Metals Inc......................... E 219 378-1930
  East Chicago *(G-3032)*
Northern Ind Indus Catings LLC............ G 574 893-4621
  Akron *(G-6)*

SIC SECTION
34 FABRICATED METAL PRODUCTS

Oerlikon Balzers Coating USA................ D 765 935-7424
  Richmond *(G-14176)*
Outland Custom Coatings LLC................ G 260 894-4818
  Ligonier *(G-11020)*
Panacea Painting & Coating Inc............. G 260 728-4222
  Decatur *(G-2875)*
Performance Coatings Spc LLC.............. G 574 606-8153
  Topeka *(G-15815)*
Powder Coating By Express LLC............ F 812 402-1010
  Evansville *(G-4250)*
Powder LLC... G 317 581-9271
  Carmel *(G-1721)*
Powdercoil Technologies LLC................ G 708 634-2343
  Crown Point *(G-2734)*
Precision Powder Coat LLC.................... G 317 483-3670
  Mooresville *(G-12236)*
Precoat Metals....................................... F 219 763-1504
  Portage *(G-13906)*
Precoat Metals Corp............................... C 219 393-3561
  La Porte *(G-10465)*
▲ Precoat Metals Corp.......................... E 317 462-7761
  Greenfield *(G-6542)*
Premier Custom Coatings LLC............... G 317 557-7841
  Greenwood *(G-6755)*
Prince Manufacturing Corp..................... D 260 357-4484
  Garrett *(G-5874)*
Pro-Kote Indy LLC.................................. G 317 872-0001
  Indianapolis *(G-9215)*
Pro-Strip Indy LLC.................................. G 317 872-0001
  Indianapolis *(G-9216)*
Procoat Inc... G 317 263-5071
  Indianapolis *(G-9218)*
Professional Bowling Ball Svc................ G 317 786-4329
  Indianapolis *(G-9220)*
Pyramid Metallizing Inc.......................... G 219 879-9967
  Michigan City *(G-11653)*
Quality Pnt Prstned Fnshes Inc.............. G 574 294-6944
  Elkhart *(G-3633)*
Quick Tanks Inc...................................... D 260 347-3850
  Kendallville *(G-10146)*
Quick Turn Anodizing LLC..................... F 877 716-1150
  Edinburgh *(G-3099)*
Quickblades... G 260 359-2072
  Huntington *(G-7359)*
Raac LLC.. E 260 925-0623
  Auburn *(G-418)*
Red Spot Paint & Varnish Co................. G 812 428-9100
  Evansville *(G-4279)*
Reed Contracting Company................... E 765 452-2638
  Kokomo *(G-10326)*
Reflective Coating LLC.......................... G 260 414-1245
  Fort Wayne *(G-5375)*
▲ Rightway Fasteners Inc..................... C 812 342-2700
  Columbus *(G-2387)*
S T Praxair Technology Inc.................... E 317 240-2500
  Indianapolis *(G-9357)*
Saran LP... C
  Indianapolis *(G-9373)*
Schafer Powder Coating Inc................... E 317 228-9987
  Whitestown *(G-16820)*
▲ Scorpion Prtctive Coatings Inc.......... F 800 483-9087
  Cloverdale *(G-2097)*
Seavac (usa) LLC................................... F 260 747-7123
  Fort Wayne *(G-5407)*
Sermatech Intl Canada Corp.................. E 317 240-2500
  Indianapolis *(G-9404)*
Smartt Innovations Inc........................... F 574 266-5432
  Elkhart *(G-3685)*
Southern Alum Finshg Co Inc................ G 800 357-9016
  Indianapolis *(G-9464)*
Sp3.. E 260 547-4150
  Decatur *(G-2885)*

Specialty Coating Systems Inc............... D 317 244-1200
  Indianapolis *(G-9470)*
▲ Specialty Coating Systems Inc.......... F 317 244-1200
  Indianapolis *(G-9469)*
Specialty Coatings LLC.......................... G 812 431-3375
  Evansville *(G-4327)*
Star Quality Awards Inc.......................... G 812 273-1740
  Madison *(G-11252)*
Steel Dynamics Inc................................ D 812 218-1490
  Jeffersonville *(G-10059)*
Steve Reiff Inc.. E 260 723-4360
  South Whitley *(G-15328)*
Stout Laser Etch LLC............................. G 574 527-9523
  Warsaw *(G-16430)*
▲ Superior Metal Tech LLC.................... D 317 897-9850
  Indianapolis *(G-9530)*
Technicoat LLC...................................... F 574 339-1745
  Grovertown *(G-6824)*
Tgr Inc.. F 765 452-8225
  Kokomo *(G-10348)*
Togs Powder Coating............................. G 574 266-2850
  Elkhart *(G-3738)*
Tri-State Powder Coating LLC................ F 812 425-7010
  Evansville *(G-4351)*
Trion Coatings LLC................................ G 312 342-2004
  South Bend *(G-15294)*
Tristate Bolt Company........................... F 260 357-5541
  Garrett *(G-5879)*
Trophy Case LLC................................... G 812 853-5087
  Newburgh *(G-13026)*
▲ Truck Stylin Unlimited...................... F 574 223-8800
  Rochester *(G-14330)*
Twin Coatings & Finishes LLC............... G 317 557-0633
  Indianapolis *(G-9663)*
Unique Specialty Services LLC.............. G 219 395-8898
  Chesterton *(G-1963)*
Universal Coatings LLC......................... G 574 520-3403
  Elkhart *(G-3762)*
Van Westrum Corporation..................... G 317 926-3200
  Indianapolis *(G-9700)*
▼ Vitracoat America Inc....................... F 574 262-2188
  Elkhart *(G-3773)*
W Kendall & Sons Inc............................ G 219 733-2412
  Wanatah *(G-16292)*
▲ Winona Powder Coating Inc............. E 574 267-8311
  Etna Green *(G-3851)*
◆ Winona Pvd Coatings LLC................. E 574 269-3255
  Warsaw *(G-16453)*
Witt Galvanizing.................................... G 574 935-4500
  Plymouth *(G-13832)*
Witt Industries Inc................................. E 765 289-3427
  Muncie *(G-12523)*
Witt Industries Inc................................. F 574 935-4500
  Plymouth *(G-13833)*
Wright Coatings Corporation................. F 317 937-6768
  Indianapolis *(G-9791)*

3482 Small arms ammunition

Adam L Hoskins..................................... G 765 580-0345
  Liberty *(G-10983)*
Armorite Ammo LLC............................. G 765 825-7527
  Connersville *(G-2425)*
Blythes Sport Shop Inc.......................... F 219 924-4403
  Griffith *(G-6795)*
Cgf Enterprises LLC.............................. G 574 889-2074
  Logansport *(G-11067)*
Dalren Enterprises LLC......................... G 502 396-0346
  Pekin *(G-13515)*
Hoosier Bullets LLC............................... G 317 694-1257
  Trafalgar *(G-15828)*
Lomatt Dynamics LLC........................... G 574 500-2517
  Leesburg *(G-10957)*

Northern Indiana Ordnance Co............... G 574 289-5938
  South Bend *(G-15173)*
Paraklese Technologies LLC.................. F 502 357-0735
  Georgetown *(G-6073)*
Sons of Thunder.................................... G 812 897-4908
  Boonville *(G-1098)*

3483 Ammunition, except for small arms, nec

Bobcat Armament and Mfg LLC............. G 317 699-6127
  Shelbyville *(G-14738)*
Lomatt Dynamics LLC........................... G 574 500-2517
  Leesburg *(G-10957)*
Pine Valley Munitions Inc...................... G 260 818-6113
  Columbia City *(G-2181)*
▲ United States Dept of Navy............... G 812 854-1762
  Crane *(G-2541)*

3484 Small arms

2nd Amendment Customs LLC.............. G 765 716-5636
  Markleville *(G-11365)*
Acme Sports Inc.................................... G 812 522-4008
  Seymour *(G-14625)*
Blythes Sport Shop Inc.......................... F 219 924-4403
  Griffith *(G-6795)*
Calumet Arsenal LLC............................. G 219 256-9885
  Whiting *(G-16833)*
CCT Enterprises LLC............................. E 260 925-1420
  Auburn *(G-375)*
CF Gunworks LLC................................. G 317 538-1122
  Frankfort *(G-5653)*
Dave Brown Customs LLC..................... G 812 727-5560
  Palmyra *(G-13479)*
Enterprise MGT Solutions LLC............... G 219 545-8544
  Merrillville *(G-11513)*
Kore Outdoor (us) Inc............................ E 800 724-6822
  Fort Wayne *(G-5156)*
Michael Hazeltine.................................. F 317 750-5091
  Greenwood *(G-6739)*
Namacle LLC... G 574 320-1436
  South Bend *(G-15158)*
Patriot Industries LLC............................ G 574 370-7899
  Bloomington *(G-943)*
Qtr Industries LLC.................................. G 260 416-8981
  Fort Wayne *(G-5360)*
Red Bull Armory LLC............................. G 757 287-7738
  Mitchell *(G-12046)*
Sisk Rifles Manufacturing LLC............... G 812 686-8067
  Tell City *(G-15517)*
Smith Group Precision LLC.................... G 855 927-6224
  Bedford *(G-673)*
Standard Issue Armory LLC................... F 812 364-1466
  Greenville *(G-6657)*
Suppress TEC LLC................................ G 812 453-5813
  Elberfeld *(G-3122)*
▼ Tippmann Arms Company LLC.......... G 260 245-0602
  Fort Wayne *(G-5485)*
Vadens Firearms & Ammun LLC............ G 317 840-5799
  Indianapolis *(G-9697)*
Wraith Arms Resolutions LLC................ G 812 380-1208
  Velpen *(G-16095)*
Zrp LLC.. G 888 824-5587
  Laotto *(G-10813)*

3489 Ordnance and accessories, nec

170 Tactical Inc..................................... G 765 793-7932
  Covington *(G-2525)*
▼ Advanced Tctcal Ord Systems LL..... G 858 228-1439
  Fort Wayne *(G-4729)*
Afsol Inc.. G 260 357-0788
  Auburn *(G-360)*
Allied Mfg Partners Inc.......................... G 260 428-2670
  Fort Wayne *(G-4745)*

Employee Codes: A=Over 500 employees, B=251-500
C=101-250, D=51-100, E=20-50, F=10-19, G=1-9

2024 Harris Indiana
Industrial Directory

34 FABRICATED METAL PRODUCTS

B & B Arms Inc .... G 317 339-4929
   Plainfield *(G-13659)*
Indiana Ordnance Works Inc .... G 812 256-4478
   Pekin *(G-13517)*
James Brummett .... G 317 724-4131
   Danville *(G-2815)*
Liberty Arms Inc .... G 574 583-5630
   Monticello *(G-12156)*
Norris Arms Co LLC .... G 574 658-4163
   Milford *(G-11801)*
Raytheon Company .... A 260 429-6000
   Fort Wayne *(G-5368)*
Rite-Way Arms LLC .... G 260 493-4517
   Fort Wayne *(G-5384)*
Sisk Rifles Manufacturing LLC .... G 812 686-8067
   Tell City *(G-15517)*
Trijent LLC .... G 502 544-4250
   Macy *(G-11196)*
Winingers Manufacturing LLC .... G 812 887-6129
   Vincennes *(G-16167)*
Zr Tactical Solutions LLC .... F 317 721-9787
   Noblesville *(G-13201)*

3491 Industrial valves

▲ Aalberts Hydrnic Flow Ctrl Inc .... E 317 257-6050
   Fishers *(G-4458)*
AMG LLC .... F 317 329-4004
   Indianapolis *(G-7513)*
Dresser LLC .... D 765 827-9200
   Connersville *(G-2436)*
◆ Dwyer Instruments LLC .... C 219 879-8868
   Michigan City *(G-11604)*
Electronics Incorporated .... E 574 256-5001
   Mishawaka *(G-11891)*
Emond Eldon .... G 219 279-2442
   Wolcott *(G-16930)*
Fitch Inc .... F 260 637-0835
   Huntertown *(G-7256)*
Flosource Inc .... E 800 752-5959
   Mooresville *(G-12208)*
Frew Process Group LLC .... G 317 565-5000
   Noblesville *(G-13081)*
Hoerbiger Service .... F 574 855-4112
   South Bend *(G-15065)*
Hoffman Sls & Specialty Co Inc .... G 317 846-6428
   Carmel *(G-1656)*
Kaman Corporation .... D 714 696-3750
   Fort Wayne *(G-5143)*
MH Vale PC .... G 219 661-0867
   Crown Point *(G-2723)*
◆ Nibco Inc .... B 574 295-3000
   Elkhart *(G-3570)*
Parker-Hannifin Corporation .... D 260 636-2104
   Albion *(G-40)*
Pentair .... G 574 278-7161
   Winamac *(G-16869)*
Picketts Place Inc .... G 317 763-1168
   Westfield *(G-16717)*
Proportion-Air Inc .... D 317 335-2602
   Mccordsville *(G-11454)*
Randall K Dike .... G 812 664-4942
   Owensville *(G-13471)*
S H Leggitt Company .... G 574 264-0230
   Elkhart *(G-3656)*
Shoemaker Inc .... F 260 625-4321
   Fort Wayne *(G-5414)*
▲ SMC Corporation of America .... B 317 899-4440
   Noblesville *(G-13176)*
▲ Specilzed Cmpnent Prts Ltd LLC .... C 260 925-2588
   Auburn *(G-425)*
▲ Stant Manufacturing Inc .... A 870 247-5480
   Connersville *(G-2468)*

Stingray Systems LLC .... G 317 238-6508
   Indianapolis *(G-9511)*
Tri-State Valve LLC .... F 901 388-1550
   Indianapolis *(G-9638)*
US Valves Inc .... G 812 476-6662
   Evansville *(G-4365)*
▲ Vernatherm LLC .... E 860 582-6776
   Columbus *(G-2411)*

3492 Fluid power valves and hose fittings

▲ Bilfinger Airvac Water Te .... D 574 223-3980
   Rochester *(G-14279)*
Cindon Inc .... F 812 853-5450
   Newburgh *(G-12998)*
Dependable Rubber Industrial .... G 765 447-5654
   Lafayette *(G-10569)*
Hydro Systems Mfg Inc .... G 260 436-4476
   Fort Wayne *(G-5088)*
▲ JM Fittings LLC .... E 260 747-9200
   Fort Wayne *(G-5137)*
▲ Kilgore Manufacturing Co Inc .... D 260 248-2002
   Columbia City *(G-2162)*
▲ Kobaltec LLC .... G 219 462-1483
   Valparaiso *(G-15988)*
M & M Svc Stn Eqp Spcalist Inc .... G 317 347-8001
   Indianapolis *(G-8801)*
Macallister Machinery Co Inc .... C 260 483-6469
   Fort Wayne *(G-5195)*
Mary Jonas .... F 317 500-0600
   Indianapolis *(G-8845)*
Metal Powder Products Co LLP .... F 317 805-3764
   Noblesville *(G-13133)*
Midwest Design Hydraulic .... G 765 714-3016
   West Lafayette *(G-16605)*
Neff Group Distributors Inc .... F 260 489-6007
   Fort Wayne *(G-5259)*
Noble Composites Inc .... G 574 533-1462
   Goshen *(G-6228)*
Nrp Jones LLC .... G 219 362-9908
   La Porte *(G-10459)*
▲ Nrp Jones LLC .... D 800 348-8868
   La Porte *(G-10460)*
P H C Industries Inc .... G
   Fort Wayne *(G-5291)*
Parker-Hannifin Corporation .... A 260 748-6000
   Fort Wayne *(G-5297)*
Proportion-Air Inc .... D 317 335-2602
   Mccordsville *(G-11454)*
River Bend Hose Specialty Inc .... E 574 233-1133
   South Bend *(G-15222)*
Seals & Components Inc .... G 708 895-5222
   La Porte *(G-10478)*
▲ Slb Corporation .... F 574 255-9774
   Mishawaka *(G-11996)*
▲ SMC Corporation of America .... B 317 899-4440
   Noblesville *(G-13176)*
▲ Techna-Fit Inc .... G 317 350-2153
   Brownsburg *(G-1408)*
▲ Terry Liquidation III Inc .... D 219 362-9908
   La Porte *(G-10489)*

3493 Steel springs, except wire

A J Kay Co .... F 224 475-0370
   South Bend *(G-14928)*
Cargo Systems Inc .... G 574 264-1600
   Elkhart *(G-3247)*
Ferguson Equipment Inc .... G 574 234-4303
   South Bend *(G-15033)*
Kokomo Spring Company Inc .... F 765 459-5156
   Kokomo *(G-10294)*
M-3 and Associates Inc .... E 574 294-3988
   Elkhart *(G-3506)*

Matthew Warren Inc .... D 574 722-8200
   Logansport *(G-11093)*
McGowan Wire Specialties Inc .... G 574 232-7110
   South Bend *(G-15145)*
Mid-West Spring Mfg Co .... G 800 424-0244
   Mentone *(G-11473)*
Muehlhausen Spring Company .... G 574 859-2481
   Flora *(G-4662)*
Myers Spring Co Inc .... E 574 753-5105
   Logansport *(G-11096)*
Pepka Spring Company Inc .... F 765 459-3114
   Kokomo *(G-10319)*
Preferred Metal Service Inc .... G 219 988-2386
   Crown Point *(G-2735)*
Specialty Wire Technologies .... F 260 750-1418
   Elkhart *(G-3692)*
Valley Tool & Die Stampings .... E 574 722-4566
   Logansport *(G-11117)*
Wellspring Components LLC .... G 260 768-7336
   Shipshewana *(G-14896)*
Winamac Coil Spring Inc .... C 574 653-2186
   Kewanna *(G-10168)*

3494 Valves and pipe fittings, nec

Air Fixtures Inc .... F 260 982-2169
   North Manchester *(G-13228)*
Ameriflo Inc .... F 317 844-2019
   Indianapolis *(G-7510)*
Ashley F Ward Inc .... G 574 294-1502
   Elkhart *(G-3196)*
Ashley F Ward Inc .... G 219 879-4177
   Michigan City *(G-11580)*
▲ Banjo Corporation .... G 765 362-7367
   Crawfordsville *(G-2546)*
Dresser LLC .... D 765 827-9200
   Connersville *(G-2436)*
◆ Eclipse Inc .... D
   Muncie *(G-12389)*
▼ Epco Products Inc .... E 260 747-8888
   Fort Wayne *(G-4956)*
Eti LLC .... F 260 368-7246
   Geneva *(G-6049)*
▲ Flotec Inc .... E 317 273-6960
   Indianapolis *(G-8206)*
Hancor Inc .... E 812 443-2080
   Brazil *(G-1144)*
Honeywell International Inc .... G 574 231-2000
   South Bend *(G-15068)*
▲ JM Fittings LLC .... E 260 747-9200
   Fort Wayne *(G-5137)*
◆ Maxon Corporation .... C 765 284-3304
   Muncie *(G-12449)*
Midwest Design Hydraulic .... G 765 714-3016
   West Lafayette *(G-16605)*
Modbar LLC .... F 206 450-4743
   Fort Wayne *(G-5239)*
◆ Nibco Inc .... B 574 295-3000
   Elkhart *(G-3570)*
Parker-Hannifin Corporation .... A 260 748-6000
   Fort Wayne *(G-5297)*
Paulus Plastic Co Inc .... G 574 834-7663
   North Webster *(G-13312)*
PHD Inc .... F 260 356-0120
   Huntington *(G-7356)*
R2b2 Industries LLC .... G 812 436-4840
   Evansville *(G-4270)*
Strahman Holdings Inc .... G 317 818-5030
   Carmel *(G-1771)*
◆ The Ford Meter Box Company Inc .... C 260 563-3171
   Wabash *(G-16217)*

3495 Wire springs

34 FABRICATED METAL PRODUCTS

A J Coil Inc .... G 574 353-7174
Tippecanoe *(G-15758)*

A J Kay Co .... F 224 475-0370
South Bend *(G-14928)*

Araymond Mfg Ctr N Amer Inc .... C 574 722-5168
Logansport *(G-11058)*

▲ Barber Manufacturing Co Inc .... D 765 643-6905
Anderson *(G-81)*

▲ Circle M Spring Inc .... E 574 267-2883
Warsaw *(G-16335)*

Drc Machining LLC .... G 812 825-5783
Bloomington *(G-859)*

Forward Lift / A Dover Company .... G 812 273-7325
Madison *(G-11221)*

▼ Hoosier Spring Co Inc .... C 574 291-7550
South Bend *(G-15070)*

Integrated Systems MGT Inc .... G 765 565-6108
Carthage *(G-1815)*

Leggett & Platt Incorporated .... D 260 347-2600
Kendallville *(G-10133)*

Mid-West Spring Mfg Co .... D 574 353-1409
Mentone *(G-11474)*

Mid-West Spring Mfg Co .... G 800 424-0244
Mentone *(G-11473)*

Myers Spring Co Inc .... E 574 753-5105
Logansport *(G-11096)*

Pepka Spring Company Inc .... F 765 459-3114
Kokomo *(G-10319)*

▲ Pimmler Holdings Inc .... G 574 583-8090
Monticello *(G-12165)*

Spring Monticello Corporation .... D 574 583-8090
Monticello *(G-12170)*

▲ Suzuki Garphyttan Corp .... D 574 232-8800
South Bend *(G-15275)*

Titus Precision Company .... G 260 244-6114
Columbia City *(G-2206)*

Valley Tool & Die Stampings .... E 574 722-4566
Logansport *(G-11117)*

Walton Industrial Park Inc .... F 574 626-2929
Walton *(G-16284)*

Winamac Coil Spring Inc .... C 574 653-2186
Kewanna *(G-10168)*

3496 Miscellaneous fabricated wire products

A J Kay Co .... F 224 475-0370
South Bend *(G-14928)*

▲ Accel International .... F 260 897-9990
Avilla *(G-471)*

Accent Wire Products .... G 765 628-3587
Greentown *(G-6644)*

Advantage Wire & Machine Inc .... G 765 698-4643
Connersville *(G-2424)*

Alliance Group Tech Inc .... D 260 375-2810
Warren *(G-16293)*

American Rigging Rental .... G 317 721-9553
Indianapolis *(G-7506)*

American Wire Rope Sling of In .... G 260 478-4700
Fort Wayne *(G-4759)*

American Wire Rope Sling of In .... G 574 257-9424
Mishawaka *(G-11841)*

American Wire Rope Sling of In .... F 877 634-2545
Indianapolis *(G-7508)*

Angola Wire Products Inc .... G 260 665-3061
Angola *(G-228)*

▲ Angola Wire Products Inc .... G 260 665-9447
Angola *(G-229)*

Automation Enclosures LLC .... G 812 453-8480
Evansville *(G-3904)*

B & G Entity Inc .... F 260 724-8874
Decatur *(G-2845)*

Belden Inc .... A 765 962-7561
Richmond *(G-14094)*

Bender Products Inc .... E 574 255-5350
Mishawaka *(G-11852)*

Benthall Bros Inc .... E 800 488-5995
Evansville *(G-3915)*

Bettner Wire Coating Dies Inc .... F 812 372-2732
Columbus *(G-2226)*

Bishop Lifting Products Inc .... G 317 634-2545
Indianapolis *(G-7631)*

◆ Braid Den Inc .... E 260 244-2995
Columbia City *(G-2126)*

Bridon-American Corporation .... D 812 749-3115
Oakland City *(G-13320)*

Cmj & Associates Corporation .... G 765 962-1947
Richmond *(G-14107)*

▲ Dekko Acquisition Parent Inc .... G 260 347-0700
Kendallville *(G-10109)*

Ecp American Steel LLC .... G 574 257-9424
Mishawaka *(G-11890)*

Ecp American Steel LLC .... E 260 478-9101
Fort Wayne *(G-4941)*

Elektrisola Incorporated .... G 317 375-8192
Indianapolis *(G-8069)*

Elevator Equipment Corporation .... D 765 966-7761
Richmond *(G-14119)*

Engineering and Industria .... E 574 722-3714
Logansport *(G-11073)*

Essex Frkawa Mgnt Wire USA LLC .... F 260 248-5500
Columbia City *(G-2146)*

Fab Solutions LLC .... G 765 744-2671
Redkey *(G-14028)*

◆ General Cage LLC .... F 765 552-5039
Anderson *(G-119)*

Grc Enterprises Inc .... E 219 932-2220
East Chicago *(G-3012)*

Group Dekko Holdings Inc .... G 800 829-3101
Fort Wayne *(G-5043)*

▲ Hessville Cable & Sling Co .... E 773 768-8181
Gary *(G-5951)*

Hewitt Manufacturing Company .... F 765 525-9829
Waldron *(G-16258)*

Hoosier Traps .... G 574 586-2401
Walkerton *(G-16267)*

Indiana Wire Products Inc .... F 812 663-7441
Greensburg *(G-6608)*

Kentuckiana Wire Rope & Supply .... F 812 282-3667
Jeffersonville *(G-10005)*

Kewanna Metal Specialties Inc .... D 574 653-2554
Kewanna *(G-10166)*

▲ Khorporate Holdings Inc .... C 260 357-3365
Laotto *(G-10807)*

Kingsford Products Inc .... F 740 862-4450
Decatur *(G-2866)*

▲ Lafayette Wire Products Inc .... D 765 474-7896
Lafayette *(G-10632)*

Lake Cable of Indiana LLC .... C 847 238-3000
Valparaiso *(G-15990)*

Lauck Manufacturing Co Inc .... F 317 787-6269
Indianapolis *(G-8727)*

Macpactor Inc .... G 502 643-7845
Jeffersonville *(G-10015)*

Madsen Wire LLC .... F 260 829-6561
Orland *(G-13368)*

Mathews Wire Inc .... F 765 659-3542
Frankfort *(G-5682)*

Merchants Metals LLC .... F 317 783-7678
Indianapolis *(G-8876)*

Mid-West Spring Mfg Co .... D 574 353-1409
Mentone *(G-11474)*

Myers Spring Co Inc .... E 574 753-5105
Logansport *(G-11096)*

Noble Wire Products Inc .... G 317 773-1926
Orland *(G-13369)*

Onspot of North America Inc .... G 203 377-0777
North Vernon *(G-13290)*

Outtadaway LLC .... G 219 866-8885
Rensselaer *(G-14062)*

Pro Tech Automation Inc .... G 317 201-3875
Monrovia *(G-12079)*

Pwt Group LLC .... E 260 490-6477
Fort Wayne *(G-5357)*

▲ R & R Engineering Co Inc .... E 765 536-2331
Summitville *(G-15429)*

Raber Buggy Shop LLC .... G 812 486-3789
Montgomery *(G-12120)*

◆ Reelcraft Industries Inc .... C 855 634-9109
Columbia City *(G-2188)*

S & J Manufacturing LLC .... G 812 662-6640
Greensburg *(G-6629)*

◆ Sandin Mfg LLC .... D 219 872-2253
Michigan City *(G-11662)*

◆ Sanlo Inc .... G 219 879-0241
Michigan City *(G-11664)*

▼ Sommer Metalcraft LLC .... D 765 362-6200
Crawfordsville *(G-2617)*

▼ Spaceguard Inc .... D 812 523-3044
Seymour *(G-14694)*

Valley Tool & Die Stampings .... E 574 722-4566
Logansport *(G-11117)*

Warnock Welding & Fabg LLC .... G 812 498-5408
Seymour *(G-14703)*

Winamac Coil Spring Inc .... C 574 653-2186
Kewanna *(G-10168)*

Wirco Inc .... C 260 897-3768
Avilla *(G-500)*

Wire-Tek Inc .... G 812 623-8300
Sunman *(G-15448)*

Yongli America LLC .... G 219 763-7920
Portage *(G-13920)*

3497 Metal foil and leaf

Avery Dennison Corporation .... D 219 696-7777
Lowell *(G-11155)*

Foil Laminating Inc .... E
Plymouth *(G-13777)*

Old Rev LLC .... G 317 580-2420
Westfield *(G-16714)*

3498 Fabricated pipe and fittings

A/C Fabricating Corp .... E 574 534-1415
Goshen *(G-6086)*

Alliance Steel LLC .... C 219 427-5400
Gary *(G-5889)*

Allied Tube & Conduit Corp .... F 765 459-8811
Kokomo *(G-10232)*

Allied Tube & Conduit Corp .... F 812 265-9255
Madison *(G-11201)*

▲ ASC Industries Inc .... E 574 264-1987
Elkhart *(G-3194)*

▲ B&J Rocket America Inc .... E 574 825-5802
Middlebury *(G-11700)*

Barry Company Inc .... G 317 578-2486
Fishers *(G-4471)*

Boyce Industries .... G 708 345-0455
Michigan City *(G-11583)*

Calpipe Industries LLC .... E 219 844-6800
Hobart *(G-7176)*

Curtis Products Inc .... C 574 289-4891
South Bend *(G-14989)*

Curtis Products Inc .... E 574 289-4891
South Bend *(G-14990)*

◆ Elkhart Products Corporation .... C 574 264-3181
Elkhart *(G-3328)*

Fabshop .... G 317 549-1681
Reelsville *(G-14031)*

34 FABRICATED METAL PRODUCTS

Globe Industrial LLC............................. F 812 301-2600
   Pekin *(G-13516)*
Globe Industries LLC............................ G 812 301-2600
   New Albany *(G-12737)*
Globe LLC.. C 812 949-2001
   New Albany *(G-12738)*
Globe Mechanical Inc........................... D 812 949-2001
   New Albany *(G-12739)*
Green Lake Tube LLC........................... F 219 397-0495
   East Chicago *(G-3013)*
▲ Green Leaf Inc.................................... C 812 877-1546
   Fontanet *(G-4699)*
Harness Machine & Fab LLC................ F 765 652-2831
   Frankfort *(G-5672)*
Hd Mechanical Inc................................ F 219 924-6050
   Griffith *(G-6806)*
Holbrook Fabrication Repr Inc.............. G 260 348-4996
   Laotto *(G-10806)*
Indiana Seal... G 317 841-3547
   Indianapolis *(G-8491)*
Industrial Tube Components Inc........... G 317 431-2188
   Lizton *(G-11049)*
Indy Tube Fabrication LLC................... G 317 883-2000
   Franklin *(G-5745)*
Jae Enterprises Inc............................... E 260 747-0568
   Fort Wayne *(G-5130)*
Jae Enterprises Inc............................... G 260 489-6249
   Fort Wayne *(G-5129)*
▲ JM Fittings LLC.................................. E 260 747-9200
   Fort Wayne *(G-5137)*
Johnson Cntrls Fire Prtction L............... G 317 826-2130
   Indianapolis *(G-8633)*
Klene Pipe Structures Inc..................... G 812 663-6445
   Greensburg *(G-6612)*
L & W Engineering Inc.......................... C 574 825-5351
   Middlebury *(G-11730)*
▲ MPS International LLC...................... E 260 824-2630
   Bluffton *(G-1043)*
National Tube Form LLC....................... C 260 478-2363
   Fort Wayne *(G-5257)*
Nelson Global Products Inc.................. C 608 719-1752
   Fort Wayne *(G-5261)*
Parker-Hannifin Corporation................. E 260 587-9102
   Ashley *(G-335)*
Plymouth Tube Company...................... D 574 946-6191
   Winamac *(G-16871)*
Porter County Fabricators Ltd............... G 219 663-4665
   Crown Point *(G-2733)*
Precision Products Group Inc............... E 260 484-4111
   Fort Wayne *(G-5340)*
Quality Hydraulic Mch Svc Inc.............. G 317 892-2596
   Danville *(G-2824)*
Randall K Dike....................................... G 812 664-4942
   Owensville *(G-13471)*
Russells Tube Forming Inc.................... E 317 241-4072
   Indianapolis *(G-9348)*
Scot Industries Inc................................. C 260 927-0262
   Auburn *(G-420)*
Siddhi Integrated Mfg Svcs Inc............. G 502 298-8640
   Clarksville *(G-2036)*
South Bend Kollel Inc............................ G 574 299-8263
   South Bend *(G-15255)*
Southwark Metal Mfg Co....................... C 317 823-5300
   Mccordsville *(G-11456)*
St Regis Culvert Inc............................... F 317 353-8065
   Indianapolis *(G-9487)*
Staples Pipe & Muffler........................... ..... 812 522-3569
   Butlerville *(G-1488)*
Star Pipe LLC.. G 317 428-7408
   Indianapolis *(G-9499)*
Steuben County Welding & Fabg.......... G 260 665-3001
   Angola *(G-295)*

Tb Plastic Extrusions Inc....................... E 574 266-7409
   Elkhart *(G-3717)*
▲ Tcb Enterprises LLC.......................... F 574 522-3971
   Middlebury *(G-11754)*
▲ Technifab Products Inc..................... E 812 442-0520
   Brazil *(G-1166)*
Thormax Enterprises LLC...................... G 812 530-7744
   Seymour *(G-14699)*
▲ Tru-Flex Real Estate Holdings LLC... D 765 893-4403
   West Lebanon *(G-16650)*
Tube Processing Corp........................... G 317 787-1321
   Indianapolis *(G-9654)*
Tube Processing Corp........................... C 317 787-5747
   Indianapolis *(G-9655)*
Tube Processing Corp........................... C 317 782-9486
   Indianapolis *(G-9656)*
Tube Processing Corp........................... ..... 317 264-7760
   Indianapolis *(G-9657)*
▲ Tube Processing Corp....................... B 317 787-1321
   Indianapolis *(G-9658)*
Uniseal Inc... E 812 425-1361
   Evansville *(G-4360)*
▲ Whipp In Holdings LLC...................... G 260 478-2363
   Fort Wayne *(G-5563)*

3499 Fabricated metal products, nec

4board LLC.. G 317 997-3354
   Indianapolis *(G-7391)*
Ad-Vance Magnetics Inc....................... E 574 223-3158
   Rochester *(G-14274)*
▲ Agi International Inc.......................... F 317 536-2415
   Indianapolis *(G-7458)*
▲ Aircom Manufacturing Inc................. B 317 545-5383
   Indianapolis *(G-7462)*
▲ Aisin Chemical Indiana LLC.............. E 812 793-2888
   Crothersville *(G-2635)*
Arrayed Additive Inc.............................. G 317 981-5982
   Indianapolis *(G-7547)*
Arroyo Industries LLC........................... G 317 605-4163
   Greenwood *(G-6671)*
Assa Abloy Door Group LLC................ G 800 826-2617
   Elkhart *(G-3197)*
Awardmakersnet Inc.............................. G 260 925-4672
   Auburn *(G-366)*
B Stevens Service LLC......................... G 812 622-2039
   Cynthiana *(G-2786)*
B6 Manufacturing LLC........................... G 317 549-4290
   Indianapolis *(G-7587)*
Barnett Industrial Inc............................. F 219 814-7500
   Valparaiso *(G-15909)*
Benz Custom Metal LLC........................ G 812 365-2613
   Marengo *(G-11261)*
Briter Products Inc................................ G 574 386-8167
   South Bend *(G-14962)*
Bway Corporation................................. G 219 462-8915
   Valparaiso *(G-15923)*
Cmbf LLC.. G 812 336-3811
   Bloomington *(G-830)*
Csi Manufacturing Inc........................... F 574 825-7891
   Middlebury *(G-11708)*
Cummings Holdings LLC....................... E 260 493-4405
   Fort Wayne *(G-4893)*
Curtis Dyna-Fog..................................... F 317 896-2561
   Westfield *(G-16681)*
Custom Metal Fabrication LLC............. G 574 257-8851
   Mishawaka *(G-11873)*
Customer 1st LLC................................. E 812 733-4638
   Borden *(G-1107)*
▲ Customer 1st LLC............................. ..... 877 768-9970
   Pekin *(G-13514)*
Davis Hezakih Corp............................... F 260 768-7300
   Shipshewana *(G-14843)*

▲ Ditto Sales Inc.................................... E 812 482-3043
   Jasper *(G-9832)*
▲ DStyle Inc... F 619 662-0560
   Jasper *(G-9833)*
Dubose Strapping Inc........................... E 765 361-0000
   Crawfordsville *(G-2564)*
E & H Bridge and Grating Inc............... G 812 277-8343
   Bedford *(G-632)*
East Chicago Shearing.......................... G 219 398-2933
   East Chicago *(G-3004)*
Ep Old Inc.. G 317 782-8362
   Indianapolis *(G-8128)*
◆ Fire King International LLC............... E 812 822-5574
   New Albany *(G-12729)*
◆ Fki Security Group LLC..................... B 812 948-8400
   New Albany *(G-12730)*
Fridge Mag... G 317 442-2872
   Cicero *(G-1996)*
GKN Sinter Metals LLC........................ C 812 883-3381
   Salem *(G-14479)*
Gleason Corporation............................. C 574 533-1141
   Goshen *(G-6150)*
Grace Manufacturing Inc....................... F 574 267-8000
   Warsaw *(G-16369)*
Great Lakes Prefabrication LLC............ G 260 489-1575
   Fort Wayne *(G-5038)*
◆ H & H Sales Company Inc................ F 260 637-3177
   Huntertown *(G-7257)*
▲ Hadady Corporation........................... E 219 322-7417
   Dyer *(G-2976)*
Hammond Group Inc............................. G 219 931-9360
   Hammond *(G-6939)*
Hand Industries Inc............................... E 574 267-3525
   Warsaw *(G-16373)*
Hg Metal Fabrication............................. G 317 491-3381
   Indianapolis *(G-8392)*
Hibbing International Friction................ F 765 529-7001
   New Castle *(G-12867)*
▲ Hosetract Industries Ltd.................... F 260 489-8828
   Fort Wayne *(G-5084)*
Huver Manufacturing Tech LLC........... G 317 460-8605
   Noblesville *(G-13098)*
Indiana State Governmen..................... E 623 326-6826
   Indianapolis *(G-8493)*
Indy Aerospace Inc............................... G 817 521-6508
   Indianapolis *(G-8522)*
Innovative 3d Mfg LLC.......................... G 317 560-5080
   Franklin *(G-5747)*
J Makes Incorporated........................... G 773 610-9867
   Griffith *(G-6809)*
JC Metal Fabrication LLC...................... G 574 340-1109
   Mishawaka *(G-11919)*
Johnson Safe Company LLC................. G 317 876-7233
   Zionsville *(G-17025)*
Jokerr Fabrication LLC......................... G 513 312-0408
   Jamestown *(G-9818)*
K C Creations... G 937 418-1859
   Indianapolis *(G-8653)*
Kimball Electronics Inc......................... D 317 545-5383
   Indianapolis *(G-8686)*
Kmsd Inc... F 219 808-7159
   Valparaiso *(G-15987)*
L & W Engineering Inc.......................... C 574 825-5351
   Middlebury *(G-11730)*
▲ Liftco Inc.. E 574 266-5551
   Elkhart *(G-3488)*
LSI Fabrication...................................... G 574 722-3101
   Peru *(G-13591)*
▲ Magnequench Inc.............................. E 765 778-7809
   Pendleton *(G-13542)*
▲ Magnets R US Inc.............................. G 574 633-0061
   South Bend *(G-15135)*

SIC SECTION
35 INDUSTRIAL AND COMMERCIAL MACHINERY AND COMPUTER EQUIPMENT

Meilink Safe Company .... D 812 941-0024
   New Albany *(G-12774)*

Metal Fab Engineering Inc .... E 574 278-7150
   Winamac *(G-16867)*

Metal Fabrication LLC .... G 812 686-9430
   Evansville *(G-4197)*

Miller Mfg Corp .... E 574 773-4136
   Nappanee *(G-12626)*

Mishawaka Art & Frame Gallery .... G 574 259-9320
   Mishawaka *(G-11953)*

Moyers Inc .... F 574 264-3119
   Elkhart *(G-3557)*

Ms Manufacturing LLC .... E 812 442-7468
   Brazil *(G-1156)*

Murpac of Fort Wayne LLC .... G 260 424-2299
   Fort Wayne *(G-5251)*

Nector Machine & Fabricating .... G 219 322-6878
   Schererville *(G-14536)*

Nst Campbellsburg LLC .... G 812 755-4501
   Noblesville *(G-13145)*

Orange Cnty Wldg & Fabrication .... G 812 653-5754
   Orleans *(G-13378)*

▲ Outsource Technologies Inc .... F 574 233-1303
   South Bend *(G-15182)*

Precision Spray LLC .... G 812 830-8443
   Vincennes *(G-16148)*

Professional Bowling Ball Svc .... G 317 786-4329
   Indianapolis *(G-9220)*

◆ PSI LLC .... G 765 483-0954
   Lebanon *(G-10935)*

R & D Metal Fabricating Inc .... G 574 533-2424
   Goshen *(G-6245)*

R&H Metalworks LLC .... G 317 513-8733
   Fairland *(G-4402)*

Rare Earth Inc .... G 574 850-1924
   Bremen *(G-1217)*

◆ Reelcraft Industries Inc .... C 855 634-9109
   Columbia City *(G-2188)*

▲ Risco Products Inc .... G 317 392-6150
   Shelbyville *(G-14791)*

◆ Rko Enterprises LLC .... G 812 273-8813
   Madison *(G-11248)*

Ronard Industries Inc .... F 219 874-4801
   Michigan City *(G-11658)*

Rose Black .... G 317 636-7459
   Indianapolis *(G-9332)*

Rowe Conveyor LLC .... G 317 602-1024
   Greenwood *(G-6761)*

▲ S C Pryor Inc .... F 317 352-1281
   Indianapolis *(G-9354)*

Sacoma Properties LLC .... F 812 526-5600
   Edinburgh *(G-3102)*

Samuel Powell .... G 812 887-6813
   French Lick *(G-5849)*

▲ Schafer Industries Inc .... D 574 234-4116
   South Bend *(G-15234)*

Schmitt Mtlwrks Fbrcations LLC .... G 812 510-3677
   Wadesville *(G-16230)*

Shrock Manufacturing Inc .... E 574 264-4126
   Elkhart *(G-3674)*

Smokers Iron Works .... G 574 674-6683
   Elkhart *(G-3687)*

Spectrum Brands Inc .... E 317 773-6627
   Noblesville *(G-13179)*

St Regis Inc .... F 317 591-3500
   Indianapolis *(G-9486)*

Stulls Mch & Fabrication Inc .... G 765 942-2717
   Ladoga *(G-10511)*

Thomas & Skinner Inc .... C 317 923-2501
   Indianapolis *(G-9592)*

Tic Toc Trophy Shop Inc .... G 574 893-4234
   Akron *(G-10)*

Timothy White .... G 765 689-8270
   Bunker Hill *(G-1444)*

Trophy Case LLC .... G 812 853-5087
   Newburgh *(G-13026)*

▲ Tru-Flex LLC .... C 765 893-4403
   West Lebanon *(G-16649)*

Tuff Stuff Sales and Svc Inc .... F 765 354-4151
   Middletown *(G-11778)*

Tusca 2 .... G 812 876-2857
   Bloomington *(G-1002)*

Twisted Mtal Fbrction Svcs Inc .... G 219 923-8045
   Munster *(G-12572)*

35 INDUSTRIAL AND COMMERCIAL MACHINERY AND COMPUTER EQUIPMENT

3511 Turbines and turbine generator sets

Allison Transmission Inc .... C 317 821-5104
   Indianapolis *(G-7488)*

Allison Transmission Inc .... A 317 242-5000
   Indianapolis *(G-7491)*

B&W Environmental .... G 260 766-4135
   Portland *(G-13929)*

Babcock .... G 219 462-8851
   Valparaiso *(G-15907)*

Caterpillar Inc .... G 765 447-6816
   Lafayette *(G-10550)*

Clayhill Wind & Solar LLC .... G 765 437-2395
   Sharpsville *(G-14709)*

Cummins Inc .... D 812 522-9366
   Seymour *(G-14645)*

Design Engineering .... G 219 926-2170
   Chesterton *(G-1919)*

Drive Process Services Inc .... G 765 741-9717
   Muncie *(G-12387)*

Falcon Manufacturing LLC .... F 317 884-3600
   Columbus *(G-2301)*

Hydration Turbine Inc .... G 317 491-0656
   Indianapolis *(G-8440)*

Iet Global Inc .... E 812 421-7810
   Evansville *(G-4114)*

▲ Integrated Energy Technologies Inc .... E 812 421-7810
   Evansville *(G-4128)*

Mantech Manifold .... G 260 479-2383
   Fort Wayne *(G-5202)*

Petal Solutions LLC .... G 765 404-7747
   West Lafayette *(G-16618)*

Power Wall Systems LLC .... G 317 348-1260
   Fishers *(G-4580)*

Prime Tech Inc .... F 317 715-1162
   Indianapolis *(G-9196)*

R W Machine Incorporated .... G 317 769-6798
   Whitestown *(G-16818)*

Siemens Energy Inc .... C 317 677-1340
   Indianapolis *(G-9424)*

Tri Aerospace LLC .... E 812 872-2400
   Terre Haute *(G-15736)*

◆ Windstream Technologies Inc .... F 812 953-1481
   North Vernon *(G-13301)*

3519 Internal combustion engines, nec

Bes Racing Engines Inc .... F 812 576-2371
   Guilford *(G-6827)*

Brazil Auto & Electric .... G 812 442-0060
   Brazil *(G-1135)*

Brunswick Corporation .... D 260 459-8200
   Fort Wayne *(G-4821)*

Carlson Motorsports .... G 765 339-4407
   Linden *(G-11030)*

Caterpillar Inc .... G 765 447-6816
   Lafayette *(G-10550)*

Ccts Technology Group Inc .... G 305 209-5743
   Indianapolis *(G-7765)*

Champion Racing Engines LLC .... G 317 335-2491
   Mccordsville *(G-11446)*

Conrad Sb LLC .... G 574 213-3743
   South Bend *(G-14981)*

▲ Cosworth LLC .... D 317 644-1037
   Indianapolis *(G-7887)*

Cummins - Allison Corp .... G 317 872-6244
   Indianapolis *(G-7922)*

◆ Cummins Americas Inc .... G 812 377-5000
   Columbus *(G-2250)*

Cummins Crosspoint LLC .... D 812 867-4400
   Evansville *(G-3999)*

Cummins Crosspoint LLC .... E 260 482-3691
   Fort Wayne *(G-4894)*

Cummins Crosspoint LLC .... E 317 484-2146
   Indianapolis *(G-7923)*

Cummins Crosspoint LLC .... E 317 244-7251
   Indianapolis *(G-7924)*

Cummins Crosspoint LLC .... E 574 252-2154
   Mishawaka *(G-11869)*

Cummins Crosspoint LLC .... E 317 243-7979
   Indianapolis *(G-7925)*

▲ Cummins Cumberland Inc .... B 317 243-7979
   Indianapolis *(G-7926)*

Cummins Dist Holdco Inc .... E 812 377-5000
   Columbus *(G-2252)*

Cummins Emission Solutions Inc .... D 615 986-2596
   Columbus *(G-2253)*

Cummins Emssion Sltons Clmbus .... E 800 286-6467
   Columbus *(G-2254)*

Cummins Inc .... G 812 377-2932
   Columbus *(G-2259)*

Cummins Inc .... G 812 524-6455
   Columbus *(G-2264)*

Cummins Inc .... G 317 460-9843
   Columbus *(G-2265)*

Cummins Inc .... G 812 377-7739
   Columbus *(G-2266)*

Cummins Inc .... E 812 374-4774
   Columbus *(G-2267)*

Cummins Inc .... E 812 377-6072
   Columbus *(G-2268)*

Cummins Inc .... B 812 377-7000
   Columbus *(G-2269)*

Cummins Inc .... G 812 312-3162
   Columbus *(G-2270)*

Cummins Inc .... G 812 377-8601
   Columbus *(G-2272)*

Cummins Inc .... F 812 378-2874
   Columbus *(G-2273)*

Cummins Inc .... F 317 610-2493
   Indianapolis *(G-7927)*

Cummins Inc .... G 317 244-7251
   Indianapolis *(G-7928)*

Cummins Inc .... D 812 522-9366
   Seymour *(G-14645)*

Cummins Inc .... G 317 751-4567
   Whiteland *(G-16782)*

Cummins Inc .... A 812 377-5000
   Columbus *(G-2271)*

Cummins Power Generation Inc .... E 574 262-4611
   Elkhart *(G-3281)*

Cummins Repair Inc .... G 260 632-4800
   Harlan *(G-7053)*

Cummins-Scania Xpi Mfg LLC .... G 812 377-5000
   Columbus *(G-2275)*

Engineered Machined Pdts Inc .... G 317 462-8894
   Greenfield *(G-6498)*

35 INDUSTRIAL AND COMMERCIAL MACHINERY AND COMPUTER EQUIPMENT — SIC SECTION

Engler Machine & Tool Inc .... F 812 386-6254
Princeton *(G-13992)*

Ertl Enterprises Inc .... F 765 622-9900
Anderson *(G-115)*

FCA North America Holdings LLC .... B 765 454-0018
Kokomo *(G-10264)*

Freedom Racing Engines .... G 317 858-9937
Pittsboro *(G-13646)*

Futurewerks LLC .... G 305 926-3633
Indianapolis *(G-8247)*

Hidea Outboard Motor Usa Inc .... G 317 286-3694
Indianapolis *(G-8397)*

Hobbs Auto Diagnostics & Repr .... G 765 606-1490
Anderson *(G-127)*

Jolliff Diesel Service LLC .... G 812 692-5725
Elnora *(G-3815)*

▲ Lingenfelter Prfmce Engrg Inc .... E 260 724-2552
Decatur *(G-2869)*

Michael Dargie .... G 765 935-2241
Richmond *(G-14165)*

Mitchell Smith Racing .... G 765 640-0237
Anderson *(G-155)*

Motorsport Price Engineering .... G 812 546-4220
Hope *(G-7229)*

Mpc Global LLC .... G 816 399-4710
Indianapolis *(G-8964)*

Powerhouse Engines LLC .... G 765 576-1418
Lynn *(G-11186)*

S & S Diesel Motorsport LLC .... G 812 216-3639
Seymour *(G-14683)*

Sequoia National LLC .... E 812 421-0095
Evansville *(G-4306)*

Spyder Controls Inc .... G 866 919-9092
South Bend *(G-15262)*

◆ Stant USA Corp .... C 765 825-3121
Connersville *(G-2470)*

Stensland Engines Inc .... G 260 623-6859
Monroeville *(G-12075)*

Torque Engineering Corporation .... F 574 264-2628
Elkhart *(G-3740)*

Unison Engine Components Inc .... C 904 739-4000
Terre Haute *(G-15738)*

W A P LLC .... E 317 421-3180
Shelbyville *(G-14813)*

Wap Inc .... F 877 421-3187
Shelbyville *(G-14814)*

3523 Farm machinery and equipment

Agri-Power Inc .... F 812 874-3316
Poseyville *(G-13976)*

Andersons Agriculture Group LP .... F 765 564-6135
Delphi *(G-2890)*

▲ Applegate Livestock Eqp Inc .... D 765 964-3715
Union City *(G-15848)*

◆ AT Ferrell Company Inc .... E 260 824-3400
Bluffton *(G-1026)*

Azland Inc .... G 765 429-6200
West Lafayette *(G-16564)*

Barry Stuckwisch .... G 812 525-1052
Seymour *(G-14631)*

Bickels Garage & Welding .... G 765 853-5457
Modoc *(G-12050)*

Bonnell Grain Handling Inc .... E 574 595-7827
Star City *(G-15396)*

Bowman & Bowman Farms Inc .... G 260 837-4171
Waterloo *(G-16515)*

BP Alternative Energy NA Inc .... G 765 884-1000
Fowler *(G-5620)*

Bruning Enterprises Inc .... G 317 835-7591
Shelbyville *(G-14742)*

Cardinal Services Inc Indiana .... D 574 267-3823
Warsaw *(G-16333)*

Carter Manufacturing Company .... G 765 563-3666
Brookston *(G-1309)*

Case Lineage Management .... G 317 721-1764
Indianapolis *(G-7754)*

▲ Case New Holland LLC .... E 765 482-5446
Lebanon *(G-10881)*

Case Weinkauff .... G 219 733-9484
Valparaiso *(G-15925)*

Cases Marine Service Inc .... G 317 379-0020
Arcadia *(G-310)*

CD & Ws Bordner Entps Inc .... G 765 268-2120
Cutler *(G-2783)*

Chief Metal Works Inc .... G 765 932-2134
Rushville *(G-14396)*

Churchill Equipment .... G 812 347-2592
Depauw *(G-2937)*

City Welding & Fabrication .... G 765 569-5403
Rockville *(G-14350)*

Cnh Industrial America LLC .... C 765 482-5409
Lebanon *(G-10884)*

Cornelius Manufacturing Inc .... D 812 636-4319
Washington *(G-16474)*

▲ Cowco Inc .... G 812 346-8993
North Vernon *(G-13260)*

CPM Acquisition Corp .... F 765 362-2600
Crawfordsville *(G-2556)*

Ctb Inc .... E 765 654-8517
Frankfort *(G-5657)*

Ctb Inc .... E 574 658-4191
Milford *(G-11791)*

◆ Ctb Inc .... A 574 658-4191
Milford *(G-11790)*

CTB MN Investment Co Inc .... A 765 654-8517
Frankfort *(G-5658)*

◆ CTB MN Investment Co Inc .... E 574 658-4191
Milford *(G-11794)*

D & H Thurston Farms LP .... G 765 847-2304
Fountain City *(G-5610)*

D A Hochstetler & Sons LLP .... F 574 642-1144
Topeka *(G-15800)*

Danko Farm Supply & Feed Inc .... G 812 870-7413
Sullivan *(G-15404)*

Davaus LLC .... G 260 245-5006
Hoagland *(G-7166)*

Davern Machine Shop .... G 765 505-1051
Dana *(G-2804)*

Delphi Products Co Inc .... F 800 382-7903
Delphi *(G-2894)*

Dpc Inc .... E 765 564-3752
Delphi *(G-2895)*

Draper Manufacturing LLC .... G 317 347-5195
Indianapolis *(G-8006)*

Dwd Miller Inc .... G 812 853-8497
Chandler *(G-1860)*

◆ Earthway Products LLC .... D 574 848-7491
Bristol *(G-1258)*

◆ Equipment Technologies Inc .... E 800 861-2142
Mooresville *(G-12204)*

Et AG Center LLC .... F 317 834-4500
Mooresville *(G-12205)*

Et Works Inc .... F 317 834-4500
Mooresville *(G-12206)*

Evelyn Dollahan .... G 574 896-2971
North Judson *(G-13211)*

▲ Farm Innovators Inc .... E 574 936-5096
Plymouth *(G-13774)*

Franklin Olin .... G 765 342-9040
Martinsville *(G-11396)*

◆ Galbreath LLC .... E 219 946-6631
Winamac *(G-16860)*

Garver Manufacturing Inc .... G 765 964-5828
Union City *(G-15854)*

▲ Gator Cases Inc .... F 260 627-8070
Columbia City *(G-2148)*

Goliath Ag LLC .... F 765 305-1141
Winchester *(G-16888)*

Greensbroom .... G 317 416-7818
Indianapolis *(G-8322)*

Greg Whitenack .... G 260 726-7321
Portland *(G-13950)*

Gvm Inc .... G 765 689-5010
Bunker Hill *(G-1441)*

Hahn Enterprises Inc .... G 574 862-4491
Wakarusa *(G-16234)*

Haines Engineering Inc .... G 260 589-3388
Berne *(G-713)*

Hampton Equipment LLC .... G 260 740-8704
Fort Wayne *(G-5049)*

Harris Farms Inc .... G 765 468-6264
Modoc *(G-12052)*

Hc Farms .... G 765 289-9909
Muncie *(G-12412)*

▲ Headsight Inc .... G 574 546-5022
Bremen *(G-1196)*

Hensler Farm Inc .... G 765 628-3411
Greentown *(G-6647)*

Hicks Farms .... G 812 852-4055
Osgood *(G-13410)*

Hog Slat Incorporated .... D 574 967-4145
Camden *(G-1520)*

Hog Slat Incorporated .... E 574 967-3776
Flora *(G-4659)*

Hog Slat Incorporated .... D 765 828-0828
Universal *(G-15875)*

Honeyville Metal Inc .... D 800 593-8377
Topeka *(G-15809)*

Hunter Industries .... G 630 200-7581
Noblesville *(G-13097)*

Hurricane Ditcher Company Inc .... F 812 886-9663
Vincennes *(G-16130)*

International A I Inc .... G 812 824-2473
Bloomington *(G-891)*

Jacobs Mfg LLC .... G 574 583-3883
Monticello *(G-12154)*

Jeffs Farm Svc .... G 812 254-1980
Washington *(G-16487)*

JI Manfcturing Fabrication Inc .... G 260 589-3723
Berne *(G-716)*

K & B Trailer Sales & Mfg Inc .... G 574 946-4382
Monterey *(G-12080)*

Kasco Mfg Co Inc .... E 317 398-7973
Shelbyville *(G-14767)*

Kenneth Fuhrman .... G 812 482-4612
Jasper *(G-9863)*

Koenig Equipment Inc .... G 765 962-7330
Richmond *(G-14154)*

Laidig Inc .... E 574 256-0204
Mishawaka *(G-11925)*

Land Enterprises .... G 317 774-9475
Noblesville *(G-13126)*

▲ Lee E Norris Cnstr & Grn Co .... G 574 353-7855
Tippecanoe *(G-15761)*

Lee Farms Enterprises Inc .... G 260 375-3319
Marion *(G-11306)*

Living Prairie Equipment LLC .... G 765 479-0759
Wolcott *(G-16933)*

Madison Manufacturing Inc .... E 574 633-4433
Bremen *(G-1204)*

McKillip Machinery Inc .... G 260 330-2842
Wabash *(G-16199)*

McM Manufacturing .... G 574 339-6994
South Bend *(G-15146)*

Millers Windmill Service .... G 574 825-2877
Middlebury *(G-11739)*

2024 Harris Indiana Industrial Directory

35 INDUSTRIAL AND COMMERCIAL MACHINERY AND COMPUTER EQUIPMENT

Modern AG Solutions LLC .... G 765 221-1011
  Pendleton *(G-13544)*

Mooresville Welding Inc .... G 317 831-2265
  Mooresville *(G-12225)*

Mssh Inc .... G 812 663-2180
  Greensburg *(G-6620)*

National Equipment Inc .... G 219 462-1205
  Valparaiso *(G-16009)*

New Holland Richmond Inc .... F 765 962-7724
  Richmond *(G-14174)*

Nichols Mfg Co Inc .... F 219 696-8577
  Lowell *(G-11174)*

Norman Wagler .... G 812 636-8015
  Odon *(G-13346)*

Onyett Welding & Machine Inc .... G 812 582-2999
  Petersburg *(G-13620)*

Original Tractor Cab Co Inc .... G 765 663-2214
  Arlington *(G-329)*

Oxbo International Corporation .... G 260 768-3217
  Shipshewana *(G-14874)*

◆ Par-Kan Company LLC .... D 260 352-2141
  Silver Lake *(G-14920)*

Perma-Green Supreme Inc .... E 219 548-3801
  Valparaiso *(G-16025)*

Peterson Mfg LLC .... G 574 876-1427
  Wheatfield *(G-16771)*

Rhinehart Development Corp .... E 260 238-4442
  Spencerville *(G-15373)*

SA Heinen LLC .... G 317 416-7818
  Indianapolis *(G-9358)*

Scott Naylor .... G 812 336-5361
  Bloomington *(G-967)*

Shobe Cases LLC .... G 317 363-9006
  Indianapolis *(G-9421)*

▼ Soilmax Inc .... E 888 764-5629
  Terre Haute *(G-15702)*

Spankys Paintball .... G 812 752-7375
  Scottsburg *(G-14580)*

Stan Clamme .... F 765 348-0008
  Hartford City *(G-7077)*

Stoffel Brothers Inc .... G 260 356-6844
  Huntington *(G-7372)*

Sun Rise Metal Shop .... G 260 463-4026
  Topeka *(G-15820)*

▲ Superb Horticulture LLC .... F 800 567-8264
  Plymouth *(G-13815)*

Swiss Perfection LLC .... F 574 457-4457
  Syracuse *(G-15481)*

Valesco Manufacturing Inc .... G 812 636-6001
  Loogootee *(G-11152)*

Valesco Manufacturing Inc .... G 765 522-2740
  Roachdale *(G-14249)*

Whitcraft Welding .... G 574 867-6021
  Grovertown *(G-6825)*

Witherspoon Farms Inc .... G 812 882-5272
  Vincennes *(G-16168)*

Wood Lighter Cases LLC .... G 812 969-3908
  Elizabeth *(G-3131)*

Writers of Vision .... G 812 239-6347
  Farmersburg *(G-4421)*

Ziggity Systems Inc .... E 574 825-5849
  Middlebury *(G-11765)*

3524 Lawn and garden equipment

Alm Services Inc .... G 765 288-6624
  Muncie *(G-12340)*

American Gardenworks Inc .... E 765 869-4033
  Fowler *(G-5617)*

Bane-Welker Equipment LLC .... F 812 234-2627
  Terre Haute *(G-15550)*

◆ Brinly-Hardy Company .... D 812 218-7200
  Jeffersonville *(G-9947)*

Deer Country Equipment LLC .... E 812 522-1922
  Seymour *(G-14646)*

Discount Power Equipment .... G 765 642-0040
  Anderson *(G-104)*

Egenolf Enterprise Inc .... F 317 501-5069
  Indianapolis *(G-8060)*

Everything Else LLC .... G 574 350-7383
  Elkhart *(G-3336)*

Forest Commodities Inc .... G 765 349-3291
  Martinsville *(G-11394)*

Graber Manufacturing .... G 812 636-7725
  Odon *(G-13337)*

Great States Corp .... G 765 288-6624
  Muncie *(G-12406)*

Husqvrna Cnsmr Otdr Prod NA .... C 812 883-3575
  Salem *(G-14483)*

▲ Lafayette Marketing Inc .... F 765 474-5374
  West Lafayette *(G-16600)*

Lastec LLC .... G 317 892-4444
  Indianapolis *(G-8725)*

Mide Products .... G 574 326-3060
  Elkhart *(G-3538)*

Midwest Equipment Mfg Inc .... F 765 436-2496
  Thorntown *(G-15753)*

Mtd Products Inc .... F 317 986-2042
  Indianapolis *(G-8970)*

Novae Corp .... F 260 982-7075
  North Manchester *(G-13245)*

▲ Novae LLC .... E 260 758-9838
  Markle *(G-11361)*

Original Tractor Cab Co Inc .... F 765 663-2214
  Arlington *(G-329)*

Palmor Products Inc .... E 800 872-2822
  Lebanon *(G-10928)*

Peters Enterprises .... G 260 493-6435
  New Haven *(G-12914)*

Rich Manufacturing Inc .... G 765 436-2744
  Lebanon *(G-10937)*

Rochester Metal Products Corp .... E 765 288-6624
  Muncie *(G-12490)*

Talon Terra LLC .... G 219 393-1400
  La Porte *(G-10487)*

▲ Textron Outdoor Power Eqp Inc .... G 704 504-6600
  Coatesville *(G-2110)*

Wheel Horse Sales & Service .... G 574 272-4242
  South Bend *(G-15305)*

Wood-Mizer Holdings Inc .... F 317 892-4444
  Lizton *(G-11052)*

◆ Wood-Mizer Holdings Inc .... C 317 271-1542
  Indianapolis *(G-9784)*

Wright Implement I LLC .... G 812 522-1922
  Seymour *(G-14707)*

3531 Construction machinery

1109 169th LLC .... G 219 671-5052
  Crown Point *(G-2647)*

A & T Cnstr & Excvtg Inc .... G 219 314-2439
  Cedar Lake *(G-1826)*

AF Ohab Company Inc .... E 317 225-4740
  Indianapolis *(G-7455)*

Altec Industries Inc .... C 317 872-3460
  Indianapolis *(G-7493)*

◆ AMA Usa Inc .... G 317 329-6590
  Indianapolis *(G-7494)*

Ameribridge LLC .... D 317 826-2000
  Indianapolis *(G-7498)*

American Industrial Co LLC .... E 317 859-9900
  Greenwood *(G-6668)*

Anthony Wise .... G 317 933-2458
  Trafalgar *(G-15825)*

▼ Asphalt Drum Mixers LLC .... E 260 637-5729
  Huntertown *(G-7249)*

◆ Asphalt Equipment Company Inc ... E 260 672-3004
  Fort Wayne *(G-4775)*

▲ Avis Industrial Corporation .... E 765 998-8100
  Upland *(G-15876)*

Birdeye Inc .... F 812 886-0598
  Vincennes *(G-16115)*

Bishop Lifting Products Inc .... G 260 478-4700
  Fort Wayne *(G-4805)*

Boarder Magic By J & A .... G 317 545-4401
  Indianapolis *(G-7652)*

Border Mgic By Wlden Entps Inc ...... G 317 628-2314
  Indianapolis *(G-7660)*

▲ Caterpillar Inc .... E 630 743-4094
  Greenfield *(G-6476)*

Caterpillar Inc .... C 765 448-5000
  Lafayette *(G-10549)*

Caterpillar Inc .... G 765 447-6816
  Lafayette *(G-10550)*

Chads LLC .... G 812 323-7377
  Ellettsville *(G-3802)*

Colby L Stanger .... G 574 536-5835
  Goshen *(G-6114)*

County of Lagrange .... F 260 499-6353
  Lagrange *(G-10732)*

Crusher Parts Direct LLC .... G 812 822-1463
  Bloomington *(G-850)*

Dyna-Fab Corporation .... E 765 893-4423
  West Lebanon *(G-16647)*

Express Steel Inc .... F 317 657-5017
  Martinsville *(G-11390)*

Galfab LLC .... F 574 946-7767
  Winamac *(G-16861)*

Harding Group LLC .... G 317 846-7401
  Indianapolis *(G-8356)*

Harding Materials Inc .... G 317 849-9666
  Indianapolis *(G-8358)*

Harrell Family LLC .... F 317 770-4550
  Indianapolis *(G-8366)*

Highland Park Services Inc .... G 317 954-0456
  Indianapolis *(G-8398)*

Howard Materials LLC .... G 317 849-9666
  Indianapolis *(G-8430)*

Hurricane Ditcher Company Inc .... F 812 886-9663
  Vincennes *(G-16130)*

▼ Indco Inc .... G 812 945-4383
  New Albany *(G-12746)*

◆ ITR America LLC .... D 219 947-8230
  Hobart *(G-7193)*

J D Digging .... G 260 589-2984
  Berne *(G-715)*

JB Bond Construction LLC .... G 219 628-4606
  Chesterton *(G-1939)*

Jeda Equipment Services Inc .... G 317 842-9377
  Fishers *(G-4550)*

◆ Jinnings Equipment LLC .... G 260 447-4343
  Fort Wayne *(G-5136)*

◆ Joyce Consulting LLC .... G 317 577-8504
  Indianapolis *(G-8641)*

Kenn Feld Group LLC .... G 260 632-4242
  Woodburn *(G-16950)*

Kentuckiana Machine and Tl Inc ...... G 502 301-9005
  Lanesville *(G-10800)*

▲ Keystone Engrg & Mfg Corp .... F 317 271-6192
  Avon *(G-532)*

Kinetics Xcavating LLC .... G 812 208-9892
  Brazil *(G-1151)*

Korte Bros Inc .... F 260 497-0500
  Fort Wayne *(G-5157)*

Lanigan Holdings LLC .... G 812 422-6912
  Evansville *(G-4161)*

Lindas Gone Buggie .... G 219 299-0174
  Hobart *(G-7199)*

Employee Codes: A=Over 500 employees, B=251-500
C=101-250, D=51-100, E=20-50, F=10-19, G=1-9

35 INDUSTRIAL AND COMMERCIAL MACHINERY AND COMPUTER EQUIPMENT

Linkel Company..G..... 812 934-5190
   Batesville *(G-596)*

Maddock Construction Eqp LLC....................E..... 812 349-3000
   Bloomington *(G-914)*

Maddox Industrial Contg LLC.........................E..... 812 544-2156
   Santa Claus *(G-14508)*

Marshall Companies Indiana...........................G..... 317 769-2666
   Lebanon *(G-10913)*

Mittler Supply Inc..G..... 765 289-6341
   Muncie *(G-12457)*

▲ Mortar Net Usa Ltd......................................G..... 800 664-6638
   Portage *(G-13893)*

Nobbe Concrete Products Inc........................G..... 765 647-4017
   Brookville *(G-1329)*

Oak & Stone Excavating & Cnstr...................G..... 812 361-6901
   Bloomington *(G-932)*

▲ Old JB LLC..C..... 812 288-0200
   Jeffersonville *(G-10029)*

Orton-Mccullough Crane Company...............G..... 260 356-7900
   Huntington *(G-7347)*

Paver Rescue Inc...G..... 317 259-4880
   Indianapolis *(G-9103)*

Premier Hydraulic Augers Inc........................E..... 260 456-8518
   Fort Wayne *(G-5344)*

Pro-Tote Systems Inc....................................F..... 574 287-6006
   South Bend *(G-15206)*

R H Marlin Excavating LLC...........................F..... 765 913-4041
   Martinsville *(G-11423)*

Ramar Industries Inc......................................G..... 765 288-7319
   Muncie *(G-12483)*

Road Alert Systems LLC................................G..... 219 669-1206
   Morocco *(G-12269)*

Road Widener LLC..G..... 844 494-3363
   Floyds Knobs *(G-4691)*

Schaefer Yard Care Ldscpg LLC...................G..... 812 215-6424
   Oakland City *(G-13322)*

Smith Excavating..G..... 812 636-0054
   Odon *(G-13351)*

Speedway Construction Pdts LLC................G..... 260 203-9806
   Fort Wayne *(G-5429)*

Square 1 Dsign Manufacture Inc...................F..... 866 647-7771
   Shelbyville *(G-14800)*

Stedman Machine Company Inc..................D..... 812 926-0038
   Aurora *(G-457)*

Summerlot Engineered Pdts Inc....................F..... 812 466-7266
   Rosedale *(G-14383)*

Templeton Coal Company Inc......................C..... 812 232-7037
   Terre Haute *(G-15726)*

Terex Advance Mixer Inc..............................D..... 260 497-0728
   Fort Wayne *(G-5475)*

Terex Corporation..G..... 574 342-0086
   Bourbon *(G-1129)*

Terex Corporation..C..... 260 497-0728
   Fort Wayne *(G-5476)*

Tmf Center Inc...E..... 765 762-3800
   Williamsport *(G-16854)*

Tmf Center Inc...C..... 765 762-1000
   Williamsport *(G-16855)*

Tracy K Hullett..G..... 765 472-3349
   Peru *(G-13606)*

Turner Paving Company.................................G..... 765 962-4408
   Richmond *(G-14221)*

Unrivaled Interiors LLC..................................G..... 317 509-0496
   Cicero *(G-2003)*

Unrivaled Interiors LLC..................................G..... 317 509-0496
   Cicero *(G-2002)*

Vires Backhoe and Dumptruc........................G..... 812 595-1630
   Deputy *(G-2942)*

Wag-Way Tool Incorporated..........................F..... 812 886-0598
   Vincennes *(G-16164)*

Wakarusa Ag LLC...F..... 574 862-1163
   Wakarusa *(G-16256)*

3532 Mining machinery

◆ Brake Supply Company Inc........................C..... 812 467-1000
   Evansville *(G-3950)*

Claymore Tools Inc...G..... 574 255-6483
   South Bend *(G-14975)*

Deister Machine Company Inc......................E..... 260 422-0354
   Fort Wayne *(G-4912)*

Deister Machine Company Inc......................E..... 260 426-7495
   Fort Wayne *(G-4913)*

▼ Deister Machine Company Inc..................C..... 260 426-7495
   Fort Wayne *(G-4914)*

Frazier Comfort Details..................................G..... 219 276-2288
   Gary *(G-5934)*

Hillenbrand Inc..A..... 812 931-5000
   Batesville *(G-590)*

◆ J W Jones Company LLC..........................E..... 765 537-2279
   Paragon *(G-13501)*

Jenmar Enterprises LLC.................................G..... 219 306-3149
   Noblesville *(G-13113)*

Jones Trucking Inc..G..... 765 537-2279
   Paragon *(G-13502)*

K-Tron America Inc..D..... 812 934-7000
   Batesville *(G-594)*

▲ Keystone Engrg & Mfg Corp......................F..... 317 271-6192
   Avon *(G-532)*

Mine System Solutions LLC..........................G..... 270 952-5422
   Boonville *(G-1091)*

Pillar Innovations LLC....................................G..... 812 474-9080
   Evansville *(G-4244)*

S & S Machine Shop Inc................................E..... 812 897-5343
   Boonville *(G-1096)*

Stedman Machine Company Inc..................D..... 812 926-0038
   Aurora *(G-457)*

Wyatt Farm Center Inc...................................G..... 574 354-2998
   Nappanee *(G-12655)*

3533 Oil and gas field machinery

Ares Division LLC...G..... 260 349-9803
   Waterloo *(G-16514)*

Daylight Engineering Inc.................................G..... 812 983-2518
   Elberfeld *(G-3111)*

▲ Diedrich Drill Inc..E..... 219 326-7788
   La Porte *(G-10401)*

Dilden Brothers Inc...E..... 765 742-1717
   Lafayette *(G-10571)*

Emquip Corporation..G..... 317 849-3977
   Indianapolis *(G-8111)*

F D McCrary Operator Inc.............................E..... 812 354-6520
   Petersburg *(G-13611)*

Fiberx Incorporated..G..... 317 501-5619
   Hammond *(G-6928)*

Gesco Group LLC..G..... 260 747-5088
   Fort Wayne *(G-5023)*

▲ Laibe Corporation.......................................D..... 317 231-2250
   Indianapolis *(G-8713)*

Llama Corporation..G..... 888 701-7432
   Decatur *(G-2870)*

◆ Lucas Oil Racing Inc..................................F..... 812 738-1147
   Corydon *(G-2504)*

M&C Tech Indiana Corporation.....................E..... 812 674-2122
   Washington *(G-16493)*

▲ Mobile Drill Operating Co LLC..................E..... 317 260-8108
   Indianapolis *(G-8940)*

Nov Inc..G..... 317 897-3099
   Indianapolis *(G-9027)*

▲ Nrp Jones LLC..D..... 800 348-8868
   La Porte *(G-10460)*

Rose-Wall Mfg Inc..G..... 317 894-4497
   Greenfield *(G-6544)*

Systems Engineering and Sls Co..................G..... 260 422-1671
   Fort Wayne *(G-5466)*

3534 Elevators and moving stairways

Braun Corporation...D..... 574 946-7413
   Winamac *(G-16856)*

Elevator Equipment Corporation....................D..... 765 966-7761
   Richmond *(G-14119)*

Elevator One LLC...G..... 317 634-8001
   Indianapolis *(G-8071)*

Haines Engineering Inc..................................G..... 260 589-3388
   Berne *(G-713)*

▲ TEC Hoist LLC...E..... 708 598-2300
   Griffith *(G-6818)*

Zeller Elevator Co...G..... 812 985-5888
   Mount Vernon *(G-12328)*

3535 Conveyors and conveying equipment

▲ 1st Source Products Inc............................F..... 812 288-7466
   Jeffersonville *(G-9919)*

Advance Fabricators Inc................................E..... 812 944-6941
   New Albany *(G-12686)*

Aggreate Systems..F..... 260 854-4711
   Rome City *(G-14373)*

Applicon Company Incorporated...................F..... 317 635-7843
   Indianapolis *(G-7532)*

▼ Banks Machine & Engrg LLC....................D..... 317 642-4980
   Shelbyville *(G-14732)*

Bastian Solutions LLC...................................F..... 317 575-9992
   Westfield *(G-16668)*

▲ Belt Tech Industrial Inc..............................E..... 812 258-5959
   Washington *(G-16473)*

Berendsen Inc...G..... 812 423-6468
   Evansville *(G-3916)*

Butterworth Industries Inc..............................E..... 765 677-6725
   Gas City *(G-6034)*

C & P Engineering and Mfg Inc.....................F..... 765 825-4293
   Connersville *(G-2430)*

C&M Conveyor Inc...C..... 812 849-5647
   Mitchell *(G-12034)*

Carman Industries Inc....................................E..... 812 288-4710
   Jeffersonville *(G-9950)*

Conveyors Inc...G..... 317 539-5472
   Danville *(G-2809)*

CPM Conveyor LLC.......................................E..... 317 875-1919
   Indianapolis *(G-7894)*

Ctb Inc...E..... 765 654-8517
   Frankfort *(G-5657)*

CTB MN Investment Co Inc..........................A..... 765 654-8517
   Frankfort *(G-5658)*

▲ Custom Conveyor Inc................................F..... 812 663-2023
   Greensburg *(G-6588)*

▲ Daifuku Intrlgistics Amer Corp..................D..... 219 777-2220
   Hobart *(G-7186)*

◆ Direct Conveyors LLC................................E..... 317 346-7777
   Franklin *(G-5725)*

Fabricated Steel Corporation.........................G..... 317 899-0012
   Indianapolis *(G-8162)*

Frontier Engineering..G..... 317 823-6885
   Indianapolis *(G-8235)*

General Material Handling Co........................G..... 317 888-5735
   Indianapolis *(G-8272)*

George Koch Sons LLC.................................D..... 812 465-9600
   Evansville *(G-4089)*

Gravel Conveyors Inc.....................................F..... 317 873-8686
   Zionsville *(G-17014)*

H & H Design & Tool Inc................................G..... 765 886-6199
   Economy *(G-3066)*

▼ Halo LLC..D..... 317 575-9992
   Carmel *(G-1647)*

◆ Hirata Corporation of America...................E..... 317 856-8600
   Indianapolis *(G-8399)*

Hoosier Conveyor Company LLC..................G..... 765 445-3337
   Knightstown *(G-10197)*

SIC SECTION 35 INDUSTRIAL AND COMMERCIAL MACHINERY AND COMPUTER EQUIPMENT

▲ Hovair Automotive LLC .... E 317 738-0485
Franklin *(G-5742)*

Indiana Im Holdings Inc .... E 260 637-3101
Fort Wayne *(G-5101)*

▲ Industrial Transmission Eqp .... E 574 936-3028
Plymouth *(G-13785)*

▲ Interntnal Mtl Hdlg Systems In .... F 812 222-4488
Greensburg *(G-6609)*

Iron Bull Manufacturing LLC .... G 765 597-2480
Marshall *(G-11374)*

▲ Keener Corporation .... C 765 825-2100
Connersville *(G-2449)*

Kelco Steel Fabrication Inc .... G 317 248-9229
Indianapolis *(G-8667)*

◆ Koehler Welding Supply Inc .... F 812 574-4103
Madison *(G-11233)*

Lauyans Holdings Inc .... E
New Albany *(G-12763)*

M Pro LLC .... G 765 459-4750
Kokomo *(G-10302)*

Mainline Conveyor Systems Inc .... F 317 831-2795
Mooresville *(G-12219)*

Manchester Inc .... G 260 982-2202
Roann *(G-14252)*

Martin Grgory Cnvyor Engrg LLC .... E 812 923-9814
Georgetown *(G-6068)*

McClamroch Ag LLC .... G 765 362-4495
Crawfordsville *(G-2588)*

▲ McGinty Conveyors Inc .... G 317 240-4315
Indianapolis *(G-8865)*

Pia Automation US Inc .... E 812 485-5500
Evansville *(G-4242)*

Prime Conveyor Inc .... E 219 736-1994
Merrillville *(G-11552)*

Rowe Conveyor LLC .... E 317 602-1024
Indianapolis *(G-9338)*

Rowe Conveyor LLC .... G 317 602-1024
Greenwood *(G-6761)*

S TEC Group Inc .... F 219 844-7030
Hammond *(G-7002)*

◆ Sager Metal Strip Company LLC ..... E 219 874-3609
Michigan City *(G-11659)*

▼ Screw Conveyor Corporation .... E 219 931-1450
Hammond *(G-7003)*

Screw Conveyor Pacific Corp .... E 219 931-1450
Hammond *(G-7004)*

▲ Shuttleworth LLC .... D 260 356-8500
Huntington *(G-7368)*

Smock Materials Handling Co .... F 317 890-3200
Indianapolis *(G-9452)*

Sparks Belting Company Inc .... G 800 451-4537
Hammond *(G-7012)*

Stahl Equipment Inc .... F 812 925-3341
Gentryville *(G-6053)*

Summerlot Engineered Pdts Inc .... F 812 466-7266
Rosedale *(G-14383)*

Systec Corporation .... D 317 890-9230
Indianapolis *(G-9542)*

◆ Vestil Manufacturing Corp .... C 260 665-7586
Angola *(G-306)*

Vibcon Corporation .... F 317 984-3543
Arcadia *(G-319)*

W M Kelley Co Inc .... D 812 945-3529
New Albany *(G-12825)*

Webber Manufacturing Company .... E 317 357-8681
Indianapolis *(G-9745)*

3536 Hoists, cranes, and monorails

Boat Lift Guys Inc .... G 260 667-3057
Angola *(G-235)*

Bryant Lift Trailer .... G 574 721-2255
Rochester *(G-14280)*

Cranewerks Inc .... D 765 663-2909
Morristown *(G-12274)*

▲ Custom Conveyor Inc .... F 812 663-2023
Greensburg *(G-6588)*

D & S Boat Lifts .... G 574 583-8972
Monticello *(G-12144)*

Dearborn Crane and Engrg Co .... E 574 259-2444
Mishawaka *(G-11882)*

Deatons Waterfront Svcs LLC .... F 317 336-7180
Fortville *(G-5591)*

Deshazo LLC .... G 317 867-7677
Westfield *(G-16685)*

Diamond Construction Svcs LLC .... G 513 314-3609
Aurora *(G-443)*

Galfab LLC .... F 574 946-7767
Winamac *(G-16861)*

▼ Hoosier Crane Service Company ..... D 574 523-2945
Elkhart *(G-3411)*

Hubbard Inc .... G 317 535-1926
Whiteland *(G-16788)*

Indiana Steel & Engrg Inc .... E 812 275-3363
Bedford *(G-647)*

Industrial Controls Corp .... G 219 884-1141
Gary *(G-5961)*

J V Crane & Engineering Inc .... E 219 942-8566
Portage *(G-13879)*

Konecranes Inc .... F 219 661-9602
Crown Point *(G-2711)*

Konecranes Inc .... G 812 479-0488
Evansville *(G-4160)*

Konecranes Inc .... G 260 451-2016
Fort Wayne *(G-5154)*

Konecranes Inc .... F 317 546-8122
Greenwood *(G-6724)*

Konecranes Inc .... E 812 941-1250
New Albany *(G-12761)*

Lakeland Pier and Lift LLC .... F 574 377-3481
Warsaw *(G-16385)*

Mooresville Welding Inc .... G 317 831-2265
Mooresville *(G-12225)*

Ohio Transmission Corporation .... G 812 466-2734
Terre Haute *(G-15655)*

Pwi .... D 574 646-2015
Nappanee *(G-12637)*

Royal ARC Welding Company .... G 260 587-3711
Ashley *(G-336)*

T & M Equipment Company Inc .... F 317 293-9255
Indianapolis *(G-9543)*

T & M Equipment Company Inc .... G 219 942-2299
Merrillville *(G-11563)*

▲ TEC Hoist LLC .... E 708 598-2300
Griffith *(G-6818)*

3537 Industrial trucks and tractors

141 Trucking LLC .... G 312 581-5121
Schererville *(G-14511)*

1st Choice Contractors LLC .... G 317 628-4721
Indianapolis *(G-7385)*

3jm Hauling LLC .... G 317 518-0750
Avon *(G-501)*

5 Star Logistics LLC .... G 708 926-4251
Highland *(G-7117)*

7r Express LLC .... G 833 611-3497
Evansville *(G-3857)*

A Divine Image Enterprise LLC .... G 317 397-8132
Indianapolis *(G-7398)*

A&J Logistic LLC .... G 708 314-6817
Dyer *(G-2965)*

Abs Freight Lines LLC .... G 317 691-6846
Indianapolis *(G-7417)*

Afr Equipment LLC .... G 888 519-9899
Laurel *(G-10824)*

All Shppers Are Prrity Trckg L .... G 317 525-6954
Indianapolis *(G-7476)*

Alta Equipment Holdings Inc .... G 269 578-3182
South Bend *(G-14939)*

Aluminum Trailer Company .... C 574 773-2440
Nappanee *(G-12579)*

AM General LLC .... A 574 258-7523
Mishawaka *(G-11840)*

▲ Ameri-Kart Corp .... C 574 848-7462
Bristol *(G-1244)*

American Industrial McHy Inc .... F 219 755-4090
Merrillville *(G-11483)*

Anderson & Anderson Trckg Inc .... G 219 661-7547
Crown Point *(G-2650)*

Aytch Logistics LLC .... G 317 443-9812
Indianapolis *(G-7581)*

B6 Transports LLC .... G 317 975-0053
Fishers *(G-4469)*

Bell Transportation LLC .... G 317 833-0745
Indianapolis *(G-7610)*

Bemcor Inc .... F 219 937-1600
Hammond *(G-6885)*

Beyond Distributions LLC .... G 631 960-1745
Indianapolis *(G-7621)*

Bills International LLC .... F 260 226-6004
Fort Wayne *(G-4800)*

Blue J Logistics LLC .... G 317 721-1784
Indianapolis *(G-7644)*

BTS Dispatching LLC .... G 317 300-4594
Indianapolis *(G-7695)*

Buhrt Engineering & Cnstr .... E 574 267-3720
Warsaw *(G-16331)*

C&C Transportation Service LLC .... F 317 677-5060
Fishers *(G-4479)*

Cade Carrier Solutions Inc .... G 312 953-5154
Hammond *(G-6889)*

Caldwells Inc .... E 765 740-4300
Morristown *(G-12272)*

Cedric Morris .... G 678 718-0012
Fishers *(G-4485)*

Century Industries LLC .... E 812 246-3371
Sellersburg *(G-14590)*

Certified Choice Truckers LLC .... G 260 615-3437
Fort Wayne *(G-4841)*

Cimc Reefer Trailer Inc .... C 219 253-2000
Monon *(G-12054)*

Citrine Dispatch LLC .... G 219 689-8293
Hammond *(G-6899)*

Clarks Big Dog Trucking LLC .... G 317 625-1388
Indianapolis *(G-7818)*

Clm Express Trucking LLC .... G 219 237-4646
Highland *(G-7130)*

Clp Towne Inc .... G 574 233-3183
South Bend *(G-14977)*

Cmoss Transport LLC .... G 317 656-1846
Indianapolis *(G-7828)*

Converto Mfg Co Inc .... G 765 478-3205
Cambridge City *(G-1492)*

Cooper Transit LLC .... G 260 797-3003
Fort Wayne *(G-4871)*

Crossroad Freight LLC .... G 239 248-4058
Indianapolis *(G-7911)*

Crossroads Frt Solutions LLC .... G 800 425-0282
Fishers *(G-4497)*

Crown Equipment Corporation .... G 574 293-1264
Elkhart *(G-3274)*

Crown Equipment Corporation .... D 812 477-5511
Evansville *(G-3998)*

Crown Equipment Corporation .... D 260 484-0055
Fort Wayne *(G-4889)*

Crown Equipment Corporation .... B 765 653-4240
Greencastle *(G-6399)*

Employee Codes: A=Over 500 employees, B=251-500
C=101-250, D=51-100, E=20-50, F=10-19, G=1-9

35 INDUSTRIAL AND COMMERCIAL MACHINERY AND COMPUTER EQUIPMENT

Crown Equipment Corporation............... E 765 520-2077
  New Castle (G-12858)
Crown Equipment Corporation............... D 317 875-7233
  Plainfield (G-13677)
D Rinker Transport LLC............................ G 765 749-4120
  Dunkirk (G-2961)
Diamonds & Pearls Trnsp LLC................. G 504 295-2701
  Indianapolis (G-7972)
Diversified Qulty Svcs Ind LLC................. G 765 644-7712
  Anderson (G-105)
DK Carrier Inc....................................... G 317 374-1835
  Greenwood (G-6688)
Dlb Transporters LLC............................. G 317 667-3368
  Indianapolis (G-7992)
Dodson Logistics LLC............................. G 937 657-7490
  Richmond (G-14115)
Dohrn Transfer Company........................ E 574 941-4484
  Plymouth (G-13771)
Dwd Trucking LLC.................................. G 317 586-3484
  Indianapolis (G-8022)
Eaton Corporation.................................. C 260 925-3800
  Auburn (G-387)
Elpers Truck Equipment LLC.................. F 812 423-5787
  Evansville (G-4031)
Exclusive Fit Trucking LLC...................... G 708 872-7593
  South Bend (G-15021)
Extreme Trailer Service LLC.................. E 812 406-1984
  Charlestown (G-1876)
Fam Express 1982 LLC.......................... G 317 628-3901
  Indianapolis (G-8163)
Felicia Fr8 LLC...................................... G 312 597-9282
  Hammond (G-6927)
Finalmile-Logistics LLC......................... G 773 259-0727
  Portage (G-13864)
First Generation Trucking LLC................ G 317 654-6272
  Indianapolis (G-8193)
First Impression Trnsp........................... G 317 682-8436
  Indianapolis (G-8194)
Forever Young Trckg Svcs LLC............... G 616 350-4053
  Indianapolis (G-8215)
Ftn Logistics LLC................................... G 317 488-7446
  Indianapolis (G-8237)
Fuentes Distributing Inc........................ G 219 808-2147
  Hammond (G-6933)
Full Throttle Enterprise Inc..................... G 317 779-3887
  Indianapolis (G-8240)
Galfab LLC.. F 574 946-7767
  Winamac (G-16861)
Generation Logistics LLC...................... G 877 238-7380
  Indianapolis (G-8273)
Genertonal Outreach Gaming LLC.......... G 872 777-6882
  Gary (G-5939)
Great Dane LLC.................................... A 812 443-4711
  Brazil (G-1143)
Green Streak Pulling Inc....................... G 812 254-6858
  Washington (G-16482)
Gypsum Express Ltd............................. G 812 247-2648
  Shoals (G-14908)
H D Eccel LLC....................................... G 574 386-2115
  South Bend (G-15056)
◆ Hirata Corporation of America............. E 317 856-8600
  Indianapolis (G-8399)
Holba Trucking and Transport................ G 219 381-4236
  Hammond (G-6946)
Hy-TEC Fiberglass Inc........................... G 260 489-6601
  Fort Wayne (G-5087)
◆ Ichinen USA Corporation..................... G 317 638-3511
  Indianapolis (G-8450)
▲ Industrial Transmission Eqp................ E 574 936-3028
  Plymouth (G-13785)
Its Family Trucking LLC......................... G 219 277-1462
  Hammond (G-6960)

Jacksons 33 Transporting LLC............... G 901 628-7803
  Indianapolis (G-8616)
JD Materials... G 219 662-1418
  Crown Point (G-2701)
Jdld Enterprises Inc.............................. G 765 481-2210
  Lebanon (G-10904)
Jet Fast Carriers LLC............................. G 219 218-3021
  Indianapolis (G-8623)
John S Cotter....................................... G 765 584-2521
  Ridgeville (G-14234)
Joyce/Dayton Corp................................ E 260 726-9361
  Portland (G-13952)
Jpc Trucking LLC................................... G 219 207-2300
  Valparaiso (G-15982)
JVI Inc... G 872 276-0823
  Hammond (G-6963)
Kath Enterprise LLC.............................. G 877 641-6990
  Gary (G-5972)
Kenneth E Ziegler.................................. G 765 675-2222
  Tipton (G-15778)
Kiyam Transport LLC............................. G 502 551-6245
  South Bend (G-15101)
Kokomo Truck Store.............................. G 765 459-5118
  Kokomo (G-10296)
Ksm Logistics LLC................................ G 574 318-2040
  South Bend (G-15108)
▲ Lafayette Wire Products Inc................ D 765 474-7896
  Lafayette (G-10632)
Laidig Inc... E 574 256-0204
  Mishawaka (G-11925)
Landgrebe Manufacturing Inc................. G 219 462-9587
  Valparaiso (G-15991)
Leggits LLC.. G 269 447-3500
  South Bend (G-15123)
Lift-A-Loft Manufacturing Inc.................. G 317 288-3691
  Muncie (G-12440)
Lifted Loads LLC................................... G 317 432-1542
  Indianapolis (G-8748)
Luna Logistics LLC................................ G 317 721-2363
  Indianapolis (G-8797)
M-Famouz Logistics LLC........................ G 219 501-1921
  Hammond (G-6974)
◆ Major Tool and Machine Inc................. C 317 636-6433
  Indianapolis (G-8820)
MHp Distribution LLC............................ F 312 731-8380
  Gary (G-5981)
Michiana Forklift Inc............................ F 574 326-3702
  Elkhart (G-3532)
Middtran Enterprises Inc....................... G 317 869-5212
  Indianapolis (G-8907)
Midwest Transit Authority LLC................ G 765 414-5097
  West Lafayette (G-16606)
Moodys Logistics Services LLC.............. G 812 512-2772
  Linton (G-11040)
Mooresville Welding Inc......................... G 317 831-2265
  Mooresville (G-12225)
Msf Express Inc................................... G 561 413-4545
  Lake Station (G-10774)
N-Complete Inc..................................... F 765 649-2244
  Anderson (G-165)
Naya Trans LLC..................................... G 317 720-8602
  Indianapolis (G-8995)
Nc2 LLC.. G 260 758-9838
  Markle (G-11359)
Nelson J Hochstetler............................. G 260 499-0315
  Lagrange (G-10756)
New Beginning Logistics LLC................. G 773 457-0925
  Merrillville (G-11547)
North Central Equipment C.................... G 574 825-2006
  Middlebury (G-11741)
O&T Alliance Group LLC........................ G 302 287-0953
  Indianapolis (G-9039)

◆ Ogden Welding Systems Inc............... E 219 322-5252
  Schererville (G-14537)
On The Go Logistics LLC....................... G 765 810-7454
  Anderson (G-173)
One Lineage Trucking Corp.................... F 708 257-6333
  Gary (G-5990)
One Little Truck LLC.............................. G 872 276-0014
  Highland (G-7149)
Only Get Better Logistics LLC................ G 317 835-5606
  Indianapolis (G-9057)
Orion Shipping Solutions Corp............... G 800 410-4910
  Indianapolis (G-9070)
Out The Box Transit Inc......................... G 317 523-0061
  Carmel (G-1713)
◆ Par-Kan Company LLC....................... D 260 352-2141
  Silver Lake (G-14920)
Pierce Tracy.. G 765 748-2361
  Anderson (G-179)
Pioneer Transport LLC........................... E 260 726-4840
  Portland (G-13960)
Powell Systems Inc............................. E 765 884-0980
  Fowler (G-5630)
Powell Systems Inc............................. G 765 884-0613
  Fowler (G-5631)
Prosperer Trucking LLC......................... G 317 551-5691
  Indianapolis (G-9232)
Qme LLC.. G 773 263-9830
  Gary (G-5998)
R & R Trucking & Freight LLC................ G 888 477-8782
  Indianapolis (G-9254)
Rance Aluminum Fabrication................. E 574 266-9028
  Elkhart (G-3639)
Renegade Dispatching LLC................... G 260 797-5423
  Fort Wayne (G-5380)
Right Direction Trckg Ex LLC................. G 502 912-2504
  Jeffersonville (G-10047)
Rlay Express Inc.................................. G 754 265-8555
  Avon (G-548)
Rowe Conveyor LLC.............................. G 317 602-1024
  Greenwood (G-6761)
S & Y Trucking LLC............................... G 317 642-6222
  Noblesville (G-13170)
S and SM Achine USA LLC.................... G 708 758-8300
  Gary (G-6006)
Safe Bird Express LLC.......................... G 607 376-7633
  Indianapolis (G-9362)
Selking International LLC.................... E 260 482-3000
  Fort Wayne (G-5408)
Selking International Inc....................... G 574 522-2001
  Elkhart (G-3668)
Shalom Trans LLC................................ E 317 712-6765
  Avon (G-550)
Showtime Conversions Inc.................... E 574 825-1130
  Middlebury (G-11752)
Smiles Motors LLC............................... G 219 801-5255
  Highland (G-7156)
Southlake Lift Truck............................. G 219 962-4695
  Gary (G-6013)
Ssm Logistics LLC............................... G 812 354-4509
  Winslow (G-16923)
Stahl Equipment Inc............................. F 812 925-3341
  Gentryville (G-6053)
Stop N Go Transport LLC...................... G 317 902-0815
  Indianapolis (G-9515)
Storageworks Inc................................. G 317 577-3511
  Fishers (G-4607)
◆ Supreme Industries Inc..................... C 574 642-3070
  Goshen (G-6265)
Tidy Janitorial Services LLC.................. G 502 807-9847
  Clarksville (G-2039)
▲ Toyota Material Handling Inc.............. D 800 381-5879
  Columbus (G-2406)

▲ Transstex LLC .... G 877 960-2644
Indianapolis (G-9631)

Truckin4ya LLC .... G 812 225-2640
Jeffersonville (G-10066)

Two Sticks Inc .... G 219 926-7910
Chesterton (G-1962)

Upshaw Freight LLC .... G 317 200-8655
Indianapolis (G-9686)

◆ Utilimaster Services LLC .... B 800 582-3454
Bristol (G-1296)

Verbott Trucking & Transportat .... G 317 363-9698
Indianapolis (G-9706)

W & M Enterprises Inc .... F 812 537-4656
Lawrenceburg (G-10865)

Wiese Holding Company .... D 317 241-8600
Indianapolis (G-9761)

Wild Hunnits Group Inc .... G 312 609-9433
Hammond (G-7034)

Xpedited Bulk Carriers LLC .... G 708 490-7539
Highland (G-7160)

Xpedited Trucking Inc .... F 463 223-7366
Carmel (G-1810)

Yes Yes Trucking LLC .... G 800 971-3633
Indianapolis (G-9801)

Youngs Freight & Logistics LLC .... G 765 639-7888
Anderson (G-219)

Zebra Express LLC .... G 317 828-9277
Indianapolis (G-9808)

Zip Zone Gone LLC .... G 812 604-0041
Evansville (G-4393)

3541 Machine tools, metal cutting type

Accutech Mold & Machine Inc .... C 260 471-6102
Fort Wayne (G-4722)

American Tool Service Inc .... F 260 493-6351
Fort Wayne (G-4758)

API International Inc .... F 317 894-1100
Greenfield (G-6463)

ARC Angle Welding/Fabrication .... F 812 619-1731
Tell City (G-15496)

Bailey Tools & Supply Inc .... G 502 635-6348
Evansville (G-3908)

Baker Prototype Engrg Inc .... G 574 266-7223
Elkhart (G-3215)

Butler Tool & Design Inc .... F 219 297-4531
Goodland (G-6080)

Capital Machine Company Inc .... F 317 638-6661
Indianapolis (G-7734)

Charleston Metal Products Inc .... F 260 837-8211
Waterloo (G-16516)

Claymore Tools Inc .... G 574 255-6483
South Bend (G-14975)

Cnm Machine Tool Repair .... G 765 552-3255
Elwood (G-3819)

Continental Diamond Tool Corp .... F 260 493-1294
New Haven (G-12899)

CPR Machining LLC .... E 574 299-0222
South Bend (G-14984)

Creative Tool Inc .... G 260 338-1222
Huntertown (G-7251)

Custom Machining Inc .... E 317 392-2328
Shelbyville (G-14749)

Cut-Pro Indexable Tooling LLC .... G 260 668-2400
Angola (G-245)

Cyberia Ltd .... G 317 721-2582
Indianapolis (G-7938)

Danubius Machine Inc .... G 219 662-7787
Crown Point (G-2673)

Dmg Mori Usa Inc .... G 317 913-0978
Indianapolis (G-7993)

Dunes Investment Inc .... F 219 764-4270
Portage (G-13860)

Eagle Precision Machining Inc .... G 260 637-4649
Huntertown (G-7255)

Edge Technologies Inc .... G 317 408-0116
Indianapolis (G-8053)

EDM Specialties Inc .... G 317 856-4700
Indianapolis (G-8056)

▼ Epco Products Inc .... E 260 747-8888
Fort Wayne (G-4956)

Express Machine .... G 812 719-5979
Cannelton (G-1536)

Extreme Tool Supply .... G 219 362-5129
La Porte (G-10407)

G & S Super Abrasives Inc .... E 260 665-5562
Angola (G-254)

GMI LLC .... G 260 209-6676
Fort Wayne (G-5028)

▲ Grinding and Polsg McHy Corp .... F 317 898-0750
Indianapolis (G-8331)

Hautau Tube Cutoff Systems LLC .... F 765 647-1600
Brookville (G-1323)

Hoosier Spline Broach Corp .... E 765 452-8273
Kokomo (G-10281)

Hy-Tech Machining Systems LLC .... E 765 649-6852
Anderson (G-131)

Indiana Handpiece Repair Inc .... G 260 436-0765
Fort Wayne (G-5100)

Indiana Oxygen Company Inc .... G 765 662-8700
Marion (G-11295)

Kaiser Tool Company Inc .... E 260 484-3620
Fort Wayne (G-5142)

Killer Machining Solutions LLC .... G 813 786-2309
Brownsburg (G-1383)

Lionshead Precision Metals LLC .... D 317 787-6358
Greenwood (G-6729)

Lmr Industries LLC .... G 219 765-4157
Hammond (G-6973)

Macallister Machinery Co Inc .... F 765 966-0759
Richmond (G-14157)

Masbez LLC .... G 855 962-7239
Frankfort (G-5681)

Maxwell Milling Indiana Inc .... G 765 489-3506
Hagerstown (G-6840)

Micro Tool & Machine Co Inc .... G 574 272-9141
Granger (G-6360)

Micro-Precision Operations .... F 260 589-2136
Berne (G-719)

◆ Milltronics Mfg Co Inc .... C 952 442-1410
Indianapolis (G-8926)

Mosey Manufacturing Co Inc .... G 765 983-8870
Richmond (G-14168)

Mosey Manufacturing Co Inc .... G 765 983-8870
Richmond (G-14169)

Mosey Manufacturing Co Inc .... G 765 983-8889
Richmond (G-14170)

Mosey Manufacturing Co Inc .... G 765 983-8870
Richmond (G-14171)

Mrg Robotics .... G 814 341-4334
Indianapolis (G-8967)

◆ Nap Asset Holdings Ltd .... D 812 482-2000
Jasper (G-9894)

Palmary America LLC .... G 317 494-1415
Franklin (G-5764)

Pathfinder Cutting Tech LLC .... F 424 342-9723
Indianapolis (G-9099)

Peerless Machinery Inc .... G 574 210-5990
South Bend (G-15188)

Qig LLC .... E 260 244-3591
Columbia City (G-2185)

R P Imel .... G 260 543-2465
Uniondale (G-15872)

Reeder & Kline Machine Co Inc .... F 317 846-6591
Carmel (G-1737)

Roeder Industries .... G 812 654-3322
Milan (G-11783)

Rx Honing Machine Corp .... G 574 259-1606
Mishawaka (G-11989)

S&S Machinery Repair LLC .... G 812 521-2368
Norman (G-13204)

Solomon M Eicher .... G 812 289-1252
Marysville (G-11436)

Specialty Tool LLC .... F 260 493-6351
Indianapolis (G-9471)

▲ Standard Locknut LLC .... C 317 399-2230
Westfield (G-16729)

Stanley Engnered Fastening LLC .... C 765 728-2433
Montpelier (G-12182)

Stedman Machine Company Inc .... D 812 926-0038
Aurora (G-457)

Surclean Inc .... F 248 791-2226
Brownsburg (G-1405)

Tascon Corp .... F 317 547-6127
Indianapolis (G-9555)

Titus Inc .... F 574 936-3345
Plymouth (G-13817)

Tom West Farms .... G 812 986-2162
Poland (G-13838)

▲ Tri-State Industries Inc .... D 219 933-1710
Hammond (G-7023)

Versatile Metal Works LLC .... F 765 754-7470
Muncie (G-12512)

White Eagle Indus Group LLC .... G 270 577-2415
Corydon (G-2523)

Whitesell Prcsion Cmpnents Inc .... C 812 282-4014
Jeffersonville (G-10075)

Winndeavor LLC .... G 219 324-2978
La Porte (G-10502)

Wood Truss Systems Inc .... G 765 751-9990
Carmel (G-1807)

Wyrco LLC .... G 317 691-2832
Fishers (G-4636)

▲ Zps America LLC .... E 317 452-4030
Indianapolis (G-9815)

3542 Machine tools, metal forming type

▲ A & M Systems Inc .... F 574 522-5000
Elkhart (G-3138)

A & M Tool Inc .... G 812 934-6533
Batesville (G-575)

A/C Fabricating Corp .... E 574 534-1415
Goshen (G-6086)

Ahern Electric Inc .... G 219 874-3508
Westville (G-16755)

Allfab LLC .... G 317 359-3539
Indianapolis (G-7482)

Altra Industrial Motion Corp .... E 219 874-5248
Michigan City (G-11577)

American Press Services .... G 937 338-3000
Union City (G-15847)

Applied Metals & Mch Works Inc .... E 260 424-4834
Fort Wayne (G-4766)

Ayco Panel .... G 765 635-8106
Jasonville (G-9822)

Beatty International Inc .... E 219 931-3000
Hammond (G-6882)

Beatty Machine & Mfg Co .... E 219 931-3000
Hammond (G-6883)

Bemcor Inc .... F 219 937-1600
Hammond (G-6885)

Beulah Inc .... G 219 309-5635
Valparaiso (G-15913)

Carver Inc .... G 260 563-7577
Wabash (G-16177)

Davis Machine and Tool Inc .... F 812 526-2674
Edinburgh (G-3076)

35 INDUSTRIAL AND COMMERCIAL MACHINERY AND COMPUTER EQUIPMENT — SIC SECTION

Die-Mensional Metal Stampg Inc............ F...... 812 265-3946
  Madison *(G-11213)*
Egenolf Machine Inc.................................... F...... 317 787-5301
  Indianapolis *(G-8061)*
Ferguson Equipment Inc............................. G...... 574 234-4303
  South Bend *(G-15033)*
Fortville Automotive Sup Inc...................... G...... 317 485-5114
  Fortville *(G-5594)*
▲ Frech U S A Inc... F...... 219 874-2812
  Michigan City *(G-11614)*
▲ Fred S Carver Inc..................................... G...... 260 563-7577
  Wabash *(G-16188)*
G & G Metal Spinners Inc........................... E...... 317 923-3225
  Indianapolis *(G-8250)*
▲ Gsw Press Automation Inc..................... G...... 419 733-5230
  North Vernon *(G-13273)*
Idra North America Inc................................ G...... 765 459-0085
  Kokomo *(G-10285)*
Independent Rail Corporation................... E...... 317 780-8480
  Indianapolis *(G-8472)*
Lionshead Precision Metals LLC............... D...... 317 787-6358
  Greenwood *(G-6729)*
Masbez LLC.. G...... 855 962-7239
  Frankfort *(G-5681)*
Masson Inc... F...... 317 632-8021
  Indianapolis *(G-8848)*
Mishawaka LLC.. F...... 574 259-1981
  Mishawaka *(G-11952)*
◆ Nachi America Inc..................................... E...... 877 622-4487
  Greenwood *(G-6743)*
Olympus Manufacturing Systems............. G...... 219 465-1520
  Valparaiso *(G-16017)*
Pbtt Inc... 810 965-3675
  Newburgh *(G-13016)*
Precision Industries Corp........................... F...... 574 522-2626
  Elkhart *(G-3615)*
Press Brake Safety LLC.............................. G...... 317 413-7593
  Zionsville *(G-17044)*
Quality Die Set Corp.................................... E...... 574 967-4411
  Logansport *(G-11104)*
Rickie Allan Pease...................................... G...... 260 244-7579
  Columbia City *(G-2191)*
Roadhog Inc.. E...... 317 858-7050
  Brownsburg *(G-1398)*
Roeder Industries.. G...... 812 654-3322
  Milan *(G-11783)*
▲ Sapp Inc... F...... 317 512-8353
  Edinburgh *(G-3103)*
Smgf LLC.. E...... 812 354-8899
  Petersburg *(G-13625)*
Southern Mechatronics Co Inc.................. G
  Brownsburg *(G-1404)*
Sullivan Engineered Services.................... G...... 812 294-1724
  Henryville *(G-7116)*
Tk Metal Forming Inc.................................. F...... 574 293-2907
  Elkhart *(G-3735)*
Toolmasters Inc... G...... 574 256-1881
  Mishawaka *(G-12014)*
Tru-Cut Machine & Tool Inc....................... G...... 260 569-1802
  Wabash *(G-16218)*
United Machine Corporation...................... G...... 219 548-8050
  Valparaiso *(G-16072)*
Versatile Metal Works LLC......................... F...... 765 754-7470
  Muncie *(G-12512)*
Vlb Group North America LLC................... E...... 317 642-3425
  Elkhart *(G-3775)*

3543 Industrial patterns

American Bronze Craft Inc......................... F...... 501 729-3018
  Indianapolis *(G-7501)*
Armour Pattern Inc..................................... G...... 219 374-9325
  Cedar Lake *(G-1827)*
Baseline Tool Company.............................. F...... 260 761-4932
  Wawaka *(G-16537)*
Charles Bane... G...... 765 855-5100
  Centerville *(G-1848)*
Charles E Obryan.. G...... 812 536-2399
  Huntingburg *(G-7274)*
Cindys Crossstitch & Patterns.................. G...... 317 410-0764
  Indianapolis *(G-7804)*
● Core-Tech Inc... D...... 260 748-4477
  Fort Wayne *(G-4877)*
Cunningham Pattern & Engrg Inc............. F...... 812 379-9571
  Columbus *(G-2276)*
Dillon Pattern Works Inc............................ F...... 765 642-3549
  Anderson *(G-103)*
Diversified Pattern Engrg Inc.................... E...... 260 897-3771
  Avilla *(G-475)*
Foley Pattern Company Inc....................... E...... 260 925-4113
  Auburn *(G-391)*
K & K Inc.. F...... 574 266-8040
  Elkhart *(G-3440)*
Maxwell Engineering Inc............................ G...... 260 745-4991
  Fort Wayne *(G-5208)*
Muncie Casting Corp.................................. E...... 765 288-2611
  Muncie *(G-12461)*
New Point Products Inc.............................. G...... 812 663-6311
  New Point *(G-12976)*
Northbend Pattern Works Inc.................... E...... 812 637-3000
  West Harrison *(G-16550)*
Northside Pattern Works Inc..................... G...... 317 290-0501
  Brownsburg *(G-1391)*
Nvsd LLC.. G...... 502 561-0007
  New Albany *(G-12785)*
Ooten Pattern Works................................... G...... 317 244-7348
  Indianapolis *(G-9061)*
Owings Patterns Inc................................... F...... 812 944-5577
  Sellersburg *(G-14609)*
Peerless Pattern & Machine Co................ G...... 765 477-7719
  Lafayette *(G-10666)*
Shells Inc... D...... 574 342-2673
  Bourbon *(G-1127)*
Standard Pattern Company Inc................. G...... 260 456-4870
  Fort Wayne *(G-5435)*
▲ Ward Pattern & Engineering Inc......... C...... 260 426-8700
  Fort Wayne *(G-5547)*
Weberdings Carving Shop Inc.................. F...... 812 934-3710
  Batesville *(G-610)*

3544 Special dies, tools, jigs, and fixtures

A & A Custom Automation Inc.................. D...... 812 464-3650
  Evansville *(G-3858)*
AAA Tool and Die Company Inc................ F...... 574 246-1222
  South Bend *(G-14931)*
Accu-Mold LLC.. E...... 269 323-0388
  Mishawaka *(G-11834)*
Accutech Mold & Machine Inc................... C...... 260 471-6102
  Fort Wayne *(G-4722)*
Acme Masking Company Inc..................... E...... 317 272-6202
  Avon *(G-503)*
▲ Acro Engineering Inc............................. E...... 812 663-6236
  Greensburg *(G-6579)*
Advanced Mold & Engineering.................. F...... 812 342-9000
  Columbus *(G-2214)*
Advanced Products Tech Inc..................... G...... 765 827-1166
  Connersville *(G-2423)*
▲ Ahaus Tool & Engineering Inc............. D...... 765 962-3573
  Richmond *(G-14084)*
▲ Aircom Manufacturing Inc.................... B...... 317 545-5383
  Indianapolis *(G-7462)*
Ajax Tool Inc.. G...... 260 747-7482
  Fort Wayne *(G-4735)*
Al-Ex Inc... G...... 574 206-0100
  Elkhart *(G-3157)*
Allegiance Tool and Die Inc....................... G...... 574 277-1819
  Granger *(G-6331)*
Allied Steel Rule Dies Inc.......................... F...... 317 634-9835
  Indianapolis *(G-7484)*
Ameri-Tek Manufacturing Inc.................... F...... 574 753-8058
  Logansport *(G-11055)*
American Steel Rule Die Inc..................... G...... 574 262-3437
  Elkhart *(G-3175)*
Apex Tool and Manufacturing................... E...... 812 425-8121
  Evansville *(G-3894)*
Applied Composites Engrg Inc................. E...... 317 243-4225
  Indianapolis *(G-7533)*
Ar-Tee Enterprises Inc............................... G...... 574 848-5543
  Bristol *(G-1246)*
Ark Model and Stampings Inc................... F...... 317 549-3394
  New Palestine *(G-12931)*
Artisan Tool & Die Inc................................ E...... 765 288-6653
  Muncie *(G-12346)*
Atkisson Enterprises Inc............................ F...... 765 675-7593
  Tipton *(G-15766)*
▲ Atlas Die LLC.. D...... 574 295-0050
  Elkhart *(G-3200)*
Aul Brothers Tool & Die Inc....................... F...... 765 759-5124
  Yorktown *(G-16968)*
Aul In The Family Tool and Die................. G...... 765 759-5161
  Yorktown *(G-16969)*
Axis Mold Inc... G...... 574 292-8904
  New Carlisle *(G-12834)*
B & B Engineering Inc................................ G...... 765 566-3460
  Bringhurst *(G-1235)*
B & D Manufacturing Inc............................ G...... 765 452-2761
  Kokomo *(G-10234)*
▲ B & J Specialty Inc................................. D...... 260 761-5011
  Wawaka *(G-16536)*
B B & H Tool of Columbus Inc.................. F...... 812 372-3707
  Columbus *(G-2224)*
B/C Precision Tool Inc................................ G...... 812 577-0642
  Greendale *(G-6439)*
B&B Tool and Molding Co Inc.................... E
  Muncie *(G-12348)*
▲ B&J Rocket America Inc......................... E...... 574 825-5802
  Middlebury *(G-11700)*
▲ Batesville Products Inc......................... D...... 513 381-2057
  Lawrenceburg *(G-10831)*
▲ Batesville Tool & Die Inc....................... B...... 812 934-5616
  Batesville *(G-584)*
▲ Beach Acquisition Co LLC..................... B...... 812 945-2688
  New Albany *(G-12698)*
Beckys Die Cutting Inc............................... G...... 260 467-1714
  Fort Wayne *(G-4792)*
Bel-Mar Products Corporation................... G...... 317 769-3262
  Whitestown *(G-16801)*
▲ Bell Machine Company Inc.................... E...... 765 654-5225
  Frankfort *(G-5652)*
Berkey Machine Corporation..................... G...... 260 761-4002
  Wawaka *(G-16538)*
Better Gutter Systems................................ G...... 765 282-2724
  Muncie *(G-12353)*
Blackerby & Associates............................. G...... 812 216-2370
  Seymour *(G-14633)*
Blessing Tool & Die Inc............................. G...... 574 875-1982
  Elkhart *(G-3226)*
BMC Marketing Corp................................... G...... 260 693-2193
  Churubusco *(G-1973)*
Bmg Inc.. G...... 812 437-3643
  Evansville *(G-3936)*
Boe Knows Mold... G...... 260 760-7136
  New Haven *(G-12894)*
Bristol Tool and Die Inc............................. F...... 574 848-5354
  Bristol *(G-1252)*
Britt Tool Inc.. D...... 812 446-0503
  Brazil *(G-1136)*

35 INDUSTRIAL AND COMMERCIAL MACHINERY AND COMPUTER EQUIPMENT

Broken Mold Customs Inc .... G 219 863-1008
  Demotte *(G-2913)*

Brownstown Qulty Tl Design Inc .... F 812 358-4593
  Brownstown *(G-1418)*

Bryan Machine Services Inc .... G 260 356-5530
  Huntington *(G-7303)*

Bryant Industries Inc .... F 812 944-6010
  New Albany *(G-12707)*

Bst Enterprises Inc .... G 260 493-4313
  New Haven *(G-12895)*

Btd Manufacturing Inc .... G 812 934-5616
  Batesville *(G-585)*

Budco Tool & Die Inc .... E 574 522-4004
  Elkhart *(G-3237)*

Burco Molding Inc .... D 317 773-5699
  Noblesville *(G-13050)*

Butler Tool & Design Inc .... F 219 297-4531
  Goodland *(G-6080)*

C & A Tool Engineering Inc .... C 260 693-2167
  Auburn *(G-372)*

C & A Tool Engineering Inc .... G 260 693-2167
  Churubusco *(G-1976)*

C & A Tool Engineering Inc .... G 260 693-2167
  Churubusco *(G-1977)*

C & A Tool Engineering Inc .... G 260 693-2167
  Churubusco *(G-1978)*

C & A Tool Engineering Inc .... G 260 693-2167
  Churubusco *(G-1979)*

C & A Tool Engineering Inc .... G 260 693-2167
  Churubusco *(G-1980)*

C & A Tool Engineering Inc .... C 260 693-2167
  Churubusco *(G-1981)*

C & A Tool Engineering Inc .... B 260 693-2167
  Churubusco *(G-1982)*

C & G Tool Inc .... G 812 524-7061
  Jonesville *(G-10083)*

C & T Engineering Inc .... F
  Seymour *(G-14635)*

C-Way Tool and Die Inc .... G 812 256-6341
  Charlestown *(G-1872)*

Center Line Mold & Tool Inc .... F 812 526-0970
  Edinburgh *(G-3070)*

Century Tool & Engr Inc .... G 317 685-0942
  Indianapolis *(G-7776)*

Chesterfield Tool & Engrg Inc .... E 765 378-5101
  Daleville *(G-2798)*

▲ Chiyoda Montrow Die Mfg Inc .... G 812 767-1885
  North Vernon *(G-13257)*

City Pattern and Foundry Company Inc. D 574 273-3000
  Granger *(G-6339)*

CL Tech Inc .... G 812 526-0995
  Edinburgh *(G-3072)*

Classic City Tool & Engineering Inc ..... F 260 925-1420
  Auburn *(G-376)*

Claymore Tools Inc .... G 574 255-6483
  South Bend *(G-14975)*

Clifty Engineering and Tool Co .... C 812 273-3272
  Madison *(G-11210)*

Collins Tl & Die Ltd Lblty Co .... G 812 273-4765
  Madison *(G-11211)*

Competition Tl & Engrg II Inc .... G 812 524-1991
  Seymour *(G-14639)*

◆ Constellation Mold Inc .... F 812 424-5338
  Evansville *(G-3982)*

Continental Machining Pdts Inc .... G 219 474-5061
  Kentland *(G-10158)*

Corydon Machine & Tool Co Inc .... E 812 738-3107
  Corydon *(G-2495)*

CPM Acquisition Corp .... F 765 362-2600
  Crawfordsville *(G-2556)*

Creative Tool and Machining .... E 812 378-3562
  Columbus *(G-2248)*

Custom Engineering Inc .... F 812 424-3879
  Evansville *(G-4003)*

Cutting Edge Wire Edm Inc .... G 765 284-3820
  Muncie *(G-12371)*

D & E Machine Inc .... G 765 653-8919
  Greencastle *(G-6402)*

D & J Tool Co Inc .... G 260 636-2682
  Albion *(G-21)*

D & M Tool Corporation .... E 812 279-8882
  Springville *(G-15384)*

D A Hochstetler & Sons LLP .... F 574 642-1144
  Topeka *(G-15800)*

D Martin Enterprises Inc .... G 219 872-8211
  Michigan City *(G-11595)*

D&D Automation Inc .... G 812 299-1045
  Terre Haute *(G-15573)*

▲ D1 Mold & Tool LLC .... F 765 378-0693
  Alexandria *(G-48)*

Davis Machine and Tool Inc .... F 812 526-2674
  Edinburgh *(G-3076)*

Dedrick Tool & Die Inc .... G 260 824-3334
  Bluffton *(G-1034)*

Defelice Engineering Inc .... G 317 834-2832
  Mooresville *(G-12201)*

▲ Delaware Dynamics LLC .... C 765 284-3335
  Muncie *(G-12378)*

▲ Delaware Machinery & Tool .... C 765 284-3335
  Muncie *(G-12380)*

◆ Delta Tool Manufacturing Inc .... G 574 223-4863
  Rochester *(G-14286)*

Delux Industries Inc .... E 812 867-0655
  Evansville *(G-4011)*

Die-Rite Machine and Tool Corp .... G 574 522-2366
  Elkhart *(G-3297)*

Dieco of Indiana Inc .... F 765 825-4151
  Connersville *(G-2435)*

Dietech Corporation .... G 260 724-8946
  Decatur *(G-2852)*

Diversified Tools and Mchs Inc .... G 260 489-0272
  Fort Wayne *(G-4919)*

Dme Manufacturing Pa Inc .... F 219 872-8211
  Michigan City *(G-11601)*

DOE Run Tooling Inc .... G 812 265-3057
  Madison *(G-11215)*

▲ Double H Manufacturing Corp .... D 215 674-4100
  Marion *(G-11281)*

Drp Mold Inc .... G 765 349-3355
  Martinsville *(G-11389)*

Duel Tool & Gage Inc .... G 317 244-0129
  Indianapolis *(G-8018)*

Dwd Industries LLC .... G 260 639-3254
  Hoagland *(G-7167)*

▲ Dwd Industries LLC .... E 260 728-9272
  Decatur *(G-2854)*

dwg Design Services Corp .... G 812 372-0864
  Columbus *(G-2292)*

Dynamic Dies Inc .... E 419 861-5613
  Indianapolis *(G-8025)*

Dynamic Dies Inc .... E 317 247-4706
  Indianapolis *(G-8026)*

Dynamic Tool Machine .... G 765 730-0167
  Yorktown *(G-16973)*

E F M Corporation .... D 812 372-4421
  Columbus *(G-2293)*

Eagle Mold & Tool .... G 574 862-1966
  Wakarusa *(G-16232)*

Elkhart Laser Products LLC .... G 574 304-7242
  Elkhart *(G-3326)*

Elkhart Tool and Die Inc .... E 574 295-8500
  Elkhart *(G-3331)*

Epw LLC .... F 574 293-5090
  Elkhart *(G-3333)*

Esteves-Dwd LLC .... D 260 728-9272
  Decatur *(G-2855)*

Evansville Tool & Die Inc .... F 812 422-7101
  Evansville *(G-4059)*

Evart Engineering Company Inc .... F 765 354-2232
  Middletown *(G-11769)*

Ex-Cut Technology LLC .... F 260 672-9602
  Roanoke *(G-14263)*

Excel Tool Inc .... E 812 522-6880
  Seymour *(G-14651)*

▲ Fayette Tool and Engineering .... D 765 825-7518
  Connersville *(G-2438)*

Fisher Tool 2 Inc .... G 812 867-8350
  Evansville *(G-4071)*

▲ Flare Precision LLC .... E 260 490-1101
  Fort Wayne *(G-4985)*

Focus Mold and Machine Inc .... F 812 422-9627
  Evansville *(G-4079)*

Foil Die International Inc .... E 260 359-9011
  Huntington *(G-7310)*

Foil Form Inc .... G 260 359-9011
  Huntington *(G-7311)*

Fort Wayne Mold & Engrg Inc .... E 260 747-9168
  Fort Wayne *(G-4998)*

▲ Fort Wayne Wire Die Inc .... C 260 747-1681
  Fort Wayne *(G-5002)*

Franklin Stamping Inds Inc .... F 765 282-5138
  Muncie *(G-12397)*

Fred Anderson .... G 765 985-2099
  Peru *(G-13583)*

Future Mold Inc .... F 812 941-8661
  New Albany *(G-12735)*

Future Tool & Engrg Co Inc .... F 812 376-8699
  Columbus *(G-2311)*

▲ Gammons Metal & Mfg Co Inc .... E 317 546-7091
  Indianapolis *(G-8258)*

Gcg Industries Inc .... E 260 482-7454
  Fort Wayne *(G-5016)*

General Motors LLC .... B 765 668-2000
  Marion *(G-11287)*

Gillum Machine & Tool Inc .... F 765 893-4426
  West Lebanon *(G-16648)*

Glaze Tool and Engineering Inc .... E 260 493-4557
  New Haven *(G-12905)*

Global Mold Solutions Inc .... F 574 259-6262
  Mishawaka *(G-11901)*

▲ Global Plastics Inc .... D 317 299-2345
  Indianapolis *(G-8290)*

Granite Engrg & Tl Co Inc .... F 812 375-9077
  Columbus *(G-2314)*

Greenwood Tool and Die Co Inc .... G 219 924-9663
  Griffith *(G-6805)*

Grimm Mold & Die Co Inc .... F 219 778-4211
  Rolling Prairie *(G-14363)*

Grotrian Tool & Die .... G 260 894-3558
  Ligonier *(G-11016)*

◆ Gta Enterprises Inc .... E 260 478-7800
  Fort Wayne *(G-5044)*

Guardian Mold Prevent Corp .... G 708 878-5788
  Dyer *(G-2975)*

◆ Gvs Technologies LLC .... F 574 293-0974
  Elkhart *(G-3393)*

H & H Design & Tool Inc .... G 765 886-6199
  Economy *(G-3066)*

H & P Tool Co Inc .... E 765 962-4504
  Richmond *(G-14129)*

H and M Tool & Die Inc .... F 812 663-8252
  Greensburg *(G-6599)*

Heritage Tool and Die Inc .... G 260 359-8121
  Huntington *(G-7318)*

Heritage Wire Die Inc .... G 260 728-9300
  Decatur *(G-2862)*

35 INDUSTRIAL AND COMMERCIAL MACHINERY AND COMPUTER EQUIPMENT — SIC SECTION

Herman Tool & Machine Inc .... F 574 594-5544
　Pierceton (G-13632)
Hermetic Coil Co Inc .... E 812 735-2400
　Bicknell (G-734)
Hewitt Tool & Die Inc .... D 765 453-3889
　Oakford (G-13319)
Highland Machine Tool Inc .... E 812 923-8884
　Floyds Knobs (G-4681)
Hipsher Tool & Die Inc .... F 260 563-4143
　Wabash (G-16192)
Hook Development Inc .... G 260 432-7771
　Fort Wayne (G-5074)
Hoosier Manufacturing LLC .... G 260 493-9990
　Fort Wayne (G-5078)
◆ Hoosier Tool & Die Co Inc .... D 812 376-8286
　Edinburgh (G-3087)
Hoosier Toolmaking & Engrg Inc .... G 260 493-9990
　Fort Wayne (G-5081)
Hopper Development Inc .... F 574 753-6621
　Logansport (G-11077)
Humphrey Tool Co Inc .... G 574 753-3853
　Logansport (G-11079)
Huntington Tool & Die Inc .... F 260 356-5940
　Van Buren (G-16085)
Huth Tool & Machine Corp .... G 260 749-9411
　Fort Wayne (G-5086)
IAm Aw TI Die Makers LL 229 .... G 574 333-5955
　Elkhart (G-3416)
Indiana Model Company Inc .... D 317 787-6358
　Indianapolis (G-8484)
Indiana Steel Rule Die Inc .... G 317 352-9859
　Indianapolis (G-8496)
Industrial Engineering Inc .... E 260 478-1514
　Fort Wayne (G-5105)
Industrial Mlding Cnslting DSI .... G 574 653-2772
　Kewanna (G-10165)
▲ Industrial Tool & Die Corp .... F 812 424-9971
　Evansville (G-4125)
Injection Mold Inc .... F 812 346-7002
　North Vernon (G-13282)
Injection Plastics & Mfg Co .... E 574 784-2070
　Lapaz (G-10816)
Inson Tool & Machine Inc .... G 812 752-3754
　Scottsburg (G-14564)
Intertech Products Inc .... D 260 982-1544
　North Manchester (G-13235)
▲ J B Tool Die & Engineering Co .... C 260 483-9586
　Fort Wayne (G-5123)
J O Wolf Tool & Die Inc .... G 260 672-2605
　Huntington (G-7333)
J P Corporation .... G 317 783-1000
　Beech Grove (G-693)
J W Model & Engineering Inc .... G 317 788-7471
　Indianapolis (G-8609)
Jacobs Machine & Tool Co Inc .... F 317 831-2917
　Mooresville (G-12217)
James Billingsley .... G 765 301-9171
　Greencastle (G-6414)
James E Barnhizer .... G 765 458-9344
　Liberty (G-10989)
Jj Machine .... G 765 723-1511
　New Ross (G-12980)
Jones Machine & Tool Inc .... E 812 364-4588
　Fredericksburg (G-5794)
Journeyman Tool & Mold Inc .... G 574 237-1880
　South Bend (G-15097)
Jpg Machine & Tool LLC .... G 812 265-4512
　Madison (G-11232)
Jus Rite Engineering Inc .... E 574 522-9600
　Elkhart (G-3438)
K & K Inc .... F 574 266-8040
　Elkhart (G-3440)

K & M Tool & Die Inc .... G 765 482-9464
　Lebanon (G-10906)
K C Machine Inc .... G 574 293-1822
　Elkhart (G-3442)
K-K Tool and Design Inc .... E 260 758-2940
　Markle (G-11356)
Kain Tool Inc .... G 260 829-6569
　Orland (G-13366)
Kazmier Tooling Inc .... G 773 586-0300
　Hammond (G-6965)
Kc Engineering Inc .... G 317 352-9742
　Indianapolis (G-8664)
Keller Tool .... G 812 873-7344
　Butlerville (G-1486)
Ken-Bar Tool & Engineering Inc .... E 765 284-4408
　Noblesville (G-13119)
Kendon Corporation .... E 765 282-1515
　Muncie (G-12433)
Kent Machine Inc .... E 765 778-7777
　Pendleton (G-13539)
Kimball Electronics Inc .... D 317 545-5383
　Indianapolis (G-8686)
King Industrial Corporation .... F 812 522-3261
　Seymour (G-14662)
Kirby Machine Company LLC .... E 317 773-6700
　Noblesville (G-13122)
Kitterman Machine Co Inc .... G 317 773-2283
　Noblesville (G-13124)
Kortzendorf Machine & Tool .... F 317 783-5449
　Greenwood (G-6725)
Kronmiller Machine & Tool Inc .... G 260 436-1355
　Fort Wayne (G-5161)
Krukemeier Machine & Tool Co .... E 317 784-7042
　Beech Grove (G-697)
L & L Engineering Co Inc .... G 317 786-6886
　Beech Grove (G-698)
Lafayette Tool & Die Inc .... G 765 429-6362
　Lafayette (G-10631)
Lake Tool & Die Inc .... G 574 457-8274
　Syracuse (G-15467)
Lb Mold Inc .... E 812 526-2030
　Edinburgh (G-3090)
Le-Hue Machine and Tool Co .... G 574 255-8404
　Mishawaka (G-11927)
Lehue Machine and Tool .... G 574 329-5456
　Osceola (G-13397)
Lex Tooling LLC .... G 765 675-6301
　Tipton (G-15779)
LH Industries Corp .... E 260 432-5563
　Fort Wayne (G-5181)
Liberty Tool and Engrg Inc .... G 765 354-9550
　Middletown (G-11772)
Little Engineering LLC .... G 317 517-3323
　Whiteland (G-16791)
Lone Star Tool & Die Weld .... G 812 346-9681
　Vernon (G-16097)
▲ Lorentson Manufacturing Co .... E 765 452-4425
　Kokomo (G-10300)
▼ Mac Machine & Metal Works Inc .... E 765 825-4121
　Connersville (G-2453)
▲ Madison Tool and Die Inc .... D 812 273-2250
　Madison (G-11239)
◆ Major Tool and Machine Inc .... C 317 636-6433
　Indianapolis (G-8820)
Makuta Inc .... F 317 642-0001
　Shelbyville (G-14773)
▲ Marian Inc .... F 317 638-6525
　Indianapolis (G-8829)
▲ Marian Worldwide Inc .... A 317 638-6525
　Indianapolis (G-8831)
Mark Tool & Die Inc .... F 765 533-4932
　Markleville (G-11369)

▲ Matchless Machine & Tool Co .... E 765 342-4550
　Martinsville (G-11412)
Matrix Manufacturing Inc .... G 260 854-4659
　Wolcottville (G-16941)
Matrix Tool Inc .... F 574 259-3093
　Mishawaka (G-11939)
Maxwell Engineering Inc .... G 260 745-4991
　Fort Wayne (G-5208)
McGinn Tool & Engineering Co .... F 317 736-5512
　Franklin (G-5755)
▲ Mdl Mold & Die Components Inc ...... G 812 373-0021
　Columbus (G-2351)
Meck Die Inc .... G 574 262-5441
　Elkhart (G-3523)
Melching Machine Inc .... E 260 622-4315
　Ossian (G-13428)
Merit Tool & Manufacturing Inc .... F 765 396-9566
　Eaton (G-3063)
Metform Tool Corporation .... E 260 745-1436
　Fort Wayne (G-5216)
▲ Michiana Global Mold Inc .... F 574 259-6262
　Mishawaka (G-11944)
Michiana Metal Fabrication Inc .... G 574 256-9010
　Elkhart (G-3533)
▲ Michiana Plastics Inc .... F 574 259-6262
　Mishawaka (G-11945)
Micro Tool & Machine Co Inc .... G 574 272-9141
　Granger (G-6360)
Midwest Mold Remediation Inc .... G 502 386-6559
　Jeffersonville (G-10019)
Midwest Stl Rule Cutng Die Inc .... E 317 780-4600
　Indianapolis (G-8914)
Midwest Tool & Die Corp .... E 260 414-1506
　Fort Wayne (G-5226)
Millennium Tool Inc .... E 812 701-5761
　Madison (G-11244)
MO Money Mold Co Inc .... G 812 256-2681
　Otisco (G-13449)
▲ Modern Drop Forge Company LLC ... B 708 489-4208
　Merrillville (G-11541)
Mold Service Inc .... G 260 868-2920
　Butler (G-1471)
Mold Stoppers of Indiana .... G 812 325-1609
　Bloomington (G-923)
Moonlight Mold & Machine Inc .... G 765 868-9860
　Kokomo (G-10313)
Morris Mold and Machine Co .... G 317 923-6653
　Indianapolis (G-8955)
Msk Mold Inc .... G 812 985-5457
　Wadesville (G-16227)
Muncie Casting Corp .... E 765 288-2611
　Muncie (G-12461)
My Pneumatic Tools and Service .... G 317 364-3324
　Greensburg (G-6621)
New Point Products Inc .... G 812 663-6311
　New Point (G-12976)
▼ Nexgen Mold & Tool Inc .... E 812 945-3375
　New Albany (G-12784)
Nixon Tool Company Inc .... E 765 966-6608
　Richmond (G-14175)
Norman Tool Inc .... G 812 867-3496
　Evansville (G-4221)
North-Side Machine & Tool Inc .... F 765 654-4538
　Frankfort (G-5686)
Northern Tool & Die LLC .... G 260 495-7314
　Fremont (G-5830)
Northside Machining Inc .... G 812 683-3500
　Huntingburg (G-7288)
O & R Precision Grinding Inc .... E 260 368-9394
　Berne (G-721)
Omega Enterprises Inc .... E 765 584-1990
　Winchester (G-16896)

SIC SECTION
35 INDUSTRIAL AND COMMERCIAL MACHINERY AND COMPUTER EQUIPMENT

Onxx Tool Inc .... G 260 897-3530
  Avilla *(G-491)*
Overton & Sons Tl & Die Co Inc .... E 317 831-4542
  Mooresville *(G-12232)*
Pace Tool & Engineering Inc .... G 812 373-9885
  Hope *(G-7230)*
Parker-Hannifin Corporation .... D 574 533-1111
  Goshen *(G-6236)*
Perfection Mold & Tool Inc .... G 574 292-0824
  South Bend *(G-15191)*
▼ Perfecto Tool & Engineering Co .... E 765 644-2821
  Anderson *(G-176)*
◆ Perm Industries Inc .... E 219 365-5000
  Saint John *(G-14456)*
Piercy Machine Co Inc .... G 317 398-9296
  Shelbyville *(G-14782)*
▲ Plastics Research and Dev Inc .... E 812 279-8885
  Springville *(G-15390)*
Ploog Engineering Co Inc .... G 219 663-2854
  Crown Point *(G-2731)*
Pontiac Engraving .... G 630 834-4424
  Plymouth *(G-13805)*
Precision Die Technologies LLC .... F 260 482-5001
  Fort Wayne *(G-5336)*
Precision Plastics Indiana Inc .... C 260 244-6114
  Columbia City *(G-2183)*
Precision Products Inc .... E 317 882-1852
  Greenwood *(G-6754)*
Precision Tool & Die Inc .... G 765 664-4786
  Marion *(G-11330)*
Precision Tubes Inc .... G 317 783-2339
  Indianapolis *(G-9187)*
Precision Welding Corp .... G 260 637-5514
  Huntertown *(G-7261)*
▼ Premier Consulting Inc .... G 260 496-9300
  Fort Wayne *(G-5343)*
Premium Mold Tool .... G 812 967-3187
  Pekin *(G-13521)*
Prestige Tooling LLC .... G 269 470-4525
  Elkhart *(G-3619)*
Price Machine & Tool Inc .... G 260 338-1081
  Huntertown *(G-7263)*
Proton Mold Tool Inc .... G 812 923-7263
  Floyds Knobs *(G-4690)*
Pt Tool Machine .... G 219 275-3633
  Brook *(G-1306)*
▲ Qmp Inc .... E 574 262-1575
  Elkhart *(G-3627)*
Quality Die Set Corp .... E 574 967-4411
  Logansport *(G-11104)*
Quality Mold and Engrg Inc .... G 812 346-6577
  Vernon *(G-16098)*
Quality Steel & Aluminium .... G 574 294-7221
  Elkhart *(G-3635)*
Quality Tool & Die Inc .... G 219 324-2511
  La Porte *(G-10469)*
Quality Tool Design Inc .... G 765 377-4055
  Connersville *(G-2464)*
Qualtech Tool & Engrg Inc .... F 260 726-6572
  Portland *(G-13965)*
R & D Mold and Engineering Inc .... G 574 257-1070
  Mishawaka *(G-11983)*
R & M Tool Engineering Inc .... G 812 352-0240
  North Vernon *(G-13294)*
Reber Machine & Tool Co Inc .... E 765 288-0297
  Muncie *(G-12485)*
Reich Tool & Design Inc .... F 574 849-6416
  Elkhart *(G-3646)*
Reliance Manufacturing LLC .... G 765 284-0151
  Muncie *(G-12489)*
Richeys Mold and Tool Inc .... G 812 752-1059
  Scottsburg *(G-14576)*

River Valley Plastics Inc .... E 574 262-5221
  Elkhart *(G-3649)*
Robert Atkins .... G 765 536-4164
  Summitville *(G-15430)*
Roembke Mfg & Design Inc .... F 260 307-1198
  Ossian *(G-13431)*
Roembke Mfg & Design Inc .... E 260 622-4135
  Ossian *(G-13432)*
Ross Engineering & Machine Inc .... E 574 586-7791
  Walkerton *(G-16276)*
Rotam Tooling Corporation .... G 260 982-8318
  North Manchester *(G-13248)*
Royer Enterprises Inc .... G 260 359-0689
  Huntington *(G-7362)*
Ruco Inc .... E 574 262-4110
  Elkhart *(G-3655)*
Sanmar Tool & Manufacturing .... G 574 232-6081
  South Bend *(G-15233)*
◆ Setco LLC .... B 812 424-2904
  Evansville *(G-4307)*
Shakour Industries Inc .... G 574 289-0100
  South Bend *(G-15239)*
Smith Machine and Tool .... G 574 223-2318
  Rochester *(G-14326)*
South Bend Form Tool Co Inc .... E 574 289-2441
  South Bend *(G-15253)*
Southern Mold and Tool Inc .... G 812 752-3333
  Scottsburg *(G-14579)*
Specialty Engrg Tl & Die LLC .... G 260 356-2678
  Huntington *(G-7369)*
Specialty Tool & Die Company .... F 765 452-9209
  Kokomo *(G-10337)*
Specialty Tooling Inc .... F 812 464-8521
  Evansville *(G-4328)*
Speedcraft Prototypes .... G 765 644-6449
  Anderson *(G-198)*
Stamina Metal Products Inc .... G 574 534-7410
  Goshen *(G-6258)*
Standard Die Supply of Indiana Inc .... D 317 236-6200
  Indianapolis *(G-9493)*
Star Tool & Die Inc .... F 574 264-3815
  Elkhart *(G-3698)*
Star Tool Inc .... E 812 372-6730
  Columbus *(G-2395)*
Stolle Tool Incorporated .... F 765 935-5185
  Richmond *(G-14209)*
Strategic Sourcing LLC .... G 812 346-6904
  North Vernon *(G-13297)*
Superior Tool & Die Co Inc .... E 574 293-2591
  Elkhart *(G-3710)*
Sure Tool & Engineering Inc .... G 260 693-2193
  Churubusco *(G-1988)*
Sutton Custom Molds Inc .... G 260 463-2772
  Lagrange *(G-10767)*
T & I Tool LLC .... G 765 489-6293
  Hagerstown *(G-6844)*
T & L Tool & Die II Inc .... G 574 722-6246
  Logansport *(G-11110)*
Taurus Tech & Engrg LLC .... E 765 282-2090
  Muncie *(G-12498)*
Tempest Tool & Machine Inc .... E 812 346-6464
  North Vernon *(G-13299)*
Thompson Machining Svcs Inc .... F 765 647-3451
  Brookville *(G-1337)*
◆ Thorgren Tool & Molding Co .... D 219 462-1801
  Valparaiso *(G-16067)*
Tl Mold Inc .... G 574 596-7875
  Elkhart *(G-3737)*
▼ Tmak Inc .... E 219 874-7661
  Michigan City *(G-11679)*
Toolcraft LLC .... E 260 749-0454
  Fort Wayne *(G-5494)*

Toolmasters Inc .... G 574 256-1881
  Mishawaka *(G-12014)*
Toppan Photomasks Inc .... C 765 854-7500
  Kokomo *(G-10350)*
Trace Engineering Inc .... G 765 354-4351
  Middletown *(G-11777)*
▼ Tree City Tool & Engrg Co Inc .... E 812 663-4196
  Greensburg *(G-6637)*
Tri State Mold .... G 859 240-7643
  Rising Sun *(G-14246)*
Triple H Tool Co .... G 812 567-4600
  Tennyson *(G-15525)*
▲ Triplex Industries Inc .... G 574 256-9253
  Mishawaka *(G-12017)*
Tuff Tool Inc .... G 262 612-8300
  Fort Wayne *(G-5512)*
United Tool & Engineering Inc .... E 574 259-1953
  Mishawaka *(G-12019)*
Valley Tool & Die Stampings .... E 574 722-4566
  Logansport *(G-11117)*
Vision Machine Works Inc .... F 574 259-6500
  Mishawaka *(G-12022)*
W W G Inc .... G 317 783-6413
  Indianapolis *(G-9733)*
Wabash Valley Tool & Engrg .... G 260 563-7690
  Wabash *(G-16222)*
Walkerton Tool & Die Inc .... E 574 586-3162
  Walkerton *(G-16279)*
Ward Corporation .... F 260 489-2281
  Fort Wayne *(G-5546)*
▲ Ward Corporation .... C 260 426-8700
  Fort Wayne *(G-5545)*
Wcm Tool & Machine Inc .... G 812 422-2315
  Evansville *(G-4380)*
Werrco Inc .... G 812 497-3500
  Brownstown *(G-1428)*
Western Consolidated Tech Inc .... D 260 495-9866
  Fremont *(G-5842)*
Wilhite Industries Inc .... G 812 853-8771
  Boonville *(G-1101)*
Wirco Inc .... C 260 897-3768
  Avilla *(G-500)*
▲ Woodburn Diamond Die Inc .... E 260 632-4217
  Woodburn *(G-16957)*
Wynn Wire Die Services Inc .... G 260 471-1395
  Fort Wayne *(G-5578)*
X-Y Tool and Die Inc .... D 260 357-3365
  Laotto *(G-10812)*

3545 Machine tool accessories

A & A Machine Service Inc .... G 317 745-7367
  Avon *(G-502)*
Advanced Prtctive Slutions LLC .... G 765 720-9574
  Coatesville *(G-2102)*
Advent Precision Inc .... G 317 908-6937
  Indianapolis *(G-7445)*
▲ Aeromet Industries Inc .... D 219 924-7442
  Griffith *(G-6787)*
Ati Inc .... E 812 520-5409
  Mount Vernon *(G-12290)*
◆ Ati Inc .... E 812 431-5409
  Mount Vernon *(G-12289)*
B & W Specialized Drilling .... G 219 746-9463
  Highland *(G-7123)*
Bel-Mar Products Corporation .... G 317 769-3262
  Whitestown *(G-16801)*
Berkey Machine Corporation .... G 260 761-4002
  Wawaka *(G-16538)*
Beverly Industrial Service Inc .... E 812 667-5047
  Dillsboro *(G-2943)*
Bristol Tool and Die Inc .... F 574 848-5354
  Bristol *(G-1252)*

Employee Codes: A=Over 500 employees, B=251-500
C=101-250, D=51-100, E=20-50, F=10-19, G=1-9

2024 Harris Indiana Industrial Directory

835

35 INDUSTRIAL AND COMMERCIAL MACHINERY AND COMPUTER EQUIPMENT

▲ Btc Lapmaster LLC .... D 317 841-2400
  Noblesville *(G-13049)*
Budco Tool & Die Inc .... E 574 522-4004
  Elkhart *(G-3237)*
Butler Tool & Design Inc .... F 219 297-4531
  Goodland *(G-6080)*
C & A Tool Engineering Inc .... C 260 693-2167
  Auburn *(G-372)*
C & A Tool Engineering Inc .... B 260 693-2167
  Churubusco *(G-1982)*
C-Way Tool and Die Inc .... G 812 256-6341
  Charlestown *(G-1872)*
Capital Machine Company Inc .... F 317 638-6661
  Indianapolis *(G-7734)*
Century Tool & Engr Inc .... G 317 685-0942
  Indianapolis *(G-7776)*
Chesterfield Tool & Engrg Inc .... E 765 378-5101
  Daleville *(G-2798)*
Chuck Stace-Allen Inc .... E 317 632-2401
  Indianapolis *(G-7803)*
Clarks Cnc LLC .... G 812 508-1773
  Springville *(G-15383)*
Claymore Tools Inc .... G 574 255-6483
  South Bend *(G-14975)*
CPR Machining LLC .... E 574 299-0222
  South Bend *(G-14984)*
Diamond Stone Technologies Inc .... F 812 276-6043
  Bedford *(G-630)*
Drake Corporation .... F 636 464-5070
  Indianapolis *(G-8005)*
Drilling & Trenching Sup Inc .... G 317 825-0919
  Shelbyville *(G-14752)*
▲ E-Collar Technologies Inc .... G 260 357-0051
  Garrett *(G-5859)*
Eagle Precision LLC .... F 260 637-4649
  Huntertown *(G-7254)*
Earthchain Magnetic Pro .... G 317 803-8034
  Indianapolis *(G-8034)*
Fairfield Manufacturing Co Inc .... G 815 508-7353
  Lafayette *(G-10577)*
▲ Fastener Equipment Corporation .... G 708 957-5100
  Valparaiso *(G-15948)*
Feddema Industries Inc .... E 260 665-6463
  Angola *(G-250)*
G & S Super Abrasives Inc .... E 260 665-5562
  Angola *(G-254)*
General Aluminum Mfg Company .... C 260 495-2600
  Fremont *(G-5822)*
General Crafts Corp .... G 574 533-1936
  Goshen *(G-6144)*
Grimm Mold & Die Co Inc .... F 219 778-4211
  Rolling Prairie *(G-14363)*
H & P Tool Co Inc .... E 765 962-4504
  Richmond *(G-14129)*
Haven Manufacturing Ind LLC .... F 260 622-4150
  Ossian *(G-13425)*
Herman Tool & Machine Inc .... F 574 594-5544
  Pierceton *(G-13632)*
Hoosier Spline Broach Corp .... E 765 452-8273
  Kokomo *(G-10281)*
◆ Hoosier Tool & Die Co Inc .... D 812 376-8286
  Edinburgh *(G-3087)*
Indiana Precision Tooling Inc .... F 812 667-5141
  Dillsboro *(G-2947)*
◆ Indiana Tool & Mfg Co Inc .... C 574 936-2112
  Plymouth *(G-13784)*
Industrial Sales & Supply Inc .... F 317 240-0560
  Indianapolis *(G-8519)*
Jones Machine & Tool Inc .... E 812 364-4588
  Fredericksburg *(G-5794)*
K-K Tool and Design Inc .... E 260 758-2940
  Markle *(G-11356)*

Kaiser Tool Company Inc .... E 260 484-3620
  Fort Wayne *(G-5142)*
Ken-Bar Tool & Engineering Inc .... E 765 284-4408
  Noblesville *(G-13119)*
Kennametal Inc .... E 574 534-2585
  Goshen *(G-6185)*
Kennametal Inc .... G 317 696-8798
  Indianapolis *(G-8670)*
Kennametal Inc .... D 812 948-2118
  New Albany *(G-12759)*
Kent Brenneke .... G 260 446-5383
  Harlan *(G-7057)*
Krukemeier Machine & Tool Co .... E 317 784-7042
  Beech Grove *(G-697)*
KTI Cutting Tools Inc .... G 260 749-1465
  Fort Wayne *(G-5163)*
Kyocera SGS Precision Tls Inc .... F 260 244-7677
  Columbia City *(G-2163)*
Liberty Tool and Engrg Inc .... G 765 354-9550
  Middletown *(G-11772)*
▲ Logansport Machine Co Inc .... E 574 735-0225
  Logansport *(G-11090)*
M4 Sciences LLC .... G 765 479-6215
  West Lafayette *(G-16603)*
M4 Sciences Corporation .... G 765 479-6215
  West Lafayette *(G-16604)*
Merit Tool & Manufacturing Inc .... F 765 396-9566
  Eaton *(G-3063)*
Micro-Precision Operations .... F 260 589-2136
  Berne *(G-719)*
Morris Mold and Machine Co .... G 317 923-6653
  Indianapolis *(G-8955)*
◆ Nachi America Inc .... E 877 622-4487
  Greenwood *(G-6743)*
Nachi Tool America Inc .... E 317 535-0320
  Greenwood *(G-6745)*
Nap Asset Holdings Ltd .... G 574 295-7651
  Elkhart *(G-3564)*
◆ Nap Asset Holdings Ltd .... D 812 482-2000
  Jasper *(G-9894)*
Nixon Tool Company Inc .... E 765 966-6608
  Richmond *(G-14175)*
Nst Technologies Mim LLC .... C 812 755-4501
  Campbellsburg *(G-1526)*
Overton & Sons Tl & Die Co Inc .... E 317 831-4542
  Mooresville *(G-12232)*
Pannell & Son Welding Inc .... G 765 948-3606
  Summitville *(G-15427)*
Petal Pushers .... G 812 396-9383
  Oaktown *(G-13328)*
Picketts Place Inc .... G 317 763-1168
  Westfield *(G-16717)*
Pontiac Engraving .... G 630 834-4424
  Plymouth *(G-13805)*
Precision Cams Inc .... G 317 634-3521
  Indianapolis *(G-9180)*
Precision Surfacing Solutions .... G 317 841-2400
  Noblesville *(G-13157)*
Precision Tubes Inc .... G 317 783-2339
  Indianapolis *(G-9187)*
Qualtech Tool & Engrg Inc .... F 260 726-6572
  Portland *(G-13965)*
R B Tool & Machinery Co .... G 574 679-0082
  Osceola *(G-13401)*
Rimsrich Tool LLC .... G 219 926-8665
  Chesterton *(G-1957)*
Rite Way Industries Inc .... E 812 206-8665
  New Albany *(G-12806)*
Riverside Tool Corp .... E 574 522-6798
  Elkhart *(G-3650)*
▲ Rusach International Inc .... F 317 638-0298
  Hope *(G-7232)*

▲ Sapp Inc .... F 317 512-8353
  Edinburgh *(G-3103)*
Scg Acquisition Company LLC .... E 574 294-1506
  Elkhart *(G-3664)*
Scheidler Machine Incorporated .... G 812 662-6555
  Greensburg *(G-6630)*
Specialty Tool LLC .... F 260 493-6351
  Indianapolis *(G-9471)*
Spectrum Services Inc .... G 574 272-7605
  Granger *(G-6380)*
Stanley Black & Decker Inc .... D 860 225-5111
  Indianapolis *(G-9495)*
Stapert Tool & Machine Co Inc .... G 317 787-2387
  Indianapolis *(G-9497)*
Superior Tool & Die Co Inc .... E 574 293-2591
  Elkhart *(G-3710)*
Surclean Inc .... F 248 791-2226
  Brownsburg *(G-1405)*
Sure Tool & Engineering Inc .... G 260 693-2193
  Churubusco *(G-1988)*
T & L Sharpening Inc .... F 574 583-3868
  Monticello *(G-12172)*
Tascon Corp .... F 317 547-6127
  Indianapolis *(G-9555)*
Teague Concrete Backhoe .... G 765 674-4692
  Jonesboro *(G-10081)*
The Akron Equipment Company .... E 260 622-4150
  Ossian *(G-13438)*
Thomas L Wehr .... G 317 835-7824
  Fairland *(G-4403)*
Toolcraft LLC .... E 260 749-0454
  Fort Wayne *(G-5494)*
▲ Tri-State Industries Inc .... D 219 933-1710
  Hammond *(G-7023)*
▲ Tsune America LLC .... F 812 378-9875
  Edinburgh *(G-3109)*
Unique Tooling LLC .... G 574 656-3585
  North Liberty *(G-13226)*
▲ W F Meyers Company Inc .... E 812 275-4485
  Bedford *(G-681)*
Ward Forging Company Inc .... G 812 923-7463
  Floyds Knobs *(G-4698)*
Whitney Tool Company Inc .... E 812 275-4491
  Bedford *(G-682)*
Willemin Macodel .... G 317 219-6113
  Noblesville *(G-13196)*
Yamaguchi Mfg Usa Inc .... G 765 973-9130
  Richmond *(G-14230)*
▲ Zps America LLC .... E 317 452-4030
  Indianapolis *(G-9815)*

3546 Power-driven handtools

Allfab LLC .... G 317 359-3539
  Indianapolis *(G-7482)*
Beckler Power Equipment .... G 260 356-1188
  Huntington *(G-7300)*
Black & Decker (us) Inc .... F 860 225-5111
  Indianapolis *(G-7636)*
Bolttech Mannings Inc .... G 219 310-8389
  Crown Point *(G-2659)*
Claymore Tools Inc .... G 574 255-6483
  South Bend *(G-14975)*
Ctsi .... E 317 868-8087
  Whiteland *(G-16781)*
▲ Diedrich Drill Inc .... E 219 326-7788
  La Porte *(G-10401)*
Drake Corporation .... F 636 464-5070
  Indianapolis *(G-8005)*
Innovative Rescue Systems LLC .... G 219 548-1028
  Valparaiso *(G-15976)*
James W Hager .... G 765 643-0188
  Alexandria *(G-54)*

35 INDUSTRIAL AND COMMERCIAL MACHINERY AND COMPUTER EQUIPMENT

Key Sheet Metal Inc.................................... G 317 546-7151
  Indianapolis *(G-8677)*

Milwaukee Electric Tool Corp..................... E 800 729-3878
  Greenwood *(G-6742)*

Otter Creek Christian Church....................... G 812 446-5300
  Brazil *(G-1159)*

Pool Shop .... G 812 446-0026
  Brazil *(G-1162)*

◆ Tippmann Sports LLC............................. D 800 533-4831
  Fort Wayne *(G-5488)*

Tippmann US Holdco Inc............................ E 260 749-6022
  Fort Wayne *(G-5489)*

Wood-Mizer Holdings Inc........................... D 812 663-5257
  Greensburg *(G-6642)*

Wynn Jones Mining Tools L L C .... G 812 858-5394
  Newburgh *(G-13030)*

3547 Rolling mill machinery

Enbi Global Inc... F 317 395-7324
  Shelbyville *(G-14754)*

Fab-Tech Industries Inc.............................. G 765 478-4191
  Cambridge City *(G-1494)*

▲ Gsw Press Automation Inc..................... G 419 733-5230
  North Vernon *(G-13273)*

Hoosier Roll Shop Services LLC................ F 219 844-8077
  Hammond *(G-6947)*

Premier Components LLC.......................... G 219 776-9372
  Hebron *(G-7105)*

Southlake Machine Corp............................ G 219 285-6150
  Morocco *(G-12270)*

Systems Contracting Corp.......................... E 765 361-2991
  Crawfordsville *(G-2621)*

Witt Industries Inc..................................... E 765 289-3427
  Muncie *(G-12523)*

3548 Welding apparatus

Best Equipment & Welding Co.................... E 317 271-8652
  Indianapolis *(G-7616)*

Blackmon Metal Fabrication LLC................ G 346 254-9500
  Gary *(G-5902)*

Bryant Machining & Welding LLC............... G 260 997-6059
  Bryant *(G-1434)*

Coleman Cable LLC................................... D 765 449-7227
  Lafayette *(G-10553)*

▲ GC Fuller Mfg Co Inc.............................. F 812 539-2831
  Lawrenceburg *(G-10838)*

Ken Anliker.. G 219 984-5676
  Chalmers *(G-1858)*

Kennametal Inc... E 574 534-2585
  Goshen *(G-6185)*

Laser Welder Company............................... G 816 807-6971
  South Bend *(G-15118)*

◆ Linde Advanced Material Techno............C 317 240-2500
  Indianapolis *(G-8758)*

Linde Gas & Equipment Inc....................... G 812 376-3314
  Columbus *(G-2343)*

◆ Manufacturing Technology Inc................C 574 230-0258
  South Bend *(G-15138)*

Microtech Holding Corp............................. G 260 490-4005
  Fort Wayne *(G-5221)*

◆ Ogden Welding Systems Inc...................E 219 322-5252
  Schererville *(G-14537)*

Precision Wldg Solutions LLC..................... G 317 698-7522
  Martinsville *(G-11422)*

Priority Steel Indus Contg LLC................... E 937 626-4361
  Greendale *(G-6453)*

S T Praxair Technology Inc......................... E 317 240-2500
  Indianapolis *(G-9357)*

Souder Deryl Co... G 765 565-6719
  Anderson *(G-195)*

▲ Tri-State Industries Inc........................... D 219 933-1710
  Hammond *(G-7023)*

Warnock Welding & Fabg LLC................... G 812 498-5408
  Seymour *(G-14703)*

3549 Metalworking machinery, nec

Aam-Equipco Inc.. G 574 272-8886
  Granger *(G-6329)*

Aaron McWhirter... G 307 256-0070
  Camby *(G-1506)*

Abell Tool Co Inc.. G 317 887-0021
  Greenwood *(G-6658)*

Arch Med Slutions - Warsaw LLC............... F 574 267-2171
  Warsaw *(G-16314)*

▼ Banks Machine & Engrg LLC.................. D 317 642-4980
  Shelbyville *(G-14732)*

Concept Machinery Inc............................... G 317 845-5588
  Indianapolis *(G-7850)*

Da-Mar Industries Inc................................. F 260 347-1662
  Kendallville *(G-10107)*

Executive Automtn Systems Inc................. E 317 545-7171
  Greenfield *(G-6503)*

Finite Filtation Company............................. G 219 789-8084
  Crown Point *(G-2684)*

George Koch Sons LLC.............................. D 812 465-9600
  Evansville *(G-4089)*

Glaze Tool and Engineering Inc.................. E 260 493-4557
  New Haven *(G-12905)*

▲ Grinding and Polsg McHy Corp.............. F 317 898-0750
  Indianapolis *(G-8331)*

▲ Gsw Press Automation Inc..................... G 419 733-5230
  North Vernon *(G-13273)*

HI Def Machining LLC................................ G 812 493-9943
  Madison *(G-11224)*

◆ Hirata Corporation of America.................E 317 856-8600
  Indianapolis *(G-8399)*

Hy-Tech Machining Systems LLC.............. E 765 649-6852
  Anderson *(G-131)*

Illinois Tool Works Inc................................ G 317 298-5000
  Indianapolis *(G-8461)*

Innovative Mold & Machine Inc.................. G 317 634-1177
  Indianapolis *(G-8557)*

Jcr Automation Inc..................................... F 260 749-6606
  New Haven *(G-12907)*

Jl Manfcturing Fabrication Inc.................... G 260 589-3723
  Berne *(G-716)*

Jle Fabricating LLC.................................... G 574 341-4034
  Argos *(G-324)*

Ken-Bar Tool & Engineering Inc................. E 765 284-4408
  Noblesville *(G-13119)*

Larrys TI Hydrlic Jack Svc LLC.................. G 317 243-8666
  Indianapolis *(G-8724)*

Maintenance Solutions Inc......................... F
  Kendallville *(G-10135)*

McBroom Electric Co Inc............................ D 317 926-3451
  Indianapolis *(G-8860)*

▲ Meriwether Tool & Engrg Inc................. E 260 744-6955
  Fort Wayne *(G-5214)*

Micro-Precision Operations........................ F 260 589-2136
  Berne *(G-719)*

Pia Automation US Inc............................... E 812 485-5500
  Evansville *(G-4242)*

Precision Automation Company.................. E 812 283-7963
  Clarksville *(G-2028)*

Quality Industrial Supplies......................... G 219 324-2654
  La Porte *(G-10468)*

▲ Rci Hv Inc... D 724 538-3180
  Chesterton *(G-1956)*

Star Tool Inc... E 812 372-6730
  Columbus *(G-2395)*

Stulls Machining Center Inc....................... G 765 942-2717
  Ladoga *(G-10510)*

Walkerton Tool & Die Inc............................ E 574 586-3162
  Walkerton *(G-16279)*

▲ Wastequip Manufacturing Co LLC.......... D 574 946-6631
  Winamac *(G-16880)*

X-Y Tool and Die Inc.................................. D 260 357-3365
  Laotto *(G-10812)*

Zim Corp... G 260 438-2110
  Auburn *(G-435)*

3552 Textile machinery

Advanced Products Tech Inc...................... G 765 827-1166
  Connersville *(G-2423)*

BR Tool LLC... G 260 452-9487
  Harlan *(G-7050)*

Lee Reed Holdings LLC.............................. G 219 255-0555
  Hammond *(G-6970)*

Machining Solutions................................... G 574 292-3227
  South Bend *(G-15132)*

Mico Industries Inc..................................... G 812 480-3015
  Evansville *(G-4202)*

Paul Miller... G 765 449-4893
  Lafayette *(G-10664)*

Precision Additive Solutions....................... G 419 320-6978
  Carmel *(G-1727)*

Sideline Equipment Inc.............................. G 574 202-0525
  Goshen *(G-6254)*

Southern Mechatronics Co Inc................... G
  Brownsburg *(G-1404)*

3553 Woodworking machinery

Allison Quality Wdwkg LLC........................ G 812 963-3359
  Evansville *(G-3881)*

Capital Machine Company Inc.................... F 317 638-6661
  Indianapolis *(G-7734)*

Core Wood Components LLC..................... G 574 370-4457
  Elkhart *(G-3268)*

Craftsman Specialties................................. G 260 705-5388
  Fort Wayne *(G-4883)*

Dsn Cabinetry Inc....................................... G 317 747-4740
  Fortville *(G-5592)*

Greypaint LLC... G 765 407-6321
  Indianapolis *(G-8327)*

▲ Grinding and Polsg McHy Corp.............. F 317 898-0750
  Indianapolis *(G-8331)*

Indiana Flame Service................................ E 219 787-7129
  Chesterton *(G-1937)*

Lozier Machinery Incorporated.................. G 812 945-2558
  New Albany *(G-12766)*

Masbez LLC.. G 855 962-7239
  Frankfort *(G-5681)*

McFeelys Inc... F 800 443-7937
  Aurora *(G-449)*

Michiana Bandsaw & Sup Co LLC............. G 574 293-5974
  Elkhart *(G-3530)*

Nobbe Concrete Products Inc..................... G 765 647-4017
  Brookville *(G-1329)*

Northtech Machine LLC.............................. F 812 967-7400
  Borden *(G-1116)*

▲ PDQ Workholding LLC........................... E 260 244-2919
  Columbia City *(G-2179)*

Rake Cabinet & Surfc Solutions................. G 812 824-8338
  Bloomington *(G-951)*

Sandman Products LLC.............................. G 574 264-7700
  Elkhart *(G-3662)*

SOWN Furnishings LLC............................. G 574 327-9029
  South Bend *(G-15259)*

Sp Holdings Inc.. F 765 284-9545
  Muncie *(G-12494)*

◆ Squirrel Daddy Inc..................................G 260 723-4946
  South Whitley *(G-15326)*

◆ Veneer Services LLC..............................F 317 346-0711
  Indianapolis *(G-9705)*

Wood-Mizer Holdings Inc........................... D 812 663-5257
  Greensburg *(G-6642)*

35 INDUSTRIAL AND COMMERCIAL MACHINERY AND COMPUTER EQUIPMENT SIC SECTION

◆ Wood-Mizer Holdings Inc .... C 317 271-1542
   Indianapolis *(G-9784)*

3554 Paper industries machinery

Bahr Bros Mfg Inc .... E 765 664-6235
   Marion *(G-11274)*

C & W Inkd .... F 317 352-1000
   Indianapolis *(G-7706)*

Corrquest Automation Inc .... G 812 596-0049
   Crandall *(G-2536)*

Custom Machining Inc .... E 317 392-2328
   Shelbyville *(G-14749)*

▲ Dovey Corporation .... E 765 649-2576
   Anderson *(G-109)*

GTW Enterprises Inc .... F 219 362-2278
   La Porte *(G-10413)*

◆ Haire Machine Corporation .... E 219 947-4545
   Merrillville *(G-11521)*

Indiana Fiber Works .... F 317 524-5711
   Indianapolis *(G-8478)*

▲ Jennerjahn Machine Inc .... D 765 998-2733
   Marion *(G-11300)*

Owens Machinery Inc .... G 812 968-3285
   Corydon *(G-2509)*

▲ Peerless Machine & Tool Corp ...... D 765 662-2586
   Marion *(G-11326)*

RPC Machinery Inc .... G 765 458-5655
   Liberty *(G-10998)*

Stickle Steam Specialties Co .... F 317 636-6563
   Indianapolis *(G-9510)*

3555 Printing trades machinery

Abacus Printingngraphics Inc .... E 915 223-5166
   Indianapolis *(G-7412)*

Acutech LLC .... F 574 262-8228
   Elkhart *(G-3153)*

▲ Blue Grass Chemical Spc LLC ..... F 812 948-1115
   New Albany *(G-12703)*

Crunchtech Holdings LLC .... G 818 583-0004
   Kendallville *(G-10106)*

Egenolf Machine Inc .... F 317 787-5301
   Indianapolis *(G-8061)*

Finzer Roller Inc .... G 219 325-8808
   La Porte *(G-10408)*

Indiana Imprint LLC .... G 812 704-2773
   French Lick *(G-5846)*

Kbc Machine .... G 317 446-6163
   Greenfield *(G-6523)*

Numerical Concepts Inc .... E 812 466-5261
   Terre Haute *(G-15654)*

▲ Perfecta USA .... F 317 862-7371
   Indianapolis *(G-9124)*

▲ Precision Rubber Plate Co Inc ..... D 317 783-3226
   Indianapolis *(G-9186)*

Print Queens LLC .... G 317 285-8934
   Indianapolis *(G-9201)*

Scalable Press Inc .... G 877 752-9060
   Indianapolis *(G-9384)*

3556 Food products machinery

▼ A M Manufacturing Co Inc .... E 219 472-7272
   Munster *(G-12526)*

American Equipment Corp .... G 888 321-0117
   Fort Wayne *(G-4753)*

Carmel Engineering Inc .... F 765 279-8955
   Kirklin *(G-10187)*

Cedar Creek Distillery LLC .... G 765 342-9000
   Martinsville *(G-11384)*

Centrifuge Support & Sups LLC ...... G 317 830-6141
   Plainfield *(G-13666)*

◆ CTB MN Investment Co Inc .... E 574 658-4191
   Milford *(G-11794)*

◆ Flavor Burst LLC .... E 317 745-2952
   Danville *(G-2812)*

Hillenbrand Inc .... A 812 931-5000
   Batesville *(G-590)*

▲ JMS Electronics Corporation .... E 574 522-0246
   Elkhart *(G-3434)*

Jua Technologies Intl Inc .... G 765 204-5533
   West Lafayette *(G-16597)*

Kaeb Sales Inc .... G 574 862-2777
   Wakarusa *(G-16236)*

Kitchen-Quip Inc .... E 260 837-8311
   Kendallville *(G-10129)*

Linco Group LLC .... G 765 418-5567
   Williamsport *(G-16851)*

▲ MD Holdings LLC .... G 317 831-7030
   Mooresville *(G-12220)*

Metzger Dairy Inc .... F 260 564-5445
   Kimmell *(G-10171)*

Mssh Inc .... G 812 663-2180
   Greensburg *(G-6620)*

Nemco Food Equipment Ltd .... G 260 399-6692
   Fort Wayne *(G-5262)*

◆ Norris Thermal Tech Inc .... G 574 353-7855
   Tippecanoe *(G-15762)*

Pacmoore Process Tech LLC .... G 317 831-2666
   Mooresville *(G-12233)*

Palmer Caning .... G 773 394-4913
   Lafayette *(G-10662)*

Rapid View LLC .... G 574 224-3373
   Rochester *(G-14315)*

◆ Reading Bakery Systems Inc .... F 317 337-0000
   Indianapolis *(G-9277)*

Roost .... G 317 842-3735
   Fishers *(G-4599)*

Skipper Rota Corporation .... F 708 331-0660
   Crown Point *(G-2758)*

Tgf Enterprises LLC .... G 440 840-9704
   Indianapolis *(G-9585)*

▲ Thomas Green LLC .... G 317 337-0000
   Indianapolis *(G-9593)*

◆ Urschel Laboratories Inc .... B 219 464-4811
   Chesterton *(G-1964)*

Urschelair Leasing LLC .... G 219 464-4811
   Chesterton *(G-1965)*

▼ Willow Way LLC .... G 765 886-4640
   Hagerstown *(G-6849)*

3559 Special industry machinery, nec

3g Concepts LLC .... G 574 267-6100
   Warsaw *(G-16306)*

651 Emergency Lighting .... G 765 748-6664
   Yorktown *(G-16967)*

▲ Alliance Winding Equipment .... E 260 478-2200
   Fort Wayne *(G-4744)*

◆ American Art Clay Co Inc .... C 317 244-6871
   Indianapolis *(G-7499)*

▲ American Feeding Systems Inc ... E 317 773-5517
   Noblesville *(G-13036)*

American Vulkan Corporation .... G 219 866-7751
   Rensselaer *(G-14042)*

AMI Industries Inc .... G 989 786-3755
   Angola *(G-226)*

Anatolia Group Ltd Partnership .... G 203 343-7808
   Indianapolis *(G-7514)*

Andritz Herr-Voss Stamco Inc .... G 219 764-8586
   Chesterton *(G-1902)*

Anodizing Technologies Inc .... G 317 253-5725
   Indianapolis *(G-7521)*

Applied Electronic Mtls LLC .... G 260 438-8632
   Fort Wayne *(G-4765)*

Automatic Fastner Tools .... G 317 784-4111
   Indianapolis *(G-7575)*

Bobcat Armament and Mfg LLC ...... G 317 699-6127
   Shelbyville *(G-14738)*

Bright Line Striping LLC .... G 765 404-1402
   Lafayette *(G-10543)*

▼ Chuck Bivens Services Inc .... F 260 747-6195
   Fort Wayne *(G-4846)*

City of Anderson .... G 765 648-6715
   Anderson *(G-93)*

Computer Age Engineering Inc .... E 765 674-8551
   Marion *(G-11278)*

Cox John .... G 765 463-6396
   West Lafayette *(G-16571)*

CPM Acquisition Corp .... F 765 362-2600
   Crawfordsville *(G-2556)*

Cutting Edge Machine & TI Inc .... D 866 514-1620
   New Paris *(G-12949)*

D W Stewart .... G 260 463-2607
   Lagrange *(G-10733)*

E & R Mfg Co Inc .... G 765 279-8826
   Kirklin *(G-10188)*

Eagle Consulting Inc .... G 317 590-0485
   Indianapolis *(G-8031)*

Engineering and Industria .... E 574 722-3714
   Logansport *(G-11073)*

Federal-Mogul Powertrain LLC .... G 574 272-5900
   South Bend *(G-15032)*

Feeding Concepts Inc .... F 317 773-2040
   Noblesville *(G-13076)*

First Gear Inc .... E 260 490-3238
   Fort Wayne *(G-4984)*

Frontier Engineering .... G 317 823-6885
   Indianapolis *(G-8235)*

Furnace Solutions Incorporated ...... G 219 738-2516
   Schererville *(G-14522)*

Globaltech Manufacturing LLC .... G 317 571-1910
   Carmel *(G-1641)*

H C Schumacher Machine Co In .... F 317 787-9361
   Indianapolis *(G-8347)*

Hermetic Coil Co Inc .... E 812 735-2400
   Bicknell *(G-734)*

Hillenbrand Inc .... A 812 931-5000
   Batesville *(G-590)*

◆ Hirata Corporation of America ..... E 317 856-8600
   Indianapolis *(G-8399)*

Honey Creek Machine Inc .... E 812 299-5255
   Terre Haute *(G-15605)*

▼ Indco Inc .... G 812 945-4383
   New Albany *(G-12746)*

Integrated Technology LLC .... F 574 300-9412
   Elkhart *(G-3428)*

J & J Engineering Inc .... F 317 462-2309
   Greenfield *(G-6520)*

Kenco Plastics Inc .... F 219 324-6621
   La Porte *(G-10433)*

Kleenflow LLC .... G 317 912-0027
   Anderson *(G-144)*

◆ Koch Enterprises Inc .... G 812 465-9800
   Evansville *(G-4159)*

Lyntech Engineering Inc .... G 574 224-2300
   Rochester *(G-14303)*

◆ Marion Glass Equipment an .... D 765 662-1172
   Marion *(G-11312)*

Mayham Mfia Cstoms Trnsprting .... G 463 248-5181
   Indianapolis *(G-8857)*

Merriman Steel and Equipment .... G 812 849-2784
   Bedford *(G-657)*

▲ Metal Technologies Inc .... D 812 384-9800
   Auburn *(G-406)*

Mid-State Automation Inc .... G 765 795-5500
   Cloverdale *(G-2089)*

Moorfeed Corporation .... E 317 545-7171
   Greenfield *(G-6532)*

SIC SECTION
35 INDUSTRIAL AND COMMERCIAL MACHINERY AND COMPUTER EQUIPMENT

◆ Mvo Usa Inc .... F 317 585-5785
Indianapolis (G-8974)

Parts Pro Auto Prfrormance LLC .... G 765 825-5545
Connersville (G-2460)

▲ Peerless Machine & Tool Corp .... D 765 662-2586
Marion (G-11326)

Pgp Corp .... D 812 285-7700
Jeffersonville (G-10036)

Plating Products Inc .... G 775 241-0416
Kokomo (G-10322)

Rexing-Goedde Electric Service .... G 812 963-5725
Wadesville (G-16229)

Safety-Kleen Systems Inc .... F 219 397-1131
East Chicago (G-3041)

▲ Service Engineering Inc .... D 317 467-2000
Greenfield (G-6550)

Shanxi-Indiana LLC .... F 219 885-2209
Gary (G-6009)

▲ Shar Systems Inc .... E 260 432-5312
Fort Wayne (G-5412)

Siddhi Integrated Mfg Svcs Inc .... G 502 298-8640
Clarksville (G-2036)

Sinden Racing Service Inc .... F 317 243-7171
Indianapolis (G-9443)

▲ SMC Corporation of America .... B 317 899-4440
Noblesville (G-13176)

Sortera Technologies Inc .... E 260 330-7100
Markle (G-11362)

Southwire Company LLC .... D 574 546-5115
Bremen (G-1222)

Sugarcube Systems Inc .... G 765 543-6709
Lafayette (G-10704)

Summit Foundry Systems Inc .... F 260 749-7740
Fort Wayne (G-5452)

Summit Industrial Tech Inc .... G 260 494-3461
Columbia City (G-2204)

Systems Engineering and Sls Co .... G 260 422-1671
Fort Wayne (G-5466)

Talon Systems Inc .... G 765 393-1711
Alexandria (G-63)

Tamco Manufacturing Co .... G 574 294-1909
Elkhart (G-3714)

▲ Technifab Products Inc .... E 812 442-0520
Brazil (G-1166)

Toco Inc .... G 317 627-8854
Greenwood (G-6775)

Trimax Machine LLC .... G 812 887-9281
Bruceville (G-1433)

Tuskin Equipment Corporation .... G 630 466-5590
Elkhart (G-3754)

▲ UFS Corporation .... F 219 464-2027
Valparaiso (G-16070)

◆ Union Tool Corp .... E 574 267-3211
Warsaw (G-16440)

Vauterbuilt Inc .... G 219 712-2384
Hebron (G-7108)

▲ Vhc Ltd .... E 765 584-2101
Winchester (G-16902)

Vibcon Corporation .... F 317 984-3543
Arcadia (G-319)

Vibromatic Company Inc .... E 317 773-3885
Noblesville (G-13193)

Watershipblue LLC .... G 317 910-8585
Indianapolis (G-9741)

Wayne Chemical Inc .... E 260 432-1120
Fort Wayne (G-5551)

Weissair .... G 260 466-7693
Angola (G-308)

Wrib Manufacturing Inc .... G 765 294-2841
Veedersburg (G-16092)

3561 Pumps and pumping equipment

3w Enterprises LLC .... G 847 366-6555
Elkhart (G-3137)

Aeromind LLC .... G 800 905-2157
Indianapolis (G-7453)

All-Pro Pump & Repair Inc .... G 317 738-4203
Morgantown (G-12252)

Allegion S&S Holding Co Inc .... E 317 429-2299
Indianapolis (G-7478)

Autoform Tool & Mfg LLC .... C 260 624-2014
Angola (G-232)

▲ Automatic Pool Covers Inc .... E 317 579-2000
Westfield (G-16666)

▲ Banjo Corporation .... C 765 362-7367
Crawfordsville (G-2546)

Dresser LLC .... D 765 827-9200
Connersville (G-2436)

▲ Dura Products Inc .... F 855 502-3872
Arcadia (G-313)

Fill-Rite Company .... E 260 747-7529
Fort Wayne (G-4982)

FL Smidth .... G 812 402-9210
Evansville (G-4073)

Flickinger Industries Inc .... E 260 432-4527
Fort Wayne (G-4986)

◆ Flint & Walling Inc .... G 800 345-9422
Kendallville (G-10111)

Flowserve Corporation .... G 219 763-1000
Portage (G-13867)

◆ Franklin Electric Co Inc .... B 260 824-2900
Fort Wayne (G-5006)

Gardner Denver Inc .... E 219 558-0354
Saint John (G-14451)

Grundfos Pumps Mfg Corp .... G 317 925-9661
Indianapolis (G-8337)

Hayward & Sams LLP .... G 260 351-4166
Stroh (G-15401)

Hoosier Fire Equipment Inc .... F 219 462-1707
Valparaiso (G-15965)

Hy-Flex Corporation .... E 765 571-5125
Knightstown (G-10198)

Jj Energy Inc .... G 630 401-7026
Lebanon (G-10905)

Mantra Enterprise LLC .... G 201 428-8709
Fishers (G-4561)

Met-Pro Technologies LLC .... G 317 293-2930
Indianapolis (G-8882)

Nst Technologies Mim LLC .... C 812 755-4501
Campbellsburg (G-1526)

Oasis Pumps Mfg Co .... G 812 783-2146
Mount Vernon (G-12313)

Ohio Transmission Corporation .... G 812 466-2734
Terre Haute (G-15655)

Parker-Hannifin Corporation .... D 260 636-2104
Albion (G-40)

PHD Inc .... F 260 356-0120
Huntington (G-7356)

Picketts Place Inc .... G 317 763-1168
Westfield (G-16717)

R B Tool & Machinery Co .... G 574 679-0082
Osceola (G-13401)

Rankin Pump and Supply Co Inc .... G 812 238-2535
Terre Haute (G-15675)

Shoemaker Welding Company .... G 574 656-4412
North Liberty (G-13223)

▲ Specialty Mfg Ind Inc .... E 812 256-4633
Charlestown (G-1894)

◆ Sterling Fluid Systems USA LLC .... C 317 925-9661
Indianapolis (G-9506)

▲ Tbk America Inc .... E 765 962-0147
Richmond (G-14210)

▲ Thrush Co Inc .... E 765 472-3351
Peru (G-13604)

Tuskin Equipment Corporation .... G 630 466-5590
Elkhart (G-3754)

◆ Tuthill Corporation .... G 260 747-7529
Fort Wayne (G-5514)

Tuthill Corporation .... C 260 747-7529
Fort Wayne (G-5515)

▲ Waterax Corporation .... G 360 574-1818
Valparaiso (G-16079)

Wee Engineer Inc .... F 765 449-4280
Dayton (G-2838)

Xylem Vue Inc .... D 574 855-1012
South Bend (G-15310)

3562 Ball and roller bearings

Casters In Motion USA Ltd LLC .... G 812 437-4627
Evansville (G-3965)

Emerson Industrial Automation .... G 574 583-9171
Monticello (G-12148)

▲ Hsm Eagle Ltd .... G 812 491-9667
Evansville (G-4112)

Jim Lemons Models .... G 317 831-5133
Camby (G-1511)

◆ McGill Manufacturing Co Inc .... A 219 465-2200
Monticello (G-12157)

Menon Bearings Limited .... G 866 556-3666
Fishers (G-4564)

◆ Nachi Technology Inc .... C 317 535-5000
Greenwood (G-6744)

NSK Corporation .... D 765 458-5000
Liberty (G-10993)

NSK Precision America Inc .... D 317 738-5000
Franklin (G-5762)

Rbc Bearings Incorporated .... G 574 935-3027
Plymouth (G-13808)

◆ Rbc Prcsion Pdts - Plymuth Inc .... D 574 935-3027
Plymouth (G-13809)

Regal Beloit America Inc .... E 219 465-2200
Monticello (G-12167)

Regal Beloit America Inc .... G 219 465-2200
Valparaiso (G-16035)

▲ Standard Locknut LLC .... C 317 399-2230
Westfield (G-16729)

Timken Company .... G 574 287-1566
South Bend (G-15282)

3563 Air and gas compressors

ABB Flexible Automation Inc .... G 317 876-9090
Indianapolis (G-7414)

◆ Abro Industries Inc .... E 574 232-8289
South Bend (G-14933)

Air Fixtures Inc .... F 260 982-2169
North Manchester (G-13228)

Atlas Copco Compressors .... G 574 264-1033
Elkhart (G-3199)

Bkb Manufacturing Inc .... G 260 982-8524
North Manchester (G-13229)

▲ Boss Industries LLC .... E 219 324-7776
La Porte (G-10390)

▲ Brama Inc .... F 317 786-7770
Indianapolis (G-7671)

Cohesant Technologies Inc .... G 317 871-7611
Indianapolis (G-7833)

Cook Compression LLC .... G 502 515-6900
Jeffersonville (G-9960)

Custom Compressor Svcs Corp .... G 219 879-4966
Michigan City (G-11592)

▲ Dekker Vacuum Technologies Inc ...... D 219 861-0661
Michigan City (G-11598)

Hitachi Global Air Pwr US LLC .... G 219 861-5207
Michigan City (G-11625)

◆ Hitachi Global Air Pwr US LLC .... C 219 879-5451
Michigan City (G-11626)

35 INDUSTRIAL AND COMMERCIAL MACHINERY AND COMPUTER EQUIPMENT — SIC SECTION

◆ K Grimmer Industries Inc............C 317 736-3800
  Leo *(G-10968)*
▲ Kobelco Cmpsr Mfg Ind Inc........D 574 295-3145
  Elkhart *(G-3459)*
◆ Linde Advanced Material Techno....C 317 240-2500
  Indianapolis *(G-8758)*
Magnum Venus Products Inc.........G 727 573-2955
  Goshen *(G-6210)*
Midwest Finishing Systems Inc......E 574 257-0099
  Mishawaka *(G-11949)*
Precisionair LLC.........................G 219 380-9267
  La Porte *(G-10464)*
◆ Roots Blowers LLC....................D 765 827-9200
  Connersville *(G-2465)*
Sullair Corporation.......................G 219 861-5005
  Michigan City *(G-11674)*
◆ Sullivan-Palatek Inc..................C 219 874-2497
  Michigan City *(G-11675)*
Systems Engineering and Sls Co....G 260 422-1671
  Fort Wayne *(G-5466)*
Vacuum Technique LLC................E 800 848-4511
  Michigan City *(G-11683)*
◆ Vanair Manufacturing Inc...........C 219 879-5100
  Michigan City *(G-11684)*
Wee Engineer Inc........................F 765 449-4280
  Dayton *(G-2838)*

3564 Blowers and fans

3-T Corp....................................F 812 424-7878
  Evansville *(G-3856)*
▲ Aero-Flo Industries Inc.............G 219 393-3555
  La Porte *(G-10378)*
Air Side Systems LLC..................G 765 778-7895
  Anderson *(G-73)*
Air-Tech Industrial Design.............G 317 797-1804
  Monrovia *(G-12076)*
Airbotx LLC...............................G 317 981-1811
  Westfield *(G-16663)*
Airjet Inc...................................D 574 264-0123
  Elkhart *(G-3155)*
◆ Anthony Group LLC..................E 317 536-7445
  Greenwood *(G-6669)*
Blocksom & Co...........................G 219 878-4458
  Trail Creek *(G-15835)*
▲ Blocksom & Co........................F 219 878-4455
  Trail Creek *(G-15836)*
CJ Magers Enterprises LLC..........G 219 778-4884
  La Porte *(G-10394)*
◆ Clarcor Air Filtration Products Inc....A 502 969-2304
  Jeffersonville *(G-9952)*
Cor-A-Vent Inc............................F 574 258-6161
  Mishawaka *(G-11865)*
◆ CTB MN Investment Co Inc.......E 574 658-4191
  Milford *(G-11794)*
Cummins Filtration Ip Inc..............G 615 514-7339
  Columbus *(G-2256)*
Dack Blower Manufacturing Inc.....G 574 867-2025
  Grovertown *(G-6823)*
Donaldson Company Inc..............A 765 659-4766
  Frankfort *(G-5660)*
Donaldson Company Inc..............G 952 887-3131
  Monticello *(G-12146)*
Dustex.......................................G 812 725-0808
  Jeffersonville *(G-9972)*
◆ Eclipse Inc..............................D
  Muncie *(G-12389)*
Eta Fabrication Inc......................F 260 897-3711
  Avilla *(G-476)*
Fan-Tastic Vent..........................G 800 521-0298
  Elkhart *(G-3342)*
FSI Filtration LLC........................G 317 264-2123
  Indianapolis *(G-8236)*

Gbi Air Systems Inc.....................G 574 272-0600
  Granger *(G-6348)*
Honeyville Metal Inc....................D 800 593-8377
  Topeka *(G-15809)*
Horner Industrial Services Inc.......F 317 634-7165
  Indianapolis *(G-8418)*
◆ Horton Fan Systems Inc...........C 317 249-9100
  Carmel *(G-1659)*
Iaire LLC...................................G 317 806-2750
  Indianapolis *(G-8447)*
Indianapolis In...........................E 855 628-3458
  Indianapolis *(G-8502)*
Kabert Industries Inc...................D 765 874-2335
  Lynn *(G-11184)*
Kch Services Inc.........................G 260 463-3100
  Lagrange *(G-10745)*
Lau Holdings LLC.......................D 574 223-3181
  Rochester *(G-14300)*
Mechanovent Corporation............G 219 326-1767
  La Porte *(G-10449)*
Midwest Purification LLC.............G 317 536-7445
  Greenwood *(G-6740)*
Natures Way..............................G 317 839-4566
  Plainfield *(G-13707)*
New York Blower Company...........E 217 347-3233
  La Porte *(G-10457)*
Pond Doctors Inc........................G 812 744-5258
  Aurora *(G-453)*
Precision Sheet Metal Inc............F 269 663-8810
  Granger *(G-6371)*
Protect Plus Industries................G 219 324-8482
  La Porte *(G-10467)*
◆ Purolator Pdts A Filtration Co....C 866 925-2247
  Jeffersonville *(G-10043)*
◆ Roots Blowers LLC..................D 765 827-9200
  Connersville *(G-2465)*
Spectrum Brands Inc...................E 317 773-6627
  Noblesville *(G-13179)*
Submicron Inc............................G 800 609-1390
  Greenfield *(G-6560)*
Terronics Development Corp Inc....G 765 552-0808
  Elwood *(G-3838)*
Thermo-Cycler Industries Inc........G 219 767-2990
  Union Mills *(G-15868)*
Universal Air Products LLC..........E 502 451-1825
  Sellersburg *(G-14619)*
Universal Blower Pac Inc..............E 317 773-7256
  Noblesville *(G-13190)*

3565 Packaging machinery

▲ A Packaging Systems LLC.........F 219 369-4131
  La Porte *(G-10372)*
All Packaging Equipment Corp......G 574 294-3371
  Elkhart *(G-3163)*
Apex Filling Systems Inc.............G 219 575-7493
  Michigan City *(G-11578)*
Blasdel Enterprises Inc................F 812 663-3213
  Greensburg *(G-6581)*
Chicago Automated Labeling Inc...G 219 531-0646
  Valparaiso *(G-15926)*
Christ Packing Systems Corp.......G 574 243-9110
  South Bend *(G-14972)*
◆ Closure Systems Intl Inc...........C 317 390-5000
  Indianapolis *(G-7825)*
Combined Technologies Inc.........G 847 968-4855
  Bristol *(G-1254)*
◆ E-Pak Machinery Inc................E 219 393-5541
  La Porte *(G-10403)*
Elf Machinery LLC.......................E 219 393-5541
  La Porte *(G-10405)*
◆ Grrk Holdings Inc....................E 317 872-0172
  Indianapolis *(G-8336)*

◆ Kwik Lok Corporation................E 260 493-1220
  New Haven *(G-12909)*
▲ Lindal North America Inc..........D 812 657-7142
  Columbus *(G-2342)*
Monosol LLC..............................G 219 763-7589
  Portage *(G-13891)*
Morgan Adhesives Company LLC....B 812 342-2004
  Columbus *(G-2357)*
Nyx LLC....................................A 734 838-3570
  New Albany *(G-12786)*
Packaging Systems Indiana Inc....G 765 449-1011
  Lafayette *(G-10661)*
Parkway Industrial Entps LLC.......F 260 622-7200
  Ossian *(G-13430)*
Powell Systems Inc.....................E 765 884-0980
  Fowler *(G-5630)*
Precision Automation Company....E 812 283-7963
  Clarksville *(G-2028)*
▲ Precision Products Group Inc....F 317 663-4590
  Indianapolis *(G-9184)*
Universal Packg Systems Inc.......C 260 829-6721
  Orland *(G-13374)*
Webber Manufacturing Company....E 317 357-8681
  Indianapolis *(G-9745)*
Whallon Machinery Inc.................E 574 643-9561
  Royal Center *(G-14394)*

3566 Speed changers, drives, and gears

▲ Aisin Drivetrain Inc..................C 812 793-2427
  Crothersville *(G-2636)*
An-Mar Wiring Systems Inc..........F 574 255-5523
  Mishawaka *(G-11842)*
▲ Auburn Gear LLC....................C 260 925-3200
  Auburn *(G-362)*
Champ Converters Incorporated...G 812 424-2602
  Evansville *(G-3968)*
Champ Torque Converters Inc......G 812 424-2602
  Evansville *(G-3969)*
▲ Dana Sac Usa Inc...................F 765 759-2300
  Yorktown *(G-16972)*
◆ Hansen Corporation.................B 812 385-3000
  Princeton *(G-13997)*
Mitsubshi Trbchrger Eng Amer I....E 317 346-5291
  Franklin *(G-5758)*
Moore Machine & Gear Inc..........E 812 963-3074
  Evansville *(G-4212)*
Nst Technologies Mim LLC..........C 812 755-4501
  Campbellsburg *(G-1526)*
Quad Plus LLC...........................G 219 844-9214
  Hammond *(G-6993)*
Regal Rexnord Corporation..........E 608 364-8800
  Fort Wayne *(G-5378)*
Rexnord Industries LLC...............G 414 643-2559
  Plainfield *(G-13722)*
▲ Sterling Electric Inc.................E 317 872-0471
  Indianapolis *(G-9505)*
Tecumseh Products Company LLC....G 812 883-3575
  Salem *(G-14502)*
United Precision Gear Co Inc.......G 317 784-4665
  Indianapolis *(G-9680)*
◆ Vanair Manufacturing Inc..........C 219 879-5100
  Michigan City *(G-11684)*

3567 Industrial furnaces and ovens

◆ Austin-Westran LLC..................E 815 234-2811
  Indianapolis *(G-7569)*
Blasdel Enterprises Inc................G 812 663-3213
  Greensburg *(G-6581)*
Brouillette Htg Coolg Plbg LLC......G 765 884-0176
  Fowler *(G-5622)*
▲ Contour Hardening Inc.............E 888 867-2184
  Indianapolis *(G-7861)*

35 INDUSTRIAL AND COMMERCIAL MACHINERY AND COMPUTER EQUIPMENT

▲ Farm Innovators Inc .... E 574 936-5096
Plymouth *(G-13774)*

George Koch Sons LLC .... D 812 465-9600
Evansville *(G-4089)*

Gillespie Mrrell Gen Contg LLC .... G 765 618-4084
Marion *(G-11288)*

Green Fast Cure LLC .... G 812 486-2510
Montgomery *(G-12101)*

▲ Heat Wagons Inc .... F 219 464-8818
Valparaiso *(G-15961)*

Hoosier Metal Polish Inc .... F 219 474-6011
Kentland *(G-10160)*

▲ IDI Fabrication Inc .... D 317 776-6577
Noblesville *(G-13100)*

Industrial Combustn Engineers .... E 219 949-5066
Gary *(G-5960)*

Infrared Technologies LLC .... E 317 326-2019
Greenfield *(G-6516)*

Light Beam Technology Inc .... G 260 635-2195
Kimmell *(G-10170)*

Midwest Finishing Systems Inc .... E 574 257-0099
Mishawaka *(G-11949)*

Power Plant Service Inc .... E 260 432-6716
Fort Wayne *(G-5328)*

Precious Technology Group LLC .... F 317 398-4411
Shelbyville *(G-14787)*

R & K Incinerator Inc .... G 260 565-3214
Decatur *(G-2878)*

◆ Rogers Engineering and Mfg Co .... E 765 478-5444
Cambridge City *(G-1503)*

Sherwood-Templeton Inc .... G 812 232-7037
Terre Haute *(G-15692)*

Templeton Coal Company Inc .... G 812 232-7037
Terre Haute *(G-15725)*

Thermal Product Solutions .... G 708 758-6530
Schererville *(G-14546)*

Thermal Tech & Temp Inc .... F 219 213-2093
Crown Point *(G-2763)*

Thermo - Transfer Inc .... F 317 398-3503
Shelbyville *(G-14805)*

Universal Door Carrier Inc .... G 317 241-3447
Indianapolis *(G-9682)*

Wax Connections Inc .... G 219 778-2325
Rolling Prairie *(G-14372)*

3568 Power transmission equipment, nec

Advanced Bearing Materials LLC .... E 812 663-3401
Greensburg *(G-6580)*

▲ Aisin Drivetrain Inc .... C 812 793-2427
Crothersville *(G-2636)*

◆ Allied Enterprises LLC .... E 765 288-8849
Muncie *(G-12339)*

Altra Industrial Motion Corp .... E 219 874-5248
Michigan City *(G-11577)*

▲ Auburn Gear LLC .... C 260 925-3200
Auburn *(G-362)*

Bearing Service Company PA .... G 773 734-5132
Griffith *(G-6794)*

▲ Bludot Inc .... G 574 277-2306
South Bend *(G-14959)*

▲ Cablecraft Motion Controls LLC .... C 260 749-5105
New Haven *(G-12897)*

Eaton Corporation .... C 260 925-3800
Auburn *(G-387)*

Eaton Corporation .... G 317 704-2520
Indianapolis *(G-8043)*

Fairfield Manufacturing Co Inc .... G 815 508-7353
Lafayette *(G-10577)*

Friskney Gear & Machine Corp .... G 260 281-2200
Corunna *(G-2482)*

G G B Inc .... G 219 733-2897
Westville *(G-16758)*

◆ Guardian Couplings LLC .... E 219 874-5248
Michigan City *(G-11617)*

◆ Guardian Ind Inc .... E 219 874-5248
Michigan City *(G-11618)*

Ktool & Fire LLC .... G 219 575-1428
La Porte *(G-10438)*

▲ Ktr Corporation .... E 219 872-9100
Michigan City *(G-11629)*

Millennium Supply Inc .... G 765 764-7000
Fowler *(G-5628)*

Monday Voigt Products Inc .... F 317 224-7920
Anderson *(G-160)*

◆ Nachi America Inc .... E 877 622-4487
Greenwood *(G-6743)*

NSK Corporation .... D 765 458-5000
Liberty *(G-10993)*

NSK Precision America Inc .... D 317 738-5000
Franklin *(G-5762)*

Odin Corporation .... G 317 849-3770
Indianapolis *(G-9041)*

Parker-Hannifin Corporation .... E 260 894-7125
Syracuse *(G-15471)*

Rexnord Industries LLC .... D 317 273-5500
Avon *(G-547)*

Rexnord Industries LLC .... G 414 643-2559
Plainfield *(G-13722)*

Siemens Industry Inc .... D 219 763-7927
Portage *(G-13914)*

Sparks Belting Company Inc .... G 800 451-4537
Hammond *(G-7012)*

◆ Star Engineering & Mch Co Inc .... E 260 824-4825
Bluffton *(G-1057)*

Steel Parts Corporation .... A 765 675-2191
Tipton *(G-15791)*

Tecumseh Products Company LLC .... G 812 883-3575
Salem *(G-14502)*

Uniseal Inc .... E 812 425-1361
Evansville *(G-4360)*

3569 General industrial machinery,

ABB Flexible Automation Inc .... G 317 876-9090
Indianapolis *(G-7414)*

▼ Action Filtration Inc .... G 812 546-6262
Hope *(G-7222)*

Advance Filter LLC .... G 317 565-7009
Anderson *(G-72)*

Advanced Lf Spport Innvtons LL .... G 574 538-1688
Goshen *(G-6090)*

▲ Agi International Inc .... F 317 536-2415
Indianapolis *(G-7458)*

Alicon LLC .... G 260 687-1259
Angola *(G-225)*

Amatrol Inc .... G 800 264-8285
Jeffersonville *(G-9929)*

Arbuckle Industries Inc .... G 317 835-7489
Fairland *(G-4396)*

Asl Technologies LLC .... G 219 733-2777
Wanatah *(G-16286)*

Automated Proc Eqp Svcs LLC .... G 219 206-2517
Union Mills *(G-15863)*

▲ Avis Industrial Corporation .... E 765 998-8100
Upland *(G-15876)*

▼ Banks Machine & Engrg LLC .... D 317 642-4980
Shelbyville *(G-14732)*

Beatty International Inc .... E 219 931-3000
Hammond *(G-6882)*

Bemcor Inc .... F 219 937-1600
Hammond *(G-6885)*

▼ Bofrebo Industries Inc .... E 219 322-1550
Schererville *(G-14516)*

▲ Boyer Machine & Tool Co Inc .... E 812 379-9581
Columbus *(G-2228)*

◆ Burgess Enterprises LLC .... G 260 615-5194
Albion *(G-20)*

Butlers General Repair .... G 812 268-5631
Sullivan *(G-15403)*

C&S Machinery Inc .... G 812 937-2160
Dale *(G-2789)*

Cardinal Services Inc Indiana .... D 574 371-1305
Warsaw *(G-16334)*

Centrifuge Chicago Corporation .... G 219 852-5200
Hammond *(G-6898)*

Clear Decision Filtration Inc .... G 219 567-2008
Francesville *(G-5637)*

Cpp Filter Corporation .... G 765 446-8416
Lafayette *(G-10560)*

Crume Industries LLC .... G 574 747-7683
Elkhart *(G-3275)*

Current Electric Inc .... F 219 872-7736
Michigan City *(G-11591)*

Deprisco Ventures Inc .... E 260 637-8660
Fort Wayne *(G-4916)*

Don Detzer LLC .... G 812 362-7599
Tennyson *(G-15523)*

Duesenburg Inc .... G 260 496-9650
Fort Wayne *(G-4931)*

◆ Elkhart Brass Manufacturi .... C 574 295-8330
Elkhart *(G-3322)*

Enpak LLC .... G 574 268-7273
Warsaw *(G-16360)*

Enviro Filtration Inc .... G 815 469-2871
Gary *(G-5929)*

Estates By Judi .... G 260 615-5195
Albion *(G-26)*

F D Deskins Company Inc .... F 317 284-4014
Fishers *(G-4520)*

Faztech LLC .... G 812 327-0926
Bloomington *(G-864)*

Filter Fabrics Inc .... F
Goshen *(G-6136)*

Filtration Plus Inc .... F 219 879-0663
Michigan City *(G-11612)*

Flow International Corporation .... F 253 850-3500
Jeffersonville *(G-9985)*

Glaze Tool and Engineering Inc .... E 260 493-4557
New Haven *(G-12905)*

GLS Machining & Design LLC .... G 765 754-8248
Alexandria *(G-52)*

Guardian Fire Systems Inc .... G 317 752-2768
Fortville *(G-5597)*

▲ Gvs Filter Technology Inc .... E 317 471-3700
Indianapolis *(G-8345)*

Gvs Filter Technology Inc .... G 317 442-3925
Zionsville *(G-17015)*

Heartland Filled Machine LLC .... G 574 223-6931
Rochester *(G-14295)*

Helmuth Quality Power System .... G 574 457-2002
Syracuse *(G-15462)*

◆ Hirata Corporation of America .... E 317 856-8600
Indianapolis *(G-8399)*

◆ Hitachi Global Air Pwr US LLC .... C 219 879-5451
Michigan City *(G-11626)*

Homer Banes .... G 765 449-8551
Lafayette *(G-10601)*

Hook Industrial Sales Inc .... D 260 432-9441
Fort Wayne *(G-5075)*

▲ Hy-Pro Corporation .... D 317 849-3535
Anderson *(G-130)*

Hy-Tech Machining Systems LLC .... E 765 649-6852
Anderson *(G-131)*

Hydro Fire Protection Inc .... E 317 780-6980
Indianapolis *(G-8442)*

Indianapolis In .... E 855 628-3458
Indianapolis *(G-8502)*

35 INDUSTRIAL AND COMMERCIAL MACHINERY AND COMPUTER EQUIPMENT — SIC SECTION

▲ Industrial Mint Wldg Machining......... E 219 393-5531
  Kingsbury (G-10179)
Jenco Engineering Inc............................ G 574 267-4608
  Warsaw (G-16380)
Joyce/Dayton Corp................................. E 260 726-9361
  Portland (G-13952)
Leasenet Incorporated............................ G 317 575-4098
  Indianapolis (G-8731)
▼ Lesac Corporation................................ E 219 879-3215
  Michigan City (G-11632)
Lube-Line Corporation............................ G 260 637-3779
  Fort Wayne (G-5192)
Lubrication Devices................................ G 574 234-4674
  South Bend (G-15130)
Lubrication Specialist Inc....................... G 317 326-4296
  Greenfield (G-6526)
Mac Industrial Holdings LLC................. F 812 838-1832
  Mount Vernon (G-12306)
▲ McCullagh Corporation......................... F 877 645-7676
  Long Beach (G-11124)
Midwest Design Hydraulic..................... G 765 714-3016
  West Lafayette (G-16605)
Midwest Fabrication LLC....................... G 574 276-5041
  Granger (G-6361)
Mixer Direct LLC..................................... D 812 202-4047
  Jeffersonville (G-10020)
Mobile Power Washing LLC.................. F 219 863-0066
  Bloomington (G-922)
◆ Nachi America Inc................................. E 877 622-4487
  Greenwood (G-6743)
Norco Industries Inc............................... G 574 262-3400
  Elkhart (G-3571)
▲ Norco Industries Inc............................. G 800 347-2232
  Elkhart (G-3572)
Perma Lubrication.................................. G 317 241-0797
  Indianapolis (G-9126)
Perma Lubrication.................................. G 219 531-9155
  Valparaiso (G-16024)
▲ Phoenix Assembly LLC......................... D 317 884-3600
  Greenwood (G-6751)
▲ Phoenix Assembly Indiana LLC........... G 317 884-3600
  Columbus (G-2378)
Pillar Innovations LLC............................ G 812 474-9080
  Evansville (G-4244)
Pittsfield Products Inc............................ D 260 488-2124
  Hamilton (G-6859)
Probotech Inc... G 317 849-6197
  Indianapolis (G-9217)
Roberson Fire & Safety Inc................... G 317 879-3119
  Indianapolis (G-9313)
Ryoei USA Inc.. F 317 912-4498
  Indianapolis (G-9352)
Safe Fleet Holdings LLC........................ G 574 849-4619
  Elkhart (G-3658)
Separation By Design Inc...................... E 812 424-1239
  Evansville (G-4305)
Shamrock Engineering Inc.................... E 812 867-0009
  Oakland City (G-13323)
Spencer Machine and Tl Co Inc............ E 812 282-6300
  Jeffersonville (G-10057)
Sprinkguard LLC.................................... F 877 274-7976
  Mishawaka (G-12006)
SRK Filters LLC..................................... G 765 647-9962
  Cedar Grove (G-1825)
Summit Manufacturing Corp.................. G 317 823-2848
  Indianapolis (G-9524)
Surclean Inc... F 248 791-2226
  Brownsburg (G-1405)
Systems Engineering and Sls Co.......... G 260 422-1671
  Fort Wayne (G-5466)
T & T Hydraulics Inc.............................. G 765 548-2355
  Rosedale (G-14384)

◆ Task Force Tips LLC.............................. C 219 462-6161
  Valparaiso (G-16064)
Thomas L Wehr....................................... G 317 835-7824
  Fairland (G-4403)
U S Filter... G 317 280-4251
  Indianapolis (G-9671)
U S Filter Distribution............................. G 317 271-1463
  Indianapolis (G-9672)
Via Development Corp........................... D 888 225-5842
  Marion (G-11347)
Vital Indus Solutions Corp..................... G 219 916-7648
  Burns Harbor (G-1457)
Wall Control Services Inc...................... G 260 450-6411
  Fort Wayne (G-5542)
Web Products... G 816 777-3735
  La Porte (G-10498)
Webber Manufacturing Company.......... E 317 357-8681
  Indianapolis (G-9745)

3571 Electronic computers

▲ 3btech Inc... E 574 233-0508
  South Bend (G-14927)
Acdc Control LLC................................... G 219 801-3900
  East Chicago (G-2988)
Apple III LLC... G 317 691-2869
  Carmel (G-1561)
Apple Terrace LLC................................. G 260 347-9400
  Kendallville (G-10089)
Apple--day Cstm Hndcrfted Pdts........... G 219 841-6602
  Valparaiso (G-15901)
Apple-Ly Ever After Inc......................... G 219 838-9397
  Highland (G-7122)
Bromire Technology............................... G 317 294-9083
  Greenfield (G-6473)
Cambridge Enterprise Inc..................... G 765 544-3402
  Merrillville (G-11496)
Computer Solutions Systems Inc.......... F 812 235-9008
  Terre Haute (G-15566)
Country Club Computer......................... G 317 271-4000
  Indianapolis (G-7889)
Cybernaut Industria LLC....................... G 317 664-5316
  Indianapolis (G-7939)
David Askew... G 574 273-0184
  Granger (G-6344)
Dcs Car Audio.. G 812 437-8488
  Evansville (G-4009)
Dec Co Ecumenical Agape Center........ G 812 222-0392
  Greensburg (G-6590)
Emmanuel Michael................................. G 806 559-5673
  Greenwood (G-6694)
Futuretek.. G 317 631-0098
  Indianapolis (G-8246)
General Dynmics Mssion Systems........ F 260 434-9500
  Fort Wayne (G-5020)
Green Apple Active LLC........................ G 910 585-1151
  Westfield (G-16693)
HP Inc.. G 317 566-6200
  Carmel (G-1662)
HP Inc.. G 317 334-3400
  Plainfield (G-13687)
Indy Web Inc... G 317 536-1201
  Indianapolis (G-8537)
Jacyl Technology Inc............................. G 260 471-6067
  Fort Wayne (G-5128)
Joseph Matthew Biaso........................... G 812 277-6871
  Mitchell (G-12041)
Keys Computers Inc.............................. G 317 750-5071
  Indianapolis (G-8678)
Kimball Electronics Inc.......................... A 812 634-4200
  Jasper (G-9865)
L5 Solutions LLC.................................... G 317 436-1044
  Indianapolis (G-8706)

Lionfish Cyber Hldngs LLC-S Ln........... G 877 732-6772
  Indianapolis (G-8766)
Milani Custom Homes LLC.................... G 219 455-5804
  Merrillville (G-11538)
Mvctc.. G 765 969-8921
  Richmond (G-14173)
Omnicell Co.. G 812 376-0747
  Columbus (G-2365)
P F Apple LLC.. G 317 773-8683
  Noblesville (G-13149)
Premium Corporation............................. E 219 258-0141
  South Bend (G-15203)
Prevail Design Systems LLC................. G 260 245-1245
  Huntertown (G-7262)
▲ Q-Edge Corporation.............................. E 317 203-6800
  Plainfield (G-13718)
Riddell Technologies LLC...................... G 219 213-9602
  Crown Point (G-2745)

3572 Computer storage devices

Emc2... G 317 435-8021
  Indianapolis (G-8102)
Integrity Qntum Innvations LLC............ G 765 537-9037
  Martinsville (G-11407)
Leroy R Sollars...................................... G 765 284-9417
  Selma (G-14622)
Quantum 7 Group LLC........................... G 812 824-9378
  Bloomington (G-950)
Quantumtech LLC................................... G 786 512-0827
  Indianapolis (G-9248)
RB Annis Instruments Inc..................... G 765 848-1621
  Greencastle (G-6428)
Scale Computing Inc............................. E 317 856-9959
  Indianapolis (G-9385)
▲ Sony Dadc US Inc.................................. A 812 462-8100
  Terre Haute (G-15706)
Techknowledgey Inc.............................. G 574 202-0362
  Goshen (G-6268)
Techknowledgey Inc.............................. G 574 971-4267
  Goshen (G-6269)

3575 Computer terminals

Binarie LLC... G 317 496-8836
  Greenwood (G-6676)
Bowmar LLC... E 260 747-3121
  Fort Wayne (G-4813)
C & P Distributing LLC.......................... F 574 256-1138
  Mishawaka (G-11857)
CIS Holdings Inc.................................... G 703 996-0500
  Indianapolis (G-7810)
Ganaway Solutions LLC........................ G 219 359-7850
  Merrillville (G-11518)
Kristopher Cox....................................... G 502 930-9162
  Scottsburg (G-14569)
Lionfish Cyber Hldngs LLC-S Ln........... G 877 732-6772
  Indianapolis (G-8766)
Loud Clear Communications LLC......... G 260 433-9479
  Auburn (G-403)
Morganblair Logistics LLC.................... G 219 249-2689
  Munster (G-12550)

3577 Computer peripheral equipment, nec

Accups LLC.. G 765 586-5021
  West Lafayette (G-16555)
Axon Network Services LLC................. G 317 818-9000
  Indianapolis (G-7580)
◆ Carson Manufacturing Co Inc............... F 317 257-3191
  Indianapolis (G-7750)
Cisco Systems Inc................................. G 317 816-5200
  Carmel (G-1588)
Clovis LLC.. G 812 944-4791
  Floyds Knobs (G-4674)

SIC SECTION
35 INDUSTRIAL AND COMMERCIAL MACHINERY AND COMPUTER EQUIPMENT

Dbisp LLC .... G 317 222-1671
  Indianapolis *(G-7957)*
Environmental Technology Inc .... E 574 233-1202
  South Bend *(G-15016)*
Federal Provider LLC .... G 317 710-3997
  Indianapolis *(G-8170)*
Impact Cnc LLC .... D 260 244-5511
  Columbia City *(G-2154)*
Laser Plus Inc .... G 574 269-1246
  Warsaw *(G-16386)*
Marteck Inc .... E 800 569-9849
  Zionsville *(G-17031)*
Midwest Office Solutions LLC .... G 262 658-2679
  Mooresville *(G-12222)*
Paradise Ink Inc .... G 812 402-4465
  Evansville *(G-4233)*
Scott Billman .... G 317 293-9921
  Indianapolis *(G-9394)*
▲ Sony Dadc US Inc .... A 812 462-8100
  Terre Haute *(G-15706)*
Syntag Rfld .... G 317 685-5292
  Indianapolis *(G-9540)*
Whyte Haus .... G 260 484-5666
  Fort Wayne *(G-5567)*
Xerox Corp .... F 765 494-6511
  Lafayette *(G-10720)*

3578 Calculating and accounting equipment

A T Systems Technologies Inc .... G 317 352-1030
  Indianapolis *(G-7403)*
Chase Beford .... G 812 277-7028
  Bedford *(G-626)*
Chase N Corydon .... F 812 738-3032
  Corydon *(G-2490)*
Chase Southport Emerson .... G 317 266-7470
  Indianapolis *(G-7787)*
Cinq LLC .... G 405 361-0097
  New Albany *(G-12713)*
Elmos .... G 574 371-2050
  Warsaw *(G-16358)*
Fairfield Gas Way .... G 260 744-2186
  Fort Wayne *(G-4973)*
Front End Digital Inc .... G 317 652-6134
  Fishers *(G-4528)*
James R McNutt .... G 317 899-6955
  Indianapolis *(G-8617)*
Retro Atm LLC .... G 317 752-6915
  Indianapolis *(G-9294)*
▲ Scales and More .... G 812 886-4245
  Vincennes *(G-16151)*
Standard Change-Makers Inc .... F 317 899-6955
  Indianapolis *(G-9492)*
▲ Standard Change-Makers Inc .... C 317 899-6955
  Indianapolis *(G-9491)*
Steven Smith .... G 317 455-1086
  Camby *(G-1514)*
Woundvision LLC .... G 317 775-6054
  Carmel *(G-1809)*

3579 Office machines, nec

Automated Bus Solutions Inc .... F 317 257-9062
  Fishers *(G-4468)*
Bach Tech Inc .... G 219 531-7424
  Valparaiso *(G-15908)*
Bastian Automation Engrg LLC .... D 317 467-2583
  Greenfield *(G-6468)*
Consultech5 .... G 219 712-2801
  Crown Point *(G-2667)*
Exaktime Innovations Inc .... F 818 222-1836
  South Bend *(G-15020)*
Glander .... G 317 889-1039
  Greenwood *(G-6707)*

Imaginestics LLC .... G 765 464-1700
  West Lafayette *(G-16594)*
◆ Martin Yale Industries LLC .... C 260 563-0641
  Wabash *(G-16198)*
Microvote General Corp .... F 317 257-4900
  Indianapolis *(G-8905)*
Pinnacle Mailing Products .... F 765 405-1194
  Yorktown *(G-16980)*
Pitney Bowes Inc .... G 260 436-7395
  Indianapolis *(G-9148)*
Pitney Bowes Inc .... G 317 769-8300
  Whitestown *(G-16814)*
Sojourn Technologies Inc .... G 317 422-1254
  Bargersville *(G-573)*
Vernon A Stevens .... G 812 626-0010
  Evansville *(G-4371)*
Voter Registration .... G 219 755-3795
  Crown Point *(G-2772)*

3581 Automatic vending machines

A Snack Above Rest LLC .... G 219 455-3335
  Gary *(G-5884)*
Ds Mgmt Group LLC .... G 317 946-8646
  Indianapolis *(G-8014)*
Evelyns Enterprise .... G 219 980-8799
  Merrillville *(G-11515)*
Key Enhancement LLC .... G 502 403-5661
  Jeffersonville *(G-10010)*
My Goodies Snack Vending LLC .... G 317 653-7395
  Anderson *(G-164)*
▲ Standard Change-Makers Inc .... C 317 899-6955
  Indianapolis *(G-9491)*
Styles Versatility LLC .... G 765 270-2217
  Lafayette *(G-10702)*
Taste of Joy LLC .... G 219 501-0157
  Merrillville *(G-11564)*
Unlimited Vending LLC .... Cinq 765 288-5952
  Muncie *(G-12510)*
Whatzthat Vending LLC .... G 317 362-9088
  Indianapolis *(G-9755)*
White House Ventures LLC .... G 260 693-3032
  Churubusco *(G-1993)*
Winbush Refreshments LLC .... G 317 762-8236
  Indianapolis *(G-9771)*
Xpressvending LLC .... G 331 264-3541
  Indianapolis *(G-9796)*

3582 Commercial laundry equipment

Brian T Klem .... G 812 342-4080
  Columbus *(G-2230)*
Chucks Cleaners LLC .... G 260 488-3362
  Hamilton *(G-6851)*
Donald L Gard .... G 219 663-7945
  Crown Point *(G-2679)*
Fresh Hamper LLC .... G 317 452-6023
  Brownsburg *(G-1370)*
Hansford Prevent LLC .... G 317 985-2346
  Indianapolis *(G-8354)*
Laundry On US LLC .... G 812 567-3653
  Terre Haute *(G-15630)*
Randolph Carpet-Tile Cleaning .... G 317 401-2300
  Cicero *(G-2000)*
Security Integrated Corp .... G 219 942-9666
  Munster *(G-12563)*

3585 Refrigeration and heating equipment

3sevens LLC .... G 502 594-2312
  Henryville *(G-7112)*
A & A Prcsion Htg Colg Rfrgn L .... G 812 401-1711
  Evansville *(G-3859)*
Advantage Engineering Inc .... D 317 887-0729
  Greenwood *(G-6660)*

Air Systems Compents LP .... G 765 483-5841
  Lebanon *(G-10873)*
All Pro Property Services LLC .... G 317 721-1227
  Indianapolis *(G-7474)*
Auto Temp Ctrl Specialists Inc .... G 812 333-2963
  Bloomington *(G-787)*
B & K Beverage Service Inc .... G 317 209-9842
  Lebanon *(G-10879)*
Caliente LLC .... E 260 426-3800
  Fort Wayne *(G-4830)*
Carrier Corporation .... D 317 243-0851
  Indianapolis *(G-7749)*
Crosspoint Power and Rfrgn LLC .... F 317 240-1967
  Indianapolis *(G-7907)*
▲ Crosspoint Solutions LLC .... E 877 826-9399
  Indianapolis *(G-7908)*
Crown Products & Services Inc .... G 317 564-4799
  Carmel *(G-1601)*
Deans Place .... G 765 282-5712
  Muncie *(G-12375)*
Delivery Concepts Inc .... E 574 522-3981
  Elkhart *(G-3289)*
Dometic Corporation .... B 260 463-7657
  Elkhart *(G-3301)*
Duncan Supply Co Inc .... G 765 446-0105
  Lafayette *(G-10572)*
Elliott-Williams Company Inc .... E 317 453-2295
  Indianapolis *(G-8097)*
Evansville Metal Products Inc .... G 812 421-6589
  Evansville *(G-4055)*
Evansville Metal Products Inc .... D 812 423-5632
  Evansville *(G-4054)*
Fletcher Heating & Cooling .... G 812 865-2984
  Paoli *(G-13494)*
▲ Flow Center Products Inc .... G 765 364-9460
  Crawfordsville *(G-2567)*
▲ Geo-Flo Corporation .... F 812 275-8513
  Bedford *(G-639)*
Grayson Thermal Systems Corp .... C 317 739-3290
  Franklin *(G-5736)*
Griffen Plmbng-Heating-Cooling .... E 574 295-2440
  Elkhart *(G-3392)*
▲ Grinon Industries LLC .... E 317 388-5100
  Indianapolis *(G-8332)*
Hitachi Astemo Indiana Inc .... C 765 213-4915
  Muncie *(G-12417)*
Hrezo Industrial Eqp & Engrg .... F 812 537-4700
  Greendale *(G-6447)*
Ilpea Industries Inc .... D 812 752-2526
  Scottsburg *(G-14561)*
Industrial Combustn Engineers .... E 219 949-5066
  Gary *(G-5960)*
Jackson Systems LLC .... C 888 359-0365
  Indianapolis *(G-8615)*
Jlb Industrial LLC .... G 765 561-1751
  Rushville *(G-14402)*
Lennox International Inc .... E 219 756-3709
  Merrillville *(G-11532)*
Lennox Nat Account Svcs LLC .... G 800 333-4001
  Indianapolis *(G-8739)*
Lennoxs Legacy Rescue Inc .... G 260 223-3115
  Decatur *(G-2868)*
M Jones Consulting LLC .... G 317 353-3823
  Monrovia *(G-12078)*
▲ Manitowoc Beverage Eqp Inc .... C 812 246-7000
  New Albany *(G-12770)*
◆ Manitowoc Beverage Systems Inc ..... C 800 367-4233
  New Albany *(G-12771)*
Master Filter Corporation .... G 317 545-3335
  Indianapolis *(G-8849)*
MD Moxie LLC .... F 260 347-1203
  Kendallville *(G-10136)*

35 INDUSTRIAL AND COMMERCIAL MACHINERY AND COMPUTER EQUIPMENT — SIC SECTION

Mr Heat Inc .... G 219 345-5629
  Demotte (G-2925)
◆ Multiplex Company Inc .... D 812 246-7000
  New Albany (G-12783)
Parker-Hannifin Corporation .... A 260 748-6000
  Fort Wayne (G-5297)
▼ Polar King International Inc .... E 260 428-2530
  Fort Wayne (G-5323)
Proair LLC .... D 574 264-5494
  Elkhart (G-3622)
Ram Services Rfrgn & Mech .... G 317 679-8541
  Indianapolis (G-9264)
Redi/Controls Inc .... G 317 494-6600
  Franklin (G-5773)
Reearth Technologies .... G 812 219-6517
  Bloomington (G-953)
Refrigeration Design Ind LLC .... G 317 498-3435
  Rushville (G-14409)
Rheem Sales Company Inc .... G 479 648-4900
  Indianapolis (G-9297)
Schnell Service Center .... G 812 683-2461
  Huntingburg (G-7290)
Stanton and Associates Inc .... G 574 247-5522
  Granger (G-6383)
Superior Distribution .... G 317 308-5525
  Indianapolis (G-9528)
Supreme Corporation .... G 260 894-9191
  Ligonier (G-11026)
◆ Supreme Corporation .... C 574 642-4888
  Goshen (G-6263)
T&S Midwest Beverage LLC .... G 317 690-1705
  Shelbyville (G-14802)
Templeton Coal Company Inc .... C 812 232-7037
  Terre Haute (G-15726)
Trane US Inc .... G 800 285-2487
  Bloomington (G-992)
Trane US Inc .... F 812 421-8725
  Evansville (G-4346)
Trane US Inc .... D 317 255-8777
  Fishers (G-4615)
Trane US Inc .... F 260 489-0884
  Fort Wayne (G-5498)
Trane US Inc .... D 765 932-7200
  Rushville (G-14415)
Trane US Inc .... G 574 282-4880
  South Bend (G-15286)
▲ Twin-Air Products Inc .... G 574 295-1129
  Elkhart (G-3755)
Validated Custom Solutions LLC .... G 317 259-7604
  Indianapolis (G-9699)
Washburn Heating & AC .... G 574 825-7697
  Middlebury (G-11757)
Waterfurnace International Inc .... B 260 478-5667
  Fort Wayne (G-5549)
Webber Manufacturing Company .... E 317 357-8681
  Indianapolis (G-9745)
Welbilt Fdsrvice Companies LLC .... B 260 459-8200
  Fort Wayne (G-5561)
Welbilt Fdsrvice Companies LLC .... B 812 406-4527
  Jeffersonville (G-10072)
Whirlpool Corporation .... D 812 426-4000
  Evansville (G-4383)

3586 Measuring and dispensing pumps

Chemical Control Systems Inc .... G 219 465-5103
  Griffith (G-6800)
Cortex Safety Technologies LLC .... G 317 414-5607
  Carmel (G-1598)
Gfi Innovations LLC .... G 847 263-9000
  Plymouth (G-13779)
▼ Indco Inc .... G 812 945-4383
  New Albany (G-12746)

Rj Fuel Services Inc .... G 812 350-2897
  Edinburgh (G-3101)
Separation By Design Inc .... E 812 424-1239
  Evansville (G-4305)

3589 Service industry machinery, nec

A&E Klassic Detailing LLC .... G 219 363-6671
  Michigan City (G-11574)
A&M Commercial Cleaning LLC .... G 765 720-3737
  Greencastle (G-6392)
Accutemp Products Inc .... D 260 493-0415
  New Haven (G-12889)
American Hydro Systems Inc .... F 866 357-5063
  Fort Wayne (G-4755)
◆ American Melt Blown Filtration .... E 219 866-3500
  Rensselaer (G-14041)
Amgi LLC .... G 317 447-1524
  New Palestine (G-12928)
Anaerobic Innovations LLC .... G 765 491-1174
  West Lafayette (G-16561)
Aqseptence Group Inc .... D 574 223-3980
  Rochester (G-14278)
Aqua Blast Corp .... F 260 728-4433
  Decatur (G-2844)
Assured Water Care Company .... G 317 997-5790
  Indianapolis (G-7555)
Astbury Water Technology Inc .... D 317 328-7153
  Indianapolis (G-7556)
▲ Bio-Response Solutions Inc .... F 317 386-3500
  Danville (G-2807)
▲ Bottom Line Management Inc .... F 812 944-7388
  Clarksville (G-2010)
Brockwood Farm .... G 812 837-9607
  Nashville (G-12664)
▲ Canature USA Inc .... G 877 771-6789
  Carmel (G-1578)
▲ Canature Watergroup USA Inc .... G 877 771-6789
  Whitestown (G-16802)
Chem-Aqua .... G 317 899-3660
  Indianapolis (G-7791)
Chemical Control Systems Inc .... G 219 465-5103
  Griffith (G-6800)
CHS Legacy Company .... G 260 456-3596
  Columbia City (G-2131)
City of Anderson .... D 765 648-6560
  Anderson (G-94)
City of Columbia City .... G 260 248-5118
  Columbia City (G-2132)
Clover Industrial Services LLC .... G 317 879-5001
  Indianapolis (G-7826)
Clute Enterprises Inc .... G 260 413-0810
  Huntertown (G-7250)
Cox Cleaning Services .... G 260 804-9001
  Fort Wayne (G-4880)
Crawford Water Care .... G 317 758-6017
  Sheridan (G-14820)
Crestwood Equity Partners LP .... G 812 265-3313
  Madison (G-11212)
Davis Water Services Inc .... G 219 394-2270
  Rensselaer (G-14050)
Earthsmarte Water Indiana Inc .... G 317 800-8442
  Indianapolis (G-8035)
Eco Water of Southern Indiana .... G 812 734-1407
  New Salisbury (G-12984)
Edelweiss Edge LLC .... G 260 399-6692
  Fort Wayne (G-4942)
Elite Hand Car Wash & More LLC .... G 317 500-8308
  Avon (G-517)
Environmental MGT & Dev Inc .... G 765 874-1539
  Lynn (G-11183)
Envmtl Franke Systems LLC .... G 260 710-6491
  Fort Wayne (G-4954)

Evoqua Water Technologies LLC .... E 317 280-4255
  Indianapolis (G-8145)
Filter Sciences LLC .... G 260 387-7709
  Fort Wayne (G-4983)
Flora Wastewater Treatment .... G 574 967-3005
  Flora (G-4658)
Fluid-Tech International Corp .... G 260 420-5000
  Fort Wayne (G-4988)
Forecast Sales Inc .... F 317 829-0147
  Indianapolis (G-8214)
Freije Treatment Systems Inc .... E 888 766-7258
  Fishers (G-4527)
Freije Treatment Systems Inc .... G 317 508-3848
  Indianapolis (G-8230)
Global Water Technologies Inc .... G 317 452-4488
  Indianapolis (G-8292)
◆ Hawk Enterprises Elkhart Inc .... G 574 294-1910
  Elkhart (G-3402)
James Morris .... G 574 387-2615
  South Bend (G-15090)
Kendle Custom Inc .... G 812 985-5917
  Evansville (G-4148)
Kirklin Waste Water Treatment .... G 765 279-5251
  Kirklin (G-10190)
Laserwash .... G 765 359-0582
  Crawfordsville (G-2584)
Leach & Sons WaterCare .... G 317 248-8954
  Danville (G-2818)
Leistner Aquatic Services Inc .... G 317 535-6099
  Morgantown (G-12260)
▼ Lonn Manufacturing Inc .... G 317 897-1440
  Indianapolis (G-8781)
M J Markiewicz & Associates .... G 765 452-6562
  Kokomo (G-10301)
Markle Water Treatment Plant .... G 260 758-3482
  Markle (G-11358)
McGuires Magic Cleaning LLC .... G 317 504-7739
  Indianapolis (G-8866)
▲ MD Holdings LLC .... G 317 831-7030
  Mooresville (G-12220)
Michiana Carwash Systems LLC .... G 574 320-2331
  Goshen (G-6219)
Michrochem LLC .... G 812 838-1832
  Mount Vernon (G-12309)
Mid State Water Treatment .... G 765 884-1220
  Fowler (G-5627)
▲ Mohawk Laboratories .... G 317 899-3660
  Indianapolis (G-8945)
Molden Associates Inc .... G 219 879-8425
  Long Beach (G-11125)
Monroe County Regional Sewer .... G 812 824-9005
  Bloomington (G-924)
New Aqua LLC .... D 317 272-3000
  Avon (G-540)
Nighthawk Enterprises LLC .... E 317 576-9235
  Indianapolis (G-9011)
Olympia Business Systems Inc .... F 800 225-5644
  Wabash (G-16206)
On The Go Portable Water Softe .... F 260 482-9614
  Bloomington (G-936)
Onesource Water .... G 866 917-7873
  Indianapolis (G-9054)
Onion Enterprises Inc .... G 317 762-6007
  Indianapolis (G-9056)
Over Globe LLC .... G 305 607-6472
  Brownsburg (G-1394)
Phoenix Pure Holdings LLC .... G 219 448-0142
  Long Beach (G-11127)
Puritan Water Conditioning .... F 765 362-6340
  Crawfordsville (G-2606)
Quantum Technologies LLC .... G 765 426-0156
  Elizabethtown (G-3132)

35 INDUSTRIAL AND COMMERCIAL MACHINERY AND COMPUTER EQUIPMENT

Rayne Water Conditioning................. G 765 742-8967
  Lafayette *(G-10677)*
Region Auto Detailing LLC................. G 219 427-6318
  East Chicago *(G-3039)*
Samco Inc................................. G 812 926-4282
  Sunman *(G-15444)*
SDP Manufacturing Inc.................... E 765 768-5000
  Dunkirk *(G-2963)*
Sewer Optical Services Inc............... G 765 242-3768
  Lebanon *(G-10940)*
SSP Technologies Inc..................... G 888 548-4668
  Chesterton *(G-1958)*
Taggarts Custom Sndblst LLC.............. G 765 825-4584
  Connersville *(G-2471)*
Technical Water Treatment Inc............ G 574 277-1949
  Granger *(G-6386)*
Thermodyne Food Svc Pdts Inc............. E 260 428-2535
  Fort Wayne *(G-5482)*
True Chem Inc............................ G 317 769-2701
  Greenwood *(G-6777)*
US Water Systems Inc..................... E 317 209-0889
  Indianapolis *(G-9688)*
Wall Control Services Inc................ G 260 450-6411
  Fort Wayne *(G-5542)*
Watcon Inc............................... G 574 287-3397
  South Bend *(G-15304)*
Water Energizers Inc..................... F 812 288-6900
  Jeffersonville *(G-10071)*
Weaver Popcorn Bulk LLC.................. E 765 357-8413
  Carmel *(G-1801)*
Western Wyne Rgonal Sewage Dst........... G 765 478-3788
  Cambridge City *(G-1505)*

3592 Carburetors, pistons, rings, valves

Federal-Mogul Powertrain LLC............. B 574 271-5954
  South Bend *(G-15031)*
Parker-Hannifin Corporation.............. E 260 587-9102
  Ashley *(G-335)*
Precision Rings Incorporated............. E 317 247-4786
  Indianapolis *(G-9185)*
Tecumseh Products Company LLC............ G 812 883-3575
  Salem *(G-14502)*
Valve Serve LLC.......................... G 260 421-1927
  Fort Wayne *(G-5526)*
▲ Victor Reinz Valve Seals LLC........... D 260 897-2827
  Avilla *(G-498)*

3593 Fluid power cylinders and actuators

Bjh Enterprises LLC...................... F 812 655-4544
  Greendale *(G-6440)*
Djs Cylinder Service Inc................. G 219 922-4819
  Griffith *(G-6802)*
Dresser LLC.............................. D 765 827-9200
  Connersville *(G-2436)*
Elevator Equipment Corporation........... D 765 966-7761
  Richmond *(G-14119)*
Enerpac Tool Group Corp.................. E 574 254-1428
  Mishawaka *(G-11894)*
▲ Five Star Hydraulics Inc............... E 219 762-1619
  Portage *(G-13866)*
Haddady Machining Company Inc............ F 708 474-8620
  East Chicago *(G-3014)*
▲ K M Specialty Pumps Inc................ F 812 925-3000
  Chandler *(G-1863)*
▲ Logansport Machine Co Inc.............. E 574 735-0225
  Logansport *(G-11090)*
Micro-Precision Operations............... F 260 589-2136
  Berne *(G-719)*
▼ Micromatic LLC......................... D 260 589-2136
  Berne *(G-720)*
PHD Inc.................................. G 260 747-6151
  Fort Wayne *(G-5309)*

PHD Inc.................................. C 260 747-6151
  Fort Wayne *(G-5310)*
▲ SMC Corporation of America............. B 317 899-4440
  Noblesville *(G-13176)*

3594 Fluid power pumps and motors

Crown Elec Svcs & Automtn Inc............ D 972 929-4700
  Portage *(G-13857)*
D A Hochstetler & Sons LLP............... F 574 642-1144
  Topeka *(G-15800)*
Dresser LLC.............................. D 765 827-9200
  Connersville *(G-2436)*
Elevator Equipment Corporation........... D 765 966-7761
  Richmond *(G-14119)*
Freudenberg-Nok General Partnr........... C 260 894-7183
  Ligonier *(G-11015)*
Gravel Conveyors Inc..................... F 317 873-8686
  Zionsville *(G-17014)*
Hydro-Gear Inc........................... G 317 821-0477
  Indianapolis *(G-8444)*
Jomar Machining & Fabg Inc............... E 574 825-9837
  Middlebury *(G-11728)*
Met-Pro Technologies LLC................. G 317 293-2930
  Indianapolis *(G-8882)*
▲ Murray Equipment Inc................... C 260 484-0382
  Fort Wayne *(G-5252)*
Nidec Motor Corporation.................. D 812 385-2564
  Princeton *(G-14007)*
Parker-Hannifin Corporation.............. E 866 247-4827
  Jeffersonville *(G-10034)*
Parker-Hannifin Corporation.............. F 219 736-0400
  Merrillville *(G-11549)*
Parker-Hannifin Corporation.............. G 317 776-7600
  Noblesville *(G-13150)*
Parker-Hannifin Corporation.............. C 574 528-9400
  Syracuse *(G-15470)*
Steel Parts Corporation.................. A 765 675-2191
  Tipton *(G-15791)*
◆ Terra Drive Systems Inc................ C 219 279-2801
  Brookston *(G-1313)*
Terry Liquidation III Inc................ F 219 362-3557
  La Porte *(G-10490)*

3596 Scales and balances, except laboratory

A H Emery Company........................ G 812 466-5265
  Terre Haute *(G-15527)*
Cullman Casting Corporation.............. G 256 735-0900
  North Vernon *(G-13262)*
▲ Indiana Scale Company Inc.............. F 812 232-0893
  Terre Haute *(G-15617)*
Powell Systems Inc....................... E 765 884-0980
  Fowler *(G-5630)*
Raco Industries LLC...................... G 812 232-3676
  Terre Haute *(G-15674)*
▲ Richards Scale Company Inc............. G 812 246-3354
  Sellersburg *(G-14612)*
Sinden Racing Service Inc................ F 317 243-7171
  Indianapolis *(G-9443)*
▲ Technical Weighing Svcs Inc............ E 219 924-3366
  Griffith *(G-6819)*
Valley Scale Company LLC................. F 812 282-5269
  Clarksville *(G-2041)*
Weights & Measures....................... G 812 349-2566
  Bloomington *(G-1008)*
Winslow Scale Company.................... E 812 466-5265
  Terre Haute *(G-15747)*

3599 Industrial machinery, nec

3d Machine Inc........................... E 219 297-3674
  Goodland *(G-6077)*
A & M Tool Inc........................... G 812 934-6533
  Batesville *(G-575)*

A & R Machine Shop LLP................... E 574 825-5686
  Middlebury *(G-11692)*
A P Machine & Tool Co Inc................ F 812 232-4939
  Terre Haute *(G-15528)*
Abrasive Waterjet Indiana LLC............ G 317 773-1631
  Noblesville *(G-13033)*
Absolute Caliber LLC..................... G 574 303-4365
  Bristol *(G-1241)*
Absolute Custom Machine LLC.............. G 812 724-2284
  Owensville *(G-13464)*
Absolute Machining LLC................... G 260 747-4568
  Fort Wayne *(G-4717)*
▲ Accraline Inc.......................... E 574 546-3484
  Bremen *(G-1170)*
Accu-Tool Inc............................ G 260 248-4529
  Columbia City *(G-2115)*
Accurate Castings Inc.................... E 224 563-3200
  Walkerton *(G-16261)*
Accurate Turning Solutions............... G 812 603-6612
  Columbus *(G-2212)*
Achates LLC.............................. F 317 852-6978
  Brownsburg *(G-1343)*
Acme Industrial Inc...................... E 260 422-6518
  Columbia City *(G-2116)*
▲ Acro Engineering Inc................... E 812 663-6236
  Greensburg *(G-6579)*
▲ Action Machine Inc..................... F 574 287-9650
  South Bend *(G-14935)*
Adept Tool and Engineering............... G 317 896-9250
  Carmel *(G-1551)*
Adkins Amusements........................ G 765 939-0285
  Richmond *(G-14083)*
Advance Machine Works Corp............... E 260 483-1183
  Fort Wayne *(G-4724)*
Advance Repair & Machining Inc........... G 765 474-8000
  Lafayette *(G-10515)*
▲ Advanced Machine & Tool Corp........... E 260 489-3572
  Fort Wayne *(G-4727)*
Advanced Metal Etching Inc............... E 260 894-4189
  Ligonier *(G-11003)*
Advantage Components Corp................ G 317 784-0299
  Brownsburg *(G-1344)*
Aegis Sales and Engineering.............. F 260 483-4160
  Fort Wayne *(G-4731)*
Aero Machine LLC......................... E 219 548-0490
  Valparaiso *(G-15893)*
Aerofab Corp............................. G 317 787-6438
  Indianapolis *(G-7452)*
▲ Aeromet Industries Inc................. D 219 924-7442
  Griffith *(G-6787)*
Agile Engineering & Mfg LLC.............. F 317 359-3360
  Indianapolis *(G-7459)*
▲ Ahaus Tool & Engineering Inc........... D 765 962-3573
  Richmond *(G-14084)*
Aj Machine Inc........................... E 260 248-4900
  Columbia City *(G-2118)*
All Points Tool & Mfg Corp............... G 574 935-3944
  Plymouth *(G-13754)*
▲ Alliance Tool & Equipment Inc.......... F 260 432-2909
  Fort Wayne *(G-4743)*
Allied Precision Machine Inc............. G 765 418-7607
  Lafayette *(G-10519)*
Allied Specialty Precision Inc........... D 574 255-4718
  Mishawaka *(G-11838)*
Alpha LLC................................ F 574 292-1805
  Warsaw *(G-16311)*
Alpha & Omega Mfg LLC.................... G 219 344-8738
  Gary *(G-5891)*
Alpha LLC................................ G 574 646-2304
  Warsaw *(G-16312)*
Alternative Machining Inc................ G 317 830-8109
  Mooresville *(G-12192)*

Employee Codes: A=Over 500 employees, B=251-500
C=101-250, D=51-100, E=20-50, F=10-19, G=1-9

2024 Harris Indiana Industrial Directory

35 INDUSTRIAL AND COMMERCIAL MACHINERY AND COMPUTER EQUIPMENT

American Industrial McHy Inc............... F 219 755-4090
  Merrillville *(G-11483)*
American Machine Works Inc............... G 219 924-3574
  Munster *(G-12529)*
American Precision Svcs Inc............... E 219 977-4451
  Gary *(G-5892)*
Amerimachine LLC............... G 260 414-1703
  Markle *(G-11354)*
▲ AMG Engineering Machining Inc....... E 317 329-4000
  Indianapolis *(G-7512)*
AMI Defense Inc............... F 219 326-1976
  La Porte *(G-10385)*
AMS Production Machining Inc............... E 317 838-9273
  Plainfield *(G-13657)*
◆ Amt Precision Parts Inc............... E 260 490-0223
  Fort Wayne *(G-4761)*
Angola Wire Products Inc............... G 260 665-3061
  Angola *(G-228)*
Anita Machine and Tool Inc............... G 765 477-6054
  Lafayette *(G-10522)*
Anne Pfeiffer Holdings Inc............... E 812 948-1422
  New Albany *(G-12689)*
Apar Technological Inc............... G 812 430-2025
  Evansville *(G-3893)*
Apex Doors Plus LLC............... G 574 370-0906
  Middlebury *(G-11696)*
Apollo Precision Machining Inc............... E 574 271-1197
  South Bend *(G-14947)*
Applied Metals & Mch Works Inc............... E 260 424-4834
  Fort Wayne *(G-4766)*
ARC EDM Incorporated............... G 765 284-3820
  Muncie *(G-12343)*
Atlas Machine and Supply Inc............... F 812 423-7762
  Evansville *(G-3901)*
Austin & Austin Inc............... F 574 586-2320
  Walkerton *(G-16264)*
Auto Center Inc............... G 317 545-3360
  Indianapolis *(G-7571)*
Auto Specialty Lafayette Inc............... G 765 446-2311
  Lafayette *(G-10531)*
Auto Truck Group LLC............... G 260 356-1610
  Huntington *(G-7299)*
Auto Truck Group LLC............... G 260 493-1800
  Roanoke *(G-14259)*
Avf Machining............... G 260 760-1531
  Butler *(G-1459)*
Axis Machine Tool Inc............... G 812 246-2600
  Sellersburg *(G-14587)*
B & C Machining Inc............... E 219 866-7091
  Rensselaer *(G-14045)*
B&B Tool and Molding Co Inc............... E
  Muncie *(G-12348)*
▲ B&J Rocket America Inc............... E 574 825-5802
  Middlebury *(G-11700)*
Badd LLC............... E 812 280-1854
  Jeffersonville *(G-9938)*
Banco Industries Inc............... G 260 347-9524
  Kendallville *(G-10096)*
▼ Banks Machine & Engrg LLC............... D 317 642-4980
  Shelbyville *(G-14732)*
Barksdale Performance............... G 219 916-5671
  Hanna *(G-7037)*
Bbs Enterprises Inc............... D 574 255-3173
  Mishawaka *(G-11848)*
Bcd and Associates LLC............... G 317 873-5394
  Indianapolis *(G-7601)*
Bcf Precision LLC............... G 888 556-2264
  Warsaw *(G-16318)*
BCI Solutions Inc............... C 574 546-2411
  Bremen *(G-1174)*
Beacon Manufacturing Inc............... G 765 753-0265
  Kokomo *(G-10237)*

Beatty International Inc............... E 219 931-3000
  Hammond *(G-6882)*
Beatty Machine & Mfg Co............... E 219 931-3000
  Hammond *(G-6883)*
Bedford Machine & Tool Inc............... E 812 275-1948
  Bedford *(G-624)*
Bel-Mar Products Corporation............... G 317 769-3262
  Whitestown *(G-16801)*
Bemcor Inc............... F 219 937-1600
  Hammond *(G-6885)*
Bemr LLC............... G 812 385-8509
  Princeton *(G-13982)*
Benz............... G 812 364-1273
  New Salisbury *(G-12983)*
Bertrand Products Inc............... E 574 234-4181
  South Bend *(G-14957)*
Best Machine Company Inc............... G 765 827-0250
  Connersville *(G-2429)*
Bishop Repair............... G 812 523-3246
  Crothersville *(G-2637)*
Blackpoint Engineering LLC............... G 765 884-4100
  Ligonier *(G-11006)*
Boggs Fabg Solutions Inc............... G 317 852-5107
  Crawfordsville *(G-2548)*
Bolinger Machine LLC............... G 317 241-2989
  Indianapolis *(G-7657)*
Bombtrack Fabrication LLC............... G 317 518-9509
  Indianapolis *(G-7659)*
Boston Tool Company Inc............... F 765 935-6282
  Richmond *(G-14100)*
Boyce Industries Group LLC............... F 317 409-3235
  Indianapolis *(G-7667)*
▲ Boyer Machine & Tool Co Inc............... E 812 379-9581
  Columbus *(G-2228)*
Brad Scher............... G 260 356-1515
  Huntington *(G-7302)*
Brent Morris............... G 812 282-6945
  Jeffersonville *(G-9946)*
Brewer Machine & Mfg Inc............... E 317 398-3505
  Shelbyville *(G-14741)*
Bristol Intgrted Tling Atmtn L............... F 574 848-5354
  Bristol *(G-1251)*
Bristol Tool and Die Inc............... F 574 848-5354
  Bristol *(G-1252)*
Browell Enterprises Inc............... F 765 447-2292
  Lafayette *(G-10546)*
Brownstown Qlty Tl Automtn LLC............... G 812 358-9059
  Brownstown *(G-1417)*
Bryan Machine Services Inc............... G 260 356-5530
  Huntington *(G-7303)*
Bryant Industries Inc............... F 812 944-6010
  New Albany *(G-12707)*
Bryant Machining & Welding LLC............... G 260 997-6059
  Bryant *(G-1434)*
Bst Enterprises Inc............... G 260 493-4313
  New Haven *(G-12895)*
Burkholder Machine LLC............... G 574 862-2004
  Goshen *(G-6105)*
Burris Engineering Inc............... F 317 862-1046
  Indianapolis *(G-7701)*
Butler Tool & Design Inc............... F 219 297-4531
  Goodland *(G-6080)*
Buxton Engineering Inc............... G 812 897-3609
  Boonville *(G-1084)*
C & P Machine Service Inc............... F 260 484-7723
  Fort Wayne *(G-4827)*
C & S Prototyping LLC............... G 812 343-8618
  Columbus *(G-2232)*
C and S Machine Inc............... G 812 687-7203
  Plainville *(G-13745)*
C M Engineering Inc............... F 812 648-2038
  Dugger *(G-2956)*

C M Grinding Incorporated............... F 574 234-6812
  South Bend *(G-14965)*
C M TEC............... G 765 284-3888
  Selma *(G-14620)*
▲ C&R Racing Incorporated............... E 317 293-4100
  Indianapolis *(G-7710)*
Cad & Machining Services Inc............... F 317 535-1067
  Whiteland *(G-16777)*
Camtool Inc............... G 765 286-9725
  Muncie *(G-12363)*
Cardemon Inc............... F 765 857-1000
  Ridgeville *(G-14233)*
Carl A Nix Welding Service Inc............... F 812 386-6281
  Princeton *(G-13987)*
Carmel Engineering Inc............... F 765 279-8955
  Kirklin *(G-10187)*
Cass County Machine Inc............... F 574 722-5714
  Logansport *(G-11066)*
Cast Metals Technology............... F 765 284-3888
  Selma *(G-14621)*
Cast Metals Technology Inc............... G 765 584-6501
  Winchester *(G-16883)*
Casting Company Inc............... G 317 509-4311
  Indianapolis *(G-7757)*
CCT Enterprises LLC............... E 260 925-1420
  Auburn *(G-375)*
Centerline Manufacturing............... G 260 348-7400
  Churubusco *(G-1983)*
Central States Fabricating............... F 574 288-5607
  South Bend *(G-14970)*
Central Tool Co Inc............... G 317 485-5344
  Fortville *(G-5588)*
Cerline Ceramic Corp............... G 765 649-7222
  Anderson *(G-92)*
Certa Craft Inc............... G 317 535-0226
  Indianapolis *(G-7778)*
Certified Automotive & Mch Sp............... G 317 897-9724
  Indianapolis *(G-7779)*
Challenge Tool & Mfg Inc............... D 260 749-9558
  New Haven *(G-12898)*
Chaos Machine Division Inc............... G 812 306-7380
  Evansville *(G-3970)*
Charleston Metal Products Inc............... F 260 281-9972
  Corunna *(G-2481)*
Charleston Metal Products Inc............... F 260 837-8211
  Waterloo *(G-16516)*
Checkered Past Racing Pdts LLC............... G 317 852-6978
  Brownsburg *(G-1359)*
Chesterfield Tool & Engrg Inc............... E 765 378-5101
  Daleville *(G-2798)*
Christie Machine Works Co Inc............... G 317 638-8840
  Indianapolis *(G-7801)*
City Pattern and Foundry Company Inc. D 574 273-3000
  Granger *(G-6339)*
CL Tech Inc............... G 812 526-0995
  Edinburgh *(G-3072)*
Classic City Tool & Engineering Inc............... F 260 925-1420
  Auburn *(G-376)*
Clifty Engineering and Tool Co............... C 812 273-3272
  Madison *(G-11210)*
Cnc Concepts Inc............... G 574 269-2301
  Warsaw *(G-16336)*
Cnc Industries Inc............... E 260 490-5700
  Fort Wayne *(G-4863)*
Cnc Machine Inc............... G 317 835-4575
  Shelbyville *(G-14746)*
Collett Partners LLC............... G 812 298-4451
  Greencastle *(G-6397)*
Collins Machining LLC............... G 812 528-5396
  North Vernon *(G-13258)*
Complete Metal Fabrication Inc............... E 812 284-4470
  Jeffersonville *(G-9957)*

SIC SECTION
35 INDUSTRIAL AND COMMERCIAL MACHINERY AND COMPUTER EQUIPMENT

Component Machine Inc .... G 317 635-8929
 Indianapolis *(G-7845)*
Conrad Machine Co Inc .... G 574 259-1190
 Osceola *(G-13387)*
▲ Contract Indus Tooling Inc .... D 765 966-1134
 Richmond *(G-14110)*
Cope Brothers Machine Shop .... G 219 663-5561
 Leroy *(G-10973)*
Corydon Machine & Tool Co Inc .... E 812 738-3107
 Corydon *(G-2495)*
Country Components Inc .... G 812 345-9594
 Edinburgh *(G-3073)*
County Line Companies LLC .... G 866 959-7866
 Kokomo *(G-10250)*
CPR Machining LLC .... E 574 299-0222
 South Bend *(G-14984)*
Crane Hill Machine Inc .... E 812 358-3534
 Seymour *(G-14641)*
Creative McHining Concepts Inc .... G 317 896-9250
 Westfield *(G-16679)*
Creative Tool and Machining .... E 812 378-3562
 Columbus *(G-2248)*
Cross Road Precision Tool Inc .... G 260 335-2772
 Union City *(G-15851)*
Crossrads Rhbilitation Ctr Inc .... C 317 897-7320
 Indianapolis *(G-7910)*
Cs Precision Machining Inc .... G 260 338-1081
 Huntertown *(G-7252)*
Cullip Industries Inc .... E 574 293-8251
 Elkhart *(G-3279)*
Culver Tool & Engineering Inc .... D 574 935-9611
 Plymouth *(G-13768)*
Cummings Machine Shop .... G 812 275-5542
 Bedford *(G-628)*
Cunningham Pattern & Engrg Inc .... F 812 379-9571
 Columbus *(G-2276)*
Custom Engineering Inc .... F 812 424-3879
 Evansville *(G-4003)*
Custom Engrg & Fabrication Inc .... E 260 745-9299
 Fort Wayne *(G-4898)*
Custom Fab & Weld Inc .... G 574 255-9689
 Mishawaka *(G-11872)*
Custom Honing Inc .... G 574 233-2846
 South Bend *(G-14991)*
Custom Keepsakes Machine EMB .... G 317 894-5506
 Indianapolis *(G-7931)*
◆ Custom Machine Mfr LLC .... E 574 251-0292
 South Bend *(G-14992)*
Custom Machining Services Inc .... G 219 462-6128
 Valparaiso *(G-15932)*
◆ Custom Machining Services Inc .... E 219 462-6128
 Valparaiso *(G-15933)*
Custom Mch Motioneering Inc .... E 574 251-0292
 South Bend *(G-14993)*
Custom Mfg Inc .... G 219 987-7716
 Demotte *(G-2914)*
Customized Machining Inc .... G 765 490-7894
 Columbus *(G-2277)*
Cutting Edge Indus Tech LLC .... G 765 471-7007
 Lafayette *(G-10566)*
Cutting Edge Machine & TI Inc .... D 866 514-1620
 New Paris *(G-12949)*
D & E Machine Inc .... G 765 653-8919
 Greencastle *(G-6402)*
D & M Precision Machining Inc .... G 219 393-5132
 Kingsbury *(G-10176)*
D & S Machine Inc .... G 317 826-2900
 Indianapolis *(G-7941)*
D E Key Machine Shop .... G 765 664-1720
 Marion *(G-11279)*
D To 3-Dimension .... G 219 793-6123
 Griffith *(G-6801)*

D&D Automation Inc .... G 812 299-1045
 Terre Haute *(G-15573)*
Da-Mar Industries Inc .... F 260 347-1662
 Kendallville *(G-10107)*
Daniel Hudelson .... G 812 865-3951
 Orleans *(G-13376)*
David L Huber .... G 812 623-4772
 Sunman *(G-15435)*
Davis Tool & Machine LLC .... F 317 896-9278
 Westfield *(G-16684)*
Dawson Machine Shop Inc .... E 812 649-4777
 Rockport *(G-14339)*
▲ Decatur Mold Tool and Engrg .... C 812 346-5188
 North Vernon *(G-13266)*
Dede Tool & Machine Inc .... G 812 232-7365
 Terre Haute *(G-15578)*
Degood Dmensional Concepts Inc .... F 574 834-5437
 North Webster *(G-13304)*
Dekalb Tool and Engrg LLC .... F 260 357-1500
 Garrett *(G-5858)*
Delbert M Dawson and Son Inc .... G 765 284-9711
 Muncie *(G-12381)*
Dependable Machine Company .... E 317 924-5378
 Indianapolis *(G-7966)*
Dependable Rubber Industrial .... G 765 447-5654
 Lafayette *(G-10569)*
Design & Mfg Solutions LLC .... F 765 478-9393
 Cambridge City *(G-1493)*
Dial-X Automated Equipment Inc .... E 260 636-7588
 Albion *(G-24)*
Die-Namic Ceramics LLC .... G 260 563-7573
 Wabash *(G-16181)*
Die-Rite Machine and Tool Corp .... G 574 522-2366
 Elkhart *(G-3297)*
Dininger Machine Service .... G 317 839-6090
 Cartersburg *(G-1813)*
Disinger Machine Shop .... G 219 567-2357
 Francesville *(G-5638)*
Diverse Fabrication Svcs LLC .... G 317 781-8800
 Indianapolis *(G-7979)*
Diverse Machine Services LLC .... G 317 670-1381
 Indianapolis *(G-7980)*
Divine Machine LLC .... G 812 709-5246
 Shoals *(G-14906)*
Djs Cylinder Service Inc .... G 219 922-4819
 Griffith *(G-6802)*
Dkl Tool & Manufacturing LLC .... G 574 289-2291
 South Bend *(G-15001)*
Don Schumacher Motor Spt Inc .... E 317 286-4380
 Brownsburg *(G-1364)*
Donald Leslie .... G 574 272-3537
 Granger *(G-6345)*
Donaldson Company Inc .... G 765 635-2285
 Anderson *(G-107)*
Dons Automotive and Mch Inc .... G 812 547-6292
 Tell City *(G-15500)*
Dunes Investment Inc .... F 219 764-4270
 Portage *(G-13860)*
Dx 4 LLC .... F 260 749-0632
 Fort Wayne *(G-4935)*
E & M Machining .... G 765 754-3613
 Frankton *(G-5790)*
Eagle Cnc Machining Inc .... F 765 289-2816
 Muncie *(G-12388)*
Eason Manufacturing Inc .... G 312 310-9430
 Griffith *(G-6803)*
Eastside Machine Shop Inc .... G 317 549-2216
 Indianapolis *(G-8040)*
Echelbarger Machining Co LLC .... G 765 252-1965
 Kokomo *(G-10261)*
Edgetek Inc .... G 812 868-1250
 Evansville *(G-4027)*

EDM Services Inc .... G 574 784-3042
 Lakeville *(G-10791)*
Eds Machine & Tool .... G 812 295-7264
 Loogootee *(G-11135)*
Eemsco Inc .... E 812 426-2224
 Evansville *(G-4028)*
Egenolf Contg & Rigging II Inc .... F 317 787-5301
 Indianapolis *(G-8059)*
Egenolf Machine Inc .... F 317 787-5301
 Indianapolis *(G-8061)*
Electro-Tech Inc .... G 219 937-0826
 Hammond *(G-6923)*
Ellis Machine Shop LLC .... G 812 779-7477
 Hazleton *(G-7094)*
Els Inc .... G 812 985-2272
 Evansville *(G-4032)*
Embree Machine Inc .... G 812 275-5729
 Springville *(G-15385)*
Emprotech Steel Services LLC .... E 219 326-6900
 La Porte *(G-10406)*
Endeavor Machined Products Inc .... G 574 232-1940
 South Bend *(G-15014)*
Endeavor Precision Inc .... G 317 903-0532
 Carmel *(G-1621)*
Endeavor Precision Inc .... G 765 557-8694
 Elwood *(G-3824)*
Engel Manufacturing Co Inc .... E 574 232-3800
 South Bend *(G-15015)*
Engineered Industrial Products .... G 317 684-4280
 Indianapolis *(G-8121)*
Esco Enterprises Indiana Inc .... F 317 241-0318
 Indianapolis *(G-8131)*
Evart Engineering Company Inc .... F 765 354-2232
 Middletown *(G-11769)*
Ex-Cut Technology LLC .... F 260 672-9602
 Roanoke *(G-14263)*
Exact-Tech Machining Inc .... F 574 970-0197
 Elkhart *(G-3337)*
Exacto Machine & Tool Inc .... G 317 872-3136
 Indianapolis *(G-8147)*
Excel Machine Company LLC .... G 317 467-0299
 Greenfield *(G-6502)*
Excel Machine Technologies Inc .... E 219 548-0708
 Valparaiso *(G-15945)*
▲ Excel Manufacturing Inc .... D 812 523-6764
 Seymour *(G-14650)*
Excel Tool & Engineering LLC .... G 765 279-8528
 Kirklin *(G-10189)*
Excel Tool Inc .... E 812 522-6880
 Seymour *(G-14651)*
Executive MGT Svcs Ind Inc .... G 317 594-6000
 Indianapolis *(G-8152)*
Express Prcsion Components Inc .... G 317 294-8138
 Indianapolis *(G-8157)*
Extreme Precision Products LLC .... G 812 839-0101
 Madison *(G-11219)*
EZ Cut Tool LLC .... G 260 748-0732
 New Haven *(G-12902)*
F B Mfg .... F 219 406-1318
 Chesterton *(G-1924)*
F S G Inc .... G 574 291-5998
 South Bend *(G-15025)*
Farmers Machine Shop Inc .... G 812 425-1238
 Evansville *(G-4065)*
Faztek LLC .... E 260 482-7544
 Fort Wayne *(G-4979)*
Feddema Industries Inc .... E 260 665-6463
 Angola *(G-250)*
Ferdinand Machine Shop .... G 812 367-2590
 Ferdinand *(G-4431)*
Ferguson Equipment Inc .... G 574 234-4303
 South Bend *(G-15033)*

Employee Codes: A=Over 500 employees, B=251-500
C=101-250, D=51-100, E=20-50, F=10-19, G=1-9

2024 Harris Indiana
Industrial Directory

35 INDUSTRIAL AND COMMERCIAL MACHINERY AND COMPUTER EQUIPMENT — SIC SECTION

Filca LLC .... G 812 637-3559
   Lawrenceburg *(G-10836)*
Fitech Inc .... E 513 398-1414
   Michigan City *(G-11613)*
Flamespray Machine Service .... G 260 726-6236
   Portland *(G-13942)*
▲ Flare Precision LLC .... E 260 490-1101
   Fort Wayne *(G-4985)*
Flenar Manufacturing LLC .... G 574 893-4070
   Rochester *(G-14291)*
Flexible Concepts Inc .... D 574 296-0941
   Elkhart *(G-3350)*
Fmt LLC .... G 260 417-5613
   Fort Wayne *(G-4989)*
Force Cnc LLC .... G 812 273-0218
   Madison *(G-11220)*
Fort Wayne Fabrication Inc .... G 260 704-6618
   Fort Wayne *(G-4993)*
Fortville Feeders Inc .... D 317 485-5195
   Fortville *(G-5595)*
Fourman Enterprises Inc .... F 812 546-5734
   Hope *(G-7225)*
Frank W Martinez .... G 574 232-6081
   South Bend *(G-15038)*
Franks Machine Shop Tool & Die .... G 574 288-6899
   South Bend *(G-15039)*
Fred Anderson .... G 765 985-2099
   Peru *(G-13583)*
Fred Brandt Co .... G 812 926-0009
   Aurora *(G-444)*
Freed Machining and Tool Inc .... G 765 538-3019
   Westpoint *(G-16744)*
Freels Machine Works Inc .... G 260 636-7948
   Albion *(G-27)*
Friskney Gear & Machine Corp .... G 260 281-2200
   Corunna *(G-2482)*
Fuhrman Precision Services Inc .... F 260 728-9600
   Decatur *(G-2857)*
Fullenkamp Machine & Mfg Inc .... F 260 726-8345
   Portland *(G-13944)*
Fulton Industries Inc .... C 574 223-4387
   Rochester *(G-14292)*
▲ Fulton Industries Inc .... E 574 968-3222
   Granger *(G-6347)*
G and P Enterprises Ind Inc .... G 812 723-3837
   Paoli *(G-13495)*
G N Holdings Inc .... E 812 372-9969
   Columbus *(G-2312)*
Garrity Tool Company LLC .... G 317 541-1400
   Indianapolis *(G-8264)*
Gary Bridge and Iron Co Inc .... G 219 884-3792
   Gary *(G-5936)*
Gem City Technologies .... F 937 252-8998
   Elkhart *(G-3369)*
Gemini Machine and Design LLC .... G 812 559-1727
   Jasper *(G-9841)*
General Machine Brokers Inc .... G 260 691-3800
   Columbia City *(G-2149)*
General Machine Solutions Inc .... F 219 378-1700
   East Chicago *(G-3011)*
▲ General Products Delaware .... B 260 668-1440
   Angola *(G-255)*
Generation Four Machine & .... G 219 297-3003
   Goodland *(G-6081)*
Gfw Fabrication .... G 260 333-7252
   Auburn *(G-394)*
Gillum Machine & Tool Inc .... F 765 893-4426
   West Lebanon *(G-16648)*
Gkd Tools LLC .... G 219 309-7758
   Valparaiso *(G-15956)*
Global Air Inc .... G 317 251-1250
   Indianapolis *(G-8288)*

Global Air Inc .... G 317 634-5300
   Indianapolis *(G-8287)*
GMI Corporation .... D 317 736-5116
   Franklin *(G-5733)*
Goad Crankshaft Service Inc .... G 812 477-1127
   Evansville *(G-4091)*
Goad Machine Works Inc .... G 812 385-8985
   Princeton *(G-13996)*
Greenwood Models Inc .... G 317 859-2988
   Greenwood *(G-6710)*
Greenwood Tool and Die Co Inc .... G 219 924-9663
   Griffith *(G-6805)*
Greg Miner .... G 765 647-1012
   Brookville *(G-1322)*
Greys Automotive Inc .... G 317 632-3562
   Indianapolis *(G-8328)*
Grimm Mold & Die Co Inc .... F 219 778-4211
   Rolling Prairie *(G-14363)*
Grindco Inc .... E 219 763-6130
   Chesterton *(G-1932)*
Griner Engineering Inc .... D 812 332-2220
   Bloomington *(G-872)*
GTC Machining LLC .... D 317 541-1400
   Indianapolis *(G-8338)*
GTC Machining LLC .... G 317 541-1400
   Indianapolis *(G-8339)*
Guardian Tech Group Ind LLC .... G 765 364-0863
   Crawfordsville *(G-2574)*
◆ Gvs Technologies LLC .... F 574 293-0974
   Elkhart *(G-3393)*
H & E Machined Specialties .... F 260 424-2527
   Fort Wayne *(G-5045)*
H & H Design & Tool Inc .... G 765 886-6199
   Economy *(G-3066)*
H&E Cutter Grinding Inc .... G 765 825-0541
   Connersville *(G-2439)*
Hadady Machining Company Inc .... F 708 474-8620
   East Chicago *(G-3014)*
Ham Enterprise LLC .... G 317 831-2902
   Martinsville *(G-11398)*
Hamblen Machine Inc .... F 812 330-6685
   Bloomington *(G-874)*
Hamilton Industrial Inc .... G 260 488-3662
   Hamilton *(G-6855)*
Hammond Machine Works Inc .... E 219 933-0479
   Hammond *(G-6942)*
Hanover Machine & Tool Inc .... G 812 265-6265
   Hanover *(G-7042)*
Hawkins Machine & Tool Inc .... G 812 522-5529
   Seymour *(G-14655)*
Hayden Corp .... G 317 501-5660
   Noblesville *(G-13093)*
Haylex Manufacturing LLC .... G 765 288-1818
   Muncie *(G-12411)*
Hdh Manufacturing Inc .... G 317 918-4088
   Indianapolis *(G-8375)*
Hdh Manufacturing Inc .... G 317 918-4088
   Indianapolis *(G-8376)*
Headco Industries Inc .... G 219 924-7758
   Highland *(G-7140)*
Headco Industries Inc .... G 574 288-4471
   South Bend *(G-15062)*
Hedgehog Manufacturing LLC .... G 260 424-9600
   Fort Wayne *(G-5059)*
Herald Machine Werks LLC .... F 219 949-0580
   Gary *(G-5950)*
Hi-Perfrmnce Sperabrasives Inc .... G 317 899-1050
   Indianapolis *(G-8395)*
Hi-Point Machine and Tool Inc .... G 574 831-5361
   New Paris *(G-12956)*
HI-Tech Turning .... G 260 997-6668
   Bryant *(G-1435)*

Highland Machine Tool Inc .... E 812 923-8884
   Floyds Knobs *(G-4681)*
◆ Highway Machine Co Inc .... E 812 385-3639
   Princeton *(G-13998)*
Hilltop Machine Shop LLC .... G 260 768-9196
   Shipshewana *(G-14851)*
Hilltop Mch Sp Haubstadt LLC .... G 812 768-5717
   Haubstadt *(G-7086)*
Hitarth LLC .... G 812 372-1744
   Columbus *(G-2317)*
Hmi Investments LLC .... E 317 736-9387
   Franklin *(G-5739)*
Hobson Tool and Machine Co .... F 317 736-4203
   Franklin *(G-5740)*
Hochbaum Machine Services Inc .... E 219 996-6830
   Hebron *(G-7100)*
Hoosier Box LLC .... G 260 210-3757
   Fort Wayne *(G-5076)*
Hoosier Industrial Supply .... G 574 535-0712
   Goshen *(G-6167)*
Hoosier Machine Company LLC .... G 317 965-5901
   Columbus *(G-2319)*
Horizon Atomtn Fabrication LLC .... G 765 896-9491
   Muncie *(G-12421)*
Horizon Plastics & Engineering .... E 574 674-5443
   Osceola *(G-13394)*
Hose Technology Inc .... E 765 762-5501
   Williamsport *(G-16848)*
▲ Hoverstream LLC .... G 317 489-0075
   Indianapolis *(G-8428)*
Hs Machine Welding .... G 812 752-2825
   Scottsburg *(G-14559)*
Hull Precision Machining Inc .... G 260 238-4372
   Spencerville *(G-15371)*
Humble Industries LLC .... G 219 702-6607
   Gary *(G-5954)*
Hunters Machining Services LLC .... G 219 405-7638
   Shelby *(G-14726)*
Huntingburg Machine Works Inc .... F 812 683-3531
   Huntingburg *(G-7282)*
Hurco International Holdings .... G 317 293-5309
   Indianapolis *(G-8437)*
Huth Tool .... G 260 749-9411
   Fort Wayne *(G-5085)*
Hyco Machine & Mold Inc .... G 574 522-5847
   Elkhart *(G-3414)*
Illiana Grinding Machining Inc .... G 219 306-0253
   East Chicago *(G-3019)*
Imco Industrial Machine Corp .... E 219 663-6100
   Crown Point *(G-2695)*
Indiana Micro Met Etching Inc .... F 574 293-3342
   Mishawaka *(G-11910)*
Indiana Model Company Inc .... D 317 787-6358
   Indianapolis *(G-8484)*
▲ Indiana Research Institute .... G 812 378-4221
   Columbus *(G-2326)*
Industrial Control Service Inc .... G 260 356-4698
   Huntington *(G-7327)*
Industrial Engineering Inc .... E 260 478-1514
   Fort Wayne *(G-5105)*
Industrial Hydraulics Inc .... E 317 247-4421
   Indianapolis *(G-8518)*
Industrial Machine .... G 812 547-5656
   Tell City *(G-15505)*
Industrial Machining Inc .... F 219 663-6100
   Crown Point *(G-2696)*
▲ Industrial Metal-Fab Inc .... E 574 288-8368
   South Bend *(G-15080)*
▲ Industrial Mint Wldg Machining .... E 219 393-5531
   Kingsbury *(G-10179)*
Industrial Pattern Works Inc .... F 219 362-4547
   La Porte *(G-10428)*

SIC SECTION
35 INDUSTRIAL AND COMMERCIAL MACHINERY AND COMPUTER EQUIPMENT

Industrial Rep Inc .... G 260 316-4973
  Fremont *(G-5823)*
Industrial Tool & Mfg Co .... G 219 932-8670
  Hammond *(G-6955)*
Indy Custom Machine Inc .... G 317 271-1544
  Indianapolis *(G-8525)*
Injection Plastics & Mfg Co .... E 574 784-2070
  Lapaz *(G-10816)*
Innovated Machine Service Inc .... G 219 462-4467
  Valparaiso *(G-15975)*
Innovative 3d Mfg LLC .... G 317 560-5080
  Franklin *(G-5747)*
▲ Innovtive Toling Solutions Inc .... F 260 487-9970
  Fort Wayne *(G-5111)*
Instrumental Machine & Dev Inc .... D 574 267-7713
  Warsaw *(G-16379)*
Integra-Tec Machining LLC .... G 574 289-2629
  South Bend *(G-15082)*
Integrity EDM LLC .... G 317 333-7630
  Tipton *(G-15775)*
Integrity Machine Systems Inc .... E 317 897-3338
  New Palestine *(G-12939)*
Iok Technology LLC .... G 812 308-1366
  Rising Sun *(G-14243)*
Iris Rubber Co Inc .... F 317 984-3561
  Cicero *(G-1997)*
Issi Engrg & Machining LLC .... F 317 240-0560
  Indianapolis *(G-8596)*
◆ J & A Machine Inc .... G 260 637-6215
  Garrett *(G-5867)*
J & H Tool Inc .... G 765 724-9691
  Alexandria *(G-53)*
▲ J & J Welding Inc .... G 812 838-4391
  Mount Vernon *(G-12303)*
J & L Tool & Machine Inc .... F 317 398-6281
  Shelbyville *(G-14763)*
J & N Metal Products LLC .... D 812 864-2600
  Brazil *(G-1150)*
J & P Machine Inc .... F 260 357-5157
  Garrett *(G-5868)*
J & R Tool Inc .... F 812 295-2557
  Loogootee *(G-11139)*
▲ J & T Marine Specialists Inc .... G 317 890-9444
  Indianapolis *(G-8600)*
▲ J B Tool Die & Engineering Co .... C 260 483-9586
  Fort Wayne *(G-5123)*
J Henrys Machine Shop LLC .... G 317 917-1052
  Indianapolis *(G-8605)*
J L Harris Machine Co Inc .... G 574 834-2866
  Leesburg *(G-10955)*
J P Corporation .... G 317 783-1000
  Beech Grove *(G-693)*
J R P Machine Products LLP .... G 260 622-4746
  Ossian *(G-13427)*
J V C Machining .... G 219 462-0363
  Valparaiso *(G-15979)*
Jacqmain Machine & Welding .... G 812 726-4409
  Vincennes *(G-16132)*
James E Trowbridge .... G 260 341-1952
  Fort Wayne *(G-5131)*
Jbd Machining .... G 765 671-9050
  Marion *(G-11299)*
Jenco Engineering Inc .... G 574 267-4608
  Warsaw *(G-16380)*
▲ Jennerjahn Machine Inc .... D 765 998-2733
  Marion *(G-11300)*
Jimco Engineering Co .... G 317 923-2290
  Indianapolis *(G-8626)*
Jj Machine .... G 765 366-8258
  Lizton *(G-11050)*
Jj Machine .... G 765 723-1511
  New Ross *(G-12980)*

Jmr Fabrication LLC .... G 317 682-7821
  Carmel *(G-1679)*
JMS Machine Inc .... G 260 244-0077
  Columbia City *(G-2161)*
Jomar Machining & Fabg Inc .... E 574 825-9837
  Middlebury *(G-11728)*
Jones Fbrication Machining Inc .... F 812 466-2237
  Terre Haute *(G-15623)*
Jones Machine & Tool Inc .... E 812 364-4588
  Fredericksburg *(G-5794)*
Jonesys Fabrication LLC .... G 317 504-6511
  Clayton *(G-2060)*
JP Machine Shop LLC .... G 574 453-7617
  Claypool *(G-2054)*
Jt Custom Machine Shop LLC .... G 812 827-1993
  Evansville *(G-4146)*
Jtledm LLC .... G 317 292-2548
  Sullivan *(G-15409)*
JW Machining LLC .... G 812 344-6753
  Columbus *(G-2332)*
K & L Machining Inc .... G 812 526-4840
  Edinburgh *(G-3088)*
K C Cmponents Wldg Fabrication .... G 317 539-6067
  Greencastle *(G-6416)*
K C Machine Inc .... G 574 293-1822
  Elkhart *(G-3442)*
K Tool .... G 574 296-9604
  Elkhart *(G-3445)*
K-Fab Inc .... G 812 663-6299
  Greensburg *(G-6611)*
K&T Performance Engrg LLC .... G 765 437-0185
  Peru *(G-13589)*
Kamplain Machine Company Inc .... G 317 388-9111
  Brownsburg *(G-1380)*
Keller Machine & Welding Inc .... E 219 464-4915
  Valparaiso *(G-15986)*
Ken Anliker .... G 219 984-5676
  Chalmers *(G-1858)*
Ken Kowalski .... G 574 633-4427
  South Bend *(G-15098)*
▲ Kens Tool & Design .... F 812 268-6653
  Sullivan *(G-15411)*
Kentuckiana Machine & Tool Inc .... G 502 593-3975
  Georgetown *(G-6065)*
Kerns Speed Shop .... G 812 275-4289
  Bedford *(G-652)*
Kiesler Machine Inc .... G 812 364-6610
  Palmyra *(G-13482)*
Kilgore Manufacturing Co .... G 260 723-5523
  South Whitley *(G-15320)*
King Investments Inc .... G 812 752-6000
  Scottsburg *(G-14568)*
King Machining Inc .... G 317 271-3132
  Avon *(G-534)*
Kings Custom Machine LLC .... G 812 477-5262
  Haubstadt *(G-7087)*
▲ Kirby Risk Corporation .... D 765 448-4567
  Lafayette *(G-10623)*
Kirk Enterprise Solutions Inc .... G 260 665-3670
  Angola *(G-268)*
Kitterman Machine Co Inc .... G 317 773-2283
  Noblesville *(G-13124)*
▲ Kobelco Cmpsr Mfg Ind Inc .... D 574 295-3145
  Elkhart *(G-3459)*
Kocsis Brothers Machine Co .... G 219 397-8400
  East Chicago *(G-3025)*
KOI Enterprises Inc .... D 812 537-2335
  Lawrenceburg *(G-10843)*
Kokomo Metal Fabricators Inc .... G 765 459-8173
  Kokomo *(G-10292)*
Koma Integration .... G 812 557-6009
  Aurora *(G-448)*

Kortzendorf Machine & Tool .... F 317 783-5449
  Greenwood *(G-6725)*
L & L Engineering Co Inc .... G 317 786-6886
  Beech Grove *(G-698)*
L & P Manufacturing Company .... G 812 405-2093
  Jonesville *(G-10085)*
L & R Machine Co Inc .... G 317 787-7251
  Beech Grove *(G-699)*
L Young Company Inc .... G 219 285-8107
  Morocco *(G-12268)*
La Porte Prcsion Mch Works LLC .... G 219 326-7000
  La Porte *(G-10440)*
Lafayette Quality Products Inc .... F 765 446-0890
  Lafayette *(G-10628)*
Lamb Machine & Tool Co .... G 317 780-9106
  Indianapolis *(G-8715)*
Laminar Fittings Inc .... G 833 855-1020
  Anderson *(G-146)*
Landis Equipment & Tool Rental .... G 812 847-2582
  Linton *(G-11037)*
Lansing Mtllizing Grinding Inc .... G 219 931-1785
  Hammond *(G-6968)*
Lathe Specialties Co Inc .... G 260 244-3629
  Columbia City *(G-2166)*
Layman Fabrication Inc .... G 812 767-2823
  North Vernon *(G-13283)*
Le-Hue Machine and Tool Co .... G 574 255-8404
  Mishawaka *(G-11927)*
Lear Machining & Waterjet Inc .... G 812 418-8111
  Columbus *(G-2338)*
Lee Machine Inc .... F 765 932-3100
  Rushville *(G-14405)*
Leer Custom Machine LLC .... G 317 385-2443
  Springville *(G-15388)*
Leis Machine Shop Inc .... G 574 278-6000
  Buffalo *(G-1439)*
Leme Inc .... E 317 788-4114
  Indianapolis *(G-8736)*
Lengacher Machine Inc .... F 260 657-3114
  Grabill *(G-6308)*
Leonard Eaton Tooling Inc .... F 574 295-5041
  Elkhart *(G-3484)*
Lg Metalworks LLC .... G 812 333-4344
  Bloomington *(G-911)*
Liberty Advance Machine Inc .... G 812 372-1010
  Columbus *(G-2341)*
Liberty Tool and Engrg Inc .... G 765 354-9550
  Middletown *(G-11772)*
Linamar Strctures USA Mich Inc .... F 260 636-7030
  Albion *(G-33)*
Linamar Strctures USA Mich Inc .... E 260 636-1069
  Albion *(G-34)*
Linden Machine Shop LLC .... G 765 339-7244
  Linden *(G-11031)*
◆ Lively Machine Company Inc .... G
  Evansville *(G-4174)*
Loading Dock Maintenance LLC .... G 260 424-3635
  Fort Wayne *(G-5188)*
Lotec Inc .... E 574 294-1506
  Elkhart *(G-3500)*
Lrt Precision Inc .... G 574 223-2578
  Rochester *(G-14302)*
Lycro Products Co Inc .... E 574 862-4981
  Wakarusa *(G-16239)*
Lynn Tool Company Inc .... G 765 874-2471
  Lynn *(G-11185)*
M & S Screw Machine Products .... G 765 853-5022
  Modoc *(G-12053)*
M G Products Inc .... E 574 293-0752
  Elkhart *(G-3505)*
M S & J Quality Screw Mch Pdts .... F 812 623-3002
  Sunman *(G-15441)*

35 INDUSTRIAL AND COMMERCIAL MACHINERY AND COMPUTER EQUIPMENT — SIC SECTION

M-Tech Machine Products LLC............ G 812 637-3500
West Harrison *(G-16549)*

M2 Water Solutions LLC............................ G 317 431-7941
Indianapolis *(G-8806)*

Machine Rebuilders & Service................ F 260 482-8168
Fort Wayne *(G-5197)*

Machine Tool Affiliates Inc...................... G 317 846-3487
Indianapolis *(G-8808)*

Machine Tool Service Inc........................ F 812 232-1912
Terre Haute *(G-15634)*

Machined Castings Spc LLC.................. F 574 223-5694
Rochester *(G-14304)*

Machining & Repr Resource Inc............ G 219 588-7395
Highland *(G-7143)*

Mactech Inc... G 219 734-6503
Portage *(G-13884)*

Magna Machine & Tool Co Inc.............. E 765 766-5388
New Castle *(G-12872)*

Maitland Engineering Inc...................... E 574 287-0155
South Bend *(G-15137)*

Major Tool and Machine Inc.................. A 317 636-6433
Indianapolis *(G-8819)*

◆ Major Tool and Machine Inc.............. C 317 636-6433
Indianapolis *(G-8820)*

Maki Precision Machining LLC............ G 219 575-7995
La Porte *(G-10447)*

Manchester Tool & Die Inc................... D 260 982-8524
North Manchester *(G-13239)*

Manchester Weld and Fab LLC............ G 260 578-5215
North Manchester *(G-13240)*

Manufactured Products Inc.................. G 765 552-2871
Elwood *(G-3831)*

Maple City Machine Inc........................ F 574 533-6742
Goshen *(G-6211)*

Margaret Machine and Tool Co............ G 219 924-0859
Griffith *(G-6813)*

▲ Marion Tool & Die Inc....................... D 812 533-9800
West Terre Haute *(G-16652)*

Maschino Industries Inc....................... G 812 346-3083
North Vernon *(G-13286)*

Master Machine Corp............................ G 317 535-6526
Indianapolis *(G-8850)*

Master Machine Inc............................... G 812 232-6583
Terre Haute *(G-15638)*

Master Metal Machining Inc................. E 574 299-0222
South Bend *(G-15139)*

Master Roll Manufacturing Inc............. G 219 393-7117
La Porte *(G-10448)*

▲ Masterbilt Incorporated.................... F 574 287-6567
South Bend *(G-15140)*

Matts Repair Inc.................................... F 219 696-6765
Lowell *(G-11171)*

Mayfield - Glenn Group Inc.................. F 219 393-7117
Kingsbury *(G-10180)*

MC Wldg & Machining Co Inc.............. G 219 393-5718
Kingsbury *(G-10181)*

McD Machine Incorporated................. G 812 339-1240
Bloomington *(G-916)*

MCI Screwdriver Systems Inc............. F 317 776-1970
Noblesville *(G-13132)*

McKinney Corporation......................... E 765 448-4800
Lafayette *(G-10644)*

Mears Machine Corp............................ E 317 745-0656
Danville *(G-2820)*

Mechancal Engrg Cntrls Atmtn C........ E 574 294-7580
Elkhart *(G-3522)*

Med Grind Inc.. G 574 965-4040
Delphi *(G-2903)*

Medtech LLC... G 330 715-6864
Charlestown *(G-1883)*

Melching Machine Inc.......................... E 260 622-4315
Ossian *(G-13428)*

Mercer Machine Company Inc............. F 317 241-9903
Camby *(G-1512)*

Merit Tool & Manufacturing Inc............ F 765 396-9566
Eaton *(G-3063)*

Mesco Manufacturing LLC................... D 812 663-3870
Greensburg *(G-6618)*

Metal Fabricated Products Co............. G 812 372-7430
Columbus *(G-2352)*

Metalcraft Precision Machining............ E 574 293-6700
Elkhart *(G-3527)*

▲ Metaltec Inc....................................... G 219 362-9811
La Porte *(G-10452)*

Metcalf Engineering Inc....................... G 765 342-6792
Indianapolis *(G-8893)*

Meyer Engineering Inc......................... F 812 663-6535
Greensburg *(G-6619)*

Meyer Oil Co... F 812 746-9525
Evansville *(G-4200)*

Michfab Machinery............................... G 260 244-6117
Columbia City *(G-2170)*

Micro Machine Works Inc.................... G 574 293-1354
Elkhart *(G-3535)*

▼ Micromatic LLC................................. D 260 589-2136
Berne *(G-720)*

Mid-States Tool & Machine Inc............ E 260 728-9797
Decatur *(G-2873)*

Mid-West Metal Products Co Inc......... E 765 741-3140
Muncie *(G-12453)*

Midcounty Machining Inc..................... G 219 992-9380
Demotte *(G-2924)*

Midwest Accurate Grinding Svc.......... F 219 696-4060
Lowell *(G-11172)*

Midwest Earthworks LLC..................... G 812 486-2443
Montgomery *(G-12115)*

Midwest Machining & Fabg.................. F 219 924-0206
Griffith *(G-6814)*

Midwest Machining LLC...................... G 212 696-7322
Nappanee *(G-12622)*

Midwest Mwi Inc................................... G 574 288-6573
Mishawaka *(G-11950)*

Midwest Precision Machining.............. G 260 459-6866
Fort Wayne *(G-5225)*

Miller Machine and Welding LLC........ G 812 882-7566
Vincennes *(G-16140)*

Miller Machine Shop Inc LLC.............. F 574 646-2900
Nappanee *(G-12625)*

Millers Wldg & Mech Svcs Inc............. G 812 923-3359
Pekin *(G-13519)*

Millwright Machine Inc......................... F 219 845-9200
Gary *(G-5983)*

Mining Machine Parts Inc.................... G 812 897-1256
Boonville *(G-1092)*

Minnich Manufacturing Inc.................. G 260 489-5357
Fort Wayne *(G-5230)*

Mitchum-Schaefer Inc.......................... E 317 546-4081
Indianapolis *(G-8935)*

Mixer Direct LLC.................................. D 812 202-4047
Jeffersonville *(G-10020)*

▲ Models LLC....................................... E 765 676-6700
Lebanon *(G-10917)*

Modern Machine & Grinding Inc......... E 219 322-1201
Dyer *(G-2978)*

Modern Machine & Tool Inc................ G 765 934-3110
Van Buren *(G-16086)*

Monroe Manufacturing Tech Inc.......... G 317 782-1005
Indianapolis *(G-8950)*

Moore Machine & Gear Inc................. E 812 963-3074
Evansville *(G-4212)*

Moore Precision Machining LLC........ G 765 265-2386
Connersville *(G-2457)*

Morehead Machinery Inc..................... G 574 651-8671
Elkhart *(G-3552)*

Morris Holding Company LLC............ C 812 446-6141
Brazil *(G-1154)*

Morris Machine & Tool........................ G 219 866-3018
Rensselaer *(G-14060)*

Morris Machine Co Inc........................ D 317 788-0371
Indianapolis *(G-8954)*

Morris Mfg & Sls Corp......................... C 812 446-6141
Brazil *(G-1155)*

Mosey Manufacturing Co Inc.............. E 765 983-8800
Richmond *(G-14172)*

Motsinger Auto Supply Inc.................. G 317 782-8484
Indianapolis *(G-8960)*

Mpp Inc... E 260 422-5426
Fort Wayne *(G-5248)*

Mqp Machining LLC............................ G 812 278-8374
Springville *(G-15389)*

Mtm Machining Inc.............................. F 219 872-8677
Michigan City *(G-11642)*

Mudhole Machine Shop LLC.............. G 765 533-4228
Middletown *(G-11775)*

Multiple Machining.............................. G 812 926-0798
Aurora *(G-450)*

Multiple Machining Inc........................ E 812 432-5946
Dillsboro *(G-2950)*

Nathan Millis Tools LLC...................... G 219 996-3305
Hebron *(G-7103)*

Nector Machine & Fabricating............. G 219 322-6878
Schererville *(G-14536)*

Nicholas Precision Works LLC........... G 260 306-3426
North Manchester *(G-13244)*

Nixon Tool Company Inc..................... E 765 966-6608
Richmond *(G-14175)*

Nmc Inc.. E 812 648-2636
Dugger *(G-2959)*

Noblitt International Corp.................... F 812 372-9969
Columbus *(G-2360)*

Noneman Machine Corp..................... G 260 632-5311
Woodburn *(G-16955)*

North-Side Machine & Tool Inc........... F 765 654-4538
Frankfort *(G-5686)*

▲ Northeast Quality Services LLC....... E 860 632-7242
West Lafayette *(G-16614)*

Northern Foundry LLC........................ G 218 263-8871
Auburn *(G-413)*

▲ Northern Indiana Manufacturing...... E 574 342-2105
Bourbon *(G-1125)*

Northside Machining Inc..................... G 812 683-3500
Huntingburg *(G-7288)*

Nortool Precision Machining Tl.......... G 574 262-3400
Elkhart *(G-3576)*

Novamatiq Inc...................................... E 260 483-1153
Fort Wayne *(G-5277)*

Numerical Concepts Inc..................... E 812 466-5261
Terre Haute *(G-15654)*

▲ Numerical Productions Inc.............. D 317 783-1362
Indianapolis *(G-9034)*

Numerix Inc.. G 260 248-2942
Columbia City *(G-2175)*

Oak View Tooling Inc.......................... F 260 244-7677
Columbia City *(G-2176)*

Oakley Industries LLC........................ G 812 246-2600
Sellersburg *(G-14608)*

Odyssey Machine Inc.......................... G 812 951-1160
Georgetown *(G-6072)*

Ogre Holdings Inc............................... F 765 675-8841
Tipton *(G-15785)*

Ohio Valley Precision Inc................... F 812 539-3687
Lawrenceburg *(G-10849)*

OHM Enterprise LLC........................... G 812 879-5455
Gosport *(G-6288)*

Oliver Machine & Tl Corp................... F 765 349-2271
Martinsville *(G-11419)*

SIC SECTION
35 INDUSTRIAL AND COMMERCIAL MACHINERY AND COMPUTER EQUIPMENT

Oliver Machine and Tool Corp .... F 765 349-2271
  Mooresville (G-12230)
Olson Custom Designs LLC .... E 317 892-6400
  Indianapolis (G-9046)
On Point Machining Inc .... G 219 393-5132
  Kingsbury (G-10183)
Opi Inc .... G
  Albion (G-38)
Ottinger Machine Co .... G 317 654-1700
  Indianapolis (G-9075)
Ottosons Industries Inc .... G 219 365-8330
  Cedar Lake (G-1835)
P & A Machine Company Inc .... G 317 634-3673
  Bargersville (G-571)
P & J Tool Co Inc .... G 317 546-4858
  Indianapolis (G-9078)
P M Fabricating Incorporated .... G 219 362-9926
  La Porte (G-10462)
P O C Industries Inc .... G 765 645-5015
  Mays (G-11445)
P T I Machining Inc .... G 765 564-9966
  Delphi (G-2905)
Pallatin Machine LLC .... G 574 703-7505
  Mishawaka (G-11969)
Pamela Taulman .... F 812 378-5008
  Columbus (G-2372)
Paradise Machine and Tool Corp .... G 317 247-4606
  Indianapolis (G-9091)
Paragon Force Inc .... D 812 384-3040
  Bloomfield (G-755)
Parametric Machining Inc .... F 260 338-1564
  Huntertown (G-7260)
Parker-Hannifin Corporation .... E 260 587-9102
  Ashley (G-335)
▲ Patriot Products LLC .... G 317 736-8007
  Franklin (G-5765)
Paynter Machine Works Inc .... G 812 883-2808
  Salem (G-14496)
Peerless Pattern & Machine Co .... G 765 477-7719
  Lafayette (G-10666)
▼ Perfecto Tool & Engineering Co .... E 765 644-2821
  Anderson (G-176)
Performance Machining Inc .... G 812 432-9180
  Dillsboro (G-2951)
Pgi Mfg LLC .... E 574 968-3222
  Granger (G-6369)
Phelps Machine Inc .... G 765 468-6791
  Parker City (G-13505)
Photon Automation Inc .... F 844 574-6866
  Greenfield (G-6538)
Photon Automation Inc .... C 844 574-6866
  Greenfield (G-6539)
Piercy Machine Co Inc .... G 317 398-9296
  Shelbyville (G-14782)
Pinson Manufacturing Co LLC .... G 217 273-8819
  Albany (G-14)
Piper Flyers II Inc .... E 317 858-9538
  Zionsville (G-17042)
Pivot Manufacturing Inc .... G 317 371-3560
  Yorktown (G-16981)
Ploog Engineering Co Inc .... G 219 663-2854
  Crown Point (G-2731)
Plymouth Foundry Inc .... E 574 936-2106
  Plymouth (G-13801)
Powder Metal Technicians Inc .... G 317 353-2812
  Franklin (G-5768)
Prairies Edge Machining Inc .... G 765 986-2222
  Williamsport (G-16852)
Prather Machining Inc .... G 812 401-7556
  Memphis (G-11466)
Precision Abrasive Machinery .... G 765 378-3315
  Daleville (G-2801)

Precision Agronomy .... G 219 552-0032
  Lowell (G-11176)
Precision Benders Incorporated .... G 574 658-9317
  Milford (G-11803)
Precision Cadcam Incorporated .... G 317 353-8058
  Indianapolis (G-9179)
Precision Cams Inc .... F 317 631-9100
  Indianapolis (G-9181)
▲ Precision Electric Inc .... E 574 256-1000
  Mishawaka (G-11977)
Precision Enterprises LLC .... G 812 873-6391
  Paris Crossing (G-13504)
Precision Fiber Solutions LLC .... G 317 421-9642
  Bargersville (G-572)
Precision Laser .... G 812 295-2200
  Loogootee (G-11147)
▼ Precision Laser Services Inc .... E 260 744-4375
  Fort Wayne (G-5339)
Precision Machined Pdts LLC .... G 260 908-4766
  Kendallville (G-10144)
Precision Medical Tech Inc .... E 574 267-6385
  Warsaw (G-16412)
Precision Services Inc .... G 812 602-8375
  Evansville (G-4255)
Pro Finish .... G 618 771-7207
  Evansville (G-4259)
Pro Finish Mold Polishing .... G 618 922-8161
  Evansville (G-4260)
Prodigy Mold & Tool Inc .... E 812 753-3029
  Haubstadt (G-7088)
Production Machining Company .... G 812 466-2885
  Terre Haute (G-15672)
Progress Group Inc .... D 219 322-3700
  Schererville (G-14539)
Promotor Engines & Components ...... G 574 533-9898
  Goshen (G-6243)
Provident Tool & Die Inc .... G 574 862-1233
  Wakarusa (G-16245)
Qig LLC .... G 260 244-3591
  Columbia City (G-2185)
Qsi Custom Machining .... G 260 636-2341
  Albion (G-42)
Quake Manufacturing Inc .... F 260 432-8023
  Fort Wayne (G-5362)
▲ Quality Machine & Tool Works .... D 812 379-2660
  Columbus (G-2383)
Quality Mch Repr & Engrg Inc .... G 317 375-1366
  Pittsboro (G-13653)
Quality Tool & Machine Co .... G 219 464-2411
  Valparaiso (G-16033)
Quicks Machine and Tool Inc .... G 812 952-2135
  Corydon (G-2513)
R & B Mold and Die Inc .... F 219 324-4176
  La Porte (G-10470)
R & D Machine Shop Inc .... G 574 946-6109
  Winamac (G-16873)
▲ Rauch Inc .... E 812 945-4063
  New Albany (G-12803)
Rayco Mch & Engrg Group Inc .... E 317 291-7848
  Indianapolis (G-9268)
Rayco Steel Process Inc .... F 574 267-7676
  Warsaw (G-16415)
RB Machine Company .... G 765 364-6716
  Crawfordsville (G-2612)
Reber Machine & Tool Co Inc .... E 765 288-0297
  Muncie (G-12485)
Reeder & Kline Machine Co Inc .... F 317 846-6591
  Carmel (G-1737)
Rehco Products Inc .... G 317 984-3319
  Arcadia (G-317)
Reliable Tool & Machine Co .... F 260 347-4000
  Kendallville (G-10148)

Reliable Tool & Machine Co .... F 260 347-4000
  Kendallville (G-10149)
Reliable Tool & Machine Co .... E 260 343-7150
  Kendallville (G-10150)
Reliance Machine Company Inc .... G 765 857-1000
  Ridgeville (G-14237)
Reliance Machine Company Inc .... D 765 284-0151
  Muncie (G-12488)
Reliant Engineering Inc .... E 317 322-9084
  Indianapolis (G-9288)
Remington Machine Inc .... F 765 724-3389
  Alexandria (G-60)
Reuer Machine & Tool Inc .... G 219 362-2894
  La Porte (G-10472)
Reynolds & Co Inc .... E 812 232-5313
  Terre Haute (G-15681)
Reynolds North .... G 812 235-5313
  Terre Haute (G-15682)
Rf Manufacturing Inc .... G 317 773-8610
  Noblesville (G-13167)
Rhodes Tool & Machine Inc .... G 812 729-7134
  Owensville (G-13472)
Rhyne Engines Inc .... G 219 845-1218
  Gary (G-6004)
Richards Complete Machine Shop ...... G 317 856-9163
  Indianapolis (G-9301)
Richters Machine & Tool .... G 260 495-5327
  Fremont (G-5833)
Rix Laser Processing .... G 812 537-9230
  Lawrenceburg (G-10857)
Rk Machine Inc .... F 812 466-0550
  Terre Haute (G-15683)
Rmt Inc .... F 260 637-4649
  Huntertown (G-7265)
Rob Passarelli .... G 317 340-8597
  Carmel (G-1743)
Rodex Machining .... G 260 768-4844
  Shipshewana (G-14884)
Rohder Machine & Tool Inc .... G 219 663-3697
  Crown Point (G-2747)
Ron Osborne Machining Inc .... G 812 637-1045
  Lawrenceburg (G-10858)
Rose Engineering Company Inc .... G 317 788-4446
  Indianapolis (G-9333)
Ross Machining .... G 765 998-2400
  Upland (G-15881)
Rotam Tooling Corporation .... G 260 982-8318
  North Manchester (G-13248)
Royal Machining & Repair LLC .... G 765 529-3545
  New Castle (G-12882)
Royalty Investments LLC .... E 812 358-3534
  Seymour (G-14682)
RPM Machinery LLC .... G 574 271-0800
  South Bend (G-15228)
Rs Precision Machining .... G 219 362-4560
  La Porte (G-10475)
Rumohr .... G 317 750-5911
  Carmel (G-1749)
Russell L Rooksberry .... G 812 659-1683
  Carlisle (G-1543)
▲ Russell Metal Products .... F 317 841-9003
  Fishers (G-4601)
Ryan Lane .... G 317 475-9730
  Indianapolis (G-9351)
S & S Components Inc .... G 812 734-1104
  Corydon (G-2514)
S Edwards Inc .... G 317 831-0261
  Mooresville (G-12240)
S&A Tooling .... G 502 836-3886
  Floyds Knobs (G-4692)
Sabina LLC .... G 574 903-4688
  Elkhart (G-3657)

35 INDUSTRIAL AND COMMERCIAL MACHINERY AND COMPUTER EQUIPMENT — SIC SECTION

San Mar..E 574 286-6884
  South Bend (G-15231)
Sardinia Machine Incorporated...............G 812 591-2091
  Westport (G-16751)
Sauers Racing Auto Machines.................G 812 265-2803
  Madison (G-11251)
Schaefer Technologies Inc.......................D 317 241-9444
  Indianapolis (G-9388)
Scheiner Art & Fabrication LLC...............G 800 998-9345
  Lawrenceburg (G-10859)
Schlatters Inc..G 219 567-9158
  Francesville (G-5645)
Scutt Tool & Die Inc..................................G 317 858-8725
  Brownsburg (G-1401)
Selco Engineering Inc..............................F
  Shelbyville (G-14795)
Select Tool and Eng Inc..........................G 574 295-6197
  Elkhart (G-3667)
Seymour Prcision Machining Inc............G 812 524-1813
  Seymour (G-14690)
Shaw Machine Works..............................G 260 356-4297
  Huntington (G-7367)
Sheridan Manufacturing Co Inc..............G 317 758-6000
  Sheridan (G-14828)
Shorts Machine Shop..............................G 765 622-6259
  Anderson (G-191)
Shull Mch & Firearms Svc Inc.................G 260 925-4198
  Butler (G-1477)
Singleton Machine Inc............................E 574 656-3400
  North Liberty (G-13225)
Sites-Workman Holdings Inc..................E 574 267-1503
  Warsaw (G-16424)
Smiths Small Engines Inc.......................G 812 232-1318
  Terre Haute (G-15699)
Snavelys Machine & Mfg Co Inc.............C 765 473-8395
  Peru (G-13601)
Sordelet Tool & Die Inc............................G 260 483-7258
  Columbia City (G-2199)
Southern Indiana Waterjet LLC...............G 812 457-3201
  Evansville (G-4324)
Sovern Machining & Welding..................G 812 392-2532
  Scipio (G-14551)
Specialty Machine and Cnc Inc...............F 765 346-0774
  Battle Ground (G-614)
Specilty Blnks Inc An Ind Corp................G 812 234-3002
  Terre Haute (G-15711)
Spencer Machine and Tl Co Inc..............E 812 282-6300
  Jeffersonville (G-10057)
Spreuer & Son Inc....................................F 260 463-3513
  Lagrange (G-10763)
Square 1 Dsign Manufacture Inc............F 866 647-7771
  Shelbyville (G-14800)
SSd Control Technology Inc....................E 574 289-5942
  South Bend (G-15264)
St Clair Group Inc.....................................D 765 435-3091
  Russellville (G-14419)
St Lenzer LLC...G 260 441-9300
  Fort Wayne (G-5434)
Stamina Metal Products Inc....................G 574 534-7410
  Goshen (G-6258)
Standish Steel Inc....................................F 812 834-5255
  Bedford (G-674)
◆ Star Engineering & Mch Co Inc............E 260 824-4825
  Bluffton (G-1057)
Star Tool & Die Inc...................................F 574 264-3815
  Elkhart (G-3698)
Stark Precision Machine LLC.................G 812 239-5291
  Terre Haute (G-15715)
Stephens Dynamics Inc..........................G 765 459-4451
  Kokomo (G-10340)
Stephens Machine Inc............................E 765 459-9770
  Kokomo (G-10342)

Stephens Machine Inc............................F 765 459-4017
  Kokomo (G-10341)
Sterling Industries Inc............................E 812 376-6560
  Columbus (G-2396)
Sterling Machine Co Inc.........................G 219 374-9360
  Cedar Lake (G-1838)
Steve Mitchell..G 574 831-4848
  New Paris (G-12969)
▲ Steve Schmidt Racing Engines..........F 317 898-1831
  Indianapolis (G-9508)
Steves Machining & Rework..................G 317 500-4627
  Franklin (G-5779)
Stoney Creek Wash Machine Shop........G 574 642-1155
  Millersburg (G-11818)
Stout Field Ind Partners.........................G 317 247-7486
  Indianapolis (G-9516)
Stout Laser Etch LLC..............................G 574 376-9296
  Warsaw (G-16429)
Stresco Machine Inc...............................G 574 773-7334
  Nappanee (G-12646)
Stulls Mch & Fabrication Inc..................G 765 942-2717
  Ladoga (G-10511)
Stump & Grind...G 812 453-2121
  Elberfeld (G-3120)
Summit Mfg & Machining Inc.................F 574 546-4571
  Bremen (G-1225)
Sun Engineering Inc...............................E 219 962-1191
  Lake Station (G-10778)
Sunman Engineering Inc........................G 812 623-4072
  Sunman (G-15446)
Superb Tooling Inc..................................F 812 367-2102
  Ferdinand (G-4449)
Superior Machine & Tool Co...................F 260 493-4517
  Fort Wayne (G-5460)
Superior Machine Incorporated.............G 574 654-8243
  New Carlisle (G-12846)
Superior Piece Parts Inc.........................F 574 277-4236
  Mishawaka (G-12011)
Superior Tool & Die Co Inc.....................E 574 293-2591
  Elkhart (G-3710)
Swansons Service Center......................G 574 858-9406
  Atwood (G-358)
Swiss Labs Machine & Engrg Inc..........G 317 346-6190
  Franklin (G-5780)
Syltech Experimental.............................G 765 489-1777
  Hagerstown (G-6843)
System Science Institute.......................G 260 436-6096
  Fort Wayne (G-5465)
T & M Precision Inc.................................G 513 253-2274
  Versailles (G-16105)
T & M Precision Inc.................................G 812 689-5769
  Versailles (G-16104)
T F & T Inc...G 765 874-1628
  Lynn (G-11188)
T K Fabricating..G 765 866-0755
  Crawfordsville (G-2622)
T K M Triple K Machining........................G 765 629-2805
  Rushville (G-14414)
T L Tate Manufacturing Inc....................G 765 452-8283
  Kokomo (G-10346)
T Shorter Manufacturing Inc..................G 574 264-4131
  Elkhart (G-3713)
T W Machine & Grinding........................G 260 799-4236
  Columbia City (G-2205)
T-Mack Machinery LLC..........................G 765 728-8655
  Montpelier (G-12183)
T-N-T Performance Mch Sp LLC............G 574 457-5056
  Syracuse (G-15483)
Taberts Machine Shop...........................G 765 464-9181
  Templeton (G-15522)
Tasco Industries Inc...............................G 219 922-6100
  Highland (G-7157)

Task Force Tips Inc.................................F 219 462-6161
  Valparaiso (G-16063)
Taurus Tech & Engrg LLC......................E 765 282-2090
  Muncie (G-12498)
Taurus Tool & Engineering Inc..............G 765 282-2090
  Muncie (G-12499)
Tech Castings LLC.................................E 765 535-4100
  Shirley (G-14902)
Technical Equipment Sales LLC............G 260 445-1008
  Fort Wayne (G-5472)
Teleios Inc...G 317 509-1596
  Carmel (G-1782)
Teresa L Powell CPA...............................G 765 962-1862
  Richmond (G-14214)
Terrel Automotive Machine Inc..............G 812 883-3859
  Salem (G-14503)
Test Rite Systems & Mfg Co LLC...........G 317 736-9192
  Franklin (G-5781)
▲ Tgm Manufacturing Inc......................F 260 758-3055
  Uniondale (G-15873)
◆ Thermwood Corporation.....................D 812 937-4476
  Dale (G-2794)
Thomas Cubit Inc...................................G 219 933-0566
  Hammond (G-7019)
▲ Thomas/Euclid Industries Inc............D 317 783-7171
  Indianapolis (G-9596)
Three Daughters Corp............................E 260 925-2128
  Auburn (G-430)
Titan Metal Worx LLC.............................E 260 422-4433
  Fort Wayne (G-5490)
Titus Inc...F 574 936-3345
  Plymouth (G-13817)
Tlk Precision Inc.....................................G 317 427-0123
  Fairland (G-4404)
▼ Tmak Inc..E 219 874-7661
  Michigan City (G-11679)
Tool Room Service..................................G 765 287-0062
  Muncie (G-12507)
Tool Source Inc.......................................G 765 778-0777
  Pendleton (G-13558)
Top Notch Tool and Engrg Inc................G 812 663-2184
  Greensburg (G-6635)
Total Tote Inc..G 260 982-8318
  North Manchester (G-13252)
Touchdown Machining Inc.....................G 812 378-0300
  Columbus (G-2405)
Tr Manufacturing LLC............................G 260 357-4679
  Garrett (G-5878)
Tradeline Fabricating Inc.......................E 812 637-1444
  Lawrenceburg (G-10862)
▼ Tree City Tool & Engrg Co Inc............E 812 663-4196
  Greensburg (G-6637)
Trg Wind..G 507 829-6695
  Noblesville (G-13183)
Tri Aerospace LLC..................................E 812 872-2400
  Terre Haute (G-15736)
Tri-K Machining Inc................................F 317 244-7724
  Danville (G-2829)
▲ Tri-State Industries Inc......................D 219 933-1710
  Hammond (G-7023)
Tri-State Machining Inc..........................G 260 422-2508
  Fort Wayne (G-5505)
Triangle Engineering Corp......................D 317 243-8549
  Indianapolis (G-9639)
Triangle Machine Inc..............................G 574 246-0165
  South Bend (G-15292)
Triple J Machining and Mfg Inc..............F 574 586-7500
  Walkerton (G-16277)
Troyer Brothers..E 260 589-2244
  Decatur (G-2887)
▲ Tru-Flex Real Estate Holdings LLC....D 765 893-4403
  West Lebanon (G-16650)

SIC SECTION
36 ELECTRONIC & OTHER ELECTRICAL EQUIPMENT & COMPONENTS

True Blue Company LLC .... E 219 324-8482
La Porte *(G-10495)*

True Precision Tech Inc .... G 765 432-2177
Kokomo *(G-10352)*

TT Machining & Fabricating LLC .... F 219 878-0399
Michigan City *(G-11681)*

Tube Form Solutions LLC .... G 574 266-5230
Elkhart *(G-3752)*

▲ Tube Form Solutions LLC .... E 574 295-5041
Elkhart *(G-3751)*

Turner Machine Co .... G 317 751-5105
Indianapolis *(G-9661)*

Turners Machining Specialties Inc .... E 812 372-9472
Columbus *(G-2407)*

Tww Fabricaton & Machine LLC .... G 985 637-8234
Brownsburg *(G-1411)*

U S Accu-Met Inc .... G 765 533-4219
Middletown *(G-11779)*

◆ Union Tool Corp .... E 574 267-3211
Warsaw *(G-16440)*

United Machine & Tool LLC .... G 260 749-8880
Fort Wayne *(G-5520)*

United Machine Corporation .... E 219 548-8050
Valparaiso *(G-16072)*

United Tool Company Inc .... F 260 563-3143
Wabash *(G-16219)*

Universal Metalcraft Inc .... E 260 547-4457
Decatur *(G-2888)*

Universal Precision Instrs Inc .... G 574 264-3997
Elkhart *(G-3763)*

Universal Tool & Engrg Co .... E 317 842-8999
Fishers *(G-4621)*

US Automation LLC .... G 260 338-1100
Huntertown *(G-7267)*

US Valves Inc .... G 812 476-6662
Evansville *(G-4365)*

Uway Extrusion LLC .... G 765 592-6089
Marshall *(G-11375)*

V I P Tooling Inc .... E 317 398-0753
Shelbyville *(G-14810)*

Val Rollers Incorporated .... G 317 542-1968
Indianapolis *(G-9698)*

Valad McHning Cntrless Grnding .... G 574 291-5541
South Bend *(G-15299)*

Valpariso Area Apprntceship Adv .... G 219 613-6226
Griffith *(G-6822)*

Value Tool & Engineering Inc .... D 574 246-1913
South Bend *(G-15301)*

Van Co .... F 574 271-8432
Mishawaka *(G-12021)*

Vanguard Machine Inc .... F 260 508-6044
Columbia City *(G-2210)*

Versatile Fabrication LLC .... G 574 293-8504
Elkhart *(G-3769)*

Vigo Machine Shop Inc .... E 812 235-8393
Terre Haute *(G-15740)*

Vincennes Welding Co Inc .... F 812 882-9682
Vincennes *(G-16160)*

Vision Machine Works Inc .... F 574 259-6500
Mishawaka *(G-12022)*

Voege Precision Mch Pdts LLC .... G 317 867-4699
Westfield *(G-16737)*

Voges Machine .... G 812 299-1546
Terre Haute *(G-15741)*

Vorzeigen Machining Inc .... E 765 827-1500
Connersville *(G-2474)*

W T Boone Enterprises Inc .... G 317 738-0275
Franklin *(G-5784)*

Wagler Machining LLC .... G 812 866-2904
Lexington *(G-10982)*

Wagner Tool Grinding Inc .... G 260 426-5145
Fort Wayne *(G-5539)*

▲ Walerko Tool and Engrg Corp .... E 574 295-2233
Elkhart *(G-3777)*

Walkerton Tool & Die Inc .... E 574 586-3162
Walkerton *(G-16279)*

Wallace Legacy 1 Inc .... E 812 944-9368
New Albany *(G-12827)*

Wallace Legacy 2 LLC .... F 812 944-9368
New Albany *(G-12828)*

Waterfield Automotive Mch Sp .... G 765 288-6262
Muncie *(G-12515)*

Waterjet Cutting Indiana Inc .... G 317 328-8444
Indianapolis *(G-9740)*

Waterjet Fabricating LLC .... G 765 288-4575
Muncie *(G-12516)*

Wauseon MCHne&mfg-Kndlvlle Div .... E 260 347-5095
Kendallville *(G-10154)*

Wayne Machine Mfrs Inc .... G 765 962-0459
Richmond *(G-14224)*

West Vigo Machine Shop Inc .... F 812 533-1961
West Terre Haute *(G-16658)*

Wg Machine & Tool .... G 317 994-5556
Lizton *(G-11051)*

Wgs Global Services LC .... G 810 239-4947
Tell City *(G-15521)*

Whitcraft Enterprises Inc .... F 260 422-6518
Fort Wayne *(G-5564)*

White Machine Inc .... G 574 267-5895
Warsaw *(G-16449)*

Wilcoxen Machine & Tool Inc .... G 317 784-4665
Indianapolis *(G-9764)*

William F Shirley .... G 812 426-2599
Evansville *(G-4385)*

Williams Tool & Machine Corp .... F 765 676-5859
Jamestown *(G-9821)*

Willis Machining Inc .... G 812 744-1100
Aurora *(G-461)*

Wilson Machine Shop Inc .... G 812 392-2774
Elizabethtown *(G-3134)*

Winn Machine Inc .... G 219 324-2978
La Porte *(G-10501)*

Wirco Inc .... C 260 897-3768
Avilla *(G-500)*

Wirecut Technologies Inc .... G 317 885-9915
Indianapolis *(G-9775)*

Wk-Rpe Inc .... G 317 739-3543
Franklin *(G-5788)*

Woehr Tool & Die .... G 408 313-1708
Elizabethtown *(G-3135)*

Wolfe and Swickard Mch Co Inc .... D 317 241-2589
Indianapolis *(G-9782)*

Woodruff Automotive LLC .... G 812 636-4908
Odon *(G-13358)*

Workrite Machine & Tool Inc .... E 260 489-4778
Fort Wayne *(G-5576)*

XYZ Machining Inc .... G 574 269-5541
Warsaw *(G-16457)*

Young Cimtech LLC .... E 812 948-1472
New Albany *(G-12832)*

Young Machine Company Inc .... G 812 944-5807
New Albany *(G-12833)*

36 ELECTRONIC & OTHER ELECTRICAL EQUIPMENT & COMPONENTS

3612 Transformers, except electric

ABB Enterprise Software Inc .... E 317 876-9090
Indianapolis *(G-7413)*

ABB Inc .... F 941 278-2200
Evansville *(G-3863)*

Ball Systems Inc .... E 317 804-2330
Westfield *(G-16667)*

▲ Coil-Tran LLC .... D 219 942-8511
Hobart *(G-7182)*

▲ Custom Magnetics Inc .... E 260 982-8508
North Manchester *(G-13231)*

Gasco LLC .... G 317 565-5000
Noblesville *(G-13083)*

General Transmission Pdts LLC .... G 574 284-2917
South Bend *(G-15043)*

Hoffmaster Electric Inc .... G 219 616-1313
Schererville *(G-14523)*

Kay Industries Inc .... G 574 236-6220
Nappanee *(G-12617)*

Protron LLC .... G 765 313-1595
Anderson *(G-181)*

R & R Regulators Inc .... F 574 522-3500
Elkhart *(G-3636)*

RB Annis Instruments Inc .... G 765 848-1621
Greencastle *(G-6428)*

Schaffner LLC .... G 317 450-3956
Indianapolis *(G-9389)*

Schneider Electric Usa Inc .... D 260 356-2060
Huntington *(G-7366)*

Weg Electric Corp .... D 260 827-2200
Bluffton *(G-1070)*

Whiting Clean Energy Inc .... E 219 473-0653
Whiting *(G-16840)*

▲ Xfmrs Inc .... A 317 834-1066
Camby *(G-1517)*

3613 Switchgear and switchboard apparatus

Advance MCS Electronics Inc .... G 574 642-3501
Ligonier *(G-11002)*

◆ Advance MCS Electronics Inc .... G 574 642-3501
Goshen *(G-6089)*

▲ American Technology Compo .... C 800 238-2687
Elkhart *(G-3177)*

Automation Control Service .... G 812 472-3292
Hardinsburg *(G-7047)*

Ayco Panel .... G 765 635-8106
Jasonville *(G-9822)*

Blinkless Power Equipment LLC .... G 317 844-7328
Indianapolis *(G-7642)*

Bonner & Associates .... G 317 571-1911
Carmel *(G-1571)*

Bryant Control Inc .... F 317 549-3355
Fishers *(G-4477)*

Burt Products Inc .... G 812 386-6890
Princeton *(G-13986)*

Caddo Connections Inc .... E 219 874-8119
La Porte *(G-10393)*

▼ Control Consultants of America .... G 219 989-3311
Hammond *(G-6905)*

Controlled Automation Inc .... F 317 770-3870
Noblesville *(G-13062)*

CTS Corporation .... G 574 293-7511
Berne *(G-707)*

▲ Custom Magnetics Inc .... E 260 982-8508
North Manchester *(G-13231)*

Direct Control Systems Inc .... G 765 282-7474
Muncie *(G-12384)*

Extrasurplus LLC .... G 252 619-8604
Gary *(G-5931)*

▼ Fabtration LLC .... F 812 989-6730
Georgetown *(G-6060)*

Hoffmaster Electric Inc .... G 219 616-1313
Schererville *(G-14523)*

Integrated Tech Resources .... G 317 757-5432
Indianapolis *(G-8569)*

Integrity Marketing Team Inc .... G 317 517-0012
Plainfield *(G-13691)*

J & J Industrial Service Inc .... G 219 362-4973
La Porte *(G-10429)*

36 ELECTRONIC & OTHER ELECTRICAL EQUIPMENT & COMPONENTS

Kouder Instrument Service Co .... G 219 374-5935
  Cedar Lake *(G-1833)*
Landis Gyr Utilities Svcs Inc .... D 765 742-1001
  Lafayette *(G-10633)*
Leman Engrg & Consulting Inc .... G 574 870-7732
  Brookston *(G-1312)*
Liberty Automation LLC .... G 574 524-0436
  Albion *(G-31)*
Maddox Engineering Inc .... F 812 903-0048
  Greenville *(G-6652)*
Mechancal Engrg Cntrls Atmtn C .... E 574 294-7580
  Elkhart *(G-3522)*
Ms Sedco Inc .... E 317 842-2545
  Indianapolis *(G-8968)*
Pinder Instruments Company Inc .... G 219 924-7070
  Munster *(G-12558)*
Protron LLC .... G 765 313-1595
  Anderson *(G-181)*
Quality Industrial Supplies .... G 219 324-2654
  La Porte *(G-10468)*
Quantum Technologies LLC .... G 765 426-0156
  Elizabethtown *(G-3132)*
Richard J Bagan Inc .... E 260 244-5115
  Columbia City *(G-2190)*
Semcor Inc .... E 219 362-0222
  La Porte *(G-10479)*
Siemens Industry Inc .... D 219 763-7927
  Portage *(G-13914)*
▲ Sigma Switches Plus Inc .... F 574 294-5776
  Elkhart *(G-3676)*
Standard Fusee Corporation .... D 765 472-4375
  Peru *(G-13602)*
Sullivan Engineered Services .... G 812 294-1724
  Henryville *(G-7116)*
Teaco Inc .... G 219 874-6234
  Michigan City *(G-11676)*
◆ Touchplate Technologies Inc .... E 260 426-1565
  Fort Wayne *(G-5497)*
Western Consolidated Tech Inc .... D 260 495-9866
  Fremont *(G-5842)*
Wpr Services LLC .... G 317 513-5269
  Fishers *(G-4635)*

3621 Motors and generators

An-Mar Wiring Systems Inc .... F 574 255-5523
  Mishawaka *(G-11842)*
B & H Electric and Supply Inc .... E 812 522-5607
  Seymour *(G-14630)*
Blinkless Power Equipment LLC .... G 317 844-7328
  Indianapolis *(G-7642)*
▲ Bluffton Motor Works LLC .... G 260 827-2200
  Bluffton *(G-1030)*
Burt Products Inc .... G 812 386-6890
  Princeton *(G-13986)*
Clipper Country .... G 765 935-2344
  Richmond *(G-14106)*
▲ Coil-Tran LLC .... D 219 942-8511
  Hobart *(G-7182)*
▲ Contour Hardening Inc .... E 888 867-2184
  Indianapolis *(G-7861)*
Controls Center Inc .... G 317 634-2665
  Indianapolis *(G-7863)*
Cummins Americas Inc .... G 800 589-9027
  Elkhart *(G-3280)*
Cummins Emssion Sltons Clmbus ...... E 800 286-6467
  Columbus *(G-2254)*
Cummins Inc .... G 812 377-2932
  Columbus *(G-2259)*
Cummins Inc .... G 812 377-8601
  Columbus *(G-2272)*
Cummins Inc .... F 812 378-2874
  Columbus *(G-2273)*

Cummins Inc .... F 317 610-2493
  Indianapolis *(G-7927)*
Cummins Inc .... G 317 244-7251
  Indianapolis *(G-7928)*
Cummins Inc .... D 812 522-9366
  Seymour *(G-14645)*
Cummins Inc .... G 317 751-4567
  Whiteland *(G-16782)*
Cummins Inc .... A 812 377-5000
  Columbus *(G-2271)*
Cummins Power Generation Inc .... E 574 262-4611
  Elkhart *(G-3281)*
▲ Custom Magnetics Inc .... E 260 982-8508
  North Manchester *(G-13231)*
D & E Auto Electric Inc .... F 219 763-3892
  Portage *(G-13858)*
Dayton-Phoenix Group Inc .... D 765 742-4410
  West Lafayette *(G-16575)*
Electric Motors and Spc .... C 260 357-4141
  Garrett *(G-5860)*
Electro Corp .... F 219 393-5571
  Kingsbury *(G-10177)*
Electrocraft Inc .... D 812 385-3013
  Princeton *(G-13991)*
Elevator Equipment Corporation .... D 765 966-7761
  Richmond *(G-14119)*
Flanders Inc .... F 812 867-7421
  Evansville *(G-4075)*
◆ Flanders Electric Motor Service LLC .. C .. 812 867-7421
  Evansville *(G-4076)*
◆ Franklin Electric Co Inc .... B 260 824-2900
  Fort Wayne *(G-5006)*
Franklin Electric Intl .... F 260 824-2900
  Fort Wayne *(G-5007)*
Futurewerks LLC .... F 305 926-3633
  Indianapolis *(G-8247)*
◆ Gillette Generators Inc .... E 574 264-9639
  Elkhart *(G-3377)*
Go Electric Inc .... G 765 400-1347
  Anderson *(G-122)*
◆ Hansen Corporation .... B 812 385-3000
  Princeton *(G-13907)*
Hendershot Service Center Inc .... F 765 653-2600
  Greencastle *(G-6412)*
I Power Energy Systems LLC .... G 765 621-9980
  Anderson *(G-132)*
Ies Subsidiary Holdings Inc .... G 330 830-3500
  South Bend *(G-15074)*
Illinois Tool Works Inc .... G 317 298-5000
  Indianapolis *(G-8461)*
Ipfw Student Housing .... G 260 481-4180
  Fort Wayne *(G-5117)*
Ipower Technologies Inc .... G 317 574-0103
  Anderson *(G-134)*
Jeannie and Rachel Heidenreich .... G 260 244-4583
  Columbia City *(G-2159)*
▲ JMS Electronics Corporation .... E 574 522-0246
  Elkhart *(G-3434)*
Jones Engineering Inc .... G 812 254-6456
  Washington *(G-16490)*
Kane Usa Inc .... E 800 547-5740
  Indianapolis *(G-8660)*
Kendrion (mishawaka) LLC .... E 574 257-2422
  Mishawaka *(G-11922)*
Leeson Electric Corporation .... E 317 821-3700
  Plainfield *(G-13697)*
Liberty Green Renewables LLP .... G 812 951-3143
  Georgetown *(G-6067)*
▲ Light Engineering .... F 317 471-1800
  Indianapolis *(G-8749)*
Lite Magnesium Products Inc .... G 765 299-3644
  Indianapolis *(G-8768)*

Marathon Electric .... G 317 837-2523
  Plainfield *(G-13699)*
Martin Diesel Services LLC .... G 570 837-6101
  Lagrange *(G-10754)*
Mighty-Quip Industries .... G 260 615-1899
  Fort Wayne *(G-5228)*
MO Trailer Corporation .... F 574 533-0824
  Goshen *(G-6226)*
Mohler Technology Inc .... E 812 897-2900
  Boonville *(G-1093)*
OH Hunt Lines Inc .... G 260 856-2125
  Cromwell *(G-2632)*
Pete D Limkemann .... G 260 403-4297
  Fort Wayne *(G-5307)*
Protron LLC .... G 765 313-1595
  Anderson *(G-181)*
Q P Inc .... F 574 295-6884
  Elkhart *(G-3626)*
Railway Unloading Services LLC .... G 219 989-7700
  Griffith *(G-6816)*
Regal Beloit America Inc .... F 260 416-5400
  Fort Wayne *(G-5377)*
▲ Regal Beloit Logistics LLC .... F 317 837-1150
  Plainfield *(G-13719)*
Regal Rexnord Corporation .... E 608 364-8800
  Fort Wayne *(G-5378)*
Regal Rexnord Corporation .... E 574 583-9171
  Monticello *(G-12168)*
Regal Rexnord Corporation .... F 317 837-2667
  Plainfield *(G-13720)*
▲ Regal-Beloit Electric Motors Inc ...... A 260 416-5400
  Fort Wayne *(G-5379)*
Ritchie Electric Motor Co LLC .... G 219 866-5185
  Rensselaer *(G-14067)*
Rpg Energy Group Inc .... F 317 614-0054
  Indianapolis *(G-9342)*
Scottorsville Sales and Svc .... G 765 250-5245
  Lafayette *(G-10688)*
Semcor Inc .... E 219 362-0222
  La Porte *(G-10479)*
Siemens Industry Inc .... D 219 763-7927
  Portage *(G-13914)*
▲ Southern Electric Coil LLC .... E 219 931-5500
  Hammond *(G-7011)*
▲ Sterling Electric Inc .... E 317 872-0471
  Indianapolis *(G-9505)*
▲ Summit/Ems Corporation .... E 574 722-1317
  Logansport *(G-11108)*
SUv Parts & Accessories Inc .... G 765 457-1345
  Kokomo *(G-10344)*
◆ Vanair Manufacturing Inc .... C 219 879-5100
  Michigan City *(G-11684)*
W W Williams Company LLC .... E 260 827-0553
  Fort Wayne *(G-5537)*

3624 Carbon and graphite products

Aerodine Composites LLC .... E 317 271-1207
  Indianapolis *(G-7450)*
Applied Composites Engrg Inc .... E 317 243-4225
  Indianapolis *(G-7533)*
Composite Specialties .... G 317 852-1408
  Brownsburg *(G-1360)*
▲ Friction Products Company LLC ..... A 765 362-3500
  Crawfordsville *(G-2568)*
Graphite Customs LLC .... G 260 402-8690
  Fort Wayne *(G-5036)*
Hickman Williams & Company .... G 219 379-5199
  La Porte *(G-10419)*
Hickman Williams & Company .... G 812 522-6293
  Seymour *(G-14656)*
Indy Prfmce Composites Inc .... G 317 858-7793
  Brownsburg *(G-1373)*

SIC SECTION
36 ELECTRONIC & OTHER ELECTRICAL EQUIPMENT & COMPONENTS

3625 Relays and industrial controls

ABB Flexible Automation Inc .... G 317 876-9090
 Indianapolis *(G-7414)*

▲ Advanced Control Tech Inc .... G 317 806-2750
 Indianapolis *(G-7437)*

Advanced Mechatronic Tech LLC .... G 920 918-0209
 Rochester *(G-14275)*

Advantage Electronics Inc .... F 317 888-1946
 Greenwood *(G-6659)*

AEL/Span LLC .... E 317 203-4602
 Plainfield *(G-13656)*

Altra Industrial Motion Corp .... E 219 874-5248
 Michigan City *(G-11577)*

◆ American Elctrnic Cmpnents Inc .... E 574 295-6330
 Elkhart *(G-3171)*

Automation & Control Svcs Inc .... F 219 558-2060
 Schererville *(G-14514)*

Axis Controls Incorporated .... G 260 414-4028
 Fort Wayne *(G-4785)*

▼ B & M Electrical Company Inc .... F 765 448-4532
 Lafayette *(G-10533)*

Bryant Control Inc .... F 317 549-3355
 Fishers *(G-4477)*

◆ Carson Manufacturing Co Inc .... F 317 257-3191
 Indianapolis *(G-7750)*

▼ Control Consultants of America .... G 219 989-3311
 Hammond *(G-6905)*

D & E Auto Electric Inc .... F 219 763-3892
 Portage *(G-13858)*

Damping Technologies Inc .... F 574 258-7916
 Mishawaka *(G-11880)*

Damping Technologies Inc .... E 574 258-7916
 Mishawaka *(G-11879)*

Danfoss Power Solutions II LLC .... G 260 248-5800
 Columbia City *(G-2136)*

Dart Controls LLC .... E 317 873-5211
 Zionsville *(G-17000)*

Direct Control Systems Inc .... G 765 282-7474
 Muncie *(G-12384)*

Doron Distribution Inc .... G 317 594-9259
 Carmel *(G-1610)*

Duesenburg Inc .... G 260 496-9650
 Fort Wayne *(G-4931)*

◆ Dwyer Instruments LLC .... C 219 879-8868
 Michigan City *(G-11604)*

E C T Franklin Control Systems .... G 765 939-2531
 Richmond *(G-14117)*

Eaton Corporation .... E 574 283-5004
 South Bend *(G-15009)*

Electro Corp .... F 219 393-5571
 Kingsbury *(G-10177)*

Electrocraft Inc .... D 812 385-3013
 Princeton *(G-13991)*

Electromechanical RES Labs .... E 812 948-8484
 New Albany *(G-12724)*

Electronics Incorporated .... G 574 256-5001
 Mishawaka *(G-11891)*

Elkhart Electronics .... G 574 679-4627
 Osceola *(G-13390)*

Enginring Cncpts Unlimited Inc .... G 317 849-8470
 Fishers *(G-4514)*

Environmental Technology Inc .... E 574 233-1202
 South Bend *(G-15016)*

Ers Automation Inc .... G 260 341-8114
 Columbia City *(G-2143)*

Flosource Inc .... E 800 752-5959
 Mooresville *(G-12208)*

Frakes Engineering Inc .... E 317 577-3000
 Indianapolis *(G-8220)*

Freelance Services LLC .... G 317 727-2669
 Pittsboro *(G-13647)*

▲ Functional Devices LLC .... E 765 883-5538
 Sharpsville *(G-14710)*

G W Enterprises .... G 260 868-2555
 Butler *(G-1464)*

General Automation Company .... F 317 849-7483
 Noblesville *(G-13085)*

Hitachi Astemo Americas Inc .... D 859 734-9451
 Ligonier *(G-11017)*

▲ Horner Apg LLC .... F 317 916-4274
 Indianapolis *(G-8414)*

Horner Industrial Services Inc .... G 260 434-1189
 Fort Wayne *(G-5083)*

Horner Industrial Services Inc .... F 317 957-4244
 Indianapolis *(G-8417)*

Horner Industrial Services Inc .... G 812 466-5281
 Terre Haute *(G-15607)*

Horner Industrial Services Inc .... G 317 639-4261
 Indianapolis *(G-8416)*

Industrial Controls Corp .... G 219 884-1141
 Gary *(G-5961)*

Innovative Battery Power Inc .... G 260 267-6582
 Fort Wayne *(G-5110)*

ITT LLC .... G 260 451-6000
 Fort Wayne *(G-5122)*

Jason Holdings Inc .... C 414 277-9300
 Richmond *(G-14147)*

▲ JMS Electronics Corporation .... E 574 522-0246
 Elkhart *(G-3434)*

Kane Usa Inc .... E 800 547-5740
 Indianapolis *(G-8660)*

Kapsch Trafficcom Usa Inc .... C 812 258-5905
 Jeffersonville *(G-10004)*

Kcma & Services LLC .... G 260 645-0885
 Waterloo *(G-16522)*

▲ Kreuter Manufacturing Co Inc .... G 574 831-4626
 New Paris *(G-12964)*

L H Controls Inc .... F 260 432-9020
 Fort Wayne *(G-5166)*

L3harris Technologies Inc .... G 260 451-6000
 Fort Wayne *(G-5171)*

Laketronics Inc .... E 260 856-4588
 Cromwell *(G-2631)*

Liberty Automation LLC .... G 574 524-0436
 Albion *(G-31)*

Master Filter Corporation .... G 317 545-3335
 Indianapolis *(G-8849)*

Micro-Precision Operations .... F 260 589-2136
 Berne *(G-719)*

Nidec Motor Corporation .... D 812 385-2564
 Princeton *(G-14007)*

Power Components of Midwest .... E 574 256-6990
 Mishawaka *(G-11976)*

Pyromation Inc .... C 260 484-2580
 Fort Wayne *(G-5358)*

Rexnord Industries LLC .... G 414 643-2559
 Plainfield *(G-13722)*

Riverside Mfg LLC .... B 260 637-4470
 Fort Wayne *(G-5386)*

Rockwell Automation Inc .... D 219 924-3002
 Munster *(G-12561)*

Rockwell Automation Inc .... G 765 481-0766
 Whitestown *(G-16819)*

Rogers Electro-Matics Inc .... F 574 457-2305
 Syracuse *(G-15477)*

SGS Cybermetrix Inc .... G 800 713-1203
 Columbus *(G-2391)*

Siemens Industry Inc .... D 219 763-7927
 Portage *(G-13914)*

▲ Sigma Switches Plus Inc .... F 574 294-5776
 Elkhart *(G-3676)*

▲ SMC Corporation of America .... B 317 899-4440
 Noblesville *(G-13176)*

Spyder Controls Inc .... G 866 919-9092
 South Bend *(G-15262)*

Teaco Inc .... G 219 874-6234
 Michigan City *(G-11676)*

Tempest Technical Sales Inc .... G 317 844-9236
 Carmel *(G-1783)*

Top of Hill Performance LLC .... G 812 637-3693
 West Harrison *(G-16552)*

◆ Touchplate Technologies Inc .... E 260 426-1565
 Fort Wayne *(G-5497)*

Touchtronics Inc .... F 574 294-2570
 Elkhart *(G-3741)*

Western Consolidated Tech Inc .... D 260 495-9866
 Fremont *(G-5842)*

Westside Automation Inc .... E 812 768-6878
 Haubstadt *(G-7093)*

Wolfe and Swickard Mch Co Inc .... D 317 241-2589
 Indianapolis *(G-9782)*

3629 Electrical industrial apparatus

▲ Amerawhip Inc .... G 317 639-5248
 Indianapolis *(G-7497)*

▲ Empro Manufacturing Co Inc .... E 317 823-3000
 Indianapolis *(G-8110)*

Enerfuel Inc .... E
 Greenfield *(G-6497)*

▲ Energy Access Incorporated .... F 317 329-1676
 Indianapolis *(G-8115)*

Envirogen Technologies LLC .... G 812 319-4496
 Evansville *(G-4042)*

Exide Technologies LLC .... G 317 876-7475
 Indianapolis *(G-8155)*

Flat Electronics LLC .... G 765 414-6635
 Fishers *(G-4524)*

Go Electric Inc .... G 765 400-1347
 Anderson *(G-122)*

Gregory Thomas Inc .... G 219 324-3801
 La Porte *(G-10412)*

▲ Kirby Risk Corporation .... D 765 448-4567
 Lafayette *(G-10623)*

Maxwell Power LLC .... G 317 998-5092
 Indianapolis *(G-8856)*

Motion & Control Entps LLC .... F 219 844-4224
 Munster *(G-12551)*

RB Annis Instruments Inc .... G 765 848-1621
 Greencastle *(G-6428)*

RES Technica LLC .... G 765 366-5089
 Oxford *(G-13477)*

Wdb Enterprises Inc .... F 219 844-4224
 Hammond *(G-7031)*

Xantrex LLC .... C 800 670-0707
 Elkhart *(G-3798)*

Xantrex LLC .... E 800 670-0707
 Elkhart *(G-3797)*

3631 Household cooking equipment

Betos Bar Inc .... G 219 397-8247
 East Chicago *(G-2993)*

◆ Onward Manufacturing Company .... E 260 358-4111
 Huntington *(G-7346)*

Sterling Manufacturing LLC .... G 260 451-9760
 Fort Wayne *(G-5442)*

Steven Ray Hughes .... G 574 491-2128
 Claypool *(G-2058)*

Thermodyne Food Svc Pdts Inc .... E 260 428-2535
 Fort Wayne *(G-5482)*

Z Grills Inc .... G 909 295-5264
 Indianapolis *(G-9806)*

3632 Household refrigerators and freezers

Freezing Systems and Svc Inc .... F 219 879-6236
 Michigan City *(G-11615)*

36 ELECTRONIC & OTHER ELECTRICAL EQUIPMENT & COMPONENTS

▼ JC Refrigeration LLC.................................. G..... 260 768-4067
Shipshewana *(G-14855)*

Whirlpool Corporation............................. D..... 812 426-4000
Evansville *(G-4383)*

3633 Household laundry equipment

▲ Accra-Pac Inc.................................... D..... 574 295-0000
Elkhart *(G-3151)*

Accra-Pac Inc....................................... G..... 574 295-0000
Elkhart *(G-3150)*

Bonzell Combs..................................... G..... 872 248-4123
Highland *(G-7125)*

Laundry On US LLC.............................. G..... 812 567-3653
Terre Haute *(G-15630)*

Megans Wash and Fold LLC................. G..... 317 903-5253
Pendleton *(G-13543)*

Whirlpool Corporation............................. E..... 317 837-5300
Plainfield *(G-13742)*

3634 Electric housewares and fans

Air Energy Systems Inc........................ G..... 317 290-8500
Indianapolis *(G-7460)*

Applied Scientific RES Inc................... G..... 219 776-4623
Merrillville *(G-11484)*

▲ Battle Creek Equipment Co................. E..... 260 495-3472
Fremont *(G-5810)*

Caprice Boyb....................................... G..... 260 442-1736
Fort Wayne *(G-4833)*

Cigar Exclusive LLC............................. G..... 317 778-2826
Fishers *(G-4487)*

Dometic Corporation............................ C..... 574 389-3759
Goshen *(G-6124)*

Electric Plus Inc................................... D..... 317 718-0100
Avon *(G-516)*

Enerlinc Inc... G..... 317 574-1009
Fortville *(G-5593)*

Exhale Fans LLC.................................. G..... 812 366-3351
Georgetown *(G-6059)*

▲ Fanimation Inc.................................... E..... 317 733-4113
Zionsville *(G-17007)*

Hoosier Roaster Llc............................. G..... 574 257-1415
Mishawaka *(G-11909)*

▲ Hyndman Industrial Pdts Inc............... E..... 260 483-6042
Fort Wayne *(G-5089)*

Janels Body Bar LLC............................ G..... 219 455-4888
Gary *(G-5968)*

Mwss Inc... G..... 574 287-3365
Elkhart *(G-3560)*

▲ Royal Spa Corporation........................ D..... 317 781-0828
Indianapolis *(G-9341)*

Scott Fetzer Company.......................... G..... 260 488-3531
Hamilton *(G-6861)*

Southeast Specialties Inc..................... G..... 706 667-0422
Indianapolis *(G-9463)*

Ward Electric LLC................................. G..... 219 462-8780
Valparaiso *(G-16078)*

3635 Household vacuum cleaners

Arden Companies LLC......................... D..... 260 747-1657
Fort Wayne *(G-4770)*

M&M Dyson Farms Inc......................... G..... 765 833-2202
Roann *(G-14251)*

Steamin Demon Inc.............................. G..... 812 288-6754
Clarksville *(G-2038)*

3639 Household appliances, nec

Appliance Pros LLC............................. G..... 812 329-2669
Heltonville *(G-7109)*

Auto-Chlor System Wash Inc................ G..... 317 334-0430
Indianapolis *(G-7573)*

Ebert Machine Company Inc................. E..... 765 473-3728
Peru *(G-13581)*

Hentz Mfg LLC..................................... G..... 260 469-0800
Fort Wayne *(G-5063)*

Keith Miller.. G..... 260 982-6858
North Manchester *(G-13237)*

◆ Sailrite Enterprises Inc........................ F..... 260 244-4647
Columbia City *(G-2195)*

◆ Solar Freeze LLC................................ E..... 260 499-4973
Lagrange *(G-10760)*

Solfire Contract Mfg Inc....................... F..... 260 755-2115
Fort Wayne *(G-5424)*

3641 Electric lamps

6605 E State LLC................................. G..... 260 433-7007
Fort Wayne *(G-4714)*

Acuity Brands Lighting Inc................... B..... 765 362-1837
Crawfordsville *(G-2543)*

◆ American Ultraviolet Company............ E..... 765 483-9514
Lebanon *(G-10874)*

Energy Saver Lights Inc...................... F..... 202 544-7868
Indianapolis *(G-8118)*

◆ International Lighting LLC................... F..... 219 989-0060
Hammond *(G-6958)*

Lampliter.. G..... 317 827-0250
Indianapolis *(G-8719)*

Lomont Holdings Co Inc...................... E..... 800 545-9023
Angola *(G-273)*

◆ Pent Plastics Inc................................. C..... 260 897-3775
Kendallville *(G-10142)*

Tap-A-Lite Inc..................................... E..... 219 932-8067
Hammond *(G-7018)*

Valeo Ltg Systems N Amer LLC........... A..... 812 523-5200
Seymour *(G-14700)*

▲ Vista Manufacturing Inc...................... E..... 574 264-0711
Elkhart *(G-3771)*

3643 Current-carrying wiring devices

▲ Advanced Control Tech Inc................. G..... 317 806-2750
Indianapolis *(G-7437)*

▲ Aearo Technologies LLC..................... A..... 612 284-1232
Indianapolis *(G-7446)*

◆ Almega/Tru-Flex Inc........................... E..... 574 546-2113
Bremen *(G-1172)*

An-Mar Wiring Systems Inc................. F..... 574 255-5523
Mishawaka *(G-11842)*

Bender Products Inc............................ E..... 574 255-5350
Mishawaka *(G-11852)*

Blackbird.. G..... 812 944-0799
New Albany *(G-12702)*

Bowmar LLC.. E..... 260 747-3121
Fort Wayne *(G-4813)*

Cloud Defensive LLC........................... G..... 813 492-5683
Chandler *(G-1859)*

▲ Cme LLC... E..... 260 623-3700
Monroeville *(G-12067)*

Coleman Cable LLC............................. E..... 574 546-5115
Bremen *(G-1180)*

▲ Connecta Corporation......................... F..... 317 923-9282
Indianapolis *(G-7852)*

Contact Fabricators Ind Inc................. G..... 317 366-7274
Middletown *(G-11768)*

Cruz Electric & Handy Svc LLC............ E..... 219 308-7117
Hobart *(G-7185)*

E M F Corp.. E..... 260 488-2479
Hamilton *(G-6852)*

▲ E M F Corp.. E..... 260 665-9541
Angola *(G-246)*

Elektrsola Dr Gerd Schldbach G........... B..... 765 477-8000
Lafayette *(G-10574)*

▲ Elkhart Supply Corp............................ E..... 574 264-4156
Elkhart *(G-3330)*

Emp Solutions Inc............................... G..... 937 608-0283
Fishers *(G-4512)*

Energypoint LLC.................................. G..... 317 275-7979
Carmel *(G-1623)*

Flagship Sign Supply LLC.................... G..... 708 474-9521
Hammond *(G-6929)*

Freudenberg-Nok General Partnr......... C..... 765 763-7246
Morristown *(G-12277)*

▲ Functional Devices LLC....................... E..... 765 883-5538
Sharpsville *(G-14710)*

Group Dekko Inc.................................. G..... 260 637-3964
Laotto *(G-10805)*

▲ Group Dekko Inc.................................. D..... 260 357-3621
Fort Wayne *(G-5042)*

Independent Protection Co................... C..... 574 831-5680
New Paris *(G-12960)*

▼ Independent Protection Co................... E..... 574 533-4116
Goshen *(G-6172)*

Kendrion (mishawaka) LLC.................. E..... 574 257-2422
Mishawaka *(G-11922)*

Kirby Risk Corporation......................... D..... 765 447-1402
Lafayette *(G-10621)*

Lapp Usa Inc....................................... C..... 973 660-9700
Brownsburg *(G-1384)*

Llama Corporation............................... G..... 888 701-7432
Decatur *(G-2870)*

Odyssian Technology LLC.................... G..... 574 257-7555
South Bend *(G-15176)*

Outman Industries Inc......................... G..... 260 467-1576
Grabill *(G-6319)*

Pent Assemblies................................. E..... 260 347-5828
Kendallville *(G-10141)*

Proterial Cable America Inc................. B..... 812 945-9011
New Albany *(G-12799)*

Rees Inc.. F..... 260 495-9811
Fremont *(G-5832)*

Tap-A-Lite Inc..................................... E..... 219 932-8067
Hammond *(G-7018)*

◆ Touchplate Technologies Inc............... E..... 260 426-1565
Fort Wayne *(G-5497)*

Ucom Inc... F..... 260 829-1294
Orland *(G-13373)*

Western Consolidated Tech Inc............ D..... 260 495-9866
Fremont *(G-5842)*

Wheelock Manufacturing Inc................ E..... 219 285-8540
Garrett *(G-5880)*

3644 Noncurrent-carrying wiring devices

Appleton Grp LLC................................ G..... 219 326-5936
La Porte *(G-10386)*

Bo-Witt Products Inc............................ E..... 812 526-5561
Edinburgh *(G-3069)*

E Squared Motorsports LLC................. G..... 317 626-2937
Avon *(G-515)*

Gund Company Inc.............................. E..... 219 374-9944
Cedar Lake *(G-1832)*

Hoffmaster Electric Inc........................ G..... 219 616-1313
Schererville *(G-14523)*

Linear Solutions Inc............................. F..... 219 237-2399
Griffith *(G-6812)*

Miller Raceway.................................... G..... 219 939-9688
Gary *(G-5982)*

Napier & Napier................................... G..... 765 580-9116
Liberty *(G-10992)*

Raceway Hand Car Wash LLC.............. G..... 260 242-9866
Kendallville *(G-10147)*

Regal Rexnord Corporation.................. E..... 574 583-9171
Monticello *(G-12168)*

Ronard Industries Inc.......................... F..... 219 874-4801
Michigan City *(G-11658)*

Surfis Inc... G..... 260 357-3475
Auburn *(G-428)*

Winona Building Products LLC............. F..... 574 822-0100
Plymouth *(G-13831)*

SIC SECTION
36 ELECTRONIC & OTHER ELECTRICAL EQUIPMENT & COMPONENTS

3645 Residential lighting fixtures

▲ A Homestead Shoppe Inc .... E 574 784-2307
   Lapaz *(G-10814)*

Arran Isle Inc .... E 574 295-4400
   Elkhart *(G-3191)*

Fashion Flooring and Ltg Inc .... G
   Valparaiso *(G-15947)*

Gleam Electrical LLC .... E 317 968-0927
   Greenwood *(G-6708)*

Lasalle Bristol Corporation .... F 574 295-4400
   Bristol *(G-1269)*

◆ Lasalle Bristol Corporation .... C 574 295-8400
   Elkhart *(G-3469)*

Metalite Corporation .... E 812 944-6600
   New Albany *(G-12776)*

Patrick Industries Inc .... F 574 295-5206
   Elkhart *(G-3588)*

Premier Mfg Group Inc .... D 203 924-6617
   Fort Wayne *(G-5345)*

Ward Industries Inc .... F 574 825-2548
   Middlebury *(G-11756)*

3646 Commercial lighting fixtures

55 West LLC .... F
   Indianapolis *(G-7392)*

Acuity Brands Inc .... G 765 362-1837
   Crawfordsville *(G-2542)*

Acuity Brands Lighting Inc .... B 765 362-1837
   Crawfordsville *(G-2543)*

Advance Leds LLC .... G 844 815-8898
   Evansville *(G-3874)*

▲ Amerlight LLC .... F 812 602-3452
   Evansville *(G-3889)*

▼ Craft Metal Products Inc .... G 317 545-3252
   Indianapolis *(G-7897)*

▲ Dream Lighting Inc .... F 574 206-4888
   Elkhart *(G-3303)*

Eco Parking Technologies LLC .... F 866 897-1234
   Indianapolis *(G-8047)*

Energy Harness Corporation .... G 239 246-1958
   Carmel *(G-1622)*

Energy Harness Corporation .... G 317 999-5561
   Indianapolis *(G-8116)*

Green Illuminating Systems Inc .... G 317 869-7430
   Noblesville *(G-13088)*

Lomont Holdings Co Inc .... E 800 545-9023
   Angola *(G-273)*

Martin Professional Inc .... G 574 294-8000
   Elkhart *(G-3516)*

Metalite Corporation .... E 812 944-6600
   New Albany *(G-12776)*

Professional Grade Svcs LLC .... G 317 688-8898
   Indianapolis *(G-9222)*

Rpg Energy Group Inc .... F 317 614-0054
   Indianapolis *(G-9342)*

Semcor Inc .... E 219 362-0222
   La Porte *(G-10479)*

Source Products Inc .... G 260 424-0864
   Columbia City *(G-2200)*

Specified Ltg Systems Ind Inc .... F 317 577-8100
   Indianapolis *(G-9472)*

Thomas Custom Lighting .... G 765 378-5472
   Chesterfield *(G-1899)*

Ward Industries Inc .... F 574 825-2548
   Middlebury *(G-11756)*

3647 Vehicular lighting equipment

Dajac Inc .... G 317 608-0500
   Sheridan *(G-14821)*

David Murray .... G 765 766-5229
   Mooreland *(G-12184)*

◆ Grote Industries Inc .... A 812 273-2121
   Madison *(G-11222)*

Grote Industries LLC .... A 812 265-8273
   Madison *(G-11223)*

J J Lites .... G 765 966-3252
   Richmond *(G-14144)*

Jtn Services Inc .... G 765 653-7158
   Greencastle *(G-6415)*

Lund International Holding Co .... E 765 742-7200
   Lafayette *(G-10641)*

North American Lighting Inc .... B 812 983-2663
   Elberfeld *(G-3116)*

Roadworks Maufacturing .... G 765 742-7200
   West Lafayette *(G-16625)*

▲ Tcb Enterprises LLC .... F 574 522-3971
   Middlebury *(G-11754)*

Techshot Lighting LLC .... G 812 923-9591
   Floyds Knobs *(G-4695)*

Valeo North America Inc .... A 812 524-5198
   Seymour *(G-14701)*

Yellow Cat LLC .... G 913 213-4570
   Bloomington *(G-1018)*

3648 Lighting equipment, nec

Always Sun Tanning Center .... G 812 238-2786
   Terre Haute *(G-15540)*

Ao Inc .... G 317 280-3000
   Avon *(G-504)*

Around Campus LLC .... G 574 360-6571
   South Bend *(G-14949)*

B&D Lighting LLC .... G 317 414-8056
   Indianapolis *(G-7586)*

Badger Daylighting Corp .... G 219 762-9177
   Portage *(G-13848)*

Blackbird .... G 812 944-0799
   New Albany *(G-12702)*

Brighter Design Inc .... G 765 447-9494
   Lafayette *(G-10544)*

Circle City Lighting Inc .... G 317 439-0824
   Noblesville *(G-13060)*

Cloud Defensive LLC .... G 813 492-5683
   Chandler *(G-1859)*

Cloud Defensive LLC .... E 812 646-1762
   Evansville *(G-3973)*

Festive Lights LLC .... G 317 998-0627
   Indianapolis *(G-8181)*

Gmp Holdings LLC .... G 317 353-6580
   Indianapolis *(G-8294)*

▲ Ikio Led Lighting LLC .... A 765 414-0835
   Indianapolis *(G-8458)*

Indiana Emergency Lighting LLC .... G 260 463-1277
   Marion *(G-11294)*

Kc Innovations LLC .... F 888 290-8920
   Loogootee *(G-11141)*

Lawncreations LLC .... G 574 536-1546
   Millersburg *(G-11815)*

Ledingedge Lighting Inc .... G 805 383-8493
   Angola *(G-272)*

Lumen Cache Inc .... F 317 222-1314
   Indianapolis *(G-8796)*

Lunarglo LLC .... G 574 294-2624
   Elkhart *(G-3503)*

Metalite Corporation .... E 812 944-6600
   New Albany *(G-12776)*

Mid-America Sound Corporation .... F 317 947-9880
   Greenfield *(G-6528)*

Nu Led Lighting .... G 317 989-7352
   Greenwood *(G-6747)*

Orka Technologies LLC .... G 812 378-9842
   Columbus *(G-2367)*

Searchlight Social LLC .... G 317 983-3802
   Kokomo *(G-10330)*

Spectrum Brands Inc .... E 317 773-6627
   Noblesville *(G-13179)*

Spotlight On Drama LLC .... G 765 643-7170
   Anderson *(G-199)*

◆ Touchplate Technologies Inc .... E 260 426-1565
   Fort Wayne *(G-5497)*

Vista Worldwide LLC .... G 574 264-0711
   Elkhart *(G-3772)*

Ward Industries Inc .... F 574 825-2548
   Middlebury *(G-11756)*

3651 Household audio and video equipment

▲ A E Techron Inc .... F 574 295-9495
   Elkhart *(G-3139)*

Adaptive Tech Solutions LLC .... G 317 762-4363
   Carmel *(G-1549)*

◆ Alpine Electronics Manufa .... A 956 217-3200
   Greenwood *(G-6665)*

American Mobile Sound Ind LLC .... G 765 288-1500
   Muncie *(G-12341)*

▲ ASA Electronics LLC .... C 574 264-3135
   Elkhart *(G-3192)*

Associated World Music LLC .... G 219 512-4511
   Crown Point *(G-2651)*

Audience Response Systems Inc .... F 812 479-7507
   Evansville *(G-3902)*

Boyer Enterprises Inc .... G 812 773-3295
   Evansville *(G-3943)*

Continntal Broadcast Group LLC .... E 317 924-1071
   Indianapolis *(G-7858)*

◆ Crown Audio Inc .... B 800 342-6939
   Elkhart *(G-3273)*

Csd Group LLC .... G 260 918-3500
   New Haven *(G-12901)*

Dage-MTI Michigan City Inc .... G 219 872-5514
   Michigan City *(G-11597)*

Damping Technologies Inc .... F 574 258-7916
   Mishawaka *(G-11880)*

Dash CAM Fusion LLC .... G 708 365-8553
   Indianapolis *(G-7953)*

Dream Systems LLC .... F 715 241-8332
   New Palestine *(G-12936)*

Ebey Sales & Service .... G 260 636-3286
   Albion *(G-25)*

◆ Electronics Research Inc .... C 812 925-6000
   Chandler *(G-1861)*

Esco Communications LLC .... D 317 298-2975
   Indianapolis *(G-8130)*

▲ Harman Embedded Audio LLC .... F 317 849-8175
   Indianapolis *(G-8363)*

Harman Professional Inc .... B 574 294-8000
   Elkhart *(G-3398)*

Haven Technologies Inc .... E 317 740-0419
   Carmel *(G-1651)*

Hole N Wall Entertainment LLC .... G 317 586-1037
   Indianapolis *(G-8402)*

Image Vault LLC .... G 812 948-8400
   New Albany *(G-12743)*

◆ Itech Holdings LLC .... E 317 567-5160
   Indianapolis *(G-8597)*

Jerome Pagell .... G 219 226-0591
   Crown Point *(G-2702)*

JP Technology Inc .... G 219 947-2525
   Crown Point *(G-2706)*

Kas Satellite & Cable Inc .... G 260 833-3941
   Angola *(G-267)*

Kelley Global Brands LLC .... G 833 554-8326
   Noblesville *(G-13118)*

◆ Klipsch Group Inc .... C 317 860-8100
   Indianapolis *(G-8695)*

Lea LLC .... F 574 216-1622
   South Bend *(G-15120)*

36 ELECTRONIC & OTHER ELECTRICAL EQUIPMENT & COMPONENTS

▲ Lexicon Incorporated............................ C 203 328-3500
  Elkhart *(G-3486)*
Loys Sales Inc....................................... G 765 552-7250
  Elwood *(G-3829)*
Mobile Communications Tech................. G 812 423-7322
  Evansville *(G-4207)*
Molden Associates Inc........................... G 219 879-8425
  Long Beach *(G-11125)*
◆ MTS Products Corp.............................. E 574 295-3142
  Elkhart *(G-3559)*
Octobers Firm Label LLC........................ G 317 778-1447
  Noblesville *(G-13147)*
Oscar Telecom Inc.................................. G 317 359-7000
  Indianapolis *(G-9073)*
RB Annis Instruments Inc....................... G 765 848-1621
  Greencastle *(G-6428)*
Record / Play Tek Inc............................. G 574 848-5233
  Bristol *(G-1284)*
▲ Skytech II LLC..................................... E 260 459-1703
  Fort Wayne *(G-5421)*
▲ Skytech-Systems Inc........................... F 260 459-1703
  Fort Wayne *(G-5422)*
Smarter Home Technology Inc............... G 815 677-6885
  Chandler *(G-1866)*
▲ Sony Dadc US Inc................................ A 812 462-8100
  Terre Haute *(G-15706)*
▲ Sports Select Usa Inc.......................... G 317 631-4011
  Indianapolis *(G-9482)*
St Joe Group Inc..................................... E 260 918-3500
  New Haven *(G-12920)*
Tech Solutions and Sales Inc................. G 317 536-5846
  Indianapolis *(G-9567)*
Technology Cons Group LLC.................. G 219 525-4064
  Merrillville *(G-11565)*
Todd Enterprise Inc................................. F 317 209-6610
  Noblesville *(G-13182)*
Total Home Control LLC......................... G 317 430-3679
  Indianapolis *(G-9623)*
▲ U-Nitt LLC... G 812 251-9980
  Carmel *(G-1792)*
Uncle Alberts Amplifier Inc..................... G 317 845-3037
  Indianapolis *(G-9676)*
Vergence LLC... F 317 547-4417
  Indianapolis *(G-9707)*
Vidicom Corporation............................... G 219 923-7475
  Hammond *(G-7029)*
▲ Weber Vintage Sound Tech Inc........... G 765 452-1249
  Kokomo *(G-10357)*
Wipbeatz LLC.. G 866 676-1465
  Indianapolis *(G-9774)*
Yongs Audio Connection LLC................. G 317 298-8333
  Indianapolis *(G-9804)*

3652 Prerecorded records and tapes

Boeke Road Baptist Church Inc............. G 812 479-5342
  Evansville *(G-3938)*
Chatterup LLC... G 317 213-6283
  Westfield *(G-16675)*
◆ Cinram Inc... A 416 298-8190
  Richmond *(G-14104)*
Cliff A Ostermeyer.................................. G 615 361-7902
  Fort Wayne *(G-4860)*
Counterpart... D 317 587-1621
  Fishers *(G-4496)*
Lifedata LLC... G 925 800-3381
  Marion *(G-11309)*
M&M Interactive Inc............................... G 317 708-1250
  Carmel *(G-1688)*
Optical Disc Solutions Inc...................... E 765 935-7574
  Richmond *(G-14177)*
Peerview Data Inc.................................. G 317 238-3234
  Indianapolis *(G-9112)*

Photonic LLC.. G 502 930-9544
  Sellersburg *(G-14610)*
Rpdm Solutions Inc................................ G 317 608-2938
  Huntington *(G-7363)*
▲ Sony Dadc US Inc................................ A 812 462-8100
  Terre Haute *(G-15706)*
▼ Voice of God Recordings Inc............... D 812 246-2137
  Jeffersonville *(G-10069)*
Wish Factory Inc..................................... F 260 745-2550
  South Whitley *(G-15332)*
▲ World Media Group Inc........................ D 317 549-8484
  Indianapolis *(G-9790)*

3661 Telephone and telegraph apparatus

Blue Byte Tech Solutions LLC................ G 574 903-5637
  Elkhart *(G-3227)*
C&D Technologies Inc............................ C 765 762-2461
  Attica *(G-345)*
Esco Communications LLC..................... D 317 298-2975
  Indianapolis *(G-8130)*
Great Deals Magazine............................ F 765 649-3302
  Anderson *(G-123)*
▲ International Resources Inc................ G 317 813-5300
  Greenwood *(G-6716)*
Nexvoo Inc.. G 866 910-8366
  Indianapolis *(G-9009)*
Omnion Power Inc................................... G 317 259-9264
  Indianapolis *(G-9049)*
Smart Choice Mobile Inc........................ E 574 830-5727
  Elkhart *(G-3684)*
Stg Networks LLC................................... G 317 667-0865
  Indianapolis *(G-9509)*
◆ Telamon International Corp................. D 317 818-6888
  Carmel *(G-1779)*
◆ Telamon Technologies Corp................ A 317 818-6888
  Carmel *(G-1781)*

3663 Radio and t.v. communications equipment

AAA Satellite Link.................................. G 765 642-7000
  Anderson *(G-71)*
Abk Tracking Inc.................................... G 812 473-9554
  Evansville *(G-3865)*
Acoustical Audio Designs LLC................ F 812 282-7522
  Jeffersonville *(G-9924)*
Anderson Shykia..................................... G 773 304-6852
  Gary *(G-5894)*
Audio-Video By Flynn.............................. G 317 408-6269
  Indianapolis *(G-7562)*
Benson Tower LLC................................. G 270 577-7598
  Evansville *(G-3914)*
Brickhouse Electronics LLC.................... F 212 643-7449
  Indianapolis *(G-7678)*
Channel 40 Network LLC....................... G 317 794-6150
  Indianapolis *(G-7785)*
Cohda Wireless America LLC................ G 248 513-2105
  Indianapolis *(G-7832)*
Commtineo LLC...................................... F 219 476-3667
  Wanatah *(G-16288)*
Corporate Systems Engrg LLC............... D 317 375-3600
  Indianapolis *(G-7878)*
◆ Crown Audio Inc................................... B 800 342-6939
  Elkhart *(G-3273)*
Destiny Solutions Inc.............................. G 502 384-0031
  Georgetown *(G-6057)*
Digital Solutions..................................... G 812 257-0333
  Washington *(G-16477)*
Ejl Tech... G 812 374-8808
  Columbus *(G-2295)*
◆ Electronics Research Inc.................... C 812 925-6000
  Chandler *(G-1861)*

Furrion LLC... G 574 361-1325
  Elkhart *(G-3360)*
Furrion LLC... G 574 327-6571
  Elkhart *(G-3361)*
Furrion LLC... G 574 327-6571
  Elkhart *(G-3362)*
Furtrieve LLC.. G 317 325-8010
  Fishers *(G-4529)*
GH Products Inc..................................... G 619 208-4823
  West Lafayette *(G-16583)*
Global Technology Group Import............ G 317 987-6902
  Indianapolis *(G-8291)*
Grand Master Llc................................... G 574 288-8273
  South Bend *(G-15048)*
Grass Valley USA LLC........................... G 765 259-1744
  Richmond *(G-14128)*
Gwin Enterprises.................................... G 317 881-6401
  Indianapolis *(G-8346)*
Harman Professional Inc....................... B 574 294-8000
  Elkhart *(G-3398)*
Haven Technologies Inc......................... E 317 740-0419
  Carmel *(G-1651)*
I E M C.. G 219 464-2890
  Valparaiso *(G-15966)*
Idonix Solutions Inc................................ G 317 544-8171
  Fishers *(G-4542)*
Indiana Department Educatio................. G 765 361-5247
  Indianapolis *(G-8477)*
Indiana Pub Brdcstg Stns Inc................. G 317 489-4477
  Indianapolis *(G-8490)*
International Rdo & Elec Corp................ G 866 262-8910
  Elkhart *(G-3429)*
Llama Corporation.................................. G 888 701-7432
  Decatur *(G-2870)*
Logikos Overview LLC............................ G 260 483-3638
  Fort Wayne *(G-5189)*
Microwave Devices Inc.......................... G 317 868-8833
  Franklin *(G-5756)*
Midwest Comm Solutions LLP................ G 800 880-5847
  Fort Wayne *(G-5224)*
Mobile King... G 317 835-9772
  Indianapolis *(G-8941)*
Motorola Solutions Inc........................... G 260 436-5331
  Fort Wayne *(G-5247)*
Motorola Solutions Inc........................... F 317 481-0914
  Indianapolis *(G-8958)*
Motorola Solutions Inc........................... G 317 716-8064
  Indianapolis *(G-8959)*
Nello Capital Inc..................................... G 574 288-3632
  South Bend *(G-15160)*
Orbital Installation Tech LLC.................. G 317 774-3668
  Noblesville *(G-13148)*
Raytheon Company................................ G 310 647-9438
  Fort Wayne *(G-5369)*
Raytheon Company................................ G 317 306-4633
  Indianapolis *(G-9275)*
RCA Corporation..................................... C 800 722-2161
  Indianapolis *(G-9276)*
Roger Miller.. G 219 531-2566
  La Porte *(G-10474)*
Ronard Industries Inc............................. F 219 874-4801
  Michigan City *(G-11658)*
Sneaky Micro Video Divisio................... G 317 925-1496
  Indianapolis *(G-9454)*
Star Tracks Command............................ G 574 596-5331
  Valparaiso *(G-16056)*
Telamon Corporation.............................. G 317 818-6888
  Whitestown *(G-16824)*
Telectro-Mek Inc..................................... G 260 747-0586
  Fort Wayne *(G-5474)*
Tu Jinghua.. G 812 327-3819
  Bloomington *(G-1000)*

SIC SECTION
36 ELECTRONIC & OTHER ELECTRICAL EQUIPMENT & COMPONENTS

W Ay-FM Media Group Inc................... G 812 945-1043
 New Albany *(G-12824)*
Woody Enterprises LLC......................... G 765 498-7300
 Bloomingdale *(G-763)*
World Rdo Mssnary Fllwship Inc........... G 574 970-4252
 Elkhart *(G-3793)*

3669 Communications equipment, nec

A Plus Datacomm.................................. G 219 472-1644
 Portage *(G-13842)*
Acterna LLC... E 317 788-9351
 Indianapolis *(G-7425)*
Ademco Inc.. G 317 359-9505
 Indianapolis *(G-7431)*
Advanced Protection Systems................ G 574 626-2939
 Walton *(G-16280)*
American Eagle Security Inc.................. G 219 980-1177
 Merrillville *(G-11482)*
American Fire Company......................... G 219 840-0630
 Valparaiso *(G-15899)*
◆ Carson Manufacturing Co Inc............. F 317 257-3191
 Indianapolis *(G-7750)*
Chasin Paper LLC.................................. G 317 429-6116
 Indianapolis *(G-7778)*
Dux Signal Kits LLC............................... G 260 623-3017
 Monroeville *(G-12068)*
Esco Communications LLC.................... D 317 298-2975
 Indianapolis *(G-8130)*
Highway Safety Services Inc.................. D 765 474-1000
 Lafayette *(G-10599)*
Kal Transportation LLC........................... G 317 615-9341
 Indianapolis *(G-8656)*
L3harris Technologies Inc...................... G 260 451-5597
 Fort Wayne *(G-5169)*
L3harris Technologies Inc...................... D 260 451-6180
 Fort Wayne *(G-5170)*
Logical Concepts................................... F 317 885-6330
 Greenwood *(G-6730)*
Makingmoves Transports LLC................ G 260 579-5584
 Fort Wayne *(G-5200)*
Master Filter Corporation....................... G 317 545-3335
 Indianapolis *(G-8849)*
Messagenet Systems Inc....................... G 317 566-1677
 Carmel *(G-1699)*
Mikes Metal Dectors............................... G 812 366-3558
 Georgetown *(G-6070)*
Molex LLC.. F 317 834-5600
 Mooresville *(G-12223)*
New Concept Metal Detector.................. G 765 447-2681
 Lafayette *(G-10658)*
Pumpalarmcom LLC............................... G 888 454-5051
 Indianapolis *(G-9239)*
SC Supply Company LLC...................... G 574 287-0252
 Mishawaka *(G-11991)*
Sentinel Alarm Inc................................. G 219 874-6051
 Trail Creek *(G-15839)*
▲ St Louis Group LLC........................... G 317 975-3121
 Indianapolis *(G-9485)*
Tct Technologies LLC............................ F 317 833-6730
 Indianapolis *(G-9563)*
Traffic Technical Support Inc.................. G 260 665-1575
 Angola *(G-302)*
Tri-Sky LLC.. G 812 746-1678
 Evansville *(G-4349)*
Tycoon Logistics LLC............................ G 317 749-1381
 Indianapolis *(G-9668)*

3671 Electron tubes

HB Connect Inc..................................... G 855 503-9159
 Fort Wayne *(G-5051)*
HB Connect Inc..................................... D 260 422-1212
 Fort Wayne *(G-5052)*

Iotron Industries USA Inc....................... E 260 212-1722
 Columbia City *(G-2157)*
J & L Uebelhor Enterprises LLC............. G 812 367-1591
 Ferdinand *(G-4436)*
Pantera Mfg Corporation........................ G 317 435-0422
 Fishers *(G-4646)*

3672 Printed circuit boards

Blue Ring Stencils LLC.......................... F 260 203-5461
 Fort Wayne *(G-4809)*
Carrier Corporation................................ F 260 358-0888
 Huntington *(G-7304)*
Cil Electronics LLC................................ E 765 457-3894
 Kokomo *(G-10244)*
▲ Compal USA (indiana) Inc.................. B 574 739-2929
 Logansport *(G-11070)*
David Kechel... G 260 627-2749
 Leo *(G-10967)*
Divsys Aerospace & Engrg LLC............. F 317 941-7777
 Indianapolis *(G-7987)*
Divsys Intl - Icape LLC.......................... E 317 405-9427
 Indianapolis *(G-7988)*
Dpict Imaging Inc.................................. G 317 436-8411
 Indianapolis *(G-8004)*
▲ Icape-Usa LLC................................... G 765 431-1271
 Indianapolis *(G-8449)*
Jtd Enterprises Inc................................ F 574 533-9438
 Goshen *(G-6180)*
◆ Key Electronics Inc............................ C 812 206-2500
 Jeffersonville *(G-10009)*
Kimball Elec Indianapolis Inc................. D 812 634-4000
 Indianapolis *(G-8684)*
Kimball Electronics Inc.......................... A 812 634-4200
 Jasper *(G-9865)*
Kimball Electronics Inc.......................... B 812 634-4000
 Jasper *(G-9866)*
Kimball Electronics Group LLC.............. G 812 634-4200
 Jasper *(G-9867)*
Kimball Electronics Mfg Inc.................... A 812 482-1600
 Jasper *(G-9869)*
▲ Kimball Electronics Tampa Inc........... G 812 634-4000
 Jasper *(G-9870)*
Pinder Instruments Company Inc............ G 219 924-7070
 Munster *(G-12558)*
Proto Engineering Llc............................ G 800 522-6752
 Mooresville *(G-12237)*
Semiconductor Test Supply LLC............. G 317 513-7393
 Martinsville *(G-11426)*
Teaco Inc... G 219 874-6234
 Michigan City *(G-11676)*
Vector Graphics Inc............................... G 317 255-9800
 Indianapolis *(G-9704)*

3674 Semiconductors and related devices

3 Micron Laser Technology LLC............. G 317 677-8958
 Indianapolis *(G-7387)*
▲ Advanced Control Tech Inc................ G 317 806-2750
 Indianapolis *(G-7437)*
Allegro Microsystems LLC...................... G 765 854-2263
 Carmel *(G-1557)*
Alliance Group Tech Inc......................... D 219 375-2810
 Warren *(G-16293)*
◆ American Ultraviolet Company............ E 765 483-9514
 Lebanon *(G-10874)*
▲ Amerlight LLC.................................... F 812 602-3452
 Evansville *(G-3889)*
▲ Autosem Inc...................................... E 574 288-8866
 South Bend *(G-14953)*
Bandgap Semiconductor LLC................. G 317 652-3250
 Noblesville *(G-13038)*
Bowmar LLC.. E 260 747-3121
 Fort Wayne *(G-4813)*

Ca Inc... E 317 844-7221
 Indianapolis *(G-7711)*
Convergent Consulting LLC.................... G 202 441-6453
 Indianapolis *(G-7864)*
▲ Dti Services Ltd Liability Co............... G 765 745-0261
 Indianapolis *(G-8015)*
Environmental Technology Inc................ E 574 233-1202
 South Bend *(G-15016)*
Express Controls.................................... G 574 831-3497
 Goshen *(G-6131)*
Federal-Mogul Powertrain LLC............... G 574 272-5900
 South Bend *(G-15032)*
Fireflies Ltd... G 219 728-6245
 Chesterton *(G-1926)*
Gen Digital Inc....................................... G 317 575-4010
 Indianapolis *(G-8268)*
Hartsock Industrial Sales Inc.................. G 317 858-8250
 Westfield *(G-16696)*
Heraeus Electro-Nite Co LLC................. C 765 473-8275
 Peru *(G-13584)*
Hoosier Cab Company LLC.................... G 812 822-2508
 Bloomington *(G-879)*
Indiana Intgrated Circuits LLC................ G 574 217-4612
 South Bend *(G-15078)*
Infineon Tech Americas Corp.................. G 866 951-9519
 Kokomo *(G-10288)*
Jdsu Acterna Holdings LLC.................... G 317 788-9351
 Indianapolis *(G-8621)*
Jones International Inc........................... G 219 746-1478
 Gary *(G-5971)*
Linear Technology LLC........................... G 317 443-1169
 Arcadia *(G-314)*
Magellan Integration Inc......................... E 812 492-4400
 Evansville *(G-4185)*
Mark Lamaster....................................... G 765 534-4185
 Noblesville *(G-13131)*
Maxim Integrated Products Inc................ G 252 227-7202
 Westfield *(G-16710)*
Microchip Technology Inc....................... G 317 842-1676
 Indianapolis *(G-8901)*
Microchip Technology Inc....................... G 317 773-8323
 Noblesville *(G-13139)*
Microscreen LLC.................................... E 574 232-4358
 South Bend *(G-15150)*
▲ Neoti LLC... F 260 494-1499
 Bluffton *(G-1045)*
Netegrity Inc.. F 219 763-6400
 Portage *(G-13898)*
Nxp Usa Inc... G 765 459-5355
 Kokomo *(G-10318)*
Paul Nelson... G 765 352-0698
 Martinsville *(G-11421)*
▲ Payne-Sparkmanm Manufacturing..... F 812 944-4893
 New Albany *(G-12792)*
Perfection Products Inc.......................... E 765 482-7786
 Lebanon *(G-10932)*
Power Components of Midwest.............. E 574 256-6990
 Mishawaka *(G-11976)*
Pyromation LLC..................................... C 260 484-2580
 Fort Wayne *(G-5358)*
◆ Qualitex Inc.. F 260 244-7839
 Columbia City *(G-2186)*
Rapid Sensors Inc................................. G 260 499-0079
 Howe *(G-7241)*
Reearth Technologies............................. G 812 219-6517
 Bloomington *(G-953)*
Sanders Pulsed Power LLC.................... G 630 313-2378
 South Bend *(G-15232)*
Semicndctor Cmponents Inds LLC......... G 765 868-5015
 Kokomo *(G-10333)*
Sunright Solar Inc.................................. G 317 503-9253
 Indianapolis *(G-9527)*

Employee Codes: A=Over 500 employees, B=251-500
C=101-250, D=51-100, E=20-50, F=10-19, G=1-9

2024 Harris Indiana
Industrial Directory

36 ELECTRONIC & OTHER ELECTRICAL EQUIPMENT & COMPONENTS

Texas Instruments Incorporated............ G 317 574-2611
Carmel *(G-1784)*

Toppan Photomasks Inc................... C 765 854-7500
Kokomo *(G-10350)*

Toyota Tsusho America Inc............... D 765 449-3500
Colburn *(G-2111)*

US Nano LLC................................. G 941 360-2161
South Bend *(G-15297)*

Viavi Solutions Inc........................... E 317 788-9351
Indianapolis *(G-9719)*

Vishay Americas Inc........................ G 765 778-4878
Pendleton *(G-13561)*

3675 Electronic capacitors

A C Mallory Capacitors LLC............... G 317 612-1000
Indianapolis *(G-7397)*

Greatbatch Ltd................................ G 260 755-7484
Warsaw *(G-16371)*

Integer Holdings Corporation............. G 260 373-1664
Fort Wayne *(G-5114)*

Kirby Risk Corporation..................... D 317 398-9713
Shelbyville *(G-14768)*

Tempest Technical Sales Inc............. G 317 844-9236
Carmel *(G-1783)*

Zepto Systems Incorporated............. G 812 323-0642
Bloomington *(G-1019)*

3676 Electronic resistors

▲ Khorporate Holdings Inc................. C 260 357-3365
Laotto *(G-10807)*

3677 Electronic coils and transformers

Andon Specialties Inc...................... G 317 983-1700
Indianapolis *(G-7516)*

Andover Coils LLC........................... D 765 447-1157
Fishers *(G-4464)*

Chemtrex LLC................................. G 317 508-4223
Noblesville *(G-13058)*

▲ Coil-Tran LLC............................... D 219 942-8511
Hobart *(G-7182)*

▲ Custom Magnetics Inc................... E 260 982-8508
North Manchester *(G-13231)*

Hermetic Coil Co Inc........................ E 812 735-2400
Bicknell *(G-734)*

Kane Usa Inc.................................. E 800 547-5740
Indianapolis *(G-8660)*

Kendrion (mishawaka) LLC................ E 574 257-2422
Mishawaka *(G-11922)*

Lesea Inc....................................... G 574 344-8215
South Bend *(G-15124)*

◆ Marshall Electric Corporation..........F 574 223-4367
Rochester *(G-14305)*

▲ Midwest Coil LLC......................... G 765 807-5429
Lafayette *(G-10648)*

Performance Mstr Coil Proc Inc......... E 765 364-1300
Crawfordsville *(G-2603)*

Q P Inc... F 574 295-6884
Elkhart *(G-3626)*

RB Annis Instruments Inc................. E 765 848-1621
Greencastle *(G-6428)*

◆ REO-Usa Inc............................... F 317 899-1395
Indianapolis *(G-9291)*

Separation Technologies Inc............. G 219 548-5814
Valparaiso *(G-16046)*

Sonicu LLC.................................... G 317 468-2345
Greenfield *(G-6556)*

▲ Southern Electric Coil LLC............. E 219 931-5500
Hammond *(G-7011)*

Tempest Technical Sales Inc............. G 317 844-9236
Carmel *(G-1783)*

◆ Tetrasolv Inc................................ F 765 643-3941
Anderson *(G-206)*

Tri-Star Filtration Inc........................ G 317 337-0940
Indianapolis *(G-9636)*

Vista Worldwide LLC........................ G 574 264-0711
Elkhart *(G-3772)*

▲ Warsaw Coil Co Inc...................... D 574 267-6041
Warsaw *(G-16443)*

▲ Xfmrs Inc.................................... A 317 834-1066
Camby *(G-1517)*

3678 Electronic connectors

Accu-Mold LLC............................... E 269 323-0388
Mishawaka *(G-11834)*

Advanced Metal Etching Inc.............. E 260 894-4189
Ligonier *(G-11003)*

Alexander Machine Inc..................... G 812 879-4982
Gosport *(G-6282)*

CTS Corporation............................. C 574 293-7511
Elkhart *(G-3277)*

Edinburgh Connector Co LLC............ E 812 526-8801
Edinburgh *(G-3082)*

Kirby Risk Corporation..................... D 765 447-1402
Lafayette *(G-10621)*

Mann Made Microwave LLC.............. G 317 407-1223
Franklin *(G-5754)*

Molex LLC..................................... F 317 834-5600
Mooresville *(G-12223)*

PMG Incorporated........................... G 574 291-3805
South Bend *(G-15198)*

RCA Corporation............................. C 800 722-2161
Indianapolis *(G-9276)*

Ronard Industries Inc....................... F 219 874-4801
Michigan City *(G-11658)*

3679 Electronic components, nec

A-1vet LLC..................................... G 317 498-1804
Indianapolis *(G-7407)*

Acterna LLC................................... E 317 788-9351
Indianapolis *(G-7425)*

Adafill Global LLC........................... G 317 798-5378
Indianapolis *(G-7427)*

Advanced Harn & Assembly LLC....... F 574 722-4040
Logansport *(G-11054)*

Alliance Group Tech Inc................... D 260 375-2810
Warren *(G-16293)*

◆ Almega/Tru-Flex Inc..................... E 574 546-2113
Bremen *(G-1172)*

◆ Alpine Electronics Manufa............. A 956 217-3200
Greenwood *(G-6665)*

▲ American Technology Compo......... C 800 238-2687
Elkhart *(G-3177)*

Assembly Masters Inc...................... G 574 293-9026
Elkhart *(G-3198)*

▲ Autosem Inc................................ E 574 288-8866
South Bend *(G-14953)*

B Q Products Inc............................. F 317 786-5500
Indianapolis *(G-7582)*

C & G Wiring Inc............................. F 574 333-3433
Elkhart *(G-3241)*

Caddo Connections Inc.................... E 219 874-8119
La Porte *(G-10393)*

◆ Carson Manufacturing Co Inc........ F 317 257-3191
Indianapolis *(G-7750)*

Circuits Repair LLC......................... G 317 512-1026
Shelbyville *(G-14745)*

Compal Electronics Na Inc................ E 574 992-8793
Logansport *(G-11069)*

Competition Electronic Systems......... G 317 291-2823
Indianapolis *(G-7844)*

CTS Elctrnic Cmponents Cal Inc........ G 574 523-3800
Elkhart *(G-3278)*

Divsys Aerospace & Engrg LLC......... F 317 941-7777
Indianapolis *(G-7987)*

Dwyer Instruments Inc..................... G 219 393-5250
La Porte *(G-10402)*

Electric-Tec LLC.............................. E 260 665-1252
Angola *(G-248)*

Electronic Services LLC................... E 765 457-3894
Kokomo *(G-10262)*

Freedom Acres Inc.......................... F 260 856-3059
Cromwell *(G-2630)*

Fruition Industries LLC..................... F 260 854-2325
Rome City *(G-14375)*

Gartech Enterprises Inc.................... F 812 794-4796
Austin *(G-465)*

◆ Green Cubes Technology LLC....... E 502 416-1060
Kokomo *(G-10273)*

Group Dekko Inc............................. E 260 854-4783
Rome City *(G-14376)*

Hartsock Industrial Sales Inc............. G 317 858-8250
Westfield *(G-16696)*

Haven Technologies Inc................... E 317 740-0419
Carmel *(G-1651)*

HB Connect Inc.............................. G 855 503-9159
Fort Wayne *(G-5051)*

HB Connect Inc.............................. D 260 422-1212
Fort Wayne *(G-5052)*

Heather Sound Amplification............. G 574 255-6100
Mishawaka *(G-11906)*

Hermac Incorporated....................... E 260 925-0312
Auburn *(G-396)*

▲ Hi-Pro Inc................................... F 260 665-5038
Angola *(G-258)*

Hymns2go LLC............................... G 317 577-0730
Fishers *(G-4540)*

Indiana Integrated Circuits In............. G 574 217-4612
South Bend *(G-15077)*

▼ Infinias LLC................................. G 317 348-1249
Indianapolis *(G-8541)*

▼ Intelliray Inc................................. G 260 547-4399
Decatur *(G-2864)*

International Fuse LLC..................... G 574 340-4042
South Bend *(G-15085)*

Investwell Electronics Inc.................. G 765 457-1911
Kokomo *(G-10289)*

Jag Wire LLC.................................. F 260 463-8537
Lagrange *(G-10744)*

▲ K I B Enterprises Corp.................. C 574 262-0518
Elkhart *(G-3443)*

Kadel Engineering Corporation.......... E 317 745-2798
Danville *(G-2816)*

Kamdoer Inc................................... E 574 293-2990
Elkhart *(G-3446)*

Kauffman Engineering LLC............... D 574 732-2154
Bremen *(G-1201)*

Kauffman Engineering LLC............... D 765 482-5640
Lebanon *(G-10907)*

Kauffman Engineering Inc................. D 574 722-3800
Logansport *(G-11086)*

Kendrion (mishawaka) LLC............... E 574 257-2422
Mishawaka *(G-11922)*

▲ Kimball Electronics Tampa Inc....... G 812 634-4000
Jasper *(G-9870)*

▲ Kirby Risk Corporation.................. D 765 448-4567
Lafayette *(G-10623)*

KK Hall Inc.................................... G 317 839-8329
Clayton *(G-2061)*

▲ Kra International LLC................... D 574 259-3550
Mishawaka *(G-11923)*

Laketronics Inc............................... E 260 856-4588
Cromwell *(G-2631)*

Leoni LLC...................................... G 574 315-0503
Mishawaka *(G-11928)*

▲ Mallory Sonalert Products Inc........ E 317 612-1000
Indianapolis *(G-8822)*

36 ELECTRONIC & OTHER ELECTRICAL EQUIPMENT & COMPONENTS

Mann Made Microwave LLC.................. G 317 407-1223
  Franklin *(G-5754)*
Microform Inc.................................. G 574 522-9851
  Elkhart *(G-3536)*
Microwave Devices Inc.................... G 317 868-8833
  Franklin *(G-5756)*
Mier Products Inc............................ E 765 457-0223
  Kokomo *(G-10307)*
▲ Mssl Wiring System Inc................. D 330 856-3366
  Portland *(G-13958)*
▲ Mursix Corporation........................ C 765 282-2221
  Yorktown *(G-16977)*
Music Store..................................... G 812 949-3004
  Clarksville *(G-2024)*
Northwind Electronics LLC............... F 317 288-0787
  Indianapolis *(G-9024)*
▲ Orion Global Sourcing Inc.............. G 812 332-3338
  Bloomington *(G-939)*
▲ Parkway Investor Group Inc.......... E 260 665-1252
  Angola *(G-281)*
Patrick Industries Inc....................... D 574 293-2990
  Elkhart *(G-3599)*
Pent Assemblies............................... E 260 347-5828
  Kendallville *(G-10141)*
Pinder Instruments Company Inc..... G 219 924-7070
  Munster *(G-12558)*
▲ Power Systems Innovations Inc..... G 812 480-4380
  Newburgh *(G-13017)*
Precision Wire Assemblies Inc......... D 765 489-6302
  Hagerstown *(G-6842)*
Precision Wire Supply LLC............... E 574 834-7545
  North Webster *(G-13313)*
Protron LLC..................................... G 765 313-1595
  Anderson *(G-181)*
▲ Quality Plas Engrg Acqstion Co..... E 574 262-2621
  Elkhart *(G-3632)*
R C Systems Inc............................... G 812 282-4898
  Jeffersonville *(G-10044)*
Rayconn LLC.................................... G 317 809-5788
  Indianapolis *(G-9269)*
Redwire Space Technologies Inc...... E 812 923-9591
  Greenville *(G-6653)*
Rtw Enterprises Inc.......................... E 574 294-3275
  Elkhart *(G-3654)*
▲ Samtec Inc..................................... A 812 944-6733
  New Albany *(G-12812)*
Schumaker Technical Assembly...... G 765 742-7176
  Lafayette *(G-10687)*
Signaling Solution Inc...................... G 812 533-1345
  Shelburn *(G-14721)*
▲ Skytech II LLC............................... E 260 459-1703
  Fort Wayne *(G-5421)*
▲ Skytech-Systems Inc..................... F 260 459-1703
  Fort Wayne *(G-5422)*
Smg Global Inc................................. G 765 250-0081
  Lafayette *(G-10691)*
Stuart Manufacturing Inc................. E 260 403-2003
  Fort Wayne *(G-5448)*
Tap-A-Lite Inc.................................. E 219 932-8067
  Hammond *(G-7018)*
Technology Dynamics....................... G 317 524-6338
  Indianapolis *(G-9569)*
Tempest Technical Sales Inc............ G 317 844-9236
  Carmel *(G-1783)*
Top Shelf Acoustics LLC................... G 317 512-4569
  Indianapolis *(G-9620)*
Toppan Photomasks Inc.................. C 765 854-7500
  Kokomo *(G-10350)*
Toyota Tsusho America Inc............. D 765 449-3500
  Colburn *(G-2111)*
Trignetra Inc.................................... G 765 637-8447
  West Lafayette *(G-16639)*

V-Tech Engineering Inc.................... F 260 824-4322
  Bluffton *(G-1067)*
Vista Worldwide LLC....................... G 574 264-0711
  Elkhart *(G-3772)*
Walton Industrial Park Inc............... F 574 626-2929
  Walton *(G-16284)*
Wattre Inc.. G 260 657-3701
  Woodburn *(G-16956)*
Wheelock Manufacturing Inc........... E 219 285-8540
  Garrett *(G-5880)*
Wilco Corporation............................ F 317 228-9320
  Indianapolis *(G-9763)*
ZF Active Safety & Elec US LLC........ D 765 429-1984
  Lafayette *(G-10721)*

3691 Storage batteries

B T Bttery Charger Systems Inc....... G 574 533-6030
  Goshen *(G-6093)*
Batteries Plus.................................. G 317 219-0007
  Noblesville *(G-13040)*
◆ Bulldog Battery Corporation.......... D 260 563-0551
  Wabash *(G-16176)*
Bw Energy & Innovation LLC............ G 214 223-2459
  Greenfield *(G-6474)*
C&D Technologies Inc....................... C 765 762-2461
  Attica *(G-345)*
Crown Battery Manufacturing Co..... G 260 423-3358
  Fort Wayne *(G-4888)*
Dd Dannar LLC................................. F 765 216-7191
  Muncie *(G-12374)*
Enpower Inc..................................... E 463 213-3200
  Indianapolis *(G-8123)*
Exide Technologies LLC................... G 317 876-7475
  Indianapolis *(G-8155)*
Greatbatch Ltd................................. G 260 755-7484
  Warsaw *(G-16371)*
Integer Holdings Corporation........... G 260 373-1664
  Fort Wayne *(G-5114)*
Johnson Controls Inc....................... F 317 917-5043
  Pittsboro *(G-13649)*
Knk Battery LLC............................... G 765 426-2016
  Otterbein *(G-13454)*
Ocella Inc.. G 845 842-8185
  Newberry *(G-12990)*
Tri-State Power Supply LLC............. G 812 537-2500
  Lawrenceburg *(G-10863)*
Trojan Battery.................................. F 317 561-5650
  Plainfield *(G-13738)*
Worldwide Battery Company LLC..... G 248 830-8537
  Elkhart *(G-3795)*
Worldwide Battery Company LLC..... G 812 475-1326
  Evansville *(G-4390)*

3692 Primary batteries, dry and wet

C&D Technologies Inc....................... C 765 762-2461
  Attica *(G-345)*
Greatbatch Ltd................................. G 260 755-7484
  Warsaw *(G-16371)*
Integer Holdings Corporation........... G 260 373-1664
  Fort Wayne *(G-5114)*
Ocella Inc.. G 845 842-8185
  Newberry *(G-12990)*

3694 Engine electrical equipment

◆ Almega/Tru-Flex Inc...................... E 574 546-2113
  Bremen *(G-1172)*
▲ Aristo LLC..................................... E
  Hobart *(G-7173)*
▼ B & M Electrical Company Inc....... F 765 448-4532
  Lafayette *(G-10533)*
Borgwarner Pds (indiana) Inc.......... C 765 778-6696
  Noblesville *(G-13045)*

Borgwarner Reman Holdings LLC..... A 800 372-5131
  Pendleton *(G-13527)*
Caddo Connections Inc.................... E 219 874-8119
  La Porte *(G-10393)*
Cds LLC... G 812 637-0900
  West Harrison *(G-16545)*
Central Steel and Wire Co LLC......... G 219 787-5000
  Portage *(G-13854)*
▲ Cpx Inc.. B 219 474-5280
  Kentland *(G-10159)*
Cummins Emssion Sltons Clmbus..... E 800 286-6467
  Columbus *(G-2254)*
Cummins Inc..................................... G 812 377-2932
  Columbus *(G-2259)*
Cummins Inc..................................... G 812 312-3162
  Columbus *(G-2270)*
Cummins Inc..................................... G 812 377-8601
  Columbus *(G-2272)*
Cummins Inc..................................... F 812 378-2874
  Columbus *(G-2273)*
Cummins Inc..................................... F 317 610-2493
  Indianapolis *(G-7927)*
Cummins Inc..................................... G 317 244-7251
  Indianapolis *(G-7928)*
Cummins Inc..................................... G 317 751-4567
  Whiteland *(G-16782)*
Cummins Inc..................................... A 812 377-5000
  Columbus *(G-2271)*
D & E Auto Electric Inc.................... F 219 763-3892
  Portage *(G-13858)*
Design Engineering.......................... G 219 926-2170
  Chesterton *(G-1919)*
E M F Corp....................................... E 260 488-2479
  Hamilton *(G-6852)*
▲ E M F Corp.................................... E 260 665-9541
  Angola *(G-246)*
East Penn Manufacturing Co............ G 317 236-6288
  Indianapolis *(G-8038)*
Federal-Mogul Powertrain LLC......... G 574 272-5900
  South Bend *(G-15032)*
GM Components Holdings LLC......... G 765 451-5011
  Kokomo *(G-10269)*
Group Dekko Inc.............................. E 574 834-2818
  North Webster *(G-13305)*
Hitachi Astemo Americas Inc........... D 859 734-9451
  Ligonier *(G-11017)*
Imp Holdings LLC............................. D 260 665-6112
  Angola *(G-263)*
Indiana Research Institute............... G 812 378-5363
  Columbus *(G-2325)*
◆ Kimball Electronics Group LLC....... C 812 634-4000
  Jasper *(G-9868)*
Kirby Risk Corporation..................... D 765 447-1402
  Lafayette *(G-10621)*
La Fontaine Generator Exchange..... G 765 981-4561
  La Fontaine *(G-10368)*
Laketronics Inc................................ E 260 856-4588
  Cromwell *(G-2631)*
Motherson Sumi Systems Limited.... A 260 726-6501
  Portland *(G-13957)*
Noel-Smyser Engineering Corp........ E 317 293-2215
  Indianapolis *(G-9020)*
◆ Old Remco Holdings LLC............... C 765 778-6499
  Pendleton *(G-13548)*
Patrick Industries Inc....................... D 260 665-6112
  Angola *(G-282)*
Qualtronics LLC................................ E 812 375-8880
  Columbus *(G-2384)*
R & R Regulators Inc........................ F 574 522-3500
  Elkhart *(G-3636)*
Spectra Prmium Mblity Sltons L....... F 800 628-5442
  Greenfield *(G-6557)*

Employee Codes: A=Over 500 employees, B=251-500
C=101-250, D=51-100, E=20-50, F=10-19, G=1-9

36 ELECTRONIC & OTHER ELECTRICAL EQUIPMENT & COMPONENTS

3695 Magnetic and optical recording media

Ziehl-Abegg Inc .... G 317 219-3014
  Noblesville *(G-13200)*

Behnke Engineering .... G 574 842-2327
  Culver *(G-2780)*
◆ Cinram Inc .... A 416 298-8190
  Richmond *(G-14104)*
RB Annis Instruments Inc .... G 765 848-1621
  Greencastle *(G-6428)*
Sony Corporation of America .... F 812 462-8726
  Terre Haute *(G-15703)*
Sony Dadc US Inc .... F 812 462-8116
  Terre Haute *(G-15704)*
Sony Dadc US Inc .... F 812 462-8784
  Terre Haute *(G-15705)*
▲ Sony Dadc US Inc .... A 812 462-8100
  Terre Haute *(G-15706)*
Tclogic LLC .... G 317 464-5152
  Indianapolis *(G-9562)*

3699 Electrical equipment and supplies, nec

Academy Energy Group LLC .... G 312 931-7443
  Newburgh *(G-12991)*
Accuracy Laser Fabrication LLC .... G 812 322-6431
  Bedford *(G-616)*
Advanced Metal Etching Inc .... E 260 894-4189
  Ligonier *(G-11003)*
Advantage Cartridge Co Inc .... F 260 747-9941
  Fort Wayne *(G-4730)*
Allegion LLC .... E 317 810-3700
  Carmel *(G-1553)*
Allied Mfg Partners Inc .... G 260 428-2670
  Fort Wayne *(G-4745)*
American Door Controls Inc .... G 812 988-4853
  Morgantown *(G-12253)*
Applied Technology Group Inc .... F 260 482-2844
  Fort Wayne *(G-4767)*
Atkore Inc .... G 219 844-6800
  Merrillville *(G-11486)*
Automated Laser Corporation .... G 260 637-4140
  Fort Wayne *(G-4781)*
Automation Consultants Inc .... G 502 552-4995
  Floyds Knobs *(G-4669)*
Automtion Ctrl Panl Sltons Inc .... F 219 961-8308
  Munster *(G-12531)*
AV Solutions Indy LLC .... G 317 509-5930
  Indianapolis *(G-7578)*
B Y M Electronics Inc .... G 574 674-5096
  Granger *(G-6335)*
Babsco Supply Inc .... G 574 267-8999
  Warsaw *(G-16316)*
Becker Elec .... G 812 362-9000
  Rockport *(G-14337)*
Best Equipment Co Inc .... E 317 823-3050
  Indianapolis *(G-7617)*
Center For Ethcal Rbtics A Nnt .... G 219 741-9374
  Hammond *(G-6897)*
Clarke Industrial Systems Inc .... E 260 489-4575
  Fishers *(G-4491)*
Conzer Security Inc .... G 317 580-9460
  Carmel *(G-1595)*
Curtis Life Research LLC .... G 317 873-4519
  Zionsville *(G-16999)*
Deprisco Ventures Inc .... E 260 637-8660
  Fort Wayne *(G-4916)*
Digiop Inc .... E 800 968-3606
  Indianapolis *(G-7974)*
Directed Photonics Inc .... G 317 877-3142
  Noblesville *(G-13072)*
E & E Garage Doors LLC .... G 317 575-9677
  Carmel *(G-1615)*

▲ E M F Corp .... E 260 665-9541
  Angola *(G-246)*
Economy Electric Htg & Coolg .... G 219 923-4441
  Highland *(G-7134)*
Electric Plus .... F 812 336-4992
  Bloomington *(G-860)*
▲ Energy Access Incorporated .... F 317 329-1676
  Indianapolis *(G-8115)*
▲ Esaote North America Inc .... D 317 813-6000
  Fishers *(G-4517)*
Expert Electrical Services LLC .... G 765 664-6642
  Marion *(G-11285)*
Fairway Laser Systems Inc .... G 219 462-6892
  Valparaiso *(G-15946)*
Frontier Electric Inc .... G 219 778-2553
  Rolling Prairie *(G-14362)*
Group Dekko Inc .... G 260 357-5988
  Garrett *(G-5866)*
Hitachi Astemo Americas Inc .... D 859 734-9451
  Ligonier *(G-11017)*
Image Vault LLC .... G 812 948-8400
  New Albany *(G-12743)*
▼ Industrial Trning Unlmted Corp .... E 812 961-8801
  Dugger *(G-2957)*
Indy Control Corporation .... G 317 787-4639
  Beech Grove *(G-692)*
Jason Incorporated .... D 847 215-1948
  Richmond *(G-14150)*
Johnson Cntrls SEC Sltions LLC .... G 800 238-2455
  Indianapolis *(G-8634)*
◆ Kimball Electronics Group LLC .... C 812 634-4000
  Jasper *(G-9868)*
Koester Metals Inc .... E 260 495-1818
  Fremont *(G-5825)*
Lancon Electric Inc .... G 260 897-3285
  Laotto *(G-10809)*
Language Company South Bend .... G 574 287-3622
  South Bend *(G-15116)*
Loud Clear Communications LLC .... G 260 433-9479
  Auburn *(G-403)*
▲ Lumen Cache Incorporated .... G 317 739-4218
  Fishers *(G-4644)*
Lynn Bros Electric Inc .... G 219 762-6386
  Portage *(G-13883)*
Magnasphere Corporation .... G 574 533-1310
  Goshen *(G-6209)*
Magnetic Instrumentation LLC .... E 317 842-7500
  Indianapolis *(G-8810)*
Marian Suzhou LLC .... G 317 638-6525
  Indianapolis *(G-8830)*
Masbez LLC .... G 855 962-7239
  Frankfort *(G-5681)*
Midwest Electrical Sales .... G 708 821-7490
  Valparaiso *(G-16002)*
Nrk Inc .... E 812 232-1800
  Terre Haute *(G-15653)*
◆ Ogden Welding Systems Inc .... E 219 322-5252
  Schererville *(G-14537)*
Ohio Valley Electric .... G 812 532-5288
  Lawrenceburg *(G-10848)*
P-Kelco Inc .... E 260 356-1376
  Huntington *(G-7352)*
Patterson Engrg & Mfg LLC .... G 217 260-1415
  Lafayette *(G-10663)*
Phil & Son Inc .... G 219 663-5757
  Crown Point *(G-2730)*
▲ Poolguard/Pbm Industries Inc .... F 812 346-2648
  North Vernon *(G-13292)*
Q P Inc .... F 574 295-6884
  Elkhart *(G-3626)*
Quality Hydraulic Mch Svc Inc .... G 317 892-2596
  Danville *(G-2824)*

Quick Panic Release LLC .... G 812 841-5733
  Terre Haute *(G-15673)*
Qumulex Inc .... E 317 207-0520
  Fishers *(G-4590)*
Rebuilding Cnslting Pckg Sltion .... G 574 389-1966
  Elkhart *(G-3641)*
Reese Forge Orna Ironwork .... G 219 775-1039
  Lake Village *(G-10782)*
Richards Electric LLC .... G 317 253-1083
  Indianapolis *(G-9302)*
Samtec Inc .... G 812 517-6081
  Scottsburg *(G-14577)*
Sandra Henry .... G 574 699-7867
  Young America *(G-16985)*
Seib Machine & Tool Co Inc .... G 812 453-6174
  Evansville *(G-4304)*
Sitewise Inc .... G 317 988-1630
  Indianapolis *(G-9444)*
Stage Ninja LLC .... G 317 829-1507
  Indianapolis *(G-9490)*
Sun Power Technologies LLC .... G 317 399-8113
  Westfield *(G-16730)*
Supernova International Inc .... G 317 969-8246
  Indianapolis *(G-9531)*
T Shorter Manufacturing Inc .... G 574 264-4131
  Elkhart *(G-3713)*
Tap-A-Lite Inc .... E 219 932-8067
  Hammond *(G-7018)*
Targamite LLC .... G 260 489-0046
  Fort Wayne *(G-5468)*
Terick Sales .... G 574 626-3173
  Walton *(G-16283)*
Thermo Cube Incorporated .... G 574 936-5096
  Plymouth *(G-13816)*
Top In Sound Inc .... G 765 649-8111
  Anderson *(G-207)*
◆ Touchplate Technologies Inc .... E 260 426-1565
  Fort Wayne *(G-5497)*
Trilithic .... G 317 536-1071
  Indianapolis *(G-9640)*
Troyer Brothers Inc .... E 260 565-2244
  Bluffton *(G-1064)*
USA Vision Systems Inc .... G 949 583-1519
  Fishers *(G-4625)*
Utility Systems Inc .... G 317 842-9000
  Indianapolis *(G-9692)*
Vincent Aliano Elc & Hvac Inc .... G 812 332-3332
  Bloomington *(G-1007)*
William D Darr .... G 574 518-0453
  Syracuse *(G-15493)*
X-Treme Lazer Tag .... G 812 238-8412
  Terre Haute *(G-15749)*
Xfmrs Holdings Inc .... F 317 834-1066
  Camby *(G-1518)*
Xwind LLC .... G 317 350-2080
  Brownsburg *(G-1414)*

37 TRANSPORTATION EQUIPMENT

3711 Motor vehicles and car bodies

1st Attack Engineering Inc .... G 260 837-2435
  Auburn *(G-359)*
7th Leadership Organization .... G 219 938-6906
  Gary *(G-5883)*
ABC Truck & Equipment LLC .... G 260 565-3307
  Bluffton *(G-1021)*
Aje Suspension Inc .... F 812 346-7356
  North Vernon *(G-13255)*
AM General Holdings LLC .... A 574 237-6222
  South Bend *(G-14940)*

SIC SECTION
37 TRANSPORTATION EQUIPMENT

AM General LLC.. A 574 258-7523
  Mishawaka *(G-11840)*

AM General LLC.. G 574 258-6699
  South Bend *(G-14941)*

◆ AM General LLC... D 574 237-6222
  South Bend *(G-14942)*

American Reliance Inds Co....................... E 260 768-4704
  Shipshewana *(G-14834)*

Andretti Technologies LLC....................... G 317 872-2700
  Indianapolis *(G-7517)*

Android Industries LLC............................. E 260 672-0112
  Roanoke *(G-14257)*

Autofarm Mobility LLC.............................. G 317 410-0070
  Daleville *(G-2795)*

▲ B & B Industries Inc............................... E 574 262-8551
  Elkhart *(G-3210)*

Badlands Pick Up Van ACC Salv............... G 574 633-2156
  Wyatt *(G-16963)*

Besi Manufacturing Inc............................. G 812 427-4114
  Vevay *(G-16106)*

Capital City Transit LLC........................... G 317 813-5800
  Mooresville *(G-12198)*

Checkered Racing & Chrome LLC............ F 812 275-2875
  Spencer *(G-15341)*

Chinook Motor Coach Corp...................... D 574 584-3756
  Peru *(G-13571)*

City of Valparaiso...................................... G 219 462-5291
  Valparaiso *(G-15928)*

Concept Cars Inc...................................... G 260 668-7553
  Angola *(G-242)*

Damon Motor Coach.................................. E 574 536-3781
  Elkhart *(G-3286)*

Delaware Employees Abenef................... G 765 284-1565
  Muncie *(G-12379)*

Discount Power Equipment....................... G 765 642-0040
  Anderson *(G-104)*

Dock Bumpers Inc.................................... G 312 597-9282
  Highland *(G-7132)*

▲ Don Schumacher Racing Corp............... E 317 858-0356
  Brownsburg *(G-1365)*

Drinan Racing Products Inc..................... G 317 486-9710
  Indianapolis *(G-8008)*

▼ Eldorado National Kansas Inc................ C 785 827-1033
  Goshen *(G-6130)*

Elringklinger Mfg Ind Inc.......................... E 734 788-1776
  Fort Wayne *(G-4947)*

Fishers Fire Station 92............................. G 317 595-3292
  Fishers *(G-4522)*

▲ Flexform Technologies LLC.................... E 574 295-3777
  Elkhart *(G-3349)*

Forest River Inc.. D 574 262-5466
  Elkhart *(G-3354)*

Franke Motorsports Inc........................... G 317 357-6995
  Indianapolis *(G-8223)*

Fred Sibley Sr.. G 574 264-2237
  Elkhart *(G-3358)*

Freightliner Cstm Chassis Corp.............. C 260 517-9678
  Wakarusa *(G-16233)*

Full Throttle Enterprise Inc..................... G 317 779-3887
  Indianapolis *(G-8240)*

Gearbox Group Inc................................... G 812 268-0322
  Sullivan *(G-15406)*

General Motors LLC................................. B 765 668-2000
  Marion *(G-11287)*

Gracie Industries LLC............................. G 260 748-0314
  Fort Wayne *(G-5032)*

Holiday House LLC.................................. F 574 206-0016
  Elkhart *(G-3408)*

Hoosier Hot Rods Classics Inc................ G 812 768-5221
  Evansville *(G-4109)*

Howerton Racecar Works Inc.................. F 317 241-0868
  Indianapolis *(G-8431)*

Independent Protection Co...................... C 574 831-5680
  New Paris *(G-12960)*

▼ Independent Protection Co..................... E 574 533-4116
  Goshen *(G-6172)*

Indiana Assemblies LLC.......................... G 812 662-2173
  Greensburg *(G-6607)*

Jbm Race Cars LLC.................................. G 812 305-3666
  Evansville *(G-4139)*

Jt Transports LLC..................................... G 317 658-1523
  Indianapolis *(G-8646)*

K & D Custom Coach Inc......................... E 574 537-1716
  Goshen *(G-6182)*

K C Cmponents Wldg Fabrication............ G 317 539-6067
  Greencastle *(G-6416)*

KFC Composite Engineering Co.............. G 219 369-9093
  La Porte *(G-10436)*

Lake Ridge Vlntr Fire Dept Inc................ G 219 980-8620
  Gary *(G-5976)*

LCI Industries... A 574 535-1125
  Elkhart *(G-3476)*

Lcm Realty LLC.. G 574 535-1125
  Elkhart *(G-3479)*

Lippert Cmponents Intl Sls Inc................ G 574 312-7480
  Elkhart *(G-3489)*

Lippert Components Inc.......................... G 574 295-1483
  Elkhart *(G-3491)*

Lippert Components Inc.......................... G 574 535-1125
  Elkhart *(G-3492)*

Lippert Components Inc.......................... D 574 535-1125
  Goshen *(G-6202)*

Lippert Components Inc.......................... G 574 537-8900
  Goshen *(G-6205)*

Lippert Components Inc.......................... G 574 849-0869
  Goshen *(G-6206)*

Lippert Components Inc.......................... F 574 971-4320
  Goshen *(G-6207)*

Lippert Components Inc.......................... E 574 312-7445
  Middlebury *(G-11734)*

Lippert Components Inc.......................... E 800 551-9149
  Mishawaka *(G-11930)*

Lippert Components Inc.......................... F 574 312-6654
  South Bend *(G-15125)*

Lippert Components Inc.......................... F 260 234-4303
  Yoder *(G-16966)*

▲ Lippert Components Inc........................ B 574 535-1125
  Elkhart *(G-3493)*

▲ Lippert Components Mfg Inc................. G 574 535-1125
  Elkhart *(G-3495)*

M-TEC Corporation................................... D 574 294-1060
  Elkhart *(G-3507)*

Mastersbilt Chassis Inc.......................... G 812 793-3666
  Crothersville *(G-2642)*

Mc Ginley Fire Apparatus........................ G 765 482-3152
  Lebanon *(G-10915)*

◆ Medix Specialty Vehicles LLC............... C 574 266-0911
  Elkhart *(G-3525)*

Mid-State Truck Equipment Inc.............. E 317 849-4903
  Fishers *(G-4566)*

Midway Specialty Vehicles LLC.............. E 574 264-2530
  Elkhart *(G-3539)*

Mirrus Corporation Inc........................... F 812 689-1411
  Versailles *(G-16102)*

Navistar Inc... G 317 787-3113
  Indianapolis *(G-8993)*

NRC Modifications Inc............................ F 574 825-3646
  Middlebury *(G-11742)*

Olson Race Cars...................................... G 765 529-6933
  New Castle *(G-12878)*

▲ Oreca North America Inc...................... G 317 517-2948
  Indianapolis *(G-9069)*

Race Cars Usa LLC.................................. G 317 508-3500
  Carmel *(G-1734)*

Rayburn Automotive Inc......................... G 317 535-8232
  Greenwood *(G-6758)*

▲ Rebel Devil Customs LLP..................... G 303 921-7131
  Sharpsville *(G-14712)*

Renewed Performance Company............ F 765 675-7586
  Tipton *(G-15789)*

Rev Recreation Group Inc...................... E 260 724-2418
  Decatur *(G-2880)*

Rev Renegade LLC................................... E 574 966-0166
  Bristol *(G-1286)*

Revenge Designs Inc.............................. G 260 724-4000
  Decatur *(G-2881)*

Richard Sheets....................................... G 574 536-8247
  Bristol *(G-1287)*

Ring-Co LLC... G 317 641-7050
  Trafalgar *(G-15831)*

Royale Phoenix Inc................................. G 574 206-1216
  Elkhart *(G-3652)*

Small World Enterprises LLC.................. G 312 550-1717
  Lake Station *(G-10776)*

Sparkling Clean Inc................................ G 812 422-4871
  Evansville *(G-4326)*

Speedsters.. G 574 546-4656
  Bremen *(G-1223)*

Spitzer Racing Enterprises..................... F 317 894-9533
  Greenfield *(G-6559)*

Stellantis... E 765 854-4201
  Kokomo *(G-10339)*

◆ Subaru Indiana Automotive Inc............. A 765 449-1111
  Lafayette *(G-10703)*

Taotao Usa Inc.. G 317 856-8628
  Indianapolis *(G-9552)*

Team Green Inc....................................... F 317 872-2700
  Indianapolis *(G-9565)*

Tesla Inc.. G 317 558-8431
  Indianapolis *(G-9579)*

Think North America Inc........................ E 313 565-6781
  Elkhart *(G-3727)*

Thor Industries Inc................................. E 574 264-2900
  Elkhart *(G-3728)*

Thor Industries Inc................................. B 574 970-7460
  Elkhart *(G-3730)*

Tidy Janitorial Services LLC................... G 502 807-9847
  Clarksville *(G-2039)*

Tony Stewart Racing Entps LLC............. G 317 858-8620
  Brownsburg *(G-1409)*

Toyota Motor Mfg Ind Inc....................... A 812 385-5153
  Princeton *(G-14016)*

◆ Toyota Motor Mfg Ind Inc..................... D 812 387-2266
  Princeton *(G-14015)*

Ty Specialized LLC................................. G 317 734-7900
  Indianapolis *(G-9667)*

U B Machine Inc...................................... F 260 493-3381
  New Haven *(G-12924)*

◆ Utilimaster Holdings Inc...................... A 800 237-7806
  Bristol *(G-1295)*

Vehicle Service Group LLC..................... C 812 273-1622
  Madison *(G-11257)*

◆ Vehicle Service Group LLC.................. C 800 640-5438
  Madison *(G-11256)*

Vuteq Usa Inc... G 812 385-2584
  Princeton *(G-14019)*

Wave Express.. G 574 642-0630
  Goshen *(G-6275)*

Wb Automotive Holdings Inc.................. G 734 604-8962
  Fort Wayne *(G-5557)*

Wethington.. G 317 594-6000
  Greenfield *(G-6571)*

Wgs Global Services LC......................... B 812 548-4446
  Tell City *(G-15520)*

3713 Truck and bus bodies

Employee Codes: A=Over 500 employees, B=251-500
C=101-250, D=51-100, E=20-50, F=10-19, G=1-9

37 TRANSPORTATION EQUIPMENT

Accubuilt Plant I .... G 574 389-9000
Elkhart (G-3152)

Accuride Emi LLC .... E 940 565-8505
Evansville (G-3868)

Arboc Specialty Vehicles LLC .... D 574 825-1720
Middlebury (G-11697)

Armor Parent Corp .... F 812 962-5000
Evansville (G-3900)

◆ Autocar LLC .... E 765 489-5499
Hagerstown (G-6833)

Bay Bridge Mfg Inc .... E 574 848-7477
Bristol (G-1249)

Bentz Transport Products Inc .... F 260 622-9100
Zionsville (G-16996)

Boice Manufacturing Inc .... D 317 773-2100
Noblesville (G-13044)

Braun Companies LLC .... E 765 332-2084
New Castle (G-12852)

▲ Braun Motor Works Inc .... G 574 205-0102
Winamac (G-16858)

Brindle Products Inc .... F 260 627-2156
Grabill (G-6290)

Chads LLC .... G 812 323-7377
Ellettsville (G-3802)

Conder Water Services .... G 812 825-9883
Bloomington (G-835)

Dana Driveshaft Products LLC .... G 260 432-2903
Marion (G-11280)

Delivery Concepts Inc .... E 574 522-3981
Elkhart (G-3289)

Delphi Body Works .... F 765 564-2212
Delphi (G-2893)

Eaton Corporation .... C 260 925-3800
Auburn (G-387)

Eaton Corporation .... G 317 704-2520
Indianapolis (G-8043)

Federal-Mogul Motorparts LLC .... G 219 872-5150
Michigan City (G-11611)

Ford Motor Company .... F 901 368-8821
Plainfield (G-13680)

Gen T LLC .... G 574 266-0911
Elkhart (G-3371)

General Motors LLC .... B 260 672-1224
Roanoke (G-14268)

Gerald S Zins .... G 812 623-4980
Osgood (G-13409)

Grahams Wrecker Service Inc .... G 317 736-4355
Whiteland (G-16787)

Gravel Conveyors Inc .... F 317 873-8686
Zionsville (G-17014)

◆ H & H Sales Company Inc .... F 260 637-3177
Huntertown (G-7257)

Hendrickson International Corp ..... C 260 349-6400
Kendallville (G-10117)

Hendrickson International Corp ..... C 765 483-5350
Lebanon (G-10896)

Independent Protection Co .... C 574 831-5680
New Paris (G-12960)

Indiana Custom Trucks LLC .... E 260 463-3244
Shipshewana (G-14852)

International Brake Inds Inc .... D 419 905-7468
South Bend (G-15084)

Kneppers Inc .... G 260 636-2180
Albion (G-30)

Kneppers Inc .... G 260 636-2180
Avilla (G-483)

▲ Kruz LLC .... E 574 772-6673
Knox (G-10214)

Lund International Holding Co .... E 765 742-7200
Lafayette (G-10641)

Luxe Trucks LLC .... F 574 522-8422
Elkhart (G-3504)

Manasek Acquisition Co LLC .... E 765 551-1600
Elwood (G-3830)

Mantra Enterprise LLC .... E 201 428-8709
Fishers (G-4561)

Marmon Highway Tech LLC .... E 317 787-0718
Indianapolis (G-8839)

▼ Mavron Inc .... F 574 267-3044
Warsaw (G-16392)

Mobility Ventures LLC .... G 734 367-3714
South Bend (G-15153)

Mooresville Welding Inc .... G 317 831-2265
Mooresville (G-12225)

Morgan Olson LLC .... C 269 659-0243
Angola (G-277)

NRC Modifications Inc .... F 574 825-3646
Middlebury (G-11742)

Original Tractor Cab Co Inc .... F 765 663-2214
Arlington (G-329)

Quality Tank Trucks & Eqp Inc .... G 317 635-0000
Indianapolis (G-9247)

▲ Ramco Engineering Inc .... E 574 266-1455
Elkhart (G-3638)

S CJ Incorporated .... F 317 822-3477
Indianapolis (G-9355)

Sharp Wraps LLC .... G 317 989-8447
Zionsville (G-17049)

Shyft Group Usa Inc .... G 574 848-2000
Bristol (G-1291)

▼ Sjc Industries Corp .... E 574 264-7511
Elkhart (G-3680)

▼ Starcraft Corporation .... G 574 534-7827
Goshen (G-6260)

Supreme Corporation .... G 574 642-4888
Goshen (G-6262)

Supreme Corporation .... G 260 894-9191
Ligonier (G-11026)

◆ Supreme Corporation .... C 574 642-4888
Goshen (G-6263)

Supreme Corporation Georgia .... G 574 228-4130
Goshen (G-6264)

◆ Supreme Industries Inc .... C 574 642-3070
Goshen (G-6265)

TLC Metals Inc .... D 317 894-8684
Greenfield (G-6566)

Townsends Disposal .... G 765 985-2126
Mexico (G-11573)

◆ Utilimaster Holdings Inc .... A 800 237-7806
Bristol (G-1295)

◆ Vanair Manufacturing Inc .... C 219 879-5100
Michigan City (G-11684)

◆ Vanguard National Trailer Corp .. E 219 253-2000
Monon (G-12058)

Wannemuehler Distribution Inc ..... F 812 422-3251
Evansville (G-4379)

Wiers Fleet Partners Inc .... F 574 936-4076
Plymouth (G-13830)

Wimmer Lime Service Inc .... F 765 948-4001
Fairmount (G-4414)

3714 Motor vehicle parts and accessories

1 Composites LLC .... G 260 665-6112
Bourbon (G-1119)

4 Piston Racing .... G 317 902-0200
Danville (G-2805)

▲ A-Fab LLC .... F 812 897-0900
Boonville (G-1078)

Acadia .... G 260 894-7125
Ligonier (G-11001)

Accuride Corporation .... C 812 962-5000
Evansville (G-3867)

Accuride Emi LLC .... E 940 565-8505
Evansville (G-3868)

▲ Action Machine Inc .... F 574 287-9650
South Bend (G-14935)

Adell Group LLC .... G 317 507-6158
Carmel (G-1550)

Advance Prtective Coatings Inc ...... G 317 228-0123
Indianapolis (G-7435)

Advanced Racg Suspensions Inc .... F 317 896-3306
Indianapolis (G-7440)

▲ Advics Manufacturing Ind LLC .... B 812 298-1617
Terre Haute (G-15533)

▲ Aero Industries Inc .... D 317 244-2433
Indianapolis (G-7448)

Aeromotive Tech Inc .... G 260 723-5646
South Whitley (G-15315)

Airfx USA LLC .... E 812 917-5573
Terre Haute (G-15536)

Airfx USA LLC .... G 812 878-8135
Brazil (G-1132)

▲ Airtek LLC .... C 219 947-1664
Hobart (G-7172)

▲ Aisin Drivetrain Inc .... C 812 793-2427
Crothersville (G-2636)

▲ Aisin USA Mfg Inc .... A 812 523-1969
Seymour (G-14627)

▲ Al-Ko Kober LLC .... C 574 294-6651
Elkhart (G-3158)

◆ All American Group Inc .... E 574 262-0123
Elkhart (G-3160)

◆ Allied Enterprises LLC .... E 765 288-8849
Muncie (G-12339)

Allied Tube & Conduit Corp .... F 812 265-9255
Madison (G-11201)

Allison Transm Holdings Inc .... A 317 242-5000
Indianapolis (G-7486)

Allison Transmission Inc .... C 317 242-5000
Indianapolis (G-7487)

Allison Transmission Inc .... C 317 821-5104
Indianapolis (G-7488)

Allison Transmission Inc .... C 317 280-6206
Indianapolis (G-7489)

Allison Transmission Inc .... D 317 242-2080
Indianapolis (G-7490)

Allison Transmission Inc .... A 317 242-5000
Indianapolis (G-7491)

▲ Allomatic Products Company ..... G 800 686-4729
Sullivan (G-15402)

AM General Holdings LLC .... A 574 237-6222
South Bend (G-14940)

AM General LLC .... A 574 258-6699
South Bend (G-14941)

◆ AM General LLC .... D 574 237-6222
South Bend (G-14942)

American Axle & Mfg Inc .... E 260 824-6800
Bluffton (G-1024)

American Axle & Mfg Inc .... E 260 495-4315
Fremont (G-5808)

Americana Development Inc .... D 574 295-3535
Elkhart (G-3179)

Amsafe Partners Inc .... D 574 266-8330
Elkhart (G-3180)

Anthony Smith .... G 765 478-5325
Cambridge City (G-1490)

Aptiv Services Us LLC .... C 765 451-0732
Carmel (G-1562)

Aptiv Services Us LLC .... A 765 451-5011
Kokomo (G-10233)

Aptiv Services Us LLC .... A 765 867-4435
Westfield (G-16665)

Ares Division LLC .... G 260 349-9803
Waterloo (G-16514)

▲ Aristo LLC .... E
Hobart (G-7173)

SIC SECTION 37 TRANSPORTATION EQUIPMENT

Armor Parent Corp................................. F 812 962-5000
   Evansville *(G-3900)*

◆ Arvin Sango Inc................................... A 812 265-2888
   Madison *(G-11203)*

▲ Attc Manufacturing Inc .... B 812 547-5060
   Tell City *(G-15497)*

▲ Atwood Mobile Products Inc............... A 574 264-2131
   Elkhart *(G-3202)*

Atwood Mobile Products LLC................. D 574 266-4848
   Elkhart *(G-3203)*

Atwood Mobile Products LLC................. D 574 264-2131
   Elkhart *(G-3204)*

Atwood Mobile Products LLC................. D 574 264-2131
   Elkhart *(G-3205)*

▲ Atwood Mobile Products LLC.............. D 574 264-2131
   Elkhart *(G-3206)*

▲ Auburn Gear LLC................................ C 260 925-3200
   Auburn *(G-362)*

Auburn Manufacturing Inc...................... E 260 925-8651
   Auburn *(G-364)*

◆ Auto Bumper Exchange Inc................. G 260 493-4408
   Fort Wayne *(G-4780)*

Autoform Tool & Mfg LLC....................... C 260 624-2014
   Angola *(G-232)*

Autoliv Asp Inc.. B 801 620-8018
   Columbia City *(G-2121)*

Automated Products Intl LLC.................. F 260 463-2515
   Lagrange *(G-10729)*

Autoneum North America Inc................. G 248 848-0100
   Jeffersonville *(G-9937)*

Avg North America Inc............................ F 765 748-3162
   Gas City *(G-6033)*

Avionic Structures Indiana Inc................. G 765 671-7865
   Marion *(G-11273)*

▲ Avis Industrial Corporation.................. E 765 998-8100
   Upland *(G-15876)*

Axis Products Inc.................................... C 574 266-8282
   Elkhart *(G-3207)*

Axle Inc... G 574 264-9434
   Elkhart *(G-3209)*

▲ B & B Manufacturing Inc..................... D 219 324-0247
   La Porte *(G-10387)*

Barry Seat Cover & Auto GL Co............. F 574 288-4603
   South Bend *(G-14956)*

Beachy Machine Inc................................ G 765 452-9051
   Kokomo *(G-10235)*

Bender Products Inc............................... E 574 255-5350
   Mishawaka *(G-11852)*

Bendix Coml Vhcl Systems LLC............. E 260 356-9720
   Huntington *(G-7301)*

Bentz Transport Products Inc................. F 260 622-9100
   Zionsville *(G-16996)*

▲ Bludot Inc... G 574 277-2306
   South Bend *(G-14959)*

▲ Borgwarner (pds) Peru Inc.................. D 765 472-2002
   Peru *(G-13568)*

Borgwarner Noblesville LLC................... G 765 451-0400
   Kokomo *(G-10240)*

Borgwarner Pds (indiana) Inc................. C 765 778-6696
   Noblesville *(G-13045)*

Borgwarner Propulsion II LLC................. G 765 236-0025
   Kokomo *(G-10241)*

Borgwarner Reman Holdings LLC.......... A 800 372-5131
   Pendleton *(G-13527)*

BRC Rubber & Plastics Inc..................... F 260 203-5300
   Churubusco *(G-1974)*

BRC Rubber & Plastics Inc..................... E 260 894-4121
   Ligonier *(G-11007)*

▲ BRC Rubber & Plastics Inc................. C 260 693-2171
   Fort Wayne *(G-4815)*

Brindle Products Inc............................... F 260 627-2156
   Grabill *(G-6290)*

BWI INDIANA INC................................... E 937 260-2460
   Greenfield *(G-6475)*

Camaco LLC... G 248 657-0246
   Portage *(G-13853)*

Cardinal Services Inc Indiana................. D 574 267-3823
   Warsaw *(G-16332)*

Cardinal Services Inc Indiana................. D 574 267-3823
   Warsaw *(G-16333)*

◆ Carlisle Indus Brake Frction I.............. B 812 336-3811
   Bloomington *(G-822)*

Carter Fuel Systems LLC....................... G 574 735-0235
   Logansport *(G-11065)*

▲ Carter Fuel Systems LLC................... B 800 342-6125
   Logansport *(G-11064)*

▲ Caterpillar Remn Powrtrn Indna......... B 317 738-2117
   Franklin *(G-5718)*

CCT Enterprises LLC............................. E 260 925-1420
   Auburn *(G-375)*

Cedar Creek Studios Inc........................ G 260 627-7320
   Leo *(G-10966)*

Champion Racing Engines LLC............. G 317 335-2491
   Mccordsville *(G-11446)*

Chemtrusion Inc..................................... E 812 280-2910
   Jeffersonville *(G-9951)*

▲ Chiyoda USA Corporation................... G 765 653-9098
   Greencastle *(G-6396)*

Coan Engineering LLC........................... E 765 456-3957
   Kokomo *(G-10246)*

Colbin Tool Company Inc....................... E 574 457-3183
   Syracuse *(G-15459)*

Component Machine Inc......................... G 317 635-8929
   Indianapolis *(G-7845)*

◆ Compositech Inc.................................. E 800 231-6755
   Indianapolis *(G-7846)*

Concept Design & Fabrication................ G 812 481-1142
   Jasper *(G-9829)*

▲ Continental Manufacturing LLC.......... E 765 778-9999
   Anderson *(G-98)*

Conversion Components Inc................... G 574 264-4181
   Elkhart *(G-3266)*

Cooper-Standard Automotive Inc........... E 260 637-5824
   Auburn *(G-380)*

Cooper-Standard Automotive Inc........... E 260 247-7703
   Fort Wayne *(G-4872)*

Covidien LP.. C 317 837-8199
   Plainfield *(G-13674)*

◆ Creative Liquid Coatings Inc............... B 260 349-1862
   Kendallville *(G-10105)*

Csr Suspension LLC.............................. G 812 346-8620
   North Vernon *(G-13261)*

Cummins Cdc Holding Inc...................... A 812 312-3162
   Columbus *(G-2251)*

Cummins Emission Solutions Inc............ D 615 986-2596
   Columbus *(G-2253)*

Cummins Engine Company Inc.............. E 812 522-9366
   Seymour *(G-14643)*

◆ Cummins Engine Holding Company.. B 812 377-5000
   Columbus *(G-2255)*

Cummins Franchise Holdco LLC............ D 812 377-5000
   Columbus *(G-2257)*

Cummins Holding Group LLC................ G 765 962-6332
   Richmond *(G-14112)*

Cummins Inc... D 812 377-5298
   Columbus *(G-2258)*

Cummins Inc... G 812 377-2932
   Columbus *(G-2259)*

Cummins Inc... G 812 377-9914
   Columbus *(G-2260)*

Cummins Inc... G 812 377-0150
   Columbus *(G-2261)*

Cummins Inc... G 765 430-0093
   Columbus *(G-2262)*

Cummins Inc... F 812 376-0742
   Columbus *(G-2263)*

Cummins Inc... G 812 377-8601
   Columbus *(G-2272)*

Cummins Inc... F 812 378-2874
   Columbus *(G-2273)*

Cummins Inc... G 260 482-3691
   Fort Wayne *(G-4895)*

Cummins Inc... F 317 610-2493
   Indianapolis *(G-7927)*

Cummins Inc... G 317 244-7251
   Indianapolis *(G-7928)*

◆ Cummins Inc.. G 812 524-6381
   Seymour *(G-14644)*

Cummins Inc... G 260 657-1436
   Woodburn *(G-16947)*

Cummins Power Systems LLC.............. A 410 590-8700
   Columbus *(G-2274)*

Cummins Sales Svc................................ G 260 482-3691
   Fort Wayne *(G-4896)*

Cummins Sales Svc................................ G 574 252-2154
   Mishawaka *(G-11870)*

Cummins-Scania Xpi Mfg LLC................ G 812 377-5000
   Columbus *(G-2275)*

Curtis-Maruyasu America Inc.................. B 812 544-2021
   Santa Claus *(G-14507)*

Cushman Performance Parts LLC.......... G 765 653-3054
   Greencastle *(G-6400)*

▲ Custom Wood Products Inc................ D 574 522-3300
   Elkhart *(G-3283)*

▲ Cvg Sprague Devices LLC................. C 614 289-5360
   Michigan City *(G-11593)*

▲ D & D Brake Sales Inc........................ E 317 485-5177
   Fortville *(G-5590)*

D & E Auto Electric Inc........................... F 219 763-3892
   Portage *(G-13858)*

Dacco/Detroit Indiana Inc....................... G 317 545-5334
   Indianapolis *(G-7945)*

Daechang Seat Co Ltd USA................... E 317 755-3663
   Indianapolis *(G-7946)*

Dallara LLC... F 317 388-5400
   Speedway *(G-15334)*

Dana Driveshaft Products LLC............... G 260 432-2903
   Marion *(G-11280)*

Dana Incorporated.................................. G 260 897-2827
   Avilla *(G-474)*

Dana Incorporated.................................. C 260 481-3597
   Fort Wayne *(G-4903)*

Dana Incorporated.................................. G 765 772-4000
   Lafayette *(G-10568)*

◆ Dana Light Axle Products LLC........... F 260 483-7174
   Fort Wayne *(G-4904)*

Danta Inc.. G 219 369-9190
   La Porte *(G-10398)*

Decker Sales Inc.................................... G 812 330-1580
   Bloomington *(G-853)*

Delco Electronics.................................... G 765 455-9713
   Kokomo *(G-10255)*

Delphi Electronics Safety........................ G 765 883-7795
   Kokomo *(G-10256)*

Delphi Technologies................................ F 765 451-0670
   Kokomo *(G-10257)*

Delphi Technologies................................ E 765 480-1993
   Kokomo *(G-10258)*

▲ Dexstar Wheel Company Inc.............. D 574 295-3535
   Elkhart *(G-3290)*

Dexter Axle Company............................ D 260 495-5100
   Fremont *(G-5820)*

Dexter Axle Company LLC..................... C 260 636-2195
   Albion *(G-23)*

Dexter Axle Company LLC..................... D 574 294-6651
   Elkhart *(G-3291)*

Employee Codes: A=Over 500 employees, B=251-500
C=101-250, D=51-100, E=20-50, F=10-19, G=1-9

37 TRANSPORTATION EQUIPMENT

Dexter Axle Company LLC .... C 574 294-6651
Elkhart *(G-3293)*

◆ Dexter Axle Company LLC .... D 574 295-7888
Elkhart *(G-3292)*

Diamet .... G 812 379-4606
Columbus *(G-2283)*

Diesel Punk Core .... G 812 631-0606
Bloomington *(G-855)*

Discount Power Equipment .... G 765 642-0040
Anderson *(G-104)*

Dometic .... C 574 266-4848
Elkhart *(G-3300)*

Dometic Corporation .... B 260 463-7657
Elkhart *(G-3301)*

Donaldson Company Inc .... A 765 659-4766
Frankfort *(G-5660)*

Double T Manufacturing Corp .... F 574 262-1340
Elkhart *(G-3302)*

Dwyer Enterprises .... G 317 573-9628
Carmel *(G-1614)*

Dynamic Axle LLC .... G 574 226-0242
Elkhart *(G-3308)*

Dynomax .... G 317 835-3813
Fishers *(G-4506)*

E-Motion LLC .... G 317 379-5761
Carmel *(G-1617)*

Eaton Corporation .... C 260 925-3800
Auburn *(G-387)*

Eaton Corporation .... G 317 704-2520
Indianapolis *(G-8043)*

Eco Vehicle Systems LLC .... E 765 964-6009
Union City *(G-15852)*

▲ Elsa LLC .... B 765 552-5200
Elwood *(G-3821)*

▲ Elsa Corporation .... B 765 552-5200
Elwood *(G-3822)*

Engineered Machined Pdts Inc .... G 317 462-8894
Greenfield *(G-6498)*

Engineered Machined Pdts Inc .... G 317 462-8894
Greenfield *(G-6499)*

◆ Enkei America Inc .... A 812 373-7000
Columbus *(G-2298)*

Enovapremier LLC .... E 812 385-0576
Princeton *(G-13993)*

◆ Exhaust Productions Inc .... D 219 942-0069
Merrillville *(G-11516)*

Fairfield Manufacturing Co Inc .... G 815 508-7353
Lafayette *(G-10577)*

◆ Fairfield Manufacturing Co Inc .... A 765 772-4000
Lafayette *(G-10576)*

Faurecia Emssons Ctrl Tech USA .... B 812 341-2000
Columbus *(G-2302)*

Faurecia Emssons Ctrl Tech USA .... A 812 348-4305
Columbus *(G-2303)*

Faurecia Emssons Ctrl Tech USA .... B 812 565-5214
Columbus *(G-2304)*

Faurecia Emssons Ctrl Tech USA .... B 812 341-2000
Columbus *(G-2305)*

Faurecia Emssons Ctrl Tech USA .... D 248 758-8160
Fort Wayne *(G-4978)*

Faurecia Exhaust Systems LLC .... C 812 341-2079
Columbus *(G-2306)*

FCA North America Holdings LLC .... B 765 454-0018
Kokomo *(G-10264)*

FCA North America Holdings LLC .... D 765 454-1705
Kokomo *(G-10265)*

FCA North America Holdings LLC .... G 765 854-4234
Kokomo *(G-10266)*

FCA US LLC .... C 765 454-1005
Kokomo *(G-10267)*

▲ FCC (adams) LLC .... B 260 589-8555
Berne *(G-711)*

▲ FCC (indiana) LLC .... A 260 726-8023
Portland *(G-13939)*

FCC (north America) Inc .... E 260 726-8023
Portland *(G-13940)*

Federal-Mogul Motorparts LLC .... G 317 875-7259
Indianapolis *(G-8171)*

Federal-Mogul Motorparts LLC .... G 219 872-5150
Michigan City *(G-11611)*

Federal-Mogul Powertrain LLC .... G 765 659-7207
Frankfort *(G-5662)*

Fenwick Motor Sports .... G 765 522-1354
Bainbridge *(G-562)*

Fiber Forged Composites LLC .... G 574 772-0107
Knox *(G-10207)*

Fisher & Company Incorporated .... D 586 746-2000
Evansville *(G-4070)*

Flex-N-Gate LLC .... G 260 665-8288
Angola *(G-251)*

Flex-N-Gate LLC .... G 765 793-5732
Covington *(G-2530)*

Flora Racing .... G 574 233-0642
South Bend *(G-15036)*

Ford Motor Company .... F 901 368-8821
Plainfield *(G-13680)*

Four Woods Laminating Inc .... E 260 593-2246
Topeka *(G-15806)*

Frank Wiss Racg Components Inc .... G 317 243-9585
Indianapolis *(G-8222)*

Freudenberg-Nok General Partnr .... C 260 894-7183
Ligonier *(G-11015)*

Freudenberg-Nok General Partnr .... G 765 763-7246
Morristown *(G-12277)*

Freudenberg-Nok General Partnr .... C 317 421-3400
Shelbyville *(G-14756)*

Freudenberg-Nok General Partnr .... C 734 354-5504
Shelbyville *(G-14757)*

▲ Friction Products Company LLC .... A 765 362-3500
Crawfordsville *(G-2568)*

FTC Products Corp .... G 219 567-2441
Francesville *(G-5642)*

◆ G E C O M Corp .... A 812 663-2270
Greensburg *(G-6595)*

G N U Inc .... C 219 464-7813
Valparaiso *(G-15952)*

Gac Enterprises Usa LLC .... F 317 839-9525
Plainfield *(G-13682)*

Gartech Enterprises Inc .... F 812 794-4796
Austin *(G-465)*

Gbj Holdings LLC .... G 317 483-1896
Highland *(G-7137)*

Gearbox Lm Holdings Inc .... G 765 362-3500
Crawfordsville *(G-2569)*

General Motors LLC .... F 260 673-2048
Roanoke *(G-14267)*

GKN Sinter Metals LLC .... C 812 883-3381
Salem *(G-14479)*

▼ Global Forming LLC .... E 317 290-1000
Indianapolis *(G-8289)*

Global Glass Inc .... F 574 294-7681
Elkhart *(G-3382)*

GM Components Holdings LLC .... G 765 451-8440
Kokomo *(G-10270)*

Graber Manufacturing .... G 812 636-7725
Odon *(G-13337)*

Grede LLC .... C 765 521-8000
New Castle *(G-12865)*

Greg Moser Engineering Inc .... E 260 726-6689
Portland *(G-13949)*

Grouper Wild LLC .... C 574 534-1499
Goshen *(G-6156)*

◆ Guardian Couplings LLC .... E 219 874-5248
Michigan City *(G-11617)*

◆ Gulf Stream Coach Inc .... C 574 773-7761
Nappanee *(G-12603)*

Hanwha Machinery America Corp .... D 574 546-2261
Bremen *(G-1195)*

Hapco Rebuilders Inc .... G 812 232-2550
Terre Haute *(G-15604)*

Hart Plastics Inc .... E 574 264-7060
Elkhart *(G-3400)*

Heads First .... G 219 785-4100
Westville *(G-16761)*

▲ Heartland Automotive .... G 765 446-2311
Lafayette *(G-10595)*

▲ Heartland Automotive Inc .... A 765 653-4263
Greencastle *(G-6409)*

Heartland Automotive LLC .... E 765 653-4263
Greencastle *(G-6410)*

Heavy Duty Manufacturing Inc .... F 260 432-2480
Fort Wayne *(G-5056)*

Hendrickson Engineering LLC .... G 765 404-9132
West Lafayette *(G-16592)*

Hendrickson International .... E 260 349-6400
Kendallville *(G-10115)*

Hendrickson International Corp .... G 260 868-2131
Butler *(G-1466)*

Hendrickson International Corp .... E 260 349-6400
Kendallville *(G-10116)*

Hendrickson International Corp .... E 260 349-6400
Kendallville *(G-10117)*

Hendrickson International Corp .... C 765 483-5350
Lebanon *(G-10896)*

Hendrickson International Corp .... C 765 483-7217
Lebanon *(G-10897)*

▲ Henman Engineering and Ma .... D 765 288-8098
Muncie *(G-12414)*

▲ Hisada America Inc .... C 812 526-0756
Edinburgh *(G-3086)*

Hitachi Astemo Americas Inc .... D 859 734-9451
Ligonier *(G-11017)*

◆ Hitachi Astemo Indiana Inc .... A 317 462-3015
Greenfield *(G-6509)*

Hoehn Engineered Products LLC .... G 260 223-9158
Decatur *(G-2863)*

Honda Dev & Mfg Amer LLC .... A 812 222-6000
Greensburg *(G-6604)*

Hoosier Industrial Supply Inc .... F 574 533-8565
Goshen *(G-6168)*

Horner Industrial Services Inc .... F 317 634-7165
Indianapolis *(G-8418)*

Icon Metal Forming LLC .... B 812 738-5900
Corydon *(G-2499)*

Ifok Inc .... F 219 477-5107
Valparaiso *(G-15968)*

IGP North America LLC .... G 812 670-3483
Jeffersonville *(G-10001)*

▲ Indiana Automotive Fas Inc .... B 317 467-0100
Greenfield *(G-6511)*

Indiana Custom Trucks LLC .... E 260 463-3244
Shipshewana *(G-14852)*

Indiana Heat Transfer Corporation .... C 574 936-3171
Salem *(G-14484)*

▲ Indiana Marujun LLC .... D 765 584-7639
Winchester *(G-16891)*

◆ Indiana Mills & Manufacturing .... B 317 896-9531
Westfield *(G-16699)*

▲ Indiana Precision Forge LLC .... E 317 421-0102
Shelbyville *(G-14760)*

Indiana Precision Technology .... G 317 462-3015
Greenfield *(G-6514)*

Indiana Research Institute .... G 812 378-5363
Columbus *(G-2325)*

▲ Indiana Transmission .... G 765 854-4201
Kokomo *(G-10287)*

37 TRANSPORTATION EQUIPMENT

Industrial Axle Company LLC.............E.....574 294-6651
  Elkhart (G-3423)
Industrial Axle Company LLC.............D.....574 295-6077
  Elkhart (G-3424)
Industrial Steering Pdts Inc................F.....260 488-1880
  Hamilton (G-6856)
◆ Indy Cylinder Head Inc....................E.....317 862-3724
  Indianapolis (G-8526)
▲ Integrated Energy Technologies Inc..E.....812 421-7810
  Evansville (G-4128)
Inter-Cntnntal Gear Brake USA...........D.....317 268-0040
  Plainfield (G-13693)
International Brake Inds Inc.................D.....419 905-7468
  South Bend (G-15084)
Interstate Power Systems Inc.............G.....952 854-2044
  Gary (G-5964)
J & L Future Fiberglass Co..................G.....574 784-2900
  Lapaz (G-10817)
Jason Incorporated..............................G.....248 455-7919
  Richmond (G-14148)
Jasper Engine Exchange Inc..............G.....812 482-1041
  Leavenworth (G-10870)
◆ Jasper Engine Exchange Inc..........A.....812 482-1041
  Jasper (G-9853)
Jasper Holdings Inc.............................F.....812 482-1041
  Jasper (G-9854)
Jasper Willow Springs Mo LLC..........G.....800 827-7455
  Jasper (G-9860)
Jlm Lubricants Usa LLC......................G.....317 500-1012
  Brownsburg (G-1377)
Joe Wade Customs.............................G.....765 548-0333
  Rosedale (G-14380)
Jrz Industries Inc.................................G.....574 834-4543
  North Webster (G-13308)
Kampco Steel Products Inc.................E.....574 294-5466
  Elkhart (G-3447)
Kautex Inc..G.....260 897-3250
  Avilla (G-481)
▲ Keihin Aircon North America..........C.....765 213-4915
  Muncie (G-12432)
Keller Performance Center.................G.....765 827-5225
  Connersville (G-2451)
Killer Camaros Custom Camaro.........G.....260 255-2425
  New Haven (G-12908)
Kinedyne..G.....260 403-5149
  Auburn (G-399)
Kinetech Inc..G.....317 441-1924
  Westfield (G-16704)
Kirby Risk Corporation........................D.....765 447-1402
  Lafayette (G-10621)
Kp Holdings LLC.................................B.....317 867-0234
  Westfield (G-16706)
◆ Kph Engineered Systems Inc.........B.....317 867-0234
  Westfield (G-16707)
Kumar Brothers Inc.............................G.....317 410-2450
  Avon (G-535)
KYB Americas Corporation.................B.....317 881-7772
  Greenwood (G-6726)
▲ KYB Americas Corporation............B.....317 736-7774
  Franklin (G-5750)
L & W Engineering Inc........................C.....574 825-5351
  Middlebury (G-11730)
Lakepark Industries Ind Inc.................D
  Shipshewana (G-14861)
Laminat LLC..G.....574 233-1534
  South Bend (G-15114)
Lances Drvshaft Components Inc......G.....219 762-2531
  Portage (G-13881)
Lau Holdings LLC................................D.....574 223-3181
  Rochester (G-14300)
LCI Industries.......................................G.....574 264-3521
  Elkhart (G-3477)

LCI Industries.......................................G.....574 312-6116
  Elkhart (G-3478)
LCI Industries.......................................A.....574 535-1125
  Elkhart (G-3476)
Lear Corporation..................................D.....260 244-1700
  Columbia City (G-2167)
Lear Corporation..................................G.....765 653-2511
  Greencastle (G-6417)
Lear Corporation..................................B.....219 852-0014
  Hammond (G-6969)
Lear Corporation..................................E.....317 481-0530
  Indianapolis (G-8730)
Lear Corporation..................................D.....574 935-3818
  Plymouth (G-13792)
Linamar Strctures USA Mich Inc.........G.....248 372-9018
  Albion (G-32)
▲ Lingenfelter Prfmce Engrg Inc........E.....260 724-2552
  Decatur (G-2869)
Lippert Components............................G.....574 226-4088
  Elkhart (G-3490)
Lippert Components Inc......................G.....574 535-1125
  Elkhart (G-3492)
Lippert Components Inc......................D.....574 535-1125
  Goshen (G-6202)
Lippert Components Inc......................G.....574 849-0869
  Goshen (G-6206)
Lippert Components Inc......................F.....574 971-4320
  Goshen (G-6207)
Lippert Components Inc......................E.....574 312-7445
  Middlebury (G-11734)
Lippert Components Inc......................E.....800 551-9149
  Mishawaka (G-11930)
Lippert Components Inc......................D.....574 537-8900
  Mishawaka (G-11931)
Lippert Components Inc......................F.....260 234-4303
  Yoder (G-16966)
▲ Lippert Components Inc.................B.....574 535-1125
  Elkhart (G-3493)
Liquivinyl LLC......................................G.....765 283-6265
  Yorktown (G-16975)
Lod LLC...G.....765 385-0631
  Fowler (G-5626)
Lund International Holding Co.............G.....888 477-3729
  Jasper (G-9884)
Madison Manufacturing Inc.................E.....574 633-4433
  Bremen (G-1204)
Magna Powertrain America Inc..........E.....765 587-1300
  Muncie (G-12443)
Magna Powertrain America Inc..........C.....765 587-1300
  Muncie (G-12444)
Make It Mobile LLC............................G.....260 562-1045
  Howe (G-7239)
Makuta Inc...F.....317 642-0001
  Shelbyville (G-14773)
▲ Mancor Indiana Inc.........................E.....765 779-4800
  Anderson (G-151)
Martinrea Industries Inc.......................C.....812 346-5750
  North Vernon (G-13285)
Mastersbilt Chassis Inc.......................G.....812 793-3666
  Crothersville (G-2642)
Meritor Inc..G.....317 279-2180
  Plainfield (G-13706)
◆ Metaldyne M&A Bluffton LLC.........D.....260 824-6800
  Bluffton (G-1042)
◆ Metaldyne Snterforged Pdts LLC....G.....812 346-1566
  North Vernon (G-13287)
Metzler Enterprise...............................G.....574 293-9267
  Elkhart (G-3529)
▲ Miasa Automotive LLC...................E.....765 751-9967
  Yorktown (G-16976)
Miata Hubs LLC...................................G.....240 298-7368
  Brownsburg (G-1388)

Midwest Auto Repair Inc.....................F.....219 322-0364
  Schererville (G-14534)
Miller Mfg Corp....................................E.....574 773-4136
  Nappanee (G-12626)
Min Ko Kyaw LLC................................F.....574 296-3500
  Elkhart (G-3545)
Mobile Dynamometer LLC..................G.....765 271-5080
  Kokomo (G-10311)
Mobility Ventures LLC.........................G.....734 367-3714
  South Bend (G-15153)
Mor/Ryde Inc.......................................C.....574 293-1581
  Elkhart (G-3551)
Morris Holding Company LLC.............C.....812 446-6141
  Brazil (G-1154)
Morris Mfg & Sls Corp........................C.....812 446-6141
  Brazil (G-1155)
Morryde International Inc....................F.....574 293-1581
  Elkhart (G-3553)
Morryde International Inc....................F.....574 293-1581
  Elkhart (G-3554)
Morryde International Inc....................C.....574 293-1581
  Elkhart (G-3555)
Mosey Manufacturing Co Inc..............C.....765 983-8889
  Richmond (G-14170)
Mosey Manufacturing Co Inc..............C.....765 983-8870
  Richmond (G-14171)
Motherson Sumi Systems Limited......A.....260 726-6501
  Portland (G-13957)
Motorama Auto Ctr Inc........................G.....317 831-0036
  Mooresville (G-12226)
Motorsport Price Engineering..............G.....812 546-4220
  Hope (G-7229)
▲ Mpt Muncie LLC..............................E.....765 587-1300
  Muncie (G-12459)
▲ Mullets Fencing and Supplies.........G.....574 646-3300
  Nappanee (G-12628)
Muncie Power Products Inc................G.....785 284-7721
  Muncie (G-12465)
◆ Muncie Power Products Inc............E.....765 284-7721
  Muncie (G-12464)
◆ Mvo Usa Inc....................................F.....317 585-5785
  Indianapolis (G-8974)
▲ Nagakura Engrg Works Co Inc.......C.....812 375-1382
  Columbus (G-2359)
Nalon Power Development LLC.........G.....317 450-7564
  Pittsboro (G-13652)
Nelson Global Products Inc................C.....317 782-9486
  Indianapolis (G-8999)
NERP LLC..G.....574 303-6377
  South Bend (G-15163)
Next Gnrtion Dlrshp Warsaw LLC.......G.....463 234-9400
  Indianapolis (G-9008)
Norco Industries Inc............................G.....574 262-3400
  Elkhart (G-3573)
North American Mfg Inc......................G.....765 948-3337
  Fairmount (G-4411)
Northern Trans & Differential...............G.....219 764-4009
  Portage (G-13900)
Northwind Electronics LLC..................F.....317 288-0787
  Indianapolis (G-9024)
NSK Corporation..................................D.....765 458-5000
  Liberty (G-10993)
NSK Precision America Inc.................D.....317 738-5000
  Franklin (G-5762)
NSK Services Inc.................................G.....812 695-2004
  Jasper (G-9899)
▲ NTN Driveshaft Inc..........................A.....812 342-7000
  Columbus (G-2362)
Nyx LLC..A.....734 838-3570
  New Albany (G-12786)
◆ Old Remco Holdings LLC.................C.....765 778-6499
  Pendleton (G-13548)

Employee Codes: A=Over 500 employees, B=251-500
C=101-250, D=51-100, E=20-50, F=10-19, G=1-9

2024 Harris Indiana
Industrial Directory

37 TRANSPORTATION EQUIPMENT

▲ Pailton Inc .... G 219 476-0085
Valparaiso (G-16021)

Pana-Pacific .... G 260 482-6607
Fort Wayne (G-5293)

Parker-Hannifin Corporation .... E 260 894-7125
Syracuse (G-15471)

Peerless Gear LLC .... G 812 883-7900
Salem (G-14497)

Perfection Wheel LLC .... G 260 358-9239
Huntington (G-7355)

Performance Brake Parts Inc .... G 260 410-1404
Grabill (G-6320)

Performance Rod & Custom Inc .... G 812 897-5805
Boonville (G-1095)

Performance Technology Inc .... G 574 862-2116
Wakarusa (G-16242)

Peterson Sanko Corp .... G 765 966-9656
Richmond (G-14182)

Phillips Company Inc .... F 812 526-8250
Edinburgh (G-3098)

▲ Phillips Company Inc .... E 812 378-3797
Columbus (G-2377)

Phinia Delphi USA LLC .... G 317 203-4602
Plainfield (G-13714)

◆ Phinia USA LLC .... B 765 778-6879
Anderson (G-177)

▲ Pierce Company Inc .... D 765 998-8100
Upland (G-15880)

◆ Pk USA Inc .... B 317 395-5500
Shelbyville (G-14784)

▲ PMG Indiana LLC .... C 812 379-4606
Columbus (G-2379)

Power Plant Service Inc .... E 260 432-6716
Fort Wayne (G-5328)

Power Train Corp Fort Wayne .... F 317 241-9393
Indianapolis (G-9167)

Pridgeon & Clay Inc .... G 317 738-4885
Franklin (G-5770)

Proto-Fab Acquisition Inc .... G 574 522-4245
Elkhart (G-3624)

Pulliam Enterprises Inc .... E 574 259-1520
Mishawaka (G-11982)

Pullman Company .... B 260 667-2200
Angola (G-290)

Quality Converters Inc .... E 260 829-6541
Orland (G-13371)

Race Engineering .... G 219 661-8904
Crown Point (G-2740)

▲ Ramco Engineering Inc .... E 574 266-1455
Elkhart (G-3638)

Rance Aluminum Fabrication .... E 574 266-9028
Elkhart (G-3639)

Raybestos Aftermarket Pdts Co .... G 765 359-1943
Crawfordsville (G-2608)

Raybestos Powertrain .... D 765 362-3500
Crawfordsville (G-2609)

Raybestos Powertrain LLC .... G 812 268-0322
Sullivan (G-15418)

Raybestos Powertrain LLC .... G 812 268-0322
Sullivan (G-15419)

Raybestos Powertrain LLC .... F 812 268-1211
Sullivan (G-15420)

Rayburn Automotive Inc .... G 317 535-8232
Greenwood (G-6758)

Rayco Mch & Engrg Group Inc .... E 317 291-7848
Indianapolis (G-9268)

Raytech Corp .... G 765 359-2882
Crawfordsville (G-2610)

▲ Raytech Powertrain LLC .... C 812 268-0322
Crawfordsville (G-2611)

▲ Reflexallen USA Inc .... E 317 870-3610
Indianapolis (G-9280)

Reliable Tool & Machine Co .... E 260 343-7150
Kendallville (G-10150)

▲ Resonac Powdered Metals Americ... E 812 663-5058
Greensburg (G-6628)

Rexnord Industries LLC .... G 414 643-2559
Plainfield (G-13722)

Rgr Engines .... G 630 488-7966
Monticello (G-12169)

Rich Bures .... G 317 270-9360
Indianapolis (G-9300)

▲ Riverside Mfg Inc .... C 260 637-4470
Fort Wayne (G-5387)

Roadwin Parts Inc .... G 630 742-4098
Hammond (G-7000)

Robert Bosch LLC .... G 260 636-1005
Albion (G-44)

Robert Bosch LLC .... G 574 654-4000
New Carlisle (G-12844)

Robert Bosch LLC .... G 574 654-4000
New Carlisle (G-12845)

Rochester Manufacturing LLC .... G 574 224-2044
Rochester (G-14318)

▲ Rt Acquisition Corp .... D 812 482-2932
Jasper (G-9907)

Ryobi Die Casting (usa) Inc .... G 317 398-3398
Shelbyville (G-14793)

▲ Ryobi Die Casting (usa) Inc .... A 317 398-3398
Shelbyville (G-14794)

S & H Metal Products Inc .... E 260 593-2565
Topeka (G-15817)

Sacoma Properties LLC .... F 812 526-5600
Edinburgh (G-3102)

Safe Fleet Mirrors .... E 574 266-3700
Elkhart (G-3659)

▼ Saldana Racing Tanks Inc .... F 317 852-4193
Indianapolis (G-9365)

◆ Shield Restraint Systems Inc .... C 574 266-8330
Elkhart (G-3673)

Smart Technologies LLC .... G 317 738-4338
Franklin (G-5777)

◆ SMI Seller Inc .... A 765 825-3121
Connersville (G-2466)

SMR Management Inc .... G 765 252-0257
Lafayette (G-10692)

Somaschini North America LLC .... E 574 968-0273
South Bend (G-15249)

▲ South Bend Clutch Inc .... E 574 256-5064
Mishawaka (G-12002)

SPD Performance Plus LLC .... G 260 433-6192
Bluffton (G-1055)

Spears Holdings Inc .... G 765 378-4908
Anderson (G-196)

▼ Specialty Rim Supply Inc .... G 812 234-3002
Terre Haute (G-15710)

Spitzer Racing Enterprises .... F 317 894-9533
Greenfield (G-6559)

Splendor Boats LLC .... F 260 352-2835
Silver Lake (G-14923)

Standard Industrial Supply Inc .... E 574 946-6661
Winamac (G-16876)

Standard Intgrted Slutions Inc .... F 574 946-6661
Winamac (G-16877)

Standard Motor Products Inc .... D 574 259-6253
Mishawaka (G-12007)

Stant Corporation .... D 765 825-3122
Connersville (G-2467)

Stant USA Corp .... B 765 825-3121
Connersville (G-2469)

◆ Stant USA Corp .... C 765 825-3121
Connersville (G-2470)

Staples Pipe & Muffler .... G 812 346-2474
North Vernon (G-13296)

Starcraft Corporation .... G 574 534-7705
Goshen (G-6259)

▼ Starcraft Corporation .... G 574 534-7827
Goshen (G-6260)

◆ State Wide Aluminum Inc .... C 574 262-2594
Elkhart (G-3699)

Steel Parts Manufacturing Inc .... C 765 675-2191
Tipton (G-15792)

Steel Tank & Fabricating Corp .... E 260 248-8971
Columbia City (G-2203)

Stephen G Morrow Inc .... G 812 876-7837
Spencer (G-15363)

Surface Generation Tech LLC .... G 765 425-2741
Anderson (G-203)

T K T Inc .... G 574 825-5233
Middlebury (G-11753)

Taylor Made Group LLC .... D 574 535-1125
Elkhart (G-3716)

Team Oneway .... G 574 387-5417
Granger (G-6385)

▲ Techna-Fit Inc .... G 317 350-2153
Brownsburg (G-1408)

Tenneco Automotive Oper Co Inc .... C 574 296-9400
Elkhart (G-3723)

Tenneco Automotive Oper Co Inc .... C 260 894-9214
Ligonier (G-11027)

Tenneco Inc .... G 317 842-5550
Indianapolis (G-9577)

The Pro Shear Corporation Corp .... G 260 408-1010
Fort Wayne (G-5481)

Thermal Ceramics Inc .... E 574 296-3500
Elkhart (G-3725)

▲ TI Automotive .... G 260 622-7372
Ossian (G-13440)

▲ TI Automotive Inc .... G 260 587-6100
Ashley (G-337)

◆ TI Automotive Ligonier Corp .... A 260 894-3163
Ligonier (G-11028)

TI Group Auto Systems LLC .... D 260 587-6100
Ashley (G-338)

TI Group Auto Systems LLC .... B 260 622-7900
Ossian (G-13441)

Timothy D Goin .... G 317 771-0404
Indianapolis (G-9606)

◆ Tire Rack Inc .... B 888 541-1777
South Bend (G-15283)

TNT Truck Accessories LLC .... G 812 305-0714
Haubstadt (G-7090)

▲ TOA (usa) LLC .... B 317 834-0522
Mooresville (G-12247)

Trans Atlantic Products LLC .... F 574 262-0165
Elkhart (G-3743)

▲ Transportation Tech Inds .... F 812 962-5000
Evansville (G-4347)

▲ Transwheel Corporation .... G 260 358-8660
Huntington (G-7374)

Transworks Inc .... G 619 441-0133
Fort Wayne (G-5501)

Tri Aerospace LLC .... E 812 872-2400
Terre Haute (G-15736)

Tru-Flex LLC .... G 812 526-5600
Edinburgh (G-3106)

▲ Tru-Flex LLC .... C 765 893-4403
West Lebanon (G-16649)

▲ Tru-Flex Real Estate Holdings LLC ..... D 765 893-4403
West Lebanon (G-16650)

Truckpro LLC .... F 765 482-6525
Lebanon (G-10948)

◆ TRW Commercial Steering .... E 765 423-5377
Lafayette (G-10710)

▲ Tsuda USA Corporation .... F 317 468-9177
Greenfield (G-6567)

SIC SECTION 37 TRANSPORTATION EQUIPMENT

Twb of Indiana.................................. G 812 342-6000
   Columbus *(G-2408)*

U B Machine Inc.............................. F 260 493-3381
   New Haven *(G-12924)*

Ultimate Sports Inc......................... G 765 423-2984
   West Lafayette *(G-16641)*

◆ Valeo Engine Cooling Inc................ A 812 663-8541
   Greensburg *(G-6638)*

▲ Valeo Ltg Systems N Amer LLC...... A 812 523-5200
   Seymour *(G-14700)*

Valeo North America Inc................. C 800 677-6004
   Greensburg *(G-6639)*

Valeo North America Inc................. B 812 663-8541
   Greensburg *(G-6640)*

Valeo North America Inc................. B 248 619-8300
   Seymour *(G-14702)*

Valley Distributing Inc.................... E 574 266-4455
   Elkhart *(G-3766)*

Vee Engineering Inc........................ D 260 424-6635
   Fort Wayne *(G-5530)*

Vehicle Service Group LLC.............. E 800 445-9262
   Madison *(G-11255)*

Vernet US Corporation..................... D 812 372-0281
   Columbus *(G-2412)*

▲ Vernet US Corporation.................... C 812 372-0281
   Columbus *(G-2413)*

Viariloc Distributors Inc................... G 317 273-0089
   Indianapolis *(G-9718)*

Viking Inc....................................... E 260 244-6141
   Columbia City *(G-2211)*

Voegele Auto Supply LLC................ G 765 647-3541
   Brookville *(G-1339)*

Vuteq Usa Inc.................................. B 502 863-6322
   Princeton *(G-14018)*

Wabash Club Raybestos Pdts Co....... G 765 359-2862
   Crawfordsville *(G-2626)*

Wabash National Corporation........... E 765 771-5300
   Lafayette *(G-10715)*

▲ Wabash National Corporation........... A 765 771-5310
   Lafayette *(G-10716)*

Wagler Competition Pdts LLC........... F 812 486-9360
   Odon *(G-13356)*

Water Pump Specialists.................... G 317 270-9360
   Indianapolis *(G-9739)*

Wayne David Incorporated............... G 317 417-7165
   Franklin *(G-5785)*

Webb Wheel Products Inc................ G 812 548-0477
   Ferdinand *(G-4451)*

Webb Wheel Products Inc................ C 812 548-0477
   Tell City *(G-15519)*

Wellspring Components LLC............ G 260 768-7336
   Shipshewana *(G-14896)*

Wetwillies Bubbles LLC.................. G 260 633-0064
   Huntertown *(G-7268)*

Wheel Group Holdings LLC............. G 317 780-1661
   Indianapolis *(G-9756)*

▲ Wheels 4 Tots Inc........................... G 219 987-6812
   Demotte *(G-2932)*

Woodys Hot Rodz LLC..................... G 812 637-1933
   Lawrenceburg *(G-10867)*

Xtrac Inc... F 317 472-2451
   Indianapolis *(G-9797)*

Ynwa Industries Inc......................... D 574 295-6641
   Elkhart *(G-3800)*

ZF Active Safety & Elec US LLC....... D 260 357-6327
   Garrett *(G-5881)*

ZF Active Safety & Elec US LLC....... E 765 429-1678
   Lafayette *(G-10722)*

ZF Active Safety & Elec US LLC....... D 765 429-1936
   Lafayette *(G-10723)*

ZF Active Safety & Elec US LLC....... A 765 423-5377
   Lafayette *(G-10724)*

ZF Automotive.................................. F 260 357-1148
   Garrett *(G-5882)*

ZF North America Inc...................... E 765 429-1622
   Lafayette *(G-10725)*

3715 Truck trailers

A1 Campers and Trlrs Mfg LLC......... G 574 227-2200
   Elkhart *(G-3143)*

▲ Agri - Traders & Repair LLC............. G 260 238-4225
   Spencerville *(G-15366)*

Agritraders Mfg Inc.......................... G 260 238-4225
   Spencerville *(G-15367)*

▼ Alloy Custom Products LLC............. D 765 564-4684
   Lafayette *(G-10520)*

Alvin J Nix..................................... G 812 347-2510
   Ramsey *(G-14023)*

Angels Wings Expedited................... F 574 339-3038
   South Bend *(G-14945)*

Arnold Brothers Construction............ G 317 775-5523
   Coatesville *(G-2103)*

Band Brothers Transport LLC............ G 317 709-4415
   Indianapolis *(G-7592)*

Bells Trucking LLC.......................... G 574 263-6030
   Goshen *(G-6099)*

Brindle Products Inc......................... F 260 627-2156
   Grabill *(G-6290)*

BSB Trans Inc.................................. G 317 919-8778
   Greenwood *(G-6677)*

C & J Services & Supplies Inc........... E 317 569-7222
   Fort Wayne *(G-4826)*

Cargo Ski Transport Inc.................... G 219 448-9888
   Crown Point *(G-2664)*

Carvers Truck and Trailer LLC.......... G 574 343-2240
   Elkhart *(G-3248)*

CDP Logistics Inc............................ G 773 968-1455
   Avon *(G-510)*

Corn Pro Inc.................................... G 812 636-4319
   Elnora *(G-3814)*

Cryogenic Indus Solutions LLC......... F 765 564-4684
   Lafayette *(G-10564)*

Delphi Body Works......................... F 765 564-2212
   Delphi *(G-2893)*

Diamond Components Inc................ E 574 358-0452
   Middlebury *(G-11711)*

Dock Bumpers Inc............................ G 312 597-9282
   Highland *(G-7132)*

Durcholz Excvtg & Cnstr Co Inc....... G 812 634-1764
   Huntingburg *(G-7278)*

Edwards Pace Co.............................. D 574 522-5337
   Elkhart *(G-3313)*

Foam X-Press LLC........................... G 260 563-5767
   Wabash *(G-16187)*

Fontaine Trailer Company................ G 574 772-6673
   Knox *(G-10208)*

Forest River Inc............................... B 574 848-1335
   Bristol *(G-1261)*

Ft Group LLC.................................. G 574 322-4369
   Bristol *(G-1263)*

Great Dane LLC............................... A 812 443-4711
   Brazil *(G-1143)*

Great Dane LLC............................... G 812 460-7706
   Terre Haute *(G-15602)*

◆ H & H Sales Company Inc............... F 260 637-3177
   Huntertown *(G-7257)*

Heartcare LLC.................................. G 260 432-7000
   Fort Wayne *(G-5055)*

Hendrickson International Corp......... C 765 483-5350
   Lebanon *(G-10896)*

Indy Asset Brokers Corporation......... G 317 502-2749
   Mooresville *(G-12213)*

Jcantave Transit LLC........................ G 855 608-2777
   Indianapolis *(G-8619)*

Kic LLC.. E 360 823-4440
   Evansville *(G-4152)*

▲ Kruz Inc... E 574 772-6673
   Knox *(G-10214)*

Kuckuck Transport LLC................... G 260 609-0316
   South Whitley *(G-15321)*

LCI Industries................................. A 574 535-1125
   Elkhart *(G-3476)*

LGS Industries LLC.......................... E 574 848-5665
   Middlebury *(G-11733)*

Liberty Trailers LLC........................ E 219 866-7141
   Rensselaer *(G-14058)*

Pace American Enterprises Inc.......... D 800 247-5767
   Middlebury *(G-11744)*

▲ Quality Steel & Alum Pdts Inc........... E 574 295-8715
   Elkhart *(G-3634)*

Rail Protection Plus LLC.................. G 812 399-1084
   New Albany *(G-12802)*

Ravens.. G 269 362-4489
   Mishawaka *(G-11984)*

Reds Custom Design LLC................. G 812 698-0763
   Taswell *(G-15495)*

Schwartzs Trailer Sales Inc............... G 317 773-2608
   Noblesville *(G-13172)*

Spartan Trailer Mfg Inc..................... G 574 309-3035
   Mishawaka *(G-12005)*

Sternberg Inc................................... E 812 867-0077
   Evansville *(G-4335)*

Strick Corporation............................ B 260 692-6121
   Monroe *(G-12062)*

Strick Trailers LLC.......................... E 260 692-6121
   Monroe *(G-12063)*

Superior Mfg Inc.............................. F 812 983-9900
   Elberfeld *(G-3121)*

Talbert Manufacturing Inc................ C 800 348-5232
   Rensselaer *(G-14071)*

▼ Travel Lite Inc................................ E 574 831-3000
   Syracuse *(G-15488)*

Truck Trailer Repair Indy LLC.......... G 317 755-2177
   Fairland *(G-4405)*

US Truck Trailer Service.................. G 574 232-2014
   South Bend *(G-15298)*

◆ Vanguard National Trailer Corp......... E 219 253-2000
   Monon *(G-12058)*

Virago Logistix Llc.......................... G 800 767-2090
   Hammond *(G-7030)*

▲ Wabash National LP........................ E 765 771-5300
   Lafayette *(G-10713)*

Wabash National Corporation........... D 800 937-4784
   Lafayette *(G-10714)*

Wabash National Corporation........... E 765 771-5300
   Lafayette *(G-10715)*

▲ Wabash National Corporation........... A 765 771-5310
   Lafayette *(G-10716)*

Wabash National Mfg LP.................. B 765 771-5310
   Lafayette *(G-10717)*

▼ Wellco Holdings Inc........................ C 574 264-9661
   Elkhart *(G-3782)*

▲ Zieman Manufacturing Comp............ C 574 535-1125
   Goshen *(G-6279)*

3716 Motor homes

Aip/Fw Funding Inc......................... G 212 627-2360
   Decatur *(G-2840)*

All American Group Inc................... G 574 262-9889
   Elkhart *(G-3159)*

All American Group Inc................... G 574 825-1720
   Middlebury *(G-11693)*

All American Group Inc................... G 574 825-5821
   Middlebury *(G-11694)*

◆ All American Group Inc................... E 574 262-0123
   Elkhart *(G-3160)*

37 TRANSPORTATION EQUIPMENT

Bison Horse Trailers LLC .... G 574 658-4161
  Milford *(G-11788)*
Coach Line Motors .... G 765 825-7893
  Connersville *(G-2431)*
Coachmen Recrtl Vhcl Co LLC .... G 574 825-5821
  Middlebury *(G-11704)*
◆ Damon Corporation .... A 574 262-2624
  Elkhart *(G-3285)*
▲ Ds Corp .... D 260 593-3850
  Topeka *(G-15804)*
Fiber-Tron Corp .... F 574 294-8545
  Elkhart *(G-3345)*
Forest River Inc .... A 574 296-7700
  Elkhart *(G-3353)*
Forest River Inc .... A 574 262-3474
  Elkhart *(G-3355)*
Forest River Inc .... C 574 642-2640
  Millersburg *(G-11812)*
Gulf Stream Coach Inc .... A 574 773-7761
  Nappanee *(G-12602)*
◆ Gulf Stream Coach Inc .... C 574 773-7761
  Nappanee *(G-12603)*
Independent Protection Co .... C 574 831-5680
  New Paris *(G-12960)*
◆ Jayco Inc .... A 574 825-5861
  Middlebury *(G-11727)*
Milford Property LLC .... F 574 970-7460
  Elkhart *(G-3543)*
Newmar Corporation .... G 574 773-7791
  Nappanee *(G-12631)*
Pen Products Miami Cor Fcilty .... G 765 689-8920
  Bunker Hill *(G-1443)*
▲ Phoenix Usa Inc .... E 574 266-2020
  Elkhart *(G-3603)*
Quality Concepts .... G 574 215-6391
  Goshen *(G-6244)*
Rev Recreation Group Inc .... D 260 724-4217
  Decatur *(G-2879)*
Southside Mini Storage .... G 574 293-3270
  Elkhart *(G-3688)*
▼ Starcraft Corporation .... G 574 534-7827
  Goshen *(G-6260)*
Thor Industries Inc .... E 574 264-2900
  Elkhart *(G-3728)*
Thor Industries Inc .... G 574 266-1111
  Elkhart *(G-3729)*
Thor Industries Inc .... F 574 262-2624
  Elkhart *(G-3731)*
Thor Industries Inc .... G 800 860-5658
  Wakarusa *(G-16254)*
Thor Industries Inc .... B 574 970-7460
  Elkhart *(G-3730)*
Thor Motor Coach Inc .... E 800 860-5658
  Wakarusa *(G-16255)*
▼ Thor Motor Coach Inc .... C 574 266-1111
  Elkhart *(G-3733)*
◆ Van Explorer Company Inc .... E 574 267-7666
  Warsaw *(G-16441)*

3721 Aircraft

Airbuoyant LLC .... G 765 623-9815
  Anderson *(G-74)*
Airplane Annuals .... G 817 528-6545
  Bainbridge *(G-558)*
Bae Systems Controls Inc .... A 260 434-5195
  Fort Wayne *(G-4787)*
Boeing Company .... G 219 977-4354
  Gary *(G-5905)*
Boeing Company .... G 317 484-1363
  Indianapolis *(G-7656)*
Charlie N83 Inc .... G 260 625-4211
  Fort Wayne *(G-4843)*

Dean Baldwin Pntg Ltd Partnr .... D 765 681-1800
  Peru *(G-13578)*
Drone Works LLC .... G 812 917-4691
  Terre Haute *(G-15579)*
Golden Age Aeroplane Works LLC .... G 812 358-5778
  Brownstown *(G-1423)*
Hoosier Helicopter Svcs Inc .... G 812 935-5296
  Bloomington *(G-880)*
Hoosier Industrial Supply .... G 574 535-0712
  Goshen *(G-6167)*
Hull Aircraft Support LLC .... G 219 324-6247
  La Porte *(G-10426)*
Infinity Drones LLC .... G 812 457-7140
  Poseyville *(G-13978)*
Mw Aircraft Inc .... G 317 873-4627
  Zionsville *(G-17034)*
Quo Vadis Aerospace LLC .... G 575 621-2372
  Indianapolis *(G-9253)*
Rollison Airplane Company Inc .... G 812 384-4972
  Bloomfield *(G-756)*
Silicis Technologies Inc .... E 317 896-5044
  Westfield *(G-16728)*
Textron Aviation Inc .... E 317 241-2893
  Indianapolis *(G-9580)*
Textron Aviation Inc .... E 317 227-3621
  Indianapolis *(G-9581)*
Thunderbird Aviation LLC .... G 847 303-3100
  Indianapolis *(G-9602)*
Tip To Tail Aerospace LLC .... G 765 437-6556
  Peru *(G-13605)*
Utilities AVI Specialists Inc .... G 219 662-8175
  Crown Point *(G-2770)*

3724 Aircraft engines and engine parts

Aerodyn Engineering LLC .... E 317 334-1523
  Indianapolis *(G-7451)*
Allens Therapuetic Services .... G 317 820-3600
  Indianapolis *(G-7481)*
Allison Transmission Inc .... A 317 242-5000
  Indianapolis *(G-7491)*
Ares Division LLC .... G 260 349-9803
  Waterloo *(G-16514)*
Bel-Mar Products Corporation .... G 317 769-3262
  Whitestown *(G-16801)*
Cuda II Inc .... F 317 839-1515
  Indianapolis *(G-7921)*
Enjet Aero Terre Haute LLC .... D 913 717-7390
  Terre Haute *(G-15586)*
GE Aviation Systems LLC .... G 765 432-5917
  Lafayette *(G-10588)*
Goodrich Corporation .... D 812 704-5200
  Jeffersonville *(G-9993)*
Honeywell International Inc .... G 812 854-4450
  Crane *(G-2538)*
Honeywell International Inc .... F 317 580-6165
  Indianapolis *(G-8408)*
Honeywell International Inc .... E 765 284-3300
  Muncie *(G-12419)*
Honeywell International Inc .... G 219 836-3803
  Munster *(G-1254C)*
Honeywell International Inc .... G 574 935-0200
  Plymouth *(G-13782)*
Honeywell International Inc .... G 574 231-3322
  South Bend *(G-15066)*
Honeywell International Inc .... A 574 231-3000
  South Bend *(G-15067)*
IBC Materials & Tech LLC .... E 765 481-2900
  Lebanon *(G-10899)*
▲ Integrated Energy Technologies Inc ... E 812 421-7810
  Evansville *(G-4128)*
Jds International Inc .... F 317 753-4427
  Noblesville *(G-13112)*

N Rolls-Royce Amercn Tech Inc .... D 317 230-4347
  Indianapolis *(G-8978)*
▲ Ngh Retail LLC .... G 219 476-0772
  Valparaiso *(G-16012)*
Nori Metals .... G 574 213-4344
  South Bend *(G-15168)*
▼ Polycraft Products Inc .... E 812 577-3401
  Greendale *(G-6452)*
Precoat Metals .... F 219 763-1504
  Portage *(G-13906)*
Robert Perez .... G 317 291-7311
  Indianapolis *(G-9314)*
Rolls-Royce Corporation .... E 812 421-7810
  Evansville *(G-4292)*
Rolls-Royce Corporation .... D 317 230-2000
  Indianapolis *(G-9326)*
Rolls-Royce Corporation .... E 317 230-4118
  Indianapolis *(G-9327)*
Rolls-Royce Corporation .... C 317 230-4118
  Indianapolis *(G-9328)*
Rolls-Royce Corporation .... E 317 657-0267
  Plainfield *(G-13723)*
Rolls-Royce Corporation .... E 317 230-2736
  Zionsville *(G-17048)*
▲ Rolls-Royce Corporation .... A 317 230-2000
  Indianapolis *(G-9329)*
Rtx Corporation .... B 260 589-7207
  Berne *(G-723)*
Rtx Corporation .... G 260 358-0888
  Huntington *(G-7364)*
Simpson Alloy Services Inc .... G 812 969-2766
  Elizabeth *(G-3129)*
Smiths Arospc Components Haute .... G 812 235-5210
  Terre Haute *(G-15698)*
Teamair Mro Ltd .... G 812 584-3733
  Moores Hill *(G-12188)*
Thermal Structures Inc .... F 951 736-9911
  Plainfield *(G-13735)*
Tri Aerospace LLC .... E 812 872-2400
  Terre Haute *(G-15736)*
Turbines Inc .... E 812 877-2587
  Terre Haute *(G-15737)*
Twigg Corporation .... G 765 342-7126
  Martinsville *(G-11431)*
Unison Engine Components Inc .... C 904 739-4000
  Terre Haute *(G-15738)*
▲ Walerko Tool and Engrg Corp .... E 574 295-2233
  Elkhart *(G-3777)*
Westerley Inc .... E
  Indianapolis *(G-9752)*

3728 Aircraft parts and equipment, nec

Aar LLC .... G 260 591-0100
  Peru *(G-13565)*
AAR Corp .... G 317 227-5000
  Indianapolis *(G-7409)*
AAR Supply Chain Inc .... F 317 227-5000
  Indianapolis *(G-7410)*
Aero Innovations LLC .... G 812 233-0384
  Terre Haute *(G-15534)*
Air Kit LLC .... G 317 745-0656
  Danville *(G-2806)*
Airman Proficiency LLC .... G 260 602-5788
  Fort Wayne *(G-4734)*
Airtomic LLC .... E 317 738-0148
  Franklin *(G-5706)*
Airtomic Repair Station .... G 317 738-0148
  Franklin *(G-5707)*
Allison Transmission Inc .... C 317 280-6206
  Indianapolis *(G-7489)*
Avt Composites .... G 317 286-7575
  Brownsburg *(G-1349)*

SIC SECTION

37 TRANSPORTATION EQUIPMENT

Avt Composites .... G 219 742-0865
  Lebanon (G-10878)
B-D Industries Inc .... F 574 295-1420
  Elkhart (G-3214)
C F Roark Wldg Engrg Co Inc .... C 317 852-3163
  Brownsburg (G-1356)
Cnc Industries Inc .... E 260 490-5700
  Fort Wayne (G-4863)
Composites Unlimited .... G 812 475-8621
  Evansville (G-3977)
Cook Aircraft Leasing Inc .... G 812 339-2044
  Bloomington (G-836)
Cuda II Inc .... F 317 839-1515
  Indianapolis (G-7921)
Dean Baldwin Pntg Ltd Partnr .... D 765 681-1800
  Peru (G-13578)
Eyc Drones LLC .... G 812 890-9068
  Vincennes (G-16124)
First Gear Inc .... E 260 490-3238
  Fort Wayne (G-4984)
Frazier Aviation LLC .... G 888 835-9269
  Cutler (G-2784)
GMI LLC .... G 260 209-6676
  Fort Wayne (G-5028)
Golden-Helvey Holdings Inc .... D 574 266-4500
  Elkhart (G-3384)
Goodrich Corporation .... D 812 704-5200
  Jeffersonville (G-9993)
HB Connect Inc .... G 855 503-9159
  Fort Wayne (G-5051)
HB Connect Inc .... D 260 422-1212
  Fort Wayne (G-5052)
Honeywell International Inc .... G 574 231-2000
  South Bend (G-15068)
Hupp & Associates Inc .... E 260 748-8282
  New Haven (G-12906)
Iasa Group LLC .... G 260 484-1322
  Fort Wayne (G-5090)
Indiana Aircraft Hardware Co .... G 317 485-6500
  Fortville (G-5600)
Indigo Industries LLC .... G 480 747-4560
  Greenwood (G-6715)
Integrated De Icing Servi .... G 317 517-1643
  Indianapolis (G-8567)
Jds International Inc .... F 317 753-4427
  Noblesville (G-13112)
Kem Krest Defense LLC .... F 574 389-2650
  Elkhart (G-3450)
L&E Engineering LLC .... A 937 746-6696
  Greenwood (G-6727)
Lift Works Inc .... G 812 797-0479
  Franklin (G-5753)
Mack Tool & Engineering Inc .... E 574 233-8424
  South Bend (G-15133)
Master Power Transmission Inc .... E 812 378-2270
  Columbus (G-2350)
Mears Machine Corp .... D 317 271-6041
  Avon (G-537)
▲ Midwest Aerospace Ltd .... F 219 365-7250
  Lowell (G-11173)
MSP Aviation Inc .... E 812 333-6100
  Bloomington (G-926)
◆ Mvo Usa Inc .... F 317 585-5785
  Indianapolis (G-8974)
Odyssian Technology LLC .... G 574 257-7555
  South Bend (G-15176)
Precision Piece Parts Inc .... G 574 255-3185
  Mishawaka (G-11978)
Pynco Inc .... E 812 275-0900
  Bedford (G-661)
Q Air Inc .... G 219 476-7048
  Valparaiso (G-16032)

Radius Aerospace Inc .... G 317 392-5000
  Shelbyville (G-14790)
Rayco Mch & Engrg Group Inc .... E 317 291-7848
  Indianapolis (G-9268)
Regent Aerospace Corporation .... C 317 837-4000
  Plainfield (G-13721)
Rjv Investments Inc .... E 574 234-1063
  South Bend (G-15223)
Rolls-Royce Corporation .... E 812 421-7810
  Evansville (G-4292)
Saab Aeronautics Indiana LLC .... E 315 445-5009
  West Lafayette (G-16627)
Safran Nclles Svcs Amricas LLC .... G 317 827-0859
  Plainfield (G-13725)
Smart Manufacturing Inc .... G 765 482-7481
  Lebanon (G-10943)
Tri Aerospace LLC .... E 812 872-2400
  Terre Haute (G-15736)
Triumph Controls LLC .... F 317 421-8760
  Shelbyville (G-14808)
Triumph Thermal Systems LLC .... G 419 273-1192
  Shelbyville (G-14809)
Tube Processing Corp .... G 317 264-7760
  Indianapolis (G-9657)
▲ Tube Processing Corp .... B 317 787-1321
  Indianapolis (G-9658)
U S S Inc .... G 260 693-1172
  Churubusco (G-1992)
Value Production Inc .... E 574 246-1913
  South Bend (G-15300)
Vertex Mdrnztion Sstinment LLC .... A 601 607-6866
  Indianapolis (G-9710)
Wolf Technical Engineering LLC .... G 800 783-9653
  Indianapolis (G-9781)

3731 Shipbuilding and repairing

Acbl Holding Corporation .... A 310 712-1850
  Jeffersonville (G-9921)
Acl Professional Services Inc .... C 812 288-0100
  Jeffersonville (G-9922)
Acl Sales Corporation .... G 812 288-0100
  Jeffersonville (G-9923)
American Barge Line Company .... G 812 288-0100
  Jeffersonville (G-9930)
American Coml Barge Line LLC .... C 812 288-0100
  Jeffersonville (G-9931)
American Commercial Lines Inc .... G 812 288-0100
  Jeffersonville (G-9932)
American Diabetes Association .... G 859 268-9129
  Indianapolis (G-7502)
Branch Express Trucking LLC .... G 574 807-2212
  South Bend (G-14961)
Cargo Skiff Corporation .... G 812 873-6349
  Butlerville (G-1482)
Commercial Barge Line Company .... E 812 288-0100
  Jeffersonville (G-9956)
▲ Corn Island Shipyard Inc .... G 812 362-8808
  Grandview (G-6327)
Estill Smith Marine Svcs Inc .... G 812 282-7944
  Jeffersonville (G-9983)
General Dynamics Corporation .... G 260 637-4773
  Fort Wayne (G-5019)
Griffin Clark LLC .... G 765 491-9059
  Bloomington (G-871)
Innovations By .... G 260 413-1869
  Fort Wayne (G-5109)
Lake Lite Inc .... G 260 918-2758
  Avilla (G-485)
Marine Builders Inc .... D 812 283-7932
  Jeffersonville (G-10016)
Paf Construction LLC .... E 812 496-4669
  Columbus (G-2371)

▲ Poseidon LLC .... C 260 422-8767
  Berne (G-722)
Rolls-Royce Corporation .... E 317 230-2000
  Indianapolis (G-9325)
Rolls-Royce Corporation .... E 317 230-8515
  West Lafayette (G-16626)
Sdf Engineering LLC .... G 317 674-2643
  Carmel (G-1755)
▼ Smoker Craft Inc .... B 574 831-2103
  New Paris (G-12968)
Tpg Mt Vernon Marine LLC .... C 317 631-0234
  Indianapolis (G-9626)
Waterways Equipment Exch Inc .... G 812 925-8104
  Chandler (G-1868)

3732 Boatbuilding and repairing

Angola Canvas Co .... F 260 665-9913
  Angola (G-227)
Atlatl Group LLC .... E 602 233-2628
  Washington (G-16472)
Boat Works .... G 574 457-4034
  Syracuse (G-15457)
Brunswick Corporation .... G 866 278-6942
  Brownsburg (G-1353)
Brunswick Corporation .... D 260 459-8200
  Fort Wayne (G-4821)
Chief Powerboats Inc .... G 219 775-7024
  Crown Point (G-2665)
Culvers Port Side Marina .... G 574 223-5090
  Rochester (G-14285)
Evansville Marine Service Inc .... E 812 424-9278
  Evansville (G-4053)
Fiberglass Pdts & Boat Repr .... G 260 627-3209
  Grabill (G-6295)
Gonzales Enterprises Inc .... G 219 841-1756
  Portage (G-13870)
Handypro of Northwest Indiana .... G 219 707-8240
  Portage (G-13875)
Harris Flotebote .... G 260 432-4555
  Fort Wayne (G-5050)
Heatherwood Enterprises Inc .... G 812 294-7270
  Memphis (G-11464)
Highwater Marine LLC .... E 574 457-2082
  Syracuse (G-15463)
▼ Highwater Marine LLC .... D 574 522-8381
  Elkhart (G-3406)
Hoosier Marine .... G 812 879-5549
  Quincy (G-14021)
Indiana Mobile Marine LLC .... G 317 961-1881
  Indianapolis (G-8483)
J & J Boat Works Inc .... G 812 667-5902
  Madison (G-11231)
J C Mfg Inc .... E 574 834-2881
  North Webster (G-13307)
Kentuckiana Yacht Services LLC .... G 812 282-7579
  Jeffersonville (G-10007)
Marine Group LLC .... C 574 622-0490
  Bristol (G-1272)
▲ Neoteric Incorporated .... F 812 234-1120
  Terre Haute (G-15650)
▼ Pontoon Boat LLC .... D 574 264-6336
  Elkhart (G-3608)
▲ Porter Inc .... A 800 736-7685
  Decatur (G-2876)
Pro Wake Watersports Indianap .... G 801 691-2153
  Noblesville (G-13159)
Pro Wake Watersports Syracuse .... G 801 691-2153
  Syracuse (G-15475)
Propaganda Motorcycles Inc .... G 765 997-8787
  Richmond (G-14188)
Robert Engle .... G 317 522-7761
  Westfield (G-16723)

Employee Codes: A=Over 500 employees, B=251-500
C=101-250, D=51-100, E=20-50, F=10-19, G=1-9

2024 Harris Indiana
Industrial Directory

37 TRANSPORTATION EQUIPMENT

Rolls-Royce Corporation .... E 317 230-2000
Indianapolis *(G-9325)*

Rolls-Royce Corporation .... E 317 230-8515
West Lafayette *(G-16626)*

Sherms Marine Inc .... F 260 563-8051
Wabash *(G-16215)*

▼ Smoker Craft Inc .... B 574 831-2103
New Paris *(G-12968)*

Sparrow Group Incorporated .... G 574 968-7335
Warsaw *(G-16428)*

Splendor Boats LLC .... F 260 352-2835
Silver Lake *(G-14923)*

▼ Sylvan Marine Inc .... B 574 831-2950
New Paris *(G-12970)*

Thunder Pro .... G 317 498-0241
Greenfield *(G-6565)*

Vanderbilt Luxury Pontoons LLC .... F 260 478-7227
Fort Wayne *(G-5527)*

▲ Veada Industries Inc .... A 574 831-4775
New Paris *(G-12973)*

Wawasee Aluminum Works Inc .... E 574 457-2082
Syracuse *(G-15490)*

West Lakes Marine Inc .... F 260 854-2525
Rome City *(G-14378)*

World Class Fiberglass .... G 317 512-3343
Fairland *(G-4406)*

Yandt Boat Works LLC .... G 219 851-8311
La Porte *(G-10503)*

Yoder Fiberglass LLC .... G 260 593-0234
Topeka *(G-15823)*

3743 Railroad equipment

2 EZ Price LLC .... G 312 912-4084
Hammond *(G-6866)*

Adams & Westlake Ltd .... E 574 264-1141
Elkhart *(G-3154)*

American Maint & Training Inc .... F 812 738-4230
Corydon *(G-2485)*

Amsted Graphite Materials LLC .... D 219 931-1900
Hammond *(G-6877)*

Arbor Preservative Systems LLC .... F 812 232-2316
Terre Haute *(G-15545)*

Autosavvy of Indianapolis LLC .... F 463 900-4685
Indianapolis *(G-7577)*

General Signals Inc .... E 812 474-4256
Evansville *(G-4088)*

▲ Hadady Corporation .... E 219 322-7417
Dyer *(G-2976)*

Horton Logistics LLC .... G 219 290-2910
Gary *(G-5953)*

Illiana Railcar Services LLC .... G 812 264-4687
Terre Haute *(G-15613)*

JP Industries Inc .... F 574 293-8763
Elkhart *(G-3436)*

Kasgro Rail Car Management .... G 812 347-3888
Corydon *(G-2503)*

MGM Enterprises .... G 219 395-1888
Chesterton *(G-1948)*

Powerrail Holdings Inc .... G 765 827-4660
Connersville *(G-2463)*

Professnal Locomotive Svcs Inc .... E 219 398-9123
East Chicago *(G-3036)*

Progress Rail Locomotive Inc .... F 765 281-2685
Muncie *(G-12479)*

Progress Rail Services Corp .... D 765 472-2002
Peru *(G-13596)*

Rolls-Royce Corporation .... E 317 230-2000
Indianapolis *(G-9325)*

Rolls-Royce Corporation .... E 317 230-8515
West Lafayette *(G-16626)*

T&S Group LLC .... G 219 310-0464
Greenwood *(G-6772)*

Tangent Rail Products Inc .... E 412 325-0202
Terre Haute *(G-15723)*

▲ Tcb Enterprises LLC .... F 574 522-3971
Middlebury *(G-11754)*

▲ Tcb Industries Inc .... F 574 522-3971
Elkhart *(G-3718)*

Transco Railway Products Inc .... E 574 753-6227
Logansport *(G-11111)*

Triple Js Express Transport .... G 317 667-2368
Indianapolis *(G-9646)*

Union Tank Car Co .... G 219 880-5248
Whiting *(G-16839)*

Veterans Fabrication LLC .... G 317 604-7704
Fishers *(G-4629)*

Wabtec Corporation .... G 317 556-4116
Plainfield *(G-13741)*

Wes Group Inc .... C 219 932-5200
Gary *(G-6028)*

Western-Cullen-Hayes Inc .... F 765 962-0526
Richmond *(G-14226)*

Yolanda Denise LLC .... G 317 457-6831
Indianapolis *(G-9803)*

3751 Motorcycles, bicycles, and parts

America Wild LLC .... G 888 485-2589
Fort Wayne *(G-4751)*

Astech Seats .... G 765 674-7448
Marion *(G-11271)*

Best Bicycle Inc .... G 812 336-2724
Bloomington *(G-804)*

Bikes-N-Trikes Incorporated .... G 317 835-4544
Boggstown *(G-1072)*

◆ Compositech Inc .... EZ 800 231-6755
Indianapolis *(G-7846)*

Custom Cycle of Indiana .... G 812 256-9089
Otisco *(G-13448)*

David Tortora .... G 317 506-6902
Carmel *(G-1605)*

Faith Forgotten Firearms LLC .... G 614 940-9145
New Albany *(G-12727)*

Iron Hawg .... G 317 462-0991
Greenfield *(G-6517)*

Jrotten Chopper Inc .... G 765 517-1779
Jonesboro *(G-10080)*

Kdz Kustoms LLC .... G 260 927-0533
Auburn *(G-398)*

Orr Motor Sports .... G 260 244-2681
Columbia City *(G-2178)*

Outdoor Performance .... F 765 732-3335
Liberty *(G-10994)*

Reality Motor Sports Inc .... G 765 662-3000
Marion *(G-11335)*

Red Hawk Choppers Inc .... G 765 307-2269
Crawfordsville *(G-2614)*

Rowe Tech .... G 317 453-0015
Indianapolis *(G-9339)*

SJ Sales Inc .... G 260 433-5947
Fort Wayne *(G-5419)*

Ss Custom Choppers LLC .... G 260 415-3793
Fort Wayne *(G-5433)*

Thugs Inc Choppers .... G 317 454-3762
Indianapolis *(G-9601)*

Time Out Trailers Inc .... G 574 294-7671
Elkhart *(G-3734)*

3761 Guided missiles and space vehicles

Cypress Springs Entps Inc .... G 812 743-8888
Wheatland *(G-16774)*

Raytheon Company .... G 310 647-9438
Fort Wayne *(G-5369)*

Raytheon Company .... G 317 306-4633
Indianapolis *(G-9275)*

3764 Space propulsion units and parts

Adranos Energetics LLC .... G 208 539-2439
West Lafayette *(G-16557)*

In Space LLC .... G 765 775-2107
Lafayette *(G-10605)*

3769 Space vehicle equipment, nec

C F Roark Wldg Engrg Co Inc .... C 317 852-3163
Brownsburg *(G-1356)*

Cypress Springs Entps Inc .... G 812 743-8888
Wheatland *(G-16774)*

◆ Major Tool and Machine Inc .... C 317 636-6433
Indianapolis *(G-8820)*

Rjv Investments Inc .... E 574 234-1063
South Bend *(G-15223)*

Thermal Ceramics Inc .... E 574 296-3500
Elkhart *(G-3725)*

3792 Travel trailers and campers

All American Group Inc .... G 574 825-5821
Middlebury *(G-11694)*

All American Group Inc .... G 574 825-8555
Middlebury *(G-11695)*

◆ All American Group Inc .... E 574 262-0123
Elkhart *(G-3160)*

Bison Coach LLC .... E 574 658-4161
Milford *(G-11787)*

Coachmen Recrtl Vhcl Co LLC .... G 574 825-5821
Middlebury *(G-11704)*

◆ Damon Corporation .... A 574 262-2624
Elkhart *(G-3285)*

Dg Manufacturing Inc .... D 574 294-7550
Elkhart *(G-3295)*

▲ Dmi Holding Corp .... C 574 534-1224
Goshen *(G-6123)*

Dna Enterprises Inc .... E 574 534-0034
Elkhart *(G-3298)*

Donald Lloyd .... G 937 304-5683
Indianapolis *(G-7996)*

▲ Ds Corp .... D 260 593-3850
Topeka *(G-15804)*

Forest River Inc .... B 574 848-1335
Bristol *(G-1261)*

Forest River Inc .... A 574 296-7700
Elkhart *(G-3353)*

Forest River Inc .... A 574 262-3474
Elkhart *(G-3355)*

Forest River Inc .... A 574 642-3112
Goshen *(G-6140)*

Forest River Inc .... C 574 533-5934
Goshen *(G-6141)*

Forest River Inc .... C 574 642-2640
Millersburg *(G-11812)*

Forest River Cherokee Inc .... G 260 593-2566
Topeka *(G-15805)*

Forest River Custom Extrusions .... G 574 975-0206
Goshen *(G-6142)*

Forks Rv Inc .... D 574 825-7467
Shipshewana *(G-14846)*

Girard Products LLC .... G 574 534-3328
Elkhart *(G-3378)*

◆ Gulf Stream Coach Inc .... C 574 773-7761
Nappanee *(G-12603)*

Gulf Stream Parts & Service .... G 574 858-2850
Etna Green *(G-3849)*

Heart Breaker Sales LLC .... G 765 489-4048
Hagerstown *(G-6837)*

Highland Ridge Rv Inc .... B 260 768-7771
Shipshewana *(G-14850)*

Homette Corporation .... G 574 294-6521
Elkhart *(G-3410)*

SIC SECTION
37 TRANSPORTATION EQUIPMENT

▼ Hy-Line Enterprises Intl Inc............... E 574 294-1112
  Elkhart *(G-3413)*

Independent Protection Co................... C 574 831-5680
  New Paris *(G-12960)*

Indiana Interstate Entps LLC................ G 260 463-8100
  Lagrange *(G-10743)*

J&K Yurts Inc.. G 317 377-9878
  Indianapolis *(G-8610)*

◆ Jayco Inc... A 574 825-5861
  Middlebury *(G-11727)*

Keystone Rv Company.......................... D 574 537-0600
  Goshen *(G-6188)*

Keystone Rv Company.......................... B 574 535-2100
  Goshen *(G-6189)*

Keystone Rv Company.......................... B 574 535-2100
  Goshen *(G-6190)*

Keystone Rv Company.......................... C 574 535-2100
  Wakarusa *(G-16237)*

Keystone Rv Company.......................... D 574 534-9430
  Goshen *(G-6191)*

Kropf Industries Inc............................ E 574 533-2171
  Goshen *(G-6192)*

◆ Kzrv LP... B 260 768-4016
  Shipshewana *(G-14856)*

Layton Homes Corporation.................. C 574 294-6521
  Elkhart *(G-3473)*

Layton Homes Corporation.................. G 574 294-6521
  Elkhart *(G-3472)*

Lippert Components Inc...................... F 574 971-4320
  Goshen *(G-6207)*

Livin Lite Corp..................................... E 574 862-2228
  Shipshewana *(G-14865)*

Lsr Conversions LLC........................... E 574 206-9610
  Elkhart *(G-3501)*

Marathon Homes Corporation.............. E 574 294-6441
  Elkhart *(G-3512)*

Newmar Corporation............................ G 574 773-7791
  Nappanee *(G-12631)*

▲ Next Gen Power Holdings LLC........... G 574 971-4490
  Elkhart *(G-3568)*

Rance Aluminum Fabrication................ E 574 266-9028
  Elkhart *(G-3639)*

▼ Recreation By Design LLC................. D 574 294-2117
  Elkhart *(G-3642)*

Skyline Corporation............................ C 574 294-2463
  Elkhart *(G-3682)*

Skyline Homes Inc.............................. G 574 294-6521
  Elkhart *(G-3683)*

▼ Starcraft Corporation....................... G 574 534-7827
  Goshen *(G-6260)*

Supreme Corporation.......................... G 260 894-9191
  Ligonier *(G-11026)*

◆ Supreme Corporation........................ C 574 642-4888
  Goshen *(G-6263)*

Switzerland Hills Inc........................... E 812 594-2810
  Patriot *(G-13511)*

Thor Industries Inc............................. G 574 584-2151
  Wakarusa *(G-16253)*

Thor Industries Inc............................. G 800 860-5658
  Wakarusa *(G-16254)*

Thor Motor Coach Inc......................... E 800 860-5658
  Wakarusa *(G-16255)*

▼ Thor Motor Coach Inc....................... C 574 266-1111
  Elkhart *(G-3733)*

TI Industries Inc................................. E 419 666-8144
  Elkhart *(G-3736)*

Trophy Homes Inc............................... E 574 264-4911
  Elkhart *(G-3748)*

▲ Wabash National LP.......................... E 765 771-5300
  Lafayette *(G-10713)*

▼ Winnebago of Indiana LLC................. C 574 825-5250
  Middlebury *(G-11759)*

Wolfpack Chassis LLC.......................... E 260 349-1887
  Kendallville *(G-10155)*

3795 Tanks and tank components

AM General LLC................................... A 574 258-7523
  Mishawaka *(G-11840)*

Jds International Inc............................ F 317 753-4427
  Noblesville *(G-13112)*

Nix Sanitary Service............................ G 812 785-1158
  Boonville *(G-1094)*

Sleegers Engineered Pdts Inc............. G 317 786-7770
  Indianapolis *(G-9448)*

Surface Generation Tech LLC.............. G 765 425-2741
  Anderson *(G-203)*

3799 Transportation equipment, nec

Alliance Rv LLC.................................... E 574 312-5215
  Elkhart *(G-3166)*

Aluminum Trailer Company................... C 574 773-2440
  Nappanee *(G-12579)*

Asanders Global LLC........................... G 224 401-4050
  Elkhart *(G-3193)*

Asw LLC.. C 260 432-1596
  Columbia City *(G-2120)*

Be Loved Transportation Inc.............. G 812 207-2610
  Bloomington *(G-800)*

Beck Industries LP............................. D 574 294-5621
  Elkhart *(G-3221)*

Beco Inc... G 765 778-3426
  Pendleton *(G-13525)*

Bridgeview Manufacturing LLC........... F 574 970-0116
  Elkhart *(G-3395)*

Buchanan Company Inc....................... G 317 919-2025
  Fort Wayne *(G-4822)*

Chubbs Steel Sales Inc....................... E 574 295-3166
  Elkhart *(G-3252)*

Collins Trailers Inc............................. G 574 294-2561
  Elkhart *(G-3257)*

Creative Manufacturing Rv LLC........... F 574 333-3302
  Elkhart *(G-3271)*

Cs Warrior Enterprise LLC................... G 317 528-0152
  Indianapolis *(G-7917)*

CTB Hauling Service LLC..................... G 317 760-3308
  Indianapolis *(G-7919)*

D Rv Luxury Suites LLC....................... F 260 562-1075
  Howe *(G-7233)*

Deluxe Akio 606 Ltd Lblty Co.............. G 708 682-2780
  Crown Point *(G-2676)*

Detroit Holdings LLC.......................... G 202 309-9681
  North Liberty *(G-13216)*

Dexter Chassis Group Inc................... D 574 266-7356
  Elkhart *(G-3294)*

Driverz For Life(d 4 L) LLC................. G 317 619-4513
  Indianapolis *(G-8010)*

Dtp Trucking LLC................................ G 463 701-8508
  Indianapolis *(G-8016)*

Durhat Transportation LLC.................. G 463 204-9119
  Greenwood *(G-6691)*

Dutch Park Homes Inc........................ E 574 642-0150
  Goshen *(G-6127)*

Eagle Freight Inc............................... G 646 634-5870
  Merrillville *(G-11509)*

East-T-West North-To-South Inc......... D 574 264-6664
  Elkhart *(G-3312)*

Ember Recrtl Vehicles Inc.................. D 844 732-4204
  Bristol *(G-1259)*

Encore Rv LLC.................................... E 574 327-6540
  Elkhart *(G-3332)*

Evolving Transport LLC...................... G 317 794-4426
  Indianapolis *(G-8143)*

Father Son Sanders Trnspt LLC.......... G 773 899-8078
  Hammond *(G-6926)*

Felicia Fr8 LLC.................................... G 312 597-9282
  Hammond *(G-6927)*

Fiber-Tron Corp................................. F 574 294-8545
  Elkhart *(G-3345)*

Fischer Fleet Wash LLC....................... G 812 661-9947
  Rockport *(G-14340)*

Flj Transport LLC............................... G 574 642-0200
  Goshen *(G-6138)*

Flywithme Delivery LLC....................... G 219 614-9384
  Indianapolis *(G-8211)*

◆ Forest River Inc............................... E 574 389-4600
  Elkhart *(G-3356)*

Frontier Carriage.............................. G 574 965-4444
  Delphi *(G-2897)*

Gardiner Rentals Bill.......................... G 765 447-5111
  Lafayette *(G-10586)*

Garry Mertz....................................... G 260 837-6451
  Waterloo *(G-16520)*

Genes Transport LLC.......................... G 404 227-5178
  Indianapolis *(G-8274)*

Global Parts Network LLC................... G 574 855-5000
  South Bend *(G-15044)*

Goods On Target Sporting Inc............. G 812 623-2300
  Sunman *(G-15438)*

Graber Manufacturing......................... G 812 636-7725
  Odon *(G-13337)*

Grand Design Rv LLC.......................... C 574 825-8000
  Middlebury *(G-11719)*

Grodin Transportation........................ G 773 614-7062
  Gary *(G-5944)*

H L Enterprise Inc.............................. G 574 294-1112
  Elkhart *(G-3395)*

Hadley Products LLC........................... G 574 266-3700
  Elkhart *(G-3396)*

Highland Ridge Rv Inc........................ B 260 768-7771
  Shipshewana *(G-14850)*

Hobbs Transport Services LLC............ G 317 607-5590
  Indianapolis *(G-8401)*

Holiday House LLC.............................. F 574 206-0016
  Elkhart *(G-3408)*

Hoosier Buggy Shop............................ G 260 593-2192
  Topeka *(G-15810)*

Hostetler Carriage............................. G 260 463-9920
  Lagrange *(G-10742)*

Huskey Parts Company LLC................. G 812 899-0950
  Washington *(G-16485)*

Hymer Group Usa LLC......................... G 574 970-7460
  Bristol *(G-1267)*

Iea Constructors Inc.......................... D 765 832-8526
  Clinton *(G-2068)*

Iea Equipment Management LLC.......... B 765 832-2800
  Clinton *(G-2069)*

Iea Management Services Inc............. G 765 832-8526
  Clinton *(G-2070)*

IKON Group.. G 574 326-3661
  Elkhart *(G-3417)*

Innovative Equipment Inc.................... G 765 572-2367
  Westpoint *(G-16745)*

▼ Intech Trailers Inc........................... D 574 221-8231
  Nappanee *(G-12614)*

JC Creations LLC................................ G 574 248-0126
  Bremen *(G-1199)*

JP Trucking Inc.................................. F 574 654-7555
  New Carlisle *(G-12841)*

Keith Kunz Motorsports LLC................ G 812 372-8494
  Columbus *(G-2333)*

Keyline Sales Inc............................... G 574 294-5611
  Elkhart *(G-3453)*

Landgrebe Manufacturing Inc.............. G 219 462-9587
  Valparaiso *(G-15991)*

Landjet International........................... G 574 970-7805
  Elkhart *(G-3468)*

37 TRANSPORTATION EQUIPMENT

Lane Wright LLC .... G 317 473-4783
  Indianapolis *(G-8722)*
Legacy Trailer Rentals LLC .... G 812 873-5218
  North Vernon *(G-13284)*
Liberty Inds Investments LLC .... D 765 246-4031
  Fillmore *(G-4455)*
Lightning Logistics Entps LLC .... G 317 333-9563
  Indianapolis *(G-8750)*
Logistick Inc .... G 800 758-5840
  South Bend *(G-15128)*
Martins Buggy Shop .... G 574 831-3699
  Nappanee *(G-12621)*
Maximum Logistics LLC .... G 317 488-1010
  Greenwood *(G-6734)*
Metalcrafters Inc .... F 574 294-2502
  Elkhart *(G-3528)*
Miller Carriage Company LLC .... G 260 768-4553
  Shipshewana *(G-14867)*
MO Trailer Corporation .... F 574 533-0824
  Goshen *(G-6226)*
Mudd-Ox Inc .... F 260 768-7221
  Shipshewana *(G-14871)*
Nexgen Group Inc .... G 574 218-6363
  Nappanee *(G-12632)*
Noble Transportation LLC .... G 317 488-7710
  Indianapolis *(G-9016)*
Norman Wagler .... G 812 636-8015
  Odon *(G-13346)*
Olympic Fiberglass Industries .... F 574 223-3101
  Rochester *(G-14310)*
On Point Precision LLC .... G 317 590-2510
  Indianapolis *(G-9052)*
Open Range Rv Company .... E 260 768-7771
  Shipshewana *(G-14872)*
P R F .... G 219 477-8660
  Portage *(G-13902)*
Parallax Group Inc .... G 800 443-4859
  Anderson *(G-175)*
Perry Miller .... G 260 894-1133
  Shipshewana *(G-14878)*
Phed Mobility LLC .... G 574 226-4104
  Elkhart *(G-3602)*
Power Freight LLC .... G 260 258-6012
  Fort Wayne *(G-5327)*
Quality Concepts .... G 574 215-6391
  Goshen *(G-6244)*
Quickspace Transportation LLC .... G 812 585-2317
  Indianapolis *(G-9250)*
Raymone Sanders Fmly Trckg LLC .... G 317 400-3545
  Indianapolis *(G-9272)*
Recreation Vhcl Technical Inst .... G 574 549-9068
  Elkhart *(G-3643)*
Recreational Customs Inc .... G 574 642-0632
  Goshen *(G-6246)*
Reset Family Solutions LLC .... G 317 699-2990
  Carthage *(G-1817)*
Ring-Co Mobile LLC .... G 317 641-7050
  Trafalgar *(G-15832)*
Rios Investment Services LLC .... G 574 514-3999
  South Bend *(G-15221)*
Safe Travels Solutions LLC .... G 317 640-4576
  Indianapolis *(G-9363)*
Schwartzs Wheel & Clip C .... G 574 546-1302
  Bremen *(G-1220)*
Seaflo Marine & Rv N Amer LLC .... E 844 473-2356
  South Bend *(G-15236)*
Shelf It Right LLC .... G 574 368-6881
  South Bend *(G-15240)*
Showhaulers Trucks Inc .... E 574 825-6764
  Middlebury *(G-11751)*
Shurtrack Transport LLC .... G 317 779-5902
  Indianapolis *(G-9423)*

Sierra Motor Corp .... D 574 848-1300
  Bristol *(G-1292)*
Slicers .... G 812 255-0655
  Vincennes *(G-16155)*
Smith Expediting Resources LLC .... G 317 935-1180
  Indianapolis *(G-9450)*
Southern Ind Lnngs Catings Inc .... G 812 206-7250
  Charlestown *(G-1893)*
Spreuer & Son Inc .... F 260 463-3513
  Lagrange *(G-10763)*
Structural Composites Ind Inc .... D 260 894-4083
  Ligonier *(G-11024)*
◆ Supreme Industries Inc .... C 574 642-3070
  Goshen *(G-6265)*
Sx4 .... G 812 967-2502
  Palmyra *(G-13486)*
▼ T I B Inc .... E 574 892-5151
  Argos *(G-327)*
Thor Industries Inc .... B 574 970-7460
  Elkhart *(G-3730)*
Thor Industries Data Center .... G 574 970-7460
  Elkhart *(G-3732)*
Three K Racing Enterprises .... G 765 482-4273
  Lebanon *(G-10946)*
TRC Mfg Inc .... G 574 262-9299
  South Bend *(G-15289)*
Trimas Corporation .... F 260 925-3700
  Auburn *(G-432)*
Use What Youve Got Ministry .... G 317 924-4124
  Indianapolis *(G-9690)*
We Greater Courier Svcs LLC .... G 317 966-1043
  Indianapolis *(G-9744)*
Wellspring Components LLC .... G 260 768-7336
  Shipshewana *(G-14896)*
Wm Express LLP .... P 773 647-5305
  Hammond *(G-7035)*
Woodberry Family Freight LLC .... G 317 665-6917
  Indianapolis *(G-9785)*
▲ Zieman Manufacturing Comp .... C 574 535-1125
  Goshen *(G-6279)*

38 MEASURING, PHOTOGRAPHIC, MEDICAL, & OPTICAL GOODS, & CLOCKS

3812 Search and navigation equipment

1st Defense .... G 317 292-3123
  Noblesville *(G-13032)*
7th Leadership Organization .... G 219 938-6906
  Gary *(G-5883)*
Aerogage Inc .... G 978 422-8224
  Martinsville *(G-11378)*
Allan Defense LLC .... G 317 525-1244
  Greenwood *(G-6664)*
Bae Systems Controls Inc .... A 260 434-5195
  Fort Wayne *(G-4787)*
Central Van Lines Inc .... C 317 849-7900
  Indianapolis *(G-7774)*
Corvette Aerospace LLC .... G 317 512-4616
  Shelbyville *(G-14747)*
Covert Defenses LLC .... G 919 749-9717
  West Lafayette *(G-16570)*
Cyclone Adg LLC .... G 520 403-2927
  New Albany *(G-12718)*
Cypress Springs Entps Inc .... G 812 743-8888
  Wheatland *(G-16774)*
Federal-Mogul Powertrain LLC .... G 574 272-5900
  South Bend *(G-15032)*
First Gear Inc .... E 260 490-3238
  Fort Wayne *(G-4984)*

Graffiti Defense LLC .... G 317 284-1788
  Fishers *(G-4533)*
Guardian Defense Inc .... G 574 265-4474
  Warsaw *(G-16372)*
H&S Defense LLC .... G 812 654-2314
  Milan *(G-11780)*
Hoosier Industrial Supply .... G 574 535-0712
  Goshen *(G-6167)*
In Defense of Women Inc .... G 574 855-1864
  Granger *(G-6353)*
Integrity Defense Services Inc .... E 812 675-4913
  Springville *(G-15387)*
Kinney Defense Solutions .... G 812 360-6189
  Bargersville *(G-569)*
L3harris Technologies Inc .... G 812 202-5171
  Crane *(G-2539)*
L3harris Technologies Inc .... G 812 202-5171
  Crane *(G-2540)*
L3harris Technologies Inc .... G 260 451-5597
  Fort Wayne *(G-5169)*
La Porte Defense Tech Corp .... G 219 362-1000
  La Porte *(G-10439)*
Lite Magnesium Products Inc .... G 765 299-3644
  Indianapolis *(G-8768)*
Lockheed Martin Corporation .... G 317 821-4000
  Indianapolis *(G-8776)*
Northwest Defense LLC .... G 931 257-0421
  Rensselaer *(G-14061)*
Outdoor Technologies LLC .... G 812 654-4399
  Milan *(G-11782)*
Pbtt Inc .... E 810 965-3675
  Newburgh *(G-13016)*
Pyromation LLC .... C 260 484-2580
  Fort Wayne *(G-5358)*
Radar Associates Corporation .... G 219 838-8030
  Munster *(G-12560)*
Raytheon Company .... A 310 647-9438
  Fort Wayne *(G-5366)*
Raytheon Company .... G 260 429-6000
  Fort Wayne *(G-5367)*
Raytheon Company .... A 260 429-6000
  Fort Wayne *(G-5368)*
Raytheon Company .... G 310 647-9438
  Fort Wayne *(G-5369)*
Raytheon Company .... C 317 306-8471
  Indianapolis *(G-9273)*
Raytheon Company .... G 317 306-7492
  Indianapolis *(G-9274)*
Raytheon Company .... G 317 306-4633
  Indianapolis *(G-9275)*
Rjv Investments Inc .... E 574 234-1063
  South Bend *(G-15223)*
Rolls-Royce Defense Svcs Inc .... D 317 230-5006
  Indianapolis *(G-9330)*
Silicis Technologies Inc .... E 317 896-5044
  Westfield *(G-16728)*
U S S Inc .... G 260 693-1172
  Churubusco *(G-1992)*
◆ Undersea Sensor Systems Inc .... E 260 248-3500
  Columbia City *(G-2209)*
United Technology Corp .... F 317 481-5784
  Indianapolis *(G-9681)*
Valor Defense Solutions Inc .... F 812 617-0362
  Odon *(G-13354)*
Value Production Inc .... E 574 246-1913
  South Bend *(G-15300)*
Xtreme ADS Limited .... E 765 644-7323
  Anderson *(G-218)*

3821 Laboratory apparatus and furniture

Ameribrace Orthopedic LLC .... G 260 704-6027
  Fort Wayne *(G-4750)*

SIC SECTION
38 MEASURING, PHOTOGRAPHIC, MEDICAL, & OPTICAL GOODS, & CLOCKS

Beckman Coulter Inc .... D 317 471-8029
   Indianapolis *(G-7606)*
Care Test Lab LLC .... G 574 326-1082
   Indianapolis *(G-7742)*
Cbf Forensics LLC .... G 708 383-8320
   Hobart *(G-7180)*
◆ Chryso Inc .... E 812 256-4220
   Charlestown *(G-1873)*
Cook Group Incorporated .... F 812 339-2235
   Bloomington *(G-838)*
Current Technologies Inc .... F 765 364-0490
   Crawfordsville *(G-2561)*
Envigo Rms Inc .... G 317 806-6080
   Greenfield *(G-6500)*
Envigo Rms Inc .... G 317 806-6060
   Greenfield *(G-6501)*
▲ Envigo Rms Inc .... C 317 806-6080
   Indianapolis *(G-8125)*
Fast Track Technologies LLC .... F 317 229-6080
   Noblesville *(G-13075)*
Harry J Kloeppel & Associates .... G 317 578-1300
   Indianapolis *(G-8368)*
Helmer Scientific LLC .... C 317 773-9073
   Noblesville *(G-13094)*
I2r .... G 812 235-6167
   Terre Haute *(G-15612)*
Integrated Instrument Svcs Inc .... F 317 248-1958
   Indianapolis *(G-8568)*
Leco Corporation .... G 574 288-9017
   South Bend *(G-15122)*
Merss Corporation .... G 317 632-7299
   Indianapolis *(G-8879)*
Modular Dvcs Acquisition LLC .... D 317 818-4480
   Indianapolis *(G-8943)*
Poly-Wood LLC .... G 877 457-3284
   Syracuse *(G-15473)*
◆ Poly-Wood LLC .... D 574 457-3284
   Syracuse *(G-15474)*
Templeton Coal Company Inc .... C 812 232-7037
   Terre Haute *(G-15726)*

3822 Environmental controls

A & A Prcsion Htg Colg Rfrgn L .... G 812 401-1711
   Evansville *(G-3859)*
Abbott Controls Inc .... G 317 697-7102
   Indianapolis *(G-7415)*
▲ Advanced Control Tech Inc .... G 317 806-2750
   Indianapolis *(G-7437)*
Advantage Engineering Inc .... D 317 887-0729
   Greenwood *(G-6660)*
Airxcel Inc .... B 574 294-5681
   Elkhart *(G-3156)*
Automated Logic Corporation .... F 765 286-1993
   Muncie *(G-12347)*
Building Temp Solutions LLC .... F 260 449-9201
   Fort Wayne *(G-4823)*
Caliente LLC .... E 260 426-3800
   Fort Wayne *(G-4830)*
Dimplex North America Limited .... F 317 890-0809
   Indianapolis *(G-7975)*
◆ Dwyer Instruments LLC .... C 219 879-8868
   Michigan City *(G-11604)*
◆ Eclipse Inc .... D
   Muncie *(G-12389)*
Elliott-Williams Company Inc .... E 317 453-2295
   Indianapolis *(G-8097)*
Gillespie Mrrell Gen Contg LLC .... G 765 618-4084
   Marion *(G-11288)*
Green Air LLC .... G 317 335-1706
   Fishers *(G-4641)*
Jackson Systems LLC .... C 888 359-0365
   Indianapolis *(G-8615)*

Johnson Controls Inc .... F 812 868-1374
   Evansville *(G-4144)*
Johnson Controls Inc .... F 317 917-5043
   Pittsboro *(G-13649)*
Johnson Sales Corp .... G 219 322-9558
   Schererville *(G-14525)*
OMI Industries Inc .... G 812 438-9218
   Rising Sun *(G-14244)*
Open Control Systems LLC .... G 317 429-0627
   Indianapolis *(G-9062)*
Pinder Instruments Company Inc .... G 219 924-7070
   Munster *(G-12558)*
Pyromation LLC .... C 260 484-2580
   Fort Wayne *(G-5358)*
Rees Inc .... F 260 495-9811
   Fremont *(G-5832)*
Ruskin .... F 574 223-3181
   Rochester *(G-14322)*
Schneider Elc Systems USA Inc .... G 317 372-2839
   Indianapolis *(G-9390)*
Seminole Energy Services .... G 219 923-2131
   Highland *(G-7153)*
Siemens Industry Inc .... E 317 381-0734
   Indianapolis *(G-9425)*
Smart Temps LLC .... G 574 217-7202
   Mishawaka *(G-11998)*
▲ SMC Corporation of America .... B 317 899-4440
   Noblesville *(G-13176)*
Spyder Controls Inc .... G 866 919-9092
   South Bend *(G-15262)*
Temperature Control Svcs LLC .... G 765 325-2439
   Lebanon *(G-10945)*
Temptek Inc .... G 317 887-6352
   Greenwood *(G-6773)*
Thatcher Engineering Corp .... D 219 949-2084
   Gary *(G-6018)*
▲ Utec Inc .... A 260 359-3514
   Huntington *(G-7377)*
Vernet US Corporation .... D 812 372-0281
   Columbus *(G-2412)*
▲ Vernet US Corporation .... C 812 372-0281
   Columbus *(G-2413)*
Vivint Inc .... B 317 983-0112
   Indianapolis *(G-9727)*
Wise Energy LLC .... G 317 475-0305
   Indianapolis *(G-9776)*

3823 Process control instruments

Advanced Boiler Ctrl Svcs Inc .... F 708 429-7066
   Crown Point *(G-2649)*
Agri-Tronix Corp .... F 317 738-4474
   Franklin *(G-5703)*
AMG LLC .... F 317 329-4004
   Indianapolis *(G-7513)*
Analyticalab Inc .... G 219 473-9777
   Whiting *(G-16831)*
Automated Drive & Design LLC .... G 812 342-0809
   Columbus *(G-2223)*
Buskirk Engineering Inc .... F 260 622-5550
   Ossian *(G-13420)*
C & K Manufacturing Inc .... F 574 264-4063
   Elkhart *(G-3242)*
Capital Tech Solutions LLC .... F 812 303-4357
   Evansville *(G-3961)*
Cec Controls Company Inc .... G 219 728-6007
   Chesterton *(G-1908)*
Cognex Corporation .... E 317 867-5079
   Westfield *(G-16677)*
Complete Controls Inc .... G 260 489-0852
   Fort Wayne *(G-4868)*
Copeland LP .... G 317 968-4250
   Greenfield *(G-6483)*

Copeland LP .... F 765 932-2956
   Rushville *(G-14397)*
Copeland LP .... C 765 932-1902
   Rushville *(G-14398)*
Cosworth Electronics LLC .... G 317 808-3800
   Indianapolis *(G-7888)*
Covidien LP .... C 317 837-8199
   Plainfield *(G-13674)*
◆ Crown Audio Inc .... B 800 342-6939
   Elkhart *(G-3273)*
Crown Elec Svcs & Automtn Inc .... D 972 929-4700
   Portage *(G-13857)*
CRS-Spv Inc .... E 502 805-0143
   Jeffersonville *(G-9965)*
Damping Technologies Inc .... F 574 258-7916
   Mishawaka *(G-11880)*
Dwyer Instruments LLC .... E 219 879-8000
   Michigan City *(G-11603)*
Dwyer Instruments Inc .... G 574 234-6853
   South Bend *(G-15007)*
Dwyer Instruments Inc .... G 219 879-8868
   South Bend *(G-15008)*
Dwyer Instruments Inc .... G 574 862-2590
   Wakarusa *(G-16231)*
Dwyer Instruments Inc .... G 219 279-2031
   Wolcott *(G-16928)*
◆ Dwyer Instruments LLC .... C 219 879-8868
   Michigan City *(G-11604)*
◆ Eclipse Inc .... D
   Muncie *(G-12389)*
Emerson Electric Co .... G 317 574-3170
   Carmel *(G-1620)*
Emerson Electric Co .... G 317 322-2055
   Indianapolis *(G-8105)*
Emerson Electric Co .... G 219 465-2411
   Valparaiso *(G-15944)*
Endress + Hauser Inc .... G 317 535-7138
   Greenwood *(G-6695)*
Endress + Hauser Inc .... G 317 535-2159
   Greenwood *(G-6696)*
▲ Endress + Hauser Inc .... C 317 535-7138
   Greenwood *(G-6697)*
◆ Endress + Hser Flwtec AG Div U .... C 317 535-7138
   Greenwood *(G-6698)*
Endress+hauser (usa) Automatio .... C 317 535-2121
   Greenwood *(G-6699)*
Endress+hauser Infoserve Inc .... G 888 363-7377
   Greenwood *(G-6700)*
◆ Endress+hauser Wetzer USA Inc .... G 317 535-1362
   Greenwood *(G-6701)*
Engineered Refr Shapes Svcs LLC .... G 765 778-8040
   Pendleton *(G-13531)*
Environmental Technology Inc .... E 574 233-1202
   South Bend *(G-15016)*
Fire Apparatus Service Inc .... G 219 985-0788
   Gary *(G-5933)*
Frew Process Group LLC .... G 317 565-5000
   Noblesville *(G-13081)*
▲ Functional Devices LLC .... E 765 883-5538
   Sharpsville *(G-14710)*
Hadady Machining Company Inc .... F 708 474-8620
   East Chicago *(G-3014)*
Harman Professional Inc .... B 574 294-8000
   Elkhart *(G-3398)*
Heraeus Electro-Nite Co LLC .... C 765 473-8275
   Peru *(G-13584)*
Hillenbrand Inc .... A 812 931-5000
   Batesville *(G-590)*
Hurco Companies Inc .... G 317 347-6208
   Indianapolis *(G-8435)*
Hurco Companies Inc .... C 317 293-5309
   Indianapolis *(G-8436)*

38 MEASURING, PHOTOGRAPHIC, MEDICAL, & OPTICAL GOODS, & CLOCKS

▲ Indev Gauging Systems Inc............. E 815 282-4463
Terre Haute (G-15615)
Indiana Instruments Inc........................ G 317 875-8032
Indianapolis (G-8479)
Indiana Thermal Solutions LLC........... F 317 570-5400
Indianapolis (G-8497)
Industrial Physics Inc........................... F 812 981-3133
New Albany (G-12747)
J & J Industrial Service Inc................... G 219 362-4973
La Porte (G-10429)
L3harris Technologies Inc.................... G 812 202-5171
Crane (G-2540)
L3harris Technologies Inc.................... G 260 451-5597
Fort Wayne (G-5169)
Leco Corporation.................................. G 574 288-9017
South Bend (G-15122)
Linda Controls LLC.............................. G 219 926-6979
Chesterton (G-1945)
Maxim Pipette Service Inc.................... G 877 536-2946
Plainfield (G-13701)
Micro Motion Inc................................... G 317 334-1893
Indianapolis (G-8900)
◆ Milltronics Mfg Co Inc......................... C 952 442-1410
Indianapolis (G-8926)
Milltronics Usa Inc................................ G 317 293-5309
Indianapolis (G-8927)
Milltronics Usa Inc................................ G 317 293-5309
Indianapolis (G-8928)
▲ Milltronics Usa Inc............................. F 317 293-5309
Indianapolis (G-8929)
Monitoring Solutions Inc....................... E 317 856-9400
Indianapolis (G-8948)
Mtcr Site Services LLC......................... G 812 598-6516
Newburgh (G-13014)
Omega Engineering LLC...................... G 317 995-1965
Indianapolis (G-9047)
Ovideon LLC... G 812 577-3274
Lawrenceburg (G-10852)
Perpetual Industries Inc....................... E 702 707-9811
Auburn (G-415)
Petal Solutions LLC.............................. G 765 404-7747
West Lafayette (G-16618)
Pyromation LLC.................................... C 260 484-2580
Fort Wayne (G-5358)
Quality Industrial Supplies.................... G 219 324-2654
La Porte (G-10468)
Ray Kammer... G 219 938-1708
Gary (G-6000)
Scadata Ventures LLC......................... F 260 373-0100
Fort Wayne (G-5401)
Siemens Industry Inc............................ D 219 763-7927
Portage (G-13914)
Surclean Inc.. F 248 791-2226
Brownsburg (G-1405)
Syscon International Inc....................... C 574 232-3900
South Bend (G-15276)
T W Brackett & Assoc LLC................... G 765 769-3000
Attica (G-355)
Technidyne Corporation....................... E 812 948-2884
New Albany (G-12821)
▲ Texmo Blank USA Inc....................... D 574 696-9990
Warsaw (G-16437)
Thermco Instrument Corporation......... F 219 362-6258
La Porte (G-10493)
Thermphyscal Prpts RES Lab Inc........ G 765 463-1581
West Lafayette (G-16637)
▲ Zs Systems LLC................................ G 765 588-4528
Lafayette (G-10727)

3824 Fluid meters and counting devices

Custom Controls & Engrg Inc............... G 812 663-0755
Greensburg (G-6587)

◆ Dwyer Instruments LLC...................... C 219 879-8868
Michigan City (G-11604)
Kendrion (mishawaka) LLC................... E 574 257-2422
Mishawaka (G-11922)
▲ Mechanical Parts & Svcs Inc............ G 219 670-1986
Valparaiso (G-16001)
Memcor Inc.. E 260 356-4300
Huntington (G-7341)
Midwest Meter Inc................................ G 574 967-0175
Flora (G-4661)
Parker Exploration & Productio............ G 812 673-4017
Wadesville (G-16228)
Phoenix America LLC........................... E 260 432-9664
Fort Wayne (G-5311)
▲ Phoenix America Inc......................... E 260 432-9664
Fort Wayne (G-5312)
Prosperus LLC...................................... G 317 786-8990
Indianapolis (G-9233)
Scalar Design Engrg & Dist LLC.......... G 765 429-5545
Lafayette (G-10685)
Speedread Technologies LLC.............. G 317 824-4544
Indianapolis (G-9477)
▲ Steiner Enterprises Inc..................... F 765 429-6409
Lafayette (G-10700)

3825 Instruments to measure electricity

Acterna LLC.. E 317 788-9351
Indianapolis (G-7425)
Advance Stores Company Inc.............. G 317 253-5034
Indianapolis (G-7436)
Advantage Electronics Inc.................... F 317 888-1946
Greenwood (G-6659)
Agilent Technologies............................ ..... 617 694-7692
Winona Lake (G-16908)
Ampac International Inc....................... G 260 424-2964
Fort Wayne (G-4760)
App Engineering Incorporated.............. F 317 536-5300
Indianapolis (G-7527)
Avid Operations Inc.............................. G 260 220-2001
Fort Wayne (G-4784)
Ball Systems Inc................................... G 317 804-2330
Westfield (G-16667)
Chance Ind Standards Lab Inc............. F 317 787-6578
Indianapolis (G-7783)
Contact Products Inc............................ G 219 838-1911
Munster (G-12536)
Copper Mountain Tech LLC.................. E 317 222-5400
Indianapolis (G-7872)
Createch/Rehder Development Co....... G 765 252-0257
West Lafayette (G-16572)
Donald Pape.. G 260 484-6088
Fort Wayne (G-4924)
Doyle Manufacturing Inc....................... G 574 848-5624
Bristol (G-1256)
Dresser LLC.. D 765 827-9200
Connersville (G-2436)
Durhat Transportation LLC................... G 463 204-9119
Greenwood (G-6691)
▲ Empro Manufacturing Co Inc............ E 317 823-3000
Indianapolis (G-8110)
Hgl Dynamics Inc.................................. G 317 782-3500
Indianapolis (G-8393)
Hilevel Technology Inc......................... G 765 349-1650
Martinsville (G-11400)
Ideal Safety & Hygiene LLC................. G 317 281-3921
Indianapolis (G-8453)
Indiana Research Institute.................... G 812 378-5363
Columbus (G-2325)
▲ Indiana Research Institute............... G 812 378-4221
Columbus (G-2326)
Jfw Industries Incorporated.................. C 317 887-1340
Indianapolis (G-8625)

Kane Usa Inc... E 800 547-5740
Indianapolis (G-8660)
Keysight Technologies Inc.................... G 260 203-2179
Fort Wayne (G-5148)
Kirby Risk Corporation.......................... D 765 447-1402
Lafayette (G-10621)
Landis Gyr Inc....................................... F 317 578-2200
Indianapolis (G-8721)
Landis+gyr Technology Inc................... G 765 742-1001
Lafayette (G-10634)
Leco Corporation.................................. G 574 288-9017
South Bend (G-15122)
Noel-Smyser Engineering Corp............ E 317 293-2215
Indianapolis (G-9020)
P&C Prime LLC..................................... F 231 420-3650
Fredericksburg (G-5795)
Precision Systems................................ G 812 283-4904
Clarksville (G-2029)
R K C Instrument................................... F 574 273-6099
South Bend (G-15213)
◆ Radian Research Inc......................... D 765 449-5500
Lafayette (G-10675)
Rail Scale Inc.. G 317 339-6486
Wilkinson (G-16844)
Renk Systems Corporation................... E 317 455-1367
Camby (G-1513)
▼ Scandigital Inc................................... G 888 333-2808
Indianapolis (G-9386)
SGS Cybermetrix Inc............................ G 800 713-1203
Columbus (G-2391)
Solid Rock LLC..................................... E 260 755-2687
Fort Wayne (G-5425)
Spectrum Industry................................. G 812 231-8355
Terre Haute (G-15712)
System Solutions Inc............................ G 317 877-7572
Cicero (G-2001)
Teaco Inc... G 219 874-6234
Michigan City (G-11676)
▲ Technical Weighing Svcs Inc............ E 219 924-3366
Griffith (G-6819)
Ticzkus Electronic and Mfg................... G 574 542-2325
Rochester (G-14328)
Utility Systems Inc................................ E 317 842-9000
Indianapolis (G-9692)
Valgotech LLC....................................... G 850 339-8877
Fishers (G-4627)
Xylem Vue Inc....................................... E 574 360-1093
Granger (G-6391)

3826 Analytical instruments

Anasazi Instruments Inc....................... F 317 861-7657
New Palestine (G-12930)
Animated Dynamics Inc........................ G 765 418-5359
West Lafayette (G-16563)
Arch Med Sltions - Elkhart LLC............ F 574 264-3997
Elkhart (G-3188)
Astbury Water Technology Inc............. G 260 668-8900
Angola (G-231)
Axis Industries Usa LLC....................... F 317 739-3390
Franklin (G-5711)
Beckman Coulter Inc............................. F 317 808-4200
Indianapolis (G-7604)
Beckman Coulter Inc............................. D 317 808-4200
Indianapolis (G-7605)
Beckman Coulter Inc............................. D 317 471-8029
Indianapolis (G-7606)
Beckman Coulter Life Sciences........... D 408 747-2000
Indianapolis (G-7607)
Capital Envmtl Entps Inc...................... G 317 240-8085
Indianapolis (G-7733)
Cubed Laboratories LLC...................... G 866 935-6165
South Bend (G-14987)

SIC SECTION
38 MEASURING, PHOTOGRAPHIC, MEDICAL, & OPTICAL GOODS, & CLOCKS

Flir Security Inc .... G 443 936-9108
  Indianapolis (G-8205)
Griffin Analytical Technologies LLC ...... E 765 775-1701
  West Lafayette (G-16588)
Inchromatics LLC .... G 317 872-7401
  Indianapolis (G-8470)
Infrared Lab Systems LLC .... G 317 896-1565
  Westfield (G-16700)
Ipheion Development Corp .... G 240 281-1619
  Indianapolis (G-8587)
Kprime Technologies LLC .... G 260 399-1337
  Fort Wayne (G-5159)
Lazar Scientific Incorporated .... G 574 271-7020
  Granger (G-6358)
Leco Corporation .... G 574 288-9017
  South Bend (G-15122)
Lk Technologies Inc .... G 812 332-4449
  Bloomington (G-912)
Lloyd Jr Frank P and Assoc .... G 317 388-9225
  Indianapolis (G-8773)
Peli Biothermal LLC .... G 763 412-4800
  Plainfield (G-13712)
Perkinelmer Hlth Sciences Inc .... G 800 385-1555
  South Bend (G-15193)
Purspec Technologies Inc .... G 765 532-2208
  West Lafayette (G-16623)
◆ R F Express Corp .... G 219 510-5193
  Valparaiso (G-16034)
Sentech Corporation .... G 317 596-1988
  Indianapolis (G-9402)
Teledyne Flir LLC .... E 412 423-2100
  West Lafayette (G-16633)
Teledyne Flir Defense Inc .... E 765 775-1701
  West Lafayette (G-16634)
Teledyne Flir Detection Inc .... E 765 775-1701
  West Lafayette (G-16635)
Templeton Coal Company Inc .... C 812 232-7037
  Terre Haute (G-15726)
Thermo Fisher Scientific Inc .... F 812 477-2760
  Evansville (G-4342)
▲ Trilithic Inc .... C 317 895-3600
  Indianapolis (G-9641)
Webber Manufacturing Company .... E 317 357-8681
  Indianapolis (G-9745)

3827 Optical instruments and lenses

AB Engineering Inc .... G 260 489-2845
  Fort Wayne (G-4716)
Better Visions PC .... F 260 244-7542
  Columbia City (G-2124)
Better Visions PC .... F 260 627-2669
  Leo (G-10963)
Corlens Inc .... G 843 822-6174
  Terre Haute (G-15568)
◆ Dave Jones Machinists LLC .... G 574 256-5500
  Mishawaka (G-11881)
General Optics LLC .... G 765 637-5578
  Zionsville (G-17012)
Motion Engineering Company Inc .... G 317 804-7990
  Westfield (G-16712)
Optical Solutions LLC LLC .... G 317 525-8308
  Fishers (G-4571)
S & S Optical Co Inc .... F 260 749-9614
  New Haven (G-12915)
Union Optical Eyecare Ctr Inc .... G 812 279-3466
  Bedford (G-679)
Vision Aid Systems Inc .... G 317 888-0323
  Greenwood (G-6778)

3829 Measuring and controlling devices, nec

Advanced Designs Corp .... F 812 333-1922
  Bloomington (G-773)

Advanced Test Concepts LLC .... E 317 328-8492
  Indianapolis (G-7442)
Ameribrace Orthopedic LLC .... G 260 704-6027
  Fort Wayne (G-4750)
◆ Ati Inc .... G 812 431-5409
  Mount Vernon (G-12289)
Avalign Technologies Inc .... G 317 865-6436
  Greenwood (G-6672)
Biodot of Indiana Inc .... G 812 945-0915
  New Albany (G-12701)
Center For Diagnostic Imaging .... F 812 234-0555
  Terre Haute (G-15557)
Chapman Environmental Controls .... G 574 674-8706
  Osceola (G-13386)
Chesterfield Tool & Engrg Inc .... E 765 378-5101
  Daleville (G-2798)
Clear Waters Serenity Center .... G 260 459-9200
  Fort Wayne (G-4858)
Containment Tech Group Inc .... G 317 862-5945
  Indianapolis (G-7855)
▲ Cvg Sprague Devices LLC .... C 614 289-5360
  Michigan City (G-11593)
Damping Technologies Inc .... F 574 258-7916
  Mishawaka (G-11880)
Deprisco Ventures Inc .... G 260 637-8660
  Fort Wayne (G-4916)
◆ Dwyer Instruments LLC .... C 219 879-8868
  Michigan City (G-11604)
Dyno One Inc .... E 812 526-0500
  Edinburgh (G-3081)
Fleming Assoc Calibration Inc .... G 317 631-4605
  Indianapolis (G-8202)
G Unit Core Inc .... G 812 526-2080
  Edinburgh (G-3084)
Hartsock Industrial Sales Inc .... G 317 858-8250
  Westfield (G-16696)
Hgl Dynamics Inc .... G 317 782-3500
  Indianapolis (G-8393)
Honeywell International Inc .... G 812 473-4163
  Evansville (G-4108)
Hoosier Industrial Supply Inc .... F 574 533-8565
  Goshen (G-6168)
Indiana Ultrasound LLC .... G 219 746-6662
  Merrillville (G-11524)
Intech Automation Systems Corp .... G 209 836-8610
  Peru (G-13587)
Iot Technologies Intl LLC .... F 317 824-4544
  Indianapolis (G-8586)
◆ J and N Enterprises Inc .... G 219 465-2700
  Valparaiso (G-15978)
▲ Lafayette Instrument Co LLC .... E 765 423-1505
  Lafayette (G-10626)
Lomont Holdings Co Inc .... E 800 545-9023
  Angola (G-273)
▲ Magwerks Corporation .... G 317 241-8011
  Danville (G-2819)
Matrix Technologies Inc .... G 765 284-3335
  Muncie (G-12448)
Mattox and Moore Inc .... G 317 632-7534
  Indianapolis (G-8852)
Micro-Precision Operations .... F 260 589-2136
  Berne (G-719)
Moyer Process & Controls Co .... G 260 495-2405
  Fremont (G-5827)
MTS Systems Corporation .... G 952 937-4000
  Alexandria (G-55)
▲ Nrp Jones LLC .... D 800 348-8868
  La Porte (G-10460)
Nuclear Measurements Corp .... G 317 546-2415
  Indianapolis (G-9032)
P C Communications Inc .... G 219 838-2546
  Highland (G-7150)

Piezotech LLC .... E 317 876-4670
  Indianapolis (G-9141)
PSL Rheotek USA Inc .... G 574 271-9417
  Granger (G-6373)
Pyromation LLC .... C 260 484-2580
  Fort Wayne (G-5358)
Robco Engineered Rbr Pdts Inc .... F 260 248-2888
  Columbia City (G-2192)
Saam Inc .... G 855 405-7773
  Indianapolis (G-9359)
Safeguard Solutions LLC .... G 317 519-0255
  Greenfield (G-6548)
Sensit Technologies LLC .... F 219 465-2700
  Valparaiso (G-16045)
Sensortec Inc .... E 260 497-8811
  Fort Wayne (G-5409)
Servoflo Corporation .... G 574 262-4171
  Elkhart (G-3670)
Sonam Technologies LLC .... G 844 887-6626
  Crown Point (G-2760)
Stout Plastic Weld .... F 219 926-7622
  Chesterton (G-1959)
Techncl Cntrls/Solutions Inc .... G 260 416-0329
  Churubusco (G-1991)
Texys America LLC .... G 317 469-4828
  Indianapolis (G-9582)
Texys Sensors LLC .... G 317 469-4828
  Indianapolis (G-9583)
Thank You Lord LLC .... G 317 319-1271
  Indianapolis (G-9586)
Therametric Technologies Inc .... F 317 565-8065
  Noblesville (G-13181)
Tmx Healthcare Tech LLC .... F 877 874-6339
  Indianapolis (G-9614)
United Leak Detection Inc .... G 317 848-4447
  Carmel (G-1795)
Vibromatic Company Inc .... E 317 773-3885
  Noblesville (G-13193)
Vibronics Inc .... G 812 853-2300
  Newburgh (G-13027)

3841 Surgical and medical instruments

34 Lives Pbc .... G 303 550-9989
  West Lafayette (G-16553)
3M Company .... B 317 692-6666
  Indianapolis (G-7388)
3M Company .... G 574 948-8103
  Plymouth (G-13750)
Accu-Mold LLC .... E 269 323-0388
  Mishawaka (G-11834)
Advanced Mbility Solutions LLC .... F 812 438-2338
  Rising Sun (G-14240)
Advanced Vscular Therapies Inc .... G 765 423-1720
  Lafayette (G-10516)
▼ Advantis Medical Inc .... C 317 859-2300
  Greenwood (G-6661)
After Action Med Dntl Sup LLC .... G 800 892-5352
  Indianapolis (G-7457)
Airgas Usa LLC .... G 317 248-8072
  Indianapolis (G-7464)
Allen Medical Systems Inc .... G 978 266-4286
  Batesville (G-576)
Allen Medical Systems Inc .... G 812 931-2512
  Batesville (G-577)
American Veteran Group LLC .... G 317 600-4749
  Westfield (G-16664)
Ameriflo2 Inc .... F 317 844-2019
  Indianapolis (G-7511)
Amplified Sciences LLC .... G 317 490-0511
  West Lafayette (G-16560)
▼ Arcamed LLC .... E 317 375-7733
  Indianapolis (G-7538)

Employee Codes: A=Over 500 employees, B=251-500
C=101-250, D=51-100, E=20-50, F=10-19, G=1-9

38 MEASURING, PHOTOGRAPHIC, MEDICAL, & OPTICAL GOODS, & CLOCKS

Ash Access Technology Inc .... G 765 742-4813
Lafayette *(G-10528)*

▼ Ats Manufacturing Inc .... G
Elkhart *(G-3201)*

Avalign Technologies Inc .... G 260 484-1500
Fort Wayne *(G-4782)*

Avalign Technologies Inc .... G 888 625-4497
Greenwood *(G-6673)*

B & J Medical LLC .... E 260 349-1275
Kendallville *(G-10094)*

Bamboo US Bidco LLC .... A 812 333-0887
Bloomington *(G-794)*

Baxter Healthcare Corporation .... G 219 942-8136
Hobart *(G-7174)*

Baxter Healthcare Corporation .... G 317 291-0620
Indianapolis *(G-7598)*

Baxter Phrm Solutions LLC .... A 812 355-7167
Bloomington *(G-799)*

Bbs Enterprises Inc .... D 574 255-3173
Mishawaka *(G-11848)*

Bcd and Associates LLC .... G 317 873-5394
Indianapolis *(G-7601)*

Bd Medical Development Inc .... G 219 310-8551
Crown Point *(G-2653)*

Becton Dickinson and Company .... D 317 561-2900
Plainfield *(G-13660)*

▲ Biomedix-Inc .... F 812 355-7000
Bloomington *(G-808)*

♦ Biomet Inc .... A 574 267-6639
Warsaw *(G-16323)*

Biomet Europe Ltd .... E 574 267-2038
Warsaw *(G-16325)*

Boston Scientific Corp .... G 951 914-2400
Indianapolis *(G-7663)*

Boston Scientific Corporation .... A 812 829-4877
Spencer *(G-15340)*

Breg Inc .... G 760 505-0521
Indianapolis *(G-7675)*

Breg Inc .... E 317 559-0479
Indianapolis *(G-7676)*

Carecycle LLC .... G 317 372-7444
Indianapolis *(G-7743)*

Catalent Pharma Solutions Inc .... D 812 355-4498
Bloomington *(G-825)*

▲ Catheter Research Inc .... C 317 872-0074
Indianapolis *(G-7760)*

Center For Dagnstc Imaging CDI ...... G 812 331-1727
Bloomington *(G-826)*

Century Pharmaceuticals Inc .... E 317 849-4210
Indianapolis *(G-7775)*

▲ Circle M Spring Inc .... E 574 267-2883
Warsaw *(G-16335)*

Circle Medical Products Inc .... G 317 271-2626
Indianapolis *(G-7809)*

CNA Tool Engineering Inc .... G 260 927-2298
Auburn *(G-377)*

Compassionate Procedures LLC .... G 317 259-4656
Indianapolis *(G-7843)*

Cook Biodevice LLC .... G 800 265-0945
Bloomington *(G-837)*

Cook Capital Equipment LLC .... F 800 457-4500
Spencer *(G-15342)*

Cook General Biotechnology LLC ...... F 317 917-3450
Indianapolis *(G-7866)*

Cook Group Incorporated .... F 812 331-1025
Ellettsville *(G-3805)*

Cook Group Incorporated .... F 812 339-2235
Bloomington *(G-838)*

Cook Incorporated .... G 812 339-2235
Bloomington *(G-839)*

Cook Incorporated .... A 812 339-2235
Bloomington *(G-841)*

Cook Incorporated .... G 812 339-2235
Ellettsville *(G-3806)*

Cook Incorporated .... G 812 829-4891
Spencer *(G-15343)*

▲ Cook Incorporated .... A 812 339-2235
Bloomington *(G-840)*

Cook Medical Holdings LLC .... G 812 339-2235
Bloomington *(G-842)*

Cook Medical Inc .... D 812 822-1402
Bloomington *(G-843)*

Cook Medical LLC .... A 812 339-2235
Bloomington *(G-844)*

Cook Medical LLC .... A 812 323-4500
Bloomington *(G-846)*

▼ Cook Medical LLC .... B 812 339-2235
Bloomington *(G-845)*

Cook Medical Technologies LLC ...... F 812 339-2235
Bloomington *(G-847)*

Cook Regentec LLC .... D 800 265-0945
Bloomington *(G-848)*

Covidien LP .... C 317 837-8199
Plainfield *(G-13674)*

Cspine Inc .... G 574 936-7893
South Bend *(G-14986)*

▲ Depuy Synthes Inc .... C 574 267-8143
Warsaw *(G-16349)*

Depuy Synthes Products Inc .... F 574 267-8143
Warsaw *(G-16350)*

Eli Lilly International Corp .... F 317 276-2000
Indianapolis *(G-8091)*

▲ Engineered Medical Systems .... D 317 246-5500
Indianapolis *(G-8122)*

▲ Esaote North America Inc .... D 317 813-6000
Fishers *(G-4517)*

Ferrellok Lifesciences LLC .... G 765 716-0056
Muncie *(G-12394)*

First Gear Inc .... E 260 490-3238
Fort Wayne *(G-4984)*

Flw Plastics Inc .... F 812 546-0050
Hope *(G-7224)*

Fort Wyne Rdlgy Assn Fundation ...... F 260 266-8120
Fort Wayne *(G-5003)*

Freudenberg Medical Mis Inc .... C 812 280-2400
Jeffersonville *(G-9987)*

GMI LLC .... G 260 209-6676
Fort Wayne *(G-5028)*

Greatbatch Ltd .... G 260 755-7300
Fort Wayne *(G-5040)*

Group Dekko Inc .... G 260 599-3405
Kendallville *(G-10114)*

Hansa Medical Products Inc .... G 317 815-0708
Carmel *(G-1649)*

Helmer Scientific LLC .... C 317 773-9073
Noblesville *(G-13094)*

Hemocleanse Inc .... F 765 742-4813
Lafayette *(G-10596)*

Holgin Technologies LLC .... F 317 774-5181
Noblesville *(G-13095)*

I V S .... G 765 914-5268
Connersville *(G-2443)*

Innotek Custom Solutions LLC .... G 260 341-8691
Fort Wayne *(G-5108)*

Innovtive Nurological Dvcs LLC ...... G 317 674-2999
Carmel *(G-1670)*

Innovtive Surgical Designs Inc .... F 812 369-4252
Spencer *(G-15351)*

Inotiv Inc .... G 812 985-5900
Mount Vernon *(G-12302)*

Inscope Medical Solutions Inc .... G 502 882-0183
New Albany *(G-12748)*

Integer Holdings Corporation .... F 317 454-8800
Indianapolis *(G-8566)*

Inventory Solutions Inc .... G 212 749-5027
Indianapolis *(G-8585)*

▲ Jemarkel Health-Tech LLC .... G 219 548-5881
Valparaiso *(G-15981)*

♦ Kilgore Manufacturing Co Inc .... D 260 248-2002
Columbia City *(G-2162)*

♦ King Systems Corporation .... B 317 776-6823
Noblesville *(G-13120)*

Lca-Vision Inc .... G 317 818-3980
Indianapolis *(G-8729)*

Lebanon Corp .... G 765 482-7273
Lebanon *(G-10910)*

LH Medical Corporation .... D 260 387-5194
Fort Wayne *(G-5183)*

Lvb Acquisition Holding LLC .... A 574 267-6639
Warsaw *(G-16389)*

Mach Medical LLC .... E 260 229-1514
Columbia City *(G-2169)*

Magitek LLC .... G 260 488-2226
Hamilton *(G-6858)*

Mattox and Moore Inc .... G 317 632-7534
Indianapolis *(G-8852)*

McClinton Life Sciences Inc .... G 317 903-4230
Indianapolis *(G-8862)*

Med Devices LLC .... G 317 508-1699
Indianapolis *(G-8869)*

Med-Cut Inc .... D 574 269-1982
Warsaw *(G-16394)*

▲ Med2950 LLC .... E 317 545-5383
Indianapolis *(G-8870)*

Medical Systems Corp Indiana .... E 317 856-1340
Indianapolis *(G-8872)*

Medline Industries LP .... G 800 633-5463
Charlestown *(G-1882)*

Medtrnic Sofamor Danek USA Inc ...... G 317 837-8142
Plainfield *(G-13702)*

Medtrnic Sofamor Danek USA Inc ...... G 574 267-6826
Warsaw *(G-16396)*

Medtronic .... G 317 837-8664
Plainfield *(G-13703)*

Micropulse Inc .... C 260 625-3304
Columbia City *(G-2171)*

Midwest Eye Services LLC .... E 833 592-7434
Wabash *(G-16201)*

Miftek Corporation .... G 765 491-3848
West Lafayette *(G-16607)*

Mira Vista Diagnostics LLC .... E 317 856-2681
Indianapolis *(G-8932)*

Nanovis LLC .... G 260 625-1502
Columbia City *(G-2173)*

Nemco Medical Ltd .... E 260 484-1500
Fort Wayne *(G-5263)*

Neurava Inc .... G 281 995-8055
Indianapolis *(G-9001)*

Newcomed Inc .... G 260 484-1500
Fort Wayne *(G-5269)*

Nexxt Spine LLC .... F 317 436-7801
Noblesville *(G-13141)*

Nginstruments LLC .... D 574 268-2112
Warsaw *(G-16401)*

Omnitech Systems Inc .... E 219 531-5532
Valparaiso *(G-16018)*

Paragon Medical Inc .... C 574 594-2140
Pierceton *(G-13637)*

▲ Paragon Medical Inc .... C 574 594-2140
Pierceton *(G-13638)*

Performance Cnc LLC .... G 574 780-4864
Bourbon *(G-1126)*

Philips Ultrasound Inc .... F 317 591-5242
Indianapolis *(G-9135)*

▲ Point Medical Corporation .... A 219 663-1775
Crown Point *(G-2732)*

SIC SECTION
38 MEASURING, PHOTOGRAPHIC, MEDICAL, & OPTICAL GOODS, & CLOCKS

▲ Polymer Technology Systems Inc ..... D 317 870-5610
　Whitestown *(G-16815)*

Precision Edge Srgcal Pdts LLC ..... D 260 624-3123
　Angola *(G-287)*

Promex Technologies LLC ..... E 317 736-0128
　Indianapolis *(G-9230)*

Prp Technologies LLC ..... G 260 433-3769
　Fort Wayne *(G-5355)*

R 2 Diagnostics Inc ..... G 574 288-4377
　South Bend *(G-15212)*

Restoration Med Polymers LLC ..... E 260 625-1573
　Columbia City *(G-2189)*

Rgr Medical Solutions Inc ..... C 317 285-9703
　Fishers *(G-4596)*

Rmi Holdings LLC ..... F 317 214-7076
　Warsaw *(G-16419)*

Rusher Medical LLC ..... G 260 341-6514
　Fort Wayne *(G-5391)*

Rx Help Centers LLC ..... G 866 478-9593
　Indianapolis *(G-9350)*

Scott G Kirk ..... G 317 843-1703
　Carmel *(G-1754)*

Single Source Medical LLC ..... E 574 656-3400
　North Liberty *(G-13224)*

Smed - Ta/Td LLC ..... G 260 625-3347
　Columbia City *(G-2198)*

Smith & Nephew Inc ..... G 800 357-6155
　Indianapolis *(G-9449)*

Smiths Medical Asd Inc ..... E 219 554-2196
　Gary *(G-6011)*

Sophysa USA Inc ..... G 219 663-7711
　Crown Point *(G-2761)*

Ste Acquisition LLC ..... G 260 925-1382
　Auburn *(G-426)*

Stryker Corporation ..... G 832 509-9988
　Mooresville *(G-12244)*

Summit Cy Precision Machining ..... G 260 258-0855
　Fort Wayne *(G-5451)*

Symmetry Medical Inc ..... C 574 267-8700
　Warsaw *(G-16434)*

▲ Symmetry Medical Inc ..... G 574 267-8700
　Warsaw *(G-16433)*

Symmetry Medical USA Inc ..... G 574 267-8700
　Warsaw *(G-16436)*

Tayco Brace Inc ..... E 574 850-7910
　South Bend *(G-15279)*

Thompson ..... G 219 942-8133
　Hobart *(G-7211)*

Tri-Pac Inc ..... C 574 855-2197
　South Bend *(G-15290)*

Tri-Pac Inc ..... C 574 855-2197
　South Bend *(G-15291)*

Universal Precision Instrs Inc ..... G 574 264-3997
　Elkhart *(G-3763)*

Vance Products Incorporated ..... C 812 829-4891
　Spencer *(G-15364)*

Vasmo Inc ..... F 317 549-3722
　Indianapolis *(G-9702)*

Verista Inc ..... A 317 849-0330
　Fishers *(G-4628)*

Vertical Power Co ..... G 574 276-8094
　Osceola *(G-13406)*

Viant ..... F 317 788-7225
　Indianapolis *(G-9716)*

Viant Medical LLC ..... E 317 454-8824
　Indianapolis *(G-9717)*

▲ Vision Training Products Inc ..... F 574 259-2070
　Mishawaka *(G-12023)*

White Surgical Inc ..... G 260 755-5800
　Fort Wayne *(G-5566)*

Yager & Associates LLC ..... G 260 413-9571
　Fort Wayne *(G-5579)*

Yosira LLC ..... G 260 241-1203
　Fort Wayne *(G-5581)*

3842 Surgical appliances and supplies

1st Choice Safety LLC ..... G 260 797-5338
　Fort Wayne *(G-4711)*

3M Company ..... B 317 692-6666
　Indianapolis *(G-7388)*

3oe Scientific LLC ..... F 317 869-7602
　Carmel *(G-1545)*

Access One By Msg Inc ..... G 260 485-7007
　Fort Wayne *(G-4718)*

▲ Accra-Pac Inc ..... D 574 295-0000
　Elkhart *(G-3151)*

Accra-Pac Inc ..... D 574 295-0000
　Elkhart *(G-3150)*

Accurate Hearing Aid Svcs LLC ..... G 219 464-1937
　Valparaiso *(G-15891)*

Active Ankle Systems Inc ..... F 812 258-0663
　Jeffersonville *(G-9925)*

Advanced Lf Spport Innvtons LL ..... G 574 538-1688
　Goshen *(G-6090)*

Advanced Orthopro Inc ..... G 812 478-3656
　Terre Haute *(G-15531)*

Advanced Orthopro Inc ..... E 317 924-4444
　Indianapolis *(G-7439)*

Advanced Wund Limb Care Ctr In ..... G 812 232-0957
　Terre Haute *(G-15532)*

▲ Aearo Technologies LLC ..... A 612 284-1232
　Indianapolis *(G-7446)*

Airgas Usa LLC ..... G 317 248-8072
　Indianapolis *(G-7464)*

American Eagle Health LLC ..... G 812 921-9224
　Floyds Knobs *(G-4668)*

American Limb & Orthopedic Co ..... G 574 522-3643
　Elkhart *(G-3173)*

American Veteran Group LLC ..... G 317 600-4749
　Westfield *(G-16664)*

Audio Diagnostics Inc ..... G 765 477-7016
　Lafayette *(G-10529)*

Automated Weapon Security Inc ..... G 860 559-7176
　Indianapolis *(G-7574)*

▲ Battle Creek Equipment Co ..... E 260 495-3472
　Fremont *(G-5810)*

Belltone Hearing Care Center ..... G 317 462-9999
　Greenfield *(G-6470)*

Biomet ..... F 574 551-8959
　Warsaw *(G-16321)*

Biomet Inc ..... F 574 371-3760
　Warsaw *(G-16322)*

◆ Biomet Inc ..... A 574 267-6639
　Warsaw *(G-16323)*

Biomet Biologics LLC ..... E 574 267-2038
　Warsaw *(G-16324)*

Biomet Europe Ltd ..... E 574 267-2038
　Warsaw *(G-16325)*

Biomet Leasing Inc ..... E 574 267-6639
　Warsaw *(G-16326)*

Biomet Orthopedics LLC ..... E 574 267-6639
　Warsaw *(G-16327)*

Biomet Sports Medicine LLC ..... D 574 267-6639
　Warsaw *(G-16328)*

Biomet Trauma LLC ..... F 574 267-6639
　Warsaw *(G-16329)*

Biomet US Reconstruction LLC ..... F 800 348-9500
　Warsaw *(G-16330)*

Bionic Prosthetics and Ortho ..... G 219 791-9200
　Elkhart *(G-3225)*

Bionic Prosthetics and Ortho ..... G 765 838-8222
　Lafayette *(G-10538)*

Bionic Prosthetics and Ortho ..... G 219 221-6119
　Michigan City *(G-11582)*

Bionic Prosthetics and Ortho ..... G 219 791-9200
　Valparaiso *(G-15914)*

Bionic Prsthtics Orthtics Grou ..... G 219 940-3104
　Merrillville *(G-11489)*

Bionic Prsthtics Orthtics Grou ..... G 219 791-9200
　Merrillville *(G-11488)*

Biopoly LLC ..... F 260 999-6135
　Fort Wayne *(G-4802)*

Bleys Prosthetics & Orthotics ..... G 812 704-3894
　Seymour *(G-14634)*

Borrv Concepts LLC ..... G 317 405-9121
　Indianapolis *(G-7661)*

Braun Corporation ..... D 574 946-7413
　Winamac *(G-16856)*

Brayden Shedron ..... G 765 480-7675
　Walton *(G-16281)*

Brewer Machine & Mfg Inc ..... E 317 398-3505
　Shelbyville *(G-14741)*

◆ Bryton Corporation ..... F 317 334-8700
　Indianapolis *(G-7694)*

Calumet Orthpd Prosthetics Co ..... G 219 942-2148
　Hobart *(G-7177)*

Center For Orthtic Prsthtic Ex ..... G 219 365-0248
　Highland *(G-7128)*

Central Brace & Limb Co Inc ..... G 765 457-4868
　Kokomo *(G-10243)*

Central Brace & Limb Co Inc ..... G 812 232-2145
　Terre Haute *(G-15558)*

Central Brace & Limb Co Inc ..... F 317 925-4296
　Indianapolis *(G-7769)*

▲ Circle City Medical Inc ..... G 317 228-1144
　Carmel *(G-1587)*

Cook Medical Holdings LLC ..... G 812 339-2235
　Bloomington *(G-842)*

Cook Medical LLC ..... A 812 339-2235
　Bloomington *(G-844)*

Cook Medical LLC ..... A 812 323-4500
　Bloomington *(G-846)*

▼ Cook Medical LLC ..... B 812 339-2235
　Bloomington *(G-845)*

Cortex Safety Technologies LLC ..... G 317 414-5607
　Carmel *(G-1598)*

Coventure I LLC ..... G 800 570-0072
　Mishawaka *(G-11867)*

Crossroads Orthotics & Cnsltn ..... G 765 359-0041
　Crawfordsville *(G-2559)*

Current Technologies Inc ..... F 765 364-0490
　Crawfordsville *(G-2561)*

Custom Outfitted Protection ..... G 317 373-2092
　Indianapolis *(G-7932)*

D J Investments Inc ..... G 765 348-3558
　Hartford City *(G-7064)*

D J Investments Inc ..... G 260 726-7346
　Portland *(G-13936)*

D J Investments Inc ..... G 765 348-4381
　Hartford City *(G-7063)*

Del Palma Orthopedics Llc ..... G 260 625-3169
　Columbia City *(G-2137)*

Depuy Inc ..... G 574 372-7010
　Winona Lake *(G-16910)*

Depuy Orthopaedics Inc ..... E 574 267-8143
　Warsaw *(G-16347)*

Depuy Products Inc ..... C 574 267-8143
　Warsaw *(G-16348)*

Depuy Synthes Sales Inc ..... G 574 267-8143
　Warsaw *(G-16351)*

Dienen Inc ..... C 574 233-3352
　South Bend *(G-14999)*

▲ Ehob LLC ..... C 317 972-4600
　Indianapolis *(G-8062)*

Equippe Advanced Mobility ..... G 317 807-6789
　Greenwood *(G-6703)*

Employee Codes: A=Over 500 employees, B=251-500
C=101-250, D=51-100, E=20-50, F=10-19, G=1-9

38 MEASURING, PHOTOGRAPHIC, MEDICAL, & OPTICAL GOODS, & CLOCKS — SIC SECTION

Fort Wayne Metals RES Pdts LLC............ G 260 747-4154
   Fort Wayne *(G-4997)*

Golden-Helvey Holdings Inc................... D 574 266-4500
   Elkhart *(G-3384)*

Great Lake Sales & Marketing.................. G 219 325-0637
   La Porte *(G-10411)*

Hanger Prsthetcs & Ortho Inc.................. F 219 844-2021
   Hammond *(G-6944)*

Hanger Prsthtics Orthotics Inc................. G 765 966-5069
   Richmond *(G-14131)*

◆ Hill-Rom Inc.. A 812 934-7777
   Batesville *(G-589)*

Howmedica Osteonics Corp..................... G 317 587-2008
   Carmel *(G-1661)*

Infinity Products Inc................................. G 317 272-3435
   Plainfield *(G-13690)*

Integrity Hearing....................................... G 317 882-9151
   Noblesville *(G-13107)*

Invacare Corporation............................... F 317 838-5500
   Plainfield *(G-13694)*

Johnsons Orthtics Prsthtics LL................ G 812 372-2800
   Columbus *(G-2331)*

▲ Kaldewei Usa Inc................................. G 866 822-2527
   Fishers *(G-4552)*

Kenney Orthopedics Carmel LLC............ G 317 993-3664
   Carmel *(G-1680)*

Kenney Orthopedics Seymour LLC......... G 812 271-1627
   Seymour *(G-14660)*

Kenney Orthpdics Blmington LLC........... G 812 727-3651
   Bloomington *(G-900)*

Kenney Orthpdics Indnpolis LLC............ G 859 241-1015
   Indianapolis *(G-8672)*

Kenney Orthpdics Indnpolis LLC............ G 317 300-0814
   Greenwood *(G-6722)*

Kenney Orthpedics Columbus LLC......... F 812 214-4623
   Columbus *(G-2334)*

Leahy Adology Hearing Aids LLC............ G 765 601-4003
   Frankfort *(G-5679)*

Lvb Acquisition Holding LLC................... A 574 267-6639
   Warsaw *(G-16389)*

Magnolia... G 317 831-3220
   Jasper *(G-9886)*

Maitland Engineering Inc........................ E 574 287-0155
   South Bend *(G-15137)*

◆ Masco Bath Corporation...................... A 317 254-5959
   Indianapolis *(G-8846)*

McMillin Hearing Aid Inc......................... G 812 847-2470
   Linton *(G-11039)*

Medical Device Bus Svcs Inc.................. G 317 596-3320
   Indianapolis *(G-8871)*

▲ Medical Device Bus Svcs Inc.............. A 574 267-8143
   Warsaw *(G-16395)*

Mobile Limb & Brace Inc........................ G 765 463-4100
   West Lafayette *(G-16610)*

Ms Wheelchair Indiana Inc..................... G 317 408-0947
   Indianapolis *(G-8969)*

Mtek Armor Group LLC........................... G 765 341-0933
   Martinsville *(G-11416)*

National Dentex LLC............................... C 317 849-5143
   Indianapolis *(G-8987)*

Nemcomed Fw LLC................................. E 260 480-5226
   Fort Wayne *(G-5264)*

Nemcomed Instrs & Implants................. F 800 255-4576
   Fort Wayne *(G-5265)*

Northern Brace Company Inc................. G 574 233-4221
   South Bend *(G-15171)*

Northern Prosthetics Inc......................... G 574 233-2459
   South Bend *(G-15174)*

Oak Brook Foot Ankle Spclsts P............. G 219 214-2047
   Michigan City *(G-11647)*

Oasis Lifestyle LLC.................................. F 574 948-0004
   Plymouth *(G-13799)*

Operation 1 Veteran Inc.......................... G 574 536-5536
   Goshen *(G-6231)*

Orthopediatrics Corp............................... G 574 268-6379
   Warsaw *(G-16404)*

Orthopediatrics US Dist.......................... E 574 268-6379
   Warsaw *(G-16405)*

Orthotic & Prosthetic Lab....................... F 812 479-6298
   Evansville *(G-4229)*

Orthotic Prosthetic Specialist................. G 219 836-8668
   Munster *(G-12555)*

OSI Specialties Inc.................................. F 317 293-4858
   Indianapolis *(G-9074)*

Paragon Medical Inc................................ C 317 570-5830
   Indianapolis *(G-9092)*

Peyton Technical Services LLC.............. F 812 738-2016
   Corydon *(G-2510)*

◆ Point Medical Corporation.................. A 219 663-1775
   Crown Point *(G-2732)*

Precision Piece Parts Inc........................ D 574 255-3185
   Mishawaka *(G-11978)*

Prevail Prsthtics Orthtics Inc.................. G 765 668-0890
   Fort Wayne *(G-5351)*

Rayco Steel Process Inc......................... F 574 267-7676
   Warsaw *(G-16415)*

Recovery Force LLC................................ G 866 604-6458
   Fishers *(G-4591)*

Rehablttion Inst Indnpolis Inc................. G 888 456-7440
   Terre Haute *(G-15678)*

Ring-Co Mobile LLC................................ G 317 641-7050
   Trafalgar *(G-15832)*

Rmi Holdings LLC.................................... F 317 214-7076
   Warsaw *(G-16419)*

Romaine Incorporated............................ F 574 294-7101
   Elkhart *(G-3651)*

Somer Inc... E 317 873-1111
   Zionsville *(G-17051)*

Standard Fusee Corporation................... D 765 472-4375
   Peru *(G-13602)*

Starkey Laboratories Inc......................... F 952 828-6934
   Plainfield *(G-13731)*

Steel Grip Inc... G 765 793-3652
   Covington *(G-2534)*

Steel Grip Inc... G 765 397-3344
   Kingman *(G-10174)*

Steris Corporation................................... D 440 354-2600
   Indianapolis *(G-9503)*

Stride Prosthetics LLC............................ G 317 520-2652
   Plainfield *(G-13732)*

Summit Pedorthics LLC........................... G 260 348-7268
   Fort Wayne *(G-5454)*

Surestep LLC... C 574 233-3352
   South Bend *(G-15274)*

▲ Symmetry Medical Inc........................ G 574 267-8700
   Warsaw *(G-16433)*

Tornier Inc.. G 574 268-0861
   Warsaw *(G-16439)*

Transcend Orthtics Prsthtics L............... G 574 233-3352
   Fort Wayne *(G-5499)*

Transcend Orthtics Prsthtics L............... G 317 300-9016
   Greenwood *(G-6776)*

Transcend Orthtics Prsthtics L............... G 317 334-1114
   Indianapolis *(G-9629)*

Transcend Orthtics Prsthtics L............... G 219 736-9960
   Merrillville *(G-11569)*

Transcend Orthtics Prsthtics L............... F 574 233-3352
   South Bend *(G-15287)*

Transmed Associates Inc........................ G 317 293-9993
   Avon *(G-555)*

Turnbow Prosthetics LLC........................ G 260 396-2234
   Columbia City *(G-2208)*

TW Enterprises LLC................................ G 513 520-8453
   Brookville *(G-1338)*

Ultra Athlete LLC..................................... G 317 520-9898
   Carmel *(G-1793)*

USA Medical Suppliers Ltd..................... G 608 782-1855
   Indianapolis *(G-9689)*

Vispalexo Inc... G 330 323-4138
   Indianapolis *(G-9723)*

Walker Family Enterprises LLC............... G 812 385-2945
   Princeton *(G-14020)*

Warsaw Orthopedic Inc........................... D 901 396-3133
   Warsaw *(G-16447)*

Wheelchair Help LLC............................... G 574 295-2220
   Elkhart *(G-3783)*

Wheelchair of Indiana............................. G 317 627-6560
   Indianapolis *(G-9757)*

Wiley Young & Associates...................... G 574 269-7006
   Warsaw *(G-16452)*

Wilsons Hearing Aid Center LLC............ G 765 747-4131
   Muncie *(G-12521)*

Wishbone Medical Inc............................. G 574 306-4006
   Warsaw *(G-16454)*

Zimmer Inc... G 574 267-2038
   Warsaw *(G-16458)*

Zimmer Inc... G 800 348-9500
   Warsaw *(G-16459)*

Zimmer Inc... G 574 267-6131
   Warsaw *(G-16460)*

Zimmer Inc... G 574 267-6131
   Warsaw *(G-16461)*

Zimmer Inc... G 574 527-7297
   Warsaw *(G-16462)*

Zimmer Inc... F 574 371-1557
   Warsaw *(G-16463)*

◆ Zimmer Inc... B 800 348-9500
   Warsaw *(G-16464)*

Zimmer Biomet... F 574 453-1326
   Fort Wayne *(G-5584)*

Zimmer Biomet Hibbard........................... F 574 267-0670
   Warsaw *(G-16465)*

Zimmer Biomet Hibbard LLC.................. G 800 352-2982
   Valparaiso *(G-16083)*

Zimmer Biomet Holdings Inc.................. G 317 872-8484
   Indianapolis *(G-9810)*

Zimmer Biomet Holdings Inc.................. A 574 267-6131
   Warsaw *(G-16466)*

Zimmer Bmet Connected Hlth LLC........ E 800 613-6131
   Warsaw *(G-16467)*

Zimmer Production Inc........................... G 574 267-6131
   Warsaw *(G-16468)*

Zimmer Production Inc........................... G 574 267-6131
   Warsaw *(G-16469)*

Zimmer Spine Inc..................................... E 800 655-2614
   Warsaw *(G-16470)*

Zimmer Us Inc.. C 574 267-6131
   Warsaw *(G-16471)*

Zollman Plastic Surgery PC..................... F 317 328-1100
   Indianapolis *(G-9813)*

3843 Dental equipment and supplies

Aero-Med LLC.. G 740 412-3855
   Indianapolis *(G-7449)*

Athena Champion Inc.............................. E 260 373-1917
   Fort Wayne *(G-4777)*

Dental Professional Laboratory.............. E 219 769-6225
   Merrillville *(G-11505)*

Fidelity Dental Handpiece Svc................ G 317 254-0277
   Indianapolis *(G-8185)*

G & H Wire Company Inc........................ D 317 346-6655
   Franklin *(G-5731)*

Growing Smiles Inc.................................. G 317 787-6404
   Indianapolis *(G-8335)*

Hayes Enterprises LLC............................ G 260 636-3262
   Albion *(G-28)*

SIC SECTION
39 MISCELLANEOUS MANUFACTURING INDUSTRIES

Kathy Zuccarelli.. G 219 865-4095
   Schererville *(G-14526)*

Knitting Mill Inc.. G 219 942-8031
   Hobart *(G-7198)*

▲ Kulzer LLC... B 574 299-5466
   South Bend *(G-15111)*

Lehi Prosthetics Dntl Lab Inc.......................... G 765 288-4613
   Muncie *(G-12439)*

LLC White Diamond... G 463 888-3585
   Indianapolis *(G-8772)*

Michael J Meyer D M D P C............................ G 812 275-7112
   Bedford *(G-658)*

National Dentex LLC....................................... C 317 849-5143
   Indianapolis *(G-8987)*

▲ Orthodontic Design & Prod Inc.................... E 317 346-6655
   Franklin *(G-5763)*

▲ Panoramic Rental Corp................................ E 800 654-2027
   Fort Wayne *(G-5294)*

Pearl Cstm Plastic Molding Inc....................... G 765 763-6961
   Gwynneville *(G-6831)*

Plaster Shak.. G 317 881-6518
   Greenwood *(G-6752)*

Protero Corporation.. E 219 393-5591
   Kingsford Heights *(G-10186)*

Rmo Inc... C 303 592-8200
   Franklin *(G-5774)*

Ronald L Miller.. G 765 662-3881
   Marion *(G-11336)*

Sellers Dental Lab... G 219 465-8719
   Valparaiso *(G-16044)*

Somer Inc.. E 317 873-1111
   Zionsville *(G-17051)*

TP Orthodontics Inc... B 219 785-2591
   La Porte *(G-10494)*

William Wsley Prof Oral Prstht....................... G 317 635-1000
   Indianapolis *(G-9766)*

3844 X-ray apparatus and tubes

American Eagle Health LLC............................ G 812 921-9224
   Floyds Knobs *(G-4668)*

CXR Company Inc... F 574 269-6020
   Warsaw *(G-16341)*

◆ Golden Engineering Inc............................... E 765 855-3493
   Centerville *(G-1849)*

Jason Holdings Inc.. C 414 277-9300
   Richmond *(G-14147)*

3845 Electromedical equipment

B & J Specialty Inc.. G 260 636-2067
   Kendallville *(G-10095)*

◆ Biomet Inc.. A 574 267-6639
   Warsaw *(G-16323)*

Biomet Europe Ltd.. E 574 267-2038
   Warsaw *(G-16325)*

Bionode LLC.. G 317 292-7686
   Indianapolis *(G-7628)*

Breath of Life Home Medic............................. F 317 896-3048
   Westfield *(G-16671)*

Cascade Metrix LLC.. G 317 572-7094
   Fishers *(G-4484)*

▲ Cliniwave Inc... G 812 923-9591
   Floyds Knobs *(G-4673)*

Cook Group Incorporated................................ F 812 339-2235
   Bloomington *(G-838)*

Covidien LP... C 317 837-8199
   Plainfield *(G-13674)*

▲ Esaote North America Inc........................... D 317 813-6000
   Fishers *(G-4517)*

Faztech LLC... G 812 327-0926
   Bloomington *(G-864)*

Laser Agent... G 317 570-0448
   Noblesville *(G-13127)*

Lvb Acquisition Holding LLC.......................... A 574 267-6639
   Warsaw *(G-16389)*

Medishield... G 502 939-9903
   New Albany *(G-12773)*

Mr-Link LLC... G 512 297-4582
   Lafayette *(G-10654)*

Nanosonics Inc.. E 844 876-7466
   Indianapolis *(G-8983)*

Orthoconcepts Inc... G 317 727-0100
   Indianapolis *(G-9072)*

Orthos Inc.. E 574 406-8145
   South Bend *(G-15181)*

Plastic Assembly Tech Inc.............................. G 317 841-1202
   Indianapolis *(G-9150)*

Purspec Technologies Inc.............................. G 765 532-2208
   West Lafayette *(G-16623)*

Radiation Physics Cnslting Inc...................... G 317 251-0193
   Indianapolis *(G-9262)*

Telamon Entp Ventures LLC.......................... F 317 818-6888
   Carmel *(G-1778)*

3851 Ophthalmic goods

▲ Aearo Technologies LLC.............................. A 612 284-1232
   Indianapolis *(G-7446)*

Armada Optical Services Inc......................... F 812 476-6623
   Evansville *(G-3899)*

City Optical Co Inc.. G 317 788-4243
   Indianapolis *(G-7814)*

City Optical Co Inc.. D 317 924-1300
   Indianapolis *(G-7813)*

Columbus Optical Service Inc........................ G 812 372-4117
   Columbus *(G-2245)*

Diversified Ophthalmics Inc........................... E 317 780-1677
   Indianapolis *(G-7985)*

Frecker Optical Inc.. F 260 747-9653
   Fort Wayne *(G-5009)*

Harmon Hrmon Uysugi Optmtrists................. F 812 723-4752
   Paoli *(G-13496)*

Hetzler Ocular Prosthetics Inc....................... G 317 598-6298
   Fishers *(G-4538)*

Jackson Vision Quest..................................... G 219 882-9397
   Gary *(G-5967)*

Kokomo Optical Company Inc........................ G 765 459-5137
   Kokomo *(G-10293)*

Luxottica of America Inc................................ G 317 293-9999
   Indianapolis *(G-8800)*

Luxottica of America Inc................................ G 219 736-0141
   Merrillville *(G-11535)*

Plainfield Eye Care... F 317 839-2368
   Plainfield *(G-13715)*

◆ Samco Group Inc... G 219 872-4413
   Michigan City *(G-11660)*

▲ Sammann Company Inc.............................. G 219 872-4413
   Michigan City *(G-11661)*

Shimp Optical Corp... G 317 636-4448
   Indianapolis *(G-9420)*

Singer Optical Company Inc.......................... F 812 423-1179
   Evansville *(G-4315)*

Spectacles of Carmel Inc............................... G 317 848-9081
   Carmel *(G-1770)*

Spectacles of Carmel Inc............................... G 317 475-9011
   Indianapolis *(G-9475)*

Tri State Optical Inc.. D 765 289-4475
   Muncie *(G-12508)*

Usv Optical Inc.. G 260 482-5033
   Fort Wayne *(G-5524)*

3861 Photographic equipment and supplies

Audio Flow LLC... G 219 230-6330
   Portage *(G-13846)*

BOM Corporation... E 765 361-0382
   Crawfordsville *(G-2549)*

Business Systems Mgt Corp.......................... G 219 938-0166
   Gary *(G-5908)*

◆ Da-Lite Screen Company LLC.................... B 574 267-8101
   Warsaw *(G-16342)*

◆ Draper Inc.. B 765 987-7999
   Spiceland *(G-15377)*

Gs Sales Inc.. G 317 595-6750
   Westfield *(G-16695)*

Heartland Film Inc.. G 317 464-9405
   Indianapolis *(G-8377)*

Image Inks Company...................................... G 317 432-5041
   Indianapolis *(G-8462)*

Insight Lpr LLC... F 855 862-5468
   Carmel *(G-1671)*

Ionpcs LLC... G 219 510-2073
   Portage *(G-13878)*

Jackson Technologies LLC............................. G 812 258-9939
   New Albany *(G-12751)*

Jeff Goshert.. G 260 672-3737
   Fort Wayne *(G-5133)*

Laser Systems.. G 219 465-1155
   Valparaiso *(G-15993)*

Lasertone Inc.. F 812 473-5945
   Evansville *(G-4162)*

Legrand AV Inc.. B 574 267-8101
   Warsaw *(G-16387)*

Mid-America Environmental LLC................... F 812 475-1644
   Evansville *(G-4204)*

Optiviz Media LLC... G 812 681-1711
   Vincennes *(G-16141)*

Smith Sound... G 765 464-2961
   West Lafayette *(G-16629)*

Success Holding Group Corp USA................. G 260 490-9990
   Ossian *(G-13435)*

Techryan Inc.. G 317 721-4835
   Plainfield *(G-13734)*

3873 Watches, clocks, watchcases, and parts

◆ Hansen Corporation..................................... B 812 385-3000
   Princeton *(G-13997)*

Smokers Iron Works.. G 574 674-6683
   Elkhart *(G-3687)*

Yoders Custom Service.................................. G 574 831-4717
   New Paris *(G-12975)*

39 MISCELLANEOUS MANUFACTURING INDUSTRIES

3911 Jewelry, precious metal

Aaland Gem Company Inc.............................. G 219 769-4492
   Merrillville *(G-11476)*

Alan W Long... G 812 265-6717
   Madison *(G-11198)*

Argentum Jewelry Inc..................................... G 812 336-3100
   Bloomington *(G-784)*

Ashleys Jewelry By Design Ltd..................... G 219 926-9039
   Chesterton *(G-1904)*

Beads To Feed LLC... G 816 299-8118
   Indianapolis *(G-7603)*

Brinker Mfg Jewelers Inc............................... F 812 476-0651
   Evansville *(G-3954)*

City of Berne... G 260 849-4038
   Berne *(G-706)*

Clarity Industry Co LLC.................................. G 678 389-5006
   Indianapolis *(G-7817)*

Collegiate Pride Inc.. G 260 726-7818
   Portland *(G-13932)*

Crystal Source.. G 812 988-7009
   Nashville *(G-12669)*

David Gonzales... G 765 284-6960
   Muncie *(G-12373)*

Employee Codes: A=Over 500 employees, B=251-500
C=101-250, D=51-100, E=20-50, F=10-19, G=1-9

39 MISCELLANEOUS MANUFACTURING INDUSTRIES

Delaurence Company .... G 219 878-8712
 Michigan City *(G-11599)*

Design Msa Inc .... G 317 817-9000
 Carmel *(G-1606)*

Downey Creations LLC .... F 317 248-9888
 Indianapolis *(G-8003)*

Ed Stump Assembly Inc .... G 574 291-0058
 South Bend *(G-15011)*

Edward E Petri Company .... G 317 636-5007
 Indianapolis *(G-8057)*

G Thrapp Jewelers Inc .... G 317 255-5555
 Indianapolis *(G-8254)*

Ginas Creative Jewelry Inc .... G 317 272-0032
 Avon *(G-521)*

Gold N Gems .... G 317 895-6002
 Indianapolis *(G-8296)*

Golden Lion Inc .... G 765 446-9557
 Lafayette *(G-10592)*

Goldstone Jewelry Inc .... G 765 742-1975
 West Lafayette *(G-16585)*

◆ Herff Jones LLC .... C 317 297-3741
 Indianapolis *(G-8383)*

Herff Jones Co Indiana - Inc .... E 317 297-3740
 Indianapolis *(G-8385)*

Intelliquote .... G 530 669-6840
 Roanoke *(G-14270)*

Interntnal Damnd Gold Exch Ltd .... G 317 872-6666
 Indianapolis *(G-8583)*

J C Sipe Inc .... G 317 848-0215
 Indianapolis *(G-8603)*

▲ Jack Forney .... G 812 334-1259
 Bloomington *(G-895)*

Janette Walker .... G 219 937-9160
 Hammond *(G-6961)*

Jewelers Boutique Inc .... G 317 788-7679
 Indianapolis *(G-8624)*

Kensington Watch Services .... G 219 306-5499
 Crown Point *(G-2708)*

Little Super Findings .... G 812 430-3353
 Evansville *(G-4173)*

Marie Lashaays LLC .... G 317 869-7939
 Indianapolis *(G-8833)*

Mark Edward Hails .... G 812 437-1030
 Evansville *(G-4189)*

O C Tanner Company .... G 317 575-8553
 Indianapolis *(G-9038)*

P&E Enterprises .... G 219 226-9524
 Crown Point *(G-2729)*

Peter Franklin Jewelers Inc .... G 260 749-4315
 New Haven *(G-12913)*

Ralph Privoznik Jewelry Art .... G 765 742-4904
 Lafayette *(G-10676)*

Rogers Enterprises Inc .... G 317 851-5500
 Greenwood *(G-6760)*

Ronaldo Designer Jewelry Inc .... F 812 972-7220
 New Albany *(G-12808)*

Stall & Kessler Inc .... G 765 742-1259
 Lafayette *(G-10698)*

Surplus Store and Exchange .... F 765 447-0200
 Lafayette *(G-10707)*

Terri Logan Studios .... G 765 966-7876
 Richmond *(G-14215)*

Tibbs Enterprises LLC .... G 574 360-9552
 Osceola *(G-13403)*

Verona LLC .... G 317 248-9888
 Indianapolis *(G-9708)*

Williams Jewelers Inc .... G 812 475-1705
 Evansville *(G-4287)*

3914 Silverware and plated ware

▲ A-1 Awards Inc .... F 317 546-9000
 Indianapolis *(G-7406)*

▲ Bruce Fox Inc .... C 812 945-3511
 New Albany *(G-12706)*

Simply Silver .... G 260 824-4667
 Bluffton *(G-1053)*

Sincerely Naiya LLC .... G 602 518-3870
 Hartford City *(G-7076)*

Stephen L Capper & Associates .... G 317 546-9000
 Indianapolis *(G-9502)*

3915 Jewelers' materials and lapidary work

Aaland Gem Company Inc .... G 219 769-4492
 Merrillville *(G-11476)*

GNB Studio Inc .... G 317 356-4834
 Indianapolis *(G-8295)*

Hendrix Co .... G 812 366-4333
 Georgetown *(G-6062)*

RC Enterprises .... G 812 279-2755
 Bedford *(G-664)*

▲ Woodburn Diamond Die Inc .... E 260 632-4217
 Woodburn *(G-16957)*

3931 Musical instruments

Ataraxis Music LLC .... G 626 945-6441
 Fishers *(G-4466)*

CJS Muzic Company-The Spot LLC .... G 219 487-9873
 Hammond *(G-6901)*

Conn-Selmer Inc .... D 574 522-1675
 Elkhart *(G-3261)*

Conn-Selmer Inc .... E 574 295-6730
 Elkhart *(G-3263)*

Conn-Selmer Inc .... D 574 295-0079
 Elkhart *(G-3264)*

◆ Conn-Selmer Inc .... D 574 522-1675
 Elkhart *(G-3262)*

Eddie S Guitars .... G 219 689-7007
 Dyer *(G-2973)*

▲ Fox Products Corporation .... C 260 723-4888
 South Whitley *(G-15318)*

▲ Gemeinhardt Musical Instr LLC .... E 574 295-5280
 Elkhart *(G-3370)*

Goulding & Wood Inc .... F 317 637-5222
 Indianapolis *(G-8309)*

Grem USA Corporation .... G 260 456-2354
 Fort Wayne *(G-5041)*

▲ Humes & Berg Mfg Co Inc .... G 219 391-5880
 East Chicago *(G-3018)*

▲ J J Babbitt Co .... G 574 315-1639
 Elkhart *(G-3431)*

Kimmel Music .... G 260 302-3082
 Kendallville *(G-10128)*

Lucas Custom Instruments LLC .... G 812 342-3093
 Columbus *(G-2347)*

Main Music .... G 812 295-2020
 Loogootee *(G-11145)*

Melvin McCullough .... G 765 577-0083
 Jamestown *(G-9819)*

Michael Duff .... G 812 336-8994
 Bloomington *(G-918)*

Patrick J Fscher Pipe Organ Sv .... G 978 314-7312
 Bloomington *(G-942)*

Plum Grove Strings LLC .... G 219 696-5401
 Lowell *(G-11175)*

▲ Rees Harps Inc .... F 812 438-3032
 Rising Sun *(G-14245)*

Sorley Horns LLC .... G 317 258-2718
 Bargersville *(G-574)*

Steinway Piano Company Inc .... D 574 522-1675
 Elkhart *(G-3700)*

Stone Custom Drum LLC .... G 260 403-7519
 Fort Wayne *(G-5445)*

Stradella String Instrs Inc .... G 219 464-3390
 Valparaiso *(G-16059)*

Sweetwater Sound LLC .... G 260 432-8176
 Fort Wayne *(G-5463)*

T Shorter Manufacturing Inc .... G 574 264-4131
 Elkhart *(G-3713)*

Uniflex Relay Systems LLC .... G 765 232-4675
 Union City *(G-15861)*

▲ Walter Piano Company Inc .... F 574 266-0615
 Elkhart *(G-3779)*

3942 Dolls and stuffed toys

Little Brown Bears .... G 219 663-9037
 Crown Point *(G-2720)*

My Sisters Doll Clothes .... G 765 459-7977
 Kokomo *(G-10315)*

Red Wagon .... G 260 768-3090
 Shipshewana *(G-14881)*

3944 Games, toys, and children's vehicles

Ahepa 157 .... G 219 864-3255
 Griffith *(G-6788)*

B & B Specialties Inc .... G 574 277-0499
 Granger *(G-6333)*

Boss Battle Games .... G 317 875-1446
 Indianapolis *(G-7662)*

▲ Chessex Manufacturing Co LLC .... F 260 471-9511
 Fort Wayne *(G-4845)*

Christopher Engle .... G 812 876-3540
 Ellettsville *(G-3803)*

Classichydros .... G 317 352-1315
 Indianapolis *(G-7820)*

Claywood Creation .... G 260 244-7719
 Columbia City *(G-2133)*

Cloak Gaming LLC .... G 502 563-8790
 Corydon *(G-2492)*

▲ Continuum Games Incorporated .... G 877 405-2662
 Indianapolis *(G-7860)*

Country Cabin LLC .... G 812 232-4635
 Terre Haute *(G-15569)*

Country Woodcrafts Inc .... G 260 244-7578
 Columbia City *(G-2135)*

Dorel Juvenile Group Inc .... C 812 372-0141
 Columbus *(G-2287)*

Dorel Juvenile Group Inc .... F 812 314-6629
 Columbus *(G-2288)*

◆ Dorel Juvenile Group Inc .... C 800 457-5276
 Columbus *(G-2289)*

◆ Dorel USA Inc .... D 812 372-0141
 Columbus *(G-2290)*

Eldon France .... G 765 793-2743
 Covington *(G-2529)*

EVS Ltd .... F 574 233-5707
 South Bend *(G-15019)*

Family Leisurecom Inc .... F 317 823-4448
 Indianapolis *(G-8164)*

Fex LLC .... G 317 308-8820
 Indianapolis *(G-8182)*

Flambeau Inc .... G 812 372-4899
 Columbus *(G-2310)*

◆ Fundex Games Ltd .... E 317 248-1080
 Indianapolis *(G-8241)*

Gener8 LLC .... G 317 253-8737
 Indianapolis *(G-8269)*

▲ Greenlight LLC .... F 317 287-0600
 Indianapolis *(G-8320)*

▲ Haan Crafts LLC .... F 765 583-4496
 Otterbein *(G-13451)*

▲ Honey and ME .... G 317 668-3924
 Franklin *(G-5741)*

Indy Products Company .... G 317 831-1114
 Mooresville *(G-12214)*

Jigsaw Creations LLC .... G 260 691-2196
 Columbia City *(G-2160)*

39 MISCELLANEOUS MANUFACTURING INDUSTRIES

K&D Crafts .... G 812 667-2575
   Dillsboro *(G-2948)*

Kan Jam LLC .... G 317 804-9129
   Westfield *(G-16703)*

KBK Magik LLC .... G 219 512-4040
   Indianapolis *(G-8663)*

Kite & Key LLC .... G 317 654-7703
   Indianapolis *(G-8689)*

Libra Elite LLC .... G 706 831-5753
   Indianapolis *(G-8745)*

Lightuptoyscom LLC .... E 812 246-1916
   Sellersburg *(G-14604)*

Lil Red Studios LLC .... G 317 443-4932
   Indianapolis *(G-8753)*

▼ Litko Aerosystems Inc .... G 219 462-9295
   Valparaiso *(G-15998)*

Ludo Fact USA LLC .... E 765 588-9137
   Lafayette *(G-10640)*

Mary Kite LLC .... G 765 749-1133
   Muncie *(G-12447)*

Mejjm Inc .... G 317 893-6929
   Indianapolis *(G-8873)*

Melissa Townsend .... G 317 797-7992
   Indianapolis *(G-8875)*

Merritt Manufacturing Inc .... G 317 409-0148
   Indianapolis *(G-8878)*

Myers Industries Inc .... F 866 429-5200
   South Bend *(G-15157)*

Nanna S Embroidery .... G 765 724-3667
   Alexandria *(G-56)*

No Limits Just Pssbilities LLC .... G 930 465-1218
   Princeton *(G-14008)*

Old Foundry Toy Works .... G 765 742-1020
   Lebanon *(G-10927)*

Ontime Toys Inc .... G 317 598-9333
   Indianapolis *(G-9058)*

◆ Peg Perego USA Inc .... D 800 671-1701
   Fort Wayne *(G-5300)*

▲ Peter Stone Company .... G 260 768-9150
   Shipshewana *(G-14879)*

Purrfectplay LLC .... G 219 926-7604
   Chesterton *(G-1955)*

Puzzles Padlocks Escape Rm LLC .... G 812 559-0767
   Jasper *(G-9904)*

Puzzles Plus LLC .... G 574 204-2054
   South Bend *(G-15209)*

Quirey Quality Engineering .... G 812 963-6097
   Evansville *(G-4268)*

RC Fun Parks LLC .... G 574 217-7715
   Granger *(G-6374)*

Red Wagon .... G 260 768-3090
   Shipshewana *(G-14881)*

Rix Products Inc .... G 812 426-1749
   Evansville *(G-4290)*

▲ Round 2 LLC .... E 574 243-3000
   South Bend *(G-15224)*

Shepherds Loft .... G 812 486-2304
   Montgomery *(G-12122)*

Sub Blanks Society LLC .... G 877 405-6406
   Fort Wayne *(G-5449)*

Suns Out Inc .... E 765 205-5645
   Marion *(G-11340)*

T & G Games Inc .... G 574 297-5455
   Monticello *(G-12171)*

Tedco Inc .... G 401 461-1118
   Indianapolis *(G-9571)*

◆ Tedco Inc .... F 765 489-4527
   Hagerstown *(G-6846)*

Tge Puzzle Pieces In Life .... G 219 345-2193
   Demotte *(G-2930)*

Tokumei LLC .... G 765 772-0073
   West Lafayette *(G-16638)*

3949 Sporting and athletic goods, nec

▲ A & JS Belts Inc .... G 219 628-0074
   Valparaiso *(G-15888)*

A Better U LLC .... G 260 704-3309
   Fort Wayne *(G-4715)*

Active Trading Intl Inc .... G 260 637-1990
   Fort Wayne *(G-4723)*

American Whitetail Inc .... F 812 937-7185
   Ferdinand *(G-4428)*

Axecalibur LLC .... G 812 822-1157
   Bloomington *(G-788)*

Bad Boys Bllard Prductions LLC .... G 702 738-4950
   Indianapolis *(G-7589)*

Battle Boards .... G 317 518-7245
   Indianapolis *(G-7597)*

▲ Battle Creek Equipment Co .... E 260 495-3472
   Fremont *(G-5810)*

Battlewear Components Inc .... G 574 262-4659
   Elkhart *(G-3217)*

Bear Komplex .... G 317 600-5833
   Crown Point *(G-2654)*

Bells of Steel Usa Inc .... G 317 981-5586
   Indianapolis *(G-7611)*

Big Shot Outfitters LLC .... G 317 736-4867
   Franklin *(G-5716)*

Bobcat Steel LLC .... G 317 699-6127
   Shelbyville *(G-14739)*

Boomerang Kidz Clothing .... G 574 992-2233
   Logansport *(G-11063)*

Boomerang Solutions .... G 812 822-2125
   Bloomington *(G-814)*

Braniff Game Birds .... G 574 784-3919
   Lakeville *(G-10788)*

Brickyard Crossing .... G 317 492-6573
   Indianapolis *(G-7679)*

Buddy Covers Inc .... G 317 846-5766
   Carmel *(G-1575)*

CCT Enterprises LLC .... E 260 925-1420
   Auburn *(G-375)*

Centurion Arms LLC .... F 619 994-5756
   Morgantown *(G-12254)*

Certor Sports LLC .... D 800 426-9784
   Plainfield *(G-13667)*

Cheercussion LLC .... F 317 762-4009
   Carmel *(G-1585)*

Chester Pool Systems Inc .... E 812 949-7333
   New Albany *(G-12712)*

Chip Ganassi Racing Teams Inc .... D 317 802-0000
   Indianapolis *(G-7798)*

CL Holding LLC .... G 317 736-4414
   Franklin *(G-5720)*

Cloud 9 Griptape LLC .... G 818 795-1082
   Dyer *(G-2970)*

Cloud Defensive LLC .... G 813 492-5683
   Chandler *(G-1859)*

Comfort Suites Baton Rouge .... G 317 247-5500
   Indianapolis *(G-7839)*

◆ Compositech Inc .... E 800 231-6755
   Indianapolis *(G-7846)*

Cover Care LLC .... D 513 297-4094
   Westfield *(G-16678)*

Crooked Stic Bows LLC .... G 812 677-2715
   Princeton *(G-13988)*

Cyc Lures .... G 574 702-1237
   Mulberry *(G-12329)*

Dauenhauer Glass Company Inc .... G 260 433-5876
   Fort Wayne *(G-4906)*

Dave Brown Customs LLC .... G 812 727-5560
   Palmyra *(G-13479)*

DCA Custom Arrows LLC .... G 317 627-0909
   Noblesville *(G-13068)*

Dead End Skateboards LLC .... G 970 699-6410
   Fort Wayne *(G-4908)*

Deer Track Archery Inc .... G 765 643-6847
   Anderson *(G-101)*

Delilah Club Covers LLC .... G 812 401-0012
   Evansville *(G-4010)*

Destro Machines LLC .... G 412 999-1619
   Carmel *(G-1607)*

▲ Diamond Billiard Products Inc ...... D 812 288-7665
   Jeffersonville *(G-9970)*

Dick Baumgartners Basket .... E 765 220-1767
   Richmond *(G-14114)*

▼ Divers Supply Company Inc .... D 317 923-4523
   Indianapolis *(G-7978)*

Dmp LLC .... G 812 699-0086
   Worthington *(G-16959)*

Drava Underwater LLC .... G 812 622-0432
   Owensville *(G-13466)*

Dropem Game Calls .... G 765 513-7667
   Kokomo *(G-10259)*

▲ Dunn-Rite Products Inc .... F 765 552-9433
   Elwood *(G-3820)*

Empire Lacrosse & Sports LLC .... G 317 497-8918
   Indianapolis *(G-7382)*

Escalade Incorporated .... D 812 467-1358
   Evansville *(G-4045)*

Escalade Inc .... G 260 569-7233
   Wabash *(G-16183)*

Fairway Custom Golf .... G 317 842-0017
   Fishers *(G-4521)*

Fanatics Lids College LLC .... E 888 814-4287
   Indianapolis *(G-8166)*

Feather Creek Calls .... G 812 229-1124
   Clinton *(G-2067)*

Federal Cartridge Company .... C 765 966-7745
   Richmond *(G-14121)*

Fencing Advisory Assoc Inc .... G 574 256-0111
   Mishawaka *(G-11896)*

Fields Outdoor Adventures LLP .... G 765 932-3964
   Rushville *(G-14400)*

Fisherman S Lurecraft Shop Inc .... F 260 829-1274
   Orland *(G-13365)*

Fishing Abilities Inc .... G 574 273-0842
   South Bend *(G-15035)*

Flambeau Inc .... G 812 372-4899
   Columbus *(G-2310)*

Fort Wayne Pools .... G 260 459-4100
   Fort Wayne *(G-5001)*

G L D Inc .... G 317 335-2760
   Mccordsville *(G-11450)*

G L D Inc .... G 317 924-7981
   Indianapolis *(G-8253)*

▲ Gameface Inc .... G 317 363-8855
   Zionsville *(G-17010)*

◆ Gared Holdings LLC .... C 317 774-9840
   Noblesville *(G-13082)*

Global Ozone Innovations LLC .... G 574 294-5797
   Elkhart *(G-3383)*

◆ Global USA Inc .... G 317 219-5647
   Westfield *(G-16692)*

Golf Plus Inc .... G 812 477-7529
   Evansville *(G-4092)*

Graphic Fx Inc .... E 812 234-0000
   Terre Haute *(G-15601)*

Grindhard Performance LLC .... G 317 334-5795
   Indianapolis *(G-8330)*

H 2 Golf LLC .... G 317 605-4720
   Carmel *(G-1646)*

Harpoon Lure Co DBA Forming T ...... G 812 371-3550
   North Vernon *(G-13275)*

Heck of A Lope .... G 260 570-3192
   Auburn *(G-395)*

Employee Codes: A=Over 500 employees, B=251-500
C=101-250, D=51-100, E=20-50, F=10-19, G=1-9

39 MISCELLANEOUS MANUFACTURING INDUSTRIES

Hercules Achievement Inc............................D 317 297-3740
  Indianapolis *(G-8382)*
Home Run LLC...G 219 531-1006
  Valparaiso *(G-15963)*
Hook & Arrow..G 260 739-6661
  Fort Wayne *(G-5073)*
Hooker Deer Drag Co LLC............................G 812 623-2706
  Sunman *(G-15439)*
Hoosier Bat Company....................................G 219 531-1006
  Valparaiso *(G-15964)*
House of Soccer Inc.....................................G 812 265-5196
  Madison *(G-11227)*
▼ Hudson Aquatic Systems LLC...................F 260 665-1635
  Angola *(G-262)*
I Run Amuck LLC...G 317 674-3339
  Indianapolis *(G-8446)*
▲ Impact Safety Inc......................................F 317 852-3067
  Indianapolis *(G-8469)*
Indiana Baton Twirling Assoc........................G 317 769-6826
  Lebanon *(G-10902)*
Indiana Sction of The Prof Glf......................F 317 738-9696
  Franklin *(G-5744)*
▲ Jay Orner Sons Billiard Co Inc.................G 317 243-0046
  Indianapolis *(G-8618)*
Kes LLC..G 812 728-8101
  Floyds Knobs *(G-4683)*
▲ Kidstuff Playsystems Inc.........................D 219 938-3331
  Gary *(G-5974)*
L&N Supply LLC...G 219 397-9500
  East Chicago *(G-3026)*
Lake House..G 574 265-6945
  Winona Lake *(G-16912)*
Learfield Sports...G 812 339-7201
  Bloomington *(G-908)*
Leisure Pool & Spa LLC................................G 812 537-0071
  Lawrenceburg *(G-10845)*
Life Less Ordinary LLC.................................G 317 727-4277
  Indianapolis *(G-8746)*
Lund Custom Calls LLC................................G 812 242-0566
  Clinton *(G-2071)*
Lure Ventures Inc..G 219 313-5425
  Mishawaka *(G-11934)*
Meredith Hughes..G 317 354-6073
  Plainfield *(G-13705)*
Mid America Powered Vehicles....................G 812 925-7745
  Chandler *(G-1864)*
▼ Midwest Gym Supply Inc........................F 812 265-4099
  Madison *(G-11242)*
◆ Mpiche LLC..F 317 636-3351
  Indianapolis *(G-8965)*
▼ Natare Corporation..................................E 317 290-8828
  Indianapolis *(G-8985)*
Nineplus Tables LLC.....................................G 317 471-7606
  Carmel *(G-1706)*
Nkg Sales..G 317 626-6555
  Indianapolis *(G-9013)*
▲ Official Sports Intl Inc............................F 574 269-1404
  Warsaw *(G-16403)*
Paraklese Technologies LLC........................F 502 357-0735
  Georgetown *(G-6073)*
Patel Ballistics Corporation..........................G 847 284-0086
  Noblesville *(G-13152)*
Pathfinder School LLC..................................G 317 791-8777
  Indianapolis *(G-9100)*
Peacock Bat Co...G 812 568-1006
  Elberfeld *(G-3117)*
PH Custom Lures LLC..................................G 765 541-0726
  Connersville *(G-2461)*
Pieniadze Inc...G 888 226-6241
  Zionsville *(G-17041)*
Pipe Dream Innovations LLC.......................G 503 910-8815
  Marion *(G-11328)*

Playfair Shuffleboard Company....................F 260 747-7288
  Fort Wayne *(G-5319)*
Popguns Inc..G 317 897-8660
  Indianapolis *(G-9163)*
Proline Bowstrings..G 513 259-3738
  Liberty *(G-10996)*
Proteq Custom Gear LLC.............................G 812 201-6002
  Brazil *(G-1164)*
Rbg Inc...G 812 866-3983
  Lexington *(G-10980)*
Reagent Chemical & RES Inc......................G 574 772-7424
  Knox *(G-10221)*
Recreation Insites LLC.................................G 317 578-0588
  Fishers *(G-4592)*
Robert J Matt..G 317 831-2400
  Mooresville *(G-12239)*
Rome Cy Area Youth Ctr Basbal..................G 260 854-4599
  Rome City *(G-14377)*
▲ Royal Spa Corporation............................D 317 781-0828
  Indianapolis *(G-9341)*
Running Company LLC.................................G 317 887-0606
  Greenwood *(G-6763)*
Ryan Piercy...G 317 796-2253
  Whiteland *(G-16794)*
S & W Swing Sets..G 260 414-6200
  New Haven *(G-12916)*
Sabre Holdings LLC.....................................F 317 222-6150
  Indianapolis *(G-9360)*
Sailor Group LLC..G 574 226-0362
  Elkhart *(G-3660)*
Sb Finishing..G 317 598-0965
  Indianapolis *(G-9382)*
Schutt Sports LLC..C 217 324-2712
  Plainfield *(G-13727)*
Schutt Sports Re LLC...................................G 217 324-3978
  Plainfield *(G-13728)*
Sea Quest Lures Inc.....................................G 219 762-4362
  Portage *(G-13911)*
Selektd Worx LLC...G 317 227-9337
  Indianapolis *(G-9401)*
Sevier Manufacturing....................................G 317 892-2784
  Brownsburg *(G-1402)*
Sharps Baton Mfg Corp...............................G 574 214-9389
  Elkhart *(G-3671)*
Shocktech USA Company.............................G 708 557-6952
  Cedar Lake *(G-1836)*
Shull Tactical Concepts Inc..........................G 260 316-9224
  Butler *(G-1478)*
Sinden Racing Service Inc...........................F 317 243-7171
  Indianapolis *(G-9443)*
Ski Inc...G 317 401-6222
  Pendleton *(G-13554)*
Sparkle Pools Inc..F 812 232-1292
  Terre Haute *(G-15707)*
Sports Plus Inc...D 260 482-8261
  Fort Wayne *(G-5431)*
Standard Fusee Corporation.........................D 765 472-4375
  Peru *(G-13602)*
Summt Outdoors...G 260 483-2519
  Fort Wayne *(G-5455)*
▲ Tarver Wolff LLC......................................G 765 265-7416
  Brookville *(G-1336)*
Thundrbird Traditional Archery....................G 812 699-1099
  Culver *(G-2782)*
Thursday Pools LLC.....................................G 317 973-0200
  Fortville *(G-5607)*
Timber Hawk Bows Inc................................G 812 837-9340
  Bloomington *(G-988)*
Tippmann Brothers LLC................................G 260 403-1911
  Fort Wayne *(G-5486)*
Titan Bats LLC..G 317 670-8380
  Carmel *(G-1787)*

Triunity LLC...G 317 703-1147
  Noblesville *(G-13185)*
Uebelhors Golf..G 317 881-4109
  Indianapolis *(G-9674)*
Unique Outdoor Products LLC.....................G 260 486-4955
  Fort Wayne *(G-5519)*
Unique Products...G 812 376-8887
  Columbus *(G-2409)*
Vanmeter and Son Lures LLC......................G 812 653-0497
  Marengo *(G-11266)*
Wedge Guys LLC..G 708 362-0731
  Cedar Lake *(G-1840)*
◆ Westfield Outdoor Inc............................C 317 334-0364
  Indianapolis *(G-9753)*
White River Outfitters LLC...........................G 812 787-0921
  Shoals *(G-14915)*
Wyatt Survival Supply LLC...........................G 765 318-2872
  Morgantown *(G-12266)*
Yourbodygetsit LLC.......................................G 317 908-7445
  Indianapolis *(G-9805)*
Zepps Predator Calls LLC............................G 574 971-8371
  Middlebury *(G-11763)*
Zepps Predator Calls LLC............................F 574 971-8371
  Middlebury *(G-11764)*

3951 Pens and mechanical pencils

▲ The Killion Corporation............................D 317 271-4536
  Indianapolis *(G-9589)*

3952 Lead pencils and art goods

Chep (usa) Inc..G 317 780-0700
  Indianapolis *(G-7795)*
Framery...G 812 537-4319
  Lawrenceburg *(G-10837)*
▲ Harcourt Industries Inc..........................E 765 629-2625
  Milroy *(G-11824)*
▲ The Killion Corporation..........................D 317 271-4536
  Indianapolis *(G-9589)*
V M Integrated..F 877 296-0621
  Indianapolis *(G-9696)*
▲ Wolfe Engineered Plastics LLC............G 812 623-8403
  Sunman *(G-15449)*
Yer Brands Inc..G 239 307-2925
  Rushville *(G-14417)*

3953 Marking devices

A & M Rubber Stamps Inc...........................G 219 836-0892
  Munster *(G-12525)*
Arben Corporation..E 812 477-7763
  Evansville *(G-3896)*
Clear Stamp Inc..G 219 324-3800
  La Porte *(G-10395)*
Heartfelt Creations Inc.................................E 574 773-3088
  Goshen *(G-6163)*
Indiana Stamp Co Inc..................................E 260 424-8973
  Fort Wayne *(G-5104)*
Koehler..G 219 462-4128
  Valparaiso *(G-15989)*
Notary Hayes LLC...G 219 292-4531
  Chesterton *(G-1950)*
Riverside Printing Co...................................G 812 275-1950
  Bedford *(G-669)*
▲ S & T Fulfillment LLC..............................E 812 466-4900
  Terre Haute *(G-15686)*
Sign A Rama...G 812 477-7763
  Evansville *(G-4310)*
Stamp Works..G 765 962-5201
  Richmond *(G-14208)*
Stampcrafter...G 574 892-5206
  Argos *(G-326)*
Toomuchfun Rubberstamps Inc..................G 260 557-4808
  Fort Wayne *(G-5495)*

39 MISCELLANEOUS MANUFACTURING INDUSTRIES

▲ Wagner Zip-Change Inc .... E 708 681-4100
Fort Wayne *(G-5540)*

3955 Carbon paper and inked ribbons

BOM Corporation .... E 765 361-0382
Crawfordsville *(G-2549)*

Gallagher Environmental Inc .... G 773 791-4670
Saint John *(G-14450)*

Lasertech Inc .... G 812 277-1321
Bedford *(G-656)*

3961 Costume jewelry

▲ Annie Oakley Enterprises Inc .... F 260 894-7100
Ligonier *(G-11004)*

Attitude of Gratitude Rocks .... G 317 331-0163
Fishers *(G-4467)*

Bivettes .... G 219 949-1742
Gary *(G-5900)*

Captured Beauty Etc LLC .... G 219 801-2572
Gary *(G-5911)*

Ch Manufacturing .... G 812 234-4600
Terre Haute *(G-15560)*

◆ Dicksons Inc .... C 812 522-1308
Seymour *(G-14647)*

Family Bracelets Direct .... G 513 312-5446
Lawrenceburg *(G-10835)*

Sisson & Son Mfg Jewelers .... G 574 967-4331
Flora *(G-4665)*

Swarovski North America Ltd .... G 317 841-0037
Indianapolis *(G-9537)*

Templeton Coal Company Inc .... G 812 232-7037
Terre Haute *(G-15725)*

Tribejewels LLC .... G 574 298-7162
South Bend *(G-15293)*

Unique Jewelry and More LLC .... G 317 244-3732
Indianapolis *(G-9677)*

3965 Fasteners, buttons, needles, and pins

Archimedes Inc .... F 260 347-3903
Kendallville *(G-10090)*

B & H Industries Corporation .... G 765 794-4428
Darlington *(G-2832)*

▲ Bollhoff Inc .... D 260 347-3903
Kendallville *(G-10097)*

Freudenberg-Nok General Partnr .... C 765 763-7246
Morristown *(G-12277)*

Frickers Inc .... G 765 965-6655
Richmond *(G-14123)*

General Fasteners Co .... G 574 343-2413
Elkhart *(G-3372)*

K&M Fasteners LLC .... G 260 525-8989
Berne *(G-717)*

▲ Rightway Fasteners Inc .... C 812 342-2700
Columbus *(G-2387)*

Scotts Fasteners & Supply LLC .... G 317 372-8743
Danville *(G-2827)*

Smart Machine Inc .... G 219 922-0706
Hammond *(G-7009)*

3991 Brooms and brushes

▲ American Way Marketing Llc .... F 574 295-6633
Elkhart *(G-3178)*

Brian Newton .... G 812 200-3149
Nashville *(G-12663)*

City of Fort Wayne .... E 260 427-1235
Fort Wayne *(G-4849)*

Jason Incorporated .... D 765 965-5333
Richmond *(G-14149)*

Midwest Finishing Systems Inc .... E 574 257-0099
Mishawaka *(G-11949)*

Reit-Price Mfg Co Incorporated .... G 765 964-3252
Union City *(G-15860)*

◆ Royal Brush Manufacturing Inc .... F 219 660-4170
Munster *(G-12562)*

3993 Signs and advertising specialties

1 Stop Signs .... G 765 748-2902
Muncie *(G-12331)*

1globalds LLC .... F 765 413-2211
Westfield *(G-16660)*

20 Minute Signs Plus Inc .... G 765 413-1046
Lafayette *(G-10512)*

8105 Georgia LLC .... G 219 757-3532
Merrillville *(G-11475)*

A Harris Verl Inc .... G 317 736-4680
Indianapolis *(G-7400)*

A One Signs & Graphics .... G 574 293-7104
Elkhart *(G-3140)*

A Plus Sign Area Ltg Spcalists .... G 765 966-4857
Richmond *(G-14080)*

A S P Parrott Signs .... G 812 325-9102
Bloomington *(G-768)*

A Sign Above .... G 317 392-2144
Laurel *(G-10823)*

A Sign Odyssey LLC .... G 219 962-1247
Lake Station *(G-10771)*

A Sign of Tymes .... G 317 251-0792
Indianapolis *(G-7402)*

A Sign-By-Design Inc .... F 317 876-7900
Lebanon *(G-10872)*

A To Z Sign Shop .... G 219 462-7489
Valparaiso *(G-15889)*

A Yard Art .... G 317 862-1486
Carmel *(G-1546)*

A-Plus Signs LLC .... G 765 966-4857
Richmond *(G-14081)*

AAA Black Signs LLC .... G 765 315-9569
Martinsville *(G-11376)*

Aardvark Vinyl Signs .... G 260 833-0800
Angola *(G-224)*

Aarvee Associates LLC .... G 312 222-5665
Indianapolis *(G-7411)*

Absograph Sign Co .... G 630 940-4093
Valparaiso *(G-15890)*

Ace Sign Company Inc .... G 812 232-4206
Terre Haute *(G-15530)*

Ace Sign Systems Inc .... G 765 288-1000
Muncie *(G-12335)*

ACS Graphics Inc .... G 260 495-7446
Fremont *(G-5806)*

ACS Sign Solution .... E 317 201-4838
Indianapolis *(G-7423)*

ACS Sign Solution .... G 317 925-2835
Indianapolis *(G-7424)*

Action Printing Sign Co .... G 219 362-9729
La Porte *(G-10375)*

Ad Vision Graphics Inc .... G 812 476-4932
Evansville *(G-3873)*

Adams Signs Inc .... G 219 972-0700
Highland *(G-7119)*

Adlink Promotions .... G 574 271-7003
Granger *(G-6330)*

ADM Custom Creations LLC .... G 765 499-0584
Hartford City *(G-7061)*

Advanced Digital Signs LLC .... G 260 704-0319
Fort Wayne *(G-4726)*

Advanced Sign & Graphics Inc .... F 765 284-8360
Muncie *(G-12336)*

Advanced Sign & Ltg Svc Inc .... G 812 430-2817
Evansville *(G-3875)*

Advantage Signs Inc .... G 219 853-1427
Hammond *(G-6868)*

Affordable Neon Services .... G 317 299-6061
Indianapolis *(G-7456)*

Affordable Sign & Neon Inc .... G 219 853-1855
Hammond *(G-6869)*

Affordable Signs Incorporated .... G 260 349-1710
Kendallville *(G-10087)*

Al Dishno Neon .... G 317 862-5374
Indianapolis *(G-7466)*

Alan Sutton Graphic Design .... G 219 567-2764
Francesville *(G-5636)*

All American Tent & Awning Inc .... E 812 232-4206
Terre Haute *(G-15537)*

Alveys Sign Co Inc .... E 812 867-2567
Evansville *(G-3883)*

American Sign Design .... G 574 287-4387
South Bend *(G-14944)*

American Spcialty Bus Intl LLC .... G 317 271-5000
Zionsville *(G-16992)*

AMS Embroidery & Signs LLC .... G 513 313-1613
Brookville *(G-1316)*

Apex Electric & Sign Inc .... G 317 326-1325
Greenfield *(G-6462)*

Apex Electric & Sign Inc .... G 317 326-1325
Morristown *(G-12271)*

Arben Corporation .... E 812 477-7763
Evansville *(G-3896)*

Arizona Sport Shirts Inc .... E 317 481-2160
Indianapolis *(G-7544)*

Art Works Sign Co Inc .... G 574 360-9290
Mishawaka *(G-11843)*

Asa Above Rest .... G 317 392-2144
Shelbyville *(G-14730)*

Asd Signs & Graphics LLC .... G 317 437-6921
Indianapolis *(G-7549)*

▲ Asempac Inc .... E 812 945-6303
New Albany *(G-12692)*

Athletic Edge Inc .... F 260 489-6613
Fort Wayne *(G-4778)*

Atrium Web Services LLC .... G 812 322-6904
Bloomington *(G-785)*

Auto & Sign Specialties Inc .... G 260 824-1987
Bluffton *(G-1027)*

Auto Art & Signs .... G 765 448-6800
Lafayette *(G-10530)*

Awards Unlimited Inc .... G 765 447-9413
Lafayette *(G-10532)*

Awning Partners Mfg Group LLC .... E 317 644-3793
Indianapolis *(G-7579)*

B & B Signs .... G 812 282-5366
Floyds Knobs *(G-4670)*

B & L Lighting and Sign Inc .... G 317 984-4206
Noblesville *(G-13037)*

▲ B2c2 LLC .... G 808 533-4128
Bloomington *(G-791)*

Baller Signs Inc .... G 260 824-1987
Bluffton *(G-1028)*

Banners Unlimited .... G 574 825-8070
Middlebury *(G-11701)*

Bassett Signs LLC .... G 812 946-0017
Jeffersonville *(G-9939)*

Baugh Enterprises Inc .... F 812 334-8189
Bloomington *(G-796)*

Baumbauer Signs .... G 260 368-7537
Geneva *(G-6048)*

Beacon Sign Company LLC .... G 317 272-2388
Avon *(G-507)*

Begley Sign Painting Inc .... G 317 835-2027
Fairland *(G-4397)*

Big Guy Signs LLC .... G 317 780-6000
Indianapolis *(G-7623)*

Bill Banner Signs .... G 765 209-2642
Falmouth *(G-4415)*

Billy R Phillips .... G 317 828-5058
Indianapolis *(G-7626)*

39 MISCELLANEOUS MANUFACTURING INDUSTRIES

Biltz Signs... G 574 594-2703
  Warsaw (G-16320)
Blumling Design & Graphics Inc............ G 765 477-7446
  Lafayette (G-10540)
Bml Graphics LLC................................. F 317 984-5500
  Tipton (G-15767)
Bo-Mar Industries Inc............................ E 317 899-1240
  Indianapolis (G-7651)
Bob Prescott.. G 219 736-7804
  Valparaiso (G-15918)
Boezeman Enterprises Inc.................... G 219 345-2732
  Demotte (G-2912)
Booth Signs Inc...................................... G 812 376-7446
  Columbus (G-2227)
Bottom Sign LLC.................................... G 812 949-7446
  New Albany (G-12704)
Boyd Sign Company............................... G 260 833-2257
  Angola (G-236)
Brett Tishner... G 765 675-2180
  Tipton (G-15769)
Brick Street Embroidery........................ G 574 453-3729
  Leesburg (G-10951)
Bright Signs and More............................ G 260 203-2444
  Fort Wayne (G-4817)
Broadway Auto Glass LLC..................... F 219 884-5277
  Merrillville (G-11493)
Broken Vessel Sign Co LLC.................... G 260 273-2780
  Decatur (G-2847)
Bully Graphics and Signs....................... G 574 870-0783
  Monticello (G-12140)
Business & Industrial Pdts Co.............. G 812 376-6149
  Columbus (G-2231)
Business Art & Designs Inc.................. G 317 782-9108
  Beech Grove (G-688)
Buttons Galore Inc................................ F 800 626-8168
  Brownsburg (G-1354)
Buy Bulk Displays................................... G 574 855-3522
  Mishawaka (G-11855)
Buy Bulk Displays LLC........................... G 574 222-4378
  Osceola (G-13384)
C & H Sign Inc Corporation.................. G 765 642-7777
  Anderson (G-86)
C4 Custom Creation LLC....................... G 574 551-3904
  Pierceton (G-13630)
Capital Custom Signs............................ G 765 689-7170
  Peru (G-13569)
Cardinal Manufacturing Co Inc............ F 317 283-4175
  Indianapolis (G-7741)
Cardinal Sign Service............................ G 812 499-0311
  Newburgh (G-12996)
Cardwell Signs LLC............................... 414 698-3992
  Sheridan (G-14819)
Castleton Village Center Inc................ G 317 577-1995
  Indianapolis (G-7758)
▲ Castleton Village Center Inc............. F 260 471-5959
  Fort Wayne (G-4837)
Chads Signs Installations Inc............... G 317 867-2737
  Noblesville (G-13056)
Christys Design & Sign Inc.................. G 317 882-5444
  Greenwood (G-6680)
Chuck Cable... G 765 981-2800
  La Fontaine (G-10367)
Classic Sign & Awning........................... G 260 665-6663
  Angola (G-241)
Clients Choice Ltd................................ G 812 853-2911
  Boonville (G-1085)
Clifford Signs Inc................................... F 765 453-0745
  Kokomo (G-10245)
Clover Signs Co..................................... F 812 442-7446
  Brazil (G-1139)
Coats Wright De Sign............................. G 317 569-5980
  Carmel (G-1591)

Cockerhams Signs & Graphics............... G 812 358-3737
  Brownsville (G-1419)
Columbus Signs..................................... G 812 376-7877
  Nashville (G-12668)
Commercial Signs Inc........................... G 260 745-2678
  Fort Wayne (G-4866)
Connectons Sign Lngage Intrprt............ G 812 449-7140
  Evansville (G-3980)
Courtney Signs...................................... F 317 653-5146
  Indianapolis (G-7890)
Creative Inc.. G 765 447-3500
  Lafayette (G-10561)
Creative Sign Resources LLC................. E 260 425-9618
  Fort Wayne (G-4885)
Creative Signs....................................... G 260 438-6352
  Fort Wayne (G-4886)
Crichlow Industries Inc......................... G 317 925-5178
  Indianapolis (G-7903)
Cumulus Intrmdate Holdings Inc............ G 765 452-5704
  Kokomo (G-10252)
Custom Creations MGT LLC.................... G 765 491-8434
  Fort Wayne (G-4897)
Custom Inspirational Signs................... G 315 715-1893
  Bicknell (G-733)
Custom Sign & Engineeri....................... E 812 401-1550
  Newburgh (G-12999)
Custom Signs Unlimited Co.................. G 260 483-4444
  Fort Wayne (G-4899)
Custombannerlab................................. G 317 956-3898
  Carmel (G-1603)
Cyclone Custom Prouducts LLC............. G 765 246-6523
  Greencastle (G-6401)
D D McKay and Associates..................... G 317 546-7446
  Indianapolis (G-7943)
D D Signs Inc... G 812 243-0084
  Terre Haute (G-15572)
Dailey Signs LLC.................................... G 317 436-7550
  Fishers (G-4500)
DBC Imaging.. G 317 757-5298
  Indianapolis (G-7956)
Debra Richard....................................... G 812 379-4927
  Columbus (G-2281)
Delaplane & Son Neon & Sign................ G 574 859-3431
  Camden (G-1519)
Designs 4 U Inc..................................... G 765 793-3026
  Covington (G-2528)
Dezigns By Cindy Ziese......................... G 219 819-8786
  Rensselaer (G-14051)
Digital Dynamics LLC........................... G 317 407-9658
  Martinsville (G-11388)
Directions Promotions.......................... G 812 746-2505
  Evansville (G-4013)
Diskey Architectural Signage................. F 260 424-0233
  Fort Wayne (G-4918)
DK Earlen Signs LLC............................. G 812 490-8423
  Newburgh (G-13000)
Doell Designs.. G 260 486-4504
  Fort Wayne (G-4921)
Don Anderson.. 574 278-7243
  Monticello (G-12145)
Doty Graphics.. G 765 763-7178
  Morristown (G-12275)
Dupre Capital LLC................................ F 812 291-1141
  Jeffersonville (G-9971)
Dxd Signs... G 219 588-4403
  Highland (G-7133)
Earl Park Sign Shop LLC........................ G 219 474-6419
  Earl Park (G-2985)
▲ Economy Signs Incorporated............. G 219 932-1233
  Hammond (G-6920)
Edinburgh Signs & Grapics.................... G 812 526-6626
  Edinburgh (G-3083)

Ehrgotts Signs & Stamps Inc................ G 317 353-2222
  Indianapolis (G-8063)
Elliott Smith Interiors LLC................... G 317 966-5101
  Zionsville (G-17005)
Embosstek... G 260 484-7700
  Fort Wayne (G-4948)
Enyart Signs... G 574 223-8254
  Rochester (G-14288)
Essential Archtctral Signs Inc.............. F 317 253-6000
  Indianapolis (G-8135)
Everywhere Signs LLC.......................... G 812 323-1471
  Bloomington (G-863)
Express Sign & Neon Llc....................... G 812 882-0104
  Vincennes (G-16123)
F & S Signage Solutions Inc.................. G 317 539-2086
  Danville (G-2811)
Fast Grafix... G 812 305-3464
  Newburgh (G-13001)
Fast Signs.. G 574 254-0545
  South Bend (G-15026)
Fastsigns.. G 260 373-0911
  Fort Wayne (G-4977)
Fastsigns.. G 317 280-3041
  Indianapolis (G-8169)
Fellers Inc... G 317 876-3008
  Indianapolis (G-8180)
Fine Guys Inc.. G 812 547-8630
  Tell City (G-15502)
First Place Trophies............................. G 812 385-3279
  Princeton (G-13994)
Flag & Banner Company Inc................. F 317 299-4880
  Indianapolis (G-8199)
Founders West Inc............................... G 812 936-7446
  Mccordsville (G-11449)
Frank Balensiefer................................. G 219 474-6419
  Earl Park (G-2986)
Freelance Lettering Inc....................... F 317 244-9272
  Indianapolis (G-8229)
Freeman Signs...................................... G 317 386-3453
  Danville (G-2813)
French Lick Auto Signs........................ G 812 936-7777
  French Lick (G-5845)
Future Signs Sales & Service................. G 765 749-5180
  Winchester (G-16887)
G C Solutions Inc.................................. G 317 334-1149
  Indianapolis (G-8252)
Gardner Graphics & Signs..................... G 765 630-8475
  Greencastle (G-6404)
Gast Sign Co.. G 219 759-4336
  Valparaiso (G-15954)
Geckos.. G 765 762-0822
  Attica (G-349)
Get Noticed Portable Signs................... G 765 649-6645
  Anderson (G-121)
Gindor Inc... G 574 642-4004
  Goshen (G-6149)
Glgraphix.. G 765 446-8600
  Lafayette (G-10590)
Golden Signworks Lighting................... G 317 358-4791
  Indianapolis (G-8299)
Good Signs... G 317 738-4663
  Franklin (G-5735)
Grace Fths Clbratory Signs LLC............ G 463 701-7673
  Indianapolis (G-8311)
▲ Grandview Aluminum Products......... F 812 649-2569
  Grandview (G-6328)
Granite Tee Signs LLC......................... G 317 670-4967
  Fort Branch (G-4703)
Graphex International.......................... G 219 696-4849
  Lowell (G-11161)
Graphic Shack Signs............................. G 765 721-4317
  Greencastle (G-6405)

39 MISCELLANEOUS MANUFACTURING INDUSTRIES

Graphic Visions .... G 812 331-7446
　Bloomington *(G-869)*
Graphically Speaking .... G 219 921-1572
　Chesterton *(G-1931)*
Graphics Emporium .... G 574 967-4627
　Bringhurst *(G-1236)*
Graphics Factory .... G 574 264-0542
　Elkhart *(G-3387)*
Graphics Systems Inc .... G 260 485-9667
　Fort Wayne *(G-5034)*
Graycraft Signs Plus Inc .... G 574 269-3780
　Warsaw *(G-16370)*
Graycraft Signs Plus Inc .... G 260 432-3760
　Fort Wayne *(G-5037)*
Grayson Graphics .... G 574 264-6466
　Elkhart *(G-3388)*
Green Sign Co Inc .... F 812 663-2550
　Greensburg *(G-6597)*
Greenfield Signs Inc .... G 317 469-3095
　Greenfield *(G-6507)*
Greenwood Light & Sign Service .... G 317 840-5729
　Boggstown *(G-1073)*
Guaranteed Lighting & Signs .... G 765 866-1229
　Crawfordsville *(G-2573)*
H L Signworks .... G 812 325-5750
　Ellettsville *(G-3808)*
◆ Hall Signs Inc .... D 812 332-9355
　Bloomington *(G-873)*
Hanks Sign Shop LLC .... G 812 367-2851
　Ferdinand *(G-4434)*
Hayes Design Company LLC .... E 574 236-5615
　South Bend *(G-15060)*
Helix Signworx LLC .... G 765 203-1381
　Anderson *(G-125)*
Hi-Rise Sign & Lighting LLC .... G 812 825-4448
　Bloomington *(G-877)*
Holloway Vinyl Signs Grap .... G 765 717-1581
　Yorktown *(G-16974)*
Hot Rod Car Care LLC .... G 317 660-2077
　Indianapolis *(G-8421)*
Hubbard Services Inc .... G 317 881-2828
　Greenwood *(G-6713)*
Huston Signs LLC .... E 317 804-9009
　Westfield *(G-16698)*
Hutchison Signs & Elec Co Inc .... E 317 894-8787
　Indianapolis *(G-8439)*
Hydrojet Signs .... G 765 584-2125
　Winchester *(G-16890)*
I F S Corp .... G 317 898-6118
　Indianapolis *(G-8445)*
▲ Icon International Inc .... D 260 482-8700
　Fort Wayne *(G-5091)*
Ideal Sign Corp .... G 219 406-2092
　Valparaiso *(G-15967)*
Illiana Signs .... G 708 862-9164
　Saint John *(G-14453)*
Image One LLC .... D 317 576-2700
　Mccordsville *(G-11451)*
Imagination Graphics .... G 812 352-8288
　North Vernon *(G-13279)*
Imperial Trophy & Awards Co .... G 260 432-8161
　Fort Wayne *(G-5096)*
In Tex Signs and Graphics .... G 812 385-2471
　Princeton *(G-14001)*
Indiana Dimensional Pdts LLC .... E 574 834-7681
　North Webster *(G-13306)*
Indiana Logo Sign Group .... G 800 950-1093
　Indianapolis *(G-8481)*
▲ Indiana Metal Craft Inc .... D 812 336-2362
　Bloomington *(G-890)*
Indiana Sign & Barricade Inc .... E 317 377-8000
　Indianapolis *(G-8492)*

Indiana Stamp Co Inc .... G 260 407-4165
　Fort Wayne *(G-5103)*
Indiana Stamp Co Inc .... E 260 424-8973
　Fort Wayne *(G-5104)*
Indiana Wrap Company LLC .... G 219 902-4997
　Merrillville *(G-11525)*
Indianapolis Signworks Inc .... E 317 872-8722
　Indianapolis *(G-8508)*
▲ Indy Imaging Inc .... E 317 917-7938
　Indianapolis *(G-8530)*
Indy Wide Format .... G 317 912-1385
　Indianapolis *(G-8538)*
Indys Pro Graphix Inc .... E 317 769-3205
　Zionsville *(G-17020)*
Indys Sign Source Inc .... G 317 372-2260
　Indianapolis *(G-8540)*
Ink Trax Promotional Solutions .... G 317 336-6921
　Mccordsville *(G-11452)*
Innovative Signs Llc .... G 317 747-4454
　Pendleton *(G-13537)*
Insign Inc .... G 317 251-0131
　Indianapolis *(G-8561)*
Integrity Sign Solutions Inc .... G 502 233-8755
　New Albany *(G-12749)*
Isf Inc .... E 317 251-1219
　Indianapolis *(G-8594)*
J R Sign Company and Services .... G 260 414-0510
　Fort Wayne *(G-5124)*
J W P Vinyl Designs .... G 812 873-8744
　Dupont *(G-2964)*
Jabra Signs & Graphics .... G 765 584-7100
　Winchester *(G-16892)*
Jacobs Advertising Inc .... G 260 854-2054
　Wolcottville *(G-16939)*
Jake Eddies Signs .... G 765 962-1892
　Richmond *(G-14146)*
James Wafford .... G 317 773-7200
　Noblesville *(G-13111)*
Jason Babbs .... G 812 595-9073
　Austin *(G-466)*
Jbl Signals and Lighting LLC .... G 574 855-2251
　South Bend *(G-15091)*
Jef Enterprises Inc .... F 812 425-0628
　Evansville *(G-4140)*
Johnny White .... G 260 441-0077
　Fort Wayne *(G-5138)*
Johnson Bros S Whitley Sign Co .... F 260 723-5161
　South Whitley *(G-15319)*
Johnson Engraving & Trophies .... G 260 982-7868
　North Manchester *(G-13236)*
Joyful Sign Company LLC .... G 317 529-1020
　Indianapolis *(G-8642)*
Joyfully Said Signs LLC .... G 574 596-9949
　Middlebury *(G-11729)*
Jrowe Signs .... G 260 668-7100
　Angola *(G-266)*
JW Signs Inc .... G 260 747-5168
　Fort Wayne *(G-5140)*
Karbach Holdings Corporation .... F 219 924-2454
　Hobart *(G-7196)*
Kay Company Inc .... E 765 659-3388
　Frankfort *(G-5677)*
Kellmark Corporation .... F 574 264-9695
　Elkhart *(G-3449)*
Kerham Inc .... E 260 483-5444
　Fort Wayne *(G-5146)*
King Signs .... G 317 882-0785
　Greenwood *(G-6723)*
Klem Signs & Restyling LLC .... G 812 357-2222
　Saint Meinrad *(G-14461)*
Klems Graphic Designs .... G 812 357-2222
　Saint Meinrad *(G-14462)*

Kokomo Thrift & Gift LLC .... G 765 553-5973
　Kokomo *(G-10295)*
Konrady Graphics Inc .... G 219 662-0436
　Crown Point *(G-2712)*
Lafayette Sign Guy LLC .... G 765 771-9900
　Lafayette *(G-10629)*
Lamar Advertising Company .... F 260 482-9566
　Fort Wayne *(G-5173)*
Landmark Signs Inc .... D 219 762-9577
　Chesterton *(G-1943)*
Legacy Sign Group LLC .... E 219 728-5102
　Westville *(G-16763)*
Legendary Designs Inc .... G 260 768-9170
　Shipshewana *(G-14864)*
Lesh Advertising Inc .... G 574 859-2141
　Camden *(G-1521)*
Lillich Sign Co Inc .... F 260 463-3930
　Lagrange *(G-10753)*
Linda Harmon De Sign Studi .... G 765 573-6138
　Marion *(G-11310)*
Link Electrical Service .... G 812 288-8184
　Jeffersonville *(G-10013)*
Literature Display Systems .... G 317 841-4398
　Indianapolis *(G-8770)*
Lloyd Werking Sign Painting .... G 765 354-2881
　Middletown *(G-11773)*
Lotus Designs LLC .... G 812 206-7281
　Charlestown *(G-1879)*
M F Y Designs Inc .... G 260 563-6662
　Wabash *(G-16196)*
▼ Margison Graphics LLC .... G 765 529-8250
　New Castle *(G-12873)*
Markle Music .... G 812 847-2103
　Linton *(G-11038)*
Marshall G Smith Sign Painting .... G 260 744-9492
　Fort Wayne *(G-5203)*
Marshall Signs .... G 260 350-1492
　Auburn *(G-404)*
Martin Signs & Crane Services .... G 317 908-9708
　Indianapolis *(G-8842)*
Masco Corporation of Indiana .... E 317 848-1812
　Indianapolis *(G-8847)*
McCaffery Sign Designs .... G 574 232-9991
　South Bend *(G-15142)*
McCord Signs LLC .... E 812 537-5516
　Lawrenceburg *(G-10846)*
Mg Electric and Sign LLC .... G 317 538-0455
　Greenfield *(G-6527)*
Michiana Signs and Lighting .... G 574 520-1254
　Mishawaka *(G-11946)*
Mid America Sign Corporation .... F 260 744-2200
　Fort Wayne *(G-5223)*
Midwest Graphix LLC .... G 812 649-2522
　Rockport *(G-14345)*
Midwest Sign Company Inc .... G 317 931-9535
　Seymour *(G-14668)*
Military Neon Signs .... G 574 258-9804
　Mishawaka *(G-11951)*
Miller Sign & Design .... G 765 457-6592
　Kokomo *(G-10308)*
Mindys Brownsburg Signs Inc .... G 317 939-0921
　Brownsburg *(G-1389)*
Mjs Businesses LLC .... G 317 845-1932
　Indianapolis *(G-8938)*
MO Signs LLC .... G 574 780-4075
　Plymouth *(G-13798)*
Monticello Signs & Scrn .... G 815 848-4111
　Monticello *(G-12158)*
Morgan Commercial Lettering .... G 260 482-6430
　Fort Wayne *(G-5243)*
Mount Graphics & Signs Inc .... G 765 483-1435
　Lebanon *(G-10920)*

Employee Codes: A=Over 500 employees, B=251-500
C=101-250, D=51-100, E=20-50, F=10-19, G=1-9

39 MISCELLANEOUS MANUFACTURING INDUSTRIES

Mullin Sign Studio .... G 219 926-8937
  Chesterton (G-1949)
Neon Accents .... G 812 537-0102
  Lawrenceburg (G-10847)
Neon Attractions Incorporated .... G 812 843-5881
  Tell City (G-15514)
▲ Neoti LLC .... F 260 494-1499
  Bluffton (G-1045)
New Hope Services Inc .... D 812 752-4892
  Scottsburg (G-14574)
New Hope Services Inc .... E 812 288-8248
  Jeffersonville (G-10022)
Next Day Signs .... G 574 259-7446
  Mishawaka (G-11965)
◆ Next Products LLC .... G 317 392-4701
  Shelbyville (G-14780)
Nitro Alley Graphix LLC .... G 317 286-3294
  Brownsburg (G-1390)
No Limit Outdoor Sign Co LLC .... G 765 457-1877
  Kokomo (G-10317)
No-Sail Splash Guard Co Inc .... G 765 522-2100
  Roachdale (G-14248)
North American Signs Inc .... D 574 234-5252
  South Bend (G-15170)
Northwest Indus Specialist Inc .... F 219 397-7446
  East Chicago (G-3033)
Nwi Signs .... G 219 796-0948
  Cedar Lake (G-1834)
▲ Olive Branch Etc Inc .... G 765 449-1884
  Lafayette (G-10660)
Ovation Communications Inc .... G 812 401-9100
  Evansville (G-4230)
Over Hill & Dale Sign Studio .... G 812 867-1664
  Evansville (G-4231)
P3 Graphix LLC .... G 812 641-1294
  Salem (G-14495)
Paint Town Graphics Inc .... E 260 422-9152
  Fort Wayne (G-5292)
Pathfinder Communications Corp .... G 574 266-5115
  South Bend (G-15187)
Pathfinder Communications Corp .... E 574 295-2500
  Elkhart (G-3587)
Paul E Shaw .... G 765 778-3383
  Pendleton (G-13550)
Peytons Barricade Sign Co LLC .... G 812 283-6461
  Jeffersonville (G-10035)
Phantom Neon LLC .... G 765 362-2221
  Crawfordsville (G-2604)
Phillips Signs & Graphics .... G 812 499-3607
  Evansville (G-4241)
Phoenix Sign Works Inc .... G 317 432-4027
  Indianapolis (G-9139)
Pink Signs LLC .... G 317 509-8805
  Mooresville (G-12235)
Pitcher Enterprises LLC .... G 574 242-1113
  Winamac (G-16870)
Pjw Inc .... G 574 295-1203
  Elkhart (G-3605)
Porter Signs .... G 812 222-0283
  Greensburg (G-6624)
Premier Sign Group Inc .... G 317 613-4411
  Indianapolis (G-9192)
Premier Signs LLC .... G 888 518-2498
  Uniondale (G-15870)
Premiere Signs Co Inc .... G 574 533-8585
  Goshen (G-6242)
Premiere Signs LLC .... G 260 543-2612
  Uniondale (G-15871)
◆ Prentice Products Inc .... E 260 747-3195
  Fort Wayne (G-5347)
Print Plus Express Inc .... G 812 466-6150
  Terre Haute (G-15671)

◆ Printing Inc Louisville KY .... F 800 237-5894
  Jeffersonville (G-10041)
Pro Signs & Graphics .... G 765 675-7446
  Tipton (G-15787)
Professional Permits .... G 574 257-2954
  Mishawaka (G-11981)
Progressive Design Apparel Inc .... E 317 293-5888
  Indianapolis (G-9225)
Pyramid Sign & Design Inc .... G 765 447-4174
  Lafayette (G-10674)
R W Moran Express Inc .... G 317 445-5861
  Indianapolis (G-9257)
R&S Sign Design .... G 765 520-5594
  New Castle (G-12881)
Ray Marketing LLC .... G 317 782-0940
  Beech Grove (G-701)
Recognition Plus .... G 812 232-2372
  Terre Haute (G-15676)
Red Hen Signs .... G 812 430-0956
  Evansville (G-4277)
▲ Reddington Design Inc .... G 574 272-0790
  South Bend (G-15217)
Reed Sign Service Inc .... G 765 459-4033
  Kokomo (G-10327)
Region Signs Inc .... F 219 473-1616
  Whiting (G-16838)
Reinforcements Design .... G 219 866-8626
  Rensselaer (G-14064)
Richard Butterfield .... G 765 754-3129
  Orestes (G-13361)
Richardson Entps Blmington LLC .... G 812 287-8179
  Bloomington (G-956)
Ricktom Promotions LLC .... G 812 430-0282
  Evansville (G-4289)
Riley Signs & Sheet Metal LLC .... G 317 359-7446
  Indianapolis (G-9307)
Rlr Associates Inc .... G 317 632-1300
  Indianapolis (G-9312)
Roesler Fine Art Services .... G 219 797-4955
  Union Mills (G-15867)
Roger Harper Signs .... G 812 945-1581
  New Albany (G-12807)
Ron Glasscock .... G 812 986-2342
  Poland (G-13837)
Ron Nawrocki .... G 260 437-5323
  Avilla (G-493)
Rookies Unlimited Inc .... G 765 536-2726
  Summitville (G-15431)
Ryan Osborne Inc .... G 317 535-4881
  Greenwood (G-6764)
Sabco Sign Co Inc .... G 317 882-3380
  Greenwood (G-6765)
Safety Vehicle Emblem Inc .... F 317 885-7565
  Indianapolis (G-9364)
Sampco Inc .... G 413 442-4043
  South Bend (G-15230)
Schaefer Sign Works .... G 317 292-9373
  Indianapolis (G-9387)
Scott Signs LLC .... G 574 533-7524
  Goshen (G-6252)
Seaton Springs Inc .... G 812 282-2440
  Clarksville (G-2035)
Selectric Signs .... G 812 378-6129
  Columbus (G-2389)
Sexton Advertising LLC .... G 812 522-4059
  Seymour (G-14688)
Shadow Signs .... G 317 481-9710
  Indianapolis (G-9412)
Shads Signs .... G 812 512-6066
  Linton (G-11046)
Shirts and Stuffs Happens .... G 812 217-8390
  Boonville (G-1097)

Sig Media LLC .... F 317 858-7624
  Indianapolis (G-9426)
Sign A Rama .... G 812 477-7763
  Evansville (G-4310)
Sign A Rama .... G 812 537-5516
  Lawrenceburg (G-10860)
Sign Arama .... G 812 657-7449
  Columbus (G-2392)
Sign Art LLC .... G 317 247-0333
  Indianapolis (G-9427)
Sign Art Quality Advertising .... G 219 763-6122
  Hobart (G-7207)
Sign Craft Industries Inc .... E 317 842-8664
  Indianapolis (G-9428)
Sign Creations .... G 574 204-2179
  Mishawaka (G-11993)
Sign Creations LLC .... G 574 855-1246
  South Bend (G-15243)
Sign Deals Delivered .... G 574 276-7404
  Bremen (G-1221)
Sign Deals Delivered Inc .... G 574 276-7404
  South Bend (G-15244)
Sign Exchange .... G 812 662-9469
  Greensburg (G-6631)
Sign Exchange .... G 812 621-2527
  Milan (G-11784)
Sign Factory .... G 574 255-7446
  Mishawaka (G-11994)
Sign For It LLC .... G 317 834-4636
  Mooresville (G-12242)
Sign Graphics Evansville Inc .... G 812 476-9151
  Evansville (G-4311)
Sign Group Inc .... G 317 228-8049
  Indianapolis (G-9429)
Sign Group Inc .... F 317 875-6969
  Indianapolis (G-9430)
Sign Guy .... G 812 345-2515
  Bloomington (G-970)
Sign Guys Inc .... G 317 875-7446
  Greenwood (G-6767)
Sign Gypsies Louisville LLC .... G 281 743-2137
  New Albany (G-12813)
Sign Here Ltd .... G 317 487-8001
  Indianapolis (G-9431)
Sign Lighting .... G 502 664-6655
  New Albany (G-12814)
Sign Masters .... G 765 525-7446
  Saint Paul (G-14469)
Sign Pro of Fort Wayne Inc .... G 260 497-8484
  Fort Wayne (G-5415)
Sign Pros .... G 765 289-2177
  Muncie (G-12492)
Sign Pros Inc .... G 765 642-1175
  Anderson (G-192)
Sign Pros of Marion .... G 765 677-1234
  Marion (G-11338)
Sign Services .... G 317 546-1111
  Indianapolis (G-9432)
Sign Solutions Inc .... F 317 881-1818
  Greenwood (G-6768)
Sign Solutions Inc .... F 317 535-5757
  Whiteland (G-16796)
Sign Source One Group Inc .... G 219 736-5865
  Hobart (G-7208)
Sign Stop LLC .... G 812 460-0119
  Terre Haute (G-15693)
Sign Store Inc .... G 812 537-0102
  Lawrenceburg (G-10861)
Sign Together .... G 812 219-2338
  Bloomington (G-971)
Sign Up 4 Fun .... G 317 800-3535
  Indianapolis (G-9433)

39 MISCELLANEOUS MANUFACTURING INDUSTRIES

Sign Write Signs LLC.................................. G 219 477-3840
Valparaiso *(G-16050)*

Sign-A-Rama... G 317 477-2400
Greenfield *(G-6551)*

Sign-Age Inc.. G 765 778-5254
Pendleton *(G-13553)*

Signart & Vinyl LLC................................. G 765 644-5290
Anderson *(G-193)*

Signature Signs....................................... G 765 717-9851
Parker City *(G-13506)*

Signcenter Inc... G 812 232-4994
Terre Haute *(G-15694)*

Signcrafters Inc....................................... G 317 579-4800
Indianapolis *(G-9434)*

Signcrafters Inc....................................... E 812 424-9011
Evansville *(G-4312)*

Signdoc Identity LLC............................... G 317 247-9670
Indianapolis *(G-9435)*

Signified Signs Inc.................................. G 219 712-7385
Crown Point *(G-2751)*

Signified Signs Inc.................................. G 219 712-7385
Portage *(G-13915)*

Signplex LLC... G 765 795-7446
Cloverdale *(G-2098)*

Signrite.. G 812 320-5245
Bloomington *(G-972)*

Signs & Designs By Lewis...................... G 574 223-9403
Rochester *(G-14325)*

Signs & Stripes By Carr.......................... G 317 432-9215
Jamestown *(G-9820)*

Signs By Design LLC.............................. G 812 853-7784
Newburgh *(G-13021)*

Signs By Don... G 219 374-6754
Cedar Lake *(G-1837)*

Signs By Sulane Inc................................ G 765 565-6773
Carthage *(G-1818)*

Signs By Susie.. G 812 385-2739
Princeton *(G-14011)*

Signs By TM LLC..................................... G 317 872-3220
Indianapolis *(G-9436)*

Signs Etc... G 574 674-9671
Osceola *(G-13402)*

Signs In Time By Greg Inc...................... G 260 749-7446
Fort Wayne *(G-5416)*

Signs Inc International............................ G 317 925-2835
Indianapolis *(G-9437)*

Signs Magic LLC..................................... G 812 473-5155
Evansville *(G-4313)*

Signs More.. G 317 392-9184
Shelbyville *(G-14799)*

Signs Now... G 812 323-2776
Bloomington *(G-973)*

Signs Now Jeffersonville......................... G 812 282-2440
Jeffersonville *(G-10054)*

Signs of Progress LLC............................ G 317 340-7225
Carmel *(G-1760)*

Signs of Seasons.................................... G 219 866-4507
Rensselaer *(G-14068)*

Signs of Times.. G 574 296-7464
Elkhart *(G-3678)*

Signs of Times LLC................................. G 812 981-3000
New Albany *(G-12815)*

Signs On Time Inc................................... F 219 661-4488
Crown Point *(G-2753)*

Signs Overnite Inc................................... G 219 365-4088
Crown Point *(G-2754)*

Signs Success... G 765 427-1437
Otterbein *(G-13455)*

Signs To Go... G 502 533-0090
Sellersburg *(G-14616)*

Signs Unlimited....................................... G 574 255-0500
Mishawaka *(G-11995)*

Signtech Sign Services Inc..................... G 574 537-8080
Goshen *(G-6255)*

Signworks... G 219 462-5353
Valparaiso *(G-16051)*

Signworks LLC.. F 317 872-8722
Indianapolis *(G-9438)*

Simko Signs LLC..................................... G 219 308-6000
Crown Point *(G-2755)*

Simple Sign Solutions Inc....................... G 317 272-5224
Noblesville *(G-13175)*

Simply Swank HM Dcor Signs LLC......... G 574 204-2339
Granger *(G-6377)*

Sister Pines Signs).................................. G 219 242-1824
Valparaiso *(G-16053)*

Sjg Enterprises Inc.................................. G 574 269-4806
Warsaw *(G-16425)*

Sky High Graphix LLC............................. G 260 267-0724
Fort Wayne *(G-5420)*

Sky High Sign Service............................. G 765 436-7012
Thorntown *(G-15755)*

Skyline Signs Inc.................................... G 765 564-4422
Delphi *(G-2908)*

Slingshot Media LLC............................... G 765 778-6848
Pendleton *(G-13555)*

Smart Displays LLC................................. G 812 322-3912
Bloomington *(G-975)*

Smith Signs Inc....................................... G 574 255-6446
Mishawaka *(G-11999)*

Sna LLC... G 317 931-1022
Indianapolis *(G-9453)*

Snep Sign Co.. G 260 982-6016
North Manchester *(G-13250)*

Snykin Inc... G 317 845-5051
Indianapolis *(G-9457)*

Sojane Technologies Inc........................ G 317 915-1059
Indianapolis *(G-9458)*

Spark Marketing LLC............................... G 219 301-0071
Dyer *(G-2983)*

Speckin Sign Service Inc........................ G 317 539-5133
Greencastle *(G-6431)*

Speedpro Imaging................................... G 765 446-8600
Lafayette *(G-10695)*

Square 1 Designs & Signs...................... G 219 552-0079
Shelby *(G-14728)*

Stackman Signs/Graphics Inc................. F 317 784-6120
Indianapolis *(G-9489)*

Stans Sign Design Inc............................ G 317 251-3838
Indianapolis *(G-9496)*

Steindler Signs & Graphix LLC............... G 219 733-2551
Wanatah *(G-16291)*

Steve Stamper... G 765 653-8786
Greencastle *(G-6432)*

Stingel Enterprises Inc............................ F 812 883-0054
Salem *(G-14501)*

◆ Stoffel Seals Corporation....................E 845 353-3800
Angola *(G-296)*

Strategic Solutions Inc........................... G 812 853-8525
Newburgh *(G-13023)*

Stritto Sign Art Company........................ G 317 356-2126
Morgantown *(G-12265)*

Sundance Signs...................................... G 765 420-7446
Lafayette *(G-10706)*

Superior Kreations Inc............................ G 765 635-3729
Anderson *(G-202)*

Supreme Signs Inc................................. G 219 384-0198
Valparaiso *(G-16062)*

Sweet Keepsakes.................................... G 219 872-8467
Trail Creek *(G-15840)*

Synergy Composites LLC........................ G 217 454-9711
Indianapolis *(G-9539)*

Tc4 LLC.. G 317 709-5429
Fishers *(G-4610)*

Team Hillman LLC................................... G 260 426-2626
Fort Wayne *(G-5470)*

Tfp Unlimited LLC................................... G 317 414-8819
Indianapolis *(G-9584)*

Tgr Inc... F 765 452-8225
Kokomo *(G-10348)*

The Baldus Company Inc........................ G 260 424-2366
Fort Wayne *(G-5480)*

▲ The Killion Corporation....................... D 317 271-4536
Indianapolis *(G-9589)*

Thousand One Inc................................... G 765 962-3636
Richmond *(G-14218)*

Timbers Custom Signs............................ G 812 866-6655
Hanover *(G-7046)*

Titan Graphics LLC.................................. G 317 496-2188
Mccordsville *(G-11457)*

Tko Enterprises Inc................................. D 317 271-1398
Plainfield *(G-13736)*

Tla Signs Inc... G 260 833-2402
Angola *(G-300)*

Todays Signs and Graphics.................... G 765 288-4771
Muncie *(G-12504)*

▲ Tower Advertising Products Inc......... D 260 593-2103
Topeka *(G-15821)*

Town & Country Industries Inc............... E 219 712-0893
Crown Point *(G-2766)*

Traffic Sign Co Inc.................................. G 317 845-9305
Indianapolis *(G-9627)*

Travis Britton.. G 317 762-6018
Indianapolis *(G-9632)*

Tremike Enterprises................................ G 317 547-6308
Indianapolis *(G-9634)*

Truck Lettering.. G 317 787-7875
Indianapolis *(G-9650)*

Ultimate Exhibits..................................... G 317 353-7374
Whitestown *(G-16828)*

Unique Signs... G 812 384-4967
Bloomfield *(G-758)*

US Signcrafters Inc................................. F 574 674-5055
Osceola *(G-13404)*

V Art Grafix LLC...................................... G 317 513-5522
Indianapolis *(G-9694)*

Van Der Weele Jon D.............................. G 574 892-5005
Argos *(G-328)*

Vince Rogers Signs Inc.......................... G 574 264-0542
Elkhart *(G-3770)*

Vinyl Creator... G 260 475-2012
Pleasant Lake *(G-13748)*

Visable Vinyl... G 765 717-9678
Hartford City *(G-7081)*

Visual Impact.. G 812 432-3524
Dillsboro *(G-2953)*

Vital Signs LLC....................................... G 219 548-1605
Valparaiso *(G-16077)*

▲ Vkf Renzel Usa Corp......................... F 219 661-6300
Crown Point *(G-2771)*

Wagner Signs Inc................................... E 317 788-0202
Indianapolis *(G-9735)*

▲ Wagner Zip-Change Inc..................... E 708 681-4100
Fort Wayne *(G-5540)*

Ward Industries Inc................................. F 574 825-2548
Middlebury *(G-11756)*

Wendell Conger....................................... G 812 282-2564
Jeffersonville *(G-10073)*

Westlund Concepts................................. F 317 819-0611
Lapel *(G-10818)*

Whiteco Industries Inc............................ A 219 769-6601
Merrillville *(G-11572)*

Whitehead Signs Inc............................... F 317 632-1800
Indianapolis *(G-9760)*

Winters Assoc Prmtnal Pdts Inc............. F 812 330-7000
Bloomington *(G-1015)*

Employee Codes: A=Over 500 employees, B=251-500
C=101-250, D=51-100, E=20-50, F=10-19, G=1-9

39 MISCELLANEOUS MANUFACTURING INDUSTRIES

Witham Anthony J Sign Prod................. G 317 984-3765
  Arcadia (G-320)
Wooden Signs.. G 317 506-6991
  Indianapolis (G-9786)
World Graffix LLC.................................. G 574 936-1927
  Plymouth (G-13834)
XI Graphics Inc....................................... F 317 738-3434
  Franklin (G-5789)
Xtreme Signs & Graphics LLC................ G 317 299-5622
  Indianapolis (G-9798)
Yard Signs... G 317 736-7446
  Trafalgar (G-15834)
Yard Signs Inc... G 317 535-7000
  Greenwood (G-6783)
Yellow Fellow Safety Signs LLC............. G 813 557-6428
  Jeffersonville (G-10077)
Yesco LLC.. G 812 469-2292
  Evansville (G-4391)
Yesco Sign & Lighting Service................ G 317 559-3374
  Indianapolis (G-9802)
Yesco Sing Lighting Service.................... G 812 577-0904
  Lawrenceburg (G-10868)
Young & Kenady Incorporated................ G 317 852-6300
  Brownsburg (G-1415)
Zeno Companies Inc................................ G 219 728-5126
  Chesterton (G-1969)
Zeno Signs LLC....................................... G 219 250-2896
  Chesterton (G-1970)

3995 Burial caskets

Astral Carrier Inc..................................... E 765 874-1406
  Lynn (G-11181)
Astral Industries Inc................................ C 765 874-2525
  Lynn (G-11182)
Aurora Casket Company LLC................. G 812 926-1110
  Aurora (G-438)
◆ Aurora Casket Company LLC............. B 800 457-1111
  Aurora (G-439)
◆ Batesville Casket Company LLC......... A 800 622-8373
  Batesville (G-580)
Batesville Casket Company Inc............... F 812 934-7010
  Batesville (G-581)
Batesville Interactive LLC...................... G 812 932-0164
  Batesville (G-582)
Batesville Services LLC........................... C 800 622-8373
  Batesville (G-583)
Cressy Memorial Group Inc.................... G 574 258-1800
  Mishawaka (G-11868)
Elder Group Inc....................................... D 765 966-7676
  Richmond (G-14118)
Hillenbrand Luxembourg Inc.................. E 812 934-7500
  Batesville (G-591)
JM Hutton & Co Inc................................ E 765 962-3506
  Richmond (G-14151)
◆ JM Hutton & Co Inc............................. D 765 962-3591
  Richmond (G-14152)
Matthews International Corp................... D 765 966-1576
  Richmond (G-14161)
Milso Industries Inc................................. F 765 966-8012
  Richmond (G-14167)
◆ Paragon Casket Inc............................... D 888 855-3601
  Richmond (G-14179)
◆ Pontone Industries LLC........................ C 765 966-8012
  Richmond (G-14183)
Romark Industries Inc............................. G 765 966-6211
  Richmond (G-14200)
◆ Tiedemann-Bevs Industries LLC......... E 765 962-4914
  Richmond (G-14219)
Vandor Corporation.................................. E 765 683-9760
  Richmond (G-14223)
◆ Werzalit of America Inc....................... D 814 362-3881
  Syracuse (G-15492)

York Group Inc.. C 765 966-1576
  Richmond (G-14232)

3996 Hard surface floor coverings, nec

▲ Eagle Flooring Brokers Inc.................. G 260 422-6100
  Fort Wayne (G-4937)
Quick Walk Systems Inc.......................... G 317 255-2247
  Indianapolis (G-9249)
Sorbashock LLC....................................... G 574 520-9784
  Fort Wayne (G-5426)

3999 Manufacturing industries, nec

4 Lens Partnerships LLC......................... G 317 490-1389
  Indianapolis (G-7390)
A J Brown Arms Company..................... G 812 384-1056
  Bloomfield (G-739)
Abboo Candle Co LLC............................ G 317 395-4404
  Fortville (G-5586)
Abbott L Abbott Nutrition....................... G 765 935-8650
  Richmond (G-14082)
ABS Mfg Rep Inc..................................... G 317 407-0406
  Carmel (G-1548)
Accra Pac Holding Co LLC..................... G 765 326-0005
  Fort Wayne (G-4719)
Accutemp Products Inc........................... G 260 493-6831
  New Haven (G-12890)
Achates LLC.. F 317 852-6978
  Brownsburg (G-1343)
Acme Firearms Mfg LLC......................... G 812 522-4008
  Seymour (G-14624)
Action Amusement................................... G 812 422-9029
  Evansville (G-3872)
Adaptive Mobility Inc.............................. F 317 347-6400
  Indianapolis (G-7429)
Adept LLC... G 812 275-8899
  Bedford (G-618)
Advance Green Mfg Co Inc..................... G 574 457-2695
  Goshen (G-6088)
Advanced Manufacturing In.................... G 260 273-9669
  Geneva (G-6047)
Advanced Mfg Solutions LLC.................. G 812 691-2030
  Shelburn (G-14716)
Advantage Manufacturing LLC............... G 317 831-2902
  Martinsville (G-11377)
Afm Industries LLC................................. E 574 910-0982
  Walkerton (G-16262)
Afraa Eyebrows....................................... G 317 881-6200
  Greenwood (G-6662)
▲ Agile Mfg Inc....................................... G 417 845-6065
  Milford (G-11785)
All Pet Supplies Inc................................. G 219 885-9670
  Gary (G-5888)
All Rvs Manufacturing Inc...................... G 574 538-1559
  Shipshewana (G-14833)
All-State Industries Inc........................... G 574 522-4245
  Elkhart (G-3165)
Alliance Studios LLC.............................. G 317 525-8487
  Indianapolis (G-7483)
Alpha Matrix LLC................................... G 812 686-1640
  Lamar (G-10794)
Always Full LLC..................................... G 317 727-9639
  Carmel (G-1559)
AM Manufacturing Company Ind........... F 800 342-6744
  Munster (G-12528)
America Corn Cutter............................... G 219 733-0885
  Wanatah (G-16285)
American Axle Manufacturi.................... F 812 418-7726
  Columbus (G-2217)
◆ American Oak Preserving Co Inc........ E 574 896-2171
  North Judson (G-13206)
Anchor Industries..................................... G 812 664-0772
  Owensville (G-13465)

Anchor Industries Inc............................... C 812 867-2421
  Evansville (G-3892)
Anglers Manufacturing............................ G 812 988-8040
  Nashville (G-12660)
Antique Candle Works Inc...................... E 765 250-8481
  Lafayette (G-10523)
Antique Candle Works LLC.................... G 765 586-6013
  Porter (G-13921)
Apex Industries LLC............................... G 260 624-5003
  Angola (G-230)
◆ ARC Industries.................................... G 812 471-1633
  Evansville (G-3897)
ARC Industries LLC................................ G 317 753-1607
  Carmel (G-1563)
ARC of Greater Boone Cnty Inc............. F 765 482-0051
  Lebanon (G-10875)
Archer Industries LLC............................. G 317 418-1260
  Indianapolis (G-7539)
Armor Contract Mfg Inc.......................... F 574 327-2962
  Elkhart (G-3189)
Artistic Stone Mfg LLC........................... G 574 546-3771
  Bremen (G-1173)
Aspire Industries..................................... F 812 542-1561
  New Albany (G-12693)
Astral Auras LLC.................................... G 219 628-5258
  Crown Point (G-2652)
Auburn Smoke N Vape LLC.................... G 260 572-6021
  Auburn (G-365)
Aunt Netts Country Candles LLC........... G 765 557-2770
  Elwood (G-3818)
Aus Embroidery Inc................................. G 317 899-1225
  Indianapolis (G-7568)
Austins Metal Mafia Inc.......................... G 812 619-6115
  Cannelton (G-1531)
Awards America Inc................................ F 219 462-7903
  Valparaiso (G-15906)
B Honey & Candles.................................. G 574 642-1145
  Shipshewana (G-14838)
B Industries Inc....................................... G 574 264-3290
  Elkhart (G-3211)
◆ B&R Manufacturing Inc....................... G 574 293-5669
  Elkhart (G-3213)
B2 Manufacturing LLC........................... G 765 993-4519
  Fountain City (G-5609)
Baerden Primitives LLC.......................... G 502 909-7045
  Clarksville (G-2007)
Bantam Industries Inc............................. G 714 561-6122
  Indianapolis (G-7596)
Barnwood Masters LLC.......................... G 260 414-9790
  Mentone (G-11469)
Basin Material Handling LLC................. G 812 849-0124
  Mitchell (G-12032)
Bask Aroma Co LLC................................ G 765 404-7582
  Lafayette (G-10535)
Bbs Celebration Center........................... G 765 730-6575
  Yorktown (G-16971)
Bdx I LLC.. F 317 741-5173
  Westfield (G-16669)
Beautybyneyadior LLC............................ G 800 988-2592
  Gary (G-5898)
Becks Bird Feeders.................................. G 765 874-1496
  Markleville (G-11367)
Beckys Orgnl Pppts Gs Cls...................... G 219 934-0895
  Highland (G-7124)
Becoming Her LLC.................................. G 317 200-0165
  Indianapolis (G-7608)
Bee Kind Candles.................................... G 765 618-5819
  Fort Wayne (G-4793)
Bells and Whistles LLC........................... G 317 315-3129
  Bloomington (G-801)
Betta Call Paul 4 Cbd LLC...................... G 317 675-6060
  Carmel (G-1567)

SIC SECTION
39 MISCELLANEOUS MANUFACTURING INDUSTRIES

Bettys Daughter Inc................................. G 317 500-1490
   Plainfield *(G-13661)*

BF Goodrich Tire Manufacturing............ G 260 493-8100
   Woodburn *(G-16946)*

Birch and Stitch LLC............................... G 317 353-7786
   Indianapolis *(G-7630)*

Birch Candle Company LLC..................... G 765 296-9425
   Dayton *(G-2837)*

Bold Solutions LLC.................................. G 708 740-8577
   Merrillville *(G-11492)*

Boudoir Lash Parlor LLC......................... G 330 259-5696
   Indianapolis *(G-7664)*

▼ Braun Corporation................................ B 574 946-6153
   Winamac *(G-16857)*

Brighttany Pollitt..................................... G 217 597-1624
   Greenfield *(G-6472)*

Brittany Bushong..................................... G 574 457-4970
   Syracuse *(G-15458)*

Brothers Industries LLC.......................... G 812 560-6224
   Greensburg *(G-6583)*

Browell Bellhousing Inc.......................... G 765 447-2292
   Lafayette *(G-10545)*

Brunk LLC... D 800 227-4156
   Goshen *(G-6101)*

Buck Hollow Cnc LLC............................. G 717 269-9322
   Brownsville *(G-1430)*

Buehrer Industries LLC........................... G 260 563-2181
   Wabash *(G-16175)*

Bunny Flaming Industries....................... G 317 554-7143
   Indianapolis *(G-7700)*

▲ Buztronics Inc..................................... E 317 876-3413
   Brownsburg *(G-1355)*

C & B Industries LLC.............................. G 260 490-3000
   Fort Wayne *(G-4824)*

C & C Industries..................................... G 260 804-6518
   Fort Wayne *(G-4825)*

C & F Industries LLC.............................. G 765 580-0378
   Liberty *(G-10984)*

C & J K Industries Inc............................. G 219 746-5760
   Munster *(G-12533)*

C & P Distributing LLC........................... F 574 256-1138
   Mishawaka *(G-11857)*

Cali Nail.. G 574 674-4126
   Osceola *(G-13385)*

Candice Jefferson................................... G 219 315-8629
   Hammond *(G-6892)*

Candle Chef LLC..................................... G 317 406-3391
   Plainfield *(G-13664)*

▲ Candles By Dar Inc............................. F 260 482-2099
   Fort Wayne *(G-4831)*

Cardis Nails.. G 812 264-9906
   Terre Haute *(G-15556)*

Carl Abbott.. G 317 590-4143
   Indianapolis *(G-7745)*

Carla Clark.. G 812 598-4687
   Evansville *(G-3964)*

Carousel Industries................................ G 317 674-8111
   Fishers *(G-4483)*

Carter Enterprises Inc............................ G 317 984-1497
   Arcadia *(G-309)*

Carters Manufacturing & Weld............... G 630 464-1520
   Knox *(G-10203)*

Casting Company Inc............................. G 317 509-4311
   Indianapolis *(G-7757)*

Cbd Revolution LLC................................ G 463 888-2806
   Indianapolis *(G-7762)*

Cbd Solutions LLC.................................. G 765 477-1900
   Lafayette *(G-10552)*

Cbdm Inc... G 317 218-3786
   Westfield *(G-16672)*

CCM Industries Inc................................. G 765 545-0597
   Winchester *(G-16884)*

Celestial Candle..................................... G 812 886-4819
   Vincennes *(G-16117)*

Centerline Manufacturing Inc................. G 260 348-7400
   Fort Wayne *(G-4839)*

Chapdells Tree & Plant Design............... G 317 845-9980
   Fishers *(G-4486)*

Christian Candle Company..................... G 317 427-8070
   Indianapolis *(G-7800)*

Churchill Cigars..................................... G 812 273-2249
   Madison *(G-11209)*

Circle S Industries LLC.......................... G 317 727-6752
   Morgantown *(G-12255)*

Clean Kutz LLC....................................... G 765 808-3232
   Muncie *(G-12366)*

Cobo Industries...................................... G 812 341-4318
   Indianapolis *(G-7830)*

Commercial Technical Svcs Inc.............. G 260 436-9898
   Fort Wayne *(G-4867)*

Containmed Inc...................................... G 317 487-8800
   Indianapolis *(G-7854)*

Coolstream Rv Ducting Inc..................... F 574 361-4271
   Elkhart *(G-3267)*

Coral Dog Candles................................. G 812 797-4050
   Bedford *(G-627)*

Corporatestars Industries LLC............... G 317 783-0614
   Indianapolis *(G-7879)*

Cosmoprof... G 317 897-0124
   Indianapolis *(G-7885)*

Cosology LLC.. G 812 630-3084
   Lamar *(G-10796)*

Country Valley Candles.......................... G 574 702-1302
   Royal Center *(G-14390)*

Covidien LP... C 317 837-8199
   Plainfield *(G-13674)*

Crichlow Industries Inc........................... G 317 925-5178
   Indianapolis *(G-7903)*

Cross Match Technologies Inc................ G 317 596-3260
   Indianapolis *(G-7905)*

Crossroads Mfg LLC............................... G 765 592-6456
   Marshall *(G-11372)*

Crr Industries LLC.................................. G 219 947-2052
   Hobart *(G-7184)*

CSM Industries LLC................................ G 219 465-2009
   Valparaiso *(G-15931)*

Csn Industries Inc.................................. G 317 697-6549
   Morgantown *(G-12257)*

Curated Luxe Co LLC.............................. G 317 797-1531
   Indianapolis *(G-7929)*

Custom Fitz LLC..................................... G 219 405-0896
   Porter *(G-13922)*

Custom Mfg & Fabrication LLC.............. G 260 908-1088
   Auburn *(G-383)*

Czech Industries LLC............................. G 317 946-1380
   Indianapolis *(G-7940)*

D A Merriman Inc................................... G 260 636-3464
   Albion *(G-22)*

D I Hair Extensions LLC......................... G 219 742-3611
   Merrillville *(G-11503)*

Damage Industries II LLC...................... G 574 256-7006
   Mishawaka *(G-11877)*

Damage Industries LLC.......................... G 574 256-7006
   Mishawaka *(G-11878)*

Damor & Co LLC..................................... G 317 790-8360
   Indianapolis *(G-7947)*

Dargo Industries..................................... G 765 716-9272
   Muncie *(G-12372)*

Daugherty Box Factory........................... G 260 375-2810
   Warren *(G-16295)*

Davis Industries Inc............................... G 317 871-0103
   Indianapolis *(G-7955)*

Dear Athletes Inc.................................... G 615 682-3332
   Noblesville *(G-13069)*

▲ Derby Industries LLC......................... G 765 778-6104
   Anderson *(G-102)*

Diamond Lush Extensions LLC.............. G 773 984-1003
   Merrillville *(G-11506)*

Diamondback Metalcrafts Inc................ G 317 363-7760
   Mooresville *(G-12202)*

Divalicious By Yours Truly LLC.............. G 219 359-6335
   Merrillville *(G-11507)*

Divine Confidence LLC........................... G 574 218-1279
   Goshen *(G-6122)*

Divine Essentials LLC............................ G 765 400-8609
   Muncie *(G-12385)*

Dj Wreath Creations LLC....................... G 317 723-3268
   Indianapolis *(G-7991)*

Dkd Mfg Inc.. G 574 298-9592
   Lakeville *(G-10790)*

DMC Distribution LLC............................ G 219 926-6401
   Porter *(G-13924)*

Dmp Industries LLC................................ G 260 413-6701
   Warsaw *(G-16353)*

Domain Industries LLC.......................... G 800 227-5337
   Fort Wayne *(G-4922)*

Down To Fabricate LLC.......................... G 812 249-1825
   Guilford *(G-6828)*

Dragon Industries Inc............................ G 574 772-2243
   Knox *(G-10205)*

Dragon Industries Incorporated............. G 574 772-3508
   Knox *(G-10206)*

Drk Global Manufacturing LLC.............. G 574 387-6264
   Mishawaka *(G-11886)*

Dropship My Bundles LLC...................... G 219 381-8061
   Gary *(G-5924)*

Dubois Manufacturing Inc..................... G 574 674-6988
   Elkhart *(G-3304)*

Due North Industries Corp..................... G 812 306-4043
   Evansville *(G-4021)*

Dw Inc... G 812 696-2149
   Farmersburg *(G-4418)*

Dynatect Manufacturing Inc................... E 219 462-0822
   Valparaiso *(G-15936)*

Dynatect Manufacturing Inc................... F 219 465-1898
   Valparaiso *(G-15937)*

E-Beam Services Inc.............................. G 765 447-6755
   Lafayette *(G-10573)*

East Industries LLC................................ G 812 273-4358
   Madison *(G-11216)*

Eastons Lettering Service...................... G 219 942-5101
   Hobart *(G-7187)*

Ebp and Associates Inc.......................... G 812 386-7062
   Princeton *(G-13990)*

▲ Edsal Inc... F 219 427-1294
   Gary *(G-5925)*

Edward Emmons..................................... G 209 352-1475
   Michigan City *(G-11606)*

Eften Inc.. G 260 982-1544
   North Manchester *(G-13233)*

Eis Packaging Machinery Inc................. G 574 870-0087
   Logansport *(G-11072)*

Elegant Eyes LLC................................... G 317 640-1995
   Greenwood *(G-6692)*

Elite Industries LLC............................... F 317 407-6869
   Indianapolis *(G-8092)*

Elkhart Brass.. E 574 266-3700
   Elkhart *(G-3320)*

Ellinger Mfg Tech LLC............................ G 574 303-2086
   Mishawaka *(G-11893)*

Emma Pearls Creations LLC.................. G 219 200-2277
   Highland *(G-7135)*

Empire Industries Inc............................. F 260 908-0996
   Butler *(G-1463)*

Energy Saver Lights Inc......................... F 202 544-7868
   Indianapolis *(G-8118)*

39 MISCELLANEOUS MANUFACTURING INDUSTRIES

Engineering and Industria................ E 574 722-3714
Logansport *(G-11073)*

Enhanced Mfg Solutions Inc................ G 812 932-1101
Batesville *(G-587)*

Enviri Corporation................ G 317 983-5353
Pittsboro *(G-13645)*

Erosion & Cnstr Solutions Inc................ E 219 885-9676
Merrillville *(G-11514)*

Estes Aws LLC................ G 317 995-9742
Indianapolis *(G-8137)*

Evo Exhibits LLC................ G 630 520-0710
Peru *(G-13582)*

Exclusive Stylez LLC................ G 470 406-2804
Indianapolis *(G-8151)*

Expressions Braids By Gwen LLC........ G 260 312-6037
Fort Wayne *(G-4968)*

Fabcore Industries LLC................ G 260 438-3431
Fort Wayne *(G-4971)*

Fancy Candle Soy LLC................ G 765 769-4042
Anderson *(G-117)*

Fast Manufacturing LLC................ G 219 778-8238
Rolling Prairie *(G-14361)*

Fcs Industries Incorporated................ G 574 288-5150
South Bend *(G-15028)*

Fenris Forge LLC................ G 260 422-9044
Fort Wayne *(G-4980)*

Fillmanns Industries LLC................ G 765 744-4772
Daleville *(G-2799)*

Fink Industries LLC................ G 219 923-2015
Highland *(G-7136)*

Fire Star Industries LLC................ G 317 432-3212
Greenwood *(G-6704)*

First Source Manufacturing................ G 574 527-7192
Pierceton *(G-13631)*

Fit Tight Covers Company Inc................ E 812 492-3370
Evansville *(G-4072)*

Fix-Ur-6 LLC................ G 812 989-4310
Floyds Knobs *(G-4677)*

Flawless Units LLC................ G 317 833-5975
Indianapolis *(G-8201)*

Flickers Candle Shop................ G 317 403-5045
Indianapolis *(G-8203)*

Foamiture................ G 574 831-4775
New Paris *(G-12953)*

Forterra Concrete Inds Inc................ E 812 426-5353
Evansville *(G-4080)*

Fortune Diversified Industries................ G 317 532-3644
Indianapolis *(G-8216)*

Fox Manufacturing LLC................ G 317 430-1493
Pendleton *(G-13533)*

Foy Industries................ G 317 727-3905
Indianapolis *(G-8218)*

Fresh Bakery Candles LLC................ G 317 899-2377
Indianapolis *(G-8232)*

Fuel Fabrication LLC................ G 219 390-7022
Crown Point *(G-2688)*

Fur Bee................ G 317 259-9498
Indianapolis *(G-8242)*

Fur Real Taxidermy LLC................ G 812 667-6365
Cross Plains *(G-2634)*

Future Manufacturing Inc................ G 260 454-0222
Huntington *(G-7312)*

Fuzion Industries................ G 812 430-4037
Evansville *(G-4082)*

FWD Technologies LLC................ G 360 907-9755
Huntington *(G-7313)*

Gale Industries Insltn Matl................ G 765 447-1191
Lafayette *(G-10583)*

Gdp Industries LLC................ G 260 414-4003
Fort Wayne *(G-5017)*

Gdt Terre Haute Mfg................ G 812 460-7706
Terre Haute *(G-15595)*

Gem Industries Inc................ G 574 773-4513
Nappanee *(G-12599)*

Gen Y Hitch................ G 574 218-6363
Bremen *(G-1192)*

Gifford Mfg Advisors LLC................ G 918 809-4116
Floyds Knobs *(G-4680)*

Ginger White LLC................ G 773 818-8740
Gary *(G-5942)*

Gladieux Trading Mfg Co................ G 260 417-6774
Fort Wayne *(G-5026)*

Glow Dr LLC................ G 317 622-6735
Noblesville *(G-13087)*

Gold Canyon Candles................ G 812 267-4477
Elizabeth *(G-3125)*

Gold Standard Truss LLC................ G 219 987-7781
Demotte *(G-2918)*

Goodlife Industries Inc................ G 317 339-6341
Indianapolis *(G-8304)*

Goodloe Industry Svc................ G 317 258-5534
Indianapolis *(G-8305)*

Goshen Mfg Co Inc................ G 574 533-1357
Goshen *(G-6152)*

Grand Products Inc................ C 317 870-3122
Indianapolis *(G-8312)*

Graphic Barn LLC................ G 812 952-3826
Lanesville *(G-10798)*

Graysville Mfg Inc................ G 812 382-4616
Sullivan *(G-15407)*

Great Lakes Waterjet Inc................ G 574 651-2158
Granger *(G-6351)*

Green Mountain Industries LLC................ G 812 585-1531
Centerpoint *(G-1844)*

Green Way Candle Company LLC................ G 574 536-3802
Goshen *(G-6155)*

Gribbins Specialty Group Inc................ G 812 422-3340
Evansville *(G-4099)*

Grit Into Grace Inc................ G 317 331-8334
Indianapolis *(G-8333)*

◆ H A Industries................ G 219 931-6304
Hammond *(G-6937)*

Hager Industries Inc................ G 317 219-6622
Noblesville *(G-13091)*

Hair Necessities................ G 812 288-5887
Clarksville *(G-2018)*

Haird Salon LLC................ G 260 804-7609
Fort Wayne *(G-5048)*

Hammertechracecars LLC................ G 765 412-8824
Avon *(G-522)*

Hart Industries Inc................ G 574 575-4657
Elkhart *(G-3399)*

Haynes Honey LLC................ G 260 563-6397
Wabash *(G-16191)*

Hdh Manfacturing................ G 317 918-4088
Indianapolis *(G-8374)*

Hefter Industries................ G 219 728-1159
Chesterton *(G-1935)*

Hensley Composites LLC................ G 574 202-3840
Mishawaka *(G-11907)*

Her Majesty Crown LLC................ G 260 218-2255
Fort Wayne *(G-5064)*

Herextensions LLC................ G 219 466-4273
East Chicago *(G-3016)*

Hestad Industries Inc................ G 574 271-7609
Granger *(G-6352)*

Hey Heys Candles LLC................ G 812 484-9956
Evansville *(G-4106)*

Hi-Def Coatings................ G 812 801-4895
Hanover *(G-7043)*

Hidden Electrical LLC................ G 317 628-4233
Westfield *(G-16697)*

HK Manufacturing Inc................ G 260 925-1680
Auburn *(G-397)*

Hlb1 LLC................ F 219 575-7534
La Porte *(G-10420)*

Hmh Manufacturing LLC................ G 765 553-5447
Kokomo *(G-10280)*

Hollowheart Industries LLC................ G 812 737-4002
Spencer *(G-15349)*

Hoosier Family Living LLC................ G 812 396-7880
Vincennes *(G-16129)*

Horizon Anim LLC................ G 317 742-4917
Indianapolis *(G-8413)*

Houghton Mifflin Harcourt Co................ C 317 359-5585
Indianapolis *(G-8425)*

Howa USA Inc................ G 765 962-7855
Richmond *(G-14137)*

Huber Industries................ G 812 537-2275
Lawrenceburg *(G-10841)*

Hungry Candle LLC................ G 773 656-1774
Indianapolis *(G-8434)*

Hurst Enterprise................ G 812 853-0901
Newburgh *(G-13006)*

Ilpea Industries Inc................ C 812 752-2526
Evansville *(G-4116)*

Incipio Devices LLC................ D 260 200-1970
Huntington *(G-7325)*

Indiana Manufacturing Inst................ G 765 494-4935
West Lafayette *(G-16595)*

Indiana Materials Proc LLC................ F 260 244-6026
Columbia City *(G-2155)*

Indigo Candles................ G 317 457-9814
Indianapolis *(G-8514)*

Indy Cbd Plus LLP................ G 317 600-6362
Indianapolis *(G-8523)*

Indy Lash and Brow LLC................ G 502 751-4947
Indianapolis *(G-8531)*

Infinite Lifts LLC................ G 260 388-2868
Huntington *(G-7328)*

Infinity Uv Inc................ G 269 625-3423
Elkhart *(G-3425)*

Ingredion Incorporated................ E 317 635-4455
Indianapolis *(G-8544)*

Innovative Slots LLC................ G 317 520-7374
Indianapolis *(G-8558)*

Insulpedia LLC................ G 317 459-4030
Fishers *(G-4548)*

International Game Technology................ G 317 731-3791
Indianapolis *(G-8577)*

Iron Men Industries Inc................ G 574 596-2251
Russiaville *(G-14423)*

J&K Generations................ G 812 508-1094
Bedford *(G-650)*

Jacobs Mfg LLC................ G 765 490-6111
Lafayette *(G-10613)*

▲ Jadco Ltd................ F 219 661-2065
Crown Point *(G-2699)*

Janelle Davis................ G 765 635-6233
Anderson *(G-139)*

Jani Industries Inc................ G 317 985-3916
Avon *(G-528)*

Jaz Industrial LLC................ F 812 305-5692
Evansville *(G-4138)*

Jcj Fabrication LLC................ G 765 621-9556
Anderson *(G-140)*

Jcs Technologies Inc................ G 317 201-5064
Fishers *(G-4549)*

Jdb Manufacturing LLC................ G 317 752-8756
Indianapolis *(G-8620)*

Jedeu Industries LLC................ G 317 660-5526
Mishawaka *(G-11920)*

Jewelry In Candles................ G 765 401-6228
Waynetown *(G-16541)*

Jewels Hair & Accessories LLC................ G 260 310-9915
Fort Wayne *(G-5135)*

SIC SECTION
39 MISCELLANEOUS MANUFACTURING INDUSTRIES

Joe May Industries LLC .... G 260 494-8735
  Huntertown *(G-7258)*

Johnson Samyra .... G 872 216-0551
  Indianapolis *(G-8635)*

Jps Candles LLC .... G 219 728-8210
  Chesterton *(G-1940)*

Jrds Industries .... G 260 729-5037
  Portland *(G-13953)*

Jwcandle Co LLC .... G 317 661-1066
  Beech Grove *(G-695)*

K & P Industries LLC .... G 317 881-9245
  Greenwood *(G-6720)*

Karma Industries Inc .... G 765 742-9200
  Lafayette *(G-10619)*

Kartistry Pro LLC .... G 317 969-7075
  Indianapolis *(G-8661)*

Kays Way .... G 219 290-0782
  Gary *(G-5973)*

Keenville & Company LLC .... G 219 916-6737
  Valparaiso *(G-15984)*

Kemco Manufacturing LLC .... G 574 546-2025
  Bremen *(G-1202)*

Kermit Usa Inc .... G 765 288-3334
  Indianapolis *(G-8674)*

Kerria Industries Inc .... G 317 852-4542
  Brownsburg *(G-1382)*

Keystone Engineering & Mfg LLC .... G 317 319-7639
  Avon *(G-531)*

Kidstar Safety .... G 800 785-6015
  Osceola *(G-13396)*

Kien Industries LLP .... G 260 471-1098
  Fort Wayne *(G-5149)*

Kill Her Set LLC .... F 317 992-2220
  Indianapolis *(G-8682)*

Kimmel Fabrication Studio LLC .... G 260 403-5691
  Fort Wayne *(G-5150)*

Kipin Industries .... G 317 510-1181
  Indianapolis *(G-8688)*

Kjs Beauty Lounge LLC .... G 317 426-0621
  Indianapolis *(G-8692)*

Kore Industries LLC .... G 773 343-5966
  Gary *(G-5975)*

Kreider Manufacturing .... G 260 894-7120
  Ligonier *(G-11018)*

Krowned By Qwan LLC .... G 317 813-9914
  Indianapolis *(G-8704)*

KS Kreations .... G 574 514-7366
  Georgetown *(G-6066)*

▼ Kt Industries LLC .... G 260 432-0027
  Fort Wayne *(G-5162)*

Kyann Manufacturing Group LLC .... G 260 724-9721
  Decatur *(G-2867)*

Lamarvis Industries LLC .... G 317 797-0483
  Terre Haute *(G-15627)*

Lambright Country Chimes Llc .... G 260 768-9138
  Shipshewana *(G-14863)*

Lamco Finishers Inc .... E 317 471-1010
  Indianapolis *(G-8717)*

Lamon Brewster Industries LLC .... G 818 668-4298
  Indianapolis *(G-8718)*

Lang Capital LLC .... G 812 325-2177
  Floyds Knobs *(G-4684)*

Larck Industries LLC .... G 574 993-5502
  Mishawaka *(G-11926)*

Larry Zoeller .... G 502 439-0812
  Lanesville *(G-10802)*

Laymon Industries LLC .... G 574 277-4536
  South Bend *(G-15119)*

Layshias Clawed Madam LLC .... G 260 257-7633
  Fort Wayne *(G-5178)*

LCI Industries .... G 574 535-1125
  Elkhart *(G-3475)*

Leland Manufacturing .... G 812 367-2068
  Ferdinand *(G-4441)*

Lennon Industries .... G 219 996-6024
  Hebron *(G-7102)*

Ler Techforce LLC .... C 812 373-0870
  Columbus *(G-2340)*

LH Industries Corp .... G 260 432-5563
  Fort Wayne *(G-5182)*

Licensed Eliquid Mfg LLC .... F 260 245-6442
  Fort Wayne *(G-5184)*

Life Essentials Inc .... F 765 423-4192
  Wolcott *(G-16932)*

Life43 LLC .... F 708 335-7329
  Merrillville *(G-11533)*

Light of Life Gel Candles .... G 574 310-3777
  Mishawaka *(G-11929)*

Lil Girls Glam LLC .... G 317 507-3443
  Indianapolis *(G-8751)*

Lil Ms One Hundred LLC .... G 765 609-9526
  Indianapolis *(G-8752)*

Linneas Lights LLC .... G 317 324-4002
  Carmel *(G-1684)*

Lippert Extrusions .... F 574 312-6467
  Elkhart *(G-3496)*

Lit By Neek .... G 317 775-5574
  Indianapolis *(G-8767)*

Lite Magnesium Products Inc .... G 765 299-3644
  Indianapolis *(G-8768)*

Little Mfg LLC .... G 812 453-8137
  Boonville *(G-1089)*

Lloyds of Indiana Inc .... G 317 251-5430
  Indianapolis *(G-8774)*

Locc Industries LLC .... G 219 575-2727
  Portage *(G-13882)*

London Hair Bundles LLC .... G 317 953-3888
  Fishers *(G-4557)*

▲ LSI Wallcovering Inc .... D 502 458-1502
  New Albany *(G-12767)*

Lsm Manufacturing LLC .... G 260 409-4030
  Grabill *(G-6311)*

Luckmann Industries .... G 317 464-0323
  Indianapolis *(G-8794)*

Lux Beauty Den LLC .... G 708 793-0871
  Merrillville *(G-11534)*

Luxurylinks LLC .... G 260 258-2814
  Fort Wayne *(G-5193)*

M & J Shelton Enterprises Inc .... G 260 745-1616
  Fort Wayne *(G-5194)*

M & M Converting Inc .... G 260 563-7411
  Wabash *(G-16195)*

M & S Curtis LLC .... G 317 946-8440
  Indianapolis *(G-8802)*

M G Industries .... G 812 362-7593
  Rockport *(G-14344)*

M2 Industries LLC .... G 812 246-0651
  Jeffersonville *(G-10014)*

Madden Engineered Products LLC .... G 574 295-4292
  Elkhart *(G-3509)*

Magic Candle Inc .... G 317 357-1101
  Indianapolis *(G-8809)*

Mallang Spa Essentials .... G 219 902-9788
  Hammond *(G-6976)*

Mane Reserved LLC .... G 219 516-5800
  Indianapolis *(G-8825)*

Manu Sangha Inc .... G 219 262-5400
  Elkhart *(G-3511)*

Manufacturing Solution Intl .... G 219 841-9434
  Chesterton *(G-1946)*

Mari Manu Corp .... G 219 804-3294
  Hammond *(G-6977)*

Mark Peiser Manufacturing Inc .... G 317 698-5376
  Brownsburg *(G-1385)*

Maron Products Inc .... G 574 254-0840
  Mishawaka *(G-11937)*

Martin Industries .... G 502 553-6599
  New Albany *(G-12772)*

Martin Industries LLC .... G 502 553-6599
  Sellersburg *(G-14605)*

Masterspas LLC .... C 260 436-9100
  Fort Wayne *(G-5207)*

◆ Masterspas LLC .... D 260 436-9100
  Fort Wayne *(G-5206)*

Maxwell Engineering Inc .... G 260 745-4991
  Fort Wayne *(G-5208)*

McPheeters and Associates Inc .... G 812 988-2840
  Freetown *(G-5804)*

ME Fabrication LLP .... G 574 594-2801
  Pierceton *(G-13634)*

ME Time Candle Co LLC .... G 317 378-5533
  Indianapolis *(G-8867)*

Medical Structures Mfg Corp .... G 574 612-0353
  Elkhart *(G-3524)*

Merrywood Group LLC .... G 765 729-5927
  Muncie *(G-12451)*

Metalworking Machinery LLC .... G 317 752-0981
  Indianapolis *(G-8892)*

Mfd Express Inc .... G 765 717-3539
  Springport *(G-15381)*

Mid America Prototyping Inc .... G 765 643-3200
  Anderson *(G-153)*

Midwest Dachshund Rescue Inc .... G 815 260-6734
  Highland *(G-7145)*

Midwest Seed Coating LLC .... G 812 949-7459
  New Albany *(G-12779)*

Milstrata Manufacturing LLC .... G 260 209-4415
  Fort Wayne *(G-5229)*

Minks & Beyond LLC .... G 219 402-7011
  Valparaiso *(G-16003)*

Mje Industries Inc .... G 219 299-3535
  Valparaiso *(G-16004)*

Mk Mfg LLC .... G 260 768-4678
  Shipshewana *(G-14870)*

Mobility Svm LLC .... E 260 434-4777
  Fort Wayne *(G-5237)*

Moco Fragrances LLC .... G 317 642-9014
  Flat Rock *(G-4656)*

Modern Biology Incorporated .... G 765 523-3338
  Lafayette *(G-10652)*

Moody Candles LLC .... G 317 535-2969
  Bargersville *(G-570)*

Moosein Industries LLC .... G 219 406-7306
  Portage *(G-13892)*

Murphys Townhouse Candles LLC .... G 260 318-0504
  Kendallville *(G-10137)*

Nail Factory LLC .... G 317 292-5637
  Indianapolis *(G-8979)*

Nakoma Products LLC .... G 317 357-5715
  Indianapolis *(G-8980)*

Nalin Manufacturing LLC .... G 812 401-9187
  Evansville *(G-4218)*

Natural Pharmaceutical Mfg LLC .... F 812 689-3309
  Osgood *(G-13413)*

Naturalee Twisted LLC .... G 317 523-1012
  Beech Grove *(G-700)*

Naturally LLC .... G 317 667-5690
  Indianapolis *(G-8991)*

Naturespire LLC .... G 463 266-0395
  Indianapolis *(G-8992)*

Neighborhood Floors & More LLC .... G 219 510-5737
  Portage *(G-13895)*

Nemcomed Instrs & Implants .... F 800 255-4576
  Fort Wayne *(G-5265)*

Netshape Technologies LLC .... E 317 805-3764
  Campbellsburg *(G-1525)*

Employee Codes: A=Over 500 employees, B=251-500
C=101-250, D=51-100, E=20-50, F=10-19, G=1-9

2024 Harris Indiana Industrial Directory

39 MISCELLANEOUS MANUFACTURING INDUSTRIES

Next Level Candles LLC .... G 574 347-1030
　South Bend *(G-15167)*

Nf Industries Inc .... G 317 738-2558
　Franklin *(G-5759)*

Nfi Industries Inc .... G 765 483-9741
　Lebanon *(G-10926)*

Night Lights Company LLC .... G 574 606-4288
　Indianapolis *(G-9010)*

Norine S Herbs .... G 574 642-4272
　Goshen *(G-6229)*

Notetech Industries LLC .... G 574 326-3188
　Elkhart *(G-3577)*

Nova Manufacturing .... G 512 750-5165
　Avon *(G-542)*

NPS Xofigo Mfg Plant 5889 .... G 317 981-4129
　Indianapolis *(G-9030)*

Nu Wave Manufacturing LLC .... G 317 989-4703
　Danville *(G-2821)*

▲ Nuwave Manufacturing .... G 317 987-8229
　Indianapolis *(G-9036)*

Omega Co .... G 317 831-4471
　Mooresville *(G-12231)*

Oreo Effect LLC .... G 574 404-4800
　South Bend *(G-15180)*

Osterfeld Industries .... G 219 926-4646
　Chesterton *(G-1952)*

Otter Creek Candle LLC .... G 812 750-4129
　Holton *(G-7219)*

Outdoor Industries .... G 574 551-5936
　Warsaw *(G-16407)*

P & M Fabrication .... G 812 232-7640
　Terre Haute *(G-15656)*

P & T Manufacturing Corp .... G 260 442-9304
　Kendallville *(G-10140)*

P P G Industries Inc .... F 812 442-5080
　Brazil *(G-1160)*

P2 Precision Mfg LLC .... G 260 609-6295
　Pierceton *(G-13636)*

Packrat Industries LLC .... G 317 295-0208
　Indianapolis *(G-9085)*

Pangaea Industries LLC .... G 574 850-5841
　South Bend *(G-15185)*

Park 100 Foods Inc .... E 765 763-6064
　Morristown *(G-12280)*

Patterson Products LLC .... G 812 309-3614
　Otwell *(G-13457)*

Paula Rosenbaum .... G 319 484-2941
　Valparaiso *(G-16022)*

Peerless Manufacturing LLC .... G 260 760-0880
　Avilla *(G-492)*

Penn & Beech Candle Co .... G 317 645-8732
　Indianapolis *(G-9114)*

Phantom Industries LLC .... G 812 276-5956
　Jeffersonville *(G-10037)*

Phtal Aoy Industries LLC .... G 260 267-0025
　Warsaw *(G-16411)*

Planet Pets .... G 812 539-7316
　Lawrenceburg *(G-10853)*

Plaquemaker Plus Inc .... G 317 594-5556
　Fishers *(G-4576)*

Plastic Recycl Export Ltd LLC .... G 301 758-6885
　Fort Wayne *(G-5318)*

Platinum Industries LLC .... G 765 744-8323
　Fishers *(G-4577)*

Polar Information Tech LLC .... G 303 725-8015
　Fishers *(G-4578)*

Politan Steel Fabrication Inc .... G 317 714-6800
　Fishers *(G-4647)*

Potorti Enterprises Inc .... G 812 989-8528
　Floyds Knobs *(G-4688)*

Preciball USA .... G 812 257-5555
　Washington *(G-16505)*

Predator Percussion LLC .... G 317 919-7659
　New Whiteland *(G-12987)*

Premium Manufacturing LLC .... G 219 258-0141
　La Porte *(G-10466)*

Premium Vinyl Mfg .... G 219 922-6501
　Griffith *(G-6815)*

Prestige Tooling LLC .... G 269 470-4525
　Elkhart *(G-3619)*

Prestoncbd LLC .... G 317 407-7068
　Carmel *(G-1728)*

Pretty Xquisite Hair LLC .... G 765 760-6948
　Muncie *(G-12478)*

Prevounce Health Inc .... F 800 618-7738
　Indianapolis *(G-9195)*

Prime Time Manufacturing .... G 574 862-3001
　Wakarusa *(G-16243)*

Pro Series Products LLC .... G 812 793-3506
　Crothersville *(G-2643)*

Procoat Products LLC .... G 812 352-6083
　North Vernon *(G-13293)*

Prominent Promotional Pdts LLC .... G 317 376-5772
　Quincy *(G-14022)*

◆ Prowler Industries LLC .... F 877 477-6953
　Greensburg *(G-6626)*

Pure Beautee Bundlez Inc .... G 574 204-3979
　Indianapolis *(G-9240)*

Pure Image Laser and Spa LLC .... G 317 306-6603
　Indianapolis *(G-9242)*

Purple Vertigo Candles LLC .... G 502 807-6619
　New Salisbury *(G-12986)*

Pwi .... D 574 646-2015
　Nappanee *(G-12637)*

Quiet Storm Productions LLC .... G 219 448-1998
　Michigan City *(G-11654)*

R M Mfg Housing Svc .... G 574 288-5207
　South Bend *(G-15214)*

R N A Industries Corp .... G 765 288-4413
　Redkey *(G-14029)*

Rappid Mfg Inc .... G 317 440-8084
　Indianapolis *(G-9266)*

Raven Industries Inc .... G 877 923-5832
　Wakarusa *(G-16246)*

Raven Lake Originals Candles .... G 765 419-1473
　Greentown *(G-6648)*

Raw Barbers and Company LLC .... G 925 383-6212
　Hammond *(G-6995)*

RE Industries Inc .... G 219 987-1764
　Demotte *(G-2928)*

Reachpoint Industries Corp .... G 219 707-3514
　Highland *(G-7152)*

Realize Inc .... F 317 915-0295
　Noblesville *(G-13165)*

Red Earth LLC .... G 260 338-1439
　Fort Wayne *(G-5373)*

Redab Industries Inc .... G 219 484-8382
　Crown Point *(G-2742)*

Redmaster Fusion LLC .... G 260 273-5819
　Fort Wayne *(G-5374)*

Resourcemfg .... G 812 574-5500
　Madison *(G-11247)*

Resourcemfg .... G 812 523-2100
　Seymour *(G-14681)*

Resourcemfg .... G 812 231-8500
　Terre Haute *(G-15679)*

Revere Industries .... G 317 638-1521
　Indianapolis *(G-9295)*

RFI Mfg Co .... G 812 207-6939
　New Albany *(G-12805)*

Ribbe Welding & Mfg Inc .... G 765 390-4044
　Kingman *(G-10173)*

Ric Corporation D/B/A .... G 260 432-0799
　Fort Wayne *(G-5382)*

Richey M A Mfg Co Sprtng Gds .... G 765 659-5389
　Frankfort *(G-5693)*

Ridge Iron LLC .... G 646 450-0092
　Plymouth *(G-13811)*

Ring Industries Inc .... G 219 204-1577
　Lake Village *(G-10783)*

Robinson Auto Parts Mfg .... G 317 921-0076
　Indianapolis *(G-9315)*

Rocca Industries LLC .... G 812 576-1011
　Brookville *(G-1333)*

Roller-Wilson Industries LLC .... G 317 377-4900
　Indianapolis *(G-9324)*

Ronlewhorn Industries LLC .... G 765 661-9343
　Indianapolis *(G-9331)*

Rosmarino Candles LLC .... G 970 218-2835
　Bloomington *(G-963)*

Rowan Industries LLC .... G 574 302-1203
　South Bend *(G-15225)*

Royal Barbie Blinks LLC .... G 765 400-6205
　Lafayette *(G-10681)*

RPM .... G 309 798-1856
　Hammond *(G-7001)*

Rustic Glow Candle Co LLC .... G 317 696-4264
　Indianapolis *(G-9349)*

S L Manufacturing LLC .... G 260 657-3392
　Grabill *(G-6323)*

Safeguard Nursery Products LLC .... G 502 648-7922
　New Albany *(G-12810)*

Sanco Industries .... G 219 426-3922
　Fort Wayne *(G-5396)*

Sanlo Manufacturing .... G 219 879-0241
　Michigan City *(G-11665)*

Satellite Industries .... G 800 328-3332
　Elkhart *(G-3663)*

Saul Goode Industries LLC .... F 317 929-1111
　Indianapolis *(G-9380)*

Scaggs Moto Designs .... G 765 426-2526
　Lafayette *(G-10684)*

Schmigbob LLC .... G 219 781-7991
　Crown Point *(G-2748)*

▲ Schwartz Manufacturing Inc .... G 260 589-3865
　Berne *(G-725)*

Seibertspace Industries LLC .... G 317 566-0014
　Carmel *(G-1757)*

Sentinel Services Inc .... E 574 360-5279
　Granger *(G-6376)*

Shark-Co Mfg LLC .... G 317 670-6397
　Lebanon *(G-10941)*

Shelovexempress LLC .... G 317 490-2097
　Evansville *(G-4309)*

Shields Mech & Fabrication LLC .... G 219 863-3972
　Demotte *(G-2929)*

Shophouse Fabrication LLC .... G 260 367-2156
　Howe *(G-7242)*

Simple Glow Candle Co .... G 260 435-0062
　Fort Wayne *(G-5418)*

Sittin Pretty LLC .... G 219 947-4121
　Crown Point *(G-2757)*

Sizzlin Sound Productions LLC .... G 765 376-0129
　Crawfordsville *(G-2615)*

SL Beauty LLC .... G 317 969-0341
　Indianapolis *(G-9446)*

SM Industries LLC .... G 219 613-5295
　Saint John *(G-14458)*

Smart Pergola .... G 317 987-7750
　Carmel *(G-1764)*

Smoke Smoke Smoke .... G 219 942-3331
　Hobart *(G-7209)*

Snake Sandbags LLC .... G 317 721-1006
　Carmel *(G-1765)*

Snowbird Industries LLC .... G 716 481-1142
　Indianapolis *(G-9455)*

SIC SECTION
39 MISCELLANEOUS MANUFACTURING INDUSTRIES

So Industries LLC .... G 765 606-7596
  Pendleton *(G-13556)*
Solae LLC .... F 219 986-6119
  Remington *(G-14039)*
Solar Freeze LLC .... E 260 499-4973
  Lagrange *(G-10761)*
Soy Magnifiscents .... G 765 746-6358
  Lafayette *(G-10694)*
Soyful Fragrant Candles LLC .... G 219 588-2685
  Gary *(G-6014)*
Sparkling Ashe LLC .... G 317 426-1824
  Indianapolis *(G-9468)*
Spear Industries Inc .... G 317 717-1957
  Greenwood *(G-6769)*
Specialty Compounds LLC .... G 574 529-0872
  Syracuse *(G-15478)*
Specialty Manufacturing .... G 317 587-4999
  Carmel *(G-1769)*
Speedhook Specialists Inc .... G 219 378-6369
  Beverly Shores *(G-732)*
Squareframe Industries LLC .... G 765 430-3301
  Lafayette *(G-10696)*
Star Manufacturing LLC .... G 574 329-6042
  Elkhart *(G-3697)*
State Beauty Supply .... G 260 755-6361
  Fort Wayne *(G-5436)*
Steel Box Co LLC .... G 812 620-7043
  Salem *(G-14500)*
Steel Green Manufacturing LLC .... E 765 481-2890
  Lebanon *(G-10944)*
Stoney Ridgs Candles .... G 574 453-6807
  Etna Green *(G-3850)*
Strobel Mfg Inc .... G 812 282-4388
  Jeffersonville *(G-10061)*
Strykeril Industries LLC .... G 219 321-0400
  Fort Wayne *(G-5447)*
Stylish Unique Salon LLC .... G 317 938-1273
  Indianapolis *(G-9519)*
Suitable Stylez .... G 765 409-9375
  Lafayette *(G-10705)*
Summerville Miniature Work Sp .... G 317 326-8355
  Greenfield *(G-6561)*
Super Spa Xclusives LLC .... G 219 448-1486
  Hammond *(G-7016)*
Sweetjoy Company LLC .... G 502 821-0511
  New Albany *(G-12820)*
Synergy Industries Inc .... G 574 320-2754
  Elkhart *(G-3711)*
▲ T & S Equipment Company .... D 260 665-9521
  Angola *(G-297)*
T S Manufacturing .... G 574 831-6647
  New Paris *(G-12971)*
Taunyas Creative Cuts .... G 812 574-7722
  Madison *(G-11253)*
Taylor Made Candles .... G 812 663-6634
  Greensburg *(G-6634)*
Tbin LLC .... G 812 491-9100
  Princeton *(G-14013)*
Teach ME Stuff .... G 317 550-6319
  Brownsburg *(G-1406)*
Tech Tronic LLC .... G 260 750-7992
  Fort Wayne *(G-5471)*
Techcom Inc .... F 812 372-0960
  Columbus *(G-2401)*
Terrapin Mfg .... G 717 339-6007
  Fort Wayne *(G-5477)*
Thanatos Manufacturing LLC .... G 260 251-8498
  Portland *(G-13969)*
The Eminence Hair Collectn LLC .... G 317 300-6051
  Indianapolis *(G-9588)*
Thermtron Mfg Inc .... G 260 622-6000
  Ossian *(G-13439)*

Thomas Products & Services Inc .... G 217 463-3999
  Clinton *(G-2079)*
Thomas Strickler .... G 574 457-2473
  Syracuse *(G-15485)*
Thomson Industries Inc .... G 574 529-2496
  Syracuse *(G-15486)*
Timberlight Manufacturing Co .... G 317 694-1317
  Indianapolis *(G-9604)*
Timothy Hoover Industries LLC .... G 812 987-6342
  Jeffersonville *(G-10064)*
Tis Holding Inc .... G 317 946-6354
  Indianapolis *(G-9609)*
Titus Mfg LLC .... G 574 286-1928
  Plymouth *(G-13818)*
Tk Elevator Corporation .... D 317 595-1125
  Indianapolis *(G-9612)*
TLC Candle Co LLC .... G 317 313-3029
  Fishers *(G-4613)*
Tmk Manufacturing LLC .... G 765 763-6754
  Morristown *(G-12281)*
Todds Hydrlcs RPR & Stl Fbrct .... G 812 466-3457
  Terre Haute *(G-15733)*
Tonis Touch LLC .... G 317 992-1280
  Plainfield *(G-13737)*
Tooties Zenergy Candles LLC .... G 317 437-9936
  Indianapolis *(G-9619)*
Topnotch Locs LLC .... G 260 557-9628
  Indianapolis *(G-9621)*
Transformation Industries LLC .... G 574 457-9320
  South Bend *(G-15288)*
Travis Industries Inc .... G 260 479-7807
  New Haven *(G-12922)*
Trellis Growing Systems LLC .... G 260 241-3128
  Fort Wayne *(G-5504)*
Tri-State Shtmtl & Mfg LLC .... G 260 402-8831
  Fort Wayne *(G-5507)*
Tri-State Veterinary Sup Inc .... G 812 477-4793
  Evansville *(G-4352)*
Trinity Displays LLC .... G 219 201-8733
  Chesterton *(G-1961)*
Troyc-Industries LLC .... G 317 531-1660
  Indianapolis *(G-9649)*
True Precision Tech Inc .... G 765 432-2177
  Kokomo *(G-10352)*
Tspdesign LLC .... G 317 785-8663
  Anderson *(G-210)*
Turning Over A New Leaf LLC .... G 765 573-3366
  Gas City *(G-6040)*
Twisod Wick Candle Company .... G 317 490-4789
  Martinsville *(G-11432)*
Twisted Wick Candle Co .... G 317 490-4789
  Nashville *(G-12681)*
Tyler Truss LLC .... D 765 221-5050
  Pendleton *(G-13559)*
Ubackoff .... G 317 557-3951
  Indianapolis *(G-9673)*
Ultimate Mfg .... G 765 517-1160
  Marion *(G-11346)*
Ultra Mfg LLC .... G 574 354-2564
  New Paris *(G-12972)*
Union City Coatings LLC .... G 765 717-3919
  Union City *(G-15862)*
Unlimited Manufacturing LLC .... G 260 515-3332
  Avilla *(G-497)*
Unplug Soy Candles .... G 217 520-2658
  Fishers *(G-4623)*
Unplug Soy Candles LLC .... G 317 650-5776
  Fortville *(G-5608)*
Upcycle Industrial Inc .... G 574 825-4990
  Middlebury *(G-11755)*
Urban Rustic Farmhouse LLC .... G 317 238-0945
  New Palestine *(G-12944)*

Vandelay Industries Ind Inc .... G 574 202-2367
  Bristol *(G-1297)*
Vandelay Properties LLC .... G 574 529-4795
  Syracuse *(G-15489)*
Vandeleigh Industries LLC .... G 574 326-3254
  Elkhart *(G-3768)*
Vemme Kart Usa LLC .... G 317 407-7172
  Mooresville *(G-12249)*
Verne Lambright .... G 260 593-0250
  Topeka *(G-15822)*
Vestil Manufacturing Corp .... G 260 665-7586
  Angola *(G-305)*
Vestil Manufacturing Corp .... G 800 348-0860
  Angola *(G-307)*
◆ Vestil Manufacturing Corp .... C 260 665-7586
  Angola *(G-306)*
Veterans Industries and Arts .... G 317 730-1815
  Indianapolis *(G-9714)*
Vickie Hildreth .... G 812 350-3575
  Columbus *(G-2414)*
Vintage Road Candles .... G 765 621-3561
  Alexandria *(G-64)*
Wagners Tree Service .... G 219 608-1525
  La Porte *(G-10497)*
Wahs Candle Studio .... G 734 846-5654
  Sharpsville *(G-14715)*
Walls Lawn & Garden Inc .... G 317 535-9059
  Whiteland *(G-16799)*
Walnut Creek Fabrication Inc .... G 765 749-1226
  Portland *(G-13975)*
Warm Glow Candle Company .... E 765 855-5483
  Centerville *(G-1855)*
Warm Glow Candle Outlet .... G 765 855-2000
  Centerville *(G-1856)*
Watchdog Manufacturing LLC .... G 574 218-6604
  Bristol *(G-1298)*
Watchdog Manufacturing LLC .... G 574 536-2445
  Elkhart *(G-3780)*
Well Done Industries LLC .... G 219 838-5201
  Lowell *(G-11180)*
Whistle Stop .... G 219 253-4100
  Monon *(G-12059)*
White Cap LLC .... G 812 425-6221
  Evansville *(G-4384)*
Wicone .... G 219 218-5199
  Hammond *(G-7033)*
Wiley Industries Incorporated .... G 317 574-1477
  Carmel *(G-1805)*
Williams Bros Hlth Care Phrm I .... E 812 335-0000
  Bloomington *(G-1012)*
Williams Bros Hlth Care Phrm I .... C 812 254-2497
  Washington *(G-16513)*
Wilson Industries .... G 313 330-0643
  New Albany *(G-12829)*
Wimmer Mfg Inc .... G 765 465-9846
  New Castle *(G-12886)*
Wink Anti Tip LLC .... G 812 305-3165
  Evansville *(G-4388)*
Wreath Inc .... G 812 939-3439
  Clay City *(G-2049)*
XYZ Model Works .... G 260 413-1873
  Decatur *(G-2889)*
Yankee Candle Company Inc .... G 812 526-5195
  Edinburgh *(G-3110)*
Yellow Cup LLC .... G 260 403-3489
  Fort Wayne *(G-5580)*
Yes Feed & Supply LLC .... G 765 361-9821
  Crawfordsville *(G-2628)*
York Tank and Mfg LLC .... F 765 401-0667
  Kingman *(G-10175)*
Young & Kenady Incorporated .... G 317 852-6300
  Brownsburg *(G-1415)*

Employee Codes: A=Over 500 employees, B=251-500
C=101-250, D=51-100, E=20-50, F=10-19, G=1-9

39 MISCELLANEOUS MANUFACTURING INDUSTRIES

Zaffer Industries LLC............................ G..... 317 910-4958
Indianapolis *(G-9807)*

40 RAILROAD TRANSPORTATION

4011 Railroads, line-haul operating

Transworks Inc..................................... G..... 619 441-0133
Fort Wayne *(G-5501)*

41 LOCAL & SUBURBAN TRANSIT & INTERURBAN HIGHWAY TRANSPORTATION

4131 Intercity and rural bus transportation

Cardinal Services Inc Indiana................ D..... 574 267-3823
Warsaw *(G-16333)*

4151 School buses

Kuharic Enterprises.............................. G..... 574 288-9410
South Bend *(G-15110)*

42 MOTOR FREIGHT TRANSPORTATION

4212 Local trucking, without storage

All American Ex Solutions LLC............. E..... 317 789-3070
Indianapolis *(G-7472)*
Band Brothers Transport LLC................ G..... 317 709-4415
Indianapolis *(G-7592)*
Blackwood Solutions LLC..................... D..... 812 676-8770
Bloomington *(G-809)*
C & C Pallets and Lumber LLC.............. G..... 765 524-3214
New Castle *(G-12855)*
Carmichael Welding Inc....................... G..... 812 825-5156
Bloomfield *(G-742)*
Dash CAM Fusion LLC......................... G..... 708 365-8553
Indianapolis *(G-7953)*
Dbisp LLC... G..... 317 222-1671
Indianapolis *(G-7957)*
Gbj Holdings LLC................................ G..... 317 483-1896
Highland *(G-7137)*
Gravel Conveyors Inc.......................... F..... 317 873-8686
Zionsville *(G-17014)*
Indiana Whitesell Corporation.............. B..... 317 279-3278
Indianapolis *(G-8500)*
▲ Industrial Mint Wldg Machining........ E..... 219 393-5531
Kingsbury *(G-10179)*
Kellers Limestone Service Inc.............. G..... 219 326-1688
La Porte *(G-10432)*
Kendallville Iron & Metal Inc................ F..... 260 347-1958
Kendallville *(G-10126)*
Krafft Gravel Inc.................................. G..... 260 238-4653
Spencerville *(G-15372)*
Lees Ready-Mix & Trucking................. E
Shelbyville *(G-14772)*
Lees Ready-Mix & Trucking Inc............ F..... 812 372-1800
Columbus *(G-2339)*
LPI Paving & Excavating...................... G..... 260 726-9564
Portland *(G-13955)*
Mnt Delivery Company........................ G..... 574 518-6250
Osceola *(G-13399)*
Paddack Brothers Inc.......................... G..... 765 659-4777
Frankfort *(G-5689)*
R & R Trucking & Freight LLC.............. G..... 888 477-8782
Indianapolis *(G-9254)*
Raymone Sanders Fmly Trckg LLC....... G..... 317 400-3545
Indianapolis *(G-9272)*
Rex Alton & Companies Inc................. F..... 812 882-8519
Vincennes *(G-16149)*

Van Duyne Block and Gravel................ G..... 574 223-6656
Rochester *(G-14331)*

4213 Trucking, except local

Accra-Pac Inc..................................... G..... 574 295-0000
Elkhart *(G-3149)*
CDP Logistics Inc................................ G..... 773 968-1455
Avon *(G-510)*
▲ Cresline Plastic Pipe Co Inc.............. E..... 812 428-9300
Evansville *(G-3994)*
▲ Frick Services Inc............................. E..... 260 761-3311
Wawaka *(G-16539)*
Full Throttle Enterprise Inc.................. G..... 317 779-3887
Indianapolis *(G-8240)*
▲ Haas Cabinet Co Inc......................... C..... 812 246-4431
Sellersburg *(G-14594)*
Jdh Logistics LLC................................ G..... 573 529-2005
Fort Branch *(G-4705)*
Jennings County Pallets Inc................. E..... 812 458-6288
Butlerville *(G-1484)*
◆ Popcorn Weaver Mfg LLC................. C..... 765 934-2101
Indianapolis *(G-9162)*
Southlake Lift Truck............................ G..... 219 962-4695
Gary *(G-6013)*
Stacks Limited.................................... G..... 765 409-5081
Lafayette *(G-10697)*
T Organization Inc.............................. E..... 463 204-5118
Greenwood *(G-6771)*
Zip Zone Gone LLC............................. G..... 812 604-0041
Evansville *(G-4393)*

4214 Local trucking with storage

Blackwood Solutions LLC..................... D..... 812 676-8770
Bloomington *(G-809)*
Kic LLC.. E..... 360 823-4440
Evansville *(G-4152)*
Simmons Equipment Sales Inc............. F..... 260 625-3308
Columbia City *(G-2197)*

4215 Courier services, except by air

Cygnus Home Service LLC................... D..... 317 882-6624
Danville *(G-2810)*
United Parcel Service Inc..................... G..... 317 776-9494
Noblesville *(G-13189)*
UPS Store 5219.................................. G..... 219 750-9597
Merrillville *(G-11570)*

4221 Farm product warehousing and storage

▲ Frick Services Inc............................. E..... 260 761-3311
Wawaka *(G-16539)*

4222 Refrigerated warehousing and storage

United States Cold Storage Inc............. E..... 765 482-2653
Lebanon *(G-10949)*

4225 General warehousing and storage

AEL/Span LLC.................................... E..... 317 203-4602
Plainfield *(G-13656)*
▲ Agi International Inc......................... F..... 317 536-2415
Indianapolis *(G-7458)*
Airxcel Inc... B..... 574 294-5681
Elkhart *(G-3156)*
Alpha Baking Co Inc........................... G..... 574 234-0188
South Bend *(G-14938)*
Bendix Coml Vhcl Systems LLC............ E..... 260 356-9720
Huntington *(G-7301)*
Bootz Manufacturing Co LLC................ C..... 812 425-4646
Evansville *(G-3942)*
Gary Bridge and Iron Co Inc................. G..... 219 884-3792
Gary *(G-5936)*
▲ Georg Utz Inc.................................. E..... 812 526-2240
Edinburgh *(G-3085)*

▲ Haas Cabinet Co Inc......................... C..... 812 246-4431
Sellersburg *(G-14594)*
Hickman Williams & Company............. G..... 219 379-5199
La Porte *(G-10419)*
Indiana Research Institute................... G..... 812 378-5363
Columbus *(G-2325)*
Indiana Whitesell Corporation.............. B..... 317 279-3278
Indianapolis *(G-8500)*
KYB Americas Corporation................... B..... 317 881-7772
Greenwood *(G-6726)*
Mark Concrete Products Inc................. G..... 317 398-8616
Shelbyville *(G-14774)*
▲ Phoenix Assembly Indiana LLC......... G..... 317 884-3600
Columbus *(G-2378)*
Pridgeon & Clay Inc............................ G..... 317 738-4885
Franklin *(G-5770)*
◆ Proedge Inc..................................... E..... 219 552-9550
Shelby *(G-14727)*
Revolution Materials (in) LLC............... D..... 812 234-2724
Terre Haute *(G-15680)*
▲ Tfi Inc... E..... 317 290-1333
Whitestown *(G-16825)*
Thormax Enterprises LLC..................... G..... 812 530-7744
Seymour *(G-14699)*
Toyota Tsusho America Inc.................. D..... 765 449-3500
Colburn *(G-2111)*
Westrock Cp LLC................................ G..... 574 936-2118
Plymouth *(G-13828)*

4226 Special warehousing and storage, nec

Coca-Cola Bottling Co......................... E..... 812 332-4434
Bloomington *(G-831)*
P-Americas LLC.................................. G..... 812 522-3421
Seymour *(G-14670)*
Quaker Chemical Corp........................ G..... 765 668-2441
Marion *(G-11332)*
Toyota Tsusho America Inc.................. D..... 765 449-3500
Colburn *(G-2111)*
Wireamerica Inc................................. G..... 260 969-1700
Fort Wayne *(G-5571)*

4231 Trucking terminal facilities

Smiles Motors LLC.............................. G..... 219 801-5255
Highland *(G-7156)*

44 WATER TRANSPORTATION

4449 Water transportation of freight

Acbl Holding Corporation..................... A..... 310 712-1850
Jeffersonville *(G-9921)*
Acl Sales Corporation.......................... G..... 812 288-0100
Jeffersonville *(G-9923)*
American Barge Line Company............. G..... 812 288-0100
Jeffersonville *(G-9930)*
American Coml Barge Line LLC............ C..... 812 288-0100
Jeffersonville *(G-9931)*
American Commercial Lines Inc........... C..... 812 288-0100
Jeffersonville *(G-9932)*
Commercial Barge Line Company......... E..... 812 288-0100
Jeffersonville *(G-9956)*

4491 Marine cargo handling

Acbl Holding Corporation..................... A..... 310 712-1850
Jeffersonville *(G-9921)*
Acl Professional Services Inc............... C..... 812 288-0100
Jeffersonville *(G-9922)*
Acl Sales Corporation.......................... G..... 812 288-0100
Jeffersonville *(G-9923)*
American Barge Line Company............. G..... 812 288-0100
Jeffersonville *(G-9930)*
American Coml Barge Line LLC............ C..... 812 288-0100
Jeffersonville *(G-9931)*

American Commercial Lines Inc............... C 812 288-0100
  Jeffersonville *(G-9932)*
Commercial Barge Line Company......... E 812 288-0100
  Jeffersonville *(G-9956)*
Culvers Port Side Marina...................... G 574 223-5090
  Rochester *(G-14285)*
Evansville Marine Service Inc................. E 812 424-9278
  Evansville *(G-4053)*
VMS Products Inc................................. G 888 321-4698
  Anderson *(G-214)*

4492 Towing and tugboat service
Evansville Marine Service Inc................. E 812 424-9278
  Evansville *(G-4053)*

4493 Marinas
Culvers Port Side Marina...................... G 574 223-5090
  Rochester *(G-14285)*
Leco Corporation.................................. G 574 288-9017
  South Bend *(G-15122)*
West Lakes Marine Inc......................... F 260 854-2525
  Rome City *(G-14378)*

45 TRANSPORTATION BY AIR

4581 Airports, flying fields, and services
Indy Aerospace Inc............................... G 817 521-6508
  Indianapolis *(G-8522)*
Mj Aircraft Inc...................................... F 765 378-7700
  Anderson *(G-156)*
Turbines Inc.. E 812 877-2587
  Terre Haute *(G-15737)*

47 TRANSPORTATION SERVICES

4724 Travel agencies
American Ex Trvl Rlted Svcs In.............. G 812 523-0106
  Seymour *(G-14629)*
▼ R Drew & Co Inc................................ G 765 420-7232
  West Lafayette *(G-16624)*
Safe Travels Solutions LLC.................... G 317 640-4576
  Indianapolis *(G-9363)*

4731 Freight transportation arrangement
Envista Concepts LLC.......................... C 317 208-9100
  Carmel *(G-1627)*
Envista Freight Managment LLC............ C 317 208-9100
  Carmel *(G-1629)*
▲ Phoenix Assembly LLC....................... D 317 884-3600
  Greenwood *(G-6751)*
▲ Phoenix Assembly Indiana LLC........... G 317 884-3600
  Columbus *(G-2378)*
T Organization Inc................................ E 463 204-5118
  Greenwood *(G-6771)*
Tpg Mt Vernon Marine LLC.................... C 317 631-0234
  Indianapolis *(G-9626)*

4741 Rental of railroad cars
▲ Transportation Tech Inds..................... F 812 962-5000
  Evansville *(G-4347)*

4783 Packing and crating
Packaging Group Corp.......................... F 219 879-2500
  Michigan City *(G-11649)*
Red Gold Inc.. G 260 726-8140
  Portland *(G-13966)*
VMS Products Inc................................. G 888 321-4698
  Anderson *(G-214)*

4785 Inspection and fixed facilities
T K Sales & Service............................. G 219 962-8982
  Gary *(G-6017)*

4789 Transportation services, nec
Aon(all or Nothing) LLC......................... G 219 405-0163
  Indianapolis *(G-7524)*
B6 Transports LLC............................... G 317 975-0053
  Fishers *(G-4469)*
Ftn Logistics LLC.................................. G 317 488-7446
  Indianapolis *(G-8237)*
Noble Transportation LLC...................... G 317 488-7710
  Indianapolis *(G-9016)*
Professnal Locomotive Svcs Inc............ E 219 398-9123
  East Chicago *(G-3036)*
Progress Rail Mfg Corp......................... C 765 281-2685
  Muncie *(G-12480)*
Progress Rail Services Corp.................. C 219 397-5326
  East Chicago *(G-3037)*
Sailor Group LLC.................................. G 574 226-0362
  Elkhart *(G-3660)*
Stop N Go Transport LLC...................... G 317 902-0815
  Indianapolis *(G-9515)*
Street Dreams Production Inc............... G 574 440-9136
  South Bend *(G-15269)*
Zip Zone Gone LLC............................... G 812 604-0041
  Evansville *(G-4393)*

48 COMMUNICATIONS

4812 Radiotelephone communication
Commtineo LLC.................................... F 219 476-3667
  Wanatah *(G-16288)*
Furtrieve LLC....................................... G 317 325-8010
  Fishers *(G-4529)*

4813 Telephone communication, except radio
Flight1 Aviation Tech Inc...................... G 404 504-7010
  Wabash *(G-16186)*
Hoosier Times Inc................................. C 812 331-4270
  Bloomington *(G-882)*
Indy Web Inc.. G 317 536-1201
  Indianapolis *(G-8537)*
Mobile Communications Tech................ G 812 423-7322
  Evansville *(G-4207)*
▲ Plum Group Inc.................................. F 617 712-3000
  Indianapolis *(G-9155)*
Scanpower LLC.................................... G 765 277-2308
  Richmond *(G-14201)*
Sky Cryptoassets LLC........................... G 949 903-6896
  Carmel *(G-1763)*
Slingshot Media LLC............................. G 765 778-6848
  Pendleton *(G-13555)*
▲ Telamon Corporation.......................... C 317 818-6888
  Carmel *(G-1777)*
Telamon Spv LLC................................. G 800 788-6680
  Carmel *(G-1780)*
Tuthill Corporation................................ C 260 747-7529
  Fort Wayne *(G-5515)*
Vectren LLC... G 812 424-6411
  Evansville *(G-4369)*

4822 Telegraph and other communications
◆ David Camp...................................... G 812 346-6255
  North Vernon *(G-13265)*
Paper Chase.. G 812 385-4757
  Princeton *(G-14009)*

4832 Radio broadcasting stations
Continntal Broadcast Group LLC........... E 317 924-1071
  Indianapolis *(G-7858)*
DMC Distribution LLC............................ G 219 926-6401
  Porter *(G-13924)*
Emmis Corporation............................... D 317 266-0100
  Indianapolis *(G-8106)*

Emmis Operating Company.................. E 317 266-0100
  Indianapolis *(G-8107)*
The Findlay Publishing Co.................... G 812 222-8000
  Batesville *(G-606)*
World Rdo Mssnary Fllwship Inc........... G 574 970-4252
  Elkhart *(G-3793)*

4833 Television broadcasting stations
Emmis Operating Company.................. E 317 266-0100
  Indianapolis *(G-8107)*
Schurz Communications Inc................. F 574 247-7237
  Mishawaka *(G-11992)*

4841 Cable and other pay television services
American Eagle Security Inc.................. G 219 980-1177
  Merrillville *(G-11482)*
Essex Frkawa Mgnt Wire USA LLC....... G 260 424-1708
  Columbia City *(G-2144)*
Times.. E 765 659-4622
  Frankfort *(G-5698)*
Vectren LLC... G 812 424-6411
  Evansville *(G-4369)*
Vision Aid Systems Inc......................... G 317 888-0323
  Greenwood *(G-6778)*
Woody Enterprises LLC........................ G 765 498-7300
  Bloomingdale *(G-763)*

4899 Communication services, nec
American Eagle Security Inc.................. G 219 980-1177
  Merrillville *(G-11482)*
Loud Clear Communications LLC.......... G 260 433-9479
  Auburn *(G-403)*
Mobile Communications Tech................ G 812 423-7322
  Evansville *(G-4207)*
Optiviz Media LLC................................ G 812 681-1711
  Vincennes *(G-16141)*
Slingshot Media LLC............................. G 765 778-6848
  Pendleton *(G-13555)*

49 ELECTRIC, GAS AND SANITARY SERVICES

4911 Electric services
Futurewerks LLC.................................. G 305 926-3633
  Indianapolis *(G-8247)*
Metergenius Inc................................... G 317 979-8257
  Indianapolis *(G-8894)*
P&C Prime LLC.................................... F 231 420-3650
  Fredericksburg *(G-5795)*
Vectren LLC... G 812 424-6411
  Evansville *(G-4369)*
Vectren LLC... A 812 491-4000
  Evansville *(G-4368)*

4922 Natural gas transmission
ANR Pipeline Company......................... G 260 463-3342
  Lagrange *(G-10728)*

4924 Natural gas distribution
◆ K Grimmer Industries Inc................... C 317 736-3800
  Leo *(G-10968)*
Vectren LLC... G 812 424-6411
  Evansville *(G-4369)*
Vectren LLC... A 812 491-4000
  Evansville *(G-4368)*

4925 Gas production and/or distribution
Citizens Energy Group.......................... F 317 261-8794
  Indianapolis *(G-7812)*
Sssi Inc... F 219 880-0818
  Gary *(G-6015)*

49 ELECTRIC, GAS AND SANITARY SERVICES

4931 Electric and other services combined

Sdf Engineering LLC .... G 317 674-2643
  Carmel *(G-1755)*

4953 Refuse systems

Aqua Utility Services LLC .... G 812 284-9243
  New Albany *(G-12690)*
Blackwood Solutions LLC .... D 812 676-8770
  Bloomington *(G-809)*
Cgs Services Inc .... G 765 763-6258
  Morristown *(G-12273)*
Circle Medical Products Inc .... G 317 271-2626
  Indianapolis *(G-7809)*
Concrete & Asphalt Recycl Inc .... G 574 237-1928
  Mishawaka *(G-11864)*
Creative Ldscp & Compost Co .... G 317 776-2909
  Noblesville *(G-13065)*
Ecobat Resources Cal Inc .... B 317 247-1303
  Indianapolis *(G-8049)*
Enviri Corporation .... F 219 397-0200
  East Chicago *(G-3007)*
Green Stream Company .... C 574 293-1949
  Elkhart *(G-3391)*
Greencycle Inc .... G 317 773-3350
  Noblesville *(G-13089)*
Hunts Maintenance Inc .... G 219 785-2333
  Westville *(G-16762)*
K & S Pallet Inc .... E 260 422-1264
  Fort Wayne *(G-5141)*
Mervis Industries Inc .... G 812 232-1251
  Terre Haute *(G-15643)*
◆ Plastic Recycling Inc .... E 317 780-6100
  Indianapolis *(G-9151)*
Recycling Center Inc .... D 765 966-8295
  Richmond *(G-14195)*
Recycling Works LLC .... F 574 293-3751
  Elkhart *(G-3644)*
Tradebe Environmental Svcs LLC .... E 800 388-7242
  Merrillville *(G-11568)*
Tradebe GP .... A 800 388-7242
  East Chicago *(G-3045)*
Winski Brothers Inc .... G 765 654-5323
  Frankfort *(G-5702)*

4959 Sanitary services, nec

County of Lagrange .... F 260 499-6353
  Lagrange *(G-10732)*
Sorbtech Inc .... G 812 944-9108
  Clarksville *(G-2037)*

4961 Steam and air-conditioning supply

Gbi Air Systems Inc .... G 574 272-0600
  Granger *(G-6348)*
Waterfurnace International Inc .... B 260 478-5667
  Fort Wayne *(G-5549)*

50 WHOLESALE TRADE - DURABLE GOODS

5012 Automobiles and other motor vehicles

Airxcel Inc .... B 574 294-5681
  Elkhart *(G-3156)*
All American Group Inc .... G 574 825-5821
  Middlebury *(G-11694)*
All American Group Inc .... G 574 825-8555
  Middlebury *(G-11695)*
Bulk Truck & Transport Service .... E 812 866-2155
  Hanover *(G-7040)*
Coachmen Recrtl Vhcl Co LLC .... G 574 825-5821
  Middlebury *(G-11704)*
▲ Dmi Holding Corp .... C 574 534-1224
  Goshen *(G-6123)*
Dna Enterprises Inc .... E 574 534-0034
  Elkhart *(G-3298)*
Fenwick Motor Sports .... G 765 522-1354
  Bainbridge *(G-562)*
Fire Apparatus Service Inc .... G 219 985-0788
  Gary *(G-5933)*
Forest River Inc .... A 574 296-7700
  Elkhart *(G-3353)*
Forest River Inc .... C 574 533-5934
  Goshen *(G-6141)*
Forest River Inc .... C 574 642-2640
  Millersburg *(G-11812)*
Grouper Wild LLC .... C 574 534-1499
  Goshen *(G-6156)*
Holiday House LLC .... F 574 206-0016
  Elkhart *(G-3408)*
Keyline Sales Inc .... G 574 294-5611
  Elkhart *(G-3453)*
Mid-State Truck Equipment Inc .... E 317 849-4903
  Fishers *(G-4566)*
Selking International LLC .... E 260 482-3000
  Fort Wayne *(G-5408)*
Selking International Inc .... G 574 522-2001
  Elkhart *(G-3668)*
Showtime Conversions Inc .... E 574 825-1130
  Middlebury *(G-11752)*
Skyline Corporation .... C 574 294-2463
  Elkhart *(G-3682)*
Sparkling Clean Inc .... G 812 422-4871
  Evansville *(G-4326)*
Thor Industries Inc .... F 574 262-2624
  Elkhart *(G-3731)*
Wabash National Corporation .... E 765 771-5300
  Lafayette *(G-10715)*
▲ Wabash National Corporation .... A 765 771-5310
  Lafayette *(G-10716)*
Wakarusa Ag LLC .... F 574 862-1163
  Wakarusa *(G-16256)*
Wee Engineer Inc .... F 765 449-4280
  Dayton *(G-2838)*

5013 Motor vehicle supplies and new parts

◆ Abro Industries Inc .... E 574 232-8289
  South Bend *(G-14933)*
▲ Action Machine Inc .... F 574 287-9650
  South Bend *(G-14935)*
Afco Performance Group LLC .... F 812 897-0900
  Boonville *(G-1079)*
◆ Allied Enterprises LLC .... E 765 288-8849
  Muncie *(G-12339)*
Asc Inc .... C 765 473-4438
  Peru *(G-13567)*
◆ Auto Bumper Exchange Inc .... G 260 493-4408
  Fort Wayne *(G-4780)*
Axis Products Inc .... C 574 266-8282
  Elkhart *(G-3207)*
▲ Ben Tire Distributors Ltd .... E 317 798-2013
  Indianapolis *(G-7612)*
◆ Boyer Machine & Tool Co Inc .... E 812 379-9581
  Columbus *(G-2228)*
◆ Brake Supply Company Inc .... C 812 467-1000
  Evansville *(G-3950)*
C & P Machine Service Inc .... F 260 484-4723
  Fort Wayne *(G-4827)*
▲ Chiyoda USA Corporation .... C 765 653-9098
  Greencastle *(G-6396)*
Chubbs Steel Sales Inc .... E 574 295-3166
  Elkhart *(G-3252)*
Conversion Components Inc .... G 574 264-4181
  Elkhart *(G-3266)*
Cummins Inc .... G 812 524-6455
  Columbus *(G-2264)*
Frank Wiss Racg Components Inc .... G 317 243-9585
  Indianapolis *(G-8222)*
Hibbing International Friction .... F 765 529-7001
  New Castle *(G-12867)*
Hoosier Fire Equipment Inc .... F 219 462-1707
  Valparaiso *(G-15965)*
Indiana Discount Tire Company .... G 574 875-8547
  Elkhart *(G-3421)*
Indiana Discount Tire Company .... G 574 549-6060
  Warsaw *(G-16377)*
Indianapolis In .... E 855 628-3458
  Indianapolis *(G-8502)*
◆ Jayco Inc .... A 574 825-5861
  Middlebury *(G-11727)*
KOI Enterprises Inc .... D 812 537-2335
  Lawrenceburg *(G-10843)*
Marmon Highway Tech LLC .... E 317 787-0718
  Indianapolis *(G-8839)*
Meritor Inc .... G 317 279-2180
  Plainfield *(G-13706)*
Mid-State Truck Equipment Inc .... E 317 849-4903
  Fishers *(G-4566)*
Midwest Mat Company .... G 765 286-0831
  Muncie *(G-12455)*
Mirrus Corporation Inc .... F 812 689-1411
  Versailles *(G-16102)*
Motsinger Auto Supply Inc .... G 317 782-8484
  Indianapolis *(G-8960)*
◆ Muncie Power Products Inc .... E 765 284-7721
  Muncie *(G-12464)*
Pfm Automotive Management Inc .... G 317 733-3977
  Zionsville *(G-17040)*
Pfm Car & Truck Castleton Inc .... E 317 577-7777
  Indianapolis *(G-9131)*
Pfm Onsite Services Inc .... G 317 784-7777
  Indianapolis *(G-9132)*
▲ Phoenix Assembly LLC .... D 317 884-3600
  Greenwood *(G-6751)*
Promotor Engines & Components .... G 574 533-9898
  Goshen *(G-6243)*
Smart Technologies LLC .... G 317 738-4338
  Franklin *(G-5777)*
◆ Stant USA Corp .... C 765 825-3121
  Connersville *(G-2470)*
Staples Pipe & Muffler .... G 812 522-3569
  Butlerville *(G-1488)*
Switzerland Hills Inc .... F 812 594-2810
  Patriot *(G-13511)*
T & M Equipment Company Inc .... F 317 293-9255
  Indianapolis *(G-9543)*
▲ Voss Automotive Inc .... D 260 373-2277
  Fort Wayne *(G-5536)*
Wb Automotive Holdings Inc .... G 734 604-8962
  Fort Wayne *(G-5557)*

5014 Tires and tubes

Bernard Burns .... G 574 382-5019
  Macy *(G-11194)*
Best-One Kentuckiana Inc .... E 812 285-5400
  Jeffersonville *(G-9941)*
▲ Cast Products LP .... E 574 294-2684
  Elkhart *(G-3249)*
Clark Tire Fishers Inc .... G 317 842-0544
  Fishers *(G-4490)*
▲ Dehco Inc .... D 574 294-2684
  Elkhart *(G-3288)*
Gentis Tire & Service Inc .... E 765 348-2400
  Hartford City *(G-7066)*
Hellmans Auto Supply Co Inc .... G 219 885-7655
  Gary *(G-5949)*

SIC SECTION
50 WHOLESALE TRADE - DURABLE GOODS

◆ Hoosier Racing Tire Corp.............................G..... 574 784-3152
  Lakeville *(G-10792)*

Hughes Tire Service Inc.................................F..... 812 883-4981
  Salem *(G-14481)*

McCord Tire Service Inc................................F..... 812 235-8016
  Terre Haute *(G-15639)*

Midwest Auto Repair Inc...............................F..... 219 322-0364
  Schererville *(G-14534)*

Midwest Mat Company..................................G..... 765 286-0831
  Muncie *(G-12455)*

Pomps Tire Service Inc..................................E..... 260 489-5252
  Fort Wayne *(G-5326)*

Portland Tire & Service Inc............................G..... 260 726-9321
  Portland *(G-13962)*

Reis Tire Sales Inc...E..... 812 425-2229
  Evansville *(G-4283)*

◆ Tire Rack Inc...B..... 888 541-1777
  South Bend *(G-15283)*

Trusty Tires Inc...G..... 812 738-4212
  Corydon *(G-2519)*

5015 Motor vehicle parts, used

▲ A-Fab LLC...F..... 812 897-0900
  Boonville *(G-1078)*

◆ Auto Bumper Exchange Inc.........................G..... 260 493-4408
  Fort Wayne *(G-4780)*

Cortex Safety Technologies LLC....................G..... 317 414-5607
  Carmel *(G-1598)*

E & M Tire Salvage Inc.................................G..... 260 745-3016
  Fort Wayne *(G-4936)*

Indiana Discount Tire Company.....................G..... 574 875-8547
  Elkhart *(G-3421)*

KOI Enterprises Inc......................................D..... 812 537-2335
  Lawrenceburg *(G-10843)*

Power Train Corp Fort Wayne.......................F..... 317 241-9393
  Indianapolis *(G-9167)*

5021 Furniture

Altstadt Business Forms Inc..........................F..... 812 425-3393
  Evansville *(G-3882)*

American Natural Resources LLC..................F..... 219 922-6444
  Griffith *(G-6790)*

Arran Isle Inc...E..... 574 295-4400
  Elkhart *(G-3191)*

C & C Mailbox Products................................G..... 765 358-4880
  Gaston *(G-6044)*

▲ Candles By Dar Inc....................................F..... 260 482-2099
  Fort Wayne *(G-4831)*

Country Woodshop LLC................................E..... 574 642-3681
  Goshen *(G-6117)*

▼ Craft Metal Products Inc...........................G..... 317 545-3252
  Indianapolis *(G-7897)*

▲ DStyle Inc..F..... 619 662-0560
  Jasper *(G-9833)*

Durogreen Outdoor LLC................................F..... 574 327-6943
  Elkhart *(G-3307)*

Family Leisurecom Inc..................................F..... 317 823-4448
  Indianapolis *(G-8164)*

▲ Ffesar Inc..G..... 812 378-4220
  Mccordsville *(G-11448)*

Furniture Distributors Inc..............................F..... 317 357-8508
  Indianapolis *(G-8243)*

▲ Global...G..... 317 494-6174
  Franklin *(G-5732)*

◆ J Squared Inc..D..... 317 866-5638
  Greenfield *(G-6521)*

◆ Jofco Inc..C..... 812 482-5154
  Jasper *(G-9861)*

◆ Jordan Manufacturing Co Inc.....................C..... 800 328-6522
  Monticello *(G-12155)*

◆ Lasalle Bristol Corporation.........................C..... 574 295-8400
  Elkhart *(G-3469)*

Lui Plus..G..... 812 309-9350
  Indianapolis *(G-8795)*

Martins Wood Works.....................................G..... 574 862-4080
  Goshen *(G-6215)*

Meilink Safe Company..................................D..... 812 941-0024
  New Albany *(G-12774)*

Oakleaf Industries Inc...................................G..... 317 414-2040
  Fishers *(G-4645)*

Pinnacle Mailing Products.............................F..... 765 405-1194
  Yorktown *(G-16980)*

Preferred Seating Company LLC...................G..... 317 782-3323
  Indianapolis *(G-9190)*

Smith & Butterfield Co Inc............................F..... 812 422-3261
  Evansville *(G-4320)*

Spectrum Finishing LLC................................G..... 260 463-7300
  Lagrange *(G-10762)*

5023 Homefurnishings

Arran Isle Inc...E..... 574 295-4400
  Elkhart *(G-3191)*

Benz Custom Metal LLC................................G..... 812 365-2613
  Marengo *(G-11261)*

Bock Engineering Company Inc....................G..... 574 522-3191
  Elkhart *(G-3229)*

◆ Brenco LLC..G..... 219 844-9570
  Schererville *(G-14517)*

▲ Candles By Dar Inc....................................F..... 260 482-2099
  Fort Wayne *(G-4831)*

Country Cabin LLC.......................................G..... 812 232-4635
  Terre Haute *(G-15569)*

▼ Craft Metal Products Inc...........................G..... 317 545-3252
  Indianapolis *(G-7897)*

Delaney Window Fashions LLC.....................G..... 317 567-7672
  Fishers *(G-4503)*

Editions Ltd Gllery Fine Art I........................G..... 317 466-9940
  Indianapolis *(G-8055)*

Faulkens Floorcover......................................F..... 574 300-4260
  South Bend *(G-15027)*

Georgia Direct Carpet Inc.............................F..... 765 966-2548
  Richmond *(G-14125)*

Lasalle Bristol Corporation............................F..... 574 295-4400
  Bristol *(G-1269)*

Lasalle Bristol Corporation............................F..... 574 936-9894
  Plymouth *(G-13791)*

◆ Lasalle Bristol Corporation.........................C..... 574 295-8400
  Elkhart *(G-3469)*

Midwest Blind & Shade Co...........................G..... 574 271-0770
  Mishawaka *(G-11947)*

◆ Onward Manufacturing Company................E..... 260 358-4111
  Huntington *(G-7346)*

Quality Drapery Corporation.........................G..... 765 481-2370
  Lebanon *(G-10936)*

◆ Santarossa Mosaic Tile Co Inc....................C..... 317 632-9494
  Indianapolis *(G-9371)*

Shaklee Authorized Distributor.....................G..... 260 471-8232
  Fort Wayne *(G-5410)*

◆ Sherwood Industries Inc............................E..... 574 262-2639
  Elkhart *(G-3672)*

Strawtown Pottery & Antq Inc......................G..... 317 984-5080
  Noblesville *(G-13180)*

Todd K Hockemeyer Inc................................G..... 260 639-3591
  Fort Wayne *(G-5492)*

◆ WC Redmon Co Inc...................................F..... 765 473-6683
  Peru *(G-13607)*

Willows and More...G..... 812 560-1088
  Westport *(G-16753)*

Zing Polymer Formations LLC.......................G..... 317 598-0480
  Fishers *(G-4637)*

5031 Lumber, plywood, and millwork

Affordable Luxury Homes Inc.......................D..... 260 758-2141
  Markle *(G-11353)*

All-Weather Products Inc..............................G..... 812 867-6403
  Evansville *(G-3880)*

Amgi LLC..G..... 317 447-1524
  New Palestine *(G-12928)*

Bee Window Incorporated.............................C..... 317 283-8522
  Fishers *(G-4473)*

Benthall Bros Inc..E..... 800 488-5995
  Evansville *(G-3915)*

Borkholder Corporation.................................E..... 574 773-4083
  Nappanee *(G-12585)*

Buckingham Pallets Inc.................................G..... 317 846-8601
  Carmel *(G-1574)*

Cardinal Glass Industries Inc........................B..... 260 495-4105
  Fremont *(G-5813)*

▲ Cast Products LP.......................................E..... 574 294-2684
  Elkhart *(G-3249)*

Chisholm Lumber & Supply Co.....................E..... 317 547-3535
  Indianapolis *(G-7799)*

Commercial Pallet Recycl Inc.......................G..... 260 668-6208
  Hudson *(G-7245)*

Commercial Pallet Recycl Inc.......................F..... 260 829-1021
  Orland *(G-13362)*

Countertop Manufacturing Inc......................E..... 765 966-4969
  Richmond *(G-14111)*

Country Woodshop LLC................................E..... 574 642-3681
  Goshen *(G-6117)*

▲ Dehco Inc..D..... 574 294-2684
  Elkhart *(G-3288)*

Dimension Plywood Inc.................................G..... 812 944-6491
  New Albany *(G-12719)*

Elko Inc..F..... 812 473-8400
  Evansville *(G-4030)*

Faulkens Floorcover......................................F..... 574 300-4260
  South Bend *(G-15027)*

Forest Products Group Inc............................F..... 765 659-1807
  Frankfort *(G-5665)*

Gordon Lumber Company..............................G..... 219 924-0500
  Griffith *(G-6804)*

Great Lakes Forest Pdts Inc.........................C..... 574 389-9663
  Elkhart *(G-3389)*

Gutter One Supply..F..... 317 872-1257
  Indianapolis *(G-8344)*

▲ Heitink Veneers Incorporated....................E..... 812 336-6436
  Bloomington *(G-876)*

Hollingsworth Sawmill Inc.............................F..... 765 883-5836
  Russiaville *(G-14422)*

Holman Lumber LLC.....................................G..... 260 337-0338
  Saint Joe *(G-14438)*

Hunter Nutrition Inc......................................F..... 765 563-1003
  Brookston *(G-1311)*

Industrial Lumber Products Inc....................G..... 219 324-7697
  La Porte *(G-10427)*

J M McCormick...G..... 317 874-4444
  Indianapolis *(G-8607)*

Jennings County Pallets Inc.........................E..... 812 458-6288
  Butlerville *(G-1484)*

K & S Pallet Inc..E..... 260 422-1264
  Fort Wayne *(G-5141)*

Kay Company Inc...E..... 765 659-3388
  Frankfort *(G-5677)*

Kinser Timber Products Inc..........................G..... 812 876-4775
  Gosport *(G-6285)*

Kountry Wood Products LLC.........................C..... 574 773-5673
  Nappanee *(G-12618)*

Lasalle Bristol Corporation............................F..... 574 293-5526
  Elkhart *(G-3470)*

Lazzaro Companies Inc................................E..... 219 980-0860
  Merrillville *(G-11529)*

▼ Mitchell Veneers Inc..................................G..... 812 941-9663
  New Albany *(G-12781)*

MJB Wood Group LLC..................................G..... 574 295-5228
  Elkhart *(G-3547)*

Employee Codes: A=Over 500 employees, B=251-500
C=101-250, D=51-100, E=20-50, F=10-19, G=1-9

50 WHOLESALE TRADE - DURABLE GOODS

National Products Inc .... E 574 457-4565
  Syracuse *(G-15469)*
North-Side Machine & Tool Inc .... F 765 654-4538
  Frankfort *(G-5686)*
Patrick Industries Inc .... D 574 294-8828
  Elkhart *(G-3592)*
▲ Patrick Industries Inc .... B 574 294-7511
  Elkhart *(G-3593)*
Patrick Industries Inc .... G 574 255-9692
  Mishawaka *(G-11971)*
Pb Metal Works .... G 765 489-1311
  Hagerstown *(G-6841)*
Phoenix Closures Inc .... F 765 658-1800
  Greencastle *(G-6424)*
Prospect Distribution Inc .... E 317 359-9551
  Indianapolis *(G-9231)*
Reeds Plastic Tops Inc .... G 765 282-1471
  Muncie *(G-12486)*
Rick Hollingshead .... G 765 833-2846
  Roann *(G-14253)*
▲ Robert Weed Plywood Corp .... B 574 848-7631
  Bristol *(G-1288)*
Servants Inc .... D 812 634-2201
  Jasper *(G-9910)*
Sims-Lohman Inc .... G 317 467-0710
  Greenfield *(G-6553)*
Spohn Associates Inc .... G 317 921-2445
  Indianapolis *(G-9480)*
Superior Laminating Inc .... G 574 361-7266
  Goshen *(G-6261)*
Therma-Tru Corp .... F 260 562-1009
  Howe *(G-7243)*
Trim-A-Door Corporation .... G 317 769-8746
  Elwood *(G-3839)*
Ufp Granger LLC .... E 574 277-7670
  Granger *(G-6387)*
US Lbm Operating Co 3009 LLC .... G 812 464-2428
  Evansville *(G-4364)*
Waninger Knneth Sons Log Tmber .... G 812 357-5200
  Fulda *(G-5850)*
Wible Lumber Inc .... E 260 351-2441
  South Milford *(G-15314)*
▲ Wolfe Engineered Plastics LLC .... G 812 623-8403
  Sunman *(G-15449)*

5032 Brick, stone, and related material

Aggrock Quarries Inc .... G 812 246-2582
  Charlestown *(G-1870)*
Amgi LLC .... G 317 447-1524
  New Palestine *(G-12928)*
Barrett Paving Materials Inc .... G 765 935-3060
  Richmond *(G-14090)*
▲ Brampton Brick Inc .... E 812 397-2190
  Farmersburg *(G-4416)*
Brickworks Supply Center LLC .... E 317 786-9208
  Carmel *(G-1573)*
Camilles Studio .... G 219 365-5902
  Cedar Lake *(G-1828)*
Cerline Ceramic Corp .... G 765 649-7222
  Anderson *(G-92)*
CMa Supply Co Fort Wayne Inc .... E 260 471-9000
  Fort Wayne *(G-4862)*
Crawford County Concrete .... G 812 739-2707
  Leavenworth *(G-10869)*
Crown Brick & Supply Inc .... E 219 663-7880
  Crown Point *(G-2668)*
Devening Block Inc .... E 812 372-4458
  Columbus *(G-2282)*
Dubois Cnty Block & Brick Inc .... F 812 482-6293
  Jasper *(G-9834)*
Evansville Block Co Inc .... E 812 422-2864
  Evansville *(G-4049)*

Garrity Stone Inc .... G 317 546-0893
  Indianapolis *(G-8263)*
Great Lakes Granite LLC .... G 708 474-8800
  Portage *(G-13872)*
Hanson Aggregates Wrp Inc .... E 502 244-7550
  Sellersburg *(G-14596)*
Hanson Agrigoods Midwest Inc .... G 317 635-9048
  Cloverdale *(G-2085)*
Heidelberg Mtls Mdwest Agg Inc .... G 765 653-7205
  Cloverdale *(G-2086)*
Heidelberg Mtls Mdwest Agg Inc .... F 765 653-1956
  Greencastle *(G-6411)*
Heidelberg Mtls Mdwest Agg Inc .... G 260 632-1410
  Woodburn *(G-16948)*
Heritage Ldscp Sup Group Inc .... E 317 849-9100
  Indianapolis *(G-8389)*
Hydro Conduit .... G 561 651-7177
  Greenfield *(G-6510)*
Ionic Cut Stone Incorporated .... G 812 829-3416
  Spencer *(G-15352)*
Irving Materials Inc .... F 765 778-4760
  Anderson *(G-136)*
Irving Materials Inc .... G 765 478-4914
  Cambridge City *(G-1496)*
Irving Materials Inc .... G 765 288-0288
  Muncie *(G-12428)*
Irving Materials Inc .... G 812 254-0820
  Washington *(G-16486)*
Irving Materials Inc .... D 317 326-3101
  Greenfield *(G-6518)*
Jones & Sons Inc .... E 812 882-2957
  Vincennes *(G-16135)*
Korte Bros Inc .... F 260 497-0500
  Fort Wayne *(G-5157)*
Kuert Concrete Inc .... F 574 293-0430
  Goshen *(G-6193)*
Kuert Concrete Inc .... E 574 232-9911
  South Bend *(G-15109)*
Larry Atwood .... G 765 525-6851
  Waldron *(G-16260)*
Majestic Block & Supply Inc .... G 317 842-6602
  Fishers *(G-4560)*
Midwest Tile and Concrete Pdts .... G 260 749-5173
  Woodburn *(G-16953)*
Minnick Services Corp .... E 260 432-5031
  Fort Wayne *(G-5231)*
Monumental Stone Works Inc .... F 765 866-0658
  New Market *(G-12927)*
Mulzer Crushed Stone Inc .... E 812 256-3346
  Charlestown *(G-1886)*
Mulzer Crushed Stone Inc .... E 812 547-3467
  Tell City *(G-15512)*
Old Dutch Sand Co Inc .... E 219 938-7020
  Gary *(G-5988)*
Ozinga Indiana Rdymx Con Inc .... F 219 949-9800
  Gary *(G-5993)*
Parke County Aggregates LLC .... G 765 245-2344
  Rockville *(G-14353)*
Plaster Shak .... G 317 881-6518
  Greenwood *(G-6752)*
Rogers Group Inc .... C 812 333-6324
  Bloomington *(G-959)*
Rogers Group Inc .... D 812 332-6341
  Bloomington *(G-960)*
Rogers Group Inc .... D 812 333-8560
  Bloomington *(G-961)*
Rogers Group Inc .... D 219 474-5125
  Kentland *(G-10163)*
Rogers Group Inc .... D 812 849-3530
  Mitchell *(G-12047)*
Rogers Group Inc .... E 765 893-4463
  Williamsport *(G-16853)*

Scotts Grant County Asp Inc .... G 765 664-2754
  Marion *(G-11337)*
Shelby Gravel Inc .... F 812 526-2731
  Edinburgh *(G-3104)*
Slater Concrete Products Inc .... G 260 347-0164
  Kendallville *(G-10152)*
U S Aggregates Inc .... E 765 564-2282
  Delphi *(G-2910)*
Wyatt Farm Center Inc .... G 574 354-2998
  Nappanee *(G-12655)*

5033 Roofing, siding, and insulation

Arran Isle Inc .... E 574 295-4400
  Elkhart *(G-3191)*
C & K United Shtmtl & Mech .... E 812 423-5090
  Evansville *(G-3958)*
▼ Craft Metal Products Inc .... E 317 545-3252
  Indianapolis *(G-7897)*
▲ Innovative Energy Inc .... E 219 696-3639
  Crown Point *(G-2697)*
Insulation Fabricators Inc .... D 219 845-2008
  Hammond *(G-6956)*
◆ Lasalle Bristol Corporation .... C 574 295-8400
  Elkhart *(G-3469)*
▲ Monument Chemical LLC .... D 317 223-2630
  Indianapolis *(G-8952)*
Patrick Industries Inc .... D 574 294-8828
  Elkhart *(G-3592)*
▲ Patrick Industries Inc .... B 574 294-7511
  Elkhart *(G-3593)*
Trivector Manufacturing Inc .... E 260 637-0141
  Fort Wayne *(G-5509)*

5039 Construction materials, nec

Bickels Garage & Welding .... G 765 853-5457
  Modoc *(G-12050)*
Biologics Modular LLC .... G 317 626-4093
  Brownsburg *(G-1350)*
Buc Construction Supply Inc .... G 574 532-9345
  Lafayette *(G-10547)*
Cbizze LLC .... G 623 204-9782
  South Bend *(G-14968)*
Creed & Dyer Precast Inc .... G 574 784-3361
  Lakeville *(G-10789)*
Erosion & Cnstr Solutions Inc .... E 219 885-9676
  Merrillville *(G-11514)*
Fencescapes LLC .... F 317 210-3912
  Avon *(G-519)*
Glass City Inc .... G 219 887-2100
  Gary *(G-5943)*
Hartford TEC Glass Co Inc .... E 765 348-1282
  Hartford City *(G-7068)*
Image One LLC .... D 317 576-2700
  Mccordsville *(G-11451)*
Indy Glass Center Inc .... E 317 591-5000
  Indianapolis *(G-8527)*
Johns Archtctral Met Solutions .... F 219 440-2116
  Crown Point *(G-2703)*
Keusch Glass Inc .... E 812 482-2566
  Jasper *(G-9864)*
Master Filter Corporation .... G 317 545-3335
  Indianapolis *(G-8849)*
Mnt Delivery Company .... G 574 518-6250
  Osceola *(G-13399)*
Morton Buildings Inc .... F 260 563-2118
  Wabash *(G-16204)*
River Valley Sheet Metal Inc .... F 574 259-2538
  Mishawaka *(G-11988)*
▲ Tuttle Aluminum & Bronze Inc .... D 317 842-2420
  Fishers *(G-4618)*

5043 Photographic equipment and supplies

SIC SECTION

50 WHOLESALE TRADE - DURABLE GOODS

Insight Lpr LLC .... F 855 862-5468
  Carmel (G-1671)
Motion Engineering Company Inc .... G 317 804-7990
  Westfield (G-16712)

5044 Office equipment

Business Systems Mgt Corp .... G 219 938-0166
  Gary (G-5908)
▲ Classic Products Corp .... E 260 484-2695
  Fort Wayne (G-4855)
Cummins - Allison Corp .... G 317 872-6244
  Indianapolis (G-7922)
◆ Fire King International LLC .... E 812 822-5574
  New Albany (G-12729)
◆ Fki Security Group LLC .... B 812 948-8400
  New Albany (G-12730)
Marketing and Retail Sales .... G 812 883-1813
  Salem (G-14489)
Meilink Safe Company .... D 812 941-0024
  New Albany (G-12774)
Office Sup of Southern Ind Inc .... G 812 283-5523
  Jeffersonville (G-10027)
Pinnacle Mailing Products .... F 765 405-1194
  Yorktown (G-16980)
▲ S C Pryor Inc .... F 317 352-1281
  Indianapolis (G-9354)

5045 Computers, peripherals, and software

American Spcialty Bus Intl LLC .... G 317 271-5000
  Zionsville (G-16992)
Business Systems Mgt Corp .... G 219 938-0166
  Gary (G-5908)
C & P Distributing LLC .... F 574 256-1138
  Mishawaka (G-11857)
Country Club Computer .... G 317 271-4000
  Indianapolis (G-7889)
Honeywell International Inc .... G 812 473-4163
  Evansville (G-4108)
Ilab LLC .... D 317 218-3258
  Indianapolis (G-8459)
L5 Solutions LLC .... G 317 436-1044
  Indianapolis (G-8706)
Maddenco Inc .... F 812 474-6245
  Evansville (G-4184)
Mirage Computers Inc .... G 260 665-5072
  Angola (G-276)
Money Tree Software Ltd .... E 541 754-3701
  Muncie (G-12458)
Osc Holdings LLC .... G 765 751-7000
  Muncie (G-12470)
S & S Programming Inc .... G 765 423-4472
  Lafayette (G-10682)
Tclogic LLC .... G 317 464-5152
  Indianapolis (G-9562)

5046 Commercial equipment, nec

Brand Sheet Metal Works Inc .... G 765 284-5594
  Muncie (G-12356)
Cottom Automated Bus Soluti .... G 317 853-6531
  Carmel (G-1599)
Csa Racking LLC .... G 414 241-3585
  Hammond (G-6908)
Delaplane & Son Neon & Sign .... G 574 859-3431
  Camden (G-1519)
▲ Indiana Scale Company Inc .... F 812 232-0893
  Terre Haute (G-15617)
Indy Hoods LLC .... F 317 731-7170
  Indianapolis (G-8529)
Lafayette Materials MGT Co Inc .... G 765 447-7400
  Lafayette (G-10627)
Markley Enterprise Inc .... D 574 295-4195
  Elkhart (G-3513)

▲ MD Holdings LLC .... G 317 831-7030
  Mooresville (G-12220)
North Central Equipment C .... G 574 825-2006
  Middlebury (G-11741)
Playfair Shuffleboard Company .... F 260 747-7288
  Fort Wayne (G-5319)
Sign Craft Industries Inc .... E 317 842-8664
  Indianapolis (G-9428)
Signdoc Identity LLC .... G 317 247-9670
  Indianapolis (G-9435)
Signrite .... G 812 320-5245
  Bloomington (G-972)
Small World Enterprises LLC .... G 312 550-1717
  Lake Station (G-10776)
Storageworks Inc .... G 317 577-3511
  Fishers (G-4607)
▲ Technical Weighing Svcs Inc .... E 219 924-3366
  Griffith (G-6819)
Thermodyne Food Svc Pdts Inc .... G 260 428-2535
  Fort Wayne (G-5482)
Unlimited Vending LLC .... G 765 288-5952
  Muncie (G-12510)
US Water Systems Inc .... E 317 209-0889
  Indianapolis (G-9688)
Whatzthat Vending LLC .... G 317 362-9088
  Indianapolis (G-9755)
Willow Way LLC .... G 765 886-4642
  Hagerstown (G-6848)
▼ Wood Technologies LLC .... E 260 627-8858
  Grabill (G-6326)

5047 Medical and hospital equipment

Active Ankle Systems Inc .... F 812 258-0663
  Jeffersonville (G-9925)
Adaptive Mobility Inc .... F 317 347-6400
  Indianapolis (G-7429)
After Action Med Dntl Sup LLC .... G 800 892-5352
  Indianapolis (G-7457)
All About Organizing .... G 513 238-8157
  Lawrenceburg (G-10827)
American Eagle Health LLC .... G 812 921-9224
  Floyds Knobs (G-4668)
Autofarm Mobility LLC .... G 317 410-0070
  Daleville (G-2795)
Belltone Hearing Care Center .... G 317 462-9999
  Greenfield (G-6470)
Breath of Life Home Medic .... G 317 896-3048
  Westfield (G-16671)
◆ Bryton Corporation .... F 317 334-8700
  Indianapolis (G-7694)
Campbell Pet Company .... G 812 692-5208
  Elnora (G-3813)
Incipio Devices LLC .... D 260 200-1970
  Huntington (G-7325)
Indy Medical Supplies LLC .... G 866 744-9013
  Zionsville (G-17019)
◆ Kilgore Manufacturing Co Inc .... D 260 248-2002
  Columbia City (G-2162)
LH Medical Corporation .... D 260 387-5194
  Fort Wayne (G-5183)
Merrill Corporation .... F 574 255-2988
  Mishawaka (G-11942)
Merss Corporation .... G 317 632-7299
  Indianapolis (G-8879)
Mwi Veterinary Supply Co .... G 317 769-7771
  Lebanon (G-10923)
Mwi Veterinary Supply Co .... G 317 769-7771
  Lebanon (G-10924)
▲ Orthodontic Design & Prod Inc .... E 317 346-6655
  Franklin (G-5763)
Plastic Assembly Tech Inc .... G 317 841-1202
  Indianapolis (G-9150)

Rgr Medical Solutions Inc .... C 317 285-9703
  Fishers (G-4596)
Sober Scientific LLC .... G 765 465-9803
  Sheridan (G-14829)
Standard Fusee Corporation .... D 765 472-4375
  Peru (G-13602)
Starkey Laboratories Inc .... F 952 828-6934
  Plainfield (G-13731)
Tayco Brace Inc .... E 574 850-7910
  South Bend (G-15279)
TW Enterprises LLC .... G 513 520-8453
  Brookville (G-1338)
▲ U-Nitt LLC .... G 812 251-9980
  Carmel (G-1792)
White Surgical Inc .... G 260 755-5800
  Fort Wayne (G-5566)
Williams Bros Hlth Care Phrm I .... E 812 335-0000
  Bloomington (G-1012)
Xennovate Medical LLC .... G 765 939-2037
  Richmond (G-14229)

5048 Ophthalmic goods

City Optical Co Inc .... D 317 924-1300
  Indianapolis (G-7813)
Diversified Ophthalmics Inc .... E 317 780-1677
  Indianapolis (G-7985)
Frecker Optical Inc .... F 260 747-9653
  Fort Wayne (G-5009)
Kokomo Optical Company Inc .... G 765 459-5137
  Kokomo (G-10293)
Singer Optical Company Inc .... F 812 423-1179
  Evansville (G-4315)
▲ Vision Training Products Inc .... F 574 259-2070
  Mishawaka (G-12023)

5049 Professional equipment, nec

American Eagle Health LLC .... G 812 921-9224
  Floyds Knobs (G-4668)
Blue Print Specialties Inc .... G 765 742-6976
  Lafayette (G-10539)
City Optical Co Inc .... G 317 788-4243
  Indianapolis (G-7814)
City Optical Co Inc .... D 317 924-1300
  Indianapolis (G-7813)
◆ Dicksons Inc .... C 812 522-1308
  Seymour (G-14647)
Eastern Engineering Supply Inc .... F 260 426-3119
  Fort Wayne (G-4938)
Lazar Scientific Incorporated .... G 574 271-7020
  Granger (G-6358)
Lk Technologies Inc .... G 812 332-4449
  Bloomington (G-912)
Maco Reprograhics LLC .... G 812 464-8108
  Evansville (G-4183)
Priority Press Inc .... G 317 848-9695
  Carmel (G-1730)
Priority Press Inc .... E 317 241-4234
  Indianapolis (G-9211)
Templeton Coal Company Inc .... G 812 232-7037
  Terre Haute (G-15725)
▲ Vision Training Products Inc .... F 574 259-2070
  Mishawaka (G-12023)
Williams Distribution LLC .... G 317 749-0006
  Indianapolis (G-9767)

5051 Metals service centers and offices

A2 Sales LLC .... E 708 924-1200
  Gary (G-5885)
Alro Steel Corporation .... E 260 749-9661
  Yoder (G-16964)
Aluminum Wldg & Mch Works Inc .... G 219 787-8066
  Chesterton (G-1901)

Employee Codes: A=Over 500 employees, B=251-500
C=101-250, D=51-100, E=20-50, F=10-19, G=1-9

2024 Harris Indiana
Industrial Directory

50 WHOLESALE TRADE - DURABLE GOODS

Ambassador Steel Corporation............. F 317 834-3434
Mooresville *(G-12193)*

Angola Wire Products Inc...................... G 260 665-3061
Angola *(G-228)*

Arran Isle Inc.. E 574 295-4400
Elkhart *(G-3191)*

Bar Processing Corporation................. F 219 931-0702
Hammond *(G-6881)*

Barks Wldg Sups & Farming Inc......... G 812 732-4366
Corydon *(G-2487)*

Beck Industries LP................................. D 574 294-5621
Elkhart *(G-3221)*

Bobcat Steel LLC................................... G 317 699-6127
Shelbyville *(G-14739)*

Burton Debiceious................................. G 317 495-0123
Indianapolis *(G-7702)*

Calpipe Industries LLC......................... E 219 844-6800
Hobart *(G-7176)*

Central Illinois Steel Company............. G 219 882-1026
Gary *(G-5915)*

Central Steel and Wire Co LLC............. G 219 787-5000
Portage *(G-13854)*

Chicago Steel Ltd Partnership.............. E 219 949-1111
Gary *(G-5918)*

Dixie Metal Spinning Corp.................... G 317 541-1330
Indianapolis *(G-7990)*

Dynamic Composites LLC.................... G 260 625-8686
Columbia City *(G-2141)*

▲ Dz Investments LLC.......................... E 317 895-4141
Indianapolis *(G-8027)*

Edcoat Limited Partnership.................. E 574 654-9105
New Carlisle *(G-12839)*

Elkhart Steel Service Inc....................... E 574 262-2552
Elkhart *(G-3329)*

Evansville Sheet Metal Works Inc......... D 812 423-7871
Evansville *(G-4057)*

Feralloy Corporation.............................. D 219 787-9698
Portage *(G-13863)*

Flexco Products Inc............................... C 574 294-2502
Elkhart *(G-3348)*

Fluid Handling Technology Inc............. G 317 216-9629
Indianapolis *(G-8207)*

Friedman Industries Inc........................ E 219 392-3400
East Chicago *(G-3008)*

G and P Enterprises Ind Inc.................. G 812 723-3837
Paoli *(G-13495)*

Gldn Rule Truss & Metal Sales............. G 812 866-1800
Lexington *(G-10976)*

▲ Global... G 317 494-6174
Franklin *(G-5732)*

Grant County Steel Inc.......................... F 765 668-7547
Marion *(G-11290)*

Gusa Holdings Inc................................. D 317 545-1221
Indianapolis *(G-8343)*

Hancor Inc.. E 812 443-2080
Brazil *(G-1144)*

Heidtman Steel Products Inc................ E 219 256-7426
East Chicago *(G-3015)*

◆ High Performance Alloys Inc............. E 765 945-8230
Windfall *(G-16905)*

Hughes Welding and Fabrication......... G 812 385-2770
Princeton *(G-13999)*

Indiana Cast Metals Assn Inc............... G 317 974-1830
Indianapolis *(G-8475)*

Jec Steel Company................................ G 574 326-3829
Goshen *(G-6179)*

Jec Steel Company................................ G 574 326-3829
Bristol *(G-1268)*

Jims Welding & Repair LLC.................. G 765 564-1797
Bringhurst *(G-1237)*

Kammerer Inc... D 260 349-9098
Kendallville *(G-10124)*

Kentuckiana Wire Rope & Supply........ F 812 282-3667
Jeffersonville *(G-10005)*

Keywest Metal.. G 219 654-4063
Hobart *(G-7197)*

◆ Lasalle Bristol Corporation................ C 574 295-8400
Elkhart *(G-3469)*

Lenex Steel Company........................... E 317 818-1622
Terre Haute *(G-15632)*

Mill Steel Co.. F 765 622-4545
Anderson *(G-154)*

Mofab Inc... G 765 649-1288
Anderson *(G-158)*

Mofab Inc... G 765 649-5577
Anderson *(G-159)*

National Material LP............................. C 219 397-5088
East Chicago *(G-3031)*

◆ New Castle Stainless Plate LLC........ D 765 529-0120
New Castle *(G-12876)*

New Process Steel LP........................... E 260 868-1445
Butler *(G-1474)*

Newco Metals Inc.................................. G 765 644-6649
Anderson *(G-168)*

Newco Metals Inc.................................. E 317 485-7721
Pendleton *(G-13546)*

Novelis Corporation.............................. C 812 462-2287
Terre Haute *(G-15652)*

Pgp Corp... D 812 285-7700
Jeffersonville *(G-10036)*

Postle Operating LLC........................... D 574 266-7720
Elkhart *(G-3612)*

▲ Postle Operating LLC........................ D 574 389-0800
Elkhart *(G-3613)*

Preferred Metal Service Inc.................. G 219 988-2386
Crown Point *(G-2735)*

Pro-Tech Tool & Stamping Inc.............. G 765 258-3613
Frankfort *(G-5691)*

▲ Quality Steel & Alum Pdts Inc........... E 574 295-8715
Elkhart *(G-3634)*

Rankin Pump and Supply Co Inc......... G 812 238-2535
Terre Haute *(G-15675)*

Reeves Manufacturing Inc.................... G 765 935-3875
Richmond *(G-14196)*

Ridge Iron LLC...................................... G 646 450-0092
Plymouth *(G-13811)*

Robinson Steel Co Inc.......................... C 219 398-4600
East Chicago *(G-3040)*

▲ Ryerson Tull Inc................................. D 219 764-3500
Burns Harbor *(G-1455)*

S&S Steel Services Inc......................... C 765 622-4545
Anderson *(G-189)*

Southern Alum Finshg Co Inc.............. G 800 357-9016
Indianapolis *(G-9464)*

Special Metals Corporation.................. B 574 262-3451
Elkhart *(G-3690)*

Spectra Metal Sales Inc........................ G 317 822-8291
Indianapolis *(G-9476)*

Steel Storage Inc................................... F 574 282-2618
South Bend *(G-15268)*

Sterling Sales and Engrg Inc................ G 765 376-0454
Veedersburg *(G-16091)*

Summerlot Engineered Pdts Inc........... F 812 466-7266
Rosedale *(G-14383)*

▼ Superior Aluminum Alloys LLC......... C 260 749-7599
New Haven *(G-12921)*

Todds Hydrlcs RPR & Stl Fbrct............ G 812 466-3457
Terre Haute *(G-15733)*

Tway Company Incorporated............... E 317 636-2591
Indianapolis *(G-9662)*

▲ U-Nitt LLC.. G 812 251-9980
Carmel *(G-1792)*

Univertical Holdings Inc....................... G 260 665-1500
Angola *(G-303)*

Upg Enterprises LLC............................. D 708 594-9200
Gary *(G-6025)*

US Metals Inc.. G 219 398-1350
East Chicago *(G-3052)*

Veterans Fabrication LLC..................... G 317 604-7704
Fishers *(G-4629)*

W & W Fabricating Inc........................... G 765 362-2182
Crawfordsville *(G-2625)*

Wegener Steel and Fabricating............. G 219 462-3911
Valparaiso *(G-16080)*

Westfield Steel Inc................................. G 812 466-3500
Terre Haute *(G-15745)*

Winski Brothers Inc............................... G 765 654-5323
Frankfort *(G-5702)*

Zimco Materials Inc............................... G 219 883-0870
Gary *(G-6029)*

5052 Coal and other minerals and ores

Al Perry Enterprises Inc........................ G 812 867-7727
Evansville *(G-3879)*

Calcean LLC.. G 812 672-4995
Seymour *(G-14636)*

Covey Rise Minerals LLC...................... G 812 897-2356
Boonville *(G-1086)*

5063 Electrical apparatus and equipment

▲ A Homestead Shoppe Inc.................. E 574 784-2307
Lapaz *(G-10814)*

Academy Energy Group LLC................ G 312 931-7443
Newburgh *(G-12991)*

Ademco Inc... G 317 359-9505
Indianapolis *(G-7431)*

Altek Inc.. G 812 385-2561
Princeton *(G-13981)*

American Fire Company....................... G 219 840-0630
Valparaiso *(G-15899)*

▲ Amerlight LLC.................................... F 812 602-3452
Evansville *(G-3889)*

Amgi LLC... G 317 447-1524
New Palestine *(G-12928)*

B & H Electric and Supply Inc.............. E 812 522-5607
Seymour *(G-14630)*

B T Bttery Charger Systems Inc........... G 574 533-6030
Goshen *(G-6093)*

Babsco Supply Inc................................ G 574 267-8999
Warsaw *(G-16316)*

Batteries Plus.. G 317 219-0007
Noblesville *(G-13040)*

Blackbird... G 812 944-0799
New Albany *(G-12702)*

Bonner & Associates............................ G 317 571-1911
Carmel *(G-1571)*

Bryant Control Inc................................. F 317 549-3355
Fishers *(G-4477)*

C & L Electric Motor Repr Inc............... G 574 533-2643
Elkhart *(G-3243)*

Controls Center Inc.............................. G 317 634-2665
Indianapolis *(G-7863)*

Crume Industries LLC........................... G 574 747-7683
Elkhart *(G-3275)*

Cummins Crosspoint LLC..................... D 812 867-4400
Evansville *(G-3999)*

Cummins Crosspoint LLC..................... E 317 243-7979
Indianapolis *(G-7925)*

Cummins Inc... G 260 482-3691
Fort Wayne *(G-4895)*

Doron Distribution Inc.......................... G 317 594-9259
Carmel *(G-1610)*

Dux Signal Kits LLC.............................. G 260 623-3017
Monroeville *(G-12068)*

Eaton Corporation................................. G 317 704-2520
Indianapolis *(G-8043)*

SIC SECTION
50 WHOLESALE TRADE - DURABLE GOODS

Electrik Connection Inc .... G 219 362-4581
La Porte (G-10404)

Electro Corp .... F 219 393-5571
Kingsbury (G-10177)

▲ Elkhart Supply Corp .... E 574 264-4156
Elkhart (G-3330)

Enyart Electric Motor Repr Inc .... G 574 288-4731
South Bend (G-15017)

Eps Enterprises Inc .... G 260 493-4913
Fort Wayne (G-4957)

Flanders Electric Mtr Svc LLC .... D 812 421-4300
Evansville (G-4078)

Gregory Thomas Inc .... G 219 324-3801
La Porte (G-10412)

Harrison Electric Inc .... F 219 879-0444
Michigan City (G-11620)

▲ Hessville Cable & Sling Co .... E 773 768-8181
Gary (G-5951)

Hoosier Fire Equipment Inc .... F 219 462-1707
Valparaiso (G-15965)

Hoosier Industrial Electric .... F 812 346-2232
North Vernon (G-13278)

▲ Horner Apg LLC .... F 317 916-4274
Indianapolis (G-8414)

Horner Electric Inc .... E 317 639-4261
Indianapolis (G-8415)

Horner Industrial Services Inc .... G 260 434-1189
Fort Wayne (G-5083)

Horner Industrial Services Inc .... C 317 639-4261
Indianapolis (G-8416)

◆ International Lighting LLC .... F 219 989-0060
Hammond (G-6958)

▲ International Resources Inc .... G 317 813-5300
Greenwood (G-6716)

Jasper Electric Motor Inc .... F 812 482-1660
Jasper (G-9851)

Jasper Electric Motor Inc .... F 812 482-1660
Jasper (G-9850)

Kamdoer Inc .... E 574 293-2990
Elkhart (G-3446)

Kirby Risk Corporation .... G 765 643-3384
Anderson (G-143)

Kirby Risk Corporation .... D 765 447-1402
Lafayette (G-10621)

Kirby Risk Corporation .... D 765 423-4205
Lafayette (G-10622)

Kirby Risk Corporation .... F 765 664-5185
Marion (G-11304)

Kirby Risk Corporation .... F 765 254-5460
Muncie (G-12435)

Kirby Risk Corporation .... D 317 398-9713
Shelbyville (G-14768)

▲ Kirby Risk Corporation .... D 765 448-4567
Lafayette (G-10623)

Lancon Electric Inc .... G 260 897-3285
Laotto (G-10809)

Logical Concepts .... F 317 885-6330
Greenwood (G-6730)

McBroom Electric Co Inc .... D 317 926-3451
Indianapolis (G-8860)

Mohler Technology Inc .... E 812 897-2900
Boonville (G-1093)

Monday Voigt Products Inc .... F 317 224-7920
Anderson (G-160)

Motor Electric Inc .... G 574 294-7123
Elkhart (G-3556)

National Handicapped Workshop .... F 765 287-8331
Muncie (G-12468)

Ocella Inc .... G 845 842-8185
Newberry (G-12990)

Patrick Industries Inc .... G 574 293-2990
Elkhart (G-3599)

Phase Three Electric Inc .... G 812 945-9922
New Albany (G-12793)

◆ Phazpak Inc .... G 260 692-6416
Monroe (G-12061)

Phil & Son Inc .... G 219 663-5757
Crown Point (G-2730)

Power Components of Midwest .... E 574 256-6990
Mishawaka (G-11976)

Robinson Industries Inc .... E 317 867-3214
Westfield (G-16724)

Rtw Enterprises Inc .... G 574 294-3275
Elkhart (G-3654)

Schneider Electric Usa Inc .... D 260 356-2060
Huntington (G-7366)

Source Products Inc .... G 260 424-0864
Columbia City (G-2200)

Tipton Engrg Elc Mtr Svcs Inc .... G 765 963-3380
Sharpsville (G-14714)

▲ Vista Manufacturing Inc .... E 574 264-0711
Elkhart (G-3771)

Wabash Valley Motor & Mch Inc .... G 812 466-7400
Terre Haute (G-15743)

Wagner Electric Fort Wayne Inc .... G 260 484-5532
Fort Wayne (G-5538)

Worldwide Battery Company LLC .... G 248 830-8537
Elkhart (G-3795)

Worldwide Battery Company LLC .... G 812 475-1326
Evansville (G-4390)

5064 Electrical appliances, television and radio

3sevens LLC .... G 502 594-2312
Henryville (G-7112)

▲ Dti Services Ltd Liability Co .... G 765 745-0261
Indianapolis (G-8015)

▲ Long Item Development Corp .... G 317 780-1077
Indianapolis (G-8780)

Pyramid Equipment Inc .... F 219 778-2591
Rolling Prairie (G-14371)

5065 Electronic parts and equipment, nec

Acterna LLC .... E 317 788-9351
Indianapolis (G-7425)

Allegion Public Ltd Company .... D 317 810-3700
Carmel (G-1554)

◆ ASA Electronics LLC .... C 574 264-3135
Elkhart (G-3192)

Brickhouse Electronics LLC .... F 212 643-7449
Indianapolis (G-7678)

▲ Coil-Tran LLC .... D 219 942-8511
Hobart (G-7182)

Copper Mountain Tech LLC .... E 317 222-5400
Indianapolis (G-7872)

▲ Dti Services Ltd Liability Co .... G 765 745-0261
Indianapolis (G-8015)

▲ Elkhart Supply Corp .... E 574 264-4156
Elkhart (G-3330)

Emergency Radio Service LLC .... G 800 377-2929
Ligonier (G-11011)

Emergency Radio Service LLC .... E 206 894-4145
Ligonier (G-11012)

Flat Electronics LLC .... G 765 414-6635
Fishers (G-4524)

▲ Harman Embedded Audio LLC .... G 317 849-8175
Indianapolis (G-8363)

Lionfish Cyber Hldngs LLC-S Ln .... G 877 732-6772
Indianapolis (G-8766)

Motion Engineering Company Inc .... G 317 840-7990
Westfield (G-16712)

R & R Regulators Inc .... F 574 522-3500
Elkhart (G-3636)

Sneaky Micro Video Divisio .... G 317 925-1496
Indianapolis (G-9454)

◆ Telamon International Corp .... D 317 818-6888
Carmel (G-1779)

▲ Xfmrs Inc .... A 317 834-1066
Camby (G-1517)

5072 Hardware

Buckaroos Inc .... G 317 899-9100
Indianapolis (G-7696)

▲ Camcar LLC .... C 574 223-3131
Rochester (G-14282)

Dbisp LLC .... G 317 222-1671
Indianapolis (G-7957)

▲ Ditto Sales Inc .... E 812 482-3043
Jasper (G-9832)

Kentuckiana Wire Rope & Supply .... F 812 282-3667
Jeffersonville (G-10005)

Onspot of North America Inc .... G 203 377-0777
North Vernon (G-13290)

Rits Ltd Brokers Inc .... G 260 348-0786
Fort Wayne (G-5385)

Standard Change-Makers Inc .... F 317 899-6955
Indianapolis (G-9492)

Tamco Manufacturing Co .... G 574 294-1909
Elkhart (G-3714)

Tartan Properties LLC .... G 317 714-7337
Indianapolis (G-9554)

▲ U-Nitt LLC .... G 812 251-9980
Carmel (G-1792)

5074 Plumbing and hydronic heating supplies

Barry Company Inc .... G 812 333-1850
Bloomington (G-795)

Barry Company Inc .... G 317 578-2486
Fishers (G-4471)

Bath Gallery Showroom .... G 219 531-2150
Valparaiso (G-15911)

▲ Cast Products LP .... E 574 294-2684
Elkhart (G-3249)

David Indus Process Pdts Inc .... G 317 577-0351
Fishers (G-4502)

▲ Dehco Inc .... D 574 294-2684
Elkhart (G-3288)

▲ Elkhart Supply Corp .... E 574 264-4156
Elkhart (G-3330)

Evoqua Water Technologies LLC .... E 317 280-4251
Indianapolis (G-8144)

Ferguson Enterprises LLC .... G 219 440-5254
Schererville (G-14521)

Flosource Inc .... E 800 752-5959
Mooresville (G-12208)

Forsyth Brothers Con Pdts Inc .... G 812 466-4080
Terre Haute (G-15590)

Frew Process Group LLC .... G 317 565-5000
Noblesville (G-13081)

Hoffman Sls & Specialty Co Inc .... G 317 846-6428
Carmel (G-1656)

Hrezo Industrial Eqp & Engrg .... F 812 537-4700
Greendale (G-6447)

Huntingburg Machine Works Inc .... F 812 683-3531
Huntingburg (G-7282)

Independent Concrete Pipe Company .. E 317 262-4920
Indianapolis (G-8471)

Lee Supply Corp .... F 812 333-4343
Bloomington (G-909)

Leeps Supply Co Inc .... E 219 756-5337
Merrillville (G-11530)

New Aqua LLC .... D 317 272-3000
Avon (G-540)

50 WHOLESALE TRADE - DURABLE GOODS

▲ Our Country Home Entps Inc............ E 260 657-5605
　Harlan *(G-7058)*
Power Plant Service Inc...................... E 260 432-6716
　Fort Wayne *(G-5328)*
▲ Spheros North America Inc............ G 734 218-7350
　Elkhart *(G-3693)*
Sun Rise Metal Shop........................... G 260 463-4026
　Topeka *(G-15820)*
Templeton Coal Company Inc............ G 812 232-7037
　Terre Haute *(G-15725)*
US Metals Inc..................................... G 219 802-8465
　Hammond *(G-7027)*
US Water Systems Inc........................ E 317 209-0889
　Indianapolis *(G-9688)*

5075 Warm air heating and air conditioning

3-T Corp... F 812 424-7878
　Evansville *(G-3856)*
▲ Aero-Flo Industries Inc................... G 219 393-3555
　La Porte *(G-10378)*
Air Energy Systems Inc...................... G 317 290-8500
　Indianapolis *(G-7460)*
◆ American Melt Blown Filtration....... E 219 866-3500
　Rensselaer *(G-14041)*
◆ Anthony Group LLC........................ E 317 536-7445
　Greenwood *(G-6669)*
▲ D & W Inc...................................... D 574 264-9674
　Elkhart *(G-3284)*
Horner Industrial Services Inc............ F 317 634-7165
　Indianapolis *(G-8418)*
Indianapolis In.................................... E 855 628-3458
　Indianapolis *(G-8502)*
◆ Koch Enterprises Inc..................... G 812 465-9800
　Evansville *(G-4159)*
Lasalle Bristol Corporation.................. F 574 293-5526
　Elkhart *(G-3470)*
Poynter Sheet Metal Inc..................... B 317 893-1193
　Greenwood *(G-6753)*
Proair LLC.. D 574 264-5494
　Elkhart *(G-3622)*
▲ Spheros North America Inc............ G 734 218-7350
　Elkhart *(G-3693)*
Superior Distribution........................... G 317 308-5525
　Indianapolis *(G-9528)*
Thermo-Cycler Industries Inc............. G 219 767-2990
　Union Mills *(G-15868)*

5078 Refrigeration equipment and supplies

Duncan Supply Co Inc........................ G 765 446-0105
　Lafayette *(G-10572)*
Elliott-Williams Company Inc............. E 317 453-2295
　Indianapolis *(G-8097)*
Refrigeration Design Ind LLC............. G 317 498-3435
　Rushville *(G-14409)*
Stanton and Associates Inc............... G 574 247-5522
　Granger *(G-6383)*
Swanel Inc... E 219 932-7676
　Hammond *(G-7017)*

5082 Construction and mining machinery

AF Ohab Company Inc....................... E 317 225-4740
　Indianapolis *(G-7455)*
◆ Brake Supply Company Inc........... C 812 467-1000
　Evansville *(G-3950)*
Carroll Distrg & Cnstr Sup Inc............ G 317 984-2400
　Noblesville *(G-13055)*
▲ Caterpillar Inc................................ E 630 743-4094
　Greenfield *(G-6476)*
Cbizze LLC... G 623 204-9782
　South Bend *(G-14968)*
Delphi Body Works.............................. F 765 564-2212
　Delphi *(G-2893)*
◆ FTC Liquidation Inc........................ F 574 295-6700
　Elkhart *(G-3359)*
Hoosier Industrial Supply Inc............. F 574 533-8565
　Goshen *(G-6168)*
◆ ITR America LLC............................ D 219 947-8230
　Hobart *(G-7193)*
Macallister Machinery Co Inc............. C 260 483-6469
　Fort Wayne *(G-5195)*
Macallister Machinery Co Inc............. F 765 966-0759
　Richmond *(G-14157)*
Masbez LLC....................................... G 855 962-7239
　Frankfort *(G-5681)*
Mining Machine Parts Inc................... G 812 897-1256
　Boonville *(G-1092)*
Mpc Global LLC.................................. G 816 399-4710
　Indianapolis *(G-8964)*
Paulus Plastic Co Inc......................... G 574 834-7663
　North Webster *(G-13312)*
Schlatters Inc..................................... G 219 567-9158
　Francesville *(G-5645)*
Simmons Equipment Sales Inc.......... F 260 625-3308
　Columbia City *(G-2197)*
Square 1 Dsign Manufacture Inc....... F 866 647-7771
　Shelbyville *(G-14800)*
Vandergriff & Associates Inc.............. G 812 422-6033
　Evansville *(G-4367)*

5083 Farm and garden machinery

A1 Campers and Trlrs Mfg LLC......... G 574 227-2200
　Elkhart *(G-3143)*
▲ Al-Ko Kober LLC............................ C 574 294-6651
　Elkhart *(G-3158)*
Bane-Welker Equipment LLC........... F 812 234-2627
　Terre Haute *(G-15550)*
Bickels Garage & Welding................. G 765 853-5457
　Modoc *(G-12050)*
Bonnell Grain Handling Inc................ E 574 595-7827
　Star City *(G-15396)*
Buffington Electric Motors.................. G 574 935-5453
　Plymouth *(G-13762)*
Chester Inc.. F 574 896-5600
　North Judson *(G-13209)*
Deer Country Equipment LLC........... E 812 522-1922
　Seymour *(G-14646)*
Delphi Products Co Inc...................... F 800 382-7903
　Delphi *(G-2894)*
▲ Dennis Polk & Associates Inc........ G 574 831-3555
　New Paris *(G-12950)*
Dexter Axle Company LLC................ C 574 294-6651
　Elkhart *(G-3293)*
Dpc Inc... E 765 564-3752
　Delphi *(G-2895)*
Hahn Enterprises Inc......................... G 574 862-4491
　Wakarusa *(G-16234)*
Jones & Sons Inc............................... E 812 299-2287
　Terre Haute *(G-15622)*
Miles Farm Supply LLC...................... D 812 359-4463
　Boonville *(G-1090)*
National Equipment Inc...................... G 219 462-1205
　Valparaiso *(G-16009)*
Schlatters Inc..................................... G 219 567-9158
　Francesville *(G-5645)*
Seaflo Marine & Rv N Amer LLC....... E 844 473-2356
　South Bend *(G-15236)*
Siteone Landscape Supply LLC........ G 219 769-2351
　Merrillville *(G-11560)*
T W Brackett & Assoc LLC................ G 765 769-3000
　Attica *(G-355)*
Wakarusa Ag LLC.............................. F 574 862-1163
　Wakarusa *(G-16256)*
Whites Welding & Machining LLC..... G 765 987-7984
　Straughn *(G-15400)*

Wright Implement I LLC..................... G 812 522-1922
　Seymour *(G-14707)*

5084 Industrial machinery and equipment

3w Enterprises LLC............................ G 847 366-6555
　Elkhart *(G-3137)*
Aam-Equipco Inc................................ G 574 272-8886
　Granger *(G-6329)*
Adept Tool and Engineering............... G 317 896-9250
　Carmel *(G-1551)*
Airgas Usa LLC.................................. G 812 362-7593
　Rockport *(G-14335)*
◆ Allied Enterprises LLC.................... E 765 288-8849
　Muncie *(G-12339)*
Aluminum Wldg & Mch Works Inc..... G 219 787-8066
　Chesterton *(G-1901)*
American Veteran Group LLC........... G 317 600-4749
　Westfield *(G-16664)*
Applicon Company Incorporated........ F 317 635-7843
　Indianapolis *(G-7532)*
Aqua Blast Corp................................. F 260 728-4433
　Decatur *(G-2844)*
Ash & Elm Cider Company LLC........ G 317 600-3164
　Indianapolis *(G-7550)*
◆ Asphalt Equipment Company Inc... E 260 672-3004
　Fort Wayne *(G-4775)*
Atlas Machine and Supply Inc........... F 812 423-7762
　Evansville *(G-3901)*
Autoform Tool & Mfg LLC................... C 260 624-2014
　Angola *(G-232)*
Ayco Panel.. G 765 635-8106
　Jasonville *(G-9822)*
B T Bttery Charger Systems Inc........ G 574 533-6030
　Goshen *(G-6093)*
▼ Banks Machine & Engrg LLC......... D 317 642-4980
　Shelbyville *(G-14732)*
Beatty International Inc...................... E 219 931-3000
　Hammond *(G-6882)*
Bemcor Inc... F 219 937-1600
　Hammond *(G-6885)*
Berendsen Inc.................................... G 812 423-6468
　Evansville *(G-3916)*
Best Equipment Co Inc...................... E 317 823-3050
　Indianapolis *(G-7617)*
Black Equipment Company S Inc...... G 812 477-6481
　Evansville *(G-3934)*
Bottcher America Corporation........... G 765 675-4449
　Tipton *(G-15768)*
◆ Brake Supply Company Inc........... C 812 467-1000
　Evansville *(G-3950)*
▲ Braun Motor Works Inc.................. G 574 205-0102
　Winamac *(G-16858)*
Buskirk Engineering Inc..................... F 260 622-5550
　Ossian *(G-13420)*
C&M Conveyor Inc............................. C 812 849-5647
　Mitchell *(G-12034)*
Capital Adhesives & Packg Corp....... F 317 834-5415
　Mooresville *(G-12197)*
Carver Inc.. G 260 563-7577
　Wabash *(G-16177)*
▲ Cast Products LP........................... G 574 294-2684
　Elkhart *(G-3249)*
Ccts Technology Group Inc............... G 305 209-5743
　Indianapolis *(G-7765)*
Clarke Industrial Systems Inc............ E 260 489-4575
　Fishers *(G-4491)*
▲ Contour Hardening Inc................... G 888 867-2184
　Indianapolis *(G-7861)*
Craft Laboratories Inc........................ E 260 432-9467
　Fort Wayne *(G-4882)*
◆ Cummins Americas Inc.................. G 812 377-5000
　Columbus *(G-2250)*

SIC SECTION
50 WHOLESALE TRADE - DURABLE GOODS

Cummins Crosspoint LLC .... D 812 867-4400
 Evansville *(G-3999)*

Cummins Crosspoint LLC .... E 260 482-3691
 Fort Wayne *(G-4894)*

Cummins Crosspoint LLC .... E 317 484-2146
 Indianapolis *(G-7923)*

Cummins Crosspoint LLC .... E 317 244-7251
 Indianapolis *(G-7924)*

Cummins Crosspoint LLC .... E 574 252-2154
 Mishawaka *(G-11869)*

Cummins Crosspoint LLC .... E 317 243-7979
 Indianapolis *(G-7925)*

▲ Cummins Cumberland Inc .... B 317 243-7979
 Indianapolis *(G-7926)*

Daniel Steffy .... G 812 726-4769
 Vincennes *(G-16118)*

▲ Dehco Inc .... D 574 294-2684
 Elkhart *(G-3288)*

▲ Dekker Vacuum Technologies Inc ..... D 219 861-0661
 Michigan City *(G-11598)*

▲ Fastener Equipment Corporation ..... G 708 957-5100
 Valparaiso *(G-15948)*

Gearbox Group Inc .... G 812 268-0322
 Sullivan *(G-15406)*

General Material Handling Co .... G 317 888-5735
 Indianapolis *(G-8272)*

Global Parts Network LLC .... G 574 855-5000
 South Bend *(G-15044)*

Grotrian Tool & Die .... G 260 894-3558
 Ligonier *(G-11016)*

◆ Hale Industries Inc .... F 317 577-0337
 Fortville *(G-5598)*

Hawkins Darryal .... G 765 282-6021
 Muncie *(G-12410)*

Headco Industries Inc .... G 219 924-7758
 Highland *(G-7140)*

Headco Industries Inc .... G 574 288-4471
 South Bend *(G-15062)*

Hoffman Sls & Specialty Co Inc .... G 317 846-6428
 Carmel *(G-1656)*

Hoosier Fire Equipment Inc .... F 219 462-1707
 Valparaiso *(G-15965)*

Hoosier Metal Polish Inc .... G 219 474-6011
 Kentland *(G-10160)*

Hope Hardwoods Inc .... F 812 546-4427
 Hope *(G-7226)*

Horner Industrial Services Inc .... F 317 634-7165
 Indianapolis *(G-8418)*

Hrezo Industrial Eqp & Engrg .... F 812 537-4700
 Greendale *(G-6447)*

▼ Indco Inc .... G 812 945-4383
 New Albany *(G-12746)*

Indiana Oxygen Company Inc .... G 765 662-8700
 Marion *(G-11295)*

Indiana Oxygen Company Inc .... D 317 290-0003
 Indianapolis *(G-8488)*

Industrial Sewing Machine Co .... G 812 425-2255
 Evansville *(G-4124)*

▲ Industrial Transmission Eqp .... E 574 936-3028
 Plymouth *(G-13785)*

Industrial Water MGT Inc .... G 317 889-0836
 Indianapolis *(G-8521)*

Interstate Power Systems Inc .... G 952 854-2044
 Gary *(G-5964)*

Jac Jmr Inc .... G 219 663-6700
 Crown Point *(G-2698)*

Jeda Equipment Services Inc .... G 317 842-9377
 Fishers *(G-4550)*

Kane Usa Inc .... E 800 547-5740
 Indianapolis *(G-8660)*

▲ Khorporate Holdings Inc .... C 260 357-3365
 Laotto *(G-10807)*

◆ Koch Enterprises Inc .... G 812 465-9800
 Evansville *(G-4159)*

Lafayette Materials MGT Co Inc .... G 765 447-7400
 Lafayette *(G-10627)*

Landis Equipment & Tool Rental .... G 812 847-2582
 Linton *(G-11037)*

Linde Gas & Equipment Inc .... G 812 376-3314
 Columbus *(G-2343)*

Linde Gas & Equipment Inc .... G 260 423-4468
 Fort Wayne *(G-5187)*

Linde Gas & Equipment Inc .... G 317 481-4550
 Indianapolis *(G-8761)*

▲ Logansport Machine Co Inc .... E 574 735-0225
 Logansport *(G-11090)*

Macallister Machinery Co Inc .... C 260 483-6469
 Fort Wayne *(G-5195)*

Macallister Machinery Co Inc .... F 765 966-0759
 Richmond *(G-14157)*

Machine Tool Service Inc .... F 812 232-1912
 Terre Haute *(G-15634)*

Magnum Venus Products Inc .... G 727 573-2955
 Goshen *(G-6210)*

Mainline Conveyor Systems Inc .... F 317 831-2795
 Mooresville *(G-12219)*

Mantra Enterprise LLC .... G 201 428-8709
 Fishers *(G-4561)*

Marquise Enterprises Ltd .... G 317 578-3400
 Indianapolis *(G-8840)*

Matheson Tri-Gas Inc .... G 812 838-5518
 Mount Vernon *(G-12307)*

Matheson Tri-Gas Inc .... G 317 892-5221
 Pittsboro *(G-13651)*

▲ McGinty Conveyors Inc .... G 317 240-4315
 Indianapolis *(G-8865)*

Mills Electric Co Inc .... G 219 931-3114
 Hammond *(G-6982)*

Mixer Direct LLC .... D 812 202-4047
 Jeffersonville *(G-10020)*

Motion & Control Entps LLC .... F 219 844-4224
 Munster *(G-12551)*

▲ Murray Equipment Inc .... C 260 484-0382
 Fort Wayne *(G-5252)*

National Consolidated Corp .... F 574 289-7885
 South Bend *(G-15159)*

▲ Novae LLC .... E 260 758-9838
 Markle *(G-11361)*

◆ Ogden Welding Systems Inc .... E 219 322-5252
 Schererville *(G-14537)*

Paradise Ink Inc .... G 812 402-4465
 Evansville *(G-4233)*

Pathfinder Cutting Tech LLC .... F 424 342-9723
 Indianapolis *(G-9099)*

Pro-Tech Tool & Stamping Inc .... G 765 258-3613
 Frankfort *(G-5691)*

Pyramid Equipment Inc .... F 219 778-2591
 Rolling Prairie *(G-14371)*

R B Tool & Machinery Co .... G 574 679-0082
 Osceola *(G-13401)*

Rankin Pump and Supply Co Inc .... G 812 238-2535
 Terre Haute *(G-15675)*

Richard J Bagan Inc .... E 260 244-5115
 Columbia City *(G-2190)*

Robinson Industries Inc .... E 317 867-3214
 Westfield *(G-16724)*

Rochester Cement Products Inc .... G 574 223-3917
 Rochester *(G-14316)*

Roeder Industries .... G 812 654-3322
 Milan *(G-11783)*

S & S Diesel Motorsport LLC .... G 812 216-3639
 Seymour *(G-14683)*

Samco Inc .... G 812 926-4282
 Sunman *(G-15444)*

Sdf Engineering LLC .... G 317 674-2643
 Carmel *(G-1755)*

Separation Technologies Inc .... G 219 548-5814
 Valparaiso *(G-16046)*

Smock Materials Handling Co .... F 317 890-3200
 Indianapolis *(G-9452)*

Specialty Tool LLC .... F 260 493-6351
 Indianapolis *(G-9471)*

Square 1 Dsign Manufacture Inc .... F 866 647-7771
 Shelbyville *(G-14800)*

SSd Control Technology Inc .... E 574 289-5942
 South Bend *(G-15264)*

Steel Tank & Fabricating Corp .... E 260 248-8971
 Columbia City *(G-2203)*

Storageworks Inc .... G 317 577-3511
 Fishers *(G-4607)*

Surclean Inc .... F 248 791-2226
 Brownsburg *(G-1405)*

Systems Engineering and Sls Co .... G 260 422-1671
 Fort Wayne *(G-5466)*

T & M Equipment Company Inc .... F 317 293-9255
 Indianapolis *(G-9543)*

T & M Equipment Company Inc .... E 219 942-2299
 Merrillville *(G-11563)*

Technical Water Treatment Inc .... G 574 277-1949
 Granger *(G-6386)*

● Terra Drive Systems Inc .... C 219 279-2801
 Brookston *(G-1313)*

Terry Liquidation III Inc .... F 219 362-3557
 La Porte *(G-10490)*

Tk Elevator Corporation .... D 317 595-1125
 Indianapolis *(G-9612)*

▲ Toyota Material Handling Inc .... D 800 381-5879
 Columbus *(G-2406)*

Troyer Brothers Inc .... E 260 565-2244
 Bluffton *(G-1064)*

▲ Tsune America LLC .... F 812 378-9875
 Edinburgh *(G-3109)*

Tway Company Incorporated .... E 317 636-2591
 Indianapolis *(G-9662)*

W M Kelley Co Inc .... D 812 945-3529
 New Albany *(G-12825)*

Waterfurnace International Inc .... B 260 478-5667
 Fort Wayne *(G-5549)*

Wdb Enterprises Inc .... F 219 844-4224
 Hammond *(G-7031)*

Western-Cullen-Hayes Inc .... F 765 962-0526
 Richmond *(G-14226)*

Wiese Holding Company .... D 317 241-8600
 Indianapolis *(G-9761)*

Z Rodz & Customs LLC .... G 574 806-5774
 Knox *(G-10229)*

5085 Industrial supplies

◆ Abro Industries Inc .... E 574 232-8289
 South Bend *(G-14933)*

Adhesive Solutions Company LLC .... G 260 691-0304
 Columbia City *(G-2117)*

Airgas Usa LLC .... G 812 474-0440
 Evansville *(G-3878)*

Airgas Usa LLC .... F 260 749-9576
 Fort Wayne *(G-4733)*

Airgas Usa LLC .... G 812 362-7593
 Rockport *(G-14335)*

Altra Industrial Motion Corp .... E 219 874-5248
 Michigan City *(G-11577)*

American Rubber Corp .... G 317 548-8455
 Anderson *(G-77)*

Avr Products Inc .... G 574 294-6101
 Bristol *(G-1247)*

▲ Barnett-Bates Corporation .... F 815 726-5223
 Anderson *(G-82)*

50 WHOLESALE TRADE - DURABLE GOODS

Bearing Service Company PA................ G 773 734-5132
  Griffith *(G-6794)*

Capital Adhesives & Packg Corp........... F 317 834-5415
  Mooresville *(G-12197)*

Clean-Seal Inc.................................... E 574 299-1888
  South Bend *(G-14976)*

Commercial Signs Inc......................... G 260 745-2678
  Fort Wayne *(G-4866)*

▲ Crown Packaging International Inc... D 219 738-1000
  Merrillville *(G-11499)*

CRS-Drs Corporation........................... G 260 478-7555
  Fort Wayne *(G-4891)*

Custom Building Products LLC............. C 765 656-0234
  Frankfort *(G-5659)*

◆ D Martin Enterprises Inc.................. F 219 872-8211
  Michigan City *(G-11596)*

Daylight Engineering Inc..................... G 812 983-2518
  Elberfeld *(G-3111)*

Dependable Rubber Industrial............. G 765 447-5654
  Lafayette *(G-10569)*

Earth First Kentuckiana Inc................. F 812 923-1227
  Charlestown *(G-1875)*

Espi Enterprises Inc............................ G 219 787-8711
  Chesterton *(G-1923)*

Exactseal Inc...................................... G 317 559-2220
  Indianapolis *(G-8148)*

◆ Fairfield Manufacturing Co Inc......... A 765 772-4000
  Lafayette *(G-10576)*

Filtration Plus Inc............................... F 219 879-0663
  Michigan City *(G-11612)*

Freudenberg-Nok General Partnr........ C 317 421-3400
  Shelbyville *(G-14756)*

▲ General Rbr Plas of Evansville......... E 812 464-5153
  Evansville *(G-4087)*

Hanwha Machinery America Corp........ D 574 546-2261
  Bremen *(G-1195)*

Headco Industries Inc......................... G 219 924-7758
  Highland *(G-7140)*

Headco Industries Inc......................... G 574 288-4471
  South Bend *(G-15062)*

Hook Industrial Sales Inc..................... D 260 432-9441
  Fort Wayne *(G-5075)*

Hoosier Industrial Supply.................... G 574 535-0712
  Goshen *(G-6167)*

Hoosier Industrial Supply Inc............... F 574 533-8565
  Goshen *(G-6168)*

Indiana Whitesell Corporation............. B 317 279-3278
  Indianapolis *(G-8500)*

Indianapolis In.................................... E 855 628-3458
  Indianapolis *(G-8502)*

Jac Jmr Inc... Jac .. 219 663-6700
  Crown Point *(G-2698)*

Kaiser Tool Company Inc.................... E 260 484-3620
  Fort Wayne *(G-5142)*

Kirby Risk Corporation........................ F 765 664-5185
  Marion *(G-11304)*

◆ Koehler Welding Supply Inc............. F 812 574-4103
  Madison *(G-11233)*

Magneco/Metrel Inc............................ D 219 885-4190
  Gary *(G-5979)*

McFeelys Inc...................................... F 800 443-7937
  Aurora *(G-449)*

Midwest Design Hydraulic................... G 765 714-3016
  West Lafayette *(G-16605)*

Mulzer Crushed Stone Inc................... E 812 547-7921
  Tell City *(G-15513)*

Nitto Inc.. G 317 879-2840
  Zionsville *(G-17037)*

NSK Corporation................................ D 765 458-5000
  Liberty *(G-10993)*

OBryan Barrel Company Inc................ E 812 479-6741
  Evansville *(G-4225)*

P H C Industries Inc............................ G
  Fort Wayne *(G-5291)*

Peter Austin Co................................... G 765 288-6397
  Muncie *(G-12474)*

Polymer Logistics Inc.......................... D 219 706-5985
  Portage *(G-13904)*

Polymod Technologies Inc................... F 260 436-1322
  Fort Wayne *(G-5325)*

▼ Press-Seal Corporation..................... C 260 436-0521
  Fort Wayne *(G-5350)*

Puck Supply & Machine LLC............... F 574 293-3333
  Elkhart *(G-3625)*

Pyro Industrial Services Inc................. E 219 787-5700
  Portage *(G-13907)*

Rankin Pump and Supply Co Inc.......... G 812 238-2535
  Terre Haute *(G-15675)*

Refractory Service Corporation........... E 219 853-0885
  Hammond *(G-6996)*

Rits Ltd Brokers Inc............................ G 260 348-0786
  Fort Wayne *(G-5385)*

River Bend Hose Specialty Inc............. E 574 233-1133
  South Bend *(G-15222)*

▲ Rusach International Inc................. F 317 638-0298
  Hope *(G-7232)*

▲ Somaschini North America LLC....... E 574 968-0273
  South Bend *(G-15249)*

Standard Die Supply of Indiana Inc...... D 317 236-6200
  Indianapolis *(G-9493)*

Stanley Black & Decker Inc................. D 860 225-5111
  Indianapolis *(G-9495)*

Stanley Engnered Fastening LLC......... C 765 728-2433
  Montpelier *(G-12182)*

Steelco Industrial Lubricants............... G 219 462-0333
  Valparaiso *(G-16057)*

▲ Terry Liquidation III Inc.................. D 219 362-9908
  La Porte *(G-10489)*

▲ Titus Tool Company Inc.................. F 206 447-1489
  Columbia City *(G-2207)*

Tri-State Power Supply LLC................ G 812 537-2500
  Lawrenceburg *(G-10863)*

Tway Company Incorporated.............. E 317 636-2591
  Indianapolis *(G-9662)*

Universal Package LLC........................ F 812 937-3605
  Ferdinand *(G-4450)*

VMS Products Inc............................... G 888 321-4698
  Anderson *(G-214)*

5087 Service establishment equipment

Bane-Clene Corp................................. G 317 546-5448
  Indianapolis *(G-7594)*

Bane-Clene Corp................................. F 317 546-5448
  Indianapolis *(G-7595)*

Bedlam Beard Company LLC............... G 317 800-9631
  Lizton *(G-11048)*

Black Lavish Essentials LLC................. G 800 214-8664
  Indianapolis *(G-7639)*

Cosmoprof.. G 317 897-0124
  Indianapolis *(G-7885)*

Divine Essentials LLC.......................... G 765 400-8609
  Muncie *(G-12385)*

Elkhart Brass Manufacturing Co.......... E 800 346-0250
  Elkhart *(G-3321)*

Evansville Assn For The Blind............. C 812 422-1181
  Evansville *(G-4047)*

G & T Industries Inc............................ G 812 634-2252
  Jasper *(G-9839)*

Hoosier Fire Equipment Inc................. F 219 462-1707
  Valparaiso *(G-15965)*

Ideal Co... G 765 457-6222
  Kokomo *(G-10284)*

Johnco Corp....................................... G 317 576-4417
  Indianapolis *(G-8632)*

Jzj Services LLC.................................. G 574 642-3182
  Goshen *(G-6181)*

Jzj Services LLC.................................. E 812 424-8268
  Evansville *(G-4147)*

Kill Her Set LLC.................................. F 317 992-2220
  Indianapolis *(G-8682)*

Kleen-Rite Supply Inc.......................... F 812 422-7483
  Evansville *(G-4156)*

Lebanon Berg Vault Co Inc.................. G 765 482-0302
  Lebanon *(G-10909)*

Maddox Engineering Inc...................... F 812 903-0048
  Greenville *(G-6652)*

Milso Industries Inc............................. F 765 966-8012
  Richmond *(G-14167)*

Modrak Products Company Inc............ F 219 838-0308
  Gary *(G-5985)*

Otter Creek Christian Church.............. G 812 446-5300
  Brazil *(G-1159)*

◆ Paragon Casket Inc......................... D 888 855-3601
  Richmond *(G-14179)*

Quality Vault Company....................... G 812 336-8127
  Bloomington *(G-949)*

Rensselaer Eagle Vault Corp................ G 219 866-5123
  Rensselaer *(G-14065)*

Roberson Fire & Safety Inc.................. G 317 879-3119
  Indianapolis *(G-9313)*

State Beauty Supply............................ G 260 755-6361
  Fort Wayne *(G-5436)*

Timberline Industries LLC................... G 812 442-0949
  Brazil *(G-1167)*

Vandor Corporation............................ E 765 683-9760
  Richmond *(G-14223)*

Whitlocks Pressure Wash.................... F 765 825-5868
  Connersville *(G-2475)*

Wildman Business Group LLC............. G 866 369-1552
  Warsaw *(G-16451)*

Williams Distribution LLC................... G 317 749-0006
  Indianapolis *(G-9767)*

5088 Transportation equipment and supplies

◆ Allied Enterprises LLC..................... E 765 288-8849
  Muncie *(G-12339)*

◆ Brake Supply Company Inc.............. C 812 467-1000
  Evansville *(G-3950)*

Full Throttle Enterprise Inc................. G 317 779-3887
  Indianapolis *(G-8240)*

Gbj Holdings LLC................................ G 317 483-1896
  Highland *(G-7137)*

General Signals Inc............................. E 812 474-4256
  Evansville *(G-4088)*

Hoosier Industrial Supply Inc............... F 574 533-8565
  Goshen *(G-6168)*

Indian Creek Outdoor Power LLC........ G 812 597-3055
  Morgantown *(G-12258)*

Indiana Aircraft Hardware Co.............. G 317 485-6500
  Fortville *(G-5600)*

Mid America Powered Vehicles............ G 812 925-7745
  Chandler *(G-1864)*

Norman Stein & Associates................. G 260 749-5468
  New Haven *(G-12912)*

▲ Porter Inc...................................... A 800 736-7685
  Decatur *(G-2876)*

R & R Regulators Inc........................... F 574 522-3500
  Elkhart *(G-3636)*

Troy Meggitt Inc................................. D 812 547-7071
  Troy *(G-15843)*

Turbines Inc....................................... E 812 877-2587
  Terre Haute *(G-15737)*

5091 Sporting and recreation goods

America Wild LLC............................... G 888 485-2589
  Fort Wayne *(G-4751)*

50 WHOLESALE TRADE - DURABLE GOODS

▲ Automatic Pool Covers Inc .... E 317 579-2000
   Westfield *(G-16666)*
B Thystrup US Corporation .... G 574 834-2554
   North Webster *(G-13302)*
Big Shot Outfitters LLC .... G 317 736-4867
   Franklin *(G-5716)*
Buddy Covers Inc .... G 317 846-5766
   Carmel *(G-1575)*
▲ Classic Products Corp .... E 260 484-2695
   Fort Wayne *(G-4855)*
Cloud Defensive LLC .... G 813 492-5683
   Chandler *(G-1859)*
Coachs Connection Inc .... G 260 356-0400
   Huntington *(G-7306)*
Crescendo Inc .... G 812 829-4759
   Spencer *(G-15344)*
Cummins Dist Holdco Inc .... E 812 377-5000
   Columbus *(G-2252)*
▲ Diamond Billiard Products Inc .... D 812 288-7665
   Jeffersonville *(G-9970)*
▲ Dunn-Rite Products Inc .... F 765 552-9433
   Elwood *(G-3820)*
Escalade Inc .... E 260 569-7233
   Wabash *(G-16183)*
Fort Wayne Pools .... C 260 459-4100
   Fort Wayne *(G-5001)*
Global Ozone Innovations LLC .... G 574 294-5797
   Elkhart *(G-3383)*
▲ Jay Orner Sons Billiard Co Inc .... G 317 243-0046
   Indianapolis *(G-8618)*
Kerham Inc .... E 260 483-5444
   Fort Wayne *(G-5146)*
Leistner Aquatic Services Inc .... G 317 535-6099
   Morgantown *(G-12260)*
Leisure Pool & Spa LLC .... G 812 537-0071
   Lawrenceburg *(G-10845)*
Lomatt Dynamics LLC .... G 574 500-2517
   Leesburg *(G-10957)*
▼ Midwest Gym Supply Inc .... F 812 265-4099
   Madison *(G-11242)*
▼ Natare Corporation .... E 317 290-8828
   Indianapolis *(G-8985)*
Ontime Toys Inc .... G 317 598-9333
   Indianapolis *(G-9058)*
Patriot Industries LLC .... G 574 370-7899
   Bloomington *(G-943)*
Playfair Shuffleboard Company .... F 260 747-7288
   Fort Wayne *(G-5319)*
Ppi Acquisition LLC .... E 765 674-8627
   Marion *(G-11329)*
Procoat Inc .... G 317 263-5071
   Indianapolis *(G-9218)*
Robert J Matt .... G 317 831-2400
   Mooresville *(G-12239)*
Sisk Rifles Manufacturing LLC .... G 812 686-8067
   Tell City *(G-15517)*
Sparkle Pools Inc .... F 812 232-1292
   Terre Haute *(G-15707)*
Sportcrafters Inc .... G 574 243-2453
   Granger *(G-6381)*
Standard Issue Armory LLC .... F 812 364-1466
   Greenville *(G-6657)*
Tippmann US Holdco Inc .... E 260 749-6022
   Fort Wayne *(G-5489)*
Uebelhors Golf .... G 317 881-4109
   Indianapolis *(G-9674)*
Wyatt Survival Supply LLC .... G 765 318-2872
   Morgantown *(G-12266)*

5092 Toys and hobby goods and supplies

◆ American Art Clay Co Inc .... C 317 244-6871
   Indianapolis *(G-7499)*
Brasilia Press Inc .... G 574 262-9700
   Elkhart *(G-3234)*
▲ Continuum Games Incorporated .... G 877 405-2662
   Indianapolis *(G-7860)*
Gener8 LLC .... G 317 253-8737
   Indianapolis *(G-8269)*
▲ Honey and ME .... G 317 668-3924
   Franklin *(G-5741)*
▼ Litko Aerosystems Inc .... G 219 462-9295
   Valparaiso *(G-15998)*
Ontime Toys Inc .... G 317 598-9333
   Indianapolis *(G-9058)*
Red Wagon .... G 260 768-3090
   Shipshewana *(G-14881)*
Summerville Miniature Work Sp .... G 317 326-8355
   Greenfield *(G-6561)*
Suns Out Inc .... E 765 205-5645
   Marion *(G-11340)*
Tokumei LLC .... G 765 772-0073
   West Lafayette *(G-16638)*

5093 Scrap and waste materials

American Scrap Processing Inc .... C 219 398-1444
   East Chicago *(G-2989)*
◆ D Martin Enterprises Inc .... F 219 872-8211
   Michigan City *(G-11596)*
Exeon Processors LLC .... F 765 674-2266
   Jonesboro *(G-10078)*
▼ J Trockman & Sons Inc .... E 812 425-5271
   Evansville *(G-4134)*
Joe W Morgan Inc .... D 812 423-5914
   Evansville *(G-4143)*
Kendallville Iron & Metal Inc .... F 260 347-1958
   Kendallville *(G-10126)*
Mervis Industries Inc .... G 765 454-5800
   Kokomo *(G-10306)*
Mervis Industries Inc .... G 812 232-1251
   Terre Haute *(G-15643)*
Newco Metals Inc .... G 765 644-6649
   Anderson *(G-168)*
Newco Metals Inc .... E 317 485-7721
   Pendleton *(G-13546)*
Omnisource LLC .... G 574 654-7561
   New Carlisle *(G-12843)*
◆ Omnisource LLC .... C 260 422-5541
   Fort Wayne *(G-5286)*
P & H Iron & Supply Inc .... F 219 853-0240
   Hammond *(G-6990)*
Plastic Recycl Export Ltd LLC .... G 301 758-6885
   Fort Wayne *(G-5318)*
Porter County Ir & Met Recycle .... F 219 996-7630
   Hebron *(G-7104)*
Recycling Center Inc .... D 765 966-8295
   Richmond *(G-14195)*
Recycling Works LLC .... F 574 293-3751
   Elkhart *(G-3644)*
Remedium Services Group LLC .... F 317 660-6868
   Carmel *(G-1741)*
Winski Brothers Inc .... G 765 654-5323
   Frankfort *(G-5702)*

5094 Jewelry and precious stones

▲ Bruce Fox Inc .... C 812 945-3511
   New Albany *(G-12706)*
Downey Creations LLC .... F 317 248-9888
   Indianapolis *(G-8003)*
First Place Trophy Inc .... G 574 293-6147
   Elkhart *(G-3347)*
▲ Gillis Company .... G 574 273-9086
   Granger *(G-6349)*
Imperial Trophy & Awards Co .... G 260 432-8161
   Fort Wayne *(G-5096)*
Nina Gail Diamonds LLC .... G 765 591-0477
   Muncie *(G-12469)*
Ram Graphics Inc .... F 765 724-7783
   Alexandria *(G-58)*
Ronaldo Designer Jewelry Inc .... F 812 972-7220
   New Albany *(G-12808)*
Surplus Store and Exchange .... F 765 447-0200
   Lafayette *(G-10707)*
▲ Tower Advertising Products Inc .... D 260 593-2103
   Topeka *(G-15821)*

5099 Durable goods, nec

◆ Abro Industries Inc .... E 574 232-8289
   South Bend *(G-14933)*
Acpi Wood Products LLC .... D 574 842-2066
   Culver *(G-2777)*
American Urn Inc .... G 812 379-5555
   Columbus *(G-2218)*
▲ American Way Marketing Llc .... F 574 295-6633
   Elkhart *(G-3178)*
Antique Stove Information .... G 574 583-6465
   Monticello *(G-12135)*
Asphalt Materials Inc .... G 317 875-4670
   Indianapolis *(G-7553)*
Bilbees Service and Supply Inc .... G 317 895-8288
   Indianapolis *(G-7625)*
Blackpoint Distribution Co LLC .... E 260 414-9096
   Leo *(G-10964)*
Blythes Sport Shop Inc .... F 219 924-4403
   Griffith *(G-6795)*
C & P Distributing LLC .... F 574 256-1138
   Mishawaka *(G-11857)*
Calumite Company LLC .... G 219 787-8667
   Portage *(G-13852)*
Conn-Selmer Inc .... E 574 295-6730
   Elkhart *(G-3263)*
Core Wood Components LLC .... G 574 370-4457
   Elkhart *(G-3268)*
▲ Economy Signs Incorporated .... G 219 932-1233
   Hammond *(G-6920)*
Fedex Office & Print Svcs Inc .... G 317 974-0378
   Indianapolis *(G-8172)*
Fedex Office & Print Svcs Inc .... G 317 917-1529
   Indianapolis *(G-8173)*
Graphic22 Inc .... G 219 921-5409
   Chesterton *(G-1930)*
K Tech Supply .... G 812 793-3352
   Crothersville *(G-2641)*
Link Electrical Service .... G 812 288-8184
   Jeffersonville *(G-10013)*
Northwest Indus Specialist Inc .... F 219 397-7446
   East Chicago *(G-3033)*
Over Hill & Dale Sign Studio .... G 812 867-1664
   Evansville *(G-4231)*
Patriot Industries LLC .... G 574 370-7899
   Bloomington *(G-943)*
◆ Peg Perego USA Inc .... D 800 671-1701
   Fort Wayne *(G-5300)*
Pine Valley Munitions Inc .... G 260 818-6113
   Columbia City *(G-2181)*
Popguns Inc .... G 317 897-8660
   Indianapolis *(G-9163)*
▲ Rees Harps Inc .... F 812 438-3032
   Rising Sun *(G-14245)*
Region Signs Inc .... F 219 473-1616
   Whiting *(G-16838)*
▲ S C Pryor Inc .... F 317 352-1281
   Indianapolis *(G-9354)*
Speedhook Specialists Inc .... G 219 378-6369
   Beverly Shores *(G-732)*
St Joe Group Inc .... E 260 918-3500
   New Haven *(G-12920)*

50 WHOLESALE TRADE - DURABLE GOODS

Traffic Sign Co Inc............................... G 317 845-9305
  Indianapolis (G-9627)
Vadens Firearms & Ammun LLC............. G 317 840-5799
  Indianapolis (G-9697)
▲ Wagner Zip-Change Inc..................... E 708 681-4100
  Fort Wayne (G-5540)
Wyatt Survival Supply LLC..................... G 765 318-2872
  Morgantown (G-12266)

51 WHOLESALE TRADE - NONDURABLE GOODS

5111 Printing and writing paper

Mecom Ltd Inc..................................... D 317 218-2600
  Indianapolis (G-8868)
Millcraft Paper Company........................ G 317 240-3500
  Indianapolis (G-8920)
Reprocomm Inc.................................... G 765 472-5700
  Peru (G-13598)

5112 Stationery and office supplies

Allison Pymnt Systems LLC DBA............. C 317 808-2400
  Indianapolis (G-7485)
Altstadt Business Forms Inc................... F 812 425-3393
  Evansville (G-3882)
Brand Prtg & Photo-Litho Co................. G 317 921-4095
  New Palestine (G-12933)
▲ Custom Forms Inc............................ F 765 463-6162
  Lafayette (G-10565)
Dbisp LLC... G 317 222-1671
  Indianapolis (G-7957)
Diversified Bus Systems Inc................... G 317 254-8668
  Indianapolis (G-7984)
Double Envelope Corp........................... G 260 434-0500
  Fort Wayne (G-4926)
Excel Business Printing Inc.................... G 317 259-1075
  Indianapolis (G-8149)
Finest Grade Products........................... G 812 421-1976
  Evansville (G-4069)
▲ Harcourt Industries Inc..................... E 765 629-2625
  Milroy (G-11824)
I4 Identity LLC..................................... G 317 662-0448
  Fishers (G-4541)
Johnco Corp.. G 317 576-4417
  Indianapolis (G-8632)
Label Tech Inc..................................... E 765 747-1234
  Muncie (G-12436)
Lasertone Inc...................................... F 812 473-5945
  Evansville (G-4162)
Maddox Engineering Inc........................ G 812 903-0048
  Greenville (G-6652)
Masson Inc.. F 317 632-8021
  Indianapolis (G-8848)
Millcraft Paper Company........................ G 317 240-3500
  Indianapolis (G-8920)
Office Sup of Southern Ind Inc............... G 812 283-5523
  Jeffersonville (G-10027)
Peerless Printing Corporation................. G 765 664-8341
  Marion (G-11327)
Perdue Printed Products Inc................... G 260 456-7575
  Fort Wayne (G-5304)
Priority Press Inc................................. G 317 848-9695
  Carmel (G-1730)
Priority Press Inc................................. E 317 241-4234
  Indianapolis (G-9211)
Rivers Resources LLC............................ G 317 572-5029
  Indianapolis (G-9310)
Smith & Butterfield Co Inc..................... F 812 422-3261
  Evansville (G-4320)
Smith & Butterfield Co Inc..................... G 812 422-3261
  Evansville (G-4321)

Stewart Graphics Inc............................. E 812 283-0455
  Jeffersonville (G-10060)
Systems & Services of Michiana............. G 574 277-3355
  South Bend (G-15278)
Systems & Services of Michiana............. G 574 273-1111
  South Bend (G-15277)

5113 Industrial and personal service paper

Farm Boy Meats of Evansville................. D 812 425-5231
  Evansville (G-4064)
▲ Gta Containers LLC........................... E 574 288-3459
  South Bend (G-15054)
Indianapolis Container Company............. G 317 580-5000
  Indianapolis (G-8503)
Millcraft Paper Company........................ G 317 240-3500
  Indianapolis (G-8920)
Orora Packaging Solutions..................... F 317 879-4628
  Indianapolis (G-9071)
▲ Precision Products Group Inc............. F 317 663-4590
  Indianapolis (G-9184)
PSC Industries Inc................................ F 812 425-9071
  Evansville (G-4263)
Servants Inc.. D 812 634-2201
  Jasper (G-9910)
Temple Inland...................................... G 765 362-1074
  Crawfordsville (G-2623)
Viking Paper Company........................... E 574 936-6300
  Plymouth (G-13825)
Westrock Cp LLC.................................. G 574 256-0318
  Mishawaka (G-12027)

5122 Drugs, proprietaries, and sundries

Aesthtcally Pleasing Skin Soak............... G 317 551-0156
  Indianapolis (G-7454)
Black Lavish Essentials LLC................... G 800 214-8664
  Indianapolis (G-7639)
Dream Beauty Lab................................ G 773 571-1817
  Marion (G-11283)
Elanco Animal Health Inc...................... A 877 352-6261
  Greenfield (G-6493)
Eli Lilly and Company............................ C 317 276-2000
  Indianapolis (G-8089)
Komodo Pharmaceuticals Inc.................. G 317 485-0023
  Fortville (G-5602)
Martin Ekwlor Phrmcuticals Inc............... F 765 962-4410
  Richmond (G-14159)
▲ Maverick Packaging Inc.................... E 574 264-2891
  Elkhart (G-3519)
North Coast Organics LLC..................... G 260 246-0289
  Fort Wayne (G-5274)
Rugged Company.................................. G 317 441-0927
  Anderson (G-187)
Seductive Lifestyle LLC......................... G 708 990-0720
  Gary (G-6008)
Tall Cotton Marketing LLC...................... G 312 320-5862
  La Porte (G-10486)
Vitamins Inc.. E 219 879-7356
  Michigan City (G-11686)
Wellsource Nutraceuticals LLC............... G 219 213-6173
  Crown Point (G-2773)

5131 Piece goods and notions

Abercrombie Textiles I LLC.................... G 574 848-5100
  Bristol (G-1240)
C M I Enterprises Inc............................ D 305 685-9651
  Elkhart (G-3244)
Custom Sewing Service......................... G 812 428-7015
  Evansville (G-4004)
Cyclone Custom Prouducts LLC............... G 765 246-6523
  Greencastle (G-6401)
Flag & Banner Company Inc................... F 317 299-4880
  Indianapolis (G-8199)

▲ Georg Utz Inc.................................. E 812 526-2240
  Edinburgh (G-3085)
◆ J Ennis Fabrics Inc (usa).................... G 877 953-6647
  Plainfield (G-13695)
Mitchell Fabrics Inc.............................. E 309 674-8631
  Lafayette (G-10651)
▲ Mpr Corporation............................... E 574 848-5100
  Bristol (G-1280)
Pearison Inc.. D 812 963-8890
  Cynthiana (G-2788)
Raine Inc... F 765 622-7687
  Anderson (G-182)
Samaron Corp....................................... E 574 970-7070
  Elkhart (G-3661)
◆ Tiedemann-Bevs Industries LLC........... E 765 962-4914
  Richmond (G-14219)

5136 Men's and boy's clothing

Arizona Sport Shirts Inc........................ E 317 481-2160
  Indianapolis (G-7544)
Locoli Inc.. E 219 515-6900
  Schererville (G-14531)
National Fdrtion State High SC............... E 317 972-6900
  Indianapolis (G-8988)
Ram Graphics Inc................................. F 765 724-7783
  Alexandria (G-58)
Smiling Cross Inc................................. G 812 323-9290
  Bloomington (G-976)
Sport Form Inc..................................... G 260 589-2200
  Berne (G-727)

5137 Women's and children's clothing

Arizona Sport Shirts Inc........................ E 317 481-2160
  Indianapolis (G-7544)
▲ Cinda B USA LLC.............................. G 260 469-0803
  Fort Wayne (G-4848)
Diaper Stone Opco LLC......................... G 866 221-2145
  Greenfield (G-6489)
Hoogies Sports House Inc..................... G 574 533-9875
  Goshen (G-6165)
Locoli Inc.. E 219 515-6900
  Schererville (G-14531)
Mammoth Hats Inc................................ F 812 849-2772
  Mitchell (G-12044)
National Fdrtion State High SC............... E 317 972-6900
  Indianapolis (G-8988)
Ontime Toys Inc................................... G 317 598-9333
  Indianapolis (G-9058)
Profit Over Romance LLC....................... G 219 900-3592
  Gary (G-5997)
Ram Graphics Inc................................. F 765 724-7783
  Alexandria (G-58)
Sport Form Inc..................................... G 260 589-2200
  Berne (G-727)

5139 Footwear

Bootmakers LLC.................................... G 765 412-7243
  West Lafayette (G-16568)
Cowpokes Inc....................................... E 765 642-3911
  Anderson (G-99)
Orb LLC... G 833 946-4672
  Indianapolis (G-9067)

5141 Groceries, general line

Albanese Conf Group Inc....................... E 219 947-3070
  Merrillville (G-11479)
◆ Albanese Conf Group Inc................... D 219 947-3070
  Merrillville (G-11480)
Mi Tierra... G 812 376-0668
  Columbus (G-2353)

5142 Packaged frozen goods

51 WHOLESALE TRADE - NONDURABLE GOODS

Cookie Please .... G 317 879-6589
Indianapolis *(G-7867)*

Farm Boy Meats of Evansville .... D 812 425-5231
Evansville *(G-4064)*

Myers Frz Foods Provisioners .... G 765 525-6304
Saint Paul *(G-14467)*

5143 Dairy products, except dried or canned

Dugdale Beef Company Inc .... E 317 291-9660
Indianapolis *(G-8019)*

Instantwhip-Indianapolis Inc .... F 317 899-1533
Indianapolis *(G-8563)*

Revival LLC .... G 812 345-4317
Indianapolis *(G-9296)*

5144 Poultry and poultry products

Jfs Milling Inc .... G 812 683-4200
Vincennes *(G-16134)*

Lambrights Inc .... G 260 463-2178
Lagrange *(G-10750)*

5145 Confectionery

Amish Country Popcorn Inc .... E 260 589-8513
Berne *(G-703)*

Combined Technologies Inc .... G 847 968-4855
Bristol *(G-1254)*

Dieng Group LLC .... G 317 699-1909
Indianapolis *(G-7973)*

Poore Brothers - Bluffton LLC .... C 260 824-2800
Bluffton *(G-1048)*

◆ **Popcorn Weaver Mfg LLC** .... G 765 934-2101
Indianapolis *(G-9162)*

◆ **Ramsey Popcorn Co Inc** .... E 812 347-2441
Ramsey *(G-14026)*

Snax In Pax Inc .... E 260 593-3066
Topeka *(G-15819)*

Swanel Inc .... E 219 932-7676
Hammond *(G-7017)*

Sweet Things Inc .... F 317 872-8720
Carmel *(G-1774)*

5146 Fish and seafoods

Dugdale Beef Company Inc .... E 317 291-9660
Indianapolis *(G-8019)*

5147 Meats and meat products

Blackpoint Distribution Co LLC .... E 260 414-9096
Leo *(G-10964)*

Dugdale Beef Company Inc .... E 317 291-9660
Indianapolis *(G-8019)*

Fisher Packing Company .... E 260 726-7355
Portland *(G-13941)*

Hobart Locker & Meat Pkg Co .... G 219 942-5952
Crown Point *(G-2693)*

▼ **Meats By Linz Inc** .... E 708 862-0830
Hammond *(G-6979)*

Merkley & Sons Inc .... E 812 482-7020
Jasper *(G-9890)*

Rices Quality Farm Meats Inc .... G 812 829-4562
Spencer *(G-15361)*

Smithland Butchering Co Inc .... G 317 729-5398
Elizabethtown *(G-3133)*

Uselman Packing Co .... G 765 832-2112
Clinton *(G-2080)*

5148 Fresh fruits and vegetables

Ready Pac Foods Inc .... C 574 935-9800
Plymouth *(G-13810)*

5149 Groceries and related products, nec

Allen Street Roasters LLC .... G 815 955-7872
La Porte *(G-10380)*

American Bottling Company .... D 260 484-4177
Fort Wayne *(G-4752)*

American Bottling Company .... C 317 875-4900
Indianapolis *(G-7500)*

American Bottling Company .... D 574 291-9000
South Bend *(G-14943)*

B S R Inc .... E 812 235-4444
Terre Haute *(G-15549)*

Bhj Usa LLC .... G 574 722-3933
Logansport *(G-11062)*

Blue Buffalo Company Ltd .... B 203 665-3500
Richmond *(G-14099)*

Buckner Inc .... E 317 570-0533
Indianapolis *(G-7699)*

▲ **Calumet Breweries Inc** .... E 219 845-2242
Hammond *(G-6891)*

Central Coca-Cola Btlg Co Inc .... G 800 241-2653
Indianapolis *(G-7770)*

Central Coca-Cola Btlg Co Inc .... E 317 243-3771
Indianapolis *(G-7772)*

◆ **Clark Foods Inc** .... E 812 949-3075
New Albany *(G-12714)*

Conagra Brands Inc .... F 219 866-3020
Rensselaer *(G-14049)*

Darlington Cookie Company .... G 800 754-2202
Indianapolis *(G-7952)*

Dieng Group LLC .... G 317 699-1909
Indianapolis *(G-7973)*

Dugdale Beef Company Inc .... E 317 291-9660
Indianapolis *(G-8019)*

◆ **Flavor Burst LLC** .... C 317 745-2952
Danville *(G-2812)*

Grabers Kountry Korner LLC .... F 812 636-4399
Odon *(G-13339)*

Grabill Country Meat 1 Inc .... F 260 627-3691
Grabill *(G-6300)*

Harlan Bakeries LLC .... C 317 272-3600
Indianapolis *(G-8361)*

▲ **Harlan Bakeries LLC** .... C 317 272-3600
Avon *(G-523)*

▲ **Harlan Bakeries-Avon LLC** .... B 317 272-3600
Avon *(G-524)*

Harvest Cafe Coffee & Tea LLC .... G 317 585-9162
Indianapolis *(G-8369)*

Hoosier Processing LLC .... G 260 422-9440
Fort Wayne *(G-5080)*

Joey Chestnut Foods LLC .... G 317 602-4830
Indianapolis *(G-8629)*

◆ **Lebermuth Company Inc** .... D 574 259-7000
South Bend *(G-15121)*

Lewis Brothers Bakeries Inc .... C 812 886-6533
Vincennes *(G-16137)*

▲ **Lewis Brothers Bakeries Inc** .... C 812 425-4642
Evansville *(G-4166)*

Mild To Wild Pepper & Herb Co .... G 317 736-8300
Greenwood *(G-6741)*

Natural Answers .... G 219 922-3663
Highland *(G-7147)*

New Aqua LLC .... D 317 272-3000
Avon *(G-540)*

Organic Bread of Heaven LLC .... F 219 883-5126
Gary *(G-5991)*

P-Americas LLC .... G 765 289-0270
Indianapolis *(G-9081)*

P-Americas LLC .... G 812 522-3421
Seymour *(G-14670)*

Passions Fruitopia LLC .... G 800 515-1891
Highland *(G-7151)*

Pepsi-Cola Metro Btlg Co Inc .... F 812 332-1200
Bloomington *(G-945)*

R D Laney Family Honey Company .... G 574 656-8701
North Liberty *(G-13220)*

Rapid View LLC .... G 574 224-3373
Rochester *(G-14315)*

Reidco Inc .... E 812 358-3000
Brownstown *(G-1426)*

Rolling Hills Springs LLC .... G 844 454-6866
Linton *(G-11044)*

Suncoast Coffee Inc .... E 317 251-3198
Indianapolis *(G-9526)*

5153 Grain and field beans

AG Plus Inc .... G 260 623-6121
Monroeville *(G-12066)*

AG Plus Inc .... E 260 723-5141
South Whitley *(G-15316)*

Archer-Daniels-Midland Company .... G 765 299-1672
Fowler *(G-5618)*

Archer-Daniels-Midland Company .... E 765 654-4411
Frankfort *(G-5649)*

B S R Inc .... E 812 235-4444
Terre Haute *(G-15549)*

Bundy Bros and Sons Inc .... F 812 966-2551
Medora *(G-11462)*

Clunette Elevator Co Inc .... F 574 858-2281
Leesburg *(G-10952)*

▲ **Frick Services Inc** .... E 260 761-3311
Wawaka *(G-16539)*

Gem Elevator Inc .... G 317 894-7722
Greenfield *(G-6505)*

Keystone Cooperative Inc .... G 765 249-2233
Michigantown *(G-11691)*

◆ **Keystone Cooperative Inc** .... C 800 525-0272
Indianapolis *(G-8680)*

Landec Ag Inc .... F 765 385-1000
Oxford *(G-13475)*

Langeland Farms Inc .... G 812 663-9546
Greensburg *(G-6614)*

Laughery Valley AG Co-Op Inc .... G 812 689-4401
Osgood *(G-13412)*

Lowes Pellets and Grain Inc .... E 812 663-7863
Greensburg *(G-6615)*

Northwest Farm Fertilizers .... G 219 785-2331
Westville *(G-16764)*

Premier AG Co-Op Inc .... E 812 522-4911
Seymour *(G-14677)*

Roy Umbarger and Sons Inc .... F 317 422-5195
Franklin *(G-5775)*

Salamonie Mills Inc .... F 260 375-2200
Warren *(G-16304)*

▼ **United Animal Health Inc** .... D 317 758-4495
Sheridan *(G-14830)*

Wallace Grain Company Inc .... F 317 758-4434
Sheridan *(G-14832)*

Wilson Fertilizer & Grain Inc .... G 574 223-3175
Rochester *(G-14333)*

5154 Livestock

D Rinker Transport LLC .... G 765 749-4120
Dunkirk *(G-2961)*

P & R Farms Llc .... G 812 326-2010
Saint Anthony *(G-14430)*

5159 Farm-product raw materials, nec

Fischer Frms Natural Foods LLC .... G 812 481-1411
Saint Anthony *(G-14428)*

◆ **Maple Leaf Inc** .... B 574 453-4455
Leesburg *(G-10958)*

5162 Plastics materials and basic shapes

A S V Plastics Inc .... F 574 264-9694
Elkhart *(G-3141)*

▲ **Ameri-Kart Corp** .... C 574 848-7462
Bristol *(G-1244)*

51 WHOLESALE TRADE - NONDURABLE GOODS

◆ American Renolit Corporation.............C 219 324-6886
La Porte *(G-10384)*

Arrowhead Plastic Engrg Inc....................F 765 396-9113
Eaton *(G-3059)*

Brunk LLC..D 800 227-4156
Goshen *(G-6101)*

Celestial Designs LLC...........................G 317 733-3110
Zionsville *(G-16997)*

CRS-Drs Corporation.............................G 260 478-7555
Fort Wayne *(G-4891)*

▲ General Rbr Plas of Evansville............E 812 464-5153
Evansville *(G-4087)*

Innovations Amplified LLC....................G 317 339-4685
Indianapolis *(G-8552)*

◆ Magnum International Inc....................E 708 889-9999
Crown Point *(G-2721)*

▲ Meyer Plastics Inc................................D 317 259-4131
Indianapolis *(G-8895)*

Nibco Inc..C 574 296-1240
Goshen *(G-6227)*

◆ Parkland Plastics Inc............................E 574 825-4336
Middlebury *(G-11745)*

Plastic Recycl Export Ltd LLC...............G 301 758-6885
Fort Wayne *(G-5318)*

Plastics Family Holdings Inc.................G 317 890-1808
Indianapolis *(G-9153)*

Polymer Logistics Inc............................D 219 706-5985
Portage *(G-13904)*

Shaw Polymers Holdings LLC...............G 219 779-9450
Crown Point *(G-2750)*

▲ Superior Indus Solutions Inc................E 317 781-4400
Indianapolis *(G-9529)*

5169 Chemicals and allied products, nec

1500 South Tibbs LLC...........................C 317 247-8141
Indianapolis *(G-7384)*

Accra-Pac Inc..G 574 295-0000
Elkhart *(G-3149)*

Adhesive Products Inc..........................G 317 899-0565
Indianapolis *(G-7432)*

Adhesive Solutions Company LLC........G 260 691-0304
Columbia City *(G-2117)*

Air Products and Chemicals Inc............G 812 466-6492
Terre Haute *(G-15535)*

Airgas Usa LLC......................................G 812 474-0440
Evansville *(G-3878)*

Airgas Usa LLC......................................G 812 362-7593
Rockport *(G-14335)*

American Sealants Inc..........................E 800 325-7040
Fort Wayne *(G-4757)*

Ampacet Corporation.............................D 812 466-5231
Terre Haute *(G-15544)*

Apg Inc...D 574 295-0000
Elkhart *(G-3185)*

B S R Inc..G 812 235-4444
Terre Haute *(G-15548)*

B S R Inc..E 812 235-4444
Terre Haute *(G-15549)*

Bane-Clene Corp....................................G 317 546-5448
Indianapolis *(G-7594)*

Bane-Clene Corp....................................F 317 546-5448
Indianapolis *(G-7595)*

Bangs Laboratories Inc.........................F 317 570-7020
Fishers *(G-4470)*

▲ Bio-Response Solutions Inc.................F 317 386-3500
Danville *(G-2807)*

▲ Cast Products LP..................................E 574 294-2684
Elkhart *(G-3249)*

Cerline Ceramic Corp............................G 765 649-7222
Anderson *(G-92)*

Continental Carbonic Pdts Inc...............G 574 273-2800
South Bend *(G-14983)*

Craft Laboratories Inc...........................E 260 432-9467
Fort Wayne *(G-4882)*

Green Tek LLC.......................................F 317 294-1614
Carmel *(G-1644)*

Hydrite Chemical Co..............................D 812 232-5411
Terre Haute *(G-15611)*

Independent Plastic Inc........................G 765 521-2251
New Castle *(G-12869)*

Indiana Oxygen Company Inc................G 765 662-8700
Marion *(G-11295)*

Indiana Oxygen Company Inc................G 317 290-0003
Indianapolis *(G-8488)*

Ink - LLC...G 317 502-6473
Franklin *(G-5746)*

J & K Supply Inc....................................G 765 448-1188
Lafayette *(G-10611)*

J 2 Systems and Supply LLC.................G 317 602-3940
Indianapolis *(G-8601)*

J&K Generations....................................G 812 508-1094
Bedford *(G-650)*

Jzj Services LLC....................................E 812 424-8268
Evansville *(G-4147)*

Kml Inc...G 260 897-3723
Laotto *(G-10808)*

◆ Koehler Welding Supply Inc.................F 812 574-4103
Madison *(G-11233)*

▲ Kolossos Inc..G 312 952-6991
Long Beach *(G-11122)*

◆ Lebermuth Company Inc......................D 574 259-7000
South Bend *(G-15121)*

Linde Gas & Equipment Inc..................G 812 376-3314
Columbus *(G-2343)*

◆ Lucas Oil Products Inc.........................C 951 270-0154
Indianapolis *(G-8793)*

◆ Magnum International Inc....................E 708 889-9999
Crown Point *(G-2721)*

Messer LLC..G 574 234-4887
South Bend *(G-15148)*

Nochar Inc..G 317 613-3046
Indianapolis *(G-9018)*

OMI Industries Inc.................................G 812 438-9218
Rising Sun *(G-14244)*

Online Packaging Incorporated............E 219 872-0925
Michigan City *(G-11648)*

Paradigm Industries Inc........................G 317 574-8590
Carmel *(G-1714)*

Pendry Coatings LLC.............................G 574 268-2956
Warsaw *(G-16410)*

Pinder Polyurethane & Plas Inc............G 219 397-8248
East Chicago *(G-3034)*

Sdf Engineering LLC.............................G 317 674-2643
Carmel *(G-1755)*

Sorbtech Inc..G 812 944-9108
Clarksville *(G-2037)*

Substrate Treatments & Lubr................F 574 258-0904
Mishawaka *(G-12010)*

▲ Superior Indus Solutions Inc................E 317 781-4400
Indianapolis *(G-9529)*

Swanel Inc..E 219 932-7676
Hammond *(G-7017)*

Tgc Auto Care Products Inc..................G 765 962-7725
Richmond *(G-14216)*

▲ Ulrich Chemical Inc..............................E 317 898-8632
Indianapolis *(G-9675)*

Warsaw Chemical Company Inc............D 574 267-3251
Warsaw *(G-16442)*

Williams Bros Hlth Care Phrm I............G 812 335-0000
Bloomington *(G-1012)*

Williams Bros Hlth Care Phrm I............C 812 254-2497
Washington *(G-16513)*

5171 Petroleum bulk stations and terminals

AMP Americas LLC................................G 312 300-6700
Fair Oaks *(G-4394)*

Hoosier Penn Oil Co Inc........................G 812 284-9433
Jeffersonville *(G-9998)*

Keystone Cooperative Inc....................G 765 249-2233
Michigantown *(G-11691)*

◆ Keystone Cooperative Inc....................C 800 525-0272
Indianapolis *(G-8680)*

Laketon Refining Corporation..............F 260 982-0703
Laketon *(G-10787)*

5172 Petroleum products, nec

Advance Energy LLC.............................G 312 665-0022
Merrillville *(G-11477)*

▲ D-A Lubricant Company Inc................E 317 923-5321
Lebanon *(G-10890)*

Hoosier Penn Oil Co Inc........................E 317 390-5406
Indianapolis *(G-8411)*

J 2 Systems and Supply LLC.................G 317 602-3940
Indianapolis *(G-8601)*

Jolliff Diesel Service LLC.....................G 812 692-5725
Elnora *(G-3815)*

◆ Koehler Welding Supply Inc.................F 812 574-4103
Madison *(G-11233)*

Laughery Valley AG Co-Op Inc.............G 812 689-4401
Osgood *(G-13412)*

Miller Industrial Fluids LLC..................E 317 634-7300
Indianapolis *(G-8921)*

Petrochoice Holdings Inc.....................E 317 634-7300
Indianapolis *(G-9130)*

Petroleum Solutions Inc.......................G 574 546-2133
Bremen *(G-1214)*

Pinnacle Oil Holdings LLC....................C 317 875-9465
Indianapolis *(G-9144)*

Pinnacle Oil Holdings LLC....................E 317 875-9465
Indianapolis *(G-9145)*

Premier AG Co-Op Inc..........................E 812 522-4911
Seymour *(G-14677)*

Spence/Banks Holdings Inc.................F 812 235-8123
Terre Haute *(G-15713)*

◆ Swift Fuels LLC.....................................G 765 464-8336
West Lafayette *(G-16632)*

Wannemuehler Distribution Inc............F 812 422-3251
Evansville *(G-4379)*

5181 Beer and ale

Barley Island Brewing Co......................G 317 770-5280
Noblesville *(G-13039)*

▲ Black Acre Brewing Company LLC.....E 317 207-6266
Indianapolis *(G-7637)*

▲ Calumet Breweries Inc.........................E 219 845-2242
Hammond *(G-6891)*

Indiana City Brewing LLC.....................F 317 643-1103
Carmel *(G-1666)*

Mishawaka Brewing Company..............G 574 256-9993
Granger *(G-6362)*

▲ Sun King Brewing Company LLC........D 317 602-3702
Indianapolis *(G-9525)*

Tavistock Restaurants LLC...................G 317 488-1230
Indianapolis *(G-9557)*

▲ Terrance A Smith Distributing..............E 765 644-3396
Anderson *(G-205)*

5182 Wine and distilled beverages

Clancys of Portage................................E 219 764-4995
Portage *(G-13856)*

Durm Vineyard Inc................................G 317 862-9463
Indianapolis *(G-8021)*

▲ Indiana Whl Wine & Lq Co Inc............G 317 667-0231
Indianapolis *(G-8501)*

Prp Wine International..........................F 317 288-0005
Indianapolis *(G-9234)*

SIC SECTION

51 WHOLESALE TRADE - NONDURABLE GOODS

▲ Vin Elite Imports Inc.................... G..... 317 264-9250
Indianapolis *(G-9720)*

5191 Farm supplies

1500 South Tibbs LLC.................... C..... 317 247-8141
Indianapolis *(G-7384)*

AG Plus Inc.................... G..... 260 623-6121
Monroeville *(G-12066)*

AG Plus Inc.................... E..... 260 723-5141
South Whitley *(G-15316)*

AG Processing A Cooperative.................... G..... 574 773-4138
Nappanee *(G-12577)*

Andersons Agriculture Group LP.................... F..... 765 564-6135
Delphi *(G-2890)*

Andersons Agriculture Group LP.................... G..... 574 626-2522
Galveston *(G-5851)*

Andersons Fertilizer Service.................... G..... 765 538-3285
Romney *(G-14379)*

Archer-Daniels-Midland Company.................... E..... 260 824-0079
Bluffton *(G-1025)*

B S R Inc.................... G..... 812 235-4444
Terre Haute *(G-15548)*

B S R Inc.................... E..... 812 235-4444
Terre Haute *(G-15549)*

▲ Belstra Milling Co Inc.................... E..... 219 987-4343
Demotte *(G-2911)*

Biodyne-Midwest LLC.................... F..... 888 970-0955
Fort Wayne *(G-4801)*

Blue River Farm Supply Inc.................... G..... 812 364-6675
Palmyra *(G-13478)*

Bristow Milling Co LLC.................... G..... 812 843-5176
Bristow *(G-1299)*

Bundy Bros and Sons Inc.................... F..... 812 966-2551
Medora *(G-11462)*

Clunette Elevator Co Inc.................... F..... 574 858-2281
Leesburg *(G-10952)*

◆ Corteva Agriscience LLC.................... A..... 317 337-3000
Indianapolis *(G-7884)*

Don Hartman Oil Co Inc.................... G..... 765 643-5026
Anderson *(G-106)*

Earth First Kentuckiana Inc.................... F..... 812 923-1227
Charlestown *(G-1875)*

Elanco Animal Health Inc.................... A..... 877 352-6261
Greenfield *(G-6493)*

Elanco International Inc.................... D..... 877 352-6261
Greenfield *(G-6494)*

Flinn Frms Bdford Feed Seed In.................... G..... 812 279-4136
Bedford *(G-636)*

▲ Frick Services Inc.................... E..... 260 761-3311
Wawaka *(G-16539)*

Helena Agri-Enterprises LLC.................... G..... 765 869-5518
Ambia *(G-66)*

Helena Agri-Enterprises LLC.................... G..... 812 654-3177
Dillsboro *(G-2946)*

Helena Agri-Enterprises LLC.................... G..... 574 268-4762
Huntington *(G-7317)*

Helena Agri-Enterprises LLC.................... G..... 765 583-4458
Otterbein *(G-13452)*

Hunter Nutrition Inc.................... F..... 765 563-1003
Brookston *(G-1311)*

International A I Inc.................... G..... 812 824-2473
Bloomington *(G-891)*

Judson Harness & Saddlery.................... G..... 765 569-0918
Rockville *(G-14352)*

Keystone Cooperative Inc.................... G..... 765 659-2596
Frankfort *(G-5678)*

Keystone Cooperative Inc.................... G..... 765 489-4141
Hagerstown *(G-6838)*

Keystone Cooperative Inc.................... G..... 765 249-2233
Michigantown *(G-11691)*

◆ Keystone Cooperative Inc.................... C..... 800 525-0272
Indianapolis *(G-8680)*

Kova Fertilizer Inc.................... E..... 812 663-5081
Greensburg *(G-6613)*

Kuntry Lumber and Farm Sup Ltd.................... F..... 260 463-3242
Lagrange *(G-10746)*

Lambrights Inc.................... G..... 260 463-2178
Lagrange *(G-10750)*

Laughery Valley AG Co-Op Inc.................... G..... 812 689-4401
Osgood *(G-13412)*

Miles Farm Supply LLC.................... D..... 812 359-4463
Boonville *(G-1090)*

Montpelier AG LLC.................... G..... 765 728-2222
Montpelier *(G-12180)*

Mulzer Crushed Stone Inc.................... E..... 812 547-7921
Tell City *(G-15513)*

◆ Mycogen Corporation.................... F..... 317 337-3000
Indianapolis *(G-8977)*

Northwest Farm Fertilizers.................... G..... 219 785-2331
Westville *(G-16764)*

Nutritional Research Assoc.................... F..... 260 723-4931
South Whitley *(G-15322)*

Pine Manor Inc.................... G..... 574 533-4186
Goshen *(G-6238)*

Premier AG Co-Op Inc.................... E..... 812 522-4911
Seymour *(G-14677)*

Roy Umbarger and Sons Inc.................... F..... 317 422-5195
Franklin *(G-5775)*

Russell E Martin.................... G..... 574 354-2563
Akron *(G-8)*

Salamonie Mills Inc.................... F..... 260 375-2200
Warren *(G-16304)*

Sun Rise Metal Shop.................... G..... 260 463-4026
Topeka *(G-15820)*

Superior AG Resources Coop Inc.................... G..... 812 724-4455
Owensville *(G-13473)*

Synergy Feeds LLC.................... E..... 260 723-5141
South Whitley *(G-15330)*

▲ U-Nitt LLC.................... G..... 812 251-9980
Carmel *(G-1792)*

Wallace Grain Company Inc.................... F..... 317 758-4434
Sheridan *(G-14832)*

Wanafeed Corporation.................... G..... 317 862-4032
Indianapolis *(G-9736)*

Wilson Fertilizer & Grain Inc.................... G..... 574 223-3175
Rochester *(G-14333)*

Winfield Solutions LLC.................... G..... 317 838-3733
Plainfield *(G-13743)*

5192 Books, periodicals, and newspapers

County West Sports.................... G..... 317 839-4076
Plainfield *(G-13673)*

Great Deals Magazine.................... F..... 765 649-3302
Anderson *(G-123)*

Hachette Book Group Inc.................... C..... 765 483-9900
Lebanon *(G-10894)*

Magazine Fulfillment Corp.................... F..... 219 874-4245
Michigan City *(G-11636)*

▲ Tom Doherty Company Inc.................... G..... 317 352-8200
Indianapolis *(G-9617)*

5193 Flowers and florists supplies

▲ Candles By Dar Inc.................... F..... 260 482-2099
Fort Wayne *(G-4831)*

▲ Jadco Ltd.................... F..... 219 661-2065
Crown Point *(G-2699)*

Salt Creek Harvest LLC.................... G..... 708 927-5569
Valparaiso *(G-16042)*

5194 Tobacco and tobacco products

Black Swan Vapors LLC.................... G..... 317 645-5210
Pendleton *(G-13526)*

Smoker Friendly.................... G..... 812 556-0244
Jasper *(G-9912)*

5198 Paints, varnishes, and supplies

Blumling Design & Graphics Inc.................... G..... 765 477-7446
Lafayette *(G-10540)*

Jack Laurie Coml Floors Inc.................... G..... 317 569-2095
Indianapolis *(G-8613)*

Mautz Paint Factory.................... G..... 574 289-2497
South Bend *(G-15141)*

5199 Nondurable goods, nec

▲ ABC Industries Inc.................... D..... 800 426-0921
Winona Lake *(G-16907)*

Abracadabra Graphics.................... G..... 812 336-1971
Bloomington *(G-771)*

Antique Candle Works Inc.................... E..... 765 250-8481
Lafayette *(G-10523)*

Apparel Plus Inc.................... G..... 812 951-2111
Georgetown *(G-6054)*

Apple Group Inc.................... E..... 765 675-4777
Tipton *(G-15764)*

Awards Unlimited Inc.................... G..... 765 447-9413
Lafayette *(G-10532)*

Baugh Enterprises Inc.................... F..... 812 334-8189
Bloomington *(G-796)*

Bbs Celebration Center.................... G..... 765 730-6575
Yorktown *(G-16971)*

Bethlehem Packg Die Cutng Inc.................... E..... 812 282-8740
New Albany *(G-12700)*

▲ Bottom Line Management Inc.................... F..... 812 944-7388
Clarksville *(G-2010)*

▲ Burston Marketing Inc.................... F..... 574 262-4005
Elkhart *(G-3238)*

Celestial Designs LLC.................... G..... 317 733-3110
Zionsville *(G-16997)*

Cluster Packaging LLC.................... G..... 612 803-1056
Crown Point *(G-2666)*

Dimo Multiservices LLC.................... F..... 463 256-0561
Avon *(G-513)*

▲ Discount Labels LLC.................... A..... 812 945-2617
New Albany *(G-12720)*

Double E Distributing Co Inc.................... G..... 812 334-2220
Bloomington *(G-858)*

Favor It Promotions Inc.................... F..... 317 733-1112
Carmel *(G-1634)*

Fisherman S Lurecraft Shop Inc.................... F..... 260 829-1274
Orland *(G-13365)*

Flag & Banner Company Inc.................... F..... 317 299-4880
Indianapolis *(G-8199)*

▲ Foam Rubber LLC.................... C..... 765 521-2000
New Castle *(G-12862)*

Foamcraft Inc.................... E..... 574 293-8569
Elkhart *(G-3352)*

Foamcraft Inc.................... E..... 574 534-4343
Goshen *(G-6139)*

Garco Graphics.................... G..... 219 980-1113
Gary *(G-5935)*

Howe House Ltd Editions Inc.................... G..... 765 742-6831
Lafayette *(G-10602)*

Huhtamaki Inc.................... D..... 765 677-0395
Marion *(G-11293)*

Innovative Concepts Group Inc.................... G..... 317 408-0292
Indianapolis *(G-8554)*

Integrity Sign Solutions Inc.................... G..... 502 233-8755
New Albany *(G-12749)*

ISI of Indiana Inc.................... G..... 317 241-2999
Indianapolis *(G-8595)*

▲ Jamil Packaging Corporation.................... E..... 574 256-2600
Mishawaka *(G-11917)*

Jer-Maur Corporation.................... G..... 812 384-8290
Bloomfield *(G-750)*

Kellmark Corporation.................... F..... 574 264-9695
Elkhart *(G-3449)*

Employee Codes: A=Over 500 employees, B=251-500
C=101-250, D=51-100, E=20-50, F=10-19, G=1-9

2024 Harris Indiana
Industrial Directory

51 WHOLESALE TRADE - NONDURABLE GOODS

Kelly Box and Packaging Corp............... D 260 432-4570
   Fort Wayne *(G-5145)*

Max of All Trades LLC........................ G 317 703-4242
   Kokomo *(G-10305)*

MHp Distribution LLC........................... F 312 731-8380
   Gary *(G-5981)*

▼ Noel Studio Inc.................................. F 317 297-1117
   Indianapolis *(G-9019)*

◆ Omnisource Marketing Group Inc........E 317 575-3300
   Indianapolis *(G-9050)*

Ontime Toys Inc.................................. G 317 598-9333
   Indianapolis *(G-9058)*

Optiviz Media LLC............................... G 812 681-1711
   Vincennes *(G-16141)*

Paust Inc... F 765 962-1507
   Richmond *(G-14180)*

Pregis LLC... G 574 936-7065
   Plymouth *(G-13806)*

Premiere Advertising.......................... G 317 722-2400
   Indianapolis *(G-9193)*

Printing Solutions Inc......................... G 812 923-0756
   Floyds Knobs *(G-4689)*

Professional Gifting Inc...................... F 800 350-1796
   Indianapolis *(G-9221)*

◆ Scott Pet Products Inc......................C 765 569-4636
   Rockville *(G-14354)*

Shilling Sales Inc................................. E 260 426-2626
   Fort Wayne *(G-5413)*

Smiling Cross Inc................................ G 812 323-9290
   Bloomington *(G-976)*

Star Quality Awards Inc...................... G 812 273-1740
   Madison *(G-11252)*

Sycamore Enterprises Inc.................. G 812 477-2266
   Evansville *(G-4339)*

T K Sales & Service............................ G 219 962-8982
   Gary *(G-6017)*

Tc4 LLC... G 317 709-5429
   Fishers *(G-4610)*

▲ Tfi Inc... E 317 290-1333
   Whitestown *(G-16825)*

Us Premier Business LLC................... G 540 822-0329
   Crown Point *(G-2769)*

Vahala Foam Inc................................. D 574 293-1287
   Elkhart *(G-3764)*

Wildman Business Group LLC............ G 866 369-1552
   Warsaw *(G-16451)*

Winters Assoc Prmtnal Pdts Inc......... F 812 330-7000
   Bloomington *(G-1015)*

Workflow Solutions LLC...................... G 502 627-0257
   New Albany *(G-12831)*

Yankee Candle Company Inc............ G 812 526-5195
   Edinburgh *(G-3110)*

Yongs Audio Connection LLC............ G 317 298-8333
   Indianapolis *(G-9804)*

52 BUILDING MATERIALS, HARDWARE, GARDEN SUPPLIES & MOBILE HOMES

5211 Lumber and other building materials

A-1 Door Specialties Inc..................... G 260 749-1635
   South Bend *(G-14930)*

Academy Inc....................................... G 574 293-7113
   Elkhart *(G-3147)*

Blue River Farm Supply Inc................ G 812 364-6675
   Palmyra *(G-13478)*

Brickworks Supply Center LLC........... E 317 786-9208
   Carmel *(G-1573)*

C & C Pallets and Lumber LLC........... G 765 524-3214
   New Castle *(G-12855)*

Carters Concrete Block Inc................. E 574 722-2644
   Fort Wayne *(G-4836)*

Classee Vinyl Windows LLC............... G 574 825-7863
   Middlebury *(G-11703)*

Concord Realstate Corp..................... F 765 423-5555
   Lafayette *(G-10554)*

Counterfitters Inc................................ G 219 531-0848
   Valparaiso *(G-15929)*

D Robertson Gravel Co Inc................. F 765 832-2768
   Clinton *(G-2065)*

Douglas Dye and Associates Inc....... G 317 844-1709
   Carmel *(G-1611)*

Eavk Legacy Inc.................................. E 812 246-4461
   New Albany *(G-12723)*

Ecpca Safe-Way LLC.......................... D 574 267-4861
   Warsaw *(G-16354)*

Elko Inc.. F 812 473-8400
   Evansville *(G-4030)*

Fergys Cabinets.................................. G 765 529-0116
   New Castle *(G-12861)*

Fitch Enterprises Inc........................... G 260 672-8462
   Roanoke *(G-14264)*

Gillespie Mrrell Gen Contg LLC.......... G 765 618-4084
   Marion *(G-11288)*

Global Stone Portage LLC.................. F 219 787-9190
   Portage *(G-13869)*

Graber Woodworks Inc....................... G 812 486-2861
   Montgomery *(G-12100)*

Gross & Sons Lumber and Veneer..... G 574 457-5214
   Syracuse *(G-15461)*

Gutter One Supply............................... F 317 872-1257
   Indianapolis *(G-8344)*

Heritage Ldscp Sup Group Inc............ E 317 849-9100
   Indianapolis *(G-8389)*

Hollingsworth Sawmill Inc................... F 765 883-5836
   Russiaville *(G-14422)*

Hoosier Interior Doors Inc................... G 574 534-3072
   Goshen *(G-6169)*

Hunter Nutrition Inc............................. F 765 563-1003
   Brookston *(G-1311)*

Hydro Conduit...................................... G 561 651-7177
   Greenfield *(G-6510)*

Innovative Corp.................................... E 317 804-5977
   Westfield *(G-16701)*

▼ Inovateus Solar LLC........................... E 574 485-1400
   South Bend *(G-15081)*

Jjs Concrete Construction LLC........... G 812 636-0173
   Montgomery *(G-12103)*

John Gebhart Woodworkings.............. G 765 492-3898
   Cayuga *(G-1823)*

K & K Fence Inc................................... E 317 359-5425
   Indianapolis *(G-8652)*

Kinser Timber Products Inc................ G 812 876-4775
   Gosport *(G-6285)*

Kline Cabinet Makers LLC.................. E 317 326-3049
   Maxwell *(G-11444)*

Kountry Wood Products LLC.............. C 574 773-5673
   Nappanee *(G-12618)*

Kuntry Lumber and Farm Sup Ltd...... F 260 463-3242
   Lagrange *(G-10746)*

Lafayette Materials MGT Co Inc......... G 765 447-7400
   Lafayette *(G-10627)*

Laminated Tops Central Ind Inc......... E 812 824-6299
   Bloomington *(G-906)*

Light House Center Inc....................... F 765 448-4502
   Lafayette *(G-10636)*

Maher Supply Inc................................ G 812 234-7699
   Terre Haute *(G-15635)*

Martins Lime Service Inc.................... G 574 784-2270
   Plymouth *(G-13796)*

▲ McIntire Concrete............................... F 765 759-7111
   Muncie *(G-12450)*

Merritt Sand and Gravel Inc................ F 260 665-2513
   Waterloo *(G-16524)*

New Castle Saw Mill........................... G 765 529-6635
   New Castle *(G-12875)*

◆ Omega Cabinets Ltd........................A 319 235-5700
   Jasper *(G-9900)*

Organized Living Inc........................... C 812 334-8839
   Bloomington *(G-938)*

Pike Lumber Company Inc.................. E 574 893-4511
   Carbon *(G-1538)*

Prairie Group....................................... F 812 877-9886
   Terre Haute *(G-15666)*

Ramco Builder and Supply LLC......... E 574 223-7802
   Rochester *(G-14314)*

Rees Inc... F 260 495-9811
   Fremont *(G-5832)*

Richardson Molding LLC.................... G 317 787-9463
   Indianapolis *(G-9303)*

Safe-Way Garage Doors LLC............. E 574 267-4861
   Warsaw *(G-16420)*

Shelby Gravel Inc................................ F 317 216-7556
   Indianapolis *(G-9418)*

Shelby Gravel Inc................................ F 317 804-8100
   Westfield *(G-16726)*

Slater Concrete Products Inc............. G 260 347-0164
   Kendallville *(G-10152)*

St Henry Tile Co Inc............................ E 260 589-2880
   Berne *(G-728)*

Steinkamp Warehouses Inc................ E 812 683-3860
   Huntingburg *(G-7292)*

Tremain Ceramic Tile & Flr Cvg.......... E 317 542-1491
   Indianapolis *(G-9633)*

Tri-State Guttertopper Inc................... G 812 455-1460
   Evansville *(G-4350)*

Tyler Truss LLC................................... D 765 221-5050
   Pendleton *(G-13559)*

United Home Supply Inc..................... G 765 288-2737
   Muncie *(G-12509)*

Woodland Manufacturing & Sup......... F 317 271-2266
   Avon *(G-557)*

Woodwright Door & Trim Inc.............. G 574 522-1667
   Elkhart *(G-3792)*

Wunder Company Inc......................... F 219 962-8573
   Lake Station *(G-10779)*

Zimco Materials Inc............................. G 219 883-0870
   Gary *(G-6029)*

Zimmer Metal Sales LLC.................... G 574 862-1800
   Goshen *(G-6280)*

5231 Paint, glass, and wallpaper stores

Doris Drapery Boutique....................... G 765 472-5850
   Peru *(G-13580)*

Glass City Inc...................................... G 219 887-2100
   Gary *(G-5943)*

Great Panes Glass Co......................... G 260 426-0203
   Fort Wayne *(G-5039)*

Greene Woodworking & Glass LLC.... G 812 755-4331
   Campbellsburg *(G-1523)*

Hinseys Pro Paint Inc.......................... G 260 407-2000
   Fort Wayne *(G-5068)*

Indiana Bevel Inc................................. G 317 596-0001
   Fishers *(G-4544)*

K M Davis Inc....................................... G 765 426-9227
   Lafayette *(G-10617)*

Mominee Studios Inc........................... G 812 473-1691
   Evansville *(G-4208)*

Moss L Glass Co Inc........................... F 765 642-4946
   Indianapolis *(G-8957)*

Oldcastle Buildingenvelope Inc........... D 317 876-1155
   Indianapolis *(G-9044)*

Otter Creek Christian Church.............. G 812 446-5300
   Brazil *(G-1159)*

54 FOOD STORES

Pool Shop .... G 812 446-0026
   Brazil *(G-1162)*
Sun Rise Metal Shop .... G 260 463-4026
   Topeka *(G-15820)*
Touch of Class Interiors .... G 765 452-5879
   Kokomo *(G-10351)*
Whitaker Glass & Mirror LLC .... G 765 482-1500
   Lebanon *(G-10950)*
Woodland Manufacturing & Sup .... F 317 271-2266
   Avon *(G-557)*

5251 Hardware stores

All-Rite Ready Mix Inc .... F 812 926-0920
   Aurora *(G-437)*
Allegion Public Ltd Company .... D 317 810-3700
   Carmel *(G-1554)*
Attica Ready Mixed Concrete .... F 765 762-2424
   Attica *(G-343)*
Barry Company Inc .... G 812 333-1850
   Bloomington *(G-795)*
Boger Cabinetry & Design Inc .... G 317 588-6954
   Fishers *(G-4476)*
CRS-Drs Corporation .... G 260 478-7555
   Fort Wayne *(G-4891)*
Dkl Tool & Manufacturing LLC .... G 574 289-2291
   South Bend *(G-15001)*
Earth First Kentuckiana Inc .... F 812 923-1227
   Charlestown *(G-1875)*
Grotrian Tool & Die .... G 260 894-3558
   Ligonier *(G-11016)*
Johnco Corp .... G 317 576-4417
   Indianapolis *(G-8632)*
Leeps Supply Co Inc .... E 219 756-5337
   Merrillville *(G-11530)*
McGrews Well Drilling Inc .... G 574 857-3875
   Rochester *(G-14306)*
Neumayr Lumber Co Inc .... F 765 764-4148
   Attica *(G-353)*
Progress Group Inc .... D 219 322-3700
   Schererville *(G-14539)*
Robinson Industries Inc .... E 317 867-3214
   Westfield *(G-16724)*
Stanley Black & Decker Inc .... D 860 225-5111
   Indianapolis *(G-9495)*
T K Sales & Service .... G 219 962-8982
   Gary *(G-6017)*
Tartan Properties LLC .... G 317 714-7337
   Indianapolis *(G-9554)*

5261 Retail nurseries and garden stores

A1 Campers and Trlrs Mfg LLC .... G 574 227-2200
   Elkhart *(G-3143)*
Agbest Cooperative Inc .... G 765 358-3388
   Gaston *(G-6043)*
Andersons Agriculture Group LP .... G 574 626-2522
   Galveston *(G-5851)*
Beckler Power Equipment .... G 260 356-1188
   Huntington *(G-7300)*
Bristow Milling Co LLC .... G 812 843-5176
   Bristow *(G-1299)*
Carmel Welding and Sup Co Inc .... E 317 846-3493
   Carmel *(G-1582)*
Deer Country Equipment LLC .... E 812 522-1922
   Seymour *(G-14646)*
Denim and Honey .... G 812 222-2009
   Greensburg *(G-6591)*
Earth First Kentuckiana Inc .... F 812 923-1227
   Charlestown *(G-1875)*
▲ Frick Services Inc .... E 260 761-3311
   Wawaka *(G-16539)*
Greencycle Inc .... G 317 773-3350
   Noblesville *(G-13089)*

Jtn Services Inc .... G 765 653-7158
   Greencastle *(G-6415)*
Keystone Cooperative Inc .... G 317 861-5080
   Fountaintown *(G-5615)*
Nachurs Alpine Solutions LLC .... G 812 738-1333
   Corydon *(G-2507)*
Pools of Fun Inc .... E 317 843-0337
   Noblesville *(G-13156)*
Sappers Market and Greenhouses .... G 219 942-4995
   Hobart *(G-7206)*
Siteone Landscape Supply LLC .... G 219 769-2351
   Merrillville *(G-11560)*
▲ U-Nitt LLC .... G 812 251-9980
   Carmel *(G-1792)*
Wanafeed Corporation .... G 317 862-4032
   Indianapolis *(G-9736)*
Wright Implement I LLC .... G 812 522-1922
   Seymour *(G-14707)*
Zionsville Towing Inc .... G 317 873-4550
   Zionsville *(G-17064)*

5271 Mobile home dealers

Delaware County Home Bldrs Inc .... G 765 289-6328
   Muncie *(G-12377)*
Light House Center Inc .... F 765 448-4502
   Lafayette *(G-10636)*
Thornes Homes Inc .... G 812 275-4656
   Bedford *(G-678)*
Willow Creek Crossing Inc .... G 219 809-8952
   La Porte *(G-10500)*

53 GENERAL MERCHANDISE STORES

5331 Variety stores

Circle Printing LLC .... G 812 663-7367
   Greensburg *(G-6584)*
Gohn Bros Manufacturing Co .... G 574 825-2400
   Middlebury *(G-11718)*

5399 Miscellaneous general merchandise

Dutch Made Inc .... G 260 657-3331
   Harlan *(G-7054)*
Zendigo Boutique LLC .... G 574 314-8328
   South Bend *(G-15312)*

54 FOOD STORES

5411 Grocery stores

Babbs Supermarket Inc .... E 812 829-2231
   Spencer *(G-15339)*
BEEFREE INC .... G 317 402-1019
   Cicero *(G-1994)*
Canary Brothers LLC .... G 317 954-1225
   Indianapolis *(G-7731)*
Food Service Distributors Inc .... G 812 267-4846
   Palmyra *(G-13480)*
Franklins Mercantile .... G 812 876-0426
   Spencer *(G-15347)*
Houchens Industries Inc .... F 812 467-7255
   Evansville *(G-4111)*
Julian Coffee Roasters Inc .... G 317 247-4208
   Zionsville *(G-17026)*
Kroger Co .... G 574 294-6092
   Elkhart *(G-3460)*
Kroger Co .... G 574 291-0740
   South Bend *(G-15107)*
Lakeshore Foods Corp .... D 219 362-8513
   La Porte *(G-10444)*
Market Place Publications .... G 219 769-7933
   Merrillville *(G-11536)*

MI Tierra .... G 812 376-0668
   Columbus *(G-2353)*
Premier AG Co-Op Inc .... E 812 522-4911
   Seymour *(G-14677)*
Rihm Inc .... G 765 478-3426
   Cambridge City *(G-1502)*
Schnuck Markets Inc .... C 812 853-9505
   Newburgh *(G-13019)*

5421 Meat and fish markets

Brook Locker Plant .... G 219 275-2611
   Brook *(G-1303)*
Dewig Bros Packing Co Inc .... E 812 768-6208
   Haubstadt *(G-7083)*
Fisher Packing Company .... E 260 726-7355
   Portland *(G-13941)*
Johns Butcher Shop Inc .... F 574 773-4632
   Nappanee *(G-12615)*
Kroger Co .... G 574 291-0740
   South Bend *(G-15107)*
Lengerich Meats Inc .... F 260 638-4123
   Zanesville *(G-16986)*
▲ Manley Meats Inc .... F 260 592-7313
   Decatur *(G-2871)*
Merkley & Sons Inc .... E 812 482-7020
   Jasper *(G-9890)*
Millers Locker Plant .... G 765 234-2381
   Crawfordsville *(G-2591)*
Moody Meats .... G 317 272-4533
   Avon *(G-538)*
Parretts Meat Proc & Catrg Inc .... F 574 967-3711
   Flora *(G-4663)*
Rices Quality Farm Meats Inc .... G 812 829-4562
   Spencer *(G-15361)*
Royal Center Locker Plant Inc .... G 574 643-3275
   Royal Center *(G-14392)*
Yoders Meats Inc .... G 260 768-4715
   Shipshewana *(G-14900)*

5441 Candy, nut, and confectionery stores

Abbotts Candy and Gifts Inc .... E 765 489-4442
   Hagerstown *(G-6832)*
Lowerys Home Made Candies Inc .... G 765 288-7300
   Muncie *(G-12441)*
Olympia Candy Kitchen LLC .... G 574 533-5040
   Goshen *(G-6230)*
Schimpffs Confectionery LLC .... F 812 283-8367
   Jeffersonville *(G-10052)*
▲ South Bend Chocolate Co Inc .... F 574 233-2577
   South Bend *(G-15251)*
Stephen Libs Candy Company Inc .... F 812 473-0048
   Evansville *(G-4331)*
Sweet Things Inc .... F 317 872-8720
   Carmel *(G-1774)*

5451 Dairy products stores

Ice Cream On Wheels Inc .... G 800 884-9793
   Griffith *(G-6808)*
Mishawaka Frozen Custard .... G 574 255-8000
   Mishawaka *(G-11956)*
Rapid View LLC .... G 574 224-3373
   Rochester *(G-14315)*
Revival LLC .... G 812 345-4317
   Indianapolis *(G-9296)*

5461 Retail bakeries

A Pinch of Sweetness LLC .... G 765 838-2358
   Lafayette *(G-10513)*
Almiras Bakery .... F 219 844-4334
   Hammond *(G-6872)*
Always Fresh Baked Goods Inc .... E 317 319-4747
   Martinsville *(G-11380)*

54 FOOD STORES

Black Rose Pastries LLC................................ G 773 708-9501
Gary (G-5901)

Blondies Cookies Inc................................... F 765 628-3978
Greentown (G-6645)

Brilliant Blondes LLC................................... F 765 288-8077
Muncie (G-12357)

Chestnut Land Company............................. G 574 271-8740
Mishawaka (G-11860)

Concannons Pastry Shop............................. F 765 288-8551
Muncie (G-12369)

Cornerstone Bread Co.................................. G 317 897-9671
Indianapolis (G-7877)

▲ Craftmark Bakery LLC............................... G 317 548-3929
Indianapolis (G-7898)

Donut Bank Inc.. E 812 426-0011
Evansville (G-4019)

Eat Da Cake LLC.. G 765 479-4985
Merrillville (G-11510)

Fingerhut Bakery Inc..................................... F 574 896-5937
North Judson (G-13212)

Ganal Corporation... G 260 749-2161
New Haven (G-12903)

Grabers Kountry Korner LLC....................... F 812 636-4399
Odon (G-13339)

Heyerly Brothers Inc..................................... F 260 622-4196
Ossian (G-13426)

Loaded Dough Cookie Co LLC.................... G 765 969-6513
Centerville (G-1851)

Moms Pound Cakes LLC............................. G 773 220-3822
Merrillville (G-11544)

Organic Bread of Heaven LLC..................... F 219 883-5126
Gary (G-5991)

Pretzels Inc.. E 574 941-2201
Plymouth (G-13807)

Richards Bakery... F 260 424-4012
Fort Wayne (G-5383)

Shipshewana Bread Box Corp..................... G 260 768-4629
Shipshewana (G-14887)

Square Donuts Inc.. G 812 232-6463
Terre Haute (G-15714)

Westfield Donuts... G 317 896-5856
Westfield (G-16739)

5499 Miscellaneous food stores

Allen Street Roasters LLC........................... G 815 955-7872
La Porte (G-10380)

Ambrotos LLC... G 413 887-1058
Otwell (G-13456)

Back To Eden Herbs Corp........................... G 317 455-1033
Camby (G-1507)

Bodycare Bodega LLC................................. G 317 643-3562
Indianapolis (G-7653)

Copper Moon Coffee LLC............................ D 317 541-9000
Lafayette (G-10555)

Ernestine Foods Inc..................................... G 219 274-0188
Crown Point (G-2681)

Herbs G&W Inc... G 574 646-2134
Nappanee (G-12609)

Max of All Trades LLC................................. G 317 703-4242
Kokomo (G-10305)

New Aqua LLC... D 317 272-3000
Avon (G-540)

Reidco Inc... E 812 358-3000
Brownstown (G-1426)

Serendipity Sanctuary................................. G 765 541-2364
Richmond (G-14203)

Utopian Coffee Company LLC..................... G 888 558-8674
Fort Wayne (G-5525)

Wellsource Nutraceuticals LLC................... G 219 213-6173
Crown Point (G-2773)

55 AUTOMOTIVE DEALERS AND GASOLINE SERVICE STATIONS

5511 New and used car dealers

American Steel Carports Inc....................... G 419 737-1331
Mount Summit (G-12284)

Autofarm Mobility LLC.................................. G 317 410-0070
Daleville (G-2795)

Ford Motor Company.................................... F 901 368-8821
Plainfield (G-13680)

General Motors LLC..................................... B 765 668-2000
Marion (G-11287)

General Motors LLC..................................... B 260 672-1224
Roanoke (G-14268)

Rolls-Royce Corporation.............................. E 317 230-2000
Indianapolis (G-9325)

Rolls-Royce Corporation.............................. E 317 230-8515
West Lafayette (G-16626)

Sternberg Inc.. E 812 867-0077
Evansville (G-4335)

♦ Subaru Indiana Automotive Inc................ A 765 449-1111
Lafayette (G-10703)

5521 Used car dealers

Coach Line Motors....................................... G 765 825-7893
Connersville (G-2431)

Futurex Industries Inc.................................. E 765 597-2221
Marshall (G-11373)

Glass City Inc... G 219 887-2100
Gary (G-5943)

Heritage Financial Group Inc...................... E 574 522-8000
Elkhart (G-3404)

Motorama Auto Ctr Inc................................ G 317 831-0036
Mooresville (G-12226)

▲ Oxford House Incorporated..................... D 765 884-3265
Fowler (G-5629)

▲ Transwheel Corporation........................... C 260 358-8660
Huntington (G-7374)

5531 Auto and home supply stores

Advance Prtective Coatings Inc.................. G 317 228-0123
Indianapolis (G-7435)

Advance Stores Company Inc.................... G 317 253-5034
Indianapolis (G-7436)

Batteries Plus... G 317 219-0007
Noblesville (G-13040)

▲ Ben Tire Distributors Ltd......................... E 317 798-2013
Indianapolis (G-7612)

Bernard Burns.. G 574 382-5019
Macy (G-11194)

Best One Tire & Svc S Bend Inc................ G 574 246-4021
South Bend (G-14958)

Best-One Lt LLC.. G 812 471-8473
Evansville (G-3928)

Best-One Tire & Auto Care of A................. G 260 665-7330
Angola (G-234)

Best-One Tire & Svc Auburn Inc................ G 260 925-2782
Auburn (G-369)

BF Goodrich Tire Manufacturing................. G 260 493-8100
Woodburn (G-16946)

Bridgestone Ret Operations LLC................ F 812 332-2119
Bloomington (G-815)

Bridgestone Ret Operations LLC................ G 260 447-2596
Columbia City (G-2127)

Bridgestone Ret Operations LLC................ G 812 477-8818
Evansville (G-3951)

Bridgestone Ret Operations LLC................ G 812 423-4451
Evansville (G-3952)

Bridgestone Ret Operations LLC................ G 317 846-6516
Indianapolis (G-7681)

Bridgestone Ret Operations LLC................ G 317 849-9120
Indianapolis (G-7682)

Bridgestone Ret Operations LLC................ G 765 447-5041
Lafayette (G-10542)

Bridgestone Ret Operations LLC................ G 317 773-2761
Noblesville (G-13048)

Bridgestone Ret Operations LLC................ G 812 232-9478
Terre Haute (G-15554)

Broadway Auto Glass LLC........................... F 219 884-5277
Merrillville (G-11493)

C & P Machine Service Inc......................... F 260 484-7723
Fort Wayne (G-4827)

Clark Tire Fishers Inc.................................. G 317 842-0544
Fishers (G-4490)

Component Machine Inc............................. G 317 635-8929
Indianapolis (G-7845)

D & D Tire Shop LLC................................... G 219 354-0402
East Chicago (G-3002)

Dales Goodyear Tire & Service.................. G 574 272-3779
South Bend (G-14995)

Daviess County Tire & Sup Inc................... G 812 254-1035
Washington (G-16475)

Daviess County Tire Inc.............................. G 812 254-1035
Washington (G-16476)

Double D... G 765 569-6822
Rockville (G-14351)

Dubois County Liners LLP.......................... G 812 634-1294
Jasper (G-9835)

E & M Tire Salvage Inc............................... G 260 745-3016
Fort Wayne (G-4936)

Engler Machine & Tool Inc.......................... F 812 386-6254
Princeton (G-13992)

Ferentino Tire USA Inc................................ G 574 316-6116
Plymouth (G-13775)

Ferguson Equipment Inc............................. G 574 234-4303
South Bend (G-15033)

Fortville Automotive Sup Inc....................... G 317 485-5114
Fortville (G-5594)

Gentis Tire & Service Inc............................ E 765 348-2400
Hartford City (G-7066)

Goodyear Tire & Rubber Company............. G 219 762-0651
Portage (G-13871)

Goodyear Tire Center.................................. G 260 726-9321
Portland (G-13946)

Greys Automotive Inc.................................. G 317 632-3562
Indianapolis (G-8328)

Hellmans Auto Supply Co Inc..................... G 219 885-7655
Gary (G-5949)

♦ Hoosier Racing Tire Corp........................ G 574 784-3152
Lakeville (G-10792)

Hoosier Tire & Retreading Inc.................... F 812 876-8286
Bloomington (G-883)

Hughes Tire Service Inc.............................. F 812 883-4981
Salem (G-14481)

Indiana Discount Tire Company.................. G 574 875-8547
Elkhart (G-3421)

J & P Custom Plating Inc............................ G 260 726-9696
Portland (G-13951)

KOI Enterprises Inc..................................... D 812 537-2335
Lawrenceburg (G-10843)

Line-X... G 812 491-9475
Evansville (G-4170)

Line-X of Schererville Inc............................ F 219 865-1000
Schererville (G-14530)

▲ Lingenfelter Prfmce Engrg Inc................ E 260 724-2552
Decatur (G-2869)

♦ Lionshead Specialty Tire & Whe............. F 574 533-6169
Goshen (G-6200)

Mastersbilt Chassis Inc............................... G 812 793-3666
Crothersville (G-2642)

McCord Tire Service Inc............................. F 812 235-8016
Terre Haute (G-15639)

SIC SECTION

56 APPAREL AND ACCESSORY STORES

Mid-State Truck Equipment Inc............... E 317 849-4903
   Fishers *(G-4566)*
Midwest Auto Repair Inc........................... F 219 322-0364
   Schererville *(G-14534)*
Mooresville Tire & Service Ctr.................. G 317 831-1215
   Mooresville *(G-12224)*
Motorsport Price Engineering................... G 812 546-4220
   Hope *(G-7229)*
Nicks Automotive Inc................................ F 765 964-6843
   Union City *(G-15856)*
Olson Race Cars....................................... G 765 529-6933
   New Castle *(G-12878)*
Parish Tire & Battery Shop........................ G 765 793-3191
   Covington *(G-2532)*
Penner Tire & Service LLC........................ G 812 653-0029
   Hardinsburg *(G-7048)*
Pomps Tire Service Inc............................. E 260 489-5252
   Fort Wayne *(G-5326)*
Portland Tire & Service Inc....................... G 260 726-9321
   Portland *(G-13962)*
Promotor Engines & Components............ G 574 533-9898
   Goshen *(G-6243)*
Pyramid Equipment Inc............................. F 219 778-2591
   Rolling Prairie *(G-14371)*
Raben Tire Co LLC.................................... G 812 465-5555
   Evansville *(G-4271)*
Reed Auto - Indy Mich LLC....................... F 317 872-1132
   Indianapolis *(G-9279)*
Reis Tire Sales Inc.................................... E 812 425-2229
   Evansville *(G-4283)*
RPM Machinery LLC.................................. G 574 271-0800
   South Bend *(G-15228)*
▲ Smith Tire Inc.. F 574 267-8261
   Warsaw *(G-16427)*
Snider Tire Inc.. D 260 824-4520
   Bluffton *(G-1054)*
Tippecanoe Tire Service Inc..................... G 765 884-0920
   Fowler *(G-5634)*
Tire Center of Portland Inc....................... G 260 726-8947
   Portland *(G-13971)*
Tri-State Power Supply LLC..................... G 812 537-2500
   Lawrenceburg *(G-10863)*
▲ Truck Stylin Unlimited.......................... F 574 223-8800
   Rochester *(G-14330)*
Trusty Tires Inc.. G 812 738-4212
   Corydon *(G-2519)*
U B Machine Inc....................................... F 260 493-3381
   New Haven *(G-12924)*
Upland Tire & Service Ctr Inc................... G 765 998-0871
   Upland *(G-15884)*
Windy City Coml Tire & Svc LLC.............. G 773 530-1246
   East Chicago *(G-3057)*
Woodward Tire Sales & Svc Inc............... G 260 432-0694
   Fort Wayne *(G-5575)*

5541 Gasoline service stations

Fairfield Gas Way..................................... G 260 744-2186
   Fort Wayne *(G-4973)*
▲ Smith Tire Inc.. F 574 267-8261
   Warsaw *(G-16427)*
West Lakes Marine Inc............................. F 260 854-4525
   Rome City *(G-14378)*

5551 Boat dealers

Culvers Port Side Marina......................... G 574 223-5090
   Rochester *(G-14285)*
Lake Lite Inc... G 260 918-2758
   Avilla *(G-485)*
▲ Porter Inc.. A 800 736-7685
   Decatur *(G-2876)*
Sherms Marine Inc................................... F 260 563-8051
   Wabash *(G-16215)*

▼ Smoker Craft Inc.................................. B 574 831-2103
   New Paris *(G-12968)*
Splendor Boats LLC.................................. F 260 352-2835
   Silver Lake *(G-14923)*
Webster Custom Canvas Inc.................... G 574 834-4497
   North Webster *(G-13314)*
West Lakes Marine Inc............................. F 260 854-2525
   Rome City *(G-14378)*

5561 Recreational vehicle dealers

Bilbees Service and Supply Inc................ G 317 895-8288
   Indianapolis *(G-7625)*
Dg Manufacturing Inc.............................. D 574 294-7550
   Elkhart *(G-3295)*
Eash LLC.. F 574 295-4450
   Elkhart *(G-3311)*
Forest River Inc....................................... C 574 533-5934
   Goshen *(G-6141)*
◆ Forest River Inc.................................... E 574 389-4600
   Elkhart *(G-3356)*
Highland Ridge Rv Inc............................. B 260 768-7771
   Shipshewana *(G-14850)*
Jag Mobile Solutions Inc......................... G 260 562-1045
   Howe *(G-7237)*
▲ Jpc LLC... F 574 293-8030
   Elkhart *(G-3437)*
Kentuckiana Yacht Services LLC............. G 812 282-7579
   Jeffersonville *(G-10007)*
Patrick Industries Inc.............................. E 574 825-4336
   Middlebury *(G-11746)*

5571 Motorcycle dealers

Atv Parts Barn LLC................................... G 812 251-6113
   Brazil *(G-1133)*
Graphics Lab Uv Printing Inc................... F 765 457-5784
   Kokomo *(G-10272)*
Iron Hawg... G 317 462-0991
   Greenfield *(G-6517)*
Orr Motor Sports...................................... G 260 244-2681
   Columbia City *(G-2178)*

5599 Automotive dealers, nec

Aluminum Trailer Company..................... C 574 773-2440
   Nappanee *(G-12579)*
Autofarm Mobility LLC............................. G 317 410-0070
   Daleville *(G-2795)*
Carlson Motorsports................................ G 765 339-4407
   Linden *(G-11030)*
Chief Metal Works Inc............................. G 765 932-2134
   Rushville *(G-14396)*
Collins Trailers Inc.................................. G 574 294-2561
   Elkhart *(G-3257)*
Holiday House LLC.................................. F 574 206-0016
   Elkhart *(G-3408)*
▼ Intech Trailers Inc................................. D 574 221-8231
   Nappanee *(G-12614)*
LGS Industries LLC................................... E 574 848-5665
   Middlebury *(G-11733)*
Mid America Powered Vehicles................ G 812 925-7745
   Chandler *(G-1864)*
Nexgen Group Inc.................................... G 574 218-6363
   Nappanee *(G-12632)*
Schwartzs Trailer Sales Inc...................... G 317 773-2608
   Noblesville *(G-13172)*
Talbert Manufacturing Inc........................ C 800 348-5232
   Rensselaer *(G-14071)*

56 APPAREL AND ACCESSORY STORES

5611 Men's and boys' clothing stores

Country Stitches Embroidery................... G 219 324-7625
   La Porte *(G-10396)*
Gohn Bros Manufacturing Co................... G 574 825-2400
   Middlebury *(G-11718)*
Golf Plus Inc... G 812 477-7529
   Evansville *(G-4092)*
Goods On Target Sporting Inc................. G 812 623-2300
   Sunman *(G-15438)*
Ladybugz Bookstore LLC......................... G 469 459-1780
   Noblesville *(G-13125)*
Mammoth Hats LLC.................................. F 812 849-2772
   Mitchell *(G-12044)*
Profit Over Romance LLC........................ G 219 900-3592
   Gary *(G-5997)*
Truu Confidence LLC............................... G 317 795-0042
   Indianapolis *(G-9653)*
Unjust LLC.. G 317 443-2584
   Fishers *(G-4622)*

5621 Women's clothing stores

Anita Lorrain LLC..................................... G 574 621-0531
   South Bend *(G-14946)*
CM Reed LLC.. G 517 546-4100
   Greendale *(G-6444)*
Formal Affairs Tuxedo Shop.................... G 574 875-6654
   Elkhart *(G-3357)*
Janelle Davis.. G 765 635-6233
   Anderson *(G-139)*
Marie Collective LLC................................ G 317 683-0408
   Indianapolis *(G-8832)*
Savage Yet Civilized LLC.......................... G 855 560-9223
   Merrillville *(G-11556)*
Signs AP & Awards On Time LLC............ G 219 661-4488
   Crown Point *(G-2752)*
Tonis Touch LLC....................................... G 317 992-1280
   Plainfield *(G-13737)*

5632 Women's accessory and specialty stores

Arm Kandy LLC... G 317 975-1576
   Indianapolis *(G-7546)*
Hidinghilda LLC.. G 260 760-7093
   Kendallville *(G-10118)*
Unique Jewelry and More LLC................. G 317 244-3732
   Indianapolis *(G-9677)*
Vera Bradley International LLC................ G 260 482-4673
   Roanoke *(G-14273)*
Zendigo Boutique LLC.............................. G 574 314-8328
   South Bend *(G-15312)*

5641 Children's and infants' wear stores

Shop Lulu Bean LLC................................. G 219 525-5336
   Merrillville *(G-11559)*

5651 Family clothing stores

Cool Cayenne LLC.................................... G 765 282-0977
   Albany *(G-12)*
Operation 1 Veteran Inc.......................... G 574 536-5536
   Goshen *(G-6231)*
Torrid LLC... F 219 769-1192
   Merrillville *(G-11567)*
Yalel Unbland LLC.................................... G 404 232-9139
   Indianapolis *(G-9799)*

5661 Shoe stores

Amos D Graber & Sons............................ F 260 749-0526
   New Haven *(G-12892)*
Buddy Covers Inc..................................... G 317 846-5766
   Carmel *(G-1575)*
Cbrk LLC... G 317 601-8546
   Indianapolis *(G-7764)*

56 APPAREL AND ACCESSORY STORES

Discount Boots & Tack .... G 812 522-9470
  Seymour *(G-14648)*

Game Plan Graphics LLC .... G 812 663-3238
  Greensburg *(G-6596)*

Integrated Orthotic Lab Inc .... G 317 852-4640
  Brownsburg *(G-1375)*

Kinney Dancewear .... G 317 581-1800
  Noblesville *(G-13121)*

5699 Miscellaneous apparel and accessories

4ink Fullfillment Services .... G 812 738-4465
  Corydon *(G-2483)*

All Things Custom LLC .... G 765 618-5332
  Sweetser *(G-15453)*

Better Blacc Wall Streetz LLC .... F 812 927-0712
  Seymour *(G-14632)*

Celestial Designs LLC .... G 317 733-3110
  Zionsville *(G-16997)*

Country Stitches Embroidery .... G 219 324-7625
  La Porte *(G-10396)*

Cowpokes Inc .... E 765 642-3911
  Anderson *(G-99)*

Dear Athletes Inc .... G 615 682-3332
  Noblesville *(G-13069)*

Dugout .... G 765 642-8528
  Anderson *(G-111)*

Eliba Collections LLC .... G 646 675-6196
  Whiteland *(G-16785)*

Formal Affairs Tuxedo Shop .... G 574 875-6654
  Elkhart *(G-3357)*

Geckos .... G 765 762-0822
  Attica *(G-349)*

Goldden Corporation .... F 765 423-4366
  Lafayette *(G-10591)*

Graphic Fx Inc .... E 812 234-0000
  Terre Haute *(G-15601)*

◆ Herff Jones LLC ....C 317 297-3741
  Indianapolis *(G-8383)*

Higgins Dyan .... G 812 876-0754
  Ellettsville *(G-3809)*

Hilltop Leather .... G 317 508-3404
  Martinsville *(G-11401)*

Hoogies Sports House Inc .... G 574 533-9875
  Goshen *(G-6165)*

◆ Hoosier Racing Tire Corp .... G 574 784-3152
  Lakeville *(G-10792)*

J B Hinchman Inc .... G 317 359-1808
  Indianapolis *(G-8602)*

Kennyleeholmescom .... G 574 612-2526
  Elkhart *(G-3451)*

Legacy Enterprises Inc .... G 219 484-9483
  Merrillville *(G-11531)*

Locoli Inc .... E 219 515-6900
  Schererville *(G-14531)*

Louies Companies Inc .... G 765 448-4300
  Lafayette *(G-10639)*

Marketing and Retail Sales .... G 812 883-1813
  Salem *(G-14489)*

Masbez LLC .... G 855 962-7239
  Frankfort *(G-5681)*

Mercantile Store .... G 812 988-6939
  Nashville *(G-12675)*

Next Level Logo Store Inc .... G 219 344-5141
  La Porte *(G-10458)*

OHaras Sports Inc .... G 219 836-5554
  Munster *(G-12554)*

Operation 1 Veteran Inc .... G 574 536-5536
  Goshen *(G-6231)*

Paul Miller .... G 765 449-4893
  Lafayette *(G-10664)*

Pretty Chique LLC .... G 317 922-5899
  Indianapolis *(G-9194)*

Professional Gifting Inc .... F 800 350-1796
  Indianapolis *(G-9221)*

Ram Graphics Inc .... F 765 724-7783
  Alexandria *(G-58)*

▲ Rivars Inc .... E 765 789-6119
  Indianapolis *(G-9309)*

Roses Square Dance Acc .... G 812 865-2821
  Orleans *(G-13382)*

Select Embroidery/Top It Off .... F 812 337-8049
  Bloomington *(G-968)*

Spobric LLC .... G 302 249-1045
  Indianapolis *(G-9479)*

Sportsmania Sales Inc .... G 317 873-5501
  Zionsville *(G-17052)*

Sugar Tree Incorporated .... G 260 417-3362
  Fort Wayne *(G-5450)*

Winning Edge of Rochester Inc .... F 574 223-6090
  Rochester *(G-14334)*

Xtreme Graphics .... G 812 989-6948
  Jeffersonville *(G-10076)*

Yalel Unbland LLC .... G 404 232-9139
  Indianapolis *(G-9799)*

57 HOME FURNITURE, FURNISHINGS AND EQUIPMENT STORES

5712 Furniture stores

A & H Enterprises LLC .... G 317 398-3070
  Shelbyville *(G-14729)*

American Natural Resources LLC .... F 219 922-6444
  Griffith *(G-6790)*

Best Chairs Incorporated .... D 812 367-1761
  Paoli *(G-13489)*

Bollock Interprises Inc .... F 765 448-6000
  Lafayette *(G-10541)*

Bowles Mattress Company Inc .... G 812 288-8614
  Jeffersonville *(G-9945)*

Carriage House Woodworking Inc ...... G 317 406-3042
  Coatesville *(G-2104)*

Chris Schwartz .... G 260 615-9574
  Grabill *(G-6292)*

Classic Kitchen and Gran LLC .... G 317 575-8883
  Westfield *(G-16676)*

Coffeys Custom Upholstery .... G 812 948-8611
  New Albany *(G-12715)*

Crossroads Furniture Co LLC .... F 765 307-2095
  Crawfordsville *(G-2558)*

Custom Cabinets & Furn LLC .... F 812 486-2503
  Montgomery *(G-12092)*

▲ Fehrenbacher Cabinets Inc .... E 812 963-3377
  Evansville *(G-4066)*

Furniture Distributors Inc .... F 317 357-8508
  Indianapolis *(G-8243)*

Futon Factory Inc .... F 317 549-8639
  Indianapolis *(G-8245)*

Graber Furniture .... G 812 295-4939
  Loogootee *(G-11136)*

Holder Bedding Inc .... G 765 642-1256
  Anderson *(G-128)*

Holder Bedding Inc .... G 765 447-7907
  Lafayette *(G-10600)*

Huntington Exteriors Inc .... F 260 356-1621
  Huntington *(G-7322)*

▲ Indiana Furniture Industries Inc .... D 812 482-5727
  Jasper *(G-9845)*

K M Davis Inc .... G 765 426-9227
  Lafayette *(G-10617)*

Lambright Woodworking LLC .... F 260 593-2721
  Topeka *(G-15811)*

Lee Supply Corp .... F 812 333-4343
  Bloomington *(G-909)*

Martins Wood Works .... G 574 862-4080
  Goshen *(G-6215)*

Oeding Corporation .... G 812 367-1271
  Ferdinand *(G-4446)*

Real Wood Works .... G 812 277-1462
  Bedford *(G-665)*

REM Industries Inc .... F 574 862-2127
  Wakarusa *(G-16247)*

Ronald Chileen Furniture .... G 574 542-4505
  Rochester *(G-14321)*

▲ Roudebush Co Inc .... G 574 595-7115
  Star City *(G-15397)*

Shearer Printing Service Inc .... E 765 457-3274
  Kokomo *(G-10334)*

Sylvia Kay Hartley .... G 317 984-3424
  Arcadia *(G-318)*

Tempur Production Usa LLC .... D 859 455-1000
  Crawfordsville *(G-2624)*

The Office Shop Inc .... E 812 934-5611
  Batesville *(G-607)*

Vans Cabinet Shop Inc .... G 574 658-9625
  Milford *(G-11808)*

Weaver Fine Furn Cabinets Inc .... G 812 342-4833
  Columbus *(G-2416)*

5713 Floor covering stores

Fashion Flooring and Ltg Inc .... G
  Valparaiso *(G-15947)*

Faulkens Floorcover .... F 574 300-4260
  South Bend *(G-15027)*

Indiana Lumber Inc .... G 812 837-9493
  Bloomington *(G-889)*

Indiana Rug Company .... G 574 252-4653
  Mishawaka *(G-11911)*

Jack Laurie Coml Floors Inc .... G 317 569-2095
  Indianapolis *(G-8613)*

K M Davis Inc .... G 765 426-9227
  Lafayette *(G-10617)*

Neighborhood Floors & More LLC ...... G 219 510-5737
  Portage *(G-13895)*

Shelby Westside Upholstering .... G 317 631-8911
  Indianapolis *(G-9419)*

Todd K Hockemeyer Inc .... G 260 639-3591
  Fort Wayne *(G-5492)*

Touch of Class Interiors .... G 765 452-5879
  Kokomo *(G-10351)*

5714 Drapery and upholstery stores

Custom Sewing Service .... G 812 428-7015
  Evansville *(G-4004)*

Designers Touch .... G 812 944-2267
  Floyds Knobs *(G-4676)*

Dixie Lee Drapery Co Inc .... G 317 783-9869
  Indianapolis *(G-7989)*

McL Window Coverings Inc .... F 317 577-2670
  Fishers *(G-4563)*

Shelby Westside Upholstering .... G 317 631-8911
  Indianapolis *(G-9419)*

5719 Miscellaneous homefurnishings

▼ Abda Incorporated .... G 317 273-8343
  Indianapolis *(G-7416)*

Doris Drapery Boutique .... G 765 472-5850
  Peru *(G-13580)*

Golden Ventures Inc .... E 317 872-2705
  Indianapolis *(G-8300)*

J P Whitt Inc .... G 765 759-0521
  Muncie *(G-12430)*

Jolar Enterprises .... G 574 875-8369
  Elkhart *(G-3435)*

K M Davis Inc .... G 765 426-9227
  Lafayette *(G-10617)*

59 MISCELLANEOUS RETAIL

Midwest Blind & Shade Co .... G 574 271-0770
  Mishawaka (G-11947)
Oasis Lifestyle LLC .... F 574 948-0004
  Plymouth (G-13799)
Otter Creek Christian Church .... G 812 446-5300
  Brazil (G-1159)
Pb Metal Works .... G 765 489-1311
  Hagerstown (G-6841)
Pool Shop .... G 812 446-0026
  Brazil (G-1162)
Sampler Inc .... F 765 663-2233
  Homer (G-7221)
Schmidt Marken Designs .... G 219 785-4238
  La Porte (G-10477)
Strawtown Pottery & Antq Inc .... G 317 984-5080
  Noblesville (G-13180)
Sun Control Center LLC .... F 260 490-9902
  Fort Wayne (G-5456)
Upanaway LLC .... G 866 218-7143
  Greenfield (G-6568)
Warsaw Cut Glass Company Inc .... G 574 267-6581
  Warsaw (G-16445)
Woodland Manufacturing & Sup .... F 317 271-2266
  Avon (G-557)

5722 Household appliance stores

3sevens LLC .... G 502 594-2312
  Henryville (G-7112)
Boger Cabinetry & Design Inc .... G 317 588-6954
  Fishers (G-4476)
Controls Center Inc .... G 317 634-2665
  Indianapolis (G-7863)
Duncan Supply Co Inc .... G 765 446-0105
  Lafayette (G-10572)
Industrial Sewing Machine Co .... G 812 425-2255
  Evansville (G-4124)
Vans TV & Appliance Inc .... F 260 927-8267
  Auburn (G-433)
Zinn Kitchens Inc .... E 574 967-4179
  Bringhurst (G-1239)

5731 Radio, television, and electronic stores

Business Systems Mgt Corp .... G 219 938-0166
  Gary (G-5908)
Loys Sales Inc .... G 765 552-7250
  Elwood (G-3829)
Michael L Jerrell .... G 812 354-9297
  Petersburg (G-13617)
RCA Corporation .... C 800 722-2161
  Indianapolis (G-9276)
Top In Sound Inc .... G 765 649-8111
  Anderson (G-207)
Van Der Weele Jon D .... G 574 892-5005
  Argos (G-328)
Vans TV & Appliance Inc .... F 260 927-8267
  Auburn (G-433)

5734 Computer and software stores

▲ 3btech Inc .... E 574 233-0508
  South Bend (G-14927)
Blue Byte Tech Solutions LLC .... G 574 903-5637
  Elkhart (G-3227)
Cbf Forensics LLC .... G 708 383-8320
  Hobart (G-7180)
Computer Solutions Systems Inc .... F 812 235-9008
  Terre Haute (G-15566)
Country Club Computer .... G 317 271-4000
  Indianapolis (G-7889)
Coy & Associates .... G 317 787-5089
  Indianapolis (G-7893)
Indiana Business People LLC .... G 317 455-4040
  Indianapolis (G-8474)

Intelligent Software Inc .... G 219 923-6166
  Munster (G-12543)
Johnco Corp .... G 317 576-4417
  Indianapolis (G-8632)
Money Tree Software Ltd .... E 541 754-3701
  Muncie (G-12458)
Riddell Technologies LLC .... G 219 213-9602
  Crown Point (G-2745)
The Office Shop Inc .... E 812 934-5611
  Batesville (G-607)
Tokumei LLC .... G 765 772-0073
  West Lafayette (G-16638)

5735 Record and prerecorded tape stores

Audio Flow LLC .... G 219 230-6330
  Portage (G-13846)

5736 Musical instrument stores

◆ Conn-Selmer Inc .... D 574 522-1675
  Elkhart (G-3262)
▲ Fox Products Corporation .... C 260 723-4888
  South Whitley (G-15318)
▲ Gemeinhardt Musical Instr LLC .... E 574 295-5280
  Elkhart (G-3370)
Markle Music .... G 812 847-2103
  Linton (G-11038)
Music Store .... G 812 949-3004
  Clarksville (G-2024)
▲ Rees Harps Inc .... F 812 438-3032
  Rising Sun (G-14245)
▲ Walter Piano Company Inc .... F 574 266-0615
  Elkhart (G-3779)

58 EATING AND DRINKING PLACES

5812 Eating places

Anns Boba Tea LLC .... G 317 681-3143
  Indianapolis (G-7520)
Axecalibur LLC .... G 812 822-1157
  Bloomington (G-788)
Barley Island Brewing Co .... G 317 770-5280
  Noblesville (G-13039)
Browns Dairy Inc .... F 219 464-4141
  Valparaiso (G-15921)
Buckner Inc .... E 317 570-0533
  Indianapolis (G-7699)
Caffeinery LLC .... G 765 896-9123
  Muncie (G-12360)
Clancys of Portage .... E 219 764-4995
  Portage (G-13856)
Deonta Walker .... G 317 970-3586
  Indianapolis (G-7965)
Dreyers Grand Ice Cream Inc .... B 260 483-3102
  Fort Wayne (G-4928)
Dugdale Beef Company Inc .... E 317 291-9660
  Indianapolis (G-8019)
Essenhaus Inc .... B 574 825-6790
  Middlebury (G-11715)
Frickers Inc .... G 765 965-6655
  Richmond (G-14123)
Grafton Peek Incorporated .... F 317 557-8377
  Greenwood (G-6709)
Harvest Cafe Coffee & Tea LLC .... G 317 585-9162
  Indianapolis (G-8369)
Harvey Hinklemeyers .... G 765 452-1942
  Kokomo (G-10276)
Heaven Sent Gurmet Cookies Inc .... G 219 980-1066
  Gary (G-5948)
Kroger Co .... G 574 291-0740
  South Bend (G-15107)

Lanthier Winery & Restaurant .... G 812 273-2409
  Madison (G-11235)
Lennies Inc .... E 812 323-2112
  Bloomington (G-910)
Masters Hand Bbq LLC .... G 260 247-5807
  Fort Wayne (G-5205)
Mayasaris LLC .... G 812 222-6292
  Greensburg (G-6616)
▼ Meats By Linz Inc .... E 708 862-0830
  Hammond (G-6979)
Mi Tierra .... G 812 376-0668
  Columbus (G-2353)
Milan Food Bank .... G 812 654-3682
  Milan (G-11781)
Mishawaka Brewing Company .... G 574 256-9993
  Granger (G-6362)
Mishawaka Frozen Custard .... G 574 255-8000
  Mishawaka (G-11956)
Olympia Candy Kitchen LLC .... G 574 533-5040
  Goshen (G-6230)
Parretts Meat Proc & Catrg Inc .... F 574 967-3711
  Flora (G-4663)
Passions Fruitopia LLC .... G 800 515-1891
  Highland (G-7151)
Pb & J Factory LLC .... G 317 504-4714
  Indianapolis (G-9107)
Richards Restaurant Inc .... F 260 997-6823
  Bryant (G-1436)
Roller-Wilson Industries LLC .... G 317 377-4900
  Indianapolis (G-9324)
Schimpffs Confectionery LLC .... F 812 283-8367
  Jeffersonville (G-10052)
Schnuck Markets Inc .... C 812 853-9505
  Newburgh (G-13019)
Smalltown Coffee Co LLC .... F 816 288-0687
  Crown Point (G-2759)
▲ South Bend Chocolate Co Inc .... F 574 233-2577
  South Bend (G-15251)
Tavistock Restaurants LLC .... G 317 488-1230
  Indianapolis (G-9557)
Turonis Forget-Me-Not Inc .... F 812 477-7500
  Evansville (G-4356)
U Want Icecream LLC .... G 317 577-4057
  Fishers (G-4619)
Upland Brewing Company Inc .... F 812 330-7421
  Bloomington (G-1005)
Wasser Brewing Company LLC .... F 765 653-3240
  Greencastle (G-6435)
Yoders Meats Inc .... G 260 768-4715
  Shipshewana (G-14900)
Zels .... G 219 864-1011
  Schererville (G-14548)

5813 Drinking places

Centerpoint Brewing Co LLC .... F 317 602-8386
  Indianapolis (G-7768)
Daredevil Brewing Company LLC .... G 765 602-1067
  Speedway (G-15336)
Frickers Inc .... G 765 965-6655
  Richmond (G-14123)
Indiana City Brewing LLC .... F 317 643-1103
  Carmel (G-1666)
Melanie Brewery Company Inc .... G 219 762-9652
  Portage (G-13886)
Mishawaka Brewing Company .... G 574 256-9993
  Granger (G-6362)
Oaken Barrel Brewing Co Inc .... E 317 887-2287
  Greenwood (G-6748)
Upland Brewing Company Inc .... F 812 330-7421
  Bloomington (G-1005)

59 MISCELLANEOUS RETAIL

59 MISCELLANEOUS RETAIL

5912 Drug stores and proprietary stores

Genoa Healthcare LLC .... G 219 427-1837
   Gary *(G-5940)*

Houchens Industries Inc .... F 812 467-7255
   Evansville *(G-4111)*

Kroger Co .... G 574 291-0740
   South Bend *(G-15107)*

Lakeshore Foods Corp .... D 219 362-8513
   La Porte *(G-10444)*

Merrill Corporation .... E 574 255-2988
   Mishawaka *(G-11942)*

Schnuck Markets Inc .... C 812 853-9505
   Newburgh *(G-13019)*

Williams Bros Hlth Care Phrm I .... E 812 335-0000
   Bloomington *(G-1012)*

Williams Bros Hlth Care Phrm I .... C 812 254-2497
   Washington *(G-16513)*

5921 Liquor stores

Big Red Liquors Inc .... G 812 339-9552
   Bloomington *(G-806)*

Brown County Wine Company Inc .... G 812 988-6144
   Nashville *(G-12666)*

Cedar Creek Winery .... G 812 988-1111
   Nashville *(G-12667)*

Crankshaft Brewing Co .... G 317 939-0138
   Brownsburg *(G-1361)*

James Lake Vineyard Inc .... G 260 495-9463
   Fremont *(G-5824)*

Lost Hollow Beer Co LLC .... G 317 796-9516
   Greencastle *(G-6420)*

▲ Oliver Wine Company Inc .... D 812 876-5800
   Bloomington *(G-935)*

Party Cask .... G 812 234-3008
   Terre Haute *(G-15657)*

Prp Wine International .... F 317 288-0005
   Indianapolis *(G-9234)*

Red Gate Farms Inc .... G 812 277-9750
   Bedford *(G-667)*

Rihm Inc .... G 765 478-3426
   Cambridge City *(G-1502)*

Wine N Vine .... G 765 282-3300
   Muncie *(G-12522)*

5932 Used merchandise stores

Cowpokes Inc .... E 765 642-3911
   Anderson *(G-99)*

Fall Creek Corporation .... G 765 482-1861
   Lebanon *(G-10893)*

Golden Lion Inc .... G 765 446-9557
   Lafayette *(G-10592)*

Northern Indiana Ordnance Co .... G 574 289-5938
   South Bend *(G-15173)*

Strawtown Pottery & Antq Inc .... G 317 984-5080
   Noblesville *(G-13180)*

5941 Sporting goods and bicycle shops

Avon Sports Apparel Corp .... G 317 887-2673
   Greenwood *(G-6674)*

Best Bicycle Inc .... G 812 336-2724
   Bloomington *(G-804)*

Bio Harness Shop .... G 812 486-2919
   Montgomery *(G-12087)*

Blythes Sport Shop Inc .... E 219 476-0026
   Valparaiso *(G-15916)*

Bobcat Armament and Mfg LLC .... G 317 699-6127
   Shelbyville *(G-14738)*

Cedar Plastics Inc .... F 765 483-3260
   Lebanon *(G-10882)*

Centurion Arms LLC .... F 619 994-5750
   Morgantown *(G-12254)*

Coachs Connection Inc .... G 260 356-0400
   Huntington *(G-7306)*

Cowpokes Inc .... E 765 642-3911
   Anderson *(G-99)*

Crescendo Inc .... G 812 829-4759
   Spencer *(G-15344)*

Deer Track Archery Inc .... G 765 643-6847
   Anderson *(G-101)*

East 40 Sports Apparel Inc .... G 812 877-3695
   Terre Haute *(G-15580)*

Fairway Custom Golf .... G 317 842-0017
   Fishers *(G-4521)*

Game Plan Graphics LLC .... G 812 663-3238
   Greensburg *(G-6596)*

Global Ozone Innovations LLC .... G 574 294-5797
   Elkhart *(G-3383)*

Golf Plus Inc .... G 812 477-7529
   Evansville *(G-4092)*

Goods On Target Sporting Inc .... G 812 623-2300
   Sunman *(G-15438)*

Hoogies Sports House Inc .... G 574 533-9875
   Goshen *(G-6165)*

Jer-Maur Corporation .... G 812 384-8290
   Bloomfield *(G-750)*

Judson Harness & Saddlery .... G 765 569-0918
   Rockville *(G-14352)*

Kerham Inc .... E 260 483-5444
   Fort Wayne *(G-5146)*

▲ Kidstuff Playsystems Inc .... D 219 938-3331
   Gary *(G-5974)*

Knoy Apparel .... G 765 448-1031
   Lafayette *(G-10624)*

Montgomery Tent & Awning Co .... F 317 357-9759
   Indianapolis *(G-8951)*

Nebo Ridge Enterprises LLC .... G 317 471-1089
   Carmel *(G-1703)*

▲ Nvb Playgrounds Inc .... G 317 826-2777
   Indianapolis *(G-9037)*

OHaras Sports Inc .... G 219 836-5554
   Munster *(G-12554)*

Pine Valley Munitions Inc .... G 260 818-6913
   Columbia City *(G-2181)*

Popguns Inc .... G 317 897-8660
   Indianapolis *(G-9163)*

Robert J Matt .... G 317 831-2400
   Mooresville *(G-12239)*

Rookies Unlimited Inc .... G 765 536-2726
   Summitville *(G-15431)*

Sabre Holdings LLC .... F 317 222-6150
   Indianapolis *(G-9360)*

▲ Schwartz Manufacturing Inc .... G 260 589-3865
   Berne *(G-725)*

Southern Indiana Collar Co .... G 812 486-3714
   Montgomery *(G-12123)*

Sportcrafters Inc .... G 574 243-2453
   Granger *(G-6381)*

Sportscenter Inc .... G 260 436-6198
   Fort Wayne *(G-5432)*

Standard Issue Armory LLC .... F 812 364-1466
   Greenville *(G-6657)*

Uebelhors Golf .... G 317 881-4109
   Indianapolis *(G-9674)*

Vadens Firearms & Ammun LLC .... G 317 840-5799
   Indianapolis *(G-9697)*

Varsity Sports Inc .... G 219 987-7200
   Demotte *(G-2931)*

Winning Edge of Rochester Inc .... F 574 223-6090
   Rochester *(G-14334)*

Xtreme Graphics .... G 812 989-6948
   Jeffersonville *(G-10076)*

5942 Book stores

Bibles For Blind Vslly Hndcppe .... G 812 466-3134
   Terre Haute *(G-15552)*

Embroidme .... G 219 465-1400
   Valparaiso *(G-15943)*

Prairie Creek Prtg & Bk Str .... G 812 636-7243
   Montgomery *(G-12119)*

5943 Stationery stores

A & H Enterprises LLC .... G 317 398-3070
   Shelbyville *(G-14729)*

Automobile Dealers Assn of Ind .... G 317 635-1441
   Indianapolis *(G-7576)*

Bryant Printing LLC .... G 765 521-3379
   New Castle *(G-12853)*

Cecils Printing & Off Sups Inc .... G 812 683-4416
   Huntingburg *(G-7273)*

Coy & Associates .... G 317 787-5089
   Indianapolis *(G-7893)*

Indiana Auto Dealers Assn Svcs .... G 317 635-1441
   Indianapolis *(G-8473)*

Inteprintations .... G 765 404-0887
   Indianapolis *(G-8571)*

Journal & Chronicle Inc .... G 812 752-5060
   Scottsburg *(G-14566)*

Marketing and Retail Sales .... G 812 883-1813
   Salem *(G-14489)*

Premier Print & Svcs Group Inc .... F 574 273-2525
   Granger *(G-6372)*

Qgraphics Inc .... G 765 564-2314
   Delphi *(G-2906)*

Scott Culbertson .... G 260 357-6430
   Garrett *(G-5876)*

Shearer Printing Service Inc .... E 765 457-3274
   Kokomo *(G-10334)*

Smith & Butterfield Co Inc .... F 812 422-3261
   Evansville *(G-4320)*

The Office Shop Inc .... E 812 934-5611
   Batesville *(G-607)*

Tippecanoe Press Inc .... G 317 392-1207
   Shelbyville *(G-14806)*

5944 Jewelry stores

Alan W Long .... G 812 265-6717
   Madison *(G-11198)*

Argentum Jewelry Inc .... G 812 336-3100
   Bloomington *(G-784)*

Ashleys Jewelry By Design Ltd .... G 219 926-9039
   Chesterton *(G-1904)*

Brinker Mfg Jewelers Inc .... F 812 476-0651
   Evansville *(G-3954)*

Collegiate Pride Inc .... G 260 726-7818
   Portland *(G-13932)*

Crystal Source .... G 812 988-7009
   Nashville *(G-12669)*

David Gonzales .... G 765 284-6960
   Muncie *(G-12373)*

Design Msa Inc .... G 317 817-9000
   Carmel *(G-1606)*

Edward E Petri Company .... G 317 636-5007
   Indianapolis *(G-8057)*

G Thrapp Jewelers Inc .... G 317 255-5555
   Indianapolis *(G-8254)*

Ginas Creative Jewelry Inc .... G 317 272-0032
   Avon *(G-521)*

Golden Lion Inc .... G 765 446-9557
   Lafayette *(G-10592)*

Goldstone Jewelry Inc .... G 765 742-1975
   West Lafayette *(G-16585)*

Interntnal Damnd Gold Exch Ltd .... G 317 872-6666
   Indianapolis *(G-8583)*

J C Sipe Inc .... G 317 848-0215
   Indianapolis *(G-8603)*

SIC SECTION 59 MISCELLANEOUS RETAIL

Jewelers Boutique Inc .... G 317 788-7679
  Indianapolis *(G-8624)*
Khamis Fine Jewelers Inc .... G 317 841-8440
  Indianapolis *(G-8681)*
Legacy Enterprises Inc .... G 219 484-9483
  Merrillville *(G-11531)*
Peter Franklin Jewelers Inc .... G 260 749-4315
  New Haven *(G-12913)*
Ralph Privoznik Jewelry Art .... G 765 742-4904
  Lafayette *(G-10676)*
Rogers Enterprises Inc .... G 317 851-5500
  Greenwood *(G-6760)*
Ronaldo Designer Jewelry Inc .... F 812 972-7220
  New Albany *(G-12808)*
Sisson & Son Mfg Jewelers .... G 574 967-4331
  Flora *(G-4665)*
Stall & Kessler Inc .... G 765 742-1259
  Lafayette *(G-10698)*
Surplus Store and Exchange .... F 765 447-0200
  Lafayette *(G-10707)*
Williams Jewelers Inc .... G 812 475-1705
  Evansville *(G-4387)*

5945 Hobby, toy, and game shops

B & B Specialties Inc .... G 574 277-0499
  Granger *(G-6333)*
Mishawaka Art & Frame Gallery .... G 574 259-9320
  Mishawaka *(G-11953)*
S & W Swing Sets .... G 260 414-6200
  New Haven *(G-12916)*
Stitch N Frame .... G 260 478-1301
  Fort Wayne *(G-5443)*
Tokumei LLC .... G 765 772-0073
  West Lafayette *(G-16638)*

5946 Camera and photographic supply stores

▲ Roi Marketing Company Inc .... G 317 644-0797
  Indianapolis *(G-9321)*

5947 Gift, novelty, and souvenir shop

Abbotts Candy and Gifts Inc .... E 765 489-4442
  Hagerstown *(G-6832)*
Alan W Long .... G 812 265-6717
  Madison *(G-11198)*
Bbs Celebration Center .... G 765 730-6575
  Yorktown *(G-16971)*
Bobby Little Creations .... G 219 313-5102
  Crown Point *(G-2658)*
Concrete Lady Inc .... E 812 256-2765
  Otisco *(G-13447)*
Cowpokes Inc .... E 765 642-3911
  Anderson *(G-99)*
Creations In Glass .... G 219 326-7941
  La Porte *(G-10397)*
Crystal Source .... G 812 988-7009
  Nashville *(G-12669)*
Custom Candy Wrappers Company .... G 574 247-0756
  Granger *(G-6340)*
Embroidme .... G 219 465-1400
  Valparaiso *(G-15943)*
Entertainment Express .... G 219 763-3610
  Portage *(G-13861)*
Friends of Third World Inc .... G 260 422-6821
  Fort Wayne *(G-5013)*
Goldden Corporation .... F 765 423-4366
  Lafayette *(G-10591)*
Kenneth Raber .... G 812 486-3102
  Montgomery *(G-12105)*
Lanthier Winery & Restaurant .... G 812 273-2409
  Madison *(G-11235)*

Lil Red Studios LLC .... G 317 443-4932
  Indianapolis *(G-8753)*
Mathews Wire Inc .... F 765 659-3542
  Frankfort *(G-5682)*
Mercantile Store .... G 812 988-6939
  Nashville *(G-12675)*
Mishawaka Art & Frame Gallery .... G 574 259-9320
  Mishawaka *(G-11953)*
Pgs LLC .... F 812 988-4030
  Nashville *(G-12678)*
Sweet Keepsakes .... G 219 872-8467
  Trail Creek *(G-15840)*

5949 Sewing, needlework, and piece goods

Custom Qlting Pllow Cshion Svc .... G 219 464-7316
  Valparaiso *(G-15934)*
Custom Sewing Service .... G 812 428-7015
  Evansville *(G-4004)*
Embroidme .... G 219 465-1400
  Valparaiso *(G-15943)*
Gohn Bros Manufacturing Co .... G 574 825-2400
  Middlebury *(G-11718)*
Hot Cake .... E 317 889-2253
  Indianapolis *(G-8419)*
▲ Indiana Ribbon Inc .... E 219 279-2112
  Wolcott *(G-16931)*
Sharps Baton Mfg Corp .... G 574 214-9389
  Elkhart *(G-3671)*
Tma Enterprises Inc .... G 317 272-0694
  Avon *(G-553)*
Varsity Sports Inc .... G 219 987-7200
  Demotte *(G-2931)*
Xtreme Graphics .... G 812 989-6948
  Jeffersonville *(G-10076)*

5961 Catalog and mail-order houses

Advance MCS Electronics Inc .... G 574 642-3501
  Ligonier *(G-11002)*
◆ Advance MCS Electronics Inc .... G 574 642-3501
  Goshen *(G-6089)*
American Legion National .... D 317 630-1200
  Indianapolis *(G-7505)*
▲ Annies Publishing LLC .... C 260 589-4000
  Berne *(G-704)*
Black Lavish Essentials LLC .... G 800 214-8664
  Indianapolis *(G-7639)*
Blessed Humbled Beginnings LLC .... G 219 255-3820
  Merrillville *(G-11490)*
Business Systems Mgt Corp .... G 219 938-0166
  Gary *(G-5908)*
Cinq LLC .... G 405 361-0097
  New Albany *(G-12713)*
Dauenhauer Glass Company Inc .... G 260 433-5876
  Fort Wayne *(G-4906)*
DMC Distribution LLC .... G 219 926-6401
  Porter *(G-13924)*
Dream Beauty Lab .... G 773 571-1817
  Marion *(G-11283)*
Favor It Promotions Inc .... F 317 733-1112
  Carmel *(G-1634)*
Gary M Brown .... G 765 831-2536
  New Castle *(G-12864)*
◆ Indiana Botanic Gardens Inc .... C 219 947-4040
  Hobart *(G-7191)*
▲ Johnny Lemas .... G 260 833-8850
  Angola *(G-264)*
Joseph Matthew Biaso .... G 812 277-6871
  Mitchell *(G-12041)*
▲ Official Sports Intl Inc .... F 574 269-1404
  Warsaw *(G-16403)*
Rose Sharon All Naturals LLC .... G 317 500-4725
  Indianapolis *(G-9334)*

▲ Roudebush Co Inc .... G 574 595-7115
  Star City *(G-15397)*
Rva LLC .... G 317 800-9800
  Fishers *(G-4602)*
Sacred Selections .... G 260 347-3758
  Kendallville *(G-10151)*
◆ Sailrite Enterprises Inc .... F 260 244-4647
  Columbia City *(G-2195)*
Shop Lulu Bean LLC .... G 219 525-5336
  Merrillville *(G-11559)*
Spagheady Inc .... G 317 499-6184
  Indianapolis *(G-9467)*
Spobric LLC .... G 302 249-1045
  Indianapolis *(G-9479)*
Summerville Miniature Work Sp .... G 317 326-8355
  Greenfield *(G-6561)*
Tokumei LLC .... G 765 772-0073
  West Lafayette *(G-16638)*
Tonis Touch LLC .... G 317 992-1280
  Plainfield *(G-13737)*
Tt2 LLC .... G 260 438-4575
  Fort Wayne *(G-5511)*
VMS Products Inc .... G 888 321-4698
  Anderson *(G-214)*
▼ Voice of God Recordings Inc .... D 812 246-2137
  Jeffersonville *(G-10069)*

5962 Merchandising machine operators

Whatzthat Vending LLC .... G 317 362-9088
  Indianapolis *(G-9755)*

5963 Direct selling establishments

3sevens LLC .... G 502 594-2312
  Henryville *(G-7112)*
A Pinch of Sweetness LLC .... G 765 838-2358
  Lafayette *(G-10513)*
Big Red Liquors Inc .... G 812 339-9552
  Bloomington *(G-806)*
Cynthia Bergstrand .... G 574 277-6160
  Granger *(G-6342)*
Deonta Walker .... G 317 970-3586
  Indianapolis *(G-7965)*
Evo Exhibits LLC .... G 630 520-0710
  Peru *(G-13582)*
Ladybugz Bookstore LLC .... G 469 459-1780
  Noblesville *(G-13125)*
Roller-Wilson Industries LLC .... G 317 377-4900
  Indianapolis *(G-9324)*

5983 Fuel oil dealers

Calumet Shreveport Fuels Llc .... D 317 328-5660
  Indianapolis *(G-7726)*
Calumet Superior LLC .... C 317 328-5660
  Indianapolis *(G-7729)*
Jolliff Diesel Service LLC .... G 812 692-5725
  Elnora *(G-3815)*
Spence/Banks Holdings Inc .... F 812 235-8123
  Terre Haute *(G-15713)*

5984 Liquefied petroleum gas dealers

Crestwood Equity Partners LP .... G 812 265-3313
  Madison *(G-11212)*
Ferrellgas LP .... G 574 936-2725
  Crawfordsville *(G-2566)*
Industrial Sewing Machine Co .... G 812 425-2255
  Evansville *(G-4124)*
Oeding Corporation .... G 812 367-1271
  Ferdinand *(G-4446)*

5989 Fuel dealers, nec

Blackwood Solutions LLC .... D 812 676-8770
  Bloomington *(G-809)*

59 MISCELLANEOUS RETAIL

▲ Carter Fuel Systems LLC................ B 800 342-6125
  Logansport (G-11064)

5992 Florists

Kroger Co.................................. G 574 291-0740
  South Bend (G-15107)
Larry Flowers Wholesale................. G 765 747-5156
  Muncie (G-12438)
Schnuck Markets Inc.................... C 812 853-9505
  Newburgh (G-13019)

5993 Tobacco stores and stands

Big Red Liquors Inc...................... G 812 339-9552
  Bloomington (G-806)
Black Swan Vapors LLC.................. G 317 645-5210
  Pendleton (G-13526)
▲ Green Nursery Inc..................... G 812 269-2220
  Bloomington (G-870)
Smoker Friendly.......................... G 812 556-0244
  Jasper (G-9912)

5995 Optical goods stores

Better Visions PC......................... F 260 244-7542
  Columbia City (G-2124)
Better Visions PC......................... F 260 627-2669
  Leo (G-10963)
City Optical Co Inc....................... D 317 924-1300
  Indianapolis (G-7813)
Columbus Optical Service Inc........... G 812 372-4117
  Columbus (G-2245)
Jackson Vision Quest.................... G 219 882-9397
  Gary (G-5967)
Kokomo Optical Company Inc........... G 765 459-5137
  Kokomo (G-10293)
Luxottica of America Inc................. G 317 293-9999
  Indianapolis (G-8800)
Luxottica of America Inc................. G 219 736-0141
  Merrillville (G-11535)
Shimp Optical Corp....................... G 317 636-4448
  Indianapolis (G-9420)
Tri State Optical Inc...................... D 765 289-4475
  Muncie (G-12508)
Usv Optical Inc........................... G 260 482-5033
  Fort Wayne (G-5524)

5999 Miscellaneous retail stores, nec

A & AS Beauty Barn LLC................ G 812 589-8559
  Evansville (G-3860)
Abundant Life Publications LLC........ G 219 730-7621
  Gary (G-5887)
Aceys Trophies & Awards............... G 574 267-1426
  Warsaw (G-16309)
Adafill Global LLC........................ G 317 798-5378
  Indianapolis (G-7427)
Advanced Lf Spport Innvtons LL....... G 574 538-1688
  Goshen (G-6090)
Advanced Orthopro Inc................. G 812 478-3656
  Terre Haute (G-15531)
Aesthtcally Pleasing Skin Soak......... G 317 551-0156
  Indianapolis (G-7454)
Airbotx LLC............................... G 317 981-1811
  Westfield (G-16663)
Allen Monument Co..................... G 317 941-7047
  Indianapolis (G-7480)
Allen Monument Co..................... G 574 240-1880
  Monticello (G-12134)
Allen Monument Company.............. G 765 362-8886
  Crawfordsville (G-2544)
American Limb & Orthopedic Co...... G 574 522-3643
  Elkhart (G-3173)
Art Ovation............................... G 317 769-4301
  Brownsburg (G-1348)

▲ Automatic Pool Covers Inc............ E 317 579-2000
  Westfield (G-16666)
Awardmakersnet Inc..................... G 260 925-4672
  Auburn (G-366)
Awards America Inc..................... F 219 462-7903
  Valparaiso (G-15906)
Awards Unlimited Inc.................... G 765 447-9413
  Lafayette (G-10532)
B S R Inc................................... G 812 235-4444
  Terre Haute (G-15548)
B S R Inc................................... E 812 235-4444
  Terre Haute (G-15549)
Barry Company Inc....................... G 812 333-1850
  Bloomington (G-795)
Bath & Body Works LLC................ F 317 209-1517
  Avon (G-506)
Bath & Body Works LLC................ F 317 468-0834
  Greenfield (G-6469)
Bath & Body Works LLC................ F 219 531-2146
  Valparaiso (G-15910)
▲ Bcw Diversified Inc.................... E 765 644-2033
  Middletown (G-11766)
Belltone Hearing Care Center........... G 317 462-9999
  Greenfield (G-6470)
Birds Nest Inc............................ G 574 247-0201
  Granger (G-6337)
Black Lavish Essentials LLC............ G 800 214-8664
  Indianapolis (G-7639)
Black Rose Pastries LLC................ G 773 708-3650
  Gary (G-5901)
Boone County Electric Inc.............. G 765 482-1430
  Lebanon (G-10880)
Brickhouse Electronics LLC............ F 212 643-7449
  Indianapolis (G-7678)
Bryan Ward............................... G 812 696-5126
  Farmersburg (G-4417)
▲ Candles By Dar Inc.................... F 260 482-2099
  Fort Wayne (G-4831)
Carl Abbott................................ G 317 590-4143
  Indianapolis (G-7745)
Carmel Trophies Plus LLC.............. G 317 844-3770
  Carmel (G-1581)
Cbizze LLC................................ G 623 204-9782
  South Bend (G-14968)
Central Brace & Limb Co Inc........... G 812 232-2145
  Terre Haute (G-15558)
Central Brace & Limb Co Inc........... F 317 925-4296
  Indianapolis (G-7769)
Classic Sign & Awning................... G 260 665-6663
  Angola (G-241)
Colophon Book Arts Supply LLC....... G 812 671-0577
  Bloomington (G-834)
Crystal Source............................ G 812 988-7009
  Nashville (G-12669)
Cybernaut Industria LLC................ G 317 664-5316
  Indianapolis (G-7939)
Cyclone Custom Prouducts LLC....... G 765 246-6523
  Greencastle (G-6401)
D J Investments Inc..................... G 765 348-3558
  Hartford City (G-7064)
D J Investments Inc..................... G 765 348-4381
  Hartford City (G-7063)
Driessen Water Inc...................... G 765 529-4905
  Muncie (G-12386)
Dwyer-Wilbert Inc........................ G 765 962-3605
  Richmond (G-14116)
Editions Ltd Gllery Fine Art I............ G 317 466-9940
  Indianapolis (G-8055)
Electric Mtr Repr & Rewind Inc......... G 812 284-5059
  Jeffersonville (G-9974)
Emma Pearls Creations LLC........... G 219 200-2277
  Highland (G-7135)

Evo Exhibits LLC......................... G 630 520-0710
  Peru (G-13582)
First Place Trophies...................... G 812 385-3279
  Princeton (G-13994)
First Place Trophy Inc................... G 574 293-6147
  Elkhart (G-3347)
Flag & Banner Company Inc........... F 317 299-4880
  Indianapolis (G-8199)
Flags International Inc................... G 574 674-5125
  Osceola (G-13392)
Flanders Electric Mtr Svc LLC.......... D 812 421-4300
  Evansville (G-4078)
Franklin Barry Gallery.................... G 317 822-8455
  Indianapolis (G-8224)
Game Plan Graphics LLC............... G 812 663-3238
  Greensburg (G-6596)
Gesco Group LLC........................ G 260 747-5088
  Fort Wayne (G-5023)
Gibbs Susie Framing & Art.............. G 765 428-2434
  Lafayette (G-10589)
Gockel Inc................................. G 574 402-0220
  Goshen (G-6151)
▲ Gvs Filter Technology Inc............. E 317 471-3700
  Indianapolis (G-8345)
H J J Inc................................... G 219 362-4421
  La Porte (G-10414)
Hanger Prsthetcs & Ortho Inc.......... F 219 844-2021
  Hammond (G-6944)
Hanger Prsthtics Orthotics Inc......... G 765 966-5069
  Richmond (G-14131)
Harris Precast Inc....................... G 219 362-2457
  La Porte (G-10416)
Herman Tool & Machine Inc............ F 574 594-5544
  Pierceton (G-13632)
High Quality Flasks LLC................. G 765 357-6392
  Lafayette (G-10598)
Home City Ice Company................ G 317 926-2451
  Indianapolis (G-8404)
Hoosier Processing LLC................ F 260 422-9440
  Fort Wayne (G-5080)
Hunter Nutrition Inc..................... F 765 563-1003
  Brookston (G-1311)
Imperial Trophy & Awards Co.......... G 260 432-8161
  Fort Wayne (G-5096)
Integrity Hearing......................... G 317 882-9151
  Noblesville (G-13107)
Jasper Electric Motor Inc............... F 812 482-1660
  Jasper (G-9850)
Jef Enterprises Inc....................... F 812 425-0628
  Evansville (G-4140)
Jer-Maur Corporation................... G 812 384-8290
  Bloomfield (G-750)
John Ley Monument Sales Inc......... G 260 347-7346
  Avilla (G-480)
Johnson Cntrls Fire Prtction L.......... G 317 826-2130
  Indianapolis (G-8633)
Johnson Engraving & Trophies......... G 260 982-7868
  North Manchester (G-13236)
Johnson Safe Company LLC............ G 317 876-7233
  Zionsville (G-17025)
Jordan Safety and Supply LLC......... G 513 315-6267
  Indianapolis (G-8638)
▲ Kids World Productions Inc........... G 317 674-6090
  Zionsville (G-17027)
◆ Koehler Welding Supply Inc.......... F 812 574-4103
  Madison (G-11233)
Koenig Equipment Inc................... G 765 962-7330
  Richmond (G-14154)
Lafayette Tents & Events LLC......... E 765 742-4277
  Lafayette (G-10630)
Larry H Poole............................. G 812 466-9345
  Terre Haute (G-15629)

62 SECURITY & COMMODITY BROKERS, DEALERS, EXCHANGES & SERVICES

Leisure Pool & Spa LLC .... G 812 537-0071
  Lawrenceburg *(G-10845)*

Linde Gas & Equipment Inc .... G 260 423-4468
  Fort Wayne *(G-5187)*

Linde Gas & Equipment Inc .... G 317 481-4550
  Indianapolis *(G-8761)*

Love-Toi LLC .... G 317 537-7635
  Anderson *(G-149)*

Majesty Hair Care System LLC .... G 317 900-6789
  Indianapolis *(G-8818)*

Mark Concrete Products Inc .... G 317 398-8616
  Shelbyville *(G-14774)*

Markle Water Treatment Plant .... G 260 758-3482
  Markle *(G-11358)*

Masterspas LLC .... C 260 436-9100
  Fort Wayne *(G-5207)*

◆ Masterspas LLC .... D 260 436-9100
  Fort Wayne *(G-5206)*

Mishawaka Art & Frame Gallery .... G 574 259-9320
  Mishawaka *(G-11953)*

Modrak Products Company Inc .... F 219 838-0308
  Gary *(G-5985)*

Mofab Inc .... G 765 649-5577
  Anderson *(G-157)*

Mold Removers LLC .... G 317 846-0977
  Indianapolis *(G-8946)*

Montgomery Tent & Awning Co .... F 317 357-9759
  Indianapolis *(G-8951)*

Mossberg & Company Inc .... F 260 755-6283
  Fort Wayne *(G-5246)*

Naturespire LLC .... G 463 266-0395
  Indianapolis *(G-8992)*

New Aqua LLC .... D 317 272-3000
  Avon *(G-540)*

New Haven Trophies & Shirts .... G 260 749-0269
  New Haven *(G-12911)*

▲ Ngh Retail LLC .... G 219 476-0772
  Valparaiso *(G-16012)*

▼ Noel Studio Inc .... F 317 297-1117
  Indianapolis *(G-9019)*

North Coast Organics LLC .... G 260 246-0289
  Fort Wayne *(G-5274)*

Northern Brace Company Inc .... G 574 233-4221
  South Bend *(G-15171)*

Northern Electric Company Inc .... E 574 289-7791
  South Bend *(G-15172)*

Northern Prosthetics Inc .... G 574 233-2459
  South Bend *(G-15174)*

Northwind Electronics LLC .... F 317 288-0787
  Indianapolis *(G-9024)*

Nose and Mustache LLC .... G 260 758-8800
  Markle *(G-11360)*

Ocella Inc .... G 845 842-8185
  Newberry *(G-12990)*

P3 Polymers LLC .... G 812 674-2051
  Washington *(G-16499)*

Parlor City Trophy & AP Inc .... G 260 824-0216
  Bluffton *(G-1047)*

Paula Rosenbaum .... G 319 484-2941
  Valparaiso *(G-16022)*

Pfortune Art & Design Inc .... G 317 872-4123
  Indianapolis *(G-9133)*

Pgs LLC .... F 812 988-4030
  Nashville *(G-12678)*

Phase Three Electric Inc .... G 812 945-9922
  New Albany *(G-12793)*

Pool Shop .... G 812 446-0026
  Brazil *(G-1162)*

Premiere Signs Co Inc .... G 574 533-8585
  Goshen *(G-6242)*

Pres-Del Electric Inc .... G 219 884-3146
  Gary *(G-5995)*

Profit Over Romance LLC .... G 219 900-3592
  Gary *(G-5997)*

Puritan Water Conditioning .... F 765 362-6340
  Crawfordsville *(G-2606)*

Pyramid Sign & Design Inc .... G 765 447-4174
  Lafayette *(G-10674)*

Quality Fire Protection .... G 269 683-0285
  South Bend *(G-15210)*

Randall Corp .... G 812 425-7122
  Evansville *(G-4272)*

Rayne Water Conditioning .... G 765 742-8967
  Lafayette *(G-10677)*

Reams Concrete .... G 812 752-3746
  Scottsburg *(G-14575)*

Recognition Plus .... G 812 232-2372
  Terre Haute *(G-15676)*

Regal Inc .... G 765 284-5722
  Muncie *(G-12487)*

Relevo Labs LLC .... G 317 900-6949
  Carmel *(G-1739)*

Ridge Iron LLC .... G 646 450-0092
  Plymouth *(G-13811)*

Roberson Fire & Safety Inc .... G 317 879-3119
  Indianapolis *(G-9313)*

Rose Sharon All Naturals LLC .... G 317 500-4725
  Indianapolis *(G-9334)*

Rose-Wall Mfg Inc .... G 317 894-4497
  Greenfield *(G-6544)*

Ruby Enterprises Inc .... G 765 649-2060
  Anderson *(G-186)*

Rugged Company .... G 317 441-0927
  Anderson *(G-187)*

Schug Awards LLC .... G 765 447-0002
  Lafayette *(G-10686)*

◆ Scott Pet Products Inc .... C 765 569-4636
  Rockville *(G-14354)*

Seductive Lifestyle LLC .... G 708 990-0720
  Gary *(G-6008)*

Serendipity Sanctuary .... G 765 541-2364
  Richmond *(G-14203)*

Shop Lulu Bean LLC .... G 219 525-5336
  Merrillville *(G-11559)*

Sign Craft Industries Inc .... E 317 842-8664
  Indianapolis *(G-9428)*

Sign Guys Inc .... G 317 875-7446
  Greenwood *(G-6767)*

Sneaky Micro Video Divisio .... G 317 925-1496
  Indianapolis *(G-9454)*

Sparkle Pools Inc .... F 812 232-1292
  Terre Haute *(G-15707)*

Specialty Shoppe .... G 574 772-7873
  Knox *(G-10225)*

Starkey Laboratories Inc .... F 952 828-6934
  Plainfield *(G-13731)*

Stitch N Frame .... G 260 478-1301
  Fort Wayne *(G-5443)*

Taylor Made Candles .... G 812 663-6634
  Greensburg *(G-6634)*

Technology Cons Group LLC .... G 219 525-4064
  Merrillville *(G-11565)*

The Office Shop Inc .... E 812 934-5611
  Batesville *(G-607)*

Thomas Monuments Inc .... G 317 244-6525
  Indianapolis *(G-9594)*

Tic Toc Trophy Shop Inc .... G 574 893-4234
  Akron *(G-10)*

Tornier Inc .... G 574 268-0861
  Warsaw *(G-16439)*

Travis Britton .... G 317 762-6018
  Indianapolis *(G-9632)*

Trek Pools LLC .... G 317 896-0493
  New Castle *(G-12883)*

Trinity Cmmnications Group Inc .... G 260 484-1029
  Fort Wayne *(G-5508)*

Twinrocker Hand Made Paper Inc .... G 765 563-3119
  Brookston *(G-1314)*

Upanaway LLC .... G 866 218-7143
  Greenfield *(G-6568)*

US Water Systems Inc .... E 317 209-0889
  Indianapolis *(G-9688)*

Van Der Weele Jon D .... G 574 892-5005
  Argos *(G-328)*

Varsity Sports Inc .... G 219 987-7200
  Demotte *(G-2931)*

▲ Vintage Chemical Inc .... G 260 745-7272
  Fort Wayne *(G-5533)*

Wanda Harrington .... G 765 642-1628
  Anderson *(G-215)*

Wasu Inc .... G 765 448-4450
  West Lafayette *(G-16645)*

▲ Wearly Monuments Inc .... F 765 284-9796
  Muncie *(G-12517)*

▲ Wilhoite Monuments Inc .... G 765 286-7423
  Muncie *(G-12520)*

Williams Bros Hlth Care Phrm I .... E 812 335-0000
  Bloomington *(G-1012)*

Williams Bros Hlth Care Phrm I .... C 812 254-2497
  Washington *(G-16513)*

Willows and More .... G 812 560-1088
  Westport *(G-16753)*

Wilsons Hearing Aid Center LLC .... G 765 747-4131
  Muncie *(G-12521)*

Winning Edge of Rochester Inc .... F 574 223-6090
  Rochester *(G-14334)*

Yankee Candle Company Inc .... G 812 526-5195
  Edinburgh *(G-3110)*

60 DEPOSITORY INSTITUTIONS

6099 Functions related to depository banking

Retro Atm LLC .... G 317 752-6915
  Indianapolis *(G-9294)*

61 NONDEPOSITORY CREDIT INSTITUTIONS

6141 Personal credit institutions

Ford Motor Company .... F 901 368-8821
  Plainfield *(G-13680)*

Heritage Financial Group Inc .... E 574 522-8000
  Elkhart *(G-3404)*

6153 Short-term business credit

Ford Motor Company .... F 901 368-8821
  Plainfield *(G-13680)*

Procard Inc .... D 303 279-2255
  Jeffersonville *(G-10042)*

6163 Loan brokers

Wallar Additions Inc .... G 574 262-1989
  Elkhart *(G-3778)*

62 SECURITY & COMMODITY BROKERS, DEALERS, EXCHANGES & SERVICES

6211 Security brokers and dealers

Calcean LLC .... G 812 672-4995
  Seymour *(G-14636)*

Cook Group Incorporated .... F 812 339-2235
  Bloomington *(G-838)*

62 SECURITY & COMMODITY BROKERS, DEALERS, EXCHANGES & SERVICES

Penn-Mar Capital LLC................................ G 463 239-2632
  Indianapolis *(G-9115)*

6221 Commodity contracts brokers, dealers

Louis Dreyfus Co AG Inds LLC.............. A
  Claypool *(G-2055)*

6231 Security and commodity exchanges

Retro Atm LLC................................... G 317 752-6915
  Indianapolis *(G-9294)*

6282 Investment advice

Horizon Publishing Company LLC......... F 219 852-3200
  Hammond *(G-6949)*
Worth Tax and Financial Svc................... G 574 267-4687
  Warsaw *(G-16456)*

63 INSURANCE CARRIERS

6399 Insurance carriers, nec

Creative Manufacturing Rv LLC.............. F 574 333-3302
  Elkhart *(G-3271)*

64 INSURANCE AGENTS, BROKERS AND SERVICE

6411 Insurance agents, brokers, and service

Cook Group Incorporated........................ F 812 339-2235
  Bloomington *(G-838)*
Haven Capital LLC................................. G 219 802-5044
  Valparaiso *(G-15960)*

65 REAL ESTATE

6512 Nonresidential building operators

Accent Complex Inc............................... G 574 522-2368
  Elkhart *(G-3148)*
All Pro Property Services LLC................ G 317 721-1227
  Indianapolis *(G-7474)*
Coach Line Motors................................ G 765 825-7893
  Connersville *(G-2431)*
Cook Group Incorporated........................ F 812 339-2235
  Bloomington *(G-838)*
◆ Jasper Engine Exchange Inc............A 812 482-1041
  Jasper *(G-9853)*
Kendalville Mall..................................... G 260 897-2697
  Avilla *(G-482)*
Tartan Properties LLC............................ G 317 714-7437
  Indianapolis *(G-9554)*

6514 Dwelling operators, except apartments

Charles Coons..................................... G 765 362-6509
  Crawfordsville *(G-2552)*
Milani Custom Homes LLC.................... G 219 455-5804
  Merrillville *(G-11538)*

6515 Mobile home site operators

Charles Coons..................................... G 765 362-6509
  Crawfordsville *(G-2552)*
Heritage Financial Group Inc................. E 574 522-8000
  Elkhart *(G-3404)*
Lakeside Manor.................................... E 219 362-3956
  La Porte *(G-10445)*
Paddack Brothers Inc............................ G 765 659-4777
  Frankfort *(G-5689)*

6519 Real property lessors, nec

Complete Property Care LLC.................. G 765 288-0890
  Muncie *(G-12368)*
Lakeside Manor.................................... E 219 362-3956
  La Porte *(G-10445)*

Napoleon Lumber Co............................ G 812 852-4545
  Napoleon *(G-12575)*

6531 Real estate agents and managers

Anderson Memorial Park Inc.................. F 765 643-3211
  Anderson *(G-78)*
Brockwood Farm.................................. G 812 837-9607
  Nashville *(G-12664)*
Caterpillar Inc...................................... G 765 447-6816
  Lafayette *(G-10550)*
Cole Energy Incorporated..................... G 317 839-9688
  Plainfield *(G-13670)*
Complete Property Care LLC.................. G 765 288-0890
  Muncie *(G-12368)*
Countryside Property LLC..................... G 800 711-5926
  Evansville *(G-3986)*
Daily Rental.. G 773 881-7762
  Munster *(G-12537)*
Gbj Holdings LLC................................. G 317 483-1896
  Highland *(G-7137)*
Heritage Financial Group Inc................. E 574 522-8000
  Elkhart *(G-3404)*
Land of Indiana Inc.............................. F 812 788-1560
  Bedford *(G-654)*
Millwork Specialties Co Inc.................... G 219 362-2960
  La Porte *(G-10453)*
Project Field Solutions Inc..................... G 317 590-7678
  Fishers *(G-4584)*
T Organization Inc............................... E 463 204-5118
  Greenwood *(G-6771)*
Thornes Homes Inc.............................. G 812 275-4656
  Bedford *(G-678)*
Tylayculture LLC.................................. G 219 678-8359
  Highland *(G-7158)*

6552 Subdividers and developers, nec

R E Casebeer & Sons Inc...................... G 812 829-3284
  Spencer *(G-15359)*
Whiteco Industries Inc.......................... A 219 769-6601
  Merrillville *(G-11572)*

6553 Cemetery subdividers and developers

Anderson Memorial Park Inc.................. F 765 643-3211
  Anderson *(G-78)*

67 HOLDING AND OTHER INVESTMENT OFFICES

6719 Holding companies, nec

Better Blacc Wall Streetz LLC................. F 812 927-0712
  Seymour *(G-14632)*
Cummins Holding Group LLC................. G 765 962-6332
  Richmond *(G-14112)*
Gbj Holdings LLC................................. G 317 483-1896
  Highland *(G-7137)*
▲ Navistar Cmponent Holdings LLC..... A 317 352-4500
  Indianapolis *(G-8994)*
▲ Rbc Holding Inc.............................. F 317 340-3845
  Greenwood *(G-6759)*
Specialty Steel Holdco Inc..................... A 877 289-2277
  Hammond *(G-7013)*
V Global Holdings LLC.......................... E 317 247-8141
  Indianapolis *(G-9695)*
Wright Horizon Enterprises LLC............. G 317 779-8182
  Westfield *(G-16741)*

6722 Management investment, open-ended

Allegion Public Ltd Company................. D 317 810-3700
  Carmel *(G-1554)*

6726 Investment offices, nec

Deedgrabbercom Inc............................ G 219 712-9722
  Munster *(G-12538)*

6732 Trusts: educational, religious, etc.

Dear Athletes Inc................................. G 615 682-3332
  Noblesville *(G-13069)*

6794 Patent owners and lessors

Cliff A Ostermeyer............................... G 615 361-7902
  Fort Wayne *(G-4860)*
▲ Crown Technology Inc..................... E 317 845-0045
  Indianapolis *(G-7914)*
Legends Maingate LLC......................... F 317 243-2000
  Indianapolis *(G-8735)*
▲ Maingate LLC.................................. D
  Indianapolis *(G-8814)*
Odyssian Technology LLC..................... G 574 257-7555
  South Bend *(G-15176)*
Rebound Project LLP............................ G 765 621-5604
  Anderson *(G-183)*

6799 Investors, nec

Deedgrabbercom Inc............................ G 219 712-9722
  Munster *(G-12538)*
Integrity Marketing Team Inc................. G 317 517-0012
  Plainfield *(G-13691)*
Penn-Mar Capital LLC........................... G 463 239-2632
  Indianapolis *(G-9115)*
Rios Investment Services LLC................ G 574 514-3999
  South Bend *(G-15221)*
Sater Enterprises................................. G 812 477-1529
  Evansville *(G-4297)*
Tylayculture LLC.................................. G 219 678-8359
  Highland *(G-7158)*

70 HOTELS, ROOMING HOUSES, CAMPS, AND OTHER LODGING PLACES

7011 Hotels and motels

Colluci Construction-Log Homes............ G 812 843-5607
  English *(G-3840)*
Rittenhouse Square.............................. G 260 824-4200
  Bluffton *(G-1051)*
Whiteco Industries Inc.......................... A 219 769-6601
  Merrillville *(G-11572)*

7032 Sporting and recreational camps

Dick Baumgartners Basket.................... E 765 220-1767
  Richmond *(G-14114)*

72 PERSONAL SERVICES

7213 Linen supply

Wildman Business Group LLC............... G 866 369-1552
  Warsaw *(G-16451)*

7215 Coin-operated laundries and cleaning

H & H Partnership Inc.......................... G 765 513-4739
  Kokomo *(G-10274)*
Laundry On US LLC.............................. G 812 567-3653
  Terre Haute *(G-15630)*

7216 Drycleaning plants, except rugs

Chucks Cleaners LLC............................ G 260 488-3362
  Hamilton *(G-6851)*

7217 Carpet and upholstery cleaning

Bane-Clene Corp.................................. G 317 546-5448
  Indianapolis *(G-7594)*

SIC SECTION

73 BUSINESS SERVICES

Bane-Clene Corp .... F 317 546-5448
 Indianapolis (G-7595)
Kings-Qlity Rstrtion Svcs LLC .... F 812 944-4347
 New Albany (G-12760)

7218 Industrial launderers

Wildman Business Group LLC .... G 866 369-1552
 Warsaw (G-16451)

7219 Laundry and garment services, nec

Country Sewing .... G 260 347-9733
 Kendallville (G-10103)

7221 Photographic studios, portrait

Kennyleeholmescom .... G 574 612-2526
 Elkhart (G-3451)
Stands Photography .... G 812 723-3922
 Paoli (G-13500)
TEC Photography .... G 812 332-9847
 Bloomington (G-985)

7231 Beauty shops

Anderson Shykia .... G 773 304-6852
 Gary (G-5894)
Beautybyneyadior LLC .... G 800 988-2592
 Gary (G-5898)
Best Electric Motor Service .... G 765 583-2408
 Otterbein (G-13450)
Bettys Daughter Inc .... G 317 500-1490
 Plainfield (G-13661)
Cali Nail .... G 574 674-4126
 Osceola (G-13385)
CD & Ws Bordner Entps Inc .... G 765 268-2120
 Cutler (G-2783)
Cheri-Theree Inc .... G 812 529-8132
 Lamar (G-10795)
Classique Hair Style .... G 317 738-2104
 Franklin (G-5721)
Divine Essentials LLC .... G 765 400-8609
 Muncie (G-12385)
Kartistry Pro LLC .... G 317 969-7075
 Indianapolis (G-8661)
Kenra Professional LLC .... F 800 428-8073
 Indianapolis (G-8673)
Kjs Beauty Lounge LLC .... G 317 426-0621
 Indianapolis (G-8692)
London Hair Bundles LLC .... G 317 953-3888
 Fishers (G-4557)
Majesty Hair Care System LLC .... G 317 900-6789
 Indianapolis (G-8818)
Naturespire LLC .... G 463 266-0395
 Indianapolis (G-8992)
Tonis Touch LLC .... G 317 992-1280
 Plainfield (G-13737)

7241 Barber shops

Cozy Cat Inc .... G 765 463-1254
 Lafayette (G-10559)
Otter Creek Christian Church .... G 812 446-5300
 Brazil (G-1159)

7261 Funeral service and crematories

◆ Aurora Casket Company LLC .... B 800 457-1111
 Aurora (G-439)
Romark Industries Inc .... G 765 966-6211
 Richmond (G-14200)

7291 Tax return preparation services

Jackson Hewitt Tax Service .... F 574 255-2200
 Mishawaka (G-11915)
P C Communications Inc .... G 219 838-2546
 Highland (G-7150)

Worth Tax and Financial Svc .... G 574 267-4687
 Warsaw (G-16456)

7299 Miscellaneous personal services

Action Embroidery Inc .... G 850 626-1796
 Charlestown (G-1869)
Always Sun Tanning Center .... G 812 238-2786
 Terre Haute (G-15540)
Beutler Meat Processing Co .... G 765 742-7285
 Lafayette (G-10536)
Country Moon Winery LLC .... G 317 773-7942
 Noblesville (G-13064)
Cruz Electric & Handy Svc LLC .... G 219 308-7117
 Hobart (G-7185)
Dave Turner .... G 765 674-3360
 Gas City (G-6035)
Formal Affairs Tuxedo Shop .... G 574 875-6654
 Elkhart (G-3357)
Grafton Peek Incorporated .... F 317 557-8377
 Greenwood (G-6709)
Higgins Dyan .... G 812 876-0754
 Ellettsville (G-3809)
Hot Cake .... E 317 889-2253
 Indianapolis (G-8419)
Louies Companies Inc .... G 765 448-4300
 Lafayette (G-10639)
Mast Services Lafayette LLC .... G 765 464-6940
 Lafayette (G-10643)
Northern Indiana Ordnance Co .... G 574 289-5938
 South Bend (G-15173)
Parretts Meat Proc & Catrg Inc .... F 574 967-3711
 Flora (G-4663)
▲ Plum Group Inc .... F 617 712-3000
 Indianapolis (G-9155)
Rackcollections LLC .... G 317 779-4302
 Indianapolis (G-9259)
Reset Family Solutions LLC .... G 317 699-2990
 Carthage (G-1817)
Selby Publishing & Printing .... G 765 453-5417
 Kokomo (G-10332)
Serendipity Sanctuary .... G 765 541-2364
 Richmond (G-14203)
Simple To Elegant LLC .... G 812 234-8700
 Terre Haute (G-15696)
Zig-Zag Crnr Qilts Baskets LLC .... G 317 326-3115
 Greenfield (G-6573)

73 BUSINESS SERVICES

7311 Advertising agencies

Baxter Design & Advertising .... G 219 464-9237
 Valparaiso (G-15912)
Charles E Watts .... G 812 547-8516
 Tell City (G-15498)
◆ Clondalkin Pharma & Healthcare Inc ... A 336 292-4555
 Indianapolis (G-7824)
Degler Mktg & Mailing Svcs .... G 317 873-5550
 Zionsville (G-17002)
Digital Design Genius .... G 317 515-3680
 Camby (G-1509)
Dow Theory Forecasts Inc .... E 219 931-6480
 Hammond (G-6915)
Em Global LLC .... G 812 258-9993
 Jeffersonville (G-9976)
Goldleaf Promotional Pdts Inc .... G 317 202-2754
 Indianapolis (G-8302)
Ovation Communications Inc .... G 812 401-9100
 Evansville (G-4230)
Printing Creations Inc .... G 765 759-9679
 Yorktown (G-16982)
Rick Singleton .... F 574 259-5555
 Mishawaka (G-11986)

Rowland Printing Co Inc .... F 317 773-1829
 Noblesville (G-13168)
Sexton Advertising LLC .... G 812 522-4059
 Seymour (G-14688)
Shilling Sales Inc .... E 260 426-2626
 Fort Wayne (G-5413)
Tremike Enterprises .... G 317 547-6308
 Indianapolis (G-9634)
Yaney Mktg Graphic Design LLC ...... G 317 776-0676
 Noblesville (G-13197)

7312 Outdoor advertising services

Lamar Advertising Company .... F 260 482-9566
 Fort Wayne (G-5173)
Sig Media LLC .... F 317 858-7624
 Indianapolis (G-9426)

7313 Radio, television, publisher representatives

Aim Media Indiana Oper LLC .... E 317 736-7101
 Franklin (G-5704)
Newspaper Holding Inc .... G 270 678-5171
 Jeffersonville (G-10024)
W Ay-FM Media Group Inc .... G 812 945-1043
 New Albany (G-12824)

7319 Advertising, nec

C & W Inkd .... F 317 352-1000
 Indianapolis (G-7706)
Linker Media Group Inc .... G 219 230-3777
 Dyer (G-2977)
Professional Gifting Inc .... F 800 350-1796
 Indianapolis (G-9221)
Sampco Inc .... G 413 442-4043
 South Bend (G-15230)
Sig Media LLC .... F 317 858-7624
 Indianapolis (G-9426)
Spark Marketing LLC .... G 219 301-0071
 Dyer (G-2983)

7322 Adjustment and collection services

Sentinel Services Inc .... E 574 360-5279
 Granger (G-6376)

7331 Direct mail advertising services

American Ex Trvl Rlted Svcs In .... G 812 523-0106
 Seymour (G-14629)
Anthony Wyne Rhblttion Ctr For .... C 317 972-1000
 Indianapolis (G-7522)
Anthony Wyne Rhblttion Ctr For .... D 260 744-6145
 Fort Wayne (G-4762)
Baugh Enterprises Inc .... F 812 334-8189
 Bloomington (G-796)
Cozy Cat Inc .... G 765 463-1254
 Lafayette (G-10559)
Crossrads Rhbilitation Ctr Inc .... C 317 897-7320
 Indianapolis (G-7910)
Data Mail Incorporated .... E 812 424-7835
 Evansville (G-4007)
Degler Mktg & Mailing Svcs .... G 317 873-5550
 Zionsville (G-17002)
Delp Printing & Mailing Inc .... G 317 872-9744
 Indianapolis (G-7963)
Faris Mailing Inc .... F 317 246-3315
 Indianapolis (G-8167)
Fineline Graphics Incorporated .... D 317 872-4490
 Indianapolis (G-8188)
Harmony Press Inc .... E 800 525-3742
 Bourbon (G-1122)
Lori Hicks .... G 574 291-6341
 South Bend (G-15129)

73 BUSINESS SERVICES

Ovation Communications Inc............... G 812 401-9100
Evansville (G-4230)

Presstime Graphics Inc....................... F 812 234-3815
Terre Haute (G-15669)

Printing Partners Inc........................... D 317 635-2282
Indianapolis (G-9206)

Printwerk Graphics & Design............... G 219 322-7722
Dyer (G-2981)

Service Graphics Inc............................ D 317 471-8246
Indianapolis (G-9408)

7334 Photocopying and duplicating services

Art Bookbinders of America.................. F 312 226-4100
Hammond (G-6880)

Blue Print Specialties Inc..................... G 765 742-6976
Lafayette (G-10539)

Blue River Printing Inc......................... G 317 392-3676
Shelbyville (G-14736)

Commercial Print Shop Inc................... G 260 724-3722
Decatur (G-2850)

Copy Solutions Inc.............................. G 260 436-2679
Fort Wayne (G-4874)

Copy-Print Shop Inc............................ E 765 447-6868
Lafayette (G-10556)

Copymat Services Inc.......................... G 765 743-5995
Lafayette (G-10557)

Creative Concept Ventures Inc.............. G 812 282-9442
Jeffersonville (G-9964)

◆ David Camp..G 812 346-6255
North Vernon (G-13265)

Dynamark Graphics Group Inc.............. E 317 328-2555
Indianapolis (G-8023)

Eastern Engineering Supply Inc............. F 260 426-3119
Fort Wayne (G-4938)

Ed Sons Inc.. F 317 897-8821
Indianapolis (G-8051)

Express Press Inc............................... G 812 882-3278
Vincennes (G-16122)

Fedex Office & Print Svcs Inc............... G 317 974-0378
Indianapolis (G-8172)

Fedex Office & Print Svcs Inc............... G 317 917-1529
Indianapolis (G-8173)

Fedex Office & Print Svcs Inc............... G 317 849-9683
Indianapolis (G-8174)

Fedex Office & Print Svcs Inc............... G 317 885-6480
Indianapolis (G-8175)

Fedex Office & Print Svcs Inc............... G 317 295-1063
Indianapolis (G-8176)

Fedex Office & Print Svcs Inc............... G 317 337-2679
Indianapolis (G-8177)

Fedex Office & Print Svcs Inc............... G 317 631-6862
Indianapolis (G-8178)

Fedex Office & Print Svcs Inc............... G 317 251-2406
Indianapolis (G-8179)

Fedex Office & Print Svcs Inc............... F 765 449-4950
Lafayette (G-10579)

Hiatt Enterprises Inc........................... G 765 289-2700
Muncie (G-12416)

Hiatt Enterprises Inc........................... F 765 289-7756
Muncie (G-12415)

J & L Dimensional Services Inc............. E 219 325-3588
La Porte (G-10430)

Maco Reprograhics LLC...................... G 812 464-8108
Evansville (G-4183)

MPS Printing Incorporated.................... G 812 273-4446
Madison (G-11245)

Mr Copy Inc....................................... G 812 334-2679
Bloomington (G-925)

Novaprints LLC.................................. F 317 577-6682
Indianapolis (G-9028)

Ovation Communications Inc............... G 812 401-9100
Evansville (G-4230)

Paper Chase....................................... G 812 385-4757
Princeton (G-14009)

Perfect Impressions Printing................. G 317 923-1756
Indianapolis (G-9121)

Printing Partners East Inc.................... G 317 356-2522
Indianapolis (G-9207)

Priority Press Inc................................ G 317 240-0103
Indianapolis (G-9212)

Randall Corp...................................... G 812 425-7122
Evansville (G-4272)

Rebecca L Hamann & Associates......... G 219 763-1233
Portage (G-13910)

Rhr Corporation.................................. G 317 788-1504
Indianapolis (G-9298)

◆ Rrc Corporation.................................. F 317 687-8325
Indianapolis (G-9343)

Service Graphics Inc........................... D 317 471-8246
Indianapolis (G-9408)

Sharp Printing Services Inc.................. G 317 842-5159
Fishers (G-4604)

Tdk Graphics Inc................................ F 219 663-7799
Crown Point (G-2762)

7335 Commercial photography

Scher Maihem Publishing Ltd............... G 260 897-2697
Avilla (G-494)

7336 Commercial art and graphic design

Annual Reports Inc.............................. G 317 736-8838
Franklin (G-5709)

Aon(all or Nothing) LLC....................... G 219 405-0163
Indianapolis (G-7524)

▲ Asempac Inc..................................... E 812 945-6303
New Albany (G-12692)

▲ Burston Marketing Inc......................... F 574 262-4005
Elkhart (G-3238)

Business Art & Designs Inc.................. G 317 782-9108
Beech Grove (G-688)

Catalent Wellness Indiana LLC............. F 812 537-5203
Greendale (G-6443)

▲ Chromasource Inc............................... C 260 420-3000
Columbia City (G-2130)

Classic Graphics Inc............................ F 260 482-3487
Fort Wayne (G-4853)

Cs Kern Inc....................................... E 765 289-8600
Muncie (G-12370)

Custom TS & Trophies........................ G 219 926-4174
Porter (G-13923)

Cyclone Custom Prouducts LLC............ G 765 246-6523
Greencastle (G-6401)

Dave Turner....................................... G 765 674-3360
Gas City (G-6035)

Debra Richard..................................... G 812 379-4927
Columbus (G-2281)

Deem & Loureiro Inc........................... G 770 652-9871
Indianapolis (G-7961)

Digital Design Genius........................... G 317 515-3680
Camby (G-1509)

Drs Graphix Group Inc......................... G 317 569-1855
Indianapolis (G-8011)

East 40 Sports Apparel Inc.................. G 812 877-3695
Terre Haute (G-15580)

Epic Graphics and Printing.................... G 219 545-1240
Gary (G-5930)

Founders West Inc.............................. G 812 936-7446
Mccordsville (G-11449)

Freckles Grphics Lafayette Inc.............. F 765 448-4692
Lafayette (G-10581)

Gibson Innovations LLC...................... G 317 561-0932
Terre Haute (G-15597)

Grace Henderson................................ G 765 661-9063
Marion (G-11289)

Graphic Visions.................................. G 812 331-7446
Bloomington (G-869)

Grayson Graphics............................... G 574 264-6466
Elkhart (G-3388)

Hetty Incorporated.............................. G 219 933-0833
Hammond (G-6945)

Hetty Incorporated.............................. G 219 836-2517
Munster (G-12539)

Hot Rod Car Care LLC........................ G 317 660-2077
Indianapolis (G-8421)

Indiana Dimensional Pdts LLC.............. E 574 834-7681
North Webster (G-13306)

Indianapolis Signworks Inc................... E 317 872-8722
Indianapolis (G-8508)

Karemar Productions........................... G 765 766-5117
Mooreland (G-12185)

Kennyleeholmescom............................ G 574 612-2526
Elkhart (G-3451)

Logo Boys Inc.................................... G 574 256-6844
Mishawaka (G-11932)

▲ Main Event Mdsg Group LLC............... F 317 570-8900
Indianapolis (G-8812)

Marketing Services Group Inc.............. B 317 381-2268
Indianapolis (G-8838)

Mid West Digital Express Inc................ F 317 733-1214
Zionsville (G-17033)

Moose Lake Products Co Inc................ F 260 432-2768
Fort Wayne (G-5242)

Optiviz Media LLC.............................. G 812 681-1711
Vincennes (G-16141)

Pam C Jones Enterprises Inc............... G 812 294-1862
Borden (G-1117)

Raging Rocket Web Design LLC........... G 219 381-5027
Crown Point (G-2741)

Reinforcements Design........................ G 219 866-8626
Rensselaer (G-14064)

Rlr Associates Inc.............................. G 317 632-1300
Indianapolis (G-9312)

Ron Glasscock................................... G 812 986-2342
Poland (G-13837)

Schaffsteins Truck Clean LLC............... F 812 464-2424
Evansville (G-4298)

Sexton Advertising LLC....................... G 812 522-4059
Seymour (G-14688)

Shadow Graphix Inc............................ G 317 481-9710
Indianapolis (G-9411)

Sig Media LLC................................... F 317 858-7624
Indianapolis (G-9426)

Smiling Cross Inc................................ G 812 323-9290
Bloomington (G-976)

Squeegeepie Merch Co LLC................. G 765 376-6358
Crawfordsville (G-2618)

Stien Designs & Graphics Inc............... G 260 347-9136
Kendallville (G-10153)

Techcom Inc...................................... F 812 372-0960
Columbus (G-2401)

Thomas E Slade Inc............................ F 812 437-5233
Evansville (G-4343)

Titan Graphics LLC............................. G 317 496-2188
Mccordsville (G-11457)

Tranter Graphics Inc............................ D 574 834-2626
Syracuse (G-15487)

Wagner Signs Inc................................ E 317 788-0202
Indianapolis (G-9735)

Whimsicals Inc................................... G 317 773-6130
Noblesville (G-13194)

World Graffix LLC............................... G 574 936-1927
Plymouth (G-13834)

▲ World Media Group Inc....................... D 317 549-8484
Indianapolis (G-9790)

Young & Kenady Incorporated.............. G 317 852-6300
Brownsburg (G-1415)

73 BUSINESS SERVICES

7338 Secretarial and court reporting

Cozy Cat Inc... G 765 463-1254
  Lafayette *(G-10559)*

Encourage Publishing LLC..................... G 812 987-6148
  New Albany *(G-12725)*

Jomark Inc... F 248 478-2600
  Angola *(G-265)*

Precisely Write Inc................................. G 317 585-7701
  Indianapolis *(G-9178)*

7342 Disinfecting and pest control services

Corteva Inc.. G 765 586-4077
  Indianapolis *(G-7882)*

Corteva Inc.. A 833 267-8382
  Indianapolis *(G-7883)*

7349 Building maintenance services, nec

A & H Enterprises LLC............................ G 317 398-3070
  Shelbyville *(G-14729)*

A 2 Z Universal Solutions....................... G 317 496-7435
  Union City *(G-15846)*

American Maint & Training Inc............... F 812 738-4230
  Corydon *(G-2485)*

Chem-Dry of Allen County...................... G 260 490-2705
  Fort Wayne *(G-4844)*

Clean By Design Inc................................ G 260 414-4444
  Fort Wayne *(G-4857)*

Complete Property Care LLC................. G 765 288-0890
  Muncie *(G-12368)*

D J Investments Inc................................ G 260 726-7346
  Portland *(G-13936)*

Hunter Venetian Blind Co....................... G 812 471-1100
  Evansville *(G-4113)*

▲ Ikio Led Lighting LLC......................... A 765 414-0835
  Indianapolis *(G-8458)*

Lady Q LLC-S... G 219 304-8404
  Indianapolis *(G-8712)*

Loves Travel Stops................................. F 574 935-4103
  Plymouth *(G-13793)*

Mold Removers LLC................................ G 317 846-0977
  Indianapolis *(G-8946)*

Onsite Construction Services................ E 312 723-8060
  Chesterton *(G-1951)*

Padgett Inc.. C 812 945-2391
  New Albany *(G-12790)*

Paradigm Industries Inc......................... G 317 574-8590
  Carmel *(G-1714)*

Poynter Sheet Metal Inc......................... B 317 893-1193
  Greenwood *(G-6753)*

Professional Grade Svcs LLC................. G 317 688-8898
  Indianapolis *(G-9222)*

Project Field Solutions Inc..................... G 317 590-7678
  Fishers *(G-4584)*

Wise Energy LLC..................................... G 317 475-0305
  Indianapolis *(G-9776)*

7352 Medical equipment rental

◆ Hill-Rom Inc... A 812 934-7777
  Batesville *(G-589)*

Williams Bros Hlth Care Phrm I............. E 812 335-0000
  Bloomington *(G-1012)*

Williams Bros Hlth Care Phrm I............. C 812 254-2497
  Washington *(G-16513)*

7353 Heavy construction equipment rental

Gesco Group LLC................................... G 260 747-5088
  Fort Wayne *(G-5023)*

GI Properties Inc.................................... G 219 763-1177
  Portage *(G-13868)*

Hampton Equipment LLC........................ G 260 740-8704
  Fort Wayne *(G-5049)*

Macallister Machinery Co Inc................. C 260 483-6469
  Fort Wayne *(G-5195)*

Macallister Machinery Co Inc................. F 765 966-0759
  Richmond *(G-14157)*

Pittman Mine Service LLC...................... G 812 847-2340
  Linton *(G-11042)*

▲ Poseidon LLC...................................... C 260 422-8767
  Berne *(G-722)*

Wyatt Farm Center Inc........................... G 574 354-2998
  Nappanee *(G-12655)*

7359 Equipment rental and leasing, nec

Aaron Company Inc................................ F 219 838-0852
  Gary *(G-5886)*

Airbotx LLC... G 317 981-1811
  Westfield *(G-16663)*

All American Tent & Awning Inc............ E 812 232-4206
  Terre Haute *(G-15537)*

Gockel Inc... G 574 402-0220
  Goshen *(G-6151)*

Goliath Ag LLC....................................... F 765 305-1141
  Winchester *(G-16888)*

▲ Heat Wagons Inc................................ F 219 464-8818
  Valparaiso *(G-15961)*

Highway Safety Services Inc................. D 765 474-1000
  Lafayette *(G-10599)*

J & J Repair.. G 574 831-3075
  Goshen *(G-6178)*

Macallister Machinery Co Inc................. F 765 966-0759
  Richmond *(G-14157)*

McL Window Coverings Inc.................... G 317 577-2670
  Fishers *(G-4563)*

Motion Engineering Company Inc.......... G 317 804-7990
  Westfield *(G-16712)*

Nix Sanitary Service............................... G 812 785-1158
  Boonville *(G-1094)*

Phil Irwin Advertising Inc....................... F 317 547-5117
  Indianapolis *(G-9134)*

Pitney Bowes Inc.................................... G 260 436-7395
  Indianapolis *(G-9148)*

Road Alert Systems LLC......................... G 219 669-1206
  Morocco *(G-12269)*

Sizzlin Sound Productions LLC.............. G 765 376-0129
  Crawfordsville *(G-2615)*

▲ Standard Change-Makers Inc............ C 317 899-6955
  Indianapolis *(G-9491)*

◆ TSF Co Inc... E 812 985-2630
  Evansville *(G-4354)*

Wdmi Inc... D 574 936-2136
  Plymouth *(G-13826)*

7361 Employment agencies

Eminence Hlth Care Stffing AGC........... G 866 350-6400
  South Bend *(G-15013)*

Vergence LLC... F 317 547-4417
  Indianapolis *(G-9707)*

7363 Help supply services

Goldenmarc LLC..................................... G 317 855-1651
  Indianapolis *(G-8301)*

Indigo Industries LLC............................. G 480 747-4560
  Greenwood *(G-6715)*

Luxly LLC.. G 617 415-8031
  Carmel *(G-1686)*

Majesty Enterprises Inc......................... G 812 752-6446
  Scottsburg *(G-14570)*

7371 Custom computer programming services

39 Degrees North LLC........................... F 855 447-3939
  Bloomington *(G-765)*

Advanced Designs Corp......................... F 812 333-1922
  Bloomington *(G-773)*

Agora Brands Group Inc......................... E 615 802-0086
  Borden *(G-1104)*

App Press LLC.. G 317 661-4759
  Indianapolis *(G-7528)*

Aunalytics Inc... D 574 307-9230
  South Bend *(G-14951)*

Authenticx Inc... D 317 296-6238
  Indianapolis *(G-7570)*

Baugh Enterprises Inc............................ F 812 334-8189
  Bloomington *(G-796)*

Benjamin Carrier.................................... G 337 366-2603
  Jeffersonville *(G-9940)*

Binarie LLC... G 317 496-8836
  Greenwood *(G-6676)*

Center For Ethcal Rbtics A Nnt............. G 219 741-9374
  Hammond *(G-6897)*

Center For The Study Knwldge D......... G 812 361-4424
  Bloomington *(G-827)*

Concrete Monkey Studios LLC.............. G 812 630-2339
  Evansville *(G-3978)*

Conversightai... F 201 294-1896
  Indianapolis *(G-7865)*

Custom Software Solutions Inc............. G 260 637-8393
  Fort Wayne *(G-4900)*

Cyberia Ltd... G 317 721-2582
  Indianapolis *(G-7938)*

Daily Peru Tribune Pubg Co................... F 765 473-6641
  Peru *(G-13577)*

Diverse Tech Services Inc..................... E 317 432-6444
  Indianapolis *(G-7982)*

Dry Heat Coffee LLC.............................. G 760 422-9865
  Indianapolis *(G-8013)*

Edutronics... G 765 529-6751
  New Castle *(G-12859)*

Eric Isaacson.. G 812 339-1811
  Bloomington *(G-862)*

Fiserv Mrtg Servicing Systems.............. C 574 282-3300
  South Bend *(G-15034)*

Flat Electronics LLC............................... G 765 414-6635
  Fishers *(G-4524)*

Flynn Media LLC..................................... G 317 536-2972
  Indianapolis *(G-8210)*

Gary M Brown... G 765 831-2536
  New Castle *(G-12864)*

Goldenmarc LLC..................................... G 317 855-1651
  Indianapolis *(G-8301)*

Ilab LLC... D 317 218-3258
  Indianapolis *(G-8459)*

Image Vault LLC..................................... G 812 948-8400
  New Albany *(G-12743)*

Imaginestics LLC.................................... G 765 464-1700
  West Lafayette *(G-16594)*

Indiana Interactive LLC.......................... E 317 233-2010
  Indianapolis *(G-8480)*

Infinite Ai Inc.. G 317 965-4850
  Carmel *(G-1669)*

Interactive Intelligence Inc.................... A 800 267-1364
  Indianapolis *(G-8575)*

Jpe Consulting LLP................................ G 574 675-9552
  Osceola *(G-13395)*

Ksn Technologies Inc............................. E 219 877-4770
  Chesterton *(G-1942)*

Leaning Palms LLC................................. G 630 886-8924
  Crown Point *(G-2715)*

Ler Techforce LLC.................................. C 812 373-0870
  Columbus *(G-2340)*

Life Less Ordinary LLC........................... G 317 727-4277
  Indianapolis *(G-8746)*

Lifedata LLC... G 925 800-3381
  Marion *(G-11309)*

73 BUSINESS SERVICES

SIC SECTION

Lord Fms Games LLC .... G ..... 317 710-2253 Indianapolis *(G-8783)*	143 Berkley LLC .... G ..... 260 414-0369 Churubusco *(G-1971)*	Captivated LLC .... G ..... 317 554-7400 Carmel *(G-1579)*
Mirage Computers Inc .... G ..... 260 665-5072 Angola *(G-276)*	250ok LLC .... E ..... 855 250-6529 Indianapolis *(G-7386)*	Carbonite Inc .... D ..... 617 587-1100 Indianapolis *(G-7737)*
Money Tree Software Ltd .... E ..... 541 754-3701 Muncie *(G-12458)*	Adalphi Corp .... G ..... 847 624-3301 Indianapolis *(G-7428)*	Carelogiq Corp .... G ..... 219 682-6327 Munster *(G-12534)*
On Call McGraw LLC .... G ..... 317 938-8777 Indianapolis *(G-9051)*	Adaptasoft Inc .... E ..... 219 567-2547 Francesville *(G-5635)*	Carleton Inc .... E ..... 574 855-3180 South Bend *(G-14967)*
▲ Paragon Medical Inc .... C ..... 574 594-2140 Pierceton *(G-13638)*	Advancing Chrsts Kngdom Globl .... G ..... 219 765-3586 Merrillville *(G-11478)*	Casper LLC .... G ..... 660 221-5906 Indianapolis *(G-7755)*
Perspicacity LLC .... G ..... 812 650-2080 Bloomington *(G-946)*	Advancing Geometrics .... G ..... 574 831-6480 Goshen *(G-6091)*	Catalyst Inc .... G ..... 317 227-3499 Plainfield *(G-13665)*
▲ Peter Stone Company .... G ..... 260 768-9150 Shipshewana *(G-14879)*	Agora Brands Group Inc .... E ..... 615 802-0086 Borden *(G-1104)*	Center For The Study Knwldge D .... G ..... 812 361-4424 Bloomington *(G-827)*
Pillar Innovations LLC .... G ..... 812 474-9080 Evansville *(G-4244)*	Allons-Y For Inv & Tech LLC .... G ..... 260 206-4445 Bloomington *(G-777)*	Cheddar Stacks Inc .... G ..... 317 566-0425 Indianapolis *(G-7790)*
Policystat LLC .... D ..... 317 644-1296 Carmel *(G-1720)*	American Academy of Sports .... G ..... 877 732-5009 Zionsville *(G-16989)*	CHG Developments LLC .... G ..... 720 480-0957 Indianapolis *(G-7797)*
Previnex LLC .... G ..... 877 212-0310 Carmel *(G-1729)*	Anabaptist Mnnnite Bblcal Smna .... D ..... 574 295-3726 Elkhart *(G-3181)*	Churchassist Technologies LLC .... G ..... 574 238-2307 Elkhart *(G-3253)*
Prevounce Health Inc .... F ..... 800 618-7738 Indianapolis *(G-9195)*	Analyswift LLC .... G ..... 801 599-5879 West Lafayette *(G-16562)*	Citybyapp Inc .... G ..... 844 843-4376 Saint John *(G-14447)*
◆ Printing Inc Louisville KY .... F ..... 800 237-5894 Jeffersonville *(G-10041)*	App Press LLC .... G ..... 317 661-4759 Indianapolis *(G-7528)*	Cleaninternet Inc .... G ..... 866 752-5326 Chesterton *(G-1913)*
Procard Inc .... D ..... 303 279-2255 Jeffersonville *(G-10042)*	Appextremes LLC .... D ..... 317 550-0148 Indianapolis *(G-7529)*	Clear Software Inc .... G ..... 317 732-8831 Zionsville *(G-16998)*
Regional Data Services Inc .... F ..... 219 661-3200 Crown Point *(G-2744)*	Application Software .... G ..... 317 814-8010 Greenfield *(G-6464)*	Clinical Architecture LLC .... E ..... 317 580-8400 Carmel *(G-1590)*
Rick Whitt .... G ..... 317 873-5507 Indianapolis *(G-9305)*	Application Software Inc .... G ..... 317 823-3525 Indianapolis *(G-7531)*	Cloud Blue .... G ..... 714 382-2767 Plainfield *(G-13669)*
Riddell Technologies LLC .... G ..... 219 213-9602 Crown Point *(G-2745)*	Aprimo Inc .... B ..... 317 663-6556 Indianapolis *(G-7535)*	Complete Cmpt Solutions Inc .... G ..... 812 923-0910 Floyds Knobs *(G-4675)*
Robocfi LLC .... G ..... 317 612-7889 Fort Wayne *(G-5388)*	Aptera Software Inc .... D ..... 260 969-1410 Fort Wayne *(G-4769)*	Compumark Industries Inc .... G ..... 219 365-0508 Saint John *(G-14448)*
Sahasra Technologies Corp .... E ..... 317 845-5326 Carmel *(G-1751)*	Artemis Intl Solutions Corp .... E ..... 708 665-3155 Valparaiso *(G-15905)*	Contango Inc .... G ..... 765 418-0756 West Lafayette *(G-16569)*
SGS Cybermetrix Inc .... G ..... 800 713-1203 Columbus *(G-2391)*	Aspire Lifestyle Inc .... SG ..... 219 814-2591 Chesterton *(G-1905)*	Conversightai .... F ..... 201 294-1896 Indianapolis *(G-7865)*
Sharpen Technologies Inc .... E ..... 855 249-3357 Indianapolis *(G-9413)*	Aunalytics Inc .... D ..... 574 307-9230 South Bend *(G-14951)*	Cooperative Ventures Ind Corp .... G ..... 317 564-4695 Carmel *(G-1596)*
Simplex Computer Services .... G ..... 260 570-7062 Auburn *(G-423)*	Authenticx Inc .... D ..... 317 296-6238 Indianapolis *(G-7570)*	Corvano LLC .... G ..... 317 403-0471 Fishers *(G-4495)*
Sk Markting Strtgies LLC DBA A .... G ..... 812 962-0900 Evansville *(G-4317)*	Baals LLC .... G ..... 260 993-0350 Fort Wayne *(G-4786)*	Crowdpixie LLC .... G ..... 317 578-3137 Fishers *(G-4498)*
Spring Ventures Infovation LLC .... G ..... 317 847-1117 Greenwood *(G-6770)*	Bauer Rey Inc .... G ..... 317 731-2812 Fishers *(G-4472)*	Crume Industries LLC .... SG ..... 574 747-7683 Elkhart *(G-3275)*
Sullivan Engineered Services .... G ..... 812 294-1724 Henryville *(G-7116)*	Big Stick Software .... G ..... 812 867-0694 Evansville *(G-3932)*	Curvo Labs Inc .... G ..... 619 316-1202 Evansville *(G-4000)*
Techknowledgey Inc .... G ..... 574 971-4267 Goshen *(G-6269)*	Blue Pillar Inc .... D ..... 317 723-6601 Indianapolis *(G-7647)*	Custom Software Solutions Inc .... G ..... 260 637-8393 Fort Wayne *(G-4900)*
Technalysis Inc .... G ..... 317 291-1985 Indianapolis *(G-9568)*	Blue Sun Ventures Ltd .... G ..... 317 426-0001 Indianapolis *(G-7649)*	Cuts Inc .... G ..... 408 334-3134 Indianapolis *(G-7937)*
Tempus Nova LLC .... F ..... 877 379-7376 Indianapolis *(G-9576)*	Bluehive Health LLC .... G ..... 260 217-5328 Fort Wayne *(G-4810)*	Cwb Software LLC .... G ..... 812 760-3431 Evansville *(G-4006)*
Tipton Engrg Elc Mtr Svcs Inc .... G ..... 765 963-3380 Sharpsville *(G-14714)*	Bolstra LLC .... G ..... 317 660-9131 Carmel *(G-1569)*	Cyber Inform LLC .... G ..... 219 688-1183 Lafayette *(G-10567)*
Tysoft LLC .... G ..... 765 405-0098 Yorktown *(G-16984)*	Bpac Inc .... F ..... 317 723-7427 Indianapolis *(G-7668)*	Dallara Research Center LLC .... G ..... 317 388-5416 Speedway *(G-15335)*
Via Development Corp .... D ..... 888 225-5842 Marion *(G-11347)*	Brad Goodman .... G ..... 765 993-2007 Brownsville *(G-1429)*	Dayspring Community Church Inc .... F ..... 260 925-4599 Auburn *(G-385)*
W T Boone Enterprises Inc .... G ..... 317 738-0275 Franklin *(G-5784)*	Brangene LLC .... G ..... 317 203-9172 Plainfield *(G-13662)*	Deberry MGT & Consulting LLC .... G ..... 317 767-4703 Indianapolis *(G-7959)*
Wall Control Services Inc .... G ..... 260 450-6411 Fort Wayne *(G-5542)*	Brightlamp Inc .... G ..... 317 285-9287 Indianapolis *(G-7685)*	Dedicated Software .... G ..... 260 341-4166 Yoder *(G-16965)*
Web Software LLC .... F ..... 765 452-3936 Kokomo *(G-10356)*	Bronze Bow Software Inc .... G ..... 260 672-9516 Roanoke *(G-14261)*	Deedgrabbercom Inc .... G ..... 219 712-9722 Munster *(G-12538)*
Wildebeest LLC .... G ..... 812 391-5631 Fort Wayne *(G-5568)*	C & S Solutions LLC .... G ..... 812 895-0048 Vincennes *(G-16116)*	Desi Technologies Inc .... G ..... 802 488-0954 South Bend *(G-14998)*
7372 Prepackaged software	Cad/CAM Technologies Inc .... G ..... 765 778-2020 Pendleton *(G-13528)*	Desk Coder LLC .... G ..... 812 406-5367 Georgetown *(G-6056)*
120 Water Audit Inc .... D ..... 888 317-1510 Zionsville *(G-16987)*	Campus Inc .... G ..... 765 674-9530 Marion *(G-11275)*	Diagnotion LLC .... G ..... 317 853-1180 Carmel *(G-1608)*

73 BUSINESS SERVICES

Company	Code	Phone
Dialing Innovations LLC	F	877 523-5384
Indianapolis (G-7969)		
Digital Design Genius	G	317 515-3680
Camby (G-1509)		
Dipt LLC	G	574 354-8471
Nappanee (G-12595)		
Diverse Tech Services Inc	E	317 432-6444
Indianapolis (G-7982)		
Donna Dalton	G	812 358-6116
Scottsburg (G-14553)		
Dotstaff LLC	E	317 806-6100
Indianapolis (G-7998)		
Eat Here Indy LLC	G	317 502-4419
Indianapolis (G-8042)		
Edutronics	G	765 529-6751
New Castle (G-12859)		
Elevate Wellness Corporation	G	317 370-9852
Zionsville (G-17004)		
Emarsys North America Inc	E	630 395-2944
Indianapolis (G-8099)		
Empirical Themes LLC	G	260 431-1437
Fort Wayne (G-4950)		
Emplify LLC	E	800 580-5344
Fishers (G-4513)		
Enghouse Networks (us) Inc	E	317 262-4666
Indianapolis (G-8119)		
Enroll Hq LLC	G	317 376-8282
Fishers (G-4515)		
Entegrata Inc	G	949 244-1646
Carmel (G-1624)		
Envista LLC	D	317 208-9100
Carmel (G-1626)		
Envista Concepts LLC	G	317 208-9100
Carmel (G-1627)		
Envista Entp Solutions LLC	C	317 208-9100
Carmel (G-1628)		
Envista Freight Managment LLC	C	317 208-9100
Carmel (G-1629)		
Eric Isaacson	G	812 339-1811
Bloomington (G-862)		
Event Odyssey Inc	G	317 483-0027
Fishers (G-4519)		
Everything Underground Inc	G	317 491-8148
Indianapolis (G-8142)		
Fanroll LLC	G	617 909-6325
Fort Wayne (G-4974)		
Farmersmarketcom LLC	G	317 523-4025
Indianapolis (G-8168)		
Finest Grade Products	G	812 421-1976
Evansville (G-4069)		
Finvantage LLC	F	317 500-4949
Carmel (G-1635)		
Fiserv Mrtg Servicing Systems	C	574 282-3300
South Bend (G-15034)		
Flight1 Aviation Tech Inc	G	404 504-7010
Wabash (G-16186)		
Flynn Media LLC	G	317 536-2972
Indianapolis (G-8210)		
Forensic Sane Software LLC	G	219 232-6576
Crown Point (G-2686)		
Frank R Komar PC	G	812 477-9110
Evansville (G-4081)		
Freehold Games LLC	G	574 656-9031
Walkerton (G-16266)		
Fwdnxt LLC	G	203 645-0736
West Lafayette (G-16581)		
Gale Force Software Corp	F	317 695-7423
Indianapolis (G-8256)		
Gametime Sporting Events LLC	G	812 406-8281
Indianapolis (G-8257)		
Gary M Brown	G	765 831-2536
New Castle (G-12864)		
Genesys Cloud Services Inc	A	317 872-3000
Indianapolis (G-8275)		
Genesys Group LLC	G	574 850-9435
Mishawaka (G-11900)		
Genesys Telecom Us Inc	B	703 673-1773
Indianapolis (G-8276)		
Givestr Inc	G	202 997-5862
Indianapolis (G-8283)		
Glidepath Com LLC	G	317 288-4459
Fishers (G-4531)		
Goengineer Inc	G	800 276-6486
South Bend (G-15045)		
Goodrich Corporation	D	812 704-5200
Jeffersonville (G-9993)		
Greenwell Software LLC	G	812 709-0214
Loogootee (G-11137)		
Groupone Health Source Inc	D	800 769-5288
Indianapolis (G-8334)		
Grumble Games LLC	G	317 941-6433
Carmel (G-1645)		
Guide Technologies LLC	G	317 844-3162
Indianapolis (G-8342)		
Hazon Learning LLC	G	765 490-6321
West Lafayette (G-16591)		
Hearsight Inc	G	208 819-8659
South Bend (G-15063)		
Hearsight LLC	G	208 819-8659
South Bend (G-15064)		
Helios LLC	E	317 554-9911
Indianapolis (G-8381)		
Help Help LLC	G	317 910-6631
Avon (G-525)		
Hot Shot Multimedia Entps LLC	G	317 537-7527
South Bend (G-15072)		
Hurco Companies Inc	C	317 293-5309
Indianapolis (G-8436)		
Hyperbole Software LLC	G	812 839-6635
Madison (G-11228)		
Identity Logix LLC	G	219 379-5560
Munster (G-12541)		
Ike Newton LLC	G	317 902-1772
Greenwood (G-6714)		
Ilab LLC	D	317 218-3258
Indianapolis (G-8459)		
Imagelaz LLC	G	574 534-0906
Goshen (G-6170)		
Imaginestics LLC	G	765 464-1700
West Lafayette (G-16594)		
Imminent Software Inc	G	317 340-4562
Carmel (G-1663)		
Indiengage LLC	G	317 331-7781
Indianapolis (G-8513)		
Indigo Bioautomation Inc	E	317 493-2400
Carmel (G-1667)		
Industrial Software LLC	G	317 862-0650
Indianapolis (G-8520)		
Infinite Ai Inc	G	317 965-4850
Carmel (G-1669)		
▲ Infologix Inc	C	260 485-7380
Noblesville (G-13106)		
Infosoft Inc	F	574 262-9800
Elkhart (G-3426)		
Infront Software LLC	G	317 501-1871
Fishers (G-4642)		
▲ Insertec Inc	D	800 556-1911
Indianapolis (G-8560)		
Insightful Apps LLC	G	812 361-1057
Zionsville (G-17021)		
Intelligent Software Inc	G	219 923-6166
Munster (G-12543)		
Intempo Software Inc	E	800 950-2221
Indianapolis (G-8570)		
Interactive Intelligence Inc	G	317 872-3000
Indianapolis (G-8572)		
Interactive Intelligence Inc	G	803 699-7778
Indianapolis (G-8573)		
Interactive Intelligence Group Inc	A	317 872-3000
Indianapolis (G-8574)		
Interactive Intelligence Inc	A	800 267-1364
Indianapolis (G-8575)		
Ip Software Inc	G	317 569-1313
Carmel (G-1673)		
It Synergistics	G	317 627-6858
Greenfield (G-6519)		
Itapmenu LLC	G	855 687-4827
Carmel (G-1674)		
Jeshsoft LLC	G	812 431-8603
Evansville (G-4142)		
JKL Software Development LLC	G	765 778-3032
Pendleton (G-13538)		
Jordan Safety and Supply LLC	G	513 315-6267
Indianapolis (G-8638)		
Jpe Consulting LLP	G	574 675-9552
Osceola (G-13395)		
Kala Mindfulness LLC	G	720 351-9664
Indianapolis (G-8657)		
Kdp LLC	G	630 362-7346
West Lafayette (G-16598)		
Kintail Inc	G	317 993-8220
Westfield (G-16705)		
Kmuet LLC	G	317 645-0421
Indianapolis (G-8697)		
Knowledge Diffusion Games LLC	G	812 361-4424
Bloomington (G-902)		
Knowledge Trading Network LLC	G	219 309-5360
Chesterton (G-1941)		
Kristine Willoughby	G	574 850-5145
South Bend (G-15106)		
Ksn Technologies Inc	E	219 877-4770
Chesterton (G-1942)		
Lactor LLC	G	765 496-6838
West Lafayette (G-16599)		
Laney Software Co	G	260 312-0759
South Bend (G-15115)		
Leaf Hut Software LLC	G	317 770-3632
Fishers (G-4555)		
Leaning Palms LLC	G	630 886-8924
Crown Point (G-2715)		
Leaselinks LLC	G	312 810-0788
Crown Point (G-2716)		
Lessonly Inc	C	317 469-9194
Indianapolis (G-8740)		
Light Stigma LLC	G	812 550-7923
Evansville (G-4169)		
Long Tail Corporation	G	260 918-0489
Fort Wayne (G-5191)		
Lord Fms Games LLC	G	317 710-2253
Indianapolis (G-8783)		
Lots of Software LLC	G	317 578-8120
Fishers (G-4558)		
Luxly LLC	G	617 415-8031
Carmel (G-1686)		
M2m Holdings Inc	D	317 249-1700
Indianapolis (G-8807)		
Maddenco Inc	F	812 474-6245
Evansville (G-4184)		
Maet LLC	G	574 220-7668
South Bend (G-15134)		
Mailgate International Inc	G	866 843-1990
Greenwood (G-6732)		
Marshall & Poe LLC	E	574 266-5244
Elkhart (G-3514)		
Masters Apps LLC	G	574 312-5233
Goshen (G-6217)		

73 BUSINESS SERVICES — SIC SECTION

Mellon Tax Service .... G 219 947-1660
  Hobart (G-7201)
Mental Rehabilitation .... G 765 414-5590
  Lafayette (G-10646)
Mesh Systems LLC .... E 317 661-4800
  Carmel (G-1698)
Mesumes Incorporated .... G 574 529-3444
  Syracuse (G-15468)
Metakite Software LLC .... G 317 441-7385
  Fishers (G-4565)
Metergenius Inc .... G 317 979-8257
  Indianapolis (G-8894)
Micro Businessware Inc .... G 502 424-6613
  Sellersburg (G-14607)
Microsoft Corporation .... F 317 705-6900
  Indianapolis (G-8904)
Mike Jones Software .... G 317 845-7479
  Indianapolis (G-8916)
▲ Milltronics Usa Inc .... F 317 293-5309
  Indianapolis (G-8929)
Mobil Trackr LLC .... G 888 504-2074
  Fishers (G-4567)
Mobile Enerlytics LLC .... G 765 464-6909
  West Lafayette (G-16609)
Money Tree Software Ltd .... E 541 754-3701
  Muncie (G-12458)
My Old KY Blog Presents LLC .... F 317 602-6641
  Indianapolis (G-8976)
Mycloud LLC .... G 317 570-8999
  Fishers (G-4568)
Myturbopc LLC .... G 574 350-9330
  Elkhart (G-3562)
Nechanna One Productions Corp .... G 317 400-8908
  Indianapolis (G-8997)
Oasis Software Solutions .... G 620 515-1240
  Fort Wayne (G-5279)
One Body Software LLC .... G 260 494-8354
  Fort Wayne (G-5287)
Onlydrams LLC .... G 219 707-6025
  Valparaiso (G-16019)
Oprato Software LLC .... G 317 573-0168
  Carmel (G-1712)
Osc Holdings LLC .... G 765 751-7000
  Muncie (G-12470)
Oxinas Partners LLC .... G 812 725-8649
  Jeffersonville (G-10032)
Patriot Software Solutions Inc .... G 317 573-5431
  Indianapolis (G-9101)
Pd Solutions Inc .... G 800 289-8787
  Nappanee (G-12635)
Performnce Sftwr Solutions Inc .... G 574 239-2444
  South Bend (G-15192)
Perq Convert LLC .... D 800 873-3117
  Indianapolis (G-9127)
Perq Multifamily Software LLC .... D 800 873-3117
  Indianapolis (G-9128)
Perspicacity LLC .... G 812 650-2080
  Bloomington (G-946)
Petroleum Jobbers Data Control .... G 574 722-4477
  Logansport (G-11102)
Phil Johnson .... G 812 457-2433
  Evansville (G-4240)
Pine Cone II LLC .... G 463 232-3138
  Carmel (G-1718)
Pineapple Software Inc .... G 812 987-8277
  Clarksville (G-2025)
▲ Plum Group Inc .... F 617 712-3000
  Indianapolis (G-9155)
Podfan LLC .... G 317 771-0475
  Indianapolis (G-9157)
Policystat LLC .... D 317 644-1296
  Carmel (G-1720)

Preferred Ppltion Hlth MGT LLC .... G 317 245-7482
  Indianapolis (G-9188)
Primary Record Inc .... G 317 270-8327
  Fishers (G-4648)
Pro It Solutions LLC .... F 574 862-0021
  Wakarusa (G-16244)
Proapse Software .... G 260 615-9839
  Fort Wayne (G-5352)
Procard Inc .... D 303 279-2255
  Jeffersonville (G-10042)
Professional Software Corp .... G 812 781-1422
  Mount Vernon (G-12316)
Pulse Analytics LLC .... G 260 615-8016
  Fishers (G-4585)
Qbank LLC .... G 317 354-5764
  Noblesville (G-13163)
Qbotix LLC .... G 562 526-5725
  Fort Wayne (G-5359)
Qlever Company LLC .... G 765 490-4694
  Rochester (G-14312)
Quality Council Indiana Inc .... G 812 533-4215
  West Terre Haute (G-16653)
Quality Data Products Inc .... G 317 595-0700
  Fishers (G-4586)
Quality Information Tech Inc .... G 317 595-0700
  Fishers (G-4587)
R O I Systems Inc .... G 260 413-6307
  Fort Wayne (G-5365)
RAD Cube LLC .... F 317 456-7560
  Indianapolis (G-9260)
Rain Network LLC .... G 909 900-7776
  South Bend (G-15216)
Rand Worldwide Inc .... G 317 572-1267
  Indianapolis (G-9265)
Rebound Project LLP .... G 765 621-5604
  Anderson (G-183)
Regional Data Services Inc .... F 219 661-3200
  Crown Point (G-2744)
Registration System LLC .... G 317 966-6919
  Fortville (G-5605)
Relational Gravity Inc .... G 317 855-7685
  Indianapolis (G-9286)
Relational Intelligence LLC .... G 317 669-8900
  Westfield (G-16722)
Renaissnce Electronic Svcs LLC .... F 317 786-2235
  Indianapolis (G-9290)
Revseller LLC .... G 800 619-6304
  Evansville (G-4287)
Rics Software Inc .... E 317 455-5338
  Indianapolis (G-9306)
Rightrez Inc .... G 812 219-1893
  Bloomington (G-958)
Roajer LLC .... G 317 348-4640
  Carmel (G-1742)
Rob Nolley Inc .... F 317 825-5211
  Shelbyville (G-14792)
Robocfi LLC .... G 317 612-7889
  Fort Wayne (G-5388)
Round Table Recording Co LLP .... G 317 981-5351
  Indianapolis (G-9336)
Rt Software .... G 317 578-8518
  Fishers (G-4600)
S & S Programming Inc .... G 765 423-4472
  Lafayette (G-10682)
Sahasra Technologies Corp .... E 317 845-5326
  Carmel (G-1751)
Salesforce Inc .... D 317 370-5737
  Indianapolis (G-9366)
Salesforcecom Inc .... F 317 981-4924
  Indianapolis (G-9367)
Seasoned Software LLC .... G 260 431-5666
  Fort Wayne (G-5406)

Secured Ftp Hosting LLC .... E 877 336-3453
  Indianapolis (G-9398)
Sedona Inc .... D 219 764-9675
  Portage (G-13912)
Sharpen Technologies Inc .... E 855 249-3357
  Indianapolis (G-9413)
Sigstr Inc .... E 317 960-3003
  Indianapolis (G-9439)
Sim2k Inc .... F 317 251-7920
  Indianapolis (G-9440)
Simcha Ai Inc .... G 415 702-5919
  Schererville (G-14544)
Simeoc LLC .... G 240 210-5685
  South Bend (G-15245)
Simma Software Inc .... G 812 418-0526
  Terre Haute (G-15695)
Simplex Computer Services .... G 260 570-7062
  Auburn (G-423)
Sk Markting Strtgies LLC DBA A .... G 812 962-0900
  Evansville (G-4317)
Sky Cryptoassets LLC .... G 949 903-6896
  Carmel (G-1763)
Skyepack LLC .... G 765 323-8568
  West Lafayette (G-16628)
Snappy Minds Llc .... G 812 661-8506
  Jasper (G-9913)
Software Informatics Group LLC .... G 317 326-2598
  Greenfield (G-6555)
Software Sales Incorporated .... G 317 258-7442
  Whitestown (G-16822)
Speak Abilities LLP .... G 303 827-8269
  West Lafayette (G-16630)
Spring Ventures Infovation LLC .... G 317 847-1117
  Greenwood (G-6770)
SS&c Technologies Inc .... F 812 266-2000
  Evansville (G-4330)
Stacks Limited .... G 765 409-5081
  Lafayette (G-10697)
Standard For Success LLC .... F 844 737-3825
  Cloverdale (G-2099)
Sterling Creek Software L L C .... G 317 567-5060
  Indianapolis (G-9504)
Stonecast Financial LLC .... G 317 537-1707
  Indianapolis (G-9514)
Straight Trippin LLC .... G 812 484-6154
  Evansville (G-4336)
Sugar Coded Software LLC .... G 858 652-0797
  Burlington (G-1446)
Supplieriq LLC .... G 574 323-0707
  South Bend (G-15273)
Tab Software Corp .... G 260 490-7132
  Fort Wayne (G-5467)
Tangoe Us Inc .... B 203 859-9300
  Indianapolis (G-9550)
Tangoe Us Inc .... C 973 257-0300
  Indianapolis (G-9551)
Tech Innovation LLC .... F 317 506-8343
  Indianapolis (G-9566)
Technalysis Inc .... G 317 291-1985
  Indianapolis (G-9568)
Tempus Nova LLC .... F 877 379-7376
  Indianapolis (G-9576)
Tgx Medical Systems LLC .... F 317 575-0300
  Carmel (G-1785)
Thornbury Software .... G 765 546-8640
  Winchester (G-16900)
Tk Software Inc .... G 317 569-8887
  Carmel (G-1788)
Toddler Timer LLC .... G 216 282-7247
  Indianapolis (G-9616)
TPC Software Inc .... G 317 844-1480
  Carmel (G-1789)

SIC SECTION
73 BUSINESS SERVICES

Trail Software Inc .... F 888 854-0933
  Indianapolis *(G-9628)*
Trh Software Inc .... G 812 264-2428
  Terre Haute *(G-15735)*
Trill Machine LLC .... G 219 730-0744
  Kentland *(G-10164)*
Trilogy Technologies LLC .... G 317 769-0215
  Whitestown *(G-16827)*
True Anlytics Mfg Slutions LLC .... G 317 995-3220
  Plainfield *(G-13739)*
Tysoft LLC .... G 765 405-0098
  Yorktown *(G-16984)*
Uva Software LLC .... G 877 927-1115
  Fishers *(G-4626)*
Vinzant Software Inc .... E 219 942-9544
  Hobart *(G-7213)*
Visual Components N Amer Corp .... G 855 823-3746
  Carmel *(G-1797)*
Vitalswap Technologies LLC .... G 725 234-0077
  Indianapolis *(G-9724)*
Waseve LLC .... G 443 204-7976
  Carmel *(G-1799)*
Wash Systems LLC .... G 317 201-2625
  Fishers *(G-4631)*
Web Software LLC .... F 765 452-3936
  Kokomo *(G-10356)*
Wentworth Software .... G 812 218-0052
  Jeffersonville *(G-10074)*
Wildebeest LLC .... G 812 391-5631
  Fort Wayne *(G-5568)*
Wingate Enterprise LLC .... G 513 293-9833
  Lawrenceburg *(G-10866)*
Wolfe Diversified Inds LLC .... F 765 683-9374
  Pendleton *(G-13562)*
Wolfgang Software .... G 317 443-5147
  Fishers *(G-4634)*
Writ Labs Inc .... G 650 560-5008
  Indianapolis *(G-9792)*
Xcelerix Corp .... F 317 208-2320
  Indianapolis *(G-9795)*
Yoder Software Inc .... G 574 302-6232
  South Bend *(G-15311)*

7373 Computer integrated systems design

Adaptive Tech Solutions LLC .... G 317 762-4363
  Carmel *(G-1549)*
Agora Brands Group Inc .... E 615 802-0086
  Borden *(G-1104)*
Binarie LLC .... G 317 496-8836
  Greenwood *(G-6676)*
Blue Byte Tech Solutions LLC .... G 574 903-5637
  Elkhart *(G-3227)*
Business Systems Mgt Corp .... G 219 938-0166
  Gary *(G-5908)*
Compumark Industries Inc .... G 219 365-0508
  Saint John *(G-14448)*
Crown Training and Dev Inc .... F 219 947-0845
  Merrillville *(G-11500)*
Cybernaut Industria LLC .... G 317 664-5316
  Indianapolis *(G-7939)*
Diverse Tech Services Inc .... E 317 432-6444
  Indianapolis *(G-7982)*
Divsys Aerospace & Engrg LLC .... F 317 941-7777
  Indianapolis *(G-7987)*
Drs Graphix Group Inc .... G 317 569-1855
  Indianapolis *(G-8011)*
Edutronics .... G 765 529-6751
  New Castle *(G-12859)*
Ers Automation Inc .... G 260 341-8114
  Columbia City *(G-2143)*
Fiserv Mrtg Servicing Systems .... C 574 282-3300
  South Bend *(G-15034)*

Flynn Media LLC .... G 317 536-2972
  Indianapolis *(G-8210)*
Frakes Engineering Inc .... E 317 577-3000
  Indianapolis *(G-8220)*
Gary M Brown .... G 765 831-2536
  New Castle *(G-12864)*
◆ Gta Enterprises Inc .... E 260 478-7800
  Fort Wayne *(G-5044)*
Knowledge Diffusion Games LLC .... G 812 361-4424
  Bloomington *(G-902)*
Long Tail Corporation .... G 260 918-0489
  Fort Wayne *(G-5191)*
▲ Lumen Cache Incorporated .... G 317 739-4218
  Fishers *(G-4644)*
Metal Fab Engineering Inc .... E 574 278-7150
  Winamac *(G-16867)*
Mirage Computers Inc .... G 260 665-5072
  Angola *(G-276)*
▲ Orion Global Sourcing Inc .... G 812 332-3338
  Bloomington *(G-939)*
Rob Nolley Inc .... F 317 825-5211
  Shelbyville *(G-14792)*
Shadow Graphix Inc .... G 317 481-9710
  Indianapolis *(G-9411)*
Vergence LLC .... F 317 547-4417
  Indianapolis *(G-9707)*

7374 Data processing and preparation

Aunalytics Inc .... D 574 307-9230
  South Bend *(G-14951)*
Big Picture Data Imaging LLC .... G 812 235-0202
  Terre Haute *(G-15553)*
Blasted Works .... G 574 583-3211
  Monticello *(G-12138)*
Blue Byte Tech Solutions LLC .... G 574 903-5637
  Elkhart *(G-3227)*
Carbonite Inc .... D 617 587-1100
  Indianapolis *(G-7737)*
Cooperative Ventures Ind Corp .... G 317 564-4695
  Carmel *(G-1596)*
Cunningham Pattern & Engrg Inc .... F 812 379-9571
  Columbus *(G-2276)*
Dx Hammond Opco LLC .... G 219 501-0905
  Whiting *(G-16834)*
Fiserv Mrtg Servicing Systems .... C 574 282-3300
  South Bend *(G-15034)*
Gieseck+dvrent Epymnts Amer In .... G 866 484-0611
  Fort Wayne *(G-5024)*
Indiana Interactive LLC .... E 317 233-2010
  Indianapolis *(G-8480)*
Long Tail Corporation .... G 260 918-0489
  Fort Wayne *(G-5191)*
NP Converters Inc .... D 812 448-2555
  Brazil *(G-1158)*
Petroleum Jobbers Data Control .... G 574 722-4477
  Logansport *(G-11102)*
Rob Nolley Inc .... F 317 825-5211
  Shelbyville *(G-14792)*
Rpg Energy Group Inc .... F 317 614-0054
  Indianapolis *(G-9342)*
Simplex Computer Services .... G 260 570-7062
  Auburn *(G-423)*
Telamon Entp Ventures LLC .... F 317 818-6888
  Carmel *(G-1778)*
Urschelair Leasing LLC .... G 219 464-4811
  Chesterton *(G-1965)*
Whiteco Industries Inc .... A 219 769-6601
  Merrillville *(G-11572)*

7375 Information retrieval services

Center For The Study Knwldge D .... G 812 361-4424
  Bloomington *(G-827)*

First Databank Inc .... G 317 571-7200
  Carmel *(G-1636)*
Fiserv Mrtg Servicing Systems .... C 574 282-3300
  South Bend *(G-15034)*
Gannett Co Inc .... G 765 423-5511
  Lafayette *(G-10584)*
Supplieriq LLC .... G 574 323-0707
  South Bend *(G-15273)*
▲ Xlibris Corporation .... B 812 671-9162
  Bloomington *(G-1017)*

7376 Computer facilities management

Computer Solutions Systems Inc .... F 812 235-9008
  Terre Haute *(G-15566)*
Rob Nolley Inc .... F 317 825-5211
  Shelbyville *(G-14792)*

7378 Computer maintenance and repair

C & P Distributing LLC .... F 574 256-1138
  Mishawaka *(G-11857)*
Compumark Industries Inc .... G 219 365-0508
  Saint John *(G-14448)*
Diverse Tech Services Inc .... E 317 432-6444
  Indianapolis *(G-7982)*
Lasertech Inc .... G 812 277-1321
  Bedford *(G-656)*
Riddell Technologies LLC .... G 219 213-9602
  Crown Point *(G-2745)*
Rob Nolley Inc .... F 317 825-5211
  Shelbyville *(G-14792)*
Simplex Computer Services .... G 260 570-7062
  Auburn *(G-423)*

7379 Computer related services, nec

Acterna LLC .... E 317 788-9351
  Indianapolis *(G-7425)*
Agora Brands Group Inc .... E 615 802-0086
  Borden *(G-1104)*
Big Picture Data Imaging LLC .... G 812 235-0202
  Terre Haute *(G-15553)*
Binarie LLC .... G 317 496-8836
  Greenwood *(G-6676)*
Blue Byte Tech Solutions LLC .... G 574 903-5637
  Elkhart *(G-3227)*
Complete Cmpt Solutions Inc .... G 812 923-0910
  Floyds Knobs *(G-4675)*
Corporate Systems Engrg LLC .... D 317 375-3600
  Indianapolis *(G-7878)*
Creative Mnds Work Pblctons LL .... G 317 759-1002
  Indianapolis *(G-7901)*
Cybernaut Industria LLC .... G 317 664-5316
  Indianapolis *(G-7939)*
Knowledge Diffusion Games LLC .... G 812 361-4424
  Bloomington *(G-902)*
Kristine Willoughby .... G 574 850-5145
  South Bend *(G-15106)*
Ksn Technologies Inc .... E 219 877-4770
  Chesterton *(G-1942)*
Ladybugz Bookstore LLC .... G 469 459-1780
  Noblesville *(G-13125)*
Mirage Computers Inc .... G 260 665-5072
  Angola *(G-276)*
Prysmian Cbles Systems USA LLC .... D 317 271-8447
  Indianapolis *(G-9236)*
Registration System LLC .... G 317 966-6919
  Fortville *(G-5605)*
Sim2k Inc .... E 317 251-7920
  Indianapolis *(G-9440)*
Sk Markting Strtgies LLC DBA A .... G 812 962-0900
  Evansville *(G-4317)*
Spring Ventures Infovation LLC .... G 317 847-1117
  Greenwood *(G-6770)*

73 BUSINESS SERVICES

Vergence LLC .... F 317 547-4417
  Indianapolis (G-9707)
Waseve LLC .... G 443 204-7976
  Carmel (G-1799)

7381 Detective and armored car services

Advanced Prtctive Slutions LLC .... G 765 720-9574
  Coatesville (G-2102)
AM General LLC .... A 574 258-7523
  Mishawaka (G-11840)
Workflow Solutions LLC .... G 502 627-0257
  New Albany (G-12831)

7382 Security systems services

American Eagle Security Inc .... G 219 980-1177
  Merrillville (G-11482)
American Fire Company .... G 219 840-0630
  Valparaiso (G-15899)
Applied Technology Group Inc .... F 260 482-2844
  Fort Wayne (G-4767)
Lionfish Cyber Hldngs LLC-S Ln .... G 877 732-6772
  Indianapolis (G-8766)
Loud Clear Communications LLC .... G 260 433-9479
  Auburn (G-403)
Phil & Son Inc .... G 219 663-5757
  Crown Point (G-2730)
Pro It Solutions LLC .... F 574 862-0021
  Wakarusa (G-16244)
▲ Roi Marketing Company Inc .... G 317 644-0797
  Indianapolis (G-9321)

7384 Photofinish laboratories

Budget Printing Centers Inc .... G 812 282-8832
  Jeffersonville (G-9948)
Graphik Mechanix Inc .... G 260 426-7001
  Fort Wayne (G-5035)
Stewart Graphics Inc .... E 812 283-0455
  Jeffersonville (G-10060)
Success Holding Group Corp USA .... G 260 490-9990
  Ossian (G-13435)

7389 Business services, nec

103 Collection LLC .... G 800 896-2945
  Schererville (G-14510)
1632 Inc .... G 219 398-4155
  East Chicago (G-2987)
1globalds LLC .... F 765 413-2211
  Westfield (G-16660)
1st Choice Contractors LLC .... G 317 628-4721
  Indianapolis (G-7385)
3jm Hauling LLC .... G 317 518-0750
  Avon (G-501)
3oe Scientific LLC .... F 317 869-7602
  Carmel (G-1545)
3sevens LLC .... G 502 594-2312
  Henryville (G-7112)
4ever Chosen LLC .... G 765 431-7548
  Kokomo (G-10230)
5 Knight LLC .... G 219 680-6661
  Anderson (G-69)
651 Emergency Lighting .... G 765 748-6664
  Yorktown (G-16967)
7th Leadership Organization .... G 219 938-6906
  Gary (G-5883)
A & A Machine Service Inc .... G 317 745-7367
  Avon (G-502)
A Snack Above Rest LLC .... G 219 455-3335
  Gary (G-5884)
A-1vet LLC .... G 317 498-1804
  Indianapolis (G-7407)
A&J Development Group LLC .... G 317 767-1182
  Indianapolis (G-7404)

A1 Deliveries LLC .... G 317 828-3951
  Indianapolis (G-7408)
Abacus Printingngraphics Inc .... E 915 223-5166
  Indianapolis (G-7412)
Accent Complex Inc .... G 574 522-2368
  Elkhart (G-3148)
Accra-Pac Inc .... G 574 295-0000
  Elkhart (G-3149)
Accuracy Laser Fabrication LLC .... G 812 322-6431
  Bedford (G-616)
Accurate Turning Solutions .... G 812 603-6612
  Columbus (G-2212)
Acdc Control LLC .... G 219 801-3900
  East Chicago (G-2988)
Ad-Vance Magnetics Inc .... E 574 223-3158
  Rochester (G-14274)
Adams Signs Inc .... G 219 972-0700
  Highland (G-7119)
Advanced Lf Spport Innvtons LL .... G 574 538-1688
  Goshen (G-6090)
Advanced Prtctive Slutions LLC .... G 765 720-9574
  Coatesville (G-2102)
Aeromind LLC .... G 800 905-2157
  Indianapolis (G-7453)
Aesthtcally Pleasing Skin Soak .... G 317 551-0156
  Indianapolis (G-7454)
Afr Equipment LLC .... G 888 519-9899
  Laurel (G-10824)
▲ Ahf Industries Inc .... C 812 936-9988
  French Lick (G-5843)
Airodapt LLC .... G 559 331-0156
  Rensselaer (G-14040)
Aje Suspension Inc .... F 812 346-7356
  North Vernon (G-13255)
Alicon LLC .... G 260 687-1259
  Angola (G-225)
All American Ex Solutions LLC .... E 317 789-3070
  Indianapolis (G-7472)
All Day Carpet Binding LLC .... G 219 851-8071
  Lafayette (G-10518)
All Things Jchari LLC .... G 260 414-4065
  Fort Wayne (G-4740)
All Things Kingdom LLC .... G 312 200-4569
  Highland (G-7120)
Allfab LLC .... G 317 359-3539
  Indianapolis (G-7482)
Allons-Y For Inv & Tech LLC .... G 260 206-4445
  Bloomington (G-777)
Alpha Matrix LLC .... G 812 686-1640
  Lamar (G-10794)
Alveys Sign Co Inc .... E 812 867-2567
  Evansville (G-3883)
American Eagle Security Inc .... G 219 980-1177
  Merrillville (G-11482)
Amish Country Dairy LLC .... G 574 323-1701
  Shipshewana (G-14835)
Ao Inc .... G 317 280-3000
  Avon (G-504)
Apg Inc .... D 574 295-0000
  Elkhart (G-3185)
Aqua Lily Products LLC .... G 951 246-9610
  Elkhart (G-3187)
▲ Asempac Inc .... E 812 945-6303
  New Albany (G-12692)
Athletic Edge Inc .... F 260 489-6613
  Fort Wayne (G-4778)
Authenticx Inc .... D 317 296-6238
  Indianapolis (G-7570)
Avari Reef Labs LLC .... G 317 201-9615
  Anderson (G-80)
B & N Rentals LLC .... G 219 850-3304
  Chesterton (G-1906)

B&C Distributor Inc .... G 609 293-3257
  Indianapolis (G-7585)
Bass Farms LLC .... G 317 401-4700
  Shelbyville (G-14734)
Bawaenterprises LLC .... G 269 228-1258
  Granger (G-6336)
Bell Transportation LLC .... G 317 833-0745
  Indianapolis (G-7610)
Best Boy Products LLC .... G 317 442-9735
  Indianapolis (G-7615)
Best Friends Inc .... G 765 985-3872
  Denver (G-2934)
Beverly Industrial Service Inc .... E 812 667-5047
  Dillsboro (G-2943)
Beyond Distributions LLC .... G 631 960-1745
  Indianapolis (G-7621)
Big Brick House Bakery LLP .... G 260 563-1071
  Fort Wayne (G-4799)
Big Bruhs Seasoning LLP .... G 502 751-5516
  Clarksville (G-2009)
Bizness As Usual Pubg LLC .... G 463 701-6433
  Indianapolis (G-7634)
Black Lavish Essentials LLC .... G 800 214-8664
  Indianapolis (G-7639)
Blackmon Metal Fabrication LLC .... G 346 254-9500
  Gary (G-5902)
Bleacherpro LLC .... G 813 394-5316
  Fort Wayne (G-4806)
Blue Dolphin Ffy LLC .... G 773 255-3591
  Hammond (G-6887)
Blueprint Restoration LLC .... G 301 730-4727
  Indianapolis (G-7650)
Borrv Concepts LLC .... G 317 405-9121
  Indianapolis (G-7661)
Botti Stdio Archtctral Arts In .... E 847 869-5933
  La Porte (G-10391)
Boudoir Lash Parlor LLC .... G 330 259-5696
  Indianapolis (G-7664)
Brangene LLC .... G 317 203-9172
  Plainfield (G-13662)
Brayden Shedron .... G 765 480-7675
  Walton (G-16281)
Browmi By Misha LLC .... G 317 801-3911
  Indianapolis (G-7689)
BTS Dispatching LLC .... G 317 300-4594
  Indianapolis (G-7695)
Bulent Gumusel .... G 812 803-5912
  Bloomington (G-818)
Byler Sawmill .... G 812 577-5761
  Bennington (G-702)
C E M Printing & Specialities .... G 269 684-6898
  South Bend (G-14964)
C Johnson Group LLC .... G 219 512-0619
  Indianapolis (G-7708)
Captivated LLC .... G 317 554-7400
  Carmel (G-1579)
Carl Abbott .... G 317 590-4143
  Indianapolis (G-7745)
Cater To You Catering LLC .... G 219 301-1091
  Hobart (G-7179)
Catherine J Bergren .... G 219 225-2819
  Gary (G-5913)
Cbrk LLC .... G 317 601-8546
  Indianapolis (G-7764)
Celestial Designs LLC .... G 317 733-3110
  Zionsville (G-16997)
Century Pharmaceuticals Inc .... E 317 849-4210
  Indianapolis (G-7775)
Certified Choice Truckers LLC .... G 260 615-3437
  Fort Wayne (G-4841)
Cfn 260 LLC .... G 260 241-5678
  Fort Wayne (G-4842)

SIC SECTION
73 BUSINESS SERVICES

Chapman Environmental Controls......... G 574 674-8706
  Osceola (G-13386)
Chef Hymie Inc............................... G 201 218-4378
  New Albany (G-12711)
CHG Developments LLC.................... G 720 480-0957
  Indianapolis (G-7797)
Chicago Steel Ltd Partnership............. E 219 949-1111
  Gary (G-5918)
Christys Design & Sign Inc................. G 317 882-5444
  Greenwood (G-6680)
CJS Muzic Company-The Spot LLC....... G 219 487-9873
  Hammond (G-6901)
Clean By Design Inc......................... G 260 414-4444
  Fort Wayne (G-4857)
Clearspring Manufacturing LLC........... F 260 593-2086
  Topeka (G-15796)
Clif Allred..................................... G 765 244-8082
  Peru (G-13573)
Cliff A Ostermeyer........................... G 615 361-7902
  Fort Wayne (G-4860)
Comptons Woodworking LLC.............. G 765 712-0568
  Cloverdale (G-2084)
▲ Concept Prints Inc......................... F 317 290-1222
  Indianapolis (G-7851)
Connies Satin Stitch Inc.................... G 219 942-1887
  Hobart (G-7183)
Cooper Transit LLC........................... G 260 797-3003
  Fort Wayne (G-4871)
Corlens Inc.................................... G 843 822-6174
  Terre Haute (G-15568)
Corner Sto LLC............................... G 219 798-2822
  Indianapolis (G-7876)
Coronado Casuals LLC...................... G 615 470-5718
  Plainfield (G-13672)
Cortex Safety Technologies LLC.......... G 317 414-5607
  Carmel (G-1598)
Costumes By Design......................... G 812 334-2029
  Bloomington (G-849)
Covington and Martin LLC.................. G 812 946-3846
  Jeffersonville (G-9963)
Crawford Water Care........................ G 317 758-6017
  Sheridan (G-14820)
Crawl Before You Walk LLC................ G 219 413-6623
  Plainfield (G-13675)
Creative Blessings Co LLC.................. G 219 293-9595
  Indianapolis (G-7900)
Creative Computer Services............... G 317 729-5779
  Franklin (G-5724)
Crossrads Rhbilitation Ctr Inc.............. C 317 897-7320
  Indianapolis (G-7910)
Crowdpixie LLC............................... G 317 578-3137
  Fishers (G-4498)
Crume Industries LLC....................... G 574 747-7683
  Elkhart (G-3275)
Culver Tool & Engineering Inc............. D 574 935-9611
  Plymouth (G-13768)
Custom Bottling & Packg Inc.............. E 877 401-7195
  Ashley (G-332)
Custom Carton Inc........................... F 260 563-7411
  Wabash (G-16179)
Custom Interior Dynamics LLC............ F 317 632-0477
  Indianapolis (G-7930)
D I Hair Extensions LLC..................... G 219 742-3611
  Merrillville (G-11503)
Dajac Inc...................................... G 317 608-0500
  Sheridan (G-14821)
Dalton Corporation........................... F 574 267-8111
  Warsaw (G-16345)
Dark Source Records LLC.................. G 616 378-6060
  Indianapolis (G-7950)
Dash CAM Fusion LLC....................... G 708 365-8553
  Indianapolis (G-7953)

Data Mail Incorporated...................... E 812 424-7835
  Evansville (G-4007)
Davenport Mfg Group LLC.................. E 260 495-1818
  Fremont (G-5819)
David M Pszonka.............................. G 219 988-2235
  Hebron (G-7098)
David Tortora................................. G 317 506-6902
  Carmel (G-1605)
Dearborn Crane and Engrg Co............. E 574 259-2444
  Mishawaka (G-11882)
Death Enn LLC................................ G 219 402-4436
  Merrillville (G-11504)
Deem & Loureiro Inc......................... G 770 652-9871
  Indianapolis (G-7961)
Deep Three Inc............................... G 260 705-2283
  Spencerville (G-15369)
Dem Guys LLC................................ G 708 552-3056
  Greenwood (G-6684)
Digistitch..................................... G 574 538-3960
  Goshen (G-6121)
Digital Design Genius....................... G 317 515-3680
  Camby (G-1509)
Dimo Multiservices LLC.................... F 463 256-0561
  Avon (G-513)
Distance Learning Systems Ind........... E 888 955-3276
  Greenwood (G-6686)
▲ Ditech Inc.................................. E 812 526-0850
  Edinburgh (G-3077)
Diverse Machine Services LLC............ G 317 670-1381
  Indianapolis (G-7980)
Diverse Sales Solutions LLC............... G 317 514-2403
  Indianapolis (G-7981)
Divine Grace Homecare..................... G 219 290-5911
  Gary (G-5923)
Divine Machine LLC.......................... G 812 709-5246
  Shoals (G-14906)
Divsys Aerospace & Engrg LLC........... F 317 941-7777
  Indianapolis (G-7987)
Dlb Transporters LLC........................ G 317 667-3368
  Indianapolis (G-7992)
Dodson Logistics LLC........................ G 937 657-7490
  Richmond (G-14115)
Doell Designs................................. G 260 486-4504
  Fort Wayne (G-4921)
Drava Underwater LLC...................... G 812 622-0432
  Owensville (G-13466)
Driessen Water Inc.......................... G 765 529-4905
  Muncie (G-12386)
Drinkgp LLC................................... G 317 410-4748
  Indianapolis (G-8009)
Driverz For Life(d 4 L) LLC................ G 317 619-4513
  Indianapolis (G-8010)
Ds Mgmt Group LLC......................... G 317 946-8646
  Indianapolis (G-8014)
Dux Signal Kits LLC.......................... G 260 623-3017
  Monroeville (G-12068)
Dx 4 LLC...................................... F 260 749-0632
  Fort Wayne (G-4935)
Dynamark Graphics Group Inc............ E 317 328-2555
  Indianapolis (G-8023)
Edwin Rahn................................... G 260 622-7178
  Ossian (G-13423)
Efurnituremax LLC........................... G 317 697-9504
  Indianapolis (G-8058)
Elegant Eyes LLC............................. G 317 640-1995
  Greenwood (G-6692)
Elite Construction Northwest.............. F 888 811-0212
  Merrillville (G-11512)
Elite Packaging LLC.......................... G 502 232-2596
  Jeffersonville (G-9975)
Elizabeth A Taylor........................... G 815 353-4798
  Freedom (G-5799)

Ellerbrock Welding LLC..................... G 559 978-2651
  New Castle (G-12860)
Em Global LLC................................ G 812 258-9993
  Jeffersonville (G-9976)
Eminence Hlth Care Stffing AGC.......... G 866 350-6400
  South Bend (G-15013)
Emmanuel Michael........................... G 806 559-5673
  Greenwood (G-6694)
Empirical Themes LLC...................... G 260 431-1437
  Fort Wayne (G-4950)
Enduring Endeavors LLC.................... G 260 410-1025
  Fort Wayne (G-4951)
Enpak LLC.................................... G 574 268-7273
  Warsaw (G-16360)
Environ Corporation......................... G 317 774-0541
  Carmel (G-1625)
Etched In Stone Engrv & EMB............. G 317 535-8160
  Whiteland (G-16786)
European Concepts LLC.................... G 888 797-9005
  Fort Wayne (G-4966)
Evans Herron................................. G 317 492-1384
  Indianapolis (G-8140)
Everything Else LLC......................... G 574 350-7383
  Elkhart (G-3336)
Exclusive Stylez LLC........................ G 470 406-2804
  Indianapolis (G-8151)
Extensive Design LLC....................... G 260 267-6752
  Fort Wayne (G-4969)
F D McCrary Operator Inc.................. G 812 354-6520
  Petersburg (G-13611)
◆ Fairfield Manufacturing Co Inc.......... A 765 772-4000
  Lafayette (G-10576)
Farwall Tsg LLC.............................. F 574 773-2108
  Nappanee (G-12596)
Father Son Sanders Trnspt LLC........... G 773 899-8078
  Hammond (G-6926)
Fedex Office & Print Svcs Inc............. G 317 974-0378
  Indianapolis (G-8172)
Fedex Office & Print Svcs Inc............. G 317 917-1529
  Indianapolis (G-8173)
Fex LLC....................................... G 317 308-8820
  Indianapolis (G-8182)
Finalmile-Logistics LLC..................... G 773 259-0727
  Portage (G-13864)
Finvantage LLC.............................. F 317 500-4949
  Carmel (G-1635)
Fischer Fleet Wash LLC..................... G 812 661-9947
  Rockport (G-14340)
Forever Young Trckg Svcs LLC............ G 616 350-4053
  Indianapolis (G-8215)
Fort Wayne Diamond Pdts Inc............. G 260 747-1681
  Fort Wayne (G-4991)
Foxxie Planner L L C........................ G 260 247-6303
  Fort Wayne (G-5004)
Freckles Grphics Lafayette Inc............ F 765 448-4692
  Lafayette (G-10581)
Freehold Games LLC........................ G 574 656-9031
  Walkerton (G-16266)
G D Cox Inc................................... G 317 398-0035
  Shelbyville (G-14758)
Galbe Magazine LLC......................... G 248 742-5231
  Carmel (G-1638)
▲ Gammons Metal & Mfg Co Inc.......... E 317 546-7091
  Indianapolis (G-8258)
Gems Quality Extensions LLC............. G 219 501-6320
  East Chicago (G-3010)
Genes Transport LLC........................ G 404 227-5178
  Indianapolis (G-8274)
Genesis Products LLC....................... C 574 266-8293
  Elkhart (G-3373)
▲ Genesis Products LLC.................... C 877 266-8292
  Goshen (G-6146)

73 BUSINESS SERVICES

Geniphys Inc .... G 317 973-0523
Zionsville (G-17013)

▲ Georg Utz Inc .... E 812 526-2240
Edinburgh (G-3085)

Gerald S Zins .... G 812 623-4980
Osgood (G-13409)

Get Right Home Solutions LLC .... G 574 374-2001
Goshen (G-6148)

Givestr Inc .... G 202 997-5862
Indianapolis (G-8283)

Gleaners Food Bank of Ind Inc .... D 317 925-0191
Indianapolis (G-8284)

Glens Pact LLC .... G 317 540-5869
Indianapolis (G-8286)

Gold Star Printing LLC .... G 260 768-7920
Shipshewana (G-14848)

Graber .... G 812 636-7699
Odon (G-13336)

Graber Box Pllet Fmly Ltd Prtn .... E 260 657-5657
Grabill (G-6296)

Graber Lumber LP .... E 260 238-4124
Spencerville (G-15370)

Graphic Fx Inc .... E 812 234-0000
Terre Haute (G-15601)

Great Lakes Waterjet Inc .... G 574 651-2158
Granger (G-6351)

Greene County Pallets Inc .... F 812 384-8362
Bloomfield (G-746)

Grnwman LLC .... G 219 359-9237
Chesterton (G-1933)

Grumble Games LLC .... G 317 941-6433
Carmel (G-1645)

H D Eccel LLC .... G 574 386-2115
South Bend (G-15056)

Hard Hustla Muzik LLC .... G 812 214-1995
Evansville (G-4103)

Hdh Manufacturing Inc .... G 317 918-4088
Indianapolis (G-8376)

Hearts Rmned Lifestyle Cir LLC .... G 800 807-0485
Gary (G-5947)

Help Help LLC .... G 317 910-6631
Avon (G-525)

Herextensions LLC .... G 219 466-4273
East Chicago (G-3016)

Hiatt Enterprises Inc .... F 765 289-7756
Muncie (G-12415)

Highway Safety Services Inc .... D 765 474-1000
Lafayette (G-10599)

HM Lowry Enterprises LLC .... G 765 524-8435
Cambridge City (G-1495)

Hmt LLC .... G 219 736-9901
Merrillville (G-11522)

Hobbs Transport Services LLC .... G 317 607-5590
Indianapolis (G-8401)

Hoehn Engineered Products LLC .... G 260 223-9158
Decatur (G-2863)

Homeland Sports LLC .... G 219 962-2315
Hobart (G-7190)

▼ Hoosier Crane Service Company ...... D 574 523-2945
Elkhart (G-3411)

Horizon Anim LLC .... G 317 742-4917
Indianapolis (G-8413)

Hush Clothing 317 LLC .... G 317 935-2184
Indianapolis (G-8438)

Huth Tool .... G 260 749-9411
Fort Wayne (G-5085)

Huth Tool & Machine Corp .... G 260 749-9411
Fort Wayne (G-5086)

Hydration Turbine Inc .... G 317 491-0656
Indianapolis (G-8440)

Idonix Solutions Inc .... G 317 544-8171
Fishers (G-4542)

Ike Newton LLC .... G 317 902-1772
Greenwood (G-6714)

Illiana Grinding Machining Inc .... G 219 306-0253
East Chicago (G-3019)

Imma Jerk LLC .... G 219 885-8613
Gary (G-5958)

Indiana Cast Metals Assn Inc .... G 317 974-1830
Indianapolis (G-8475)

Indiana Chemical LLC .... G 317 912-3800
Indianapolis (G-8476)

Indiengage LLC .... G 317 331-7781
Indianapolis (G-8513)

Innovations By .... G 260 413-1869
Fort Wayne (G-5109)

▲ Insertec Inc .... D 800 556-1911
Indianapolis (G-8560)

Interntional Pipe Cons Sls LLC .... F 765 388-2222
New Castle (G-12870)

Interntnal Damnd Gold Exch Ltd .... G 317 872-6666
Indianapolis (G-8583)

Intimusic LLC .... G 574 210-4562
South Bend (G-15086)

Its Family Trucking LLC .... G 219 277-7162
Hammond (G-6960)

J P Corporation .... G 317 783-1000
Beech Grove (G-693)

Jacksons 33 Transporting LLC .... G 901 628-7803
Indianapolis (G-8616)

James Harper .... G 812 267-4251
Depauw (G-2939)

Jaszy Drinks LLC .... G 219 742-5013
Gary (G-5969)

Jcantave Transit LLC .... G 855 608-2777
Indianapolis (G-8619)

Jeshsoft LLC .... G 812 431-8603
Evansville (G-4142)

Jet Fast Carriers LLC .... G 219 218-3021
Indianapolis (G-8623)

Jknk Ventures Inc .... E 812 246-0900
Sellersburg (G-14603)

Jle Fabricating LLC .... G 574 341-4034
Argos (G-324)

John F Semrau .... G 765 337-8831
Medaryville (G-11459)

Johnny Graber Woodworking .... G 260 466-4957
Grabill (G-6305)

JP Industries Inc .... F 574 293-8763
Elkhart (G-3436)

Jtex Cnstr & Consulting LLC .... G 812 486-9123
Velpen (G-16093)

Just Perfection LLC .... G 347 559-5878
Indianapolis (G-8650)

K C Creations .... G 937 418-1859
Indianapolis (G-8653)

Kala Mindfulness LLC .... G 720 351-9664
Indianapolis (G-8657)

Keenville & Company LLC .... G 219 916-6737
Valparaiso (G-15984)

Kelwood Designs LLC .... G 574 862-2472
Goshen (G-6184)

Kessler Concepts Inc .... F 317 630-9901
Indianapolis (G-8675)

Khamis Fine Jewelers Inc .... G 317 841-8440
Indianapolis (G-8681)

Kinetics Xcavating LLC .... G 812 208-9892
Brazil (G-1151)

King Investments Inc .... G 812 752-6000
Scottsburg (G-14568)

L M Corporation .... E 574 535-0581
Goshen (G-6194)

Lady Q LLC-S .... G 219 304-8404
Indianapolis (G-8712)

Ladybugz Bookstore LLC .... G 469 459-1780
Noblesville (G-13125)

Lakeland Pier and Lift LLC .... F 574 377-3481
Warsaw (G-16385)

Lamco Finishers Inc .... E 317 471-1010
Indianapolis (G-8717)

Lane Wright LLC .... G 317 473-4783
Indianapolis (G-8722)

Laser Marking Technologies .... G 812 852-7999
Osgood (G-13411)

Leach & Sons WaterCare .... G 317 248-8954
Danville (G-2818)

Leaning Palms LLC .... G 630 886-8924
Crown Point (G-2715)

Legacy Trailer Rentals LLC .... G 812 873-5218
North Vernon (G-13284)

Leistner Aquatic Services Inc .... G 317 535-6099
Morgantown (G-12260)

Lewis & Lee Presents LLC .... G 219 484-5298
Hammond (G-6971)

Lg Metalworks LLC .... G 812 333-4344
Bloomington (G-911)

Lgndz Customs LLC .... G 765 293-9303
Marion (G-11308)

Ligonier Woodworking .... G 260 894-9969
Ligonier (G-11019)

Lions Quarter LLC .... G 219 932-5531
Hammond (G-6972)

Little Super Findings .... G 812 430-3353
Evansville (G-4173)

Lj Motive LLC .... F 219 588-5480
Hobart (G-7200)

LLC 2 Holdings Limited LLC .... G 317 319-9825
Zionsville (G-17030)

London Hair Bundles LLC .... G 317 953-3888
Fishers (G-4557)

Lord Fms Games LLC .... G 317 710-2253
Indianapolis (G-8783)

Loves Enterprise LLC .... G 219 307-9191
Gary (G-5978)

Lovett Entertainment LLC .... G 773 208-9608
Schererville (G-14532)

Lulus Prom and Bridal LLC .... G 812 772-2013
Tell City (G-15509)

Lux Beauty Den LLC .... G 708 793-0871
Merrillville (G-11534)

Luxetrend LLC .... G 502 208-9344
Evansville (G-4178)

Maddox Engineering Inc .... F 812 903-0048
Greenville (G-6652)

Magaws of Boston .... G 765 935-6170
Richmond (G-14158)

Magical Moments LLC .... G 463 209-5766
Greenwood (G-6731)

Mains Enterprises Inc .... G 765 425-0162
Wilkinson (G-16843)

Makingmoves Transports LLC .... G 260 579-5584
Fort Wayne (G-5200)

Mammoth Hats Inc .... F 812 849-2772
Mitchell (G-12044)

Mantra Enterprise LLC .... G 201 428-8709
Fishers (G-4561)

Marie Collective LLC .... G 317 683-0408
Indianapolis (G-8832)

Markle Water Treatment Plant .... G 260 758-3482
Markle (G-11358)

Marshall G Smith Sign Painting .... G 260 744-9492
Fort Wayne (G-5203)

Martin Uniforms LLC .... G 317 408-9186
Indianapolis (G-8843)

Mast Services Lafayette LLC .... G 765 464-6940
Lafayette (G-10643)

SIC SECTION   73 BUSINESS SERVICES

Company	Code	Phone
Masters Apps LLC	G	574 312-5233
Goshen (G-6217)		
Maurices Sgnture Chsecakes LLC	G	708 879-0031
Valparaiso (G-16000)		
Maury Boyd & Associates Inc	F	317 849-6110
Indianapolis (G-8853)		
McGuires Magic Cleaning LLC	G	317 504-7739
Indianapolis (G-8866)		
Meadowlark Wdwkg Cabinetry LLC	G	765 541-3660
Connersville (G-2456)		
Megans Wash and Fold LLC	G	317 903-5253
Pendleton (G-13543)		
Melissa Lambino	G	317 506-5274
Indianapolis (G-8874)		
Mellon Tax Service	G	219 947-1660
Hobart (G-7201)		
Melvin McCullough	G	765 577-0083
Jamestown (G-9819)		
Menard Inc	C	812 466-1234
Terre Haute (G-15641)		
Michael Cary Ross	G	765 631-2565
Martinsville (G-11413)		
Michael Filley	G	956 443-6364
Owensburg (G-13463)		
Michael Hazeltine	F	317 750-5091
Greenwood (G-6739)		
Michael Holland	G	317 538-1776
Indianapolis (G-8897)		
Micro Businessware Inc	G	502 424-6613
Sellersburg (G-14607)		
Midwest Accurate Grinding Svc	F	219 696-4060
Lowell (G-11172)		
Midwest Design Hydraulic	G	765 714-3016
West Lafayette (G-16605)		
Midwest Electrical Sales	G	708 821-7490
Valparaiso (G-16002)		
Midwest Tire & Service LLC	G	502 377-3722
Salem (G-14492)		
Midwestern Structures LLC	G	574 835-9733
Muncie (G-12456)		
Modular Green Systems LLC	G	260 547-4121
Craigville (G-2535)		
Moodys Logistics Services LLC	G	812 512-2772
Linton (G-11040)		
Morganblair Logistics LLC	G	219 249-2689
Munster (G-12550)		
MTA Technology LLC	F	765 447-2221
Lafayette (G-10655)		
Murphy Mill Services LLC	G	219 246-9290
Valparaiso (G-16006)		
Muzfeed Inc	G	815 252-7676
Fort Wayne (G-5253)		
Mvctc	G	765 969-8921
Richmond (G-14173)		
My Goodies Snack Vending LLC	G	317 653-7395
Anderson (G-164)		
My Old KY Blog Presents LLC	F	317 602-6641
Indianapolis (G-8976)		
Myfoodmixer LLC	G	219 229-7036
Michigan City (G-11644)		
Naporamic LLC	G	463 249-8265
Indianapolis (G-8984)		
National Handicapped Workshop	F	765 287-8331
Muncie (G-12468)		
National Products LLC	G	219 393-5536
Kingsbury (G-10182)		
Naya Trans LLC	G	317 720-8602
Indianapolis (G-8995)		
Nelson J Hochstetler	G	260 499-0315
Lagrange (G-10756)		
New Aqua LLC	D	317 272-3000
Avon (G-540)		
Next Level Candles LLC	G	574 347-1030
South Bend (G-15167)		
Next Reformation Publishing Co	G	317 650-1364
Plainfield (G-13708)		
Nicholas Mendel	G	574 870-8856
Delphi (G-2904)		
Nka Cabinet Designs LLC	G	765 490-4661
Lafayette (G-10659)		
No Limits Just Pssbilities LLC	G	930 465-1218
Princeton (G-14008)		
No More Bugs	G	317 658-6096
Indianapolis (G-9014)		
Nobleman Logistics LLC	G	317 340-7406
Indianapolis (G-9017)		
Noblesville Pack & Ship	G	317 776-6306
Noblesville (G-13144)		
North Coast Organics LLC	G	260 246-0289
Fort Wayne (G-5274)		
Nut House Woodworks LLC	G	317 345-7177
Summitville (G-15426)		
Oakleaf Industries Inc	G	317 414-2040
Fishers (G-4645)		
Octobers Firm Label LLC	G	317 778-1447
Noblesville (G-13147)		
▲ Olive Branch Etc Inc	G	765 449-1884
Lafayette (G-10660)		
Olson Custom Designs LLC	E	317 892-6400
Indianapolis (G-9046)		
Olympus Management LLC	G	317 412-7977
Westfield (G-16715)		
Omega One Connect Inc	G	317 626-3445
Indianapolis (G-9048)		
On Point Precision LLC	G	317 590-2510
Indianapolis (G-9052)		
On The Go Portable Water Softe	F	260 482-9614
Bloomington (G-936)		
Only Get Better Logistics LLC	G	317 835-5606
Indianapolis (G-9057)		
Ontime Toys Inc	G	317 598-9333
Indianapolis (G-9058)		
Operation 1 Veteran Inc	G	574 536-5536
Goshen (G-6231)		
▲ Orion Global Sourcing Inc	G	812 332-3338
Bloomington (G-939)		
Out The Box Transit Inc	G	317 523-0061
Carmel (G-1713)		
Outstnding Trdshow Exhbt Svcs	F	888 735-4348
North Judson (G-13213)		
Over Globe LLC	G	305 607-6472
Brownsburg (G-1394)		
Owen County Pallet LLC	G	812 384-6568
Worthington (G-16962)		
Owens Machinery Inc	G	812 968-3285
Corydon (G-2509)		
Owens Property Solutions LLC	G	708 374-2626
Gary (G-5992)		
Oxinas Partners LLC	G	812 725-8649
Jeffersonville (G-10032)		
P & J Tool Co Inc	G	317 546-4858
Indianapolis (G-9078)		
P&C Prime LLC	F	231 420-3650
Fredericksburg (G-5795)		
P413 Corporation	G	317 769-0679
Zionsville (G-17039)		
Paige Marschall	G	574 277-1631
Granger (G-6368)		
Pappas Construction LLC	G	219 314-7068
Hobart (G-7203)		
Paris Black Fashion LLC	G	317 529-7119
Greencastle (G-6423)		
Part Solutions LLC	G	219 477-5101
South Bend (G-15186)		
Passions Fruitopia LLC	G	800 515-1891
Highland (G-7151)		
Pathfinder Services Inc	E	260 356-0500
Huntington (G-7354)		
Patrick Industries Inc	G	574 293-1521
Elkhart (G-3589)		
Performers Edition LLC	G	317 429-1300
Indianapolis (G-9125)		
Peterson Mfg LLC	G	574 876-1427
Wheatfield (G-16771)		
Pgp Corp	D	812 285-7700
Jeffersonville (G-10036)		
Polley Tech LLC	G	812 524-0688
Seymour (G-14675)		
PostNet Postal & Business Svcs	G	317 462-7118
Greenfield (G-6541)		
Potorti Enterprises Inc	G	812 989-8528
Floyds Knobs (G-4688)		
▲ Precision Products Group Inc	F	317 663-4590
Indianapolis (G-9184)		
Premium Corporation	E	219 258-0141
South Bend (G-15203)		
Presidential Bath & Fix LLC	G	812 259-9817
Evansville (G-4257)		
Print It Inc	G	317 774-6848
Indianapolis (G-9200)		
Priority Detailing	G	812 591-0299
Westport (G-16750)		
Proapse Software	G	260 615-9839
Fort Wayne (G-5352)		
Professional Gifting Inc	F	800 350-1796
Indianapolis (G-9221)		
Profit Over Romance LLC	G	219 900-3592
Gary (G-5997)		
Progress Rail Mfg Corp	C	765 281-2685
Muncie (G-12480)		
Progress Rail Services Corp	C	219 397-5326
East Chicago (G-3037)		
Puritan Water Conditioning	F	765 362-6340
Crawfordsville (G-2606)		
Purspec Technologies Inc	G	765 532-2208
West Lafayette (G-16623)		
Qualtronics LLC	E	812 375-8880
Columbus (G-2384)		
Quickspace Transportation LLC	G	812 585-2317
Indianapolis (G-9250)		
R&H Metalworks LLC	G	317 513-8733
Fairland (G-4402)		
Rackcollections LLC	G	317 779-4302
Indianapolis (G-9259)		
Rai LLC	G	765 227-0111
Indianapolis (G-9263)		
Rakk LLC	G	812 271-4300
Austin (G-470)		
Ramifications LLC	G	765 729-5484
Muncie (G-12484)		
Rapar Inc	G	812 254-9886
Washington (G-16506)		
▲ Rauch Inc	E	812 945-4063
New Albany (G-12803)		
Rayes Rpid Rslts - MBL DRG ALC	G	317 721-1065
Indianapolis (G-9270)		
RC Enterprise LLC	G	317 935-5628
Carmel (G-1735)		
Red Bull Armory LLC	G	757 287-7738
Mitchell (G-12046)		
Reed Sign Service Inc	G	765 459-4033
Kokomo (G-10327)		
Reloaded Activewear LLC	G	317 652-7394
Indianapolis (G-9289)		
Renegade Dispatching LLC	G	260 797-5423
Fort Wayne (G-5380)		

Employee Codes: A=Over 500 employees, B=251-500
C=101-250, D=51-100, E=20-50, F=10-19, G=1-9

73 BUSINESS SERVICES

Respect Da Flava LLC .... G 765 243-1629
Indianapolis *(G-9293)*

Rf Manufacturing Inc .... G 317 773-8610
Noblesville *(G-13167)*

Ricktom Promotions LLC .... G 812 430-0282
Evansville *(G-4289)*

Riverside Tool Corp .... E 574 522-6798
Elkhart *(G-3650)*

Rlay Express Inc .... G 754 265-8555
Avon *(G-548)*

Rlr Associates Inc .... G 317 632-1300
Indianapolis *(G-9312)*

Road Alert Systems LLC .... G 219 669-1206
Morocco *(G-12269)*

Rob Nolley Inc .... F 317 825-5211
Shelbyville *(G-14792)*

Rob Passarelli .... G 317 340-8597
Carmel *(G-1743)*

▲ Roi Marketing Company Inc .... G 317 644-0797
Indianapolis *(G-9321)*

Ronald Lee Allen .... G 812 644-7649
Loogootee *(G-11150)*

Rookies Unlimited Inc .... G 765 536-2726
Summitville *(G-15431)*

Roost .... G 317 842-3735
Fishers *(G-4599)*

Rose & Petal LLC .... G 260 704-5731
Fort Wayne *(G-5389)*

Rose Sharon All Naturals LLC .... G 317 500-4725
Indianapolis *(G-9334)*

Rowe Tech 317 453-0015
Indianapolis *(G-9339)*

◆ Royal Adhesives & Sealants LLC .... D 574 246-5000
South Bend *(G-15226)*

Royal Barbie Blinks LLC .... G 765 400-6205
Lafayette *(G-10681)*

Rt Smart Solutions LLC .... F 317 435-2200
Indianapolis *(G-9345)*

RTC .... G 260 503-9770
Columbia City *(G-2193)*

Rubenstein LLC .... G 317 946-2752
Indianapolis *(G-9346)*

Rustic Fisher Creations LLC .... G 574 279-5754
North Liberty *(G-13222)*

Sampco Inc .... G 413 442-4043
South Bend *(G-15230)*

Sams Tech Tire LLC .... G 219 942-7317
Hobart *(G-7205)*

Samuel Powell .... G 812 887-6813
French Lick *(G-5849)*

Schuler Precision Tool LLC .... G 260 982-2704
North Manchester *(G-13249)*

Selektd Worx LLC .... G 317 227-9337
Indianapolis *(G-9401)*

Sengo LLC .... G 574 383-9833
South Bend *(G-15238)*

Sentinel Services Inc .... E 574 360-5279
Granger *(G-6376)*

▲ Sepro Corporation .... E 317 580-8282
Carmel *(G-1758)*

Service Graphics Inc .... D 317 471-8246
Indianapolis *(G-9408)*

Setser Fabricating LLC .... G 812 546-2169
Columbus *(G-2390)*

Sewer Optical Services Inc .... G 765 242-3768
Lebanon *(G-10940)*

Shalom Trans LLC .... E 317 712-6765
Avon *(G-550)*

SHE Publishing LLC .... G 219 515-8032
Indianapolis *(G-9414)*

Shelovexempress LLC .... G 317 490-2097
Evansville *(G-4309)*

Short 9th LLC .... G 270 313-5665
Indianapolis *(G-9422)*

Shurtrack Transport LLC .... G 317 779-5902
Indianapolis *(G-9423)*

Signs AP & Awards On Time LLC .... G 219 661-4488
Crown Point *(G-2752)*

Sills Custom Works & Fab LLC .... G 219 200-9813
Knox *(G-10224)*

Silverthorn Handyman Svcs LLC .... G 812 896-4201
Salem *(G-14498)*

Simply Saidahs LLC .... G 317 650-4256
Carmel *(G-1762)*

Sky Cryptoassets LLC .... G 949 903-6896
Carmel *(G-1763)*

SL Beauty LLC .... G 317 969-0341
Indianapolis *(G-9446)*

Smiling Cross Inc .... G 812 323-9290
Bloomington *(G-976)*

Snappy Minds Llc .... G 812 661-8506
Jasper *(G-9913)*

Solid Rock LLC .... G 260 755-2687
Fort Wayne *(G-5425)*

Spagheady Inc .... G 317 499-6184
Indianapolis *(G-9467)*

Spark Marketing LLC .... G 219 301-0071
Dyer *(G-2983)*

Speak Abilities LLP .... G 303 827-8269
West Lafayette *(G-16630)*

Specialized Printed Products .... G 260 483-7075
Fort Wayne *(G-5428)*

Specialty Shoppe .... G 574 772-7873
Knox *(G-10225)*

Spectrum Marketing .... G 765 643-5566
Anderson *(G-197)*

Sprinkguard LLC .... F 877 274-7976
Mishawaka *(G-12006)*

Sprinter Xpress Delivery LLC .... G 317 496-5959
Indianapolis *(G-9483)*

Squeegeepie Merch Co LLC .... G 765 376-6358
Crawfordsville *(G-2618)*

Star Quality Awards Inc .... G 812 273-1740
Madison *(G-11252)*

◆ Steel Dynamics Inc .... B 260 969-3500
Fort Wayne *(G-5438)*

Steele Roofing Co LLC .... G 219 243-1563
Valparaiso *(G-16058)*

Stem Point LLC .... G 352 870-0122
Franklin *(G-5778)*

Stien Designs & Graphics Inc .... G 260 347-9136
Kendallville *(G-10153)*

Still Safety Products LLC .... G 855 249-0009
Evanston *(G-3855)*

Study Studsters LLC .... G 574 635-1018
Elkhart *(G-3702)*

Sugarcube Systems Inc .... G 765 543-6709
Lafayette *(G-10704)*

Suitable Stylez .... G 765 409-9375
Lafayette *(G-10705)*

Suncoast Coffee Inc .... E 317 251-3198
Indianapolis *(G-9526)*

T & M Equipment Company Inc .... F 317 293-9255
Indianapolis *(G-9543)*

T&S Group LLC .... G 219 310-0364
Greenwood *(G-6772)*

Tanguero Inc .... G 415 236-2642
Bloomington *(G-983)*

▲ Tasus Corporation .... C 812 333-6500
Bloomington *(G-984)*

Tc4 LLC .... G 317 709-5429
Fishers *(G-4610)*

Tdk Graphics Inc .... F 219 663-7799
Crown Point *(G-2762)*

Teaco Inc .... G 219 874-6234
Michigan City *(G-11676)*

Tgf Enterprises LLC .... G 440 840-9704
Indianapolis *(G-9585)*

Thegoosecompany LLC .... G 708 280-7512
Munster *(G-12570)*

Timelessmusicgroup LLC .... G 317 721-6671
Carmel *(G-1786)*

Timothy D Goin .... G 317 771-0404
Indianapolis *(G-9606)*

Tj Constructions LLC .... G 470 406-2804
Indianapolis *(G-9611)*

Todd Enterprise Inc .... F 317 209-6610
Noblesville *(G-13182)*

Tooties Zenergy Candles LLC .... G 317 437-9936
Indianapolis *(G-9619)*

Touch of Class Interiors .... G 765 452-5879
Kokomo *(G-10351)*

Travis Britton .... G 317 762-6018
Indianapolis *(G-9632)*

Trevares D Smith .... G 765 603-0468
Marion *(G-11343)*

Tri-Pac Inc .... C 574 855-2197
South Bend *(G-15291)*

Tri-State Metal Inc .... E 219 397-0470
East Chicago *(G-3047)*

Trill Machine LLC .... G 219 730-0744
Kentland *(G-10164)*

Trinity Displays LLC .... G 219 201-8733
Chesterton *(G-1961)*

Triumphant Jrney MBL Ntary Svc .... G 608 208-5604
Madison *(G-11254)*

True Analytics Mfg Slutions LLC .... G 317 995-3220
Plainfield *(G-13739)*

True Chem Inc .... G 317 769-2701
Greenwood *(G-6777)*

Tspdesign LLC .... G 317 785-8663
Anderson *(G-210)*

Tt2 LLC .... G 260 438-4575
Fort Wayne *(G-5511)*

Turn & Burn Welding Inc .... G 812 766-0641
Otwell *(G-13458)*

TW Enterprises LLC .... G 513 520-8453
Brookville *(G-1338)*

Uinspire LLC .... G 574 575-6949
Elkhart *(G-3756)*

Ultima Plastics LLC .... G 812 459-1430
Evansville *(G-4358)*

Underdog Diner LLP .... G 812 598-2970
Evansville *(G-4359)*

Unique Global Solutions LLC .... G 765 779-5030
Anderson *(G-212)*

Universal Packg Systems Inc .... C 260 829-6721
Orland *(G-13374)*

Unrivaled Interiors LLC .... G 317 509-0496
Cicero *(G-2003)*

Upshaw Freight LLC .... G 317 200-8655
Indianapolis *(G-9686)*

Urban Rustic Farmhouse LLC .... G 317 238-0945
New Palestine *(G-12944)*

Verbott Trucking & Transportat .... G 317 363-9698
Indianapolis *(G-9706)*

Vicksmetal Armco Associates .... E 765 659-5555
Frankfort *(G-5700)*

Virago Logistix Llc .... G 800 767-2090
Hammond *(G-7030)*

Visable Vinyl .... G 765 717-9678
Hartford City *(G-7081)*

Wagner Signs Inc .... E 317 788-0202
Indianapolis *(G-9735)*

Wall Control Services Inc .... G 260 450-6411
Fort Wayne *(G-5542)*

75 AUTOMOTIVE REPAIR, SERVICES AND PARKING

Walton Industrial Park Inc .... F 574 626-2929
   Walton *(G-16284)*

Warnock Welding & Fabg LLC .... G 812 498-5408
   Seymour *(G-14703)*

▲ Warsaw Metal Products Inc .... F 574 269-6211
   Pierceton *(G-13642)*

Watcon Inc .... G 574 287-3397
   South Bend *(G-15304)*

▲ Web Industries Fort Wayne Inc .... E 260 432-0027
   Fort Wayne *(G-5559)*

Westlund Concepts .... F 317 819-0611
   Lapel *(G-10818)*

Whimsicals Inc .... G 317 773-6130
   Noblesville *(G-13194)*

Whitehead Signs Inc .... F 317 632-1800
   Indianapolis *(G-9760)*

Wildebeest LLC .... G 812 391-5631
   Fort Wayne *(G-5568)*

Williams Woodshop .... G 574 686-2324
   Camden *(G-1522)*

Wisemed Inc .... G 317 644-1169
   Indianapolis *(G-9778)*

Witham Anthony J Sign Prod .... G 317 984-3765
   Arcadia *(G-320)*

Wm Express LLP .... G 773 647-5305
   Hammond *(G-7035)*

Woodberry Family Freight LLC .... G 317 665-6917
   Indianapolis *(G-9785)*

Wyatt Survival Supply LLC .... G 765 318-2872
   Morgantown *(G-12266)*

Xpedited Trucking Inc .... F 463 223-7366
   Carmel *(G-1810)*

Xpressvending LLC .... G 331 264-3541
   Indianapolis *(G-9796)*

Youngs Freight & Logistics LLC .... G 765 639-7888
   Anderson *(G-219)*

Zachary T Laffin .... G 317 480-2248
   Greenfield *(G-6572)*

▲ Zojila Ltd Liability Company .... G 765 404-3767
   Lafayette *(G-10726)*

75 AUTOMOTIVE REPAIR, SERVICES AND PARKING

7513 Truck rental and leasing, without drivers

Carmel Welding and Sup Co Inc .... E 317 846-3493
   Carmel *(G-1582)*

Imel John .... G 317 873-8764
   Zionsville *(G-17017)*

Landis Equipment & Tool Rental .... G 812 847-2582
   Linton *(G-11037)*

Mid-State Truck Equipment Inc .... E 317 849-4903
   Fishers *(G-4566)*

Stout Plastic Weld .... F 219 926-7622
   Chesterton *(G-1959)*

Upland Tire & Service Ctr Inc .... G 765 998-0871
   Upland *(G-15884)*

7514 Passenger car rental

Perma Lubrication .... G 317 241-0797
   Indianapolis *(G-9126)*

7515 Passenger car leasing

Ford Motor Company .... F 901 368-8421
   Plainfield *(G-13680)*

7519 Utility trailer rental

Grand Design Rv LLC .... G 574 825-8000
   Middlebury *(G-11719)*

Imel John .... G 317 873-8764
   Zionsville *(G-17017)*

7532 Top and body repair and paint shops

Alveys Sign Co Inc .... E 812 867-2567
   Evansville *(G-3883)*

Barry Seat Cover & Auto GL Co .... F 574 288-4603
   South Bend *(G-14956)*

Bearcat Corp .... E 574 533-0448
   Goshen *(G-6098)*

C M I Enterprises Inc .... D 305 685-9651
   Elkhart *(G-3244)*

Fiedeke Vinyl Coverings Inc .... F 574 534-3408
   Goshen *(G-6135)*

Hoosier Hot Rods Classics Inc .... G 812 768-5221
   Evansville *(G-4109)*

Hot Rod Car Care LLC .... G 317 660-2077
   Indianapolis *(G-8421)*

Independent Protection Co .... C 574 831-5680
   New Paris *(G-12960)*

▼ Independent Protection Co .... E 574 533-4116
   Goshen *(G-6172)*

Indiana Custom Trucks LLC .... E 260 463-3244
   Shipshewana *(G-14852)*

Love Upholstery LLC .... G 812 639-3789
   Jasper *(G-9883)*

Marmon Highway Tech LLC .... E 317 787-0718
   Indianapolis *(G-8839)*

Martin Signs & Crane Services .... G 317 908-9708
   Indianapolis *(G-8842)*

Mosiers Tarps LLC .... G 260 563-3332
   Wabash *(G-16205)*

Nicks Automotive Inc .... F 765 964-6843
   Union City *(G-15856)*

Northern Ind Indus Catings LLC .... G 574 893-4621
   Akron *(G-6)*

Pyramid Sign & Design Inc .... G 765 447-4174
   Lafayette *(G-10674)*

Schaffsteins Truck Clean LLC .... F 812 464-2424
   Evansville *(G-4298)*

Showtime Conversions Inc .... E 574 825-1130
   Middlebury *(G-11752)*

Steve Reiff Inc .... E 260 723-4360
   South Whitley *(G-15328)*

▲ Twin-Air Products Inc .... F 574 295-1129
   Elkhart *(G-3755)*

7533 Auto exhaust system repair shops

▲ Airtek LLC .... C 219 947-1664
   Hobart *(G-7172)*

Auto Specialty Lafayette Inc .... G 765 446-2311
   Lafayette *(G-10531)*

Mighty Muffler LLC .... G 765 966-6833
   Richmond *(G-14166)*

Reed Auto - Indy Mich LLC .... F 317 872-1132
   Indianapolis *(G-9279)*

7534 Tire retreading and repair shops

Atr Tire and Repair LLC .... G 574 349-4462
   New Paris *(G-12946)*

Auto Express Vale .... E 317 897-6618
   Indianapolis *(G-7572)*

Bandag Warranty .... G 800 523-6366
   Indianapolis *(G-7593)*

▲ Ben Tire Distributors Ltd .... E 317 798-2013
   Indianapolis *(G-7612)*

Bernard Burns .... G 574 382-5019
   Macy *(G-11194)*

Best One Tire & Svc S Bend Inc .... G 574 246-4021
   South Bend *(G-14958)*

Best-One Kentuckiana Inc .... G 812 282-4799
   Jeffersonville *(G-9942)*

Best-One Kentuckiana Inc .... E 812 285-5400
   Jeffersonville *(G-9941)*

Best-One Lt LLC .... G 812 471-8473
   Evansville *(G-3928)*

Best-One Tire & Auto Care of A .... G 260 665-7330
   Angola *(G-234)*

Best-One Tire & Svc Auburn Inc .... G 260 925-2782
   Auburn *(G-369)*

Bridgestone Ret Operations LLC .... F 812 332-2119
   Bloomington *(G-815)*

Bridgestone Ret Operations LLC .... G 260 447-2596
   Columbia City *(G-2127)*

Bridgestone Ret Operations LLC .... G 812 477-8818
   Evansville *(G-3951)*

Bridgestone Ret Operations LLC .... F 812 423-4451
   Evansville *(G-3952)*

Bridgestone Ret Operations LLC .... G 317 846-6516
   Indianapolis *(G-7681)*

Bridgestone Ret Operations LLC .... G 317 849-9120
   Indianapolis *(G-7682)*

Bridgestone Ret Operations LLC .... G 765 447-5041
   Lafayette *(G-10542)*

Bridgestone Ret Operations LLC .... G 317 773-2761
   Noblesville *(G-13048)*

Bridgestone Ret Operations LLC .... G 812 232-9478
   Terre Haute *(G-15554)*

Clark Tire Fishers Inc .... G 317 842-0544
   Fishers *(G-4490)*

Cunningham Tire Services Inc .... G 765 473-9200
   Peru *(G-13576)*

Custom Tire Cutting Inc .... G 812 745-9140
   Oaktown *(G-13326)*

D & D Tire Shop LLC .... G 219 354-0402
   East Chicago *(G-3002)*

Dales Goodyear Tire & Service .... G 574 272-3779
   South Bend *(G-14995)*

Daviess County Tire & Sup Inc .... G 812 254-1035
   Washington *(G-16475)*

Daviess County Tire Inc .... G 812 254-1035
   Washington *(G-16476)*

Double D .... G 765 569-6822
   Rockville *(G-14351)*

E & M Tire Salvage Inc .... G 260 745-3016
   Fort Wayne *(G-4936)*

Gentis Tire & Service Inc .... E 765 348-2400
   Hartford City *(G-7066)*

Goodyear Tire Center .... G 260 726-9321
   Portland *(G-13946)*

Hellmans Auto Supply Co Inc .... G 219 885-7655
   Gary *(G-5949)*

Hoosier Tire & Retreading Inc .... F 812 876-8286
   Bloomington *(G-883)*

Hughes Tire Service Inc .... F 812 883-4981
   Salem *(G-14481)*

Indiana Discount Tire Company .... G 574 875-8547
   Elkhart *(G-3421)*

Indiana Discount Tire Company .... G 574 549-6060
   Warsaw *(G-16377)*

K Tech Supply .... G 812 793-3352
   Crothersville *(G-2641)*

Leonards Auto Service .... G 812 879-4802
   Gosport *(G-6286)*

Lopez Tires & Wheels LLC .... G 219 654-4586
   Lake Station *(G-10773)*

Loves Travel Stops .... F 574 935-4103
   Plymouth *(G-13793)*

McCord Tire Service Inc .... F 812 235-8016
   Terre Haute *(G-15639)*

Midwest Tire & Service LLC .... G 502 377-3722
   Salem *(G-14492)*

Mighty Muffler LLC .... G 765 966-6833
   Richmond *(G-14166)*

75 AUTOMOTIVE REPAIR, SERVICES AND PARKING

Mooresville Tire & Service Ctr................ G 317 831-1215
  Mooresville *(G-12224)*
Parish Tire & Battery Shop...................... G 765 793-3191
  Covington *(G-2532)*
Paul Nunez Road Service....................... G 765 584-1628
  Winchester *(G-16898)*
Penner Tire & Service LLC..................... G 812 653-0029
  Hardinsburg *(G-7048)*
Pfm Automotive Management Inc........... G 317 733-3977
  Zionsville *(G-17040)*
Pfm Car & Truck Castleton Inc................ E 317 577-7777
  Indianapolis *(G-9131)*
Pfm Onsite Services Inc......................... G 317 784-7777
  Indianapolis *(G-9132)*
Pomps Tire Service Inc.......................... E 260 489-5252
  Fort Wayne *(G-5326)*
Portland Tire & Service Inc..................... G 260 726-9321
  Portland *(G-13962)*
Premier Bandage 3 Inc........................... F 574 257-0248
  South Bend *(G-15202)*
R T Tire & Auto-Lebanon......................... G 317 443-6025
  Sheridan *(G-14826)*
Raben Tire Co LLC.................................. F 812 465-5555
  Evansville *(G-4271)*
Reed Auto - Indy Mich LLC..................... F 317 872-1132
  Indianapolis *(G-9279)*
Reis Tire Sales Inc................................. E 812 425-2229
  Evansville *(G-4283)*
Ricks Motorcycle Tire Svc LLC............... G 219 369-1028
  Mill Creek *(G-11809)*
▲ Smith Tire Inc...................................... F 574 267-8261
  Warsaw *(G-16427)*
Snider Tire Inc....................................... D 260 824-4520
  Bluffton *(G-1054)*
Superior Axle LLC.................................. E 574 295-1905
  Elkhart *(G-3707)*
Taylor Tire Treading Co Inc.................... G 317 634-9476
  Indianapolis *(G-9559)*
Tippecanoe Tire Service Inc................... G 765 884-0920
  Fowler *(G-5634)*
Tire Center of Portland Inc..................... G 260 726-8947
  Portland *(G-13971)*
Tire Central and Service Avon................ G 317 966-0662
  Indianapolis *(G-9608)*
Tires Enterprises Corp............................ F 866 807-4930
  Gary *(G-6019)*
Trusty Tires Inc...................................... G 812 738-4212
  Corydon *(G-2519)*
Upland Tire & Service Ctr Inc................. G 765 998-0871
  Upland *(G-15884)*
Windy City Coml Tire & Svc LLC............ G 773 530-1246
  East Chicago *(G-3057)*
Woodward Tire Sales & Svc Inc............. G 260 432-0694
  Fort Wayne *(G-5575)*

7536 Automotive glass replacement shops

Barry Seat Cover & Auto GL Co............. F 574 288-4603
  South Bend *(G-14956)*
Broadway Auto Glass LLC...................... F 219 884-5277
  Merrillville *(G-11493)*

7537 Automotive transmission repair shops

Hobbs Auto Diagnostics & Repr............. G 765 606-1490
  Anderson *(G-127)*
◆ Metaldyne M&A Bluffton LLC.............. D 260 824-6800
  Bluffton *(G-1042)*
Mikesmobimech LLC.............................. G 317 753-0492
  Indianapolis *(G-8918)*
Northern Trans & Differential.................. G 219 764-4009
  Portage *(G-13900)*
Tecumseh Products Company LLC........ G 812 883-3575
  Salem *(G-14502)*

Truckpro LLC... F 765 482-6525
  Lebanon *(G-10948)*

7538 General automotive repair shops

Auto Center Inc...................................... G 317 545-3360
  Indianapolis *(G-7571)*
Auto Express Vale.................................. E 317 897-6618
  Indianapolis *(G-7572)*
Auto Specialty Lafayette Inc................... G 765 446-2311
  Lafayette *(G-10531)*
Awol Metal Contorsion LLC.................... G 260 909-0411
  Kendallville *(G-10093)*
Barry Seat Cover & Auto GL Co............. F 574 288-4603
  South Bend *(G-14956)*
Bills Gar & Auto Refinishing................... G 765 296-4978
  Lafayette *(G-10537)*
Bridgestone Ret Operations LLC............ G 317 773-2761
  Noblesville *(G-13048)*
C & P Machine Service Inc..................... F 260 484-7723
  Fort Wayne *(G-4827)*
Ccts Technology Group Inc.................... G 305 209-5743
  Indianapolis *(G-7765)*
CD & Ws Bordner Entps Inc................... G 765 268-2120
  Cutler *(G-2783)*
Chappos Inc... G 219 942-8101
  Hobart *(G-7181)*
Cummins Crosspoint LLC....................... E 317 243-7979
  Indianapolis *(G-7925)*
▲ Cummins Cumberland Inc................... B 317 243-7979
  Indianapolis *(G-7926)*
Dons Automotive and Mch Inc................ G 812 547-6292
  Tell City *(G-15500)*
Hendershot Service Center Inc............... F 765 653-2600
  Greencastle *(G-6412)*
Hobbs Auto Diagnostics & Repr............. G 765 606-1490
  Anderson *(G-127)*
Indian Creek Outdoor Power LLC........... G 812 597-3055
  Morgantown *(G-12258)*
Indiana Mobile Marine LLC..................... G 317 961-1881
  Indianapolis *(G-8483)*
◆ Jasper Engine Exchange Inc..............A 812 482-1041
  Jasper *(G-9853)*
Jolliff Diesel Service LLC........................ G 812 692-5725
  Elnora *(G-3815)*
Kerns Speed Shop.................................. G 812 275-4289
  Bedford *(G-652)*
Leonards Auto Service............................ G 812 879-4802
  Gosport *(G-6286)*
Macallister Machinery Co Inc.................. C 260 483-6469
  Fort Wayne *(G-5195)*
Marmon Highway Tech LLC.................... E 317 787-0718
  Indianapolis *(G-8839)*
Midwest Auto Repair Inc......................... F 219 322-0364
  Schererville *(G-14534)*
Mikesmobimech LLC.............................. G 317 753-0492
  Indianapolis *(G-8918)*
Mitchell Smith Racing............................. G 765 640-0237
  Anderson *(G-155)*
Mooresville Tire & Service Ctr................ G 317 831-1215
  Mooresville *(G-12224)*
Morgan Automotive................................. G 765 378-0593
  Chesterfield *(G-1897)*
OHM Automotive LLC............................. G 812 879-5455
  Bloomington *(G-934)*
Performance Technology Inc.................. G 574 862-2116
  Wakarusa *(G-16242)*
Pfm Automotive Management Inc........... G 317 733-3977
  Zionsville *(G-17040)*
Pfm Car & Truck Castleton Inc................ E 317 577-7777
  Indianapolis *(G-9131)*
Pfm Onsite Services Inc......................... G 317 784-7777
  Indianapolis *(G-9132)*

Pyramid Equipment Inc........................... F 219 778-2591
  Rolling Prairie *(G-14371)*
Reed Auto - Indy Mich LLC..................... F 317 872-1132
  Indianapolis *(G-9279)*
Sauers Racing Auto Machines................ G 812 265-2803
  Madison *(G-11251)*
Schnell Service Center........................... G 812 683-2461
  Huntingburg *(G-7290)*
Selking International LLC........................ E 260 482-3000
  Fort Wayne *(G-5408)*
Selking International Inc......................... G 574 522-2001
  Elkhart *(G-3668)*
Three K Racing Enterprises................... G 765 482-4273
  Lebanon *(G-10946)*
Tire Central and Service Avon................ G 317 966-0662
  Indianapolis *(G-9608)*
Upland Tire & Service Ctr Inc................. G 765 998-0871
  Upland *(G-15884)*
Woodruff Automotive LLC...................... G 812 636-4908
  Odon *(G-13358)*
Woodward Tire Sales & Svc Inc............. G 260 432-0694
  Fort Wayne *(G-5575)*

7539 Automotive repair shops, nec

Anthony Smith.. G 765 478-5325
  Cambridge City *(G-1490)*
Auto Specialty Lafayette Inc................... G 765 446-2311
  Lafayette *(G-10531)*
▼ B & M Electrical Company Inc............ F 765 448-4532
  Lafayette *(G-10533)*
BCI Solutions Inc.................................... C 574 546-2411
  Bremen *(G-1174)*
Best Weld Inc... G 765 641-7720
  Anderson *(G-83)*
Brent Morris.. G 812 282-6945
  Jeffersonville *(G-9946)*
Bridgestone Ret Operations LLC............ G 317 773-2761
  Noblesville *(G-13048)*
CCT Enterprises LLC............................. E 260 925-1420
  Auburn *(G-375)*
Champ Torque Converters Inc................ G 812 424-2602
  Evansville *(G-3969)*
Champion Racing Engines LLC............. G 317 335-2491
  Mccordsville *(G-11446)*
Deans Place... G 765 282-5712
  Muncie *(G-12375)*
Forks Rv Inc... D 574 825-7467
  Shipshewana *(G-14846)*
Frank Wiss Racg Components Inc......... G 317 243-9585
  Indianapolis *(G-8222)*
Greg Moser Engineering Inc................... E 260 726-6689
  Portland *(G-13949)*
H & E Machined Specialties................... F 260 424-2527
  Fort Wayne *(G-5045)*
Jeannie and Rachel Heidenreich............ G 260 244-4583
  Columbia City *(G-2159)*
Lances Drvshaft Components Inc.......... G 219 762-2531
  Portage *(G-13881)*
Mc Ginley Fire Apparatus....................... G 765 482-3152
  Lebanon *(G-10915)*
Midwest Auto Repair Inc......................... F 219 322-0364
  Schererville *(G-14534)*
Mighty Muffler LLC................................. G 765 966-6833
  Richmond *(G-14166)*
Mikesmobimech LLC.............................. G 317 753-0492
  Indianapolis *(G-8918)*
Morgan Automotive................................. G 765 378-0593
  Chesterfield *(G-1897)*
Next Gnrtion Dlrshp Warsaw LLC.......... G 463 234-9400
  Indianapolis *(G-9008)*
▲ Numerical Productions Inc.................. D 317 783-1362
  Indianapolis *(G-9034)*

SIC SECTION

76 MISCELLANEOUS REPAIR SERVICES

Parish Tire & Battery Shop .... G 765 793-3191
  Covington (G-2532)
Reed Auto - Indy Mich LLC .... F 317 872-1132
  Indianapolis (G-9279)
Rugged Steel Works LLC .... F 260 444-4241
  Fort Wayne (G-5390)
S & S Diesel Motorsport LLC .... G 812 216-3639
  Seymour (G-14683)
Three Daughters Corp .... E 260 925-2128
  Auburn (G-430)
Waterfield Automotive Mch Sp .... G 765 288-6262
  Muncie (G-12515)

7542 Carwashes

Paulus Plastic Co Inc .... G 574 834-7663
  North Webster (G-13312)
Schaffsteins Truck Clean LLC .... F 812 464-2424
  Evansville (G-4298)
Whitlocks Pressure Wash .... F 765 825-5868
  Connersville (G-2475)

7549 Automotive services, nec

A 2 Z Universal Solutions .... G 317 496-7435
  Union City (G-15846)
Auto Specialty Lafayette Inc .... G 765 446-2311
  Lafayette (G-10531)
Chads LLC .... G 812 323-7377
  Ellettsville (G-3802)
Deans Place .... G 765 282-5712
  Muncie (G-12375)
Esco Enterprises Indiana Inc .... F 317 241-0318
  Indianapolis (G-8131)
Gorrepati Service Systems .... G 317 299-7590
  Indianapolis (G-8308)
Grahams Wrecker Service Inc .... G 317 736-4355
  Whiteland (G-16787)
Hendershot Service Center Inc .... F 765 653-2600
  Greencastle (G-6412)
Illinois Lubricants LLC .... G 260 436-2444
  Fort Wayne (G-5092)
K & D Custom Coach Inc .... E 574 537-1716
  Goshen (G-6182)
▲ Lingenfelter Prfmce Engrg Inc .... E 260 724-2552
  Decatur (G-2869)
Mitchell Smith Racing .... G 765 640-0237
  Anderson (G-155)
Parish Tire & Battery Shop .... G 765 793-3191
  Covington (G-2532)
◆ Qualitex Inc .... F 260 244-7839
  Columbia City (G-2186)
Rhyne Engines Inc .... G 219 845-1218
  Gary (G-6004)
Sparkling Clean Inc .... G 812 422-4871
  Evansville (G-4326)
Wilson Enterprises Inc .... G 765 362-1089
  Crawfordsville (G-2627)
Zionsville Towing Inc .... G 317 873-4550
  Zionsville (G-17064)

76 MISCELLANEOUS REPAIR SERVICES

7623 Refrigeration service and repair

Expert Electrical Services LLC .... G 765 664-6642
  Marion (G-11285)
▼ JC Refrigeration LLC .... G 260 768-4067
  Shipshewana (G-14855)

7629 Electrical repair shops

Advantage Cartridge Co Inc .... F 260 747-9941
  Fort Wayne (G-4730)

Agri-Tronix Corp .... F 317 738-4474
  Franklin (G-5703)
Baseline Tool Company .... F 260 761-4932
  Wawaka (G-16537)
Best Equipment Co Inc .... E 317 823-3050
  Indianapolis (G-7617)
Chance Ind Standards Lab Inc .... F 317 787-6578
  Indianapolis (G-7783)
Cinq LLC .... G 405 361-0097
  New Albany (G-12713)
Columbus Signs .... G 812 376-7877
  Nashville (G-12668)
Cummins - Allison Corp .... G 317 872-6244
  Indianapolis (G-7922)
Egenolf Machine Inc .... F 317 787-5301
  Indianapolis (G-8061)
Horner Industrial Services Inc .... G 812 466-5281
  Terre Haute (G-15607)
Horner Industrial Services Inc .... C 317 639-4261
  Indianapolis (G-8416)
I E M C .... G 219 464-2890
  Valparaiso (G-15966)
Johnson Bros S Whitley Sign Co .... F 260 723-5161
  South Whitley (G-15319)
Kouder Instrument Service Co .... G 219 374-5935
  Cedar Lake (G-1833)
Lasertone Inc .... F 812 473-5945
  Evansville (G-4162)
Mid-America Environmental LLC .... F 812 475-1644
  Evansville (G-4204)
Ohio Transmission Corporation .... G 812 466-2734
  Terre Haute (G-15655)
Peter Austin Co .... G 765 288-6397
  Muncie (G-12474)
R C Systems Inc .... G 812 282-4898
  Jeffersonville (G-10044)
Richard J Bagan Inc .... E 260 244-5115
  Columbia City (G-2190)
Shearer Printing Service Inc .... F 765 457-3274
  Kokomo (G-10334)
Sign Group Inc .... F 317 875-6969
  Indianapolis (G-9430)
Teaco Inc .... G 219 874-6234
  Michigan City (G-11676)
The Office Shop Inc .... E 812 934-5611
  Batesville (G-607)
United Machine Corporation .... E 219 548-8050
  Valparaiso (G-16072)
Vandergriff & Associates Inc .... G 812 422-6033
  Evansville (G-4367)
Vertical Steel Maintenance LLC .... G 912 710-0626
  Indianapolis (G-9711)

7631 Watch, clock, and jewelry repair

Ginas Creative Jewelry Inc .... G 317 272-0032
  Avon (G-521)
GNB Studio Inc .... G 317 356-4834
  Indianapolis (G-8295)
Golden Lion Inc .... G 765 446-9557
  Lafayette (G-10592)
Goldstone Jewelry Inc .... G 765 742-1975
  West Lafayette (G-16585)
Interntnal Damnd Gold Exch Ltd .... G 317 872-6666
  Indianapolis (G-8583)
Kensington Watch Services .... G 219 306-5499
  Crown Point (G-2708)
Khamis Fine Jewelers Inc .... G 317 841-8440
  Indianapolis (G-8681)
Mark Edward Hails .... G 812 437-1030
  Evansville (G-4189)
Rogers Enterprises Inc .... G 317 851-5500
  Greenwood (G-6760)

Sisson & Son Mfg Jewelers .... G 574 967-4331
  Flora (G-4665)
Stall & Kessler Inc .... G 765 742-1259
  Lafayette (G-10698)
Williams Jewelers Inc .... G 812 475-1705
  Evansville (G-4387)

7641 Reupholstery and furniture repair

Aaron Company Inc .... F 219 838-0852
  Gary (G-5886)
Antique Stove Information .... G 574 583-6465
  Monticello (G-12135)
Claridges Wood Shop .... G 812 536-2569
  Stendal (G-15398)
Coffeys Custom Upholstery .... G 812 948-8611
  New Albany (G-12715)
Columbus Cstm Cbinets Furn LLC .... G 812 379-9411
  Columbus (G-2242)
Covers of Indiana Inc .... G 317 244-0291
  Indianapolis (G-7891)
Deer Ridgewood Craft LLC .... G 812 535-3744
  West Terre Haute (G-16651)
Douglas Dye and Associates Inc .... G 317 844-1709
  Carmel (G-1611)
Industrial Sewing Machine Co .... G 812 425-2255
  Evansville (G-4124)
Kasnak Restorations Inc .... G 317 852-9770
  Brownsburg (G-1381)
Love Upholstery LLC .... G 812 639-3789
  Jasper (G-9883)
Rhyne & Associates Inc .... F 317 786-4459
  Indianapolis (G-9299)
Shelby Westside Upholstering .... G 317 631-8911
  Indianapolis (G-9419)
Spectrum Marketing .... G 765 643-5566
  Anderson (G-197)
Z Rodz & Customs LLC .... G 574 806-5774
  Knox (G-10229)

7692 Welding repair

104 Welding .... G 219 393-0801
  La Porte (G-10370)
A & A Industries Inc .... G 812 663-5584
  Greensburg (G-6577)
AAA Welding Inc .... G 574 293-5294
  Elkhart (G-3144)
Aarons Welding LLC .... G 574 529-3885
  Warsaw (G-16308)
ABC Fix-N-Fab Welding LLC .... G 765 230-6492
  Covington (G-2526)
ABF Welding & Pipe LLC .... G 765 977-7349
  Cambridge City (G-1489)
Absolute Fabrication Inc .... G 574 848-0300
  Elkhart (G-3146)
Absolute Welding Inc .... F 812 923-8001
  Borden (G-1103)
AC Welding Mscellaneous Ir Inc .... G 317 491-2898
  Indianapolis (G-7419)
Accu-Built Tooling and Weld .... G 574 825-7878
  Goshen (G-6087)
Ace Welding and Machine Inc .... G 812 379-9625
  Columbus (G-2213)
▲ Acro Engineering Inc .... E 812 663-6236
  Greensburg (G-6579)
Action Welding & Machine Svcs .... G 219 766-0406
  Kouts (G-10360)
Acwelding & Misc Iron Inc .... G 317 491-2898
  Indianapolis (G-7426)
Advanced Welding and Engrg .... G 317 820-3595
  Indianapolis (G-7443)
Allfab LLC .... G 317 359-3539
  Indianapolis (G-7482)

76 MISCELLANEOUS REPAIR SERVICES

American Machine & Fabg Co Inc............. G 812 944-4136
  New Albany *(G-12688)*
Amos D Graber & Sons............................. F 260 749-0526
  New Haven *(G-12892)*
Amos Welding LLC..................................... G 765 561-2359
  Rushville *(G-14395)*
Angel ARC Welding.................................... G 812 322-9027
  Columbus *(G-2220)*
Annette Balfour... G 765 286-1910
  Muncie *(G-12342)*
APL Welding & Fabrication LLC............. G 765 572-1088
  Westpoint *(G-16742)*
Applied Metals & Mch Works Inc........... E 260 424-4834
  Fort Wayne *(G-4766)*
ARC Angle Welding/Fabrication.............. F 812 619-1731
  Tell City *(G-15496)*
Arcpro Welding & Prop Repair................ G 812 867-6383
  Evansville *(G-3898)*
Area Welding Inc LLC............................... G 219 669-0981
  Dyer *(G-2967)*
Area Welding Innovations LLC.............. G 219 789-2209
  Gary *(G-5895)*
Ash Welding.. G 219 808-7139
  Hebron *(G-7096)*
Atp Welding Inc... G 765 483-9273
  Lebanon *(G-10877)*
Auto Truck Group LLC............................. G 260 356-1610
  Huntington *(G-7299)*
Auto Truck Group LLC............................. G 260 493-1800
  Roanoke *(G-14259)*
Automated Welding Services Inc............ G 812 464-8784
  Evansville *(G-3903)*
B C Welding Inc... G 574 272-9008
  Granger *(G-6334)*
B&M Millwright Inc.................................... G 765 883-8177
  Russiaville *(G-14420)*
Bair Welding LLC....................................... G 260 485-1452
  Fort Wayne *(G-4788)*
Bare Bones Custom Welding................... G 502 773-2338
  New Albany *(G-12695)*
Bargers Welding Shop.............................. G 812 889-2095
  Lexington *(G-10974)*
Barks Wldg Sups & Farming Inc............ G 812 732-4366
  Corydon *(G-2487)*
Bates Machine Inc..................................... G 574 264-3997
  Elkhart *(G-3216)*
Beards Welding & Fabrication................ G 317 374-4779
  Franklin *(G-5713)*
Beasley Fabricating & McHnng.............. G 219 297-4000
  Goodland *(G-6079)*
Beasley Welding... G 812 883-2573
  Salem *(G-14474)*
Bel-Mar Products Corporation................ G 317 769-3262
  Whitestown *(G-16801)*
Bergren & Associates............................... G 219 852-1500
  Hammond *(G-6886)*
Best Equipment & Welding Co................ E 317 271-8652
  Indianapolis *(G-7616)*
Bever Wldg & Fabrication LLC............... G 765 524-4597
  Knightstown *(G-10194)*
Beyond Welding Inspection Inc.............. G 812 849-4410
  Mitchell *(G-12033)*
Boat Worx of Monticello........................... G 574 297-7961
  Monticello *(G-12139)*
Bobs Welding & Repair LLC................... G 765 744-4192
  Farmland *(G-4422)*
Bontrager Welding..................................... G 260 463-8950
  Lagrange *(G-10730)*
Bordners Aut Serv.................................... G 260 483-4064
  Fort Wayne *(G-4812)*
Brand Sheet Metal Works Inc................. G 765 284-5594
  Muncie *(G-12356)*

Brazing Preforms LLC.............................. G 317 705-6455
  Noblesville *(G-13047)*
Bryant Welding & Fabrication................. G 765 935-4281
  Richmond *(G-14101)*
Buchanan Iron Works Inc........................ G 219 785-4480
  Westville *(G-16757)*
Butlers General Repair............................. G 812 268-5631
  Sullivan *(G-15403)*
C & C Welding & Fabg Inc...................... G 812 384-8089
  Bloomfield *(G-741)*
C-Mar Welding.. G 260 410-8104
  New Haven *(G-12896)*
C-Way Tool and Die Inc........................... G 812 256-6341
  Charlestown *(G-1872)*
C&W Fabrication LLC............................... D 812 282-0488
  Jeffersonville *(G-9949)*
Calumet Welding Center Inc................... G 219 923-9353
  Griffith *(G-6798)*
Camm Machine and Welding LLC......... G 812 347-2040
  Ramsey *(G-14024)*
Campbells Welding & Machine.............. G 574 643-6705
  Royal Center *(G-14389)*
Carmel Welding and Sup Co Inc........... E 317 846-3493
  Carmel *(G-1582)*
Carmichael Welding Inc........................... G 812 825-5156
  Bloomfield *(G-742)*
Century Tool & Engr Inc.......................... G 317 685-0942
  Indianapolis *(G-7776)*
Certified Welding Company Inc............. G 765 522-3238
  Bainbridge *(G-561)*
Cesars Welding LLC.................................. G 317 938-8830
  Indianapolis *(G-7780)*
Chappos Inc.. G 219 942-8101
  Hobart *(G-7181)*
Chesterfield Tool & Engrg Inc................ E 765 378-5101
  Daleville *(G-2798)*
Chief Metal Works Inc.............................. G 765 932-2134
  Rushville *(G-14396)*
City Welding & Fabrication..................... G 765 569-5403
  Rockville *(G-14350)*
Clearspring Welding................................. G 260 463-8754
  Wolcottville *(G-16936)*
Cline Brothers Welding Inc..................... G 812 738-3537
  Corydon *(G-2491)*
Clinton Parker... G 219 877-5096
  Hammond *(G-6903)*
CM Welding Inc.. G 765 258-4024
  Frankfort *(G-5654)*
Collins Tl & Die Ltd Lblty Co................... G 812 273-4765
  Madison *(G-11211)*
Conley Welding Specialties Inc............. G 260 343-9051
  Kendallville *(G-10101)*
Constant Voltage Welding Inc................ G 765 339-7914
  New Richmond *(G-12977)*
Continental Welding Sup Corp............... G 812 232-2488
  Terre Haute *(G-15567)*
Country Welding... G 812 358-4402
  Seymour *(G-14640)*
Country Welding LLC................................ G 260 352-2938
  Silver Lake *(G-14919)*
Craig Welding and Mfg Inc..................... E 574 353-7912
  Mentone *(G-11472)*
Crow Welding and Fabrication............... G 317 619-3190
  Indianapolis *(G-7913)*
Custom Fab & Weld Inc........................... G 574 277-8877
  Granger *(G-6341)*
Custom Machining Services Inc............ G 219 462-6128
  Valparaiso *(G-15932)*
◆ Custom Machining Services Inc........ E 219 462-6128
  Valparaiso *(G-15933)*
D & J Fabrication and Welding.............. G 260 414-0300
  Auburn *(G-384)*

D & S Metal Fab & Welding LLC........... G 317 862-2503
  Indianapolis *(G-7942)*
D&M Repair and Welding LLC............... G 765 533-4565
  Markleville *(G-11368)*
Da-Mar Industries Inc............................... F 260 347-1662
  Kendallville *(G-10107)*
Dalam Welding LLC................................... G 260 593-0167
  Topeka *(G-15801)*
Darlage Metalworx LLC............................ G 812 341-5530
  Columbus *(G-2278)*
Davids Inc.. F 812 376-6870
  Columbus *(G-2280)*
Davis Custom Welding............................. G 765 847-2407
  Richmond *(G-14113)*
Davis Tool & Machine LLC..................... F 317 896-9278
  Westfield *(G-16684)*
Davron Fabricating.................................... G 765 339-7303
  New Richmond *(G-12978)*
DB&h Welding and Fabrication.............. G 765 617-8474
  Wilkinson *(G-16842)*
Diamond Welding....................................... G 765 741-2760
  Muncie *(G-12383)*
Dianne Forrest Welding Company........ G 219 381-1667
  Gary *(G-5922)*
Ditech Inc... E 812 379-9756
  Edinburgh *(G-3078)*
DLM Fabrication... G 219 393-8820
  Chesterton *(G-1920)*
Dons Specialty Welding LLC.................. G 260 557-3492
  Fort Wayne *(G-4925)*
Douglas Drudge... G 574 566-2210
  Claypool *(G-2052)*
Downeys Welding Repair........................ G 765 778-4727
  Pendleton *(G-13530)*
Drake Enterprises LLC............................. G 317 460-5991
  Pittsboro *(G-13644)*
Dransfield & Associates Wldg............... G 317 736-6281
  Franklin *(G-5726)*
Du-Mar Welding LLC................................ G 574 223-9889
  Rochester *(G-14287)*
Dunes Investment Inc............................... F 219 764-4270
  Portage *(G-13860)*
E & H Industrial Services LLC............... F 317 569-8819
  Carmel *(G-1616)*
E & H Industrial Services Inc................. E 317 670-4456
  Indianapolis *(G-8028)*
E Z Welding... G 574 892-6417
  Argos *(G-321)*
East Side Welding Inc............................. G 317 823-4065
  Indianapolis *(G-8039)*
Ebwa Industries Inc.................................. F 317 637-5860
  Indianapolis *(G-8044)*
Eckstein Welding & Fabrication............. G 812 934-2059
  Batesville *(G-586)*
Edco Welding and Hydraulic Inc........... F 317 783-2323
  Indianapolis *(G-8052)*
Eds Crane Service.................................... G 317 535-7385
  Whiteland *(G-16783)*
Egenolf Machine Inc................................. F 317 787-5301
  Indianapolis *(G-8061)*
Ellerbrock Welding LLC........................... G 559 978-2651
  New Castle *(G-12860)*
Epic Welding LLC...................................... G 502 554-6326
  Jeffersonville *(G-9979)*
Ernies Welding Shop LLC....................... G 812 326-2600
  Saint Anthony *(G-14427)*
▲ Ernstberger Enterprises Inc................ D 812 282-0488
  Jeffersonville *(G-9981)*
Evers Welding Company Inc.................. G 812 576-2232
  Guilford *(G-6829)*
Fabcreation... G 812 246-6222
  Sellersburg *(G-14593)*

SIC SECTION
76 MISCELLANEOUS REPAIR SERVICES

Fancil Welding LLC .... G 574 267-8627
  Warsaw *(G-16361)*
Farmway Welding .... G 574 498-6147
  Argos *(G-322)*
Fayette Welding Service Inc .... G 317 852-2929
  Brownsburg *(G-1366)*
▲ Flare Precision LLC .... E 260 490-1101
  Fort Wayne *(G-4985)*
Flynn Welding & Inspection LLC .... G 812 327-7437
  Solsberry *(G-14925)*
Four Star Welding .... G 574 825-3856
  Middlebury *(G-11716)*
Freedom Industrial Welding LLC .... G 812 686-9802
  Rockport *(G-14341)*
Friths Custom Weld .... G 812 937-2618
  Dale *(G-2790)*
Frye Welding LLC .... G 260 908-4766
  Kendallville *(G-10112)*
Fullenkamp Machine & Mfg Inc .... F 260 726-8345
  Portland *(G-13944)*
Galbreath Industrial Svcs LLC .... G 574 737-8159
  Logansport *(G-11074)*
Galloweld LLC .... G 219 215-2006
  Hammond *(G-6934)*
Gary Simons .... G 812 852-4316
  Osgood *(G-13408)*
Garys Welding & Machining LLC .... G 812 279-6780
  Bedford *(G-637)*
General Sheet Metal Works Inc .... E 574 288-0611
  South Bend *(G-15042)*
Georges Welding & Mech Svc .... G 219 989-0781
  Gary *(G-5941)*
Gibson Brothers Welding Inc .... F 765 948-5775
  Fairmount *(G-4410)*
Gilleys Repair and Welding .... G 812 374-6009
  Columbus *(G-2313)*
Gilleys Wldg & Fabrication LLC .... G 765 720-0554
  Fillmore *(G-4453)*
Gillum Machine & Tool Inc .... F 765 893-4426
  West Lebanon *(G-16648)*
GL Custom Welding LLC .... G 260 593-0253
  Topeka *(G-15807)*
Glens Mobile Welding .... G 219 663-2668
  Crown Point *(G-2689)*
Glicks Miracles Inc .... G 260 436-6671
  Fort Wayne *(G-5027)*
Gravelton Machine Shop Inc .... G 574 773-3413
  Nappanee *(G-12600)*
Greenwood Models Inc .... G 317 859-2988
  Greenwood *(G-6710)*
H & H Design & Tool Inc .... G 765 886-6199
  Economy *(G-3066)*
H & S Fabrication LLC .... G 260 724-3656
  Decatur *(G-2860)*
Hammond Machine Works Inc .... E 219 933-0479
  Hammond *(G-6942)*
Hartware Technologies .... G 317 439-5816
  Carmel *(G-1650)*
Hasty Welding .... G 765 482-8925
  Lebanon *(G-10895)*
Heise Welding Service .... G 574 652-4631
  Burrows *(G-1458)*
Hepton Welding LLC .... G 800 570-4238
  Nappanee *(G-12608)*
Herman Tool & Machine Inc .... F 574 594-5544
  Pierceton *(G-13632)*
Hershberger Welding .... G 574 642-3994
  Millersburg *(G-11813)*
Hetsco .... G 317 530-5331
  Greenwood *(G-6711)*
Hickory Corner Custom Wldg LLC ...... G 812 890-2926
  Vincennes *(G-16128)*

Highball Fabricators LLC .... G 574 831-6647
  New Paris *(G-12957)*
Highland Machine Tool Inc .... E 812 923-8884
  Floyds Knobs *(G-4681)*
Hill Top Welding LLC .... G 765 585-2549
  Attica *(G-351)*
Himes Casting Repair .... G 317 831-2571
  Mooresville *(G-12209)*
Hite Welding & Chassis .... G 765 741-0046
  Muncie *(G-12418)*
Hively Welding Company Inc .... G 219 843-5111
  Medaryville *(G-11458)*
Hochstetler Welding .... G 260 463-2793
  Lagrange *(G-10741)*
Hochstetler Welding LLC .... G 574 773-0600
  Nappanee *(G-12612)*
Hoke Weld .... G 812 569-0587
  Paoli *(G-13497)*
Hollers Welding Llc .... G 812 825-9834
  Bloomington *(G-878)*
Hoosier Machine & Welding Inc .... F 317 638-6286
  Indianapolis *(G-8410)*
Hoosier Spline Broach Corp .... E 765 452-8273
  Kokomo *(G-10281)*
Hoosier Welding .... G 765 521-4539
  New Castle *(G-12868)*
Hubbard Welding .... G 317 539-2758
  Clayton *(G-2059)*
Huehls Salcoating Lawncare LLC .... G 317 782-4069
  Indianapolis *(G-8433)*
Huffman Metalworks LLC .... G 574 835-0783
  Brookville *(G-1325)*
Hughes Welding and Fabrication .... G 812 385-2770
  Princeton *(G-13999)*
Huntington Sheet Metal Inc .... D 260 356-9011
  Huntington *(G-7323)*
I M S I Rental Svcs & Repair .... G 765 522-1223
  North Salem *(G-13254)*
▲ Impact Racing Inc .... D 317 852-3067
  Indianapolis *(G-8468)*
▲ Imperial Stamping Corporation .... D 574 294-3780
  Elkhart *(G-3419)*
▼ Indiana Industrial Svcs LLC .... D 317 769-6099
  Whitestown *(G-16810)*
Indiana Mobile Welding LLC .... G 317 771-8900
  Noblesville *(G-13102)*
Indianplis Wldg Fbrication LLC .... G 317 999-7856
  Indianapolis *(G-8512)*
▲ Industrial Mint Wldg Machining .... E 219 393-5531
  Kingsbury *(G-10179)*
Innovative Metalworks LLC .... G 260 839-0295
  Sidney *(G-14916)*
Innovative Welding LLC .... G 574 642-4537
  Goshen *(G-6175)*
Instate Welding Service Inc .... G 260 437-2894
  Fort Wayne *(G-5112)*
IWP LLC .... G 812 756-0303
  Holton *(G-7218)*
J & J Repair .... G 574 831-3075
  Goshen *(G-6178)*
J & J Welding .... G 219 872-7282
  Michigan City *(G-11627)*
▲ J & J Welding Inc .... E 812 838-4391
  Mount Vernon *(G-12303)*
J & R Welding .... G 574 862-1590
  Wakarusa *(G-16235)*
J A Smit Inc .... G 812 424-8141
  Evansville *(G-4133)*
James Conner Welding LLC .... G 765 230-0455
  Darlington *(G-2833)*
Jarrod Zachary Weld .... G 765 230-6424
  Crawfordsville *(G-2582)*

Jbs Welding .... G 317 946-8676
  Greenwood *(G-6718)*
Jerry Lambert .... G 765 378-7599
  Daleville *(G-2800)*
Jims Welding & Repair LLC .... G 765 564-1797
  Bringhurst *(G-1237)*
Jlr Mechanical Inc .... G 502 551-6879
  Clarksville *(G-2021)*
Joe Woodrow .... G 765 866-0436
  New Market *(G-12926)*
Johns Portable Siiop Weld .... G 574 936-1702
  Plymouth *(G-13789)*
Johns Welding and Fabrication .... G 574 936-1702
  Plymouth *(G-13790)*
Johnsons Welding Inc .... G 317 835-2438
  Boggstown *(G-1074)*
Jomar Machining & Fabg Inc .... E 574 825-9837
  Middlebury *(G-11728)*
JRS Custom Fabrication .... G 317 852-4964
  Brownsburg *(G-1378)*
K & B Trailer Sales & Mfg Inc .... G 574 946-4382
  Monterey *(G-12080)*
K & M Weld Fab .... G 219 362-3736
  Rolling Prairie *(G-14366)*
K C Cmponents Wldg Fabrication .... G 317 539-6067
  Greencastle *(G-6416)*
K-K Tool and Design Inc .... E 260 758-2940
  Markle *(G-11356)*
Kammerer Inc .... D 260 349-9098
  Kendallville *(G-10124)*
Kammerer Inc .... F 260 347-0389
  Kendallville *(G-10123)*
Kark Welding .... G 574 400-3989
  Granger *(G-6357)*
Kc Mig Welding LLC .... G 317 739-1051
  Fishers *(G-4553)*
Kevin Chumbley Enterprises .... G 502 548-2544
  Palmyra *(G-13481)*
Kleihege Welding Machine .... G 812 849-5056
  Mitchell *(G-12042)*
Klingerman Welding .... G 574 342-7375
  Bourbon *(G-1123)*
Knepps Custom Welding .... G 765 525-5130
  Saint Paul *(G-14466)*
Knip Welding .... G 219 987-5123
  Demotte *(G-2921)*
Kocsis Brothers Machine Co .... G 219 397-8400
  East Chicago *(G-3025)*
Kortzendorf Machine & Tool .... F 317 783-5449
  Greenwood *(G-6725)*
Kyle Fabrication & Welding LLC .... G 317 627-8537
  Franklin *(G-5751)*
Kz Welding .... G 260 350-7397
  Hudson *(G-7247)*
L & C Welding LLC .... G 260 593-3410
  Shipshewana *(G-14857)*
L & L Engineering Co Inc .... G 317 786-6886
  Beech Grove *(G-698)*
L & R Machine Co Inc .... G 317 787-7251
  Beech Grove *(G-699)*
L L Welding .... G 812 499-2961
  Tell City *(G-15506)*
L&N Welding LLC .... G 317 372-9554
  Danville *(G-2817)*
Lane Shady Welding LLC .... G 574 825-5553
  Middlebury *(G-11732)*
Larry Shorts Welding .... G 812 664-4910
  Owensville *(G-13470)*
Lauck Manufacturing Co Inc .... F 317 787-6269
  Indianapolis *(G-8727)*
Lawson Welding Shop .... G 812 448-8984
  Harmony *(G-7059)*

Employee Codes: A=Over 500 employees, B=251-500
C=101-250, D=51-100, E=20-50, F=10-19, G=1-9

76 MISCELLANEOUS REPAIR SERVICES

Lee Crawford Welding .... G 317 490-8009
  Indianapolis (G-8732)
Lengachers Welding LLC .... G 260 438-9033
  Grabill (G-6310)
Leons Fabrication Inc .... F 219 365-5272
  Schererville (G-14528)
Linden Machine Shop LLC .... G 765 339-7244
  Linden (G-11031)
Little Creations LLC .... G 765 868-9656
  Kokomo (G-10299)
Loading Dock Maintenance LLC .... G 260 424-3635
  Fort Wayne (G-5188)
Lockwood Welding Incorporated .... G 260 925-2086
  Waterloo (G-16523)
Lozano Wldg & Fabrication LLC .... G 812 550-1706
  Evansville (G-4175)
Lozano Wldg & Fabrication LLC .... G 812 629-2000
  Newburgh (G-13012)
M & M Service Co Wldg & Repr .... G 812 328-6195
  Freelandville (G-5803)
◆ Major Tool and Machine Inc .... C 317 636-6433
  Indianapolis (G-8820)
Manier Wldg & Fabrication LLC .... G 765 675-6078
  Tipton (G-15782)
◆ Manufacturing Technology Inc .... C 574 230-0258
  South Bend (G-15138)
Mapco .... G 765 795-3179
  Cloverdale (G-2088)
Martin Welding Shop .... G 574 862-2578
  Wakarusa (G-16240)
Martinez Custom Welding .... G 574 377-2251
  Warsaw (G-16391)
Mattox Machine & Welding Inc .... G 812 883-6460
  Salem (G-14490)
Matts Repair Inc .... F 219 696-6765
  Lowell (G-11171)
McGinn Tool & Engineering Co .... F 317 736-5512
  Franklin (G-5755)
Melching Machine Inc .... E 260 622-4315
  Ossian (G-13428)
Mengel Welding Company .... G 219 987-4079
  Demotte (G-2923)
Mervin M Burkholder .... G 574 862-4144
  Wakarusa (G-16241)
Metal Head Welding .... G 812 582-4234
  Winslow (G-16920)
Metcalf Engineering Inc .... G 765 342-6792
  Indianapolis (G-8893)
Mg Iron Welding Inc .... G 708 916-1344
  Hammond (G-6980)
Microtech Welding Corp .... G 574 268-5314
  Warsaw (G-16398)
Microtech Welding Corp .... F 260 490-4005
  Fort Wayne (G-5222)
Midwest Machining & Fabg .... F 219 924-0206
  Griffith (G-6814)
Midwest Welding Fabrication .... G 574 226-8306
  Elkhart (G-3542)
Midwest Welding Fabrication .... G 260 355-9354
  Warren (G-16301)
Mikesmobimech LLC .... G 317 753-0492
  Indianapolis (G-8918)
Miller Custom Metals LLC .... G 219 279-2671
  Wolcott (G-16934)
Miller Machine and Welding LLC .... G 812 882-7566
  Vincennes (G-16140)
Miller Welding .... G 765 628-2463
  Kokomo (G-10309)
Miller Welding LLC .... G 812 381-0800
  Bloomfield (G-753)
Millers Wldg & Mech Svcs Inc .... G 812 923-3359
  Pekin (G-13519)

Misner Welding & Cnstr Inc .... G 812 648-2980
  Dugger (G-2958)
Mitchum-Schaefer Inc .... E 317 546-4081
  Indianapolis (G-8935)
Modern Wldg & Boiler Works Inc .... G 812 232-5039
  Terre Haute (G-15647)
Monogram Metal Shop LLC .... G 260 797-3307
  Grabill (G-6316)
Montgomery Welding Inc .... G 812 486-3710
  Montgomery (G-12116)
▲ Moores Welding Service Inc .... G 260 627-2177
  Leo (G-10969)
Mooresville Welding Inc .... G 317 831-2265
  Mooresville (G-12225)
Morgan Nye .... G 812 738-4587
  Corydon (G-2505)
Morris Machine & Tool .... G 219 866-3018
  Rensselaer (G-14060)
Motsinger Auto Supply Inc .... G 317 782-8484
  Indianapolis (G-8960)
Mrrx Mobile Railcar Repair LLC .... G 812 251-0055
  Clinton (G-2072)
Mtm Machining Inc .... F 219 872-8677
  Michigan City (G-11642)
Mullets Welding LLC .... G 574 773-0189
  Nappanee (G-12629)
Ncs Welding Inc .... G 574 946-7485
  Winamac (G-16868)
Nector Machine & Fabricating .... G 219 322-6878
  Schererville (G-14536)
Neil Silke .... G 574 999-4866
  Fort Wayne (G-5260)
Newlins Wldg & Tank Maint LLC .... G 765 245-2741
  Montezuma (G-12082)
Newton Wldg & Fabrication LLC .... G 765 365-5129
  Crawfordsville (G-2594)
Nichols Mfg Co Inc .... F 219 696-8577
  Lowell (G-11174)
Nix & Company LLC .... G 219 595-5541
  Munster (G-12552)
Nk Welding Products Inc .... G 260 424-1901
  Fort Wayne (G-5273)
Noble County Welding Inc .... F 260 897-4082
  Avilla (G-490)
Northeast Enterprises Inc .... G 260 485-8011
  Fort Wayne (G-5275)
Northside Machining Inc .... G 812 683-3500
  Huntingburg (G-7288)
Northside Wldg Fabrication LLC .... G 317 844-2240
  Carmel (G-1708)
O & R Precision Grinding Inc .... E 260 368-9394
  Berne (G-721)
Oakes .... G 765 384-5317
  Marion (G-11322)
OBrien Jack & Pat Enterprises .... G 765 653-5070
  Greencastle (G-6422)
OHM Automotive LLC .... G 812 879-5455
  Bloomington (G-934)
On Site Welding & Maintenance .... G 812 755-4184
  Campbellsburg (G-1527)
On The Spot Welding LLC .... G 317 746-6699
  Indianapolis (G-9053)
On-Site Wldg Mllright Svcs LLC .... G 317 843-9773
  Carmel (G-1711)
Onyett Welding & Machine Inc .... G 812 582-2999
  Petersburg (G-13620)
Overton & Sons Tl & Die Co Inc .... E 317 831-4542
  Mooresville (G-12232)
Owens Machine & Welding .... G 574 583-9566
  Monticello (G-12163)
Pannell & Son Welding Inc .... G 765 948-3606
  Summitville (G-15427)

Parsons Welding Service .... G 812 597-4914
  Morgantown (G-12262)
Patrick Welding LLC .... G 812 557-7299
  New Albany (G-12791)
Peerless Pattern & Machine Co .... G 765 477-7719
  Lafayette (G-10666)
Penn Central Welding LLC .... G 260 463-2490
  Lagrange (G-10757)
Pfeiffer Welding & Fabrication .... G 765 434-1983
  Sharpsville (G-14711)
Phipps Sons Welding .... G 219 776-3810
  Gary (G-5994)
Portable Welding Solutions .... G 714 381-1690
  Indianapolis (G-9164)
▲ Powerweld Inc .... G 219 462-8700
  Valparaiso (G-16029)
Prairie Welding & Repair .... G 574 858-0509
  Leesburg (G-10959)
Precision Pulse LLC .... G 765 472-6002
  Peru (G-13593)
Precision Tubes Inc .... G 317 783-2339
  Indianapolis (G-9187)
Precision Welding Corp .... G 260 637-5514
  Huntertown (G-7261)
Professional Sndblst & Wldg .... G 574 355-9825
  Logansport (G-11103)
Pyramid Equipment .... G 219 778-4253
  Rolling Prairie (G-14370)
Pyramid Equipment Inc .... F 219 778-2591
  Rolling Prairie (G-14371)
Pyro Micro Welding LLC .... G 812 431-3330
  Evansville (G-4267)
Quality Die Set Corp .... E 574 967-4411
  Logansport (G-11104)
R & M Welding & Fabricating Sp .... G 812 295-9130
  Loogootee (G-11148)
R & R Welding .... G 260 424-3635
  Fort Wayne (G-5364)
Raber Buggy Shop LLC .... G 812 486-3789
  Montgomery (G-12120)
Red Forge Inc .... G 812 934-9641
  Batesville (G-602)
Ribbe Welding & Mfg Inc .... G 765 390-4044
  Kingman (G-10173)
Richard Myers Mllwrght .... G 765 883-8177
  Russiaville (G-14425)
Robert L Wehr .... G 812 482-2673
  Jasper (G-9905)
Robert Warrick .... G 765 294-4335
  Veedersburg (G-16090)
Roberts C Wldg Trck Hvy Equip .... G 812 623-1525
  Sunman (G-15443)
Rods Welding Shop .... G 812 859-4250
  Coal City (G-2101)
Roembke Mfg & Design Inc .... F 260 622-4030
  Ossian (G-13433)
Roger Baber Portable Wldg LLC .... G 574 859-4520
  Galveston (G-5853)
◆ Rogers Engineering and Mfg Co .... E 765 478-5444
  Cambridge City (G-1503)
Ron Mendenhall .... G 765 866-8283
  Ladoga (G-10509)
Rons General Repair .... G 765 732-3805
  West College Corner (G-16543)
Royers General Wldg & Repr LLC .... G 574 862-2707
  Goshen (G-6250)
Russs Custom Welding Corp .... G 765 795-5795
  Cloverdale (G-2096)
Rusty Shelden Duwane .... G 812 890-5780
  Washington (G-16508)
S-Tech Inc .... G 812 793-3506
  Crothersville (G-2645)

SIC SECTION
76 MISCELLANEOUS REPAIR SERVICES

Saliwnchik Sons Wldg Fbrction............. G..... 219 362-9009
  La Porte *(G-10476)*

Schenk and Sons Tree Svc Inc................ G..... 812 985-3954
  Mount Vernon *(G-12321)*

Schuler Precision Tool LLC.................. G..... 260 982-2704
  North Manchester *(G-13249)*

Seib Machine & Tool Co Inc.................. G..... 812 453-6174
  Evansville *(G-4304)*

Seiler Excavating Inc........................ G..... 260 925-0507
  Auburn *(G-422)*

Shank Welding Inc............................ G..... 260 897-2068
  Avilla *(G-495)*

Shipshe Welding............................... G..... 260 768-7267
  Shipshewana *(G-14886)*

Shoemaker Welding Company................. G..... 574 656-4412
  North Liberty *(G-13223)*

Shucks Wldg & Fabrication LLC............. G..... 317 409-8526
  Atlanta *(G-342)*

Sifford Custom Welding...................... G..... 765 969-3473
  Lynn *(G-11187)*

Six Mile Welding LLC........................ G..... 260 768-3126
  Lagrange *(G-10759)*

Skipper Rota Corporation................... F..... 708 331-0660
  Crown Point *(G-2758)*

Slabaugh Welding LLC........................ G..... 574 773-5410
  Milford *(G-11806)*

Smith Welding................................ G..... 765 438-4173
  Tipton *(G-15790)*

Snyders Prtble Wldg Fbrication............. G..... 574 258-4015
  Mishawaka *(G-12001)*

Southwest Welding LLC....................... G..... 574 862-4453
  Wakarusa *(G-16252)*

Sovern Machining & Welding................. G..... 812 392-2532
  Scipio *(G-14551)*

Speedcraft Prototypes....................... G..... 765 644-6449
  Anderson *(G-198)*

◆ **Star Engineering & Mch Co Inc**............ E..... 260 824-4825
  Bluffton *(G-1057)*

Starkey Welding Inc.......................... G..... 765 932-2005
  Rushville *(G-14413)*

Stephens Welding LLC........................ G..... 812 925-6033
  Chandler *(G-1867)*

Stolle Tool Incorporated................... F..... 765 935-5185
  Richmond *(G-14209)*

Stoltzfus Custom Welding LLC............... G..... 765 569-2362
  Rockville *(G-14356)*

Stonebraker Welding Servi................... G..... 574 453-7630
  Leesburg *(G-10961)*

Stout Plastic Weld........................... F..... 219 926-7622
  Chesterton *(G-1959)*

Stowers Wldg Indus Piping LLC.............. G..... 765 279-5002
  Kirklin *(G-10192)*

Stricker Welding LLC........................ G..... 812 207-3800
  Memphis *(G-11467)*

Strike & Walk Da Cup Wldg LLC.............. G..... 219 455-4683
  Hammond *(G-7015)*

Summerlot Engineered Pdts Inc.............. F..... 812 466-7266
  Rosedale *(G-14383)*

Summers Metals & More....................... G..... 812 689-7088
  Osgood *(G-13417)*

Sun Engineering Inc.......................... E..... 219 962-1191
  Lake Station *(G-10778)*

SW Watkins Limited........................... D..... 260 484-4844
  Fort Wayne *(G-5462)*

Swags Welding Services LLC................. G..... 260 417-7510
  Churubusco *(G-1989)*

T & E Welding Inc............................ F..... 812 324-0140
  Petersburg *(G-13627)*

T K Sales & Service.......................... G..... 219 962-8982
  Gary *(G-6017)*

Tactical Wldg Fabrication LLC.............. G..... 317 457-5340
  Indianapolis *(G-9547)*

TAs Welding and Grn Svcs LLC............... G..... 765 210-4274
  Wabash *(G-16216)*

Taylor Welding............................... G..... 765 659-2955
  Frankfort *(G-5697)*

Teck Machine LLC............................. G..... 574 773-7004
  Nappanee *(G-12648)*

Ted Bostick................................... G..... 765 458-6555
  Liberty *(G-10999)*

Tegeler Welding Services LLC............... G..... 765 409-6446
  Richmond *(G-14213)*

Terhune Welding Shop........................ G..... 260 565-3446
  Bluffton *(G-1063)*

Terrys Welding Inc........................... G..... 765 564-3331
  Delphi *(G-2909)*

Tfp Inc....................................... G..... 219 513-9572
  Griffith *(G-6820)*

Thomas Cubit Inc............................. G..... 219 933-0566
  Hammond *(G-7019)*

Thrasher Welding and Mch Sp................ G..... 260 475-5550
  Angola *(G-298)*

Titus Inc..................................... F..... 574 936-3345
  Plymouth *(G-13817)*

TNT Fabricating LLC......................... G..... 574 540-2465
  Plymouth *(G-13819)*

Todds Wldg & Stl Fabrication............... G..... 812 824-2407
  Bloomington *(G-990)*

Toolcraft LLC................................ E..... 260 749-0454
  Fort Wayne *(G-5494)*

Total Concepts Design Inc................... D..... 812 752-6534
  Scottsburg *(G-14582)*

Town Welder................................... G..... 219 945-1311
  Crown Point *(G-2767)*

Tradeline Fabricating Inc................... E..... 812 637-1444
  Lawrenceburg *(G-10862)*

Tri-Esco Inc.................................. F..... 765 446-7937
  Colburn *(G-2112)*

Tube Processing Corp........................ G..... 317 264-7760
  Indianapolis *(G-9657)*

▲ **Tube Processing Corp**..................... B..... 317 787-1321
  Indianapolis *(G-9658)*

Turn & Burn Welding Inc..................... G..... 812 766-0641
  Otwell *(G-13458)*

Turners Machining Specialties Inc.......... E..... 812 372-9472
  Columbus *(G-2407)*

▲ **Tuttle Aluminum & Bronze Inc**............. D..... 317 842-2420
  Fishers *(G-4618)*

Two Guys Mechanical Contrs Inc............. E..... 574 946-7671
  Winamac *(G-16878)*

Tyco Welding.................................. G..... 812 988-8770
  Nashville *(G-12682)*

Ultimate Wldg Fabrication LLC.............. G..... 317 379-2676
  Noblesville *(G-13188)*

United Industrial & Wldg LLC............... G..... 812 526-4050
  Columbus *(G-2410)*

United Tool Company Inc..................... F..... 260 563-3143
  Wabash *(G-16219)*

Uptgraft Welding............................. G..... 260 824-4624
  Bluffton *(G-1065)*

Uskert Welding................................ G..... 219 759-2794
  Valparaiso *(G-16073)*

Velazquez Wldg Solutions LLC............... G..... 812 391-9892
  New Albany *(G-12822)*

Vincennes Welding Co Inc.................... F..... 812 882-9682
  Vincennes *(G-16160)*

Vision Machine Works Inc.................... G..... 574 259-6500
  Mishawaka *(G-12022)*

Weavers Welding............................... G..... 812 438-3425
  Aurora *(G-459)*

Welders Choice................................ G..... 219 880-5470
  Hammond *(G-7032)*

Welding Center................................ G..... 219 921-1509
  Chesterton *(G-1968)*

Welding Plus LLC.............................. G..... 317 902-0883
  Indianapolis *(G-9746)*

Welding Shop.................................. G..... 260 593-2544
  Ligonier *(G-11029)*

Welding Unlimited LLC....................... G..... 812 582-0777
  Petersburg *(G-13628)*

Weldors Inc................................... G..... 765 289-9074
  Muncie *(G-12518)*

Welshco LLC................................... G..... 219 767-2786
  Union Mills *(G-15869)*

West Vigo Machine Shop Inc................. F..... 812 533-1961
  West Terre Haute *(G-16658)*

Whites Welding & Machining LLC............. G..... 765 987-7984
  Straughn *(G-15400)*

William F Shirley............................. G..... 812 426-2599
  Evansville *(G-4385)*

Williams Weld Service LLC................... G..... 812 865-3298
  Orleans *(G-13383)*

Wilson Machine Shop Inc..................... G..... 812 392-2774
  Elizabethtown *(G-3134)*

Wilson Welding & Piping LLC................ G..... 317 397-4865
  Greenwood *(G-6781)*

Wrib Manufacturing Inc...................... G..... 765 294-2841
  Veedersburg *(G-16092)*

Wws Fabricating Inc.......................... G..... 765 506-7341
  Marion *(G-11352)*

X-Y Tool and Die Inc......................... D..... 260 357-3365
  Laotto *(G-10812)*

Yoders & Sons Repair Shop................... G..... 260 593-2727
  Topeka *(G-15824)*

York & Sons Welding LLC..................... G..... 812 577-6352
  Moores Hill *(G-12189)*

Zimmer Welding LLC........................... G..... 317 632-5212
  Indianapolis *(G-9812)*

Zionsville Towing Inc........................ G..... 317 873-4550
  Zionsville *(G-17064)*

7694 Armature rewinding shops

Altek Inc..................................... G..... 812 385-2561
  Princeton *(G-13981)*

Atv Parts Barn LLC........................... G..... 812 251-6113
  Brazil *(G-1133)*

B & D Electric Inc........................... F..... 812 254-2122
  Shoals *(G-14903)*

Best Electric Motor Service................. G..... 765 583-2408
  Otterbein *(G-13450)*

Black Equipment Company S Inc............... C..... 812 477-6481
  Evansville *(G-3934)*

Boone County Electric Inc................... G..... 765 482-1430
  Lebanon *(G-10880)*

Buffington Electric Motors.................. G..... 574 935-5453
  Plymouth *(G-13762)*

C & L Electric Motor Repr Inc............... G..... 574 533-2643
  Elkhart *(G-3243)*

C&C Electric Motors LLC..................... G..... 574 656-3898
  North Liberty *(G-13215)*

Columbus Industrial Electric................ F..... 812 372-8414
  Columbus *(G-2244)*

Eemsco Inc.................................... E..... 812 426-2224
  Evansville *(G-4028)*

Electric Motor Services Inc................. E..... 219 931-2850
  Hammond *(G-6922)*

Electric Mtr Repr & Rewind Inc.............. G..... 812 284-5059
  Jeffersonville *(G-9974)*

Electrical Motor Products Inc............... G..... 877 455-1599
  Fort Wayne *(G-4944)*

Electrik Connection Inc..................... G..... 219 362-4581
  La Porte *(G-10404)*

Electro Corp................................. F..... 219 393-5571
  Kingsbury *(G-10177)*

Enyart Electric Motor Repr Inc.............. G..... 574 288-4731
  South Bend *(G-15017)*

Employee Codes: A=Over 500 employees, B=251-500
C=101-250, D=51-100, E=20-50, F=10-19, G=1-9

76 MISCELLANEOUS REPAIR SERVICES

Eps Enterprises Inc.................................. G 260 493-4913
  Fort Wayne *(G-4957)*
Evans Enterprises LLC............................. G 317 986-2073
  Indianapolis *(G-8141)*
Flanders Inc.. F 812 867-7421
  Evansville *(G-4075)*
◆ Flanders Electric Motor Service LLC..C 812 867-7421
  Evansville *(G-4076)*
Flanders Electric Mtr Svc LLC................ E 812 867-4014
  Evansville *(G-4077)*
Flanders Electric Mtr Svc LLC................ D 812 421-4300
  Evansville *(G-4078)*
Gary Electric Motor Service Co.............. F 219 884-6555
  Valparaiso *(G-15953)*
Gorrepati Service Systems...................... G 317 299-7590
  Indianapolis *(G-8308)*
Gottman Electric Company Inc............... G 812 838-0037
  Mount Vernon *(G-12297)*
Harrison Electric Inc.............................. F 219 879-0444
  Michigan City *(G-11620)*
Hoosier Industrial Electric..................... F 812 346-2232
  North Vernon *(G-13278)*
▲ Horner Apg LLC................................. F 317 916-4274
  Indianapolis *(G-8414)*
Horner Electric Inc................................ E 317 639-4261
  Indianapolis *(G-8415)*
Horner Industrial Services Inc................ G 260 434-1189
  Fort Wayne *(G-5083)*
Horner Industrial Services Inc................ G 812 466-5281
  Terre Haute *(G-15607)*
Horner Industrial Services Inc................ C 317 639-4261
  Indianapolis *(G-8416)*
Ies Subsidiary Holdings Inc.................... G 219 937-0100
  Hammond *(G-6953)*
Ies Subsidiary Holdings Inc.................... G 330 830-3500
  South Bend *(G-15074)*
Illiana Electrical Svcs LLC...................... G 219 276-1743
  Valparaiso *(G-15969)*
Illiana Indus Elc Mtr Svcs Inc................. F 219 286-3654
  Valparaiso *(G-15970)*
Indian Creek Outdoor Power LLC........... G 812 597-3055
  Morgantown *(G-12258)*
Industrial Motor & Tool LLC................... G 574 534-8282
  Goshen *(G-6174)*
Integrated Power Services LLC.............. F 812 665-4400
  Poseyville *(G-13979)*
Jasper Electric Motor Inc....................... F 812 482-1660
  Jasper *(G-9851)*
Jasper Electric Motor Inc....................... F 812 482-1660
  Jasper *(G-9850)*
Kesters Electric Motor Svc LLC.............. G 574 269-2889
  Warsaw *(G-16382)*
Kiemle-Hankins Company...................... F 219 213-2643
  Crown Point *(G-2709)*
Kirby Risk Corporation........................... G 765 643-3384
  Anderson *(G-143)*
Kirby Risk Corporation........................... D 765 423-4205
  Lafayette *(G-10622)*
Kirby Risk Corporation........................... F 765 664-5185
  Marion *(G-11304)*
Kirby Risk Corporation........................... F 765 254-5460
  Muncie *(G-12435)*
▲ Kirby Risk Corporation...................... D 765 448-4567
  Lafayette *(G-10623)*
Kochs Electric Inc.................................. E 317 639-5624
  Indianapolis *(G-8700)*
Kw Maintenance Services LLC............... E 574 232-2051
  South Bend *(G-15113)*
Machine Rebuilders & Service................ F 260 482-8168
  Fort Wayne *(G-5197)*
Magnetech Industrial Svcs Inc............... G 219 937-0100
  Hammond *(G-6975)*

McBroom Electric Co Inc........................ D 317 926-3451
  Indianapolis *(G-8860)*
Mills Electric Co Inc............................... G 219 931-3114
  Hammond *(G-6982)*
Mohler Technology Inc........................... E 812 897-2900
  Boonville *(G-1093)*
Morgan Automotive................................ G 765 378-0593
  Chesterfield *(G-1897)*
Motor Electric Inc................................... G 574 294-7123
  Elkhart *(G-3556)*
Northern Electric Company Inc.............. E 574 289-7791
  South Bend *(G-15172)*
P H C Industries Inc.............................. G
  Fort Wayne *(G-5291)*
Peter Austin Co...................................... G 765 288-6397
  Muncie *(G-12474)*
Phase Three Electric Inc........................ G 812 945-9922
  New Albany *(G-12793)*
▲ Phazpak Inc.. G 260 692-6416
  Monroe *(G-12061)*
▲ Precision Electric Inc........................ E 574 256-1000
  Mishawaka *(G-11977)*
Pres-Del Electric Inc............................. G 219 884-3146
  Gary *(G-5995)*
Q P Inc.. F 574 295-6884
  Elkhart *(G-3626)*
Quality Forklift Repair LLC.................... G 574 702-5733
  Rochester *(G-14313)*
Quality Repair Services Inc................... F 317 881-0205
  Greenwood *(G-6756)*
Reliable Indus Sls & Svc LLC................. G 219 929-8295
  Valparaiso *(G-16037)*
Ritchie Electric Motor Co LLC............... G 219 866-5185
  Rensselaer *(G-14067)*
Robinson Industries Inc......................... E 317 867-3214
  Westfield *(G-16724)*
Ronald Holloway.................................... G 574 223-6825
  Plymouth *(G-13812)*
Spina Enterprises Inc............................ G 219 879-0444
  Michigan City *(G-11670)*
Tipton Electric Motor Services.............. G 765 963-3380
  Sharpsville *(G-14713)*
Tipton Engrg Elc Mtr Svcs Inc................ G 765 963-3380
  Sharpsville *(G-14714)*
Wabash Valley Motor & Mch Inc............. G 812 466-7400
  Terre Haute *(G-15743)*
Wagner Electric Fort Wayne Inc............. G 260 484-5532
  Fort Wayne *(G-5538)*
Wright Repairs Inc................................. F 765 674-3300
  Gas City *(G-6042)*

7699 Repair services, nec

3-T Corp.. F 812 424-7878
  Evansville *(G-3856)*
Accu-Built Tooling and Weld.................. G 574 825-7878
  Goshen *(G-6087)*
Altek Inc... G 812 385-2561
  Princeton *(G-13981)*
Aluminum Wldg & Mch Works Inc.......... G 219 787-8066
  Chesterton *(G-1901)*
▲ American Flame LLC......................... D 260 459-1703
  Fort Wayne *(G-4754)*
American Machine & Fabg Co Inc.......... G 812 944-4136
  New Albany *(G-12688)*
American Natural Resources LLC......... F 219 922-6444
  Griffith *(G-6790)*
American Pallet & Recycl Inc................. G 219 322-4391
  Dyer *(G-2966)*
Amos D Graber & Sons........................... F 260 749-0526
  New Haven *(G-12892)*
Applied Metals & Mch Works Inc........... E 260 424-4834
  Fort Wayne *(G-4766)*

Automation Consultants Inc................... G 502 552-4995
  Floyds Knobs *(G-4669)*
B & C Machining Inc............................... E 219 866-7091
  Rensselaer *(G-14045)*
B & H Electric and Supply Inc................ E 812 522-5607
  Seymour *(G-14630)*
Bastian Automation Engrg LLC.............. D 317 467-2583
  Greenfield *(G-6468)*
Bickels Garage & Welding...................... G 765 853-5457
  Modoc *(G-12050)*
Bikes-N-Trikes Incorporated................. G 317 835-4544
  Boggstown *(G-1072)*
Bio Harness Shop................................... G 812 486-2919
  Montgomery *(G-12087)*
Black Equipment Company S Inc............ C 812 477-6481
  Evansville *(G-3934)*
Blasted Works... G 574 583-3211
  Monticello *(G-12138)*
Bonnell Grain Handling Inc................... E 574 595-7827
  Star City *(G-15396)*
Boyd Machine and Repair Co................. E 260 635-2195
  Kimmell *(G-10169)*
Broadway Auto Glass LLC...................... F 219 884-5277
  Merrillville *(G-11493)*
Buffington Electric Motors..................... G 574 935-5453
  Plymouth *(G-13762)*
Buhrt Engineering & Cnstr..................... E 574 267-3720
  Warsaw *(G-16331)*
Bulk Truck & Transport Service............. E 812 866-2155
  Hanover *(G-7040)*
C & P Distributing LLC.......................... F 574 256-1138
  Mishawaka *(G-11857)*
C & T Engineering Inc........................... F
  Seymour *(G-14635)*
Certified Clipper Inc.............................. G 317 894-3787
  Greenfield *(G-6478)*
Cindon Inc... F 812 853-5450
  Newburgh *(G-12998)*
Clm Pallet Recycling Inc........................ G 317 485-4080
  Fortville *(G-5589)*
Color Glo.. G 812 926-2639
  Aurora *(G-441)*
Complete Controls Inc........................... G 260 489-0852
  Fort Wayne *(G-4868)*
Cox Cleaning Services........................... G 260 804-9001
  Fort Wayne *(G-4880)*
Cummins Repair Inc............................... G 260 632-4800
  Harlan *(G-7053)*
▲ Customer 1st LLC.............................. G 877 768-9970
  Pekin *(G-13514)*
CXR Company Inc.................................. F 574 269-6020
  Warsaw *(G-16341)*
D&D Automation Inc............................... G 812 299-1045
  Terre Haute *(G-15573)*
Dave Brown Customs LLC..................... G 812 727-5560
  Palmyra *(G-13479)*
▲ Decatur Mold Tool and Engrg............ C 812 346-5188
  North Vernon *(G-13266)*
Deer Country Equipment LLC................ E 812 522-1922
  Seymour *(G-14646)*
Dependable Rubber Industrial.............. G 765 447-5654
  Lafayette *(G-10569)*
Dx 4 LLC... F 260 749-0632
  Fort Wayne *(G-4935)*
Eis Packaging Machinery Inc................. G 574 870-0087
  Logansport *(G-11072)*
Evansville Assn For The Blind............... C 812 422-1181
  Evansville *(G-4047)*
Fabcreation.. G 812 246-6222
  Sellersburg *(G-14593)*
Fairway Custom Golf.............................. G 317 842-0017
  Fishers *(G-4521)*

SIC SECTION
76 MISCELLANEOUS REPAIR SERVICES

Fayette Welding Service Inc.................. G 317 852-2929
   Brownsburg *(G-1366)*

Fibertech Plastics LLC......................... D 812 983-2642
   Elberfeld *(G-3113)*

Fidelity Dental Handpiece Svc................ G 317 254-0277
   Indianapolis *(G-8185)*

Fire Apparatus Service Inc.................... G 219 985-0788
   Gary *(G-5933)*

▲ Five Star Hydraulics Inc.................... E 219 762-1619
   Portage *(G-13866)*

Flamespray Machine Service.................. G 260 726-6236
   Portland *(G-13942)*

Flanders Electric Mtr Svc LLC................. D 812 421-4300
   Evansville *(G-4078)*

Fourman Enterprises Inc...................... F 812 546-5734
   Hope *(G-7225)*

Gary Bridge and Iron Co Inc................... G 219 884-3792
   Gary *(G-5936)*

Gary M Brown.................................. G 765 831-2536
   New Castle *(G-12864)*

Goudy Bros Boiler Co Inc...................... G 765 459-4416
   Kokomo *(G-10271)*

Goulding & Wood Inc........................... F 317 637-5222
   Indianapolis *(G-8309)*

Gravelton Machine Shop Inc................... G 574 773-3413
   Nappanee *(G-12600)*

Grayson Thermal Systems Corp................ C 317 739-3290
   Franklin *(G-5736)*

Green Stream Company........................ C 574 293-1949
   Elkhart *(G-3391)*

Griffin Clark LLC................................ G 765 491-9059
   Bloomington *(G-871)*

Halyard Corporation........................... E 219 515-2820
   Portage *(G-13873)*

Hamilton Bros Inc.............................. F 317 241-2571
   Indianapolis *(G-8353)*

Hayward & Sams LLP........................... G 260 351-4166
   Stroh *(G-15401)*

Heads First..................................... G 219 785-4100
   Westville *(G-16761)*

Heartland Filled Machine LLC.................. G 574 223-6931
   Rochester *(G-14295)*

Highball Fabricators LLC....................... G 574 831-6647
   New Paris *(G-12957)*

Hmt LLC.. G 219 736-9901
   Merrillville *(G-11522)*

Hobbs Auto Diagnostics & Repr............... G 765 606-1490
   Anderson *(G-127)*

Hoosier Buggy Shop............................ G 260 593-2192
   Topeka *(G-15810)*

Horner Industrial Services Inc................. G 260 434-1189
   Fort Wayne *(G-5083)*

Horner Industrial Services Inc................. G 812 466-5281
   Terre Haute *(G-15607)*

Horner Industrial Services Inc................. C 317 639-4261
   Indianapolis *(G-8416)*

Hunter Venetian Blind Co...................... G 812 471-1100
   Evansville *(G-4113)*

Image Plus Original LLC........................ G 800 226-7316
   Indianapolis *(G-8463)*

Indiana Handpiece Repair Inc.................. G 260 436-0765
   Fort Wayne *(G-5100)*

Indiana Mobile Welding LLC.................... G 317 771-8900
   Noblesville *(G-13102)*

Industrial Controls Corp....................... G 219 884-1141
   Gary *(G-5961)*

Industrial Hydraulics Inc....................... E 317 247-4421
   Indianapolis *(G-8518)*

Iron Hawg..................................... G 317 462-0991
   Greenfield *(G-6517)*

J & J Pallet Corp............................... E 812 944-8670
   New Albany *(G-12750)*

▲ Jay Orner Sons Billiard Co Inc............... G 317 243-0046
   Indianapolis *(G-8618)*

Jeda Equipment Services Inc.................. G 317 842-9377
   Fishers *(G-4550)*

JL Walter & Associates Inc.................... D 317 524-3600
   Indianapolis *(G-8628)*

K & S Farm Machine Shop Inc.................. F 812 663-8567
   Greensburg *(G-6610)*

▲ K M Specialty Pumps Inc.................... F 812 925-3000
   Chandler *(G-1863)*

Ken Kowalski.................................. G 574 633-4427
   South Bend *(G-15098)*

Kochs Electric Inc.............................. E 317 639-5624
   Indianapolis *(G-8700)*

Line-X.. G 812 491-9475
   Evansville *(G-4170)*

Lomatt Dynamics LLC.......................... G 574 500-2517
   Leesburg *(G-10957)*

Macallister Machinery Co Inc.................. C 260 483-6469
   Fort Wayne *(G-5195)*

Mantra Enterprise LLC......................... G 201 428-8709
   Fishers *(G-4561)*

Markle Music................................... G 812 847-2103
   Linton *(G-11038)*

Merss Corporation............................. G 317 632-7299
   Indianapolis *(G-8879)*

Metal Fab Engineering Inc..................... E 574 278-7150
   Winamac *(G-16867)*

Mid America Powered Vehicles................ G 812 925-7745
   Chandler *(G-1864)*

Mikesmobimech LLC........................... G 317 753-0492
   Indianapolis *(G-8918)*

Millers Wood Specialties Inc................... E 765 478-3248
   Cambridge City *(G-1499)*

Mnbkc LLC..................................... F 317 956-6558
   Indianapolis *(G-8939)*

Mnt Delivery Company......................... G 574 518-6250
   Osceola *(G-13399)*

Morgan Automotive............................ G 765 378-0593
   Chesterfield *(G-1897)*

Morris Mold and Machine Co................... G 317 923-6653
   Indianapolis *(G-8955)*

Motion & Control Entps LLC................... F 219 844-4224
   Munster *(G-12551)*

Mrrx Mobile Railcar Repair LLC................. G 812 251-0055
   Clinton *(G-2072)*

Mtr Machining Concept Inc.................... G 260 587-3381
   Ashley *(G-334)*

◆ Nap Asset Holdings Ltd...................... D 812 482-2000
   Jasper *(G-9894)*

Nestor Sales LLC............................... G 574 295-5535
   Elkhart *(G-3566)*

Newlins Wldg & Tank Maint LLC................ G 765 245-2741
   Montezuma *(G-12082)*

Odyssey Machine Inc.......................... G 812 951-1160
   Georgetown *(G-6072)*

Orton-Mccullough Crane Company............ G 260 356-7900
   Huntington *(G-7347)*

Ottosons Industries Inc........................ G 219 365-8330
   Cedar Lake *(G-1835)*

Peerless Machinery Inc........................ G 574 210-5990
   South Bend *(G-15188)*

Perry Products Inc............................. G 260 316-8816
   Angola *(G-283)*

Pgc Mulch LLC................................. G 812 455-0700
   Evansville *(G-4236)*

Phil & Son Inc.................................. G 219 663-5757
   Crown Point *(G-2730)*

Power Plant Service Inc........................ E 260 432-6716
   Fort Wayne *(G-5328)*

Progress Group Inc............................ D 219 322-3700
   Schererville *(G-14539)*

Protron LLC.................................... G 765 313-1595
   Anderson *(G-181)*

Pwi Corp....................................... E 574 646-2015
   Nappanee *(G-12638)*

Randall Corp................................... G 812 425-7122
   Evansville *(G-4272)*

Rankin Pump and Supply Co Inc............... G 812 238-2535
   Terre Haute *(G-15675)*

Recovery Force LLC........................... G 866 604-6458
   Fishers *(G-4591)*

▲ Refractory Service Corporation.............. E 219 397-7108
   East Chicago *(G-3038)*

Reynolds & Co Inc............................. E 812 232-5313
   Terre Haute *(G-15681)*

Robert J Matt.................................. G 317 831-2400
   Mooresville *(G-12239)*

Rx Honing Machine Corp....................... G 574 259-1606
   Mishawaka *(G-11989)*

S & R Welding Inc.............................. G 317 710-0360
   Indianapolis *(G-9353)*

▲ S C Pryor Inc................................ F 317 352-1281
   Indianapolis *(G-9354)*

Skips Bumper Repair.......................... G 773 289-2255
   Gary *(G-6010)*

Smiths Small Engines Inc...................... G 812 232-1318
   Terre Haute *(G-15699)*

Southlake Machine Corp....................... G 219 285-6150
   Morocco *(G-12270)*

Spectrum Services Inc......................... G 574 272-7605
   Granger *(G-6380)*

Standard Change-Makers Inc.................. F 317 899-6955
   Indianapolis *(G-9492)*

Stanley Black & Decker Inc.................... D 860 225-5111
   Indianapolis *(G-9495)*

Storageworks Inc.............................. G 317 577-3511
   Fishers *(G-4607)*

Sunburst Stained Glass Co Inc................. G 812 853-0460
   Newburgh *(G-13024)*

Sunrise Wood Products LLC.................... G 260 463-4822
   Lagrange *(G-10765)*

Surclean Inc................................... F 248 791-2226
   Brownsburg *(G-1405)*

T & L Sharpening Inc........................... F 574 583-3868
   Monticello *(G-12172)*

T & M Equipment Company Inc................. F 317 293-9255
   Indianapolis *(G-9543)*

T & M Equipment Company Inc................. E 219 942-2299
   Merrillville *(G-11563)*

T & T Hydraulics Inc........................... G 765 548-2355
   Rosedale *(G-14384)*

Tank Construction & Service Co............... F 317 509-6294
   Whitestown *(G-16823)*

Tarpenning-Lafollette Co Inc.................. E 317 780-1500
   Indianapolis *(G-9553)*

▲ Technical Weighing Svcs Inc................. E 219 924-3366
   Griffith *(G-6819)*

Thornes Homes Inc........................... G 812 275-4656
   Bedford *(G-678)*

Tk Elevator Corporation....................... D 317 595-1125
   Indianapolis *(G-9612)*

Todds Hydrlcs RPR & Stl Fbrct................ G 812 466-3457
   Terre Haute *(G-15733)*

Tradebe Environmental Svcs LLC.............. E 800 388-7242
   Merrillville *(G-11568)*

Tradebe GP.................................... A 800 388-7242
   East Chicago *(G-3045)*

Tradebe Industrial Svcs LLC................... D 800 388-7242
   East Chicago *(G-3046)*

Tri-State Valve LLC............................ F 901 388-1550
   Indianapolis *(G-9638)*

▼ Trifab & Construction Inc.................... G 219 845-1300
   Hammond *(G-7024)*

Employee Codes: A=Over 500 employees, B=251-500
C=101-250, D=51-100, E=20-50, F=10-19, G=1-9

76 MISCELLANEOUS REPAIR SERVICES

Troy Meggitt Inc... D 812 547-7071
  Troy *(G-15843)*
Twigg Corporation.................................... G 765 342-7126
  Martinsville *(G-11431)*
U S Accu-Met Inc....................................... G 765 533-4219
  Middletown *(G-11779)*
Uncle Alberts Amplifier Inc..................... G 317 845-3037
  Indianapolis *(G-9676)*
Valley Scale Company LLC..................... F 812 282-5269
  Clarksville *(G-2041)*
Valley Sharpening Inc.............................. G 574 674-9077
  Osceola *(G-13405)*
Wall Control Services Inc........................ G 260 450-6411
  Fort Wayne *(G-5542)*
▲ Walter Piano Company Inc................... F 574 266-0615
  Elkhart *(G-3779)*
Wdb Enterprises Inc................................. F 219 844-4224
  Hammond *(G-7031)*
Whitcraft Welding...................................... G 574 867-6021
  Grovertown *(G-6825)*
Whitlocks Pressure Wash........................ F 765 825-5868
  Connersville *(G-2475)*
Wright Implement I LLC......................... G 812 522-1922
  Seymour *(G-14707)*
X-L Box Inc... F 219 763-3736
  Valparaiso *(G-16082)*
Zionsville Towing Inc................................ G 317 873-4550
  Zionsville *(G-17064)*

78 MOTION PICTURES

7812 Motion picture and video production

Bird Publishing Company....................... G 219 462-6330
  Valparaiso *(G-15915)*
Heart Breaker Sales LLC......................... G 765 489-4048
  Hagerstown *(G-6837)*
Motion Engineering Company Inc......... G 317 804-7990
  Westfield *(G-16712)*
National Fdrtion State High SC............. E 317 972-6900
  Indianapolis *(G-8988)*
Sizzlin Sound Productions LLC............. G 765 376-0129
  Crawfordsville *(G-2615)*
Technology Cons Group LLC................ G 219 525-4064
  Merrillville *(G-11565)*
Top In Sound Inc...................................... G 765 649-8111
  Anderson *(G-207)*

7819 Services allied to motion pictures

Hard Hustla Muzik LLC............................ G 812 214-1995
  Evansville *(G-4103)*

7822 Motion picture and tape distribution

Sweetwater Sound LLC.......................... G 260 432-8176
  Fort Wayne *(G-5463)*

7841 Video tape rental

Royal Inc.. F 812 424-4925
  Evansville *(G-4295)*

79 AMUSEMENT AND RECREATION SERVICES

7911 Dance studios, schools, and halls

Tanguero Inc... G 415 236-2642
  Bloomington *(G-983)*

7922 Theatrical producers and services

Hard Hustla Muzik LLC............................ G 812 214-1995
  Evansville *(G-4103)*
Mid-America Sound Corporation........... F 317 947-9880
  Greenfield *(G-6528)*

Patchwork Costumes LLC....................... G 317 750-6162
  Indianapolis *(G-9097)*
Trinity Cmmnications Group Inc............ G 260 484-1029
  Fort Wayne *(G-5508)*
Whiteco Industries Inc............................. A 219 769-6601
  Merrillville *(G-11572)*

7929 Entertainers and entertainment groups

Anderson Shykia...................................... G 773 304-6852
  Gary *(G-5894)*
Axecalibur LLC.. G 812 822-1157
  Bloomington *(G-788)*
CJS Muzic Company-The Spot LLC....... G 219 487-9873
  Hammond *(G-6901)*
Entertainment Express............................. G 219 763-3610
  Portage *(G-13861)*
Hard Hustla Muzik LLC............................ G 812 214-1995
  Evansville *(G-4103)*
Heart Breaker Sales LLC......................... G 765 489-4048
  Hagerstown *(G-6837)*
Lions Quarter LLC................................... G 219 932-5531
  Hammond *(G-6972)*
Michael Duff... G 812 336-8994
  Bloomington *(G-918)*
Roajer LLC... G 317 348-4640
  Carmel *(G-1742)*
Tanguero Inc... G 415 236-2642
  Bloomington *(G-983)*
Tyler Truss Systems Inc.......................... F 765 221-5050
  Pendleton *(G-13560)*

7941 Sports clubs, managers, and promoters

Athletes Management & Services........... G 317 925-8200
  Indianapolis *(G-7559)*
Diamond Hoosier....................................... G 317 773-1411
  Noblesville *(G-13070)*

7948 Racing, including track operation

Chip Ganassi Racing Teams Inc............ D 317 802-0000
  Indianapolis *(G-7798)*
Team Green Inc... F 317 872-2700
  Indianapolis *(G-9565)*

7991 Physical fitness facilities

Tylayculture LLC....................................... G 219 678-8359
  Highland *(G-7158)*
Worth Tax and Financial Svc.................. G 574 267-4687
  Warsaw *(G-16456)*
Zendigo Boutique LLC............................. G 574 314-8328
  South Bend *(G-15312)*

7992 Public golf courses

Stone Quary.. E 765 473-5578
  Peru *(G-13603)*

7993 Coin-operated amusement devices

Coach Line Motors................................... G 765 825-7893
  Connersville *(G-2431)*

7997 Membership sports and recreation clubs

Country Club Computer........................... G 317 271-4000
  Indianapolis *(G-7889)*

7999 Amusement and recreation, nec

Black Rose Pastries LLC......................... G 773 708-3650
  Gary *(G-5901)*
Dear Athletes Inc...................................... G 615 682-3332
  Noblesville *(G-13069)*
Elizabeth A Taylor..................................... G 815 353-4798
  Freedom *(G-5799)*

Global Ozone Innovations LLC.............. G 574 294-5797
  Elkhart *(G-3383)*
Hamilton County Business Mag............. G 317 774-7747
  Noblesville *(G-13092)*
Leistner Aquatic Services Inc................. G 317 535-6099
  Morgantown *(G-12260)*
Mid America Powered Vehicles.............. G 812 925-7745
  Chandler *(G-1864)*

80 HEALTH SERVICES

8011 Offices and clinics of medical doctors

Advanced Mbility Solutions LLC............ F 812 438-2338
  Rising Sun *(G-14240)*
Advanced Orthopro Inc.......................... E 317 924-4444
  Indianapolis *(G-7439)*
Fort Wyne Rdlgy Assn Fundation.......... F 260 266-8120
  Fort Wayne *(G-5003)*
Groupone Health Source Inc................. D 800 769-5288
  Indianapolis *(G-8334)*
Zollman Plastic Surgery PC.................... F 317 328-1100
  Indianapolis *(G-9813)*

8021 Offices and clinics of dentists

National Dentex LLC............................... C 317 849-5143
  Indianapolis *(G-8987)*
Somer Inc.. E 317 873-1111
  Zionsville *(G-17051)*

8042 Offices and clinics of optometrists

City Optical Co Inc.................................. D 317 924-1300
  Indianapolis *(G-7813)*
Harmon Hrmon Uysugi Optmtrists........ F 812 723-4752
  Paoli *(G-13496)*
Lca-Vision Inc.. G 317 818-3980
  Indianapolis *(G-8729)*
Luxottica of America Inc......................... G 317 293-9999
  Indianapolis *(G-8800)*
Plainfield Eye Care................................... F 317 839-2368
  Plainfield *(G-13715)*
Union Optical Eyecare Ctr Inc................ G 812 279-3466
  Bedford *(G-679)*

8049 Offices of health practitioner

Audio Diagnostics Inc.............................. G 765 477-7016
  Lafayette *(G-10529)*
Natural Answers.. G 219 922-3663
  Highland *(G-7147)*
Sidney & Janice Bond............................. G 812 366-8160
  Floyds Knobs *(G-4693)*
Vergence LLC.. F 317 547-4417
  Indianapolis *(G-9707)*

8071 Medical laboratories

Center For Diagnostic Imaging............... F 812 234-0555
  Terre Haute *(G-15557)*
Mira Vista Diagnostics LLC................... E 317 856-2681
  Indianapolis *(G-8932)*
Sober Scientific LLC................................ G 765 465-9803
  Sheridan *(G-14829)*
Toralgen Inc... G 812 820-3374
  Indianapolis *(G-9622)*

8072 Dental laboratories

Dental Professional Laboratory.............. E 219 769-6225
  Merrillville *(G-11505)*
National Dentex LLC............................... C 317 849-5143
  Indianapolis *(G-8987)*
Sellers Dental Lab.................................... G 219 465-8719
  Valparaiso *(G-16044)*
Somer Inc.. E 317 873-1111
  Zionsville *(G-17051)*

SIC SECTION

William Wsley Prof Oral Prstht................ G..... 317 635-1000
  Indianapolis (G-9766)

8082 Home health care services

Borrv Concepts LLC................................ G..... 317 405-9121
  Indianapolis (G-7661)
Vergence LLC.. F..... 317 547-4417
  Indianapolis (G-9707)

8099 Health and allied services, nec

Audio Diagnostics Inc............................ G..... 765 477-7016
  Lafayette (G-10529)
Eminence Hlth Care Stffing AGC............. G..... 866 350-6400
  South Bend (G-15013)
Workflow Solutions LLC.......................... G..... 502 627-0257
  New Albany (G-12831)

81 LEGAL SERVICES

8111 Legal services

Eaton Corporation................................. G..... 317 704-2520
  Indianapolis (G-8043)
Enterprise MGT Solutions LLC................. G..... 219 545-8544
  Merrillville (G-11513)
Triumphant Jrney MBL Ntary Svc............ G..... 608 208-5604
  Madison (G-11254)

82 EDUCATIONAL SERVICES

8211 Elementary and secondary schools

Boeke Road Baptist Church Inc.............. G..... 812 479-5342
  Evansville (G-3938)
Lionfish Cyber Hldngs LLC-S Ln.............. G..... 877 732-6772
  Indianapolis (G-8766)
Pathfinder School LLC............................ G..... 317 791-8777
  Indianapolis (G-9100)

8221 Colleges and universities

Anabaptist Mnnnite Bblcal Smna............. D..... 574 295-3726
  Elkhart (G-3181)
Ball State University............................... G..... 765 285-8218
  Muncie (G-12349)
◆ St Meinrad Archabbey......................... D..... 812 357-6611
  Saint Meinrad (G-14464)
Trustees Indiana University..................... G..... 812 855-7995
  Bloomington (G-995)
Trustees Indiana University..................... G..... 812 855-3439
  Bloomington (G-997)
Trustees Indiana University..................... G..... 812 856-4186
  Bloomington (G-998)
Trustees Indiana University..................... F..... 812 855-4848
  Bloomington (G-999)
University Notre Dame Du Lac................ F..... 574 631-7471
  Notre Dame (G-13317)
University Notre Dame Du Lac................ E..... 574 631-6346
  Notre Dame (G-13318)

8231 Libraries

Center For The Study Knwldge D............ G..... 812 361-4424
  Bloomington (G-827)
Pages Editorial Services Inc................... F..... 765 674-4212
  Marion (G-11323)

8243 Data processing schools

Cad/CAM Technologies Inc.................... G..... 765 778-2020
  Pendleton (G-13528)
Gary M Brown....................................... G..... 765 831-2536
  New Castle (G-12864)
Joseph Matthew Biaso.......................... G..... 812 277-6871
  Mitchell (G-12041)

8249 Vocational schools, nec

Crown Training and Dev Inc................... F..... 219 947-0845
  Merrillville (G-11500)
Nechanna One Productions Corp............ G..... 317 400-8908
  Indianapolis (G-8997)
Strike & Walk Da Cup Wldg LLC.............. G..... 219 455-4683
  Hammond (G-7015)

8299 Schools and educational services

Advanced Prtctive Slutions LLC.............. G..... 765 720-9574
  Coatesville (G-2102)
Apologia Eductl Ministries Inc................ E..... 765 608-3280
  Anderson (G-79)
Center For Ethcal Rbtics A Nnt............... G..... 219 741-9374
  Hammond (G-6897)
Friends of Third World Inc...................... G..... 260 422-6821
  Fort Wayne (G-5013)
Kcma & Services LLC............................. G..... 260 645-0885
  Waterloo (G-16522)
▲ Lakota Language Consortium............. F..... 888 525-6828
  Bloomington (G-905)
Loys Sales Inc....................................... G..... 765 552-7250
  Elwood (G-3829)
Plum Grove Strings LLC......................... G..... 219 696-5401
  Lowell (G-11175)
Tanguero Inc... G..... 415 236-2642
  Bloomington (G-983)
Worth Tax and Financial Svc.................. G..... 574 267-4687
  Warsaw (G-16456)

83 SOCIAL SERVICES

8322 Individual and family services

Advanced Community Enhancement...... G..... 513 615-6730
  Guilford (G-6826)
ARC of Greater Boone Cnty Inc.............. F..... 765 482-0051
  Lebanon (G-10875)
Cyberia Ltd... G..... 317 721-2582
  Indianapolis (G-7938)
Fresh Start Inc..................................... F..... 812 254-3398
  Washington (G-16479)
Knox Cnty Assn For Rmrkble Ctz............ D..... 812 886-4312
  Vincennes (G-16136)
Mishawaka Frozen Custard.................... G..... 574 255-8000
  Mishawaka (G-11956)
New Hope Services Inc......................... D..... 812 752-4892
  Scottsburg (G-14574)
New Hope Services Inc......................... E..... 812 288-8248
  Jeffersonville (G-10022)
Rva LLC.. G..... 317 800-9800
  Fishers (G-4602)

8331 Job training and related services

Anthony Wyne Rhblttion Ctr For............ D..... 260 744-6145
  Fort Wayne (G-4762)
ARC of Greater Boone Cnty Inc.............. F..... 765 482-0051
  Lebanon (G-10875)
Cabinetmaker Inc.................................. G..... 812 723-3461
  Paoli (G-13490)
Cardinal Services Inc Indiana................. D..... 574 267-3823
  Warsaw (G-16333)
Cooperative Ventures Ind Corp.............. G..... 317 564-4695
  Carmel (G-1596)
Cyberia Ltd... G..... 317 721-2582
  Indianapolis (G-7938)
Evansville Arc Inc.................................. D..... 812 471-1633
  Evansville (G-4046)
Lionfish Cyber Hldngs LLC-S Ln.............. G..... 877 732-6772
  Indianapolis (G-8766)
New Hope Services Inc......................... D..... 812 752-4892
  Scottsburg (G-14574)
New Hope Services Inc......................... E..... 812 288-8248
  Jeffersonville (G-10022)

Pathfinder Services Inc......................... E..... 260 356-0500
  Huntington (G-7354)
▲ Rauch Inc... E..... 812 945-4063
  New Albany (G-12803)
Rise Inc.. D..... 260 665-9408
  Angola (G-292)
Success Holding Group Intl Inc.............. G..... 260 450-1982
  Ossian (G-13436)

8361 Residential care

Cardinal Services Inc Indiana................. D..... 574 267-3823
  Warsaw (G-16333)
Fresh Start Inc..................................... F..... 812 254-3398
  Washington (G-16479)

84 MUSEUMS, ART GALLERIES AND BOTANICAL AND ZOOLOGICAL GARDENS

8412 Museums and art galleries

Editions Ltd Gllery Fine Art I.................. G,.... 317 466-9940
  Indianapolis (G-8055)
Framery... G..... 812 537-4319
  Lawrenceburg (G-10837)

86 MEMBERSHIP ORGANIZATIONS

8611 Business associations

▼ Abda Incorporated............................. G..... 317 273-8343
  Indianapolis (G-7416)
American Maint & Training Inc............... F..... 812 738-4230
  Corydon (G-2485)
Automobile Dealers Assn of Ind............. G..... 317 635-1441
  Indianapolis (G-7576)
News-Banner Publications Inc............... E..... 260 824-0224
  Bluffton (G-1046)
Squeegeepie Merch Co LLC................... G..... 765 376-6358
  Crawfordsville (G-2618)
Super Blend Inc.................................... G..... 260 463-7486
  Lagrange (G-10766)

8621 Professional organizations

34 Lives Pbc.. G..... 303 550-9989
  West Lafayette (G-16553)
American Academy of Sports................. G..... 877 732-5009
  Zionsville (G-16989)
American School Health Assn................ G..... 703 506-7675
  Bloomington (G-779)
Indiana State Medical Assn................... E..... 317 261-2060
  Indianapolis (G-8494)

8631 Labor organizations

Dist Council 91..................................... G..... 812 962-9191
  Evansville (G-4014)

8641 Civic and social associations

American Legion National...................... D..... 317 630-1200
  Indianapolis (G-7505)
Hoosier Tribune Corp............................ G..... 907 570-8888
  Carmel (G-1658)

8661 Religious organizations

Advancing Chrsts Kngdom Globl............ G..... 219 765-3586
  Merrillville (G-11478)
Boeke Road Baptist Church Inc.............. G..... 812 479-5342
  Evansville (G-3938)
Catholic Press of Evansville................... G..... 812 424-5536
  Evansville (G-3966)
Christian Sound & Song Inc................... G..... 574 294-2893
  Elkhart (G-3251)

86 MEMBERSHIP ORGANIZATIONS

Dayspring Community Church Inc......... F 260 925-4599
  Auburn *(G-385)*
Fresh Start Inc.................................... F 812 254-3398
  Washington *(G-16479)*
Gospel Echoes Team Association......... G 574 533-0221
  Goshen *(G-6153)*
Old Paths Tract Society Inc.................. G 812 247-2560
  Shoals *(G-14909)*
Otter Creek Christian Church................ G 812 446-5300
  Brazil *(G-1159)*
Temple-Inland Inc................................ G 765 675-6732
  Tipton *(G-15793)*
Wesleyan Church Corporation.............. E 317 774-7900
  Fishers *(G-4632)*
World Rdo Mssnary Fllwship Inc.......... G 574 970-4252
  Elkhart *(G-3793)*

8699 Membership organizations, nec

Academy of Mdel Aronautics Inc......... D 765 287-1256
  Muncie *(G-12334)*
American Diabetes Association............ G 859 268-9129
  Indianapolis *(G-7502)*
▼ World Missionary Press Inc.............. E 574 831-2111
  New Paris *(G-12974)*

87 ENGINEERING, ACCOUNTING, RESEARCH, AND MANAGEMENT SERVICES

8711 Engineering services

7th Leadership Organization................. G 219 938-6906
  Gary *(G-5883)*
Accucast Inc....................................... G 317 849-5521
  Fishers *(G-4459)*
Advanced Welding and Engrg.............. G 317 820-3595
  Indianapolis *(G-7443)*
Aerodyn Engineering LLC................... E 317 334-1523
  Indianapolis *(G-7451)*
AM General Holdings LLC................... A 574 237-6222
  South Bend *(G-14940)*
◆ AM General LLC.............................. D 574 237-6222
  South Bend *(G-14942)*
Apex AG Solutions LLC....................... F 765 305-1930
  Winchester *(G-16882)*
Arroyo Industries LLC......................... G 317 605-4163
  Greenwood *(G-6671)*
Barger Engineering Inc....................... G 812 476-3077
  Evansville *(G-3909)*
Behnke Engineering............................ G 574 842-2327
  Culver *(G-2780)*
Binarie LLC.. G 317 496-8836
  Greenwood *(G-6676)*
Biosafe Engineering LLC..................... E 317 858-8099
  Indianapolis *(G-7629)*
Butler Tool & Design Inc..................... F 219 297-4531
  Goodland *(G-6080)*
Computer Age Engineering Inc............ E 765 674-8551
  Marion *(G-11278)*
Crown Elec Svcs & Automtn Inc.......... D 972 929-4700
  Portage *(G-13857)*
Crown Training and Dev Inc................ F 219 947-0845
  Merrillville *(G-11500)*
Crume Industries LLC......................... G 574 747-7683
  Elkhart *(G-3275)*
▲ Daifuku Intrlgistics Amer Corp......... D 219 777-2220
  Hobart *(G-7186)*
Damping Technologies Inc.................. F 574 258-7916
  Mishawaka *(G-11880)*
Damping Technologies Inc.................. E 574 258-7916
  Mishawaka *(G-11879)*

Daylight Engineering Inc..................... G 812 983-2518
  Elberfeld *(G-3111)*
Design Engineering............................. G 219 926-2170
  Chesterton *(G-1919)*
Direct Control Systems Inc.................. G 765 282-7474
  Muncie *(G-12384)*
Divsys Aerospace & Engrg LLC........... F 317 941-7777
  Indianapolis *(G-7987)*
Drake Enterprises LLC........................ G 317 460-5991
  Pittsboro *(G-13644)*
Duesenburg Inc.................................. G 260 496-9650
  Fort Wayne *(G-4931)*
Durhat Transportation LLC.................. G 463 204-9119
  Greenwood *(G-6691)*
Engnered Refr Shapes Svcs LLC......... G 765 778-8040
  Pendleton *(G-13531)*
Enterprise MGT Solutions LLC............. G 219 545-8544
  Merrillville *(G-11513)*
Future Mold Inc.................................. F 812 941-8661
  New Albany *(G-12735)*
Gmp Holdings LLC.............................. G 317 353-6580
  Indianapolis *(G-8294)*
▼ Halo LLC.. D 317 575-9992
  Carmel *(G-1647)*
Hautau Tube Cutoff Systems LLC........ F 765 647-1600
  Brookville *(G-1323)*
Hgl Dynamics Inc............................... G 317 782-3500
  Indianapolis *(G-8393)*
◆ Hirata Corporation of America......... E 317 856-8600
  Indianapolis *(G-8399)*
Hrezo Industrial Eqp & Engrg.............. F 812 537-4700
  Greendale *(G-6447)*
Imagineering Enterprises Inc............... E 317 635-8565
  Indianapolis *(G-8464)*
Imagineering Enterprises Inc............... E 574 287-0642
  South Bend *(G-15075)*
▲ Imagineering Enterprises Inc.......... D 574 287-2941
  South Bend *(G-15076)*
In Space LLC..................................... G 765 775-2107
  Lafayette *(G-10605)*
Indigo Industries LLC......................... G 480 747-4560
  Greenwood *(G-6715)*
Industrial Combustn Engineers............ E 219 949-5066
  Gary *(G-5960)*
Indy Hoods LLC.................................. F 317 731-7170
  Indianapolis *(G-8529)*
Ipheion Development Corp.................. G 240 281-1619
  Indianapolis *(G-8587)*
Ironworks Engineering LLC................. G 317 296-9359
  New Palestine *(G-12940)*
Jackson Systems LLC........................ C 888 359-0365
  Indianapolis *(G-8615)*
JMS Engineered Plastics Inc............... G 574 277-3228
  South Bend *(G-15093)*
JMS Engineered Plastics Inc............... D 574 277-3228
  South Bend *(G-15094)*
K&T Performance Engrg LLC............... G 765 437-0185
  Peru *(G-13589)*
Klinge Enameling Company Inc........... E 317 359-8291
  Indianapolis *(G-8694)*
▲ KYB Americas Corporation.............. B 317 736-7774
  Franklin *(G-5750)*
Leman Engrg & Consulting Inc............ G 574 870-7732
  Brookston *(G-1312)*
▲ Lingenfelter Prfmce Engrg Inc........ E 260 724-2552
  Decatur *(G-2869)*
Llama Corporation.............................. G 888 701-7432
  Decatur *(G-2870)*
Lyntech Engineering Inc..................... G 574 224-2900
  Rochester *(G-14303)*
Maddox Engineering Inc..................... F 812 903-0048
  Greenville *(G-6652)*

SIC SECTION

Meridian Resources LLC..................... G 812 463-2281
  Carmel *(G-1697)*
Mesh Systems LLC............................ E 317 661-4800
  Carmel *(G-1698)*
Metal Fab Engineering Inc.................. E 574 278-7150
  Winamac *(G-16867)*
Metal Technologies Inc Alabama......... D 260 925-4717
  Auburn *(G-408)*
Midwest Finishing Systems Inc........... E 574 257-0099
  Mishawaka *(G-11949)*
Mobility Ventures LLC........................ G 734 367-3714
  South Bend *(G-15153)*
Modern Forge Companies LLC............ A 708 388-1806
  Merrillville *(G-11542)*
Moore Engineering & Prod Co............. F 812 479-1051
  Evansville *(G-4211)*
▼ Natare Corporation......................... E 317 290-8828
  Indianapolis *(G-8985)*
Odyssian Technology LLC................... G 574 257-7555
  South Bend *(G-15176)*
Oilfield Research Inc.......................... G 812 424-2907
  Evansville *(G-4226)*
Pia Automation US Inc....................... E 812 485-5500
  Evansville *(G-4242)*
Precision Surveillance Corp................. G 219 397-4295
  East Chicago *(G-3035)*
Quantum Technologies LLC................. G 765 426-0156
  Elizabethtown *(G-3132)*
Rd Rubber Products Inc..................... G 260 357-3571
  Garrett *(G-5875)*
◆ Ring-R Inc..................................... G 260 565-3347
  Decatur *(G-2882)*
Rob Passarelli................................... G 317 340-8597
  Carmel *(G-1743)*
Robert Perez...................................... G 317 291-7311
  Indianapolis *(G-9314)*
Robinson Engineering & Oil Co............ F 812 477-1575
  Evansville *(G-4291)*
◆ Royal Adhesives & Sealants LLC..... D 574 246-5000
  South Bend *(G-15226)*
S TEC Group Inc................................ F 219 844-7030
  Hammond *(G-7002)*
Scalar Design Engrg & Dist LLC.......... G 765 429-5545
  Lafayette *(G-10685)*
Selco Engineering Inc........................ F
  Shelbyville *(G-14795)*
◆ Setco LLC..................................... B 812 424-2904
  Evansville *(G-4307)*
SGS Cybermetrix Inc.......................... G 800 713-1203
  Columbus *(G-2391)*
Specialty Blanks Inc........................... G 812 232-8775
  Terre Haute *(G-15708)*
Specialty Tooling Inc.......................... F 812 464-8521
  Evansville *(G-4328)*
Stedman Machine Company Inc.......... D 812 926-0038
  Aurora *(G-457)*
▲ Stratikore Inc................................. G 574 807-0028
  La Porte *(G-10485)*
▲ Superior Indus Solutions Inc........... E 317 781-4400
  Indianapolis *(G-9529)*
T R Bulger Inc................................... G 219 879-8525
  Trail Creek *(G-15841)*
Technalysis Inc.................................. G 317 291-1985
  Indianapolis *(G-9568)*
▲ Telamon Corporation...................... C 317 818-6888
  Carmel *(G-1777)*
Wolf Technical Engineering LLC.......... G 800 783-9653
  Indianapolis *(G-9781)*
Woody Enterprises LLC...................... G 765 498-7300
  Bloomingdale *(G-763)*
World Rdo Mssnary Fllwship Inc.......... G 574 970-4252
  Elkhart *(G-3793)*

87 ENGINEERING, ACCOUNTING, RESEARCH, AND MANAGEMENT SERVICES

Wpr Services LLC .... G 317 513-5269
  Fishers *(G-4635)*
Xtreme ADS Limited .... E 765 644-7323
  Anderson *(G-218)*

8712 Architectural services

7th Leadership Organization .... G 219 938-6906
  Gary *(G-5883)*
Architura Corporation .... G 317 348-1000
  Indianapolis *(G-7541)*
Deem & Loureiro Inc .... G 770 652-9871
  Indianapolis *(G-7961)*
Meyer Custom Woodworking Inc .... G 812 695-2021
  Dubois *(G-2954)*
◆ Werzalit of America Inc .... D 814 362-3881
  Syracuse *(G-15492)*

8713 Surveying services

Tmx Healthcare Tech LLC .... F 877 874-6339
  Indianapolis *(G-9614)*

8721 Accounting, auditing, and bookkeeping

Frank R Komar PC .... G 812 477-9110
  Evansville *(G-4081)*
Groupone Health Source Inc .... D 800 769-5288
  Indianapolis *(G-8334)*
Lil Red Studios LLC .... G 317 443-4932
  Indianapolis *(G-8753)*
Sentinel Services Inc .... E 574 360-5279
  Granger *(G-6376)*

8731 Commercial physical research

Ampacet Corporation .... E 812 466-9828
  Terre Haute *(G-15543)*
Bangs Laboratories Inc .... F 317 570-7020
  Fishers *(G-4470)*
Biokorf LLC .... G 765 727-0782
  West Lafayette *(G-16565)*
Biopoly LLC .... F 260 999-6135
  Fort Wayne *(G-4802)*
Catalent Indiana LLC .... B 812 355-6746
  Bloomington *(G-824)*
▲ Contour Hardening Inc .... E 888 867-2184
  Indianapolis *(G-7861)*
Cook Medical Holdings LLC .... G 812 339-2235
  Bloomington *(G-842)*
◆ Corteva Agriscience LLC .... A 317 337-3000
  Indianapolis *(G-7884)*
Durhat Transportation LLC .... G 463 204-9119
  Greenwood *(G-6691)*
Eli Lilly International Corp .... F 317 276-2000
  Indianapolis *(G-8091)*
Faztech LLC .... G 812 327-0926
  Bloomington *(G-864)*
IBC Materials & Tech LLC .... E 765 481-2900
  Lebanon *(G-10899)*
Inotiv Inc .... G 812 985-5900
  Mount Vernon *(G-12302)*
Kp Pharmaceutical Tech Inc .... E 812 330-8121
  Bloomington *(G-903)*
MBX Biosciences Inc .... E 317 659-0200
  Carmel *(G-1695)*
◆ Mycogen Corporation .... F 317 337-3000
  Indianapolis *(G-8977)*
Naturegenic Inc .... G 765 807-5525
  West Lafayette *(G-16612)*
Pfizer Inc .... D 212 733-2323
  Terre Haute *(G-15660)*
Polymod Technologies Inc .... F 260 436-1322
  Fort Wayne *(G-5325)*
Pynco Inc .... E 812 275-0900
  Bedford *(G-661)*

Silicis Technologies Inc .... E 317 896-5044
  Westfield *(G-16728)*

8732 Commercial nonphysical research

Americas Coml Trnsp RES Co LLC .... F 812 379-2085
  Columbus *(G-2219)*
Applied Scientific RES Inc .... G 219 776-4623
  Merrillville *(G-11484)*
Enviri Corporation .... G 317 983-5353
  Pittsboro *(G-13645)*
▲ SealCorpUSA Inc .... D 866 868-0791
  Evansville *(G-4303)*
Sk Markting Strtgies LLC DBA A .... G 812 962-0900
  Evansville *(G-4317)*
Tgf Enterprises LLC .... G 440 840-9704
  Indianapolis *(G-9585)*
Trinity Cmmnications Group Inc .... G 260 484-1029
  Fort Wayne *(G-5508)*
Waseve LLC .... G 443 204-7976
  Carmel *(G-1799)*

8733 Noncommercial research organizations

Ampacet Corporation .... E 812 466-9828
  Terre Haute *(G-15543)*
Ash Access Technology Inc .... G 765 742-4813
  Lafayette *(G-10528)*
Center For The Study Knwldge D .... G 812 361-4424
  Bloomington *(G-827)*
Cyberia Ltd .... G 317 721-2582
  Indianapolis *(G-7938)*

8734 Testing laboratories

Acterna LLC .... E 317 788-9351
  Indianapolis *(G-7425)*
Bundoo Laboratories LLC .... G 317 978-5574
  Beech Grove *(G-687)*
Cortex Safety Technologies LLC .... G 317 414-5607
  Carmel *(G-1598)*
Divsys Aerospace & Engrg LLC .... F 317 941-7777
  Indianapolis *(G-7987)*
Divsys Intl - Icape LLC .... E 317 405-9427
  Indianapolis *(G-7988)*
Eminence Hlth Care Stffing AGC .... G 866 350-6400
  South Bend *(G-15013)*
Flynn Welding & Inspection LLC .... G 812 327-7437
  Solsberry *(G-14925)*
▲ Indiana Research Institute .... G 812 378-4221
  Columbus *(G-2326)*
Integrated Instrument Svcs Inc .... F 317 248-1958
  Indianapolis *(G-8568)*
Mold Removers LLC .... G 317 846-0977
  Indianapolis *(G-8946)*
Moseley Laboratories Inc .... F 317 866-8460
  Greenfield *(G-6533)*
Northern Indiana Ordnance Co .... G 574 289-5938
  South Bend *(G-15173)*
Odyssian Technology LLC .... G 574 257-7555
  South Bend *(G-15176)*
Qig LLC .... E 260 244-3591
  Columbia City *(G-2185)*
Radon Environmental Inc .... G 317 843-0804
  Elkhart *(G-3637)*
Rapid View LLC .... G 574 224-3373
  Rochester *(G-14315)*
Thermphyscal Prpts RES Lab Inc .... G 765 463-1581
  West Lafayette *(G-16637)*

8741 Management services

▲ Agi International Inc .... F 317 536-2415
  Indianapolis *(G-7458)*
Agora Brands Group Inc .... E 615 802-0086
  Borden *(G-1104)*

Assured General Contg LLC .... G 260 740-4744
  Fort Wayne *(G-4776)*
Automated Laser Corporation .... G 260 637-4140
  Fort Wayne *(G-4781)*
Central Coca-Cola Btlg Co Inc .... E 800 241-2653
  Bloomington *(G-828)*
Central Coca-Cola Btlg Co Inc .... E 800 241-2653
  Indianapolis *(G-7770)*
Central Coca-Cola Btlg Co Inc .... E 812 482-7475
  Jasper *(G-9827)*
Central Coca-Cola Btlg Co Inc .... E 260 726-7126
  Portland *(G-13930)*
Central Coca-Cola Btlg Co Inc .... E 800 241-2653
  Shelbyville *(G-14744)*
Commtineo LLC .... F 219 476-3667
  Wanatah *(G-16288)*
Crown Training and Dev Inc .... F 219 947-0845
  Merrillville *(G-11500)*
Fretina Corporation .... F 812 547-6471
  Tell City *(G-15504)*
Hgmc Supply Inc .... F 317 351-9500
  Indianapolis *(G-8394)*
▲ Indiana Scale Company Inc .... F 812 232-0893
  Terre Haute *(G-15617)*
LH Industries Corp .... E 260 432-5563
  Fort Wayne *(G-5181)*
Paragon Force Inc .... D 812 384-3040
  Bloomfield *(G-755)*
Patrick Industries Inc .... G 574 293-1521
  Elkhart *(G-3597)*
▲ Phoenix Assembly LLC .... G 317 884-3600
  Greenwood *(G-6751)*
▲ Phoenix Assembly Indiana LLC .... G 317 884-3600
  Columbus *(G-2378)*
Pittman Mine Service LLC .... G 812 847-2340
  Linton *(G-11042)*
Triumphant Jrney MBL Ntary Svc .... G 608 208-5604
  Madison *(G-11254)*

8742 Management consulting services

Adafill Global LLC .... G 317 798-5378
  Indianapolis *(G-7427)*
Advanced Prtctive Slutions LLC .... G 765 720-9574
  Coatesville *(G-2102)*
▲ Agi International Inc .... F 317 536-2415
  Indianapolis *(G-7458)*
American Eagle Health LLC .... G 812 921-9224
  Floyds Knobs *(G-4668)*
American Veteran Group LLC .... G 317 600-4749
  Westfield *(G-16664)*
Appextremes LLC .... D 317 550-0148
  Indianapolis *(G-7529)*
Arroyo Industries LLC .... G 317 605-4163
  Greenwood *(G-6671)*
Aspire Lifestyle Inc .... G 219 814-2591
  Chesterton *(G-1905)*
Assured General Contg LLC .... G 260 740-4744
  Fort Wayne *(G-4776)*
Blackpoint Distribution Co LLC .... E 260 414-9096
  Leo *(G-10964)*
Carelogiq Corp .... G 219 682-6327
  Munster *(G-12534)*
Christian Sound & Song Inc .... G 574 294-2893
  Elkhart *(G-3251)*
Citizens By-Products Coal Co .... F 317 927-4738
  Indianapolis *(G-7811)*
Clinical Architecture LLC .... E 317 580-8400
  Carmel *(G-1590)*
Deberry MGT & Consulting LLC .... G 317 767-4703
  Indianapolis *(G-7959)*
Denver Marketing Co LLC .... G 866 692-2326
  Indianapolis *(G-7964)*

87 ENGINEERING, ACCOUNTING, RESEARCH, AND MANAGEMENT SERVICES — SIC SECTION

Destiny Solutions Inc .... G 502 384-0031
  Georgetown *(G-6057)*
Digital Carvings LLC .... G 812 269-6123
  Ellettsville *(G-3807)*
Dimo Multiservices LLC .... F 463 256-0561
  Avon *(G-513)*
▲ Ditech Inc .... E 812 526-0850
  Edinburgh *(G-3077)*
Dock Bumpers Inc .... G 312 597-9282
  Highland *(G-7132)*
Eli Lilly International Corp .... F 317 276-2000
  Indianapolis *(G-8091)*
Em Global LLC .... G 812 258-9993
  Jeffersonville *(G-9976)*
Emarsys North America Inc .... E 630 395-2944
  Indianapolis *(G-8099)*
Enpak LLC .... G 574 268-7273
  Warsaw *(G-16360)*
Enterprise MGT Solutions LLC .... G 219 545-8544
  Merrillville *(G-11513)*
Envista LLC .... D 317 208-9100
  Carmel *(G-1626)*
Envista Entp Solutions LLC .... C 317 208-9100
  Carmel *(G-1628)*
Evo Exhibits LLC .... G 630 520-0710
  Peru *(G-13582)*
Finvantage LLC .... F 317 500-4949
  Carmel *(G-1635)*
Froet Group LLC .... F 317 414-2538
  Whitestown *(G-16807)*
General Automation Company .... F 317 849-7483
  Noblesville *(G-13085)*
▲ Georg Utz Inc .... E 812 526-2240
  Edinburgh *(G-3085)*
Gibson Nehemiah Group Inc .... F 317 643-3838
  Muncie *(G-12401)*
Giles Agency Incorporated .... G 317 842-5546
  Indianapolis *(G-8281)*
Heritage Financial Group Inc .... E 574 522-8000
  Elkhart *(G-3404)*
Holic LLC .... E 765 444-8115
  Middletown *(G-11770)*
Ike Newton LLC .... G 317 902-1772
  Greenwood *(G-6714)*
Indiana Home Pro LLC .... G 812 968-4822
  Corydon *(G-2501)*
Innovations Amplified LLC .... G 317 339-4685
  Indianapolis *(G-8552)*
Jam Printing Inc .... F 765 649-9292
  Anderson *(G-138)*
Jtex Cnstr & Consulting LLC .... G 812 486-9123
  Velpen *(G-16093)*
Kennyleeholmescom .... G 574 612-2526
  Elkhart *(G-3451)*
Liberty Automation LLC .... G 574 524-0436
  Albion *(G-31)*
Life Path Numerology Center .... G 317 638-9752
  Indianapolis *(G-8747)*
Machining & Repr Resource Inc .... G 219 588-7395
  Highland *(G-7143)*
Maddox Industrial Contg LLC .... E 812 544-2156
  Santa Claus *(G-14508)*
McNeil Coatings Cons Inc .... G 317 885-1557
  Greenwood *(G-6736)*
Mpp Holdings Inc .... G 317 805-3764
  Noblesville *(G-13140)*
Northern Indiana Ordnance Co .... G 574 289-5938
  South Bend *(G-15273)*
Pinnacle Oil Holdings LLC .... C 317 875-9465
  Indianapolis *(G-9144)*
Pinnacle Oil Holdings LLC .... E 317 875-9465
  Indianapolis *(G-9145)*

▲ Plum Group Inc .... F 617 712-3000
  Indianapolis *(G-9155)*
◆ Printing Inc Louisville KY .... F 800 237-5894
  Jeffersonville *(G-10041)*
Project Field Solutions Inc .... G 317 590-7678
  Fishers *(G-4584)*
Quantum Technologies LLC .... G 765 426-0156
  Elizabethtown *(G-3132)*
Raging Rocket Web Design LLC .... G 219 381-5027
  Crown Point *(G-2741)*
Rios Investment Services LLC .... G 574 514-3999
  South Bend *(G-15221)*
Rogers Marketing & Prtg Inc .... G 317 838-7203
  Avon *(G-549)*
▲ Roi Marketing Company Inc .... G 317 644-0797
  Indianapolis *(G-9321)*
Sentinel Services Inc .... E 574 360-5279
  Granger *(G-6376)*
Sexton Advertising LLC .... G 812 522-4059
  Seymour *(G-14688)*
Sk Markting Strtgies LLC DBA A .... G 812 962-0900
  Evansville *(G-4317)*
Smith Consulting Inc .... E 765 728-5980
  Montpelier *(G-12181)*
Sorbtech Inc .... G 812 944-9108
  Clarksville *(G-2037)*
Spark Marketing LLC .... G 219 301-0071
  Dyer *(G-2983)*
Spring Ventures Infovation LLC .... G 317 847-1117
  Greenwood *(G-6770)*
Stonecast Financial LLC .... G 317 537-1707
  Indianapolis *(G-9514)*
Supplieriq LLC .... G 574 323-0707
  South Bend *(G-15273)*
Tgf Enterprises LLC .... G 440 840-9704
  Indianapolis *(G-9585)*
Tippmann US Holdco Inc .... E 260 749-6022
  Fort Wayne *(G-5489)*
Tmx Healthcare Tech LLC .... F 877 874-6339
  Indianapolis *(G-9614)*
Triumphant Jrney MBL Ntary Svc .... G 608 208-5604
  Madison *(G-11254)*
Utilities AVI Specialists Inc .... G 219 662-8175
  Crown Point *(G-2770)*
Vivid Social Group LLC .... G 317 447-7319
  Indianapolis *(G-9726)*
Waseve LLC .... G 443 204-7976
  Carmel *(G-1799)*
Winfield Solutions LLC .... G 317 838-3733
  Plainfield *(G-13743)*

8743 Public relations services

Annual Reports Inc .... G 317 736-8838
  Franklin *(G-5709)*
Digital Design Genius .... G 317 515-3680
  Camby *(G-1509)*
Gs Sales Inc .... G 317 595-6750
  Westfield *(G-16695)*
Kamrex Inc .... E 317 204-3779
  Avon *(G-530)*
Kessler Concepts Inc .... F 317 630-9901
  Indianapolis *(G-8675)*
Minute Print It Inc .... G 765 482-9019
  Lebanon *(G-10916)*
Plaquemaker Plus Inc .... G 317 594-5556
  Fishers *(G-4576)*
Printing Creations Inc .... G 765 759-9679
  Yorktown *(G-16982)*

8744 Facilities support services

Fiserv Mrtg Servicing Systems .... C 574 282-3300
  South Bend *(G-15034)*

Johnson Controls Inc .... F 812 868-1374
  Evansville *(G-4144)*
Johnson Controls Inc .... F 317 917-5043
  Pittsboro *(G-13649)*

8748 Business consulting, nec

A Page Beyond LLC .... G 317 589-8218
  Fishers *(G-4638)*
Abundant Life Publications LLC .... G 219 730-7621
  Gary *(G-5887)*
▲ Agi International Inc .... F 317 536-2415
  Indianapolis *(G-7458)*
Agora Brands Group Inc .... E 615 802-0086
  Borden *(G-1104)*
Al Perry Enterprises Inc .... G 812 867-7727
  Evansville *(G-3879)*
American Eagle Health LLC .... G 812 921-9224
  Floyds Knobs *(G-4668)*
Anaerobic Innovations LLC .... G 765 491-1174
  West Lafayette *(G-16561)*
Asphalt Materials Inc .... G 317 875-4670
  Indianapolis *(G-7553)*
Assurance Waste Management LLC .... G 765 341-4431
  Cloverdale *(G-2082)*
Aunalytics Inc .... D 574 307-9230
  South Bend *(G-14951)*
Automobile Dealers Assn of Ind .... G 317 635-1441
  Indianapolis *(G-7576)*
Binarie LLC .... G 317 496-8836
  Greenwood *(G-6676)*
Carelogiq Corp .... G 219 682-6327
  Munster *(G-12534)*
Commtineo LLC .... F 219 476-3667
  Wanatah *(G-16288)*
Corvano LLC .... G 317 403-0471
  Fishers *(G-4495)*
Cr Publications .... G 219 931-6700
  Hammond *(G-6906)*
Crown Training and Dev Inc .... F 219 947-0845
  Merrillville *(G-11500)*
Cybernaut Industria LLC .... G 317 664-5316
  Indianapolis *(G-7939)*
Detroit Holdings LLC .... G 202 309-9681
  North Liberty *(G-13216)*
Dieng Group LLC .... G 317 699-1909
  Indianapolis *(G-7973)*
DMC Distribution LLC .... G 219 926-6401
  Porter *(G-13924)*
Drake Enterprises LLC .... G 317 460-5991
  Pittsboro *(G-13644)*
Encourage Publishing LLC .... G 812 987-6148
  New Albany *(G-12725)*
Enterprise MGT Solutions LLC .... G 219 545-8544
  Merrillville *(G-11513)*
F D Deskins Company Inc .... F 317 284-4014
  Fishers *(G-4520)*
Goldenmarc LLC .... G 317 855-1651
  Indianapolis *(G-8301)*
Indiana Auto Dealers Assn Svcs .... G 317 635-1441
  Indianapolis *(G-8473)*
Indigo Industries LLC .... G 480 747-4560
  Greenwood *(G-6715)*
Indy Web Inc .... G 317 536-1201
  Indianapolis *(G-8537)*
Ingroup .... G 317 817-9997
  Indianapolis *(G-8547)*
Ipheion Development Corp .... G 240 281-1619
  Indianapolis *(G-8587)*
Jdh Logistics LLC .... G 573 529-2005
  Fort Branch *(G-4705)*
John R Bowen & Associates .... G 812 544-2267
  Newburgh *(G-13010)*

Ksn Technologies Inc.................................. E 219 877-4770
  Chesterton *(G-1942)*
Nebo Ridge Enterprises LLC.................... G 317 471-1089
  Carmel *(G-1703)*
P J J T Distributors Inc............................. G 812 254-2218
  Washington *(G-16498)*
Peerless Gear LLC.................................. G 812 883-7900
  Salem *(G-14497)*
Pyrotek Incorporated............................... D 260 248-4141
  Columbia City *(G-2184)*
RAD Cube LLC.. F 317 456-7560
  Indianapolis *(G-9260)*
◆ Radian Research Inc.............................. D 765 449-5500
  Lafayette *(G-10675)*
Rebound Project LLP................................ G 765 621-5604
  Anderson *(G-183)*
Registration System LLC.......................... G 317 966-6919
  Fortville *(G-5605)*
Road Alert Systems LLC.......................... G 219 669-1206
  Morocco *(G-12269)*
Sailor Group LLC..................................... G 574 226-0362
  Elkhart *(G-3660)*
Samaron Corp... E 574 970-7070
  Elkhart *(G-3661)*
Sentinel Services Inc................................ E 574 360-5279
  Granger *(G-6376)*
Sk Markting Strtgies LLC DBA A............... G 812 962-0900
  Evansville *(G-4317)*
Sorbtech Inc... G 812 944-9108
  Clarksville *(G-2037)*
Spring Ventures Infovation LLC................. G 317 847-1117
  Greenwood *(G-6770)*
Standard For Success LLC...................... F 844 737-3825
  Cloverdale *(G-2099)*
TMI.. G 574 533-4741
  Goshen *(G-6270)*
Trinette Clark Agency Corp...................... G 317 671-6097
  Indianapolis *(G-9643)*
Turning Over A New Leaf LLC.................. G 765 573-3366
  Gas City *(G-6040)*
Vanessa Collins LLC................................ G 219 985-5705
  Floyds Knobs *(G-4697)*
Vigo Coal Operating Co Inc...................... C 812 759-8446
  Evansville *(G-4374)*

89 SERVICES, NOT ELSEWHERE CLASSIFIED

8999 Services, nec

1632 Inc.. G 219 398-4155
  East Chicago *(G-2987)*
CJS Muzic Company-The Spot LLC......... G 219 487-9873
  Hammond *(G-6901)*
Encourage Publishing LLC....................... G 812 987-6148
  New Albany *(G-12725)*
Fabcreation... G 812 246-6222
  Sellersburg *(G-14593)*
Franklin Barry Gallery............................... G 317 822-8455
  Indianapolis *(G-8224)*
Gibbs Susie Framing & Art....................... G 765 428-2434
  Lafayette *(G-10589)*
Grace Henderson...................................... G 765 661-9063
  Marion *(G-11289)*
Hot Shot Multimedia Entps LLC................ G 317 537-7527
  South Bend *(G-15072)*
Innovative Chem Resources Inc............... G 317 695-6001
  Indianapolis *(G-8553)*
Ipheion Development Corp....................... G 240 281-1619
  Indianapolis *(G-8587)*
Magaws of Boston.................................... G 765 935-6170
  Richmond *(G-14158)*
Meridian Resources LLC.......................... G 812 463-2281
  Carmel *(G-1697)*
Mycloud LLC... G 317 570-8999
  Fishers *(G-4568)*
Patchwork Costumes LLC........................ G 317 750-6162
  Indianapolis *(G-9097)*
Precisely Write Inc................................... G 317 585-7701
  Indianapolis *(G-9178)*
Telamon Entp Ventures LLC..................... F 317 818-6888
  Carmel *(G-1778)*
▲ Trilithic Inc.. C 317 895-3600
  Indianapolis *(G-9641)*

Tylayculture LLC....................................... G 219 678-8359
  Highland *(G-7158)*

91 EXECUTIVE, LEGISLATIVE & GENERAL GOVERNMENT, EXCEPT FINANCE

9121 Legislative bodies

City of Anderson....................................... G 765 648-6715
  Anderson *(G-93)*

92 JUSTICE, PUBLIC ORDER AND SAFETY

9224 Fire protection

Centre Township....................................... E 765 482-1729
  Lebanon *(G-10883)*
City of Valparaiso..................................... G 219 462-5291
  Valparaiso *(G-15928)*

95 ADMINISTRATION OF ENVIRONMENTAL QUALITY AND HOUSING PROGRAMS

9532 Urban and community development

Road Alert Systems LLC.......................... G 219 669-1206
  Morocco *(G-12269)*

97 NATIONAL SECURITY AND INTERNATIONAL AFFAIRS

9711 National security

Dla Document Services............................ G 812 854-1465
  Crane *(G-2537)*

ALPHABETIC SECTION

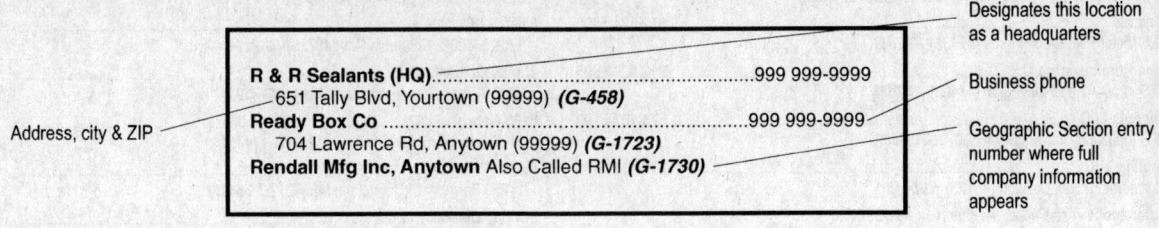

- Designates this location as a headquarters
- Business phone
- Geographic Section entry number where full company information appears
- Address, city & ZIP

R & R Sealants (HQ)...999 999-9999
  651 Tally Blvd, Yourtown (99999) *(G-458)*
Ready Box Co 999 999-9999
  704 Lawrence Rd, Anytown (99999) *(G-1723)*
Rendall Mfg Inc, Anytown Also Called RMI *(G-1730)*

See footnotes for symbols and codes identification.
- Companies listed alphabetically.
- Complete physical or mailing address.

.dwg Tooling Technologies, Columbus Also Called: dwg Design Services Corp *(G-2292)*
(ebs Cmpstes Engnred Bnded Str..................................... 574 266-3471
  3506 Henke St Elkhart (46514) *(G-3136)*
(SISTER COMPANY OF ENDRESS + HAUSER INC, GREENWOOD, IN), Greenwood Also Called: Endress+hauser (usa) Automatio *(G-6699)*
1 Composites LLC... 260 665-6112
  606 W Center St Bourbon (46504) *(G-1119)*
1 Stop Signs.. 765 748-2902
  900 E Streeter Ave Muncie (47303) *(G-12331)*
1 Up, Kokomo Also Called: Web Software LLC *(G-10356)*
101 Tool & Die LLC... 260 203-2981
  3418 Delray Dr Fort Wayne (46815) *(G-4708)*
103 Collection LLC... 800 896-2945
  7402 Nature View Dr Schererville (46375) *(G-14510)*
104 Welding.. 219 393-0801
  2721 S State Road 104 La Porte (46350) *(G-10370)*
10x Engineered Materials LLC....................................... 260 209-1207
  1162 Manchester Ave Wabash (46992) *(G-16170)*
11/18 Pro Aluminum LLC... 260 204-3577
  817 W Berry St Apt 3 Fort Wayne (46802) *(G-4709)*
110495 - Pacmoore Process Tech, Mooresville Also Called: Pacmoore Process Tech LLC *(G-12233)*
1109 169th LLC... 219 671-5052
  1109 Churchill Ln Crown Point (46307) *(G-2647)*
12 Stone Ventures Inc.. 765 573-4605
  9488 N W 100 Converse (46919) *(G-2476)*
12-05 Distillery LLC... 317 402-4818
  636 Virginia Ave Indianapolis (46203) *(G-7383)*
120 Water Audit Inc.. 888 317-1510
  250 S Elm St Zionsville (46077) *(G-16987)*
1205 Distillery.. 317 804-5675
  120 Camilla Ct Westfield (46074) *(G-16659)*
12154 Holding Corp... 260 563-8371
  3837 Mill St Wabash (46992) *(G-16171)*
123carportz.. 574 376-0470
  1321 E Jefferson Blvd Mishawaka (46545) *(G-11833)*
141 Trucking LLC... 312 581-5121
  3141 Amber Way Schererville (46375) *(G-14511)*
143 Berkley LLC.. 260 414-0369
  6455 E Mcguire Rd Churubusco (46723) *(G-1971)*
1500 South Tibbs LLC... 317 247-8141
  201 N Illinois St Ste 1800 Indianapolis (46204) *(G-7384)*
1632 Inc... 219 398-4155
  4202 Baring Ave East Chicago (46312) *(G-2987)*
170 Tactical Inc... 765 793-7932
  406 Liberty St Covington (47932) *(G-2525)*
18 Threads LLC... 260 409-2923
  6121 W Jefferson Blvd Fort Wayne (46804) *(G-4710)*
18th Street Distillery LLC... 219 803-0820
  5417 Oakley Ave Ste 1 Hammond (46320) *(G-6865)*
1970, Fishers Also Called: Disaster Masters Inc *(G-4504)*
1globalds LLC.. 765 413-2211
  16750 Glen Way Westfield (46062) *(G-16660)*

1st Attack Engineering Inc... 260 837-2435
  5709 County Road 35 Auburn (46706) *(G-359)*
1st Choice Contractors LLC... 317 628-4721
  3510 Delmar Rd Indianapolis (46220) *(G-7385)*
1st Choice Machining & Tooling, Madison Also Called: Extreme Precision Products LLC *(G-11219)*
1st Choice Safety LLC.. 260 797-5338
  4642 Pleasant Valley Dr Fort Wayne (46825) *(G-4711)*
1st Defense.. 317 292-3123
  6613 Crossbridge Dr Noblesville (46062) *(G-13032)*
1st Place Trophy Shop, Elkhart Also Called: First Place Trophy Inc *(G-3347)*
1st Source Products Inc.. 812 288-7466
  2822 Sable Mill Ln Jeffersonville (47130) *(G-9919)*
1z2z Imprints.. 303 918-8979
  3815 E Tamarron Dr Bloomington (47408) *(G-764)*
2 EZ Price LLC... 312 912-4084
  4126 Towle Ave Hammond (46327) *(G-6866)*
20 Minute Signs Plus Inc... 765 413-1046
  3032 E 800 S Lafayette (47909) *(G-10512)*
20/20 Custom Molded Plas LLC....................................... 260 565-2020
  785 Decker Dr Bluffton (46714) *(G-1020)*
243 Quarry... 765 653-4100
  8090 S State Road 243 Cloverdale (46120) *(G-2081)*
250ok LLC.. 855 250-6529
  9247 N Meridian St Ste 301 Indianapolis (46260) *(G-7386)*
2nd Amendment Customs LLC.. 765 716-5636
  1572 E Us Highway 36 Markleville (46056) *(G-11365)*
3 Micron Laser Technology LLC...................................... 317 677-8958
  8174 E 21st St Indianapolis (46219) *(G-7387)*
3-D Services... 574 933-4819
  16357 14th Rd Plymouth (46563) *(G-13749)*
3-K Racing, Lebanon Also Called: Three K Racing Enterprises *(G-10946)*
3-T Corp... 812 424-7878
  2206 N Grand Ave Evansville (47711) *(G-3856)*
323ink LLC... 812 282-3620
  2818 Sable Mill Ln Jeffersonville (47130) *(G-9920)*
34 Lives Pbc... 303 550-9989
  1281 Win Hentschel Blvd Ste 2574 West Lafayette (47906) *(G-16553)*
37 Pipe & Supply LLC... 812 275-5676
  8987 S.R. 37 Bedford (47421) *(G-615)*
39 Degrees, Bloomington Also Called: 39 Degrees North LLC *(G-765)*
39 Degrees North LLC... 855 447-3939
  908 N Walnut St Bloomington (47404) *(G-765)*
3b Photonics LLC... 574 702-2620
  2721 E County Road 650 N Logansport (46947) *(G-11053)*
3b Tech Computers, South Bend Also Called: 3btech Inc *(G-14927)*
3btech Inc... 574 233-0508
  3431 William Richardson Dr Ste B South Bend (46628) *(G-14927)*
3c Coman Ltd... 317 650-5156
  800 W Ohio St Fortville (46040) *(G-5585)*
3d Machine Inc... 219 297-3674
  215 S Newton St Goodland (47948) *(G-6077)*

ALPHABETIC SECTION

3d Parts Mfg LLC.. 317 860-6941
3248 Dr Martin Luther King Jr Blvd Anderson (46013) *(G-68)*

3d Stone Inc.. 812 824-5805
6700 S Victor Pike Bloomington (47403) *(G-766)*

3d Stone Purchaser Inc... 812 824-5805
6700 S Victor Pike Bloomington (47403) *(G-767)*

3g Concepts LLC.. 574 267-6100
3824 S Industrial Dr Warsaw (46580) *(G-16306)*

3jm Hauling LLC... 317 518-0750
10143 Morning Light Dr Avon (46123) *(G-501)*

3M, Indianapolis Also Called: 3M Company *(G-7388)*

3M, Plymouth Also Called: 3M Company *(G-13750)*

3M Company.. 765 348-3200
304 S 075 E Hartford City (47348) *(G-7060)*

3M Company.. 317 692-6666
5457 W 79th St Indianapolis (46268) *(G-7388)*

3M Company.. 574 948-8103
2925 Gary Dr Plymouth (46563) *(G-13750)*

3oe Scientific LLC.. 317 869-7602
424 W Main St Carmel (46032) *(G-1545)*

3rd Rock Energy Services LLC............................. 314 750-2722
12658 Watford Way Fishers (46037) *(G-4456)*

3rivers Soap Company LLC.................................. 260 418-0241
1935 E State Blvd Fort Wayne (46805) *(G-4712)*

3sevens LLC.. 502 594-2312
110 Ash St Henryville (47126) *(G-7112)*

3stax Printing & EMB LLC..................................... 317 612-7122
5699 E 71st St Indianapolis (46220) *(G-7389)*

3w Enterprises, Elkhart Also Called: 3w Enterprises LLC *(G-3137)*

3w Enterprises LLC.. 847 366-6555
2727 Industrial Pkwy Elkhart (46516) *(G-3137)*

4 Bar M Inc... 765 653-7119
9825 W Mount Carmel Rd Gosport (47433) *(G-6281)*

4 Lens Partnerships LLC...................................... 317 490-1389
7242 Crest Ln Indianapolis (46256) *(G-7390)*

4 Piston Racing.. 317 902-0200
200 Colin Ct Danville (46122) *(G-2805)*

411 Newspaper.. 219 922-8846
1130 Camellia Dr Munster (46321) *(G-12524)*

421 Pallet & Crate... 765 249-5088
888 S Us Highway 421 Frankfort (46041) *(G-5647)*

47tee LLC... 317 373-8070
10526 Blue Springs Ln Fishers (46037) *(G-4457)*

4board LLC.. 317 997-3354
802 N Meridian St Indianapolis (46204) *(G-7391)*

4d Manufacturing, North Judson Also Called: Evelyn Dollahan *(G-13211)*

4ever Chosen LLC.. 765 431-7548
2300 S Berkley Rd Kokomo (46902) *(G-10230)*

4ink, Corydon Also Called: 4ink Fullfillment Services *(G-2483)*

4ink Fullfillment Services..................................... 812 738-4465
2070 Highway 337 Nw # 101 Corydon (47112) *(G-2483)*

5 Knight LLC... 219 680-6661
2223 Sheridan St Anderson (46016) *(G-69)*

5 Star Logistics LLC... 708 926-4251
3105 Amy Ct Highland (46322) *(G-7117)*

500 Line, Syracuse Also Called: Tranter Graphics Inc *(G-15487)*

502 Mold Polishing LLC....................................... 502 436-0239
1007 Wagon Trl Greenville (47124) *(G-6650)*

55 West LLC
5935 W 84th St Ste D Indianapolis (46278) *(G-7392)*

5m Poultry LLC.. 812 890-5558
10977 S County Road 500 E Carlisle (47838) *(G-1539)*

6 Twenty-Six Inc... 260 471-2002
1907 Production Rd Fort Wayne (46808) *(G-4713)*

651 Emergency Lighting...................................... 765 748-6664
1801 S Lindell Dr Yorktown (47396) *(G-16967)*

6605 E State LLC... 260 433-7007
2311 Forest Glade Fort Wayne (46845) *(G-4714)*

7 Up Bottling Co, Indianapolis Also Called: American Bottling Company *(G-7500)*

7lo, Gary Also Called: 7th Leadership Organization *(G-5883)*

7r Express LLC... 833 611-3497
815 John St Ste 110 Evansville (47713) *(G-3857)*

7th Leadership Organization................................. 219 938-6906
6775 Ash Pl Gary (46403) *(G-5883)*

80/20 LLC... 260 248-8030
1701 S 400 E Columbia City (46725) *(G-2114)*

80of80 Group LLC.. 812 814-1167
7022 W 10th St Indianapolis (46214) *(G-7393)*

8105 Georgia LLC.. 219 757-3532
8105 Georgia St Merrillville (46410) *(G-11475)*

85th & Pine LLC... 219 781-1327
14259 Fortress Ct Saint John (46373) *(G-14445)*

8th Day Distillery LLC.. 317 690-2202
1080 E Beechwood Ln Indianapolis (46227) *(G-7394)*

911 Led Lights, Mooreland Also Called: David Murray *(G-12184)*

A & A Custom Automation Inc (PA)....................... 812 464-3650
2125 Bergdolt Rd Evansville (47711) *(G-3858)*

A & A Industries Inc... 812 663-5584
201 S Monfort St Greensburg (47240) *(G-6577)*

A & A Machine Service Inc................................... 317 745-7367
4830 E Main St Avon (46123) *(G-502)*

A & A Prcsion Htg Colg Rfrgn L........................... 812 401-1711
1272 Maxwell Ave Evansville (47711) *(G-3859)*

A & A Sheet Metal Products (PA).......................... 219 326-1288
5122 N State Road 39 La Porte (46350) *(G-10371)*

A & AS Beauty Barn LLC..................................... 812 589-8559
1127 Lincoln Ave Apt 629 Evansville (47714) *(G-3860)*

A & B Fabricating, Mentone Also Called: A & B Fabricating & Maint Inc *(G-11468)*

A & B Fabricating & Maint Inc.............................. 574 353-1012
516 N Morgan St Mentone (46539) *(G-11468)*

A & D Building, Evansville Also Called: Red Spot Paint & Varnish Co *(G-4280)*

A & E Publications LLC....................................... 317 795-4308
125 E 86th St Indianapolis (46240) *(G-7395)*

A & H Enterprises LLC... 317 398-3070
60 E Washington St Shelbyville (46176) *(G-14729)*

A & JS Belts Inc... 219 628-0074
215 Sauk Trl Valparaiso (46385) *(G-15888)*

A & L Spcialty Foods H C Trnsp, Indianapolis Also Called: Park 100 Foods Inc *(G-9093)*

A & M Innovations LLC.. 317 306-6118
37 Erins Ct Whiteland (46184) *(G-16776)*

A & M Rubber Stamps Inc.................................... 219 836-0892
424 Hickory Ln Munster (46321) *(G-12525)*

A & M Systems Inc... 574 522-5000
4121 Eastland Dr Elkhart (46516) *(G-3138)*

A & M Tool Inc.. 812 934-6533
23102 Vote Rd Batesville (47006) *(G-575)*

A & M Woodworking... 574 642-4555
5545 S 1125 W Millersburg (46543) *(G-11810)*

A & R Machine Shop LLP.................................... 574 825-5686
14719 County Road 20 Middlebury (46540) *(G-11692)*

A & S Logging Inc.. 574 896-3136
2340 E 800 S North Judson (46366) *(G-13205)*

A & T Cnstr & Excvtg Inc..................................... 219 314-2439
10212 W 128th Ave Cedar Lake (46303) *(G-1826)*

A & T Concrete Supply Inc................................... 812 753-4252
81 E State Road 168 Fort Branch (47648) *(G-4701)*

A 2 Z Universal Solutions.................................... 317 496-7435
1350 W State Road 28 Union City (47390) *(G-15846)*

A A A Mudjackers Inc.. 317 574-1990
5925 W 300 N Sharpsville (46068) *(G-14708)*

A AMP R Woodworking.. 574 849-1477
15006 County Road 28 Goshen (46528) *(G-6084)*

A and R Erectors Incorporated............................. 317 271-3429
1605 Country Club Rd Indianapolis (46234) *(G-7396)*

A B I Dept, North Judson Also Called: Chester Inc *(G-13209)*

A B R Imagery, Bloomington Also Called: Abr Images Inc *(G-770)*

A Better U LLC.. 260 704-3309
3419 Bass Rd Fort Wayne (46808) *(G-4715)*

A C C, Fort Wayne Also Called: Applied Coating Converting LLC *(G-4764)*

A C Mallory Capacitors LLC (PA)......................... 317 612-1000
4411 S High School Rd Indianapolis (46241) *(G-7397)*

A D I Screen Printing... 765 457-8580
6776 W 00 Ns Kokomo (46901) *(G-10231)*

ALPHABETIC SECTION — A&J Woodworking LLC

A Divine Image Enterprise LLC... 317 397-8132
9114 Key Ln Indianapolis (46234) *(G-7398)*

A E I, Indianapolis *Also Called: Aerodyn Engineering LLC (G-7451)*

A E Techron Inc... 574 295-9495
2507 Warren St Elkhart (46516) *(G-3139)*

A G A Gas Inc... 317 783-2331
5825 Elmwood Ave Indianapolis (46203) *(G-7399)*

A Great Stitch... 317 698-3743
800 Lane 440 Lake James Angola (46703) *(G-223)*

A H Emery Company.. 812 466-5265
1355 Aberdeen St Terre Haute (47804) *(G-15527)*

A Harris Verl Inc... 317 736-4680
112 W Saint Clair St Indianapolis (46204) *(G-7400)*

A Homestead Shoppe Inc (PA)................................. 574 784-2307
330 E Vandalia St Lapaz (46537) *(G-10814)*

A J Brown Arms Company....................................... 812 384-1056
709 N Washington St Bloomfield (47424) *(G-739)*

A J Coil Inc.. 574 353-7174
20015 Apple Rd Tippecanoe (46570) *(G-15758)*

A J Kay Co... 224 475-0370
4604 S Burnett Dr South Bend (46614) *(G-14928)*

A J Schnell Wood Works LLC................................. 317 370-8890
9894 Equestrian Way Zionsville (46077) *(G-16988)*

A J Witham Sign Production, Arcadia *Also Called: Witham Anthony J Sign Prod (G-320)*

A Lit'le Bit of Heaven Farm, Arcadia *Also Called: Debra Schneider (G-312)*

A Little Unique Embroider... 812 246-0592
12106 Columbus Mann Rd Sellersburg (47172) *(G-14586)*

A M A, Muncie *Also Called: Academy of Mdel Aronautics Inc (G-12334)*

A M A C O, Indianapolis *Also Called: American Art Clay Co Inc (G-7499)*

A M Manufacturing Co Inc.. 219 472-7272
9200 Calumet Ave Ste Nw07 Munster (46321) *(G-12526)*

A M T, Fort Wayne *Also Called: Advanced Machine & Tool Corp (G-4727)*

A New Covenant Woodwork LLC............................ 812 737-2929
4305 Hooptown Rd Se Laconia (47135) *(G-10504)*

A One Pallet Inc.. 859 282-6137
100 Brown St Greendale (47025) *(G-6436)*

A One Signs & Graphics... 574 293-7104
726 Middleton Run Rd Elkhart (46516) *(G-3140)*

A P M, Scottsburg *Also Called: American Plastic Molding Corp (G-14552)*

A P Machine & Tool Co Inc...................................... 812 232-4939
1301 Elm St Terre Haute (47807) *(G-15528)*

A Packaging Systems LLC...................................... 219 369-4131
1500 Lake St La Porte (46350) *(G-10372)*

A Packs, La Porte *Also Called: A Packaging Systems LLC (G-10372)*

A Page Beyond LLC.. 317 589-8218
13009 Fairfax Ct Fishers (46055) *(G-4638)*

A Pallet Company.. 317 687-9020
1305 Bedford St Indianapolis (46221) *(G-7401)*

A Pinch of Sweetness LLC...................................... 765 838-2358
2415 Sagamore Pkwy S Lafayette (47905) *(G-10513)*

A Plus Datacomm... 219 472-1644
3282 Roswell Dr Portage (46368) *(G-13842)*

A Plus Metals LLC... 915 341-0650
4353 E 250 N Rockville (47872) *(G-14349)*

A Plus Printing, Brazil *Also Called: Innovative Printing Svcs Inc (G-1147)*

A Plus Sign Area Ltg Spcalists................................. 765 966-4857
920 Progress Dr Richmond (47374) *(G-14080)*

A Pro-Build Company, Mooresville *Also Called: Carter Lee Building Component (G-12199)*

A R. Martin Woodworks, Fishers *Also Called: Robert M Kolarich (G-4597)*

A Raymond Tinnerman, Logansport *Also Called: Araymond Mfg Ctr N Amer Inc (G-11058)*

A Rental Center, Linton *Also Called: Landis Equipment & Tool Rental (G-11037)*

A S I, Bloomington *Also Called: Author Solutions LLC (G-786)*

A S I, Madison *Also Called: Arvin Sango Inc (G-11203)*

A S M Inc... 260 724-8220
125 W Grant St Decatur (46733) *(G-2839)*

A S P Parrott Signs.. 812 325-9102
1820 S Walnut St Bloomington (47401) *(G-768)*

A S V Plastics Inc.. 574 264-9694
419 Roske Dr Elkhart (46516) *(G-3141)*

A Shade Faster Products LLC................................. 574 584-5744
23035 Lake Shore Dr Elkhart (46514) *(G-3142)*

A Shutter In Time LLC... 317 512-6753
9780 W 450 S Manilla (46150) *(G-11259)*

A Sign Above... 317 392-2144
25033 Us Highway 52 Laurel (47024) *(G-10823)*

A Sign Odyssey LLC.. 219 962-1247
727 Central Ave Lake Station (46405) *(G-10771)*

A Sign of Tymes... 317 251-0792
2881 E 56th St Indianapolis (46220) *(G-7402)*

A Sign-By-Design Inc... 317 876-7900
501 W Noble St Lebanon (46052) *(G-10872)*

A Snack Above Rest LLC.. 219 455-3335
466 Johnson St Gary (46402) *(G-5884)*

A T C, Elkhart *Also Called: American Technology Components Incorporated (G-3177)*

A T C Specialists, Bloomington *Also Called: Auto Temp Ctrl Specialists Inc (G-787)*

A T G, Fort Wayne *Also Called: Applied Technology Group Inc (G-4767)*

A T L, Indianapolis *Also Called: Philips Ultrasound Inc (G-9135)*

A T Systems Technologies Inc................................ 317 352-1030
68 N Gale St Indianapolis (46201) *(G-7403)*

A Taste of Court Valjean LLC.................................. 812 802-8584
3011 Southeast Blvd Evansville (47714) *(G-3861)*

A To Z Sheet Metal, Indianapolis *Also Called: Bright Sheet Metal Company Inc (G-7684)*

A To Z Sign Shop... 219 462-7489
55 Us Highway 30 Bldg B Valparaiso (46383) *(G-15889)*

A U I, Columbus *Also Called: American Urn Inc (G-2218)*

A W Manufacturing, Angola *Also Called: Angola Wire Products Inc (G-228)*

A W T, Indianapolis *Also Called: Astbury Water Technology Inc (G-7556)*

A Wild Hare LLC.. 812 988-9453
44 N Van Buren St Nashville (47448) *(G-12658)*

A Yard Art... 317 862-1486
305 3rd Ave Ne Carmel (46032) *(G-1546)*

A-1 Awards Inc.. 317 546-9000
2500 N Ritter Ave Indianapolis (46218) *(G-7406)*

A-1 Door Specialties Inc.. 260 749-1635
630 E Bronson St Ste 1 South Bend (46601) *(G-14930)*

A-1 Graphics Inc.. 765 289-1851
2500 W 7th St Muncie (47302) *(G-12332)*

A-1 Machine, Terre Haute *Also Called: Rk Machine Inc (G-15683)*

A-1 Pallet, Clarksville *Also Called: A-1 Pallet Co Inc Clarksville (G-2005)*

A-1 Pallet Co Inc Clarksville..................................... 812 288-6339
1507 Progress Way Clarksville (47129) *(G-2005)*

A-1 Pallet Co of Clarksville (PA)............................... 812 288-6339
940 Cottonwood Dr Clarksville (47129) *(G-2006)*

A-1 Screenprinting LLC... 812 558-0286
512 E Kirkwood Ave Bloomington (47408) *(G-769)*

A-1 Screenprinting LLC... 765 588-3851
314 W State St West Lafayette (47906) *(G-16554)*

A-1vet LLC.. 317 498-1804
4411 Dunn St Indianapolis (46226) *(G-7407)*

A-Fab LLC... 812 897-0900
977 Hyrock Blvd Boonville (47601) *(G-1078)*

A-Lert Construction Service, Garrett *Also Called: Centurion Industries Inc (G-5855)*

A-Plus Signs LLC.. 765 966-4857
920 Progress Dr Richmond (47374) *(G-14081)*

A-R-T Printing.. 812 235-8600
1309 N 19th St Terre Haute (47807) *(G-15529)*

A-Rose Consultants LLC.. 765 650-8700
805 E Washington St Frankfort (46041) *(G-5648)*

A/C Fabricating Corp.. 574 534-1415
1821 Century Dr Goshen (46528) *(G-6086)*

A&A Screen Printing.. 765 473-8783
311 W 8th St Peru (46970) *(G-13564)*

A&E Klassic Detailing LLC....................................... 219 363-6671
1620 E Michigan Blvd Michigan City (46360) *(G-11574)*

A&J Construction HM Rmdlg LLC............................ 574 514-5127
1251 N Eddy St South Bend (46617) *(G-14929)*

A&J Development Group LLC.................................. 317 767-1182
633 N Livingston Ave Indianapolis (46222) *(G-7404)*

A&J Logistic LLC... 708 314-6817
905 Joliet St Dyer (46311) *(G-2965)*

A&J Woodworking LLC.. 574 642-4551
12263 County Road 36 Goshen (46528) *(G-6085)*

ALPHABETIC SECTION

A&M Commercial Cleaning LLC...765 720-3737
1138 Avenue D St Greencastle (46135) *(G-6392)*
A&M Tool & Die, Summitville *Also Called: Robert Atkins (G-15430)*
A&R Sawmill LLC..765 238-8829
9450 Clyde Oler Rd Greens Fork (47345) *(G-6574)*
A+ Images Inc..317 405-8955
5700 W Minnesota St Ste A5 Indianapolis (46241) *(G-7405)*
A1 Campers and Trlrs Mfg LLC..574 227-2200
30063 Tower Rd Elkhart (46516) *(G-3143)*
A1 Deliveries LLC...317 828-3951
2926 Medford Ave Indianapolis (46222) *(G-7408)*
A1 Iron & Aluminum Co, South Bend *Also Called: Ironcraft Co Inc (G-15088)*
A1 Pallet, Evansville *Also Called: A1 Pallets Inc (G-3862)*
A1 Pallet Liquidators...765 356-4020
2700 Indiana Ave Anderson (46012) *(G-70)*
A1 Pallets Inc..812 425-0381
1801 W Maryland St Evansville (47712) *(G-3862)*
A2 Sales LLC (PA)..708 924-1200
2700 E 5th Ave Gary (46402) *(G-5885)*
Aa Truck Sleeper LLC, Fort Wayne *Also Called: Domain Industries LLC (G-4922)*
AAA Black Signs LLC..765 315-9569
347 E Mahalasville Rd Martinsville (46151) *(G-11376)*
AAA Galvanizing - Joliet Inc..260 488-4477
7825 S Homestead Dr Hamilton (46742) *(G-6850)*
AAA Galvanizing - Joliet Inc..765 289-3427
2415 S Walnut St Muncie (47302) *(G-12333)*
AAA Galvanizing - Joliet Inc..574 935-4500
2631 Jim Neu Dr Plymouth (46563) *(G-13751)*
AAA Satellite Link...765 642-7000
1529 W 2nd St Anderson (46016) *(G-71)*
AAA State of Play.com, Indianapolis *Also Called: Nvb Playgrounds Inc (G-9037)*
AAA Tool and Die Company Inc (PA).....................................574 246-1222
25101 Cleveland Rd South Bend (46628) *(G-14931)*
AAA Welding Inc...574 293-5294
28338 County Road 24 Elkhart (46517) *(G-3144)*
Aacoa, Elkhart *Also Called: Bonnell Aluminum Elkhart Inc (G-3232)*
Aaland Gem Company Inc...219 769-4492
8102 Georgia St Merrillville (46410) *(G-11476)*
Aalberts Hydrnic Flow Ctrl Inc..317 257-6050
9982 E 121st St Fishers (46037) *(G-4458)*
Aalberts Surface Technologies, North Vernon *Also Called: Atmosphere Annealing LLC (G-13256)*
Aalberts Surface Technologies, Wabash *Also Called: Al-Fe Heat Treating LLC (G-16173)*
AAM Bluffton, Bluffton *Also Called: American Axle & Mfg Inc (G-1024)*
AAM Powertrain, Fremont *Also Called: American Axle & Mfg Inc (G-5808)*
Aam-Equipco Inc (PA)..574 272-8886
12838 Loop Ct Granger (46530) *(G-6329)*
Aar LLC...260 591-0100
150 E Washington Ave Peru (46970) *(G-13565)*
AAR Aircraft Services, Indianapolis *Also Called: AAR Corp (G-7409)*
AAR Corp...317 227-5000
2825 West Perimeter Rd Ste 101 Indianapolis (46241) *(G-7409)*
AAR Defense Systems Logistics, Indianapolis *Also Called: AAR Supply Chain Inc (G-7410)*
AAR Supply Chain Inc...317 227-5000
2825 West Perimeter Rd Indianapolis (46241) *(G-7410)*
Aardvark Furniture, West Lafayette *Also Called: Wasu Inc (G-16645)*
Aardvark Graphics..574 267-4799
4121 Deer Run N Warsaw (46582) *(G-16307)*
Aardvark Straws, Fort Wayne *Also Called: Hoffmaster Group Inc (G-5070)*
Aardvark Vinyl Signs...260 833-0800
1875 W 275 N Angola (46703) *(G-224)*
Aaron Company Inc..219 838-0852
4835 W 45th Ave Gary (46408) *(G-5886)*
Aaron Dickinson...317 503-0922
1789 W 200 N Greenfield (46140) *(G-6457)*
Aaron McWhirter..307 256-0070
6272 E Pemboke Ct Camby (46113) *(G-1506)*
Aarons Welding LLC..574 529-3885
6421 E Mckenna Rd Warsaw (46582) *(G-16308)*
Aarvee Associates LLC..312 222-5665
9541 Valparaiso Ct Indianapolis (46268) *(G-7411)*

AB Engineering Inc...260 489-2845
5822 Kruse Dr Fort Wayne (46818) *(G-4716)*
AB&b Services LLC..317 405-7219
550 Congressional Blvd Carmel (46032) *(G-1547)*
Abacus Printingngraphics Inc...915 223-5166
425 Blue Spring Dr Ste 103 Indianapolis (46239) *(G-7412)*
ABB Enterprise Software Inc..317 876-9090
6530 Corporate Dr Indianapolis (46278) *(G-7413)*
ABB ENTERPRISE SOFTWARE INC., Indianapolis *Also Called: ABB Enterprise Software Inc (G-7413)*
ABB Flexible Automation Inc..317 876-9090
8401 Northwest Blvd Indianapolis (46278) *(G-7414)*
ABB Inc..941 278-2200
401 N Congress Ave Evansville (47715) *(G-3863)*
ABB Robotics, Indianapolis *Also Called: ABB Flexible Automation Inc (G-7414)*
Abboo Candle Co LLC..317 395-4404
10091 N Balfer Dr W Fortville (46040) *(G-5586)*
Abbott Inc..765 647-2523
1049 Main St Brookville (47012) *(G-1315)*
Abbott Controls Inc...317 697-7102
5777 W 74th St Indianapolis (46278) *(G-7415)*
Abbott Industrial Sewing LLC...574 383-1588
1044 Eclipse Pl South Bend (46628) *(G-14932)*
Abbott L Abbott Nutrition..765 935-8650
4200 W Industries Rd Richmond (47374) *(G-14082)*
Abbott's Candy Shop, Hagerstown *Also Called: Abbotts Candy and Gifts Inc (G-6832)*
Abbotts Candy and Gifts Inc (PA)...765 489-4442
48 E Walnut St Hagerstown (47346) *(G-6832)*
Abbp LLC..812 402-2000
616 N Norman Ave Evansville (47711) *(G-3864)*
Abby Grace's Gifts, Newburgh *Also Called: Trophy Case LLC (G-13026)*
ABC, Winona Lake *Also Called: ABC Industries Inc (G-16907)*
ABC Embroidery, Albion *Also Called: ABC Embroidery Inc (G-16)*
ABC Embroidery Inc...260 636-7311
3008 S 50 W Albion (46701) *(G-16)*
ABC Fix-N-Fab Welding LLC...765 230-6492
1106 N Portland Arch Rd Covington (47932) *(G-2526)*
ABC Industries Inc (PA)..800 426-0921
301 Kings Hwy Winona Lake (46590) *(G-16907)*
ABC Truck & Equipment LLC...260 565-3307
941 N Main St # B Bluffton (46714) *(G-1021)*
Abda Incorporated...317 273-8343
1159 Country Club Rd Indianapolis (46224) *(G-7416)*
Abell Tool Co Inc..317 887-0021
446 Park 800 Dr Greenwood (46143) *(G-6658)*
Abercrombie Textiles I LLC...574 848-5100
103 Hinsdale Farm Rd Bristol (46507) *(G-1240)*
ABERDEEN WOODS APARTMENTS, Jeffersonville *Also Called: New Hope Services Inc (G-10022)*
ABF Welding & Pipe LLC...765 977-7349
308 N 3rd St Cambridge City (47327) *(G-1489)*
ABI, Terre Haute *Also Called: Advics Manufacturing Ind LLC (G-15533)*
ABI Plastics LLC...574 294-1700
2510 Middlebury St Elkhart (46516) *(G-3145)*
Abk Tracking Inc..812 473-9554
1201 N Weinbach Ave Evansville (47711) *(G-3865)*
ABM Advanced Bearing Mtls LLC..812 663-3401
1515 W Main St Greensburg (47240) *(G-6578)*
Abr Enterprises LLC...808 352-4658
11027 Barrymore Run Roanoke (46783) *(G-14255)*
Abr Images Inc..866 342-4764
3808 W Vernal Pike Bloomington (47404) *(G-770)*
Abracadabra Graphics...812 336-1971
5144 E State Road 45 Bloomington (47408) *(G-771)*
Abrasive & Tooling Division, Noblesville *Also Called: Precision Surfacing Solutions (G-13157)*
Abrasive Processing & Tech LLC (PA)...................................317 485-5157
712 E Ohio St Fortville (46040) *(G-5587)*
Abrasive Waterjet Indiana LLC..317 773-1631
15513 Stony Creek Way Noblesville (46060) *(G-13033)*
Abro, South Bend *Also Called: Abro Industries Inc (G-14933)*
Abro Industries Inc (PA)...574 232-8289
3580 Blackthorn Ct South Bend (46628) *(G-14933)*

ALPHABETIC SECTION

Abs Freight Lines LLC.. 317 691-6846
1138 W 33rd St Indianapolis (46208) *(G-7417)*

ABS Mfg Rep Inc... 317 407-0406
1950 E Greyhound Pass Ste 18 Carmel (46033) *(G-1548)*

Absograph Sign Co.. 630 940-4093
125 Windridge Rd Valparaiso (46385) *(G-15890)*

Absolute Caliber LLC... 574 303-4365
50839 Oak Tree Ln Bristol (46507) *(G-1241)*

Absolute Coins, Borden Also Called: Absolute Custom Coins Inc *(G-1102)*

Absolute Custom Coins Inc.. 812 733-4043
130 East St Borden (47106) *(G-1102)*

Absolute Custom Machine LLC................................. 812 724-2284
5954 S 1075 W Owensville (47665) *(G-13464)*

Absolute Fabrication Inc... 574 848-0300
1651 Toledo Rd Elkhart (46516) *(G-3146)*

Absolute Machining LLC.. 260 747-4568
3834 Vanguard Dr Fort Wayne (46809) *(G-4717)*

Absolute Printing Equipment, Indianapolis Also Called: Perfecta USA *(G-9124)*

Absolute Stone Polsg Repr LLC................................ 317 709-9539
3801 Crest Point Dr Westfield (46062) *(G-16661)*

Absolute Welding Inc.. 812 923-8001
130 East St Borden (47106) *(G-1103)*

Abstrakt Group LLC... 800 200-8994
7022 W 10th St Ste A Indianapolis (46214) *(G-7418)*

Abtrex Industries Inc (PA).. 734 728-0550
59640 Market St South Bend (46614) *(G-14934)*

Abundant Life Publications LLC................................ 219 730-7621
320 Roosevelt St Gary (46404) *(G-5887)*

AC Printing Inc... 708 418-9100
2647 Highway Ave Highland (46322) *(G-7118)*

AC Welding Mscellaneous Ir Inc................................ 317 491-2898
2625 S Lockburn St Indianapolis (46241) *(G-7419)*

Academy Energy Group LLC (PA)............................. 312 931-7443
106 State St Ste C Newburgh (47630) *(G-12991)*

Academy Inc... 574 293-7113
21291 Buckingham Rd Elkhart (46516) *(G-3147)*

Academy of Mdel Aronautics Inc.............................. 765 287-1256
5161 E Memorial Dr Muncie (47302) *(G-12334)*

Acadia... 260 894-7125
1201 Gerber St Ligonier (46767) *(G-11001)*

Acbl Holding Corporation (PA).................................. 310 712-1850
1701 E Market St Jeffersonville (47130) *(G-9921)*

Accel International... 260 897-9990
302 Progress Way Avilla (46710) *(G-471)*

Accelerated Curing Inc.. 260 726-3202
304 E 100 N Portland (47371) *(G-13926)*

Accent Bicycles, Carmel Also Called: David Tortora *(G-1605)*

Accent Complex Inc... 574 522-2368
515 East St Elkhart (46516) *(G-3148)*

Accent Limestone & Carving Inc............................... 812 876-7040
5900 N Maple Grove Rd Bloomington (47404) *(G-772)*

Accent Limestone & Carving Inc............................... 812 829-5663
2255 Wood Dr Spencer (47460) *(G-15338)*

Accent Printing, Elkhart Also Called: Accent Complex Inc *(G-3148)*

Accent Wire Products.. 765 628-3587
324 Shamrock Ave Greentown (46936) *(G-6644)*

Access Cell Phones, Mishawaka Also Called: Jackson Hewitt Tax Service *(G-11915)*

Access One By Msg Inc.. 260 485-7007
5120 Speedway Dr Fort Wayne (46825) *(G-4718)*

Accessindiana, Indianapolis Also Called: Indiana Interactive LLC *(G-8480)*

Accessories By Sherwood, Elkhart Also Called: Sherwood Industries Inc *(G-3672)*

Acclaim Graphics Inc... 812 424-5035
908 N Garvin St Evansville (47711) *(G-3866)*

Accounting Department, Fishers Also Called: United Turf Alliance LLC *(G-4620)*

Accra Pac, Elkhart Also Called: Accra-Pac Inc *(G-3149)*

Accra Pac Holding Co LLC....................................... 765 326-0005
6435 W Jefferson Blvd Ste 151 Fort Wayne (46804) *(G-4719)*

Accra-Pac Inc.. 574 295-0000
711 Middleton Run Rd Elkhart (46516) *(G-3149)*

Accra-Pac Inc (DH).. 574 295-0000
2730 Middlebury St Elkhart (46516) *(G-3150)*

Accra-Pac Inc.. 574 295-0000
1919 Superior St Elkhart (46516) *(G-3151)*

Accraline Inc.. 574 546-3484
1420 W Bike St Bremen (46506) *(G-1170)*

Accraline Inc-Metal Surgeons, Bremen Also Called: Accraline Inc *(G-1170)*

Accu-Built Tooling and Weld..................................... 574 825-7878
17821 County Road 14 Goshen (46528) *(G-6087)*

Accu-Label Inc... 260 482-5223
2021 Research Dr Fort Wayne (46808) *(G-4720)*

Accu-Mold LLC.. 269 323-0388
1702 E 7th St Mishawaka (46544) *(G-11834)*

Accu-Tool Inc... 260 248-4529
831 E Short St Columbia City (46725) *(G-2115)*

Accubuilt Plant I.. 574 389-9000
2811 Tuscany Dr Elkhart (46514) *(G-3152)*

Accuburn Williamsport Inc.. 765 762-1100
304 W Washington St Williamsport (47993) *(G-16845)*

Accucast Inc.. 317 849-5521
13352 Kimberlite Dr Fishers (46038) *(G-4459)*

Accucast Industries... 219 929-1137
1631 Pioneer Trl Chesterton (46304) *(G-1900)*

Accucraft Imaging Inc... 219 933-3007
5920 Hohman Ave Hammond (46320) *(G-6867)*

Accugear Inc.. 260 497-6600
6710 Innovation Blvd Fort Wayne (46818) *(G-4721)*

Accuprint of Kentuckiana Inc.................................... 812 944-8603
4101 Reas Ln New Albany (47150) *(G-12685)*

Accups LLC... 765 586-5021
1050 Roxboro St West Lafayette (47906) *(G-16555)*

Accuracy Laser Fabrication LLC.............................. 812 322-6431
2120 Dixie Hwy Bedford (47421) *(G-616)*

Accurate Castings Inc (PA)....................................... 219 362-8531
118 Koomler Dr La Porte (46350) *(G-10373)*

Accurate Castings Inc... 219 393-3122
3232 3rd Rd La Porte (46350) *(G-10374)*

Accurate Castings Inc... 224 563-3200
104 Fulmer St Walkerton (46574) *(G-16261)*

Accurate Hearing Aid Svcs LLC............................... 219 464-1937
2150 Smoke Rd Valparaiso (46385) *(G-15891)*

Accurate Manufactured Products, Indianapolis Also Called: Accurate Mnfctred Pdts Group I *(G-7420)*

Accurate Mnfctred Pdts Group I............................... 317 472-9000
8090 Woodland Dr Indianapolis (46278) *(G-7420)*

Accurate Publishing Co.. 219 836-1397
8445 Manor Ave Apt 301 Munster (46321) *(G-12527)*

Accurate Turning Solutions....................................... 812 603-6612
4141 W Carr Hill Rd Columbus (47201) *(G-2212)*

Accuride Corporation.. 812 962-5000
7140 Office Cir Evansville (47715) *(G-3867)*

Accuride Emi LLC... 940 565-8505
7140 Office Cir Evansville (47715) *(G-3868)*

Accutech Mold & Machine Inc................................. 260 471-6102
2817 Goshen Rd Fort Wayne (46808) *(G-4722)*

Accutemp, New Haven Also Called: Accutemp Products Inc *(G-12889)*

Accutemp Products Inc (PA).................................... 260 493-0415
11919 John Adams Dr New Haven (46774) *(G-12889)*

Accutemp Products Inc.. 260 493-6831
12004 Lincoln Hwy E New Haven (46774) *(G-12890)*

Acdc Control LLC... 219 801-3900
5614 Homerlee Ave East Chicago (46312) *(G-2988)*

Ace Extrusion LLC (PA).. 812 868-8640
14020 Highway 57 Evansville (47725) *(G-3869)*

Ace Extrusion LLC.. 812 436-4840
701 N 9th Ave Evansville (47712) *(G-3870)*

Ace Extrusion LLC.. 812 463-5230
1800 W Maryland St Evansville (47712) *(G-3871)*

Ace Hardware, Kentland Also Called: Prmi 1 Inc *(G-10162)*

Ace Metal Sales, Marysville Also Called: Solomon M Eicher *(G-11436)*

Ace Mobility Inc... 317 241-2444
9850 E 30th St Indianapolis (46229) *(G-7421)*

Ace Printing... 812 275-3412
68 Miami Dr Bedford (47421) *(G-617)*

(PA)=Parent Co (HQ)=Headquarters (DH)=Div Headquarters

Ace Sign & Awning, Terre Haute *Also Called: All American Tent & Awning Inc (G-15537)*
Ace Sign Company Inc..812 232-4206
1140 3rd Ave Terre Haute (47807) *(G-15530)*
Ace Sign Systems Inc..765 288-1000
3621 W Royerton Rd Muncie (47304) *(G-12335)*
Ace Tool & Engineering Co, Mooresville *Also Called: S Edwards Inc (G-12240)*
Ace Welding and Machine Inc..812 379-9625
2461 N Indianapolis Rd Columbus (47201) *(G-2213)*
Acell Inc...765 464-8198
3589 Sagamore Pkwy N Ste 220 Lafayette (47904) *(G-10514)*
Aceys Trophies & Awards..574 267-1426
222 W Prairie St Warsaw (46580) *(G-16309)*
Achates LLC...317 852-6978
481 Southpoint Cir Brownsburg (46112) *(G-1343)*
Aci Construction Company Inc.....................................317 549-1833
5108 Topp Dr Indianapolis (46218) *(G-7422)*
Acl Professional Services Inc......................................812 288-0100
1701 Utica Pike Jeffersonville (47130) *(G-9922)*
Acl Sales Corporation..812 288-0100
1701 E Market St Jeffersonville (47130) *(G-9923)*
Acme Cabinet Corporation..219 924-1800
1331 E Main St Griffith (46319) *(G-6785)*
Acme Coatings, Avon *Also Called: Big Dipper Inc (G-508)*
Acme Firearms Mfg LLC...812 522-4008
800 E Tipton St Seymour (47274) *(G-14624)*
Acme Industrial Inc...260 422-6518
2380 E Cardinal Dr Columbia City (46725) *(G-2116)*
Acme Masking Company Inc..317 272-6202
240 Production Dr Avon (46123) *(G-503)*
Acme Sports Inc...812 522-4008
800 E Tipton St Seymour (47274) *(G-14625)*
Acorn Ridge Highlands, Warsaw *Also Called: Hand Industries Inc (G-16373)*
Acorn Woodworks...317 867-4377
16116 Ditch Rd Westfield (46074) *(G-16662)*
Acoustical Audio Designs LLC.....................................812 282-7522
2008 Coopers Ln Jeffersonville (47130) *(G-9924)*
Acpi Wood Products LLC...574 842-2066
515 W Mill St Culver (46511) *(G-2777)*
Acra-Line Products Inc..765 675-8841
641 Cleveland St Tipton (46072) *(G-15763)*
Acro Biomedical Co Ltd...317 286-6788
12175 Visionary Way Ste 1160 Fishers (46038) *(G-4460)*
Acro Engineering Inc..812 663-6236
1120 W Washington St Greensburg (47240) *(G-6579)*
ACS, Griffith *Also Called: ACS Technical Products Inc (G-6786)*
ACS Graphics Inc..260 495-7446
103 N Wayne St Fremont (46737) *(G-5806)*
ACS Sign Solution..317 201-4838
115 E 21st St Indianapolis (46202) *(G-7423)*
ACS Sign Solution (PA)..317 925-2835
1110 E 22nd St Indianapolis (46202) *(G-7424)*
ACS Sign Systems, Indianapolis *Also Called: ACS Sign Solution (G-7423)*
ACS Technical Products Inc..219 924-4370
420 S Colfax St Griffith (46319) *(G-6786)*
Act, Indianapolis *Also Called: Advanced Control Tech Inc (G-7437)*
Act Research, Columbus *Also Called: Americas Coml Trnsp RES Co LLC (G-2219)*
Actega North America Inc..800 426-4657
650 W 67th Pl Schererville (46375) *(G-14512)*
Acterna LLC...317 788-9351
5808 Churchman Byp Indianapolis (46203) *(G-7425)*
Action Amusement...812 422-9029
1405 Allens Ln Evansville (47710) *(G-3872)*
Action Cooling Towers Inc...219 285-2660
2649 S 500 W Morocco (47963) *(G-12267)*
Action Embroidery Inc...850 626-1796
300 Pike St Charlestown (47111) *(G-1869)*
Action Filtration Inc (PA)...812 546-6262
221 Raymond St Hope (47246) *(G-7222)*
Action Machine Inc...574 287-9650
1847 Prairie Ave South Bend (46613) *(G-14935)*
Action Plus Shopper & Shoppers, Demotte *Also Called: Kankakee Valley Post News (G-2920)*

Action Printing Sign Co..219 362-9729
238 W Johnson Rd La Porte (46350) *(G-10375)*
Action Welding & Machine Svcs..................................219 766-0406
1101 W Daumer Rd Kouts (46347) *(G-10360)*
Active Ankle Systems Inc..812 258-0663
233 Quartermaster Ct Jeffersonville (47130) *(G-9925)*
Active Trading Intl Inc...260 637-1990
6015 2 Highway Drive Ste G Fort Wayne (46818) *(G-4723)*
Acuity Brands Inc...765 362-1837
1304 E Elmore St Crawfordsville (47933) *(G-2542)*
Acuity Brands Lighting Inc..765 362-1837
1615 E Elmore St Crawfordsville (47933) *(G-2543)*
Acura Pharmaceutical Tech.......................................574 842-3305
16235 State Road 17 Culver (46511) *(G-2778)*
Acutech LLC..574 262-8228
53905 County Road 9 Ste C Elkhart (46514) *(G-3153)*
Acwelding & Misc Iron Inc...317 491-2898
2209 E Beecher St Ste B Indianapolis (46203) *(G-7426)*
Ad Vision Graphics Inc..812 476-4932
1820 N Hoosier Ave Evansville (47715) *(G-3873)*
Ad-Sign & Display Division, Indianapolis *Also Called: Phil Irwin Advertising Inc (G-9134)*
Ad-Vance Magnetics Inc..574 223-3158
625 Monroe St Rochester (46975) *(G-14274)*
Adafill Global LLC...317 798-5378
735 Shelby St Ste 33 Indianapolis (46203) *(G-7427)*
Adalphi Corp..847 624-3301
9668 Spruance Ct Indianapolis (46256) *(G-7428)*
Adam L Hoskins...765 580-0345
3922 N County Road 250 W Liberty (47353) *(G-10983)*
Adams & Westlake Ltd..574 264-1141
940 N Michigan St Elkhart (46514) *(G-3154)*
Adams Signs Inc..219 972-0700
9020 Ohio Pl Highland (46322) *(G-7119)*
Adams Smith (PA)..219 661-2812
10431 Floyd St Crown Point (46307) *(G-2648)*
Adamswells Phonebooks LLC....................................260 622-6046
125 N Johnson St Bluffton (46714) *(G-1022)*
Adaptasoft Inc..219 567-2547
106 E Montgomery St Francesville (47946) *(G-5635)*
Adaptek Systems, Fort Wayne *Also Called: Deprisco Ventures Inc (G-4916)*
Adaptive Mobility Inc..317 347-6400
7040 Guion Rd Indianapolis (46268) *(G-7429)*
Adaptive Tech Solutions LLC.....................................317 762-4363
14915 Silver Thorne Way Carmel (46033) *(G-1549)*
Adcomm Bindery, Roachdale *Also Called: No-Sail Splash Guard Co Inc (G-14248)*
Addenda LLC (HQ)...317 290-5007
5929 Lakeside Blvd Indianapolis (46278) *(G-7430)*
Addivant USA LLC..765 497-6020
1435 Win Hentschel Blvd Ste 115 West Lafayette (47906) *(G-16556)*
Adell Group LLC...317 507-6158
1385 Sierra Spgs 5 Carmel (46280) *(G-1550)*
Ademco Inc..317 359-9505
3160 N Shadeland Ave Indianapolis (46226) *(G-7431)*
Adept LLC..812 275-8899
677 Guthrie Rd Bedford (47421) *(G-618)*
Adept Tool and Engineering......................................317 896-9250
11307 Green St Carmel (46033) *(G-1551)*
Adhesive Products Inc..317 899-0565
8736 E 33rd St Indianapolis (46226) *(G-7432)*
Adhesive Solutions Company LLC (PA)......................260 691-0304
4201 N 450 E Columbia City (46725) *(G-2117)*
ADI Global Distribution, Indianapolis *Also Called: Ademco Inc (G-7431)*
Adidas North America Inc...219 878-5822
601 Wabash St Ste 1205 Michigan City (46360) *(G-11575)*
Adidas Outlet Store Mich Cy, Michigan City *Also Called: Adidas North America Inc (G-11575)*
Adjust Your Crown Hair Care Pd...............................317 970-1144
5332 Penway St Indianapolis (46224) *(G-7433)*
Adkev Inc..574 583-4420
1207 N 6th St Monticello (47960) *(G-12132)*
Adkev Inc (PA)..219 297-4484
664 S Iroquois St Goodland (47948) *(G-6078)*

ALPHABETIC SECTION — Advanced Welding and Engrg

Adkins Amusements 765 939-0285
903 N D St Richmond (47374) *(G-14083)*

Adkins Sawmill Inc 812 849-4036
2929 Fleenor Rd Mitchell (47446) *(G-12029)*

Adlake, Elkhart Also Called: Adams & Westlake Ltd *(G-3154)*

Adlink Promotions 574 271-7003
52074 N Lakeshore Dr Granger (46530) *(G-6330)*

ADM, Beech Grove Also Called: ADM Milling Co *(G-685)*

ADM, Beech Grove Also Called: Archer-Daniels-Midland Company *(G-686)*

ADM, Bluffton Also Called: Archer-Daniels-Midland Company *(G-1025)*

ADM, Crawfordsville Also Called: Archer-Daniels-Midland Company *(G-2545)*

ADM, Frankfort Also Called: Archer-Daniels-Midland Company *(G-5649)*

ADM, Huntertown Also Called: Asphalt Drum Mixers LLC *(G-7249)*

ADM, Mount Vernon Also Called: ADM Milling Co *(G-12286)*

ADM, Nappanee Also Called: Archer-Daniels-Midland Company *(G-12580)*

ADM, Rensselaer Also Called: Archer-Daniels-Midland Company *(G-14043)*

ADM, Rensselaer Also Called: Archer-Daniels-Midland Company *(G-14044)*

ADM Custom Creations LLC 765 499-0584
6 Belfast Ct Hartford City (47348) *(G-7061)*

ADM Grain, Fowler Also Called: Archer-Daniels-Midland Company *(G-5618)*

ADM Grain Co, New Haven Also Called: Archer-Daniels-Midland Company *(G-12893)*

ADM Milling Co 317 783-3321
854 Bethel Ave Beech Grove (46107) *(G-685)*

ADM Milling Co 812 838-4445
614 W 2nd St Mount Vernon (47620) *(G-12286)*

Administrative Office, Indianapolis Also Called: Guide Technologies LLC *(G-8342)*

Adranos Energetics LLC 208 539-2439
137 Prophet Dr West Lafayette (47906) *(G-16557)*

Adrian Orchards Inc 317 784-0550
500 W Epler Ave Indianapolis (46217) *(G-7434)*

Advance Aero Inc 317 513-6071
135 E Harrison St Mooresville (46158) *(G-12190)*

Advance Auto Parts, Indianapolis Also Called: Advance Stores Company Inc *(G-7436)*

Advance Cabinetry and Millwork, Mishawaka Also Called: Trim-A-Door Corporation *(G-12016)*

Advance Energy, Merrillville Also Called: Advance Energy LLC *(G-11477)*

Advance Energy LLC 312 665-0022
8650 Mississippi St Merrillville (46410) *(G-11477)*

Advance Fabricators Inc 812 944-6941
980 Progress Blvd New Albany (47150) *(G-12686)*

Advance Filter LLC 317 565-7009
4515 Dr Martin Luther King Jr Blvd Anderson (46013) *(G-72)*

Advance Green Mfg Co Inc 574 457-2695
2482 E Kercher Rd Goshen (46526) *(G-6088)*

Advance Leader, Kendallville Also Called: Kpc Media Group Inc *(G-10130)*

Advance Leds LLC 844 815-8898
118 W Missouri St Evansville (47710) *(G-3874)*

Advance Machine Works Corp 260 483-1183
2620 Independence Dr Fort Wayne (46808) *(G-4724)*

Advance MCS Electronics Inc (PA) 574 642-3501
67928 Us Highway 33 Goshen (46526) *(G-6089)*

Advance MCS Electronics Inc 574 642-3501
11034 County Rd Ligonier (46767) *(G-11002)*

Advance Protection System, Walton Also Called: Advanced Protection Systems *(G-16280)*

Advance Prtective Coatings Inc 317 228-0123
8448 Moller Rd Indianapolis (46268) *(G-7435)*

Advance Repair & Machining Inc 765 474-8000
3311 Imperial Pkwy Ste B Lafayette (47909) *(G-10515)*

Advance Stores Company Inc 317 253-5034
5125 N Keystone Ave Indianapolis (46205) *(G-7436)*

Advanced Assembly, Columbia City Also Called: Lear Corporation *(G-2167)*

Advanced Bearing Materials LLC 812 663-3401
1515 W Main St Greensburg (47240) *(G-6580)*

Advanced Boiler Ctrl Svcs Inc (PA) 708 429-7066
7515 Cline Ave Crown Point (46307) *(G-2649)*

Advanced Building Concepts, Linton Also Called: Indiana Operations LLC *(G-11035)*

Advanced Cabinet Systems, Marion Also Called: J G Bowers Inc *(G-11297)*

Advanced Cabinet Systems Inc 765 677-8000
1629 S Joaquin Dr Marion (46953) *(G-11268)*

Advanced Community Enhancement 513 615-6730
19412 Collier Ridge Rd Guilford (47022) *(G-6826)*

Advanced Control Tech Inc 317 806-2750
6805 Hillsdale Ct Indianapolis (46250) *(G-7437)*

Advanced Cryotechnology, Indianapolis Also Called: Cook General Biotechnology LLC *(G-7866)*

Advanced Cutting Systems Inc 260 423-3394
3700 E Pontiac St Fort Wayne (46803) *(G-4725)*

Advanced Designs Corp (PA) 812 333-1922
1169 W 2nd St Bloomington (47403) *(G-773)*

Advanced Digital Imaging 765 491-9434
1231 Cumberland Ave Ste A West Lafayette (47906) *(G-16558)*

Advanced Digital Signs LLC 260 704-0319
5031 Charlotte Ave Fort Wayne (46815) *(G-4726)*

Advanced Drainage Systems Inc 812 443-2080
2340 E Us Highway 40 Brazil (47834) *(G-1131)*

Advanced Drainage Systems Inc 317 917-7960
420 S Belmont Ave Indianapolis (46222) *(G-7438)*

Advanced Engineering Inc 260 356-8077
5299 N Mishler Rd Huntington (46750) *(G-7296)*

Advanced Harn & Assembly LLC 574 722-4040
830 Old State Rd 25 Logansport (46947) *(G-11054)*

Advanced Lf Spport Innvtons LL 574 538-1688
59125 County Road 21 Goshen (46528) *(G-6090)*

Advanced Machine & Tool Corp (PA) 260 489-3572
3706 Transportation Dr Fort Wayne (46818) *(G-4727)*

Advanced Manufacturing In 260 273-9669
500 W Line St Geneva (46740) *(G-6047)*

Advanced Mbility Solutions LLC 812 438-2338
4669 Cass Union Rd Rising Sun (47040) *(G-14240)*

Advanced Mechatronic Tech LLC 920 918-0209
4756 S Wabash Rd Rochester (46975) *(G-14275)*

Advanced Metal Etching In 260 894-4189
801 Gerber St Ligonier (46767) *(G-11003)*

Advanced Metal Fabricators Inc 574 259-1263
1204 E 6th St Mishawaka (46544) *(G-11835)*

Advanced Mfg Solutions LLC 812 691-2030
227 E County Road 500 N Shelburn (47879) *(G-14716)*

Advanced Mold & Engineering 812 342-9000
7980 S International Dr Columbus (47201) *(G-2214)*

Advanced Mtlwrking Prctces LLC 317 337-0441
4511 W 99th St Carmel (46032) *(G-1552)*

Advanced Orthopro Inc (HQ) 317 924-4444
1820 N Illinois St Indianapolis (46202) *(G-7439)*

Advanced Orthopro Inc 812 478-3656
3185 S 3rd Pl Terre Haute (47802) *(G-15531)*

Advanced Products Tech Inc 765 827-1166
5430 Western Ave Connersville (47331) *(G-2423)*

Advanced Protection Systems 574 626-2939
6257 S County Road 900 E Walton (46994) *(G-16280)*

Advanced Protective Tech LLC (PA) 888 531-4527
310 N 400 E Valparaiso (46383) *(G-15892)*

Advanced Prtctive Slutions LLC 765 720-9574
639 Gettysburg Coatesville (46121) *(G-2102)*

Advanced Racg Suspensions Inc 317 896-3306
1698 Midwest Blvd Indianapolis (46214) *(G-7440)*

Advanced Radiant Systems, Fortville Also Called: Hale Industries Inc *(G-5598)*

Advanced Services LLC 317 780-6909
5426 Elmwood Ave Indianapolis (46203) *(G-7441)*

Advanced Sign & Graphics Inc 765 284-8360
3000 S Walnut St Muncie (47302) *(G-12336)*

Advanced Sign & Ltg Svc Inc 812 430-2817
13350 N Green River Rd Evansville (47725) *(G-3875)*

Advanced Systems Intgrtion LLC 260 447-5555
4534 Allen Martin Dr Fort Wayne (46806) *(G-4728)*

Advanced Tctcal Ord Systems LL 858 228-1439
2713 W Ferguson Rd Fort Wayne (46809) *(G-4729)*

Advanced Test Concepts LLC 317 328-8492
4037 Guion Ln Indianapolis (46268) *(G-7442)*

Advanced Vscular Therapies In 765 423-1720
1125 N 13th St Lafayette (47904) *(G-10516)*

Advanced Welding and Engrg 317 820-3595
8155 Crawfordsville Rd Indianapolis (46214) *(G-7443)*

ALPHABETIC SECTION

Advanced Wund Limb Care Ctr In... 812 232-0957
303 S 14th St Terre Haute (47807) *(G-15532)*

Advancing Chrsts Kngdom Globl... 219 765-3586
6220 Broadway Merrillville (46410) *(G-11478)*

Advancing Geometrics... 574 831-6480
20544 County Road 138 Goshen (46526) *(G-6091)*

Advantage Cartridge Co Inc... 260 747-9941
10319 Liberty Mills Rd Fort Wayne (46804) *(G-4730)*

Advantage Components Corp... 317 784-0299
6320 Wings Ct Brownsburg (46112) *(G-1344)*

Advantage Electronics Inc... 317 888-1946
525 E Stop 18 Rd Greenwood (46143) *(G-6659)*

Advantage Embroidery Inc... 765 471-0188
1059 E 400 S Bringhurst (46913) *(G-1234)*

Advantage Engineering Inc (PA)... 317 887-0729
525 E Stop 18 Rd Greenwood (46142) *(G-6660)*

Advantage Manufacturing Inc... 773 626-2200
1385 N Bendix Dr South Bend (46628) *(G-14936)*

Advantage Manufacturing LLC... 317 237-4289
1802 W 10th St Indianapolis (46222) *(G-7444)*

Advantage Manufacturing LLC... 317 831-2902
30 Robb Hill Rd Martinsville (46151) *(G-11377)*

Advantage Print Solutions... 812 473-5945
700 N Weinbach Ave Evansville (47711) *(G-3876)*

Advantage Productions... 219 879-6892
7256 W Oakmeadow Dr La Porte (46350) *(G-10376)*

Advantage Signs Inc... 219 853-1427
6223 Hohman Ave Hammond (46324) *(G-6868)*

Advantage Thermal Service, Kendallville Also Called: MD Moxie LLC *(G-10136)*

Advantage Wire & Machine Inc... 765 698-4643
5480 Industrial Ave Connersville (47331) *(G-2424)*

Advantex Inc... 812 339-6479
5981 E State Road 45 Bloomington (47408) *(G-774)*

Advantis, Greenwood Also Called: Advantis Medical Inc *(G-6661)*

Advantis Medical Inc... 317 859-2300
2121 Southtech Dr Ste 600 Greenwood (46143) *(G-6661)*

Advent Precision Inc... 317 908-6937
1740 Industry Dr Ste E Indianapolis (46219) *(G-7445)*

Adventureglass, North Webster Also Called: B Thystrup US Corporation *(G-13302)*

Advertiser, Hebron Also Called: Russ Print Shp/Hbron Advrtser *(G-7106)*

Advics Manufacturing Ind LLC... 812 298-1617
10550 James Adams St Terre Haute (47802) *(G-15533)*

Ae Sport, Fort Wayne Also Called: Amanda Elizabeth LLC *(G-4748)*

Ae Techron, Elkhart Also Called: A E Techron Inc *(G-3139)*

Aearo Company, Indianapolis Also Called: Aearo Technologies LLC *(G-7446)*

Aearo Technologies LLC (DH)... 612 284-1232
7911 Zionsville Rd Indianapolis (46268) *(G-7446)*

Aearo Technologies LLC... 317 692-6666
7911 Zionsville Rd Indianapolis (46268) *(G-7447)*

AEC America, Columbus Also Called: Indiana Research Institute *(G-2325)*

Aef Emblem, Carmel Also Called: Favor It Promotions Inc *(G-1634)*

AEG, Newburgh Also Called: Academy Energy Group LLC *(G-12991)*

Aegis Sales and Engineering... 260 483-4160
5411 Industrial Rd Fort Wayne (46825) *(G-4731)*

AEL/Span LLC... 317 203-4602
6032 Gateway Dr Plainfield (46168) *(G-13656)*

Aero Industries Inc (PA)... 317 244-2433
4243 W Bradbury Ave Indianapolis (46241) *(G-7448)*

Aero Innovations LLC... 812 233-0384
7750 State Road 42 Terre Haute (47803) *(G-15534)*

Aero Machine LLC... 219 548-0490
1251 Transport Dr Ste A Valparaiso (46383) *(G-15893)*

Aero Metals Inc (PA)... 219 326-1976
1201 E Lincolnway La Porte (46350) *(G-10377)*

Aero-Flo Industries Inc... 219 393-3555
3999 E Hupp Rd Bldg R34 La Porte (46350) *(G-10378)*

Aero-Med LLC... 740 412-3855
5110 W 74th St Indianapolis (46268) *(G-7449)*

Aerodine Composites LLC... 317 271-1207
1755 Midwest Blvd Indianapolis (46214) *(G-7450)*

Aerodyn Engineering LLC (PA)... 317 334-1523
1919 S Girls School Rd Indianapolis (46241) *(G-7451)*

Aerofab, Indianapolis Also Called: Tube Processing Corp *(G-9658)*

Aerofab Corp... 317 787-6438
3750 Shelby St Indianapolis (46227) *(G-7452)*

Aerogage Inc... 978 422-8224
1010 N Park Ave Martinsville (46151) *(G-11378)*

Aeromet Industries Inc... 219 924-7442
739 S Arbogast St Griffith (46319) *(G-6787)*

Aeromind LLC... 800 905-2157
835 N Capitol Ave Indianapolis (46204) *(G-7453)*

Aeromotive Mfg Inc... 765 552-0668
8421 N 750 W Elwood (46036) *(G-3817)*

Aeromotive Tech Inc... 260 723-5646
4835 W 800 S South Whitley (46787) *(G-15315)*

Aesthtcally Pleasing Skin Soak... 317 551-0156
2454 Wigeon Ct Indianapolis (46234) *(G-7454)*

Aet Films, Rosedale Also Called: Taghleef Industries Inc *(G-14385)*

AF Ohab Company Inc... 317 225-4740
2346 S Lynhurst Dr Ste 302 Indianapolis (46241) *(G-7455)*

Afco Performance Group LLC (PA)... 812 897-0900
977 Hyrock Blvd Boonville (47601) *(G-1079)*

Afco Racing Products, Boonville Also Called: Afco Performance Group LLC *(G-1079)*

Afequip.com, Indianapolis Also Called: AF Ohab Company Inc *(G-7455)*

Affinis Group LLC (PA)... 317 831-3830
1050 Indianapolis Rd Mooresville (46158) *(G-12191)*

Affordable Computer Repair, Yoder Also Called: Dedicated Software *(G-16965)*

Affordable Luxury Homes Inc... 260 758-2141
49 S 500 E Markle (46770) *(G-11353)*

Affordable Neon Services... 317 299-6061
7051 Crawfordsville Rd Indianapolis (46214) *(G-7456)*

Affordable Screen Printing EMB... 574 278-7885
8262 N Kiger Dr Monticello (47960) *(G-12133)*

Affordable Sign & Neon Inc... 219 853-1855
534 Conkey St Ste 1 Hammond (46324) *(G-6869)*

Affordable Signs Incorporated... 260 349-1710
700 S Orchard St Kendallville (46755) *(G-10087)*

Afm Industries LLC... 574 910-0982
72960 Poplar Rd Walkerton (46574) *(G-16262)*

AFP, Indianapolis Also Called: American Family Pharmacy LLC *(G-7503)*

Afr Equipment LLC... 888 519-9899
13046 Bulltown Rd Laurel (47024) *(G-10824)*

Afraa Eyebrows... 317 881-6200
888 N Us Highway 31 N Greenwood (46142) *(G-6662)*

Afsol Inc... 260 357-0788
6869 County Road 11a Auburn (46706) *(G-360)*

Aftco Manufacturing, Yorktown Also Called: Aul In The Family Tool and Die *(G-16969)*

After Action Med Dntl Sup LLC... 800 892-5352
4444 Decatur Blvd Ste 100 Indianapolis (46241) *(G-7457)*

After Hours Embroidery... 812 926-9355
406 2nd St Aurora (47001) *(G-436)*

Aftermath Cidery and Winery... 219 299-8463
454 Greenwich St Valparaiso (46383) *(G-15894)*

AG Apparel and Screen Prtg LLC... 260 483-3817
5515 Planeview Dr Fort Wayne (46825) *(G-4732)*

AG Plus Inc... 260 623-6121
306 W South St Monroeville (46773) *(G-12066)*

AG Plus Inc (PA)... 260 723-5141
401 N Main St South Whitley (46787) *(G-15316)*

AG Printing Specialists LLC... 866 445-6824
2880 Us Highway 231 S Ste 200 Lafayette (47909) *(G-10517)*

AG Processing A Cooperative... 574 773-4138
302 S Main St Nappanee (46550) *(G-12577)*

Agalite Seattle... 800 269-8343
1126 S Lafayette Blvd South Bend (46601) *(G-14937)*

Agate Workshop... 812 333-0900
103 N College Ave Bloomington (47404) *(G-775)*

Agbest Cooperative Inc... 765 358-3388
430 S Sycamore St Gaston (47342) *(G-6043)*

Aggreate Systems (PA)... 260 854-4711
102 Industry Bnd Rome City (46784) *(G-14373)*

ALPHABETIC SECTION

Aggreate Systems.. 260 854-4711
  106 Industry Bnd Rome City (46784) *(G-14374)*

Aggregate Service, Plymouth *Also Called: Stone Quary* *(G-13814)*

Aggrock Quarries Inc.. 812 246-2582
  5421 County Road 403 Charlestown (47111) *(G-1870)*

Agi International Inc.. 317 536-2415
  2525 N Shadeland Ave Ste D5 Indianapolis (46219) *(G-7458)*

Agi Logistics, Indianapolis *Also Called: Agi International Inc* *(G-7458)*

Agile Engineering & Mfg LLC................................ 317 359-3360
  3902 E 16th St Ste A Indianapolis (46201) *(G-7459)*

Agile Mfg Inc... 417 845-6065
  720 Industrial Park Road Milford (46542) *(G-11785)*

Agilent Technologies.. 617 694-7692
  1000 Park Ave Winona Lake (46590) *(G-16908)*

Agora Brands Group Inc...................................... 615 802-0086
  116 West St Borden (47106) *(G-1104)*

Agrati - Park Forest LLC...................................... 219 531-2202
  4001 Redbow Dr Valparaiso (46383) *(G-15895)*

Agri - Traders & Repair LLC................................. 260 238-4225
  16702 Campbell Rd Spencerville (46788) *(G-15366)*

Agri-Power Inc... 812 874-3316
  10100 Highway 165 Poseyville (47633) *(G-13976)*

Agri-Tronix Corp... 317 738-4474
  2001 N Morton St Franklin (46131) *(G-5703)*

Agricon LLC.. 219 261-2157
  3823 W 1800 S Remington (47977) *(G-14032)*

Agricor Inc.. 765 662-0606
  1626 S Joaquin Dr Marion (46953) *(G-11269)*

Agriselect Evansville LLC.................................... 812 453-2235
  11401 N Green River Rd Evansville (47725) *(G-3877)*

Agritraders Mfg Inc... 260 238-4225
  16702 Campbell Rd Spencerville (46788) *(G-15367)*

Agsync, Wakarusa *Also Called: Raven Industries Inc* *(G-16246)*

Ah Medora Lfg LLC... 346 440-1416
  546 S County Road 870 W Medora (47260) *(G-11460)*

Ahaus, Richmond *Also Called: Ahaus Tool & Engineering Inc* *(G-14084)*

Ahaus Tool & Engineering Inc............................. 765 962-3573
  200 Industrial Pkwy Richmond (47374) *(G-14084)*

Ahepa 157... 219 864-3255
  1400 S Broad St Griffith (46319) *(G-6788)*

Ahern Electric Inc.. 219 874-3508
  11527 W 50 N Westville (46391) *(G-16755)*

Ahf Industries Inc.. 812 936-9988
  8647 W State Road 56 French Lick (47432) *(G-5843)*

Aibmr Life Sciences Inc...................................... 812 822-1400
  205 N College Ave Ste 513 Bloomington (47404) *(G-776)*

Ail, Evansville *Also Called: Lasertone Inc* *(G-4162)*

Aim Media Indiana Oper LLC.............................. 812 358-2111
  116 E Cross St Brownstown (47220) *(G-1416)*

Aim Media Indiana Oper LLC.............................. 812 372-7811
  2980 N National Rd Ste A Columbus (47201) *(G-2215)*

Aim Media Indiana Oper LLC (PA)...................... 812 372-7811
  2980 N National Rd # A Columbus (47201) *(G-2216)*

Aim Media Indiana Oper LLC.............................. 317 736-7101
  30 S Water St Ste A Franklin (46131) *(G-5704)*

Aim Media Indiana Oper LLC.............................. 812 736-7101
  30 S Water St Ste A Franklin (46131) *(G-5705)*

Aim Media Indiana Oper LLC.............................. 317 462-5528
  22 W New Rd Greenfield (46140) *(G-6458)*

Aim Media Indiana Oper LLC.............................. 317 462-5528
  22 W New Rd Greenfield (46140) *(G-6459)*

Aim Media Indiana Oper LLC.............................. 317 462-5528
  22 W New Rd Greenfield (46140) *(G-6460)*

Aim Media Indiana Oper LLC.............................. 812 988-2221
  147 E Main St Nashville (47448) *(G-12659)*

Aim Media Indiana Oper LLC.............................. 765 778-2324
  104 W High St Pendleton (46064) *(G-13524)*

Aim Media Indiana Oper LLC.............................. 812 522-4871
  100 Saint Louis Ave Seymour (47274) *(G-14626)*

Aip/Fw Funding Inc (PA)..................................... 212 627-2360
  1031 E Us Highway 224 Decatur (46733) *(G-2840)*

Air & Energy, Mishawaka *Also Called: River Valley Sheet Metal Inc* *(G-11988)*

Air Energy Systems Inc (PA)............................... 317 290-8500
  4790 W 73rd St Indianapolis (46268) *(G-7460)*

Air Filters Sales & Service, Jeffersonville *Also Called: Purolator Pdts A Filtration Co* *(G-10043)*

Air Fixtures Inc... 260 982-2169
  1108 N Sycamore St North Manchester (46962) *(G-13228)*

Air In Motion Publishers LLC............................... 317 850-0149
  1963 Clark Rd Indianapolis (46224) *(G-7461)*

Air Kit LLC.. 317 745-0656
  2985 S County Road 300 E Danville (46122) *(G-2806)*

Air Products, Terre Haute *Also Called: Air Products and Chemicals Inc* *(G-15535)*

Air Products and Chemicals Inc........................... 812 466-6492
  5901 N 13th St Terre Haute (47805) *(G-15535)*

Air Ride Technologies, Jasper *Also Called: Rt Acquisition Corp* *(G-9907)*

Air Side Systems LLC... 765 778-7895
  3620 W 73rd St Anderson (46011) *(G-73)*

Air Support Medical, Hope *Also Called: Flw Plastics Inc* *(G-7224)*

Air Support Medical Company, Hope *Also Called: Eclipse Molding Company LLC* *(G-7223)*

Air Systems Compents LP................................... 765 483-5841
  843 Indianapolis Ave Lebanon (46052) *(G-10873)*

Air Vac Sewer Systems, Rochester *Also Called: Aqseptence Group Inc* *(G-14278)*

Air-Tech Industrial Design................................... 317 797-1804
  580 W Main St Monrovia (46157) *(G-12076)*

Airborne Services, Fishers *Also Called: Kevin M Walters* *(G-4554)*

Airbotx LLC.. 317 981-1811
  16525 Southpark Dr Westfield (46074) *(G-16663)*

Airbuoyant LLC.. 765 623-9815
  1508 E 7th St Anderson (46012) *(G-74)*

Aircom Manufacturing Inc.................................... 317 545-5383
  6205 E 30th St Indianapolis (46219) *(G-7462)*

Airfeet Insoles, Greenwood *Also Called: Airfeet LLC* *(G-6663)*

Airfeet LLC... 317 441-1817
  191 Us Highway 31 S Ste C Greenwood (46142) *(G-6663)*

Airfx USA LLC (PA)... 812 878-8135
  1484 E County Road 600 N Brazil (47834) *(G-1132)*

Airfx USA LLC.. 812 917-5573
  501 S Airport Street Terre Haute (47803) *(G-15536)*

Airgas, Evansville *Also Called: Airgas Usa LLC* *(G-3878)*

Airgas, Indianapolis *Also Called: Airgas Inc* *(G-7463)*

Airgas Inc.. 317 632-7106
  1441 Bates St Indianapolis (46201) *(G-7463)*

Airgas Puritan Medical, Indianapolis *Also Called: Airgas Usa LLC* *(G-7464)*

Airgas Usa LLC.. 812 474-0440
  2300 N Burkhardt Rd Evansville (47715) *(G-3878)*

Airgas Usa LLC.. 260 749-9576
  4935 New Haven Ave Fort Wayne (46803) *(G-4733)*

Airgas Usa LLC.. 317 248-8072
  5430 W Morris St Indianapolis (46241) *(G-7464)*

Airgas Usa LLC.. 812 362-7593
  6500 N Us Highway 231 Rockport (47635) *(G-14335)*

Airjet Inc.. 574 264-0123
  2101 Kinro Ct Elkhart (46514) *(G-3155)*

Airlift Services International, Alexandria *Also Called: Energy Inc* *(G-51)*

Airman Proficiency LLC...................................... 260 602-5788
  210 Grove St Fort Wayne (46805) *(G-4734)*

Airodapt LLC.. 559 331-0156
  809 E Stewart Dr Rensselaer (47978) *(G-14040)*

Airomat, Fort Wayne *Also Called: Life Management Inc* *(G-5185)*

Airplane Annuals... 817 528-6545
  517 E County Road 825 N Bainbridge (46105) *(G-558)*

Airtek LLC.. 219 947-1664
  4410 W 37th Ave Frnt Hobart (46342) *(G-7172)*

Airtomic LLC.. 317 738-0148
  75 Linville Way Franklin (46131) *(G-5706)*

Airtomic Repair Station....................................... 317 738-0148
  75 Linville Way Franklin (46131) *(G-5707)*

Airvac, Rochester *Also Called: Bilfinger Airvac Water Technologies Inc* *(G-14279)*

Airxcel Inc.. 574 294-5681
  1136 Verdant St Elkhart (46516) *(G-3156)*

Aisin Chemical Indiana LLC 812 793-2888
  1004 Industrial Way Crothersville (47229) *(G-2635)*
Aisin Drivetrain Inc 812 793-2427
  1001 Industrial Way Crothersville (47229) *(G-2636)*
Aisin USA Mfg Inc 812 523-1969
  1700 E 4th Street Rd Seymour (47274) *(G-14627)*
Aj Express Broker Service 812 866-1380
  73 N Rogers Rd Madison (47250) *(G-11197)*
Aj Machine Inc 260 248-4900
  2441 E Business 30 Columbia City (46725) *(G-2118)*
Aj Masonry & Son LLC 260 569-0082
  65 Noble St Wabash (46992) *(G-16172)*
Aj Screen Printing LLC 574 274-4333
  9545 Tyler Rd Bremen (46506) *(G-1171)*
Ajax Tool Inc 260 747-7482
  2828 Commercial Rd Fort Wayne (46809) *(G-4735)*
Aje Suspension Inc 812 346-7356
  6235 N County Road 275 W North Vernon (47265) *(G-13255)*
Ajem Welding 812 595-3541
  261 E State Road 256 Austin (47102) *(G-462)*
AJS Gyros To Go 812 951-1715
  441 Rocky Meadow Rd Ne New Salisbury (47161) *(G-12982)*
AK Industries Inc 574 936-6022
  2055 Pidco Dr Plymouth (46563) *(G-13752)*
AK Supply Inc 317 895-0410
  6321 E 30th St Ste 206 Indianapolis (46219) *(G-7465)*
AK Tool and Die Inc 574 286-9010
  13990 Early Rd Mishawaka (46545) *(G-11836)*
Aker Composite Solutions Inc 574 935-0908
  2900 Gary Dr Plymouth (46563) *(G-13753)*
Akina, West Lafayette *Also Called: Akina Inc (G-16559)*
Akina Inc 765 464-0501
  3495 Kent Ave Ste M200 West Lafayette (47906) *(G-16559)*
Akka Plastics Inc 812 849-9256
  1100 Teke Burton Dr Mitchell (47446) *(G-12030)*
Akron Concrete Products Inc (PA) 574 893-4841
  321 N Maple St Akron (46910) *(G-1)*
Akzo Nobel Coatings Inc 574 372-2000
  1102 Leiter Dr Warsaw (46580) *(G-16310)*
Al Dishno Neon 317 862-5374
  5249 Hickory Rd Indianapolis (46239) *(G-7466)*
Al Perry Enterprises Inc (PA) 812 867-7727
  9203 Petersburg Rd Evansville (47725) *(G-3879)*
Al-Ex Inc 574 206-0100
  3170 Windsor Ct Elkhart (46514) *(G-3157)*
Al-Fe Heat Treating LLC 260 563-8321
  200 Wedcor Ave Wabash (46992) *(G-16173)*
Al-Ko Kober, Elkhart *Also Called: Al-Ko Kober LLC (G-3158)*
Al-Ko Kober, Elkhart *Also Called: Dexter Axle Company LLC (G-3291)*
Al-Ko Kober LLC 574 294-6651
  21611 Protecta Dr Elkhart (46516) *(G-3158)*
Al's, La Porte *Also Called: Lakeshore Foods Corp (G-10444)*
Alan Daily 574 595-6253
  7300 S 600 E Star City (46985) *(G-15394)*
Alan Sutton Graphic Design 219 567-2764
  4635 S 1450 W Francesville (47946) *(G-5636)*
Alan Sword LLC 812 913-1412
  2908 River Heritage Trl Jeffersonville (47130) *(G-9926)*
Alan W Long 812 265-6717
  120 E Main St Madison (47250) *(G-11198)*
Alani Nutrition LLC 502 509-4922
  351 Logistics Ave Jeffersonville (47130) *(G-9927)*
Alaninu, Jeffersonville *Also Called: Alani Nutrition LLC (G-9927)*
Albanese Candy Retail, Merrillville *Also Called: Albanese Conf Group Inc (G-11479)*
Albanese Conf Group Inc 219 947-3070
  5441 E Lincoln Hwy Merrillville (46410) *(G-11479)*
Albanese Conf Group Inc (PA) 219 947-3070
  5441 E Lincoln Hwy Merrillville (46410) *(G-11480)*
Albany Metal Treating Inc 765 789-6470
  400 S Gray St Albany (47320) *(G-11)*
Alberding Woodworking Inc 260 728-9526
  7050 N 200 W Decatur (46733) *(G-2841)*

Albertson Seed Sales 765 267-0680
  3868 W County Road 1200 S Russellville (46175) *(G-14418)*
Albion New ERA, Albion *Also Called: All Printing and Publications (G-17)*
Albrecht Incorporated (PA) 260 422-9440
  1025 Osage St Fort Wayne (46808) *(G-4736)*
Albright's Raw Dog Food, Fort Wayne *Also Called: Albrecht Incorporated (G-4736)*
Albrights Raw Pet Food, Fort Wayne *Also Called: Hoosier Processing LLC (G-5080)*
Alcatraz Brewing Co., Indianapolis *Also Called: Tavistock Restaurants LLC (G-9557)*
Alcoa Corporation 812 853-6111
  4400 W State Route 66 Newburgh (47630) *(G-12992)*
Alcoa Corporation 812 842-3350
  4700 Darlington Rd Newburgh (47630) *(G-12993)*
Alcoa Corporation 765 983-9200
  1701 Williamsburg Pike Richmond (47374) *(G-14085)*
Alcoa Csi, Crawfordsville *Also Called: Closure Systems Intl Hldngs In (G-2553)*
Alcoa Newco, Newburgh *Also Called: Warrick Newco LLC (G-13028)*
Alcoa Power Generating Inc 812 842-3350
  4700 Darlington Rd Newburgh (47630) *(G-12994)*
Alconex Specialty Products 260 744-3446
  4201 Piper Dr Fort Wayne (46809) *(G-4737)*
Alconex Specialty Products (PA) 260 744-3446
  7255 Chalfant Rd Fort Wayne (46818) *(G-4738)*
Alconex Specialty Products, Fort Wayne *Also Called: Alconex Specialty Products (G-4737)*
ALE Enterprises Inc 317 856-2981
  4623 S High School Rd Indianapolis (46241) *(G-7467)*
Alebro LLC 317 876-9212
  7690 Zionsville Rd Indianapolis (46268) *(G-7468)*
Aleph Bet Document Centre, New Haven *Also Called: Samuel Wahli (G-12917)*
Alex Mid West, La Porte *Also Called: Alexandria Mw LLC (G-10379)*
Alex Virok DBA Intec 317 770-7559
  6281 Saw Mill Dr Noblesville (46062) *(G-13034)*
Alexander Machine Inc 812 879-4982
  7847 Jones Rd Gosport (47433) *(G-6282)*
Alexander Screw Products Inc 317 898-5313
  8750 Pendleton Pike Indianapolis (46226) *(G-7469)*
Alexander Thompson 218 577-7627
  3348 169th St G137 Hammond (46323) *(G-6870)*
Alexandria Extrsion Mdmrica LL 317 545-1221
  4925 Aluminum Dr Indianapolis (46218) *(G-7470)*
Alexandria Mw LLC 219 324-9541
  4747 W State Road 2 Ste B La Porte (46350) *(G-10379)*
Alexandria Times-Tribune, Alexandria *Also Called: Elwood Publishing Company Inc (G-50)*
Alexandria Tribune, The, Tipton *Also Called: Elwood Publishing Company Inc (G-15772)*
Alexson LLC 219 210-3642
  292 E Us Highway 20 Michigan City (46360) *(G-11576)*
Algalco LLC 317 361-2787
  6532 Castle Knoll Ct Indianapolis (46250) *(G-7471)*
Alh Building Systems, Markle *Also Called: Affordable Luxury Homes Inc (G-11353)*
Alicon LLC 260 687-1259
  4720 W 200 N Angola (46703) *(G-225)*
Alig LLC 812 362-7593
  6500 N Us Highway 231 Rockport (47635) *(G-14336)*
All 4u Printing LLC 317 845-2955
  6710 W 425 S Morgantown (46160) *(G-12251)*
All About Organizing 513 238-8157
  253 Charles A Liddle Dr Ste 1 Lawrenceburg (47025) *(G-10827)*
All American Ex Solutions LLC 317 789-3070
  5101 Decatur Blvd Ste W Indianapolis (46241) *(G-7472)*
All American Group Inc 260 724-7391
  309 S 13th St Decatur (46733) *(G-2842)*
All American Group Inc 574 262-9889
  1251 N Nappanee St Elkhart (46514) *(G-3159)*
All American Group Inc (HQ) 574 262-0123
  2831 Dexter Dr Elkhart (46514) *(G-3160)*
All American Group Inc 574 262-0123
  2831 Dexter Dr Elkhart (46514) *(G-3161)*
All American Group Inc 574 825-1720
  51165 Greenfield Pkwy Middlebury (46540) *(G-11693)*
All American Group Inc 574 825-5821
  423 N Main St Middlebury (46540) *(G-11694)*

ALPHABETIC SECTION — Allied Applications LLC

All American Group Inc 574 825-8555
   14489 Us Highway 20 Middlebury (46540) *(G-11695)*

All American Homes LLC (DH) 574 266-3044
   2831 Dexter Dr Elkhart (46514) *(G-3162)*

All American Homes Indiana LLC 260 724-9171
   1418 S 13th St Decatur (46733) *(G-2843)*

All American Tent & Awning Inc 812 232-4206
   1140 3rd Ave Terre Haute (47807) *(G-15537)*

All Around Construction LLC 219 902-0742
   5807 Hayes St Merrillville (46410) *(G-11481)*

All Day Carpet Binding LLC 219 851-8071
   3814 Rushgrove Dr Lafayette (47909) *(G-10518)*

All Glass LLC 260 969-1839
   221 Grandstand Way Fort Wayne (46825) *(G-4739)*

All Good Things LLC 812 871-2844
   5997 E Risks Ridge Rd Madison (47250) *(G-11199)*

All Good Things Soaps and 812 801-4700
   318 W Main St Madison (47250) *(G-11200)*

All Gussied Up Embroidery 317 517-1557
   12207 Beckley Rd Indianapolis (46229) *(G-7473)*

All Packaging Equipment Corp 574 294-3371
   1749 Fieldhouse Ave Elkhart (46517) *(G-3163)*

All Pet Supplies Inc 219 885-9670
   3982 Broadway Gary (46408) *(G-5888)*

All Points Tool & Mfg Corp 574 935-3944
   2743 Pioneer Dr Plymouth (46563) *(G-13754)*

All Printing and Publications 260 636-2727
   407 S Orange St Albion (46701) *(G-17)*

All Pro Property Services LLC 317 721-1227
   9175 Harrison Park Ct Indianapolis (46216) *(G-7474)*

All Pro Shearing Inc 317 691-1005
   1905 Lawton Ave Indianapolis (46203) *(G-7475)*

All Rvs Manufacturing Inc 574 538-1559
   1055 N 625 W Shipshewana (46565) *(G-14833)*

All Shppers Are Prrity Trckg L 317 525-6954
   5953 Wixson Ct Indianapolis (46254) *(G-7476)*

All Star Manufacturing Inc 574 293-8141
   18243 W Shore Cir Culver (46511) *(G-2779)*

All State Manufacturing Co Inc 812 466-2276
   4024 2nd Pkwy Terre Haute (47804) *(G-15538)*

All Steel Carports Inc 765 284-0694
   2200 N Granville Ave Muncie (47303) *(G-12337)*

All Steel Crprts Buildings LLC 765 284-0694
   2200 N Granville Ave Muncie (47303) *(G-12338)*

All Things Custom LLC 765 618-5332
   102 S Main St Sweetser (46987) *(G-15453)*

All Things Jchari LLC 260 414-4065
   6937 Huguenard Rd Apt 101 Fort Wayne (46818) *(G-4740)*

All Things Kingdom LLC 312 200-4569
   9409 Southmoor Ave Apt 19 Highland (46322) *(G-7120)*

All Time Low Magazine LLC 317 286-7221
   9996 Olympic Cir Indianapolis (46234) *(G-7477)*

All You Naturally LLC 574 215-5425
   1501 Cedar St Elkhart (46514) *(G-3164)*

All-Phase Construction Co LLC 317 345-7057
   10182 Orange Blossom Trl Fishers (46038) *(G-4461)*

All-Pro Pump & Repair Inc 317 738-4203
   7907 W 500 S Morgantown (46160) *(G-12252)*

All-Rite Ready Mix Inc 812 926-0920
   10513 Morgan Branch Rd Aurora (47001) *(G-437)*

All-State Industries Inc 574 522-4245
   409 Roske Dr Unit B Elkhart (46516) *(G-3165)*

All-Terrain Conversions LLC 260 758-2525
   13534 Lafayette Center Rd Roanoke (46783) *(G-14256)*

All-Weather Products Inc 812 867-6403
   8346 Baumgart Rd Evansville (47725) *(G-3880)*

Allan Copley Designs, Jasper *Also Called: DStyle Inc (G-9833)*

Allan Defense LLC 317 525-1244
   2828 Coventry Ln Greenwood (46143) *(G-6664)*

Allegheny Coatings, Fremont *Also Called: Allegheny Coatings RE LLC (G-5807)*

Allegheny Coatings RE LLC 260 495-4445
   302 E Mcswain Dr Fremont (46737) *(G-5807)*

Allegheny Ludlum Corp 412 394-2800
   250 E Lafayette St Portland (47371) *(G-13927)*

Allegiance Tool and Die Inc 574 277-1819
   12888 Industrial Park Dr Granger (46530) *(G-6331)*

Allegion, Carmel *Also Called: Schlage Lock Company LLC (G-1752)*

Allegion LLC 317 810-3700
   11819 Pennsylvania St Carmel (46032) *(G-1553)*

Allegion Public Ltd Company 317 810-3700
   11819 Pennsylvania St Carmel (46032) *(G-1554)*

Allegion S&S Holding Co Inc (HQ) 317 810-3700
   11819 Pennsylvania St Carmel (46032) *(G-1555)*

Allegion S&S Holding Co Inc 317 429-2299
   8506 E 30th St Indianapolis (46219) *(G-7478)*

Allegion US Holding Co Inc (HQ) 317 810-3700
   11819 Pennsylvania St Carmel (46032) *(G-1556)*

Allegra Marketing Print Mail 317 643-6248
   8025 Castleway Dr Ste 103 Indianapolis (46278) *(G-7479)*

Allegra Print & Imaging, Elkhart *Also Called: Nea LLC (G-3565)*

Allegra Print & Imaging, Indianapolis *Also Called: Wise Printing Inc (G-9777)*

Allegra Print & Imaging, Warsaw *Also Called: Hugh K Eagan (G-16375)*

Allegro Microsystems LLC 765 854-2263
   11711 Pennsylvania St Ste 240 Carmel (46032) *(G-1557)*

Allen Apr Plastics Repair Inc 260 482-8523
   3685 Lima Rd Fort Wayne (46805) *(G-4741)*

Allen C Terhune & Associates 765 948-4164
   122 S Main St Fairmount (46928) *(G-4407)*

Allen Fabricators Inc 260 458-0008
   10106 Smith Rd Fort Wayne (46809) *(G-4742)*

Allen Medical Systems Inc 978 266-4286
   1069 State Road 46 E Batesville (47006) *(G-576)*

Allen Medical Systems Inc 812 931-2512
   93 N Coonhunters Rd Batesville (47006) *(G-577)*

Allen Monument Co 317 941-7047
   5234 Madison Ave Indianapolis (46227) *(G-7480)*

Allen Monument Co 574 240-1880
   706 N Main St Ste H Monticello (47960) *(G-12134)*

Allen Monument Co, Indianapolis *Also Called: Allen Monument Co (G-7480)*

Allen Monument Co, Monticello *Also Called: Allen Monument Co (G-12134)*

Allen Monument Company (PA) 765 362-8886
   212 Hamilton St Crawfordsville (47933) *(G-2544)*

Allen Street Roasters LLC 815 955-7872
   415 Allen St La Porte (46350) *(G-10380)*

Allen-Davis Enterprises Inc 574 303-2173
   920 Brook Run Dr Apt 3b Mishawaka (46544) *(G-11837)*

Allens Therapuetic Services 317 820-3600
   450 E 96th St Ste 500 Indianapolis (46240) *(G-7481)*

Allergan Sales LLC 888 786-6471
   1250 Patrol Rd Charlestown (47111) *(G-1871)*

Allfab LLC 317 359-3539
   1414 Sadlier Circle West Dr Indianapolis (46239) *(G-7482)*

Alliance Aluminum Products Inc 574 848-4300
   1649 Commerce Dr Bristol (46507) *(G-1242)*

Alliance Feed LLC 260 244-6100
   2560 S 600 E Columbia City (46725) *(G-2119)*

Alliance Group Tech Inc 260 375-2810
   311 9th St Warren (46792) *(G-16293)*

Alliance Machine, Boonville *Also Called: Sons of Thunder (G-1098)*

Alliance Rv LLC 574 312-5215
   301 Benchmark Dr Elkhart (46516) *(G-3166)*

Alliance Steel, Gary *Also Called: A2 Sales LLC (G-5885)*

Alliance Steel LLC 219 427-5400
   2700 E 5th Ave Gary (46402) *(G-5889)*

Alliance Steel Corporation 708 924-1200
   2700 E 5th Ave Gary (46402) *(G-5890)*

Alliance Studios LLC 317 525-8487
   5634 Nuckols Ct Indianapolis (46237) *(G-7483)*

Alliance Tool & Equipment Inc 260 432-2909
   3919 Engle Rd Fort Wayne (46804) *(G-4743)*

Alliance Winding Equipment (PA) 260 478-2200
   3939 Vanguard Dr Fort Wayne (46809) *(G-4744)*

Allied Applications LLC 502 817-6478
   723 Quarry Rd Nw Corydon (47112) *(G-2484)*

(PA)=Parent Co (HQ)=Headquarters (DH)=Div Headquarters

Allied Enterprises LLC — 765 288-8849
3228 W Kilgore Ave Muncie (47304) *(G-12339)*

Allied Mfg Partners Inc — 260 428-2670
4410 New Haven Ave Fort Wayne (46803) *(G-4745)*

Allied Mineral Products Inc — 219 923-5875
1950 N Griffith Blvd Ste D Griffith (46319) *(G-6789)*

ALLIED MINERAL PRODUCTS, INC., Griffith *Also Called: Allied Mineral Products Inc* *(G-6789)*

Allied Precision Machine Inc — 765 418-7607
3900 E 450 S Lafayette (47909) *(G-10519)*

Allied Specialty Precision Inc — 574 255-4718
815 E Lowell Ave Mishawaka (46545) *(G-11838)*

Allied Steel Rule Dies Inc — 317 634-9835
5811 W Minnesota St Indianapolis (46241) *(G-7484)*

Allied Tube & Conduit Corp — 765 459-8811
101 E Broadway St Kokomo (46901) *(G-10232)*

Allied Tube & Conduit Corp — 812 265-9255
4004 N Us 421 Madison (47250) *(G-11201)*

Allin Plastic Engraving Inc — 219 972-2223
2845 Garfield Ave Hammond (46322) *(G-6871)*

Allison Parts Distribution, Indianapolis *Also Called: Allison Transmission Inc (G-7488)*

Allison Pymnt Systems LLC DBA (HQ) — 317 808-2400
2200 Production Dr Indianapolis (46241) *(G-7485)*

Allison Quality Wdwkg LLC — 812 963-3359
9701 Saint Wendel Rd Evansville (47720) *(G-3881)*

Allison Transm Holdings Inc (PA) — 317 242-5000
1 Allison Way Indianapolis (46222) *(G-7486)*

Allison Transmission, Indianapolis *Also Called: Allison Transm Holdings Inc (G-7486)*

Allison Transmission, Indianapolis *Also Called: Allison Transmission Inc (G-7490)*

Allison Transmission Inc — 317 242-5000
901 Grande Ave Indianapolis (46222) *(G-7487)*

Allison Transmission Inc — 317 821-5104
5902 Decatur Blvd Indianapolis (46241) *(G-7488)*

Allison Transmission Inc — 317 280-6206
6040 W 62nd St Indianapolis (46278) *(G-7489)*

Allison Transmission Inc — 317 242-2080
2840 Fortune Cir W Ste A Indianapolis (46241) *(G-7490)*

Allison Transmission Inc — 317 242-5000
1 Allison Way Indianapolis (46222) *(G-7491)*

Allison Transmission Division, Indianapolis *Also Called: Allison Transmission Inc (G-7487)*

Allomatic Products Company (DH) — 800 686-4729
609 E Chaney St Sullivan (47882) *(G-15402)*

Allons-Y For Inv & Tech LLC — 260 206-4445
1161 S Adams St Apt 11 Bloomington (47403) *(G-777)*

Alloy Custom Products, Lafayette *Also Called: Cryogenic Indus Solutions LLC (G-10564)*

Alloy Custom Products LLC — 765 564-4684
9701 Old State Road 25 N Lafayette (47905) *(G-10520)*

Alloy Engineering & Casting Co, Avilla *Also Called: Illinois Ni Cast LLC (G-478)*

Allsports — 812 883-3561
210 N Main St Salem (47167) *(G-14470)*

Allstade Business Forms, Evansville *Also Called: Altstadt Business Forms Inc (G-3882)*

Allstate Mfg, Terre Haute *Also Called: All State Manufacturing Co Inc (G-15538)*

Allterrain Paving & Cnstr LLC — 502 265-4731
2235 Corydon Pike New Albany (47150) *(G-12687)*

Alm Services Inc — 765 288-6624
2100 N Granville Ave Muncie (47303) *(G-12340)*

Almco Steel Products Corp — 260 824-1118
59 N Oak Street Ext Bluffton (46714) *(G-1023)*

Almega Wire Products, Bremen *Also Called: Almega/Tru-Flex Inc (G-1172)*

Almega/Tru-Flex Inc — 574 546-2113
3917 State Road 106 Bremen (46506) *(G-1172)*

Almet Inc — 260 493-1556
300 Hartzell Rd New Haven (46774) *(G-12891)*

Almiras Bakery — 219 844-4334
2635 169th St Hammond (46323) *(G-6872)*

Almix, Fort Wayne *Also Called: Asphalt Equipment Company Inc (G-4775)*

Almost Famous Printing — 219 793-6388
1309 119th St Whiting (46394) *(G-16830)*

Alocit USA — 317 631-9111
1128 S West St Indianapolis (46225) *(G-7492)*

Alpha LLC — 574 292-1805
3000 N Airport Rd Warsaw (46582) *(G-16311)*

Alpha & Omega Mfg LLC — 219 344-8738
1408 W 47th Ave Gary (46408) *(G-5891)*

Alpha Baking Co Inc — 219 324-7440
360 N Fail Rd La Porte (46350) *(G-10381)*

Alpha Baking Co Inc — 574 234-0188
1133 S Main St South Bend (46601) *(G-14938)*

Alpha Laser and Imaging, Evansville *Also Called: Mid-America Environmental LLC (G-4204)*

Alpha LLC — 574 646-2304
3000 N Airport Rd 7a Warsaw (46582) *(G-16312)*

Alpha Loop Inc — 317 710-0076
5950 Lincoln Rd Martinsville (46151) *(G-11379)*

Alpha Matrix LLC — 812 686-1640
9946 N County Road 475 E Lamar (47550) *(G-10794)*

Alpha Systems, Elkhart *Also Called: Patrick Industries Inc (G-3588)*

AlphaGraphics, Carmel *Also Called: Kile Enterprises Inc (G-1681)*

AlphaGraphics, Elkhart *Also Called: Printed By Erik Inc (G-3621)*

AlphaGraphics, Elkhart *Also Called: Summit LLC (G-3705)*

Alphajak LLC — 574 800-4810
118 N Race St Mishawaka (46544) *(G-11839)*

Alpine Electronics Manufacturing of America Inc — 956 217-3200
421 N Emerson Ave Greenwood (46143) *(G-6665)*

Alpine Enterprises — 574 773-5475
12844 N 700 W Nappanee (46550) *(G-12578)*

Alro Steel Corporation — 260 749-9661
2912 Pleasant Center Rd Yoder (46798) *(G-16964)*

Als Woodcraft Inc — 812 967-4458
435 E Main St Borden (47106) *(G-1105)*

Alsip Pallet Company Inc — 219 322-3288
1154 Thiel Dr Schererville (46375) *(G-14513)*

Alsons Corporation — 800 421-0001
55 E 111th St Carmel (46280) *(G-1558)*

Alta Equipment Holdings Inc — 269 578-3182
3502 W Mcgill St South Bend (46628) *(G-14939)*

Altair Nanotechnologies Inc — 317 333-7617
3019 Enterprise Dr Anderson (46013) *(G-75)*

Altec Engineering Inc (PA) — 574 293-1965
2401 W Mishawaka Rd Elkhart (46517) *(G-3167)*

Altec Industries Inc — 317 872-3460
5201 W 84th St Indianapolis (46268) *(G-7493)*

Altec LLC — 812 282-8256
242 America Pl Jeffersonville (47130) *(G-9928)*

Altek Inc — 812 385-2561
1603 E Broadway St Princeton (47670) *(G-13981)*

Altek Mfg. Co., Clarksville *Also Called: Precision Automation Company (G-2028)*

Alternative Container, Indianapolis *Also Called: Jenson Industries Inc (G-8622)*

Alternative Fuel Solutions LLC — 260 224-1965
8380 N 200 W Huntington (46750) *(G-7297)*

Alternative Machining Inc — 317 830-8109
29 S Franklin St Mooresville (46158) *(G-12192)*

Alterra Plastics LLC — 812 271-1890
2213 Killion Ave Seymour (47274) *(G-14628)*

Altivity Packaging, Scottsburg *Also Called: Multi-Color Corporation (G-14572)*

Altra Industrial Motion Corp — 219 874-5248
300 Indiana Highway 212 Michigan City (46360) *(G-11577)*

Altstadt Business Forms Inc (PA) — 812 425-3393
1550 Baker Ave Evansville (47710) *(G-3882)*

Aludyne North America LLC — 260 925-4711
1200 Power Dr Auburn (46706) *(G-361)*

Aludyne North America LLC — 574 594-9681
5 Arnolt Dr Pierceton (46562) *(G-13629)*

Alum-Elec Structures Inc — 260 347-9362
250 W Grove St Kendallville (46755) *(G-10088)*

Alumina Products Incorporated — 727 934-9781
1400 N 14th St Terre Haute (47807) *(G-15539)*

Aluminum Conversion Inc — 260 856-2180
204 Parkway Cromwell (46732) *(G-2629)*

Aluminum Dynamics LLC (HQ) — 260 969-3500
7575 W Jefferson Blvd Fort Wayne (46804) *(G-4746)*

Aluminum Extrusions — 574 206-0100
3170 Windsor Ct Elkhart (46514) *(G-3168)*

ALPHABETIC SECTION — American Cook Systems

Aluminum Insights LLC 574 534-5547
104 E Innovation Blvd Syracuse (46567) *(G-15454)*

Aluminum Trailer Company (HQ) 574 773-2440
751 N Tomahawk Trl Nappanee (46550) *(G-12579)*

Aluminum Wldg & Mch Works Inc 219 787-8066
225 W Dunes Hwy Chesterton (46304) *(G-1901)*

Alumnitec, Jeffersonville *Also Called: Altec LLC (G-9928)*

Alveys Sign Co Inc 812 867-2567
13100 Highway 57 Evansville (47725) *(G-3883)*

Alvin J Nix 812 347-2510
2820 Fairdale Rd Nw Ramsey (47166) *(G-14023)*

Always Fresh Baked Goods Inc 317 319-4747
560 E Washington St Martinsville (46151) *(G-11380)*

Always Full LLC 317 727-9639
1105 W 136th St Carmel (46032) *(G-1559)*

Always Sun Tanning Center (PA) 812 238-2786
1420 N 25th St Terre Haute (47803) *(G-15540)*

AM General, South Bend *Also Called: AM General LLC (G-14942)*

AM General Holdings LLC 574 237-6222
105 N Niles Ave South Bend (46617) *(G-14940)*

AM General LLC 574 258-7523
13200 Mckinley Hwy Mishawaka (46545) *(G-11840)*

AM General LLC 574 258-6699
711 W Chippewa Ave South Bend (46614) *(G-14941)*

AM General LLC (HQ) 574 237-6222
105 N Niles Ave South Bend (46617) *(G-14942)*

AM Manufacturing Company Ind 800 342-6744
9200 Calumet Ave Ste Nw7 Munster (46321) *(G-12528)*

AM Publishing Inc 317 806-0001
11650 Lantern Rd Ste 103 Fishers (46038) *(G-4462)*

AM Stabilizers, Valparaiso *Also Called: AM Stabilizers Corporation (G-15896)*

AM Stabilizers Corporation 219 844-3980
705 Silhavy Rd Valparaiso (46383) *(G-15896)*

Am-Safe Commercial Products, Elkhart *Also Called: Amsafe Partners Inc (G-3180)*

AMA Design Print 219 462-8683
389 E Us Highway 30 Valparaiso (46383) *(G-15897)*

AMA Usa Inc 317 329-6590
5350 Lakeview Parkway South Dr Ste D Indianapolis (46268) *(G-7494)*

Amalgamated Incorporated 260 489-2549
6211 Discount Dr Fort Wayne (46818) *(G-4747)*

Amanda Elizabeth LLC 602 317-9633
3711 Vanguard Dr Ste C Fort Wayne (46809) *(G-4748)*

Amatrol Inc 800 264-8285
1638 Production Rd Jeffersonville (47130) *(G-9929)*

Amatsigroup Inc (DH) 617 576-2005
2458 N Chamberlain St Terre Haute (47805) *(G-15541)*

Amazing Well Drill Pump Plbg 317 384-9132
3015 Radford Dr Indianapolis (46226) *(G-7495)*

Ambandash 260 415-1709
3826 Walden Run Fort Wayne (46815) *(G-4749)*

Ambassador Steel Corporation 317 834-3434
149 Sycamore Ln Mooresville (46158) *(G-12193)*

AMBASSADOR STEEL CORPORATION, Mooresville *Also Called: Ambassador Steel Corporation (G-12193)*

Ambre Blends 317 257-0202
7825 E 89th St Indianapolis (46256) *(G-7496)*

Ambrosia Orchard Inc 260 639-4101
14025 Us Highway 27 Hoagland (46745) *(G-7165)*

Ambrotos LLC 413 887-1058
8640 E County Road 200 N Otwell (47564) *(G-13456)*

Ambu, Noblesville *Also Called: King Systems Corporation (G-13120)*

AMC Acquisition Corporation 215 572-0738
4840 Beck Dr Elkhart (46516) *(G-3169)*

Amcor Flexibles North Amer Inc 812 466-2213
1350 N Fruitridge Ave Terre Haute (47804) *(G-15542)*

Amcor Pet Packaging NA, Greenwood *Also Called: Amcor Rigid Packaging Usa LLC (G-6666)*

Amcor Phrm Packg USA LLC 812 591-2332
1108 N State Road 3 Westport (47283) *(G-16748)*

Amcor Rigid Packaging Usa LLC 317 736-4313
3201 Bearing Dr Franklin (46131) *(G-5708)*

Amcor Rigid Packaging Usa LLC 317 736-4313
800 Commerce Parkway West Dr Greenwood (46143) *(G-6666)*

Amerawhip Inc 317 639-5248
1735 W 18th St Indianapolis (46202) *(G-7497)*

Amercan, Fort Wayne *Also Called: Scotia Corporation (G-5404)*

Ameri-Can Engineering, Argos *Also Called: T I B Inc (G-327)*

Ameri-Kan, Fort Wayne *Also Called: Rugged Steel Works LLC (G-5390)*

Ameri-Kart Corp 225 642-7874
1667 Commerce Dr Bristol (46507) *(G-1243)*

Ameri-Kart Corp (HQ) 574 848-7462
1667 Commerce Dr Bristol (46507) *(G-1244)*

Ameri-Kart(mi) Corp 269 641-5811
1667 Commerce Dr Bristol (46507) *(G-1245)*

Ameri-Tek Manufacturing Inc 574 753-8058
3332 Billiard Dr Logansport (46947) *(G-11055)*

Ameribrace Orthopedic LLC 260 704-6027
14504 Lima Rd Fort Wayne (46818) *(G-4750)*

Ameribridge LLC 317 826-2000
5425 Poindexter Dr Indianapolis (46235) *(G-7498)*

America Corn Cutter 219 733-0885
9203 Twin Acres Dr Wanatah (46390) *(G-16285)*

America Wild LLC 888 485-2589
327 Ley Rd Fort Wayne (46825) *(G-4751)*

American Academy of Sports 877 732-5009
9264 Greenthread Ln Zionsville (46077) *(G-16989)*

American Adventures Inc 574 875-6850
2809 Ferndale Rd Elkhart (46517) *(G-3170)*

American Art Clay Co Inc (PA) 317 244-6871
6060 Guion Rd Indianapolis (46254) *(G-7499)*

American Axle & Mfg Inc 260 824-6800
131 W Harvest Rd Bluffton (46714) *(G-1024)*

American Axle & Mfg Inc 260 495-4315
307 S Tillotson St Fremont (46737) *(G-5808)*

American Axle Manufacturi 812 418-7726
2805 Norcross Dr Columbus (47201) *(G-2217)*

American Barge Line Company (DH) 812 288-0100
1701 E Mkt St Jeffersonville (47130) *(G-9930)*

American Beverage Marketers, New Albany *Also Called: Clark Foods Inc (G-12714)*

American Binders LLC 260 827-7799
134 Green Dr Ste D Avilla (46710) *(G-472)*

American Bottling Company 260 484-4177
2711 Independence Dr Fort Wayne (46808) *(G-4752)*

American Bottling Company 317 875-4900
5430 W 81st St Indianapolis (46268) *(G-7500)*

American Bottling Company 574 291-9000
4610 S Burnett Dr South Bend (46614) *(G-14943)*

American Bottling Company 765 987-7800
6083 State Rd Spiceland (47385) *(G-15376)*

American Bronze Craft Inc (PA) 501 729-3018
5520 Kopetsky Dr Ste A Indianapolis (46217) *(G-7501)*

American Business Forms I 317 852-8956
328 Acre Ave Brownsburg (46112) *(G-1345)*

American Cabinet Refacing Inc 317 875-7453
10650 Bennett Pkwy Ste 300 Zionsville (46077) *(G-16990)*

American Classifieds 317 782-8111
1776 Windward Dr Greenwood (46143) *(G-6667)*

American Co 812 250-9575
2131 Covert Ave Evansville (47714) *(G-3884)*

American Colors Clothing 812 822-0476
314 E Kirkwood Ave Bloomington (47408) *(G-778)*

American Coml Barge Line LLC (DH) 812 288-0100
1701 E Market St Jeffersonville (47130) *(G-9931)*

American Commercial Barge Line, Jeffersonville *Also Called: American Commercial Lines Inc (G-9932)*

American Commercial Lines Inc (HQ) 812 288-0100
1701 E Market St Jeffersonville (47130) *(G-9932)*

AMERICAN COMMUNICATIONS NETWOR, Hagerstown *Also Called: Brian Bex Report Inc (G-6834)*

American Containers Inc (PA) 574 936-4068
2526 Western Ave Plymouth (46563) *(G-13755)*

American Cook Systems, Fort Wayne *Also Called: American Equipment Corp (G-4753)*

American Corrugated.. 812 425-4056
  3410 Claremont Ave Evansville (47712) *(G-3885)*

American Crane & Millwright....................................... 765 452-5000
  6132 Industrial Dr Gas City (46933) *(G-6030)*

American Diabetes Association................................... 859 268-9129
  8604 Allisonville Rd Ste 140 Indianapolis (46250) *(G-7502)*

American Direct Sales LLC... 877 462-2621
  711 Garfield Ave Valparaiso (46383) *(G-15898)*

American Door Controls Inc... 812 988-4853
  51 W State Road 45 Morgantown (46160) *(G-12253)*

American Dream Nut Butter... 317 326-9363
  12033 Logan Hunter Trl Noblesville (46060) *(G-13035)*

American Eagle Health LLC.. 812 921-9224
  2572 Campion Rd Floyds Knobs (47119) *(G-4668)*

American Eagle Security Inc.. 219 980-1177
  6111 Harrison St Ste 126 Merrillville (46410) *(G-11482)*

American Elctrnic Cmpnents Inc................................... 574 295-6330
  913 10th St Elkhart (46516) *(G-3171)*

American Elite Printing LLC... 765 513-0889
  15541 Slip Anchor Ln Fishers (46040) *(G-4639)*

American Elkhart LLC.. 574 293-0333
  2304 Charlotte Ave Elkhart (46517) *(G-3172)*

American Equipment Corp... 888 321-0117
  10827 La Cabreah Ln Fort Wayne (46845) *(G-4753)*

American Ex Trvl Rlted Svcs In..................................... 812 523-0106
  709 A Ave E Seymour (47274) *(G-14629)*

American Express, Seymour Also Called: American Ex Trvl Rlted Svcs In *(G-14629)*

American Fabricating... 812 897-0900
  1302 N Rockport Rd Boonville (47601) *(G-1080)*

American Fabricators Inc... 219 844-4744
  5832 Cline Ave Hammond (46323) *(G-6873)*

American Family Pharmacy LLC.................................. 317 334-1933
  3250 N Post Rd Ste 285 Indianapolis (46226) *(G-7503)*

American Feeding Systems Inc.................................... 317 773-5517
  15425 Endeavor Dr Noblesville (46060) *(G-13036)*

American Fibertech Corporation................................... 219 261-3586
  250 Main St Lafayette (47901) *(G-10521)*

American Fibertech Corporation................................... 812 849-6095
  3159 Fleenor Rd Mitchell (47446) *(G-12031)*

American Fibertech Corporation (PA)........................... 219 261-3586
  4 N New York St Remington (47977) *(G-14033)*

American Fire Company... 219 840-0630
  2603 Oakwood Dr Valparaiso (46383) *(G-15899)*

American Flame LLC... 260 459-1703
  9230 Conservation Way Fort Wayne (46809) *(G-4754)*

American Gardenworks Inc.. 765 869-4033
  407 S Adeway Fowler (47944) *(G-5617)*

American Heritage Shutters LLC.................................. 317 598-6908
  9450 Timberline Dr Indianapolis (46256) *(G-7504)*

American Home Fragrance, South Bend Also Called: Lebermuth Company Inc *(G-15121)*

American Hosiery, Hobart Also Called: J J P Enterprise *(G-7194)*

American Hydraulic Hoses, Newburgh Also Called: Cindon Inc *(G-12998)*

American Hydro Systems Inc....................................... 866 357-5063
  7201 Engle Rd Fort Wayne (46804) *(G-4755)*

American Hydroformers Inc... 260 428-2660
  4410 New Haven Ave Fort Wayne (46803) *(G-4756)*

American Industrial Co LLC... 317 859-9900
  1400 American Way Greenwood (46143) *(G-6668)*

American Industrial McHy Inc...................................... 219 755-4090
  4015 W 83rd Pl Merrillville (46410) *(G-11483)*

American Keeper Corporation...................................... 765 521-2080
  3300 S Commerce Dr New Castle (47362) *(G-12849)*

American Label Products Inc....................................... 317 873-9850
  4949 W 106th St Zionsville (46077) *(G-16991)*

American Legion National Headquarters (PA).............. 317 630-1200
  700 N Pennsylvania St Indianapolis (46204) *(G-7505)*

American Licorice Company (PA)................................. 219 324-1400
  1914 Happiness Way La Porte (46350) *(G-10382)*

American Limb & Orthopedic Co.................................. 574 522-3643
  3614 S Nappanee St Ste 122 Elkhart (46517) *(G-3173)*

American Machine & Fabg Co Inc................................ 812 944-4136
  1223 E 8th St New Albany (47150) *(G-12688)*

American Machine Works Inc...................................... 219 924-3574
  570 Progress Ave Munster (46321) *(G-12529)*

American Maint & Training Inc..................................... 812 738-4230
  300 E Walnut St Corydon (47112) *(G-2485)*

American Melt Blown Filtration..................................... 219 866-3500
  1030 E Elm St Rensselaer (47978) *(G-14041)*

American Millwork, Elkhart Also Called: AMC Acquisition Corporation *(G-3169)*

American Millwork LLC.. 574 295-4158
  4840 Beck Dr Elkhart (46516) *(G-3174)*

American Mobile Power, Fairmount Also Called: North American Mfg Inc *(G-4411)*

American Mobile Sound Ind LLC.................................. 765 288-1500
  2418 W 7th St Muncie (47302) *(G-12341)*

American Natural Resources LLC................................ 219 922-6444
  120 N Broad St Griffith (46319) *(G-6790)*

American Natural Resources Str, Griffith Also Called: American Natural Resources LLC *(G-6790)*

American Oak Preserving Co Inc (PA).......................... 574 896-2171
  601 Mulberry St North Judson (46366) *(G-13206)*

American Pallet & Recycl Inc (PA)................................ 219 322-4391
  1203 Sheffield Ave Dyer (46311) *(G-2966)*

American Performance Engrg, Peru Also Called: K&T Performance Engrg LLC *(G-13589)*

American Plastic Molding Corp..................................... 813 752-7000
  965 S Elm St Scottsburg (47170) *(G-14552)*

American Precision Svcs Inc.. 219 977-4451
  7110 W 21st Ave Gary (46406) *(G-5892)*

American Press Services... 937 338-3000
  935 W Pearl St Union City (47390) *(G-15847)*

American Printing.. 219 836-5600
  8208 Calumet Ave Munster (46321) *(G-12530)*

American Printing & Advg Inc (PA)............................... 219 937-1844
  5324 Hohman Ave Hammond (46320) *(G-6874)*

American Printing Company (PA)................................. 574 533-5399
  2331 Eisenhower Dr N Goshen (46526) *(G-6092)*

American Printing Indiana LLC..................................... 765 825-7600
  1047 Broadway St Anderson (46012) *(G-76)*

American Reliance Inds Co... 260 768-4704
  860 N Tuscany Dr Shipshewana (46565) *(G-14834)*

American Renolit, La Porte Also Called: American Renolit Corp La *(G-10383)*

American Renolit Corp La.. 856 241-4901
  1207 E Lincolnway La Porte (46350) *(G-10383)*

American Renolit Corporation (DH).............................. 219 324-6886
  1207 E Lincolnway La Porte (46350) *(G-10384)*

American Resources Corporation (PA)......................... 317 855-9926
  12115 Visionary Way Fishers (46038) *(G-4463)*

American Rigging Rental... 317 721-9553
  1717 W 10th St Indianapolis (46222) *(G-7506)*

American Roller Company LLC.................................... 574 586-3101
  201 Industrial Park Dr Walkerton (46574) *(G-16263)*

American Rubber Corp.. 317 548-8455
  1136 Dilts St Anderson (46017) *(G-77)*

American School Health Assn...................................... 703 506-7675
  3011 S Xavier Ct Bloomington (47401) *(G-779)*

American Scrap Processing Inc................................... 219 398-1444
  3601 Canal St East Chicago (46312) *(G-2989)*

American Sealants Inc (HQ).. 800 325-7040
  9190 Yeager Ln Fort Wayne (46809) *(G-4757)*

American Senior Homecare... 317 849-4968
  4519 E 82nd St Ofc Indianapolis (46250) *(G-7507)*

American Sign Design... 574 287-4387
  1702 Lincoln Way W South Bend (46628) *(G-14944)*

American Spcialty Bus Intl LLC.................................... 317 271-5000
  5701 S 800 E Zionsville (46077) *(G-16992)*

American Speedy Printing, Indianapolis Also Called: Smitson Cmmnications Group LLC *(G-9451)*

American Speedy Printing, Valparaiso Also Called: D-J Printing Specialists Inc *(G-15935)*

American Sportworks, Columbia City Also Called: Asw LLC *(G-2120)*

American Stair Corp.. 815 886-9600
  3510 Calumet Ave Hammond (46320) *(G-6875)*

American Stair Corporation Inc.................................... 800 872-7824
  3510 Calumet Ave Hammond (46320) *(G-6876)*

American Stave Company LLC.................................... 812 883-9374
  5170 W State Road 56 Salem (47167) *(G-14471)*

ALPHABETIC SECTION — Anatolia Group Ltd Partnership

American Steel Carports Inc 419 737-1331
404 W Main St Mount Summit (47361) *(G-12284)*

American Steel Rule Die Inc 574 262-3437
3401 Reedy Dr Elkhart (46514) *(G-3175)*

American Stonecast Pdts Inc 574 206-0097
4315 Wyland Dr Elkhart (46516) *(G-3176)*

American Sunspace, Elkhart Also Called: Wallar Additions Inc *(G-3778)*

American Technology Components Incorporated 800 238-2687
1147 N Michigan St Elkhart (46514) *(G-3177)*

American Tool Service Inc (PA) 260 493-6351
7007 Trafalgar Dr Fort Wayne (46803) *(G-4758)*

American Translifts Company, Brownsburg Also Called: Tru Bore Company *(G-1410)*

American Trucker, New Palestine Also Called: Informa Business Media Inc *(G-12938)*

American Ultraviolet Company (PA) 765 483-9514
212 S Mount Zion Rd Lebanon (46052) *(G-10874)*

American Urn Inc 812 379-5555
2315 N Cherry St Columbus (47201) *(G-2218)*

American Veteran Group LLC 317 600-4749
17020 Emerald Green Cir Westfield (46074) *(G-16664)*

American Vulkan Corporation 219 866-7751
317 S Weston St Rensselaer (47978) *(G-14042)*

American Way Marketing Llc 574 295-6633
400 Pine Creek Ct Elkhart (46516) *(G-3178)*

American Wedge Company 812 883-1086
215 N Tarr Ave Salem (47167) *(G-14472)*

American Whitetail Inc 812 937-7185
8478 E State Road 62 Ferdinand (47532) *(G-4428)*

American Window and Glass Inc (PA) 812 464-9400
2715 Lynch Rd Evansville (47711) *(G-3886)*

American Wire Rope & Sling, Indianapolis Also Called: American Wire Rope Sling of In *(G-7508)*

American Wire Rope Sling of In 260 478-4700
3122 Engle Rd Fort Wayne (46809) *(G-4759)*

American Wire Rope Sling of In (HQ) 877 634-2545
5760 Dividend Rd Indianapolis (46241) *(G-7508)*

American Wire Rope Sling of In 574 257-9424
5005 Lincolnway E Mishawaka (46544) *(G-11841)*

American Woodmark Corporation 765 677-1690
5300 Eastside Parkway Dr Gas City (46933) *(G-6031)*

Americana Development Inc 574 295-3535
400 Collins Rd Elkhart (46516) *(G-3179)*

Americas Cabinet Co Ind Inc 317 788-9533
7367 E Us Highway 40 Greenfield (46140) *(G-6461)*

Americas Coml Trnsp RES Co LLC 812 379-2085
4440 Middle Rd Columbus (47203) *(G-2219)*

Americhef USA, Kendallville Also Called: Kitchen-Quip Inc *(G-10129)*

Americraft Carton Inc 812 537-1784
102 Industrial Dr Lawrenceburg (47025) *(G-10828)*

AMERICRAFT CARTON, INC., Lawrenceburg Also Called: Americraft Carton Inc *(G-10828)*

Amerifab Inc 317 231-0100
3501 E 9th St Indianapolis (46201) *(G-7509)*

Ameriflo Inc 317 844-2019
4496 Saguaro Trl Indianapolis (46268) *(G-7510)*

Ameriflo2 Inc 317 844-2019
4496 Saguaro Trl Indianapolis (46268) *(G-7511)*

Ameriforce Media LLC 812 961-9478
304 W Kirkwood Ave Apt 100 Bloomington (47404) *(G-780)*

Amerimachine LLC 260 414-1703
10415 N 300 W-90 Markle (46770) *(G-11354)*

Ameriqual Foods, Evansville Also Called: Ameriqual Group LLC *(G-3887)*

Ameriqual Group LLC 812 867-1444
18200 Highway 41 N Evansville (47725) *(G-3887)*

Ameriqual Group LLC (DH) 812 867-1444
18200 Highway 41 N Evansville (47725) *(G-3888)*

Ameriqual Packaging, Evansville Also Called: Ameriqual Group LLC *(G-3888)*

Ameristamp Sign-A-Rama, Evansville Also Called: Arben Corporation *(G-3896)*

Ameristeel, Muncie Also Called: Tishler Industries Inc *(G-12502)*

Amerlight LLC (PA) 812 602-3452
2800 Lynch Rd Ste B Evansville (47711) *(G-3889)*

AMG Engineering Machining Inc 317 329-4000
4030 Guion Ln Indianapolis (46268) *(G-7512)*

AMG LLC 317 329-4004
4030 Guion Ln Indianapolis (46268) *(G-7513)*

Amgi LLC 317 447-1524
2345 S Briarwood Dr New Palestine (46163) *(G-12928)*

AMI Defense Inc 219 326-1976
1201 E Lincolnway La Porte (46350) *(G-10385)*

AMI Industries Inc 989 786-3755
1501 Wohlert St Angola (46703) *(G-226)*

Amish Country Dairy LLC 574 323-1701
1360 N 850 W Shipshewana (46565) *(G-14835)*

Amish Country Popcorn Inc 260 589-8513
5433 S 150 E Berne (46711) *(G-703)*

Amish Woodworking LLC 574 941-4439
8870 State Road 17 Plymouth (46563) *(G-13756)*

Amkus Rescue Systems, Valparaiso Also Called: Innovative Rescue Systems LLC *(G-15976)*

Amor Couture, Anderson Also Called: Janelle Davis *(G-139)*

Amorlai Organics LLC 219 595-9102
9445 Indianapolis Blvd Ste 1272 Highland (46322) *(G-7121)*

Amos D Graber & Sons 260 749-0526
5229 Bruick Rd New Haven (46774) *(G-12892)*

Amos Welding LLC 765 561-2359
2117 E 700 N Rushville (46173) *(G-14395)*

Amos-Hill Associates Inc 812 526-2671
112 Shelby Ave Edinburgh (46124) *(G-3067)*

AMP, Carmel Also Called: Advanced Mtlwrking Prctces LLC *(G-1552)*

AMP Americas LLC 312 300-6700
5431 E 600 N Fair Oaks (47943) *(G-4394)*

AMP CNG, Fair Oaks Also Called: AMP Americas LLC *(G-4394)*

Ampac International Inc 260 424-2964
1118 Cedar St Fort Wayne (46803) *(G-4760)*

Ampacet Corporation 812 466-9828
3801 N Fruitridge Ave Terre Haute (47804) *(G-15543)*

Ampacet Corporation 812 466-5231
3701 N Fruitridge Ave Terre Haute (47804) *(G-15544)*

Ampacet Research & Development, Terre Haute Also Called: Ampacet Corporation *(G-15543)*

Amplified Sciences LLC 317 490-0511
3000 Kent Ave West Lafayette (47906) *(G-16560)*

Amrosia Metal Fabrication Inc 812 425-5707
1701 N Kentucky Ave Evansville (47711) *(G-3890)*

AMS Embroidery & Signs LLC 513 313-1613
110 S Main St Unit A Brookville (47012) *(G-1316)*

AMS Pro Sound and Lightingame, Muncie Also Called: American Mobile Sound Ind LLC *(G-12341)*

AMS Production Machining Inc 317 838-9273
800 Andico Rd Plainfield (46168) *(G-13657)*

Amsafe Partners Inc 574 266-8330
3802 Gallatin Way Elkhart (46514) *(G-3180)*

Amsted Graphite Materials LLC 219 931-1900
4831 Hohman Ave Hammond (46327) *(G-6877)*

Amsted Rail International Inc 800 621-8442
4831 Hohman Ave Hammond (46327) *(G-6878)*

Amt, Rochester Also Called: Advanced Mechatronic Tech LLC *(G-14275)*

Amt Parts International, Fort Wayne Also Called: Amt Precision Parts Inc *(G-4761)*

Amt Precision Parts Inc 260 490-0223
3606 Transportation Dr Fort Wayne (46818) *(G-4761)*

Amtek Wholesale Signs, Salem Also Called: Stingel Enterprises Inc *(G-14501)*

An Squared LLC 317 517-7139
1375 S 700 W New Palestine (46163) *(G-12929)*

An-Mar Wiring Systems Inc 574 255-5523
711 E Grove St Mishawaka (46545) *(G-11842)*

Anabaptist Mnnnite Bblcal Smna 574 295-3726
3003 Benham Ave Elkhart (46517) *(G-3181)*

Anaerobic Innovations LLC 765 491-1174
2221 Huron Rd West Lafayette (47906) *(G-16561)*

Analyswift LLC 801 599-5879
444 Jennings St West Lafayette (47906) *(G-16562)*

Analyticalab Inc (PA) 219 473-9777
1404 119th St Ste A Whiting (46394) *(G-16831)*

Anasazi Instruments Inc 317 861-7657
23 S Westside Dr # A New Palestine (46163) *(G-12930)*

Anatolia Group Ltd Partnership 203 343-7808
640 E Michigan St Indianapolis (46202) *(G-7514)*

(PA)=Parent Co (HQ)=Headquarters (DH)=Div Headquarters

Anchor Enterprises... 812 282-7220
  10 Arctic Spgs Jeffersonville (47130) *(G-9933)*
Anchor Glass Container Corp.. 812 537-1655
  200 Belleview Dr Greendale (47025) *(G-6437)*
Anchor Glass Container Corp.. 765 584-6101
  603 E North St Winchester (47394) *(G-16881)*
Anchor Industries.. 812 664-0772
  9248 W 280 S Owensville (47665) *(G-13465)*
Anchor Industries Inc (PA).. 812 867-2421
  1100 Burch Dr Evansville (47725) *(G-3891)*
Anchor Industries Inc.. 812 867-2421
  7701 Highway 41 N Evansville (47725) *(G-3892)*
Anchor Seals Incorporated.. 412 299-6900
  219 Virginia St Gary (46402) *(G-5893)*
Anchor Seals Incorporated, Gary Also Called: Anchor Seals Incorporated *(G-5893)*
Ancient Cellars... 503 437-4827
  360 W 63rd St Indianapolis (46260) *(G-7515)*
Anco Products, Elkhart Also Called: API Indiana Inc *(G-3186)*
Andersen Corporation... 260 694-6861
  219 W State Road 218 Poneto (46781) *(G-13839)*
Anderson Shykia.. 773 304-6852
  4025 Kentucky St Gary (46409) *(G-5894)*
Anderson & Anderson Trckg Inc................................... 219 661-7547
  104 W Hack Ct Crown Point (46307) *(G-2650)*
Anderson Amish Cabinets LLC...................................... 317 575-9277
  14545 John Paul Way Carmel (46032) *(G-1560)*
Anderson Creations Inc... 574 223-8932
  371 E 450 N Rochester (46975) *(G-14276)*
Anderson Fab Llc... 317 534-7306
  9199 Huggin Hollow Rd Martinsville (46151) *(G-11381)*
Anderson Machine Tool, Peru Also Called: Fred Anderson *(G-13583)*
Anderson Memorial Park Inc... 765 643-3211
  6805 Dr Martin Luther King Jr Blvd Anderson (46013) *(G-78)*
Anderson Parking Authority, Anderson Also Called: City of Anderson *(G-93)*
Anderson Products... 765 794-4242
  700 E Rd Darlington (47940) *(G-2831)*
Anderson Silver Plating Co... 574 294-6447
  541 Industrial Pkwy Elkhart (46516) *(G-3182)*
Andersons Agriculture Group LP.................................. 765 564-6135
  3902 N Anderson Dr Delphi (46923) *(G-2890)*
Andersons Agriculture Group LP.................................. 574 626-2522
  8086 E 900 Galveston (46932) *(G-5851)*
Andersons Agriculture Group LP.................................. 574 753-4974
  2345 S 400 E Logansport (46947) *(G-11056)*
Andersons Clymers Ethanol LLC................................... 574 722-2627
  3389 W County Road 300 S Logansport (46947) *(G-11057)*
Andersons Fertilizer Service... 765 538-3285
  527 W 1150 S Romney (47981) *(G-14379)*
Andis Logging Inc.. 812 723-2357
  76 W County Road 550 S Paoli (47454) *(G-13487)*
Andon Specialties Inc.. 317 983-1700
  5736 W 79th St Indianapolis (46278) *(G-7516)*
Andover Coils, Fishers Also Called: Andover Coils LLC *(G-4464)*
Andover Coils LLC... 765 447-1157
  13865 Black Canyon Ct Fishers (46038) *(G-4464)*
Andre Corp.. 574 293-0207
  3406 S Main St 8 Elkhart (46517) *(G-3183)*
Andre Renee Writes Pubg Co LLC................................ 219 746-4329
  Hammond (46323) *(G-6879)*
Andresen Graphic Processors....................................... 317 291-7071
  10843 E County Road 950 N Brownsburg (46112) *(G-1346)*
Andretti Technologies LLC.. 317 872-2700
  7615 Zionsville Rd Indianapolis (46268) *(G-7517)*
Andritz Herr-Voss Stamco Inc....................................... 219 764-8586
  1079 Lot #1, Industry Drive Chesterton (46304) *(G-1902)*
Android Industries LLC.. 260 672-0112
  12808 Stonebridge Rd # 110 Roanoke (46783) *(G-14257)*
Android Industries Fort Wayne, Roanoke Also Called: Android Industries LLC *(G-14257)*
Andys Global Inc.. 317 595-8825
  8445 Castlewood Dr Ste C Indianapolis (46250) *(G-7518)*
Anew Company Inc.. 574 293-9088
  4811 Eastland Dr Elkhart (46516) *(G-3184)*

Anewco, Elkhart Also Called: Anew Company Inc *(G-3184)*
Angel ARC Welding.. 812 322-9027
  7551 Hartshaven Ln Columbus (47201) *(G-2220)*
Angels Wings Expedited.. 574 339-3038
  1246 Echo Dr South Bend (46614) *(G-14945)*
Angies Printing LLC... 765 966-6237
  1751 Sheridan St Richmond (47374) *(G-14086)*
Anglers Manufacturing... 812 988-8040
  217 Salt Creek Rd Nashville (47448) *(G-12660)*
Angola Canvas Co... 260 665-9913
  2301 N Wayne St Angola (46703) *(G-227)*
Angola Wire Products Inc... 260 665-3061
  1300 Wohlert St Angola (46703) *(G-228)*
Angola Wire Products Inc (PA)..................................... 260 665-9447
  803 Wohlert St Angola (46703) *(G-229)*
Animalsinkcom LLC... 317 496-8467
  7489 Windridge Way Brownsburg (46112) *(G-1347)*
Animated Dynamics Inc... 765 418-5359
  1281 Win Hentschel Blvd West Lafayette (47906) *(G-16563)*
Anippe... 317 979-1110
  11486 Enclave Blvd Fishers (46038) *(G-4465)*
Anita Cole... 907 479-2245
  3071 Dutch Mill St Portage (46368) *(G-13843)*
Anita Lorrain LLC... 574 621-0531
  52303 Emmons Rd Ste 20 South Bend (46637) *(G-14946)*
Anita Machine and Tool Inc.. 765 477-6054
  510 Elston Rd Lafayette (47909) *(G-10522)*
Anliker Machine, Chalmers Also Called: Ken Anliker *(G-1858)*
Anndys Paradise LLC... 317 258-7531
  7105 Knobwood Dr Apt A Indianapolis (46260) *(G-7519)*
Anne Pfeiffer Holdings Inc.. 812 948-1422
  325 Park East Blvd New Albany (47150) *(G-12689)*
Annette Balfour.. 765 286-1910
  2201 E Memorial Dr Rear Muncie (47302) *(G-12342)*
Annie Oakley Enterprises Inc.. 260 894-7100
  300 Johnson St Ligonier (46767) *(G-11004)*
Annies Publishing LLC... 260 589-4000
  306 E Parr Rd Berne (46711) *(G-704)*
Anns Boba Tea LLC... 317 681-3143
  3827 N Mithoefer Rd Ste B7 Pmb B8 Indianapolis (46235) *(G-7520)*
Annual Reports Inc.. 317 736-8838
  1250 Park Ave Franklin (46131) *(G-5709)*
Annual Reports Services, Franklin Also Called: Annual Reports Inc *(G-5709)*
Anodizing Technologies Inc.. 317 253-5725
  5868 N New Jersey St Indianapolis (46220) *(G-7521)*
Anodyne Medical Device Inc (DH)................................ 954 340-0500
  1069 State Road 46 E Batesville (47006) *(G-578)*
ANR Pipeline Company.. 260 463-3342
  2255 W Us Highway 20 Lagrange (46761) *(G-10728)*
Anthony D Etienne Logging... 812 843-5872
  15502 N State Road 66 Magnet (47520) *(G-11258)*
Anthony Group LLC... 317 536-7445
  2011 Southtech Dr Ste 100 Greenwood (46143) *(G-6669)*
Anthony Smith.. 765 478-5325
  9 E Front St Cambridge City (47327) *(G-1490)*
Anthony Wise.. 317 933-2458
  5655 S 50 W Trafalgar (46181) *(G-15825)*
Anthony Wyne Rhblttion Ctr For (PA).......................... 260 744-6145
  8515 Bluffton Rd Fort Wayne (46809) *(G-4762)*
Anthony Wyne Rhblttion Ctr For................................... 317 972-1000
  2762 Rand Rd Indianapolis (46241) *(G-7522)*
Anthonyjean LLC.. 317 513-4981
  2000 Dockside Dr Greenwood (46143) *(G-6670)*
Antique Candle Works Inc.. 765 250-8481
  1611 Schuyler Ave Lafayette (47904) *(G-10523)*
Antique Candle Works LLC... 765 586-6013
  913 Waverly Rd Porter (46304) *(G-13921)*
Antique Stove Information.. 574 583-6465
  421 N Main St Monticello (47960) *(G-12135)*
Antiques At 200 East LLC... 812 933-0863
  1211 Lammers Pike Batesville (47006) *(G-579)*

ALPHABETIC SECTION

Antler Creek Woodworking LLC 812 636-0188
　9100 N 1025 E Odon (47562) *(G-13330)*

Anton Alexander, Fort Wayne *Also Called: European Concepts LLC (G-4966)*

Antreasian Design Inc 317 546-3234
　3124 Ridgeview Dr Indianapolis (46226) *(G-7523)*

Ao Inc 317 280-3000
　9227 E Us Highway 36 Avon (46123) *(G-504)*

Aoc LLC 219 465-4384
　2552 Industrial Dr Valparaiso (46383) *(G-15900)*

AON, Indianapolis *Also Called: Aon(all or Nothing) LLC (G-7524)*

Aon(all or Nothing) LLC 219 405-0163
　2003 Lisa Walk Dr Indianapolis (46227) *(G-7524)*

AP Lazer, Indianapolis *Also Called: Supernova International Inc (G-9531)*

Apar Technological Inc 812 430-2025
　305 S Welworth Ave Evansville (47714) *(G-3893)*

APC Paving, New Albany *Also Called: Allterrain Paving & Cnstr LLC (G-12687)*

Apex AG Solutions LLC 765 305-1930
　130 S 100 E Winchester (47394) *(G-16882)*

Apex Doors Plus LLC 574 370-0906
　420 N Main St Middlebury (46540) *(G-11696)*

Apex Electric & Sign Inc 317 326-1325
　4328 E State Road 234 Greenfield (46140) *(G-6462)*

Apex Electric & Sign Inc (PA) 317 326-1325
　500 N Range Line Rd Morristown (46161) *(G-12271)*

Apex Engineered Entps LLC 317 346-7148
　2590 E 200 S Franklin (46131) *(G-5710)*

Apex Filling Systems Inc 219 575-7493
　1001 Eastwood Rd Michigan City (46360) *(G-11578)*

Apex Industries LLC 260 624-5003
　309 W Stocker St Angola (46703) *(G-230)*

Apex Procurement LLC 574 304-2679
　4802 E State Road 14 Claypool (46510) *(G-2050)*

Apex Tool and Manufacturing 812 425-8121
　2306 N New York Ave Evansville (47711) *(G-3894)*

Apexx Engineering, Montgomery *Also Called: Apexx Enterprises LLC (G-12085)*

Apexx Enterprises LLC 812 486-2443
　6654 E Us Highway 50 Montgomery (47558) *(G-12085)*

Apg Inc 574 295-0000
　2825 Middlebury St Elkhart (46516) *(G-3185)*

API, Lagrange *Also Called: Automated Products Intl LLC (G-10729)*

API Indiana Inc 574 293-5574
　2500 17th St Elkhart (46517) *(G-3186)*

API International Inc 317 894-1100
　6219 W Stoner Dr Greenfield (46140) *(G-6463)*

APL Welding & Fabrication LLC 765 572-1088
　7436 Turner Rd Westpoint (47992) *(G-16742)*

Apollo America 812 284-3300
　701 Port Rd Jeffersonville (47130) *(G-9934)*

Apollo Design Technology Inc 260 497-9191
　4012 Merchant Rd Fort Wayne (46818) *(G-4763)*

Apollo Otdoor Cstm Designs Inc 317 430-1373
　1848 Stout Field East Dr Indianapolis (46241) *(G-7525)*

Apollo Precision Machining Inc 574 271-1197
　4085 Ralph Jones Dr South Bend (46628) *(G-14947)*

Apollo Prtg & Graphics Ctr Inc 574 287-3707
　731 S Michigan St South Bend (46601) *(G-14948)*

Apologia Eductl Ministries Inc 765 608-3280
　1106 Meridian St Ste 340 Anderson (46016) *(G-79)*

Apotex Corp 317 334-1314
　5110 W 74th St Indianapolis (46268) *(G-7526)*

Apotex Corp 317 839-6550
　2516 Airwest Blvd Plainfield (46168) *(G-13658)*

Apothecare Rx, Indianapolis *Also Called: Skinny & Co Inc (G-9445)*

App Engineering Incorporated 317 536-5300
　5234 Elmwood Ave Indianapolis (46203) *(G-7527)*

App Press LLC 317 661-4759
　435 Virginia Ave Unit 607 Indianapolis (46203) *(G-7528)*

Appalachian Log Structures 812 744-5711
　10994 Chesterville Rd Moores Hill (47032) *(G-12186)*

Apparel Design Group 812 339-3355
　671 S Landmark Ave Bloomington (47403) *(G-781)*

Apparel Plus Inc 812 951-2111
　1175 Copperfield Dr Georgetown (47122) *(G-6054)*

Appextremes LLC 317 550-0148
　54 Monument Cir Ste 200 Indianapolis (46204) *(G-7529)*

Apple Group Inc 765 675-4777
　122 N East St Tipton (46072) *(G-15764)*

Apple III LLC 317 691-2869
　3928 Kitty Hawk Ct Carmel (46033) *(G-1561)*

Apple Press Inc 317 253-7752
　6327 Ferguson St Indianapolis (46220) *(G-7530)*

Apple Terrace LLC 260 347-9400
　515 Professional Way Kendallville (46755) *(G-10089)*

Apple--day Cstm Hndcrfted Pdts 219 841-6602
　2005 Worthington Dr Valparaiso (46383) *(G-15901)*

Apple-Ly Ever After Inc 219 838-9397
　3542 Highway Ave Highland (46322) *(G-7122)*

Applegate, Union City *Also Called: Applegate Livestock Eqp Inc (G-15848)*

Applegate Livestock Eqp Inc (DH) 765 964-3715
　902 S State Road 32 Union City (47390) *(G-15848)*

Appleton Electric Division, La Porte *Also Called: Appleton Grp LLC (G-10386)*

Appleton Grp LLC 219 326-5936
　2362 N Us Highway 35 La Porte (46350) *(G-10386)*

Appliance Pros LLC 812 329-2669
　3730 State Road 58 E Heltonville (47436) *(G-7109)*

Application Software 317 814-8010
　117 Wood St Greenfield (46140) *(G-6464)*

Application Software Inc 317 823-3525
　9801 Fall Creek Rd Ste 101 Indianapolis (46256) *(G-7531)*

Applicon Company Incorporated 317 635-7843
　450 N Somerset Ave Indianapolis (46222) *(G-7532)*

Applied Coating Converting LLC 260 436-4455
　3736 N Wells St Fort Wayne (46808) *(G-4764)*

Applied Composites Engrg Inc 317 243-4225
　705 S Girls School Rd Indianapolis (46231) *(G-7533)*

Applied Electronic Mtls LLC 260 438-8632
　9609 Ardmore Ave Fort Wayne (46809) *(G-4765)*

Applied Fabricators Inc 317 284-0685
　7185 W 200 N Greenfield (46140) *(G-6465)*

Applied Laboratories Inc (HQ) 812 372-2607
　1600 W Brian Dr Columbus (47201) *(G-2221)*

Applied Logic Electronics LLC 317 633-7300
　2525 N Shadeland Ave Ste C6 Indianapolis (46219) *(G-7534)*

Applied Metals & Mch Works Inc 260 424-4834
　1036 Saint Marys Ave Fort Wayne (46808) *(G-4766)*

Applied Scientific RES Inc 219 776-4623
　2036 W 86th Ln Merrillville (46410) *(G-11484)*

Applied Technology Group Inc 260 482-2844
　2230 W Coliseum Blvd Fort Wayne (46808) *(G-4767)*

Applied Thermal Tech Inc 574 269-7116
　2169 N 100 E Warsaw (46582) *(G-16313)*

Apr Plastic Fabricating Inc 260 482-8523
　3685 Lima Rd Fort Wayne (46805) *(G-4768)*

Apr Plastics Inc 812 258-8888
　3350 Claremont Ave Evansville (47712) *(G-3895)*

Aprimo Inc 317 663-6556
　135 N Pennsylvania St Ste 2300 Indianapolis (46204) *(G-7535)*

APS Kreative Kustomz LLC 317 384-1267
　3709 N Shadeland Ave Indianapolis (46226) *(G-7536)*

Apsco of Indiana, Fort Wayne *Also Called: Shank Brothers Inc (G-5411)*

Aptera Software Inc 260 969-1410
　113 W Berry St Ste 3 Fort Wayne (46802) *(G-4769)*

Aptiv Services Us LLC 765 451-0732
　13085 Hamilton Crossing Blvd Ste X Carmel (46032) *(G-1562)*

Aptiv Services Us LLC 765 451-5011
　2705 S Goyer Rd Kokomo (46902) *(G-10233)*

Aptiv Services Us LLC 765 867-4435
　17001 Oak Ridge Rd Westfield (46074) *(G-16665)*

Aqseptence Group Inc 574 208-5866
　4079 N Old Us Highway 31 Rochester (46975) *(G-14277)*

Aqseptence Group Inc 574 223-3980
　4217 N Old Us Highway 31 Rochester (46975) *(G-14278)*

AQSEPTENCE GROUP, INC.   ALPHABETIC SECTION

AQSEPTENCE GROUP, INC., Rochester Also Called: Aqseptence Group Inc *(G-14277)*
Aqua Blast Corp.. 260 728-4433
  1025 W Commerce Dr Decatur (46733) *(G-2844)*
Aqua Lily Products LLC (PA)... 951 246-9610
  1806 Conant St Elkhart (46516) *(G-3187)*
Aqua Systems, Avon Also Called: New Aqua LLC *(G-540)*
Aqua Utility Services LLC... 812 284-9243
  1829 E Spring St Ste 106 New Albany (47150) *(G-12690)*
Aquabee Coolers LLC... 615 947-7962
  5293 N Targhee Ct Bloomington (47404) *(G-782)*
Aquathin A Wtr Prfction Evnsvl, Evansville Also Called: Kendle Custom Inc *(G-4148)*
Aquestive Therapeutics Inc... 219 762-4143
  6465 Ameriplex Dr Portage (46368) *(G-13844)*
Aquestive Therapeutics Inc... 219 762-3165
  6560 Melton Rd Portage (46368) *(G-13845)*
AR Shot It LLC.. 317 654-0187
  5409 Ashbourne Ln Indianapolis (46226) *(G-7537)*
Ar-Tee Enterprises Inc.. 574 848-5543
  19874 County Road 6 Bristol (46507) *(G-1246)*
Aratana, Greenfield Also Called: Aratana Therapeutics Inc *(G-6466)*
Aratana Therapeutics Inc (HQ).................................... 913 353-1000
  2500 Innovation Way N Greenfield (46140) *(G-6466)*
Araymond Mfg Ctr N Amer Inc..................................... 574 722-5168
  800 W County Road 250 S Logansport (46947) *(G-11058)*
Arben Corporation... 812 477-7763
  1300 N Royal Ave Evansville (47715) *(G-3896)*
Arboc Specialty Vehicles LLC...................................... 574 825-1720
  51165 Greenfield Pkwy Middlebury (46540) *(G-11697)*
Arbor Industries Inc.. 574 825-2375
  117 14th Ave Middlebury (46540) *(G-11698)*
Arbor Preservative Systems LLC................................. 812 232-2316
  2901 Ohio Blvd Terre Haute (47803) *(G-15545)*
Arboramerica Inc.. 765 572-1212
  7852 W 200 S Westpoint (47992) *(G-16743)*
Arbuckle Industries Inc... 317 835-7489
  4990 N 550 W Fairland (46126) *(G-4396)*
ARC Angle Welding/Fabrication................................... 812 619-1731
  535 10th St Apt 8 Tell City (47586) *(G-15496)*
ARC EDM Incorporated.. 765 284-3820
  1800 W Mt Pleasant Blvd Muncie (47302) *(G-12343)*
ARC Industries.. 812 471-1633
  615 W Virginia St Evansville (47710) *(G-3897)*
ARC Industries LLC.. 317 753-1607
  6561 Iroquois Ln Carmel (46033) *(G-1563)*
ARC of Greater Boone Cnty Inc.................................... 765 482-0051
  912 W Main St Lebanon (46052) *(G-10875)*
ARC Rehab Services, Lebanon Also Called: ARC of Greater Boone Cnty Inc *(G-10875)*
Arcamed LLC.. 317 375-7733
  5101 Decatur Blvd Ste A Indianapolis (46241) *(G-7538)*
Arcane Wonders... 469 964-9050
  384 S Main St Roanoke (46783) *(G-14258)*
Arcelormittal.. 219 787-7432
  506 Rainier Ct Valparaiso (46385) *(G-15902)*
Arcelormittal Holdings LLC (HQ)................................. 219 399-1200
  3210 Watling St East Chicago (46312) *(G-2990)*
Arcelormittal Indiana Harbor W, East Chicago Also Called: Indiana Arcelormittal Harbor LLC *(G-3020)*
Arch Chemicals Inc... 219 464-3949
  2852 Raystone Dr Valparaiso (46383) *(G-15903)*
Arch Med Sltions - Elkhart LLC.................................... 574 264-3997
  2921 Lavanture Pl Elkhart (46514) *(G-3188)*
Arch Med Slutions - Warsaw LLC................................ 574 267-2171
  2070 N Cessna Rd Warsaw (46582) *(G-16314)*
Arch Wood Protection Inc.. 219 464-3949
  2852 Raystone Dr Valparaiso (46383) *(G-15904)*
Archer Industries LLC... 317 418-1260
  3245 N College Ave Indianapolis (46205) *(G-7539)*
Archer Products Inc.. 317 899-0700
  8756 E 33rd St Indianapolis (46226) *(G-7540)*
Archer-Daniels-Midland Company............................... 317 783-3321
  854 Bethel Ave Beech Grove (46107) *(G-686)*
Archer-Daniels-Midland Company............................... 260 824-0079
  1800 W Western Ave Bluffton (46714) *(G-1025)*
Archer-Daniels-Midland Company............................... 765 362-2965
  3696 E 510 S Crawfordsville (47933) *(G-2545)*
Archer-Daniels-Midland Company............................... 765 299-1672
  203 E Railroad St Fowler (47944) *(G-5618)*
Archer-Daniels-Midland Company............................... 765 654-4411
  2191 W County Road 0 N/S Frankfort (46041) *(G-5649)*
Archer-Daniels-Midland Company............................... 574 773-4138
  252 S Jackson St Nappanee (46550) *(G-12580)*
Archer-Daniels-Midland Company............................... 260 749-0022
  356 Hartzell Rd New Haven (46774) *(G-12893)*
Archer-Daniels-Midland Company............................... 219 866-2810
  1201 W State Road 114 Rensselaer (47978) *(G-14043)*
Archer-Daniels-Midland Company............................... 219 866-3939
  9179 W State Road 14 Rensselaer (47978) *(G-14044)*
Archibald Brothers Intl Inc... 812 941-8267
  209 Quality Ave Ste 1 New Albany (47150) *(G-12691)*
Archibald Frozen Desserts, New Albany Also Called: Archibald Brothers Intl Inc *(G-12691)*
Archimedes Inc (DH).. 260 347-3903
  2705 Marion Dr Kendallville (46755) *(G-10090)*
Architctral Opning Cnslting LL.................................... 502 836-5545
  15212 Gum Corner Rd Otisco (47163) *(G-13446)*
Architectural Plywood, New Albany Also Called: Dimension Plywood Inc *(G-12719)*
Architectural Stone Sales Inc...................................... 812 279-2421
  1728 30th St Bedford (47421) *(G-619)*
Architura Corporation... 317 348-1000
  9880 Westpoint Dr Ste 400 Indianapolis (46256) *(G-7541)*
Arco Electric Products, Shelbyville Also Called: Kirby Risk Corporation *(G-14768)*
Arconic Forgings & Extrusions, Lafayette Also Called: Arconic US LLC *(G-10525)*
Arconic US LLC.. 765 447-1707
  160 N 36th St Lafayette (47905) *(G-10524)*
Arconic US LLC.. 765 771-3600
  3131 Main St Lafayette (47905) *(G-10525)*
Arconic US LLC.. 412 553-2500
  3131 Main St Lafayette (47905) *(G-10526)*
Arcosa Lightweight, Mooresville Also Called: Arcosa Lw Hpb LLC *(G-12194)*
Arcosa Lw Hpb LLC... 317 831-0710
  6618 N Tidewater Rd Mooresville (46158) *(G-12194)*
Arcpro Welding & Prop Repair..................................... 812 867-6383
  14121 Bickmeier Rd Evansville (47725) *(G-3898)*
Arctic Glacier USA Inc... 800 562-1990
  2404 U St Bedford Bedford (47421) *(G-620)*
Arctic Ice Express Inc.. 812 333-0423
  2423 W Industrial Park Dr Bloomington (47404) *(G-783)*
Ardagh Glass Inc.. 765 768-7891
  524 E Center St Dunkirk (47336) *(G-2960)*
Ardagh Glass Inc (HQ)... 317 558-1002
  10194 Crosspoint Blvd 410 Indianapolis (46256) *(G-7542)*
Ardagh Glass Inc.. 765 662-1172
  123 E Mckinley St Marion (46952) *(G-11270)*
Ardagh Glass Inc.. 610 341-7885
  1509 S Macedonia Ave Muncie (47302) *(G-12344)*
ARDAGH GLASS INC., Dunkirk Also Called: Ardagh Glass Inc *(G-2960)*
Ardagh Glass Packaging Inc.. 317 558-1002
  10194 Crosspoint Blvd 410 Indianapolis (46256) *(G-7543)*
Ardagh Is Services, Marion Also Called: Ardagh Glass Inc *(G-11270)*
Arden Companies LLC... 260 747-1657
  3510 Piper Dr Fort Wayne (46809) *(G-4770)*
Arden/Benhar Mills, Fort Wayne Also Called: Arden Companies LLC *(G-4770)*
Ardena Company... 219 926-1018
  1423 Parmaker Chesterton (46304) *(G-1903)*
Area Welding Inc LLC.. 219 669-0981
  1503 215th St Dyer (46311) *(G-2967)*
Area Welding Innovations LLC..................................... 219 789-2209
  4705 Roosevelt St Gary (46408) *(G-5895)*
Ares Division LLC.. 260 349-9803
  345 Cobblers Way Waterloo (46793) *(G-16514)*
Areva Pharmaceuticals Inc.. 855 853-4760
  7112 Areva Dr Ne Georgetown (47122) *(G-6055)*
Argentum Jewelry Inc.. 812 336-3100
  205 N College Ave Ste 100 Bloomington (47404) *(G-784)*

ALPHABETIC SECTION — Ascot Enterprises Inc

Arion Roofing & Shtmtl Inc 317 525-1984
  1686 S Hiland Dr Frankfort (46041) *(G-5650)*

Aristo LLC
  4410 W 37th Ave Frnt Hobart (46342) *(G-7173)*

Aristo Catalyst Technology, Hobart *Also Called: Aristo LLC (G-7173)*

Aristocrat Inc 812 634-0460
  1 Masterbrand Cabinets Dr Jasper (47546) *(G-9824)*

Aristoline Cabinets Inc 260 482-9719
  5803 Industrial Rd Fort Wayne (46825) *(G-4771)*

Arizona Isotope Science RES 702 219-1243
  7796 S Innovation Way Bunker Hill (46914) *(G-1440)*

Arizona Sport Shirts Inc 317 481-2160
  100 Gasoline Aly Ste Az Indianapolis (46222) *(G-7544)*

Ark Model and Stampings Inc 317 549-3394
  5894 W 600 S New Palestine (46163) *(G-12931)*

Arkley Biotek LLC 317 331-7580
  4444 Decatur Blvd Ste 300 Indianapolis (46241) *(G-7545)*

Arm Kandy LLC 317 975-1576
  6100 N Keystone Ave Ste 459 Indianapolis (46220) *(G-7546)*

Armada Optical Services Inc 812 476-6623
  701 N Weinbach Ave Ste 410 Evansville (47711) *(G-3899)*

Armco 219 981-8864
  6071 Broadway Merrillville (46410) *(G-11485)*

Armor Coat LLC 260 210-1307
  328 Hauenstein Rd Huntington (46750) *(G-7298)*

Armor Contract Mfg Inc 574 327-2962
  300 Comet Ave Elkhart (46514) *(G-3189)*

Armor Group 574 293-1791
  300 Comet Ave Elkhart (46514) *(G-3190)*

Armor Metal Group Madison Inc, Madison *Also Called: Armor Products Inc (G-11202)*

Armor Parent Corp (HQ) 812 962-5000
  7140 Office Cir Evansville (47715) *(G-3900)*

Armor Products Inc 502 228-1458
  4600 N Mason Montgomery Rd Madison (47250) *(G-11202)*

Armored Locks Inc 219 798-6502
  6841 W Bleck Rd Michigan City (46360) *(G-11579)*

Armorite Ammo LLC 765 825-7527
  901 W 21st St Connersville (47331) *(G-2425)*

Armour Fire Protection, Indianapolis *Also Called: Carl Abbott (G-7745)*

Armour Pattern Inc 219 374-9325
  9121 W 133rd Ave Cedar Lake (46303) *(G-1827)*

Armstrongs 219 977-8368
  1189 Gerry St Gary (46406) *(G-5896)*

Arneys Freeze-Dried Treats LLC 812 801-1386
  7312 Mill Run Rd Apt B Fort Wayne (46819) *(G-4772)*

Arnold Brothers Construction 317 775-5523
  7483 W County Road 350 S Coatesville (46121) *(G-2103)*

Arnold Family Woodworks 765 246-6593
  3294 E County Road 50 S Fillmore (46128) *(G-4452)*

Around Campus LLC 574 360-6571
  319 Lamonte Ter South Bend (46616) *(G-14949)*

Arran Isle Inc (HQ) 574 295-4400
  601 County Road 17 Elkhart (46516) *(G-3191)*

Arrayed Additive Inc 317 981-5982
  6119 Guion Rd Indianapolis (46254) *(G-7547)*

Arrow Container LLC 317 882-6444
  6550 E 30th St Ste 130 Indianapolis (46219) *(G-7548)*

Arrow Metals Inc 765 825-4443
  1527 Vermont Ave Connersville (47331) *(G-2426)*

Arrow Vault Co Inc 765 742-1704
  1312 Underwood St Lafayette (47904) *(G-10527)*

Arrowhead Composites, Muncie *Also Called: Arrowhead Plastic Engrg Inc (G-12345)*

Arrowhead Plastic Engrg Inc 765 396-9113
  1155 N Hartford St Eaton (47338) *(G-3059)*

Arrowhead Plastic Engrg Inc (PA) 765 286-0533
  2909 S Hoyt Ave Muncie (47302) *(G-12345)*

Arrowhead Plastic Products, Eaton *Also Called: Arrowhead Plastic Engrg Inc (G-3059)*

Arroyo Industries LLC 317 605-4163
  5324 Crooked Stick Ct Greenwood (46142) *(G-6671)*

Art Bookbinders of America 312 226-4100
  5920 Hohman Ave Hammond (46320) *(G-6880)*

Art Gallery, The, La Porte *Also Called: H J J Inc (G-10414)*

Art Ovation 317 769-4301
  7615 S State Road 267 Brownsburg (46112) *(G-1348)*

Art Works, Mishawaka *Also Called: Art Works Sign Co Inc (G-11843)*

Art Works Sign Co Inc 574 360-9290
  55581 Currant Rd Mishawaka (46545) *(G-11843)*

Artcraft Printers, South Bend *Also Called: Overgaards Artcraft Printers (G-15183)*

Artek Inc 260 484-4222
  3311 Enterprise Rd Fort Wayne (46808) *(G-4773)*

Artemis International Inc 260 436-6899
  3711 Vanguard Dr Ste A Fort Wayne (46809) *(G-4774)*

Artemis Intl Solutions Corp 708 665-3155
  2600 Roosevelt Rd Ste 200-6 Valparaiso (46383) *(G-15905)*

Artful Living 317 764-7232
  645 Mcnamara Ct Carmel (46032) *(G-1564)*

Artisan Interiors Inc (PA) 574 825-9494
  526 S Main St Middlebury (46540) *(G-11699)*

Artisan Tool & Die Inc 765 288-6653
  3805 W State Road 28 Muncie (47303) *(G-12346)*

Artisanz Fabrication & Machine 317 956-2384
  130 Scranton Ct Zionsville (46077) *(G-16993)*

Artisanz Fabrication and Mch 765 859-5118
  1209 W South St Lebanon (46052) *(G-10876)*

Artistic Carton 260 925-6060
  301 S Progress Dr E Kendallville (46755) *(G-10091)*

Artistic Coatings LLC 260 463-5253
  5654 N State Road 5 Shipshewana (46565) *(G-14836)*

Artistic Composite Pallets LLC 317 960-5813
  4518 W 99th St Carmel (46032) *(G-1565)*

Artistic Expressions Pubg Inc 317 502-6213
  111 E South C St Gas City (46933) *(G-6032)*

Artistic Stone Mfg LLC 574 546-3771
  5958 4th Rd Bremen (46506) *(G-1173)*

Artys Logging Inc 812 969-3124
  7800 E Highway 11 Se Elizabeth (47117) *(G-3123)*

Arvin Sango Inc (HQ) 812 265-2888
  2905 Wilson Ave Madison (47250) *(G-11203)*

Arvin's Creative Woodworking, Winslow *Also Called: William R Arvin (G-16926)*

Arxada, Valparaiso *Also Called: Arch Wood Protection Inc (G-15904)*

AS Logging LLC 812 613-0577
  1760 N Belcher Rd Taswell (47175) *(G-15494)*

As You Wish Custom 502 216-3144
  2100 Elk Pointe Blvd Jeffersonville (47130) *(G-9935)*

Asa Above Rest 317 392-2144
  702 E Washington St Shelbyville (46176) *(G-14730)*

ASA Electronics LLC (PA) 574 264-3135
  2602 Marina Dr Elkhart (46514) *(G-3192)*

Asahi TEC America Corporation 765 962-8399
  1757 Sheridan St Richmond (47374) *(G-14087)*

Asanders Global LLC 224 401-4050
  2125 Toledo Rd Apt 145 Elkhart (46516) *(G-3193)*

Asbury Hall, Evansville *Also Called: Sycamore Enterprises Inc (G-4339)*

ASC, Lebanon *Also Called: Air Systems Compents LP (G-10873)*

Asc Inc 765 472-5331
  N Miami Industrial Park Peru (46970) *(G-13566)*

Asc Inc (PA) 765 473-4438
  100 N Park Ave Peru (46970) *(G-13567)*

ASC Industries Inc 574 264-1987
  23325 County Road 6 Elkhart (46514) *(G-3194)*

Aschulman, Evansville *Also Called: Lyondllbsell Advnced Plymers I (G-4179)*

Ascl Printwear LLC 317 507-0548
  1238 Eton Way Avon (46123) *(G-505)*

Ascot Enterprises Inc 877 773-7751
  53706 County Road 9 Elkhart (46514) *(G-3195)*

Ascot Enterprises Inc 574 658-3000
  1002 N Old State Road 15 Milford (46542) *(G-11786)*

Ascot Enterprises Inc 574 773-7751
  1901 Cheyenne St Nappanee (46550) *(G-12581)*

Ascot Enterprises Inc (PA) 877 773-7751
  503 S Main St Nappanee (46550) *(G-12582)*

Ascot Enterprises Inc 260 593-3733
  129 Roy St Topeka (46571) *(G-15795)*

Ascot Plant 10 — ALPHABETIC SECTION

Ascot Plant 10, Nappanee *Also Called: Ascot Enterprises Inc (G-12581)*

Asd Signs & Graphics LLC 317 437-6921
2020 Churchman Ave Indianapolis (46203) *(G-7549)*

Asempac Inc 812 945-6303
5300 Foundation Blvd New Albany (47150) *(G-12692)*

Asf Keystones, Hammond *Also Called: Amsted Graphite Materials LLC (G-6877)*

ASG Unlimited, Indianapolis *Also Called: Midwest Empire LLC (G-8908)*

Ash & Elm Cider Company LLC 317 600-3164
2112 E Washington St Indianapolis (46201) *(G-7550)*

Ash Access Technology Inc 765 742-4813
3601 Sagamore Pkwy N Ste B Lafayette (47904) *(G-10528)*

Ash Welding 219 808-7139
296 W State Road 8 Hebron (46341) *(G-7096)*

Ash-Lin Inc 317 861-1540
386 E Brookville Rd Fountaintown (46130) *(G-5613)*

ASHA, Bloomington *Also Called: American School Health Assn (G-779)*

Ashley F Ward Inc 574 294-1502
56883 Elk Ct Elkhart (46516) *(G-3196)*

Ashley F Ward Inc 219 879-4177
2031 Tryon Rd Michigan City (46360) *(G-11580)*

Ashley Industrial Molding Inc (PA) 260 587-9155
310 S Wabash St Ashley (46705) *(G-330)*

Ashley Industrial Molding Inc 260 349-1982
100 S Progress Dr W Kendallville (46755) *(G-10092)*

Ashley Machine, Greensburg *Also Called: Mssh Inc (G-6620)*

Ashley Ward, Elkhart *Also Called: Ashley F Ward Inc (G-3196)*

Ashley Worldwide Inc (PA) 574 259-2481
13388 State Road 23 Granger (46530) *(G-6332)*

Ashleys Elements LLC 765 480-2168
588 S 100 E Tipton (46072) *(G-15765)*

Ashleys Jewelry By Design Ltd 219 926-9039
2450 Idaho St Chesterton (46304) *(G-1904)*

Asi Limited
4485 S Perry Worth Rd Whitestown (46075) *(G-16800)*

Asl Technologies LLC 219 733-2777
10525 W Us Highway 30 Bldg 3d Wanatah (46390) *(G-16286)*

Asphalt Cutbacks Inc 219 398-4230
3000 Gary Rd East Chicago (46312) *(G-2991)*

Asphalt Drum Mixers LLC 260 637-5729
1 Adm Pkwy Huntertown (46748) *(G-7249)*

Asphalt Equipment Company Inc (PA) 260 672-3004
13333 Us Highway 24 W Fort Wayne (46814) *(G-4775)*

Asphalt Materials Inc 317 243-8304
7901 W Morris St Indianapolis (46231) *(G-7551)*

Asphalt Materials Inc (HQ) 317 872-6010
8720 Robbins Rd Indianapolis (46268) *(G-7552)*

Asphalt Materials Inc 317 875-4670
5400 W 86th St Indianapolis (46268) *(G-7553)*

Aspire Industries 812 542-1561
5329 Foundation Blvd New Albany (47150) *(G-12693)*

Aspire Lifestyle Inc 219 814-2591
709 Plaza Dr Ste 2-154 Chesterton (46304) *(G-1905)*

Assa Abloy Door Group LLC 800 826-2617
53518 Cr 9n, Ste.B Elkhart (46514) *(G-3197)*

Assalys House Garlic LLC 219 310-5934
8529 E 181st Ave Hebron (46341) *(G-7097)*

Assembly Masters Inc 574 293-9026
56624 Elk Park Dr Elkhart (46516) *(G-3198)*

Assmann, Garrett *Also Called: Assmann Corporation America (G-5854)*

Assmann Corporation America (PA) 260 357-3181
300 N Taylor Rd Garrett (46738) *(G-5854)*

Associated Cnstr Publications 317 660-2395
1028 Shelby St Indianapolis (46203) *(G-7554)*

Associated Label Inc 812 877-3682
8402 E Davis Ave Terre Haute (47805) *(G-15546)*

Associated Mfg & Packg, Crawfordsville *Also Called: Yes Feed & Supply LLC (G-2628)*

Associated World Music LLC 219 512-4511
2125 W 96th Pl Crown Point (46307) *(G-2651)*

Assurance Waste Management LLC 765 341-4431
11048 W Awbrey Rd Cloverdale (46120) *(G-2082)*

Assured General Contg LLC 260 740-4744
3907 Evergreen Ln Fort Wayne (46815) *(G-4776)*

Assured Water Care Company 317 997-5790
304 Crosby Dr Indianapolis (46227) *(G-7555)*

Astar Inc 574 234-2137
645 Wilber St South Bend (46628) *(G-14950)*

Astbury Water Technology Inc 260 668-8900
601 W 400 N Angola (46703) *(G-231)*

Astbury Water Technology Inc (PA) 317 328-7153
5940 W Raymond St Indianapolis (46241) *(G-7556)*

Astec Corp 317 872-7550
7750 Zionsville Rd Ste 650 Indianapolis (46268) *(G-7557)*

Astech Seats 765 674-7448
314 S Washington St Marion (46952) *(G-11271)*

Astellas Pharma Us Inc 574 595-7569
6946 E 450 S Star City (46985) *(G-15395)*

Astral Auras LLC 219 628-5258
9800 Connecticut Dr Crown Point (46307) *(G-2652)*

Astral Carrier Inc 765 874-1406
7375 S Us Highway 27 Lynn (47355) *(G-11181)*

Astral Industries Inc (DH) 765 874-2525
7375 S Us Highway 27 Lynn (47355) *(G-11182)*

Astrazeneca Pharmaceuticals LP 240 252-0125
6400 William Keck Byp Mount Vernon (47620) *(G-12287)*

Astrazeneca Pharmaceuticals LP 812 429-5000
4601 Highway 62 E Mount Vernon (47620) *(G-12288)*

Asw LLC 260 432-1596
2499 S 600 E Ste 102 Columbia City (46725) *(G-2120)*

AT Ferrell Company Inc (PA) 260 824-3400
1440 S Adams St Bluffton (46714) *(G-1026)*

At The Barn Winery 513 310-8810
1726 Einsel Rd Lawrenceburg (47025) *(G-10829)*

Ataraxis Music LLC 626 945-6441
9128 Technology Ln Fishers (46038) *(G-4466)*

Atc Plastics LLC (PA) 317 469-7552
450 E 96th St Ste 500 Indianapolis (46240) *(G-7558)*

Atc Trailers, Nappanee *Also Called: Aluminum Trailer Company (G-12579)*

Atco-Gary Metal Tech LLC 219 885-3232
1931 E Main St Griffith (46319) *(G-6791)*

Athena Branding Solutions, Quincy *Also Called: Prominent Promotional Pdts LLC (G-14022)*

Athena Champion Inc 260 373-1917
2621 Corrinado Ct Fort Wayne (46808) *(G-4777)*

Athletes Management & Services 317 925-8200
3750 Guion Rd Ste 315 Indianapolis (46222) *(G-7559)*

Athletic Edge Inc 260 489-6613
1133 Old Bridge Pl Fort Wayne (46825) *(G-4778)*

ATI 317 238-3073
6635 E 30th St Indianapolis (46219) *(G-7560)*

Ati Inc (DH) 812 431-5409
103 Brown St Mount Vernon (47620) *(G-12289)*

Ati Inc 812 520-5409
204a Main St Mount Vernon (47620) *(G-12290)*

ATI Flat Rlled Pdts Hldngs LLC 765 529-9570
516 W State Road 38 New Castle (47362) *(G-12850)*

ATI Flat Rolled Products, New Castle *Also Called: ATI Flat Rlled Pdts Hldngs LLC (G-12850)*

Atkins Quarry 972 653-5550
1415 Quarry Rd Jeffersonville (47130) *(G-9936)*

Atkisson Enterprises Inc 765 675-7593
632 Mill St Tipton (46072) *(G-15766)*

Atkore Inc 219 844-6800
2400 E 69th Ave Merrillville (46410) *(G-11486)*

Atlas Copco Compressors 574 264-1033
831 E Windsor Ave Unit 8 Elkhart (46514) *(G-3199)*

Atlas Copco Vacuum, Michigan City *Also Called: Vacuum Technique LLC (G-11683)*

Atlas Die LLC (HQ) 574 295-0050
2000 Middlebury St Elkhart (46516) *(G-3200)*

Atlas Foundry Company Inc 765 662-2525
601 N Henderson Ave Marion (46952) *(G-11272)*

Atlas Machine and Supply Inc 812 423-7762
5001 Hitch Peters Rd Evansville (47711) *(G-3901)*

Atlatl Group LLC 602 233-2628
1987 Troy Rd Washington (47501) *(G-16472)*

Atm, Angola *Also Called: Autoform Tool & Mfg LLC (G-232)*

ALPHABETIC SECTION

Atmosphere Annealing LLC 812 346-1275
　1300 Indtl Dr North Vernon (47265) *(G-13256)*

Atmosphere Dynamics Corp 317 392-6262
　1107 Saint Joseph St Shelbyville (46176) *(G-14731)*

Atomic Filament, Kendallville *Also Called: Crunchtech Holdings LLC (G-10106)*

Atp Steel & Welding Supplies, Lebanon *Also Called: Atp Welding Inc (G-10877)*

Atp Welding Inc 765 483-9273
　930 Hendricks Dr Lebanon (46052) *(G-10877)*

Atr Tire and Repair LLC 574 349-4462
　21925 County Road 50 New Paris (46553) *(G-12946)*

Atrium Web Services LLC 812 322-6904
　3709 E Devonshire Ln Bloomington (47408) *(G-785)*

Ats Manufacturing Inc
　2026 Sterling Ave Elkhart (46516) *(G-3201)*

Attc, Tell City *Also Called: Attc Manufacturing Inc (G-15497)*

Attc Manufacturing Inc 812 547-5060
　10455 State Road 37 Tell City (47586) *(G-15497)*

Attica Ready Mixed Concrete (PA) 765 762-2424
　104 W Sycamore St Attica (47918) *(G-343)*

Attitude of Gratitude Rocks 317 331-0163
　11057 Allisonville Rd Ste 153 Fishers (46038) *(G-4467)*

Atv Parts Barn LLC 812 251-6113
　10997 N Meridian Street Rd Brazil (47834) *(G-1133)*

Atwood Concrete Construction, Waldron *Also Called: Larry Atwood (G-16260)*

Atwood Mobile Products, Elkhart *Also Called: Atwood Mobile Products Inc (G-3202)*

Atwood Mobile Products Inc 574 264-2131
　1120 N Main St Elkhart (46514) *(G-3202)*

Atwood Mobile Products LLC 574 266-4848
　5155 Verdant St Elkhart (46516) *(G-3203)*

Atwood Mobile Products LLC 574 264-2131
　2040 Toledo Rd Elkhart (46516) *(G-3204)*

Atwood Mobile Products LLC 574 264-2131
　2701 Ada Dr Elkhart (46514) *(G-3205)*

Atwood Mobile Products LLC (DH) 574 264-2131
　1120 N Main St Elkhart (46514) *(G-3206)*

Atwood Solutions, Elkhart *Also Called: Atwood Mobile Products LLC (G-3206)*

Aubry Lane LLC 317 644-6372
　120 E Market St Ste 100 Indianapolis (46204) *(G-7561)*

Auburn Gear, Auburn *Also Called: Auburn Gear LLC (G-362)*

Auburn Gear LLC (PA) 260 925-3200
　400 E Auburn Dr Auburn (46706) *(G-362)*

Auburn Hardwood Molding 260 925-5959
　1109 W Auburn Dr Auburn (46706) *(G-363)*

Auburn Manufacturing Inc 260 925-8651
　1000 W Auburn Dr Auburn (46706) *(G-364)*

Auburn Smoke N Vape LLC 260 572-6021
　1029 W 7th St Auburn (46706) *(G-365)*

Audience Response Systems Inc 812 479-7507
　5611 E Morgan Ave Ste C Evansville (47715) *(G-3902)*

Audio Diagnostics Inc 765 477-7016
　2320 Concord Rd Ste A Lafayette (47909) *(G-10529)*

Audio Flow LLC 219 230-6330
　2121 Yule St Portage (46368) *(G-13846)*

Audio-Video By Flynn 317 408-6269
　4911 Carrollton Ave Indianapolis (46205) *(G-7562)*

Audiodiagnostics, Lafayette *Also Called: Audio Diagnostics Inc (G-10529)*

Audiovox Spclized Applications, Elkhart *Also Called: ASA Electronics LLC (G-3192)*

Audubon Workshop 812 537-3583
　5200 Schenley Pl Greendale (47025) *(G-6438)*

August Gill Apparel LLC 317 342-2800
　5534 Saint Joe Rd Fort Wayne (46835) *(G-4779)*

Augustin Prtg & Design Svcs (PA) 765 966-7130
　211 Nw 7th St Richmond (47374) *(G-14088)*

Aul Brothers Tool & Die Inc 765 759-5124
　101 S Buckingham Rd Yorktown (47396) *(G-16968)*

Aul In The Family Tool and Die 765 759-5161
　9801 W Jackson St Yorktown (47396) *(G-16969)*

Aunalytics Inc (PA) 574 307-9230
　460 Stull St Ste 100 South Bend (46601) *(G-14951)*

Aunt Lindas Embroidery 574 256-0508
　621 E Broadway St # C Mishawaka (46545) *(G-11844)*

Aunt Millie's Bakeries, Fort Wayne *Also Called: Perfection Bakeries Inc (G-5306)*

Aunt Millies Bakeries, Valparaiso *Also Called: Perfection Bakeries Inc (G-16023)*

Aunt Netts Country Candles LLC 765 557-2770
　7374 West State Rd Elwood (46036) *(G-3818)*

Auntie Anne's, Mishawaka *Also Called: Chestnut Land Company (G-11860)*

Auntie Anne's, Muncie *Also Called: Brilliant Blondes LLC (G-12357)*

Aurora Casket Company LLC 812 926-1110
　50 Factory Aurora (47001) *(G-438)*

Aurora Casket Company LLC (HQ) 800 457-1111
　10944 Marsh Rd Aurora (47001) *(G-439)*

Aurora Services Inc 260 463-4901
　7155 N 675 W Shipshewana (46565) *(G-14837)*

Aurorium, Indianapolis *Also Called: AURORIUM LLC (G-7566)*

Aurorium Foreign Holdings LLC (PA) 317 247-8141
　201 N Illinois St Ste 1800 Indianapolis (46204) *(G-7563)*

Aurorium Holdings LLC (PA) 317 247-8141
　201 N Illinois St Ste 1800 Indianapolis (46204) *(G-7564)*

Aurorium LLC 317 247-8141
　201 N Illinois St Indianapolis (46204) *(G-7565)*

AURORIUM LLC (HQ) 317 247-8141
　201 N Illinois St Ste 1800 Indianapolis (46204) *(G-7566)*

Aurorium Ppc Holdings LLC 317 247-8141
　201 N Illinois St Ste 1800 Indianapolis (46204) *(G-7567)*

Aus Embroidery Inc 317 899-1225
　8745 Rawles Ave Ste C Indianapolis (46219) *(G-7568)*

Austin & Austin Inc (PA) 574 586-2320
　648 Stephens St Walkerton (46574) *(G-16264)*

Austin Powder Company 812 342-1237
　13468 W Old Nashville Rd Columbus (47201) *(G-2222)*

Austin Tri-Hawk Automotive Inc 812 794-0062
　2001 West Just Industrial Parkway Austin (47102) *(G-463)*

Austin-Westran LLC (PA) 815 234-2811
　2876 Wooded Glen Ct Indianapolis (46268) *(G-7569)*

Austins Metal Mafia Inc 812 619-6115
　8175 Boyd Rd Cannelton (47520) *(G-1531)*

Authenticx Inc 317 296-6238
　9405 Delegates Row Indianapolis (46240) *(G-7570)*

Author Solutions LLC (PA) 812 339-6000
　1663 S Liberty Dr Bloomington (47403) *(G-786)*

Auto & Sign Specialties Inc 260 824-1987
　3124 E State Road 124 Bluffton (46714) *(G-1027)*

Auto Art & Signs 765 448-6800
　420 Sagamore Pkwy N Lafayette (47904) *(G-10530)*

Auto Bumper Exchange Inc 260 493-4408
　2321 Bremer Rd Fort Wayne (46803) *(G-4780)*

Auto Center Inc 317 545-3360
　5461 Massachusetts Ave Indianapolis (46218) *(G-7571)*

Auto Express Vale 317 897-6618
　9065 Pendleton Pike Indianapolis (46236) *(G-7572)*

Auto Extras Inc 574 855-2370
　1002 S Lafayette Blvd South Bend (46601) *(G-14952)*

Auto Specialty Lafayette Inc 765 446-2311
　313 Teal Rd Lafayette (47905) *(G-10531)*

Auto Temp Ctrl Specialists Inc 812 333-2963
　1001 S Walnut St Bloomington (47401) *(G-787)*

Auto Truck Group LLC 260 356-1610
　1640 Riverfork Dr Huntington (46750) *(G-7299)*

Auto Truck Group LLC 260 493-1800
　14014 Hitzfield Ct Roanoke (46783) *(G-14259)*

Auto Wood Restoration 219 797-3775
　24 S Pennsylvania St Hanna (46340) *(G-7036)*

Auto-Chlor System Wash Inc 317 334-0430
　6040 W 79th St Indianapolis (46278) *(G-7573)*

Autocar LLC (DH) 765 489-5499
　551 S Washington St Hagerstown (47346) *(G-6833)*

Autocar Trucks, Hagerstown *Also Called: Autocar LLC (G-6833)*

Autofarm Mobility LLC 317 410-0070
　9004 S County Road 800 W Daleville (47334) *(G-2795)*

Autoform Tool & Mfg LLC 260 624-2014
　1501 Wohlert St Angola (46703) *(G-232)*

Autoliv Asp Inc 801 620-8018
　5627 E Rail Connect Dr Columbia City (46725) *(G-2121)*

Autoliv Steering Whl Faciltty, Columbia City *Also Called: Autoliv Asp Inc (G-2121)*

Automated Bus Solutions Inc... 317 257-9062
8700 North St Ste 400 Fishers (46038) *(G-4468)*

Automated Drive & Design LLC... 812 342-0809
6350 Inwood Dr Columbus (47201) *(G-2223)*

Automated Egg Producers, North Manchester *Also Called: Midwest Poultry Services LP (G-13243)*

Automated Fuels, Terre Haute *Also Called: Spence/Banks Holdings Inc (G-15713)*

Automated Laser Corporation.. 260 637-4140
14224 Plank St Fort Wayne (46818) *(G-4781)*

Automated Logic - Indiana, Muncie *Also Called: Automated Logic Corporation (G-12347)*

Automated Logic Corporation.. 765 286-1993
117 N High St Muncie (47305) *(G-12347)*

Automated Proc Eqp Svcs LLC.. 219 206-2517
952 W 1150 S Union Mills (46382) *(G-15863)*

Automated Products Intl LLC... 260 463-2515
2840 N State Road 9 Lagrange (46761) *(G-10729)*

Automated Routing Inc.. 812 357-2429
16920 N State Road 545 Saint Meinrad (47577) *(G-14460)*

Automated Systems Technology, Mitchell *Also Called: C&M Conveyor Inc (G-12034)*

Automated Weapon Security Inc.. 860 559-7176
9324 E 10th St Indianapolis (46229) *(G-7574)*

Automated Welding Services Inc.. 812 464-8784
1401 Wimberg Rd Evansville (47710) *(G-3903)*

Automatic Fastner Tools... 317 784-4111
3250 Payne Dr Indianapolis (46227) *(G-7575)*

Automatic Pool Covers Inc.. 317 579-2000
17397 Oak Ridge Rd Ste 100 Westfield (46074) *(G-16666)*

Automation & Control Svcs Inc.. 219 558-2060
2440 Ontario St Schererville (46375) *(G-14514)*

Automation Consultants Inc.. 502 552-4995
4003 Kendall Ct Floyds Knobs (47119) *(G-4669)*

Automation Control Service.. 812 472-3292
8349 W Radcliff Rd Hardinsburg (47125) *(G-7047)*

Automation Enclosures LLC.. 812 453-8480
815 John St Ste 140 Evansville (47713) *(G-3904)*

Automobile Dealers Assn of Ind (PA).. 317 635-1441
150 W Market St Ste 812 Indianapolis (46204) *(G-7576)*

Automotive Vibration Division, Ligonier *Also Called: Freudenberg-Nok General Partnr (G-11015)*

Automtic Pool Cver Prfssionals, Westfield *Also Called: Cover Care LLC (G-16678)*

Automtion Ctrl Panl Sltons Inc... 219 961-8308
514 Jenna Dr Munster (46321) *(G-12531)*

Autoneum North America Inc... 248 848-0100
100 River Ridge Pkwy Jeffersonville (47130) *(G-9937)*

Autonomy House Publications, Monticello *Also Called: Antique Stove Information (G-12135)*

Autosavvy of Indianapolis LLC... 463 900-4685
5333 W Pike Plaza Rd Indianapolis (46254) *(G-7577)*

Autosem Inc.. 574 288-8866
1701 S Main St South Bend (46613) *(G-14953)*

Autumn Makers Mobile HM Subdv... 765 759-7878
2800 S Andrews Rd Yorktown (47396) *(G-16970)*

AV Solutions Indy LLC.. 317 509-5930
4929 Evanston Ave Indianapolis (46205) *(G-7578)*

Avalign Delivery Systems Div, Greenwood *Also Called: Avalign Technologies Inc (G-6673)*

Avalign Instrs & Implants Div, Fort Wayne *Also Called: Nemcomed Fw LLC (G-5264)*

Avalign Technologies Inc... 260 484-1500
8727 Clinton Park Dr Fort Wayne (46825) *(G-4782)*

Avalign Technologies Inc... 317 865-6436
2121 Southtech Dr Ste 600 Greenwood (46143) *(G-6672)*

Avalign Technologies Inc... 888 625-4497
2121 Southtech Dr Ste 600 Greenwood (46143) *(G-6673)*

Avari Labs, Anderson *Also Called: Avari Reef Labs LLC (G-80)*

Avari Reef Labs LLC.. 317 201-9615
5217 S 100 E Anderson (46013) *(G-80)*

Avbf, Indianapolis *Also Called: Audio-Video By Flynn (G-7562)*

Ave Maria Press Inc... 574 287-2831
1865 Moreau Dr Notre Dame (46556) *(G-13315)*

Aventine Renewable Energy... 812 838-9598
7201 Port Rd Mount Vernon (47620) *(G-12291)*

Aventine Renewable Fuels, Mount Vernon *Also Called: Aventine Renewable Energy (G-12291)*

Avery Dennison Corporation... 260 481-4500
3011 Independence Dr Fort Wayne (46808) *(G-4783)*

Avery Dennison Corporation... 317 462-1988
870 Anderson Blvd Greenfield (46140) *(G-6467)*

Avery Dennison Corporation... 219 696-7777
270 Westmeadow Pl Lowell (46356) *(G-11155)*

Avery Dennison Fasson, Greenfield *Also Called: Avery Dennison Corporation (G-6467)*

Avf Machining.. 260 760-1531
5850 County Road 24 Butler (46721) *(G-1459)*

Avg North America Inc... 765 748-3162
5133 Eastside Parkway Dr Gas City (46933) *(G-6033)*

Avid Operations Inc... 260 220-2001
1210 Lynn Ave Fort Wayne (46805) *(G-4784)*

Avient Corporation.. 574 267-1100
3454 N Detroit St (State Rd 15) Warsaw (46582) *(G-16315)*

Avionic Structures Indiana Inc.. 765 671-7865
4589 N Wabash Rd Marion (46952) *(G-11273)*

Avionics Mounts Inc... 812 988-2949
4510 State Road 46 E Nashville (47448) *(G-12661)*

Avis Industrial Corporation (PA)... 765 998-8100
1909 S Main St Upland (46989) *(G-15876)*

Avon Sports Apparel Corp... 317 887-2673
3115 Meridian Parke Dr Ste D Greenwood (46142) *(G-6674)*

Avr Products Inc... 574 294-6101
53689 Pheasant Ridge Dr Bristol (46507) *(G-1247)*

Avt Composites... 317 286-7575
1652 E Northfield Dr Ste 2400 Brownsburg (46112) *(G-1349)*

Avt Composites... 219 742-0865
2970 S 500 W Lebanon (46052) *(G-10878)*

Awardmakersnet Inc... 260 925-4672
1916 Wayne St Auburn (46706) *(G-366)*

Awards America Inc... 219 462-7903
397 E Us Highway 30 Valparaiso (46383) *(G-15906)*

Awards Unlimited Inc... 765 447-9413
3031 Union St Lafayette (47904) *(G-10532)*

Awning Innovations, Mccordsville *Also Called: Image One LLC (G-11451)*

Awning Partners Mfg Group LLC... 317 644-3793
1160 W 16th St Indianapolis (46202) *(G-7579)*

Awningtec Usa Incorporated.. 812 734-0423
3265 Highway 62 Nw Corydon (47112) *(G-2486)*

Awol Metal Contorsion LLC.. 260 909-0411
439 Prospect Ave Kendallville (46755) *(G-10093)*

Awrc, Fort Wayne *Also Called: Anthony Wyne Rhbltton Ctr For (G-4762)*

Axe Head Threads LLC.. 317 607-6330
2320 S Richman Way New Palestine (46163) *(G-12932)*

Axecalibur LLC.. 812 822-1157
3604 W 3rd St Bloomington (47404) *(G-788)*

Axiom Yachts, Washington *Also Called: Atlatl Group LLC (G-16472)*

Axis Controls Incorporated.. 260 414-4028
6100 Lower Huntington Rd Fort Wayne (46809) *(G-4785)*

Axis Fiber Solutions, Whiteland *Also Called: Ctsi (G-16781)*

Axis Industries Usa LLC... 317 739-3390
1400 Commerce Pkwy Franklin (46131) *(G-5711)*

Axis Machine and Tool, Sellersburg *Also Called: Oakley Industries LLC (G-14608)*

Axis Machine Tool Inc.. 812 246-2600
1229 Bringham Dr Sellersburg (47172) *(G-14587)*

Axis Mold Inc... 574 292-8904
53450 Tamarack Rd New Carlisle (46552) *(G-12834)*

Axis Products Inc.. 574 266-8282
21611 Protecta Dr Elkhart (46516) *(G-3207)*

Axis Unlimited LLC... 574 370-8923
3403 Reedy Dr Elkhart (46514) *(G-3208)*

Axle Inc... 574 264-9434
53664 County Road 9 Elkhart (46514) *(G-3209)*

Axon Network Services LLC... 317 818-9000
9245 N Meridian St Ste 225 Indianapolis (46260) *(G-7580)*

Axtrom Inds Pallet Div LLC... 812 859-4873
170 Mt Calvery Rd Freedom (47431) *(G-5797)*

Axtrom Industries/Pallat Div, Freedom *Also Called: Axtrom Inds Pallet Div LLC (G-5797)*

ALPHABETIC SECTION — B&B Manufacturing

Ayco Panel 765 635-8106
   4641 N County Road 825 E Jasonville (47438) *(G-9822)*

Aynes Custom Upholstery, Freedom *Also Called: Aynes Upholstery LLC (G-5798)*

Aynes Upholstery LLC 812 829-1321
   3220 Dunn Rd Freedom (47431) *(G-5798)*

Aytch Logistics LLC 317 443-9812
   2304 E 34th St Indianapolis (46218) *(G-7581)*

Azami Press 765 242-7988
   859 N Main St Frankfort (46041) *(G-5651)*

Azland Inc 765 429-6200
   345 Burnetts Rd Ste 300 West Lafayette (47906) *(G-16564)*

Aztec Printing Inc (PA) 812 422-1462
   9800 Highway 66 Wadesville (47638) *(G-16226)*

Azteca Milling LP 812 867-3190
   15700 Highway 41 N Evansville (47725) *(G-3905)*

Azteca Milling Co, Evansville *Also Called: Azteca Milling LP (G-3905)*

Azz Galvanizing - Muncie, Muncie *Also Called: AAA Galvanizing - Joliet Inc (G-12333)*

Azz Galvanizing Hamilton, Hamilton *Also Called: AAA Galvanizing - Joliet Inc (G-6850)*

Azz Galvanizing Plymouth, Plymouth *Also Called: AAA Galvanizing - Joliet Inc (G-13751)*

B & A Cnstr & Design Inc 812 683-4600
   772 W 3rd St Huntingburg (47542) *(G-7270)*

B & B Arms Inc 317 339-4929
   3921 Clarks Creek Rd Plainfield (46168) *(G-13659)*

B & B Engineering Inc 765 566-3460
   7102 E 300 S Bringhurst (46913) *(G-1235)*

B & B Industries Inc 574 262-8551
   1121 D I Dr Elkhart (46514) *(G-3210)*

B & B Manufacturing Inc 219 324-0247
   712 N Fail Rd La Porte (46350) *(G-10387)*

B & B Molders LLC 574 259-7838
   58471 Fir Rd Mishawaka (46544) *(G-11845)*

B & B Powder Coating 260 726-4290
   6353 S Us Highway 27 Portland (47371) *(G-13928)*

B & B Sawmill Inc 812 834-5072
   7142 Leatherwood Rd Bedford (47421) *(G-621)*

B & B Signs 812 282-5366
   5060 Buck Creek Rd Floyds Knobs (47119) *(G-4670)*

B & B Specialties Inc 574 277-0499
   14234 Cleveland Rd Granger (46530) *(G-6333)*

B & B Washer Assemblies, Liberty *Also Called: Larry G Byrd (G-10990)*

B & C Machining Inc 219 866-7091
   320 E Merritt St Rensselaer (47978) *(G-14045)*

B & D Electric Inc 812 254-2122
   8633 Us Highway 50 Shoals (47581) *(G-14903)*

B & D Manufacturing Inc 765 452-2761
   2100 E Carter St Kokomo (46901) *(G-10234)*

B & G Box, Farmersburg *Also Called: Bryan Ward (G-4417)*

B & G Entity Inc 260 724-8874
   125 W Grant St Decatur (46733) *(G-2845)*

B & G Woodworking, Attica *Also Called: Gloria J Burnworth (G-350)*

B & H, Seymour *Also Called: B & H Electric and Supply Inc (G-14630)*

B & H Electric and Supply Inc (PA) 812 522-5607
   740 C Ave E Seymour (47274) *(G-14630)*

B & H Industries Corporation 765 794-4428
   6425 E South St Darlington (47940) *(G-2832)*

B & J Medical LLC 260 349-1275
   4268 E Us Highway 6 Kendallville (46755) *(G-10094)*

B & J Specialty Inc 260 636-2067
   4268 E Us Highway 6 Kendallville (46755) *(G-10095)*

B & J Specialty Inc (PA) 260 761-5011
   7919 N 100 E Wawaka (46794) *(G-16536)*

B & K Beverage Service Inc 317 209-9842
   3005 E 100 N Lebanon (46052) *(G-10879)*

B & L Custom Cabinets Inc 765 379-2471
   7427 N County Road 300 W Rossville (46065) *(G-14386)*

B & L Lighting and Sign Inc 317 984-4206
   21570 Anchor Bay Dr Noblesville (46062) *(G-13037)*

B & L Shtmtl Rofg A Tcta Amer 812 332-4309
   1301 N Monroe St Bloomington (47404) *(G-789)*

B & M Electrical Company Inc 765 448-4532
   710 Navco Dr Lafayette (47905) *(G-10533)*

B & M Steel & Welding Inc 765 964-5868
   1251 S Jackson Pike Union City (47390) *(G-15849)*

B & N Rentals LLC 219 850-3304
   1506 Washington Ave Chesterton (46304) *(G-1906)*

B & W Specialized Drilling 219 746-9463
   9002 Indianapolis Blvd Ste B Highland (46322) *(G-7123)*

B and C Enterprises 260 691-2171
   5095 W 450 S Albion (46701) *(G-18)*

B B & H Tool of Columbus Inc 812 372-3707
   2775 Roadway Dr Columbus (47201) *(G-2224)*

B B Mining Inc (PA) 812 845-2717
   11700 Water Tank Rd Cynthiana (47612) *(G-2785)*

B C I, Shelbyville *Also Called: Installed Building Pdts LLC (G-14762)*

B C T, Indianapolis *Also Called: Templeton Myers Inc (G-9575)*

B C Welding Inc 574 272-9008
   12801 Industrial Park Dr Granger (46530) *(G-6334)*

B D Custom Manufacturing Inc 574 848-0925
   1100 Bloomingdale Dr Bristol (46507) *(G-1248)*

B G Hoadley Quarries Inc (PA) 812 332-1447
   3211 W Arlington Rd Bloomington (47404) *(G-790)*

B Happy Peanut Butter LLC 317 733-3831
   10830 Bennett Pkwy Ste F Zionsville (46077) *(G-16994)*

B Honey & Candles 574 642-1145
   2260 N 1000 W Shipshewana (46565) *(G-14838)*

B I P C O, Columbus *Also Called: Business & Industrial Pdts Co (G-2231)*

B Industries Inc 574 264-3290
   4000 E Bristol St Ste 3 Elkhart (46514) *(G-3211)*

B K & M Inc 219 924-0184
   210 S Lindberg St Griffith (46319) *(G-6792)*

B L, Bloomington *Also Called: B & L Shtmtl Rofg A Tcta Amer (G-789)*

B N Oil LLC 859 816-2244
   622 Arch St Lawrenceburg (47025) *(G-10830)*

B Nickell Woodworking LLC 574 333-2863
   4848 Beck Dr Elkhart (46516) *(G-3212)*

B Nutty LLC 844 426-8889
   6370 Ameriplex Dr Ste 102 Portage (46368) *(G-13847)*

B Plus Enterprises Inc 219 733-9404
   122 S Illinois St Wanatah (46390) *(G-16287)*

B Q Products Inc 317 786-5500
   6233 Brookville Rd Indianapolis (46219) *(G-7582)*

B S M, Gary *Also Called: Business Systems Mgt Corp (G-5908)*

B S R Inc 812 235-4444
   2612 Prairieton Rd Terre Haute (47802) *(G-15547)*

B S R Inc 812 235-4444
   3130 S State Road 63 Terre Haute (47802) *(G-15548)*

B S R Inc (PA) 812 235-4444
   200 W Voorhees St Terre Haute (47802) *(G-15549)*

B Stevens Service LLC 812 622-2039
   10470 Evansville St Cynthiana (47612) *(G-2786)*

B T Bttery Charger Systems Inc 574 533-6030
   17189 County Road 22 Goshen (46528) *(G-6093)*

B T Door 574 534-1726
   1206 Abbington Ct Goshen (46526) *(G-6094)*

B Thystrup US Corporation 574 834-2554
   201 E Epworth Forest Rd North Webster (46555) *(G-13302)*

B Walter & Company Inc 260 563-2181
   655 Factory St Wabash (46992) *(G-16174)*

B Word LLC 317 654-6873
   8818 Cardinal Flower Ln Indianapolis (46231) *(G-7583)*

B Y M Electronics Inc 574 674-5096
   10288 Anderson Rd Granger (46530) *(G-6335)*

B-D Industries Inc 574 295-1420
   1715 Fieldhouse Ave Elkhart (46517) *(G-3214)*

B-Hive Printing 812 897-3905
   804 W Main St Boonville (47601) *(G-1081)*

B.N.W. Industries, Tippecanoe *Also Called: Lee E Norris Cnstr & Grn Co (G-15761)*

B/C Precision Tool Inc 812 577-0642
   1000b Schenley Pl Greendale (47025) *(G-6439)*

B&B Goodiez 765 338-6833
   911 1/2 Western Ave Connersville (47331) *(G-2427)*

B&B Manufacturing, La Porte *Also Called: B & B Manufacturing Inc (G-10387)*

ALPHABETIC SECTION

B&B Tool and Molding Co Inc
624 S Jefferson St Muncie (47305) *(G-12348)*

B&B Urban Eats Corporation.. 317 998-9848
3445 Welch Dr Indianapolis (46224) *(G-7584)*

B&C Distributor Inc (PA).. 609 293-3257
3950 Culligan Ave Ste A Indianapolis (46218) *(G-7585)*

B&D Lighting LLC... 317 414-8056
5635 Hickory Rd Indianapolis (46239) *(G-7586)*

B&F Plastics Inc... 765 962-6125
540 N 8th St Richmond (47374) *(G-14089)*

B&H Capital Inc.. 812 376-9301
3460 Commerce Dr Columbus (47201) *(G-2225)*

B&J Rocket America Inc.. 574 825-5802
325 N Main St Middlebury (46540) *(G-11700)*

B&M Millwright Inc... 765 883-8177
2719 S 1280 W Russiaville (46979) *(G-14420)*

B&M Plastics Inc.. 812 422-0888
2300 Lynch Rd Evansville (47711) *(G-3906)*

B&M Steel Fabrication, Union City Also Called: B & M Steel & Welding Inc *(G-15849)*

B&M Wood Inc.. 574 535-0024
2108 Eisenhower Dr N Goshen (46526) *(G-6095)*

B&R Manufacturing Inc.. 574 293-5669
2503 Marina Dr Elkhart (46514) *(G-3213)*

B&W Environmental... 260 766-4135
1423 E State Road 26 Portland (47371) *(G-13929)*

B&W Packaging Mfg LLC.. 812 280-9578
4140 Capital Dr New Albany (47150) *(G-12694)*

B2 Manufacturing LLC.. 765 993-4519
606 Century Dr Fountain City (47341) *(G-5609)*

B2c2 LLC... 808 533-4128
2664 S Sunflower Dr Bloomington (47403) *(G-791)*

B6 Manufacturing LLC.. 317 549-4290
4701 Massachusetts Ave Indianapolis (46218) *(G-7587)*

B6 Transports LLC.. 317 975-0053
11 Municipal Dr Ste 200 Fishers (46038) *(G-4469)*

Ba Romines Sheetmetal Inc.. 260 657-5500
11827 Hood St Harlan (46743) *(G-7049)*

Baals LLC.. 260 993-0350
118 W Columbia St Ste 402 Fort Wayne (46802) *(G-4786)*

Babbs Super-Value, Spencer Also Called: Babbs Supermarket Inc *(G-15339)*

Babbs Supermarket Inc.. 812 829-2231
459 W Morgan St Spencer (47460) *(G-15339)*

Babcock... 219 462-8851
67 Sanctuary Dr Valparaiso (46385) *(G-15907)*

Babcocks Coatings LLC... 812 624-2120
8410 Kneer Rd Evansville (47720) *(G-3907)*

Babsco Electric, Warsaw Also Called: Babsco Supply Inc *(G-16316)*

Babsco Supply Inc.. 574 267-8999
2361 Shelby Dr Warsaw (46580) *(G-16316)*

Baby Gender Plus, Merrillville Also Called: Indiana Ultrasound LLC *(G-11524)*

Bacchus Winery Golf Vinyrd LLC...................................... 574 732-4663
14 Golfview Dr Logansport (46947) *(G-11059)*

Bacchus Winery LLC... 574 722-1416
820 Golden Bear Ter Logansport (46947) *(G-11060)*

Bach Tech Inc... 219 531-7424
67 S 500 W Valparaiso (46385) *(G-15908)*

Back Alley Creations LLC.. 219 306-6590
927 Tyler Ave Dyer (46311) *(G-2968)*

Back To Eden Herbs Corp.. 317 455-1033
8411 Windfall Ln Ste 60 Camby (46113) *(G-1507)*

Back To Eden Herbs Shop, Camby Also Called: Back To Eden Herbs Corp *(G-1507)*

Backwoods Vynl Werks LLC... 765 607-1292
2008 S 22nd St Lafayette (47905) *(G-10534)*

Backyard Company.. 317 727-0298
5621 Woodland Trace Blvd Indianapolis (46237) *(G-7588)*

Bad Boys Bllard Prductions LLC....................................... 702 738-4950
9041 Matterhorn Rd Indianapolis (46234) *(G-7589)*

Bada Boom Fireworks LLC.. 219 472-6700
4601 Cleveland St Gary (46408) *(G-5897)*

Badd LLC... 812 280-1854
4750 New Middle Rd Jeffersonville (47130) *(G-9938)*

Badger Daylighting Corp.. 219 762-9177
5597 Old Porter Rd Ste D Portage (46368) *(G-13848)*

Badlands Accessories Salvage, Wyatt Also Called: Badlands Pick Up Van ACC Salv *(G-16963)*

Badlands Pick Up Van ACC Salv...................................... 574 633-2156
66521 State Rd 331 Wyatt (46595) *(G-16963)*

Bae Systems Controls Inc... 260 434-5195
4250 Airport Expy Fort Wayne (46809) *(G-4787)*

Baerden Primitives LLC.. 502 909-7045
2316 Gutford Rd Clarksville (47129) *(G-2007)*

Bag Corporation.. 317 699-5523
3039 E 38th St Indianapolis (46218) *(G-7590)*

Bagbarn Co.. 847 850-2592
975 Industrial Dr Ste 11 Madison (47250) *(G-11204)*

Bags By Brenda.. 765 779-4287
3674 E 575 S Markleville (46056) *(G-11366)*

Bahr Bros Mfg Inc... 765 664-6235
2545 S Lincoln Blvd Marion (46953) *(G-11274)*

Bahr Brothers Manufacturing, Marion Also Called: Bahr Bros Mfg Inc *(G-11274)*

Bailey Tools & Supply Inc... 502 635-6348
5716 E Morgan Ave Ste 9 Evansville (47715) *(G-3908)*

Bains Packing and Rfrgn... 260 244-5209
3922 E Old Trail Rd Columbia City (46725) *(G-2122)*

Bains' Packing & Refrigeration, Columbia City Also Called: Bains Packing and Rfrgn *(G-2122)*

Bair Welding LLC.. 260 485-1452
7745 Trier Rd Fort Wayne (46815) *(G-4788)*

Baird Home Corporation.. 812 883-1141
1401 W Mulberry St Salem (47167) *(G-14473)*

Baird Homes of Distinction, Salem Also Called: Baird Home Corporation *(G-14473)*

Baird Ice Cream Co.. 812 283-3345
110 N Randolph Ave Clarksville (47129) *(G-2008)*

Bake-A-Batch, Hammond Also Called: Debra M Lewis *(G-6912)*

Baked With Billie LLC... 317 517-1575
653 Temperance Ave Indianapolis (46203) *(G-7591)*

Baker Metalworks... 260 572-9353
5843 County Road 59 Saint Joe (46785) *(G-14436)*

Baker Petrolite LLC... 219 473-5329
2831 Indian Airforce Blvd Whiting (46394) *(G-16832)*

Baker Prototype Engrg Inc... 574 266-7223
53050 Elkhart East Blvd Elkhart (46514) *(G-3215)*

Bakesmart, Indianapolis Also Called: Blue Sun Ventures Ltd *(G-7649)*

Balboa Press... 812 671-9756
1663 S Liberty Dr Bloomington (47403) *(G-792)*

Bald Spot Racing LLC.. 317 402-7188
4629 Northwestern Dr Zionsville (46077) *(G-16995)*

Bald Spot Sports, Zionsville Also Called: Bald Spot Racing LLC *(G-16995)*

Baldwin Logging Inc... 812 834-1040
11763 State Road 58 E Norman (47264) *(G-13202)*

Ball Brass and Aluminum Foundry Inc............................. 260 925-3515
525 Hazel St Auburn (46706) *(G-367)*

Ball Corporation.. 574 583-9418
1104 N 6th St Monticello (47960) *(G-12136)*

Ball Inc... 317 736-8236
1900 Commerce Pkwy Franklin (46131) *(G-5712)*

Ball Metal Beverage Cont Corp... 574 583-9418
501 N 6th St Monticello (47960) *(G-12137)*

Ball Metal Beverage Cont Div, Monticello Also Called: Ball Metal Beverage Cont Corp *(G-12137)*

Ball State Daily News, Muncie Also Called: Ball State University *(G-12349)*

Ball State University... 765 285-8218
276 Park Journalism Bldg Muncie (47306) *(G-12349)*

Ball Systems Inc... 317 804-2330
16469 Southpark Dr Westfield (46074) *(G-16667)*

Ball Systems Technologies, Westfield Also Called: Ball Systems Inc *(G-16667)*

Baller Signs, Bluffton Also Called: Auto & Sign Specialties Inc *(G-1027)*

Baller Signs Inc... 260 824-1987
3124 E State Road 124 Bluffton (46714) *(G-1028)*

Bamar Plastics Inc.. 574 234-4066
1702 Robinson St South Bend (46613) *(G-14954)*

Bamboo US Bidco LLC... 812 355-5289
1801 N Curry Pike Bloomington (47404) *(G-793)*

ALPHABETIC SECTION

Bamboo US Bidco LLC.. 812 333-0887
  2000 N Curry Pike Bloomington (47402) *(G-794)*
Ban Transit, Lagrange *Also Called: Nelson J Hochstetler (G-10756)*
Banco Industries Inc.. 260 347-9524
  11542 N State Road 3 Kendallville (46755) *(G-10096)*
Band Brothers Transport LLC..................................... 317 709-4415
  2415 Penny Ct Indianapolis (46229) *(G-7592)*
Band Shoppe, Cynthiana *Also Called: Pearison Inc (G-2788)*
Bandag Warranty... 800 523-6366
  9302 E 30th St Indianapolis (46229) *(G-7593)*
Bandgap Semiconductor, Noblesville *Also Called: Bandgap Semiconductor LLC (G-13038)*
Bandgap Semiconductor LLC..................................... 317 652-3250
  176 W Logan St Ste 231 Noblesville (46060) *(G-13038)*
Bane-Clene Corp.. 317 546-5448
  4533 Millersville Rd Indianapolis (46205) *(G-7594)*
Bane-Clene Corp (PA)... 317 546-5448
  3940 N Keystone Ave Indianapolis (46205) *(G-7595)*
Bane-Welker Equipment LLC..................................... 812 234-2627
  300 W Margaret Dr Terre Haute (47802) *(G-15550)*
Banes Machine Shop, Lafayette *Also Called: Homer Banes (G-10601)*
Bangs Laboratories Inc... 317 570-7020
  9025 Technology Dr Fishers (46038) *(G-4470)*
Banjo Corporation.. 765 362-7367
  150 Banjo Dr Crawfordsville (47933) *(G-2546)*
Banks Machine & Engrg LLC...................................... 317 642-4980
  1677 W 400 N Shelbyville (46176) *(G-14732)*
Banner Graphic, Greencastle *Also Called: Truth Publishing Company Inc (G-6434)*
Banner Publications, Borden *Also Called: Green Banner Publications Inc (G-1109)*
Banners Unlimited.. 574 825-8070
  509 S Main St Middlebury (46540) *(G-11701)*
Bantam Inc.. 574 387-3890
  1822 S Bend Ave South Bend (46637) *(G-14955)*
Bantam Industries Inc... 714 561-6122
  2346 S Lynhurst Dr Ste 601 Indianapolis (46241) *(G-7596)*
Banyan Tree, The, Michigan City *Also Called: Delaurence Company (G-11599)*
Bar Keepers Friend, Indianapolis *Also Called: Servaas Laboratories Inc (G-9406)*
Bar Processing Corporation....................................... 219 931-0702
  4527 Columbia Ave Hammond (46327) *(G-6881)*
Bar Processing of Indiana, Hammond *Also Called: Bar Processing Corporation (G-6881)*
Bar Steel Service Center, Indianapolis *Also Called: Mitchel & Scott Machine Co (G-8933)*
Bar-Wal Products... 574 457-5311
  6537 E Waco Dr Syracuse (46567) *(G-15455)*
Barber & Ross of Indiana, Knox *Also Called: Scp Building Products LLC (G-10223)*
Barber Manufacturing Co Inc (PA)............................. 765 643-6905
  1824 Brown St Anderson (46016) *(G-81)*
Barbs Homemade Noodles... 812 486-3762
  787 S 700 E Montgomery (47558) *(G-12086)*
Bare Bones Custom Welding...................................... 502 773-2338
  245 Merrywood Ln New Albany (47150) *(G-12695)*
Bare Metal Inc.. 812 948-1313
  4160 Capital Dr New Albany (47150) *(G-12696)*
Barger Engineering Inc... 812 476-3077
  2116 Lincoln Ave Evansville (47714) *(G-3909)*
Bargers Welding Shop.. 812 889-2095
  6791 E State Road 362 Lexington (47138) *(G-10974)*
Baril Coatings Usa LLC.. 260 665-8431
  401 Growth Pkwy Angola (46703) *(G-233)*
Barker Kitchen & Bath Cabinets................................. 812 493-4693
  4240 S Carmel Rd Hanover (47243) *(G-7039)*
Barkman Custom Woodworking................................. 574 773-9212
  30235 Us Highway 6 Nappanee (46550) *(G-12583)*
Barks Wldg Sups & Farming Inc................................ 812 732-4366
  6125 Highway 135 Sw Corydon (47112) *(G-2487)*
Barksdale Performance... 219 916-5671
  4655 W Volk Rd Hanna (46340) *(G-7037)*
Barley Island Brewing Co... 317 770-5280
  5855 E 211th St Ste 32 Noblesville (46062) *(G-13039)*
Barnes Executive Trnsp, Carmel *Also Called: Luxly LLC (G-1686)*
Barnett Bates, Anderson *Also Called: Forged Alliance Inc (G-118)*
Barnett Industrial Inc.. 219 814-7500
  3012 Grand Trunk Rd Valparaiso (46383) *(G-15909)*

Barnett-Bates Corporation.. 815 726-5223
  1415 Fairview St Anderson (46016) *(G-82)*
Barnhizer Machining and Wldg, Liberty *Also Called: James E Barnhizer (G-10989)*
Barns Unlimited LLC... 765 489-6282
  3434 S County Road 950 E New Castle (47362) *(G-12851)*
Barnwood Masters LLC.. 260 414-9790
  207 N Tucker St Mentone (46539) *(G-11469)*
Baron Embroidery Corp.. 260 484-8700
  103 S Main St Auburn (46706) *(G-368)*
Barrett Custom Knives.. 574 533-4297
  18943 County Road 18 Goshen (46528) *(G-6096)*
Barrett Manufacturing Inc.. 812 753-5808
  901 E John St Fort Branch (47648) *(G-4702)*
Barrett Paving Materials Inc...................................... 765 935-3060
  5834 Inke Rd Richmond (47374) *(G-14090)*
Barrington Packaging Systems I............................... 847 382-8066
  19 W South St Shelbyville (46176) *(G-14733)*
Barry A Wilcox... 260 495-3677
  207 S Wayne St Fremont (46737) *(G-5809)*
Barry Company Inc.. 812 333-1850
  2037 S Yost Ave Bloomington (47403) *(G-795)*
Barry Company Inc.. 317 578-2486
  13317 Britton Park Rd Fishers (46038) *(G-4471)*
Barry Seat Cover & Auto GL Co................................. 574 288-4603
  1924 S Michigan St South Bend (46613) *(G-14956)*
Barry Stuckwisch.. 812 525-1052
  1330 N State Road 11 Seymour (47274) *(G-14631)*
Barry Stuckwisch Mowing, Seymour *Also Called: Barry Stuckwisch (G-14631)*
Bartel Printing Company Inc..................................... 574 267-7421
  310 Cedar St Warsaw (46580) *(G-16317)*
Bartons Screen Printing... 812 422-4303
  1938 N Green River Rd Evansville (47715) *(G-3910)*
Bartons Teez.. 812 422-4303
  1938 N Green River Rd Evansville (47715) *(G-3911)*
Baseline Tool Company.. 260 761-4932
  8458 N Baseline Rd Wawaka (46794) *(G-16537)*
Basic Elements LLC... 219 838-1325
  1305 Macarthur Blvd Munster (46321) *(G-12532)*
Basiloid Products, Bicknell *Also Called: M&M Fabrication LLC (G-735)*
Basin Energy Inc.. 812 983-2519
  514 Se 1st St Evansville (47713) *(G-3912)*
Basin Material Handling LLC..................................... 812 849-0124
  240 S Meridian Rd Mitchell (47446) *(G-12032)*
Bask Aroma Co LLC.. 765 404-7582
  8600 Patience Ln Lafayette (47905) *(G-10535)*
Basket Buddy, Fort Wayne *Also Called: Walter Ostermeyer (G-5543)*
Bass Farms LLC.. 317 401-4700
  5522 S 75 W Shelbyville (46176) *(G-14734)*
Bassett Signs LLC.. 812 946-0017
  5812 Bates Ct Jeffersonville (47130) *(G-9939)*
Basteel Perimeter Systems, Frankfort *Also Called: Bell Machine Company Inc (G-5652)*
Bastian Automation Engrg LLC................................. 317 467-2583
  315 W New Rd Greenfield (46140) *(G-6468)*
Bastian Sltons Advnced Mfg Ctr, Westfield *Also Called: Bastian Solutions LLC (G-16668)*
Bastian Solutions, Greenfield *Also Called: Bastian Automation Engrg LLC (G-6468)*
Bastian Solutions LLC... 317 575-9992
  1821 Bastian Ct Westfield (46074) *(G-16668)*
Bastins Custom Fabricating LLC.............................. 765 987-8385
  5002 W County Road 450 S Knightstown (46148) *(G-10193)*
Bat Signs & Graphics, Tipton *Also Called: Brett Tishner (G-15769)*
Bates Machine Inc.. 574 264-3997
  2921 Lavanture Pl Elkhart (46514) *(G-3216)*
Bates Technologies, LLC, Noblesville *Also Called: Btc Lapmaster LLC (G-13049)*
Batesville Casket Company LLC (HQ)..................... 800 622-8373
  1 Batesville Blvd Batesville (47006) *(G-580)*
Batesville Casket Company Inc................................. 812 934-7010
  100 Eastern Ave Batesville (47006) *(G-581)*
Batesville Interactive LLC.. 812 932-0164
  1 Batesville Blvd Batesville (47006) *(G-582)*
Batesville Interactive, Inc., Batesville *Also Called: Batesville Interactive LLC (G-582)*

Batesville Management Services, Batesville *Also Called: Batesville Casket Company LLC* *(G-580)*

Batesville Products Inc..812 926-4230
10367 Randall Ave Aurora (47001) *(G-440)*

Batesville Products Inc (PA).......................................513 381-2057
434 Margaret St Lawrenceburg (47025) *(G-10831)*

Batesville Services LLC (HQ)....................................800 622-8373
1 Batesville Blvd Batesville (47006) *(G-583)*

Batesville Tool & Die Inc..812 934-5616
177 Six Pine Ranch Rd Batesville (47006) *(G-584)*

Bath & Body Works, Greenfield *Also Called: Bath & Body Works LLC (G-6469)*

Bath & Body Works LLC..317 209-1517
10343 E Us Highway 36 Avon (46123) *(G-506)*

Bath & Body Works LLC..317 468-0834
1519 N State St Greenfield (46140) *(G-6469)*

Bath & Body Works LLC..219 531-2146
2410 Laporte Ave Ste 140 Valparaiso (46383) *(G-15910)*

Bath Gallery Showroom...219 531-2150
709 Morthland Dr Valparaiso (46383) *(G-15911)*

Batteries Plus..317 219-0007
2640 Conner St Noblesville (46060) *(G-13040)*

Battisti Customs, Elkhart *Also Called: Forest River Inc (G-3354)*

Battle Boards LLC...317 518-7245
4851 W Minnesota St Indianapolis (46241) *(G-7597)*

Battle Creek Equipment Co (PA)..............................260 495-3472
702 S Reed Rd Fremont (46737) *(G-5810)*

Battle Creek Health Eqp Co, Fremont *Also Called: Battle Creek Equipment Co (G-5810)*

Battlefield Tech Unlimited, Danville *Also Called: James Brummett (G-2815)*

Battlewear Components Inc......................................574 262-4659
1421 Lawndale Rd Elkhart (46514) *(G-3217)*

Bauer Rey Inc..317 731-2812
11057 Allisonville Rd Ste 240 Fishers (46038) *(G-4472)*

Baugh Enterprises Inc...812 334-8189
125 S Westplex Ave Bloomington (47404) *(G-796)*

Bauman Harnish Rubber Co, Garrett *Also Called: Griffith Rbr Mills of Garrett (G-5864)*

Baumbauer Signs...260 368-7537
967 Sw High St Geneva (46740) *(G-6048)*

Bavettes Meat Company LLC....................................312 590-7141
10794 Standish Pl Noblesville (46060) *(G-13041)*

Bawaenterprises LLC..269 228-1258
30836 Oakcrest Dr Granger (46530) *(G-6336)*

Bawling Acres Woodworking LLC............................260 768-3214
155 S 1000 W Middlebury (46540) *(G-11702)*

Baxter, Batesville *Also Called: Allen Medical Systems Inc (G-577)*

Baxter Biosciences, Bloomington *Also Called: Bamboo US Bidco LLC (G-793)*

Baxter Design & Advertising....................................219 464-9237
656 Franklin St Valparaiso (46383) *(G-15912)*

Baxter Healthcare Corporation.................................219 942-8136
428 N Liberty St Hobart (46342) *(G-7174)*

Baxter Healthcare Corporation.................................317 291-0620
6812 Corporate Dr Indianapolis (46278) *(G-7598)*

Baxter Intl..812 355-4283
3249 S Southern Oaks Dr Bloomington (47401) *(G-797)*

Baxter Lumber LLC...812 873-6868
12876 W Deputy Pike Rd Deputy (47230) *(G-2940)*

Baxter Phrm Solutions LLC (HQ).............................812 333-0887
927 S Curry Pike Bloomington (47403) *(G-798)*

Baxter Phrm Solutions LLC......................................812 355-7167
927 S Curry Pike Bloomington (47403) *(G-799)*

Baxter Printing Incorporated....................................219 923-1999
311 N Broad St Griffith (46319) *(G-6793)*

Bay Bridge Manufacturing, Bristol *Also Called: Bay Bridge Mfg Inc (G-1249)*

Bay Bridge Mfg Inc..574 848-7477
1301 Commerce Dr Bristol (46507) *(G-1249)*

Bay Valley Foods LLC...574 935-3097
1430 Western Ave Plymouth (46563) *(G-13757)*

Bayer Great Lakes Prod Co LLC..............................317 945-7121
908 N Independence St Windfall (46076) *(G-16903)*

Bayer Healthcare LLC...574 262-6136
3400 Middlebury St Elkhart (46516) *(G-3218)*

Bayer Healthcare LLC...574 252-4735
4100 Edison Lakes Pkwy Mishawaka (46545) *(G-11846)*

Bayer Healthcare LLC...574 252-4734
3930 Edison Lakes Pkwy Mishawaka (46545) *(G-11847)*

Bayview Estates...574 457-4136
400 S Harkless Dr Syracuse (46567) *(G-15456)*

Bbliss & Jus Be Zany...215 251-9235
446 Blue Spring Dr Indianapolis (46239) *(G-7599)*

Bbs Celebration Center..765 730-6575
1019 S Yorkchester Dr Yorktown (47396) *(G-16971)*

Bbs Enterprises Inc...574 255-3173
55980 Russell Industrial Pkwy Mishawaka (46545) *(G-11848)*

Bc Countertops Inc...317 637-4427
1343 Sadlier Circle South Dr Indianapolis (46239) *(G-7600)*

Bcd and Associates LLC..317 873-5394
8904 Bash St Ste M Indianapolis (46256) *(G-7601)*

Bcf Precision LLC...888 556-2264
930 Executive Dr Warsaw (46580) *(G-16318)*

Bch Image USA Inc...812 326-1025
4582 S Cross St Saint Anthony (47575) *(G-14426)*

BCI Solutions Inc..574 546-2411
500 N Baltimore St Bremen (46506) *(G-1174)*

Bcw Diversified Inc...765 644-2033
8984 W Sr236 Middletown (47356) *(G-11766)*

Bcw Supplies, Middletown *Also Called: Bcw Diversified Inc (G-11766)*

Bd Medical Development Inc...................................219 310-8551
1140 Millennium Dr Crown Point (46307) *(G-2653)*

Bdc Enterprise LLC...317 395-6740
1628 S Miller St Shelbyville (46176) *(G-14735)*

Bdl Supply, Indianapolis *Also Called: Buckeye Diamond Logistics Inc (G-7698)*

Bdx I LLC..317 741-5173
17219 Foundation Pkwy Westfield (46074) *(G-16669)*

Be Body Butters LLC..317 362-9248
5345 Brendon Park Dr Indianapolis (46226) *(G-7602)*

Be Loved Transportation Inc...................................812 207-2610
2514 S Rogers St Bloomington (47403) *(G-800)*

Bea MA Bkes Spclty Dsserts LLC............................219 302-6716
3329 E 73rd Ave Merrillville (46410) *(G-11487)*

Beach Acquisition Co LLC.......................................812 945-2688
999 Progress Blvd New Albany (47150) *(G-12697)*

Beach Acquisition Co LLC (HQ)..............................812 945-2688
3900 Green Valley Rd New Albany (47150) *(G-12698)*

Beach House Beverages LLC..................................260 969-1064
624 W Wayne St Fort Wayne (46802) *(G-4789)*

Beacher Business Printers, Michigan City *Also Called: Montgomery & Associates Inc (G-11641)*

Beachfront Furniture Inc..574 875-0817
60874 Ridgepoint Ct Elkhart (46517) *(G-3219)*

Beachlers Sugar Bush, Claypool *Also Called: Silas Beachler (G-2057)*

Beachwood Lumber Co Inc......................................574 858-9325
7878 W Old Road 30 Warsaw (46580) *(G-16319)*

Beachwood Manufacturing, Warsaw *Also Called: Beachwood Lumber Co Inc (G-16319)*

Beachy Machine Inc..765 452-9051
175 E North St Kokomo (46901) *(G-10235)*

Beachy Machine Shop LLC......................................765 452-9051
3884 E 400 N Kokomo (46901) *(G-10236)*

Beachy Performance Parts, Kokomo *Also Called: Beachy Machine Inc (G-10235)*

Beacon House..219 756-2131
7203 Starling Dr Schererville (46375) *(G-14515)*

Beacon Industries Inc...812 526-0100
912 S Walnut St Edinburgh (46124) *(G-3068)*

Beacon Manufacturing Inc.......................................765 753-0265
2200 N Calumet St Kokomo (46901) *(G-10237)*

Beacon Sign Company LLC.....................................317 272-2388
9305 E Us Highway 36 Avon (46123) *(G-507)*

Beads To Feed LLC..816 299-8118
8888 Keystone Xing Ste 1300 Indianapolis (46240) *(G-7603)*

Beams of Grace Press..574 238-1644
68080 County Road 23 New Paris (46553) *(G-12947)*

Beams Seatbelts Inc...574 970-2667
3802 Gallatin Way Elkhart (46514) *(G-3220)*

Bear Arms Holsters..260 310-2376
1149 Grant Ave Fort Wayne (46803) *(G-4790)*

ALPHABETIC SECTION

Bear Creek Farms, Bryant *Also Called: Richards Restaurant Inc (G-1436)*
Bear Enterprise, Hammond *Also Called: Brittany Hornsby (G-6888)*
Bear Hollow Wood Carvers.. 812 936-3030
  469 S Maple St French Lick (47432) *(G-5844)*
Bear Hollow Wood Carvers LLC.. 812 843-5549
  25895 Old State Road 37 Saint Croix (47576) *(G-14433)*
Bear Komplex... 317 600-5833
  1001 E Summit St Crown Point (46307) *(G-2654)*
Bear Wallow Distillery.. 812 657-4923
  4484 Old State Road 46 Nashville (47448) *(G-12662)*
Bearcat Anodizing LLC.. 574 533-0448
  2431 E Kercher Rd Goshen (46526) *(G-6097)*
Bearcat Corp.. 574 533-0448
  2431 E Kercher Rd Goshen (46526) *(G-6098)*
Beards Welding & Fabrication.. 317 374-4779
  8321 W Shelby 250 S Franklin (46131) *(G-5713)*
Bearing Headquarters Co, Highland *Also Called: Headco Industries Inc (G-7140)*
Bearing Headquarters Co, South Bend *Also Called: Headco Industries Inc (G-15062)*
Bearing Service Company PA... 773 734-5132
  1951 N Griffith Blvd Griffith (46319) *(G-6794)*
Bears Den EMB & More LLC.. 260 724-4070
  530 E 900 N Decatur (46733) *(G-2846)*
Beasley Fabricating & McHnng... 219 297-4000
  11237 S State Road 55 Goodland (47948) *(G-6079)*
Beasley Welding.. 812 883-2573
  310 S Canton South Boston Rd Salem (47167) *(G-14474)*
Beast Custom Athletic Printing... 765 610-6802
  418 W Fifth St Fairmount (46928) *(G-4408)*
Beatty International Inc (PA).. 219 931-3000
  940 150th St Hammond (46327) *(G-6882)*
Beatty Machine & Mfg Co.. 219 931-3000
  940 150th St Hammond (46327) *(G-6883)*
Beattys Custom Woods.. 574 722-2752
  824 14th St Logansport (46947) *(G-11061)*
Beautiful Brides By TEC, Bloomington *Also Called: TEC Photography (G-985)*
Beautybyneyadior LLC.. 800 988-2592
  2007 Harrison St Gary (46407) *(G-5898)*
Beaver Gravel Corporation.. 317 773-0679
  16101 River Rd Noblesville (46062) *(G-13042)*
Beaver Materials, Noblesville *Also Called: Beaver Gravel Corporation (G-13042)*
Beaver Products Inc... 317 773-0679
  16101 River Rd Noblesville (46062) *(G-13043)*
Beaver Readi-Mix, Noblesville *Also Called: Ma-Ri-Al Corp (G-13129)*
Beazer East Inc... 260 490-9006
  1820 W Washington Center Rd Fort Wayne (46818) *(G-4791)*
Beazer East Inc... 812 883-2191
  1510 W Market St Salem (47167) *(G-14475)*
Beck Industries LP... 574 294-5621
  28707 La Rue St Elkhart (46516) *(G-3221)*
Becker Elec... 812 362-9000
  6500 N Us Highway 231 Rockport (47635) *(G-14337)*
Beckett Bronze Company Inc (PA).. 765 282-2261
  401 W 23rd St Muncie (47302) *(G-12350)*
Beckett Bronze Company Inc... 765 282-2261
  106 E 20th St Muncie (47302) *(G-12351)*
Beckler Power Equipment... 260 356-1188
  1255 S Jefferson St Huntington (46750) *(G-7300)*
Beckman Coulter Inc.. 317 808-4200
  7451 Winton Dr Indianapolis (46268) *(G-7604)*
Beckman Coulter Inc.. 317 808-4200
  5350 Lakeview Parkway South Dr Ste A Indianapolis (46268) *(G-7605)*
Beckman Coulter Inc.. 317 471-8029
  5355 W 76th St Indianapolis (46268) *(G-7606)*
Beckman Coulter Life Sciences.. 408 747-2000
  5350 Lakeview Pkwy S Dr Indianapolis (46268) *(G-7607)*
Becks Bird Feeders.. 765 874-1496
  8909 S State Road 109 Markleville (46056) *(G-11367)*
Beckys Die Cutting Inc... 260 467-1714
  701 Sherman Blvd Fort Wayne (46808) *(G-4792)*
Beckys Orgnl Pppts Gs Cls.. 219 934-0895
  9326 Idlewild Dr Highland (46322) *(G-7124)*

Beco, Pendleton *Also Called: Beco Inc (G-13525)*
Beco Inc... 765 778-3426
  6642 S State Road 67 Pendleton (46064) *(G-13525)*
Becoming Her LLC... 317 200-0165
  8319 Michigan Rd Indianapolis (46268) *(G-7608)*
Becoming Press LLC.. 317 823-9983
  18847 Goldwater Rd Westfield (46062) *(G-16670)*
Becton Dickinson and Company... 317 561-2900
  2350 Reeves Rd Plainfield (46168) *(G-13660)*
Bedford Crane Service LLC... 812 275-4411
  957 J St Bedford (47421) *(G-622)*
Bedford Cut Stone Co, Bedford *Also Called: Architectural Stone Sales Inc (G-619)*
Bedford Limestone Suppliers.. 812 279-9120
  1319 Breckenridge Rd Bedford (47421) *(G-623)*
Bedford Machine & Tool Inc.. 812 275-1948
  2103 John Williams Blvd Bedford (47421) *(G-624)*
Bedford Stonecrafters Inc... 812 275-2646
  3160 Mitchell Rd Bedford (47421) *(G-625)*
Bedlam Beard Company LLC... 317 800-9631
  6427 N County Road 200 W Lizton (46149) *(G-11048)*
Bee Kind Candles.. 765 618-5819
  1409 Sinclair St Fort Wayne (46808) *(G-4793)*
Bee Window Incorporated... 317 283-8522
  115 Shadowlawn Dr Fishers (46038) *(G-4473)*
Beebe Cabinet Co Inc... 574 293-3580
  22695 State Road 120 Elkhart (46516) *(G-3222)*
Beecher Hairston LLC... 317 714-6703
  3621 N Drexel Ave Indianapolis (46218) *(G-7609)*
Beechys Molding Plus LLC.. 260 768-7030
  1365 N 500 W Shipshewana (46565) *(G-14839)*
BEEFREE INC.. 317 402-1019
  20935 State Road 19 Cicero (46034) *(G-1994)*
Beeline Woodworking... 260 894-3806
  9687 N 700 W Ligonier (46767) *(G-11005)*
Beemsterboer Slag Corp... 219 392-1930
  3210 Watling St East Chicago (46312) *(G-2992)*
Beemsterboer Slag Corp (PA).. 773 785-6000
  3411 Sheffield Ave Hammond (46327) *(G-6884)*
Beer and Slabaugh Inc.. 574 773-3413
  23965 Us Highway 6 Nappanee (46550) *(G-12584)*
Begley Sign Painting Inc... 317 835-2027
  220 N Murnan Ln Fairland (46126) *(G-4397)*
Beh IL Corp.. 219 886-2710
  201 Mississippi St Gary (46402) *(G-5899)*
Behning Inc... 260 672-2663
  287 N Main St Roanoke (46783) *(G-14260)*
Behnke Engineering.. 574 842-2327
  321 E Washington St Culver (46511) *(G-2780)*
Bel-Mar Products Corporation... 317 769-3262
  5 E Pierce St Whitestown (46075) *(G-16801)*
Belcher Tobiah.. 765 513-2211
  906 Danbury Dr Kokomo (46901) *(G-10238)*
Belcher Printing Services.. 812 305-1093
  11437 Middle Mount Vernon Rd Evansville (47712) *(G-3913)*
Belden, Richmond *Also Called: Belden Wire & Cable Company LLC (G-14095)*
Belden Cdt, Richmond *Also Called: Belden Inc (G-14094)*
Belden Inc.. 317 818-6300
  401 Pennsylvania Pkwy Carmel (46280) *(G-1566)*
Belden Inc.. 978 537-9961
  2200 Us Highway 27 S Richmond (47374) *(G-14091)*
Belden Inc.. 724 222-7060
  2200 Us Highway 27 S Richmond (47374) *(G-14092)*
Belden Inc.. 765 983-5200
  2200 Us Highway 27 S Richmond (47374) *(G-14093)*
Belden Inc.. 765 962-7561
  350 Nw N St Richmond (47374) *(G-14094)*
Belden Wire & Cable Company LLC (HQ).............................. 765 983-5200
  2200 Us Highway 27 S Richmond (47374) *(G-14095)*
Belgian Horse Winery LLC... 765 779-3002
  7122 W County Road 625 N Middletown (47356) *(G-11767)*
Bell Graphics and Design LLC.. 765 827-5441
  3207 Iowa Ave Connersville (47331) *(G-2428)*

Bell Machine Company Inc 765 654-5225
1400 Magnolia Ave Frankfort (46041) *(G-5652)*

Bell Transportation LLC 317 833-0745
11333 Fairweather Pl Indianapolis (46229) *(G-7610)*

Bell-Horn, Carmel *Also Called: Circle City Medical Inc (G-1587)*

Bella Food Sales LLC 574 229-8803
56288 Erickson Dr Mishawaka (46545) *(G-11849)*

Bellahauss Distributers 260 485-4343
4767 Evard Rd Fort Wayne (46835) *(G-4794)*

Bello Custom Woodcrafts 574 314-5973
4014 Fir Rd Mishawaka (46545) *(G-11850)*

Bells and Whistles LLC 317 315-3129
3747 E Stipp Rd Bloomington (47401) *(G-801)*

Bells of Steel Usa Inc 317 981-5586
6002 Corporate Way Indianapolis (46278) *(G-7611)*

Bells Trucking LLC 574 263-6030
531 Broadmore Est Goshen (46528) *(G-6099)*

Belltone Hearing Care Center 317 462-9999
1789 N State St Greenfield (46140) *(G-6470)*

Belmont Sand, Indianapolis *Also Called: Marietta Martin Materials Inc (G-8834)*

Belstra Milling Co Inc (PA) 219 987-4343
424 15th St Se Demotte (46310) *(G-2911)*

Belstra Milling Co Inc 219 766-2284
207 E Mentor St Kouts (46347) *(G-10361)*

Belt Tech Industrial Inc (PA) 812 258-5959
1996 S 300 W Washington (47501) *(G-16473)*

Bemcor Inc 219 937-1600
940 150th St Hammond (46327) *(G-6885)*

Bemis Distillers LLC 317 619-0711
3374 Shore Dr Greenwood (46143) *(G-6675)*

Bemr LLC 812 385-8509
333 S 2nd Ave Princeton (47670) *(G-13982)*

Ben Tire Distributors Ltd (PA) 317 798-2013
9465 Counselors Row Ste 112 Indianapolis (46240) *(G-7612)*

Benakovich Builders 219 204-2777
10725 W State Road 47 Thorntown (46071) *(G-15750)*

Benchmark Chemical Corp 317 875-0051
8425 Zionsville Rd Indianapolis (46268) *(G-7613)*

Benchmark Fabricated Steel, Terre Haute *Also Called: Benchmark Inc (G-15551)*

Benchmark Inc 812 238-0659
4149 4th Pkwy Terre Haute (47804) *(G-15551)*

Bender Mold & Machine Inc 574 255-5176
55951 Russell Industrial Pkwy Mishawaka (46545) *(G-11851)*

Bender Plastics, Mishawaka *Also Called: Bender Products Inc (G-11852)*

Bender Products Inc 574 255-5350
55951 Russell Industrial Pkwy Mishawaka (46545) *(G-11852)*

Bendix Coml Vhcl Systems LLC 260 356-9720
1850 Riverfork Dr Huntington (46750) *(G-7301)*

Benham Sawmill LLC 812 723-2644
150 W County Road 250 N Paoli (47454) *(G-13488)*

Benjamin Carrier 337 366-2603
6 Fay Ave Jeffersonville (47130) *(G-9940)*

Bennett Printing 812 966-2917
1245 S County Road 925 W Medora (47260) *(G-11461)*

Bennington, Elkhart *Also Called: Pontoon Boat LLC (G-3608)*

Bens Creative Ventures LLC 574 279-1057
5534 Saint Joe Rd Fort Wayne (46835) *(G-4795)*

Bens Quarry LLC 812 824-3730
303 E Ingram Rd Springville (47462) *(G-15382)*

Benson Tower LLC 270 577-7598
10833 Sunset Dr Evansville (47712) *(G-3914)*

Bent Industrial Services LLC 260 352-0106
9730 S State Road 15 Silver Lake (46982) *(G-14917)*

Bent Tree Custom Sawing LLC 260 693-9781
9309 Bryie Rd Churubusco (46723) *(G-1972)*

Bentcil Company, The, Indianapolis *Also Called: The Killion Corporation (G-9589)*

Benthall Bros Inc (PA) 800 488-5995
15 Read St Evansville (47710) *(G-3915)*

Benton Review Newspaper 765 884-1902
204 N Adams Ave Fowler (47944) *(G-5619)*

Bentz Transport Products Inc 260 622-9100
3943 Weston Pointe Dr Zionsville (46077) *(G-16996)*

Bentz Woodworking 765 525-4946
6850 S State Road 9 Waldron (46182) *(G-16257)*

Benz 812 364-1273
1920 Flatwood Rd Ne New Salisbury (47161) *(G-12983)*

Benz Custom Metal LLC 812 365-2613
4640 E Valeene Rd Marengo (47140) *(G-11261)*

Berean Builders Publishing Inc 765 287-5157
3001 W Woodbridge Dr Muncie (47304) *(G-12352)*

Berendsen Inc 812 423-6468
460 E Sycamore St Evansville (47713) *(G-3916)*

Berg 219 226-4350
393 Golden Oak Ct Crown Point (46307) *(G-2655)*

Berg Bows, Bloomington *Also Called: Michael Duff (G-918)*

Berger Table Pads Inc 317 631-2577
1501 W Market St Indianapolis (46222) *(G-7614)*

Bergren & Associates 219 852-1500
481 Fayette St Hammond (46320) *(G-6886)*

Berkey Machine Corporation 260 761-4002
7037a N Triplett St Wawaka (46794) *(G-16538)*

Bernard Burns 574 382-5019
6093 S Old Us Highway 31 Macy (46951) *(G-11194)*

Berne, Ossian *Also Called: Berne Apparel Company (G-13419)*

Berne Apparel Company (PA) 260 622-1500
2501 E 850 N Ossian (46777) *(G-13419)*

Berne Locker Storage 260 589-2806
206 High St Berne (46711) *(G-705)*

Berne Ready Mix, Berne *Also Called: St Henry Tile Co Inc (G-728)*

Bernell, Mishawaka *Also Called: Vision Training Products Inc (G-12023)*

BERRY, Evansville *Also Called: Berry Global Group Inc (G-3921)*

Berry, Evansville *Also Called: Setco LLC (G-4307)*

Berry Film Products Co Inc 812 306-2690
101 Oakley St Evansville (47710) *(G-3917)*

Berry Global Inc 812 334-7090
4100 W Profile Pkwy Bloomington (47404) *(G-802)*

Berry Global Inc (HQ) 812 424-2904
101 Oakley St Evansville (47710) *(G-3918)*

Berry Global Inc 812 867-6671
3245 Kansas Rd Evansville (47725) *(G-3919)*

Berry Global Inc 812 421-3136
1900 Commerce Pkwy Franklin (46131) *(G-5714)*

Berry Global Inc 260 495-2000
701 E Depot St Fremont (46737) *(G-5811)*

Berry Global Inc 812 558-3510
10485 E 1250 N Odon (47562) *(G-13331)*

Berry Global Inc 812 386-1525
889 W Gach Rd Princeton (47670) *(G-13983)*

Berry Global Inc 765 966-1414
630 Commerce Rd Richmond (47374) *(G-14096)*

Berry Global Escrow Corp 812 424-2904
101 Oakley St Evansville (47710) *(G-3920)*

Berry Global Group Inc (PA) 812 424-2904
101 Oakley St Evansville (47710) *(G-3921)*

Berry Global Group Inc 812 868-7429
889 W Gach Rd Princeton (47670) *(G-13984)*

Berry Plas Technical Svcs Inc 812 424-2904
101 Oakley St Evansville (47710) *(G-3922)*

Berry Plastics, Evansville *Also Called: Berry Global Inc (G-3918)*

Berry Plastics Escrow Corp 812 424-2904
101 Oakley St Evansville (47710) *(G-3923)*

Berry Plastics Group Inc 812 424-2904
101 Oakley St Evansville (47710) *(G-3924)*

Berry Plastics Ik LLC 641 648-5047
101 Oakley St Evansville (47710) *(G-3925)*

Berry Plastics Opco Inc 812 402-2903
9845 Hedden Rd Evansville (47725) *(G-3926)*

Berry Plastics Opco Inc (DH) 812 424-2904
101 Oakley St Evansville (47710) *(G-3927)*

Bert R Huncilman & Son Inc 812 945-3544
115 Security Pkwy New Albany (47150) *(G-12699)*

Bertelsmann Pubg Group Inc 410 386-7717
1019 N State Road 47 Crawfordsville (47933) *(G-2547)*

ALPHABETIC SECTION

Bertrand Products Inc... 574 234-4181
2323 Foundation Dr South Bend (46628) *(G-14957)*

Beryl Martin, Griffith *Also Called: Ccmp Inc (G-6799)*

Bes Racing Engines Inc.. 812 576-2371
27545 State Route 1 Guilford (47022) *(G-6827)*

Besi Manufacturing Inc.. 812 427-4114
503 Vineyard St Vevay (47043) *(G-16106)*

Besse Veneers Inc... 906 428-3113
718 E Park St Trafalgar (46181) *(G-15826)*

Best Barn Pizza, Medaryville *Also Called: John F Semrau (G-11459)*

Best Beers LLC... 812 332-1234
1100 S Strong Dr Bloomington (47403) *(G-803)*

Best Bicycle Inc.. 812 336-2724
4012 E 10th St Bloomington (47408) *(G-804)*

Best Blinds.. 260 490-4422
8534 Fritz Rd Fort Wayne (46818) *(G-4796)*

Best Boy & Co., Indianapolis *Also Called: Best Boy Products LLC (G-7615)*

Best Boy Products LLC.. 317 442-9735
7337 Glenview Dr E Indianapolis (46250) *(G-7615)*

Best Chairs, Ferdinand *Also Called: Best Chairs Incorporated (G-4429)*

Best Chairs Incorporated... 812 367-1761
Highway 66 E Cannelton (47520) *(G-1532)*

Best Chairs Incorporated (PA)...................................... 812 367-1761
1 Best Dr Ferdinand (47532) *(G-4429)*

Best Chairs Incorporated... 812 367-1761
1700 W Willowcreek Rd Paoli (47454) *(G-13489)*

Best Custom Cabinet Refacing...................................... 260 459-1448
6821 S 275 W Columbia City (46725) *(G-2123)*

Best Electric, Otterbein *Also Called: Best Electric Motor Service (G-13450)*

Best Electric Motor Service.. 765 583-2408
11430 E Us Hwy 52 Otterbein (47970) *(G-13450)*

Best Equipment & Welding Co...................................... 317 271-8652
1960 Midwest Blvd Indianapolis (46214) *(G-7616)*

Best Equipment Co Inc (PA).. 317 823-3050
5550 Poindexter Dr Indianapolis (46235) *(G-7617)*

Best Formed Plastics LLC... 574 293-6128
21209 Protecta Dr Elkhart (46516) *(G-3223)*

Best Friends Inc... 765 985-3872
252 W Harrison St Denver (46926) *(G-2934)*

Best Machine Company Inc... 765 827-0250
1830 Virginia Ave Connersville (47331) *(G-2429)*

Best One Tire & Svc S Bend Inc.................................... 574 246-4021
4411 Quality Dr South Bend (46628) *(G-14958)*

Best Tires & Wheels.. 317 306-3379
320 N Morton St Franklin (46131) *(G-5715)*

Best Vineyards LLC... 812 969-9463
8373 Morgans Ln Se Elizabeth (47117) *(G-3124)*

Best Weld Inc... 765 641-7720
1315 W 18th St Anderson (46016) *(G-83)*

Best-One Kentuckiana Inc (PA)..................................... 812 285-5400
3215 Industrial Pkwy Jeffersonville (47130) *(G-9941)*

Best-One Kentuckiana Inc... 812 282-4799
1402 Truckers Blvd Jeffersonville (47130) *(G-9942)*

Best-One Lt LLC.. 812 471-8473
6640 Toney Ln Evansville (47715) *(G-3928)*

Best-One Tire & Auto Care of A..................................... 260 665-7330
1101 N Wayne St Angola (46703) *(G-234)*

Best-One Tire & Svc Auburn Inc.................................... 260 925-2782
1712 Wayne St Auburn (46706) *(G-369)*

Bestway Foam, Indianapolis *Also Called: Foamcraft Inc (G-8212)*

Beta Steel Corp.. 219 787-0001
6500 S Boundary Rd Portage (46368) *(G-13849)*

Bethlehem Packg Die Cutng Inc.................................... 812 282-8740
802 E 8th St New Albany (47150) *(G-12700)*

Betos Bar Inc... 219 397-8247
1301 E Chicago Ave East Chicago (46312) *(G-2993)*

Betta Call Paul 4 Cbd LLC... 317 675-6060
1015 Oswego Rd Carmel (46032) *(G-1567)*

Better Blacc Wall Streetz LLC....................................... 812 927-0712
6248 Knollview Way # 816 Seymour (47274) *(G-14632)*

Better Built Barns Inc... 812 477-2001
4415 E Morgan Ave Evansville (47715) *(G-3929)*

Better Built Products, Lowell *Also Called: V N C Inc (G-11179)*

Better Gutter Systems.. 765 282-2724
1435 S Kinney Ave Muncie (47302) *(G-12353)*

Better Surplus, Henryville *Also Called: 3sevens LLC (G-7112)*

Better Visions PC... 260 244-7542
513 N Line St Columbia City (46725) *(G-2124)*

Better Visions PC... 260 627-2669
10529 Hosler Rd Ste A Leo (46765) *(G-10963)*

Better Way Partners LLC... 574 831-3340
70891 County Road 23 New Paris (46553) *(G-12948)*

Better Way Products.. 574 546-2868
3659 Destiny Dr Bremen (46506) *(G-1175)*

Better Way Products, New Paris *Also Called: Better Way Partners LLC (G-12948)*

Bettner Wire Coating Dies Inc.. 812 372-2732
1230 Jackson St Columbus (47201) *(G-2226)*

Bettys Daughter Inc... 317 500-1490
2685 E Main St Ste 108 Plainfield (46168) *(G-13661)*

Betzdearborn Division, Valparaiso *Also Called: Veolia Wts Usa Inc (G-16075)*

Beulah Inc.. 219 309-5635
808 N 360 W Valparaiso (46385) *(G-15913)*

Beunerfarm Publishing Inc... 317 514-1505
418 S Sheridan Ave Indianapolis (46219) *(G-7618)*

Beutler Meat Processing Co.. 765 742-7285
802 Wabash Ave Lafayette (47905) *(G-10536)*

Bev Can Printers LLC.. 219 617-6181
1705 State St Bldg B La Porte (46350) *(G-10388)*

Beveled Glass & Ltg Designs, Indianapolis *Also Called: Larry Robertson Associates (G-8723)*

Bever Wldg & Fabrication LLC...................................... 765 524-4597
9653 S County Road 575 W Knightstown (46148) *(G-10194)*

Beverly Harris... 317 910-0542
8401 Moller Rd Unit 681161 Indianapolis (46268) *(G-7619)*

Beverly Industrial Service Inc... 812 667-5047
4233 S Farmers Retreat Rd Dillsboro (47018) *(G-2943)*

Bex Screen Printing Inc... 317 791-0375
5602 Elmwood Ave Ste 214 Indianapolis (46203) *(G-7620)*

Beyond Distributions LLC.. 631 960-1745
10427 Hornton St Indianapolis (46236) *(G-7621)*

Beyond Monograms LLC... 812 746-2624
525 Locust St Mount Vernon (47620) *(G-12292)*

Beyond The Countertops, Indianapolis *Also Called: Bc Countertops Inc (G-7600)*

Beyond Welding Inspection Inc...................................... 812 849-4410
2041 Clover Ln Mitchell (47446) *(G-12033)*

BF Goodrich, Woodburn *Also Called: Michelin North America Inc (G-16951)*

BF Goodrich Tire Manufacturing.................................... 260 493-8100
18906 Old 24 Woodburn (46797) *(G-16946)*

Bhar Incorporated.. 260 749-5168
6509 Moeller Rd Fort Wayne (46806) *(G-4797)*

Bhar Printing Incorporated... 317 899-1020
929 W 16th St Indianapolis (46202) *(G-7622)*

Bhaura Inc.. 260 745-5700
4226 Lafayette St Fort Wayne (46806) *(G-4798)*

Bhj Usa LLC... 574 722-3933
81 E Industrial Blvd Logansport (46947) *(G-11062)*

Bi-State Asphalt... 765 832-5000
14516 S 200 E Clinton (47842) *(G-2064)*

Bibles For Blind Vslly Hndcppe...................................... 812 466-3134
3228 E Rose Hill Ave Terre Haute (47805) *(G-15552)*

Biblical Enterprises Inc... 812 391-0071
3428 S Burks Ct Bloomington (47401) *(G-805)*

Biblical Publishing Svcs Inc... 219 213-2078
307 E Clark St Crown Point (46307) *(G-2656)*

Bickels Garage & Welding... 765 853-5457
5520 W 900 S Modoc (47358) *(G-12050)*

Biddle Precision Components Inc.................................. 317 758-4451
701 S Mn St Sheridan (46069) *(G-14817)*

Biela Printing.. 219 874-8094
1004 Kentucky St Michigan City (46360) *(G-11581)*

Big B Distributors Inc... 812 425-5235
2727 N Kentucky Ave Evansville (47711) *(G-3930)*

Big Brick House Bakery LLP.. 260 563-1071
4322 Marvin Dr Fort Wayne (46806) *(G-4799)*

Big Bruhs Seasoning LLP.. 502 751-5516
209 Altra Dr Clarksville (47129) *(G-2009)*

Big Cone Inc.. 812 424-1416
102 W Franklin St Evansville (47710) *(G-3931)*

Big Creek LLC.. 812 876-0835
8636 W Mount Carmel Rd Gosport (47433) *(G-6283)*

Big Dipper Inc.. 317 272-6202
240 Production Dr Avon (46123) *(G-508)*

Big Dog Adhesives LLC.. 574 350-2237
435 Harrison St Elkhart (46516) *(G-3224)*

Big Guy Signs LLC.. 317 780-6000
5575 Elmwood Ave Ste C Indianapolis (46203) *(G-7623)*

Big Inch Fabricators Cnstr Inc.. 765 245-9353
6127 W Us Highway 36 Montezuma (47862) *(G-12081)*

Big Picture Data Imaging LLC.. 812 235-0202
608 N 13th St Terre Haute (47807) *(G-15553)*

Big Red, Indianapolis Also Called: Brama Inc *(G-7671)*

Big Red Liquors Inc.. 812 339-9552
435 S Walnut St Bloomington (47401) *(G-806)*

Big Shot Outfitters LLC.. 317 736-4867
2777 N Morton St Franklin (46131) *(G-5716)*

Big Stick Software.. 812 867-0694
3415 E Boonville New Harmony Rd Evansville (47725) *(G-3932)*

Bigasspizzacutter.com, Indianapolis Also Called: Tgf Enterprises LLC *(G-9585)*

Bigg Dawg Construction LLC.. 317 506-1436
3330 N Bancroft St Indianapolis (46218) *(G-7624)*

Bike Jerseys .com, Bloomington Also Called: Best Bicycle Inc *(G-804)*

Bikes-N-Trikes Incorporated.. 317 835-4544
6597 W 300 N Boggstown (46110) *(G-1072)*

Bilbees Service and Supply Inc.. 317 895-8288
8777 E 16th St Indianapolis (46219) *(G-7625)*

Bilfinger Airvac Water Technologies Inc.. 574 223-3980
4217 N Old Us 31 Rochester (46975) *(G-14279)*

Bill Banner Signs.. 765 209-2642
10697 N 600 E Falmouth (46127) *(G-4415)*

Bill's Garage & Hot Rod Parts, Lafayette Also Called: Bills Gar & Auto Refinishing *(G-10537)*

Bills Furniture.. 317 695-8347
1509 E Elliston Dr Bloomington (47401) *(G-807)*

Bills Gar & Auto Refinishing.. 765 296-4978
5219 S 900 E Lafayette (47905) *(G-10537)*

Bills Industries LLC.. 765 629-0227
7794 S 175 W Milroy (46156) *(G-11821)*

Bills International LLC.. 260 226-6004
3330 S Anthony Blvd Fort Wayne (46806) *(G-4800)*

Bills Pallets, Cloverdale Also Called: Billy D Snider *(G-2083)*

Bills Printing.. 765 962-7674
1310 Nw 5th St Richmond (47374) *(G-14097)*

Billy D Snider.. 765 795-6426
294 Bubble Loo Rd Cloverdale (46120) *(G-2083)*

Billy R Phillips.. 317 828-5058
1844 Winton Ave Indianapolis (46224) *(G-7626)*

Billy R Ransom.. 812 897-5921
665 Heritage Ln Boonville (47601) *(G-1082)*

Billy R Ransom Logging, Boonville Also Called: Billy R Ransom *(G-1082)*

Biltz Signs.. 574 594-2703
5843 E Mckenna Rd Warsaw (46582) *(G-16320)*

Bimbo Bakeries Usa Inc.. 317 570-1741
6935 Lake Plaza Dr Ste D Indianapolis (46220) *(G-7627)*

Bimbo Bakeries USA, Inc, Indianapolis Also Called: Bimbo Bakeries Usa Inc *(G-7627)*

Binarie, Greenwood Also Called: Binarie LLC *(G-6676)*

Binarie LLC.. 317 496-8836
863 Silverleaf Dr Greenwood (46143) *(G-6676)*

Bingo Bugle.. 765 348-2859
2301 N 100 E Hartford City (47348) *(G-7062)*

Bio Harness Shop.. 812 486-2919
5913 E 350 N Montgomery (47558) *(G-12087)*

Bio-Alternative LLC.. 765 793-5731
11778 S 600 W Covington (47932) *(G-2527)*

Bio-Response Solutions Inc.. 317 386-3500
200 Colin Ct Danville (46122) *(G-2807)*

Biodot of Indiana Inc.. 812 945-0915
3081 Autumn Hill Trl New Albany (47150) *(G-12701)*

Biodyne-Midwest LLC.. 888 970-0955
3850 Concept Ct Ste 101 Fort Wayne (46808) *(G-4801)*

Biodyne-Usa, Fort Wayne Also Called: Biodyne-Midwest LLC *(G-4801)*

Biokorf LLC.. 765 727-0782
1008 Ravinia Rd West Lafayette (47906) *(G-16565)*

Biologics Modular LLC.. 317 626-4093
1533 E Northfield Dr Ste 600 Brownsburg (46112) *(G-1350)*

Biomedix-Inc.. 812 355-7000
3895 W Vernal Pike Bloomington (47404) *(G-808)*

Biomet.. 574 551-8959
320 Hepler Dr Warsaw (46580) *(G-16321)*

Biomet, Warsaw Also Called: Biomet Sports Medicine LLC *(G-16328)*

Biomet, Inc.. 574 371-3760
56 E Bell Dr Warsaw (46582) *(G-16322)*

Biomet Inc (HQ).. 574 267-6639
345 E Main St Warsaw (46580) *(G-16323)*

Biomet Biologics LLC.. 574 267-2038
56 E Bell Dr Warsaw (46582) *(G-16324)*

Biomet Europe Ltd.. 574 267-2038
56 E Bell Dr Warsaw (46582) *(G-16325)*

Biomet Leasing Inc.. 574 267-6639
56 E Bell Dr Warsaw (46582) *(G-16326)*

Biomet Orthopedics LLC.. 574 267-6639
56 E Bell Dr Warsaw (46582) *(G-16327)*

Biomet Sports Medicine LLC.. 574 267-6639
56 E Bell Dr Warsaw (46581) *(G-16328)*

Biomet Trauma LLC.. 574 267-6639
56 E Bell Dr Warsaw (46582) *(G-16329)*

Biomet US Reconstruction LLC.. 800 348-9500
56 E Bell Dr Warsaw (46582) *(G-16330)*

Bionic Prosthetics & Orthotics, Merrillville Also Called: Bionic Prsthtics Orthtics Grou *(G-11488)*

Bionic Prosthetics and Ortho.. 219 791-9200
3130a Windsor Ct Elkhart (46514) *(G-3225)*

Bionic Prosthetics and Ortho.. 765 838-8222
5 Executive Dr Ste D-2 Lafayette (47905) *(G-10538)*

Bionic Prosthetics and Ortho.. 219 221-6119
1200 S Woodland Ave Ste A Michigan City (46360) *(G-11582)*

Bionic Prosthetics and Ortho.. 219 791-9200
1101 Glendale Blvd Valparaiso (46383) *(G-15914)*

Bionic Prsthtics Orthtics Grou (PA).. 219 791-9200
8695 Connecticut St Ste E Merrillville (46410) *(G-11488)*

Bionic Prsthtics Orthtics Grou.. 219 940-3104
3803 E Lincoln Hwy Merrillville (46410) *(G-11489)*

Bionode LLC.. 317 292-7686
7987 Clearwater Pkwy Indianapolis (46240) *(G-7628)*

Biopoly LLC.. 260 999-6135
7136 Gettysburg Pike Fort Wayne (46804) *(G-4802)*

Biosafe Engineering LLC.. 317 858-8099
5750 W 80th St Indianapolis (46278) *(G-7629)*

Bioscience Vaccines Inc.. 765 464-5890
1425 Innovation Pl West Lafayette (47906) *(G-16566)*

Biota Biosciences Inc.. 765 702-3744
16239 Wagner Rd Cambridge City (47327) *(G-1491)*

Biotta Juices, Fishers Also Called: Caj Food Products Inc *(G-4481)*

Birch and Stitch LLC.. 317 353-7786
1701 Redbay Dr Indianapolis (46234) *(G-7630)*

Birch Candle Company LLC.. 765 296-9425
731 S St Dayton (47941) *(G-2837)*

Birch Wood.. 260 432-0011
8151 Glencarin Blvd Fort Wayne (46804) *(G-4803)*

Bird and Cleaver LLC.. 260 579-2799
4036 Fernbank Dr Fort Wayne (46815) *(G-4804)*

Bird Publishing Company.. 219 462-6330
1600 Edgewater Beach Rd Valparaiso (46383) *(G-15915)*

Birdeye Inc.. 812 886-0598
483 N Mount Zion Rd Vincennes (47591) *(G-16115)*

Birds Nest Inc.. 574 247-0201
421 E University Dr Granger (46530) *(G-6337)*

Bishop Lifting Products Inc.. 260 478-4700
3122 Engle Rd Fort Wayne (46809) *(G-4805)*

ALPHABETIC SECTION — Blue Flame

Bishop Lifting Products Inc 317 634-2545
5760 Dividend Rd Indianapolis (46241) *(G-7631)*

Bishop Repair 812 523-3246
4514 S County Road 700 E Crothersville (47229) *(G-2637)*

Bison Coach LLC 574 658-4161
1002 N Old State Road 15 Milford (46542) *(G-11787)*

Bison Horse Trailers LLC 574 658-4161
804 S Higbee St Milford (46542) *(G-11788)*

Bittersweet LLC 317 254-0677
1912 Broad Ripple Ave Indianapolis (46220) *(G-7632)*

Bituminous Materials & Sup LP 317 228-8203
5400 W 86th St Indianapolis (46268) *(G-7633)*

Bivettes 219 949-1742
3636 W 19th Ave Gary (46404) *(G-5900)*

Bixlers Logging, Lexington Also Called: Keith Bixler *(G-10978)*

Bizcard 317 436-8649
1253 N Blue Spruce Ct Greenfield (46140) *(G-6471)*

Bizness As Usual Pubg LLC 463 701-6433
3524 Bodelva Ln Indianapolis (46228) *(G-7634)*

BJ Corporation of Indiana LLC 317 507-6672
3605 Commercial Dr Indianapolis (46222) *(G-7635)*

Bjh Enterprises LLC 812 655-4544
890 Rudolph Way Greendale (47025) *(G-6440)*

Bk Royston Publishing LLC 502 802-5385
3117 Wooded Way Jeffersonville (47130) *(G-9943)*

Bkb Custom Cabinetry LLC 317 439-9427
5055 Oakridge Dr Mooresville (46158) *(G-12195)*

Bkb Manufacturing Inc 260 982-8524
607 S Wabash Rd North Manchester (46962) *(G-13229)*

Black & Decker (us) Inc 860 225-5111
10475 Crosspoint Blvd Ste 400 Indianapolis (46256) *(G-7636)*

Black Acre Brewing Company LLC 317 207-6266
5632 E Washington St Indianapolis (46219) *(G-7637)*

Black and Gold Energy LLC 812 618-6744
514 Se 1st St Evansville (47713) *(G-3933)*

Black Bear Recrtl Vehicles, Middlebury Also Called: Grand Design Rv LLC *(G-11719)*

Black Beauty Mining Div, Lynnville Also Called: Peabody Midwest Mining LLC *(G-11192)*

Black Dog Printing LLC 812 955-0577
711 S 9th St Richmond (47374) *(G-14098)*

Black Equipment Company S Inc 812 477-6481
1187 Burch Dr Evansville (47725) *(G-3934)*

Black Gold Ventures Ind LLC 260 820-0771
2829 E State Road 124 Bluffton (46714) *(G-1029)*

Black Hustle Holdings Corp 800 988-7067
838 N Delaware St Ste 191090 Indianapolis (46204) *(G-7638)*

Black Jewell Popcorn, Columbus Also Called: LLC Black Jewell *(G-2344)*

Black Lavish Essentials LLC 800 214-8664
8888 Keystone Xing Ste 1300 Indianapolis (46240) *(G-7639)*

Black Panther Mining LLC 812 745-2920
12661 N Agri Care Rd Oaktown (47561) *(G-13325)*

Black Plate Catering 317 255-8030
6033 Moon Shadow Dr Indianapolis (46259) *(G-7640)*

Black Rose Pastries LLC 773 708-3650
1315 Marshall Pl Gary (46404) *(G-5901)*

Black Swan Vapors LLC 317 645-5210
118 W State St Pendleton (46064) *(G-13526)*

Blackbird 812 944-0799
1636 Slate Run Rd New Albany (47150) *(G-12702)*

Blackerby & Associates 812 216-2370
444 Persimmon Dr Seymour (47274) *(G-14633)*

Blackfoot Powder Coating 812 531-9315
5729 N State Road 59 Brazil (47834) *(G-1134)*

Blackmon Metal Fabrication LLC 346 254-9500
840 E 44th Ave Gary (46409) *(G-5902)*

Blackpoint Distribution Co LLC 260 414-9096
15718 Viberg Rd Leo (46765) *(G-10964)*

Blackpoint Engineering LLC 765 884-4100
494 W Us Highway 6 Ligonier (46767) *(G-11006)*

Blackthorn Design Studio, Columbus Also Called: Debra Richard *(G-2281)*

Blackwell Limestone, Norman Also Called: Justin Blackwell *(G-13203)*

Blackwood Solutions LLC 812 676-8770
1901 S Liberty Dr Bloomington (47403) *(G-809)*

Blair Industries LLC 765 215-2735
1900 W Mt Pleasant Blvd Ste A Muncie (47302) *(G-12354)*

Blaney Sealcoating 219 241-3622
6752 W Forrester Rd La Porte (46350) *(G-10389)*

Blasdel Enterprises, Greensburg Also Called: Blasdel Enterprises Inc *(G-6581)*

Blasdel Enterprises Inc 812 663-3213
495 W Mckee St Greensburg (47240) *(G-6581)*

Blasted Works 574 583-3211
214 N Main St Monticello (47960) *(G-12138)*

Bleacherpro LLC 813 394-5316
4703 Collbran Ct Fort Wayne (46835) *(G-4806)*

Blehm Plastics 317 736-4090
2140 Earlywood Dr Franklin (46131) *(G-5717)*

Blended LLC 317 268-8005
148 1/2 S Washington St Danville (46122) *(G-2808)*

Blessed Humbled Beginnings LLC 219 255-3820
5164 E 81st Ave Ste 183 Merrillville (46410) *(G-11490)*

Blessing Enterprises Inc 219 736-9800
1420 E 91st Dr Merrillville (46410) *(G-11491)*

Blessing Tool & Die Inc 574 875-1982
24366 County Road 45 Elkhart (46516) *(G-3226)*

Bleu Rooster Designs 317 845-0889
7444 River Highlands Dr Fishers (46038) *(G-4474)*

Bleys Prosthetics & Orthotics 812 704-3894
50 Hancock St Seymour (47274) *(G-14634)*

Blinds At Home LLC 317 489-8133
4709 N Capitol Ave Indianapolis (46208) *(G-7641)*

Blinds Plus LLC 812 825-1932
Stanford (47463) *(G-15393)*

Blinkless Power Equipment LLC 317 844-7328
8802 Bash St Ste F Indianapolis (46256) *(G-7642)*

Blitz, Jeffersonville Also Called: Blitz Manufacturing Co Ind *(G-9944)*

Blitz Manufacturing Co Ind 812 284-2548
263 America Pl Jeffersonville (47130) *(G-9944)*

Blocksom & Co 219 878-4458
110 Menke Rd Trail Creek (46360) *(G-15835)*

Blocksom & Co (PA) 219 878-4455
110 Menke Rd Trail Creek (46360) *(G-15836)*

Blondies Cookies Inc (PA) 765 628-3978
100 W Main St Greentown (46936) *(G-6645)*

Bloom Pharmaceutical 260 615-2633
2831 Union Chapel Rd Fort Wayne (46845) *(G-4807)*

Bloomers Woodworking Inc 317 502-9360
1834 N Shortridge Rd Indianapolis (46219) *(G-7643)*

Bloomfield Mfg Co Inc 812 384-4441
46 W Spring St Bloomfield (47424) *(G-740)*

Blooming Bath, Greenfield Also Called: Upanaway LLC *(G-6568)*

Bloomington Asphalt & Cnstr, Bloomington Also Called: Rogers Group Inc *(G-962)*

Bloomington Brewing Co, Bloomington Also Called: Lennies Inc *(G-910)*

Bloomington Con Surfaces Corp 812 345-0011
3650 S Kingsbury Ave Bloomington (47401) *(G-810)*

Bloomington Cookies LLC 812 668-7779
1155 S College Mall Rd Ste B Bloomington (47401) *(G-811)*

Bloomington Crushed Stone, Bloomington Also Called: Rogers Group Inc *(G-961)*

Bloomington Letter Shop 812 824-6363
5717 S Rogers St Bloomington (47403) *(G-812)*

Bloomington Stitchery LLC 208 371-9598
325 W Persimmon Ct Bloomington (47403) *(G-813)*

Bludot Inc 574 277-2306
4335 Meghan Beeler Ct South Bend (46628) *(G-14959)*

Blue Bell Mattress Company LLC 260 749-9393
3434 S Maplecrest Rd Fort Wayne (46803) *(G-4808)*

Blue Buffalo Company Ltd 203 665-3500
4748 W Industries Rd Richmond (47374) *(G-14099)*

Blue Byte Tech Solutions LLC 574 903-5637
28571 County Road 16 Elkhart (46516) *(G-3227)*

Blue Creek Trail Map Co 765 455-9867
3506 Hawthorne Ln Kokomo (46902) *(G-10239)*

Blue Dolphin Ffy LLC 773 255-3591
3348 169th St Ste G137 Hammond (46323) *(G-6887)*

Blue Flame, Madison Also Called: Crestwood Equity Partners LP *(G-11212)*

Blue Grass Chemical Spc LLC (PA) 812 948-1115
895 Industrial Blvd New Albany (47150) *(G-12703)*

Blue Heron Vineyards LLC 812 619-6045
5330 Blue Heron Ln Cannelton (47520) *(G-1533)*

Blue J Logistics LLC 317 721-1784
4859 Leone Dr Indianapolis (46226) *(G-7644)*

Blue Marble Cocktails Inc 888 400-3090
6008 Corporate Way Indianapolis (46278) *(G-7645)*

Blue Moon Oil Company LLC 317 892-2499
10359 N County Road 650 E Brownsburg (46112) *(G-1351)*

Blue Octopus Printing Company 317 247-1997
2431 Directors Row Indianapolis (46241) *(G-7646)*

Blue Pillar Inc 317 723-6601
9025 River Rd Ste 150 Indianapolis (46240) *(G-7647)*

Blue Print Specialties Inc 765 742-6976
1500 Union St Lafayette (47904) *(G-10539)*

Blue Print University Inc 317 446-8715
5326 W 16th St Speedway (46224) *(G-15333)*

Blue Ribbon Products Inc 317 972-7970
8188 Allison Ave Indianapolis (46268) *(G-7648)*

Blue Ring Stencils LLC 260 203-5461
2248 Research Dr Fort Wayne (46808) *(G-4809)*

Blue River Farm Supply Inc 812 364-6675
14485 Greene St Ne Palmyra (47164) *(G-13478)*

Blue River Printing Inc 317 392-3676
55 E Washington St Shelbyville (46176) *(G-14736)*

Blue River Services Inc 812 738-2437
101 N Mulberry St Corydon (47112) *(G-2488)*

Blue River Stamping Inc 317 395-5600
600 Northridge Dr Shelbyville (46176) *(G-14737)*

Blue River Timber LLC 812 291-0411
2997 Gethsemane Church Rd Evansville (47712) *(G-3935)*

Blue River Wood Products, Salem *Also Called: American Stave Company LLC (G-14471)*

Blue Sky Life Stories LLC 574 298-1254
53641 Michael Ct Elkhart (46514) *(G-3228)*

Blue Sun Ventures Ltd 317 426-0001
525 S Meridian St Indianapolis (46225) *(G-7649)*

Bluehive Health LLC 260 217-5328
1690 Broadway Ste 550 Fort Wayne (46802) *(G-4810)*

Blueprint Restoration LLC 301 730-4727
3320 Montgomery Dr Indianapolis (46227) *(G-7650)*

Bluewater Thermal Solutions, South Bend *Also Called: Harbor Metals LLC (G-15058)*

Bluffton Motor Works LLC (HQ) 260 827-2200
410 E Spring St Bluffton (46714) *(G-1030)*

Bluffton Plant, Bluffton *Also Called: Metaldyne M&A Bluffton LLC (G-1042)*

Bluffton Rubber 260 824-4501
810 Lancaster St Bluffton (46714) *(G-1031)*

Blume Metal Sales LLC 765 490-0600
695 W State Road 18 Brookston (47923) *(G-1308)*

Blumenau Alpacas 219 713-6171
19950 Austin St Lowell (46356) *(G-11156)*

Blumling Design & Graphics Inc 765 477-7446
3228 Olympia Dr Ste C Lafayette (47909) *(G-10540)*

Blush and Bobby Pins LLC 317 789-5166
600 E Carmel Dr Ste 249 Carmel (46032) *(G-1568)*

Blush Bath Bombs By Amor 219 313-3993
6650 Rohrman Rd Crown Point (46307) *(G-2657)*

Blush Salon Boutique 317 523-1635
11631 Maple St Fishers (46038) *(G-4475)*

Blythes Sport Shop Inc (PA) 219 924-4403
138 N Broad St Griffith (46319) *(G-6795)*

Blythes Sport Shop Inc 219 476-0026
2810 Calumet Ave Valparaiso (46383) *(G-15916)*

Bm Creations Inc 219 922-8935
1313 E Main St Griffith (46319) *(G-6796)*

BMC Marketing Corp 260 693-2193
300 E Pleasant St Churubusco (46723) *(G-1973)*

Bmg Inc 812 437-3643
10334 Hedden Rd Evansville (47725) *(G-3936)*

Bmi Refractory Services Inc 219 885-2209
201 Mississippi St Gary (46402) *(G-5903)*

Bmk Investments Inc 574 282-2538
3615 W Mcgill St South Bend (46628) *(G-14960)*

Bmk Printing, South Bend *Also Called: Bmk Investments Inc (G-14960)*

Bml Graphics LLC 317 984-5500
4484 S State Road 19 Tipton (46072) *(G-15767)*

Bmr Group, Kimmell *Also Called: Boyd Machine and Repair Co (G-10169)*

Bo-Mar Industries Inc 317 899-1240
3838 S Arlington Ave Indianapolis (46203) *(G-7651)*

Bo-Witt Products Inc 812 526-5561
500 N Walnut St Edinburgh (46124) *(G-3069)*

Boarder Magic By J & A 317 545-4401
902 W Banta Rd Indianapolis (46217) *(G-7652)*

Boardworks Inc 219 464-8111
369 E Us Highway 30 Valparaiso (46383) *(G-15917)*

Boat Lift Guys Inc 260 667-3057
207 Hoosier Dr Ste 1 Angola (46703) *(G-235)*

Boat Works 574 457-4034
6348 E Trusdell Ave Syracuse (46567) *(G-15457)*

Boat Worx of Monticello 574 297-7961
624 S Main St Monticello (47960) *(G-12139)*

Bob Prescott 219 736-7804
101 W 78th Pl Valparaiso (46385) *(G-15918)*

Bobby Little Creations 219 313-5102
610 W Joliet St Crown Point (46307) *(G-2658)*

Bobcat Armament and Mfg LLC 317 699-6127
1640 E State Road 44 Ste A Shelbyville (46176) *(G-14738)*

Bobcat Steel LLC 317 699-6127
1640 E State Road 44 Shelbyville (46176) *(G-14739)*

Bobilyn Printing 219 926-7087
615 E 900 N Westville (46391) *(G-16756)*

Bobs Welding & Repair LLC 765 744-4192
6447 W 250 S Farmland (47340) *(G-4422)*

Bock Engineering Company Inc 574 522-3191
4307 Wyland Dr Elkhart (46516) *(G-3229)*

Bock Industries Inc 574 295-8070
29851 County Road 20 Elkhart (46517) *(G-3230)*

Body Panels Co 812 962-6262
1101 N Governor St Evansville (47711) *(G-3937)*

BODY PANELS CO, Evansville *Also Called: Body Panels Co (G-3937)*

Bodycare Bodega LLC 317 643-3562
3960 Southeastern Ave Indianapolis (46203) *(G-7653)*

Bodycare Bodega, The, Indianapolis *Also Called: Bodycare Bodega LLC (G-7653)*

Bodycote Testing Group Inc 219 882-4283
2090 E 15th Ave Gary (46402) *(G-5904)*

Bodycote Thermal Proc Inc 574 295-2491
908 County Road 1 N Elkhart (46514) *(G-3231)*

Bodycote Thermal Proc Inc 260 423-1691
3715 E Washington Blvd Fort Wayne (46803) *(G-4811)*

Bodycote Thermal Proc Inc 812 662-0500
1930 N Montgomery Rd Greensburg (47240) *(G-6582)*

Bodycote Thermal Proc Inc 317 924-4321
500 W 21st St Indianapolis (46202) *(G-7654)*

Boe Knows Mold 260 760-7136
488 Courtney Dr New Haven (46774) *(G-12894)*

Boehrnger Mnnheim Phrmctcals C 317 521-2000
9115 Hague Rd Indianapolis (46256) *(G-7655)*

Boeing, Gary *Also Called: Boeing Company (G-5905)*

Boeing, Indianapolis *Also Called: Boeing Company (G-7656)*

Boeing Company 219 977-4354
6309 Airport Rd Gary (46406) *(G-5905)*

Boeing Company 317 484-1363
2745 S Hoffman Rd Indianapolis (46241) *(G-7656)*

Boeke Road Baptist Church Inc 812 479-5342
2601 S Boeke Rd Evansville (47714) *(G-3938)*

Boezeman Enterprises Inc 219 345-2732
9941 N 1200 W Demotte (46310) *(G-2912)*

Boezeman Signs Graphic Design, Demotte *Also Called: Boezeman Enterprises Inc (G-2912)*

Bofrebo Industries Inc 219 322-1550
1145 Birch Dr Schererville (46375) *(G-14516)*

Boger Cabinetry & Design Inc 317 588-6954
9721 Kincaid Dr Fishers (46037) *(G-4476)*

ALPHABETIC SECTION

Boggs Fabg Solutions Inc... 317 852-5107
3902 W Offield Monument Rd Crawfordsville (47933) *(G-2548)*

Boice Manufacturing Inc... 317 773-2100
1699 S 8th St Noblesville (46060) *(G-13044)*

Boilers Inc... 765 742-5855
2605 Yeager Rd West Lafayette (47906) *(G-16567)*

Bold Solutions LLC.. 708 740-8577
7452 Hendricks St Merrillville (46410) *(G-11492)*

Bolinger Machine LLC... 317 241-2989
23 N Alton Ave Indianapolis (46222) *(G-7657)*

Bollhoff Inc (DH)... 260 347-3903
2705 Marion Dr Kendallville (46755) *(G-10097)*

Bollock Interprises Inc.. 765 448-6000
900 Farabee Ct Lafayette (47905) *(G-10541)*

Bollygood Inc.. 317 215-5616
1075 Broad Ripple Ave Pmb 334 Indianapolis (46220) *(G-7658)*

Bolstra LLC.. 317 660-9131
12400 N Meridian St Ste 120 Carmel (46032) *(G-1569)*

Bolt Custom Trucks, Fort Wayne Also Called: Gracie Industries LLC *(G-5032)*

Bolttech Mannings Inc... 219 310-8389
1170 Arrowhead Ct Crown Point (46307) *(G-2659)*

Bolttech Mannings, Inc., Crown Point Also Called: Bolttech Mannings Inc *(G-2659)*

Bolttech-Mannings Inc... 219 682-5864
1403 Boca Lago Dr Valparaiso (46383) *(G-15919)*

BOM Corporation... 765 361-0382
3370 E State Road 32 Crawfordsville (47933) *(G-2549)*

Bomarko, Plymouth Also Called: Bomarko Inc *(G-13758)*

Bomarko Inc (PA)... 574 936-9901
1955 N Oak Dr Plymouth (46563) *(G-13758)*

Bombtrack Fabrication... 317 286-7711
45 Mardale Dr Ste G Brownsburg (46112) *(G-1352)*

Bombtrack Fabrication LLC.. 317 518-9509
11058 Mallard Way Indianapolis (46278) *(G-7659)*

Bonaccorsi Wine Company LLC..................................... 310 777-3704
12586 Pembrooke Cir Carmel (46032) *(G-1570)*

Bonar Inc... 260 636-7430
307 Woods Dr Albion (46701) *(G-19)*

Bonar Well Drilling, Albion Also Called: Bonar Inc *(G-19)*

Bondline Adhesives Inc.. 812 423-4651
500 N Woods Ave Evansville (47712) *(G-3939)*

Bonnell Aluminum Inc.. 815 351-6802
508 Wilson St Kentland (47951) *(G-10157)*

Bonnell Aluminum Elkhart Inc.. 574 262-4685
2551 County Road 10 W Elkhart (46514) *(G-3232)*

Bonnell Grain Handling Inc.. 574 595-7827
3191 E 800 S Star City (46985) *(G-15396)*

Bonner & Associates... 317 571-1911
12310 Windsor Dr Carmel (46033) *(G-1571)*

Bontrager Welding... 260 463-8950
3035 W 100 S # B Lagrange (46761) *(G-10730)*

Bonzell Combs.. 872 248-4123
9445 Indianapolis Blvd Highland (46322) *(G-7125)*

Boogie Bonez Bbq, Noblesville Also Called: Shawn Ferguson *(G-13174)*

Book of US LLC.. 331 256-5953
8041 Pine Island Ct Apt B38 Crown Point (46307) *(G-2660)*

Boomerang Kidz Clothing... 574 992-2233
825 18th St Logansport (46947) *(G-11063)*

Boomerang Solutions... 812 822-2125
416 S Washington St Bloomington (47401) *(G-814)*

Boomers.. 765 741-4031
2627 S Walnut St Muncie (47302) *(G-12355)*

Boondocks Logging LLC.. 812 247-3363
12471 Sanders Ln Shoals (47581) *(G-14904)*

Boone County Electric Inc.. 765 482-1430
2607 Viceroy Ln Lebanon (46052) *(G-10880)*

Booth Signs Inc... 812 376-7446
1307 12th St Columbus (47201) *(G-2227)*

Bootmakers LLC... 765 412-7243
2550 Kent Ave Ste 2 West Lafayette (47906) *(G-16568)*

Bootz Industries, Evansville Also Called: Bootz Manufacturing Co LLC *(G-3940)*

Bootz Industries, Evansville Also Called: Bootz Manufacturing Co LLC *(G-3941)*

Bootz Manufacturing Co LLC... 812 423-5019
1600 N 1st Ave Evansville (47710) *(G-3940)*

Bootz Manufacturing Co LLC (HQ)................................. 812 423-5401
1400 Park St Evansville (47710) *(G-3941)*

Bootz Manufacturing Co LLC... 812 425-4646
2301 W Maryland St Evansville (47712) *(G-3942)*

Bootz Plumbing, Evansville Also Called: Bootz Manufacturing Co LLC *(G-3942)*

Border Mgic By Wlden Entps Inc................................... 317 628-2314
2532 W Morris St Indianapolis (46221) *(G-7660)*

Bordners Aut Serv... 260 483-4084
3510 Eleanor Ave Apt A Fort Wayne (46805) *(G-4812)*

Bordners Truck Repair & Algnmt, Cutler Also Called: CD & Ws Bordner Entps Inc *(G-2783)*

Borgwarner (pds) Peru Inc (DH)..................................... 765 472-2002
588 W 7th St Peru (46970) *(G-13568)*

Borgwarner Noblesville LLC... 765 451-0400
2151 E Lincoln Rd Kokomo (46902) *(G-10240)*

Borgwarner Pds (indiana) Inc (HQ)................................ 765 778-6696
13975 Borgwarner Dr Noblesville (46060) *(G-13045)*

Borgwarner Power Drive System, Noblesville Also Called: Borgwarner Pds (indiana) Inc *(G-13045)*

Borgwarner Propulsion II LLC.. 765 236-0025
1501 E 200 N Kokomo (46901) *(G-10241)*

Borgwarner Reman Holdings LLC................................. 800 372-5131
600 Corporation Dr Pendleton (46064) *(G-13527)*

Borkholder Building Supply, Nappanee Also Called: Borkholder Corporation *(G-12585)*

Borkholder Corporation (PA)... 574 773-4083
786 Us Highway 6 Nappanee (46550) *(G-12585)*

Borkholder Lavon.. 574 773-3714
492 Us Highway 6 Nappanee (46550) *(G-12586)*

Borkholder Wood Products Inc..................................... 574 546-2613
2060 5th Rd Bremen (46506) *(G-1176)*

Borman Distributing Inc.. 219 713-8523
650 E 119th Pl Crown Point (46307) *(G-2661)*

Borrv Concepts LLC (PA)... 317 405-9121
6420 Cotton Bay Dr N Indianapolis (46254) *(G-7661)*

Bosch Auto Proving Ground, New Carlisle Also Called: Robert Bosch LLC *(G-12845)*

Bosch Automotive, Albion Also Called: Robert Bosch LLC *(G-44)*

Bosch Braking System, New Carlisle Also Called: Robert Bosch LLC *(G-12844)*

Bose Knife Works.. 812 397-5114
7252 N County Road 300 E Shelburn (47879) *(G-14717)*

Boss Battle Games.. 317 875-1446
10202 E Washington St Ste 500 Indianapolis (46229) *(G-7662)*

Boss Industries LLC.. 219 324-7776
1761 Genesis Dr La Porte (46350) *(G-10390)*

Boston Scientific Corp... 951 914-2400
111 Monument Cir Ste 2900 Indianapolis (46204) *(G-7663)*

Boston Scientific Corporation.. 812 829-4877
780 Brookside Dr Spencer (47460) *(G-15340)*

Boston Tool Company Inc... 765 935-6282
800 S 9th St Richmond (47374) *(G-14100)*

Botanic Choice, Hobart Also Called: Indiana Botanic Gardens Inc *(G-7191)*

Bottcher America Corporation....................................... 765 675-4449
717 Industrial Dr Tipton (46072) *(G-15768)*

Botti Stdio Archtctral Arts In (PA).................................. 847 869-5933
1500 Lake St La Porte (46350) *(G-10391)*

Bottom Line Management Inc....................................... 812 944-7388
1410 Johnson Ln Clarksville (47129) *(G-2010)*

Bottom Line Rv, Middlebury Also Called: Jayco Inc *(G-11727)*

Bottom Sign LLC... 812 949-7446
4239 Earnings Way New Albany (47150) *(G-12704)*

Boudoir Lash Parlor LLC... 330 259-5696
1534 Lancashire Ct Indianapolis (46260) *(G-7664)*

Bowell Ty & Michelle, Greendale Also Called: Ty Bowells Farrier Service *(G-6456)*

Bowen Printing Inc.. 574 936-3924
200 S Michigan St Plymouth (46563) *(G-13759)*

Bowers Envelope Company Inc..................................... 317 253-4321
5331 N Tacoma Ave Indianapolis (46220) *(G-7665)*

Bowers Record Sleeve Bag Div, Indianapolis Also Called: Bowers Envelope Company Inc *(G-7665)*

Bowles Mattress Company Inc (PA)............................... 812 288-8614
1220 Watt St Jeffersonville (47130) *(G-9945)*

(PA)=Parent Co (HQ)=Headquarters (DH)=Div Headquarters

Bowman & Bowman Farms Inc — 260 837-4171
4678 County Road 22 Waterloo (46793) *(G-16515)*

Bowman E&M, Petersburg Also Called: Solar Sources Underground LLC *(G-13626)*

Bowmans Hoof Trimming — 574 522-2838
28824 Country Ln Elkhart (46514) *(G-3233)*

Bowmans Tin Shop Inc — 574 936-3234
1576 Hoham Dr Plymouth (46563) *(G-13760)*

Bowmar LLC — 260 747-3121
8000 Bluffton Rd Fort Wayne (46809) *(G-4813)*

Bowsman Tank Co — 260 244-7129
115 W Spencer St Columbia City (46725) *(G-2125)*

Bowtie Woodworks LLC — 765 667-1934
4820 Broadway St Indianapolis (46205) *(G-7666)*

Boy-Conn Printers Incorporated — 219 462-2665
803 Glendale Blvd Valparaiso (46383) *(G-15920)*

Boyce Industries — 708 345-0455
1655 N 500 E Michigan City (46360) *(G-11583)*

Boyce Industries Group LLC — 317 409-3235
5373 W 86th St Indianapolis (46268) *(G-7667)*

Boyd Machine and Repair Co — 260 635-2195
3794 W 50 S Kimmell (46760) *(G-10169)*

Boyd Sign Company — 260 833-2257
495 Lane 298 Crooked Lk Angola (46703) *(G-236)*

Boyer Enterprises Inc — 812 773-3295
12311 Edgewater Dr Evansville (47720) *(G-3943)*

Boyer Machine & Tool Co Inc — 812 379-9581
1080 S Gladstone Ave Columbus (47201) *(G-2228)*

BP Alternative Energy NA Inc — 765 884-1000
91 S 100 E Fowler (47944) *(G-5620)*

BP Wind Energy North Amer Inc — 765 884-1000
91 S 100 E Fowler (47944) *(G-5621)*

Bpac Inc — 317 723-7427
9025 River Rd Ste 150 Indianapolis (46240) *(G-7668)*

Bpc Manufacturing Operation — 574 936-9894
1755 N Oak Dr Plymouth (46563) *(G-13761)*

Bprex Brazil Holding Inc — 812 306-2764
101 Oakley St Evansville (47710) *(G-3944)*

Bprex Closure Systems LLC — 812 424-2904
101 Oakley St Evansville (47710) *(G-3945)*

Bprex Closures LLC (DH) — 812 424-2904
101 Oakley St Evansville (47710) *(G-3946)*

Bprex Closures LLC — 812 867-6671
3245 Kansas Rd Evansville (47725) *(G-3947)*

Bprex Closures LLC — 812 386-1525
889 W Gach Rd Princeton (47670) *(G-13985)*

Bprex Healthcare Packaging Inc — 812 424-2904
101 Oakley St Evansville (47710) *(G-3948)*

BR Tool LLC — 260 452-9487
14310 State Road 101 Harlan (46743) *(G-7050)*

Brackett Heating & AC Inc — 812 476-1138
5233 Old Boonville Hwy Evansville (47715) *(G-3949)*

Brad Bugher — 765 883-8112
360 W Main St Russiaville (46979) *(G-14421)*

Brad Goodman — 765 993-2007
3855 N County Road 550 E Brownsville (47325) *(G-1429)*

Brad Scher — 260 356-1515
1910 William St Huntington (46750) *(G-7302)*

Braden Sutphin Ink Co — 317 352-8781
1340 Sadlier Circle East Dr Indianapolis (46239) *(G-7669)*

Bradford Press Inc — 574 876-3601
302 W 3rd St Mishawaka (46544) *(G-11853)*

Brahm Corporation — 317 502-3133
3555 Sedgemoor Cir Carmel (46032) *(G-1572)*

Braid Den Inc — 260 244-2995
4532 E Park 30 Dr Columbia City (46725) *(G-2126)*

Brainstorm Print, Indianapolis Also Called: Brainstorm Print LLC *(G-7670)*

Brainstorm Print LLC — 317 466-1600
2603 55th Pl Indianapolis (46220) *(G-7670)*

Brake Supply Company Inc (HQ) — 812 467-1000
5501 Foundation Blvd Evansville (47725) *(G-3950)*

Bralin Laser Services Inc — 260 357-6511
2233 County Road 72 Auburn (46706) *(G-370)*

Brama Inc — 317 786-7770
5855 Kopetsky Dr Ste I Indianapolis (46217) *(G-7671)*

Brampton Brick Inc — 812 397-2190
1256 E County Road 950 N Farmersburg (47850) *(G-4416)*

Branch Express Trucking LLC — 574 807-2212
1149 Wilber St South Bend (46628) *(G-14961)*

Brand Prtg & Photo-Litho Co (PA) — 317 921-4095
4793 W Meadow Lake Dr New Palestine (46163) *(G-12933)*

Brand Quick Printing, New Palestine Also Called: Brand Prtg & Photo-Litho Co *(G-12933)*

Brand Restaurant Equipment, Muncie Also Called: Brand Sheet Metal Works Inc *(G-12356)*

Brand Sheet Metal Works Inc — 765 284-5594
907 S Burlington Dr Muncie (47302) *(G-12356)*

Branded By Jdh, Warsaw Also Called: Aardvark Graphics *(G-16307)*

Brandenberger Door Mfg — 260 657-1494
14633 Antwerp Rd Grabill (46741) *(G-6289)*

Branding Stitch LLC — 765 468-8463
104 N Main St Ste 2 Farmland (47340) *(G-4423)*

Brandt's, Aurora Also Called: Fred Brandt Co *(G-444)*

Brandwise LLC — 317 574-0066
16170 Sundew Dr Noblesville (46062) *(G-13046)*

Brandywine Creek — 317 868-0563
12524 Southeastern Ave Indianapolis (46259) *(G-7672)*

Brandywine Creek Vnyrds Wnery — 317 403-5669
8437 W 1200 N New Palestine (46163) *(G-12934)*

Brangene LLC — 317 203-9172
815 Walton Dr Plainfield (46168) *(G-13662)*

Braniff Game Birds — 574 784-3919
67510 Mulberry Rd Lakeville (46536) *(G-10788)*

Branik Inc — 260 467-1808
3626 Illinois Rd Fort Wayne (46804) *(G-4814)*

Brasilia Press Inc — 574 262-9700
2911 Moose Trl Elkhart (46514) *(G-3234)*

Brass Products Division, Albion Also Called: Parker-Hannifin Corporation *(G-40)*

Bratco Inc — 812 536-4071
502 N 2nd St Holland (47541) *(G-7214)*

Braun Companies LLC — 765 332-2084
7813 E State Road 38 New Castle (47362) *(G-12852)*

Braun Corporation — 574 946-7413
627 W 11th St Winamac (46996) *(G-16856)*

Braun Corporation (DH) — 574 946-6153
631 W 11th St Winamac (46996) *(G-16857)*

Braun Motor Works Inc (PA) — 574 205-0102
144 S 100 W Winamac (46996) *(G-16858)*

Braunability, Winamac Also Called: Braun Corporation *(G-16857)*

Bray Logging — 812 863-7947
6399 E State Road 58 Owensburg (47453) *(G-13459)*

Brayden Shedron — 765 480-7675
403 N Davis St Walton (46994) *(G-16281)*

Brazeway LLC — 317 392-2533
1109 Lincoln St Shelbyville (46176) *(G-14740)*

Brazil Auto & Electric — 812 442-0060
1106 N Harrison St Brazil (47834) *(G-1135)*

Brazil Industrial Coatings, Brazil Also Called: P P G Industries Inc *(G-1160)*

Brazing Preforms LLC — 317 705-6455
15402 Stony Creek Way Noblesville (46060) *(G-13047)*

BRC Rubber & Plastics Inc — 260 827-0871
810 Lancaster St Bluffton (46714) *(G-1032)*

BRC Rubber & Plastics Inc — 260 203-5300
589 S Main St Churubusco (46723) *(G-1974)*

BRC Rubber & Plastics Inc (PA) — 260 693-2171
1029a W State Blvd Fort Wayne (46808) *(G-4815)*

BRC Rubber & Plastics Inc — 260 894-4121
1497 Gerber St Ligonier (46767) *(G-11007)*

BRC Rubber & Plastics Inc — 765 728-8510
623 W Monroe St Montpelier (47359) *(G-12177)*

BRC Rubber Group, Fort Wayne Also Called: BRC Rubber & Plastics Inc *(G-4815)*

BRC Rubber Plastics Inc — 260 894-7263
502 N Cavin St Ligonier (46767) *(G-11008)*

Bread Box Bake Shop, Shipshewana Also Called: Shipshewana Bread Box Corp *(G-14887)*

Breadmansrt Llc — 219 238-9169
3500 W 22nd Ave Gary (46404) *(G-5906)*

ALPHABETIC SECTION — Bristol-Myers Squibb Company

Breast Diagnostic Center, Fort Wayne *Also Called: Fort Wyne Rdlgy Assn Fundation (G-5003)*

Breath of Life, Westfield *Also Called: Breath of Life Home Medical Equipment and Respiratory Systems Inc (G-16671)*

Breath of Life Home Medical Equipment and Respiratory Systems Inc 317 896-3048
430 Alpha Dr Ste 100 Westfield (46074) *(G-16671)*

Breckenridge Recrtl Pk Trlrs, Elkhart *Also Called: Damon Corporation (G-3285)*

Bredensteiner & Associates 317 921-2226
1920 Dr Martin Luther King Jr St Ste A Indianapolis (46202) *(G-7673)*

Bredensteiner Imaging Inc 317 921-1900
1920 Dr Martin Luther King Jr St Ste A Indianapolis (46202) *(G-7674)*

Breg Inc 760 505-0521
3055 N Meridian St Indianapolis (46208) *(G-7675)*

Breg Inc 317 559-0479
2835 Fortune Cir W Indianapolis (46241) *(G-7676)*

Breiner Company Inc 317 272-2521
259 Production Dr Avon (46123) *(G-509)*

Bremen Castings, Inc., Bremen *Also Called: BCI Solutions Inc (G-1174)*

Bremen Composites LLC 574 546-3791
425 Industrial Dr Bremen (46506) *(G-1177)*

Bremen Corporation (HQ) 574 546-4238
405 Industrial Dr Bremen (46506) *(G-1178)*

Bremen Wire Products, Bremen *Also Called: Kauffman Engineering LLC (G-1201)*

Bremtown Fine Cstm Cbnetry Inc 574 546-2781
1456 State Rd 331 Bremen (46506) *(G-1179)*

Brenco Exotic Woods, Schererville *Also Called: Brenco LLC (G-14517)*

Brenco LLC (PA) 219 844-9570
526 Turnberry Dr Schererville (46375) *(G-14517)*

Brendacurtis Recipe Books LLC 574 216-2261
425 Blue Spring Dr Ste 101 Indianapolis (46239) *(G-7677)*

Brenmeer LLC 260 267-0249
5716 Wald Rd Fort Wayne (46818) *(G-4816)*

Brent Devers 812 657-3786
1207 Washington St Columbus (47201) *(G-2229)*

Brent Morris 812 282-6945
508 Hemlock Rd Jeffersonville (47130) *(G-9946)*

Brethren In Chrst Mdia Mnstrie 574 267-7400
1104 Kings Hwy Winona Lake (46590) *(G-16909)*

Brett Tishner 765 675-2180
213 Armstrong St Tipton (46072) *(G-15769)*

Brewer Machine & Mfg Inc 317 398-3505
1501 Miller Ave Shelbyville (46176) *(G-14741)*

Brewers Contg & Wdwrk LLC 812 620-8961
4901 S Eastern School Rd Pekin (47165) *(G-13512)*

Briali Vineyards, Fremont *Also Called: Briali Vineyards LLC (G-5812)*

Briali Vineyards LLC 260 316-5156
102 W State Road 120 Fremont (46737) *(G-5812)*

Brian Bex Report Inc 765 489-5566
100 N Woodpecker Rd Hagerstown (47346) *(G-6834)*

Brian Newton 812 200-3149
58 E Main St Ste 4 # 483 Nashville (47448) *(G-12663)*

Brian T Klem 812 342-4080
4270 W Jonathan Moore Pike Columbus (47201) *(G-2230)*

Brianza USA Corp 574 855-9520
3503 Cooper Dr Elkhart (46514) *(G-3235)*

Brick 812 522-8636
309 Walnut St Jonesville (47247) *(G-10082)*

Brick Street Embroidery 574 453-3729
205 E Prairie St Leesburg (46538) *(G-10951)*

Brickhouse Electronics LLC 212 643-7449
5718 W 79th St Indianapolis (46278) *(G-7678)*

Brickhouse Security, Indianapolis *Also Called: Brickhouse Electronics LLC (G-7678)*

Brickworks Supply Center LLC 317 786-9208
430 W Carmel Dr Carmel (46032) *(G-1573)*

Brickyard Crossing 317 492-6573
2572 Moller Rd Indianapolis (46224) *(G-7679)*

Brics 317 257-5757
901 E 64th St Indianapolis (46220) *(G-7680)*

Bridgestone Ret Operations LLC 812 332-2119
219 S Walnut St Bloomington (47404) *(G-815)*

Bridgestone Ret Operations LLC 260 447-2596
651 Country Side Dr Columbia City (46725) *(G-2127)*

Bridgestone Ret Operations LLC 812 477-8818
4611 Washington Ave Evansville (47714) *(G-3951)*

Bridgestone Ret Operations LLC 812 423-4451
4401 N 1st Ave Evansville (47710) *(G-3952)*

Bridgestone Ret Operations LLC 317 846-6516
1300 E 86th St Ste 2 Indianapolis (46240) *(G-7681)*

Bridgestone Ret Operations LLC 317 849-9120
6020 E 82nd St Ofc Indianapolis (46250) *(G-7682)*

Bridgestone Ret Operations LLC 765 447-5041
2415 Sagamore Pkwy S Lafayette (47905) *(G-10542)*

Bridgestone Ret Operations LLC 317 773-2761
249 N 10th St Noblesville (46060) *(G-13048)*

Bridgestone Ret Operations LLC 812 232-9478
940 Wabash Ave Terre Haute (47807) *(G-15554)*

Bridgeview Eye Partners, Wabash *Also Called: Midwest Eye Services LLC (G-16201)*

Bridgeview Manufacturing LLC 574 970-0116
5321 Beck Dr Elkhart (46516) *(G-3236)*

Bridon American Oakland, Oakland City *Also Called: Bridon-American Corporation (G-13320)*

Bridon-American Corporation 812 749-3115
11698 E 200 S Oakland City (47660) *(G-13320)*

Briggs Exploration Prod Co LLC 812 249-0564
4424 Vogel Rd Ste 404 Evansville (47715) *(G-3953)*

Bright Corp 765 642-3114
1313 E Main St Griffith (46319) *(G-6797)*

Bright Line Striping LLC 765 404-1402
1620 N 15th St Lafayette (47904) *(G-10543)*

Bright Sheet Metal Company Inc 317 783-3181
1930 S State Ave Indianapolis (46203) *(G-7683)*

Bright Sheet Metal Company Inc (PA) 317 291-7600
4212 W 71st St Ste A Indianapolis (46268) *(G-7684)*

Bright Signs and More 260 203-2444
2410 W Jefferson Blvd Fort Wayne (46802) *(G-4817)*

Brighter Design Inc 765 447-9494
1650 Skyline Rd Lafayette (47905) *(G-10544)*

Brightlamp Inc 317 285-9287
1230 Hoyt Ave Indianapolis (46203) *(G-7685)*

Brighton Mills, West Harrison *Also Called: H Nagel & Son Co (G-16546)*

Brighttany Pollitt 217 597-1624
2181 N West Bay Dr Apt D Greenfield (46140) *(G-6472)*

Brill Stuff LLC 502 889-9705
122 Spickert Knob Rd New Albany (47150) *(G-12705)*

Brilliant Blondes LLC 765 288-8077
3501 N Granville Ave Ste 3 Muncie (47303) *(G-12357)*

Brim Concrete Inc 765 564-4975
2485 W Gravel Pit Rd Delphi (46923) *(G-2891)*

Brinco Manufacturing Inc 574 213-1008
51650 County Road 133 Bristol (46507) *(G-1250)*

Brindle Products Inc (PA) 260 627-2156
13633 David Dr Grabill (46741) *(G-6290)*

Brinker Mfg Jewelers Inc 812 476-0651
111 S Green River Rd Evansville (47715) *(G-3954)*

Brinkman Press Inc 317 722-0305
6945 Hawthorn Park Dr Indianapolis (46220) *(G-7686)*

Brinly-Hardy Company (PA) 812 218-7200
3230 Industrial Pkwy Jeffersonville (47130) *(G-9947)*

Bristol Intgrted Tling Atmtn L 574 848-5354
689 Commerce Dr Bristol (46507) *(G-1251)*

Bristol Myers 812 428-1927
2400 W Lloyd Expy Evansville (47712) *(G-3955)*

Bristol Pallet 574 862-1862
64466 State Road 19 Goshen (46526) *(G-6100)*

Bristol Tool and Die, Bristol *Also Called: Bristol Intgrted Tling Atmtn L (G-1251)*

Bristol Tool and Die Inc 574 848-5354
710 Commerce Dr Bristol (46507) *(G-1252)*

Bristol Ventures LLC 765 649-8452
2698 N 400 W Anderson (46011) *(G-84)*

Bristol-Myers Squibb, Evansville *Also Called: Bristol-Myers Squibb Company (G-3956)*

Bristol-Myers Squibb, Fort Wayne *Also Called: Bristol-Myers Squibb Company (G-4818)*

Bristol-Myers Squibb, Mount Vernon *Also Called: Bristol-Myers Squibb Company (G-12293)*

Bristol-Myers Squibb Company 812 429-5505
7503 Highway 57 Evansville (47725) *(G-3956)*

Bristol-Myers Squibb Company... 260 432-2764
7527 Aboite Center Rd Fort Wayne (46804) *(G-4818)*

Bristol-Myers Squibb Company... 812 307-2000
6400 William Keck Byp Mount Vernon (47620) *(G-12293)*

Bristow Milling Co LLC... 812 843-5176
4721 Water St Bristow (47515) *(G-1299)*

Briter Products Inc... 574 386-8167
1901 N Bendix Dr South Bend (46628) *(G-14962)*

Britt Tool Inc.. 812 446-0503
949 E National Ave Brazil (47834) *(G-1136)*

Brittany Bushong... 574 457-4970
808 S Huntington St Syracuse (46567) *(G-15458)*

Brittany Hornsby... 219 789-0984
7240 Northcote Ave Hammond (46324) *(G-6888)*

Broad Ripple Chip Co LLC... 317 590-7687
5060 E 62nd St Ste 124 Indianapolis (46220) *(G-7687)*

Broadway Auto Glass LLC... 219 884-5277
6491 Broadway Merrillville (46410) *(G-11493)*

Broadway Press LLC.. 765 644-8813
2112 Broadway St Anderson (46012) *(G-85)*

Brock Grain Systems, Milford Also Called: Ctb Inc *(G-11790)*

Brocks Incorporated... 765 721-3068
6541 N Us Highway 231 Bainbridge (46105) *(G-559)*

Brockwood Farm... 812 837-9607
7867 Axsom Branch Rd Nashville (47448) *(G-12664)*

Brogan Pharmaceuticals LLC.. 219 644-3693
9800 Connecticut Dr Crown Point (46307) *(G-2662)*

Broken Mold Customs Inc... 219 863-1008
1207 Daisy St Se Demotte (46310) *(G-2913)*

Broken Tee LLC.. 812 559-0741
904 Reyling Dr Unit 4 Jasper (47546) *(G-9825)*

Broken Vessel Sign Co LLC.. 260 273-2780
3710 N Hickory Rd Decatur (46733) *(G-2847)*

Bromire Technology... 317 294-9083
120 Lake View Ct N Greenfield (46140) *(G-6473)*

Bronze Bow Software Inc... 260 672-9516
7717 Aboite Rd Roanoke (46783) *(G-14261)*

Brook Locker Plant... 219 275-2611
243 W Main St Brook (47922) *(G-1303)*

Brookfield Sand & Gravel Inc (PA)....................................... 317 835-2235
8587 N 850 W Fairland (46126) *(G-4398)*

Brooks Publications Inc.. 317 756-9830
305 N East St Indianapolis (46202) *(G-7688)*

Brookville Democrat, Brookville Also Called: Whitewater Publications Inc *(G-1341)*

Brookville Tool Co, Brookville Also Called: Greg Miner *(G-1322)*

Brookwood Cabinet Company Inc.. 260 749-5012
5912 Old Maumee Rd Fort Wayne (46803) *(G-4819)*

Broomcorn Johnny's, Nashville Also Called: Brian Newton *(G-12663)*

Brothers Industries LLC.. 812 560-6224
803 E Washington St Greensburg (47240) *(G-6583)*

Brouillette Htg Coolg Plbg LLC... 765 884-0176
403 W 5th St Fowler (47944) *(G-5622)*

Browell Bellhousing Inc... 765 447-2292
711 N 31st St Lafayette (47904) *(G-10545)*

Browell Enterprises Inc... 765 447-2292
711 N 31st St Lafayette (47904) *(G-10546)*

Browmi By Misha LLC.. 317 801-3911
8022 E 46th St Indianapolis (46226) *(G-7689)*

Brown & Brown Fuel.. 219 984-5173
5774 S State Road 43 Chalmers (47929) *(G-1857)*

Brown County Forest Products, Nashville Also Called: Jwb Group LLC *(G-12672)*

Brown County Kettle Corn LLC... 812 558-4536
245 Van Buren St Nashville (47448) *(G-12665)*

Brown County Wine Company Inc (PA)................................ 812 988-6144
4520 State Road 46 E Nashville (47448) *(G-12666)*

Brown Ridge Studio... 812 335-0643
625 N Lwer Brdie Glyan Rd Bloomington (47408) *(G-816)*

Browning, William Logging, Brookville Also Called: William Browning *(G-1342)*

Browns Dairy Inc (PA).. 219 464-4141
57 Monroe St Valparaiso (46383) *(G-15921)*

Browns Simply Printings... 317 490-7493
126 S Jefferson St Mooresville (46158) *(G-12196)*

Browns Woodworking Limited.. 260 693-2868
4966 N 550 E Churubusco (46723) *(G-1975)*

Brownsburg Custom Cabinets Inc.. 317 271-1887
1747 Country Club Rd Indianapolis (46234) *(G-7690)*

Brownstown Qlty TI Automtn LLC.. 812 358-9059
593 S State Road 135 Brownstown (47220) *(G-1417)*

Brownstown Qulty TI Design Inc.. 812 358-4593
1408 E State Road 250 Brownstown (47220) *(G-1418)*

Bruce A Hodson.. 765 212-7757
4309 N Ruppert Rd Attica (47918) *(G-344)*

Bruce Fox Inc (PA).. 812 945-3511
1909 Mcdonald Ln New Albany (47150) *(G-12706)*

Bruce Payne... 260 492-2259
810 Lakeridge Pl Fort Wayne (46819) *(G-4820)*

Bruco Industries, Fort Wayne Also Called: Mettle Holdings Incorporated *(G-5217)*

Brulin, Indianapolis Also Called: Brulin & Company Inc *(G-7691)*

Brulin, Indianapolis Also Called: Brulin Holding Company Inc *(G-7692)*

Brulin & Company Inc.. 317 923-3211
2920 Dr Andrew J Brown Ave Indianapolis (46205) *(G-7691)*

Brulin Holding Company Inc (PA)... 317 923-3211
2920 Dr Andrew J Brown Ave Indianapolis (46205) *(G-7692)*

Brummett Enterprises LLC.. 812 325-6993
3101 W Arlington Rd Bloomington (47404) *(G-817)*

Bruning Enterprises Inc.. 317 835-7591
7718 N State Road 9 Shelbyville (46176) *(G-14742)*

Brunk LLC (PA).. 800 227-4156
803 Logan St Goshen (46528) *(G-6101)*

Brunk Plastic Services, Goshen Also Called: Brunk LLC *(G-6101)*

Bruno Cb Inc... 317 619-7467
9465 Counselors Row Ste 200 Indianapolis (46240) *(G-7693)*

Brunsman Graphic Design, Connersville Also Called: Bell Graphics and Design LLC *(G-2428)*

Brunswick Corporation.. 866 278-6942
4857 N Ronald Reagan Pkwy Brownsburg (46112) *(G-1353)*

Brunswick Corporation.. 260 459-8200
1111 N Hadley Rd Fort Wayne (46804) *(G-4821)*

Bryan Janky... 708 921-7676
453 Andover Dr Valparaiso (46385) *(G-15922)*

Bryan Machine Services Inc... 260 356-5530
345 Commerce Dr Huntington (46750) *(G-7303)*

Bryan Snyder Inc.. 574 238-4481
2213 Cambridge Dr Goshen (46528) *(G-6102)*

Bryan Ward.. 812 696-5126
247 W Hampton Dr Farmersburg (47850) *(G-4417)*

Bryant Control Inc.. 317 549-3355
9925 E 126th St Ste 130 Fishers (46038) *(G-4477)*

Bryant Ice Co Inc... 765 459-4543
824 S Armstrong St Kokomo (46901) *(G-10242)*

Bryant Industries Inc... 812 944-6010
201b E 18th St New Albany (47150) *(G-12707)*

Bryant Lift Trailer.. 574 721-2255
2917 Barrett Rd Rochester (46975) *(G-14280)*

Bryant Machining & Welding LLC... 260 997-6059
1015 E State Road 67 Bryant (47326) *(G-1434)*

Bryant Printing LLC... 765 521-3379
2601 Broad St New Castle (47362) *(G-12853)*

Bryant Trucking, Richmond Also Called: Bryant Welding & Fabrication *(G-14101)*

Bryant Welding & Fabrication... 765 935-4281
2693 N Round Barn Rd Richmond (47374) *(G-14101)*

Bryant's LP Gas, Hillsboro Also Called: Nicholas Bryant *(G-7161)*

Bryton Corporation.. 317 334-8700
4001 Methanol Ln Indianapolis (46268) *(G-7694)*

BSB Trans Inc... 317 919-8778
711 Legacy Blvd Greenwood (46143) *(G-6677)*

Bsbw Cultured Marble Inc... 812 246-5619
860 S Penn Ave Sellersburg (47172) *(G-14588)*

BSC Vntres Acquisition Sub LLC.. 260 665-7521
100 Woodhull Dr Angola (46703) *(G-237)*

Bst Corp... 812 925-7911
1066 Hunter Blvd Boonville (47601) *(G-1083)*

Bst Enterprises Inc.. 260 493-4313
1900 Summit St New Haven (46774) *(G-12895)*

ALPHABETIC SECTION — Business Health

BT Management Inc 219 794-9546
  8605 Indiana Pl Merrillville (46410) *(G-11494)*

BT&f LLC 574 272-6128
  12441 Beckley St Ste 8 Granger (46530) *(G-6338)*

Btc Lapmaster LLC 317 841-2400
  14560 Bergen Blvd Noblesville (46060) *(G-13049)*

Btd Manufacturing Inc (PA) 812 934-5616
  177 Six Pine Ranch Rd Batesville (47006) *(G-585)*

Btq Manufacturing Inc (DH) 574 223-4311
  2516 E State Road 14 Rochester (46975) *(G-14281)*

BTS Dispatching LLC 317 300-4594
  988 N Boehning St Indianapolis (46219) *(G-7695)*

Buc Construction Supply Inc 574 532-9345
  2304 Brothers Dr Ste E Lafayette (47909) *(G-10547)*

Buchan Logging Inc 260 749-4697
  3333 E 600 N Decatur (46733) *(G-2848)*

Buchan Saw Mill, Decatur *Also Called: Buchan Logging Inc (G-2848)*

Buchanan Company Inc 317 919-2025
  4610 Industrial Rd Fort Wayne (46825) *(G-4822)*

Buchanan Iron Works Inc 219 785-4480
  103 Greenway St Westville (46391) *(G-16757)*

Buck Creek Winery, Indianapolis *Also Called: Durm Vineyard Inc (G-8021)*

Buck Hollow Cnc LLC 717 269-9322
  579 N County Road 500 E Brownsville (47325) *(G-1430)*

Buckaroos Inc (PA) 317 899-9100
  9800 Crosspoint Blvd Indianapolis (46256) *(G-7696)*

Buckeye Corrugated Inc 317 856-3701
  4001 S High School Rd Indianapolis (46241) *(G-7697)*

Buckeye Diamond Logistics Inc 317 524-9304
  217 S Belmont Ave Ste E Indianapolis (46222) *(G-7698)*

Buckingham Pallets Inc 317 846-8601
  12325 Camberly Ln Carmel (46033) *(G-1574)*

Buckner Inc (PA) 317 570-0533
  9922 E 79th St Indianapolis (46256) *(G-7699)*

Bucktown Metal Works, Carlisle *Also Called: Russell L Rooksberry (G-1543)*

Bud LLC 574 534-5300
  3352 Maple City Dr Goshen (46526) *(G-6103)*

Budco Tool & Die Inc 574 522-4004
  56935 Elk Ct Elkhart (46516) *(G-3237)*

Buddy Covers Inc 317 846-5766
  201 W Greyhound Pass Carmel (46032) *(G-1575)*

Buddy Eugene Publishing LLC 574 223-6048
  2031 S 650 E Akron (46910) *(G-2)*

Budget Blinds, Muncie *Also Called: J P Whitt Inc (G-12430)*

Budget Inks LLC 877 636-4657
  45 S Public Sq Angola (46703) *(G-238)*

Budget Instant Print, Jeffersonville *Also Called: Budget Printing Centers Inc (G-9948)*

Budget Printing Centers Inc (PA) 812 282-8832
  902 E 10th St Jeffersonville (47130) *(G-9948)*

Buehler's Buy Low 4182, Evansville *Also Called: Houchens Industries Inc (G-4111)*

Buehrer Industries LLC 260 563-2181
  655 Factory St Wabash (46992) *(G-16175)*

Buffington Custom Kitchens, Seymour *Also Called: Phoenix Custom Kitchens Inc (G-14674)*

Buffington Electric Motors 574 935-5453
  2520 Lake Ave Plymouth (46563) *(G-13762)*

Buffington Farm Service, Plymouth *Also Called: Buffington Electric Motors (G-13762)*

Bugher Fabricating, Russiaville *Also Called: Brad Bugher (G-14421)*

Buhrt Engineering & Cnstr 574 267-3720
  27 E 250 N Warsaw (46582) *(G-16331)*

Builders Concrete & Supply Co Inc 317 570-6201
  9170 E 131st St Fishers (46038) *(G-4478)*

Builders Iron Works Inc 574 254-1553
  1016 E 12th St Mishawaka (46544) *(G-11854)*

Building Indiana 219 226-0300
  1255 Erie Ct Ste C Crown Point (46307) *(G-2663)*

Building Temp Solutions LLC 260 449-9201
  3811 Fourier Dr Fort Wayne (46825) *(G-4823)*

Buis Enterprises Inc 317 839-7394
  6987 S County Road 750 E Plainfield (46168) *(G-13663)*

Bulent Gumusel 812 803-5912
  3366 S Oaklawn Cir Bloomington (47401) *(G-818)*

Bulk Truck & Transport Service 812 866-2155
  659 W Lagrange Rd Hanover (47243) *(G-7040)*

Bull Moose Tube, Elkhart *Also Called: Bock Industries Inc (G-3230)*

Bulldog, Hobart *Also Called: ITR America LLC (G-7193)*

Bulldog Battery Corporation (PA) 260 563-0551
  98 E Canal St Wabash (46992) *(G-16176)*

Bully Graphics and Signs 574 870-0783
  6242 E 700 N Monticello (47960) *(G-12140)*

Bully Products Inc 574 312-0511
  2701 Lismore Dr Goshen (46526) *(G-6104)*

Bundoo Laboratories LLC 317 978-5574
  17 N 5th Ave Beech Grove (46107) *(G-687)*

Bundy Bros and Sons Inc 812 966-2551
  3 David St Medora (47260) *(G-11462)*

Bunge North America East LLC 260 724-2101
  1200 N 2nd St Decatur (46733) *(G-2849)*

Bunny Beautiful Cosmetics LLC 219 433-1698
  3416 Elm St East Chicago (46312) *(G-2994)*

Bunny Flaming Industries 317 554-7143
  1741 S Delaware St Indianapolis (46225) *(G-7700)*

Burco, Noblesville *Also Called: Burco Molding Inc (G-13050)*

Burco Molding Inc 317 773-5699
  15015 Herriman Blvd Noblesville (46060) *(G-13050)*

Burgess Auction Resale, Albion *Also Called: Burgess Enterprises LLC (G-20)*

Burgess Enterprises LLC 260 615-5194
  441 S 400 E Albion (46701) *(G-20)*

Burkert-Walton Inc 812 425-7157
  1561 Allens Ln Evansville (47710) *(G-3957)*

Burkes Garden Wood Pdts LLC 765 344-1724
  4774 S 1000 E Brazil (47834) *(G-1137)*

Burkholder Machine LLC 574 862-2004
  25354 County Road 40 Goshen (46526) *(G-6105)*

Burks Door & Sash Inc 317 844-2484
  599 3rd Ave Sw Carmel (46032) *(G-1576)*

Burlington Grain & Prod Co LLC 866 767-2627
  210 S Main St Sheridan (46069) *(G-14818)*

Burns Buildings, Macy *Also Called: Burns Construction Inc (G-11195)*

Burns Cabinets and Disp Inc 260 897-2219
  140 Green Dr Avilla (46710) *(G-473)*

Burns Construction Inc 574 382-2315
  6676 S Old Us Highway 31 Macy (46951) *(G-11195)*

Burns Tire Service, Macy *Also Called: Bernard Burns (G-11194)*

Burris Engineering Inc 317 862-1046
  5430 S Franklin Rd Indianapolis (46239) *(G-7701)*

Burst of Beauty LLC 708 970-2181
  1329 Williams St Gary (46404) *(G-5907)*

Burston Marketing Inc 574 262-4005
  2802 Frederic Dr Elkhart (46514) *(G-3238)*

Burt Products Inc 812 386-6890
  315 S West St Princeton (47670) *(G-13986)*

Burton Debiceious (PA) 317 495-0123
  3827 N Mitthoefer Rd Unit C9 Indianapolis (46235) *(G-7702)*

Burton Lumber Co Inc 812 866-4438
  13980 W Polk Rd Lexington (47138) *(G-10975)*

Busakshamban, Fort Wayne *Also Called: Trellborg Sling Sltions US Inc (G-5503)*

Busche Enterprise, Albion *Also Called: Linamar Strctures USA Mich Inc (G-33)*

Bush Pilot Beard Balm 574 535-4949
  217 S Cottage Ave Goshen (46528) *(G-6106)*

Bush Trophy Case & Embroidery, Anderson *Also Called: Wanda Harrington (G-215)*

Bushwood Ventures Htc LLC 317 523-0991
  9693 Reston Ln Fishers (46055) *(G-4640)*

Business & Industrial Pdts Co 812 376-6149
  3552 Mockingbird Dr Columbus (47203) *(G-2231)*

Business Art & Designs Inc 317 782-9108
  402 Main St Beech Grove (46107) *(G-688)*

Business Connection LLC 219 762-5660
  2708 Willowcreek Rd Portage (46368) *(G-13850)*

Business Forms Designs Inc 317 353-6647
  1333 N Huber St Indianapolis (46219) *(G-7703)*

Business Health 219 762-7105
  5715 Independence Ave Portage (46368) *(G-13851)*

Business Pple Mag Grter Fort W, Fort Wayne Also Called: Michiana Bus Publications Inc (G-5220)

Business Systems Mgt Corp.. 219 938-0166
8414 Maple Ave Gary (46403) *(G-5908)*

Business To Business, Mishawaka Also Called: Michiana Executive Journal (G-11943)

Buskirk Engineering, Ossian Also Called: Buskirk Engineering Inc (G-13420)

Buskirk Engineering Inc... 260 622-5550
7224 E 900 N Ossian (46777) *(G-13420)*

Busters Cement Products Inc (PA)..................................... 765 529-0287
3450 S Spiceland Rd New Castle (47362) *(G-12854)*

Butcher Block Inc... 219 696-9111
17918 Grant Pl Lowell (46356) *(G-11157)*

Butler Bulletin, Auburn Also Called: Kpc Media Group Inc (G-401)

Butler Mill Service Company, Butler Also Called: Levy Environmental Services Co (G-1470)

Butler Tool & Design Inc.. 219 297-4531
641 S Newton St Goodland (47948) *(G-6080)*

Butler Vineyards (PA).. 812 332-6660
6200 E Robinson Rd Bloomington (47408) *(G-819)*

Butler Vineyards... 219 929-1400
401 Broadway Chesterton (46304) *(G-1907)*

Butler Winery, Bloomington Also Called: Butler Vineyards (G-819)

Butler-Macdonald Inc... 317 872-5115
5955 W 80th St Indianapolis (46278) *(G-7704)*

Butlers General Repair.. 812 268-5631
1259 W State Road 154 Sullivan (47882) *(G-15403)*

Butterfield Foods, Noblesville Also Called: Butterfield Foods LLC (G-13051)

Butterfield Foods LLC.. 317 776-4775
635 Westfield Rd Noblesville (46060) *(G-13051)*

Buttermilk Ridge Publishing, Noblesville Also Called: Yaney Mktg Graphic Design LLC (G-13197)

Butterworth Industries Inc.. 765 677-6725
5050 Eastside Parkway Dr Gas City (46933) *(G-6034)*

Buttons Galore Inc... 800 626-8168
110 E College Ave Brownsburg (46112) *(G-1354)*

Buxton Engineering Inc.. 812 897-3609
1322 S Rockport Rd Boonville (47601) *(G-1084)*

Buy Bulk Displays.. 574 855-3522
3505 N Home St Mishawaka (46545) *(G-11855)*

Buy Bulk Displays LLC... 574 222-4378
1610 3rd St Osceola (46561) *(G-13384)*

Buztronics Inc.. 317 876-3413
464 Southpoint Cir Ste 100 Brownsburg (46112) *(G-1355)*

Buzzi Unicem, Carmel Also Called: Lone Star Industries Inc (G-1685)

Buzzi Unicem USA Inc... 317 706-3352
10333 N Meridian St Ste 235 Carmel (46290) *(G-1577)*

Buzzi Unicem USA Inc... 574 674-8873
55284 Corwin Rd Elkhart (46514) *(G-3239)*

Buzzi Unicem USA Inc... 765 653-9766
3301 S County Road 150 W Greencastle (46135) *(G-6393)*

Buzzi Unicem USA Inc... 317 780-9860
1112 W Thompson Rd Indianapolis (46217) *(G-7705)*

Bw Energy & Innovation LLC (PA)..................................... 214 223-2459
1752 Fields Blvd Greenfield (46140) *(G-6474)*

Bw Manufacturing, Kokomo Also Called: Mier Products Inc (G-10307)

Bw Wholesale LLC... 775 856-3522
336 N Windsong Ln Greenwood (46142) *(G-6678)*

Bway Corporation.. 219 462-8915
4002 Montdale Park Dr Valparaiso (46383) *(G-15923)*

Bwi Group, Greenfield Also Called: BWI INDIANA INC (G-6475)

BWI INDIANA INC.. 937 260-2460
989 Opportunity Pkwy Greenfield (46140) *(G-6475)*

Bwt LLC.. 574 232-3338
802 Fellows St South Bend (46601) *(G-14963)*

Bwxt Nclear Oprtions Group Inc....................................... 812 838-1200
1400 Old Highway 69 S Mount Vernon (47620) *(G-12294)*

By The Sword Inc... 877 433-9368
304 E Sunset Dr Huntingburg (47542) *(G-7271)*

By-Pass Paint Shop Inc (PA)... 574 264-5334
1132 N Nappanee St Elkhart (46514) *(G-3240)*

Bybee Stone Company Inc... 812 876-2215
6293 N Matthews Dr Ellettsville (47429) *(G-3801)*

Bye Buy Cci Inc.. 260 925-0623
1937 Jacob St Auburn (46706) *(G-371)*

Byler Family Wood Working... 574 825-3339
60845 State Road 13 Goshen (46528) *(G-6107)*

Byler Sawmill... 812 577-5761
9435 State Road 250 Bennington (47011) *(G-702)*

C & A Tool Engineering Inc.. 260 693-2167
1015 W 15th St Auburn (46706) *(G-372)*

C & A Tool Engineering Inc.. 260 693-2167
105 S Main St Churubusco (46723) *(G-1976)*

C & A Tool Engineering Inc.. 260 693-2167
118 N Main St Churubusco (46723) *(G-1977)*

C & A Tool Engineering Inc.. 260 693-2167
100 Cole St Churubusco (46723) *(G-1978)*

C & A Tool Engineering Inc.. 260 693-2167
411 S Mulberry St Churubusco (46723) *(G-1979)*

C & A Tool Engineering Inc.. 260 693-2167
119 S Mulberry St Churubusco (46723) *(G-1980)*

C & A Tool Engineering Inc.. 260 693-2167
101 N Main St Churubusco (46723) *(G-1981)*

C & A Tool Engineering Inc (HQ)..................................... 260 693-2167
4100 N Us 33 Churubusco (46723) *(G-1982)*

C & A TOOL ENGINEERING INC., Auburn Also Called: C & A Tool Engineering Inc (G-372)

C & A TOOL ENGINEERING INC., Churubusco Also Called: C & A Tool Engineering Inc (G-1976)

C & A TOOL ENGINEERING INC., Churubusco Also Called: C & A Tool Engineering Inc (G-1977)

C & A TOOL ENGINEERING INC., Churubusco Also Called: C & A Tool Engineering Inc (G-1978)

C & A TOOL ENGINEERING INC., Churubusco Also Called: C & A Tool Engineering Inc (G-1979)

C & A TOOL ENGINEERING INC., Churubusco Also Called: C & A Tool Engineering Inc (G-1980)

C & A TOOL ENGINEERING INC., Churubusco Also Called: C & A Tool Engineering Inc (G-1981)

C & B Industries LLC... 260 490-3000
9009 Coldwater Rd Fort Wayne (46825) *(G-4824)*

C & C Industries.. 260 804-6518
10214 Chestnut Plaza Dr Fort Wayne (46814) *(G-4825)*

C & C Iron Inc.. 219 769-2511
6409 Hendricks St Merrillville (46410) *(G-11495)*

C & C Mailbox Products.. 765 358-4880
18100 N County Road 925 W Gaston (47342) *(G-6044)*

C & C Pallets and Lumber LLC... 765 524-3214
1611 S County Road 275 W New Castle (47362) *(G-12855)*

C & C Welding & Fabg Inc... 812 384-8089
32 W Judson St Bloomfield (47424) *(G-741)*

C & F Industries LLC... 765 580-0378
5282 W Booth Rd Liberty (47353) *(G-10984)*

C & G Salsa Company LLC.. 317 569-9099
5282 E 156th St Noblesville (46062) *(G-13052)*

C & G Tool Inc... 812 524-7061
706 W Chestnut St Jonesville (47247) *(G-10083)*

C & G Wiring Inc... 574 333-3433
1823 Leer Dr Elkhart (46514) *(G-3241)*

C & H Sign Inc Corporation... 765 642-7777
805 Morton St Anderson (46016) *(G-86)*

C & J Cabinets.. 574 255-5812
3203 York St Mishawaka (46544) *(G-11856)*

C & J K Industries Inc... 219 746-5760
230 Timrick Dr Munster (46321) *(G-12533)*

C & J Plating & Grinding LLC.. 765 288-8728
411 E 3rd St Muncie (47302) *(G-12358)*

C & J Security Solutions, Fort Wayne Also Called: C & J Services & Supplies Inc (G-4826)

C & J Services & Supplies Inc.. 317 569-7222
5201 Investment Dr Fort Wayne (46808) *(G-4826)*

C & K Manufacturing Inc... 574 264-4063
25943 Forest Hill Ave Elkhart (46514) *(G-3242)*

C & K United Shtmtl & Mech.. 812 423-5090
2805 Lincoln Ave Ste C Evansville (47714) *(G-3958)*

C & L Electric Motor Repr Inc... 574 533-2643
2910 Airport Pkwy Elkhart (46514) *(G-3243)*

ALPHABETIC SECTION — Cabinets & Furniture

C & L Lumber Inc.. 812 536-2171
8836 W State Road 64 Huntingburg (47542) *(G-7272)*

C & L Sheet Metal LLC.. 812 449-9126
2263 E Tennessee St Evansville (47711) *(G-3959)*

C & P Distributing LLC.. 574 256-1138
2500 Miracle Ln Ste D Mishawaka (46545) *(G-11857)*

C & P Engineering and Mfg Inc................................ 765 825-4293
1605 Kentucky Ave Connersville (47331) *(G-2430)*

C & P Machine Service Inc...................................... 260 484-7723
445 Council Dr Fort Wayne (46825) *(G-4827)*

C & P Woodworking Inc.. 260 637-3088
7108 County Road 17 Auburn (46706) *(G-373)*

C & R, Indianapolis Also Called: C&R Racing Incorporated *(G-7710)*

C & R Cnstr & Consulting LLC................................ 812 738-4493
598 Schwartz Rd Nw Corydon (47112) *(G-2489)*

C & R Construction, Corydon Also Called: C & R Cnstr & Consulting LLC *(G-2489)*

C & R Plating Corp.. 586 755-4900
302 Factory St Columbia City (46725) *(G-2128)*

C & R Woodworks... 317 422-9603
8880 Huggin Hollow Rd Martinsville (46151) *(G-11382)*

C & S Prototyping LLC.. 812 343-8618
3345 Commerce Dr Columbus (47201) *(G-2232)*

C & S Solutions LLC.. 812 895-0048
2064 N Old Highway 41 Vincennes (47591) *(G-16116)*

C & T Engineering Inc
322 Thompson Rd Seymour (47274) *(G-14635)*

C & W Inkd.. 317 352-1000
6300 Brookville Rd Bldg B Indianapolis (46219) *(G-7706)*

C A E, Marion Also Called: Computer Age Engineering Inc *(G-11278)*

C A Lakey Family Saw Mill Inc................................ 765 378-7528
9491 S County Road 900 W Daleville (47334) *(G-2796)*

C and S Machine Inc... 812 687-7203
122 Main St Plainville (47568) *(G-13745)*

C C Cook and Son Lbr Co Inc................................. 765 672-4235
6236 W Us Highway 40 Reelsville (46171) *(G-14030)*

C D C P Inc.. 219 766-2284
207 E Mentor St Kouts (46347) *(G-10362)*

C D I, Fort Wayne Also Called: Complete Drives Inc *(G-4869)*

C D I, Leesburg Also Called: Composite Designs Inc *(G-10953)*

C E Kersting & Sons.. 574 896-2766
6800 S 300 W North Judson (46366) *(G-13207)*

C E M Printing & Specialities.................................. 269 684-6898
50750 Marie Ct South Bend (46637) *(G-14964)*

C E R Metal Marking Corp...................................... 219 924-9710
2224 Industrial Dr Ste C Highland (46322) *(G-7126)*

C F Roark Wldg Engrg Co Inc................................. 317 852-3163
136 N Green St Brownsburg (46112) *(G-1356)*

C Fabco/L Inc.. 219 785-4181
9811 W State Road 2 Ste 1 La Porte (46350) *(G-10392)*

C H Ellis LLC.. 317 636-3351
2432 Southeastern Ave Indianapolis (46201) *(G-7707)*

C Is For Cookie LLP.. 574 538-9841
67209 County Road 27 Goshen (46526) *(G-6108)*

C J P Corporation.. 219 924-1685
9445 Indianapolis Blvd Ste A Highland (46322) *(G-7127)*

C Johnson Group LLC... 219 512-0619
8734 Navigator Dr Apt 1305 Indianapolis (46237) *(G-7708)*

C M Engineering Inc.. 812 648-2038
8112 E Main St Dugger (47848) *(G-2956)*

C M Grinding Incorporated...................................... 574 234-6812
55643 Fairview Ave South Bend (46628) *(G-14965)*

C M I Automotive of Indiana, Elkhart Also Called: C M I Enterprises Inc *(G-3244)*

C M I Enterprises Inc... 305 685-9651
2904 Leer Ct Elkhart (46514) *(G-3244)*

C M TEC... 765 284-3888
11200 E State Road 32 Selma (47383) *(G-14620)*

C Milligan Investments LLC..................................... 219 241-5811
1208 Pine Creek Rd Valparaiso (46383) *(G-15924)*

C N J Well Drilling.. 317 892-2100
1721 Laurel St Indianapolis (46203) *(G-7709)*

C R Graphics.. 317 881-6192
485 E Pearl St Greenwood (46143) *(G-6679)*

C S I, Indianapolis Also Called: Closure Systems Intl Inc *(G-7825)*

C-Level, Plainfield Also Called: Infinity Products Inc *(G-13690)*

C-Mar Welding... 260 410-8104
16808 Notestine Rd New Haven (46774) *(G-12896)*

C-P Industries, Granger Also Called: City Pattern and Foundry Company Inc *(G-6339)*

C-Point Inc... 260 478-9551
3522 W Ferguson Rd Ste A Fort Wayne (46809) *(G-4828)*

C-Way Tool and Die Inc... 812 256-6341
103 Industrial Way Charlestown (47111) *(G-1872)*

C. H. Ellis, Indianapolis Also Called: C H Ellis LLC *(G-7707)*

C.J. Boots Casket Company, Richmond Also Called: Vandor Corporation *(G-14223)*

C.P.i, Bloomington Also Called: Circle - Prosco Inc *(G-829)*

C&C Electric Motors LLC.. 574 656-3898
1011 Industrial Pkwy North Liberty (46554) *(G-13215)*

C&C Transportation Service LLC............................ 317 677-5060
10744 Springston Ct Fishers (46037) *(G-4479)*

C&D Technologies Inc.. 765 762-2461
200 W Main St Attica (47918) *(G-345)*

C&F Fabricating LLC... 765 362-5922
1831 E Elmore St Crawfordsville (47933) *(G-2550)*

C&H Plastic Letters & Signs, Anderson Also Called: C & H Sign Inc Corporation *(G-86)*

C&M Conveyor Inc.. 812 849-5647
4598 State Road 37 Mitchell (47446) *(G-12034)*

C&M Fine Pack, Fort Wayne Also Called: D&W Fine Pack LLC *(G-4902)*

C&M Woodworking LLC... 260 403-4555
10225 Donald Ave Leo (46765) *(G-10965)*

C&P Machine, Fort Wayne Also Called: C & P Machine Service Inc *(G-4827)*

C&R Racing Incorporated (HQ).............................. 317 293-4100
6950 Guion Rd Indianapolis (46268) *(G-7710)*

C&S Machinery Inc... 812 937-2160
5440 E 2150 N Dale (47523) *(G-2789)*

C&W Fabrication LLC... 812 282-0488
211 Eastern Blvd Jeffersonville (47130) *(G-9949)*

C4 Custom Creation LLC.. 574 551-3904
6328 E Old Road 30 Pierceton (46562) *(G-13630)*

C4 Polymers Inc.. 440 543-3866
1407 S Meeker Ave Muncie (47302) *(G-12359)*

C5 Printing & Graphic Design, Connersville Also Called: Codybro LLC *(G-2432)*

CA, Indianapolis Also Called: Ca Inc *(G-7711)*

Ca Inc... 317 844-7221
250 E 96th St Ste 375 Indianapolis (46240) *(G-7711)*

Caa Inc... 574 537-0933
16255 County Road 22 Goshen (46528) *(G-6109)*

Cabinet and Stone Expo... 317 879-1688
8227 Northwest Blvd Ste 205 Indianapolis (46278) *(G-7712)*

Cabinet and Stone Expo LLC................................. 317 879-1688
5775 W 79th St Indianapolis (46278) *(G-7713)*

Cabinet Barn 2com... 317 421-1750
1648 E State Road 44 Shelbyville (46176) *(G-14743)*

Cabinet Barn Inc... 812 246-5237
105 Adkins Ct Sellersburg (47172) *(G-14589)*

Cabinet Crafters Corp... 765 724-7074
120 S Sheridan St Alexandria (46001) *(G-47)*

Cabinet Expressions... 317 366-7669
15503 Outside Trl Noblesville (46060) *(G-13053)*

Cabinet Fctories Outl Richmond............................. 765 966-3875
633 S H St Richmond (47374) *(G-14102)*

Cabinetmaker Inc.. 812 723-3461
1714 E Owl Hollow Rd Paoli (47454) *(G-13490)*

Cabinetmaker, The, Paoli Also Called: Cabinetmaker Inc *(G-13490)*

Cabinetry Green, Fishers Also Called: Cabinetry Green LLC *(G-4480)*

Cabinetry Green LLC.. 317 842-1550
13818 Promise Rd Fishers (46038) *(G-4480)*

Cabinetry Ideas Inc... 317 722-1300
6113 Allisonville Rd Indianapolis (46220) *(G-7714)*

Cabinetry Solutions LLC... 574 326-3699
2933 Thorne Dr Elkhart (46514) *(G-3245)*

Cabinets & Counters Inc.. 812 858-3300
7387 Savannah Dr Newburgh (47630) *(G-12995)*

Cabinets & Furniture, Grabill Also Called: Graber Cabinetry LLC *(G-6297)*

Cabinets By Rick Inc 812 945-2220
1630 Grant Line Rd New Albany (47150) *(G-12708)*

Cabinets Inc 219 322-3900
1220 Birch Dr Schererville (46375) *(G-14518)*

Cabinets Plus By Ptrick Geer I 765 642-0329
6406 Production Dr Anderson (46013) *(G-87)*

Cabinets To Go, Indianapolis *Also Called: Cabinets To Go LLC (G-7715)*

Cabinets To Go LLC 317 486-0888
3150 Rand Rd Indianapolis (46241) *(G-7715)*

Cabinets Unlimited Corporation 219 558-2210
10067 Raven Wood Dr Saint John (46373) *(G-14446)*

Cabinets Unlimited Inc 260 925-5555
5471 County Road 51 Saint Joe (46785) *(G-14437)*

Cable Sign Painting, La Fontaine *Also Called: Chuck Cable (G-10367)*

Cablecraft Motion Controls LLC (HQ) 260 749-5105
2110 Summit St New Haven (46774) *(G-12897)*

Cac Wallpanels LLC 260 437-4003
14329 Rupert Rd Harlan (46743) *(G-7051)*

Cad & Machining Services Inc 317 535-1067
518 Williamson St Whiteland (46184) *(G-16777)*

Cad/CAM Technologies Inc 765 778-2020
178 S Heritage Way Pendleton (46064) *(G-13528)*

Caddo Connections Inc 219 874-8119
2833 N Goldring Rd La Porte (46350) *(G-10393)*

Cade Carrier Solutions Inc 312 953-5154
6430 Moraine Ave Hammond (46324) *(G-6889)*

Caffeinery LLC 765 896-9123
401 S Walnut St Muncie (47305) *(G-12360)*

Caicos Solutions LLC 317 314-3776
3410 N High School Rd Ste G Pmb 1017 Indianapolis (46224) *(G-7716)*

Caine Publishing LLC 312 215-5253
2721 Floral Trl Long Beach (46360) *(G-11121)*

Caj Food Products Inc 888 524-6882
11650 Olio Rd Ste 1000 Fishers (46037) *(G-4481)*

Cal Pipe Manufacturing Inc 219 844-6800
6451 Northwind Pkwy Hobart (46342) *(G-7175)*

Calbrite Industries 219 844-6800
2207 165th St Hammond (46320) *(G-6890)*

Calcar Quarries Incorporated 812 723-2109
731 Ne Main St Paoli (47454) *(G-13491)*

Calcean, Seymour *Also Called: Calcean LLC (G-14636)*

Calcean LLC 812 672-4995
2213 Killion Ave Seymour (47274) *(G-14636)*

Calcium Products, Swayzee *Also Called: Irving Materials Inc (G-15451)*

Caldwell Gravel Sales Tm, Morristown *Also Called: Cgs Services Inc (G-12273)*

Caldwells Inc 765 740-4300
10911 N 600 E Morristown (46161) *(G-12272)*

Calf-Teria, Spencerville *Also Called: Rhinehart Development Corp (G-15373)*

Calhoun Logging Corporation 260 839-0268
9543 S State Road 13 Claypool (46510) *(G-2051)*

Cali Nail 574 674-4126
941 Lincolnway W Osceola (46561) *(G-13385)*

Cali Nail Salon, Osceola *Also Called: Cali Nail (G-13385)*

Calico Precision Molding LLC 260 484-4500
1211 Progress Rd Fort Wayne (46808) *(G-4829)*

Caliente LLC 260 426-3800
315 E Wallace St Fort Wayne (46803) *(G-4830)*

California Colors Inc 317 435-1351
508 Conner Creek Dr Fishers (46038) *(G-4482)*

California Pellet Mill Company, Crawfordsville *Also Called: CPM Acquisition Corp (G-2556)*

California Sugars LLC 219 886-9151
911 Virginia St Gary (46402) *(G-5909)*

Call Leader, Elwood *Also Called: Elwood Publishing Company Inc (G-3823)*

Callisons Inc 574 896-5074
7675 S 100 W North Judson (46366) *(G-13208)*

Calpipe Industries LLC 219 844-6800
6451 Northwind Pkwy Hobart (46342) *(G-7176)*

Calumet, Indianapolis *Also Called: Calumet Missouri LLC (G-7722)*

Calumet, Indianapolis *Also Called: Calumet Spclty Pdts Prtners LP (G-7728)*

Calumet Inc (PA) 317 328-5660
2780 Waterfront Parkway East Dr Ste 200 Indianapolis (46214) *(G-7717)*

Calumet Wilbert Vault Co Inc 219 980-1173
1920 W 41st Ave Gary (46408) *(G-5910)*

Calumet Arsenal LLC 219 256-9885
1517 Fischrupp Ave 2nd Fl Whiting (46394) *(G-16833)*

Calumet Breweries Inc 219 845-2242
6535 Osborne Ave Hammond (46320) *(G-6891)*

Calumet Finance Corp 317 328-5660
2780 Waterfront Parkway Indianapolis (46214) *(G-7718)*

Calumet Gp LLC 317 328-5660
2780 Waterfront Parkway East Dr Ste 200 Indianapolis (46214) *(G-7719)*

Calumet International Inc 317 328-5660
2780 Waterfront Parkway East Dr Ste 200 Indianapolis (46214) *(G-7720)*

Calumet Karns City Ref LLC (DH) 317 328-5660
2780 Waterfront Parkway East Dr Ste 200 Indianapolis (46214) *(G-7721)*

Calumet Missouri LLC (DH) 318 795-3800
2780 Waterfront Parkway East Dr Indianapolis (46214) *(G-7722)*

Calumet Operating LLC (DH) 317 328-5660
2780 Waterfront Pkwy Indianapolis (46214) *(G-7723)*

Calumet Orthpd Prosthetics Co 219 942-2148
7554 Grand Blvd Hobart (46342) *(G-7177)*

Calumet Pallet Company Inc 219 932-4550
4333 Ohio St Michigan City (46360) *(G-11584)*

Calumet Paralogics LLC 765 587-4618
301 S Butterfield Rd Muncie (47303) *(G-12361)*

Calumet Press, The, Hammond *Also Called: Ckmt Associates Inc (G-6902)*

Calumet Refining LLC (DH) 317 328-5660
2780 Waterfront Parkway East Dr Ste 200 Indianapolis (46214) *(G-7724)*

Calumet Refining LLC 765 587-4618
301 S Butterfield Rd Muncie (47303) *(G-12362)*

Calumet Shreveport Llc 317 328-5660
2780 Waterfront Parkway East Dr Indianapolis (46214) *(G-7725)*

Calumet Shreveport Fuels Llc 317 328-5660
2780 Waterfront Parkway East Dr Indianapolis (46214) *(G-7726)*

Calumet Shreveport Ref LLC (DH) 317 328-5660
2780 Waterfront Parkway East Dr Ste 200 Indianapolis (46214) *(G-7727)*

Calumet Spcialty Pdts Partners, Indianapolis *Also Called: Calumet Refining LLC (G-7724)*

Calumet Spclty Pdts Prtners LP (HQ) 317 328-5660
1060 N Capitol Ave Ste 6-401 Indianapolis (46204) *(G-7728)*

Calumet Superior LLC 317 328-5660
2780 Waterfront Parkway East Dr Indianapolis (46214) *(G-7729)*

Calumet Surface Hardening, Hammond *Also Called: D & D Industries Inc (G-6910)*

Calumet Welding Center Inc 219 923-9353
1947 N Griffith Blvd Griffith (46319) *(G-6798)*

Calumite Company LLC 219 787-8667
1605 Adler Cir Ste I Portage (46368) *(G-13852)*

CAM Metal Fabrication LLC 260 982-6280
911 W Main St North Manchester (46962) *(G-13230)*

Camaco LLC 248 657-0246
6515 Ameriplex Dr Ste B Portage (46368) *(G-13853)*

Cambridge Enterprise Inc 765 544-3402
5931 Roosevelt Pl Merrillville (46410) *(G-11496)*

Cambridge Molding Inc 574 546-4311
1574 Us Highway 6 Nappanee (46550) *(G-12587)*

Camcar LLC 574 223-3131
4366 N Old Us Highway 31 Rochester (46975) *(G-14282)*

Camera Art, Indianapolis *Also Called: Herff Jones LLC (G-8383)*

Camilles Studio 219 365-5902
11650 Wicker Ave Cedar Lake (46303) *(G-1828)*

Camm Machine and Welding LLC 812 347-2040
10035 Buffalo Trace Rd Nw Ramsey (47166) *(G-14024)*

Camo Diva, Fort Wayne *Also Called: Sugar Tree Incorporated (G-5450)*

Camoplast Crocker, Howe *Also Called: Exo-S US LLC (G-7235)*

Campbell Logging LLC 812 972-6280
9100 W State Road 64 Birdseye (47513) *(G-738)*

Campbell Pet Company 812 692-5208
120 N Odon St Elnora (47529) *(G-3813)*

Campbell Printing Company 219 866-5913
125 N Van Rensselaer St Rensselaer (47978) *(G-14046)*

Campbell Road Sawmill LP 260 238-4252
17127 Campbell Rd Spencerville (46788) *(G-15368)*

Campbells Welding & Machine 574 643-6705
202 E Day St Royal Center (46978) *(G-14389)*

ALPHABETIC SECTION — Carecycle LLC

Campus Inc 765 674-9530
   1500 S Western Ave Marion (46953) *(G-11275)*

Camtool, Muncie *Also Called: Camtool Inc (G-12363)*

Camtool Inc 765 286-9725
   3690 S Hoyt Ave Muncie (47302) *(G-12363)*

Can-Clay Corp
   402 Washington St Cannelton (47520) *(G-1534)*

Cana Inc (PA) 574 266-6566
   29194 Phillips St Elkhart (46514) *(G-3246)*

Cana Cabinetry, Elkhart *Also Called: Cana Inc (G-3246)*

Canary Brothers LLC 317 954-1225
   900 N College Ave Indianapolis (46202) *(G-7730)*

Canary Brothers LLC (PA) 317 954-1225
   3832 E 82nd St Indianapolis (46240) *(G-7731)*

Canature, Carmel *Also Called: Canature USA Inc (G-1578)*

Canature USA Inc (PA) 877 771-6789
   9760 Mayflower Park Dr Ste 110 Carmel (46032) *(G-1578)*

Canature Watergroup USA Inc (HQ) 877 771-6789
   6353 Commerce Dr Ste 300 Whitestown (46075) *(G-16802)*

Candice Jefferson 219 315-8629
   220 Wildwood Rd Apt 201 Hammond (46324) *(G-6892)*

Candied Cakes 800 261-0823
   4415 Mountbatten Ct Indianapolis (46254) *(G-7732)*

Candle Chef LLC 317 406-3391
   890 Ridgewood Dr Bldg 202-D Plainfield (46168) *(G-13664)*

Candles By Dar Inc (PA) 260 482-2099
   8308 Riveroak Dr Fort Wayne (46825) *(G-4831)*

Candy Com 317 939-0102
   1207 E Northfield Dr Brownsburg (46112) *(G-1357)*

Canines Choice Inc 765 662-2633
   1019 E 26th St Marion (46953) *(G-11276)*

Cannelburg Proc Plant LLC 812 486-3223
   204 S Main St Cannelburg (47519) *(G-1529)*

Cannon Fabrication Company 765 629-2277
   7957 S State Road 3 Milroy (46156) *(G-11822)*

Cannon Timber LLC 219 754-1088
   418 E Oneida St La Crosse (46348) *(G-10364)*

Canpack US LLC 272 226-7225
   2451 W Fuson Rd Muncie (47302) *(G-12364)*

Canterbury R V, Elkhart *Also Called: Dna Enterprises Inc (G-3298)*

Canvas & Conversation LLC 812 425-5960
   8515 Edinborough Rd Evansville (47725) *(G-3960)*

Canvas Mw LLC (DH) 630 560-3703
   500 Blaine St Michigan City (46360) *(G-11585)*

Canvas Shop LLC 260 768-7755
   850 Taylor Dr Shipshewana (46565) *(G-14840)*

Canvas Vinyl Creations Inc 317 371-4227
   20230 Hague Rd 189 Noblesville (46062) *(G-13054)*

Capco LLC 812 375-1700
   1349 Arcadia Dr Columbus (47201) *(G-2233)*

Cape Sandy Quarry, Leavenworth *Also Called: Mulzer Crushed Stone Inc (G-10871)*

Capeable Sensory Products LLC 260 387-5939
   6411 Highview Dr Fort Wayne (46818) *(G-4832)*

Capeable Weighted Products, Fort Wayne *Also Called: Capeable Sensory Products LLC (G-4832)*

Capital Adhesives & Packg Corp 317 834-5415
   1260 S Old State Road 67 Mooresville (46158) *(G-12197)*

Capital City Transit LLC 317 813-5800
   5657 E State Road 144 Mooresville (46158) *(G-12198)*

Capital Custom Signs 765 689-7170
   1251 N Lancer St Peru (46970) *(G-13569)*

Capital Envmtl Entps Inc 317 240-8085
   3440b S Post Rd Indianapolis (46239) *(G-7733)*

Capital Industries, Shelbyville *Also Called: Banks Machine & Engrg LLC (G-14732)*

Capital Machine Company Inc 317 638-6661
   2801 Roosevelt Ave Indianapolis (46218) *(G-7734)*

Capital Machines International, Indianapolis *Also Called: Capital Machine Company Inc (G-7734)*

Capital Tech Solutions LLC 812 303-4357
   1112 S Villa Dr Evansville (47714) *(G-3961)*

Capitol City Container Corp 317 875-0290
   8240 Zionsville Rd Indianapolis (46268) *(G-7735)*

Capitol Source Network 260 248-9747
   366 E 600 N Columbia City (46725) *(G-2129)*

Caprice Boyb 260 442-1736
   702 Tennessee Ave Fort Wayne (46805) *(G-4833)*

Capricorn Foods LLC 219 670-1872
   6412 Forest Ave Hammond (46324) *(G-6893)*

Caps Inc 773 859-0111
   6945 Forest Ave Hammond (46324) *(G-6894)*

Capstone Commerce Company, Indianapolis *Also Called: Egenolf Enterprise Inc (G-8060)*

Capstone Rail LLC 877 242-4252
   2302 Columbus Ave Anderson (46016) *(G-88)*

Captivated LLC 317 554-7400
   5483 Kenwood Pl Carmel (46033) *(G-1579)*

Captive Holdings LLC 812 424-2904
   101 Oakley St Evansville (47710) *(G-3962)*

Captive Plastics LLC (DH) 812 424-2904
   101 Oakley St Evansville (47710) *(G-3963)*

Captive-Aire Systems Inc 317 852-3770
   20 Airport Rd Ste 500 Brownsburg (46112) *(G-1358)*

Captive-Aire Systems Inc 352 467-4439
   1515 Brookville Crossing Way Indianapolis (46239) *(G-7736)*

Captured Beauty Etc LLC 219 801-2572
   1809 Chase St Gary (46404) *(G-5911)*

Car-TEC, Ridgeville *Also Called: Cardemon Inc (G-14233)*

Car-X Muffler & Brake, Indianapolis *Also Called: Gorrepati Service Systems (G-8308)*

Carb-Rite, Schneider *Also Called: EJ Bognar Incorporated (G-14549)*

Carbonite Inc (HQ) 617 587-1100
   8470 Allison Pointe Blvd Ste 300 Indianapolis (46250) *(G-7737)*

Carcapsule USA Inc 219 945-9493
   4590 W 61st Ave Hobart (46342) *(G-7178)*

Card Calender Publishing Llc 812 234-5999
   200 Arcadia Terre Haute (47803) *(G-15555)*

Cardboard Apothecary 574 309-3007
   60215 Emerald Dr South Bend (46614) *(G-14966)*

Cardcarecom 574 315-5294
   16540 Jackson Rd Mishawaka (46544) *(G-11858)*

Cardemon Inc 765 857-1000
   108 W 2nd St Ridgeville (47380) *(G-14233)*

Carden Jennings Publishing 317 490-7080
   8363 Basswood Dr Apt 1a Indianapolis (46268) *(G-7738)*

Cardina L G, Fremont *Also Called: Cardinal Glass Industries Inc (G-5813)*

Cardinal, Indianapolis *Also Called: Cardinal Manufacturing Co Inc (G-7741)*

Cardinal Container Corp 317 898-2715
   750 S Post Rd Indianapolis (46239) *(G-7739)*

Cardinal Ethanol LLC (PA) 765 964-3137
   1554 N 600 E Union City (47390) *(G-15850)*

Cardinal Glass Industries Inc 260 495-4105
   301 E Mcswain Dr Fremont (46737) *(G-5813)*

Cardinal Health 414 LLC 317 981-4100
   4343 W 62nd St Indianapolis (46268) *(G-7740)*

Cardinal Manufacturing Co Inc 317 283-4175
   1095 E 52nd St Indianapolis (46205) *(G-7741)*

Cardinal Publishers Group, Indianapolis *Also Called: Tom Doherty Company Inc (G-9617)*

Cardinal Services Inc Indiana 574 267-3823
   504 N Bay Dr Warsaw (46580) *(G-16332)*

Cardinal Services Inc Indiana (PA) 574 267-3823
   504 N Bay Dr Warsaw (46580) *(G-16333)*

Cardinal Services Inc Indiana 574 371-1305
   1770 E Smith St Warsaw (46580) *(G-16334)*

Cardinal Sign Service 812 499-0311
   5268 Epworth Rd Newburgh (47630) *(G-12996)*

Cardinal Spirits LLC 812 202-6789
   922 S Morton St Bloomington (47403) *(G-820)*

Cardis Nails 812 264-9906
   1458 S 7th St Unit 2 Terre Haute (47802) *(G-15556)*

Cardwell Signs LLC 414 698-3992
   112 Arrowhead St Sheridan (46069) *(G-14819)*

Care Test Lab LLC 574 326-1082
   2346 S Lynhurst Dr Ste 606 Indianapolis (46241) *(G-7742)*

Carecycle LLC 317 372-7444
   8302 E 33rd St Indianapolis (46226) *(G-7743)*

Carelogiq Corp... 219 682-6327
  10326 Sandy Ln Munster (46321) *(G-12534)*

Carenotes, Saint Meinrad *Also Called: St Meinrad Archabbey (G-14464)*

Cargill, Dana *Also Called: Cargill Incorporated (G-2803)*

Cargill, Hammond *Also Called: Cargill Incorporated (G-6895)*

Cargill, Mentone *Also Called: Cargill Incorporated (G-11471)*

Cargill Incorporated...................................... 765 665-3326
  225 E Briarwood Ave Dana (47847) *(G-2803)*

Cargill Incorporated...................................... 402 533-4227
  1100 Indianapolis Blvd Hammond (46320) *(G-6895)*

Cargill Incorporated...................................... 574 353-7623
  104 N Etna St Mentone (46539) *(G-11470)*

Cargill Incorporated...................................... 574 353-7621
  104 N Etna St Mentone (46539) *(G-11471)*

Cargill Dry Corn Ingrdents Inc........................ 317 632-1481
  1730 W Michigan St Indianapolis (46222) *(G-7744)*

Cargill Hybrid Seeds, Carmel *Also Called: Dow Agrosciences LLC (G-1612)*

Cargo Ski Transport Inc................................. 219 448-9888
  9528 Cleveland St Crown Point (46307) *(G-2664)*

Cargo Skiff Corporation................................. 812 873-6349
  1280 N County Road 500 E Butlerville (47223) *(G-1482)*

Cargo Systems Inc....................................... 574 264-1600
  2603 Glenview Dr Elkhart (46514) *(G-3247)*

Cargo Towing Solutions, Greendale *Also Called: Bjh Enterprises LLC (G-6440)*

Carl A Nix Welding Service Inc....................... 812 386-6281
  4827 W State Road 64 Princeton (47670) *(G-13987)*

Carl Abbott... 317 590-4143
  6725 Shelley St Indianapolis (46219) *(G-7745)*

Carl Buddig Company.................................... 708 210-3130
  215 45th St Munster (46321) *(G-12535)*

Carl Fox Cabinets Inc.................................... 812 342-3020
  704 W Chestnut St Jonesville (47247) *(G-10084)*

Carl Hugness Publishing................................ 812 273-2472
  318 Mulberry St Madison (47250) *(G-11205)*

Carla Clark... 812 598-4687
  2507 Graham Ave Evansville (47714) *(G-3964)*

Carleton Inc (PA)... 574 855-3180
  1251 N Eddy St Ste 202 South Bend (46617) *(G-14967)*

Carlex Glass America LLC............................. 260 925-5656
  1900 Center St Auburn (46706) *(G-374)*

Carlex Glass America LLC............................. 260 894-7750
  860 W Us Highway 6 Ligonier (46767) *(G-11009)*

Carlex Glass Ind Inc-Auburn, Auburn *Also Called: Carlex Glass America LLC (G-374)*

Carlisle Companies Inc.................................. 812 334-8793
  1031 E Hillside Dr Bloomington (47401) *(G-821)*

Carlisle Indus Brake Frction I........................ 812 336-3811
  1031 E Hillside Dr Bloomington (47401) *(G-822)*

Carlisle Mine.. 812 398-2200
  1466 E State Road 58 Carlisle (47838) *(G-1540)*

Carlson Motorsports...................................... 765 339-4407
  215 N High St Linden (47955) *(G-11030)*

Carlson Racing, Linden *Also Called: Carlson Motorsports (G-11030)*

Carlton Ventures Inc..................................... 317 637-2590
  1815 N Meridian St Ste 100 Indianapolis (46202) *(G-7746)*

Carlton West Oil Company LLC...................... 812 375-9689
  3237 Nugent Blvd Columbus (47203) *(G-2234)*

Carman Industries Inc (PA)........................... 812 288-4710
  1005 W Riverside Dr Jeffersonville (47130) *(G-9950)*

Carmel Engineering Inc................................. 765 279-8955
  413 E Madison St Kirklin (46050) *(G-10187)*

Carmel Indiana... 317 575-9942
  881 3rd Ave Sw Ste 101 Carmel (46032) *(G-1580)*

Carmel Sand & Gravel, Carmel *Also Called: Martin Marietta Materials Inc (G-1692)*

Carmel Trophies Plus, Carmel *Also Called: Carmel Trophies Plus LLC (G-1581)*

Carmel Trophies Plus LLC............................. 317 844-3770
  411 N Rangeline Rd Carmel (46032) *(G-1581)*

Carmel Welding and Sup Co Inc..................... 317 846-3493
  550 S Rangeline Rd Carmel (46032) *(G-1582)*

Carmeuse Lime Inc...................................... 219 949-1450
  1 N Carmeuse Ln Gary (46406) *(G-5912)*

Carmeuse Lime & Stone, Gary *Also Called: Carmeuse Lime Inc (G-5912)*

Carmichael Solutions, Indianapolis *Also Called: Carmichael Solutions LLC (G-7747)*

Carmichael Solutions LLC............................. 317 356-2883
  8227 Northwest Blvd Ste 130 Indianapolis (46278) *(G-7747)*

Carmichael Welding Inc................................. 812 825-5156
  9136 E State Road 54 Bloomfield (47424) *(G-742)*

Carol Burt.. 765 282-5383
  605 E County Road 700 N Muncie (47303) *(G-12365)*

Carol Butler.. 201 292-4364
  8324 Lamplighter Ct Fort Wayne (46835) *(G-4834)*

Carother's Printing Company, South Bend *Also Called: Kill-N-Em Inc (G-15100)*

Carousel Industries....................................... 317 674-8111
  10419 Corning Way Fishers (46038) *(G-4483)*

Carousel Winery... 812 849-1005
  6058 Lawrenceport Rd Mitchell (47446) *(G-12035)*

Carousel Winery, Bedford *Also Called: Red Gate Farms Inc (G-667)*

Carpenter Co Inc.. 317 297-2900
  5751 W 56th St Indianapolis (46254) *(G-7748)*

Carpenter Realtors, Indianapolis *Also Called: Carpenter Co Inc (G-7748)*

Carr Custom Painted Mtcyc, Jamestown *Also Called: Signs & Stripes By Carr (G-9820)*

Carr Logging.. 812 863-7585
  9322 E State Road 58 Owensburg (47453) *(G-13460)*

Carrara Industries Inc.................................. 765 643-3430
  1619 W 5th St Anderson (46016) *(G-89)*

Carrera Manufacturing Inc............................. 260 726-9800
  2085 Commerce Dr Bluffton (46714) *(G-1033)*

Carriage House Woodworking........................ 765 352-8514
  439 E Morgan St Martinsville (46151) *(G-11383)*

Carriage House Woodworking Inc................... 317 406-3042
  8043 S Putnam County Rd Coatesville (46121) *(G-2104)*

Carrier, Indianapolis *Also Called: United Technology Corp (G-9681)*

Carrier Corporation....................................... 260 358-0888
  3650 W 200 N Huntington (46750) *(G-7304)*

Carrier Corporation....................................... 317 243-0851
  7310 W Morris St Indianapolis (46231) *(G-7749)*

Carroll County Comet, Delphi *Also Called: Carroll Papers Inc (G-2892)*

Carroll County Comet, Flora *Also Called: Carroll Papers Inc (G-4657)*

Carroll Distrg & Cnstr Sup Inc....................... 317 984-2400
  20935 Cicero Rd. (Sr 19) Noblesville (46060) *(G-13055)*

Carroll Papers Inc.. 765 564-2222
  114 E Franklin St Delphi (46923) *(G-2892)*

Carroll Papers Inc (PA)................................. 574 967-4135
  14 E Main St Flora (46929) *(G-4657)*

Carson Manufacturing Co Inc........................ 317 257-3191
  5451 N Rural St Indianapolis (46220) *(G-7750)*

Cartec Company, Ridgeville *Also Called: Reliance Machine Company Inc (G-14237)*

Carter & Carter Publishing LLC...................... 317 882-0748
  7521 Gunyon Ct Indianapolis (46237) *(G-7751)*

Carter Cabinet Company Inc......................... 317 985-5782
  5928 W 600 S New Palestine (46163) *(G-12935)*

Carter Engineered Quality, Logansport *Also Called: Carter Fuel Systems LLC (G-11064)*

Carter Enterprises Inc.................................. 317 984-1497
  119 W Main St Arcadia (46030) *(G-309)*

Carter Fuel Systems LLC (DH)...................... 800 342-6125
  101 E Industrial Blvd Logansport (46947) *(G-11064)*

Carter Fuel Systems LLC.............................. 574 735-0235
  91 E Industrial Blvd Logansport (46947) *(G-11065)*

Carter Lee Building Component..................... 317 834-5380
  9028 N Old State Road 67 Mooresville (46158) *(G-12199)*

Carter Manufacturing Company...................... 765 563-3666
  896 E Carter Ct Brookston (47923) *(G-1309)*

Carter Septic Tank Inc.................................. 574 583-5796
  1720 N Buckeye St Monticello (47960) *(G-12141)*

Carter-Lee Building Components.................... 317 639-5431
  1717 W Washington St Indianapolis (46222) *(G-7752)*

Carters LLC... 260 432-3568
  2200 Lafontain St Fort Wayne (46802) *(G-4835)*

Carters Concrete Block Inc (PA).................... 574 722-2644
  2200 Lafontain St Fort Wayne (46802) *(G-4836)*

Carters Concrete Block Inc........................... 574 583-7811
  1846 N Francis St Monticello (47960) *(G-12142)*

ALPHABETIC SECTION — CCI Big Boy Products

Carters Manufacturing & Weld 630 464-1520
3270 S County Road 210 Knox (46534) *(G-10203)*

Cartesian Corp 765 742-0293
230 Walnut St Lafayette (47905) *(G-10548)*

Carton Craft Corporation 812 949-4393
2549 Charlestown Rd Ste 1 New Albany (47150) *(G-12709)*

Cartridge World Chicago, Saint John Also Called: Gallagher Environmental Inc *(G-14450)*

Carver, Wabash Also Called: Fred S Carver Inc *(G-16188)*

Carver Inc 260 563-7577
1569 Morris St Wabash (46992) *(G-16177)*

Carver Non-Woven Indiana LLC 260 627-0033
706 E Depot St Fremont (46737) *(G-5814)*

Carver Non-Woven Tech LLC 260 627-0033
706 E Depot St Fremont (46737) *(G-5815)*

Carvers Truck and Trailer LLC 574 343-2240
2946 Jami St Elkhart (46514) *(G-3248)*

Cascade Metrix LLC 317 572-7094
12321 Hawks Nest Dr Fishers (46037) *(G-4484)*

Cascades Holding US Inc 219 697-2900
3126 E 500 S Brook (47922) *(G-1304)*

Cascades Moulded Pulp-Indiana, Brook Also Called: Cascades Holding US Inc *(G-1304)*

Case Indy Products Inc 317 677-0200
407 Ansley Ct Indianapolis (46234) *(G-7753)*

Case Lineage Management 317 721-1764
12125 E 65th St Unit 36838 Indianapolis (46236) *(G-7754)*

Case New Holland LLC 765 482-5446
420 S Enterprise Blvd Lebanon (46052) *(G-10881)*

Case Weinkauff 219 733-9484
671 E 100 S Valparaiso (46383) *(G-15925)*

Cases Marine Service Inc 317 379-0020
6281 E 261st St Arcadia (46030) *(G-310)*

Cash & Carry Lumber Co Inc 765 378-7575
14113 W Main St Daleville (47334) *(G-2797)*

Cash Concrete Products Inc 765 653-4887
State Road 240 Greencastle (46135) *(G-6394)*

Cash Concrete Products Inc (PA) 765 653-4007
1541 S County Road 450 E Greencastle (46135) *(G-6395)*

Cash Logging LLC 812 843-5335
20198 N State Road 66 Mount Pleasant (47520) *(G-12283)*

Casper LLC 660 221-5906
4310 Stout Field North Dr Indianapolis (46241) *(G-7755)*

Cass County Byproducts, Logansport Also Called: Bhj Usa LLC *(G-11062)*

Cass County Machine Inc 574 722-5714
2915 Green Hills Dr Logansport (46947) *(G-11066)*

Cassie Cakes LLC 219 308-3320
3824 170th St Hammond (46323) *(G-6896)*

Cast Metals Technology 765 284-3888
11200 E State Road 32 Selma (47383) *(G-14621)*

Cast Metals Technology Inc 765 584-6501
1036 N Old Highway 27 Winchester (47394) *(G-16883)*

Cast Products LP (DH) 574 294-2684
5400 Beck Dr Elkhart (46516) *(G-3249)*

Cast Products LP 574 255-9619
1711 Clover Rd Mishawaka (46545) *(G-11859)*

Cast Stone 317 617-1088
5236 Basin Park Dr Indianapolis (46239) *(G-7756)*

Casters In Motion USA Ltd LLC 812 437-4627
1513 N Cullen Ave Evansville (47715) *(G-3965)*

Casting Company Inc 317 509-4311
8047 Raindance Trl Indianapolis (46239) *(G-7757)*

Casting Service, La Porte Also Called: Kennametal Inc *(G-10435)*

Castleton Village Center Inc (PA) 260 471-5959
6321 Huguenard Rd Ste A Fort Wayne (46818) *(G-4837)*

Castleton Village Center Inc 317 577-1995
450 E 96th St Indianapolis (46240) *(G-7758)*

Cat People Press LLC 260 750-8652
1836 Glenwood Ave Fort Wayne (46805) *(G-4838)*

Catalent Indiana LLC 812 355-6746
3770 W Jonathan Dr Bloomington (47404) *(G-823)*

Catalent Indiana LLC (DH) 812 355-6746
1300 S Patterson Dr Bloomington (47403) *(G-824)*

Catalent Pharma Services, Bloomington Also Called: Catalent Pharma Solutions Inc *(G-825)*

Catalent Pharma Solutions Inc 812 355-4498
1300 S Patterson Dr Bloomington (47403) *(G-825)*

Catalent Wellness LLC (DH) 800 344-6225
601 Rudolph Way Greendale (47025) *(G-6441)*

Catalent Wellness Holdings LLC (HQ) 800 344-6225
601 Rudolph Way Greendale (47025) *(G-6442)*

Catalent Wellness Indiana LLC 812 537-5203
601 Rudolph Way Greendale (47025) *(G-6443)*

Catalpa Valley, North Vernon Also Called: Daniel Shade *(G-13263)*

Catalyst Inc (PA) 317 227-3499
2680 E Main St Ste 324 Plainfield (46168) *(G-13665)*

Catalyst USA, Plainfield Also Called: Catalyst Inc *(G-13665)*

Catchrs LLC 310 902-9723
365 E 75th St Indianapolis (46240) *(G-7759)*

Catco, Hobart Also Called: Airtek LLC *(G-7172)*

Cater To You Catering LLC 219 301-1091
994 Deer Cross Trl Hobart (46342) *(G-7179)*

Caterpillar, Greenfield Also Called: Caterpillar Inc *(G-6476)*

Caterpillar, Lafayette Also Called: Caterpillar Inc *(G-10549)*

Caterpillar, Lafayette Also Called: Caterpillar Inc *(G-10550)*

Caterpillar Authorized Dealer, Fort Wayne Also Called: Macallister Machinery Co Inc *(G-5195)*

Caterpillar Authorized Dealer, Richmond Also Called: Macallister Machinery Co Inc *(G-14157)*

Caterpillar Inc 630 743-4094
6719 W 350 N Greenfield (46140) *(G-6476)*

Caterpillar Inc 765 448-5000
3701 South St Lafayette (47905) *(G-10549)*

Caterpillar Inc 765 447-6816
1451 Veterans Memorial Pkwy E Lafayette (47905) *(G-10550)*

Caterpillar Remn Powrtrn Indna (HQ) 317 738-2117
751 International Dr Franklin (46131) *(G-5718)*

Catherine J Bergren 219 225-2819
862 Floyd St Gary (46403) *(G-5913)*

Catheter Research Inc 317 872-0074
6102 Victory Way Indianapolis (46278) *(G-7760)*

Catholic Church School Market, Tell City Also Called: Charles E Watts *(G-15498)*

Catholic Moment 765 742-2050
610 Lingle Ave Lafayette (47901) *(G-10551)*

Catholic Press of Evansville 812 424-5536
4200 N Kentucky Ave Evansville (47711) *(G-3966)*

Catholic Woodworker 317 413-4276
14844 Admiral Way N Carmel (46032) *(G-1583)*

Cause Printing Company 765 573-3330
2812 Theater Ave Huntington (46750) *(G-7305)*

Cave & Co. Printing, Westfield Also Called: Damalak Printing Inc *(G-16683)*

Cave Company Printing Inc 812 863-4333
5282 S Black Ankle Rd Bloomfield (47424) *(G-743)*

Cave Quarries Inc 812 936-7743
1156 N County Road 425 W Paoli (47454) *(G-13492)*

Cavity Factofy LLC 317 937-5385
8144 Crackling Ln Indianapolis (46259) *(G-7761)*

CB Fabrication 765 649-1336
425 Sycamore St Anderson (46016) *(G-90)*

Cbd Revolution LLC 463 888-2806
10202 E Washington St Ste 446 Indianapolis (46229) *(G-7762)*

Cbd Solutions LLC 765 477-1900
2469 State St Lafayette (47905) *(G-10552)*

Cbdm Inc 317 218-3786
14655 N Gray Rd Westfield (46062) *(G-16672)*

Cbf Forensics LLC 708 383-8320
201 N Linda St Hobart (46342) *(G-7180)*

Cbfc LLC (PA) 317 677-1577
7698 Zionsville Rd Indianapolis (46268) *(G-7763)*

Cbizze LLC 623 204-9782
1709 Pulaski St South Bend (46613) *(G-14968)*

Cbrk LLC 317 601-8546
6025 W 46th St Indianapolis (46254) *(G-7764)*

Ccd Northwoods LLC 219 690-1868
12805 W 159th Ave Lowell (46356) *(G-11158)*

CCI Big Boy Products, Warsaw Also Called: Cardinal Services Inc Indiana *(G-16332)*

CCI Contract Manufacturing, Warsaw *Also Called: Cardinal Services Inc Indiana (G-16334)*

CCM Industries Inc... 765 545-0597
610 N 100 E Winchester (47394) *(G-16884)*

Ccmp Inc... 219 922-8935
1313 E Main St Griffith (46319) *(G-6799)*

Ccoa of Indiana, Hammond *Also Called: Control Consultants of America (G-6905)*

CCT Enterprises LLC.. 260 925-1420
530 North St Auburn (46706) *(G-375)*

Ccts Technology Group Inc... 305 209-5743
8403 N Illinois St Indianapolis (46260) *(G-7765)*

CD & Ws Bordner Entps Inc.. 765 268-2120
6559 S State Road 75 Cutler (46920) *(G-2783)*

CD Grafix LLC.. 812 945-4443
632 Providence Way Ste 3 Clarksville (47129) *(G-2011)*

Cdb Screen Printing Inc... 765 472-4404
2131 W Otter Creek Dr Peru (46970) *(G-13570)*

CDP Logistics Inc... 773 968-1455
1943 Collingwood Dr Avon (46123) *(G-510)*

Cds LLC.. 812 637-0900
99 Mill St West Harrison (47060) *(G-16545)*

Ce Systems Inc.. 812 372-8234
1045 S Gladstone Ave Columbus (47201) *(G-2235)*

Ceadogs LLC-S.. 219 779-1352
100 N Montgomery St Gary (46403) *(G-5914)*

Cec Controls Company Inc.. 219 728-6007
100 Brown Ave Chesterton (46304) *(G-1908)*

Cecils Printing & Off Sups Inc.. 812 683-4416
319 E 4th St Huntingburg (47542) *(G-7273)*

Cedar Creek Distillery LLC... 765 342-9000
3820 Leonard Rd Martinsville (46151) *(G-11384)*

Cedar Creek Sawmill LLC.. 260 627-3985
15010 Page Rd Grabill (46741) *(G-6291)*

Cedar Creek Studios Inc.. 260 627-7320
7030 Hosler Rd Leo (46765) *(G-10966)*

Cedar Creek Winery.. 765 342-9000
3820 Leonard Rd Martinsville (46151) *(G-11385)*

Cedar Creek Winery.. 812 988-1111
36 E Franklin St Nashville (47448) *(G-12667)*

Cedar Creek Woodworking LLC... 812 687-7556
8374 N 650 E Odon (47562) *(G-13332)*

Cedar Plastics Inc.. 765 483-3260
1016 W Main St Rear Lebanon (46052) *(G-10882)*

Cedar Shack.. 219 682-5531
11300 W 131st Pl Cedar Lake (46303) *(G-1829)*

Cedar Woodworking.. 812 486-2765
7932 E 625 N Montgomery (47558) *(G-12088)*

Cedric Morris.. 678 718-0012
9783 E 116th St Fishers (46037) *(G-4485)*

Cei, Columbus *Also Called: Columbus Engineering Inc (G-2243)*

Celanese Corporation... 812 421-8900
2300 Lynch Rd Evansville (47711) *(G-3967)*

Celebration Ice LLC... 812 634-9801
31 S Clay St Jasper (47546) *(G-9826)*

Celebration Station, Merrillville *Also Called: Whiteco Industries Inc (G-11572)*

Celestial Candle.. 812 886-4819
138 E 17th St Vincennes (47591) *(G-16117)*

Celestial Designs, Zionsville *Also Called: Celestial Designs LLC (G-16997)*

Celestial Designs LLC.. 317 733-3110
80 N First St Zionsville (46077) *(G-16997)*

Cellofoam North America Inc.. 317 535-9008
150 Crossroads Dr Whiteland (46184) *(G-16778)*

Cemex... 317 351-9912
1051 S Emerson Ave Indianapolis (46203) *(G-7766)*

Cemex Materials LLC.. 317 891-7500
6662 W 350 N Greenfield (46140) *(G-6477)*

Cemex Materials LLC.. 317 891-3015
1501 S Holt Rd Indianapolis (46241) *(G-7767)*

Cemex Materials LLC.. 317 769-5601
4360 Whitelick Dr Whitestown (46075) *(G-16803)*

Centennial Graphics Group, Clarksville *Also Called: Centennial Group Inc (G-2012)*

Centennial Group Inc.. 812 948-2886
1330 Woerner Ave Clarksville (47129) *(G-2012)*

Center Concrete Inc.. 800 453-4224
4225 County Road 79 Butler (46721) *(G-1460)*

CENTER CONCRETE INC, Butler *Also Called: Center Concrete Inc.(G-1460)*

Center For Dagnstc Imaging CDI... 812 331-7727
3802 W Industrial Blvd Ste 4 Bloomington (47403) *(G-826)*

Center For Diagnostic Imaging... 812 234-0555
4313 S 7th St Terre Haute (47802) *(G-15557)*

Center For Ethcal Rbtics A Nnt... 219 741-9374
5530 Sohl Ave Hammond (46320) *(G-6897)*

Center For Orthtic Prsthtic Ex... 219 365-0248
2213 Main St Unit 1c-102 Highland (46322) *(G-7128)*

Center For The Study Knwldge D.. 812 361-4424
1441 S Fenbrook Ln Ste 300 Bloomington (47401) *(G-827)*

Center Line Mold & Tool Inc.. 812 526-0970
703 S Eisenhower Dr Edinburgh (46124) *(G-3070)*

Centerline Manufacturing.. 260 348-7400
18628 Wappes Rd Churubusco (46723) *(G-1983)*

Centerline Manufacturing Inc... 260 348-7400
4611 Newaygo Rd Ste E Fort Wayne (46808) *(G-4839)*

Centerline Woodworking.. 260 768-4116
695 S 600 W Lagrange (46761) *(G-10731)*

Centerpoint Brewing, Indianapolis *Also Called: Centerpoint Brewing Co LLC (G-7768)*

Centerpoint Brewing Co LLC.. 317 602-8386
1125 Brookside Ave Ste B1 Indianapolis (46202) *(G-7768)*

Central Bakery, Valparaiso *Also Called: Indiana Grocery Group LLC (G-15971)*

Central Brace & Limb Co Inc (PA)....................................... 317 925-4296
1901 N Capitol Ave Indianapolis (46202) *(G-7769)*

Central Brace & Limb Co Inc.. 765 457-4868
802 S Berkley Rd Ste B Kokomo (46901) *(G-10243)*

Central Brace & Limb Co Inc.. 812 232-2145
500 E Springhill Dr Ste G Terre Haute (47802) *(G-15558)*

Central Coca-Cola Btlg Co Inc.. 765 642-9951
3200 E 38th St Anderson (46013) *(G-91)*

Central Coca-Cola Btlg Co Inc.. 800 241-2653
1701 S Liberty Dr Bloomington (47403) *(G-828)*

Central Coca-Cola Btlg Co Inc.. 260 478-2978
5010 Airport Expy Fort Wayne (46809) *(G-4840)*

Central Coca-Cola Btlg Co Inc.. 800 241-2653
8351 Northwest Blvd Indianapolis (46278) *(G-7770)*

Central Coca-Cola Btlg Co Inc.. 317 398-0129
5000 W 25th St Indianapolis (46224) *(G-7771)*

Central Coca-Cola Btlg Co Inc.. 317 243-3771
3830 Hanna Cir Indianapolis (46241) *(G-7772)*

Central Coca-Cola Btlg Co Inc.. 812 482-7475
641 Wernsing Rd Jasper (47546) *(G-9827)*

Central Coca-Cola Btlg Co Inc.. 260 726-7126
1617 N Meridian St Portland (47371) *(G-13930)*

Central Coca-Cola Btlg Co Inc.. 800 241-2653
405 N Harrison St Shelbyville (46176) *(G-14744)*

Central Coca-Cola Btlg Co Inc.. 574 291-1511
1400 W Ireland Rd South Bend (46614) *(G-14969)*

Central Concrete Supply LLC... 812 481-2331
801 E 230s Jasper (47546) *(G-9828)*

Central Illinois Steel Company... 219 882-1026
50 N Bridge St Gary (46404) *(G-5915)*

Central Indiana Ethanol LLC... 765 384-4001
12911 N Meridian St Ste 101 Carmel (46032) *(G-1584)*

Central Indiana Ethanol LLC (PA)....................................... 765 384-4001
2955 W Delphi Pike Marion (46952) *(G-11277)*

Central Indiana Woodworkers.. 317 407-9228
1702 Misty Lake Dr Indianapolis (46260) *(G-7773)*

Central Rubber & Plastics Inc... 574 534-6411
17416 County Road 34 Goshen (46528) *(G-6110)*

Central Services Print Shop, South Bend *Also Called: City South Bend Building Corp (G-14973)*

Central States Fabricating.. 574 288-5607
3015 N Kenmore St South Bend (46628) *(G-14970)*

Central States Mfg Inc.. 219 879-4770
2051 Tryon Rd Michigan City (46360) *(G-11586)*

Central Steel and Wire Co LLC.. 219 787-5000
501 George Nelson Dr Portage (46368) *(G-13854)*

ALPHABETIC SECTION

Central Steel Coil Processing, Portage *Also Called: Central Steel and Wire Co LLC (G-13854)*
Central Tool Co Inc 317 485-5344
  767 W Garden St Fortville (46040) *(G-5588)*
Central Van Lines Inc 317 849-7900
  8010 Castleton Rd Indianapolis (46250) *(G-7774)*
Central Wire Industries, Michigan City *Also Called: Sanlo Inc (G-11664)*
Centre Township 765 482-1729
  525 Ransdell Rd Lebanon (46052) *(G-10883)*
Centrifuge Chicago, Hammond *Also Called: Centrifuge Chicago Corporation (G-6898)*
Centrifuge Chicago Corporation 219 852-5200
  6015 Hump Rd Hammond (46320) *(G-6898)*
Centrifuge Support & Sups LLC 317 830-6141
  1418 Dallas Dr Plainfield (46168) *(G-13666)*
Centrum Force Fabrication 574 295-5367
  204 W Clinton St Goshen (46526) *(G-6111)*
Centura Solid Surfacing Inc 317 867-5555
  3525 W State Road 32 Westfield (46074) *(G-16673)*
Centurion Arms LLC 619 994-5756
  8985 N Carmel Ridge Rd Morgantown (46160) *(G-12254)*
Centurion Industries Inc (PA) 260 357-6665
  1107 N Taylor Rd Garrett (46738) *(G-5855)*
Century Concrete Inc 765 739-6210
  3725 W Us Highway 36 Bainbridge (46105) *(G-560)*
Century Foam, Elkhart *Also Called: Century Foam Inc (G-3250)*
Century Foam Inc (PA) 574 293-5547
  2600 S Nappanee St Elkhart (46517) *(G-3250)*
Century Grave & Vault Service 812 967-2110
  2807 S Franklin School Rd Pekin (47165) *(G-13513)*
Century Industries LLC 812 246-3371
  299 Prather Ln Sellersburg (47172) *(G-14590)*
Century Marble Co Inc 317 867-5555
  3525 W State Road 32 Westfield (46074) *(G-16674)*
Century Memorial, Bainbridge *Also Called: Century Concrete Inc (G-560)*
Century Pharmaceuticals Inc 317 849-4210
  10377 Hague Rd Indianapolis (46256) *(G-7775)*
Century Steel Fabricating Inc 317 834-1295
  4421 E County Line Rd Camby (46113) *(G-1508)*
Century Tool & Engr Inc 317 685-0942
  1330 Deloss St Indianapolis (46203) *(G-7776)*
Century Tube, Madison *Also Called: Allied Tube & Conduit Corp (G-11201)*
Century Tube LLC 812 265-9255
  4004 N Us 421 Madison (47250) *(G-11206)*
Cenveo Worldwide Limited 800 995-9500
  4115 Profit Ct New Albany (47150) *(G-12710)*
Ceramic Fiber Enterprises Inc 765 362-2179
  503 W 300 N Crawfordsville (47933) *(G-2551)*
Ceramica Inc 317 546-0087
  6695 E 34th St Indianapolis (46226) *(G-7777)*
Cereplast Inc 310 615-1900
  2213 Killion Ave Seymour (47274) *(G-14637)*
Cerline Ceramic Corp 765 649-7222
  1415 Fairview St Anderson (46016) *(G-92)*
Cerro Wire LLC 812 793-2929
  1002 Industrial Way Crothersville (47229) *(G-2638)*
Certa Craft Inc 317 535-0226
  3902 E 16th St Ste A Indianapolis (46201) *(G-7778)*
Certainteed LLC 812 645-0400
  1001 W Industrial Dr Terre Haute (47802) *(G-15559)*
Certified Automotive & Mch Sp 317 897-9724
  8340 E Washington St Indianapolis (46219) *(G-7779)*
Certified Choice Truckers LLC 260 615-3437
  1211 Bethany Ln Fort Wayne (46825) *(G-4841)*
Certified Clipper Inc 317 894-3787
  6790 W 300 N Greenfield (46140) *(G-6478)*
Certified Welding Company Inc 765 522-3238
  5355 E County Road 500 N Bainbridge (46105) *(G-561)*
Certor Sports LLC (PA) 800 426-9784
  9400 Bradford Rd Plainfield (46168) *(G-13667)*
Cervantes-Screens, Fredericksburg *Also Called: Screens (G-5796)*
Cervella, Carmel *Also Called: Innovtive Nurological Dvcs LLC (G-1670)*
Cesars Welding LLC 317 938-8830
  1213 N Sherman Dr Indianapolis (46201) *(G-7780)*

CF Gunworks LLC 317 538-1122
  1157 S County Road 1000 E Frankfort (46041) *(G-5653)*
Cfn 260 LLC 260 241-5678
  5625 Breconshire Dr Fort Wayne (46804) *(G-4842)*
Cgenetech Inc 317 295-1925
  7940 Crestway Dr Apt 1010 Indianapolis (46236) *(G-7781)*
Cgf Enterprises LLC 574 889-2074
  5438 N County Road 75 W Logansport (46947) *(G-11067)*
Cgm, Whitestown *Also Called: Precast Solutions Inc (G-16816)*
Cgs Services Inc 765 763-6258
  2920 E Us Highway 52 Morristown (46161) *(G-12273)*
CH Ellis Co Inc (PA) 317 636-3351
  2432 Southeastern Ave Indianapolis (46201) *(G-7782)*
Ch Manufacturing 812 234-4600
  4411 S Trudys Pl Terre Haute (47802) *(G-15560)*
Chad Simons 219 405-1620
  803 Shannon Dr Chesterton (46304) *(G-1909)*
Chad's Towing and Recovery, Ellettsville *Also Called: Chads LLC (G-3802)*
Chads LLC 812 323-7377
  6679 W Mcneely St Ellettsville (47429) *(G-3802)*
Chads Signs Installations Inc (PA) 317 867-2737
  555 Park 32 West Dr Noblesville (46062) *(G-13056)*
Challenge Plastic Products Inc 812 526-0582
  110 W Industrial Dr Edinburgh (46124) *(G-3071)*
Challenge Tool & Mfg Inc 260 749-9558
  11725 Lincoln Hwy E New Haven (46774) *(G-12898)*
Challenger Design, Nappanee *Also Called: HB International LLC (G-12606)*
Challenger Door Plant 58, Nappanee *Also Called: HB International LLC (G-12604)*
Chameleon Lifestyles LLC 317 468-3246
  1678 E Grey Feather Trl Greenfield (46140) *(G-6479)*
Champ Converters, Evansville *Also Called: Champ Torque Converters Inc (G-3969)*
Champ Converters Incorporated 812 424-2602
  1914 N Denby Ave Evansville (47711) *(G-3968)*
Champ Torque Converters Inc 812 424-2602
  1914 N Denby Ave Evansville (47711) *(G-3969)*
Champion Racing Engines LLC 317 335-2491
  5002 W State Road 234 Mccordsville (46055) *(G-11446)*
Champion Target 765 966-7745
  232 Industrial Pkwy Richmond (47374) *(G-14103)*
Champion Wood Products Inc 812 282-9460
  840 S Penn Ave Ste A Sellersburg (47172) *(G-14591)*
Champions Image 317 501-3617
  19122 Timothy Ln Noblesville (46060) *(G-13057)*
Chance Abrasives 219 871-0977
  217 Twilight Dr Michigan City (46360) *(G-11587)*
Chance Ind Standards Lab Inc 317 787-6578
  2919 Shelby St Indianapolis (46203) *(G-7783)*
Chanel J Luxury Collection LLC 470 210-4706
  4407 Lakefield Trce Indianapolis (46254) *(G-7784)*
Channel 40 Network LLC 317 794-6150
  4248 Royalty Dr Apt E Indianapolis (46254) *(G-7785)*
Chaos Machine Division Inc 812 306-7380
  424 N Willow Rd Evansville (47711) *(G-3970)*
Chapdells Tree & Plant Design 317 845-9980
  11480 E 111th St Fishers (46037) *(G-4486)*
Chapman Environmental Controls 574 674-8706
  10463 Pleasant Valley Ct Osceola (46561) *(G-13386)*
Chapmans Cider Company LLC 260 444-1194
  300 Industrial Dr Angola (46703) *(G-239)*
Chappelle Canvas and Uphl 765 505-3925
  3655 E Grant Ave Terre Haute (47805) *(G-15561)*
Chappelles Sheet Metal Shop 812 246-2121
  14504 State Road 60 Borden (47106) *(G-1106)*
Chappos Inc 219 942-8101
  101 N Wabash St Hobart (46342) *(G-7181)*
Charles Bane 765 855-5100
  2009 Willow Grove Rd Centerville (47330) *(G-1848)*
Charles Coons 765 362-6509
  2401 Indianapolis Rd Crawfordsville (47933) *(G-2552)*
Charles E Obryan 812 536-2399
  8999 S 500w Huntingburg (47542) *(G-7274)*

Charles E Watts — 812 547-8516
42 Zurich Way Tell City (47586) *(G-15498)*

Charles Kolb Logging — 765 458-7766
7096 S Snowden Rd Liberty (47353) *(G-10985)*

Charles Kolb Sons Logging — 765 647-4309
1135 John St Brookville (47012) *(G-1317)*

Charles Stewart — 812 801-9694
3519 N Shun Pike Rd Madison (47250) *(G-11207)*

Charles W Knies Sawmill, Huntingburg Also Called: Knies Sawmill Inc *(G-7285)*

Charles Wnngs DBA Dassault AVI — 928 276-4983
6871 Pierson Dr Indianapolis (46241) *(G-7786)*

Charleston, Bremen Also Called: Patrick Industries Inc *(G-1212)*

Charleston Metal Products Inc — 260 281-9972
1746 Us Highway 6 Corunna (46730) *(G-2481)*

Charleston Metal Products Inc — 260 837-8211
350 Grant St Waterloo (46793) *(G-16516)*

Charleston Metal Products Inc (PA) — 260 837-8211
350 Grant St Waterloo (46793) *(G-16517)*

Charlie N83 Inc — 260 625-4211
12207 Illinois Rd Fort Wayne (46814) *(G-4843)*

Charmaran Company LLC — 260 347-3347
1451 Stonebraker Dr Kendallville (46755) *(G-10098)*

Chart Lifecycle Inc — 317 535-4315
1725 N Graham Rd Franklin (46131) *(G-5719)*

Chase Beford — 812 277-7028
1602 I St Bedford (47421) *(G-626)*

Chase Manufacturing LLC (PA) — 574 546-4776
506 S Oakland Ave Nappanee (46550) *(G-12588)*

Chase N Corydon — 812 738-3032
1881 Old Highway 135 Nw Corydon (47112) *(G-2490)*

Chase Plastic Services Inc — 574 239-4090
5245 Dylan Dr South Bend (46628) *(G-14971)*

Chase Southport Emerson — 317 266-7470
7120 Emblem Dr Indianapolis (46237) *(G-7787)*

Chasin Paper LLC — 317 429-6116
5282 Jonathan Trce Apt 2c Indianapolis (46226) *(G-7788)*

Chateau De Pique Inc (PA) — 812 522-9296
101 N Poplar St Seymour (47274) *(G-14638)*

Chateau Thomas Winery Inc (PA) — 317 837-9463
6291 Cambridge Way Plainfield (46168) *(G-13668)*

Chatter House Press — 317 514-4133
7915 S Emerson Ave Ste B303 Indianapolis (46237) *(G-7789)*

Chatterup LLC — 317 213-6283
16272 Dandborn Dr Westfield (46074) *(G-16675)*

Che's Da'zines and Printz, South Bend Also Called: Esther Reid *(G-15018)*

Checkered Past Racing Pdts LLC — 317 852-6978
481 Southpoint Cir Ste 8 Brownsburg (46112) *(G-1359)*

Checkered Racing & Chrome LLC — 812 275-2875
2221 N St Rd Spencer (47460) *(G-15341)*

Cheddar Stacks Inc — 317 566-0425
5875 Castle Creek Parkway North Dr Ste 310 Indianapolis (46250) *(G-7790)*

Cheercussion LLC — 317 762-4009
1091 3rd Ave Sw Carmel (46032) *(G-1585)*

Cheetah Building Products — 812 466-1234
4600 N 13th St Terre Haute (47805) *(G-15562)*

Chef Hymie Grande, New Albany Also Called: Chef Hymie Inc *(G-12711)*

Chef Hymie Inc — 201 218-4378
13 Wynn Gate Ct New Albany (47150) *(G-12711)*

Chef Mikes Private Chef Catrg, Michigan City Also Called: Myfoodmixer LLC *(G-11644)*

Chegar Manufacturing Company — 765 945-7444
951 N Independence St Windfall (46076) *(G-16904)*

Chem Tech Inc — 574 848-1001
501 Bloomingdale Dr Bristol (46507) *(G-1253)*

Chem-Aqua — 317 899-3660
8401 E 33rd St Indianapolis (46226) *(G-7791)*

Chem-Dry, Fort Wayne Also Called: Chem-Dry of Allen County *(G-4844)*

Chem-Dry of Allen County — 260 490-2705
10214 Chestnut Plaza Dr Fort Wayne (46814) *(G-4844)*

Chem-Elec, North Webster Also Called: Chematics Inc *(G-13303)*

Chematics Inc — 574 834-2406
4519 Highway 13 S North Webster (46555) *(G-13303)*

Chemcoaters LLC — 219 977-1929
700 Chase St Gary (46404) *(G-5916)*

Chemical Control Systems Inc (PA) — 219 465-5103
403 Industrial Dr Griffith (46319) *(G-6800)*

Chemical Ingrdent Ppe Jn-San D, Indianapolis Also Called: Williams Distribution LLC *(G-9767)*

Chemicals Inc USA — 317 334-1000
8194 Allison Ave Indianapolis (46268) *(G-7792)*

Chemque Inc — 800 268-6111
6107 Guion Rd Indianapolis (46254) *(G-7793)*

Chemstation, Carmel Also Called: Paradigm Industries Inc *(G-1714)*

Chemtec LLC — 812 499-8408
5309 Ellington Ct Newburgh (47630) *(G-12997)*

Chemtrade Solutions LLC — 317 917-0319
1598 S Senate Ave Indianapolis (46225) *(G-7794)*

Chemtrex LLC — 317 508-4223
6315 Edenshall Ln Noblesville (46062) *(G-13058)*

Chemtrusion Inc — 812 280-2910
1403 Port Rd Jeffersonville (47130) *(G-9951)*

Chemtrusion-Indiana, Jeffersonville Also Called: Chemtrusion Inc *(G-9951)*

Chep (usa) Inc — 317 780-0700
606 W Troy Ave Indianapolis (46225) *(G-7795)*

Cheri-Theree Inc — 812 529-8132
Lamar (47550) *(G-10795)*

Cherished Woodcraft — 317 502-4451
627 W South St Greenfield (46140) *(G-6480)*

Cherry Hill Shopping Park, Connersville Also Called: Coach Line Motors *(G-2431)*

Cherry Hill Vineyard LLC — 317 846-5170
10236 Ditch Rd Carmel (46032) *(G-1586)*

Chesapeake Recycling Inc — 574 946-6602
1600 S Us Highway 35 Winamac (46996) *(G-16859)*

Chessex, Fort Wayne Also Called: Chessex Manufacturing Co LLC *(G-4845)*

Chessex Manufacturing Co LLC — 260 471-9511
3415 Centennial Dr Fort Wayne (46808) *(G-4845)*

Chester Inc — 574 896-5600
6020 S 500 W North Judson (46366) *(G-13209)*

Chester Pool Systems Inc — 812 949-7333
5311 Foundation Blvd New Albany (47150) *(G-12712)*

Chesterfield Tool & Engrg Inc — 765 378-5101
13710 W Commerce Rd Daleville (47334) *(G-2798)*

Chesterton Printing Co — 219 250-2896
102 Brown Ave Chesterton (46304) *(G-1910)*

Chestnut Land Company — 574 271-8740
6501 Grape Rd Ste 670a Mishawaka (46545) *(G-11860)*

Cheyenne Enterprises LLC — 317 253-7795
6100 N Keystone Ave Ste 105 Indianapolis (46220) *(G-7796)*

CHG Developments LLC — 720 480-0957
1075 Broad Ripple Ave # 202 Indianapolis (46220) *(G-7797)*

Chicago Automated Labeling Inc — 219 531-0646
44 N 450 E Valparaiso (46383) *(G-15926)*

Chicago Bifold — 708 532-4365
2640 Condit St Highland (46322) *(G-7129)*

Chicago Case Company, Indianapolis Also Called: Mpiche LLC *(G-8965)*

Chicago Cold Rolling LLC — 219 787-2021
250 W Us Highway 12 Chesterton (46304) *(G-1911)*

Chicago Crusader News Group — 219 885-4357
1549 Broadway Gary (46407) *(G-5917)*

Chicago Flame Hardening Co — 773 768-3608
5200 Railroad Ave Ste 1 East Chicago (46312) *(G-2995)*

Chicago Steel Ltd Partnership — 219 949-1111
700 Chase St Gary (46404) *(G-5918)*

Chicken and Salsa Inc — 812 480-6580
1513 S Green River Rd Evansville (47715) *(G-3971)*

Chief Automotive Technologies, Madison Also Called: Vehicle Service Group LLC *(G-11255)*

Chief Automotive Technologies, Madison Also Called: Vehicle Service Group LLC *(G-11256)*

Chief Industries Inc — 219 866-4121
1225 E Maple St Rensselaer (47978) *(G-14047)*

Chief Metal Works Inc — 765 932-2134
1705 W Us Highway 52 Rushville (46173) *(G-14396)*

Chief Powerboats Inc — 219 775-7024
280 Wood St Crown Point (46307) *(G-2665)*

ALPHABETIC SECTION — CIT

Chikol Equities, Granger *Also Called: Sentinel Services Inc (G-6376)*
CHILDREN'S BETTER HEALTH INSTI, Indianapolis *Also Called: Saturday Evening Post Soc Inc (G-9379)*
   Childrens Outreach 317 535-7014
      26 Erins Ct Whiteland (46184) *(G-16779)*
   Chillers Microcreamery LLC 812 987-1298
      Floyds Knobs (47119) *(G-4671)*
   Chinook Motor Coach Corp 574 584-3756
      1482 N Eel River Cemetery Rd Peru (46970) *(G-13571)*
   Chip Ganassi Racing Teams Inc 317 802-0000
      7777 Woodland Dr Indianapolis (46278) *(G-7798)*
   Chisholm Lumber & Supply Co 317 547-3535
      3419 Roosevelt Ave Indianapolis (46218) *(G-7799)*
   Chiyoda Montrow Die Mfg Inc 812 767-1885
      640 Ertel Ln North Vernon (47265) *(G-13257)*
   Chiyoda USA Corporation 765 653-9098
      2200 E State Road 240 Greencastle (46135) *(G-6396)*
Chocolate Moose, The, Bloomington *Also Called: Penguin Enterprises LLC (G-944)*
Chore-Time Plty Prod Systems, Milford *Also Called: Ctb Inc (G-11791)*
   Chris Schwartz 260 615-9574
      13631 Spencerville Rd Grabill (46741) *(G-6292)*
   Christ Packing Systems Corp 574 243-9110
      316 S Eddy St South Bend (46617) *(G-14972)*
   Christian Candle Company 317 427-8070
      1509 Mary Dr Indianapolis (46241) *(G-7800)*
   Christian Sound & Song Inc 574 294-2893
      56718 Coppergate Dr Elkhart (46516) *(G-3251)*
   Christie Machine Works Co Inc 317 638-8840
      425 W Mccarty St Indianapolis (46225) *(G-7801)*
   Christina Ann Clark 317 778-7832
      10547 Moqui Ct Indianapolis (46235) *(G-7802)*
   Christman Logging 502 525-2649
      7641 N Bacon Ridge Rd Madison (47250) *(G-11208)*
   Christopher Engle 812 876-3540
      7251 W State Road 46 Ellettsville (47429) *(G-3803)*
Christy Minerals, Valparaiso *Also Called: Christy Refractories Co Llc (G-15927)*
   Christy Refractories Co Llc 219 464-2856
      402 Wall St Valparaiso (46383) *(G-15927)*
   Christys Design & Sign Inc 317 882-5444
      500 Polk St Ste 17 Greenwood (46143) *(G-6680)*
Chromasource, Columbia City *Also Called: Chromasource Inc (G-2130)*
   Chromasource Inc 260 420-3000
      2433 S Cr 600 E Columbia City (46725) *(G-2130)*
   Chrome Deposit Corporation (HQ) 219 763-1571
      6640 Melton Rd Portage (46368) *(G-13855)*
Chronicle-Tribune, Marion *Also Called: Paxton Media Group LLC (G-11324)*
Chrysler Foundry, Kokomo *Also Called: FCA North America Holdings LLC (G-10264)*
Chrysler Transmission, Kokomo *Also Called: FCA North America Holdings LLC (G-10265)*
   Chryso Inc 812 256-4220
      10600 Highway 62 Unit 7 Charlestown (47111) *(G-1873)*
   CHS Legacy Company 260 456-3596
      2921 E Crescent Ave Columbia City (46725) *(G-2131)*
   Chubbs Steel Sales Inc 574 295-3166
      57832 County Road 3 Elkhart (46517) *(G-3252)*
   Chuck Bivens Services Inc 260 747-6195
      10216 Airport Dr Fort Wayne (46809) *(G-4846)*
   Chuck Cable 765 981-2800
      1 Rennaker St La Fontaine (46940) *(G-10367)*
   Chuck Shane Gravel LLC 574 893-4110
      7930 W State Road 114 Silver Lake (46982) *(G-14918)*
   Chuck Stace-Allen Inc 317 632-2401
      2246 W Minnesota St Ste 50 Indianapolis (46221) *(G-7803)*
   Chucks Cleaners LLC 260 488-3362
      3820 E Bellefontaine Rd Hamilton (46742) *(G-6851)*
   Chuppville Carving 574 354-7642
      11726 N 1000 W Nappanee (46550) *(G-12589)*
   Churchassist Technologies LLC 574 238-2307
      23879 Banyan Cir Elkhart (46516) *(G-3253)*
   Churchill Cigars 812 273-2249
      605 W 2nd St Madison (47250) *(G-11209)*
   Churchill Equipment 812 347-2592
      4880 Adams Rd Nw Depauw (47115) *(G-2937)*

   Ci Publishing Ecomm LLC 317 679-1866
      5534 Saint Joe Rd Fort Wayne (46835) *(G-4847)*
   Cibus Fresh LLC 317 674-8379
      15510 Stony Creek Way Noblesville (46060) *(G-13059)*
   Ciderleaf Tea Company Inc 812 375-1937
      4525 Progress Dr Columbus (47201) *(G-2236)*
Cie, Marion *Also Called: Central Indiana Ethanol LLC (G-11277)*
   Cigar Exclusive LLC 317 778-2826
      12995 Star Dr Fishers (46037) *(G-4487)*
   Cil Electronics LLC 765 457-3894
      1942 S Elizabeth St Kokomo (46902) *(G-10244)*
Cimbar Performance Mineral, Mount Vernon *Also Called: United Minerals and Prpts Inc (G-12325)*
   Cimc Reefer Trailer Inc 219 253-2000
      285 E Water Tower Dr Monon (47959) *(G-12054)*
   Cimentos N Votorantim Amer Inc 812 384-9463
      993 In 54 Bloomfield (47424) *(G-744)*
Cimtech, New Albany *Also Called: Anne Pfeiffer Holdings Inc (G-12689)*
Cinda B, Fort Wayne *Also Called: Cinda B USA LLC (G-4848)*
   Cinda B USA LLC 260 469-0803
      1530 Progress Rd Fort Wayne (46808) *(G-4848)*
   Cindon Inc 812 853-5450
      8400 Golden Dr Newburgh (47630) *(G-12998)*
   Cindys Crosstitch & Patterns 317 410-0764
      2265 Reformers Ave Indianapolis (46203) *(G-7804)*
   Cindys Embroidery 574 551-4521
      202 W Walnut St Akron (46910) *(G-3)*
   Cindys In Stitches Inc 317 841-1408
      9836 N By Northeast Blvd Fishers (46037) *(G-4488)*
   Cinq LLC 405 361-0097
      802 E 8th St New Albany (47150) *(G-12713)*
Cinq5, New Albany *Also Called: Cinq LLC (G-12713)*
   Cinram Inc 416 298-8190
      1600 Rich Rd Richmond (47374) *(G-14104)*
   Circle - Prosco Inc (PA) 812 339-3653
      401 N Gates Dr Bloomington (47404) *(G-829)*
Circle City Copperworks, Greenfield *Also Called: Applied Fabricators Inc (G-6465)*
Circle City Cryogenics, Indianapolis *Also Called: Circle City Heat Treating Inc (G-7805)*
   Circle City Heat Treating Inc 317 440-9102
      2243 Massachusetts Ave Indianapolis (46218) *(G-7805)*
Circle City Kombucha, Indianapolis *Also Called: Circle City Sonorans LLC (G-7807)*
   Circle City Lighting Inc 317 439-0824
      21570 Anchor Bay Dr Noblesville (46062) *(G-13060)*
   Circle City Medical Inc 317 228-1144
      10850 Ruby Ct Carmel (46032) *(G-1587)*
   Circle City Rebar LLC 317 917-8566
      4002 Industrial Blvd Indianapolis (46254) *(G-7806)*
   Circle City Sonorans LLC 317 395-3693
      1050 E Washington St Indianapolis (46202) *(G-7807)*
   Circle City Woodworking 765 637-6687
      5574 Alcott Ln Indianapolis (46221) *(G-7808)*
   Circle M Spring Inc 574 267-2883
      930 Executive Dr Warsaw (46580) *(G-16335)*
   Circle Medical Products Inc 317 271-2626
      8202 Indy Ln Indianapolis (46214) *(G-7809)*
   Circle Printing LLC 812 663-7367
      130 W Main St Greensburg (47240) *(G-6584)*
   Circle S Industries LLC 317 727-6752
      1780 S Hickey Rd Morgantown (46160) *(G-12255)*
Circle Y Farms, Springville *Also Called: Robert L Young (G-15391)*
   Circles Legacy Publishing LLC 219 322-1278
      3419 Violet Ln Dyer (46311) *(G-2969)*
   Circuits Repair LLC 317 512-1026
      212 Francis St Shelbyville (46176) *(G-14745)*
   CIS Holdings Inc 703 996-0500
      8888 Keystone Xing Ste 600 Indianapolis (46240) *(G-7810)*
Cisco Systems, Carmel *Also Called: Cisco Systems Inc (G-1588)*
   Cisco Systems Inc 317 816-5200
      11711 N Meridian St Ste 250 Carmel (46032) *(G-1588)*
CIT, Richmond *Also Called: Contract Indus Tooling Inc (G-14110)*

Citadel Architectural Pdts LLC 800 446-8828
   6198 W Airport Blvd Greenfield (46140) *(G-6481)*

Citgo, Huntingburg *Also Called: Hucks Food Fuel (G-7281)*

Citiview Publications LLC 502 296-1623
   132 Lee Dr Floyds Knobs (47119) *(G-4672)*

Citizens By-Products Coal Co (HQ) 317 927-4738
   2020 N Meridian St Indianapolis (46202) *(G-7811)*

Citizens Energy Group 317 261-8794
   366 Kentucky Ave Indianapolis (46225) *(G-7812)*

Citrine Dispatch LLC 219 689-8293
   7603 Catalpa Ave Hammond (46324) *(G-6899)*

City of Anderson 765 648-6715
   1035 Main St Anderson (46016) *(G-93)*

City of Anderson 765 648-6560
   2801 Gene Gustin Way Anderson (46011) *(G-94)*

City of Berne 260 849-4038
   428 Wind Ridge Trl Berne (46711) *(G-706)*

City of Columbia City 260 248-5118
   925 E Van Buren St Columbia City (46725) *(G-2132)*

City of Fort Wayne 260 427-1235
   1701 Lafayette St Fort Wayne (46803) *(G-4849)*

City of Valparaiso 219 462-5291
   2065 Cumberland Dr Valparaiso (46383) *(G-15928)*

City Optical Co Inc (PA) 317 924-1300
   2839 Lafayette Rd Indianapolis (46222) *(G-7813)*

City Optical Co Inc 317 788-4243
   3636 S East St Indianapolis (46227) *(G-7814)*

City Pattern and Foundry Company Inc 574 273-3000
   12767 Industrial Park Dr Granger (46530) *(G-6339)*

City South Bend Building Corp 574 235-9977
   1045 W Sample St South Bend (46619) *(G-14973)*

City Supply Inc 574 259-6028
   1807 N Cedar St Mishawaka (46545) *(G-11861)*

City Vision Center, Columbia City *Also Called: Better Visions PC (G-2124)*

City Vision Center, Leo *Also Called: Better Visions PC (G-10963)*

City Welding & Fabrication 765 569-5403
   255 N Dormeyer Ave Rockville (47872) *(G-14350)*

City Wineworks 765 460-5563
   69 N Broadway Peru (46970) *(G-13572)*

Citybyapp Inc 844 843-4376
   9440 W 103rd Pl Saint John (46373) *(G-14447)*

Cives Corporation 219 279-4000
   337 N 700 W Wolcott (47995) *(G-16927)*

Cives Steel Company, Wolcott *Also Called: Cives Corporation (G-16927)*

Civic Press Inc 219 750-9361
   8520 Broadway Merrillville (46410) *(G-11497)*

Civic Spark Media LLC 765 357-4335
   400 N A St Unit 9 Richmond (47375) *(G-14105)*

CJ Logging LLC 812 360-0163
   2336 S Conservation Club Rd Morgantown (46160) *(G-12256)*

CJ Magers Enterprises LLC 219 778-4884
   5505 N 300 E La Porte (46350) *(G-10394)*

CJ Printing 219 924-1685
   9445 Indianapolis Blvd Ste F Hammond (46322) *(G-6900)*

CJ Sweets, Indianapolis *Also Called: C Johnson Group LLC (G-7708)*

CJS Muzic Company-The Spot LLC 219 487-9873
   5258 Hohman Ave Hammond (46320) *(G-6901)*

Cjs Stop N Go 317 877-0681
   5855 E 211th St Ste 34 Noblesville (46062) *(G-13061)*

CK Products, Fort Wayne *Also Called: CK Products LLC (G-4850)*

CK Products LLC 260 484-2517
   6230 Innovation Blvd Fort Wayne (46818) *(G-4850)*

Ckh Two Inc 317 841-7800
   9160 Ford Cir Fishers (46038) *(G-4489)*

Ckmt Associates Inc 219 924-2820
   6405 Olcott St Hammond (46320) *(G-6902)*

CL Holding LLC 317 736-4414
   1441 Amy Ln Franklin (46131) *(G-5720)*

CL Tech Inc 812 526-0995
   216 N Main St Edinburgh (46124) *(G-3072)*

Clabber Girl, Terre Haute *Also Called: Hulman & Company (G-15609)*

Clabber Girl Corporation 812 232-9446
   900 Wabash Ave Terre Haute (47807) *(G-15563)*

Claeys Candy Inc 574 287-1818
   5229 Nimtz Pkwy South Bend (46628) *(G-14974)*

Claires Cabinet Refinishing 317 495-5406
   6207 Broadway St Indianapolis (46220) *(G-7815)*

Clancys of Portage 219 764-4995
   2542 Portage Mall Portage (46368) *(G-13856)*

Clarcor Air Filtration Products Inc 502 969-2304
   100 River Ridge Cir Jeffersonville (47130) *(G-9952)*

Claridges Wood Shop 812 536-2569
   9424 S County Road 400 E Stendal (47585) *(G-15398)*

Clarios LLC 260 485-9999
   6010 Brandy Chase Cv Fort Wayne (46815) *(G-4851)*

Clarios LLC 260 479-4400
   8710 Indianapolis Rd Fort Wayne (46809) *(G-4852)*

Clarios LLC 317 638-7611
   5920 Castleway West Dr Indianapolis (46250) *(G-7816)*

Clarity Industry Co LLC 678 389-5006
   827 Laclede St Indianapolis (46241) *(G-7817)*

Clark Foods Inc (PA) 812 949-3075
   810 Progress Blvd New Albany (47150) *(G-12714)*

Clark Millworks 260 665-1270
   1587 S Old Us Highway 27 Angola (46703) *(G-240)*

Clark Tire Fishers Inc 317 842-0544
   12371 Reynolds Dr Fishers (46038) *(G-4490)*

Clark's Snacks, New Albany *Also Called: Jones Popcorn Inc (G-12755)*

Clarke Harland Corp 812 283-9598
   237 America Pl Jeffersonville (47130) *(G-9953)*

Clarke Harland Corp 812 283-9598
   240 America Pl Jeffersonville (47130) *(G-9954)*

Clarke Industrial Systems Inc 260 489-4575
   9084 Technology Dr Ste 150 Fishers (46038) *(G-4491)*

Clarks Big Dog Trucking LLC 317 625-1388
   2701 Highland Pl Indianapolis (46208) *(G-7818)*

Clarks Cnc LLC 812 508-1773
   1718 S Jackson Pike Springville (47462) *(G-15383)*

Classee Vinyl Windows LLC 574 825-7863
   59323 County Road 35 Middlebury (46540) *(G-11703)*

Classic, Fort Wayne *Also Called: Classic Products Corp (G-4855)*

Classic Baluster, Brazil *Also Called: Burkes Garden Wood Pdts LLC (G-1137)*

Classic Buildings Inc 812 944-5821
   2709 Blackiston Mill Rd Clarksville (47129) *(G-2013)*

Classic Cabinets LLC 317 507-3775
   723 S Rangeline Rd Carmel (46032) *(G-1589)*

Classic Chemical Corp 812 934-3289
   7750 Zionsville Rd Ste 700 Indianapolis (46268) *(G-7819)*

Classic City Tool & Engineering Inc 260 925-1420
   1101 W Auburn Dr Auburn (46706) *(G-376)*

Classic Graphics Inc 260 482-3487
   4211 Earth Dr Fort Wayne (46809) *(G-4853)*

Classic Industries Inc 812 421-4006
   2308 Commercial Ct Evansville (47720) *(G-3972)*

Classic Kitchen and Gran LLC 317 575-8883
   17408 Tiller Ct Ste 300 Westfield (46074) *(G-16676)*

Classic LLC 260 241-4353
   11512 Carroll Lynn Dr Fort Wayne (46818) *(G-4854)*

Classic Manufacturing Co LLC 765 344-1619
   4774 S 1000 E Brazil (47834) *(G-1138)*

Classic Products Corp (PA) 260 484-2695
   4617 Industrial Rd Fort Wayne (46825) *(G-4855)*

Classic Rock Face Block Inc 260 704-3113
   520 Southview Ave Fort Wayne (46806) *(G-4856)*

Classic Sign & Awning 260 665-6663
   Angola (46703) *(G-241)*

Classic Truss WD Cmponents Inc 812 944-5821
   2709 Blackiston Mill Rd Clarksville (47129) *(G-2014)*

Classichydros 317 352-1315
   940 N Audubon Rd Indianapolis (46219) *(G-7820)*

Classico Seating, Carmel *Also Called: Hanco Inc (G-1648)*

Classique Hair Style 317 738-2104
   50 S Water St Franklin (46131) *(G-5721)*

ALPHABETIC SECTION — Clover Printing LLC

Classy Stitches..317 856-3261
   5336 Honey Manor Dr Indianapolis (46221) *(G-7821)*

Clay Critters, West Lafayette Also Called: R Drew & Co Inc *(G-16624)*

Clayhill Wind & Solar LLC...765 437-2395
   3660 W 500 S Sharpsville (46068) *(G-14709)*

Claymore Tools Inc...574 255-6483
   5501 Abshire Dr South Bend (46614) *(G-14975)*

Claywood Creation...260 244-7719
   111 S Briarwood Ln Columbia City (46725) *(G-2133)*

CLC, Kendallville Also Called: Creative Liquid Coatings Inc *(G-10105)*

CLC Embroidery LLC (PA)...219 395-9600
   332 Wake Robin Dr Chesterton (46304) *(G-1912)*

Clean Air of Evansville, Evansville Also Called: 3-T Corp *(G-3856)*

Clean By Design Inc...260 414-4444
   1509 Holly Ridge Run Fort Wayne (46845) *(G-4857)*

CLEAN EXHAUST, Indianapolis Also Called: Ccts Technology Group Inc *(G-7765)*

Clean Kutz LLC..765 808-3232
   2851 N Oakwood Ave Muncie (47304) *(G-12366)*

Clean Lines Painting LLC..708 200-2210
   120 Poplar St Michigan City (46360) *(G-11588)*

Clean-Seal Inc...574 299-1888
   20900 Ireland Rd South Bend (46614) *(G-14976)*

Cleaninternet Inc...866 752-5326
   1070 S Calumet Rd Unit 892 Chesterton (46304) *(G-1913)*

Cleanroomsusa, Brownsburg Also Called: Biologics Modular LLC *(G-1350)*

Clear Decision Filtration Inc......................................219 567-2008
   4571 S 1450 W Francesville (47946) *(G-5637)*

Clear Software Inc...317 732-8831
   112 N Ninth St Zionsville (46077) *(G-16998)*

Clear Stamp Inc...219 324-3800
   24 Industrial Pkwy La Porte (46350) *(G-10395)*

Clear View Cstm Wndows Dors In..............................812 877-1000
   9630 E Us Highway 40 Terre Haute (47803) *(G-15564)*

Clear Waters Serenity Center...................................260 459-9200
   3207 Covington Rd Fort Wayne (46802) *(G-4858)*

Clearline Operations LLC..765 381-8361
   3301 W Mt Pleasant Blvd Muncie (47302) *(G-12367)*

Clearspring Manufacturing LLC..................................260 593-2086
   4225 W 350 S Topeka (46571) *(G-15796)*

Clearspring Welding...260 463-8754
   1497 W 550 S Wolcottville (46795) *(G-16936)*

Cleaver Enterprises Inc..260 625-5822
   11334 Bay Pines Ct Fort Wayne (46814) *(G-4859)*

Cleer Vision Tempered Glass, Elkhart Also Called: Cleer Vision Windows Inc *(G-3254)*

Cleer Vision Windows Inc...574 262-0449
   3401 County Road 6 E Elkhart (46514) *(G-3254)*

Cleveland-Cliffs Burns Harbor (DH)...........................219 787-2120
   250 W Us Highway 12 Burns Harbor (46304) *(G-1449)*

Cleveland-Cliffs Burns Hbr LLC.................................219 787-2120
   250 W Us Highway 12 Burns Harbor (46304) *(G-1450)*

Cleveland-Cliffs Inc..219 787-2120
   250 W Us Highway 12 Burns Harbor (46304) *(G-1451)*

Cleveland-Cliffs Inc..574 654-1000
   30755 Edison Rd New Carlisle (46552) *(G-12835)*

Cleveland-Cliffs Indiana Harbor, East Chicago Also Called: Cleveland-Cliffs Indiana Hbr *(G-2996)*

Cleveland-Cliffs Indiana Hbr.....................................219 399-1200
   3210 Watling St East Chicago (46312) *(G-2996)*

Cleveland-Cliffs Kote Inc (DH)..................................574 654-1000
   30755 Edison Rd New Carlisle (46552) *(G-12836)*

Cleveland-Cliffs Kote LP...574 654-1000
   30755 Edison Rd New Carlisle (46552) *(G-12837)*

Cleveland-Cliffs Steel Corp......................................812 362-6000
   6500 N Us Highway 231 Rockport (47635) *(G-14338)*

Cleveland-Cliffs Steel LLC..219 787-2120
   250 W Us Highway 12 Chesterton (46304) *(G-1914)*

Cleveland-Cliffs Steel LLC..219 399-6500
   3001 E Columbus Dr East Chicago (46312) *(G-2997)*

Cleveland-Cliffs Steel LLC..312 346-0300
   3300 Dickey Rd East Chicago (46312) *(G-2998)*

Cleveland-Cliffs Steel LLC..219 399-1000
   3001 Dickey Rd East Chicago (46312) *(G-2999)*

Cleveland-Cliffs Steel LLC..219 399-1200
   3210 Watling St East Chicago (46312) *(G-3000)*

Cleveland-Cliffs Tek L.P., New Carlisle Also Called: Cleveland-Cliffs New Crlsle l LP *(G-12838)*

Clevelnd-Clffs Mnorca Mine Inc.................................219 787-2002
   Chesterton (46304) *(G-1915)*

Clevelnd-Clffs Mnorca Mine Inc (DH)........................219 399-1200
   3210 Watling St East Chicago (46312) *(G-3001)*

Clevelnd-Clffs New Crlsle l LP..................................574 654-1000
   30755 Edison Rd New Carlisle (46552) *(G-12838)*

Clevelnd-Clffs Tblar Cmpnnts L.................................812 341-3200
   150 W 450 S Columbus (47201) *(G-2237)*

Clients Choice Ltd..812 853-2911
   2144 Wildwood Dr Boonville (47601) *(G-1085)*

Clif Allred...765 244-8082
   5090 E 100 S Peru (46970) *(G-13573)*

Clif Bar & Company...510 596-6451
   7575 Georgetown Rd Indianapolis (46268) *(G-7822)*

CLIF BAR & COMPANY, Indianapolis Also Called: Clif Bar & Company *(G-7822)*

Cliff A Ostermeyer..615 361-7902
   1727 N Glendale Dr Fort Wayne (46804) *(G-4860)*

Clifford Signs Inc...765 453-0745
   3040 S Lafountain St Kokomo (46902) *(G-10245)*

Clifty Engineering and Tool Co..................................812 273-3272
   2949 Clifty Dr Madison (47250) *(G-11210)*

Climate Systems Division, Fort Wayne Also Called: Parker-Hannifin Corporation *(G-5297)*

Cline Brothers Welding Inc.......................................812 738-3537
   3490 Highway 62 Ne Corydon (47112) *(G-2491)*

Clinical Architecture LLC (PA)..................................317 580-8400
   11611 N Meridian St Ste 500 Carmel (46032) *(G-1590)*

Clinical Scrubs LLC...317 607-3991
   9961 Ellis Dr Indianapolis (46235) *(G-7823)*

Cliniwave Inc...812 923-9591
   5605 Featheringill Rd Floyds Knobs (47119) *(G-4673)*

Clinton Custom Wood Turning...................................574 535-0543
   62172 County Road 33 Goshen (46528) *(G-6112)*

Clinton Harness Shop LLC.......................................574 533-9797
   13705 State Road 4 Goshen (46528) *(G-6113)*

Clinton Parker...219 877-5096
   6341 Indianapolis Blvd Hammond (46320) *(G-6903)*

Clipper Country...765 935-2344
   1539 S 9th St Richmond (47374) *(G-14106)*

Clm Express Trucking LLC.......................................219 237-4646
   9445 Indianapolis Blvd Ste 1148 Highland (46322) *(G-7130)*

Clm Pallet Recycling Inc (PA)...................................317 485-4080
   3103 W 1000 N Fortville (46040) *(G-5589)*

Cloak Gaming LLC..502 563-8790
   2225 Heritage Way Nw Apt 75 Corydon (47112) *(G-2492)*

Clondalkin Pharma & Healthcare Inc.........................336 292-4555
   6454 Saguaro Ct Indianapolis (46268) *(G-7824)*

Closure Systems Intl Hldngs In.................................765 364-6300
   1604 E Elmore St Crawfordsville (47933) *(G-2553)*

Closure Systems Intl Inc..765 364-6300
   1205 E Elmore St Crawfordsville (47933) *(G-2554)*

Closure Systems Intl Inc (HQ)..................................317 390-5000
   7820 Innovation Blvd Ste 100 Indianapolis (46278) *(G-7825)*

Cloud 9 Griptape LLC..818 795-1082
   2710 Hillcrest Dr Dyer (46311) *(G-2970)*

Cloud Blue..714 382-2767
   501 Airtech Pkwy Plainfield (46168) *(G-13669)*

Cloud Defensive, Chandler Also Called: Cloud Defensive LLC *(G-1859)*

Cloud Defensive LLC...813 492-5683
   612 Grace Way Chandler (47610) *(G-1859)*

Cloud Defensive LLC...812 646-1762
   6045 Wedeking Ave Evansville (47715) *(G-3973)*

Cloudmaker Glass Studio, Michigan City Also Called: Cloudmaker Studio Inc *(G-11589)*

Cloudmaker Studio Inc..219 879-1724
   4987 W Us Highway 20 Michigan City (46360) *(G-11589)*

Clover Industrial Services LLC..................................317 879-5001
   1555 S Franklin Rd Ste D Indianapolis (46239) *(G-7826)*

Clover Printing LLC...260 657-3003
   16840 State Road 37 Harlan (46743) *(G-7052)*

(PA)=Parent Co (HQ)=Headquarters (DH)=Div Headquarters

Clover Sheet Metal Company... 574 293-5912
28298 Clay St Elkhart (46517) *(G-3255)*

Clover Signs Co... 812 442-7446
100 N Meridian St Brazil (47834) *(G-1139)*

Cloverleaf Farms Dairy.. 219 938-5140
6401 Melton Rd Gary (46403) *(G-5919)*

Clovis LLC... 812 944-4791
3333 Buffalo Trl Floyds Knobs (47119) *(G-4674)*

Clown Room, The, Lexington *Also Called: Rbg Inc (G-10980)*

Clp Towne Inc... 574 233-3183
24805 Us Highway 20 South Bend (46628) *(G-14977)*

Club Cyberia, Indianapolis *Also Called: Cyberia Ltd (G-7938)*

Clunette Elevator Co Inc.. 574 858-2281
4316 W 600 N Leesburg (46538) *(G-10952)*

Cluster Packaging LLC.. 612 803-1056
10769 Bdwy Ave Ste 146 Crown Point (46307) *(G-2666)*

Clutch Graphics.. 812 244-9673
14650 N Oak St Carbon (47837) *(G-1537)*

Clute Enterprises Inc... 260 413-0810
18706 Coldwater Rd Huntertown (46748) *(G-7250)*

CM Reed LLC (PA)... 517 546-4100
18463 Running Deer Ln Greendale (47025) *(G-6444)*

CM Tech (PA).. 765 584-6501
1036 N Old Highway 27 Winchester (47394) *(G-16885)*

CM Welding Inc.. 765 258-4024
238 W County Road 425 N Frankfort (46041) *(G-5654)*

CMa Steel & Fabrication Inc.. 260 207-9000
3333 Independence Dr Fort Wayne (46808) *(G-4861)*

CMA Supply, Fort Wayne *Also Called: CMa Supply Co Fort Wayne Inc (G-4862)*

CMa Supply Co Fort Wayne Inc.. 260 471-9000
3333 Independence Dr Fort Wayne (46808) *(G-4862)*

Cmbf LLC.. 812 336-3811
1031 E Hillside Dr Bloomington (47401) *(G-830)*

Cme LLC... 260 623-3700
21600 Monroeville Rd Monroeville (46773) *(G-12067)*

Cmg Inc... 317 890-1999
455 Rawles Ct Indianapolis (46229) *(G-7827)*

CMI, Columbus *Also Called: Cummins Power Systems LLC (G-2274)*

CMI Pgi Holdings LLC (HQ)... 812 377-5000
500 Jackson St Columbus (47201) *(G-2238)*

Cmj & Associates Corporation.. 765 962-1947
160 Fort Wayne Ave Richmond (47374) *(G-14107)*

Cmoss Transport LLC... 317 656-1846
3413 Luewan Dr Indianapolis (46235) *(G-7828)*

CMS, Whiteland *Also Called: Cad & Machining Services Inc (G-16777)*

CMS Technologies Inc... 219 395-8272
147 N Jackson Blvd Ste 1x Chesterton (46304) *(G-1916)*

CNA Tool Engineering Inc.. 260 927-2298
1015 W 15th St Auburn (46706) *(G-377)*

Cnc Concepts Inc... 574 269-2301
3019 S County Farm Rd Warsaw (46580) *(G-16336)*

Cnc Industries Inc.. 260 490-5700
3810 Fourier Dr Fort Wayne (46818) *(G-4863)*

Cnc Machine Inc... 317 835-4575
1380 N 450 W Shelbyville (46176) *(G-14746)*

Cnc Metalworking, Fort Wayne *Also Called: Toolcraft LLC (G-5494)*

Cnh Industrial America LLC... 765 482-5409
400 S Enterprise Blvd Lebanon (46052) *(G-10884)*

Cnh Industrial Parts and Svc, Lebanon *Also Called: Cnh Industrial America LLC (G-10884)*

Cnhi LLC... 765 640-4893
1133 Jackson St Anderson (46016) *(G-95)*

Cnhi LLC... 812 944-6481
221 Spring St Jeffersonville (47130) *(G-9955)*

Cnhi LLC... 574 936-3101
218 N Michigan St Plymouth (46563) *(G-13763)*

Cnm Machine Tool Repair... 765 552-3255
9833 W Sunset Ln Elwood (46036) *(G-3819)*

Cns Custom Woodworks Inc... 812 350-2431
1053 Hummingbird Ln Columbus (47203) *(G-2239)*

CO-OP TRADING, Fort Wayne *Also Called: Friends of Third World Inc (G-5013)*

Co-Packaging, Portage *Also Called: MSI Express Inc (G-13894)*

Co-Tronics Inc.. 574 722-3850
2935 W 100 N Peru (46970) *(G-13574)*

Coach Line Motors... 765 825-7893
2516 Western Ave Connersville (47331) *(G-2431)*

Coach Monay Publishing LLC... 463 256-5096
3250a W 86th St Indianapolis (46268) *(G-7829)*

Coachmen Recreational Vehicle, Elkhart *Also Called: All American Group Inc (G-3159)*

Coachmen Recrtl Vhcl Co LLC.. 574 825-5821
423 N Main St Middlebury (46540) *(G-11704)*

Coachs Connection Inc... 260 356-0400
200 E Park Dr Huntington (46750) *(G-7306)*

Coan Engineering LLC... 765 456-3957
2277 E North St Kokomo (46901) *(G-10246)*

Coast OEM LLC.. 765 553-5904
2500 N Union St Kokomo (46901) *(G-10247)*

Coast To Coast, Huntington *Also Called: Transwheel Corporation (G-7374)*

Coasterstone, Carmel *Also Called: Dsh Indiana Inc (G-1613)*

Coats Wright De Sign... 317 569-5980
200 S Rangeline Rd Ste 122 Carmel (46032) *(G-1591)*

Coblentz Cabinet LLC.. 812 687-7525
8876 E 800 N Montgomery (47558) *(G-12089)*

Cobo Industries.. 812 341-4318
6831 Ridge Vale Pl Apt 2b Indianapolis (46237) *(G-7830)*

Coca Cola Bottling Company I... 812 376-3381
1334 Washington St Columbus (47201) *(G-2240)*

Coca Cola Btlg Co Kokomo Ind (PA)....................................... 765 457-4421
2305 Davis Rd Kokomo (46901) *(G-10248)*

Coca Cola Btlg Co Kokomo Ind... 574 936-3220
1701 Pidco Dr Plymouth (46563) *(G-13764)*

Coca-Cola, Anderson *Also Called: Central Coca-Cola Btlg Co Inc (G-91)*

Coca-Cola, Bloomington *Also Called: Central Coca-Cola Btlg Co Inc (G-828)*

Coca-Cola, Bloomington *Also Called: Coca-Cola Bottling Co (G-831)*

Coca-Cola, Columbus *Also Called: Coca Cola Bottling Company I (G-2240)*

Coca-Cola, Evansville *Also Called: Coca-Cola Consolidated Inc (G-3974)*

Coca-Cola, Indianapolis *Also Called: Central Coca-Cola Btlg Co Inc (G-7770)*

Coca-Cola, Indianapolis *Also Called: Central Coca-Cola Btlg Co Inc (G-7771)*

Coca-Cola, Indianapolis *Also Called: Central Coca-Cola Btlg Co Inc (G-7772)*

Coca-Cola, Jasper *Also Called: Central Coca-Cola Btlg Co Inc (G-9827)*

Coca-Cola, Kokomo *Also Called: Coca Cola Btlg Co Kokomo Ind (G-10248)*

Coca-Cola, Portland *Also Called: Central Coca-Cola Btlg Co Inc (G-13930)*

Coca-Cola, Portland *Also Called: Coca-Cola Bottling Co Portland (G-13931)*

Coca-Cola, Shelbyville *Also Called: Central Coca-Cola Btlg Co Inc (G-14744)*

Coca-Cola, South Bend *Also Called: Central Coca-Cola Btlg Co Inc (G-14969)*

Coca-Cola, South Bend *Also Called: Coca-Cola Enterprises (G-14978)*

Coca-Cola Bottling Co.. 812 332-4434
1701 S Liberty Dr Box 2 Bloomington (47403) *(G-831)*

Coca-Cola Bottling Co.. 800 688-2053
1700 Industries Rd Richmond (47374) *(G-14108)*

Coca-Cola Bottling Co Portland... 260 729-6124
1617 N Meridian St Portland (47371) *(G-13931)*

Coca-Cola Consolidated Inc.. 812 228-3200
3223 Interstate Dr Evansville (47715) *(G-3974)*

Coca-Cola Enterprises... 574 291-1511
1700 W Ireland Rd South Bend (46614) *(G-14978)*

Cochran Custom Woodworking LLC....................................... 765 523-3220
9036 Vine St Stockwell (47983) *(G-15399)*

Cockerhams Signs & Graphics... 812 358-3737
1130 S County Road 150 W Brownstown (47220) *(G-1419)*

Cocoaloca Cosmetics LLC.. 352 246-6629
5337 Stonehedge Blvd Fort Wayne (46835) *(G-4864)*

Codeclouds, Fort Wayne *Also Called: Long Tail Corporation (G-5191)*

Codeweld Inc.. 317 784-4140
905 E Edgewood Ave Indianapolis (46227) *(G-7831)*

Codybro LLC.. 765 827-5441
3207 Iowa Ave Connersville (47331) *(G-2432)*

Coeus Technology Inc... 765 203-2304
2701 Entp Dr Ste 230 Anderson (46013) *(G-96)*

Coffee Lomont & Moyer Inc... 260 422-7825
1205 W Main St Fort Wayne (46808) *(G-4865)*

Coffey Connection LLC..317 300-9639
  1000 S Morgantown Rd Greenwood (46143) *(G-6681)*

Coffeys Custom Upholstery..812 948-8611
  610 Silver St New Albany (47150) *(G-12715)*

Coffman Dallas Log & Excvtg......................................812 738-1528
  2045 Dixie Rd Sw Corydon (47112) *(G-2493)*

Coffman Dallas Logging, Corydon Also Called: Coffman Dallas Log & Excvtg *(G-2493)*

Coffman Logging..812 732-4857
  2190 Lickford Bridge Rd Sw Corydon (47112) *(G-2494)*

Cognex Corporation..317 867-5079
  804 Allen Ct Westfield (46074) *(G-16677)*

Cohda Wireless America LLC......................................248 513-2105
  450 E 96th St Ste 500 Indianapolis (46240) *(G-7832)*

Cohesant Technologies Inc...317 871-7611
  5845 W 82nd St Ste 102 Indianapolis (46278) *(G-7833)*

Coil-Tran LLC (HQ)...219 942-8511
  160 S Illinois St Hobart (46342) *(G-7182)*

Cois Coillte Woodworking LLC...................................812 340-3718
  2116 S Smith Rd Bloomington (47401) *(G-832)*

Cola Voce Music Inc..317 466-0624
  4600 Sunset Ave Indianapolis (46208) *(G-7834)*

Colbert Packaging Corporation..................................574 295-6605
  1511 W Lusher Ave Elkhart (46517) *(G-3256)*

Colbin Tool Company Inc..574 457-3183
  1021 N Indiana Ave Syracuse (46567) *(G-15459)*

Colby L Stanger...574 536-5835
  15504 County Road 42 Goshen (46528) *(G-6114)*

Cold Heading Co..260 495-7003
  900 S Cassell St Fremont (46737) *(G-5816)*

Cold Heading Co..260 495-4222
  401 E Sidel St Fremont (46737) *(G-5817)*

Cold Heading Co..260 587-3231
  103 W State Road 4 Hudson (46747) *(G-7244)*

Cold Pressed Juice, Michigan City Also Called: Rays Juice Company *(G-11656)*

Cole Energy Incorporated...317 839-9688
  660 Andico Rd Plainfield (46168) *(G-13670)*

Coleman Cable LLC..574 546-5115
  515 Enterprise Dr Bremen (46506) *(G-1180)*

Coleman Cable LLC..765 449-7227
  3400 Union St Lafayette (47905) *(G-10553)*

Coleman Logging...765 458-7219
  2529 S Us Highway 27 Liberty (47353) *(G-10986)*

Coleman Sawmill Supply...812 865-4001
  260 S 6th St Orleans (47452) *(G-13375)*

Collective Press Inc..812 325-1385
  401 W 6th St Ste J Bloomington (47404) *(G-833)*

Collective Publishing LLC..317 418-0503
  12313 Ostara Ct Fishers (46037) *(G-4492)*

Colleen Coble Incorporated.......................................260 563-2028
  53 Highland Dr Wabash (46992) *(G-16178)*

College Network Inc (PA)...800 395-3276
  3815 River Crossing Pkwy Ste 260 Indianapolis (46240) *(G-7835)*

Collegiate Pride Inc..260 726-7818
  807 N Meridian St Portland (47371) *(G-13932)*

Collett Partners LLC..812 298-4451
  944 W County Road 350 N Greencastle (46135) *(G-6397)*

Collier's Glass Block Windows, South Bend Also Called: Colliers Glassblock Inc *(G-14979)*

Colliers Glassblock Inc..574 288-8682
  824 Park Ave South Bend (46616) *(G-14979)*

Collins Caviar Company...269 231-5100
  113 York St Michigan City (46360) *(G-11590)*

Collins Machining LLC..812 528-5396
  4600 W Sunset Blvd North Vernon (47265) *(G-13258)*

Collins Tl & Die Ltd Lblty Co......................................812 273-4765
  2902 Wilson Ave Madison (47250) *(G-11211)*

Collins Trailers Inc...574 294-2561
  1053 Middleton Run Rd Elkhart (46516) *(G-3257)*

Colluci Construction-Log Homes...............................812 843-5607
  10591 Oriental Rd English (47118) *(G-3840)*

Colonial Baking Co Inc...812 232-4466
  660 N 1st St Terre Haute (47807) *(G-15565)*

Colophon Book Arts Supply LLC................................812 671-0577
  5400 N Brummetts Creek Rd Bloomington (47408) *(G-834)*

Color Glo...812 926-2639
  5083 Country Hills Dr Aurora (47001) *(G-441)*

Color Master Inc (PA)..260 868-2320
  810 S Broadway St Butler (46721) *(G-1461)*

Color-Box, Richmond Also Called: Menasha Packaging Company LLC *(G-14163)*

Color-Box LLC...765 966-7588
  623 S G St Richmond (47374) *(G-14109)*

Colorcon, Indianapolis Also Called: Colorcon Inc *(G-7837)*

Colorcon Inc...317 545-6211
  6585 E 30th St Indianapolis (46219) *(G-7836)*

Colorcon Inc...317 545-6211
  3702 E 21st St Indianapolis (46218) *(G-7837)*

Colored Threads, Indianapolis Also Called: Table Thyme Designs LLC *(G-9546)*

Colorimetric, Elkhart Also Called: Cast Products LP *(G-3249)*

Colorimetric Inc..574 255-9619
  1711 Clover Rd Mishawaka (46545) *(G-11862)*

Colormax Digital Imaging Inc (PA)............................812 477-3805
  626 Court St Evansville (47708) *(G-3975)*

Colormax Imaging, Evansville Also Called: Colormax Digital Imaging Inc *(G-3975)*

Colorrush Inc...317 374-3494
  1802 W 51st St Indianapolis (46228) *(G-7838)*

Colorworks, Indianapolis Also Called: Gammons Metal & Mfg Co Inc *(G-8258)*

Columbia City Mill Service, Columbia City Also Called: Levy Environmental Services Co *(G-2168)*

Columbia City Plastics Inc..260 244-0065
  831 E Short St Columbia City (46725) *(G-2134)*

Columbia City Ready Mix, Columbia City Also Called: Speedway Redi Mix Inc *(G-2201)*

Columbus Cabinetry LLC..812 447-1005
  1117 16th St Columbus (47201) *(G-2241)*

Columbus Cstm Cbinets Furn LLC..............................812 379-9411
  4475 Middle Rd Columbus (47203) *(G-2242)*

Columbus Engineering Inc...812 342-1231
  6600 S 50 W Columbus (47201) *(G-2243)*

Columbus Industrial Electric.....................................812 372-8414
  1625 N Indianapolis Rd Columbus (47201) *(G-2244)*

Columbus Optical Service Inc....................................812 372-4117
  2475 Cottage Ave Columbus (47201) *(G-2245)*

Columbus Pallet Corp...812 372-7272
  1520 14th St Columbus (47201) *(G-2246)*

Columbus Signs..812 376-7877
  3770 Reed Hollow Rd Nashville (47448) *(G-12668)*

Columbus Transfer Station, Columbus Also Called: Darling Ingredients Inc *(G-2279)*

Columbus Vault Co...812 372-3210
  3100 S Us Highway 31 Columbus (47201) *(G-2247)*

Columbus Wholesale Optical, Columbus Also Called: Columbus Optical Service Inc *(G-2245)*

Colwell Inc (HQ)..260 347-1981
  2605 Marion Dr Kendallville (46755) *(G-10099)*

Colwell Inc...260 347-1981
  231 S Progress Dr E Kendallville (46755) *(G-10100)*

Coman Publishing Company......................................574 255-9800
  54377 30th St South Bend (46635) *(G-14980)*

Combi Institiute Inc..602 269-2288
  12570 Lynnwood Blvd Carmel (46033) *(G-1592)*

Combined Technologies Inc (PA)..............................847 968-4855
  503 Bloomingdale Dr Bristol (46507) *(G-1254)*

Comfort Suites Baton Rouge......................................317 247-5500
  5701 Progress Rd Indianapolis (46241) *(G-7839)*

Commercial Aircraft, Fort Wayne Also Called: Bae Systems Controls Inc *(G-4787)*

Commercial Barge Line Company (DH)......................812 288-0100
  1701 E Market St Jeffersonville (47130) *(G-9956)*

Commercial Coatings Assoc LLC...............................812 773-3526
  800 E Oregon St Evansville (47711) *(G-3976)*

Commercial Electric Co Inc.......................................260 726-9357
  600 E Votaw St Portland (47371) *(G-13933)*

Commercial Finishing Corp..317 267-0377
  7199 English Ave Indianapolis (46219) *(G-7840)*

Commercial Pallet Recycl Inc....................................260 668-6208
  7430 S 800 W Hudson (46747) *(G-7245)*

Commercial Pallet Recycl Inc (PA)..260 829-1021
5235 N State Road 327 Orland (46776) *(G-13362)*

Commercial Print Shop Inc..260 724-3722
210 S 2nd St Decatur (46733) *(G-2850)*

Commercial Printing Service, Connersville Also Called: Tatman Inc *(G-2472)*

Commercial Review, The, Portland Also Called: Graphic Printing Co Inc *(G-13947)*

Commercial School of Lettering, Fort Wayne Also Called: Commercial Signs Inc *(G-4866)*

Commercial Signs Inc..260 745-2678
513 E Hawthorne St Fort Wayne (46806) *(G-4866)*

Commercial Structures Corp..574 773-7931
65213 County Road 31 Goshen (46528) *(G-6115)*

Commercial Structures Corp (PA)..574 773-7931
655 N Tomahawk Trl Nappanee (46550) *(G-12590)*

Commercial Technical Svcs Inc..260 436-9898
2809 Carrington Dr Fort Wayne (46804) *(G-4867)*

Commercial Trucks, Mooresville Also Called: Indy Asset Brokers Corporation *(G-12213)*

Commodity Blenders LLC..260 375-3202
10643 S Hartford City Rd Warren (46792) *(G-16294)*

Commodity Brokers Company, Indianapolis Also Called: Ontime Toys Inc *(G-9058)*

Commodore Homes LLC..574 533-7100
58096 County Road 7 Elkhart (46517) *(G-3258)*

Common Collabs LLC..574 249-9182
508 Lane St North Judson (46366) *(G-13210)*

Common Sense Producing LLC..317 622-1682
1041 N Village Greene Dr Greenfield (46140) *(G-6482)*

Commtineo LLC..219 476-3667
10525 W Us Highway 30 Bldg 4c Wanatah (46390) *(G-16288)*

Community Holdings Indiana Inc..765 622-1212
1133 Jackson St Anderson (46016) *(G-97)*

Community Holdings Indiana Inc..812 663-3111
135 S Franklin St Greensburg (47240) *(G-6585)*

Community Holdings Indiana Inc..765 457-4130
620 S Berkley Rd Kokomo (46901) *(G-10249)*

Community Holdings Indiana Inc..765 482-4650
117 E Washington St Lebanon (46052) *(G-10885)*

Community Holdings Indiana Inc..317 873-6397
117 E Washington St Lebanon (46052) *(G-10886)*

Community Holdings Indiana Inc..574 722-5000
517 E Broadway Logansport (46947) *(G-11068)*

Community Papers Inc..317 241-7363
2191 Real Quiet Dr Indianapolis (46234) *(G-7841)*

Compal Electronics Na Inc..574 992-8793
1 Technology Way Logansport (46947) *(G-11069)*

Compal USA, Logansport Also Called: Compal USA (indiana) Inc *(G-11070)*

Compal USA (indiana) Inc..574 739-2929
1 Technology Way Logansport (46947) *(G-11070)*

Companion Publications LLC..317 294-8189
5640 Rawles Ave Indianapolis (46219) *(G-7842)*

Compassionate Procedures LLC..317 259-4656
8140 Morningside Dr Indianapolis (46240) *(G-7843)*

Competition Electronic Systems..317 291-2823
5706 Hollister Dr Indianapolis (46224) *(G-7844)*

Competition TI & Engrg II Inc..812 524-1991
2600 Montgomery Dr Seymour (47274) *(G-14639)*

Competitive Pallet Service, Jeffersonville Also Called: Ernest A Cooper *(G-9980)*

Complete Cmpt Solutions Inc..812 923-0910
4801 Paoli Pike Ste 104 Floyds Knobs (47119) *(G-4675)*

Complete Controls Inc..260 489-0852
3923 Option Pass Fort Wayne (46818) *(G-4868)*

Complete Drives Inc (PA)..260 489-6033
6419 Discount Dr Fort Wayne (46818) *(G-4869)*

Complete Finish Inc..260 587-3588
200 S Parker Dr Ashley (46705) *(G-331)*

Complete Metal Fabrication Inc..812 284-4470
801 Trey St Jeffersonville (47130) *(G-9957)*

Complete Packaging Group Inc..765 547-1300
9021 State Road 101 Brookville (47012) *(G-1318)*

Complete Printing Service, Decatur Also Called: Commercial Print Shop Inc *(G-2850)*

Complete Property Care LLC..765 288-0890
806 W Jackson St Muncie (47305) *(G-12368)*

Complete Prtg Solutions Inc..812 285-9200
2199 Hamburg Pike Jeffersonville (47130) *(G-9958)*

Complex Plastics LLC..574 389-9911
23153 Circle Ln Elkhart (46514) *(G-3259)*

Complex Plastics LLC..603 305-3043
2630 Sterling Ave Elkhart (46516) *(G-3260)*

Complex Structures Group LLC..219 947-3939
4433 E 83rd Ave Merrillville (46410) *(G-11498)*

Component Machine Inc..317 635-8929
1631 Gent Ave Indianapolis (46202) *(G-7845)*

Composite Designs Inc..574 453-2902
306 School St Leesburg (46538) *(G-10953)*

Composite Specialties..317 852-1408
464 Johnson Ln Ste D Brownsburg (46112) *(G-1360)*

Composite Tech Assemblies LLC..574 948-0004
904 Markley Dr Plymouth (46563) *(G-13765)*

Compositech Inc..800 231-6755
5315 Walt Pl Indianapolis (46254) *(G-7846)*

Composites Syndicate LLC..260 484-3139
8301 Clinton Park Dr Fort Wayne (46825) *(G-4870)*

Composites Unlimited..812 475-8621
1250 S Green River Rd Evansville (47715) *(G-3977)*

Composition LLC..317 979-7214
14048 Woodlark Dr Fishers (46038) *(G-4493)*

Comptons Woodworking LLC..765 712-0568
11275 S Meridian Line Rd Cloverdale (46120) *(G-2084)*

Compucomics..812 876-1480
6079 N Holly Dr Ellettsville (47429) *(G-3804)*

Compumark Industries Inc..219 365-0508
9853 Northcote Ave Saint John (46373) *(G-14448)*

Computer Age Engineering Inc..765 674-8551
867 E 38th St Marion (46953) *(G-11278)*

Computer Solutions Systems Inc..812 235-9008
19 S 6th St Ste 900 Terre Haute (47807) *(G-15566)*

Computer Technology..812 283-5094
1101 Watt St Jeffersonville (47130) *(G-9959)*

Comtineo, Wanatah Also Called: Commtineo LLC *(G-16288)*

Conagra Brands Inc..765 563-3182
162 E 900 S Brookston (47923) *(G-1310)*

Conagra Brands Inc..317 329-3700
4300 W 62nd St Indianapolis (46268) *(G-7847)*

Conagra Brands Inc..402 240-5000
7579 Georgetown Rd Indianapolis (46268) *(G-7848)*

Conagra Brands Inc..740 387-2722
750 E Drexel Pkwy Rensselaer (47978) *(G-14048)*

Conagra Brands Inc..219 866-3020
750 E Drexel Pkwy Rensselaer (47978) *(G-14049)*

Conagra Dairy Foods Company..317 329-3700
4300 W 62nd St Indianapolis (46268) *(G-7849)*

Concannons Pastry Shop..765 288-8551
4801 N Baker Ln Muncie (47304) *(G-12369)*

Concept Assembly Solutions LLC..574 855-2534
55625 Currant Rd Mishawaka (46545) *(G-11863)*

Concept Cabinet Shop..765 653-1080
508 S Bloomington St Greencastle (46135) *(G-6398)*

CONCEPT CABINET SHOP, Greencastle Also Called: Concept Cabinet Shop *(G-6398)*

Concept Cars Inc..260 668-7553
1280 N 290 W Angola (46703) *(G-242)*

Concept Design & Fabrication..812 481-1142
352 S Saint Charles St Jasper (47546) *(G-9829)*

Concept Machinery Inc..317 845-5588
1219 N Delaware St Indianapolis (46202) *(G-7850)*

Concept Prints Inc..317 290-1222
6707 Guion Rd Indianapolis (46268) *(G-7851)*

Concept Tool & Engineering Inc..812 352-0055
508 5th St North Vernon (47265) *(G-13259)*

Concepts Cabinet Shop Inc (PA)..317 272-7430
7599 E Us Highway 36 Avon (46123) *(G-511)*

Concepts In Stone & Tile Inc..574 267-4712
118 N Buffalo St Warsaw (46580) *(G-16337)*

Concord Realstate Corp..765 423-5555
308 Erie St Lafayette (47904) *(G-10554)*

Concord Window Manufacturing, Lafayette Also Called: Concord Realstate Corp *(G-10554)*

ALPHABETIC SECTION — Convergent Consulting LLC

Concrete & Asphalt Recycl Inc (DH) 574 237-1928
2010 Went Ave Mishawaka (46545) *(G-11864)*

Concrete Construction, Seymour *Also Called: Scruggs Construction Inc* *(G-14687)*

Concrete Lady Inc (PA) 812 256-2765
4910 Highway 3 Otisco (47163) *(G-13447)*

Concrete Monkey Studios LLC 812 630-2339
236 Calle Del Prado Evansville (47712) *(G-3978)*

Concrete Supply LLC (PA) 812 474-6715
4300 Vogel Rd Evansville (47715) *(G-3979)*

Conder Water Services 812 825-9883
7691 W Kirksville Rd Bloomington (47403) *(G-835)*

Confluence Pharmaceuticals LLC 317 379-7498
27628 Will Parker Rd Arcadia (46030) *(G-311)*

Conforce International Inc 765 473-3061
2935 W 100 N Peru (46970) *(G-13575)*

Conforce USA, Peru *Also Called: Conforce International Inc* *(G-13575)*

Conforma Clad Inc 812 948-2118
501 Park East Blvd New Albany (47150) *(G-12716)*

Conga, Indianapolis *Also Called: Appextremes LLC* *(G-7529)*

Conger Signs, Jeffersonville *Also Called: Wendell Conger* *(G-10073)*

Conley Welding Specialties Inc 260 343-9051
605 S Orchard St Kendallville (46755) *(G-10101)*

Conn-Selmer Inc 574 522-1675
2415 Industrial Pkwy Elkhart (46516) *(G-3261)*

Conn-Selmer Inc (DH) 574 522-1675
600 Industrial Pkwy Elkhart (46516) *(G-3262)*

Conn-Selmer Inc 574 295-6730
500 Industrial Pkwy Elkhart (46516) *(G-3263)*

Conn-Selmer Inc 574 295-0079
1000 Industrial Pkwy Elkhart (46516) *(G-3264)*

Connecta Corporation 317 923-9282
3363 Boulevard Pl Indianapolis (46208) *(G-7852)*

Connection LLC 260 593-3999
128 S Main St Topeka (46571) *(G-15797)*

Connectons Sign Lngage Intrprt 812 449-7140
4500 Taylor Ave Evansville (47714) *(G-3980)*

Connectronics, Edinburgh *Also Called: Edinburgh Connector Co LLC* *(G-3082)*

Conner Saw Mill, Walton *Also Called: Conner Sawmill Inc* *(G-16282)*

Conner Sawmill Inc 574 626-3227
300 North St Walton (46994) *(G-16282)*

Connersville Paint Mfgco 765 825-4111
196 Water St Connersville (47331) *(G-2433)*

Connies Satin Stitch Inc 219 942-1887
829 E 3rd St Hobart (46342) *(G-7183)*

Conopco Inc 219 659-3200
1200 Calumet Ave Hammond (46320) *(G-6904)*

Conover Custom Fabrication Inc 317 784-1904
2625 S Pennsylvania St Indianapolis (46225) *(G-7853)*

Conrad Machine Co Inc 574 259-1190
55858 Season Ct Osceola (46561) *(G-13387)*

Conrad Sb LLC 574 213-3743
2025 S William St South Bend (46613) *(G-14981)*

Consolidated Printing Svcs Inc 765 468-6033
201 E Henry St Farmland (47340) *(G-4424)*

Consolidated Recycling Co Inc 812 547-7951
2406 Lynch Rd Evansville (47711) *(G-3981)*

Constant Voltage Welding Inc 765 339-7914
3231 W 1100 N New Richmond (47967) *(G-12977)*

Constellation Mold Inc 812 424-5338
4825 Hitch Peters Rd Evansville (47711) *(G-3982)*

Construction, Avon *Also Called: Fencescapes LLC* *(G-519)*

Construction, Evansville *Also Called: Empire Contractors Inc* *(G-4035)*

Construction, Evansville *Also Called: Tri-State Guttertopper Inc* *(G-4350)*

Construction, Fort Wayne *Also Called: Assured General Contg LLC* *(G-4776)*

Construction, Fort Wayne *Also Called: Kreative Concepts LLC* *(G-5160)*

Construction, Hobart *Also Called: Noble Project Services LLC* *(G-7202)*

Construction, Indianapolis *Also Called: Rai LLC* *(G-9263)*

Construction, Lafayette *Also Called: Mast Services Lafayette LLC* *(G-10643)*

Construction, Michigan City *Also Called: Clean Lines Painting LLC* *(G-11588)*

Construction, Thorntown *Also Called: Benakovich Builders* *(G-15750)*

Construction Bus Media LLC (HQ) 847 359-6493
350 Monon Blvd Carmel (46032) *(G-1593)*

Consultech5 .... 219 712-2801
3056 Sunrise Dr Crown Point (46307) *(G-2667)*

Contact Concealment, La Porte *Also Called: Shadowhouse Jiu-Jitsu Inc* *(G-10481)*

Contact Fabricators Ind Inc 317 366-7274
8896 W State Road 236 Middletown (47356) *(G-11768)*

Contact Products Inc 219 838-1911
8736 Schreiber Dr Munster (46321) *(G-12536)*

Container Service Corp 574 232-7474
2811 Viridian Dr South Bend (46628) *(G-14982)*

Containmed Inc (PA) 317 487-8800
1841 Ludlow Ave Indianapolis (46201) *(G-7854)*

Containment Tech Group Inc (PA) 317 862-5945
5460 Victory Dr Ste 300 Indianapolis (46203) *(G-7855)*

Contango Inc 765 418-0756
1281 Win Hentschel Blvd Ste 1300 West Lafayette (47906) *(G-16569)*

Contech Engnered Solutions LLC 317 407-4914
10130 Bahamas Cir Fishers (46037) *(G-4494)*

Contech Engnered Solutions LLC 317 842-7766
7164 Graham Rd Ste 120 Indianapolis (46250) *(G-7856)*

Contech Engnered Solutions LLC 812 849-3933
Metric Industrial Pk Mitchell (47446) *(G-12036)*

Contech Engnered Solutions LLC 812 849-3933
200 John R Williams Ave Mitchell (47446) *(G-12037)*

Contego International Inc 317 580-0665
334 W Greyhound Pass Carmel (46032) *(G-1594)*

Contego International Inc (PA) 574 223-5989
1013 Arthur St Rochester (46975) *(G-14283)*

Contemporary Books Inc 317 753-5247
7965 Mallard Lndg Indianapolis (46278) *(G-7857)*

Continental Advantage Eqp, Evansville *Also Called: Brake Supply Company Inc* *(G-3950)*

Continental Carbonic Pdts Inc 574 273-2800
4075 Ralph Jones Dr South Bend (46628) *(G-14983)*

Continental Diamond Tool Corp (PA) 260 493-1294
10511 Rose Ave New Haven (46774) *(G-12899)*

Continental Industries Inc (PA) 574 262-4511
100 W Windsor Ave Elkhart (46514) *(G-3265)*

Continental Machining Pdts Inc 219 474-5061
306 S 3rd St Kentland (47951) *(G-10158)*

Continental Manufacturing LLC 765 778-9999
1524 Jackson St Anderson (46016) *(G-98)*

Continental Register Co, Elkhart *Also Called: Continental Industries Inc* *(G-3265)*

Continental Welding Sup Corp 812 232-2488
1317 Poplar St Terre Haute (47807) *(G-15567)*

Continntal Broadcast Group LLC 317 924-1071
1800 N Meridian St Ste 201 Indianapolis (46202) *(G-7858)*

Continntal Crpntry Cmpnnts LLC 219 733-0367
9702 W Us Highway 30 Wanatah (46390) *(G-16289)*

Continuous Care Trnsp LLC 463 336-0555
10932 Freeman Ct Indianapolis (46234) *(G-7859)*

Continuum Games Incorporated 877 405-2662
1240 Brookville Way Ste J Indianapolis (46239) *(G-7860)*

Contitech Usa Inc 260 925-0700
725 W 15th St Auburn (46706) *(G-378)*

Contitech Usa Inc 260 925-0700
207 S West St Auburn (46706) *(G-379)*

Contols and Data Services, Indianapolis *Also Called: Rolls-Royce Corporation* *(G-9326)*

Contour Hardening Inc (PA) 888 867-2184
8401 Northwest Blvd Indianapolis (46278) *(G-7861)*

Contract Indus Tooling Inc (PA) 765 966-1134
2351 Production Ct Richmond (47374) *(G-14110)*

Control Consultants of America (PA) 219 989-3311
3800 179th St Hammond (46323) *(G-6905)*

Control Key Plus 317 567-2194
4015 E 82nd St Indianapolis (46250) *(G-7862)*

Controlled Automation Inc 317 770-3870
15421 Stony Creek Way Ste A Noblesville (46060) *(G-13062)*

Controls Center Inc 317 634-2665
1125 Western Dr Indianapolis (46241) *(G-7863)*

Convergent Consulting LLC 202 441-6453
6226 N Delaware St Indianapolis (46220) *(G-7864)*

(PA)=Parent Co (HQ)=Headquarters (DH)=Div Headquarters

ALPHABETIC SECTION

Conversightai... 201 294-1896
1220 Waterway Blvd Indianapolis (46202) *(G-7865)*

Conversion Components Inc............................. 574 264-4181
51174 Creek Haven Dr Elkhart (46514) *(G-3266)*

Conversions By Bearcat, Goshen *Also Called: Bearcat Corp (G-6098)*

Converto Mfg Co Inc.................................... 765 478-3205
220 S Green St Cambridge City (47327) *(G-1492)*

Conveyors Inc... 317 539-5472
3434 S State Road 39 Danville (46122) *(G-2809)*

Conzer Security Inc..................................... 317 580-9460
1089 3rd Ave Sw Ste 200 Carmel (46032) *(G-1595)*

Cook Aircraft Leasing Inc.............................. 812 339-2044
750 N Daniels Way Bloomington (47404) *(G-836)*

Cook Biodevice LLC..................................... 800 265-0945
750 N Daniels Way Bloomington (47404) *(G-837)*

Cook Capital Equipment LLC............................ 800 457-4500
1100 W Morgan St Spencer (47460) *(G-15342)*

Cook Compression LLC................................... 502 515-6900
2540 Centennial Blvd Jeffersonville (47130) *(G-9960)*

Cook Endoscopy, Bloomington *Also Called: Cook Incorporated (G-840)*

Cook General Biotechnology LLC........................ 317 917-3450
1102 Indiana Ave Indianapolis (46202) *(G-7866)*

Cook Group Incorporated (PA).......................... 812 339-2235
750 N Daniels Way Bloomington (47404) *(G-838)*

Cook Group Incorporated............................... 812 331-1025
6300 N Matthews Dr Ellettsville (47429) *(G-3805)*

Cook Incorporated...................................... 812 339-2235
1025 W Acuff Rd Bloomington (47404) *(G-839)*

Cook Incorporated (HQ)................................. 812 339-2235
750 N Daniels Way Bloomington (47404) *(G-840)*

Cook Incorporated...................................... 812 339-2235
1700 N Curry Pike Bloomington (47404) *(G-841)*

Cook Incorporated...................................... 812 339-2235
6600 W Mcneely St Ellettsville (47429) *(G-3806)*

Cook Incorporated...................................... 812 829-4891
1100 W Morgan St Spencer (47460) *(G-15343)*

Cook Medical, Bloomington *Also Called: Cook Incorporated (G-841)*

Cook Medical, Bloomington *Also Called: Cook Medical LLC (G-845)*

Cook Medical, Ellettsville *Also Called: Cook Group Incorporated (G-3805)*

Cook Medical Holdings LLC (HQ)........................ 812 339-2235
750 N Daniels Way Bloomington (47404) *(G-842)*

Cook Medical Inc....................................... 812 822-1402
301 N Curry Pike Bloomington (47404) *(G-843)*

Cook Medical LLC....................................... 812 339-2235
400 N Daniels Way Bloomington (47404) *(G-844)*

Cook Medical LLC (HQ).................................. 812 339-2235
750 N Daniels Way Bloomington (47404) *(G-845)*

Cook Medical LLC....................................... 812 323-4500
1800 N Curry Pike Bloomington (47404) *(G-846)*

Cook Medical Technologies LLC......................... 812 339-2235
750 N Daniels Way Bloomington (47404) *(G-847)*

Cook Polymer Technology, Bloomington *Also Called: Cook Medical LLC (G-846)*

Cook Polymer Technology, Bloomington *Also Called: Sabin Corporation (G-965)*

Cook Regentec, Bloomington *Also Called: Cook Regentec LLC (G-848)*

Cook Regentec LLC...................................... 800 265-0945
500 W Simpson Chapel Rd Bloomington (47404) *(G-848)*

Cook Urological, Spencer *Also Called: Cook Incorporated (G-15343)*

Cook Urological, Spencer *Also Called: Vance Products Incorporated (G-15364)*

Cookie Please... 317 879-6589
3444b Washington Blvd Indianapolis (46205) *(G-7867)*

Cool Cayenne.. 260 376-0977
601 N Meridian St Portland (47371) *(G-13934)*

Cool Cayenne LLC....................................... 765 282-0977
7020 E County Road 900 N Albany (47320) *(G-12)*

Cool Planet Awning Co, Indianapolis *Also Called: Cool Planet LLC (G-7868)*

Cool Planet LLC... 317 927-9000
340 S Mitthoeffer Rd Indianapolis (46229) *(G-7868)*

Coolstream Rv Ducting Inc.............................. 574 361-4271
2019 W Lusher Ave Elkhart (46517) *(G-3267)*

Coomer & Sons Sawmill, Frankfort *Also Called: Coomer & Sons Sawmill Inc (G-5655)*

Coomer & Sons Sawmill Inc.............................. 765 659-2846
184 Roy Scott Pkwy Frankfort (46041) *(G-5655)*

Cooper, Auburn *Also Called: Cooper-Standard Automotive Inc (G-380)*

Cooper, Bremen *Also Called: Cooper-Standard Automotive Inc (G-1181)*

Cooper, Fort Wayne *Also Called: Cooper-Standard Automotive Inc (G-4872)*

Cooper, Topeka *Also Called: Cooper-Standard Automotive Inc (G-15798)*

Cooper Transit LLC..................................... 260 797-3003
14105 Aloes Psge Fort Wayne (46845) *(G-4871)*

Cooper-Standard Automotive Inc........................ 260 637-5824
725 W 11th St Auburn (46706) *(G-380)*

Cooper-Standard Automotive Inc........................ 574 546-5938
501 High Rd Bremen (46506) *(G-1181)*

Cooper-Standard Automotive Inc........................ 260 247-7703
9910 Dupont Circle Dr E Fort Wayne (46825) *(G-4872)*

Cooper-Standard Automotive Inc........................ 260 593-2156
324 Morrow St Topeka (46571) *(G-15798)*

Cooper's Custom Hardwoods, Crawfordsville *Also Called: Coopers Wood Heat Supply LLC (G-2555)*

Cooperative Ventures Ind Corp.......................... 317 564-4695
11550 N Meridian St Ste 180 Carmel (46032) *(G-1596)*

Coopers Canvas.. 317 292-2165
9355 Rawles Ave Indianapolis (46229) *(G-7869)*

Coopers Wood Heat Supply LLC.......................... 765 918-1039
3506 W Offield Monument Rd Crawfordsville (47933) *(G-2555)*

Cope Brothers Machine Shop............................ 219 663-5561
5301 East State Rd 231 Leroy (46355) *(G-10973)*

Copeland LP... 317 968-4250
6579 W 350 N Ste A Greenfield (46140) *(G-6483)*

Copeland LP... 765 932-2956
616 Conrad Harcourt Way Rushville (46173) *(G-14397)*

Copeland LP... 765 932-1902
500 Conrad Harcourt Way Rushville (46173) *(G-14398)*

Copia Vineyards and Winery LLC......................... 805 835-6094
435 Virginia Ave Unit 707 Indianapolis (46203) *(G-7870)*

Copies Plus LLC... 317 545-5083
5845 Lawton Loop East Dr Ste 201 Indianapolis (46216) *(G-7871)*

Copper Kttle Fudge Popcorn LLC........................ 260 417-1036
4714 Union Chapel Rd Fort Wayne (46845) *(G-4873)*

Copper Moon Coffee LLC (PA)........................... 317 541-9000
1503 Veterans Memorial Pkwy E Lafayette (47905) *(G-10555)*

Copper Moon World Coffees, Lafayette *Also Called: Copper Moon Coffee LLC (G-10555)*

Copper Mountain Tech LLC (PA)......................... 317 222-5400
631 E New York St Indianapolis (46202) *(G-7872)*

Copy Quick, Fort Wayne *Also Called: Classic Graphics Inc (G-4853)*

Copy Solutions Inc..................................... 260 436-2679
6338 W Jefferson Blvd Fort Wayne (46804) *(G-4874)*

Copy-Print Shop Inc.................................... 765 447-6868
627 S Earl Ave Ste A Lafayette (47904) *(G-10556)*

Copyfire Typesetting Inc............................... 317 894-0408
1513 Touchstone Dr Indianapolis (46239) *(G-7873)*

Copymat Services Inc................................... 765 743-5995
20 N Salisbury St Lafayette (47906) *(G-10557)*

Cor-A-Vent Inc.. 574 258-6161
945 E 6th St Mishawaka (46544) *(G-11865)*

Cor-A-Vent Inc (PA).................................... 574 255-1910
2529 Lincolnway W Mishawaka (46544) *(G-11866)*

Coral Dog Candles...................................... 812 797-4050
2412 M St Bedford (47421) *(G-627)*

Corange International
9115 Hague Rd Indianapolis (46256) *(G-7874)*

Corbetts Custom Cabinetry LLC......................... 812 670-6211
6104 Carr Cir Jeffersonville (47130) *(G-9961)*

Core Biologic LLC...................................... 888 390-8838
3201 Stellhorn Rd Fort Wayne (46815) *(G-4875)*

Core Laboratories LP................................... 260 312-0455
1726 Saint Joe River Dr Fort Wayne (46805) *(G-4876)*

Core Minerals Operating Co Inc......................... 812 759-6950
25 Nw Riverside Dr Ste 310 Evansville (47708) *(G-3983)*

Core Wood Components LLC.............................. 574 370-4457
2995 Paul Dr Ste A Elkhart (46514) *(G-3268)*

Core-Tech Inc... 260 748-4477
6000 Maumee Rd Fort Wayne (46803) *(G-4877)*

ALPHABETIC SECTION — Country Embroidery

Corebiologic LLC.. 260 437-0353
4415 Winding Brook Rd Fort Wayne (46814) *(G-4878)*

Coreslab Strctres Indnplis Inc............................... 317 353-2118
1030 S Kitley Ave Indianapolis (46203) *(G-7875)*

Coreslab Structures, Indianapolis Also Called: Coreslab Strctres Indnplis Inc *(G-7875)*

Corey Kerst... 765 585-3026
945 N Milligan Hill Rd Attica (47918) *(G-346)*

Corlens Inc.. 843 822-6174
129 Lakeshore Terre Haute (47803) *(G-15568)*

Corn Flour Producers Llc.. 812 875-3113
7383 N 100 W Worthington (47471) *(G-16958)*

Corn Island Shipyard Inc.. 812 362-8808
9447 Indiana 66 Grandview (47615) *(G-6327)*

Corn Pro Inc.. 812 636-4319
5344 E 1250 N Elnora (47529) *(G-3814)*

Cornelius Manufacturing Inc................................... 812 636-4319
1912 E Us Hwy 50 Washington (47501) *(G-16474)*

Corner Cabinet.. 317 859-6336
405 E Main St Greenwood (46143) *(G-6682)*

Corner Sto LLC... 219 798-2822
4725 Madison Ave Apt 56 Indianapolis (46227) *(G-7876)*

Cornerstone Bread Co.. 317 897-9671
840 N Meridian St Indianapolis (46204) *(G-7877)*

Cornerstone Business Prtg LLC............................. 574 642-4060
801 Wayne St Ste 11 Middlebury (46540) *(G-11705)*

Cornerstone Cabinets... 317 718-0050
206 S County Rd 300 East Plainfield (46168) *(G-13671)*

Cornerstone Fllwship Kndllvlle............................... 260 347-0615
110 S Oak St Kendallville (46755) *(G-10102)*

Cornerstone Mill Work.. 260 357-0754
106 N Randolph St Garrett (46738) *(G-5856)*

Cornerstone Moulding Inc...................................... 574 546-4249
1586 3rd Rd Bremen (46506) *(G-1182)*

Coronado Casuals LLC.. 615 470-5718
2680 E Main St Ste 228 Plainfield (46168) *(G-13672)*

Coronado Stone, Jeffersonville Also Called: Coronado Stone Inc *(G-9962)*

Coronado Stone Inc... 812 284-2845
4306 Charlestown Pike Jeffersonville (47130) *(G-9962)*

Corporate Office, Brazil Also Called: Indiana Oxide Corporation *(G-1145)*

Corporate Packaging Solutions, Indianapolis Also Called: Cps Inc *(G-7895)*

Corporate Printing, Zionsville Also Called: Mid West Digital Express Inc *(G-17033)*

Corporate Shirts Direct Inc..................................... 317 474-6033
2141 Holiday Ln Franklin (46131) *(G-5722)*

Corporate Systems Engineering, Indianapolis Also Called: Corporate Systems Engrg LLC *(G-7878)*

Corporate Systems Engrg LLC.............................. 317 375-3600
1215 Brookville Way Indianapolis (46239) *(G-7878)*

Corporatestars Industries LLC................................ 317 783-0614
5528 Grassy Bank Dr Indianapolis (46237) *(G-7879)*

Corr-Wood Manufacturing Inc................................ 812 867-0700
10501 Hedden Rd Evansville (47725) *(G-3984)*

Correct Construction, Portage Also Called: Gl Properties Inc *(G-13868)*

Corrosion Technologies Inc.................................... 317 894-0627
6268 W Stoner Dr Ste C Greenfield (46140) *(G-6484)*

Corrquest Automation Inc...................................... 812 596-0049
2060 Highway 335 Ne Crandall (47114) *(G-2536)*

Corrugated Concepts, Indianapolis Also Called: Corrugated Concepts LLC *(G-7880)*

Corrugated Concepts LLC..................................... 317 290-1140
7225 Woodland Dr Ste 200 Indianapolis (46278) *(G-7880)*

Corsi Cabinet Company Inc................................... 317 786-1434
6111 Churchman Byp Indianapolis (46203) *(G-7881)*

Corsica Scents LLC.. 603 219-1287
12574 Meeting House Rd Carmel (46032) *(G-1597)*

Corteva Inc.. 765 586-4077
9146 Zionsville Rd Indianapolis (46268) *(G-7882)*

Corteva Inc (PA)... 833 267-8382
9330 Zionsville Rd Indianapolis (46268) *(G-7883)*

Corteva Agriscience, Indianapolis Also Called: Corteva Inc *(G-7882)*

Corteva Agriscience, Indianapolis Also Called: Corteva Inc *(G-7883)*

CORTEVA AGRISCIENCE, Indianapolis Also Called: Eidp Inc *(G-8064)*

Corteva Agriscience LLC (HQ)............................... 317 337-3000
9330 Zionsville Rd Indianapolis (46268) *(G-7884)*

Cortex Safety Technologies LLC............................ 317 414-5607
421 S Rangeline Rd Carmel (46032) *(G-1598)*

Corvano LLC... 317 403-0471
11309 Guy St Fishers (46038) *(G-4495)*

Corvette Aerospace LLC.. 317 512-4616
130 Rampart St Shelbyville (46176) *(G-14747)*

Cory Pmp LLC... 574 223-3177
401 E 4th St Rochester (46975) *(G-14284)*

Cory Williamson.. 812 242-0400
6745 S County Road 200 E Clay City (47841) *(G-2042)*

Corydon Democrat, The, Corydon Also Called: OBannon Publishing Company *(G-2508)*

Corydon Machine & Tool Co Inc............................. 812 738-3107
615 Quarry Rd Nw Corydon (47112) *(G-2495)*

Cosco Home & Office Pdts Div, Columbus Also Called: Dorel Juvenile Group Inc *(G-2289)*

Cosmoprof.. 317 897-0124
9455 E Washington St Indianapolis (46229) *(G-7885)*

Cosmos Superior Foods LLC.................................. 317 975-2747
10611 E 59th St Indianapolis (46236) *(G-7886)*

Cosology LLC.. 812 630-3084
11573 N State Road 245 Lamar (47550) *(G-10796)*

Costume Delights, Ellettsville Also Called: Higgins Dyan *(G-3809)*

Costumes By Design.. 812 334-2029
1912 S Montclair Ave Bloomington (47401) *(G-849)*

Cosworth, Indianapolis Also Called: Cosworth Electronics LLC *(G-7888)*

Cosworth LLC... 317 644-1037
5355 W 86th St Indianapolis (46268) *(G-7887)*

Cosworth Electronics LLC...................................... 317 808-3800
5355 W 86th St Indianapolis (46268) *(G-7888)*

Cottom Automated Bus Soluti................................ 317 853-6531
13295 Illinois St Ste 313 Carmel (46032) *(G-1599)*

Cottonwood Corp (PA)... 260 820-0415
1412 Evergreen Ct Ossian (46777) *(G-13421)*

Cottonwood Farm, Ossian Also Called: Cottonwood Corp *(G-13421)*

Couden Woodworks Inc... 317 370-0835
23808 Couden Rd Noblesville (46060) *(G-13063)*

Cougar Bag Eb LLC... 317 831-9720
3310 Hancel Cir Mooresville (46158) *(G-12200)*

Counter Column LLC.. 815 564-7569
1000 Sagamore Pkwy N Ste 102 Lafayette (47904) *(G-10558)*

Counter Design Co Inc... 812 477-1243
2381 N Cullen Ave Evansville (47715) *(G-3985)*

Counterfitters Inc.. 219 531-0848
359 Franklin St Ste C Valparaiso (46383) *(G-15929)*

Counterpart.. 317 587-1621
12115 Visionary Way Fishers (46038) *(G-4496)*

Countertop Connections Inc................................... 317 822-9858
3042 Hudson St Franklin (46131) *(G-5723)*

Countertop Manufacturing Inc................................ 765 966-4969
1600 Nw 11th St Richmond (47374) *(G-14111)*

Countertop Shoppe Inc.. 574 936-1423
505 W Jefferson St Plymouth (46563) *(G-13766)*

Country Cabin LLC... 812 232-4635
5125 S Us Highway 41 Terre Haute (47802) *(G-15569)*

Country Cabinets LLC.. 260 694-6777
3900 W State Road 218 Poneto (46781) *(G-13840)*

Country Charm.. 765 572-2588
2721 E Flint Rd Attica (47918) *(G-347)*

Country Club Computer.. 317 271-4000
8247 Indy Ct Indianapolis (46214) *(G-7889)*

Country Components Inc.. 812 345-9594
8990 S Edinburgh Rd Edinburgh (46124) *(G-3073)*

Country Corner Woodworks LLC............................ 574 825-6782
13775 County Road 22 Middlebury (46540) *(G-11706)*

Country Craft Cabinets LLC................................... 574 596-8624
17090 State Road 120 Bristol (46507) *(G-1255)*

Country Craftsman Wdwkg LLC............................. 574 773-4911
8563 W 1100 N Nappanee (46550) *(G-12591)*

Country Embroidery... 765 833-9002
4795 W 800 N Roann (46974) *(G-14250)*

Country Estate Mobile Home Pk   **ALPHABETIC SECTION**

Country Estate Mobile Home Pk, Frankfort *Also Called: Paddack Brothers Inc* *(G-5689)*

Country Folk Works, Rochester *Also Called: Anderson Creations Inc* *(G-14276)*

Country Hritg Wnery Vinyrd Inc 260 637-2980
185 County Road 68 Laotto (46763) *(G-10803)*

Country Lane Woodworking LLC 574 642-0662
66991 County Road 43 Millersburg (46543) *(G-11811)*

Country Maid, La Crosse *Also Called: La Braid Inc* *(G-10366)*

Country Meadow Wood Products, Shipshewana *Also Called: Orla Bontrater* *(G-14873)*

Country Mill Cabinet Co Inc 260 693-9289
7590 E 400 S Laotto (46763) *(G-10804)*

Country Moon Winery, Noblesville *Also Called: Country Moon Winery LLC* *(G-13064)*

Country Moon Winery LLC 317 773-7942
16222 Prairie Baptist Rd Noblesville (46060) *(G-13064)*

Country Sewing 260 347-9733
8929 E 1125 N Kendallville (46755) *(G-10103)*

Country Stitches Embroidery 219 324-7625
606 E 400 N La Porte (46350) *(G-10396)*

Country Stone 260 837-7134
2280 County Road 27 Waterloo (46793) *(G-16518)*

Country Stones and The Gravel, Waterloo *Also Called: Wilhelm Gravel Co Inc* *(G-16534)*

Country Valley Candles 574 702-1302
9813 W County Road 900 N Royal Center (46978) *(G-14390)*

Country View Cabinets LLC 574 825-3150
11770 County Road 32 Goshen (46528) *(G-6116)*

Country View Furn Mfg & Uphl 812 636-5024
8659 N 1000 E Odon (47562) *(G-13333)*

Country Welding 812 358-4402
233 Western Pkwy Seymour (47274) *(G-14640)*

Country Welding LLC 260 352-2938
11706 S 600 W Silver Lake (46982) *(G-14919)*

Country Woodcrafts Inc 260 244-7578
2283 E State Road 205 Columbia City (46725) *(G-2135)*

Country Woodshop LLC 574 642-3681
62870 County Road 43 Goshen (46528) *(G-6117)*

Country Woodworking LLC 812 636-6004
7650 E 1000 N Odon (47562) *(G-13334)*

Countrymark Cooperative, Mount Vernon *Also Called: Countrymark Ref Logistics LLC* *(G-12295)*

Countrymark Log Homes Inc 866 468-3301
5112 Parks Ridge Rd Vevay (47043) *(G-16107)*

Countrymark Ref Logistics LLC 812 838-4341
1200 Refinery Rd Mount Vernon (47620) *(G-12295)*

Countryroad Carriage, Shipshewana *Also Called: Perry Miller* *(G-14878)*

Countryside Cabinetry LLC 765 597-2391
2881 E Lucas Rd Marshall (47859) *(G-11371)*

Countryside Printing LLC 812 486-2454
7243 E 300 N Montgomery (47558) *(G-12090)*

Countryside Property LLC 800 711-5926
1033 E Walnut St Evansville (47714) *(G-3986)*

Countryside Sawmill 812 486-2991
8753 E 450 N Montgomery (47558) *(G-12091)*

Countryside Tool 260 357-3839
1723 South Rd Garrett (46738) *(G-5857)*

County Line Cabinetry LLC 574 642-1202
705 N 1200 W Middlebury (46540) *(G-11707)*

County Line Companies LLC 866 959-7866
4815 S 100 W Kokomo (46902) *(G-10250)*

County Line Woodworking 574 935-7107
11594 N 1100 W Bremen (46506) *(G-1183)*

County Materials Corp 317 323-6000
119 N Main St Maxwell (46154) *(G-11443)*

County Materials Corp 317 769-5503
6142 S Indianapolis Rd Whitestown (46075) *(G-16804)*

County of Lagrange 260 499-6353
300 E Factory St Lagrange (46761) *(G-10732)*

County of Steuben 260 833-2401
100 Lane 101 Crooked Lk Angola (46703) *(G-243)*

County West Sports 317 839-4076
1702 E Main St Plainfield (46168) *(G-13673)*

Couragio Press LLC 260 471-5603
2226 Lawndale Dr Fort Wayne (46805) *(G-4879)*

Courier Printing Co Allen Cnty 260 627-2728
13720 Main St Grabill (46741) *(G-6293)*

Courier-Times Inc 765 529-1111
201 S 14th St New Castle (47362) *(G-12856)*

Court & Commercial Records, Indianapolis *Also Called: IBJ Corporation* *(G-8448)*

Courtney Signs 317 653-5146
2410 Enterprise St Indianapolis (46219) *(G-7890)*

Covalence Coated Products, Evansville *Also Called: Covalnce Spcialty Coatings LLC* *(G-3988)*

Covalnce Spcalty Adhesives LLC (DH) 812 424-2904
101 Oakley St Evansville (47710) *(G-3987)*

Covalnce Spcialty Coatings LLC (DH) 812 424-2904
101 Oakley St Evansville (47710) *(G-3988)*

Coventure I LLC 800 570-0072
5776 Grape Rd Mishawaka (46545) *(G-11867)*

Cover Care LLC 513 297-4094
17397 Oak Ridge Rd Ste 100 Westfield (46074) *(G-16678)*

Coverite, Monticello *Also Called: Coverite-Custom Covers* *(G-12143)*

Coverite-Custom Covers 574 278-7152
8593 N State Road 39 Monticello (47960) *(G-12143)*

Covers of Indiana Inc 317 244-0291
5050 W Mooresville Rd Indianapolis (46221) *(G-7891)*

Covert Defenses LLC 919 749-9717
1195 S Sharon Chapel Rd West Lafayette (47906) *(G-16570)*

Covestro LLC 765 659-4721
3110 W State Road 28 Frankfort (46041) *(G-5656)*

Covey Rise Minerals LLC 812 897-2356
1617 S 1st St Boonville (47601) *(G-1086)*

Covia Holdings Corporation 812 683-2179
1405 Industrial Park Dr Huntingburg (47542) *(G-7275)*

COVIA HOLDINGS CORPORATION, Huntingburg *Also Called: Covia Holdings Corporation* *(G-7275)*

Covidien LP 317 837-8199
2824 Airwest Blvd Plainfield (46168) *(G-13674)*

Covington and Martin LLC 812 946-3846
1513 Clairview Dr Jeffersonville (47130) *(G-9963)*

Cowco Inc 812 346-8993
3780 S State Highway 7 North Vernon (47265) *(G-13260)*

Cowpokes Inc 765 642-3911
1812 E 53rd St Anderson (46013) *(G-99)*

Cowpokes Western Outfitters, Anderson *Also Called: Cowpokes Inc* *(G-99)*

Cox Cleaning Services 260 804-9001
6435 W Jefferson Blvd Num 140 Fort Wayne (46804) *(G-4880)*

Cox Interior, Indianapolis *Also Called: Cox Interior Inc* *(G-7892)*

Cox Interior Inc 317 896-2227
9333 Castlegate Dr Indianapolis (46256) *(G-7892)*

Cox John 765 463-6396
140 Tamiami Ct West Lafayette (47906) *(G-16571)*

Coy & Associates 317 787-5089
2305 E Banta Rd Indianapolis (46227) *(G-7893)*

Cozy Cat Inc 765 463-1254
2101 Indian Trail Dr Lafayette (47906) *(G-10559)*

Cozy Cottage LLC 812 838-6891
1808 Greenbrier Ct Mount Vernon (47620) *(G-12296)*

Cp Inc 765 825-4111
27100 Hall Rd Connersville (47331) *(G-2434)*

CP Polymer Solutions LLC 812 426-1350
2301 Saint Joseph Ind Park Dr Evansville (47720) *(G-3989)*

CPC 812 358-5010
811 Bloomington Rd Brownstown (47220) *(G-1420)*

Cpg - Ohio LLC 260 829-6721
9880 W Maple St Orland (46776) *(G-13363)*

CPI Aircraft Interiors, New Albany *Also Called: Custom Plywood Inc* *(G-12717)*

CPI Card Group - Indiana Inc 260 424-4920
613 High St Fort Wayne (46808) *(G-4881)*

CPI Holding Corporation 812 424-2904
101 Oakley St Evansville (47710) *(G-3990)*

CPM Acquisition Corp 765 362-2600
1114 E Wabash Ave Crawfordsville (47933) *(G-2556)*

CPM Conveyor LLC 317 875-1919
2260 Distributors Dr Indianapolis (46241) *(G-7894)*

ALPHABETIC SECTION — Cresline Plastic Pipe Co Inc

Cpp Filter Corporation.. 765 446-8416
730 Farabee Ct Lafayette (47905) *(G-10560)*

CPR Machining LLC.. 574 299-0222
4520 S Burnett Dr South Bend (46614) *(G-14984)*

Cps Inc.. 317 804-2300
5645 W 82nd St # 100 Indianapolis (46278) *(G-7895)*

Cpx Inc.. 219 474-5280
410 E Kent St Kentland (47951) *(G-10159)*

Cr Publications.. 219 931-6700
640 Conkey St Hammond (46324) *(G-6906)*

Cr Publications.. 219 931-6700
7103 Kennedy Ave Hammond (46323) *(G-6907)*

CRA-Wal Inc.. 317 856-3701
4001 S High School Rd Indianapolis (46241) *(G-7896)*

Craddock Finishing, Evansville Also Called: Craddock Furniture Corporation *(G-3991)*

Craddock Furniture Corporation.. 812 425-2691
1400 W Illinois St Evansville (47710) *(G-3991)*

Craft Laboratories Inc.. 260 432-9467
1901 Lakeview Dr Fort Wayne (46808) *(G-4882)*

Craft Metal Products Inc.. 317 545-3252
2751 N Emerson Ave Indianapolis (46218) *(G-7897)*

Craftech Building Systems Inc.. 574 773-4167
2676 E Market St Nappanee (46550) *(G-12592)*

Crafted Vanity Company.. 219 293-6063
1933 Hendricks St Gary (46404) *(G-5920)*

Craftline Printing, Fort Wayne Also Called: C-Point Inc *(G-4828)*

Craftmark Bakery LLC.. 317 548-3929
5202 Exploration Dr Indianapolis (46241) *(G-7898)*

Craftsman Lithograph, Roanoke Also Called: Behning Inc *(G-14260)*

Craftsman Specialties.. 260 705-5388
6535 Felger Rd Fort Wayne (46818) *(G-4883)*

Craig Hydraulic Enterprises.. 812 432-5108
9790 Front St Dillsboro (47018) *(G-2944)*

Craig Welding and Mfg Inc.. 574 353-7912
5158 N 825 E Mentone (46539) *(G-11472)*

Craigs Printing Co.. 812 358-5010
811 Bloomington Rd Brownstown (47220) *(G-1421)*

Crane Composites Inc.. 574 295-9391
21067 Protecta Dr Elkhart (46516) *(G-3269)*

Crane Composites Inc.. 815 467-8600
2424 E Kercher Rd Goshen (46526) *(G-6118)*

Crane Hill Machine Inc.. 812 358-3534
2476 E Us Highway 50 Seymour (47274) *(G-14641)*

Crane Pro Services, Crown Point Also Called: Konecranes Inc *(G-2711)*

Crane Pro Services, Greenwood Also Called: Konecranes Inc *(G-6724)*

Cranehill Mch & Fabrication, Seymour Also Called: Royalty Investments LLC *(G-14682)*

Cranewerks Inc.. 765 663-2909
511 N Range Line Rd Morristown (46161) *(G-12274)*

Crankshaft Brewing Co.. 317 939-0138
1630 E Northfield Dr Brownsburg (46112) *(G-1361)*

Crates & Pallets, Fountaintown Also Called: Ash-Lin Inc *(G-5613)*

Crawal Division, Indianapolis Also Called: CRA-Wal Inc *(G-7896)*

Crawford County Concrete.. 812 739-2707
7172 S Tower Rd Leavenworth (47137) *(G-10869)*

Crawford Industries LLC (HQ).. 800 428-0840
1414 Crawford Dr Crawfordsville (47933) *(G-2557)*

Crawford Water Care.. 317 758-6017
22902 Mulebarn Rd Sheridan (46069) *(G-14820)*

Crawl Before You Walk LLC.. 219 413-6623
270 Double Creek Dr Plainfield (46168) *(G-13675)*

Crazy Skates USA, Indianapolis Also Called: Sabre Holdings LLC *(G-9360)*

Createc Corporation.. 317 566-0022
6835 Guion Rd Ste A Indianapolis (46268) *(G-7899)*

Createch/Rehder Development Co.. 765 252-0257
2139 Klondike Rd West Lafayette (47906) *(G-16572)*

Creations In Canvas Vinyl.. 317 984-5712
1669 Cape Charles Ct Cicero (46034) *(G-1995)*

Creations In Glass.. 219 326-7941
725 Pine Lake Ave La Porte (46350) *(G-10397)*

Creative Blessings Co LLC.. 219 293-9595
4723 Round Lake Rd Apt H Indianapolis (46205) *(G-7900)*

Creative Cabinets.. 574 264-9041
30034 County Road 10 Elkhart (46514) *(G-3270)*

Creative Coatings, Fort Wayne Also Called: Creative Powder Coatings LLC *(G-4884)*

Creative Computer Services.. 317 729-5779
4223 S Shelby 750 W Franklin (46131) *(G-5724)*

Creative Concept Ventures Inc.. 812 282-9442
590 Missouri Ave Jeffersonville (47130) *(G-9964)*

Creative Concepts Cabinetry.. 812 522-0204
335 W Brown St Seymour (47274) *(G-14642)*

Creative Construction Pubg Inc.. 765 743-9704
2720 S River Rd West Lafayette (47906) *(G-16573)*

Creative Finishing LLC.. 812 591-8111
6417 S County Road 220 Sw Greensburg (47240) *(G-6586)*

Creative Foam Corporation.. 574 546-4238
405 Industrial Dr Bremen (46506) *(G-1184)*

Creative Inc.. 765 447-3500
150 N 36th St Lafayette (47905) *(G-10561)*

Creative Industries Inc.. 317 248-1102
5280 Oakbrook Dr Plainfield (46168) *(G-13676)*

Creative Ldsc & Compost Co.. 317 776-2909
18377 Deshane Ave Noblesville (46060) *(G-13065)*

Creative Ldscpg & Compost Co, Noblesville Also Called: Creative Ldscp & Compost Co *(G-13065)*

Creative Liquid Coatings Inc.. 260 349-1862
221 S Progress Dr W Kendallville (46755) *(G-10104)*

Creative Liquid Coatings Inc (PA).. 260 349-1862
2620 Marion Dr Kendallville (46755) *(G-10105)*

Creative Machining Concept, Westfield Also Called: Creative McHining Concepts Inc *(G-16679)*

Creative Manufacturing Rv LLC.. 574 333-3302
330 E Windsor Ave Elkhart (46514) *(G-3271)*

Creative McHining Concepts Inc.. 317 896-9250
17018 Westfield Park Rd Westfield (46074) *(G-16679)*

Creative Metal Works Wrought.. 812 883-2008
1901 E State Road 56 Salem (47167) *(G-14476)*

Creative Mnds Work Pblctons LL.. 317 759-1002
8063 Madison Ave Pmb 587 Indianapolis (46227) *(G-7901)*

Creative Powder Coatings LLC.. 260 489-3580
7505 Freedom Way Fort Wayne (46818) *(G-4884)*

Creative Sign Resources LLC (PA).. 260 425-9618
4707 E Washington Blvd Fort Wayne (46803) *(G-4885)*

Creative Signs.. 260 438-6352
4117 Merchant Rd Fort Wayne (46818) *(G-4886)*

Creative Tool and Machining.. 812 378-3562
4010 Middle Rd Columbus (47203) *(G-2248)*

Creative Tool Inc.. 260 338-1222
2403 W Shoaff Rd Huntertown (46748) *(G-7251)*

Creative Wood Designs Inc.. 260 894-4533
710 Gerber St Ligonier (46767) *(G-11010)*

Creative Woodworks LLC.. 260 450-1742
9771 Maysville Rd Fort Wayne (46815) *(G-4887)*

Creative Works Inc.. 317 834-4770
5767 Dividend Rd Indianapolis (46241) *(G-7902)*

Creative Works Theme Factory, Indianapolis Also Called: Creative Works Inc *(G-7902)*

Creed & Dyer Precast Inc.. 574 784-3361
68186 Us Highway 31 Lakeville (46536) *(G-10789)*

Creekside Embroidery.. 574 656-8333
26181 Stanton Rd Walkerton (46574) *(G-16265)*

Cregg Custom Cabinets.. 812 342-3605
12230 W 525 S Columbus (47201) *(G-2249)*

Crenshaw Paving, Michigantown Also Called: Crenshaw Paving Incorporated *(G-11689)*

Crenshaw Paving Incorporated.. 765 249-2342
7304 E County Road 100 N Michigantown (46057) *(G-11689)*

Crescendo Inc.. 812 829-4759
56 E Jefferson St Spencer (47460) *(G-15344)*

Crescent Plastics Inc.. 812 428-9305
600 N Cross Pointe Blvd Evansville (47715) *(G-3992)*

Crescnt-Crsln-Wbash Plas Fndti.. 812 428-9300
600 N Cross Pointe Blvd Evansville (47715) *(G-3993)*

Cresline Plastic Pipe Co Inc (PA).. 812 428-9300
600 N Cross Pointe Blvd Evansville (47715) *(G-3994)*

Cresline-Northwest LLC (PA)...812 428-9300
600 N Cross Pointe Blvd Evansville (47715) *(G-3995)*

Cresline-West Inc (PA)..812 428-9300
600 N Cross Pointe Blvd Evansville (47715) *(G-3996)*

Cressy Memorial Group Inc...574 258-1800
3925 Glaser Ct Mishawaka (46545) *(G-11868)*

Crestview Woodworking LLC..260 768-4707
6825 W 450 N Shipshewana (46565) *(G-14841)*

Crestwood Equity Partners LP..812 265-3313
3625 Clifty Dr Madison (47250) *(G-11212)*

Cretaceous Cures..317 379-7744
15541 Wildflower Ln Westfield (46074) *(G-16680)*

Crichlow Industries Inc..317 925-5178
6848 Hawthorn Park Dr Indianapolis (46220) *(G-7903)*

Crickys Country Cabinets LLC...812 486-3705
1831 N 950 E Loogootee (47553) *(G-11129)*

Crisman Sand Company Inc...219 462-3114
736 N 400 E Valparaiso (46383) *(G-15930)*

Criss, Charles, Lamar *Also Called: Cheri-Theree Inc (G-10795)*

Criterion Catalyst Technologys, Michigan City *Also Called: Shell Catalysts & Tech LP (G-11667)*

Criterion Press Inc..317 236-1570
1400 N Meridian St Indianapolis (46202) *(G-7904)*

Crone Logging LLC...765 346-0025
4005 Parker Rd Martinsville (46151) *(G-11386)*

Crone Lumber Co Inc...765 342-1160
501 N Park Ave Martinsville (46151) *(G-11387)*

Crooked Stic Bows LLC...812 677-2715
214 E Emerson St Princeton (47670) *(G-13988)*

Crop and Drop Granite Surfaces, Portage *Also Called: Great Lakes Granite LLC (G-13872)*

Crosbie Foundry Company Inc..574 262-1502
1600 Mishawaka St Elkhart (46514) *(G-3272)*

Cross Country Hardwood LLC...812 571-4226
10071 Bill Peelman Rd Vevay (47043) *(G-16108)*

Cross Match Technologies Inc..317 596-3260
8440 Allison Pointe Blvd Indianapolis (46250) *(G-7905)*

Cross Printwear Inc...317 293-1776
3466 N Raceway Rd Indianapolis (46234) *(G-7906)*

Cross Road Precision Tool Inc..260 335-2772
7747 E 800 S Union City (47390) *(G-15851)*

Cross Rv Sales, Lagrange *Also Called: Indiana Interstate Entps LLC (G-10743)*

Cross-Cut Wood Shop, The, Nappanee *Also Called: FM Holdings LLC (G-12597)*

Crossfire Press Corporation..765 987-7164
980 W Fair Oaks Rd New Castle (47362) *(G-12857)*

Crosspoint Polymer Tech LLC...812 426-1350
2301 Saint Joseph Ind Park Dr Evansville (47720) *(G-3997)*

Crosspoint Power and Rfrgn LLC (PA)................................317 240-1967
4301 W Morris St Indianapolis (46241) *(G-7907)*

Crosspoint Solutions, Indianapolis *Also Called: Cummins Crosspoint LLC (G-7924)*

Crosspoint Solutions LLC...877 826-9399
2601 Fortune Cir E Ste 300c Indianapolis (46241) *(G-7908)*

Crossrads Cntrtops Cbnetry LLC...317 908-9254
606 S Audubon Rd Indianapolis (46219) *(G-7909)*

Crossrads Rhbilitation Ctr Inc...317 897-7320
8302 E 33rd St Indianapolis (46226) *(G-7910)*

Crossroad Freight LLC..239 248-4058
12255 Country Side Dr Indianapolis (46229) *(G-7911)*

Crossroads Biologicals LLC...765 239-9113
331 Cromwell Ct Lafayette (47909) *(G-10562)*

Crossroads Door & Hardware Inc.......................................812 234-9751
1301 Eagle St Terre Haute (47807) *(G-15570)*

Crossroads Farms Dairy, Indianapolis *Also Called: Kroger Limited Partnership II (G-8703)*

Crossroads Frt Solutions LLC..800 425-0282
11 Municipal Dr Ste 200 Fishers (46038) *(G-4497)*

Crossroads Furniture Co LLC...765 307-2095
121 N Washington St Crawfordsville (47933) *(G-2558)*

Crossroads Galvanizing LLC..765 421-6741
4877 E Old 350 S Lafayette (47905) *(G-10563)*

Crossroads Imprints Inc...765 482-2931
107 W Main St Lebanon (46052) *(G-10887)*

Crossroads Lighting, Indianapolis *Also Called: Gmp Holdings LLC (G-8294)*

Crossroads Mfg LLC..765 592-6456
1882 E State Road 236 Marshall (47859) *(G-11372)*

Crossroads Orthotics & Cnsltn...765 359-0041
821 S Washington St Crawfordsville (47933) *(G-2559)*

Crossroads Solar Entps LLC..607 759-1058
251 E Sample St Ste 100 South Bend (46601) *(G-14985)*

Crossroads Sourcing Group Ltd...847 940-4123
737 Edison Way Carmel (46032) *(G-1600)*

Crosswind Pharmacy...812 381-4815
4838 Fletcher Ave Indianapolis (46203) *(G-7912)*

Crothersville Times..812 793-2188
510 Moore St Ste 100 Crothersville (47229) *(G-2639)*

Crow Welding and Fabrication..317 619-3190
2410 W County Line Rd Indianapolis (46217) *(G-7913)*

Crowd Factor, Lafayette *Also Called: Goldden Corporation (G-10591)*

Crowdpixie LLC...317 578-3137
7594 Timber Springs Dr N Fishers (46038) *(G-4498)*

Crowdreviewscom LLC..239 227-2428
1913 N Michigan St Ste F # 218 Plymouth (46563) *(G-13767)*

Crown Audio Inc..800 342-6939
1718 W Mishawaka Rd Elkhart (46517) *(G-3273)*

Crown Battery Manufacturing Co.......................................260 423-3358
3000 E Washington Blvd Fort Wayne (46803) *(G-4888)*

Crown Brick & Supply Inc (PA)..219 663-7880
820 Thomas St Crown Point (46307) *(G-2668)*

Crown Broadcast Irec, Elkhart *Also Called: International Rdo & Elec Corp (G-3429)*

Crown Cork & Seal, Crawfordsville *Also Called: Crown Cork & Seal Usa Inc (G-2560)*

Crown Cork & Seal Usa Inc..765 362-3200
400 N Walnut St Crawfordsville (47933) *(G-2560)*

Crown E.S.A., Portage *Also Called: Crown Elec Svcs & Automtn Inc (G-13857)*

Crown Elec Svcs & Automtn Inc (DH)................................972 929-4700
5960 Southport Rd Portage (46368) *(G-13857)*

Crown Equipment Corporation..574 293-1264
1125 Herman St Elkhart (46516) *(G-3274)*

Crown Equipment Corporation..812 477-5511
2540 Diego Dr Evansville (47715) *(G-3998)*

Crown Equipment Corporation..260 484-0055
9110 Avionics Dr Fort Wayne (46809) *(G-4889)*

Crown Equipment Corporation..765 653-4240
2600 State Rd 240 E Greencastle (46135) *(G-6399)*

Crown Equipment Corporation..765 520-2077
1817 I Ave New Castle (47362) *(G-12858)*

Crown Equipment Corporation..317 875-7233
2495 E Perry Rd Plainfield (46168) *(G-13677)*

Crown Group Co..260 432-6900
4301 Engle Ridge Dr Fort Wayne (46804) *(G-4890)*

Crown International, Elkhart *Also Called: Crown Audio Inc (G-3273)*

Crown Lift Trucks, Elkhart *Also Called: Crown Equipment Corporation (G-3274)*

Crown Lift Trucks, Evansville *Also Called: Crown Equipment Corporation (G-3998)*

Crown Lift Trucks, Greencastle *Also Called: Crown Equipment Corporation (G-6399)*

Crown Lift Trucks, New Castle *Also Called: Crown Equipment Corporation (G-12858)*

Crown Lift Trucks, Plainfield *Also Called: Crown Equipment Corporation (G-13677)*

Crown Lift Trucks-Ft Wayne, Fort Wayne *Also Called: Crown Equipment Corporation (G-4889)*

Crown Mtal Fbricators Erectors..219 661-8277
1031 E Summit St Crown Point (46307) *(G-2669)*

Crown Packaging International Inc (PA)............................219 738-1000
8919 Colorado St Merrillville (46410) *(G-11499)*

Crown Point Graphics, Indianapolis *Also Called: Mejjm Inc (G-8873)*

Crown Point Printing LLC..219 226-0900
1082 Breuckman Dr Crown Point (46307) *(G-2670)*

Crown Point Shopping News..219 663-4212
112 W Clark St Crown Point (46307) *(G-2671)*

Crown Products & Services Inc (PA)..................................317 564-4799
12821 E New Market St Ste 310 Carmel (46032) *(G-1601)*

Crown Technology Inc..317 845-0045
7513 E 96th St Indianapolis (46256) *(G-7914)*

Crown Training and Dev Inc...219 947-0845
2642 E 84th Pl Merrillville (46410) *(G-11500)*

Crown Unlimited Machine, Bluffton *Also Called: MPS International LLC (G-1043)*

Crr Industries LLC..219 947-2052
8414 Old Lincoln Hwy Hobart (46342) *(G-7184)*

ALPHABETIC SECTION — Cummins

CRS-Drs Corporation 260 478-7555
  4004 Lower Huntington Rd Fort Wayne (46809) (G-4891)
CRS-Spv Inc 502 805-0143
  4555 New Middle Rd Jeffersonville (47130) (G-9965)
Crumbl- Bloomington, Bloomington Also Called: Bloomington Cookies LLC (G-811)
Crume Industries LLC 574 747-7683
  1329 Freda Dr A Elkhart (46514) (G-3275)
Crunchtech Holdings LLC 818 583-0004
  6928 N 400 E Kendallville (46755) (G-10106)
Crusher Parts Direct LLC 812 822-1463
  3905 W Farmer Ave Bloomington (47403) (G-850)
Crust N More Inc 317 890-7878
  6815 E 34th St Indianapolis (46226) (G-7915)
Cruz Electric & Handy Svc LLC 219 308-7117
  541 N Wisconsin St Hobart (46342) (G-7185)
Cryogenic Indus Solutions LLC 765 564-4684
  9701 Old State Road 25 N Lafayette (47905) (G-10564)
Cryogenic Support Systems Inc 765 764-4961
  1903 W State Road 63 Williamsport (47993) (G-16846)
Cryovac LLC 317 876-4100
  7950 Allison Ave Indianapolis (46268) (G-7916)
Cryovac Division, Indianapolis Also Called: Cryovac LLC (G-7916)
Crystal Colors, South Bend Also Called: Sugarpaste (G-15272)
Crystal Graphics Inc 317 535-9202
  530 E Main St Whiteland (46184) (G-16780)
Crystal Industries Inc 574 264-6166
  28870 Phillips St Elkhart (46514) (G-3276)
Crystal Lake LLC 574 858-2514
  6500 W Crystal Lake Rd Warsaw (46580) (G-16338)
Crystal Lake LLC (PA) 574 267-3101
  4217 W Old Road 30 Warsaw (46580) (G-16339)
Crystal Shadows 574 269-2722
  1080 W 200 S Warsaw (46580) (G-16340)
Crystal Source 812 988-7009
  150 S Old School Way Nashville (47448) (G-12669)
Crystal Valley Farms LLC (PA) 260 829-6550
  9622 W 350 N Orland (46776) (G-13364)
Cs Kern Inc 765 289-8600
  3401 S Hamilton Ave Muncie (47302) (G-12370)
Cs Precision Machining Inc 260 338-1081
  16335 Lima Rd Ste 6a Huntertown (46748) (G-7252)
Cs Technology, Terre Haute Also Called: Computer Solutions Systems Inc (G-15566)
Cs Warrior Enterprise LLC 317 528-0152
  5868 E 71st St Indianapolis (46220) (G-7917)
Csa Racking LLC 414 241-3585
  6650 Arizona Ave Hammond (46323) (G-6908)
Csc-Indiana LLC 708 625-3255
  2190 Summit St New Haven (46774) (G-12900)
Csd Group LLC 260 918-3500
  3003 Ryan Rd New Haven (46774) (G-12901)
Csg, Merrillville Also Called: Complex Structures Group LLC (G-11498)
Csi, Crawfordsville Also Called: Closure Systems Intl Inc (G-2554)
Csi Electronics, Kokomo Also Called: Cil Electronics LLC (G-10244)
Csi Manufacturing Inc 574 825-7891
  209 York Dr Middlebury (46540) (G-11708)
Csi Signs, Noblesville Also Called: Chads Signs Installations Inc (G-13056)
CSM Industries LLC 219 465-2009
  472 Ridgeland Ave Valparaiso (46385) (G-15931)
Csn Industries Inc 317 697-6549
  1797 S Conservation Club Rd Morgantown (46160) (G-12257)
Cspine Inc 574 936-7893
  3501 Miller Dr South Bend (46634) (G-14986)
Csr Associates LLC 317 255-2247
  5315 N Pennsylvania St Indianapolis (46220) (G-7918)
Csr Suspension LLC 812 346-8620
  485 S County Road 575 W North Vernon (47265) (G-13261)
CST, Crown Point Also Called: Cargo Ski Transport Inc (G-2664)
CT Polymers LLC 574 598-6132
  12340 Elm Rd Bourbon (46504) (G-1120)
Ctb Inc 765 654-8517
  1750 W State Road 28 Frankfort (46041) (G-5657)
Ctb Inc 574 658-4191
  410 N Higbee St Milford (46542) (G-11789)
Ctb Inc (HQ) 574 658-4191
  611 N Higbee St Milford (46542) (G-11790)
Ctb Inc 574 658-4191
  410 N Higbee St Milford (46542) (G-11791)
CTB Hauling Service LLC 317 760-3308
  6511 Crandall Cir Indianapolis (46260) (G-7919)
CTB Inc Employee Benefit Tr A 574 658-5132
  Milford (46542) (G-11792)
CTB International Corp 574 658-9431
  State Road 15 North Milford (46542) (G-11793)
CTB MN Investment Co Inc 765 654-8517
  1750 W State Road 28 Frankfort (46041) (G-5658)
CTB MN Investment Co Inc (HQ) 574 658-4191
  611 N Higbee St Milford (46542) (G-11794)
Cte Solutions, Plymouth Also Called: Culver Tool & Engineering Inc (G-13768)
CTI, Bristol Also Called: Combined Technologies Inc (G-1254)
Ctm, New Haven Also Called: Challenge Tool & Mfg Inc (G-12898)
Cto Publishing Inc 765 210-8290
  306 S Main St Apt 207 Kokomo (46901) (G-10251)
Ctp Corporation, Indianapolis Also Called: Nelson Global Products Inc (G-8999)
Ctp Division Nelson Globl Pdts, Greenwood Also Called: Nelson Global Products Inc (G-6746)
CTS Corporation 574 293-7511
  406 E Parr Rd Berne (46711) (G-707)
CTS Corporation 574 293-7511
  905 N West Blvd Elkhart (46514) (G-3277)
CTS Elctrnic Cmponents Cal Inc 574 523-3800
  905 N West Blvd Elkhart (46514) (G-3278)
Ctsi 317 868-8087
  4671 N Graham Rd Whiteland (46184) (G-16781)
Ctsi, Fort Wayne Also Called: Commercial Technical Svcs Inc (G-4867)
CUARTETO TANGUERO, Bloomington Also Called: Tanguero Inc (G-983)
Cubed Laboratories LLC 866 935-6165
  1162 E Lasalle Ave South Bend (46617) (G-14987)
Cuda II Inc (PA) 317 514-0885
  1910 S Girls School Rd Indianapolis (46241) (G-7920)
Cuda II Inc 317 839-1515
  1910 S Girls School Rd Indianapolis (46241) (G-7921)
Culligan, Muncie Also Called: Driessen Water Inc (G-12386)
Cullip Industries Inc 574 293-8251
  300 Comet Ave Elkhart (46514) (G-3279)
Cullip Tool & Die, Elkhart Also Called: Cullip Industries Inc (G-3279)
Cullman Casting Corporation 256 735-0900
  3750 N County Road 75 W Mount Vernon (47265) (G-13262)
Culpeper Wood Preservers, Shelbyville Also Called: Jefferson Homebuilders Inc (G-14765)
Cultor Food Science 812 299-6700
  100 Pfizer Dr Terre Haute (47802) (G-15571)
Culture Wars, South Bend Also Called: Ultramontane Associates Inc (G-15295)
Culver, Middlebury Also Called: Culver Duck Farms Inc (G-11709)
Culver Duck Farms Inc 574 825-9537
  12215 County Road 10 Middlebury (46540) (G-11709)
Culver Tool & Engineering Inc 574 935-9611
  1901 Walter Glaub Dr Plymouth (46563) (G-13768)
Culvers Port Side Marina 574 223-5090
  1409 Wentzel St Rochester (46975) (G-14285)
Cumberland Millwork & Supply 260 471-6936
  5736 Industrial Rd Fort Wayne (46825) (G-4892)
CUMBERLAND MILLWORK & SUPPLY INC, Fort Wayne Also Called: Cumberland Millwork & Supply (G-4892)
Cummings Holdings LLC 260 493-4405
  1432 E Gump Rd Fort Wayne (46845) (G-4893)
Cummings Machine Shop 812 275-5542
  1200 K St Bedford (47421) (G-628)
Cummings Production Machining, Fort Wayne Also Called: Cummings Holdings LLC (G-4893)
Cummins, Columbus Also Called: Cummins Cdc Holding Inc (G-2251)
Cummins, Columbus Also Called: Cummins Dist Holdco Inc (G-2252)
Cummins, Columbus Also Called: Cummins Emission Solutions Inc (G-2253)

Cummins   ALPHABETIC SECTION

Cummins, Columbus *Also Called: Cummins Engine Holding Company (G-2255)*
Cummins, Columbus *Also Called: Cummins Franchise Holdco LLC (G-2257)*
Cummins, Columbus *Also Called: Cummins Inc (G-2271)*
Cummins, Columbus *Also Called: Cummins-Scania Xpi Mfg LLC (G-2275)*
Cummins, Elkhart *Also Called: Cummins Americas Inc (G-3280)*
Cummins, Evansville *Also Called: Cummins Crosspoint LLC (G-3999)*
Cummins, Fort Wayne *Also Called: Cummins Crosspoint LLC (G-4894)*
Cummins, Fort Wayne *Also Called: Cummins Inc (G-4895)*
Cummins, Harlan *Also Called: Cummins Repair Inc (G-7053)*
Cummins, Indianapolis *Also Called: Cummins Crosspoint LLC (G-7925)*
Cummins, Indianapolis *Also Called: Cummins Cumberland Inc (G-7926)*
Cummins, Mishawaka *Also Called: Cummins Crosspoint LLC (G-11869)*
Cummins, Woodburn *Also Called: Cummins Inc (G-16947)*

Cummins - Allison Corp 317 872-6244
5696 W 74th St Indianapolis (46278) *(G-7922)*

Cummins Americas Inc (HQ) 812 377-5000
500 Jackson St Columbus (47201) *(G-2250)*

Cummins Americas Inc 800 589-9027
5125 Beck Dr Elkhart (46516) *(G-3280)*

Cummins Cdc Holding Inc 812 312-3162
500 Jackson St Columbus (47201) *(G-2251)*

Cummins Clmbus Mdrnge Eng Plan, Columbus *Also Called: Cummins Inc (G-2266)*

Cummins Crosspoint LLC 812 867-4400
7901 Highway 41 N Evansville (47725) *(G-3999)*

Cummins Crosspoint LLC 260 482-3691
3415 W Coliseum Blvd Fort Wayne (46808) *(G-4894)*

Cummins Crosspoint LLC 317 484-2146
4557 W Bradbury Ave Ste 3 Indianapolis (46241) *(G-7923)*

Cummins Crosspoint LLC 317 244-7251
3621 W Morris St Indianapolis (46241) *(G-7924)*

Cummins Crosspoint LLC (HQ) 317 243-7979
111 Monument Cir Ste 601 Indianapolis (46204) *(G-7925)*

Cummins Crosspoint LLC 574 252-2154
3025 N Home St Mishawaka (46545) *(G-11869)*

Cummins Cumberland Inc 317 243-7979
2601 Fortune Cir E Ste 300c Indianapolis (46241) *(G-7926)*

Cummins Dist Holdco Inc (HQ) 812 377-5000
500 Jackson St Columbus (47201) *(G-2252)*

Cummins Emission Solutions Inc (HQ) 615 986-2596
500 Jackson St Columbus (47201) *(G-2253)*

Cummins Emssion Sltons Clmbus 800 286-6467
500 Jackson St Columbus (47201) *(G-2254)*

Cummins Engine, Columbus *Also Called: Cummins Americas Inc (G-2250)*

Cummins Engine Company Inc 812 522-9366
800 E 3rd St Seymour (47274) *(G-14643)*

Cummins Engine Holding Company 812 377-5000
500 Jackson St Columbus (47201) *(G-2255)*

Cummins Filtration Ip Inc 615 514-7339
500 Jackson St Columbus (47201) *(G-2256)*

Cummins Franchise Holdco LLC 812 377-5000
500 Jackson St Columbus (47201) *(G-2257)*

Cummins Fuel Systems, Columbus *Also Called: Cummins Inc (G-2268)*

Cummins Holding Group LLC 765 962-6332
3712 National Rd W Richmond (47374) *(G-14112)*

Cummins Inc 812 377-5298
7660 S International Dr Columbus (47201) *(G-2258)*

Cummins Inc 812 377-2932
910 S Marr Rd Columbus (47201) *(G-2259)*

Cummins Inc 812 377-9914
5175 N Warren Dr Ste 100 Columbus (47203) *(G-2260)*

Cummins Inc 812 377-0150
2879 Prairie Stream Way Columbus (47203) *(G-2261)*

Cummins Inc 765 430-0093
525 Jackson St Columbus (47201) *(G-2262)*

Cummins Inc 812 376-0742
1350 Arcadia Dr Columbus (47201) *(G-2263)*

Cummins Inc 812 524-6455
1825 W 450 S Columbus (47201) *(G-2264)*

Cummins Inc 317 460-9843
4303 Washington St Columbus (47203) *(G-2265)*

Cummins Inc 812 377-7739
2725 W County Road 450 Columbus (47201) *(G-2266)*

Cummins Inc 812 374-4774
3540 W 450 S Columbus (47201) *(G-2267)*

Cummins Inc 812 377-6072
1460 N National Rd Columbus (47201) *(G-2268)*

Cummins Inc 812 377-7000
1900 Mckinley Ave Columbus (47201) *(G-2269)*

Cummins Inc 812 312-3162
500 Jackson St Columbus (47201) *(G-2270)*

Cummins Inc (PA) 812 377-5000
500 Jackson St Columbus (47201) *(G-2271)*

Cummins Inc 812 377-8601
2851 State St Columbus (47201) *(G-2272)*

Cummins Inc 812 378-2874
301 Jackson St Columbus (47201) *(G-2273)*

Cummins Inc 260 482-3691
3415 W Coliseum Blvd Fort Wayne (46808) *(G-4895)*

Cummins Inc 317 610-2493
301 E Market St Indianapolis (46204) *(G-7927)*

Cummins Inc 317 244-7251
3621 W Morris St Indianapolis (46241) *(G-7928)*

Cummins Inc 812 524-6381
845 A Ave E Seymour (47274) *(G-14644)*

Cummins Inc 812 522-9366
800 E 3rd St Seymour (47274) *(G-14645)*

Cummins Inc 317 751-4567
5635 N Graham Rd Whiteland (46184) *(G-16782)*

Cummins Inc 260 657-1436
20329 Notestine Rd Woodburn (46797) *(G-16947)*

Cummins Onan, Elkhart *Also Called: Cummins Power Generation Inc (G-3281)*

Cummins Power Generation Inc 574 262-4611
5125 Beck Dr Ste A Elkhart (46516) *(G-3281)*

Cummins Power Systems LLC 410 590-8700
500 Jackson St Columbus (47201) *(G-2274)*

Cummins Repair Inc 260 632-4800
11110 Scipio Rd Harlan (46743) *(G-7053)*

Cummins Sales and Service, Columbus *Also Called: Cummins Inc (G-2270)*
Cummins Sales and Service, Indianapolis *Also Called: Cummins Inc (G-7927)*

Cummins Sales Svc 260 482-3691
3415 W Coliseum Blvd Fort Wayne (46808) *(G-4896)*

Cummins Sales Svc 574 252-2154
3025 N Home St Mishawaka (46545) *(G-11870)*

Cummins Technical Center, Columbus *Also Called: Cummins Inc (G-2269)*
Cummins-Allison, Indianapolis *Also Called: Cummins - Allison Corp (G-7922)*

Cummins-Scania Xpi Mfg LLC (PA) 812 377-5000
1460 N National Rd Columbus (47201) *(G-2275)*

Cumulus Intrmdate Holdings Inc 765 452-5704
4834 N Parkway Kokomo (46901) *(G-10252)*

Cunningham Optical One, Muncie *Also Called: Tri State Optical Inc (G-12508)*

Cunningham Pattern & Engrg Inc 812 379-9571
4399 N Us Hwy 31 Columbus (47201) *(G-2276)*

Cunningham Precision, Columbus *Also Called: Ce Systems Inc (G-2235)*

Cunningham Tire Services Inc 765 473-9200
452 W 14th St Peru (46970) *(G-13576)*

Cupkas Bee Good Meadery LLC 260 927-3837
112 N Main St Auburn (46706) *(G-381)*

Cupkas Bee Good Meadery LLC (PA) 260 927-3837
819 N Indiana Ave Auburn (46706) *(G-382)*

Cupprint LLC 574 323-5250
635 S Lafayette Blvd Ste Aa South Bend (46601) *(G-14988)*

Curated Luxe Co LLC 317 797-1531
5928 Keensburg Dr Indianapolis (46228) *(G-7929)*

Curia Indiana LLC 765 463-0112
3065 Kent Ave West Lafayette (47906) *(G-16574)*

Current Electric Inc 219 872-7736
301 Chapala Pkwy Michigan City (46360) *(G-11591)*

Current Publishing LLC 317 489-4444
30 S Rangeline Rd Carmel (46032) *(G-1602)*

Current Technologies Inc 765 364-0490
Frontage Rd Crawfordsville (47933) *(G-2561)*

ALPHABETIC SECTION — Custom Poly Packaging

Curtis Dyna-Fog 317 896-2561
  525 Park St Westfield (46074) *(G-16681)*

Curtis Honeycutt LLC 317 645-7540
  957 Hannibal St Noblesville (46060) *(G-13066)*

Curtis Life Research LLC 317 873-4519
  7000 Hull Rd Zionsville (46077) *(G-16999)*

Curtis Products Inc 574 289-4891
  722 Carroll St South Bend (46601) *(G-14989)*

Curtis Products Inc (PA) 574 289-4891
  401 N Bendix Dr South Bend (46628) *(G-14990)*

Curtis Tom Tool and Dye 574 293-3832
  622 Jay Dee St Elkhart (46514) *(G-3282)*

Curtis-Maruyasu America Inc 812 544-2021
  48 S Buffaloville Rd Santa Claus (47579) *(G-14507)*

Curvo Labs Inc (PA) 619 316-1202
  58 Adams Ave Evansville (47713) *(G-4000)*

Cushman Performance Parts LLC 765 653-3054
  1556 N County Road 175 W Greencastle (46135) *(G-6400)*

Custom Blacksmith Shop 765 292-2745
  29579 N State Road 19 Atlanta (46031) *(G-341)*

Custom Blacksmithing, Atlanta *Also Called: Custom Blacksmith Shop (G-341)*

Custom Blind and Shade Company 812 867-9280
  21 W Sunrise Dr Evansville (47710) *(G-4001)*

Custom Blind Co 812 867-9280
  21 W Sunrise Dr Evansville (47710) *(G-4002)*

Custom Bottling & Packg Inc 877 401-7195
  101 S Parker Dr Ashley (46705) *(G-332)*

Custom Building Products LLC 765 656-0234
  3800 W State Road 28 Frankfort (46041) *(G-5659)*

Custom Built Barns Inc (PA) 765 457-9037
  2312 N Plate St Kokomo (46901) *(G-10253)*

Custom Built Storage Sheds, Kokomo *Also Called: Custom Built Barns Inc (G-10253)*

Custom Cabinets & Furn LLC 812 486-2503
  4578 N 875 E Montgomery (47558) *(G-12092)*

Custom Candy Wrappers Company 574 247-0756
  52092 Larkspur Cir Granger (46530) *(G-6340)*

Custom Carton Inc 260 563-7411
  3758 W Old 24 Wabash (46992) *(G-16179)*

Custom Cast Stone Inc 317 896-1700
  734 E 169th St Westfield (46074) *(G-16682)*

Custom Coating Inc, Auburn *Also Called: Raac LLC (G-418)*

Custom Coatings 317 392-7908
  2446 N Michigan Rd Shelbyville (46176) *(G-14748)*

Custom Compressor Svcs Corp 219 879-4966
  104 Woodland Ct Ste A Michigan City (46360) *(G-11592)*

Custom Controls & Engrg Inc 812 663-0755
  346 E North St Greensburg (47240) *(G-6587)*

Custom Conveyor Inc 812 663-2023
  4858 E State Road 46 Greensburg (47240) *(G-6588)*

Custom Covers Inc 765 481-7800
  4548 W 50 S Lebanon (46052) *(G-10888)*

Custom Creations By Heather 574 302-7525
  210 E 13th St Mishawaka (46544) *(G-11871)*

Custom Creations MGT LLC 765 491-8434
  5534 Saint Joe Rd Fort Wayne (46835) *(G-4897)*

Custom Crimp, Valparaiso *Also Called: Custom Machining Services Inc (G-15933)*

Custom Cycle of Indiana 812 256-9089
  4914 Highway 3 Otisco (47163) *(G-13448)*

Custom Design Laminates Inc 574 674-9174
  10055 Mckinley Hwy Osceola (46561) *(G-13388)*

Custom Door Manufacturing 812 636-3667
  8076 N 1100 E Loogootee (47553) *(G-11130)*

Custom Draperies of Indiana 219 924-2500
  7205 Calumet Ave Hammond (46324) *(G-6909)*

Custom Embroideries LLC 708 257-0415
  2109 Southlake Mall Merrillville (46410) *(G-11501)*

Custom Embroidery 317 459-6603
  11695 Sunnybrook Pl Fishers (46038) *(G-4499)*

Custom Engineering Inc 812 424-3879
  1900 Lynch Rd Evansville (47711) *(G-4003)*

Custom Engrg & Fabrication Inc 260 745-9299
  2211 Freeman St Fort Wayne (46802) *(G-4898)*

Custom Expressions, Fort Wayne *Also Called: Athletic Edge Inc (G-4778)*

Custom Fab & Weld Inc (PA) 574 277-8877
  16915 Cleveland Rd Granger (46530) *(G-6341)*

Custom Fab & Weld Inc 574 255-9689
  1030 N Merrifield Ave Mishawaka (46545) *(G-11872)*

Custom Fiber Composites LLC 765 376-1360
  7285 S State Road 267 Lebanon (46052) *(G-10889)*

Custom Fitz LLC 219 405-0896
  10 Wagner Rd Porter (46304) *(G-13922)*

Custom Forms Inc 765 463-6162
  1400 Canal Rd Ste B Lafayette (47904) *(G-10565)*

Custom Formulating & Blending, Bristol *Also Called: F B C Inc (G-1260)*

Custom Golf By Uebelhor, Indianapolis *Also Called: Uebelhors Golf (G-9674)*

Custom Honing Inc 574 233-2846
  24840 Us Highway 20 South Bend (46628) *(G-14991)*

Custom Imprint, Merrillville *Also Called: BT Management Inc (G-11494)*

Custom Imprint Corporation 800 378-3397
  8605 Indiana Pl Merrillville (46410) *(G-11502)*

Custom Ink Writers 260 202-9350
  5451 E 400 S Portland (47371) *(G-13935)*

Custom Inspirational Signs 315 715-1893
  12008 E Ragsdale Rd Bicknell (47512) *(G-733)*

Custom Interior Dynamics, Indianapolis *Also Called: Custom Interior Dynamics LLC (G-7930)*

Custom Interior Dynamics LLC 317 632-0477
  3314 Prospect St Indianapolis (46203) *(G-7930)*

Custom Keepsakes Machine EMB 317 894-5506
  915 Tanninger Dr Indianapolis (46239) *(G-7931)*

Custom Kraft Pack LLC 502 595-8146
  100 Technology Way Jeffersonville (47130) *(G-9966)*

Custom Machine Mfr LLC 574 251-0292
  4111 Technology Dr South Bend (46628) *(G-14992)*

Custom Machine Shop, Lafayette *Also Called: Browell Enterprises Inc (G-10546)*

Custom Machining Inc (PA) 317 392-2328
  1204 Hale Rd Shelbyville (46176) *(G-14749)*

Custom Machining Services Inc 219 462-6128
  318 N 400 E Valparaiso (46383) *(G-15932)*

Custom Machining Services Inc (HQ) 219 462-6128
  326 N 400 E Valparaiso (46383) *(G-15933)*

Custom Magnetics Inc (PA) 260 982-8508
  801 W Main St North Manchester (46962) *(G-13231)*

Custom Manufacturing Solutions, Bloomington *Also Called: OHM Automotive LLC (G-934)*

Custom Manufacturing Solutions, Gosport *Also Called: OHM Enterprise LLC (G-6288)*

Custom Mch Motioneering Inc 574 251-0292
  4111 Technology Dr South Bend (46628) *(G-14993)*

Custom Metal Fabrication LLC 574 257-8851
  603 W 9th St Mishawaka (46544) *(G-11873)*

Custom Metal Industries, Greenfield *Also Called: Edwards Steel Inc (G-6492)*

Custom Mfg & Fabrication LLC 260 908-1088
  5536 County Road 31 Auburn (46706) *(G-383)*

Custom Mfg Inc 219 987-7716
  10020 N 1100 W Demotte (46310) *(G-2914)*

Custom Millwork & Display Inc 574 289-4000
  2102 W Washington St Ste 1 South Bend (46628) *(G-14994)*

Custom Motorcycles, Fort Wayne *Also Called: Hinseys Pro Paint Inc (G-5068)*

Custom Mtal Fnshng-Indiana LLC 765 489-4089
  9705 State Road 38 Hagerstown (47346) *(G-6835)*

Custom Outfitted Protection 317 373-2092
  9309 Memorial Park Dr 1b Indianapolis (46216) *(G-7932)*

Custom Packaging Inc 317 876-9559
  7248 Haverhill Ct Indianapolis (46250) *(G-7933)*

Custom Pallet Recycl Trnsp LLC 317 903-4447
  2222 Hillside Ave Indianapolis (46218) *(G-7934)*

Custom Plastics LLC 574 259-2340
  1950 E Mckinley Ave Mishawaka (46545) *(G-11874)*

Custom Plywood Inc (PA) 812 944-7300
  301 Quality Ave New Albany (47150) *(G-12717)*

Custom Polish & Chrome 260 665-7448
  114 Lange Ln Angola (46703) *(G-244)*

Custom Polishing, Lynnville *Also Called: Doug Wilcox (G-11189)*

Custom Poly Packaging, Fort Wayne *Also Called: D & M Enterprises LLC (G-4901)*

Custom Precision Components

Custom Precision Components, Ossian *Also Called: Roembke Mfg & Design Inc (G-13433)*
Custom Printing Co, Brownstown *Also Called: CPC (G-1420)*
Custom Prints and Tees LLC 317 891-4550
  7915 S Emerson Ave Indianapolis (46237) *(G-7935)*
Custom Qlting Pllow Cshion Svc 219 464-7316
  102 Harmel Dr Valparaiso (46383) *(G-15934)*
Custom Sewing Service 812 428-7015
  2644 N Heidelbach Ave Evansville (47711) *(G-4004)*
Custom Sheds Plus LLC 260 215-3988
  13836 County Road 48 Syracuse (46567) *(G-15460)*
Custom Sign & Engineeri 812 401-1550
  5344 Vann Rd Newburgh (47630) *(G-12999)*
Custom Signs, Lawrenceburg *Also Called: Neon Accents (G-10847)*
Custom Signs Unlimited Co 260 483-4444
  1410 Goshen Ave Fort Wayne (46808) *(G-4899)*
Custom Software Solutions Inc 260 637-8393
  1737 Traders Xing Fort Wayne (46845) *(G-4900)*
Custom Sound Designs, New Haven *Also Called: St Joe Group Inc (G-12920)*
Custom Stitcher 219 306-7784
  19504 Clark St Lowell (46356) *(G-11159)*
Custom Tables & Cabinets 812 486-3831
  5127 E 300 N Montgomery (47558) *(G-12093)*
Custom Tire Cutting Inc 812 745-9140
  8258 E Freelandville Rd Oaktown (47561) *(G-13326)*
Custom TS & Trophies 219 926-4174
  30 E Burwell Dr Porter (46304) *(G-13923)*
Custom Tube Co, Fort Wayne *Also Called: Jae Enterprises Inc (G-5129)*
Custom Tube Co, Fort Wayne *Also Called: Jae Enterprises Inc (G-5130)*
Custom Urethanes Inc 219 924-1644
  10010 Express Dr Highland (46322) *(G-7131)*
Custom Wood Creations LLC 765 860-1983
  2913 E Center Rd Kokomo (46902) *(G-10254)*
Custom Wood Floor, Evansville *Also Called: Custom Woodworking (G-4005)*
Custom Wood Products Inc 574 522-3300
  1901 W Hively Ave Elkhart (46517) *(G-3283)*
Custom Woodwork Design LLC 317 254-1358
  6303 N Oakland Ave Indianapolis (46220) *(G-7936)*
Custom Woodworking 812 339-6601
  732 S Village Dr Bloomington (47403) *(G-851)*
Custom Woodworking 812 422-6786
  3314 Kratzville Rd Evansville (47710) *(G-4005)*
Custom-Flex, West Lebanon *Also Called: Tru-Flex LLC (G-16649)*
Custombannerlab 317 956-3898
  614 S Rangeline Rd Carmel (46032) *(G-1603)*
Customer 1st LLC 812 733-4638
  21005 Souders Rd Borden (47106) *(G-1107)*
Customer 1st LLC (PA) 877 768-9970
  8899 E Daily Rd Lot 51 Pekin (47165) *(G-13514)*
Customer 1st Safes & Services, Pekin *Also Called: Customer 1st LLC (G-13514)*
Customized Machining Inc 765 490-7894
  8101 Sunset Ct Columbus (47201) *(G-2277)*
Cut-Pro Indexable Tooling LLC 260 668-2400
  212 Growth Pkwy Angola (46703) *(G-245)*
Cuts Inc 408 334-3134
  830 Massachusetts Ave Ste 1500 Indianapolis (46204) *(G-7937)*
Cutting Edge Indus Tech LLC 765 471-7007
  3323 Concord Rd Ste 2 Lafayette (47909) *(G-10566)*
Cutting Edge Machine & TI Inc 866 514-1620
  19149 County Road 146 New Paris (46553) *(G-12949)*
Cutting Edge Wire Edm Inc 765 284-3820
  1800 W Mt Pleasant Blvd Muncie (47302) *(G-12371)*
Cvg Sprague Devices LLC (HQ) 614 289-5360
  527 W Us Highway 20 Michigan City (46360) *(G-11593)*
Cwb Software LLC 812 760-3431
  9811 Cove Ct Evansville (47711) *(G-4006)*
CXR Company Inc 574 269-6020
  2599 N Fox Farm Rd Warsaw (46580) *(G-16341)*
Cyber Inform LLC 219 688-1183
  5536 Lux Blvd Lafayette (47905) *(G-10567)*
Cyberia Ltd 317 721-2582
  6800 E 30th St Indianapolis (46219) *(G-7938)*

Cybernaut Industria LLC 317 664-5316
  7640 Gunyon Dr Indianapolis (46237) *(G-7939)*
Cyc Lures 574 702-1237
  7929 W County Road 550 N Mulberry (46058) *(G-12329)*
Cyclone Adg LLC 520 403-2927
  166 Mills Ln New Albany (47150) *(G-12718)*
Cyclone Custom Prouducts LLC 765 246-6523
  4982 E County Road 325 S Greencastle (46135) *(G-6401)*
Cyclone Manufacturing Co Inc 260 774-3311
  151 N Washington St Urbana (46990) *(G-15885)*
Cygnus Home Service LLC 317 882-6624
  2700 E Main St Danville (46122) *(G-2810)*
Cylicron LLC 812 283-4600
  5171 Maritime Jeffersonville (47130) *(G-9967)*
Cynthia Bergstrand 574 277-6160
  50648 Glen Meadow Ln Granger (46530) *(G-6342)*
Cynthia Rogers, Indianapolis *Also Called: Csr Associates LLC (G-7918)*
Cypress Springs Entps Inc 812 743-8888
  11536 E Lucky Point Rd Wheatland (47597) *(G-16774)*
Czech Industries LLC 317 946-1380
  10 S New Jersey St Ste 300 Indianapolis (46204) *(G-7940)*
D & B Cabinet Sales Inc 317 392-2870
  660 E Jackson St Shelbyville (46176) *(G-14750)*
D & D Brake Sales Inc 317 485-5177
  State Road 234 & County Rd 200 W Fortville (46040) *(G-5590)*
D & D Industries Inc 219 844-5600
  6805 Mccook Ave Hammond (46323) *(G-6910)*
D & D Mouldings & Millwork LLC 317 770-5500
  15509 Stony Creek Way Noblesville (46060) *(G-13067)*
D & D Tire Shop LLC 219 354-0402
  4707 Tod Ave East Chicago (46312) *(G-3002)*
D & E Auto Electric Inc 219 763-3892
  5665 Old Porter Rd Portage (46368) *(G-13858)*
D & E Cabinets 812 486-2961
  8835 E 650 N Montgomery (47558) *(G-12094)*
D & E Machine Inc 765 653-8919
  944 W County Road 350 N Greencastle (46135) *(G-6402)*
D & E Printing Company Inc 317 852-9048
  2 E Main St Brownsburg (46112) *(G-1362)*
D & E Workshop 260 593-0195
  9680 W 700 S Topeka (46571) *(G-15799)*
D & H Thurston Farms LP 765 847-2304
  8307 Gifford Rd Fountain City (47341) *(G-5610)*
D & J Custom Embroidery 219 874-9061
  707 E 11th St Michigan City (46360) *(G-11594)*
D & J Fabrication and Welding 260 414-0300
  2471 County Road 64 Auburn (46706) *(G-384)*
D & J Tool Co Inc 260 636-2682
  300 S 7th St Albion (46701) *(G-21)*
D & L Industrial Finishes Inc 765 458-5157
  215 Brownsville Ave Liberty (47353) *(G-10987)*
D & M Enterprises LLC 260 483-4008
  3216 Congressional Pkwy Fort Wayne (46808) *(G-4901)*
D & M Precision Machining Inc 219 393-5132
  1 Kingsbury Industrial Park, 7111 Union Center Road Kingsbury (46345) *(G-10176)*
D & M Printing Inc 812 847-4837
  1089 1st St Se Linton (47441) *(G-11034)*
D & M Sales LLC 574 825-9024
  13487 County Road 22 Middlebury (46540) *(G-11710)*
D & M Systems Inc 812 327-2384
  6516 S Thomas Ct Owensburg (47453) *(G-13461)*
D & M Tool Corporation (HQ) 812 279-8882
  699 Washboard Rd Springville (47462) *(G-15384)*
D & S Boat Lifts 574 583-8972
  4285 E Chalmers Rd Monticello (47960) *(G-12144)*
D & S Enterprises 812 354-6108
  132 W Branch St Petersburg (47567) *(G-13609)*
D & S Machine Inc 317 826-2900
  10640 Deme Dr Ste R Indianapolis (46236) *(G-7941)*
D & S Machine Products Inc 812 926-6250
  6965 Us Highway 50 Aurora (47001) *(G-442)*

ALPHABETIC SECTION — Dallara Research Center LLC

D & S Metal Fab & Welding LLC 317 862-2503
  6217 S Carroll Rd Indianapolis (46259) *(G-7942)*

D & T Tool Special Machine 260 597-7216
  8405 N 675 E Ossian (46777) *(G-13422)*

D & V Precision Sheetmetal 317 462-2601
  205 S 400 W Greenfield (46140) *(G-6485)*

D & W Inc 574 264-9674
  941 Oak St Elkhart (46514) *(G-3284)*

D A Hochstetler & Sons LLP 574 642-1144
  4165 S 500 W Topeka (46571) *(G-15800)*

D A Merriman Inc 260 636-3464
  2259 E State Road 8 Albion (46701) *(G-22)*

D and D Custom Concrete Inc 574 274-6013
  14369 Douglas Rd Mishawaka (46545) *(G-11875)*

D and R Custom Logging, Warsaw *Also Called: Graber Ronald D Yoder & (G-16368)*

D C C, Elkhart *Also Called: Quality Plas Engrg Acqstion Co (G-3632)*

D D McKay and Associates 317 546-7446
  4068 Pendleton Way Indianapolis (46226) *(G-7943)*

D D Signs Inc 812 243-0084
  1720 N 1st St Terre Haute (47804) *(G-15572)*

D E Key Machine Shop 765 664-1720
  1442 E 450 N Marion (46952) *(G-11279)*

D H Gravel Company 765 893-4914
  7794 S State Road 263 Williamsport (47993) *(G-16847)*

D I Hair Extensions LLC 219 742-3611
  7450 Noble St Merrillville (46410) *(G-11503)*

D J Investments Inc (PA) 765 348-4381
  0660 E 200 S Hartford City (47348) *(G-7063)*

D J Investments Inc 765 348-3558
  1608 N Cherry St Hartford City (47348) *(G-7064)*

D J Investments Inc 260 726-7346
  111 W North St Ste C Portland (47371) *(G-13936)*

D K Enterprises LLC 260 356-9011
  1675 Riverfork Dr Huntington (46750) *(G-7307)*

D L Miller Woodworking 260 562-9329
  5345 N 400 W Shipshewana (46565) *(G-14842)*

D M Sales & Engineering Inc 317 783-5493
  1325 Sunday Dr Indianapolis (46217) *(G-7944)*

D Martin Enterprises Inc 219 872-8211
  310 Commerce Sq Michigan City (46360) *(G-11595)*

D Martin Enterprises Inc (PA) 219 872-8211
  320 Commerce Sq Michigan City (46360) *(G-11596)*

D N D Oil Company, Crawfordsville *Also Called: Dnd Dust Control Inc (G-2563)*

D P Woods Unlimited 765 362-3625
  2407 N Everett St Crawfordsville (47933) *(G-2562)*

D R G Publishing 260 589-4000
  306 E Parr Rd Berne (46711) *(G-708)*

D Rinker Transport LLC 765 749-4120
  9975 W 200 S Dunkirk (47336) *(G-2961)*

D Robertson Gravel Co Inc 765 832-2768
  3499 E 1850 S Clinton (47842) *(G-2065)*

D Rv Luxury Suites LLC 260 562-1075
  1000 Interchange Dr Howe (46746) *(G-7233)*

D S Custom Tees 219 802-3127
  2548 Marshalltown Dr Gary (46407) *(G-5921)*

D S M, Evansville *Also Called: Envalior Engineering Materials Inc (G-4039)*

D Terrell & Company, Washington *Also Called: Douglas P Terrell (G-16478)*

D Timber Inc 219 374-8085
  14405 Clark St Crown Point (46307) *(G-2672)*

D To 3-Dimension 219 793-6123
  633 N Colfax St Griffith (46319) *(G-6801)*

D W Stewart 260 463-2607
  104 E Wayne St Lagrange (46761) *(G-10733)*

D-10 Services Inc 317 889-7235
  887 Jennifer Dr Greenwood (46143) *(G-6683)*

D-A Lubricant Company, Lebanon *Also Called: D-A Lubricant Company Inc (G-10890)*

D-A Lubricant Company Inc (PA) 317 923-5321
  801 Edwards Dr Lebanon (46052) *(G-10890)*

D-J Printing Specialists Inc 219 465-1164
  2600 Roosevelt Rd Ste 200-4 Valparaiso (46383) *(G-15935)*

D&A Transportation, South Bend *Also Called: Pro-Tote Systems Inc (G-15206)*

D&D Automation Inc 812 299-1045
  1207 E Dallas Dr Terre Haute (47802) *(G-15573)*

D&D Manufacturing, Union Mills *Also Called: Hot Stamping & Printing (G-15865)*

D&J Custom Embroidery, Michigan City *Also Called: D & J Custom Embroidery (G-11594)*

D&J Printing, North Manchester *Also Called: Dale Flora (G-13232)*

D&M Plywood Sales, Middlebury *Also Called: D & M Sales LLC (G-11710)*

D&M Repair and Welding LLC 765 533-4565
  10261 E 1100 N Markleville (46056) *(G-11368)*

D&W Fine Pack LLC 260 432-3027
  7707 Vicksburg Pike Fort Wayne (46804) *(G-4902)*

D1 Mold & Tool LLC 765 378-0693
  8201 N State Road 9 Alexandria (46001) *(G-48)*

DA Inc (DH) 812 730-2130
  1800 Patrol Rd Charlestown (47111) *(G-1874)*

Da-Lite, Warsaw *Also Called: Legrand AV Inc (G-16387)*

Da-Lite Screen Company LLC 574 267-8101
  3100 N Detroit St Warsaw (46582) *(G-16342)*

Da-Mar Industries Inc (PA) 260 347-1662
  201 W Ohio St Kendallville (46755) *(G-10107)*

Dacco/Detroit Indiana Inc 317 545-5334
  514 W Merrill St Indianapolis (46225) *(G-7945)*

Dack Blower Manufacturing Inc 574 867-2025
  10660 E Us Highway 30 Grovertown (46531) *(G-6823)*

Dads Custom Intercooler Tanks 765 243-9070
  4473 N 700 E Van Buren (46991) *(G-16084)*

Dads Root Beer Company LLC 812 482-5352
  950 S Saint Charles St Jasper (47546) *(G-9830)*

Daechang Seat Co Ltd USA 317 755-3663
  8150 Woodland Dr Indianapolis (46278) *(G-7946)*

Daed Toolworks 317 861-7419
  3255 W Birdsong Ct Greenfield (46140) *(G-6486)*

Dage-MTI, Michigan City *Also Called: Dage-MTI Michigan City Inc (G-11597)*

Dage-MTI Michigan City Inc 219 872-5514
  106 Woodside Dr Michigan City (46360) *(G-11597)*

Daifuku Intrlgistics Amer Corp (DH) 219 777-2220
  6300 Northwind Pkwy Hobart (46342) *(G-7186)*

Dailey Signs LLC 317 436-7550
  10087 Allisonville Rd Ste G Fishers (46038) *(G-4500)*

Daily Co 574 546-5126
  4502 W Shore Dr Bremen (46506) *(G-1185)*

Daily II Larry 765 884-9355
  702 N Lincoln Ave Fowler (47944) *(G-5623)*

Daily Money Managers Ind LLC 317 797-0012
  Carmel (46033) *(G-1604)*

Daily Peru Tribune Pubg Co 765 473-6641
  11 S Broadway Peru (46970) *(G-13577)*

Daily Rental 773 881-7762
  8327 Oakwood Ave Munster (46321) *(G-12537)*

Dairychem Laboratories Inc (PA) 317 849-8400
  9120 Technology Ln Fishers (46038) *(G-4501)*

Dairyland Woodworks LLC 715 271-2110
  2131 N 700 W Warsaw (46580) *(G-16343)*

Daisy Tees LLC 574 259-1933
  4224 Anchor Dr Mishawaka (46544) *(G-11876)*

Dajac Inc 317 608-0500
  805 Wesco Pkwy Sheridan (46069) *(G-14821)*

Dalam Welding LLC 260 593-0167
  7665 S 200 W Topeka (46571) *(G-15801)*

Dale Flora 260 982-7233
  5249 E 1250 N North Manchester (46962) *(G-13232)*

Dale's Auto Service, South Bend *Also Called: Dales Goodyear Tire & Service (G-14995)*

Dales Goodyear Tire & Service 574 272-3779
  50942 Indiana State Route 933 South Bend (46637) *(G-14995)*

Dalex, Terre Haute *Also Called: Dalex Fbrication Machining Inc (G-15574)*

Dalex Fbrication Machining Inc 812 232-7081
  925 N Fruitridge Ave Ste 3 Terre Haute (47803) *(G-15574)*

Dallara LLC 317 388-5400
  1201 Main St Speedway (46224) *(G-15334)*

Dallara Indycar Factory, Speedway *Also Called: Dallara LLC (G-15334)*

Dallara Research Center LLC 317 388-5416
  1201 Main St Ste B Speedway (46224) *(G-15335)*

Dallas Group of America Inc — ALPHABETIC SECTION

Dallas Group of America Inc..812 283-6675
1402 Fabricon Blvd Jeffersonville (47130) *(G-9968)*

Dallas Towing Service, Evansville *Also Called: Sparkling Clean Inc (G-4326)*

Dalren Enterprises LLC..502 396-0346
3180 S Pixley Knob Rd Pekin (47165) *(G-13515)*

Daltech Enterprises Inc...260 527-4590
810 S Broad St Fremont (46737) *(G-5818)*

Daltech Force, Fremont *Also Called: Daltech Enterprises Inc (G-5818)*

Dalton Corp Kndllvlle Mfg Fclt...260 637-6047
200 W Ohio St Kendallville (46755) *(G-10108)*

Dalton Corp Warsaw Mfg Fcilty......................................574 267-8111
Lincoln & Jefferson St Warsaw (46581) *(G-16344)*

Dalton Corporation...574 267-8111
1900 E Jefferson St Warsaw (46580) *(G-16345)*

Dalton Foundries, Warsaw *Also Called: Dalton Corporation (G-16345)*

Damage Industries II LLC...574 256-7006
55685 Currant Rd Mishawaka (46545) *(G-11877)*

Damage Industries LLC..574 256-7006
55685 Currant Rd Ste D Mishawaka (46545) *(G-11878)*

Damalak Printing Inc...317 896-5337
104 W Main St Westfield (46074) *(G-16683)*

Damon Corporation..574 262-2624
2958 Gateway Dr Elkhart (46514) *(G-3285)*

Damon Motor Coach...574 536-3781
604 Middleton Run Rd Elkhart (46516) *(G-3286)*

Damor & Co LLC..317 790-8360
3812 Screech Owl Cir Indianapolis (46228) *(G-7947)*

Damping Technologies Inc (PA).....................................574 258-7916
55656 Currant Rd Mishawaka (46545) *(G-11879)*

Damping Technologies Inc...574 258-7916
12970 Mckinley Hwy Ste 1 Mishawaka (46545) *(G-11880)*

Dan Barnett Woodworking LLC......................................765 724-7828
1570 E 1100 N Alexandria (46001) *(G-49)*

Dan St. Germain, Kendallville *Also Called: Creative Liquid Coatings Inc (G-10104)*

Dana, Yorktown *Also Called: Dana Sac Usa Inc (G-16972)*

Dana Driveshaft Products LLC......................................260 432-2903
400 S Miller Ave Marion (46953) *(G-11280)*

Dana Fairfield, Lafayette *Also Called: Fairfield Manufacturing Co Inc (G-10576)*

Dana Fairfield, Lafayette *Also Called: Fairfield Manufacturing Co Inc (G-10577)*

Dana Incorporated...260 897-2827
301 Progress Way Avilla (46710) *(G-474)*

Dana Incorporated...260 481-3597
2100 W State Blvd Fort Wayne (46808) *(G-4903)*

Dana Incorporated...765 772-4000
2400 Sagamore Pkwy S Lafayette (47903) *(G-10568)*

Dana Light Axle Products, Fort Wayne *Also Called: Dana Light Axle Products LLC (G-4904)*

Dana Light Axle Products LLC (DH)...............................260 483-7174
2100 W State Blvd Fort Wayne (46808) *(G-4904)*

Dana Sac Usa Inc (DH)..765 759-2300
14141 W Brevini Dr Ste 10 Yorktown (47396) *(G-16972)*

Dana Sealing Products, Avilla *Also Called: Victor Reinz Valve Seals LLC (G-498)*

Dance Sophisticates Inc..317 634-7728
1605 Prospect St Indianapolis (46203) *(G-7948)*

Dance World Bazaar Corporation...................................812 663-7679
1553 N Commerce East Dr Greensburg (47240) *(G-6589)*

Dancing Crane Publishing LLC......................................812 675-2362
9591 E Mineral-Koleen Rd Owensburg (47453) *(G-13462)*

Danco Anodizing, Warsaw *Also Called: Riepen LLC (G-16418)*

Danfoss Power Solutions II LLC....................................260 248-5800
1380 S Williams Dr Columbia City (46725) *(G-2136)*

Daniel Hudelson...812 865-3951
27 W Quarry Rd Orleans (47452) *(G-13376)*

Daniel Publications...574 269-2825
2212 E 225 S Warsaw (46580) *(G-16346)*

Daniel Shade..812 346-6285
2400 S County Road 550 W North Vernon (47265) *(G-13263)*

Daniel Steffy..812 726-4769
3572 N Bruceville Rd Vincennes (47591) *(G-16118)*

Daniels Vineyard LLC...317 894-6860
6311 W Stoner Dr Greenfield (46140) *(G-6487)*

Danisco USA, Terre Haute *Also Called: Danisco USA Inc (G-15576)*

Danisco USA Inc...812 299-6700
11 W Litesse Dr Terre Haute (47802) *(G-15575)*

Danisco USA Inc...812 299-6700
33 W Litesse Dr Terre Haute (47802) *(G-15576)*

Danko Farm Supply & Feed Inc.....................................812 870-7413
755 W Washington St Sullivan (47882) *(G-15404)*

Danny Webb Plumbing...574 936-2746
18391 6th Rd Plymouth (46563) *(G-13769)*

Danta Inc...219 369-9190
3202 E 400 S La Porte (46350) *(G-10398)*

Danta Welding, La Porte *Also Called: Danta Inc (G-10398)*

Danubius Machine Inc..219 662-7787
11205 Delaware Pkwy Crown Point (46307) *(G-2673)*

Danwood Industries..219 369-1484
7606 S Young Rd La Porte (46350) *(G-10399)*

Danzer Services Inc (PA)...812 526-2601
206 S Holland St Edinburgh (46124) *(G-3074)*

Danzer Veneer Americas Inc...812 526-6789
206 S Holland St Edinburgh (46124) *(G-3075)*

Dappered Man LLC..317 520-1194
1060 E Main St Ste 417 Brownsburg (46112) *(G-1363)*

Darden Corporation Corp...317 376-5724
7847 Swallowtail Dr Indianapolis (46214) *(G-7949)*

Daredevil Brewing Co, Speedway *Also Called: Daredevil Brewing Company LLC (G-15336)*

Daredevil Brewing Company LLC..................................765 602-1067
1151 Main St Speedway (46224) *(G-15336)*

Dargie Racing Engines, Richmond *Also Called: Michael Dargie (G-14165)*

Dargo Industries...765 716-9272
4121 W Pickell St Muncie (47303) *(G-12372)*

Dark Source Records LLC...616 378-6060
5017 E 41st St Indianapolis (46226) *(G-7950)*

Darlage Metalworx LLC..812 341-5530
1647 Washington St Columbus (47201) *(G-2278)*

Darlage Sawmill..812 358-3574
1564 S County Road 100 E Brownstown (47220) *(G-1422)*

Darling Ingredients Inc...317 708-3070
345 Water St Columbus (47201) *(G-2279)*

Darling Ingredients Inc...317 784-4486
700 W Southern Ave Indianapolis (46225) *(G-7951)*

Darling Ingredients Inc...812 659-3399
7358 S Griffin Rd Newberry (47449) *(G-12988)*

Darling Ingredients Inc...913 321-9328
12091 Plymouth Goshen Trl Plymouth (46563) *(G-13770)*

Darlington Cookie Company (PA)..................................800 754-2202
10475 Crosspoint Blvd Ste 110 Indianapolis (46256) *(G-7952)*

Darlington Farms, Fort Wayne *Also Called: Ellison Bakery LLC (G-4946)*

Darlington Farms, Indianapolis *Also Called: Darlington Cookie Company (G-7952)*

Darlite Designs, Fort Wayne *Also Called: Candles By Dar Inc (G-4831)*

Darner Golden Publishing LLC......................................812 675-0897
202 Heltonville Rd W Bedford (47421) *(G-629)*

Dart Controls LLC..317 873-5211
5000 W 106th St Zionsville (46077) *(G-17000)*

Dash CAM Fusion LLC..708 365-8553
8465 Keystone Xing Ste 115 Indianapolis (46240) *(G-7953)*

Data Label Inc (PA)...800 457-0676
1000 Spruce St Terre Haute (47807) *(G-15577)*

Data Mail Incorporated..812 424-7835
1014 Main St Evansville (47708) *(G-4007)*

Data Print Initiatives LLC...260 489-2665
1710 Dividend Rd Fort Wayne (46808) *(G-4905)*

Datagraphic Printing, Chesterton *Also Called: Four Part Inc (G-1928)*

Daubert Vci Inc..574 772-9310
1805 Pacific Ave Knox (46534) *(G-10204)*

Dauenhauer Glass Company Inc...................................260 433-5876
12230 Chesterbrook Ct Fort Wayne (46845) *(G-4906)*

Daugherty Box Factory..260 375-2810
311 9th St Warren (46792) *(G-16295)*

Daugherty Cabinets...574 272-9205
51719 Gumwood Rd Granger (46530) *(G-6343)*

Davaus LLC...260 245-5006
14508 Bruick Ln Hoagland (46745) *(G-7166)*

ALPHABETIC SECTION

Dave Brown Customs LLC 812 727-5560
11138 S Locust Creek Dr Palmyra (47164) *(G-13479)*

Dave Jones Machinists LLC 574 256-5500
1212 N Merrifield Ave Mishawaka (46545) *(G-11881)*

Dave OMara Paving Inc (PA) 812 346-1214
1100 E O And M Ave North Vernon (47265) *(G-13264)*

Dave Turner 765 674-3360
109 E South D St Gas City (46933) *(G-6035)*

Davenport Mfg Group LLC 260 495-1818
301 W Water St Fremont (46737) *(G-5819)*

Davern Machine Shop 765 505-1051
1248 E 500 S Dana (47847) *(G-2804)*

Daves Custom Design, Granger *Also Called: David Askew (G-6344)*

David Alan Chocolatier, Lebanon *Also Called: Lebanon Corp (G-10910)*

David Askew 574 273-0184
51931 Pennyroyal Ln Granger (46530) *(G-6344)*

David Camp 812 346-6255
101 Hoosier St North Vernon (47265) *(G-13265)*

David Company, Fishers *Also Called: David Indus Process Pdts Inc (G-4502)*

David Edward Furniture Inc (DH) 812 482-1600
1600 Royal St Jasper (47546) *(G-9831)*

David Fleming 414 202-6586
1409 Butternut Ln Indianapolis (46234) *(G-7954)*

David Gonzales 765 284-6960
701 E Mcgalliard Rd Muncie (47303) *(G-12373)*

David Indus Process Pdts Inc 317 577-0351
10142 Brooks School Rd Ste 102 Fishers (46037) *(G-4502)*

David Kechel 260 627-2749
12921 Leo Rd Leo (46765) *(G-10967)*

David L Huber 812 623-4772
12218 N Schneider Rd Sunman (47041) *(G-15435)*

David L Phillips 312 937-0299
3603 W Woodcliff Ct Bloomington (47403) *(G-852)*

David L Phillips Services, Bloomington *Also Called: David L Phillips (G-852)*

David M Pszonka 219 988-2235
93 S 695 W Hebron (46341) *(G-7098)*

David Murray 765 766-5229
6645 E County Road 600 N Mooreland (47360) *(G-12184)*

David Tortora 317 506-6902
11700 Oak Tree Way Carmel (46032) *(G-1605)*

David W Imhoff 574 862-4375
62480 County Road 9 Goshen (46526) *(G-6119)*

Davids Inc 812 376-6870
905 S Gladstone Ave Columbus (47201) *(G-2280)*

Davies-Imperial Coatings Inc 219 933-0877
1275 State St Hammond (46320) *(G-6911)*

Daviess County Metal Sales 812 486-4299
9929 E Us Highway 50 Cannelburg (47519) *(G-1530)*

Daviess County Tire & Sup Inc 812 254-1035
879 S State Road 57 Washington (47501) *(G-16475)*

Daviess County Tire Inc 812 254-1035
879 S State Road 57 Washington (47501) *(G-16476)*

Davis Cabinet & Design, Hagerstown *Also Called: Davis Cabinet and Flooring LLC (G-6836)*

Davis Cabinet and Flooring LLC 765 530-8170
10 Paul R Foulke Pkwy Hagerstown (47346) *(G-6836)*

Davis Chocolate, Mishawaka *Also Called: Deco Chem Inc (G-11883)*

Davis Custom Welding 765 847-2407
3526 Whitewater Rd Richmond (47374) *(G-14113)*

Davis Exteriors Inc 260 786-1600
2272 E N 800 Andrews (46702) *(G-221)*

Davis Hezakih Corp 260 768-7300
255 E Main St Shipshewana (46565) *(G-14843)*

Davis Hotel, Shipshewana *Also Called: Davis Hezakih Corp (G-14843)*

Davis Industries Inc 317 871-0103
4090 Westover Dr Indianapolis (46268) *(G-7955)*

Davis Machine and Tool Inc 812 526-2674
920 S Walnut St Edinburgh (46124) *(G-3076)*

Davis Tool & Machine LLC 317 896-9278
19224 Eagletown Rd Westfield (46074) *(G-16684)*

Davis Vachon Artworks 260 489-9160
227 W Wallen Rd Fort Wayne (46825) *(G-4907)*

Davis Water Conditioning, Rensselaer *Also Called: Davis Water Services Inc (G-14050)*

Davis Water Services Inc 219 394-2270
4898 S 1000 W Rensselaer (47978) *(G-14050)*

Davis Wholesale Supply, Indianapolis *Also Called: Alebro LLC (G-7468)*

Davron Fabricating 765 339-7303
3873 W 750 N New Richmond (47967) *(G-12978)*

Dawghouse Grub Pub LLC 765 778-2727
104 W State St Pendleton (46064) *(G-13529)*

Dawn Food Products Inc 800 333-3296
9601 Georgia St Crown Point (46307) *(G-2674)*

Dawn Food Products Frozen Div, Crown Point *Also Called: Dawn Food Products Inc (G-2674)*

Dawson Machine Shop Inc 812 649-4777
614 N State Road 161 Rockport (47635) *(G-14339)*

Dawson Sheet Metal, Muncie *Also Called: Delbert M Dawson and Son Inc (G-12381)*

Daylight Engineering Inc 812 983-2518
11022 Elberfeld Rd Elberfeld (47613) *(G-3111)*

Dayson Geological Consulting 812 868-0957
501 Caranza Ct Evansville (47711) *(G-4008)*

Dayspring Community Church Inc 260 925-4599
2305 N Indiana Ave Auburn (46706) *(G-385)*

Dayton-Phoenix Group Inc 765 742-4410
4750 Swisher Rd West Lafayette (47906) *(G-16575)*

Db Polishing 574 518-2443
6445 W 1350 N Nappanee (46550) *(G-12593)*

Db Schenker, Indianapolis *Also Called: Flir Security Inc (G-8205)*

DB&h Welding and Fabrication 765 617-8474
8296 N Main Cross St Wilkinson (46186) *(G-16842)*

DBC Imaging 317 757-5298
5583 W 74th St Indianapolis (46268) *(G-7956)*

Dbfederal, Indianapolis *Also Called: Dbisp LLC (G-7957)*

Dbisp LLC (PA) 317 222-1671
777 Beachway Dr Ste 102 Indianapolis (46224) *(G-7957)*

DC Coaters Inc 765 675-6006
550 Industrial Dr Tipton (46072) *(G-15770)*

DC Construction Services Inc 317 577-0276
9465 Counselors Row Indianapolis (46240) *(G-7958)*

Dc's Mobile Electronics, Evansville *Also Called: Dcs Car Audio (G-4009)*

DCA Custom Arrows LLC 317 627-0909
5861 Daw St Noblesville (46062) *(G-13068)*

Dcs Car Audio 812 437-8488
1732 W Franklin St Ste A Evansville (47712) *(G-4009)*

Dd Dannar LLC 765 216-7191
4620 W Bethel Ave Ste 1 Muncie (47304) *(G-12374)*

De Harts Pallet & Lbr Mfg Co, Austin *Also Called: Dehart Pallet & Lumber Co (G-464)*

Dead End Skateboards LLC 970 699-6410
7713 Placer Run Fort Wayne (46815) *(G-4908)*

Dean Baldwin Pntg Ltd Partnr 765 681-1800
1395 N Hoosier Blvd Peru (46970) *(G-13578)*

Dean Co Inc 317 891-2518
6153 W 400 N Greenfield (46140) *(G-6488)*

Deans Place 765 282-5712
4203 E Jackson St Muncie (47303) *(G-12375)*

Dear Athletes Foundation The, Noblesville *Also Called: Dear Athletes Inc (G-13069)*

Dear Athletes Inc 615 682-3332
5561 Village Winds Dr Apt D Noblesville (46062) *(G-13069)*

Dearborn Coatings LLC 513 600-9580
25768 Mount Pleasant Rd Lawrenceburg (47025) *(G-10832)*

Dearborn Crane and Engrg Co (PA) 574 259-2444
1133 E 5th St Mishawaka (46544) *(G-11882)*

Dearborn Overhead Crane, Mishawaka *Also Called: Dearborn Crane and Engrg Co (G-11882)*

Death Enn LLC 219 402-4436
2264 W 60th Dr Merrillville (46410) *(G-11504)*

Death Studios 219 362-4321
431 Pine Lake Ave La Porte (46350) *(G-10400)*

Deatons Waterfront Svcs LLC 317 336-7180
3253 W 1000 N Fortville (46040) *(G-5591)*

Debamc Inc 765 608-2100
6501 Production Dr Anderson (46013) *(G-100)*

Debbies Handmade Soap 765 747-5090
1140 E County Road 500 S Muncie (47302) *(G-12376)*

Deberry MGT & Consulting LLC	317 767-4703
10475 Crosspoint Blvd Ste 250 Indianapolis (46256) *(G-7959)*	
Debra Collins	317 873-1977
480 Benderfield Dr Zionsville (46077) *(G-17001)*	
Debra Lindhorst	260 375-3285
103 N Wayne St Warren (46792) *(G-16296)*	
Debra M Lewis	219 937-4240
6630 Jefferson Ave Hammond (46324) *(G-6912)*	
Debra Richard	812 379-4927
4927 Denny Columbus (47201) *(G-2281)*	
Debra Schneider	317 420-9360
25610 Salem Church Rd Arcadia (46030) *(G-312)*	
Debrand Inc (PA)	260 969-8333
10105 Auburn Park Dr Fort Wayne (46825) *(G-4909)*	
Debrand Fine Chocolates, Fort Wayne Also Called: Debrand Inc *(G-4909)*	
Dec Co Ecumenical Agape Center	812 222-0392
1533 N Commerce West Dr Greensburg (47240) *(G-6590)*	
Dec-O-Art Inc	574 294-6451
3914 Lexington Park Dr Elkhart (46514) *(G-3287)*	
Decatur Daily Democrat, Decatur Also Called: Decatur Publishing Co Inc *(G-2851)*	
Decatur Mold Tool and Engrg	812 346-5188
3330 N State Highway 7 North Vernon (47265) *(G-13266)*	
Decatur Plastic Products Inc	812 352-6050
655 Montrow Pkwy North Vernon (47265) *(G-13267)*	
Decatur Plastic Products Inc (PA)	812 346-5159
3250 N State Highway 7 North Vernon (47265) *(G-13268)*	
Decatur Publishing Co Inc	260 724-2121
141 S 2nd St Decatur (46733) *(G-2851)*	
Decatur Wire Die, Hoagland Also Called: Dwd Industries LLC *(G-7167)*	
Decker Sales Inc	812 330-1580
5100 E Four Boys Trl Bloomington (47408) *(G-853)*	
Deco Chem Inc	574 255-2366
3502 N Home St Mishawaka (46545) *(G-11883)*	
Deco Coatings Inc	317 889-9290
1428 W Henry St Ste B1 Indianapolis (46221) *(G-7960)*	
Decora Cabinets, Jasper Also Called: Masterbrand Cabinets LLC *(G-9888)*	
Dede Tool & Machine Inc	812 232-7365
799 W Springhill Dr Terre Haute (47802) *(G-15578)*	
Dedicated Software	260 341-4166
6018 Hamilton Rd Yoder (46798) *(G-16965)*	
Dedrick Tool & Die Inc	260 824-3334
2929 E State Road 124 Bluffton (46714) *(G-1034)*	
Dee Scents LLC	765 275-2242
110 E South St Wingate (47994) *(G-16906)*	
Deedgrabbercom Inc	219 712-9722
9812 Twin Creek Blvd Munster (46321) *(G-12538)*	
Deem & Loureiro Inc	770 652-9871
8111 Bayberry Ct Indianapolis (46250) *(G-7961)*	
Deep Three Inc	260 705-2283
17607 Rupert Rd Spencerville (46788) *(G-15369)*	
Deer Country Equipment LLC	812 522-1922
1250 W 2nd St Seymour (47274) *(G-14646)*	
Deer Creek Custom LLC	812 719-5902
11833 Deer Creek Rd Tell City (47586) *(G-15499)*	
Deer Creek Village	574 699-6327
2934 S 300 W Trlr 220 Peru (46970) *(G-13579)*	
Deer Ridgewood Craft LLC	812 535-3744
5330 Yuma Rd West Terre Haute (47885) *(G-16651)*	
Deer Run Sawmill LLC	812 732-4608
8242 Valley City Mauckport Rd Sw Mauckport (47142) *(G-11437)*	
Deer Track Archery Inc	765 643-6847
648 W 500 S Anderson (46013) *(G-101)*	
Deerwood Group	219 866-5521
792 E State Road 16 Monon (47959) *(G-12055)*	
Defelice Engineering Inc	317 834-2832
7451 N Ridgeway Ln Mooresville (46158) *(G-12201)*	
Defining Trndstting Cstm Print	260 755-1038
2050 Lafayette St Fort Wayne (46803) *(G-4910)*	
Deflecto LLC (DH)	317 849-9555
7035 W 86th St Indianapolis (46250) *(G-7962)*	
Deg Corp	219 663-7900
1150 E Summit St Crown Point (46307) *(G-2675)*	
Degler Mktg & Mailing Svcs	317 873-5550
8930 Cooper Rd Zionsville (46077) *(G-17002)*	
Degood Dmensional Concepts Inc	574 834-5437
7815 N State Road 13 North Webster (46555) *(G-13304)*	
Dehart Pallet & Lumber Co	812 794-2974
2737 E State Road 256 Austin (47102) *(G-464)*	
Dehco Inc (HQ)	574 294-2684
5400 Beck Dr Elkhart (46516) *(G-3288)*	
Deister Concentrator, Fort Wayne Also Called: Deister Concentrator Na LLC *(G-4911)*	
Deister Concentrator Na LLC	260 747-2700
3210 Freeman St Fort Wayne (46802) *(G-4911)*	
Deister Machine Company Inc	260 422-0354
1604 E Berry St Fort Wayne (46803) *(G-4912)*	
Deister Machine Company Inc	260 426-7495
901 Glasgow Ave Fort Wayne (46803) *(G-4913)*	
Deister Machine Company Inc (PA)	260 426-7495
1933 E Wayne St Fort Wayne (46803) *(G-4914)*	
Deka Battery, Indianapolis Also Called: East Penn Manufacturing Co *(G-8038)*	
Dekalb Metal Finishing Inc	260 925-1820
625 W 15th St Auburn (46706) *(G-386)*	
Dekalb Molded Plastics Company (PA)	260 868-2105
550 W Main St Butler (46721) *(G-1462)*	
Dekalb Tool and Engrg LLC	260 357-1500
700 E Quincy St Garrett (46738) *(G-5858)*	
Dekker Vacuum Technologies Inc	219 861-0661
935 S Woodland Ave Michigan City (46360) *(G-11598)*	
Dekko Acquisition Parent Inc (PA)	260 347-0700
6928 N 400 E Kendallville (46755) *(G-10109)*	
Dekko Techinal Center, Laotto Also Called: Group Dekko Inc *(G-10805)*	
Del Palma Orthopedics Llc	260 625-3169
5865 E State Road 14 Columbia City (46725) *(G-2137)*	
Delaco Kasle Proc Ind LLC	812 280-8800
5146 Maritime Jeffersonville (47130) *(G-9969)*	
Delaney Window Fashions LLC	317 567-7672
14297 Delaney Dr Fishers (46038) *(G-4503)*	
Delaplane & Son Neon & Sign	574 859-3431
7768 E 550 N Camden (46917) *(G-1519)*	
Delaplane Son Neon & Sign Svc, Camden Also Called: Delaplane & Son Neon & Sign *(G-1519)*	
Delaurence Company	219 878-8712
223 W 6th St Michigan City (46360) *(G-11599)*	
Delaware County Home Bldrs Inc	765 289-6328
2411 N Dr Martin Luther King Jr Blvd Muncie (47303) *(G-12377)*	
Delaware County Mobile Homes, Muncie Also Called: Delaware County Home Bldrs Inc *(G-12377)*	
Delaware Dynamics LLC	765 284-3335
700 S Mulberry St Muncie (47302) *(G-12378)*	
Delaware Employees Abenef	765 284-1565
700 S Mulberry St Muncie (47302) *(G-12379)*	
Delaware Machinery, Muncie Also Called: Matrix Technologies Inc *(G-12448)*	
Delaware Machinery & Tool Company Inc	765 284-3335
700 S Mulberry St Muncie (47302) *(G-12380)*	
Delbert Kemp	812 486-3325
3540 N 700 E Montgomery (47558) *(G-12095)*	
Delbert M Dawson and Son Inc	765 284-9711
1405 W Kilgore Ave Muncie (47305) *(G-12381)*	
Delco Electronics	765 455-9713
3700 Orleans Dr Kokomo (46902) *(G-10255)*	
Delilah Club Covers LLC	812 401-0012
4812 Tippecanoe Dr Evansville (47715) *(G-4010)*	
Delivery Concepts Inc (PA)	574 522-3981
29301 County Road 20 Elkhart (46517) *(G-3289)*	
Delmar Knepp Logging	812 486-2565
10293 E 600 N Loogootee (47553) *(G-11131)*	
Deloro Stellite Holdings Corporation	574 534-2585
1201 Eisenhower Dr N Goshen (46526) *(G-6120)*	
Delp Printing & Mailing Inc	317 872-9744
7750 Zionsville Rd Ste 200 Indianapolis (46268) *(G-7963)*	
Delphi, Carmel Also Called: Aptiv Services Us LLC *(G-1562)*	
Delphi, Kokomo Also Called: Aptiv Services Us LLC *(G-10233)*	
Delphi Body Works	765 564-2212
313 S Washington St Delphi (46923) *(G-2893)*	

ALPHABETIC SECTION — Dexter Chassis Group Inc

Delphi Electronics Safety 765 883-7795
  1705 Greenacres Dr Kokomo (46901) *(G-10256)*
Delphi Pdts & Svc Solutions, Plainfield Also Called: AEL/Span LLC *(G-13656)*
Delphi Powertrain, Plainfield Also Called: Phinia Delphi USA LLC *(G-13714)*
Delphi Products Co Inc 800 382-7903
  2065 W Us Highway 421 Delphi (46923) *(G-2894)*
Delphi Products Company, Delphi Also Called: Dpc Inc *(G-2895)*
Delphi Technologies 765 451-0670
  5514 Four Mile Dr Kokomo (46901) *(G-10257)*
Delphi Technologies 765 480-1993
  1008 Pinoak Dr Kokomo (46901) *(G-10258)*
Delphos Herald of Indiana Inc (HQ) 812 537-0063
  126 W High St Lawrenceburg (47025) *(G-10833)*
Delphos Herald of Indiana Inc 812 438-2011
  235 Main St Rising Sun (47040) *(G-14241)*
Delta Tool Manufacturing Inc 574 223-4863
  1090 W 325 S Rochester (46975) *(G-14286)*
Delux Illumination 219 331-9525
  217 S 13th St Chesterton (46304) *(G-1917)*
Delux Industries Inc 812 867-0655
  8230 Carrington Dr Evansville (47711) *(G-4011)*
Deluxe Akio 606 Ltd Lblty Co 708 682-2780
  525 W 93rd Pl Apt 213 Crown Point (46307) *(G-2676)*
Deluxe Detail LLC 574 292-8968
  1509 Berkshire Dr South Bend (46614) *(G-14996)*
Deluxe Wheel Company 219 395-8003
  1457 N Veden Rd Chesterton (46304) *(G-1918)*
Dem Guys LLC 708 552-3056
  2945 Sentiment Ln Greenwood (46143) *(G-6684)*
Demotte Decorative Stone Inc 219 987-5461
  6611 W State Road 10 Demotte (46310) *(G-2915)*
Demotte Yard, Demotte Also Called: Legacy Vulcan LLC *(G-2922)*
Denim and Honey 812 222-2009
  217 N Broadway St Greensburg (47240) *(G-6591)*
Denneycreative 260 494-0862
  56 W Market St Ste 6 Wabash (46992) *(G-16180)*
Dennis Cooper 847 970-2667
  1024 Autumn Trce Shelbyville (46176) *(G-14751)*
Dennis Etiennes Logging Inc 812 843-4518
  14370 Ureka Rd Cannelton (47520) *(G-1535)*
Dennis K Marvell 812 779-5107
  3700 W 250 N Patoka (47666) *(G-13507)*
Dennis Polk & Associates Inc 574 831-3555
  4916 N Sr 15 New Paris (46553) *(G-12950)*
Dennys Woodcraft Inc 812 883-0770
  5498 E State Road 56 Salem (47167) *(G-14477)*
Dental Enterprises, Kingsford Heights Also Called: Protero Corporation *(G-10186)*
Dental Handpiece Service, Indianapolis Also Called: Fidelity Dental Handpiece Svc *(G-8185)*
Dental Professional Laboratory 219 769-6225
  8040 Cleveland Pl Merrillville (46410) *(G-11505)*
Dentisse Inc 260 444-3046
  10542 Coldwater Rd Ste B Fort Wayne (46845) *(G-4915)*
Denver Marketing Co LLC 866 692-2326
  8235 E 96th St Ste 110 Indianapolis (46256) *(G-7964)*
Deonta Walker 317 970-3586
  5528 Dollar Hide North Dr Indianapolis (46221) *(G-7965)*
Dependable Machine Company 317 924-5378
  1846 E 30th St Indianapolis (46218) *(G-7966)*
Dependable Metal Treating Inc 260 347-5744
  902 Dowling St Kendallville (46755) *(G-10110)*
Dependable Rubber Industrial 765 447-5654
  201 Farabee Dr S Lafayette (47905) *(G-10569)*
Deprisco Ventures Inc 260 637-8660
  14224 Plank St Fort Wayne (46818) *(G-4916)*
Depuy Inc 574 372-7010
  2809 William Dr Winona Lake (46590) *(G-16910)*
Depuy Orthopaedics Inc (DH) 574 267-8143
  700 Orthopaedic Dr Warsaw (46582) *(G-16347)*
Depuy Products Inc (HQ) 574 267-8143
  700 Orthopaedic Dr Warsaw (46582) *(G-16348)*
Depuy Synthes, Warsaw Also Called: Depuy Orthopaedics Inc *(G-16347)*
Depuy Synthes Inc (DH) 574 267-8143
  700 Orthopaedic Dr Warsaw (46582) *(G-16349)*
Depuy Synthes Products Inc 574 267-8143
  700 Orthopaedic Dr Warsaw (46582) *(G-16350)*
Depuy Synthes Sales Inc 574 267-8143
  700 Orthopaedic Dr Warsaw (46582) *(G-16351)*
Derby Inc 574 233-4500
  24350 State Road 23 South Bend (46614) *(G-14997)*
Derby Industries, South Bend Also Called: Derby Inc *(G-14997)*
Derby Industries LLC 765 778-6104
  4301 W 73rd St Anderson (46011) *(G-102)*
Descon, Brownsburg Also Called: Young & Kenady Incorporated *(G-1415)*
Deshazo LLC 317 867-7677
  1022 Kendall Ct Ste 2 Westfield (46074) *(G-16685)*
Desi Technologies Inc 802 488-0954
  54608 Twyckenham Dr South Bend (46637) *(G-14998)*
Design & Mfg Solutions LLC 765 478-9393
  15421 W Hunnicut Rd Cambridge City (47327) *(G-1493)*
Design Engineering 219 926-2170
  600 River Dr Chesterton (46304) *(G-1919)*
Design Engineering Company, Chesterton Also Called: Design Engineering *(G-1919)*
Design Msa Inc 317 817-9000
  200 S Rangeline Rd Ste 217 Carmel (46032) *(G-1606)*
Designers Touch 812 944-2267
  5008 Lakeview Dr Floyds Knobs (47119) *(G-4676)*
Designs 4 U Inc 765 793-3026
  1350 W 100 N Covington (47932) *(G-2528)*
Designs By Kim 574 268-9904
  408 E Lynnwood Dr S Warsaw (46580) *(G-16352)*
Desirable Scents 317 504-4976
  3843 Daisy Dr Lafayette (47905) *(G-10570)*
Desk Coder LLC 812 406-5367
  6170 Park St Georgetown (47122) *(G-6056)*
Destiny Solutions Inc 502 384-0031
  8265 State Road 64 Georgetown (47122) *(G-6057)*
Destro Machines LLC 412 999-1619
  15015 Silver Thorne Way Carmel (46033) *(G-1607)*
Detroit Holdings LLC 202 309-9681
  24803 Stanton Rd North Liberty (46554) *(G-13216)*
Detroit Salt Company LC 313 841-5144
  1575 W Senate Ave Indianapolis (46201) *(G-7967)*
Detweilers Cabinet Shop 765 629-2698
  6053 W State Road 244 Milroy (46156) *(G-11823)*
Deutsch Kase Haus Inc, Middlebury Also Called: Middlebury Cheese Company LLC *(G-11737)*
Developmental Natural Res 317 543-4886
  8750 Sugar Pine Pt Indianapolis (46256) *(G-7968)*
Devening Block Inc (PA) 812 372-4458
  895 Jonesville Rd Columbus (47201) *(G-2282)*
Devil Doc Coffee 317 417-8486
  6576 Kings Ct Avon (46123) *(G-512)*
Dewig Bros Packing Co Inc 812 768-6208
  100 E Maple St Haubstadt (47639) *(G-7083)*
Dewig Deer Processing, Owensville Also Called: Kenny Dewig Meats Sausage Inc *(G-13469)*
Dexstar Wheel, Elkhart Also Called: Americana Development Inc *(G-3179)*
Dexstar Wheel Company Inc 574 295-3535
  400 Collins Rd Elkhart (46516) *(G-3290)*
Dexter Axle, Elkhart Also Called: Dexter Axle Company LLC *(G-3292)*
Dexter Axle, Fremont Also Called: Dexter Axle Company *(G-5820)*
Dexter Axle Company 260 495-5100
  301 W Pearl St Fremont (46737) *(G-5820)*
Dexter Axle Company LLC 260 636-2195
  500 S 7th St Albion (46701) *(G-23)*
Dexter Axle Company LLC 574 294-6651
  21611 Protecta Dr Elkhart (46516) *(G-3291)*
Dexter Axle Company LLC (HQ) 574 295-7888
  2900 Industrial Pkwy Elkhart (46516) *(G-3292)*
Dexter Axle Company LLC 574 294-6651
  21608 Protecta Dr Elkhart (46516) *(G-3293)*
Dexter Axle Division, Albion Also Called: Dexter Axle Company LLC *(G-23)*
Dexter Chassis Group Inc 574 266-7356
  2501 Jeanwood Dr Elkhart (46514) *(G-3294)*

Dexterous Mold and Tool Inc 812 422-8046
2535 Locust Creek Dr Evansville (47720) *(G-4012)*

Dezigns By Cindy Ziese 219 819-8786
5270 W 300 N Rensselaer (47978) *(G-14051)*

Df Global Mfg, Indianapolis *Also Called: Mary Jonas (G-8845)*

Dg Manufacturing Inc 574 294-7550
28564 Holiday Pl Elkhart (46517) *(G-3295)*

Dg Timber Inc 812 295-9876
15562 Half Moon Rd Loogootee (47553) *(G-11132)*

DH Machine Inc 574 773-9211
352 N Tomahawk Trl Nappanee (46550) *(G-12594)*

Dhgraphix and Apparel Co LLC 317 908-2634
500 Polk St Ste 13 Greenwood (46143) *(G-6685)*

Diagnotion LLC 317 853-1180
11611 N Meridian St Ste 455 Carmel (46032) *(G-1608)*

Dial-X Automated Equipment Inc 260 636-7588
3903 S State Road 9 Albion (46701) *(G-24)*

Dialectical Publishing LLC 812 650-1094
3008 E Daniel St Bloomington (47401) *(G-854)*

Dialing Innovations LLC 877 523-5384
6401 S East St Ste C Indianapolis (46227) *(G-7969)*

Diamet 812 379-4606
8841 W 450 S Columbus (47201) *(G-2283)*

Diamond Billiard Products Inc 812 288-7665
4700 New Middle Rd Jeffersonville (47130) *(G-9970)*

Diamond Components Inc 574 358-0452
109 14th Ave Ste 1 Middlebury (46540) *(G-11711)*

Diamond Construction Svcs LLC 513 314-3609
6534 Hartford Pike Aurora (47001) *(G-443)*

Diamond Hoosier 317 773-1411
518 Sunset Dr Noblesville (46060) *(G-13070)*

Diamond J Construction LLC 260 433-5571
14910 Towne Gardens Dr Huntertown (46748) *(G-7253)*

Diamond Lush Extensions LLC 773 984-1003
5164 E 81st Ave Merrillville (46410) *(G-11506)*

Diamond Manufacturing Company 219 874-2374
600 Royal Rd Michigan City (46360) *(G-11600)*

Diamond Mfg Co Midwest, Michigan City *Also Called: Diamond Manufacturing Company (G-11600)*

Diamond Mining Lead 317 340-7760
929 Evening Dr Ste A Indianapolis (46201) *(G-7970)*

Diamond Plastics Corporation 765 287-9234
4100 Niles Rd Muncie (47302) *(G-12382)*

Diamond Specialty Vehicles, Middlebury *Also Called: Diamond Components Inc (G-11711)*

Diamond State Naturals LLC 479 970-4755
10783 Caval Cade Ct Indianapolis (46234) *(G-7971)*

Diamond Stone Technologies Inc 812 276-6043
2237 Industrial Dr Bedford (47421) *(G-630)*

Diamond Waterjet 219 713-1727
3468 Watling St East Chicago (46312) *(G-3003)*

Diamond Welding 765 741-2760
4401 S Delaware Dr Muncie (47302) *(G-12383)*

Diamondback Metalcrafts Inc 317 363-7760
980 Westbrook Dr Mooresville (46158) *(G-12202)*

Diamonds & Pearls Trnsp LLC 504 295-2701
4368 N Audubon Rd Indianapolis (46226) *(G-7972)*

Dianas Beauty Salon 812 699-7904
595 Forest Dr Bloomfield (47424) *(G-745)*

Diane Vander Vliet 574 389-9360
56045 Riverdale Dr Elkhart (46514) *(G-3296)*

Dianne Forrest Welding Company 219 381-1667
5101 Vermont St Gary (46409) *(G-5922)*

Diaper Stone Opco LLC 866 221-2145
7284 W 200 N Greenfield (46140) *(G-6489)*

Dick Baumgartners Basket 765 220-1767
707 Beeson Rd Richmond (47374) *(G-14114)*

Dick's Sign Shop, Orestes *Also Called: Richard Butterfield (G-13361)*

Dickey Consumer Products Inc 317 773-8330
15268 Stony Creek Way Ste 100 Noblesville (46060) *(G-13071)*

Dickinson Woodworking LLC 317 519-5254
1789 W 200 N Greenfield (46140) *(G-6490)*

Dicksons Inc 812 522-1308
709 B Ave E Seymour (47274) *(G-14647)*

Dicksons Inspirational Gifts, Seymour *Also Called: Dicksons Inc (G-14647)*

Diddlebug Publishing LLC 574 612-2389
520 Garfield St Osceola (46561) *(G-13389)*

Die-Mensional Metal Stampg Inc 812 265-3946
1404 W Niblo Rd Jpg Madison (47250) *(G-11213)*

Die-Mensional Metal Stampings, Madison *Also Called: Die-Mensional Metal Stampg Inc (G-11213)*

Die-Namic Ceramics LLC 260 563-7573
948 Manchester Ave Wabash (46992) *(G-16181)*

Die-Rite Machine and Tool Corp 574 522-2366
129 Rush Ct Elkhart (46516) *(G-3297)*

Dieco of Indiana Inc 765 825-4151
5130 Western Ave Connersville (47331) *(G-2435)*

Diedrich Drill Inc 219 326-7788
5 Fisher St La Porte (46350) *(G-10401)*

Dienen Inc (PA) 574 233-3352
17530 Dugdale Dr South Bend (46635) *(G-14999)*

Dieng Group LLC 317 699-1909
3167 N Delaware St Indianapolis (46205) *(G-7973)*

Diesel Punk Core 812 631-0606
3520 S Mcdougal St Bloomington (47403) *(G-855)*

Diesel Rx Products, Shelbyville *Also Called: Wap Inc (G-14814)*

Dietech Corporation 260 724-8946
1001 W Commerce Dr Decatur (46733) *(G-2852)*

Dietrich Industries Inc 219 931-6344
1435 165th Street Hammond (46320) *(G-6913)*

Digger Specialties Inc 574 546-2811
3639 Destiny Dr Bremen (46506) *(G-1186)*

Digger Specialties Inc (PA) 574 546-5999
3446 Us Highway 6 Bremen (46506) *(G-1187)*

Digiop Inc 800 968-3606
9340 Priority Way West Dr Indianapolis (46240) *(G-7974)*

Digistitch 574 538-3960
16123 County Road 40 Goshen (46528) *(G-6121)*

Digital Carvings LLC 812 269-6123
927 E Meadowlands Dr Ellettsville (47429) *(G-3807)*

Digital Color Graphics, Indianapolis *Also Called: Diversfied Cmmnctons Group Inc (G-7983)*

Digital Design Genius 317 515-3680
9174 Bainbridge Dr Camby (46113) *(G-1509)*

Digital Dynamics LLC 317 407-9658
5660 Perry Rd Martinsville (46151) *(G-11388)*

Digital Helium LLC 219 365-4038
9301 W 94th Pl Saint John (46373) *(G-14449)*

Digital Image Editions 812 876-4770
117 E Wylie Rd Bloomington (47408) *(G-856)*

Digital Printing Incorporated 812 265-2205
7122 W Interstate Block Rd Madison (47250) *(G-11214)*

Digital Solutions 812 257-0333
402 S State Road 57 Washington (47501) *(G-16477)*

Dilden Bros Well & Drilling, Lafayette *Also Called: Dilden Brothers Inc (G-10571)*

Dilden Brothers Inc 765 742-1717
1426 Canal Rd Lafayette (47904) *(G-10571)*

Dillman Farm Incorporated 812 825-5525
4955 W State Road 45 Bloomington (47403) *(G-857)*

Dillon Pattern Works Inc 765 642-3549
1010 W 21st St Anderson (46016) *(G-103)*

Dimension Plywood Inc 812 944-6491
415 Industrial Blvd New Albany (47150) *(G-12719)*

Dimensional Imprinting Inc 260 417-0202
13579 Whitaker Dr Milton (47357) *(G-11832)*

Dimo Multiservices LLC 463 256-0561
7998 Cobblesprings Dr Avon (46123) *(G-513)*

Dimplex North America Limited 317 890-0809
221 S Franklin Rd Ste 300 Indianapolis (46219) *(G-7975)*

Dininger Machine Service 317 839-6090
6398 Amber Pass Cartersburg (46168) *(G-1813)*

Dintec Agrichemicals 317 337-7870
9330 Zionsville Rd Indianapolis (46268) *(G-7976)*

Dior Publishing 765 471-2249
606 Hillcrest Rd West Lafayette (47906) *(G-16576)*

ALPHABETIC SECTION

Dipt, Nappanee *Also Called: Dipt LLC (G-12595)*

Dipt LLC.. 574 354-8471
110 S Main St Nappanee (46550) *(G-12595)*

Direct Cnnect Prtg Dgital Svcs, Indianapolis *Also Called: Rhr Corporation (G-9298)*

Direct Control Systems Inc... 765 282-7474
8409 W Greenview Dr Muncie (47304) *(G-12384)*

Direct Conveyors LLC... 317 346-7777
551 Earlywood Dr Franklin (46131) *(G-5725)*

Direct Innovations LLC... 812 343-6085
4251 Fairlawn Dr Columbus (47203) *(G-2284)*

Direct Path Alliance, Greenwood *Also Called: Arroyo Industries LLC (G-6671)*

Direct Point LLC.. 260 705-2279
200 6th St Fort Wayne (46808) *(G-4917)*

Direct Printing Co... 317 831-1047
106 David Ln Mooresville (46158) *(G-12203)*

Directed Photonics Inc... 317 877-3142
7178 Oakbay Dr Noblesville (46062) *(G-13072)*

Directions Promotions... 812 746-2505
1363 E Chandler Ave Evansville (47714) *(G-4013)*

Dirig Sheet Metal, Fort Wayne *Also Called: SW Watkins Limited (G-5462)*

Dirty Squeegee Screen Prtg LLC... 574 358-0003
57319 County Road 35 Middlebury (46540) *(G-11712)*

Disaster Masters Inc.. 317 385-2216
12621 Walrond Rd Fishers (46037) *(G-4504)*

Discount Boots & Tack.. 812 522-9770
1931 N Ewing St Seymour (47274) *(G-14648)*

Discount Copier Service, Noblesville *Also Called: Discount Copy Services Inc (G-13073)*

Discount Copy Services Inc.. 317 773-8783
100 Mensa Dr Noblesville (46062) *(G-13073)*

Discount Labels, New Albany *Also Called: Cenveo Worldwide Limited (G-12710)*

Discount Labels LLC.. 812 945-2617
4115 Profit Ct New Albany (47150) *(G-12720)*

Discount Power Equipment... 765 642-0040
2650 E State Road 236 Anderson (46017) *(G-104)*

Discount Tire, Elkhart *Also Called: Indiana Discount Tire Company (G-3421)*

Discount Tire, Warsaw *Also Called: Indiana Discount Tire Company (G-16377)*

Discover Putnam County... 765 653-4026
20 S Jackson St Greencastle (46135) *(G-6403)*

Disinger Machine Shop... 219 567-2357
4045 S 1450 W Francesville (47946) *(G-5638)*

Diskey Architectural Signage... 260 424-0233
450 E Brackenridge St Fort Wayne (46802) *(G-4918)*

Diskit Sales Division, Lafayette *Also Called: Perry Foam Products Inc (G-10667)*

Displaysource, Fort Wayne *Also Called: Icon International Inc (G-5091)*

Dist Council 91... 812 962-9191
409 Millner Industrial Dr Evansville (47710) *(G-4014)*

Distance Learning Systems, Greenwood *Also Called: Distance Learning Systems Ind (G-6686)*

Distance Learning Systems Ind.. 888 955-3276
107 N State Road 135 Ste 302 Greenwood (46142) *(G-6686)*

Distillery 64 LLC... 502 536-7485
800 E 8th St Ste 107 New Albany (47150) *(G-12721)*

Distinct Images Inc.. 317 613-4413
6830 Hawthorn Park Dr Indianapolis (46220) *(G-7977)*

Distinctive Kitchen & Bath Inc... 317 882-7100
1480 Olive Branch Parke Ln Ste 500 Greenwood (46143) *(G-6687)*

Distributeurs De Monnaie Std, Indianapolis *Also Called: Standard Change-Makers Inc (G-9491)*

Distributor, Indianapolis *Also Called: Indianapolis In (G-8502)*

Ditech Inc (PA)... 812 526-0850
1000 S Main St Edinburgh (46124) *(G-3077)*

Ditech Inc.. 812 379-9756
1151 S Walnut St Edinburgh (46124) *(G-3078)*

Ditto Sales Inc.. 812 424-4098
1817 W Virginia St Evansville (47712) *(G-4015)*

Ditto Sales Inc (PA)... 812 482-3043
2332 Cathy Ln Jasper (47546) *(G-9832)*

Diva This Diva That Inc... 219 533-0077
1251 N Eddy St South Bend (46617) *(G-15000)*

Divaero, Indianapolis *Also Called: Divsys Aerospace & Engrg LLC (G-7987)*

Divalicious By Yours Truly LLC.. 219 359-6335
759 E 81st Ave Merrillville (46410) *(G-11507)*

Divers Supply Company Inc... 317 923-4523
50 W 33rd St Indianapolis (46208) *(G-7978)*

Diverse Fabrication Svcs LLC.. 317 781-8800
1721 S Franklin Rd Ste 100 Indianapolis (46239) *(G-7979)*

Diverse Machine Services LLC... 317 670-1381
2705 Chamberlin Dr Indianapolis (46227) *(G-7980)*

Diverse Managed Services, Indianapolis *Also Called: Diverse Tech Services Inc (G-7982)*

Diverse Sales Solutions LLC.. 317 514-2403
4947 Oakbrook Ct Indianapolis (46254) *(G-7981)*

Diverse Tech Services Inc.. 317 432-6444
7135 Waldemar Dr Indianapolis (46268) *(G-7982)*

Diverse Woodworking LLC... 812 366-3000
505 Maplewood Blvd Georgetown (47122) *(G-6058)*

Diversfied Cmmnctns Group Inc.. 317 755-3191
5550 N Delaware St Indianapolis (46220) *(G-7983)*

Diversified Bus Systems Inc.. 317 254-8668
1398 N Shadeland Ave Ste 2233 Indianapolis (46219) *(G-7984)*

Diversified Ophthalmics Inc... 317 780-1677
4555 Independence Sq Indianapolis (46203) *(G-7985)*

Diversified Pattern Engrg Inc... 260 897-3771
100 Progress Way Avilla (46710) *(G-475)*

Diversified Qulty Svcs Ind LLC... 765 644-7712
1315 W 18th St Anderson (46016) *(G-105)*

Diversified Tools and Mchs Inc.. 260 489-0272
2701 W Wallen Rd Fort Wayne (46818) *(G-4919)*

Diversified Wood Products, Jeffersonville *Also Called: HI Tech Veneer LLC (G-9995)*

Diversity - Vuteq LLC.. 812 761-0210
825 E 350 S Princeton (47670) *(G-13989)*

Diversity Press LLC... 317 241-4234
4026 W 10th St Indianapolis (46222) *(G-7986)*

Divine Confidence LLC.. 574 218-1279
2932 Elkhart Rd Apt 308 Goshen (46526) *(G-6122)*

Divine Essentials LLC.. 765 400-8609
2815 N Oakwood Ave Muncie (47304) *(G-12385)*

Divine Grace Homecare.. 219 290-5911
4224 Connecticut St Gary (46409) *(G-5923)*

Divine Heritage Barns LLC... 812 709-0066
4849 E Us Highway 52 Rushville (46173) *(G-14399)*

Divine Machine.. 812 388-6323
9999 Eagles Nest Ln Shoals (47581) *(G-14905)*

Divine Machine LLC.. 812 709-5246
17246 N Sr 450 Shoals (47581) *(G-14906)*

Division 60, Indianapolis *Also Called: Gardner Glass Products Inc (G-8260)*

Divsys Aerospace & Engrg LLC.. 317 941-7777
8174 Zionsville Rd Indianapolis (46268) *(G-7987)*

Divsys Intl - Icape LLC.. 317 405-9427
8102 Zionsville Rd Indianapolis (46268) *(G-7988)*

Dixie Lee Drapery Co Inc.. 317 783-9869
2434 Madison Ave Indianapolis (46225) *(G-7989)*

Dixie Metal Spinning Corp.. 317 541-1330
4730 Industrial Pkwy Indianapolis (46226) *(G-7990)*

Dj Wreath Creations LLC.. 317 723-3268
6829 Meadowgreen Dr Indianapolis (46236) *(G-7991)*

Djs Cylinder Service Inc... 219 922-4819
223 S Lindberg St Griffith (46319) *(G-6802)*

DK Carrier Inc.. 317 374-1835
777 Fireside Dr Greenwood (46143) *(G-6688)*

DK Earlen Signs LLC.. 812 490-8423
2699 Anvil Ct Newburgh (47630) *(G-13000)*

Dkd Mfg Inc... 574 298-9592
64695 Us Highway 31 Lakeville (46536) *(G-10790)*

Dkl Tool & Manufacturing LLC... 574 289-2291
25855 Northwood Dr South Bend (46619) *(G-15001)*

Dkm Embroidery Inc... 260 471-4070
3203 Caprice Ct Fort Wayne (46808) *(G-4920)*

Dla Construction... 404 992-0805
3467 Highland Ct Crown Point (46307) *(G-2677)*

Dla Document Services.. 812 854-1465
300 Highway 361 Bldg 18 Crane (47522) *(G-2537)*

ALPHABETIC SECTION

Dlb Custom Extrusions LLC... 812 423-6405
1618 Lynch Rd Evansville (47711) *(G-4016)*

Dlb Transporters LLC... 317 667-3368
3043 N White River Parkway East Dr Indianapolis (46208) *(G-7992)*

Dlicous Dsserts By Deedee LLC................................. 317 515-1858
411 S Taylor St South Bend (46601) *(G-15002)*

DLM Fabrication.. 219 393-8820
122 Washington Ave Chesterton (46304) *(G-1920)*

Dmb Embroidery LLC... 812 592-3301
111 E Center Cross St Edinburgh (46124) *(G-3079)*

DMC Distribution LLC... 219 926-6401
172 S 19th St Porter (46304) *(G-13924)*

DMD Pharmaceuticals, Noblesville *Also Called: Dickey Consumer Products Inc (G-13071)*

Dme Manufacturing Pa Inc... 219 872-8211
310 Commerce Sq Michigan City (46360) *(G-11601)*

Dmg Mori Usa Inc.. 317 913-0978
6848 Hillsdale Ct Indianapolis (46250) *(G-7993)*

Dmi Holding Corp (HQ)... 574 534-1224
2164 Caragana Ct Goshen (46526) *(G-6123)*

Dmp Industries LLC... 260 413-6701
1411 E Springhill Rd Warsaw (46580) *(G-16353)*

Dmp LLC... 812 699-0086
2868 W 325 N Worthington (47471) *(G-16959)*

Dna Designs LLC.. 812 329-1310
121 Robin Hood Ln Bedford (47421) *(G-631)*

Dna Enterprises Inc... 574 534-0034
21710 County Road 10 Elkhart (46514) *(G-3298)*

Dnd Dust Control Inc... 765 362-3774
2209 Indianapolis Rd Crawfordsville (47933) *(G-2563)*

Dnh Woodworking.. 260 593-0439
4885 S 900 W Topeka (46571) *(G-15802)*

Dnm Converters & Cores... 502 599-5225
107 E Lynnwood Dr Clarksville (47129) *(G-2015)*

Do It Best, Attica *Also Called: Neumayr Lumber Co Inc (G-353)*

Do It Best, Merrillville *Also Called: Leeps Supply Co Inc (G-11530)*

Dobbins Interior Woodworks..................................... 812 221-0058
5916 E County Road 300 S Dillsboro (47018) *(G-2945)*

Dock Bumpers Inc... 312 597-9282
9445 Indianapolis Blvd Highland (46322) *(G-7132)*

Dockside... 574 400-0848
1835 Lincoln Way E South Bend (46613) *(G-15003)*

Docu-Tech Services Inc (PA).................................... 219 769-1715
1442 E 86th Pl Merrillville (46410) *(G-11508)*

Docutech Document Service..................................... 219 690-3038
1601 Northview Dr Lowell (46356) *(G-11160)*

Dodd Sawmills Incorporated..................................... 812 268-4811
85 E County Road 450 N Sullivan (47882) *(G-15405)*

Dodge Heating and Coolg Contrs, Angola *Also Called: Knox Inc (G-269)*

Dodson Logistics LLC... 937 657-7490
2526 Nw A St Richmond (47374) *(G-14115)*

DOE Run Tooling Inc... 812 265-3057
8550 E Doe Run Rd Madison (47250) *(G-11215)*

Doehler Dry Ingrdent Sltons LL.................................. 574 797-0364
1852 N Home St Mishawaka (46545) *(G-11884)*

Doehler Dry Ingrdent Solutions, Mishawaka *Also Called: Doehler Dry Ingrdent Sltons LL (G-11884)*

Doell Designs.. 260 486-4504
5211 Stellhorn Rd Fort Wayne (46815) *(G-4921)*

Doerr Printing Co... 317 568-0135
4222 E 18th St Indianapolis (46218) *(G-7994)*

Dog Ear Publishing.. 317 228-3656
8888 Keystone Xing Ste 1300 Indianapolis (46240) *(G-7995)*

Doglicious, Marion *Also Called: Canines Choice Inc (G-11276)*

Dohrn Transfer Company... 574 941-4484
14555 Lincoln Hwy Plymouth (46563) *(G-13771)*

DOHRN TRANSFER COMPANY, Plymouth *Also Called: Dohrn Transfer Company (G-13771)*

Domain Industries LLC... 800 227-5337
3900 Transportation Dr Fort Wayne (46818) *(G-4922)*

Domaindress LLC.. 812 430-4856
331 Inwood Dr Evansville (47711) *(G-4017)*

Domar Machine & Tool Inc.. 574 295-8871
56740 Elk Park Dr Elkhart (46516) *(G-3299)*

Domco LLC.. 317 902-4404
10741 Downing St Carmel (46033) *(G-1609)*

Dometic... 574 266-4848
5155 Verdant St Elkhart (46516) *(G-3300)*

Dometic, Elkhart *Also Called: Dometic Corporation (G-3301)*

Dometic Corporation.. 260 463-7657
5155 Verdant St Elkhart (46516) *(G-3301)*

Dometic Corporation.. 574 389-3759
2482 Century Dr Goshen (46528) *(G-6124)*

Dominion Building Products, Elkhart *Also Called: Assa Abloy Door Group LLC (G-3197)*

Domore Seating, Elkhart *Also Called: Lexington LLC (G-3487)*

Doms Froyo LLC.. 574 855-1120
560 W Ireland Rd Ste 1 South Bend (46614) *(G-15004)*

Don Anderson... 574 278-7243
10739 N 650 E Monticello (47960) *(G-12145)*

Don Detzer LLC.. 812 362-7599
12859 N County Road 125 W Tennyson (47637) *(G-15523)*

Don Hartman Oil Co Inc... 765 643-5026
4193 Alexandria Pike Anderson (46012) *(G-106)*

Don Jones Oil Company, Vincennes *Also Called: Pioneer Oil Company Inc (G-16144)*

Don R Fruchey Inc... 260 493-3626
2121 Wayne Haven St Fort Wayne (46803) *(G-4923)*

Don Schumacher Motor Spt Inc................................. 317 286-4380
1681 E Northfield Dr Ste B Brownsburg (46112) *(G-1364)*

Don Schumacher Racing Corp.................................. 317 858-0356
1681 E Northfield Dr Ste A Brownsburg (46112) *(G-1365)*

Don Taylor... 219 662-0597
9524 Cleveland St Crown Point (46307) *(G-2678)*

Don's Truck -N- Go, Indianapolis *Also Called: Donald Lloyd (G-7996)*

Donald H & Susan K Minch....................................... 260 726-9486
2825 W 400 N Portland (47371) *(G-13937)*

Donald L Gard... 219 663-7945
11629 Burr St Crown Point (46307) *(G-2679)*

Donald Leslie.. 574 272-3537
16780 Brick Rd Granger (46530) *(G-6345)*

Donald Lloyd... 937 304-5683
2040 Theodore Dr Indianapolis (46214) *(G-7996)*

Donald Pape.. 260 484-6088
3327 Collegiate Ct Rear Fort Wayne (46805) *(G-4924)*

Donaldson Co, Monticello *Also Called: Donaldson Company Inc (G-12146)*

Donaldson Company Inc... 765 635-2285
6810 Layton Rd Anderson (46011) *(G-107)*

Donaldson Company Inc... 765 659-4766
3260 W State Road 28 Frankfort (46041) *(G-5660)*

Donaldson Company Inc... 952 887-3131
303 N 6th St Monticello (47960) *(G-12146)*

Donaldson Country Home, Lebanon *Also Called: Donaldsons Chocolates Inc (G-10891)*

Donaldson Hydraulic Filters, Anderson *Also Called: Donaldson Company Inc (G-107)*

Donaldsons Chocolates Inc...................................... 765 482-3334
600 S State Road 39 Lebanon (46052) *(G-10891)*

Donna Dalton... 812 358-6116
5319 N Mount Rd Scottsburg (47170) *(G-14553)*

Donna McCormick.. 574 278-3152
8593 N State Road 39 Monticello (47960) *(G-12147)*

Dons Automotive and Mch Inc.................................. 812 547-6292
1047 6th St Tell City (47586) *(G-15500)*

Dons Specialty Welding LLC..................................... 260 557-3492
924 Mildred Ave Fort Wayne (46808) *(G-4925)*

Dontstoptillyougetenough LLC.................................. 812 250-8262
235 N Burkhardt Rd Evansville (47715) *(G-4018)*

Donut Bank Inc (PA)... 812 426-0011
1031 E Diamond Ave Evansville (47711) *(G-4019)*

Donut Bank Bakery, Evansville *Also Called: Donut Bank Inc (G-4019)*

Doodles and Dreams Pubg LLC................................ 317 796-6059
795 Bloor Ln Zionsville (46077) *(G-17003)*

Door Service Supply.. 317 496-0391
4075 Primrose Path Greenwood (46142) *(G-6689)*

Doors & Drawers Inc... 574 533-3509
2302 Dierdorff Rd Goshen (46526) *(G-6125)*

Dorel Home Furnishings Inc.................................... 812 372-0141
2525 State St Columbus (47201) *(G-2285)*

ALPHABETIC SECTION — Draper Manufacturing LLC

Dorel Juvenile Group Inc 812 372-0141
505 S Cherry St Columbus (47201) *(G-2286)*

Dorel Juvenile Group Inc 812 372-0141
2525 State St Columbus (47201) *(G-2287)*

Dorel Juvenile Group Inc 812 314-6629
500 S Gladstone Ave Columbus (47201) *(G-2288)*

Dorel Juvenile Group Inc (DH) 800 457-5276
2525 State St Columbus (47201) *(G-2289)*

Dorel USA Inc (HQ) 812 372-0141
2525 State St Columbus (47201) *(G-2290)*

Doris Drapery Boutique 765 472-5850
68 N Broadway Peru (46970) *(G-13580)*

Dorma 317 468-6742
215 W New Rd Greenfield (46140) *(G-6491)*

Dormakaba USA Inc 317 806-4605
6161 E 75th St Indianapolis (46250) *(G-7997)*

Doron Distribution Inc 317 594-9259
1277 Helford Ln Carmel (46032) *(G-1610)*

DOT America Inc 260 244-5700
335 Towerview Dr Columbia City (46725) *(G-2138)*

Dotstaff, Indianapolis *Also Called: Dotstaff LLC (G-7998)*

Dotstaff LLC 317 806-6100
9800 Crosspoint Blvd Indianapolis (46256) *(G-7998)*

Dotted Lime Resale LLC 317 908-3905
4232 Zachary Ln Westfield (46062) *(G-16686)*

Doty Graphics 765 763-7178
9038 N State Road 9 Morristown (46161) *(G-12275)*

Doty, Leroy E. Builder, Crown Point *Also Called: Leroy E Doty Cabinet Shop (G-2717)*

Double D 765 569-6822
214 E Ohio St Rockville (47872) *(G-14351)*

Double E Distributing Co Inc 812 334-2220
2214 E Rock Creek Dr Bloomington (47401) *(G-858)*

Double E Dstrbtng Co, Bloomington *Also Called: Double E Distributing Co Inc (G-858)*

Double E Enterprise Inc 812 689-0671
205 Western Ave Osgood (47037) *(G-13407)*

Double E Woodworking LLC 260 593-0522
9880 W 700 S Topeka (46571) *(G-15803)*

Double Envelope Corp 260 434-0500
10804 Lake Shasta Ct Fort Wayne (46804) *(G-4926)*

Double H Manufacturing Corp 215 674-4100
2548 W 26th St Marion (46953) *(G-11281)*

Double H Plastics, Marion *Also Called: Double H Manufacturing Corp (G-11281)*

Double H Plastics Inc 765 664-9090
2548 W 26th St Marion (46953) *(G-11282)*

Double J Woodworking 812 290-8877
1184 Carroll Ave Lawrenceburg (47025) *(G-10834)*

Double L Woodworking LLC 260 768-3155
12478 County Road 34 Goshen (46528) *(G-6126)*

Double T Leather Inc 765 393-3676
3320 Columbus Ave Anderson (46013) *(G-108)*

Double T Manufacturing Corp 574 262-1340
27139 County Road 6 Elkhart (46514) *(G-3302)*

Doug Wilcox 812 476-1957
1188 W State Route 68 Lynnville (47619) *(G-11189)*

Douglas Drudge 574 566-2210
1384 W 600 S Claypool (46510) *(G-2052)*

Douglas Dumpster and Svcs LLC 630 460-8727
6212 Us Highway 6 Unit 294 Portage (46368) *(G-13859)*

Douglas Dye and Associates Inc 317 844-1709
501 Industrial Dr Carmel (46032) *(G-1611)*

Douglas Estes 219 718-0911
783 S 250 W Hebron (46341) *(G-7099)*

Douglas K Gresham 812 445-3174
1540 N County Road 900 W Seymour (47274) *(G-14649)*

Douglas P Terrell 812 254-1976
1289 S State Road 57 Washington (47501) *(G-16478)*

Dove Printing Services Inc 317 469-7546
7410 E 33rd St Indianapolis (46226) *(G-7999)*

Dover Chemical Corporation 219 852-0042
3000 Sheffield Ave Hammond (46327) *(G-6914)*

Dovey Corporation 765 649-2576
3220 W 25th St Anderson (46011) *(G-109)*

Dow Agroscience 765 743-0015
1281 Win Hentschel Blvd West Lafayette (47906) *(G-16577)*

Dow Agrosciences 765 775-2918
3400 Kent Ave Ste 100 West Lafayette (47906) *(G-16578)*

Dow Agrosciences LLC 317 846-7873
457 3rd Ave Sw Carmel (46032) *(G-1612)*

Dow Agrosciences LLC 317 252-5602
5110 E 69th St Indianapolis (46220) *(G-8000)*

DOW AGROSCIENCES LLC, Indianapolis *Also Called: Dow Agrosciences LLC (G-8000)*

Dow Chemical, Indianapolis *Also Called: Dow Chemical Company (G-8001)*

Dow Chemical Company 317 337-3819
9330 Zionsville Rd Indianapolis (46268) *(G-8001)*

Dow Elanco Sciences 317 337-3691
9330 Zionsville Rd Indianapolis (46268) *(G-8002)*

Dow Theory Forecasts Inc 219 931-6480
7412 Calumet Ave Hammond (46324) *(G-6915)*

Down Range Industries LLC 219 895-0834
11214 Daisy Ln Cedar Lake (46303) *(G-1830)*

Down To Fabricate LLC 812 249-1825
5016 Main St Guilford (47022) *(G-6828)*

Downey Creations LLC 317 248-9888
1811 Executive Dr Ste R Indianapolis (46241) *(G-8003)*

Downeys Welding Repair 765 778-4727
105 Bess Blvd Pendleton (46064) *(G-13530)*

Doyle Logging Etienne, Magnet *Also Called: Anthony D Etienne Logging (G-11258)*

Doyle Manufacturing Inc 574 848-5624
2108 Blakesley Pkwy Bristol (46507) *(G-1256)*

Doyle Pitner 574 699-6046
201 S California St Galveston (46932) *(G-5852)*

Dp Construction, Galveston *Also Called: Doyle Pitner (G-5852)*

Dpc Inc 765 564-3752
2065 W Us Highway 421 Delphi (46923) *(G-2895)*

Dpi, Madison *Also Called: Digital Printing Incorporated (G-11214)*

Dpict Imaging Inc 317 436-8411
7400 N Shadeland Ave Ste 255 Indianapolis (46250) *(G-8004)*

Dpp, North Vernon *Also Called: Decatur Plastic Products Inc (G-13268)*

Dps Printing LLC 260 503-9681
950 Liberty Dr Columbia City (46725) *(G-2139)*

Dr Pepper, South Bend *Also Called: Dr Pepper Snapple Group (G-15005)*

Dr Pepper Bottling Co 765 647-3576
261 Webers Ln Brookville (47012) *(G-1319)*

Dr Pepper Snapple Group 574 291-9000
4610 S Burnett Dr South Bend (46614) *(G-15005)*

Dr Pepper Snapple Group I 260 484-4177
2711 Independence Dr Fort Wayne (46808) *(G-4927)*

Dr Restorations Inc 317 646-7150
4252 N Raceway Rd Clermont (46234) *(G-2063)*

Dr Tavel Premium Optical, Indianapolis *Also Called: City Optical Co Inc (G-7814)*

Dr Tavel's One Hour Optical, Indianapolis *Also Called: City Optical Co Inc (G-7813)*

Dragon ESP Ltd 574 893-1569
8857 E State Road 14 Akron (46910) *(G-4)*

Dragon Industries Inc 574 772-2243
2180 E 400 S Knox (46534) *(G-10205)*

Dragon Industries Incorporated 574 772-3508
2120 E State Road 10 Knox (46534) *(G-10206)*

Dragon Printing LLC 317 919-9619
5075 Olive Branch Rd Greenwood (46143) *(G-6690)*

Dragonwood LLC 765 947-0097
11965 W 150 N Kempton (46049) *(G-10086)*

Drake Corporation 636 464-5070
9930 E 56th St Indianapolis (46236) *(G-8005)*

Drake Enterprises LLC 317 460-5991
6135 E County Road 900 N Pittsboro (46167) *(G-13644)*

Dransfield & Associates Wldg 317 736-6281
8955 W Shelby Franklin (46131) *(G-5726)*

Draper Inc (PA) 765 987-7999
411 S Pearl St Spiceland (47385) *(G-15377)*

Draper Manufacturing, Indianapolis *Also Called: Draper Manufacturing LLC (G-8006)*

Draper Manufacturing LLC 317 347-5195
4008 W 10th St Indianapolis (46222) *(G-8006)*

Drapery Gallery, Lafayette *Also Called: K M Davis Inc (G-10617)*

Drava Underwater LLC..812 622-0432
509 N 2nd St Ste B Owensville (47665) *(G-13466)*

Drc Machining LLC..812 825-5783
13968 Thacker Rd Bloomington (47403) *(G-859)*

Dream Beauty Lab...773 571-1817
1023 S Maple St Marion (46953) *(G-11283)*

Dream Center Evansville Inc..812 401-5558
16 W Morgan Ave Evansville (47710) *(G-4020)*

Dream Fishing/Lure, The, Plainfield *Also Called: Meredith Hughes (G-13705)*

Dream Lighting Inc..574 206-4888
2111 Industrial Pkwy Elkhart (46516) *(G-3303)*

Dream Mill, Elwood *Also Called: Aunt Netts Country Candles LLC (G-3818)*

Dream Systems, New Palestine *Also Called: Dream Systems LLC (G-12936)*

Dream Systems LLC...715 241-8332
7316 W Beyers Ct New Palestine (46163) *(G-12936)*

Dream Theory Publishing LLC..317 598-0320
11145 Harriston Dr Fishers (46037) *(G-4505)*

Dresser LLC...765 827-9200
900 W Mount St Connersville (47331) *(G-2436)*

Dresser Roots Blowers & Cmpsr, Connersville *Also Called: Dresser LLC (G-2436)*

Drew It Yourself Wood Working.......................................317 250-6548
12605 Cold Stream Rd Noblesville (46060) *(G-13074)*

Drews Deer Processing..812 279-6246
8122 Us Highway 50 W Mitchell (47446) *(G-12038)*

Drews Parts LLC..317 800-8713
705 E School St Anderson (46012) *(G-110)*

Dreyers Grand Ice Cream Inc..260 483-3102
3426 N Wells St Fort Wayne (46808) *(G-4928)*

DRG, Berne *Also Called: Dynamic Resource Group Inc (G-709)*

Dribot LLC...317 885-6330
203 W Morris St Indianapolis (46225) *(G-8007)*

Driessen Water Inc...765 529-4905
1509 N Wheeling Ave Muncie (47303) *(G-12386)*

Drike Inc...574 259-8822
315 Union St Mishawaka (46544) *(G-11885)*

Drilling & Trenching Sup Inc..317 825-0919
860 Elston Dr Shelbyville (46176) *(G-14752)*

Drilling World, Shelbyville *Also Called: Drilling & Trenching Sup Inc (G-14752)*

Drillmaster Corp..732 919-3088
8900 Highway 65 Ste 5 Cynthiana (47612) *(G-2787)*

Drinan Racing Products Inc..317 486-9710
100 Gasoline Aly Ste F Indianapolis (46222) *(G-8008)*

Drinkgp LLC..317 410-4748
5707 Brockton Dr Apt 115 Indianapolis (46220) *(G-8009)*

Drive Process Services Inc..765 741-9717
6017 W Hellis Dr Muncie (47304) *(G-12387)*

Driverz For Life(d 4 L) LLC...317 619-4513
3151 N New Jersey St Indianapolis (46205) *(G-8010)*

Drk Global Manufacturing LLC...................................574 387-6264
1921 N Cedar St Mishawaka (46545) *(G-11886)*

Drone Works LLC..812 917-4691
933 S 5th St Apt 3 Terre Haute (47807) *(G-15579)*

Dropem Game Calls...765 513-7667
1003 N Forest Dr Kokomo (46901) *(G-10259)*

Dropship My Bundles LLC..219 381-8061
1021 Willard St Gary (46404) *(G-5924)*

Drp Mold Inc...765 349-3355
70 James Baldwin Dr Martinsville (46151) *(G-11389)*

Drs Graphix Group Inc..317 569-1855
3855 E 96th St Ste P Indianapolis (46240) *(G-8011)*

Drshopecom LLC...800 255-1510
5740 Thunderbird Rd Ste C Indianapolis (46236) *(G-8012)*

Drug Plastics and Glass Co Inc.................................765 385-0035
5 Bottle Dr Oxford (47971) *(G-13474)*

Drug Plastics Closures Inc..812 526-0555
2875 W 800 N Edinburgh (46124) *(G-3080)*

Dry Inc..503 977-9204
7201 Engle Rd Fort Wayne (46804) *(G-4929)*

Dry Cleaners Secret, Fort Wayne *Also Called: Dry Inc (G-4929)*

Dry Heat Coffee LLC..760 422-9865
6255 Carrollton Ave Ste 30091 Indianapolis (46220) *(G-8013)*

Ds Corp..260 593-3850
1115 W Lake St Topeka (46571) *(G-15804)*

Ds Mgmt Group LLC..317 946-8646
7533 Prairie View Dr Indianapolis (46256) *(G-8014)*

Ds Products Inc...260 563-9030
202 Wedcor Ave Wabash (46992) *(G-16182)*

Ds Smith Rapak, Indianapolis *Also Called: Grrk Holdings Inc (G-8336)*

DS Woods Custom Cabinets....................................260 692-6565
2231 N Us Highway 27 Decatur (46733) *(G-2853)*

Dse Inc..812 376-0310
2651 Cessna Dr Columbus (47203) *(G-2291)*

Dsh Indiana Inc...317 704-8130
4250 W 99th St Carmel (46032) *(G-1613)*

DSM Enterprises LLC..317 698-3317
3025 N 550 E Lebanon (46052) *(G-10892)*

DSM Precision Manufacturing, Brownsburg *Also Called: Don Schumacher Motor Spt Inc (G-1364)*

DSM Publications...312 730-7375
5430 White Oak Ave Hammond (46320) *(G-6916)*

Dsn Cabinetry Inc..317 747-4740
1373 W 850 N Fortville (46040) *(G-5592)*

DStyle Inc...619 662-0560
1600 Royal St Jasper (47546) *(G-9833)*

Dti Services Ltd Liability Co...................................765 745-0261
5935 W 84th St Ste A Indianapolis (46278) *(G-8015)*

Dtp Trucking LLC..463 701-8508
11526 Stoeppelwerth Dr Indianapolis (46229) *(G-8016)*

Du-Mar Welding LLC..574 223-9889
2858 E 650 N Rochester (46975) *(G-14287)*

Dual Machine Corporation....................................317 921-9850
1951 Bloyd Ave Indianapolis (46218) *(G-8017)*

Dualtech Inc..317 738-9043
450 Blue Chip Ct Franklin (46131) *(G-5727)*

Dub City Tires, East Chicago *Also Called: D & D Tire Shop LLC (G-3002)*

Dubois Cnty Block & Brick Inc..............................812 482-6293
2208 Newton St Jasper (47546) *(G-9834)*

Dubois Co Block & Brick, Jasper *Also Called: Dubois Cnty Block & Brick Inc (G-9834)*

Dubois County Free Press LLC.............................812 639-9651
4288 W 630s Huntingburg (47542) *(G-7276)*

Dubois County Liners LLP...................................812 634-1294
555 E 12th Ave Jasper (47546) *(G-9835)*

Dubois Manufacturing Inc...................................574 674-6988
30561 Old Us 20 Elkhart (46514) *(G-3304)*

Dubois Wood Products Inc (PA).........................812 683-3613
707 E 6th St Huntingburg (47542) *(G-7277)*

Dubois-Spncer Cunties Pubg Inc (PA)...............812 367-2041
113 W 6th St Ferdinand (47532) *(G-4430)*

Dubose Strapping Inc...765 361-0000
4414 E 400 S Crawfordsville (47933) *(G-2564)*

Dud(e)s N Roses LLC..260 739-9053
4325 Oakhurst Dr Fort Wayne (46815) *(G-4930)*

Due North Industries Corp.................................812 306-4043
5215 James Ave Evansville (47712) *(G-4021)*

Duel Tool & Gage Inc..317 244-0129
1553 S Concord St Indianapolis (46241) *(G-8018)*

Duesenburg Inc..260 496-9650
3330 Congressional Pkwy Fort Wayne (46808) *(G-4931)*

Dugdale Beef Company Inc...............................317 291-9660
4224 W 71st St Indianapolis (46268) *(G-8019)*

Dugout...765 642-8528
2203 Broadway St Anderson (46012) *(G-111)*

Dulcius Vineyards LLC......................................260 602-9259
2573 W 500 S-57 Columbia City (46725) *(G-2140)*

Duley Press Inc..574 259-5203
2906 N Home St Mishawaka (46545) *(G-11887)*

Dump & Go, Elkhart *Also Called: Quality Steel & Alum Pdts Inc (G-3634)*

Duncan Supply Co Inc.......................................765 446-0105
510 Morland Dr Lafayette (47905) *(G-10572)*

Duncan Systems, Mishawaka *Also Called: Lippert Components Inc (G-11930)*

Dune Ridge Winery LLC....................................219 548-4605
1240 W Beam St Chesterton (46304) *(G-1921)*

ALPHABETIC SECTION — Dynamark Graphics Group Inc

Duneland Alpacas Ltd 219 877-4417
1394 N County Line Rd Michigan City (46360) *(G-11602)*

Dunes Investment Inc 219 764-4270
6672 Melton Rd Portage (46368) *(G-13860)*

Dungan Aerial Service Inc 765 827-1355
4290 N County Road 450 W Connersville (47331) *(G-2437)*

Dunham Rbr Blting Corp A Belt, Fort Wayne *Also Called: CRS-Drs Corporation (G-4891)*

Dunham Rubber Belting Corp 317 604-5313
1689 N Michigan Rd Shelbyville (46176) *(G-14753)*

Dunn-Rite Products Inc (PA) 765 552-9433
2200 S J St Elwood (46036) *(G-3820)*

Duplicast Metalworks Inc 317 926-0745
1809 Cornell Ave Indianapolis (46202) *(G-8020)*

Dupont, Kokomo *Also Called: Toppan Photomasks Inc (G-10350)*

Dupont, Valparaiso *Also Called: Eidp Inc (G-15938)*

Dupont and Tonkel Partners LLC 260 444-2264
10501 Day Lily Dr Fort Wayne (46825) *(G-4932)*

Dupont Circle III 260 489-9508
9910 Dupont Circle Dr E Fort Wayne (46825) *(G-4933)*

Dupont Commons LLC 260 637-3215
10050 Bent Creek Blvd Fort Wayne (46825) *(G-4934)*

Dupont De Nemours Inc 219 261-2124
600 Harrington St Remington (47977) *(G-14034)*

Dupont Nutrition & Health, Terre Haute *Also Called: Eidp Inc (G-15583)*

Dupouy Enterprises LLC 765 453-1466
2215 Carr Dr Kokomo (46902) *(G-10260)*

Dupre Capital LLC 812 291-1141
215 Quartermaster Ct Jeffersonville (47130) *(G-9971)*

Dura Products Inc 855 502-3872
504 Demoss Ave Arcadia (46030) *(G-313)*

Dura-Vent Corp 574 936-2432
1435 N Michigan St Ste 3 Plymouth (46563) *(G-13772)*

Durakool, Elkhart *Also Called: American Elctrnic Cmpnents Inc (G-3171)*

Duramark, Westfield *Also Called: Duramark Technologies Inc (G-16687)*

Duramark Technologies Inc (PA) 317 867-5700
16450 Southpark Dr Westfield (46074) *(G-16687)*

Duramold, South Bend *Also Called: Duramold Castings Inc (G-15006)*

Duramold Castings Inc 574 251-1611
1901 N Bendix Dr South Bend (46628) *(G-15006)*

Duratech, Noblesville *Also Called: Fast Track Technologies LLC (G-13075)*

Durcholz Excvtg & Cnstr Co In, Huntingburg *Also Called: Durcholz Excvtg & Cnstr Co Inc (G-7278)*

Durcholz Excvtg & Cnstr Co Inc 812 634-1764
4308 S State Road 162 Huntingburg (47542) *(G-7278)*

Durhat Transportation LLC 463 204-9119
335 Lake Ridge Ln Greenwood (46142) *(G-6691)*

Durm Vineyard Inc 317 862-9463
11747 Indian Creek Rd S Indianapolis (46259) *(G-8021)*

Duro Inc 574 293-6860
24478 County Road 45 Elkhart (46516) *(G-3305)*

Duro Recycling Inc 574 522-2572
24478 County Road 45 Elkhart (46516) *(G-3306)*

Durogreen Outdoor LLC 574 327-6943
4540 Pine Creek Rd Elkhart (46516) *(G-3307)*

Durusa LLC 574 312-0923
12980-F Ste 310 Granger (46530) *(G-6346)*

Dustex 812 725-0808
3428 Charlestown Pike Jeffersonville (47130) *(G-9972)*

Dusty Barn Distillery, Mount Vernon *Also Called: Southern In Distillery (G-12322)*

Dutch Country Organics LLC 574 536-7403
407 N Main St Middlebury (46540) *(G-11713)*

Dutch Country Woodworking Inc 260 499-4847
200 Industrial Pkwy Lagrange (46761) *(G-10734)*

Dutch Craft Woodwork LLC 812 486-3675
4876 N 775 E Montgomery (47558) *(G-12096)*

Dutch Kettle LLC 574 546-4033
6375 Fir Rd Bremen (46506) *(G-1188)*

Dutch Made Inc (PA) 260 657-3311
10415 Roth Rd Grabill (46741) *(G-6294)*

Dutch Made Inc 260 657-3331
16836 State Road 37 Harlan (46743) *(G-7054)*

Dutch Maid Bakery, Goshen *Also Called: Miller Distributions Inc (G-6224)*

Dutch Park Homes Inc 574 642-0150
2249 Lincolnway E Goshen (46526) *(G-6127)*

Dutch Waffle Company LLC 574 312-4578
16834 Mill Pond Trl Plymouth (46563) *(G-13773)*

Dutchcraft Corporation 260 463-8366
50 S 375 W Lagrange (46761) *(G-10735)*

Dutchland LLC 812 254-5400
1099 Seals Rd Loogootee (47553) *(G-11133)*

Dutchmaid Woodworking LLC 260 768-7442
2320 N 700 W Shipshewana (46565) *(G-14844)*

Dutchtown Homes Inc 812 354-2197
6518 N County Road 500 E Petersburg (47567) *(G-13610)*

Dux Signal Kits LLC 260 623-3017
23132 Monroeville Rd Monroeville (46773) *(G-12068)*

Dvs Refractories, Gary *Also Called: Shanxi-Indiana LLC (G-6009)*

Dw Inc 812 696-2149
220 E Hampton St Farmersburg (47850) *(G-4418)*

Dwd Industries LLC (DH) 260 728-9272
1921 Patterson St Decatur (46733) *(G-2854)*

Dwd Industries LLC 260 639-3254
11117 English St Hoagland (46745) *(G-7167)*

Dwd Miller Inc 812 853-8497
10399 Telephone Rd Chandler (47610) *(G-1860)*

Dwd Trucking LLC 317 586-3484
2715 Cabin Hill Rd Indianapolis (46229) *(G-8022)*

dwg Design Services Corp 812 372-0864
1220 Washington St Columbus (47201) *(G-2292)*

DWG Global Services LLC 469 605-0567
1986 Devonshire Ave Avon (46123) *(G-514)*

Dwight Smith Logging 812 834-5546
815 Roberts Ln Heltonville (47436) *(G-7110)*

Dwyer Enterprises 317 573-9628
12075 Waterford Ln Carmel (46033) *(G-1614)*

Dwyer Instruments LLC 219 879-8000
102 Indiana Highway 212 Michigan City (46360) *(G-11603)*

Dwyer Instruments Inc 219 393-5250
3999 E Hupp Rd La Porte (46350) *(G-10402)*

Dwyer Instruments Inc 574 234-6853
1440 Ignition Dr South Bend (46601) *(G-15007)*

Dwyer Instruments Inc 219 879-8868
6850 Enterprise Dr South Bend (46628) *(G-15008)*

Dwyer Instruments Inc 574 862-2590
55 Ward St Wakarusa (46573) *(G-16231)*

Dwyer Instruments Inc 219 279-2031
204 E Sherry Ln Wolcott (47995) *(G-16928)*

Dwyer Instruments Inc, South Bend *Also Called: Dwyer Instruments Inc (G-15007)*

DWYER INSTRUMENTS INC, South Bend *Also Called: Dwyer Instruments Inc (G-15008)*

DWYER INSTRUMENTS INC, Wakarusa *Also Called: Dwyer Instruments Inc (G-16231)*

DWYER INSTRUMENTS INC, Wolcott *Also Called: Dwyer Instruments Inc (G-16928)*

Dwyer Instruments LLC (HQ) 219 879-8868
102 Indiana Highway 212 Michigan City (46360) *(G-11604)*

Dwyer-Wilbert Inc 765 962-3605
1014 National Rd W Richmond (47374) *(G-14116)*

Dwyer-Wilbert Monument, Richmond *Also Called: Dwyer-Wilbert Inc (G-14116)*

Dx 4 LLC 260 749-0632
3518 S Maplecrest Rd Fort Wayne (46806) *(G-4935)*

Dx Hammond Opco LLC (PA) 219 501-0905
100-500 Indianapolis Blvd Whiting (46394) *(G-16834)*

Dxd Signs 219 588-4403
9231 Spring St Highland (46322) *(G-7133)*

Dye Woodworks, Carmel *Also Called: Douglas Dye and Associates Inc (G-1611)*

Dyer Signwerks Inc 219 322-7722
1000 Richard Rd Dyer (46311) *(G-2971)*

Dyer Vault Company Inc 219 865-2521
1750 Sheffield Ave Dyer (46311) *(G-2972)*

Dyna-Fab Corporation 765 893-4423
3893 S State Road 263 West Lebanon (47991) *(G-16647)*

Dynamark Graphics Group Inc (PA) 317 328-2555
7210 Zionsville Rd Indianapolis (46268) *(G-8023)*

Dynamark Graphics Group Inc 317 569-1855
3855 E 96th St Ste L Indianapolis (46240) *(G-8024)*

ALPHABETIC SECTION

Dynamic Aerospace and Defense, Elkhart *Also Called: Dynamic Metals LLC (G-3310)*

Dynamic Axle LLC.. 574 226-0242
25863 Northland Crossing Dr Elkhart (46514) *(G-3308)*

Dynamic Composites LLC...................................... 260 625-8686
2670 S 700 E Columbia City (46725) *(G-2141)*

Dynamic Designs Scottys...................................... 219 809-7268
3409 Franklin St Michigan City (46360) *(G-11605)*

Dynamic Dies Inc... 419 861-5613
2801 Fortune Cir E Ste I Indianapolis (46241) *(G-8025)*

Dynamic Dies Inc... 317 247-4706
2321 Executive Dr Indianapolis (46241) *(G-8026)*

Dynamic Fabrication LLC...................................... 812 305-5576
2214 Saint Joseph Ind Park Dr Evansville (47720) *(G-4022)*

Dynamic Fabrication LLC...................................... 812 305-5576
1331 Grove St Evansville (47710) *(G-4023)*

Dynamic Finish Solutions LLC............................... 574 529-0121
1319 W North St Bremen (46506) *(G-1189)*

Dynamic Industrial Group LLC............................... 574 295-5525
54347 Highland Blvd Elkhart (46514) *(G-3309)*

Dynamic Metals LLC (PA)..................................... 574 262-2497
54347 Highland Blvd Elkhart (46514) *(G-3310)*

Dynamic Packg Solutions Inc................................ 574 848-1410
406 Kesco Dr Bristol (46507) *(G-1257)*

Dynamic Resource Group Inc................................ 260 589-4000
269 S Jefferson St Berne (46711) *(G-709)*

Dynamic Tool Machine.. 765 730-0167
4750 S County Road 500 W Yorktown (47396) *(G-16973)*

Dynatect Manufacturing Inc.................................. 219 462-0822
386 E State Road 2 Valparaiso (46383) *(G-15936)*

Dynatect Manufacturing Inc.................................. 219 465-1898
386 E State Road 2 Valparaiso (46383) *(G-15937)*

Dyno Nobel Inc.. 260 731-4431
7860 W 400 N Pennville (47369) *(G-13563)*

Dyno One Inc.. 812 526-0500
14671 N 250 W Edinburgh (46124) *(G-3081)*

Dynomax... 317 835-3813
11797 Belle Plaine Blvd Fishers (46037) *(G-4506)*

Dytec-Nci LLC... 317 919-0000
8500 E 116th St Unit 6156 Fishers (46038) *(G-4507)*

Dz Investments LLC... 317 895-4141
3131 N Franklin Rd Ste E Indianapolis (46226) *(G-8027)*

E & B Paving Inc (HQ)... 765 643-5358
286 W 300 N Anderson (46012) *(G-112)*

E & B Paving Inc.. 765 674-5848
3888 S Garthwaite Rd Marion (46953) *(G-11284)*

E & D Tire & Repair LLC..................................... 812 486-6493
11326 E 600 N Loogootee (47553) *(G-11134)*

E & E Garage Doors LLC..................................... 317 575-9677
10155 N College Ave Carmel (46280) *(G-1615)*

E & H Bridge and Grating Inc.............................. 812 277-8343
1 Lavender Ln Bedford (47421) *(G-632)*

E & H Bridge Inc.. 812 279-2308
8136 State Road 158 Bedford (47421) *(G-633)*

E & H Industrial Services LLC............................. 317 569-8819
963 Orlando St Carmel (46032) *(G-1616)*

E & H Industrial Services Inc............................... 317 670-4456
5671 Guion Rd Indianapolis (46254) *(G-8028)*

E & L Construction Inc.. 765 525-7081
1375 N 800 E Manilla (46150) *(G-11260)*

E & M Machining... 765 754-3613
204 S Washington St Frankton (46044) *(G-5790)*

E & M Tire Salvage Inc.. 260 745-3016
2609 S Clinton St Fort Wayne (46803) *(G-4936)*

E & R Fabricating Inc.. 812 275-0388
8854 State Road 37 Bedford (47421) *(G-634)*

E & R Mfg Co Inc... 765 279-8826
504 N Illinois St Kirklin (46050) *(G-10188)*

E & S Wood Creations LLC................................. 260 768-3033
2030 N 450 W Lagrange (46761) *(G-10736)*

E C T Franklin Control Systems......................... 765 939-2531
1831 W Main St Richmond (47374) *(G-14117)*

E D H Inc.. 219 712-5145
925 Central Ave Rm D Lake Station (46405) *(G-10772)*

E F M Corporation... 812 372-4421
1480 14th St Columbus (47201) *(G-2293)*

E Fab Inc.. 317 786-9593
513 National Ave Ste A Indianapolis (46227) *(G-8029)*

E G Ammerman Jr.. 812 623-3504
825 N Meridian St Sunman (47041) *(G-15436)*

E L M, Indianapolis *Also Called: Ewing Light Metals Co Inc (G-8146)*

E M C, Sheridan *Also Called: Biddle Precision Components Inc (G-14817)*

E M Cummings Veneers Inc............................... 812 944-2269
601 E 4th St New Albany (47150) *(G-12722)*

E M F, Angola *Also Called: E M F Corp (G-246)*

E M F Corp (PA).. 260 665-9541
505 Pokagon Trl Angola (46703) *(G-246)*

E M F Corp... 260 488-2479
7335 S Enterprise Dr Hamilton (46742) *(G-6852)*

E M P, Greenfield *Also Called: Engineered Machined Pdts Inc (G-6499)*

E M S, Indianapolis *Also Called: Engineered Medical Systems (G-8122)*

E M Woodworking... 812 486-2696
6000 N 450 E Montgomery (47558) *(G-12097)*

E P I, Indianapolis *Also Called: Epi Printers Inc (G-8129)*

E P I, Kingsbury *Also Called: Environmental Products Inc (G-10178)*

E P I, Merrillville *Also Called: Exhaust Productions Inc (G-11516)*

E S A I, South Bend *Also Called: Ed Stump Assembly Inc (G-15011)*

E S C O, Elkhart *Also Called: Elkhart Supply Corp (G-3330)*

E S I, Garrett *Also Called: Enzyme Solutions Inc (G-5861)*

E Squared Motorsports LLC............................... 317 626-2937
1511 N County Road 600 E Avon (46123) *(G-515)*

E Z Choice... 219 852-4281
5529 Calumet Ave Hammond (46320) *(G-6917)*

E Z Welding... 574 892-6417
20954 Michigan Rd Argos (46501) *(G-321)*

E-Beam Services Inc.. 765 447-6755
3400 Union St Lafayette (47905) *(G-10573)*

E-Collar Technologies Inc................................... 260 357-0051
2120 Forrest Park Dr Garrett (46738) *(G-5859)*

E-Commerce, Lizton *Also Called: Bedlam Beard Company LLC (G-11048)*

E-Motion LLC... 317 379-5761
493 Ironwood Dr Carmel (46033) *(G-1617)*

E-Pak Machinery Inc... 219 393-5541
1535 S State Road 39 La Porte (46350) *(G-10403)*

E-Tank Ltd... 317 296-0510
999 W Troy Ave Indianapolis (46225) *(G-8030)*

EAB INDUSTRIES, Evansville *Also Called: Evansville Assn For The Blind (G-4047)*

Eagle Bearing, Ltd., Evansville *Also Called: Hsm Eagle Ltd (G-4112)*

Eagle Cnc Machining Inc..................................... 765 289-2816
801 W Riggin Rd Muncie (47303) *(G-12388)*

Eagle Consulting Inc... 317 590-0485
7968 Zionsville Rd Indianapolis (46268) *(G-8031)*

Eagle Crusher Co, Aurora *Also Called: Stedman Machine Company Inc (G-457)*

Eagle Flooring Brokers Inc.................................. 260 422-6100
220 Fernhill Ave Fort Wayne (46805) *(G-4937)*

Eagle Freight Inc.. 646 634-5870
6111 Harrison St Ste 119 Merrillville (46410) *(G-11509)*

Eagle Industries Inc... 812 282-1393
131 E Court Ave Ste 200 Jeffersonville (47130) *(G-9973)*

Eagle Magnetic Company Inc............................. 317 297-1030
7417 Crawfordsville Rd Indianapolis (46214) *(G-8032)*

Eagle Mold & Tool.. 574 862-1966
1011 E Waterford St Wakarusa (46573) *(G-16232)*

Eagle Packaging Inc.. 260 281-2333
2301 W Wilden Ave Goshen (46528) *(G-6128)*

Eagle Pet Products Inc.. 574 259-7834
1025 W 11th St Mishawaka (46544) *(G-11888)*

Eagle Precision LLC.. 260 637-4649
2420 W Shoaff Rd Huntertown (46748) *(G-7254)*

Eagle Precision Machining Inc............................ 260 637-4649
2420 W Shoaff Rd Huntertown (46748) *(G-7255)*

Eagle River Coal, Evansville *Also Called: Eagle River Coal LLC (G-4024)*

ALPHABETIC SECTION

Eagle River Coal LLC 618 252-0490
250 N Cross Pointe Blvd Evansville (47715) *(G-4024)*

Eagle Tile, Fort Wayne *Also Called: Eagle Flooring Brokers Inc (G-4937)*

Earl Park Sign Shop LLC 219 474-6419
208 S Locust St Earl Park (47942) *(G-2985)*

Earl's Indy, Indianapolis *Also Called: Esco Enterprises Indiana Inc (G-8131)*

Earth Essentials LLC 260 479-0115
11012 Barrymore Run Roanoke (46783) *(G-14262)*

Earth First, Charlestown *Also Called: Earth First Kentuckiana Inc (G-1875)*

Earth First Kentuckiana Inc (PA) 812 923-1227
5511 County Road 403 Charlestown (47111) *(G-1875)*

Earth Mama Compost 317 759-4589
10830 Lafayette Rd Indianapolis (46278) *(G-8033)*

Earthcare LLC 812 455-9258
3311 E Powell Ave Evansville (47714) *(G-4025)*

Earthchain Magnetic Pro 317 803-8034
9930 E 56th St Indianapolis (46236) *(G-8034)*

Earthly-Love 708 896-0191
267 Dyer Blvd Hammond (46320) *(G-6918)*

Earthsmarte Water Indiana Inc 317 800-8442
8481 Bash St Ste 1200 Indianapolis (46250) *(G-8035)*

Earthway Products LLC 574 848-7491
1009 Maple St Bristol (46507) *(G-1258)*

Earthwise Plastics, Gas City *Also Called: Earthwise Plastics Inc (G-6036)*

Earthwise Plastics Inc 765 673-0308
100 Earthwise Way Gas City (46933) *(G-6036)*

Eash Design, Elkhart *Also Called: Eash LLC (G-3311)*

Eash LLC 574 295-4450
301 Benchmark Dr Elkhart (46516) *(G-3311)*

Easley Enterprises Inc 317 636-4516
205 N College Ave Indianapolis (46202) *(G-8036)*

Easley Winery, Indianapolis *Also Called: Easley Enterprises Inc (G-8036)*

Eason Manufacturing Inc 312 310-9430
601 Industrial Dr Ste B Griffith (46319) *(G-6803)*

East 40 Sports Apparel Inc 812 877-3695
215 Deming Ln Terre Haute (47803) *(G-15580)*

East Cast Erosion Holdings LLC (HQ) 812 867-4873
4609 E Boonville New Harmony Rd Evansville (47725) *(G-4026)*

East Chicago Shearing 219 398-2933
4303 Kennedy Ave East Chicago (46312) *(G-3004)*

East Coast Plastics, Michigan City *Also Called: Lighthouse Industries Inc (G-11633)*

East Coast Treasure Finds LLC 845 879-8744
4000 W 106th St Ste 125-154 Carmel (46032) *(G-1618)*

East Fork Studio & Press Inc 765 458-6103
104 Ne First St Brownsville (47325) *(G-1431)*

East Heat Wood Pellets LLC 317 638-4840
217 S Belmont Ave Ste E Indianapolis (46222) *(G-8037)*

East Industries LLC 812 273-4358
831 W Main St Madison (47250) *(G-11216)*

East Penn Manufacturing Co 317 236-6288
918 S Senate Ave Indianapolis (46225) *(G-8038)*

East Side Welding Inc 317 823-4065
10148 Pendleton Pike Indianapolis (46236) *(G-8039)*

East-T-West North-To-South Inc 574 264-6664
3000 County Road 6 W Elkhart (46514) *(G-3312)*

Eastern Banner Supply Corp 812 448-2222
932 W National Ave Brazil (47834) *(G-1140)*

Eastern Engineering Supply Inc 260 426-3119
1239 N Wells St Fort Wayne (46808) *(G-4938)*

Eastern Red Cedar Products LLC (PA) 812 365-2495
9611 S County Road 425 E Marengo (47140) *(G-11262)*

Easterwood, Warsaw *Also Called: Indiana Vac-Form Inc (G-16378)*

Eastlake Metals LLC 219 655-5526
2230 Indianapolis Blvd Whiting (46394) *(G-16835)*

Eastons Lettering Service 219 942-5101
514 E 3rd St Hobart (46342) *(G-7187)*

Eastside Machine Shop Inc 317 549-2216
4500 Dunn St Indianapolis (46226) *(G-8040)*

Eastside Vice Cmnty News Mdia 317 356-2222
195 N Shortridge Rd Indianapolis (46219) *(G-8041)*

Easywater, Fishers *Also Called: Freije Treatment Systems Inc (G-4527)*

Eat Da Cake LLC 765 479-4985
3764 W 92nd Ct Merrillville (46410) *(G-11510)*

Eat Here Indy LLC (PA) 317 502-4419
5255 Winthrop Ave Ste 110 Indianapolis (46220) *(G-8042)*

Eaton Corporation 260 925-3800
201 Brandon St Auburn (46706) *(G-387)*

Eaton Corporation 317 704-2520
7365 Winton Dr Indianapolis (46268) *(G-8043)*

Eaton Corporation 574 283-5004
2930 Foundation Dr South Bend (46628) *(G-15009)*

Eaton Septic Tank Company 765 396-3275
14601 N State Road 3n Eaton (47338) *(G-3060)*

Eavk Legacy Inc (PA) 812 246-4461
6000 Grant Line Rd New Albany (47150) *(G-12723)*

Ebc LLC 812 234-4111
1075 Crawford St Terre Haute (47807) *(G-15581)*

Ebenezer Press LLC 260 482-2864
2121 Kenwood Ave Fort Wayne (46805) *(G-4939)*

Ebenezer Sportswear, Gas City *Also Called: Dave Turner (G-6035)*

Ebert Machine Company Inc 765 473-3728
2177 S State Road 19 Peru (46970) *(G-13581)*

Ebey Sales & Service 260 636-3286
1037 E Baseline Rd Albion (46701) *(G-25)*

Ebony & Co Inc 260 246-4691
3721 Plaza Dr Fort Wayne (46806) *(G-4940)*

Ebp and Associates Inc 812 386-7062
115 S Hall St Princeton (47670) *(G-13990)*

Ebsc, Elkhart *Also Called: (ebs Cmpstes Engnred Bnded Str (G-3136)*

Ebwa Industries Inc 317 637-5860
1556 Deloss St Indianapolis (46201) *(G-8044)*

Echelbarger Machining Co LLC 765 252-1965
2614 Precision Dr Kokomo (46902) *(G-10261)*

Echelbrger Precision Machining, Kokomo *Also Called: Echelbarger Machining Co LLC (G-10261)*

Echo Engrg & Prod Sups Inc (PA) 317 876-8848
7150 Winton Dr Ste 300 Indianapolis (46268) *(G-8045)*

Echo Supply, Indianapolis *Also Called: Echo Engrg & Prod Sups Inc (G-8045)*

Echo, The, Bluffton *Also Called: News-Banner Publications Inc (G-1046)*

Eckart America Corporation 219 864-4861
650 W 67th Pl Ste 200 Schererville (46375) *(G-14519)*

Eckco Plastics Inc 574 258-5552
56599 Twin Branch Dr Mishawaka (46545) *(G-11889)*

Eckhart & Company Inc 317 347-2665
4011 W 54th St Indianapolis (46254) *(G-8046)*

Eckhart Woodworking Inc 260 692-6218
424 S Van Buren St Monroe (46772) *(G-12060)*

Eckstein Welding & Fabrication 812 934-2059
11385 N Delaware Rd Batesville (47006) *(G-586)*

Eclipse Inc (HQ) 201 E 18th St Muncie (47302) *(G-12389)*

Eclipse Imports, Indianapolis *Also Called: Futon Factory Inc (G-8245)*

Eclipse Molding Company LLC 812 546-0050
199 Raymond St Hope (47246) *(G-7223)*

Eco Golf, Knox *Also Called: Hoosier Custom Plastics LLC (G-10210)*

Eco Owl Press LLC 574 703-3941
626 Portage Ave South Bend (46616) *(G-15010)*

Eco Parking Technologies LLC 866 897-1234
8001 Castleway Dr Indianapolis (46250) *(G-8047)*

Eco Partners Inc 317 450-3346
515 Twin Oaks Dr Carmel (46032) *(G-1619)*

Eco Services Operations Corp 219 932-7651
2000 Michigan St Hammond (46320) *(G-6919)*

Eco Vehicle Systems LLC 765 964-6009
1274 S State Road 32 Union City (47390) *(G-15852)*

Eco Water of Southern Indiana 812 734-1407
7685 Highway 135 Ne New Salisbury (47161) *(G-12984)*

Eco-Bat America LLC 317 247-1303
7870 W Morris St Indianapolis (46231) *(G-8048)*

Ecobat Resources Cal Inc 317 247-1303
7870 W Morris St Indianapolis (46231) *(G-8049)*

Ecojacks LLC 574 306-0414
503 E Broad St South Whitley (46787) *(G-15317)*

Ecolab Equipment Care ALPHABETIC SECTION

Ecolab Equipment Care, Fishers Also Called: Ecolab Inc *(G-4508)*

Ecolab Inc.. 317 567-2876
11973 Exit 5 Pkwy Fishers (46037) *(G-4508)*

Ecolab Inc.. 260 359-3280
970 E Tipton St Huntington (46750) *(G-7308)*

Ecolab Inc.. 260 375-4710
2847 E 600 S Warren (46792) *(G-16297)*

Economy Dumpster... 317 308-7774
6116 Burlington Ave Indianapolis (46220) *(G-8050)*

Economy Electric Htg & Coolg... 219 923-4441
9031 Grace St Highland (46322) *(G-7134)*

Economy Offset Printers Inc.. 574 534-6270
2516 Industrial Park Dr Ste A Goshen (46526) *(G-6129)*

Economy Signs, Hammond Also Called: Economy Signs Incorporated *(G-6920)*

Economy Signs Incorporated... 219 932-1233
546 Conkey St Hammond (46324) *(G-6920)*

Econotec Inc... 812 299-1642
4677 E Mclean Dr Terre Haute (47802) *(G-15582)*

Ecowater, New Salisbury Also Called: Eco Water of Southern Indiana *(G-12984)*

Ecp American Steel LLC (HQ).. 260 478-9101
3122 Engle Rd Fort Wayne (46809) *(G-4941)*

Ecp American Steel LLC... 574 257-9424
5005 Lincolnway E Ste B Mishawaka (46544) *(G-11890)*

Ecpca Safe-Way LLC (PA)... 574 267-4861
3814 E Us Highway 30 Warsaw (46580) *(G-16354)*

ECR Fuel, Ladoga Also Called: Emerald Cast Rnewable Fuel LLC *(G-10507)*

Ect, Richmond Also Called: E C T Franklin Control Systems *(G-14117)*

Ecu, Fishers Also Called: Enginring Cncpts Unlimited Inc *(G-4514)*

Ed Henry & Son... 765 675-7235
3340 S 400 W Tipton (46072) *(G-15771)*

Ed Lloyd Co.. 812 342-2505
13240 S 100 W Columbus (47201) *(G-2294)*

Ed Nickels... 219 887-6128
5793 Taney Pl Merrillville (46410) *(G-11511)*

Ed Sons Inc (PA)... 317 897-8821
8335 Pendleton Pike Indianapolis (46226) *(G-8051)*

Ed Stump Assembly Inc... 574 291-0058
60856 Us 31 S South Bend (46614) *(G-15011)*

Edco Welding and Hydraulic Inc.. 317 783-2323
1815 Kentucky Ave Indianapolis (46221) *(G-8052)*

Edcoat Limited Partnership... 574 654-9105
30350 Edison Rd New Carlisle (46552) *(G-12839)*

Eddie S Guitars... 219 689-7007
2111 Northwinds Dr Dyer (46311) *(G-2973)*

Edelweiss Edge LLC... 260 399-6692
5316 Hopkinton Dr Fort Wayne (46814) *(G-4942)*

Eden Foods Inc.. 765 396-3344
201 E Babb Rd Eaton (47338) *(G-3061)*

Eder Bros LLC.. 219 718-3335
1243 Primrose Ln Schererville (46375) *(G-14520)*

Edge Manufacturing Inc.. 260 827-0482
1274 S Adams St Bluffton (46714) *(G-1035)*

Edge Technologies Inc.. 317 408-0116
4455 W 62nd St Indianapolis (46268) *(G-8053)*

Edgeband USA, Jeffersonville Also Called: Pleasant Hill Veneer Corp *(G-10039)*

Edgetek Inc.. 812 868-1250
10600 Highway 57 Evansville (47725) *(G-4027)*

Edgewood Building Supply, Carmel Also Called: Brickworks Supply Center LLC *(G-1573)*

Edgewood Metal Fab LLC.. 574 546-5947
1265 B Rd Bremen (46506) *(G-1190)*

Edibleindy, Indianapolis Also Called: Rubenstein LLC *(G-9346)*

Edinburgh Connector Co LLC.. 812 526-8801
908 S Walnut St Edinburgh (46124) *(G-3082)*

Edinburgh Signs & Grapics... 812 526-6626
500 1/2 W Center Cross St Edinburgh (46124) *(G-3083)*

Editarts... 317 702-1215
4503 N College Ave Indianapolis (46205) *(G-8054)*

Editions Ltd Gllery Fine Art I... 317 466-9940
838 E 65th St Indianapolis (46220) *(G-8055)*

EDM Services Inc... 574 784-3042
18599 Osborne Rd Lakeville (46536) *(G-10791)*

EDM Specialties Inc.. 317 856-4700
7746 Milhouse Rd Indianapolis (46241) *(G-8056)*

EDS, Indianapolis Also Called: Endowment Development Services *(G-8114)*

EDS, Jeffersonville Also Called: Energy Delivery Solutions LLC *(G-9977)*

Eds Crane Service... 317 535-7385
660 Parkway St Whiteland (46184) *(G-16783)*

Eds Machine & Tool... 812 295-7264
1250 Mount Pleasant Rd Loogootee (47553) *(G-11135)*

EDS Teez LLC.. 224 518-3388
6312 Madison Ave Apt 2 Hammond (46324) *(G-6921)*

Eds Wood Craft... 812 768-6617
300 E Gibson St Haubstadt (47639) *(G-7084)*

Edsal Inc.. 219 427-1294
700 Chase St Ste 400 Gary (46404) *(G-5925)*

Edsal Manufacturing Co LLC.. 773 254-0600
700 Chase St Ste 400 Gary (46404) *(G-5926)*

Edutronics.. 765 529-6751
3707 S Memorial Dr New Castle (47362) *(G-12859)*

Edw C Levy Co.. 765 364-9251
New Core Rd Crawfordsville (47933) *(G-2565)*

Edward E Petri Company... 317 636-5007
20 N Meridian St Ste 206 Indianapolis (46204) *(G-8057)*

Edward Emmons.. 209 352-1475
11576 W 400 N Michigan City (46360) *(G-11606)*

Edwards Pace Co.. 574 522-5337
28858 Ventura Dr Elkhart (46517) *(G-3313)*

Edwards Steel Inc... 317 462-9451
2042 E Main St Greenfield (46140) *(G-6492)*

Edwin Coe LLC.. 260 438-7678
6675 E Us Highway 33 Churubusco (46723) *(G-1984)*

Edwin Coe Spirits, Churubusco Also Called: Edwin Coe LLC *(G-1984)*

Edwin Rahn.. 260 622-7178
706 Millside Ct Ossian (46777) *(G-13423)*

Edys Grd Ice Cream, Fort Wayne Also Called: Dreyers Grand Ice Cream Inc *(G-4928)*

Eemsco, Evansville Also Called: Eemsco Inc *(G-4028)*

Eemsco Inc.. 812 426-2224
600 W Eichel Ave Evansville (47710) *(G-4028)*

Efficient Plas Solutions Inc... 574 965-4690
9745 N 850 W Delphi (46923) *(G-2896)*

Efil Pharmaceuticals Corp... 765 491-7247
3706 Litchfield Pl West Lafayette (47906) *(G-16579)*

EFP, Elkhart Also Called: Efp LLC *(G-3314)*

Efp LLC (HQ).. 574 295-4690
223 Middleton Run Rd Elkhart (46516) *(G-3314)*

Efp LLC.. 812 602-0019
14636 Foundation Ave Evansville (47725) *(G-4029)*

Eften Inc.. 260 982-1544
906 W Hanley Rd North Manchester (46962) *(G-13233)*

Efurnituremax LLC.. 317 697-9504
8070 Castleton Rd # 117 Indianapolis (46250) *(G-8058)*

Egenolf Contg & Rigging II Inc... 317 787-5301
350 Wisconsin St Indianapolis (46225) *(G-8059)*

Egenolf Enterprise Inc... 317 501-5069
2855 N Evanklin Rd Ste Indianapolis (46226) *(G-8060)*

Egenolf Machine Inc.. 317 787-5301
2916 Bluff Rd Ste A Indianapolis (46225) *(G-8061)*

Egg Innovations, Warsaw Also Called: Egg Innovations LLC *(G-16355)*

Egg Innovations LLC (PA)... 574 267-7545
4799 W 100 N Warsaw (46580) *(G-16355)*

Egg Innvtons Organic Feeds LLC... 800 337-1951
578 Jefferson St Gary (46402) *(G-5927)*

Egglife Foods Inc... 219 261-5500
911 N 1200 W Wolcott (47995) *(G-16929)*

Eggpress LLC.. 574 267-2847
4217 W Old Road 30 Warsaw (46580) *(G-16356)*

EH Baare Corporation (PA)... 765 778-7895
3620 W 73rd St Anderson (46011) *(G-113)*

Ehob LLC... 317 972-4600
250 N Belmont Ave Indianapolis (46222) *(G-8062)*

Ehrgotts Signs & Stamps Inc... 317 353-2222
12001 E Washington St Ste B Indianapolis (46229) *(G-8063)*

ALPHABETIC SECTION — Elengas Customwear

Eichers Sawmill 260 624-5882
  6395 E 450 S Hamilton (46742) *(G-6853)*

Eidp Inc (HQ) 833 267-8382
  974 Centre Rd Bldg 735 Indianapolis (46268) *(G-8064)*

Eidp Inc 812 299-6700
  11 W Litesse Dr Terre Haute (47802) *(G-15583)*

Eidp Inc 219 462-4587
  218 N 250 W Valparaiso (46385) *(G-15938)*

Eight Ten Twelve LLC 317 773-8532
  954 Conner St Indianapolis (46201) *(G-8065)*

Eiler Marketing, Jeffersonville *Also Called: Em Global LLC (G-9976)*

Eis Fibercoating Inc 574 722-5192
  616 E Main St Logansport (46947) *(G-11071)*

Eis Packaging Machinery Inc 574 870-0087
  4754 E County Road 75 N Logansport (46947) *(G-11072)*

Eiseles Honey LLC 317 896-5830
  8146 Zionsville Rd Indianapolis (46268) *(G-8066)*

EJ Bognar Incorporated 412 344-9900
  23810 Highland St Schneider (46376) *(G-14549)*

EJ Brooks Company (HQ) 800 348-4777
  409 Hoosier Dr Angola (46703) *(G-247)*

Ej Usa Inc 765 744-1184
  201 N Illinois St Ste 1900 Indianapolis (46204) *(G-8067)*

Eje Industries LLC 574 326-3269
  2610 Sterling Ave Elkhart (46516) *(G-3315)*

Ejl Tech 812 374-8808
  461 S Mapleton St Ste B Columbus (47201) *(G-2295)*

Ekmi, Fort Wayne *Also Called: Elringklinger Mfg Ind Inc (G-4947)*

Ekos Manufacturing LLC 847 630-9717
  365 S Post Rd Indianapolis (46219) *(G-8068)*

El Mexicano Inc 260 456-6843
  2301 Fairfield Ave Ste 102 Fort Wayne (46807) *(G-4943)*

El Mexicano Newspaper, Fort Wayne *Also Called: El Mexicano Inc (G-4943)*

El Popular, Valparaiso *Also Called: El Popular Sausage Factory LLC (G-15939)*

El Popular Inc 219 397-3728
  910 E Chicago Ave East Chicago (46312) *(G-3005)*

El Popular Sausage Factory LLC 219 476-7040
  1251 Transport Dr Ste C Valparaiso (46383) *(G-15939)*

El Shaddai Inc 260 359-9080
  2819 Wal Mart Dr Ste D Huntington (46750) *(G-7309)*

Elan Corp PLC 317 442-1502
  11237 Wedgefield Ct Fishers (46037) *(G-4509)*

Elanco Animal Health, Fishers *Also Called: Eli Lilly and Company (G-4511)*

Elanco Animal Health, Greenfield *Also Called: Elanco Animal Health Inc (G-6493)*

Elanco Animal Health, Indianapolis *Also Called: Eli Lilly and Company (G-8074)*

Elanco Animal Health, Indianapolis *Also Called: Eli Lilly and Company (G-8075)*

Elanco Animal Health, Indianapolis *Also Called: Eli Lilly and Company (G-8077)*

Elanco Animal Health, Indianapolis *Also Called: Eli Lilly and Company (G-8080)*

Elanco Animal Health, Indianapolis *Also Called: Eli Lilly and Company (G-8082)*

Elanco Animal Health, Indianapolis *Also Called: Eli Lilly and Company (G-8085)*

Elanco Animal Health, Indianapolis *Also Called: Eli Lilly and Company (G-8087)*

Elanco Animal Health Inc (PA) 877 352-6261
  2500 Innovation Way N Greenfield (46140) *(G-6493)*

Elanco Anmal Hlth A Div Eli Ll, Plainfield *Also Called: Eli Lilly and Company (G-13678)*

Elanco International Inc (HQ) 877 352-6261
  2500 Innovation Way N Greenfield (46140) *(G-6494)*

Elanco US Inc 765 832-4400
  10500 S State Road 63 Clinton (47842) *(G-2066)*

Elanco US Inc (HQ) 877 352-6261
  2500 Innovation Way N Greenfield (46140) *(G-6495)*

Elanco US Inc 812 242-5999
  1445 S 1st St Terre Haute (47802) *(G-15584)*

Elder Group Inc 765 966-7676
  4251 W Industries Rd Richmond (47374) *(G-14118)*

Eldon France 765 793-2743
  1484 S Stringtown Rd Covington (47932) *(G-2529)*

Eldorado National Kansas Inc (HQ) 785 827-1033
  2367 Century Dr Goshen (46528) *(G-6130)*

Electonic Systems Division, Fort Wayne *Also Called: L3harris Technologies Inc (G-5170)*

Electri-Cable Assemblies, Fort Wayne *Also Called: Premier Mfg Group Inc (G-5345)*

Electri-Tec, Angola *Also Called: Electric-Tec LLC (G-248)*

Electri-Tec, Angola *Also Called: Parkway Investor Group Inc (G-281)*

Electric Coating Tech LLC 219 378-1930
  4407 Railroad Ave East Chicago (46312) *(G-3006)*

Electric Motor Services Inc (PA) 219 931-2850
  6350 Indianapolis Blvd Hammond (46320) *(G-6922)*

Electric Motors and Spc 260 357-4141
  701 W King St Garrett (46738) *(G-5860)*

Electric Mtr Repr & Rewind Inc 812 284-5059
  1502 Research Dr Jeffersonville (47130) *(G-9974)*

Electric Plus 812 336-4992
  1030 W 17th St Bloomington (47404) *(G-860)*

Electric Plus Inc 317 718-0100
  173 S County Road 525 E Avon (46123) *(G-516)*

Electric Power Service, Fort Wayne *Also Called: Eps Enterprises Inc (G-4957)*

Electric-Tec LLC 260 665-1252
  509 Growth Pkwy Angola (46703) *(G-248)*

Electrical Motor Products Inc 877 455-1599
  15009 Dunton Rd Fort Wayne (46845) *(G-4944)*

Electrical Technology Service, Martinsville *Also Called: Franklin Olin (G-11396)*

Electrik Connection Inc 219 362-4581
  106 Washington St La Porte (46350) *(G-10404)*

Electro Corp 219 393-5571
  1st Rd Kingsbury Industrial Park Kingsbury (46345) *(G-10177)*

Electro Seal Corporation 219 926-8606
  914 Broadway Chesterton (46304) *(G-1922)*

Electro-Coat Technologies 574 266-7356
  2501 Jeanwood Dr Elkhart (46514) *(G-3316)*

Electro-Spec Inc 317 738-9199
  1800 Commerce Pkwy Franklin (46131) *(G-5728)*

Electro-Tech Inc 219 937-0826
  5334 Sohl Ave Hammond (46320) *(G-6923)*

Electrocoat Technologies, Elkhart *Also Called: Dexter Chassis Group Inc (G-3294)*

Electrocraft Inc 812 385-3013
  901 S 1st St Princeton (47670) *(G-13991)*

Electromechanical RES Labs 812 948-8484
  2560 Charlestown Rd New Albany (47150) *(G-12724)*

Electron Beam Welding, Indianapolis *Also Called: Ebwa Industries Inc (G-8044)*

Electronic Services LLC 765 457-3894
  1942 S Elizabeth St Kokomo (46902) *(G-10262)*

Electronic Tool Associates, Elkhart *Also Called: Learman Electronic Tool Assoc (G-3481)*

Electronics Incorporated 574 256-5001
  56790 Magnetic Dr Mishawaka (46545) *(G-11891)*

Electronics Research Inc (PA) 812 925-6000
  7777 Gardner Rd Chandler (47610) *(G-1861)*

Elegan Customwear, Valparaiso *Also Called: Elegan Sportswear Inc (G-15941)*

Elegan Graphics 219 462-9921
  5905 Murvihill Rd Valparaiso (46383) *(G-15940)*

Elegan Sportswear Inc 219 464-8416
  212 Lincolnway Valparaiso (46383) *(G-15941)*

Elegant Eyes LLC 317 640-1995
  1271 Barngate Cir Greenwood (46142) *(G-6692)*

Elegant Needleworks Inc 765 284-9427
  7500 N Janna Dr Muncie (47303) *(G-12390)*

Elektrisola Incorporated 317 375-8192
  2400 N Shadeland Ave Ste B Indianapolis (46219) *(G-8069)*

Elektrsola Dr Gerd Schldbach G 260 421-5400
  4300 New Haven Ave Fort Wayne (46803) *(G-4945)*

Elektrsola Dr Gerd Schldbach G 765 477-8000
  2800 Concord Rd Lafayette (47909) *(G-10574)*

Element Armament 317 530-9013
  51 N Us Highway 31 Whiteland (46184) *(G-16784)*

Element Armament LLC 317 442-7924
  5120 N 400 W Bargersville (46106) *(G-565)*

Element Clumbus 812 526-2329
  8800 N Us Highway 31 Columbus (47201) *(G-2296)*

Elemental S A Protection 765 717-7325
  509 N Forest Ave Muncie (47304) *(G-12391)*

Elements Elearning LLC 317 986-2113
  4543 Melbourne Rd Indianapolis (46228) *(G-8070)*

Elengas Customwear 317 577-1677
  12463 Norman Pl Fishers (46037) *(G-4510)*

Elevate Wellness Corporation.. 317 370-9852 480 W Poplar St Zionsville (46077) *(G-17004)*		**Elite Printing Inc (PA)**.. 317 257-2744 2138 E 52nd St Indianapolis (46205) *(G-8094)*	
Elevated Cnstr Group LLC... 708 731-7232 405 Florence St Hammond (46324) *(G-6924)*		**Elite Protective Coatings**.. 317 476-1712 3632 Woodland Streams Dr Greenwood (46143) *(G-6693)*	
Elevator Equipment Corporation...................................... 765 966-7761 2230 Nw 12th St Richmond (47374) *(G-14119)*		**Elite Transit LLC**.. 317 507-2126 9210 Tenor Dr Indianapolis (46231) *(G-8095)*	
Elevator One LLC... 317 634-8001 120 E Market St Indianapolis (46204) *(G-8071)*		**Elixir Industries**.. 574 259-7133 5201 Lincolnway E Mishawaka (46544) *(G-11892)*	
Elf Machinery LLC.. 219 393-5541 1535 S State Road 39 La Porte (46350) *(G-10405)*		**Elizabeth A Taylor**.. 815 353-4798 7675 Ault Rd Freedom (47431) *(G-5799)*	
Elgin Fastener Group LLC... 812 689-8917 1415 S Benham Rd Versailles (47042) *(G-16099)*		**Elkcases Inc**... 574 295-7700 23143 Heaton Vis Elkhart (46514) *(G-3317)*	
Eli Lilly and Company... 317 748-1622 12023 Quarry Ct Fishers (46037) *(G-4511)*		**Elkhart Bedding Co Inc**... 574 293-6200 2124 Sterling Ave Elkhart (46516) *(G-3318)*	
Eli Lilly and Company... 317 276-2000 Lilly Corporate Center Indianapolis (46285) *(G-8072)*		**Elkhart Binding Inc**.. 574 522-5455 51784 State Road 19 Elkhart (46514) *(G-3319)*	
Eli Lilly and Company... 317 276-7907 1280 S Dakota St Indianapolis (46225) *(G-8073)*		**Elkhart Brass**.. 574 266-3700 1302 W Beardsley Ave Elkhart (46514) *(G-3320)*	
Eli Lilly and Company... 317 276-2118 639 S Delaware St Indianapolis (46225) *(G-8074)*		**Elkhart Brass Manufacturing Co**.. 800 346-0250 1302 W Beardsley Ave Elkhart (46514) *(G-3321)*	
Eli Lilly and Company... 317 276-2000 2301 Executive Dr Indianapolis (46241) *(G-8075)*		**Elkhart Brass Manufacturing Company Inc (DH)**.................... 574 295-8330 1302 W Beardsley Ave Elkhart (46514) *(G-3322)*	
Eli Lilly and Company... 317 276-2000 450 S Meridian St Indianapolis (46225) *(G-8076)*		**Elkhart Bristol Corp**... 574 264-7600 1850 E Bristol St Elkhart (46514) *(G-3323)*	
Eli Lilly and Company... 317 276-5925 1402 S Dakota St Indianapolis (46225) *(G-8077)*		**Elkhart Cases Inc**.. 574 295-7700 23143 Heaton Vis Elkhart (46514) *(G-3324)*	
Eli Lilly and Company... 317 276-2000 427 S Illinois St Indianapolis (46225) *(G-8078)*		**Elkhart County Gravel Inc**.. 574 825-7913 56570 County Road 35 Middlebury (46540) *(G-11714)*	
Eli Lilly and Company... 317 651-7790 1223 S Harding St Indianapolis (46221) *(G-8079)*		**Elkhart County Gravel Inc (PA)**.. 574 831-2815 19242 Us Highway 6 New Paris (46553) *(G-12951)*	
Eli Lilly and Company... 317 277-0147 30 S Meridian St 5th Fl Indianapolis (46204) *(G-8080)*		**Elkhart County Gravel Inc**.. 574 831-2815 2042 W 300 N Warsaw (46582) *(G-16357)*	
Eli Lilly and Company... 317 276-2000 1223 W Morris St Indianapolis (46221) *(G-8081)*		**Elkhart Electronics**.. 574 679-4627 59425 Apple Rd Osceola (46561) *(G-13390)*	
Eli Lilly and Company... 317 276-2000 2401 Directors Row Indianapolis (46241) *(G-8082)*		**Elkhart Hinge Co Inc**... 574 293-2841 1839 W Lusher Ave Elkhart (46517) *(G-3325)*	
Eli Lilly and Company... 317 276-2000 1400 W Raymond St Indianapolis (46221) *(G-8083)*		**Elkhart Laser Products LLC**... 574 304-7242 116 Parker Ave Elkhart (46516) *(G-3326)*	
Eli Lilly and Company... 317 276-7907 355 E Merrill St Indianapolis (46225) *(G-8084)*		**Elkhart Plastics Inc**... 574 370-1079 316 Lake Shore Dr Michigan City (46360) *(G-11607)*	
Eli Lilly and Company... 317 276-2000 1555 S Harding St Indianapolis (46221) *(G-8085)*		**Elkhart Plating Corp**.. 574 294-1800 1913 14th St Elkhart (46516) *(G-3327)*	
Eli Lilly and Company... 317 277-1307 1 Lilly Corporate Ctr Indianapolis (46285) *(G-8086)*		**Elkhart Products Corporation (HQ)**... 574 264-3181 1255 Oak St Elkhart (46514) *(G-3328)*	
Eli Lilly and Company... 317 276-2000 1200 Kentucky Ave Indianapolis (46221) *(G-8087)*		**Elkhart Steel Service Inc (PA)**... 574 262-2552 23321 C R 106 Elkhart (46514) *(G-3329)*	
Eli Lilly and Company (PA).. 317 276-2000 Lilly Corporate Ctr Indianapolis (46285) *(G-8088)*		**Elkhart Supply Corp**.. 574 264-4156 1126 Kent St Elkhart (46514) *(G-3330)*	
Eli Lilly and Company... 317 276-2000 893 S Delaware St Indianapolis (46225) *(G-8089)*		**Elkhart Tool and Die Inc**... 574 295-8500 2400 15th St Elkhart (46517) *(G-3331)*	
Eli Lilly and Company... 317 433-3624 2222 Stanley Rd Plainfield (46168) *(G-13678)*		**Elkhart Tri-Went Industrial, Geneva** Also Called: Eti LLC *(G-6049)*	
Eli Lilly and Company... 812 242-5900 1445 S 1st St Terre Haute (47802) *(G-15585)*		**Elkhart Truth, The, Elkhart** Also Called: Truth Publishing Company Inc *(G-3750)*	
Eli Lilly Interamerica Inc (HQ)... 317 276-2000 Lilly Corporate Center Indianapolis (46285) *(G-8090)*		**Elkhart Yard, Elkhart** Also Called: Legacy Vulcan LLC *(G-3483)*	
Eli Lilly International Corp (HQ).. 317 276-2000 893 S Delaware St Indianapolis (46225) *(G-8091)*		**Elko Inc**... 812 473-8400 940 N Boeke Rd Evansville (47711) *(G-4030)*	
Eliba Collections LLC... 646 675-6196 512 Genisis Dr Whiteland (46184) *(G-16785)*		**Elko Plastic Fabricators Div, Evansville** Also Called: Elko Inc *(G-4030)*	
Elite Construction Northwest... 888 811-0212 5164 E 81st Ave Ste 13 Merrillville (46410) *(G-11512)*		**Ellerbrock Welding LLC**.. 559 978-2651 277 N Hillsboro Rd New Castle (47362) *(G-12860)*	
Elite Crete Systems Inc (PA).. 219 465-7671 1151 Transport Dr Valparaiso (46383) *(G-15942)*		**Ellinger Mfg Tech LLC**... 574 303-2086 55015 Currant Rd Mishawaka (46545) *(G-11893)*	
Elite Hand Car Wash & More LLC..................................... 317 500-8308 8403 E Us Highway 36 Ste C Avon (46123) *(G-517)*		**Elliott Co of Indianapolis**.. 317 291-1213 9200 Zionsville Rd Indianapolis (46268) *(G-8096)*	
Elite Industries LLC... 317 407-6869 6331 Muirfield Way Indianapolis (46237) *(G-8092)*		**Elliott Company, Indianapolis** Also Called: Elliott Co of Indianapolis *(G-8096)*	
Elite Packaging LLC.. 502 232-2596 100 Technology Way Jeffersonville (47130) *(G-9975)*		**Elliott Mfg & Fabrication**... 812 865-0516 2302 W Coffee Dr N Paoli (47454) *(G-13493)*	
Elite Printing Inc.. 317 781-9701 4239 Madison Ave Indianapolis (46227) *(G-8093)*		**Elliott Smith Interiors LLC**.. 317 966-5101 7650 W 96th St Zionsville (46077) *(G-17005)*	
		Elliott-Williams Company Inc... 317 453-2295 3500 E 20th St Indianapolis (46218) *(G-8097)*	
		Ellis Machine Shop LLC... 812 779-7477 1318 E 870 N Hazleton (47640) *(G-7094)*	

ALPHABETIC SECTION — Empire Industries Inc

Ellison Bakery LLC 800 711-8091
4108 W Ferguson Rd Fort Wayne (46809) *(G-4946)*

Elm Packaging, Decatur *Also Called: Tp/Elm Acquisition Sbusid Inc (G-2886)*

Elmers Service LLC 260 463-8287
1880 W 300 N Howe (46746) *(G-7234)*

Elmos 574 371-2050
1900 Plaza Dr Warsaw (46580) *(G-16358)*

Elmotec-Statolmat 260 758-8300
10214 Chestnut Dr Ste 211 Markle (46770) *(G-11355)*

Elpers Truck Equipment LLC 812 423-5787
8136 Baumgart Rd Evansville (47725) *(G-4031)*

Elringklinger Mfg Ind Inc 734 788-1776
2677 Persistence Dr Fort Wayne (46808) *(G-4947)*

Els Inc 812 985-2272
10435 Upper Mount Vernon Rd Evansville (47712) *(G-4032)*

Elsa, Elwood *Also Called: Elsa LLC (G-3821)*

Elsa, Elwood *Also Called: Elsa Corporation (G-3822)*

Elsa LLC 765 552-5200
1240 S State Road 37 Elwood (46036) *(G-3821)*

Elsa Corporation (DH) 765 552-5200
1240 S State Road 37 Elwood (46036) *(G-3822)*

Elsie Manufacturing Company 260 837-8841
600 W Maple St Waterloo (46793) *(G-16519)*

Elucence Products, Indianapolis *Also Called: Kenra Professional LLC (G-8673)*

Elvin L Nuest Sales and Servic 219 863-5216
420 S Bill St Francesville (47946) *(G-5639)*

Elwood Fuel and Cigs LLC 317 244-5744
1050 S High School Rd Indianapolis (46241) *(G-8098)*

Elwood Operations, Richmond *Also Called: Mosey Manufacturing Co Inc (G-14169)*

Elwood Publishing Company Inc 765 724-4469
1 Harrison Sq Alexandria (46001) *(G-50)*

Elwood Publishing Company Inc (HQ) 765 552-3355
317 S Anderson St Elwood (46036) *(G-3823)*

Elwood Publishing Company Inc 765 675-2115
116 S Main St Ste A Tipton (46072) *(G-15772)*

Elysian Company LLC 574 267-2259
110 E Center St Warsaw (46580) *(G-16359)*

Em Black Oxide 574 233-4933
3702 W Sample St Ste 4052 South Bend (46619) *(G-15012)*

Em Global LLC 812 258-9993
326 E Court Ave Jeffersonville (47130) *(G-9976)*

Em Printing & Embroidery LLC 812 373-0082
2221 Pear Tree Ct Columbus (47201) *(G-2297)*

EM&s, Garrett *Also Called: Electric Motors and Spc (G-5860)*

Emarsys North America Inc 630 395-2944
10 W Market St Ste 1350 Indianapolis (46204) *(G-8099)*

Ember Recrtl Vehicles Inc 844 732-4204
710 Commerce Dr Bristol (46507) *(G-1259)*

Embosstek 260 484-7700
7525 Maplecrest Rd Fort Wayne (46835) *(G-4948)*

Embree Machine Inc 812 275-5729
1435 Greer Ln Springville (47462) *(G-15385)*

Embroidered Planet 812 599-7951
314 E 1st St Madison (47250) *(G-11217)*

Embroidery By Jackie 765 438-6240
11489 E County Road 600 N Forest (46039) *(G-4700)*

Embroidery Concepts 812 988-6499
4689 Point Idalawn Dr Unionville (47468) *(G-15874)*

Embroidery Design Inc 260 625-5538
2205 Braemar Dr Fort Wayne (46814) *(G-4949)*

Embroidery Designs, Monticello *Also Called: Unique Graphic Designs Inc (G-12175)*

Embroidery Express, Terre Haute *Also Called: Mary Duncan (G-15636)*

Embroidery N Beyond 540 903-4861
2048 Whitetail Ct Avon (46123) *(G-518)*

Embroidery Plus Inc 317 243-3445
5514 W Washington St Indianapolis (46241) *(G-8100)*

Embroidery Sew Into It LLC 317 734-3891
9130 Otis Ave Ste C Indianapolis (46216) *(G-8101)*

Embroidery Solutions LLC 812 923-9152
8301 Pekin Rd Ste 1 Greenville (47124) *(G-6651)*

Embroidery Unlimited 812 265-4575
220 E Main St Madison (47250) *(G-11218)*

Embroidme 219 465-1400
2254 Morthland Dr Valparaiso (46385) *(G-15943)*

Embroidme, Avon *Also Called: Tma Enterprises Inc (G-553)*

EMC Precision Machining II LLC 317 758-4451
701 S Main St Sheridan (46069) *(G-14822)*

EMC Stamping, La Porte *Also Called: Dwyer Instruments Inc (G-10402)*

Emc2 .... 317 435-8021
3539 N Colorado Ave Indianapolis (46218) *(G-8102)*

Emco Gears Inc 317 243-3836
703 S Girls School Rd Indianapolis (46231) *(G-8103)*

Emerald Cast Rnewable Fuel LLC 765 942-5019
329 W College St Ladoga (47954) *(G-10507)*

Emerge Curriculum Pubg LLC 317 523-2687
5330 E 38th St Indianapolis (46218) *(G-8104)*

Emergency Radio Service LLC 800 377-2929
9144 N 900 W Ligonier (46767) *(G-11011)*

Emergency Radio Service LLC (PA) 206 894-4145
592 W Perry Rd Ligonier (46767) *(G-11012)*

Emerson, Carmel *Also Called: Emerson Electric Co (G-1620)*

Emerson, Indianapolis *Also Called: Emerson Electric Co (G-8105)*

Emerson, Valparaiso *Also Called: Emerson Electric Co (G-15944)*

Emerson Climate Technologies, Greenfield *Also Called: Copeland LP (G-6483)*

Emerson Electric Co 317 574-3170
1517 Springmill Ponds Blvd Carmel (46032) *(G-1620)*

Emerson Electric Co 317 322-2055
8320 Brookville Rd Ste E Indianapolis (46239) *(G-8105)*

Emerson Electric Co 219 465-2411
2300 Evans Ave Valparaiso (46383) *(G-15944)*

Emerson Industrial Automation 574 583-9171
705 N 6th St Monticello (47960) *(G-12148)*

Emery Winslow Scale Co., Terre Haute *Also Called: A H Emery Company (G-15527)*

Emge Foods LLC 317 894-7777
5593 W Us Highway 40 Greenfield (46140) *(G-6496)*

Emi LLC 812 437-9100
5701 Old Boonville Hwy Evansville (47715) *(G-4033)*

EMI Quality Plating, Evansville *Also Called: Emi LLC (G-4033)*

EMI Quality Plating, Evansville *Also Called: Evantek Manufacturing Inds LLC (G-4061)*

Eminence Hlth Care Stffing AGC 866 350-6400
2015 W Western Ave Ste 201 South Bend (46619) *(G-15013)*

EMJ Metals 317 838-8899
2301 Airwest Blvd Plainfield (46168) *(G-13679)*

Emma Pearls Creations LLC 219 200-2277
2158 45th St Highland (46322) *(G-7135)*

Emmantony Productions 765 649-5967
1730 Lora St Anderson (46013) *(G-114)*

Emmanuel Michael 806 559-5673
2027 Prairie Sky Ln Greenwood (46143) *(G-6694)*

Emmis Communications, Indianapolis *Also Called: Emmis Corporation (G-8106)*

Emmis Corporation (PA) 317 266-0100
40 Monument Cir Ste 700 Indianapolis (46204) *(G-8106)*

Emmis Operating Company (HQ) 317 266-0100
40 Monument Cir Ste 700 Indianapolis (46204) *(G-8107)*

Emmis Publishing LP (HQ) 317 266-0100
40 Monument Cir Ste 100 Indianapolis (46204) *(G-8108)*

Emmis Publishing Corporation (HQ) 317 266-0100
40 Monument Cir Ste 700 Indianapolis (46204) *(G-8109)*

Emmons Model Aircraft Company, Michigan City *Also Called: Edward Emmons (G-11606)*

Emond Eldon 219 279-2442
3522 N 900 W Wolcott (47995) *(G-16930)*

Emond's Drainage Service, Wolcott *Also Called: Emond Eldon (G-16930)*

Emp, Fishers *Also Called: Enterprise Marking Pdts Inc (G-4516)*

Emp, Greenfield *Also Called: Engineered Machined Pdts Inc (G-6498)*

Emp of Evansville 812 962-1309
4 Chestnut St Evansville (47713) *(G-4034)*

Emp Solutions Inc 937 608-0283
11650 Lantern Rd Ste 105 Fishers (46038) *(G-4512)*

Empire Contractors Inc 812 424-3865
2200 Lexington Rd Evansville (47720) *(G-4035)*

Empire Industries Inc 260 908-0996
5631 County Road 16 Butler (46721) *(G-1463)*

Empire Lacross & Sports LLC 317 497-8918
9700 Lake Shore Dr E B Indianapolis (46280) *(G-7382)*

Empirical Themes LLC 260 431-1437
12103 Thornapple Cv Fort Wayne (46845) *(G-4950)*

Emplify LLC 800 580-5344
8626 E 116th St Fishers (46038) *(G-4513)*

Empro Manufacturing Co Inc 317 823-3000
10920 E 59th St Indianapolis (46236) *(G-8110)*

Emprotech Steel Services LLC 219 326-6900
3234 N State Road 39 La Porte (46350) *(G-10406)*

Emquip Corporation 317 849-3977
4359 E 75th St Indianapolis (46250) *(G-8111)*

Enbi, Shelbyville *Also Called: Enbi Global Inc (G-14754)*

Enbi Global Inc (PA) 317 395-7324
1703 Mccall Dr Shelbyville (46176) *(G-14754)*

ENBI INDIANA INC (PA) 317 398-3267
1703 Mccall Dr Shelbyville (46176) *(G-14755)*

Encom Polymers, Evansville *Also Called: Encom Polymers LLC (G-4036)*

Encom Polymers LLC 812 421-7700
4825 N Spring St Evansville (47711) *(G-4036)*

Enconco Inc 317 251-1251
6450 Rucker Rd Indianapolis (46220) *(G-8112)*

Encore Rv LLC 574 327-6540
2702 Ada Dr Elkhart (46514) *(G-3332)*

Encorr Sheets LLC 317 290-1140
3600 Woodview Trce Ste 300 Indianapolis (46268) *(G-8113)*

Encourage Books, New Albany *Also Called: Encourage Publishing LLC (G-12725)*

Encourage Publishing LLC 812 987-6148
1116 Creekview Cir New Albany (47150) *(G-12725)*

Encouragement Today, Greenfield *Also Called: Brighttany Pollitt (G-6472)*

Endeavor Machined Products Inc 574 232-1940
1705 N Bendix Dr South Bend (46628) *(G-15014)*

Endeavor Precision Inc 317 903-0532
5304 Woodfield Dr Carmel (46033) *(G-1621)*

Endeavor Precision Inc 765 557-8694
2635 S F St Elwood (46036) *(G-3824)*

Endless Creations 812 623-0190
224 Nieman St Sunman (47041) *(G-15437)*

Endowment Development Services 317 542-9829
921 E 86th St Indianapolis (46240) *(G-8114)*

Endress + Hauser Inc 317 535-7138
2413 Endress Pl Greenwood (46143) *(G-6695)*

Endress + Hauser Inc 317 535-2159
2350 Endress Pl Greenwood (46143) *(G-6696)*

Endress + Hauser Inc (DH) 317 535-7138
2350 Endress Pl Greenwood (46143) *(G-6697)*

Endress + Hser Flwtec AG Div U 317 535-7138
2330 Endress Pl Greenwood (46143) *(G-6698)*

Endress+hauser (usa) Automatio 317 535-2121
2340 Endress Pl Greenwood (46143) *(G-6699)*

Endress+hauser Infoserve Inc 888 363-7377
2350 Endress Pl Greenwood (46143) *(G-6700)*

Endress+hauser Wetzer USA Inc 317 535-1362
2413 Endress Pl Greenwood (46143) *(G-6701)*

Endresshauser, Greenwood *Also Called: Endress + Hser Flwtec AG Div U (G-6698)*

Endresshauser USA, Greenwood *Also Called: Endress + Hauser Inc (G-6697)*

Enduring Endeavors LLC 260 410-1025
13033 Sutters Pkwy Fort Wayne (46845) *(G-4951)*

Enduring Graphics, Valparaiso *Also Called: National Equipment Inc (G-16009)*

Endustra Filter Manufacturers, Schererville *Also Called: Bofrebo Industries Inc (G-14516)*

Enerfuel Inc
3023 N Distribution Way # 100 Greenfield (46140) *(G-6497)*

Energy Access Incorporated 317 329-1676
5595 W 74th St Indianapolis (46268) *(G-8115)*

Energy Delivery Solutions LLC 502 271-8753
3315 Industrial Pkwy Jeffersonville (47130) *(G-9977)*

Energy Drilling LLC 618 943-5314
1290 N State Road 67 Vincennes (47591) *(G-16119)*

Energy Harness Corporation 239 246-1958
13335 Mercer St Carmel (46032) *(G-1622)*

Energy Harness Corporation 317 999-5561
5225 Exploration Dr Indianapolis (46241) *(G-8116)*

Energy House, Loogootee *Also Called: Kc Innovations LLC (G-11141)*

Energy Inc 765 948-3504
8201 N State Road 9 Alexandria (46001) *(G-51)*

Energy Quest Inc 317 827-9212
8553 Bash St Ste 107 Indianapolis (46250) *(G-8117)*

Energy Saver Lights Inc 202 544-7868
2530 Brandywine Ct Indianapolis (46241) *(G-8118)*

Energypoint LLC 317 275-7979
12400 N Meridian St Ste 180 Carmel (46032) *(G-1623)*

Enerlinc Inc 317 574-1009
315 N Madison St Fortville (46040) *(G-5593)*

Enerpac Tool Group Corp 574 254-1428
1217 E 7th St Mishawaka (46544) *(G-11894)*

Engel Manufacturing, South Bend *Also Called: Engel Manufacturing Co Inc (G-15015)*

Engel Manufacturing Co Inc 574 232-3800
411 W Indiana Ave South Bend (46613) *(G-15015)*

Enghouse Networks (us) Inc (HQ) 317 262-4666
333 N Alabama St Ste 240 Indianapolis (46204) *(G-8119)*

Engineered Conveyors Inc (PA) 765 459-4545
1055 Home Ave Kokomo (46902) *(G-10263)*

Engineered Dock Systems Inc 317 803-2443
3010 W Morris St Indianapolis (46241) *(G-8120)*

Engineered Industrial Products 317 684-4280
5652 W 74th St Indianapolis (46278) *(G-8121)*

Engineered Machined Pdts Inc 317 462-8894
317 462-8894 Greenfield (46140) *(G-6498)*

Engineered Machined Pdts Inc 317 462-8894
125 N Blue Rd Greenfield (46140) *(G-6499)*

Engineered Medical Systems 317 246-5500
2055 Executive Dr Indianapolis (46241) *(G-8122)*

Engineered Models, Indianapolis *Also Called: Enconco Inc (G-8112)*

Engineered Products, Fort Wayne *Also Called: Ecp American Steel LLC (G-4941)*

Engineered Products Inc 219 662-2080
1203 E Summit St Crown Point (46307) *(G-2680)*

Engineering Aggregates Corp 765 249-3073
803 Main St Michigantown (46057) *(G-11690)*

Engineering and Industrial Services LLC 574 722-3714
2095 S County Road 150 E Logansport (46947) *(G-11073)*

Enginered Refr Shapes Svcs LLC (PA) 765 778-8040
3370 W 1000 S Pendleton (46064) *(G-13531)*

Enginred Plstic Components Inc 812 752-6742
640 N Wilson Rd Scottsburg (47170) *(G-14554)*

Enginring Cncpts Unlimited Inc 317 849-8470
8950 Technology Dr Fishers (46038) *(G-4514)*

Engle Enterprises, Westfield *Also Called: Robert Engle (G-16723)*

Englehardt Custom Wdwkg LLC 812 425-9282
4125 Kedzie Ave Evansville (47712) *(G-4037)*

Engler Machine & Tool Inc 812 386-6254
1106 W 150 S Princeton (47670) *(G-13992)*

English Resources Inc 812 423-6716
816 Nw 2nd St Evansville (47708) *(G-4038)*

Engraving and Stamp Center Inc 812 336-0606
218 N Madison St Bloomington (47404) *(G-861)*

Enhanced Embroidery 812 448-8452
3318 W County Road 900 N Brazil (47834) *(G-1141)*

Enhanced Mfg Solutions Inc 812 932-1101
23 Hillcrest Estates Dr Batesville (47006) *(G-587)*

Enifiy, New Castle *Also Called: Gary M Brown (G-12864)*

Enjet Aero Terre Haute LLC 913 717-7390
501 S Airport St Terre Haute (47803) *(G-15586)*

Enjoy Life Foods, Jeffersonville *Also Called: Enjoy Life Natural Brands LLC (G-9978)*

Enjoy Life Natural Brands LLC 844 624-7162
301 Salem Rd Jeffersonville (47130) *(G-9978)*

Enkei America Inc (PA) 812 373-7000
2900 Inwood Dr Columbus (47201) *(G-2298)*

Enkei America Moldings Inc 812 373-7000
2680 Norcross Dr Columbus (47201) *(G-2299)*

Enmac Inc 812 298-8711
13200 S Us Highway 41 Terre Haute (47802) *(G-15587)*

Enovapremier LLC 812 385-0576
858 E 350 S Princeton (47670) *(G-13993)*

ALPHABETIC SECTION — Ernie's Welding Shop

Enpak LLC 574 268-7273
939 E Pound Dr N Warsaw (46582) *(G-16360)*

Enpower Inc 463 213-3200
8740 Hague Rd Bldg 7 Indianapolis (46256) *(G-8123)*

Enroll Hq LLC 317 376-8282
12175 Visionary Way Ste 710 Fishers (46038) *(G-4515)*

Entegrata Inc 949 244-1646
1950 E Greyhound Pass Ste 18 Carmel (46033) *(G-1624)*

Enterprise Marking Pdts Inc 317 867-7600
12840 Ford Dr Fishers (46038) *(G-4516)*

Enterprise MGT Solutions LLC (PA) 219 545-8544
1900 W 62nd Ave Merrillville (46410) *(G-11513)*

Entertainment Express 219 763-3610
3460 Anthony Dr Portage (46368) *(G-13861)*

Entourage Yearbooks 317 552-2207
5321 N College Ave Indianapolis (46220) *(G-8124)*

Envalior Engineering Materials Inc (DH) ... 800 333-4237
2267 W Mill Rd Evansville (47720) *(G-4039)*

Envalior Engineering Mtls Inc 812 435-7500
2267 W Mill Rd Evansville (47720) *(G-4040)*

Envalior Engineering Mtls Inc 812 435-7500
1100 E Louisiana St Evansville (47711) *(G-4041)*

Envelope Service Inc 260 432-6277
7101 Lincoln Pkwy Fort Wayne (46804) *(G-4952)*

Envigo Rms Inc 317 806-6080
6825 W 400 N Ste 170 Greenfield (46140) *(G-6500)*

Envigo Rms Inc 317 806-6060
671 S Meridian Rd Greenfield (46140) *(G-6501)*

Envigo Rms Inc (DH) 317 806-6080
8520 Allison Pointe Blvd Ste 400 Indianapolis (46250) *(G-8125)*

Enviri Corporation 219 397-0200
5222 Indianapolis Blvd East Chicago (46312) *(G-3007)*

Enviri Corporation 219 944-6250
7100 W 9th Ave Gary (46406) *(G-5928)*

Enviri Corporation 317 983-5353
8000 N County Road 225 E Pittsboro (46167) *(G-13645)*

Enviro Filters, Gary *Also Called: Enviro Filtration Inc (G-5929)*

Enviro Filtration Inc (PA) 815 469-2871
4719 Roosevelt St Gary (46408) *(G-5929)*

Enviro Group Inc 317 882-9360
290 Noble St Ste A Greenwood (46142) *(G-6702)*

Enviro Ink 260 748-0636
6926 Quemetco Ct Ste A Fort Wayne (46803) *(G-4953)*

Envirogen Technologies LLC 812 319-4496
1133 E Virginia St Evansville (47711) *(G-4042)*

Enviromental Services Pdts Mfg, Akron *Also Called: Dragon ESP Ltd (G-4)*

Environ Corporation 317 774-0541
550 Congressional Blvd Ste 115 Carmel (46032) *(G-1625)*

Environment Tech of Fort Wayne, South Bend *Also Called: Environmental Technology Inc (G-15016)*

Environmental MGT & Dev Inc 765 874-1539
105 West Sherman Street Lynn (47355) *(G-11183)*

Environmental Products Inc 219 393-3446
Fourth Road Kingsbury Kingsbury (46345) *(G-10178)*

Environmental Technology Inc 574 233-1202
1850 N Sheridan St South Bend (46628) *(G-15016)*

Enviropeel USA 317 631-9100
1128 S West St Indianapolis (46225) *(G-8126)*

Enviropeel USA, Indianapolis *Also Called: Precision Cams Inc (G-9181)*

Enviroplas LLC 812 868-0808
15220 Foundation Ave Evansville (47725) *(G-4043)*

Enviroplas LLC 812 868-0808
10100 Hedden Rd Evansville (47725) *(G-4044)*

Envirotech Extrusion Inc 765 966-8068
4810 Woodside Dr Richmond (47374) *(G-14120)*

Envision Graphics Inc 260 925-2266
118 W 9th St Auburn (46706) *(G-388)*

Envista LLC (PA) 317 208-9100
11555 N Meridian St Ste 300 Carmel (46032) *(G-1626)*

Envista Concepts LLC 317 208-9100
11711 N Meridian St Ste 415 Carmel (46032) *(G-1627)*

Envista Entp Solutions LLC 317 208-9100
11711 N Meridian St Ste 415 Carmel (46032) *(G-1628)*

Envista Freight Managment LLC 317 208-9100
11711 N Meridian St Ste 415 Carmel (46032) *(G-1629)*

Envmtl Franke Systems LLC 260 710-6491
1303 Big Horn Pl Fort Wayne (46825) *(G-4954)*

Enyart Electric Motor Repr Inc 574 288-4731
1313 Prairie Ave South Bend (46613) *(G-15017)*

Enyart Signs 574 223-8254
2155 N Old Us Highway 31 Rochester (46975) *(G-14288)*

Enyart Signs of All Kinds, Rochester *Also Called: Enyart Signs (G-14288)*

Enzyme Solutions Inc 800 523-1323
10219 River Rapids Run Fort Wayne (46845) *(G-4955)*

Enzyme Solutions Inc (PA) 260 553-9100
2105 Forrest Park Dr Garrett (46738) *(G-5861)*

Eorigami Publishing LLC 317 842-9659
8614 Amy Ln Indianapolis (46256) *(G-8127)*

EP Graphics Inc (HQ) 877 589-2145
169 S Jefferson St Berne (46711) *(G-710)*

Ep Old Inc 317 782-8362
520 S Post Rd Indianapolis (46239) *(G-8128)*

Epc-Columbia Inc 812 752-6742
640 N Wilson Rd Scottsburg (47170) *(G-14555)*

Epco Products Inc 260 747-8888
3736 Vanguard Dr Fort Wayne (46809) *(G-4956)*

Epi Printers Inc 317 579-4870
7502 E 86th St Indianapolis (46256) *(G-8129)*

Epic Graphics and Printing 219 545-1240
201 E 5th Ave Gary (46402) *(G-5930)*

Epic Welding LLC 502 554-6326
5815 New Chapel Rd Jeffersonville (47130) *(G-9979)*

Eps Enterprises Inc 260 493-4913
5423 State Road 930 Fort Wayne (46803) *(G-4957)*

Epw LLC 574 293-5090
1500 W Hively Ave Ste A Elkhart (46517) *(G-3333)*

Equipment Technologies, Mooresville *Also Called: Et Works Inc (G-12206)*

Equipment Technologies Inc (PA) 800 861-2142
2201 Hancel Pkwy Mooresville (46158) *(G-12204)*

Equippe Advanced Mobility 317 807-6789
3209 W Smith Valley Rd Ste 146 Greenwood (46142) *(G-6703)*

Equippe Mobility Resources, Greenwood *Also Called: Equippe Advanced Mobility (G-6703)*

Erapsco 386 740-5361
4868 E Park 30 Dr Columbia City (46725) *(G-2142)*

Erbeco, Fort Wayne *Also Called: Bloom Pharmaceutical (G-4807)*

ERC Mining Indiana Corp 812 665-9780
15127 W 700 N Jasonville (47438) *(G-9823)*

Eric Isaacson 812 339-1811
416 E University St Bloomington (47401) *(G-862)*

Eric Isaacson Software, Bloomington *Also Called: Eric Isaacson (G-862)*

Erie Haven Concrete, Fort Wayne *Also Called: Erie-Haven Inc (G-4959)*

Erie Haven Inc 260 665-2052
1310 W Maumee St Angola (46703) *(G-249)*

Erie-Haven Inc 260 478-1674
1204 S Union St Auburn (46706) *(G-389)*

Erie-Haven Inc 260 353-1133
235 S Adams St Bluffton (46714) *(G-1036)*

Erie-Haven Inc 260 483-3865
4708 Industrial Rd Fort Wayne (46825) *(G-4958)*

Erie-Haven Inc (PA) 260 478-1674
3909 Limestone Dr Fort Wayne (46809) *(G-4959)*

Erj Composites LLC 574 360-3517
1600 W 6th St Mishawaka (46544) *(G-11895)*

Erl, New Albany *Also Called: Electromechanical RES Labs (G-12724)*

Erler Industries Inc (PA) 812 346-4421
418 Stockwell St North Vernon (47265) *(G-13269)*

Ernest A Cooper 812 284-0436
1502 Production Rd Jeffersonville (47130) *(G-9980)*

Ernestine Foods Inc 219 274-0188
9800 Connecticut Dr Crown Point (46307) *(G-2681)*

Ernestine's Food Gallery, Hammond *Also Called: On-Time LLC (G-6989)*

Ernie's Welding Shop, Saint Anthony *Also Called: Ernies Welding Shop LLC (G-14427)*

Ernies Welding Shop LLC 812 326-2600
3854 E 450 S Saint Anthony (47575) *(G-14427)*

Ernst Enterprises Inc 260 726-8282
1125 W Water St Portland (47371) *(G-13938)*

Ernst Enterprises Inc 812 284-5205
4710 Utica Sellersburg Rd Sellersburg (47172) *(G-14592)*

Ernst Enterprises Inc 765 584-5700
1041 N Old Highway 27 Winchester (47394) *(G-16886)*

Ernstberger Enterprises Inc 812 282-0488
211 Eastern Blvd Jeffersonville (47130) *(G-9981)*

Erny Sheet Metal Inc 812 482-1044
1020 2nd Ave Jasper (47546) *(G-9836)*

Erosion & Cnstr Solutions Inc 219 885-9676
4088 W 82nd Ct Merrillville (46410) *(G-11514)*

Erosion Construction Services, Merrillville Also Called: Erosion & Cnstr Solutions Inc *(G-11514)*

Erp Iron Ore LLC 574 270-8608
64 E 100 N Reynolds (47980) *(G-14072)*

Ers Automation Inc 260 341-8114
1420 S 500 E Columbia City (46725) *(G-2143)*

Ers Holding Company Inc (PA) 260 894-4145
9144 N 900 W Ligonier (46767) *(G-11013)*

Ers Tower LLC 260 894-4145
9144 N 900 W Ligonier (46767) *(G-11014)*

Ers-Oci Wireless, Ligonier Also Called: Emergency Radio Service LLC *(G-11011)*

Ers-Oci Wireless, Ligonier Also Called: Emergency Radio Service LLC *(G-11012)*

Erss, Pendleton Also Called: Enginered Refr Shapes Svcs LLC *(G-13531)*

Ertel Cellars Winery Inc 812 933-1500
3794 E County Road 1100 N Batesville (47006) *(G-588)*

Ertl Enterprises Inc 765 622-9900
2316 Jefferson St Anderson (46016) *(G-115)*

Ertl Fabricating Inc 765 393-1376
2316 Jefferson St Anderson (46016) *(G-116)*

Es Deicing 260 422-2020
3500 Meyer Rd Fort Wayne (46806) *(G-4960)*

Esaote North America Inc 317 813-6000
11907 Exit 5 Pkwy Fishers (46037) *(G-4517)*

Esarey Hardwood Creations LLC 419 610-6486
534 Hoffman Dr New Albany (47150) *(G-12726)*

Esc Promotions, Pendleton Also Called: Wolfe Diversified Inds LLC *(G-13562)*

Escalade, Evansville Also Called: Escalade Incorporated *(G-4045)*

Escalade Incorporated (PA) 812 467-1358
817 Maxwell Ave Evansville (47711) *(G-4045)*

Escalade Inc 260 569-7233
251 Wedcor Ave Wabash (46992) *(G-16183)*

Esco Communications LLC (HQ) 317 298-2975
8940 Vincennes Cir Indianapolis (46268) *(G-8130)*

Esco Enterprises Indiana Inc 317 241-0318
302 Gasoline Aly Indianapolis (46222) *(G-8131)*

Esco Industries Inc 574 522-4500
1701 Conant St Elkhart (46516) *(G-3334)*

Esii - Embroidery Sew Into It 317 734-3891
9130 Otis Ave Ste C Indianapolis (46216) *(G-8132)*

Eskape Press LLC 765 659-1237
2587 S County Road 180 E Frankfort (46041) *(G-5661)*

Espi Enterprises Inc 219 787-8711
307 Melton Rd Ste B Chesterton (46304) *(G-1923)*

Essence In Harmony 317 727-6420
438 W Stop 11 Rd Indianapolis (46217) *(G-8133)*

Essence Scents LLC 317 679-5627
10839 Teeter Ct Indianapolis (46236) *(G-8134)*

Essenhaus Inc 574 825-6790
240 W Us Highway 20 Middlebury (46540) *(G-11715)*

Essenhaus Foods, Middlebury Also Called: Essenhaus Inc *(G-11715)*

Essential Archtctral Signs Inc 317 253-6000
6464 Rucker Rd Indianapolis (46220) *(G-8135)*

Essex 317 201-7099
5105 Plantation Dr Indianapolis (46250) *(G-8136)*

Essex Brownell LLC 260 424-1708
1601 Wall St Fort Wayne (46802) *(G-4961)*

Essex Brownell Llc, Fort Wayne Also Called: Essex Brownell LLC *(G-4961)*

Essex Frkawa Mgnt Wire USA LLC 260 424-1708
2499 S 600 E Columbia City (46725) *(G-2144)*

Essex Frkawa Mgnt Wire USA LLC 260 248-5500
2601 S 600 E Columbia City (46725) *(G-2145)*

Essex Frkawa Mgnt Wire USA LLC 260 248-5500
2580 S 600 St E Columbia City (46725) *(G-2146)*

Essex Frkawa Mgnt Wire USA LLC 260 461-4000
1700 Taylor Fort Wayne (46802) *(G-4962)*

Essex Frkawa Mgnt Wire USA LLC 260 461-4000
1601 Wall St Fort Wayne (46802) *(G-4963)*

Essex Frkawa Mgnt Wire USA LLC 260 461-4183
1700 Taylor St Fort Wayne (46802) *(G-4964)*

Essex Frkawa Mgnt Wire USA LLC 317 738-4365
3200 Essex Dr Franklin (46131) *(G-5729)*

Essex Services Inc 260 461-4000
1601 Wall St Fort Wayne (46802) *(G-4965)*

Essex Wire & Cable Division, Columbia City Also Called: Essex Frkawa Mgnt Wire USA LLC *(G-2144)*

Estates By Judi 260 615-5195
441 S 400 E Albion (46701) *(G-26)*

Esteem Style Wear, Indianapolis Also Called: Sarah Johnson Nettles *(G-9372)*

Estes Aws LLC 317 995-9742
470 S Mitthoefer Rd Indianapolis (46229) *(G-8137)*

Estes Design and Mfg Inc 317 899-2203
470 S Mitthoeffer Rd Indianapolis (46229) *(G-8138)*

Estes Waste Solutions LLC 812 283-6400
5005 Hamburg Pike Jeffersonville (47130) *(G-9982)*

Esteves Group USA, Decatur Also Called: Esteves-Dwd LLC *(G-2855)*

Esteves-Dwd LLC 260 728-9272
1921 Patterson St Decatur (46733) *(G-2855)*

Esther Reid 314 504-6659
2121 Inglewood Pl South Bend (46616) *(G-15018)*

Estill Smith Marine Svcs Inc 812 282-7944
4210 E Hwy 62 Jeffersonville (47130) *(G-9983)*

Et AG Center LLC 317 834-4500
2201 Hancel Pkwy Mooresville (46158) *(G-12205)*

Et Sprayers, Mooresville Also Called: Equipment Technologies Inc *(G-12204)*

Et Works Inc (HQ) 317 834-4500
2201 Hancel Pkwy Mooresville (46158) *(G-12206)*

Eta Engineering, Avilla Also Called: Eta Fabrication Inc *(G-476)*

Eta Fabrication Inc 260 897-3711
10605 E Baseline Rd Avilla (46710) *(G-476)*

Etcetera Press 317 845-9999
11480 E 111th St Fishers (46037) *(G-4518)*

Etched In Stone Engrv & EMB 317 535-8160
459 E Main St Whiteland (46184) *(G-16786)*

Ethels Kitchen LLC 317 441-2712
3533 N Audubon Rd Indianapolis (46218) *(G-8139)*

Eti Fab Inc 574 233-1202
17055 Oak Ridge Rd Westfield (46074) *(G-16688)*

Eti LLC (HQ) 260 368-7246
700 Rainbow Rd Geneva (46740) *(G-6049)*

Ettensohn & Company, Tell City Also Called: Ettensohn & Company LLC *(G-15501)*

Ettensohn & Company LLC 812 547-5491
9018 State Road 237 Tell City (47586) *(G-15501)*

Etter Tire Service, Fowler Also Called: Tippecanoe Tire Service Inc *(G-5634)*

Euclid Machine Co, Indianapolis Also Called: Thomas/Euclid Industries Inc *(G-9596)*

Euronique Inc 812 983-3337
7633 Saint Johns Rd Elberfeld (47613) *(G-3112)*

European Concepts LLC 888 797-9005
5607 Newland Pl Fort Wayne (46835) *(G-4966)*

Evangel Press, Winona Lake Also Called: Brethren In Chrst Mdia Mnstrie *(G-16909)*

Evangeline Orchard & Winery 574 278-6301
10737 N 800 E Monticello (47960) *(G-12149)*

Evans Herron 317 492-1384
702 Yosemite Dr Indianapolis (46217) *(G-8140)*

Evans Adhesive Corporation 812 859-4245
7140 State Highway 246 Spencer (47460) *(G-15345)*

Evans Enterprises LLC 317 986-2073
7644 Bancaster Dr Indianapolis (46268) *(G-8141)*

Evans Limestone Co 812 279-9744
1201 Limestone Dr Bedford (47421) *(G-635)*

ALPHABETIC SECTION

Evans Metal Products Co Inc.. 574 264-2166
  2400 Johnson St Elkhart (46514) *(G-3335)*
Evansville Arc Inc.. 812 471-1633
  2515 Kotter Ave Evansville (47715) *(G-4046)*
Evansville Assn For The Blind.. 812 422-1181
  500 N 2nd Ave Evansville (47710) *(G-4047)*
Evansville Bindery Inc... 812 423-2222
  221 E Columbia St Evansville (47711) *(G-4048)*
Evansville Block Co Inc... 812 422-2864
  1700 W Franklin St Ste 14 Evansville (47712) *(G-4049)*
Evansville Corp Design Inc... 812 426-0911
  401 Nw 4th St Evansville (47708) *(G-4050)*
Evansville Courier, Evansville *Also Called: Evansville Courier Co (G-4051)*
Evansville Courier Co (DH).. 812 464-7500
  300 E Walnut St Evansville (47713) *(G-4051)*
Evansville Lithograph Co Inc.. 812 477-0506
  3112 E Walnut St Evansville (47714) *(G-4052)*
Evansville Living, Evansville *Also Called: Tucker Publishing Group Inc (G-4355)*
Evansville Marine Service Inc (PA)....................................... 812 424-9278
  2300 Broadway Ave Evansville (47712) *(G-4053)*
Evansville Materials, Evansville *Also Called: Mulzer Crushed Stone Inc (G-4216)*
Evansville Metal Products Inc (PA)....................................... 812 423-5632
  119 Ladonna Blvd Evansville (47711) *(G-4054)*
Evansville Metal Products Inc... 812 421-6589
  2086 N 6th Ave Evansville (47710) *(G-4055)*
Evansville Pallets... 812 550-0199
  2203 N Kentucky Ave Evansville (47711) *(G-4056)*
Evansville Sales, Evansville *Also Called: Berendsen Inc (G-3916)*
Evansville Sheet Metal Works Inc... 812 423-7871
  1901 W Maryland St Evansville (47712) *(G-4057)*
Evansville Thunderbolts.. 812 435-0872
  1 Se Martin Luther King Jr Blvd Evansville (47708) *(G-4058)*
Evansville Tool & Die Inc.. 812 422-7101
  4900 N Saint Joseph Ave Evansville (47720) *(G-4059)*
Evansville-Baumgart - Flanders, Evansville *Also Called: Flanders Electric Motor Service LLC (G-4076)*
Evansvlle Print Specialist Inc.. 812 423-5831
  2217 W Franklin St Evansville (47712) *(G-4060)*
Evantek Manufacturing Inds LLC.. 812 437-9100
  5701 Old Boonville Hwy Evansville (47715) *(G-4061)*
Evart Engineering Company Inc... 765 354-2232
  1340 State St Middletown (47356) *(G-11769)*
Evecxia Therapeutics Inc.. 919 597-8762
  20267 Chatham Creek Dr Westfield (46074) *(G-16689)*
Evelyn Dollahan... 574 896-2971
  520 E 625 S North Judson (46366) *(G-13211)*
Evelyns Enterprise.. 219 980-8799
  2525 W 59th Pl Merrillville (46410) *(G-11515)*
Evening World, Spencer *Also Called: Spencer Evening World (G-15362)*
Event Odyssey Inc... 317 483-0027
  11549 Yard St Fishers (46037) *(G-4519)*
Everett Charles Technologies, Munster *Also Called: Contact Products Inc (G-12536)*
Evers Welding Company Inc... 812 576-2232
  7218 Wolf Creek Rd Guilford (47022) *(G-6829)*
Everybody, Crawfordsville *Also Called: Nathaniel Bowman (G-2592)*
Everyone's News, La Porte *Also Called: Advantage Productions (G-10376)*
Everything Else LLC... 574 350-7383
  1322 W Lexington Ave Elkhart (46514) *(G-3336)*
Everything Under Sun LLC.. 812 438-3397
  3379 Nelson Rd Rising Sun (47040) *(G-14242)*
Everything Under The Sun, Rising Sun *Also Called: Everything Under Sun LLC (G-14242)*
Everything Underground Inc... 317 491-8148
  4410 Rhapsody Ln Indianapolis (46235) *(G-8142)*
Everywhere Signs LLC... 812 323-1471
  2630 N Walnut St Bloomington (47404) *(G-863)*
Evia Custom Cabinets LLC.. 317 987-5504
  14221 Avian Way Carmel (46033) *(G-1630)*
EVille Iron Street Rods Ltd... 812 428-3764
  Evansville (47730) *(G-4062)*
Evo Exhibits LLC.. 630 520-0710
  1105 American Pkwy Peru (46970) *(G-13582)*

Evolving Transport LLC... 317 794-4426
  502 Bernard Ave Indianapolis (46208) *(G-8143)*
Evonik Corporation.. 765 477-4300
  1650 Lilly Rd Lafayette (47909) *(G-10575)*
Evoqua Water Technologies LLC.. 317 280-4251
  6125 Guion Rd Indianapolis (46254) *(G-8144)*
Evoqua Water Technologies LLC.. 317 280-4255
  6111 Guion Rd Indianapolis (46254) *(G-8145)*
EVS Ltd.. 574 233-5707
  24500 Research Dr South Bend (46628) *(G-15019)*
Ewing Light Metals Co Inc... 317 926-4591
  3451 Terrace Ave Indianapolis (46203) *(G-8146)*
Ewing Printing Company Inc.. 812 882-2415
  516 Vigo St Vincennes (47591) *(G-16120)*
Ex-Cut Technology LLC... 260 672-9602
  5130 E 900 N Roanoke (46783) *(G-14263)*
Exact Shtmtl & Skylights Inc... 219 670-3520
  763 Seminole Ct Crown Point (46307) *(G-2682)*
Exact-Tech Machining Inc.. 574 970-0197
  1140 County Road 6 W Elkhart (46514) *(G-3337)*
Exactifab... 812 420-2723
  10309 N Industrial Park Dr Brazil (47834) *(G-1142)*
Exacto Machine & Tool Inc.. 317 872-3136
  3402 W 79th St Indianapolis (46268) *(G-8147)*
Exactseal Inc... 317 559-2220
  7601 E 88th Pl Ste 3b Indianapolis (46256) *(G-8148)*
Exaktime Innovations Inc... 818 222-1836
  310 W South St Ste 200 South Bend (46601) *(G-15020)*
Excel Business Printing Inc... 317 259-1075
  6302 Rucker Rd Ste A Indianapolis (46220) *(G-8149)*
Excel Finishings LLC... 260 768-7667
  4510 W 200 N Lagrange (46761) *(G-10737)*
Excel Machine Company LLC.. 317 467-0299
  3103 W Us Highway 40 Greenfield (46140) *(G-6502)*
Excel Machine Technologies Inc.. 219 548-0708
  405 Elm St Valparaiso (46383) *(G-15945)*
Excel Manufacturing Inc... 812 523-6764
  1705 E 4th Street Rd Seymour (47274) *(G-14650)*
Excel Tool & Engineering LLC... 765 279-8528
  307 S Main St Kirklin (46050) *(G-10189)*
Excel Tool Inc.. 812 522-6880
  2020 1st Ave Seymour (47274) *(G-14651)*
Excell, Lagrange *Also Called: E & S Wood Creations LLC (G-10736)*
Excell Color Graphics Inc... 260 482-2720
  2623 Camino Ct Fort Wayne (46808) *(G-4967)*
Excell Usa Inc... 812 895-1687
  1065 E Beckes Ln Vincennes (47591) *(G-16121)*
Excellon Technologies, Fort Wayne *Also Called: HB Connect Inc (G-5051)*
Excellon Technologies, Fort Wayne *Also Called: HB Connect Inc (G-5052)*
Excenart, West Lafayette *Also Called: Viper USA Inc (G-16642)*
Except As A Child Pubg LLC... 317 658-0075
  6131 N Pershing Ave Indianapolis (46228) *(G-8150)*
Exchange Publishing Corp.. 574 831-2138
  19401 Industrial Dr New Paris (46553) *(G-12952)*
Exclusive Fit Trucking LLC.. 708 872-7593
  53429 Ba J Er Ln South Bend (46635) *(G-15021)*
Exclusive Reality, Clermont *Also Called: Dr Restorations Inc (G-2063)*
Exclusive Stylez LLC... 470 406-2804
  2018 Winter Ave Indianapolis (46218) *(G-8151)*
Executive Automtn Systems Inc... 317 545-7171
  4162 N Ems Blvd Greenfield (46140) *(G-6503)*
EXECUTIVE MANAGEMENT SERVICES OF INDIANA, INC., Indianapolis *Also Called: Executive MGT Svcs Ind Inc (G-8152)*
Executive MGT Svcs Ind Inc.. 317 594-6000
  1605 Prospect St Indianapolis (46203) *(G-8152)*
Executive Polishing, Indianapolis *Also Called: Evans Herron (G-8140)*
Exelead Inc (HQ)... 317 347-2800
  6925 Guion Rd Indianapolis (46268) *(G-8153)*
Exelead Inc.. 317 612-2900
  6102 Victory Way Indianapolis (46278) *(G-8154)*
Exelis Inc., Electronic, Crane *Also Called: L3harris Technologies Inc (G-2539)*

(PA)=Parent Co (HQ)=Headquarters (DH)=Div Headquarters

Exemplary Foam   ALPHABETIC SECTION

Exemplary Foam, Elkhart *Also Called: Exemplary Foam Inc (G-3338)*

Exemplary Foam Inc (PA).. 574 295-8888
1235 W Hively Ave Elkhart (46517) *(G-3338)*

Exemplary Foam South LLC... 423 302-0962
2600 S Nappanee St Elkhart (46517) *(G-3339)*

Exeon Processors LLC (PA)... 765 674-2266
232 W Pearl St Jonesboro (46938) *(G-10078)*

Exhale Fans LLC... 812 366-3351
6370 Forest Grove Dr Ne Georgetown (47122) *(G-6059)*

Exhaust Productions Inc... 219 942-0069
2777 E 83rd Pl Merrillville (46410) *(G-11516)*

Exhibit A Plastics LLC... 765 386-6702
4170 S State Road 75 Coatesville (46121) *(G-2105)*

Exide Technologies LLC... 317 876-7475
5945 W 84th St Ste B Indianapolis (46278) *(G-8155)*

Exo-S US LLC (DH).. 260 562-4100
6505 N State Road 9 Howe (46746) *(G-7235)*

Exotic Metal Treating Inc.. 317 784-8565
6234 E Hanna Ave Indianapolis (46203) *(G-8156)*

Expedition Log Homes... 219 663-5555
11091 Marion Pl Crown Point (46307) *(G-2683)*

Experimental Nylon Products.. 574 674-8747
1610 3rd St Osceola (46561) *(G-13391)*

Expert Electrical Services LLC... 765 664-6642
2916 E Bocock Rd Marion (46952) *(G-11285)*

Expert Woodworks.. 219 345-2705
9126 N 200 E Lake Village (46349) *(G-10780)*

Exploding Brain Press.. 219 393-0796
607 Franklin St Michigan City (46360) *(G-11608)*

Explorer Sport Trucks, Warsaw *Also Called: Van Explorer Company Inc (G-16441)*

Express Binding Inc.. 317 269-8114
1769 E 106th St Carmel (46032) *(G-1631)*

Express Controls... 574 831-3497
24471 County Road 142 Goshen (46526) *(G-6131)*

Express Machine... 812 719-5979
6115 Sugar Maple Rd Cannelton (47520) *(G-1536)*

Express Motors.. 812 437-9495
1059 E Riverside Dr Evansville (47714) *(G-4063)*

Express Prcsion Components Inc... 317 294-8138
2750 S Arlington Ave Indianapolis (46203) *(G-8157)*

Express Press, South Bend *Also Called: Systems & Services of Michiana (G-15277)*

Express Press 4, South Bend *Also Called: Express Press Indiana Inc (G-15022)*

Express Press Inc.. 812 882-3278
2129 Washington Ave Vincennes (47591) *(G-16122)*

Express Press Indiana Inc.. 219 874-2223
3505 W Mcgill St South Bend (46628) *(G-15022)*

Express Press Indiana Inc (PA).. 574 277-3355
325 N Dixie Way South Bend (46637) *(G-15023)*

Express Print, Frankfort *Also Called: Smith Business Supply Inc (G-5694)*

Express Printing & Copies, North Vernon *Also Called: David Camp (G-13265)*

Express Printing & Copying... 219 762-3508
2554 Portage Mall Portage (46368) *(G-13862)*

Express Sign & Neon Llc.. 812 882-0104
119 S 15th St Vincennes (47591) *(G-16123)*

Express Signs, Vincennes *Also Called: Express Press Inc (G-16122)*

Express Steel Inc... 317 657-5017
9240 N Waverly Park Rd Martinsville (46151) *(G-11390)*

Expressions Braids By Gwen LLC... 260 312-6037
3442 Stellhorn Rd Ste 4 Fort Wayne (46815) *(G-4968)*

Expressions Custom Tees.. 317 205-6229
12407 Rose Haven Dr Indianapolis (46235) *(G-8158)*

Extensive Design LLC... 260 267-6752
10007 Northbrook Valley Dr Apt 3 Fort Wayne (46825) *(G-4969)*

Exton Inc... 574 533-0447
2134 Dierdorff Rd 27 Goshen (46526) *(G-6132)*

Extra, The, Shelbyville *Also Called: Shelbyville Newspapers Inc (G-14798)*

Extrasurplus LLC... 252 619-8604
504 Broadway Ste 316 Gary (46402) *(G-5931)*

Extreme Finishes LLC... 812 524-2442
105 S Obrien St Seymour (47274) *(G-14652)*

Extreme Precision Products LLC... 812 839-0101
11388 N West Fork Rd Madison (47250) *(G-11219)*

Extreme Tool Supply... 219 362-5129
6348 W 100 S La Porte (46350) *(G-10407)*

Extreme Trailer Service LLC.. 812 406-1984
117 Industrial Way Charlestown (47111) *(G-1876)*

Exxon, South Bend *Also Called: Exxon Mobil Corporation (G-15024)*

Exxon Mobil Corporation... 574 217-7630
3323 Prairie Ave South Bend (46614) *(G-15024)*

Eyb Promotions... 812 376-3212
3490 Commerce Dr Columbus (47201) *(G-2300)*

Eyc Drones LLC... 812 890-9068
1834 S Old Us 41 Ste 1 Vincennes (47591) *(G-16124)*

EZ Cut Tool LLC.. 260 748-0732
110 Rose Ave New Haven (46774) *(G-12902)*

Ez Services LLC.. 317 965-3013
4106 Dunedin Ct Westfield (46062) *(G-16690)*

F & F Machine Specialties, Mishawaka *Also Called: Bbs Enterprises Inc (G-11848)*

F & F Screw Machine Products.. 574 293-0362
4302 Wyland Dr Elkhart (46516) *(G-3340)*

F & N Woodworking, Lagrange *Also Called: F & N Woodworking LLC (G-10738)*

F & N Woodworking LLC... 260 463-8938
2105 W 450 S Lagrange (46761) *(G-10738)*

F & S Signage Solutions Inc.. 317 539-2086
2765 S County Road 250 W Danville (46122) *(G-2811)*

F B C Inc (PA).. 574 848-5288
1123 Commerce Dr Bristol (46507) *(G-1260)*

F B Mfg... 219 406-1318
864 N Calumet Ave Chesterton (46304) *(G-1924)*

F D Deskins Company Inc.. 317 284-4014
12554 Spire View Dr Fishers (46037) *(G-4520)*

F D McCrary Operator Inc... 812 354-6520
4295 W County Road 350 N Petersburg (47567) *(G-13611)*

F G Metal.. 260 580-0361
721 Runnion Ave Fort Wayne (46808) *(G-4970)*

F Hoffmann-La Roche Ltd (PA).. 317 370-8578
2701 Castle Hill Dr Apt 921 Indianapolis (46250) *(G-8159)*

F Hoffmann-La Roche Ltd.. 317 370-8578
9115 Hague Rd Indianapolis (46256) *(G-8160)*

F J Rettig & Sons Inc.. 260 563-6603
485 W Canal St Wabash (46992) *(G-16184)*

F Robert Gardner Co Inc... 317 634-2333
1621 E New York St Indianapolis (46201) *(G-8161)*

F S G Inc.. 574 291-5998
222 E Walter St South Bend (46614) *(G-15025)*

F W A Decks & Fencing.. 219 865-3275
2401 Hickory Dr Dyer (46311) *(G-2974)*

Fab Con, Bedford *Also Called: Sigma Steel Inc (G-672)*

Fab Solutions LLC... 765 744-2671
10135 W 800 S Redkey (47373) *(G-14028)*

Fab-Tech Industries Inc... 765 478-4191
14271 W Us Highway 40 Cambridge City (47327) *(G-1494)*

Fabco Publishing, Indianapolis *Also Called: Flag & Banner Company Inc (G-8199)*

Fabcore Industries LLC.. 260 438-3431
928 Pencross Dr Fort Wayne (46845) *(G-4971)*

Fabcreation.. 812 246-6222
7412 Highway 31 E Sellersburg (47172) *(G-14593)*

Fabri-Tech Inc.. 317 849-7755
8236 N 600 W Mccordsville (46055) *(G-11447)*

Fabric Services, Bristol *Also Called: Mpr Corporation (G-1280)*

Fabricated Metals Corp.. 219 734-6896
2180 N State Road 149 Chesterton (46304) *(G-1925)*

Fabricated Metals Corp (PA).. 219 871-0230
4991a W Us Highway 20 Michigan City (46360) *(G-11609)*

Fabricated Steel Corporation... 317 899-0012
9809 Park Davis Dr Indianapolis (46235) *(G-8162)*

Fabshop.. 317 549-1681
8732 W County Road 1075 S Reelsville (46171) *(G-14031)*

Fabstar Inc... 765 230-0261
200 E Maple St Cayuga (47928) *(G-1821)*

Fabtration LLC... 812 989-6730
526 Maplewood Blvd Georgetown (47122) *(G-6060)*

Fabtron Corporation.. 260 925-5770
1820 Sprott St Auburn (46706) *(G-390)*

ALPHABETIC SECTION

Faerber's Bee Window, Fishers *Also Called: Bee Window Incorporated* **(G-4473)**

Faes Cabinet LLC.. 567 259-8571
916 W Coliseum Blvd Ste 4 Fort Wayne (46808) **(G-4972)**

Fairfield Gas Way... 260 744-2186
4230 Fairfield Ave Fort Wayne (46807) **(G-4973)**

Fairfield Manufacturing Co Inc (HQ)......................... 765 772-4000
2400 Sagamore Pkwy S Lafayette (47903) **(G-10576)**

Fairfield Manufacturing Co Inc................................. 815 508-7353
2309 Concord Rd Lafayette (47909) **(G-10577)**

Fairmont Door Corp... 260 563-6307
209 S Huntington St Wabash (46992) **(G-16185)**

Fairmount News... 765 948-4164
122 S Main St Fairmount (46928) **(G-4409)**

Fairview Fittings & Mfg... 574 206-8884
23845 County Road 6 Elkhart (46514) **(G-3341)**

Fairview Woodworking.. 260 768-3255
8655 W 100 S Shipshewana (46565) **(G-14845)**

Fairway Custom Golf... 317 842-0017
12500 Brooks School Rd Fishers (46037) **(G-4521)**

Fairway Laser Systems Inc..................................... 219 462-6892
950 Transport Dr Valparaiso (46383) **(G-15946)**

Faith Forgotten Firearms LLC................................. 614 940-9145
1812 Corydon Pike New Albany (47150) **(G-12727)**

Faith Music Missions, Evansville *Also Called: Boeke Road Baptist Church Inc* **(G-3938)**

Faith Nicole Publications LLC................................. 708 238-3101
477 Roosevelt Ct Hammond (46320) **(G-6925)**

Faith Walkers.. 219 873-1900
7358 W Johnson Rd Michigan City (46360) **(G-11610)**

Faith Walkers Screen Printing, Michigan City *Also Called: Faith Walkers* **(G-11610)**

Falcon Manufacturing LLC..................................... 317 884-3600
6200 S International Dr Columbus (47201) **(G-2301)**

Fall Creek Corporation... 765 482-1861
917 E Walnut St Lebanon (46052) **(G-10893)**

Fall Creek Enterprises, Lebanon *Also Called: Fall Creek Corporation* **(G-10893)**

Falls Cities Printing Inc.. 812 949-9051
323 Vincennes St New Albany (47150) **(G-12728)**

Fam Express 1982 LLC.. 317 628-3901
1534 N Emerson Ave Indianapolis (46219) **(G-8163)**

Family Bracelets Direct.. 513 312-5446
21939 Wilbur Dr Lawrenceburg (47025) **(G-10835)**

Family Design, Gary *Also Called: Aaron Company Inc* **(G-5886)**

Family Leisurecom Inc... 317 823-4448
11811 Pendleton Pike Indianapolis (46236) **(G-8164)**

Family Vineyard LLC.. 812 322-1720
3944 N Delaware St Indianapolis (46205) **(G-8165)**

Fan-Tastic Vent.. 800 521-0298
1120 N Main St Elkhart (46514) **(G-3342)**

Fanatics.. 317 844-5478
12011 Hoover Rd Carmel (46032) **(G-1632)**

Fanatics Lids College LLC...................................... 888 814-4287
7676 Interactive Way Ste 300 Indianapolis (46278) **(G-8166)**

Fancil Welding LLC... 574 267-8627
721 S Buffalo St Warsaw (46580) **(G-16361)**

Fancil Welding Service, Warsaw *Also Called: Fancil Welding LLC* **(G-16361)**

Fancy Bee Clothing Co., Gary *Also Called: Catherine J Bergren* **(G-5913)**

Fancy Candle Soy LLC.. 765 769-4042
1078 E 500 S Anderson (46013) **(G-117)**

Fanfare Sales, Indianapolis *Also Called: Frances Monforte* **(G-8221)**

Fanim Industries Inc.. 888 567-2055
10983 Bennett Pkwy Zionsville (46077) **(G-17006)**

Fanimation, Zionsville *Also Called: Fanim Industries Inc* **(G-17006)**

Fanimation Inc... 317 733-4113
10983 Bennett Pkwy Zionsville (46077) **(G-17007)**

Fanroll LLC (PA).. 617 909-6325
3236 Illinois Rd Fort Wayne (46802) **(G-4974)**

Farbest Farms Inc... 812 481-1034
4689 S 400w Huntingburg (47542) **(G-7279)**

Farbest Foods Inc.. 812 683-4200
1155 W 12th Ave Ste B Jasper (47546) **(G-9837)**

Farbest Foods Intl Inc.. 812 683-4200
4689 S 400w Huntingburg (47542) **(G-7280)**

Faris Mailing Inc.. 317 246-3315
701 N Holt Rd Ste 3 Indianapolis (46222) **(G-8167)**

Farm Boy Meats of Evansville................................. 812 425-5231
2761 N Kentucky Ave Evansville (47711) **(G-4064)**

Farm Fab.. 574 862-4775
65511 County Road 9 Goshen (46526) **(G-6133)**

Farm Innovators Inc... 574 936-5096
2255 Walter Glaub Dr Plymouth (46563) **(G-13774)**

Farmer Automatic America Inc............................... 574 857-3116
5571 S State Road 25 Rochester (46975) **(G-14289)**

Farmer Legacy Inc... 574 264-4625
25575 Woodlawn Ave Elkhart (46514) **(G-3343)**

Farmers Exchange, New Paris *Also Called: Exchange Publishing Corp* **(G-12952)**

Farmers Machine Shop Inc.................................... 812 425-1238
1511 E Virginia St Ste C Evansville (47711) **(G-4065)**

Farmersmarketcom LLC.. 317 523-4025
115 Pope Ave Apt O Indianapolis (46202) **(G-8168)**

Farmland Lumber, South Whitley *Also Called: Steve Reiff Inc* **(G-15328)**

Farmway Welding.. 574 498-6147
20097 Gumwood Rd Argos (46501) **(G-322)**

Farmweek, Knightstown *Also Called: Mayhill Publications Inc* **(G-10199)**

Farwall Tsg LLC.. 574 773-2108
302 Dal Mar Way Nappanee (46550) **(G-12596)**

Fas Plastic Enterprises Inc..................................... 812 265-2928
3408 W State Road 56 Hanover (47243) **(G-7041)**

Fashion City.. 260 744-6753
1108 E Pontiac St Ste 2 Fort Wayne (46803) **(G-4975)**

Fashion Flooring and Lighting, Valparaiso *Also Called: Fashion Flooring and Ltg Inc* **(G-15947)**

Fashion Flooring and Ltg Inc
2510 Beech St Valparaiso (46383) **(G-15947)**

Fasi Coatings, Gary *Also Called: Fasi Coatings LLC* **(G-5932)**

Fasi Coatings LLC... 219 985-0788
3905 W Ridge Rd Gary (46408) **(G-5932)**

Fasi Codings, Gary *Also Called: Fire Apparatus Service Inc* **(G-5933)**

Faske Wood Moulding Inc...................................... 812 923-5601
10215 Saint Johns Rd Borden (47106) **(G-1108)**

Fasson Roll North America Div, Fort Wayne *Also Called: Avery Dennison Corporation* **(G-4783)**

Fast Grafix.. 812 305-3464
5942 Jeffrey Ln Newburgh (47630) **(G-13001)**

Fast Holster LLC... 317 727-5243
10376 Harrow Pl Carmel (46280) **(G-1633)**

Fast Land Food, Kokomo *Also Called: H & H Partnership Inc* **(G-10274)**

Fast Manufacturing LLC... 219 778-8238
3956 E 800 N Rolling Prairie (46371) **(G-14361)**

Fast Print Incorporated.. 260 484-5487
3050 E State Blvd Fort Wayne (46805) **(G-4976)**

Fast Signs... 574 254-0545
2411 Mishawaka Ave South Bend (46615) **(G-15026)**

Fast Track Technologies LLC.................................. 317 229-6080
18882 Mallery Rd Noblesville (46060) **(G-13075)**

Fastener Equipment Corporation............................ 708 957-5100
3604 Meadowlark Dr Valparaiso (46383) **(G-15948)**

Fastsigns.. 260 373-0911
3014 N Clinton St Fort Wayne (46805) **(G-4977)**

Fastsigns.. 317 280-3041
9668 Allisonville Rd Indianapolis (46250) **(G-8169)**

Fastsigns, Bloomington *Also Called: B2c2 LLC* **(G-791)**

Fastsigns, Bloomington *Also Called: Richardson Entps Blmington LLC* **(G-956)**

Fastsigns, Columbus *Also Called: Booth Signs Inc* **(G-2227)**

Fastsigns, Greenwood *Also Called: Hubbard Services Inc* **(G-6713)**

Fastsigns, Indianapolis *Also Called: G C Solutions Inc* **(G-8252)**

Fastsigns, Indianapolis *Also Called: I F S Corp* **(G-8445)**

Fastsigns, Indianapolis *Also Called: Snykin Inc* **(G-9457)**

Fastsigns, Jeffersonville *Also Called: Dupre Capital LLC* **(G-9971)**

Fastsigns, South Bend *Also Called: Fast Signs* **(G-15026)**

Fastsigns, South Bend *Also Called: Pathfinder Communications Corp* **(G-15187)**

Fasttimes Fabrication Cus..................................... 574 858-9222
115 S Walnut St Etna Green (46524) **(G-3848)**

Father Son Sanders Trnspt LLC 773 899-8078
7925 Belmont Ave Hammond (46324) *(G-6926)*

Faulkenberg Printing Co Inc 317 638-1359
1670 Amy Ln Franklin (46131) *(G-5730)*

Faulkens Floorcover 574 300-4260
2045 N Meade St South Bend (46628) *(G-15027)*

Faulkner Fabricating Inc 574 342-0022
4050 Lincoln Hwy Bourbon (46504) *(G-1121)*

Faurecia Emissions Control TEC, Columbus *Also Called: Faurecia Exhaust Systems LLC (G-2306)*

Faurecia Emissions Ctrl Tech, Columbus *Also Called: Faurecia Emssons Ctrl Tech USA (G-2305)*

Faurecia Emssons Ctrl Tech USA 812 341-2000
830 W 450 S Columbus (47201) *(G-2302)*

Faurecia Emssons Ctrl Tech USA 812 348-4305
601 S Gladstone Ave Columbus (47201) *(G-2303)*

Faurecia Emssons Ctrl Tech USA 812 565-5214
17th Street Warehouse Columbus (47201) *(G-2304)*

Faurecia Emssons Ctrl Tech USA 812 341-2000
950 W 450 S Bldg 1 Columbus (47201) *(G-2305)*

Faurecia Emssons Ctrl Tech USA 248 758-8160
4510 Airport Express Way Fort Wayne (46809) *(G-4978)*

Faurecia Exhaust Systems LLC 812 341-2079
950 W 450 S Columbus (47201) *(G-2306)*

Favor It Promotions Inc 317 733-1112
4250 W 99th St Carmel (46032) *(G-1634)*

Fayette Tool and Engineering 765 825-7518
5432 Western Ave Connersville (47331) *(G-2438)*

Fayette Welding Service Inc 317 852-2929
7555 S State Road 267 Brownsburg (46112) *(G-1366)*

Faztech LLC 812 327-0926
7069 S Leisure Ln Bloomington (47401) *(G-864)*

Faztek LLC 260 482-7544
12788 Bluffton Rd Fort Wayne (46809) *(G-4979)*

Fbapower, Richmond *Also Called: Scanpower LLC (G-14201)*

Fbsa LLC (PA) 800 443-4540
7346 W 400 N Rochester (46975) *(G-14290)*

Fca LLC 765 448-1775
3517 Crouch St Lafayette (47905) *(G-10578)*

FCA North America Holdings LLC 765 454-0018
1947 S Elizabeth St Kokomo (46902) *(G-10264)*

FCA North America Holdings LLC 765 454-1705
2401 S Reed Rd Kokomo (46902) *(G-10265)*

FCA North America Holdings LLC 765 854-4234
3660 State Rd 931 Kokomo (46901) *(G-10266)*

FCA Packaging, Lafayette *Also Called: Fca LLC (G-10578)*

FCA US LLC 765 454-1005
1001 E Boulevard Kokomo (46902) *(G-10267)*

FCC (adams) LLC (HQ) 260 589-8555
936 E Parr Rd Berne (46711) *(G-711)*

FCC (indiana) LLC 260 726-8023
555 Industrial Dr Portland (47371) *(G-13939)*

FCC (north America) Inc (HQ) 260 726-8023
555 Industrial Dr Portland (47371) *(G-13940)*

FCC North America, Berne *Also Called: FCC (adams) LLC (G-711)*

Fci Flavors, Portage *Also Called: First Creative Ingredients Inc (G-13865)*

Fcs Industries Incorporated 574 288-5150
4300 Quality Dr South Bend (46628) *(G-15028)*

Fdc Graphics Films Inc (PA) 800 634-7523
3820 William Richardson Dr South Bend (46628) *(G-15029)*

FDS Northwood LLC 765 289-2481
420 S Ohio Ave Muncie (47302) *(G-12392)*

Feather Creek Calls 812 229-1124
860 E 1375 S Clinton (47842) *(G-2067)*

Feddema Industries Inc 260 665-6463
1305 Wohlert St Angola (46703) *(G-250)*

Federal Cartridge Company 765 966-7745
232 Industrial Pkwy Richmond (47374) *(G-14121)*

Federal Mogul, South Bend *Also Called: Federal-Mogul Powertrain LLC (G-15031)*

Federal Process Corp 574 288-0607
6851 Enterprise Dr South Bend (46628) *(G-15030)*

Federal Provider LLC 317 710-3997
55 Monument Cir Ste 744 Indianapolis (46204) *(G-8170)*

Federal-Mogul, Frankfort *Also Called: Federal-Mogul Powertrain LLC (G-5662)*

Federal-Mogul, Indianapolis *Also Called: Federal-Mogul Motorparts LLC (G-8171)*

Federal-Mogul, Michigan City *Also Called: Federal-Mogul Motorparts LLC (G-11611)*

Federal-Mogul Motorparts LLC 317 875-7259
8325 N Norfolk St 100 Indianapolis (46268) *(G-8171)*

Federal-Mogul Motorparts LLC 219 872-5150
402 Royal Rd Michigan City (46360) *(G-11611)*

Federal-Mogul Powertrain LLC 765 659-7207
2845 W State Road 28 Frankfort (46041) *(G-5662)*

Federal-Mogul Powertrain LLC 574 271-5954
3605 Cleveland Rd South Bend (46628) *(G-15031)*

Federal-Mogul Powertrain LLC 574 272-5900
5435 Dylan Dr Ste 200 South Bend (46628) *(G-15032)*

Federated Auto Parts, Lawrenceburg *Also Called: KOI Enterprises Inc (G-10843)*

Federated Media, Elkhart *Also Called: Pathfinder Communications Corp (G-3587)*

Fedex, Indianapolis *Also Called: Fedex Office & Print Svcs Inc (G-8172)*

Fedex, Indianapolis *Also Called: Fedex Office & Print Svcs Inc (G-8173)*

Fedex, Indianapolis *Also Called: Fedex Office & Print Svcs Inc (G-8174)*

Fedex, Indianapolis *Also Called: Fedex Office & Print Svcs Inc (G-8175)*

Fedex, Indianapolis *Also Called: Fedex Office & Print Svcs Inc (G-8176)*

Fedex, Indianapolis *Also Called: Fedex Office & Print Svcs Inc (G-8177)*

Fedex, Indianapolis *Also Called: Fedex Office & Print Svcs Inc (G-8178)*

Fedex, Indianapolis *Also Called: Fedex Office & Print Svcs Inc (G-8179)*

Fedex, Lafayette *Also Called: Fedex Office & Print Svcs Inc (G-10579)*

Fedex Office & Print Svcs Inc 317 974-0378
10 S West St Indianapolis (46204) *(G-8172)*

Fedex Office & Print Svcs Inc 317 917-1529
50 S Capitol Ave Indianapolis (46204) *(G-8173)*

Fedex Office & Print Svcs Inc 317 849-9683
4825 E 82nd St Ste 200 Indianapolis (46250) *(G-8174)*

Fedex Office & Print Svcs Inc 317 885-6480
8231 Us 31 Indianapolis (46227) *(G-8175)*

Fedex Office & Print Svcs Inc 317 295-1063
5030 W Pike Plaza Rd Indianapolis (46254) *(G-8176)*

Fedex Office & Print Svcs Inc 317 337-2679
3269 W 86th St Ste A Indianapolis (46268) *(G-8177)*

Fedex Office & Print Svcs Inc 317 631-6862
120 Monument Cir Ste 107 Indianapolis (46204) *(G-8178)*

Fedex Office & Print Svcs Inc 317 251-2406
1050 Broad Ripple Ave Indianapolis (46220) *(G-8179)*

Fedex Office & Print Svcs Inc 765 449-4950
3520 South St Lafayette (47905) *(G-10579)*

Fedex Office Print & Ship Ctr, Tell City *Also Called: Firehouse Printing LLC (G-15503)*

Feeding Concepts Inc 317 773-2040
15235 Herriman Blvd Noblesville (46060) *(G-13076)*

Fehrenbacher Cabinets Inc 812 963-3377
8944 Big Cynthiana Rd Evansville (47720) *(G-4066)*

Fehring F N & Son Printers 219 933-0439
450 N 325 E Valparaiso (46383) *(G-15949)*

Fehring Printers, Valparaiso *Also Called: Fehring F N & Son Printers (G-15949)*

Felicia Fr8 LLC 312 597-9282
3831 Hohman Ave Pmb 1058 Hammond (46327) *(G-6927)*

Fellers Inc 317 876-3008
7768 Moller Rd Indianapolis (46268) *(G-8180)*

FELLERS INC, Indianapolis *Also Called: Fellers Inc (G-8180)*

Fellwocks Automotive 812 867-3658
10004 Darmstadt Rd Evansville (47710) *(G-4067)*

Femyer Drapery Shop 765 282-3398
4409 W Burton Dr Muncie (47304) *(G-12393)*

Fencescapes LLC 317 210-3912
1385 Balsam Fir Pass Avon (46123) *(G-519)*

Fencing Advisory Assoc Inc 574 256-0111
109 Lincolnway W Mishawaka (46544) *(G-11896)*

Fender 4 Star Meat Processing, Spencer *Also Called: Fender 4 Star Meats Processing (G-15346)*

Fender 4 Star Meats Processing 812 829-3240
1494 Rocky Hill Rd Spencer (47460) *(G-15346)*

ALPHABETIC SECTION — Finish Alternatives

Fenders Inc 574 293-3717
  5304 Beck Dr Elkhart (46516) *(G-3344)*

Fenestration Products LLC 317 831-5314
  101 Linel Dr Mooresville (46158) *(G-12207)*

Fenris Forge LLC 260 422-9044
  706 Lawton Pl Fort Wayne (46805) *(G-4980)*

Fenwick Motor Sports 765 522-1354
  112 S Washington St Bainbridge (46105) *(G-562)*

Fenwick Pharma LLC 765 412-1889
  5315 Shootingstar Ln West Lafayette (47906) *(G-16580)*

Feralloy Corporation 219 787-9698
  6755 Waterway Dr Portage (46368) *(G-13863)*

Ferco Aerospace, Greenwood *Also Called: L&E Engineering LLC (G-6727)*

Ferdinand Machine Shop 812 367-2590
  825 Main St Ferdinand (47532) *(G-4431)*

Ferdinand Processing Inc 812 367-2073
  1182 E 5th St Ferdinand (47532) *(G-4432)*

Ferentino Tire USA Inc 574 316-6116
  400 Lake Ave Plymouth (46563) *(G-13775)*

Ferguson Enterprises LLC 219 440-5254
  574 Kennedy Ave Schererville (46375) *(G-14521)*

Ferguson Equipment Inc 574 234-4303
  25170 Edison Rd South Bend (46628) *(G-15033)*

Ferguson Waterworks, Schererville *Also Called: Ferguson Enterprises LLC (G-14521)*

Fergys Cabinets 765 529-0116
  2506 Grand Ave New Castle (47362) *(G-12861)*

Ferree Logging LLC 812 786-1676
  2150 Leonard Rd Nw Corydon (47112) *(G-2496)*

Ferrellgas, Crawfordsville *Also Called: Ferrellgas LP (G-2566)*

Ferrellgas LP 574 936-2725
  2111b Indianapolis Rd Crawfordsville (47933) *(G-2566)*

Ferrellok Lifesciences LLC 765 716-0056
  3905 N Linden St Muncie (47304) *(G-12394)*

Ferret, Inc., Elkhart *Also Called: Smco Inc (G-3686)*

Ferrill-Fisher Incorporated 812 935-9000
  8768 N Wayport Rd Bloomington (47404) *(G-865)*

Ferry Street Woodworks 812 427-9663
  319 Ferry St Vevay (47043) *(G-16109)*

Festive Lights LLC 317 998-0627
  4617 E 16th St Indianapolis (46201) *(G-8181)*

Fetzer Publishing 765 966-9169
  327 Hazelwood Ln Richmond (47374) *(G-14122)*

Fex Labs, Indianapolis *Also Called: Fex LLC (G-8182)*

Fex LLC 317 308-8820
  4909 Sunview Cir Apt 1218 Indianapolis (46237) *(G-8182)*

Ff - Top of Pie LLC 317 876-1951
  5000 Anson Blvd Whitestown (46075) *(G-16805)*

Ffd Publishing LLC 260 423-2119
  1730 Kensington Blvd Fort Wayne (46805) *(G-4981)*

Ffeine, Crown Point *Also Called: Roast Haus Coffee LLC (G-2746)*

Ffesar Inc 812 378-4220
  6564 W Black Tail Way Mccordsville (46055) *(G-11448)*

Fiber Bond, Trail Creek *Also Called: Gaius Julius Crassus Inc (G-15838)*

Fiber Bond Operating LLC 219 879-4541
  110 Menke Rd Trail Creek (46360) *(G-15837)*

Fiber By-Products Corp
  61801 County Road 127 Goshen (46528) *(G-6134)*

Fiber Forged Composites LLC 574 772-0107
  1517 S 100 W Knox (46534) *(G-10207)*

Fiber Technologies LLC 812 569-4641
  2517 E Caray Ct Bloomington (47401) *(G-866)*

Fiber-Tron Corp 574 294-8545
  29877 Old Us 33 Elkhart (46516) *(G-3345)*

Fiberglas & Plastic Fabg 317 549-1779
  2832 N Webster Ave Indianapolis (46219) *(G-8183)*

Fiberglass Pdts & Boat Repr 260 627-3209
  12401 Bay Heights Blvd Grabill (46741) *(G-6295)*

Fibergrate Composite 317 752-2500
  8148 Castle Lake Rd Indianapolis (46256) *(G-8184)*

Fibertech, Remington *Also Called: American Fibertech Corporation (G-14033)*

Fibertech Plastics, Elberfeld *Also Called: Fibertech Plastics LLC (G-3113)*

Fibertech Plastics LLC 812 983-2642
  11744 Blue Bell Rd Elberfeld (47613) *(G-3113)*

Fiberx Incorporated 317 501-5619
  7150 Indianapolis Blvd Hammond (46324) *(G-6928)*

Fiberx Products, Hammond *Also Called: Fiberx Incorporated (G-6928)*

Fibrosan Inc 574 612-4736
  2926 Paul Dr Elkhart (46514) *(G-3346)*

Fickle Peach Inc 765 282-5211
  117 E Charles St Muncie (47305) *(G-12395)*

Fideli Publishing 888 343-3542
  119 W Morgan St Martinsville (46151) *(G-11391)*

Fidelity Dental Handpiece Svc 317 254-0277
  4330 Black Oak Dr Indianapolis (46228) *(G-8185)*

Fiedeke Vinyl Coverings Inc 574 534-3408
  811 Eisenhower Dr N Goshen (46526) *(G-6135)*

Field Construction 574 664-2010
  5222 E County Road 650 N Twelve Mile (46988) *(G-15844)*

Field Rubber Products Inc 317 773-3787
  3211 Conner St Noblesville (46060) *(G-13077)*

Fielders Choice Direct, Oxford *Also Called: Landec Ag Inc (G-13475)*

Fields Outdoor Adventures LLP 765 932-3964
  126 S Perkins St Rushville (46173) *(G-14400)*

Fierce Publishing 765 251-3262
  501 Fletcher Ave Apt B Indianapolis (46203) *(G-8186)*

Figg Publishing Inc 317 797-2022
  8103 E Us Highway 36 Ste W Avon (46123) *(G-520)*

Figid Press LLC 717 809-0092
  1299 Spring Lake Dr Brownsburg (46112) *(G-1367)*

Figtree Print LLC 978 503-1779
  10101 Brook Meadow Dr Evansville (47711) *(G-4068)*

Filca LLC 812 637-3559
  22806 Stateline Rd Lawrenceburg (47025) *(G-10836)*

Fill-Rite Company 260 747-7529
  8825 Aviation Dr Fort Wayne (46809) *(G-4982)*

Fill-Rite Division, Fort Wayne *Also Called: Tuthill Corporation (G-5515)*

Fillmanns Industries LLC 765 744-4772
  3921 S Highbanks Rd Daleville (47334) *(G-2799)*

Filmtech Inc 888 399-7442
  3830 E County Road 200 S Greensburg (47240) *(G-6592)*

Filson Earthwork Company 317 774-3180
  21785 Riverwood Ave Noblesville (46062) *(G-13078)*

Filter Fabrics Inc
  63023 Lakeside Dr Goshen (46528) *(G-6136)*

Filter Sciences LLC 260 387-7709
  327 Ley Rd Fort Wayne (46825) *(G-4983)*

Filtration Parts Incorporated 704 661-8135
  513 N Melville St Rensselaer (47978) *(G-14052)*

Filtration Plus Inc 219 879-0663
  4208 N 900 W Michigan City (46360) *(G-11612)*

Finalmile-Logistics LLC 773 259-0727
  3125 Yukon St Portage (46368) *(G-13864)*

Financial Publishing Div, South Bend *Also Called: Carleton Inc (G-14967)*

Financial Times-Prentice Hall, Indianapolis *Also Called: Pearson Education Inc (G-9110)*

Findley Foster Corp 812 524-7279
  14 S County Road 1250 E Seymour (47274) *(G-14653)*

Fine Guys Inc 812 547-8630
  1002 Tell St Tell City (47586) *(G-15502)*

Fine Print, Bloomington *Also Called: Wraco Enterprises Inc (G-1016)*

Fine Woodworks 765 346-2630
  4045 Cramer Rd Martinsville (46151) *(G-11392)*

Fineline Digital Group Inc 317 872-4490
  8081 Zionsville Rd Indianapolis (46268) *(G-8187)*

Fineline Graphics Incorporated 317 872-4490
  8081 Zionsville Rd Indianapolis (46268) *(G-8188)*

Fineline Printing Group, Indianapolis *Also Called: Fineline Graphics Incorporated (G-8188)*

Finest Grade Products 812 421-1976
  2949 Arlington Ave Evansville (47712) *(G-4069)*

Fingerhut Bakery Inc (PA) 574 896-5937
  119 Lane St North Judson (46366) *(G-13212)*

Finish Alternatives 317 440-2899
  705 Northfield Ct Indianapolis (46227) *(G-8189)*

Finite Filtation Company   ALPHABETIC SECTION

Finite Filtation Company.. 219 789-8084
   120 Las Olas Ct Crown Point (46307) *(G-2684)*

Fink Industries LLC... 219 923-2015
   8750 Johnston St Highland (46322) *(G-7136)*

Finley Creek Vineyards LLC.. 317 769-5483
   795 S Us 421 Zionsville (46077) *(G-17008)*

Finvantage LLC.. 317 500-4949
   275 Medical Dr Unit 633 Carmel (46082) *(G-1635)*

Finvantage Solutions, Carmel *Also Called: Finvantage LLC (G-1635)*

Finzer Roller Inc.. 219 325-8808
   1164 E 150 N La Porte (46350) *(G-10408)*

Finzer Roller Inc.. 219 325-8808
   235 Factory St La Porte (46350) *(G-10409)*

Fire Apparatus Service Inc... 219 985-0788
   3905 W Ridge Rd Gary (46408) *(G-5933)*

Fire King International LLC (PA)....................................... 812 822-5574
   900 Park Pl New Albany (47150) *(G-12729)*

Fire King Security Group, New Albany *Also Called: Fki Security Group LLC (G-12730)*

Fire Star Industries LLC.. 317 432-3212
   4644 Brentridge Pkwy Greenwood (46143) *(G-6704)*

Fired Up Tees LLC.. 317 412-4113
   6740 W 150 N Bargersville (46106) *(G-566)*

Fireflies Ltd... 219 728-6245
   1505 S Calumet Rd Chesterton (46304) *(G-1926)*

Firehouse Printing LLC... 812 547-3109
   711 Humboldt St Tell City (47586) *(G-15503)*

Firesmoke Org.. 317 690-2542
   323 N Delaware St Indianapolis (46204) *(G-8190)*

Firestone, Bloomington *Also Called: Bridgestone Ret Operations LLC (G-815)*

Firestone, Columbia City *Also Called: Bridgestone Ret Operations LLC (G-2127)*

Firestone, Evansville *Also Called: Bridgestone Ret Operations LLC (G-3951)*

Firestone, Evansville *Also Called: Bridgestone Ret Operations LLC (G-3952)*

Firestone, Indianapolis *Also Called: Bridgestone Ret Operations LLC (G-7681)*

Firestone, Indianapolis *Also Called: Bridgestone Ret Operations LLC (G-7682)*

Firestone, Lafayette *Also Called: Bridgestone Ret Operations LLC (G-10542)*

Firestone, Noblesville *Also Called: Bridgestone Ret Operations LLC (G-13048)*

Firestone, Terre Haute *Also Called: Bridgestone Ret Operations LLC (G-15554)*

First Age Woodworking LLC.. 765 667-1847
   5725 Carry Back Dr Indianapolis (46237) *(G-8191)*

First Class Printing.. 317 808-2222
   6800 E 30th St Indianapolis (46219) *(G-8192)*

First Creative Ingredients Inc... 219 764-0202
   6625 Daniel Burnham Dr Ste D Portage (46368) *(G-13865)*

First Databank Inc.. 317 571-7200
   10 E Main St Carmel (46032) *(G-1636)*

First Flash Line, Fort Wayne *Also Called: Moose Lake Products Co Inc (G-5242)*

First Gear Engineering & Tech, Fort Wayne *Also Called: First Gear Inc (G-4984)*

First Gear Inc.. 260 490-3238
   4321 Goshen Rd Fort Wayne (46818) *(G-4984)*

First Generation Trucking LLC.. 317 654-6272
   8445 Country Meadows Dr Indianapolis (46234) *(G-8193)*

First Image.. 219 791-9900
   1447 E 86th Pl Merrillville (46410) *(G-11517)*

First Impression Trnsp... 317 682-8436
   2654 N Harding St Indianapolis (46208) *(G-8194)*

First Impressions Embroidary... 574 276-0750
   4763 Fir Rd Bremen (46506) *(G-1191)*

First Metals & Plastics Inc... 812 379-4400
   3805 Jonesville Rd Columbus (47201) *(G-2307)*

First Metals & Plastics Technologies Inc........................... 812 379-4400
   3805 Jonesville Rd Columbus (47201) *(G-2308)*

First Miracle LLC... 812 472-3527
   8518 S Kays Chapel Rd Fredericksburg (47120) *(G-5793)*

First Place Trophies... 812 385-3279
   1595 E State Road 64 Princeton (47670) *(G-13994)*

First Place Trophy Inc.. 574 293-6147
   24888 County Road 20 Elkhart (46517) *(G-3347)*

First Quality Printing Inc.. 317 506-8633
   5410 Radnor Rd Indianapolis (46226) *(G-8195)*

First Quality Printing Center... 317 546-5531
   5498 Emerson Way Indianapolis (46226) *(G-8196)*

First Source Manufacturing... 574 527-7192
   6511 E Pierceton Rd Pierceton (46562) *(G-13631)*

Fischer Fleet Wash LLC.. 812 661-9947
   204 S Lincoln Ave Rockport (47635) *(G-14340)*

Fischer Frms Natural Foods LLC....................................... 812 481-1411
   4630 S Cross St Saint Anthony (47575) *(G-14428)*

Fischer Woodcraft Incorporated.. 317 627-6035
   1024 Timber Grove Pl Beech Grove (46107) *(G-689)*

Fiserv Mrtg Servicing Systems (HQ).................................. 574 282-3300
   3575 Moreau Ct # 2 South Bend (46628) *(G-15034)*

Fish Factory... 219 929-9375
   676 Mississinewa Rd Chesterton (46304) *(G-1927)*

Fisher & Company Incorporated....................................... 586 746-2000
   2301 Saint George Rd Evansville (47711) *(G-4070)*

Fisher Clinical Services Inc.. 317 277-0337
   1220 W Morris St Indianapolis (46221) *(G-8197)*

Fisher Dynamics Evansville, Evansville *Also Called: Fisher & Company Incorporated (G-4070)*

Fisher Packing Company... 260 726-7355
   300 W Walnut St Portland (47371) *(G-13941)*

Fisher Specialties, Harlan *Also Called: Fisher Specialties Inc (G-7055)*

Fisher Specialties Inc... 260 385-8251
   11515 Roberts Rd Harlan (46743) *(G-7055)*

Fisher Tool 2 Inc.. 812 867-8350
   8231 Burch Park Dr Evansville (47725) *(G-4071)*

Fisherman S Lurecraft Shop Inc.. 260 829-1274
   10195 W State Road 120 Orland (46776) *(G-13365)*

Fishers Fire Station 92... 317 595-3292
   11595 Brooks School Rd Fishers (46037) *(G-4522)*

Fishers Laser Carvers LLC.. 317 845-0500
   11918 Halla Pl Fishers (46038) *(G-4523)*

Fishers Sun Herald, Fishers *Also Called: Topics Newspapers Inc (G-4614)*

Fishing Abilities Inc... 574 273-0842
   22770 Adams Rd South Bend (46628) *(G-15035)*

Fit Tight Covers Company Inc... 812 492-3370
   1200 N Willow Rd Ste 100 Evansville (47711) *(G-4072)*

Fitch Enterprises Inc.. 260 672-8462
   7477 E State Road 114 92 Roanoke (46783) *(G-14264)*

Fitch Inc.. 260 637-0835
   3708 Mccomb Rd Huntertown (46748) *(G-7256)*

Fitech Divison, Michigan City *Also Called: Ashley F Ward Inc (G-11580)*

Fitech Inc.. 513 398-1414
   2031 Tryon Rd Michigan City (46360) *(G-11613)*

Fitesa Indiana LLC... 812 466-0202
   1069 Crawford St Terre Haute (47807) *(G-15588)*

Fitesa Indiana LLC... 812 466-0266
   3400-A Fort Harrison Rd Terre Haute (47804) *(G-15589)*

Fitzpatrick Sons Woodworks LLC...................................... 219 987-2223
   9190 W 1100 N Demotte (46310) *(G-2916)*

Five Dmensions Restoration LLC....................................... 347 490-8904
   7020 Pershing Rd Indianapolis (46268) *(G-8198)*

Five Star Fab & Erectors LLC... 812 614-9558
   806 E Randall St Greensburg (47240) *(G-6593)*

Five Star Hydraulics Inc... 219 762-1619
   1210 Crisman Rd Portage (46368) *(G-13866)*

Five Star Sheets LLC... 574 654-8058
   54370 Smilax Rd New Carlisle (46552) *(G-12840)*

Five Starr Inc.. 812 367-1554
   453 W 9th St Ferdinand (47532) *(G-4433)*

Fives N Amercn Combustn Inc.. 219 662-9600
   730 N Main St Crown Point (46307) *(G-2685)*

Fix-Ur-6 LLC.. 812 989-4310
   3330 Old Hill Rd Floyds Knobs (47119) *(G-4677)*

Fizz Wizz.. 812 718-9045
   851 N State St North Vernon (47265) *(G-13270)*

Fki Security Group LLC.. 812 948-8400
   101 Security Pkwy New Albany (47150) *(G-12730)*

FL Smidth... 812 402-9210
   1315 N Cullen Ave Ste 102 Evansville (47715) *(G-4073)*

Flag & Banner Company Inc... 317 299-4880
   5450 Lafayette Rd Ste 5 Indianapolis (46254) *(G-8199)*

Flags International Inc 574 674-5125
10845 Mckinley Hwy Osceola (46561) *(G-13392)*

Flagship Sign Supply, Hammond Also Called: Flagship Sign Supply LLC *(G-6929)*

Flagship Sign Supply LLC 708 474-9521
532 Conkey St Hammond (46324) *(G-6929)*

Flagstone Village LLC 219 989-3265
1402 173rd St Hammond (46324) *(G-6930)*

Flair Exchange LLC 765 210-4604
5266 E 100 S Tipton (46072) *(G-15773)*

Flair Interiors Inc 574 534-2163
1010 Eisenhower Dr S Goshen (46526) *(G-6137)*

Flair Molded Plastics Inc 812 425-6155
2521 Lynch Rd Evansville (47711) *(G-4074)*

Flambeau Inc 812 372-4899
4325 Middle Rd Columbus (47203) *(G-2309)*

Flambeau Inc 812 372-4899
4325 Middle Rd Columbus (47203) *(G-2310)*

Flamco, Fishers Also Called: Aalberts Hydrnic Flow Ctrl Inc *(G-4458)*

Flamespray Machine Service 260 726-6236
237 E Votaw St Portland (47371) *(G-13942)*

Flanders Inc 812 867-7421
8101 Baumgart Rd Evansville (47725) *(G-4075)*

Flanders Electric Motor Service LLC (PA) 812 867-7421
8101 Baumgart Rd Evansville (47725) *(G-4076)*

Flanders Electric Mtr Svc LLC 812 867-4014
500 E Buena Vista Rd Evansville (47711) *(G-4077)*

Flanders Electric Mtr Svc LLC 812 421-4300
1050 E Maryland St Evansville (47711) *(G-4078)*

Flannigan Press LLC 317 776-4914
10422 Magenta Dr Noblesville (46060) *(G-13079)*

Flare Precision LLC 260 490-1101
6210 Discount Dr Fort Wayne (46818) *(G-4985)*

Flat Electronics LLC (PA) 765 414-6635
9783 E 116th St Pmb 3040 Fishers (46037) *(G-4524)*

Flat Rock 219 852-5262
6732 Calumet Ave Hammond (46324) *(G-6931)*

Flat Roll Div - Jeffersonville, Jeffersonville Also Called: Steel Dynamics Inc *(G-10059)*

Flavor Burst, Danville Also Called: Flavor Burst LLC *(G-2812)*

Flavor Burst LLC 317 745-2952
499 Commerce Dr Danville (46122) *(G-2812)*

Flavor Imperium LLC 765 499-0854
6139 Robin Run Apt A Indianapolis (46254) *(G-8200)*

Flawless Units LLC 317 833-5975
6919 E 10th St Indianapolis (46219) *(G-8201)*

Fleetwood Homes, Decatur Also Called: Rev Recreation Group Inc *(G-2879)*

Fleetwood Homes, Decatur Also Called: Rev Recreation Group Inc *(G-2880)*

Fleming Air Flow, Indianapolis Also Called: Fleming Assoc Calibration Inc *(G-8202)*

Fleming and Sons Home Imprv 765 717-6690
621 N Mulberry St Muncie (47305) *(G-12396)*

Fleming Assoc Calibration Inc 317 631-4605
2318 E 45th St Indianapolis (46205) *(G-8202)*

FLEming&sonz, Indianapolis Also Called: David Fleming *(G-7954)*

Flenar Manufacturing LLC 574 893-4070
2906 Ft Wayne Rd Rochester (46975) *(G-14291)*

Fletcher Heating & Cooling 812 865-2984
2049 W County Road 500 N Paoli (47454) *(G-13494)*

Flex Appeals Family and Frien 219 863-3830
9985 Arrowhead Ln Demotte (46310) *(G-2917)*

Flex-N-Gate LLC 260 665-8288
3000 Woodhull Dr Angola (46703) *(G-251)*

Flex-N-Gate LLC 765 793-5732
11778 S 600 W Covington (47932) *(G-2530)*

Flexaust, Warsaw Also Called: Flexaust Inc *(G-16362)*

Flexaust Inc (DH) 574 267-7909
1510 Armstrong Rd Warsaw (46580) *(G-16362)*

Flexco Products Inc 574 294-2502
2415 Bryant St Elkhart (46516) *(G-3348)*

Flexform Technologies LLC 574 295-3777
4955 Beck Dr Elkhart (46516) *(G-3349)*

Flexible Concepts Inc 574 296-0941
1620 Middlebury St Elkhart (46516) *(G-3350)*

Flexible Materials Inc (PA) 812 280-7000
3101 Hamburg Pike Ste B Jeffersonville (47130) *(G-9984)*

Flexible Technologies Inc 574 936-2432
1435 N Michigan St Ste 3 Plymouth (46563) *(G-13776)*

Flexseals Mfg LLC 574 293-0333
28255 Charlotte Ave Bldg 1 Elkhart (46517) *(G-3351)*

Flickers Candle Shop 317 403-5045
2310 E Loretta Dr Indianapolis (46227) *(G-8203)*

Flickinger Industries Inc 260 432-4527
1801 Carlton Ave Fort Wayne (46802) *(G-4986)*

Flight Dept, South Bend Also Called: Leco Corporation *(G-15122)*

Flight1 Aviation Tech Inc 404 504-7010
1677 King St Wabash (46992) *(G-16186)*

Flinn Frms Bdford Feed Seed In 812 279-4136
917 17th St Bedford (47421) *(G-636)*

Flint & Walling Inc (HQ) 800 345-9422
95 N Oak St Kendallville (46755) *(G-10111)*

Flint CPS Inks North Amer LLC 317 870-4422
4910 W 78th St Indianapolis (46268) *(G-8204)*

Flint Group US LLC 574 269-4603
3025 E Old Road 30 Warsaw (46582) *(G-16363)*

Flint Ink North America Div, Warsaw Also Called: Flint Group US LLC *(G-16363)*

Flir Detection, West Lafayette Also Called: Teledyne Flir Detection Inc *(G-16635)*

Flir Security Inc 443 936-9108
5250 W 76th St Indianapolis (46268) *(G-8205)*

Flir Systems, West Lafayette Also Called: Teledyne Flir Defense Inc *(G-16634)*

Flj Transport LLC 574 642-0200
1025 Lantern Ln Goshen (46526) *(G-6138)*

Floating Docks Mfg Co, Indianapolis Also Called: Engineered Dock Systems Inc *(G-8120)*

Flodder Sawmill LLC 765 628-0280
10861 E 100 N Greentown (46936) *(G-6646)*

Flomatic International, New Albany Also Called: Manitowoc Beverage Eqp Inc *(G-12770)*

Floor Works Mfg & Fab 812 394-2311
6224 W Walnut Fairbanks (47849) *(G-4395)*

Flora Racing 574 233-0642
3319 W Sample St South Bend (46619) *(G-15036)*

Flora Wastewater Treatment 574 967-3005
507 N Division St Flora (46929) *(G-4658)*

Floral Beverages, Gas City Also Called: Heartland Harvest Proc LLC *(G-6038)*

Floral-Guard, Indianapolis Also Called: Servaas Manufacturing Corp *(G-9407)*

Flosource Inc 800 752-5959
1405 Hancel Pkwy Mooresville (46158) *(G-12208)*

Flotec Inc 317 273-6960
7625 W New York St Indianapolis (46214) *(G-8206)*

Flow Center Products Inc 765 364-9460
2065 S Nucor Rd Crawfordsville (47933) *(G-2567)*

Flow International Corporation 253 850-3500
1635 Production Rd Jeffersonville (47130) *(G-9985)*

Flowers Baking Co Ohio LLC 502 350-4700
1601 W 37th Ave Hobart (46342) *(G-7188)*

Flowears Baking Co Ohio LLC 502 350-4700
1006 E 22nd St Marion (46953) *(G-11286)*

Flowers Baking Co Ohio LLC 502 350-4700
1133 S Main St South Bend (46601) *(G-15037)*

Flowers Bkg Co Bardstown LLC 502 350-4700
1531 W Tipton St Seymour (47274) *(G-14654)*

Flowserve, Portage Also Called: Flowserve Corporation *(G-13867)*

Flowserve Corporation 219 763-1000
6675 Daniel Burnham Dr Ste F Portage (46368) *(G-13867)*

Floyd County Brewing Co LLC 502 724-3202
129 W Main St New Albany (47150) *(G-12731)*

Flp Woodworks 260 424-3904
1510 Boone St Fort Wayne (46808) *(G-4987)*

Fluid Handling Technology Inc 317 216-9629
7692 Zionsville Rd Indianapolis (46268) *(G-8207)*

Fluid-Tech International Corp 260 420-5000
820 Schick St Fort Wayne (46803) *(G-4988)*

Flutes Inc (PA) 317 870-6010
8252 Zionsville Rd Indianapolis (46268) *(G-8208)*

Flutes Inc 844 317-2021
1102 W Hanna Ave Indianapolis (46217) *(G-8209)*

Flw Plastics Inc 812 546-0050
199 Raymond St Hope (47246) *(G-7224)*

Flying Pig Woodworks LLC 219 242-5557
5076 W Madura Rd Union Mills (46382) *(G-15864)*

Flying Turtle Publishing Inc 219 221-8488
7216 Birch Ave Hammond (46324) *(G-6932)*

Flying W Trophy Div, Indianapolis Also Called: Professional Bowling Ball Svc *(G-9220)*

Flyinneedle Embroidery Inc 260 672-0742
3132 E 900 N Roanoke (46783) *(G-14265)*

Flynn & Sons Sand & Gravel LLC 812 636-4400
11971 N Us Highway 231 Odon (47562) *(G-13335)*

Flynn Interactive, Indianapolis Also Called: Flynn Media LLC *(G-8210)*

Flynn Media LLC 317 536-2972
9334 Champton Dr Indianapolis (46256) *(G-8210)*

Flynn Welding & Inspection LLC 812 327-7437
9405 N Newark Rd Solsberry (47459) *(G-14925)*

Flyover Enterprises Inc 317 417-1747
1068 Chipmunk Ln Pendleton (46064) *(G-13532)*

Flywithme Delivery LLC 219 614-9384
4350 Madison Ave Apt 110 Indianapolis (46227) *(G-8211)*

FM Holdings LLC 574 773-2814
2051 Cheyenne St Ste 1 Nappanee (46550) *(G-12597)*

Fmt LLC 260 417-5613
1525 Mayfield Rd Fort Wayne (46825) *(G-4989)*

Foam Fabricators, New Albany Also Called: Foam Fabricators Inc *(G-12732)*

Foam Fabricators Inc 812 948-1696
950 Progress Blvd New Albany (47150) *(G-12732)*

Foam Rubber LLC 765 521-2000
2600 Troy Ave New Castle (47362) *(G-12862)*

Foam Rubber Products, New Castle Also Called: Foam Rubber LLC *(G-12862)*

Foam X-Press LLC 260 563-5767
675 E 250 S Wabash (46992) *(G-16187)*

Foamcraft Inc 574 293-8569
900 Industrial Pkwy Elkhart (46516) *(G-3352)*

Foamcraft Inc 574 534-4343
2506 Industrial Park Dr Goshen (46526) *(G-6139)*

Foamcraft Inc (PA) 317 545-3626
9230 Harrison Park Ct Indianapolis (46216) *(G-8212)*

Foamcraft Inc 812 849-3350
100 N Industrial Pkwy Mitchell (47446) *(G-12039)*

Foamex, Auburn Also Called: Fxi Inc *(G-392)*

Foamex, Fort Wayne Also Called: Foamex LP *(G-4990)*

Foamex, Fort Wayne Also Called: Fxi Inc *(G-5015)*

Foamex LP 800 417-4257
8520 Temple Drive Fort Wayne (46809) *(G-4990)*

Foamfab, Elkhart Also Called: Exemplary Foam South LLC *(G-3339)*

Foamiture 574 831-4775
19240 Tarman Rd New Paris (46553) *(G-12953)*

Focal Point Cabinetry, Osceola Also Called: Custom Design Laminates Inc *(G-13388)*

Focus Mold and Machine Inc 812 422-9627
1145 Indy Ct Evansville (47725) *(G-4079)*

Fog Foundry Frankfort 765 670-6445
58 W Clinton St Frankfort (46041) *(G-5663)*

Fogwell Technologies Inc 260 410-1898
10525 W Yoder Rd Roanoke (46783) *(G-14266)*

Foil Die International, Huntington Also Called: Foil Die International Inc *(G-7310)*

Foil Die International Inc 260 359-9011
1054 W 900 N Huntington (46750) *(G-7310)*

Foil Form Inc 260 359-9011
1054 W 900 N Huntington (46750) *(G-7311)*

Foil Laminating Inc
1000 Pidco Dr Plymouth (46563) *(G-13777)*

Foley Pattern Company Inc 260 925-4113
500 W 11th St Auburn (46706) *(G-391)*

Folk Art To Go 317 753-8553
8152 Meadow Bend Dr Indianapolis (46259) *(G-8213)*

Fontaine Trailer Company 574 772-6673
1201 W Culver Rd Knox (46534) *(G-10208)*

Fontaine Trailer Company, Knox Also Called: Fontaine Trailer Company *(G-10208)*

Fontaine Truck Equipment Co, Indianapolis Also Called: Marmon Highway Tech LLC *(G-8839)*

Fontana Fasteners Inc (DH) 765 654-0477
3595 W State Road 28 Frankfort (46041) *(G-5664)*

Food Service Distributors Inc 812 267-4846
14820 N Martin Mathis Rd Ne Palmyra (47164) *(G-13480)*

Foods Alive Inc 260 488-4497
1600 Wohlert St Angola (46703) *(G-252)*

Foppers Gourmet Pet Treat Bky, Logansport Also Called: Nick-Em Builders LLC *(G-11100)*

Foppers Pet Treat Bakery, Logansport Also Called: Nick-Em Builders LLC *(G-11099)*

For Bare Feet LLC 812 322-9317
1201 S Ohio St Martinsville (46151) *(G-11393)*

For The Love of Words LLC 317 550-8805
625 E Freeport Rd Morristown (46161) *(G-12276)*

Force Cnc LLC 812 273-0218
940 Lanier Dr Madison (47250) *(G-11220)*

Ford, Plainfield Also Called: Ford Motor Company *(G-13680)*

Ford Motor Company 901 368-8821
2675 Reeves Rd Plainfield (46168) *(G-13680)*

Ford Sawmills Inc 812 324-2134
2019 E Old Terre Haute Rd Vincennes (47591) *(G-16125)*

Forecast Sales Inc 317 829-0147
2719 Tobey Dr Indianapolis (46219) *(G-8214)*

Forefront Foam LLC 574 343-1146
1015 Saint Jerome St Mishawaka (46544) *(G-11897)*

Foremost Fabricators, Goshen Also Called: Bud LLC *(G-6103)*

Foremost Fabricators, Goshen Also Called: Patrick Industries Inc *(G-6237)*

Foremost Flexible Fabricating 812 663-4756
824 N Michigan Ave Greensburg (47240) *(G-6594)*

Foremost Flexible Products, Greensburg Also Called: Foremost Flexible Fabricating *(G-6594)*

Forensic Sane Software LLC 219 232-6576
5201 Fountain Dr Ste B Crown Point (46307) *(G-2686)*

Foresee LLC 219 226-9663
158 N Main St Crown Point (46307) *(G-2687)*

Forest Commodities Inc (PA) 765 349-3291
1789 S Old State Road 67 Martinsville (46151) *(G-11394)*

Forest Products Group Inc 765 659-1807
901 Blinn Ave Frankfort (46041) *(G-5665)*

Forest Products Group Ind Div, Frankfort Also Called: Forest Products Group Inc *(G-5665)*

Forest Products Mfg Co (PA) 812 482-5625
51 E 30th St Jasper (47546) *(G-9838)*

Forest River, Elkhart Also Called: Forest River Inc *(G-3356)*

Forest River Inc 574 848-1335
17645 Commerce Dr Bristol (46507) *(G-1261)*

Forest River Inc 574 296-7700
3603 S Nappanee St Elkhart (46517) *(G-3353)*

Forest River Inc 574 262-5466
3601 County Road 6 E Elkhart (46514) *(G-3354)*

Forest River Inc 574 262-3474
2745 Northland Dr Elkhart (46514) *(G-3355)*

Forest River Inc (HQ) 574 389-4600
900 County Road 1 N Elkhart (46514) *(G-3356)*

Forest River Inc 574 642-3112
2367 Century Dr Goshen (46528) *(G-6140)*

Forest River Inc 574 533-5934
3010 College Ave Goshen (46528) *(G-6141)*

Forest River Inc 574 642-2640
201 W Elm St Millersburg (46543) *(G-11812)*

Forest River Cherokee Inc 260 593-2566
402 Lehman Ave Topeka (46571) *(G-15805)*

Forest River Custom Extrusions 574 975-0206
712 Eisenhower Dr S Goshen (46526) *(G-6142)*

Forever Young Trckg Svcs LLC 616 350-4053
6444 Grandview Dr Indianapolis (46260) *(G-8215)*

Forge Racks and Dunnage, Connersville Also Called: Keener Metal Fabricating LLC *(G-2450)*

Forged Alliance Inc 815 726-5223
1415 Fairview St Anderson (46016) *(G-118)*

Forks Rv Inc 574 825-7467
11280 W Us Highway 20 Shipshewana (46565) *(G-14846)*

Form Wood Industries Inc 812 284-3676
1601 Production Rd Jeffersonville (47130) *(G-9986)*

Form/TEC Plastics Incorporated 765 342-2300
1000 Industrial Dr Martinsville (46151) *(G-11395)*

ALPHABETIC SECTION — Franke Motorsports Inc

Formal, Elkhart *Also Called: Formal Affairs Tuxedo Shop (G-3357)*

Formal Affairs Tuxedo Shop 574 875-6654
23797 Us Highway 33 Elkhart (46517) *(G-3357)*

Formflex, Bloomingdale *Also Called: Futurex Industries Inc (G-760)*

Forro Press Inc 317 576-1797
12210 Driftstone Dr Fishers (46037) *(G-4525)*

Forsyth Brothers Con Pdts Inc (PA) 812 466-4080
4500 N Fruitridge St Terre Haute (47805) *(G-15590)*

Forsyth Puttmann LLC 812 466-2925
4500 N Fruitridge St Terre Haute (47805) *(G-15591)*

Fort Meyers, Fort Wayne *Also Called: United Oil Corp (G-5521)*

Fort Wayne Business Weekly, Fort Wayne *Also Called: Kpc Media Group Inc (G-5158)*

Fort Wayne Diamond Pdts Inc 260 747-1681
2625 E Pontiac St Fort Wayne (46803) *(G-4991)*

Fort Wayne Fabrication 260 459-8848
3303 Freeman St Fort Wayne (46802) *(G-4992)*

Fort Wayne Fabrication Inc 260 704-6618
1624 Simons St Fort Wayne (46803) *(G-4993)*

Fort Wayne Metals, Columbia City *Also Called: Fort Wayne Metals RES Pdts LLC (G-2147)*

Fort Wayne Metals, Fort Wayne *Also Called: Fort Wayne Metals RES Pdts LLC (G-4995)*

Fort Wayne Metals, Fort Wayne *Also Called: Fort Wayne Metals RES Pdts LLC (G-4996)*

Fort Wayne Metals RES Pdts 260 747-4154
3401 Mcarthur Dr Fort Wayne (46809) *(G-4994)*

Fort Wayne Metals RES Pdts LLC 260 747-4154
2300 E Cardinal Dr Columbia City (46725) *(G-2147)*

Fort Wayne Metals RES Pdts LLC 260 747-4154
9823 Ardmore Ave Fort Wayne (46809) *(G-4995)*

Fort Wayne Metals RES Pdts LLC (PA) 260 747-4154
9609 Ardmore Ave Fort Wayne (46809) *(G-4996)*

Fort Wayne Metals RES Pdts LLC 260 747-4154
9307 Avionics Dr Fort Wayne (46809) *(G-4997)*

FORT WAYNE METALS RESEARCH PRODUCTS CORP, Fort Wayne *Also Called: Fort Wayne Metals RES Pdts (G-4994)*

Fort Wayne Mold & Engrg Inc 260 747-9168
4501 Earth Dr Fort Wayne (46809) *(G-4998)*

Fort Wayne Newspapers Inc 260 461-8444
600 W Main St Fort Wayne (46802) *(G-4999)*

Fort Wayne Plastics Inc 260 432-2520
510 Sumpter St Fort Wayne (46804) *(G-5000)*

Fort Wayne Pools 260 459-4100
6930 Gettysburg Pike Fort Wayne (46804) *(G-5001)*

Fort Wayne Wire Die Inc (PA) 260 747-1681
2424 American Way Fort Wayne (46809) *(G-5002)*

Fort Wyne Rdlgy Assn Fundation 260 266-8120
3707 New Vision Dr Fort Wayne (46845) *(G-5003)*

Forterra Concrete Inds Inc 812 426-5353
1213 Stanley Ave Evansville (47711) *(G-4080)*

Forterra Concrete Inds Inc 859 254-4242
4360 Whitelick Dr Whitestown (46075) *(G-16806)*

Fortune Diversified Industries 317 532-3644
6809 Corporate Dr Indianapolis (46278) *(G-8216)*

Fortville Automotive Sup Inc 317 485-5114
305 W Broadway St Fortville (46040) *(G-5594)*

Fortville Feeders Inc (PA) 317 485-5195
750 E Broadway St Fortville (46040) *(G-5595)*

Forward Lift / A Dover Company 812 273-7325
996 Industrial Dr Madison (47250) *(G-11221)*

Fostrom Press LLC 812 945-0071
2234 Balmer Fenwick Rd Floyds Knobs (47119) *(G-4678)*

Founders West Inc 812 936-7446
8049 N 600 W Mccordsville (46055) *(G-11449)*

Foundry Services Inc 317 955-8112
10482 Winghaven Dr Noblesville (46060) *(G-13080)*

Fountain Acres Foods 765 847-1897
1140 W Whitewater Rd Fountain City (47341) *(G-5611)*

Fountain County Neighbor 765 762-2411
113 S Perry St Attica (47918) *(G-348)*

Fountaintown Forge Inc 317 861-5403
5513 S 100 E Fountaintown (46130) *(G-5614)*

Four Corners Winery LLC 219 730-5311
294 E 600 N Valparaiso (46383) *(G-15950)*

Four Daughters LLC 805 868-7456
3000 Overlook Trce New Albany (47150) *(G-12733)*

Four Part Inc 219 926-7777
132 S Calumet Rd Chesterton (46304) *(G-1928)*

Four Quarters RE LLC 765 474-2295
728 Cherokee Ave Lafayette (47905) *(G-10580)*

Four Season Oil Inc 317 215-1214
1237 American Ave Plainfield (46168) *(G-13681)*

Four Star Fabricators Inc 812 354-9995
810 S Ind Park Dr Petersburg (47567) *(G-13612)*

Four Star Field Services Inc 812 354-9995
804 S Industrial Park Dr Ste 10 Petersburg (47567) *(G-13613)*

Four Star Printing 765 620-9728
1001 E Sigler St Frankton (46044) *(G-5791)*

Four Star Screen Printing LLC 765 533-3006
1379 N Cadiz Pike New Castle (47362) *(G-12863)*

Four Star Welding 574 825-3856
11400 W 300n Middlebury (46540) *(G-11716)*

Four Woods Laminating Inc (PA) 260 593-2246
7550 W 500 S Topeka (46571) *(G-15806)*

Fourman Enterprises Inc 812 546-5734
701 South St Hope (47246) *(G-7225)*

Fowler Ridge IV Wind Farm LLC 765 884-1029
2870 W State Road 18 Fowler (47944) *(G-5624)*

Fox Manufacturing Inc 317 430-1493
12910 Bristow Ln Pendleton (46064) *(G-13533)*

Fox Products Corporation 260 723-4888
6110 S State Road 5 South Whitley (46787) *(G-15318)*

Fox Studios Inc 317 253-0135
6027 Gladden Dr Indianapolis (46220) *(G-8217)*

Fox Uniform Inc 317 350-2684
468 Southpoint Cir Ste 100 Brownsburg (46112) *(G-1368)*

Foxxie Planner L L C 260 247-6303
1416 Rosemont Dr Fort Wayne (46808) *(G-5004)*

Foy Industries 317 727-3905
6953 Dean Rd Indianapolis (46220) *(G-8218)*

Fr Chinook LLC 317 356-1666
7441 Chinook Cir Indianapolis (46219) *(G-8219)*

Frakes Engineering Inc 317 577-3000
7950 Castleway Dr Ste 160 Indianapolis (46250) *(G-8220)*

Frakes Industrial Sales & Svc, Westfield *Also Called: Robinson Industries Inc (G-16724)*

Frame Shop, The, Indianapolis *Also Called: Franklin Barry Gallery (G-8224)*

Framed Art Division, Elkhart *Also Called: Keyline Sales Inc (G-3453)*

Framery 812 537-4319
84 E High St Lawrenceburg (47025) *(G-10837)*

Frances Monforte 317 875-0880
8788 Robbins Rd Indianapolis (46268) *(G-8221)*

Francesville Vulcan Materials 219 567-9155
14530 W 700 S Francesville (47946) *(G-5640)*

Francine Bond Insur Agcy Inc 317 262-2250
316 Prebster Dr Brownsburg (46112) *(G-1369)*

Francisco Mining, Francisco *Also Called: Peabody Midwest Mining LLC (G-5646)*

Franco Corporation 765 675-6691
600 Industrial Dr Tipton (46072) *(G-15774)*

Frank Balensiefer 219 474-6419
208 S Locust St Earl Park (47942) *(G-2986)*

Frank Balensiefer Painting, Earl Park *Also Called: Frank Balensiefer (G-2986)*

Frank H Monroe Heating & Coolg 812 945-2566
595 Industrial Blvd New Albany (47150) *(G-12734)*

Frank Miller, Union City *Also Called: Frank Miller Lumber Co Inc (G-15853)*

Frank Miller Lumber Co Inc (PA) 800 345-2643
1690 Frank Miller Rd Union City (47390) *(G-15853)*

Frank R Komar PC 812 477-9110
4111 Washington Ave Evansville (47714) *(G-4081)*

Frank W Martinez 574 232-6081
54555 Pine Rd South Bend (46628) *(G-15038)*

Frank Wiss Racg Components Inc 317 243-9585
140 Gasoline Aly Indianapolis (46222) *(G-8222)*

Franke & Associates, Indianapolis *Also Called: Franke Motorsports Inc (G-8223)*

Franke Motorsports Inc 317 357-6995
6501 E Troy Ave Indianapolis (46203) *(G-8223)*

Franke Plating Works Inc   **ALPHABETIC SECTION**

Franke Plating Works Inc 260 422-8477
   1918 E Wayne St Fort Wayne (46803) *(G-5005)*

Frankfort Masonry & Supply, Fort Wayne *Also Called: Carters Concrete Block Inc (G-4836)*

Frankfort Newspaper 859 254-2385
   251 E Clinton St Frankfort (46041) *(G-5666)*

Frankfort Plastics Inc 931 510-0525
   2021 W County Road 0 Ns Frankfort (46041) *(G-5667)*

Franklin Barry Gallery 317 822-8455
   617 Massachusetts Ave Indianapolis (46204) *(G-8224)*

Franklin Cornucopia, Greenwood *Also Called: Mild To Wild Pepper & Herb Co (G-6741)*

FRANKLIN ELECTRIC, Fort Wayne *Also Called: Franklin Electric Co Inc (G-5006)*

Franklin Electric Co Inc (PA) 260 824-2900
   9255 Coverdale Rd Fort Wayne (46809) *(G-5006)*

Franklin Electric Intl (HQ) 260 824-2900
   9255 Coverdale Rd Fort Wayne (46809) *(G-5007)*

Franklin Garage Ltd 260 442-2439
   1312 Franklin Ave Fort Wayne (46808) *(G-5008)*

Franklin Olin 765 342-9040
   6425 Hall School Rd Martinsville (46151) *(G-11396)*

Franklin Publishing Inc 800 634-1993
   5373 Ashby Ct Greenwood (46143) *(G-6705)*

Franklin Stamping Inds Inc 765 282-5138
   105 W Fuson Rd Muncie (47302) *(G-12397)*

Franklin Township Civic League 317 862-1774
   8822 Southeastern Ave Indianapolis (46239) *(G-8225)*

FRANKLIN TOWNSHIP INFORMER, Indianapolis *Also Called: Franklin Township Civic League (G-8225)*

Franklin Well Service LLC 877 943-4680
   400 Main St Vincennes (47591) *(G-16126)*

Franklins Mercantile 812 876-0426
   7115 Kimberly Ln Spencer (47460) *(G-15347)*

Franks Machine Shop Tool & Die 574 288-6899
   24133 State Road 2 South Bend (46619) *(G-15039)*

Fratco, Monticello *Also Called: Fratco Inc (G-12150)*

Fratco Inc 800 854-7120
   4385 S 1450 W Francesville (47946) *(G-5641)*

Fratco Inc (PA) 800 854-7120
   105 W Broadway St Monticello (47960) *(G-12150)*

Frazier Aviation LLC 888 835-9269
   7237 S State Road 75 Cutler (46920) *(G-2784)*

Frazier Comfort Details 219 276-2288
   1500 W 46th Ave Gary (46408) *(G-5934)*

Frech U S A Inc 219 874-2812
   6000 Ohio St Michigan City (46360) *(G-11614)*

Frecker Optical Inc 260 747-9653
   7115 Old Trail Rd Fort Wayne (46809) *(G-5009)*

Freckles Grphics Lafayette Inc 765 448-4692
   3835 Fortune Dr Lafayette (47905) *(G-10581)*

Fred Anderson 765 985-2099
   4757 N 400 E Peru (46970) *(G-13583)*

Fred Brandt Co 812 926-0009
   N Hogan Rd Aurora (47001) *(G-444)*

Fred D McCrary 812 354-6520
   4295 W County Road 350 N Petersburg (47567) *(G-13614)*

Fred S Carver Inc (DH) 260 563-7577
   1569 Morris St Wabash (46992) *(G-16188)*

Fred Schock Company Inc 765 647-4648
   Brookville (47012) *(G-1320)*

Fred Sibley Enterprises, Elkhart *Also Called: Fred Sibley Sr (G-3358)*

Fred Sibley Sr 574 264-2237
   25551 Homewood Ave Elkhart (46514) *(G-3358)*

Fred Smith Store Fixtures 812 347-2363
   3700 Commerce Way Nw Corydon (47112) *(G-2497)*

Fred Smith Store Fixtures Inc 812 347-2363
   6405 Highway 337 Nw Depauw (47115) *(G-2938)*

Freda Inc 260 665-8431
   401 Growth Pkwy Angola (46703) *(G-253)*

Freddie Powell 574 658-3345
   339 S 30th St Lafayette (47904) *(G-10582)*

Freds Custom Furniture 260 726-2519
   2612 S Blaine Pike Portland (47371) *(G-13943)*

Freduenberg-Nok Sealing Tech, Shelbyville *Also Called: Freudenberg-Nok General Partnr (G-14757)*

Freeband Custom Paint LLC 219 216-2553
   3156 Watergate Pl Indianapolis (46224) *(G-8226)*

Freed Machining and Tool Inc 765 538-3019
   6033 W 800 S Westpoint (47992) *(G-16744)*

Freedman Mobility Seating, Rochester *Also Called: Fbsa LLC (G-14290)*

Freedom Acres Inc 260 856-3059
   458 Olive St Cromwell (46732) *(G-2630)*

Freedom Corrugated LLC 317 290-1140
   5505 W 74th St Indianapolis (46268) *(G-8227)*

Freedom Industrial Welding LLC 812 686-9802
   709 N 7th St Rockport (47635) *(G-14341)*

Freedom Intentional LLC 219 576-2699
   5690 Cheval Ln Indianapolis (46235) *(G-8228)*

Freedom Lumber Company, Monroeville *Also Called: Monrovlle Box Pllet WD Pdts LL (G-12071)*

Freedom Racing Engines 317 858-9937
   2400 Commerce Way Pittsboro (46167) *(G-13646)*

Freedom Valley Cabinets 717 606-2811
   7483 Old Glory Ln Freedom (47431) *(G-5800)*

Freehold Games LLC 574 656-9031
   69080 Sycamore Rd Walkerton (46574) *(G-16266)*

Freelance Lettering Inc 317 244-9272
   4 Gasoline Aly Ste A Indianapolis (46222) *(G-8229)*

Freelance Services LLC 317 727-2669
   6151 Canterbury Ct Pittsboro (46167) *(G-13647)*

Freels Machine Works Inc 260 636-7948
   489 S 75 E Albion (46701) *(G-27)*

Freeman Signs 317 386-3453
   2949 E Main St Danville (46122) *(G-2813)*

Freeport Minerals Corporation 260 421-5400
   2131 S Coliseum Blvd Fort Wayne (46803) *(G-5010)*

Freeze Dried Partners LLC 800 783-1326
   11650 Olio Rd Ste 1000 Fishers (46037) *(G-4526)*

Freezing Systems and Svc Inc 219 879-6236
   107 Freyer Rd Michigan City (46360) *(G-11615)*

Freight Transport, Indianapolis *Also Called: Safe Bird Express LLC (G-9362)*

Freightliner Cstm Chassis Corp 260 517-9678
   66540 State Road 19 Wakarusa (46573) *(G-16233)*

Freije Treatment Systems Inc 888 766-7258
   9910 N By Northeast Blvd Ste 200 Fishers (46037) *(G-4527)*

Freije Treatment Systems Inc 317 508-3848
   7435 E 86th St Indianapolis (46256) *(G-8230)*

Frema Holdings LLC 317 822-8002
   1030 E New York St Indianapolis (46202) *(G-8231)*

Fremont Coatings Div 260 495-4445
   302 E Mcswain Dr Fremont (46737) *(G-5821)*

Fremont Plastics, Fremont *Also Called: Sonoco Teq LLC (G-5835)*

French International Coatings 574 505-0774
   15205 E 200 S Akron (46910) *(G-5)*

French Lick Auto Signs (PA) 812 936-7777
   9451 W State Road 56 French Lick (47432) *(G-5845)*

Fresh Bakery Candles, Indianapolis *Also Called: Fresh Bakery Candles LLC (G-8232)*

Fresh Bakery Candles LLC 317 899-2377
   223 Belmar Ave Indianapolis (46219) *(G-8232)*

Fresh Fenix LLC (PA) 260 385-2584
   1627 Short St Fort Wayne (46808) *(G-5011)*

Fresh Fenix LLC 260 385-2584
   1620 Broadway Fort Wayne (46802) *(G-5012)*

Fresh Hamper LLC 317 452-6023
   3135 N State Road 267 Ste B Brownsburg (46112) *(G-1370)*

Fresh News LLC 219 929-5558
   509 S Park Dr Chesterton (46304) *(G-1929)*

Fresh Printz Incorporated 812 352-6400
   61 Norris Ave North Vernon (47265) *(G-13271)*

Fresh Start Inc 812 254-3398
   113 N Industrial Park Rd Washington (47501) *(G-16479)*

Fretina Corporation 812 547-6471
   2001 Main St Tell City (47586) *(G-15504)*

Freudenberg Medical Mis Inc (DH) 812 280-2400
   2301 Centennial Blvd Jeffersonville (47130) *(G-9987)*

Freudenberg-Nok General Partnr.. 260 894-7183
  1497 Gerber St Ligonier (46767) *(G-11015)*

Freudenberg-Nok General Partnr.. 765 763-7246
  487 W Main St Morristown (46161) *(G-12277)*

Freudenberg-Nok General Partnr.. 317 421-3400
  1700 Miller Ave Shelbyville (46176) *(G-14756)*

Freudenberg-Nok General Partnr.. 734 354-5504
  877 Miller Ave Ste B Shelbyville (46176) *(G-14757)*

Frew Process Group LLC... 317 565-5000
  605 Sheridan Rd Ste 100 Noblesville (46060) *(G-13081)*

Frick Services Inc (PA).. 260 761-3311
  3154 W Depot St Wawaka (46794) *(G-16539)*

Frickers Inc... 765 965-6655
  3237 Chester Blvd Richmond (47374) *(G-14123)*

Friction Products Company LLC.. 765 362-3500
  1204 Darlington Ave Crawfordsville (47933) *(G-2568)*

Friction-Free LLC.. 317 385-6975
  6520 Royal Oakland Pl Indianapolis (46236) *(G-8233)*

Fridge Mag... 317 442-2872
  1025 Freshwater Ln Cicero (46034) *(G-1996)*

Friedman Industries Inc.. 219 392-3400
  4303 Kennedy Ave East Chicago (46312) *(G-3008)*

Friends of Third World Inc (PA)... 260 422-6821
  611 W Wayne St Fort Wayne (46802) *(G-5013)*

Friskney Gear & Machine Corp.. 260 281-2200
  106 N Bridge St Corunna (46730) *(G-2482)*

Friskney Gear Division, Corunna *Also Called: Friskney Gear & Machine Corp (G-2482)*

Friths Custom Weld.. 812 937-2618
  9 E Elm St Dale (47523) *(G-2790)*

Frito Lay.. 574 269-1410
  2162 N Cessna Rd Warsaw (46582) *(G-16364)*

Frito-Lay, Frankfort *Also Called: Frito-Lay North America Inc (G-5668)*

Frito-Lay, Frankfort *Also Called: Frito-Lay North America Inc (G-5669)*

Frito-Lay North America Inc.. 765 659-4517
  2611 W County Road 0 Ns Frankfort (46041) *(G-5668)*

Frito-Lay North America Inc.. 765 659-1831
  323 S County Road 300 W Frankfort (46041) *(G-5669)*

Fritz Distribution LLC.. 463 207-8210
  1015 W 31st St Apt 213 Indianapolis (46208) *(G-8234)*

Froet Group LLC.. 317 414-2538
  7529 E State Road 32 Whitestown (46075) *(G-16807)*

Frogs Leap... 812 235-5759
  100 N Fruitridge Ave Ste 2 Terre Haute (47803) *(G-15592)*

From Trees To These Inc.. 260 592-7397
  6188 E 25 N Decatur (46733) *(G-2856)*

From Woods... 765 468-7387
  1279 S 1000 W Farmland (47340) *(G-4425)*

Front End Digital Inc.. 317 652-6134
  11899 Stepping Stone Dr Fishers (46037) *(G-4528)*

Front Line Manufacturing, Warsaw *Also Called: Frontline Mfg Inc (G-16365)*

Front Porch Sugarhouse... 574 831-5753
  69515 County Road 21 New Paris (46553) *(G-12954)*

Front Porch Sugarhouse, New Paris *Also Called: Michael Ramer (G-12965)*

Frontier Carriage.. 574 965-4444
  7872 W 1000 N Delphi (46923) *(G-2897)*

Frontier Electric Inc... 219 778-2553
  3074 N 350 E Rolling Prairie (46371) *(G-14362)*

Frontier Engineering... 317 823-6885
  12469 E 65th St Indianapolis (46236) *(G-8235)*

Frontier Woodworks... 260 463-2049
  3350 E 200 S Lagrange (46761) *(G-10739)*

Frontline Mfg Inc.. 574 269-6751
  2466 W 200 N Warsaw (46580) *(G-16365)*

Frontline Mfg Inc (PA).. 574 453-2902
  1445 Polk Dr Warsaw (46582) *(G-16366)*

Frostbite Press LLC.. 812 216-1372
  6679 S County Road 1025 E Crothersville (47229) *(G-2640)*

Frozen Garden LLC.. 219 286-3578
  315 E 316 N Ste C Valparaiso (46383) *(G-15951)*

Frugal Times... 317 326-4165
  2309 W 100 N Greenfield (46140) *(G-6504)*

Fruit Hills Winery Orchrd LLC... 574 848-9463
  55503 State Road 15 Bristol (46507) *(G-1262)*

Fruition Industries LLC... 260 854-2325
  105 Warmer Dr Rome City (46784) *(G-14375)*

Frye Welding LLC.. 260 908-4766
  6065 E Leighty Rd Kendallville (46755) *(G-10112)*

Frys Digistitch.. 574 831-6854
  19061 Oak St New Paris (46553) *(G-12955)*

FSI, Schererville *Also Called: Furnace Solutions Incorporated (G-14522)*

FSI Filtration LLC (PA)... 317 264-2123
  1550 Indiana Ave Indianapolis (46202) *(G-8236)*

Ft Group LLC... 574 322-4369
  19224 County Road 8 Bristol (46507) *(G-1263)*

Ft Wayne Reader.. 260 420-8580
  1301 Lafayette St Ste 202 Fort Wayne (46802) *(G-5014)*

FTC Liquidation Inc.. 574 295-6700
  24615 County Road 45 Ste 4 Elkhart (46516) *(G-3359)*

FTC Products Corp.. 219 567-2441
  Hwy 421 N One Half Mile Francesville (47946) *(G-5642)*

Fti Inc... 812 983-2642
  11744 Blue Bell Rd Elberfeld (47613) *(G-3114)*

Ftic, Jamestown *Also Called: Fukai Toyotetsu Indiana Corp (G-9817)*

Ftn Logistics LLC.. 317 488-7446
  3622 Cedar Pine Pl Indianapolis (46235) *(G-8237)*

Fuel Bladder Distributors Inc.. 317 852-9156
  3800 N State Road 267 Ste B Brownsburg (46112) *(G-1371)*

Fuel Fabrication LLC.. 219 390-7022
  14727 Reeder Ct Crown Point (46307) *(G-2688)*

Fuel Recovery Service Inc... 317 372-3029
  125 W South St Unit 2690 Indianapolis (46206) *(G-8238)*

Fuel Vm LLC.. 317 828-6060
  Indianapolis (46250) *(G-8239)*

Fuentes Distributing Inc... 219 808-2147
  6811 New Hampshire Ave Hammond (46323) *(G-6933)*

Fuhrman Precision Services Inc.. 260 728-9600
  10484 N 200 W Decatur (46733) *(G-2857)*

Fukai Toyotetsu Indiana Corp... 765 676-4800
  1100 N Lebanon St Jamestown (46147) *(G-9817)*

Full Circle Printing & Mktg, Avon *Also Called: Jt Printing LLC (G-529)*

Full Court Press, Indianapolis *Also Called: Hardingpoorman Inc (G-8359)*

Full Court Press Printing, Indianapolis *Also Called: Hardingpoorman Group Inc (G-8360)*

Full Metal Solutions LLC.. 812 725-9660
  295a America Pl Jeffersonville (47130) *(G-9988)*

Full Tank Freedom Inc... 317 485-7887
  720 E Broadway St Fortville (46040) *(G-5596)*

Full Throttle Enterprise Inc... 317 779-3887
  6115 Allisonville Rd Indianapolis (46220) *(G-8240)*

Fullenkamp Machine, Portland *Also Called: Fullenkamp Machine & Mfg Inc (G-13944)*

Fullenkamp Machine & Mfg Inc.. 260 726-8345
  1507 N Meridian St Portland (47371) *(G-13944)*

Fuller Architectural Hardwoods, Daleville *Also Called: Cash & Carry Lumber Co Inc (G-2797)*

Fullifillment Center, Peru *Also Called: Asc Inc (G-13566)*

Fully Promoted.. 317 884-9290
  996 S State Road 135 Ste B Greenwood (46143) *(G-6706)*

Fully Promoted, Muncie *Also Called: Fully Promoted Muncie (G-12398)*

Fully Promoted Muncie... 765 281-8870
  2201 N Granville Ave Muncie (47303) *(G-12398)*

Fulton Industries, Granger *Also Called: Pgi Mfg LLC (G-6369)*

Fulton Industries Inc (PA).. 574 968-3222
  51565 Bittersweet Rd Ste B Granger (46530) *(G-6347)*

Fulton Industries Inc... 574 223-4387
  2903 Ft Wayne Rd 25 Rochester (46975) *(G-14292)*

Functional Devices LLC... 765 883-5538
  101 Commerce Dr Sharpsville (46068) *(G-14710)*

Fundex Games Ltd.. 317 248-1080
  1901 W 16th St Indianapolis (46202) *(G-8241)*

Funky Monkey Snacks, Fishers *Also Called: Freeze Dried Partners LLC (G-4526)*

Fur Bee.. 317 259-9498
  6552 Cornell Ave Indianapolis (46220) *(G-8242)*

Fur Real Taxidermy LLC... 812 667-6365
  4339 E County Road 900 S Cross Plains (47017) *(G-2634)*

Furnace Solutions Incorporated — ALPHABETIC SECTION

Furnace Solutions Incorporated 219 738-2516
  5314 Gull Dr Schererville (46375) *(G-14522)*

Furniture Distributors Inc 317 357-8508
  6405 Brookville Rd Indianapolis (46219) *(G-8243)*

Furniture Manufacturer, Indianapolis Also Called: Tls By Design LLC *(G-9613)*

Furniture Sales & Marketing 317 849-1508
  7219 Knollvalley Ln Indianapolis (46256) *(G-8244)*

Furrion LLC 574 361-1325
  2572 Links Dr Apt 3a Elkhart (46514) *(G-3360)*

Furrion LLC 574 327-6571
  1121 Herman St Elkhart (46516) *(G-3361)*

Furrion LLC (DH) 574 327-6571
  52567 Independence Ct Elkhart (46514) *(G-3362)*

Furtrieve LLC 317 325-8010
  9783 E 116th St Pmb 67 Fishers (46037) *(G-4529)*

Fusion Designs, Goshen Also Called: Country Woodshop LLC *(G-6117)*

Fusonweaver Publishing LLC 260 251-3946
  931 W Walnut St Portland (47371) *(G-13945)*

Futaba Indiana America Corp 812 895-4700
  3320 S Keller Rd Vincennes (47591) *(G-16127)*

Futon Factory Inc (PA) 317 549-8639
  5920 E 34th St Indianapolis (46218) *(G-8245)*

Future Fiberglass, Lapaz Also Called: J & L Future Fiberglass Co *(G-10817)*

Future Foam Inc 574 294-7694
  1900 W Lusher Ave Elkhart (46517) *(G-3363)*

Future Form Plastics 574 293-4004
  612 Kollar St Elkhart (46514) *(G-3364)*

Future Manufacturing Inc 260 454-0222
  1700 Riverfork Dr Huntington (46750) *(G-7312)*

Future Mold Inc 812 941-8661
  100 Galvin Way New Albany (47150) *(G-12735)*

Future Signs Sales & Service 765 749-5180
  709 S Main St Winchester (47394) *(G-16887)*

Future Tool & Engrg Co Inc 812 376-8699
  3400 Scott Dr Columbus (47201) *(G-2311)*

Futuretek 317 631-0098
  535 N Livingston Ave Indianapolis (46222) *(G-8246)*

Futurewerks LLC 305 926-3633
  9112 Sargent Rd Indianapolis (46256) *(G-8247)*

Futurex Industries Inc 765 498-8900
  80 E Smith St Bloomingdale (47832) *(G-759)*

Futurex Industries Inc (PA) 765 498-3900
  70 N Main St Bloomingdale (47832) *(G-760)*

Futurex Industries Inc 765 597-2221
  101 E Guion St Marshall (47859) *(G-11373)*

Futurex Industries Inc 812 299-5708
  10000 S Carlisle St Terre Haute (47802) *(G-15593)*

Fuzion Industries 812 430-4037
  2200 W Maryland St Evansville (47712) *(G-4082)*

Fuzion Products LLC 317 536-0745
  6312 Southeastern Ave Indianapolis (46203) *(G-8248)*

Fuzzys Spirits LLC 317 489-6572
  9455 Delegates Row Indianapolis (46240) *(G-8249)*

Fuzzys Vodka, Indianapolis Also Called: Fuzzys Spirits LLC *(G-8249)*

FWD Technologies LLC 360 907-9755
  7872 N 100 E Huntington (46750) *(G-7313)*

Fwdnxt LLC 203 645-0736
  923 Windsor Dr West Lafayette (47906) *(G-16581)*

Fwp, Fort Wayne Also Called: Fort Wayne Plastics Inc *(G-5000)*

Fxi Inc 260 925-1073
  2211 Wayne St Auburn (46706) *(G-392)*

Fxi Inc 260 747-7485
  3005 Commercial Rd Fort Wayne (46809) *(G-5015)*

Fxi Auburn 260 925-1073
  2211 Wayne St Auburn (46706) *(G-393)*

Fyberdyne Laboratories 574 291-9438
  19644 Gilmer St South Bend (46614) *(G-15040)*

G & B Directional Boring LLC 574 538-8132
  2620 N 850 W Shipshewana (46565) *(G-14847)*

G & G Metal Spinners Inc 317 923-3225
  1717 Cornell Ave Indianapolis (46202) *(G-8250)*

G & H Diversified Mfg LP 713 849-2111
  1705 Midwest Blvd Indianapolis (46214) *(G-8251)*

G & H Wire Company Inc (PA) 317 346-6655
  40 Linville Way Franklin (46131) *(G-5731)*

G & J 765 457-9889
  1252 N Main St Kokomo (46901) *(G-10268)*

G & J Publishing LLC 765 914-3378
  11146 Liberty Pike Brookville (47012) *(G-1321)*

G & L Machine LLP 260 488-2100
  5920 County Road 4 Hamilton (46742) *(G-6854)*

G & P Machinery, Indianapolis Also Called: Grinding and Polsg McHy Corp *(G-8331)*

G & R Woodworking LLC 812 687-7701
  7747 N 775 E Montgomery (47558) *(G-12098)*

G & S Rural Woodworking 765 348-7781
  1102 S 200 E Hartford City (47348) *(G-7065)*

G & S Super Abrasives Inc 260 665-5562
  1601 Wohlert St Angola (46703) *(G-254)*

G & T Industries Inc 812 634-2252
  2741 Cathy Ln Jasper (47546) *(G-9839)*

G & T Industries Inc 812 634-2252
  290 E 30th St Jasper (47546) *(G-9840)*

G and G Peppers LLC 765 358-4519
  12245 N County Road 450 W Gaston (47342) *(G-6045)*

G and P Enterprises Ind Inc 812 723-3837
  782 N Greenbriar Dr Paoli (47454) *(G-13495)*

G C I, Nappanee Also Called: Grrreat Creations *(G-12601)*

G C Solutions Inc 317 334-1149
  3702 W 86th St Ste B Indianapolis (46268) *(G-8252)*

G D C, Goshen Also Called: Gdc Inc *(G-6143)*

G D Cox Inc 317 398-0035
  105 S Harrison St Shelbyville (46176) *(G-14758)*

G E C O M Corp (DH) 812 663-2270
  1025 E Barachel Ln Greensburg (47240) *(G-6595)*

G G B Inc 219 733-2897
  7512 S 800 W Westville (46391) *(G-16758)*

G L D Inc (PA) 317 924-7981
  6427 N Ewing St Indianapolis (46220) *(G-8253)*

G L D Inc 317 335-2760
  13206 Fairwood Dr Mccordsville (46055) *(G-11450)*

G N Holdings Inc 812 372-9969
  4735 N Indianapolis Rd Columbus (47203) *(G-2312)*

G N U Inc 219 464-7813
  2252 Industrial Dr Valparaiso (46383) *(G-15952)*

G Thrapp Jewelers Inc 317 255-5555
  3810 E 79th St Indianapolis (46240) *(G-8254)*

G Unit Core Inc 812 526-2080
  1015 S Walnut St Edinburgh (46124) *(G-3084)*

G W Enterprises 260 868-2555
  7063 County Road 24 Butler (46721) *(G-1464)*

G.F. Munich Welding, Jeffersonville Also Called: C&W Fabrication LLC *(G-9949)*

G&H Orthodontics, Franklin Also Called: G & H Wire Company Inc *(G-5731)*

G&S Research Inc 317 815-1443
  3511 E Carmel Dr Carmel (46033) *(G-1637)*

G2 House of Styles, Seymour Also Called: Better Blacc Wall Streetz LLC *(G-14632)*

G4 Tool and Technology Inc 574 970-0844
  2907 Paul Dr Elkhart (46514) *(G-3365)*

Gabhart Logging LLC 812 365-2425
  4532 E Goodman Ridge Rd Marengo (47140) *(G-11263)*

Gabriel Products Inc 502 291-5388
  2303 Cypress Pt Jeffersonville (47130) *(G-9989)*

Gabriel V Fulkerson 502 727-0038
  5498 Ponderosa Rd Ne Lanesville (47136) *(G-10797)*

Gac Enterprises Usa LLC 317 839-9525
  849 Whitaker Rd Ste D Plainfield (46168) *(G-13682)*

GAF 219 872-1111
  505 N Roeske Ave Michigan City (46360) *(G-11616)*

GAF, Michigan City Also Called: GAF *(G-11616)*

GAF Materials, Michigan City Also Called: Standard Industries Inc *(G-11672)*

GAF Materials, Mount Vernon Also Called: Standard Industries Inc *(G-12323)*

Gaius Julius Crassus Inc 219 879-4541
  110 Menke Rd Trail Creek (46360) *(G-15838)*

ALPHABETIC SECTION

Galaxy Container LLC 574 936-6300
   1001 Pidco Dr Plymouth (46563) *(G-13778)*

Galbe Magazine LLC 248 742-5231
   10540 Combs Ave Carmel (46280) *(G-1638)*

Galbreath Industrial Svcs LLC 574 737-8159
   801 Erie Ave Logansport (46947) *(G-11074)*

Galbreath LLC (DH) 219 946-6631
   480 E 150 S Winamac (46996) *(G-16860)*

Gale Enameling Co Inc 317 839-7474
   10095 Old National Rd Indianapolis (46231) *(G-8255)*

Gale Force Software Corp 317 695-7423
   8720 Castle Creek Parkway East Dr Ste 200 Indianapolis (46250) *(G-8256)*

Gale Industries Insltn Matl 765 447-1191
   150 N 36th St Lafayette (47905) *(G-10583)*

Galfab LLC (DH) 574 946-7767
   612 W 11th St Winamac (46996) *(G-16861)*

Gallagher Drilling, Evansville *Also Called: Victor R Gallagher (G-4373)*

Gallagher Drilling Inc (PA) 812 477-6746
   115 Se 3rd St Fl 2 Evansville (47708) *(G-4083)*

Gallagher Environmental Inc 773 791-4670
   9111 Hibiscus Dr Saint John (46373) *(G-14450)*

Gallery of Kitchens, Vincennes *Also Called: Warren Homes Inc (G-16165)*

Galleyware Company Inc 302 996-9480
   10505 Bennett Pkwy Ste 200 Zionsville (46077) *(G-17009)*

Galloway Fabricating 574 453-3802
   3776 E 750 N Leesburg (46538) *(G-10954)*

Galloweld LLC 219 215-2006
   3831 Hohman Ave Hammond (46327) *(G-6934)*

Galvanized Division, Bristol *Also Called: Quality Galvanized Pdts Inc (G-1283)*

Game Face Brands, Zionsville *Also Called: Pieniadze Inc (G-17041)*

Game Plan Graphics LLC 812 663-3238
   102 E Washington St Greensburg (47240) *(G-6596)*

Gameface Inc 317 363-8855
   1555 W Oak St Ste 100 Zionsville (46077) *(G-17010)*

Gamer Energy LLC 317 660-9262
   13644 N Meridian St Carmel (46032) *(G-1639)*

Gametime Sporting Events LLC 812 406-8281
   8520 Allison Pointe Blvd Ste 223 Indianapolis (46250) *(G-8257)*

Gammons Metal & Mfg Co Inc 317 546-7091
   2900 N Richardt Ave Indianapolis (46219) *(G-8258)*

Ganal Corporation 260 749-2161
   915 Lincoln Hwy E New Haven (46774) *(G-12903)*

Ganaway Solutions LLC 219 359-7850
   5475 Broadway Merrillville (46410) *(G-11518)*

Gannett Co Inc 765 423-5511
   1501 Veterans Memorial Pkwy E Lafayette (47905) *(G-10584)*

Gannett Media Corp 765 423-5512
   300 Main St Ste 314 Lafayette (47901) *(G-10585)*

Gannett Media Corp 765 962-1575
   1175 North Dr Richmond (47374) *(G-14124)*

Gannon Mtal Fbrcators Erectors 219 398-0299
   418 E Chicago Ave East Chicago (46312) *(G-3009)*

Gapco Inc 317 787-6440
   1817 Inisheer Ct Indianapolis (46217) *(G-8259)*

Gaptooth Publishing 574 551-6386
   403 S Union St Warsaw (46580) *(G-16367)*

Garco Graphics 219 980-1113
   4730 Broadway Gary (46408) *(G-5935)*

Garden of Remedies Inc 463 241-5991
   8411 Windfall Ln Camby (46113) *(G-1510)*

Gardiner Rentals Bill 765 447-5111
   510 Veterans Memorial Pkwy E Lafayette (47905) *(G-10586)*

Gardner Denver Inc 219 558-0354
   9495 Keilman St Ste 2b Saint John (46373) *(G-14451)*

Gardner Glass Products Inc 317 464-0881
   1705 Lafayette Rd Indianapolis (46222) *(G-8260)*

Gardner Graphics & Signs 765 630-8475
   1221 S Bloomington St Greencastle (46135) *(G-6404)*

Gardner Mirror Corp 317 464-0881
   1705 Lafayette Rd Indianapolis (46222) *(G-8261)*

Gardner Woodcrafts, Plainfield *Also Called: George Gardner (G-13683)*

Gared Holdings LLC 317 774-9840
   9200 E 146th St Ste A Noblesville (46060) *(G-13082)*

Gared Sports, Noblesville *Also Called: Gared Holdings LLC (G-13082)*

Garmco (usa) Inc 352 404-8998
   300 N Meridian St Ste 1100 Indianapolis (46204) *(G-8262)*

Garphik Mechanix, Fort Wayne *Also Called: Wayne Press Incorporated (G-5553)*

Garphyttan Wire, South Bend *Also Called: Suzuki Garphyttan Corp (G-15275)*

Garrett Printing, Garrett *Also Called: Scott Culbertson (G-5876)*

Garrett Products 260 357-5988
   1605 Dekko Dr Garrett (46738) *(G-5862)*

Garrett Prtg & Graphics Inc 812 422-6005
   1405 N 1st Ave Evansville (47710) *(G-4084)*

Garrity Stone Inc 317 546-0893
   3137 N Ritter Ave Indianapolis (46218) *(G-8263)*

Garrity Tool Company LLC 317 541-1400
   3555 Developers Rd Ste A Indianapolis (46227) *(G-8264)*

Garrity Tool Company, LLC, Indianapolis *Also Called: GTC Machining LLC (G-8339)*

Garry Mertz 260 837-6451
   702 County Road 39 Waterloo (46793) *(G-16520)*

Gartech Enterprises Inc 812 794-4796
   3037 W State Road 256 Austin (47102) *(G-465)*

Gartland Foundry Company Inc 812 232-0226
   330 Grant St Terre Haute (47802) *(G-15594)*

Garver Manufacturing Inc 765 964-5828
   224 N Columbia St Rear Union City (47390) *(G-15854)*

Gary Bridge and Iron Co Inc 219 884-3792
   3700 Roosevelt St Gary (46408) *(G-5936)*

Gary Crusader, Gary *Also Called: Chicago Crusader News Group (G-5917)*

Gary E Ellsworth 260 639-3078
   14221 Franke Rd Hoagland (46745) *(G-7168)*

Gary Electric Motor Service Co 219 884-6555
   393 E Us Highway 30 Valparaiso (46383) *(G-15953)*

Gary M Brown 765 831-2536
   719 Vine St New Castle (47362) *(G-12864)*

Gary Metal Mfg LLC 219 885-3232
   2700 E 5th Ave Gary (46402) *(G-5937)*

Gary Poppins LLC 866 354-1300
   4055 E 250 N Knox (46534) *(G-10209)*

Gary Poppins Popcorn, Knox *Also Called: Gary Poppins LLC (G-10209)*

Gary Printing Inc 219 886-1767
   1950 W 11th Ave Gary (46404) *(G-5938)*

Gary Ratcliff 765 538-3170
   9950 Us Highway 231 S Lafayette (47909) *(G-10587)*

Gary Simons 812 852-4316
   3018 W County Road 700 N Osgood (47037) *(G-13408)*

Gary's Welding and Machining, Bedford *Also Called: Garys Welding & Machining LLC (G-637)*

Garyrae Inc 574 255-7141
   800 Cleveland St Mishawaka (46544) *(G-11898)*

Garys Welding & Machining LLC 812 279-6780
   411 County Complex Rd Bedford (47421) *(G-637)*

Gas City B & K Inc 765 674-9651
   928 E Main St Gas City (46933) *(G-6037)*

Gasco, Noblesville *Also Called: Gasco LLC (G-13083)*

Gasco LLC 317 565-5000
   15305 Stony Creek Way Noblesville (46060) *(G-13083)*

Gaska Tape Inc 574 294-5431
   1810 W Lusher Ave Elkhart (46517) *(G-3366)*

Gast Sign Co 219 759-4336
   499 W Us Highway 30 Valparaiso (46385) *(G-15954)*

Gateway Builders & Properties 574 295-9944
   1001 Parkway Ave Ste 1 Elkhart (46516) *(G-3367)*

Gator Buckets, Crawfordsville *Also Called: New Market Plastics Inc (G-2593)*

Gator Buckets, Lebanon *Also Called: Cedar Plastics Inc (G-10882)*

Gator Cases, Columbia City *Also Called: Gator Cases Inc (G-2148)*

Gator Cases Inc 260 627-8070
   2499 S 600 E Columbia City (46725) *(G-2148)*

Gauger Woodworking Plus 812 421-8223
   2012 Koring Rd Evansville (47720) *(G-4085)*

Gaunt Family LLC 812 473-3167
   7001 Red Wing Dr Evansville (47715) *(G-4086)*

Gbi Air Systems Inc 574 272-0600
  50867 Post Rd Granger (46530) *(G-6348)*
Gbj Holdings LLC 317 483-1896
  9445 Indianapolis Blvd Ste 1092 Highland (46322) *(G-7137)*
Gbo Corporation 574 825-7670
  106 Industrial Pkwy E Middlebury (46540) *(G-11717)*
GC Fuller Mfg Co Inc 812 539-2831
  1 Shurlite Dr Lawrenceburg (47025) *(G-10838)*
Gcam Inc 714 738-6462
  5341 E Thompson Rd Indianapolis (46237) *(G-8265)*
Gcg Industries Inc 260 482-7454
  4636 Newaygo Rd Fort Wayne (46808) *(G-5016)*
GCI LLC 317 574-4970
  484 E Carmel Dr Ste 142 Carmel (46032) *(G-1640)*
GCI Slingers LLC 317 873-8686
  5005 W 106th St Zionsville (46077) *(G-17011)*
Gdc Inc 574 533-3128
  22428 Elkhart East Blvd Elkhart (46514) *(G-3368)*
Gdc Inc (PA) 574 533-3128
  815 Logan St Goshen (46528) *(G-6143)*
Gdp Industries LLC 260 414-4003
  7431 Regina Dr Fort Wayne (46815) *(G-5017)*
Gdt Terre Haute Mfg 812 460-7706
  4955 N 13th St Bldg 12 Terre Haute (47805) *(G-15595)*
GE, Lafayette *Also Called: GE Aviation Systems LLC (G-10588)*
GE Aviation Systems LLC 765 432-5917
  3700 Us Highway 52 S Lafayette (47905) *(G-10588)*
Gear Up Awards, Terre Haute *Also Called: Larry H Poole (G-15629)*
Gearbox Group Inc 812 268-0322
  609 E Chaney St Sullivan (47882) *(G-15406)*
Gearbox Lm Holdings Inc (PA) 765 362-3500
  711 Tech Dr Crawfordsville (47933) *(G-2569)*
Geberts Cleaning Service 812 254-4658
  216 Apraw Rd Washington (47501) *(G-16480)*
Gebhart's Woodworking & Lumber, Cayuga *Also Called: John Gebhart Woodworkings (G-1823)*
Geckos 765 762-0822
  111 S Perry St Attica (47918) *(G-349)*
Gehl Industries Inc 574 773-7663
  9547 W 1050 N Nappanee (46550) *(G-12598)*
Geiger & Peters Inc 317 322-7740
  761 S Sherman Dr Indianapolis (46203) *(G-8266)*
Gem City Junction LLC 765 659-6733
  63 E Clinton St Frankfort (46041) *(G-5670)*
Gem City Technologies 937 252-8998
  54347 Highland Blvd Elkhart (46514) *(G-3369)*
Gem Elevator Inc 317 894-7722
  768 N 400 W Greenfield (46140) *(G-6505)*
Gem Industries Inc 574 773-4513
  1400 Northwood Dr Nappanee (46550) *(G-12599)*
Gem-Rose Corporation 317 773-6400
  597 Christian Ave Noblesville (46060) *(G-13084)*
Gema, Indianapolis *Also Called: ITW Gema (G-8598)*
Gema USA Inc 317 298-5000
  4141 W 54th St Indianapolis (46254) *(G-8267)*
Gemeinhardt Musical Instr LLC 574 295-5280
  3302 S Nappanee St Elkhart (46517) *(G-3370)*
Gemini Machine and Design LLC 812 559-1727
  1321 W Magnolia St Jasper (47546) *(G-9841)*
Gemini Oil LLC 260 571-8388
  1323 W 600 S Warren (46792) *(G-16298)*
Gems Quality Extensions LLC 219 501-6320
  1211 W 149th St Apt 2f East Chicago (46312) *(G-3010)*
Gemstone, Elkhart *Also Called: Newlett Inc (G-3567)*
Gemstone Musical Instruments, Elkhart *Also Called: Gemeinhardt Musical Instr LLC (G-3370)*
Gen Digital Inc 317 575-4010
  8888 Keystone Xing Ste 1300 Indianapolis (46240) *(G-8268)*
Gen Enterprises 574 498-6777
  3500 18b Rd Tippecanoe (46570) *(G-15759)*
Gen T LLC 574 266-0911
  3008 Mobile Dr Elkhart (46514) *(G-3371)*

Gen Y Hitch 574 218-6363
  621 E Plymouth St Bremen (46506) *(G-1192)*
Gen-Twelve Corporation 260 483-7075
  10917 Smokey Ridge Pl Fort Wayne (46818) *(G-5018)*
Gen-Y Hitch, Nappanee *Also Called: Nexgen Group Inc (G-12632)*
Gener8 LLC 317 253-8737
  1901 W 16th St Indianapolis (46202) *(G-8269)*
General Alum & Chemical, Indianapolis *Also Called: Chemtrade Solutions LLC (G-7794)*
General Aluminum Mfg Company 260 495-2600
  303 E Swager St Fremont (46737) *(G-5822)*
General Aluminum Mfg Company 260 356-3900
  1345 Henry St Huntington (46750) *(G-7314)*
General Automation Company 317 849-7483
  9520 E 206th St Noblesville (46060) *(G-13085)*
General Cage LLC 765 552-5039
  1106 Meridian St Ste 325 Anderson (46016) *(G-119)*
General Cnstr & Consulting LLC 812 340-5673
  2200 N Dr Martin Luther King Jr Blvd Muncie (47303) *(G-12399)*
General Contractor, Kokomo *Also Called: Max of All Trades LLC (G-10305)*
General Crafts Corp 574 533-1936
  602 E Madison St Goshen (46526) *(G-6144)*
General Devices Co Inc 317 897-7000
  1410 S Post Rd Ste 100 Indianapolis (46239) *(G-8270)*
General Dynamics Corporation 260 637-4773
  1124 Falcon Creek Pkwy Fort Wayne (46845) *(G-5019)*
General Dynmics Mssion Systems 260 434-9500
  1700 Magnavox Way Ste 200 Fort Wayne (46804) *(G-5020)*
General Electric Betz, East Chicago *Also Called: Veolia Wts Usa Inc (G-3053)*
General Fabricators Inc 317 787-9354
  5230 S Harding St Indianapolis (46217) *(G-8271)*
General Fasteners Co 574 343-2413
  2701 Decio Dr Elkhart (46514) *(G-3372)*
General Freight Trucking, Indianapolis *Also Called: Lifted Loads LLC (G-8748)*
General Machine & Saw Co Ind, South Bend *Also Called: General Mch & Saw Co of Ind (G-15041)*
General Machine Brokers Inc 260 691-3800
  1295 E 600 N Columbia City (46725) *(G-2149)*
General Machine Solutions Inc 219 378-1700
  3550 Canal St East Chicago (46312) *(G-3011)*
General Material Handling Co 317 888-5735
  1302 Kings Cove Ct Indianapolis (46260) *(G-8272)*
General Mch & Saw Co of Ind 574 232-6077
  3636 Gagnon St South Bend (46628) *(G-15041)*
General Mills, Fishers *Also Called: General Mills Inc (G-4530)*
General Mills Inc 317 509-3709
  12222 Bedrock Ct Fishers (46037) *(G-4530)*
General Motors, Bedford *Also Called: General Motors LLC (G-638)*
General Motors, Roanoke *Also Called: General Motors LLC (G-14267)*
General Motors, Roanoke *Also Called: General Motors LLC (G-14268)*
General Motors LLC 812 279-7321
  105 Gm Dr Bedford (47421) *(G-638)*
General Motors LLC 765 668-2000
  2400 W 2nd St Marion (46952) *(G-11287)*
General Motors LLC 260 673-2048
  12808 Stonebridge Rd Roanoke (46783) *(G-14267)*
General Motors LLC 260 672-1224
  12200 Lafayette Center Rd Roanoke (46783) *(G-14268)*
General Mrgans Scrnprint Shppe, Corydon *Also Called: Blue River Services Inc (G-2488)*
General Optics LLC 765 637-5578
  11955 Eaglerun Way Zionsville (46077) *(G-17012)*
General Products, Angola *Also Called: General Products Delaware Corporation (G-255)*
General Products Delaware Corporation 260 668-1440
  1411 Wohlert St Angola (46703) *(G-255)*
General Rbr Plas of Evansville (PA) 812 464-5153
  1902 N Kentucky Ave Evansville (47711) *(G-4087)*
General Sheet Metal Works Inc (PA) 574 288-0611
  25101 Cleveland Rd South Bend (46628) *(G-15042)*
General Signals Inc 812 474-4256
  5611 E Morgan Ave Evansville (47715) *(G-4088)*
General Stamping & Metalworks, South Bend *Also Called: General Sheet Metal Works Inc (G-15042)*

General Transmission Pdts LLC.. 574 284-2917
105 N Niles Ave South Bend (46617) *(G-15043)*

Generation Four Machine &.. 219 297-3003
319 N Newton St Goodland (47948) *(G-6081)*

Generation Logistics LLC.. 877 238-7380
201 N Illinois St Ste 1600 Indianapolis (46204) *(G-8273)*

Generations Collision Services, Whiteland Also Called: Grahams Wrecker Service Inc *(G-16787)*

Genertonal Outreach Gaming LLC.. 872 777-6882
1934 W 5th Ave Apt 202 Gary (46404) *(G-5939)*

Genes Transport LLC.. 404 227-5178
11266 Echo Grove Ct Indianapolis (46236) *(G-8274)*

Genesis Molding Inc.. 574 256-9271
55901 Currant Rd Mishawaka (46545) *(G-11899)*

Genesis Plastics and Engineering LLC.. 812 752-6742
640 N Wilson Rd Scottsburg (47170) *(G-14556)*

Genesis Plastics Solutions LLC.. 812 283-4435
2200 Centennial Blvd Jeffersonville (47130) *(G-9990)*

Genesis Products LLC.. 574 266-8293
3130 Tuscany Dr Elkhart (46514) *(G-3373)*

Genesis Products LLC.. 574 262-4054
2924 County Road 6 E Elkhart (46514) *(G-3374)*

Genesis Products LLC.. 877 266-8292
2608 Almac Ct Elkhart (46514) *(G-3375)*

Genesis Products LLC.. 574 533-5089
1846 Eisenhower Dr S Goshen (46526) *(G-6145)*

Genesis Products LLC (PA).. 877 266-8292
1853 Eisenhower Dr S Goshen (46526) *(G-6146)*

Genesis Products, Plant 2, Elkhart Also Called: Genesis Products LLC *(G-3373)*

Genesys, Indianapolis Also Called: Genesys Telecom Us Inc *(G-8276)*

Genesys Cloud Services Inc.. 317 872-3000
7601 Interactive Way Indianapolis (46278) *(G-8275)*

Genesys Group LLC.. 574 850-9435
713 N Main St Mishawaka (46545) *(G-11900)*

Genesys Telecom Us Inc.. 703 673-1773
7601 Interactive Way Indianapolis (46278) *(G-8276)*

Geneva Manufacturing Inc.. 260 368-7555
6120 Highview Dr Fort Wayne (46818) *(G-5021)*

Geniphys, Zionsville Also Called: Geniphys Inc *(G-17013)*

Geniphys Inc.. 317 973-0523
10307 Oak Ridge Dr Zionsville (46077) *(G-17013)*

Genoa Healthcare LLC.. 219 427-1837
1100 W 6th Ave Gary (46402) *(G-5940)*

Genpak LLC.. 812 256-7040
251 Paul Garrett Ave Jeffersonville (47130) *(G-9991)*

Genpak LLC.. 812 752-3111
845 S Elm St Scottsburg (47170) *(G-14557)*

Genrich Custom Cabinetry Mllwk.. 317 351-0991
2525 N Shadeland Ave Indianapolis (46219) *(G-8277)*

Gensic Creative Metals, Fort Wayne Also Called: Coffee Lomont & Moyer Inc *(G-4865)*

Gentec LLC.. 260 436-7333
3905 Goeglein Rd Fort Wayne (46815) *(G-5022)*

Genteq, Fort Wayne Also Called: Regal Beloit America Inc *(G-5377)*

Gentis Tire & Service Inc.. 765 348-2400
219 N Walnut St Hartford City (47348) *(G-7066)*

Gentry Well & Pump Service LLC.. 260 563-1907
8939 S 100 W Wabash (46992) *(G-16189)*

Gentrys Cabinet Inc.. 765 643-6611
415 Main St Anderson (46016) *(G-120)*

Geo Pfaus Sons Company Inc.. 800 732-8645
800 Wall St Jeffersonville (47130) *(G-9992)*

Geo-Flo Corporation.. 812 275-8513
905 Williams Park Dr Bedford (47421) *(G-639)*

Geocel Holdings Corporation.. 574 264-0645
2504 Marina Dr Elkhart (46514) *(G-3376)*

Geon Performance Solutions LLC.. 812 466-5116
3915 1st Pkwy Terre Haute (47804) *(G-15596)*

Georg Utz Inc.. 812 526-2240
14000 N 250 W Edinburgh (46124) *(G-3085)*

George Gardner.. 317 270-8036
256 N Center St Plainfield (46168) *(G-13683)*

George Koch Sons LLC (HQ).. 812 465-9600
10 S 11th Ave Evansville (47712) *(G-4089)*

George P Stewart Printing Co.. 317 924-5143
2901 N Tacoma Ave Indianapolis (46218) *(G-8278)*

George Voyles Logging, Salem Also Called: George Voyles Sawmill Inc *(G-14478)*

George Voyles Sawmill Inc.. 812 472-3968
4887 W Apple Ln Salem (47167) *(G-14478)*

Georges Custom Wood Wkg Inc.. 812 944-3344
614 Maple Ln New Albany (47150) *(G-12736)*

Georges Welding & Mech Svc.. 219 989-0781
2630 Colfax St Gary (46406) *(G-5941)*

Georgetown Truss Company Inc.. 812 951-2647
9627 State Road 64 Georgetown (47122) *(G-6061)*

Georgia Direct Carpet Inc.. 765 966-2548
5200 National Rd E Richmond (47374) *(G-14125)*

Georgia Direct Crpt & Cabinets, Richmond Also Called: Georgia Direct Carpet Inc *(G-14125)*

Georgia-Pacific, Richmond Also Called: Color-Box LLC *(G-14109)*

Georgia-Pacific, Wheatfield Also Called: Georgia-Pacific LLC *(G-16766)*

Georgia-Pacific, Wheatfield Also Called: Georgia-Pacific LLC *(G-16767)*

Georgia-Pacific Corrugated III LLC (DH)   5645 W 82nd St Indianapolis (46278) *(G-8279)*

Georgia-Pacific LLC.. 219 776-0069
604 Na Sandifer Rd Wheatfield (46392) *(G-16766)*

Georgia-Pacific LLC.. 219 956-3100
484 E 1400 N Wheatfield (46392) *(G-16767)*

Ger, Valparaiso Also Called: Global Energy Resources LLC *(G-15957)*

Gerald S Zins.. 812 623-4980
910 E County Road 875 N Osgood (47037) *(G-13409)*

Gerard.. 219 924-6388
9311 Southmoor Ave Highland (46322) *(G-7138)*

Gerardot Performance Pdts Inc.. 260 623-3048
108 W Barnhart St Monroeville (46773) *(G-12069)*

Gerber Manufacturing, Granger Also Called: Ashley Worldwide Inc *(G-6332)*

Gerdau Ameristeel Texas, Muncie Also Called: Gerdau Ameristeel US Inc *(G-12400)*

Gerdau Ameristeel US Inc.. 765 286-5454
1810 S Macedonia Ave Muncie (47302) *(G-12400)*

Gerdau Macsteel Inc.. 260 356-9520
25 Commercial Rd Huntington (46750) *(G-7315)*

Gerdau McSteel Atmsphere Annli.. 812 346-1275
1300 Industrial Dr North Vernon (47265) *(G-13272)*

GES Services LLC.. 812 270-3090
2705 N Red Bank Rd Evansville (47720) *(G-4090)*

Gesco Group LLC (PA).. 260 747-5088
4422 Earth Dr Fort Wayne (46809) *(G-5023)*

Gessner Woodworking.. 812 389-2594
106 N 1000 E Celestine (47521) *(G-1841)*

Get Down Get Arund Prcous Mtls.. 219 243-2105
9954 W Us Highway 6 Westville (46391) *(G-16759)*

Get Lathered.. 317 201-7291
5129 E 68th St Indianapolis (46220) *(G-8280)*

Get Noticed Portable Signs.. 765 649-6645
1842 Lowell Ave Anderson (46011) *(G-121)*

Get Printing Inc.. 574 533-6827
432 Blackport Dr Goshen (46528) *(G-6147)*

Get Published Inc.. 812 334-5279
1663 S Liberty Dr Ste 200 Bloomington (47403) *(G-867)*

Get Right Home Solutions LLC.. 574 374-2001
275 Winchester Trl Goshen (46526) *(G-6148)*

Gettelfinger Holdings LLC.. 812 923-9065
5773 Scottsville Rd Floyds Knobs (47119) *(G-4679)*

Gfi Innovations, Plymouth Also Called: Gfi Innovations LLC *(G-13779)*

Gfi Innovations LLC.. 847 263-9000
2940 Miller Dr Plymouth (46563) *(G-13779)*

Gfw Fabrication.. 260 333-7252
1905 Jacob St Auburn (46706) *(G-394)*

Gh LLC.. 765 775-3776
3000 Kent Ave West Lafayette (47906) *(G-16582)*

GH Products Inc.. 619 208-4823
3917 Sunnycroft Pl West Lafayette (47906) *(G-16583)*

Ghk Truss LLC (PA).. 812 282-6600
521 N Clark Blvd Clarksville (47129) *(G-2016)*

Ghost Forge L T D — ALPHABETIC SECTION

Ghost Forge L T D (PA)..765 362-8654
1009 S Elm St Crawfordsville (47933) *(G-2570)*

Ghost Frge Rubenesque Fashions, Crawfordsville Also Called: Ghost Forge L T D *(G-2570)*

GI Properties Inc (PA)...219 763-1177
6610 Melton Rd Portage (46368) *(G-13868)*

Giant Paw Prints Inc...219 241-9299
549 N 300 E Valparaiso (46383) *(G-15955)*

Giant Paw Prints Rescue......................................219 241-9299
857 Main St Westville (46391) *(G-16760)*

Gibbs Susie Framing & Art...................................765 428-2434
514 Main St Lafayette (47901) *(G-10589)*

Gibson Brothers Welding Inc................................765 948-5775
1520 W 900 S Fairmount (46928) *(G-4410)*

Gibson County Coal LLC......................................812 385-1816
3455 S 700 W Owensville (47665) *(G-13467)*

Gibson County Meats LLC...................................812 724-2333
9208 W State Road 165 Owensville (47665) *(G-13468)*

Gibson County Sand & Grav Inc...........................812 851-5800
2997 W State Road 68 Haubstadt (47639) *(G-7085)*

Gibson Innovations LLC......................................317 561-0932
2017 N 26th St Terre Haute (47804) *(G-15597)*

Gibson Nehemiah Group Inc................................317 643-3838
801 N Mulberry St Muncie (47305) *(G-12401)*

Gieseck+dvrent Epymnts Amer In........................866 484-0611
2621 Corrinado Ct Fort Wayne (46808) *(G-5024)*

Gifford Mfg Advisors LLC....................................918 809-4116
3570 Lafayette Pkwy Floyds Knobs (47119) *(G-4680)*

Gifts That Last, Madison Also Called: Alan W Long *(G-11198)*

Gilberts Machine, Uniondale Also Called: Tgm Manufacturing Inc *(G-15873)*

Giles Agency Incorporated...................................317 842-5546
7002 Graham Rd Ste 219 Indianapolis (46220) *(G-8281)*

Giles Chemical Corporation.................................812 537-4852
200 Brown St Greendale (47025) *(G-6445)*

Giles Manufacturing, Greendale Also Called: Giles Chemical Corporation *(G-6445)*

Giles Manufacturing Company.............................812 537-4852
200 Brown St Greendale (47025) *(G-6446)*

Gill Carbide Saw & Tl Svc LLC.............................317 698-6787
8471 Waverly Rd Martinsville (46151) *(G-11397)*

Gillespie Mrrell Gen Contg LLC...........................765 618-4084
1240 S Adams St Marion (46953) *(G-11288)*

Gillette Generators Inc..574 264-9639
2921 Thorne Dr Elkhart (46514) *(G-3377)*

Gilleys Repair and Welding.................................812 374-6009
1501 Wrenwood Dr Columbus (47201) *(G-2313)*

Gilleys Wldg & Fabrication LLC...........................765 720-0554
390 N County Road 475 E Fillmore (46128) *(G-4453)*

Gillis Company...574 273-9086
51093 Bittersweet Rd Granger (46530) *(G-6349)*

Gillum Machine & Tool Inc..................................765 893-4426
3365 W State Road 28 West Lebanon (47991) *(G-16648)*

Gilpin Inc...260 724-9155
1819 Patterson St Decatur (46733) *(G-2858)*

Gilpin Custom Woodworking LLC.......................260 413-6618
10611 Coopers Hawk Trce Roanoke (46783) *(G-14269)*

Ginas Creative Jewelry Inc.................................317 272-0032
8100 E Us Highway 36 Ste 7 Avon (46123) *(G-521)*

Ginas Essentials..812 406-3276
7705 Carrol Rd Nabb (47147) *(G-12574)*

Gindor Inc..574 642-4004
66101 Us Highway 33 Goshen (46526) *(G-6149)*

Ginger White LLC..773 818-8740
7429 Ash Ave Gary (46403) *(G-5942)*

Gingerbread House Publications........................260 622-4868
11216 N 500 E Ossian (46777) *(G-13424)*

Giraffe-X Graphics Inc.......................................317 546-4944
5746 Wheeler Rd Indianapolis (46216) *(G-8282)*

Girard Products LLC...574 534-3328
4800 Beck Dr Elkhart (46516) *(G-3378)*

Girard Systems, Elkhart Also Called: Girard Products LLC *(G-3378)*

Girls...812 299-1382
6860 E Manor Dr Terre Haute (47802) *(G-15598)*

Girod Truss LLC..260 442-8240
17007 Doty Rd New Haven (46774) *(G-12904)*

Girtz Engineering, Monticello Also Called: Girtz Industries Inc *(G-12151)*

Girtz Industries Inc...844 464-4789
5262 N East Shafer Dr Monticello (47960) *(G-12151)*

Givestr Inc...202 997-5862
6198 Meridian Street West Dr Indianapolis (46208) *(G-8283)*

Gkb Holdings Inc...260 471-7744
909 Production Rd Fort Wayne (46808) *(G-5025)*

Gkd Tools LLC..219 309-7758
1152 West St Valparaiso (46385) *(G-15956)*

GKN Aerospace Muncie Inc..............................765 747-7147
3901 S Delaware Dr Muncie (47302) *(G-12402)*

GKN Sinter Metals LLC....................................812 883-3381
198 S Imperial Dr Salem (47167) *(G-14479)*

GL Custom Welding LLC..................................260 593-0253
5760 S State Road 5 Topeka (46571) *(G-15807)*

Gladieux Trading Mfg Co.................................260 417-6774
6414 Popp Rd Fort Wayne (46845) *(G-5026)*

Glander...317 889-1039
1678 Ashwood Dr Greenwood (46143) *(G-6707)*

Glas-Col LLC..812 235-6167
711 Hulman St Terre Haute (47802) *(G-15599)*

Glas-Col Div, Terre Haute Also Called: Templeton Coal Company Inc *(G-15725)*

Glas-Master, Pendleton Also Called: Fox Manufacturing LLC *(G-13533)*

Glasgow Daily Times, Jeffersonville Also Called: Newspaper Holding Inc *(G-10024)*

Glasrite Div, Indianapolis Also Called: PSC Industries Inc *(G-9237)*

Glass City, Gary Also Called: Glass City Inc *(G-5943)*

Glass City Inc..219 887-2100
4980 Broadway Gary (46408) *(G-5943)*

Glass Molders Pottery Pla...............................812 398-6222
2126 E County Road 7 Se Carlisle (47838) *(G-1541)*

Glass Surgeons Inc...219 374-2500
12604 Havenwood Pass Cedar Lake (46303) *(G-1831)*

Glassic Design, Fishers Also Called: May First Inc *(G-4562)*

Glasswing Press LLC.....................................937 554-1784
18046 Forreston Oak Dr Noblesville (46062) *(G-13086)*

Glaze Tool and Engineering Inc.......................260 493-4557
1610 Summit St New Haven (46774) *(G-12905)*

Glcc Laurel LLC..765 497-6100
1 Geddes Way West Lafayette (47906) *(G-16584)*

Gldn Rule Truss & Metal Sales.......................812 866-1800
4886 S 850 W Lexington (47138) *(G-10976)*

Gleam Electrical LLC....................................317 968-0927
1313 Millstone Ct Greenwood (46143) *(G-6708)*

Gleaners Food Bank of Ind Inc......................317 925-0191
3737 Waldemere Ave Indianapolis (46241) *(G-8284)*

Gleason Corporation....................................574 533-1141
612 E Reynolds St Goshen (46526) *(G-6150)*

Glen-Gery Corporation.................................317 784-2505
5518 Shelby St Indianapolis (46227) *(G-8285)*

Glenmark Industries Inc...............................574 936-5788
1100 Pidco Dr Plymouth (46563) *(G-13780)*

Glens Mobile Welding..................................219 663-2668
12207 Burr St Crown Point (46307) *(G-2689)*

Glens Pact LLC...317 540-5869
7018 Patrick Pl Indianapolis (46256) *(G-8286)*

Glgraphix..765 446-8600
311 Sagamore Pkwy N Ste 6 Lafayette (47904) *(G-10590)*

Glicks Miracles Inc.....................................260 436-6671
5732 Glendale Rd Fort Wayne (46804) *(G-5027)*

Glidden Professional Paint Ctr, Carmel Also Called: PPG Architectural Finishes Inc *(G-1722)*

Glidden Professional Paint Ctr, Fort Wayne Also Called: PPG Architectural Finishes Inc *(G-5330)*

Glidden Professional Paint Ctr, Fort Wayne Also Called: PPG Architectural Finishes Inc *(G-5331)*

Glidden Professional Paint Ctr, Indianapolis Also Called: PPG Architectural Finishes Inc *(G-9168)*

Glidden Professional Paint Ctr, Indianapolis Also Called: PPG Architectural Finishes Inc *(G-9169)*

Glidden Professional Paint Ctr, Lafayette Also Called: PPG Architectural Finishes Inc *(G-10669)*

ALPHABETIC SECTION

Glidepath Com LLC.. 317 288-4459
  12175 Visionary Way Fishers (46038) *(G-4531)*

Glittered Pig LLC... 812 779-6154
  107 S Spring St Princeton (47670) *(G-13995)*

Global... 317 494-6174
  600 Ironwood Dr Ste N Franklin (46131) *(G-5732)*

Global Air Inc (PA)... 317 634-5300
  913 Bates St Indianapolis (46202) *(G-8287)*

Global Air Inc.. 317 251-1251
  6450 Rucker Rd Indianapolis (46220) *(G-8288)*

Global Building Products LLC... 574 296-6868
  1121 Herman St Elkhart (46516) *(G-3379)*

Global Composites Inc... 574 522-9956
  58190 County Road 3 Elkhart (46517) *(G-3380)*

Global Composites Inc... 574 294-7681
  56807 Elk Park Dr Elkhart (46516) *(G-3381)*

Global Energy Resources LLC.. 219 712-2556
  5206 Garden Gtwy Valparaiso (46383) *(G-15957)*

Global Forming LLC.. 317 290-1000
  913 Bates St Indianapolis (46202) *(G-8289)*

Global Glass Inc.. 574 294-7681
  28967 Old Us 33 Elkhart (46516) *(G-3382)*

Global Harvest Foods LLC.. 219 984-6110
  10 E 100 S Reynolds (47980) *(G-14073)*

Global Medical Industries, Fort Wayne *Also Called: GMI LLC (G-5028)*

Global Mold Solutions Inc... 574 259-6262
  1702 E 7th St Mishawaka (46544) *(G-11901)*

Global Moulding, Elkhart *Also Called: Global Composites Inc (G-3380)*

Global Odor Ctrl Tech Mid Amer, Dillsboro *Also Called: Craig Hydraulic Enterprises (G-2944)*

Global Ozone Innovations LLC... 574 294-5797
  425 Pine Creek Ct Elkhart (46516) *(G-3383)*

Global Packaging LLC.. 317 896-2089
  16707 Southpark Dr Westfield (46074) *(G-16691)*

Global Parts Network LLC... 574 855-5000
  5102 Dylan Dr South Bend (46628) *(G-15044)*

Global Plastics Inc.. 317 299-2345
  6739 Guion Rd Indianapolis (46268) *(G-8290)*

Global Precision Parts, Wabash *Also Called: Ds Products Inc (G-16182)*

Global Stone Portage LLC... 219 787-9190
  6600 Us Highway 12 Portage (46368) *(G-13869)*

Global Technology Group Import.. 317 987-6902
  1209 S High School Rd Indianapolis (46241) *(G-8291)*

Global USA Inc.. 317 219-5647
  17401 Tiller Ct Ste A Westfield (46074) *(G-16692)*

Global Water Technologies Inc... 317 452-4488
  351 W 10th St Ste 537 Indianapolis (46202) *(G-8292)*

Globaltech Manufacturing LLC... 317 571-1910
  14465 Welford Way Carmel (46032) *(G-1641)*

Globe Asphalt Paving Co Inc.. 317 568-4344
  6445 E 30th St Indianapolis (46219) *(G-8293)*

Globe Industrial LLC... 812 301-2600
  242 S Voyles Rd Pekin (47165) *(G-13516)*

Globe Industries LLC.. 812 301-2600
  20 W 7th St New Albany (47150) *(G-12737)*

Globe LLC... 812 949-2001
  20 W 7th St New Albany (47150) *(G-12738)*

Globe Mechanical Inc... 812 949-2001
  20 W 7th St New Albany (47150) *(G-12739)*

Gloria J Burnworth.. 765 366-3950
  2875 N 70 W Attica (47918) *(G-350)*

Glovers Ice Cream Inc.. 765 654-6712
  705 W Clinton St Frankfort (46041) *(G-5671)*

Glow Dr LLC.. 317 622-6735
  16751 Clover Rd Noblesville (46060) *(G-13087)*

GLS, Alexandria *Also Called: GLS Machining & Design LLC (G-52)*

GLS Machining & Design LLC... 765 754-8248
  12516 N 300 W Alexandria (46001) *(G-52)*

Glue-Lam Erectors Inc... 317 878-9717
  723 E Park St Trafalgar (46181) *(G-15827)*

Glynn Johnson, Indianapolis *Also Called: Von Duprin LLC (G-9729)*

GM Components Holdings LLC.. 765 451-5011
  2150 E Lincoln Rd Kokomo (46902) *(G-10269)*

GM Components Holdings LLC.. 765 451-8440
  2100 E Lincoln Rd Kokomo (46902) *(G-10270)*

GMI, Eaton *Also Called: Graphic Menus Inc (G-3062)*

GMI, Franklin *Also Called: GMI Corporation (G-5733)*

GMI Corporation... 317 736-5116
  700 International Dr Franklin (46131) *(G-5733)*

GMI Group, Plymouth *Also Called: Glenmark Industries Inc (G-13780)*

GMI LLC... 260 209-6676
  1830 Wayne Trce Ste 110 Fort Wayne (46803) *(G-5028)*

Gmp Holdings LLC.. 317 353-6580
  2525 N Shadeland Ave Bldg 30 # 6 Indianapolis (46219) *(G-8294)*

Gmv LLC.. 765 635-4842
  9621 Bramblewood Way Carmel (46032) *(G-1642)*

GNB Studio Inc.. 317 356-4834
  5410 E Washington St Indianapolis (46219) *(G-8295)*

Go Electric Inc... 765 400-1347
  1920 Purdue Pkwy Ste 400 Anderson (46016) *(G-122)*

Go Print LLC... 765 778-1111
  1260 W 700 S Pendleton (46064) *(G-13534)*

Goad Crankshaft Service Inc.. 812 477-1127
  3514 E Morgan Ave Evansville (47715) *(G-4091)*

Goad Machine Works Inc... 812 385-8985
  3746 E 50 N Princeton (47670) *(G-13996)*

Goatee Shirt Printing LLC.. 219 916-2443
  1039 N 200 W Valparaiso (46385) *(G-15958)*

Gockel Inc... 574 402-0220
  62360 County Road 33 Goshen (46528) *(G-6151)*

Gockle, Goshen *Also Called: Gockel Inc (G-6151)*

Godfrey & Wing Inc... 765 284-5050
  3416 S Hoyt Ave Muncie (47302) *(G-12403)*

Godfrey Marine, Elkhart *Also Called: Highwater Marine LLC (G-3406)*

Goengineer Inc... 800 276-6486
  1251 N Eddy St Ste 200 South Bend (46617) *(G-15045)*

Goengineer, Inc., South Bend *Also Called: Goengineer Inc (G-15045)*

Goetz Printing... 812 243-2086
  415 Barton Ave Terre Haute (47803) *(G-15600)*

Goetz Printing & Copy Center, Terre Haute *Also Called: Goetz Printing (G-15600)*

Gogolaks Engraving.. 219 972-3995
  8620 Beech Ave Hammond (46321) *(G-6935)*

Gohn Bros Manufacturing Co.. 574 825-2400
  105 S Main St Middlebury (46540) *(G-11718)*

Goings Properties LLC... 765 294-2380
  450 E Division Rd Veedersburg (47987) *(G-16087)*

Gold & Black Illustrated, West Lafayette *Also Called: Boilers Inc (G-16567)*

Gold Bond Building Pdts LLC.. 812 247-2424
  9720 Us Highway 50 Shoals (47581) *(G-14907)*

Gold Canyon Candles... 812 267-4477
  3793 Doolittle Hill Rd Se Elizabeth (47117) *(G-3125)*

Gold Medal Awards, Bunker Hill *Also Called: Timothy White (G-1444)*

Gold N Gems... 317 895-6002
  10202 E Washington St Ste 1325 Indianapolis (46229) *(G-8296)*

Gold Seale Woodworking... 765 744-4159
  4100 W Robinwood Dr Muncie (47304) *(G-12404)*

Gold Standard Truss LLC.. 219 987-7781
  817 15th St Se Demotte (46310) *(G-2918)*

Gold Star Printing LLC.. 260 768-7920
  2075 N 735 W Shipshewana (46565) *(G-14848)*

Goldden Corporation (PA).. 765 423-4366
  3601 Sagamore Pkwy N Ste E Lafayette (47904) *(G-10591)*

Golden Age Aeroplane Works LLC... 812 358-5778
  2375 E State Road 250 Brownstown (47220) *(G-1423)*

Golden Beam Metals LLC.. 317 806-2750
  8122 Dean Rd Indianapolis (46240) *(G-8297)*

Golden Engineering Inc.. 765 855-3493
  6364 Means Rd Centerville (47330) *(G-1849)*

Golden Lion Inc.. 765 446-9557
  3416 State Road 38 E Lafayette (47905) *(G-10592)*

Golden Lion Jewelers, Lafayette *Also Called: Golden Lion Inc (G-10592)*

Golden Press Studio... 765 318-7936
  98 W Adams St Franklin (46131) *(G-5734)*

Golden Pride Hair Company LLC 812 777-9604
7576 Ivywood Dr Apt B Indianapolis (46250) *(G-8298)*

Golden Signworks Lighting 317 358-4791
7019 Brookville Rd Indianapolis (46239) *(G-8299)*

Golden Thread LLC 765 557-7801
516 N Anderson St Ste C Elwood (46036) *(G-3825)*

Golden Valley Microwave Foods, Rensselaer *Also Called: Conagra Brands Inc* *(G-14048)*

Golden Ventures Inc 317 872-2705
7687 Winton Dr Indianapolis (46268) *(G-8300)*

Golden-Helvey Holdings Inc 574 266-4500
1020 County Road 6 W Elkhart (46514) *(G-3384)*

Goldenmarc LLC 317 855-1651
10475 Crosspoint Blvd Ste 250 Indianapolis (46256) *(G-8301)*

Goldleaf Promotional Pdts Inc 317 202-2754
6630 Ferguson St Indianapolis (46220) *(G-8302)*

Goldman Machine Services 812 359-5440
5233 W County Road 600 N Richland (47634) *(G-14078)*

Goldshield Fiber Glass Inc 260 728-2476
2004 Patterson St Decatur (46733) *(G-2859)*

Goldstar Truss LLC 765 366-2679
2302 S Us Highway 41 Veedersburg (47987) *(G-16088)*

Goldstone Jewelry Inc 765 742-1975
3617 Montclair St West Lafayette (47906) *(G-16585)*

Golf Plus Inc 812 477-7529
5601 E Virginia St Evansville (47715) *(G-4092)*

Golfo Di Napoli LLC 260 479-9890
7916 S Warren Rd Warren (46792) *(G-16299)*

Goliath Ag LLC 765 305-1141
2230 E State Road 32 Winchester (47394) *(G-16888)*

Gonzales Enterprises Inc 219 841-1756
2681 Teresa St Portage (46368) *(G-13870)*

Gonzalez Pallets 317 644-1242
105 S Denny St Indianapolis (46201) *(G-8303)*

Good Earth Compost LLC 812 824-7928
650 E Empire Mill Rd Bloomington (47401) *(G-868)*

Good Earth Publications Inc 540 460-6459
815 College Ave Richmond (47374) *(G-14126)*

Good Impressions Printing, Zionsville *Also Called: Zogman Enterprises Inc* *(G-17065)*

Good Morning Publishing Co 317 782-8381
415 Main St Beech Grove (46107) *(G-690)*

Good News Network LLC 812 219-2376
1950 Pecan Ct Crown Point (46307) *(G-2690)*

Good Poppi LLC 812 319-1660
640 Kirkwood Dr Evansville (47715) *(G-4093)*

Good Signs 317 738-4663
368 S Main St Ste 1 Franklin (46131) *(G-5735)*

Goodar & Harris LLC 312 465-3899
4433 N Candlewick Ln West Lafayette (47906) *(G-16586)*

Goodlife Industries Inc 317 339-6341
3925 E 26th St Indianapolis (46218) *(G-8304)*

Goodloe Industry Svc 317 258-5534
3101 N Campbell Ave Indianapolis (46218) *(G-8305)*

Goodman & Wolfe, Terre Haute *Also Called: Mervis Industries Inc* *(G-15643)*

Goodrich Corporation 812 704-5200
510 Patrol Rd Jeffersonville (47130) *(G-9993)*

Goodrick Timber 765 778-7442
3102 Market St Pendleton (46064) *(G-13535)*

Goods On Target Sporting Inc 812 623-2300
14224 N Rosfeld Rd Sunman (47041) *(G-15438)*

Goodtime Technology Dev Ltd 317 876-3661
5150 W 76th St Indianapolis (46268) *(G-8306)*

Goodyear, Portage *Also Called: Goodyear Tire & Rubber Company* *(G-13871)*

Goodyear, Portland *Also Called: Goodyear Tire Center* *(G-13946)*

Goodyear Tire & Rubber Company 219 762-0651
6791 Melton Rd Portage (46368) *(G-13871)*

Goodyear Tire Center 260 726-9321
210 S Meridian St Portland (47371) *(G-13946)*

Goose Graphics L L C 260 563-4516
4943 Coventry Pkwy Fort Wayne (46804) *(G-5029)*

Goosecreek Woodworking LLC 317 557-9189
6140 W 1100 N Carthage (46115) *(G-1814)*

Gordon D Browning 765 458-7792
1617 E Swain Rd Liberty (47353) *(G-10988)*

Gordon Lumber Company 219 924-0500
806 W Avenue H Griffith (46319) *(G-6804)*

Gorganite Publishing LLC 812 480-2787
5534 Saint Joe Rd Fort Wayne (46835) *(G-5030)*

Gorilla Plastic Rbr Group LLC 317 635-9616
3401 Newton Ave Indianapolis (46201) *(G-8307)*

Gorrepati Service Systems 317 299-7590
3653 Lafayette Rd Indianapolis (46222) *(G-8308)*

Goshen Mfg Co Inc 574 533-1357
612 E Reynolds St Goshen (46526) *(G-6152)*

Gospel Echoes Team Association (PA) 574 533-0221
1809 E Monroe St Ste C Goshen (46528) *(G-6153)*

Gosport Manufacturing Co Inc 800 457-4406
11 Lousisa St Gosport (47433) *(G-6284)*

Gottman Electric Company Inc 812 838-0037
3350 Old Highway 62 Mount Vernon (47620) *(G-12297)*

Goudy Bros Boiler Co Inc 765 459-4416
100 W Spraker St Kokomo (46901) *(G-10271)*

Goulding & Wood Inc 317 637-5222
823 Massachusetts Ave Indianapolis (46204) *(G-8309)*

Gov 6 Corp 317 847-4942
450 E 96th St Ste 500 Indianapolis (46240) *(G-8310)*

Govparts LLC 260 449-9741
1810 S Anthony Blvd Fort Wayne (46803) *(G-5031)*

Gowdy Woodworking, Elkhart *Also Called: Gowdy Woodworks* *(G-3385)*

Gowdy Woodworks 574 293-4399
906 Plum St Elkhart (46514) *(G-3385)*

Goyal Products, Fort Wayne *Also Called: Alliance Winding Equipment* *(G-4744)*

Gpi Midwest LLC 260 925-6060
301 S Progress Dr E Kendallville (46755) *(G-10113)*

Gps America, Marion *Also Called: Marion Glass Equipment and Technology Company Inc* *(G-11312)*

Gra-Rock Redi Mix Precast LLC 765 395-7275
5925 E 1050 S Amboy (46911) *(G-67)*

Graber 812 636-7699
6608 E 1000 N Odon (47562) *(G-13336)*

Graber Box Pllet Fmly Ltd Prtn 260 657-5657
16301 Trammel Rd Grabill (46741) *(G-6296)*

Graber Cabinetry LLC 260 627-2243
15210 Grabill Rd Grabill (46741) *(G-6297)*

Graber Furniture 812 295-4939
6377 N 1200 E Loogootee (47553) *(G-11136)*

Graber Lumber LP 260 238-4124
17528 Cuba Rd Spencerville (46788) *(G-15370)*

Graber Manufacturing 812 636-7725
Ct Rd 1050 N Odon (47562) *(G-13337)*

Graber Manufacturing LLC 260 657-3400
12836 Cuba Rd Grabill (46741) *(G-6298)*

Graber Manufacturing & Repair, Odon *Also Called: Graber Manufacturing* *(G-13337)*

Graber Ronald D Yoder & 574 268-9512
1515 Fox Farm Rd Warsaw (46580) *(G-16368)*

Graber Steel & Fab LLC 812 636-8418
8528 N 900 E Odon (47562) *(G-13338)*

Graber Thermoloc Windows LLC 812 486-3273
9058 E 500 N Montgomery (47558) *(G-12099)*

Graber Woodworks Inc 812 486-2861
5155 N 900 E Montgomery (47558) *(G-12100)*

Grabers Kountry Korner LLC 812 636-4399
8902 N 900 E Odon (47562) *(G-13339)*

Grabers Portable Band Mill 812 636-4158
10722 N 1000 E Odon (47562) *(G-13340)*

Grabill Cabinet Co, Grabill *Also Called: Schertz Craftsmen Inc* *(G-6324)*

Grabill Canning Company LLC 815 692-6036
13211 West St Grabill (46741) *(G-6299)*

Grabill Country Meat 1 Inc 260 627-3691
13211 West St Grabill (46741) *(G-6300)*

Grabill Country Meats, Grabill *Also Called: Grabill Canning Company LLC* *(G-6299)*

Grabill Home Food Service, Grabill *Also Called: Grabill Country Meat 1 Inc* *(G-6300)*

Grabill Truss Incorporated 260 627-0933
14005 David Ln Grabill (46741) *(G-6301)*

ALPHABETIC SECTION

Grabill Truss Manufacturing, Grabill *Also Called: Grabill Truss Incorporated (G-6301)*
Grable Burial Vault Svc Inc 574 753-4514
  322 Highland St Logansport (46947) *(G-11075)*
Grace Amazing Graphics 812 737-2841
  250 W Old Highway 11 Sw Laconia (47135) *(G-10505)*
Grace Fths Clbratory Signs LLC 463 701-7673
  3713 Newcastle Ct Indianapolis (46235) *(G-8311)*
Grace Henderson 765 661-9063
  204 S Nebraska St Marion (46952) *(G-11289)*
Grace Island Spcalty Foods Inc 260 357-3336
  5840 County Road 11 Garrett (46738) *(G-5863)*
Grace Manufacturing Inc 574 267-8000
  1500 W Center St Warsaw (46580) *(G-16369)*
Grace Steel LLC 574 387-4612
  2920 W Sample St South Bend (46619) *(G-15046)*
Grace Steel Corporation (PA) 574 218-6600
  21601 Durham Way Bristol (46507) *(G-1264)*
Grace To Grow Publications 219 932-0711
  507 State St Hammond (46320) *(G-6936)*
Gracie Industries LLC 260 748-0314
  3900 Transportation Dr Fort Wayne (46818) *(G-5032)*
Gracies Paw Prints 317 910-9969
  10053 Parkshore Dr Fishers (46038) *(G-4532)*
Graef Custom Homes LLC 574 807-5859
  52792 Red Fox Trl South Bend (46628) *(G-15047)*
Grafac Apparel, Evansville *Also Called: Grafac Industries Inc (G-4094)*
Grafac Industries Inc 812 474-0930
  2315 E Morgan Ave Evansville (47711) *(G-4094)*
Grafco Industries Ltd Partnr (HQ) 812 424-2904
  101 Oakley St Evansville (47710) *(G-4095)*
Grafcor Inc 765 966-7030
  601 Nw 5th St Richmond (47374) *(G-14127)*
Graffiti Defense LLC 317 284-1788
  12488 Brandamore Ln Fishers (46037) *(G-4533)*
Grafton Peek Incorporated 317 557-8377
  410 E Main St Greenwood (46143) *(G-6709)*
Graham Feed Company, Terre Haute *Also Called: B S R Inc (G-15547)*
Graham Feed Company, Terre Haute *Also Called: B S R Inc (G-15548)*
Graham Feed Company, Terre Haute *Also Called: B S R Inc (G-15549)*
Grahams Wrecker Service Inc 317 736-4355
  300 White St Whiteland (46184) *(G-16787)*
Grain Millers, Marion *Also Called: Agricor Inc (G-11269)*
Grain Processing Corporation 812 257-0480
  1443 S 300 W Washington (47501) *(G-16481)*
Grampas Cedar Works LLC 317 372-0816
  8456 N Baltimore Rd Monrovia (46157) *(G-12077)*
Grand Design Rv LLC (HQ) 574 825-8000
  11333 County Road 2 Middlebury (46540) *(G-11719)*
Grand Master Llc 574 288-8273
  1619 Miami St South Bend (46613) *(G-15048)*
Grand Products Inc 317 870-3122
  1650 S Girls School Rd Indianapolis (46231) *(G-8312)*
Grandma Irma Sauces Corp 773 688-9029
  417 W 81st Ave Merrillville (46410) *(G-11519)*
Grandpas Beef Jerky LLC 317 258-3209
  12310 Eddington Pl Fishers (46037) *(G-4534)*
Grandview Aluminum Products 812 649-2569
  110 W 4th St Grandview (47615) *(G-6328)*
Granger Gazette Inc 574 277-2679
  50841 Stonebridge Dr Granger (46530) *(G-6350)*
Granite and Marble, Westfield *Also Called: Absolute Stone Polsg Repr LLC (G-16661)*
Granite Engrg & Tl Co Inc (PA) 812 375-9077
  51 S Us Highway 31 Columbus (47201) *(G-2314)*
Granite Tee Signs LLC 317 670-4967
  7913 S Andee Ln Fort Branch (47648) *(G-4703)*
Granitech 574 674-6988
  3954 Lexington Park Dr Elkhart (46514) *(G-3386)*
Grannys LLC 812 969-3058
  7156 Black Creek Rd Elizabeth (47117) *(G-3126)*
Grant County Steel, Marion *Also Called: Grant County Steel Inc (G-11290)*
Grant County Steel Inc 765 668-7547
  2201 S Branson St Marion (46953) *(G-11290)*

Grape Arbor Publishing LLC 317 219-9337
  66 Rosewalk Cir Apt 1b Carmel (46032) *(G-1643)*
Graphex International 219 696-4849
  792 W 181st Ave Lowell (46356) *(G-11161)*
Graphic 2000 Forms Labels 260 387-5943
  8327 Norwood Ct Fort Wayne (46835) *(G-5033)*
Graphic 22, Chesterton *Also Called: Graphic22 Inc (G-1930)*
Graphic Barn LLC 812 952-3826
  6636 Riley Ridge Rd Lanesville (47136) *(G-10798)*
Graphic Enterprises, Brookville *Also Called: Huelseman Printing Co (G-1324)*
Graphic Expressions 219 663-2085
  6707 Broadway Merrillville (46410) *(G-11520)*
Graphic Expressions Inc 317 577-9622
  13025 New Britton Dr Fishers (46038) *(G-4535)*
Graphic Fx Inc 812 234-0000
  1130 Walnut St Terre Haute (47807) *(G-15601)*
Graphic Menus Inc 765 396-3003
  16555 N State Road 3n Eaton (47338) *(G-3062)*
Graphic Packaging Holding Co 219 324-6160
  115 Koomler Dr La Porte (46350) *(G-10410)*
Graphic Printing Co Inc (PA) 260 726-8141
  309 W Main St Portland (47371) *(G-13947)*
Graphic Shack Signs 765 721-4317
  3216 S County Road 675 E Greencastle (46135) *(G-6405)*
Graphic Visions 812 331-7446
  1314 W Kirkwood Ave Bloomington (47404) *(G-869)*
Graphic Vsons Screen Prtg Sgns, Bloomington *Also Called: Graphic Visions (G-869)*
Graphic22 Inc 219 921-5409
  1505 S Calumet Rd Ste 2 Chesterton (46304) *(G-1930)*
Graphically Speaking 219 921-1572
  349 Sand Creek Dr Chesterton (46304) *(G-1931)*
Graphics 55, Alexandria *Also Called: Robert Burkhart (G-62)*
Graphics Emporium 574 967-4627
  2540 E 200 S Bringhurst (46913) *(G-1236)*
Graphics Factory 574 264-0542
  400 W Crawford St Elkhart (46514) *(G-3387)*
Graphics Lab Uv Printing Inc 765 457-5784
  1041 S Union St Kokomo (46902) *(G-10272)*
Graphics Output, Fort Wayne *Also Called: Two B Enterprises Inc (G-5518)*
Graphics Plus, Avilla *Also Called: Ron Nawrocki (G-493)*
Graphics Systems Inc 260 485-9667
  8421 Mayhew Rd Fort Wayne (46835) *(G-5034)*
Graphics Unlimited 765 288-6816
  500 S Celia Ave # B Muncie (47303) *(G-12405)*
Graphics Unlmted McRpublishing 260 665-3443
  740 E 50 N Angola (46703) *(G-256)*
Graphie-Tees, South Bend *Also Called: Mito-Craft Inc (G-15152)*
Graphik Mechanix Inc 260 426-7001
  1716 S Harrison St Fort Wayne (46802) *(G-5035)*
Graphite Customs LLC 260 402-8690
  9323 Parkway Dr Fort Wayne (46804) *(G-5036)*
Graphix Unlimited Inc 574 546-3770
  3947 State Road 106 Bremen (46506) *(G-1193)*
Grass Valley, Richmond *Also Called: Grass Valley USA LLC (G-14128)*
Grass Valley USA LLC 765 259-1744
  1411 Nw 11th St Richmond (47374) *(G-14128)*
Grateful Heart Enterprises LLC 765 838-2266
  5082 Glacier Way Lafayette (47909) *(G-10593)*
Grateful Heart Gallery & Gifts, Lafayette *Also Called: Grateful Heart Enterprises LLC (G-10593)*
Gravel Conveyors Inc (PA) 317 873-8686
  5005 W 106th St Zionsville (46077) *(G-17014)*
Gravel Doctor Indianapolis LLC 317 399-4585
  7611 Dornock Dr Indianapolis (46237) *(G-8313)*
Gravelton Machine Shop Inc 574 773-3413
  23965 Us Highway 6 Nappanee (46550) *(G-12600)*
Graves Media & Pubg Group LLC 317 679-4072
  1312 Scotland Blvd Indianapolis (46231) *(G-8314)*
Graveyardgarlic LLC 502 523-8148
  8888 Keystone Xing Indianapolis (46240) *(G-8315)*
Graybull Organic Wines Inc 317 797-2186
  8435 Georgetown Rd Ste 600 Indianapolis (46268) *(G-8316)*

Graycraft Signs Plus, Warsaw *Also Called: Sjg Enterprises Inc (G-16425)*
Graycraft Signs Plus Inc (PA)... 260 432-3760
  2428 Getz Rd Fort Wayne (46804) *(G-5037)*
Graycraft Signs Plus Inc... 574 269-3780
  3304 Lake City Hwy Warsaw (46580) *(G-16370)*
Grayson Automotive Systems, Franklin *Also Called: Grayson Thermal Systems Corp (G-5736)*
Grayson Graphics.. 574 264-6466
  3008 Mobile Dr Elkhart (46514) *(G-3388)*
Grayson Thermal Systems Corp... 317 739-3290
  980 Hurricane Rd Franklin (46131) *(G-5736)*
Graysville Mfg Inc... 812 382-4616
  4391 N County Road 875 W Sullivan (47882) *(G-15407)*
Grc Enterprises Inc.. 219 932-2220
  3477 Watling St East Chicago (46312) *(G-3012)*
Greaseco, Valparaiso *Also Called: Times 10 Associates LLC (G-16068)*
Great American Puzzle Factory, Indianapolis *Also Called: Fundex Games Ltd (G-8241)*
Great Dane LLC.. 812 443-4711
  2664 E Us Highway 40 Brazil (47834) *(G-1143)*
Great Dane LLC.. 812 460-7706
  4955 N 13th St Terre Haute (47805) *(G-15602)*
Great Dane Trailers, Brazil *Also Called: Great Dane LLC (G-1143)*
Great Dane Trailers, Terre Haute *Also Called: Great Dane LLC (G-15602)*
Great Deals Magazine... 765 649-3302
  1232 Broadway St Ste 300 Anderson (46012) *(G-123)*
Great Deals Racing... 765 288-4608
  8081 W Mccolm Rd Gaston (47342) *(G-6046)*
Great Lake Sales & Marketing.. 219 325-0637
  3735 W Pawnee Dr La Porte (46350) *(G-10411)*
Great Lakes Forest Pdts Inc (PA).. 574 389-9663
  21861 Protecta Dr Elkhart (46516) *(G-3389)*
Great Lakes Granite LLC... 708 474-8800
  6050 Eagle Ave Portage (46368) *(G-13872)*
Great Lakes Lamination Inc (PA)... 574 389-9663
  1103 Maple St Bristol (46507) *(G-1265)*
Great Lakes Lamination Inc... 574 389-9663
  21861 Protecta Dr Elkhart (46516) *(G-3390)*
Great Lakes Prefabrication LLC.. 260 489-1575
  4334 Ardmore Ave Fort Wayne (46802) *(G-5038)*
Great Lakes Steel Corporation... 574 273-7000
  4100 Edison Lakes Pkwy Mishawaka (46545) *(G-11902)*
Great Lakes Waterjet Inc.. 574 651-2158
  53100 Corydon Ct Granger (46530) *(G-6351)*
Great Panes Glass Co.. 260 426-0203
  1307 N Wells St Fort Wayne (46808) *(G-5039)*
Great States Corp.. 765 288-6624
  2100 N Granville Ave Muncie (47303) *(G-12406)*
Greatbatch Ltd... 260 755-7300
  4545 Kroemer Rd Fort Wayne (46818) *(G-5040)*
Greatbatch Ltd... 260 755-7484
  265 E Bell Dr Ste A Warsaw (46582) *(G-16371)*
Greatbatch Medical, Fort Wayne *Also Called: Greatbatch Ltd (G-5040)*
Greatbatch Medical, Fort Wayne *Also Called: Integer Holdings Corporation (G-5114)*
Greatbatch Medical, Indianapolis *Also Called: Integer Holdings Corporation (G-8566)*
Greatbatch Medical, Warsaw *Also Called: Greatbatch Ltd (G-16371)*
Greazy Pickle LLC... 260 726-9200
  211 W Main St Portland (47371) *(G-13948)*
Grede LLC... 765 521-8000
  2700 Plum St New Castle (47362) *(G-12865)*
Green Air LLC... 317 335-1706
  13967 Hawkstone Dr Fishers (46040) *(G-4641)*
Green Apple Active LLC (PA).. 910 585-1151
  17304 Tilbury Way Westfield (46074) *(G-16693)*
Green Banner Publications Inc (PA)... 812 967-3176
  215 Money Hollow Rd Borden (47106) *(G-1109)*
Green City Cabinets, Odon *Also Called: Southern Indiana Wdwkg LLC (G-13352)*
Green Cow Power LLC... 219 984-5915
  24130 County Road 40 Goshen (46526) *(G-6154)*
Green Cubes Tech, Kokomo *Also Called: Green Cubes Technology LLC (G-10273)*
Green Cubes Technology LLC (PA)... 502 416-1060
  2121 E Boulevard Kokomo (46902) *(G-10273)*

Green Earth Polymers Inc... 812 602-4070
  4825 N Spring St Evansville (47711) *(G-4096)*
Green Fast Cure LLC.. 812 486-2510
  5461 E 300 N Montgomery (47558) *(G-12101)*
Green Forest Sawmill LLC.. 812 745-3335
  407 W Main St Oaktown (47561) *(G-13327)*
Green Illuminating Systems Inc... 317 869-7430
  10330 Pleasant St Ste 600 Noblesville (46060) *(G-13088)*
Green Lake Tube LLC (PA)... 219 397-0495
  4500 Euclid Ave East Chicago (46312) *(G-3013)*
Green Leaf Inc.. 812 877-1546
  9490 N Baldwin St Fontanet (47851) *(G-4699)*
Green Leafs LLC... 812 483-6383
  2100 Lakes Edge Dr Newburgh (47630) *(G-13002)*
Green Mountain Industries LLC... 812 585-1531
  603 W State Road 46 Centerpoint (47840) *(G-1844)*
Green Nursery Inc... 812 269-2220
  101 W Kirkwood Ave Ste 107 Bloomington (47404) *(G-870)*
Green Nursery, The, Bloomington *Also Called: Green Nursery Inc (G-870)*
Green Plains Grain Company LLC... 812 985-7480
  8999 W Franklin Rd Mount Vernon (47620) *(G-12298)*
Green Plains Inc... 812 985-7480
  8999 W Franklin Rd Mount Vernon (47620) *(G-12299)*
Green Plains Mount Vernon, Mount Vernon *Also Called: Green Plains Grain Company LLC (G-12298)*
Green Plus Plastics LLC... 317 672-2410
  3131 N Franklin Rd Ste L Indianapolis (46226) *(G-8317)*
Green Sign Co Inc.. 812 663-2550
  1045 E Freeland Rd Greensburg (47240) *(G-6597)*
Green Streak Pulling Inc... 812 254-6858
  1312 E 200 N Washington (47501) *(G-16482)*
Green Stream Company.. 574 293-1949
  29414 Phillips St Elkhart (46514) *(G-3391)*
Green Tech... 260 350-0089
  2305 W 200 S Lagrange (46761) *(G-10740)*
Green Tech America Inc.. 765 588-3834
  606 Riley Ln West Lafayette (47906) *(G-16587)*
Green Tek LLC.. 317 294-1614
  4925 Jennings Dr Carmel (46033) *(G-1644)*
Green Tree Plastics LLC... 812 402-4127
  1107 E Virginia St Evansville (47711) *(G-4097)*
Green Way Candle Company LLC... 574 536-3802
  63 Greenway Dr Goshen (46526) *(G-6155)*
Greencastle Offset Inc... 765 653-4026
  20 S Jackson St Greencastle (46135) *(G-6406)*
Greencastle Offset Printing, Greencastle *Also Called: Greencastle Offset Inc (G-6406)*
Greencycle, Indianapolis *Also Called: Greencycle of Indiana Inc (G-8318)*
Greencycle, Whitestown *Also Called: Greencycle of Indiana Inc (G-16808)*
Greencycle Inc... 317 773-3350
  2695 Cicero Rd Noblesville (46060) *(G-13089)*
Greencycle of Indiana Inc... 317 780-8175
  1103 W Troy Ave Indianapolis (46225) *(G-8318)*
Greencycle of Indiana Inc... 317 769-5668
  4227 S Perry Worth Rd Whitestown (46075) *(G-16808)*
Greene County Pallets Inc.. 812 384-8362
  1338 N Harv-Wright Rd Bloomfield (47424) *(G-746)*
Greene Woodworking & Glass LLC.. 812 755-4331
  10136 W Suder Ln Campbellsburg (47108) *(G-1523)*
Greenfield Gravel Inc.. 317 326-4003
  2605 W 200 N Greenfield (46140) *(G-6506)*
Greenfield Signs Inc.. 317 469-3095
  716 W Main St Greenfield (46140) *(G-6507)*
Greenleaf Foods Spc Inc... 317 554-4322
  8735 E 33rd St Bldg B Indianapolis (46226) *(G-8319)*
Greenlight Collectibles, Indianapolis *Also Called: Greenlight LLC (G-8320)*
Greenlight LLC.. 317 287-0600
  5901 Lakeside Blvd Indianapolis (46278) *(G-8320)*
Greenline Screen Printing.. 317 572-1155
  6830 Hawthorn Park Dr Indianapolis (46220) *(G-8321)*
Greenman's Printing & Imaging, Angola *Also Called: Jomark Inc (G-265)*
Greens Groomer, Indianapolis *Also Called: SA Heinen LLC (G-9358)*

Greensboro Sand & Gravel LLC.................................. 765 624-9342
4497 W County Road 350 S Knightstown (46148) *(G-10195)*

Greensbroom.. 317 416-7818
4555 W Bradbury Ave Ste 1 Indianapolis (46241) *(G-8322)*

Greensburg Daily News, Greensburg Also Called: Community Holdings Indiana Inc *(G-6585)*

Greensburg Printing Co Inc... 812 663-8265
116 N Franklin St Greensburg (47240) *(G-6598)*

Greensgroomer Worldwide Inc... 317 388-0695
3890 N Raceway Rd Indianapolis (46234) *(G-8323)*

Greensgroomer Worldwide Inc (PA)................................ 317 388-0695
10930 E Us Highway 136 Indianapolis (46234) *(G-8324)*

Greensignco.com, Greensburg Also Called: Green Sign Co Inc *(G-6597)*

Greenwell Software LLC.. 812 709-0214
9750 N 1300 E Loogootee (47553) *(G-11137)*

Greenwood Ladies Auxiliary 252...................................... 317 788-8458
4619 Anita Dr Indianapolis (46217) *(G-8325)*

Greenwood Light & Sign Service..................................... 317 840-5729
7955 W 400 N Boggstown (46110) *(G-1073)*

Greenwood Models Inc.. 317 859-2988
350 Commerce Parkway West Dr Greenwood (46143) *(G-6710)*

Greenwood Tool and Die Co Inc..................................... 219 924-9663
231 S Lindberg St Griffith (46319) *(G-6805)*

Grefco Minerals Inc... 765 362-6000
2510 N Concord Rd Crawfordsville (47933) *(G-2571)*

Greg Abplanalp Logging LLC.. 812 873-8463
1395 N County Road 615 E Butlerville (47223) *(G-1483)*

Greg Miner... 765 647-1012
10068 Oxford Pike Brookville (47012) *(G-1322)*

Greg Moser Engineering Inc... 260 726-6689
102 Performance Dr Portland (47371) *(G-13949)*

Greg Samples... 812 595-3033
5043 N Elk Creek Rd Scottsburg (47170) *(G-14558)*

Greg Whitenack.. 260 726-7321
1338 W 100 N Portland (47371) *(G-13950)*

Gregory Thomas Inc (PA).. 219 324-3801
1823 N Circle View Ln La Porte (46350) *(G-10412)*

Greif Inc.. 740 657-6606
3719 W 96th St Indianapolis (46268) *(G-8326)*

Grem USA Corporation.. 260 456-2354
315 E Wallace St Fort Wayne (46803) *(G-5041)*

Greypaint LLC.. 765 407-6321
3055 Pawnee Dr Indianapolis (46235) *(G-8327)*

Greys Automotive Inc.. 317 632-3562
1604 W Minnesota St Indianapolis (46221) *(G-8328)*

Greystone Logistics Inc... 812 459-9978
9747 Morris Dr Evansville (47720) *(G-4098)*

Gribbins Specialty Group Inc (PA).................................. 812 422-3340
1400 E Columbia St Evansville (47711) *(G-4099)*

Grider & Co Construction LLC... 310 986-7533
5607 N Oxford St Indianapolis (46220) *(G-8329)*

Griffen Plmbng-Heating-Cooling..................................... 574 295-2440
2310 Toledo Rd Elkhart (46516) *(G-3392)*

Griffen Plumbing & Heating, Elkhart Also Called: Griffen Plmbng-Heating-Cooling *(G-3392)*

Griffin Analytical Technologies LLC............................... 765 775-1701
3000 Kent Ave Ste E1 West Lafayette (47906) *(G-16588)*

Griffin Clark LLC... 765 491-9059
2738 S Pinehurst Dr Bloomington (47403) *(G-871)*

Griffin Industries LLC.. 812 379-9528
345 Water St Columbus (47201) *(G-2315)*

Griffin Industries LLC.. 812 659-3399
7358 S Griffin Rd Newberry (47449) *(G-12989)*

Griffin Trailers, Elkhart Also Called: Chubbs Steel Sales Inc *(G-3252)*

Griffith Rbr Mills of Garrett (HQ)...................................... 260 357-3125
400 N Taylor Rd Garrett (46738) *(G-5864)*

Griffith Rbr Mills of Garrett... 260 357-0876
507 N Lee St Garrett (46738) *(G-5865)*

Grimm Mold & Die Co Inc... 219 778-4211
200 S Depot St Rolling Prairie (46371) *(G-14363)*

Grindco Inc... 219 763-6130
288 W 1050 N Chesterton (46304) *(G-1932)*

Grindhard Performance LLC.. 317 334-5795
6020 E 82nd St Indianapolis (46250) *(G-8330)*

Grinding and Polsg McHy Corp....................................... 317 898-0750
2801 Tobey Dr Indianapolis (46219) *(G-8331)*

Grinds Manufacturing LLC.. 510 763-1088
17065 Oak Ridge Rd Westfield (46074) *(G-16694)*

Griner Engineering Inc.. 812 332-2220
2500 N Curry Pike Bloomington (47404) *(G-872)*

Grinon Industries LLC (PA).. 317 388-5100
7649 Winton Dr Indianapolis (46268) *(G-8332)*

Grip-Tite, Granger Also Called: BT&f LLC *(G-6338)*

Grit Into Grace Inc... 317 331-8334
859 N Parker Ave Indianapolis (46201) *(G-8333)*

Grizzly Ridge Hardwoods LLC.. 574 546-3600
1820 Dogwood Rd Bremen (46506) *(G-1194)*

Grnwman LLC.. 219 359-9237
1212 Jefferson Ave Chesterton (46304) *(G-1933)*

Gro-Tec Inc.. 765 853-1246
10324 W Us Highway 36 Modoc (47358) *(G-12051)*

Grodin Transportation... 773 614-7062
307 Marshall St Gary (46404) *(G-5944)*

Gross & Sons Lumber and Veneer................................. 574 457-5214
8516 E 1250 N Syracuse (46567) *(G-15461)*

Grote Industries Inc (PA)... 812 273-2121
2600 Lanier Dr Madison (47250) *(G-11222)*

Grote Industries LLC... 812 265-8273
2600 Lanier Dr Madison (47250) *(G-11223)*

Grotrian Tool & Die.. 260 894-3558
300 Sroufe St Ligonier (46767) *(G-11016)*

Ground Pounder of Indiana, Georgetown Also Called: Paraklese Technologies LLC *(G-6073)*

Groundbreakers, Indianapolis Also Called: Hydro Vac Services LLC *(G-8443)*

Group Dekko Inc (DH)... 260 357-3621
7310 Innovation Blvd # 104 Fort Wayne (46818) *(G-5042)*

Group Dekko Inc.. 260 357-5988
1605 Dekko Dr Garrett (46738) *(G-5866)*

Group Dekko Inc.. 260 599-3405
6928 N 400e Dock 101 Kendallville (46755) *(G-10114)*

Group Dekko Inc.. 260 637-3964
11913 E 450 S Laotto (46763) *(G-10805)*

Group Dekko Inc.. 574 834-2818
8701 E Backwater Rd North Webster (46555) *(G-13305)*

Group Dekko Inc.. 260 854-4783
105 Warrner Dr Rome City (46784) *(G-14376)*

Group Dekko Holdings Inc (HQ)..................................... 800 829-3101
7310 Innovation Blvd Ste 104 Fort Wayne (46818) *(G-5043)*

Grouper Wild LLC... 574 534-1499
910 Eisenhower Dr S Goshen (46526) *(G-6156)*

Groupone Health Source Inc... 800 769-5288
11715 Fox Rd Ste 400 # 178 Indianapolis (46236) *(G-8334)*

Growing Child Inc... 765 463-1696
1325 Palmer Dr West Lafayette (47906) *(G-16589)*

Growing Smiles Inc.. 317 787-6404
7210 Madison Ave Apt O Indianapolis (46227) *(G-8335)*

Growlers.. 219 924-0245
2816 Highway Ave Highland (46322) *(G-7139)*

Grrk Holdings Inc... 317 872-0172
7430 New Augusta Rd Indianapolis (46268) *(G-8336)*

Grrreat Creations.. 574 773-5331
597 Shawnee St Nappanee (46550) *(G-12601)*

Grumble Games LLC.. 317 941-6433
12975 Limberlost Dr Carmel (46033) *(G-1645)*

Grundfos Pumps Mfg Corp... 317 925-9661
2005 Dr Martin Luther King Jr St Indianapolis (46202) *(G-8337)*

Grundy Woodworks.. 765 337-4596
600 W Main St Crawfordsville (47933) *(G-2572)*

Gryphon Print Studio LLC.. 574 514-1644
3702 W Sample St South Bend (46619) *(G-15049)*

Gs Sales Inc.. 317 595-6750
2802 Pyrenean Pl Westfield (46074) *(G-16695)*

Gsw Press, North Vernon Also Called: Gsw Press Automation Inc *(G-13273)*

Gsw Press Automation Inc.. 419 733-5230
5100 N State Highway 7 North Vernon (47265) *(G-13273)*

Gt Automation Group, Fort Wayne Also Called: Gta Enterprises Inc *(G-5044)*

Gt Industries, North Vernon *Also Called: Gt Industries Inc (G-13274)*
Gt Industries Inc..734 241-7242
  3765 N State Highway 3 North Vernon (47265) *(G-13274)*
Gt Stamping Inc..574 533-4108
  1025 S 10th St Goshen (46526) *(G-6157)*
Gta Containers Inc..574 288-3459
  3300 W Sample St Ste 1200 South Bend (46619) *(G-15050)*
Gta Containers Inc..574 288-3459
  445 N Sheridan St South Bend (46619) *(G-15051)*
Gta Containers Inc..574 288-3459
  4201 Linden Ave South Bend (46619) *(G-15052)*
Gta Containers LLC..574 288-3459
  4201 Linden Ave South Bend (46619) *(G-15053)*
Gta Containers LLC (PA)..574 288-3459
  4201 Linden Ave South Bend (46619) *(G-15054)*
GTA CONTAINERS, INC., South Bend *Also Called: Gta Containers Inc (G-15051)*
Gta Drum Inc..574 288-3459
  1410 Napier St South Bend (46601) *(G-15055)*
Gta Drums, South Bend *Also Called: Gta Containers Inc (G-15052)*
Gta Enterprises Inc...260 478-7800
  9305 Yeager Ln Fort Wayne (46809) *(G-5044)*
GTC Machining LLC..317 541-1400
  3555 Developers Rd Indianapolis (46227) *(G-8338)*
GTC Machining LLC..317 541-1400
  3555 Developers Rd Ste A Indianapolis (46227) *(G-8339)*
Gti Static Solutions, La Porte *Also Called: Gregory Thomas Inc (G-10412)*
GTW Enterprises Inc..219 362-2278
  1164 E 150 N La Porte (46350) *(G-10413)*
Guaranteed Lighting & Signs...765 866-1229
  6490 S 200 W Crawfordsville (47933) *(G-2573)*
Guardian Couplings LLC..219 874-5248
  300 Indiana Highway 212 Michigan City (46360) *(G-11617)*
Guardian Defense Inc...574 265-4474
  3765 S Britney Dr Warsaw (46580) *(G-16372)*
Guardian Enterprises LLC..317 416-8926
  9465 Counselors Row Ste 200 Indianapolis (46240) *(G-8340)*
Guardian Fire Systems Inc..317 752-2768
  435 W Broadway St Fortville (46040) *(G-5597)*
Guardian Ind Inc..219 874-5248
  300 Indiana Highway 212 Michigan City (46360) *(G-11618)*
Guardian Industries, Michigan City *Also Called: Altra Industrial Motion Corp (G-11577)*
Guardian Industries, Michigan City *Also Called: Guardian Ind Inc (G-11618)*
Guardian Mold Prevent Corp...708 878-5788
  906 Jackson Pl Dyer (46311) *(G-2975)*
Guardian Tech Group Ind LLC...765 364-0863
  1100 E Elmore St Crawfordsville (47933) *(G-2574)*
Gud Wazh Laundromat, Highland *Also Called: Bonzell Combs (G-7125)*
Guide Book Publishing...317 259-0599
  5929 Haverford Ave Indianapolis (46220) *(G-8341)*
Guide Engineering, Fort Wayne *Also Called: Novamatiq Inc (G-5277)*
Guide Technologies LLC..317 844-3162
  250 E 96th St Ste 525 Indianapolis (46240) *(G-8342)*
Gulf Stream Coach Inc..574 773-7761
  2404 E Market St Nappanee (46550) *(G-12602)*
Gulf Stream Coach Inc (PA)...574 773-7761
  503 S Oakland Ave Nappanee (46550) *(G-12603)*
Gulf Stream Coach Plant 59, Nappanee *Also Called: Gulf Stream Coach Inc (G-12602)*
Gulf Stream Parts & Service...574 858-2850
  330 N Tower St Etna Green (46524) *(G-3849)*
Gumena LLC..574 339-6510
  13738 Jefferson Blvd Mishawaka (46545) *(G-11903)*
Gund Company Inc...219 374-9944
  10501 W 133rd Ave Cedar Lake (46303) *(G-1832)*
Gusa Holdings Inc...317 545-1221
  4925 Aluminum Dr Indianapolis (46218) *(G-8343)*
Gutierrez Mexican Bky Mkt Inc..574 534-9979
  122 S Main St Goshen (46526) *(G-6158)*
Gutman, Anthony & Mary, Versailles *Also Called: T & M Precision Inc (G-16104)*
Gutter One Supply..317 872-1257
  8026 Woodland Dr Indianapolis (46278) *(G-8344)*

Guy Cardboard...812 989-4809
  2860 N Highway 11 Se Elizabeth (47117) *(G-3127)*
Guys Wood N Things..812 689-0433
  340 N County Road 300 W Holton (47023) *(G-7216)*
Gvm Inc...765 689-5010
  8497 S Us Highway 31 Bunker Hill (46914) *(G-1441)*
Gvs Filter Technology Inc..317 471-3700
  5353 W 79th St Indianapolis (46268) *(G-8345)*
Gvs Filter Technology Inc..317 442-3925
  4522 Winterspring Cres Zionsville (46077) *(G-17015)*
Gvs Technologies LLC..574 293-0974
  5308 Beck Dr Elkhart (46516) *(G-3393)*
Gwaltney Drilling Inc...812 254-5085
  101 Se 3rd St Washington (47501) *(G-16483)*
Gwin Enterprises...317 881-6401
  7294 S Delaware St Indianapolis (46227) *(G-8346)*
Gypsum Express Ltd..812 247-2648
  9720 Us Highway 50 Shoals (47581) *(G-14908)*
Gypsy Moon Ragdolls Inc..260 589-2852
  423 Wabash St Berne (46711) *(G-712)*
H & A Products Inc...574 226-0079
  28761 Holiday Pl Elkhart (46517) *(G-3394)*
H & E Machined Specialties..260 424-2527
  1321 E Wallace St Fort Wayne (46803) *(G-5045)*
H & H Commercial Heat Treating....................................765 288-3618
  2200 E 8th St Muncie (47302) *(G-12407)*
H & H Design & Tool Inc..765 886-6199
  222 2nd St Economy (47339) *(G-3066)*
H & H Home Improvement Inc..812 288-8700
  1120 N Taggart Ave Clarksville (47129) *(G-2017)*
H & H Manufacturing Inc...812 664-3582
  499 N 150 W Patoka (47666) *(G-13508)*
H & H Metal Products Inc..812 256-0444
  104 Industrial Way Charlestown (47111) *(G-1877)*
H & H Partnership Inc..765 513-4739
  174 E North St Kokomo (46901) *(G-10274)*
H & H Sales Company Inc...260 637-3177
  16339 Lima Rd Huntertown (46748) *(G-7257)*
H & M Bay Inc...410 463-5430
  3410 Meyer Rd Fort Wayne (46803) *(G-5046)*
H & M Pallet, Milroy *Also Called: Milroy Pallet Inc (G-11828)*
H & N Machine Division of, Waterloo *Also Called: Charleston Metal Products Inc (G-16516)*
H & P Tool Co Inc..765 962-4504
  610 S G St Richmond (47374) *(G-14129)*
H & R Industrial, Kokomo *Also Called: H & R Industrial LLC (G-10275)*
H & R Industrial LLC...765 868-8408
  832 S Berkley Rd Kokomo (46901) *(G-10275)*
H & S Custom Countertops Inc......................................812 422-6314
  5705 E Morgan Ave Evansville (47715) *(G-4100)*
H & S Fabrication LLC..260 724-3656
  5342 N 400 W Decatur (46733) *(G-2860)*
H & W Molders Inc...812 423-9340
  1031 W Tennessee St Evansville (47710) *(G-4101)*
H 2 Golf LLC..317 605-4720
  3435 Briar Creek Ln Carmel (46033) *(G-1646)*
H A Industries...219 931-6304
  4527 Columbia Ave Hammond (46327) *(G-6937)*
H A King Co Inc...260 482-6376
  3210 Clairmont Ct Fort Wayne (46808) *(G-5047)*
H A P Industries Inc...765 948-3385
  7220 S 200 W Jonesboro (46938) *(G-10079)*
H and M Tool & Die Inc..812 663-8252
  242 W Mckee St Greensburg (47240) *(G-6599)*
H C J B World Radio, Elkhart *Also Called: World Rdo Mssnary Fllwship Inc (G-3793)*
H C Schumacher Machine Co In....................................317 787-9361
  3619 S Arlington Ave Indianapolis (46203) *(G-8347)*
H D Eccel LLC..574 386-2115
  19221 Cleveland Rd South Bend (46637) *(G-15056)*
H D I, Logansport *Also Called: Hopper Development Inc (G-11077)*
H H Pallet...765 505-1682
  1977 N 175 W Crawfordsville (47933) *(G-2575)*

ALPHABETIC SECTION

H H Pallet.. 765 323-3117
3450 E State Road 32 Crawfordsville (47933) *(G-2576)*

H J J Inc.. 219 362-4421
1533 Weller Ave La Porte (46350) *(G-10414)*

H L Enterprise, Elkhart *Also Called: H L Enterprise Inc (G-3395)*

H L Enterprise Inc.. 574 294-1112
5321 Beck Dr Elkhart (46516) *(G-3395)*

H L Signworks... 812 325-5750
616 N Robin Dr Ellettsville (47429) *(G-3808)*

H M C, Princeton *Also Called: Highway Machine Co Inc (G-13998)*

H M C Screen Printing Inc... 317 773-8532
954 Conner St Noblesville (46060) *(G-13090)*

H Nagel & Son Co (PA)... 513 665-4550
707 Harrison Brookville Rd Unit 220 West Harrison (47060) *(G-16546)*

H P Oil, Jeffersonville *Also Called: Hoosier Penn Oil Co Inc (G-9998)*

H P Oil Co, Indianapolis *Also Called: Hoosier Penn Oil Co Inc (G-8411)*

H P Products, Hartford City *Also Called: Harold Precision Products Inc (G-7067)*

H P Schmitt Packing Co Inc..................................... 260 724-3146
976 Waynesboro Rd Decatur (46733) *(G-2861)*

H T D, Edinburgh *Also Called: Hoosier Tool & Die Co Inc (G-3087)*

H W Molders... 812 423-3552
1500 W Missouri St Evansville (47710) *(G-4102)*

H-C Liquidating Corp.. 574 535-9300
1002 Eisenhower Dr N Goshen (46526) *(G-6159)*

H&E Cutter Grinding Inc... 765 825-0541
6251 Industrial Ave N Connersville (47331) *(G-2439)*

H&G Legacy Co... 317 241-9233
3637 Farnsworth St Indianapolis (46241) *(G-8348)*

H&H Media LLC... 317 213-0480
1805 Sheffield Ct Anderson (46011) *(G-124)*

H&S Defense LLC... 812 654-2314
1455 N County Road 525 E Milan (47031) *(G-11780)*

H3r Garage LLC.. 317 519-1368
11125 Baycreek Dr Indianapolis (46236) *(G-8349)*

Haan Crafts LLC... 765 583-4496
506 E 2nd St Otterbein (47970) *(G-13451)*

Haas Cabinet Co Inc (PA).. 812 246-4431
625 W Utica St Sellersburg (47172) *(G-14594)*

Hachette Book Group Inc.. 765 483-9900
121 N Enterprise Blvd Lebanon (46052) *(G-10894)*

Hackett & Hackett LLC.. 574 370-7191
1234 N Eddy St Apt 454 South Bend (46617) *(G-15057)*

Hackett Publishing Company.................................. 317 635-9250
832 Pierson St Indianapolis (46204) *(G-8350)*

Hackett Publishing Company (PA)......................... 317 635-9250
3333 Massachusetts Ave Indianapolis (46218) *(G-8351)*

Hackman Borthers Show Feed, Brownstown *Also Called: Mark Hackman (G-1425)*

Hackney Home Furnishings Inc............................. 317 895-4300
9420 E 33rd St Indianapolis (46235) *(G-8352)*

Hadady Corporation (PA).. 219 322-7417
1832 Lake St Dyer (46311) *(G-2976)*

Hadady Machining Company Inc (PA)................... 708 474-8620
4809 Tod Ave East Chicago (46312) *(G-3014)*

Hadley Products LLC... 574 266-3700
319 Roske Dr Elkhart (46516) *(G-3396)*

Hagemier Products... 812 526-0377
6181 S 550 E Franklin (46131) *(G-5737)*

Hager Industries Inc.. 317 219-6622
230 Riverwood Dr Noblesville (46062) *(G-13091)*

Hagerstown Plastics Inc... 765 939-3849
621 S J St Richmond (47374) *(G-14130)*

Hahn Enterprises Inc... 574 862-4491
911 E Waterford St Wakarusa (46573) *(G-16234)*

Hails' Jewelry Service, Evansville *Also Called: Mark Edward Hails (G-4189)*

Haines Engineering Inc... 260 589-3388
6262 S 550 E Berne (46711) *(G-713)*

Hair Necessities.. 812 288-5887
711 E Lewis And Clark Pkwy Ste 105 Clarksville (47129) *(G-2018)*

Hair of Ferret.. 219 663-1599
339 Maple Ln Crown Point (46307) *(G-2691)*

Haird Salon LLC... 260 804-7609
420 Lillian Ave Fort Wayne (46808) *(G-5048)*

Haire Machine Corporation..................................... 219 947-4545
3019 E 84th Pl Merrillville (46410) *(G-11521)*

Halal Processing Solutions.................................... 832 385-2394
2100 E Willard St Muncie (47302) *(G-12408)*

Hale Industries Inc... 317 577-0337
315 N Madison St Fortville (46040) *(G-5598)*

Hall Signs Inc.. 812 332-9355
4495 W Vernal Pike Bloomington (47404) *(G-873)*

HALLADOR, Terre Haute *Also Called: Hallador Energy Company (G-15603)*

Hallador Energy Company (PA).............................. 812 299-2800
1183 E Canvasback Dr Terre Haute (47802) *(G-15603)*

Halo LLC (PA)... 317 575-9992
10585 N Meridian St Fl 3 Carmel (46290) *(G-1647)*

Halox Division, Hammond *Also Called: Icl Specialty Products Inc (G-6951)*

Halsen Brothers Shtmtl Inc..................................... 574 583-3358
300 Tioga Rd Monticello (47960) *(G-12152)*

Halstab, Hammond *Also Called: Hammond Group Inc (G-6938)*

Halstab Division, Hammond *Also Called: Hammond Group Inc (G-6939)*

Halyard Corporation... 219 515-2820
6610 Shepherd Ave Portage (46368) *(G-13873)*

Ham Enterprise LLC... 317 831-2902
160 E Morgan St Martinsville (46151) *(G-11398)*

Ham Enterprises Machine Co................................. 765 342-7966
4590 Jordan Rd Martinsville (46151) *(G-11399)*

Hamblen Machine Inc.. 812 330-6685
1830 S Walnut St Bloomington (47401) *(G-874)*

Hamilton Bros Inc... 317 241-2571
1840 Midwest Blvd Indianapolis (46214) *(G-8353)*

Hamilton Canvas Inc.. 219 763-1686
2305 Hamstrom Rd Ste F Portage (46368) *(G-13874)*

Hamilton County Business Mag............................. 317 774-7747
1095 Mulberry St Noblesville (46060) *(G-13092)*

Hamilton Industrial Inc.. 260 488-3662
6610 S State Road 1 Hamilton (46742) *(G-6855)*

Hamilton Iron Works Inc.. 574 533-3784
208 W Lincoln Ave Goshen (46526) *(G-6160)*

Hammer Marketing... 317 841-1567
9635 Woodlands Dr Fishers (46037) *(G-4536)*

Hammer Plastics Incorporated............................... 574 255-7230
1015 E 12th St Mishawaka (46544) *(G-11904)*

Hammertechracecars LLC....................................... 765 412-8824
6396 Granny Smith Ln Avon (46123) *(G-522)*

Hammond Drapery, Hammond *Also Called: Custom Draperies of Indiana (G-6909)*

Hammond Group Inc (PA)....................................... 219 931-9360
2901 Carlson Dr Ste 200 Hammond (46323) *(G-6938)*

Hammond Group Inc.. 219 931-9360
3100 Michigan St Hammond (46323) *(G-6939)*

Hammond Group Inc.. 219 845-0031
2323 165th St Hammond (46320) *(G-6940)*

Hammond Lead Products, Hammond *Also Called: Hammond Group Inc (G-6940)*

Hammond Lead Products Llc................................. 219 931-9360
2901 Carlson Dr Hammond (46323) *(G-6941)*

Hammond Machine Works Inc................................ 219 933-0479
5047 Columbia Ave Hammond (46327) *(G-6942)*

Hammond Steel Components LLC......................... 630 816-1343
3200 Sheffield Ave Hammond (46327) *(G-6943)*

Hammond Works, Hammond *Also Called: Dover Chemical Corporation (G-6914)*

Hampels Woodland Products.................................. 574 293-2124
61292 County Road 7 Elkhart (46517) *(G-3397)*

Hampton Equipment LLC.. 260 740-8704
7127 Hessen Cassel Rd Fort Wayne (46816) *(G-5049)*

Hampton Ironworks Inc... 219 929-6448
542 Dunewood Dr Chesterton (46304) *(G-1934)*

Hamster Press Klingel-Engle Pu, Ellettsville *Also Called: Christopher Engle (G-3803)*

Hanco Inc
1374 Clay Spring Dr Carmel (46032) *(G-1648)*

Hancor Inc... 812 443-2080
2340 E Us Highway 40 Brazil (47834) *(G-1144)*

Hand Industries Inc.. 574 267-3525
315 S Hand Ave Warsaw (46580) *(G-16373)*

Handle Bar, The, Kokomo *Also Called: G & J (G-10268)*

Handmade Natural Products | ALPHABETIC SECTION

Handmade Natural Products, Evansville *Also Called: Rosies Holistic Lifestyle LLC (G-4293)*
Handson (HQ) 812 246-4481
   4700 Utica Sellersburg Rd Sellersburg (47172) *(G-14595)*
Handstitched Memories 765 430-4346
   56 Jester Ct Lafayette (47905) *(G-10594)*
Handyman and Tree Service, Bedford *Also Called: Quick To Fix LLC (G-662)*
Handypro of Northwest Indiana 219 707-8240
   6212 Us Highway 6 Ste 225 Portage (46368) *(G-13875)*
Hanger Bolt & Stud Co Inc 317 462-4477
   165 W New Rd Greenfield (46140) *(G-6508)*
Hanger Prsthetcs & Ortho Inc 219 844-2021
   7324 Indianapolis Blvd Hammond (46324) *(G-6944)*
Hanger Prsthtics Orthotics Inc 765 966-5069
   4821 Old National Rd E Ste A Richmond (47374) *(G-14131)*
Hanks Sign Shop LLC 812 367-2851
   330 Main St Ferdinand (47532) *(G-4434)*
Hanover Machine & Tool Inc 812 265-6265
   3408 W State Road 56 Hanover (47243) *(G-7042)*
Hansa Medical Products Inc 317 815-0708
   2000 W 106th St Carmel (46032) *(G-1649)*
Hansen Corporation 812 385-3000
   901 S 1st St Princeton (47670) *(G-13997)*
Hansford Prevent LLC 317 985-2346
   5658 Buck Pond Ct Indianapolis (46237) *(G-8354)*
Hanson Aggregates, Charlestown *Also Called: Aggrock Quarries Inc (G-1870)*
Hanson Aggregates Wrp Inc 502 244-7550
   301 Highway 31 Sellersburg (47172) *(G-14596)*
Hanson Agrigoods Midwest Inc 317 635-9048
   8950 S State Road 243 Cloverdale (46120) *(G-2085)*
Hanson Pipe Precast 219 873-9509
   302 Elmwood Dr Michigan City (46360) *(G-11619)*
Hanwha Machinery America Corp 574 546-2261
   431 N Birkey St Bremen (46506) *(G-1195)*
Hapco Rebuilders Inc 812 232-2550
   129 N 2nd St Terre Haute (47807) *(G-15604)*
Happy Buddah 765 998-3008
   62 E Berry Ave Upland (46989) *(G-15877)*
Happy Tees LLC 317 465-0122
   628 E 63rd St Indianapolis (46220) *(G-8355)*
Happy Valley Sand & Gravel, Plainfield *Also Called: Happy Valley Sand and Grav Inc (G-13684)*
Happy Valley Sand and Grav Inc 317 839-6800
   4232 E Us Highway 40 Plainfield (46168) *(G-13684)*
Harbisonwalker Intl Inc 219 881-4440
   76 N Bridge St Gary (46404) *(G-5945)*
Harbor Metals LLC 574 232-3338
   802 Fellows St South Bend (46601) *(G-15058)*
Harcourt Industries Inc 765 629-2625
   7765 S 175 W Milroy (46156) *(G-11824)*
Harcourt Outlines, Milroy *Also Called: Harcourt Industries Inc (G-11824)*
Hard Hustla Muzik LLC 812 214-1995
   800 Sycamore St # 329 Evansville (47708) *(G-4103)*
Hard Surface Fabrications Inc 574 259-4843
   2302 E 3rd St Mishawaka (46544) *(G-11905)*
Hard Truth Distilling Co LLC 812 720-4840
   418 Old State Road 46 Nashville (47448) *(G-12670)*
Hard Truth Hills, Nashville *Also Called: Hard Truth Distilling Co LLC (G-12670)*
Hard Workin Hard Livin, Fort Wayne *Also Called: Custom Creations MGT LLC (G-4897)*
Harder Woods 402 572-0433
   64844 County Road 35 Goshen (46528) *(G-6161)*
Hardesty Printing Co Inc (PA) 574 223-4553
   1218 N State Road 25 Rochester (46975) *(G-14293)*
Hardesty Printing Co Inc 574 267-7591
   411 W Market St Warsaw (46580) *(G-16374)*
Harding Group, Indianapolis *Also Called: Howard Materials LLC (G-8430)*
Harding Group LLC 317 846-7401
   5145 E 96th St Indianapolis (46240) *(G-8356)*
Harding Group LLC 317 536-8364
   1100 S Tibbs Ave Indianapolis (46241) *(G-8357)*
Harding Materials Inc 317 849-9666
   10151 Hague Rd Indianapolis (46256) *(G-8358)*

Hardingpoorman Inc 317 876-3355
   4923 W 78th St Indianapolis (46268) *(G-8359)*
Hardingpoorman Group Inc 317 876-3355
   4923 W 78th St Indianapolis (46268) *(G-8360)*
Hardwood Door Mfg LLC 812 486-3313
   5084 N 575 E Montgomery (47558) *(G-12102)*
Hardwood Flooring, Vevay *Also Called: Cross Country Hardwood LLC (G-16108)*
Hardwoods By Bill LLC 219 465-5346
   2902 Kickbush Dr Valparaiso (46385) *(G-15959)*
Hare Canvas Products, Markle *Also Called: Nose and Mustache LLC (G-11360)*
Harl Plastics, Elkhart *Also Called: Hart Plastics Inc (G-3400)*
Harlan Bakeries, Avon *Also Called: Harlan Bakeries LLC (G-523)*
Harlan Bakeries, Indianapolis *Also Called: Harlan Bakeries LLC (G-8361)*
Harlan Bakeries LLC (PA) 317 272-3600
   7597 E Us Highway 36 Avon (46123) *(G-523)*
Harlan Bakeries LLC 317 272-3600
   404 S Kitley Ave Indianapolis (46219) *(G-8361)*
Harlan Bakeries-Avon LLC 317 272-3600
   7597 E Us Highway 36 Avon (46123) *(G-524)*
Harlan Cabinets Inc 260 657-5154
   12707 Spencerville Rd Harlan (46743) *(G-7056)*
Harlan Development Company 317 352-1583
   404 S Kitley Ave Indianapolis (46219) *(G-8362)*
Harman Embedded Audio LLC 317 849-8175
   6602 E 75th St Ste 520 Indianapolis (46250) *(G-8363)*
Harman Professional Inc 574 294-8000
   1718 W Mishawaka Rd Elkhart (46517) *(G-3398)*
Harman Specialty Group, Elkhart *Also Called: Lexicon Incorporated (G-3486)*
Harmon Hrmon Uysugi Optmtrists (PA) 812 723-4752
   488 W Hospital Rd Ste 1 Paoli (47454) *(G-13496)*
Harmony Marketing Group, Bourbon *Also Called: Harmony Press Inc (G-1122)*
Harmony Press Inc (PA) 800 525-3742
   115 N Main St Bourbon (46504) *(G-1122)*
Harmony Winery 317 585-9463
   18 N Jefferson St Knightstown (46148) *(G-10196)*
Harness Machine & Fab LLC 765 652-2831
   7734 S 500 E Frankfort (46041) *(G-5672)*
Harold Mailand 317 266-8398
   928 N Alabama St Indianapolis (46202) *(G-8364)*
Harold Precision Products Inc 765 348-2710
   1600 Gilkey Ave Hartford City (47348) *(G-7067)*
Harpercollins Publishers LLC 800 242-7737
   2700 N Richardt Ave Indianapolis (46219) *(G-8365)*
Harpercollins Publishers LLC 219 324-4880
   2205 E Lincolnway La Porte (46350) *(G-10415)*
Harpercollins Publishers LLC 317 839-4307
   716 Airtech Pkwy Plainfield (46168) *(G-13685)*
Harpercollins Publishers LLC 317 406-8777
   700 Airtech Pkwy Plainfield (46168) *(G-13686)*
Harpercollins Return Center, La Porte *Also Called: Harpercollins Publishers LLC (G-10415)*
Harpers Headstone Care, Depauw *Also Called: James Harper (G-2939)*
Harpoon Lure Co DBA Forming T 812 371-3550
   1080 N County Road 700 W North Vernon (47265) *(G-13275)*
Harpring Steel Inc 812 256-6326
   109 Industrial Way Charlestown (47111) *(G-1878)*
Harps On Main, Rising Sun *Also Called: Rees Harps Inc (G-14245)*
Harrell Family LLC 317 770-4550
   6802 Hillsdale Ct Indianapolis (46250) *(G-8366)*
Harrington Noodles Inc 574 546-3861
   2915 Commerce St Plymouth (46563) *(G-13781)*
Harris Burial Service Inc 812 939-3605
   1440 W County Road 800 S Clay City (47841) *(G-2043)*
Harris City Stone Co, Laurel *Also Called: New Point Stone Co Inc (G-10825)*
Harris City Stone Company, Greensburg *Also Called: New Point Stone Co Inc (G-6622)*
Harris Farms Inc 765 468-6264
   10575 W 400 S Modoc (47358) *(G-12052)*
Harris Flotebote 260 432-4555
   1111 N Hadley Rd Fort Wayne (46804) *(G-5050)*
Harris Kayot, Fort Wayne *Also Called: Brunswick Corporation (G-4821)*
Harris Oil Co, Evansville *Also Called: Michael R Harris (G-4201)*

ALPHABETIC SECTION — HB International LLC

Harris Precast Inc (PA) 219 362-2457
   1877 W Severs Rd La Porte (46350) *(G-10416)*

Harris Precast Inc 219 362-9671
   703 N Fail Rd La Porte (46350) *(G-10417)*

Harris Stone Service Inc 765 522-6241
   5581 N County Road 25 W Bainbridge (46105) *(G-563)*

Harris Sugar Bush LLC (PA) 765 653-5108
   999 E County Road 325 N Greencastle (46135) *(G-6407)*

Harrison Concrete 812 275-6682
   1218 7th St Bedford (47421) *(G-640)*

Harrison Electric Inc 219 879-0444
   10855 W 400 N Michigan City (46360) *(G-11620)*

Harrison Hauling Inc 574 862-3196
   64341 County Road 11 Goshen (46526) *(G-6162)*

Harrison Press 513 367-4582
   126 W High St Lawrenceburg (47025) *(G-10839)*

Harrison Sand and Gravel Co (PA) 812 663-2021
   992 S County Road 800 E Greensburg (47240) *(G-6600)*

Harrison Sand and Gravel Co 812 656-8149
   4215 Harrison Brookville Rd West Harrison (47060) *(G-16547)*

Harry & Izzys Northside LLC 317 915-8045
   4050 E 82nd St Indianapolis (46250) *(G-8367)*

Harry J Kloeppel & Associates 317 578-1300
   6974 Hillsdale Ct Indianapolis (46250) *(G-8368)*

Harry S Watts 219 879-1606
   10585 W 100 N Michigan City (46360) *(G-11621)*

Harsco Pittsboro, Pittsboro Also Called: Enviri Corporation *(G-13645)*

Hart Industries Inc 574 575-4657
   2907 Park Six Ct Elkhart (46514) *(G-3399)*

Hart Plastics Inc 574 264-7060
   2907 Park Six Ct Elkhart (46514) *(G-3400)*

Hartford Bakery Inc (HQ) 812 425-4642
   500 N Fulton Ave Evansville (47710) *(G-4104)*

Hartford City News Times 765 348-0110
   123 W Franklin St Winchester (47394) *(G-16889)*

Hartford Heat Treatment 812 725-8272
   37 W 5th St New Albany (47150) *(G-12740)*

Hartford TEC Glass Co Inc (PA) 765 348-1282
   735 E Water St Hartford City (47348) *(G-7068)*

Hartland Products Inc 219 778-9034
   5022 E Oak Knoll Rd Rolling Prairie (46371) *(G-14364)*

Hartley Interiors, Arcadia Also Called: Sylvia Kay Hartley *(G-318)*

Hartley J Company Inc 812 376-9708
   110 S 1000 E Hartsville (47244) *(G-7082)*

Hartman Logging 765 653-3889
   1158 W Us Highway 40 Greencastle (46135) *(G-6408)*

Hartsock Industrial Sales Inc 317 858-8250
   480 Enterprise Dr Westfield (46074) *(G-16696)*

Hartson-Kennedy Cabinet Top Co (PA) 765 668-8144
   522 W 22nd St Marion (46953) *(G-11291)*

Hartware Technologies 317 439-5816
   13099 Tarkington Cmn Carmel (46033) *(G-1650)*

Hartwell's Premium Products, Greenwood Also Called: Grafton Peek Incorporated *(G-6709)*

Hartzells Homemade Ice Cream 812 332-3502
   107 N Dunn St Bloomington (47408) *(G-875)*

Harvest Cafe Coffee & Tea LLC 317 585-9162
   2225 E 54th St Ste A Indianapolis (46220) *(G-8369)*

Harvey Hinklemeyers 765 452-1942
   1554 S Dixon Rd Kokomo (46902) *(G-10276)*

Harvey Industries, Wabash Also Called: Harvey Industries LLC *(G-16190)*

Harvey Industries LLC 260 563-8371
   3837 Mill St Wabash (46992) *(G-16190)*

Hassenplug & Son Sand & Gravel 574 223-5230
   1515 W 450 N Rochester (46975) *(G-14294)*

Hasser Enterprises Inc 765 583-1444
   8023 Us Highway 52 W West Lafayette (47906) *(G-16590)*

Hasty Welding 765 482-8925
   104 E Superior St Lebanon (46052) *(G-10895)*

Hat Plug US 574 575-2520
   1230 N Nappanee St Elkhart (46514) *(G-3401)*

Hatch Prints 312 952-1908
   901 N Saint Peter St South Bend (46617) *(G-15059)*

Haus Love Inc 317 601-6521
   5901 N College Ave Indianapolis (46220) *(G-8370)*

Hautau Tube Cutoff Systems LLC 765 647-1600
   11199 State Road 101 Brookville (47012) *(G-1323)*

Hautefirebeauty, Fort Wayne Also Called: Caprice Boyb *(G-4833)*

Haven Capital LLC 219 802-5044
   5 Washington St Valparaiso (46383) *(G-15960)*

Haven Manufacturing Ind LLC 260 622-4150
   6935 N State Road 1 Ossian (46777) *(G-13425)*

Haven Technologies Inc (PA) 317 740-0419
   873 W Carmel Dr Carmel (46032) *(G-1651)*

Hawaiian Smoothie LLC 317 881-7290
   12395 Eddington Pl Fishers (46037) *(G-4537)*

Hawk Enterprises Elkhart Inc (PA) 574 294-1910
   2902 Park Six Ct Elkhart (46514) *(G-3402)*

Hawk Precision Components Inc 812 755-4501
   596 W Oak St Campbellsburg (47108) *(G-1524)*

Hawker Beechcraft Svcs, Indianapolis Also Called: Textron Aviation Inc *(G-9581)*

Hawkins Inc 765 288-8930
   4601 S Delaware Dr Muncie (47302) *(G-12409)*

Hawkins Darryal 765 282-6021
   1001 E 18th St Muncie (47302) *(G-12410)*

Hawkins Industrial Resource Co, Muncie Also Called: Hawkins Darryal *(G-12410)*

Hawkins Machine & Tool Inc 812 522-5529
   2166 N County Road 900 E Seymour (47274) *(G-14655)*

Hawkins Print Shop, La Porte Also Called: Riden Inc *(G-10473)*

Hawthorne Products Inc 765 768-6585
   16828 N State Road 167n Dunkirk (47336) *(G-2962)*

Hayabusa LLC 317 594-1188
   5025 E 82nd St Indianapolis (46250) *(G-8371)*

Hayden Corp 317 501-5660
   6192 Stonehenge Blvd Noblesville (46062) *(G-13093)*

Hayes Design Company LLC 574 236-5615
   1247 Mishawaka Ave South Bend (46615) *(G-15060)*

Hayes Enterprises LLC 260 636-3262
   2174 N River Rd W Albion (46701) *(G-28)*

Haylex Manufacturing LLC 765 288-1818
   4401 S Delaware Dr Muncie (47302) *(G-12411)*

Haymons Publishing LLC 219 484-8510
   5100 Vermont St Gary (46409) *(G-5946)*

Haynes, Kokomo Also Called: Haynes International Inc *(G-10278)*

Haynes Honey LLC 260 563-6397
   1269 E 500 S Wabash (46992) *(G-16191)*

Haynes International Inc 765 457-3790
   2000 W Defenbaugh St Kokomo (46902) *(G-10277)*

Haynes International Inc (PA) 765 456-6000
   1020 W Park Ave Kokomo (46904) *(G-10278)*

Haynes International Inc 765 450-4310
   527 E Lincoln Rd Kokomo (46902) *(G-10279)*

Haynes International Inc 219 326-8530
   3238 N State Road 39 La Porte (46350) *(G-10418)*

Hayward & Sams LLP 260 351-4166
   4250 E 1175 S Stroh (46789) *(G-15401)*

Haywood Printing Co 812 384-8639
   2015 W State Road 54 Bloomfield (47424) *(G-747)*

Haywood Printing Co Inc 765 742-4085
   1801 W 18th St Indianapolis (46202) *(G-8372)*

Hazon Learning LLC 765 490-6321
   1281 Win Hentschel Blvd Rm 2935 West Lafayette (47906) *(G-16591)*

HB, Lafayette Also Called: Holder Bedding Inc *(G-10600)*

HB Connect Inc 855 503-9159
   2701 S Coliseum Blvd Fort Wayne (46803) *(G-5051)*

HB Connect Inc 260 422-1212
   1105 Sherman Blvd Fort Wayne (46808) *(G-5052)*

HB Gutters LLC 765 414-5698
   2444 E 100 N Winamac (46996) *(G-16862)*

HB International LLC 574 773-8200
   501 S Oakland Ave Nappanee (46550) *(G-12604)*

HB International LLC (DH) 574 773-0470
   1205 E Lincoln St Nappanee (46550) *(G-12605)*

HB International LLC 574 773-8200
   24785 Us Highway 6 Nappanee (46550) *(G-12606)*

Hc Farms..	765 289-9909
1010 E County Road 700 N Muncie (47303) *(G-12412)*	
Hco Holding I Corporation....................................	317 248-1344
4351 W Morris St Indianapolis (46241) *(G-8373)*	
Hd Car Detailing...	574 298-3975
50880 Indiana State Route 933 Ste 2 South Bend (46637) *(G-15061)*	
Hd Mechanical Inc..	219 924-6050
507 Industrial Dr Griffith (46319) *(G-6806)*	
HD Williams Co...	812 372-6476
201 W County Rd 100 S New Castle (47362) *(G-12866)*	
Hd Woodworking...	260 310-9327
7950 Rothman Rd Fort Wayne (46835) *(G-5053)*	
Hdh Manfacturing...	317 918-4088
1715 Expo Ln Indianapolis (46214) *(G-8374)*	
Hdh Manufacturing Inc..	317 918-4088
4008 W 10th St Indianapolis (46222) *(G-8375)*	
Hdh Manufacturing Inc (PA)..................................	317 918-4088
3534 Nolen Dr Indianapolis (46234) *(G-8376)*	
Headco Industries Inc...	219 924-7558
9922 Express Dr Highland (46322) *(G-7140)*	
Headco Industries Inc...	574 288-4471
1625 Commerce Dr South Bend (46628) *(G-15062)*	
Headlands Ltd..	260 426-9884
9125 E 480 S Wolcottville (46795) *(G-16937)*	
Heads 1st, Westville Also Called: Heads First *(G-16761)*	
Heads First..	219 785-4100
7 Plain St Westville (46391) *(G-16761)*	
Heads Up Bundles, Hammond Also Called: Candice Jefferson *(G-6892)*	
Headsight Inc...	574 546-5022
4845 3b Rd Bremen (46506) *(G-1196)*	
Heagy Vineyards LLC..	317 752-4484
10330 Holaday Dr Carmel (46032) *(G-1652)*	
Healey Custom Cabinetry LLC.............................	574 946-4000
802 N Us Highway 35 Winamac (46996) *(G-16863)*	
Health and Wellness, Indianapolis Also Called: Cbd Revolution LLC *(G-7762)*	
Hearing Aid Outlet, Hartford City Also Called: D J Investments Inc *(G-7063)*	
Hearing Aid Outlet, Hartford City Also Called: D J Investments Inc *(G-7064)*	
Hearing Aid Outlet, Portland Also Called: D J Investments Inc *(G-13936)*	
Hearsight Inc..	208 819-8659
410 Howard St South Bend (46617) *(G-15063)*	
Hearsight LLC...	208 819-8659
410 Howard St South Bend (46617) *(G-15064)*	
Heart Breaker Sales LLC..	765 489-4048
10094 Lacy Rd Hagerstown (47346) *(G-6837)*	
Heart Breaker Video Dis Jockey, Hagerstown Also Called: Heart Breaker Sales LLC *(G-6837)*	
Heart Struggle LLC...	812 480-2580
5534 Saint Joe Rd Fort Wayne (46835) *(G-5054)*	
Heartcare LLC...	260 432-7000
7806 W Jefferson Blvd Ste D Fort Wayne (46804) *(G-5055)*	
Heartfelt Creations Inc...	574 773-3088
2147 Eisenhower Dr N Goshen (46526) *(G-6163)*	
Hearthcraft, Clarksville Also Called: Bottom Line Management Inc *(G-2010)*	
Hearthglow Inc...	260 839-3205
3902 E State Road 14 Claypool (46510) *(G-2053)*	
Hearthside Food Solutions LLC...........................	219 878-1522
502 W Us Highway 20 Michigan City (46360) *(G-11622)*	
Hearthside Food Solutions LLC...........................	812 877-1588
9445 Us Hwy 40 Seelyville (47878) *(G-14585)*	
Heartland Adhesives Inc..	219 310-8645
7519 Boardwalk Crown Point (46307) *(G-2692)*	
Heartland Aluminum Inc...	260 375-4652
1750 Riverfork Dr Huntington (46750) *(G-7316)*	
Heartland Automotive..	765 446-2311
3700 David Howarth Dr Lafayette (47909) *(G-10595)*	
Heartland Automotive, Greencastle Also Called: Heartland Automotive LLC *(G-6410)*	
Heartland Automotive Inc......................................	765 653-4263
300 S Warren Dr Greencastle (46135) *(G-6409)*	
Heartland Automotive LLC.....................................	765 653-4263
300 S Warren Dr Greencastle (46135) *(G-6410)*	
Heartland Castings Inc...	260 837-8311
675 E Union St Waterloo (46793) *(G-16521)*	
Heartland Express LLC...	317 422-1438
465 S Baldwin St Bargersville (46106) *(G-567)*	
Heartland Filled Machine LLC...............................	574 223-6931
5176 State Road 110 Rochester (46975) *(G-14295)*	
Heartland Film Inc..	317 464-9405
1043 Virginia Ave Ste 2 Indianapolis (46203) *(G-8377)*	
Heartland Food Products Group, Carmel Also Called: Tc Heartland LLC *(G-1776)*	
Heartland Food Products Group, Indianapolis Also Called: Tc Heartland LLC *(G-9560)*	
Heartland Harvest Proc LLC (PA).........................	260 228-0736
4861 S 600 E Bldg A Gas City (46933) *(G-6038)*	
Heartland Harvest Proc LLC..................................	260 228-0736
1532 N 325 W Hartford City (47348) *(G-7069)*	
Heartland Industries Inc..	317 569-1718
861 N Rangeline Rd Carmel (46032) *(G-1653)*	
Heartland Metal LLC...	574 773-0509
5481 W 1350 N Nappanee (46550) *(G-12607)*	
Heartland Pet Food Mfg Ind LLC..........................	765 209-4140
4748 W Industries Rd Richmond (47374) *(G-14132)*	
Heartland Printworks, Indianapolis Also Called: Virtu Fine Art Services Inc *(G-9722)*	
Heartland Shutter Company LLC.........................	317 710-3350
4920 Mccray St Indianapolis (46224) *(G-8378)*	
Heartland Table Pads LLC.....................................	888 487-2377
401 N Main St Wolcottville (46795) *(G-16938)*	
Hearts Remained, Gary Also Called: Hearts Rmned Lifestyle Cir LLC *(G-5947)*	
Hearts Rmned Lifestyle Cir LLC...........................	800 807-0485
1052 N County Line Rd Gary (46403) *(G-5947)*	
Heat Exchanger Design Inc...................................	317 686-9000
901 E Beecher St Indianapolis (46203) *(G-8379)*	
Heat Treatment, Griffith Also Called: Legacy Heat Treatment LLC *(G-6811)*	
Heat Wagons Inc..	219 464-8818
342 N Co Rd 400 E Valparaiso (46383) *(G-15961)*	
Heather Sound Amplification................................	574 255-6100
1717 E 6th St Mishawaka (46544) *(G-11906)*	
Heatherwood Enterprises Inc...............................	812 294-7270
1210 Harvest Ridge Blvd Memphis (47143) *(G-11464)*	
Heaven Sent Gourmet Cookies Inc.....................	219 980-1066
3745 Broadway Gary (46409) *(G-5948)*	
Heavy Duty Manufacturing Inc.............................	260 432-2480
4317 Clubview Dr Fort Wayne (46804) *(G-5056)*	
Heb Development LLC...	616 363-3825
200 N State Road 59 Centerpoint (47840) *(G-1845)*	
Hebron Ventures Global, Fort Wayne Also Called: Hebron Ventures North America *(G-5057)*	
Hebron Ventures North America...........................	260 437-7733
344 Field St Fort Wayne (46805) *(G-5057)*	
Heck of A Lope..	260 570-3192
4809 County Road 51 Auburn (46706) *(G-395)*	
Heckaman Homes, Nappanee Also Called: Craftech Building Systems Inc *(G-12592)*	
Heckley Printing Inc...	260 434-1370
6134 Constitution Dr Fort Wayne (46804) *(G-5058)*	
Heco, Chesterton Also Called: Grindco Inc *(G-1932)*	
Hedgehog Manufacturing LLC..............................	260 424-9600
1031 Columbia Ave Fort Wayne (46805) *(G-5059)*	
Hedgehog Press LLC..	260 387-5237
1136 Columbia Ave Fort Wayne (46805) *(G-5060)*	
Hefter Industries...	219 728-1159
133 S Calumet Rd Chesterton (46304) *(G-1935)*	
HEIDELBERG MATERIALS SOUTHWEST AGG LLC, Fort Wayne Also Called: Heidelberg Mtls Sthwest Agg LL *(G-5062)*	
HEIDELBERG MATERIALS SOUTHWEST AGG LLC, Sellersburg Also Called: Heidelberg Mtls Sthwest Agg LL *(G-14598)*	
Heidelberg Mtls Mdwest Agg Inc..........................	765 653-7205
State Road 243 Cty Rd 900 S Cloverdale (46120) *(G-2086)*	
Heidelberg Mtls Mdwest Agg Inc..........................	260 747-3105
6100 Ardmore Ave Fort Wayne (46809) *(G-5061)*	
Heidelberg Mtls Mdwest Agg Inc..........................	765 653-1956
70 Veterans Memorial Hwy Greencastle (46135) *(G-6411)*	
Heidelberg Mtls Mdwest Agg Inc..........................	812 889-2120
313 S State Road 203 Lexington (47138) *(G-10977)*	
Heidelberg Mtls Mdwest Agg Inc..........................	812 346-6100
610 S County Road 250 E North Vernon (47265) *(G-13276)*	
Heidelberg Mtls Mdwest Agg Inc..........................	812 246-1942
5417 State Rd 403 Sellersburg (47172) *(G-14597)*	

Heidelberg Mtls Mdwest Agg Inc 812 689-5017
  606 W County Road 300 S Versailles (47042) *(G-16100)*

Heidelberg Mtls Mdwest Agg Inc 260 632-1410
  22821 Dawkins Rd Woodburn (46797) *(G-16948)*

Heidelberg Mtls Mdwest Agg Inc 260 632-4252
  17831 Us Highway 24 Woodburn (46797) *(G-16949)*

Heidelberg Mtls Sthast Agg LLC 317 788-4086
  4200 S Harding St Indianapolis (46217) *(G-8380)*

Heidelberg Mtls Sthwest Agg LL 260 665-2626
  260 E 300 N Angola (46703) *(G-257)*

Heidelberg Mtls Sthwest Agg LL 260 747-5011
  7320 Lower Huntington Rd Fort Wayne (46809) *(G-5062)*

Heidelberg Mtls Sthwest Agg LL 812 246-4481
  4700 Utica Sellersburg Rd Sellersburg (47172) *(G-14598)*

Heidelberg Mtls US Cem LLC 574 753-5121
  3084 W County Road 225 S Logansport (46947) *(G-11076)*

Heidelberg Mtls US Cem LLC 812 849-2191
  180 N Meridian Rd Mitchell (47446) *(G-12040)*

Heidelberg Mtls US Cem LLC 812 246-5472
  Hwy 31 Sellersburg (47172) *(G-14599)*

Heidenreich Woodworking Inc 317 861-9331
  4175 S Kelly Dr New Palestine (46163) *(G-12937)*

Heidtman Steel Products Inc 419 691-4646
  4400 County Road 59 Butler (46721) *(G-1465)*

Heidtman Steel Products Inc 219 256-7426
  4407 Railroad Ave East Chicago (46312) *(G-3015)*

Heinold Feeds, Kouts *Also Called: C D C P Inc (G-10362)*

Heise Welding Service 574 652-4631
  1 Bk South Of Main Burrows (46916) *(G-1458)*

Heitink Veneers Incorporated 812 336-6436
  1141 N Sunrise Greetings Ct Bloomington (47404) *(G-876)*

Helena Agri-Enterprises LLC 765 869-5518
  210 N 1st St Ambia (47917) *(G-66)*

Helena Agri-Enterprises LLC 812 654-3177
  5262 E Us Highway 50 Dillsboro (47018) *(G-2946)*

Helena Agri-Enterprises LLC 574 268-4762
  321 Thurman Poe Way Huntington (46750) *(G-7317)*

Helena Agri-Enterprises LLC 765 583-4458
  502 W Oxford St Otterbein (47970) *(G-13452)*

Helgeson Steel Inc 574 293-5576
  1130 Verdant St Ste 1 Elkhart (46516) *(G-3403)*

Helios LLC 317 554-9911
  8001 Woodland Dr Indianapolis (46278) *(G-8381)*

Helios Software, Indianapolis *Also Called: Helios LLC (G-8381)*

Helivin LLC 800 680-7281
  7532 Peachwood Dr Ste 307 Newburgh (47630) *(G-13003)*

Helix Signworx LLC 765 203-1381
  530 W 6th St Anderson (46016) *(G-125)*

Hellman's Tire Service, Gary *Also Called: Hellmans Auto Supply Co Inc (G-5949)*

Hellmans Auto Supply Co Inc 219 885-7655
  612 E 5th Ave Gary (46402) *(G-5949)*

Hello Nature Usa Inc (PA) 765 615-1900
  1800 Purdue Pkwy Anderson (46016) *(G-126)*

Helmer Scientific, Noblesville *Also Called: Helmer Scientific LLC (G-13094)*

Helmer Scientific LLC 317 773-9073
  14400 Bergen Blvd Noblesville (46060) *(G-13094)*

Helming Bros Inc 812 634-9797
  1030 Fairview Ave Jasper (47546) *(G-9842)*

Helmsburg Sawmill Inc 812 988-6161
  2230 State Road 45 Nashville (47448) *(G-12671)*

Helmuth Quality Power System 574 457-2002
  100 S Huntington St Syracuse (46567) *(G-15462)*

Helmuths Woodworking LLC 574 825-0073
  61095 E County Line Rd Shipshewana (46565) *(G-14849)*

Help Help LLC 317 910-6631
  1935 Acorn Ct Avon (46123) *(G-525)*

Help4u Publications LLC 219 771-0189
  86 E Oak Hill Rd Chesterton (46304) *(G-1936)*

Helping Hands 219 696-4564
  516 Michigan Ave Lowell (46356) *(G-11162)*

Helping Hrts Helping Hands Inc 248 980-5090
  411 E Warren St Middlebury (46540) *(G-11720)*

Helsel, Campbellsburg *Also Called: Nst Technologies Mim LLC (G-1526)*

Helvie and Sons Inc 765 674-1372
  5418 S Lincoln Blvd Marion (46953) *(G-11292)*

Hemocleanse Inc (PA) 765 742-4813
  3601 Sagamore Pkwy N Ste B Lafayette (47904) *(G-10596)*

Henager, Elberfeld *Also Called: James G Henager (G-3115)*

Hendershot Service Center Inc 765 653-2600
  711 N Jackson St Greencastle (46135) *(G-6412)*

Hendrickson Engineering LLC 765 404-9132
  3080 Hamilton St West Lafayette (47906) *(G-16592)*

Hendrickson International 260 349-6400
  101 S Progress Dr W Kendallville (46755) *(G-10115)*

Hendrickson International Corp 260 868-2131
  201 W Cherry St Butler (46721) *(G-1466)*

Hendrickson International Corp 260 349-6400
  220 S Progress Dr W Kendallville (46755) *(G-10116)*

Hendrickson International Corp 260 349-6400
  101 S Progress Dr W Kendallville (46755) *(G-10117)*

Hendrickson International Corp 765 483-5350
  180 N Mount Zion Rd Lebanon (46052) *(G-10896)*

Hendrickson International Corp 765 483-7217
  210 N Enterprise Blvd Lebanon (46052) *(G-10897)*

Hendrickson Suspension, Butler *Also Called: Hendrickson International Corp (G-1466)*

Hendrickson Trailer, Lebanon *Also Called: Hendrickson International Corp (G-10897)*

Hendrickson Trailer Suspension, Lebanon *Also Called: Hendrickson International Corp (G-10896)*

Hendrickson Truck Suspension, Kendallville *Also Called: Hendrickson International Corp (G-10116)*

Hendrix Co 812 366-4333
  3025 E Whiskey Run Rd Ne Georgetown (47122) *(G-6062)*

Henkel US Operations Corp 765 284-5050
  3416 S Hoyt Ave Muncie (47302) *(G-12413)*

Henman Engineering and Machine Inc 765 288-8098
  3301 W Mt Pleasant Blvd Muncie (47302) *(G-12414)*

Hennessey Montage Prints 317 841-7562
  6471 Brauer Ln Carmel (46033) *(G-1654)*

Hennessy Sheet Metal 219 365-7058
  9791 Rambling Rose Ln Saint John (46373) *(G-14452)*

Henry Fligeltaub Co Div, Evansville *Also Called: Joe W Morgan Inc (G-4143)*

Henry Holsters LLC 812 369-2266
  224 State Highway 43 Spencer (47460) *(G-15348)*

Henry Street LLC 317 788-7225
  1001 Hurricane St Ste 5 Franklin (46131) *(G-5738)*

Henschen Sand and Gravel 260 367-2636
  4635 N 800 E Howe (46746) *(G-7236)*

Hensler Farm Inc 765 628-3411
  652 Villa Manor Ct Greentown (46936) *(G-6647)*

Hensley Composites LLC 574 202-3840
  1927 N Cedar St Mishawaka (46545) *(G-11907)*

Hensley Custom Cabinetry 219 843-5331
  3281 E 400 N Rensselaer (47978) *(G-14053)*

Hensley Fabricating & Eqp Co 574 498-6514
  17624 State Road 331 Tippecanoe (46570) *(G-15760)*

Hensley Hydra-Haulers, Tippecanoe *Also Called: Hensley Fabricating & Eqp Co (G-15760)*

Hentz Mfg LLC 260 469-0800
  1530 Progress Rd Fort Wayne (46808) *(G-5063)*

Hepton Welding LLC 800 570-4238
  9352 W Hepton Rd Nappanee (46550) *(G-12608)*

Her Majesty Crown LLC 260 218-2255
  429 E Dupont Rd # 1118 Fort Wayne (46825) *(G-5064)*

Heraeus Electro-Nite Co LLC 765 473-8275
  1025 Industrial Pkwy Peru (46970) *(G-13584)*

Herald Argus 219 362-2161
  422 Franklin St Ste B Michigan City (46360) *(G-11623)*

Herald Bulletin, The, Anderson *Also Called: Community Holdings Indiana Inc (G-97)*

Herald Machine Werks LLC 219 949-0580
  7100 Industrial Hwy Gary (46406) *(G-5950)*

Herald Times, Bloomington *Also Called: Hoosier Times Inc (G-882)*

Herb Rahman & Sons Inc 812 367-2513
  9426 E County Road 2100 N Ferdinand (47532) *(G-4435)*

Herbert Vernon Sawmill, Greensburg *Also Called: Herberts Sawmill Inc (G-6601)*

Herberts Sawmill Inc... 812 663-9347
  3438 E County Road 700 S Greensburg (47240) *(G-6601)*
Herbs G&W Inc.. 574 646-2134
  10517 W 1100 N Nappanee (46550) *(G-12609)*
Herbs Rebel Inc.. 812 762-4400
  247 S Franklin St Bloomfield (47424) *(G-748)*
Herco, Bicknell *Also Called: Hermetic Coil Co Inc (G-734)*
Herculean Meal Prep, Indianapolis *Also Called: Canary Brothers LLC (G-7730)*
Herculean Meal Prep, Indianapolis *Also Called: Canary Brothers LLC (G-7731)*
Hercules Achievement Inc.. 317 297-3740
  4501 W 62nd St Indianapolis (46268) *(G-8382)*
Herextensions LLC... 219 466-4273
  4728 Baring Ave East Chicago (46312) *(G-3016)*
Herff Jones LLC (HQ)... 317 297-3741
  4501 W 62nd St Indianapolis (46268) *(G-8383)*
Herff Jones LLC.. 317 612-3400
  4625 W 62nd St Indianapolis (46268) *(G-8384)*
Herff Jones Co Indiana - Inc.. 317 297-3740
  4625 W 62nd St Indianapolis (46268) *(G-8385)*
Heritage Aggregates LLC.. 317 434-4600
  3719 W 96th St Indianapolis (46268) *(G-8386)*
Heritage Aggregates LLC (PA)..................................... 317 872-6010
  5400 W 86th St Indianapolis (46268) *(G-8387)*
Heritage Aggregates LLC.. 765 436-7665
  6990 N 875 W Thorntown (46071) *(G-15751)*
Heritage Arms, Huntington *Also Called: Heritage Tool and Die Inc (G-7318)*
Heritage Asphalt Llc... 317 872-6010
  5400 W 86th St Indianapolis (46268) *(G-8388)*
Heritage Custom Products... 812 425-8639
  1915 W Illinois St Evansville (47712) *(G-4105)*
Heritage Distributing Company.................................... 317 413-6514
  6350 S 175 W Columbus (47201) *(G-2316)*
Heritage Financial Group Inc (PA)................................ 574 522-8000
  120 W Lexington Ave Ste 200 Elkhart (46516) *(G-3404)*
Heritage Flower Company, Crown Point *Also Called: Jadco Ltd (G-2699)*
Heritage Group Safety, Indianapolis *Also Called: Asphalt Materials Inc (G-7553)*
Heritage Hardwoods KY Inc (PA)................................. 812 288-5855
  1507 Production Rd Jeffersonville (47130) *(G-9994)*
Heritage Lake Community Svcs................................... 317 766-4118
  26 Gettysburg Coatesville (46121) *(G-2106)*
Heritage Ldscp Sup Group Inc..................................... 317 849-9100
  5272 E 65th St Indianapolis (46220) *(G-8389)*
Heritage Log Homes... 812 427-2591
  10648 Stevens Rd Vevay (47043) *(G-16110)*
Heritage Log Homes, Moores Hill *Also Called: Appalachian Log Structures (G-12186)*
Heritage Products Inc... 765 364-9002
  2000 Smith Ave Crawfordsville (47933) *(G-2577)*
Heritage Tool and Die Inc... 260 359-8121
  679 W Markle Rd Huntington (46750) *(G-7318)*
Heritage Unlimited LLC (PA).. 574 538-8021
  11641 County Road 30 Goshen (46528) *(G-6164)*
Heritage Wire Die Inc... 260 728-9300
  10484 N 200 W Decatur (46733) *(G-2862)*
Heritage-Crystal Clean Inc... 317 390-3642
  3970 W 10th St Indianapolis (46222) *(G-8390)*
Hermac Incorporated.. 260 925-0312
  540 North St Auburn (46706) *(G-396)*
Herman Tool & Machine Inc... 574 594-5544
  2 Arnolt Dr Pierceton (46562) *(G-13632)*
Hermans' Christmas Land, Pierceton *Also Called: Herman Tool & Machine Inc (G-13632)*
Hermetic Coil Co Inc.. 812 735-2400
  12005 E Davis Ln Bicknell (47512) *(G-734)*
Heron Blue Publications LLC....................................... 317 696-0674
  11157 Valeside Cres Carmel (46032) *(G-1655)*
Herr-Voss Stamco Roll Center, Chesterton *Also Called: Rci Hv Inc (G-1956)*
Herrera Seamless Gutters, Berne *Also Called: Santos Herrera (G-724)*
Herrero Printing Co, Wolcottville *Also Called: Headlands Ltd (G-16937)*
Hershberger Welding.. 574 642-3994
  11520 W 700 S Millersburg (46543) *(G-11813)*
Hessit Works Inc.. 812 829-6246
  4181 S Us Highway 231 Freedom (47431) *(G-5801)*

Hessville Cable & Sling Co.. 773 768-8181
  1601 Cline Ave Gary (46406) *(G-5951)*
Hestad Industries Inc... 574 271-7609
  52265 Wood Haven Dr Granger (46530) *(G-6352)*
Hetsco... 317 530-5331
  2620 Endress Pl Greenwood (46143) *(G-6711)*
Hetty Incorporated.. 219 933-0833
  6937 Calumet Ave Hammond (46324) *(G-6945)*
Hetty Incorporated (PA).. 219 836-2517
  8244 Calumet Ave Munster (46321) *(G-12539)*
Hetzler Ocular Prosthetics Inc (PA)............................. 317 598-6298
  10173 Allisonville Rd Ste 200 Fishers (46038) *(G-4538)*
Hewitt Manufacturing Company................................... 765 525-9829
  5365 S 600 E Waldron (46182) *(G-16258)*
Hewitt Molding, Oakford *Also Called: Hewitt Tool & Die Inc (G-13319)*
Hewitt Tool & Die Inc... 765 453-3889
  1138 E 400 S Oakford (46965) *(G-13319)*
Hey Heys Candles LLC.. 812 484-9956
  2827 Egmont St Evansville (47712) *(G-4106)*
Heyerly Bakery, Ossian *Also Called: Heyerly Brothers Inc (G-13426)*
Heyerly Brothers Inc.. 260 622-4196
  107 N Jefferson St Ossian (46777) *(G-13426)*
Heywood Williams Inc.. 574 295-8400
  601 County Road 17 Elkhart (46516) *(G-3405)*
Hf Chlor-Alkali LLC (PA).. 317 591-0000
  9307 E 56th St Indianapolis (46216) *(G-8391)*
Hf Group LLC... 260 982-2107
  1010 N Sycamore St North Manchester (46962) *(G-13234)*
Hg Metal Fabrication.. 317 491-3381
  1426 N Graham Ave Indianapolis (46219) *(G-8392)*
Hg Metals, Indianapolis *Also Called: Hgmc Supply Inc (G-8394)*
Hgl Dynamics Inc... 317 782-3500
  6979 Corporate Cir Indianapolis (46278) *(G-8393)*
Hgmc Supply Inc.. 317 351-9500
  5402 Massachusetts Ave Indianapolis (46218) *(G-8394)*
HH Rellim Inc... 812 662-9944
  3494 E Base Rd Greensburg (47240) *(G-6602)*
HI Def Machining LLC.. 812 493-9943
  3508 N Sr 7 Madison (47250) *(G-11224)*
HI Tech Veneer, Jeffersonville *Also Called: JDC Veneers Inc (G-10003)*
HI Tech Veneer LLC... 812 284-9775
  276 America Pl Jeffersonville (47130) *(G-9995)*
Hi-Def Coatings.. 812 801-4895
  6607 W State Road 56 Hanover (47243) *(G-7043)*
Hi-Perfrmnce Sperabrasives Inc.................................. 317 899-1050
  9133 Pendleton Pike Ste G Indianapolis (46236) *(G-8395)*
Hi-Point Machine and Tool Inc..................................... 574 831-5361
  19519 Industrial Dr # 2 New Paris (46553) *(G-12956)*
Hi-Pro Inc... 260 665-5038
  1410 Wohlert St Ste C Angola (46703) *(G-258)*
Hi-Rise & Sign Services, Bloomington *Also Called: Hi-Rise Sign & Lighting LLC (G-877)*
Hi-Rise Sign & Lighting LLC.. 812 825-4448
  6524 W Ison Rd Bloomington (47403) *(G-877)*
Hi-Tech Concrete Inc... 765 477-5550
  3691 S 500 E Lafayette (47905) *(G-10597)*
Hi-Tech Foam Products LLC (PA)............................... 317 737-2298
  550 Bell St Indianapolis (46202) *(G-8396)*
Hi-Tech Hydraulics, Rensselaer *Also Called: B & C Machining Inc (G-14045)*
Hi-Tech Label Inc... 765 659-1800
  357 E Washington St Frankfort (46041) *(G-5673)*
HI-Tech Turning.. 260 997-6668
  303 N Hendricks St Bryant (47326) *(G-1435)*
Hi-Temp Refractories, Crawfordsville *Also Called: Ht Enterprises Inc (G-2578)*
Hiatt Enterprises Inc (PA).. 765 289-7756
  1716 N Wheeling Ave Ste 1 Muncie (47303) *(G-12415)*
Hiatt Enterprises Inc.. 765 289-2700
  506 N Mckinley Ave Muncie (47303) *(G-12416)*
Hiatt Printing, Muncie *Also Called: Hiatt Enterprises Inc (G-12415)*
Hiatt Printing, Muncie *Also Called: Hiatt Enterprises Inc (G-12416)*
Hibbing International Friction...................................... 765 529-7001
  2001 Troy Ave New Castle (47362) *(G-12867)*

ALPHABETIC SECTION

Hickman Williams & Company 219 379-5199
  2321 W Progress Dr La Porte (46350) *(G-10419)*
Hickman Williams & Company 812 522-6293
  2083 Upper Heiskell Ct Seymour (47274) *(G-14656)*
Hickman Williams & Co, La Porte *Also Called: Hickman Williams & Company (G-10419)*
Hickory Corner Custom Wldg LLC 812 890-2926
  5041 S Hickory Corner Rd Vincennes (47591) *(G-16128)*
Hickory Furniture Designs Inc 765 642-0700
  403 S Noble St Shelbyville (46176) *(G-14759)*
Hickory Hill Soap 574 825-9853
  13993 County Road 12 Middlebury (46540) *(G-11721)*
Hickory Valley Woodworking LLC 812 486-2857
  10432 E 625 N Loogootee (47553) *(G-11138)*
Hicks Farms 812 852-4055
  3871 W County Road 1050 N Osgood (47037) *(G-13410)*
Hidden Electrical LLC 317 628-4233
  15287 Decl Dr Westfield (46074) *(G-16697)*
Hidea Outboard Motor Usa Inc 317 286-3694
  7043 Girls School Ave Indianapolis (46241) *(G-8397)*
Hidinghilda LLC 260 760-7093
  1511 Brookview Blvd Kendallville (46755) *(G-10118)*
Hielo Services LLC 219 973-1952
  3011 Crabapple Ln Hobart (46342) *(G-7189)*
Higgins Dyan 812 876-0754
  5680 W Mcneely St Ellettsville (47429) *(G-3809)*
High Caliber Cabinetry LLC 812 246-5550
  7617 Old State Road 60 Ste 1 Sellersburg (47172) *(G-14600)*
High Note Publishing 765 313-1699
  571 S 1400 E34 Swayzee (46986) *(G-15450)*
High Performance Alloys Inc (PA) 765 945-8230
  1985 E 500 N Windfall (46076) *(G-16905)*
High Quality Flasks LLC 765 357-6392
  3732 Navarre Ct Lafayette (47905) *(G-10598)*
High Tech Fabricators Inc 260 744-4467
  1211 E Wallace St Fort Wayne (46803) *(G-5065)*
High Value Metal Inc 812 522-6468
  101 Blish St Seymour (47274) *(G-14657)*
Highball Fabricators LLC 574 831-6647
  68563 County Road 17 New Paris (46553) *(G-12957)*
Highland Computer Forms Inc 260 665-6268
  1510 Wohlert St Angola (46703) *(G-259)*
Highland Machine Tool Inc 812 923-8884
  3461 E Luther Rd Floyds Knobs (47119) *(G-4681)*
Highland Park Services Inc 317 954-0456
  5345 Winthrop Ave Indianapolis (46220) *(G-8398)*
Highland Ridge Rv Inc 260 768-7771
  3195 N State Road 5 Shipshewana (46565) *(G-14850)*
Highmark Pack Systems, Fort Wayne *Also Called: Highmark Technologies LLC (G-5066)*
Highmark Technologies LLC 260 483-0012
  8343 Clinton Park Dr Fort Wayne (46825) *(G-5066)*
Hightec Solar Inc 219 814-4279
  1000 Indiana Highway 212 Michigan City (46360) *(G-11624)*
Hightech Signs, Fort Wayne *Also Called: Castleton Village Center Inc (G-4837)*
Hightech Signs, Indianapolis *Also Called: Castleton Village Center Inc (G-7758)*
Highwater Marine LLC (PA) 574 522-8381
  4500 Middlebury St Elkhart (46516) *(G-3406)*
Highwater Marine LLC 574 457-2082
  300 E Chicago St Syracuse (46567) *(G-15463)*
Highway Machine Co Inc 812 385-3639
  3010 S Old Us Highway 41 Princeton (47670) *(G-13998)*
Highway Press Inc 812 283-6462
  2199 Hamburg Pike Jeffersonville (47130) *(G-9996)*
Highway Safety Services Inc 765 474-1000
  4121 S 500 E Lafayette (47905) *(G-10599)*
Highway Sign Service, Geneva *Also Called: Baumbauer Signs (G-6048)*
Hiler Industries, La Porte *Also Called: Accurate Castings Inc (G-10373)*
Hilevel Technology Inc 765 349-1650
  4529 E Hacker Creek Rd Martinsville (46151) *(G-11400)*
HILEVEL TECHNOLOGY INC., Martinsville *Also Called: Hilevel Technology Inc (G-11400)*
Hilex Poly Co LLC 812 346-1066
  1001 2nd St North Vernon (47265) *(G-13277)*

Hill and Griffith, Indianapolis *Also Called: H&G Legacy Co (G-8348)*
Hill Construction Co LLC 812 843-3279
  11266 Ohio Rd Saint Croix (47576) *(G-14434)*
Hill Top Welding LLC 765 585-2549
  217 N State Road 55 Attica (47918) *(G-351)*
Hill-Rom, Batesville *Also Called: Hill-Rom Inc (G-589)*
Hill-Rom Inc (DH) 812 934-7777
  1069 State Road 46 E Batesville (47006) *(G-589)*
Hillcrest Enterprises LLC (PA) 812 875-2500
  11267 Coal City Arney Rd Worthington (47471) *(G-16960)*
Hillcrest Mobile Homes Court, Crawfordsville *Also Called: Charles Coons (G-2552)*
Hillcrest Pallet Incorporated 812 883-3636
  5445 W Kansas Church Rd Salem (47167) *(G-14480)*
Hillenbrand, Batesville *Also Called: Hillenbrand Inc (G-590)*
Hillenbrand Inc (PA) 812 931-5000
  1 Batesville Blvd Batesville (47006) *(G-590)*
Hillenbrand Luxembourg Inc (DH) 812 934-7500
  1 Batesville Blvd Batesville (47006) *(G-591)*
Hills Pet Nutrition Inc 765 935-7071
  2325 Union Pike Richmond (47374) *(G-14133)*
Hillshire Brands Company 260 456-4802
  1108 E Pontiac St Fort Wayne (46803) *(G-5067)*
Hilltop Basic Resources Inc 812 594-2293
  14208 State Road 156 Patriot (47038) *(G-13510)*
Hilltop Leather 317 508-3404
  1820 Observatory Rd Martinsville (46151) *(G-11401)*
Hilltop Machine Shop LLC 260 768-9196
  10515 W Us Highway 20 Shipshewana (46565) *(G-14851)*
Hilltop Mch Sp Haubstadt LLC 812 768-5717
  4958 E 1200 S Haubstadt (47639) *(G-7086)*
Hilltop Metal Fabricating LLC 574 773-4975
  71024 County Road 13 Nappanee (46550) *(G-12610)*
Hilltop Specialties LLC 574 773-4975
  71024 County Road 13 Nappanee (46550) *(G-12611)*
Hilltop Wood Working 270 604-1962
  4406 W County Road 1050 S Madison (47250) *(G-11225)*
Him Gentlemans Boutique 812 924-7441
  314 Pearl St New Albany (47150) *(G-12741)*
Himes Casting Repair 317 831-2571
  171 Center Dr Mooresville (46158) *(G-12209)*
Hinchman Racing Uniforms, Indianapolis *Also Called: J B Hinchman Inc (G-8602)*
Hinen Printing Co 260 248-8984
  117 W Market St Columbia City (46725) *(G-2150)*
Hingecraft Corporation 574 293-6543
  3601 Lexington Park Dr Elkhart (46514) *(G-3407)*
Hinsdale Farms Ltd 574 848-0344
  605 Kesco Dr Bristol (46507) *(G-1266)*
Hinseys Pro Paint Inc 260 407-2000
  6931 Quemetco Ct Fort Wayne (46803) *(G-5068)*
Hinshaw Roofing & Sheet Metal Co Inc 765 659-3311
  2452 S State Road 39 Frankfort (46041) *(G-5674)*
Hinshaw Tool & Die, Lynn *Also Called: T F & T Inc (G-11188)*
Hipsher Tool & Die Inc 260 563-4143
  1593 S State Road 115 Wabash (46992) *(G-16192)*
Hirata Corporation of America (HQ) 317 856-8600
  5625 Decatur Blvd Indianapolis (46241) *(G-8399)*
His, Anderson *Also Called: Don Hartman Oil Co Inc (G-106)*
His Love Kept ME Pubg LLC 408 893-5908
  2310 Fescue Pl Apt D Indianapolis (46260) *(G-8400)*
His Word Is My Sword LLC 260 433-9911
  7719 Allison Ave Fort Wayne (46819) *(G-5069)*
Hisada America Inc 812 526-0756
  1191 S Walnut St Edinburgh (46124) *(G-3086)*
Hitachi Astemo Americas Inc 859 734-9451
  925 N Main St Ligonier (46767) *(G-11017)*
Hitachi Astemo Indiana Inc (HQ) 317 462-3015
  400 W New Rd Greenfield (46140) *(G-6509)*
Hitachi Astemo Indiana Inc 765 213-4915
  4400 N Superior Dr Muncie (47303) *(G-12417)*
Hitachi Global Air Pwr US LLC 219 861-5207
  1100 Kieffer Rd Michigan City (46360) *(G-11625)*

Hitachi Global Air Pwr US LLC — ALPHABETIC SECTION

Hitachi Global Air Pwr US LLC (HQ) 219 879-5451
1 Sullair Way Michigan City (46360) *(G-11626)*

Hitarth LLC 812 372-1744
1609 Cottage Ave Ste G Columbus (47201) *(G-2317)*

Hitchcock Tool LLC 513 276-7345
710 Nw 5th St Richmond (47374) *(G-14134)*

Hite Welding & Chassis 765 741-0046
1715 E 18th St Muncie (47302) *(G-12418)*

Hites Hardwood Lumber Corp 574 278-7783
309 S East St Buffalo (47925) *(G-1438)*

Hittler Insurance LLC 260 519-1275
301 Erie Stone Rd Huntington (46750) *(G-7319)*

Hitzer Inc 260 589-8536
269 E Main St Berne (46711) *(G-714)*

Hively Welding Company Inc 219 843-5111
14695 W State Road 14 Medaryville (47957) *(G-11458)*

Hjr Oil Inc 317 849-4503
11361 Rainbow Falls Ln Fishers (46037) *(G-4539)*

HK Manufacturing Inc 260 925-1680
203 Hunters Rdg Auburn (46706) *(G-397)*

HK Petroleum Ltd 229 366-1313
606 E Main St Madison (47250) *(G-11226)*

Hlb1 LLC 219 575-7534
9977 N State Road 39 La Porte (46350) *(G-10420)*

HM Lowry Enterprises LLC 765 524-8435
13072 W Us Highway 40 Cambridge City (47327) *(G-1495)*

Hmh, Indianapolis Also Called: Houghton Mifflin Harcourt Co *(G-8425)*

Hmh Manufacturing LLC 765 553-5447
832 S Berkley Rd Kokomo (46901) *(G-10280)*

Hmi Investments LLC 317 736-9387
291 Province St Franklin (46131) *(G-5739)*

Hmi Machinery, Topeka Also Called: Honeyville Metal Inc *(G-15809)*

Hmi North, Indianapolis Also Called: Harding Group LLC *(G-8356)*

Hmi South, Indianapolis Also Called: Harding Group LLC *(G-8357)*

HMS Zoo Diets Inc 260 824-5157
43 Sunrise Way Bluffton (46714) *(G-1037)*

Hmt LLC 219 736-9901
4100 W 82nd Ave Merrillville (46410) *(G-11522)*

Hobart Cleaners, Munster Also Called: Security Integrated Corp *(G-12563)*

Hobart Electronics, Hobart Also Called: Coil-Tran LLC *(G-7182)*

Hobart Locker & Meat Pkg Co 219 942-5952
8602 Randolph St Crown Point (46307) *(G-2693)*

Hobbs Auto Diagnostics & Repr 765 606-1490
3594 N State Road 9 Anderson (46012) *(G-127)*

Hobbs Transport Services LLC 317 607-5590
4450 N Vinewood Ave Indianapolis (46254) *(G-8401)*

Hobson Tool and Machine Co 317 736-4203
3061 N Morton St Franklin (46131) *(G-5740)*

Hochbaum Machine Services Inc 219 996-6830
11 Wood Ct Hebron (46341) *(G-7100)*

Hochstetler Welding 260 463-2793
2520 W 350 N Lagrange (46761) *(G-10741)*

Hochstetler Welding LLC 574 773-0600
7262 W 1350 N Nappanee (46550) *(G-12612)*

Hochstetler Woodworking LLC 260 593-3255
3085 S 600 W Topeka (46571) *(G-15808)*

Hoehn Engineered Products LLC 260 223-9158
5853 N Piqua Rd Decatur (46733) *(G-2863)*

Hoehn Hardwoods 812 968-3242
2285 Fogel Rd Se Corydon (47112) *(G-2498)*

Hoehn Plastics Inc 812 874-3646
11481 W 925 S Poseyville (47633) *(G-13977)*

Hoerbiger Service 574 855-4112
2834 Southridge Dr South Bend (46614) *(G-15065)*

Hoffman La Roche, Indianapolis Also Called: F Hoffmann-La Roche Ltd *(G-8159)*

Hoffman La Roche, Indianapolis Also Called: F Hoffmann-La Roche Ltd *(G-8160)*

Hoffman Quality Graphics 574 223-5738
2096 Sycamore Dr Rochester (46975) *(G-14296)*

Hoffman Sls & Specialty Co Inc 317 846-6428
3222 Birch Canyon Dr Carmel (46033) *(G-1656)*

Hoffmaster Electric Inc 219 616-1313
1635 Hartley Dr Schererville (46375) *(G-14523)*

Hoffmaster Group Inc 855 230-5281
2701 S Coliseum Blvd Ste 1148 Fort Wayne (46803) *(G-5070)*

Hog Slat Incorporated 574 967-4145
200 N Meridian Line Rd Camden (46917) *(G-1520)*

Hog Slat Incorporated 574 967-3776
315 S Sycamore St Ste 11 Flora (46929) *(G-4659)*

Hog Slat Incorporated 765 828-0828
18506 S Rangeline Rd Universal (47884) *(G-15875)*

Hogan Stamping LLC 812 656-8222
305 Maple St West Harrison (47060) *(G-16548)*

Hoke Weld 812 569-0587
1194 E County Road 450 S Paoli (47454) *(G-13497)*

Holba Trucking and Transport 219 381-4236
3241 176th St Hammond (46323) *(G-6946)*

Holbrook Fabrication Repr Inc 260 348-4996
10447 E Swan Rd Laotto (46763) *(G-10806)*

Holbrook Manufacturing, Franklin Also Called: Hmi Investments LLC *(G-5739)*

Holcim - Mwr Inc 260 665-2052
1310 W Maumee St Angola (46703) *(G-260)*

Holcim (us) Inc 219 378-1193
3210 Watling St East Chicago (46312) *(G-3017)*

Holder Bedding Inc 765 642-1256
1923 W 8th St Anderson (46016) *(G-128)*

Holder Bedding Inc (PA) 765 447-7907
230 Farabee Dr N Lafayette (47905) *(G-10600)*

Hole N Wall Entertainment LLC 317 586-1037
9165 Otis Ave Ste 225 Indianapolis (46216) *(G-8402)*

Holgin Technologies LLC 317 774-5181
15335 Endeavor Dr Ste 100 Noblesville (46060) *(G-13095)*

Holic LLC 765 444-8115
710 Norfleet Dr W Middletown (47356) *(G-11770)*

Holiday House LLC 574 206-0016
25771 Miner Rd Elkhart (46514) *(G-3408)*

Holiday House Trailers, Elkhart Also Called: Holiday House LLC *(G-3408)*

Holland Colours Americas Inc 765 935-0329
1501 Progress Dr Richmond (47374) *(G-14135)*

Holland Metal Fab Inc 574 522-1434
1550 W Lusher Ave Elkhart (46517) *(G-3409)*

Hollands Deer Processing LLC 765 472-5876
1848 W Lovers Lane Rd Peru (46970) *(G-13585)*

Hollers Welding Llc 812 825-9834
13983 E Gardner Rd Bloomington (47403) *(G-878)*

Hollingshead Mixer Company LLC 260 897-4397
200 Dekko Dr Avilla (46710) *(G-477)*

Hollingsworth & Associates, Osceola Also Called: R B Tool & Machinery Co *(G-13401)*

Hollingsworth Lumber, Russiaville Also Called: Hollingsworth Sawmill Inc *(G-14422)*

Hollingsworth Sawmill Inc 765 883-5836
6810 W 400 S Russiaville (46979) *(G-14422)*

Holloway Electric Motor Svc, Plymouth Also Called: Ronald Holloway *(G-13812)*

Holloway House Inc 317 485-4272
309 Business Park Dr Fortville (46040) *(G-5599)*

Holloway Vinyl Signs Grap 765 717-1581
4100 S Native Ct Yorktown (47396) *(G-16974)*

Hollowheart Industries LLC 812 737-4002
5916 N Us Highway 231 Spencer (47460) *(G-15349)*

Hollys Cstm Canvas & Uphl LLC 317 550-6818
5564 E Orchard Rd Mooresville (46158) *(G-12210)*

Holm Industries, Scottsburg Also Called: Ilpea Industries Inc *(G-14562)*

Holm Industries Warehouses, Scottsburg Also Called: Ilpea Industries Inc *(G-14560)*

Holman Lumber LLC 260 337-0338
6878 County Road 62 Saint Joe (46785) *(G-14438)*

Holman Sptic Tank Sls Rdymix I 812 689-1913
4896 S Old Michigan Rd Holton (47023) *(G-7217)*

Holman's Septic Tank Sales, Holton Also Called: Holman Sptic Tank Sls Rdymix I *(G-7217)*

Holmes & Company LLC 260 244-6149
807 E Ellsworth St Columbia City (46725) *(G-2151)*

Holscher Products Inc 765 884-8021
407 W Main St Fowler (47944) *(G-5625)*

Holsum of Fort Wayne Inc (HQ) 260 456-2130
136 Murray St Fort Wayne (46803) *(G-5071)*

Holsum of Fort Wayne Inc 219 362-4561
800 Boyd Blvd La Porte (46350) *(G-10421)*

ALPHABETIC SECTION — Hoosier Box LLC

Holzer Ready Mix LLC 317 306-9327
  405 S Shortridge Rd Indianapolis (46219) *(G-8403)*

Holzer Site Mix LLC, Indianapolis *Also Called: Holzer Ready Mix LLC (G-8403)*

Home - Little Creek Winery 812 319-3951
  4116 Koressel Rd Evansville (47720) *(G-4107)*

Home City Ice, Attica *Also Called: Home City Ice Company (G-352)*

Home City Ice Company 765 762-6096
  200 S Market St Attica (47918) *(G-352)*

Home City Ice Company 317 926-2451
  2000 Dr Martin Luther King Jr St Indianapolis (46202) *(G-8404)*

Home City Ice Company 317 926-2451
  3602 W Washington St Indianapolis (46241) *(G-8405)*

Home Cookies, Pittsboro *Also Called: Hometown Products (G-13648)*

Home Design Products, Alexandria *Also Called: Resin Partners Inc (G-61)*

Home Design Products, Anderson *Also Called: Resin Partners Inc (G-185)*

Home Foods, Noblesville *Also Called: Home Snack Foods LLC (G-13096)*

Home Guard Industries Inc 260 627-6060
  13101 Main St Grabill (46741) *(G-6302)*

Home Mag Pub Indianapolis 317 810-1341
  301 E Carmel Dr Ste C100 Carmel (46032) *(G-1657)*

Home Mountain Printing, Valparaiso *Also Called: Home Mountain Publishing Co Inc (G-15962)*

Home Mountain Publishing Co Inc 219 462-6601
  3602 Enterprise Ave Valparaiso (46383) *(G-15962)*

Home News Enterprises LLC 800 876-7811
  333 2nd St Columbus (47201) *(G-2318)*

Home Phone Inc 812 941-8551
  414 Spring St Jeffersonville (47130) *(G-9997)*

Home Publishing LLC 317 886-1137
  9465 Counselors Row Ste 200 Indianapolis (46240) *(G-8406)*

Home Reserve LLC 260 969-6939
  3015 Cannongate Dr Fort Wayne (46808) *(G-5072)*

Home Reserve.com, Fort Wayne *Also Called: Home Reserve LLC (G-5072)*

Home Run LLC 219 531-1006
  312 N 325 E Ste B Valparaiso (46383) *(G-15963)*

Home Snack Foods LLC 317 764-6644
  16591 Meadow Wood Dr Noblesville (46062) *(G-13096)*

Home Works, Lafayette *Also Called: James A Andrew Inc (G-10614)*

Homecrest Cabinetry, Goshen *Also Called: H-C Liquidating Corp (G-6159)*

Homeland Sports LLC 219 962-2315
  4697 E 36th Ave Hobart (46342) *(G-7190)*

Homelife Forever Inc 765 307-0416
  1197 E State Road 236 Roachdale (46172) *(G-14247)*

Homemark Cabinetry LLC 678 234-4519
  4747 Western Ave Connersville (47331) *(G-2440)*

Homeowners Equity & Rlty Corp 219 981-1700
  306 W Ridge Rd Bldg 300 Gary (46408) *(G-5952)*

Homer Banes 765 449-8551
  520 S Earl Ave Lafayette (47904) *(G-10601)*

Homes & Lifestyles Magazine 574 674-6639
  11859 Lincolnway Osceola (46561) *(G-13393)*

Homeshield, Richmond *Also Called: Imperial Products LLC (G-14138)*

Homestead Barns LLC 740 624-0997
  2794 N County Road 50 E Greencastle (46135) *(G-6413)*

Homestead Properties Inc 812 866-4415
  10214 W Deputy Pike Rd Deputy (47230) *(G-2941)*

Homestead Shoppe, Lapaz *Also Called: A Homestead Shoppe Inc (G-10814)*

Hometown Embroidery LLC 765 778-7533
  176 Oxford Ave Pendleton (46064) *(G-13536)*

Hometown Energy LLC 812 663-3391
  1430 W Main St Greensburg (47240) *(G-6603)*

Hometown Food Service, Kendallville *Also Called: Jeff Snyder (G-10120)*

Hometown Products 317 625-2447
  9339 N County Road 150 E Pittsboro (46167) *(G-13648)*

Hometown Shirts & Graphix LLC 765 564-3066
  101 S Washington St Delphi (46923) *(G-2898)*

Homette Corporation (HQ) 574 294-6521
  200 Nibco Pkwy Ste 200 Elkhart (46516) *(G-3410)*

Honda Dev & Mfg Amer LLC 812 222-6000
  2755 N Michigan Ave Greensburg (47240) *(G-6604)*

Honey & Salt LLC 317 625-1135
  309 Poplar Rd Indianapolis (46219) *(G-8407)*

Honey and ME 317 668-3924
  2908 N Graham Rd # A Franklin (46131) *(G-5741)*

Honey Creek Machine Inc 812 299-5255
  1537 W Harlan Dr Terre Haute (47802) *(G-15605)*

Honey Pot Development 260 318-0001
  730 E Mitchell St Kendallville (46755) *(G-10119)*

Honeyville Metal Inc 800 593-8377
  4200 S 900 W Topeka (46571) *(G-15809)*

Honeywell, Crane *Also Called: Honeywell International Inc (G-2538)*

Honeywell, Evansville *Also Called: Honeywell International Inc (G-4108)*

Honeywell, Indianapolis *Also Called: Honeywell International Inc (G-8408)*

Honeywell, Muncie *Also Called: Honeywell International Inc (G-12419)*

Honeywell, Munster *Also Called: Honeywell International Inc (G-12540)*

Honeywell, Plymouth *Also Called: Honeywell International Inc (G-13782)*

Honeywell, South Bend *Also Called: Honeywell International Inc (G-15066)*

Honeywell, South Bend *Also Called: Honeywell International Inc (G-15067)*

Honeywell, South Bend *Also Called: Honeywell International Inc (G-15068)*

Honeywell Authorized Dealer, Evansville *Also Called: Jack Frost LLC (G-4136)*

Honeywell Authorized Dealer, Indianapolis *Also Called: Abbott Controls Inc (G-7415)*

Honeywell Authorized Dealer, Michigan City *Also Called: Paniccia Heating & Cooling Inc (G-11650)*

Honeywell Authorized Dealer, Middlebury *Also Called: Washburn Heating & AC (G-11757)*

Honeywell Authorized Dealer, Monticello *Also Called: Halsen Brothers Shtmtl Inc (G-12152)*

Honeywell Authorized Dealer, New Albany *Also Called: Frank H Monroe Heating & Coolg (G-12734)*

Honeywell Friction Materials, Fortville *Also Called: D & D Brake Sales Inc (G-5590)*

Honeywell International Inc 812 854-4450
  3330n 138b Crane (47522) *(G-2538)*

Honeywell International Inc 812 473-4163
  101 Plaza Dr Ste 103 Evansville (47715) *(G-4108)*

Honeywell International Inc 317 580-6165
  6826 Hillsdale Ct Indianapolis (46250) *(G-8408)*

Honeywell International Inc 765 284-3300
  201 E 18th St Muncie (47302) *(G-12419)*

Honeywell International Inc 219 836-3803
  9200 Calumet Ave Ste N510 Munster (46321) *(G-12540)*

Honeywell International Inc 574 935-0200
  504 E Garro St Plymouth (46563) *(G-13782)*

Honeywell International Inc 574 231-3322
  717 N Bendix Dr South Bend (46628) *(G-15066)*

Honeywell International Inc 574 231-3000
  3520 Westmoor St South Bend (46628) *(G-15067)*

Honeywell International Inc 574 231-2000
  3520 Westmoor St South Bend (46628) *(G-15068)*

Hoogie's, Goshen *Also Called: Hoogies Sports House Inc (G-6165)*

Hoogies Sports House Inc 574 533-9875
  825 Logan St Goshen (46528) *(G-6165)*

Hook & Arrow 260 739-6661
  7536 Winchester Rd Fort Wayne (46819) *(G-5073)*

Hook Development Inc 260 432-7771
  2731 Brooklyn Ave Fort Wayne (46802) *(G-5074)*

Hook Industrial Sales Inc (PA) 260 432-9441
  2731 Brooklyn Ave Fort Wayne (46802) *(G-5075)*

Hooker Corner Winery LLC 765 585-1225
  444 W State Road 26 Pine Village (47975) *(G-13643)*

Hooker Deer Drag Co LLC 812 623-2706
  27499 Lawrenceville Rd Sunman (47041) *(G-15439)*

Hoop-It Embroidery 260 224-6577
  3869 W 608 N Huntington (46750) *(G-7320)*

Hoople Country Kitchens Inc 812 649-2351
  714 N 5th St Rockport (47635) *(G-14342)*

Hoosier Bat Company 219 531-1006
  1556 W Lincolnway Ste 2 Valparaiso (46385) *(G-15964)*

Hoosier Bat Company, Valparaiso *Also Called: Home Run LLC (G-15963)*

Hoosier Box and Skid Inc 574 256-2111
  2401 Schumacher Dr Mishawaka (46545) *(G-11908)*

Hoosier Box LLC 260 210-3757
  7909 Grassland Ct Fort Wayne (46825) *(G-5076)*

Hoosier Buggy Shop... 260 593-2192
  5345 W 600 S Topeka (46571) *(G-15810)*
Hoosier Bullets & Training, Trafalgar Also Called: Hoosier Bullets LLC *(G-15828)*
Hoosier Bullets LLC.. 317 694-1257
  6620 S 200 W Trafalgar (46181) *(G-15828)*
Hoosier Cab Company LLC.. 812 822-2508
  500 S Morton St Ste 20 Bloomington (47403) *(G-879)*
Hoosier Container Inc.. 765 966-2541
  1001 Indiana Ave Richmond (47374) *(G-14136)*
Hoosier Conveyor Company LLC...................................... 765 445-3337
  100 W Morgan St Knightstown (46148) *(G-10197)*
Hoosier Crane, Elkhart Also Called: Hoosier Crane Service Company *(G-3411)*
Hoosier Crane Service Company....................................... 574 523-2945
  3500 Charlotte Ave Elkhart (46517) *(G-3411)*
Hoosier Custom Plastics LLC... 574 772-2120
  201 Hamilton Dr Knox (46534) *(G-10210)*
Hoosier Custom Woodworking.. 574 642-3764
  67348 County Road 33 Millersburg (46543) *(G-11814)*
Hoosier Daddy Custom Tees... 218 308-3544
  5364 Central Ave Portage (46368) *(G-13876)*
Hoosier Engineering Co Inc... 260 694-6887
  7726 S Meridian Rd Poneto (46781) *(G-13841)*
Hoosier Ethanol Energy LLC... 260 407-6161
  110 W Berry St Ste 1200 Fort Wayne (46802) *(G-5077)*
Hoosier Family Living LLC... 812 396-7880
  Vincennes (47591) *(G-16129)*
Hoosier Fiberglass Industries.. 812 232-5027
  2011 S 3rd St Terre Haute (47802) *(G-15606)*
Hoosier Fire Equipment Inc (PA)... 219 462-1707
  4009 Montdale Park Dr Valparaiso (46383) *(G-15965)*
Hoosier Gasket Corporation (PA).. 317 545-2000
  2400 Enterprise Park Pl Indianapolis (46218) *(G-8409)*
Hoosier Helicopter Svcs Inc... 812 935-5296
  7900 N Thames Dr Bloomington (47408) *(G-880)*
Hoosier Horse Review LLC... 765 212-1320
  7301 S County Road 400 W Muncie (47302) *(G-12420)*
Hoosier Hot Rods Classics Inc... 812 768-5221
  5209 N Kerth Ave Evansville (47711) *(G-4109)*
Hoosier House Furnishings LLC... 574 975-0357
  220 Blackport Dr Goshen (46528) *(G-6166)*
Hoosier Industrial Electric... 812 346-2232
  1003 Rodgers Park Dr North Vernon (47265) *(G-13278)*
Hoosier Industrial Supply.. 574 535-0712
  2516 Industrial Park Dr Goshen (46526) *(G-6167)*
Hoosier Industrial Supply Inc.. 574 533-8565
  1223 N Chicago Ave Ste 2 Goshen (46528) *(G-6168)*
Hoosier Interior Doors Inc... 574 534-3072
  523 E Lincoln Ave Goshen (46528) *(G-6169)*
Hoosier Jiffy Print.. 260 563-8715
  675 Stitt St Wabash (46992) *(G-16193)*
Hoosier Jiffy Print, Marion Also Called: L & L Press Inc *(G-11305)*
Hoosier Locavore, Morristown Also Called: Locavore Productions LLC *(G-12279)*
Hoosier Machine & Welding Inc.. 317 638-6286
  451 Arbor Ave Indianapolis (46221) *(G-8410)*
Hoosier Machine Company LLC... 317 965-5901
  2875 N State Road 9 Columbus (47203) *(G-2319)*
Hoosier Manufacturing LLC... 260 493-9990
  9312 Avionics Dr Fort Wayne (46809) *(G-5078)*
Hoosier Marine.. 812 879-5549
  10151 N Us Highway 231 Quincy (47456) *(G-14021)*
Hoosier Metal Polish Inc... 219 474-6011
  304 N Fairground Rd Kentland (47951) *(G-10160)*
Hoosier Miracle Inc (PA)... 765 473-4438
  300 N Park Ave Peru (46970) *(G-13586)*
Hoosier Molded Products Inc... 574 235-7900
  3603 Progress Dr South Bend (46628) *(G-15069)*
Hoosier Pallet LLC... 765 629-2899
  4126 W 900 S Milroy (46156) *(G-11825)*
Hoosier Penn Oil Co Inc (PA)... 317 390-5406
  4060 W 10th St Indianapolis (46222) *(G-8411)*
Hoosier Penn Oil Co Inc.. 812 284-9433
  2990 Industrial Pkwy Jeffersonville (47130) *(G-9998)*

Hoosier Plastics Inc.. 812 232-5027
  2535 N 200 W Angola (46703) *(G-261)*
Hoosier Powder Coating LLC.. 574 253-7737
  9583 W 1350 N Nappanee (46550) *(G-12613)*
Hoosier Press Inc... 765 649-3716
  1027 Meridian St Anderson (46016) *(G-129)*
Hoosier Pride Plastics Inc.. 260 497-7080
  6120 Highview Dr Fort Wayne (46818) *(G-5079)*
Hoosier Processing LLC.. 260 422-9440
  1025 Osage St Fort Wayne (46808) *(G-5080)*
Hoosier Racing Tire Corp (DH)... 574 784-3152
  65465 State Road 931 Lakeville (46536) *(G-10792)*
Hoosier Ready Mix, Washington Also Called: Hoosier Ready Mix LLC *(G-16484)*
Hoosier Ready Mix LLC... 812 254-7625
  1115 S 300 W Washington (47501) *(G-16484)*
Hoosier Reclaimed Timber... 812 322-3912
  5660 N Murat Rd Bloomington (47408) *(G-881)*
Hoosier Roaster Llc... 574 257-1415
  2212 Lincolnway W Mishawaka (46544) *(G-11909)*
Hoosier Roll Shop Services LLC... 219 844-8077
  7020 Cline Ave Hammond (46323) *(G-6947)*
Hoosier Sealing Supply Co, Indianapolis Also Called: Long Jim Jay Jr *(G-8779)*
Hoosier Spline Broach Corp.. 765 452-8273
  1401 Touby Pike Kokomo (46901) *(G-10281)*
Hoosier Spring Co Inc.. 574 291-7550
  4604 S Burnett Dr South Bend (46614) *(G-15070)*
Hoosier Stamping LLC... 812 426-2778
  7988 Gardner Rd Chandler (47610) *(G-1862)*
Hoosier Stamping & Mfg Corp (DH).................................... 812 426-2778
  700 Schrader Dr Evansville (47712) *(G-4110)*
Hoosier Tank and Mfg LLC... 574 232-8368
  1710 N Sheridan St South Bend (46628) *(G-15071)*
Hoosier Times Inc... 812 275-3372
  2139 16th St Bedford (47421) *(G-641)*
Hoosier Times Inc... 812 332-4401
  301 Main St Beech Grove (46107) *(G-691)*
Hoosier Times Inc (DH).. 812 331-4270
  1840 S Walnut St Bloomington (47401) *(G-882)*
Hoosier Times Inc... 765 342-3311
  60 S Jefferson St Martinsville (46151) *(G-11402)*
Hoosier Tire, Lakeville Also Called: Hoosier Racing Tire Corp *(G-10792)*
Hoosier Tire & Retreading Inc.. 812 876-8286
  5200 W State Road 46 Bloomington (47404) *(G-883)*
Hoosier Tool & Die Co Inc.. 812 376-8286
  224 N Pleasant St Edinburgh (46124) *(G-3087)*
Hoosier Toolmaking & Engrg Inc... 260 493-9990
  6930 Derek Dr Fort Wayne (46803) *(G-5081)*
Hoosier Traps.. 574 586-2401
  20112 W 3b Rd Walkerton (46574) *(G-16267)*
Hoosier Tribune Corp... 907 570-8888
  12659 Enclave Ct Carmel (46032) *(G-1658)*
Hoosier Tribune, The, Carmel Also Called: Hoosier Tribune Corp *(G-1658)*
Hoosier Trim Products LLC.. 317 271-4007
  1850 Expo Ln Indianapolis (46214) *(G-8412)*
Hoosier Wallbeds Incorporated.. 812 747-7154
  23036 Stateline Rd Lawrenceburg (47025) *(G-10840)*
Hoosier Washer... 317 460-8354
  4711 S 375 E Waldron (46182) *(G-16259)*
Hoosier Welding... 765 521-4539
  1726 S County Road 125 W New Castle (47362) *(G-12868)*
Hoosier Wheel, Evansville Also Called: Hoosier Stamping & Mfg Corp *(G-4110)*
Hoosier Wood Creations Inc... 574 831-6330
  19881 County Road 146 New Paris (46553) *(G-12958)*
Hoosier Wood Works.. 812 325-9823
  118 E Ridgeview Dr Bloomington (47401) *(G-884)*
Hoover Sheet Metal, Indianapolis Also Called: Sanbar of Indiana Inc *(G-9369)*
Hoover Well Drilling Inc... 574 831-4901
  20477 County Road 46 New Paris (46553) *(G-12959)*
Hope Hardwoods Inc... 812 546-4427
  1006 Seminary St Hope (47246) *(G-7226)*
Hope Star Journal, Hope Also Called: Indiana News Media LLC *(G-7228)*

ALPHABETIC SECTION

Hopkins & Woods, Indianapolis *Also Called: Metcalf Engineering Inc (G-8893)*

Hopkins Gravel Sand & Concrete... 317 831-2704
540 State Road 267 Mooresville (46158) *(G-12211)*

Hopper Development Inc... 574 753-6621
1332 18th St Logansport (46947) *(G-11077)*

Hopwood Cellars Winery LLC... 317 873-4099
12 E Cedar St Zionsville (46077) *(G-17016)*

Horizon Anim LLC... 317 742-4917
7834 Gilmore Rd Indianapolis (46219) *(G-8413)*

Horizon Atomtn Fabrication LLC... 765 896-9491
3620 S Hoyt Ave Muncie (47302) *(G-12421)*

Horizon Biotechnologies LLC... 317 534-2540
1740 S Morgantown Rd Greenwood (46143) *(G-6712)*

Horizon Farms LLC... 765 427-3685
6942 E 350 N Monticello (47960) *(G-12153)*

Horizon Management Svcs Inc (PA).. 219 852-3200
7412 Calumet Ave Hammond (46324) *(G-6948)*

Horizon Plastics, Osceola *Also Called: Horizon Plastics & Engineering (G-13394)*

Horizon Plastics & Engineering... 574 674-5443
1243 3rd St Osceola (46561) *(G-13394)*

Horizon Publications Inc... 260 244-5153
927 W Connexion Way Columbia City (46725) *(G-2152)*

Horizon Publishing Co, Hammond *Also Called: Horizon Publishing Company LLC (G-6949)*

Horizon Publishing Company LLC.. 219 852-3200
7412 Calumet Ave Ste 1 Hammond (46324) *(G-6949)*

Horizon Terra Incorporated (DH)... 812 280-0000
101 River Ridge Cir Jeffersonville (47130) *(G-9999)*

Horn Pre-Cast Inc... 812 372-4458
895 Jonesville Rd Columbus (47201) *(G-2320)*

Horneco Fabrication Inc... 260 672-2064
13020 Redding Dr Fort Wayne (46814) *(G-5082)*

Horner Advanced Products Group, Indianapolis *Also Called: Horner Apg LLC (G-8414)*

Horner Apg LLC (PA).. 317 916-4274
59 S State Ave Indianapolis (46201) *(G-8414)*

Horner Electric, Fort Wayne *Also Called: Horner Industrial Services Inc (G-5083)*

Horner Electric Inc... 317 639-4261
1521 E Washington St Indianapolis (46201) *(G-8415)*

Horner Industrial Group, Indianapolis *Also Called: Horner Industrial Services Inc (G-8416)*

Horner Industrial Services Inc... 260 434-1189
4421 Ardmore Ave Fort Wayne (46809) *(G-5083)*

Horner Industrial Services Inc (PA).. 317 639-4261
1521 E Washington St Indianapolis (46201) *(G-8416)*

Horner Industrial Services Inc... 317 957-4244
940 S West St Indianapolis (46225) *(G-8417)*

Horner Industrial Services Inc... 317 634-7165
2045 E Washington St Indianapolis (46201) *(G-8418)*

Horner Industrial Services Inc... 812 466-5281
3601 Scherer Rd Terre Haute (47804) *(G-15607)*

Horoho Printing Company Inc... 765 452-8862
500 N Philips St Kokomo (46901) *(G-10282)*

Horse N Around Animal & Tack... 765 618-2032
7288 S 825 E Upland (46989) *(G-15878)*

Horton, Carmel *Also Called: Horton Fan Systems Inc (G-1659)*

Horton Fan Systems Inc... 317 249-9100
201 W Carmel Dr Carmel (46032) *(G-1659)*

Horton Logistics LLC... 219 290-2910
3758 Polk St Gary (46408) *(G-5953)*

Hose Assemblies, Mishawaka *Also Called: Slb Corporation (G-11996)*

Hose Technology Inc.. 765 762-5501
2520 E Us Hwy 41 Williamsport (47993) *(G-16848)*

Hosetract Industries Ltd.. 260 489-8828
6433 Discount Dr Fort Wayne (46818) *(G-5084)*

Hostetler Carriage... 260 463-9920
3200 W 300 S Lagrange (46761) *(G-10742)*

Hot Cake... 317 889-2253
6845 Bluff Rd Indianapolis (46217) *(G-8419)*

Hot Heart Press LLC... 317 846-6057
10617 Jordan Rd Carmel (46032) *(G-1660)*

Hot Off Press.. 317 253-5987
5838 Bonnie Brae St Indianapolis (46228) *(G-8420)*

Hot Off Press.. 260 591-8331
832 Manchester Ave Wabash (46992) *(G-16194)*

Hot Rod Car Care LLC... 317 660-2077
7266 E 86th St Indianapolis (46250) *(G-8421)*

Hot Shot Multimedia Entps LLC... 317 537-7527
1610 Hilltop Dr South Bend (46614) *(G-15072)*

Hot Shot USA, South Bend *Also Called: Hot Shot Multimedia Entps LLC (G-15072)*

Hot Stamping & Printing.. 219 767-2429
6601 W 900 S Union Mills (46382) *(G-15865)*

Hotel Tango Distillery, Indianapolis *Also Called: Hotel Tango Whiskey Inc (G-8422)*

Hotel Tango Whiskey Inc... 317 653-1806
951 W Morris St Ste E Indianapolis (46221) *(G-8422)*

Hotel Vanities Intl LLC.. 317 787-2330
400 N Johnson Rd Indianapolis (46237) *(G-8423)*

Hotel Vanities Intl LLC (PA).. 317 787-2330
5514 Stockwell Ct Indianapolis (46237) *(G-8424)*

Hotmix Inc (PA)... 812 926-1471
110 Forest Ave Aurora (47001) *(G-445)*

Hotmix Inc.. 812 663-2020
992 S County Road 800 E Greensburg (47240) *(G-6605)*

Hotricity LLC... 765 212-0411
3008 E Tanner Dr Muncie (47302) *(G-12422)*

Houchens Industries Inc.. 812 467-7255
4635 N 1st Ave Evansville (47710) *(G-4111)*

Houck Industries Inc... 812 663-5675
814 E Randall St Greensburg (47240) *(G-6606)*

Houghton Mifflin Harcourt Co.. 317 359-5585
2700 N Richardt Ave Indianapolis (46219) *(G-8425)*

Houghton Mifflin Harcourt Pubg... 317 359-5585
2700 N Richardt Ave Indianapolis (46219) *(G-8426)*

House of Delrenee LLC.. 219 670-1153
9052 Woodmoss Ln Indianapolis (46250) *(G-8427)*

House of Fara Incorporated.. 219 362-8544
4747 W State Road 2 Ste A La Porte (46350) *(G-10422)*

House of Soccer Inc... 812 265-5196
404 E Main St Madison (47250) *(G-11227)*

HOUSE OF SOCCER, INC., Madison *Also Called: House of Soccer Inc (G-11227)*

Housefield Marketing, Indianapolis *Also Called: Omnisource Marketing Group Inc (G-9050)*

Housz of Drake, Fishers *Also Called: Rva LLC (G-4602)*

Hovair Automotive, Franklin *Also Called: Hovair Automotive LLC (G-5742)*

Hovair Automotive LLC.. 317 738-0485
211 Province St Franklin (46131) *(G-5742)*

Hoverstream LLC... 317 489-0075
4801 Van Cleave St Indianapolis (46226) *(G-8428)*

How You Perceive Ever (PA)... 301 579-4973
7399 N Shadeland Ave Ste 299 Indianapolis (46250) *(G-8429)*

Howa USA Inc... 765 962-7855
1767 Sheridan St Richmond (47374) *(G-14137)*

Howard & Sons Cement Pdts Inc... 574 293-1906
2912 Oakland Ave Elkhart (46517) *(G-3412)*

Howard Logging.. 260 327-3862
680 N 850 W-92 Pierceton (46562) *(G-13633)*

Howard Materials LLC... 317 849-9666
2916 Kentucky Ave Indianapolis (46221) *(G-8430)*

Howard Pblctions Vidette Times, Valparaiso *Also Called: Lee Publications Inc (G-15994)*

Howard Print Shop LLC... 765 453-6161
2111 W Alto Rd Kokomo (46902) *(G-10283)*

Howden Compressors Inc... 610 313-9800
900 W Mount St Connersville (47331) *(G-2441)*

Howe House Limited Editions, Lafayette *Also Called: Howe House Ltd Editions Inc (G-10602)*

Howe House Ltd Editions Inc (PA).. 765 742-6831
624 South St Lafayette (47901) *(G-10602)*

Howe Industries, Indianapolis *Also Called: CH Ellis Co Inc (G-7782)*

Hower Tool Division, Ossian *Also Called: The Akron Equipment Company (G-13438)*

Howerton Racecar Works Inc... 317 241-0868
360 Gasoline Aly Indianapolis (46222) *(G-8431)*

Howerton Racing Products, Indianapolis *Also Called: Howerton Racecar Works Inc (G-8431)*

Howey Political Report, The, Indianapolis *Also Called: Newslink Inc (G-9007)*

Howmedica Osteonics Corp... 317 587-2008
12348 Hancock St Carmel (46032) *(G-1661)*

Howmet Aerospace Inc.. 317 241-9393
2334 Production Dr Indianapolis (46241) *(G-8432)*

Howmet Aerospace Inc

ALPHABETIC SECTION

Howmet Aerospace Inc.. 219 326-7400
  1110 E Lincolnway La Porte (46350) *(G-10423)*
Howmet Aerospace Inc.. 812 853-6111
  State Highway 66 Newburgh (47630) *(G-13004)*
Howmet Aerospace Inc.. 412 553-4545
  2792 Laura Lynn Ln Newburgh (47630) *(G-13005)*
HOWMET AEROSPACE INC, Newburgh Also Called: Howmet Aerospace Inc *(G-13005)*
Howmet Corporation.. 219 325-4143
  926 E Lincolnway La Porte (46350) *(G-10424)*
Howse Ov Drmrs LLC.. 574 366-2406
  1251 N Eddy St South Bend (46617) *(G-15073)*
HP, Carmel Also Called: HP Inc *(G-1662)*
HP, Plainfield Also Called: HP Inc *(G-13687)*
HP Inc.. 317 566-6200
  201 W 103rd St Ste 240 Carmel (46290) *(G-1662)*
HP Inc.. 317 334-3400
  1301 Smith Rd Ste 101 Plainfield (46168) *(G-13687)*
Hpalloy, Windfall Also Called: High Performance Alloys Inc *(G-16905)*
Hpc International Inc.. 219 922-4868
  5261 Fountain Dr Ste A Crown Point (46307) *(G-2694)*
Hpi Wire Assemblies, Angola Also Called: Hi-Pro Inc *(G-258)*
Hpp Mold & Tool, Fort Wayne Also Called: Hoosier Pride Plastics Inc *(G-5079)*
Hr Agri-Power, Poseyville Also Called: Agri-Power Inc *(G-13976)*
Hrezo Engineering, Greendale Also Called: Hrezo Industrial Eqp & Engrg *(G-6447)*
Hrezo Industrial Eqp & Engrg.. 812 537-4700
  1025 Ridge Ave Greendale (47025) *(G-6447)*
Hrr Enterprises Inc... 219 362-9050
  1755 Genesis Dr La Porte (46350) *(G-10425)*
Hs Custom Manufacturing, Centerville Also Called: Scheffler Hartmut Romanus *(G-1853)*
Hs Machine Welding... 812 752-2825
  733 W Bellevue Ave Scottsburg (47170) *(G-14559)*
Hs Processing, Butler Also Called: Heidtman Steel Products Inc *(G-1465)*
Hsm Eagle Ltd.. 812 491-9667
  6149 Wedeking Ave Evansville (47715) *(G-4112)*
Ht Enterprises Inc... 765 794-4174
  5070 N Old State Road 55 Crawfordsville (47933) *(G-2578)*
HTI.. 574 722-2814
  500 W Clinton St Ste 2 Logansport (46947) *(G-11078)*
Hu/Man Tech, Noblesville Also Called: Huver Manufacturing Tech LLC *(G-13098)*
Hub City Stl & Fabrication LLC.................................... 260 760-0370
  4487 S Arba Pike Union City (47390) *(G-15855)*
Hubbard & Cravens Coffee, Indianapolis Also Called: Suncoast Coffee Inc *(G-9526)*
Hubbard Feeds, Shipshewana Also Called: Ridley USA Inc *(G-14883)*
Hubbard Inc.. 317 535-1926
  6774 N Us Highway 31 Whiteland (46184) *(G-16788)*
Hubbard Services Inc... 317 881-2828
  1280 Us Highway 31 N Ste T Greenwood (46142) *(G-6713)*
Hubbard Welding.. 317 539-2758
  10114 S County Road 100 W Clayton (46118) *(G-2059)*
Hubcaps Galore Inc.. 812 944-5200
  311 W Main St New Albany (47150) *(G-12742)*
Huber Industries... 812 537-2275
  434 Margaret St Lawrenceburg (47025) *(G-10841)*
Huber Industries, Aurora Also Called: Batesville Products Inc *(G-440)*
Huber Orchards Inc.. 812 923-9463
  19816 Huber Rd Borden (47106) *(G-1110)*
Huber's Orchard & Winery, Borden Also Called: Huber Orchards Inc *(G-1110)*
Huckleberry Winery.. 317 850-4445
  3057 Amber Way Bargersville (46106) *(G-568)*
Hucks Food Fuel... 812 683-5566
  601 N Main St Huntingburg (47542) *(G-7281)*
Hudec Construction Company...................................... 219 922-9811
  148 N Ivanhoe Ct Griffith (46319) *(G-6807)*
Hudec Woodworking Company, Griffith Also Called: Hudec Construction Company *(G-6807)*
Hudelson Fabrication, Orleans Also Called: Lana Hudelson *(G-13377)*
Hudelson Machine & Sharpening, Orleans Also Called: Daniel Hudelson *(G-13376)*
Hudson Aquatic Systems LLC..................................... 260 665-1635
  1100 Wohlert St Angola (46703) *(G-262)*
Hudson Industries Inc... 260 587-3288
  105 W State Road 4 Hudson (46747) *(G-7246)*

Huehls Salcoating Lawncare LLC................................. 317 782-4069
  312 E Epler Ave Indianapolis (46227) *(G-8433)*
Huelseman Printing Co... 765 647-3947
  9085 Bath Rd Brookville (47012) *(G-1324)*
Huffman Metalworks LLC.. 574 835-0783
  16098 Messerschmidt Rd Brookville (47012) *(G-1325)*
Hugh K Eagan... 574 269-5411
  201 W Center St Warsaw (46580) *(G-16375)*
Hughes Custom Smokers, Claypool Also Called: Steven Ray Hughes *(G-2058)*
Hughes Tire Service Inc... 812 883-4981
  209 S Water St Salem (47167) *(G-14481)*
Hughes Welding and Fabrication.................................. 812 385-2770
  906 Virgil Blvd Princeton (47670) *(G-13999)*
Huhtamaki Inc... 219 972-4264
  6629 Indianapolis Blvd Hammond (46320) *(G-6950)*
Huhtamaki Inc... 765 677-0395
  1001 E 38th St Ste B Marion (46953) *(G-11293)*
Huhtamaki Foodservice, Hammond Also Called: Huhtamaki Inc *(G-6950)*
Hull Aircraft Support LLC.. 219 324-6247
  602 Lakeside St La Porte (46350) *(G-10426)*
Hull Precision Machining Inc.. 260 238-4372
  6974 State Road 1 Spencerville (46788) *(G-15371)*
Hulletts Backhoe Service, Peru Also Called: Tracy K Hullett *(G-13606)*
Hulman & Company... 812 232-9446
  4780 E Margaret Dr Terre Haute (47803) *(G-15608)*
Hulman & Company (PA)... 812 232-9446
  900 Wabash Ave Terre Haute (47807) *(G-15609)*
Humble Industries LLC... 219 702-6607
  772 Buchanan St Gary (46402) *(G-5954)*
Humes & Berg Mfg Co Inc.. 219 391-5880
  4801 Railroad Ave East Chicago (46312) *(G-3018)*
Humphrey Tool Co Inc.. 574 753-3853
  120 Water St Logansport (46947) *(G-11079)*
Hungry Candle LLC.. 773 656-1774
  1243 S East St Indianapolis (46225) *(G-8434)*
Hunt Club Distillery.. 317 441-7194
  3774 W State Road 47 Sheridan (46069) *(G-14823)*
Hunt Wesson Foods, Rensselaer Also Called: Conagra Brands Inc *(G-14049)*
Hunter Industries.. 630 200-7581
  5477 Cottage Grove Ln Noblesville (46062) *(G-13097)*
Hunter Nutrition Inc.. 765 563-1003
  200 Ns St Brookston (47923) *(G-1311)*
Hunter Sheep Nutrition, Brookston Also Called: Hunter Nutrition Inc *(G-1311)*
Hunter Venetian Blind Co... 812 471-1100
  2419 Hialeah Dr Evansville (47715) *(G-4113)*
Hunters Machining Services LLC................................. 219 405-7638
  1305 W 231st Ave Shelby (46377) *(G-14726)*
Hunters Ridge Winery LLC... 812 967-9463
  9945 E Garrison Hollow Rd Salem (47167) *(G-14482)*
Huntingburg Machine Works Inc................................... 812 683-3531
  309 N Main St Huntingburg (47542) *(G-7282)*
Huntington County Tab Inc... 260 356-1107
  1670 Etna Ave Huntington (46750) *(G-7321)*
Huntington Exteriors Inc... 260 356-1621
  1700 N Broadway St Huntington (46750) *(G-7322)*
Huntington Sheet Metal Inc (PA).................................. 260 356-9011
  1675 Riverfork Dr Huntington (46750) *(G-7323)*
Huntington Sheet Metal Inc.. 260 356-9011
  2060 Old Us Highway 24 Huntington (46750) *(G-7324)*
Huntington Tool & Die Inc.. 260 356-5940
  9742 E 700 N Van Buren (46991) *(G-16085)*
Hunts Maintenance Inc... 219 785-2333
  107 Greenway St Westville (46391) *(G-16762)*
Huntsman Intl Trdg Corp.. 812 334-7090
  4100 W Profile Pkwy Bloomington (47404) *(G-885)*
Hupp & Associates Inc... 260 748-8282
  1690 Summit St Ste B New Haven (46774) *(G-12906)*
Hupp Aerospace Defense, New Haven Also Called: Hupp & Associates Inc *(G-12906)*
HURCO, Indianapolis Also Called: Hurco Companies Inc *(G-8436)*
Hurco Companies Inc... 317 347-6208
  7220 Winton Dr Indianapolis (46268) *(G-8435)*

ALPHABETIC SECTION

Hurco Companies Inc (PA) 317 293-5309
  1 Technology Way Indianapolis (46268) *(G-8436)*
Hurco International Holdings (HQ) 317 293-5309
  1 Technology Way Indianapolis (46268) *(G-8437)*
Hurco Usa, Inc., Indianapolis *Also Called: Milltronics Usa Inc (G-8929)*
Hurricane Compressor Company, Leo *Also Called: K Grimmer Industries Inc (G-10968)*
Hurricane Ditcher Company Inc 812 886-9663
  2425 S Cathlinette Rd Vincennes (47591) *(G-16130)*
Hurst Custom Cabinets Inc 812 683-3378
  1003 S Cherry St Huntingburg (47542) *(G-7283)*
Hurst Enterprise 812 853-0901
  7866 Owens Dr Newburgh (47630) *(G-13006)*
Hurst Manufacturing Division, Princeton *Also Called: Nidec Motor Corporation (G-14007)*
Hush Clothing 317 LLC 317 935-2184
  5111 Kingman Dr Indianapolis (46226) *(G-8438)*
Huskey Parts Company LLC 812 899-0950
  615 W Hefron St Washington (47501) *(G-16485)*
Husqvrna Cnsmr Otdr Prod NA 812 883-3575
  1555 S Jackson St Salem (47167) *(G-14483)*
Hussleaire LLC 312 889-4866
  3960 Southeastern Ave Gary (46404) *(G-5955)*
Huston Signs LLC 317 804-9009
  E 181st St Westfield (46074) *(G-16698)*
Hutchison Signs & Elec Co Inc 317 894-8787
  215 S Munsie St Indianapolis (46229) *(G-8439)*
Huth Tool 260 749-9411
  6930 Derek Dr Fort Wayne (46803) *(G-5085)*
Huth Tool & Machine Corp 260 749-9411
  6930 Derek Dr Fort Wayne (46803) *(G-5086)*
Huthone LLC 260 248-2384
  707 Burke St Columbia City (46725) *(G-2153)*
Huver Manufacturing Tech LLC 317 460-8605
  10210 Carmine Dr Noblesville (46060) *(G-13098)*
Hux Oil Corp 812 894-2096
  5451 Riley Rd Terre Haute (47802) *(G-15610)*
Hy-Flex Corporation 765 571-5125
  8774 In 109 Knightstown (46148) *(G-10198)*
Hy-Line Enterprises Intl Inc 574 294-1112
  25369 Vernon Xing Elkhart (46514) *(G-3413)*
Hy-Line North America LLC 260 375-3041
  1029 Mill Site Dr Warren (46792) *(G-16300)*
Hy-Pro Corporation 317 849-3535
  6810 Layton Rd Anderson (46011) *(G-130)*
Hy-Pro Filtration, Anderson *Also Called: Hy-Pro Corporation (G-130)*
Hy-TEC Fiberglass Inc 260 489-6601
  2201 Suppliers Ct Fort Wayne (46818) *(G-5087)*
Hy-Tech Machining Systems LLC 765 649-6852
  2900 S Scatterfield Rd Anderson (46013) *(G-131)*
Hyco Machine & Mold Inc 574 522-5847
  121 Rush Ct Elkhart (46516) *(G-3414)*
Hyderabad House, Carmel *Also Called: Nineplus Tables LLC (G-1706)*
Hydration Turbine Inc 317 491-0656
  5433 Brendonridge Rd Indianapolis (46226) *(G-8440)*
Hydraulic Press Brick Company (HQ) 317 290-1140
  3600 Woodview Trce Ste 300 Indianapolis (46268) *(G-8441)*
Hydraulic Press Brick Company 317 290-1140
  6618 N Tidewater Rd Mooresville (46158) *(G-12212)*
Hydrite Chemical Co 812 232-5411
  2250 S 13th St Terre Haute (47802) *(G-15611)*
Hydro Conduit 561 651-7177
  6662 W 350 N Greenfield (46140) *(G-6510)*
Hydro Conduit of Texas LP 317 769-2261
  4360 Whitelick Dr Whitestown (46075) *(G-16809)*
Hydro Extrusion Usa LLC 765 825-1141
  5120 Western Ave Connersville (47331) *(G-2442)*
Hydro Extrusion Usa LLC 574 262-2667
  3406 Reedy Dr Elkhart (46514) *(G-3415)*
Hydro Extrusion Usa LLC 888 935-5757
  400 S Main St North Liberty (46554) *(G-13217)*
Hydro Fire Protection Inc 317 780-6980
  8603 Bluff Rd Indianapolis (46217) *(G-8442)*

Hydro Systems Mfg Inc 260 436-4476
  3632 Illinois Rd Ofc Fort Wayne (46804) *(G-5088)*
Hydro Vac Services LLC 317 345-2120
  6435 E 30th St Indianapolis (46219) *(G-8443)*
Hydro-Gear Inc 317 821-0477
  7330 Woodland Dr Indianapolis (46278) *(G-8444)*
Hydrojet Signs 765 584-2125
  707 N Co Rd 400 E Winchester (47394) *(G-16890)*
Hydrojet Signs and Fabricating, Winchester *Also Called: Hydrojet Signs (G-16890)*
Hydroxyl Rentals, Westfield *Also Called: Airbotx LLC (G-16663)*
Hymer Group Usa LLC 574 970-7460
  1220 Maple St Bristol (46507) *(G-1267)*
Hymns To Go, Fishers *Also Called: Hymns2go LLC (G-4540)*
Hymns2go LLC 317 577-0730
  10315 Stonebridge Ct Fishers (46037) *(G-4540)*
Hyndman Industrial Pdts Inc 260 483-6042
  4031 Merchant Rd Ste A Fort Wayne (46818) *(G-5089)*
Hype Magazine, The, Indianapolis *Also Called: How You Perceive Ever (G-8429)*
Hypeauditor, Indianapolis *Also Called: Stonecast Financial LLC (G-9514)*
Hyperbole Creations, Madison *Also Called: Hyperbole Software LLC (G-11228)*
Hyperbole Software LLC 812 839-6635
  9383 E Tate Ridge Rd Madison (47250) *(G-11228)*
Hytek Hose & Coupling Div, La Porte *Also Called: Terry Liquidation III Inc (G-10489)*
I A S, Peru *Also Called: Intech Automation Systems Corp (G-13587)*
I B P, Logansport *Also Called: Tyson Fresh Meats Inc (G-11115)*
I B P, Washington *Also Called: Tyson Fresh Meats Inc (G-16511)*
I B P Hog Buying Station, Linden *Also Called: Tyson Fresh Meats Inc (G-11033)*
I B P Hog Buying Station, Rossville *Also Called: Tyson Fresh Meats Inc (G-14388)*
I C R, Indianapolis *Also Called: Innovative Chem Resources Inc (G-8553)*
I C S, Huntington *Also Called: Industrial Control Service Inc (G-7327)*
I D I, Logansport *Also Called: Indiana Dimension Inc (G-11082)*
I E M C 219 464-2890
  1150 Lincolnway Ste 1 Valparaiso (46385) *(G-15966)*
I E Products, Fort Wayne *Also Called: Mad Dasher Inc (G-5198)*
I F S Corp 317 898-6118
  9433 E Washington St Indianapolis (46229) *(G-8445)*
I M I, Anderson *Also Called: Irving Materials Inc (G-135)*
I M I, Bedford *Also Called: Irving Materials Inc (G-649)*
I M I, Bloomington *Also Called: Irving Materials Inc (G-892)*
I M I, Bluffton *Also Called: Irving Materials Inc (G-1039)*
I M I, Brookville *Also Called: Irving Materials Inc (G-1327)*
I M I, Cambridge City *Also Called: Irving Materials Inc (G-1496)*
I M I, Connersville *Also Called: Irving Materials Inc (G-2446)*
I M I, Crawfordsville *Also Called: Irving Materials Inc (G-2581)*
I M I, Elwood *Also Called: Irving Materials Inc (G-3826)*
I M I, Greenfield *Also Called: Irving Materials Inc (G-6518)*
I M I, Huntingburg *Also Called: Irving Materials Inc (G-7284)*
I M I, Huntington *Also Called: Irving Materials Inc (G-7331)*
I M I, Indianapolis *Also Called: Irving Materials Inc (G-8589)*
I M I, Indianapolis *Also Called: Irving Materials Inc (G-8590)*
I M I, Indianapolis *Also Called: Irving Materials Inc (G-8591)*
I M I, Kokomo *Also Called: Irving Materials Inc (G-10290)*
I M I, Lafayette *Also Called: Irving Materials Inc (G-10610)*
I M I, Logansport *Also Called: Irving Materials Inc (G-11084)*
I M I, Marion *Also Called: Irving Materials Inc (G-11296)*
I M I, Mooresville *Also Called: Irving Materials Inc (G-12216)*
I M I, Muncie *Also Called: Irving Materials Inc (G-12428)*
I M I, Noblesville *Also Called: Irving Materials Inc (G-13108)*
I M I, Noblesville *Also Called: Irving Materials Inc (G-13109)*
I M I, Spencer *Also Called: Irving Materials Inc (G-15353)*
I M I, Springport *Also Called: Irving Materials Inc (G-15380)*
I M I, Tipton *Also Called: Irving Materials Inc (G-15777)*
I M I, Washington *Also Called: Irving Materials Inc (G-16486)*
I M I, West Lafayette *Also Called: Irving Materials Inc (G-16596)*
I M I, Whiteland *Also Called: Irving Materials Inc (G-16790)*
I M L, Winchester *Also Called: Indiana Marujun LLC (G-16891)*

I M S I   ALPHABETIC SECTION

I M S I, North Salem *Also Called: I M S I Rental Svcs & Repair (G-13254)*

I M S I Rental Svcs & Repair.. 765 522-1223
  13118 N County Road 900 E North Salem (46165) *(G-13254)*

I MI Erie Stone.. 765 728-5335
  5067 E Cummins Rd Montpelier (47359) *(G-12178)*

I N C O M Wholesale Supply... 574 722-2442
  2865 E Market St Logansport (46947) *(G-11080)*

I Noodles.. 765 447-2288
  111 N Chauncey Ave West Lafayette (47906) *(G-16593)*

I P Callison & Sons, North Judson *Also Called: Callisons Inc (G-13208)*

I P F, Shelbyville *Also Called: Indiana Precision Forge LLC (G-14760)*

I Power, Anderson *Also Called: Ipower Technologies Inc (G-134)*

I Power Energy Systems LLC... 765 621-9980
  4640 Dr Martin Luther King Jr Blvd Anderson (46013) *(G-132)*

I Run Amuck LLC... 317 674-3339
  8105 Halyard Way Indianapolis (46236) *(G-8446)*

I S M A Report, Indianapolis *Also Called: Indiana State Medical Assn (G-8494)*

I T Equipment, Plymouth *Also Called: Industrial Transmission Eqp (G-13785)*

I V S... 765 914-5268
  7079 S County Road 200 E Connersville (47331) *(G-2443)*

I W I, Fishers *Also Called: Ckh Two Inc (G-4489)*

I-69 Trailer Center, Markle *Also Called: Novae LLC (G-11361)*

I2r.. 812 235-6167
  711 Hulman St Terre Haute (47802) *(G-15612)*

I2s, Indianapolis *Also Called: Integrated Instrument Svcs Inc (G-8568)*

I4 Identity LLC... 317 662-0448
  12463 Duval Dr Fishers (46037) *(G-4541)*

Iaire LLC (PA).. 317 806-2750
  6805 Hillsdale Ct Indianapolis (46250) *(G-8447)*

IAm Aw TI Die Makers LL 229... 574 333-5955
  2618 Lowell Ave Elkhart (46516) *(G-3416)*

Iasa Group LLC (PA).. 260 484-1322
  1905 Production Rd Fort Wayne (46808) *(G-5090)*

IBC Advanced Alloys, Franklin *Also Called: IBC US Holdings Inc (G-5743)*

IBC Advanced Alloys Copper, Franklin *Also Called: Nonferrous Products Inc (G-5761)*

IBC Coatings Technologies Ltd.. 317 418-3725
  902 Hendricks Dr Lebanon (46052) *(G-10898)*

IBC Materials & Tech LLC... 765 481-2900
  823 Hendricks Dr Lebanon (46052) *(G-10899)*

IBC US Holdings Inc.. 317 738-2558
  401 Arvin Rd Franklin (46131) *(G-5743)*

Ibc-Sputtek Inc.. 765 482-9802
  902 Hendricks Dr Lebanon (46052) *(G-10900)*

IBJ Corporation.. 317 634-6200
  1 Monument Cir Ste 300 Indianapolis (46204) *(G-8448)*

Ibr, Ashley *Also Called: Welder On Way LLC (G-340)*

Ican Mobile Canning, Logansport *Also Called: Ican Solutions LLC (G-11081)*

Ican Solutions LLC.. 574 355-6500
  5294 E Division Rd Logansport (46947) *(G-11081)*

Icape Group, Indianapolis *Also Called: Icape-Usa LLC (G-8449)*

Icape-Usa LLC (HQ).. 765 431-1271
  8102 Zionsville Rd Indianapolis (46268) *(G-8449)*

Icbo, Indianapolis *Also Called: International Code Council Inc (G-8576)*

Ice Cream On Wheels Inc.. 800 884-9793
  2011 N Griffith Blvd Griffith (46319) *(G-6808)*

Ice Cream Specialties Inc... 765 474-2989
  2600 Concord Rd Lafayette (47909) *(G-10603)*

Ice Cream Specialties Inc... 219 980-0800
  6510 Broadway Merrillville (46410) *(G-11523)*

Icf/Eco, Warsaw *Also Called: Indiana Coated Fabrics Inc (G-16376)*

Ichinen USA Corporation... 317 638-3511
  735 Saint Paul St Indianapolis (46203) *(G-8450)*

Icl Specialty Products Inc.. 219 933-1560
  6530 Schneider St Hammond (46320) *(G-6951)*

Icl Specialty Products Inc.. 219 933-1560
  1326 Summer St Hammond (46320) *(G-6952)*

Icon Beauty Supply Inc.. 317 209-6550
  14350 Mundy Dr Ste 800-268 Noblesville (46060) *(G-13099)*

Icon International Inc... 260 482-8700
  8333 Clinton Park Dr Fort Wayne (46825) *(G-5091)*

Icon Metal Forming LLC... 812 738-5900
  2190 Landmark Ave Ne Corydon (47112) *(G-2499)*

ICP Liquidating Company.. 419 841-3361
  2050 S Harding St Indianapolis (46221) *(G-8451)*

Ics Inks LLP... 317 690-9254
  6101 Drawbridge Ln Indianapolis (46250) *(G-8452)*

Ics-Cargo Clean, Alton *Also Called: Industrial Container Svcs LLC (G-65)*

Ict, Franklin *Also Called: Innovative Casting Tech Inc (G-5748)*

Ict, Shipshewana *Also Called: Indiana Custom Trucks LLC (G-14852)*

ID Graphics Incorporated... 765 649-9988
  416 W 11th St Anderson (46016) *(G-133)*

Ideal Inc.. 765 457-6222
  1037 S Union St Kokomo (46902) *(G-10284)*

Ideal Coatings LLC.. 574 358-0182
  11431 County Road 10 Middlebury (46540) *(G-11722)*

Ideal Janitor Supply, Kokomo *Also Called: Ideal Inc (G-10284)*

Ideal Pro Cnc Inc... 260 693-1954
  6231 N 650 E Churubusco (46723) *(G-1985)*

Ideal Safety & Hygiene LLC... 317 281-3921
  818 Canyon Rd Indianapolis (46217) *(G-8453)*

Ideal Sign Corp.. 219 406-2092
  507 N 325 W Valparaiso (46385) *(G-15967)*

Ideal Testing and Services LLC... 812 431-8500
  3410 N High School Rd Ste G Indianapolis (46224) *(G-8454)*

Idemitsu Lubricants Amer Corp (DH)................................... 812 284-3300
  701 Port Rd Jeffersonville (47130) *(G-10000)*

Identity Logix LLC.. 219 379-5560
  10048 Wellington Ter Munster (46321) *(G-12541)*

Identitylogix, Munster *Also Called: Identity Logix LLC (G-12541)*

Idgas Inc... 317 839-1133
  915 Corey Ln Plainfield (46168) *(G-13688)*

IDI, Noblesville *Also Called: Industrial Dictrics Hldngs Inc (G-13104)*

IDI Composites International, Noblesville *Also Called: Industrial Dielectrics Inc (G-13103)*

IDI Fabrication Inc (PA)... 317 776-6577
  14444 Herriman Blvd Noblesville (46060) *(G-13100)*

Idonix Solutions Inc... 317 544-8171
  12377 Berry Patch Ln Fishers (46037) *(G-4542)*

Idp, North Webster *Also Called: Indiana Dimensional Pdts LLC (G-13306)*

Idra North America Inc.. 765 459-0085
  1510 Ann St Kokomo (46901) *(G-10285)*

Idx - Louisville, Jeffersonville *Also Called: Horizon Terra Incorporated (G-9999)*

Iea Constructors Inc.. 765 832-8526
  3900 White Ave Clinton (47842) *(G-2068)*

IEA CONSTRUCTORS, INC., Clinton *Also Called: Iea Constructors Inc (G-2068)*

Iea Equipment Management LLC.. 765 832-2800
  3900 White Ave Clinton (47842) *(G-2069)*

Iea Management Services Inc.. 765 832-8526
  3900 White Ave Clinton (47842) *(G-2070)*

Ierc, Elkhart *Also Called: CTS Elctrnic Cmponents Cal Inc (G-3278)*

Ies Subsidiary Holdings Inc... 219 937-0100
  1825 Summer St Hammond (46320) *(G-6953)*

Ies Subsidiary Holdings Inc... 330 830-3500
  1125 S Walnut St South Bend (46619) *(G-15074)*

Iet Global Inc... 812 421-7810
  225 W Morgan Ave Ste A Evansville (47710) *(G-4114)*

Ifc Fence LLC.. 219 977-4000
  3245 W 46th Ave Gary (46408) *(G-5956)*

Ifok Inc.. 219 477-5107
  447 E Us Highway 6 Valparaiso (46383) *(G-15968)*

Ifp Automation, Fishers *Also Called: Clarke Industrial Systems Inc (G-4491)*

Ifs Coatings... 317 471-5122
  5335 W 74th St Indianapolis (46268) *(G-8455)*

Igetpaid LLC.. 708 916-2967
  4645 Buchanan St Gary (46408) *(G-5957)*

Igh Steel Fabrication Inc.. 765 482-7534
  1001 Ransdell Rd Lebanon (46052) *(G-10901)*

Igotkickz LLC... 812 893-7674
  4913 Rolling Ridge Dr Evansville (47712) *(G-4115)*

IGP North America LLC... 812 670-3483
  702 N Shore Dr Ste 500 Jeffersonville (47130) *(G-10001)*

ALPHABETIC SECTION — Impact Safety Inc

Ihs Campaign For Ind Exprnce... 317 234-5232
450 W Ohio St Indianapolis (46202) *(G-8456)*

Iic, South Bend *Also Called: Indiana Intgrated Circuits LLC (G-15078)*

Iiiimpressions That Count Inc.. 317 423-0581
917 Greer St Indianapolis (46203) *(G-8457)*

Ike Newton LLC.. 317 902-1772
949 Fry Rd Greenwood (46142) *(G-6714)*

Ikelite Underwater Systems, Indianapolis *Also Called: Divers Supply Company Inc (G-7978)*

Ikio Led Lighting, Indianapolis *Also Called: Ikio Led Lighting LLC (G-8458)*

Ikio Led Lighting LLC... 765 414-0835
8470 Allison Pointe Blvd Ste 128 Indianapolis (46250) *(G-8458)*

IKON Group... 574 326-3661
330 E Windsor Ave Elkhart (46514) *(G-3417)*

Ikonik Graphix, Delphi *Also Called: Nicholas Mendel (G-2904)*

Ilab LLC... 317 218-3258
5432 Wood Hollow Dr Indianapolis (46239) *(G-8459)*

Ilc Resources, Cloverdale *Also Called: Iowa Limestone Company (G-2087)*

Illiana Electrical Svcs LLC.. 219 276-1743
501 Garfield Ave Valparaiso (46383) *(G-15969)*

Illiana Grinding Machining Inc.. 219 306-0253
4450 Euclid Ave East Chicago (46312) *(G-3019)*

Illiana Indus Elc Mtr Svcs Inc.. 219 286-3654
393 E Us Highway 30 Valparaiso (46383) *(G-15970)*

Illiana Railcar Services LLC.. 812 264-4687
5110 N 15th St Terre Haute (47805) *(G-15613)*

Illiana Remedial Action Inc... 219 844-4862
6550 Osborne Ave Hammond (46320) *(G-6954)*

Illiana Signs... 708 862-9164
11525 Upper Peninsula Ln Saint John (46373) *(G-14453)*

Illinois Agri-News... 317 726-5391
2575 55th Pl Ste A Indianapolis (46220) *(G-8460)*

Illinois Lubricants LLC... 260 436-2444
1300 Airport North Office Park Ste A Fort Wayne (46825) *(G-5092)*

Illinois Ni Cast LLC.. 260 897-3768
105 Progress Way Avilla (46710) *(G-478)*

Illinois Tool Works Inc.. 317 298-5000
4141 W 54th St Indianapolis (46254) *(G-8461)*

Illuminated Image, Angola *Also Called: Lomont Holdings Co Inc (G-273)*

Ilpea Industries Inc.. 812 752-2526
2500 Lynch Rd Evansville (47711) *(G-4116)*

Ilpea Industries Inc.. 812 414-2728
1320 S Main St Scottsburg (47170) *(G-14560)*

Ilpea Industries Inc.. 812 752-2526
745 S Gardner St Scottsburg (47170) *(G-14561)*

Ilpea Industries Inc (HQ).. 812 752-2526
745 S Gardner St Scottsburg (47170) *(G-14562)*

IM Impressed... 219 838-7959
9540 Fran Lin Pkwy Munster (46321) *(G-12542)*

Im Indiana Holdings Inc... 260 478-1674
6300 Ardmore Ave Fort Wayne (46809) *(G-5093)*

Ima Inox Market America LLC... 765 896-4411
4401 S Cowan Rd Muncie (47302) *(G-12423)*

Image LLC... 260 436-6125
6838 Covington Creek Trl Fort Wayne (46804) *(G-5094)*

Image Builders/Rowland Prtg, Noblesville *Also Called: Rowland Printing Co Inc (G-13168)*

Image Inks Company... 317 432-5041
7363 Red Rock Rd Indianapolis (46236) *(G-8462)*

Image One LLC (PA)... 317 576-2700
7795 N 200 W Mccordsville (46055) *(G-11451)*

Image Plus Original LLC.. 800 226-7316
5160 E 65th St Ste 100 Indianapolis (46220) *(G-8463)*

Image Vault LLC.. 812 948-8400
101 Security Pkwy New Albany (47150) *(G-12743)*

Imagelaz LLC.. 574 534-0906
2106 Lisa Ct Goshen (46528) *(G-6170)*

Imagination Graphics... 812 423-6503
2323 W Franklin St Evansville (47712) *(G-4117)*

Imagination Graphics... 812 352-8288
3855a N State Highway 3 North Vernon (47265) *(G-13279)*

Imagination Set In Stone LLC.. 812 660-0031
5698 W County Road 600 N Richland (47634) *(G-14079)*

Imagine Like God LLC... 574 575-5023
1020 E Beardsley Ave Elkhart (46514) *(G-3418)*

Imagine Metals.. 574 971-3902
2102 E Lincoln Ave Goshen (46528) *(G-6171)*

Imagineering Enterprises Inc... 317 635-8565
2719 N Emerson Ave Ste A Indianapolis (46218) *(G-8464)*

Imagineering Enterprises Inc... 574 287-0642
3722 Foundation Ct South Bend (46628) *(G-15075)*

Imagineering Enterprises Inc (PA)................................... 574 287-2941
1302 W Sample St South Bend (46619) *(G-15076)*

Imagineering Finishing Tech, South Bend *Also Called: Imagineering Enterprises Inc (G-15075)*

Imagineering Finishing Tech, South Bend *Also Called: Imagineering Enterprises Inc (G-15076)*

Imaginestics LLC... 765 464-1700
1801 Kalberer Rd Ste A100 West Lafayette (47906) *(G-16594)*

IMC, Indianapolis *Also Called: Indiana Model Company Inc (G-8484)*

Imco, Crown Point *Also Called: Imco Industrial Machine Corp (G-2695)*

Imco Industrial Machine Corp.. 219 663-6100
1201 S Main St Crown Point (46307) *(G-2695)*

IMD, Warsaw *Also Called: Instrumental Machine & Dev Inc (G-16379)*

Imel John... 317 873-8764
4901 W 106th St Zionsville (46077) *(G-17017)*

Imel Machining Co, Uniondale *Also Called: R P Imel (G-15872)*

Imh Fabrication LLC... 317 252-5566
2073 Dr Andrew J Brown Ave Indianapolis (46202) *(G-8465)*

Imh Fabrication LLC (PA).. 317 508-7462
1929 Columbia Ave Indianapolis (46202) *(G-8466)*

Imh Products, Indianapolis *Also Called: Imh Fabrication LLC (G-8466)*

Imhoff's Leather Works, Goshen *Also Called: David W Imhoff (G-6119)*

IMI Bloomfield.. 812 384-0045
9 E Judson St Bloomfield (47424) *(G-749)*

IMI Irving Material, Greenwood *Also Called: Irving Materials Inc (G-6717)*

IMI Riving Materials Inc.. 812 753-4201
79 E State Road 168 Fort Branch (47648) *(G-4704)*

IMI South LLC.. 812 284-9732
1221 Highway 31 E Clarksville (47129) *(G-2019)*

IMI South LLC.. 812 738-4173
3060 Cline Rd Nw Corydon (47112) *(G-2500)*

IMI South LLC.. 812 273-1428
3650 N Sr 7 Madison (47250) *(G-11229)*

IMI South LLC.. 812 945-6605
1732 Lincoln Ave New Albany (47150) *(G-12744)*

IMI Southwest Inc (HQ)... 812 424-3554
1816 W Lloyd Expy Evansville (47712) *(G-4118)*

IMI Southwest Inc.. 260 432-3973
201 S Thomas Rd Fort Wayne (46808) *(G-5095)*

Imma Jerk LLC... 219 885-8613
1742 Hayes St Gary (46404) *(G-5958)*

Immi, Westfield *Also Called: Indiana Mills & Manufacturing (G-16699)*

Imminent Software Inc... 317 340-4562
6575 Brauer Ln Carmel (46033) *(G-1663)*

Immunotek Bio Centers LLC.. 337 500-1294
3859 W Washington St Indianapolis (46241) *(G-8467)*

Immunotek Bio Centers LLC.. 337 500-1294
1665 E 10th St Jeffersonville (47130) *(G-10002)*

Imp Holdings LLC.. 260 665-6112
409 Growth Pkwy Angola (46703) *(G-263)*

Impact, Frankfort *Also Called: Keystone Cooperative Inc (G-5678)*

Impact Cnc LLC (PA).. 260 244-5511
2651 S 600 E Columbia City (46725) *(G-2154)*

Impact Forge Group Inc... 812 342-5527
2705 Norcross Dr Columbus (47201) *(G-2321)*

Impact Forge Group Inc (DH).. 812 342-4437
2805 Norcross Dr Columbus (47201) *(G-2322)*

Impact Molding Elkhart, Elkhart *Also Called: Indiana Plastics LLC (G-3422)*

Impact Racing Inc.. 317 852-3067
7991 W 21st St Ste A2 Indianapolis (46214) *(G-8468)*

Impact Safety Inc... 317 852-3067
7991 W 21st St Ste D1 Indianapolis (46214) *(G-8469)*

Impact Trailers, Bristol *Also Called: Ft Group LLC* **(G-1263)**

Imperial Designs.. 765 985-2712
  6599 N State Road 19 Denver (46926) **(G-2935)**

Imperial Fabrics, Nappanee *Also Called: Ascot Enterprises Inc* **(G-12582)**

Imperial Petroleum Inc.. 812 867-1433
  11600 German Pines Dr Darmstadt (47725) **(G-2836)**

Imperial Products LLC.. 765 966-0322
  451 Industrial Pkwy Richmond (47374) **(G-14138)**

Imperial Stamping Company, Elkhart *Also Called: Imperial Stamping Corporation* **(G-3419)**

Imperial Stamping Corporation... 574 294-3780
  4801 Middlebury St Elkhart (46516) **(G-3419)**

Imperial Steel Tank, Gary *Also Called: Refax Inc* **(G-6002)**

Imperial Trophy & Awards Co.. 260 432-8161
  2405 W Jefferson Blvd Fort Wayne (46802) **(G-5096)**

Impression Printing... 765 342-6977
  389 E Walnut St Martinsville (46151) **(G-11403)**

Impressions LLC... 765 490-2575
  3007 1/2 Kossuth St Lafayette (47904) **(G-10604)**

Impressions Printing Inc... 812 634-2574
  508 Jackson St Jasper (47546) **(G-9843)**

Impressive Printing.. 812 913-1101
  515 E Daisy Ln New Albany (47150) **(G-12745)**

Imprint It All... 812 234-0024
  1419 S 25th St Terre Haute (47803) **(G-15614)**

Impulse of Jasper Inc.. 812 481-2880
  613 Main St Jasper (47546) **(G-9844)**

IMS Surface Conditioning... 219 881-0155
  1 N Buchanan St Gary (46402) **(G-5959)**

Imw, Kingsbury *Also Called: Industrial Mint Wldg Machining* **(G-10179)**

In Business For Life Inc.. 317 691-6169
  12400 N Meridian St Ste 150 Carmel (46032) **(G-1664)**

In Case of Emergency Press.. 812 650-3352
  1112 S Morton St Bloomington (47403) **(G-886)**

In Cloudbrst Lawn Sprnklr Svcs.. 260 492-8400
  1707 Brandywine Trl Fort Wayne (46845) **(G-5097)**

In Defense of Women Inc... 574 855-1864
  52075 Avanelle St Granger (46530) **(G-6353)**

In Ductile LLC... 317 776-8000
  1600 S 8th St Noblesville (46060) **(G-13101)**

In Space LLC... 765 775-2107
  820 Roberts St Lafayette (47904) **(G-10605)**

In Stitches Inc... 574 294-2121
  135 Easy Shopping Pl Elkhart (46516) **(G-3420)**

In Stitches Custom Embroidery... 812 385-2877
  129 E Broadway St Princeton (47670) **(G-14000)**

In Stitchz & Signz LLC... 574 892-5956
  11189 State Road 10 Argos (46501) **(G-323)**

In Tex Signs and Graphics... 812 385-2471
  533 N Main St Princeton (47670) **(G-14001)**

In The Am LLC... 408 836-8200
  319 Angelina Way Avon (46123) **(G-526)**

In-Fab Inc... 812 279-8144
  2030 John Williams Blvd Bedford (47421) **(G-642)**

In-Print.. 219 956-3001
  886 E 900 N Wheatfield (46392) **(G-16768)**

In, Technology Center, Indianapolis *Also Called: Prysmian Cbles Systems USA LLC* **(G-9236)**

Incense Incense.. 317 544-9444
  5599 Springhollow Ct Avon (46123) **(G-527)**

Inchromatics LLC... 317 872-7401
  1545 Trace Ln Indianapolis (46260) **(G-8470)**

Incipio Devices LLC... 260 200-1970
  3650 W 200 N Huntington (46750) **(G-7325)**

Incog Biopharma Services Inc... 812 320-4236
  12050 Exit 5 Pkwy Fishers (46037) **(G-4543)**

Indalex Inc... 765 457-1117
  1500 E Murden St Kokomo (46901) **(G-10286)**

Indco Inc.. 812 945-4383
  4040 Earnings Way New Albany (47150) **(G-12746)**

Independent Cabinets.. 502 594-6026
  12910 Highway 60 Memphis (47143) **(G-11465)**

Independent Concrete Pipe, Indianapolis *Also Called: Independent Concrete Pipe Company* **(G-8471)**

Independent Concrete Pipe Company............................... 317 262-4920
  2050 S Harding St Indianapolis (46221) **(G-8471)**

Independent Limestone Co LLC.. 812 824-4951
  6001 S Rockport Rd Bloomington (47403) **(G-887)**

Independent Pallet LLC.. 502 356-2757
  3001 Progress Way Sellersburg (47172) **(G-14601)**

Independent Plastic Inc.. 765 521-2251
  3060 S Commerce Dr New Castle (47362) **(G-12869)**

Independent Protection Co (PA).. 574 533-4116
  1607 S Main St Goshen (46526) **(G-6172)**

Independent Protection Co.. 574 831-5680
  67895 Industrial Dr New Paris (46553) **(G-12960)**

Independent Rail Corporation.. 317 780-8480
  6233 Brookville Rd Indianapolis (46219) **(G-8472)**

Independent Water Tech, Whitestown *Also Called: Canature Watergroup USA Inc* **(G-16802)**

Indev Gauging Systems Inc... 815 282-4463
  5350 N 13th St Terre Haute (47805) **(G-15615)**

Indian Creek Outdoor Power LLC...................................... 812 597-3055
  250 W Mulberry St Morgantown (46160) **(G-12258)**

Indian Trail Wines LLC... 574 889-2509
  7540 N County Road 350 W Royal Center (46978) **(G-14391)**

Indiana Aircraft Hardware Co... 317 485-6500
  221 S Main St Fortville (46040) **(G-5600)**

Indiana Arcelormittal Harbor LLC...................................... 219 399-1200
  3210 Watling St East Chicago (46312) **(G-3020)**

Indiana Architectural Plywood (PA)................................... 317 878-4822
  750 E Park St Trafalgar (46181) **(G-15829)**

Indiana Artisan Inc.. 317 607-8715
  22 N Rangeline Rd Carmel (46032) **(G-1665)**

Indiana Assemblies LLC.. 812 662-2173
  1424 W Main St Greensburg (47240) **(G-6607)**

Indiana Auto Dealers Assn Svcs....................................... 317 635-1441
  150 W Market St Ste 812 Indianapolis (46204) **(G-8473)**

Indiana Automotive Fas Inc... 317 467-0100
  1300 Anderson Blvd Greenfield (46140) **(G-6511)**

Indiana Baking Co... 260 483-5997
  9025 Sunburst Ln Fort Wayne (46804) **(G-5098)**

Indiana Barrier Wall LLC.. 260 747-5777
  7107 Smith Rd Fort Wayne (46809) **(G-5099)**

Indiana Baton Twirling Assoc.. 317 769-6826
  6920 S 280 E Lebanon (46052) **(G-10902)**

Indiana Bevel Inc.. 317 596-0001
  8605 South St Fishers (46038) **(G-4544)**

Indiana Botanic Gardens Inc.. 219 947-4040
  3401 W 37th Ave Hobart (46342) **(G-7191)**

Indiana Box Company.. 317 462-7743
  2200 Royal Dr Greenfield (46140) **(G-6512)**

Indiana Box Company (DH)... 260 356-9660
  1200 Riverfork Dr Huntington (46750) **(G-7326)**

Indiana Brick Co., Carmel *Also Called: Southfield Corporation* **(G-1767)**

Indiana Bridge, Muncie *Also Called: Indiana Bridge Inc* **(G-12424)**

Indiana Bridge Inc.. 765 288-1985
  1810 S Macedonia Ave Muncie (47302) **(G-12424)**

Indiana Business People LLC.. 317 455-4040
  7176 Lakeview Parkway West Dr Indianapolis (46268) **(G-8474)**

Indiana Cardinal, Evansville *Also Called: Martin Holding Company LLC* **(G-4190)**

Indiana Carton Company Inc.. 574 546-3848
  1721 W Bike St Bremen (46506) **(G-1197)**

Indiana Cast Metals Assn Inc... 317 974-1830
  Indianapolis (46244) **(G-8475)**

Indiana Cast Stone Company.. 317 847-5429
  4288 Freedom Rd Spencer (47460) **(G-15350)**

Indiana Chemical Inc.. 317 912-3800
  8070 Castleton Rd Unit 413-414 Indianapolis (46250) **(G-8476)**

Indiana City Brewing LLC... 317 643-1103
  1036 W 136th St Carmel (46032) **(G-1666)**

Indiana Clipper Blade Co, Greenfield *Also Called: Certified Clipper Inc* **(G-6478)**

Indiana Coal Mining Institute... 812 232-5011
  322 S 6th St Terre Haute (47807) **(G-15616)**

Indiana Coated Fabrics Inc.. 574 269-1280
  102 Enterprise Dr Warsaw (46580) **(G-16376)**

ALPHABETIC SECTION — Indiana Oxide Corporation

Indiana Coatings Division, Fort Wayne *Also Called: PPG Industries Inc (G-5334)*
Indiana Custom Embroidery, Indianapolis *Also Called: Profit Finders Incorporated (G-9223)*
Indiana Custom Fabrication Inc 812 727-8900
  113 High St Hope (47246) *(G-7227)*
Indiana Custom Machining, Columbus *Also Called: Pamela Taulman (G-2372)*
Indiana Custom Trucks LLC 260 463-3244
  1095 N 925 W Shipshewana (46565) *(G-14852)*
Indiana Cut Stone Inc 812 275-0264
  616 Guthrie Rd Bedford (47421) *(G-643)*
Indiana Daily Student, Bloomington *Also Called: Trustees Indiana University (G-996)*
Indiana Department Educatio 765 361-5247
  100 N Senate Ave Rm N248 Indianapolis (46204) *(G-8477)*
Indiana Dimension Inc 574 739-2319
  1621 W Market St Logansport (46947) *(G-11082)*
Indiana Dimensional Pdts LLC 574 834-7681
  7224 N State Road 13 North Webster (46555) *(G-13306)*
Indiana Discount Tire Company 574 875-8547
  3711 S Main St Elkhart (46517) *(G-3421)*
Indiana Discount Tire Company 574 549-6060
  857 N Parker St Warsaw (46582) *(G-16377)*
Indiana Distribution Center, Indianapolis *Also Called: Ole Mexican Foods Inc (G-9045)*
Indiana Division, Whiteland *Also Called: Cellofoam North America Inc (G-16778)*
Indiana Drilling Company Inc (PA) 812 477-1575
  1410 N Cullen Ave Evansville (47715) *(G-4119)*
Indiana Ductile, Noblesville *Also Called: In Ductile LLC (G-13101)*
Indiana Emergency Lighting LLC 260 463-1277
  10709 E 100 S Marion (46953) *(G-11294)*
Indiana Fabric Solutions Inc 812 279-0255
  2030 John Williams Blvd Bedford (47421) *(G-644)*
Indiana Factory Outlet Mar Inc 260 799-4764
  3450 S 1100 W-57 Larwill (46764) *(G-10819)*
Indiana Fan & Fabrication, Indianapolis *Also Called: Horner Industrial Services Inc (G-8418)*
Indiana Fencing Academy, Mishawaka *Also Called: Fencing Advisory Assoc Inc (G-11896)*
Indiana Fiber Works 317 524-5711
  625 E 11th St Indianapolis (46202) *(G-8478)*
Indiana Fine Blanking 574 772-3850
  1200 Kloeckner Dr Knox (46534) *(G-10211)*
Indiana Fine Blanking, Knox *Also Called: Mpi Engineered Tech Win LLC (G-10216)*
Indiana Flame Service 219 787-7129
  250 W Us Highway 12 Chesterton (46304) *(G-1937)*
Indiana Furniture, Jasper *Also Called: Indiana Furniture Industries Inc (G-9845)*
Indiana Furniture Industries Inc (PA) 812 482-5727
  1224 Mill St Jasper (47546) *(G-9845)*
Indiana Galvanizing LLC 574 822-9102
  51702 Lovejoy Dr Middlebury (46540) *(G-11723)*
Indiana Gratings Inc 765 342-7191
  210 W Douglas St Martinsville (46151) *(G-11404)*
Indiana Gravel LLC 574 538-7152
  66541 Us Highway 33 Goshen (46526) *(G-6173)*
Indiana Green Burial LLC 812 961-1960
  219 Terre Haute Rd Worthington (47471) *(G-16961)*
Indiana Grocery Group LLC 219 462-5147
  555 Coolwood Dr Valparaiso (46385) *(G-15971)*
Indiana Handpiece Repair Inc 260 436-0765
  9530 Old Grist Mill Pl Fort Wayne (46835) *(G-5100)*
Indiana Harbor, East Chicago *Also Called: Cleveland-Cliffs Steel LLC (G-3000)*
Indiana Harbor Coke Company LP 219 397-5769
  3210 Watling St East Chicago (46312) *(G-3021)*
Indiana Heat Transfer Corporation 574 936-3171
  500 West Harrison Street Salem (47167) *(G-14484)*
Indiana Home Pro LLC 812 968-4822
  200 S Capitol Ave Corydon (47112) *(G-2501)*
Indiana Im Holdings Inc (PA) 260 637-3101
  13415 Coldwater Rd Fort Wayne (46845) *(G-5101)*
Indiana Imprint LLC 812 704-2773
  7352 S Meadows Ln French Lick (47432) *(G-5846)*
Indiana Industrial Svcs LLC (PA) 317 769-6099
  5294 Performance Way Whitestown (46075) *(G-16810)*
Indiana Instruments Inc 317 875-8032
  8032 Gordon Dr Indianapolis (46278) *(G-8479)*

Indiana Integrated Circuits In 574 217-4612
  1400 E Angela Blvd South Bend (46617) *(G-15077)*
Indiana Interactive LLC 317 233-2010
  151 W Ohio St # 100 Indianapolis (46204) *(G-8480)*
Indiana Interstate Entps LLC 260 463-8100
  1695 E Us Highway 20 Lagrange (46761) *(G-10743)*
Indiana Intgrated Circuits LLC 574 217-4612
  1400 E Angela Blvd Unit 107 South Bend (46617) *(G-15078)*
Indiana Knitwear Corporation (PA) 317 462-4413
  230 E Osage St Greenfield (46140) *(G-6513)*
Indiana Labor News, Indianapolis *Also Called: Labor News Inc (G-8710)*
Indiana Law Journal, Bloomington *Also Called: Trustees Indiana University (G-995)*
Indiana Lime Stone Co, Bedford *Also Called: Indiana Lmstone Acqisition LLC (G-645)*
Indiana Limestone Company, Bloomington *Also Called: Indiana Lmstone Acqisition LLC (G-888)*
Indiana Limestone Company, Oolitic *Also Called: Victor Oolitic Stone Company (G-13360)*
Indiana Lmstone Acqisition LLC 812 275-5556
  7056 State Road 158 Bedford (47421) *(G-645)*
Indiana Lmstone Acqisition LLC (DH) 812 275-3341
  120 W 7th St Ste 210 Bloomington (47404) *(G-888)*
Indiana Logo Sign Group 800 950-1093
  600 E 96th St Ste 460 Indianapolis (46240) *(G-8481)*
Indiana Lumber Inc 812 837-9493
  8215 S State Road 446 Bloomington (47401) *(G-889)*
Indiana Manufacturing Inst 765 494-4935
  1105 Challenger Ave West Lafayette (47906) *(G-16595)*
Indiana Marine Products, Angola *Also Called: Imp Holdings LLC (G-263)*
Indiana Marine Products, Angola *Also Called: Patrick Industries Inc (G-282)*
Indiana Marujun LLC 765 584-7639
  200 Inks Dr Winchester (47394) *(G-16891)*
Indiana Masonry LLC 317 937-4275
  955 Burbank Rd Indianapolis (46219) *(G-8482)*
Indiana Materials Proc LLC 260 244-6026
  5750 E Rail Connect Dr Columbia City (46725) *(G-2155)*
Indiana Media Group, Anderson *Also Called: Cnhi LLC (G-95)*
Indiana Metal Craft Inc 812 336-2362
  4602 W Innovation Dr Bloomington (47404) *(G-890)*
Indiana Metal Stamping Co 574 936-2964
  500 W Harrison St Plymouth (46563) *(G-13783)*
Indiana Micro Met Etching Inc 574 293-3342
  1906 Clover Rd Mishawaka (46545) *(G-11910)*
Indiana Mills & Manufacturing (PA) 317 896-9531
  18881 Immi Way Westfield (46074) *(G-16699)*
Indiana Mobile Marine LLC 317 961-1881
  3720 Tade Ln Indianapolis (46234) *(G-8483)*
Indiana Mobile Welding LLC 317 771-8900
  245 Riverwood Dr Noblesville (46062) *(G-13102)*
Indiana Model Company Inc 317 787-6358
  6136 E Hanna Ave Indianapolis (46203) *(G-8484)*
Indiana Nanotech LLC 317 385-1578
  7750 Centerstone Dr Indianapolis (46259) *(G-8485)*
Indiana Natural Infusions LLC (PA) 847 754-9277
  287 Westmeadow Pl Lowell (46356) *(G-11163)*
Indiana News Media LLC 812 703-2025
  10132 N Hickory Ln Columbus (47203) *(G-2323)*
Indiana News Media LLC (PA) 812 546-4940
  645 Harrison St Hope (47246) *(G-7228)*
Indiana Newspapers LLC 317 444-3800
  8278 Georgetown Rd Indianapolis (46268) *(G-8486)*
Indiana Newspapers LLC (DH) 317 444-4000
  130 S Meridian St Indianapolis (46225) *(G-8487)*
Indiana Newspapers LLC 765 213-5700
  220 S Walnut St Muncie (47305) *(G-12425)*
Indiana Newspapers LLC 812 886-9955
  702 Main St Vincennes (47591) *(G-16131)*
Indiana Operations LLC 812 847-8924
  325 Se 12th Street Linton (47441) *(G-11035)*
Indiana Ordnance Works Inc (PA) 812 256-4478
  11020 E Fitzpatrick Ln Pekin (47165) *(G-13517)*
Indiana Oxide Corporation 812 446-2525
  10665 N State Road 59 Brazil (47834) *(G-1145)*

Indiana Oxygen Company Inc

ALPHABETIC SECTION

Indiana Oxygen Company Inc (PA).................................. 317 290-0003
6099 Corporate Way Indianapolis (46278) *(G-8488)*

Indiana Oxygen Company Inc.. 765 662-8700
2215 S Western Ave Marion (46953) *(G-11295)*

Indiana Packers Corporation (HQ)................................. 765 564-3680
6755 W 100 N Delphi (46923) *(G-2899)*

Indiana Pallet Company... 219 398-4223
724 E Chicago Ave East Chicago (46312) *(G-3022)*

Indiana Petroleum Contractors (PA).............................. 812 477-1575
1410 N Cullen Ave Evansville (47715) *(G-4120)*

Indiana Plastics LLC.. 574 294-3253
2221 Industrial Pkwy Elkhart (46516) *(G-3422)*

Indiana Polymers Inc... 219 762-9550
333 W 806 N Valparaiso Valparaiso (46385) *(G-15972)*

Indiana Powder Coatings Inc... 615 347-2787
9413 N Tower Rd Brazil (47834) *(G-1146)*

Indiana PQ Stucco LLC... 317 685-0246
325 S Oakland Ave Indianapolis (46201) *(G-8489)*

Indiana Precast Inc... 812 372-7771
895 Jonesville Rd Columbus (47201) *(G-2324)*

Indiana Precision Forge LLC.. 317 421-0102
302 Northbrook Dr Shelbyville (46176) *(G-14760)*

Indiana Precision Plastics Inc.. 765 762-2452
701 State Road 28 E Williamsport (47993) *(G-16849)*

Indiana Precision Technology.. 317 462-3015
400 W New Rd Greenfield (46140) *(G-6514)*

Indiana Precision Tooling Inc... 812 667-5141
4233 S Farmers Retreat Rd Dillsboro (47018) *(G-2947)*

Indiana Pub Brdcstg Stns Inc... 317 489-4477
1630 N Meridian St Ste 2105 Indianapolis (46202) *(G-8490)*

Indiana Quarriers & Carvers... 812 935-8383
562 Kentucky Hollow Rd Bedford (47421) *(G-646)*

Indiana Refractories Inc.. 260 426-3286
1815 S Anthony Blvd Fort Wayne (46803) *(G-5102)*

Indiana Research Institute... 812 378-5363
1402 Hutchins Ave Columbus (47201) *(G-2325)*

Indiana Research Institute (PA)..................................... 812 378-4221
4571 N Long Rd Columbus (47203) *(G-2326)*

Indiana Review, Bloomington Also Called: Trustees Indiana University *(G-997)*

Indiana Ribbon Inc.. 219 279-2112
106 N 2nd St Wolcott (47995) *(G-16931)*

Indiana Rmnce Writers Amer Inc................................... 317 695-5255
11807 Allisonville Rd 552 Fishers (46038) *(G-4545)*

Indiana Rug Company.. 574 252-4653
900 Cleveland St Mishawaka (46544) *(G-11911)*

Indiana Scale Company Inc... 812 232-0893
1607 Maple Ave Terre Haute (47804) *(G-15617)*

Indiana Sction of The Prof Glf....................................... 317 738-9696
2625 Hurricane Rd Franklin (46131) *(G-5744)*

Indiana Seal... 317 841-3547
9329 Castlegate Dr Indianapolis (46256) *(G-8491)*

Indiana Service Pros LLC.. 317 658-4673
839 Shelbys Crst Shelbyville (46176) *(G-14761)*

Indiana Sign & Barricade Inc... 317 377-8000
5240 E 25th St Indianapolis (46218) *(G-8492)*

Indiana Signworks, Fort Wayne Also Called: Indiana Stamp Co Inc *(G-5103)*

Indiana Soap Company.. 317 448-5295
3252 W Sunset Dr N Greenfield (46140) *(G-6515)*

Indiana Southern Millwork Inc (PA)................................ 812 346-6129
819 Buckeye St North Vernon (47265) *(G-13280)*

Indiana Southern Mold Corp.. 812 346-2622
2945 N State Highway 3 North Vernon (47265) *(G-13281)*

Indiana Spike & Rail Co LLC.. 812 352-7349
39 N Pike St Vernon (47282) *(G-16096)*

Indiana Stamp Co Inc... 260 407-4165
1319 Production Rd Fort Wayne (46808) *(G-5103)*

Indiana Stamp Co Inc (PA)... 260 424-8973
1319 Production Rd Fort Wayne (46808) *(G-5104)*

Indiana Standards Laboratory, Indianapolis Also Called: Chance Ind Standards Lab Inc *(G-7783)*

Indiana State Governmen.. 623 326-6826
101 W Ohio St Ste 500 Indianapolis (46204) *(G-8493)*

Indiana State Medical Assn... 317 261-2060
322 Canal Walk Indianapolis (46202) *(G-8494)*

Indiana Steel & Engrg Inc (PA)....................................... 812 275-3363
957 J St Bedford (47421) *(G-647)*

Indiana Steel Fabricating Inc (PA)................................. 317 247-4545
4545 W Bradbury Ave Indianapolis (46241) *(G-8495)*

Indiana Steel Fabricating Inc... 765 742-1031
925 S 1st St Lafayette (47905) *(G-10606)*

Indiana Steel Rule & Die, Indianapolis Also Called: Indiana Steel Rule Die Inc *(G-8496)*

Indiana Steel Rule Die Inc... 317 352-9859
6331 English Ave Indianapolis (46219) *(G-8496)*

Indiana Stone Works... 812 279-0448
11438 Us Highway 50 W Bedford (47421) *(G-648)*

Indiana Team Yearbook.. 812 858-7113
6999 Cottage Ln Newburgh (47630) *(G-13007)*

Indiana Thermal Solutions LLC...................................... 317 570-5400
6872 Hillsdale Ct Bldg 375 Indianapolis (46250) *(G-8497)*

Indiana Ticket Company, Muncie Also Called: Muncie Novelty Company Inc *(G-12463)*

Indiana Tool Inc... 765 825-7117
6260 Industrial Ave N Connersville (47331) *(G-2444)*

Indiana Tool & Mfg Co Inc.. 574 936-2112
6100 Michigan Rd Plymouth (46563) *(G-13784)*

Indiana Transmission.. 765 854-4201
3660 Us Highway 31 N Kokomo (46901) *(G-10287)*

Indiana Tube Corporation (DH)...................................... 812 467-7155
2100 Lexington Rd Evansville (47720) *(G-4121)*

Indiana Ultrasound LLC.. 219 746-6662
2055 W 64th Pl Merrillville (46410) *(G-11524)*

Indiana Univ Schl Medicine.. 317 278-6518
980 W Walnut St Indianapolis (46202) *(G-8498)*

Indiana Vac-Form Inc.. 574 269-1725
2030 N Boeing Rd Warsaw (46582) *(G-16378)*

Indiana Veneers, Indianapolis Also Called: Indiana Veneers Corp *(G-8499)*

Indiana Veneers Corp... 317 926-2458
1121 E 24th St Indianapolis (46205) *(G-8499)*

Indiana Whiskey Co.. 574 339-1737
1115 W Sample St South Bend (46619) *(G-15079)*

Indiana Whitesell Corporation....................................... 317 279-3278
5101 Decatur Blvd Ste W Indianapolis (46241) *(G-8500)*

Indiana Whl Wine & Lq Co Inc....................................... 317 667-0231
1240 Brookville Way Ste J Indianapolis (46239) *(G-8501)*

Indiana Wire Assembly, Hamilton Also Called: E M F Corp *(G-6852)*

Indiana Wire Die Co, Huntington Also Called: Royer Enterprises Inc *(G-7362)*

Indiana Wire Products Inc... 812 663-7441
915 N Ireland St Greensburg (47240) *(G-6608)*

Indiana Wood Products Inc.. 574 825-2129
58228 County Road 43 Middlebury (46540) *(G-11724)*

Indiana Wrap Company LLC.. 219 902-4997
6200 Broadway Merrillville (46410) *(G-11525)*

Indianapolis In... 855 628-3458
8520 E 33rd St Indianapolis (46226) *(G-8502)*

Indianapolis - Pipe, Indianapolis Also Called: Cemex Materials LLC *(G-7767)*

Indianapolis Badge Name Plate, Indianapolis Also Called: Crichlow Industries Inc *(G-7903)*

Indianapolis Container Company................................... 317 580-5000
Indianapolis (46268) *(G-8503)*

Indianapolis Division, Mccordsville Also Called: Southwark Metal Mfg Co *(G-11456)*

Indianapolis Fabrications LLC....................................... 317 600-3522
1125 Brookside Ave Ste G50 Indianapolis (46202) *(G-8504)*

Indianapolis Gatorade.. 317 821-6400
5858 Decatur Blvd Indianapolis (46241) *(G-8505)*

Indianapolis I&I, Indianapolis Also Called: Paragon Medical Inc *(G-9092)*

Indianapolis Industrial Pdts... 317 359-3078
2320 Duke St Indianapolis (46205) *(G-8506)*

Indianapolis Metal Spinning Co..................................... 317 273-7440
1924 Midwest Blvd Indianapolis (46214) *(G-8507)*

Indianapolis Power... 317 834-3871
6075 High St Martinsville (46151) *(G-11405)*

Indianapolis Recorder, Indianapolis Also Called: George P Stewart Printing Co *(G-8278)*

Indianapolis Signworks Inc.. 317 872-8722
5349 W 86th St Indianapolis (46268) *(G-8508)*

ALPHABETIC SECTION — Indy Custom Machine Inc

Indianapolis Social SEC Off.. 800 772-1213
5515 N Post Rd Indianapolis (46216) *(G-8509)*

Indianapolis Star, Indianapolis *Also Called: Indiana Newspapers LLC (G-8486)*

Indianapolis Star, The, Indianapolis *Also Called: Indiana Newspapers LLC (G-8487)*

Indianapolis Thermal Proc, Indianapolis *Also Called: Ooley Products Inc (G-9059)*

Indianapolis Welding Co, Indianapolis *Also Called: Christie Machine Works Co Inc (G-7801)*

Indianapolis Wood Products... 812 752-6944
1273 S Gardner St Scottsburg (47170) *(G-14563)*

Indianapolis Woodworking... 317 345-4180
6745 Barrington Pl Fishers (46038) *(G-4546)*

Indianapolis, In Plant, Indianapolis *Also Called: Prysmian Cbles Systems USA LLC (G-9235)*

Indianna.. 219 947-9533
1931 Northwind Pkwy Hobart (46342) *(G-7192)*

Indianplis Legislative Insight... 317 955-9997
200 W Washington St Ste M12 Indianapolis (46204) *(G-8510)*

Indianplis Press CLB Fndtion I... 317 701-1130
615 N Alabama St Ste 119 Indianapolis (46204) *(G-8511)*

Indianplis Wldg Fbrication LLC.. 317 999-7856
10565 E Southport Rd Indianapolis (46259) *(G-8512)*

Indiengage LLC... 317 331-7781
634 E New York St Indianapolis (46202) *(G-8513)*

Indierail, Indianapolis *Also Called: Independent Rail Corporation (G-8472)*

Indigo Bioautomation Inc.. 317 493-2400
385 City Center Dr Ste 200 Carmel (46032) *(G-1667)*

Indigo Candles... 317 457-9814
640 E 16th St Indianapolis (46202) *(G-8514)*

Indigo Industries LLC.. 480 747-4560
3209 Smith Valley Rd Greenwood (46142) *(G-6715)*

Indilabel LLC... 317 839-8814
2198 Reeves Rd Ste 4c Plainfield (46168) *(G-13689)*

Indilex Aluminum Solutions... 765 825-1141
5120 Western Ave Connersville (47331) *(G-2445)*

Indiwoodworks Company.. 317 283-6931
348 W 44th St Indianapolis (46208) *(G-8515)*

Induction Iron Incorporated... 813 969-3300
403 N 7th Ave Evansville (47710) *(G-4122)*

Industrial Adhesives Indiana... 317 271-2100
8202 Indy Ln Indianapolis (46214) *(G-8516)*

Industrial and Coml Contg Inc... 219 405-8599
3206 Cascade Dr Valparaiso (46383) *(G-15973)*

Industrial Anodizing Co Inc... 317 637-4641
1610 W Washington St Indianapolis (46222) *(G-8517)*

Industrial Axle Company LLC.. 574 294-6651
21611 Protecta Dr Elkhart (46516) *(G-3423)*

Industrial Axle Company LLC (DH)...................................... 574 295-6077
21608 Protecta Dr Elkhart (46516) *(G-3424)*

Industrial Chemical & Envmt Co, Valparaiso *Also Called: Thomas R Clark (G-16065)*

Industrial Combustion Engnrs, Gary *Also Called: Industrial Combustn Engineers (G-5960)*

Industrial Combustn Engineers... 219 949-5066
7000 W 21st Ave Gary (46406) *(G-5960)*

Industrial Container Svcs LLC... 812 283-7659
6213 Gheens Mill Road Alton (47137) *(G-65)*

Industrial Control Service Inc.. 260 356-4698
1321 W Park Dr Huntington (46750) *(G-7327)*

Industrial Controls Corp... 219 884-1141
3821 Vermont St Gary (46409) *(G-5961)*

Industrial Contrs Shtmtl Div, Evansville *Also Called: Sterling Industrial LLC (G-4333)*

Industrial Dielectrics Inc... 317 773-1766
407 S 7th St Noblesville (46060) *(G-13103)*

Industrial Dlctrics Hldngs Inc (PA)....................................... 317 773-1766
15389 North Pointe Blvd Noblesville (46060) *(G-13104)*

Industrial Elec Maint Co, Valparaiso *Also Called: I E M C (G-15966)*

Industrial Engineering Inc.. 260 478-1514
4430 Tielker Rd Fort Wayne (46809) *(G-5105)*

Industrial Engineering NC, Fort Wayne *Also Called: Industrial Engineering Inc (G-5105)*

Industrial Hydraulics Inc.. 317 247-4421
1005 Western Dr Indianapolis (46241) *(G-8518)*

Industrial Lumber Products Inc... 219 324-7697
251 N State Road 39 La Porte (46350) *(G-10427)*

Industrial Machine.. 812 547-5656
1645 Main St Tell City (47586) *(G-15505)*

Industrial Machine & Tool, New Albany *Also Called: Bryant Industries Inc (G-12707)*

Industrial Machining Inc... 219 663-6100
1201 Merrillville Rd Crown Point (46307) *(G-2696)*

Industrial Metal-Fab Inc... 574 288-8368
2806 W Sample St South Bend (46619) *(G-15080)*

Industrial Mint Wldg Machining (PA).................................... 219 393-5531
2nd & Hupp Rd Kingsbury (46345) *(G-10179)*

Industrial Mlding Cnslting DSI... 574 653-2772
630 E Main St Kewanna (46939) *(G-10165)*

Industrial Motor & Tool LLC.. 574 534-8282
60282 County Road 21 Goshen (46528) *(G-6174)*

Industrial Organic Inks Inc.. 219 878-0613
1608 Fox Point Dr Chesterton (46304) *(G-1938)*

Industrial Pallet, Lafayette *Also Called: American Fibertech Corporation (G-10521)*

Industrial Pallet, Mitchell *Also Called: American Fibertech Corporation (G-12031)*

Industrial Pattern Works Inc... 219 362-4547
119 Koomler Dr La Porte (46350) *(G-10428)*

Industrial Physics Inc.. 812 981-3133
100 Quality Ave New Albany (47150) *(G-12747)*

Industrial Plastics Group LLC... 812 831-4053
911 E Virginia St Evansville (47711) *(G-4123)*

Industrial Plating Inc... 765 447-5036
120 N 36th St Lafayette (47905) *(G-10607)*

Industrial Products Div, Akron *Also Called: Sonoco Products Company (G-9)*

Industrial Rep Inc... 260 316-4973
1184 E State Road 120 Fremont (46737) *(G-5823)*

Industrial Sales & Supply Inc.. 317 240-0560
5640 Professional Cir Indianapolis (46241) *(G-8519)*

Industrial Services Co, Evansville *Also Called: Van Zandt Enterprises Inc (G-4366)*

Industrial Sewing Machine Co... 812 425-2255
2750 N Burkhardt Rd Ste 107 Evansville (47715) *(G-4124)*

Industrial Software LLC... 317 862-0650
7657 Stones River Ct Indianapolis (46259) *(G-8520)*

Industrial Steel and Sup Corp... 219 865-0500
645 65th St Ste 5 Schererville (46375) *(G-14524)*

Industrial Steel Cnstr Inc.. 219 885-5610
86 N Bridge St Gary (46404) *(G-5962)*

Industrial Steel Co Division, Elkhart *Also Called: Flexco Products Inc (G-3348)*

Industrial Steering Pdts Inc (PA)... 260 488-1880
7790 S Homestead Dr Hamilton (46742) *(G-6856)*

Industrial Tool & Die Corp.. 812 424-9971
2201 Lexington Rd Evansville (47720) *(G-4125)*

Industrial Tool & Mfg Co.. 219 932-8670
4901 Calumet Ave Hammond (46327) *(G-6955)*

Industrial Transmission Eqp... 574 936-3028
2033 Western Ave Plymouth (46563) *(G-13785)*

Industrial Trning Unlmted Corp... 812 961-8801
8184 E Station Dugger (47848) *(G-2957)*

Industrial Tube Components Inc.. 317 431-2188
6114 N County Road 50 W Lizton (46149) *(G-11049)*

Industrial Water MGT Inc... 317 889-0836
5365 W Minnesota St Indianapolis (46241) *(G-8521)*

Industrial Woodkraft Inc (PA).. 812 897-4893
811 Hyrock Blvd Boonville (47601) *(G-1087)*

Industrial Woodkraft Inc.. 812 827-6544
251 E 30th St Jasper (47546) *(G-9846)*

Indy Aerospace Inc... 817 521-6508
2801 Fortune Cir E Ste J Indianapolis (46241) *(G-8522)*

Indy Asset Brokers Corporation.. 317 502-2749
11762 N Smokey Row Rd Mooresville (46158) *(G-12213)*

Indy Auto Graphics, Indianapolis *Also Called: Hot Rod Car Care LLC (G-8421)*

Indy Cbd Plus LLP.. 317 600-6362
10911 Parker Dr Indianapolis (46231) *(G-8523)*

Indy Color Printing LLC... 317 371-8829
6220 Hardegan St Indianapolis (46227) *(G-8524)*

Indy Composite Works Inc... 317 280-9766
4960 Markham Way Apt 532 Zionsville (46077) *(G-17018)*

Indy Control Corporation... 317 787-4639
308 Main St Beech Grove (46107) *(G-692)*

Indy Custom Machine Inc.. 317 271-1544
8267 Indy Ct Indianapolis (46214) *(G-8525)*

Indy Cylinder Head Inc   **ALPHABETIC SECTION**

Indy Cylinder Head Inc 317 862-3724
   8621 Southeastern Ave Ste B Indianapolis (46239) *(G-8526)*

Indy Glass Center Inc 317 591-5000
   6366 E 32nd Ct Indianapolis (46226) *(G-8527)*

Indy Hanger, Indianapolis *Also Called: Innovative Fabrication LLC (G-8555)*

Indy High Btu LLC 317 749-0732
   2319 Kentucky Ave Indianapolis (46221) *(G-8528)*

Indy Hoods LLC 317 731-7170
   1367 Sadlier Circle South Dr Indianapolis (46239) *(G-8529)*

Indy Imaging Inc 317 917-7938
   1300 W 16th St Indianapolis (46202) *(G-8530)*

Indy Lash and Brow LLC 502 751-4947
   7404 Franklin Parke Ct Indianapolis (46259) *(G-8531)*

Indy Medical Supplies LLC 866 744-9013
   650 S 800 E Zionsville (46077) *(G-17019)*

Indy Metal Finishing Co 317 858-5353
   468 Southpoint Cir Ste 500 Brownsburg (46112) *(G-1372)*

Indy Parts Inc 317 243-7171
   2 Gasoline Aly # A Indianapolis (46222) *(G-8532)*

Indy Powder Coating Inc 317 244-2231
   4300 W 10th St Indianapolis (46222) *(G-8533)*

Indy Powder Coatings LLC 317 236-7177
   10482 Winghaven Dr Noblesville (46060) *(G-13105)*

Indy Prfmce Composites Inc 317 858-7793
   1185 E Northfield Dr Ste A Brownsburg (46112) *(G-1373)*

Indy Products Company 317 831-1114
   1225 Indianapolis Rd Mooresville (46158) *(G-12214)*

Indy Side Piece LLC 317 426-3927
   6015 E 34th St Indianapolis (46226) *(G-8534)*

Indy Stud Welding Inc 317 416-3617
   2654 Allen Ave Indianapolis (46203) *(G-8535)*

Indy Tube Fabrication LLC 317 883-2000
   398 Cincinnati St Franklin (46131) *(G-5745)*

Indy W EMB Silk Screening LLC 317 634-4906
   1417 E Riverside Dr Indianapolis (46202) *(G-8536)*

Indy Web Inc 317 536-1201
   3151 Madison Ave Indianapolis (46227) *(G-8537)*

Indy Wide Format 317 912-1385
   8905 Stonebriar Dr Indianapolis (46259) *(G-8538)*

Indy Wiring Services LLC 317 371-7044
   150 Gasoline Aly Brownsburg (46112) *(G-1374)*

Indycoast Partners LLC 317 454-1050
   2258 Finchley Rd Carmel (46032) *(G-1668)*

Indys Infant Center LLC 317 717-3622
   2842 Boulevard Pl Indianapolis (46208) *(G-8539)*

Indys Pro Graphix Inc 317 769-3205
   11275 E 300 S Zionsville (46077) *(G-17020)*

Indys Sign Source Inc 317 372-2260
   5501 W 86th St Ste C Indianapolis (46268) *(G-8540)*

Infineon Tech Americas Corp 866 951-9519
   2529 Commerce Dr Ste H Kokomo (46902) *(G-10288)*

Infinias LLC 317 348-1249
   9340 Priority Way West Dr Indianapolis (46240) *(G-8541)*

Infinite Ai Inc 317 965-4850
   1950 E Greyhound Pass Ste 18-169 Carmel (46033) *(G-1669)*

Infinite Lifts LLC 260 388-2868
   615 Arthur St Huntington (46750) *(G-7328)*

Infinitprint Solutions Inc 765 962-1507
   217 S 4th St Richmond (47374) *(G-14139)*

Infinity Drones LLC 812 457-7140
   5700 High School Rd Poseyville (47633) *(G-13978)*

Infinity Molding & Assembly Inc 812 838-0370
   5520 Industrial Rd Mount Vernon (47620) *(G-12300)*

Infinity Performance Inc 317 479-1017
   7002 N Park Ave Indianapolis (46220) *(G-8542)*

Infinity Plastics Group Ltd 812 838-0370
   5520 Industrial Rd Mount Vernon (47620) *(G-12301)*

Infinity Products Inc 317 272-3435
   2340 E Perry Rd Ste 109 Plainfield (46168) *(G-13690)*

Infinity Uv Inc 269 625-3423
   4240 Pine Creek Rd Elkhart (46516) *(G-3425)*

Info Publishing Impact LLC 317 912-3642
   9869 Worthington Blvd Fishers (46038) *(G-4547)*

Info-Lite, Indianapolis *Also Called: Sojane Technologies Inc (G-9458)*

Infobind Systems Inc 260 248-4989
   3619 Centennial Dr Fort Wayne (46808) *(G-5106)*

Infologix Inc 260 485-7380
   14670 Cumberland Rd Noblesville (46060) *(G-13106)*

Informa Business Media Inc 317 233-1310
   4639 W Stonehaven Ln New Palestine (46163) *(G-12938)*

Infosoft Inc 574 262-9800
   2911 Moose Trl Elkhart (46514) *(G-3426)*

Infrared Lab Systems LLC 317 896-1565
   17408 Tiller Ct Ste 1900 Westfield (46074) *(G-16700)*

Infrared Technologies LLC 317 326-2019
   6531 E 200 N Greenfield (46140) *(G-6516)*

Infront Software LLC 317 501-1871
   10785 Harbor Bay Ct Fishers (46040) *(G-4642)*

Ingenus LLC 317 430-1855
   5664 Fen Ct Indianapolis (46220) *(G-8543)*

Ingleside Holdings L P 574 273-7000
   4100 Edison Lakes Pkwy Mishawaka (46545) *(G-11912)*

Ingram Road Quarry LLC 812 824-3730
   303 E Ingram Rd Springville (47462) *(G-15386)*

Ingredion Incorporated 317 635-4455
   1050 W Raymond St Indianapolis (46221) *(G-8544)*

Ingredion Incorporated 317 635-4455
   1515 Drover St Indianapolis (46221) *(G-8545)*

Ingredion Incorporated 317 295-4122
   5521 W 74th St Indianapolis (46268) *(G-8546)*

Ingredion Incorporated 800 713-0208
   319 Warrior Trl Whiteland (46184) *(G-16789)*

Ingroup 317 817-9997
   200 W Washington St Ste M12 Indianapolis (46204) *(G-8547)*

Inhabit Inc 317 636-1699
   211 S Ritter Ave Ste B Indianapolis (46219) *(G-8548)*

Injection Mold Inc 812 346-7002
   134 E O And M Ave North Vernon (47265) *(G-13282)*

Injection Plastics 574 784-2070
   12798 2a Road Lapaz (46537) *(G-10815)*

Injection Plastics & Mfg Co 574 784-2070
   12140 Us Hwy 6 E Lapaz (46537) *(G-10816)*

Ink - LLC 317 502-6473
   290 Fairway Lakes Dr Franklin (46131) *(G-5746)*

Ink Dawgz LLC 219 781-6972
   380 S 100 W Valparaiso (46385) *(G-15974)*

Ink Spot 260 482-4492
   215 W State Blvd Fort Wayne (46808) *(G-5107)*

Ink Spot Tattoo 260 244-0025
   302 S Main St Columbia City (46725) *(G-2156)*

Ink Trax Promotional Solutions 317 336-6921
   6157 Terra Ln Mccordsville (46055) *(G-11452)*

Ink Well, Indianapolis *Also Called: Carlton Ventures Inc (G-7746)*

Inkworks Studio LLC 812 401-6203
   767 S Green River Rd Evansville (47715) *(G-4126)*

Inland Container 317 876-0768
   4030 Vincennes Rd Indianapolis (46268) *(G-8549)*

Inland Paper Board & Packaging 317 879-9710
   5461 W 79th St Indianapolis (46268) *(G-8550)*

Inline Cleaning Systems, Logansport *Also Called: Engineering and Industrial Services LLC (G-11073)*

Inline Shirt Printing LLC 765 647-6356
   5062 State Road 252 Brookville (47012) *(G-1326)*

Innerprint Inc 317 509-6511
   12940 Rocky Pointe Rd Fishers (46055) *(G-4643)*

Innocor Foam Tech - Acp Inc 574 294-7694
   1900 W Lusher Ave Elkhart (46517) *(G-3427)*

Innoleo LLC 561 994-8905
   6510 Telecom Dr Ste 165 Indianapolis (46278) *(G-8551)*

Innomark Communications, Richmond *Also Called: Grafcor Inc (G-14127)*

Innotek Custom Solutions LLC 260 341-8691
   429 E Dupont Rd Ste 49 Fort Wayne (46825) *(G-5108)*

ALPHABETIC SECTION — Integrated Power Services LLC

Innovated Machine Service Inc 219 462-4467
514 E 400 S Valparaiso (46383) *(G-15975)*

Innovations Amplified LLC 317 339-4685
2255 Colfax Ln Indianapolis (46260) *(G-8552)*

Innovations By 260 413-1869
2611 Lincroft Dr Fort Wayne (46845) *(G-5109)*

Innovative 3d Mfg LLC 317 560-5080
600 International Dr Franklin (46131) *(G-5747)*

Innovative Battery Power Inc 260 267-6582
10827 Middleford Pl Fort Wayne (46818) *(G-5110)*

Innovative Casting Tech, Franklin Also Called: Dualtech Inc *(G-5727)*

Innovative Casting Tech Inc 317 738-5966
2100 Earlywood Dr Franklin (46131) *(G-5748)*

Innovative Chem Resources Inc 317 695-6001
6464 Rucker Rd Indianapolis (46220) *(G-8553)*

Innovative Composites Ltd 574 857-2224
5408 State St Ste 25 Rochester (46975) *(G-14297)*

Innovative Concepts Group Inc 317 408-0292
8624 Quarterhorse Dr Indianapolis (46256) *(G-8554)*

Innovative Consumer Packaging, Crawfordsville Also Called: Crawford Industries LLC *(G-2557)*

Innovative Corp 317 804-5977
17401 Tiller Ct Ste H Westfield (46074) *(G-16701)*

Innovative Energy Inc 219 696-3639
1204 Erie Ct Crown Point (46307) *(G-2697)*

Innovative Equipment Inc 765 572-2367
9227 W 600 S Westpoint (47992) *(G-16745)*

Innovative Fabrication LLC 317 215-5988
1440 Brookville Way Indianapolis (46239) *(G-8555)*

Innovative Home Offices, Westfield Also Called: Innovative Corp *(G-16701)*

Innovative Media Sciences Inc 317 366-4371
36 Parkview Ave Indianapolis (46201) *(G-8556)*

Innovative Metalworks LLC 260 839-0295
106 S Main St Sidney (46562) *(G-14916)*

Innovative Mold & Machine Inc 317 634-1177
2702 Brill Rd Indianapolis (46225) *(G-8557)*

Innovative Packaging Inc 260 356-6577
1312 Flaxmill Rd Huntington (46750) *(G-7329)*

Innovative Packaging Assoc Inc 260 356-6577
1312 Flaxmill Rd Huntington (46750) *(G-7330)*

Innovative Printing Svcs Inc 812 443-1007
219 W Church St Brazil (47834) *(G-1147)*

Innovative Rescue Systems LLC (PA) 219 548-1028
4201 Montdale Dr Valparaiso (46383) *(G-15976)*

Innovative Signs Llc 317 747-4454
9571 W Quarter Moon Dr Pendleton (46064) *(G-13537)*

Innovative Slots LLC 317 520-7374
2652 Brill Rd Indianapolis (46225) *(G-8558)*

Innovative Welding LLC 574 642-4537
64640 County Road 37 Goshen (46528) *(G-6175)*

Innovtive Cating Solutions Inc 317 879-2222
7950 Georgetown Rd Ste 200 Indianapolis (46268) *(G-8559)*

Innovtive Nurological Dvcs LLC 317 674-2999
13295 Illinois St Ste 312 Carmel (46032) *(G-1670)*

Innovtive Surgical Designs Inc 812 369-4252
3206 Hardscrabble Rd Spencer (47460) *(G-15351)*

Innovtive Toling Solutions Inc 260 487-9970
6225 Commodity Ct Fort Wayne (46818) *(G-5111)*

Inotiv Inc 812 985-5900
10424 Middle Mount Vernon Rd Mount Vernon (47620) *(G-12302)*

Inovateus Solar LLC 574 485-1400
19890 State Line Rd South Bend (46637) *(G-15081)*

Insana Tees 219 801-5104
2808 Woodward St Portage (46368) *(G-13877)*

Insane Wayne's Metal Art, French Lick Also Called: Samuel Powell *(G-5849)*

Inscope Medical Solutions Inc 502 882-0183
110 E Market St New Albany (47150) *(G-12748)*

Insertec Inc (PA) 800 556-1911
4011 W 54th St Indianapolis (46254) *(G-8560)*

Inside Systems 317 831-3772
1053 E Jessup Way Mooresville (46158) *(G-12215)*

Insight Equity Holdings LLC 219 378-1930
4407 Railroad Ave East Chicago (46312) *(G-3023)*

Insight Group, Indianapolis Also Called: Indianplis Legislative Insight *(G-8510)*

Insight Lpr LLC 855 862-5468
11350 N Meridian St Ste 200 Carmel (46032) *(G-1671)*

Insightful Apps LLC 812 361-1057
1357 James Ct Zionsville (46077) *(G-17021)*

Insign Inc 317 251-0131
5812 Linton Ln Indianapolis (46220) *(G-8561)*

Insignia Promotions, Elkhart Also Called: In Stitches Inc *(G-3420)*

Inson Tool & Machine Inc 812 752-3754
833 S Gardner St Scottsburg (47170) *(G-14564)*

Inspire LLC 317 339-7718
6503 Ferguson St Indianapolis (46220) *(G-8562)*

Inspired Fire GL Stdio Gllery 765 474-1981
2124 State Road 25 W Lafayette (47909) *(G-10608)*

Installed Building Pdts LLC 317 398-3216
886 W Mausoleum Rd Shelbyville (46176) *(G-14762)*

Instant Copy, Lafayette Also Called: Twin Prints Inc *(G-10711)*

Instant Warehouse 765 342-3430
1290 Morton Ave Martinsville (46151) *(G-11406)*

Instantwhip-Indianapolis Inc 317 899-1533
9125 Burk Rd Indianapolis (46229) *(G-8563)*

Instate Welding Service Inc 260 437-2894
4911 Industrial Rd Fort Wayne (46825) *(G-5112)*

Institute of Mennonite Studies, Elkhart Also Called: Anabaptist Mnnnite Bblcal Smna *(G-3181)*

Instru-Med, Warsaw Also Called: Med-Cut Inc *(G-16394)*

Instrumental Machine & Dev Inc 574 267-7713
2098 N Pound Dr W Warsaw (46582) *(G-16379)*

Insty-Prints 317 788-1504
930 E Hanna Ave Indianapolis (46227) *(G-8564)*

Insty-Prints, Indianapolis Also Called: Printing Partners East Inc *(G-9207)*

Insty-Prints, Jeffersonville Also Called: Creative Concept Ventures Inc *(G-9964)*

Insul-Coustic Corporation 260 420-1480
2701 S Coliseum Blvd Ste 1286 Fort Wayne (46803) *(G-5113)*

Insulation Fabricators Inc (DH) 219 845-2008
2501 165th St Ste 3 Hammond (46320) *(G-6956)*

Insulation Specialties of Amer 219 733-2502
1095 Kabert Dr Wanatah (46390) *(G-16290)*

Insulpedia LLC 317 459-4030
11430 Idlewood Dr Fishers (46037) *(G-4548)*

Insultech, Indianapolis Also Called: Insultech LLC *(G-8565)*

Insultech LLC 317 389-5134
2681 Rand Rd Indianapolis (46241) *(G-8565)*

Insurance, Clarksville Also Called: Tidy Janitorial Services LLC *(G-2039)*

Insurance Publishing Plus, Carmel Also Called: Rough Notes Company Inc *(G-1746)*

Intat Precision Inc 765 932-5323
2148 N State Road 3 Rushville (46173) *(G-14401)*

Intech Automation Systems Corp 209 836-8610
206 N Grant St Peru (46970) *(G-13587)*

Intech Trailers Inc 574 221-8231
29286 County Road 52 Nappanee (46550) *(G-12614)*

Integer Holdings Corporation 260 373-1664
4545 Kroemer Rd Fort Wayne (46818) *(G-5114)*

Integer Holdings Corporation 317 454-8800
3737 N Arlington Ave Indianapolis (46218) *(G-8566)*

Integra-Tec Machining LLC 574 289-2629
3702 W Sample St Ste 4045 South Bend (46619) *(G-15082)*

Integral Technologies Inc 812 550-1770
2605 Eastside Park Rd Ste 1 Evansville (47715) *(G-4127)*

Integrated Custom Components, Fort Wayne Also Called: Iasa Group LLC *(G-5090)*

Integrated De Icing Servi 317 517-1643
7899 S Service Rd Ste H Indianapolis (46241) *(G-8567)*

Integrated Energy Technologies Inc 812 421-7810
225 W Morgan Ave Ste A Evansville (47710) *(G-4128)*

Integrated Instrument Svcs Inc 317 248-1958
5601 Fortune Cir S Ste A Indianapolis (46241) *(G-8568)*

Integrated Orthotic Lab Inc 317 852-4640
1630 E Northfield Dr Ste 400 Brownsburg (46112) *(G-1375)*

Integrated Power Services LLC 812 665-4400
6751 Frontage Rd Poseyville (47633) *(G-13979)*

Integrated Sealing Systems Div, Syracuse *Also Called: Parker-Hannifin Corporation* *(G-15471)*

Integrated Systems MGT Inc.. 765 565-6108
7002 W 1000 N # B Carthage (46115) *(G-1815)*

Integrated Tech Resources.. 317 757-5432
2445 Directors Row Ste J Indianapolis (46241) *(G-8569)*

Integrated Technology LLC.. 574 300-9412
221 W Lexington Ave Elkhart (46516) *(G-3428)*

Integrative Flavors, Michigan City *Also Called: Williams West & Witts Pdts Co* *(G-11687)*

Integrity, Plainfield *Also Called: Integrity Rttional Molding LLC* *(G-13692)*

Integrity Defense Services Inc.. 812 675-4913
1463 S State Road 45 Springville (47462) *(G-15387)*

Integrity EDM LLC.. 317 333-7630
641 Cleveland St Tipton (46072) *(G-15775)*

Integrity Fiber Supply LLC (HQ).. 317 290-1140
10 W Carmel Dr Ste 300 Carmel (46032) *(G-1672)*

Integrity Hearing (PA).. 317 882-9151
5628 Merritt Cir Noblesville (46062) *(G-13107)*

Integrity Machine Systems Inc.. 317 897-3338
22 S Westside Dr New Palestine (46163) *(G-12939)*

Integrity Marketing Team Inc.. 317 517-0012
4067 Cheltonham Ct Plainfield (46168) *(G-13691)*

Integrity Qntum Innvations LLC.. 765 537-9037
6830 Hancock Ridge Rd Martinsville (46151) *(G-11407)*

Integrity Rttional Molding LLC.. 317 837-1101
701 N Carr Rd Plainfield (46168) *(G-13692)*

Integrity Sign Solutions Inc.. 502 233-8755
4302 Security Pkwy New Albany (47150) *(G-12749)*

Integrity Woodcrafting.. 260 562-2067
4285 N 500 W Shipshewana (46565) *(G-14853)*

Intellectual Quality LLC.. 708 979-3127
5004 Trotter Dr Lafayette (47905) *(G-10609)*

Intelligent Software Inc.. 219 923-6166
9609 Cypress Ave Munster (46321) *(G-12543)*

Intelliquote.. 530 669-6840
13548 Zubrick Rd Roanoke (46783) *(G-14270)*

Intelliray Inc.. 260 547-4399
10262 N 550 W Decatur (46733) *(G-2864)*

Intempo Software Inc.. 800 950-2221
8777 Purdue Rd Ste 340 Indianapolis (46268) *(G-8570)*

Inteplast Building Products.. 574 825-5845
219 W Us Highway 20 Middlebury (46540) *(G-11725)*

Inteplast Group Corporation.. 219 220-2528
3505 W Us Highway 24 Remington (47977) *(G-14035)*

Inteprintations.. 765 404-0887
8909 Stonewall Dr Indianapolis (46231) *(G-8571)*

Inter Print At Ions.. 765 404-0887
10630 E County Road 750 N Brownsburg (46112) *(G-1376)*

Inter-Cntnntal Gear Brake USA.. 317 268-0040
923 Whitaker Rd Plainfield (46168) *(G-13693)*

Interactions Incorporated.. 574 722-6207
1031 N 3rd St Logansport (46947) *(G-11083)*

Interactive Engineering Inc.. 574 272-5851
15925 Fair Banks Ct Granger (46530) *(G-6354)*

Interactive Intelligence Inc.. 317 872-3000
7601 Interactive Way Indianapolis (46278) *(G-8572)*

Interactive Intelligence Inc.. 803 699-7778
7601 Interactive Way Indianapolis (46278) *(G-8573)*

Interactive Intelligence Group Inc.. 317 872-3000
7601 Interactive Way Indianapolis (46278) *(G-8574)*

Interactive Intelligence Inc.. 800 267-1364
7601 Interactive Way Indianapolis (46278) *(G-8575)*

Interactive Surface Tech LLC.. 812 246-0900
1511 Avco Blvd Sellersburg (47172) *(G-14602)*

Interchurch Print Shop, Indianapolis *Also Called: Perfect Impressions Printing* *(G-9121)*

Interebar Fabricators LLC.. 630 701-9204
4531 Columbia Ave Ste C Hammond (46327) *(G-6957)*

Interfaith Resources, Heltonville *Also Called: Special Ideas Incorporated* *(G-7111)*

Interior Fixs & Mllwk Co Inc.. 812 446-0933
995 E Barnett St Knightsville (47857) *(G-10202)*

Interlight, Hammond *Also Called: International Lighting LLC* *(G-6958)*

Intermetco Processing Inc.. 812 423-5914
1901 W Louisiana St Evansville (47710) *(G-4129)*

Internal Honing Service, Paoli *Also Called: G and P Enterprises Ind Inc* *(G-13495)*

International A I Inc.. 812 824-2473
7909 S Fairfax Rd Bloomington (47401) *(G-891)*

International Bakers Service.. 574 287-7111
1902 N Sheridan St South Bend (46628) *(G-15083)*

International Brake Inds Inc.. 419 905-7468
4300 Quality Dr South Bend (46628) *(G-15084)*

International Code Council Inc.. 317 879-1677
1223 S Richland St Indianapolis (46221) *(G-8576)*

International English Inc.. 260 868-2670
3597 County Road 75 Butler (46721) *(G-1467)*

International Food Tech Inc.. 812 853-9432
8499 Spencer Dr Newburgh (47630) *(G-13008)*

International Fuel Systems.. 317 345-3302
751 International Dr Franklin (46131) *(G-5749)*

International Fuse LLC.. 574 340-4042
2206 Mishawaka Ave South Bend (46615) *(G-15085)*

International Game Technology.. 317 731-3791
1302 N Meridian St Indianapolis (46202) *(G-8577)*

International Infusion LP.. 708 710-9200
8618 Jefferson Ave Munster (46321) *(G-12544)*

International Label Mfg LLC.. 812 235-5071
1925 S 13th St Terre Haute (47802) *(G-15618)*

International Lighting LLC.. 219 989-0060
7939 New Jersey Ave Hammond (46323) *(G-6958)*

International Metals Proc, Indianapolis *Also Called: Dz Investments LLC* *(G-8027)*

International Mill Service Inc.. 219 881-0155
1 N Broadway Gary (46402) *(G-5963)*

International Paper, Butler *Also Called: International Paper Company* *(G-1468)*
International Paper, Cayuga *Also Called: International Paper Company* *(G-1822)*
International Paper, Crawfordsville *Also Called: International Paper Company* *(G-2579)*
International Paper, Crawfordsville *Also Called: International Paper Company* *(G-2580)*
International Paper, Fort Wayne *Also Called: International Paper Company* *(G-5115)*
International Paper, Hammond *Also Called: International Paper Company* *(G-6959)*
International Paper, Indianapolis *Also Called: International Paper Company* *(G-8578)*
International Paper, Indianapolis *Also Called: International Paper Company* *(G-8579)*
International Paper, Indianapolis *Also Called: International Paper Company* *(G-8580)*
International Paper, Indianapolis *Also Called: International Paper Company* *(G-8581)*
International Paper, Indianapolis *Also Called: International Paper Company* *(G-8582)*
International Paper, Saint Anthony *Also Called: International Paper Company* *(G-14429)*
International Paper, Terre Haute *Also Called: International Paper Company* *(G-15619)*
International Paper, Tipton *Also Called: International Paper Company* *(G-15776)*

International Paper Company.. 260 868-2151
2626 County Road 71 Butler (46721) *(G-1468)*

International Paper Company.. 765 492-3341
2585 E 200 N Cayuga (47928) *(G-1822)*

International Paper Company.. 765 359-0107
1823 E Elmore St Crawfordsville (47933) *(G-2579)*

International Paper Company.. 765 364-5342
801 N Englewood Dr Crawfordsville (47933) *(G-2580)*

International Paper Company.. 260 747-9111
3904 W Ferguson Rd Fort Wayne (46809) *(G-5115)*

International Paper Company.. 219 844-6509
2501 165th St Ste 3 Hammond (46320) *(G-6959)*

International Paper Company.. 317 870-0192
5012 W 79th St Indianapolis (46268) *(G-8578)*

International Paper Company.. 317 481-4000
7536 Miles Dr Indianapolis (46231) *(G-8579)*

International Paper Company.. 317 715-9080
8501 Moller Rd Indianapolis (46268) *(G-8580)*

International Paper Company.. 317 871-6999
4901 W 79th St Indianapolis (46268) *(G-8581)*

International Paper Company.. 317 390-3300
2135 Stout Field East Dr Indianapolis (46241) *(G-8582)*

International Paper Company.. 812 326-2125
3565 E 550 S St Rt 6 Saint Anthony (47575) *(G-14429)*

International Paper Company.. 800 643-7244
320 S 25th St Ste 2 Terre Haute (47803) *(G-15619)*

ALPHABETIC SECTION — Irvine Window Coverings

International Paper Company 765 675-6732
815 Industrial Dr Tipton (46072) *(G-15776)*

International Rdo & Elec Corp 866 262-8910
2515 Toledo Rd Elkhart (46516) *(G-3429)*

International Resources Inc 317 813-5300
545 Christy Dr Ofc 7304 Greenwood (46143) *(G-6716)*

International Steel Company 812 425-3311
2138 N 6th Ave Evansville (47710) *(G-4130)*

International Wire Group Inc 574 546-4680
833 Legner St Bremen (46506) *(G-1198)*

International Wood Inc 812 883-5778
300 W Hackberry St Salem (47167) *(G-14485)*

International Wood Inc 260 248-1491
2425 E Us Highway 6 Albion (46701) *(G-29)*

Interntional Pipe Cons Sls LLC 765 388-2222
900 New York Ave New Castle (47362) *(G-12870)*

Interntnal Damnd Gold Exch Ltd 317 872-6666
6010 W 86th St Ste 114 Indianapolis (46278) *(G-8583)*

Interntnal Mtl Hdlg Systems In 812 222-4488
806 E Randall St Greensburg (47240) *(G-6609)*

Interntonal Revolving Door Div, Evansville *Also Called: International Steel Company (G-4130)*

Interrachem LLC 812 858-3147
5722 Prospect Dr Newburgh (47630) *(G-13009)*

Interrachem, LLC, Newburgh *Also Called: Interrachem LLC (G-13009)*

Interstate Block Corporation 812 273-1742
3148 Clifty Dr Madison (47250) *(G-11230)*

Interstate Castings, Indianapolis *Also Called: Kitley Company (G-8691)*

Interstate Forestry, Plymouth *Also Called: Interstate Forestry Inc (G-13786)*

Interstate Forestry Inc 574 936-1284
10200 W County Line Rd Plymouth (46563) *(G-13786)*

Interstate Gravel, Williamsport *Also Called: Rogers Group Inc (G-16853)*

Interstate Power Systems Inc 952 854-2044
2601 E 15th Ave Gary (46402) *(G-5964)*

Interstate Powersystems, Gary *Also Called: Interstate Power Systems Inc (G-5964)*

Interstate Steel Erectors Inc (PA) 765 754-7508
1110 E Sigler St Frankton (46044) *(G-5792)*

Interstate Steel Fabricating, Frankton *Also Called: Interstate Steel Erectors Inc (G-5792)*

Interstate Truss LLC 260 463-6124
4875 N 675 W Shipshewana (46565) *(G-14854)*

Intertech Products Inc (HQ) 260 982-1544
906 W Hanley Rd North Manchester (46962) *(G-13235)*

Intervention Diagnostics Inc 317 432-6091
6925 Hawthorn Park Dr Indianapolis (46220) *(G-8584)*

Intimus International NA, Wabash *Also Called: Olympia Business Systems Inc (G-16206)*

Intimusic LLC 574 210-4562
56601 Sonora Ave South Bend (46619) *(G-15086)*

Intratek Engineering, Fort Wayne *Also Called: Intratek Inc (G-5116)*

Intratek Inc 260 484-3377
3209 Clearfield Ct Fort Wayne (46808) *(G-5116)*

Intri-Cut Tool, Roanoke *Also Called: Ex-Cut Technology LLC (G-14263)*

Invacare Corporation 317 838-5500
1100 Whitaker Rd Plainfield (46168) *(G-13694)*

Inventory Solutions Inc 212 749-5027
4305 Saguaro Trl Indianapolis (46268) *(G-8585)*

Inventure Electronics, Goshen *Also Called: Jtd Enterprises Inc (G-6180)*

Inventure Foods Inc 260 824-2800
705 W Dustman Rd Bluffton (46714) *(G-1038)*

Investwell Electronics Inc 765 457-1911
329 E Firmin St Kokomo (46902) *(G-10289)*

Invign LLC 574 971-5498
2514 Messick Dr S Goshen (46526) *(G-6176)*

Inwood Office Environment, Jasper *Also Called: Inwood Office Furniture Inc (G-9847)*

Inwood Office Furniture Inc 812 482-6121
1108 E 15th St Jasper (47546) *(G-9847)*

INX International Ink Co 765 939-6625
1056 Industries Rd Richmond (47374) *(G-14140)*

INX INTERNATIONAL INK CO, Richmond *Also Called: INX International Ink Co (G-14140)*

INX LLC 219 779-0508
4491 Roosevelt St Gary (46408) *(G-5965)*

Io Hvac Controls, Indianapolis *Also Called: Jackson Systems LLC (G-8615)*

Iok Tech, Rising Sun *Also Called: Iok Technology LLC (G-14243)*

Iok Technology LLC 812 308-1366
3293 Salem Ridge Rd Rising Sun (47040) *(G-14243)*

Ioni 2 Inc 219 261-2115
18325 S 580 W Remington (47977) *(G-14036)*

Ionic Cut Stone Incorporated 812 829-3416
1201 Kelley Farm Dr Spencer (47460) *(G-15352)*

Ionpcs LLC 219 510-2073
2867 Carmel St Portage (46368) *(G-13878)*

Iot Technologies Intl LLC 317 824-4544
4525 Saguaro Trl Indianapolis (46268) *(G-8586)*

Iotron Industries USA Inc 260 212-1722
4394 E Park 30 Dr Columbia City (46725) *(G-2157)*

Iowa Limestone Company 317 981-7919
8114 S State Road 243 Cloverdale (46120) *(G-2087)*

Ip Corporation 574 259-1505
1460 E 12th St Mishawaka (46544) *(G-11913)*

Ip Corporation 574 234-1105
1545 S Olive St South Bend (46619) *(G-15087)*

Ip Moulding Inc 574 825-5845
219 W Us Highway 20 Middlebury (46540) *(G-11726)*

Ip Software Inc 317 569-1313
10333 N Meridian St Carmel (46290) *(G-1673)*

Ipfw Student Housing 260 481-4180
2101 E Coliseum Blvd Ste 100 Fort Wayne (46805) *(G-5117)*

Ipg, Evansville *Also Called: Industrial Plastics Group LLC (G-4123)*

Ipheion Custom Technologies, Indianapolis *Also Called: Ipheion Development Corp (G-8587)*

Ipheion Development Corp 240 281-1619
3421 Breckenridge Dr Indianapolis (46228) *(G-8587)*

Ipower Technologies Inc 317 574-0103
4640 Dr Martin Luther King Jr Blvd Anderson (46013) *(G-134)*

Ips, Evansville *Also Called: Smith & Butterfield Co Inc (G-4321)*

Ips Indiana, Indianapolis *Also Called: Ips-Integrated Prj Svcs LLC (G-8588)*

Ips-Integrated Prj Svcs LLC 317 247-1200
320 N Meridian St Ste 212 Indianapolis (46204) *(G-8588)*

Ira William Scott 219 241-5674
407 Center St Valparaiso (46385) *(G-15977)*

IRD Group Inc 812 425-3311
2138 N 6th Ave Evansville (47710) *(G-4131)*

Ireco Metals Inc 574 936-2146
1433 Western Ave Plymouth (46563) *(G-13787)*

Iris Rubber Co Inc 317 984-3561
10 E Jackson St Cicero (46034) *(G-1997)*

Iron Baluster LLC 574 975-0288
1722 Eisenhower Dr N # B Goshen (46526) *(G-6177)*

Iron Bull Manufacturing LLC 765 597-2480
5947 N 350 E Marshall (47859) *(G-11374)*

Iron Dynamics Inc 260 868-8800
4500 County Road 59 Butler (46721) *(G-1469)*

Iron Hawg 317 462-0991
5191 E Us Highway 40 Greenfield (46140) *(G-6517)*

Iron Men Industries Inc 574 596-2251
6086 W 250 S Russiaville (46979) *(G-14423)*

Iron Out Inc 260 483-2519
3404 Conestoga Dr Fort Wayne (46808) *(G-5118)*

Iron Out Inc (PA) 800 654-0791
6714 Pointe Inverness Way Ste 200 Fort Wayne (46804) *(G-5119)*

Iron Timbers LLC 812 614-0467
342 Harvest Ct Versailles (47042) *(G-16101)*

Ironcraft Co Inc 574 272-0866
50655 Indiana State Route 933 South Bend (46637) *(G-15088)*

Ironhorse Detailing Inc 812 939-3300
8445 S State Road 59 Clay City (47841) *(G-2044)*

Ironmonger Spring Division, Walton *Also Called: Walton Industrial Park Inc (G-16284)*

Ironworks Engineering LLC 317 296-9359
3683 W 1100 N New Palestine (46163) *(G-12940)*

Iroquois Bio-Energy Co LLC (HQ) 219 866-2928
751 W State Road 114 Rensselaer (47978) *(G-14054)*

Irvine Shade & Door Inc (PA) 574 522-1446
1000 Verdant St Elkhart (46516) *(G-3430)*

Irvine Window Coverings, Elkhart *Also Called: Irvine Shade & Door Inc (G-3430)*

Irving Materials

ALPHABETIC SECTION

Irving Materials, New Albany *Also Called: IMI South LLC (G-12744)*

Irving Materials Inc..765 644-8819
1601 N Scatterfield Rd Anderson (46012) *(G-135)*

Irving Materials Inc..765 778-4760
5002 S State Road 67 Anderson (46013) *(G-136)*

Irving Materials Inc..812 275-7450
1307 Bundy Ln Bedford (47421) *(G-649)*

Irving Materials Inc..812 333-8530
1800 N Kinser Pike Bloomington (47404) *(G-892)*

Irving Materials Inc..260 824-3428
2321 E 150 N Bluffton (46714) *(G-1039)*

Irving Materials Inc..812 443-4661
305 N Murphy Ave Brazil (47834) *(G-1148)*

Irving Materials Inc..765 647-6533
1352 Fairfield Ave Brookville (47012) *(G-1327)*

Irving Materials Inc..765 478-4914
14413 W Us Highway 40 Cambridge City (47327) *(G-1496)*

Irving Materials Inc..765 825-2581
1998 S State Road 121 Connersville (47331) *(G-2446)*

Irving Materials Inc..765 362-6904
3350 E State Road 32 Crawfordsville (47933) *(G-2581)*

Irving Materials Inc..765 552-5041
2500 S D St Elwood (46036) *(G-3826)*

Irving Materials Inc..812 424-3551
6000 Oak Grove Rd Evansville (47715) *(G-4132)*

Irving Materials Inc..317 326-3101
6300 Ardmore Ave Fort Wayne (46809) *(G-5120)*

Irving Materials Inc..765 654-5333
28 W St Rd Frankfort (46041) *(G-5675)*

Irving Materials Inc (PA)..317 326-3101
8032 N State Road 9 Greenfield (46140) *(G-6518)*

Irving Materials Inc..317 888-0157
6695 W Smith Valley Rd Greenwood (46142) *(G-6717)*

Irving Materials Inc..812 683-4444
615 W 12th St Huntingburg (47542) *(G-7284)*

Irving Materials Inc..260 356-7214
500 Erie Stone Rd Huntington (46750) *(G-7331)*

Irving Materials Inc..317 843-2944
5244 E 96th St Indianapolis (46240) *(G-8589)*

Irving Materials Inc..317 872-0152
4700 W 96th St Indianapolis (46268) *(G-8590)*

Irving Materials Inc..317 783-3381
4200 S Harding St Ste X Indianapolis (46217) *(G-8591)*

Irving Materials Inc..317 243-7391
4330 W Morris St Indianapolis (46241) *(G-8592)*

Irving Materials Inc..317 899-2187
3130 N Post Rd Indianapolis (46226) *(G-8593)*

Irving Materials Inc..765 452-4044
1315 S Dixon Rd Kokomo (46902) *(G-10290)*

Irving Materials Inc..765 922-7285
1420 S Union St Kokomo (46902) *(G-10291)*

Irving Materials Inc..765 423-2533
2903 Old State Road 25 N Lafayette (47905) *(G-10610)*

Irving Materials Inc..765 462-5620
417 Sw St Lebanon (46052) *(G-10903)*

Irving Materials Inc..574 722-3420
2245 S County Road 150 E Logansport (46947) *(G-11084)*

Irving Materials Inc..765 674-2271
3892 S Garthwaite Rd Marion (46953) *(G-11296)*

Irving Materials Inc..765 342-3369
1502 Rogers Rd Martinsville (46151) *(G-11408)*

Irving Materials Inc..765 728-5335
5067 E Cummins Rd Montpelier (47359) *(G-12179)*

Irving Materials Inc..317 831-0224
501 N Samuel Moore Pkwy Mooresville (46158) *(G-12216)*

Irving Materials Inc..765 836-4007
4304 E County Road 350 N Muncie (47303) *(G-12426)*

Irving Materials Inc..765 288-5566
4312 E County Road 350 N Muncie (47303) *(G-12427)*

Irving Materials Inc..765 288-0288
4304 E County Road 350 N Muncie (47303) *(G-12428)*

Irving Materials Inc..317 770-1745
17050 River Rd Noblesville (46062) *(G-13108)*

Irving Materials Inc..317 773-3640
12798 State Road 38 E Noblesville (46060) *(G-13109)*

Irving Materials Inc..574 936-2975
10988 11th Rd Plymouth (46563) *(G-13788)*

Irving Materials Inc..219 261-2441
318 W South St Remington (47977) *(G-14037)*

Irving Materials Inc..812 883-4242
784 N Wilson Rd Scottsburg (47170) *(G-14565)*

Irving Materials Inc..812 829-9445
947 W State Highway 46 Spencer (47460) *(G-15353)*

Irving Materials Inc..765 755-3447
1078 E Luray Rd Springport (47386) *(G-15380)*

Irving Materials Inc..765 922-7931
6455 W 600 S Swayzee (46986) *(G-15451)*

Irving Materials Inc..765 922-7991
6377 W 600 S Swayzee (46986) *(G-15452)*

Irving Materials Inc..765 675-6327
929 E Jefferson St Tipton (46072) *(G-15777)*

Irving Materials Inc..812 254-0820
611 W Main St Washington (47501) *(G-16486)*

Irving Materials Inc..765 743-3806
301 Ahlers Dr West Lafayette (47906) *(G-16596)*

Irving Materials Inc..317 535-7566
600 Tracy Rd Whiteland (46184) *(G-16790)*

Irving Materials Inc..574 946-3754
1132 S Us Highway 35 Winamac (46996) *(G-16864)*

Irving Materials Inc..260 356-7214
500 Erie Stone Rd Huntington (46750) *(G-7332)*

Irwin Hodson Group Indiana LLC...260 482-8052
2980 E Coliseum Blvd Ste 102 Fort Wayne (46805) *(G-5121)*

Isd Precision, Spencer *Also Called: Innovtive Surgical Designs Inc (G-15351)*

Isf Inc...317 251-1219
6468 Rucker Rd Indianapolis (46220) *(G-8594)*

Isg Burns Harbor Services LLC..219 787-2120
250 W Us Highway 12 Burns Harbor (46304) *(G-1452)*

Ishkadiddle Publishing LLC..765 744-8588
2405 N Moors St Muncie (47304) *(G-12429)*

ISI of Indiana Inc..317 241-2999
5342 W Vermont St Indianapolis (46224) *(G-8595)*

Isolatek International, Huntington *Also Called: Usmpc Buyer Inc (G-7376)*

Issi Engrg & Machining LLC...317 240-0560
5640 Professional Cir Indianapolis (46241) *(G-8596)*

Ist Liquidating Inc..812 358-3894
848 W Sweet St Brownstown (47220) *(G-1424)*

It Synergistics..317 627-6858
1283 S Harmony Trl Greenfield (46140) *(G-6519)*

It's Tops, Mishawaka *Also Called: Drike Inc (G-11885)*

Italmac USA Inc..574 243-0217
12743 Heather Park Dr Ste 104 Granger (46530) *(G-6355)*

Itamco Company, Plymouth *Also Called: Indiana Tool & Mfg Co Inc (G-13784)*

Itapmenu LLC...855 687-4827
14300 Clay Terrace Blvd Ste 200 Carmel (46032) *(G-1674)*

Itech Digital, Indianapolis *Also Called: Itech Holdings LLC (G-8597)*

Itech Holdings LLC..317 567-5160
6330 E 75th St Ste 132 Indianapolis (46250) *(G-8597)*

Itera LLC...574 538-3838
19260 County Road 46 Ste 3 New Paris (46553) *(G-12961)*

Itestout.com, Indianapolis *Also Called: College Network Inc (G-7835)*

ITR America LLC (PA)...219 947-8230
6301 Northwind Pkwy Hobart (46342) *(G-7193)*

Its, Westpoint *Also Called: Innovative Equipment Inc (G-16745)*

Its Family Trucking LLC..219 277-7162
7121 Alexander Ave Hammond (46323) *(G-6960)*

Its Personal Laser Engraving...812 934-6657
3243 County Rd 1150 E Batesville (47006) *(G-592)*

Itsuwa America Inc..812 375-0323
1349 Arcadia Dr Columbus (47201) *(G-2327)*

Itsuwa Usa LLC..812 375-0323
1349 Arcadia Dr Columbus (47201) *(G-2328)*

ALPHABETIC SECTION

ITT Communications Systems, Fort Wayne *Also Called: ITT LLC (G-5122)*

ITT LLC.. 260 451-6000
   1919 W Cook Rd Fort Wayne (46818) *(G-5122)*

ITW Gema... 317 298-5000
   4141 W 54th St Indianapolis (46254) *(G-8598)*

ITW Gema, Indianapolis *Also Called: Illinois Tool Works Inc (G-8461)*

Iu East Business Office.. 765 973-8218
   2325 Chester Blvd Richmond (47374) *(G-14141)*

Iu International Svc Ctr.. 812 855-9086
   601 E Kirkwood Ave Bloomington (47405) *(G-893)*

Iuniverse, Bloomington *Also Called: Get Published Inc (G-867)*

Iuniverse Inc... 812 330-2909
   1663 S Liberty Dr Bloomington (47403) *(G-894)*

IVc Industrial Coatings Inc.. 812 442-5080
   2831 E Industrial Park Dr Brazil (47834) *(G-1149)*

Ivy Hill Packaging Division, Indianapolis *Also Called: Multi Packaging Solutions Inc (G-8971)*

IWP LLC.. 812 756-0303
   7207 W Versailles St Holton (47023) *(G-7218)*

J & A Machine Inc.. 260 637-6215
   219 E Quincy St Garrett (46738) *(G-5867)*

J & B Pallet, Warsaw *Also Called: Meagan Inc (G-16393)*

J & B Sales & Induction Srvcs... 765 965-2500
   420 S M St Richmond (47374) *(G-14142)*

J & C Printing Co, Scottsburg *Also Called: Journal & Chronicle Inc (G-14566)*

J & F Steel Corporation... 219 764-3500
   310 Tech Dr Burns Harbor (46304) *(G-1453)*

J & H Tool Inc.. 765 724-9691
   109 S Clinton St Alexandria (46001) *(G-53)*

J & J Boat Works Inc.. 812 667-5902
   502 Miles Ridge Rd Madison (47250) *(G-11231)*

J & J Engineering Inc.. 317 462-2309
   610 W Osage St Greenfield (46140) *(G-6520)*

J & J Industrial Service Inc... 219 362-4973
   2204 E Lincolnway Bldg D La Porte (46350) *(G-10429)*

J & J Oil Well Service Inc... 812 354-9007
   7558 W County Road 225 N Petersburg (47567) *(G-13615)*

J & J Pallet Corp.. 812 288-4487
   640 Miller Ave Clarksville (47129) *(G-2020)*

J & J Pallet Corp (PA)... 812 944-8670
   2234 E Market St New Albany (47150) *(G-12750)*

J & J Printing Co.. 765 642-6642
   2107 State St Anderson (46012) *(G-137)*

J & J Repair.. 574 831-3075
   22064 County Road 142 Goshen (46526) *(G-6178)*

J & J Welding... 219 872-7282
   4100 W 700 N Michigan City (46360) *(G-11627)*

J & J Welding Inc... 812 838-4391
   1114 W 4th St Mount Vernon (47620) *(G-12303)*

J & J Winery.. 765 969-1188
   3415 National Rd W Richmond (47374) *(G-14143)*

J & J Woodcrafters.. 765 436-2466
   2416 N State Road 75 Thorntown (46071) *(G-15752)*

J & K Associates Inc... 317 255-3588
   6302 Rucker Rd Ste C Indianapolis (46220) *(G-8599)*

J & K Supply Inc.. 765 448-1188
   3515 Coleman Ct Lafayette (47905) *(G-10611)*

J & L Dimensional Services Inc... 219 325-3588
   16 Industrial Pkwy La Porte (46350) *(G-10430)*

J & L Future Fiberglass Co... 574 784-2900
   211 W Randolph St Lapaz (46537) *(G-10817)*

J & L Tool & Machine Inc... 317 398-6281
   1441 Miller Ave Shelbyville (46176) *(G-14763)*

J & L Uebelhor Enterprises LLC.. 812 367-1591
   1440 Virginia St Ferdinand (47532) *(G-4436)*

J & N Metal Products LLC.. 812 864-2600
   33 N County Road 250 W Brazil (47834) *(G-1150)*

J & P Custom Plating Inc.. 260 726-9696
   807 N Meridian St Portland (47371) *(G-13951)*

J & P Machine Inc.. 260 357-5157
   1213 S Franklin St Garrett (46738) *(G-5868)*

J & R Tool Inc... 812 295-2557
   1444 Us Highway 50 Loogootee (47553) *(G-11139)*

J & R Welding... 574 862-1590
   29823 County Road 40 Wakarusa (46573) *(G-16235)*

J & T Marine Specialists Inc.. 317 890-9444
   810 S Mitthoeffer Rd Indianapolis (46239) *(G-8600)*

J 2 Systems and Supply LLC.. 317 602-3940
   3820 N Keystone Ave Indianapolis (46205) *(G-8601)*

J A Davis.. 812 354-9129
   802 E Mccoy St Petersburg (47567) *(G-13616)*

J A Smit Inc... 812 424-8141
   1500 N Fulton Ave Evansville (47710) *(G-4133)*

J and G Enterprises.. 219 778-4319
   5556 E 300 N Rolling Prairie (46371) *(G-14365)*

J and N Enterprises Inc.. 219 465-2700
   851 Transport Dr Valparaiso (46383) *(G-15978)*

J B Enterprises, Elkhart *Also Called: Collins Trailers Inc (G-3257)*

J B Hinchman Inc.. 317 359-1808
   100 Gasoline Aly Ste A Indianapolis (46222) *(G-8602)*

J B Tool Die & Engineering Co.. 260 483-9586
   1509 Dividend Rd Fort Wayne (46808) *(G-5123)*

J Borinstein Inc.. 317 252-0875
   5936 N Brandywine Rd Shelbyville (46176) *(G-14764)*

J C Mfg Inc (PA).. 574 834-2881
   7248 N State Road 13 North Webster (46555) *(G-13307)*

J C Penney Optical, Fort Wayne *Also Called: Usv Optical Inc (G-5524)*

J C Sipe Inc.. 317 848-0215
   2949 River Bay Dr N Indianapolis (46240) *(G-8603)*

J C Sipe Jewelers, Indianapolis *Also Called: J C Sipe Inc (G-8603)*

J Coffey Metal Masters Inc.. 317 780-1864
   2514 Bethel Ave Indianapolis (46203) *(G-8604)*

J D Digging.. 260 589-2984
   2636 E State Road 218 Berne (46711) *(G-715)*

J Ennis Fabrics Inc (usa).. 877 953-6647
   853 Columbia Rd Ste 125 Plainfield (46168) *(G-13695)*

J G Bowers Inc... 765 677-1000
   1629 S Joaquin Dr Marion (46953) *(G-11297)*

J G Cabinet & Counter Inc.. 260 723-4275
   2571 S State Road 5 Larwill (46764) *(G-10820)*

J Game Ventures LLC.. 812 241-7096
   3105 Garden View Ter Apt F Danville (46122) *(G-2814)*

J H J Inc... 574 256-6966
   15314 Harrison Rd Mishawaka (46544) *(G-11914)*

J Henrys Machine Shop LLC.. 317 917-1052
   1111 S East St Indianapolis (46225) *(G-8605)*

J J Babbitt Co... 574 315-1639
   2201 Industrial Pkwy Elkhart (46516) *(G-3431)*

J J Lites.. 765 966-3252
   4469 Webster Rd Richmond (47374) *(G-14144)*

J J P Enterprise... 219 947-3154
   442 Quail Dr Hobart (46342) *(G-7194)*

J J Powerwashing, South Bend *Also Called: James Morris (G-15090)*

J Jacoby Inc (PA)... 317 877-9275
   285 Westchester Blvd Noblesville (46062) *(G-13110)*

J Jarrett Engineering Inc... 812 268-3338
   603 S County Road 450 E Sullivan (47882) *(G-15408)*

J Jones Machine LLC.. 765 366-8258
   8876 E 400 S New Ross (47968) *(G-12979)*

J L Harris Machine Co Inc.. 574 834-2866
   4953 N 700 E Leesburg (46538) *(G-10955)*

J L Mfg & Fab, Berne *Also Called: Jl Manfcturing Fabrication Inc (G-716)*

J L Squared Inc.. 317 354-1513
   1347 Sadlier Circle South Dr Indianapolis (46239) *(G-8606)*

J L Wickey Corp.. 260 627-3109
   10107 Graber Rd Grabill (46741) *(G-6303)*

J M Hutton... 765 935-4817
   751 S O St Richmond (47374) *(G-14145)*

J M Hutton & Company, Richmond *Also Called: JM Hutton & Co Inc (G-14152)*

J M McCormick.. 317 874-4444
   8214 Allison Ave Indianapolis (46268) *(G-8607)*

J M Woodworking Co Inc.. 260 627-8362
   10832 Witmer Rd Grabill (46741) *(G-6304)*

J Makes Incorporated... 773 610-9867
   1820 Norwood Dr Griffith (46319) *(G-6809)*

J Miller Cabinet Company, Columbia City *Also Called: J Miller Cabinet Company Inc (G-2158)*

J Miller Cabinet Company Inc... 260 691-2032
5874 N 350 E Columbia City (46725) *(G-2158)*

J O Mory Sheet Metal Division, Avilla *Also Called: JO Mory Inc (G-479)*

J O Wolf Tool & Die Inc... 260 672-2605
550 Condit St Huntington (46750) *(G-7333)*

J P Corporation... 317 783-1000
227 Main St Beech Grove (46107) *(G-693)*

J P Whitt Inc.. 765 759-0521
827 S Tillotson Ave Muncie (47304) *(G-12430)*

J Pinto Wood and Veneer Corp... 317 389-0440
68 N Gale St Ste B Indianapolis (46201) *(G-8608)*

J Plus Products Inc... 317 660-1003
4000 W 106th St Ste 125-217 Carmel (46032) *(G-1675)*

J R and D Exploration Inc... 812 677-2895
1938 W Brumfield Ave Princeton (47670) *(G-14002)*

J R Newby... 765 664-3501
405 N Henderson Ave Marion (46952) *(G-11298)*

J R P Machine Products LLP.. 260 622-4746
420 Carol Ann Ln Ossian (46777) *(G-13427)*

J R Sign Company and Services.. 260 414-0510
2811 Autumn Leaf Ln Fort Wayne (46808) *(G-5124)*

J Robert Switzer... 765 474-1307
1020 Beck Ln Lafayette (47909) *(G-10612)*

J Squared Inc (PA)... 317 866-5638
2588 Jannetides Blvd Greenfield (46140) *(G-6521)*

J T Custom Woodcraft, Middletown *Also Called: Jeff Goodnight (G-11771)*

J T D Spiral Inc... 260 497-1300
6212 Highview Dr Fort Wayne (46818) *(G-5125)*

J T Woodworking LLC.. 513 543-1130
20531 Heather Ct Lawrenceburg (47025) *(G-10842)*

J Tees... 812 524-9292
9389 N County Road 100 E Seymour (47274) *(G-14658)*

J Trockman & Sons Inc.. 812 425-5271
1017 Bayse St Evansville (47714) *(G-4134)*

J V C Machining... 219 462-0363
766 N 500 E Valparaiso (46383) *(G-15979)*

J V Crane & Engineering Inc.. 219 942-8566
3084 Edgewood St Portage (46368) *(G-13879)*

J W Hicks Inc (PA)... 219 736-2212
8955 Louisiana St Merrillville (46410) *(G-11526)*

J W Jones Company LLC... 765 537-2279
2468 S State Road 67 Paragon (46166) *(G-13501)*

J W Model & Engineering Inc... 317 788-7471
5508 Elmwood Ave Ste 406 Indianapolis (46203) *(G-8609)*

J W P Vinyl Designs... 812 873-8744
5210 E Private Road 415 S Dupont (47231) *(G-2964)*

J-N Sheet Metal Company Inc.. 260 436-7916
2828 Covington Rd Fort Wayne (46802) *(G-5126)*

J.R. Graber Wood Box Division, Grabill *Also Called: JR Graber & Sons LLC (G-6306)*

J&J Sprts Screen Prtg Sprit Wr.. 812 909-2686
3012 Covert Ave Ste B Evansville (47714) *(G-4135)*

J&J Welding, Michigan City *Also Called: J & J Welding (G-11627)*

J&K Generations.. 812 508-1094
1233 Brown Station Rd Bedford (47421) *(G-650)*

J&K Yurts Inc.. 317 377-9878
4375 Sellers St Indianapolis (46226) *(G-8610)*

J&P Custom Designs Inc... 317 253-2198
550 W 65th St Indianapolis (46260) *(G-8611)*

J2 S&S, Indianapolis *Also Called: J 2 Systems and Supply LLC (G-8601)*

J4 Printing LLC... 260 417-5382
1008 Orlando Dr Fort Wayne (46825) *(G-5127)*

Jabra Signs & Graphics... 765 584-7100
406 S Brown St Winchester (47394) *(G-16892)*

Jac Jmr Inc... 219 663-6700
1421 E Summit St Crown Point (46307) *(G-2698)*

Jack Forney.. 812 334-1259
512 W 15th St Bloomington (47404) *(G-895)*

Jack Frost LLC... 812 477-7244
1401 N Fares Ave Evansville (47711) *(G-4136)*

Jack Howard.. 317 788-7643
1915 S State Ave Indianapolis (46203) *(G-8612)*

Jack Laurie Coml Floors Inc... 317 569-2095
7998 Georgetown Rd Indianapolis (46268) *(G-8613)*

Jack Mix... 812 923-8679
3400 Lawrence Banet Rd Floyds Knobs (47119) *(G-4682)*

Jack O'Brien Welding Service, Greencastle *Also Called: OBrien Jack & Pat Enterprises (G-6422)*

Jackie Collection LLC.. 219 678-8176
1400 E 51st Pl Gary (46409) *(G-5966)*

Jackson Brothers Lumber Co.. 812 847-7812
59 State Rd S Linton (47441) *(G-11036)*

Jackson Group Inc.. 317 791-9000
5804 Churchman Byp Indianapolis (46203) *(G-8614)*

Jackson Hewitt Tax Service.. 574 255-2200
922 S Beiger St Mishawaka (46544) *(G-11915)*

Jackson Hewitt Tax Service, Warsaw *Also Called: Worth Tax and Financial Svc (G-16456)*

Jackson Seed Service LLC.. 812 480-6555
14510 Old State Rd Evansville (47725) *(G-4137)*

Jackson Systems LLC... 888 359-0365
5418 Elmwood Ave Indianapolis (46203) *(G-8615)*

Jackson Technologies LLC... 812 258-9939
3007 Charlestown Xing Ste B200 New Albany (47150) *(G-12751)*

Jackson Vision Quest.. 219 882-9397
521 Broadway Gary (46402) *(G-5967)*

Jackson-Jennings LLC.. 812 522-4911
103 Community Dr Seymour (47274) *(G-14659)*

Jacksons 33 Transporting LLC.. 901 628-7803
3172 N Capitol Ave Indianapolis (46208) *(G-8616)*

Jacksons Woodworks LLC.. 765 623-0638
1609 N E St Elwood (46036) *(G-3827)*

Jacob Adams... 765 564-2314
108 E Main St Delphi (46923) *(G-2900)*

Jacobs & Brichford LLC... 765 692-0056
2957 S State Road 1 Connersville (47331) *(G-2447)*

Jacobs Advertising Inc.. 260 854-2054
6170 S 520 E Wolcottville (46795) *(G-16939)*

Jacobs Company LLC.. 317 818-8500
10661 Winterwood Carmel (46032) *(G-1676)*

Jacobs Machine & Tool Co Inc.. 317 831-2917
315 E Washington St Mooresville (46158) *(G-12217)*

Jacobs Mfg LLC... 765 490-6111
218 Trowbridge Dr Lafayette (47909) *(G-10613)*

Jacobs Mfg LLC... 574 583-3883
806 N 1st St Monticello (47960) *(G-12154)*

Jacqmain Machine & Welding... 812 726-4409
1070 N Mcclure Rd Vincennes (47591) *(G-16132)*

Jacyl Technology Inc (PA)... 260 471-6067
6020 Huguenard Rd Fort Wayne (46818) *(G-5128)*

Jacyl Web Design, Fort Wayne *Also Called: Jacyl Technology Inc (G-5128)*

Jadco Ltd... 219 661-2065
401 N Jackson St Crown Point (46307) *(G-2699)*

Jae Enterprises Inc (PA)... 260 489-6249
7707 Freedom Way Fort Wayne (46818) *(G-5129)*

Jae Enterprises Inc.. 260 747-0568
8000 Baer Rd Fort Wayne (46809) *(G-5130)*

Jaeger-Ntek Sling Slutions Inc.. 219 324-1111
115 Koomler Dr La Porte (46350) *(G-10431)*

Jag Metal... 812 235-7200
1633 Harding Ave Terre Haute (47802) *(G-15620)*

Jag Metal Spinning Inc.. 812 533-5501
1022 Crawford St Sandford (47885) *(G-14506)*

Jag Mobile Solutions Inc... 260 562-1045
770 E State Road 120 Howe (46746) *(G-7237)*

Jag Wire LLC... 260 463-8537
130 E 200 N Lagrange (46761) *(G-10744)*

Jake Eddies Signs... 765 962-1892
923 N E St Richmond (47374) *(G-14146)*

Jam Printing Inc.. 765 649-9292
1200 Meridian St Anderson (46016) *(G-138)*

James A Andrew Inc.. 765 269-9807
665 Maple Point Dr Lafayette (47904) *(G-10614)*

James Billingsley.. 765 301-9171
101 Percy L Julian Dr Greencastle (46135) *(G-6414)*

ALPHABETIC SECTION

James Brummett.. 317 724-4131
  212 Woodberry Dr Danville (46122) *(G-2815)*

James Conner Welding LLC................................ 765 230-0455
  5133 N 700 E Darlington (47940) *(G-2833)*

James David Inc.. 260 744-0579
  11323 Nightingale Cv Roanoke (46783) *(G-14271)*

James E Barnhizer.. 765 458-9344
  2302 Omar Fields Dr Liberty (47353) *(G-10989)*

James E Trowbridge... 260 341-1952
  2629 Carroll Rd Fort Wayne (46818) *(G-5131)*

James Electronics Div., North Manchester *Also Called: Custom Magnetics Inc* *(G-13231)*

James F Reilly 3 Ent... 574 277-8267
  1969 E Mckinley Ave Mishawaka (46545) *(G-11916)*

James G Henager.. 812 795-2230
  8837 S State Road 57 Elberfeld (47613) *(G-3115)*

James Harper.. 812 267-4251
  426 E Main St Nw Depauw (47115) *(G-2939)*

James Lake Vineyard Inc.................................... 260 495-9463
  6208 N Van Guilder Rd Fremont (46737) *(G-5824)*

James McBryde... 206 504-4689
  1251 N Eddy St South Bend (46617) *(G-15089)*

James Morris.. 574 387-2615
  1042 N Elmer St South Bend (46628) *(G-15090)*

James R McNutt.. 317 899-6955
  3130 N Mitthoefer Rd Indianapolis (46235) *(G-8617)*

James Smith.. 260 414-1237
  1320 Goshen Ave Fort Wayne (46808) *(G-5132)*

James W Hager... 765 643-0188
  5731 N 100 E Alexandria (46001) *(G-54)*

James Wafford.. 317 773-7200
  1720 S 10th St Noblesville (46060) *(G-13111)*

Jamil Packaging Corporation (PA)..................... 574 256-2600
  1420 Industrial Dr Mishawaka (46544) *(G-11917)*

Jamplast Inc.. 812 838-8562
  7451 Highway 62 E Mount Vernon (47620) *(G-12304)*

Janco Engineered Products LLC....................... 574 255-3169
  1217 E 7th St Mishawaka (46544) *(G-11918)*

Janelle Davis... 765 635-6233
  1604 S Madison Ave Anderson (46016) *(G-139)*

Janels Body Bar LLC... 219 455-4888
  1116 Broadway Gary (46407) *(G-5968)*

Janesville Acoustics, Richmond *Also Called: Jason Incorporated* *(G-14148)*

Janets Embroidery... 219 261-2812
  9515 W 1600 S Goodland (47948) *(G-6082)*

Janette Walker.. 219 937-9160
  1050 Eaton St Hammond (46320) *(G-6961)*

Jani Industries Inc... 317 985-3916
  2256 N County Road 800 E Avon (46123) *(G-528)*

Janice Cabinetry LLC.. 219 741-8120
  1066 Farrell St Valparaiso (46385) *(G-15980)*

Janis Buhl... 765 478-5448
  26 W Church St Cambridge City (47327) *(G-1497)*

Jans Sewing Things.. 812 945-8113
  201 Hausfeldt Ln New Albany (47150) *(G-12752)*

Jarrod Zachary Weld... 765 230-6424
  3384 E State Road 32 Crawfordsville (47933) *(G-2582)*

Jason, Richmond *Also Called: Jason Holdings Inc* *(G-14147)*

Jason Babbs... 812 595-9073
  3869 N Whitsett Rd Austin (47102) *(G-466)*

Jason Holdings Inc (PA)..................................... 414 277-9300
  833 E Michigan St Ste 900 Richmond (47374) *(G-14147)*

Jason Incorporated... 248 455-7919
  2350 Salisbury Rd N Richmond (47374) *(G-14148)*

Jason Incorporated... 765 965-5333
  2350 Salisbury Rd N Richmond (47374) *(G-14149)*

Jason Incorporated... 847 215-1948
  2350 Salisbury Rd N Richmond (47374) *(G-14150)*

Jason Sword LLC... 502 550-4183
  1405 Valley View Rd New Albany (47150) *(G-12753)*

Jasper Chair Company....................................... 812 482-5239
  534 E 8th St Jasper (47546) *(G-9848)*

Jasper Desk Company Inc................................. 812 482-4132
  415 E 6th St Jasper (47546) *(G-9849)*

Jasper Electric Motor Inc (HQ)......................... 812 482-1660
  815 Wernsing Rd Jasper (47546) *(G-9850)*

Jasper Electric Motor Inc.................................. 812 482-1660
  733 W Division Rd Jasper (47546) *(G-9851)*

Jasper EMB & Screen Prtg................................ 812 482-4787
  310 Main St Jasper (47546) *(G-9852)*

Jasper EMB & Screenprinting, Jasper *Also Called: Jasper EMB & Screen Prtg* *(G-9852)*

Jasper Engine Exchange Inc (PA).................... 812 482-1041
  815 Wernsing Rd Jasper (47546) *(G-9853)*

Jasper Engine Exchange Inc............................. 812 482-1041
  6400 E Industrial Ln Leavenworth (47137) *(G-10870)*

Jasper Engines & Transmissions, Jasper *Also Called: Jasper Engine Exchange Inc* *(G-9853)*

Jasper Equipment Company LLC..................... 219 866-0600
  701 N Melville St Rensselaer (47978) *(G-14055)*

Jasper Group, Paoli *Also Called: Jasper Seating Company Inc* *(G-13498)*

Jasper Group Brands, Jasper *Also Called: Jasper Seating Company Inc* *(G-9858)*

Jasper Holdings Inc (PA)................................... 812 482-1041
  815 Wernsing Rd Jasper (47546) *(G-9854)*

Jasper Plastics Solutions, Syracuse *Also Called: Jp Incorporated - Indiana* *(G-15465)*

Jasper Rubber Products Inc.............................. 812 482-3242
  1093 1st Ave W Jasper (47546) *(G-9855)*

Jasper Rubber Products Inc (DH).................... 812 482-3242
  1010 1st Ave W Jasper (47546) *(G-9856)*

Jasper Seating Company Inc............................. 812 936-9977
  8084 W County Road 25 S French Lick (47432) *(G-5847)*

Jasper Seating Company Inc............................. 812 771-4500
  932 Mill St Jasper (47546) *(G-9857)*

Jasper Seating Company Inc (PA).................... 812 482-3204
  225 Clay St Jasper (47546) *(G-9858)*

Jasper Seating Company Inc............................. 812 723-1323
  1352 W Hospital Rd Paoli (47454) *(G-13498)*

Jasper Veneer Inc.. 812 482-4245
  810 W 14th St Jasper (47546) *(G-9859)*

Jasper Willow Springs Mo LLC........................ 800 827-7455
  815 Wernsing Rd Jasper (47546) *(G-9860)*

Jaszy Drinks LLC.. 219 742-5013
  1572 Ralston St Gary (46406) *(G-5969)*

Jay C Food 84.. 812 886-9311
  1400 Washington Ave Vincennes (47591) *(G-16133)*

Jay Costas Companies Inc................................ 219 663-4364
  1492 N Main St Crown Point (46307) *(G-2700)*

Jay Orner Sons Billiard Co Inc (PA)................ 317 243-0046
  6333 Rockville Rd Indianapolis (46214) *(G-8618)*

Jayco Inc (HQ)... 574 825-5861
  903 S Main St Middlebury (46540) *(G-11727)*

Jays Woodworking Direct LLC.......................... 219 345-3335
  387 E 800 N Lake Village (46349) *(G-10781)*

Jaz Industrial LLC... 812 305-5692
  13040 Reising Ln Evansville (47720) *(G-4138)*

JB Bond Construction LLC............................... 219 628-4606
  252 E Burdick Rd Chesterton (46304) *(G-1939)*

JB Graphics Inc.. 317 819-0008
  250 W Tansey Xing Westfield (46074) *(G-16702)*

Jbd Machining... 765 671-9050
  1702 W Jeffras Ave Marion (46952) *(G-11299)*

Jbj Custom Woodworking Inc........................... 260 450-7295
  22221 S County Line Rd E Monroeville (46773) *(G-12070)*

Jbl Signals and Lighting LLC............................ 574 855-2251
  4316 Technology Dr South Bend (46628) *(G-15091)*

Jbm Race Cars LLC.. 812 305-3666
  7901 Newburgh Rd Evansville (47715) *(G-4139)*

Jbs New Third Publishing LLC.......................... 812 262-8595
  2 Fairhurst Ct Terre Haute (47802) *(G-15621)*

Jbs Powder Coating LLC.................................... 812 952-1204
  7320 Thomas Ave Ne Lanesville (47136) *(G-10799)*

Jbs United Inc... 317 758-2609
  322 S Main St Sheridan (46069) *(G-14824)*

Jbs United Inc... 765 296-4539
  3503 W County Road 300 N Frankfort (46041) *(G-5676)*

Jbs Welding...	317 946-8676
1350 N Harvey Rd Greenwood (46143) *(G-6718)*	
JC Creations LLC..	574 248-0126
219 W Dewey St Bremen (46506) *(G-1199)*	
JC Metal Fabrication LLC.....................................	574 340-1109
15393 Kelly Rd Mishawaka (46544) *(G-11919)*	
JC Moag Corporation..	812 284-8400
4835 Research Blvd Ne Georgetown (47122) *(G-6063)*	
JC Printing...	574 721-9000
301 Burlington Ave Logansport (46947) *(G-11085)*	
JC Refrigeration LLC..	260 768-4067
6495 W 200 N Shipshewana (46565) *(G-14855)*	
Jcantave Transit LLC..	855 608-2777
7375 Mariner Way Apt 311 Indianapolis (46214) *(G-8619)*	
Jci Jones Chemicals Inc.......................................	317 787-8382
600 Bethel Ave Beech Grove (46107) *(G-694)*	
Jcj Fabrication LLC...	765 621-9556
1653 W 500 S Anderson (46013) *(G-140)*	
Jcmz Enterprises Inc..	812 372-0288
725 S Mapleton St Columbus (47201) *(G-2329)*	
Jcr Automation Inc...	260 749-6606
1426 Ryan Rd New Haven (46774) *(G-12907)*	
Jcs Technologies Inc..	317 201-5064
13872 Wendessa Dr Fishers (46038) *(G-4549)*	
JD Engineered Products LLC...............................	260 316-2907
2725 E 500 S Hamilton (46742) *(G-6857)*	
JD Materials...	219 662-1418
11563 Baker St Crown Point (46307) *(G-2701)*	
Jdb Manufacturing LLC...	317 752-8756
1010 E Sumner Ave Indianapolis (46227) *(G-8620)*	
JDC Veneers Inc...	812 284-9775
276 America Pl Jeffersonville (47130) *(G-10003)*	
Jdh Logistics LLC...	573 529-2005
313 E Park St Fort Branch (47648) *(G-4705)*	
Jdld Enterprises Inc...	765 481-2210
507 Indianapolis Ave Lebanon (46052) *(G-10904)*	
Jds International Inc..	317 753-4427
15321 Herriman Blvd Noblesville (46060) *(G-13112)*	
Jds Pughs Cabinets Inc.......................................	317 835-2910
4195 W Pitcher Dr Trafalgar (46181) *(G-15830)*	
Jdsu Acterna Holdings LLC..................................	317 788-9351
5808 Churchman Byp Indianapolis (46203) *(G-8621)*	
JE Mnnix Well Srvcing Mini E................................	765 855-5464
5997 Smoker Rd Centerville (47330) *(G-1850)*	
Jeannie and Rachel Heidenreich..........................	260 244-4583
1240 N Airport Rd Columbia City (46725) *(G-2159)*	
Jeans Extrusions Inc..	812 883-2581
201 Jeans Dr Salem (47167) *(G-14486)*	
Jec Steel Company (PA)......................................	574 326-3829
1151 Bloomingdale Dr Bristol (46507) *(G-1268)*	
Jec Steel Company...	574 326-3829
57587 County Road 29 Goshen (46528) *(G-6179)*	
Jeco Plastic Products LLC..................................	317 839-4943
885 Andico Rd Plainfield (46168) *(G-13696)*	
Jeda Equipment Services Inc..............................	317 842-9377
13270 Summerwood Ln Fishers (46038) *(G-4550)*	
Jedeu Industries LLC..	317 660-5526
154 Eastgate Cir Mishawaka (46544) *(G-11920)*	
Jef Enterprises Inc (PA).......................................	812 425-0628
1200 W Columbia St Evansville (47710) *(G-4140)*	
Jeff Goodnight...	765 779-4867
5444 S County Road 350 E Middletown (47356) *(G-11771)*	
Jeff Goshert..	260 672-3737
11301 Us Highway 24 W Fort Wayne (46814) *(G-5133)*	
Jeff Hurst Custom Wdwkg Inc..............................	812 367-1430
8134 S State Road 162 Ferdinand (47532) *(G-4437)*	
Jeff Hury Hrdwood Flors Pntg S...........................	812 204-8650
629 S Norman Ave Evansville (47714) *(G-4141)*	
Jeff Snyder..	260 349-0405
3273 N Old State Road 3 Kendallville (46755) *(G-10120)*	
Jefferson Homebuilders Inc.................................	317 398-3125
701 W Mausoleum Rd Shelbyville (46176) *(G-14765)*	
Jeffs Farm Svc..	812 254-1980
1328 N 300 W Washington (47501) *(G-16487)*	
Jem Printing Inc..	812 376-9264
808 3rd St Ste C Columbus (47201) *(G-2330)*	
Jemarkel Health-Tech LLC..................................	219 548-5881
2701 Beech St Ste R Valparaiso (46383) *(G-15981)*	
Jenco Engineering Inc...	574 267-4608
27 E 250 N Warsaw (46582) *(G-16380)*	
Jenmar Enterprises LLC.......................................	219 306-3149
19268 Chicory Ct Noblesville (46060) *(G-13113)*	
Jennerjahn Machine Inc.......................................	765 998-2733
701 N Miller Ave Marion (46952) *(G-11300)*	
Jennings County Pallets Inc................................	812 458-6288
5195 E Us Highway 50 Butlerville (47223) *(G-1484)*	
Jennings County Pallets Inc................................	812 458-6288
5195 E Us Highway 50 Butlerville (47223) *(G-1485)*	
Jensen Cabinet Inc...	260 456-2131
205 Murray St Fort Wayne (46803) *(G-5134)*	
Jensen Publications Inc.......................................	317 514-8864
7333 Fox Hollow Rdg Zionsville (46077) *(G-17022)*	
Jenson Industries Inc..	317 871-0122
8219 Zionsville Rd Indianapolis (46268) *(G-8622)*	
Jenstar Asphalt LLC..	219 963-6263
3003 E 15th Pl Gary (46403) *(G-5970)*	
Jer-Maur Corporation..	812 384-8290
119 E Main St Bloomfield (47424) *(G-750)*	
Jerden Industries Inc...	812 332-1762
1104 S Morton St Bloomington (47403) *(G-896)*	
Jeremy Parker...	765 284-5414
3501 N Granville Ave Ste 95 Muncie (47303) *(G-12431)*	
Jerico Metal Specialties Inc................................	812 339-3182
1111 W 17th St Ste 1 Bloomington (47404) *(G-897)*	
Jerome Pagell...	219 226-0591
1752 Broadacre Rd Crown Point (46307) *(G-2702)*	
Jerrels & Company LLC.......................................	317 691-6045
135 Parkview Rd Carmel (46032) *(G-1677)*	
Jerry Hillenburg Co...	317 422-8884
8365 Woodlawn Dr Martinsville (46151) *(G-11409)*	
Jerry L Fuelling...	317 709-6978
8470 E 300 S Zionsville (46077) *(G-17023)*	
Jerry Lambert...	765 378-7599
10010 S County Road 900 W Daleville (47334) *(G-2800)*	
Jerry Lewis Cnstr & Excvtg, Greencastle *Also Called: Lewis Jerry Cnstr & Excvtg (G-6418)*	
Jerry Oppered..	574 269-5363
2534 S Country Club Rd Warsaw (46580) *(G-16381)*	
Jeshsoft LLC...	812 431-8603
414 Mount Ashley Rd Evansville (47711) *(G-4142)*	
Jessen Manufacturing Co Inc..............................	574 295-3836
1409 W Beardsley Ave Elkhart (46514) *(G-3432)*	
Jessup Paper Box LLC...	765 588-9137
4775 Dale Dr Lafayette (47905) *(G-10615)*	
Jet Black, Kokomo *Also Called: Dupouy Enterprises LLC (G-10260)*	
Jet City Specialties, Ligonier *Also Called: Blackpoint Engineering LLC (G-11006)*	
Jet Engineering, Warsaw *Also Called: Symmetry Medical Mfg Inc (G-16435)*	
Jet Fast Carriers LLC...	219 218-3021
8818 Cardinal Flower Ln Indianapolis (46231) *(G-8623)*	
Jet Technologies Inc..	574 264-3613
53893 N Park Ave Elkhart (46514) *(G-3433)*	
Jewelers Boutique Inc..	317 788-7679
3320 Madison Ave Indianapolis (46227) *(G-8624)*	
Jewelry In Candles...	765 401-6228
6188 W Division Rd Waynetown (47990) *(G-16541)*	
Jewels Hair & Accessories LLC...........................	260 310-9915
3215 Bowser Ave Fort Wayne (46806) *(G-5135)*	
Jewett Printing, Farmersburg *Also Called: Jewett Publications Inc (G-4420)*	
Jewett Printing LLC..	812 232-0087
219 W Main St Farmersburg (47850) *(G-4419)*	
Jewett Publications Inc.......................................	812 232-0087
219 W Main St Farmersburg (47850) *(G-4420)*	
Jezroc Metalworks LLC..	317 417-1132
205 S 1100 E Zionsville (46077) *(G-17024)*	

ALPHABETIC SECTION

Jfs Milling Inc..812 683-4200
3672 S Keller Rd Vincennes (47591) *(G-16134)*

Jfw Industries Incorporated..................................317 887-1340
5134 Commerce Square Dr Indianapolis (46237) *(G-8625)*

Jl Woodworking LLC..317 910-2976
5770 Osprey Way Carmel (46033) *(G-1678)*

Jiffy Lube, Fort Wayne Also Called: Illinois Lubricants LLC *(G-5092)*

Jigsaw Creations LLC..260 691-2196
5867 N 350 E Columbia City (46725) *(G-2160)*

Jim Graber Logging LLC......................................812 636-7000
10514 N 1000 E Odon (47562) *(G-13341)*

Jim Lemons Cnstr & Models, Camby Also Called: Jim Lemons Models *(G-1511)*

Jim Lemons Models...317 831-5133
13575 N Western Rd Camby (46113) *(G-1511)*

Jim McCarter Logging...812 321-5661
2752 S Enley Rd Wheatland (47597) *(G-16775)*

Jim Rhodes Logging..812 739-4221
2121 W State Road 62 English (47118) *(G-3841)*

Jimco Engineering Co..317 923-2290
3315 Sutherland Ave Indianapolis (46218) *(G-8626)*

Jims Welding & Repair LLC.................................765 564-1797
2359 E 400 S Bringhurst (46913) *(G-1237)*

Jinnings Equipment LLC.....................................260 447-4343
4434 Allen Martin Dr Fort Wayne (46806) *(G-5136)*

Jj Energy Inc..630 401-7026
621 Indianapolis Ave Lebanon (46052) *(G-10905)*

Jj Machine...765 366-8258
921 Walnut Grove Ct Lizton (46149) *(G-11050)*

Jj Machine...765 723-1511
8834 E 400 S New Ross (47968) *(G-12980)*

Jjs Concrete Construction LLC............................812 636-0173
9149 E 800 N Montgomery (47558) *(G-12103)*

Jjs Enterprise LLC..812 736-0062
2689 Breckenridge Rd Ne Corydon (47112) *(G-2502)*

JKL Software Development LLC..........................765 778-3032
210 E Water St Pendleton (46064) *(G-13538)*

Jknk Ventures Inc..812 246-0900
1511 Avco Blvd Sellersburg (47172) *(G-14603)*

Jkp Printing Inc...574 246-1650
1701 Linden Ave South Bend (46628) *(G-15092)*

JKS Music Publishing LLC..................................888 461-8703
3817 Maplewood Dr Lafayette (47905) *(G-10616)*

Jl 2 Incorporated...317 783-3340
4109 Five Points Rd Indianapolis (46239) *(G-8627)*

Jl Manfcturing Fabrication Inc.............................260 589-3723
3633 E 800 S Berne (46711) *(G-716)*

Jl Vincent Enterprises, Rochester Also Called: Vickery Tape & Label Co Inc *(G-14332)*

JL Walter & Associates Inc..................................317 524-3600
2099 Montcalm St Indianapolis (46202) *(G-8628)*

Jlb Industrial LLC..765 561-1751
5066 S The Farm Rd Rushville (46173) *(G-14402)*

Jle Fabricating LLC...574 341-4034
402 West St Argos (46501) *(G-324)*

Jlm Lubricants Usa LLC......................................317 500-1012
1110 Windhaven Cir Apt B Brownsburg (46112) *(G-1377)*

Jlm Pharmatech, Seymour Also Called: Pd Sub LLC *(G-14673)*

Jlr Mechanical Inc...502 551-6879
2020 Hospitality Way Clarksville (47129) *(G-2021)*

Jlr Welding & Fabrication, Clarksville Also Called: Jlr Mechanical Inc *(G-2021)*

JM Fittings LLC...260 747-9200
7815 Inverness Glens Dr Fort Wayne (46804) *(G-5137)*

JM Hutton & Co Inc...765 962-3506
1117 N E St Richmond (47374) *(G-14151)*

JM Hutton & Co Inc (PA).....................................765 962-3591
1501 S 8th St Richmond (47374) *(G-14152)*

JM Hutton & Company, Richmond Also Called: JM Hutton & Co Inc *(G-14151)*

JM Woodworking Enterprise LLC........................574 773-0444
3701 W 1350 N Milford (46542) *(G-11795)*

JM Woodworking LLC...574 354-7093
12198 N Syracuse Webster Rd Syracuse (46567) *(G-15464)*

Jmr Fabrication LLC..317 682-7821
10636 Winterwood Carmel (46032) *(G-1679)*

JMS Electronics Corporation...............................574 522-0246
4400 Wyland Dr Elkhart (46516) *(G-3434)*

JMS Engineered Plastics Inc...............................574 277-3228
1705 Commerce Dr South Bend (46628) *(G-15093)*

JMS Engineered Plastics Inc (PA).......................574 277-3228
52275 Indiana State Route 933 South Bend (46637) *(G-15094)*

JMS Machine Inc...260 244-0077
307 Diamond Ave Columbia City (46725) *(G-2161)*

JMS Mold & Engineering Co Inc..........................574 272-0198
50941 Indiana State Route 933 South Bend (46637) *(G-15095)*

Jmt, Mooresville Also Called: Jacobs Machine & Tool Co Inc *(G-12217)*

Jnj Blue Enterprise LLC (PA)..............................502 593-8464
3012 Charlestown Xing New Albany (47150) *(G-12754)*

Jnp Custom Designs, Indianapolis Also Called: J&P Custom Designs Inc *(G-8611)*

JO Mory Inc...260 897-3541
201 Progress Way Avilla (46710) *(G-479)*

JO Mory Inc...260 347-3753
621 Professional Way Kendallville (46755) *(G-10121)*

Joans Tshirt Printing LLC...................................812 934-2616
103 N Main St Batesville (47006) *(G-593)*

Job Shop Coatings Inc..317 462-9714
18 E Pierson St Greenfield (46140) *(G-6522)*

Jobsite Mobile Offices, Rochester Also Called: Jobsite Trailer Corporation *(G-14298)*

Jobsite Trailer Corporation..................................574 224-4000
1393 N Lucas St Rochester (46975) *(G-14298)*

Jodo Investments Inc..765 651-0200
3112 S Boots St Marion (46953) *(G-11301)*

Joe May Industries LLC......................................260 494-8735
2650 Stonecrop Rd Huntertown (46748) *(G-7258)*

Joe W Morgan Inc...812 423-5914
1719 W Louisiana St Evansville (47710) *(G-4143)*

Joe Wade Customs...765 548-0333
324 N Main St Rosedale (47874) *(G-14380)*

Joe Woodrow..765 866-0436
107 W Main St New Market (47965) *(G-12926)*

Joey Chestnut Eats, Indianapolis Also Called: Joey Chestnut Foods LLC *(G-8629)*

Joey Chestnut Foods LLC...................................317 602-4830
101 W Washington St Ste 1250 Indianapolis (46204) *(G-8629)*

Jofco Inc..812 482-5154
225 Clay St Jasper (47546) *(G-9861)*

Jofco, International, Jasper Also Called: Jofco Inc *(G-9861)*

John Bowen, Newburgh Also Called: John R Bowen & Associates *(G-13010)*

John Collier Logging Inc.....................................317 539-9663
9874 E Us Highway 40 Fillmore (46128) *(G-4454)*

John Davern, Dana Also Called: Davern Machine Shop *(G-2804)*

John Deere Authorized Dealer, Seymour Also Called: Deer Country Equipment LLC
(G-14646)

John Deere Landscapes, Merrillville Also Called: Siteone Landscape Supply LLC *(G-11560)*

John F Semrau..765 337-8831
2617 N Us Highway 421 Medaryville (47957) *(G-11459)*

John G Wagler..812 709-1681
9639 N 1150 E Odon (47562) *(G-13342)*

John Gebhart Woodworkings...............................765 492-3898
5352 N Fable St Cayuga (47928) *(G-1823)*

John King..317 801-3080
6515 Olivia Ln Indianapolis (46226) *(G-8630)*

John Ley Monument Sales Inc............................260 347-7346
101 Progress Way Avilla (46710) *(G-480)*

John R Bowen & Associates................................812 544-2267
7777 Ashwood Ct Newburgh (47630) *(G-13010)*

John S Cotter..765 584-2521
1858 E 700 N Ridgeville (47380) *(G-14234)*

John Wiley & Sons Inc...317 572-3000
9200 Keystone Xing Ste 800 Indianapolis (46240) *(G-8631)*

Johnco Corp..317 576-4417
8770 Commerce Park Pl Ste F Indianapolis (46268) *(G-8632)*

Johnny Graber Woodworking...............................260 466-4957
11522 Notestine Rd Grabill (46741) *(G-6305)*

Johnny Lemas...260 833-8850
2314 N 200 W Angola (46703) *(G-264)*

Johnny Long..812 698-2516
1360 S 125 E Washington (47501) *(G-16488)*

Johnny White.. 260 441-0077
6607 Hanna St Fort Wayne (46816) *(G-5138)*

Johnny White Signs, Fort Wayne *Also Called: Johnny White (G-5138)*

Johnny's Savory Sauces, Washington *Also Called: Johnny Long (G-16488)*

Johns Archtctral Met Solutions.................................. 219 440-2116
800 E Porter St Crown Point (46307) *(G-2703)*

Johns Butcher Shop Inc.. 574 773-4632
158 N Main St Nappanee (46550) *(G-12615)*

Johns Manville Corporation...................................... 574 546-4666
1215 W Dewey St Bremen (46506) *(G-1200)*

Johns Manville Corporation...................................... 765 973-5200
814 Richmond Ave Richmond (47374) *(G-14153)*

Johns Portable Siiop Weld....................................... 574 936-1702
10476 Muckshaw Rd Plymouth (46563) *(G-13789)*

Johns Welding and Fabrication.................................. 574 936-1702
1203 N Michigan St Plymouth (46563) *(G-13790)*

Johnson & Johnson.. 732 524-0400
10284 Seagrave Dr Fishers (46037) *(G-4551)*

Johnson & Johnson Incorporated................................ 317 539-8420
9440 S State Road 39 Mooresville (46158) *(G-12218)*

Johnson Bros S Whitley Sign Co................................ 260 723-5161
304 N Calhoun St South Whitley (46787) *(G-15319)*

Johnson Brothers Sign Co., South Whitley *Also Called: Johnson Bros S Whitley Sign Co (G-15319)*

Johnson Cntrls Fire Prtction L.................................. 317 826-2130
1255 N Senate Ave Indianapolis (46202) *(G-8633)*

Johnson Cntrls SEC Sltions LLC................................ 800 238-2455
10405 Crosspoint Blvd Indianapolis (46256) *(G-8634)*

Johnson Contrls Authorized Dlr, Lafayette *Also Called: Duncan Supply Co Inc (G-10572)*

Johnson Controls, Crown Point *Also Called: Johnson Controls Inc (G-2704)*

Johnson Controls, Evansville *Also Called: Johnson Controls Inc (G-4144)*

Johnson Controls, Fort Wayne *Also Called: Clarios LLC (G-4851)*

Johnson Controls, Indianapolis *Also Called: Controls Center Inc (G-7863)*

Johnson Controls, Pittsboro *Also Called: Johnson Controls Inc (G-13649)*

Johnson Controls, Rockport *Also Called: Johnson Controls Inc (G-14343)*

Johnson Controls Inc... 219 736-7105
2293 N Main St Crown Point (46307) *(G-2704)*

Johnson Controls Inc... 812 868-1374
8401 N Kentucky Ave Ste H Evansville (47725) *(G-4144)*

Johnson Controls Inc... 317 917-5043
314 Brixton Woods West Dr Pittsboro (46167) *(G-13649)*

Johnson Controls Inc... 812 362-6901
6500 N Us Highway 231 Rockport (47635) *(G-14343)*

Johnson Controls SEC Solutions, Indianapolis *Also Called: Johnson Cntrls SEC Sltions LLC (G-8634)*

Johnson Engraving & Trophies.................................. 260 982-7868
1302 Beckley St North Manchester (46962) *(G-13236)*

Johnson Hardware, Elkhart *Also Called: L E Johnson Products Inc (G-3462)*

Johnson Safe Company LLC...................................... 317 876-7233
8750 E 200 S Zionsville (46077) *(G-17025)*

Johnson Sales Corp.. 219 322-9558
1145 Birch Dr Schererville (46375) *(G-14525)*

Johnson Samyra.. 872 216-0551
11531 Planewood Ct Indianapolis (46235) *(G-8635)*

Johnsons Burial Designs... 317 549-2148
3950 N Layman Ave Indianapolis (46226) *(G-8636)*

Johnsons Orthtics Prsthtics LL.................................. 812 372-2800
941 25th St Columbus (47201) *(G-2331)*

Johnsons Welding Inc.. 317 835-2438
7908 W 525 N Boggstown (46110) *(G-1074)*

Jokerr Fabrication LLC... 513 312-0408
409 W Mill St Jamestown (46147) *(G-9818)*

Jolar Enterprises.. 574 875-8369
58052 Ox Bow Dr Elkhart (46516) *(G-3435)*

Jolene D Pavey.. 765 473-6171
4641 S 50 W Peru (46970) *(G-13588)*

Jolliff Diesel Service LLC.. 812 692-5725
7325 E 1500 N Elnora (47529) *(G-3815)*

Jomar Machining & Fabg Inc.................................... 574 825-9637
13393 County Road 22 Middlebury (46540) *(G-11728)*

Jomark Inc.. 248 478-2600
40 Lane 274 Crooked Lk Angola (46703) *(G-265)*

Jones & Sons Inc... 812 299-2287
3527 Erie Canal Rd Terre Haute (47802) *(G-15622)*

Jones & Sons Inc... 812 882-2957
784 S 6th Street Rd Vincennes (47591) *(G-16135)*

JONES & SONS, INC., Terre Haute *Also Called: Jones & Sons Inc (G-15622)*

JONES & SONS, INC., Vincennes *Also Called: Jones & Sons Inc (G-16135)*

Jones & Webb Associates Inc.................................. 317 236-9755
2544 Andy Dr Indianapolis (46229) *(G-8637)*

Jones and Sons Inc (PA)....................................... 812 254-4731
1262 S State Road 57 Washington (47501) *(G-16489)*

Jones Engineering Inc... 812 254-6456
897 W 150 S Washington (47501) *(G-16490)*

Jones Fbrication Machining Inc................................. 812 466-2237
5600 N Us Highway 41 Terre Haute (47805) *(G-15623)*

Jones International Inc... 219 746-1478
437 Connecticut St Gary (46402) *(G-5971)*

Jones Machine & Tool Inc...................................... 812 364-4588
14710 N Crossroad Nw Fredericksburg (47120) *(G-5794)*

Jones Popcorn Inc.. 812 941-8810
125 Quality Ave New Albany (47150) *(G-12755)*

Jones Trucking Inc.. 765 537-2279
2468 S State Road 67 Paragon (46166) *(G-13502)*

Jonesville Desk, North Vernon *Also Called: Indiana Southern Millwork Inc (G-13280)*

Jonesys Fabrication LLC.. 317 504-6511
9913 S County Road 25 W Clayton (46118) *(G-2060)*

Jordan Manufacturing Co Inc (PA)........................... 800 328-6522
1200 S 6th St Monticello (47960) *(G-12155)*

Jordan Safety and Supply LLC (PA)......................... 513 315-6267
4614 Radnor Rd Indianapolis (46226) *(G-8638)*

Jorh Frame, Crown Point *Also Called: Jorh Frame & Moulding Co Inc (G-2705)*

Jorh Frame & Moulding Co Inc................................ 708 747-3440
2909 Morningside Dr Crown Point (46307) *(G-2705)*

Josam, Michigan City *Also Called: Josam Company (G-11628)*

Josam Company (HQ).. 219 872-5531
525 W Us Highway 20 Michigan City (46360) *(G-11628)*

Joseph Fisher... 765 435-7231
6492 E 850 N Waveland (47989) *(G-16535)*

Joseph M Schmidt.. 260 223-3498
7741 N 200 E Decatur (46733) *(G-2865)*

Joseph Matthew Biaso... 812 277-6871
615 W Warren St # A Mitchell (47446) *(G-12041)*

Joseph Northern.. 574 309-5508
2621 Prast Blvd South Bend (46628) *(G-15096)*

Josh Rowland... 574 596-6754
6221 Strathaven Rd Noblesville (46062) *(G-13114)*

Jossey-Bass Publishers... 877 762-2974
10475 Crosspoint Blvd Indianapolis (46256) *(G-8639)*

Journal & Chronicle Inc.. 812 752-5060
39 E Wardell St Scottsburg (47170) *(G-14566)*

Journal and Courier, Lafayette *Also Called: Gannett Media Corp (G-10585)*

Journal of Teaching Writing.................................... 317 274-0092
425 University Blvd Indianapolis (46202) *(G-8640)*

Journal Reporter, Gas City *Also Called: Twin City Journal Reporter (G-6041)*

Journeyman Tool & Mold Inc.................................. 574 237-1880
23755 Kern Rd South Bend (46614) *(G-15097)*

Joyce Consulting LLC.. 317 577-8504
9132 Sargent Manor Ct Indianapolis (46256) *(G-8641)*

Joyce/Dayton Corp.. 260 726-9361
1621 N Meridian St Portland (47371) *(G-13952)*

Joyful Sign Company LLC...................................... 317 529-1020
4205 Devon Court West Dr Indianapolis (46226) *(G-8642)*

Joyfully Said Signs LLC... 574 596-9949
402 E Warren St Middlebury (46540) *(G-11729)*

Jp Incorporated - Indiana....................................... 574 457-2062
501 W Railroad Ave Syracuse (46567) *(G-15465)*

JP Custom Cabinetry Inc....................................... 219 956-3587
13467 Whippoorwill Ln Wheatfield (46392) *(G-16769)*

JP Industries Inc.. 574 293-8763
726 Middleton Run Rd Elkhart (46516) *(G-3436)*

ALPHABETIC SECTION — K & L Machining Inc

JP Machine Shop LLC 574 453-7617
2661 E 1000 S Claypool (46510) *(G-2054)*

JP Ownership Group Inc 317 791-1122
5804 Churchman Byp Indianapolis (46203) *(G-8643)*

JP Signs, Dupont *Also Called: J W P Vinyl Designs (G-2964)*

JP Technology Inc 219 947-2525
10769 Broadway Crown Point (46307) *(G-2706)*

JP Trucking Inc 574 654-7555
54340 Smilax Rd New Carlisle (46552) *(G-12841)*

Jpc LLC 574 293-8030
2926 Paul Dr Elkhart (46514) *(G-3437)*

Jpc Mat, Elkhart *Also Called: Jpc LLC (G-3437)*

Jpc Trucking LLC 219 207-2300
2106 Morthland Dr Valparaiso (46383) *(G-15982)*

Jpe Consulting LLP 574 675-9552
10451 Dunn Rd Osceola (46561) *(G-13395)*

Jpg Machine & Tool LLC 812 265-4512
1263 W Jpg Woodfill Rd Ste 212 Madison (47250) *(G-11232)*

Jps Candles LLC 219 728-8210
1735 Indian Boundary Rd Chesterton (46304) *(G-1940)*

Jpt Enterprises Inc 260 672-1605
6435 W Jefferson Blvd Fort Wayne (46804) *(G-5139)*

JR Graber & Sons LLC (PA) 260 657-1071
15822 Trammel Rd Grabill (46741) *(G-6396)*

JR Grber Sons Fmly Ltd Prtnr 260 657-1071
15822 Trammel Rd Grabill (46741) *(G-6307)*

Jrds Industries 260 729-5037
1700 N Meridian St Portland (47371) *(G-13953)*

Jri Woodworks 812 401-1234
1601 Florence St Evansville (47710) *(G-4145)*

Jrotten Chopper Inc 765 517-1779
6563 Wheeling Pike Jonesboro (46938) *(G-10080)*

Jrowe Signs 260 668-7100
311 S Superior St Angola (46703) *(G-266)*

Jrp Machine Co 317 955-1905
1607 Deloss St Ste B Indianapolis (46201) *(G-8644)*

Jrs Custom Cabinets Co 219 696-7205
16855 Mississippi St Lowell (46356) *(G-11164)*

JRS Custom Fabrication 317 852-4964
602 E Main St Brownsburg (46112) *(G-1378)*

Jrs Polishing LLC 574 306-2351
1446 E 225 S Winona Lake (46590) *(G-16911)*

Jrs Wood Shop 765 498-2663
6950 W 1025 N Kingman (47952) *(G-10172)*

Jrxgra-50, Grabill *Also Called: JR Grber Sons Fmly Ltd Prtnr (G-6307)*

Jrz Industries Inc 574 834-4543
133 S East St North Webster (46555) *(G-13308)*

Jsi, French Lick *Also Called: Jasper Seating Company Inc (G-5847)*

Jt Composites LLC (PA) 317 297-9520
312 Gasoline Aly Ste C Indianapolis (46222) *(G-8645)*

Jt Custom Machine Shop LLC 812 827-1993
3065 Cottage Dr Evansville (47711) *(G-4146)*

Jt Printing LLC 317 271-7700
77 Park Place Blvd Avon (46123) *(G-529)*

Jt Transports LLC 317 658-1523
5625 N German Church Rd # 3194 Indianapolis (46235) *(G-8646)*

Jtd Enterprises Inc 574 533-9438
609 N Harrison St Goshen (46528) *(G-6180)*

Jtex Cnstr & Consulting LLC 812 486-9123
9841 E County Road 850 S Velpen (47590) *(G-16093)*

JTI Inc 317 797-9698
1801 S Lynhurst Dr Indianapolis (46241) *(G-8647)*

Jtledm LLC 317 292-2548
2816 N County Rd 800 W Sullivan (47882) *(G-15409)*

Jtm Home & Building 219 690-1445
16005 Chestnut St Lowell (46356) *(G-11165)*

Jtn Services Inc 765 653-7158
4421 S Us Highway 231 Greencastle (46135) *(G-6415)*

Jua Technologies Intl Inc 765 204-5533
1281 Win Hentschel Blvd Ste 1300 West Lafayette (47906) *(G-16597)*

Judd Associates, Bloomington *Also Called: Richard M Judd (G-955)*

Judkins Sr Renaldo G 812 944-4251
2315 Birch Dr Clarksville (47129) *(G-2022)*

Judson Harness & Saddlery 765 569-0918
4889 E 350 N Rockville (47872) *(G-14352)*

Julian Coffee Roasters, Zionsville *Also Called: Julian Coffee Roasters Inc (G-17026)*

Julian Coffee Roasters Inc 317 247-4208
10830 Bennett Pkwy Ste N Zionsville (46077) *(G-17026)*

Julie Edwards Ceramics 317 681-9523
957 N Graham Ave Indianapolis (46219) *(G-8648)*

Julie Stergen 317 888-6146
157 Sycamore Ln Greenwood (46142) *(G-6719)*

Jupiter Aluminum Corporation 219 932-3322
205 E Carey St Fairland (46126) *(G-4399)*

Jupiter Aluminum Corporation (PA) 219 932-3322
1745 165th St Ste 6 Hammond (46320) *(G-6962)*

Jupiter Coil Coating, Fairland *Also Called: Jupiter Aluminum Corporation (G-4399)*

Jus Rite Engineering Inc 574 522-9600
56977 Elk Ct Elkhart (46516) *(G-3438)*

Jushi USA Fiberglass 574 293-0061
3310 Middlebury St Elkhart (46516) *(G-3439)*

Just For Granite LLC 317 842-8255
5277 Emco Dr Indianapolis (46220) *(G-8649)*

Just For Karts, Covington *Also Called: Eldon France (G-2529)*

Just Install LLC 317 607-3911
20962 Hinkle Rd Noblesville (46062) *(G-13115)*

Just Monograms LLC 812 827-3693
535 University Dr Jasper (47546) *(G-9862)*

Just Perfection LLC 347 559-5878
6613 Meadowlark Dr Indianapolis (46226) *(G-8650)*

Just Phone Rentals.com, Greenwood *Also Called: International Resources Inc (G-6716)*

Just Standout LLC 317 531-6956
951 E 86th St Ste 200e Indianapolis (46240) *(G-8651)*

Justin Blackwell 812 834-6350
7071 State Road 446 Norman (47264) *(G-13203)*

JVI Inc 872 276-0823
47 Ruth St Apt 2 Hammond (46320) *(G-6963)*

JW Hicks Inc 574 772-7755
20 Kloeckner Dr Knox (46534) *(G-10212)*

JW Machining LLC 812 344-6753
12775 W Becks Grove Rd Columbus (47201) *(G-2332)*

JW Packaging LLC 317 414-9038
204 W Railroad St Converse (46919) *(G-2477)*

JW Signs Inc 260 747-5168
2511 Alma Ave Fort Wayne (46809) *(G-5140)*

JW Woodworking Inc 574 831-3033
72057 County Road 17 New Paris (46553) *(G-12962)*

Jwb Group LLC 812 371-7344
357 Brown Hill Rd Nashville (47448) *(G-12672)*

Jwcandle Co LLC 317 661-1066
4344 Malden Ct Apt C Beech Grove (46107) *(G-695)*

Jzj Services LLC (PA) 812 424-8268
210 S Morton Ave Evansville (47713) *(G-4147)*

Jzj Services LLC 574 642-3182
63410 County Road 33 Goshen (46528) *(G-6181)*

K & B Trailer Sales & Mfg Inc 574 946-4382
93 E 800 N Monterey (46960) *(G-12080)*

K & D Custom Coach Inc 574 537-1716
408 High Park Ave Goshen (46526) *(G-6182)*

K & I Hard Chrome Inc 812 948-1166
1900 E Main St New Albany (47150) *(G-12756)*

K & I Sash & Door, Evansville *Also Called: US Lbm Operating Co 3009 LLC (G-4364)*

K & K Cabinets & Supply 317 852-4808
1640 S Green St Ste A Brownsburg (46112) *(G-1379)*

K & K Fence Inc 317 359-5425
6520 Brookville Rd Indianapolis (46219) *(G-8652)*

K & K Inc 574 266-8040
2617 Glenview Dr Elkhart (46514) *(G-3440)*

K & K Industries Inc 812 486-3281
8518 E 550 N Montgomery (47558) *(G-12104)*

K & L Machining Inc 812 526-4840
6973 S Us Highway 31 Edinburgh (46124) *(G-3088)*

K & M Tool & Die — ALPHABETIC SECTION

K & M Tool & Die, Lebanon *Also Called: K & M Tool & Die Inc (G-10906)*

K & M Tool & Die Inc 765 482-9464
406 S Patterson St Lebanon (46052) *(G-10906)*

K & M Weld Fab 219 362-3736
3381 N 300 E Rolling Prairie (46371) *(G-14366)*

K & M Woodworking, Montgomery *Also Called: Kenneth Raber (G-12105)*

K & N Carpet, Fort Wayne *Also Called: Todd K Hockemeyer Inc (G-5492)*

K & P Industries LLC 317 881-9245
1200 Tanglewood Dr Greenwood (46142) *(G-6720)*

K & P Products, Mishawaka *Also Called: Vision Machine Works Inc (G-12022)*

K & S Farm Machine Shop Inc 812 663-8567
4620 S County Road 550 E Greensburg (47240) *(G-6610)*

K & S Pallet Inc 260 422-1264
1025 Osage St Fort Wayne (46808) *(G-5141)*

K A Components, Otterbein *Also Called: Kerkhoff Associates Inc (G-13453)*

K and S Pallets, Fort Wayne *Also Called: K & S Pallet Inc (G-5141)*

K C Cmponents Wldg Fabrication 317 539-6067
5334 E County Road 600 S Greencastle (46135) *(G-6416)*

K C Creations 937 418-1859
11612 Breckenridge Ct Indianapolis (46236) *(G-8653)*

K C Designs Printing, Bloomington *Also Called: Kc Designs (G-899)*

K C Form Plastics LLC 574 333-2523
1009 Borg Rd Elkhart (46514) *(G-3441)*

K C Machine Inc 574 293-1822
56850 Elk Park Dr Elkhart (46516) *(G-3442)*

K Diamond Sheet Metal 765 671-9847
934 S Nebraska St Marion (46953) *(G-11302)*

K Grimmer Industries Inc 317 736-3800
17301 Juniper Ln Leo (46765) *(G-10968)*

K I B Electronics, Elkhart *Also Called: K I B Enterprises Corp (G-3443)*

K I B Enterprises Corp 574 262-0518
1147 N Michigan St Elkhart (46514) *(G-3443)*

K Irpcheadstart Program 219 345-2011
10448 N 450 E Demotte (46310) *(G-2919)*

K M Davis Inc 765 426-9227
919b Main St Lafayette (47901) *(G-10617)*

K M I, Fremont *Also Called: Koester Metals Inc (G-5825)*

K M Specialty Pumps Inc 812 925-3000
8055 State Route 62 W Chandler (47610) *(G-1863)*

K Q Servicing LLC 812 486-9244
22383 Third Rd Loogootee (47553) *(G-11140)*

K S Mold Inc 260 357-5141
4650 Chester Dr Elkhart (46516) *(G-3444)*

K S Oil Corp 812 453-3026
8681 Waterford Dr Mount Vernon (47620) *(G-12305)*

K Tech Specialty Coatings Inc 260 587-3888
111 W Garfield St Ashley (46705) *(G-333)*

K Tech Supply 812 793-3352
12740 E County Road 400 S Crothersville (47229) *(G-2641)*

K Tool 574 296-9604
700 W Beardsley Ave Ste 17 Elkhart (46514) *(G-3445)*

K W Deer Processing 812 824-2492
1715 E Rayletown Rd Bloomington (47401) *(G-898)*

K Willoughby Consulting, South Bend *Also Called: Kristine Willoughby (G-15106)*

K-Fab Inc 812 663-6299
1940 N Montgomery Rd Greensburg (47240) *(G-6611)*

K-K Tool and Design Inc 260 758-2940
50 Countryside Dr Markle (46770) *(G-11356)*

K-TEC Corp 317 398-6684
850 Elston Dr Shelbyville (46176) *(G-14766)*

K-Tron America Inc 812 934-7000
1 Batesville Blvd Batesville (47006) *(G-594)*

K&A Sheet Metal LLC 317 300-1518
5333 Commerce Square Dr Ste E Indianapolis (46237) *(G-8654)*

K&D Crafts 812 667-2575
13020 Southfork Rd Dillsboro (47018) *(G-2948)*

K&D&s Trucking and Reality LLC 847 791-6848
823 174th Pl Hammond (46324) *(G-6964)*

K&M Fasteners LLC 260 525-8989
365 W Compromise St Berne (46711) *(G-717)*

K&T Performance Engrg LLC 765 437-0185
1975 N Lancer St Peru (46970) *(G-13589)*

K2 Industrial Services Inc (DH) 219 933-1100
2552 Industrial Dr Highland (46322) *(G-7141)*

K2 Mold LLC 574 293-4613
60232 State Road 15 Lot 12 Goshen (46528) *(G-6183)*

K2 Plastics Inc 574 773-2243
26400 County Road 50 Nappanee (46550) *(G-12616)*

Ka Crown Point Inc 219 595-5276
1650 Blue Heron Ct Crown Point (46307) *(G-2707)*

Kabert Industries Inc 765 874-2335
514 W Church St Lynn (47355) *(G-11184)*

KABERT INDUSTRIES INC, Lynn *Also Called: Kabert Industries Inc (G-11184)*

Kable Tool & Engineering 260 726-9670
530 E 300 N Portland (47371) *(G-13954)*

Kadel Engineering Corporation 317 745-2798
1627 E Main St Danville (46122) *(G-2816)*

Kadet Products Inc 765 552-7341
2403 S J St Elwood (46036) *(G-3828)*

Kaeb Sales Inc 574 862-2777
27481 County Road 40 Wakarusa (46573) *(G-16236)*

Kain Tool Inc 260 829-6569
9775 W Maple St Orland (46776) *(G-13366)*

Kairos Specialty Metals Corp 765 836-5540
404 W Main St Mount Summit (47361) *(G-12285)*

Kaiser Aluminum Warrick LLC 412 315-2900
4000 W State Route 66 Newburgh (47630) *(G-13011)*

Kaiser Pickles LLC 812 954-5115
6965 Us Highway 50 Aurora (47001) *(G-446)*

Kaiser Press Inc 317 619-7092
2525 E 91st St Indianapolis (46240) *(G-8655)*

Kaiser Tool Company Inc 260 484-3620
3620 Centennial Dr Fort Wayne (46808) *(G-5142)*

Kaizen Woodworks 714 350-6281
13371 Kingsfield Ct Granger (46530) *(G-6356)*

Kal Transportation LLC 317 615-9341
1110 Aqua Vista Dr Indianapolis (46229) *(G-8656)*

Kala Mindfulness LLC 720 351-9664
2951 Cooperland Ct Indianapolis (46268) *(G-8657)*

Kaldewei Usa Inc 866 822-2527
14074 Trade Center Dr Ste 148 Fishers (46038) *(G-4552)*

Kaleidoscope Inc 765 423-1951
1214 North St Lafayette (47904) *(G-10618)*

Kalems Enterprises Inc 317 399-1645
8455 Castlewood Dr Ste H Indianapolis (46250) *(G-8658)*

Kalenborn Abresist Corporation (HQ) 800 348-0717
5541 N State Road 13 Urbana (46990) *(G-15886)*

Kaley Centerless Grinding, South Bend *Also Called: Valad McHning Cntrless Grnding (G-15299)*

Kalustyan Corporation 908 688-6111
1650 Northwind Pkwy Hobart (46342) *(G-7195)*

Kaman Automation, Fort Wayne *Also Called: Kaman Corporation (G-5143)*

Kaman Corporation 714 696-3750
213 W Wayne St Fort Wayne (46802) *(G-5143)*

Kamdoer Inc 574 293-2990
4027 Timber Ct Elkhart (46514) *(G-3446)*

Kammerer Dynamics Inc 260 349-9098
5780 E Concrete Dr Kendallville (46755) *(G-10122)*

Kammerer Inc (PA) 260 347-0389
2348 E Kammerer Rd Kendallville (46755) *(G-10123)*

Kammerer Inc 260 349-9098
303 W Wayne St Kendallville (46755) *(G-10124)*

Kampco Steel Products Inc 574 294-5466
57533 County Road 3 Elkhart (46517) *(G-3447)*

Kamplain Machine Company Inc 317 388-9111
7785 Maloney Rd Brownsburg (46112) *(G-1380)*

Kamps Inc 317 634-8360
1905 S Belmont Ave Indianapolis (46221) *(G-8659)*

Kamrex Inc 317 204-3779
7367 Business Center Dr Avon (46123) *(G-530)*

Kan Jam LLC 317 804-9129
17401 Tiller Ct Ste A Westfield (46074) *(G-16703)*

ALPHABETIC SECTION — Kellco

Kane Usa Inc 800 547-5740
7601 E 88th Pl Ste 888 Indianapolis (46256) *(G-8660)*

Kaniewski & Odle Trckg & Repr, Williamsport *Also Called: Cryogenic Support Systems Inc (G-16846)*

Kankakee Valley Post News 219 987-5111
827 S Halleck St Demotte (46310) *(G-2920)*

Kankakee Valley Publishing Co 219 866-5111
117 N Van Rensselaer St Rensselaer (47978) *(G-14056)*

Kanoff Enterprises 574 575-6787
928 W Berry Ave Mishawaka (46545) *(G-11921)*

Kant Slam Door Check Company, Bloomfield *Also Called: Bloomfield Mfg Co Inc (G-740)*

Kapsch Trafficcom Usa Inc 812 258-5905
107 Quartermaster Ct Jeffersonville (47130) *(G-10004)*

Karbach Holdings Corporation 219 924-2454
1701 Northwind Pkwy Hobart (46342) *(G-7196)*

Karemar Productions 765 766-5117
6789 E State Road 36 Mooreland (47360) *(G-12185)*

Kark Welding 574 400-3989
51285 Bittersweet Rd Ste F Granger (46530) *(G-6357)*

Karma Industries Inc 765 742-9200
525 Wabash Ave Lafayette (47905) *(G-10619)*

Kartistry Pro LLC 317 969-7075
5555 N Tacoma Ave Ste 208 Indianapolis (46220) *(G-8661)*

Karton King, Bloomington *Also Called: Big Red Liquors Inc (G-806)*

Kas Satellite & Cable Inc (PA) 260 833-3941
60 Lane 165 Jimmerson Lk Angola (46703) *(G-267)*

Kasco Mfg Co Inc 317 398-7973
170 W 600 N Shelbyville (46176) *(G-14767)*

Kasgro Rail Car Management 812 347-3888
209 N Capitol Ave Corydon (47112) *(G-2503)*

Kasnak Designs, Brownsburg *Also Called: Kasnak Restorations Inc (G-1381)*

Kasnak Restorations Inc 317 852-9770
5505 N County Road 1000 E Brownsburg (46112) *(G-1381)*

Kasting Printing Service 317 881-9411
7146 S Meridian St Indianapolis (46217) *(G-8662)*

Kat Tales Embroidery 219 299-2693
3503 Sunset Dr Valparaiso (46383) *(G-15983)*

Katalyst Corporation 317 783-6500
176 Schaff St Beech Grove (46107) *(G-696)*

Katalyst Industrial Coatings, Beech Grove *Also Called: Katalyst Corporation (G-696)*

Kath Enterprise LLC 877 641-6990
4308 E 6th Ave Gary (46403) *(G-5972)*

Katherine Mackey 765 825-0634
409 Ridge Rd Connersville (47331) *(G-2448)*

Kathy Zuccarelli 219 865-4095
1314 Eagle Ridge Dr Schererville (46375) *(G-14526)*

Katies Candy LLC 800 558-9898
8126 Van Buren Ave Munster (46321) *(G-12545)*

Kauffman Engineering LLC 574 732-2154
510 E 2nd St Bremen (46506) *(G-1201)*

Kauffman Engineering LLC 765 482-5640
202 S Mount Zion Rd Lebanon (46052) *(G-10907)*

Kauffman Engineering Inc 574 722-3800
830 S State Road 25 Logansport (46947) *(G-11086)*

KAUFFMAN ENGINEERING INC, Logansport *Also Called: Kauffman Engineering Inc (G-11086)*

Kautex Inc 260 897-3250
210 Green Dr Avilla (46710) *(G-481)*

Kawneer Company Inc 317 882-2314
1040 Sierra Dr Ste 1500 Greenwood (46143) *(G-6721)*

Kay Company Inc 765 659-3388
509 W Barner St Frankfort (46041) *(G-5677)*

Kay Industries, Nappanee *Also Called: Kay Industries Inc (G-12617)*

Kay Industries Inc (PA) 574 236-6220
207 E Market St Nappanee (46550) *(G-12617)*

Kayco, Frankfort *Also Called: Kay Company Inc (G-5677)*

Kays Way 219 290-0782
5058 Massachusetts St Gary (46409) *(G-5973)*

Kaze, Georgetown *Also Called: Kaze Energy LLC (G-6064)*

Kaze Energy LLC 502 664-5519
6108 Deer Trace Ct Georgetown (47122) *(G-6064)*

Kazmier Tooling Inc 773 586-0300
3039 169th Pl Hammond (46323) *(G-6965)*

Kbc Machine 317 446-6163
408 Woodland East Dr Greenfield (46140) *(G-6523)*

Kbi Inc 765 763-6114
2618 E Us Highway 52 Morristown (46161) *(G-12278)*

KBK Magik LLC 219 512-4040
730 Lansdowne Rd Indianapolis (46234) *(G-8663)*

Kbs Coatings, Valparaiso *Also Called: Advanced Protective Tech LLC (G-15892)*

Kbshimmer Bath and Body Inc 317 979-2307
2820 S State Road 63 Terre Haute (47802) *(G-15624)*

Kc Designs 812 876-4020
2801 W Bristol Dr Bloomington (47404) *(G-899)*

Kc Engineering Inc 317 352-9742
5602 Elmwood Ave Ste 118 Indianapolis (46203) *(G-8664)*

Kc Innovations LLC 888 290-8920
11720 W 250n Loogootee (47553) *(G-11141)*

Kc Mig Welding LLC 317 739-1051
189 S Sunblest Blvd Fishers (46038) *(G-4553)*

KCARC, Vincennes *Also Called: Knox Cnty Assn For Rmrkble Ctz (G-16136)*

Kcc Inc 317 632-5258
1511 Bates St Indianapolis (46201) *(G-8665)*

Kch Services Inc 260 463-3100
202 W Central Ave Lagrange (46761) *(G-10745)*

Kcma & Services LLC 260 645-0885
1954 County Road 43 Waterloo (46793) *(G-16522)*

Kd Dids Quilting 317 460-0646
8184 Sedge Grass Rd Noblesville (46060) *(G-13116)*

Kdp LLC 630 362-7346
1301 Palmer Dr West Lafayette (47906) *(G-16598)*

Kds Industries LLC 574 333-2720
21790 Beck Dr Elkhart (46516) *(G-3448)*

Kdz Kustoms LLC 260 927-0533
521 Ley Dr Auburn (46706) *(G-398)*

Kdz Motorcycle Sales and Svc, Auburn *Also Called: Kdz Kustoms LLC (G-398)*

Keco Engineered Coatings Inc (PA) 317 356-7279
1030 S Kealing Ave Indianapolis (46203) *(G-8666)*

Keefer Printing Company Inc 260 424-4543
3824 Transportation Dr Fort Wayne (46818) *(G-5144)*

Keen Screen 812 989-8885
120 Edgemont Dr New Albany (47150) *(G-12757)*

Keen Screen 812 945-5336
3314 Grant Line Rd New Albany (47150) *(G-12758)*

Keener Corporation 765 825-2100
950 Conwell St Connersville (47331) *(G-2449)*

Keener Metal Fabricating LLC (PA) 765 825-2100
950 Conwell St Connersville (47331) *(G-2450)*

Keenville & Company LLC 219 916-6737
1703 Vale Park Rd Valparaiso (46383) *(G-15984)*

Keihin Aircon North America 765 213-4915
4400 N Superior Dr Muncie (47303) *(G-12432)*

Keil Chemical Corporation 219 931-2630
3000 Sheffield Ave Hammond (46327) *(G-6966)*

Keith Bixler 812 866-1637
352 S Getty Rd Lexington (47138) *(G-10978)*

Keith Ison 765 938-1460
615 Conrad Harcourt Way Rushville (46173) *(G-14403)*

Keith Kunz Motorsports LLC 812 372-8494
4575 Kelly St Columbus (47203) *(G-2333)*

Keith Miller 260 982-6858
701 N Mill St North Manchester (46962) *(G-13237)*

Keith Smith 317 336-6746
6516 W Deer Crossing Blvd Mccordsville (46055) *(G-11453)*

Kelby J Waldrip 812 824-2492
18826 Fairfield Blvd Noblesville (46060) *(G-13117)*

Kelco Steel Fabrication Inc 317 248-9229
3827 W Troy Ave Indianapolis (46241) *(G-8667)*

Keline Manufacturing, Elkhart *Also Called: JP Industries Inc (G-3436)*

Kelk Publishing LLC 812 268-6356
249 W Washington St Sullivan (47882) *(G-15410)*

Kellco, Georgetown *Also Called: Kentuckiana Machine & Tool Inc (G-6065)*

Keller Crescent Co

ALPHABETIC SECTION

Keller Crescent Co, Indianapolis *Also Called: Clondalkin Pharma & Healthcare Inc (G-7824)*
Keller Logging LLC 219 309-0379
   210 W 375 S Valparaiso (46385) *(G-15985)*
Keller Machine & Welding Inc 219 464-4915
   5705 Murvihill Rd Valparaiso (46383) *(G-15986)*
Keller Performance Center 765 827-5225
   300 E 30th St Connersville (47331) *(G-2451)*
Keller Tool 812 873-7344
   1085 N County Road 500 E Butlerville (47223) *(G-1486)*
Keller Tools, Butlerville *Also Called: Keller Tool (G-1486)*
Kellers Limestone Service Inc 219 326-1688
   2074 N 50 W La Porte (46350) *(G-10432)*
Kelley Global Brands LLC 833 554-8326
   632 Longford Way Noblesville (46062) *(G-13118)*
Kellmark Corporation 574 264-9695
   2501 Ada Dr Elkhart (46514) *(G-3449)*
Kellog, Seelyville *Also Called: Hearthside Food Solutions LLC (G-14585)*
Kellum Imprints Inc 812 347-2546
   1675 Highway 64 Nw Ramsey (47166) *(G-14025)*
Kellum Imprints & Trophies, Ramsey *Also Called: Kellum Imprints Inc (G-14025)*
Kelly Bixler Logging 812 752-6636
   4769 S Underwood Rd Scottsburg (47170) *(G-14567)*
Kelly Box and Packaging Corp (PA) 260 432-4570
   2801 Covington Rd Fort Wayne (46802) *(G-5145)*
Kelly Box and Packaging Corp 317 804-7044
   3035 N Shadeland Ave Ste 400 Indianapolis (46226) *(G-8668)*
Kelsie Pierce 812 279-1335
   234 Rawlins Mill Rd Bedford (47421) *(G-651)*
Kelvion Products Inc 865 606-6027
   2401 Directors Row Indianapolis (46241) *(G-8669)*
Kelwood Designs LLC 574 862-2472
   25440 County Road 138 Goshen (46526) *(G-6184)*
Kem Krest Defense LLC 574 389-2650
   3221 Magnum Dr Elkhart (46516) *(G-3450)*
Kemco International Inc 260 829-1263
   9915 W Maple St Orland (46776) *(G-13367)*
Kemco Manufacturing LLC 574 546-2025
   617 E Plymouth St Bremen (46506) *(G-1202)*
Kemira Water Solutions Inc 219 397-2646
   3761 Canal St East Chicago (46312) *(G-3024)*
Kemper Tool Inc 812 744-8633
   11804 Long Branch Rd Moores Hill (47032) *(G-12187)*
Ken Anliker 219 984-5676
   2785 S 75 W Chalmers (47929) *(G-1858)*
Ken Co Hartland, Rolling Prairie *Also Called: Hartland Products Inc (G-14364)*
Ken Duikhoff 765 668-8697
   3112 S Washington St Marion (46953) *(G-11303)*
Ken Kowalski 574 633-4427
   26237 Swallow Ct South Bend (46619) *(G-15098)*
Ken-Bar Tool & Engineering Inc 765 284-4408
   101 Minnow Ln Noblesville (46060) *(G-13119)*
Ken's Cycle Service, South Bend *Also Called: Ken Kowalski (G-15098)*
Kenco Plastics Inc 219 324-6621
   809 Pine Lake Ave La Porte (46350) *(G-10433)*
Kenco Plastics Inc (PA) 219 362-7565
   2022 W 450 N La Porte (46350) *(G-10434)*
Kendallville Custom Printing 260 347-9233
   1307 N Lima Rd Kendallville (46755) *(G-10125)*
Kendallville Iron & Metal Inc 260 347-1958
   243 E Lisbon Rd Kendallville (46755) *(G-10126)*
Kendallville Publishing Co Inc 260 347-0400
   102 N Main St Kendallville (46755) *(G-10127)*
Kendallville Mall 260 897-2697
   109 N Baum St Avilla (46710) *(G-482)*
Kendle Custom Inc 812 985-5917
   11711 Boberg Rd Evansville (47712) *(G-4148)*
Kendon Corporation 765 282-1515
   3904 S Hoyt Ave Muncie (47302) *(G-12433)*
Kendrion (mishawaka) LLC 574 257-2422
   56733 Magnetic Dr Mishawaka (46545) *(G-11922)*
Kenley Corporation 765 825-7150
   5540 Western Ave Connersville (47331) *(G-2452)*

Kenn Feld Group LLC (PA) 260 632-4242
   4724 N State Road 101 Woodburn (46797) *(G-16950)*
Kennametal Consora Clad, New Albany *Also Called: Kennametal Inc (G-12759)*
Kennametal Inc 574 534-2585
   1201 Eisenhower Dr N Goshen (46526) *(G-6185)*
Kennametal Inc 317 696-8798
   9217 Backwater Dr Indianapolis (46250) *(G-8670)*
Kennametal Inc 219 362-1000
   300 Philadelphia St La Porte (46350) *(G-10435)*
Kennametal Inc 812 948-2118
   501 Park East Blvd New Albany (47150) *(G-12759)*
Kennametal Stellite, Goshen *Also Called: Kennametal Stellite LP (G-6186)*
Kennametal Stellite LP 574 534-9532
   1201 Eisenhower Dr N Goshen (46526) *(G-6186)*
Kennedy Expressline Inc 574 272-9072
   2933 Council Oak Dr South Bend (46628) *(G-15099)*
Kennedy Metal Products Inc 219 322-9388
   1050 Kennedy Ave Schererville (46375) *(G-14527)*
Kennedy Tank & Mfg Co 317 787-1311
   833 E Sumner Ave Indianapolis (46227) *(G-8671)*
Kenneth E Ziegler 765 675-2222
   2899 E 150 S Tipton (46072) *(G-15778)*
Kenneth Fuhrman 812 482-4612
   6711 N 550w Jasper (47546) *(G-9863)*
Kenneth Raber 812 486-3102
   2436 N 750 E Montgomery (47558) *(G-12105)*
Kenney Orthopedics, Bloomington *Also Called: Kenney Orthpdics Blmington LLC (G-900)*
Kenney Orthopedics Carmel LLC (HQ) 317 993-3664
   10435 N Pennsylvania St Carmel (46280) *(G-1680)*
Kenney Orthopedics Seymour LLC (HQ) 812 271-1627
   629 E Tipton St Seymour (47274) *(G-14660)*
Kenney Orthpdics Blmington LLC 812 727-3651
   474 S Landmark Ave Bloomington (47403) *(G-900)*
Kenney Orthpdics Indnpolis LLC (HQ) 317 300-0814
   521 E County Line Rd Ste B Greenwood (46143) *(G-6722)*
Kenney Orthpdics Indnpolis LLC 859 241-1015
   1801 Senate Blvd Ste 420 Indianapolis (46202) *(G-8672)*
Kenney Orthpedics Columbus LLC 812 214-4623
   2525 California St Ste B Columbus (47201) *(G-2334)*
Kenny Dewig Meats Sausage Inc 812 724-2333
   9208 W State Road 165 Owensville (47665) *(G-13469)*
Kennyleeholmescom 574 612-2526
   25855 Kiser Ct Elkhart (46514) *(G-3451)*
Kenra Professional LLC (HQ) 800 428-8073
   7445 Company Dr Indianapolis (46237) *(G-8673)*
Kens Foods Inc 765 505-7900
   917 Edwards Dr Lebanon (46052) *(G-10908)*
Kens Tool & Design 812 268-6653
   2437 N Section St Sullivan (47882) *(G-15411)*
Kensington Watch Services 219 306-5499
   146 N Main St Crown Point (46307) *(G-2708)*
Kent Brenneke 260 446-5383
   14038 Scipio Rd Harlan (46743) *(G-7057)*
Kent Machine Inc 765 778-7777
   8677 S State Road 9 Pendleton (46064) *(G-13539)*
Kent Mercantile, Hanover *Also Called: Pates Processing LLC (G-7044)*
Kent Nutrition Group Inc 574 722-5368
   2407 S 400 E Logansport (46947) *(G-11087)*
Kentner Creek, Wabash *Also Called: West Plains Distribution LLC (G-16224)*
Kentuckiana Machine & Tool Inc 502 593-3975
   518 Maplewood Blvd Georgetown (47122) *(G-6065)*
Kentuckiana Machine and TI Inc 502 301-9005
   4550 Lazy Creek Rd Ne Lanesville (47136) *(G-10800)*
Kentuckiana Wire Rope & Supply 812 282-3667
   3335 Industrial Pkwy Jeffersonville (47130) *(G-10005)*
Kentuckiana Wood Products Inc 812 288-7989
   1275 Meigs Ave Jeffersonville (47130) *(G-10006)*
Kentuckiana Yacht Services LLC 812 282-7579
   700 E Market St Jeffersonville (47130) *(G-10007)*
Kentucky Ave Mine, Indianapolis *Also Called: Martin Marietta Materials Inc (G-8841)*
Kentucky Concrete Indiana LLC 812 282-6671
   2220 Hamburg Pike Jeffersonville (47130) *(G-10008)*

ALPHABETIC SECTION — Kilgore Manufacturing Co

Kentucky Wood Floors LLC 812 256-2164
533 Louis Smith Rd Borden (47106) *(G-1111)*

Kep Chem Inc 574 739-0501
616 Center Ave Logansport (46947) *(G-11088)*

Keppler Steel and Fabricating 765 289-1529
1401 S Macedonia Ave Muncie (47302) *(G-12434)*

Kerham Inc 260 483-5444
205 E Collins Rd Fort Wayne (46825) *(G-5146)*

Kerkhoff Associates Inc (PA) 765 583-4491
21 W Oxford St Otterbein (47970) *(G-13453)*

Kermit Usa Inc 765 288-3334
221 S Franklin Rd Ste 710 Indianapolis (46219) *(G-8674)*

Kern's Speed & Racing Products, Bedford Also Called: Kerns Speed Shop *(G-652)*

Kerns Speed Shop 812 275-4289
203 Newton St Bedford (47421) *(G-652)*

Kerr Group LLC 812 424-2904
315 Se 2nd St Evansville (47713) *(G-4149)*

Kerria Industries Inc 317 852-4542
668 Albatross Ln Brownsburg (46112) *(G-1382)*

Kerry Inc 812 464-9151
1615 N Fulton Ave Evansville (47710) *(G-4150)*

Kerry Inc 812 464-9151
1515 Park St Evansville (47710) *(G-4151)*

Kerst Pallet, Attica Also Called: Corey Kerst *(G-346)*

Kes LLC 812 728-8101
5013 Lakeview Dr Floyds Knobs (47119) *(G-4683)*

Kessington LLC 574 266-4500
1020 County Road 6 W Elkhart (46514) *(G-3452)*

Kessington Machine Products, Elkhart Also Called: Kessington LLC *(G-3452)*

Kessler Concepts Inc 317 630-9901
225 E 10th St Indianapolis (46202) *(G-8675)*

Kesters Electric Motor Svc LLC 574 269-2889
1408 Armstrong Rd Warsaw (46580) *(G-16382)*

Ketch Publishing 812 327-0072
4675 N Benton Dr Bloomington (47408) *(G-901)*

Keter North America Inc 765 298-6800
6435 S Scatterfield Rd Anderson (46013) *(G-141)*

Keter North America, Inc., Anderson Also Called: Keter North America Inc *(G-141)*

Keter Us Inc (DH) 317 575-4700
6435 S Scatterfield Rd Anderson (46013) *(G-142)*

Kettle Processed Foods, Morristown Also Called: Park 100 Foods Inc *(G-12280)*

Keurig Dr Pepper Inc 812 522-3823
1450 Schleter Rd Seymour (47274) *(G-14661)*

Keusch Glass Inc 812 482-2566
403 E 23rd St Jasper (47546) *(G-9864)*

Kevin Chumbley Enterprises 502 548-2544
3637 E Wetzel Rd Palmyra (47164) *(G-13481)*

Kevin Koch 574 971-8094
211 E Washington St Goshen (46528) *(G-6187)*

Kevin M Walters 317 565-9564
11220 Hearthstone Dr Fishers (46037) *(G-4554)*

Kewanna Metal Specialties Inc (PA) 574 653-2554
419 W Main St Kewanna (46939) *(G-10166)*

Kewanna Screen Printing Inc 574 653-2683
109 Toner St Kewanna (46939) *(G-10167)*

Key Electronics Inc 812 206-2500
2533 Centennial Blvd Jeffersonville (47130) *(G-10009)*

Key Enhancement LLC 502 403-5661
3310 E 10th St Ste 4 Jeffersonville (47130) *(G-10010)*

Key Made Now 317 664-8582
317 N Kenyon St Indianapolis (46219) *(G-8676)*

Key Millwork Inc 260 426-6501
1830 Wayne Trce Fort Wayne (46803) *(G-5147)*

Key Sheet Metal Inc 317 546-7151
1128 E Maryland St Indianapolis (46202) *(G-8677)*

Keyline Sales Inc 574 294-5611
2601 Marina Dr Elkhart (46514) *(G-3453)*

Keys Computers Inc 317 750-5071
8443 La Habra Ln Bldg 1 Indianapolis (46236) *(G-8678)*

Keys R US 317 616-0267
3210 E Thompson Rd Indianapolis (46227) *(G-8679)*

Keysight Technologies Inc 260 203-2179
1200 Airport North Office Park Ste D Fort Wayne (46825) *(G-5148)*

Keystone Concrete Inc (PA) 260 693-6437
12628 Us Highway 33 N Churubusco (46723) *(G-1986)*

Keystone Cooperative Inc 317 861-5080
1124 W Railroad St Fountaintown (46130) *(G-5615)*

Keystone Cooperative Inc 765 659-2596
411b Eb Kellyb Road Frankfort (46041) *(G-5678)*

Keystone Cooperative Inc 765 489-4141
4379 Jacksonburg Rd Hagerstown (47346) *(G-6838)*

Keystone Cooperative Inc (PA) 800 525-0272
770 N High School Rd Indianapolis (46214) *(G-8680)*

Keystone Cooperative Inc 765 249-2233
805 East St Michigantown (46057) *(G-11691)*

Keystone Engineering & Mfg LLC 317 319-7639
9786 E County Road 200 N Avon (46123) *(G-531)*

Keystone Engrg & Mfg Corp (PA) 317 271-6192
9786 E County Road 200 N Avon (46123) *(G-532)*

Keystone Industrial Flrg LLC 317 403-8747
7029 E County Road 200 N Avon (46123) *(G-533)*

Keystone Plant 35, Wakarusa Also Called: Keystone Rv Company *(G-16237)*

Keystone Rv Company 574 537-0600
2164 Caragana Ct Goshen (46526) *(G-6188)*

Keystone Rv Company 574 535-2100
2425 Davis Dr Goshen (46526) *(G-6189)*

Keystone Rv Company 574 535-2100
17400 Hackberry Dr Goshen (46526) *(G-6190)*

Keystone Rv Company (HQ) 574 534-9430
2642 Hackberry Dr Goshen (46526) *(G-6191)*

Keystone Rv Company 574 535-2100
608 Nelsons Pkwy Wakarusa (46573) *(G-16237)*

Keywest Metal 219 513-8429
2034 N Griffith Blvd Griffith (46319) *(G-6810)*

Keywest Metal 219 654-4063
6338 E 35th Ave Hobart (46342) *(G-7197)*

KFC Composite Engineering Co 219 369-9093
3451 S State Road 104 La Porte (46350) *(G-10436)*

Kh, Crown Point Also Called: Kiemle-Hankins Company *(G-2709)*

Khamis Fine Jewelers Inc 317 841-8440
9763 Fall Creek Rd Indianapolis (46256) *(G-8681)*

Khorporate Holdings Inc (PA) 260 357-3365
6492 State Road 205 Laotto (46763) *(G-10807)*

Kia Dos, Gary Also Called: Anderson Shykia *(G-5894)*

Kibbechem Inc 574 266-1234
22243 Innovation Dr Elkhart (46514) *(G-3454)*

Kic, Evansville Also Called: Kic LLC *(G-4152)*

Kic LLC 360 823-4440
7140 Office Cir Evansville (47715) *(G-4152)*

Kids At Heart Publishing Llc 765 478-5773
219 W Main St Cambridge City (47327) *(G-1498)*

Kids Place, Scottsburg Also Called: New Hope Services Inc *(G-14574)*

Kids World Productions Inc 317 674-6090
11551 Willow Bend Dr Zionsville (46077) *(G-17027)*

Kidstar Safety 800 785-6015
54846 Beech Rd Osceola (46561) *(G-13396)*

Kidstuff Playsystems Inc 219 938-3331
5400 Miller Ave Gary (46403) *(G-5974)*

Kiel Media LLC 219 544-2060
16 E Main St La Crosse (46348) *(G-10365)*

Kiemle-Hankins Company 219 213-2643
1011 E Summit St Crown Point (46307) *(G-2709)*

Kien Industries LLP 260 471-1098
4752 Trier Rd Fort Wayne (46815) *(G-5149)*

Kiesler Machine Inc 812 364-6610
13700 Chrissy Ln Ne Palmyra (47164) *(G-13482)*

Kihm Metal Technologies, Brazil Also Called: Ms Manufacturing LLC *(G-1156)*

Kik Cusrtom Products, Elkhart Also Called: Accra-Pac Inc *(G-3150)*

Kile Enterprises Inc 317 844-6629
1051 3rd Ave Sw Carmel (46032) *(G-1681)*

Kilgore Manufacturing Co 260 723-5523
602 Hathaway Dr South Whitley (46787) *(G-15320)*

Kilgore Manufacturing Co Inc.. 260 248-2002
  445 S Line St Columbia City (46725) *(G-2162)*
Kilgore Mfg Plant No 1, Columbia City *Also Called: Kilgore Manufacturing Co Inc (G-2162)*
Kill Her Set LLC... 317 992-2220
  6920 Eagle Highlands Way Ste 100 Indianapolis (46254) *(G-8682)*
Kill-N-Em Inc.. 574 233-6655
  2118 Franklin St South Bend (46613) *(G-15100)*
Killer Camaros Custom Camaro... 260 255-2425
  4762 Zelt Cv 1/2 New Haven (46774) *(G-12908)*
Killer Car Customs, New Haven *Also Called: Killer Camaros Custom Camaro (G-12908)*
Killer Machining Solutions LLC... 813 786-2309
  1650 E Northfield Dr Ste 1400 Brownsburg (46112) *(G-1383)*
Kim Plant 2, Muncie *Also Called: Hitachi Astemo Indiana Inc (G-12417)*
Kim Print LLC.. 812 223-5333
  6604 Heron Neck Dr Apt N Indianapolis (46217) *(G-8683)*
Kimalco Inc.. 812 463-3105
  213 W Division St Ste J Evansville (47710) *(G-4153)*
Kimalco Mattress, Evansville *Also Called: Kimalco Inc (G-4153)*
Kimball Corporate, The, Jasper *Also Called: Kimball Electronics Group LLC (G-9868)*
Kimball Elec Indianapolis Inc.. 812 634-4000
  2950 N Catherwood Ave Indianapolis (46219) *(G-8684)*
Kimball Electronics, Jasper *Also Called: Kimball Electronics Inc (G-9866)*
Kimball Electronics Inc.. 317 357-3175
  2402 N Shadeland Ave Indianapolis (46219) *(G-8685)*
Kimball Electronics Inc.. 317 545-5383
  6205 E 30th St Indianapolis (46219) *(G-8686)*
Kimball Electronics Inc.. 812 634-4200
  1038 E 15th St Jasper (47546) *(G-9865)*
Kimball Electronics Inc (PA)... 812 634-4000
  1205 Kimball Blvd Jasper (47546) *(G-9866)*
Kimball Electronics Group LLC.. 812 634-4200
  1600 Royal St Jasper (47546) *(G-9867)*
Kimball Electronics Group LLC (HQ)... 812 634-4000
  1205 Kimball Blvd Jasper (47546) *(G-9868)*
Kimball Electronics Mfg Inc.. 812 482-1600
  1600 Royal St Jasper (47549) *(G-9869)*
Kimball Electronics Tampa Inc (DH)... 812 634-4000
  1205 Kimball Blvd Jasper (47546) *(G-9870)*
Kimball Furniture Group LLC.. 812 482-8401
  1620 Cherry St Jasper (47546) *(G-9871)*
Kimball Furniture Group LLC (DH)... 812 482-1600
  1600 Royal St Jasper (47546) *(G-9872)*
Kimball Furniture Group LLC.. 812 482-8517
  1180 E 16th St Jasper (47546) *(G-9873)*
Kimball Furniture Group LLC.. 812 634-3526
  340 11th Ave Jasper (47546) *(G-9874)*
Kimball Hospitality Inc.. 812 482-8090
  1180 E 16th St Jasper (47546) *(G-9875)*
Kimball Hospitality Inc (DH)... 812 482-8090
  1600 Royal St Jasper (47546) *(G-9876)*
Kimball Inc.. 812 482-1600
  1600 Royal St Jasper (47546) *(G-9877)*
Kimball International, Jasper *Also Called: Kimball International Inc (G-9878)*
Kimball International Inc (HQ)... 812 482-1600
  1600 Royal St Jasper (47546) *(G-9878)*
Kimball International Inc.. 812 937-3284
  1600 Royal St Jasper (47546) *(G-9879)*
Kimball International Transit (DH)... 812 634-3346
  1001 Hrj Ln Jasper (47546) *(G-9880)*
Kimball Intl Brands Inc (DH)... 812 482-1600
  1600 Royal St Jasper (47546) *(G-9881)*
Kimball Office, Jasper *Also Called: Kimball Furniture Group LLC (G-9871)*
Kimber Creek Ltd, Zionsville *Also Called: Mgtc Inc (G-17032)*
Kimmel Fabrication Studio LLC.. 260 403-5691
  2727 Lofty Dr Ste 4 Fort Wayne (46808) *(G-5150)*
Kimmel Music... 260 302-3082
  221 S Morton St Kendallville (46755) *(G-10128)*
Kinco, Seymour *Also Called: King Industrial Corporation (G-14662)*
Kindful, Indianapolis *Also Called: Trail Software Inc (G-9628)*
Kindred Biosciences Inc (HQ)... 650 701-7901
  2500 Innovation Way N Greenfield (46140) *(G-6524)*

Kinedyne.. 260 403-5149
  3486 County Road 36 Auburn (46706) *(G-399)*
Kinetech LLC... 317 441-1924
  16840 Joliet Rd Westfield (46074) *(G-16704)*
Kinetech NM, Westfield *Also Called: Kinetech LLC (G-16704)*
Kinetics Xcavating LLC... 812 208-9892
  8391 N County Road 100 E Brazil (47834) *(G-1151)*
King Industrial Corporation.. 812 522-3261
  105 S Obrien St Seymour (47274) *(G-14662)*
King Investments Inc... 812 752-6000
  505 E Mcclain Ave Scottsburg (47170) *(G-14568)*
King Machining Inc... 317 271-3132
  5574 Station Hill Dr Avon (46123) *(G-534)*
King of Mountain Kom EMB LLC... 812 799-0611
  1998 Creekstone Dr Columbus (47201) *(G-2335)*
King of Tarpaulins The, Gosport *Also Called: Gosport Manufacturing Co Inc (G-6284)*
King Signs... 317 882-0785
  722 N Hawey Rd Greenwood (46142) *(G-6723)*
King Systems Corporation... 317 776-6823
  15011 Herriman Blvd Noblesville (46060) *(G-13120)*
King Tut Inc... 317 938-9907
  4720 Pebblepointe Pass Zionsville (46077) *(G-17028)*
King's Antenna Service, Angola *Also Called: Kas Satellite & Cable Inc (G-267)*
King's Copies, Indianapolis *Also Called: Rrc Corporation (G-9343)*
Kingery Group Inc.. 317 823-9585
  6574 Breckenridge Dr Indianapolis (46236) *(G-8687)*
Kingmaker Foods, Indianapolis *Also Called: Cbfc LLC (G-7763)*
Kings Custom Machine LLC... 812 477-5262
  1832 E Sierra Dr Haubstadt (47639) *(G-7087)*
Kings-Qlity Rstrtion Svcs LLC.. 812 944-4347
  1818 E Market St New Albany (47150) *(G-12760)*
Kingsbury Castings Div, La Porte *Also Called: Accurate Castings Inc (G-10374)*
Kingsford, Decatur *Also Called: Kingsford Products Inc (G-2866)*
Kingsford Products Inc (PA).. 740 862-4450
  1819 Patterson St Decatur (46733) *(G-2866)*
Kinko's, Lafayette *Also Called: Kinkos Inc (G-10620)*
Kinkos Inc... 765 449-4950
  3520 South St Lafayette (47905) *(G-10620)*
Kinney Dancewear... 317 581-1800
  14753 Hazel Dell Xing Ste 600 Noblesville (46062) *(G-13121)*
Kinney Defense Solutions... 812 360-6189
  933 Quarterhorse Run Bargersville (46106) *(G-569)*
Kinro, Elkhart *Also Called: Kinro Manufacturing Inc (G-3456)*
Kinro Manufacturing Inc.. 803 385-5171
  Elkhart (46515) *(G-3455)*
Kinro Manufacturing Inc.. 574 535-1125
  3501 County Road 6 E Elkhart (46514) *(G-3456)*
Kinro Manufacturing Inc (HQ)... 574 535-1125
  3501 County Road 6 E Elkhart (46514) *(G-3457)*
Kinser Timber Products Inc... 812 876-4775
  8283 W Hedrick Rd Gosport (47433) *(G-6285)*
Kinser Trucking, Gosport *Also Called: Kinser Timber Products Inc (G-6285)*
Kintail Inc.. 317 993-8220
  17399 Dovehouse Ln Westfield (46074) *(G-16705)*
Kinzie Mill Work... 765 564-4355
  852 S 800 W Delphi (46923) *(G-2901)*
Kipin Industries... 317 510-1181
  2950 Prospect St Indianapolis (46203) *(G-8688)*
Kipps Plumbing Inc... 219 661-9320
  800 E North St Ste 1 Crown Point (46307) *(G-2710)*
Kirby, Hamilton *Also Called: Scott Fetzer Company (G-6861)*
Kirby Machine Company LLC.. 317 773-6700
  1709 Cherry St Noblesville (46060) *(G-13122)*
Kirby Risk Corporation... 765 643-3384
  633 Broadway St Anderson (46012) *(G-143)*
Kirby Risk Corporation... 765 447-1402
  3574 Mccarty Ln Lafayette (47905) *(G-10621)*
Kirby Risk Corporation... 765 423-4205
  714 S 1st St Lafayette (47905) *(G-10622)*
Kirby Risk Corporation (PA).. 765 448-4567
  1815 Sagamore Pkwy N Lafayette (47904) *(G-10623)*

ALPHABETIC SECTION

Kirby Risk Corporation 765 664-5185
1221 S Adams St Marion (46953) *(G-11304)*

Kirby Risk Corporation 765 254-5460
1619 S Walnut St Muncie (47302) *(G-12435)*

Kirby Risk Corporation 317 398-9713
2325 E Michigan Rd Shelbyville (46176) *(G-14768)*

Kirby Risk Electric Motor Repr, Lafayette Also Called: Kirby Risk Corporation *(G-10622)*

Kirby Risk Electrical Supply, Anderson Also Called: Kirby Risk Corporation *(G-143)*

Kirby Risk Electrical Supply, Lafayette Also Called: Kirby Risk Corporation *(G-10623)*

Kirby Risk Servicenter, Lafayette Also Called: Kirby Risk Corporation *(G-10621)*

Kirby Tool and Die Inc 812 369-7779
2716 N Pierce Dr Solsberry (47459) *(G-14926)*

Kirchoff Custom Sports Inc 812 434-0355
311 Eissler Rd Evansville (47711) *(G-4154)*

Kirk Enterprise Solutions Inc 260 665-3670
333 Hoosier Dr Angola (46703) *(G-268)*

Kirklin Waste Water Treatment 765 279-5251
800 North Main Street Kirklin (46050) *(G-10190)*

Kisco, Cedar Lake Also Called: Kouder Instrument Service Co *(G-1833)*

Kistner Enterprises Inc 317 773-7733
623 Westfield Rd Noblesville (46060) *(G-13123)*

Kitchen & Bath Fixtures 574 296-7617
3601 Charlotte Ave Elkhart (46517) *(G-3458)*

Kitchen & Baths By Untd HM Sup, Muncie Also Called: United Home Supply Inc *(G-12509)*

Kitchen Kompact Inc 812 282-6681
911 E 11th St Jeffersonville (47130) *(G-10011)*

Kitchen Queen LLC 812 662-8399
58 W County Rd 650 N Saint Paul (47272) *(G-14465)*

Kitchen-Quip Inc 260 837-8311
338 S Oak St Kendallville (46755) *(G-10129)*

Kitchen/Bath Design Center, Harlan Also Called: Dutch Made Inc *(G-7054)*

Kitchens By Gregory Ltd 219 769-1551
8680 Louisiana St Merrillville (46410) *(G-11527)*

Kite & Key LLC 317 654-7703
5825 Alpine Ave Indianapolis (46224) *(G-8689)*

Kite Greyhound LLC 317 577-5600
30 S Meridian St Indianapolis (46204) *(G-8690)*

Kitley Company 317 546-2427
3823 Massachusetts Ave Indianapolis (46218) *(G-8691)*

Kitterman Machine Co Inc 317 773-2283
87 S 8th St Noblesville (46060) *(G-13124)*

Kitwana Kouture LLC 812 589-7135
705 Se 3rd St Apt B Evansville (47713) *(G-4155)*

Kiyam Transport LLC 502 551-6245
1251 N Eddy St Ste 200 South Bend (46617) *(G-15101)*

Kjs Associates, Indianapolis Also Called: Magnetic Instrumentation LLC *(G-8810)*

Kjs Beauty Lounge LLC 317 426-0621
3639 N Raceway Rd Indianapolis (46234) *(G-8692)*

KK Hall Inc 317 839-8329
6774 S County Road 400 E Clayton (46118) *(G-2061)*

Klabunde LLC 765 635-1101
9662 S State Road 13 Fortville (46040) *(G-5601)*

Kleeman Cabinetry 812 926-0428
9814 Hueseman Rd Aurora (47001) *(G-447)*

Kleen-Rite Supply Inc 812 422-7483
1101 E Diamond Ave Evansville (47711) *(G-4156)*

Kleenflow LLC 317 912-0027
4515 Dr Martin Luther King Jr Blvd Anderson (46013) *(G-144)*

Kleerblue Solutions 800 320-2122
1601 Buchanan Rd Evansville (47720) *(G-4157)*

Kleihege Welding Machine 812 849-5056
746 Parks Implement Rd Mitchell (47446) *(G-12042)*

Klem Signs & Restyling LLC 812 357-2222
15875 N State Road 545 Saint Meinrad (47577) *(G-14461)*

Klems Graphic Designs 812 357-2222
15875 N State Road 545 Saint Meinrad (47577) *(G-14462)*

Klene Pipe Structures Inc 812 663-6445
515 N Anderson St Greensburg (47240) *(G-6612)*

Klh Audio, Noblesville Also Called: Kelley Global Brands LLC *(G-13118)*

Klh Holding Corporation (HQ) 317 634-3976
2002 Lafayette Rd Indianapolis (46222) *(G-8693)*

Klincher Locknut, Indianapolis Also Called: Dual Machine Corporation *(G-8017)*

Kline Cabinet Makers LLC 317 326-3049
16 S Main St Maxwell (46154) *(G-11444)*

Klinge Coatings, Indianapolis Also Called: Klinge Enameling Company Inc *(G-8694)*

Klinge Enameling Company Inc 317 359-8291
5001 Prospect St Indianapolis (46203) *(G-8694)*

Klingerman Welding 574 342-7375
409 W Jackson St Bourbon (46504) *(G-1123)*

Klipsch, Indianapolis Also Called: Klipsch Group Inc *(G-8695)*

Klipsch Group Inc (HQ) 317 860-8100
3502 Woodview Trce Ste 200 Indianapolis (46268) *(G-8695)*

Klomp Construction Company 219 308-8372
9160 W 106th Ave Saint John (46373) *(G-14454)*

Klosterman Baking Co 317 359-5545
5867 Churchman Rd Indianapolis (46203) *(G-8696)*

KLOSTERMAN BAKING CO., Indianapolis Also Called: Klosterman Baking Co *(G-8696)*

Klotz Synthetic Lubricants LLC 260 490-0489
7424 Freedom Way Fort Wayne (46818) *(G-5151)*

KMC Controls, New Paris Also Called: Kreuter Manufacturing Co Inc *(G-12964)*

KMC Corporation 574 267-7033
602 Leiter Dr Warsaw (46580) *(G-16383)*

KMC Enterprises Inc 765 584-1533
1094 N Old Highway 27 Winchester (47394) *(G-16893)*

Kmi, Palmyra Also Called: Kiesler Machine Inc *(G-13482)*

Kml Inc (PA) 260 897-3723
108 S Main St Laotto (46763) *(G-10808)*

Kmls LLC 317 845-2955
6710 W 425 S Morgantown (46160) *(G-12259)*

Kmm Creative LLC 813 764-9294
5534 Saint Joe Rd Fort Wayne (46835) *(G-5152)*

Kms, Hobart Also Called: Knitting Mill Inc *(G-7198)*

Kmsd Inc 219 808-7159
5705 Murvihill Rd Valparaiso (46383) *(G-15987)*

Kmuet LLC 317 645-0421
2815 Ralston Ave Indianapolis (46218) *(G-8697)*

Kn Platech America Corporation 317 392-7707
1755 Mccall Dr Shelbyville (46176) *(G-14769)*

Knapke & Sons Inc 260 639-0112
14525 Bruick Ln Hoagland (46745) *(G-7169)*

Knapp Engraving, Montgomery Also Called: Cedar Woodworking *(G-12088)*

Knauf Insulation Inc (HQ) 317 398-4434
1 Knauf Dr Shelbyville (46176) *(G-14770)*

Knepp Logging LLC 812 486-3741
2946 N 900 E Loogootee (47553) *(G-11142)*

Kneppers Inc 260 636-2180
575 Weber Rd Albion (46701) *(G-30)*

Kneppers Inc (PA) 260 636-2180
1390 N 750 E Avilla (46710) *(G-483)*

Knepps Custom Welding 765 525-5130
7586 N County Road 450 W Saint Paul (47272) *(G-14466)*

Knepps Logging Bandmilling 812 486-7721
5220 N 650 E Montgomery (47558) *(G-12106)*

Knepps Woodworking 812 486-3546
6161 E 350 N Montgomery (47558) *(G-12107)*

Knies Sawmill Inc 812 683-3402
2238 E 550s Huntingburg (47542) *(G-7285)*

Knight Davis Publishing LLC 812 568-9646
1245 W Wortman Rd Evansville (47725) *(G-4158)*

Knights Woodworking LLC 812 988-2106
3991 State Road 46 W Nashville (47448) *(G-12673)*

Knip Welding 219 987-5123
8446 W 1000 N Demotte (46310) *(G-2921)*

Knit Knot Crochet 765 730-9416
503 N George St Ridgeville (47380) *(G-14235)*

Knitting Mill Inc 219 942-8031
291 N County Line Rd Hobart (46342) *(G-7198)*

Knk Battery LLC 765 426-2016
9117 E State Road 26 Otterbein (47970) *(G-13454)*

Knorr Brake Truck Systems Co 260 356-9720
1230 Sabine St Huntington (46750) *(G-7334)*

Knothole Woodworks LLC 317 600-8151
223 W Henry Rd Kirklin (46050) *(G-10191)*

Knots & Spots Inc 574 946-6000
5341 N Us Highway 35 Winamac (46996) *(G-16865)*

Knotted Strands Crochet 574 232-9127
733 Roland Ct South Bend (46601) *(G-15102)*

Know Wonder Publishing LLC 317 506-4611
2844 Medford Ave Indianapolis (46222) *(G-8698)*

Knowledge Diffusion Games, Bloomington *Also Called: Knowledge Diffusion Games LLC (G-902)*

Knowledge Diffusion Games LLC 812 361-4424
1441 S Fenbrook Ln Ste 100 Bloomington (47401) *(G-902)*

Knowledge Trading Network LLC 219 309-5360
346 E 1200 N Chesterton (46304) *(G-1941)*

Knox, Knox *Also Called: Knox Fertilizer Company Inc (G-10213)*

Knox City Sand & Gravel, Vincennes *Also Called: Rogers Group Inc (G-16150)*

Knox Cnty Assn For Rmrkble Ctz (PA) 812 886-4312
2525 N 6th St Vincennes (47591) *(G-16136)*

Knox Enterprises Inc 317 714-3073
1 Technology Way Indianapolis (46268) *(G-8699)*

Knox Fertilizer Company Inc 574 772-6275
2660 E 100 S Knox (46534) *(G-10213)*

Knox Inc 260 665-6617
101 Fox Lake Rd Angola (46703) *(G-269)*

Knoy Apparel 765 448-1031
1164 S Creasy Ln Lafayette (47905) *(G-10624)*

Knu LLC (PA) 812 367-1761
824 W 23rd St Ferdinand (47532) *(G-4438)*

Kobaltec LLC 219 462-1483
1450 Clark Rd Valparaiso (46385) *(G-15988)*

Kobelco Cmpsr Mfg Ind Inc 574 295-3145
3000 Hammond Ave Elkhart (46516) *(G-3459)*

Koch Enterprises, Evansville *Also Called: Koch Enterprises Inc (G-4159)*

Koch Enterprises Inc (PA) 812 465-9800
14 S 11th Ave Evansville (47712) *(G-4159)*

Koch Foods 574 457-4384
4823 E 1200 N Syracuse (46567) *(G-15466)*

Koch House of Design, Goshen *Also Called: Kevin Koch (G-6187)*

Koch Industries Inc 260 356-7191
502 E Hosler Rd Huntington (46750) *(G-7335)*

KOCH INDUSTRIES, INC., Huntington *Also Called: Koch Industries Inc (G-7335)*

Kochs Electric Inc 317 639-5624
202 E Palmer St Indianapolis (46225) *(G-8700)*

Kocsis Brothers Machine Co 219 397-8400
4321 Railroad Ave East Chicago (46312) *(G-3025)*

Koehler 219 462-4128
1905 Whitney Ave Valparaiso (46383) *(G-15989)*

Koehler Welding Supply Inc 812 574-4103
2352 Michigan Rd Madison (47250) *(G-11233)*

Koenig Equipment Inc 765 962-7330
3421 State Road 38 Richmond (47374) *(G-14154)*

Koester Metals Inc 260 495-1818
301 W Water St Fremont (46737) *(G-5825)*

Koetter Sawmill, Borden *Also Called: Koetter Woodworking (G-1112)*

Koetter Woodworking 812 923-8875
533 Louis Smith Rd Borden (47106) *(G-1112)*

Koetter Woodworking Inc (PA) 812 923-8875
533 Louis Smith Rd Borden (47106) *(G-1113)*

KOI Enterprises Inc 812 537-2335
601 Saint Clair St Lawrenceburg (47025) *(G-10843)*

Kokoku Wire Industries Corp 574 287-5610
406 Manitou Pl South Bend (46616) *(G-15103)*

Kokomo Casting Plant, Kokomo *Also Called: FCA US LLC (G-10267)*

Kokomo Electronic Assembly, Kokomo *Also Called: GM Components Holdings LLC (G-10270)*

Kokomo Metal Fabricators Inc 765 459-8173
1931 E North St Kokomo (46901) *(G-10292)*

Kokomo Optical Company Inc 765 459-5137
501 E Lincoln Rd Kokomo (46902) *(G-10293)*

Kokomo Perspective Wilson Advg, Kokomo *Also Called: Wilson Media Group Inc (G-10359)*

Kokomo Power Electronics, Kokomo *Also Called: Borgwarner Propulsion II LLC (G-10241)*

Kokomo Press LLC 317 575-9903
5534 Saint Joe Rd Fort Wayne (46835) *(G-5153)*

Kokomo Sand, Russiaville *Also Called: Martin Marietta Materials Inc (G-14424)*

Kokomo Spring Company Inc 765 459-5156
320 Rainbow Dr Kokomo (46902) *(G-10294)*

Kokomo Thrift & Gift LLC 765 553-5973
1016 S Main St Kokomo (46902) *(G-10295)*

Kokomo Truck Store 765 459-5118
901 E Markland Ave Kokomo (46901) *(G-10296)*

Koldcare, Elkhart *Also Called: Romaine Incorporated (G-3651)*

Kolossos, Long Beach *Also Called: Kolossos Inc (G-11122)*

Kolossos Inc 312 952-6991
2715 Duffy Ln Long Beach (46360) *(G-11122)*

Koma Integration 812 557-6009
10778 Randall Ave Aurora (47001) *(G-448)*

Komodo Pharmaceuticals Inc 317 485-0023
8064 W 1000 S Fortville (46040) *(G-5602)*

Komun Scents 317 308-0714
4635 Falcon Run Way Indianapolis (46254) *(G-8701)*

Konecranes Inc 219 661-9602
1255 Erie Ct Ste B Crown Point (46307) *(G-2711)*

Konecranes Inc 812 479-0488
2400 Kotter Ave Evansville (47715) *(G-4160)*

Konecranes Inc 260 451-2016
3939 Fourier Dr Ste D Fort Wayne (46818) *(G-5154)*

Konecranes Inc 317 546-8122
134 S Park Blvd Greenwood (46143) *(G-6724)*

Konecranes Inc 812 941-1250
900 Progress Blvd New Albany (47150) *(G-12761)*

Konrady Graphics Inc 219 662-0436
4070 Bush Hill Ct Crown Point (46307) *(G-2712)*

Konrady Plastics Inc 219 763-7001
1780 Coppes Ct Portage (46368) *(G-13880)*

Koomler & Sons Inc 260 482-7641
3820 Superior Ridge Dr Fort Wayne (46808) *(G-5155)*

Koontz-Wagner Custom Controls Holdings LLC 574 387-5802
3801 Voorde Dr Ste B South Bend (46628) *(G-15104)*

Koontz-Wagner Electric, South Bend *Also Called: Koontz-Wagner Custom Controls Holdings LLC (G-15104)*

Koontz-Wagner Maintenance Svcs, South Bend *Also Called: Kw Maintenance Services LLC (G-15113)*

Kopelov Cut Stone Inc 812 675-0099
2321 39th St Bedford (47421) *(G-653)*

Kopy Kat, Jeffersonville *Also Called: Office Sup of Southern Ind Inc (G-10027)*

Kore Industries LLC 773 343-5966
518 S Hancock St Unit 2671 Gary (46403) *(G-5975)*

Kore Outdoor (us) Inc 800 724-6822
4230 Lake Ave Fort Wayne (46815) *(G-5156)*

Korte Bros Inc 260 497-0500
620 W Cook Rd Fort Wayne (46825) *(G-5157)*

Kortzendorf Machine & Tool 317 783-5449
646 Macy Way Greenwood (46142) *(G-6725)*

Kostyo Woodworking Inc 812 466-7350
3399 Fort Harrison Rd Terre Haute (47804) *(G-15625)*

Kouder Instrument Service Co 219 374-5935
9003 W 142nd Pl Cedar Lake (46303) *(G-1833)*

Kountry Kraft Wood Pdts LLC 574 831-6736
68604 County Road 15 New Paris (46553) *(G-12963)*

Kountry Wood Products LLC (PA) 574 773-5673
352 Shawnee St Nappanee (46550) *(G-12618)*

Kousei Usa Inc 812 373-7315
2396 Norcross Dr Ste C Columbus (47201) *(G-2336)*

Kova Fertilizer Inc (PA) 812 663-5081
1330 N Anderson St Greensburg (47240) *(G-6613)*

Kovenz Memorial Shop, La Porte *Also Called: Harris Precast Inc (G-10416)*

Kozs Quality Printing Inc 219 696-6711
17934 Grant Pl # A Lowell (46356) *(G-11166)*

Kp Holdings LLC 317 867-0234
2000 E 196th St Westfield (46074) *(G-16706)*

Kp Pharmaceutical Tech Inc 812 330-8121
1212 W Rappel Ave Bloomington (47404) *(G-903)*

Kpc Media Group, Angola *Also Called: Kpc Media Group Inc (G-270)*

Kpc Media Group Inc 678 645-0000
45 S Public Sq Angola (46703) *(G-270)*

ALPHABETIC SECTION

Kpc Media Group Inc 260 925-2611
  118 W 9th St Auburn (46706) *(G-400)*
Kpc Media Group Inc 260 868-5501
  118 W 9th St Auburn (46706) *(G-401)*
Kpc Media Group Inc 260 426-2640
  6418 Lima Rd Fort Wayne (46818) *(G-5158)*
Kpc Media Group Inc (PA) 260 347-0400
  102 N Main St Kendallville (46755) *(G-10130)*
Kph Engineered Systems Inc 317 867-0234
  2000 E 196th St Westfield (46074) *(G-16707)*
Kprime Technologies LLC 260 399-1337
  9318 Airport Dr Ste F Fort Wayne (46809) *(G-5159)*
Kra International LLC (PA) 574 259-3550
  1810 Clover Rd Mishawaka (46545) *(G-11923)*
Krafft Gravel Inc (PA) 260 238-4653
  6031 County Road 68 Spencerville (46788) *(G-15372)*
Kraft Foods, Kendallville *Also Called: Kraft Heinz Foods Company (G-10131)*
Kraft Heinz Foods Company 260 347-1300
  151 W Ohio St Kendallville (46755) *(G-10131)*
Krafty Bravo LLC 317 366-3485
  1251 N Eddy St Ste 200 South Bend (46617) *(G-15105)*
Kraigs Custom Woodworking 574 904-7501
  1810 E 12th St Mishawaka (46544) *(G-11924)*
Kramer Furn & Cab Makers Inc 812 526-2711
  12600 N Presidential Way Edinburgh (46124) *(G-3089)*
Krazy Klothes Ltd (PA) 317 687-8310
  1101 S Illinois St Indianapolis (46225) *(G-8702)*
Kreamo Bakers, South Bend *Also Called: Alpha Baking Co Inc (G-14938)*
Kreative Concepts LLC 260 579-0922
  808 Colerick St Fort Wayne (46806) *(G-5160)*
Kreider Manufacturing 260 894-7120
  405 Gerber St Ligonier (46767) *(G-11018)*
Kremers Urban Phrmcuticals Inc (HQ) 1101 C Ave W Seymour (47274) *(G-14663)*
Kretler Tool & Engineering Inc 260 897-2662
  104 Well St Avilla (46710) *(G-484)*
Kreuter Manufacturing Co Inc (PA) 574 831-4626
  19476 Industrial Dr New Paris (46553) *(G-12964)*
Kristine Willoughby 574 850-5145
  23700 Marquette Blvd Lot 5 South Bend (46628) *(G-15106)*
Kristopher Cox 502 930-9162
  101 N 5th St Apt 16 Scottsburg (47170) *(G-14569)*
Krocs Butcher Shop LLC 812 208-8116
  3000 Kussner St Terre Haute (47802) *(G-15626)*
Kroger, Elkhart *Also Called: Kroger Co (G-3460)*
Kroger, South Bend *Also Called: Kroger Co (G-15107)*
Kroger Co 574 294-6092
  130 W Hively Ave Elkhart (46517) *(G-3460)*
Kroger Co 574 291-0740
  1217 E Ireland Rd South Bend (46614) *(G-15107)*
Kroger Limited Partnership II 765 364-5200
  800 N Englewood Dr Crawfordsville (47933) *(G-2583)*
Kroger Limited Partnership II 317 229-7600
  400 S Shortridge Rd Indianapolis (46219) *(G-8703)*
Kronmiller Machine & Tool Inc 260 436-1355
  2230 Lakeview Dr Fort Wayne (46808) *(G-5161)*
Kropf Industries Inc 574 533-2171
  58647 State Road 15 Goshen (46528) *(G-6192)*
Krowned By Qwan LLC 317 813-9914
  6101 N Keystone Ave Indianapolis (46220) *(G-8704)*
Krs, Evansville *Also Called: Kleen-Rite Supply Inc (G-4156)*
Krukemeier Machine & Tool Co 317 784-7042
  4949 Subway St Beech Grove (46107) *(G-697)*
Kruz, Knox *Also Called: Kruz Inc (G-10214)*
Kruz Inc (PA) 574 772-6673
  1201 W Culver Rd Knox (46534) *(G-10214)*
KS Kreations 574 514-7366
  7700 Greenbrier Rd Ne Georgetown (47122) *(G-6066)*
Ksm Logistics LLC 574 318-2040
  2009 N Brookfield St South Bend (46628) *(G-15108)*
Ksn Technologies Inc 219 877-4770
  364 Indian Boundary Rd Ste A Chesterton (46304) *(G-1942)*

Kt Cakes 812 442-6047
  13699 N Rock Run Church Rd Rosedale (47874) *(G-14381)*
Kt Industries LLC 260 432-0027
  3925 Ardmore Ave Fort Wayne (46802) *(G-5162)*
Kt Soap Products LLC 219 344-5871
  1709 Genesis Dr La Porte (46350) *(G-10437)*
KTI Cutting Tool, Fort Wayne *Also Called: KTI Cutting Tools Inc (G-5163)*
KTI Cutting Tools Inc 260 749-1465
  7007 Trafalgar Dr Fort Wayne (46803) *(G-5163)*
Ktool & Fire LLC 219 575-1428
  1503 Monroe St La Porte (46350) *(G-10438)*
Ktr Corporation 219 872-9100
  122 Anchor Rd Michigan City (46360) *(G-11629)*
Kubota Authorized Dealer, Terre Haute *Also Called: Bane-Welker Equipment LLC (G-15550)*
Kuckuck Transport LLC 260 609-0316
  2165 S 625 W South Whitley (46787) *(G-15321)*
Kueber Cabinet Shop, Mount Vernon *Also Called: Robert C Kueber (G-12317)*
Kuehne Nagel, Plainfield *Also Called: Rolls-Royce Corporation (G-13723)*
Kuehnert Dairy Inc 260 489-3766
  6532 W Cook Rd Fort Wayne (46818) *(G-5164)*
Kuert Concrete, South Bend *Also Called: Kuert Concrete Inc (G-15109)*
Kuert Concrete Inc 574 293-0430
  18370 Us Highway 20 Goshen (46528) *(G-6193)*
Kuert Concrete Inc 574 223-2414
  1101 W 13th St Rochester (46975) *(G-14299)*
Kuert Concrete Inc (PA) 574 232-9911
  5909 Nimtz Pkwy South Bend (46628) *(G-15109)*
Kuert Concrete Inc 574 453-3993
  155 W 600 N Warsaw (46582) *(G-16384)*
Kuharic Enterprises 574 288-9410
  57890 Crumstown Hwy South Bend (46619) *(G-15110)*
Kulzer LLC 574 299-5466
  4315 S Lafayette Blvd South Bend (46614) *(G-15111)*
Kumar Brothers Inc 317 410-2450
  432 Huron Ter Apt B Avon (46123) *(G-535)*
Kumas Dumpster Rentals LLC 662 422-1508
  8145 Mount Ct Apt C Crown Point (46307) *(G-2713)*
Kuntry Lumber and Farm Sup Ltd 260 463-3242
  2875 S 00 E W Lagrange (46761) *(G-10746)*
Kuri TEC Manufacturing Inc 765 764-6000
  2600 E Us Hwy 41 Williamsport (47993) *(G-16850)*
Kurvy Kurves Kouture LLC 812 340-6090
  1100 N Crescent Rd Apt A208 Bloomington (47404) *(G-904)*
Kustom Kilms LLC 317 512-5813
  2410 Chestnut St Columbus (47201) *(G-2337)*
Kustom Tool, Fort Wayne *Also Called: James E Trowbridge (G-5131)*
Kvk US Technologies Inc 765 529-1100
  1016 S 25th St New Castle (47362) *(G-12871)*
Kw Custom Controls LLC 312 343-3920
  4755 Ameritech Dr South Bend (46628) *(G-15112)*
Kw Maintenance Services LLC 574 232-2051
  3801 Voorde Dr Ste B South Bend (46628) *(G-15113)*
Kwik Kopy Business Center 130, Evansville *Also Called: Ovation Communications Inc (G-4230)*
Kwik Kopy Printing 219 663-7799
  1180 N Main St Crown Point (46307) *(G-2714)*
Kwik Lok Corporation 260 493-1220
  1222 Ryan Rd New Haven (46774) *(G-12909)*
Kyann Manufacturing Group LLC 260 724-9721
  5232 N 375 E Decatur (46733) *(G-2867)*
KYB Americas Corporation (HQ) 317 736-7774
  2625 N Morton St Franklin (46131) *(G-5750)*
KYB Americas Corporation 317 881-7772
  850 N Graham Rd Ste C Greenwood (46143) *(G-6726)*
Kyle Fabrication & Welding LLC 317 627-8537
  200 W King St Franklin (46131) *(G-5751)*
Kyocera SGS Precision Tls Inc 260 244-7677
  201 Towerview Dr Columbia City (46725) *(G-2163)*
Kys, Jeffersonville *Also Called: Kentuckiana Yacht Services LLC (G-10007)*
Kz Welding 260 350-7397
  7754 W 400 S Hudson (46747) *(G-7247)*

Kzrv LP 260 768-4016
985 N 900 W Shipshewana (46565) *(G-14856)*

L & C Welding LLC 260 593-3410
11705 W 300 S Shipshewana (46565) *(G-14857)*

L & D Custom Woodworking LLC 812 486-2958
3610 N 900 E Montgomery (47558) *(G-12108)*

L & L Engineering Co Inc 317 786-6886
4925 Subway St Beech Grove (46107) *(G-698)*

L & L Fittings Mfg, Fort Wayne *Also Called: JM Fittings LLC (G-5137)*

L & L Press Inc 765 664-3162
1417 W Kem Rd Marion (46952) *(G-11305)*

L & L Woodworking LLC 574 535-4613
13614 N 700 W Nappanee (46550) *(G-12619)*

L & N Woodworking LLC 260 768-7008
2240 N 925 W Shipshewana (46565) *(G-14858)*

L & P Manufacturing Company 812 405-2093
207 Rodgers Ln Jonesville (47247) *(G-10085)*

L & R Machine Co Inc 317 787-7251
3136 S Emerson Ave Beech Grove (46107) *(G-699)*

L & R Marine LLC 260 768-8094
8755 W 250 N Shipshewana (46565) *(G-14859)*

L & S Lumber 765 886-1452
7501 State Road 38 Greens Fork (47345) *(G-6575)*

L & W Engineering Inc 574 825-5351
107 Industrial Pkwy E Middlebury (46540) *(G-11730)*

L & W Printing Services, Franklin *Also Called: Lesha and Wade Printing Svcs (G-5752)*

L & W Woodworking LLC 260 463-8938
4635 S 200 W Wolcottville (46795) *(G-16940)*

L and P Brothers 219 313-6946
7238 Oakdale Ave Hammond (46324) *(G-6967)*

L B Foster Company 260 244-2887
2658 S 700 E Columbia City (46725) *(G-2164)*

L E, Indianapolis *Also Called: Light Engineering (G-8749)*

L E Johnson Products Inc 574 293-5664
1133 Lusher Ave Elkhart (46516) *(G-3461)*

L E Johnson Products Inc (PA) 574 293-5664
2100 Sterling Ave Elkhart (46516) *(G-3462)*

L H Carbide Corporation (HQ) 260 432-5563
4420 Clubview Dr Fort Wayne (46804) *(G-5165)*

L H Controls Inc 260 432-9020
4420 Clubview Dr Fort Wayne (46804) *(G-5166)*

L H Stamping Corporation (HQ) 260 432-5563
4420 Clubview Dr Fort Wayne (46804) *(G-5167)*

L J T, South Bend *Also Called: Lock Joint Tube LLC (G-15127)*

L L Welding 812 499-2961
806 22nd St Tell City (47586) *(G-15506)*

L M Corporation 574 535-0581
416 Steury Ave Goshen (46528) *(G-6194)*

L M Products Inc 765 643-3802
1325 Meridian St Anderson (46016) *(G-145)*

L R Green Co Inc 317 781-4200
5650 Elmwood Ave Indianapolis (46203) *(G-8705)*

L R Nisley & Sons 574 642-1245
62724 County Road 35 Goshen (46528) *(G-6195)*

L S Manufacturing, Elkhart *Also Called: Patrick Industries Inc (G-3594)*

L Young Company Inc (PA) 219 285-8107
2673 W State Road 114 Morocco (47963) *(G-12268)*

L-Source Ltd LLC 260 459-1971
4630 W Jefferson Blvd Ste 6 Fort Wayne (46804) *(G-5168)*

L&E Engineering LLC 937 746-6696
254 N Graham Rd Greenwood (46143) *(G-6727)*

L&N Supply LLC 219 397-9500
4016 Deodar St East Chicago (46312) *(G-3026)*

L&N Welding LLC 317 372-9554
121 Commerce Dr Ste 306 Danville (46122) *(G-2817)*

L&S Sanitation Service 765 932-5410
270 S 100 W Rushville (46173) *(G-14404)*

L3harris Technologies Inc 812 202-5171
27548 N 1400 E Crane (47522) *(G-2539)*

L3harris Technologies Inc 812 202-5171
27548 N 1400 E Crane (47522) *(G-2540)*

L3harris Technologies Inc 260 451-5597
1919 W Cook Rd Fort Wayne (46818) *(G-5169)*

L3harris Technologies Inc 260 451-6180
1919 W Cook Rd Fort Wayne (46818) *(G-5170)*

L3harris Technologies Inc 260 451-6000
7310 Innovation Blvd Fort Wayne (46818) *(G-5171)*

L5 Solutions LLC 317 436-1044
7950 Castleway Dr Ste 160 Indianapolis (46250) *(G-8706)*

La Braid Inc 219 754-2501
9404 W 2100 S La Crosse (46348) *(G-10366)*

La Farga, New Haven *Also Called: Sdi Lafarga LLC (G-12919)*

La Fontaine Generator Exchange 765 981-4561
202 Logan St La Fontaine (46940) *(G-10368)*

La Grange County, Lagrange *Also Called: County of Lagrange (G-10732)*

La Grange Publishing Co Inc 260 463-3243
State Rte 9 S Lagrange (46761) *(G-10747)*

La Michoacana 574 293-9799
1854 Woodland Dr Elkhart (46514) *(G-3463)*

La Ola Latino Americana 317 822-0345
2401 W Washington St Indianapolis (46222) *(G-8707)*

La Porte Defense Tech Corp 219 362-1000
300 Philadelphia St La Porte (46350) *(G-10439)*

La Porte Prcsion Mch Works LLC 219 326-7000
1756 Genesis Dr La Porte (46350) *(G-10440)*

La Porte Smokes and Beverages 219 575-7754
609 E Lincolnway La Porte (46350) *(G-10441)*

La Porte Technologies LLC (PA) 219 362-1000
300 Philadelphia St La Porte (46350) *(G-10442)*

La Voz De Ind Blingual Newsppr, Indianapolis *Also Called: La Voz De Indiana Inc (G-8709)*

La Voz De Indiana Inc 317 636-7970
6332 Hollister Dr Apt 2005 Indianapolis (46224) *(G-8708)*

La Voz De Indiana Inc 317 423-0957
2911 W Washington St Ste B Indianapolis (46222) *(G-8709)*

LA Woodworking LLC 574 825-5580
10328 County Road 24 Middlebury (46540) *(G-11731)*

La-Z-Boy Contract Furniture, Ferdinand *Also Called: Knu LLC (G-4438)*

La-Z-Boy Inc 812 367-0190
1 Best Dr Ferdinand (47532) *(G-4439)*

Label Logic, Elkhart *Also Called: Label Logic Inc (G-3464)*

Label Logic Inc 574 266-6007
516 Pine Creek Ct Elkhart (46516) *(G-3464)*

Label Tech Inc 765 747-1234
2601 S Walnut St Muncie (47302) *(G-12436)*

Labels Unlimited, New Albany *Also Called: Discount Labels LLC (G-12720)*

Labor News Inc 317 251-1287
4280 Kessler Lane East Dr Indianapolis (46220) *(G-8710)*

Lacap Container Corp 317 835-4282
521 One Half E Hendricks St Shelbyville (46176) *(G-14771)*

Lacay Fabrication and Mfg Inc 574 288-4678
2801 Glenview Dr Elkhart (46514) *(G-3465)*

Laced Cake LLC 317 520-6235
7408 Bentley Dr Indianapolis (46214) *(G-8711)*

Laconia Laser Engraving 812 786-3641
2825 Mosquito Creek Rd Se Laconia (47135) *(G-10506)*

Lacopa International Inc 317 410-1483
5028 Hill Valley Dr Pittsboro (46167) *(G-13650)*

Lactor LLC 765 496-6838
3221 Covington St West Lafayette (47906) *(G-16599)*

Ladifrog's Clerical Services, South Bend *Also Called: Lori Hicks (G-15129)*

Lady Q LLC-S 219 304-8404
8520 Allison Pointe Blvd Indianapolis (46250) *(G-8712)*

Ladybugz Bookstore LLC 469 459-1780
14350 Mundy Dr Noblesville (46060) *(G-13125)*

Lafayette Furniture 765 446-9777
3812 Fortune Dr Lafayette (47905) *(G-10625)*

Lafayette Instrument Co LLC (PA) 765 423-1505
3700 Sagamore Pkwy N Lafayette (47904) *(G-10626)*

Lafayette Interior Fashions, West Lafayette *Also Called: Lafayette Venetian Blind Inc (G-16601)*

Lafayette Marketing Inc 765 474-5374
3180 W 250 N West Lafayette (47906) *(G-16600)*

ALPHABETIC SECTION

Lafayette Materials MGT Co Inc 765 447-7400
635 Erie St Lafayette (47904) *(G-10627)*

Lafayette Quality Products Inc 765 446-0890
111 Farabee Dr S Lafayette (47905) *(G-10628)*

Lafayette Sign Guy LLC 765 771-9900
310 Farabee Dr S Lafayette (47905) *(G-10629)*

Lafayette Tents & Events LLC 765 742-4277
3320 S 460 E Lafayette (47905) *(G-10630)*

Lafayette Tool & Die Inc 765 429-6362
1836 Monon Ave Lafayette (47904) *(G-10631)*

Lafayette Venetian Blind Inc (PA) 765 464-2500
3000 Klondike Rd West Lafayette (47906) *(G-16601)*

Lafayette Wire Products Inc 765 474-7896
2700 Concord Rd Lafayette (47909) *(G-10632)*

Laff Worx LLC 812 267-0430
2475 E Whiskey Run Rd Ne New Salisbury (47161) *(G-12985)*

Lafontaine Gravel Inc 765 981-4849
1244 E 1050 S La Fontaine (46940) *(G-10369)*

Lagnaippe LLC 812 288-9291
802 E 8th St New Albany (47150) *(G-12762)*

Lagrange Products Inc 260 495-3025
607 S Wayne St Fremont (46737) *(G-5826)*

Lagwana Printing Inc (PA) 260 463-4901
4425 W Us Highway 20 Ste 3 Lagrange (46761) *(G-10748)*

Lagwana Printing Inc 260 463-4901
2465 N 850 W Shipshewana (46565) *(G-14860)*

Laibe Corporation 317 231-2250
1414 Bates St Indianapolis (46201) *(G-8713)*

Laidig Inc 574 256-0204
14535 Dragoon Trl Mishawaka (46544) *(G-11925)*

Laird Plastics, Indianapolis Also Called: Plastics Family Holdings Inc *(G-9153)*

Lake Air Balance 219 988-2449
639 W 250 S Hebron (46341) *(G-7101)*

Lake Cable of Indiana LLC 847 238-3000
2700 Evans Ave Valparaiso (46383) *(G-15990)*

Lake Copper Conductors LLC 847 238-3000
4430 Eastland Dr Elkhart (46516) *(G-3466)*

Lake County Sand & Gravel LLC 219 988-4540
2115 W Lincoln Hwy Merrillville (46410) *(G-11528)*

Lake Effect Embroidery 219 785-4551
6313 W 450 S La Porte (46350) *(G-10443)*

Lake Effect Pharma LLC 315 694-1111
1800 N Capitol Ave Ste E504 Indianapolis (46202) *(G-8714)*

Lake House 574 265-6945
720 E Canal St Winona Lake (46590) *(G-16912)*

Lake Lite Inc 260 918-2758
100 Industrial Dr Avilla (46710) *(G-485)*

Lake Ridge Vlntr Fire Dept Inc 219 980-8620
2301 W 47th Ave Gary (46408) *(G-5976)*

Lake Tool & Die Inc 574 457-8274
1009 W Brooklyn St Syracuse (46567) *(G-15467)*

Lakeland Pallets Inc 574 674-5906
2505 Middlebury St Elkhart (46516) *(G-3467)*

Lakeland Pier and Lift LLC 574 377-3481
1401 N Antler Dr Warsaw (46582) *(G-16385)*

Lakeland Technology, Warsaw Also Called: Sites-Workman Holdings Inc *(G-16424)*

Lakemaster Inc 765 288-3718
2407 S Walnut St Muncie (47302) *(G-12437)*

Lakepark Industries Ind Inc
750 E Middlebury St Shipshewana (46565) *(G-14861)*

Laker Winery LLC 812 934-4633
13654 Tangman Rd Sunman (47041) *(G-15440)*

Lakeshore Foods Corp 219 362-8513
702 E Lincolnway Ste 1 La Porte (46350) *(G-10444)*

Lakeshore Graphics, Crown Point Also Called: Adams Smith *(G-2648)*

Lakeside Book Company, Indianapolis Also Called: Lsc Communications Book LLC *(G-8789)*

Lakeside Book Company, Indianapolis Also Called: Lsc Communications Book LLC *(G-8790)*

Lakeside Book Company, Indianapolis Also Called: Lsc Communications Book LLC *(G-8791)*

Lakeside Book Company, Plainfield Also Called: Lsc Communications Book LLC *(G-13698)*

Lakeside Embroidery 260 691-3289
735 E Spear Rd Columbia City (46725) *(G-2165)*

Lakeside Foods 219 924-4860
9130 O Day Dr Highland (46322) *(G-7142)*

Lakeside Manor 219 362-3956
196 W Mcclung Rd La Porte (46350) *(G-10445)*

Lakeside Woodworking 812 687-7901
10915 Hauser Rd Freedom (47431) *(G-5802)*

Lakestreet Enterprises LLC 260 768-7991
75 N 700 W Lagrange (46761) *(G-10749)*

Laketon Refining Corporation 260 982-0703
2784 W Lukens Lake Rd Laketon (46943) *(G-10787)*

Laketronics Inc 260 856-4588
2 Moore St Cromwell (46732) *(G-2631)*

Lakeview Engineered Pdts Inc 260 432-3479
2500 W Jefferson Blvd Fort Wayne (46802) *(G-5172)*

Lakeview Woodworking 574 642-1335
10190 County Road 34 Goshen (46528) *(G-6196)*

Lakota Language Consortium 888 525-6828
1720 N Kinser Pike Bloomington (47404) *(G-905)*

LAKOTA LANGUAGE CONSORTIUM, Bloomington Also Called: Lakota Language Consortium *(G-905)*

Lamar Advertising Company 260 482-9566
4511 Executive Blvd Fort Wayne (46808) *(G-5173)*

Lamarvis Industries LLC 317 797-0483
1457 S 13th 1/2 St Terre Haute (47802) *(G-15627)*

Lamaster Radiation Consulting, Noblesville Also Called: Mark Lamaster *(G-13131)*

Lamb Machine & Tool Co 317 780-9106
3619 S Arlington Ave Indianapolis (46203) *(G-8715)*

LAMB Woodworking LLC 260 768-7992
5510 W 200 N Shipshewana (46565) *(G-14862)*

Lambel Corporation 317 849-6828
7902 E 88th St Indianapolis (46256) *(G-8716)*

Lambert Metal Finishing Inc 260 493-0529
6912 Derek Dr Fort Wayne (46803) *(G-5174)*

Lambert Wood Works LLC 812 952-4204
3745 Crandall Lanesville Rd Ne Lanesville (47136) *(G-10801)*

Lambright Aluminum, Topeka Also Called: Verne Lambright *(G-15822)*

Lambright Country Chimes Llc 260 768-9138
8340 W Us Highway 20 Unit 3 Shipshewana (46565) *(G-14863)*

Lambright Woodworking LLC 260 593-2721
7785 W 300 S Topeka (46571) *(G-15811)*

Lambrights Inc 260 463-2178
2450 W Us Highway 20 Lagrange (46761) *(G-10750)*

Lamco Finishers Inc 317 471-1010
8260 Zionsville Rd Indianapolis (46268) *(G-8717)*

Lami-Crafts Inc 812 232-3012
2806 S 7th St Terre Haute (47802) *(G-15628)*

Laminar Fittings Inc 833 855-1020
1136 Dilts St Bldg 3 Anderson (46017) *(G-146)*

Laminat LLC 574 233-1534
1404 Honan Dr South Bend (46614) *(G-15114)*

Laminated Tops Central Ind Inc 812 824-6299
711 E Dillman Rd Bloomington (47401) *(G-906)*

Laminique Inc 765 482-4222
105 Bennington Dr Zionsville (46077) *(G-17029)*

Lammco, Lafayette Also Called: Lafayette Materials MGT Co Inc *(G-10627)*

Lamon Brewster Industries LLC 818 668-4298
1248 Munsee Cir Indianapolis (46228) *(G-8718)*

Lamonicos Cnstr & Maint LLC 219 951-8554
1173 Van Buren St Gary (46407) *(G-5977)*

Lamplitter 317 827-0250
9521 Valparaiso Ct Indianapolis (46268) *(G-8719)*

Lana Hudelson 812 865-3951
27 W Quarry Rd Orleans (47452) *(G-13377)*

Lance Snyder 717 632-4477
9040 Orly Rd Ste 100 Indianapolis (46241) *(G-8720)*

Lances Drvshaft Components Inc 219 762-2531
2076 Dombey Rd Portage (46368) *(G-13881)*

Lancon Electric Inc 260 897-3285
101 S Main St Laotto (46763) *(G-10809)*

Land Enterprises 317 774-9475
7116 Summer Oak Dr Noblesville (46062) *(G-13126)*

Land O'Lakes

Land O'Lakes, Flora *Also Called: Land OLakes Inc (G-4660)*
Land O'Lakes, Richmond *Also Called: Land OLakes Inc (G-14155)*
Land of Indiana Inc... 812 788-1560
   10 Pinewood Dr Bedford (47421) *(G-654)*
Land OLakes Inc.. 574 967-3064
   95 S 200 E Flora (46929) *(G-4660)*
Land OLakes Inc.. 765 962-9561
   505 N 4th St Richmond (47374) *(G-14155)*
Landec Ag Inc (HQ).. 765 385-1000
   201 N Michigan St Oxford (47971) *(G-13475)*
Landgrebe Manufacturing Inc..................................... 219 462-9587
   208 N 250 W Valparaiso (46385) *(G-15991)*
Landis Equipment & Tool Rental................................. 812 847-2582
   390 S Main St Linton (47441) *(G-11037)*
Landis Gyr Inc.. 317 578-2200
   8002 N Shadeland Ave Indianapolis (46250) *(G-8721)*
Landis Gyr Utilities Svcs Inc....................................... 765 742-1001
   2800 Duncan Rd Lafayette (47904) *(G-10633)*
Landis Plastics... 765 966-1414
   630 Commerce Rd Richmond (47374) *(G-14156)*
Landis+gyr Technology Inc.. 765 742-1001
   2800 Duncan Rd Lafayette (47904) *(G-10634)*
Landjet International.. 574 970-7805
   21240 Protecta Dr Elkhart (46516) *(G-3468)*
Landmark Home & Land Company (PA)..................... 219 874-4065
   1902 Washington St Michigan City (46360) *(G-11630)*
Landmark Signs Inc... 219 762-9577
   7424 Industrial Ave Chesterton (46304) *(G-1943)*
Landmark Signs Group, Chesterton *Also Called: Landmark Signs Inc (G-1943)*
Landmark Wood Products Inc.................................... 812 338-2641
   118 W Sawmill Rd English (47118) *(G-3842)*
Landsberg Indianapolis Div 1015, Indianapolis *Also Called: Orora Packaging Solutions (G-9071)*
Landscape Products, Frankfort *Also Called: Ostler Enterprises Inc (G-5688)*
Lane Byler Inc.. 260 920-4377
   5858 County Road 35 Auburn (46706) *(G-402)*
Lane Legacy Vineyard.. 937 902-7738
   12330 Whitcomb Rd Brookville (47012) *(G-1328)*
Lane Shady Welding LLC... 574 825-5553
   56322 Cr35 Middlebury (46540) *(G-11732)*
Lane Wright LLC.. 317 473-4783
   1006 W 35th St Indianapolis (46208) *(G-8722)*
Laney Software Co.. 260 312-0759
   17144 Moonlite Dr South Bend (46614) *(G-15115)*
Lang Capital LLC... 812 325-2177
   4100 Sylvan Dr Floyds Knobs (47119) *(G-4684)*
Langeland Farms Inc... 812 663-9546
   3806 S County Road 550 E Greensburg (47240) *(G-6614)*
Langley Fine Art Prints.. 219 872-0087
   2019 Somerset Rd Long Beach (46360) *(G-11123)*
Language Company South Bend................................ 574 287-3622
   2002 Mishawaka Ave South Bend (46615) *(G-15116)*
Lanigan Holdings LLC.. 812 422-6912
   3400 Claremont Ave Evansville (47712) *(G-4161)*
Lannett Company, Inc, Seymour *Also Called: Kremers Urban Phrmcuticals Inc (G-14663)*
Lansing Metalizing & Grinding, Hammond *Also Called: Lansing Mtlizing Grinding Inc (G-6968)*
Lansing Mtlizing Grinding Inc..................................... 219 931-1785
   4742 Calumet Ave Hammond (46327) *(G-6968)*
Lanthier Winery LLC.. 502 663-2399
   2612 Franks Dr Madison (47250) *(G-11234)*
Lanthier Winery & Restaurant.................................... 812 273-2409
   123 Mill St Madison (47250) *(G-11235)*
Laotto Brewing LLC... 260 897-3152
   7530 E Swan Rd Avilla (46710) *(G-486)*
Lape Steel, Elkhart *Also Called: Elkhart Steel Service Inc (G-3329)*
Lapell Post, Pendleton *Also Called: Pendleton Times (G-13552)*
Lapis Services Inc... 219 464-9131
   1101 Cumberland Xing Valparaiso (46383) *(G-15992)*
Lapp Usa Inc... 973 660-9700
   1665 W Northfield Dr Brownsburg (46112) *(G-1384)*

ALPHABETIC SECTION

Laptop Publishing LLC.. 317 379-5716
   3531 Rolling Springs Dr Carmel (46033) *(G-1682)*
Larck Industries LLC... 574 993-5502
   55685 Currant Rd Ste D Mishawaka (46545) *(G-11926)*
Largus Printing, Munster *Also Called: Largus Speedy Print Corp (G-12546)*
Largus Speedy Print Corp.. 219 922-8414
   732 45th St Munster (46321) *(G-12546)*
Larry Atwood.. 765 525-6851
   6597 S 250 E Waldron (46182) *(G-16260)*
Larry Conover... 317 787-4020
   227 N East St Pendleton (46064) *(G-13540)*
Larry Flowers Wholesale.. 765 747-5156
   2948 S Chippewa Ln Muncie (47302) *(G-12438)*
Larry G Byrd... 765 458-7285
   2312 W County Road 250 S Liberty (47353) *(G-10990)*
Larry Graber Cabinets.. 812 486-2713
   9407 E 500 N Montgomery (47558) *(G-12109)*
Larry H Poole.. 812 466-9345
   7826 E Rose Hill Ave Terre Haute (47805) *(G-15629)*
Larry Robertson Associates..................................... 812 537-4090
   1056 Millwood Ct Indianapolis (46260) *(G-8723)*
Larry Shorts Welding.. 812 664-4910
   9956 W 450 S Owensville (47665) *(G-13470)*
Larry Zoeller... 502 439-0812
   7509 Geswein Rd Lanesville (47136) *(G-10802)*
Larrys Canvas Cleaning... 260 463-2220
   909 S Poplar St Lagrange (46761) *(G-10751)*
Larrys Marine Canvas.. 252 725-2902
   2107 Park Ave Bedford (47421) *(G-655)*
Larrys Tl Hydrlic Jack Svc LLC................................. 317 243-8666
   702 S Lynhurst Dr Indianapolis (46241) *(G-8724)*
Las Arribes LLC... 317 892-9463
   8768 N Wayport Rd Bloomington (47404) *(G-907)*
Lasalle Bristol, Elkhart *Also Called: Lasalle Bristol Corporation (G-3469)*
Lasalle Bristol Corporation....................................... 574 295-4400
   1203 N Division St Bristol (46507) *(G-1269)*
Lasalle Bristol Corporation (DH)............................... 574 295-8400
   601 County Road 17 Elkhart (46516) *(G-3469)*
Lasalle Bristol Corporation....................................... 574 293-5526
   3933 E Jackson Blvd Elkhart (46516) *(G-3470)*
Lasalle Bristol Corporation....................................... 574 936-9894
   1755 N Oak Dr Plymouth (46563) *(G-13791)*
Lasalles Landing Vineyard LLC................................ 574 277-2711
   51739 Lilac Rd South Bend (46628) *(G-15117)*
Laser Agent... 317 570-0448
   15402 Stony Creek Way Noblesville (46060) *(G-13127)*
Laser Graphx Inc.. 574 834-4443
   7196 N State Road 13 North Webster (46555) *(G-13309)*
Laser Images, Fort Wayne *Also Called: Kaiser Tool Company Inc (G-5142)*
Laser Marking Technologies.................................... 812 852-7999
   873 W County Road 600 N Osgood (47037) *(G-13411)*
Laser Plus Inc.. 574 269-1246
   3950 N Blue Heron Dr Warsaw (46582) *(G-16386)*
Laser Systems... 219 465-1155
   104 Billings St Ste A Valparaiso (46383) *(G-15993)*
Laser Welder Company.. 816 807-6971
   1507 S Olive St South Bend (46619) *(G-15118)*
Laser Welder LLC, Fort Wayne *Also Called: Neil Silke (G-5260)*
Lasertech Inc... 812 277-1321
   4684 Dixie Hwy Bedford (47421) *(G-656)*
Lasertone Inc... 812 473-5945
   700 N Weinbach Ave Ste 101 Evansville (47711) *(G-4162)*
Laserwash.. 765 359-0582
   1529 S Washington St Crawfordsville (47933) *(G-2584)*
Lasher Lumber Inc... 812 836-2618
   15147 State Road 145 Tell City (47586) *(G-15507)*
Lasikplus Vision Center, Indianapolis *Also Called: Lca-Vision Inc (G-8729)*
Lassus Bros Oil Inc.. 260 625-4003
   10225 Illinois Rd Fort Wayne (46814) *(G-5175)*
Lastec, Indianapolis *Also Called: Wood-Mizer Holdings Inc (G-9784)*
Lastec, Lizton *Also Called: Wood-Mizer Holdings Inc (G-11052)*

ALPHABETIC SECTION

Lastec LLC.. 317 892-4444
  8180 W 10th St Indianapolis (46214) *(G-8725)*
Latch Gard Co Inc.. 574 862-2373
  1900 Fieldhouse Ave Elkhart (46517) *(G-3471)*
Lathe Specialties Co Inc...................................... 260 244-3629
  2299 E Business 30 Columbia City (46725) *(G-2166)*
Lather Up LLC... 260 638-4978
  2040 W 900 N-90 Markle (46770) *(G-11357)*
Laticrete International Inc.................................... 317 298-8510
  4620 W 84th St Ste 200 Indianapolis (46268) *(G-8726)*
Lattice Works, Evansville *Also Called: Plastic Extrusions Company (G-4245)*
Lau Holdings LLC... 574 223-3181
  510 N State Road 25 Rochester (46975) *(G-14300)*
Lauck Manufacturing Co Inc................................ 317 787-6269
  735 Bacon St Indianapolis (46227) *(G-8727)*
Laudeman Place Inc... 574 546-4404
  1851 Dogwood Rd Bremen (46506) *(G-1203)*
Lauer Log Homes Inc.. 260 486-7010
  6630 Reed Rd Fort Wayne (46835) *(G-5176)*
Laughery Gravel Co, Osgood *Also Called: Schmaltz Ready Mix Concrete (G-13415)*
Laughery Sawmill... 812 432-5649
  10678 W Laughery Creek Rd Dillsboro (47018) *(G-2949)*
Laughery Valley AG Co-Op, Osgood *Also Called: Laughery Valley AG Co-Op Inc (G-13412)*
Laughery Valley AG Co-Op Inc (PA)................... 812 689-4401
  336 N Buckeye St Osgood (47037) *(G-13412)*
Laundry On US LLC... 812 567-3653
  2333 S Fruitridge Ave Terre Haute (47803) *(G-15630)*
Laundry Room, The, Columbus *Also Called: Brian T Klem (G-2230)*
Lauyans Holdings Inc
  620 Durgee Rd New Albany (47150) *(G-12763)*
Lava Lips.. 317 965-6629
  6821 Grosvenor Pl Indianapolis (46220) *(G-8728)*
Lavender Patch Fabr Quilts LLC.......................... 574 848-0011
  20615 Baltimore Oriole Dr Bristol (46507) *(G-1270)*
Lawncreations LLC.. 574 536-1546
  10592 County Rd Millersburg (46543) *(G-11815)*
Lawrence Cnty Fabrication Corp.......................... 812 849-0124
  240 S Meridian Rd Mitchell (47446) *(G-12043)*
Lawrence Industries Inc...................................... 260 432-9693
  10403 Arbor Trl Fort Wayne (46804) *(G-5177)*
Lawrence Shirks... 574 223-5118
  4920 State Road 110 Rochester (46975) *(G-14301)*
Lawrenceburg Mini Barns.................................... 513 290-5794
  535 W Eads Pkwy Lawrenceburg (47025) *(G-10844)*
Lawrenco Steel Inc.. 812 466-7115
  4000 E Evans Ave Terre Haute (47805) *(G-15631)*
Lawson Design Inc.. 812 967-2810
  2109 S Casey Rd Henryville (47126) *(G-7113)*
Lawson Welding Shop... 812 448-8984
  10516 North County 200e Harmony (47853) *(G-7059)*
Layman Fabrication Inc....................................... 812 767-2823
  895 W County Road 350 N North Vernon (47265) *(G-13283)*
Laymon Industries LLC.. 574 277-4536
  51878 Westwood Forest Dr South Bend (46628) *(G-15119)*
Layshias Clawed Madam LLC............................. 260 257-7633
  1415 Sinclair St Fort Wayne (46808) *(G-5178)*
Layton Elkhart, Elkhart *Also Called: Layton Homes Corporation (G-3473)*
Layton Homes Corporation (HQ)......................... 574 294-6521
  2520 Bypass Rd Elkhart (46514) *(G-3472)*
Layton Homes Corporation.................................. 574 294-6521
  411 County Road 15 Elkhart (46516) *(G-3473)*
Lazar Scientific Incorporated.............................. 574 271-7020
  12692 Sandy Dr Ste 116 Granger (46530) *(G-6358)*
Lazy Dog Press, Lafayette *Also Called: Lazy Dog Press LLC (G-10635)*
Lazy Dog Press LLC.. 510 227-9404
  815 Wabash Ave Lafayette (47905) *(G-10635)*
Lazzaro Companies Inc....................................... 219 980-0860
  5880 Broadway Merrillville (46410) *(G-11529)*
Lazzerini Corporation... 574 206-4769
  1011 Herman St Elkhart (46516) *(G-3474)*
Lb Mold, Edinburgh *Also Called: Lb Mold Inc (G-3090)*

Lb Mold Inc.. 812 526-2030
  1031 S Main St Edinburgh (46124) *(G-3090)*
Lb Woodworking, Nappanee *Also Called: Borkholder Lavon (G-12586)*
Lbw Printing & Dtp.. 260 347-9053
  1219 N Lima Rd Kendallville (46755) *(G-10132)*
Lc Covers LLC... 260 463-2220
  909 S Poplar St Lagrange (46761) *(G-10752)*
Lc Screen Printing LLC....................................... 812 687-7476
  7654 N 650 E Montgomery (47558) *(G-12110)*
Lca-Vision Inc... 317 818-3980
  8930 Keystone Xing Indianapolis (46240) *(G-8729)*
Lcf Enterprises LLC... 260 483-3248
  10050 Bent Creek Blvd Fort Wayne (46825) *(G-5179)*
LCI Industries... 574 535-1125
  1722 W Mishawaka Rd Elkhart (46517) *(G-3475)*
LCI Industries (PA).. 574 535-1125
  3501 County Road 6 E Elkhart (46514) *(G-3476)*
LCI Industries... 574 264-3521
  3407 Cooper Dr Elkhart (46514) *(G-3477)*
LCI Industries... 574 312-6116
  3308 Charlotte Ave Elkhart (46517) *(G-3478)*
Lcm Realty LLC... 574 535-1125
  3501 County Road 6 E Elkhart (46514) *(G-3479)*
Lcm Realty IV LLC... 574 312-6182
  2469 E Kercher Rd Goshen (46526) *(G-6197)*
Le Air Co Inc... 812 988-1313
  1313 Timber Crest Rd Nashville (47448) *(G-12674)*
Le Kem of Indiana Inc.. 812 932-5536
  1863 Lammers Pike Batesville (47006) *(G-595)*
Le-Hue Machine and Tool Co.............................. 574 255-8404
  1915 N Cedar St Mishawaka (46545) *(G-11927)*
Lea LLC... 574 216-1622
  635 S Lafayette Blvd Bldg 113 South Bend (46601) *(G-15120)*
Leach & Sons WaterCare (PA)............................. 317 248-8954
  671 E Main St # E Danville (46122) *(G-2818)*
Leach and Sons Water Systems, Danville *Also Called: Leach & Sons WaterCare (G-2818)*
Leader Publishing Co of Salem........................... 812 883-3281
  117 E Walnut St 119 Salem (47167) *(G-14487)*
Leaf Hut Software LLC.. 317 770-3632
  8430 Weaver Woods Pl Fishers (46038) *(G-4555)*
League of Fancy Hats LLC.................................. 260 355-7115
  8588 N 100 E Huntington (46750) *(G-7336)*
Leahy Adology Hearing Aids LLC........................ 765 601-4003
  1303 S Jackson St Frankfort (46041) *(G-5679)*
Leaning Palms LLC... 630 886-8924
  735 Quinlan Ct Crown Point (46307) *(G-2715)*
Leap Frogz Ink LLC... 317 786-2441
  872 N State Road 135 # D Greenwood (46142) *(G-6728)*
Lear Corporation.. 260 244-1700
  2101 S 600 E Columbia City (46725) *(G-2167)*
Lear Corporation.. 765 653-2511
  750 S Fillmore Rd Greencastle (46135) *(G-6417)*
Lear Corporation.. 219 852-0014
  2204 Michigan St Hammond (46320) *(G-6969)*
Lear Corporation.. 317 481-0530
  4409 W Morris St Indianapolis (46241) *(G-8730)*
Lear Corporation.. 574 935-3818
  2000 Walter Glaub Dr Plymouth (46563) *(G-13792)*
Lear Machining & Waterjet, Columbus *Also Called: Lear Machining & Waterjet Inc (G-2338)*
Lear Machining & Waterjet Inc............................ 812 418-8111
  4056 N Long Rd Columbus (47203) *(G-2338)*
Learfield Sports.. 812 339-7201
  1710 N Kinser Pike Bloomington (47404) *(G-908)*
Learman Elctrnic Tl Assctesinc............................ 574 293-4641
  58211 County Road 105 Elkhart (46517) *(G-3480)*
Learman Electronic Tool Assoc........................... 574 226-0420
  1513 S 6th St Elkhart (46516) *(G-3481)*
Learning Cedar Woodworking.............................. 574 862-1864
  28388 County Road 30 Elkhart (46517) *(G-3482)*
Learnlab, Dugger *Also Called: Industrial Trning Unlmted Corp (G-2957)*
Leaselinks LLC.. 312 810-0788
  631 W South St Crown Point (46307) *(G-2716)*

Leasenet Incorporated 317 575-4098
  8888 Keystone Xing Ste 1300 Indianapolis (46240) *(G-8731)*
Leather Yoder Company LLC 260 833-4030
  2064 N 130 W Angola (46703) *(G-271)*
Lebanon Berg Vault Co, Lebanon *Also Called: Lebanon Berg Vault Co Inc (G-10909)*
Lebanon Berg Vault Co Inc 765 482-0302
  730 E Elm St Lebanon (46052) *(G-10909)*
Lebanon Corp 765 482-7273
  1700 N Lebanon St Lebanon (46052) *(G-10910)*
Lebanon In Distribution Center, Lebanon *Also Called: Prysmian Cbles Systems USA LLC (G-10934)*
Lebanon Reporter, The, Lebanon *Also Called: Community Holdings Indiana Inc (G-10885)*
Lebermuth Company Inc (PA) 574 259-7000
  4004 Technology Dr South Bend (46628) *(G-15121)*
Leclere Manufacturing Inc 812 683-5627
  2905 Newton St Jasper (47546) *(G-9882)*
Leco Corporation 574 288-9017
  4100 Lathrop St South Bend (46628) *(G-15122)*
Ledgerwood & Sons Sawmill LLC 812 939-8212
  246 Pleasant View Rd Coal City (47427) *(G-2100)*
Ledingedge Lighting Inc 805 383-8493
  505 Pokagon Trl Angola (46703) *(G-272)*
Lee Crawford Welding 317 490-8009
  2836 Newhart St Indianapolis (46217) *(G-8732)*
Lee E Norris Cnstr & Grn Co (PA) 574 353-7855
  7930 N 700 E Tippecanoe (46570) *(G-15761)*
Lee Enterprises Inc Times 219 933-3200
  601 45th St Munster (46321) *(G-12547)*
Lee Farms Enterprises Inc 260 375-3319
  10912 W 1000 S 90 Marion (46952) *(G-11306)*
Lee Machine Inc 765 932-3100
  505 E 11th St Rushville (46173) *(G-14405)*
Lee Publications Inc 219 462-5151
  1111 Glendale Blvd Valparaiso (46383) *(G-15994)*
Lee Reed Embroidery, Hammond *Also Called: Lee Reed Holdings LLC (G-6970)*
Lee Reed Holdings LLC 219 255-0555
  4737 Towle Ave Hammond (46327) *(G-6970)*
Lee Supply Corp 812 333-4343
  1821 W 3rd St Bloomington (47404) *(G-909)*
LEE SUPPLY CORP., Bloomington *Also Called: Lee Supply Corp (G-909)*
Lee's Double D Tire & Muffler, Rockville *Also Called: Double D (G-14351)*
Lee's Ready Mix, Shelbyville *Also Called: Lees Ready-Mix & Trucking (G-14772)*
Lee's Ready-Mix, Columbus *Also Called: Lees Ready-Mix & Trucking Inc (G-2339)*
Lee's Wood Products, Elkhart *Also Called: Duro Inc (G-3305)*
Leed Samples-Fulfillment 812 867-4340
  9700 Highway 57 Evansville (47725) *(G-4163)*
Leed Selling Tools Corp (PA) 812 867-4340
  9700 Highway 57 Evansville (47725) *(G-4164)*
Leed Selling Tools Corp 812 482-7888
  5312 W Ireland Center St Ireland (47545) *(G-9816)*
Leed Thermal Processing Inc 317 637-5102
  1718 N Luett Ave Indianapolis (46222) *(G-8733)*
Leepoxy Plastics Inc 260 747-7411
  3706 W Ferguson Rd Fort Wayne (46809) *(G-5180)*
Leeps Supply Co Inc (PA) 219 756-5337
  8001 Tyler St Merrillville (46410) *(G-11530)*
Leer Custom Machine LLC 317 385-2443
  301 Pinewood Ln Springville (47462) *(G-15388)*
Lees Ready-Mix & Trucking (PA) 701 Hodell St Ste 101 Shelbyville (46176) *(G-14772)*
Lees Ready-Mix & Trucking Inc 812 372-1800
  1460 Blessing Rd Columbus (47201) *(G-2339)*
Leesburg Stop-N-Go LLC 574 453-3004
  101 S Main St Leesburg (46538) *(G-10956)*
Leeson Electric Corporation 317 821-3700
  9899 Bradford Rd Plainfield (46168) *(G-13697)*
Legacy, Indianapolis *Also Called: Legacy Resources Co LP (G-8734)*
Legacy Enterprises Inc 219 484-9483
  903 W 67th Pl Merrillville (46410) *(G-11531)*
Legacy Heat Treatment LLC 219 237-4500
  801 E Main St Ste 16 Griffith (46319) *(G-6811)*

Legacy Resources Co LP (PA) 317 328-5660
  2780 Waterfront Parkway East Dr Ste 200 Indianapolis (46214) *(G-8734)*
Legacy Screen Printing Promoti 219 262-4000
  1086 N State Road 149 Chesterton (46304) *(G-1944)*
Legacy Screen Prtg Prmtons LLC 219 262-4000
  100 Anchor Rd Ste 5 Michigan City (46360) *(G-11631)*
Legacy Sign Group LLC 219 728-5102
  7933 W Us Highway 6 Westville (46391) *(G-16763)*
Legacy Trailer Rentals LLC 812 873-5218
  5565 S Base Rd North Vernon (47265) *(G-13284)*
Legacy Vulcan LLC 219 987-3040
  832 15th St Se - Sr231 Demotte (46310) *(G-2922)*
Legacy Vulcan LLC 574 293-1536
  2500 W Lusher Ave Elkhart (46517) *(G-3483)*
Legacy Vulcan LLC 219 567-9155
  14530 W 700 S Francesville (47946) *(G-5643)*
Legacy Vulcan LLC 219 696-5467
  9331 W 205th Ave Lowell (46356) *(G-11167)*
Legacy Vulcan LLC 219 253-6686
  6857 N Us Highway 421 Monon (47959) *(G-12056)*
Legacy Vulcan LLC 219 462-5832
  651 Axe Ave Valparaiso (46383) *(G-15995)*
Legacy Vulcan LLC 219 465-3066
  4105 Montdale Park Dr Valparaiso (46383) *(G-15996)*
Legacy Wood Creations LLC 574 773-4405
  24675 County Road 54 Nappanee (46550) *(G-12620)*
Legend Valley Products, Winamac *Also Called: Braun Motor Works Inc (G-16858)*
Legendary Designs Inc 260 768-9170
  2685 N 850 W Shipshewana (46565) *(G-14864)*
Legends Global Merchandise, Indianapolis *Also Called: Legends Maingate LLC (G-8735)*
Legends Maingate LLC 317 243-2000
  7900 Rockville Rd Indianapolis (46214) *(G-8735)*
Leggett & Platt Incorporated 219 866-7181
  1132 N Cullen St Rensselaer (47978) *(G-14057)*
Leggett & Platt 0714, Kouts *Also Called: Leggett & Platt Incorporated (G-10363)*
Leggett & Platt Incorporated 260 347-2600
  2225 Production Rd Kendallville (46755) *(G-10133)*
Leggett & Platt Incorporated 219 766-2261
  State Road 8 Kouts (46347) *(G-10363)*
Leggits LLC 269 447-3500
  1931 Malvern Way South Bend (46614) *(G-15123)*
Legrand AV Inc 574 267-8101
  3100 N Detroit St Warsaw (46582) *(G-16387)*
Lehi Prosthetics Dntl Lab Inc 765 288-4613
  1501 W Jackson St Muncie (47303) *(G-12439)*
Lehman Manufacturing, Kentland *Also Called: Hoosier Metal Polish Inc (G-10160)*
Lehmans Slid Surfc Fabrication, Nappanee *Also Called: Willie Lehman (G-12654)*
Lehue Machine and Tool 574 329-5456
  55981 Wynneywood Dr Osceola (46561) *(G-13397)*
Leibering Dimension Inc 812 367-2971
  514 W 8th St Ferdinand (47532) *(G-4440)*
Lein Corporation 765 674-6950
  3301 S Hamaker St Marion (46953) *(G-11307)*
Leis Machine Shop Inc 574 278-6000
  6033 E Hwy 16 Buffalo (47925) *(G-1439)*
Leistner Aquatic Services Inc 317 535-6099
  7657 N State Road 135 Morgantown (46160) *(G-12260)*
Leisure Pool & Spa LLC 812 537-0071
  159 Florence Dr Lawrenceburg (47025) *(G-10845)*
Leland Manufacturing 812 367-2068
  1 Best Dr Ferdinand (47532) *(G-4441)*
Leman Engrg & Consulting Inc 574 870-7732
  520 E 1050 S Brookston (47923) *(G-1312)*
Lemar Industries Corporat 515 266-7264
  611 N Higbee St Milford (46542) *(G-11796)*
Leme Inc (PA) 317 788-4114
  6107 Churchman Byp Indianapolis (46203) *(G-8736)*
Lemonwire LLC 317 243-1758
  5616 W 74th St Ste A Indianapolis (46278) *(G-8737)*
Lenex Steel Company (PA) 317 818-1622
  450 E 96th St Ste 100 Indianapolis (46240) *(G-8738)*

ALPHABETIC SECTION — Libertyworks

Lenex Steel Company.. 317 818-1622
2325 S 6th St Terre Haute (47802) *(G-15632)*

Lengacher Machine Inc.. 260 657-3114
17305 Grabill Rd Grabill (46741) *(G-6308)*

Lengacher Meats LLC.. 260 627-8060
13601 Antwerp Rd Grabill (46741) *(G-6309)*

Lengachers Welding LLC.. 260 438-9033
13817 Antwerp Rd Grabill (46741) *(G-6310)*

Lengerich Meats Inc.. 260 638-4123
3095 Van Horn Zanesville (46799) *(G-16986)*

Lennies Inc.. 812 323-2112
514 E Kirkwood Ave Bloomington (47408) *(G-910)*

Lennon Industries.. 219 996-6024
1102 Norbeh Dr Hebron (46341) *(G-7102)*

Lennox, Merrillville Also Called: Lennox International Inc *(G-11532)*

Lennox International Inc.. 219 756-3709
3977 W 83rd Pl Merrillville (46410) *(G-11532)*

Lennox Nat Account Svcs LLC.. 800 333-4001
1345 Brookville Way Ste Q Indianapolis (46239) *(G-8739)*

Lennoxs Legacy Rescue Inc.. 260 223-3115
4777 N 375 E Decatur (46733) *(G-2868)*

Lenscrafters, Indianapolis Also Called: Luxottica of America Inc *(G-8800)*

Lenscrafters, Merrillville Also Called: Luxottica of America Inc *(G-11535)*

Leonard Eaton Tooling Inc.. 574 295-5041
435 Roske Dr Elkhart (46516) *(G-3484)*

Leonards Auto Service.. 812 879-4802
7566 Smith Rd Gosport (47433) *(G-6286)*

Leoni LLC.. 574 315-0503
1015 W 7th St Mishawaka (46544) *(G-11928)*

Leons Fabrication Inc.. 219 365-5272
8850 Parrish Ave Schererville (46375) *(G-14528)*

Lep Special Fasteners, Frankfort Also Called: Fontana Fasteners Inc *(G-5664)*

Lepark Mold & Tool.. 574 262-0518
1147 N Michigan St Elkhart (46514) *(G-3485)*

Ler Techforce LLC (PA).. 812 373-0870
305 Franklin St Columbus (47201) *(G-2340)*

Leroy E Doty Cabinet Shop.. 219 663-1139
4514 W 105th Ave Crown Point (46307) *(G-2717)*

Leroy R Sollars.. 765 284-9417
305 1 2 Rd N Selma (47383) *(G-14622)*

Lesac Corporation (PA).. 219 879-3215
700 W Michigan Blvd Michigan City (46360) *(G-11632)*

Lesea Inc.. 574 344-8215
3801 Voorde Dr South Bend (46628) *(G-15124)*

Lesh Advertising Inc.. 574 859-2141
6938 E State Road 218 Camden (46917) *(G-1521)*

Lesha and Wade Printing Svcs.. 317 738-4992
4242 E 500 S Franklin (46131) *(G-5752)*

Leslie Lathe Tool Co, Granger Also Called: Donald Leslie *(G-6345)*

Leslie Nuss.. 219 462-3499
3161 Heavilin Rd Valparaiso (46385) *(G-15997)*

Lessonly Inc.. 317 469-9194
1129 E 16th St Indianapolis (46202) *(G-8740)*

Letica Corporation.. 812 421-3136
101 Oakley St Evansville (47710) *(G-4165)*

Letter Pro, Pendleton Also Called: Paul E Shaw *(G-13550)*

Letter Shop, The, Evansville Also Called: Randall Corp *(G-4272)*

Letterkenny Press Inc.. 317 752-4375
5032 Beaumont Way South Dr Indianapolis (46250) *(G-8741)*

Level Set Cabinet Works LLC.. 812 787-0830
2835 E 250 S Washington (47501) *(G-16491)*

Levy Environmental Services Co.. 260 868-5123
4506 County Road 59 Butler (46721) *(G-1470)*

Levy Environmental Services Co.. 260 625-4930
2734 S 800 E Columbia City (46725) *(G-2168)*

Lewger Machine & Tool, Kendallville Also Called: Da-Mar Industries Inc *(G-10107)*

Lewis & Lee Presents LLC.. 219 484-5298
3916 Torrence Ave Hammond (46327) *(G-6971)*

LEWIS BAKERIES, Evansville Also Called: Lewis Brothers Bakeries Inc *(G-4166)*

Lewis Bakeries, La Porte Also Called: Holsum of Fort Wayne Inc *(G-10421)*

Lewis Bakeries, Vincennes Also Called: Lewis Brothers Bakeries Inc *(G-16137)*

Lewis Brothers Bakeries Inc (PA).. 812 425-4642
500 N Fulton Ave Evansville (47710) *(G-4166)*

Lewis Brothers Bakeries Inc.. 812 886-6533
2792 S Old Decker Rd Vincennes (47591) *(G-16137)*

Lewis Jerry Cnstr & Excvtg.. 765 653-2800
1249 N Jackson St Greencastle (46135) *(G-6418)*

Lewis Property Solutions LLC.. 574 361-0168
1403 Pike Dr Bristol (46507) *(G-1271)*

Lewis Sealing & Cleaning.. 317 783-1424
1601 E Sumner Ave Indianapolis (46227) *(G-8742)*

Lex Tooling LLC.. 765 675-6301
604 Berryman Pike Tipton (46072) *(G-15779)*

Lexicon Incorporated.. 203 328-3500
1718 W Mishawaka Rd Elkhart (46517) *(G-3486)*

Lexington LLC.. 574 295-8166
2503 Banks Ct Elkhart (46514) *(G-3487)*

Lexington Pharmaceuticals.. 317 870-0370
8496 Georgetown Rd Indianapolis (46268) *(G-8743)*

Lexington Phrmcticals Labs LLC.. 317 566-9750
14300 Clay Terrace Blvd Ste 249 Carmel (46032) *(G-1683)*

Lexington Steel, Gary Also Called: Upg Enterprises LLC *(G-6025)*

Lfab, Indianapolis Also Called: Indianapolis Fabrications LLC *(G-8504)*

Lg Metalworks LLC.. 812 333-4344
4200 N Mount Gilead Rd Bloomington (47408) *(G-911)*

Lgenia Inc.. 317 861-8850
412 S Maple St Ste 104 Fortville (46040) *(G-5603)*

Lgin LLC.. 260 562-2233
6825 N 375 E Howe (46746) *(G-7238)*

Lgndz Customs LLC.. 765 293-9303
3402 S Landess St Marion (46953) *(G-11308)*

LGS Industries LLC (HQ).. 574 848-5665
11550 Harter Dr Middlebury (46540) *(G-11733)*

LGS Plumbing Inc.. 219 663-2177
1110 E Summit St Crown Point (46307) *(G-2718)*

LH Industries Corp (PA).. 260 432-5563
4420 Clubview Dr Fort Wayne (46804) *(G-5181)*

LH Industries Corp.. 260 432-5563
4503 Ardon Ct Fort Wayne (46816) *(G-5182)*

LH Medical Corporation.. 260 387-5194
6932 Gettysburg Pike Fort Wayne (46804) *(G-5183)*

Lh Stamping, Fort Wayne Also Called: LH Industries Corp *(G-5182)*

LI, Lafayette Also Called: Lafayette Instrument Co LLC *(G-10626)*

Liberation.. 219 736-7329
5308 Gull Dr Schererville (46375) *(G-14529)*

Liberty Advance Machine Inc.. 812 372-1010
3210 Scott Dr Columbus (47201) *(G-2341)*

Liberty Arms Inc.. 574 583-5630
6942 E 350 N Monticello (47960) *(G-12156)*

Liberty Automation LLC.. 574 524-0436
4890 N 150 E Albion (46701) *(G-31)*

Liberty Book & Bb Manufactures (PA).. 317 633-1450
901 E Maryland St Indianapolis (46202) *(G-8744)*

Liberty Cut Stone Inc.. 812 935-5515
9921 N Liberty Hollow Rd Gosport (47433) *(G-6287)*

Liberty Forge, Liberty Also Called: Ted Bostick *(G-10999)*

Liberty Green Renewables LLP.. 812 951-3143
5019 Georges Hill Rd Ne Georgetown (47122) *(G-6067)*

Liberty Herald.. 765 458-5114
10 N Market St Liberty (47353) *(G-10991)*

Liberty Inds Investments LLC.. 765 246-4031
130 E Cemetery Rd Fillmore (46128) *(G-4455)*

Liberty Screen Printing.. 812 273-4358
831 W Main St Madison (47250) *(G-11236)*

Liberty Signs, Monticello Also Called: Don Anderson *(G-12145)*

Liberty Tool and Engrg Inc.. 765 354-9550
277 N 11th St Middletown (47356) *(G-11772)*

Liberty Trailers, Fillmore Also Called: Liberty Inds Investments LLC *(G-4455)*

Liberty Trailers LLC.. 219 866-7141
1628 W State Road 114 Rensselaer (47978) *(G-14058)*

Libertyworks, Indianapolis Also Called: N Rolls-Royce Amercn Tech Inc *(G-8978)*

Libra Elite LLC — ALPHABETIC SECTION

Libra Elite LLC..706 831-5753
9702 E Washington St Ste 400-116 Indianapolis (46229) *(G-8745)*

Licar America LLC..812 256-6400
600 Patrol Rd Ste 300 Jeffersonville (47130) *(G-10012)*

Licensed Eliquid Mfg LLC......................................260 245-6442
6746 E State Blvd Fort Wayne (46815) *(G-5184)*

Lid, Indianapolis Also Called: Long Item Development Corp *(G-8780)*

Life Essentials, Wolcott Also Called: Life Essentials Inc *(G-16932)*

Life Essentials Inc..765 423-4192
5364 S Us Highway 231 Wolcott (47995) *(G-16932)*

Life Garden Publishing Inc....................................812 246-2113
908 Sunset Cir Borden (47106) *(G-1114)*

Life Less Ordinary LLC..317 727-4277
9032 Sargent Creek Dr Indianapolis (46256) *(G-8746)*

Life Management Inc..260 747-7408
2916 Engle Rd Fort Wayne (46809) *(G-5185)*

Life Path Business Sevices, Indianapolis Also Called: Life Path Numerology Center *(G-8747)*

Life Path Numerology Center................................317 638-9752
108 S Elder Ave Indianapolis (46222) *(G-8747)*

Life Sentences Publishing LLC..............................765 437-0149
434 Kentucky Ave Tipton (46072) *(G-15780)*

Life Spice and Ingredients LLC.............................708 301-0447
260 Westmeadow Pl Lowell (46356) *(G-11168)*

Life43 LLC...708 335-7329
5162 E 81st Ave Merrillville (46410) *(G-11533)*

Lifedata LLC..925 800-3381
1800 N Wabash Rd Ste 300 Marion (46952) *(G-11309)*

Lifespice Ingredients, Lowell Also Called: Life Spice and Ingredients LLC *(G-11168)*

Lifoam Industries LLC...410 889-1023
9999 E 121st St Fishers (46037) *(G-4556)*

Lift Works Inc...812 797-0479
1726 S Centerline Rd Franklin (46131) *(G-5753)*

Lift-A-Loft Manufacturing Inc................................317 288-3691
9501 S Center Rd Muncie (47302) *(G-12440)*

Liftco Inc...574 266-5551
3301 Reedy Dr Elkhart (46514) *(G-3488)*

Lifted Loads LLC..317 432-1542
7936 Bach Dr Indianapolis (46239) *(G-8748)*

Liggett Group LLC..812 479-7635
1836 N Colony Rd Evansville (47715) *(G-4167)*

Light & Ink Corporation...812 421-1400
1018 E Diamond Ave Evansville (47711) *(G-4168)*

Light Beam Technology Inc...................................260 635-2195
3794 W 50 S Kimmell (46760) *(G-10170)*

Light Engineering...317 471-1800
7951 Zionsville Rd Indianapolis (46268) *(G-8749)*

Light House Center Inc (PA).................................765 448-4502
3918 Harry Ave Lafayette (47905) *(G-10636)*

Light House Woodworking DBA.............................260 704-0589
5553 County Road 79a Saint Joe (46785) *(G-14439)*

Light of Life Gel Candles..574 310-3777
819 Kline St Mishawaka (46544) *(G-11929)*

Light Printing Co..815 429-3724
9054 S 335 E Brook (47922) *(G-1305)*

Light Stigma LLC..812 550-7923
10701 Greenleaf Dr Evansville (47712) *(G-4169)*

Lightcrafters Nanotech LLC..................................610 844-8341
9188 Vigo St Crown Point (46307) *(G-2719)*

Lighthouse Industries Inc......................................772 429-1774
107 Eastwood Rd Ste D Michigan City (46360) *(G-11633)*

Lighthouse Industries Inc (PA).............................219 879-1550
107 Eastwood Rd Ste B Michigan City (46360) *(G-11634)*

Lighthuse Cstm Frmng Fine Art, Marion Also Called: Grace Henderson *(G-11289)*

Lighting, Fort Wayne Also Called: Vlc Services LLC *(G-5535)*

Lighting Studio, The, Lafayette Also Called: Brighter Design Inc *(G-10544)*

Lightning Logistics Entps LLC..............................317 333-9563
8520 Allison Pointe Blvd Indianapolis (46250) *(G-8750)*

Lightning Printing..765 362-5999
115 N Washington St Crawfordsville (47933) *(G-2585)*

Lightuptoyscom LLC (PA).....................................812 246-1916
8512 Commerce Park Dr Sellersburg (47172) *(G-14604)*

Ligonier Woodworking...260 894-9969
1068 E Perry Rd Ligonier (46767) *(G-11019)*

Lil Girl's Glam Spa Bus, Indianapolis Also Called: Lil Girls Glam LLC *(G-8751)*

Lil Girls Glam LLC...317 507-3443
2333 Rostock Ct Indianapolis (46229) *(G-8751)*

Lil Ms One Hundred LLC.......................................765 609-9526
2515 Village Cir W Indianapolis (46229) *(G-8752)*

Lil Red Studios LLC...317 443-4932
8113 States Bend Dr Indianapolis (46239) *(G-8753)*

Lila J Athletic Wear..502 619-2898
3415 Royal Lake Dr Floyds Knobs (47119) *(G-4685)*

Lillich Sign Co Inc..260 463-3930
1333 Industrial Dr N Lagrange (46761) *(G-10753)*

Lillsun Manufacturing Co Inc................................260 356-6514
1350 Harris St Huntington (46750) *(G-7337)*

Lilly, Indianapolis Also Called: Eli Lilly and Company *(G-8088)*

Lilly Research Laboratories..................................317 276-0127
1 Lilly Corporate Ctr Indianapolis (46285) *(G-8754)*

Lilly Technology Center - N, Indianapolis Also Called: Eli Lilly and Company *(G-8081)*

Lilly Usa LLC..317 276-2000
Lilly Corporate Center Indianapolis (46285) *(G-8755)*

Lilly Ventures..317 651-3050
Lilly Corporate Center Dc 10 Indianapolis (46285) *(G-8756)*

Lily Group Inc...812 268-5459
103 N Court St Sullivan (47882) *(G-15412)*

Limanis Pop Up Concessions LLC.........................317 966-1507
137 Production Dr Avon (46123) *(G-536)*

Lime City Manufacturing, Huntington Also Called: Reber Enterprises LLC *(G-7360)*

Limitless Woodworking LLC..................................317 702-1763
21218 Cyntheanne Rd Noblesville (46060) *(G-13128)*

Limon Woodworking LLC......................................317 362-9179
4002 Bertrand Rd Indianapolis (46222) *(G-8757)*

Linamar Strctures USA Mich Inc..........................248 372-9018
1510 Progress Dr Albion (46701) *(G-32)*

Linamar Strctures USA Mich Inc..........................260 636-7030
1612 Progress Dr Albion (46701) *(G-33)*

Linamar Strctures USA Mich Inc..........................260 636-1069
600 S 7th St Albion (46701) *(G-34)*

Linamar Strctures USA Mich Inc..........................260 636-7030
100 Progress Way Avilla (46710) *(G-487)*

Linco Group LLC..765 418-5567
2310 W Division Rd Williamsport (47993) *(G-16851)*

Lincoln Industries Inc..812 897-0715
110 W Division St Boonville (47601) *(G-1088)*

Lincoln Printing, Fort Wayne Also Called: Lincoln Printing Corporation *(G-5186)*

Lincoln Printing Corporation.................................260 424-5200
10351 Dawsons Creek Blvd Ste D Fort Wayne (46825) *(G-5186)*

Linda Controls LLC...219 926-6979
402 E 1500 N Chesterton (46304) *(G-1945)*

Linda Harmon De Sign Studi..................................765 573-6138
407 S Washington St Marion (46953) *(G-11310)*

Lindal North America Inc......................................812 657-7142
6010 S International Dr Columbus (47201) *(G-2342)*

Lindas Gone Buggie..219 299-0174
28 E 36th Pl Hobart (46342) *(G-7199)*

Linde Advanced Material Techno (DH).................317 240-2500
1500 Polco St Indianapolis (46222) *(G-8758)*

Linde Advanced Mtl Tech Inc................................317 240-2500
1555 Main St Indianapolis (46224) *(G-8759)*

Linde Gas & Equipment Inc...................................812 376-3314
111 S National Rd Columbus (47201) *(G-2343)*

Linde Gas & Equipment Inc...................................260 423-4468
1725 Edsall Ave Fort Wayne (46803) *(G-5187)*

Linde Gas & Equipment Inc...................................574 537-1366
2502 Dierdorff Rd Goshen (46526) *(G-6198)*

Linde Gas & Equipment Inc...................................317 782-4661
5720 Kopetsky Dr Ste N Indianapolis (46217) *(G-8760)*

Linde Gas & Equipment Inc...................................317 481-4550
1400 Polco St Indianapolis (46222) *(G-8761)*

Linde Gas North America, Indianapolis Also Called: Linde Gas & Equipment Inc *(G-8760)*

Linde Inc..317 984-7002
1420 Bayswater Ln Cicero (46034) *(G-1998)*

ALPHABETIC SECTION

Linde Inc.. 219 391-5100
  4550 Kennedy Ave East Chicago (46312) *(G-3027)*
Linde Inc.. 317 881-6825
  5255 E Stop 11 Rd Ste 490 Indianapolis (46237) *(G-8762)*
Linde Inc.. 765 456-1128
  2100 E Lincoln Rd Kokomo (46902) *(G-10297)*
Linde Inc.. 219 326-7808
  3076 N State Road 39 La Porte (46350) *(G-10446)*
Linde Inc.. 812 524-0173
  1625 Bateman Dr Seymour (47274) *(G-14664)*
Linden Machine Shop, Linden Also Called: Linden Machine Shop LLC *(G-11031)*
Linden Machine Shop LLC.. 765 339-7244
  220 N Main St Linden (47955) *(G-11031)*
Line-X... 812 491-9475
  1804 Stringtown Rd Evansville (47711) *(G-4170)*
Line-X, Jasper Also Called: Dubois County Liners LLP *(G-9835)*
Line-X, Schererville Also Called: Line-X of Schererville Inc *(G-14530)*
Line-X of Indy, Indianapolis Also Called: Advance Prtective Coatings Inc *(G-7435)*
Line-X of Schererville Inc... 219 865-1000
  2041 Us Highway 41 Schererville (46375) *(G-14530)*
Linear Publishing Corp... 317 722-8500
  921 E 86th St Ste 108 Indianapolis (46240) *(G-8763)*
Linear Solutions Inc.. 219 237-2399
  149 S Colfax St Griffith (46319) *(G-6812)*
Linear Technology LLC.. 317 443-1169
  18 Point Ln Arcadia (46030) *(G-314)*
Linel Signature, Mooresville Also Called: Fenestration Products LLC *(G-12207)*
Liner Products LLC... 812 723-0244
  1468 W Hospital Rd Paoli (47454) *(G-13499)*
Lingenfelter Prfmce Engrg Inc.. 260 724-2552
  1557 Winchester Rd Decatur (46733) *(G-2869)*
Lingenfelter Racing, Decatur Also Called: Lingenfelter Prfmce Engrg Inc *(G-2869)*
Linguistics Club, Bloomington Also Called: Trustees Indiana University *(G-999)*
Link Electrical Service.. 812 288-8184
  1018 E 7th St Jeffersonville (47130) *(G-10013)*
Link Engineering LLC (PA)... 765 457-1166
  1719 N Main St Kokomo (46901) *(G-10298)*
Link Graphics, Evansville Also Called: Light & Ink Corporation *(G-4168)*
Link Printing Services LLC (PA).. 317 826-9852
  7370 Royal Oakland Dr Indianapolis (46236) *(G-8764)*
Link Printing Services LLC.. 317 902-6374
  11216 Fall Creek Rd Indianapolis (46256) *(G-8765)*
Linkel Company (PA)... 812 934-5190
  1081 Morris Rd Batesville (47006) *(G-596)*
Linker Media Group Inc.. 219 230-3777
  905 Joliet St Dyer (46311) *(G-2977)*
Linneas Lights LLC.. 317 324-4002
  839 W Carmel Dr Carmel (46032) *(G-1684)*
Linton Daily Citizen, Linton Also Called: Russ Publishing *(G-11045)*
Lionfish Cyber Hldngs LLC-S Ln..................................... 877 732-6772
  101 W Ohio St Ste 2000 Indianapolis (46204) *(G-8766)*
Lionfish Cyber Security, Indianapolis Also Called: Lionfish Cyber Hldngs LLC-S Ln *(G-8766)*
Lions Pride Customs LLC.. 765 490-8296
  6598 E 900 S Lafayette (47909) *(G-10637)*
Lions Quarter LLC... 219 932-5531
  635 165th St Hammond (46324) *(G-6972)*
Lionshead Alloys LLC (PA)... 574 533-6169
  305 Steury Ave Goshen (46528) *(G-6199)*
Lionshead Precision Metals LLC...................................... 317 787-6358
  1222 S Graham Rd Greenwood (46143) *(G-6729)*
Lionshead Specialty Tire & Whe (PA).............................. 574 533-6169
  305 Steury Ave Goshen (46528) *(G-6200)*
Lipper Components, Goshen Also Called: Lippert Components Inc *(G-6202)*
Lippert, Elkhart Also Called: Lippert Components Inc *(G-3493)*
Lippert Cmponents Intl Sls Inc.. 574 312-7480
  3501 County Road 6 E Elkhart (46514) *(G-3489)*
Lippert Components... 574 226-4088
  625 Bower St Elkhart (46514) *(G-3490)*
Lippert Components Inc.. 574 295-1483
  3308 Charlotte Ave Elkhart (46517) *(G-3491)*
Lippert Components Inc.. 574 535-1125
  57912 Charlotte Ave Elkhart (46517) *(G-3492)*
Lippert Components Inc (HQ)... 574 535-1125
  3501 County Road 6 E Elkhart (46514) *(G-3493)*
Lippert Components Inc.. 574 295-8166
  2503 Banks Ct Elkhart (46514) *(G-3494)*
Lippert Components Inc.. 574 534-8177
  2602 College Ave Goshen (46528) *(G-6201)*
Lippert Components Inc.. 574 535-1125
  2703 College Ave Goshen (46528) *(G-6202)*
Lippert Components Inc.. 574 537-8900
  1701 Century Dr Goshen (46528) *(G-6203)*
Lippert Components Inc.. 574 536-7803
  1302 Eisenhower Dr N Goshen (46526) *(G-6204)*
Lippert Components Inc.. 574 537-8900
  2703 College Ave Goshen (46528) *(G-6205)*
Lippert Components Inc.. 574 849-0869
  65781 Sourwood Goshen (46526) *(G-6206)*
Lippert Components Inc.. 574 971-4320
  16840 Skyview Rd Goshen (46526) *(G-6207)*
Lippert Components Inc.. 574 312-7445
  51040 Greenfield Pkwy Middlebury (46540) *(G-11734)*
Lippert Components Inc.. 800 551-9149
  408 S Byrkit St Mishawaka (46544) *(G-11930)*
Lippert Components Inc.. 574 537-8900
  401 S Beiger St Mishawaka (46544) *(G-11931)*
Lippert Components Inc.. 574 312-6654
  1280 S Olive St South Bend (46619) *(G-15125)*
Lippert Components Inc.. 260 234-4303
  2909 Pleasant Center Rd Yoder (46798) *(G-16966)*
Lippert Components Mfg Inc (DH).................................. 574 535-1125
  3501 County Road 6 E Elkhart (46514) *(G-3495)*
Lippert Extrusions.. 574 312-6467
  1722 W Mishawaka Rd Elkhart (46517) *(G-3496)*
Lippert Interior Solutions, Goshen Also Called: Lippert Components Inc *(G-6201)*
Liquid Filter Housings Inc... 414 530-8584
  513 N Melville St Rensselaer (47978) *(G-14059)*
Liquid Ninja Energy LLC... 812 746-2830
  6050 Wedeking Ave Ste 14 Evansville (47715) *(G-4171)*
Liquidspring LLC.. 765 474-7816
  4899 E 400 S Lafayette (47905) *(G-10638)*
Liquivinyl LLC... 765 283-6265
  7405 W Augusta Blvd Yorktown (47396) *(G-16975)*
Lit By Neek... 317 775-5574
  10949 Minuteman Ct Indianapolis (46234) *(G-8767)*
Lite Magnesium Products Inc... 765 299-3644
  6119 Guion Rd Indianapolis (46254) *(G-8768)*
Liteauto Inc.. 317 813-5045
  10475 Crosspoint Blvd Ste 250 Indianapolis (46256) *(G-8769)*
Literature Display Systems.. 317 841-4398
  7035 E 86th St Indianapolis (46250) *(G-8770)*
Literature Sales... 219 873-3093
  613 Franklin St Michigan City (46360) *(G-11635)*
Litho Press Inc... 317 634-6468
  1747 Massachusetts Ave Indianapolis (46201) *(G-8771)*
Lithocraft Inc... 812 948-1608
  1502 Beeler St New Albany (47150) *(G-12764)*
Lithogrphic Communications LLC................................... 219 924-9779
  9701 Indiana Pkwy Munster (46321) *(G-12548)*
Lithotone Inc (PA)... 574 294-5521
  1313 W Hively Ave Elkhart (46517) *(G-3497)*
Litko Aerosystems Inc... 219 462-9295
  2006 Warbler Dr Valparaiso (46383) *(G-15998)*
Litko Game Accessories, Valparaiso Also Called: Litko Aerosystems Inc *(G-15998)*
Little Bird Picture Framing.. 812 437-0285
  100 N Saint Joseph Ave Evansville (47712) *(G-4172)*
Little Brown Bears... 219 663-9037
  317 S Main St Crown Point (46307) *(G-2720)*
Little Cabin Embroidery.. 812 719-3888
  9225 Sunset Rd Tell City (47586) *(G-15508)*
Little Creations LLC.. 765 868-9656
  800 N Washington St Kokomo (46901) *(G-10299)*

Little Engineering LLC   ALPHABETIC SECTION

Little Engineering LLC 317 517-3323
   6406 N 75 W Whiteland (46184) *(G-16791)*

Little Leaf Records, Valparaiso *Also Called: Leslie Nuss (G-15997)*

Little Mfg LLC 812 453-8137
   2122 N State Route 61 Boonville (47601) *(G-1089)*

Little Nugget, Indianapolis *Also Called: CHG Developments LLC (G-7797)*

Little Super Findings 812 430-3353
   5115 Pollack Ave Evansville (47715) *(G-4173)*

Live Proud Spirits, Carmel *Also Called: Proud Spirits Inc (G-1731)*

Lively Machine Company Inc
   4404 Upper Mount Vernon Rd Evansville (47712) *(G-4174)*

Livin Lite Corp 574 862-2228
   985 N 900 W Shipshewana (46565) *(G-14865)*

Livin' Lite Rv, Shipshewana *Also Called: Livin Lite Corp (G-14865)*

Living Prairie Equipment LLC 765 479-0759
   2768 N 1000 W Wolcott (47995) *(G-16933)*

Livings Graphics Inc 574 264-4114
   2111 Cassopolis St Elkhart (46514) *(G-3498)*

Lj Motive LLC 219 588-5480
   6163 Oregon St Hobart (46342) *(G-7200)*

Ljt Texas LLC (DH) 800 257-6859
   515 W Ireland Rd South Bend (46614) *(G-15126)*

Lk Technologies Inc 812 332-4449
   1590 S Liberty Dr Ste A Bloomington (47403) *(G-912)*

Llama Corporation 888 701-7432
   2937 E 900 N Decatur (46733) *(G-2870)*

LLC, Muncie *Also Called: Gibson Nehemiah Group Inc (G-12401)*

LLC 2 Holdings Limited LLC 317 319-9825
   1868 Corniche Dr Zionsville (46077) *(G-17030)*

LLC Black Jewell 800 948-2302
   417 Washington St Columbus (47201) *(G-2344)*

LLC Tipton Mills
   835 S Mapleton St Columbus (47201) *(G-2345)*

LLC Ward Stone 812 587-0272
   1610 W State Road 252 Flat Rock (47234) *(G-4654)*

LLC White Diamond 463 888-3585
   5610 Crawfordsville Rd Ste 1904 Indianapolis (46224) *(G-8772)*

Lloyd & Mona Sulivan 812 522-9191
   2169 N County Road 400 E Seymour (47274) *(G-14665)*

Lloyd Jr Frank P and Assoc 317 388-9225
   4461 Sylvan Rd Indianapolis (46228) *(G-8773)*

Lloyd Werking Sign Painting 765 354-2881
   243 High St Middletown (47356) *(G-11773)*

Lloyds of Indiana Inc 317 251-5430
   2507 Roosevelt Ave Indianapolis (46218) *(G-8774)*

Lm Sugarbush LLC 812 967-4491
   29618 Green Rd Borden (47106) *(G-1115)*

LMC Workholding, Logansport *Also Called: Logansport Machine Co Inc (G-11090)*

Lmr Industries LLC 219 765-4157
   930 165th St Hammond (46324) *(G-6973)*

Loaded Dough Cookie Co LLC 765 969-6513
   306 Deerfield Way Centerville (47330) *(G-1851)*

Loading Dock Maintenance LLC 260 424-3635
   5032 Moeller Rd Fort Wayne (46806) *(G-5188)*

Locavore Productions LLC 317 371-2970
   6559 E 1200 N Morristown (46161) *(G-12279)*

Locc Industries LLC 219 575-2727
   23 Beach Ln Portage (46368) *(G-13882)*

Lock Joint Tube LLC (DH) 574 299-5326
   515 W Ireland Rd South Bend (46614) *(G-15127)*

Lock Joint Tube Texas, South Bend *Also Called: Ljt Texas LLC (G-15126)*

Lockerbie Square Cab Co Inc 317 635-1134
   4350 W 10th St Indianapolis (46222) *(G-8775)*

Lockheed Martin, Indianapolis *Also Called: Lockheed Martin Corporation (G-8776)*

Lockheed Martin Corporation 317 821-4000
   5101 Decatur Blvd Ste A Indianapolis (46241) *(G-8776)*

Lockwood Welding Incorporated 260 925-2086
   2450 County Road 32 Waterloo (46793) *(G-16523)*

Locoli Inc (PA) 219 515-6900
   1650 Us Highway 41 Ste E Schererville (46375) *(G-14531)*

Lod LLC 765 385-0631
   1153 N Us Highway 41 Fowler (47944) *(G-5626)*

Lodos Theranostics LLC 765 427-2492
   132 Vigo Ct West Lafayette (47906) *(G-16602)*

Loewenstein Furniture Inc 800 521-5381
   1204 E 6th St Huntingburg (47542) *(G-7286)*

Log Home Construction Indiana, Manilla *Also Called: E & L Construction Inc (G-11260)*

Logan Stampings Inc (PA) 574 722-3101
   40 E Industrial Blvd Logansport (46947) *(G-11089)*

Logan Stampings Inc 574 722-3101
   1105 American Pkwy Peru (46970) *(G-13590)*

Logan Street Signs and Banners, Noblesville *Also Called: James Wafford (G-13111)*

Logansport Machine Co Inc 574 735-0225
   1200 W Linden Ave Logansport (46947) *(G-11090)*

Loggers Incorporated 812 939-2797
   7755 S County Rd 50 Clay City (47841) *(G-2045)*

Logging 812 216-3544
   10680 W Seymour Rd Seymour (47274) *(G-14666)*

Logic Furniture, Goshen *Also Called: Wieland Designs Inc (G-6276)*

Logic Furniture LLC 574 975-0007
   1149 Monroe St Indianapolis (46229) *(G-8777)*

Logical Concepts 317 885-6330
   494 S Emerson Ave Ste E1 Greenwood (46143) *(G-6730)*

Logikos Overview LLC 260 483-3638
   9812 Dawsons Creek Blvd Fort Wayne (46825) *(G-5189)*

Logistick Inc 800 758-5840
   19880 State Line Rd South Bend (46637) *(G-15128)*

Logo Apparel Plus, Floyds Knobs *Also Called: Gettelfinger Holdings LLC (G-4679)*

Logo Boys Inc 574 256-6844
   3102 N Home St Mishawaka (46545) *(G-11932)*

Logo Connxtion, Terre Haute *Also Called: Vco Inc (G-15739)*

Logo USA Corporation (PA) 317 867-8518
   320 Parkway Cir Westfield (46074) *(G-16708)*

Logo Zone Inc 574 753-7569
   731 Lakeview Dr Logansport (46947) *(G-11091)*

Logos, Tell City *Also Called: Fine Guys Inc (G-15502)*

Logos Express Inc 317 272-1200
   1225 Ransdell Ct Lebanon (46052) *(G-10911)*

Logowear LLC 317 462-3376
   910 Meadow Ln Greenfield (46140) *(G-6525)*

Lomatt Dynamics LLC 574 500-2517
   106 W Van Buren St Leesburg (46538) *(G-10957)*

Lomont Holdings Co Inc 800 545-9023
   1825 W Maumee St Angola (46703) *(G-273)*

London Hair Bundles, Fishers *Also Called: London Hair Bundles LLC (G-4557)*

London Hair Bundles LLC 317 953-3888
   13813 Wendessa Dr Fishers (46038) *(G-4557)*

Londynn Nailed You, Indianapolis *Also Called: Johnson Samyra (G-8635)*

Lone Star Industries Inc (DH) 317 706-3314
   10401 N Meridian St Ste 120 Carmel (46290) *(G-1685)*

Lone Star Industries Inc 574 674-8873
   55284 Corwin Rd Elkhart (46514) *(G-3499)*

Lone Star Industries Inc 260 482-4559
   4805 Investment Dr Fort Wayne (46808) *(G-5190)*

Lone Star Industries Inc 765 653-9766
   3301 S County Road 150 W Greencastle (46135) *(G-6419)*

Lone Star Industries Inc 317 780-9860
   1112 W Thompson Rd Indianapolis (46217) *(G-8778)*

Lone Star Tool & Die Weld 812 346-9681
   432 4th St Mt Vernon (47282) *(G-16097)*

Long Jim Jay Jr 317 446-4409
   5822 Rahke Rd Indianapolis (46217) *(G-8779)*

Long Item Development Corp 317 780-1077
   2210 National Ave Indianapolis (46227) *(G-8780)*

Long Leather Works LLC 812 336-5309
   518 W 4th St Bloomington (47404) *(G-913)*

Long Tail Corporation (PA) 260 918-0489
   4630 W Jefferson Blvd Ste 1 Fort Wayne (46804) *(G-5191)*

Longhorn Marketing Group 765 650-4430
   1950 E Walnut St Frankfort (46041) *(G-5680)*

Longhorn Sand and Gravel LLC 574 532-2788
   30430 Osborne Rd North Liberty (46554) *(G-13218)*

Lonn Manufacturing Inc 317 897-1440
   5450 W 84th St Indianapolis (46268) *(G-8781)*

ALPHABETIC SECTION — Lucent Polymers Inc

Loogootee Tribune Inc 812 295-2500
514 N John F Kennedy Ave Loogootee (47553) *(G-11143)*

Look Trailers, Middlebury *Also Called: LGS Industries LLC (G-11733)*

Loon Creek Leather LLC 260 356-0726
750 N Marion Rd Huntington (46750) *(G-7338)*

Lopez Tires & Wheels LLC 219 654-4586
3020 Fairview Ave Lake Station (46405) *(G-10773)*

Lord Corporation 317 259-4161
5101 E 65th St Indianapolis (46220) *(G-8782)*

Lord Fms Games LLC 317 710-2253
7244 Rooses Way Indianapolis (46217) *(G-8783)*

Lorentson Manufacturing Co (PA) 765 452-4425
1111 Rank Pkwy Kokomo (46901) *(G-10300)*

Lori Hicks 574 291-6341
310 Barbie St South Bend (46614) *(G-15129)*

Lost Hollow Beer Co LLC 317 796-9516
102 E Franklin St Greencastle (46135) *(G-6420)*

Lost Legends Publishing LLC 765 606-5342
158 Chariot Dr Anderson (46013) *(G-147)*

Lost Realms Publishing LLC 319 230-3666
1231 Redwood Dr Anderson (46011) *(G-148)*

Lotec Inc 574 294-1506
2000 Industrial Pkwy Elkhart (46516) *(G-3500)*

Lots of Software LLC 317 578-8120
13534 Kelsey Ln Fishers (46038) *(G-4558)*

Lotus Designs LLC 812 206-7281
113 Industrial Way Charlestown (47111) *(G-1879)*

Louanna Stilwell 812 631-0647
6451 S County Road 1075 E Velpen (47590) *(G-16094)*

Loud Clear Communications LLC 260 433-9479
6439 County Road 29 Auburn (46706) *(G-403)*

Loughmiller Mch TI Design Inc 812 295-3903
12851 E 150 N Loogootee (47553) *(G-11144)*

Louies Companies Inc 765 448-4300
2415 Sagamore Pkwy S Lafayette (47905) *(G-10639)*

Louis Dreyfus Co AG Inds LLC
7344 S State Road 15 Claypool (46510) *(G-2055)*

Louisiana-Pacific Corporation 574 825-5845
219 W Us Highway 20 Middlebury (46540) *(G-11735)*

Louisville Division, New Albany *Also Called: Konecranes Inc (G-12761)*

Louisville Veneer Corp 502 500-7176
301 E Elm St New Albany (47150) *(G-12765)*

Loutsa Inc 317 273-0123
7435 W 10th St Indianapolis (46214) *(G-8784)*

Love Handle LLC 317 384-1102
11702 Maze Rd Indianapolis (46259) *(G-8785)*

Love To Stitch LLC 812 342-8565
1097 Westview Point Dr Columbus (47201) *(G-2346)*

Love Upholstery LLC 812 639-3789
5265 W Oak Ridge Dr Jasper (47546) *(G-9883)*

Love-Toi LLC 317 537-7635
1251 Flint Ct Anderson (46013) *(G-149)*

Love2readlove2write Pubg LLC 317 550-9755
5936 Copeland Lakes Dr Indianapolis (46221) *(G-8786)*

Loves Enterprise LLC 219 307-9191
3589 Delaware St Gary (46409) *(G-5978)*

Loves Travel Stops 574 935-4103
2952 Gary Dr Plymouth (46563) *(G-13793)*

Lovett Entertainment LLC 773 208-9608
1825 Lakeview Ct Schererville (46375) *(G-14532)*

Lovett Pallet Recycling LLC 317 638-4840
217 S Belmont Ave Ste E Indianapolis (46222) *(G-8787)*

Low Vision Store, Greenwood *Also Called: Vision Aid Systems Inc (G-6778)*

Lowell Concrete Products Inc 219 696-3339
9312 W 181st Ave Lowell (46356) *(G-11169)*

Lowell Quarry, Lowell *Also Called: Legacy Vulcan LLC (G-11167)*

Lowery's Candies, Muncie *Also Called: Lowerys Home Made Candies Inc (G-12441)*

Lowerys Home Made Candies Inc 765 288-7300
6255 W Kilgore Ave Muncie (47304) *(G-12441)*

Lowes Pellets and Grain Inc (PA) 812 663-7863
2372 W State Road 46 Greensburg (47240) *(G-6615)*

Loy's Music Center, Elwood *Also Called: Loys Sales Inc (G-3829)*

Loyal Mfg Corp 317 359-3185
1121 S Shortridge Rd Indianapolis (46239) *(G-8788)*

Loys Sales Inc 765 552-7250
715 S 22nd St Elwood (46036) *(G-3829)*

Lozano Wldg & Fabrication LLC 812 550-1706
3816 E Morgan Ave Evansville (47715) *(G-4175)*

Lozano Wldg & Fabrication LLC 812 629-2000
7120 Savannah Dr Newburgh (47630) *(G-13012)*

Lozier Machinery Incorporated 812 945-2558
695 Industrial Blvd New Albany (47150) *(G-12766)*

LP Middlebury, Middlebury *Also Called: Louisiana-Pacific Corporation (G-11735)*

LPI Paving & Excavating (PA) 260 726-9564
1401 W Votaw St Portland (47371) *(G-13955)*

Lrt Precision Inc 574 223-2578
1703 Jefferson St Rochester (46975) *(G-14302)*

Lsc Communications Inc 765 364-2247
600 W State Road 32 Crawfordsville (47933) *(G-2586)*

Lsc Communications Inc 812 234-1585
200 Hulman St Terre Haute (47802) *(G-15633)*

Lsc Communications Book LLC 317 715-2406
5532 W 74th St Ste 14 N Indianapolis (46268) *(G-8789)*

Lsc Communications Book LLC 317 715-2406
5536 W 74th St Indianapolis (46268) *(G-8790)*

Lsc Communications Book LLC (HQ) 317 715-2402
5550 W 74th St Indianapolis (46268) *(G-8791)*

Lsc Communications Book LLC 317 406-8783
716 Airtech Pkwy Plainfield (46168) *(G-13698)*

Lsc Communications Us LLC 812 256-3396
100 Quality Ct Charlestown (47111) *(G-1880)*

Lsc Communications Us LLC 765 362-1300
600 W State Road 32 Crawfordsville (47933) *(G-2587)*

Lsc Communications Us LLC 574 267-7101
2801 W Old Road 30 Warsaw (46580) *(G-16388)*

LSI, Granger *Also Called: Lazar Scientific Incorporated (G-6358)*

LSI Fabrication 574 722-3101
1105 American Pkwy Peru (46970) *(G-13591)*

LSI Metal Fabrication Inc 574 722-3101
1100 E Main St Logansport (46947) *(G-11092)*

LSI Wallcovering, New Albany *Also Called: LSI Wallcovering Inc (G-12767)*

LSI Wallcovering Inc (PA) 502 458-1502
2073 Mcdonald Ave New Albany (47150) *(G-12767)*

Lsm Manufacturing LLC 260 409-4030
15303 Roth Rd Grabill (46741) *(G-6311)*

Lsr Conversions LLC 574 206-9610
25771 Miner Rd Elkhart (46514) *(G-3501)*

Lt Metal Masters Inc 317 780-1864
2514 Bethel Ave Indianapolis (46203) *(G-8792)*

LTI Holdings Inc 574 389-1878
53208 Columbia Dr Elkhart (46514) *(G-3502)*

Lubber Dubbers 812 475-1725
6240 E Virginia St Evansville (47715) *(G-4176)*

Lube-Line Corporation (PA) 260 637-3779
906 Carroll Rd Fort Wayne (46845) *(G-5192)*

Lubrication Devices 574 234-4674
719 W North Shore Dr South Bend (46617) *(G-15130)*

Lubrication Devices Mfg, South Bend *Also Called: Lubrication Devices (G-15130)*

Lubrication Specialist Inc 317 326-4296
5231 N Sugar Hills Dr Greenfield (46140) *(G-6526)*

Lucas Custom Instruments LLC 812 342-3093
13360 W Becks Grove Rd Columbus (47201) *(G-2347)*

Lucas Oil, Corydon *Also Called: Lucas Oil Racing Inc (G-2504)*

Lucas Oil, Indianapolis *Also Called: Lucas Oil Products Inc (G-8793)*

Lucas Oil Pro Plling Prmotions 812 246-3350
5511 County Road 403 Charlestown (47111) *(G-1881)*

Lucas Oil Products Inc (PA) 951 270-0154
1310 E 96th St Indianapolis (46240) *(G-8793)*

Lucas Oil Racing Inc 812 738-1147
3199 Harrison Way Nw Corydon (47112) *(G-2504)*

Lucent Polymers Acquisition, Evansville *Also Called: Lucent Polymers Inc (G-4177)*

Lucent Polymers Inc 812 421-2216
1700 Lynch Rd Evansville (47711) *(G-4177)*

Luckmann Industries.. 317 464-0323
 3135 Jackson St Indianapolis (46222) *(G-8794)*

Lucky Man Wdwkg Hndyman Svcs L........................ 810 247-3099
 13011 Blalock Dr Fishers (46037) *(G-4559)*

Ludo Fact USA LLC (DH)... 765 588-9137
 4775 Dale Dr Lafayette (47905) *(G-10640)*

Ludwick Graphics Inc (PA)...................................... 574 233-2165
 1312 Honan Dr South Bend (46614) *(G-15131)*

Lue Manufacturing Corporation.............................. 574 862-4249
 27667 County Road 40 Wakarusa (46573) *(G-16238)*

Lui Plus.. 812 309-9350
 7933 Valley Stream Dr Indianapolis (46237) *(G-8795)*

Luick Quality Gage & Tool, Muncie Also Called: Haylex Manufacturing LLC *(G-12411)*

Lululemon... 574 271-3260
 6501 Grape Rd Spc 289 Mishawaka (46545) *(G-11933)*

Lulus Prom and Bridal LLC..................................... 812 772-2013
 1408 Main St Tell City (47586) *(G-15509)*

Lumber WD Furn Mg Sell WD Flrg, South Whitley Also Called: Ecojacks LLC *(G-15317)*

Lume Deodorant.. 623 227-8724
 5102 Barack Obama Way New Albany (47150) *(G-12768)*

Lumen Cache Incorporated..................................... 317 739-4218
 13402 Chrisfield Ln Fishers (46055) *(G-4644)*

Lumen Cache Inc... 317 222-1314
 11216 Fall Creek Rd Ste 110 Indianapolis (46256) *(G-8796)*

Luna Logistics LLC... 317 721-2363
 8355 Weathervane Cir Indianapolis (46239) *(G-8797)*

Lunarglo LLC.. 574 294-2624
 22385 Via Pompeii Elkhart (46516) *(G-3503)*

Lund Custom Calls LLC... 812 242-0566
 801 S 4th St Clinton (47842) *(G-2071)*

Lund International Holding Co................................ 888 477-3729
 2415 Cathy Ln Jasper (47546) *(G-9884)*

Lund International Holding Co................................ 765 742-7200
 3565 E 300 N Lafayette (47905) *(G-10641)*

Lure Ventures Inc... 219 313-5325
 532 Ballard Ave Mishawaka (46544) *(G-11934)*

Lush & Luxe Creations LLC................................... 317 561-0574
 4841 Industrial Pkwy Indianapolis (46226) *(G-8798)*

Lux Beauty Den LLC.. 708 793-0871
 5164 E 81st Ave Pmb 2022 Merrillville (46410) *(G-11534)*

Luxe Fashion Palace LLC....................................... 317 379-1372
 11705 Sinclair Dr Indianapolis (46235) *(G-8799)*

Luxe Trucks LLC... 574 522-8422
 3504 Henke St Elkhart (46514) *(G-3504)*

Luxetrend LLC.. 502 208-9344
 1014 Mary St Apt 2 Evansville (47710) *(G-4178)*

Luxly LLC.. 617 415-8031
 14549 Brackney Ln Carmel (46032) *(G-1686)*

Luxottica of America Inc... 317 293-9999
 4020 Lafayette Rd Indianapolis (46254) *(G-8800)*

Luxottica of America Inc... 219 736-0141
 2212 Southlake Mall Merrillville (46410) *(G-11535)*

Luxurylinks LLC.. 260 258-2814
 848 Dolphin Dr Fort Wayne (46816) *(G-5193)*

Luxxeen America Corporation............................... 888 589-9336
 3850 Birkdale Dr Carmel (46033) *(G-1687)*

Lvb Acquisition Holding LLC................................. 574 267-6639
 56 E Bell Dr Warsaw (46582) *(G-16389)*

Lycro Products Co Inc... 574 862-4981
 66557 State Road 19 Wakarusa (46573) *(G-16239)*

Lynn Beck... 765 523-2260
 9950 S 1000 E Clarks Hill (47930) *(G-2004)*

Lynn Bros Electric Inc... 219 762-6386
 5685 Old Porter Rd Portage (46368) *(G-13883)*

Lynn Tool Company Inc... 765 874-2471
 107 Elm St Lynn (47355) *(G-11185)*

Lyntech Engineering Inc.. 574 224-2300
 2516 E State Road 14 Rochester (46975) *(G-14303)*

Lyondllbsell Advnced Plymers I............................. 219 392-3375
 4404 Euclid Ave East Chicago (46312) *(G-3028)*

Lyondllbsell Advnced Plymers I............................. 812 202-1968
 820 E Columbia St Evansville (47711) *(G-4179)*

Lyondllbsell Advnced Plymers I............................. 713 309-7148
 5001 Ohara Dr Evansville (47711) *(G-4180)*

Lyondllbsell Advnced Plymers I............................. 812 253-5203
 15000 Us Hwy 41 Evansville (47725) *(G-4181)*

Lyondllbsell Advnced Plymers I............................. 574 935-5131
 1301 Flora St Plymouth (46563) *(G-13794)*

M & C LLC... 812 482-7447
 3626 N Newton St Jasper (47546) *(G-9885)*

M & D Draperies.. 812 886-4608
 2022 Jackson Dr Vincennes (47591) *(G-16138)*

M & D Woodworking... 260 450-0484
 11522 Antwerp Rd Grabill (46741) *(G-6312)*

M & H Woodworking LLC.. 812 486-2570
 3591 N 775 E Montgomery (47558) *(G-12111)*

M & J Shelton Enterprises Inc................................ 260 745-1616
 2131 Fairfield Ave Fort Wayne (46802) *(G-5194)*

M & K Services, South Bend Also Called: Northern Indiana Ordnance Co *(G-15173)*

M & M Converting Inc... 260 563-7411
 3758 W Old 24 Wabash (46992) *(G-16195)*

M & M Custom Embroidery..................................... 407 334-5076
 3489 S 700 E Walkerton (46574) *(G-16268)*

M & M Printing, Clarksville Also Called: Mike Mugler *(G-2023)*

M & M Service Co, Freelandville Also Called: M & M Service Co Wldg & Repr *(G-5803)*

M & M Service Co Wldg & Repr............................. 812 328-6195
 Hwy 159 S Freelandville (47535) *(G-5803)*

M & M Svc Stn Eqp Spcalist Inc............................. 317 347-8001
 2228 Yandes St Indianapolis (46205) *(G-8801)*

M & M Tabletops LLC.. 502 396-9236
 4218 Payne Koehler Rd New Albany (47150) *(G-12769)*

M & M Woodworking.. 812 486-2418
 4192 E 350 N Washington (47501) *(G-16492)*

M & S Curtis LLC... 317 946-8440
 10015 Chester Dr Indianapolis (46240) *(G-8802)*

M & S Indus Met Fabricators, Huntington Also Called: M & S Indus Met Fbricators Inc *(G-7339)*

M & S Indus Met Fbricators Inc.............................. 260 356-0300
 5 Commercial Rd Huntington (46750) *(G-7339)*

M & S Screw Machine Products............................. 765 853-5022
 S Main St Modoc (47358) *(G-12053)*

M & S Steel Corp... 260 357-5184
 217 E Railroad St Garrett (46738) *(G-5869)*

M A C Corporation.. 317 545-3341
 4717 Massachusetts Ave Indianapolis (46218) *(G-8803)*

M A Studio Inc.. 574 275-2200
 3153 S 900 W San Pierre (46374) *(G-14505)*

M and M Embroidery.. 317 504-2235
 3553 Lowry Rd Indianapolis (46222) *(G-8804)*

M B S, New Albany Also Called: Manitowoc Beverage Systems Inc *(G-12771)*

M Bryant Denisa.. 317 350-3878
 3650 W 86th St Indianapolis (46268) *(G-8805)*

M E C, Westfield Also Called: Motion Engineering Company Inc *(G-16712)*

M F Y Designs Inc... 260 563-6662
 1051 N State Road 15 Wabash (46992) *(G-16196)*

M G Industries.. 812 362-7593
 6500 N Us Highway 231 Rockport (47635) *(G-14344)*

M G Products Inc... 574 293-0752
 4707 Chester Dr Elkhart (46516) *(G-3505)*

M J Markiewicz & Associates................................. 765 452-6562
 1768 N 300 W Kokomo (46901) *(G-10301)*

M Jones Consulting LLC... 317 353-3823
 208 E Main St Monrovia (46157) *(G-12078)*

M L X Graphics, Terre Haute Also Called: Phoenix Color Corp *(G-15661)*

M M Printing Plus.. 574 658-9345
 634 E Beer Rd Milford (46542) *(G-11797)*

M P L, Fairland Also Called: Marstone Products Ltd *(G-4400)*

M Pro LLC... 765 459-4750
 4812 N Parkway Kokomo (46901) *(G-10302)*

M Ross Masson, Indianapolis Also Called: Masson Inc *(G-8848)*

M S & J Quality Screw Mch Pdts............................ 812 623-3002
 8925 E County Road 1000 N Sunman (47041) *(G-15441)*

M S Aronstam Jewelers, Carmel Also Called: Design Msa Inc *(G-1606)*

ALPHABETIC SECTION — Mafco & Poseidon Barge

M S Powder Coating.. 260 356-0300
5 Commercial Rd Huntington (46750) *(G-7340)*

M U Holdings Inc.. 317 596-9786
815 W Jefferson St Bldg 4 Tipton (46072) *(G-15781)*

M-3 & Associates, Elkhart *Also Called: Wait Industries LLC (G-3776)*

M-3 and Associates Inc.. 574 294-3988
2500 Ada Dr Elkhart (46514) *(G-3506)*

M-Famouz Logistics LLC.. 219 501-1921
6616 Jefferson Ave Hammond (46324) *(G-6974)*

M-TEC Corporation... 574 294-1060
701 Collins Rd Elkhart (46516) *(G-3507)*

M-Tech Machine Products LLC.............................. 812 637-3500
27755 Daugherty Ln Ste A West Harrison (47060) *(G-16549)*

M.A.S. Products, Elkhart *Also Called: Mid America Screw Products (G-3537)*

M&C Tech Indiana Corporation............................. 812 674-2122
1928 Technology Dr Washington (47501) *(G-16493)*

M&C Wndrink Rverside Farms Inc......................... 928 897-0061
24121 Whitcomb St Lowell (46356) *(G-11170)*

M&M Dyson Farms Inc... 765 833-2202
6651 N 400 W Roann (46974) *(G-14251)*

M&M Fabrication LLC.. 812 692-5511
7382 Russell Dr Bicknell (47512) *(G-735)*

M&M Interactive Inc.. 317 708-1250
1661 Gotland Dr Carmel (46032) *(G-1688)*

M&M Performance Inc... 574 536-6103
16077 Prairie Rose Ave Goshen (46528) *(G-6208)*

M2 Industries LLC... 812 246-0651
2200 Utica Pike Apt 4 Jeffersonville (47130) *(G-10014)*

M2 Water Solutions LLC.. 317 431-7941
951 E 86th St Ste 200d Indianapolis (46240) *(G-8806)*

M2i LLC.. 765 618-2162
3809 N 400 W Marion (46952) *(G-11311)*

M2m Holdings Inc.. 317 249-1700
450 E 96th St Ste 300 Indianapolis (46240) *(G-8807)*

M4 Sciences LLC... 765 479-6215
4840 Us Highway 231 N West Lafayette (47906) *(G-16603)*

M4 Sciences Corporation...................................... 765 479-6215
4840 Us Highway 231 N West Lafayette (47906) *(G-16604)*

MA Metal Co Inc.. 812 526-2666
216 N Main St Edinburgh (46124) *(G-3091)*

MA Publishing Inc.. 812 217-0925
2205 Bellemeade Ave Apt A Evansville (47714) *(G-4182)*

Ma-Ri-Al Corp.. 317 773-0679
16101 River Rd Noblesville (46062) *(G-13129)*

Maax Aker Plastics, Plymouth *Also Called: Maax Inc (G-13795)*

Maax Inc.. 574 936-3838
1001 N Oak Dr Plymouth (46563) *(G-13795)*

Mac Industrial Holdings LLC................................. 812 838-1832
901 E 3rd St Mount Vernon (47620) *(G-12306)*

Mac Industrial Services, Mount Vernon *Also Called: Michrochem LLC (G-12309)*

Mac Machine & Metal Works Inc........................... 765 825-4121
100 N Grand Ave Connersville (47331) *(G-2453)*

Macallister Machinery Co Inc................................ 260 483-6469
2500 W Coliseum Blvd Fort Wayne (46808) *(G-5195)*

Macallister Machinery Co Inc................................ 765 966-0759
4791 Old National Rd E Richmond (47374) *(G-14157)*

Macdesign Inc... 317 580-9390
1009 3rd Ave Sw Carmel (46032) *(G-1689)*

Macednian Ptrtic Orgnztion of............................... 260 422-5900
124 W Wayne St Ste 204 Fort Wayne (46802) *(G-5196)*

MACEDONIAN TRIBUNE, Fort Wayne *Also Called: Macednian Ptrtic Orgnztion of (G-5196)*

Mach 1 Paper and Poly Pdts Inc............................ 574 522-4500
1801 Minnie St Elkhart (46516) *(G-3508)*

Mach Medical LLC... 260 229-1514
4707 E Park 30 Dr Columbia City (46725) *(G-2169)*

Machine Elements Inc... 219 508-3968
244 Crabapple Ln Valparaiso (46383) *(G-15999)*

Machine Keys Inc.. 765 228-4208
3809 N Chadam Ln Apt 1b Muncie (47304) *(G-12442)*

Machine Rebuilders & Service.............................. 260 482-8168
646 Pentolina Dr Fort Wayne (46845) *(G-5197)*

Machine Shop, Battle Ground *Also Called: Specialty Machine and Cnc Inc (G-614)*

Machine Tool Affiliates Inc.................................... 317 846-3487
8401 E 75th St Indianapolis (46256) *(G-8808)*

Machine Tool Service Inc...................................... 812 232-1912
117 Elm St Terre Haute (47807) *(G-15634)*

Machined Castings Spc LLC................................. 574 223-5694
290 Blacketor Dr Rochester (46975) *(G-14304)*

Machining, Brownsville *Also Called: Buck Hollow Cnc LLC (G-1430)*

Machining & Repr Resource Inc............................ 219 588-7395
3236 Strong St Highland (46322) *(G-7143)*

Machining Solutions... 574 292-3227
942 S 27th St South Bend (46615) *(G-15132)*

Mack Tool & Engineering Inc................................ 574 233-8424
2820 Viridian Dr South Bend (46628) *(G-15133)*

Mackey's Drapes, Connersville *Also Called: Katherine Mackey (G-2448)*

Maco Press Inc.. 317 846-5754
560 3rd Ave Sw Carmel (46032) *(G-1690)*

Maco Reprograhics LLC.. 812 464-8108
600 Court St Evansville (47708) *(G-4183)*

Macor.. 574 255-2658
1025 W 11th St Mishawaka (46544) *(G-11935)*

Macpactor Inc.. 502 643-7845
414 Spring St Jeffersonville (47130) *(G-10015)*

Macs Express Inc.. 765 865-9700
428 E Center Rd Kokomo (46902) *(G-10303)*

Mactac, Columbus *Also Called: Morgan Adhesives Company LLC (G-2357)*

Mactech Inc... 219 734-6503
5589 Old Porter Rd Portage (46368) *(G-13884)*

Mad Dasher Inc... 260 747-0545
4410 Tielker Rd Fort Wayne (46809) *(G-5198)*

Mad Media LLC.. 317 210-5609
501 E 6th St Sheridan (46069) *(G-14825)*

Madden Engineered Products LLC........................ 574 295-4292
1317 Princeton St Elkhart (46516) *(G-3509)*

Maddenco Inc.. 812 474-6245
4847 E Virginia St Ste G Evansville (47715) *(G-4184)*

Maddock Construction Eqp LLC............................ 812 349-3000
239 W Grimes Ln Bloomington (47403) *(G-914)*

Maddox Engineering Inc.. 812 903-0048
6670 Buttontown Rd Greenville (47124) *(G-6652)*

Maddox Industrial Contg LLC................................ 812 544-2156
1377 W Ruby Winkler Santa Claus (47579) *(G-14508)*

Made of, Greenfield *Also Called: Diaper Stone Opco LLC (G-6489)*

Made-Rite Manufacturing Inc................................ 812 967-2652
3967 E Sullivan Ln Salem (47167) *(G-14488)*

Mader Mill Inc... 812 876-9754
3720 State Highway 43 Spencer (47460) *(G-15354)*

Madison Cabinets Inc.. 260 639-3915
14727 Bruick Dr Hoagland (46745) *(G-7170)*

Madison County Cabinets Inc................................ 765 778-4646
9592 W 650 S Pendleton (46064) *(G-13541)*

Madison Courier... 812 265-3641
310 Courier Sq Madison (47250) *(G-11237)*

Madison Iron and Wood, Madison *Also Called: Charles Stewart (G-11207)*

Madison Manufacturing Inc................................... 574 633-4433
66990 State Road 331 Bremen (46506) *(G-1204)*

Madison Millwork Inc.. 765 649-7883
707 Jackson St Anderson (46016) *(G-150)*

Madison Precision Products Inc............................ 812 273-4702
94 E 400 N Madison (47250) *(G-11238)*

Madison Printing & Mailing, Michigan City *Also Called: Thomas Madison (G-11678)*

Madison Railroad, Madison *Also Called: Mayors Office City of Madison (G-11240)*

Madison Tool and Die Inc...................................... 812 273-2250
3000 Michigan Rd Madison (47250) *(G-11239)*

Madison, The, Mishawaka *Also Called: J H J Inc (G-11914)*

Madsen Wire LLC.. 260 829-6561
101 Madsen St Orland (46776) *(G-13368)*

Maet LLC... 574 220-7668
242 1234 N Eddy St South Bend (46617) *(G-15134)*

Mafco & Poseidon Barge....................................... 260 589-9000
750 E Parr Rd Berne (46711) *(G-718)*

Mafcote Wabash Paper Coating 260 563-4181
301 Wedcor Ave Wabash (46992) *(G-16197)*

Magaws of Boston 765 935-6170
5774 State Road 227 S Richmond (47374) *(G-14158)*

Magaws of Boston The, Richmond Also Called: Magaws of Boston *(G-14158)*

Magazine Fulfillment Corp 219 874-4245
613 Franklin St Michigan City (46360) *(G-11636)*

Magellan Integration Inc 812 492-4400
318 Main St Ste 322 Evansville (47708) *(G-4185)*

Magic Candle Inc 317 357-1101
203 S Audubon Rd Indianapolis (46219) *(G-8809)*

Magic Company 260 747-1502
405 Lower Huntington Rd Fort Wayne (46819) *(G-5199)*

Magic Premium Snacks, Fort Wayne Also Called: Magic Company *(G-5199)*

Magical Moments LLC 463 209-5766
1687 Honey Ln Greenwood (46143) *(G-6731)*

Magie Brothers, Indianapolis Also Called: Calumet Karns City Ref LLC *(G-7721)*

Magitek LLC 260 488-2226
5618 County Road 6 Hamilton (46742) *(G-6858)*

Magna Machine & Tool Co Inc 765 766-5388
3722 N Messick Rd New Castle (47362) *(G-12872)*

Magna Powertrain America Inc 765 587-1300
1400 W Fuson Rd Muncie (47302) *(G-12443)*

Magna Powertrain America Inc 765 587-1300
4701 S Cowan Rd Muncie (47302) *(G-12444)*

Magna-Tech Manufacturing Corporation 765 284-5050
3416 S Hoyt Ave Muncie (47302) *(G-12445)*

Magnasphere Corporation 574 533-1310
2556 Southside Park Dr Goshen (46526) *(G-6209)*

Magneco/Metrel Inc 219 885-4190
201 Mississippi St Gary (46402) *(G-5979)*

Magnequench Inc (DH) 765 778-7809
237 S Pendleton Ave Ste C Pendleton (46064) *(G-13542)*

Magnetech Industrial Svcs Inc 219 937-0100
1825 Summer St Hammond (46320) *(G-6975)*

Magnetic Concepts Corporation 317 580-4021
17005 Westfield Park Rd Ste 100 Westfield (46074) *(G-16709)*

Magnetic Instrumentation, Indianapolis Also Called: Utility Systems Inc *(G-9692)*

Magnetic Instrumentation LLC 317 842-7500
8431 Castlewood Dr Indianapolis (46250) *(G-8810)*

Magnets R US Inc 574 633-0061
63300 State Road 331 South Bend (46614) *(G-15135)*

Magnifiscents 317 549-3880
5207 E 38th St Indianapolis (46218) *(G-8811)*

Magnolia 317 831-3220
311 W 36th St Jasper (47546) *(G-9886)*

Magnum Exploration Inc 812 673-4914
4301 Romaine Rd New Harmony (47631) *(G-12887)*

Magnum Industries, Goshen Also Called: Magnum Venus Products Inc *(G-6210)*

Magnum International Inc 708 889-9999
11494 Broadway Crown Point (46307) *(G-2721)*

Magnum Venus Products Inc 727 573-2955
320 N Main St Goshen (46528) *(G-6210)*

Magwerks, Danville Also Called: Magwerks Corporation *(G-2819)*

Magwerks Corporation 317 241-8011
501 Commerce Dr Danville (46122) *(G-2819)*

Mahan Technical Design LLC 765 341-0533
400 E Mahalasville Rd Martinsville (46151) *(G-11410)*

Maher Cnstr Roofg & Siding, Terre Haute Also Called: Maher Supply Inc *(G-15635)*

Maher Supply Inc 812 234-7699
910 N 10th St Terre Haute (47807) *(G-15635)*

Mahogany Scents 574 271-1364
53154 Bracken Fern Dr South Bend (46637) *(G-15136)*

Mahoney Foundries Inc (PA) 260 347-1768
209 W Ohio St Kendallville (46755) *(G-10134)*

Mailboxes and Parcel Depot, Jasper Also Called: M & C LLC *(G-9885)*

Mailgate International Inc 866 843-1990
3209 W Smith Valley Rd Greenwood (46142) *(G-6732)*

Mailgate SC, Greenwood Also Called: Mailgate International Inc *(G-6732)*

Mailroom LLC 765 254-0000
1305 N Granville Ave Muncie (47303) *(G-12446)*

Main Event Mdsg Group LLC 317 570-8900
6880 Hillsdale Ct Indianapolis (46250) *(G-8812)*

Main Music 812 295-2020
12958 E Us Highway 50 Loogootee (47553) *(G-11145)*

Main One Media, Indianapolis Also Called: Main1media LLC *(G-8813)*

Main Street Sports, Bloomfield Also Called: Jer-Maur Corporation *(G-750)*

Main1media LLC 317 841-7000
8459 Castlewood Dr Ste D Indianapolis (46250) *(G-8813)*

Maingate LLC ....
7900 Rockville Rd Ste X Indianapolis (46214) *(G-8814)*

Mainline Conveyor Systems Inc 317 831-2795
3301 Hancel Cir Mooresville (46158) *(G-12219)*

Mains Enterprises Inc 765 425-0162
9762 N Nashville Rd Wilkinson (46186) *(G-16843)*

Mainstreet Marketing Entps LLC 765 482-6815
900 W Main St Lebanon (46052) *(G-10912)*

Maintenance Solutions Inc
313 W Rush St Kendallville (46755) *(G-10135)*

Maitland Engineering Inc 574 287-0155
2713 Foundation Dr South Bend (46628) *(G-15137)*

Majestic Block & Supply Inc 317 842-6602
7711 Loma Ct Fishers (46038) *(G-4560)*

Majestic Creations LLC 317 258-2794
8094 Stonebranch East Dr Indianapolis (46256) *(G-8815)*

Majestic Draperies Inc 574 257-8465
59193 Green Valley Pkwy Elkhart (46517) *(G-3510)*

Majestic Marble Imports Inc 317 237-4400
1100 E Maryland St Indianapolis (46202) *(G-8816)*

Majestic Water Company 317 790-2448
3815 River Crossing Pkwy Ste 100 Indianapolis (46240) *(G-8817)*

Majesty Enterprises Inc 812 752-6446
2068 S Jimtown Ln Scottsburg (47170) *(G-14570)*

Majesty Express, Scottsburg Also Called: Majesty Enterprises Inc *(G-14570)*

Majesty Hair Care, Indianapolis Also Called: Majesty Hair Care System LLC *(G-8818)*

Majesty Hair Care System LLC 317 900-6789
4010 W 86th St Ste N Indianapolis (46268) *(G-8818)*

Major Tool and Machine Inc 317 636-6433
2045 Doctor Andrew Indianapolis (46202) *(G-8819)*

Major Tool and Machine Inc (HQ) 317 636-6433
1458 E 19th St Indianapolis (46218) *(G-8820)*

Mak Steel Services LLC 812 525-8879
1191 King Ave Seymour (47274) *(G-14667)*

Make It Black Seal Coating 219 629-6230
3764 Louisiana St Gary (46409) *(G-5980)*

Make It Mobile LLC 260 562-1045
770 E State Road 120 Howe (46746) *(G-7239)*

Make Your Mark - Custom EMB 812 664-0026
106 N 1st Ave Princeton (47670) *(G-14003)*

Makers Hand Woodworking 317 797-8776
6100 E Pottery Rd Albany (47320) *(G-13)*

Maki Precision Machining LLC 219 575-7995
720 Boyd Blvd La Porte (46350) *(G-10447)*

Makingmoves Transports LLC 260 579-5584
6322 Millhollow Ln Fort Wayne (46815) *(G-5200)*

Makit, Warsaw Also Called: Jerry Oppered *(G-16381)*

Maks Plastic LLC 574 215-1800
13077 Mckinley Hwy Mishawaka (46545) *(G-11936)*

Makuta Inc 317 642-0001
2155 Intelliplex Dr Shelbyville (46176) *(G-14773)*

Maley & Wertz Inc (PA) 812 425-3358
900 E Columbia St Evansville (47711) *(G-4186)*

Maley & Wertz Lumber, Evansville Also Called: Maley & Wertz Inc *(G-4186)*

Malibu C, Indianapolis Also Called: Malibu Wellness Inc *(G-8821)*

Malibu Wellness Inc 317 624-7560
6050 E Hanna Ave Ste 1 Indianapolis (46203) *(G-8821)*

Mallang Spa Essentials 219 902-9788
923 Field St Hammond (46320) *(G-6976)*

Mallory Sonalert, Indianapolis Also Called: Mallory Sonalert Products Inc *(G-8822)*

Mallory Sonalert Products Inc 317 612-1000
4411 S High School Rd Indianapolis (46241) *(G-8822)*

Mama Fox Tee Company 260 438-4054
1712 Glen Elm Dr Fort Wayne (46845) *(G-5201)*

Mamas Soul Rollin LLC..256 479-4171
731 Lynn St Indianapolis (46222) *(G-8823)*

Mammoth Hats Inc..812 849-2772
1773 Huron Williams Rd Mitchell (47446) *(G-12044)*

Man Child Property Dev LLC...317 205-4109
4035 Sunshine Ave Indianapolis (46228) *(G-8824)*

Manar Inc (PA)...812 526-2891
905 S Walnut St Edinburgh (46124) *(G-3092)*

Manar Medical Inc..812 526-6734
906 S Walnut St Edinburgh (46124) *(G-3093)*

Manasek Acquisition Co LLC..765 551-1600
11700 N State Road 37 Elwood (46036) *(G-3830)*

Manchester Inc..260 982-2202
6973 E 975 N Roann (46974) *(G-14252)*

Manchester Industries Inc VA..765 489-4521
63 Paul R Foulke Pkwy Hagerstown (47346) *(G-6839)*

Manchester North News Journal...260 982-6383
1306 State Road 114 W North Manchester (46962) *(G-13238)*

Manchester Tool & Die Inc...260 982-8524
601 S Wabash Rd North Manchester (46962) *(G-13239)*

Manchester Weld and Fab LLC...260 578-5215
612 W 4th St North Manchester (46962) *(G-13240)*

Manchild Property Development, Indianapolis Also Called: Man Child Property Dev LLC *(G-8824)*

Mancor Indiana Inc..765 779-4800
7825 American Way Anderson (46013) *(G-151)*

Mandala Screen Printing Inc...574 946-6290
950 E 250 N Winamac (46996) *(G-16866)*

Mane Reserved LLC..219 516-5800
333 N Alabama St Indianapolis (46204) *(G-8825)*

Manic Meadery..219 614-1846
1003 E Summit St Crown Point (46307) *(G-2722)*

Manier Wldg & Fabrication LLC..765 675-6078
859 Market Rd Tipton (46072) *(G-15782)*

Manitou Plastics, Kewanna Also Called: Industrial Mlding Cnslting DSI *(G-10165)*

Manitowoc Beverage Eqp Inc (DH).......................................812 246-7000
645 Park East Blvd Ste 5 New Albany (47150) *(G-12770)*

Manitowoc Beverage Systems Inc (DH)...............................800 367-4233
645 Park East Blvd Ste 5 New Albany (47150) *(G-12771)*

Manitowoc Kitchencare, Jeffersonville Also Called: Welbilt Fdsrvice Companies LLC *(G-10072)*

Manley Meats Inc..260 592-7313
302 S 400 E Decatur (46733) *(G-2871)*

Mann Made Microwave LLC..317 407-1223
240 N Forsythe St Franklin (46131) *(G-5754)*

Mannon L Walters Inc...812 867-5946
6015 Heckel Rd Evansville (47725) *(G-4187)*

Mannon Oil LLC..812 867-5946
6015 Heckel Rd Evansville (47725) *(G-4188)*

Manolos Wines, Bloomington Also Called: Las Arribes LLC *(G-907)*

Manorwood Homes, Elkhart Also Called: The Commodore Corporation *(G-3724)*

Manta Rugs..765 869-5940
305 N Harrison St Boswell (47921) *(G-1118)*

Mantech Manifold..260 479-2383
9105 Clubridge Dr Fort Wayne (46809) *(G-5202)*

Mantra Enterprise LLC..201 428-8709
12694 Balbo Pl Fishers (46037) *(G-4561)*

Manu Sangha Inc..219 262-5400
3400 County Road 6 E Elkhart (46514) *(G-3511)*

Manufactured Products Inc...765 552-2871
2700 S K St Elwood (46036) *(G-3831)*

Manufacturing, Indianapolis Also Called: Turner Machine Co *(G-9661)*

Manufacturing, La Porte Also Called: Hlb1 LLC *(G-10420)*

Manufacturing, Logansport Also Called: Eis Packaging Machinery Inc *(G-11072)*

Manufacturing, Mooresville Also Called: Diamondback Metalcrafts Inc *(G-12202)*

Manufacturing, South Bend Also Called: Ferguson Equipment Inc *(G-15033)*

Manufacturing Facility, Evansville Also Called: Bprex Closures LLC *(G-3947)*

Manufacturing Solution Intl...219 841-9434
1145 Max Mochal Hwy Chesterton (46304) *(G-1946)*

Manufacturing Technology, Indianapolis Also Called: Monroe Manufacturing Tech Inc *(G-8950)*

Manufacturing Technology Inc (PA).....................................574 230-0258
1702 W Washington St South Bend (46628) *(G-15138)*

Mapco..765 795-3179
7230 E County Road 1000 S Cloverdale (46120) *(G-2088)*

Maple City Machine Inc...574 533-6742
1762 E Kercher Rd Goshen (46526) *(G-6211)*

Maple Hill Naturals LLC...765 427-9413
508 Fairington Ave Lafayette (47905) *(G-10642)*

Maple Lane Metals LLC...260 627-0987
13428 Springfield Center Rd Grabill (46741) *(G-6313)*

Maple Leaf Inc (PA)..574 453-4455
101 E Church St Leesburg (46538) *(G-10958)*

Maple Leaf Inc..260 982-8655
11241 N 400 W North Manchester (46962) *(G-13241)*

Maple Leaf Farms, Leesburg Also Called: Maple Leaf Inc *(G-10958)*

Maple Leaf Farms Inc (HQ)..574 453-4500
9166 N 200 E Milford (46542) *(G-11798)*

Maple Leaf Farms Inc...574 658-4121
9179 N 200 E Milford (46542) *(G-11799)*

Maple Leaf Graphics Inc..317 410-0321
13540 Kensington Pl Carmel (46032) *(G-1691)*

Maple Leaf Printing Co Inc...574 534-7790
301 W Lincoln Ave Goshen (46526) *(G-6212)*

Maple-Hunter Decals...812 894-9759
8075 St Rd 46 Riley (47871) *(G-14239)*

Maplehurst Bakeries, Brownsburg Also Called: Weston Foods US Holdings LLC *(G-1413)*

Mar-Kan Marketing Inc..317 228-9335
3402 W 79th St Indianapolis (46268) *(G-8826)*

Marathon Electric..317 837-2523
9899 Bradford Rd Plainfield (46168) *(G-13699)*

Marathon Homes Corporation...574 294-6441
4420 Pine Creek Rd Elkhart (46516) *(G-3512)*

Marathon Oil, Fort Wayne Also Called: Fairfield Gas Way *(G-4973)*

Marble Uniques, Tipton Also Called: M U Holdings Inc *(G-15781)*

Marc Woodworking, Indianapolis Also Called: Marc Woodworking Inc *(G-8827)*

Marc Woodworking Inc..317 635-9663
1719 English Ave Indianapolis (46201) *(G-8827)*

Marco Plastics Inc..812 333-0062
1616 S Huntington Dr Bloomington (47401) *(G-915)*

Marcotte Cabinets...574 520-1342
51286 Ironwood Rd Granger (46530) *(G-6359)*

Marengo Candy Barn Inc..812 365-2141
376 S Bradley St Marengo (47140) *(G-11264)*

Margaret Machine and Tool Co..219 924-0859
206 S Lindberg St Griffith (46319) *(G-6813)*

Margco International LLC...317 568-4274
6445 E 30th St Indianapolis (46219) *(G-8828)*

Margison Graphics LLC...765 529-8250
1813 S Memorial Dr New Castle (47362) *(G-12873)*

Margison Sign Company, New Castle Also Called: Margison Graphics LLC *(G-12873)*

Mari Manu Corp...219 804-3294
2929 Carlson Dr Hammond (46323) *(G-6977)*

Mariah Foods Corp..812 378-3366
1333 Indiana Ave Columbus (47201) *(G-2348)*

Mariah Retail Store..812 372-8712
52 Stadler Dr Columbus (47201) *(G-2349)*

Marian Inc (HQ)..317 638-6525
1011 E Saint Clair St Indianapolis (46202) *(G-8829)*

Marian Suzhou LLC (PA)..317 638-6525
1011 E Saint Clair St Indianapolis (46202) *(G-8830)*

Marian Worldwide Inc (PA)..317 638-6525
1011 E Saint Clair St Indianapolis (46202) *(G-8831)*

Marie Collective LLC..317 683-0408
7893 Hunters Path Indianapolis (46214) *(G-8832)*

Marie Lashaays LLC..317 869-7939
2042 Titleist Ln Indianapolis (46229) *(G-8833)*

Marietta Martin Materials Inc..317 789-4020
5620 S Belmont Ave Indianapolis (46217) *(G-8834)*

Marietta Martin Materials Inc..765 459-3194
2400 W 50 S Kokomo (46902) *(G-10304)*

Marietta Martin Materials Inc..317 831-7391
8520 N Waverly Park Rd Martinsville (46151) *(G-11411)*

Marietta Martin Materials Inc... 317 776-4460
  15215 River Rd Noblesville (46062) *(G-13130)*
Marine Builders Inc.... 812 283-7932
  5821 Utica Pike Jeffersonville (47130) *(G-10016)*
Marine Group LLC... 574 622-0490
  11 Lakota Ln Bristol (46507) *(G-1272)*
Marine Mooring Inc.... 574 594-5787
  3404 N 600 E Warsaw (46582) *(G-16390)*
Marine Precast, Decatur *Also Called: Prestress Services Inc (G-2877)*
Marion Glass Equipment and Technology Company Inc............ 765 662-1172
  123 E Mckinley St Marion (46952) *(G-11312)*
Marion Manufacturing, West Terre Haute *Also Called: Marion Tool & Die Inc (G-16652)*
Marion Metal Products Inc.... 765 662-8333
  401 N Henderson Ave Marion (46952) *(G-11313)*
Marion Paper Box Company.. 765 664-6435
  600 E 18th St Marion (46953) *(G-11314)*
Marion Quarters At Fort.... 317 672-4841
  5747 N Post Rd Indianapolis (46216) *(G-8835)*
Marion Steel Fabrication Inc... 765 664-1478
  1819 S Branson St Marion (46953) *(G-11315)*
Marion Steel Fabrication Inc (PA)................................... 765 664-1478
  333 W 4th St Marion (46952) *(G-11316)*
Marion Tent & Awning Co... 765 664-7722
  225 W Swayzee St Marion (46952) *(G-11317)*
Marion Tool & Die Inc (PA)... 812 533-9800
  1126 W National Ave West Terre Haute (47885) *(G-16652)*
Marion-Kay Spices, Brownstown *Also Called: Reidco Inc (G-1426)*
Marion, In Plant, Marion *Also Called: Prysmian Cbles Systems USA LLC (G-11331)*
Maritime Design Services, Carmel *Also Called: Sdf Engineering LLC (G-1755)*
Mark A Morin Logging Inc.... 812 327-4917
  757 N Walnut St West Baden Springs (47469) *(G-16542)*
Mark Concrete Products Inc... 317 398-8616
  1126 Miller Ave Shelbyville (46176) *(G-14774)*
Mark Dekonindk... 260 357-5443
  176 County Road 52 Avilla (46710) *(G-488)*
Mark Edward Hails.... 812 437-1030
  440 Tyler Ave Evansville (47715) *(G-4189)*
Mark Foster... 574 965-4558
  6954 N 980 W Delphi (46923) *(G-2902)*
Mark Hackman.. 812 522-8257
  3640 S County Road 400 E Brownstown (47220) *(G-1425)*
Mark Lamaster... 765 534-4185
  16271 E 191st St Noblesville (46060) *(G-13131)*
Mark Middleton... 812 967-2853
  5691 S Olive Branch Rd Pekin (47165) *(G-13518)*
Mark Miller... 317 626-9441
  249 Byrkit St Indianapolis (46217) *(G-8836)*
Mark Miller Backflow, Indianapolis *Also Called: Mark Miller (G-8836)*
Mark Parmenter.. 812 829-6583
  358 S East St Spencer (47460) *(G-15355)*
Mark Peiser Manufacturing Inc...................................... 317 698-5376
  3800 A Hway 267 N Brownsburg (46112) *(G-1385)*
Mark Tool & Die Inc.... 765 533-4932
  50 W Main St Markleville (46056) *(G-11369)*
Mark-Line Industries LLC... 574 825-5851
  51687 County Road 133 Bristol (46507) *(G-1273)*
Mark's Woodshop, Avilla *Also Called: Mark Dekonindk (G-488)*
Marked LLC... 317 777-3625
  4445 Greenmeadow Cir Indianapolis (46235) *(G-8837)*
Market Place Publications.. 219 769-7733
  7091 Broadway Ste D Merrillville (46410) *(G-11536)*
Marketing and Retail Sales... 812 883-1813
  1318 S Jackson St Salem (47167) *(G-14489)*
Marketing Kreativo.. 574 370-5410
  22541 Briarhill Dr Goshen (46528) *(G-6213)*
Marketing Services Group Inc...................................... 317 381-2268
  2601 S Holt Rd Indianapolis (46241) *(G-8838)*
Markfore Shurtz Unlimited, Fort Wayne *Also Called: Kerham Inc (G-5146)*
Markle Classic Signs, Linton *Also Called: Markle Music (G-11038)*
Markle Music... 812 847-2103
  1796 S State Road 59 Linton (47441) *(G-11038)*

Markle Water Treatment Plant...................................... 260 758-3482
  460 Parkview Dr Markle (46770) *(G-11358)*
Markley Enterprise Inc.... 574 295-4195
  2605 Whipple Ave Elkhart (46516) *(G-3513)*
Marley-Wylain Company, The, Michigan City *Also Called: Canvas Mw LLC (G-11585)*
Marmon Highway Tech LLC... 317 787-0718
  2770 Bluff Rd Indianapolis (46225) *(G-8839)*
Marner Door Manufacturing LLC................................... 812 486-3128
  4254 N 525 E Montgomery (47558) *(G-12112)*
Maron Products Inc.... 574 254-0840
  1015 Saint Jerome St Mishawaka (46544) *(G-11937)*
Maron Products Incorporated...................................... 574 259-1971
  1301 Industrial Dr Mishawaka (46544) *(G-11938)*
Marque, Elkhart *Also Called: Sjc Industries Corp (G-3680)*
Marquise Enterprises Ltd.. 317 578-3400
  7330 E 86th St Ste 100 Indianapolis (46256) *(G-8840)*
Marshall & Poe Bus Cons & CP, Elkhart *Also Called: Marshall & Poe LLC (G-3514)*
Marshall & Poe LLC (PA)... 574 266-5244
  818 Erwin St Elkhart (46514) *(G-3514)*
Marshall Companies Indiana...................................... 317 769-2666
  6850 S 280 E Lebanon (46052) *(G-10913)*
Marshall Crane, Lebanon *Also Called: Marshall Companies Indiana (G-10913)*
Marshall Electric Corporation (PA)............................... 574 223-4367
  425 N State Road 25 Rochester (46975) *(G-14305)*
Marshall G Smith Sign Painting................................... 260 744-9492
  472 Wiebke St Fort Wayne (46806) *(G-5203)*
Marshall Gas Controls, Elkhart *Also Called: S H Leggitt Company (G-3656)*
Marshall Signs.. 260 350-1492
  1270 Rohm Dr Auburn (46706) *(G-404)*
Marson International LLC... 574 295-4222
  1001 Sako Ct Elkhart (46516) *(G-3515)*
Marstone Products Ltd.. 800 466-7465
  203 N Edgerton St Fairland (46126) *(G-4400)*
Marteck Inc.... 800 569-9849
  10505 Bennett Pkwy Ste 200 Zionsville (46077) *(G-17031)*
Marteck of California, Zionsville *Also Called: Robert Copeland (G-17047)*
Martell & Co... 317 752-2847
  1674 Harvest Meadow Dr Greenwood (46143) *(G-6733)*
Martin Diesel Services LLC....................................... 570 837-6101
  214 E Marquis Rd N Lagrange (46761) *(G-10754)*
Martin Ekwlor Phrmcuticals Inc................................... 765 962-4410
  2800 Se Pwy Richmond (47374) *(G-14159)*
Martin Grgory Cnvyor Engrg LLC................................. 812 923-9814
  1549 Pirtle Dr Georgetown (47122) *(G-6068)*
Martin Holding Company LLC.................................... 812 401-9988
  605 W Eichel Ave Evansville (47710) *(G-4190)*
Martin Industries... 502 553-6599
  4235 Earnings Way New Albany (47150) *(G-12772)*
Martin Industries LLC... 502 553-6599
  Sellersburg (47172) *(G-14605)*
Martin Marietta Aggregates, Carmel *Also Called: Martin Marietta Materials Inc (G-1693)*
Martin Marietta Aggregates, Kokomo *Also Called: Marietta Martin Materials Inc (G-10304)*
Martin Marietta Aggregates, Martinsville *Also Called: Marietta Martin Materials Inc (G-11411)*
Martin Marietta Materials Inc..................................... 317 846-8540
  11010 Hazel Dell Pkwy Carmel (46280) *(G-1692)*
Martin Marietta Materials Inc..................................... 317 573-4460
  12220 N Meridian St Ste 100 Carmel (46032) *(G-1693)*
Martin Marietta Materials Inc..................................... 317 846-5942
  9825 Gray Rd Carmel (46280) *(G-1694)*
Martin Marietta Materials Inc..................................... 317 244-4460
  2605 Kentucky Ave Indianapolis (46221) *(G-8841)*
Martin Marietta Materials Inc..................................... 765 883-8172
  3891 S 500 W Russiaville (46979) *(G-14424)*
Martin Professional Inc... 574 294-8000
  1718 W Mishawaka Rd Elkhart (46517) *(G-3516)*
Martin Signs, Indianapolis *Also Called: Martin Signs & Crane Services (G-8842)*
Martin Signs & Crane Services.................................. 317 908-9708
  7204 E 46th St Indianapolis (46226) *(G-8842)*
Martin Truss Mfg LLC... 574 862-4457
  62332 County Road 1 Elkhart (46517) *(G-3517)*

ALPHABETIC SECTION

Martin Uniforms LLC... 317 408-9186
6057 Lakeside Manor Ave Indianapolis (46254) *(G-8843)*

Martin Welding Shop.. 574 862-2578
27585 County Road 40 Wakarusa (46573) *(G-16240)*

Martin Yale Industries LLC.. 260 563-0641
251 Wedcor Ave Wabash (46992) *(G-16198)*

Martinez Custom Welding... 574 377-2251
2063 E Riverside Dr Warsaw (46582) *(G-16391)*

Martinrea Industries Inc.. 812 346-5750
505 Industrial Dr North Vernon (47265) *(G-13285)*

Martins Buggy Shop.. 574 831-3699
24070 County Road 46 Nappanee (46550) *(G-12621)*

Martins Lime Service Inc.. 574 784-2270
2551 Michigan Rd Plymouth (46563) *(G-13796)*

Martins Mini Barns LLC.. 574 238-0045
25707 State Road 119 Goshen (46526) *(G-6214)*

Martins Wood Works... 574 862-4080
66227 County Road 9 Goshen (46526) *(G-6215)*

Martinson Cabinet Shop... 219 926-1566
1245 W Us Highway 20 Chesterton (46304) *(G-1947)*

Martinson Custom Kitchens, Chesterton *Also Called: Martinson Cabinet Shop (G-1947)*

Martinsville Milling Co Inc... 317 253-2581
8510 Olde Mill Circle East Dr Indianapolis (46260) *(G-8844)*

Martys Desktop Publish... 715 520-7682
29200 County Road 20 # 69 Elkhart (46517) *(G-3518)*

Marv Kahlig & Sons Inc.. 260 335-2212
3229 S 500 E Portland (47371) *(G-13956)*

Marvell Logging Company LLC... 812 779-5107
3700 W 250 N Patoka (47666) *(G-13509)*

Marvelous Woodworking LLC.. 317 679-5890
5475 S 175 W Lebanon (46052) *(G-10914)*

Marwood Sales Co... 812 288-8344
2901 Hamburg Pike Jeffersonville (47130) *(G-10017)*

Mary Duncan.. 812 238-3637
601 W Honey Creek Dr Terre Haute (47802) *(G-15636)*

Mary Jonas... 317 500-0600
2104 Dr Andrew J Brown Ave Indianapolis (46202) *(G-8845)*

Mary Kite LLC.. 765 749-1133
4300 W University Ave Muncie (47304) *(G-12447)*

Marys Gift Baskets LLC.. 502 819-3022
9039 Richland Dr Georgetown (47122) *(G-6069)*

Masbez LLC.. 855 962-7239
509 W Barner St Frankfort (46041) *(G-5681)*

Maschino Industries Inc... 812 346-3083
1405 S County Road 750 W North Vernon (47265) *(G-13286)*

Maschino Woodworks Inc.. 812 230-7428
739 N Forest Dr Terre Haute (47803) *(G-15637)*

Masco, Indianapolis *Also Called: Masco Corporation of Indiana (G-8847)*

Masco Bath Corporation... 317 254-5959
8445 Keystone Xing Indianapolis (46240) *(G-8846)*

Masco Bath South, Indianapolis *Also Called: Masco Bath Corporation (G-8846)*

Masco Corporation of Indiana.. 317 848-1812
300 S Carroll Rd Indianapolis (46229) *(G-8847)*

Mason Corporation... 219 865-8040
1049 Us Highway 41 Schererville (46375) *(G-14533)*

Masonite Corporation... 574 586-3192
105 Industrial Park Dr Walkerton (46574) *(G-16269)*

Masonite International Corp.. 574 586-3192
111 Muskin Dr Walkerton (46574) *(G-16270)*

Massey-Null Inc... 260 447-7900
4519 Allen Martin Dr Fort Wayne (46806) *(G-5204)*

Masson Inc... 317 632-8021
567 N Highland Ave Indianapolis (46202) *(G-8848)*

Mast Services Lafayette LLC... 765 464-6940
14 Torchwood Ct Lafayette (47905) *(G-10643)*

Mast Woodworking... 812 636-7938
9922 E 1000 N Odon (47562) *(G-13343)*

Master Brand Cabinets, Goshen *Also Called: Masterbrand Cabinets LLC (G-6216)*

Master Built Racing Accessory, Crothersville *Also Called: Mastersbilt Chassis Inc (G-2642)*

Master Enterprises, Indianapolis *Also Called: Master Filter Corporation (G-8849)*

Master Filter Corporation.. 317 545-3335
4195 Millersville Rd Indianapolis (46205) *(G-8849)*

Master Machine Corp... 317 535-6526
3902 E 16th St Ste A Indianapolis (46201) *(G-8850)*

Master Machine Inc.. 812 232-6583
600 E Voorhees St Terre Haute (47802) *(G-15638)*

Master Manufacturing Company... 812 425-1561
4703 Ohara Dr Evansville (47711) *(G-4191)*

Master Metal Engineering, South Bend *Also Called: Master Metal Machining Inc (G-15139)*

Master Metal Machining Inc.. 574 299-0222
4520 S Burnett Dr South Bend (46614) *(G-15139)*

Master Piece Krafts LLC.. 260 768-4330
4875 N 675 W Shipshewana (46565) *(G-14866)*

Master Power Transmission Inc... 812 378-2270
3300 10th St Columbus (47201) *(G-2350)*

Master Roll Manufacturing Inc.. 219 393-7117
3999 Hupp Rd Bldg R-2-3 La Porte (46350) *(G-10448)*

Master Spas, Fort Wayne *Also Called: Masterspas LLC (G-5206)*

Masterbilt Incorporated... 574 287-6567
3801 Voorde Dr South Bend (46628) *(G-15140)*

Masterbrand Inc (PA)... 812 482-2527
1 Masterbrand Cabinets Dr Jasper (47546) *(G-9887)*

Masterbrand Cabinets LLC... 812 482-2527
6385 East State Road 164 Celestine (47521) *(G-1842)*

Masterbrand Cabinets LLC... 812 367-1104
328 Main St Ferdinand (47532) *(G-4442)*

Masterbrand Cabinets LLC... 812 367-1104
614 W 3rd St Ferdinand (47532) *(G-4443)*

Masterbrand Cabinets LLC... 574 535-9300
1002 Eisenhower Dr N Goshen (46526) *(G-6216)*

Masterbrand Cabinets LLC... 812 482-2527
1009 N Geiger St Huntingburg (47542) *(G-7287)*

Masterbrand Cabinets LLC... 812 482-2513
1491 S Meridian Rd Jasper (47546) *(G-9888)*

Masterbrand Cabinets LLC... 765 966-3940
1340 Rose City Blvd Richmond (47374) *(G-14160)*

Masterbrand US Holdings Corp.. 812 482-2527
1 Masterbrand Cabinets Dr Jasper (47546) *(G-9889)*

Mastercraft Inc (PA)... 260 463-8702
711 S Poplar St Lagrange (46761) *(G-10755)*

Mastercraft Safety, Indianapolis *Also Called: Impact Racing Inc (G-8468)*

Masterguard LLC, Covington *Also Called: Flex-N-Gate LLC (G-2530)*

Masters Apps LLC.. 574 312-5233
2807 S Main St Goshen (46526) *(G-6217)*

Masters Hand Bbq LLC.. 260 247-5807
2753 Freeman St Fort Wayne (46802) *(G-5205)*

Mastersbilt Chassis Inc... 812 793-3666
6520 S Us Highway 31 Crothersville (47229) *(G-2642)*

Masterspas LLC (PA)... 260 436-9100
6927 Lincoln Pkwy Fort Wayne (46804) *(G-5206)*

Masterspas LLC.. 260 436-9100
510 Sumpter St Fort Wayne (46804) *(G-5207)*

Mat Matrs of Indiana Inc.. 260 624-2882
205 Industrial Dr Angola (46703) *(G-274)*

Mata Custom Woodworking... 812 987-2676
923 Penn St Jeffersonville (47130) *(G-10018)*

Matalco Bluffton LLC.. 260 353-3100
1390 S Adams St Bluffton (46714) *(G-1040)*

Matam Corp.. 317 264-9908
1434 N New Jersey St Indianapolis (46202) *(G-8851)*

Matchless, Richmond *Also Called: Osborn LLC (G-14178)*

Matchless Machine & Tool Co... 765 342-4550
55 James Baldwin Dr Martinsville (46151) *(G-11412)*

Matco Pallets... 260 223-0585
2001 N St Rd 101 Decatur (46733) *(G-2872)*

Material Sciences, East Chicago *Also Called: Electric Coating Tech LLC (G-3006)*

Material Sciences, East Chicago *Also Called: New Star Metals Inc (G-3032)*

Matheson Tri-Gas Inc... 812 838-5518
1101 Holler Rd Mount Vernon (47620) *(G-12307)*

Matheson Tri-Gas Inc... 317 892-5221
8000 N County Road 225 E Pittsboro (46167) *(G-13651)*

Mathews Wire Inc... 765 659-3542
358 N Columbia St Frankfort (46041) *(G-5682)*

Matjack Division Indianapolis, Indianapolis *Also Called: Indianapolis Industrial Pdts (G-8506)*

Matrix Label Systems Inc 317 839-1973
  4692 S County Road 600 E Plainfield (46168) *(G-13700)*

Matrix Manufacturing Inc 260 854-4659
  4935 S 300 E Wolcottville (46795) *(G-16941)*

Matrix Technologies Inc 765 284-3335
  700 S Mulberry St Muncie (47302) *(G-12448)*

Matrix Tool Inc 574 259-3093
  1210 S Merrifield Ave Mishawaka (46544) *(G-11939)*

Matrixx-Qtr Inc 812 429-0901
  15000 Highway 41 N Evansville (47725) *(G-4192)*

Matthew Schlachter 812 686-5486
  24170 Cattail Rd Bristow (47515) *(G-1300)*

Matthew Warren Inc 574 722-8200
  500 E Ottawa St Logansport (46947) *(G-11093)*

Matthew Warren Spring, Logansport *Also Called: Matthew Warren Inc (G-11093)*

Matthews Aurora Fnrl Solutions, Aurora *Also Called: Aurora Casket Company LLC (G-439)*

Matthews International Corp 765 966-1576
  620 S J St Richmond (47374) *(G-14161)*

Mattox and Moore Inc 317 632-7534
  1503 E Riverside Dr Indianapolis (46202) *(G-8852)*

Mattox Machine & Welding Inc 812 883-6460
  504 Cox Ferry Rd Salem (47167) *(G-14490)*

Matts Repair Inc 219 696-6765
  9412 W 181st Ave Lowell (46356) *(G-11171)*

Maul Technology, Winchester *Also Called: Vhc Ltd (G-16902)*

Maul Technology Co 765 584-2101
  300 W Martin St Winchester (47394) *(G-16894)*

Maumee Machine & Tool, Harlan *Also Called: Kent Brenneke (G-7057)*

Maureen Sharp 765 379-3644
  153 N Gaddis St Rossville (46065) *(G-14387)*

Maurer Constructors Inc 812 236-5950
  10109 N Harmony Border St Brazil (47834) *(G-1152)*

Maurer Specialty Pools and Con 574 320-2429
  1310 E 6th St Mishawaka (46544) *(G-11940)*

Maurices Sgnture Chsecakes LLC 708 879-0031
  889 Thoreau Trl Valparaiso (46383) *(G-16000)*

Maury Boyd & Associates Inc 317 849-6110
  9900 Westpoint Dr Ste 120 Indianapolis (46256) *(G-8853)*

Mauser Packaging Solutions 317 297-4638
  6061 Guion Rd Indianapolis (46254) *(G-8854)*

MAUSER PACKAGING SOLUTIONS, Indianapolis *Also Called: Mauser Packaging Solutions (G-8854)*

Mautz Paint Factory 574 289-2497
  1201 S Main St South Bend (46601) *(G-15141)*

Maverick Molding, Mishawaka *Also Called: Paul Tirotta (G-11972)*

Maverick Packaging Inc 574 264-2891
  3505 Reedy Dr Elkhart (46514) *(G-3519)*

Mavrick Entrmt Netwrk Inc 317 779-1237
  480 Southpoint Cir Brownsburg (46112) *(G-1386)*

Mavron, Warsaw *Also Called: Mavron Inc (G-16392)*

Mavron Inc 574 267-3044
  152 S Zimmer Rd Warsaw (46580) *(G-16392)*

Mavtv Motorsports, Brownsburg *Also Called: Mavrick Entrmt Netwrk Inc (G-1386)*

Max Katz Bag Company Inc 317 635-9561
  235 S Lasalle St Indianapolis (46201) *(G-8855)*

Max of All Trades LLC 317 703-4242
  801 N Mccann St Kokomo (46901) *(G-10305)*

Maxcare Bionics, Avon *Also Called: Transmed Associates Inc (G-555)*

Maxim Integrated Products Inc 252 227-7202
  16848 Southpark Dr Westfield (46074) *(G-16710)*

MAXIM INTEGRATED PRODUCTS, INC., Westfield *Also Called: Maxim Integrated Products Inc (G-16710)*

Maxim Pipette Service Inc 877 536-2946
  4310 Saratoga Pkwy Ste 100 Plainfield (46168) *(G-13701)*

Maximum Business Solutions Inc 219 933-1809
  5930 Hohman Ave Ste 201 Hammond (46320) *(G-6978)*

Maximum Logistics LLC 317 488-1010
  1237 Southlake Ave E Greenwood (46143) *(G-6734)*

Maxon Corporation (HQ) 765 284-3304
  201 E 18th St Muncie (47302) *(G-12449)*

Maxon, A Honeywell Company, Muncie *Also Called: Maxon Corporation (G-12449)*

Maxwell Engineering Inc 260 745-4991
  616 E Wallace St Fort Wayne (46803) *(G-5208)*

Maxwell Milling Indiana Inc 765 489-3506
  4359 N State Road 1 Hagerstown (47346) *(G-6840)*

Maxwell Power LLC 317 998-5092
  5868 E 71st St # 712 Indianapolis (46220) *(G-8856)*

May and Co Inc 317 236-6500
  3210 Greensview Dr Greenwood (46143) *(G-6735)*

May First Inc 317 330-1000
  10497 Silver Ridge Cir Fishers (46038) *(G-4562)*

May Suu Mon LLC 786 556-8295
  5125 Standish Dr Fort Wayne (46806) *(G-5209)*

Mayasaris LLC (PA) 812 222-6292
  213 N Broadway St Greensburg (47240) *(G-6616)*

Mayasaris LLC 812 593-2881
  1570 W Commerce Dr Ste 302 Greensburg (47240) *(G-6617)*

Mayco International LLC 765 348-5780
  1701 W Mcdonald St Hartford City (47348) *(G-7070)*

Mayco Intl Hartford Cy, Hartford City *Also Called: Mayco International LLC (G-7070)*

Mayes Powder Coating LLC 317 403-6549
  49 N Railroad St Whiteland (46184) *(G-16792)*

Mayfield - Glenn Group Inc 219 393-7117
  3999 Hupp Rd Bldg R23 Kingsbury (46345) *(G-10180)*

Mayham Mfia Cstoms Trnsprting 463 248-5181
  3102 E Minnesota St Indianapolis (46203) *(G-8857)*

Mayhill Publications Inc (PA) 765 345-5133
  27 N Jefferson St Knightstown (46148) *(G-10199)*

Mayors Office City of Madison 812 273-4248
  950 Industrial Dr Madison (47250) *(G-11240)*

Mays+red Spot Coatings LLC 317 558-2024
  5611 E 71st St Indianapolis (46220) *(G-8858)*

Mbci Inc 317 835-2201
  1780 Mccall Dr Shelbyville (46176) *(G-14775)*

Mbciindy 317 398-4400
  1780 Mccall Dr Shelbyville (46176) *(G-14776)*

Mbpc Progressive Consultants 765 301-1864
  401 Longcastle Dr Apt 3 Greencastle (46135) *(G-6421)*

Mbsi Holdings LLC 574 295-1214
  58120 County Road 3 Elkhart (46517) *(G-3520)*

Mbv-Midwest LLC 800 400-3090
  7520 Georgetown Rd Bldg 131 Indianapolis (46268) *(G-8859)*

Mbx, Carmel *Also Called: MBX Biosciences Inc (G-1695)*

MBX Biosciences Inc 317 659-0200
  11711 N Meridian St Ste 300 Carmel (46032) *(G-1695)*

Mc Cord Tire & Auto Service, Terre Haute *Also Called: McCord Tire Service Inc (G-15639)*

Mc Coy Bolt Works Inc 260 482-4476
  2811 Congressional Pkwy Fort Wayne (46808) *(G-5210)*

Mc Custom Cabinets Inc 502 641-1528
  2157 W Salem Rd Underwood (47177) *(G-15845)*

Mc Ginley Fire Apparatus 765 482-3152
  901 W Washington St Lebanon (46052) *(G-10915)*

Mc Kay Printing Services, Long Beach *Also Called: Pagels-Kelley Enterprises LLC (G-11126)*

Mc Metalcraft Inc 574 259-8101
  1210 Willow St Mishawaka (46545) *(G-11941)*

MC Wldg & Machining Co Inc 219 393-5718
  I Kingsbury Industrial Park Kingsbury (46345) *(G-10181)*

MCB Accessories, Greenfield *Also Called: TLC Metals Inc (G-6566)*

McBeth Designs Inc 317 848-7313
  820 W Main St Carmel (46032) *(G-1696)*

McBroom Electric Co Inc 317 926-3451
  800 W 16th St Indianapolis (46202) *(G-8860)*

McBroom Industrial Services, Indianapolis *Also Called: McBroom Electric Co Inc (G-8860)*

McC, Pendleton *Also Called: Madison County Cabinets Inc (G-13541)*

McCaffery Sign Designs 574 232-9991
  1310 S Main St Ste 2 South Bend (46601) *(G-15142)*

McCallister Industries Inc 317 417-7365
  1417 N Harding St Ste C Indianapolis (46202) *(G-8861)*

McCallister's Custom Iron, Indianapolis *Also Called: McCallister Industries Inc (G-8861)*

McCammon Engineering Corp 812 356-4455
  1863 W County Road 500 S Sullivan (47882) *(G-15413)*

ALPHABETIC SECTION — Med-Pharm Pharmacy

McClamroch Ag LLC 765 362-4495
115 W 580 N Crawfordsville (47933) *(G-2588)*

McClinton Life Sciences Inc 317 903-4230
8110 Woodland Dr Indianapolis (46278) *(G-8862)*

McClure Concrete 765 525-6098
3139 E Vandalia Rd Flat Rock (47234) *(G-4655)*

McCombs and Son Company 765 825-4581
201 W 6th St Connersville (47331) *(G-2454)*

McCombs Fabrication LLC 765 265-0594
1400 Madison St Connersville (47331) *(G-2455)*

McCord Signs LLC (PA) 812 537-5516
1090 W Eads Pkwy Lawrenceburg (47025) *(G-10846)*

McCord Tire Service Inc 812 235-8016
3503 S Us Highway 41 Terre Haute (47802) *(G-15639)*

McCormack Prtg Impressions Inc 765 675-9556
618 Oak St Tipton (46072) *(G-15783)*

McCormick & Company Inc 410 527-6189
2741 Foundation Dr South Bend (46628) *(G-15143)*

McCormick & Company Inc 574 234-8101
3425 Lathrop St South Bend (46628) *(G-15144)*

McCracken Curve Distillery LLC 812 486-3651
5663 E Old Us Highway 50 Montgomery (47558) *(G-12113)*

McCrary, Fred D Oil Co, Petersburg Also Called: Fred D McCrary *(G-13614)*

McCreary Concrete Products Inc 765 932-3058
875 Industrial Dr Tipton (46072) *(G-15784)*

McCrocklin Mobility, Daleville Also Called: Autofarm Mobility LLC *(G-2795)*

McCrory Publishing 260 485-1812
2530 Deerwood Dr Fort Wayne (46825) *(G-5211)*

McCullagh Corporation 877 645-7676
2302 Florimond Dr Long Beach (46360) *(G-11124)*

McCullugh Archlogical Svcs LLC 260 402-3462
410 N Arsenal Ave Indianapolis (46201) *(G-8863)*

McD Machine Incorporated 812 339-1240
2345 W Industrial Park Dr Bloomington (47404) *(G-916)*

McDowell Enterprises Inc 574 293-1042
2010 Superior St Elkhart (46516) *(G-3521)*

McElroy Metal Mill Inc 317 823-6895
10504 E 59th St Indianapolis (46236) *(G-8864)*

McElroy Metal Service Center, Indianapolis Also Called: McElroy Metal Mill Inc *(G-8864)*

McFall Family Meats LLC 812 547-6546
1414 20th St Tell City (47586) *(G-15510)*

McFeelys Inc 800 443-7937
340 2nd St Aurora (47001) *(G-449)*

McGill Manufacturing Co Inc 219 465-2200
705 N 6th St Monticello (47960) *(G-12157)*

McGill Manufacturing Company, Valparaiso Also Called: Regal Beloit America Inc *(G-16035)*

McGinn Tool & Engineering Co 317 736-5512
1001 Yandes St Franklin (46131) *(G-5755)*

McGinty Conveyors Inc 317 240-4315
5002 W Washington St Indianapolis (46241) *(G-8865)*

McGowan Wire Specialties Inc 574 232-7110
600 United Dr South Bend (46601) *(G-15145)*

McGrews Well Drilling Inc 574 857-3875
7413 S 125 W Rochester (46975) *(G-14306)*

McGuires Magic Cleaning LLC 317 504-7739
5344 Traditions Dr Indianapolis (46235) *(G-8866)*

MCI Screwdriver Systems Inc 317 776-1970
14800 Herriman Blvd Noblesville (46060) *(G-13132)*

McIntire Concrete 765 759-7111
4701 W County Road 1000 N Muncie (47303) *(G-12450)*

McKillip Machinery Inc 260 330-2842
697 W 50 N Wabash (46992) *(G-16199)*

McKinney Corporation 765 448-4800
4710 Fastline Dr Lafayette (47905) *(G-10644)*

McL Window Coverings Inc (PA) 317 577-2670
11815 Technology Ln Fishers (46038) *(G-4563)*

McLaughlin Furnace Group, Avilla Also Called: McLaughlin Services LLC *(G-489)*

McLaughlin Services LLC (PA) 260 897-4328
150 Eagle Dr Avilla (46710) *(G-489)*

McLean's Screen Printing, Greensburg Also Called: Dance World Bazaar Corporation *(G-6589)*

McM Manufacturing 574 339-6994
1902 S Main St South Bend (46613) *(G-15146)*

McMillan Express 260 447-7648
3505 Wayne Trce Fort Wayne (46806) *(G-5212)*

McMillin Hearing Aid Inc 812 847-2470
2160 E State Highway 54 Linton (47441) *(G-11039)*

McNeil Coatings Cons Inc 317 885-1557
1132 Kay Dr Greenwood (46142) *(G-6736)*

MCP Performance Plastic, Portage Also Called: MCP Usa Inc *(G-13885)*

MCP Usa Inc 219 734-6598
6750 Daniel Burnham Dr Ste E Portage (46368) *(G-13885)*

McPheeters and Associates Inc 812 988-2840
7517 Becks Grove Rd Freetown (47235) *(G-5804)*

McPubs Inc 317 539-6461
2785 S County Road 1000 E Coatesville (46121) *(G-2107)*

MD Holdings LLC 317 831-7030
451 E County Line Rd Mooresville (46158) *(G-12220)*

MD Laird Inc 317 842-6338
2947 S Emerson Ave Greenwood (46143) *(G-6737)*

MD Moxie LLC 260 347-1203
5966 E Concrete Dr Kendallville (46755) *(G-10136)*

Md/Lf Incorporated 765 575-8130
187 S Denny Dr New Castle (47362) *(G-12874)*

Mdl Mold & Die Components Inc 812 373-0021
1130 Industrial Rd Ste B Columbus (47203) *(G-2351)*

Mdl Woodworking LLC 260 242-1824
1011 W Packard Ave Fort Wayne (46807) *(G-5213)*

ME Fabrication LLP 574 594-2801
8214 E 200 N Pierceton (46562) *(G-13634)*

ME Time Candle Co LLC 317 378-5533
4928 E 62nd St Apt E Indianapolis (46220) *(G-8867)*

Mead Johnson & Company LLC (DH) 812 429-5000
2400 W Lloyd Expy Evansville (47721) *(G-4193)*

Mead Johnson & Company LLC 812 429-5000
62 West State Rd Mount Vernon (47620) *(G-12308)*

Mead Johnson Nutrition, Evansville Also Called: Mead Johnson & Company LLC *(G-4193)*

Mead Johnson Nutritionals, Mount Vernon Also Called: Mead Johnson & Company LLC *(G-12308)*

Meadowlark Wdwkg Cabinetry LLC 765 541-3660
105 W 24th St Connersville (47331) *(G-2456)*

Meagan Inc 574 267-8626
711 S Buffalo St Warsaw (46580) *(G-16393)*

Mears Machine Corp (PA) 317 271-6041
9973 E Us Highway 36 Avon (46123) *(G-537)*

Mears Machine Corp 317 745-0656
2983 S County Road 300 E Danville (46122) *(G-2820)*

Measure Press Inc 812 473-0361
526 S Lincoln Park Dr Evansville (47714) *(G-4194)*

Meats By Linz Inc (PA) 708 862-0830
628 Hoffman St Hammond (46327) *(G-6979)*

Meca, Elkhart Also Called: Mechancal Engrg Cntrls Atmtn C *(G-3522)*

Mechancal Engrg Cntrls Atmtn C 574 294-7580
57236 Nagy Dr Elkhart (46517) *(G-3522)*

Mechanical Parts & Svcs Inc 219 670-1986
304 Burlington Beach Rd Valparaiso (46383) *(G-16001)*

Mechanovent Corporation 219 326-1767
171 Factory St La Porte (46350) *(G-10449)*

Meck Die Inc 574 262-5441
29029 Phillips St Elkhart (46514) *(G-3523)*

Mecom, Indianapolis Also Called: Mecom Ltd Inc *(G-8868)*

Mecom Ltd Inc 317 218-2600
500 E 96th St Ste 360 Indianapolis (46240) *(G-8868)*

Med Devices LLC 317 508-1699
6335 Old Orchard Rd Indianapolis (46226) *(G-8869)*

Med Grind Inc 574 965-4040
7848 N Us Highway 421 Delphi (46923) *(G-2903)*

Med Pad Incorporated 812 422-6154
1411 Timberlake Rd Evansville (47710) *(G-4195)*

Med-Cut Inc 574 269-1982
727 N Detroit St Warsaw (46580) *(G-16394)*

Med-Pharm Pharmacy 812 232-2086
2723 S 7th St Ste M Terre Haute (47802) *(G-15640)*

Med2950 LLC 317 545-5383
2950 N Catherwood Ave Indianapolis (46219) *(G-8870)*

Medallion Cabinetry 574 842-2066
515 W Mill St Culver (46511) *(G-2781)*

Medical Device Bus Svcs Inc 317 596-3320
8904 Bash St Ste A Indianapolis (46256) *(G-8871)*

Medical Device Bus Svcs Inc (HQ) 574 267-8143
700 Orthopaedic Dr Warsaw (46582) *(G-16395)*

Medical Manufacturing, Indianapolis *Also Called: Ameriflo2 Inc (G-7511)*

Medical Structures Mfg Corp 574 612-0353
1803 Minnie St Elkhart (46516) *(G-3524)*

Medical Systems Corp Indiana 317 856-1340
6352 Airway Dr Indianapolis (46241) *(G-8872)*

Medical Systems Division, Merrillville *Also Called: Parker-Hannifin Corporation (G-11549)*

Medishield 502 939-9903
1598 Rector Ln New Albany (47150) *(G-12773)*

Medix Specialty Vehicles LLC 574 266-0911
3008 Mobile Dr Elkhart (46514) *(G-3525)*

Medlin Custom Woodworking Inc 765 939-0923
245 S 3rd St Richmond (47374) *(G-14162)*

Medline Industries LP 800 633-5463
251 Hilton Dr Charlestown (47111) *(G-1882)*

Medtech LLC 330 715-6864
3322 Nine Penny Ln Charlestown (47111) *(G-1883)*

Medtric LLC 765 427-7234
4129 Nauset Dr Lafayette (47909) *(G-10645)*

Medtrnic Sofamor Danek USA Inc 317 837-8142
1620 Hawthorne Dr Ste 400 Plainfield (46168) *(G-13702)*

Medtrnic Sofamor Danek USA Inc 574 267-6826
2500 Silveus Xing Warsaw (46582) *(G-16396)*

Medtronic 317 837-8664
2824 Airwest Blvd Plainfield (46168) *(G-13703)*

Medtronic, Plainfield *Also Called: Medtrnic Sofamor Danek USA Inc (G-13702)*

Medtronic, Warsaw *Also Called: Medtrnic Sofamor Danek USA Inc (G-16396)*

Medventure Technology, Jeffersonville *Also Called: Freudenberg Medical Mis Inc (G-9987)*

Meer Enterprises Inc 574 522-7527
21700 Protecta Dr Elkhart (46516) *(G-3526)*

Meese Inc (HQ) 800 829-4535
1745 Cragmont St Madison (47250) *(G-11241)*

Megan Inc 574 267-8626
711 S Buffalo St Warsaw (46580) *(G-16397)*

Megans Wash and Fold LLC 317 903-5253
108 Shamrock Cir Apt 26 Pendleton (46064) *(G-13543)*

Meggitt Control Systems, Troy *Also Called: Troy Meggitt Inc (G-15843)*

Meggitt Sensing Systems, Indianapolis *Also Called: Piezotech LLC (G-9141)*

Meier Winery & Vinyard LLC 812 382-4220
4251 N State Road 63 Sullivan (47882) *(G-15414)*

Meilink Safe Company 812 941-0024
101 Security Pkwy New Albany (47150) *(G-12774)*

Mejjm Inc 317 893-6929
4371 Sellers St Indianapolis (46226) *(G-8873)*

Mel-Rhon Inc 574 546-4559
124 E Plymouth St Bremen (46506) *(G-1205)*

Melanie Brewery Company Inc 219 762-9652
146 Shore Dr Portage (46368) *(G-13886)*

Melaninwisdomgarment 574 315-3081
2509 Sampson St South Bend (46614) *(G-15147)*

Melay LLC 614 726-0565
1624 S Waterleaf Dr Apt 203 Westfield (46074) *(G-16711)*

Melching Machine Inc 260 622-4315
1630 Baker Dr Ossian (46777) *(G-13428)*

Melissa Lambino 317 506-5274
524 E 11th St Apt 2 Indianapolis (46202) *(G-8874)*

Melissa Townsend 317 797-7992
623 S Gerrard Dr Indianapolis (46241) *(G-8875)*

Mellon Tax Service 219 947-1660
101 Center St Hobart (46342) *(G-7201)*

Mels Guitars and Repair, Jamestown *Also Called: Melvin McCullough (G-9819)*

Melting Point Metalworks LLC 317 984-0037
70 Mardale Dr Ste D Brownsburg (46112) *(G-1387)*

Melvin McCullough 765 577-0083
52 W Jefferson St Jamestown (46147) *(G-9819)*

Memcor Inc 260 356-4300
1320 Flaxmill Rd Huntington (46750) *(G-7341)*

Memcor-Truohm, Huntington *Also Called: Memcor Inc (G-7341)*

Memorial Arts Studio, San Pierre *Also Called: M A Studio Inc (G-14505)*

Menard Inc 812 466-1234
4600 N 13th St Terre Haute (47805) *(G-15641)*

Menasha Packaging Company LLC 877 818-2016
1056 Industries Rd Richmond (47374) *(G-14163)*

Mendenhall Powder Coating, Ladoga *Also Called: Ron Mendenhall (G-10509)*

Mendozas Incorporated 219 791-9034
7425 Madison St Merrillville (46410) *(G-11537)*

Mengel Welding Company 219 987-4079
12510 N 600 W Demotte (46310) *(G-2923)*

Menon Bearings Limited 866 556-3666
10849 Windermere Blvd Fishers (46037) *(G-4564)*

Mental Rehabilitation 765 414-5590
1322 Fairfax Dr Lafayette (47909) *(G-10646)*

Mepco, Evansville *Also Called: Moore Engineering & Prod Co (G-4211)*

Mercantile 1, Nashville *Also Called: Mercantile Store (G-12675)*

Mercantile Store (PA) 812 988-6939
44 N Van Buren St Nashville (47448) *(G-12675)*

Mercer Machine Company Inc 317 241-9903
10356 Leases Corner Ct Camby (46113) *(G-1512)*

Merchants Metals, Indianapolis *Also Called: Merchants Metals LLC (G-8876)*

Merchants Metals LLC 317 783-7678
6701 Bluff Rd Indianapolis (46217) *(G-8876)*

Merck Sharp & Dohme LLC 908 740-4000
2150 Stanley Rd Plainfield (46168) *(G-13704)*

Mercury Marine, Brownsburg *Also Called: Brunswick Corporation (G-1353)*

Meredith Hughes 317 354-6073
2106 Crown Plaza Blvd Plainfield (46168) *(G-13705)*

Merediths Inc 765 966-5084
800 S 7th St Richmond (47374) *(G-14164)*

Meridian Brick LLC 812 894-2454
5601 E Price Dr Terre Haute (47802) *(G-15642)*

Meridian Metalform Inc 812 422-1524
1025 W Tennessee St Evansville (47710) *(G-4196)*

Meridian Resources LLC 812 463-2281
13329 Dumbarton St Carmel (46032) *(G-1697)*

Merin Interiors Indianapolis 317 251-6603
1145 Woodmere Dr Indianapolis (46260) *(G-8877)*

Merit Tool & Manufacturing Inc 765 396-9566
120 N Hartford St Eaton (47338) *(G-3063)*

Meritor Inc 317 279-2180
849 Whitaker Rd Plainfield (46168) *(G-13706)*

Meriwether Tool & Engrg Inc 260 744-6955
10108 Smith Rd Fort Wayne (46809) *(G-5214)*

Merkley & Sons Inc 812 482-7020
3994 W 180n Jasper (47546) *(G-9890)*

Merkley Packing Co, Jasper *Also Called: Merkley & Sons Inc (G-9890)*

Merrill Corporation 574 255-2988
606 N Main St Mishawaka (46545) *(G-11942)*

Merrill Manufacturing Inc 812 752-6688
1052 S Bond St Scottsburg (47170) *(G-14571)*

Merrill Pharmacy, Mishawaka *Also Called: Merrill Corporation (G-11942)*

Merrillville Awning & Tent, Merrillville *Also Called: Blessing Enterprises Inc (G-11491)*

Merriman Kiln & Mill Service, Bedford *Also Called: Merriman Steel and Equipment (G-657)*

Merriman Steel and Equipment 812 849-2784
10430 Tunnelton Rd Bedford (47421) *(G-657)*

Merritt Manufacturing Inc 317 409-0148
1350c W Southport Rd Ste 218 Indianapolis (46217) *(G-8878)*

Merritt Sand and Gravel Inc (PA) 260 665-2513
2007 County Road 39 Waterloo (46793) *(G-16524)*

Merrywood Group LLC 765 729-5927
3709 W Woodstock Ln Muncie (47302) *(G-12451)*

Merss Corporation 317 632-7299
1017 W 23rd St Indianapolis (46208) *(G-8879)*

Mertz Custom Trailer Mfg, Waterloo *Also Called: Garry Mertz (G-16520)*

Mervin Knepps Molding 812 486-2971
6349 N 900 E Montgomery (47558) *(G-12114)*

Mervin M Burkholder.. 574 862-4144
26253 County Road 42 Wakarusa (46573) *(G-16241)*

Mervis & Sons, Kokomo Also Called: Mervis Industries Inc *(G-10306)*

Mervis Industries Inc... 765 454-5800
990 E Carter St Kokomo (46901) *(G-10306)*

Mervis Industries Inc... 812 232-1251
830 S 13th St Terre Haute (47807) *(G-15643)*

Mes Legacy Pc Inc.. 317 769-5503
5759 W 85th St Indianapolis (46278) *(G-8880)*

Mesco Manufacturing LLC.. 812 663-3870
900 E Randall St Greensburg (47240) *(G-6618)*

Mesh Systems LLC (PA).. 317 661-4800
801 Congressional Blvd Ste 300 Carmel (46032) *(G-1698)*

Meshberger Brothers Stone Corporation......................... 260 334-5311
6311 W State Road 218-1 Bluffton (46714) *(G-1041)*

Meshberger Stone Inc, Indianapolis Also Called: Heritage Aggregates LLC *(G-8387)*

Message The, Evansville Also Called: Catholic Press of Evansville *(G-3966)*

Messagenet Systems Inc.. 317 566-1677
1905 S New Market St Ste 269 Carmel (46032) *(G-1699)*

Messenger, Auburn Also Called: Messenger LLC *(G-405)*

Messenger LLC... 260 925-1700
318 E 7th St Auburn (46706) *(G-405)*

Messenger, The, Attica Also Called: Fountain County Neighbor *(G-348)*

Messer LLC.. 908 464-8100
1045 Harding Ct Indianapolis (46217) *(G-8881)*

Messer LLC.. 219 324-0498
7996 N State Road 39 La Porte (46350) *(G-10450)*

Messer LLC.. 574 234-4887
3809 W Calvert St South Bend (46613) *(G-15148)*

Mestek Inc... 317 831-5314
101 Linel Dr Mooresville (46158) *(G-12221)*

Mesumes Incorporated.. 574 529-3444
1204 N Algonquin Dr Syracuse (46567) *(G-15468)*

Met-Pak Specialties Corp... 260 420-2217
9910 Airport Dr Fort Wayne (46809) *(G-5215)*

Met-Pro Technologies LLC... 317 293-2930
6040 Guion Rd Indianapolis (46254) *(G-8882)*

Metafab... 317 217-1546
226 Lincoln St Indianapolis (46225) *(G-8883)*

Metakite Software LLC... 317 441-7385
8430 Weaver Woods Pl Fishers (46038) *(G-4565)*

Metal Art Inc.. 765 354-4571
7730 N Raider Rd Middletown (47356) *(G-11774)*

Metal Dynamics Ltd... 812 949-7998
30 E 10th St New Albany (47150) *(G-12775)*

Metal Etching Tech Associates, Fort Wayne Also Called: Blue Ring Stencils LLC *(G-4809)*

Metal Fab Engineering Inc... 574 278-7150
9341 S State Road 39 Winamac (46996) *(G-16867)*

Metal Fabricated Products Co.. 812 372-7430
925 S Marr Rd Columbus (47201) *(G-2352)*

Metal Fabrication LLC.. 812 686-9430
1001 Mount Auburn Rd Evansville (47720) *(G-4197)*

Metal Fabricators Plus, Indianapolis Also Called: Metal Fabricators Plus LLC *(G-8884)*

Metal Fabricators Plus LLC... 317 757-3672
4701 Rockville Rd Ste E Indianapolis (46222) *(G-8884)*

Metal Finishing Co Inc... 317 546-9004
3901 E 26th St Indianapolis (46218) *(G-8885)*

Metal Forming Industries, Russellville Also Called: St Clair Group Inc *(G-14419)*

Metal Head Welding.. 812 582-4234
211 N Main St Winslow (47598) *(G-16920)*

Metal Improvement Company LLC................................. 317 875-6030
5945 W 84th St Ste D Indianapolis (46278) *(G-8886)*

Metal Masters, Indianapolis Also Called: J Coffey Metal Masters Inc *(G-8604)*

Metal Masters Inc... 812 421-9162
4600 Broadway Ave Evansville (47712) *(G-4198)*

Metal Plate Polishing, Fort Wayne Also Called: Mpp Inc *(G-5248)*

Metal Powder Products LLC... 317 214-8120
111 Monument Cir Ste 3200 Indianapolis (46204) *(G-8887)*

Metal Powder Products Co LLP..................................... 317 805-3764
14670 Cumberland Rd Noblesville (46060) *(G-13133)*

Metal Powder Products LLC (PA)................................... 317 805-3764
14670 Cumberland Rd Noblesville (46060) *(G-13134)*

Metal Sales Manufacturing Corp.................................... 812 246-1866
7800 Highway 60 Sellersburg (47172) *(G-14606)*

Metal Services LLC... 219 787-1514
250 W Us Highway 12 Burns Harbor (46304) *(G-1454)*

Metal Services LLC... 219 397-0650
3001 Dickey Rd East Chicago (46312) *(G-3029)*

Metal Solutions Inc... 317 781-6734
5756 Churchman Rd Indianapolis (46203) *(G-8888)*

Metal Source LLC... 260 563-8833
1733 S Wabash St Wabash (46992) *(G-16200)*

Metal Spinners Inc (PA).. 260 665-2158
914 Wohlert St Angola (46703) *(G-275)*

Metal Tech - Mnnpolis Die Cast, Auburn Also Called: Minneapolis Die Casting LLC *(G-411)*

Metal Technologies, Auburn Also Called: Metal Technologies Indiana LLC *(G-409)*

Metal Technologies, Auburn Also Called: West Allis Gray Iron *(G-434)*

Metal Technologies Inc (PA).. 812 384-9800
1537 W Auburn Dr Auburn (46706) *(G-406)*

Metal Technologies Inc.. 812 384-9800
Rr #1, Sr 54 E Bloomfield (47424) *(G-751)*

Metal Technologies Auburn LLC.................................... 260 527-1410
1537 W Auburn Dr Auburn (46706) *(G-407)*

Metal Technologies Inc Alabama (PA)............................. 260 925-4717
1401 S Grandstaff Dr Auburn (46706) *(G-408)*

Metal Technologies Indiana LLC.................................... 260 925-4717
1401 S Grandstaff Dr Auburn (46706) *(G-409)*

Metalcraft, Elkhart Also Called: Metalcraft Precision Machining *(G-3527)*

Metalcraft Inc... 260 761-3001
3330 W Us Highway 6 Wawaka (46794) *(G-16540)*

Metalcraft Precision Machining..................................... 574 293-6700
56854 Elk Ct Elkhart (46516) *(G-3527)*

Metalcrafters Inc... 574 294-2502
2415 Bryant St Elkhart (46516) *(G-3528)*

Metaldyne M&A Bluffton LLC...................................... 260 824-6800
131 W Harvest Rd Bluffton (46714) *(G-1042)*

Metaldyne North Vernon, North Vernon Also Called: Metaldyne Snterforged Pdts LLC *(G-13287)*

Metaldyne Snterforged Pdts LLC (DH)........................... 812 346-1566
3100 N State Highway 3 North Vernon (47265) *(G-13287)*

Metalfor LLC.. 812 212-2248
1358 Tekulve Rd Batesville (47006) *(G-597)*

Metalite Corporation... 812 944-6600
1815 Troy St New Albany (47150) *(G-12776)*

Metalized Coatings LLC... 219 851-0683
1540 Genesis Dr La Porte (46350) *(G-10451)*

Metallic Dice Games, Fort Wayne Also Called: Fanroll LLC *(G-4974)*

Metallic Seals Inc... 317 780-0773
2735 Brill Rd Indianapolis (46225) *(G-8889)*

Metallurgical Processing, Fort Wayne Also Called: Bodycote Thermal Proc Inc *(G-4811)*

Metals and Additives LLC.. 812 446-2525
10665 N State Road 59 Brazil (47834) *(G-1153)*

Metals and Additives LLC (PA)..................................... 317 290-5007
5929 Lakeside Blvd Indianapolis (46278) *(G-8890)*

Metaltec Inc... 219 362-9811
11 Pine Lake Ave Ste C La Porte (46350) *(G-10452)*

Metalure Pigments Facility, Schererville Also Called: Eckart America Corporation *(G-14519)*

Metalworking Lubricants Co... 317 269-2444
1509 S Senate Ave Indianapolis (46225) *(G-8891)*

Metalworking Machinery LLC....................................... 317 752-0981
11126 Baycreek Dr Indianapolis (46236) *(G-8892)*

Metcalf Engineering Inc... 765 342-6792
405 W Raymond St Indianapolis (46225) *(G-8893)*

Metergenius Inc.. 317 979-8257
5621 Indianola Ave Indianapolis (46220) *(G-8894)*

Metform Tool Corporation... 260 745-1436
2424 American Way Fort Wayne (46809) *(G-5216)*

Metheny Enterprises Inc.. 317 692-9900
145 Stony Creek Overlook Noblesville (46060) *(G-13135)*

Metl-Span LLC... 317 398-1100
1717 Mccall Dr Shelbyville (46176) *(G-14777)*

Metro Area Printing — ALPHABETIC SECTION

Metro Area Printing, Indianapolis *Also Called: Kalems Enterprises Inc (G-8658)*
Metro Plastics Tech Inc 317 776-0860
17145 Metro Park Ct Noblesville (46060) *(G-13136)*
Metro Plastics Technologies, Noblesville *Also Called: Metro Plastics Tech Inc (G-13136)*
Metro Printed Products Inc 317 885-0077
1001 Commerce Parkway South Dr Ste H Greenwood (46143) *(G-6738)*
Metropolitan Printing Svcs LLC 812 332-7279
720 S Morton St Bloomington (47403) *(G-917)*
Metropolitan Printing, Rrd, Bloomington *Also Called: Metropolitan Printing Svcs LLC (G-917)*
Mettle Creek, Cambridge City *Also Called: Western Wayne News (G-1504)*
Mettle Holdings Incorporated (PA) 260 447-3880
4630 Allen Martin Dr Fort Wayne (46806) *(G-5217)*
Mettle Holdings Incorporated 260 447-3880
4532 Allen Martin Dr Fort Wayne (46806) *(G-5218)*
Metzgas Exterior, Columbus *Also Called: Michael D Metz (G-2354)*
Metzger Dairy Inc 260 564-5445
4837 W 100 S Kimmell (46760) *(G-10171)*
Metzler Enterprise 574 293-9267
2745 Homer Ave Elkhart (46517) *(G-3529)*
Meuth Concrete, Princeton *Also Called: Meuth Construction Supply Inc (G-14004)*
Meuth Construction Supply, Evansville *Also Called: Meuth Construction Supply Inc (G-4199)*
Meuth Construction Supply Inc 812 424-8554
2201 Bergdolt Rd Evansville (47711) *(G-4199)*
Meuth Construction Supply Inc 270 826-8554
200 Tennessee St Princeton (47670) *(G-14004)*
Mexabilly Brothers LLC 765 621-6334
1410 Chesterfield Dr Anderson (46012) *(G-152)*
Meyer Custom Woodworking Inc 812 695-2021
2657 E State Road 56 Dubois (47527) *(G-2954)*
Meyer Engineering Inc 812 663-6535
1420 W Main St Greensburg (47240) *(G-6619)*
Meyer Foods Inc 317 773-6594
18247 Pennington Rd Noblesville (46060) *(G-13137)*
Meyer Ice Cream LLC 812 941-8267
209 Quality Ave Ste 3 New Albany (47150) *(G-12777)*
Meyer Oil Co 812 746-9525
19920 Ruffian Way Evansville (47725) *(G-4200)*
Meyer Plastics Inc 260 482-4595
3410 Congressional Pkwy Fort Wayne (46808) *(G-5219)*
Meyer Plastics Inc (PA) 317 259-4131
5968 Sunnyside Rd Indianapolis (46236) *(G-8895)*
Mfd Express Inc 765 717-3539
8463 N County Road 200 W Springport (47386) *(G-15381)*
Mg Electric and Sign LLC 317 538-0455
3885 W 100 S Greenfield (46140) *(G-6527)*
Mg Impressions LLC 317 219-5118
15320 Herriman Blvd Noblesville (46060) *(G-13138)*
Mg Iron Welding Inc 708 916-1344
809 May St Hammond (46320) *(G-6980)*
MGM Enterprises 219 395-1888
1493 Hogan Ave Chesterton (46304) *(G-1948)*
Mgpi Processing Inc 812 532-4100
7 Ridge Ave Greendale (47025) *(G-6448)*
Mgtc Inc 317 780-0609
5757 Kopetsky Dr Ste D Indianapolis (46217) *(G-8896)*
Mgtc Inc (DH) 317 873-8697
11541 Trail Ridge Pl Zionsville (46077) *(G-17032)*
MH Vale PC 219 661-0867
3805 W 107th Ln Crown Point (46307) *(G-2723)*
MHp Distribution LLC 312 731-8380
300 S Henry St Gary (46403) *(G-5981)*
Mhp Holdings Inc (HQ) 574 825-9524
101 Joan Dr Middlebury (46540) *(G-11736)*
MI Tierra 812 376-0668
1461 Central Ave Columbus (47201) *(G-2353)*
Miami Gardens Millwork 812 208-4541
11437 E Us Highway 40 Terre Haute (47803) *(G-15644)*
Miasa Automotive LLC 765 751-9967
2101 S West St Yorktown (47396) *(G-16976)*
Miata Hubs LLC 240 298-7368
9572 Edgewater Ct Brownsburg (46112) *(G-1388)*

Mica Shop Inc 574 533-1102
2122 Lincolnway E Goshen (46526) *(G-6218)*
Michael and Sons Incorporated (PA) 812 876-4736
2606 E Calvertville Rd Bloomfield (47424) *(G-752)*
Michael Cary Ross 765 631-2565
805 Riverview Dr Martinsville (46151) *(G-11413)*
Michael D Metz 812 526-9606
6615 W Ohio Ridge Rd Columbus (47201) *(G-2354)*
Michael Dargie 765 935-2241
1700 Nw 11th St Richmond (47374) *(G-14165)*
Michael Deom Professional 812 836-2206
9394 Abner Rd Tell City (47586) *(G-15511)*
Michael Duff 812 336-8994
4615 E State Road 45 Bloomington (47408) *(G-918)*
Michael Filley (PA) 956 443-6364
10736 E Main St Owensburg (47453) *(G-13463)*
Michael Greene 317 753-7226
1001 E Main St Unit 12 Ladoga (47954) *(G-10508)*
Michael Hazeltine 317 750-5091
2704 Monarchy Ln Greenwood (46143) *(G-6739)*
Michael Holland 317 538-1776
1167 N Mitthoefer Rd Indianapolis (46229) *(G-8897)*
Michael J Meyer D M D P C 812 275-7112
1504 Dental Dr Bedford (47421) *(G-658)*
Michael L Baker 812 967-2160
8779 E New Philadelphia Rd Salem (47167) *(G-14491)*
Michael L Jerrell 812 354-9297
4703 N County Road 175 E Petersburg (47567) *(G-13617)*
Michael L Reynolds 812 528-7844
8274 W County Road 425 S Medora (47260) *(G-11463)*
Michael Montgomery 317 478-6080
5340 Holly Springs Ct Indianapolis (46254) *(G-8898)*
Michael R Harris 812 425-9411
20 Nw 1st St Rear 208 Evansville (47708) *(G-4201)*
Michael Ramer 574 538-8010
69515 County Road 21 New Paris (46553) *(G-12965)*
Michael Skaggs 812 732-8809
Rr 1 Mauckport (47142) *(G-11438)*
Michele L Gravel 317 889-0521
8607 Depot Dr Indianapolis (46217) *(G-8899)*
Michelin North America Inc 260 493-8100
18906 Us Highway 24 Woodburn (46797) *(G-16951)*
Michfab Machinery 260 244-6117
201 Towerview Dr Columbia City (46725) *(G-2170)*
Michiana Bandsaw & Sup Co LLC 574 293-5974
2115 E Jackson Blvd Elkhart (46516) *(G-3530)*
Michiana Bus Publications Inc 260 497-0433
7729 Westfield Dr Fort Wayne (46825) *(G-5220)*
Michiana Carwash Systems LLC 574 320-2331
15228 County Road 22 Goshen (46528) *(G-6219)*
Michiana Column & Truss LLC 574 862-2828
27608 County Road 36 # A Goshen (46526) *(G-6220)*
Michiana Compressor, Elkhart *Also Called: Michiana Forklift Inc (G-3532)*
Michiana Directional Drilling, Bristol *Also Called: Niblock Excavating Inc (G-1281)*
Michiana Elkhart Inc 574 206-0620
51505 State Road 19 Elkhart (46514) *(G-3531)*
Michiana Executive Journal 574 256-6666
203 N Main St Mishawaka (46544) *(G-11943)*
Michiana Forklift Inc 574 326-3702
2921 Moose Trl Elkhart (46514) *(G-3532)*
Michiana Global Mold Inc 574 259-6262
1702 E 7th St Mishawaka (46544) *(G-11944)*
Michiana Laminated Products 260 562-2871
7130 N 050 E Howe (46746) *(G-7240)*
Michiana Metal Fabrication Inc 574 256-9010
1227 W Beardsley Ave Elkhart (46514) *(G-3533)*
Michiana Metal Finishing Inc 574 206-0666
2805 Frederic Dr Elkhart (46514) *(G-3534)*
Michiana Pallet Recycle Inc 574 232-8566
55022 Pear Rd South Bend (46628) *(G-15149)*
Michiana Plastics Inc 574 259-6262
1702 E 7th St Mishawaka (46544) *(G-11945)*

Michiana Signs and Lighting.. 574 520-1254
1035 E Mckinley Ave Mishawaka (46545) *(G-11946)*

Michigan City Baking, Michigan City Also Called: Hearthside Food Solutions LLC *(G-11622)*

Michigan City Brewing Co Inc.. 219 879-4677
208 Wabash St Michigan City (46360) *(G-11637)*

Michigan City News Dispatch, Michigan City Also Called: News Dispatch *(G-11645)*

Michigan City Paper Box Co.. 219 872-8383
1206 Pine St Michigan City (46360) *(G-11638)*

Michigan Stone Company Div, Michigantown Also Called: Engineering Aggregates Corp *(G-11690)*

Michrochem LLC... 812 838-1832
901 E 3rd St Mount Vernon (47620) *(G-12309)*

Micka Cabinets... 219 838-5450
8328 Kennedy Ave Highland (46322) *(G-7144)*

Mico Industries LLC... 812 480-3015
2301 Lexington Rd Evansville (47720) *(G-4202)*

Micro Businessware Inc.. 502 424-6613
8508 Starview Ct Sellersburg (47172) *(G-14607)*

Micro Machine Works Inc.. 574 293-1354
835 Lillian Ave Elkhart (46516) *(G-3535)*

Micro Motion Inc... 317 334-1893
8525 Northwest Blvd Indianapolis (46278) *(G-8900)*

MICRO MOTION INC, Indianapolis Also Called: Micro Motion Inc *(G-8900)*

Micro Tool & Machine Co Inc.. 574 272-9141
51836 Purdue Ct Granger (46530) *(G-6360)*

Micro-Precision Operations... 260 589-2136
525 Berne St Berne (46711) *(G-719)*

Microchip Technology Inc... 317 842-1676
9114 Sargent Creek Dr Indianapolis (46256) *(G-8901)*

Microchip Technology Inc... 317 773-8323
9779 E 146th St Ste 130 Noblesville (46060) *(G-13139)*

Microform Inc... 574 522-9851
21053 Protecta Dr Ste A Elkhart (46516) *(G-3536)*

Micromatic LLC (PA).. 260 589-2136
525 Berne St Berne (46711) *(G-720)*

Micrometl Corporation (PA).. 317 524-5400
3035 N Shadeland Ave Ste 300 Indianapolis (46226) *(G-8902)*

Micronutrients Division, Indianapolis Also Called: Micronutrients USA LLC *(G-8903)*

Micronutrients USA LLC... 317 486-5880
1550 Research Way Indianapolis (46231) *(G-8903)*

Micropulse Inc (PA)... 260 625-3304
5865 E State Road 14 Columbia City (46725) *(G-2171)*

Microscreen LLC.. 574 232-4358
1106 High St South Bend (46601) *(G-15150)*

Microsoft, Indianapolis Also Called: Microsoft Corporation *(G-8904)*

Microsoft Corporation.. 317 705-6900
8702 Keystone Xing Ste 66 Indianapolis (46240) *(G-8904)*

Microtech Holding Corp... 260 490-4005
3601 Focus Dr Fort Wayne (46818) *(G-5221)*

Microtech Welding Corp (PA)... 260 490-4005
3601 Focus Dr Fort Wayne (46818) *(G-5222)*

Microtech Welding Corp... 574 268-5314
265 E Bell Dr Warsaw (46582) *(G-16398)*

Microvote General Corp.. 317 257-4900
7144 Lakeview Parkway West Dr Indianapolis (46268) *(G-8905)*

Microwave Devices Inc.. 317 868-8833
240 N Forsythe St Franklin (46131) *(G-5756)*

Microwave Plant, Garrett Also Called: Griffith Rbr Mills of Garrett *(G-5865)*

Microworks Inc... 219 661-8620
2200 W 97th Pl Crown Point (46307) *(G-2724)*

Mid America Coop Education... 317 726-6910
6302 Rucker Rd Indianapolis (46220) *(G-8906)*

Mid America Powered Vehicles.. 812 925-7745
1699 S Stevenson Station Rd Chandler (47610) *(G-1864)*

Mid America Print Council Inc.. 765 463-3971
2217 Miami Trl Lafayette (47906) *(G-10647)*

Mid America Prototyping Inc.. 765 643-3200
428 E 21st St Anderson (46016) *(G-153)*

Mid America Screw Products.. 574 294-6905
21559 Protecta Dr Elkhart (46516) *(G-3537)*

Mid America Sign Corporation (PA)................................. 260 744-2200
1319 Production Rd Fort Wayne (46808) *(G-5223)*

Mid Continent Cabinetry.. 866 527-0141
1 Masterbrand Cabinets Dr Jasper (47546) *(G-9891)*

Mid Continent Cabinetry, Jasper Also Called: Norcraft Companies LP *(G-9897)*

Mid Mountain Materials Inc.. 812 550-5867
1176 E Diamond Ave Evansville (47711) *(G-4203)*

Mid State Water Treatment.. 765 884-1220
1009 E 5th St Fowler (47944) *(G-5627)*

Mid Valley Supply Co, Indianapolis Also Called: M & M Svc Stn Eqp Spcalist Inc *(G-8801)*

Mid West Digital Express Inc... 317 733-1214
10815 Deandra Dr Zionsville (46077) *(G-17033)*

Mid-America Environmental LLC..................................... 812 475-1644
5815 Metro Center Dr Evansville (47715) *(G-4204)*

Mid-America Golf Car, Chandler Also Called: Mid America Powered Vehicles *(G-1864)*

Mid-America Sound, Greenfield Also Called: Mid-America Sound Corporation *(G-6528)*

Mid-America Sound Corporation..................................... 317 947-9880
6643 W 400 N Greenfield (46140) *(G-6528)*

Mid-City Plating Co Inc.. 765 289-2374
921 E Charles St Muncie (47305) *(G-12452)*

Mid-County Machining, Demotte Also Called: Midcounty Machining Inc *(G-2924)*

Mid-Mountain Materials, Evansville Also Called: Mid Mountain Materials Inc *(G-4203)*

Mid-State Automation Inc.. 765 795-5500
12389 Camp Otto Rd Cloverdale (46120) *(G-2089)*

Mid-State Truck Equipment Inc.. 317 849-4903
11020 Allisonville Rd Fishers (46038) *(G-4566)*

Mid-States Rubber Products Inc...................................... 812 385-3473
1232 S Race St Princeton (47670) *(G-14005)*

Mid-States Tool & Machine Inc.. 260 728-9797
2220 Patterson St Decatur (46733) *(G-2873)*

Mid-West Homes For Pets, Muncie Also Called: Mid-West Metal Products Co Inc *(G-12454)*

Mid-West Metal Products Co Inc...................................... 765 741-3140
3500 S Hoyt Ave Muncie (47302) *(G-12453)*

Mid-West Metal Products Co Inc (PA)............................. 888 741-1044
3142 S Cowan Rd Muncie (47302) *(G-12454)*

Mid-West Spring and Stamping, Mentone Also Called: Mid-West Spring Mfg Co *(G-11473)*

Mid-West Spring Mfg Co (PA).. 800 424-0244
105 N Etna St Mentone (46539) *(G-11473)*

Mid-West Spring Mfg Co.. 574 353-1409
105 N Etna St Mentone (46539) *(G-11474)*

Midas Muffler, Indianapolis Also Called: Reed Auto - Indy Mich LLC *(G-9279)*

Midcountry Media Inc... 765 345-5133
27 N Jefferson St Knightstown (46148) *(G-10200)*

Midcounty Machining Inc... 219 992-9380
11694 Lilac Ct Demotte (46310) *(G-2924)*

Middlebury Cheese Company LLC (HQ)......................... 574 825-9511
11275 W 250 N Middlebury (46540) *(G-11737)*

Middlebury Hardwood Pdts Inc, Middlebury Also Called: Mhp Holdings Inc *(G-11736)*

Middletown Enterprises Inc.. 765 348-3100
105 N Wabash Ave Hartford City (47348) *(G-7071)*

Middtran Enterprises Inc.. 317 869-5212
7399 N Shadeland Ave Pmb 323 Indianapolis (46250) *(G-8907)*

Mide Products.. 574 326-3060
53848 N Park Ave Elkhart (46514) *(G-3538)*

Mide Products LLC.. 574 333-5906
22420 Forsythia Dr Goshen (46528) *(G-6221)*

Midland Metal Products, Hammond Also Called: Midland Metal Products Co *(G-6981)*

Midland Metal Products Co... 773 927-5700
1401 165th St Hammond (46320) *(G-6981)*

Midnite Grafix... 812 386-9430
3437 S 125 E Princeton (47670) *(G-14006)*

Midway Products Group Inc.. 734 241-7242
105 W State Road 4 Hudson (46747) *(G-7248)*

Midway Specialty Vehicles LLC....................................... 574 264-2530
2940 Dexter Dr Elkhart (46514) *(G-3539)*

Midwest Accurate Grinding Svc...................................... 219 696-4060
17211 Morse St Lowell (46356) *(G-11172)*

Midwest Aerospace Ltd... 219 365-7250
10653 W 181st Ave Lowell (46356) *(G-11173)*

Midwest Aerospace Casting LLC.................................... 708 597-1300
899 E 99th Ct Crown Point (46307) *(G-2725)*

Midwest Auto Repair Inc.. 219 322-0364
1901 Lincolnwood Rd Schererville (46375) *(G-14534)*

Midwest Bale Ties Inc — 765 364-0113
1200 E Wabash Ave Crawfordsville (47933) *(G-2589)*

Midwest Bio-Products Inc — 765 793-3426
618 Liberty St Covington (47932) *(G-2531)*

Midwest Blind & Shade Co — 574 271-0770
4115 Grape Rd Mishawaka (46545) *(G-11947)*

Midwest Cabinet Solutions Inc — 765 664-3938
1001 E 24th St Marion (46953) *(G-11318)*

Midwest Caviar LLC — 812 338-3610
439 E State Road 64 English (47118) *(G-3843)*

Midwest Coil LLC — 765 807-5429
2304 Brothers Dr Ste A Lafayette (47909) *(G-10648)*

Midwest Color Printing LLC — 812 822-2947
2458 S Walnut St Bloomington (47401) *(G-919)*

Midwest Comm Solutions LLP — 800 880-5847
4801 Hartman Rd Fort Wayne (46807) *(G-5224)*

Midwest Country Cabinets — 812 486-8580
5973 N 1200 E Loogootee (47553) *(G-11146)*

Midwest Custom Chemicals Inc — 812 858-3147
5722 Prospect Dr Newburgh (47630) *(G-13013)*

Midwest Custom Finishing Inc — 219 874-0099
800 Royal Rd Michigan City (46360) *(G-11639)*

Midwest Custom Finishing Inc (PA) — 574 258-0099
1906 Clover Rd Mishawaka (46545) *(G-11948)*

Midwest Dachshund Rescue Inc — 815 260-6734
2023 Ridgewood St Highland (46322) *(G-7145)*

Midwest Design Hydraulic — 765 714-3016
4807 Homewood Dr West Lafayette (47906) *(G-16605)*

Midwest Division, Francesville Also Called: Legacy Vulcan LLC *(G-5643)*

Midwest Division - Bluffton, Fort Wayne Also Called: W W Williams Company LLC *(G-5537)*

Midwest Earthworks LLC — 812 486-2443
973 S 800 E Montgomery (47558) *(G-12115)*

Midwest Electrical Sales — 708 821-7490
961 Sheffield Dr Valparaiso (46385) *(G-16002)*

MIDWEST ELECTRICAL SALES, Valparaiso Also Called: Midwest Electrical Sales *(G-16002)*

Midwest Empire LLC — 317 786-7446
3747 S Meridian St Indianapolis (46217) *(G-8908)*

Midwest Energy Partners, Indianapolis Also Called: Midwest Energy Partners LLC *(G-8909)*

Midwest Energy Partners LLC — 317 600-3235
201 S Capitol Ave Ste 510 Indianapolis (46225) *(G-8909)*

Midwest Equipment Mfg Inc — 765 436-2496
5225 Serum Plant Rd Thorntown (46071) *(G-15753)*

Midwest Eye Services LLC — 833 592-7434
835 N Cass St Wabash (46992) *(G-16201)*

Midwest Fabrication LLC — 574 276-5041
16100 Branchwood Ln Granger (46530) *(G-6361)*

Midwest Fade Control — 219 926-5043
4901 Tazer Dr Lafayette (47905) *(G-10649)*

Midwest Fast Structures LLC — 812 886-3060
2341 S Old Decker Rd Vincennes (47591) *(G-16139)*

Midwest Film Factory, Avilla Also Called: Scher Maihem Publishing Ltd *(G-494)*

Midwest Finishing Systems Inc — 574 257-0099
55770 Evergreen Plaza Dr Mishawaka (46545) *(G-11949)*

Midwest Garage Doors LLC — 317 739-2534
839 Shelbys Crst Shelbyville (46176) *(G-14778)*

Midwest Gasket Corporation — 765 629-2221
100 S Railroad St Milroy (46156) *(G-11826)*

Midwest Graphics Inc — 317 780-4600
5550 Elmwood Ct Indianapolis (46203) *(G-8910)*

Midwest Graphix LLC — 812 649-2522
1540 S County Road 100 W Ste D Rockport (47635) *(G-14345)*

Midwest Gym Supply Inc (PA) — 812 265-4099
775 Scott Ct Madison (47250) *(G-11242)*

Midwest Indus Met Fbrction Inc — 260 356-5262
281 Thurman Poe Way Huntington (46750) *(G-7342)*

Midwest Industrial Metal — 260 358-0373
2080 Old Us Highway 24 Huntington (46750) *(G-7343)*

Midwest Industrial Tanks, Elkhart Also Called: Axis Unlimited LLC *(G-3208)*

Midwest Leather LLC — 435 257-7880
10914 Page Rd Grabill (46741) *(G-6314)*

Midwest Logging & Veneer — 765 342-2774
50 Rose St Martinsville (46151) *(G-11414)*

Midwest Machine & Design, Montgomery Also Called: Midwest Earthworks LLC *(G-12115)*

Midwest Machining & Fabg — 219 924-0206
711 W Main St Griffith (46319) *(G-6814)*

Midwest Machining LLC — 212 696-7322
10485 W 1350 N Nappanee (46550) *(G-12622)*

Midwest Manufacturing, Terre Haute Also Called: Menard Inc *(G-15641)*

Midwest Mat Company — 765 286-0831
2204 N Dr Martin Luther King Jr Blvd Muncie (47303) *(G-12455)*

Midwest Metal Solutions Inc — 317 769-6489
6145 S Indianapolis Rd Whitestown (46075) *(G-16811)*

Midwest Metal Works Inc — 812 981-0810
921 Progress Blvd New Albany (47150) *(G-12778)*

Midwest Meter Inc — 574 967-0175
200 Commercial Dr Flora (46929) *(G-4661)*

Midwest Minis, Indianapolis Also Called: Midwest Minis LLC *(G-8911)*

Midwest Minis LLC — 317 500-3294
3116 Elizabeth St Indianapolis (46234) *(G-8911)*

Midwest Mold Remediation Inc — 502 386-6559
912 Webster Blvd Jeffersonville (47130) *(G-10019)*

Midwest Municipal Supply, Owensville Also Called: Randall K Dike *(G-13471)*

Midwest Mwi Inc — 574 288-6573
1201 Industrial Dr Mishawaka (46544) *(G-11950)*

Midwest Nonwovens Indiana LLC — 317 241-8956
4760 Kentucky Ave Ste A Indianapolis (46221) *(G-8912)*

Midwest Office Solutions LLC — 262 658-2679
5825 E County Road 800 S Mooresville (46158) *(G-12222)*

Midwest Parenting Publications, Indianapolis Also Called: Linear Publishing Corp *(G-8763)*

Midwest Pediatric Cardiology, Munster Also Called: Midwest Pediatric Crdiolgy PC *(G-12549)*

Midwest Pediatric Crdiolgy PC — 219 836-1355
800 Macarthur Blvd Ste 3 Munster (46321) *(G-12549)*

Midwest Pipecoating Inc — 219 322-4564
925 Kennedy Ave Schererville (46375) *(G-14535)*

Midwest Plastics Company Inc — 574 264-4994
1603 E Lake Dr W Elkhart (46514) *(G-3540)*

Midwest Plastics Company Inc (PA) — 574 674-0161
401 Lincolnway W Osceola (46561) *(G-13398)*

Midwest Poultry Services LP (PA) — 574 353-7651
800 Wabash Rd North Manchester (46962) *(G-13242)*

Midwest Poultry Services LP — 260 982-8122
500 Strauss Provimi Rd North Manchester (46962) *(G-13243)*

Midwest Precision Machining — 260 459-6866
3626 Illinois Rd Fort Wayne (46804) *(G-5225)*

Midwest Printing — 812 238-1641
1925 S 13th St Terre Haute (47802) *(G-15645)*

Midwest Purification LLC — 317 536-7445
2011 Southtech Dr # 130 Greenwood (46143) *(G-6740)*

Midwest Roll Forming & Mfg Inc — 574 594-2100
1 Arnolt Dr Pierceton (46562) *(G-13635)*

Midwest Rubber Sales Inc — 765 468-7105
2135 N 900 W Farmland (47340) *(G-4426)*

Midwest Sandbags LLC — 847 366-6555
2727 Industrial Pkwy Elkhart (46516) *(G-3541)*

Midwest Seed Coating LLC — 812 949-7459
2020 E Main St New Albany (47150) *(G-12779)*

Midwest Shade & Drapery Co — 317 849-2131
1422 Sadlier Circle West Dr Indianapolis (46239) *(G-8913)*

Midwest Sheet Metal Inc — 574 223-3332
2467 E 200 N Rochester (46975) *(G-14307)*

Midwest Sign Company Inc — 317 931-9535
819 N Obrien St Seymour (47274) *(G-14668)*

Midwest Spring & Stamping, Mentone Also Called: Mid-West Spring Mfg Co *(G-11474)*

Midwest Stl Rule Cutng Die Inc — 317 780-4600
5570 Elmwood Ct Indianapolis (46203) *(G-8914)*

Midwest Surface Prep LLC — 317 726-1336
5835 White Oak Ct Indianapolis (46220) *(G-8915)*

Midwest Tile & Concrete Pdts, Woodburn Also Called: Midwest Tile and Concrete Pdts *(G-16952)*

Midwest Tile and Concrete Pdts — 260 749-5173
4309 Webster Rd Woodburn (46797) *(G-16952)*

Midwest Tile and Concrete Pdts (PA) — 260 749-5173
4309 Webster Rd Woodburn (46797) *(G-16953)*

ALPHABETIC SECTION — Miller Poultry

Midwest Tire & Auto Repair, Schererville Also Called: Midwest Auto Repair Inc (G-14534)

Midwest Tire & Service LLC 502 377-3722
3381 N Griffin Ct Salem (47167) (G-14492)

Midwest Tool & Die Corp 260 414-1506
1126 Sunset Lake Cv Fort Wayne (46845) (G-5226)

Midwest Transit Authority LLC 765 414-5097
4410 Crossbow Ct West Lafayette (47906) (G-16606)

Midwest Tube Mills Inc (PA) 812 265-1553
2906 Clifty Dr Madison (47250) (G-11243)

Midwest Water Controls, Gary Also Called: Ray Kammer (G-6000)

Midwest Welding Fabrication 574 226-8306
30182 Blue Spruce Dr Elkhart (46514) (G-3542)

Midwest Welding Fabrication 260 355-9354
1138 E 600 S Warren (46792) (G-16301)

Midwest Wheelcoaters LLC 219 874-0099
800 Royal Rd Michigan City (46360) (G-11640)

Midwest Willys LLC 765 362-2247
3708 S 100 E Crawfordsville (47933) (G-2590)

Midwest-Tek Inc 812 981-3551
4345 Security Pkwy New Albany (47150) (G-12780)

Midwestern Pallet Service Inc 260 563-1526
3632 W Old 24 Wabash (46992) (G-16202)

Midwestern Pet Foods Inc (PA) 812 867-7466
9634 Hedden Rd Evansville (47725) (G-4205)

Midwestern Structures LLC 574 835-9733
9500 N Wheeling Ave Muncie (47304) (G-12456)

Mier Products Inc 765 457-0223
1500 Ann St Kokomo (46901) (G-10307)

Miftek, West Lafayette Also Called: Miftek Corporation (G-16607)

Miftek Corporation 765 491-3848
1231 Cumberland Ave Ste H West Lafayette (47906) (G-16607)

Mightier Press 260 609-6582
10088 Chapmans Cv Fort Wayne (46835) (G-5227)

Mighty Muffler LLC 765 966-6833
1440 Nw 5th St Richmond (47374) (G-14166)

Mighty-Quip Industries 260 615-1899
921 E Dupont Rd 894 Fort Wayne (46825) (G-5228)

Mignone Communications, Berne Also Called: EP Graphics Inc (G-710)

Mignone Communications Incorporated 260 358-0266
880 E State St Huntington (46750) (G-7344)

Mik Mocha Prints LLC 812 376-8891
4637 Clairmont Dr Columbus (47203) (G-2355)

Mike Fisher Logging 812 357-2169
6480 E 850 S Ferdinand (47532) (G-4444)

Mike Gross 574 529-2201
68080 County Road 23 New Paris (46553) (G-12966)

Mike Jones Software 317 845-7479
8903 Powderhorn Ln Indianapolis (46256) (G-8916)

Mike Mugler 812 945-4266
1907 Majestic Meadows Dr Clarksville (47129) (G-2023)

Mike-Sells West Virginia Inc 317 241-7422
5767 Dividend Rd Indianapolis (46241) (G-8917)

Mikes Creative Woodworks LLC 502 649-3665
2405 Arrowhead Dr Charlestown (47111) (G-1884)

Mikes Metal Dectors 812 366-3558
9350 Indian Bluff Rd Ne Georgetown (47122) (G-6070)

Mikesmobimech LLC 317 753-0492
3921 E Washington St Indianapolis (46201) (G-8918)

Mikro Furniture 812 877-9550
7975 E Chandler Ave Terre Haute (47803) (G-15646)

Milagro Packaging, Princeton Also Called: Southland Container Corp (G-14012)

Milan Food Bank 812 654-3682
201 Josephine St Milan (47031) (G-11781)

Milani Custom Homes LLC 219 455-5804
5222 Connecticut St Merrillville (46410) (G-11538)

Mild To Wild Pepper & Herb Co 317 736-8300
305 Sunbeam Ln Greenwood (46143) (G-6741)

Miles Farm Service, Boonville Also Called: Miles Farm Supply LLC (G-1090)

Miles Farm Supply LLC 812 359-4463
7187 State Hwy 66 E Boonville (47601) (G-1090)

Miles Printing, Indianapolis Also Called: Miles Printing Corporation (G-8919)

Miles Printing Corporation 317 243-8571
4923 W 78th St Indianapolis (46268) (G-8919)

Miles Systems Mfg Inc 574 988-0067
7385 N Walker Rd New Carlisle (46552) (G-12842)

Milestone Cabinetry 219 947-0600
2916 E 83rd Pl Merrillville (46410) (G-11539)

Milestone Contractors LP 812 579-5248
3410 S 650 E Columbus (47203) (G-2356)

Milestone Contractors LP 765 772-7500
3301 S 460 E Lafayette (47905) (G-10650)

Milestone Contractors N Inc 219 924-5900
24358 State Road 23 South Bend (46614) (G-15151)

MILESTONE CONTRACTORS NORTH, INC., South Bend Also Called: Milestone Contractors N Inc (G-15151)

Milford Property LLC 574 970-7460
601 E Beardsley Ave Elkhart (46514) (G-3543)

Military Facilitie, Crane Also Called: United States Dept of Navy (G-2541)

Military Neon Signs 574 258-9804
3304 Wild Cherry Rdg W Mishawaka (46544) (G-11951)

Military Thermals, Fort Wayne Also Called: Enduring Endeavors LLC (G-4951)

Mill Creek Lumber Co 765 347-8546
729 E Water St Hartford City (47348) (G-7072)

Mill Steel Co 765 622-4545
444 E 29th St Anderson (46016) (G-154)

Millcraft Paper Company 317 240-3500
2735 Fortune Cir W Ste A Indianapolis (46241) (G-8920)

Millenium Sheet Metal Inc 574 935-9101
6730 W County Line Rd Plymouth (46563) (G-13797)

Millennial Fireworks 812 732-5126
10645 Highway 135 Sw Mauckport (47142) (G-11439)

Millennium Supply Inc 765 764-7000
407 S Adeway Fowler (47944) (G-5628)

Millennium Tool Inc 812 701-5761
619 Thomas Hill Rd Madison (47250) (G-11244)

Miller Block Co, Evansville Also Called: Evansville Block Co Inc (G-4049)

Miller Brothers Builders Inc 574 533-8602
1819 E Monroe St Goshen (46528) (G-6222)

Miller Cabinetry & Furn LLC 260 657-5052
16016 Trammel Rd Grabill (46741) (G-6315)

Miller Cabins and Barns LLC 574 773-7661
30695 County Road 150 Nappanee (46550) (G-12623)

Miller Carriage Company LLC 260 768-4553
3035 N 850 W Shipshewana (46565) (G-14867)

Miller Chemical Tech & MGT, Franklin Also Called: Miller Chemical Tech & MGT Inc (G-5757)

Miller Chemical Tech & MGT Inc 317 560-5437
980 Hurricane Rd Ste B Franklin (46131) (G-5757)

Miller Creations 574 903-9961
62909 Fairview Dr Goshen (46528) (G-6223)

Miller Custom Metals LLC 219 279-2671
1530 N 800 W Wolcott (47995) (G-16934)

Miller Distributions Inc 574 533-1940
508 W Lincoln Ave Ste D Goshen (46526) (G-6224)

Miller Door & Trim Inc 574 533-8141
2249 Lincolnway E Goshen (46526) (G-6225)

Miller Express Inc 765 572-2303
7724 S 700 W Westpoint (47992) (G-16746)

Miller Hardwoods LLC 574 773-9371
8760 W 1350 N Nappanee (46550) (G-12624)

Miller Industrial Fluids, Indianapolis Also Called: Petrochoice Holdings Inc (G-9130)

Miller Industrial Fluids LLC 317 634-7300
1751 W Raymond St Indianapolis (46221) (G-8921)

Miller Machine and Welding LLC 812 882-7566
2610 S Old Decker Rd Vincennes (47591) (G-16140)

Miller Machine Shop Inc 574 646-2900
10780 W 1100 N Nappanee (46550) (G-12625)

Miller Maid Cabinets Inc 317 780-8280
6815 S Emerson Ave Ste D Indianapolis (46237) (G-8922)

Miller Meat Poultry, Orland Also Called: Crystal Valley Farms LLC (G-13364)

Miller Mfg Corp 574 773-4136
901 E Lincoln St Nappanee (46550) (G-12626)

Miller Poultry, Orland Also Called: Pine Manor Inc (G-13370)

Miller Raceway... 219 939-9688 4900 Melton Rd Gary (46403) *(G-5982)*	**Milroy Spindle Shop**.. 765 629-2176 2221 W 1000 S Milroy (46156) *(G-11829)*
Miller Sign & Design... 765 457-6592 1820 N Purdum St Kokomo (46901) *(G-10308)*	**Milso Industries, Richmond** *Also Called: Milso Industries Inc (G-14167)*
Miller Steel Fabricators..................................... 260 768-7321 3235 N 675 W Shipshewana (46565) *(G-14868)*	**Milso Industries Inc**.. 765 966-8012 401 Industrial Pkwy Richmond (47374) *(G-14167)*
Miller Veneers Inc... 317 638-2326 3724 E 13th St Indianapolis (46201) *(G-8923)*	**Milstrata Manufacturing LLC**............................. 260 209-4415 7525 Maplecrest Rd Ste 156 Fort Wayne (46835) *(G-5229)*
Miller Waste Mills Inc... 507 454-6900 8111 Zionsville Rd Indianapolis (46268) *(G-8924)*	**Miltec Circuits, Leo** *Also Called: David Kechel (G-10967)*
Miller Welding.. 765 628-2463 3305 N 700 E Kokomo (46901) *(G-10309)*	**Milwaukee Ductile Iron Inc**............................... 260 925-4717 1401 S Grandstaff Dr Auburn (46706) *(G-410)*
Miller Welding LLC... 812 381-0800 2139 S Iron Mountain Rd Bloomfield (47424) *(G-753)*	**Milwaukee Electric Tool Corp**........................... 800 729-3878 2198 Southtech Dr Greenwood (46143) *(G-6742)*
Millercarlson, Carmel *Also Called: Cortex Safety Technologies LLC (G-1598)*	**Milwaukee Tool, Greenwood** *Also Called: Milwaukee Electric Tool Corp (G-6742)*
Millers Custom Cabinets................................... 260 768-7830 8170 W State Road 120 Shipshewana (46565) *(G-14869)*	**Min Ko Kyaw LLC**... 574 296-3500 2730 Industrial Pkwy Elkhart (46516) *(G-3545)*
Millers Custom Care Candes............................ 574 658-4976 12711 N 400 W Milford (46542) *(G-11800)*	**Minds Eye Graphics Inc**..................................... 260 724-2050 958 Yorktown Rd Decatur (46733) *(G-2874)*
Millers Locker Plant... 765 234-2381 1979 N Summer Dr Crawfordsville (47933) *(G-2591)*	**Mindys Brownsburg Signs Inc**........................... 317 939-0921 237 Harts Ford Way Brownsburg (46112) *(G-1389)*
Millers Mill... 574 825-2010 55514 County Road 8 Middlebury (46540) *(G-11738)*	**Mine System Solutions LLC**............................. 270 952-5422 2355 Eby Rd Boonville (47601) *(G-1091)*
Millers Mini-Barns LLC...................................... 812 883-8072 6073 S West Washington School Rd Salem (47167) *(G-14493)*	**Mining Machine Parts Inc**.................................. 812 897-1256 420 S 3rd St Boonville (47601) *(G-1092)*
Millers Saw Mill.. 812 883-5246 76 E Miller Sawmill Rd Salem (47167) *(G-14494)*	**Mining Media Inc**.. 317 802-7116 6043 Primrose Ave Indianapolis (46220) *(G-8930)*
Millers Windmill Service.................................... 574 825-2877 14386 County Road 14 Middlebury (46540) *(G-11739)*	**Minks & Beyond LLC**.. 219 402-7011 2106 Morthland Dr Valparaiso (46383) *(G-16003)*
Millers Wldg & Mech Svcs Inc........................... 812 923-3359 9556 Voylcs Rd Pckin (47165) *(G-13519)*	**Minneapolis Die Casting LLC**........................... 763 536-5500 1401 S Grandstaff Dr Auburn (46706) *(G-411)*
Millers Wood Specialties Inc............................. 765 478-3248 850 E Church St Cambridge City (47327) *(G-1499)*	**Minnich Manufacturing Inc**................................ 260 489-5357 2421 W Wallen Rd Fort Wayne (46818) *(G-5230)*
Millers Woodnthings Inc.................................... 574 825-2996 11894 County Rd 14 Middlebury (46540) *(G-11740)*	**Minnick Services, Fort Wayne** *Also Called: Minnick Services Corp (G-5231)*
Milliner Printing Company Inc........................... 260 563-5717 425 S Wabash St Wabash (46992) *(G-16203)*	**Minnick Services Corp (PA)**............................... 260 432-5031 222 N Thomas Rd Fort Wayne (46808) *(G-5231)*
Millipore Sigma... 317 453-5490 6925 Guion Rd Indianapolis (46268) *(G-8925)*	**Minnix J E Well Servicing**.................................. 765 855-5464 5997 Smoker Rd Centerville (47330) *(G-1852)*
Millmade Incorporated....................................... 812 424-7778 9 N Kentucky Ave Evansville (47711) *(G-4206)*	**Mint City Sewing & Tack LLC**........................... 574 546-2230 2320 4c Rd Bremen (46506) *(G-1206)*
Millmark Enterprises Inc................................... 574 389-9904 1935 Markle Ave Elkhart (46517) *(G-3544)*	**Minteq International Inc**..................................... 219 886-9555 1 N Broadway Gary (46402) *(G-5984)*
Millrose Custom Woodworking......................... 812 699-5101 12 S Harrison St Bloomfield (47424) *(G-754)*	**Minteq International Inc**..................................... 219 771-9093 1789 Schiller St Portage (46368) *(G-13887)*
Mills Custom Powder Coating........................... 812 766-0308 1444 E County Road 475 S Winslow (47598) *(G-16921)*	**MINTEQ INTERNATIONAL INC., Portage** *Also Called: Minteq International Inc (G-13887)*
Mills Electric Co Inc... 219 931-3114 4828 Calumet Ave Hammond (46327) *(G-6982)*	**Minteq Shapes and Services Inc (HQ)**............. 219 762-4863 1789 Schiller St Portage (46368) *(G-13888)*
Mills River Publishing Company...................... 765 561-3445 611 N Harrison St Rushville (46173) *(G-14406)*	**Minute Print It Inc**... 765 482-9019 312 W South St Lebanon (46052) *(G-10916)*
Milltronics Mfg Co Inc....................................... 952 442-1410 2920 Fortune Cir W Indianapolis (46241) *(G-8926)*	**Minuteman Press**.. 317 209-1677 6377 Rockville Rd Indianapolis (46214) *(G-8931)*
Milltronics Usa Inc... 317 293-5309 2920 Fortune Cir W Ste C Indianapolis (46241) *(G-8927)*	**Minuteman Press, Indianapolis** *Also Called: Print Sharp Enterprises Inc (G-9203)*
Milltronics Usa Inc... 317 293-5309 7220 Winton Dr Indianapolis (46268) *(G-8928)*	**Minuteman Press, Indianapolis** *Also Called: Printing Concepts Inc (G-9205)*
Milltronics Usa Inc (HQ).................................... 317 293-5309 1 Technology Way Indianapolis (46268) *(G-8929)*	**Minuteman Press, Portage** *Also Called: Business Connection LLC (G-13850)*
Millwood Box & Pallet.. 765 628-7330 4665 E 600 N Kokomo (46901) *(G-10310)*	**Minuteman Press, Schererville** *Also Called: Quality Printing of NW Ind (G-14540)*
Millwork Specialties Co Inc............................... 219 362-2960 1405 Lake St La Porte (46350) *(G-10453)*	**Mira Vista Diagnostics LLC**............................... 317 856-2681 4705 Decatur Blvd Indianapolis (46241) *(G-8932)*
Millwright Machine Inc...................................... 219 845-9200 899 Grant St Gary (46404) *(G-5983)*	**Mirage Computers Inc**.. 260 665-5072 1220 S Wayne St Angola (46703) *(G-276)*
Millwright Riggers Inc (mri).............................. 765 673-4000 2703 W 9th St Marion (46953) *(G-11319)*	**Mirrus Corporation Inc**...................................... 812 689-1411 225 N Us Highway 421 Versailles (47042) *(G-16102)*
Milroy Canning Company.................................. 765 629-2221 100 S Railroad St Milroy (46156) *(G-11827)*	**Mirteq Holdings Inc**.. 260 490-3706 2246 Research Dr Fort Wayne (46808) *(G-5232)*
Milroy Pallet Inc.. 765 629-2919 3018 W 1050 S Milroy (46156) *(G-11828)*	**Mirwec Coating, Bloomington** *Also Called: Mirwec Film Incorporated (G-920)*
	Mirwec Film Incorporated................................. 812 331-7194 601 S Liberty Dr Bloomington (47403) *(G-920)*
	Mis Amores, Indianapolis *Also Called: Deonta Walker (G-7965)*
	Mishawaka LLC.. 574 259-1981 609 E Jefferson Blvd Mishawaka (46545) *(G-11952)*
	Mishawaka Art & Frame Gallery....................... 574 259-9320 110 N Main St Mishawaka (46544) *(G-11953)*
	Mishawaka Brewing Company.......................... 574 256-9993 408 W Cleveland Rd Granger (46530) *(G-6362)*

ALPHABETIC SECTION — Mobius Learning

Mishawaka Devision, Mishawaka *Also Called: Ncp Coatings Inc (G-11964)*

Mishawaka Door LLC... 574 259-2822
58743 Executive Dr Mishawaka (46544) *(G-11954)*

Mishawaka Food Pantry Inc................................ 574 220-6213
315 Lincolnway W Mishawaka (46544) *(G-11955)*

Mishawaka Frozen Custard.................................. 574 255-8000
3921 N Main St Mishawaka (46545) *(G-11956)*

Mishawaka Sheet Metal, Elkhart *Also Called: Patrick Industries Inc (G-3600)*

Mishawaka Sheet Metal LLC.................................. 574 294-5959
28505 C R 20 W Elkhart (46517) *(G-3546)*

Mishawaka Whse & Distrg LLC............................... 574 259-6011
2017 Elder Rd Mishawaka (46545) *(G-11957)*

Misner Welding & Cnstr Inc.................................. 812 648-2980
6922 E County Road 425 S Dugger (47848) *(G-2958)*

Miss Print, Hammond *Also Called: Hetty Incorporated (G-6945)*

Miss Print, Munster *Also Called: Hetty Incorporated (G-12539)*

Mission 1 Communications, Ligonier *Also Called: Ers Tower LLC (G-11014)*

Mission Woodworking Inc..................................... 574 848-5697
502 Kesco Dr Bristol (46507) *(G-1274)*

Mississippi Lime Company.................................... 800 437-5463
570 E Boundary Rd Portage (46368) *(G-13889)*

Mister Hicbachi... 812 339-6288
4400 E 3rd St Bloomington (47401) *(G-921)*

Misty Harbor, Bristol *Also Called: Marine Group LLC (G-1272)*

Mitchel & Scott Machine Co.................................. 317 639-5331
1841 Ludlow Ave Indianapolis (46201) *(G-8933)*

Mitchel & Scott Machine Co, Indianapolis *Also Called: Mitchel Group Incorporated (G-8934)*

Mitchel Group Incorporated (PA).......................... 317 639-5331
1841 Ludlow Ave Indianapolis (46201) *(G-8934)*

Mitchell L Kline... 812 449-6518
13833 N County Road 1100 E Evanston (47531) *(G-3853)*

Mitchell Crushed Stone, Mitchell *Also Called: Rogers Group Inc (G-12047)*

Mitchell Fabrics Inc... 309 674-8631
3532 Coleman Ct Ste B Lafayette (47905) *(G-10651)*

Mitchell Marketing Group Inc................................ 317 816-7010
2621 Towne Dr Carmel (46032) *(G-1700)*

Mitchell Smith Auto Service, Anderson *Also Called: Mitchell Smith Racing (G-155)*

Mitchell Smith Racing... 765 640-0237
4570 W State Road 32 Anderson (46011) *(G-155)*

Mitchell Veneers Inc... 812 941-9663
4250 Earnings Way New Albany (47150) *(G-12781)*

Mitchell-Fleming Printing Inc................................ 317 462-5467
420 W Osage St Greenfield (46140) *(G-6529)*

Mitchum-Schaefer Inc.. 317 546-4081
4901 W Raymond St Indianapolis (46241) *(G-8935)*

Mito Material Solutions Inc (PA)........................... 855 344-6486
8902 Vincenness Cir Ste B Indianapolis (46268) *(G-8936)*

Mito-Craft Inc... 574 287-4555
505 S Logan St South Bend (46615) *(G-15152)*

Mitsubishi Chemical Advncd Mtr........................... 260 479-4100
2710 American Way Fort Wayne (46809) *(G-5233)*

Mitsubsh Chem Advnced Mtls In........................... 260 479-4700
4115 Polymer Pl Fort Wayne (46809) *(G-5234)*

Mitsubshi Trbchrger Eng Amer I........................... 317 346-5291
1200 N Mitsubishi Pkwy Ste A Franklin (46131) *(G-5758)*

Mittal Steel -Ihw- 3 Sp, East Chicago *Also Called: Clevelnd-Cliffs Mnorca Mine Inc (G-3001)*

Mittera Charlestown, Charlestown *Also Called: Mittera Group Inc (G-1885)*

Mittera Group Inc... 812 256-3396
100 Quality Ct Charlestown (47111) *(G-1885)*

Mittler Supply Inc... 317 290-0121
6810 Guion Rd Indianapolis (46268) *(G-8937)*

Mittler Supply Inc... 765 289-6341
810 S Liberty St Muncie (47302) *(G-12457)*

Mix On Site.. 765 607-2140
2252 Us Highway 52 W West Lafayette (47906) *(G-16608)*

Mixer Direct, Jeffersonville *Also Called: Mixer Direct LLC (G-10020)*

Mixer Direct LLC... 812 202-4047
4650 New Middle Rd Jeffersonville (47130) *(G-10020)*

Mj Aircraft Inc... 765 378-7700
262 Airport Rd Anderson (46017) *(G-156)*

Mj Finishing LLC... 574 646-2080
5311 E County Line Rd Bremen (46506) *(G-1207)*

MJB Wood Group LLC.. 574 295-5228
1600 Fieldhouse Ave Ste A Elkhart (46517) *(G-3547)*

Mje Industries Inc... 219 299-3535
460 Lincolnway Unit 343 Valparaiso (46384) *(G-16004)*

Mjs Apparel EMB Screenprinting........................... 260 357-0199
1308 S Randolph St Garrett (46738) *(G-5870)*

Mjs Businesses LLC.. 317 845-1932
8444 Castlewood Dr Indianapolis (46250) *(G-8938)*

Mjs Concrete.. 260 341-5640
19427 Notestine Rd Woodburn (46797) *(G-16954)*

Mk Interiors, Indianapolis *Also Called: American Heritage Shutters LLC (G-7504)*

Mk List, Winona Lake *Also Called: Watermelon World Publishing (G-16917)*

Mk Mfg LLC.. 260 768-4678
8895 W 250 N Shipshewana (46565) *(G-14870)*

Mkmclain Inc.. 260 478-1636
7105 Ardmore Ave Fort Wayne (46809) *(G-5235)*

Mla Printing Inc.. 219 398-8888
6331 Cleveland St Merrillville (46410) *(G-11540)*

MM&m Electrical Supply, Cedar Lake *Also Called: Gund Company Inc (G-1832)*

Mnbkc LLC... 317 956-6558
7953 E Southport Rd Indianapolis (46259) *(G-8939)*

Mnt Delivery Company.. 574 518-6250
72 Sunnycrest Dr Osceola (46561) *(G-13399)*

MO Money Mold Co Inc...................................... 812 256-2681
4818 Highway 3 Otisco (47163) *(G-13449)*

MO Signs LLC.. 574 780-4075
1842 W Jefferson St Plymouth (46563) *(G-13798)*

MO Trailer Corporation....................................... 574 533-0824
2211 W Wilden Ave Goshen (46528) *(G-6226)*

MO Trailers, Goshen *Also Called: MO Trailer Corporation (G-6226)*

Mo-Wood Products Inc (HQ)................................ 812 482-5625
51 E 30th St Jasper (47546) *(G-9892)*

Moan Racing Products LLC.................................. 317 644-3100
4812 S 50 W Greenfield (46140) *(G-6530)*

Mobel Inc (PA).. 812 367-1214
2130 Industrial Park Rd Ferdinand (47532) *(G-4445)*

Mobex Global, Albion *Also Called: Mobex Global US Inc (G-35)*

Mobex Global US Inc.. 319 269-3848
1563 State Route #8 Albion (46701) *(G-35)*

Mobil Trackr, Fishers *Also Called: Mobil Trackr LLC (G-4567)*

Mobil Trackr LLC.. 888 504-2074
12175 Visionary Way Fishers (46038) *(G-4567)*

Mobilcraft Wood Products, Elkhart *Also Called: Patrick Industries Inc (G-3597)*

Mobile Communications Tech.............................. 812 423-7322
945 N Peerless Rd Evansville (47712) *(G-4207)*

Mobile Disposal.. 260 267-6348
5310 Oak Chase Run Fort Wayne (46845) *(G-5236)*

Mobile Drill Intl, Indianapolis *Also Called: Mobile Drill Operating Co LLC (G-8940)*

Mobile Drill Operating Co LLC............................. 317 260-8108
3807 Madison Ave Indianapolis (46227) *(G-8940)*

Mobile Dynamometer LLC................................... 765 271-5080
1309 E Markland Ave Kokomo (46901) *(G-10311)*

Mobile Enerlytics LLC... 765 464-6909
1281 Win Hentschel Blvd Ste 1707 West Lafayette (47906) *(G-16609)*

Mobile King.. 317 835-9772
1638 Shelby St Indianapolis (46203) *(G-8941)*

Mobile Limb & Brace Inc.................................... 765 463-4100
2041 Klondike Rd West Lafayette (47906) *(G-16610)*

Mobile Power Washing LLC................................. 219 863-0066
4693 N Brookbank Dr Bloomington (47404) *(G-922)*

Mobile/Modular Express II LLC............................ 574 295-1214
58120 County Road 3 Elkhart (46517) *(G-3548)*

Mobili Fiver Usa Corp... 219 900-3751
135 N Pennsylvania St Ste 1610 Indianapolis (46204) *(G-8942)*

Mobility Svm LLC... 260 434-4777
505 Avenue Of Autos Fort Wayne (46804) *(G-5237)*

Mobility Ventures LLC... 734 367-3714
105 N Niles Ave South Bend (46617) *(G-15153)*

Mobius Learning, Carmel *Also Called: Cooperative Ventures Ind Corp (G-1596)*

(PA)=Parent Co (HQ)=Headquarters (DH)=Div Headquarters

Mockenhaupt Publishing Inc   **ALPHABETIC SECTION**

Mockenhaupt Publishing Inc 315 778-0067
   1901 Pemberton Dr Fort Wayne (46805) *(G-5238)*

Moco Fragrances LLC 317 642-9014
   1756 W 850 S Flat Rock (47234) *(G-4656)*

Modbar LLC 206 450-4743
   628 Leesburg Rd Fort Wayne (46808) *(G-5239)*

Model 1, Indianapolis Also Called: Next Gnrtion Dlrshp Warsaw LLC *(G-9008)*

Modele LLC 219 300-6929
   9445 Indianapolis Blvd Highland (46322) *(G-7146)*

Models LLC (PA) 765 676-6700
   2275 S 500 W Lebanon (46052) *(G-10917)*

Modern AG Solutions LLC 765 221-1011
   738 N Pendleton Ave Pendleton (46064) *(G-13544)*

Modern Biology Incorporated 765 523-3338
   2211 South St Lafayette (47904) *(G-10652)*

Modern Door Corporation 574 586-3117
   1300 Virginia St Walkerton (46574) *(G-16271)*

Modern Drop Forge Company LLC (PA) 708 489-4208
   8757 Colorado St Merrillville (46410) *(G-11541)*

Modern Forge Companies LLC (PA) 708 388-1806
   8757 Colorado St Merrillville (46410) *(G-11542)*

Modern Forge Indiana LLC 219 945-5945
   8757 Colorado St Merrillville (46410) *(G-11543)*

Modern Graphics, Peru Also Called: Reprocomm Inc *(G-13598)*

Modern Machine & Grinding Inc 219 322-1201
   2001 Clark Rd Dyer (46311) *(G-2978)*

Modern Machine & Tool Inc 765 934-3110
   106 W Main St Van Buren (46991) *(G-16086)*

Modern Materials Inc 574 223-4509
   435 N State Road 25 Rochester (46975) *(G-14308)*

Modern Muscle Car Factory Inc 574 329-6390
   30446 County Road 12 Elkhart (46514) *(G-3549)*

Modern Wldg & Boiler Works Inc 812 232-5039
   3500 Plum St Terre Haute (47803) *(G-15647)*

Modernfold Inc (DH) 800 869-9685
   215 W New Rd Greenfield (46140) *(G-6531)*

Modernfold of Nevada, Greenfield Also Called: Modernfold Inc *(G-6531)*

Modrak Products Company Inc 219 838-0308
   3700 Clark Rd Gary (46408) *(G-5985)*

Modroto, Madison Also Called: Meese Inc *(G-11241)*

Modular Builders Inc 574 223-4934
   2756 Ft Wayne Rd Rochester (46975) *(G-14309)*

Modular Devices, Indianapolis Also Called: Modular Dvcs Acquisition LLC *(G-8943)*

Modular Dvcs Acquisition LLC 317 818-4480
   1515 Brookville Crossing Way Indianapolis (46239) *(G-8943)*

Modular Green Systems LLC 260 547-4121
   5889 N 700 W-1 Craigville (46731) *(G-2535)*

Moeller Printing Co Inc 317 353-2224
   4401 E New York St Indianapolis (46201) *(G-8944)*

Mofab Inc 765 649-5577
   619 W 14th St Anderson (46016) *(G-157)*

Mofab Inc 765 649-1288
   1424 Fairview St Anderson (46016) *(G-158)*

Mofab Inc (PA) 765 649-5577
   1415 Fairview St Anderson (46016) *(G-159)*

Mohawk Group LLC 765 250-5458
   2550 Yeager Rd Apt 2-1 West Lafayette (47906) *(G-16611)*

Mohawk Laboratories 317 899-3660
   8401 E 33rd St Indianapolis (46226) *(G-8945)*

Mohler Technology Inc 812 897-2900
   2355 Eby Rd Boonville (47601) *(G-1093)*

Mokb Presents, Indianapolis Also Called: My Old KY Blog Presents LLC *(G-8976)*

Molargik Woodworking Inc 260 357-6625
   1116 S Hamsher St Garrett (46738) *(G-5871)*

Mold Removers LLC 317 846-0977
   1020 E 86th St Indianapolis (46240) *(G-8946)*

Mold Service Inc 260 868-2920
   2911 County Road 59 Butler (46721) *(G-1471)*

Mold Stoppers of Indiana 812 325-1609
   1135 N Logan Rd Bloomington (47404) *(G-923)*

Molded Acstcal Pdts Easton Inc 610 253-7135
   3733 Lexington Park Dr Elkhart (46514) *(G-3550)*

Molded Acstcal Pdts Easton Inc 574 968-3124
   13065 Anderson Rd Granger (46530) *(G-6363)*

Molded Foam LLC 574 848-1500
   1203 S Division St Bristol (46507) *(G-1275)*

Molded Foam Products, Bristol Also Called: Molded Foam LLC *(G-1275)*

Molded Foam Products Inc 574 848-1500
   1203 S Division St Bristol (46507) *(G-1276)*

Molden Associates Inc 219 879-8425
   1804 Lake Shore Dr Long Beach (46360) *(G-11125)*

Molding Products Division, South Bend Also Called: Ip Corporation *(G-15087)*

Molex LLC 317 834-5600
   1500 Hancel Pkwy Mooresville (46158) *(G-12223)*

Molti Gusti LLC 317 660-5692
   3812 Vanguard Cir Carmel (46032) *(G-1701)*

Momentive Performance Mtls, Garrett Also Called: Momentive Performance Mtls Inc *(G-5872)*

Momentive Performance Mtls Inc 612 499-3902
   3206 Teramo Cv Fort Wayne (46814) *(G-5240)*

Momentive Performance Mtls Inc 260 357-2000
   420 N Taylor Rd Garrett (46738) *(G-5872)*

Momentum Foot & Ankle Clinics, Michigan City Also Called: Oak Brook Foot Ankle Spclsts P *(G-11647)*

Mominee Studios Inc 812 473-1691
   5001 Lincoln Ave Evansville (47715) *(G-4208)*

Moms Pound Cakes LLC 773 220-3822
   7713 Colorado St Merrillville (46410) *(G-11544)*

Monarch Distributing LLC 800 382-9851
   430 Fintail Dr Indianapolis (46219) *(G-8947)*

Monarch Distributing Company, Indianapolis Also Called: Monarch Distributing LLC *(G-8947)*

Monarch Elite Naturals LLC 219 201-1816
   2692 W 60th Dr Merrillville (46410) *(G-11545)*

Monday Voigt Products Inc 317 224-7920
   804 Hazlett St Anderson (46016) *(G-160)*

Money Tree Software Ltd 541 754-3701
   115 S Walnut St Muncie (47305) *(G-12458)*

Monitoring Solutions Inc 317 856-9400
   4404 Guion Rd Indianapolis (46254) *(G-8948)*

Monkey Hollow 812 998-2112
   11534 E County Road 1740 N Saint Meinrad (47577) *(G-14463)*

Monofoilusa LLC 317 340-9951
   2635 S F St Elwood (46036) *(G-3832)*

Monogram Comfort Foods LLC 574 848-0344
   605 Kesco Dr Bristol (46507) *(G-1277)*

Monogram Food Solutions LLC 574 848-0344
   605 Kesco Dr Bristol (46507) *(G-1278)*

Monogram Frozen Foods LLC 574 848-0344
   605 Kesco Dr Bristol (46507) *(G-1279)*

Monogram Metal Shop LLC 260 797-3307
   11213 Witmer Rd Grabill (46741) *(G-6316)*

Monogrammed Mrs LLC 317 605-8471
   5415 N Pennsylvania St Indianapolis (46220) *(G-8949)*

Monon Meat Packing Company 219 253-6363
   402 N Railroad St Monon (47959) *(G-12057)*

Monosol, Portage Also Called: Monosol LLC *(G-13890)*

Monosol LLC 219 324-9459
   1609 Genesis Dr La Porte (46350) *(G-10454)*

Monosol LLC 765 485-5400
   155 S Mount Zion Rd Lebanon (46052) *(G-10918)*

Monosol LLC (DH) 219 762-3165
   707 E 80th Pl Ste 301 Merrillville (46410) *(G-11546)*

Monosol LLC 219 762-3165
   1701 County Line Rd Portage (46368) *(G-13890)*

Monosol LLC 219 763-7589
   1500 Louis Sullivan Dr Portage (46368) *(G-13891)*

Monroe County Regional Sewer 812 824-9005
   Bloomington (47404) *(G-924)*

Monroe Manufacturing Tech Inc 317 782-1005
   5508 Elmwood Ave Ste 422 Indianapolis (46203) *(G-8950)*

Monrovlle Box Pllet WD Pdts LL 260 623-3128
   20009 Monroeville Rd Monroeville (46773) *(G-12071)*

Monsanto, Evansville Also Called: Monsanto Company *(G-4209)*

Monsanto, Reynolds Also Called: Monsanto Company *(G-14074)*

Monsanto, Union Mills *Also Called: Monsanto Company (G-15866)*
Monsanto, Windfall *Also Called: Bayer Great Lakes Prod Co LLC (G-16903)*
Monsanto Company 229 759-0034
   737 Rusher Ln Evansville (47725) *(G-4209)*
Monsanto Company 323 265-1025
   6025 W 300 S Lafayette (47909) *(G-10653)*
Monsanto Company 574 870-0397
   371 N Diener Rd Reynolds (47980) *(G-14074)*
Monsanto Company 219 733-2938
   10201 S 700 W Union Mills (46382) *(G-15866)*
MONSANTO COMPANY, Lafayette *Also Called: Monsanto Company (G-10653)*
Monsanto Whitestown Seed 317 692-9485
   5224 Performance Way Whitestown (46075) *(G-16812)*
Montech USA, Columbia City *Also Called: Richard J Bagan Inc (G-2190)*
Montezuma Jewelry, Muncie *Also Called: David Gonzales (G-12373)*
Montgomery & Associates Inc 219 879-0088
   911 Franklin St Michigan City (46360) *(G-11641)*
Montgomery Tent & Awning Co 317 357-9759
   5054 E 10th St Indianapolis (46201) *(G-8951)*
Montgomery Welding Inc 812 486-3710
   6216 E Us Highway 50 Montgomery (47558) *(G-12116)*
Monticello Signs & Scrn 815 848-4111
   728 N Main St Monticello (47960) *(G-12158)*
Monticello Vault Burial Co 574 583-3206
   2304 N 750 E Monticello (47960) *(G-12159)*
Montpelier AG LLC 765 728-2222
   240 W Windsor St Montpelier (47359) *(G-12180)*
Montrow Group 812 352-7356
   950 W Jfk Dr North Vernon (47265) *(G-13288)*
Monument Chemical LLC (PA) 317 223-2630
   6510 Telecom Dr Ste 425 Indianapolis (46278) *(G-8952)*
Monument Lighthouse Chart 317 657-0160
   8503 Summertree Ln Indianapolis (46256) *(G-8953)*
Monumental Stone Works Inc 765 866-0658
   105 S 3rd St New Market (47965) *(G-12927)*
Moo-Over LLC 260 224-2108
   207 W Van Buren St Columbia City (46725) *(G-2172)*
Moody Candles LLC 317 535-2969
   4162 W Whiteland Rd Bargersville (46106) *(G-570)*
Moody Meats 317 272-4533
   235 N Avon Ave Avon (46123) *(G-538)*
Moodys Logistics Services LLC 812 512-2772
   609 A St Ne Linton (47441) *(G-11040)*
Moon Fabricating Corp 765 459-4194
   700 W Morgan St Kokomo (46901) *(G-10312)*
Mooney Copy Service Inc 812 423-6626
   40 E Sycamore St Evansville (47713) *(G-4210)*
Moonlight Mold & Machine Inc 765 868-9860
   924 Millbrook Ln Kokomo (46901) *(G-10313)*
Moonshine Leather Company Inc 812 988-1326
   38 S Van Buren St Nashville (47448) *(G-12676)*
Moore Designs Unlmtd 812 354-2233
   234 E Harvest Ln Petersburg (47567) *(G-13618)*
Moore Engineering & Prod Co (PA) 812 479-1051
   2104 Lincoln Ave Evansville (47714) *(G-4211)*
Moore Machine & Gear, Evansville *Also Called: Moore Machine & Gear Inc (G-4212)*
Moore Machine & Gear Inc 812 963-3074
   10920 N Saint Joseph Ave Evansville (47720) *(G-4212)*
Moore Metal Works & A/C LLC 812 422-9473
   3712 Upper Mount Vernon Rd Evansville (47712) *(G-4213)*
Moore Precision Machining LLC (PA) 765 265-2386
   1400 Madison St Connersville (47331) *(G-2457)*
Moore Services Incorporated 317 571-9800
   403 Industrial Dr Carmel (46032) *(G-1702)*
Moore Shirts LLC 317 350-4342
   5534 Saint Joe Rd Fort Wayne (46835) *(G-5241)*
Moore-Langen Printing Company Inc 812 234-1585
   200 Hulman St Terre Haute (47802) *(G-15648)*
Moores Country Wood Crafting 317 984-3326
   507 Demoss Ave Arcadia (46030) *(G-315)*
Moores Pie Shop Inc 765 457-2428
   115 W Elm St Kokomo (46901) *(G-10314)*

Moores Welding Service Inc 260 627-2177
   13131 Leo Rd Leo (46765) *(G-10969)*
Mooresville Goodyear Tire, Mooresville *Also Called: Mooresville Tire & Service Ctr (G-12224)*
Mooresville Times 317 831-0280
   78 N Main St Martinsville (46151) *(G-11415)*
Mooresville Tire & Service Ctr 317 831-1215
   432 N Monroe St Mooresville (46158) *(G-12224)*
Mooresville Welding Inc 317 831-2265
   220 E Washington St Mooresville (46158) *(G-12225)*
Moorfeed Corporation 317 545-7171
   4162 N Ems Blvd Greenfield (46140) *(G-6532)*
Moorfeed Corporation, Greenfield *Also Called: Executive Automtn Systems Inc (G-6503)*
Moose Lake Products Co Inc 260 432-2768
   6528 Constitution Dr Fort Wayne (46804) *(G-5242)*
Moose Lodge 219 362-2446
   925 Boyd Blvd La Porte (46350) *(G-10455)*
Moose Lodge No 492, La Porte *Also Called: Moose Lodge (G-10455)*
Moosein Industries LLC 219 406-7306
   1256 Camelot Mnr Portage (46368) *(G-13892)*
Mor-Ryde Service Center, Elkhart *Also Called: Mor/Ryde Inc (G-3551)*
Mor/Ryde Inc 574 293-1581
   1966 Sterling Ave Elkhart (46516) *(G-3551)*
More Wallace, Indianapolis *Also Called: R R Donnelley Inc (G-9256)*
Morehead Machinery Inc 574 651-8671
   30924 County Road 8 Elkhart (46514) *(G-3552)*
Morgan Adhesives Company LLC 812 342-2004
   2576 Norcross Dr Columbus (47201) *(G-2357)*
Morgan Automotive 765 378-0593
   4443 State Road 32 E Chesterfield (46017) *(G-1897)*
Morgan Commercial Lettering 260 482-6430
   434 Merkler St Fort Wayne (46825) *(G-5243)*
Morgan County Sand & Gravel Co, Martinsville *Also Called: Rogers Group Inc (G-11424)*
Morgan Excavating 812 385-6036
   5268 S 875 E Oakland City (47660) *(G-13321)*
Morgan Foods Inc 812 794-1170
   90 W Morgan St Austin (47102) *(G-467)*
Morgan Francis Flagpoles & ACC, Indianapolis *Also Called: Superior Metal Tech LLC (G-9530)*
Morgan Nye 812 738-4587
   442 Quarry Rd Nw Corydon (47112) *(G-2505)*
Morgan Nye Welding, Corydon *Also Called: Morgan Nye (G-2505)*
Morgan Olson LLC 269 659-0243
   300 Growth Pkwy Angola (46703) *(G-277)*
Morgan Thermal Ceramics, Elkhart *Also Called: Thermal Ceramics Inc (G-3725)*
Morganblair Logistics LLC 219 249-2689
   8330 Columbia Ave Munster (46321) *(G-12550)*
Moriroku Technology N Amer Inc 765 221-7576
   3511 W 73rd St Anderson (46011) *(G-161)*
Morning Song Wild Bird Feed, Reynolds *Also Called: Scotts Miracle-Gro Company (G-14076)*
Morris Holding Company LLC (PA) 812 446-6141
   1015 E Mechanic St Brazil (47834) *(G-1154)*
Morris Machine & Tool 219 866-3018
   828 N Scott St Rensselaer (47978) *(G-14060)*
Morris Machine Co Inc 317 788-0371
   6480 S Belmont Ave Indianapolis (46217) *(G-8954)*
Morris Machine Shop, Jeffersonville *Also Called: Brent Morris (G-9946)*
Morris Mfg & Sls Corp 812 446-6141
   1015 E Mechanic St Brazil (47834) *(G-1155)*
Morris Mold and Machine Co 317 923-6653
   4015 Ferguson Rd Indianapolis (46239) *(G-8955)*
Morris Printing Company Inc 317 639-5553
   1502 N College Ave Indianapolis (46202) *(G-8956)*
Morris Sheet Metal Corp 260 497-1300
   6212 Highview Dr Fort Wayne (46818) *(G-5244)*
Morryde International Inc 574 293-1581
   1536 Grant St Elkhart (46514) *(G-3553)*
Morryde International Inc 574 293-1581
   23208 Cooper Dr Elkhart (46514) *(G-3554)*
Morryde International Inc (PA) 574 293-1581
   1966 Sterling Ave Elkhart (46516) *(G-3555)*

Morse Metal Fab Inc 574 674-6237
  51111 Bittersweet Rd Granger (46530) *(G-6364)*
Mortar Net Usa Ltd. 800 664-6638
  6575 Daniel Burnham Dr Ste G Portage (46368) *(G-13893)*
Mortgageserv, South Bend *Also Called: Fiserv Mrtg Servicing Systems (G-15034)*
Morton Buildings Inc. 765 653-9781
  6215 S Us Highway 231 Cloverdale (46120) *(G-2090)*
Morton Buildings Inc. 800 447-7436
  Us-231 Jasper (47546) *(G-9893)*
Morton Buildings Inc. 260 563-2118
  1873 S State Road 115 Wabash (46992) *(G-16204)*
Morton Salt Inc. 219 477-0061
  7024 Parrot Rd New Haven (46774) *(G-12910)*
Moseley Laboratories Inc. 317 866-8460
  6108 W Stoner Dr Greenfield (46140) *(G-6533)*
Moser Engineering, Portland *Also Called: Greg Moser Engineering Inc (G-13949)*
Moses Leathers 260 203-8799
  810 Schick St Fort Wayne (46803) *(G-5245)*
Mosey Manufacturing Co Inc 765 983-8870
  534 N 17th St Richmond (47374) *(G-14168)*
Mosey Manufacturing Co Inc 765 983-8870
  1700 N F St Richmond (47374) *(G-14169)*
Mosey Manufacturing Co Inc 765 983-8889
  1700 N F St Richmond (47374) *(G-14170)*
Mosey Manufacturing Co Inc 765 983-8870
  1700 N F St Richmond (47374) *(G-14171)*
Mosey Manufacturing Co Inc (PA) 765 983-8800
  262 Fort Wayne Ave Richmond (47374) *(G-14172)*
Mosey Manufacturing Plant 7, Richmond *Also Called: Mosey Manufacturing Co Inc (G-14170)*
Mosey Plant II, Richmond *Also Called: Mosey Manufacturing Co Inc (G-14171)*
Mosier Log Homes, Corydon *Also Called: Mosier Pallet & Lumber Co (G-2506)*
Mosier Pallet & Lumber Co 812 366-4817
  3600 Tee Rd Ne Corydon (47112) *(G-2506)*
Mosiers Tarps LLC 260 563-3332
  4021 S State Road 15 Wabash (46992) *(G-16205)*
Moss Glass, Indianapolis *Also Called: Moss L Glass Co Inc (G-8957)*
Moss L Glass Co Inc 765 642-4946
  5265 E 82nd St Indianapolis (46250) *(G-8957)*
Mossberg & Company Inc 260 755-6283
  3202 Clearfield Ct Fort Wayne (46808) *(G-5246)*
Mossberg & Company Inc 574 236-1094
  4100 Technology Dr South Bend (46628) *(G-15154)*
Mossberg & Company Inc (PA) 574 289-9253
  301 E Sample St South Bend (46601) *(G-15155)*
Mossberg Co 574 850-6285
  301 E Sample St South Bend (46601) *(G-15156)*
Mossberg Industries, Laotto *Also Called: Khorporate Holdings Inc (G-10807)*
Mossberg Industries Inc (HQ) 260 357-5141
  204 N 2nd St Garrett (46738) *(G-5873)*
Mossbev, South Bend *Also Called: Mossberg & Company Inc (G-15155)*
Mossman Metal Works 765 676-6055
  3595 W 200 S Lebanon (46052) *(G-10919)*
Motherson Sumi Systems Limited 260 726-6501
  700 Industrial Dr Portland (47371) *(G-13957)*
Motion & Control Entps LLC 219 844-4224
  616 Progress Ave Munster (46321) *(G-12551)*
Motion Engineering Company Inc 317 804-7990
  17338 Westfield Park Rd Ste 4 Westfield (46074) *(G-16712)*
Motivated Entrepreneur, The, Syracuse *Also Called: Mesumes Incorporated (G-15468)*
Motor Electric Inc. 574 294-7123
  4700 Eastland Dr Elkhart (46516) *(G-3556)*
Motorama Auto Ctr Inc (PA) 317 831-0036
  10509 N Old State Road 67 Mooresville (46158) *(G-12226)*
Motorama Kart Parts, Mooresville *Also Called: Motorama Auto Ctr Inc (G-12226)*
Motorola, Fort Wayne *Also Called: Motorola Solutions Inc (G-5247)*
Motorola, Indianapolis *Also Called: Motorola Solutions Inc (G-8958)*
Motorola Solutions Inc 260 436-5331
  3304 Mallard Cove Ln Fort Wayne (46804) *(G-5247)*
Motorola Solutions Inc 317 481-0914
  2461 Directors Row Ste C Indianapolis (46241) *(G-8958)*
Motorola Solutions Inc (PA) 317 716-8064
  2461 Directors Row Ste C Indianapolis (46241) *(G-8959)*
Motorsport Price Engineering 812 546-4220
  205 Main St Hope (47246) *(G-7229)*
Motsinger Auto Supply Inc 317 782-8484
  345 W Hanna Ave Indianapolis (46217) *(G-8960)*
Mougeotte Publishing Inc 765 649-3302
  1232 Broadway St Ste 300 Anderson (46012) *(G-162)*
Mould-Rite Inc. 812 967-3200
  5885 E Old Pekin Rd Pekin (47165) *(G-13520)*
Mount Graphics & Signs Inc 765 483-1435
  1101 S Lebanon St Lebanon (46052) *(G-10920)*
Mountjoy Wooding 317 897-6792
  1221 Schleicher Ave Indianapolis (46229) *(G-8961)*
Mountville Mats. 574 753-8858
  5270 E Country Club Rd Logansport (46947) *(G-11094)*
Mouron & Company Inc. 317 243-7955
  1025 Western Dr Indianapolis (46241) *(G-8962)*
Movie Poster Print. 812 679-7301
  4114 Washington St Columbus (47203) *(G-2358)*
Moyer Process & Controls Co 260 495-2405
  105 N Wayne St Fremont (46737) *(G-5827)*
Moyers Inc. 574 264-3119
  3502 Reedy Dr Elkhart (46514) *(G-3557)*
Mp Constructions LLC 888 520-7005
  8888 Keystone Xing Indianapolis (46240) *(G-8963)*
Mp Global Products LLC 866 751-3765
  890 Central Ct New Albany (47150) *(G-12782)*
Mpc Global LLC 816 399-4710
  6300 Southeastern Ave Indianapolis (46203) *(G-8964)*
Mpi Engineered Tech LLC 574 772-3850
  1200 Kloeckner Dr Knox (46534) *(G-10215)*
Mpi Engineered Tech Win LLC 574 772-3850
  1200 Kloeckner Dr Knox (46534) *(G-10216)*
Mpi Products Holdings LLC (DH) 248 237-3007
  1200 Kloeckner Dr Knox (46534) *(G-10217)*
Mpi Products LLC 248 237-3007
  1200 Kloeckner Dr Knox (46534) *(G-10218)*
Mpiche LLC (PA) 317 636-3351
  2432 Southeastern Ave Indianapolis (46201) *(G-8965)*
Mpm, Petersburg *Also Called: Michael L Jerrell (G-13617)*
Mpp, Campbellsburg *Also Called: Netshape Technologies LLC (G-1525)*
Mpp, Noblesville *Also Called: Metal Powder Products LLC (G-13134)*
Mpp, Noblesville *Also Called: Nst Technologies Mim LLC (G-13146)*
Mpp Holdings Inc 317 805-3764
  14670 Cumberland Rd Noblesville (46060) *(G-13140)*
Mpp Inc. 260 422-5426
  2413 Meyer Rd Fort Wayne (46803) *(G-5248)*
Mpr Corporation 574 848-5100
  103 Hinsdale Farm Rd Bristol (46507) *(G-1280)*
MPS, Wabash *Also Called: Midwestern Pallet Service Inc (G-16202)*
MPS Egg Farms, North Manchester *Also Called: Midwest Poultry Services LP (G-13242)*
MPS Indianapolis Inc. 317 241-2020
  2020 Production Dr Indianapolis (46241) *(G-8966)*
MPS International LLC 260 824-2630
  941 N Main St Bluffton (46714) *(G-1043)*
MPS Printing Incorporated 812 273-4446
  339 Clifty Dr Madison (47250) *(G-11245)*
Mpt Muncie LLC 765 587-1300
  4701 S Cowan Rd Muncie (47302) *(G-12459)*
Mpt Muncie East, Muncie *Also Called: Magna Powertrain America Inc (G-12443)*
Mqp Machining LLC 812 278-8374
  6581 State Road 54 W Springville (47462) *(G-15389)*
Mr Copy Inc. 812 334-2679
  501 E 10th St Bloomington (47408) *(G-925)*
Mr Copyrite 219 462-1108
  308 Lincolnway Valparaiso (46383) *(G-16005)*
Mr Fuel 317 531-0891
  140 Holwager Dr Spiceland (47385) *(G-15378)*
Mr Heat Inc. 219 345-5629
  11735 N State Road 55 Demotte (46310) *(G-2925)*

ALPHABETIC SECTION — Mulzer Crushed Stone Inc

Mr Pin Shi Peter Lee 574 264-9754
  23329 Century Dr Elkhart (46514) *(G-3558)*
Mr Tintz 219 844-5500
  6806 Indianapolis Blvd Ste D Hammond (46324) *(G-6983)*
Mr Trophy, Argos Also Called: Van Der Weele Jon D *(G-328)*
Mr-Link LLC 512 297-4582
  408 Brunswick Dr Apt 13 Lafayette (47909) *(G-10654)*
Mr. Canary Company, Carmel Also Called: Mitchell Marketing Group Inc *(G-1700)*
Mr2 Performance LLC 765 483-9371
  722 W Pearl St Lebanon (46052) *(G-10921)*
Mrg Robotics 814 341-4334
  6328 Moonstruck Pkwy Indianapolis (46259) *(G-8967)*
Mrrx Mobile Railcar Repair LLC 812 251-0055
  1020 W Trinity Ave Clinton (47842) *(G-2072)*
Mrs International, Fort Wayne Also Called: Machine Rebuilders & Service *(G-5197)*
Mrs T'S Bakery, Bremen Also Called: Mel-Rhon Inc *(G-1205)*
Ms Manufacturing LLC 812 442-7468
  301 N Murphy Ave Brazil (47834) *(G-1156)*
Ms Sedco Inc 317 842-2545
  7898 Zionsville Rd Indianapolis (46268) *(G-8968)*
Ms Wheelchair Indiana Inc 317 408-0947
  9106 Tansel Ct Indianapolis (46234) *(G-8969)*
MSC Property Management Div, La Porte Also Called: Millwork Specialties Co Inc *(G-10453)*
Msca LLC 574 583-6220
  303 N 6th St Monticello (47960) *(G-12160)*
Msd Group LLC 260 444-4658
  9025 Coldwater Rd Ste 400 Fort Wayne (46825) *(G-5249)*
Msf Express Inc 561 413-4545
  1242 E 28th Ave Lake Station (46405) *(G-10774)*
MSI Express Inc 219 871-9882
  6515 Ameriplex Dr Portage (46368) *(G-13894)*
Msk Mold Inc 812 985-5457
  2591 Juanita Ave Wadesville (47638) *(G-16227)*
MSP, Bloomington Also Called: MSP Aviation Inc *(G-926)*
MSP Aviation Inc 812 333-6100
  239 W Grimes Ln Bloomington (47403) *(G-926)*
Mss, Boonville Also Called: Mine System Solutions LLC *(G-1091)*
Mssh Inc 812 663-2180
  901 N Carver St Greensburg (47240) *(G-6620)*
Mssl Wiring System Inc (HQ) 330 856-3366
  700 Industrial Dr Portland (47371) *(G-13958)*
Mt Olive Manufacturing LLC 317 834-8525
  3304 Hancel Cir Mooresville (46158) *(G-12227)*
MT Publishing Company Inc 812 468-8022
  209 Nw 8th St Evansville (47708) *(G-4214)*
Mt Vernon Coal Transfer Co 812 838-5531
  3300 Bluff Rd Mount Vernon (47620) *(G-12310)*
Mt Vernon Transfer Trml LLC 812 838-5531
  3300 Bluff Rd Mount Vernon (47620) *(G-12311)*
Mt. Olive Manufacturing, Inc., Mooresville Also Called: Mt Olive Manufacturing LLC *(G-12227)*
Mt. Vernon Barge Service, Indianapolis Also Called: Tpg Mt Vernon Marine LLC *(G-9626)*
MTA Technology LLC 765 447-2221
  2624 Salem St Lafayette (47904) *(G-10655)*
Mtcr Site Services LLC 812 598-6516
  6033 Vann Rd Newburgh (47630) *(G-13014)*
Mtd, Fort Wayne Also Called: Midwest Tool & Die Corp *(G-5226)*
Mtd Products, Indianapolis Also Called: Mtd Products Inc *(G-8970)*
Mtd Products Inc 317 986-2042
  7868 Zionsville Rd Indianapolis (46268) *(G-8970)*
Mtek, Martinsville Also Called: Mtek Armor Group LLC *(G-11416)*
Mtek Armor Group LLC 765 341-0933
  501 Rogers Rd Martinsville (46151) *(G-11416)*
Mtek Weapon Systems, Martinsville Also Called: Mahan Technical Design LLC *(G-11410)*
MTI, South Bend Also Called: Manufacturing Technology Inc *(G-15138)*
MTI Mexico Machining LLC 260 925-4717
  1401 S Grandstaff Dr Auburn (46706) *(G-412)*
Mtm Machining Inc 219 872-8677
  311 Indiana Highway 212 Michigan City (46360) *(G-11642)*
Mtr Machining Concept Inc 260 587-3381
  2878 W 800 S Ashley (46705) *(G-334)*

MTS Products Corp 574 295-3142
  28672 Holiday Pl Elkhart (46517) *(G-3559)*
MTS Systems Corporation 952 937-4000
  1611 S Harrison St Alexandria (46001) *(G-55)*
Mudd-Ox Inc 260 768-7221
  8525 W 750 N Shipshewana (46565) *(G-14871)*
Mudhole Machine Shop LLC 765 533-4228
  5121 N County Road 200 W Middletown (47356) *(G-11775)*
Muehlhausen Spring Company 574 859-2481
  488 N 705 E Flora (46929) *(G-4662)*
Muhlen Sohn Inc 765 640-9674
  3019 Enterprise Dr Anderson (46013) *(G-163)*
Muhlen Sohn Industries, L.P., Anderson Also Called: Muhlen Sohn Inc *(G-163)*
Mulhern Belting Inc 201 337-5700
  910 Indiana Highway 212 Michigan City (46360) *(G-11643)*
Mullet Custom Interior LLC 574 773-9442
  106 3b Rd Nappanee (46550) *(G-12627)*
Mullets Fencing and Supplies 574 646-3300
  7749 W 1000 N Nappanee (46550) *(G-12628)*
Mullets Welding LLC 574 773-0189
  12848 N 700 W Nappanee (46550) *(G-12629)*
Mullin Sign Studio 219 926-8937
  48 E 1050 N Chesterton (46304) *(G-1949)*
Mullis Custom Framing LLC 317 627-4024
  246 Victory Hl Coatesville (46121) *(G-2108)*
Multi Fiber LLC 260 353-1510
  1000 W Wiley Ave Bluffton (46714) *(G-1044)*
Multi Packaging Solutions Inc 317 241-2020
  2020 Production Dr Indianapolis (46241) *(G-8971)*
Multi Packaging Solutions Ind, Indianapolis Also Called: MPS Indianapolis Inc *(G-8966)*
Multi-Color Corporation 513 396-5600
  2281 S Us Highway 31 Scottsburg (47170) *(G-14572)*
Multi-Color Corporation 812 752-0586
  2281 S Us Highway 31 Scottsburg (47170) *(G-14573)*
Multi-Wall Packaging Corp 219 882-0070
  1 N Bridge St Gary (46404) *(G-5986)*
Multimatic Indiana Inc (DH) 260 868-1000
  201 Re Jones Rd Butler (46721) *(G-1472)*
Multimatic Indiana Inc 260 749-3700
  2808 S Maplecrest Rd Fort Wayne (46803) *(G-5250)*
Multiple Machining 812 926-0798
  312 3rd St Aurora (47001) *(G-450)*
Multiple Machining Inc 812 432-5946
  10150 Lenover St Dillsboro (47018) *(G-2950)*
Multiple Resource Solution 317 862-2584
  6925 S Carroll Rd Indianapolis (46259) *(G-8972)*
Multiplex Company Inc (DH) 812 246-7000
  645 Park East Blvd Ste 5 New Albany (47150) *(G-12783)*
Multiseal, Evansville Also Called: Multiseal Inc *(G-4215)*
Multiseal Inc 812 428-3422
  4320 Hitch Peters Rd Evansville (47711) *(G-4215)*
Mulzer Crushed Stone, English Also Called: Mulzer Crushed Stone Inc *(G-3844)*
Mulzer Crushed Stone Inc 812 256-3346
  15602 Charlestown Bethlehem Rd Charlestown (47111) *(G-1886)*
Mulzer Crushed Stone Inc 812 937-2442
  4590 E Aw Mulzer Dr Dale (47523) *(G-2791)*
Mulzer Crushed Stone Inc 812 365-2145
  Old Hwy #64 E English (47118) *(G-3844)*
Mulzer Crushed Stone Inc 844 480-6803
  900 Nw Riverside Dr Evansville (47708) *(G-4216)*
Mulzer Crushed Stone Inc 812 739-4777
  19925 S Alton Fredonia Rd Leavenworth (47137) *(G-10871)*
Mulzer Crushed Stone Inc 812 732-1002
  9610 River Rd Sw Mauckport (47142) *(G-11440)*
Mulzer Crushed Stone Inc 812 838-3472
  10700 Highway 69 S Mount Vernon (47620) *(G-12312)*
Mulzer Crushed Stone Inc 812 354-9650
  204 W Illinois St Petersburg (47567) *(G-13619)*
Mulzer Crushed Stone Inc 812 547-3467
  3rd Lafayette St Tell City (47586) *(G-15512)*
Mulzer Crushed Stone Inc (DH) 812 547-7921
  534 Mozart St Tell City (47586) *(G-15513)*

Mulzer Security, Charlestown *Also Called: Mulzer Crushed Stone Inc (G-1886)*

Muncie Cabinet Discounters.. 765 216-7367
4205 N Wheeling Ave Muncie (47304) *(G-12460)*

Muncie Casting Corp.. 765 288-2611
1406 E 18th St Muncie (47302) *(G-12461)*

Muncie Manufacturing Plant, Muncie *Also Called: Spartech LLC (G-12495)*

Muncie Metal Spinning Inc.. 765 288-1937
1100 E 20th St Muncie (47302) *(G-12462)*

Muncie Novelty Company Inc... 765 288-8301
9610 N State Road 67 Muncie (47303) *(G-12463)*

Muncie Power Products Inc (HQ)... 765 284-7721
201 E Jackson St Ste 500 Muncie (47305) *(G-12464)*

Muncie Power Products Inc.. 785 284-7721
342 N Pershing Dr Muncie (47305) *(G-12465)*

Muncie Sand & Gravel Inc.. 765 282-6422
4210 E Mcgalliard Rd Muncie (47303) *(G-12466)*

Munster Steel Co Inc... 219 924-5198
1501 Huehn St Hammond (46327) *(G-6984)*

Muro Pallets Corporation... 219 803-0500
141 141st St Hammond (46327) *(G-6985)*

Murpac of Fort Wayne LLC... 260 424-2299
3405 Meyer Rd Ste 135 Fort Wayne (46803) *(G-5251)*

Murphy Mill Services LLC.. 219 246-9290
154 Curtis Dr Valparaiso (46383) *(G-16006)*

Murphys Townhouse Candles LLC....................................... 260 318-0504
226 S Park Ave Kendallville (46755) *(G-10137)*

Murray Equipment Inc... 260 484-0382
2515 Charleston Pl Fort Wayne (46808) *(G-5252)*

Murrays Tin Cup... 260 349-1002
2004 W North St Kendallville (46755) *(G-10138)*

Mursix, Yorktown *Also Called: Mursix Corporation (G-16977)*

Mursix Corporation (PA).. 765 282-2221
2401 N Executive Park Dr Yorktown (47396) *(G-16977)*

Musculoskeletal Publ Analis Inc.. 574 269-4861
1691 S Meadow Dr Warsaw (46580) *(G-16399)*

Music Store... 812 949-3004
307 W Lewis And Clark Pkwy Clarksville (47129) *(G-2024)*

Music Town Distributors, Fort Wayne *Also Called: Cliff A Ostermeyer (G-4860)*

Mustard Seed Woodworking LLC... 765 336-4423
325 Lafayette Ave Lebanon (46052) *(G-10922)*

Muzfeed Inc... 815 252-7676
6304 Tanbark Trl Fort Wayne (46835) *(G-5253)*

Mv-1, South Bend *Also Called: Mobility Ventures LLC (G-15153)*

Mvctc... 765 969-8921
240 E Farlow Rd Richmond (47374) *(G-14173)*

Mvgreene Distributing, Ladoga *Also Called: Michael Greene (G-10508)*

Mvk Pharmaceuticals LLC.. 317 374-2178
1800 N Capitol Ave Ste E504 Indianapolis (46202) *(G-8973)*

Mvo USA, Indianapolis *Also Called: Mvo Usa Inc (G-8974)*

Mvo Usa Inc... 317 585-5785
8804 Bash St Ste A Indianapolis (46256) *(G-8974)*

Mvp Dumpsters Inc.. 317 502-3155
8093 S 600 W Pendleton (46064) *(G-13545)*

Mw Aircraft Inc... 317 873-4627
9730 Soaring Hawk Cir Zionsville (46077) *(G-17034)*

Mwf LLC... 812 936-5303
3000 S Walnut Street Pike Apt F6 Bloomington (47401) *(G-927)*

Mwi Animal Health, Lebanon *Also Called: Mwi Veterinary Supply Co (G-10924)*

Mwi Animal Health- Lebanon, Lebanon *Also Called: Mwi Veterinary Supply Co (G-10923)*

Mwi Veterinary Supply Co.. 317 769-7771
5025 In-267 Ste 100 Lebanon (46052) *(G-10923)*

Mwi Veterinary Supply Co.. 317 769-7771
5025 S State Road 267 Rm 100 Lebanon (46052) *(G-10924)*

Mwss Inc.. 574 287-3365
2810 Bridger Ct Elkhart (46514) *(G-3560)*

Mx5 & Associates Inc... 574 226-0733
24615 County Road 45 Ste 2 Elkhart (46516) *(G-3561)*

My Charisma, Indianapolis *Also Called: Melissa Townsend (G-8875)*

My Daily Wedding Deals LLC.. 812 603-6149
4822 Crystal River Ct Indianapolis (46240) *(G-8975)*

My Felicity Creations LLC.. 317 363-3269
1125 Robb Hill Rd Martinsville (46151) *(G-11417)*

My Goodies Snack Vending LLC... 317 653-7395
1905 E Balsam Ct Anderson (46011) *(G-164)*

My Old KY Blog Presents LLC.. 317 602-6641
1043 Virginia Ave Ste 217 Indianapolis (46203) *(G-8976)*

My Pneumatic Tools and Service.. 317 364-3324
7032 E Shelby County Road 1100 S Greensburg (47240) *(G-6621)*

My Sisters Doll Clothes... 765 459-7977
1038 Springwater Rd Kokomo (46902) *(G-10315)*

Mycloud LLC... 317 570-8999
8595 Babson Ct Fishers (46038) *(G-4568)*

Mycogen Corporation (HQ).. 317 337-3000
9330 Zionsville Rd Indianapolis (46268) *(G-8977)*

Myers, Saint Paul *Also Called: Myers Frz Foods Provisioniers (G-14467)*

Myers Cabinet Company.. 765 342-7781
409 E Pike St Martinsville (46151) *(G-11418)*

Myers Design Inc... 317 955-2450
6061 Logansport Rd Logansport (46947) *(G-11095)*

Myers Enterprises Inc... 812 636-7350
102 W Main St Odon (47562) *(G-13344)*

Myers Frz Foods Provisioniers.. 765 525-6304
405 W Dorsey St Saint Paul (47272) *(G-14467)*

Myers Industries Inc... 866 429-5200
3300 N Kenmore St South Bend (46628) *(G-15157)*

Myers Spring Co Inc... 574 753-5105
720 Water St Logansport (46947) *(G-11096)*

Myers Wood Products... 765 597-2147
1287 E 1200 N Bloomingdale (47832) *(G-761)*

Myfin Inc... 812 287-8579
101 N College Ave Bloomington (47404) *(G-928)*

Myfoodmixer LLC... 219 229-7036
3212 Salem Ct Apt 3 Michigan City (46360) *(G-11644)*

Mystique Winery and Vinyrd LLC.. 812 922-5612
13000 Gore Rd Lynnville (47619) *(G-11190)*

Mytex Polymers, Jeffersonville *Also Called: Mytex Polymers US Corp (G-10021)*

Mytex Polymers US Corp (DH)... 812 280-2900
1403 Port Rd Jeffersonville (47130) *(G-10021)*

Myturbopc LLC.. 574 350-9330
55348 Osborn Ave Ste C Elkhart (46514) *(G-3562)*

Mz Ventur Partners, Nappanee *Also Called: Wyatt Farm Center Inc (G-12655)*

N & R Woodworking Llc.. 812 787-0644
10546 N 700 E Odon (47562) *(G-13345)*

N E W Interstate Concrete Inc.. 812 234-5983
2223 E Margaret Dr Terre Haute (47802) *(G-15649)*

N K Hurst Co Inc.. 317 634-6425
10505 Bennett Pkwy Ste 100 Zionsville (46077) *(G-17035)*

N R S, Fort Wayne *Also Called: National Rcreation Systems Inc (G-5256)*

N Rolls-Royce Amercn Tech Inc.. 317 230-4347
2059 S Tibbs Ave Ste Sc Indianapolis (46241) *(G-8978)*

N T F, Fort Wayne *Also Called: National Tube Form LLC (G-5257)*

N Y B, La Porte *Also Called: New York Blower Company (G-10457)*

N Y X, Mishawaka *Also Called: Nyx Fort Wayne LLC (G-11968)*

N-Complete Inc.. 765 649-2244
804 Lincoln St Anderson (46016) *(G-165)*

N.E.W. Indiana Co., Columbus *Also Called: Nagakura Engrg Works Co Inc (G-2359)*

N.G.D. Global, Muncie *Also Called: Nina Gail Diamonds LLC (G-12469)*

N2 Publishing.. 812 449-0408
6709 E Oak St Evansville (47715) *(G-4217)*

N2 Publishing, Anderson *Also Called: H&H Media LLC (G-124)*

N2 Publishing, Greenwood *Also Called: Anthonyjean LLC (G-6670)*

NA Holding-Lime City LLC... 260 212-2294
3601 Focus Dr Fort Wayne (46818) *(G-5254)*

Nachi, Greenwood *Also Called: Nachi Technology Inc (G-6744)*

Nachi America Inc (HQ).. 877 622-4487
715 Pushville Rd Greenwood (46143) *(G-6743)*

Nachi Technology Inc... 317 535-5000
713 Pushville Rd Greenwood (46143) *(G-6744)*

Nachi Tool America Inc... 317 535-0320
717 Pushville Rd Greenwood (46143) *(G-6745)*

Nachurs Alpine Solutions LLC 812 738-1333
3185 Cline Rd Nw Corydon (47112) *(G-2507)*

Nacjam Interior Blinds Inc 765 449-8035
5021 Saddle Dr Lafayette (47905) *(G-10656)*

Nagakura Engrg Works Co Inc 812 375-1382
630 S Mapleton St Columbus (47201) *(G-2359)*

Nai Print Solutions 317 392-1207
168 W Hendricks St Shelbyville (46176) *(G-14779)*

Nail Factory LLC 317 292-5637
1122 E 16th St Unit 110 Indianapolis (46202) *(G-8979)*

Nakoma Products LLC 317 357-5715
2855 N Franklin Rd Ste A7 Indianapolis (46219) *(G-8980)*

Nalc LLC 502 548-9590
8090 S State Road 243 Cloverdale (46120) *(G-2091)*

Nalin Manufacturing LLC 812 401-9187
2108 E Virginia St Evansville (47711) *(G-4218)*

Nalon Power Development LLC 317 450-7564
10342 N County Road 471 E Pittsboro (46167) *(G-13652)*

Namacle LLC 574 320-1436
17911 Turners Dr South Bend (46635) *(G-15158)*

Nampac, Indianapolis *Also Called: North America Packaging Corp (G-9021)*

Namsou Lims LLC 347 641-5886
2002 High Eagle Trl Apt 1025 Indianapolis (46224) *(G-8981)*

Nanas Cakes and Sweets LLC 317 694-4271
3136 N Tacoma Ave Indianapolis (46218) *(G-8982)*

Nancy Ferber 219 548-3645
143 Woodland Hickory Ct Valparaiso (46385) *(G-16007)*

Nanna S Embroidery 765 724-3667
169 E State Road 28 Alexandria (46001) *(G-56)*

Nano X Labs, LLC, Crown Point *Also Called: Lightcrafters Nanotech LLC (G-2719)*

Nanochem Technologies LLC 574 970-2436
1203 Kent St Elkhart (46514) *(G-3563)*

Nanosonics Inc 844 876-7466
7205 E 87th St Indianapolis (46256) *(G-8983)*

Nanovis LLC (PA) 260 625-1502
5865 E State Road 14 Columbia City (46725) *(G-2173)*

Nanshan Amer Advnced Alum Tech 765 838-8645
3600 Us Highway 52 S Lafayette (47905) *(G-10657)*

Nap Asset Holdings Ltd 574 295-7651
900 Instamatic Dr Elkhart (46516) *(G-3564)*

Nap Asset Holdings Ltd (PA) 812 482-2000
1180 Wernsing Rd Jasper (47546) *(G-9894)*

NAPA Autoparts Fortville, Fortville *Also Called: Fortville Automotive Sup Inc (G-5594)*

Napier & Napier 765 580-9116
2369 S Us Highway 27 Liberty (47353) *(G-10992)*

Napolean Quarry, Batesville *Also Called: New Point Stone Co Inc (G-598)*

Napoleon Lumber Co 812 852-4545
Us Hwy 421 S Napoleon (47034) *(G-12575)*

Naporamic LLC 463 249-8265
11308 Narrowleaf Dr Indianapolis (46235) *(G-8984)*

Naptown Etching Inc 317 733-8776
7313 Mayflower Park Dr Zionsville (46077) *(G-17036)*

Narrow Gate Publishing LLC 219 464-8579
113 Shorewood Dr Valparaiso (46385) *(G-16008)*

Nasco Industries Inc 812 254-7393
3 Ne 21st St Washington (47501) *(G-16494)*

Nasg Indiana LLC 765 381-4310
3401 W 8th St Muncie (47302) *(G-12467)*

Nash Sheet Metal Co 812 397-5306
4295 E County Road 800 N Shelburn (47879) *(G-14718)*

Nashville Tasting Room 812 720-7080
26 Honeysuckle Ln Nashville (47448) *(G-12677)*

Natalie Anderson LLC 812 951-3532
2007 Brookstone Way Georgetown (47122) *(G-6071)*

Natare, Indianapolis *Also Called: Natare Corporation (G-8985)*

Natare Corporation (PA) 317 290-8828
5905 W 74th St Indianapolis (46278) *(G-8985)*

Natcon, South Bend *Also Called: National Consolidated Corp (G-15159)*

Nates Beef Jerky 765 348-6569
9642 E 811 S Upland (46989) *(G-15879)*

Nates LLC 765 400-4613
2224 Meridian St Anderson (46016) *(G-166)*

Nathan Millis Tools LLC 219 996-3305
115 Poplar Ct Hebron (46341) *(G-7103)*

Nathaniel Bowman 765 365-2358
1107 Durham Dr Crawfordsville (47933) *(G-2592)*

National Athc Sportswear Inc 260 436-2248
3911 Option Pass Fort Wayne (46818) *(G-5255)*

National Caster Acquisition 574 273-7000
4100 Edison Lakes Pkwy Mishawaka (46545) *(G-11958)*

National Casting Corporation 574 273-7000
4100 Edison Lakes Pkwy Mishawaka (46545) *(G-11959)*

National Chimney Supply-VT Inc 317 636-0552
2147c Fletcher Ave Indianapolis (46203) *(G-8986)*

National Coating Line Corp 574 273-7000
4100 Edison Lakes Pkwy Mishawaka (46545) *(G-11960)*

National Consolidated Corp 574 289-7885
25855 State Road 2 South Bend (46619) *(G-15159)*

National Dentex LLC 317 849-5143
8840 Commerce Park Pl Indianapolis (46268) *(G-8987)*

NATIONAL EMBLEM SALES DIV, Indianapolis *Also Called: American Legion National Headquarters (G-7505)*

National Equipment Inc 219 462-1205
358 Harrison Blvd Valparaiso (46383) *(G-16009)*

National Fdrtion State High SC (PA) 317 972-6900
690 W Washington St Indianapolis (46204) *(G-8988)*

National Group, The, Lafayette *Also Called: Copy-Print Shop Inc (G-10556)*

National Gypsum Co, Shoals *Also Called: Proform Finishing Products LLC (G-14910)*

National Gypsum Company, Clinton *Also Called: Ng Operations LLC (G-2073)*

National Gypsum Company, Rensselaer *Also Called: Proform Finishing Products LLC (G-14063)*

National Handicapped Workshop 765 287-8331
5900 W Kilgore Ave Muncie (47304) *(G-12468)*

National Lib Bindery Co of Ind 317 636-5606
55 S State Ave Ste 100 Indianapolis (46201) *(G-8989)*

National Material Company LLC 219 397-5088
4506 Cline Ave East Chicago (46312) *(G-3030)*

National Material LP 219 397-5088
4506 Cline Ave East Chicago (46312) *(G-3031)*

National Mtls Procurement Corp 574 273-7000
4100 Edison Lakes Pkwy Mishawaka (46545) *(G-11961)*

National Printfast, Indianapolis *Also Called: Kingery Group Inc (G-8687)*

National Printing Converters, Brazil *Also Called: NP Converters Inc (G-1158)*

National Products Inc 574 457-4565
201 E Medusa St Syracuse (46567) *(G-15469)*

National Products LLC 219 393-5536
1st Rd Kingsbury Industrial Pk Kingsbury (46345) *(G-10182)*

National Rcreation Systems Inc 260 482-6023
1300 Airport North Office Park Ste D Fort Wayne (46825) *(G-5256)*

National Screen Printing Co, Indianapolis *Also Called: Kessler Concepts Inc (G-8675)*

Natniel Steel Funding Corp 574 273-7000
4100 Edison Lakes Pkwy Mishawaka (46545) *(G-11962)*

National Steel Pellet Company 574 273-7000
4100 Edison Lakes Pkwy Mishawaka (46545) *(G-11963)*

National Stock Dog Registry, Butler *Also Called: International English Inc (G-1467)*

National Tube Form, Fort Wayne *Also Called: Nelson Global Products Inc (G-5261)*

National Tube Form, Fort Wayne *Also Called: Whipp In Holdings LLC (G-5563)*

National Tube Form LLC 260 478-2363
3405 Engle Rd Fort Wayne (46809) *(G-5257)*

Nationwide Publishing Company 260 312-3924
12110 Glen Lake Dr Fort Wayne (46814) *(G-5258)*

Natural Answers 219 922-3663
2300 Ramblewood Dr Ste C Highland (46322) *(G-7147)*

Natural Coating Systems 765 642-2464
3220 W 25th St Anderson (46011) *(G-167)*

Natural Essentials 310 493-6509
3812 Screech Owl Cir Indianapolis (46228) *(G-8990)*

Natural Pharmaceutical Mfg LLC 812 689-3309
117 S Walnut St Osgood (47037) *(G-13413)*

Naturalee Twisted LLC 317 523-1012
5 Kiefer Ct Beech Grove (46107) *(G-700)*

Naturally LLC 317 667-5690
1235 E 52nd St Apt A11 Indianapolis (46205) *(G-8991)*

Naturegenic Inc   **ALPHABETIC SECTION**

Naturegenic Inc (PA)...765 807-5525
   1281 Win Hentschel Blvd Ste 1573 West Lafayette (47906) *(G-16612)*

Natures Alpine Solutions, Corydon *Also Called: Nachurs Alpine Solutions LLC (G-2507)*

Natures Way...317 839-4566
   6246 E County Road 700 S Plainfield (46168) *(G-13707)*

Naturespire LLC...463 266-0395
   10301 Medallion Dr Apt 150 Indianapolis (46231) *(G-8992)*

Natursutten, Greenfield *Also Called: Pebble Natursutten LLC (G-6536)*

Navistar, Indianapolis *Also Called: Navistar Inc (G-8993)*

Navistar Inc...317 787-3113
   1429 Harding Ct Indianapolis (46217) *(G-8993)*

Navistar Cmponent Holdings LLC...317 352-4500
   5565 Brookville Rd Indianapolis (46219) *(G-8994)*

Naya Trans LLC...317 720-8602
   7498 Rockleigh Ave Apt A Indianapolis (46214) *(G-8995)*

Nays Custom Canvas...317 523-4279
   104 Sawgrass Ct Lebanon (46052) *(G-10925)*

NC Coatings LLC...574 213-4754
   30338 County Road 56 Nappanee (46550) *(G-12630)*

Nc2 LLC...260 758-9838
   1 Novae Pkwy Markle (46770) *(G-11359)*

Ncd Indianapolis, Indianapolis *Also Called: New Carbon Company LLC (G-9002)*

Ncd Sbcp, South Bend *Also Called: New Carbon Company LLC (G-15164)*

NCH Corporation...317 899-3660
   8401 E 33rd St Indianapolis (46226) *(G-8996)*

Ncp Coatings Inc...574 255-9678
   1413 Clover Rd Mishawaka (46545) *(G-11964)*

Ncs Welding Inc...574 946-7485
   827 E 25 S Winamac (46996) *(G-16868)*

Nea LLC...574 295-0024
   131 W Marion St Elkhart (46516) *(G-3565)*

Neal Tire & Auto Service, Indianapolis *Also Called: Ben Tire Distributors Ltd (G-7612)*

Nebo Ridge Bicycles, Carmel *Also Called: Nebo Ridge Enterprises LLC (G-1703)*

Nebo Ridge Enterprises LLC...317 471-1089
   4335 W 106th St Ste 900 Carmel (46032) *(G-1703)*

Nechanna One Productions Corp...317 400-8908
   11252 Redskin Ln Apt G Indianapolis (46235) *(G-8997)*

Nector Machine & Fabricating...219 322-6878
   595 Kennedy Ave Schererville (46375) *(G-14536)*

Needles Contract EMB Inc...812 491-9636
   2913 E Mulberry St Evansville (47714) *(G-4219)*

Neely Publishing LLC...574 271-7978
   17145 Barryknoll Way Granger (46530) *(G-6365)*

Neenah Foundry Company...317 875-7245
   5950 W 82nd St Indianapolis (46278) *(G-8998)*

Neeta Sweet Cupcakes n Minis...574 286-7032
   52101 Goldenrod Ln Granger (46530) *(G-6366)*

Neff Engineering, Fort Wayne *Also Called: Neff Group Distributors Inc (G-5259)*

Neff Group Distributors Inc (PA)...260 489-6007
   7114 Innovation Blvd Fort Wayne (46818) *(G-5259)*

Neighborhood Floors & More LLC...219 510-5737
   5822 Us Highway 6 Ste A Portage (46368) *(G-13895)*

Neil Silke...574 999-4866
   5534 Saint Joe Rd Fort Wayne (46835) *(G-5260)*

Nello, South Bend *Also Called: Nello Capital Inc (G-15160)*

Nello Capital Inc (PA)...574 288-3632
   105 E Jefferson Blvd Ste 525 South Bend (46601) *(G-15160)*

Nello Corporation, South Bend *Also Called: Nello Inc (G-15161)*

Nello Inc (HQ)...574 288-3632
   1201 S Sheridan St South Bend (46619) *(G-15161)*

Nelmar Engraving Company, Avon *Also Called: Nelmar Printing Co (G-539)*

Nelmar Printing Co...317 504-7840
   573 Othello Way Avon (46123) *(G-539)*

Nelsen Steel...708 308-6749
   1501 Boca Lago Dr Valparaiso (46383) *(G-16010)*

Nelson Acquisition LLC...574 753-6377
   130 E Industrial Blvd Logansport (46947) *(G-11097)*

Nelson Brothers...812 250-7520
   7525 E Virginia St Evansville (47715) *(G-4220)*

Nelson Global Products Inc...608 719-1752
   3405 Engle Rd Fort Wayne (46809) *(G-5261)*

Nelson Global Products Inc...317 787-5747
   2615 Endress Pl Greenwood (46143) *(G-6746)*

Nelson Global Products Inc...317 782-9486
   2840 Fortune Cir W Ste A Indianapolis (46241) *(G-8999)*

Nelson J Hochstetler...260 499-0315
   2080 E 050 N Lagrange (46761) *(G-10756)*

Nelson Salomon Cruz Ramos LLC...765 863-2885
   821 W Park Ave Kokomo (46901) *(G-10316)*

Nelson Tube Company, Logansport *Also Called: Nelson Acquisition LLC (G-11097)*

Nemco Food Equipment Ltd...260 399-6692
   5316 Hopkinton Dr Fort Wayne (46814) *(G-5262)*

Nemco Medical Ltd...260 484-1500
   8727 Clinton Park Dr Fort Wayne (46825) *(G-5263)*

Nemcomed Fw LLC...260 480-5226
   8727 Clinton Park Dr Fort Wayne (46825) *(G-5264)*

Nemcomed Instrs & Implants...800 255-4576
   8727 Clinton Park Dr Fort Wayne (46825) *(G-5265)*

Neo Industries LLC...219 762-6075
   1775 Willowcreek Rd Portage (46368) *(G-13896)*

Neo Industries LLC (HQ)...574 217-4078
   1400 E Angela Blvd South Bend (46617) *(G-15162)*

Neo Industries (indiana) Inc...219 762-6075
   1775 Willowcreek Rd Portage (46368) *(G-13897)*

Neodyne Technologies, Indianapolis *Also Called: Robert Perez (G-9314)*

Neon Accents...812 537-0102
   101 W Eads Pkwy Lawrenceburg (47025) *(G-10847)*

Neon Amenities Incorporated...765 759-9133
   4060 S County Road 550 W Yorktown (47396) *(G-16978)*

Neon Attractions Incorperated...812 843-5881
   535 10th St Tell City (47586) *(G-15514)*

Neon Services, Indianapolis *Also Called: Billy R Phillips (G-7626)*

Neoteric Hovercraft, Terre Haute *Also Called: Neoteric Incorporated (G-15650)*

Neoteric Incorporated...812 234-1120
   1649 Tippecanoe St Terre Haute (47807) *(G-15650)*

Neoti, Bluffton *Also Called: Neoti LLC (G-1045)*

Neoti LLC...260 494-1499
   910 Lancaster St Bluffton (46714) *(G-1045)*

Neptune Flotation LLC...317 588-3600
   11405 Pennsylvania St Ste 106 Carmel (46032) *(G-1704)*

NERP LLC...574 303-6377
   58016 Crumstown Hwy South Bend (46619) *(G-15163)*

Nestor Sales LLC...574 295-5535
   205 County Road 17 Elkhart (46516) *(G-3566)*

Netegrity Inc...219 763-6400
   5787 Us Highway 6 Portage (46368) *(G-13898)*

Netshape Technologies LLC...317 805-3764
   596 W Oak St Campbellsburg (47108) *(G-1525)*

Neu Scrapbooking Store, Indianapolis *Also Called: Neu Scrapbooking Store LLC (G-9000)*

Neu Scrapbooking Store LLC...317 781-7970
   5309 Kit Dr Indianapolis (46237) *(G-9000)*

Neumayr Lumber Co Inc...765 764-4148
   401 S Union St Attica (47918) *(G-353)*

Neurava Inc...281 995-8055
   1220 Waterway Blvd Indianapolis (46202) *(G-9001)*

New Albany Tribune, Jeffersonville *Also Called: Cnhi LLC (G-9955)*

New Aqua LLC (HQ)...317 272-3000
   7785 E Us Highway 36 Avon (46123) *(G-540)*

New Beginning Logistics LLC...773 457-0325
   5164 E 81st Ave Merrillville (46410) *(G-11547)*

New Beginnings Art Foundry...219 326-7059
   57 Keston Elm Dr La Porte (46350) *(G-10456)*

New Carbon Company LLC...574 247-2270
   1840 Executive Dr Bldg 21 Indianapolis (46241) *(G-9002)*

New Carbon Company LLC...574 247-2270
   24355 Edison Rd South Bend (46628) *(G-15164)*

New Castle Courier Times, New Castle *Also Called: Courier-Times Inc (G-12856)*

New Castle Foundry, New Castle *Also Called: Grede LLC (G-12865)*

New Castle Saw Mill...765 529-6635
   2910 Outer Dr New Castle (47362) *(G-12875)*

New Castle Stainless Plate LLC...765 529-0120
   549 W State Road 38 New Castle (47362) *(G-12876)*

ALPHABETIC SECTION

New Century Publishing..................317 366-9691
1040 E 86th St Ste 42a Indianapolis (46240) *(G-9003)*

New Concept Metal Detector..................765 447-2681
511 N Earl Ave Lafayette (47904) *(G-10658)*

New Dalton Foundry LLC (PA)..................574 267-8111
1900 E Jefferson St Warsaw (46580) *(G-16400)*

New Day Meadery LLC..................317 602-7030
1125 Brookside Ave Ste D1 Indianapolis (46202) *(G-9004)*

New Elements LLC..................219 465-1389
212 Morthland Dr Valparaiso (46383) *(G-16011)*

New End Zone Sporting Goods..................812 254-1895
3089 E. National Hwy Washington (47501) *(G-16495)*

New Energy Corp..................574 233-3116
3201 W Calvert St South Bend (46613) *(G-15165)*

New England Sheets LLC..................978 487-2500
3600 Woodview Trce Ste 300 Indianapolis (46268) *(G-9005)*

New Haven Bakery, New Haven *Also Called: Ganal Corporation (G-12903)*

New Haven Trophies & Shirts..................260 749-0269
710 Broadway St New Haven (46774) *(G-12911)*

New Holland Richmond Inc..................765 962-7724
3100 W Industries Rd Richmond (47374) *(G-14174)*

New Hope Services Inc (PA)..................812 288-8248
725 Wall St Jeffersonville (47130) *(G-10022)*

New Hope Services Inc..................812 752-4892
1642 W Mcclain Ave Ste 1 Scottsburg (47170) *(G-14574)*

New Horizons Baking Co LLC..................260 495-7055
700 W Water St Fremont (46737) *(G-5828)*

New Image Cabinet Coating..................812 228-4666
5506 Briarhill Dr Floyds Knobs (47119) *(G-4686)*

New Image Prtg & Design Inc..................260 969-0410
3233 Lafayette St Fort Wayne (46806) *(G-5266)*

New Market Plastics Inc (PA)..................317 758-5494
3206 S Us Highway 231 Crawfordsville (47933) *(G-2593)*

New Market Welding, New Market *Also Called: Joe Woodrow (G-12926)*

New Millennium Bldg Systems LLC..................260 868-6000
6115 County Road 42 Butler (46721) *(G-1473)*

New Millennium Bldg Systems LLC (HQ)..................260 969-3500
1690 Broadway Ste 19 Fort Wayne (46802) *(G-5267)*

New Nello Operating Co LLC..................574 288-3632
1201 S Sheridan St South Bend (46619) *(G-15166)*

New Palestine Awards, New Palestine *Also Called: NP Awards LLC (G-12941)*

New Philosopher Prss..................812 964-0786
5156 N Brummetts Creek Rd Bloomington (47408) *(G-929)*

New Point Products Inc..................812 663-6311
8563 E State Rte 46 New Point (47263) *(G-12976)*

New Point Products Martguild, New Point *Also Called: New Point Products Inc (G-12976)*

New Point Stone Co Inc..................812 852-4225
8792 N County Road 300 W Batesville (47006) *(G-598)*

New Point Stone Co Inc (PA)..................812 663-2021
992 S County Road 800 E Greensburg (47240) *(G-6622)*

New Point Stone Co Inc..................765 698-2227
24031 Derbyshire Rd Laurel (47024) *(G-10825)*

New Process, Fort Wayne *Also Called: New Process Graphics LLC (G-5268)*

New Process Graphics LLC..................260 489-1700
310 W Cook Rd Fort Wayne (46825) *(G-5268)*

New Process Steel LP..................260 868-1445
4258 County Road 61 Butler (46721) *(G-1474)*

New Readers Press..................317 514-6515
6414 Woodhaven Ct Avon (46123) *(G-541)*

New Star Metals Inc..................219 378-1930
4407 Railroad Ave Ste 3a East Chicago (46312) *(G-3032)*

New Style of Crossroads LLC..................260 593-3800
9585 W 700 S Topeka (46571) *(G-15812)*

New Time Inc..................219 655-5041
1464 Indianapolis Blvd Whiting (46394) *(G-16836)*

New York Blower Company..................217 347-3233
171 Factory St La Porte (46350) *(G-10457)*

New-Indy Containerboard, Hartford City *Also Called: New-Indy Hartford City LLC (G-7073)*

New-Indy Hartford City LLC (DH)..................765 348-5440
501 S Spring St Hartford City (47348) *(G-7073)*

Newco Metals Inc..................765 644-6649
1515 E 22nd St Anderson (46016) *(G-168)*

Newco Metals Inc (PA)..................317 485-7721
7268 S State Road 13 Pendleton (46064) *(G-13546)*

Newco Metals Processing, Bedford *Also Called: Recycling Services Indiana Inc (G-666)*

Newcomed Inc..................260 484-1500
8727 Clinton Park Dr Fort Wayne (46825) *(G-5269)*

Newell Industrial LLC..................260 636-3336
200 E Park Dr Albion (46701) *(G-36)*

Newlett Inc..................574 294-8899
435 Harrison St Elkhart (46516) *(G-3567)*

Newlins Wldg & Tank Maint LLC..................765 245-2741
5360 U S Hwy 36 E Montezuma (47862) *(G-12082)*

Newmar Corporation (HQ)..................574 773-7791
355 Delaware St Nappanee (46550) *(G-12631)*

Newpark Resources Inc..................765 546-9473
205 S Walnut St Ridgeville (47380) *(G-14236)*

Newport Pallet Inc..................217 497-8220
1888 S State Rd 63 Newport (47966) *(G-13031)*

Newport Pallet Inc..................765 505-9463
1110 W Industrial Dr Hillsdale (47854) *(G-7163)*

News & Tribune, Jeffersonville *Also Called: Southern Indiana Bus Source (G-10056)*

News 4 U Magazine, Evansville *Also Called: Emp of Evansville (G-4034)*

News and Tribune..................812 206-2168
221 Spring St Jeffersonville (47130) *(G-10023)*

News Dispatch (HQ)..................219 874-7211
422 Franklin St Ste B Michigan City (46360) *(G-11645)*

News Examiner Circulation Dept..................765 825-2914
406 N Central Ave Connersville (47331) *(G-2458)*

News Herald Newspaper, Marion *Also Called: News-Herald Inc (G-11320)*

News Journal, North Manchester *Also Called: Manchester North News Journal (G-13238)*

News Publishing, Tell City *Also Called: News Publishing Company LLC (G-15515)*

News Publishing Company LLC..................812 649-4440
541 Main St Rockport (47635) *(G-14346)*

News Publishing Company LLC (DH)..................502 633-4334
542 7th St Tell City (47586) *(G-15515)*

News Publishing Company Inc (DH)..................260 461-8444
600 W Main St Fort Wayne (46802) *(G-5270)*

News Reminder..................574 583-5121
114 S Main St Monticello (47960) *(G-12161)*

News-Banner Publications Inc..................260 824-0224
125 N Johnson St Bluffton (46714) *(G-1046)*

News-Gazette..................765 584-4501
123 W Franklin St Winchester (47394) *(G-16895)*

News-Herald Inc..................765 425-8903
120 E 4th St Marion (46952) *(G-11320)*

News-Sentinel, Fort Wayne *Also Called: Fort Wayne Newspapers Inc (G-4999)*

News-Sun, The, Fairmount *Also Called: Allen C Terhune & Associates (G-4407)*

News-Times, Winchester *Also Called: Hartford City News Times (G-16889)*

Newsletter Express Ltd..................317 876-8916
3500 Depauw Blvd Ste 1000 Indianapolis (46268) *(G-9006)*

Newslink Inc..................317 202-0210
6255 Evanston Ave Indianapolis (46220) *(G-9007)*

Newsnow Dubois County..................812 827-6131
511 Newton St Jasper (47546) *(G-9895)*

Newspaper Holding Inc..................270 678-5171
221 Spring St Jeffersonville (47130) *(G-10024)*

Newspaper Holding Inc..................812 231-4200
222 S 7th St Terre Haute (47807) *(G-15651)*

Newspaper Holding Inc..................812 254-0480
102 E Van Trees St Washington (47501) *(G-16496)*

Newspaper Solutions, Avon *Also Called: Ao Inc (G-504)*

Newton Business Forms..................812 256-5399
104 Bates Dr Charlestown (47111) *(G-1887)*

Newton County Stone Co, Kentland *Also Called: Rogers Group Inc (G-10163)*

Newton Wldg & Fabrication LLC..................765 365-5129
1020 E College St Crawfordsville (47933) *(G-2594)*

Newtons Legacy Wdwkg Engrv LLC..................812 322-3360
2920 N Hartstrait Rd Bloomington (47404) *(G-930)*

Nexgen Group Inc..................574 218-6363
3400 W Market St Nappanee (46550) *(G-12632)*

Nexgen Mold & Tool Inc..................812 945-3375
4300 Security Pkwy New Albany (47150) *(G-12784)*

(PA)=Parent Co (HQ)=Headquarters (DH)=Div Headquarters

Next Day Signs 574 259-7446
13565 Us 20 Mishawaka (46545) *(G-11965)*

Next Day Signs, Greenwood *Also Called: Sign Guys Inc (G-6767)*

Next Day Signs, Indianapolis *Also Called: D D McKay and Associates (G-7943)*

Next Day Signs & Images, Mishawaka *Also Called: Next Day Signs (G-11965)*

Next Gen Power Holdings LLC 574 971-4490
3002 Coast Ct Elkhart (46514) *(G-3568)*

Next Gnrtion Dlrshp Warsaw LLC 463 234-9400
9225 Priority Way West Dr Ste 300 Indianapolis (46240) *(G-9008)*

Next Level Candles LLC 574 347-1030
521 Cottage Grove Ave South Bend (46616) *(G-15167)*

Next Level Logo Store Inc 219 344-5141
811 Fairfield Ave La Porte (46350) *(G-10458)*

Next Offset Solutions Inc 773 844-1784
203 Gardenia Dr West Lafayette (47906) *(G-16613)*

Next Phase Graphics 260 627-6259
16825 Lima Rd Huntertown (46748) *(G-7259)*

Next Products LLC 317 392-4701
2201 E Michigan Rd Shelbyville (46176) *(G-14780)*

Next Reformation Publishing Co 317 650-1364
4086 Hennessey Dr Plainfield (46168) *(G-13708)*

Nexvoo Inc 866 910-8366
8517 Oakmont Ln Indianapolis (46260) *(G-9009)*

Nexxt Spine LLC 317 436-7801
14425 Bergen Blvd Ste B Noblesville (46060) *(G-13141)*

Nf Friction Composites Inc 574 516-1131
1441 Holland St Logansport (46947) *(G-11098)*

Nf Industries Inc 317 738-2558
401 Arvin Rd Franklin (46131) *(G-5759)*

Nfi Industries Inc 765 483-9741
510 S Enterprise Blvd Lebanon (46052) *(G-10926)*

Ng Instruments, Inc., Warsaw *Also Called: Nginstruments LLC (G-16401)*

Ng Operations LLC 765 828-0898
75 Ivy Ln Clinton (47842) *(G-2073)*

Ng Operations LLC 765 828-0371
2230 N Main St Clinton (47842) *(G-2074)*

NG OPERATIONS, LLC, Clinton *Also Called: Ng Operations LLC (G-2074)*

Ngh Retail LLC 219 476-0772
315 E 316 N Ste A Valparaiso (46383) *(G-16012)*

Ngh Retail LLC 219 476-0772
301 W 550 N Valparaiso (46385) *(G-16013)*

Nginstruments LLC 574 268-2112
4643 N State Road 15 Warsaw (46582) *(G-16401)*

Nhi-Jrj Corp 574 293-9690
316 Roske Dr Elkhart (46516) *(G-3569)*

Nhk Seating of America Inc 765 605-2443
2195 W Barner St Frankfort (46041) *(G-5683)*

Nhk Seating of America Inc (DH) 765 659-4781
2298 W State Road 28 Frankfort (46041) *(G-5684)*

Niagara Bottling LLC 909 230-5000
350 Logistics Ave Jeffersonville (47130) *(G-10025)*

Niagara Bottling LLC 909 758-5313
1250 Whitaker Rd Plainfield (46168) *(G-13709)*

Niagara Lasalle Corporation (HQ) 219 853-6000
1412 150th St Hammond (46327) *(G-6986)*

Nibco, Elkhart *Also Called: Nibco Inc (G-3570)*

Nibco Inc 812 256-8500
204 Pike St Charlestown (47111) *(G-1888)*

Nibco Inc (PA) 574 295-3000
1516 Middlebury St Elkhart (46516) *(G-3570)*

Nibco Inc 574 296-1240
701 Eisenhower Dr N Goshen (46526) *(G-6227)*

Niblock Excavating Inc (PA) 574 848-4437
906 Maple St Bristol (46507) *(G-1281)*

Niblock Excavating Inc 260 248-2100
1080 Spartan Dr Ste C Columbia City (46725) *(G-2174)*

Nice-Pak Products Inc 845 365-1700
1 Nice Pak Rd Mooresville (46158) *(G-12228)*

Nice-Pak Products Inc 317 839-0373
381 Airtech Pkwy Plainfield (46168) *(G-13710)*

Nicholas Bryant 765 366-0108
2539 E School House Rd Hillsboro (47949) *(G-7161)*

Nicholas Mendel 574 870-8856
101 S Washington St Delphi (46923) *(G-2904)*

Nicholas Precision Works LLC 260 306-3426
1101 Taylor St North Manchester (46962) *(G-13244)*

Nichols Mfg Co Inc 219 696-8577
1006 W 203rd Ave Lowell (46356) *(G-11174)*

Nichols Operating LLC 812 753-3600
8157 S 100 W Fort Branch (47648) *(G-4706)*

Nicholson and Sons Prtg Inc 812 283-1200
209 Eastern Blvd Jeffersonville (47130) *(G-10026)*

Nicholson Printing, Jeffersonville *Also Called: Nicholson and Sons Prtg Inc (G-10026)*

Nick-Em Builders LLC 574 992-8313
501 N Park Ave Logansport (46947) *(G-11099)*

Nick-Em Builders LLC (PA) 574 516-1060
1005 W Broadway Logansport (46947) *(G-11100)*

Nickel Enterprises, Elkhart *Also Called: Patrick Industries Inc (G-3596)*

Nickprint Inc (PA) 317 489-3033
484 E Carmel Dr Carmel (46032) *(G-1705)*

Nicks Automotive Inc 765 964-6843
2741 N 700 E Union City (47390) *(G-15856)*

Nicorr LLC 574 342-0700
4050 Lincoln Hwy Bourbon (46504) *(G-1124)*

Nicosin Extursion Inc 812 442-6751
2058 W County Road 1200 N Brazil (47834) *(G-1157)*

Nidec Motor Corporation 812 385-2564
1551 E Broadway St Princeton (47670) *(G-14007)*

Nielsen Company 812 889-3493
1602 S 1066 W Lexington (47138) *(G-10979)*

Nielsen Enterprises Inc 574 277-3748
51950 Chicory Ln Granger (46530) *(G-6367)*

Night Lights Company LLC 574 606-4288
1323 Lemans Cir Apt 606 Indianapolis (46205) *(G-9010)*

Nighthawk Enterprises LLC 317 576-9235
8658 Castle Park Dr Ste 101 Indianapolis (46256) *(G-9011)*

Nightkrawler Kustoms LLC 812 599-0251
1690 W State Highway 250 Paris Crossing (47270) *(G-13503)*

Nik-O-Lok Company, Indianapolis *Also Called: Standard Change-Makers Inc (G-9492)*

Nike, Michigan City *Also Called: Nike Inc (G-11646)*

Nike Inc 219 879-1320
917 Lighthouse Pl Michigan City (46360) *(G-11646)*

Nina Gail Diamonds LLC 765 591-0477
2013 S Lazy Creek Dr Muncie (47302) *(G-12469)*

Ninas Scrub Boutique LLC 833 445-1955
1735 Lockerbie Ct Anderson (46011) *(G-169)*

Nineplus Tables LLC 317 471-7606
14238 Chariots Whisper Dr Carmel (46074) *(G-1706)*

Ninth Avenue Foods, Columbus *Also Called: Heritage Distributing Company (G-2316)*

Nippon Steel Pipe America Inc (DH) 812 523-0842
1515 E 4th Street Rd Seymour (47274) *(G-14669)*

Nipro Phrmpckging Amricas Corp 812 591-2332
1108 N State Road 3 Westport (47283) *(G-16749)*

Nisco, Topeka *Also Called: Nishikawa Cooper LLC (G-15813)*

Nishikawa Cooper LLC 260 593-2156
501 High Rd Bremen (46506) *(G-1208)*

Nishikawa Cooper LLC 260 593-2156
2785 Persistence Dr Fort Wayne (46808) *(G-5271)*

Nishikawa Cooper LLC 248 978-6953
5120 Investment Dr Fort Wayne (46808) *(G-5272)*

Nishikawa Cooper LLC (DH) 260 593-2156
324 Morrow St Topeka (46571) *(G-15813)*

Nishikawa of America Inc (HQ) 260 593-2156
324 Morrow St Topeka (46571) *(G-15814)*

Nisley, L R & Sons, Goshen *Also Called: L R Nisley & Sons (G-6195)*

Nistem, Zionsville *Also Called: Nitto Inc (G-17037)*

Nitas Scrubs Zone LLC 317 204-6576
11533 Signet Ln Indianapolis (46235) *(G-9012)*

Nite Owl Promotions Inc 812 876-3888
7011 N Red Hill Rd Ellettsville (47429) *(G-3810)*

Nitrex Inc 317 346-7700
350 Blue Chip Ct Franklin (46131) *(G-5760)*

Nitro Alley Graphix LLC 317 286-3294
1185 E Northfield Dr Ste A Brownsburg (46112) *(G-1390)*

ALPHABETIC SECTION — North American Stamping Group

Nitto Inc 317 879-2840
10505 Bennett Pkwy Ste 300 Zionsville (46077) *(G-17037)*

Nix & Company LLC 219 595-5541
417 Mayfair Ct Munster (46321) *(G-12552)*

Nix Sanitary Service 812 785-1158
703 S 2nd St Boonville (47601) *(G-1094)*

Nixon Tool Company Inc 765 966-6608
301 N 3rd St Richmond (47374) *(G-14175)*

NJ Logging LLC 812 597-0782
1766 W Three Story Hill Rd Morgantown (46160) *(G-12261)*

Nk Welding Products Inc 260 424-1901
302 W Superior St Fort Wayne (46802) *(G-5273)*

Nka Cabinet Designs LLC 765 490-4661
90 Professional Ct Lafayette (47905) *(G-10659)*

Nkahoots Bdy Bath Butters LLC 317 559-2442
1412 E Main St Crawfordsville (47933) *(G-2595)*

Nkg Sales 317 626-6555
12136 Pepperwood Dr Indianapolis (46236) *(G-9013)*

Nlmk, Portage Also Called: Nlmk Indiana LLC *(G-13899)*

Nlmk Indiana LLC 219 787-8200
6500 S Boundary Rd Portage (46368) *(G-13899)*

Nmc Inc 812 648-2636
8068 E Main St Dugger (47848) *(G-2959)*

Nna Beverages, Indianapolis Also Called: Mbv-Midwest LLC *(G-8859)*

No Fan Clothing LLC 312 371-7648
12610 Misty Ridge Ct Fishers (46037) *(G-4569)*

No Limit Outdoor Sign Co LLC 765 457-1877
2501 N Apperson Way Kokomo (46901) *(G-10317)*

No Limits Just Pssbilities LLC 930 465-1218
1509 Cottonwood Dr Princeton (47670) *(G-14008)*

No More Bugs 317 658-6096
5008 Bonnie Brae St Indianapolis (46228) *(G-9014)*

No-Load Fund Investor Inc 317 571-1471
10534 Coppergate Carmel (46032) *(G-1707)*

No-Sail Splash Guard Co Inc 765 522-2100
10254 N Us Highway 231 Roachdale (46172) *(G-14248)*

Noah Worcester Derm Society 317 257-5907
8365 Keystone Xing Indianapolis (46240) *(G-9015)*

Noahvpn, Carmel Also Called: Sky Cryptoassets LLC *(G-1763)*

Nob Hill Vineyards LLC 260 402-6070
844 S Clear Lake Dr Fremont (46737) *(G-5829)*

Nobbe Concrete Products Inc 765 647-4017
11177 Us Highway 52 Brookville (47012) *(G-1329)*

Noble Composites Inc 574 533-1462
2424 E Kercher Rd Goshen (46526) *(G-6228)*

Noble County Welding Inc 260 897-4082
635 S Van Scoyoc St Avilla (46710) *(G-490)*

Noble Industrial Fabrications, Avilla Also Called: Noble County Welding Inc *(G-490)*

Noble Industries Inc 317 773-1926
17575 Presley Dr Noblesville (46060) *(G-13142)*

Noble Project Services LLC 219 484-9669
822 W 39th Pl Hobart (46342) *(G-7202)*

Noble Transportation LLC 317 488-7710
3701 Rome Ter Indianapolis (46228) *(G-9016)*

Noble Wire Products Inc 317 773-1926
Noblesville (46061) *(G-13143)*

Noble Wire Products Inc 317 773-1926
101 Madsen St Orland (46776) *(G-13369)*

Noble Woodworks 765 525-4226
8988 S 475 E Saint Paul (47272) *(G-14468)*

Nobleman Logistics LLC 317 340-7406
4514 Brookhollow Blvd Indianapolis (46254) *(G-9017)*

Noblesville Pack & Ship 317 776-6306
199 N 9th St Noblesville (46060) *(G-13144)*

Noblesville Sand & Gravel, Noblesville Also Called: Marietta Martin Materials Inc *(G-13130)*

Noblitt Fabricating, Columbus Also Called: Noblitt International Corp *(G-2360)*

Noblitt Fabricating, Columbus Also Called: Noblitt International Corp *(G-2361)*

Noblitt International Corp 812 372-9969
4572 N Long Rd Columbus (47203) *(G-2360)*

Noblitt International Corp 812 372-9969
4735 N Indianapolis Rd Columbus (47203) *(G-2361)*

Nochar Inc 317 613-3046
1311 W 96th St Ste 240 Indianapolis (46260) *(G-9018)*

Noel Studio Inc 317 297-1117
8533 Zionsville Rd Indianapolis (46268) *(G-9019)*

Noel-Smyser Engineering Corp 317 293-2215
4005 Industrial Blvd Indianapolis (46254) *(G-9020)*

Nolan Co, Jeffersonville Also Called: Eagle Industries Inc *(G-9973)*

Noneman Machine Corp 260 632-5311
4517 Bull Rapids Rd Woodburn (46797) *(G-16955)*

Nonferrous Products Inc 317 738-2558
401 Arvin Rd Franklin (46131) *(G-5761)*

Noodle Shop Co - Colorado Inc 219 548-0921
71 Silhavy Rd Ste 101 Valparaiso (46383) *(G-16014)*

Nor-Cote International, Crawfordsville Also Called: Nor-Cote International Inc *(G-2597)*

Nor-Cote International Inc 800 488-9180
506 Lafayette Ave Crawfordsville (47933) *(G-2596)*

Nor-Cote International Inc (PA) 800 488-9180
605 Lafayette Ave Crawfordsville (47933) *(G-2597)*

Norco Industries Inc 574 262-3400
2600 Jeanwood Dr Elkhart (46514) *(G-3571)*

Norco Industries Inc 800 347-2232
2800 Northland Dr Elkhart (46514) *(G-3572)*

Norco Industries Inc 574 262-3400
2600 Jeanwood Dr Elkhart (46514) *(G-3573)*

Norcraft Companies Inc (DH) 800 297-0661
1 Masterbrand Cabinets Dr Jasper (47546) *(G-9896)*

Norcraft Companies LP (DH) 812 482-2527
1 Masterbrand Cabinets Dr Jasper (47546) *(G-9897)*

Norcraft Holding LLC 812 482-2527
1 Masterbrand Cabinets Dr Jasper (47546) *(G-9898)*

Nori Metals 574 213-4344
1420 S Walnut St South Bend (46619) *(G-15168)*

Norine S Herbs 574 642-4272
14746 County Road 34 Goshen (46528) *(G-6229)*

Norlightspresscom 812 675-8054
762 State Road 458 Bedford (47421) *(G-659)*

Norman Stein & Associates 260 749-5468
9520 Paulding Rd New Haven (46774) *(G-12912)*

Norman Tool Inc 812 867-3496
15415 Old State Rd Evansville (47725) *(G-4221)*

Norman Wagler 812 636-8015
Rd 700 E Rr1 33a Odon (47562) *(G-13346)*

Norres North America Inc 855 667-7370
701 W Chippewa Ave Ste 200 South Bend (46614) *(G-15169)*

Norris Arms Co LLC 574 658-4163
405 N Old State Road 15 Milford (46542) *(G-11801)*

Norris Thermal Tech Inc 574 353-7855
7930 N 700 E Tippecanoe (46570) *(G-15762)*

Norstam Veneers Inc 812 732-4391
2990 Overlook Dr Sw Mauckport (47142) *(G-11441)*

North America Frac Sand Inc (PA) 260 490-9990
215 N Jefferson St Ossian (46777) *(G-13429)*

North America Packaging Corp 317 291-2396
6061 Guion Rd Indianapolis (46254) *(G-9021)*

North America Packaging Corp 219 462-8915
4002 Montdale Park Dr Valparaiso (46383) *(G-16015)*

North American Composites, Mishawaka Also Called: Ip Corporation *(G-11913)*

North American Extrusn & Assem 260 636-3336
200 E Park Dr Albion (46701) *(G-37)*

North American Ink 765 659-6000
2642 W State Road 28 Frankfort (46041) *(G-5685)*

North American Latex Corp 812 268-6608
49 Industrial Park Dr Sullivan (47882) *(G-15415)*

North American Lighting, Elberfeld Also Called: North American Lighting Inc *(G-3116)*

North American Lighting Inc 812 983-2663
11833 Industrial Park Dr Elberfeld (47613) *(G-3116)*

North American Mfg Inc 765 948-3337
619 E Jefferson St Fairmount (46928) *(G-4411)*

North American Signs Inc (PA) 574 234-5252
3601 Lathrop St South Bend (46628) *(G-15170)*

North American Stamping Group, Muncie Also Called: Nasg Indiana LLC *(G-12467)*

(PA)=Parent Co (HQ)=Headquarters (DH)=Div Headquarters

North Central Equipment C   **ALPHABETIC SECTION**

North Central Equipment C 574 825-2006
   59871 E County Line Rd Middlebury (46540) *(G-11741)*

North Central Ind Shavings LLC 765 395-3875
   307 E Dunn St Converse (46919) *(G-2478)*

North Central Pallets Inc 574 892-6142
   13990 State Road 10 Argos (46501) *(G-325)*

North Coast Organics LLC 260 246-0289
   629 E Washington Blvd Fort Wayne (46802) *(G-5274)*

North Indianapolis Quarry, Carmel *Also Called: Martin Marietta Materials Inc (G-1694)*

North Star Distributing, Lafayette *Also Called: Ice Cream Specialties Inc (G-10603)*

North Star Distributing, Merrillville *Also Called: Ice Cream Specialties Inc (G-11523)*

North Star Stone Inc 219 464-7272
   312 N 325 E Valparaiso (46383) *(G-16016)*

North Vernon Division, North Vernon *Also Called: Martinrea Industries Inc (G-13285)*

North Vernon Industry (HQ) 812 346-8772
   3750 N County Road 75 W North Vernon (47265) *(G-13289)*

North Webster Construction Inc 574 834-4448
   7240 N State Road 13 North Webster (46555) *(G-13310)*

North Woods Village, Mishawaka *Also Called: True North Group LLC (G-12018)*

North-Side Machine & Tool Inc 765 654-4538
   1604 N County Road 0 Ew Frankfort (46041) *(G-5686)*

Northbend Pattern Works Inc 812 637-3000
   28080 Ziegler Blvd West Harrison (47060) *(G-16550)*

Northeast Bottling Co 260 343-0208
   250 W Vine St Kendallville (46755) *(G-10139)*

Northeast Enterprises Inc 260 485-8011
   6428 Saint Joe Center Rd Ste A Fort Wayne (46835) *(G-5275)*

Northeast Quality Services LLC 860 632-7242
   719 Bexley Rd West Lafayette (47906) *(G-16614)*

Northeast Welding, Fort Wayne *Also Called: Northeast Enterprises Inc (G-5275)*

Northeast Woodworking 260 665-1986
   1450 N 140 W Angola (46703) *(G-278)*

Northedge Steel LLC 336 594-0171
   900 New York Ave New Castle (47362) *(G-12877)*

Northedge Steel LLC 765 444-6021
   13901 W Jackson St Yorktown (47396) *(G-16979)*

Northern Box Company Inc 574 264-2161
   1328 Mishawaka St Elkhart (46514) *(G-3574)*

Northern Brace Company Inc (PA) 574 233-4221
   610 N Michigan St Ste 104 South Bend (46601) *(G-15171)*

Northern Brace Nthrn Prsthtics, South Bend *Also Called: Northern Brace Company Inc (G-15171)*

Northern Division, Indianapolis *Also Called: Altec Industries Inc (G-7493)*

Northern Electric Company Inc 574 289-7791
   116 N Hill St South Bend (46617) *(G-15172)*

Northern Foundry LLC 218 263-8871
   1401 S Grandstaff Dr Auburn (46706) *(G-413)*

Northern Ind Indus Catings LLC 574 893-4621
   619 E Main St Akron (46910) *(G-6)*

Northern Indiana Axle LLC 574 773-3039
   1780 W Market St Nappanee (46550) *(G-12633)*

Northern Indiana Axle Co, Nappanee *Also Called: Mullets Fencing and Supplies (G-12628)*

Northern Indiana Manufacturing (PA) 574 342-2105
   202 S Ecker Ave Bourbon (46504) *(G-1125)*

Northern Indiana Mfg, Chesterton *Also Called: Electro Seal Corporation (G-1922)*

Northern Indiana Oil LLC 317 966-0288
   8553 Zionsville Rd Indianapolis (46268) *(G-9022)*

Northern Indiana Ordnance Co 574 289-5938
   60161 Mayflower Rd South Bend (46614) *(G-15173)*

Northern Indiana Packg Co Inc (DH) 260 356-9660
   1200 Riverfork Dr Huntington (46750) *(G-7345)*

Northern Indiana Truss LLC 574 858-0505
   2208 N 500 W Warsaw (46580) *(G-16402)*

Northern Prosthetics Inc 574 233-2459
   610 N Michigan St Ste 104 South Bend (46601) *(G-15174)*

Northern Tool & Die LLC 260 495-7314
   501 E Depot St Fremont (46737) *(G-5830)*

Northern Trans & Differential 219 764-4009
   6641 Melton Rd Portage (46368) *(G-13900)*

Northern Wood Products Inc 574 586-3068
   3573 Thorn Rd Walkerton (46574) *(G-16272)*

Northfield Block Company 800 424-0190
   901 E Troy Ave Indianapolis (46203) *(G-9023)*

Northside Machine, Dugger *Also Called: Nmc Inc (G-2959)*

Northside Machining Inc 812 683-3500
   304 W 12th St Huntingburg (47542) *(G-7288)*

Northside Pattern Works Inc 317 290-0501
   10222 Terri Ln Brownsburg (46112) *(G-1391)*

Northside Wldg Fabrication LLC 317 844-2240
   375 E 106th St Carmel (46280) *(G-1708)*

Northtech Machine LLC 812 967-7400
   102 Walnut St Borden (47106) *(G-1116)*

Northwest Alum Fabricators Inc 219 844-4354
   6103 Kennedy Ave Hammond (46323) *(G-6987)*

Northwest Defense LLC 931 257-0421
   335 E 550 N Rensselaer (47978) *(G-14061)*

Northwest Farm Fertilizers 219 785-2331
   4725 S Us Highway 421 Westville (46391) *(G-16764)*

Northwest Ind Backflow Testers 219 663-8390
   5910 E 129th Ave Crown Point (46307) *(G-2726)*

Northwest Ind Fabrication LLC 219 613-7461
   8900 Mississippi St Ste C Merrillville (46410) *(G-11548)*

Northwest Indiana Newsppr Inc 574 722-5000
   517 E Broadway Logansport (46947) *(G-11101)*

Northwest Indus Specialist Inc 219 397-7446
   4333 Indianapolis Blvd East Chicago (46312) *(G-3033)*

Northwest Interiors Inc 574 294-2326
   405 Pine Creek Ct Elkhart (46516) *(G-3575)*

Northwest News, Fort Wayne *Also Called: Northwest News & Printing (G-5276)*

Northwest News & Printing 260 637-9003
   3306 Independence Dr Fort Wayne (46808) *(G-5276)*

Northwind Electronics LLC 317 288-0787
   8875 Bash St Indianapolis (46256) *(G-9024)*

Northwind Pharmaceuticals LLC 317 436-8522
   9402 Uptown Dr Ste 1200 Indianapolis (46256) *(G-9025)*

Northwind Pharmaceuticals LLC 800 722-0772
   212 W 10th St Ste A310 Indianapolis (46202) *(G-9026)*

Norton Packaging Inc 574 867-6002
   5190 N Industrial Pkwy Hamlet (46532) *(G-6864)*

Nortool Precision Machining Tl 574 262-3400
   2600 Jeanwood Dr Elkhart (46514) *(G-3576)*

Nose and Mustache LLC 260 758-8800
   300 N Tracy St Markle (46770) *(G-11360)*

Not For Profit 501c3 RES Inst, Bloomington *Also Called: Center For The Study Knwldge D (G-827)*

Notary Hayes LLC 219 292-4531
   1050 Broadway Ste 19 Chesterton (46304) *(G-1950)*

Notetech Industries LLC 574 326-3188
   21125 Protecta Dr Elkhart (46516) *(G-3577)*

Notre Dame Press, Notre Dame *Also Called: University Notre Dame Du Lac (G-13318)*

Nouvex, New Albany *Also Called: Poly Group LLC (G-12796)*

Nov Inc 317 897-3099
   9870 E 30th St Indianapolis (46229) *(G-9027)*

Nov Oak Woodworking 812 422-1973
   913 Washington Ave Evansville (47713) *(G-4222)*

Nova, Evansville *Also Called: Nova Polymers Incorporated (G-4223)*

Nova Manufacturing 512 750-5165
   1153 S Avon Ave Avon (46123) *(G-542)*

Nova Packaging Group Inc 765 651-2600
   2409 W 2nd St Marion (46952) *(G-11321)*

Nova Pak, Marion *Also Called: Nova Packaging Group Inc (G-11321)*

Nova Polymers Incorporated 812 476-0339
   2650 Eastside Park Rd Evansville (47715) *(G-4223)*

Novae Corp 260 982-7075
   11870 N 650 E North Manchester (46962) *(G-13245)*

NOVAE CORP., North Manchester *Also Called: Novae Corp (G-13245)*

Novae LLC (PA) 260 758-9838
   1 Novae Pkwy Markle (46770) *(G-11361)*

Novamatiq Inc 260 483-1153
   1515 Dividend Rd Fort Wayne (46808) *(G-5277)*

Novaprints, Indianapolis *Also Called: Novaprints LLC (G-9028)*

Novaprints LLC 317 577-6682
   7805 E 89th St Indianapolis (46256) *(G-9028)*

ALPHABETIC SECTION

Novartis Corporation 317 852-3839
  30 Lakeshore Pl Brownsburg (46112) *(G-1392)*

Novelis Corporation 812 462-2287
  5901 N 13th St Terre Haute (47805) *(G-15652)*

Novels By Nellotie 812 583-1196
  393 Sonny Dorsett Rd Mitchell (47446) *(G-12045)*

Novo Nrdisk RES Ctr Indnplis I 541 520-8030
  5225 Exploration Dr Indianapolis (46241) *(G-9029)*

NP Awards LLC 317 861-0825
  5188 W Windmill Way New Palestine (46163) *(G-12941)*

NP Converters Inc 812 448-2555
  18 S Murphy Ave Brazil (47834) *(G-1158)*

Npm Holdings Inc 812 689-3309
  117 S Walnut St Osgood (47037) *(G-13414)*

Npp Packaging Graphics 317 522-2010
  610 White Oak Ct Zionsville (46077) *(G-17038)*

NPS Xofigo Mfg Plant 5889 .... 317 981-4129
  4343 W 62nd St Indianapolis (46268) *(G-9030)*

Npx One LLC 201 791-7600
  7950 Allison Ave Indianapolis (46268) *(G-9031)*

NPX One, LLC, Indianapolis *Also Called: Npx One LLC (G-9031)*

NRC Modifications Inc 574 825-3646
  51045 Greenfield Pkwy Middlebury (46540) *(G-11742)*

Nrk Inc 812 232-1800
  924 Lafayette Ave Terre Haute (47804) *(G-15653)*

Nrp Jones LLC 219 362-9908
  28 Industrial Pkwy La Porte (46350) *(G-10459)*

Nrp Jones LLC (PA) 800 348-8868
  302 Philadelphia St La Porte (46350) *(G-10460)*

NS Holdings Corporation 574 273-7000
  4100 Edison Lakes Pkwy Mishawaka (46545) *(G-11966)*

NS Land Company 574 273-7000
  4100 Edison Lakes Parkway Mishawaka (46545) *(G-11967)*

Nsci 317 820-6526
  301 American Way N Carmel (46032) *(G-1709)*

Nsignia Screen Printing 260 420-0500
  512 W Superior St Fort Wayne (46802) *(G-5278)*

Nsignia Screenprinting, Fort Wayne *Also Called: Brenmeer LLC (G-4816)*

NSK Corporation 765 458-5000
  1112 E Kitchel Rd Liberty (47353) *(G-10993)*

NSK Corporation, Liberty Plant, Liberty *Also Called: NSK Corporation (G-10993)*

NSK Prcsion Amer Bllscrew Plan, Franklin *Also Called: NSK Precision America Inc (G-5762)*

NSK Precision America Inc 317 738-5000
  3450 Bearing Dr Franklin (46131) *(G-5762)*

NSK Services Inc 812 695-2004
  5384 N Kellerville Rd Jasper (47546) *(G-9899)*

Nspire LLC 219 301-2446
  1325 Bigger St Gary (46404) *(G-5987)*

Nst Campbellsburg LLC 812 755-4501
  14670 Cumberland Rd Noblesville (46060) *(G-13145)*

Nst Technologies Mim LLC 812 755-4501
  596 W Oak St Campbellsburg (47108) *(G-1526)*

Nst Technologies Mim LLC (HQ) 812 248-9273
  14670 Cumberland Rd Noblesville (46060) *(G-13146)*

Ntk Prcsion Axle Corp - Andrso 765 221-7800
  7635 S Layton Rd Anderson (46011) *(G-170)*

Ntk Precision Axle Corporation 765 656-1000
  741 S County Road 200 W Frankfort (46041) *(G-5687)*

NTN Driveshaft Inc 812 342-7000
  8251 S International Dr Columbus (47201) *(G-2362)*

Nu Led Lighting 317 989-7352
  1147 Old Vines Ct Greenwood (46143) *(G-6747)*

Nu Wave Manufacturing LLC 317 989-4703
  3173 E Main St Danville (46122) *(G-2821)*

Nuaxon Bioscience Inc 812 762-4400
  899 S College Mall Rd Unit 161 Bloomington (47401) *(G-931)*

Nuclear Measurements Corp 317 546-2415
  2460 N Arlington Ave Indianapolis (46239) *(G-9032)*

Nucor Building Systems, Waterloo *Also Called: Nucor Corporation (G-16526)*

Nucor Corporation 765 364-1323
  4537 S Nucor Rd Crawfordsville (47933) *(G-2598)*

Nucor Corporation 260 337-1800
  6610 County Road 60a Saint Joe (46785) *(G-14440)*

Nucor Corporation 260 337-1606
  6730 County Road 60 Saint Joe (46785) *(G-14441)*

Nucor Corporation 260 337-1808
  County Road 60 Saint Joe (46785) *(G-14442)*

Nucor Corporation 260 837-7891
  305 Industrial Pkwy Waterloo (46793) *(G-16525)*

Nucor Corporation 260 837-7891
  250 Industrial Pkwy Waterloo (46793) *(G-16526)*

Nucor Corporation 260 837-7891
  250 Industrial Pkwy Waterloo (46793) *(G-16527)*

Nucor Fastener, Saint Joe *Also Called: Nucor Corporation (G-14441)*

Nucor Harris Rebar Midwest LLC 317 831-2456
  149 Sycamore Ln Mooresville (46158) *(G-12229)*

Nucor Rebar Fabrication S LLC (PA) 260 925-5440
  1342 S Grandstaff Dr Auburn (46706) *(G-414)*

Nucor Steel Corp 765 364-1323
  4537 S Nucor Rd Crawfordsville (47933) *(G-2599)*

Nucor Tubular Products 812 265-7548
  4004 N Us 421 Madison (47250) *(G-11246)*

Nuevopoly LLC 317 260-0026
  8481 Bash St Ste 700 Indianapolis (46250) *(G-9033)*

Nugent Sand Company 812 372-7508
  5205 W State Road 46 Columbus (47201) *(G-2363)*

Nukemed Inc 765 437-1631
  3358 W 800 S Bunker Hill (46914) *(G-1442)*

Nukemed Inc 574 271-2800
  17490 Dugdale Dr South Bend (46635) *(G-15175)*

Numark Industries Company Ltd 317 718-2502
  7124 E County Road 150 S Ste B Avon (46123) *(G-543)*

Numerical Concepts Inc 812 466-5261
  4040 1st Pkwy Terre Haute (47804) *(G-15654)*

Numerical Productions Inc 317 783-1362
  3901 S Arlington Ave Indianapolis (46203) *(G-9034)*

Numerix Inc 260 248-2942
  406 Diamond Ave Ste B Columbia City (46725) *(G-2175)*

Nunez Farm & Road Svc, Winchester *Also Called: Paul Nunez Road Service (G-16898)*

Nupointe Energy LLC 765 981-2664
  1323 W 600 S Warren (46792) *(G-16302)*

Nussmeier Engraving Company 812 425-1339
  933 Main St Evansville (47708) *(G-4224)*

Nut House Woodworks LLC 317 345-7177
  247 E 1550 N Summitville (46070) *(G-15426)*

Nutramaize, West Lafayette *Also Called: Nutramaize LLC (G-16615)*

Nutramaize LLC 765 273-8274
  1281 Win Hentschel Blvd Unit 046 West Lafayette (47906) *(G-16615)*

Nutritional Research Assoc (PA) 260 723-4931
  407 E Broad St South Whitley (46787) *(G-15322)*

Nuvo Inc 317 254-2400
  3951 N Meridian St Ste 200 Indianapolis (46208) *(G-9035)*

Nuvo Newsweekly, Indianapolis *Also Called: Nuvo Inc (G-9035)*

Nuwave Manufacturing 317 987-8229
  68 N Gale St Ste G Indianapolis (46201) *(G-9036)*

Nvb Playgrounds Inc 317 826-2777
  10859 E Washington St # 100 Indianapolis (46229) *(G-9037)*

Nvsd LLC 502 561-0007
  2235 Corydon Pike New Albany (47150) *(G-12785)*

Nwhoodtales Corp 708 858-0598
  2436 Wicker Ave Highland (46322) *(G-7148)*

Nwi Print & Mail LLC 219 916-1358
  1050 Flagstone Dr Dyer (46311) *(G-2979)*

Nwi Signs 219 796-0948
  10726 W 151st Ave Cedar Lake (46303) *(G-1834)*

Nwitimescom 219 933-3200
  601 45th St Munster (46321) *(G-12553)*

Nxp Semiconductors, Kokomo *Also Called: Nxp Usa Inc (G-10318)*

Nxp Usa Inc 765 459-5355
  2733 Albright Rd Kokomo (46902) *(G-10318)*

Nyx LLC 734 838-3570
  3900 Green Valley Rd New Albany (47150) *(G-12786)*

Nyx Fort Wayne LLC.. 260 484-0595
  616 W Mckinley Ave Mishawaka (46545) *(G-11968)*
Nyx New Albany, New Albany Also Called: Beach Acquisition Co LLC *(G-12698)*
Nyxperimental LLC... 765 684-7077
  580 Locust St Middletown (47356) *(G-11776)*
Nyxperimental LLC... 914 506-0266
  634 N Pendleton Ave Pendleton (46064) *(G-13547)*
O & P Lab, Evansville Also Called: Orthotic & Prosthetic Lab *(G-4229)*
O & R Precision Grinding Inc.. 260 368-9394
  225 Heritage Trl Berne (46711) *(G-721)*
O C Tanner Company.. 317 575-8553
  3850 Priority Way South Dr Ste 116 Indianapolis (46240) *(G-9038)*
O D P, Franklin Also Called: Orthodontic Design & Prod Inc *(G-5763)*
O-M Distributors Inc... 219 853-1900
  724 Hoffman St Hammond (46327) *(G-6988)*
O'SULLIVANS ITALIAN PUB, Fort Wayne Also Called: Tfs Inc *(G-5478)*
O&T Alliance Group LLC.. 302 287-0953
  7432 River Walk Dr Indianapolis (46214) *(G-9039)*
O3 Solutions, Huntertown Also Called: Clute Enterprises Inc *(G-7250)*
Oak & Stone Excavating & Cnstr.................................. 812 361-6901
  7811 W Eller Rd Bloomington (47403) *(G-932)*
Oak Brook Foot Ankle Spclsts P................................... 219 214-2047
  10176 W 400 N Ste D Michigan City (46360) *(G-11647)*
Oak Hill Winery LLC... 765 395-3632
  111 E Marion St Converse (46919) *(G-2479)*
Oak Security Group LLC... 317 585-9830
  10640 E 59th St Ste 200 Indianapolis (46236) *(G-9040)*
Oak Tree Experimental Farm, Washington Also Called: Perdue Farms Inc *(G-16501)*
Oak View Tooling Inc... 260 244-7677
  724 E Swihart St Columbia City (46725) *(G-2176)*
Oaken Barrel Brewing Co Inc...................................... 317 887-2287
  50 Airport Pkwy Ste L Greenwood (46143) *(G-6748)*
Oakenbarrel.com, Greenwood Also Called: Oaken Barrel Brewing Co Inc *(G-6748)*
Oakes... 765 384-5317
  2728 N 500 W Marion (46952) *(G-11322)*
Oakleaf Industries Inc.. 317 414-2040
  9914 Soaring Eagle Ln Fishers (46055) *(G-4645)*
Oakley Brothers Distillery... 765 274-5590
  34 W 8th St Anderson (46016) *(G-171)*
Oakley Industries LLC.. 812 246-2600
  1229 Bringham Dr Ste B Sellersburg (47172) *(G-14608)*
Oaklief LLC... 765 642-9010
  3211 Jay Dr Anderson (46012) *(G-172)*
Oasis Bath, Plymouth Also Called: Oasis Lifestyle LLC *(G-13799)*
Oasis Lifestyle, Plymouth Also Called: Composite Tech Assemblies LLC *(G-13765)*
Oasis Lifestyle LLC.. 574 948-0004
  1400 Pidco Dr Plymouth (46563) *(G-13799)*
Oasis Pumps Mfg Co.. 812 783-2146
  3001 Curtis Rd Mount Vernon (47620) *(G-12313)*
Oasis Software Solutions.. 620 515-1240
  1910 Saint Joe Center Rd Fort Wayne (46825) *(G-5279)*
OBannon Publishing Company.................................... 812 738-4552
  117 W Walnut St Corydon (47112) *(G-2508)*
Obelisk Re-Play Opco LLC.. 866 228-1485
  7284 W 200 N Greenfield (46140) *(G-6534)*
OBrien Jack & Pat Enterprises..................................... 765 653-5070
  1208 W County Road 125 S Greencastle (46135) *(G-6422)*
OBryan Barrel Company Inc.. 812 479-6741
  5501 Old Boonville Hwy Evansville (47715) *(G-4225)*
Observer, The, Notre Dame Also Called: University Notre Dame Du Lac *(G-13317)*
Occasions Group Inc... 812 623-2225
  957 N Meridian St Sunman (47041) *(G-15442)*
Occoutdoors Inc.. 317 862-2584
  6597 W 300 N Boggstown (46110) *(G-1075)*
Oce Corporate Printing Div... 260 436-7395
  6915 Innovation Blvd Fort Wayne (46818) *(G-5280)*
Ocella Inc.. 845 842-8185
  7970 S Energy Dr Newberry (47449) *(G-12990)*
Ocella Tech, Newberry Also Called: Ocella Inc *(G-12990)*
Oconnorwoodworking.. 812 364-1022
  3059 W May Dr Palmyra (47164) *(G-13483)*

Octobers Firm Label LLC.. 317 778-1447
  57 Lions Creek Ct S Noblesville (46062) *(G-13147)*
Odb Inc.. 260 673-0062
  7203 Wintergreen Dr Fort Wayne (46814) *(G-5281)*
Odin Corporation... 317 849-3770
  6736 E 82nd St Indianapolis (46250) *(G-9041)*
Odon Journal, Odon Also Called: Myers Enterprises Inc *(G-13344)*
Odon Saw Mill, Odon Also Called: Odon Sawmill Inc *(G-13347)*
Odon Sawmill Inc... 812 636-7314
  304 S Gum St Odon (47562) *(G-13347)*
Odyssey Machine, Georgetown Also Called: Odyssey Machine Inc *(G-6072)*
Odyssey Machine Inc... 812 951-1160
  9627 State Road 64 Georgetown (47122) *(G-6072)*
Odyssian Technology LLC.. 574 257-7555
  511 E Colfax Ave South Bend (46617) *(G-15176)*
Oeding Corporation.. 812 367-1271
  443 W 16th St Ferdinand (47532) *(G-4446)*
Oehlers Woods... 317 848-2698
  1481 W 136th St Carmel (46032) *(G-1710)*
OEM Solution Center, Indianapolis Also Called: Cummins Crosspoint LLC *(G-7923)*
Oerlikon Balzers Coating USA..................................... 765 935-7424
  1580 Progress Dr Richmond (47374) *(G-14176)*
Oesterling Chimney Sweep Inc................................... 812 372-3512
  2360 N National Rd Columbus (47201) *(G-2364)*
Off The Pallet LLC... 317 674-2711
  3276 E State Road 32 Westfield (46074) *(G-16713)*
Office Furniture Liquidators, Evansville Also Called: Evansville Corp Design Inc *(G-4050)*
Office Hub, Shelbyville Also Called: A & H Enterprises LLC *(G-14729)*
Office Sup of Southern Ind Inc (PA)............................ 812 283-5523
  417 Spring St Jeffersonville (47130) *(G-10027)*
Official Sports Intl Inc.. 574 269-1404
  4120 Corridor Dr Warsaw (46582) *(G-16403)*
Offset House Inc... 317 849-5155
  9374 Castlegate Dr Indianapolis (46256) *(G-9042)*
Offset House Printing, Indianapolis Also Called: Offset House Inc *(G-9042)*
Offset One Inc... 260 456-8828
  1609 S Calhoun St Fort Wayne (46802) *(G-5282)*
Ofs Brands, Huntingburg Also Called: Ofs Brands Holdings Inc *(G-7289)*
Ofs Brands Holdings Inc (PA)..................................... 800 521-5381
  1204 E 6th St Huntingburg (47542) *(G-7289)*
Ogden Welding Systems Inc....................................... 219 322-5252
  372 Division St Schererville (46375) *(G-14537)*
Oger, Greenfield Also Called: Wethington *(G-6571)*
Ogre Holdings Inc.. 765 675-8841
  641 Cleveland St Tipton (46072) *(G-15785)*
OH Hunt Lines Inc... 260 856-2125
  591 N Jefferson St Cromwell (46732) *(G-2632)*
Ohana Donuts and Ice Cream LLC (PA)....................... 317 288-0922
  11640 Brooks School Rd Ste 100 Fishers (46037) *(G-4570)*
OHaras Sports Inc... 219 836-5554
  1844 45th St Munster (46321) *(G-12554)*
Ohio County News, The, Rising Sun Also Called: Delphos Herald of Indiana Inc *(G-14241)*
Ohio River Trading Co.. 765 653-4100
  8090 S State Road 243 Cloverdale (46120) *(G-2092)*
Ohio River Veneer LLC... 812 824-7928
  650 E Empire Mill Rd Bloomington (47401) *(G-933)*
Ohio Transmission Corporation................................... 812 466-2734
  1502 Lafayette Ave Terre Haute (47804) *(G-15655)*
Ohio Valley Caviar... 812 338-4367
  1927 E Shelton Rd English (47118) *(G-3845)*
Ohio Valley Creative Enrgy Inc................................... 502 468-9787
  626 Albany St New Albany (47150) *(G-12787)*
Ohio Valley Door Corp... 812 945-5285
  2143 Willow St New Albany (47150) *(G-12788)*
Ohio Valley Electric... 812 532-5288
  800 Aep Dr Lawrenceburg (47025) *(G-10848)*
Ohio Valley Precision Inc... 812 539-3687
  42 Doughty Rd Lawrenceburg (47025) *(G-10849)*
Ohio Valley Ready Mix, Jeffersonville Also Called: Kentucky Concrete Indiana LLC *(G-10008)*
Ohio Valley Ready Mix Inc... 812 282-6671
  2220 Hamburg Pike Jeffersonville (47130) *(G-10028)*

ALPHABETIC SECTION

Ohio Vly Fuel Injction Svc Inc 812 987-5857
  5905 Stacy Rd Charlestown (47111) *(G-1889)*

Ohio Vly Screen Prtrs EMB Engr 812 539-3307
  139 W Tate St Ste 3 Lawrenceburg (47025) *(G-10850)*

OHM Automotive LLC 812 879-5455
  3748 S Claybridge Dr Bloomington (47401) *(G-934)*

OHM Enterprise LLC 812 879-5455
  2534 State Highway 67 Gosport (47433) *(G-6288)*

Oil and Go, Crown Point *Also Called: Jay Costas Companies Inc (G-2700)*

Oil Palace, Indianapolis *Also Called: Oil Palace Limited (G-9043)*

Oil Palace Limited 317 679-9187
  4525 Lafayette Rd Ste L Indianapolis (46254) *(G-9043)*

Oil Technology Inc 219 322-2724
  1112 Us Highway 41 # 208 Schererville (46375) *(G-14538)*

Oilfield Research Inc 812 424-2907
  7825 Old Orchard Trl Evansville (47712) *(G-4226)*

Okos Family Farms LLC 765 567-2750
  4505 Pretty Prairie Rd Battle Ground (47920) *(G-613)*

Old Bob's, Avon *Also Called: Woodland Manufacturing & Sup (G-557)*

Old Capital Printing LLC 812 946-9444
  3314 Grant Line Rd Ste 3 New Albany (47150) *(G-12789)*

Old Dutch Sand Co Inc 219 938-7020
  4600 E 15th Ave Gary (46403) *(G-5988)*

Old Fort Distillery Inc 260 705-5128
  12311 Saint Joe Rd Grabill (46741) *(G-6317)*

Old Fort Tee Company LLC 248 506-3762
  4930 Woodhurst Blvd Fort Wayne (46807) *(G-5283)*

Old Foundry Toy Works 765 742-1020
  6325 N 500 E Lebanon (46052) *(G-10927)*

Old Guy Woodcrafters LLC 574 527-9044
  1312 Freedom Pkwy Winona Lake (46590) *(G-16913)*

Old Hickory Furniture, Shelbyville *Also Called: Old Hickory Furniture Company Inc (G-14781)*

Old Hickory Furniture Company Inc (PA) 317 398-3151
  403 S Noble St Shelbyville (46176) *(G-14781)*

Old Hoosier Meats 574 825-2940
  101 Wayne St Middlebury (46540) *(G-11743)*

Old Ip Inc 574 294-3253
  2221 Industrial Pkwy Elkhart (46516) *(G-3578)*

Old JB LLC 812 288-0200
  1701 E Market St Jeffersonville (47130) *(G-10029)*

OLD PATHS TRACT SOCIETY, Shoals *Also Called: Old Paths Tract Society Inc (G-14909)*

Old Paths Tract Society Inc 812 247-2560
  11298 Old Paths Ln Shoals (47581) *(G-14909)*

Old Plastics Company Inc 812 699-0379
  12759 W 300 N Linton (47441) *(G-11041)*

Old Remco Holdings LLC (DH) 765 778-6499
  600 Corporation Dr Pendleton (46064) *(G-13548)*

Old Rev LLC (PA) 317 580-2420
  16855 Southpark Dr Ste 100 Westfield (46074) *(G-16714)*

Old World Fudge & Cds Dogs LLC 260 610-2249
  206 Raleigh Ct Columbia City (46725) *(G-2177)*

Oldcastle Buildingenvelope Inc 317 876-1155
  8441 Bearing Dr Indianapolis (46268) *(G-9044)*

Olde York Potato Chips Inc
  918 W Cook Rd Fort Wayne (46825) *(G-5284)*

Oldenburg Pallet Inc 812 933-0568
  19349 Tony Rd Batesville (47006) *(G-599)*

Ole Mexican Foods Inc 574 359-7262
  5945 W 84th St Indianapolis (46278) *(G-9045)*

Olive Branch Etc Inc 765 449-1884
  181 Sagamore Pkwy S Ste B Lafayette (47905) *(G-10660)*

Oliver Machine & Tl Corp 765 349-2271
  110 Industrial Dr Martinsville (46151) *(G-11419)*

Oliver Machine and Tool Corp 765 349-2271
  110 Industrial Dr Mooresville (46158) *(G-12230)*

Oliver Wine Company Inc (HQ) 812 876-5800
  200 E Winery Rd Bloomington (47404) *(G-935)*

Oliver Winery, Bloomington *Also Called: Oliver Wine Company Inc (G-935)*

Olken Company, Michigan City *Also Called: Ronard Industries Inc (G-11658)*

Olon Industries Inc (us) 812 256-6400
  600 Patrol Rd Jeffersonville (47130) *(G-10030)*

Olon Industries Inc (us) 812 254-0427
  2510 E National Hwy Washington (47501) *(G-16497)*

Olson Custom Designs LLC 317 892-6400
  4825 W 79th St Indianapolis (46268) *(G-9046)*

Olson Race Cars 765 529-6933
  129 N 26th St New Castle (47362) *(G-12878)*

Olympia Business Systems Inc 800 225-5644
  251 Wedcor Ave Wabash (46992) *(G-16206)*

Olympia Candy Kitchen LLC 574 533-5040
  136 N Main St Goshen (46526) *(G-6230)*

Olympic Fiberglass Industries 574 223-3101
  1235 E 4th St Rochester (46975) *(G-14310)*

Olympus Management LLC 317 412-7977
  17062 Olympus Ct Westfield (46062) *(G-16715)*

Olympus Manufacturing Systems 219 465-1520
  4703 N Calumet Ave Valparaiso (46383) *(G-16017)*

Omco, Piercton *Also Called: Midwest Roll Forming & Mfg Inc (G-13635)*

Omega, Bristol *Also Called: Reshcor Inc (G-1285)*

Omega Cabinetry, Jasper *Also Called: Omega Cabinets Ltd (G-9900)*

Omega Cabinets Ltd (HQ) 319 235-5700
  1 Masterbrand Cabinets Dr Jasper (47546) *(G-9900)*

Omega Co 317 831-4471
  12494 N Woodlawn Dr Mooresville (46158) *(G-12231)*

Omega Engineering LLC 317 995-1965
  6731 Winnock Dr Indianapolis (46220) *(G-9047)*

Omega Enterprises Inc 765 584-1990
  732 W Washington St Winchester (47394) *(G-16896)*

Omega National Products LLC 574 295-5353
  1010 Rowe St Elkhart (46516) *(G-3579)*

Omega One Connect Inc 317 626-3445
  3825 E 78th St Indianapolis (46240) *(G-9048)*

Omega Process Solutions LLC 574 546-5606
  860 Legner St # 870 Bremen (46506) *(G-1209)*

Omega Products Inc 574 546-5606
  870 Legner St Bremen (46506) *(G-1210)*

OMI Industries, Rising Sun *Also Called: OMI Industries Inc (G-14244)*

OMI Industries Inc 812 438-9218
  1300 Barbour Way Rising Sun (47040) *(G-14244)*

Omicron Biochemicals Inc 574 287-6910
  115 S Hill St South Bend (46617) *(G-15177)*

Omni Auto Parts, Fort Wayne *Also Called: Omnisource LLC (G-5286)*

Omni Oxide, Indianapolis *Also Called: Metals and Additives LLC (G-8890)*

Omni Plastics, Evansville *Also Called: Omni Plastics LLC (G-4227)*

Omni Plastics LLC 812 422-0888
  2300 Lynch Rd Evansville (47711) *(G-4227)*

Omni Tech Intrmdate Hldngs LLC (PA) 786 201-2094
  779 Rudolph Way Greendale (47025) *(G-6449)*

Omni Technologies Inc (PA) 812 537-4102
  779 Rudolph Way Greendale (47025) *(G-6450)*

Omni Technologies Inc 812 539-4144
  80 Brown St Greendale (47025) *(G-6451)*

Omnicell Co 812 376-0747
  1015 Rocky Ford Rd Columbus (47203) *(G-2365)*

Omnimax International LLC 574 848-7432
  5201 Investment Dr Fort Wayne (46808) *(G-5285)*

Omnimax International LLC 574 773-7981
  2341 E Market St Nappanee (46550) *(G-12634)*

Omnion Power Inc 317 259-9264
  3148 E 48th St Indianapolis (46205) *(G-9049)*

Omnisource LLC (HQ) 260 422-5541
  7575 W Jefferson Blvd Fort Wayne (46804) *(G-5286)*

Omnisource LLC 574 654-7561
  54450 Smilax Rd New Carlisle (46552) *(G-12843)*

Omnisource Marketing Group Inc 317 575-3300
  8925 N Meridian St Ste 150 Indianapolis (46260) *(G-9050)*

Omnitech Systems Inc 219 531-5532
  450 Campbell St Ste 2 Valparaiso (46385) *(G-16018)*

Omr North America Inc 317 510-9700
  4755 Gilman St Speedway (46224) *(G-15337)*

On Call McGraw LLC 317 938-8777
  1507 N Downey Ave Indianapolis (46219) *(G-9051)*

On Point Machining Inc..219 393-5132
  7111 Union Center Rd Kingsbury (46345) *(G-10183)*
On Point Precision LLC..317 590-2510
  3633 N Grant Ave Indianapolis (46218) *(G-9052)*
On Semiconductor, Kokomo *Also Called: Semicndctor Cmponents Inds LLC (G-10333)*
On Site Welding & Maintenance..................................812 755-4184
  7632 E County Road 240 N Campbellsburg (47108) *(G-1527)*
On Target, Sunman *Also Called: Goods On Target Sporting Inc (G-15438)*
On The Ball Rmdlg & Repr LLP......................................812 910-9408
  212 W 9th St Bicknell (47512) *(G-736)*
On The Go Logistics LLC..765 810-7454
  1426 Dewey St Anderson (46016) *(G-173)*
On The Go Portable Water Softe...................................260 482-9614
  3905 W Roll Ave Bloomington (47403) *(G-936)*
On The Spot Welding LLC..317 746-6699
  1936 S Lynhurst Dr Ste D Indianapolis (46241) *(G-9053)*
On-Site Wldg Mllright Svcs LLC.....................................317 843-9773
  9844 Chambray Dr Carmel (46280) *(G-1711)*
On-Time LLC...708 890-0230
  6507 Ohio Ave Hammond (46323) *(G-6989)*
Oncite LLC..765 874-1500
  6741 E 500 S Union City (47390) *(G-15857)*
One Body Software LLC..260 494-8354
  12022 Waterside Ct Fort Wayne (46814) *(G-5287)*
One Eight Seven, Gary *Also Called: One Eight Seven Incorporated (G-5989)*
One Eight Seven Incorporated......................................219 886-2060
  1050 Michigan St Gary (46402) *(G-5989)*
One Lineage Trucking Corp...708 257-6333
  636 Mckinley St Gary (46404) *(G-5990)*
One Little Truck LLC...872 276-0014
  2343 81st St Highland (46322) *(G-7149)*
One Source Fabrication LLC...574 259-6011
  325 S Lafayette Blvd South Bend (46601) *(G-15178)*
One Source Labs, New Albany *Also Called: Workflow Solutions LLC (G-12831)*
One-Stop Travel Shop Inc...812 339-9496
  317 E Dodds St Bloomington (47401) *(G-937)*
ONeal Wood Products Inc...765 342-2709
  1120 Lenvoil Rd Martinsville (46151) *(G-11420)*
Onesource Water..866 917-7873
  1060 N Capitol Ave Ste E230 Indianapolis (46204) *(G-9054)*
Onfield Apparel Group LLC...317 895-7249
  8677 Impact Ct Indianapolis (46219) *(G-9055)*
Onion Enterprises Inc..317 762-6007
  5705 W 73rd St Indianapolis (46278) *(G-9056)*
Online Packaging Incorporated....................................219 872-0925
  124 Tri Quad Dr Michigan City (46360) *(G-11648)*
Only Alpha, Fort Wayne *Also Called: Trivector Manufacturing Inc (G-5509)*
Only Get Better Logistics LLC.......................................317 835-5606
  6022 Morning Dove Dr Indianapolis (46228) *(G-9057)*
Onlydrams LLC..219 707-6025
  814 N 400 E Valparaiso (46383) *(G-16019)*
Onsite Construction Services.......................................312 723-8060
  416 Jefferson Ave Chesterton (46304) *(G-1951)*
Onspot of North America Inc (HQ)...............................203 377-0777
  1075 Rodgers Park Dr North Vernon (47265) *(G-13290)*
Onsyte Mobile Labs LLC..800 570-6844
  1251 N Eddy St Ste 200 South Bend (46617) *(G-15179)*
Ontime Toys Inc (PA)...317 598-9333
  9190 Corporation Dr Ste 106 Indianapolis (46256) *(G-9058)*
ONu Acres LLC..765 565-1355
  9350 W 800 N Carthage (46115) *(G-1816)*
Onward Manufacturing Company (DH).......................260 358-4111
  1000 E Market St Huntington (46750) *(G-7346)*
Onxx Tool Inc..260 897-3530
  135 Nicholas Pl Avilla (46710) *(G-491)*
Onyett Fabricators, Petersburg *Also Called: Smgf LLC (G-13625)*
Onyett Welding & Machine Inc.....................................812 582-2999
  409 N 8th St Petersburg (47567) *(G-13620)*
Onyett, A.B. & Sons, Petersburg *Also Called: Onyett Welding & Machine Inc (G-13620)*
Ooley Products Inc..317 787-9351
  405 W Raymond St Indianapolis (46225) *(G-9059)*

Ooshirts Inc..317 246-9083
  7800 Records St Ste C Indianapolis (46226) *(G-9060)*
Ooten Pattern Works..317 244-7348
  1101 N Eleanor St Indianapolis (46214) *(G-9061)*
Op1vet, Goshen *Also Called: Operation 1 Veteran Inc (G-6231)*
Open Control Systems LLC..317 429-0627
  905 N Capitol Ave Ste 200 Indianapolis (46204) *(G-9062)*
Open Gate Design & Decor, Anderson *Also Called: Open Gate LLC (G-174)*
Open Gate LLC..765 734-1314
  2834 N 900 W Anderson (46011) *(G-174)*
Open Kitchen LLC...317 974-9966
  4022 Shelby St Indianapolis (46227) *(G-9063)*
Open Range Rv, Shipshewana *Also Called: Highland Ridge Rv Inc (G-14850)*
Open Range Rv Company..260 768-7771
  3195 N State Road 5 Shipshewana (46565) *(G-14872)*
Operation 1 Veteran Inc..574 536-5536
  20201 Eagle Hill Ln Goshen (46528) *(G-6231)*
Opflex, Indianapolis *Also Called: Opflex Solutions Inc (G-9064)*
Opflex Environmental Tech, Indianapolis *Also Called: Opflex Technologies LLC (G-9065)*
Opflex Solutions Inc..800 568-7036
  733 S West St Indianapolis (46225) *(G-9064)*
Opflex Technologies LLC (HQ).....................................518 568-7036
  733 S West St Indianapolis (46225) *(G-9065)*
Opflex Technologies LLC..317 731-6123
  2525 N Shadeland Ave Indianapolis (46219) *(G-9066)*
Opi Inc
  71 E 400 S Ste A Albion (46701) *(G-38)*
Opportunities Inc...574 518-0606
  6122 N 675 E North Webster (46555) *(G-13311)*
Oprato Software LLC...317 573-0168
  14155 Wicksworth Way Carmel (46032) *(G-1712)*
Opta (usa) Inc...716 446-8888
  5th Rd Bldg 4 Kingsbury (46345) *(G-10184)*
Opta Minerals (holdco) Inc...574 586-9559
  205 Plymouth Laporte Tr State Hwy 104 Walkerton (46574) *(G-16273)*
Optical Disc Solutions Inc..765 935-7574
  1767 Sheridan St Richmond (47374) *(G-14177)*
Optical Solutions LLC LLC...317 525-8308
  Fishers (46038) *(G-4571)*
Optiviz Media LLC..812 681-1711
  1420 Wheeler St Vincennes (47591) *(G-16141)*
Optum Pharmacy 702 LLC..812 256-8600
  1050 Patrol Rd Jeffersonville (47130) *(G-10031)*
Orange Cnty Wldg & Fabrication.................................812 653-5754
  6063 N County Road 200 E Orleans (47452) *(G-13378)*
Orange County Processing...812 865-2028
  5028 N State Road 37 Orleans (47452) *(G-13379)*
Orano Med LLC...469 638-0632
  1145 E Northfield Dr Brownsburg (46112) *(G-1393)*
Orb, Indianapolis *Also Called: Orb LLC (G-9067)*
Orb LLC...833 946-4672
  8016 Sandi Ct Indianapolis (46260) *(G-9067)*
Orbital Installation Tech LLC..317 774-3668
  9750 E 150th St Ste 1200 Noblesville (46060) *(G-13148)*
Orchard Lane Cabinets..574 825-7568
  14425 County Road 126 Goshen (46528) *(G-6232)*
Orchid Systems, Carmel *Also Called: Messagenet Systems Inc (G-1699)*
Ordonez Construccion Svcs LLC..................................317 771-1213
  825 S Fleming St Indianapolis (46241) *(G-9068)*
Oreca, Indianapolis *Also Called: Oreca North America Inc (G-9069)*
Oreca North America Inc..317 517-2948
  3950 Guion Ln Indianapolis (46268) *(G-9069)*
Oreo Effect LLC...574 404-4800
  1233 Woodfield Ave South Bend (46615) *(G-15180)*
Org Chem Group LLC (PA)..812 464-4446
  2406 Lynch Rd Evansville (47711) *(G-4228)*
Organi Gro, New Castle *Also Called: Md/Lf Incorporated (G-12874)*
Organic Bread of Heaven, Gary *Also Called: Organic Bread of Heaven LLC (G-5991)*
Organic Bread of Heaven LLC......................................219 883-5126
  2700 W 5th Ave Gary (46404) *(G-5991)*

ALPHABETIC SECTION — Overgaards Artcraft Printers

Organized Living Inc..812 334-8839
1500 S Strong Dr Bloomington (47403) *(G-938)*

Original Brdford Soap Wrks Inc..................................812 342-6854
7667 S International Dr Columbus (47201) *(G-2366)*

Original Tractor Cab Co Inc......................................765 663-2214
6849 West Front St Arlington (46104) *(G-329)*

Orion Global Sourcing Inc..812 332-3338
1516 S Walnut St Bloomington (47401) *(G-939)*

Orion Safety Products, Peru *Also Called: Standard Fusee Corporation (G-13602)*

Orion Shipping Solutions Corp...................................800 410-4910
201 N Illinois St Ste 1600 Indianapolis (46204) *(G-9070)*

Orka Technologies LLC...812 378-9842
2182 W 500 N Columbus (47201) *(G-2367)*

Orla Bontrater..260 768-7553
1310 S 900 W Shipshewana (46565) *(G-14873)*

Ornamental Division, Anderson *Also Called: Mofab Inc (G-157)*

Ornamental Division, Anderson *Also Called: Mofab Inc (G-158)*

Orora Packaging Solutions.......................................317 879-4628
4635 W 84th St Ste 500 Indianapolis (46268) *(G-9071)*

Orpro Prosthetics & Orthotics, Richmond *Also Called: Hanger Prsthtics Orthotics Inc (G-14131)*

Orr Cabinet Co...260 636-7757
300 E Washington St Albion (46701) *(G-39)*

Orr Cabinetry, Albion *Also Called: Orr Cabinet Co (G-39)*

Orr Motor Sports...260 244-2681
3151 S State Road 9 Columbia City (46725) *(G-2178)*

Orthoconcepts Inc..317 727-0100
10947 Echo Grove Cir Indianapolis (46236) *(G-9072)*

Orthodontic Design & Prod Inc (PA).............................317 346-6655
40 Linville Way Franklin (46131) *(G-5763)*

Orthopediatrics, Warsaw *Also Called: Orthopediatrics Corp (G-16404)*

Orthopediatrics Corp (PA)..574 268-6379
2850 Frontier Dr Warsaw (46582) *(G-16404)*

Orthopediatrics US Dist..574 268-6379
2850 Frontier Dr Warsaw (46582) *(G-16405)*

Orthopedic Precision Instrs, Albion *Also Called: Opi Inc (G-38)*

Orthos Inc...574 406-8145
100 E Wayne St Ste 410 South Bend (46601) *(G-15181)*

Orthotic & Prosthetic Lab..812 479-6298
125 N Weinbach Ave Ste 310 Evansville (47711) *(G-4229)*

Orthotic Prosthetic Specialist...................................219 836-8668
625 Ridge Rd Ste D Munster (46321) *(G-12555)*

Orton Crane, Huntington *Also Called: Orton-Mccullough Crane Company (G-7347)*

Orton-Mccullough Crane Company.................................260 356-7900
1244 E Market St Huntington (46750) *(G-7347)*

Orville Redenbacher Popcorn, Brookston *Also Called: Conagra Brands Inc (G-1310)*

Osborn LLC (HQ)...414 277-9300
2350 N Salisbury Rd Richmond (47374) *(G-14178)*

Osborn Manufacturing Corp......................................574 267-6156
960 N Lake St Warsaw (46580) *(G-16406)*

Osc Holdings LLC..765 751-7000
1150 W Kilgore Ave Muncie (47305) *(G-12470)*

Oscar Telecom Inc..317 359-7000
5812 Hartle Dr Indianapolis (46216) *(G-9073)*

Osgood Journal, Versailles *Also Called: Ripley Publishing Co Inc (G-16103)*

OSI Specialties Inc..317 293-4858
6299 Guion Rd Indianapolis (46268) *(G-9074)*

Osr Inc..812 342-7642
6893 S International Dr Columbus (47201) *(G-2368)*

Osram Inc..317 847-6268
310 E Main St Westfield (46074) *(G-16716)*

Ossian Plant, Ossian *Also Called: TI Group Auto Systems LLC (G-13441)*

Osterfeld Industries...219 926-4646
1050 Broadway # Stsuite8 Chesterton (46304) *(G-1952)*

Osterholt Construction Inc......................................260 672-3493
3648 N Norwood Rd Huntington (46750) *(G-7348)*

Osterholt Truss, Huntington *Also Called: Osterholt Construction Inc (G-7348)*

Ostler Enterprises Inc...765 656-1275
1624 W Armstrong Rd Frankfort (46041) *(G-5688)*

Otech, Rolling Prairie *Also Called: OTech Corporation (G-14367)*

OTech Corporation...219 778-8001
4744 E Oak Knoll Rd Rolling Prairie (46371) *(G-14367)*

Otis Dynamic Enterprises LLC (PA)..............................860 978-6003
5534 Saint Joe Rd Fort Wayne (46835) *(G-5288)*

Otp Industrial Solutions, Terre Haute *Also Called: Ohio Transmission Corporation (G-15655)*

Ottenweller Co Inc (PA)...260 484-3166
3011 Congressional Pkwy Fort Wayne (46808) *(G-5289)*

Ottenweller Company LLC..260 245-0197
2321 Bremer Rd Fort Wayne (46803) *(G-5290)*

Otter Creek Candle LLC..812 750-4129
2303 N Old Michigan Rd Holton (47023) *(G-7219)*

Otter Creek Christian Church....................................812 446-5300
6299 N Crow St Brazil (47834) *(G-1159)*

Ottinger Machine Co...317 654-1700
2900 N Richardt Ave Indianapolis (46219) *(G-9075)*

Ottinger Machine Shop, Indianapolis *Also Called: Ottinger Machine Co (G-9075)*

Ottosons Industries Inc..219 365-8330
12742 Wicker Ave Ste B Cedar Lake (46303) *(G-1835)*

Our Brown County, Nashville *Also Called: Singing Pines Projects Inc (G-12680)*

Our Country Home, Grabill *Also Called: Our Country Home Entps Inc (G-6318)*

Our Country Home Entps Inc.....................................260 657-5605
13101 Main St Grabill (46741) *(G-6318)*

Our Country Home Entps Inc (PA)................................260 657-5605
12120 Water St Harlan (46743) *(G-7058)*

Our Daily Brew, Fort Wayne *Also Called: Odb Inc (G-5281)*

Our Sunday Visitor Apps LLC....................................800 348-2440
200 Noll Plz Huntington (46750) *(G-7349)*

Our Sunday Visitor Inc (PA).....................................260 359-2564
200 Noll Plz Huntington (46750) *(G-7350)*

Our Times Newspaper, Evansville *Also Called: SLM Mrkting Communications Inc (G-4319)*

Ourobio, Indianapolis *Also Called: Transfoam LLC (G-9630)*

Out of Box Solutions Inc..317 605-8719
755 Fletcher Ave Indianapolis (46203) *(G-9076)*

Out The Box Transit Inc...317 523-0061
13295 Illinois St Carmel (46032) *(G-1713)*

Outdoor Industries..574 551-5936
221 S Hand Ave Warsaw (46580) *(G-16407)*

Outdoor Performance...765 732-3335
2920 S Us Highway 27 Liberty (47353) *(G-10994)*

Outdoor Roomscapes Inc...574 965-2009
11965 W 800 N Monticello (47960) *(G-12162)*

Outdoor Technologies LLC.......................................812 654-4399
2780 N County Road 450 E Milan (47031) *(G-11782)*

Outfield Prsnlzed Spt Blls Inc..................................219 661-8942
12880 Jefferson Dr Crown Point (46307) *(G-2727)*

Outfitter...765 289-6456
2704 N Walnut St Muncie (47303) *(G-12471)*

Outfitter, Muncie *Also Called: Outfitter (G-12471)*

Outfitters Inc..765 778-9097
880 S Pendleton Ave Pendleton (46064) *(G-13549)*

Outland Custom Coatings LLC....................................260 894-4818
4310 N 750 W Ligonier (46767) *(G-11020)*

Outman Industries Inc...260 467-1576
13737 Main St Grabill (46741) *(G-6319)*

Outsource Technologies Inc.....................................574 233-1303
1832 N Kenmore St South Bend (46628) *(G-15182)*

Outstanding Tradeshow Exhibit, North Judson *Also Called: Outstnding Trdshow Exhbt Svcs (G-13213)*

Outstnding Trdshow Exhbt Svcs..................................888 735-4348
5235 W State Road 10 Ste 1 North Judson (46366) *(G-13213)*

Outtadaway LLC..219 866-8885
503 W Washington St Rensselaer (47978) *(G-14062)*

Ovation Communications Inc.....................................812 401-9100
1326 N Weinbach Ave Evansville (47711) *(G-4230)*

Over Globe LLC (PA)...305 607-6472
3105 Nw 107th Ave Ste 506 Brownsburg (46112) *(G-1394)*

Over Hill & Dale Sign Studio....................................812 867-1664
12730 Highway 57 Evansville (47725) *(G-4231)*

Over Top Roofing and Rmdlg LLC.................................513 704-5422
254 Charles A Liddle Dr Ste 5 Lawrenceburg (47025) *(G-10851)*

Overgaards Artcraft Printers....................................574 234-8464
2213 S Michigan St South Bend (46613) *(G-15183)*

Overton & Sons Tl & Die Co Inc (PA).. 317 831-4542
   1250 S Old State Road 67 Mooresville (46158) *(G-12232)*
Overton Industries, Mooresville *Also Called: Overton & Sons Tl & Die Co Inc (G-12232)*
Ovideon LLC.. 812 577-3274
   135 Short St Side Lawrenceburg (47025) *(G-10852)*
Owen County Pallet LLC.. 812 384-6568
   9611 Stahl Rd Worthington (47471) *(G-16962)*
Owen Valley Winery LLC.. 812 828-0883
   491 Timber Ridge Rd Spencer (47460) *(G-15356)*
Owen Woodworking.. 317 331-6936
   3012 S State Road 39 Danville (46122) *(G-2822)*
Owens Corning, Angola *Also Called: Owens Corning Sales LLC (G-279)*
Owens Corning, Brookville *Also Called: Owens Corning Sales LLC (G-1330)*
Owens Corning, Brookville *Also Called: Owens Corning Sales LLC (G-1331)*
Owens Corning, Valparaiso *Also Called: Owens Corning Sales LLC (G-16020)*
Owens Corning Sales LLC.. 260 665-7318
   1211 Wohlert St Angola (46703) *(G-279)*
Owens Corning Sales LLC.. 765 647-2857
   6102 Holland Rd Brookville (47012) *(G-1330)*
Owens Corning Sales LLC.. 765 647-4131
   128 W 8th St Brookville (47012) *(G-1331)*
Owens Corning Sales LLC.. 219 465-4324
   2552 Industrial Dr Valparaiso (46383) *(G-16020)*
Owens Corning Sales LLC.. 260 563-2111
   3711 Mill St Wabash (46992) *(G-16207)*
Owens Corning Sales Therm, Wabash *Also Called: Owens Corning Sales LLC (G-16207)*
Owens Fuel Center... 260 358-1211
   2718 Guilford St Huntington (46750) *(G-7351)*
Owens Machine & Welding.. 574 583-9566
   1110 N 6th St Monticello (47960) *(G-12163)*
Owens Machinery Inc... 812 968-3285
   3194 Fogel Rd Se Corydon (47112) *(G-2509)*
Owens Property Solutions LLC.. 708 374-2626
   1308 Delaware St Gary (46407) *(G-5992)*
Owings Patterns Inc.. 812 944-5577
   3011 Progress Way Sellersburg (47172) *(G-14609)*
Ox Industries Inc... 765 396-3317
   800 S Romy St Ste A Eaton (47338) *(G-3064)*
Oxbo International Corporation.. 260 768-3217
   10605 W 750 N Shipshewana (46565) *(G-14874)*
Oxbow Carbon & Minerals.. 219 473-0359
   2815 Indianapolis Blvd Whiting (46394) *(G-16837)*
Oxford Cabinet Company LLC.. 765 223-2101
   141 S Us Highway 27 Liberty (47353) *(G-10995)*
Oxford House, Fowler *Also Called: Oxford House Incorporated (G-5629)*
Oxford House Incorporated.. 765 884-3265
   606 W State Road 18 Fowler (47944) *(G-5629)*
Oxford Industries Inc.. 317 569-0866
   8701 Keystone Xing Ste 14b Indianapolis (46240) *(G-9077)*
Oxinas Partners LLC.. 812 725-8649
   607 N Shore Dr Ste 101 Jeffersonville (47130) *(G-10032)*
Ozinga, Goshen *Also Called: Ozinga Bros Inc (G-6234)*
Ozinga - Concrete.. 574 291-7100
   715 W Ireland Rd South Bend (46614) *(G-15184)*
Ozinga Bros, Goshen *Also Called: Ozinga Bros Inc (G-6233)*
Ozinga Bros Inc.. 574 546-2550
   524 N Bowen Ave Bremen (46506) *(G-1211)*
Ozinga Bros Inc.. 219 662-0925
   1211 E Summit St Crown Point (46307) *(G-2728)*
Ozinga Bros Inc.. 574 971-8239
   1700 Egbert Ave Goshen (46528) *(G-6233)*
Ozinga Bros Inc.. 574 642-4455
   65723 Us Highway 33 Goshen (46526) *(G-6234)*
Ozinga Bros Inc.. 219 949-9800
   1575 Adler Cir Ste B Portage (46368) *(G-13901)*
Ozinga Bros Inc.. 219 956-3418
   11607 N State Road 49 Wheatfield (46392) *(G-16770)*
Ozinga Inc.. 219 324-2286
   708 N Fail Rd La Porte (46350) *(G-10461)*
Ozinga Indiana Rdymx Con Inc... 219 949-9800
   400 Blaine St Gary (46406) *(G-5993)*
Ozinga Ready Mix, Portage *Also Called: Ozinga Bros Inc (G-13901)*
Ozinga Ready Mix, Wheatfield *Also Called: Ozinga Bros Inc (G-16770)*
P & A Machine Company Inc.. 317 634-3673
   4985 Kerrington Blvd Bargersville (46106) *(G-571)*
P & E Products.. 765 969-2644
   637 W 17th St Connersville (47331) *(G-2459)*
P & H Iron & Supply Inc... 219 853-0240
   1435 Summer St Hammond (46320) *(G-6990)*
P & J Industries Inc... 260 894-7143
   1494 Gerber St Ligonier (46767) *(G-11021)*
P & J Sectional Housing.. 260 982-7231
   14385 N 200 E North Manchester (46962) *(G-13246)*
P & J Tool Co Inc.. 317 546-4858
   3525 Massachusetts Ave Indianapolis (46218) *(G-9078)*
P & M Fabrication... 812 232-7640
   2820 S Center St Terre Haute (47802) *(G-15656)*
P & R Farms Llc... 812 326-2010
   5195 E State Road 64 Saint Anthony (47575) *(G-14430)*
P & T Manufacturing Corp... 260 442-9304
   1451 Stonebraker Dr Kendallville (46755) *(G-10140)*
P A Rogers Printing Service.. 317 823-7627
   10748 Oyster Bay Ct Indianapolis (46236) *(G-9079)*
P C Communications Inc... 219 838-2546
   2301 Ridgewood St Highland (46322) *(G-7150)*
P D F, Brazil *Also Called: Process Development & Fabrication Inc (G-1163)*
P D Q, Columbia City *Also Called: PDQ Workholding LLC (G-2179)*
P DS Monogramming... 812 894-2363
   1712 E County Road 650 N Shelburn (47879) *(G-14719)*
P F Apple LLC... 317 773-8683
   19541 Heather Ln Noblesville (46060) *(G-13149)*
P H C Industries Inc
   3115 Pittsburg St Fort Wayne (46803) *(G-5291)*
P H Drew Incorporated.. 317 297-5152
   2450 N Raceway Rd Indianapolis (46234) *(G-9080)*
P J J T Distributors Inc... 812 254-2218
   501 N Meridian St Washington (47501) *(G-16498)*
P Js Custom Embroidering LLC... 219 787-9161
   252 Haglund Rd Chesterton (46304) *(G-1953)*
P M Fabricating Incorporated... 219 362-9926
   2008 Ohio St La Porte (46350) *(G-10462)*
P M I LLC... 812 374-3856
   12595 N Executive Dr Edinburgh (46124) *(G-3094)*
P M P Design, Fishers *Also Called: Plaquemaker Plus Inc (G-4576)*
P O C Industries Inc... 765 645-5015
   8944 N Crossway Mays (46155) *(G-11445)*
P P G Industries Inc... 812 442-5080
   2831 E Industrial Park Dr Brazil (47834) *(G-1160)*
P R F.. 219 477-8660
   6737 Central Ave Ste D Portage (46368) *(G-13902)*
P S C Fabricating, Evansville *Also Called: PSC Industries Inc (G-4263)*
P T I Machining Inc.. 765 564-9966
   5395 W 200 N Delphi (46923) *(G-2905)*
P-Americas LLC.. 812 794-4455
   1402 W State Road 256 Austin (47102) *(G-468)*
P-Americas LLC.. 812 332-1200
   214 W 17th St Bloomington (47404) *(G-940)*
P-Americas LLC.. 765 647-3576
   261 Webers Ln Brookville (47012) *(G-1332)*
P-Americas LLC.. 765 289-0270
   1104 S Post Rd Indianapolis (46239) *(G-9081)*
P-Americas LLC.. 219 836-1800
   9300 Calumet Ave Munster (46321) *(G-12556)*
P-Americas LLC.. 812 522-3421
   1811 1st Ave Seymour (47274) *(G-14670)*
P-Kelco Inc.. 260 356-1376
   465 N Broadway St Huntington (46750) *(G-7352)*
P-Kelco Inc (PA).. 260 356-6326
   245 Erie St Huntington (46750) *(G-7353)*
P.sprayz, Indianapolis *Also Called: Michael Montgomery (G-8898)*
P&C Prime LLC... 231 420-3650
   9879 S Bullington Rd Fredericksburg (47120) *(G-5795)*

ALPHABETIC SECTION

P&E Enterprises.. 219 226-9524
3936 S Lakeshore Dr Crown Point (46307) *(G-2729)*

P&M Beverage Imports, Plainfield *Also Called: Pepito Miller Bev Imports LLC (G-13713)*

P&Y Farm Fresh Market LLC.................................. 812 767-1902
800 S County Road 600 E Butlerville (47223) *(G-1487)*

P2 Precision Mfg LLC.. 260 609-6295
7815 E 500 S Pierceton (46562) *(G-13636)*

P3 Graphix LLC.. 812 641-1294
4225 E Quaker Rd Salem (47167) *(G-14495)*

P3 Polymers LLC.. 812 674-2051
110 E Main St Washington (47501) *(G-16499)*

P413 Corporation (PA)... 317 769-0679
7163 Whitestown Pkwy Zionsville (46077) *(G-17039)*

Pac Banner Works, Mishawaka *Also Called: Plastimatic Arts Corp (G-11975)*

Pace American Enterprises Inc (HQ)...................... 800 247-5767
11550 Harter Dr Middlebury (46540) *(G-11744)*

Pace Tool & Engineering Inc................................ 812 373-9885
19905 E County Road 640 N Hope (47246) *(G-7230)*

Pacemaker Buildings, North Webster *Also Called: North Webster Construction Inc (G-13310)*

Pacheco Winery Ltd Lblty Co............................... 812 799-0683
602 3rd St Columbus (47201) *(G-2369)*

Pacific Beach Peanut BTR LLC.............................. 858 522-9297
9402 Uptown Dr Ste 1200 Indianapolis (46256) *(G-9082)*

Pack Printing LLC... 317 437-9779
1916 Haynes Ave Indianapolis (46240) *(G-9083)*

Packaging Corporation America............................ 812 376-9301
3460 Commerce Dr Columbus (47201) *(G-2370)*

Packaging Corporation America............................ 812 526-5919
12599 N Presidential Way Edinburgh (46124) *(G-3095)*

Packaging Corporation America............................ 765 674-9781
520 S 1st St Gas City (46933) *(G-6039)*

Packaging Corporation America............................ 317 247-0193
7752 W Morris St Indianapolis (46231) *(G-9084)*

Packaging Corporation America............................ 812 482-4598
240 S Truman Rd Jasper (47546) *(G-9901)*

Packaging Corporation America............................ 812 522-3100
2200 D Ave E Seymour (47274) *(G-14671)*

Packaging Corporation America............................ 812 522-3100
2209 Killion Ave Seymour (47274) *(G-14672)*

Packaging Corporation America............................ 812 882-7631
408 E Saint Clair St Vincennes (47591) *(G-16142)*

Packaging Group Corp (PA).................................. 219 879-2500
2125 E Us Highway 12 Ste C Michigan City (46360) *(G-11649)*

Packaging Lgstics Slutions LLC............................ 502 807-8346
300 Missouri Ave Jeffersonville (47130) *(G-10033)*

Packaging Logic, La Porte *Also Called: Pli LLC (G-10463)*

Packaging Systems Indiana Inc (PA)..................... 765 449-1011
3532 Crouch St Lafayette (47905) *(G-10661)*

Packerware, Evansville *Also Called: Berry Film Products Co Inc (G-3917)*

Packrat Industries LLC....................................... 317 295-0208
8464 Flatwood Ct Indianapolis (46278) *(G-9085)*

Pacmoore Process Tech LLC................................ 317 831-2666
100 Pacmoore Pkwy Mooresville (46158) *(G-12233)*

Pacmoore Products Inc...................................... 317 831-2666
100 Pacmoore Pkwy Mooresville (46158) *(G-12234)*

Pactiv LLC.. 574 936-7065
1411 Pidco Dr Plymouth (46563) *(G-13800)*

Pacvan Inc... 317 791-2020
2995 S Harding St Ste 1 Indianapolis (46225) *(G-9086)*

Paddack Brothers Inc... 765 659-4777
4410 W Old State Road 28 Frankfort (46041) *(G-5689)*

Padgett Inc.. 812 945-2391
901 E 4th St New Albany (47150) *(G-12790)*

Paf Construction LLC... 812 496-4669
4840 Progress Dr Columbus (47201) *(G-2371)*

Pag Holdings Inc... 814 446-2525
10665 N State Road 59 Brazil (47834) *(G-1161)*

Pag Holdings LLC (HQ)....................................... 317 290-5006
5929 Lakeside Blvd Indianapolis (46278) *(G-9087)*

PAG HOLDINGS, INC., Brazil *Also Called: Pag Holdings Inc (G-1161)*

Pag Holdings, Inc., Indianapolis *Also Called: Pag Holdings LLC (G-9087)*

Pagels-Kelley Enterprises LLC............................. 219 872-8552
2718 Roslyn Trl Long Beach (46360) *(G-11126)*

Pages, Marion *Also Called: Pages Editorial Services Inc (G-11323)*

Pages Editorial Services Inc............................... 765 674-4212
113 E Old Kokomo Rd Marion (46953) *(G-11323)*

Paige Marschall.. 574 277-1631
12622 Alexander Dr Granger (46530) *(G-6368)*

Paige's Custom Lettering, Granger *Also Called: Paige Marschall (G-6368)*

Pailton Inc... 219 476-0085
2901 Bertholet Blvd Valparaiso (46383) *(G-16021)*

Paint Town Graphics Inc.................................... 260 422-9152
1828 W Main St Fort Wayne (46808) *(G-5292)*

Paklab, Orland *Also Called: Universal Packg Systems Inc (G-13374)*

Palibrio... 812 671-9757
1663 S Liberty Dr Bloomington (47403) *(G-941)*

Palladin Services Inc... 317 745-6741
1425 N County Road 200 W Danville (46122) *(G-2823)*

Palladium Item, The, Richmond *Also Called: Gannett Media Corp (G-14124)*

Pallatin Machine LLC... 574 703-7505
1902 W 6th St Mishawaka (46544) *(G-11969)*

Pallet Builder Inc.. 765 948-3345
1520 W 900 S Fairmount (46928) *(G-4412)*

Pallet Builder Inc (PA)....................................... 765 584-1441
112 Inks Dr Winchester (47394) *(G-16897)*

Pallet Depot... 317 897-1774
9226 E 33rd St Indianapolis (46235) *(G-9088)*

Pallet Recyclers LLC.. 812 402-0095
4200 Upper Mount Vernon Rd Evansville (47712) *(G-4232)*

Pallet Subs LLC.. 260 768-4021
5345 W 200 N Shipshewana (46565) *(G-14875)*

Palletone Inc.. 260 768-4021
5345 W 200 N Shipshewana (46565) *(G-14876)*

Palletone of Indiana Inc.................................... 260 768-4021
5345 W 200 N Shipshewana (46565) *(G-14877)*

Pallets R US, Roann *Also Called: Rick Hollingshead (G-14253)*

Palmary America LLC... 317 494-1415
1880 Northwood Plz Franklin (46131) *(G-5764)*

Palmer Caning.. 773 394-4913
3204 Olympia Dr Ste A Lafayette (47909) *(G-10662)*

Palmetto Planters LLC....................................... 765 396-4446
1153 N Hartford St Eaton (47338) *(G-3065)*

Palmor Products Inc... 800 872-2822
1990 John Bart Rd Lebanon (46052) *(G-10928)*

Pam C Jnes Typography Graphics, Borden *Also Called: Pam C Jones Enterprises Inc (G-1117)*

Pam C Jones Enterprises Inc.............................. 812 294-1862
3007 Crone Rd Borden (47106) *(G-1117)*

Pamela Taulman.. 812 378-5008
982 S Marr Rd Columbus (47201) *(G-2372)*

Pana-Pacific... 260 482-6607
918 E State Blvd Fort Wayne (46805) *(G-5293)*

Panacea Painting & Coating Inc........................... 260 728-4222
1013 W Commerce Dr Decatur (46733) *(G-2875)*

Panda Prints... 574 322-1050
19647 County Road 8 Bristol (46507) *(G-1282)*

Pandora Printing.. 574 551-9624
1831 Rosemont Ave Warsaw (46580) *(G-16408)*

Panel Solutions Inc (PA).................................... 574 389-8494
5015 Verdant St Elkhart (46516) *(G-3580)*

Panel Solutions Inc... 574 295-0222
5015 Verdant St Elkhart (46516) *(G-3581)*

Panel Solutions/Tape Tech, Elkhart *Also Called: Panel Solutions Inc (G-3580)*

Pangaea Industries LLC..................................... 574 850-5841
3702 W Sample St Ste 4060 # 4060 South Bend (46619) *(G-15185)*

Paniccia Heating & Cooling Inc........................... 219 872-2198
5076 N Bleck Rd Michigan City (46360) *(G-11650)*

Pannell & Son Welding Inc................................. 765 948-3606
207 N Summit St Summitville (46070) *(G-15427)*

Panolam Industries Inc..................................... 574 264-0702
25603 Borg Rd Elkhart (46514) *(G-3582)*

Panoramic Rental Corp...................................... 800 654-2027
4321 Goshen Rd Fort Wayne (46818) *(G-5294)*

Pantera Mfg Corporation.. 317 435-0422
10609 Serra Vista Pt Fishers (46040) *(G-4646)*

Panther Graphics LLC.. 317 223-3845
5740 Decatur Blvd Indianapolis (46241) *(G-9089)*

Panther Werks, Bedford *Also Called: Smith Group Precision LLC (G-673)*

Paper Chase.. 812 385-4757
503 W State St Princeton (47670) *(G-14009)*

Paper of Montgomery County.. 765 361-8888
201 E Jefferson St Ste 200 Crawfordsville (47933) *(G-2600)*

Paper of Wabash County Inc.. 260 563-8326
606 N State Road 13 Wabash (46992) *(G-16208)*

Paper Products, Muncie *Also Called: Larry Flowers Wholesale (G-12438)*

Paper Street Press.. 765 894-0027
1841 King Eider Dr West Lafayette (47906) *(G-16616)*

Papercharm Scrpbking Stdio LLC................................. 317 624-2878
6101 N Keystone Ave Ste 100 Indianapolis (46220) *(G-9090)*

Papers Inc.. 574 534-2591
134 S Main St Goshen (46526) *(G-6235)*

Papers Inc.. 574 269-2932
114 W Market St Warsaw (46580) *(G-16409)*

Paperworks Industries Inc.. 260 569-3352
455 Factory St Wabash (46992) *(G-16209)*

Paperworks Industries Inc.. 260 563-3102
455 Factory St Wabash (46992) *(G-16210)*

Paperworks Wabash Inc... 260 569-3303
455 Factory St Wabash (46992) *(G-16211)*

Pappas Construction LLC.. 219 314-7068
2310 Pembroke Dr N Hobart (46342) *(G-7203)*

Par Digital Imaging Inc... 317 787-3330
1134 Sweetbriar Dr Greenwood (46143) *(G-6749)*

Par-Kan Company LLC... 260 352-2141
2915 W 900 S Silver Lake (46982) *(G-14920)*

Paradigm Industries Inc... 317 574-8590
12236 Hancock St Carmel (46032) *(G-1714)*

Paradise Ink, Evansville *Also Called: Paradise Ink Inc (G-4233)*

Paradise Ink Inc.. 812 402-4465
619 N Burkhardt Rd Ste G Evansville (47715) *(G-4233)*

Paradise Machine and Tool Corp.................................. 317 247-4606
6820 W Minnesota St Indianapolis (46241) *(G-9091)*

Paragon Casket Inc.. 888 855-3601
1751 S 8th St Richmond (47374) *(G-14179)*

Paragon Force Inc.. 812 384-3040
280 Northgate Blvd Ste A Bloomfield (47424) *(G-755)*

Paragon Manufacturing Inc... 260 665-1492
700 Wohlert St Angola (46703) *(G-280)*

Paragon Medical Inc.. 317 570-5830
7350 E 86th St Indianapolis (46256) *(G-9092)*

Paragon Medical Inc.. 574 594-2140
22 Pequignot Dr Pierceton (46562) *(G-13637)*

Paragon Medical Inc (HQ)... 574 594-2140
8 Matchett Dr Pierceton (46562) *(G-13638)*

Paragon Printing Center Inc.. 574 533-5835
11194 River Oaks Ln W Osceola (46561) *(G-13400)*

Paragon Tube Corporation... 260 424-1266
1605 Winter St Fort Wayne (46803) *(G-5295)*

Paraklese Technologies LLC.. 502 357-0735
7600 State Rd 64 Ste Alpha 2 Georgetown (47122) *(G-6073)*

Parallax Group Inc... 800 443-4859
600 Broadway St Anderson (46012) *(G-175)*

Paralogics, Muncie *Also Called: Calumet Paralogics LLC (G-12361)*

Paralogics LLC... 765 587-4618
301 S Butterfield Rd Muncie (47303) *(G-12472)*

Parametric Machining Inc... 260 338-1564
16335 Lima Rd Ste 3 Huntertown (46748) *(G-7260)*

Paramount Plastics Inc.. 574 264-2143
2810 Jeanwood Dr Elkhart (46514) *(G-3583)*

Paramount Tube Division, Fort Wayne *Also Called: Precision Products Group Inc (G-5340)*

Paramount Tube Division, Indianapolis *Also Called: Precision Products Group Inc (G-9184)*

Paratex Products, Trail Creek *Also Called: Blocksom & Co (G-15835)*

Parco Incorporated... 260 451-0810
9100 Front St Fort Wayne (46818) *(G-5296)*

Parent Co. Glassteel, Goshen *Also Called: Stability America Inc (G-6257)*

Paris Black Fashion LLC... 317 529-7119
3084 W Us Highway 40 Greencastle (46135) *(G-6423)*

Parish Tire & Battery Shop... 765 793-3191
416 3rd St Covington (47932) *(G-2532)*

Park 100 Foods Inc.. 317 549-4545
6908 E 30th St Indianapolis (46219) *(G-9093)*

Park 100 Foods Inc.. 765 763-6064
205 Central Pkwy Morristown (46161) *(G-12280)*

Park 100 Foods Inc (PA)... 765 675-3480
326 E Adams St Tipton (46072) *(G-15786)*

PARK DEVELOPEMENT, Anderson *Also Called: Anderson Memorial Park Inc (G-78)*

Park Embroidery Designs LLC..................................... 317 780-1515
5230 Park Emerson Dr Ste L Indianapolis (46203) *(G-9094)*

Park Ohio, Huntington *Also Called: General Aluminum Mfg Company (G-7314)*

Parke County Aggregates LLC..................................... 765 245-2344
5081 N State Road 59 Rockville (47872) *(G-14353)*

Parke County Sentinel, Rockville *Also Called: Torch Newspapers Inc (G-14359)*

Parke County Wood You Like...................................... 317 575-9530
12224 Castle Ct Carmel (46033) *(G-1715)*

Parker Exploration & Productio.................................... 812 673-4017
2940 Donner Rd Wadesville (47638) *(G-16228)*

Parker Hvac Filtration, Jeffersonville *Also Called: Parker-Hannifin Corporation (G-10034)*

Parker Seal Service Ctr, Noblesville *Also Called: Parker-Hannifin Corporation (G-13150)*

Parker-Hannifin Corporation... 260 636-2104
903 N Orange St Albion (46701) *(G-40)*

Parker-Hannifin Corporation... 260 587-9102
201 S Parker Dr Ashley (46705) *(G-335)*

Parker-Hannifin Corporation... 260 748-6000
5417 State Road 930 Fort Wayne (46803) *(G-5297)*

Parker-Hannifin Corporation... 574 533-1111
1525 S 10th St Goshen (46526) *(G-6236)*

Parker-Hannifin Corporation... 866 247-4827
100 River Ridge Cir Jeffersonville (47130) *(G-10034)*

Parker-Hannifin Corporation... 219 736-0400
1201 E 86th Pl Ste H Merrillville (46410) *(G-11549)*

Parker-Hannifin Corporation... 317 776-7600
14425 Bergen Blvd Ste C Noblesville (46060) *(G-13150)*

Parker-Hannifin Corporation... 574 528-9400
501 S Sycamore St Syracuse (46567) *(G-15470)*

Parker-Hannifin Corporation... 260 894-7125
501 S Sycamore St Syracuse (46567) *(G-15471)*

Parking Bumper Company, Universal *Also Called: Hog Slat Incorporated (G-15875)*

Parkland Plastics, Middlebury *Also Called: Patrick Industries Inc (G-11746)*

Parkland Plastics Inc... 574 825-4336
104 Yoder Dr Middlebury (46540) *(G-11745)*

Parkway Industrial Entps LLC...................................... 260 622-7200
420 Industrial Pkwy Ossian (46777) *(G-13430)*

Parkway Investor Group Inc... 260 665-1252
509 Growth Pkwy Angola (46703) *(G-281)*

Parlor City Trophy & AP Inc... 260 824-0216
125 N Main St Bluffton (46714) *(G-1047)*

Parr Corp.. 574 264-9614
3200 County Road 6 E Elkhart (46514) *(G-3584)*

Parr Holdings LLC... 423 468-1855
3200 County Road 6 E Elkhart (46514) *(G-3585)*

Parr Technologies, Elkhart *Also Called: Parr Holdings LLC (G-3585)*

Parr Technologies LLC.. 574 264-9614
3200 County Road 6 E Elkhart (46514) *(G-3586)*

Parretts Meat Proc & Catrg Inc................................... 574 967-3711
603 Railroad St Flora (46929) *(G-4663)*

Parretts Mt Proc Hog Roasting, Flora *Also Called: Parretts Meat Proc & Catrg Inc (G-4663)*

Parrot Press Inc... 260 422-6402
520 Spring St Fort Wayne (46808) *(G-5298)*

Parsley Seal Coating Stripping, Ellettsville *Also Called: Parsleys Seal Coating Inc (G-3811)*

Parsleys Seal Coating Inc.. 812 876-5450
305 S Ridge Springs Ln Ellettsville (47429) *(G-3811)*

Parsolex, West Lafayette *Also Called: Parsolex Gmp Center Inc (G-16617)*

Parsolex Gmp Center Inc... 765 464-8414
3000 Kent Ave Ste 1510 West Lafayette (47906) *(G-16617)*

ALPHABETIC SECTION — Paust Printers

Parson Adhesives Inc 812 401-7277
2545 Eastside Park Rd Evansville (47715) *(G-4234)*

Parsons Welding Service 812 597-4914
9655 N Haasetown Rd Morgantown (46160) *(G-12262)*

Part Solutions LLC 219 477-5101
52167 Farmington Sqr South Bend (46624) *(G-15186)*

Partlow Farms LLC 317 919-8064
15486 Herriman Blvd Noblesville (46060) *(G-13151)*

Partners Marketing, Indianapolis *Also Called: Printing Partners Inc (G-9206)*

Parts Cleaning Tech LLC 317 243-4205
2263 Distributors Dr Indianapolis (46241) *(G-9095)*

Parts Pro Auto Prfrormance LLC 765 825-5545
510 E 5th St Connersville (47331) *(G-2460)*

Party Cask 812 234-3008
1652 S 25th St Terre Haute (47803) *(G-15657)*

Party Cask Southeast, Terre Haute *Also Called: Party Cask (G-15657)*

Pasou Foods Inc 574 457-4092
1103 S Huntington St Syracuse (46567) *(G-15472)*

Passions Fruitopia LLC 800 515-1891
9445 Indianapolis Blvd Ste 1026 Highland (46322) *(G-7151)*

Pasteleria Gresil LLC 317 299-8801
5348 W 38th St Indianapolis (46254) *(G-9096)*

Patchwork Costumes, Indianapolis *Also Called: Patchwork Costumes LLC (G-9097)*

Patchwork Costumes LLC 317 750-6162
6091 Parrington Dr Indianapolis (46236) *(G-9097)*

Patco Distribution, East Chicago *Also Called: Universal Services Inc (G-3051)*

Patel Ballistics Corporation 847 284-0086
7024 Bladstone Rd Noblesville (46062) *(G-13152)*

Pates Processing LLC 812 866-4710
4251 S 850 W Hanover (47243) *(G-7044)*

Pates Slaughtering & Proc 812 866-4710
Off Hwy 62 Hanover (47243) *(G-7045)*

Path Bright Publications LLC 888 505-6780
9801 Fall Creek Rd Ste 115 Indianapolis (46256) *(G-9098)*

Pathfinder Communications Corp (PA) 574 295-2500
421 S 2nd St Ste 100 Elkhart (46516) *(G-3587)*

Pathfinder Communications Corp 574 266-5115
2409 Mishawaka Ave South Bend (46615) *(G-15187)*

Pathfinder Cutting Tech LLC 424 342-9723
5623 W 74th St Indianapolis (46278) *(G-9099)*

Pathfinder School LLC (PA) 317 791-8777
6050 Churchman Byp Indianapolis (46203) *(G-9100)*

Pathfinder Services Inc (PA) 260 356-0500
2824 Theater Ave Huntington (46750) *(G-7354)*

Patora Fine Jewelers, Indianapolis *Also Called: Interntnal Damnd Gold Exch Ltd (G-8583)*

Patria Press LLC 317 508-7239
7117 Koldyke Dr Fishers (46038) *(G-4572)*

Patricia J Nickels Inc 502 489-4358
8324 Cypress Dr Charlestown (47111) *(G-1890)*

Patrick, Elkhart *Also Called: Patrick Industries Inc (G-3593)*

Patrick Industries Inc 260 665-6112
409 Growth Pkwy Angola (46703) *(G-282)*

Patrick Industries Inc 574 546-5222
1849 Dogwood Rd Bremen (46506) *(G-1212)*

Patrick Industries Inc 574 295-5206
5120 Beck Dr Elkhart (46516) *(G-3588)*

Patrick Industries Inc 574 293-1521
1926 W Lusher Ave Elkhart (46517) *(G-3589)*

Patrick Industries Inc 574 294-1975
2300 W Mishawaka Rd Elkhart (46517) *(G-3590)*

Patrick Industries Inc 574 295-9660
4906 Hoffman St Ste B Elkhart (46516) *(G-3591)*

Patrick Industries Inc 574 294-8828
1012 Borg Rd Elkhart (46514) *(G-3592)*

Patrick Industries Inc (PA) 574 294-7511
107 W Franklin St Elkhart (46516) *(G-3593)*

Patrick Industries Inc 574 294-8828
56741 Elk Park Dr Elkhart (46516) *(G-3594)*

Patrick Industries Inc 574 266-8400
1515 Leininger Ave Elkhart (46517) *(G-3595)*

Patrick Industries Inc 574 294-5758
3905 Lexington Park Dr Elkhart (46514) *(G-3596)*

Patrick Industries Inc 574 293-1521
1930 W Lusher Ave Elkhart (46517) *(G-3597)*

Patrick Industries Inc 574 522-7710
1808 W Hively Ave Elkhart (46517) *(G-3598)*

Patrick Industries Inc 574 293-2990
2520 Industrial Pkwy Elkhart (46516) *(G-3599)*

Patrick Industries Inc 574 294-5959
28505 C R 20 W Elkhart (46517) *(G-3600)*

Patrick Industries Inc 574 534-5300
3352 Maple City Dr Goshen (46526) *(G-6237)*

Patrick Industries Inc 574 825-4336
104 Yoder Dr Middlebury (46540) *(G-11746)*

Patrick Industries Inc 574 255-9692
5020 Lincolnway E Mishawaka (46544) *(G-11970)*

Patrick Industries Inc 574 255-9692
5020 Lincolnway E Mishawaka (46544) *(G-11971)*

Patrick J Fscher Pipe Organ Sv 978 314-7312
510 E University St Bloomington (47401) *(G-942)*

Patrick Welding LLC 812 557-7299
1820 Rita Dr New Albany (47150) *(G-12791)*

Patriot Inc 317 462-5172
343 N Windswept Rd Greenfield (46140) *(G-6535)*

Patriot Industries, Bloomington *Also Called: Patriot Industries LLC (G-943)*

Patriot Industries LLC 574 370-7899
8917 N Old State Road 37 Bloomington (47408) *(G-943)*

Patriot Label Inc 812 877-1611
9192 E Hwy 40 Terre Haute (47803) *(G-15658)*

Patriot Packaging LLC 812 346-0700
1002 Rodgers Park Dr North Vernon (47265) *(G-13291)*

Patriot Plant, Patriot *Also Called: Hilltop Basic Resources Inc (G-13510)*

Patriot Porcelain LLC 574 583-5128
114 Constitution Plz Monticello (47960) *(G-12164)*

Patriot Products, Franklin *Also Called: Patriot Products LLC (G-5765)*

Patriot Products LLC 317 736-8007
2011 Earlywood Dr Franklin (46131) *(G-5765)*

Patriot Software Solutions Inc 317 573-5431
1311 W 96th St Ste 220 Indianapolis (46260) *(G-9101)*

Pattern Inc 317 733-8302
941 N Meridian St Indianapolis (46204) *(G-9102)*

Patterson Engrg & Mfg LLC 217 260-1415
517 N Admirals Pointe Dr Lafayette (47909) *(G-10663)*

Patterson Products LLC 812 309-3614
8446 W Himsel Rd Otwell (47564) *(G-13457)*

Paul Applegate 574 656-8664
27884 Quinn Rd North Liberty (46554) *(G-13219)*

Paul E Potts 812 354-3241
8689 W Private Road 375 N Hazleton (47640) *(G-7095)*

Paul E Shaw 765 778-3383
521 Taylor St Pendleton (46064) *(G-13550)*

Paul H Rohe Company Inc 812 926-1471
110 Forest Ave Aurora (47001) *(G-451)*

Paul Knepp Saw Mill, Montgomery *Also Called: Paul Knepp Sawmill Inc (G-12117)*

Paul Knepp Sawmill Inc 812 486-3773
3589 N 900 E Montgomery (47558) *(G-12117)*

Paul Miller 765 449-4893
1516 Sherwood Dr Lafayette (47909) *(G-10664)*

Paul Nelson 765 352-0698
4009 E Rembrandt Dr Martinsville (46151) *(G-11421)*

Paul Nunez Road Service 765 584-1628
2711 E 500 N Winchester (47394) *(G-16898)*

Paul Tirotta 574 255-4101
1701 E 6th St Mishawaka (46544) *(G-11972)*

Paula Rosenbaum 319 484-2941
2752 Hearthstone Dr Valparaiso (46383) *(G-16022)*

Pauls Seating Inc 574 522-0630
56912 Elk Ct Elkhart (46516) *(G-3601)*

Paulus Plastic Co Inc 574 834-7663
304 E George St North Webster (46555) *(G-13312)*

Paust Inc (PA) 765 962-1507
14 N 10th St Richmond (47374) *(G-14180)*

Paust Printers, Richmond *Also Called: Paust Inc (G-14180)*

Paver Rescue Inc 317 259-4880
  9386 Castlegate Dr Indianapolis (46256) *(G-9103)*

Pavers Inc 317 271-0823
  2900 N County Road 900 E Indianapolis (46234) *(G-9104)*

Paving Plus Company 317 784-1857
  3541 Brehob Rd Indianapolis (46217) *(G-9105)*

Paws Depot, Elnora *Also Called: Campbell Pet Company (G-3813)*

Pax Custom Woodworking LLC 805 300-3720
  8418 Castle Farms Rd Indianapolis (46256) *(G-9106)*

Paxton Media Group, Frankfort *Also Called: Times (G-5698)*

Paxton Media Group LLC 765 664-5111
  610 S Adams St Marion (46953) *(G-11324)*

Paxxal Inc 317 296-7724
  14425 Bergen Blvd Ste A Noblesville (46060) *(G-13153)*

Payne George A Petroleum Engr 812 853-3813
  5844 Sharon Rd Newburgh (47630) *(G-13015)*

Payne-Sparkmanm Manufacturing 812 944-4893
  2571 Roanoke Ave New Albany (47150) *(G-12792)*

Payne's Die Cutting, Fort Wayne *Also Called: Bruce Payne (G-4820)*

Paynes Fine Cabrinetry 765 589-9176
  7705 E 300 N Lafayette (47905) *(G-10665)*

Paynter Machine Works Inc 812 883-2808
  1302 E Hackberry St Salem (47167) *(G-14496)*

Paytons Barbecue Inc 765 294-2716
  119 E Washington St Veedersburg (47987) *(G-16089)*

Pb & J Factory LLC 317 504-4714
  1220 Waterway Blvd Indianapolis (46202) *(G-9107)*

Pb Metal Works 765 489-1311
  50 Paul R Foulke Pkwy Hagerstown (47346) *(G-6841)*

Pbp Publishing LLC 574 707-1010
  5534 Saint Joe Rd Fort Wayne (46835) *(G-5299)*

Pbtt, Newburgh *Also Called: Pbtt Inc (G-13016)*

Pbtt Inc 810 965-3675
  5622 Vann Rd Newburgh (47630) *(G-13016)*

PC Imprints LLC 812 622-0855
  10521 Emge Rd Poseyville (47633) *(G-13980)*

PCA, Columbus *Also Called: Packaging Corporation America (G-2370)*

PCA, Edinburgh *Also Called: Packaging Corporation America (G-3095)*

PCA, Indianapolis *Also Called: Packaging Corporation America (G-9084)*

PCA, Jasper *Also Called: Packaging Corporation America (G-9901)*

PCA, Seymour *Also Called: Packaging Corporation America (G-14672)*

PCA Publishing Inc 317 658-2055
  8845 Jackson St Indianapolis (46231) *(G-9108)*

PCA Suthern Ind Corrugated LLC 812 376-9301
  3460 Commerce Dr Columbus (47201) *(G-2373)*

PCA/Gas City 323, Gas City *Also Called: Packaging Corporation America (G-6039)*

PCI By Ray Marketing, Beech Grove *Also Called: Ray Marketing LLC (G-701)*

PD Kangaroo Inc 317 417-7143
  1241 N New Jersey St Indianapolis (46202) *(G-9109)*

Pd Solutions Inc 800 289-8787
  504 S Oakland Ave Nappanee (46550) *(G-12635)*

Pd Sub LLC 812 524-0534
  2223 Killion Ave Seymour (47274) *(G-14673)*

Pdb II Inc 219 865-1888
  2661 Tower Ct Dyer (46311) *(G-2980)*

Pdi, Columbus *Also Called: Phillips Company Inc (G-2377)*

PDQ Workholding LLC 260 244-2919
  1100 S Williams Dr # 1 Columbia City (46725) *(G-2179)*

Peabody Bear Run Mining LLC 314 342-7676
  7255 E County Road 600 S Carlisle (47838) *(G-1542)*

Peabody Energy Corporation 314 342-3400
  566 Dickeyville Rd Lynnville (47619) *(G-11191)*

Peabody Midwest Mining LLC 812 782-3209
  County Rd 850 E Francisco (47649) *(G-5646)*

Peabody Midwest Mining LLC (HQ) 812 297-7661
  566 Dickeyville Rd Lynnville (47619) *(G-11192)*

Peabody Midwest Mining LLC 812 254-7714
  1281 S 300 W Washington (47501) *(G-16400)*

Peace Love Cupcakes 812 239-1591
  3833 N 25th St Terre Haute (47805) *(G-15659)*

Peace Valley Cabinets Inc 812 486-3831
  5127 E 300 N Montgomery (47558) *(G-12118)*

Peace Water Winery LLC 317 810-1330
  22400 Cammack Rd Noblesville (46062) *(G-13154)*

Peacock Bat Co 812 568-1006
  8466 Susott Rd Elberfeld (47613) *(G-3117)*

Peacock Logging Inc 812 794-3579
  2376 E Harrod Rd Austin (47102) *(G-469)*

Peacock Plastics Inc 765 935-9178
  4124 High St Richmond (47374) *(G-14181)*

Peafield Products Inc 317 839-8473
  4692 S County Road 600 E Plainfield (46168) *(G-13711)*

Peak Toolworks, Jasper *Also Called: Nap Asset Holdings Ltd (G-9894)*

Peanut Butter Ministries Inc 260 627-0777
  13631 Leo Rd Leo (46765) *(G-10970)*

Pearison Inc 812 963-8890
  8900 Highway 65 Cynthiana (47612) *(G-2788)*

Pearl Cstm Plastic Molding Inc 765 763-6961
  7072 E Mulberry St Gwynneville (46144) *(G-6831)*

Pearl Custom Plastic, Gwynneville *Also Called: Pearl Cstm Plastic Molding Inc (G-6831)*

Pearl Screen Printing 812 429-1686
  428 Nw 3rd St Evansville (47708) *(G-4235)*

Pearson Education Inc 317 428-3049
  800 E 96th St Ste 300 Indianapolis (46240) *(G-9110)*

Pearson Education Inc 765 483-6738
  150 Pearson Parkway Lebanon (46052) *(G-10929)*

Pearson Printing Company 765 664-8769
  3239 S Washington St Marion (46953) *(G-11325)*

Peas In A Pod Publications LLC 812 923-5365
  3909 Knable Ct Floyds Knobs (47119) *(G-4687)*

Pebble Natursutten LLC 866 228-1473
  7284 W 200 N Greenfield (46140) *(G-6536)*

Peepers By Peeperspecs, Michigan City *Also Called: Sammann Company Inc (G-11661)*

Peepers Reading Glasses, Michigan City *Also Called: Samco Group Inc (G-11660)*

Peer Foods, Columbus *Also Called: Mariah Foods Corp (G-2348)*

Peer Foods, Greenfield *Also Called: Peer Foods Group Inc (G-6537)*

Peer Foods Group Inc 773 927-1440
  Columbus (47202) *(G-2374)*

Peer Foods Group Inc 812 703-2081
  3013 W Presidential Way Edinburgh (46124) *(G-3096)*

Peer Foods Group Inc 317 894-7777
  5593 W Us Highway 40 Greenfield (46140) *(G-6537)*

Peer Foods Group Inc 317 735-4283
  1825 Stout Field Ter Indianapolis (46241) *(G-9111)*

Peerless Gear, Salem *Also Called: Husqvrna Cnsmr Otdr Prod NA (G-14483)*

Peerless Gear LLC 812 883-7900
  1555 S Jackson St Salem (47167) *(G-14497)*

Peerless Machine & Tool Corp 765 662-2586
  1804 W 2nd St Marion (46952) *(G-11326)*

Peerless Machinery Inc 574 210-5990
  4406 Technology Dr South Bend (46628) *(G-15188)*

Peerless Manufacturing LLC (PA) 260 760-0880
  2084 N 800 E Avilla (46710) *(G-492)*

Peerless Pattern & Machine Co 765 477-7719
  3521 Coleman Ct Lafayette (47905) *(G-10666)*

Peerless Printing & Off Sups, Marion *Also Called: Peerless Printing Corporation (G-11327)*

Peerless Printing Corporation 765 664-8341
  513 S Washington St Marion (46953) *(G-11327)*

Peerless Pump Company, Indianapolis *Also Called: Sterling Fluid Systems USA LLC (G-9506)*

Peerview Data Inc 317 238-3234
  5255 Winthrop Ave Indianapolis (46220) *(G-9112)*

Peg Perego USA Inc 800 671-1701
  3625 Independence Dr Fort Wayne (46808) *(G-5300)*

Peli Biothermal LLC 763 412-4800
  915 Airtech Pkwy Ste 102 Plainfield (46168) *(G-13712)*

Peli Biothermal Service Center, Plainfield *Also Called: Peli Biothermal LLC (G-13712)*

Pems, Monroe *Also Called: Phazpak Inc (G-12061)*

Pen & Pink 317 372-6465
  2435 Shelby St Indianapolis (46203) *(G-9113)*

Pen It Publications LLC 812 392-2658
  5110 W County Road 400 N Scipio (47273) *(G-14550)*

ALPHABETIC SECTION — Perfection Bakeries Inc

Pen Products Miami Cor Fcilty 765 689-8920
3063w 800 S Bunker Hill (46914) *(G-1443)*

Pendleton Door Company 765 778-4164
8680 S 750 W Pendleton (46064) *(G-13551)*

Pendleton Times 765 778-2324
6837 S State Road 67 Pendleton (46064) *(G-13552)*

Pendry Coatings LLC 574 268-2956
1119 Seymour Midwest Dr Warsaw (46580) *(G-16410)*

Pengad/Indy, Muncie Also Called: Pengad/West Inc *(G-12473)*

Pengad/West Inc 765 286-3000
1106 E Seymour St Ste A Muncie (47302) *(G-12473)*

Penguin Enterprises LLC 812 333-0475
401 S Walnut St Bloomington (47401) *(G-944)*

Penguin Petes 812 838-9670
1809 Westridge Dr Mount Vernon (47620) *(G-12314)*

Penguin Random House LLC 800 733-3000
1019 N State Road 47 Crawfordsville (47933) *(G-2601)*

Penguin Random House LLC 765 362-5125
1021 N State Road 47 Crawfordsville (47933) *(G-2602)*

Penguin Random House LLC 800 672-7836
199 Pearson Pkwy Lebanon (46052) *(G-10930)*

Penn & Beech Candle Co 317 645-8732
1219 N New Jersey St Indianapolis (46202) *(G-9114)*

Penn Central Welding LLC 260 463-2490
1245 S 100 E Lagrange (46761) *(G-10757)*

Penn Tool, Indianapolis Also Called: Precision Tubes Inc *(G-9187)*

Penn-Mar Capital LLC 463 239-2632
10475 Crosspoint Blvd Ste 250 Indianapolis (46256) *(G-9115)*

Penner Tire & Service LLC 812 653-0029
390 E Us Highway 150 Hardinsburg (47125) *(G-7048)*

Pennplastics LLC 574 286-0705
945 E 6th St Mishawaka (46544) *(G-11973)*

Pennville Custom Cabinetry, Portland Also Called: Commercial Electric Co Inc *(G-13933)*

Pens By Maisie Inc 574 287-6178
309 E Pokagon St South Bend (46617) *(G-15189)*

Pent Assemblies 260 347-5828
6928 N 400 E Kendallville (46755) *(G-10141)*

Pent Plastics Inc (PA) 260 897-3775
6928 N 400 E Kendallville (46755) *(G-10142)*

Pentair 574 278-7161
9449 S 550 W Winamac (46996) *(G-16869)*

Pentera Group Inc 317 543-2055
921 E 86th St Ste 100 Indianapolis (46240) *(G-9116)*

Pentzer Printing Inc 812 372-2896
4505 Kelly St Columbus (47203) *(G-2375)*

Penway Inc 812 526-2645
900 S Walnut St Edinburgh (46124) *(G-3097)*

Penz Inc 574 255-4736
1320 S Merrifield Ave Mishawaka (46544) *(G-11974)*

People's Exchange, The, Lagrange Also Called: Lagwana Printing Inc *(G-10748)*

Pepcon Concrete Inc 765 964-6572
1567 Frank Miller Rd Union City (47390) *(G-15858)*

Pepito Miller Bev Imports LLC 317 416-3215
4188 Scioto Dr Plainfield (46168) *(G-13713)*

Pepka Spring Company Inc 765 459-3114
810 S Waugh St Kokomo (46901) *(G-10319)*

Peppers Ridge LLC 812 499-3743
4304 N County Road 200 W Rockport (47635) *(G-14347)*

Pepsi 3449 .... 317 760-7335
5510 Exploration Dr Indianapolis (46241) *(G-9117)*

Pepsi Beverages Co., Fort Wayne Also Called: Pepsi Beverages Company *(G-5301)*

Pepsi Beverages Company 260 428-9156
4433 Gulfstream Dr Fort Wayne (46809) *(G-5301)*

Pepsi Beverages Company 219 836-1800
9300 Calumet Ave Munster (46321) *(G-12557)*

Pepsi Bottling Ventures LLC 765 659-7313
2611 W County Road 0 Ns Frankfort (46041) *(G-5690)*

Pepsi-Cola 812 634-1844
2811 Market St Jasper (47546) *(G-9902)*

Pepsi-Cola, Bloomington Also Called: Pepsi-Cola Metro Btlg Co Inc *(G-945)*

Pepsi-Cola, Frankfort Also Called: Pepsi Bottling Ventures LLC *(G-5690)*

Pepsi-Cola, Logansport Also Called: Interactions Incorporated *(G-11083)*

Pepsi-Cola Metro Btlg Co Inc 812 332-1200
214 W 17th St Bloomington (47404) *(G-945)*

Pepsico 260 750-9106
4692 Craftsbury Cir Apt A Fort Wayne (46818) *(G-5302)*

Pepsico 317 821-6400
5858 Decatur Blvd Indianapolis (46241) *(G-9118)*

Pepsico 317 334-0153
3124 Perry Blvd Whitestown (46075) *(G-16813)*

Pepsico, Austin Also Called: P-Americas LLC *(G-468)*

Pepsico, Bloomington Also Called: P-Americas LLC *(G-940)*

Pepsico, Brookville Also Called: P-Americas LLC *(G-1332)*

Pepsico, Fort Wayne Also Called: Pepsico Inc *(G-5303)*

Pepsico, Indianapolis Also Called: P-Americas LLC *(G-9081)*

Pepsico, Indianapolis Also Called: Pepsi 3449 *(G-9117)*

Pepsico, Indianapolis Also Called: Pepsico *(G-9118)*

Pepsico, Jasper Also Called: Pepsi-Cola *(G-9902)*

Pepsico, Knightstown Also Called: Pepsico Inc *(G-10201)*

Pepsico, Logansport Also Called: Wp Beverages LLC *(G-11120)*

Pepsico, Munster Also Called: P-Americas LLC *(G-12556)*

Pepsico, Munster Also Called: Pepsi Beverages Company *(G-12557)*

Pepsico, Seymour Also Called: P-Americas LLC *(G-14670)*

Pepsico Inc 260 579-3461
3939 N Wells St Fort Wayne (46808) *(G-5303)*

Pepsico Inc 317 830-4011
9101 Orly Rd Indianapolis (46241) *(G-9119)*

Pepsico Inc 765 345-7668
7870 W County Road 850 S Knightstown (46148) *(G-10201)*

Pepsico Beverage Sales LLC 574 314-6001
5435 Dylan Dr Ste 100 South Bend (46628) *(G-15190)*

Perdue Farms, Lebanon Also Called: Perdue Farms Inc *(G-10931)*

Perdue Farms, Thorntown Also Called: Perdue Farms Inc *(G-15754)*

Perdue Farms, Vincennes Also Called: Perdue Farms Inc *(G-16143)*

Perdue Farms, Washington Also Called: Perdue Farms Inc *(G-16502)*

Perdue Farms Inc 765 325-2997
5490 N 500 E Lebanon (46052) *(G-10931)*

Perdue Farms Inc 765 436-7990
4586 N Us Highway 52 Thorntown (46071) *(G-15754)*

Perdue Farms Inc 812 886-0593
500 Perdue Rd Vincennes (47591) *(G-16143)*

Perdue Farms Inc 757 787-5210
100 W 400 N Washington (47501) *(G-16501)*

Perdue Farms Inc 812 254-8500
65 S 200 W Washington (47501) *(G-16502)*

Perdue Farms Inc 812 254-8515
65 S 200 W Washington (47501) *(G-16503)*

Perdue Printed Products Inc 260 456-7575
1707 S Harrison St Fort Wayne (46802) *(G-5304)*

Perfect Apparel LLC 317 389-5553
8443 Flatwood Ct Indianapolis (46278) *(G-9120)*

Perfect Impressions Printing 317 923-1756
3901 N Meridian St Ste 15 Indianapolis (46208) *(G-9121)*

Perfect Manufacturing LLC 317 924-5284
450 W 16th Pl Indianapolis (46202) *(G-9122)*

Perfect Pallets Inc (PA) 888 553-5559
450 W 16th Pl Indianapolis (46202) *(G-9123)*

Perfect Pig Inc 219 984-5355
332 W 100 N Reynolds (47980) *(G-14075)*

Perfect Plastic Printing Corp 317 888-9447
3967 Woodmore Dr Greenwood (46142) *(G-6750)*

Perfect Seating 317 564-8173
1016 3rd Ave Sw Carmel (46032) *(G-1716)*

Perfect Twist Pretzels LLC 574 248-1715
401 E Market St Nappanee (46550) *(G-12636)*

Perfect World Denim LLC 260 449-9099
212 Pearl St Fort Wayne (46802) *(G-5305)*

Perfecta USA 317 862-7371
5505 S Franklin Rd Indianapolis (46239) *(G-9124)*

Perfection Bakeries Inc (PA) 260 424-8245
6230 Bluffton Rd Fort Wayne (46809) *(G-5306)*

Perfection Bakeries Inc 219 789-4816
2650 Barley Rd Valparaiso (46383) *(G-16023)*

Perfection Mold & Tool Inc 574 292-0824
22255 Barking Deer Run South Bend (46628) *(G-15191)*

Perfection Products Inc 765 482-7786
1320 Indianapolis Ave Lebanon (46052) *(G-10932)*

Perfection Wheel LLC 260 358-9239
255 N Briant St Huntington (46750) *(G-7355)*

Perfecto Tool & Engineering Co 765 644-2821
1124 W 53rd St Anderson (46013) *(G-176)*

Performance, Dillsboro Also Called: Performance Machining Inc *(G-2951)*

Performance Brake Parts Inc 260 410-1404
10709 Steury Ln Grabill (46741) *(G-6320)*

Performance Cnc LLC 574 780-4864
1338 12th Rd Bourbon (46504) *(G-1126)*

Performance Coatings Spc LLC 574 606-8153
7030 W 665 S Topeka (46571) *(G-15815)*

Performance Machining Inc 812 432-9180
13350 Us Highway 50 Dillsboro (47018) *(G-2951)*

Performance Minerals Corp (PA) 219 365-8356
10220 Wicker Ave Ste 3 Saint John (46373) *(G-14455)*

Performance Mstr Coil Proc Inc 765 364-1300
3752 E 350 S Crawfordsville (47933) *(G-2603)*

Performance Organics, South Bend Also Called: James McBryde *(G-15089)*

Performance Powder Coating 765 438-5224
1124 S Union St Kokomo (46902) *(G-10320)*

Performance Rod & Custom Inc 812 897-5805
6200 N State Route 61 Boonville (47601) *(G-1095)*

Performance Technology Inc 574 862-2116
65251 State Road 19 Wakarusa (46573) *(G-16242)*

Performance Tool Inc 260 726-6572
103 Performance Dr Portland (47371) *(G-13959)*

Performer's Edition, Indianapolis Also Called: Performers Edition LLC *(G-9125)*

Performers Edition LLC 317 429-1300
230 E Ohio St Indianapolis (46204) *(G-9125)*

Performnce Sftwr Solutions Inc 574 239-2444
6561 Lonewolf Dr Ste 200 South Bend (46628) *(G-15192)*

Perkinelmer Hlth Sciences Inc 800 385-1555
2633 Foundation Dr South Bend (46628) *(G-15193)*

Perm Industries Inc 219 365-5000
9660 Industrial Dr Saint John (46373) *(G-14456)*

Perm Machine & Tool Co, Saint John Also Called: Perm Industries Inc *(G-14456)*

Perma Lubrication 317 241-0797
2346 S Lynhurst Dr Ste J Indianapolis (46241) *(G-9126)*

Perma Lubrication 219 531-9155
2503 Chicago St Ste A Valparaiso (46383) *(G-16024)*

Perma-Green Supreme Inc 219 548-3801
5609 Murvihill Rd Valparaiso (46383) *(G-16025)*

Permabase Building Pdts LLC 765 828-0898
75 Ivy Ln Clinton (47842) *(G-2075)*

Permalatt Products Inc (PA) 574 546-6311
3462 Us Highway 6 Bremen (46506) *(G-1213)*

Permawick Company Inc 812 376-0703
3110 Permawick Dr Columbus (47201) *(G-2376)*

Permo Wick, Columbus Also Called: Vernet US Corporation *(G-2412)*

Perpetual Industries Inc 702 707-9811
2193 Rotunda Dr Auburn (46706) *(G-415)*

Perq Convert LLC 800 873-3117
5868 E 71st St Ste E-672 Indianapolis (46220) *(G-9127)*

Perq Multifamily Software LLC 800 873-3117
5868 E 71st St Ste E-672 Indianapolis (46220) *(G-9128)*

Perry Equipment, Crawfordsville Also Called: McClamroch Ag LLC *(G-2588)*

Perry Foam Products Inc (PA) 765 474-3404
2335 S 30th St Lafayette (47909) *(G-10667)*

Perry Material Sales, Terre Haute Also Called: Prairie Group *(G-15666)*

Perry Miller 260 894-1133
2195 N 675 W Shipshewana (46565) *(G-14878)*

Perry Products Inc 260 316-8816
959 Growth Pkwy Angola (46703) *(G-283)*

Personal Impressions Inc 317 485-4409
325 W Broadway St Fortville (46040) *(G-5604)*

Personal Record Media LLC 317 507-4459
9760 Highpoint Ridge Dr Unit 102 Fishers (46037) *(G-4573)*

Perspicacity LLC 812 650-2080
4718 E Donington Dr Bloomington (47401) *(G-946)*

Peru Hardwood Products Inc 765 473-4844
2678 N Mexico Rd Peru (46970) *(G-13592)*

Peru Tribune, Peru Also Called: Daily Peru Tribune Pubg Co *(G-13577)*

Petal Pushers 812 396-9383
2276 E Cardinal Rd Oaktown (47561) *(G-13328)*

Petal Solutions LLC 765 404-7747
5164 Flowermound Dr West Lafayette (47906) *(G-16618)*

Pete D Limkemann 260 403-4297
724 S Doyle Rd Fort Wayne (46803) *(G-5307)*

Pete's Peaches, Washington Also Called: Southern Indiana Chemical Inc *(G-16509)*

Peter Austin Co 765 288-6397
900 W 1st St Muncie (47305) *(G-12474)*

Peter Franklin Jewelers Inc (PA) 260 749-4315
507 Broadway St New Haven (46774) *(G-12913)*

Peter Stone Company 260 768-9150
805 E North Village Dr Shipshewana (46565) *(G-14879)*

Peters & Marske, Michigan City Also Called: Mtm Machining Inc *(G-11642)*

Peters Enterprises 260 493-6435
217 State Road 930 W New Haven (46774) *(G-12914)*

Peters Equipment, New Haven Also Called: Peters Enterprises *(G-12914)*

Peterson Mfg LLC 574 876-1427
2848 W 1700 N Wheatfield (46392) *(G-16771)*

Peterson Sanko Corp 765 966-9656
505 Industrial Pkwy Richmond (47374) *(G-14182)*

Petnet Indiana LLC 865 218-2000
1345 W 16th St Rm 1 Indianapolis (46202) *(G-9129)*

Petoskey Plastics Inc 765 348-9808
1100 W Grant St Hartford City (47348) *(G-7074)*

Petrochoice Holdings Inc 317 634-7300
1751 W Raymond St Indianapolis (46221) *(G-9130)*

Petrogas International Corp 260 484-0859
2444 Woodland Trl Auburn (46706) *(G-416)*

Petroleum Jobbers Data Control 574 722-4477
2938 N County Road 275 E Logansport (46947) *(G-11102)*

Petroleum Solutions Inc 574 546-2133
809 Douglas Rd Bremen (46506) *(G-1214)*

Pettigrew 260 868-2032
7725 County Road 32 Butler (46721) *(G-1475)*

Pettit Printing Inc 260 563-2346
789 S Carroll St Wabash (46992) *(G-16212)*

Peyton Technical Services LLC 812 738-2016
1548 Highway 62 Nw Corydon (47112) *(G-2510)*

Peytons Barricade Sign Co LLC 812 283-6461
814 Spring St Jeffersonville (47130) *(G-10035)*

PFC Farm Services Inc 260 235-0817
3204 N 250 E Fremont (46737) *(G-5831)*

Pfeiffer Welding & Fabrication 765 434-1983
10373 W 650 N Sharpsville (46068) *(G-14711)*

Pfeiffer Winery & Vineyard Inc 812 952-2650
940 Saint Peters Church Rd Ne Corydon (47112) *(G-2511)*

Pfizer, South Bend Also Called: Pfizer Inc *(G-15194)*

Pfizer, Terre Haute Also Called: Pfizer Inc *(G-15660)*

Pfizer Inc 574 232-9927
6879 Enterprise Dr Ste 500 South Bend (46628) *(G-15194)*

Pfizer Inc 212 733-2323
411 E Dallas Dr Terre Haute (47802) *(G-15660)*

Pfm Automotive Management Inc 317 733-3977
4902 W 106th St Zionsville (46077) *(G-17040)*

Pfm Car & Truck Care, Indianapolis Also Called: Pfm Car & Truck Castleton Inc *(G-9131)*

Pfm Car & Truck Castleton Inc 317 577-7777
9501 Corporation Dr Indianapolis (46256) *(G-9131)*

Pfm Onsite, Indianapolis Also Called: Pfm Onsite Services Inc *(G-9132)*

Pfm Onsite Services Inc 317 784-7777
1402 W Hanna Ave Indianapolis (46217) *(G-9132)*

Pfortune Art & Design, Indianapolis Also Called: Pfortune Art & Design Inc *(G-9133)*

Pfortune Art & Design Inc 317 872-4123
9549 Valparaiso Ct Indianapolis (46268) *(G-9133)*

ALPHABETIC SECTION — Phonozoic

Pgc Landscaping & Mulch, Evansville Also Called: Pgc Mulch LLC *(G-4236)*
Pgc Mulch LLC.. 812 455-0700
1501 N 7th Ave Evansville (47710) *(G-4236)*
Pgi Mfg LLC (PA).. 574 968-3222
51565 Bittersweet Rd # B Granger (46530) *(G-6369)*
Pgp Corp.. 812 285-7700
701 Loop Rd Jeffersonville (47130) *(G-10036)*
Pgp International Inc.. 812 867-5129
5404 Foundation Blvd Evansville (47725) *(G-4237)*
Pgp International Inc.. 812 449-0650
1901 N New York Ave Evansville (47711) *(G-4238)*
Pgs LLC (PA)... 812 988-4030
120 E Main St Nashville (47448) *(G-12678)*
PH Custom Lures LLC.. 765 541-0726
3984 S County Road 350 E Connersville (47331) *(G-2461)*
Phan Gear Prints LLC.. 260 450-2539
2301 Fairfield Ave Apt 702 Fort Wayne (46807) *(G-5308)*
Phantom Industries LLC...................................... 812 276-5956
734 Spring St Jeffersonville (47130) *(G-10037)*
Phantom Neon LLC.. 765 362-2221
100 E North St Crawfordsville (47933) *(G-2604)*
Phantom Signs, Crawfordsville Also Called: Phantom Neon LLC *(G-2604)*
Pharma Form Finders LLC................................... 317 362-1191
11164 Muirfield Trce Fishers (46037) *(G-4574)*
Pharmaprinter Inc.. 765 543-1520
1201 Cumberland Ave Ste 105 West Lafayette (47906) *(G-16619)*
Pharos Tribune, Logansport Also Called: Community Holdings Indiana Inc *(G-11068)*
Pharos-Tribune, Logansport Also Called: Northwest Indiana Newsppr Inc *(G-11101)*
Phase Three Electric Inc...................................... 812 945-9922
2115 E Market St New Albany (47150) *(G-12793)*
Phasefour LLP... 812 583-7247
715 S Burkhardt Rd Evansville (47715) *(G-4239)*
Phazpak Inc... 260 692-6416
259 N Van Buren St Monroe (46772) *(G-12061)*
PHD Inc... 260 747-6151
9030 Clubridge Dr Fort Wayne (46809) *(G-5309)*
PHD Inc (HQ)... 260 747-6151
9009 Clubridge Dr Fort Wayne (46809) *(G-5310)*
PHD Inc... 260 356-0120
4763 N Us Highway 24 E Huntington (46750) *(G-7356)*
Phed Mobility LLC.. 574 226-4104
55335 Corwin Rd Elkhart (46514) *(G-3602)*
Phelps Dodge, Fort Wayne Also Called: Freeport Minerals Corporation *(G-5010)*
Phelps Machine Inc.. 765 468-6791
150 South Fulton St Parker City (47368) *(G-13505)*
Phend and Brown Inc (PA).................................... 574 658-4166
367 E 1250 N Milford (46542) *(G-11802)*
Phenix, Fort Wayne Also Called: Precision Products Group Inc *(G-5341)*
Phil & Son Inc.. 219 663-5757
871 N Madison St Crown Point (46307) *(G-2730)*
Phil Etienne Timber, Saint Croix Also Called: Phil Etiennes Timber Harvest *(G-14435)*
Phil Etiennes Timber Harvest............................... 812 843-5132
25993 Saint Croix Rd Saint Croix (47576) *(G-14435)*
Phil Irwin Advertising Inc..................................... 317 547-5117
5995 E 30th St Indianapolis (46218) *(G-9134)*
Phil Johnson.. 812 457-2433
512 S Green River Rd Evansville (47715) *(G-4240)*
Philip Konrad & Sons Inc..................................... 574 772-3966
1315 E State Road 10 Knox (46534) *(G-10219)*
Philip Pins... 219 769-1059
3701 W 79th Pl Merrillville (46410) *(G-11550)*
Philipps Wood Processing................................... 812 357-2824
8942 E County Road 1850 N Ferdinand (47532) *(G-4447)*
Philips Ultrasound Inc.. 317 591-5242
7518 E 39th St Indianapolis (46226) *(G-9135)*
Phillip D Kennedy Publishing............................... 317 872-6366
9256 Holyoke Ct Indianapolis (46268) *(G-9136)*
Phillip Westrick... 219 232-8337
101 E Lincoln St Kentland (47951) *(G-10161)*
Phillips Brothers Printers, Huntington Also Called: Mignone Communications Incorporated *(G-7344)*

Phillips Company Inc (PA).................................... 812 378-3797
6330 E 100 S Columbus (47201) *(G-2377)*
Phillips Company Inc... 812 526-8250
1045 S Walnut St Edinburgh (46124) *(G-3098)*
Phillips Diversified Services................................ 260 248-2975
309 N Washington St Columbia City (46725) *(G-2180)*
Phillips Feed Service Inc..................................... 610 250-2099
1936 S Lynhurst Dr, Indianapolis, In 46241, United States. Indianapolis (46241) *(G-9137)*
Phillips Pattern & Casting Inc (PA)...................... 765 288-2319
1001 W Riggin Rd Muncie (47303) *(G-12475)*
Phillips Pet Food & Supplies, Indianapolis Also Called: Phillips Feed Service Inc *(G-9137)*
Phillips Signs & Graphics.................................... 812 499-3607
4800 Tecumseh Ln Evansville (47715) *(G-4241)*
Phinia Delphi USA LLC.. 317 203-4602
6032 Gateway Dr Plainfield (46168) *(G-13714)*
Phinia USA LLC (DH)... 765 778-6879
6512 Production Dr Anderson (46013) *(G-177)*
Phipps Sons Welding... 219 776-3810
2126 W Ridge Rd Gary (46408) *(G-5994)*
PHM Brands LLC... 219 879-7356
1700 E Us Highway 12 Michigan City (46360) *(G-11651)*
Phoenix America LLC... 260 432-9664
4717 Clubview Dr Fort Wayne (46804) *(G-5311)*
Phoenix America Inc.. 260 432-9664
4717 Clubview Dr Fort Wayne (46804) *(G-5312)*
Phoenix Assembly LLC (HQ)................................ 317 884-3600
164 S Park Blvd Greenwood (46143) *(G-6751)*
Phoenix Assembly Indiana LLC............................ 317 884-3600
6200 S International Dr Columbus (47201) *(G-2378)*
Phoenix Brands LLC (PA).................................... 203 975-0319
2601 Fortune Cir E Ste 102b Indianapolis (46241) *(G-9138)*
Phoenix Closures Inc... 765 658-1800
2000 S Jackson St Greencastle (46135) *(G-6424)*
Phoenix Color, Terre Haute Also Called: Phoenix Color Corp *(G-15662)*
Phoenix Color Corp... 812 238-1551
200 Hulman St Terre Haute (47802) *(G-15661)*
Phoenix Color Corp... 812 234-1585
200 Hulman St Terre Haute (47802) *(G-15662)*
Phoenix Corporation.. 513 727-4763
1821 165th St Hammond (46320) *(G-6991)*
Phoenix Custom Kitchens Inc.............................. 812 523-1890
6600 N Us Highway 31 Seymour (47274) *(G-14674)*
Phoenix Fbrcators Erectors LLC (PA)................... 317 271-7002
182 S County Road 900 E Avon (46123) *(G-544)*
Phoenix Infiniti LLC... 260 443-2782
9723 W Cove Ct Fort Wayne (46804) *(G-5313)*
Phoenix Int Publications...................................... 317 796-2375
4792 E 400 S Ste B Lafayette (47905) *(G-10668)*
Phoenix Metals, Hammond Also Called: Phoenix Corporation *(G-6991)*
Phoenix Natural Resources Inc (HQ).................... 636 537-0283
Rte 5 Jasper (47546) *(G-9903)*
Phoenix Press Inc... 765 644-3959
1047 Broadway St Anderson (46012) *(G-178)*
Phoenix Pure Holdings LLC................................. 219 448-0142
2511 Fairway Dr Long Beach (46360) *(G-11127)*
Phoenix Safe International, Lebanon Also Called: PSI LLC *(G-10935)*
Phoenix Services LLC.. 219 787-0019
1190 E Loop Dr Portage (46368) *(G-13903)*
Phoenix Services LLC.. 219 399-7808
280 Scotscraig Dr Valparaiso (46385) *(G-16026)*
PHOENIX SERVICES, LLC, Portage Also Called: Phoenix Services LLC *(G-13903)*
Phoenix Sign Works Inc....................................... 317 432-4027
5345 Lexington Ave Indianapolis (46219) *(G-9139)*
Phoenix Stamping Group LLC.............................. 404 699-2882
2701 S Coliseum Blvd Ste 1326 Fort Wayne (46803) *(G-5314)*
Phoenix Usa Inc.. 574 266-2020
3504 Cooper Dr Elkhart (46514) *(G-3603)*
Phoenix Woodworking Co LLC............................. 317 340-0726
3865 Penzance Pl Carmel (46032) *(G-1717)*
Phonozoic.. 812 331-0047
1208 W 8th St Bloomington (47404) *(G-947)*

Photo Screen Service Inc 317 636-7712
  1505 Southeastern Ave Indianapolis (46201) *(G-9140)*
Photo Specialties 812 944-5111
  232 Maevi Dr New Albany (47150) *(G-12794)*
Photograv, Goshen *Also Called: Imagelaz LLC (G-6170)*
Photon Automation Inc 844 574-6866
  275 Center St Greenfield (46140) *(G-6538)*
Photon Automation Inc (PA) 844 574-6866
  501 W New Rd Greenfield (46140) *(G-6539)*
Photonic LLC 502 930-9544
  611 Beau Vista Pl Sellersburg (47172) *(G-14610)*
Photoprose Productions Inc 316 371-4634
  1528 Scott St Jeffersonville (47130) *(G-10038)*
Phtal Aoy Industries LLC 260 267-0025
  810 S Buffalo St Ste D Warsaw (46580) *(G-16411)*
Phyllis Kennedy Hardware, Indianapolis *Also Called: Phillip D Kennedy Publishing (G-9136)*
Phytoption LLC 765 490-7738
  3316 Morgan St West Lafayette (47906) *(G-16620)*
Pia Automation US Inc (DH) 812 485-5500
  5825 Old Boonville Hwy Evansville (47715) *(G-4242)*
Piccolo Printing 888 901-8648
  729 S Green River Rd Evansville (47715) *(G-4243)*
Picketts Place Inc 317 763-1168
  17041 Westfield Park Rd Westfield (46074) *(G-16717)*
Pickle Bites LLC 773 780-7559
  7451 Olcott Ave Hammond (46323) *(G-6992)*
Pickled Pedaler 317 877-0624
  5713 Mahogany Dr Noblesville (46062) *(G-13155)*
Pickslays Woodworking 530 388-8697
  1313 Wooster Rd Winona Lake (46590) *(G-16914)*
Picture It Inc 260 463-7373
  4425 W Us Highway 20 Ste 1 Lagrange (46761) *(G-10758)*
Picture Perfect Printing 765 482-4241
  1301 Ashley Dr Lebanon (46052) *(G-10933)*
Picture This & Stitch That 219 797-4006
  2222 W 1200 S Hanna (46340) *(G-7038)*
Piece Vallet Cabinets, Montgomery *Also Called: Custom Tables & Cabinets (G-12093)*
Pieniadze Inc 888 226-6241
  1555 W Oak St Ste 100 Zionsville (46077) *(G-17041)*
Pierce Company Inc (HQ) 765 998-8100
  35 North 8th St Upland (46989) *(G-15880)*
Pierce Oil Co Inc 812 268-6356
  115 W Jackson St Sullivan (47882) *(G-15416)*
Pierce Tracy 765 748-2361
  4663 State Road 32 E Anderson (46017) *(G-179)*
Pierceton Case & Tray, Pierceton *Also Called: Paragon Medical Inc (G-13638)*
Pierceton I&I, Pierceton *Also Called: Paragon Medical Inc (G-13637)*
Pierceton Rubber Products Inc 574 594-3002
  3076 S 900 E Pierceton (46562) *(G-13639)*
Piercy Machine Co Inc 317 398-9296
  945 W 300 S Shelbyville (46176) *(G-14782)*
Piercy Sports, Whiteland *Also Called: Ryan Piercy (G-16794)*
Piezotech LLC (HQ) 317 876-4670
  8431 Georgetown Rd Ste 300 Indianapolis (46268) *(G-9141)*
Pigeon Switch Pottery 812 567-4124
  1896 Pigeon Switch Tennyson (47637) *(G-15524)*
Pike County Publishing Corp (PA) 812 354-8500
  820 E Poplar St Petersburg (47567) *(G-13621)*
Pike Lumber Company Inc 574 893-4511
  440 W County Rd1450 N Carbon (47837) *(G-1538)*
Pike Lumber Company Inc (PA) 574 893-4511
  719 Front St Akron (46910) *(G-7)*
Pike Publishing 812 354-4701
  407 E Walnut St Petersburg (47567) *(G-13622)*
Pilkington North America Inc 317 346-0621
  1001 Hurricane St Franklin (46131) *(G-5766)*
Pilkington North America Inc 317 392-7000
  300 Northridge Dr Shelbyville (46176) *(G-14783)*
Pilkington North America Inc 574 273-5457
  3725 Cleveland Rd Ste 100 South Bend (46628) *(G-15195)*
Pillar Innovations LLC 812 474-9080
  9844 Hedden Rd Evansville (47725) *(G-4244)*

Pillsbury, New Albany *Also Called: Pillsbury Company LLC (G-12795)*
Pillsbury Company LLC 812 944-8411
  707 Pillsbury Ln New Albany (47150) *(G-12795)*
Pilot News, Plymouth *Also Called: Cnhi LLC (G-13763)*
Pimmler Holdings Inc (PA) 574 583-8090
  3137 S Freeman Rd Monticello (47960) *(G-12165)*
Pin Oak Group LLC 260 637-7778
  3150 Mallard Cove Ln Fort Wayne (46804) *(G-5315)*
Pin Point Av LLC 317 750-3120
  8226 Kentallen Ct Indianapolis (46236) *(G-9142)*
Pin-Up Curls LLC 260 241-5871
  1835 Marietta Dr Fort Wayne (46804) *(G-5316)*
Pinder Industries, Munster *Also Called: Pinder Instruments Company Inc (G-12558)*
Pinder Instruments Company Inc 219 924-7070
  9751 Indiana Pkwy Ste A Munster (46321) *(G-12558)*
Pinder Polyurethane & Plas Inc 219 397-8248
  481 E 151st St East Chicago (46312) *(G-3034)*
Pine Cone II LLC 463 232-3138
  11555 N Meridian St Ste 560 Carmel (46032) *(G-1718)*
Pine Manor Inc 574 533-4186
  321 S 3rd St Goshen (46526) *(G-6238)*
Pine Manor Inc (HQ) 800 532-4186
  9622 W 350 N Orland (46776) *(G-13370)*
Pine Valley Munitions Inc 260 818-6113
  555 N Line St Columbia City (46725) *(G-2181)*
Pineapple Software Inc 812 987-8277
  1801 Creekside Dr Clarksville (47129) *(G-2025)*
Pinetree Woodcraft LLC 765 886-1177
  3734 Sugar Grove Rd Greens Fork (47345) *(G-6576)*
Ping Custom Drapery Workroom 317 984-3251
  11313 E 234th St Cicero (46034) *(G-1999)*
Ping's Custom Drapery, Cicero *Also Called: Ping Custom Drapery Workroom (G-1999)*
Pingleton Logging Inc 765 653-2878
  525 S County Road 550 W Greencastle (46135) *(G-6425)*
Pingleton Sawmill Inc 765 653-2878
  525 S County Road 550 W Greencastle (46135) *(G-6426)*
Pink Signs LLC 317 509-8805
  502 State Road 267 Mooresville Mooresville (46158) *(G-12235)*
Pinnacle Equipment Company Inc 317 259-1180
  1616 Milburn St Indianapolis (46202) *(G-9143)*
Pinnacle Mailing Products 765 405-1194
  7701 W Kilgore Ave Ste 5 Yorktown (47396) *(G-16980)*
Pinnacle Oil, Indianapolis *Also Called: Pinnacle Oil Holdings LLC (G-9145)*
Pinnacle Oil, Indianapolis *Also Called: Pinnacle Oil Inc (G-9146)*
Pinnacle Oil Holdings LLC 317 875-9465
  8175 Allison Ave Indianapolis (46268) *(G-9144)*
Pinnacle Oil Holdings LLC (PA) 317 875-9465
  5009 W 81st St Indianapolis (46268) *(G-9145)*
Pinnacle Oil Inc 317 875-9465
  5009 W 81st St Indianapolis (46268) *(G-9146)*
Pinnacle Oil Trading LLC 317 875-9465
  5009 W 81st St Indianapolis (46268) *(G-9147)*
Pinnacle Textile Inds LLC 574 223-4311
  2516 E State Road 14 Rochester (46975) *(G-14311)*
Pinpoint Printer 812 577-0630
  541 Green Blvd Aurora (47001) *(G-452)*
Pinson Manufacturing Co LLC 217 273-8819
  500 W Walnut St Albany (47320) *(G-14)*
Pioneer Cane & Handle Co 812 859-4415
  3016 E River Rd Clay City (47841) *(G-2046)*
Pioneer Metal Finishing LLC 574 287-7239
  2424 Foundation Dr South Bend (46628) *(G-15196)*
Pioneer Oil Company Inc 812 494-2800
  400 Main St Vincennes (47591) *(G-16144)*
Pioneer Oilfield Services LLC 812 882-0999
  1290 N State Road 67 Vincennes (47591) *(G-16145)*
Pioneer Plastics Corporation 574 264-0702
  25603 Borg Rd Elkhart (46514) *(G-3604)*
Pioneer Transport LLC 260 726-4840
  1617 N Meridian St Portland (47371) *(G-13960)*
PIP Marketing Signs Print 317 843-5755
  11711 Pennsylvania St Ste 107 Carmel (46032) *(G-1719)*

ALPHABETIC SECTION

PIP Printing, Carmel *Also Called: PIP Marketing Signs Print (G-1719)*
PIP Printing, Columbus *Also Called: Jem Printing Inc (G-2330)*
PIP Printing, Greenwood *Also Called: MD Laird Inc (G-6737)*
PIP Printing, Indianapolis *Also Called: Drs Graphix Group Inc (G-8011)*
PIP Printing, Indianapolis *Also Called: Dynamark Graphics Group Inc (G-8023)*
PIP Printing, Indianapolis *Also Called: Dynamark Graphics Group Inc (G-8024)*
PIP Printing, Indianapolis *Also Called: Ed Sons Inc (G-8051)*
PIP Printing, New Albany *Also Called: Lagnaippe LLC (G-12762)*
PIP Printing, Noblesville *Also Called: Kistner Enterprises Inc (G-13123)*
PIP Printing & Marketting Svcs, Anderson *Also Called: Jam Printing Inc (G-138)*
Pipe Creek Jr 765 922-7991
  6377 W 600 S Sims (46986) *(G-14924)*
Pipe Dream Innovations LLC 503 910-8815
  4201 S Washington St # 3269 Marion (46953) *(G-11328)*
Pipeconx, Evansville *Also Called: Ace Extrusion LLC (G-3870)*
Pipeconx, Evansville *Also Called: R2b2 Industries LLC (G-4270)*
Piper Flyers II Inc 317 858-9538
  230 Woodstock Ct Zionsville (46077) *(G-17042)*
Piro, Fishers *Also Called: Piro Shoes LLC (G-4575)*
Piro Shoes LLC 888 849-0916
  8327 Weaver Woods Pl Fishers (46038) *(G-4575)*
Pitcher Enterprises LLC 574 242-1113
  524 N Plymouth Rd Winamac (46996) *(G-16870)*
Pitney Bowes, Indianapolis *Also Called: Pitney Bowes Inc (G-9148)*
Pitney Bowes, Whitestown *Also Called: Pitney Bowes Inc (G-16814)*
Pitney Bowes Inc 260 436-7395
  5071 W 74th St Indianapolis (46268) *(G-9148)*
Pitney Bowes Inc 317 769-8300
  5490 Industrial Ct Whitestown (46075) *(G-16814)*
Pittman Mine Service LLC 812 847-2340
  2878 N State Road 59 Linton (47441) *(G-11042)*
Pittsfield of Indiana, Hamilton *Also Called: Pittsfield Products Inc (G-6859)*
Pittsfield Products Inc 260 488-2124
  7365 S Enterprise Dr Hamilton (46742) *(G-6859)*
Pivot Manufacturing Inc 317 371-3560
  2401 N Executive Park Dr Ste 1000 Yorktown (47396) *(G-16981)*
Pizo Operating Company LLC 317 243-0811
  7901 W Morris St Indianapolis (46231) *(G-9149)*
Pjkellynet 765 457-5864
  4814 N Parkway Kokomo (46901) *(G-10321)*
Pjw Inc 574 295-1203
  56199 Parkway Ave Elkhart (46516) *(G-3605)*
Pk USA Inc (HQ) 317 395-5500
  600 Northridge Dr Shelbyville (46176) *(G-14784)*
Pl Porter, Westfield *Also Called: Kph Engineered Systems Inc (G-16707)*
Placon Corporation 608 278-4920
  2901 Oakland Ave Elkhart (46517) *(G-3606)*
Plainfield Eye Care 317 839-2368
  900 Edwards Dr Plainfield (46168) *(G-13715)*
Plainfield Winery Tstng Rm 317 837-9463
  6291 Cambridge Way Plainfield (46168) *(G-13716)*
Planet Goshen LLC 574 830-5797
  2616 Peddlers Village Rd Goshen (46526) *(G-6239)*
Planet Pets 812 539-7316
  1099 W Eads Pkwy Lawrenceburg (47025) *(G-10853)*
Plank & Stella, Indianapolis *Also Called: Melissa Lambino (G-8874)*
Planks Printing Service Inc 574 533-1739
  505 S 9th St Goshen (46526) *(G-6240)*
Plant 83, Elkhart *Also Called: Lippert Components Inc (G-3492)*
Plaquemaker Plus Inc 317 594-5556
  10080 E 121st St Ste 118 Fishers (46037) *(G-4576)*
Plas-Tech Molding & Design Inc 260 761-3006
  7037 N Triplett St B Brimfield (46794) *(G-1233)*
Plaster Shak 317 881-6518
  1797 Old State Road 37 Greenwood (46143) *(G-6752)*
Plastic Assembly Tech Inc 317 841-1202
  8445 Castlewood Dr Ste B Indianapolis (46250) *(G-9150)*
Plastic Cardz LLC 260 431-6380
  12721 Us Highway 24 W Fort Wayne (46814) *(G-5317)*

Plastic Composites Co., Fort Wayne *Also Called: Composites Syndicate LLC (G-4870)*
Plastic Dynamics Inc (PA) 574 272-4576
  52060 Larkspur Cir Granger (46530) *(G-6370)*
Plastic Extrusions Company 812 479-3232
  6500 Newburgh Rd Evansville (47715) *(G-4245)*
Plastic Molding Mfg Inc 574 234-9036
  5102 Dylan Dr South Bend (46628) *(G-15197)*
Plastic Moldings Company Llc 317 392-4139
  1451 Miller Ave Shelbyville (46176) *(G-14785)*
Plastic Pipe Technologies LLC 317 674-5944
  2907 S Wollenweber Rd New Palestine (46163) *(G-12942)*
Plastic Processors Inc 260 488-3999
  7450 S Homestead Dr Hamilton (46742) *(G-6860)*
Plastic Project Resource LLC 812 390-9790
  3302 N Meadow Dr Hope (47246) *(G-7231)*
Plastic Recycl Export Ltd LLC 301 758-6885
  6167 Stoney Creek Dr Fort Wayne (46825) *(G-5318)*
Plastic Recycling Inc (PA) 317 780-6100
  7601 Rockville Rd Indianapolis (46214) *(G-9151)*
Plastic Top Fabricators Inc 317 786-4367
  1302 W Troy Ave Indianapolis (46225) *(G-9152)*
Plastic Works, Fort Wayne *Also Called: Meyer Plastics Inc (G-5219)*
Plasticraft-Complete Acrylics 765 610-9502
  4441 S Scatterfield Rd Anderson (46013) *(G-180)*
Plastics Family Holdings Inc 317 890-1808
  3439 N Shadeland Ave Ste 5 Indianapolis (46226) *(G-9153)*
Plastics Research and Dev Inc 812 279-8885
  747 Washboard Rd Springville (47462) *(G-15390)*
Plastimatic Arts Corp 574 254-9000
  3622 N Home St Mishawaka (46545) *(G-11975)*
Plating Products Inc 775 241-0416
  1020 S Main St Kokomo (46902) *(G-10322)*
Platinum Display Group 317 731-5026
  5855 Kopetsky Dr Indianapolis (46217) *(G-9154)*
Platinum Equity, Jeffersonville *Also Called: Acbl Holding Corporation (G-9921)*
Platinum Feeds and Supply LLC 812 593-7232
  6140 W County Road 240 Nw Greensburg (47240) *(G-6623)*
Platinum Industries LLC 765 744-8323
  11625 Suncatcher Dr Fishers (46037) *(G-4577)*
Play 2 Win Screenprinting LLC 765 426-0679
  8975 E 200 S Oxford (47971) *(G-13476)*
Playfair Shuffleboard Company 260 747-7288
  7021 Bluffton Rd Fort Wayne (46809) *(G-5319)*
Pleasant Hill Veneer Corp 812 725-8924
  278c America Pl Ste C Jeffersonville (47130) *(G-10039)*
Plexiclass Awards Disc Tropies, Elkhart *Also Called: Smokers Iron Works (G-3687)*
Pli LLC 219 326-1350
  239 Factory St La Porte (46350) *(G-10463)*
Pliant LLC 253 872-2253
  101 Oakley St Evansville (47710) *(G-4246)*
PLM Holdings Inc 812 232-0624
  3956 S State Road 63 Terre Haute (47802) *(G-15663)*
Ploog Engineering Co Inc 219 663-2854
  814 N Indiana Ave Crown Point (46307) *(G-2731)*
Pls, Jeffersonville *Also Called: Packaging Lgstics Slutions LLC (G-10033)*
Plum Group Inc (HQ) 617 712-3000
  101 W Washington St Indianapolis (46204) *(G-9155)*
Plum Grove Music, Lowell *Also Called: Plum Grove Strings LLC (G-11175)*
Plum Grove Strings LLC 219 696-5401
  1107 E 181st Ave Lowell (46356) *(G-11175)*
Plum Voice, Indianapolis *Also Called: Plum Group Inc (G-9155)*
Plumrose, Elkhart *Also Called: Plumrose Usa Inc (G-3607)*
Plumrose Usa Inc 574 295-8190
  24402 County Road 45 Elkhart (46516) *(G-3607)*
Pluto, French Lick *Also Called: Ahf Industries Inc (G-5843)*
Plymouth Foundry Inc 574 936-2106
  523 W Harrison St Plymouth (46563) *(G-13801)*
Plymouth Molding Group LLC 574 933-4189
  2925 Commerce St Plymouth (46563) *(G-13802)*
Plymouth Oil and Gas Inc 574 875-4808
  57592 Hearthstone Ct Goshen (46528) *(G-6241)*

Plymouth Pallet Company Inc 574 935-5553
1145 Markley Dr Plymouth (46563) *(G-13803)*

Plymouth Pdts Acquisition Inc 574 936-4757
1800 Jim Neu Dr Ste 7 Plymouth (46563) *(G-13804)*

Plymouth Transfer Station, Plymouth *Also Called: Darling Ingredients Inc (G-13770)*

Plymouth Tube Company 574 946-6191
572 W State Road 14 Winamac (46996) *(G-16871)*

Plz Corp 317 788-0750
6501 Julian Ave Indianapolis (46219) *(G-9156)*

PMC, Saint John *Also Called: Performance Minerals Corp (G-14455)*

PMC, Shelbyville *Also Called: Plastic Moldings Company Llc (G-14785)*

PMG Incorporated 574 291-3805
5534 Colonial Ln South Bend (46614) *(G-15198)*

PMG Indiana LLC (DH) 812 379-4606
1751 Arcadia Dr Columbus (47201) *(G-2379)*

Pmp Enterprise, Centerville *Also Called: Charles Bane (G-1848)*

Pocket Press LLC 888 237-2110
4101 S Harrison St Fort Wayne (46807) *(G-5320)*

Poco A Poco LLC 317 443-5753
7611 Hursh Rd Leo (46765) *(G-10971)*

Podfan LLC 317 771-0475
6507 Carrollton Ave Indianapolis (46220) *(G-9157)*

Poet Bprocessing - Cloverdale, Cloverdale *Also Called: Poet Brfining - Cloverdale LLC (G-2093)*

Poet Borefining - Portland LLC 260 726-2681
1542 S 200 W Portland (47371) *(G-13961)*

Poet Bprcessing - N Manchester, North Manchester *Also Called: Poet Brfining - N Mnchester LLC (G-13247)*

Poet Bprocessing - Shelbyville, Shelbyville *Also Called: Poet Brfining - Shelbyville LLC (G-14786)*

Poet Brfining - Alexandria LLC 765 724-4384
13179 N 100 E Alexandria (46001) *(G-57)*

Poet Brfining - Cloverdale LLC 765 795-3235
2265 E County Road 800 S Cloverdale (46120) *(G-2093)*

Poet Brfining- Portland 18200, Portland *Also Called: Poet Borefining - Portland LLC (G-13961)*

Poet Brfning - N Mnchester LLC 260 774-3532
868 E 800 N North Manchester (46962) *(G-13247)*

Poet Brfning - Shelbyville LLC 317 699-4199
2373 W 300 N Shelbyville (46176) *(G-14786)*

Poet Brfnng- Alexandria 21200, Alexandria *Also Called: Poet Brfining - Alexandria LLC (G-57)*

Point Biopharma Global Inc (HQ) 317 543-9957
4850 W 78th St Indianapolis (46268) *(G-9158)*

Point Biopharma Inc 833 544-2637
4850 W 78th St Indianapolis (46268) *(G-9159)*

Point Biopharma USA Inc 317 543-9957
4850 W 78th St Indianapolis (46268) *(G-9160)*

Point Machine Products Inc 574 289-2429
621 S Scott St South Bend (46601) *(G-15199)*

Point Medical Corporation 219 663-1775
871 E Summit St Crown Point (46307) *(G-2732)*

Poiry Partners, Fort Wayne *Also Called: Poiry Partners LLC (G-5322)*

Poiry Partners LLC 260 436-7070
7337 W Jefferson Blvd Fort Wayne (46804) *(G-5321)*

Poiry Partners LLC (PA) 260 424-1030
2535 Wayne Trce Fort Wayne (46803) *(G-5322)*

Poland Chapel Historical Soc 213 977-2280
5251 N Candlestick Corner Rd Centerpoint (47840) *(G-1846)*

Polar Ice, Indianapolis *Also Called: Home City Ice Company (G-8405)*

Polar Information Tech LLC 303 725-8015
7083 Koldyke Dr Fishers (46038) *(G-4578)*

Polar King International Inc 260 428-2530
4424 New Haven Ave Fort Wayne (46803) *(G-5323)*

Polar Kraft Boats, Syracuse *Also Called: Wawasee Aluminum Works Inc (G-15490)*

Polar Seal Inc 260 356-2369
4461 W 500 N Huntington (46750) *(G-7357)*

Policystat LLC 317 644-1296
550 Congressional Blvd Ste 100 Carmel (46032) *(G-1720)*

Politan Steel Fabrication Inc 317 714-6800
15133 Clove Hitch Ct Fishers (46040) *(G-4647)*

Polk, Dennis Equipment, New Paris *Also Called: Dennis Polk & Associates Inc (G-12950)*

Polley Tech LLC 812 524-0688
333 S State Road 11 Seymour (47274) *(G-14675)*

Poly Group LLC 812 590-4750
3000 Technology Ave Ste 2221 New Albany (47150) *(G-12796)*

Poly HI Solidur Inc 260 479-4100
2710 American Way Fort Wayne (46809) *(G-5324)*

Poly Pro Tools, Zionsville *Also Called: Remco Products Corporation (G-17046)*

Poly-Seal LLC (HQ) 812 306-2573
101 Oakley St Evansville (47710) *(G-4247)*

Poly-Wood LLC 877 457-3284
925a Polywood Way Syracuse (46567) *(G-15473)*

Poly-Wood LLC (HQ) 574 457-3284
1000 Polywood Way Syracuse (46567) *(G-15474)*

Polycon Industries Inc 219 738-1000
8919 Colorado St Merrillville (46410) *(G-11551)*

Polycraft Products Inc (PA) 812 577-3401
897 Rudolph Way Greendale (47025) *(G-6452)*

Polyfusion LLC 260 624-7659
395 Lane 101 Angola (46703) *(G-284)*

Polyfusion LLC 260 624-7659
959 Growth Pkwy Ste D Angola (46703) *(G-285)*

Polygon Company 574 586-3145
Tenesse St Walkerton (46574) *(G-16274)*

Polygon Company (PA) 574 586-3145
103 Industrial Park Dr Walkerton (46574) *(G-16275)*

Polymath Publishing LLC 317 410-5551
6043 N Oxford St Indianapolis (46220) *(G-9161)*

Polymer Logistics Inc 219 706-5985
6750 Daniel Burnham Dr Portage (46368) *(G-13904)*

Polymer Science Inc (PA) 574 583-3751
2577 S Freeman Rd Monticello (47960) *(G-12166)*

Polymer Technology Systems Inc (HQ) 317 870-5610
4600 Anson Blvd Whitestown (46075) *(G-16815)*

Polymicrospheres Division, Indianapolis *Also Called: Vasmo Inc (G-9702)*

Polymod Technologies Inc 260 436-1322
4146 Engleton Dr Fort Wayne (46804) *(G-5325)*

Polyram Compounds LLC 812 401-5830
15000 Foundation Ave Evansville (47725) *(G-4248)*

Polytec Packaging Solution, Fort Wayne *Also Called: Calico Precision Molding LLC (G-4829)*

Polytek Development Corp 317 494-6420
2140 Earlywood Dr Franklin (46131) *(G-5767)*

Polyweave Industries Inc 812 467-0300
11 S Kentucky Ave Evansville (47714) *(G-4249)*

Pom By ARI LLC 312 978-1668
612 Broadmoor Ave Munster (46321) *(G-12559)*

Pomps Tire Service Inc 260 489-5252
2720 Goshen Rd Fort Wayne (46808) *(G-5326)*

Pond Champs, Fort Wayne *Also Called: Sanco Industries Inc (G-5397)*

Pond Doctor, Aurora *Also Called: Pond Doctors Inc (G-453)*

Pond Doctors Inc 812 744-5258
11343 Coyote Run Rd Aurora (47001) *(G-453)*

Ponderosa Cabinet Company LLC 260 349-2509
7817 E Cree Lake Dr N Kendallville (46755) *(G-10143)*

Pontiac Engraving 630 834-4424
900 W Garro St Plymouth (46563) *(G-13805)*

Pontone Industries LLC 765 966-8012
401 Industrial Pkwy Richmond (47374) *(G-14183)*

Pontoon Boat LLC 574 264-6336
2805 Decio Dr Elkhart (46514) *(G-3608)*

Pontoonstuff Inc 574 970-0003
1165 Fremont Ct Elkhart (46516) *(G-3609)*

Pool Enterprises, Nashville *Also Called: Helmsburg Sawmill Inc (G-12671)*

Pool Shop 812 446-0026
1202 W Hendrix St Brazil (47834) *(G-1162)*

Poolguard, North Vernon *Also Called: Poolguard/Pbm Industries Inc (G-13292)*

Poolguard/Pbm Industries Inc 812 346-2648
1150 W Jfk Dr North Vernon (47265) *(G-13292)*

Pools of Fun Inc 317 843-0337
14765 Hazel Dell Xing Noblesville (46062) *(G-13156)*

Poore Brothers - Bluffton LLC 260 824-2800
705 W Dustman Rd Bluffton (46714) *(G-1048)*

ALPHABETIC SECTION

Popcorn Weaver Mfg LLC (PA) 765 934-2101
9365 Counselors Row Indianapolis (46240) *(G-9162)*

Pope Steel 317 498-0504
4496 E 100 N Greenfield (46140) *(G-6540)*

Popguns Inc 317 897-8660
30 S Post Rd Indianapolis (46219) *(G-9163)*

Poppy Co 317 442-2491
10915 N State Road 267 Brownsburg (46112) *(G-1395)*

Poptique Popcorn LLC 260 244-3745
120 W Walker Way Ste C Columbia City (46725) *(G-2182)*

Porchlight, Fishers *Also Called: Porchlight Group Inc (G-4579)*

Porchlight Group Inc 317 804-1166
7 Launch Way Ste 610 Fishers (46038) *(G-4579)*

Portable Welding Solutions 714 381-1690
805 Olin Ave Indianapolis (46222) *(G-9164)*

Portage Custom Wear LLC 219 841-9070
2294 Swanson Rd Portage (46368) *(G-13905)*

Portee Publishing LLC 812 259-5446
501 N Meridian St Washington (47501) *(G-16504)*

Porter Case Inc 219 289-2616
3718 W Western Ave South Bend (46619) *(G-15200)*

Porter County Fabricators Ltd 219 663-4665
13405 Montgomery St Crown Point (46307) *(G-2733)*

Porter County Ir & Met Recycle 219 996-7630
552 S 600 W Ste 1 Hebron (46341) *(G-7104)*

Porter Engineered Systems, Westfield *Also Called: Porter Systems Inc (G-16718)*

Porter Inc 800 736-7685
2200 W Monroe St Decatur (46733) *(G-2876)*

Porter Paints, Avon *Also Called: PPG Architectural Finishes Inc (G-545)*

Porter Paints, Carmel *Also Called: PPG Architectural Finishes Inc (G-1723)*

Porter Paints, Carmel *Also Called: PPG Architectural Finishes Inc (G-1724)*

Porter Paints, Evansville *Also Called: PPG Architectural Finishes Inc (G-4251)*

Porter Paints, Fort Wayne *Also Called: PPG Architectural Finishes Inc (G-5332)*

Porter Paints, Vincennes *Also Called: PPG Architectural Finishes Inc (G-16146)*

Porter Signs 812 222-0283
305 E 5th St Greensburg (47240) *(G-6624)*

Porter Systems Inc (DH) 519 737-1678
2000 E 196th St Westfield (46074) *(G-16718)*

Portland Division, Portland *Also Called: Joyce/Dayton Corp (G-13952)*

Portland Tire & Service Inc 260 726-9321
210 S Meridian St Portland (47371) *(G-13962)*

Poseidon Barge, Berne *Also Called: Poseidon LLC (G-722)*

Poseidon LLC 260 422-8767
725 E Parr Rd Berne (46711) *(G-722)*

Posey County News 812 682-3950
801 North St New Harmony (47631) *(G-12888)*

Positron Corporation (PA) 574 295-8777
4614 Wyland Dr Elkhart (46516) *(G-3610)*

Post and Mail, Columbia City *Also Called: Horizon Publications Inc (G-2152)*

Poster Display Co, Indianapolis *Also Called: L R Green Co Inc (G-8705)*

Posters 2 Prints LLC (PA) 800 598-5837
9900 Westpoint Dr Ste 138 Indianapolis (46256) *(G-9165)*

Posters 2 Prints LLC 317 414-8972
10428 Starboard Way Indianapolis (46256) *(G-9166)*

Posters 2 Prints LLC 317 769-3784
9389 Timberwolf Ln Zionsville (46077) *(G-17043)*

Postle Aluminum, Elkhart *Also Called: Postle Operating LLC (G-3612)*

Postle Aluminum Company LLC (HQ) 574 389-0800
511 Pine Creek Ct Elkhart (46516) *(G-3611)*

Postle Operating LLC 574 266-7720
1503 Pierina Dr Elkhart (46514) *(G-3612)*

Postle Operating LLC (HQ) 574 389-0800
511 Pine Creek Ct Elkhart (46516) *(G-3613)*

Postmasters, Indianapolis *Also Called: Anthony Wyne Rhblttion Ctr For (G-7522)*

PostNet, Greenfield *Also Called: PostNet Postal & Business Svcs (G-6541)*

PostNet Postal & Business Svcs 317 462-7118
1547 N State St Greenfield (46140) *(G-6541)*

Potorti Enterprises Inc 812 989-8528
4618 Shadyview Dr Floyds Knobs (47119) *(G-4688)*

Poultry Press 765 827-0932
943 N My Ln Connersville (47331) *(G-2462)*

Powco Inc 765 334-4210
2583 S State Road 1 Cambridge City (47327) *(G-1500)*

Powder Blue 918 835-2629
723 Quarry Rd Nw Corydon (47112) *(G-2512)*

Powder Coating By Express LLC 812 402-1010
1400 N Fares Ave Evansville (47711) *(G-4250)*

Powder Cting / Hlscher Pwdr Ct, Fowler *Also Called: Holscher Products Inc (G-5625)*

Powder LLC 317 581-9271
1791 Hourglass Dr Carmel (46032) *(G-1721)*

Powder Metal Technicians Inc 317 353-2812
1565 Graham St Franklin (46131) *(G-5768)*

Powder Processing & Tech LLC 219 462-4141
5103 Evans Ave Valparaiso (46383) *(G-16027)*

Powdercoil Technologies LLC 708 634-2343
9800 Connecticut Dr Crown Point (46307) *(G-2734)*

Powdertech Corp 219 462-4141
5103 Evans Ave Valparaiso (46383) *(G-16028)*

Powell Paving Company, Cambridge City *Also Called: Powco Inc (G-1500)*

Powell Systems Inc 765 884-0980
83 S Meridian Rd Fowler (47944) *(G-5630)*

Powell Systems Inc 765 884-0613
604 E 9th St Fowler (47944) *(G-5631)*

Powell Woodworking LLC 812 279-5029
196 Bartlettsville Rd Bedford (47421) *(G-660)*

Power Components of Midwest 574 256-6990
56641 Twin Branch Dr Mishawaka (46545) *(G-11976)*

Power Freight, Fort Wayne *Also Called: Power Freight LLC (G-5327)*

Power Freight LLC 260 258-6012
4825 Devonshire Dr Fort Wayne (46806) *(G-5327)*

Power Gear, Mishawaka *Also Called: Enerpac Tool Group Corp (G-11894)*

Power Plant Service Inc 260 432-6716
2500 W Jefferson Blvd Fort Wayne (46802) *(G-5328)*

Power Systems Innovations Inc 812 480-4380
3247 Commerce Dr Newburgh (47630) *(G-13017)*

Power Train, Lebanon *Also Called: Truckpro LLC (G-10948)*

Power Train Corp Fort Wayne (PA) 317 241-9393
2334 Production Dr Indianapolis (46241) *(G-9167)*

Power Wall Systems LLC 317 348-1260
11253 Tall Trees Dr Fishers (46038) *(G-4580)*

Powerclean Inc (PA) 260 483-1375
6808 Metro Park Dr E Fort Wayne (46818) *(G-5329)*

Powerclean Industrial Services, Fort Wayne *Also Called: Powerclean Inc (G-5329)*

Powerhouse Engines LLC 765 576-1418
10771 S 100 E Lynn (47355) *(G-11186)*

Powerrail Holdings Inc 765 827-4660
1321 N Illinois Ave Connersville (47331) *(G-2463)*

Powerrail Mfg, Connersville *Also Called: Powerrail Holdings Inc (G-2463)*

Powers Farms, Angola *Also Called: Powers Hardwoods (G-286)*

Powers Hardwoods 260 665-5498
8090 E 40 S Angola (46703) *(G-286)*

Powers Welding Shop, Evansville *Also Called: J A Smit Inc (G-4133)*

Powerweld Inc (PA) 219 462-8700
2501 Beech St Valparaiso (46383) *(G-16029)*

Poynter, Greenwood *Also Called: Poynter Sheet Metal Inc (G-6753)*

Poynter Sheet Metal Inc 317 893-1193
775 Commerce Parkway West Dr Greenwood (46143) *(G-6753)*

PPG 4312, Clarksville *Also Called: PPG Industries Inc (G-2026)*

PPG 4313, New Albany *Also Called: PPG Industries Inc (G-12797)*

PPG 4361, Indianapolis *Also Called: PPG Industries Inc (G-9172)*

PPG 4363, Indianapolis *Also Called: PPG Industries Inc (G-9171)*

PPG 4364, Indianapolis *Also Called: PPG Industries Inc (G-9174)*

PPG 4365, Indianapolis *Also Called: PPG Industries Inc (G-9173)*

PPG 4366, Avon *Also Called: PPG Industries Inc (G-546)*

PPG 4369, Carmel *Also Called: PPG Industries Inc (G-1725)*

PPG 4371, Westfield *Also Called: PPG Industries Inc (G-16719)*

PPG 4378, Terre Haute *Also Called: PPG Industries Inc (G-15665)*

PPG 4379, Vincennes *Also Called: PPG Industries Inc (G-16147)*

PPG 4380, Evansville *Also Called: PPG Industries Inc (G-4253)*

PPG 4382, Evansville *Also Called: PPG Industries Inc (G-4254)*

PPG 4383, Fort Wayne Also Called: PPG Industries Inc *(G-5333)*
PPG 5547, Indianapolis Also Called: PPG Industries Inc *(G-9175)*
PPG 9259, Fishers Also Called: PPG Industries Inc *(G-4582)*
PPG Aerospace, Indianapolis Also Called: PRC - Desoto International Inc *(G-9177)*

PPG Architectural Finishes Inc 317 745-0427
   5201 E Us Highway 36 Ste 209 Avon (46123) *(G-545)*
PPG Architectural Finishes Inc 317 575-8011
   148 W Carmel Dr Carmel (46032) *(G-1722)*
PPG Architectural Finishes Inc 317 575-8011
   148 W Carmel Dr Carmel (46032) *(G-1723)*
PPG Architectural Finishes Inc 317 471-8250
   10111 N Michigan Rd Carmel (46032) *(G-1724)*
PPG Architectural Finishes Inc 812 473-0339
   2211 N Burkhardt Rd Ste C Evansville (47715) *(G-4251)*
PPG Architectural Finishes Inc 260 436-1854
   826 Lawrence Dr Fort Wayne (46804) *(G-5330)*
PPG Architectural Finishes Inc 260 436-1854
   826 Lawrence Dr Fort Wayne (46804) *(G-5331)*
PPG Architectural Finishes Inc 260 373-2373
   2510 Independence Dr Fort Wayne (46808) *(G-5332)*
PPG Architectural Finishes Inc 317 634-2547
   1435 Brookville Way Ste E Indianapolis (46239) *(G-9168)*
PPG Architectural Finishes Inc 317 787-9393
   7025 Madison Ave Indianapolis (46227) *(G-9169)*
PPG Architectural Finishes Inc 765 447-9334
   15 N Earl Ave Lafayette (47904) *(G-10669)*
PPG Architectural Finishes Inc 812 232-0672
   1700 Wabash Ave Terre Haute (47807) *(G-15664)*
PPG Architectural Finishes Inc 812 882-0440
   417 Main St Vincennes (47591) *(G-16146)*
PPG Holdings Inc 317 663-4590
   8770 Guion Rd Ste A Indianapolis (46268) *(G-9170)*
PPG Industries Inc 317 745-0427
   5201 E Us Highway 36 Ste 209 Avon (46123) *(G-546)*
PPG Industries Inc 317 870-0345
   10111 N Michigan Rd Carmel (46032) *(G-1725)*
PPG Industries Inc 812 948-9253
   319 E Lewis And Clark Pkwy Clarksville (47129) *(G-2026)*
PPG Industries Inc 812 867-6601
   424 E Inglefield Rd Evansville (47725) *(G-4252)*
PPG Industries Inc 812 424-4774
   306 N 7th Ave Evansville (47710) *(G-4253)*
PPG Industries Inc 812 473-0339
   2211 N Burkhardt Rd Ste D Evansville (47715) *(G-4254)*
PPG Industries Inc 317 598-9448
   10564 E 96th St Ste 6 Fishers (46037) *(G-4581)*
PPG Industries Inc 317 577-2344
   7275 E 116th St Fishers (46038) *(G-4582)*
PPG Industries Inc 260 373-2373
   2510 Independence Dr Fort Wayne (46808) *(G-5333)*
PPG Industries Inc 260 432-6900
   4301 Engle Rd Fort Wayne (46804) *(G-5334)*
PPG Industries Inc 317 251-9494
   2311 E 53rd St Indianapolis (46220) *(G-9171)*
PPG Industries Inc 317 267-0511
   952 N Delaware St Indianapolis (46202) *(G-9172)*
PPG Industries Inc 317 897-3836
   10009 E Washington St Indianapolis (46229) *(G-9173)*
PPG Industries Inc 317 787-9393
   7025 Madison Ave Indianapolis (46227) *(G-9174)*
PPG Industries Inc 317 546-5714
   6951 E 30th St Ste E Indianapolis (46219) *(G-9175)*
PPG Industries Inc 765 282-0316
   2701 N Wheeling Ave Muncie (47303) *(G-12476)*
PPG Industries Inc 812 944-4164
   3314 Grant Line Rd Ste 1 New Albany (47150) *(G-12797)*
PPG Industries Inc 812 232-0672
   1700 Wabash Ave Terre Haute (47807) *(G-15665)*
PPG Industries Inc 812 882-0440
   417 Main St Vincennes (47591) *(G-16147)*
PPG Industries Inc 317 867-5934
   3132 E State Road 32 Westfield (46074) *(G-16719)*

Ppi Acquisition LLC 765 674-8627
   1424 W 35th St Marion (46953) *(G-11329)*
PQ LLC 812 288-7186
   1101 Quartz Rd Clarksville (47129) *(G-2027)*
Praire Material, Bloomfield Also Called: Cimentos N Votorantim Amer Inc *(G-744)*
Prairie Creek Book Store, Montgomery Also Called: Prairie Creek Prtg & Bk Str *(G-12119)*
Prairie Creek Prtg & Bk Str 812 636-7243
   9309 E 800 N Montgomery (47558) *(G-12119)*
Prairie Gold Rush 812 342-3608
   17390 S State Road 58 Seymour (47274) *(G-14676)*
Prairie Group 812 877-9886
   5222 E Margaret Dr Terre Haute (47803) *(G-15666)*
Prairie Group Inc 812 824-1355
   7100 S Old State Road 37 Bloomington (47403) *(G-948)*
Prairie Preservation Guild Ltd 765 884-1902
   111 E 5th St Fowler (47944) *(G-5632)*
Prairie Sun Vineyard LLC 219 741-5918
   3131 N 700 E Rolling Prairie (46371) *(G-14368)*
Prairie Welding & Repair 574 858-0509
   3360 W 700 N Leesburg (46538) *(G-10959)*
Prairies Edge Machining Inc 765 986-2222
   4920 W Division Rd Williamsport (47993) *(G-16852)*
Prairieton Printing 812 299-9611
   3878 W Newton Dr Terre Haute (47802) *(G-15667)*
Praiseworthy Press LLC 765 536-2077
   151 W Indiana St Summitville (46070) *(G-15428)*
Prather Machining Inc 812 401-7556
   13403 Columbus Mann Rd Memphis (47143) *(G-11466)*
Pratt (jet Corr) Inc 219 548-9191
   3155 S State Road 49 Valparaiso (46383) *(G-16030)*
Pratt Industries USA, Valparaiso Also Called: Pratt (jet Corr) Inc *(G-16030)*
Pratt Paper (in) LLC 219 477-1040
   3050 Anthony Pratt Dr Valparaiso (46383) *(G-16031)*
Pratt Visual Solutions Company 800 428-7728
   3035 N Shadeland Ave Indianapolis (46226) *(G-9176)*
Pratt-Kulsrud LLC 317 844-9122
   13021 Abraham Run Carmel (46033) *(G-1726)*
Praxair, Cicero Also Called: Linde Inc *(G-1998)*
Praxair, Columbus Also Called: Linde Gas & Equipment Inc *(G-2343)*
Praxair, Fort Wayne Also Called: Linde Gas & Equipment Inc *(G-5187)*
Praxair, Indianapolis Also Called: Linde Advanced Material Techno *(G-8758)*
Praxair, Indianapolis Also Called: Linde Advanced Mtl Tech Inc *(G-8759)*
Praxair, Indianapolis Also Called: Linde Gas & Equipment Inc *(G-8761)*
Praxair, Indianapolis Also Called: Linde Inc *(G-8762)*
Praxair, Kokomo Also Called: Linde Inc *(G-10297)*
Praxair, La Porte Also Called: Linde Inc *(G-10446)*
Praxair, Seymour Also Called: Linde Inc *(G-14664)*
Praxair Distribution, Goshen Also Called: Linde Gas & Equipment Inc *(G-6198)*
PRC - Desoto International Inc 317 290-1600
   6022 Corporate Way Indianapolis (46278) *(G-9177)*
Prd, Springville Also Called: Plastics Research and Dev Inc *(G-15390)*
Pre-Owned Auto Center, Indianapolis Also Called: Auto Center Inc *(G-7571)*
Precast Solutions Inc 317 545-6557
   6145 S Indianapolis Rd Whitestown (46075) *(G-16816)*
Precast Specialties Inc 260 623-6131
   111 Utility Dr Monroeville (46773) *(G-12072)*
Preciball USA 812 257-5555
   219 E Main St Ste 4x Washington (47501) *(G-16505)*
Precious Gems Metals 260 563-4780
   112 W Market St Wabash (46992) *(G-16213)*
Precious Technology Group LLC (PA) 317 398-4411
   1111 W Mckay Rd Shelbyville (46176) *(G-14787)*
Precise Manufacturing, Fort Wayne Also Called: Whitcraft Enterprises Inc *(G-5564)*
Precise Plate, Columbus Also Called: Precise Tooling Solutions Inc *(G-2380)*
Precise Title Inc 219 987-2286
   8917 24th St Sw Demotte (46310) *(G-2926)*
Precise Tooling Solutions Inc 812 378-0247
   3150 Scott Dr Columbus (47201) *(G-2380)*
Precisely Write Inc 317 585-7701
   9801 Fall Creek Rd # 202 Indianapolis (46256) *(G-9178)*

ALPHABETIC SECTION — Preferred Popcorn LLC

Precision Abrasive Machinery..765 378-3315
14200 W Commerce Rd Daleville (47334) *(G-2801)*

Precision Additive Solutions...419 320-6978
12950 Old Meridian St Apt 2005 Carmel (46032) *(G-1727)*

Precision Agronomy...219 552-0032
23305 Whitcomb St Lowell (46356) *(G-11176)*

Precision Automation Company..812 283-7963
2120 Addmore Ln Clarksville (47129) *(G-2028)*

Precision Battery Fabrication, Wabash Also Called: Bulldog Battery Corporation *(G-16176)*

Precision Benders Incorporated..574 658-9317
411 N Old State Road 15 Milford (46542) *(G-11803)*

Precision Buffing & Polsg Inc...574 262-3430
54194 Adams St Elkhart (46514) *(G-3614)*

Precision Building, Elkhart Also Called: Precision Buffing & Polsg Inc *(G-3614)*

Precision Cadcam Incorporated...317 353-8058
8446 Brookville Rd Indianapolis (46239) *(G-9179)*

Precision Cams Inc..317 634-3521
522 S Harding St Indianapolis (46221) *(G-9180)*

Precision Cams Inc (PA)..317 631-9100
3510 E Raymond St Indianapolis (46203) *(G-9181)*

Precision Colors LLC...260 969-6402
2617 Meyer Rd Fort Wayne (46803) *(G-5335)*

Precision Cryogenic Systems..317 273-2800
7804 Rockville Rd Indianapolis (46214) *(G-9182)*

Precision Design, Young America Also Called: Sandra Henry *(G-16985)*

Precision Die Technologies LLC...260 482-5001
4716 Speedway Dr Fort Wayne (46825) *(G-5336)*

Precision Edge Srgcal Pdts LLC..260 624-3123
1910 N Wayne St Angola (46703) *(G-287)*

Precision Electric Inc...574 256-1000
1508 W 6th St Mishawaka (46544) *(G-11977)*

Precision Electronics, Mishawaka Also Called: Precision Electric Inc *(G-11977)*

Precision Enterprises LLC..812 873-6391
9775 S County Road 550 W Paris Crossing (47270) *(G-13504)*

Precision Fabrication Inc...260 422-4448
710 Hanover St Fort Wayne (46803) *(G-5337)*

Precision Fiber Solutions LLC..317 421-9642
3950 W Smokey Row Rd Bargersville (46106) *(G-572)*

Precision Gage LLC..260 925-4717
1401 S Grandstaff Dr Auburn (46706) *(G-417)*

Precision Heat Treating Corp...260 749-5125
2711 Adams Center Rd Fort Wayne (46803) *(G-5338)*

Precision Industries Corp..574 522-2626
601 Wagner Ave Elkhart (46516) *(G-3615)*

Precision Label Incorporated...812 877-3811
8890 E Davis Ave Terre Haute (47805) *(G-15668)*

Precision Laser...812 295-2200
11919 E 250 N Loogootee (47553) *(G-11147)*

Precision Laser Services Inc..260 744-4375
14730 Lima Rd Fort Wayne (46818) *(G-5339)*

Precision Machined Pdts LLC..260 908-4766
6065 E Leighty Rd Kendallville (46755) *(G-10144)*

Precision Medical Inds Inc...260 234-3112
907 Weber Rd Albion (46701) *(G-41)*

Precision Medical Tech Inc..574 267-6385
2059 N Pound Dr W Warsaw (46582) *(G-16412)*

Precision Mill Work & Plastics, South Bend Also Called: Precision Millwork & Plas Inc *(G-15201)*

Precision Millwork & Plas Inc..574 243-8720
3311 William Richardson Dr South Bend (46628) *(G-15201)*

Precision Piece Parts Inc...574 255-3185
712 S Logan St Mishawaka (46544) *(G-11978)*

Precision Plastics, Columbia City Also Called: Precision Plastics Indiana Inc *(G-2183)*

Precision Plastics Indiana Inc...260 244-6114
900 W Connexion Way Columbia City (46725) *(G-2183)*

Precision Polishing & Buffing...317 352-0165
1038 S Kealing Ave Indianapolis (46203) *(G-9183)*

Precision Powder Coat LLC...317 483-3670
141 E South St Ste E Mooresville (46158) *(G-12236)*

Precision Print LLC...765 789-8799
10910 E County Road 500 N Albany (47320) *(G-15)*

Precision Products Group, Indianapolis Also Called: PPG Holdings Inc *(G-9170)*

Precision Products Group Inc..260 484-4111
1430 Progress Rd Fort Wayne (46808) *(G-5340)*

Precision Products Group Inc..260 424-3734
2701 S Coliseum Blvd Ste 1148 Fort Wayne (46803) *(G-5341)*

Precision Products Group Inc (PA)......................................317 663-4590
8770 Guion Rd Ste A Indianapolis (46268) *(G-9184)*

Precision Products Inc (PA)...317 882-1852
1701 Industrial Dr Greenwood (46143) *(G-6754)*

Precision Pulse LLC..765 472-6002
323 W 5th St Peru (46970) *(G-13593)*

Precision Rings Incorporated...317 247-4786
5611 Progress Rd Indianapolis (46241) *(G-9185)*

Precision Rubber Plate Co Inc...317 783-3226
5620 Elmwood Ave Indianapolis (46203) *(G-9186)*

Precision Services Inc...812 602-8375
6601 W Mill Rd Evansville (47720) *(G-4255)*

Precision Sheet Metal Inc..269 663-8810
51963 Bellflower Ln Granger (46530) *(G-6371)*

Precision Spray LLC...812 830-8443
2474 N Palomino Dr Vincennes (47591) *(G-16148)*

Precision Stamping Inc...574 522-8987
720 Collins Rd Elkhart (46516) *(G-3616)*

Precision Stitch Indiana Inc...765 473-6734
404 W Canal St Peru (46970) *(G-13594)*

Precision Stmping Slutions LLC...317 501-4436
10823 Turne Grv Fishers (46037) *(G-4583)*

Precision Surfacing Solutions...317 841-2400
14560 Bergen Blvd Ste 800 Noblesville (46060) *(G-13157)*

Precision Surveillance Corp...219 397-4295
3468 Watling St East Chicago (46312) *(G-3035)*

Precision Systems...812 283-4904
478 Accrusia Ave Clarksville (47129) *(G-2029)*

Precision Tank & Equipment Co..260 894-4002
215 Heckner Dr Ligonier (46767) *(G-11022)*

Precision Technologies I LLC..260 668-7500
200 Industrial Dr Angola (46703) *(G-288)*

Precision Tool, New Paris Also Called: Steve Mitchell *(G-12969)*

Precision Tool & Die Inc...765 664-4786
1735 W Factory Ave Marion (46952) *(G-11330)*

Precision Tubes Inc..317 783-2339
5730 Kopetsky Dr Ste C Indianapolis (46217) *(G-9187)*

Precision Utilities Group Inc..260 485-8300
5916 E State Blvd Fort Wayne (46815) *(G-5342)*

Precision Welding Corp..260 637-5514
16403 Lima Rd Huntertown (46748) *(G-7261)*

Precision Wire Assemblies Inc...765 489-6302
551 E Main St Hagerstown (47346) *(G-6842)*

Precision Wire Service, North Webster Also Called: Precision Wire Supply LLC *(G-13313)*

Precision Wire Supply LLC..574 834-7545
7493 E 800 N North Webster (46555) *(G-13313)*

Precision Wire Technologies, Fort Wayne Also Called: Pwt Group LLC *(G-5357)*

Precision Wldg Solutions LLC..317 698-7522
1369 Crabapple Ct Martinsville (46151) *(G-11422)*

Precision Wood Products, Mishawaka Also Called: Garyrae Inc *(G-11898)*

Precision Woodcrafters, Decatur Also Called: A S M Inc *(G-2839)*

Precisionair, La Porte Also Called: Precisionair LLC *(G-10464)*

Precisionair LLC...219 380-9267
1828 N Summit Dr La Porte (46350) *(G-10464)*

Precoat Metals..219 763-1504
6144 Us Highway 12 Portage (46368) *(G-13906)*

PRECOAT METALS, Portage Also Called: Precoat Metals *(G-13906)*

Precoat Metals Corp (DH)...317 462-7761
1950 E Main St Greenfield (46140) *(G-6542)*

Precoat Metals Corp...219 393-3561
858 E Hupp Rd La Porte (46350) *(G-10465)*

Predator Percussion LLC...317 919-7659
1174 Dark Star Ct New Whiteland (46184) *(G-12987)*

Preferred Metal Service Inc...219 988-2386
1146 Sunnyslope Dr Crown Point (46307) *(G-2735)*

Preferred Popcorn LLC..308 850-6631
3055 W Bradford Rd Ne Palmyra (47164) *(G-13484)*

(PA)=Parent Co (HQ)=Headquarters (DH)=Div Headquarters

Preferred Ppltion Hlth MGT LLC...317 245-7482
9951 Crosspoint Blvd Ste 300 Indianapolis (46256) *(G-9188)*

Preferred Print..317 371-8829
6220 Hardegan St Indianapolis (46227) *(G-9189)*

Preferred Seating Company LLC..317 782-3323
633 Yosemite Dr Indianapolis (46217) *(G-9190)*

Preferred Shtmtl Fbrcation LLC..317 494-6232
299 Cincinnati St Franklin (46131) *(G-5769)*

Preferred Tank & Tower Inc (PA)...270 826-7950
5444 E Indiana St Pmb 374 Evansville (47715) *(G-4256)*

Pregis LLC..574 936-7065
1411 Pidco Dr Plymouth (46563) *(G-13806)*

Premier AG, Seymour *Also Called: Premier AG Co-Op Inc (G-14677)*

Premier AG Co-Op Inc (PA)..812 522-4911
811 W 2nd St Seymour (47274) *(G-14677)*

Premier Bandage 3 Inc...574 257-0248
4411 Quality Dr South Bend (46628) *(G-15202)*

Premier Claim Services, Indianapolis *Also Called: Renaissnce Electronic Svcs LLC (G-9290)*

Premier Components LLC..219 776-9372
346 S 725 W Hebron (46341) *(G-7105)*

Premier Concepts Inc...574 269-7570
2371 N Rainbow Dr Warsaw (46582) *(G-16413)*

Premier Consulting Inc (PA)...260 496-9300
1415 Profit Dr Fort Wayne (46808) *(G-5343)*

Premier Custom Coatings LLC..317 557-7841
4676 Rainmaker Row Greenwood (46143) *(G-6755)*

Premier Fiberglass Co Inc..574 264-5457
55080 Phillips St Elkhart (46514) *(G-3617)*

Premier Forge Group LLC (PA)..800 727-8121
250 E Lafayette St Portland (47371) *(G-13963)*

Premier Frozen Desserts...812 580-8866
8090 E County Road 100 S Seymour (47274) *(G-14678)*

Premier Homes, Clarksville *Also Called: Classic Buildings Inc (G-2013)*

Premier Hydraulic Augers Inc...260 456-8518
2707 Lofty Dr Fort Wayne (46808) *(G-5344)*

Premier Label Company Inc...765 289-5000
1205 E Washington St Muncie (47305) *(G-12477)*

Premier Lumber Company Inc...219 801-6018
6717 Atcheson Dr Chesterton (46304) *(G-1954)*

Premier Mfg Group Inc..203 924-6617
7310 Innovation Blvd Ste 104 Fort Wayne (46818) *(G-5345)*

Premier Paving..302 396-8851
3384 Preakness St Whitestown (46075) *(G-16817)*

Premier Powder Coating, Huntington *Also Called: P-Kelco Inc (G-7353)*

Premier Print & Svcs Group Inc..574 273-2525
6910 N Main St Unit 11 Granger (46530) *(G-6372)*

Premier Printing...765 459-8339
1708 W Taylor St Kokomo (46901) *(G-10323)*

Premier Prints LLC..812 987-1129
3018 Seminole Dr Jeffersonville (47130) *(G-10040)*

Premier Scrap Processing LLC..317 242-9502
6051 Central Ave Indianapolis (46220) *(G-9191)*

Premier Sign Group Inc...317 613-4411
740 E 52nd St Ste 7 Indianapolis (46205) *(G-9192)*

Premier Signs LLC..888 518-2498
726 W Us Highway 224 Uniondale (46791) *(G-15870)*

Premier Wire Die, Fort Wayne *Also Called: Premier Consulting Inc (G-5343)*

Premiere Advertising...317 722-2400
2704 E 62nd St Ste B Indianapolis (46220) *(G-9193)*

Premiere Services, Goshen *Also Called: Premiere Signs Co Inc (G-6242)*

Premiere Signs Co Inc...574 533-8585
400 N Main St Goshen (46528) *(G-6242)*

Premiere Signs LLC..260 543-2612
888 W Railroad St Uniondale (46791) *(G-15871)*

Premium Corporation..219 258-0141
1019 Royal Vineyards South Bend (46637) *(G-15203)*

Premium Manufacturing LLC..219 258-0141
28 Richmond St La Porte (46350) *(G-10466)*

Premium Mold Tool..812 967-3187
4225 S Hickory Grove Rd Pekin (47165) *(G-13521)*

Premium Vinyl Mfg...219 922-6501
231 S Lindberg St Griffith (46319) *(G-6815)*

Prentice Products, Fort Wayne *Also Called: Prentice Products Holdings LLC (G-5346)*

Prentice Products Holdings LLC..260 747-3195
310 W Cook Rd Fort Wayne (46825) *(G-5346)*

Prentice Products Inc..260 747-3195
4236 W Ferguson Rd Fort Wayne (46809) *(G-5347)*

Pres-Del Electric Inc...219 884-3146
4172 Broadway Gary (46408) *(G-5995)*

Preserving Past..574 835-0833
3764 E Jackson Blvd Elkhart (46516) *(G-3618)*

Presidential Bath & Fix LLC..812 259-9817
215 Wedeking Ave Evansville (47711) *(G-4257)*

Press 96, Carmel *Also Called: Priority Press Inc (G-1730)*

Press A Button LLC..630 400-1704
15478 Harmon Pl Noblesville (46060) *(G-13158)*

Press A Dent..260 760-1585
614 Constance Ave Fort Wayne (46805) *(G-5348)*

Press Brake Safety LLC..317 413-7593
1938 S 925 E Zionsville (46077) *(G-17044)*

Press Dispatch, Petersburg *Also Called: Pike County Publishing Corp (G-13621)*

Press Ganey Holdings Inc..574 387-4764
1739 Winston Dr South Bend (46635) *(G-15204)*

Press-Seal Corporation..260 436-0521
2801 W State Blvd Fort Wayne (46808) *(G-5349)*

Press-Seal Corporation (PA)..260 436-0521
2424 W State Blvd Fort Wayne (46808) *(G-5350)*

Presstime Graphics Inc..812 234-3815
1016 Poplar St Terre Haute (47807) *(G-15669)*

Prestige Printing Inc..812 372-2500
1307 12th St Columbus (47201) *(G-2381)*

Prestige Tooling LLC...269 470-4525
419 Harrison St Elkhart (46516) *(G-3619)*

Preston Leaderbrand...812 828-0883
491 Timber Ridge Rd Spencer (47460) *(G-15357)*

Prestoncbd LLC (PA)...317 407-7068
13391 Mercer St Carmel (46032) *(G-1728)*

Prestress Services Inc...260 724-7117
7855 Nw Winchester Rd Decatur (46733) *(G-2877)*

Pretty Chique LLC...317 922-5899
4203 Millersville Rd Ste 300 Indianapolis (46205) *(G-9194)*

Pretty Incredible, Jeffersonville *Also Called: Printing Inc Louisville KY (G-10041)*

Pretty Xquisite Hair LLC..765 760-6948
3813 N Chadam Ln Apt 1a Muncie (47304) *(G-12478)*

Pretzels LLC (PA)...800 456-4838
123 W Harvest Rd Bluffton (46714) *(G-1049)*

Pretzels Inc...574 941-2201
2910 Commerce St Plymouth (46563) *(G-13807)*

PRETZELS INC, Plymouth *Also Called: Pretzels Inc (G-13807)*

Prevail Design Systems LLC..260 245-1245
5130 Willow Bluff Trl Huntertown (46748) *(G-7262)*

Prevail Prsthtics Orthtics Inc...765 668-0890
7735 W Jefferson Blvd # C Fort Wayne (46804) *(G-5351)*

Prevention Response Technology, Rushville *Also Called: Prt Inc (G-14407)*

Previnex, Carmel *Also Called: Previnex LLC (G-1729)*

Previnex LLC..877 212-0310
38 W Main St Carmel (46032) *(G-1729)*

Prevounce Health Inc..800 618-7738
3250 N Post Rd Ste 180 Indianapolis (46226) *(G-9195)*

Price Machine & Tool Inc (PA)..260 338-1081
16335 Lima Rd Ste 9a Huntertown (46748) *(G-7263)*

Pridgeon & Clay Inc...317 738-4885
150 Arvin Rd Franklin (46131) *(G-5770)*

Primal Prints LLC..260 494-8435
15115 Hidden Oaks Run Huntertown (46748) *(G-7264)*

Primary Pdts Ingrdnts Amrcas L...765 448-7123
2245 Sagamore Pkwy N Lafayette (47904) *(G-10670)*

Primary Pdts Ingrdnts Amrcas L...765 474-5474
3300 Us Highway 52 S Lafayette (47905) *(G-10671)*

Primary Record Inc...317 270-8327
9678 Reston Ln Fishers (46055) *(G-4648)*

Prime Conveyor Inc..219 736-1994
8903 Louisiana St Merrillville (46410) *(G-11552)*

ALPHABETIC SECTION — Pro Pallet LLC

Prime Source LLC 812 867-8921
   4609 E Boonville New Harmony Rd Evansville (47725) *(G-4258)*

Prime Tech Inc 317 715-1162
   3131 N Franklin Rd Ste B Indianapolis (46226) *(G-9196)*

Prime Time Manufacturing 574 862-3001
   66149 State Road 19 Wakarusa (46573) *(G-16243)*

Primed & Ready LLC 317 694-2028
   5036 E 65th St Indianapolis (46220) *(G-9197)*

Primet Fluid Power, Munster Also Called: Motion & Control Entps LLC *(G-12551)*

Primex, Richmond Also Called: Primex Plastics Corporation *(G-14186)*

Primex Clor Cmpnding Addtves C 800 222-5116
   1235 N F St Richmond (47374) *(G-14184)*

Primex Design Fabrication Corp 765 935-2990
   400 Industrial Pkwy Richmond (47374) *(G-14185)*

Primex Plastics Corporation (HQ) 765 966-7774
   1235 N F St Richmond (47374) *(G-14186)*

Primix Corporation 574 858-0069
   510 East Main Street Atwood (46502) *(G-357)*

Primmient, Lafayette Also Called: Primary Pdts Ingrdnts Amrcas L *(G-10671)*

Prince Manufacturing, Garrett Also Called: Prince Manufacturing Corp *(G-5874)*

Prince Manufacturing Corp 260 357-4484
   320 N Taylor Rd Garrett (46738) *(G-5874)*

Princess Palayse 317 937-9394
   2829 Schofield Ave Indianapolis (46218) *(G-9198)*

Princeton Daily Clarion, Princeton Also Called: Princeton Publishing Inc *(G-14010)*

Princeton Publishing Inc 812 385-2525
   100 N Gibson St Princeton (47670) *(G-14010)*

Prinit Press, Richmond Also Called: Augustin Prtg & Design Svcs *(G-14088)*

Print 2 Finish LLC 812 256-5515
   231 Butler Ave Charlestown (47111) *(G-1891)*

Print Center Inc 219 874-9683
   2016 Oriole Trl Long Beach (46360) *(G-11128)*

Print Ideas 317 299-8766
   2233 Country Club Rd Indianapolis (46234) *(G-9199)*

Print It Inc 317 774-6848
   7349 N Shadeland Ave Indianapolis (46250) *(G-9200)*

Print It Plus Inc 812 466-7446
   2151 Lafayette Ave Ste 101 Terre Haute (47805) *(G-15670)*

Print It Wear It Inc 317 946-1456
   679 Brent Woods Dr Shelbyville (46176) *(G-14788)*

Print Management Solutions Inc 574 234-7269
   1833 Hass Dr South Bend (46635) *(G-15205)*

Print My Merch LLC 765 269-6772
   14208 Dragoon Trl Mishawaka (46544) *(G-11979)*

Print Plus Express Inc 812 466-6150
   7623 N 42nd St Terre Haute (47805) *(G-15671)*

Print Queens LLC 317 285-8934
   2004 Fernway St Indianapolis (46218) *(G-9201)*

Print Resources Inc 317 833-7000
   1500 E Riverside Dr Indianapolis (46202) *(G-9202)*

Print Sharp Enterprises Inc 317 899-2754
   9105 E 56th St Ste E Indianapolis (46216) *(G-9203)*

Print Shop Inc 574 264-0023
   51748 State Road 19 Elkhart (46514) *(G-3620)*

Print Solutions of Indiana 219 988-4186
   1744 Beachview Ct Crown Point (46307) *(G-2736)*

Print Source Corporation 260 824-3911
   213 E Perry St Bluffton (46714) *(G-1050)*

Print Tech, Evansville Also Called: Acclaim Graphics Inc *(G-3866)*

Print2promo Group Inc 219 778-4649
   7592 E 400 N Rolling Prairie (46371) *(G-14369)*

Printcraft Press Inc 765 457-2141
   524 S Union St Kokomo (46901) *(G-10324)*

Printcrafters Inc 812 838-4106
   304 W 4th St Mount Vernon (47620) *(G-12315)*

Printed By Erik Inc 574 295-1203
   22158 Elkhart East Blvd Elkhart (46514) *(G-3621)*

Printers Group 317 835-7720
   4485 W 600 N Fairland (46126) *(G-4401)*

Printers Plus, Elkhart Also Called: Livings Graphics Inc *(G-3498)*

Printing All Stars 812 288-9291
   802 E 8th St New Albany (47150) *(G-12798)*

Printing Center Inc 317 545-8518
   3503 N Shadeland Ave Indianapolis (46226) *(G-9204)*

Printing Company LLC 812 367-2668
   8765 S Club Rd Ferdinand (47532) *(G-4448)*

Printing Complex, The, Indianapolis Also Called: Printing Center Inc *(G-9204)*

Printing Concepts Inc 317 899-2754
   4371 Sellers St Indianapolis (46226) *(G-9205)*

Printing Creations Inc 765 759-9679
   2410 S Vine St Yorktown (47396) *(G-16982)*

Printing Impression 812 537-4077
   21073 Alpine Dr Lawrenceburg (47025) *(G-10854)*

Printing In Time Inc 502 807-3545
   8213 Lotticks Corner Rd Se Elizabeth (47117) *(G-3128)*

Printing Inc Louisville KY 800 237-5894
   1600 Dutch Ln Ste A Jeffersonville (47130) *(G-10041)*

Printing Partners Inc (PA) 317 635-2282
   929 W 16th St Indianapolis (46202) *(G-9206)*

Printing Partners East Inc 317 356-2522
   929 W 16th St Indianapolis (46202) *(G-9207)*

Printing Place Inc 260 665-8444
   1500 N Wayne St Ste B Angola (46703) *(G-289)*

Printing Services Inc 317 300-0363
   5333 Commerce Square Dr Indianapolis (46237) *(G-9208)*

Printing Solutions Inc 812 923-0756
   6220 Sarles Creek Rd Floyds Knobs (47119) *(G-4689)*

Printing Technologies Inc 800 428-3786
   6266 Morenci Trl Indianapolis (46268) *(G-9209)*

Printpack Inc 812 663-5091
   930 E Barachel Ln Ste 200 Greensburg (47240) *(G-6625)*

Printsource 317 507-6526
   6139 Riverview Dr Indianapolis (46208) *(G-9210)*

Printwerk Graphics & Design 219 322-7722
   1000 Richard Rd Dyer (46311) *(G-2981)*

Printwise LLC 765 244-1983
   149 W Canal St Peru (46970) *(G-13595)*

Printworks Inc 317 535-1250
   655 Tracy Rd Whiteland (46184) *(G-16793)*

Priority Business Forms, Indianapolis Also Called: Priority Press Inc *(G-9211)*

Priority Detailing 812 591-0299
   3484 W Laytons Dr Westport (47283) *(G-16750)*

Priority Plastics Inc (PA) 260 726-7000
   500 Industrial Dr Portland (47371) *(G-13964)*

Priority Press Inc 317 848-9695
   9609 N College Ave Carmel (46280) *(G-1730)*

Priority Press Inc (PA) 317 241-4234
   4026 W 10th St Indianapolis (46222) *(G-9211)*

Priority Press Inc 317 240-0103
   4026 W 10th St Indianapolis (46222) *(G-9212)*

Priority Printing LLC 317 241-4234
   4026 W 10th St Indianapolis (46222) *(G-9213)*

Priority Steel Indus Contg LLC 937 626-4361
   777 E Eads Pkwy Greendale (47025) *(G-6453)*

Prized Possession 317 842-1498
   6606 Avalon Forest Dr Indianapolis (46250) *(G-9214)*

Prmi 1 Inc 219 474-5022
   102 S 4th St Kentland (47951) *(G-10162)*

Pro Door Manufacturing LLC 317 839-3050
   6030 Gateway Dr Plainfield (46168) *(G-13717)*

Pro Door Mfg, Plainfield Also Called: Pro Door Manufacturing LLC *(G-13717)*

Pro Finish 618 771-7207
   4825 Hitch Peters Rd Evansville (47711) *(G-4259)*

Pro Finish Mold Polishing 618 922-8161
   9918 Massey Dr Evansville (47725) *(G-4260)*

Pro Industies, Franklin Also Called: CL Holding LLC *(G-5720)*

Pro It Solutions LLC 574 862-0021
   111 W Waterford St Wakarusa (46573) *(G-16244)*

Pro Laminators, Sellersburg Also Called: Jknk Ventures Inc *(G-14603)*

Pro Link 765 225-1051
   400 Fairlane Dr Crawfordsville (47933) *(G-2605)*

Pro Pallet LLC 219 292-3389
   1584 Blaine St Gary (46406) *(G-5996)*

Pro Prints — ALPHABETIC SECTION

Pro Prints 812 932-3800
  394 Northside Dr Batesville (47006) *(G-600)*
Pro Prints Gear, Marion *Also Called: Ppi Acquisition LLC (G-11329)*
Pro Series Products LLC 812 793-3506
  208 N Armstrong St Crothersville (47229) *(G-2643)*
Pro Signs & Graphics 765 675-7446
  704 W Jefferson St Tipton (46072) *(G-15787)*
Pro Stop Mechanical Shop, Camby *Also Called: Aaron McWhirter (G-1506)*
Pro Tech Automation Inc 317 201-3875
  8236 N Hall Rd Monrovia (46157) *(G-12079)*
Pro Traument Scale, Franklin *Also Called: Agri-Tronix Corp (G-5703)*
Pro Wake Watersports Indianap 801 691-2153
  9175 E 146th St Noblesville (46060) *(G-13159)*
Pro Wake Watersports Syracuse 801 691-2153
  1309 S Harkless Dr Syracuse (46567) *(G-15475)*
Pro-Blast Equip, Fort Wayne *Also Called: Professional Metal Refinishing (G-5353)*
Pro-Chem-Co Inc 219 962-8554
  2319 Ripley St Lake Station (46405) *(G-10775)*
Pro-Fab Sheet Metal Ind Inc
  880 E 99th Ct Ste B Crown Point (46307) *(G-2737)*
Pro-Form Plastics Inc 812 522-4433
  11624 E State Road 250 Crothersville (47229) *(G-2644)*
Pro-Form Plastics Inc 812 522-4433
  15200 S Jonesville Rd Columbus (47201) *(G-2382)*
Pro-Kote Indy LLC 317 872-0001
  8813 Robbins Rd Indianapolis (46268) *(G-9215)*
Pro-Mark Bldg Solutions LLC 812 798-1178
  575 N 1000 W Linton (47441) *(G-11043)*
Pro-Motor Engines, Goshen *Also Called: Promotor Engines & Components (G-6243)*
Pro-Strip Indy LLC 317 872-0001
  4020 Millersville Rd Indianapolis (46205) *(G-9216)*
Pro-Tech Tool & Stamping Inc 765 258-3613
  890 E County Road 600 N Frankfort (46041) *(G-5691)*
Pro-Tex-All, Evansville *Also Called: Jzj Services LLC (G-4147)*
Pro-Tote Systems Inc 574 287-6006
  1705 S Olive St South Bend (46613) *(G-15206)*
Proair LLC 574 264-5494
  2900 County Road 6 W Elkhart (46514) *(G-3622)*
Proapse Software 260 615-9839
  604 Constance Ave Fort Wayne (46805) *(G-5352)*
Probotech Inc 317 849-6197
  6848 Hawthorn Park Dr Indianapolis (46220) *(G-9217)*
Procard Inc 303 279-2255
  1 Heartland Way Jeffersonville (47130) *(G-10042)*
Process Development & Fabrication Inc 812 443-6000
  10102 N Murphy Rd Brazil (47834) *(G-1163)*
Process Systems & Services (PA) 812 427-2331
  13395 Innovation Dr Florence (47020) *(G-4666)*
Proco, Fort Wayne *Also Called: Protective Coatings Inc (G-5354)*
Procoat Inc 317 263-5071
  920 E New York St Indianapolis (46202) *(G-9218)*
Procoat Products LLC 812 352-6083
  604 W Montrow Industrial Pkwy North Vernon (47265) *(G-13293)*
Prodigy Mold & Tool Inc 812 753-3029
  88 E 1100 S Haubstadt (47639) *(G-7088)*
Product Engineering Company, Columbus *Also Called: E F M Corporation (G-2293)*
Production Dynamics, Valparaiso *Also Called: Task Force Tips Inc (G-16063)*
Production Machining Company 812 466-2885
  4850 N 13th St Terre Haute (47805) *(G-15672)*
Production Partners Inc 574 229-5960
  1710 Clover Rd Ste 3 Mishawaka (46545) *(G-11980)*
Production Plant, Kokomo *Also Called: Borgwarner Noblesville LLC (G-10240)*
Production Plastic Molding 317 872-4669
  3402 W 79th St Indianapolis (46268) *(G-9219)*
Production Plating, Indianapolis *Also Called: Progressive Plating Company (G-9226)*
Production Systems Assoc, Huntingburg *Also Called: Masterbrand Cabinets LLC (G-7287)*
Productivity Fabricators Inc 765 966-2896
  2332 Flatley Rd Richmond (47374) *(G-14187)*
Productivity Resources Inc 317 245-4040
  325 Pickwick Ct Noblesville (46062) *(G-13160)*

Proedge Inc 219 552-9550
  23326 Shelby Rd Shelby (46377) *(G-14727)*
Profab Custom Metal Works Inc 812 865-3999
  7040 N State Road 337 Orleans (47452) *(G-13380)*
Professional Bowling Ball Svc 317 786-4329
  2630 Madison Ave Indianapolis (46225) *(G-9220)*
Professional Custom Knife, Shelburn *Also Called: Bose Knife Works (G-14717)*
Professional Design LLC 765 529-1590
  1220 Church St New Castle (47362) *(G-12879)*
Professional Gifting Inc 800 350-1796
  6366 Guilford Ave # 300 Indianapolis (46220) *(G-9221)*
Professional Grade Services, Indianapolis *Also Called: Professional Grade Svcs LLC (G-9222)*
Professional Grade Svcs LLC 317 688-8898
  10428 Windward Dr Indianapolis (46234) *(G-9222)*
Professional Metal Refinishing 260 436-2828
  2415 W State Blvd Fort Wayne (46808) *(G-5353)*
Professional Pallets LLC 859 393-4328
  100 Brown St Greendale (47025) *(G-6454)*
Professional Permits 574 257-2954
  2319 Lincolnway E Mishawaka (46544) *(G-11981)*
Professional Services Sector, Auburn *Also Called: Perpetual Industries Inc (G-415)*
Professional Sndblst & Wldg 574 355-9825
  4747 E Division Rd Logansport (46947) *(G-11103)*
Professional Software Corp 812 781-1422
  109 E 2nd St Mount Vernon (47620) *(G-12316)*
Professionally Polished LLC 219 779-7664
  1716 Beachview Ct Crown Point (46307) *(G-2738)*
Professnal Locomotive Svcs Inc 219 398-9123
  4949 Huish Dr East Chicago (46312) *(G-3036)*
Profit Finders Incorporated 317 251-7792
  7750 Records St Indianapolis (46226) *(G-9223)*
Profit Over Romance LLC 219 900-3592
  1400 W 19th Pl Gary (46407) *(G-5997)*
Proform, Fort Wayne *Also Called: Dx 4 LLC (G-4935)*
Proform Finishing Products LLC 219 866-7570
  1325 E Maple St Rensselaer (47978) *(G-14063)*
Proform Finishing Products LLC 812 247-2424
  9720 Us Highway 50 Shoals (47581) *(G-14910)*
Proforma Corporate Solutions, Granger *Also Called: Nielsen Enterprises Inc (G-6367)*
Proforma Premier Printing 317 842-9181
  10252 Eastwind Ct Indianapolis (46256) *(G-9224)*
Proforma Print Promo Group 574 931-2941
  3702 W Sample St South Bend (46619) *(G-15207)*
Proforma Viking, Fort Wayne *Also Called: Viking Business Ventures Inc (G-5532)*
Progress Examiner 812 865-3242
  233 S 2nd St Orleans (47452) *(G-13381)*
Progress Group Inc 219 322-3700
  918 Kennedy Ave Schererville (46375) *(G-14539)*
Progress Rail Locomotive Inc 765 281-2685
  3500 S Cowan Rd Muncie (47302) *(G-12479)*
Progress Rail Mfg Corp 765 281-2685
  3500 S Cowan Rd Muncie (47302) *(G-12480)*
Progress Rail Services Corp 219 397-5326
  175 W Chicago Ave East Chicago (46312) *(G-3037)*
Progress Rail Services Corp 765 472-2002
  405 Life Rd Peru (46970) *(G-13596)*
Progress Tool & Die Shop, Tipton *Also Called: Atkisson Enterprises Inc (G-15766)*
Progressive Design Apparel Inc 317 293-5888
  7260 Georgetown Rd Indianapolis (46268) *(G-9225)*
Progressive Plastics Inc 765 552-2004
  2200 S J St Elwood (46036) *(G-3833)*
Progressive Plating Company 317 923-2413
  2064 Columbia Ave Indianapolis (46202) *(G-9226)*
Progressive Printing Co Inc 765 653-3814
  115 N Jackson St Ste 1 Greencastle (46135) *(G-6427)*
Project Field Solutions Inc 317 590-7678
  11 Municipal Dr Ste 200 Fishers (46038) *(G-4584)*
Project House 317 691-4237
  9149 Lantern Ln Indianapolis (46256) *(G-9227)*
Project One Studio, Indianapolis *Also Called: Projectione LLC (G-9228)*

ALPHABETIC SECTION

Projectione LLC.. 812 480-6006
3151 Kirkbride Way Apt C Indianapolis (46222) *(G-9228)*

Prokuma Incorporated... 812 461-1681
110 N Main St Evansville (47711) *(G-4261)*

Proline Bowstrings.. 513 259-3738
1957 S Hubble Rd Liberty (47353) *(G-10996)*

Proline Spray Foam Inc... 317 981-2158
3880 Pendleton Way Ste 700 Indianapolis (46226) *(G-9229)*

Prolon Inc... 574 522-8900
1040 Sako Ct Elkhart (46516) *(G-3623)*

Promex Technologies LLC.................................... 317 736-0128
7510 E 82nd St Indianapolis (46256) *(G-9230)*

Prominent Promotional Pdts LLC.......................... 317 376-5772
10550 Millgrove Rd Quincy (47456) *(G-14022)*

Promotor Engines & Components......................... 574 533-9898
1814 Lincolnway E Goshen (46526) *(G-6243)*

Propaganda Motorcycles Inc................................. 765 997-8787
1304 Rose City Blvd Richmond (47374) *(G-14188)*

Property Management, Jasper Also Called: Kimball Inc *(G-9877)*

Prophalt Sealcoating LLC..................................... 502 356-3238
331 Vest Rd Henryville (47126) *(G-7114)*

Proportion-Air Inc (PA)... 317 335-2602
8250 N 600 W Mccordsville (46055) *(G-11454)*

Proprint Forms LLC.. 317 861-8701
2603 S Hillview Dr New Palestine (46163) *(G-12943)*

Proseries Products, Scottsburg Also Called: King Investments Inc *(G-14568)*

Prospect Distribution Inc...................................... 317 359-9551
6312 Southeastern Ave Indianapolis (46203) *(G-9231)*

Prosperer Trucking LLC....................................... 317 551-5691
6620 Hollow Run Dr Indianapolis (46214) *(G-9232)*

Prosperus LLC... 317 786-8990
5644 S Meridian St Ste E Indianapolis (46217) *(G-9233)*

Prosthetic Solutions Indiana, Terre Haute Also Called: Rehablttion Inst Indnpolis Inc *(G-15678)*

Protec Panel & Truss Mfg LLC.............................. 574 281-9080
323 High Rd Bremen (46506) *(G-1215)*

Protech Powder Coatings Inc............................... 814 456-1243
215 Brownsville Ave Liberty (47353) *(G-10997)*

Protect Plus Industries... 219 324-8482
229 Factory St La Porte (46350) *(G-10467)*

Protective Coatings Inc.. 260 424-2900
1602 Birchwood Ave Fort Wayne (46803) *(G-5354)*

Proteq Custom Gear LLC..................................... 812 201-6002
3057 W County Road 1200 N Brazil (47834) *(G-1164)*

Proterial Cable America Inc.................................. 812 945-9011
5300 Grant Line Rd New Albany (47150) *(G-12799)*

Protero Corporation.. 219 393-5591
605 Grayton Rd Kingsford Heights (46346) *(G-10186)*

Protherm Supply Inc... 812 492-3386
1409 E Maryland St Evansville (47711) *(G-4262)*

Proto Engineering Llc.. 800 522-6752
319 Harlan Dr Mooresville (46158) *(G-12237)*

Proto-Fab Acquisition Inc..................................... 574 522-4245
1615 Elreno St Elkhart (46516) *(G-3624)*

Proton Mold Tool Inc.. 812 923-7263
6126 Saint Marys Rd Floyds Knobs (47119) *(G-4690)*

Protron LLC.. 765 313-1595
1812 Mounds Rd Ste X Anderson (46016) *(G-181)*

Proud Spirits Inc... 301 775-0386
111 W Main St Ste 100 Carmel (46032) *(G-1731)*

Provident Tool & Die Inc...................................... 574 862-1233
66100 State Road 19 Wakarusa (46573) *(G-16245)*

Provisa International Inc...................................... 812 207-9137
6303 21st Century Dr Charlestown (47111) *(G-1892)*

Prowler Industries LLC.. 877 477-6953
1220 N Liberty Cir E Greensburg (47240) *(G-6626)*

Proximity Controls, Michigan City Also Called: Dwyer Instruments LLC *(G-11604)*

Proximo Distillers LLC... 201 204-1718
220 Shipping St Lawrenceburg (47025) *(G-10855)*

Proximo Distillers Indiana, Lawrenceburg Also Called: Proximo Distillers LLC *(G-10855)*

Prp Technologies LLC... 260 433-3769
3201 Stellhorn Rd Fort Wayne (46815) *(G-5355)*

Prp Wine International... 317 288-0005
8310 Allison Pointe Blvd Ste 205 Indianapolis (46250) *(G-9234)*

Prt Inc.. 765 938-3333
700 W 5th St Rushville (46173) *(G-14407)*

Pryor Safe & Lock, Indianapolis Also Called: S C Pryor Inc *(G-9354)*

Prysmian Cbles Systems USA LLC..................... 317 271-8447
7950 Rockville Rd Indianapolis (46214) *(G-9235)*

Prysmian Cbles Systems USA LLC..................... 317 271-8447
7920 Rockville Rd Indianapolis (46214) *(G-9236)*

Prysmian Cbles Systems USA LLC..................... 765 483-1760
311 S Enterprise Blvd Lebanon (46052) *(G-10934)*

Prysmian Cbles Systems USA LLC..................... 765 664-2321
440 E 8th St Marion (46953) *(G-11331)*

PSC, East Chicago Also Called: Precision Surveillance Corp *(G-3035)*

PSC Industries Inc... 812 425-9071
900 E Virginia St Evansville (47711) *(G-4263)*

PSC Industries Inc... 317 547-5439
6790 E 32nd St Indianapolis (46226) *(G-9237)*

PSI, Monticello Also Called: Polymer Science Inc *(G-12166)*

PSI Group Inc.. 317 297-3211
5071 W 74th St Indianapolis (46268) *(G-9238)*

PSI LLC (PA)... 765 483-0954
382 N Mount Zion Rd Lebanon (46052) *(G-10935)*

PSI Molded Plastics, South Bend Also Called: PSI Molded Plastics Ind Inc *(G-15208)*

PSI Molded Plastics Ind Inc................................. 574 288-2100
3615 Voorde Dr South Bend (46628) *(G-15208)*

PSL Rheotek USA Inc... 574 271-9417
12692 Sandy Dr Ste 115 Granger (46530) *(G-6373)*

Pssi, South Bend Also Called: Performnce Sftwr Solutions Inc *(G-15192)*

Pt Tool Machine... 219 275-3633
5183 E 894 S Brook (47922) *(G-1306)*

Ptc Alliance Corporation...................................... 765 259-3334
1480 Nw 11th St Richmond (47374) *(G-14189)*

Ptc Tubular Products LLC (HQ)........................... 765 259-3334
1480 Nw 11th St Richmond (47374) *(G-14190)*

PTG Inc... 317 892-4625
5838 E County Road 800 N Brownsburg (46112) *(G-1396)*

PTG Silicones Inc.. 812 948-8719
827 Progress Blvd New Albany (47150) *(G-12800)*

Pts Diagnostics, Whitestown Also Called: Polymer Technology Systems Inc *(G-16815)*

Publishers Consulting Corp................................. 219 874-4245
613 Franklin St Michigan City (46360) *(G-11652)*

Publishers Sovereign Grace................................ 765 296-5538
307 S Glick St Mulberry (46058) *(G-12330)*

Puck Supply & Machine LLC............................... 574 293-3333
56644 Elk Park Dr Elkhart (46516) *(G-3625)*

Pucl Bindley Bioscience Ctr................................ 765 496-3975
1203 W State St West Lafayette (47907) *(G-16621)*

Pudders LLC.. 317 402-3507
18 Public Sq Shelbyville (46176) *(G-14789)*

Pugh's Cabinets, Trafalgar Also Called: Jds Pughs Cabinets Inc *(G-15830)*

Pulaski County Press Inc..................................... 574 946-6628
114 W Main St Winamac (46996) *(G-16872)*

Pull Rite, Mishawaka Also Called: Pulliam Enterprises Inc *(G-11982)*

Pulliam Enterprises Inc....................................... 574 259-1520
13790 Jefferson Blvd Mishawaka (46545) *(G-11982)*

Pullman Company... 260 667-2200
503 Weatherhead St Angola (46703) *(G-290)*

Pulse Analytics LLC.. 260 615-8016
12764 Tamworth Dr Fishers (46037) *(G-4585)*

Pulse Energy... 812 268-6700
3137 N Old 41 Sullivan (47882) *(G-15417)*

Pulse Energy Systems LLC................................ 618 392-5502
420 Nw 5th St Ste 2b Evansville (47708) *(G-4264)*

Pumpalarmcom... 888 454-5051
203 W Morris St Indianapolis (46225) *(G-9239)*

Pumpkin Patch Market Inc.................................. 574 825-3312
10532 Us Highway 20 Middlebury (46540) *(G-11747)*

Punjab Empire Inc... 765 987-8786
981 Sheets Ct Greenfield (46140) *(G-6543)*

Punkish Press LLC.. 812 626-1028
18762 Long Walk Ln Noblesville (46060) *(G-13161)*

Pur-SE, Greendale *Also Called: CM Reed LLC (G-6444)*
PURDUE EXPONENT, THE, West Lafayette *Also Called: Purdue Student Pubg Foundation (G-16622)*
Purdue Student Pubg Foundation... 765 743-1111
  460 Northwestern Ave West Lafayette (47906) *(G-16622)*
Purdy Concrete Inc (PA).. 765 477-7687
  3633 Old Us Highway 231 S Lafayette (47909) *(G-10672)*
Purdy Materials Inc.. 765 474-8993
  3633 Us Highway 231 S Lafayette (47909) *(G-10673)*
Pure Beautee Bundlez Inc... 574 204-3979
  6929 E 10th St Ste 200 Indianapolis (46219) *(G-9240)*
Pure Creative Publishing LLC.. 765 860-8999
  5534 Saint Joe Rd Fort Wayne (46835) *(G-5356)*
Pure Edible Oils, Indianapolis *Also Called: Northern Indiana Oil LLC (G-9022)*
Pure Elements LLC.. 317 503-0411
  8415 Southern Springs Dr Indianapolis (46237) *(G-9241)*
Pure Flow Airdog, Shelbyville *Also Called: W A P LLC (G-14813)*
Pure Image Laser and Spa LLC... 317 306-6603
  8350 S Emerson Ave Ste 120 Indianapolis (46237) *(G-9242)*
Purewal Publishing LLC... 317 703-6899
  176 W Logan St Noblesville (46060) *(G-13162)*
Purina Animal Nutrition LLC.. 812 424-5501
  2124 Lynch Rd Evansville (47711) *(G-4265)*
Purina Animal Nutrition LLC.. 765 659-4791
  2472 W State Road 28 Frankfort (46041) *(G-5692)*
Purina Animal Nutrition LLC.. 574 658-4137
  346 W 1350 N Milford (46542) *(G-11804)*
Purina Animal Nutrition LLC.. 765 373-9377
  1700 Industries Rd Richmond (47374) *(G-14191)*
Purina Animal Nutrition LLC.. 765 962-9561
  505 N 4th St Richmond (47374) *(G-14192)*
Purina Animal Nutrition LLC.. 765 962-9561
  415 N 6th & Neff St Richmond (47374) *(G-14193)*
Purina Mills, Evansville *Also Called: Purina Mills LLC (G-4266)*
Purina Mills, Milford *Also Called: Purina Mills LLC (G-11805)*
Purina Mills LLC... 812 424-5501
  2124 Lynch Rd Evansville (47711) *(G-4266)*
Purina Mills LLC... 574 658-4137
  346 W 1350 N Milford (46542) *(G-11805)*
Puritan Water Conditioning... 765 362-6340
  216 Lafayette Ave Crawfordsville (47933) *(G-2606)*
Purolator Pdts A Filtration Co (PA).. 866 925-2247
  100 River Ridge Cir Jeffersonville (47130) *(G-10043)*
Purple Door Press... 219 690-1046
  8833 W 156th Ct Lowell (46356) *(G-11177)*
Purple Vertigo Candles LLC... 502 807-6619
  1145 Old State Road 64 Ne New Salisbury (47161) *(G-12986)*
Purrfectplay LLC.. 219 926-7604
  790 Graham Dr Chesterton (46304) *(G-1955)*
Purspec Technologies, West Lafayette *Also Called: Purspec Technologies Inc (G-16623)*
Purspec Technologies Inc... 765 532-2208
  1281 Win Hentschel Blvd West Lafayette (47906) *(G-16623)*
Push Enterprises, Kokomo *Also Called: Belcher Tobiah (G-10238)*
Putnam Plastics Inc (PA).. 765 795-6102
  30 W Stardust Rd Cloverdale (46120) *(G-2094)*
Puzzles Padlocks Escape Rm LLC... 812 559-0767
  402 Mccrillus St Jasper (47546) *(G-9904)*
Puzzles Plus LLC... 574 204-2054
  1837 Thornhill Dr South Bend (46614) *(G-15209)*
Pvm, Columbia City *Also Called: Pine Valley Munitions Inc (G-2181)*
Pw Apparel, Kentland *Also Called: Phillip Westrick (G-10161)*
Pwi.. 574 646-2015
  7930 W 1000 N Nappanee (46550) *(G-12637)*
Pwi Corp... 574 646-2015
  7930 W 1000 N Nappanee (46550) *(G-12638)*
Pwt Group LLC.. 260 490-6477
  6320 Highview Dr Fort Wayne (46818) *(G-5357)*
Pylo Health, Indianapolis *Also Called: Prevounce Health Inc (G-9195)*
Pynco Inc.. 812 275-0900
  2605 35th St Bedford (47421) *(G-661)*

Pyramid Equipment... 219 778-4253
  8 S Depot St Rolling Prairie (46371) *(G-14370)*
PYRAMID EQUIPMENT, Rolling Prairie *Also Called: Pyramid Equipment (G-14370)*
Pyramid Equipment Inc (PA)... 219 778-2591
  211 S Prairie St Rolling Prairie (46371) *(G-14371)*
Pyramid Metallizing Inc.. 219 879-9967
  3155 W Dunes Hwy Michigan City (46360) *(G-11653)*
Pyramid Plastic Group Inc.. 260 327-3145
  1560 N State Road 5 Larwill (46764) *(G-10821)*
Pyramid Sign & Design Inc... 765 447-4174
  515 Farabee Dr S Lafayette (47905) *(G-10674)*
Pyrimont Operating Solutions, Fishers *Also Called: Front End Digital Inc (G-4528)*
Pyro Industrial Services Inc.. 219 787-5700
  6610 Shepherd Ave Portage (46368) *(G-13907)*
Pyro Micro Welding LLC... 812 431-3330
  1901 Orchard Rd Evansville (47720) *(G-4267)*
Pyro Shield Inc.. 219 661-8600
  1171 Erie Ct Crown Point (46307) *(G-2739)*
Pyromation LLC... 260 484-2580
  5211 Industrial Rd Fort Wayne (46825) *(G-5358)*
Pyrotek Incorporated... 260 248-4141
  4447 E Park 30 Dr Columbia City (46725) *(G-2184)*
Pzm Indiana LLC... 317 337-0441
  4511 W 99th St Carmel (46032) *(G-1732)*
Q Air Inc.. 219 476-7048
  4008 Murvihill Rd. Valparaiso (46383) *(G-16032)*
Q C I, Orland *Also Called: Quality Converters Inc (G-13371)*
Q P Inc... 574 295-6884
  530 E Lexington Ave Ste 155 Elkhart (46516) *(G-3626)*
Q-Edge Corporation.. 317 203-6800
  1301 Smith Rd Ste 101 Plainfield (46168) *(G-13718)*
Qbank LLC... 317 354-5764
  2117 Dakota Dr Noblesville (46062) *(G-13163)*
Qbc Catering LLC... 812 364-4293
  2124 E County Line Rd S Palmyra (47164) *(G-13485)*
Qbotix LLC.. 562 526-5725
  1355 Getz Rd Ste E Fort Wayne (46804) *(G-5359)*
Qci, West Terre Haute *Also Called: Quality Council Indiana Inc (G-16653)*
Qfs Holdings LLC.. 317 634-2543
  2457 E Washington St Ste B Indianapolis (46201) *(G-9243)*
Qgraphics Inc (PA).. 765 564-2314
  108 E Main St Delphi (46923) *(G-2906)*
Qgraphics Inc... 574 967-3733
  103 W Walnut St Flora (46929) *(G-4664)*
Qig LLC.. 260 244-3591
  225 Towerview Dr Columbia City (46725) *(G-2185)*
Qlever Company LLC.. 765 490-4694
  3363 E 550 S Ste 590 Rochester (46975) *(G-14312)*
Qme LLC.. 773 263-9830
  2262 W 17th Ave Gary (46404) *(G-5998)*
Qmp Inc.. 574 262-1575
  2925 Stephen Pl Elkhart (46514) *(G-3627)*
Qpoly LLC... 574 386-4671
  56977 Elk Ct Elkhart (46516) *(G-3628)*
Qsi Custom Machining... 260 636-2341
  1512 Progress Dr Albion (46701) *(G-42)*
Qtg Pepsi Co Larry Davi... 317 830-4020
  9101 Orly Rd Indianapolis (46241) *(G-9244)*
Qtr Industries LLC... 260 416-8981
  1035 Sutton Dr Unit B Fort Wayne (46804) *(G-5360)*
Quad 4, Elkhart *Also Called: Quad 4 Plastics Inc (G-3629)*
Quad 4 Plastics Inc.. 574 293-8660
  1840 Borneman Ave Elkhart (46517) *(G-3629)*
Quad Plus LLC.. 219 844-9214
  3535 165th St Hammond (46323) *(G-6993)*
Quad/Graphics Inc.. 260 748-5300
  6502 Nelson Rd Fort Wayne (46803) *(G-5361)*
QUAD/GRAPHICS INC., Fort Wayne *Also Called: Quad/Graphics Inc (G-5361)*
Quadrant Engrg Plastic Pdts, Fort Wayne *Also Called: Mitsubishi Chemical Advncd Mtr (G-5233)*
Quake Manufacturing Inc.. 260 432-8023
  3923 Engle Rd Fort Wayne (46804) *(G-5362)*

ALPHABETIC SECTION

Quaker Chemical Corp 765 668-2441
  2400 W 2nd St Marion (46952) *(G-11332)*
Quaker Oats, Indianapolis Also Called: Quaker Oats Company *(G-9245)*
Quaker Oats, Muncie Also Called: Quaker Oats Company *(G-12481)*
Quaker Oats Company 317 821-6442
  5858 Decatur Blvd Indianapolis (46241) *(G-9245)*
Quaker Oats Company 765 288-1503
  3300 S Hoyt Ave Muncie (47302) *(G-12481)*
Qualitex Inc 260 244-7839
  4185 E Park 30 Dr Columbia City (46725) *(G-2186)*
Quality Coatings Inc 812 925-3314
  1700 N State St Chandler (47610) *(G-1865)*
Quality Concepts 574 215-6391
  14206 State Road 4 Goshen (46528) *(G-6244)*
Quality Converters Inc 260 829-6541
  9675 W Maple St Orland (46776) *(G-13371)*
Quality Council Indiana Inc 812 533-4215
  602 W Paris Ave West Terre Haute (47885) *(G-16653)*
Quality Data Products Inc 317 595-0700
  10142 Brooks School Rd Ste 210 Fishers (46037) *(G-4586)*
Quality Die Set Corp 574 967-4411
  600 Water St Logansport (46947) *(G-11104)*
Quality Drapery Corporation 765 481-2370
  1334 W Main St Lebanon (46052) *(G-10936)*
Quality Engineered Pdts Inc 574 294-6943
  56802 Elk Ct Elkhart (46516) *(G-3630)*
Quality Fabricated Solutions, Indianapolis Also Called: Qfs Holdings LLC *(G-9243)*
Quality Fabrication Ind Inc 765 529-9776
  3174 S Commerce Dr New Castle (47362) *(G-12880)*
Quality Fence Ltd 260 768-4986
  6450 W 275 N Shipshewana (46565) *(G-14880)*
Quality Fire Protection 269 683-0285
  5320 S Main St South Bend (46614) *(G-15210)*
Quality Forklift Repair LLC 574 702-5733
  4662 E State Road 14 Rochester (46975) *(G-14313)*
Quality Fuel Solutions 574 293-1423
  1001 Sako Ct Elkhart (46516) *(G-3631)*
Quality Galvanized Pdts Inc 574 848-5151
  19473 County Road 8 Bristol (46507) *(G-1283)*
Quality Graphics Corp 219 845-7084
  7801 Northcote Ave Hammond (46324) *(G-6994)*
Quality Hardwood Products Inc 260 982-2043
  3902 E State Road 14 Claypool (46510) *(G-2056)*
Quality Hardwood Sales, Nappanee Also Called: Ufp Nappanee LLC *(G-12649)*
Quality Hardwood Sales LLC 574 773-2505
  493 Shawnee St Nappanee (46550) *(G-12639)*
Quality Hydraulic Mch Svc Inc 317 892-2596
  4905 E County Road 450 N Danville (46122) *(G-2824)*
Quality Imagination Corp 317 753-0042
  4405 Massachusetts Ave Indianapolis (46218) *(G-9246)*
Quality Imprssons Print Design, Crown Point Also Called: Jac Jmr Inc *(G-2698)*
Quality Industrial Service, Michigan City Also Called: Tmak Inc *(G-11679)*
Quality Industrial Services, La Porte Also Called: Quality Industrial Supplies *(G-10468)*
Quality Industrial Supplies 219 324-2654
  517 Brighton St La Porte (46350) *(G-10468)*
Quality Information Tech Inc 317 595-0700
  10142 Brooks School Rd Ste 210 Fishers (46037) *(G-4587)*
Quality Inspection and Gage, Columbia City Also Called: Qig LLC *(G-2185)*
Quality Machine & Tool Works 812 379-2660
  1201 Michigan Ave Columbus (47201) *(G-2383)*
Quality Mch Repr & Engrg Inc 317 375-1366
  4406 Quail Creek Trce N Pittsboro (46167) *(G-13653)*
Quality Metal Products, Elkhart Also Called: Qmp Inc *(G-3627)*
Quality Mold and Engrg Inc 812 346-6577
  230 N State Highways 3 & 7 Vernon (47282) *(G-16098)*
Quality Molded Products Inc 574 272-3733
  19850 State Line Rd South Bend (46637) *(G-15211)*
Quality Pallet 765 348-4840
  1506 W Park Ave Hartford City (47348) *(G-7075)*
Quality Pallet 765 212-2215
  1000 E Seymour St Muncie (47302) *(G-12482)*

Quality Pallet Recycling LLC 317 840-5990
  3964 W 700 S Rushville (46173) *(G-14408)*
Quality Pallets Inc 812 873-6818
  8740 W County Road 700 S Commiskey (47227) *(G-2421)*
Quality Plas Engrg Acqstion Co 574 262-2621
  2507 Decio Dr Elkhart (46514) *(G-3632)*
Quality Pnt Prstned Fnshes Inc 574 294-6944
  28827 Old Us 33 Elkhart (46516) *(G-3633)*
Quality Printing, Anderson Also Called: Phoenix Press Inc *(G-178)*
Quality Printing of NW Ind 219 322-6677
  2315 Us Highway 41 Schererville (46375) *(G-14540)*
Quality Repair Services Inc 317 881-0205
  411 Knight Dr Greenwood (46142) *(G-6756)*
Quality Steel & Alum Pdts Inc 574 295-8715
  28620 County Road 20 Elkhart (46517) *(G-3634)*
Quality Steel & Aluminium 574 294-7221
  56741 Elk Park Dr Elkhart (46516) *(G-3635)*
Quality Steel Treating Co Inc 317 357-8691
  641 Cleveland St Tipton (46072) *(G-15788)*
Quality Surfaces Inc 812 876-5838
  2087 Franklin Rd Spencer (47460) *(G-15358)*
Quality Tank Trucks & Eqp Inc 317 635-0000
  3301 Moore Ave Indianapolis (46201) *(G-9247)*
Quality Tool & Die Inc 219 324-2511
  521 Brighton St La Porte (46350) *(G-10469)*
Quality Tool & Machine Co 219 464-2411
  393 S State Road 49 Valparaiso (46383) *(G-16033)*
Quality Tool Design Inc 765 377-4055
  1645 E County Road 175 N Connersville (47331) *(G-2464)*
Quality Tooling, Sunman Also Called: David L Huber *(G-15435)*
Quality Vault Company 812 336-8127
  1908 W Allen St Bloomington (47403) *(G-949)*
Qualtech Tool & Engrg Inc 260 726-6572
  103 Performance Dr Portland (47371) *(G-13965)*
Qualtronics LLC 812 375-8880
  4775 Progress Dr Columbus (47201) *(G-2384)*
Quanex Heat Treat 260 356-9520
  25 Commercial Rd Huntington (46750) *(G-7358)*
Quanex Homeshield LLC 765 966-0322
  451 Industrial Pkwy Richmond (47374) *(G-14194)*
Quantum 7 Group LLC 812 824-9378
  3523 E Harbor Dr Bloomington (47401) *(G-950)*
Quantum Technologies LLC 765 426-0156
  7135 E 750 S Elizabethtown (47232) *(G-3132)*
Quantumtech LLC 786 512-0827
  5042 Brandywine Dr Apt 322 Indianapolis (46241) *(G-9248)*
Queen City Candy, LLC, Greendale Also Called: Catalent Wellness Indiana LLC *(G-6443)*
Queen City Press 317 840-1135
  9623 Wandering Woods Ct Fishers (46037) *(G-4588)*
Quemetco, Indianapolis Also Called: Eco-Bat America LLC *(G-8048)*
Quest Energy Inc 317 318-5737
  8856 South St Fishers (46038) *(G-4589)*
Quick Panic Release LLC 812 841-5733
  2216 Dutch Ln Terre Haute (47802) *(G-15673)*
Quick Tanks Inc 260 347-3850
  545 Krueger St Kendallville (46755) *(G-10145)*
Quick Tanks Inc 260 347-3850
  522 Krueger St Kendallville (46755) *(G-10146)*
Quick To Fix LLC 812 660-2044
  518 16th St Bedford (47421) *(G-662)*
Quick Turn Anodizing LLC 877 716-1150
  6973 S Us Highway 31 Edinburgh (46124) *(G-3099)*
Quick Walk Systems Inc 317 255-2247
  5315 N Pennsylvania St Indianapolis (46220) *(G-9249)*
Quickblades 260 359-2072
  1640 Riverfork Dr Ste A Huntington (46750) *(G-7359)*
Quicks Machine and Tool Inc 812 952-2135
  5523 Corydon Ridge Rd Ne Corydon (47112) *(G-2513)*
Quicksign, Indianapolis Also Called: Sign Craft Industries Inc *(G-9428)*
Quickspace Transportation LLC 812 585-2317
  6701 N College Ave Apt 503 Indianapolis (46220) *(G-9250)*

ALPHABETIC SECTION

Quiet Storm Productions LLC 219 448-1998
2320 Normandy Dr Apt 3d Michigan City (46360) *(G-11654)*

Quikcut LLC 260 447-3880
4630 Allen Martin Dr Fort Wayne (46806) *(G-5363)*

Quikrete, Indianapolis *Also Called: Quikrete Companies LLC (G-9252)*

Quikrete Companies LLC 317 241-8237
1501 S Holt Rd Indianapolis (46241) *(G-9251)*

Quikrete Companies LLC 317 251-2281
3100 E 56th St Indianapolis (46220) *(G-9252)*

Quikset Bollard Company 502 648-6734
2234 E Market St New Albany (47150) *(G-12801)*

Quilt Bug 812 926-3092
11860 Creekside Aurora (47001) *(G-454)*

Quilters Garden 812 539-4939
9 E Center St Lawrenceburg (47025) *(G-10856)*

Quintel Inc 219 322-3399
628 Gatlin Rd Schererville (46375) *(G-14541)*

Quirey Quality Engineering 812 963-6097
2251 Commercial Ct Evansville (47720) *(G-4268)*

Qumulex Inc 317 207-0520
9059 Technology Ln Fishers (46038) *(G-4590)*

Quo Vadis Aerospace LLC 575 621-2372
1951 W Edgewood Ave Indianapolis (46217) *(G-9253)*

R & B Fine Printing Inc 219 365-9490
9720 Industrial Dr Saint John (46373) *(G-14457)*

R & B Mold and Die Inc 219 324-4176
1560 Lake St La Porte (46350) *(G-10470)*

R & D Machine Shop Inc 574 946-6109
935 N Us Highway 35 Winamac (46996) *(G-16873)*

R & D Metal Fabricating Inc 574 533-2424
414 N Main St Ste 414 Goshen (46528) *(G-6245)*

R & D Mold and Engineering Inc 574 257-1070
1710 Clover Rd Mishawaka (46545) *(G-11983)*

R & E Pallet Inc 219 873-9671
1843 E Us Highway 12 Michigan City (46360) *(G-11655)*

R & J Excvtg & Sealcoating LLC 812 799-1849
1240 11th St Columbus (47201) *(G-2385)*

R & K Incinerator Inc 260 565-3214
6125 W 100 S Decatur (46733) *(G-2878)*

R & M Tool Engineering Inc 812 352-0240
3355 N 4th St North Vernon (47265) *(G-13294)*

R & M Welding & Fabricating Sp (PA) 812 295-9130
1192 State Road 550 Loogootee (47553) *(G-11148)*

R & R, Columbia City *Also Called: R & R Manufacturing (G-2187)*

R & R Custom Woodworking Inc 574 773-5436
30480 County Road 52 Nappanee (46550) *(G-12640)*

R & R Engineering Co Inc 765 536-2331
801 S Main St Summitville (46070) *(G-15429)*

R & R Manufacturing 260 244-5621
1150 W 150 N Columbia City (46725) *(G-2187)*

R & R Plastics Inc 219 393-5505
4th Rd Kingsbury Industrial Park Kingsbury (46345) *(G-10185)*

R & R Regulators Inc 574 522-3500
24545 County Road 45 Elkhart (46516) *(G-3636)*

R & R Technologies LLC (PA) 812 526-2655
7560 E County Line Rd Edinburgh (46124) *(G-3100)*

R & R Trucking & Freight LLC 888 477-8782
6101 N Keystone Ave Ste 100 Indianapolis (46220) *(G-9254)*

R & R Welding 260 424-3635
1238 E Lewis St Fort Wayne (46803) *(G-5364)*

R & S Plating Inc 317 925-2396
2302 Bloyd Ave Indianapolis (46218) *(G-9255)*

R & T Farm Supply, Akron *Also Called: Russell E Martin (G-8)*

R 2 Diagnostics Inc 574 288-4377
1801 Commerce Dr South Bend (46628) *(G-15212)*

R B Tool & Machinery Co 574 679-0082
10120 Glenwood Ave Osceola (46561) *(G-13401)*

R Booe & Son Hardwoods Inc 812 835-2663
481 N Meridian Rd Centerpoint (47840) *(G-1847)*

R C Systems Inc 812 282-4897
Jeffersonville (47131) *(G-10044)*

R D Laney Family Honey Company 574 656-8701
25725 New Rd North Liberty (46554) *(G-13220)*

R D-N-P Drilling Inc 219 956-3481
3759 W 900 N Wheatfield (46392) *(G-16772)*

R Drew & Co Inc 765 420-7232
4866 N 9th Street Rd West Lafayette (47906) *(G-16624)*

R E Casebeer & Sons Inc 812 829-3284
661 W Market St Spencer (47460) *(G-15359)*

R F Express Corp 219 510-5193
2601 Vale Park Rd Valparaiso (46383) *(G-16034)*

R H Marlin Excavating LLC 765 913-4041
2502 W Clover Ln Martinsville (46151) *(G-11423)*

R J Hanlon Company Inc 317 867-0028
345 E 175th St Westfield (46074) *(G-16720)*

R J Hanlon Company Inc (PA) 317 867-2900
17408 Tiller Ct Ste 600 Westfield (46074) *(G-16721)*

R J Smithey LLC 317 435-8473
2213 Running Brook Pl Greenwood (46143) *(G-6757)*

R K C Instrument 574 273-6099
4245 Meghan Beeler Ct South Bend (46628) *(G-15213)*

R M I, Warsaw *Also Called: Rmi Holdings LLC (G-16419)*

R M Mfg Housing Svc 574 288-5207
1001 S Mayflower Rd L South Bend (46619) *(G-15214)*

R N A Industries Corp 765 288-4413
251 E Sheridan St Redkey (47373) *(G-14029)*

R O I Systems Inc 260 413-6307
9181 Lima Rd Fort Wayne (46818) *(G-5365)*

R P Imel 260 543-2465
1501 W Us Highway 224 Uniondale (46791) *(G-15872)*

R P Wakefield Company Inc 260 837-8841
600 W Maple St Waterloo (46793) *(G-16528)*

R R Donnelley & Sons Company 260 624-2350
611 W Mill St Angola (46703) *(G-291)*

R R Donnelley & Sons Company 765 362-1300
1009 Sloan St Crawfordsville (47933) *(G-2607)*

R R Donnelley & Sons Company 812 523-1800
709 A Ave E Seymour (47274) *(G-14679)*

R R Donnelley & Sons Company 574 267-7101
2801 W Old Road 30 Warsaw (46580) *(G-16414)*

R R Donnelley Inc 317 614-2508
201 S Capitol Ave Ste 201 Indianapolis (46225) *(G-9256)*

R R M, Rochester *Also Called: Rochester Rttional Molding Inc (G-14320)*

R S C, East Chicago *Also Called: Refractory Service Corporation (G-3038)*

R T P Company, Indianapolis *Also Called: Miller Waste Mills Inc (G-8924)*

R T Tire & Auto-Lebanon 317 443-6025
24518 Jerkwater Rd Sheridan (46069) *(G-14826)*

R T W Refractory Inc 812 468-4299
3141 Broadway Ave Evansville (47712) *(G-4269)*

R W Machine Incorporated 317 769-6798
3463 S 500 E Whitestown (46075) *(G-16818)*

R W Moran Express Inc 317 445-5861
6214 Morenci Trl Ste 200 Indianapolis (46268) *(G-9257)*

R&H Metalworks LLC 317 513-8733
8142 N 700 W Fairland (46126) *(G-4402)*

R&S Sign Design 765 520-5594
3963 S State Road 103 New Castle (47362) *(G-12881)*

R2 Pharma LLC 317 810-6205
11550 N Meridian St Ste 290 Carmel (46032) *(G-1733)*

R2b2 Industries LLC 812 436-4840
701 N 9th Ave Evansville (47712) *(G-4270)*

R3 Composites Corp (PA) 260 627-0033
14123 Roth Rd Grabill (46741) *(G-6321)*

Raac LLC 260 925-0623
1937 Jacob St Auburn (46706) *(G-418)*

Raad Custom Woodworking LLC 765 432-1385
2651 Sea Biscuit Ln Kokomo (46901) *(G-10325)*

Rab Wood Products 574 206-5001
1507 S Olive St Ste B South Bend (46619) *(G-15215)*

Rabb and Howe Cabinet Top Co 317 926-6442
2571 Winthrop Ave Indianapolis (46205) *(G-9258)*

Raben Tire Co LLC 812 465-5555
1108 N Fares Ave Evansville (47711) *(G-4271)*

ALPHABETIC SECTION — Ravens

Raber Buggy Shop LLC 812 486-3789
7209 E 300 N Montgomery (47558) *(G-12120)*

Raber Wheel Works LLC 812 486-2786
7226 E 300 N Montgomery (47558) *(G-12121)*

Race Cars Usa LLC 317 508-3500
1530 Woodlake Ct Carmel (46032) *(G-1734)*

Race Engineering 219 661-8904
725 E Goldsborough St Ste 4 Crown Point (46307) *(G-2740)*

Racestar Publications 219 987-2096
9054 Holmes Ter E Demotte (46310) *(G-2927)*

Raceway Hand Car Wash LLC 260 242-9866
606 Fairview Blvd Kendallville (46755) *(G-10147)*

Racing Fuel Ignite 765 733-0833
2950 W Delphi Pike Marion (46952) *(G-11333)*

Rack Hub LLC 260 571-7028
3276 N 500 E Urbana (46990) *(G-15887)*

Rackcollections LLC 317 779-4302
317 N Hamilton Ave Indianapolis (46201) *(G-9259)*

Raco Industries LLC 812 232-3676
1607 Maple Ave Terre Haute (47804) *(G-15674)*

RAD Cube LLC (PA) 317 456-7560
9449 Priority Way West Dr Ste 110 Indianapolis (46240) *(G-9260)*

RAD Fabrication Llc 317 903-0065
940 E Michigan St Indianapolis (46202) *(G-9261)*

Radar Associates Corporation 219 838-8030
1117 Melbrook Dr Munster (46321) *(G-12560)*

Radel Wood Products Inc 765 472-2940
1630 W Logansport Rd Peru (46970) *(G-13597)*

Radian Research Inc 765 449-5500
3852 Fortune Dr Lafayette (47905) *(G-10675)*

Radiant Energy Distribution, Monrovia *Also Called: M Jones Consulting LLC (G-12078)*

Radiation Physics Cnslting Inc 317 251-0193
7022 Warwick Rd Indianapolis (46220) *(G-9262)*

Radiator Specialty Company 574 546-5606
860 Legner St 870 Bremen (46506) *(G-1216)*

Radio and Broadcasting Towers, Evansville *Also Called: Benson Tower LLC (G-3914)*

Radio Resources, La Porte *Also Called: Roger Miller (G-10474)*

Radio Station Wrbi, Batesville *Also Called: The Findlay Publishing Co (G-606)*

Radius Aerospace Inc 317 392-5000
850 Elston Dr Shelbyville (46176) *(G-14790)*

Radon Environmental Inc 317 843-0804
2320 Broadmoor Dr Elkhart (46514) *(G-3637)*

Raemarie Essentials LLC 219 248-5482
5481 Sand Ave Portage (46368) *(G-13908)*

Raging Rocket Web Design LLC 219 381-5027
9800 Connecticut Dr Crown Point (46307) *(G-2741)*

Rahn Printing, Ossian *Also Called: Edwin Rahn (G-13423)*

Rai LLC (PA) 765 227-0111
3638 Lombardy Pl Indianapolis (46226) *(G-9263)*

Rail Protection Plus LLC 812 399-1084
3913 Horne Ave New Albany (47150) *(G-12802)*

Rail Scale Inc 317 339-6486
5303 N 800 E Wilkinson (46186) *(G-16844)*

Railway Unloading Services LLC 219 989-7700
2001 N Cline Ave Griffith (46319) *(G-6816)*

Rain Network LLC 909 900-7776
23232 Amber Valley Dr South Bend (46628) *(G-15216)*

Rain Song Farms LLC 317 640-4534
19539 Pilgrim Rd Noblesville (46060) *(G-13164)*

Rain Song Winery, Noblesville *Also Called: Rain Song Farms LLC (G-13164)*

Rainbow Printing LLC 812 275-3372
2139 16th St Bedford (47421) *(G-663)*

Raine Inc 765 622-7687
6401 S Madison Ave Anderson (46013) *(G-182)*

Rainmaker Polymers LLC (PA) 574 268-0010
2986 E Prestwick Rd Winona Lake (46590) *(G-16915)*

Rake Cabinet & Surfc Solutions 812 824-8338
705 E Dillman Rd Bloomington (47401) *(G-951)*

Rakk LLC 812 271-4300
491 W Main St Austin (47102) *(G-470)*

Ralph Privoznik Jewelry Art 765 742-4904
1010 Main St Lafayette (47901) *(G-10676)*

Ralph Ransom Logging, Newburgh *Also Called: Ralph Ransom Veneers (G-13018)*

Ralph Ransom Veneers 812 858-9956
6599 Heathervale Ct Newburgh (47630) *(G-13018)*

Ralph West, Boonville *Also Called: S & S Machine Shop Inc (G-1096)*

Ralston Yard, Valparaiso *Also Called: Legacy Vulcan LLC (G-15995)*

Ram Apparel, Alexandria *Also Called: Ram Graphics Inc (G-58)*

Ram Graphics Inc 765 724-7783
1509 S Longwood Dr Alexandria (46001) *(G-58)*

Ram North America Inc 317 984-1971
25415 State Road 19 Arcadia (46030) *(G-316)*

Ram Services Rfrgn & Mech 317 679-8541
5170 Atherton North Dr Indianapolis (46219) *(G-9264)*

Ramar Industries Inc 765 288-7319
6200 N Wheeling Ave Muncie (47304) *(G-12483)*

Ramco, Portage *Also Called: Anita Cole (G-13843)*

Ramco Builder and Supply LLC 574 223-7802
4572 N Old Us Highway 31 Rochester (46975) *(G-14314)*

Ramco Engineering Inc 574 266-1455
2805 Frederic Dr Elkhart (46514) *(G-3638)*

Ramco Supply, Rochester *Also Called: Ramco Builder and Supply LLC (G-14314)*

Ramifications LLC 765 729-5484
11559 S County Road 300 W Muncie (47302) *(G-12484)*

Ramo & Co LLC 219 381-1843
2572 Van Buren St Gary (46407) *(G-5999)*

Ramsey Popcorn Co Inc 812 347-2441
5645 Clover Valley Rd Nw Ramsey (47166) *(G-14026)*

Rance Aluminum Fabrication 574 266-9028
3012 Mobile Dr Elkhart (46514) *(G-3639)*

Rand Worldwide Inc 317 572-1267
8604 Allisonville Rd Indianapolis (46250) *(G-9265)*

Randall Corp 812 425-7122
1105 E Virginia St Evansville (47711) *(G-4272)*

Randall K Dike 812 664-4942
5038 S State Road 65 Owensville (47665) *(G-13471)*

Randall Lowe Sons Sawmill LLC 812 936-2254
6543 W County Road 875 S French Lick (47432) *(G-5848)*

Randolph Carpet-Tile Cleaning 317 401-2300
59 W Armitage Dr Cicero (46034) *(G-2000)*

Randys Tooling & Wdwkg LLC 812 326-2204
6017 S 500e Saint Anthony (47575) *(G-14431)*

Rankin Pump and Supply Co Inc 812 238-2535
130 N 11th St Terre Haute (47807) *(G-15675)*

Rapar Inc 812 254-9886
705 W National Hwy Washington (47501) *(G-16506)*

Rapid Ribbons, Goshen *Also Called: Planks Printing Service Inc (G-6240)*

Rapid Rule Co Inc 574 784-2273
69159 Pine Rd North Liberty (46554) *(G-13221)*

Rapid Sensors Inc 260 499-0079
6060 N 160 W Howe (46746) *(G-7241)*

Rapid View LLC 574 224-3373
491 Apache Dr Rochester (46975) *(G-14315)*

Rappid Mfg Inc 317 440-8084
8219 Indy Ct Indianapolis (46214) *(G-9266)*

Rare Earth Inc 574 850-1924
68114 Lake Trl Bremen (46506) *(G-1217)*

Rasure Prints LLC 812 454-6222
4001 Wood Castle Rd Evansville (47711) *(G-4273)*

Ratcliff Enterprises, Lafayette *Also Called: Gary Ratcliff (G-10587)*

Ratech Industries, Crown Point *Also Called: Innovative Energy Inc (G-2697)*

Rathburn Tool & Manufacturing, Auburn *Also Called: Three Daughters Corp (G-430)*

Ratner Steel Supply Co 219 787-6700
655 George Nelson Dr Portage (46368) *(G-13909)*

Rauch Inc (PA) 812 945-4063
845 Park Pl New Albany (47150) *(G-12803)*

RAUCH INDUSTRIES, New Albany *Also Called: Rauch Inc (G-12803)*

Raven Industries Inc 877 923-5832
29769 County Road 40 Wakarusa (46573) *(G-16246)*

Raven Lake Originals Candles 765 419-1473
489 S 950 E Greentown (46936) *(G-6648)*

Ravens 269 362-4489
605 W Edison Rd Ste F Mishawaka (46545) *(G-11984)*

Raver Ready Mix Concrete LLC 812 662-7900
3013 N Huntersville Rd Batesville (47006) *(G-601)*

Raw Barbers and Company LLC 925 383-6212
7450 California Ave Hammond (46323) *(G-6995)*

Ray Envelope Company Inc 317 353-6251
450 S Kitley Ave Indianapolis (46219) *(G-9267)*

Ray Kammer 219 938-1708
6805 Forest Ave Gary (46403) *(G-6000)*

Ray Marketing LLC 317 782-0940
619 Memorial Dr Beech Grove (46107) *(G-701)*

Ray's Wood Products, Martinsville *Also Called: Terry L Ray (G-11430)*

Raybestos, Sullivan *Also Called: Raybestos Powertrain LLC (G-15420)*

Raybestos Aftermarket Pdts Co 765 359-1943
204 Maple St Crawfordsville (47933) *(G-2608)*

Raybestos Powertrain 765 362-3500
1204 Darlington Ave Crawfordsville (47933) *(G-2609)*

Raybestos Powertrain LLC 812 268-0322
609 E Chaney St Sullivan (47882) *(G-15418)*

Raybestos Powertrain LLC 812 268-0322
110 Industrial Park Dr Sullivan (47882) *(G-15419)*

Raybestos Powertrain LLC 812 268-1211
312 S St Clair St Sullivan (47882) *(G-15420)*

Rayburn Automotive Inc 317 535-8232
1120 Meriman Dr Greenwood (46143) *(G-6758)*

Rayco Marketing 574 293-8416
29675 Old Us 20 Elkhart (46514) *(G-3640)*

Rayco Mch & Engrg Group Inc 317 291-7848
970 Western Dr Indianapolis (46241) *(G-9268)*

Rayco Steel Process Inc 574 267-7676
207 S Lincoln St Warsaw (46580) *(G-16415)*

Rayconn LLC 317 809-5788
2122 Dr Martin Luther King Jr St Unit A3 Indianapolis (46202) *(G-9269)*

Rayes Rpid Rslts - MBL DRG ALC 317 721-1065
532 Chase St Indianapolis (46221) *(G-9270)*

Raymond Little Print Shop 317 246-9083
2900 N Shadeland Ave Ste B1 Indianapolis (46218) *(G-9271)*

Raymond Truex 574 858-2260
5383 W 400 N Warsaw (46582) *(G-16416)*

Raymone Sanders Fmly Trckg LLC 317 400-3545
5414 Calder Way Apt 411 Indianapolis (46226) *(G-9272)*

Rayne Water Conditioning 765 742-8967
2706 Elk St Lafayette (47904) *(G-10677)*

Rays Juice Company 219 809-7400
1555 Delaware St Michigan City (46360) *(G-11656)*

Rays Logging LLC 812 935-5307
746 Cuba Rd Spencer (47460) *(G-15360)*

Raytech Corp 765 359-2882
711 Tech Dr Crawfordsville (47933) *(G-2610)*

Raytech Powertrain, Crawfordsville *Also Called: Raytech Powertrain LLC (G-2611)*

Raytech Powertrain LLC 812 268-0322
204 Maple St Crawfordsville (47933) *(G-2611)*

Raytheon, Fort Wayne *Also Called: Raytheon Company (G-5366)*

Raytheon, Fort Wayne *Also Called: Raytheon Company (G-5367)*

Raytheon, Fort Wayne *Also Called: Raytheon Company (G-5368)*

Raytheon, Fort Wayne *Also Called: Raytheon Company (G-5369)*

Raytheon, Indianapolis *Also Called: Raytheon Company (G-9273)*

Raytheon, Indianapolis *Also Called: Raytheon Company (G-9274)*

Raytheon, Indianapolis *Also Called: Raytheon Company (G-9275)*

Raytheon Company 310 647-9438
5001 Us Highway 30 W Fort Wayne (46818) *(G-5366)*

Raytheon Company 260 429-6000
1320 Production Rd Fort Wayne (46808) *(G-5367)*

Raytheon Company 260 429-6000
1010 Production Rd Fort Wayne (46808) *(G-5368)*

Raytheon Company 310 647-9438
1010 Production Rd Fort Wayne (46808) *(G-5369)*

Raytheon Company 317 306-8471
3939 Priority Way South Dr Ste 100 Indianapolis (46240) *(G-9273)*

Raytheon Company 317 306-7492
623 Midnight Ct Indianapolis (46239) *(G-9274)*

Raytheon Company 317 306-4633
6125 E 21st St Indianapolis (46219) *(G-9275)*

RB Annis Instruments Inc 765 848-1621
117 W Franklin St Greencastle (46135) *(G-6428)*

RB Apparel, Bloomington *Also Called: RB Concepts (G-952)*

RB Concepts 317 735-2172
8451 S Marcy Ct Bloomington (47401) *(G-952)*

RB Machine Company 765 364-6716
2907 S 550 E Crawfordsville (47933) *(G-2612)*

Rbc Bearings Incorporated 574 935-3027
2912 Gary Dr Plymouth (46563) *(G-13808)*

Rbc Holding Inc 317 340-3845
1006 Old Eagle Way Greenwood (46143) *(G-6759)*

Rbc Prcsion Pdts - Plymouth Inc (DH) 574 935-3027
2928 Gary Dr Plymouth (46563) *(G-13809)*

Rbg Inc 812 866-3983
9186 W Henry Rd Lexington (47138) *(G-10980)*

Rbk Development Inc 574 267-5879
1058 W 400 N Warsaw (46582) *(G-16417)*

Rbm Manufacturing Inc 765 364-6933
566 S 200 E Crawfordsville (47933) *(G-2613)*

Rbs Tees Co 812 522-8675
1102 Gaiser Dr Seymour (47274) *(G-14680)*

RC Canada Dry Bottling Company, Seymour *Also Called: Keurig Dr Pepper Inc (G-14661)*

RC Cola, Evansville *Also Called: Royal Crown Bottling Corp (G-4294)*

RC Enterprise LLC 317 935-5628
581 S Rangeline Rd Carmel (46032) *(G-1735)*

RC Enterprises 812 279-2755
2611 16th St 301 Bedford (47421) *(G-664)*

RC Fun Parks LLC 574 217-7715
12990 Adams Rd Granger (46530) *(G-6374)*

RC Property Preservation LLC 765 660-3808
3117 S Adams St Marion (46953) *(G-11334)*

RC Systems, Jeffersonville *Also Called: R C Systems Inc (G-10044)*

RC Transportation LLC 812 424-7978
1100 Independence Ave Evansville (47714) *(G-4274)*

RCA Commercial Electronics, Indianapolis *Also Called: Dti Services Ltd Liability Co (G-8015)*

RCA Commerical Electronics, Indianapolis *Also Called: RCA Corporation (G-9276)*

RCA Corporation 800 722-2161
5935 W 84th St Ste A Indianapolis (46278) *(G-9276)*

Rcate Plbg Mech Ltd Lblty Co 812 613-0386
7907 Hillside Dr Sellersburg (47172) *(G-14611)*

Rci Hv Inc 724 538-3180
1079 Industry Dr Chesterton (46304) *(G-1956)*

RCO-Reed Corporation 317 736-8014
1050 Eastview Dr Franklin (46131) *(G-5771)*

Rd Rubber Products Inc 260 357-3571
1600 South Rd Garrett (46738) *(G-5875)*

RD Smith Manufacturing Inc 260 829-6709
5990 N State Road 327 Orland (46776) *(G-13372)*

Rdb Environmental LLC (PA) 708 362-3618
2953 In-14 Francesville (47946) *(G-5644)*

Rdd Properties Inc 317 870-1940
300 E Railroad St Waterloo (46793) *(G-16529)*

RE Industries Inc 219 987-1764
1328 15th St Se Ste 4 Demotte (46310) *(G-2928)*

RE Wilson LLC 317 730-4846
235 Wakefield Way Zionsville (46077) *(G-17045)*

RE Winset Music, Kendallville *Also Called: Sacred Selections (G-10151)*

Re-Play, Greenfield *Also Called: Obelisk Re-Play Opco LLC (G-6534)*

REA Magnet Wire, Fort Wayne *Also Called: Elektrsola Dr Gerd Schldbach G (G-4945)*

REA Magnet Wire, Lafayette *Also Called: Elektrsola Dr Gerd Schldbach G (G-10574)*

REA Magnet Wire Company Inc (PA) 800 732-9473
3400 E Coliseum Blvd Ste 200 Fort Wayne (46805) *(G-5370)*

Reachpoint Industries Corp 219 707-3514
2419 81st St Highland (46322) *(G-7152)*

Reading Bakery Systems Inc 317 337-0000
7517 Winton Dr Indianapolis (46268) *(G-9277)*

Ready Pac Foods Inc 574 935-9800
2050 N Oak Dr Plymouth (46563) *(G-13810)*

ALPHABETIC SECTION — Redrum Incorporated

Ready Set Go Inc 765 564-2847
   4280 W 700 N Delphi (46923) *(G-2907)*

Reagent Chemical & RES Inc 574 772-7424
   317 Kloeckner Dr Knox (46534) *(G-10220)*

Reagent Chemical & RES Inc 574 772-7424
   1705 Pacific Ave Knox (46534) *(G-10221)*

Reagent Chemical & Research, Inc., Knox *Also Called: Reagent Chemical & RES Inc* *(G-10220)*

Real Alloy Recycling LLC 260 563-2409
   305 Dimension Ave Wabash (46992) *(G-16214)*

Real Estate Sign Services, Indianapolis *Also Called: Insign Inc (G-8561)*

Real Log Homes, Attica *Also Called: Country Charm (G-347)*

Real Wood Works 812 277-1462
   2802 North South Poor Farm Rd Bedford (47421) *(G-665)*

Reality Gaming, Scottsburg *Also Called: Kristopher Cox (G-14569)*

Reality Motor Sports Inc 765 662-3000
   2021 S Western Ave Marion (46953) *(G-11335)*

Realize Inc 317 915-0295
   15515 Endeavor Dr Noblesville (46060) *(G-13165)*

Really Good Stuff Inc 812 402-8275
   9951 Hedden Rd Evansville (47725) *(G-4275)*

Reams Concrete 812 752-3746
   32 W Leota Rd Scottsburg (47170) *(G-14575)*

Rebar, Fort Wayne *Also Called: Rebar Corp of Indiana (G-5371)*

Rebar Corp of Indiana 260 471-2002
   5601 Industrial Rd Fort Wayne (46825) *(G-5371)*

Rebecca L Hamann & Associates 219 763-1233
   5069 Stagecoach Rd Portage (46368) *(G-13910)*

Rebel Devil Customs LLP 303 921-7131
   4819 N 900 W Sharpsville (46068) *(G-14712)*

Reber Enterprises LLC 260 356-6826
   1470 Etna Ave Huntington (46750) *(G-7360)*

Reber Machine & Tool Co Inc 765 288-0297
   1112 S Liberty St Muncie (47302) *(G-12485)*

Rebound Project LLP 765 621-5604
   1125 N Madison Ave Anderson (46011) *(G-183)*

Rebuilding Cnsltng Pckg Slton 574 389-1966
   636 Kollar St Elkhart (46514) *(G-3641)*

Reckitt Benckiser LLC 812 429-5000
   2400 W Lloyd Expy Evansville (47712) *(G-4276)*

Reckon Plating Inc 260 744-4339
   5300 Hanna St Fort Wayne (46806) *(G-5372)*

Reckon With It Tees Stuff LLC 765 585-3610
   1853 S Towpath Rd Covington (47932) *(G-2533)*

Recognition Plus 812 232-2372
   25 S 6th St Terre Haute (47807) *(G-15676)*

Recon Power Bikes, Fort Wayne *Also Called: America Wild LLC (G-4751)*

Reconserve of Indiana Inc 812 299-2191
   3315 Hancel Cir Mooresville (46158) *(G-12238)*

Record / Play Tek Inc 574 848-5233
   110 E Vistula St Bristol (46507) *(G-1284)*

Recovery Force LLC 866 604-6458
   10022 Lantern Rd Ste 100 Fishers (46037) *(G-4591)*

Recreation By Design LLC 574 294-2117
   57420 County Road 3 Elkhart (46517) *(G-3642)*

Recreation Insites LLC 317 578-0588
   12237 Westmorland Dr Fishers (46037) *(G-4592)*

Recreation Nation, Elkhart *Also Called: Dehco Inc (G-3288)*

Recreation Vhcl Technical Inst 574 549-9068
   3333 Middlebury St Elkhart (46516) *(G-3643)*

Recreational Customs Inc 574 642-0632
   67928 Us Highway 33 Goshen (46526) *(G-6246)*

Recycle Design Inc 765 374-0316
   804 Hazlett St Anderson (46016) *(G-184)*

Recycled New, Elkhart *Also Called: Duro Recycling Inc (G-3306)*

Recycling Center Inc 765 966-8295
   630 S M St Richmond (47374) *(G-14195)*

Recycling Services Indiana Inc 812 279-8114
   1202 Breckenridge Rd Bedford (47421) *(G-666)*

Recycling Works LLC 574 293-3751
   605 Mason St Elkhart (46516) *(G-3644)*

Red Beard Beef Jerky 574 596-7054
   1530 Cassopolis St Ste B Elkhart (46514) *(G-3645)*

Red Bull Armory LLC 757 287-7738
   440 Peaceful Valley Rd Mitchell (47446) *(G-12046)*

Red Chair Designs 317 852-9880
   10185 Terri Ln Brownsburg (46112) *(G-1397)*

Red Earth Industrial, Fort Wayne *Also Called: Red Earth LLC (G-5373)*

Red Earth LLC 260 338-1439
   Fort Wayne (46845) *(G-5373)*

Red Forge Inc 812 934-9641
   4552 State Road 46 E Batesville (47006) *(G-602)*

Red Gate Farms Inc 812 277-9750
   8987 State Road 37 Bedford (47421) *(G-667)*

Red Gold, Elwood *Also Called: Red Gold Inc (G-3837)*

Red Gold Inc 765 557-5500
   900 N D St Elwood (46036) *(G-3834)*

Red Gold Inc 765 557-5500
   622 S 22nd St Elwood (46036) *(G-3835)*

Red Gold Inc 765 552-3386
   490 S 22nd St Elwood (46036) *(G-3836)*

Red Gold Inc 260 368-9017
   705 Williams St Geneva (46740) *(G-6050)*

Red Gold Inc 765 557-5500
   901 W 1200 S Geneva (46740) *(G-6051)*

Red Gold Inc 260 726-8140
   957 W 200 S Portland (47371) *(G-13966)*

Red Gold Inc (PA) 765 557-5500
   1520 S 22nd St Elwood (46036) *(G-3837)*

Red Gold LP 765 754-8750
   2595 W State Road 28 Alexandria (46001) *(G-59)*

Red Gold/Elwood, Elwood *Also Called: Red Gold Inc (G-3836)*

Red Hawk Choppers Inc 765 307-2269
   419 Lafayette Ave Crawfordsville (47933) *(G-2614)*

Red Hen Signs 812 430-0956
   306 Boehne Ave Evansville (47712) *(G-4277)*

Red Line Graphics Incorporated (PA) 317 784-3777
   6430 S Belmont Ave Indianapolis (46217) *(G-9278)*

Red Rover Wholesale, Fort Wayne *Also Called: Big Brick House Bakery LLP (G-4799)*

Red Spot Paint & Varnish Co 812 428-9100
   1001 E Louisiana St Evansville (47711) *(G-4278)*

Red Spot Paint & Varnish Co 812 428-9100
   1016 E Columbia St Evansville (47711) *(G-4279)*

Red Spot Paint & Varnish Co 812 428-9100
   1111 E Louisiana St Evansville (47711) *(G-4280)*

Red Spot Paint & Varnish Co (HQ) 812 428-9100
   1107 E Louisiana St Evansville (47711) *(G-4281)*

Red Spot Uv/Vm Research, Evansville *Also Called: Red Spot Paint & Varnish Co (G-4278)*

Red Star, Larwill *Also Called: Red Star Contract Mfg Inc (G-10822)*

Red Star Contract Mfg Inc 260 327-3145
   1560 N State Road 5 Larwill (46764) *(G-10822)*

Red Stitch Creative LLC 202 255-8940
   3547 Tahoe Rd Carmel (46033) *(G-1736)*

Red Storm Athletics Inc 765 464-3336
   156 Sagamore Pkwy W Lafayette (47906) *(G-10678)*

Red Wagon 260 768-3090
   255 N Harrison St Ste 206 Shipshewana (46565) *(G-14881)*

Redab Industries Inc 219 484-8382
   10425 Maine Dr Crown Point (46307) *(G-2742)*

Reddington Design Inc 574 272-0790
   4221 Ralph Jones Ct South Bend (46628) *(G-15217)*

Redhawk Choppers, Crawfordsville *Also Called: Red Hawk Choppers Inc (G-2614)*

Redhead Publishing LLC 317 535-7400
   4129 N 75 W Franklin (46131) *(G-5772)*

Redi/Controls Inc 317 494-6600
   161 R J Pkwy Franklin (46131) *(G-5773)*

Redlin Custom Woodworking LLC 317 578-1852
   8507 Barstow Dr Fishers (46038) *(G-4593)*

Redmaster Fusion LLC 260 273-5819
   9308 Madina Pkwy Fort Wayne (46825) *(G-5374)*

Redmon, Peru *Also Called: WC Redmon Co Inc (G-13607)*

Redrum Incorporated 859 489-1516
   225 Conner St New Albany (47150) *(G-12804)*

Reds Custom Design LLC 812 698-0763
3910 W State Road 64 Taswell (47175) *(G-15495)*

Redspot Paint and Varnish Co 812 428-9100
1107 East La St Evansville (47711) *(G-4282)*

Redwire Space Technologies Inc 812 923-9591
7200 Highway 150 Greenville (47124) *(G-6653)*

Reearth Technologies 812 219-6517
706 W Allen St Bloomington (47403) *(G-953)*

Reed Auto - Indy Mich LLC 317 872-1132
8530 Michigan Rd Indianapolis (46268) *(G-9279)*

Reed Contracting Company 765 452-2638
113 W Jefferson St Kokomo (46901) *(G-10326)*

Reed Manufacturing Services, Franklin Also Called: RCO-Reed Corporation *(G-5771)*

Reed Minerals 219 944-6250
7100 W 9th Ave Gary (46406) *(G-6001)*

Reed Quarries Inc 812 332-2771
2950 N Prow Rd Bloomington (47404) *(G-954)*

Reed Sign Service Inc 765 459-4033
113 W Jefferson St Kokomo (46901) *(G-10327)*

Reeder & Kline Machine Co Inc 317 846-6591
14042 Plantation Wood Ln Carmel (46033) *(G-1737)*

Reeders Cleaners Inc 812 945-4833
1205 Eastern Blvd Clarksville (47129) *(G-2030)*

Reeds Plastic Tops Inc 765 282-1471
2150 E Memorial Dr Muncie (47302) *(G-12486)*

Reelcraft Industries Inc 855 634-9109
2842 E Business 30 Columbia City (46725) *(G-2188)*

Reelement Technologies Corp 317 855-9926
12115 Visionary Way Fishers (46038) *(G-4594)*

Rees Inc 260 495-9811
405 S Reed Rd Fremont (46737) *(G-5832)*

Rees Harps Inc 812 438-3052
222 Main St Rising Sun (47040) *(G-14245)*

Reese Forge Orna Ironwork 219 775-1039
6873 W 700 N Lake Village (46349) *(G-10782)*

Reeves Feed & Grain LLC 812 453-3313
12407 Upper Griffin Rd Griffin (47616) *(G-6784)*

Reeves Manufacturing Inc 765 935-3875
1214 Sheridan St Richmond (47374) *(G-14196)*

Refax Inc 219 977-0414
3240 W 5th Ave Gary (46406) *(G-6002)*

Refax Wear Products Inc 219 977-0414
3240 W 5th Ave Gary (46406) *(G-6003)*

Reflective Coating, Fort Wayne Also Called: Reflective Coating LLC *(G-5375)*

Reflective Coating LLC 260 414-1245
1240 W Main St Fort Wayne (46808) *(G-5375)*

Reflectix Inc 765 533-4332
1 School St Markleville (46056) *(G-11370)*

Reflexallen USA Inc 317 870-3610
2655 Fortune Cir W Ste A Indianapolis (46241) *(G-9280)*

Refractory Engineers Inc 317 273-2000
1750 Midwest Blvd Indianapolis (46214) *(G-9281)*

Refractory Service Corporation (PA) 219 397-7108
4900 Cline Ave East Chicago (46312) *(G-3038)*

Refractory Service Corporation 219 853-0885
4902 Calumet Ave Hammond (46327) *(G-6996)*

Refractory Specialists LLC 260 969-1099
3525 Metro Dr N Fort Wayne (46818) *(G-5376)*

Refresco Beverages, Greendale Also Called: Refresco Beverages US Inc *(G-6455)*

Refresco Beverages US Inc 812 537-7300
2000 Schenley Pl Greendale (47025) *(G-6455)*

Refreshment Services Inc 812 466-0602
3875 4th Pkwy Terre Haute (47804) *(G-15677)*

Refrigeration Design Ind LLC 317 498-3435
319 E 350 S Rushville (46173) *(G-14409)*

Refrigeration Sys of Evans, Evansville Also Called: Evansville Metal Products Inc *(G-4054)*

Reg Prof Reporter, Portage Also Called: Rebecca L Hamann & Associates *(G-13910)*

Regal Beloit America Inc 260 416-5400
1946 W Cook Rd Fort Wayne (46818) *(G-5377)*

Regal Beloit America Inc 219 465-2200
705 N 6th St Monticello (47960) *(G-12167)*

Regal Beloit America Inc 219 465-2200
2300 Evans Ave Valparaiso (46383) *(G-16035)*

Regal Beloit Logistics LLC 317 837-1150
9899 Bradford Rd Plainfield (46168) *(G-13719)*

Regal Bowait, Plainfield Also Called: Regal Beloit Logistics LLC *(G-13719)*

Regal Inc 765 284-5722
305 N Gray St Muncie (47303) *(G-12487)*

Regal Manufacturing Company 765 334-8118
502 S Green St Cambridge City (47327) *(G-1501)*

Regal Marketing, Muncie Also Called: Regal Inc *(G-12487)*

Regal Mills Odon 812 295-2299
2805 N 1200 E Loogootee (47553) *(G-11149)*

Regal Mold & Die, Elkhart Also Called: Ruco Inc *(G-3655)*

Regal Rexnord Corporation 608 364-8800
1946 W Cook Rd Fort Wayne (46818) *(G-5378)*

Regal Rexnord Corporation 574 583-9171
705 N 6th St Monticello (47960) *(G-12168)*

Regal Rexnord Corporation 317 837-2667
9899 Bradford Rd Plainfield (46168) *(G-13720)*

Regal-Beloit Electric Motors Inc 260 416-5400
1946 W Cook Rd Fort Wayne (46818) *(G-5379)*

Regenbogen Woodworks LLC 317 902-8221
431 Rainbow Ln Indianapolis (46260) *(G-9282)*

Regent Aerospace Corporation 317 837-4000
2501 E Perry Rd Plainfield (46168) *(G-13721)*

Regin Manufacturing, Indianapolis Also Called: AMG LLC *(G-7513)*

Region Auto Detailing LLC 219 427-6318
4317 Ivy St East Chicago (46312) *(G-3039)*

Region Communications Inc 219 662-8888
7590 E 109th Ave Crown Point (46307) *(G-2743)*

Region Design Co LLC 219 851-1308
1334 W 300 N La Porte (46350) *(G-10471)*

Region Signs Inc 219 473-1616
1345 119th St Whiting (46394) *(G-16838)*

Regional Data Services Inc 219 661-3200
1260 Arrowhead Ct Crown Point (46307) *(G-2744)*

Regional Development Company 219 476-0504
1757 Thornapple Cir Valparaiso (46385) *(G-16036)*

Register Publication, Lawrenceburg Also Called: Delphos Herald of Indiana Inc *(G-10833)*

Registration System LLC 317 966-6919
412 S Maple St Ste 230 Fortville (46040) *(G-5605)*

Rehabltition Inst Indnpolis Inc 888 456-7440
3501 S 3rd Pl Terre Haute (47802) *(G-15678)*

Rehco Products Inc 317 984-3319
700 S East St Arcadia (46030) *(G-317)*

Reiberg Ceramics 317 283-8441
5723 N Meridian St Indianapolis (46208) *(G-9283)*

Reich Tool & Design Inc 574 849-6416
1635 Woodfield Ct Elkhart (46514) *(G-3646)*

REICH TOOL & DESIGN, INC, Elkhart Also Called: Reich Tool & Design Inc *(G-3646)*

Reidco Inc 812 358-3000
1351 W Us Highway 50 Brownstown (47220) *(G-1426)*

Reilly Industries Inc 317 247-8141
1500 S Tibbs Ave Indianapolis (46241) *(G-9284)*

Reinforcements Design 219 866-8626
3195 1/2 W Clark St Rensselaer (47978) *(G-14064)*

Reis Tire Sales Inc 812 425-2229
1512 W Columbia St Evansville (47710) *(G-4283)*

Reiss Orna & Structurall Pdts 317 925-2371
3739 N Illinois St Indianapolis (46208) *(G-9285)*

Reit Price Co 765 964-3252
532 W Chestnut St Union City (47390) *(G-15859)*

Reit-Price Mfg Co Incorporated 765 964-3252
522 W Chestnut St Union City (47390) *(G-15860)*

Relational Gravity 317 855-7685
12623 Tealwood Dr Indianapolis (46236) *(G-9286)*

Relational Intelligence LLC 317 669-8900
14948 Annabel Ct Westfield (46074) *(G-16722)*

Relaxura LLC 317 333-1324
5726 High Timber Ln Indianapolis (46235) *(G-9287)*

Relevo, Carmel Also Called: Relevo Inc *(G-1738)*

ALPHABETIC SECTION — Revenge Designs Inc

Relevo Inc 317 644-0099
5883 William Conner Way Carmel (46033) *(G-1738)*

Relevo Labs LLC 317 900-6949
5883 William Conner Way Carmel (46033) *(G-1739)*

Reliable Diagnstc Bus Lab LLC 219 401-3122
5164 E 81st Ave Merrillville (46410) *(G-11553)*

Reliable Indus Sls & Svc LLC 219 929-8295
1707 Whittier Park Dr Valparaiso (46383) *(G-16037)*

Reliable Metalcraft, Mishawaka Also Called: Mc Metalcraft Inc *(G-11941)*

Reliable Prod Machining & Wldg, Kendallville Also Called: Reliable Tool & Machine Co *(G-10150)*

Reliable Tool & Machine Co 260 347-4000
902 S Main St Kendallville (46755) *(G-10148)*

Reliable Tool & Machine Co 260 347-4000
800 Weston Ave Kendallville (46755) *(G-10149)*

Reliable Tool & Machine Co (PA) 260 343-7150
301 W Ohio St Kendallville (46755) *(G-10150)*

Reliance Machine Company Inc (PA) 765 284-0151
4605 S Walnut St Muncie (47302) *(G-12488)*

Reliance Machine Company Inc 765 857-1000
108 W 2nd St Ridgeville (47380) *(G-14237)*

Reliance Manufacturing LLC 765 284-0151
4605 S Walnut St Muncie (47302) *(G-12489)*

Reliant Engineering Inc 317 322-9084
1329 Sadlier Circle West Dr Indianapolis (46239) *(G-9288)*

Reliv 317 507-1548
12738 Kiawah Dr Carmel (46033) *(G-1740)*

Reloaded Activewear LLC 317 652-7394
4738 E 34th St Indianapolis (46218) *(G-9289)*

Relx Inc 317 849-9806
9737 Pine Ridge East Dr Fishers (46038) *(G-4595)*

REM Industries Inc 574 862-2127
902 Nelsons Pkwy Wakarusa (46573) *(G-16247)*

Remco Products Corporation 317 876-9856
4735 W 106th St Zionsville (46077) *(G-17046)*

Remedium Services Group LLC 317 660-6868
11711 N College Ave Ste 170 Carmel (46032) *(G-1741)*

Remington Machine Inc 765 724-3389
6 Twin Oaks St Alexandria (46001) *(G-60)*

Remmler Drilling & Pump Svc, Greensburg Also Called: Remmler Well Drilling LLC *(G-6627)*

Remmler Well Drilling LLC 812 663-8178
3970 N County Rd 500 N Greensburg (47240) *(G-6627)*

Remodel Construction, Pekin Also Called: Brewers Contg & Wdwrk LLC *(G-13512)*

Renaissnce Electronic Svcs LLC 317 786-2235
6510 Telecom Dr Ste 300 Indianapolis (46278) *(G-9290)*

Renegade Dispatching LLC 260 797-5423
2737 W Washington Center Rd Fort Wayne (46818) *(G-5380)*

Renegade Rv, Bristol Also Called: Rev Renegade LLC *(G-1286)*

Renewed Performance Company 765 675-7586
1095 Development Dr Tipton (46072) *(G-15789)*

Renk Systems Corporation 317 455-1367
8880 Union Mills Dr Camby (46113) *(G-1513)*

Reno LLC 708 846-7821
7350 Jeffrey St Schererville (46375) *(G-14542)*

Renobi, Westfield Also Called: Kintail Inc *(G-16705)*

Renolit, La Porte Also Called: American Renolit Corporation *(G-10384)*

Renovera, Pbc., West Lafayette Also Called: 34 Lives Pbc *(G-16553)*

Rensselaer Eagle Vault Corp 219 866-5123
250 N Mckinley Ave Rensselaer (47978) *(G-14065)*

Rensselaer Print Co 219 866-5000
116 N Cullen St Rensselaer (47978) *(G-14066)*

Rensselaer Republican, Rensselaer Also Called: Kankakee Valley Publishing Co *(G-14056)*

Rensselaer Septic Tanks, Rensselaer Also Called: Rensselaer Eagle Vault Corp *(G-14065)*

Rentown Cabinets LLC 574 546-2569
2735 Birch Rd Bremen (46506) *(G-1218)*

REO-Usa Inc 317 899-1395
8450 E 47th St Indianapolis (46226) *(G-9291)*

Repeal 1205 LLC 317 402-4818
7254 Whitehall Dr Indianapolis (46256) *(G-9292)*

Replas of Texas Inc 812 421-3600
15000 Highway 41 N Evansville (47725) *(G-4284)*

Reprocomm Inc 765 423-2578
1400 Teal Rd Ste 1 Lafayette (47905) *(G-10679)*

Reprocomm Inc (PA) 765 472-5700
179 N Miami St Peru (46970) *(G-13598)*

Republic Inc 812 342-8028
333 2nd St Columbus (47201) *(G-2386)*

Republican 317 745-2777
6 E Main St Danville (46122) *(G-2825)*

Republican Newspaper, Danville Also Called: Republican *(G-2825)*

RES Technica LLC 765 366-5089
3776 S 875 E Oxford (47971) *(G-13477)*

Reschcor Inc (PA) 574 295-2413
2123 Blakesley Pkwy Bristol (46507) *(G-1285)*

Reschcor Inc 574 295-2413
2711 Industrial Pkwy Elkhart (46516) *(G-3647)*

Resco Products Inc 219 844-7830
5501 Kennedy Ave Hammond (46323) *(G-6997)*

Research, Indianapolis Also Called: Indiana Nanotech LLC *(G-8485)*

Reset Family Solutions LLC 317 699-2990
501 N East St Carthage (46115) *(G-1817)*

Residual Pays Daily 260 267-1617
2313 Florida Dr Apt C15 Fort Wayne (46805) *(G-5381)*

Residue Regency Pad, Evansville Also Called: Residue West Inc *(G-4285)*

Residue West Inc 731 587-9596
2625 Kotter Ave Evansville (47715) *(G-4285)*

Resin Partners Inc 765 724-7761
602 S Fairview St Alexandria (46001) *(G-61)*

Resin Partners Inc (DH) 765 298-6800
6435 S Scatterfield Rd Anderson (46013) *(G-185)*

Resistance Wire, Fort Wayne Also Called: Hyndman Industrial Pdts Inc *(G-5089)*

Resonac Powdered Metals Americ (DH) 812 663-5058
1024 E Barachel Ln Greensburg (47240) *(G-6628)*

RESOURCE CONNECTION, Huntington Also Called: Pathfinder Services Inc *(G-7354)*

Resourcemfg 812 574-5500
220 Clifty Dr Ste P Madison (47250) *(G-11247)*

Resourcemfg 812 523-2100
105 W 2nd St Ste 102 Seymour (47274) *(G-14681)*

Resourcemfg 812 231-8500
2501 Ohio Blvd Terre Haute (47803) *(G-15679)*

Respect Da Flava LLC 765 243-1629
5580 Revolutionary Dr Indianapolis (46254) *(G-9293)*

Responsble Enrgy Oprations LLC 812 354-8776
625 N 9th St Petersburg (47567) *(G-13623)*

Resprin Inc 219 996-5864
53 Jefferson St Valparaiso (46383) *(G-16038)*

Restonic, New Albany Also Called: Woodland Standard Inc *(G-12830)*

Restoration Med Polymers LLC 260 625-1573
4474 E Park 30 Dr Columbia City (46725) *(G-2189)*

Retail, Merrillville Also Called: Shop Lulu Bean LLC *(G-11559)*

Retail Truck and Turf Eqp, Fishers Also Called: Mid-State Truck Equipment Inc *(G-4566)*

Rethceif Packaging, Ossian Also Called: Parkway Industrial Entps LLC *(G-13430)*

Retrieving With Evie 812 455-5292
2515 Glenn Ave Evansville (47711) *(G-4286)*

Retro Atm LLC 317 752-6915
5325 E 82nd St Pmb 145 Indianapolis (46250) *(G-9294)*

Rettigs Industrial Supply, Wabash Also Called: F J Rettig & Sons Inc *(G-16184)*

Reuer Machine & Tool Inc 219 362-2894
1733 E State Road 2 La Porte (46350) *(G-10472)*

Rev Group, Decatur Also Called: Goldshield Fiber Glass Inc *(G-2859)*

Rev Recreation Group Inc 260 724-4217
1803 Winchester St Decatur (46733) *(G-2879)*

Rev Recreation Group Inc 260 724-2418
1420 Patterson St Decatur (46733) *(G-2880)*

Rev Renegade LLC 574 966-0166
52216 State Road 15 Bristol (46507) *(G-1286)*

Revelation Medical Devices, Auburn Also Called: Ste Acquisition LLC *(G-426)*

Revele, Indianapolis Also Called: Groupone Health Source Inc *(G-8334)*

Revenge Designs, Decatur Also Called: Revenge Designs Inc *(G-2881)*

Revenge Designs Inc 260 724-4000
1040 S 11th St Decatur (46733) *(G-2881)*

Revere Industries..317 638-1521
111 Monument Cir Ste 3200 Indianapolis (46204) *(G-9295)*

Revere Plastics Systems LLC..................................812 670-2240
5171 Maritime Jeffersonville (47130) *(G-10045)*

Reversible Rollers, Chesterfield Also Called: Smiths Enterprises Inc *(G-1898)*

Revival Food Co, Indianapolis Also Called: Revival LLC *(G-9296)*

Revival LLC..812 345-4317
4315 N Park Ave Indianapolis (46205) *(G-9296)*

Revolution Materials (in) LLC (DH)...........................812 234-2724
300 N Fruitridge Ave Terre Haute (47803) *(G-15680)*

Revolver LLC...317 418-1824
13904 Town Center Blvd Ste 800 Noblesville (46060) *(G-13166)*

Revseller LLC..800 619-6304
5444 E Indiana St Pmb 215 Evansville (47715) *(G-4287)*

Rex Alton & Companies Inc....................................812 882-8519
2341 S Old Decker Rd Vincennes (47591) *(G-16149)*

Rex Alton Trucking, Vincennes Also Called: Rex Alton & Companies Inc *(G-16149)*

Rex Byers Htg & Coolg Systems..............................765 459-8858
4108 Cartwright Dr Kokomo (46902) *(G-10328)*

Rexam, Princeton Also Called: Bprex Closures LLC *(G-13985)*

Rexford Rand Corp (PA)..219 872-5561
2123 E Us Highway 12 Michigan City (46360) *(G-11657)*

Rexing-Goedde Electric Service..............................812 963-5725
13100 St Wendel Rd Wadesville (47638) *(G-16229)*

Rexnord Industries LLC..317 273-5500
1304 Turfway Dr Avon (46123) *(G-547)*

Rexnord Industries LLC..414 643-2559
9899 Bradford Rd Plainfield (46168) *(G-13722)*

Reynolds & Co Inc..812 232-5313
1916 S 25th St Terre Haute (47802) *(G-15681)*

Reynolds North...812 235-5313
1025 N Fruitridge Ave Terre Haute (47804) *(G-15682)*

Rf Manufacturing Inc..317 773-8610
1780 S 10th St Noblesville (46060) *(G-13167)*

Rfbp Inc
3245 Kansas Rd Evansville (47725) *(G-4288)*

Rfc LLC...812 284-0650
1205 N Access Dr Jeffersonville (47130) *(G-10046)*

RFI, Columbus Also Called: Rightway Fasteners Inc *(G-2387)*

RFI Mfg Co..812 207-6939
2505 Glenwood Ct New Albany (47150) *(G-12805)*

Rgr Engines..630 488-7966
3540 E 425 N Monticello (47960) *(G-12169)*

Rgr Medical Solutions Inc..317 285-9703
11807 Allisonville Rd Ste 137 Fishers (46038) *(G-4596)*

RH Yoder Enterprises LLC......................................574 825-6183
2375 S 1100 W Shipshewana (46565) *(G-14882)*

Rheem Sales Company Inc.....................................479 648-4900
1240 Brookville Way Indianapolis (46239) *(G-9297)*

Rhi Magnesita...219 237-2420
2929 Carlson Dr Ste 201 Hammond (46323) *(G-6998)*

Rhinehart Development Corp..................................260 238-4442
5345 County Road 68 Spencerville (46788) *(G-15373)*

Rhinehart Finishing LLC...260 238-4442
5345 County Road 68 Spencerville (46788) *(G-15374)*

Rhino Shipping Solutions, Fishers Also Called: Rhino Shipping Solutions LLC *(G-4649)*

Rhino Shipping Solutions LLC................................317 721-9476
10432 Crestmoor Ln Fishers (46040) *(G-4649)*

Rhodes Tool & Machine Inc....................................812 729-7134
7864 W State Road 165 Owensville (47665) *(G-13472)*

Rhondas Tasty Treats LLC.....................................574 315-4011
706 S 29th St South Bend (46615) *(G-15218)*

Rhr Corporation..317 788-1504
930 E Hanna Ave Indianapolis (46227) *(G-9298)*

Rhyne & Associates Inc..317 786-4459
3560 Madison Ave Indianapolis (46227) *(G-9299)*

Rhyne Competition Engines, Gary Also Called: Rhyne Engines Inc *(G-6004)*

Rhyne Engines Inc..219 845-1218
5733 W 25th Ave Gary (46406) *(G-6004)*

Rhyne, R E & Company, Indianapolis Also Called: Rhyne & Associates Inc *(G-9299)*

Ribbe Welding & Mfg Inc..765 390-4044
4526 S Odd St Kingman (47952) *(G-10173)*

Ric Corporation D/B/A...260 432-0799
6215 Constitution Dr Fort Wayne (46804) *(G-5382)*

Ricca Chemical Company LLC..............................812 932-1161
1490 Lammers Pike Batesville (47006) *(G-603)*

Rices Quality Farm Meats Inc.................................812 829-4562
1294 Freeman Rd Spencer (47460) *(G-15361)*

Rich Beauty, Syracuse Also Called: Brittany Bushong *(G-15458)*

Rich Bures..317 270-9360
5108 W Vermont St Indianapolis (46224) *(G-9300)*

Rich Glas Products, Jonesboro Also Called: H A P Industries Inc *(G-10079)*

Rich Halstead..219 462-8888
302 Morgan Blvd Valparaiso (46383) *(G-16039)*

Rich Manufacturing Inc...765 436-2744
1990 John Bart Rd Lebanon (46052) *(G-10937)*

Richard Butterfield..765 754-3129
23 N Superior Orestes (46063) *(G-13361)*

Richard J Bagan Inc...260 244-5115
1280 S Williams Dr Columbia City (46725) *(G-2190)*

Richard K Williams...616 745-9319
201 S Orange St Albion (46701) *(G-43)*

Richard M Judd..916 704-3364
508 W 3rd St Bloomington (47404) *(G-955)*

Richard Myers Mllwrght..765 883-8177
2719 S 1280 W Russiaville (46979) *(G-14425)*

Richard Sheets...574 536-8247
15569 State Road 120 Bristol (46507) *(G-1287)*

Richard Squier Pallets Inc.....................................260 281-2434
2522 Us Highway 6 Waterloo (46793) *(G-16530)*

Richards Bakery...260 424-4012
1130 N Wells St Fort Wayne (46808) *(G-5383)*

Richards Complete Machine Shop.........................317 856-9163
6403 W Thompson Rd Indianapolis (46221) *(G-9301)*

Richards Electric LLC...317 253-1083
1949 Herford Dr Indianapolis (46229) *(G-9302)*

Richards Liquidation Corp......................................574 807-8588
1655 E 12th St Mishawaka (46544) *(G-11985)*

Richards Printery..812 406-0295
9357 Arthur Coffman Rd Greenville (47124) *(G-6654)*

Richards Restaurant Inc...260 997-6823
8341 N 400 E Bryant (47326) *(G-1436)*

Richards Scale Company Inc.................................812 246-3354
820 S Penn Ave Sellersburg (47172) *(G-14612)*

Richardson Entps Blmington LLC...........................812 287-8179
2454 S Walnut St Bloomington (47401) *(G-956)*

Richardson Molding LLC..317 787-9463
5601 S Meridian St Ste B Indianapolis (46217) *(G-9303)*

Richardson Woodworking.......................................765 689-8348
6395 S Strawtown Pike Peru (46970) *(G-13599)*

Richcraft Wood Product, Bloomington Also Called: Richcraft Wood Products LLC *(G-957)*

Richcraft Wood Products LLC................................812 320-7884
4655 W Richland Plaza Dr Bloomington (47404) *(G-957)*

Richeson Cabinent, Indianapolis Also Called: Richeson Contracting Inc *(G-9304)*

Richeson Contracting Inc.......................................317 889-5995
5325 Commerce Square Dr Indianapolis (46237) *(G-9304)*

Richey M A Mfg Co Sprtng Gds..............................765 659-5389
401 S Prairie Ave Frankfort (46041) *(G-5693)*

Richeys Mold and Tool Inc.....................................812 752-1059
101 E Owen St Scottsburg (47170) *(G-14576)*

Richmond Baking Co..765 962-8535
520 N 6th St Richmond (47374) *(G-14197)*

Richmond Baking Georgia Inc................................765 962-8535
520 N 6th St Richmond (47374) *(G-14198)*

Richmond Casting Company..................................765 935-4090
1775 Rich Rd Richmond (47374) *(G-14199)*

Richters Machine & Tool..260 495-5327
4395 E 300 N Fremont (46737) *(G-5833)*

Rick Black Associates LLC....................................765 838-3498
3233 E 200 N Lafayette (47905) *(G-10680)*

Rick Hollingshead..765 833-2846
7076 W 900 N Roann (46974) *(G-14253)*

Rick Singleton..574 259-5555
203 N Main St Mishawaka (46544) *(G-11986)*

ALPHABETIC SECTION

Rick Whitt... 317 873-5507
316 N Kealing Ave Indianapolis (46201) *(G-9305)*

Rick's Tool Company, Columbia City *Also Called: Rickie Allan Pease (G-2191)*

Rickie Allan Pease.. 260 244-7579
406 Diamond Ave Columbia City (46725) *(G-2191)*

Rickles Pickles LLC.. 260 495-9024
103 W Toledo St Fremont (46737) *(G-5834)*

Ricks Motorcycle Tire Svc LLC.............................. 219 369-1028
7117 E Division Rd Mill Creek (46365) *(G-11809)*

Ricktom Promotions LLC..................................... 812 430-0282
4528 Moray Dr Evansville (47714) *(G-4289)*

Rics Software Inc.. 317 455-5338
129 E Market St Ste 1100 Indianapolis (46204) *(G-9306)*

Riddell Technologies, Crown Point *Also Called: Riddell Technologies LLC (G-2745)*

Riddell Technologies LLC..................................... 219 213-9602
1351 W 95th Ct Crown Point (46307) *(G-2745)*

Riddle Ridge Woodworks..................................... 812 596-4503
1731 E Denton Rd English (47118) *(G-3846)*

Riden Inc... 219 362-5511
315 Lincolnway La Porte (46350) *(G-10473)*

Ridge Iron LLC.. 646 450-0092
1911 Western Ave Plymouth (46563) *(G-13811)*

Ridge Winery Inc.. 812 427-3380
227 Parks Ridge Rd Vevay (47043) *(G-16111)*

Ridley USA Inc... 260 768-4103
135 Main St Shipshewana (46565) *(G-14883)*

Riegsecker Woodworks Inc.................................. 574 642-3504
15600 County Road 38 Goshen (46528) *(G-6247)*

Rieke LLC (HQ)... 260 925-3700
500 W 7th St Auburn (46706) *(G-419)*

Rieke Packaging Systems, Auburn *Also Called: Rieke LLC (G-419)*

Riepen LLC... 574 269-5900
2450 Deelyn Dr Warsaw (46580) *(G-16418)*

Rieth-Riley Cnstr Co Inc...................................... 574 875-5183
7500 W 5th Ave Gary (46406) *(G-6005)*

Rieth-Riley Cnstr Co Inc...................................... 574 288-8321
25200 State Road 23 South Bend (46614) *(G-15219)*

Right Angle Stl & Fabrication............................... 574 773-7148
401 E Lincoln St Nappanee (46550) *(G-12641)*

Right Angle Stl Fbrication Inc.............................. 574 862-2432
29508 County Road 38 Wakarusa (46573) *(G-16248)*

Right Direction Trckg Ex LLC............................... 502 912-2504
1250 Veterans Pkwy Jeffersonville (47129) *(G-10047)*

Rightcolors LLC.. 812 675-8775
2190 Coveyville Rd Bedford (47421) *(G-668)*

Rightrez Inc... 812 219-1893
3010 E David Dr Bloomington (47401) *(G-958)*

Rightway Fasteners Inc....................................... 812 342-2700
7945 S International Dr Columbus (47201) *(G-2387)*

Rihm Foods, Cambridge City *Also Called: Rihm Inc (G-1502)*

Rihm Inc (PA)... 765 478-3426
8360 E County Road 950 S Cambridge City (47327) *(G-1502)*

Riley Signs & Sheet Metal LLC............................. 317 359-7446
5800 Massachusetts Ave Indianapolis (46218) *(G-9307)*

Rim Molding and Engrg Inc.................................. 574 294-1932
56855 Ferrettie Ct Mishawaka (46545) *(G-11987)*

Rimedion Inc.. 415 513-5535
5742 W 74th St Indianapolis (46278) *(G-9308)*

Rimsmith Tool LLC... 219 926-8665
830 Sidewalk Rd Chesterton (46304) *(G-1957)*

Ring Industries Inc... 219 204-1577
3572 W State Road 10 Lot 13 Lake Village (46349) *(G-10783)*

Ring-Co LLC... 317 641-7050
8402 S 250 W Trafalgar (46181) *(G-15831)*

Ring-Co Mobile LLC.. 317 641-7050
8402 S 250 W Trafalgar (46181) *(G-15832)*

Ring-R Engineering, Decatur *Also Called: Ring-R Inc (G-2882)*

Ring-R Inc... 260 565-3347
6691 W State Road 124 Decatur (46733) *(G-2882)*

Rink Printing Company....................................... 574 232-7935
814 S Main St South Bend (46601) *(G-15220)*

Rink Riverside Printing, South Bend *Also Called: Rink Printing Company (G-15220)*

Rinker Materials, Greenfield *Also Called: Cemex Materials LLC (G-6477)*

Rinker Materials, Indianapolis *Also Called: Quikrete Companies LLC (G-9251)*

Rios Investment Services LLC.............................. 574 514-3999
20266 Richard Ave South Bend (46637) *(G-15221)*

Ripley Publishing Co Inc...................................... 812 689-6364
115 S Washington St Versailles (47042) *(G-16103)*

Risco Products Inc... 317 392-6150
1344 N Michigan Rd Shelbyville (46176) *(G-14791)*

Rise Inc... 260 665-9408
907 S Wayne St Angola (46703) *(G-292)*

Ristance, Mishawaka *Also Called: Standard Motor Products Inc (G-12007)*

Ritchie Electric Motor Co LLC.............................. 219 866-5185
615 N Mckinley Ave Rensselaer (47978) *(G-14067)*

Rite Products Inc... 260 627-6465
13601 Roth Rd Grabill (46741) *(G-6322)*

Rite Way Industries Inc...................................... 812 206-8665
4201 Reas Ln New Albany (47150) *(G-12806)*

Rite-Way Arms LLC... 260 493-4517
6911 Trafalgar Dr Fort Wayne (46803) *(G-5384)*

Rite-Way Steel Inc... 574 262-3465
25687 Woodlawn Ave Elkhart (46514) *(G-3648)*

Ritecount, Vincennes *Also Called: Scales and More (G-16151)*

Rits Ltd Brokers Inc... 260 348-0786
3339 Stone Blvd Fort Wayne (46802) *(G-5385)*

Rittenhouse Square.. 260 824-4200
312 S Main St Bluffton (46714) *(G-1051)*

Ritter's Frozen Custard, Mishawaka *Also Called: Mishawaka Frozen Custard (G-11956)*

Rivars Inc.. 765 789-6119
3925 River Crossing Pkwy Ste 300 Indianapolis (46240) *(G-9309)*

River Bend Hose Specialty, South Bend *Also Called: River Bend Hose Specialty Inc (G-15222)*

River Bend Hose Specialty Inc............................. 574 233-1133
1111 S Main St South Bend (46601) *(G-15222)*

River Cement Sales Company............................. 812 285-1003
1350 Bates Bowyer Ave Jeffersonville (47130) *(G-10048)*

RIVER CEMENT SALES COMPANY, Jeffersonville *Also Called: River Cement Sales Company (G-10048)*

River Valley Plastics Inc..................................... 574 262-5221
1090 D I Dr Elkhart (46514) *(G-3649)*

River Valley Sheet Metal Inc............................... 574 259-2538
58785 Executive Dr Mishawaka (46544) *(G-11988)*

Rivera Screenprinting.. 812 663-0816
1010 E State Road 46 Burney (47240) *(G-1448)*

Rivers Resources LLC... 317 572-5029
7114 Lakeview Parkway West Dr Indianapolis (46268) *(G-9310)*

Riverside Mfg LLC.. 260 637-4470
14510 Lima Rd Fort Wayne (46818) *(G-5386)*

Riverside Mfg Inc (PA)....................................... 260 637-4470
14510 Lima Rd Fort Wayne (46818) *(G-5387)*

Riverside Petroleum Ind LLC............................... 812 639-0859
2873 N State Road 57 Washington (47501) *(G-16507)*

Riverside Printing Co... 812 275-1950
1407 I St Bedford (47421) *(G-669)*

Riverside Tool Corp (HQ).................................... 574 522-6798
3504 Henke St Elkhart (46514) *(G-3650)*

Rix Laser Processing.. 812 537-9230
252 Charles A Liddle Dr Lawrenceburg (47025) *(G-10857)*

Rix Products, Evansville *Also Called: Rix Products Inc (G-4290)*

Rix Products Inc.. 812 426-1749
3747 Hogue Rd Evansville (47712) *(G-4290)*

Rj Fuel Services Inc... 812 350-2897
6815 W State Road 252 Edinburgh (46124) *(G-3101)*

Rj Partners of Indiana Inc
2457 E Washington St Indianapolis (46201) *(G-9311)*

Rjv Investments Inc... 574 234-1063
2411 Foundation Dr South Bend (46628) *(G-15223)*

Rk Machine Inc.. 812 466-0550
3170 N 25th St Terre Haute (47804) *(G-15683)*

Rkdjrt Inc.. 812 354-8899
3377 N State Road 57 Petersburg (47567) *(G-13624)*

Rko Enterprises LLC 812 273-8813
2850 Clifty Dr Madison (47250) *(G-11248)*

Rl Strahm Woodworking Inc 260 623-3228
18609 Paulding Rd Monroeville (46773) *(G-12073)*

Rlay Express Inc 754 265-8555
230 Oxmoor Way Apt I Avon (46123) *(G-548)*

Rlr Associates Inc 317 632-1300
1302 N Illinois St Indianapolis (46202) *(G-9312)*

Rmg Cabinetry Inc 219 712-6129
6809 Columbia Ave Ste C Hammond (46324) *(G-6999)*

Rmi Holdings LLC 317 214-7076
4130 Corridor Dr Warsaw (46582) *(G-16419)*

Rmo Inc (PA) 303 592-8200
2165 Earlywood Dr Franklin (46131) *(G-5774)*

Rmt Inc 260 637-4649
2420 W Shoaff Rd Huntertown (46748) *(G-7265)*

Ro-Vic Wood Products Inc 812 283-9199
254c America Pl Jeffersonville (47130) *(G-10049)*

Road Alert Systems LLC 219 669-1206
112 E State St Morocco (47963) *(G-12269)*

Road Runner Expediting, Greenwood Also Called: Franklin Publishing Inc *(G-6705)*

Road Widener LLC 844 494-3363
4620 Williamsburg Sta Floyds Knobs (47119) *(G-4691)*

Roadhog Inc 317 858-7050
464 Southpoint Cir Ste A Brownsburg (46112) *(G-1398)*

Roadwin Parts Inc 630 742-4098
3640 179th St Hammond (46323) *(G-7000)*

Roadworks Manufacturing, Lafayette Also Called: Lund International Holding Co *(G-10641)*

Roadworks Maufacturing 765 742-7200
2482 Klondike Rd West Lafayette (47906) *(G-16625)*

Roajer LLC 317 348-4640
13865 Barberry Ct Carmel (46033) *(G-1742)*

Roann Publishers 574 831-2795
22425 County Road 42 Goshen (46526) *(G-6248)*

Roast Haus Coffee LLC 224 544-9550
1085 Millennium Dr Crown Point (46307) *(G-2746)*

Rob Nolley Inc 317 825-5211
30 E Washington St Ste 400 Shelbyville (46176) *(G-14792)*

Rob Passarelli 317 340-8597
219 E Admiral Way S Carmel (46032) *(G-1743)*

Robco Engineered Rbr Pdts Inc 260 248-2888
707 E Short St Columbia City (46725) *(G-2192)*

Roberson Fire & Safety Inc 317 879-3119
5603 W 74th St Indianapolis (46278) *(G-9313)*

Robert Atkins (PA) 765 536-4164
303 E North Main St Summitville (46070) *(G-15430)*

Robert Bosch LLC 260 636-1005
1613 Progress Dr Albion (46701) *(G-44)*

Robert Bosch LLC 574 654-4000
32104 State Road 2 New Carlisle (46552) *(G-12844)*

Robert Bosch LLC 574 654-4000
32104 State Road 2 New Carlisle (46552) *(G-12845)*

Robert Burkhart 219 448-0365
434 W State Road 28 Alexandria (46001) *(G-62)*

Robert C Kueber 812 838-5813
20 Highway 62 W Mount Vernon (47620) *(G-12317)*

Robert Cody Jacobs 812 606-5195
1635 Lucas Hollow Rd Nashville (47448) *(G-12679)*

Robert Copeland 951 245-0041
10505 Bennett Pkwy Ste 200 Zionsville (46077) *(G-17047)*

Robert D Meadows 812 797-8294
3568 Peerless Rd Bedford (47421) *(G-670)*

Robert Engle 317 522-7761
4243 Bullfinch Way Westfield (46062) *(G-16723)*

Robert J Matt 317 831-2400
246 E Washington St Mooresville (46158) *(G-12239)*

Robert J Stankovich 317 844-0886
12412 Windbush Way Carmel (46033) *(G-1744)*

Robert L Wehr 812 482-2673
1527 W 100s Jasper (47546) *(G-9905)*

Robert L Young 812 863-4475
4436 S Young Dr Springville (47462) *(G-15391)*

Robert M Kolarich 317 596-9753
10688 Adam Ct Fishers (46037) *(G-4597)*

Robert Perez 317 291-7311
3945 Guion Ln Ste A Indianapolis (46268) *(G-9314)*

Robert S Froman 765 565-6819
3395 N Henderson Rd Rushville (46173) *(G-14410)*

Robert W Sheffer 219 464-2095
4411 Evans Ave Valparaiso (46383) *(G-16040)*

Robert Warrick 765 294-4335
100 N Eagle St Veedersburg (47987) *(G-16090)*

Robert Weed Plywood Corp 574 848-7631
705 Maple St Bristol (46507) *(G-1288)*

Roberts C Wldg Trck Hvy Equip 812 623-1525
8448 E County Road 1100 N Sunman (47041) *(G-15443)*

Robertson Crushed Stone Inc 812 633-4881
6300 Hwy 64 Nw Milltown (47145) *(G-11820)*

Robinson Auto Parts Mfg 317 921-0076
830 E 38th St Indianapolis (46205) *(G-9315)*

Robinson Engineering & Oil Co (PA) 812 477-1575
1410 N Cullen Ave Evansville (47715) *(G-4291)*

Robinson Industries Inc 317 867-3214
17111 Westfield Park Rd Westfield (46074) *(G-16724)*

Robinson Steel Co Inc 219 398-4600
4303 Kennedy Ave East Chicago (46312) *(G-3040)*

Robocfi LLC 317 612-7889
505 Roxbury Ct Fort Wayne (46807) *(G-5388)*

Rocca Industries LLC 812 576-1011
28847 Central Dr Brookville (47012) *(G-1333)*

Roche Applied Sciences, Indianapolis Also Called: Roche Diagnostics Corporation *(G-9318)*

Roche Diabetes Care Inc 317 521-2000
9115 Hague Rd Indianapolis (46256) *(G-9316)*

Roche Diagnostics Corp 317 521-2000
9344 Castlegate Dr Bldg F Indianapolis (46256) *(G-9317)*

Roche Diagnostics Corporation 317 521-2000
7988 Centerpoint Dr Indianapolis (46256) *(G-9318)*

Roche Diagnostics Corporation (DH) 800 428-5076
9115 Hague Rd Indianapolis (46256) *(G-9319)*

Roche Diagnostics Puerto Rico, Indianapolis Also Called: Corange International *(G-7874)*

Roche Operations Ltd 787 285-0170
9115 Hague Rd # C Indianapolis (46256) *(G-9320)*

Rochester Cement Products Inc 574 223-3917
2184 Sweetgum Rd Rochester (46975) *(G-14316)*

Rochester Concrete Plant, Rochester Also Called: Kuert Concrete Inc *(G-14299)*

Rochester Homes Inc (PA) 574 223-4321
1345 N Lucas St Rochester (46975) *(G-14317)*

Rochester Manufacturing LLC 574 224-2044
2903 Ft Wayne Rd Rochester (46975) *(G-14318)*

Rochester Metal Products Corp 765 288-6624
2100 N Granville Ave Muncie (47303) *(G-12490)*

Rochester Metal Products Corp (PA) 574 223-3164
616 Indiana Ave Rochester (46975) *(G-14319)*

Rochester Plant, Rochester Also Called: Fulton Industries Inc *(G-14292)*

Rochester Rttional Molding Inc 574 223-8844
1952 E Lucas St Rochester (46975) *(G-14320)*

Rock Creek 2019 Inc 812 933-0388
1646 Lammers Pike Batesville (47006) *(G-604)*

Rock Creek Stone LLC 260 694-6880
781 N 500 W Bluffton (46714) *(G-1052)*

Rock Equipment, Paragon Also Called: J W Jones Company LLC *(G-13501)*

Rock Garden Engraving 765 647-3357
268 Main St Brookville (47012) *(G-1334)*

Rock Hard Stnes Cstm Prtg Rhns 219 613-0112
9242 Bigger St Merrillville (46410) *(G-11554)*

Rock Hollow Golf Club, Peru Also Called: Stone Quary *(G-13603)*

Rock N' Roll Alley, Lafayette Also Called: Paul Miller *(G-10664)*

Rock Run Industries LLC 574 361-0848
11665 W 600 S Millersburg (46543) *(G-11816)*

Rock-Tenn Paperboard Products, Columbus Also Called: Westrock Rkt LLC *(G-2418)*

Rockport Roll Shop LLC 812 362-6419
6500 N Us Highway 231 Rockport (47635) *(G-14348)*

Rockport Works, Rockport Also Called: Cleveland-Cliffs Steel Corp *(G-14338)*

ALPHABETIC SECTION

Rocktenn-Knox, Knox *Also Called: Westrock Cp LLC (G-10228)*
Rockwell Automation Inc.. 219 924-3002
225 45th St Munster (46321) *(G-12561)*
Rockwell Automation Inc.. 765 481-0766
4255 S 500 E Whitestown (46075) *(G-16819)*
Rockwell Diversified Woodworks.. 317 758-4797
26715 Dunbar Rd Sheridan (46069) *(G-14827)*
Rocky Mountain Orthodontics, Franklin *Also Called: Rmo Inc (G-5774)*
Rod Welding and Auto, Coal City *Also Called: Rods Welding Shop (G-2101)*
Rodeswood LLC... 574 457-4496
14852 County Road 50 Syracuse (46567) *(G-15476)*
Rodex Machining.. 260 768-4844
7400 W 650 N Shipshewana (46565) *(G-14884)*
Rodman's Auto Wood Restoration, Hanna *Also Called: Auto Wood Restoration (G-7036)*
Rodney Sloan Logging Inc... 812 934-5321
1324 E Salem Rd Batesville (47006) *(G-605)*
Rods Welding Shop.. 812 859-4250
2135 Beech Church Rd Coal City (47427) *(G-2101)*
Roebic Laboratories Inc.. 317 578-0135
8280 Courtney Dr Fishers (46038) *(G-4598)*
Roeder Industries... 812 654-3322
406 W Carr St Milan (47031) *(G-11783)*
Roembke, Ossian *Also Called: Roembke Mfg & Design Inc (G-13432)*
Roembke Mfg & Design Inc.. 260 307-1198
425 Industrial Pkwy Ossian (46777) *(G-13431)*
Roembke Mfg & Design Inc (PA).. 260 622-4135
1580 Baker Dr Ossian (46777) *(G-13432)*
Roembke Mfg & Design Inc.. 260 622-4030
1580 Baker Dr Ossian (46777) *(G-13433)*
Roesler Fine Art Services... 219 797-4955
11888 S Hunsley Rd Union Mills (46382) *(G-15867)*
Roger Baber Portable Wldg LLC.. 574 859-4520
9132 County Rd 50 S Galveston (46932) *(G-5853)*
Roger Harper Signs... 812 945-1581
617 Indiana Ave New Albany (47150) *(G-12807)*
Roger Miller.. 219 531-2566
230 Whispering Blvd La Porte (46350) *(G-10474)*
Rogers & Hollands Jewelers, Greenwood *Also Called: Rogers Enterprises Inc (G-6760)*
Rogers Cabinetry... 574 664-9931
2527 N County Road 925 E Logansport (46947) *(G-11105)*
Rogers Electro-Matics Inc.. 574 457-2305
405 W Chicago St Syracuse (46567) *(G-15477)*
Rogers Engineering and Mfg Co.. 765 478-5444
112 S Center St Cambridge City (47327) *(G-1503)*
Rogers Enterprises Inc... 317 851-5500
1251 Us Highway 31 N Greenwood (46142) *(G-6760)*
Rogers Group Inc... 812 333-6324
550 S Adams St Bloomington (47403) *(G-959)*
Rogers Group Inc... 812 332-6341
2944 E Covenanter Dr Bloomington (47401) *(G-960)*
Rogers Group Inc... 812 333-8560
1100 N Oard Rd Bloomington (47404) *(G-961)*
Rogers Group Inc... 812 333-8550
1110 N Oard Rd Bloomington (47404) *(G-962)*
Rogers Group Inc... 219 474-5125
235 E Us Highway 24 Kentland (47951) *(G-10163)*
Rogers Group Inc... 765 342-6898
1500 Rogers Rd Martinsville (46151) *(G-11424)*
Rogers Group Inc... 812 849-3530
3020 State Road 60 W Mitchell (47446) *(G-12047)*
Rogers Group Inc... 812 275-7860
938 Sieboldt Quarry Rd Springville (47462) *(G-15392)*
Rogers Group Inc... 812 882-3640
1200 S 6th St Vincennes (47591) *(G-16150)*
Rogers Group Inc... 765 893-4463
3255 W 650 S Williamsport (47993) *(G-16853)*
Rogers Marketing & Prtg Inc.. 317 838-7203
7588 E County Road 100 S Avon (46123) *(G-549)*
ROH Custom Cabinetry LLC.. 260 802-1158
6784 W State Road 114 Lot 21 Silver Lake (46982) *(G-14921)*
Rohder Machine & Tool Inc.. 219 663-3697
1023 E Summit St Crown Point (46307) *(G-2747)*

Rohe, Paul H, Aurora *Also Called: Valley Asphalt Corporation (G-458)*
Rohrs Custom Metal.. 812 689-3764
2426 N Old Michigan Rd Holton (47023) *(G-7220)*
Roi Marketing and Safety, Indianapolis *Also Called: Roi Marketing Company Inc (G-9321)*
Roi Marketing Company Inc.. 317 644-0797
9511 Angola Ct Ste 261 Indianapolis (46268) *(G-9321)*
Roka Farms, Indianapolis *Also Called: Roka Urban Ag LLC (G-9322)*
Roka Urban Ag LLC... 317 513-8828
6845 Massachusetts Ave Indianapolis (46226) *(G-9322)*
Rol Publications.. 812 366-4154
3600 Amy Ln Ne Greenville (47124) *(G-6655)*
Roll Coater Inc... 317 652-1102
9908 Blue Ridge Way Indianapolis (46234) *(G-9323)*
Roller-Wilson Industries LLC.. 317 377-4900
2730 Hillside Ave Indianapolis (46218) *(G-9324)*
Rollie Williams Paint Spot... 812 827-2488
1391 Cherry St Jasper (47546) *(G-9906)*
Rollin Mini Barns LLC.. 812 687-7581
6950 E 800 N Odon (47562) *(G-13348)*
Rolling Hills Springs LLC... 844 454-6866
2897 N 1375 W Linton (47441) *(G-11044)*
Rollison Airplane Company Inc.. 812 384-4972
County Road 300 S Bloomfield (47424) *(G-756)*
Rolls-Royce Corporation.. 812 421-7810
225 W Morgan Ave Ste A Evansville (47710) *(G-4292)*
Rolls-Royce Corporation.. 317 230-2000
2601 W Raymond St Indianapolis (46241) *(G-9325)*
Rolls-Royce Corporation.. 317 230-2000
7661 North Perimeter Rd Ste 1x Indianapolis (46241) *(G-9326)*
Rolls-Royce Corporation.. 317 230-4118
2359 S Tibbs Ave Indianapolis (46241) *(G-9327)*
Rolls-Royce Corporation.. 317 230-4118
1875 S Tibbs Ave Indianapolis (46241) *(G-9328)*
Rolls-Royce Corporation (DH)... 317 230-2000
450 S Meridian St Indianapolis (46225) *(G-9329)*
Rolls-Royce Corporation.. 317 657-0267
3051 Midfield Ct Ste 190 Plainfield (46168) *(G-13723)*
Rolls-Royce Corporation.. 317 230-8515
1801 Newman Rd Ste 1700 West Lafayette (47906) *(G-16626)*
Rolls-Royce Corporation.. 317 230-2736
11747 Shadowwood Ct Zionsville (46077) *(G-17048)*
Rolls-Royce Defense Svcs Inc... 317 230-5006
450 S Meridian St Indianapolis (46225) *(G-9330)*
Rolls-Royce Performance Bldg, Indianapolis *Also Called: Rolls-Royce Corporation (G-9327)*
Rollway Bearing, Monticello *Also Called: Regal Beloit America Inc (G-12167)*
Romaine Incorporated... 574 294-7101
2026 Sterling Ave Elkhart (46516) *(G-3651)*
Romanart Incorporated.. 219 736-9150
7302 Taft St Merrillville (46410) *(G-11555)*
Romark Industries Inc... 765 966-6211
1751 S 8th St Richmond (47374) *(G-14200)*
Rome Cy Area Youth Ctr Basbal....................................... 260 854-4599
705 Kelly Street Ext Rome City (46784) *(G-14377)*
Romotech, New Paris *Also Called: Rotational Molding Tech Inc (G-12967)*
Ron Glasscock... 812 986-2342
3282 N County Road 700 E Poland (47868) *(G-13837)*
Ron Mendenhall.. 765 866-8283
751 W 1150 S Ladoga (47954) *(G-10509)*
Ron Nawrocki.. 260 437-5323
1415 S 650 E Avilla (46710) *(G-493)*
Ron Osborne Machining Inc... 812 637-1045
25660 Mount Pleasant Rd Lawrenceburg (47025) *(G-10858)*
Ronald Chileen Furniture.. 574 542-4505
9369 Ohio St Rochester (46975) *(G-14321)*
Ronald Holloway.. 574 223-6825
420 Klinger St Plymouth (46563) *(G-13812)*
Ronald L Miller.. 765 662-3881
1102 N Wabash Ave Marion (46952) *(G-11336)*
Ronald Lee Allen... 812 644-7649
8271 S 1125 E Loogootee (47553) *(G-11150)*
Ronald Wright Logging LLC.. 812 338-2665
61 S Pleasant Hill Rd English (47118) *(G-3847)*

Ronaldo, New Albany *Also Called: Ronaldo Designer Jewelry Inc (G-12808)*

Ronaldo Designer Jewelry Inc (PA)..812 972-7220
115 E Spring St Ste 102 New Albany (47150) *(G-12808)*

Ronard Industries Inc..219 874-4801
1005 E Michigan Blvd Michigan City (46360) *(G-11658)*

Ronlewhorn Industries LLC...765 661-9343
4226 Sunset Ave Indianapolis (46208) *(G-9331)*

Ronnie Elmore Jr...765 719-1681
1193 E State Road 42 Cloverdale (46120) *(G-2095)*

Rons General Repair..765 732-3805
403 Ramsey St West College Corner (47003) *(G-16543)*

Roof Masters Plus LLC..765 572-1321
7800 W 650 S Westpoint (47992) *(G-16747)*

Rookies Unlimited Inc..765 536-2726
103 South Mn Summitville (46070) *(G-15431)*

Rookstools Pier Shop Inc..574 453-4771
2931 E Armstrong Rd Leesburg (46538) *(G-10960)*

Roomworks LLC...317 846-2090
200 S Rangeline Rd Ste 116 Carmel (46032) *(G-1745)*

Roost..317 842-3735
7371 E 116th St Fishers (46038) *(G-4599)*

Roots Blowers LLC (HQ)...765 827-9200
900 W Mount St Connersville (47331) *(G-2465)*

Rose & Petal LLC...260 704-5731
6625 Pointe Inverness Way Fort Wayne (46804) *(G-5389)*

Rose Black..317 636-7459
1357 W 18th St Ste 101 Indianapolis (46202) *(G-9332)*

Rose Engineering Company Inc...317 788-4446
1105 Martin St Indianapolis (46227) *(G-9333)*

Rose HI Lawn Care Ldscpg Snow..812 230-0024
920 N 25th St Terre Haute (47803) *(G-15684)*

Rose Sharon All Naturals LLC..317 500-4725
1220 Waterway Blvd Indianapolis (46202) *(G-9334)*

Rose True Graphics...812 844-1559
4432 Upper South Point Dr Loogootee (47553) *(G-11151)*

Rose-Wall Mfg Inc..317 894-4497
5827 W Us Highway 40 Greenfield (46140) *(G-6544)*

Roses Square Dance Acc...812 865-2821
448 E Liberty Rd Orleans (47452) *(G-13382)*

Rosies Holistic Lifestyle LLC...812 682-1212
5642 Ryan Ln Evansville (47712) *(G-4293)*

Roskovenski Sand & Gravel Inc...765 832-6748
3200 E 1850 S Clinton (47842) *(G-2076)*

Rosmarino Candles LLC...970 218-2835
310 S High St Bloomington (47401) *(G-963)*

Ross Engineering & Machine Inc..574 586-7791
70100 Stephens St Walkerton (46574) *(G-16276)*

Ross Machining...765 998-2400
8855 E 500 S Upland (46989) *(G-15881)*

Ross Solutions, Martinsville *Also Called: Michael Cary Ross (G-11413)*

Ross-Gage Inc (PA)..317 283-2323
4011 W 54th St Indianapolis (46254) *(G-9335)*

Rosskovenski Concrete & Rdymx...765 832-6103
12927 S State Road 63 Clinton (47842) *(G-2077)*

Rossroads Rv, Topeka *Also Called: Ds Corp (G-15804)*

Rosswyvern Press LLC...859 421-0864
2224 Birch Dr Clarksville (47129) *(G-2031)*

Rotadyne, La Porte *Also Called: Finzer Roller Inc (G-10409)*

Rotam Tooling, North Manchester *Also Called: Total Tote Inc (G-13252)*

Rotam Tooling Corporation (PA)..260 982-8318
11606 N State Road 15 North Manchester (46962) *(G-13248)*

Rotation Dynamics, La Porte *Also Called: Finzer Roller Inc (G-10408)*

Rotational Molding Tech Inc...574 831-6450
67742 County Road 23 Ste 1 New Paris (46553) *(G-12967)*

Roteck Enterprises Inc..219 322-4132
13801 77th Ave Dyer (46311) *(G-2982)*

Roth Bioscience LLC...574 533-3351
1303 Eisenhower Dr S Goshen (46526) *(G-6249)*

Roto-Fab LLC..260 375-4480
587 E 1000 S Warren (46792) *(G-16303)*

Roudebush Co Inc...574 595-7115
583 S State Rd 119 Star City (46985) *(G-15397)*

Rough Notes Company Inc (PA)..317 582-1600
11690 Technology Dr Carmel (46032) *(G-1746)*

Round 2 LLC...574 243-3000
4073 Meghan Beeler Ct South Bend (46628) *(G-15224)*

Round Table Recording Co LLP...317 981-5351
6345 Carrollton Ave Indianapolis (46220) *(G-9336)*

Round Town Brewery LLC..317 657-6397
950 S White River Pky West Dr Indianapolis (46204) *(G-9337)*

Round World Products Inc...317 257-7352
75 Executive Dr Ste B Carmel (46032) *(G-1747)*

Row Printing Inc...317 796-3289
7177 Golden Oak Brownsburg (46112) *(G-1399)*

Row Printing Inc...317 441-4301
5860 Walkabout Way Brownsburg (46112) *(G-1400)*

Rowan Industries LLC...574 302-1203
52555 Kenilworth Rd South Bend (46637) *(G-15225)*

Rowe Conveyor LLC (PA)..317 602-1024
1729 Us Highway 31 S Ste F Greenwood (46143) *(G-6761)*

Rowe Conveyor LLC..317 602-1024
5719 Garden Dr Indianapolis (46217) *(G-9338)*

Rowe Tech..317 453-0015
4327 Carrollton Ave Indianapolis (46205) *(G-9339)*

Rowland Printing Co Inc...317 773-1829
199 N 9th St Noblesville (46060) *(G-13168)*

Roy Umbarger and Sons Inc..317 422-5195
186 S 600 E Franklin (46131) *(G-5775)*

Royal, Indianapolis *Also Called: Royal Food Products Inc (G-9340)*

Royal & Langnickel Brush Mfg, Munster *Also Called: Royal Brush Manufacturing Inc (G-12562)*

Royal Adhesives & Sealants LLC (HQ)...574 246-5000
2001 W Washington St South Bend (46628) *(G-15226)*

Royal ARC Welding Company..260 587-3711
640 County Road 27 Ashley (46705) *(G-336)*

Royal Barbie Blinks LLC...765 400-6205
408 Brunswick Dr Lafayette (47909) *(G-10681)*

Royal Box Group LLC..317 462-7743
2200 Royal Dr Greenfield (46140) *(G-6545)*

Royal Box Group LLC..765 728-2416
1200 Riverfork Dr Huntington (46750) *(G-7361)*

Royal Brush Manufacturing Inc (PA)..219 660-4170
515 45th St Munster (46321) *(G-12562)*

Royal Center Locker Plant Inc...574 643-3275
104 S Chicago St Royal Center (46978) *(G-14392)*

Royal Couture Treats Btq Ltd..812 914-9057
216 Pearl St New Albany (47150) *(G-12809)*

Royal Crown Bottling Corp (HQ)...812 424-7978
1100 Independence Ave Evansville (47714) *(G-4294)*

Royal Design Custom Kitchens &...260 593-0508
9685 W 300 S Topeka (46571) *(G-15816)*

Royal Elastomers, South Bend *Also Called: Royal Adhesives & Sealants LLC (G-15226)*

Royal Feeds, Evansville *Also Called: Royal Inc (G-4295)*

Royal Food Products Inc..317 782-2660
7001 Hawthorn Park Dr Ste A Indianapolis (46220) *(G-9340)*

Royal Holdings Inc (HQ)...574 246-5000
2001 W Washington St South Bend (46628) *(G-15227)*

Royal Inc...812 424-4925
1210 N Fulton Ave Evansville (47710) *(G-4295)*

Royal Machining & Repair LLC..765 529-3545
1524 Grand Ave Ste B New Castle (47362) *(G-12882)*

Royal Rubber Company, South Bend *Also Called: Rubber Shop Inc (G-15229)*

Royal Spa Corporation (PA)...317 781-0828
2041 W Epler Ave Indianapolis (46217) *(G-9341)*

Royal Spa Manufacturing, Indianapolis *Also Called: Royal Spa Corporation (G-9341)*

Royale Phoenix Inc..574 206-1216
53972 N Park Ave Elkhart (46514) *(G-3652)*

Royalty, Seymour *Also Called: Crane Hill Machine Inc (G-14641)*

Royalty Investments LLC..812 358-3534
2476 E Us Highway 50 Seymour (47274) *(G-14682)*

Royer Corporation...800 457-8997
805 East St Madison (47250) *(G-11249)*

Royer Enterprises Inc..260 359-0689
6780 N 362 W Huntington (46750) *(G-7362)*

ALPHABETIC SECTION

Royers General Wldg & Repr LLC 574 862-2707
26354 County Road 38 Goshen (46526) *(G-6250)*

Royster Clark Closed 812 397-2617
2745 W State Road 48 Shelburn (47879) *(G-14720)*

RPC Machinery Inc 765 458-5655
424 N Industrial Park Rd Liberty (47353) *(G-10998)*

Rpdm Solutions Inc 317 608-2938
925 Poplar St Huntington (46750) *(G-7363)*

Rpf Inc 317 727-6386
6643 W Boggstown Rd Boggstown (46110) *(G-1076)*

Rpg Energy Group Inc 317 614-0054
5610 Dividend Rd Indianapolis (46241) *(G-9342)*

Rph On Call LLC 317 622-4800
1115 N 300 W Greenfield (46140) *(G-6546)*

RPI Components Inc 574 536-2283
2503 Whipple Ave Elkhart (46516) *(G-3653)*

RPM 309 798-1856
3142 174th Ct Hammond (46323) *(G-7001)*

RPM Machinery LLC 574 271-0800
3953 Ralph Jones Dr South Bend (46628) *(G-15228)*

RPM Tool, Princeton Also Called: Bemr LLC *(G-13982)*

RPS Printing Services, Plainfield Also Called: Buis Enterprises Inc *(G-13663)*

Rpt, Bristol Also Called: Record / Play Tek Inc *(G-1284)*

Rrc Corporation 317 687-8325
1002 E Garfield Dr Indianapolis (46203) *(G-9343)*

Rs Pallet Inc 574 596-8777
19816 County Road 6 Bristol (46507) *(G-1289)*

Rs Precision Machining 219 362-4560
7909 N Wilhelm Rd La Porte (46350) *(G-10475)*

Rs Used Oil Services Inc 866 778-7336
4501 W 99th St Ste 1000 Carmel (46032) *(G-1748)*

Rst Custom Woodworking LL 317 602-2490
1015 E 42nd St Indianapolis (46205) *(G-9344)*

Rt Acquisition Corp 812 482-2932
350 S Saint Charles St Jasper (47546) *(G-9907)*

Rt Smart Solutions LLC 317 435-2200
4901 W 36th St Indianapolis (46224) *(G-9345)*

Rt Software 317 578-8518
13534 Kelsey Ln Fishers (46038) *(G-4600)*

RTC 260 503-9770
1901 N Airport Rd Columbia City (46725) *(G-2193)*

RTC Threaders, Columbia City Also Called: RTC *(G-2193)*

Rtees LLC 317 345-7445
7013 Stonecreek Dr Plainfield (46168) *(G-13724)*

Rtp Enterprise Inc 317 258-3213
15158 Proud Truth Dr Noblesville (46060) *(G-13169)*

Rtw Enterprises Inc 574 294-3275
2924 County Road 6 E Elkhart (46514) *(G-3654)*

Rtx Corporation 260 589-7207
917 Liechty Rd Berne (46711) *(G-723)*

Rtx Corporation 260 358-0888
3650 W 200 N Huntington (46750) *(G-7364)*

Rubber Products Distrs Inc (PA) 317 883-6700
1741 Keaton Way Ste C Greenwood (46143) *(G-6762)*

Rubber Shop Inc 574 291-6440
500 W Chippewa Ave South Bend (46614) *(G-15229)*

Rubenstein LLC 317 946-2752
7982 Fishback Rd Indianapolis (46278) *(G-9346)*

Rubicon Foods LLC 317 826-8793
7320 E 86th St Ste 400 Indianapolis (46256) *(G-9347)*

Ruby Enterprises Inc 765 649-2060
1150 W 29th St Anderson (46016) *(G-186)*

Ruco Inc 574 262-4110
1817 Leer Dr Elkhart (46514) *(G-3655)*

Rudys Food & Fuel LLC 812 547-2530
740 9th St Tell City (47586) *(G-15516)*

Rug Works, Elkhart Also Called: Bock Engineering Company Inc *(G-3229)*

Rugged Company 317 441-0927
3404 Clark St Anderson (46013) *(G-187)*

Rugged Steel Works LLC 260 444-4241
4325 Meyer Rd Fort Wayne (46806) *(G-5390)*

Rumohr 317 750-5911
3930 Madeline Ln Carmel (46033) *(G-1749)*

Running Around Screen Prtg LLC 260 248-1216
227 W Van Buren St Columbia City (46725) *(G-2194)*

Running Company LLC 317 887-0606
1251 N Us Highway 31 N Spc 112 Greenwood (46142) *(G-6763)*

Running Vines Winery 219 617-2429
15 Washington St Valparaiso (46383) *(G-16041)*

Rusach International Inc 317 638-0298
100 Raymond St Hope (47246) *(G-7232)*

Rush County Stone Co Inc 765 629-2211
5814 W State Road 244 Milroy (46156) *(G-11830)*

Rush County Wood Products 765 629-0603
2437 W 900 S Milroy (46156) *(G-11831)*

Rush Hour Station 812 323-7874
421 E 3rd St Bloomington (47401) *(G-964)*

Rusher Medical LLC 260 341-6514
6028 Heywood Cv Fort Wayne (46815) *(G-5391)*

Ruskin 574 223-3181
510 N State Road 25 Rochester (46975) *(G-14322)*

Russ Print Shp/Hbron Advrtser 219 996-3142
131 N Main St Hebron (46341) *(G-7106)*

Russ Publishing 812 847-4487
79 S Main St Linton (47441) *(G-11045)*

Russell Beeman Logging Inc 765 387-0064
4935 E County Road 67 Anderson (46017) *(G-188)*

Russell E Martin 574 354-2563
7585 E 350 S Akron (46910) *(G-8)*

Russell L Rooksberry 812 659-1683
6142 S State Road 159 Carlisle (47838) *(G-1543)*

Russell Metal Products 317 841-9003
9238 Alton Ct Fishers (46037) *(G-4601)*

Russell's Septic Tank Service, Mount Vernon Also Called: Russells Excvtg Sptc Tnks Inc *(G-12318)*

Russells Excvtg Sptic Tnks Inc 812 838-2471
6800 Leonard Rd S Mount Vernon (47620) *(G-12318)*

Russells Tube Forming Inc 317 241-4072
220 Gasoline Aly Indianapolis (46222) *(G-9348)*

Russs Custom Welding Corp 765 795-5795
673 W County Road 1000 S Cloverdale (46120) *(G-2096)*

Rust Publishing In LLC 765 653-5151
100 N Jackson St Greencastle (46135) *(G-6429)*

Rustic Creations LLC 574 349-8156
71703 County Road 9 Nappanee (46550) *(G-12642)*

Rustic Fisher Creations LLC 574 279-5754
67679 Sycamore Rd North Liberty (46554) *(G-13222)*

Rustic Glow Candle Co LLC 317 696-4264
7605 Indian Lake Rd Indianapolis (46236) *(G-9349)*

Rusty Shelden Duwane 812 890-5780
209 Se 2nd St Washington (47501) *(G-16508)*

Ruwaldt Packing Company Inc 219 942-2911
6510 E Ridge Rd Hobart (46342) *(G-7204)*

Rva LLC 317 800-9800
11393 Hawkshead Ln Apt 201 Fishers (46037) *(G-4602)*

Rvp, Elkhart Also Called: River Valley Plastics Inc *(G-3649)*

Rwh Woodworking LLC 317 714-5179
1166 S 25 E # F Greenfield (46140) *(G-6547)*

Rx Help Centers LLC 866 478-9593
3905 Vincennes Rd Ste 200 Indianapolis (46268) *(G-9350)*

Rx Honing Machine Corp 574 259-1606
1301 E 5th St Mishawaka (46544) *(G-11989)*

Ryan Fuelling 260 403-6450
6928 Nighthawk Dr Fort Wayne (46835) *(G-5392)*

Ryan Lane 317 475-9730
5548 Broadway St Indianapolis (46220) *(G-9351)*

Ryan Osborne Inc 317 535-4881
3667 Woodland Streams Dr Greenwood (46143) *(G-6764)*

Ryan Piercy 317 796-2253
3180 E 600 N Whiteland (46184) *(G-16794)*

Ryerson Tull Inc (DH) 219 764-3500
310 Tech Dr Burns Harbor (46304) *(G-1455)*

Ryobi, Rushville *Also Called: T K M Triple K Machining (G-14414)*
Ryobi, Shelbyville *Also Called: Ryobi Die Casting (usa) Inc (G-14794)*
Ryobi Die Casting (usa) Inc 317 398-3398
525 Industrial Park Dr Shelbyville (46176) *(G-14793)*
Ryobi Die Casting (usa) Inc (HQ) 317 398-3398
800 W Mausoleum Rd Shelbyville (46176) *(G-14794)*
Ryobi Press Parts 800 901-3304
478 Gradle Dr Ste C Carmel (46032) *(G-1750)*
Ryoei USA Inc 317 912-4498
5524 Fortune Cir S Indianapolis (46241) *(G-9352)*
S & G Excavating Inc (PA) 812 234-4848
545 E Margaret Dr Terre Haute (47802) *(G-15685)*
S & H Cabinets 574 773-7465
70932 County Road 3 Nappanee (46550) *(G-12643)*
S & H Metal Products Inc 260 593-2565
122 Redman Dr Topeka (46571) *(G-15817)*
S & J Manufacturing LLC 812 662-6640
712 S Christy Rd Greensburg (47240) *(G-6629)*
S & M Precast Inc 812 246-6258
16700 Sima Gray Rd Henryville (47126) *(G-7115)*
S & R Welding Inc 317 710-0360
113 Pennsylvania Ct Indianapolis (46225) *(G-9353)*
S & S Components Inc 812 734-1104
1050 Driftwood Dr Ne Corydon (47112) *(G-2514)*
S & S Diesel Motorsport LLC 812 216-3639
1471 W Tipton St Seymour (47274) *(G-14683)*
S & S Machine Co, Evansville *Also Called: William F Shirley (G-4385)*
S & S Machine Shop Inc (PA) 812 897-5343
298 Essex Dr Boonville (47601) *(G-1096)*
S & S Optical Co Inc 260 749-9614
416 Ann St New Haven (46774) *(G-12915)*
S & S Precast Inc 574 946-4123
840 W 25 S Winamac (46996) *(G-16874)*
S & S Programming Inc 765 423-4472
625 S Earl Ave Ste D Lafayette (47904) *(G-10682)*
S & T Fulfillment LLC 812 466-4900
351 S Airport St Terre Haute (47803) *(G-15686)*
S & W Electric, La Porte *Also Called: Electrik Connection Inc (G-10404)*
S & W Swing Sets 260 414-6200
17007 Doty Rd New Haven (46774) *(G-12916)*
S & Y Trucking LLC 317 642-6222
15499 Border Dr Noblesville (46060) *(G-13170)*
S and SM Achine USA LLC 708 758-8300
3110 W 5th Ave Gary (46406) *(G-6006)*
S C Pryor Inc 317 352-1281
5424 Brookville Rd Indianapolis (46219) *(G-9354)*
S CJ Incorporated 317 822-3477
2021 W Raymond St Indianapolis (46221) *(G-9355)*
S E P, Rosedale *Also Called: Summerlot Engineered Pdts Inc (G-14383)*
S Edwards Inc 317 831-0261
292 W Harrison St Mooresville (46158) *(G-12240)*
S G I, Indianapolis *Also Called: Service Graphics Inc (G-9408)*
S G I, Indianapolis *Also Called: Sign Group Inc (G-9430)*
S H Leggitt Company 574 264-0230
831 E Windsor Ave Unit 9 Elkhart (46514) *(G-3656)*
S L Manufacturing LLC 260 657-3392
18535 Hurshtown Rd Grabill (46741) *(G-6323)*
S L Thomas Family Winery Inc 812 273-3755
208 E 2nd St Madison (47250) *(G-11250)*
S M Smith LLC - S Stngel Mnged 219 802-6064
3098 Hanley St Gary (46406) *(G-6007)*
S P X Corp 574 594-9681
5 Arnolt Dr Pierceton (46562) *(G-13640)*
S R Wood Inc 812 288-9201
1801 Progress Way Clarksville (47129) *(G-2032)*
S S & E Enterprises 260 749-0026
1906 Kendawa Dr Fort Wayne (46815) *(G-5393)*
S S M Inc 317 357-4552
4000 Southeastern Ave Indianapolis (46203) *(G-9356)*
S T Laminating, Elkhart *Also Called: Double T Manufacturing Corp (G-3302)*
S T Praxair Technology Inc 317 240-2500
1500 Polco St Indianapolis (46222) *(G-9357)*

S TEC Group Inc (PA) 219 844-7030
2345 167th St Hammond (46323) *(G-7002)*
S U S, Logansport *Also Called: SUS Cast Products Inc (G-11109)*
S-Tech Inc 812 793-3506
208 N Armstrong St Crothersville (47229) *(G-2645)*
S.B.I., Brownsburg *Also Called: Fuel Bladder Distributors Inc (G-1371)*
S.E.S., Henryville *Also Called: Sullivan Engineered Services (G-7116)*
S&A Tooling 502 836-3886
300 Lafollette Sta S Ste 302 # 283 Floyds Knobs (47119) *(G-4692)*
S&K Sheet Metal LLC 260 623-3398
107 Webster St Monroeville (46773) *(G-12074)*
S&S Machinery Repair LLC 812 521-2368
12807 W Us Highway 50 Norman (47264) *(G-13204)*
S&S Steel Services Inc 765 622-4545
444 E 29th St Anderson (46016) *(G-189)*
SA Heinen LLC 317 416-7818
3890 N Raceway Rd Indianapolis (46234) *(G-9358)*
Saab Aeronautics Indiana LLC 315 445-5009
2099 Hypersonic Pkwy West Lafayette (47906) *(G-16627)*
Saam Inc 855 405-7773
55 Monument Cir Fl 7 Indianapolis (46204) *(G-9359)*
Sabco Sign Co Inc 317 882-3380
1620 W Smith Valley Rd Ste C Greenwood (46142) *(G-6765)*
Sabert Corporation 260 222-0758
8510 Ardmore Ave Fort Wayne (46809) *(G-5394)*
Sabert Corporation 260 747-3149
3511 Engle Rd Fort Wayne (46809) *(G-5395)*
Sabic Innovative Plas US LLC 812 372-0197
945 S Marr Rd Columbus (47201) *(G-2388)*
Sabic Innovative Plas US LLC 812 831-4054
2101 Hwy 69 S Mount Vernon (47620) *(G-12319)*
Sabic Innovative Plastics, Mount Vernon *Also Called: Sabic Innvtive Plas Mt Vrnon L (G-12320)*
Sabic Innvtive Plas Mt Vrnon L 812 838-4385
1 Lexan Ln Mount Vernon (47620) *(G-12320)*
Sabin Corporation 812 323-4500
3800 W Constitution Ave Bloomington (47403) *(G-965)*
Sabina LLC 574 903-4688
127 S Main St Elkhart (46516) *(G-3657)*
Sabre Holdings LLC 317 222-6150
2801 Fortune Cir E Ste B Indianapolis (46241) *(G-9360)*
Sabre Integrated Services 317 844-9100
800 E 96th St Indianapolis (46240) *(G-9361)*
Sabre Manufacturing LLC 574 772-5380
5420 E State Road 8 Knox (46534) *(G-10222)*
Saco Industries Inc 219 690-9900
17151 Morse St Lowell (46356) *(G-11178)*
Sacoma Properties LLC 812 526-5600
955 S Walnut St Edinburgh (46124) *(G-3102)*
Sacred Selections 260 347-3758
112 N Shore Dr Kendallville (46755) *(G-10151)*
Safe Bird Express LLC 607 376-7633
3039 N Post Rd Indianapolis (46226) *(G-9362)*
Safe Fleet, Elkhart *Also Called: Safe Fleet Mirrors (G-3659)*
Safe Fleet Holdings LLC 574 849-4619
3802 Gallatin Way Elkhart (46514) *(G-3658)*
Safe Fleet Mirrors 574 266-3700
319 Roske Dr Elkhart (46516) *(G-3659)*
Safe Travels Solutions LLC 317 640-4576
8939 New Church Blvd Indianapolis (46231) *(G-9363)*
Safe-Way Door, Warsaw *Also Called: Ecpca Safe-Way LLC (G-16354)*
Safe-Way Garage Doors LLC 574 267-4861
3814 E Us Hwy 3 Warsaw (46580) *(G-16420)*
Safeguard Nursery Products LLC 502 648-7922
100 Galvin Way New Albany (47150) *(G-12810)*
Safeguard Solutions LLC 317 519-0255
635 N State St Greenfield (46140) *(G-6548)*
Safety 1st Cosco, Columbus *Also Called: Dorel USA Inc (G-2290)*
Safety First, Columbus *Also Called: Dorel Juvenile Group Inc (G-2287)*
Safety Vehicle Emblem Inc 317 885-7565
5235 Commerce Cir Indianapolis (46237) *(G-9364)*

ALPHABETIC SECTION

Safety-Kleen, East Chicago *Also Called: Safety-Kleen Systems Inc (G-3041)*
Safety-Kleen Systems Inc 219 397-1131
  601 Riley Rd East Chicago (46312) *(G-3041)*
Safetynet LLC 502 609-3339
  2241 State St New Albany (47150) *(G-12811)*
Safran Nclles Svcs Amricas LLC (HQ) 317 827-0859
  845 Airtech Pkwy Ste 172 Plainfield (46168) *(G-13725)*
Sagamore Ready-Mix LLC 765 759-8999
  8700 S County Road 600 W Daleville (47334) *(G-2802)*
Sagamore Ready-Mix LLC (PA) 317 570-6201
  9170 E 131st St Fishers (46038) *(G-4603)*
Sager Metal Strip Company LLC 219 874-3609
  100 Boone Dr Michigan City (46360) *(G-11659)*
Sahasra Technologies Corp (PA) 317 845-5326
  1119 Keystone Way Ste 301 Carmel (46032) *(G-1751)*
Sailor Group LLC 574 226-0362
  1400 W Bristol St Elkhart (46514) *(G-3660)*
Sailor Logistic, Elkhart *Also Called: Sailor Group LLC (G-3660)*
Sailrite Enterprises Inc 260 244-4647
  2390 E 100 S Columbia City (46725) *(G-2195)*
Saimax Products Inc 248 299-5585
  2545 Eastside Park Rd Evansville (47715) *(G-4296)*
Saint Adrian Meats Sausage LLC 317 403-3305
  6115 E State Road 47 Lebanon (46052) *(G-10938)*
Saint-Gobain Abrasives Inc 317 837-0700
  1001 Perry Rd Plainfield (46168) *(G-13726)*
Salabell Publishing LLC 219 865-6906
  320 King Henry Dr Schererville (46375) *(G-14543)*
Salamonie Mills Inc 260 375-2200
  525 N Wayne St Warren (46792) *(G-16304)*
Saldana Racing Products, Indianapolis *Also Called: Saldana Racing Tanks Inc (G-9365)*
Saldana Racing Tanks Inc 317 852-4193
  3754 N Raceway Rd Indianapolis (46234) *(G-9365)*
Salem Fast Printing Service, Salem *Also Called: Marketing and Retail Sales (G-14489)*
Salem Leader, The, Salem *Also Called: Leader Publishing Co of Salem (G-14487)*
Salesforce Inc 317 370-5737
  111 Monument Cir Ste 2000 Indianapolis (46204) *(G-9366)*
SALESFORCE.COM, INC., Indianapolis *Also Called: Salesforcecom Inc (G-9367)*
Salesforcecom Inc 317 981-4924
  111 Monument Cir Ste 2000 Indianapolis (46204) *(G-9367)*
Salesman Sawmill Inc 812 382-9154
  3396 N County Road 550 W Sullivan (47882) *(G-15421)*
Saliwnchik Sons Wldg Fbrction 219 362-9009
  3707 N Us Highway 35 La Porte (46350) *(G-10476)*
Salon Canvas LLC 574 703-7018
  52245 Woodsedge Dr Granger (46530) *(G-6375)*
Salt Creek Harvest, Valparaiso *Also Called: Salt Creek Harvest LLC (G-16042)*
Salt Creek Harvest LLC 708 927-5569
  314 W 700 N Valparaiso (46385) *(G-16042)*
Salt Creek Winery, Freetown *Also Called: Twin Willows LLC (G-5805)*
Sam Mouron Equipment Co Inc 317 776-1799
  15535 Stony Creek Way Noblesville (46060) *(G-13171)*
Sam's Tech Supply, Hobart *Also Called: Sams Tech Tire LLC (G-7205)*
Sam's Windmill Service, Middlebury *Also Called: Millers Windmill Service (G-11739)*
Samaron Corp 574 970-7070
  3310 Magnum Dr Elkhart (46516) *(G-3661)*
Samco Inc 812 279-8131
  1000 U St Bedford (47421) *(G-671)*
Samco Group Inc (PA) 219 872-4413
  9935 N Us Highway 12 E Michigan City (46360) *(G-11660)*
Samco Inc 812 926-4282
  19992 N Manchester Rd Sunman (47041) *(G-15444)*
Sammann Company Inc 219 872-4413
  9935 E Us Highway 12 Michigan City (46360) *(G-11661)*
Sampan Group LLC 812 280-6094
  202 Ash St Jeffersonville (47130) *(G-10050)*
Sampan Screen Print, Jeffersonville *Also Called: Sampan Screen Print New Image (G-10051)*
Sampan Screen Print New Image 812 282-8499
  202 Ash St Jeffersonville (47130) *(G-10051)*
Sampco Inc 413 442-4043
  915 W Ireland Rd South Bend (46614) *(G-15230)*

Sampco of Indiana, South Bend *Also Called: Sampco Inc (G-15230)*
Sampler Inc (PA) 765 663-2233
  7138 W 235 S Homer (46146) *(G-7221)*
Sampson Fiberglass Inc 574 255-4356
  2424 N Home St Mishawaka (46545) *(G-11990)*
Sams Tech Tire LLC 219 942-7317
  435 S Shelby St Hobart (46342) *(G-7205)*
Sams Technical Publishing LLC 800 428-7267
  9850 E 30th St Indianapolis (46229) *(G-9368)*
Samtec Inc (PA) 812 944-6733
  520 Park East Blvd New Albany (47150) *(G-12812)*
Samtec Inc 812 517-6081
  861 S Lake Rd S Scottsburg (47170) *(G-14577)*
Samtec USA, New Albany *Also Called: Samtec Inc (G-12812)*
Samuel Powell 812 887-6813
  395 N County Road 1075 W French Lick (47432) *(G-5849)*
Samuel Wahli 260 749-2288
  13539 Old 24 E New Haven (46774) *(G-12917)*
San Jo Steel Inc 317 888-6227
  610 W Main St Greenwood (46142) *(G-6766)*
San Mar 574 286-6884
  54555 Pine Rd South Bend (46628) *(G-15231)*
Sanbar of Indiana Inc 317 375-6220
  1721 S Franklin Rd Ste 100 Indianapolis (46239) *(G-9369)*
Sanco Industries 219 426-3922
  409 E Cook Rd Ste 200 Fort Wayne (46825) *(G-5396)*
Sanco Industries Inc 260 467-1791
  1819 S Calhoun St Fort Wayne (46802) *(G-5397)*
Sanco Industries Inc (PA) 260 426-6281
  1819 S Calhoun St Fort Wayne (46802) *(G-5398)*
Sand Dcl LLC 260 459-9565
  5618 W Jefferson Blvd Fort Wayne (46804) *(G-5399)*
Sander Processing Incorporated (PA) 812 481-0044
  6614 E State Road 164 Celestine (47521) *(G-1843)*
Sanders & Crosley LLC 812 268-4472
  662 E Leach St Sullivan (47882) *(G-15422)*
Sanders Pulsed Power LLC 630 313-2378
  1400 E Angela Blvd Ste 310 South Bend (46617) *(G-15232)*
Sandin Mfg LLC 219 872-2253
  250 Indiana Highway 212 Michigan City (46360) *(G-11662)*
Sandman Products, Elkhart *Also Called: Sandman Products LLC (G-3662)*
Sandman Products LLC 574 264-7700
  2604 Glenview Dr Elkhart (46514) *(G-3662)*
Sandpaper Studio LLC 317 435-7479
  6403 N 300 E Whiteland (46184) *(G-16795)*
Sandra Henry 574 699-7867
  1475 Denmark St Young America (46998) *(G-16985)*
Sandusky Abrasive Wheel Co 219 879-6601
  532 W 4th St Michigan City (46360) *(G-11663)*
Sandusky-Chicago Abrasive Whl, Michigan City *Also Called: Sandusky Abrasive Wheel Co (G-11663)*
Sandwabi Woodworking LLC 765 891-0774
  1416 Victoria Dr Lebanon (46052) *(G-10939)*
Sandy Island Press 812 360-7288
  1215 E Fairwood Dr Bloomington (47408) *(G-966)*
Sandy Little Coal Company Inc 812 529-8216
  12568 N State Road 245 Evanston (47531) *(G-3854)*
Sangsin Indiana Inc 765 432-4143
  700 E Firmin St Kokomo (46902) *(G-10329)*
Saniserv 317 831-7030
  451 E County Line Rd Mooresville (46158) *(G-12241)*
Saniserv, Mooresville *Also Called: MD Holdings LLC (G-12220)*
Sanitation Equipment, Elkhart *Also Called: Global Ozone Innovations LLC (G-3383)*
Sanlo Inc 219 879-0241
  400 Indiana Highway 212 Michigan City (46360) *(G-11664)*
Sanlo Manufacturing 219 879-0241
  400 Indiana Highway 212 Michigan City (46360) *(G-11665)*
Sanmar Tool & Manufacturing 574 232-6081
  54555 Pine Rd South Bend (46628) *(G-15233)*
Sanofi US Services Inc 317 228-5750
  5225 W 81st St Indianapolis (46268) *(G-9370)*

Sanoh America Inc 419 425-2600
3701 David Howarth Dr Ste C Lafayette (47909) *(G-10683)*

Sansher Corporation 260 484-2000
8005 N Clinton St Fort Wayne (46825) *(G-5400)*

Santarossa Mosaic Tile Co Inc (PA) 317 632-9494
2707 Roosevelt Ave Indianapolis (46218) *(G-9371)*

Santos Herrera 260 849-3454
654 Fulton St Berne (46711) *(G-724)*

Sapp Inc 317 512-8353
600 S Kyle St Edinburgh (46124) *(G-3103)*

Sapp USA, Edinburgh Also Called: Sapp Inc *(G-3103)*

Sapper's Farm Market, Hobart Also Called: Sappers Market and Greenhouses *(G-7206)*

Sappers Market and Greenhouses 219 942-4995
1155 S Lake Park Ave Hobart (46342) *(G-7206)*

Sarah Johnson Nettles 317 778-0023
1226 N Illinois St # 404 Indianapolis (46202) *(G-9372)*

Saran LP
820 S Post Rd Indianapolis (46239) *(G-9373)*

Saratoga, Saratoga Also Called: Town of Saratoga *(G-14509)*

Sardinia Machine Incorporated 812 591-2091
12337 S State Road 3 Westport (47283) *(G-16751)*

Sargent Controls & Aerospace, Franklin Also Called: Airtomic Repair Station *(G-5707)*

Sasaki Coating North Amer Inc 317 956-2232
6330 Corporate Dr Ste B Indianapolis (46278) *(G-9374)*

Sassy Organics Collection LLC 231 942-0751
7840 Gilmore Rd Indianapolis (46219) *(G-9375)*

Sassy Scrubz LLC 463 224-5693
7535 Bayview Club Dr Apt 1c Indianapolis (46250) *(G-9376)*

Satco Inc 317 856-0301
4221 S High School Rd Indianapolis (46241) *(G-9377)*

Satek Winery, Fremont Also Called: James Lake Vineyard Inc *(G-5824)*

Satellite Industries 800 328-3332
5313 Beck Dr Elkhart (46516) *(G-3663)*

Sater Enterprises 812 477-1529
5401 Vogel Rd Ste 430 Evansville (47715) *(G-4297)*

Satin & Stems 765 318-2211
808 Canyon Rd Indianapolis (46217) *(G-9378)*

Saturday Evening Post Soc Inc 317 634-1100
3520 Guion Rd Ste 200 Indianapolis (46222) *(G-9379)*

Saturn Petcare Inc 812 263-5646
1400 E Polymer Dr Terre Haute (47802) *(G-15687)*

Saturn Petcare Inc 812 872-5646
100 E Saturn Petcare Dr Terre Haute (47802) *(G-15688)*

Saturn Petcare Inc 812 872-5646
93 E Dallas Dr Terre Haute (47802) *(G-15689)*

Saturn Wheel Company Inc 260 375-4720
507 E 9th St Warren (46792) *(G-16305)*

Sauers Racing Auto Machines 812 265-2803
1532 E Telegraph Hill Rd Madison (47250) *(G-11251)*

Saul Goode Industries LLC 317 929-1111
2024 Bluff Rd Indianapolis (46225) *(G-9380)*

Sav-or Pack, Avon Also Called: Rogers Marketing & Prtg Inc *(G-549)*

Savage Yet Civilized LLC 855 560-9223
5475 Broadway Merrillville (46410) *(G-11556)*

Saver Systems, Richmond Also Called: Merediths Inc *(G-14164)*

Savor Flavor LLC 812 667-1030
13721 Prosperity Ridge Rd Dillsboro (47018) *(G-2952)*

Sawdust Farms Woodworking LLC 574 946-3399
6518 W 300 S Winamac (46996) *(G-16875)*

Sawmill Pride LLC 317 442-2958
5056 Milton St Coatesville (46121) *(G-2109)*

SAWs Woodworking LLC 574 773-4216
72990 County Road 101 Nappanee (46550) *(G-12644)*

Say Help, Avon Also Called: Help Help LLC *(G-525)*

Saybolt 812 944-5001
1223 Providence Way Clarksville (47129) *(G-2033)*

Saybolt LP 812 282-7242
905 Eastern Blvd Ste C Clarksville (47129) *(G-2034)*

Sazzys Place LLC 317 414-6332
9124 Venona Way Indianapolis (46234) *(G-9381)*

Sb Finishing 317 598-0965
6844 Hawthorn Park Dr Indianapolis (46220) *(G-9382)*

SC Supply Company LLC 574 287-0252
14396 Sage Ct Mishawaka (46545) *(G-11991)*

Scadata Scientific, LLC, Fort Wayne Also Called: Scadata Ventures LLC *(G-5401)*

Scadata Ventures LLC 260 373-0100
1700 Magnavox Way Ste 100 Fort Wayne (46804) *(G-5401)*

Scaggs Moto Designs 765 426-2526
3521 Coleman Ct Lafayette (47905) *(G-10684)*

Scalable Press 510 396-5226
7800 Records St Indianapolis (46226) *(G-9383)*

Scalable Press Inc 877 752-9060
4805 Punjab Dr Indianapolis (46218) *(G-9384)*

Scalar Design Engrg & Dist LLC 765 429-5545
836 Shawnee Ave Lafayette (47905) *(G-10685)*

Scale Computing Inc (PA) 317 856-9959
525 S Meridian St Ste 3e Indianapolis (46225) *(G-9385)*

Scales and More 812 886-4245
1098 E Beckes Ln Vincennes (47591) *(G-16151)*

Scandigital Inc 888 333-2808
9900 Westpoint Dr Ste 138 Indianapolis (46256) *(G-9386)*

Scandinavian Sleep Products, Greenwood Also Called: May and Co Inc *(G-6735)*

Scanpower LLC 765 277-2308
822 E Main St Richmond (47374) *(G-14201)*

Scepter Inc 812 735-2600
6467 N Scepter Rd Bicknell (47512) *(G-737)*

Scg Acquisition Company LLC 574 294-1506
2000 Industrial Pkwy Elkhart (46516) *(G-3664)*

Schacht-Pfister Inc 260 356-9775
232 E Washington St Ste 3 Huntington (46750) *(G-7365)*

Schaefer Farms & Excavating, Oakland City Also Called: Schaefer Yard Care Ldscpg LLC *(G-13322)*

Schaefer Sign Works 317 292-9373
5658 W 73rd St Indianapolis (46278) *(G-9387)*

Schaefer Technologies, Indianapolis Also Called: Mitchum-Schaefer Inc *(G-8935)*

Schaefer Technologies Inc 317 241-9444
4901 W Raymond St Indianapolis (46241) *(G-9388)*

Schaefer Yard Care Ldscpg LLC 812 215-6424
4280 S State Road 57 Oakland City (47660) *(G-13322)*

Schafer Gear Works-South Bend, South Bend Also Called: Schafer Industries Inc *(G-15234)*

Schafer Industries Inc (PA) 574 234-4116
4701 Nimtz Pkwy South Bend (46628) *(G-15234)*

Schafer Powder Coating Inc 317 228-9987
5450 Industrial Ct Whitestown (46075) *(G-16820)*

Schafer Power Washing 812 866-1956
8420 W Polk Rd Lexington (47138) *(G-10981)*

Schaffner LLC 317 450-3956
7016 Cricklewood Rd Indianapolis (46220) *(G-9389)*

Schaffner Manufacturing Co 601 366-9902
2350 Salisbury Rd N Richmond (47374) *(G-14202)*

Schaffsteins Truck Clean LLC 812 464-2424
601 N 9th Ave Evansville (47712) *(G-4298)*

Schatzi Press 317 335-2335
10004 Springstone Rd Fishers (46055) *(G-4650)*

Scheffler Hartmut Romanus 765 855-2917
7798 George Doherty Rd Centerville (47330) *(G-1853)*

Scheidler Machine Incorporated 812 662-6555
3551 N Old Us Highway 421 Greensburg (47240) *(G-6630)*

Scheiner Art & Fabrication LLC 800 998-9345
998 Geneva Ct Lawrenceburg (47025) *(G-10859)*

Schell & Kampeter Inc 765 570-4262
2530 N State Road 3 Rushville (46173) *(G-14411)*

Schenk and Sons Tree Svc Inc 812 985-3954
11018 Altheide Rd Mount Vernon (47620) *(G-12321)*

Scher Machine, Huntington Also Called: Brad Scher *(G-7302)*

Scher Maihem Publishing Ltd 260 897-2697
109 N Baum St Avilla (46710) *(G-494)*

Scherer Indus Group Horner Elc, Indianapolis Also Called: Horner Electric Inc *(G-8415)*

Schergers Kttle Jams Jellies - 800 447-6475
120 N Morton St Shipshewana (46565) *(G-14885)*

Schertz Craftsmen Inc 877 472-2782
13844 Sawmill Rd Grabill (46741) *(G-6324)*

Schick Sand & Gravel, Muncie Also Called: Muncie Sand & Gravel Inc *(G-12466)*

ALPHABETIC SECTION — Scott Pet Products Inc

Schimpffs Confectionery LLC 812 283-8367
347 Spring St Jeffersonville (47130) *(G-10052)*

Schindler Woodwork 513 314-5943
6006 English Hill Rd Cedar Grove (47016) *(G-1824)*

Schlabach Hardwoods LLC 574 642-1157
11186 County Road 34 Goshen (46528) *(G-6251)*

Schlage Lock Company LLC (HQ) 317 810-3700
11819 Pennsylvania St Carmel (46032) *(G-1752)*

Schlatters Inc 219 567-9158
16179 W 500 S Francesville (47946) *(G-5645)*

Schmalbach-Lubeca, Franklin Also Called: Amcor Rigid Packaging Usa LLC *(G-5708)*

Schmaltz Ready Mix Concrete (PA) 812 689-5140
705 Tanglewood Rd Osgood (47037) *(G-13415)*

Schmidt Cabinetry & Furn LLC 574 862-2200
903 Nelsons Pkwy Wakarusa (46573) *(G-16249)*

Schmidt Contracting Inc 812 482-3923
1111 Maurice St Jasper (47546) *(G-9908)*

Schmidt Marken Designs 219 785-4238
3403 S Wozniak Rd La Porte (46350) *(G-10477)*

Schmigbob LLC 219 781-7991
5366 E 111th Ave Crown Point (46307) *(G-2748)*

Schmitt Bennett 812 459-8523
20101 Old Princeton Rd Haubstadt (47639) *(G-7089)*

Schmitt Mtlwrks Fbrcations LLC 812 510-3677
9121 Damm Rd Wadesville (47638) *(G-16230)*

Schmucker Woodworking LLC 260 413-9784
13131 Ehle Rd New Haven (46774) *(G-12918)*

Schmuckers Wood Shop 260 485-1434
9966 Eby Rd Fort Wayne (46835) *(G-5402)*

Schnabeltier, Rochester Also Called: Rapid View LLC *(G-14315)*

Schneider Elc Systems USA Inc 317 372-2839
101 W Ohio St Indianapolis (46204) *(G-9390)*

Schneider Electric, Huntington Also Called: Schneider Electric Usa Inc *(G-7366)*

Schneider Electric Usa Inc 260 356-2060
6 Commercial Rd Huntington (46750) *(G-7366)*

Schneiders Wood Shop Inc 812 522-4621
5910 N Us Highway 31 Seymour (47274) *(G-14684)*

Schnell Service Center 812 683-2461
209 N Cherry St Huntingburg (47542) *(G-7290)*

Schnuck Markets Inc 812 853-9505
8301 Bell Oaks Dr Newburgh (47630) *(G-13019)*

Schnucks, Newburgh Also Called: Schnuck Markets Inc *(G-13019)*

Scholars Inn Bakehouse, Bloomington Also Called: Sib Inc *(G-969)*

Scholastic Education 260 437-1485
1120 Lake Pointe Cv Fort Wayne (46845) *(G-5403)*

School Datebooks, Lafayette Also Called: Sdi Innovations Inc *(G-10689)*

Schott Gemtron Corporation 812 882-2680
2000 Chestnut St Vincennes (47591) *(G-16152)*

Schouten Metal Craft Inc 317 546-2639
2211 E 44th St Indianapolis (46205) *(G-9391)*

Schrock 812 636-7842
11981 N 1000 E Odon (47562) *(G-13349)*

Schrock Aggregate Company Inc (HQ) 574 862-4167
111 Industrial Dr Wakarusa (46573) *(G-16250)*

Schrock Excavating Inc (PA) 574 862-4167
111 Industrial Dr Wakarusa (46573) *(G-16251)*

Schrock Metal Fab LLC 574 825-5653
54039 County Road 43 Middlebury (46540) *(G-11748)*

Schroeder Log Home Supply Inc 574 825-1054
409 W Berry St Middlebury (46540) *(G-11749)*

Schroer Drapery 812 523-3633
5542 E State Road 250 Brownstown (47220) *(G-1427)*

Schuckers Orna Ir Works Co 812 422-7057
2211 Glenview Dr Evansville (47720) *(G-4299)*

Schug Awards LLC 765 447-0002
229 S 30th St Lafayette (47909) *(G-10686)*

Schuhler Woodworking LLC 317 626-0452
414 Western Dr Danville (46122) *(G-2826)*

Schuler Precision Tool, North Manchester Also Called: Schuler Precision Tool LLC *(G-13249)*

Schuler Precision Tool LLC 260 982-2704
6177 W State Road 114 North Manchester (46962) *(G-13249)*

Schult Homes Corp 574 825-5880
221 W Us Highway 20 Middlebury (46540) *(G-11750)*

Schumaker Technical Assembly 765 742-7176
681 N 36th St Lafayette (47905) *(G-10687)*

Schurz Communications Inc (HQ) 574 247-7237
1301 E Douglas Rd Ste 200 Mishawaka (46545) *(G-11992)*

Schurz Communications Inc 574 235-6496
225 W Colfax Ave South Bend (46626) *(G-15235)*

Schuster Sheet Metal Inc 574 293-4802
418 Roske Dr Elkhart (46516) *(G-3665)*

Schutt Sports LLC 217 324-2712
9400 Bradford Rd Plainfield (46168) *(G-13727)*

Schutt Sports Re LLC 217 324-3978
9400 Bradford Rd Plainfield (46168) *(G-13728)*

Schutte Lithography Inc 812 469-3500
1207 Harrelton Ct Evansville (47714) *(G-4300)*

Schwan Products LLC 260 350-4764
9560 W 700 S Topeka (46571) *(G-15818)*

Schwan's Home Service, Danville Also Called: Cygnus Home Service LLC *(G-2810)*

Schwartz Elmer D Mfg Co, Berne Also Called: Schwartz Manufacturing Inc *(G-725)*

Schwartz Manufacturing Inc 260 589-3865
1261 W 200 S Berne (46711) *(G-725)*

Schwartz Wheel Co 574 546-0101
2750 3b Rd Bremen (46506) *(G-1219)*

Schwartz Woodworking 260 593-3193
4810 S 950 W Millersburg (46543) *(G-11817)*

Schwartz Woodworking LLC 260 854-9457
7240 S 075 W # B Wolcottville (46795) *(G-16942)*

Schwartz's Custom Woodworking, Grabill Also Called: Chris Schwartz *(G-6292)*

Schwartz's Wheel Repair, Bremen Also Called: Schwartzs Wheel & Clip C *(G-1220)*

Schwartzs Trailer Sales Inc 317 773-2608
117 Cicero Rd Noblesville (46060) *(G-13172)*

Schwartzs Wheel & Clip C 574 546-1302
4199 Cedar Rd Bremen (46506) *(G-1220)*

Schwartzville Pallet 260 244-4144
4861 W 300 S Columbia City (46725) *(G-2196)*

Schwarz Partners LP (PA) 317 290-1140
10 W Carmel Dr Ste 300 Carmel (46032) *(G-1753)*

Schwarz Partners Packaging LLC 812 523-6600
2245 Killion Ave Seymour (47274) *(G-14685)*

Schwarz Pharma 812 523-3457
1101 C Ave W Seymour (47274) *(G-14686)*

SCI, Ligonier Also Called: Structural Composites Ind Inc *(G-11024)*

Science Fiction Public, East Chicago Also Called: 1632 Inc *(G-2987)*

Scoop Entertainment Source 317 475-0615
2021 E 52nd St Ste 204 Indianapolis (46205) *(G-9392)*

Scoop LLC 317 713-2141
241 N Pennsylvania St Ste 300 Indianapolis (46204) *(G-9393)*

Scorpion Prtctve Coatings Inc 800 483-9087
6184 S Us Highway 231 Cloverdale (46120) *(G-2097)*

Scot Industries Inc 260 927-0262
1729 W Auburn Dr Auburn (46706) *(G-420)*

Scotia Corporation 260 479-8800
7707 Freedom Way Fort Wayne (46818) *(G-5404)*

Scott Bernth 219 926-4836
509 E 1100 N Otis (46391) *(G-13445)*

Scott Billman 317 293-9921
5411 Maplewood Dr Indianapolis (46224) *(G-9394)*

Scott Culbertson 260 357-6430
1202 S Hamsher St Garrett (46738) *(G-5876)*

Scott Fetzer Company 260 488-3531
7715 S Homestead Dr Hamilton (46742) *(G-6861)*

Scott G Kirk 317 843-1703
14165 Warbler Way N Carmel (46033) *(G-1754)*

Scott Naylor 812 336-5361
7170 N Old State Road 37 Bloomington (47408) *(G-967)*

Scott Pet Products Inc 765 569-4702
370 W Vermillion Rise Run Hillsdale (47854) *(G-7164)*

Scott Pet Products Inc (PA) 765 569-4636
1543 N Us Highway 41 Rockville (47872) *(G-14354)*

Scott Pet Products Inc 765 569-4636
840 N Us Highway 41 Rockville (47872) *(G-14355)*

Scott Printing LLC 812 306-7477
11545 Bohannon Dr Evansville (47725) *(G-4301)*

Scott Signs LLC 574 533-7524
600 E Jackson St Goshen (46526) *(G-6252)*

Scott Steel Services Inc 219 663-4740
1203 E Summit St Crown Point (46307) *(G-2749)*

Scott's Custom Cabinents, Otis Also Called: Scott Bernth *(G-13445)*

Scottorsville Sales and Svc 765 250-5245
602 S Earl Ave Lafayette (47904) *(G-10688)*

Scotts Fasteners & Supply LLC 317 372-8743
1945 W County Road 300 S Danville (46122) *(G-2827)*

Scotts Grant County Asp Inc 765 664-2754
2686 S 300 W Marion (46953) *(G-11337)*

Scotts Miracle-Gro Company 219 984-6110
10 E 100 S Reynolds (47980) *(G-14076)*

Scottsburg Stoneware LLC 812 752-6353
445 S Whippoorwill Ln Scottsburg (47170) *(G-14578)*

Scout Mountain Farm - Hideaway 812 738-7196
2145 Scout Mountain Rd Nw Corydon (47112) *(G-2515)*

Scp Building Products LLC 574 772-2955
1001 W Culver Rd Knox (46534) *(G-10223)*

Scp Holdings Inc 260 925-2588
1700 S Indiana Ave Auburn (46706) *(G-421)*

Scp Limited, Auburn Also Called: Specilzed Cmpnent Prts Ltd LLC *(G-425)*

Scramboosay LLC 317 654-0595
5441 Kelvington Ln Indianapolis (46254) *(G-9395)*

Scrapbook Nook 812 967-3306
205 W State Road 60 Pekin (47165) *(G-13522)*

Scrapwood Sawmill 574 223-2725
3488 S Wabash Rd Rochester (46975) *(G-14323)*

Screen Printing, Granger Also Called: Sir Graphics Inc *(G-6379)*

Screen Printing, Richmond Also Called: Black Dog Printing LLC *(G-14098)*

Screen Printing Super Store 317 804-9904
17408 Tiller Ct Ste 100 Westfield (46074) *(G-16725)*

Screen Tech Designs, Columbus Also Called: Dse Inc *(G-2291)*

Screenbroidery LLC 317 546-1900
15255 Endeavor Dr Ste 200 Noblesville (46060) *(G-13173)*

Screenprint Special Tees LLC 317 396-0349
4353 W 96th St Ste 200 Indianapolis (46268) *(G-9396)*

Screens 812 472-3274
6750 W Nesmith Rd Fredericksburg (47120) *(G-5796)*

Screw Conveyor, Hammond Also Called: Screw Conveyor Pacific Corp *(G-7004)*

Screw Conveyor Corporation (PA) 219 931-1450
700 Hoffman St Hammond (46327) *(G-7003)*

Screw Conveyor Pacific Corp (PA) 219 931-1450
700 Hoffman St Hammond (46327) *(G-7004)*

Screw Machine Products, La Porte Also Called: Nrp Jones LLC *(G-10460)*

Scrubs2therescue LLC 317 748-7677
5348 Crittenden Ave Indianapolis (46220) *(G-9397)*

Scruggs Construction Inc 812 528-8178
110 S Chestnut St Seymour (47274) *(G-14687)*

Scurvy Palace Publishing LLC 317 809-4591
6149 New Harmony Rd Martinsville (46151) *(G-11425)*

Scutt Tool & Die Inc 317 858-8725
3245 N State Road 267 Brownsburg (46112) *(G-1401)*

SD, Kokomo Also Called: Stephens Machine Inc *(G-10341)*

Sdbd Incorporated 260 376-1134
10211 Hosler Rd Leo (46765) *(G-10972)*

Sdf Engineering LLC 317 674-2643
13786 Langley Dr Carmel (46032) *(G-1755)*

Sdg Elkhart LLC 574 294-4646
314 W High St Elkhart (46516) *(G-3666)*

Sdgs Rubs & Spices LLC 773 531-5497
1722 171st St Hammond (46324) *(G-7005)*

SDI, Fort Wayne Also Called: Steel Dynamics Inc *(G-5438)*

Sdi Innovations Inc (PA) 765 471-8883
2880 Us Highway 231 S Ste 200 Lafayette (47909) *(G-10689)*

Sdi Lafarga LLC 260 748-6565
1640 Ryan Rd New Haven (46774) *(G-12919)*

Sdn Specialty Wallcoverin 812 736-1806
9219 Dawn Dr Georgetown (47122) *(G-6074)*

SDP Manufacturing Inc 765 768-5000
400 Industrial Dr Dunkirk (47336) *(G-2963)*

Se-Cur-All Cabinets, La Porte Also Called: A & A Sheet Metal Products *(G-10371)*

Sea Quest Lures Inc 219 762-4362
2141 Whippoorwill St Portage (46368) *(G-13911)*

Sea Salt & Cinnamon LLC 727 481-4024
228 N Monroe St Muncie (47305) *(G-12491)*

Seaflo, South Bend Also Called: Seaflo Marine & Rv N Amer LLC *(G-15236)*

Seaflo Marine & Rv N Amer LLC 844 473-2356
3602 W Sample St South Bend (46619) *(G-15236)*

Seal Corp 812 868-0790
1179 E Diamond Ave Evansville (47711) *(G-4302)*

Seal Jet Unlimited, La Porte Also Called: Seals & Components Inc *(G-10478)*

Seal Products LLC 260 436-5628
3702 Vanguard Dr Fort Wayne (46809) *(G-5405)*

Seal Tec Inc 812 282-4388
3131 Industrial Pkwy Jeffersonville (47130) *(G-10053)*

SealCorpUSA Inc 866 868-0791
1175 E Diamond Ave Evansville (47711) *(G-4303)*

Seals & Components Inc 708 895-5222
6436 W Laura Ln La Porte (46350) *(G-10478)*

Sealwrap Systems LLC 317 462-3310
325 E Main St Greenfield (46140) *(G-6549)*

Sealy Components, Rensselaer Also Called: Leggett & Platt Incorporated *(G-14057)*

Searchlight Social LLC 317 983-3802
1694 S 200 E Kokomo (46902) *(G-10330)*

Seasoned Software LLC 260 431-5666
13030 Callison Ct Fort Wayne (46845) *(G-5406)*

Seat Tech, Goshen Also Called: Seating Technology Inc *(G-6253)*

Seating Technologies, Goshen Also Called: Zieman Manufacturing Company Inc *(G-6279)*

Seating Technology Inc 574 971-4100
2703 College Ave Goshen (46528) *(G-6253)*

Seaton Springs Inc 812 282-2440
632 Eastern Blvd Ste B Clarksville (47129) *(G-2035)*

Seavac (usa) Inc 260 747-7123
9304 Yeager Ln Fort Wayne (46809) *(G-5407)*

Sechler's Fine Pickles, Saint Joe Also Called: Sechlers Pickles Inc *(G-14443)*

Sechlers Pickles Inc (PA) 260 337-5461
5686 State Rd 1 Saint Joe (46785) *(G-14443)*

Second Cycle LLC 765 432-8178
1233 W Jackson St Ste A Kokomo (46901) *(G-10331)*

Secured Ftp Hosting LLC 877 336-3453
525 S Meridian St # 3b Indianapolis (46225) *(G-9398)*

Security Integrated Corp 219 942-9666
109 Leicester Rd Munster (46321) *(G-12563)*

Security Paks Intl LLC 317 536-2662
11405 Pennsylvania St Ste 106 Carmel (46032) *(G-1756)*

Sedona Inc 219 764-9675
3195 Willowcreek Rd Portage (46368) *(G-13912)*

Seductive Lifestyle Inc 708 990-0720
1128 Burr St Gary (46406) *(G-6008)*

Seedline International Inc 765 795-2500
5409 S County Road 250 E Greencastle (46135) *(G-6430)*

Sego Woodworking 317 431-9087
5839 Garden Dr Indianapolis (46217) *(G-9399)*

Segundo Deluxe LLC 260 414-7820
2725 S Kenmore Rd Indianapolis (46203) *(G-9400)*

Segura Publishing Company 574 631-3143
1045 W Washington St South Bend (46601) *(G-15237)*

Seib Machine & Tool Co Inc 812 453-6174
14314 Bender Rd Evansville (47720) *(G-4304)*

Seibertspace Industries LLC 317 566-0014
13476 Spotswood St Carmel (46032) *(G-1757)*

Seibs Welding, Evansville Also Called: Seib Machine & Tool Co Inc *(G-4304)*

Seiler & Sons 812 858-9598
5922 Seiler Rd Newburgh (47630) *(G-13020)*

Seiler Excavating Inc 260 925-0507
6310 County Road 31 Auburn (46706) *(G-422)*

Seismic Vision LLC 219 548-8704
967 Misty Glen Dr Valparaiso (46385) *(G-16043)*

Selby Publishing & Printing 765 453-5417
3405 Zartman Rd Kokomo (46902) *(G-10332)*

Selco Engineering Inc
　1677 W 400 N Shelbyville (46176) *(G-14795)*

Select Embroidery, Bloomington *Also Called: Select Embroidery/Top It Off (G-968)*

Select Embroidery/Top It Off.. 812 337-8049
　1713 N College Ave Ste 3 Bloomington (47404) *(G-968)*

Select Gourmet Popcorn.. 812 212-2202
　9632 N County Road 800 E Sunman (47041) *(G-15445)*

Select Tool and Eng Inc.. 574 295-6197
　59753 Park Side Dr Elkhart (46517) *(G-3667)*

Selectric Signs.. 812 378-6129
　3055 State St Columbus (47201) *(G-2389)*

Selektd Worx LLC.. 317 227-9337
　1453 Woodlawn Ave Indianapolis (46203) *(G-9401)*

Self Reliance Outfitters, Indianapolis *Also Called: Pathfinder School LLC (G-9100)*

Selking International LLC (HQ)... 260 482-3000
　2807 Goshen Rd Fort Wayne (46808) *(G-5408)*

Selking International Inc... 574 522-2001
　836 Verdant St Elkhart (46516) *(G-3668)*

Selking International Inc, Elkhart *Also Called: Selking International Inc (G-3668)*

Sellers Dental Lab... 219 465-8719
　378 E 400 N Valparaiso (46383) *(G-16044)*

Sellersburg Metals & Wldg Co... 812 248-0811
　1000 Service Dr Sellersburg (47172) *(G-14613)*

Selmer Paris, Elkhart *Also Called: Conn-Selmer Inc (G-3262)*

Semcor Inc.. 219 362-0222
　1500 Genesis Dr La Porte (46350) *(G-10479)*

Semcor Manufacturing, La Porte *Also Called: Semcor Inc (G-10479)*

Semicndctor Cmponents Inds LLC.. 765 868-5015
　1708 Mollee Ct Kokomo (46902) *(G-10333)*

Semiconductor Test Supply, Martinsville *Also Called: Semiconductor Test Supply LLC (G-11426)*

Semiconductor Test Supply LLC.. 317 513-7393
　400 E Mahalasville Rd Martinsville (46151) *(G-11426)*

Seminole Energy Services... 219 923-2131
　8244 Kennedy Ave Highland (46322) *(G-7153)*

Seminole Stone Inc.. 812 634-7115
　1503 S Meridian Rd Jasper (47546) *(G-9909)*

Semmaterials LP.. 574 267-5076
　2820 Durbin St Warsaw (46580) *(G-16421)*

Senefoods, Indianapolis *Also Called: Dieng Group LLC (G-7973)*

Sengo LLC... 574 383-9833
　219 David St South Bend (46637) *(G-15238)*

Sengo Products, South Bend *Also Called: Sengo LLC (G-15238)*

Senior Lf Auto Rv Publications, Milford *Also Called: The Papers Inc (G-11807)*

Senoj, Gary *Also Called: Jones International Inc (G-5971)*

Sensit Technologies, Valparaiso *Also Called: J and N Enterprises Inc (G-15978)*

Sensit Technologies LLC (HQ).. 219 465-2700
　851 Transport Dr Valparaiso (46383) *(G-16045)*

Sensortec Inc.. 260 497-8811
　7620 Disalle Blvd Fort Wayne (46825) *(G-5409)*

Sentech Corporation.. 317 596-1988
　8358 Masters Rd Indianapolis (46250) *(G-9402)*

Sentimental Stitches... 317 694-1244
　9722 Oakhaven Ct Indianapolis (46256) *(G-9403)*

Sentinel Alarm Inc... 219 874-6051
　2815 E Michigan Blvd Trail Creek (46360) *(G-15839)*

Sentinel Services Inc... 574 360-5279
　51618 Autumn Ridge Dr Granger (46530) *(G-6376)*

Separation By Design Inc.. 812 424-1239
　1601 Buchanan Rd Evansville (47720) *(G-4305)*

Separation Technologies Inc... 219 548-5814
　463 E Us Highway 30 Ste 4 Valparaiso (46383) *(G-16046)*

Sepracor Inc.. 317 513-6257
　13923 Ash Stone Ct Fishers (46040) *(G-4651)*

Sepro Corporation (PA)... 317 580-8282
　11550 N Meridian St Ste 600 Carmel (46032) *(G-1758)*

Sequoia National LLC (PA)... 812 421-0095
　1712 Read St Evansville (47710) *(G-4306)*

Ser North America LLC.. 765 639-0300
　3025 Dr Martin Luther King Jr Blvd Anderson (46016) *(G-190)*

Seraphim Coffee.. 765 409-1942
　1 Berwick Dr Lafayette (47909) *(G-10690)*

Seraphim Lux LLC... 872 201-8273
　8714 Polk St Merrillville (46410) *(G-11557)*

Serenade Foods, Milford *Also Called: Maple Leaf Farms Inc (G-11798)*

Serenade Foods, Milford *Also Called: Maple Leaf Farms Inc (G-11799)*

Serendipity Sanctuary.. 765 541-2364
　532 N 19th St Richmond (47374) *(G-14203)*

Sermatech Intl Canada Corp... 317 240-2500
　1500 Polco St Indianapolis (46222) *(G-9404)*

Sermatech-Aeroforge, Muncie *Also Called: GKN Aerospace Muncie Inc (G-12402)*

Servaas Inc (PA)... 317 633-2020
　3520 Guion Rd Ste 200 Indianapolis (46222) *(G-9405)*

Servaas Laboratories Inc... 317 636-7760
　5240 Walt Pl Indianapolis (46254) *(G-9406)*

Servaas Manufacturing Corp.. 317 253-0454
　4897 Kessler Boulevard East Dr Indianapolis (46220) *(G-9407)*

Servants Inc (PA).. 812 634-2201
　3145 Lottes Dr Jasper (47546) *(G-9910)*

Service Engineering Inc... 317 467-2000
　2190 W Main St Greenfield (46140) *(G-6550)*

Service Graphics Inc... 317 471-8246
　8350 Allison Ave Indianapolis (46268) *(G-9408)*

Service Printers Inc... 574 266-6710
　28574 Phillips St Elkhart (46514) *(G-3669)*

Service Steel Framing Inc... 260 868-5853
　206 Depot St Butler (46721) *(G-1476)*

Service/Sales, Mitchell *Also Called: Joseph Matthew Biaso (G-12041)*

Services Everyone Needs Today.. 260 368-9262
　11725 S 650 W Geneva (46740) *(G-6052)*

Servoflo Corporation.. 574 262-4171
　54503 Saddle Brook Xing Elkhart (46514) *(G-3670)*

Sesco, Fort Wayne *Also Called: Systems Engineering and Sls Co (G-5466)*

Setco LLC (DH)... 812 424-2904
　101 Oakley St Evansville (47710) *(G-4307)*

Setser Fabricating LLC... 812 546-2169
　15601 E 225 N Columbus (47203) *(G-2390)*

Sevenoks Inc.. 800 523-8715
　3539 Monroe St La Porte (46350) *(G-10480)*

Sevier Manufacturing.. 317 892-2784
　103 Oak Hill Dr Brownsburg (46112) *(G-1402)*

Sew Beautiful Embroidry... 812 793-2245
　5084 S County Road 1060 E Crothersville (47229) *(G-2646)*

Sew Creative... 260 622-6263
　401 Ingle Dr Ossian (46777) *(G-13434)*

Sewer Optical Services Inc... 765 242-3768
　1825 John Bart Rd Lebanon (46052) *(G-10940)*

Sexton, Bloomington *Also Called: Quality Vault Company (G-949)*

Sexton & Associates, Seymour *Also Called: Sexton Advertising LLC (G-14688)*

Sexton Advertising LLC... 812 522-4059
　312 W 2nd St Seymour (47274) *(G-14688)*

Sexton Plywood & Veneer Co.. 812 454-0488
　227 Rosemarie Ct Evansville (47715) *(G-4308)*

Sexton Vault Company, Bloomington *Also Called: Wilbert Sexton Corporation (G-1011)*

Seymour Division, Seymour *Also Called: Packaging Corporation America (G-14671)*

Seymour Manufacturing Co Inc (HQ)................................... 812 522-2900
　500 N Broadway St Seymour (47274) *(G-14689)*

Seymour Midwest LLC... 574 267-7875
　1037 Seymour Midwest Dr Bldg C Warsaw (46580) *(G-16422)*

Seymour Midwest LLC (PA)... 574 267-7875
　2666 S Country Club Rd Warsaw (46580) *(G-16423)*

Seymour Prcision Machining Inc.. 812 524-1813
　1733 1st Ave Seymour (47274) *(G-14690)*

Seymour Trbune A Cal Ltd Prtnr.. 812 522-4871
　100 Saint Louis Ave Seymour (47274) *(G-14691)*

Sg Solutions LLC... 812 535-6000
　444 W Sandford Ave West Terre Haute (47885) *(G-16654)*

Sg Trading Post, Fort Wayne *Also Called: Dkm Embroidery Inc (G-4920)*

SGS Cybermetrix Inc (HQ)... 800 713-1203
　2860 N National Rd A Columbus (47201) *(G-2391)*

SGS Tool, Columbia City Also Called: Kyocera SGS Precision Tls Inc (G-2163)

Sha-Do Corp.. 574 848-9296
1501 Bloomingdale Dr Bristol (46507) (G-1290)

Shaal John... 812 882-2396
503 Grouseland Dr Vincennes (47591) (G-16153)

Shackelford Graphics.. 317 783-3582
7522 Honnen Dr N Indianapolis (46256) (G-9409)

Shade By Design Inc.. 317 602-3513
6321 E 30th St Ste 206 Indianapolis (46219) (G-9410)

Shade Tree Press.. 765 548-2421
8945 S Coxville Rd Rosedale (47874) (G-14382)

Shadow Graphix Inc... 317 481-9710
4703 W Vermont St Indianapolis (46222) (G-9411)

Shadow Screen Printing.................................... 812 234-3104
1521 Maple Ave Terre Haute (47804) (G-15690)

Shadow Signs.. 317 481-9710
4703 W Vermont St Indianapolis (46222) (G-9412)

Shadowhouse Jiu-Jitsu Inc................................ 219 873-4556
3707 N Promenade Cir La Porte (46350) (G-10481)

Shads Signs.. 812 512-6066
60 S Main St Linton (47441) (G-11046)

Shady Creek Vineyard LLC................................ 219 874-9463
2030 Tryon Rd Michigan City (46360) (G-11666)

Shady Oaks Logging LLC.................................. 317 902-9741
7705 Gartner Dr Morgantown (46160) (G-12263)

Shafer Stoneware.. 765 855-2409
610 N Morton Ave Centerville (47330) (G-1854)

Shaklee Authorized Distributor............................ 260 471-8232
3330 Thames Dr Fort Wayne (46815) (G-5410)

Shakour Industries Inc...................................... 574 289-0100
1319 Wayne St N South Bend (46615) (G-15239)

Shalom Trans LLC... 317 712-6765
297 Shiloh Crossing Dr Avon (46123) (G-550)

Shamrock Cabinets Inc..................................... 812 482-7969
5785 W 150n Jasper (47546) (G-9911)

Shamrock Engineering Inc................................. 812 867-0009
1020 W Morton St Oakland City (47660) (G-13323)

Shank Brothers Inc.. 260 744-4802
3710 Piper Dr Fort Wayne (46809) (G-5411)

Shank Welding Inc... 260 897-2068
7056 E 100 N Avilla (46710) (G-495)

Shannon Door, Carmel Also Called: Burks Door & Sash Inc (G-1576)

Shanxi-Indiana LLC.. 219 885-2209
201 Mississippi St Gary (46402) (G-6009)

Shape Man, Mishawaka Also Called: South Bend Screen Process Inc (G-12003)

Shape Shifters Inc... 812 400-0580
420 N State Road 45 Bloomfield (47424) (G-757)

Shar Systems Inc.. 260 432-5312
3210 Freeman St Fort Wayne (46802) (G-5412)

Shark-Co Mfg LLC... 317 670-6397
1231 Indianapolis Ave Lebanon (46052) (G-10941)

Sharon K Utter.. 765 349-8991
140 Hammans St Martinsville (46151) (G-11427)

Sharon S Cheesecakes..................................... 219 477-5773
2214 Dixon Dr Valparaiso (46383) (G-16047)

Sharon Sperry... 219 736-0121
1106 W 73rd Ave Merrillville (46410) (G-11558)

Sharon's Tolebooth, Merrillville Also Called: Sharon Sperry (G-11558)

Sharp Printing, Fishers Also Called: Sharp Printing Services Inc (G-4604)

Sharp Printing Services Inc................................ 317 842-5159
11100 Allisonville Rd Fishers (46038) (G-4604)

Sharp Wraps LLC.. 317 989-8447
2114 Williams Glen Blvd Zionsville (46077) (G-17049)

Sharp's Creations, Elkhart Also Called: Sharps Baton Mfg Corp (G-3671)

Sharp's Woodshop, Shelbyville Also Called: Vernon Sharp (G-14812)

Sharpen, Indianapolis Also Called: Sharpen Technologies Inc (G-9413)

Sharpen Technologies Inc (PA)........................... 855 249-3357
101 W Washington St Ste 600e Indianapolis (46204) (G-9413)

Sharps Baton Mfg Corp..................................... 574 214-9389
57330 Orchard Ridge Dr Elkhart (46516) (G-3671)

Shaw Machine Shop, Huntington Also Called: Shaw Machine Works (G-7367)

Shaw Machine Works....................................... 260 356-4297
1024 2nd St Huntington (46750) (G-7367)

Shaw Polymers Holdings LLC (PA)...................... 219 779-9450
400 N Indiana Ave Crown Point (46307) (G-2750)

Shawn Ferguson.. 269 300-7090
12160 E 216th St Noblesville (46060) (G-13174)

SHE Publishing LLC... 219 515-8032
5625 N German Church Rd Indianapolis (46235) (G-9414)

Shear Line Golf, Noblesville Also Called: Triunity LLC (G-13185)

Shearer Business Products, Kokomo Also Called: Shearer Printing Service Inc (G-10334)

Shearer Printing Service Inc............................... 765 457-3274
107 W Markland Ave Kokomo (46901) (G-10334)

Shed Craft Creations LLC.................................. 765 993-1161
1204 S Huntsville Rd Winchester (47394) (G-16899)

Sheet Metal Models Inc..................................... 317 783-1303
2702 National Ave Indianapolis (46227) (G-9415)

Sheet Metal Models/Machine TI, Indianapolis Also Called: Sheet Metal Models Inc (G-9415)

Sheet Metal Services Inc................................... 219 924-1206
9944 Express Dr Highland (46322) (G-7154)

Sheet Mtal Wkrs Lcal 20 Apprnt.......................... 317 541-0050
2828 E 45th St Ste A Indianapolis (46205) (G-9416)

Sheets LLC... 317 290-1140
10 W Carmel Dr Ste 300 Carmel (46032) (G-1759)

Shelburne Engraving.. 317 873-6257
8888 W 96th St Zionsville (46077) (G-17050)

Shelby Custom Cabinets Inc............................... 317 398-0344
3081 S Miller St Shelbyville (46176) (G-14796)

Shelby Gravel, Rushville Also Called: Shelby Gravel Inc (G-14412)

Shelby Gravel Inc... 812 526-2731
7520 E 650 S Edinburgh (46124) (G-3104)

Shelby Gravel Inc... 317 738-3445
451 Arvin Rd Franklin (46131) (G-5776)

Shelby Gravel Inc... 317 784-6678
2701 S Emerson Ave Indianapolis (46203) (G-9417)

Shelby Gravel Inc... 317 216-7556
10770 E County Road 300 N Indianapolis (46234) (G-9418)

Shelby Gravel Inc... 765 932-3292
982 S Flatrock River Rd Rushville (46173) (G-14412)

Shelby Gravel Inc (PA)...................................... 317 398-4485
157 E Rampart St Shelbyville (46176) (G-14797)

Shelby Gravel Inc... 317 804-8100
17701 Spring Mill Rd Westfield (46074) (G-16726)

Shelby Materials, Indianapolis Also Called: Shelby Gravel Inc (G-9418)

Shelby Materials, Shelbyville Also Called: Shelby Gravel Inc (G-14797)

Shelby Upholstering Interiors, Indianapolis Also Called: Shelby Westside Upholstering (G-9419)

Shelby Westside Upholstering............................ 317 631-8911
3136 W 16th St Indianapolis (46222) (G-9419)

Shelbyville Newspapers Inc................................ 317 398-6631
123 E Washington St Shelbyville (46176) (G-14798)

Shelbyville Plant, Shelbyville Also Called: Pilkington North America Inc (G-14783)

Shelden Welding & Fabrication, Washington Also Called: Rusty Shelden Duwane (G-16508)

Shelf It Right LLC... 574 368-6881
2015 W Western Ave Ste 333 South Bend (46619) (G-15240)

Shelf Tag Supply Corporation............................. 317 580-4030
611 3rd Ave Sw Westfield (46074) (G-16727)

Shell, Richmond Also Called: Shell Pipe Line Corporation (G-14204)

Shell Catalysts & Tech LP.................................. 219 874-6211
1800 E Us Highway 12 Michigan City (46360) (G-11667)

Shell Pipe Line Corporation................................ 765 962-1329
1221 S 9th St Richmond (47374) (G-14204)

Shells Inc... 574 342-2673
502 Old Us Highway 30 E Bourbon (46504) (G-1127)

Shelovexempress LLC...................................... 317 490-2097
235 N Burkhardt Rd Evansville (47715) (G-4309)

Shelton Enterprises, Fort Wayne Also Called: M & J Shelton Enterprises Inc (G-5194)

Shenango LLC.. 812 235-2058
1200 College Ave Terre Haute (47802) (G-15691)

Shepherd & David LLC...................................... 317 769-4751
1640 N Us 421 Whitestown (46075) (G-16821)

ALPHABETIC SECTION — Sign A Rama

Shepherds Loft.. 812 486-2304
  8008 E 625 N Montgomery (47558) *(G-12122)*

Sheridan Manufacturing Co Inc....................................... 317 758-6000
  508 S Main St Sheridan (46069) *(G-14828)*

Sherman Enterprises Inc... 260 636-6225
  4426 S 100 W Albion (46701) *(G-45)*

Sherms Marine Inc.. 260 563-8051
  8662 S 400 W Wabash (46992) *(G-16215)*

Sherwood Industries Inc... 574 262-2639
  1805 Leer Dr Elkhart (46514) *(G-3672)*

Sherwood Plastics, Bristol *Also Called: Ameri-Kart Corp (G-1243)*

Sherwood-Templeton Inc.. 812 232-7037
  701 Wabash Ave Ste 501 Terre Haute (47807) *(G-15692)*

Sherwood-Templeton Coal Co Inc, Terre Haute *Also Called: Sherwood-Templeton Inc (G-15692)*

Sheung T Cheng... 646 220-2195
  5833 Pinstrip Ave Portage (46368) *(G-13913)*

Shidler Associates... 574 232-7357
  6851 Enterprise Dr South Bend (46628) *(G-15241)*

Shield, Elkhart *Also Called: Shield Restraint Systems Inc (G-3673)*

Shield Restraint Systems Inc (HQ)................................. 574 266-8330
  3802 Gallatin Way Elkhart (46514) *(G-3673)*

Shields Designs, Martinsville *Also Called: Form/TEC Plastics Incorporated (G-11395)*

Shields Mech & Fabrication LLC.................................... 219 863-3972
  11474 Chateau Ln Demotte (46310) *(G-2929)*

Shilling Sales Inc.. 260 426-2626
  414 E Wayne St Fort Wayne (46802) *(G-5413)*

Shiloh Custom Woodworks.. 812 636-0100
  9394 E 1000 N Odon (47562) *(G-13350)*

Shiloh Industries Hot Stamping, Goshen *Also Called: Grouper Wild LLC (G-6156)*

Shiloh Susiebell LLC.. 574 936-8412
  304 Webster Ave Plymouth (46563) *(G-13813)*

Shimp Optical Corp.. 317 636-4448
  932 S Meridian St Ste 101 Indianapolis (46225) *(G-9420)*

Shinabargar Custom Stairs... 219 462-1735
  176 Goodview Dr Valparaiso (46385) *(G-16048)*

Shipping Plus, Boonville *Also Called: B-Hive Printing (G-1081)*

Shipshe Welding.. 260 768-7267
  8435 W Us Highway 20 Shipshewana (46565) *(G-14886)*

Shipshewana Bread Box Corp....................................... 260 768-4629
  140 One Half N Morton St Shipshewana (46565) *(G-14887)*

Shipshewana Woodworks LLC...................................... 260 768-7034
  7720 W 200 N Shipshewana (46565) *(G-14888)*

Shirks Wood Products, Rochester *Also Called: Lawrence Shirks (G-14301)*

Shirt Print Ave.. 812 882-9610
  2038 Washington Ave Vincennes (47591) *(G-16154)*

Shirts and Stuffs Happens... 812 217-8390
  956 W Main St Boonville (47601) *(G-1097)*

Shoals News... 812 247-2828
  311 High St Shoals (47581) *(G-14911)*

Shobe Cases LLC.. 317 363-9006
  26 W Washington St Apt 1001 Indianapolis (46204) *(G-9421)*

Shocktech USA Company.. 708 557-6952
  8603 W 132nd Pl Cedar Lake (46303) *(G-1836)*

Shodas Tees & Gifts.. 260 418-8448
  403 S Main St South Whitley (46787) *(G-15323)*

Shoemaker Inc.. 260 625-4321
  12120 Yellow River Rd Fort Wayne (46818) *(G-5414)*

Shoemaker Welding Company....................................... 574 656-4412
  65508 State Road 23 North Liberty (46554) *(G-13223)*

Shop Lulu Bean LLC.. 219 525-5336
  2032 W 81st Ave Merrillville (46410) *(G-11559)*

Shophouse Fabrication LLC.. 260 367-2156
  4925 N 900 E Howe (46746) *(G-7242)*

Shopping Guide News Inc... 574 223-5417
  617 Main St Rochester (46975) *(G-14324)*

Shore Measuring Systems, Attica *Also Called: T W Brackett & Assoc LLC (G-355)*

Shoreline East Inc.. 219 878-9991
  301 W Us Highway 20 Ste C Michigan City (46360) *(G-11668)*

Shoremet LLC... 219 390-3336
  3601 Enterprise Ave Valparaiso (46383) *(G-16049)*

Short 9th LLC... 270 313-5665
  6453 Waterloo Ln Indianapolis (46268) *(G-9422)*

Shorts Machine Shop... 765 622-6259
  509 E 29th St Anderson (46016) *(G-191)*

Shotmizer Unit Dose Packaging, Kokomo *Also Called: Link Engineering LLC (G-10298)*

Shouse Sawmill Inc.. 812 743-2017
  4679 S State Road 241 Monroe City (47557) *(G-12065)*

Showersleeve & Castcover Co, Mishawaka *Also Called: Coventure I LLC (G-11867)*

Showhaulers, Middlebury *Also Called: Showhaulers Trucks Inc (G-11751)*

Showhaulers Trucks Inc.. 574 825-6764
  114 Industrial Pkwy E Middlebury (46540) *(G-11751)*

Showtime Conversions Inc... 574 825-1130
  116 Industrial Pkwy E Middlebury (46540) *(G-11752)*

Shreve Manufacturing, Elkhart *Also Called: Elkhart Brass Manufacturing Co (G-3321)*

Shrock Manufacturing Inc... 574 264-4126
  2746 Jami St Elkhart (46514) *(G-3674)*

Shucks Wldg & Fabrication LLC.................................... 317 409-8526
  4588 S 200 E Atlanta (46031) *(G-342)*

Shull Mch & Firearms Svc Inc....................................... 260 925-4198
  3877 County Road 49 Butler (46721) *(G-1477)*

Shull Tactical Concepts Inc.. 260 316-9224
  3877 County Road 49 Butler (46721) *(G-1478)*

Shur Ply, Lagrange *Also Called: Dutch Country Woodworking Inc (G-10734)*

Shurtrack Transport LLC... 317 779-5902
  10417 Lookout Ln Indianapolis (46234) *(G-9423)*

Shuttleworth LLC (DH)... 260 356-8500
  10 Commercial Rd Huntington (46750) *(G-7368)*

Shuttleworth North America, Huntington *Also Called: Shuttleworth LLC (G-7368)*

Shyft Group Usa Inc.. 574 848-2000
  603 Earthway Blvd Bristol (46507) *(G-1291)*

Sib Inc... 812 331-6029
  573 W Simpson Chapel Rd Bloomington (47404) *(G-969)*

Siddhi Integrated Mfg Svcs Inc..................................... 502 298-8640
  1513 Lynch Ln Clarksville (47129) *(G-2036)*

Sideline Equipment Inc.. 574 202-0525
  64701 Cr35 Goshen (46528) *(G-6254)*

Siders & Son Gravel.. 574 893-4110
  225 N Washington St Roann (46974) *(G-14254)*

Sidney & Janice Bond... 812 366-8160
  4424 Erin Dr Floyds Knobs (47119) *(G-4693)*

Sieboldt Quarry, Springville *Also Called: Rogers Group Inc (G-15392)*

Siemens Energy Inc... 317 677-1340
  201 S Capitol Ave Ste 910 Indianapolis (46225) *(G-9424)*

Siemens Hlthcare Dgnostics Inc.................................. 574 262-6139
  3400 Middlebury St Elkhart (46516) *(G-3675)*

Siemens Industrial Services, Portage *Also Called: Siemens Industry Inc (G-13914)*

Siemens Industry Inc... 317 381-0734
  7800 Col H Weir Cook Mem Dr Indianapolis (46241) *(G-9425)*

Siemens Industry Inc... 219 763-7927
  6625 Daniel Burnham Dr Portage (46368) *(G-13914)*

Siemer Milling Company.. 513 814-9216
  707 Harrison Brookville Rd West Harrison (47060) *(G-16551)*

Sierra Interiors, Bristol *Also Called: Sierra Motor Corp (G-1292)*

Sierra Machine... 574 232-5694
  26378 Lakeview Dr South Bend (46619) *(G-15242)*

Sierra Motor Corp... 574 848-1300
  19224 County Road 8 Bristol (46507) *(G-1292)*

Sifford Custom Welding... 765 969-3473
  246 W 1000 S Lynn (47355) *(G-11187)*

Sig Media LLC.. 317 858-7624
  3750 Wallace Ave Indianapolis (46218) *(G-9426)*

Sigma South Division, Elkhart *Also Called: Sigma Switches Plus Inc (G-3676)*

Sigma Steel Inc (PA).. 812 275-4489
  1218 5th St Bedford (47421) *(G-672)*

Sigma Switches Plus Inc... 574 294-5776
  4703 Wyland Dr Elkhart (46516) *(G-3676)*

Sigma Wire International LLC....................................... 574 295-9660
  4906 Hoffman St Ste B Elkhart (46516) *(G-3677)*

Sign A Rama.. 812 477-7763
  1300 N Royal Ave Evansville (47715) *(G-4310)*

(PA)=Parent Co (HQ)=Headquarters (DH)=Div Headquarters

Sign A Rama — ALPHABETIC SECTION

Sign A Rama.. 812 537-5516
1090 W Eads Pkwy Lawrenceburg (47025) *(G-10860)*

Sign Arama.. 812 657-7449
3192 Washington St Columbus (47201) *(G-2392)*

Sign Art, Hobart *Also Called: Sign Art Quality Advertising (G-7207)*

Sign Art Etc, Lafayette *Also Called: Olive Branch Etc Inc (G-10660)*

Sign Art LLC.. 317 247-0333
2525 N Shadeland Ave Ste A9 Indianapolis (46219) *(G-9427)*

Sign Art Quality Advertising................................... 219 763-6122
5474 Us Hwy 6 Hobart (46342) *(G-7207)*

Sign Craft Industries Inc... 317 842-8664
8816 Corporation Dr Indianapolis (46256) *(G-9428)*

Sign Creations... 574 204-2179
919 Saint Jerome St Mishawaka (46544) *(G-11993)*

Sign Creations LLC... 574 855-1246
55234 Holmes Rd South Bend (46628) *(G-15243)*

Sign Deals Delivered... 574 276-7404
2949 2b Rd Bremen (46506) *(G-1221)*

Sign Deals Delivered Inc... 574 276-7404
19355 Sundale Dr South Bend (46614) *(G-15244)*

Sign Designs, South Bend *Also Called: McCaffery Sign Designs (G-15142)*

Sign Exchange.. 812 662-9469
3242 S Us Highway 421 Greensburg (47240) *(G-6631)*

Sign Exchange.. 812 621-2527
1022 S County Road 625 E Milan (47031) *(G-11784)*

Sign Experts, Lafayette *Also Called: Creative Inc (G-10561)*

Sign Fab, Indianapolis *Also Called: Isf Inc (G-8594)*

Sign Factory.. 574 255-7446
55811 Elder Rd Mishawaka (46545) *(G-11994)*

Sign Factory, Indianapolis *Also Called: Mjs Businesses LLC (G-8938)*

Sign For It LLC.. 317 834-4636
68 W Main St Mooresville (46158) *(G-12242)*

Sign Graphics Evansville Inc.................................... 812 476-9151
6020 Feltman Dr Evansville (47711) *(G-4311)*

Sign Group Inc.. 317 228-8049
5370 W 84th St Indianapolis (46268) *(G-9429)*

Sign Group Inc (PA).. 317 875-6969
5370 W 84th St Indianapolis (46268) *(G-9430)*

Sign Guy.. 812 345-2515
4079 N Brookwood Dr Bloomington (47404) *(G-970)*

Sign Guys Inc.. 317 875-7446
80 S Serenity Way Greenwood (46142) *(G-6767)*

Sign Gypsies, New Albany *Also Called: Sign Gypsies Louisville LLC (G-12813)*

Sign Gypsies Louisville LLC..................................... 281 743-2137
1009 Silver St New Albany (47150) *(G-12813)*

Sign Here Ltd.. 317 487-8001
4444 Decatur Blvd Ste 1200 Indianapolis (46241) *(G-9431)*

Sign Lighting... 502 664-6655
1663 Kenwood Ave New Albany (47150) *(G-12814)*

Sign Masters... 765 525-7446
207 S Taylor St Saint Paul (47272) *(G-14469)*

Sign Pro, Fort Wayne *Also Called: Sign Pro of Fort Wayne Inc (G-5415)*

Sign Pro, Kokomo *Also Called: Cumulus Intrmdate Holdings Inc (G-10252)*

Sign Pro of Fort Wayne Inc....................................... 260 497-8484
7710 Lima Rd Fort Wayne (46818) *(G-5415)*

Sign Pros... 765 289-2177
3509 W County Road 400 N Muncie (47304) *(G-12492)*

Sign Pros Inc... 765 642-1175
633 Jackson St Anderson (46016) *(G-192)*

Sign Pros of Marion... 765 677-1234
4260 S 400 W Marion (46953) *(G-11338)*

Sign Services.. 317 546-1111
1305 W 29th St Indianapolis (46208) *(G-9432)*

Sign Solutions Inc.. 317 881-1818
505 Commerce Parkway West Dr Greenwood (46143) *(G-6768)*

Sign Solutions Inc.. 317 535-5757
121 Crossroads Dr Whiteland (46184) *(G-16796)*

Sign Source One Group Inc...................................... 219 736-5865
3429 Michigan St Hobart (46342) *(G-7208)*

Sign Stop LLC... 812 460-0119
1515 S 3rd St Terre Haute (47802) *(G-15693)*

Sign Store Inc... 812 537-0102
101 W Eads Pkwy Lawrenceburg (47025) *(G-10861)*

Sign Together... 812 219-2338
2103 S Georgetown Rd Bloomington (47401) *(G-971)*

Sign Up 4 Fun... 317 800-3535
11729 Tidewater Dr S Indianapolis (46236) *(G-9433)*

Sign Write Signs LLC... 219 477-3840
1451 Joliet Rd Valparaiso (46385) *(G-16050)*

Sign-A-Rama... 317 477-2400
1302 W Main St Greenfield (46140) *(G-6551)*

Sign-A-Rama, Evansville *Also Called: Sign A Rama (G-4310)*

Sign-A-Rama, Indianapolis *Also Called: A Harris Verl Inc (G-7400)*

Sign-A-Rama, Lawrenceburg *Also Called: Sign A Rama (G-10860)*

Sign-Age Inc.. 765 778-5254
178 S Heritage Way Pendleton (46064) *(G-13553)*

Signal 10 Supply, Walton *Also Called: Brayden Shedron (G-16281)*

Signaling Solution Inc... 812 533-1345
6274 N County Road 25 E Shelburn (47879) *(G-14721)*

Signart & Vinyl LLC.. 765 644-5290
5132 W State Road 32 Anderson (46011) *(G-193)*

Signature Formulations LLC.................................... 317 878-1086
3 Trafalgar Sq Trafalgar (46181) *(G-15833)*

Signature Metals Inc... 317 335-2207
6315 Pin Oak Dr Mccordsville (46055) *(G-11455)*

Signature Signs.. 765 717-9851
10610 W State Road 32 Parker City (47368) *(G-13506)*

Signcenter Inc.. 812 232-4994
333 N Fruitridge Ave Terre Haute (47803) *(G-15694)*

Signcrafters Inc (PA)... 812 424-9011
1508 Stringtown Rd Evansville (47711) *(G-4312)*

Signcrafters Inc.. 317 579-4800
7602 E 88th Pl Indianapolis (46256) *(G-9434)*

Signdoc Identity LLC... 317 247-9670
3150 Rand Rd Indianapolis (46241) *(G-9435)*

Signet Cabinetry Inc.. 812 248-0612
1400 Service Dr Sellersburg (47172) *(G-14614)*

Signet Millwork LLC... 812 248-0612
1400 Service Dr Sellersburg (47172) *(G-14615)*

Signgrafx & Engraving, Richmond *Also Called: Thousand One Inc (G-14218)*

Signified Signs Inc... 219 712-7385
8356 E 137th Ave Crown Point (46307) *(G-2751)*

Signified Signs Inc... 219 712-7385
Portage (46368) *(G-13915)*

Signplex LLC... 765 795-7446
4 W Market St Cloverdale (46120) *(G-2098)*

Signrite.. 812 320-5245
2351 W Thrasher Rd Bloomington (47403) *(G-972)*

Signs & Designs By Lewis... 574 223-9403
2220 W 2nd St Rochester (46975) *(G-14325)*

Signs & Stripes By Carr... 317 432-9215
8970 W Us Highway 136 Jamestown (46147) *(G-9820)*

Signs AP & Awards On Time LLC............................. 219 661-4488
10740 Broadway Crown Point (46307) *(G-2752)*

Signs By Design LLC... 812 853-7784
4133 Merchant Dr Ste 5 Newburgh (47630) *(G-13021)*

Signs By Don... 219 374-6754
12998 Oakdale Pl Cedar Lake (46303) *(G-1837)*

Signs By Sulane Inc... 765 565-6773
5920 W 850 N Carthage (46115) *(G-1818)*

Signs By Susie.. 812 385-2739
4288 S Old State Road 65 Princeton (47670) *(G-14011)*

Signs By TM LLC.. 317 872-3220
6246 La Pas Trl Indianapolis (46268) *(G-9436)*

Signs By Tmrrow Indianapolis NW, Indianapolis *Also Called: Aarvee Associates LLC (G-7411)*

Signs By Tomorrow, Valparaiso *Also Called: Bob Prescott (G-15918)*

Signs Etc... 574 674-9671
10170 Glenwood Ave Osceola (46561) *(G-13402)*

Signs In Time, Fort Wayne *Also Called: Signs In Time By Greg Inc (G-5416)*

Signs In Time By Greg Inc... 260 749-7446
4306 Lake Ave Fort Wayne (46815) *(G-5416)*

Signs Inc International.. 317 925-2835
2525 N Shadeland Ave Ste A9 Indianapolis (46219) *(G-9437)*

ALPHABETIC SECTION — Simtra Biopharma Solutions

Signs Magic LLC 812 473-5155
716 N Weinbach Ave Evansville (47711) *(G-4313)*

Signs More 317 392-9184
628 Highpointe Blvd Shelbyville (46176) *(G-14799)*

Signs Now 812 323-2776
2500 W Industrial Park Dr Bloomington (47404) *(G-973)*

Signs Now, Clarksville *Also Called: Seaton Springs Inc (G-2035)*

Signs Now, Evansville *Also Called: Signs Magic LLC (G-4313)*

Signs Now Jeffersonville 812 282-2440
590 Missouri Ave Ste 104 Jeffersonville (47130) *(G-10054)*

Signs of Progress LLC 317 340-7225
5363 Randolph Crescent Dr Carmel (46033) *(G-1760)*

Signs of Seasons 219 866-4507
2675 W Clark St Rensselaer (47978) *(G-14068)*

Signs of Times 574 296-7464
2201 S Nappanee St Elkhart (46517) *(G-3678)*

Signs of Times, Poland *Also Called: Ron Glasscock (G-13837)*

Signs of Times LLC 812 981-3000
714 Mount Tabor Rd New Albany (47150) *(G-12815)*

Signs On Time Inc 219 661-4488
10740 Broadway Crown Point (46307) *(G-2753)*

Signs Overnite Inc 219 365-4088
8304 Cline Ave Crown Point (46307) *(G-2754)*

Signs Success 765 427-1437
107 E Us Highway 52 Otterbein (47970) *(G-13455)*

Signs To Go 502 533-0090
7904 Old State Road 60 Sellersburg (47172) *(G-14616)*

Signs Unlimited 574 255-0500
4121 Lincolnway E Mishawaka (46544) *(G-11995)*

Signtech, Goshen *Also Called: Signtech Sign Services Inc (G-6255)*

Signtech Sign Services Inc 574 537-8080
1508 Bashor Rd Goshen (46528) *(G-6255)*

Signworks 219 462-5353
2003 Calumet Ave Valparaiso (46383) *(G-16051)*

Signworks LLC 317 872-8722
5349 W 86th St Indianapolis (46268) *(G-9438)*

Sigstr Inc 317 960-3003
20 N Meridian St Ste 400 # 4 Indianapolis (46204) *(G-9439)*

Sil Magazine, Marengo *Also Called: Sil Publishing Co LLC (G-11265)*

Sil Publishing Co LLC 812 989-8871
2176 Ne Trestle Lane Marengo (47140) *(G-11265)*

Sila Seal, Indianapolis *Also Called: Meyer Plastics Inc (G-8895)*

Silas Beachler 260 578-1625
9569 S 600 E Claypool (46510) *(G-2057)*

Silberline Mfg Co Inc 260 728-2111
2010 Guy Brown Dr Decatur (46733) *(G-2883)*

Silberline of Indiana, Decatur *Also Called: Silberline Mfg Co Inc (G-2883)*

Silca, Indianapolis *Also Called: Aeromind LLC (G-7453)*

Silcotec, La Porte *Also Called: Silcotec Inc (G-10482)*

Silcotec Inc 219 324-4411
707 Boyd Blvd La Porte (46350) *(G-10482)*

Silgan, Hammond *Also Called: Silgan Containers Mfg Corp (G-7006)*

Silgan, La Porte *Also Called: Silgan Containers Mfg Corp (G-10483)*

Silgan, Ligonier *Also Called: Silgan Plastics LLC (G-11023)*

Silgan, Seymour *Also Called: Silgan Plastics LLC (G-14692)*

Silgan, Seymour *Also Called: Silgan Plastics LLC (G-14693)*

Silgan Closures, Evansville *Also Called: Silgan White Cap LLC (G-4314)*

Silgan Containers Mfg Corp 219 845-1500
2501 165th St Ste 2 Hammond (46320) *(G-7006)*

Silgan Containers Mfg Corp 219 362-7002
300 N Fail Rd La Porte (46350) *(G-10483)*

Silgan Plastics LLC 260 894-7814
910 Gerber St Ligonier (46767) *(G-11023)*

Silgan Plastics LLC 812 522-0900
3779 N County Road 850 E Seymour (47274) *(G-14692)*

Silgan Plastics LLC 812 522-0900
S O Brien St Seymour (47274) *(G-14693)*

Silgan White Cap LLC 812 425-6222
2201 W Maryland St Evansville (47712) *(G-4314)*

Silgan White Cap LLC 765 983-9200
1701 Williamsburg Pike Richmond (47374) *(G-14205)*

Silhouette Body Sculpt LLC 219 237-2391
9219 Indianapolis Blvd Ste 200 Highland (46322) *(G-7155)*

Silicis Technologies Inc 317 896-5044
17225 Westfield Park Rd Westfield (46074) *(G-16728)*

Silk Mountain Creations Inc 317 815-1660
1117 S Rangeline Rd Carmel (46032) *(G-1761)*

Sills Custom Works & Fab LLC 219 200-9813
6082 E 25 N Knox (46534) *(G-10224)*

Silva Military Solutions, Fort Wayne *Also Called: Innovations By (G-5109)*

Silverthorn Handyman Svcs LLC 812 896-4201
3395 W State Road 60 Salem (47167) *(G-14498)*

Silverwood Signs, Greencastle *Also Called: Steve Stamper (G-6432)*

Sim2k Inc 317 251-7920
7160 Graham Rd Indianapolis (46250) *(G-9440)*

Siman Promotions Inc 260 637-5621
904 Mill Pointe Fort Wayne (46845) *(G-5417)*

Simcha Ai Inc 415 702-5919
326 W Us Highway 30 Schererville (46375) *(G-14544)*

Simco of Southern Indiana 812 890-6225
2585 W Heidelberg Rd Sw Corydon (47112) *(G-2516)*

Simeoc LLC 240 210-5685
18125 Chipstead Dr South Bend (46637) *(G-15245)*

Simko & Sons Inc 219 933-9100
4545 Ash Ave Hammond (46327) *(G-7007)*

Simko Industrial Fabricators 219 933-9100
4545 Ash Ave Hammond (46327) *(G-7008)*

Simko Signs LLC 219 308-6000
7570 E 109th Ave Crown Point (46307) *(G-2755)*

Simma Software Inc 812 418-0526
5940 S Ernest St Terre Haute (47802) *(G-15695)*

Simmons Equipment Sales Inc 260 625-3308
6025 S State Road 9 Columbia City (46725) *(G-2197)*

Simmons Winery & Farm Mkt Inc 812 546-0091
8111 E 450 N Columbus (47203) *(G-2393)*

Simon and Sons 812 852-3636
5802 N Us Highway 421 Osgood (47037) *(G-13416)*

Simon S Pit Stop, Osgood *Also Called: Gary Simons (G-13408)*

Simone-Chrisette Pubg LLC 317 985-9851
10838 Tallow Wood Ln Indianapolis (46236) *(G-9441)*

Simple Glow Candle Co 260 435-0062
9501 Chapmans Blvd Fort Wayne (46835) *(G-5418)*

Simple Sign Solutions Inc 317 272-5224
9985 Waterside Dr Noblesville (46060) *(G-13175)*

Simple To Elegant LLC 812 234-8700
1601 S 3rd St Terre Haute (47802) *(G-15696)*

Simplex Computer Services 260 570-7062
1405 Willow Dr Auburn (46706) *(G-423)*

Simplified Imaging LLC 219 663-5122
1126 Arrowhead Ct Crown Point (46307) *(G-2756)*

Simply Amazing 219 464-9621
2801 Evans Ave Valparaiso (46383) *(G-16052)*

Simply Good Foods Usa Inc 317 622-4154
3023 N Distribution Way Unit 200 Greenfield (46140) *(G-6552)*

Simply Natural By J LLC 317 464-7299
2269 Tradewinds Dr Apt H Indianapolis (46229) *(G-9442)*

Simply Saidahs LLC 317 650-4256
4000 W 106th St Ste 125-130 Carmel (46032) *(G-1762)*

Simply Sdahs Natural Skin Care, Carmel *Also Called: Simply Saidahs LLC (G-1762)*

Simply Silver 260 824-4667
1165 Fawncrest Ct Bluffton (46714) *(G-1053)*

Simply Swank HM Dcor Signs LLC 574 204-2339
12650 Adams Rd Granger (46530) *(G-6377)*

Simpson Aerospace Services, Elizabeth *Also Called: Simpson Alloy Services Inc (G-3129)*

Simpson Alloy Services Inc 812 969-2766
7017 Old Highway 111 Se Elizabeth (47117) *(G-3129)*

Sims, Clarksville *Also Called: Siddhi Integrated Mfg Svcs Inc (G-2036)*

Sims Cabinet Co Inc (PA) 317 634-1747
778 Robertson Ct Danville (46122) *(G-2828)*

Sims-Lohman Inc 317 467-0710
725 E Main St Greenfield (46140) *(G-6553)*

Simtra Biopharma Solutions, Bloomington *Also Called: Baxter Phrm Solutions LLC (G-798)*

Simtra Biopharma Solutions

ALPHABETIC SECTION

Simtra Biopharma Solutions, Bloomington Also Called: Baxter Phrm Solutions LLC *(G-799)*
Sincerely Different LLC.. 574 292-1727
51860 Sharon Ct Granger (46530) *(G-6378)*
Sincerely Naiya LLC.. 602 518-3870
213 E Kickapoo St Hartford City (47348) *(G-7076)*
Sinclair Glass, Hartford City Also Called: Middletown Enterprises Inc *(G-7071)*
Sinden Racing Service Inc.. 317 243-7171
1201 Main St Indianapolis (46224) *(G-9443)*
Sinflex Paper Co Inc.. 765 789-6688
301 S Butterfield Rd Muncie (47303) *(G-12493)*
Singer Optical Company Inc... 812 423-1179
1401 N Royal Ave Evansville (47715) *(G-4315)*
Singing Pines Projects Inc.. 812 988-8807
2499 State Road 45 Nashville (47448) *(G-12680)*
Single Inc.. 812 877-2220
96 Woodbine Terre Haute (47803) *(G-15697)*
Single Source Medical LLC.. 574 656-3400
791 Industrial Pkwy North Liberty (46554) *(G-13224)*
Singles Ministry, The, Tippecanoe Also Called: Gen Enterprises *(G-15759)*
Singleton Machine Inc.. 574 656-3400
791 Industrial Pkwy North Liberty (46554) *(G-13225)*
Sir Graphics Inc.. 574 272-9330
12599 Industrial Park Dr Granger (46530) *(G-6379)*
Sirmax North America Inc.. 765 639-0300
2915 Dr Martin Luther King Jr Blvd Anderson (46016) *(G-194)*
Sisco Box, Evansville Also Called: Sisco Corporation *(G-4316)*
Sisco Corporation.. 812 422-2090
1231 E Michigan St Evansville (47711) *(G-4316)*
Sisk Rifles Manufacturing LLC.. 812 686-8067
914 S Boundary Way Tell City (47586) *(G-15517)*
Sisson & Son Mfg Jewelers.. 574 967-4331
7 W Main St Flora (46929) *(G-4665)*
Sisson Steel Inc.. 812 354-8701
739 S State Road 61 Winslow (47598) *(G-16922)*
Sissys Ceramics.. 951 550-7728
30803 County Road 20 Elkhart (46517) *(G-3679)*
Sister Pines Signs... 219 242-1824
875 Thoreau Trl Valparaiso (46383) *(G-16053)*
Sit Can Happen LLC.. 812 346-4188
130 N County Road 400 W North Vernon (47265) *(G-13295)*
Site Enhancement Services, South Bend Also Called: North American Signs Inc *(G-15170)*
Siteone Landscape Supply LLC.. 219 769-2351
4068 W 82nd Ct Merrillville (46410) *(G-11560)*
Sites-Workman Holdings Inc... 574 267-1503
1195 Polk Dr Warsaw (46582) *(G-16424)*
Sitesuccess Inc... 219 808-4076
521 Saint Andrews Dr Schererville (46375) *(G-14545)*
Sitewise Inc... 317 988-1630
4440 S High School Rd Indianapolis (46241) *(G-9444)*
Sittin Pretty LLC.. 219 947-4121
9470 Randolph St Crown Point (46307) *(G-2757)*
Six Mile Welding LLC... 260 768-3126
40 S 600 W Lagrange (46761) *(G-10759)*
Six Six Graphics, Brownsburg Also Called: Six Six Sublimation LLC *(G-1403)*
Six Six Sublimation LLC... 317 858-5211
1531 E Northfield Dr Ste 300 Brownsburg (46112) *(G-1403)*
Sizzlin Sound Productions LLC... 765 376-0129
2297 E Traction Rd Crawfordsville (47933) *(G-2615)*
SJ Sales Inc.. 260 433-5947
6715 Wood Glen Ct Fort Wayne (46814) *(G-5419)*
Sjc Industries Corp.. 574 264-7511
1110 D I Dr Elkhart (46514) *(G-3680)*
Sjg Enterprises Inc.. 574 269-4806
3304 Lake City Hwy Warsaw (46580) *(G-16425)*
SJS Components LLC... 260 578-0192
6778 S State Road 13 Warsaw (46580) *(G-16426)*
Sk Beer, Indianapolis Also Called: Sun King Brewing Company LLC *(G-9525)*
Sk Marktng Strtgies LLC DBA A....................................... 812 962-0900
10400 W Boonville New Harmony Rd Evansville (47720) *(G-4317)*
Ski Inc... 317 401-6222
204 Lucky Ln Pendleton (46064) *(G-13554)*

Skinny & Co Inc... 888 865-4278
5762 W 74th St Ste 117 Indianapolis (46278) *(G-9445)*
Skipper Rota Corporation... 708 331-0660
130 E 168th St Crown Point (46307) *(G-2758)*
Skips Bumper Repair... 773 289-2255
520 W Ridge Rd Gary (46408) *(G-6010)*
Skjodt Ink, Carmel Also Called: Maple Leaf Graphics Inc *(G-1691)*
Skjodt-Barrett Foods Inc.. 765 482-6856
401 S Enterprise Blvd Lebanon (46052) *(G-10942)*
Sky Cryptoassets LLC... 949 903-6896
14530 Baldwin Ln Carmel (46032) *(G-1763)*
Sky High Graphix LLC... 260 267-0724
1501 S Clinton St Fort Wayne (46866) *(G-5420)*
Sky High Sign Service... 765 436-7012
6716 N 1075 W Thorntown (46071) *(G-15755)*
Sky Thunder LLC... 812 397-0102
6521 N Us Highway 41 Shelburn (47879) *(G-14722)*
Skyepack LLC... 765 323-8568
3000 Kent Ave West Lafayette (47906) *(G-16628)*
Skyline Champion Corporation... 574 294-6521
2520 Bypass Rd Elkhart (46515) *(G-3681)*
Skyline Corporation... 574 294-2463
401 County Road 15 Elkhart (46516) *(G-3682)*
Skyline Homes Inc (HQ).. 574 294-6521
2520 Bypass Rd Elkhart (46514) *(G-3683)*
Skyline Mainsfield, Elkhart Also Called: Homette Corporation *(G-3410)*
Skyline Signs & Awnings, Delphi Also Called: Skyline Signs Inc *(G-2908)*
Skyline Signs Inc... 765 564-4422
1989 W Mill St Delphi (46923) *(G-2908)*
Skytech II LLC... 260 459-1703
9230 Conservation Way Fort Wayne (46809) *(G-5421)*
Skytech-Systems Inc... 260 459-1703
9230 Conservation Way Fort Wayne (46809) *(G-5422)*
Skyway Fuels Inc.. 219 575-7624
1131 S Redbud Dr La Porte (46350) *(G-10484)*
SL Beauty LLC.. 317 969-0341
2212 Emrich Ln Indianapolis (46222) *(G-9446)*
SL Terrastar Group LLC.. 317 702-7240
55 S State Ave Ste 318 Indianapolis (46201) *(G-9447)*
Slabach Logging LLC.. 260 768-4644
7615 W 200 N Shipshewana (46565) *(G-14889)*
Slabaugh Meat Processing LLC....................................... 574 773-0381
72700 County Road 101 Nappanee (46550) *(G-12645)*
Slabaugh Metal Fab LLC... 574 342-0554
1860 12th Rd Bourbon (46504) *(G-1128)*
Slabaugh Storage Barns Inc.. 260 768-7989
9550 W 375 N Shipshewana (46565) *(G-14890)*
Slabaugh Welding LLC.. 574 773-5410
3942 W 1350 N Milford (46542) *(G-11806)*
Slade Print, Evansville Also Called: Thomas E Slade Inc *(G-4343)*
Slate Mechanical Inc... 765 452-9611
4602 W 100 N Kokomo (46901) *(G-10335)*
Slater Concrete Products Inc... 260 347-0164
322 E Wayne St Kendallville (46755) *(G-10152)*
Slater Publishing Co, Westville Also Called: WAr - LLC- Westville Prtg *(G-16765)*
Slatile Roofing and Shtmtl Co.. 574 233-7485
1703 S Ironwood Dr Ste A South Bend (46613) *(G-15246)*
Slavica Publishers... 812 856-4186
1430 N Willis Dr Bloomington (47404) *(G-974)*
Slavica Publishers, Bloomington Also Called: Trustees Indiana University *(G-998)*
Slb Corporation... 574 255-9774
1906 E Mckinley Ave Mishawaka (46545) *(G-11996)*
Sld of The Adidas Group, Indianapolis Also Called: Sports Licensed Division *(G-9481)*
Sledgehammer Printing Corp... 812 629-2160
4956 State Route 261 Newburgh (47630) *(G-13022)*
Sleegers, Indianapolis Also Called: Sleegers Engineered Pdts Inc *(G-9448)*
Sleegers Engineered Pdts Inc.. 317 786-7770
5855 Kopetsky Dr Ste I Indianapolis (46217) *(G-9448)*
SLEEP EASY TECHNOLOGY INC................................... 208 241-3264
1400 E Angela Blvd Unit 147 South Bend (46617) *(G-15247)*
Sleepmadecom LLC.. 662 350-0999
2625 Kotter Ave Evansville (47715) *(G-4318)*

ALPHABETIC SECTION

Slicers 812 255-0655
  2715 Washington Ave Vincennes (47591) *(G-16155)*

Slingshot Media LLC 765 778-6848
  600 Corporation Dr Pendleton (46064) *(G-13555)*

SLM Mrkting Communications Inc 812 426-7993
  605 S Evans Ave Evansville (47713) *(G-4319)*

Sloan, Rodney Logging, Batesville *Also Called: Rodney Sloan Logging Inc (G-605)*

Slon Inc 765 884-1792
  206 N Harrison Ave Fowler (47944) *(G-5633)*

SM Industries LLC 219 613-5295
  13701 Limerick Dr Saint John (46373) *(G-14458)*

Small Parts Inc 574 739-6236
  112 E Mildred St Logansport (46947) *(G-11106)*

Small Parts Inc (HQ) 574 753-6323
  600 Humphrey St Logansport (46947) *(G-11107)*

Small Repairs/Mobile For Ind, Clinton *Also Called: Mrrx Mobile Railcar Repair LLC (G-2072)*

Small Town Printers LLC 812 596-1536
  6265 Sand Hill Rd Se Elizabeth (47117) *(G-3130)*

Small World Enterprises LLC 312 550-1717
  3822 Central Ave Lake Station (46405) *(G-10776)*

Smalltown Coffee Co LLC 816 288-0687
  306 E Goldsborough St Crown Point (46307) *(G-2759)*

Smart Choice Mobile Inc 574 830-5727
  4542 Elkhart Rd Elkhart (46517) *(G-3684)*

Smart Displays LLC 812 322-3912
  5660 N Murat Rd Bloomington (47408) *(G-975)*

Smart Machine Inc 219 922-0706
  9941 Express Dr Hammond (46322) *(G-7009)*

Smart Manufacturing Inc 765 482-7481
  228 W 700 S Lebanon (46052) *(G-10943)*

Smart Pergola 317 987-7750
  12958 Brighton Ave Carmel (46032) *(G-1764)*

Smart Products, Muncie *Also Called: Sp Holdings Inc (G-12494)*

Smart Systems 800 348-0823
  303 S Byrkit St Mishawaka (46544) *(G-11997)*

Smart Technologies LLC 317 738-4338
  317 E Creekside Ct W Franklin (46131) *(G-5777)*

Smart Temps LLC 574 217-7202
  435 Park Place Cir Ste 100 Mishawaka (46545) *(G-11998)*

Smarter Home Technology Inc 815 677-6885
  355 Fuquay Rd Chandler (47610) *(G-1866)*

Smartfile, Indianapolis *Also Called: Secured Ftp Hosting LLC (G-9398)*

Smartt Innovations Inc 574 266-5432
  54160 Adams St Elkhart (46514) *(G-3685)*

SMC, Noblesville *Also Called: SMC Corporation of America (G-13176)*

SMC Corporation of America (HQ) 317 899-4440
  10100 Smc Blvd Noblesville (46060) *(G-13176)*

Smco Inc 574 295-1482
  2505 Laura Ct Elkhart (46517) *(G-3686)*

Smed - Ta/Td LLC 260 625-3347
  4707 E Park 30 Dr Columbia City (46725) *(G-2198)*

Smg Global Inc 765 250-0081
  3701 David Howarth Dr Ste B Lafayette (47909) *(G-10691)*

Smgf LLC 812 354-8899
  3377 N State Road 57 Petersburg (47567) *(G-13625)*

SMI Seller Inc 765 825-3121
  Connersville (47331) *(G-2466)*

Smile Promotions, Bloomington *Also Called: Smiling Cross Inc (G-976)*

Smiles Motors LLC 219 801-5255
  2646 Highway Ave Highland (46322) *(G-7156)*

Smiling Cross Inc 812 323-9290
  700 S College Ave Ste A Bloomington (47403) *(G-976)*

Smith & Butterfield, Evansville *Also Called: Smith & Butterfield Inc (G-4320)*

Smith & Butterfield Co Inc (DH) 812 422-3261
  2800 Lynch Rd Ste D Evansville (47711) *(G-4320)*

Smith & Butterfield Co Inc 812 422-3261
  2800 Lynch Rd Ste D Evansville (47711) *(G-4321)*

Smith & Nephew Inc 800 357-6155
  8434 Georgetown Rd Indianapolis (46268) *(G-9449)*

Smith Brothers Berne Inc (PA) 260 589-2131
  356 Monroe St Berne (46711) *(G-726)*

Smith Business Supply Inc 765 654-4442
  358 N Columbia St Frankfort (46041) *(G-5694)*

Smith Consulting Inc 765 728-5980
  850 W Huntington St Montpelier (47359) *(G-12181)*

Smith Custom Cabinets 812 342-4797
  1196 N Nelson Ridge Rd Columbus (47201) *(G-2394)*

Smith Excavating 812 636-0054
  10122 E 1400 N Odon (47562) *(G-13351)*

Smith Expediting Resources LLC 317 935-1180
  8520 Allison Pointe Blvd Ste 220 Indianapolis (46250) *(G-9450)*

Smith Graphics & Design, Mishawaka *Also Called: Smith Signs Inc (G-11999)*

Smith Group Precision LLC 855 927-6224
  2124 Dixie Hwy Bedford (47421) *(G-673)*

Smith Machine and Tool 574 223-2318
  3392 Wabash Ave Rochester (46975) *(G-14326)*

Smith Metal Finishing, Fort Wayne *Also Called: Lambert Metal Finishing Inc (G-5174)*

Smith Printing, Linton *Also Called: D & M Printing Inc (G-11034)*

Smith Ready Mix Inc (PA) 219 462-3191
  251 Lincolnway Valparaiso (46383) *(G-16054)*

Smith Signs Inc 574 255-6446
  317 Capital Ave Mishawaka (46544) *(G-11999)*

Smith Sound 765 464-2961
  2340 Sagamore Pkwy W Lot 4 West Lafayette (47906) *(G-16629)*

Smith Technologies 317 839-6766
  5832 Oberlies Way Plainfield (46168) *(G-13729)*

Smith Tire Inc 574 267-8261
  2335 N Detroit St Ste A Warsaw (46580) *(G-16427)*

Smith Welding 765 438-4173
  3170 S 110 W Tipton (46072) *(G-15790)*

Smith, M G Sign Painting, Fort Wayne *Also Called: Marshall G Smith Sign Painting (G-5203)*

Smith's Radiator Service, Cambridge City *Also Called: Anthony Smith (G-1490)*

Smith's Small Engines, Terre Haute *Also Called: Smiths Small Engines Inc (G-15699)*

Smithfield Direct LLC 812 867-6644
  8426 Baumgart Rd Evansville (47725) *(G-4322)*

Smithfield Direct LLC 765 473-3086
  3311 S State Road 19 Peru (46970) *(G-13600)*

Smithfield Foods, Greenfield *Also Called: Smithfield Foods Inc (G-6554)*

Smithfield Foods Inc 812 446-2328
  195 N Sherman St Brazil (47834) *(G-1165)*

Smithfield Foods Inc 317 891-1888
  3271 N Distribution Way Greenfield (46140) *(G-6554)*

Smithland Butchering Co Inc 317 729-5398
  11420 S Us Highway 31 Elizabethtown (47232) *(G-3133)*

Smiths Arospc Components Haute 812 235-5210
  333 S 3rd St Terre Haute (47807) *(G-15698)*

Smiths Enterprises Inc 765 378-6267
  1124 Dilts St Chesterfield (46017) *(G-1898)*

Smiths Medical Asd Inc 219 554-2196
  5700 W 23rd Ave Gary (46406) *(G-6011)*

Smiths Small Engines Inc 812 232-1318
  1515 N 25th St Terre Haute (47803) *(G-15699)*

Smiths Woodcraft 765 395-8044
  4804 N 1300 E 34 Converse (46919) *(G-2480)*

Smitson Cmmnications Group LLC 317 876-8916
  3500 Depauw Blvd Ste 1000 Indianapolis (46268) *(G-9451)*

Smock Materials Handling Co 317 890-3200
  3420 Park Davis Cir Indianapolis (46235) *(G-9452)*

Smoke Smoke Smoke 219 942-3331
  1165 W 37th Ave Hobart (46342) *(G-7209)*

Smoked Bros LLC 360 440-6948
  7007 Windsong Ct Georgetown (47122) *(G-6075)*

Smoked Q LLC 260 494-5029
  921 E Dupont Rd Fort Wayne (46825) *(G-5423)*

Smoker Craft Inc (PA) 574 831-2103
  68143 Clunette St New Paris (46553) *(G-12968)*

Smoker Friendly 812 556-0244
  1925 Newton St Jasper (47546) *(G-9912)*

Smokers Iron Works 574 674-6683
  30907 County Road 16 Elkhart (46516) *(G-3687)*

Smor Cases Inc 574 291-0346
  4622 S Burnett Dr South Bend (46614) *(G-15248)*

SMR Management Inc — ALPHABETIC SECTION

SMR Management Inc.. 765 252-0257
  2139 Klondike Rd Lafayette (47906) *(G-10692)*
SMR MANAGEMENT INC, Lafayette Also Called: SMR Management Inc *(G-10692)*
SMS Group Inc... 219 880-0256
  201 Mississippi St Ste 12a Gary (46402) *(G-6012)*
SMS Technical Services, Gary Also Called: SMS Group Inc *(G-6012)*
Smurfit Stone Container, Wabash Also Called: Paperworks Industries Inc *(G-16210)*
Sna LLC... 317 931-1022
  8309 Hampton Cir E Indianapolis (46256) *(G-9453)*
Snake Sandbags LLC... 317 721-1006
  1300 E 86th St Unit 90165 Carmel (46290) *(G-1765)*
Snapple Beverage Corp.. 812 424-7978
  1100 Independence Ave Evansville (47714) *(G-4323)*
Snappy Minds Llc... 812 661-8506
  1330 Cobblestone Rd Jasper (47546) *(G-9913)*
Snavely Machine, Peru Also Called: Snavelys Machine & Mfg Co Inc *(G-13601)*
Snavelys Machine & Mfg Co Inc................................. 765 473-8395
  1070 Industrial Pkwy Peru (46970) *(G-13601)*
Snax In Pax Inc.. 260 593-3066
  204 Hawpatch Dr Topeka (46571) *(G-15819)*
Sneaky Micro Video Divisio.. 317 925-1496
  3216 N Pennsylvania St Indianapolis (46205) *(G-9454)*
Snep Sign Co.. 260 982-6016
  14767 N State Road 13 North Manchester (46962) *(G-13250)*
Snider Tire, Bluffton Also Called: Snider Tire Inc *(G-1054)*
Snider Tire Inc... 260 824-4520
  1400 W Wiley Ave Bluffton (46714) *(G-1054)*
Snodgrass Sheet Metal, Indianapolis Also Called: Bright Sheet Metal Company Inc *(G-7683)*
Snow Management Group.. 574 252-5253
  14009 Jefferson Blvd Mishawaka (46545) *(G-12000)*
Snowbird Industries LLC.. 716 481-1142
  1116 N Linwood Ave Indianapolis (46201) *(G-9455)*
Snyders Prtble Wldg Fbrication................................... 574 258-4015
  Mishawaka (46546) *(G-12001)*
Snyders-Lance Inc.. 317 270-7599
  10100 Lantern Rd Fishers (46037) *(G-4605)*
Snyders-Lance Inc.. 317 858-2209
  9040 Orly Rd Indianapolis (46241) *(G-9456)*
Snyders-Lance Inc.. 812 285-0939
  125 Peacely St Jeffersonville (47130) *(G-10055)*
Snykin Inc... 317 845-5051
  3915 E 96th St Indianapolis (46240) *(G-9457)*
So Industries LLC... 765 606-7596
  4197 W 950 S Pendleton (46064) *(G-13556)*
Soap Guy, The, La Porte Also Called: Tall Cotton Marketing LLC *(G-10486)*
Soapequipment.com, Hagerstown Also Called: Willow Way LLC *(G-6849)*
Soapy Soap Co.. 812 269-8812
  2001 N Hunt St Terre Haute (47805) *(G-15700)*
Soapy Soap Company.. 812 269-8812
  2001 N Hunt St Terre Haute (47805) *(G-15701)*
Sober Scientific LLC (PA)... 765 465-9803
  17739 Joliet Rd Sheridan (46069) *(G-14829)*
Sochatti, Indianapolis Also Called: True Essence Foods Inc *(G-9651)*
Society For Ethnmusicology Inc................................... 812 855-6672
  800 E 3rd St Bloomington (47405) *(G-977)*
Sofamor/Danek Group Mfg Div, Warsaw Also Called: Warsaw Orthopedic Inc *(G-16447)*
Soft Stop, Anderson Also Called: Ruby Enterprises Inc *(G-186)*
Softexpert Usa LLC.. 260 925-7674
  625 W 15th St Auburn (46706) *(G-424)*
Software Informatics Group LLC................................ 317 326-2598
  869 N 300 W Greenfield (46140) *(G-6555)*
Software Sales Incorporated...................................... 317 258-7442
  3370 S 450 E Whitestown (46075) *(G-16822)*
Soil-Max, Terre Haute Also Called: Soilmax Inc *(G-15702)*
Soilmax Inc... 888 764-5629
  1201 S 1st St Terre Haute (47802) *(G-15702)*
Sojane Technologies Inc.. 317 915-1059
  9002 N Meridian St Ste 210 Indianapolis (46260) *(G-9458)*
Sojourn Technologies Inc... 317 422-1254
  3485 W 100 N Bargersville (46106) *(G-573)*

Sol Melanin Beauty LLC... 317 354-3977
  7801 Knue Rd Indianapolis (46250) *(G-9459)*
Solae... 260 724-2101
  1200 N 2nd St Decatur (46733) *(G-2884)*
Solae, Remington Also Called: Dupont De Nemours Inc *(G-14034)*
Solae LLC.. 800 325-7108
  413 N Cressy Ave Remington (47977) *(G-14038)*
Solae LLC (PA)... 219 986-6119
  310 N Cressy Ave Remington (47977) *(G-14039)*
Solar Freeze LLC.. 260 499-4973
  214 E Marquis Rd N Lagrange (46761) *(G-10760)*
Solar Freeze LLC.. 260 499-4973
  214 E Marquis Rd N Lagrange (46761) *(G-10761)*
Solar Sources Underground LLC................................. 812 354-2808
  1592 N State Road 61 Petersburg (47567) *(G-13626)*
Solas Ray Lighting, Anderson Also Called: Continental Manufacturing LLC *(G-98)*
Solas Ray Lighting, Indianapolis Also Called: 55 West LLC *(G-7392)*
Solema USA Inc... 765 361-0806
  315 Glenn St Crawfordsville (47933) *(G-2616)*
Solfire, Fort Wayne Also Called: Solfire Contract Mfg Inc *(G-5424)*
Solfire Contract Mfg Inc... 260 755-2115
  4939 Decatur Rd Fort Wayne (46806) *(G-5424)*
Solid Base Waterproofing, Greencastle Also Called: K C Cmponents Wldg Fabrication *(G-6416)*
Solid Rock LLC.. 260 755-2687
  6201 Discount Dr Fort Wayne (46818) *(G-5425)*
Solid Rock Gbc.. 260 723-4806
  213 Reed St South Whitley (46787) *(G-15324)*
Solid Surface Craftsmen Inc...................................... 317 535-2333
  100 Crossroads Dr Ste D Whiteland (46184) *(G-16797)*
Solomon M Eicher.. 812 289-1252
  7809 Henderson Rd Marysville (47141) *(G-11436)*
Soltek, Evansville Also Called: Boyer Enterprises Inc *(G-3943)*
Solutions For Print LLC.. 812 584-2701
  9530 N 100 W Fountaintown (46130) *(G-5616)*
Somaschini North America LLC................................ 574 968-0273
  4601 Nimtz Pkwy South Bend (46628) *(G-15249)*
Somer Inc... 317 873-1111
  11707 N Michigan Rd Zionsville (46077) *(G-17051)*
Somer Dental Laboratories, Zionsville Also Called: Somer Inc *(G-17051)*
Somersaults LLC... 317 747-7496
  10285 Normandy Ct Fishers (46040) *(G-4652)*
Somersaults Life Archives, Fishers Also Called: Somersaults LLC *(G-4652)*
Somethin Sweet Llc... 317 804-4894
  2717 Coldstream Ln Apt 2d Indianapolis (46220) *(G-9460)*
Sommer, Crawfordsville Also Called: Sommer Metalcraft LLC *(G-2617)*
Sommer Awning Group, Indianapolis Also Called: Awning Partners Mfg Group LLC *(G-7579)*
Sommer Letter Company LLC................................... 260 414-6686
  3916 E North County Line Rd Huntertown (46748) *(G-7266)*
Sommer Metalcraft LLC... 765 362-6200
  315 Poston Dr Crawfordsville (47933) *(G-2617)*
Sonam Technologies LLC.. 844 887-6626
  9800 Connecticut Dr Crown Point (46307) *(G-2760)*
Sonicu LLC... 317 468-2345
  11 American Legion Pl Greenfield (46140) *(G-6556)*
Sonlite Pallet Services Inc.. 219 798-5003
  2404 E 73rd Ave Merrillville (46410) *(G-11561)*
Sonny Scaffolds Inc (PA).. 317 831-3900
  319 Harlan Dr Mooresville (46158) *(G-12243)*
Sonobuoy Tech Systems, Columbia City Also Called: Erapsco *(G-2142)*
Sonoco Products, Edinburgh Also Called: Sonoco Products Company *(G-3105)*
Sonoco Products Company.. 574 598-2731
  1535 S State Road 19 Akron (46910) *(G-9)*
Sonoco Products Company.. 812 526-5511
  6502 S Us Highway 31 Edinburgh (46124) *(G-3105)*
Sonoco Prtective Solutions Inc.................................. 260 726-9333
  1619 N Meridian St Portland (47371) *(G-13967)*
Sonoco Teq LLC.. 260 495-9842
  500 W Water St Fremont (46737) *(G-5835)*
Sons of Thunder... 812 897-4908
  1233 Mount Gilead Rd Boonville (47601) *(G-1098)*

Sony Corporation of America.. 812 462-8726
  1800 N Fruitridge Ave Terre Haute (47804) *(G-15703)*
Sony Dadc, Terre Haute *Also Called: Sony Dadc US Inc (G-15706)*
Sony Dadc US Inc.. 812 462-8116
  3181 N Fruitridge Ave Terre Haute (47804) *(G-15704)*
Sony Dadc US Inc.. 812 462-8784
  1600 N Fruitridge Ave Terre Haute (47804) *(G-15705)*
Sony Dadc US Inc (DH)... 812 462-8100
  1800 N Fruitridge Ave Terre Haute (47804) *(G-15706)*
Sonya V Glutenfree, Michigan City *Also Called: Alexson LLC (G-11576)*
Sophistcted Lving Indianapolis.. 317 565-4555
  200 S Rangeline Rd Ste 212 Carmel (46032) *(G-1766)*
Sophysa USA Inc... 219 663-7711
  503 E Summit St Ste 5 Crown Point (46307) *(G-2761)*
Sorbashock LLC... 574 520-9784
  204 Barouche Pl Fort Wayne (46845) *(G-5426)*
Sorbtech Inc... 812 944-9108
  1305 Veterans Pkwy Ste 1000 Clarksville (47129) *(G-2037)*
Sordelet Tool & Die Inc.. 260 483-7258
  2765 E Crescent Ave Columbia City (46725) *(G-2199)*
Sorg Millwork.. 260 639-3223
  10744 S Us Highway 27 Fort Wayne (46816) *(G-5427)*
Sorley Horns LLC... 317 258-2718
  7295 W 350 N Bargersville (46106) *(G-574)*
Sortera Technologies Inc... 260 330-7100
  5224 E Asher Dr Markle (46770) *(G-11362)*
Souder Deryl Co... 765 565-6719
  2918 Harbur Blvd Anderson (46011) *(G-195)*
Souder Walling, Anderson *Also Called: Souder Deryl Co (G-195)*
Soulbrain Mi Inc.. 248 869-3079
  2141 Touby Pike Kokomo (46901) *(G-10336)*
Sound & Graphics... 219 963-7293
  925 Central Ave Rm D Lake Station (46405) *(G-10777)*
Sound Mind Treats.. 317 809-5832
  7646 Sand Pt Apt B Indianapolis (46240) *(G-9461)*
Sound System... 317 407-4092
  5219 Five Points Rd Indianapolis (46239) *(G-9462)*
Source Hospitality Mfg Group, Washington *Also Called: Troy Stuart (G-16510)*
Source Products Inc.. 260 424-0864
  9875 S Washington Rd Columbia City (46725) *(G-2200)*
South Bend Brew Werks LLC... 801 209-2987
  321 S Main St Ste 105 South Bend (46601) *(G-15250)*
South Bend Chocolate Co Inc (PA).. 574 233-2577
  3300 W Sample St Ste 110 South Bend (46619) *(G-15251)*
South Bend Clutch Inc... 574 256-5064
  709 W Jefferson Blvd Mishawaka (46545) *(G-12002)*
South Bend Ethanol LLC.. 574 703-3360
  3201 W Calvert St South Bend (46613) *(G-15252)*
South Bend Form Tool Co Inc.. 574 289-2441
  408 W Indiana Ave South Bend (46613) *(G-15253)*
South Bend Heat Treat Inc.. 574 288-4794
  1331 Northside Blvd South Bend (46615) *(G-15254)*
South Bend Kollel Inc.. 574 299-8263
  3016 Caroline St South Bend (46614) *(G-15255)*
South Bend Metal Products Co, South Bend *Also Called: Shakour Industries Inc (G-15239)*
South Bend Screen Process Inc (PA)....................................... 574 254-9000
  3622 N Home St Mishawaka (46545) *(G-12003)*
South Bend Smoke Time, South Bend *Also Called: South Bend Smoke Time Inc (G-15256)*
South Bend Smoke Time Inc... 574 318-4837
  1841 S Bend Ave South Bend (46637) *(G-15256)*
South Bend Tribune Corp.. 574 971-5651
  114 S Main St Goshen (46526) *(G-6256)*
South Bend Tribune Corp (DH).. 574 235-6161
  225 W Colfax Ave South Bend (46626) *(G-15257)*
South Bend Woodworks LLC... 574 232-8875
  707 S Scott St South Bend (46601) *(G-15258)*
South Gibson Star-Times Inc... 812 753-3553
  203 S Mccreary St Fort Branch (47648) *(G-4707)*
South Shore Slag LLC (PA)... 219 881-6544
  3411 Sheffield Ave Hammond (46327) *(G-7010)*
South Whtley Trbune Prcton New.. 260 723-4771
  113 S State St South Whitley (46787) *(G-15325)*

South Wire, Bremen *Also Called: Coleman Cable LLC (G-1180)*
Southcorp Packaging North Amer, Valparaiso *Also Called: North America Packaging Corp (G-16015)*
Southeast Specialties Inc.. 706 667-0422
  2210 National Ave Indianapolis (46227) *(G-9463)*
Southeast Wood Treating Inc.. 765 962-4077
  5353 S D St Richmond (47374) *(G-14206)*
SOUTHEAST WOOD TREATING, INC., Richmond *Also Called: Southeast Wood Treating Inc (G-14206)*
Southeastern Supply Co, Indianapolis *Also Called: Prospect Distribution Inc (G-9231)*
Southern Alum Finshg Co Inc.. 800 357-9016
  5302 W 78th St Indianapolis (46268) *(G-9464)*
Southern Electric Coil LLC.. 219 931-5500
  5025 Columbia Ave Hammond (46327) *(G-7011)*
Southern Fuel LLC... 219 689-3552
  1250 N Mckinley Ave Rensselaer (47978) *(G-14069)*
Southern In Distillery.. 812 454-0135
  6861 Carson School Rd Mount Vernon (47620) *(G-12322)*
Southern Ind Lnngs Catings Inc... 812 206-7250
  113 Industrial Way Charlestown (47111) *(G-1893)*
Southern Indiana Bus Source... 812 206-6397
  221 Spring St Jeffersonville (47130) *(G-10056)*
Southern Indiana Chemical Inc (PA).. 812 687-7118
  358 E 900 N Washington (47501) *(G-16509)*
Southern Indiana Collar Co... 812 486-3714
  1692 N 725 E Montgomery (47558) *(G-12123)*
Southern Indiana Collar Mfg Co, Montgomery *Also Called: Southern Indiana Collar Co (G-12123)*
Southern Indiana Hardwoods Inc.. 812 326-2053
  2739 S Saint Anthony Rd W Huntingburg (47542) *(G-7291)*
Southern Indiana Sawmill LLC... 502 664-5723
  3325 N Highland Rd Salem (47167) *(G-14499)*
Southern Indiana Supply Inc... 812 482-2267
  1059 Wernsing Rd Jasper (47546) *(G-9914)*
Southern Indiana Treating, Huntingburg *Also Called: Steinkamp Warehouses Inc (G-7292)*
Southern Indiana Vinyl Window, Odon *Also Called: Vernon Greyber (G-13355)*
Southern Indiana Waterjet LLC.. 812 457-3201
  2286 Commercial Ct Evansville (47720) *(G-4324)*
Southern Indiana Wdwkg LLC... 812 636-0127
  9798 E 1200 N Odon (47562) *(G-13352)*
Southern Mechatronics Co Inc
  708 S Locust Ln Brownsburg (46112) *(G-1404)*
Southern Mold and Tool Inc.. 812 752-3333
  915 S Elm St Scottsburg (47170) *(G-14579)*
Southfield Corporation.. 812 824-1355
  7100 S Old State Road 37 Bloomington (47403) *(G-978)*
Southfield Corporation.. 317 846-6060
  430 W Carmel Dr Carmel (46032) *(G-1767)*
Southfield Corporation.. 317 773-5340
  15215 River Rd Noblesville (46060) *(G-13177)*
Southlake Lift Truck.. 219 962-4695
  3601 Arizona St Gary (46405) *(G-6013)*
Southlake Machine Corp... 219 285-6150
  112 N Polk St Morocco (47963) *(G-12270)*
Southland Container Corp... 812 385-0774
  Rr 1 Box 174 Princeton (47670) *(G-14012)*
Southland Metals Inc.. 574 252-4441
  4042 Southampton Dr Mishawaka (46544) *(G-12004)*
Southside Mini Storage... 574 293-3270
  2031 W Mishawaka Rd Elkhart (46517) *(G-3688)*
Southside Plating Works Inc... 219 293-5508
  2010 Superior St Elkhart (46516) *(G-3689)*
Southside Publishing, Indianapolis *Also Called: Southsider (G-9465)*
Southside Solidification Svcs, Carmel *Also Called: Remedium Services Group LLC (G-1741)*
Southside Times, Beech Grove *Also Called: Hoosier Times Inc (G-691)*
Southside Times The, Avon *Also Called: Times Leader Publications LLC (G-552)*
Southsider... 317 781-0023
  6025 Madison Ave Ste B Indianapolis (46227) *(G-9465)*
Southwark Metal Mfg Co... 317 823-5300
  5671 W 600 N Mccordsville (46055) *(G-11456)*
Southwest Grafix and AP Inc... 812 425-5104
  2229 W Franklin St Evansville (47712) *(G-4325)*

Southwest Welding LLC 574 862-4453
  28125 County Road 42 Wakarusa (46573) *(G-16252)*
Southwire Company LLC 574 546-5115
  515 Copperfield Way Bremen (46506) *(G-1222)*
Southwire Company LLC 765 449-7227
  3400 Union St Lafayette (47905) *(G-10693)*
Southwire Company LLC 317 445-2722
  600 Perry Rd Ste 100 Plainfield (46168) *(G-13730)*
Southwire East Insulating, Bremen *Also Called: Southwire Company LLC (G-1222)*
Southwire Senator Wire, Plainfield *Also Called: Southwire Company LLC (G-13730)*
Sovern Machining & Welding 812 392-2532
  4540 W County Road 740 N Scipio (47273) *(G-14551)*
SOWN Furnishings LLC 574 327-9029
  1808 Coachmans Trl South Bend (46637) *(G-15259)*
Soy Creamy, Valparaiso *Also Called: Paula Rosenbaum (G-16022)*
Soy Magnifiscents 765 746-6358
  651 N 7th St Apt 2 Lafayette (47901) *(G-10694)*
Soy-Yer Dough, Rushville *Also Called: Yer Brands Inc (G-14417)*
Soyful Fragrant Candles LLC 219 588-2685
  1129 Baker St Gary (46404) *(G-6014)*
Sp Holdings Inc 765 284-9545
  3401 N Commerce Dr Muncie (47303) *(G-12494)*
Sp3 .... 260 547-4150
  3531 W Us Highway 224 Decatur (46733) *(G-2885)*
Space Kraft 317 871-6999
  4901 W 79th St Indianapolis (46268) *(G-9466)*
Spaceguard Inc 812 523-3044
  711 S Commerce Dr Seymour (47274) *(G-14694)*
Spaceguard Products, Seymour *Also Called: Spaceguard Inc (G-14694)*
Spagheady Inc 317 499-6184
  6419 Hunters Green Ct Indianapolis (46278) *(G-9467)*
Spankys Paintball 812 752-7375
  2799 E State Road 356 Scottsburg (47170) *(G-14580)*
Spark Marketing LLC 219 301-0071
  2010 Georgia Ave Dyer (46311) *(G-2983)*
Sparkle Pools Inc 812 232-1292
  2225 N 25th St Terre Haute (47804) *(G-15707)*
Sparkling Ashe LLC 317 426-1824
  4610 Karen Dr Indianapolis (46226) *(G-9468)*
Sparkling Clean Inc 812 422-4871
  1018 Bayse St Evansville (47714) *(G-4326)*
Sparkman Pallet & Lumber Inc 812 873-6052
  9197 N Jake Gayle Rd Commiskey (47227) *(G-2422)*
Sparks Belting Company Inc 800 451-4537
  3420 179th St # 3b Hammond (46323) *(G-7012)*
Sparrow Group Incorporated 574 968-7335
  911 Hawthorn Dr Warsaw (46582) *(G-16428)*
Spartan Trailer Mfg Inc 574 309-3035
  1207 Lincolnway W Mishawaka (46544) *(G-12005)*
Spartech LLC 765 281-5100
  1401 E Memorial Dr Muncie (47302) *(G-12495)*
Spartech Plastics, Warsaw *Also Called: Avient Corporation (G-16315)*
Spaulding Products and Mfg Co, West Lafayette *Also Called: Cox John (G-16571)*
Spawn Mate, New Albany *Also Called: Spawn Mate Inc (G-12816)*
Spawn Mate Inc 812 948-2174
  2049 Indiana Ave New Albany (47150) *(G-12816)*
SPD Performance Plus LLC 260 433-6192
  476 N 500 W Bluffton (46714) *(G-1055)*
Speak Abilities LLP 303 827-8269
  221 W Wood St Apt 6 West Lafayette (47906) *(G-16630)*
Spear Industries Inc 317 717-1957
  943 Maple Stone Dr Greenwood (46143) *(G-6769)*
Spears Holdings Inc 765 378-4908
  3574 E State Road 236 Anderson (46017) *(G-196)*
Special Cutting Tools, Angola *Also Called: Feddema Industries Inc (G-250)*
Special Fabrication Services 812 384-5384
  418 East Hgwy 57 Elnora (47529) *(G-3816)*
Special Ideas Incorporated 812 834-5691
  511 Diamond Rd Heltonville (47436) *(G-7111)*
Special Metals Corporation 574 262-3451
  2900 Higgins Blvd Elkhart (46514) *(G-3690)*

Special Projects Corp 219 874-7184
  1 Buckingham Ct Michigan City (46360) *(G-11669)*
Special Tees, Roachdale *Also Called: Homelife Forever Inc (G-14247)*
Speciality Manufacturing, Charlestown *Also Called: Specialty Mfg Ind Inc (G-1894)*
Specialized Printed Products (PA) 260 483-7075
  6716 Metro Park Dr E Fort Wayne (46818) *(G-5428)*
Specialized Wood Products Inc 574 522-6376
  4221 Middlebury St Elkhart (46516) *(G-3691)*
Specialty Adhesive Film Co (PA) 812 926-0156
  10510 Randall Ave Aurora (47001) *(G-455)*
Specialty Blanks Inc 812 232-8775
  500 S 9th St Terre Haute (47807) *(G-15708)*
Specialty Coating Systems Inc (DH) 317 244-1200
  7645 Woodland Dr Indianapolis (46278) *(G-9469)*
Specialty Coating Systems Inc 317 244-1200
  7645 Woodland Dr Indianapolis (46278) *(G-9470)*
Specialty Coatings LLC 812 431-3375
  3301 N 1st Ave # B Evansville (47710) *(G-4327)*
Specialty Compounds Inc 574 529-0872
  501 W Railroad Ave Syracuse (46567) *(G-15478)*
Specialty Engrg Tl & Die LLC 260 356-2678
  875 E State St Huntington (46750) *(G-7369)*
Specialty Food Group LLC 219 531-2142
  463 E Us Highway 30 Valparaiso (46383) *(G-16055)*
Specialty Machine and Cnc Inc 765 346-0774
  100 W 1250 S Battle Ground (47920) *(G-614)*
Specialty Manufacturers Inc 317 241-1111
  11595 N Meridian St Ste 705 Carmel (46032) *(G-1768)*
Specialty Manufacturing 317 587-4999
  11595 N Meridian St # 705 Carmel (46032) *(G-1769)*
Specialty Mfg Ind Inc 812 256-4633
  15412 Highway 62 Ste 2 Charlestown (47111) *(G-1894)*
Specialty Products & Polymers 269 684-5931
  50869 Hawthorne Meadow Dr South Bend (46628) *(G-15260)*
Specialty Rim Supply, Terre Haute *Also Called: Specilty Blnks Inc An Ind Corp (G-15711)*
Specialty Rim Supply Inc 812 234-3002
  1033 Crawford St Terre Haute (47807) *(G-15709)*
Specialty Rim Supply Inc (PA) 812 234-3002
  500 S 9th St Terre Haute (47807) *(G-15710)*
Specialty Shoppe 574 772-7873
  640 S 800 E Knox (46534) *(G-10225)*
Specialty Steel Holdco Inc 877 289-2277
  1412 150th St Hammond (46327) *(G-7013)*
Specialty Steel Works Inc (PA) 877 289-2277
  1412 150th St Hammond (46327) *(G-7014)*
Specialty Tool & Die Company 765 452-9209
  1614 Rank Parkway Ct Kokomo (46901) *(G-10337)*
Specialty Tool LLC 260 493-6351
  6011 E Hanna Ave Ste D Indianapolis (46203) *(G-9471)*
Specialty Tooling Inc 812 464-8521
  2391 Lexington Rd Evansville (47720) *(G-4328)*
Specialty Wire Technologies 260 750-1418
  23651 Wilshire Blvd E Elkhart (46516) *(G-3692)*
Specification Products Inc 888 881-1726
  1718 Pleasant St Noblesville (46060) *(G-13178)*
Specified Ltg Systems Ind Inc 317 577-8100
  8904 Bash St Ste B Indianapolis (46256) *(G-9472)*
Specilty Blnks Inc An Ind Corp 812 234-3002
  1033 Crawford St Terre Haute (47807) *(G-15711)*
Specilty Stnless Stl Fbrction 317 430-3490
  7626 Normandy Blvd Indianapolis (46278) *(G-9473)*
Specilty Stnless Stl Fbrction (PA) 317 337-9800
  4337 W 96th St Ste 500 Indianapolis (46268) *(G-9474)*
Specilzed Cmpnent Prts Ltd LLC 260 925-2588
  1700 S Indiana Ave Auburn (46706) *(G-425)*
Speckin Sign Service Inc 317 539-5133
  845 Indianapolis Rd Greencastle (46135) *(G-6431)*
Spectacles of Carmel Inc 317 848-9081
  30 1st St Sw Carmel (46032) *(G-1770)*
Spectacles of Carmel Inc 317 475-9011
  7945 Lieber Rd Indianapolis (46260) *(G-9475)*

ALPHABETIC SECTION

Spectra Metal Sales Inc.. 317 822-8291
1711 W New York St Indianapolis (46222) *(G-9476)*

Spectra Prmium Mblity Sltons L (PA)................................ 800 628-5442
3052 N Distribution Way Greenfield (46140) *(G-6557)*

Spectra Prmium Mblity Sltons U....................................... 800 628-5442
3052 N Distribution Way Greenfield (46140) *(G-6558)*

Spectron MRC LLC.. 574 271-2800
17490 Dugdale Dr South Bend (46635) *(G-15261)*

Spectronrx, Bunker Hill Also Called: Nukemed Inc *(G-1442)*

Spectronrx, South Bend Also Called: Nukemed Inc *(G-15175)*

Spectrum Brands Inc... 317 773-6627
20975 Creek Rd Noblesville (46060) *(G-13179)*

Spectrum Finishing LLC... 260 463-7300
1340 Industrial Dr N Lagrange (46761) *(G-10762)*

Spectrum Industry.. 812 231-8355
500 8th Ave Terre Haute (47804) *(G-15712)*

Spectrum Marketing.. 765 643-5566
1629 Pearl St Anderson (46016) *(G-197)*

Spectrum MGT Holdg Co LLC... 812 941-6899
1608 Vance Ave New Albany (47150) *(G-12817)*

Spectrum Print and Mktg LLC... 317 908-7471
7575 E County Road 150 S Avon (46123) *(G-551)*

Spectrum Service, Granger Also Called: Spectrum Services Inc *(G-6380)*

Spectrum Services Inc... 574 272-7605
12911 Industrial Park Dr Unit 7 Granger (46530) *(G-6380)*

Speedcraft Prototypes... 765 644-6449
141 W 14th St Anderson (46016) *(G-198)*

Speedgrip Chuck, Elkhart Also Called: Lotec Inc *(G-3500)*

Speedgrip Chuck Company, Elkhart Also Called: Scg Acquisition Company LLC *(G-3664)*

Speedhook Specialists Inc.. 219 378-6369
845 E Lake Front Dr Beverly Shores (46301) *(G-732)*

Speedpro Imaging.. 765 446-8600
311 Sagamore Pkwy N Ste 6 Lafayette (47904) *(G-10695)*

Speedpro Imaging, Indianapolis Also Called: DBC Imaging *(G-7956)*

Speedread Technologies, Indianapolis Also Called: Speedread Technologies LLC *(G-9477)*

Speedread Technologies LLC... 317 824-4544
4525 Saguaro Trl Indianapolis (46268) *(G-9477)*

Speedsters.. 574 546-4656
119 N Liberty Dr Bremen (46506) *(G-1223)*

Speedway Construction Pdts LLC................................. 260 203-9806
4817 Industrial Rd Fort Wayne (46825) *(G-5429)*

Speedway Redi Mix Inc... 260 665-5999
260 E 300 N Angola (46703) *(G-293)*

Speedway Redi Mix Inc... 260 244-7205
400 S Whitley St Columbia City (46725) *(G-2201)*

SPEEDWAY REDI MIX INC, Angola Also Called: Speedway Redi Mix Inc *(G-293)*

Speedway Redi-Mix Inc (PA).. 260 496-8877
4820 Industrial Rd Fort Wayne (46825) *(G-5430)*

Speedway Redi-Mix Inc.. 260 356-5600
1217 W Park Dr Huntington (46750) *(G-7370)*

Speedway Sand & Gravel Inc.. 574 893-7355
2896 S 1600 E Silver Lake (46982) *(G-14922)*

Speedy Stitch Embroidery... 812 597-4654
550 S State Road 135 Morgantown (46160) *(G-12264)*

Speedy-Screen LLC.. 317 910-0724
11109 Keough Dr Indianapolis (46236) *(G-9478)*

Spence/Banks Holdings Inc (PA)................................... 812 235-8123
700 N 1st St Terre Haute (47807) *(G-15713)*

Spencer Cnty Journal-Democrat, Rockport Also Called: News Publishing Company LLC *(G-14346)*

Spencer County Leader, Ferdinand Also Called: Dubois-Spncer Cunties Pubg Inc *(G-4430)*

Spencer Evening World (PA)... 812 829-2255
114 E Franklin St Spencer (47460) *(G-15362)*

Spencer Industries Inc (PA).. 812 937-4561
902 Buffaloville Rd Dale (47523) *(G-2792)*

Spencer Logging... 812 595-0987
5297 N State Road 39 Scottsburg (47170) *(G-14581)*

Spencer Machine and TI Co Inc..................................... 812 282-6300
6205 Gheens Mill Rd Jeffersonville (47130) *(G-10057)*

Spencer Printing Inc... 765 288-6111
4404 S Madison St Muncie (47302) *(G-12496)*

Spencer Strainer Systems, Jeffersonville Also Called: Spencer Machine and TI Co Inc *(G-10057)*

Sperry & Rice Manufacturing Company LLC............... 765 647-4141
9146 Us Highway 52 Brookville (47012) *(G-1335)*

Spheros North America Inc... 734 218-7350
22150 Challenger Dr Elkhart (46514) *(G-3693)*

SPI Industries, South Bend Also Called: Quality Molded Products Inc *(G-15211)*

Spi-Binding Company Inc.. 765 794-4992
610 South St Darlington (47940) *(G-2834)*

Spiceland Wood Products, Spiceland Also Called: Spiceland Wood Products Inc *(G-15379)*

Spiceland Wood Products Inc.. 765 987-8156
609 S Pearl St Spiceland (47385) *(G-15379)*

Spider Tie.. 574 596-3073
501 W Railroad Ave Syracuse (46567) *(G-15479)*

Spin Zone Cycling, Granger Also Called: Sportcrafters Inc *(G-6381)*

Spina Enterprises Inc... 219 879-0444
10855 W 400 N Michigan City (46360) *(G-11670)*

Spiral-Fab Inc... 812 427-3006
14679 Upper Tinker Rd Vevay (47043) *(G-16112)*

Spiritbuilding Publishing... 765 623-2238
15591 N State Road 9 Summitville (46070) *(G-15432)*

Spiritual Book Associates, Notre Dame Also Called: Ave Maria Press Inc *(G-13315)*

Spirrow Therapeutics LLC... 317 750-8879
132 Vigo Ct West Lafayette (47906) *(G-16631)*

Spitzer Enterprises, Greenfield Also Called: Dean Co Inc *(G-6488)*

Spitzer Racing Enterprises... 317 894-9533
6135 W 400 N Greenfield (46140) *(G-6559)*

Splendor Boats LLC... 260 352-2835
9526 S State Road 15 Silver Lake (46982) *(G-14923)*

Spobric LLC.. 302 249-1045
8911 Himebaugh Ln Indianapolis (46231) *(G-9479)*

Spohn Associates Inc... 317 921-2445
3935 N Meridian St Indianapolis (46208) *(G-9480)*

Sport Form Inc... 260 589-2200
151 W Main St Berne (46711) *(G-727)*

Sportcrafters Inc (PA).. 574 243-2453
51345 Bittersweet Rd Granger (46530) *(G-6381)*

Sports Licensed Division... 317 895-7000
8677 Logo Athletic Ct Indianapolis (46219) *(G-9481)*

Sports Locker Room, Shelbyville Also Called: G D Cox Inc *(G-14758)*

Sports Plus, Fort Wayne Also Called: Sports Plus Inc *(G-5431)*

Sports Plus Inc... 260 482-8261
4201 Coldwater Rd Fort Wayne (46805) *(G-5431)*

Sports Screen Impact... 812 926-9355
718 Green Blvd Aurora (47001) *(G-456)*

Sports Select Usa Inc... 317 631-4011
1920 N Shadeland Ave Indianapolis (46219) *(G-9482)*

Sports Unlimited Printed AP... 574 772-4239
6 S Cleveland St Knox (46534) *(G-10226)*

Sportscenter Inc.. 260 436-6198
5511 Coventry Ln Fort Wayne (46804) *(G-5432)*

Sportsmania Sales Inc... 317 873-5501
260 S First St Ste 4 Zionsville (46077) *(G-17052)*

Spotlight On Drama LLC.. 765 643-7170
3551 W 8th Street Rd Anderson (46011) *(G-199)*

Spotlight Strategies, Franklin Also Called: XI Graphics Inc *(G-5789)*

Spray Inc... 812 346-3197
6492 E State Road 258 Seymour (47274) *(G-14695)*

Spray Sand & Gravel Inc.. 812 522-5417
6492 E State Road 258 Seymour (47274) *(G-14696)*

Spray Sand & Gravel Inc (PA)... 812 523-8081
1635 Murray Hill Dr Seymour (47274) *(G-14697)*

Spray Sand and Gravel, Seymour Also Called: Spray Inc *(G-14695)*

Spreuer & Son Inc.. 260 463-3513
115 E Spring St Lagrange (46761) *(G-10763)*

Sprigati LLC.. 219 484-9455
8250 Baring Ave Munster (46321) *(G-12564)*

Spring Monticello Corporation.. 574 583-8090
3137 S Freeman Rd Monticello (47960) *(G-12170)*

Spring Ventures Infovation LLC...................................... 317 847-1117
1846 Saratoga Dr Greenwood (46143) *(G-6770)*

Sprinkguard LLC 877 274-7976
5776 Grape Rd Ste 51 Mishawaka (46545) *(G-12006)*

Sprinter Xpress Delivery LLC 317 496-5959
3654 Katelyn Ln Indianapolis (46228) *(G-9483)*

Sprunger Engineering, Elkhart *Also Called: Elkcases Inc (G-3317)*

Sprunger Engineering, Elkhart *Also Called: Elkhart Cases Inc (G-3324)*

Spunlite, Muncie *Also Called: Muncie Metal Spinning Inc (G-12462)*

Spurlino Mtls Indianapolis LLC 765 339-4055
11528 N Us Highway 231 Linden (47955) *(G-11032)*

SPX Corporation 219 879-6561
500 Blaine St Michigan City (46360) *(G-11671)*

SPX Corporation 812 849-5647
4598 State Road 37 Mitchell (47446) *(G-12048)*

SPX CORPORATION, Mitchell *Also Called: SPX Corporation (G-12048)*

Spyder Controls Inc 866 919-9092
1251 N Eddy St Ste 200 South Bend (46617) *(G-15262)*

Square 1 Design, Shelbyville *Also Called: Square 1 Dsign Manufacture Inc (G-14800)*

Square 1 Designs & Signs 219 552-0079
23316 Shelby Rd Shelby (46377) *(G-14728)*

Square 1 Dsign Manufacture Inc 866 647-7771
1 Clark Rd Shelbyville (46176) *(G-14800)*

Square Donuts Inc 812 232-6463
935 Wabash Ave Terre Haute (47807) *(G-15714)*

Squareframe Industries LLC 765 430-3301
25 Executive Dr Ste G Lafayette (47905) *(G-10696)*

Squeegeepie Merch Co LLC 765 376-6358
600 Mill St Crawfordsville (47933) *(G-2618)*

Squeeze Play, Muncie *Also Called: Jeremy Parker (G-12431)*

Squirrel Daddy Inc 260 723-4946
405 W Buffalo St South Whitley (46787) *(G-15326)*

Sr Petroleum Inc 574 383-5879
15482 Bryanton Ct Granger (46530) *(G-6382)*

Sr Wood, Clarksville *Also Called: S R Wood Inc (G-2032)*

Srae Construction LLC 219 216-1902
2754 N County Road 825 W Royal Center (46978) *(G-14393)*

Srg Global Evansville, Evansville *Also Called: Srg Global Trim Inc (G-4329)*

Srg Global Trim Inc (DH) 812 473-6200
601 N Congress Ave Evansville (47715) *(G-4329)*

SRK Filters LLC 765 647-9962
5010 Beesley Rd Cedar Grove (47016) *(G-1825)*

Ss Custom Choppers LLC 260 415-3793
804 W Wildwood Ave Fort Wayne (46807) *(G-5433)*

Ss Elevations LLC 574 310-5442
1143 E Ireland Rd Ste 1073 South Bend (46614) *(G-15263)*

SS&c Technologies Inc 812 266-2000
110 N Fulton Ave Evansville (47710) *(G-4330)*

Ssci, West Lafayette *Also Called: Curia Indiana LLC (G-16574)*

SSd Control Technology Inc 574 289-5942
1801 S Main St South Bend (46613) *(G-15264)*

Ssi, Fort Wayne *Also Called: System Science Institute (G-5465)*

Ssm Logistics LLC 812 354-4509
6242 E State Road 56 Winslow (47598) *(G-16923)*

SSP Technologies Inc 888 548-4668
709 Plaza Dr Ste 2 Chesterton (46304) *(G-1958)*

Sssi Inc 219 880-0818
1 N Broadway Gary (46402) *(G-6015)*

St Augustines Press Inc (PA) 574 291-3500
17917 Killington Way South Bend (46614) *(G-15265)*

St Clair Group Inc 765 435-3091
7903 W County Road 1325 N Russellville (46175) *(G-14419)*

St Clair Press 317 612-9100
1203 E Saint Clair St Indianapolis (46202) *(G-9484)*

St Henry Tile Co Inc 260 589-2880
155 E Buckeye St Berne (46711) *(G-728)*

St Henry Tile Co Inc 765 966-7771
1000 N F St Richmond (47374) *(G-14207)*

St Joe Group Inc 260 918-3500
3003 Ryan Rd New Haven (46774) *(G-12920)*

St John Sports, Schererville *Also Called: Locoli Inc (G-14531)*

St Lenzer LLC 260 441-9300
4520 Ellenwood Dr Fort Wayne (46806) *(G-5434)*

St Louis Group LLC 317 975-3121
8888 Keystone Xing Ste 650 Indianapolis (46240) *(G-9485)*

St Meinrad Archabbey (PA) 812 357-6611
200 Hill Dr Saint Meinrad (47577) *(G-14464)*

St Regis Inc (PA) 317 591-3500
3233 N Post Rd Indianapolis (46226) *(G-9486)*

St Regis Culvert Inc 317 353-8065
1101 S Kitley Ave Indianapolis (46203) *(G-9487)*

ST&I, Mishawaka *Also Called: Substrate Treatments & Lubr (G-12010)*

Staab Sheet Metal Inc 317 241-2553
2720 S Tibbs Ave Ste 1x Indianapolis (46241) *(G-9488)*

Stability America Inc 574 642-3029
2928 Elder Dr Goshen (46526) *(G-6257)*

Stackman Signs/Graphics Inc 317 784-6120
5520 S Harding St Indianapolis (46217) *(G-9489)*

Stacks Limited 765 409-5081
4570 Duckhorn Ln Lafayette (47909) *(G-10697)*

Stacy Publishing Inc 812 923-1111
6901 Georgetown Greenville Rd Greenville (47124) *(G-6656)*

Stadry Enclosure Co 812 284-2244
213 Riverwood Dr Jeffersonville (47130) *(G-10058)*

Stafco, Columbia City *Also Called: Steel Tank & Fabricating Corp (G-2203)*

Stafford Gravel Inc 260 868-2503
4225 County Road 79 Butler (46721) *(G-1479)*

Stage Door Graphics 317 398-9011
207 S Harrison St Shelbyville (46176) *(G-14801)*

Stage Ninja LLC 317 829-1507
707 E Murry St Indianapolis (46227) *(G-9490)*

Stahl Equipment Inc 812 925-3341
14094 N Base Rd Gentryville (47537) *(G-6053)*

Stalcop LLC (PA) 765 436-7926
1217 W Main St Thorntown (46071) *(G-15756)*

Stalcop Cold US, Thorntown *Also Called: Stalcop LLC (G-15756)*

Stall & Kessler Inc 765 742-1259
333 Columbia St Lafayette (47901) *(G-10698)*

Stall Kessler's Diamond Center, Lafayette *Also Called: Stall & Kessler Inc (G-10698)*

Staltari Enterprises Inc 574 522-1988
236 Marshall Blvd Elkhart (46516) *(G-3694)*

Stamina Metal Products Inc 574 534-7410
901 E Madison St Goshen (46528) *(G-6258)*

Stamp N Scrap Ink Corp 219 440-7239
1043 Sheffield Ave Dyer (46311) *(G-2984)*

Stamp Works 765 962-5201
121 S 5th St Richmond (47374) *(G-14208)*

Stampcrafter 574 892-5206
324 Weidner Ave Argos (46501) *(G-326)*

Stampede Enterprises Inc 574 232-5997
24545 State Road 23 South Bend (46614) *(G-15266)*

Stamping Plant, Batesville *Also Called: Batesville Casket Company Inc (G-581)*

Stan Clamme 765 348-0008
725 E Water St Hartford City (47348) *(G-7077)*

Stanbio Laboratory LP 830 249-0772
1814 Leer Dr Elkhart (46514) *(G-3695)*

Standard Change-Makers Inc (PA) 317 899-6955
3130 N Mitthoefer Rd Indianapolis (46235) *(G-9491)*

Standard Change-Makers Inc 317 899-6955
3130 N Mitthoefer Rd Indianapolis (46235) *(G-9492)*

Standard Coal Lab, Washington *Also Called: Peabody Midwest Mining LLC (G-16500)*

Standard Die Supply of Indiana Inc 317 236-6200
927 S Pennsylvania St Indianapolis (46225) *(G-9493)*

Standard Fertilizer Company 812 663-8391
2006 S County Road 60 Sw Greensburg (47240) *(G-6632)*

Standard For Success LLC 844 737-3825
10741 S County Road 850 E Cloverdale (46120) *(G-2099)*

Standard Fusee Corporation 765 472-4375
3157 N 500 W Peru (46970) *(G-13602)*

Standard Industrial Supply Inc 574 946-6661
100 Michigan Winamac (46996) *(G-16876)*

Standard Industries Inc 219 872-1111
505 N Roeske Ave Michigan City (46360) *(G-11672)*

Standard Industries Inc 812 838-4861
901 Givens Rd Mount Vernon (47620) *(G-12323)*

ALPHABETIC SECTION — Steel Dynamics Inc

Standard Intgrted Slutions Inc 574 946-6661
  100 Michigan Winamac (46996) *(G-16877)*

Standard Issue Armory LLC 812 364-1466
  8600 Highway 150 Greenville (47124) *(G-6657)*

Standard Label Co Inc 574 522-3548
  4200 Wyland Dr Elkhart (46516) *(G-3696)*

Standard Locknut LLC 317 399-2230
  1045 E 169th St Westfield (46074) *(G-16729)*

Standard Motor Products Inc 574 259-6253
  1718 N Home St Mishawaka (46545) *(G-12007)*

Standard Pattern Company Inc 260 456-4870
  2136 Lafayette St Fort Wayne (46803) *(G-5435)*

Standard Plastic Corporation 260 824-0214
  850 Decker Dr Bluffton (46714) *(G-1056)*

Standish Steel Inc 812 834-5255
  280 Standish Steel Dr Bedford (47421) *(G-674)*

Standout Creations LLC 765 203-9110
  1078 E 500 S Anderson (46013) *(G-200)*

Standout Socks 317 531-6950
  3704 Ontario Cir Indianapolis (46268) *(G-9494)*

Stands Photography 812 723-3922
  792 S Ridgecrest Ln Paoli (47454) *(G-13500)*

Stanger Excavating, Goshen Also Called: Colby L Stanger *(G-6114)*

Stanley Black & Decker Inc 860 225-5111
  6161 E 75th St Indianapolis (46250) *(G-9495)*

Stanley Engnered Fastening LLC 765 728-2433
  7345 N 400 E Montpelier (47359) *(G-12182)*

Stanley Hydraulic Tools AP, Indianapolis Also Called: Stanley Black & Decker Inc *(G-9495)*

Stanley Oliver Products LLC 260 499-3506
  3545 E 100 N Lagrange (46761) *(G-10764)*

Stans Sign Design Inc 317 251-3838
  6373 Rucker Rd Indianapolis (46220) *(G-9496)*

Stant Corporation 765 825-3122
  1620 Columbia Ave Connersville (47331) *(G-2467)*

Stant Manufacturing Inc 870 247-5480
  1620 Columbia Ave Connersville (47331) *(G-2468)*

Stant USA Corp 765 825-3121
  1620 Columbia Ave Connersville (47331) *(G-2469)*

Stant USA Corp (HQ) 765 825-3121
  1620 Columbia Ave Connersville (47331) *(G-2470)*

Stanton and Associates Inc 574 247-5522
  6910 N Main St Unit 15 Granger (46530) *(G-6383)*

Stapert Tool & Machine Co Inc 317 787-2387
  2958 Carson Ave Indianapolis (46203) *(G-9497)*

Staples Pipe & Muffler (PA) 812 522-3569
  1365 S County Road 650 E Butlerville (47223) *(G-1488)*

Staples Pipe & Muffler 812 346-2474
  523 Hoosier St North Vernon (47265) *(G-13296)*

Star, Crown Point Also Called: Crown Point Shopping News *(G-2671)*

Star Case Manufacturing Co LLC 219 922-4440
  648 Superior Ave Munster (46321) *(G-12565)*

Star Engineering & Mch Co Inc 260 824-4825
  1717 Lancaster St Bluffton (46714) *(G-1057)*

Star Manufacturing LLC 574 329-6042
  2772 Faith Ave Elkhart (46514) *(G-3697)*

Star Nail 765 453-0743
  1500 E Markland Ave Kokomo (46901) *(G-10338)*

Star Nova US LLC (PA) 269 830-5802
  3702 W Sample St South Bend (46619) *(G-15267)*

Star Packaging Company Inc 317 357-3707
  6124 Brokenhurst Rd Indianapolis (46220) *(G-9498)*

Star Pipe LLC 317 428-7408
  6119 Guion Rd Indianapolis (46254) *(G-9499)*

Star Quality Awards Inc 812 273-1740
  322 Crestwood Dr Madison (47250) *(G-11252)*

Star Technology Inc 260 837-7833
  200 Executive Dr Waterloo (46793) *(G-16531)*

Star Tool & Die Inc 574 264-3815
  53088 Faith Ave Elkhart (46514) *(G-3698)*

Star Tool Inc 812 372-6730
  4489 Middle Rd Columbus (47203) *(G-2395)*

Star Tools, Columbus Also Called: Star Tool Inc *(G-2395)*

Star Tracks Command 574 596-5331
  3705 Chimney Hill Dr Valparaiso (46383) *(G-16056)*

Star Water Systems, Kendallville Also Called: Flint & Walling Inc *(G-10111)*

Star Weld, Rushville Also Called: Starkey Welding Inc *(G-14413)*

Starburst Sales, North Judson Also Called: American Oak Preserving Co Inc *(G-13206)*

Starcraft, Goshen Also Called: Starcraft Corporation *(G-6260)*

Starcraft Accessories, Goshen Also Called: Starcraft Corporation *(G-6259)*

Starcraft Bus, Goshen Also Called: Forest River Inc *(G-6140)*

Starcraft Corporation 574 534-7705
  2006 Century Dr Goshen (46528) *(G-6259)*

Starcraft Corporation (HQ) 574 534-7827
  1123 S Indiana Ave Goshen (46526) *(G-6260)*

Starcraft Tire and Wheel, Mishawaka Also Called: Richards Liquidation Corp *(G-11985)*

Stark Precision Machine LLC 812 239-5291
  1205 E Dallas Dr Terre Haute (47802) *(G-15715)*

Stark Truss Company Inc 219 866-2772
  1317 N Owen St Rensselaer (47978) *(G-14070)*

Starkey Global Dist Ctr, Plainfield Also Called: Starkey Laboratories Inc *(G-13731)*

Starkey Laboratories Inc 952 828-6934
  3810 Plainfield Rd Ste 112 Plainfield (46168) *(G-13731)*

Starkey Welding Inc 765 932-2005
  709 W 1st St Rushville (46173) *(G-14413)*

Starlight Printing 812 486-3905
  3792 N 525 E Montgomery (47558) *(G-12124)*

Starline Mfg LLC 765 847-1306
  11262 Arba Pike Fountain City (47341) *(G-5612)*

Starquest Products, Elkhart Also Called: Kinro Manufacturing Inc *(G-3457)*

State Beauty Supply 260 755-6361
  3822 Lafayette St Fort Wayne (46806) *(G-5436)*

State Cleaning Solutions 812 336-4817
  8813 Boehning Ln Indianapolis (46219) *(G-9500)*

State Gear Co., Indianapolis Also Called: Precision Cams Inc *(G-9180)*

State Line Woodworking 260 768-4577
  6520 N 675 W Shipshewana (46565) *(G-14891)*

State Plating, Indianapolis Also Called: Wrr Inc *(G-9794)*

State Wide Aluminum Inc 574 262-2594
  3518 County Road 6 E Elkhart (46514) *(G-3699)*

State Wide Window, Elkhart Also Called: State Wide Aluminum Inc *(G-3699)*

Stateline Woodturnings LLC 260 768-4507
  7005 W 650 N Shipshewana (46565) *(G-14892)*

States Engineering, Fort Wayne Also Called: Chuck Bivens Services Inc *(G-4846)*

Static Media Inc (PA) 212 366-4500
  79 Madison Ave Fl 2 Fishers (46038) *(G-4606)*

Static Pen Publishing LLC 765 609-0202
  10 N Tahoe Ct Lafayette (47909) *(G-10699)*

Statzer C Mark, Wabash Also Called: Tru-Cut Machine & Tool Inc *(G-16218)*

Stay Put Doggy LLC 812 591-8232
  401 E Paul St Westport (47283) *(G-16752)*

Ste Acquisition LLC 260 925-1382
  1105 W Auburn Dr Auburn (46706) *(G-426)*

Stealth Energy Group LLC 316 260-0064
  6807 Wellington Cir Zionsville (46077) *(G-17053)*

Stealth Furniture, Spencerville Also Called: Deep Three Inc *(G-15369)*

Steamin Demon Inc 812 288-6754
  1041 S Clark Blvd Clarksville (47129) *(G-2038)*

Steckler Grassfed LLC 812 683-3098
  21477 N County Road 600 E Dale (47523) *(G-2793)*

Stedman Machine Company Inc 812 926-0038
  129 Franklin St Aurora (47001) *(G-457)*

Steel Avenue Inc
  3848 Cottage Ave Mishawaka (46544) *(G-12008)*

Steel Box Co LLC 812 620-7043
  521 S Tristin Ct Salem (47167) *(G-14500)*

Steel Dynamics Inc 260 868-8000
  4500 County Road 59 Butler (46721) *(G-1480)*

Steel Dynamics Inc 866 740-8700
  2601 S County Rd 700 E Columbia City (46725) *(G-2202)*

Steel Dynamics Inc 260 969-3500
  6714 Pointe Inverness Way Fort Wayne (46804) *(G-5437)*

Steel Dynamics Inc (PA) 260 969-3500
7575 W Jefferson Blvd Fort Wayne (46804) *(G-5438)*

Steel Dynamics Inc 812 218-1490
5134 Loop Rd Jeffersonville (47130) *(G-10059)*

Steel Dynamics Inc 317 892-7000
8000 N County Road 225 E Pittsboro (46167) *(G-13654)*

Steel Dynamics Columbus LLC 260 969-3500
7575 W Jefferson Blvd Fort Wayne (46804) *(G-5439)*

Steel Dynamics Engineered Bar, Pittsboro Also Called: Steel Dynamics Inc *(G-13654)*

STEEL DYNAMICS HEARTLAND LLC 812 299-8866
455 W Industrial Dr Terre Haute (47802) *(G-15716)*

Steel Dynamics Sls N Amer Inc 260 868-8000
4500 County Road 59 Butler (46721) *(G-1481)*

Steel Dynamics Sls N Amer Inc (HQ) 260 969-3500
7575 W Jefferson Blvd Fort Wayne (46804) *(G-5440)*

Steel Green Manufacturing LLC 765 481-2890
824 S State Road 39 Lebanon (46052) *(G-10944)*

Steel Grip Inc 765 793-3652
1200 Pearl St Covington (47932) *(G-2534)*

Steel Grip Inc 765 397-3344
42233 S Kingman Rd Kingman (47952) *(G-10174)*

Steel Grip Safety Apparel, Kingman Also Called: Steel Grip Inc *(G-10174)*

Steel Manufacturing, East Chicago Also Called: Green Lake Tube LLC *(G-3013)*

Steel Parts Corporation 765 675-2191
801 Berryman Pike Tipton (46072) *(G-15791)*

Steel Parts Manufacturing Inc (HQ) 765 675-2191
801 Berryman Pike Tipton (46072) *(G-15792)*

Steel Services Inc 317 783-5255
3551 S Lynhurst Dr Indianapolis (46241) *(G-9501)*

Steel Storage Inc 574 282-2618
1408 Elwood Ave Ste A South Bend (46628) *(G-15268)*

Steel Tank & Fabricating Corp 260 248-8971
365 S James St Columbia City (46725) *(G-2203)*

Steel Technologies LLC 765 362-3110
3560 S Nucor Rd Crawfordsville (47933) *(G-2619)*

Steel Technologies LLC 812 663-9704
1811 N Montgomery Rd Greensburg (47240) *(G-6633)*

Steel Technologies LLC 502 245-2110
5830 Southport Rd Portage (46368) *(G-13916)*

Steelco Industrial Lubricants 219 462-0333
358 Ruge St Valparaiso (46385) *(G-16057)*

Steele Roofing Co LLC 219 243-1563
349-1 W 100 S Valparaiso (46385) *(G-16058)*

Steelmaster, Middlebury Also Called: Gbo Corporation *(G-11717)*

Steeltech Partners LLC 812 849-0124
240 S Meridian Rd Mitchell (47446) *(G-12049)*

Steffy Wood Products, Angola Also Called: Steffy Wood Products Inc *(G-294)*

Steffy Wood Products Inc 260 665-8016
701 W Mill St Angola (46703) *(G-294)*

Steindler Signs & Graphix LLC 219 733-2551
105 Koselke St Wanatah (46390) *(G-16291)*

Steiner Enterprises Inc 765 429-6409
3532 Coleman Ct Ste B Lafayette (47905) *(G-10700)*

Steinkamp Warehouses Inc 812 683-3860
1000 N Main St Huntingburg (47542) *(G-7292)*

Steinway Piano Company Inc (DH) 574 522-1675
600 Industrial Pkwy Elkhart (46516) *(G-3700)*

Stella-Jones Corporation 812 789-5331
3818 S County Road 50 E Winslow (47598) *(G-16924)*

Stellantis 765 854-4201
3660 Us Highway 31 N Kokomo (46901) *(G-10339)*

Stem Point LLC 352 870-0122
4828 E 300 N Franklin (46131) *(G-5778)*

Stems & Stitches 260 503-4955
6711 W 200 S South Whitley (46787) *(G-15327)*

Stemwood Corp 812 945-6646
2710 Grant Line Rd New Albany (47150) *(G-12818)*

Stenidy Industries Inc 317 873-5343
10305 Cottonwood Ct Zionsville (46077) *(G-17054)*

Stensland Engines Inc 260 623-6859
4933 Morgan Rd Monroeville (46773) *(G-12075)*

Stephen G Morrow Inc 812 876-7837
2632 Schooling Rd Spencer (47460) *(G-15363)*

Stephen L Capper & Associates 317 546-9000
2500 N Ritter Ave Indianapolis (46218) *(G-9502)*

Stephen Libs Candy Company Inc 812 473-0048
6225 Vogel Rd Evansville (47715) *(G-4331)*

Stephen Libs Finer Chocolate, Evansville Also Called: Stephen Libs Candy Company Inc *(G-4331)*

Stephens Dynamics Inc 765 459-4451
1600 Dodge St Kokomo (46902) *(G-10340)*

Stephens Machine Inc (PA) 765 459-4017
1600 Dodge St Kokomo (46902) *(G-10341)*

Stephens Machine Inc 765 459-9770
1801 S Berkley Rd Kokomo (46902) *(G-10342)*

Stephens Welding LLC 812 925-6033
1000 S State St Chandler (47610) *(G-1867)*

Sterigenics, Columbia City Also Called: Iotron Industries USA Inc *(G-2157)*

Steris Corporation 440 354-2600
6015 W 79th St Indianapolis (46278) *(G-9503)*

Steritech-Usa Inc 260 745-7272
2007 Bremer Rd Fort Wayne (46803) *(G-5441)*

Sterling Berry Corporation 812 424-2904
101 Oakley St Evansville (47710) *(G-4332)*

Sterling Creek Software L L C 317 567-5060
8888 Keystone Xing Indianapolis (46240) *(G-9504)*

Sterling Electric Inc (PA) 317 872-0471
7997 Allison Ave Indianapolis (46268) *(G-9505)*

Sterling Fluid Systems USA LLC (DH) 317 925-9661
2005 Dr Martin Luther King Jr St Indianapolis (46202) *(G-9506)*

Sterling Impressions Inc 317 329-9773
7016 Coffman Rd Indianapolis (46268) *(G-9507)*

Sterling Industrial LLC 812 423-7832
1001 Mount Auburn Rd Evansville (47720) *(G-4333)*

Sterling Industrial LLC (PA) 812 479-5447
401 Nw 1st St Evansville (47708) *(G-4334)*

Sterling Industries Inc 812 376-6560
4015 N Long Rd Columbus (47203) *(G-2396)*

Sterling Machine Co Inc 219 374-9360
10501 W 133rd Ave Lot 6 Cedar Lake (46303) *(G-1838)*

Sterling Manufacturing Inc 260 451-9760
144 E Collins Rd Fort Wayne (46825) *(G-5442)*

Sterling Sales and Engrg Inc 765 376-0454
324 S Sterling Ave Veedersburg (47987) *(G-16091)*

Sternberg Inc 812 867-0077
8950 N Kentucky Ave Evansville (47725) *(G-4335)*

Sternberg International Isuzu, Evansville Also Called: Sternberg Inc *(G-4335)*

Sterno Delivery, La Porte Also Called: Sevenoks Inc *(G-10480)*

Steuben County Parks, Angola Also Called: County of Steuben *(G-243)*

Steuben County Welding & Fabg 260 665-3001
2797 Woodhull Dr Angola (46703) *(G-295)*

Steve Mitchell 574 831-4848
69420 County Road 27 New Paris (46553) *(G-12969)*

Steve Reiff Inc (PA) 260 723-4360
5650 W 800 S South Whitley (46787) *(G-15328)*

Steve Schmidt Racing Engines 317 898-1831
8560 E 30th St Indianapolis (46219) *(G-9508)*

Steve Stamper 765 653-8786
210 Elizabeth St Greencastle (46135) *(G-6432)*

Steve Weaver Art 574 546-3530
113 N Center St Bremen (46506) *(G-1224)*

Steve's Automotive Center, Spencer Also Called: Stephen G Morrow Inc *(G-15363)*

Steven Block 765 749-5394
7805 N Tanglewood Ln Muncie (47304) *(G-12497)*

Steven Ray Hughes 574 491-2128
5972 S 450 W Claypool (46510) *(G-2058)*

Steven Smith 317 455-1086
13965 N State Road 67 Camby (46113) *(G-1514)*

Steves Machining & Rework 317 500-4627
1299 Paris Dr Franklin (46131) *(G-5779)*

Steves Pallets 260 856-2047
3868 N 1025 W Cromwell (46732) *(G-2633)*

ALPHABETIC SECTION — Strick Trailers LLC

Steves Pallets Inc 574 457-3620
12661 N Pleasant Grove Rd Syracuse (46567) *(G-15480)*

Steves Woodworking LLC 317 507-4194
5500 Lincoln Rd Martinsville (46151) *(G-11428)*

Stewart Graphics Inc (PA) 812 283-0455
1419 Fabricon Blvd Jeffersonville (47130) *(G-10060)*

Stg Networks LLC 317 667-0865
5536 W Raymond St Indianapolis (46241) *(G-9509)*

Stickle Steam Specialties Co 317 636-6563
2215 Valley Ave Indianapolis (46218) *(G-9510)*

Stien Designs & Graphics Inc 260 347-9136
106 S Main St Kendallville (46755) *(G-10153)*

Stiffler Handy Product, Indianapolis Also Called: Alexander Screw Products Inc *(G-7469)*

Still Safety Products LLC 855 249-0009
9285 N Cr600 East Evanston (47531) *(G-3855)*

Still Safety Sling, Evanston Also Called: Still Safety Products LLC *(G-3855)*

Stillions Saw Mill 812 824-6542
7208 S Rockport Rd Bloomington (47403) *(G-979)*

Stillions Sawmill, Bloomington Also Called: Stillions Saw Mill *(G-979)*

Stines Printing Inc 260 356-5994
549 Warren St Huntington (46750) *(G-7371)*

Stingel Enterprises Inc 812 883-0054
1002 Webb St Salem (47167) *(G-14501)*

Stingray Systems LLC 317 238-6508
5701 Elmwood Ave Indianapolis (46203) *(G-9511)*

Stingray Valves, Indianapolis Also Called: Stingray Systems LLC *(G-9511)*

Stitch Glitch 765 274-1435
2210 Crestwood Dr Anderson (46016) *(G-201)*

Stitch N Frame 260 478-1301
4220 Bluffton Rd Fort Wayne (46809) *(G-5443)*

Stitch N Time, Seymour Also Called: Lloyd & Mona Sulivan *(G-14665)*

Stitchery Garden LLC 765 450-4695
4410 S 00 Ew Ste A Kokomo (46902) *(G-10343)*

Stlogics, Carmel Also Called: Sahasra Technologies Corp *(G-1751)*

Stoffel Brothers Inc 260 356-6844
6195 N 200 W Huntington (46750) *(G-7372)*

Stoffel Seals Corporation (DH) 845 353-3800
409 Hoosier Dr Angola (46703) *(G-296)*

Stogdill Sports 812 524-7081
1244 Hickory Hill Rd Seymour (47274) *(G-14698)*

Stolle Tool Incorporated 765 935-5185
4693 Webster Rd Richmond (47374) *(G-14209)*

Stolls Woodworking LLC 812 486-5117
8779 N 1025 E Odon (47562) *(G-13353)*

Stoltzfus Custom Welding LLC 765 569-2362
5044 N Judson Rd Rockville (47872) *(G-14356)*

Stolz Structural Inc 812 983-4720
7735 Saint Johns Rd Elberfeld (47613) *(G-3118)*

Stoncor Group Inc 260 747-9724
4115 Polymer Pl Fort Wayne (46809) *(G-5444)*

Stone Artisans Ltd 317 362-0107
7952 Zionsville Rd Indianapolis (46268) *(G-9512)*

Stone Artisans Ltd 847 219-7862
3820 E 62nd St Indianapolis (46220) *(G-9513)*

Stone City Ironworks Inc 812 279-3023
1519 G St Bedford (47421) *(G-675)*

Stone City Products Inc 812 275-3373
1206 7th St Bedford (47421) *(G-676)*

Stone Coal Services LLC 812 455-8215
5344 Gander Rd Elberfeld (47613) *(G-3119)*

Stone Custom Drum LLC 260 403-7519
2701 S Coliseum Blvd Fort Wayne (46803) *(G-5445)*

Stone Quary (PA) 765 473-5578
350 N 150 W Peru (46970) *(G-13603)*

Stone Quary 574 936-2975
10988 11th Rd Plymouth (46563) *(G-13814)*

Stone Sand & Concrete Sales, Tell City Also Called: Mulzer Crushed Stone Inc *(G-15512)*

Stone Surface Solutions, Noblesville Also Called: J Jacoby Inc *(G-13110)*

Stone-Street Quarries Inc 260 639-6511
5536 Hoagland Rd Hoagland (46745) *(G-7171)*

Stonebraker Welding Servi 574 453-7630
38 Ems T32c Ln Leesburg (46538) *(G-10961)*

Stonecast Financial LLC 317 537-1707
9165 Otis Ave Ste 238 Indianapolis (46216) *(G-9514)*

Stonefly Press LLC 812 369-4147
3001 S Forrester St Bloomington (47401) *(G-980)*

Stonehard, Fort Wayne Also Called: Stoncor Group Inc *(G-5444)*

Stoney Acres Woodworking LLC 260 768-4367
2685 S 1000 W Shipshewana (46565) *(G-14893)*

Stoney Creek Wash Machine Shop 574 642-1155
66365 E County Line Rd Millersburg (46543) *(G-11818)*

Stoney Creek Winery LLC 574 642-4454
10315 County Road 146 Millersburg (46543) *(G-11819)*

Stoney Ridgs Candles 574 453-6807
7630 W 640 N Etna Green (46524) *(G-3850)*

Stop N Go Transport LLC 317 902-0815
7821 Palawan Dr Indianapolis (46239) *(G-9515)*

Storageworks Inc 317 577-3511
12000 Exit 5 Pkwy Fishers (46037) *(G-4607)*

Stork News Northwest Indiana 219 808-5221
2880 Tulip Ln Hobart (46342) *(G-7210)*

Storm Trailers, Elkhart Also Called: H & A Products Inc *(G-3394)*

Stotlar Hill LLC 260 497-0808
4723 E Washington Blvd Fort Wayne (46803) *(G-5446)*

Stout Field Ind Partners 317 247-7486
4001 E Minnesota St Indianapolis (46203) *(G-9516)*

Stout Laser Etch LLC 574 376-9296
2345 S Sunrise Cir Warsaw (46580) *(G-16429)*

Stout Laser Etch LLC 574 527-9523
2345 S Sunrise Cir Warsaw (46580) *(G-16430)*

Stout Plastic Weld 219 926-7622
425 S 15th St Chesterton (46304) *(G-1959)*

Stoutco Inc (PA) 574 848-4411
1 Stoutco Dr Bristol (46507) *(G-1293)*

Stowers Wldg Indus Piping LLC 765 279-5002
6103 S County Road 980 E Kirklin (46050) *(G-10192)*

Stradella String Instrs Inc 219 464-3390
120 Sylvan Dr Valparaiso (46385) *(G-16059)*

Strahman Holdings Inc (HQ) 317 818-5030
10201 N Illinois St Ste 200 Carmel (46290) *(G-1771)*

Straight Trippin LLC 812 484-6154
2424 Antilles Dr Evansville (47725) *(G-4336)*

Stranco Inc 219 874-5221
1306 W Us Highway 20 Michigan City (46360) *(G-11673)*

Strand Diagnostics LLC 317 455-2100
5770 Decatur Blvd Ste A Indianapolis (46241) *(G-9517)*

Strategic Solutions Inc 812 853-8525
4133 Merchant Dr Ste 6 Newburgh (47630) *(G-13023)*

Strategic Sourcing LLC 812 346-6904
3320 N State Highway 7 North Vernon (47265) *(G-13297)*

Strategic Tanks Incorporated 574 807-2403
Notre Dame (46556) *(G-13316)*

Stratikore Inc 574 807-0028
1714 E Lincolnway La Porte (46350) *(G-10485)*

Strauss Veal Feeds Inc (PA) 260 982-8611
600 Strauss Provimi Rd North Manchester (46962) *(G-13251)*

Strawtown Pottery & Antq Inc 317 984-5080
12738 Strawtown Ave Noblesville (46060) *(G-13180)*

Streamside Woodshop LLC 260 768-7887
2275 N 925 W Shipshewana (46565) *(G-14894)*

Street Department, Fort Wayne Also Called: City of Fort Wayne *(G-4849)*

Street Dreams Production Inc 574 440-9136
1218 W Washington St South Bend (46601) *(G-15269)*

Streetscape Products Limited, Greensburg Also Called: HH Rellim Inc *(G-6602)*

Stresco Machine Inc 574 773-7334
2365 Beech Rd Nappanee (46550) *(G-12646)*

Strescore Inc 574 233-1117
24445 State Road 23 South Bend (46614) *(G-15270)*

Streven Distilling Company LLC 574 527-4061
733 N Detroit St Warsaw (46580) *(G-16431)*

Strick Corporation 260 692-6121
301 N Polk St Monroe (46772) *(G-12062)*

Strick Trailers LLC 260 692-6121
301 N Polk St Monroe (46772) *(G-12063)*

Stricker Welding LLC 812 207-3800
506 Fairview Rd Memphis (47143) *(G-11467)*

Stride Prosthetics LLC 317 520-2652
2498 Perry Crossing Way Ste 210 Plainfield (46168) *(G-13732)*

Strike & Walk Da Cup Wldg LLC 219 455-4683
6333 Kennedy Ave Hammond (46323) *(G-7015)*

Stritto Sign Art Company 317 356-2126
6639 Allender Trce Morgantown (46160) *(G-12265)*

Strobel Mfg Inc 812 282-4388
6516 Longview Beach Rd Jeffersonville (47130) *(G-10061)*

Strobel Technologies, Jeffersonville *Also Called: Seal Tec Inc (G-10053)*

Stroh Fixit Shop, Stroh *Also Called: Hayward & Sams LLP (G-15401)*

Strohbeck Cabinet Install 812 923-5013
4339 Country View Dr Floyds Knobs (47119) *(G-4694)*

Strong Stitches 260 450-1456
503 S Main St Laotto (46763) *(G-10810)*

Structral Cmpnnts Fbrction Inc 765 342-9188
60 James Baldwin Dr Martinsville (46151) *(G-11429)*

Structural Composites LLC 574 294-7511
107 W Franklin St Elkhart (46516) *(G-3701)*

Structural Composites Ind Inc 260 894-4083
1118 Gerber St Ligonier (46767) *(G-11024)*

Structural Iron & Fab Inc 260 758-2273
480 W Scott St Markle (46770) *(G-11363)*

Stryker Cdc2, Mooresville *Also Called: Stryker Corporation (G-12244)*

Stryker Corporation 832 509-9988
2496 Westpoint Blvd Mooresville (46158) *(G-12244)*

Strykeril Industries LLC 219 321-0400
5534 Saint Joe Rd Fort Wayne (46835) *(G-5447)*

Stryten Energy LLC 812 342-0139
2405 Norcross Dr Columbus (47201) *(G-2397)*

STS Packaging 317 210-0305
2630 Westpoint Blvd Mooresville (46158) *(G-12245)*

Stuart Integrated Systems, Fort Wayne *Also Called: Stuart Manufacturing Inc (G-5448)*

Stuart Manufacturing Inc 260 403-2003
1830 Wayne Trce Unit 407 Fort Wayne (46803) *(G-5448)*

Studabker Spclty Woodworks LLC 260 273-1326
4755 E 300 S Bluffton (46714) *(G-1058)*

Studio A Advertising, Mishawaka *Also Called: Rick Singleton (G-11986)*

Studio Digital Salsa LLC 317 439-8994
7820 Lincoln Trl Plainfield (46168) *(G-13733)*

Studio Indiana 812 332-5073
430 N Sewell Rd Bloomington (47408) *(G-981)*

Studio Printers 574 772-0900
310 Franklin St North Judson (46366) *(G-13214)*

Study Studsters LLC 574 635-1018
616 Mcdonald St Elkhart (46516) *(G-3702)*

Stulls Machining Center Inc 765 942-2717
209 E College St Ladoga (47954) *(G-10510)*

Stulls Mch & Fabrication Inc 765 942-2717
213 E Locust St Ladoga (47954) *(G-10511)*

Stump & Grind 812 453-2121
8827 S State Road 57 Elberfeld (47613) *(G-3120)*

Stump Home Specialties Mfg Inc 574 291-0050
2220 S Main St South Bend (46613) *(G-15271)*

Stump Printing Co 260 723-5171
111 E Broad St South Whitley (46787) *(G-15329)*

Sturm Heat Treating Inc 317 357-2368
1110 S Drexel Ave Indianapolis (46203) *(G-9518)*

Styled-Rite, Gary *Also Called: Trim-A-Seal of Indiana Inc (G-6022)*

Styles Kitchen LLC 765 405-6875
3117 Coppergate Dr Apt 8 Lafayette (47909) *(G-10701)*

Styles Versatility LLC 765 270-2217
1601 Vinton St Lafayette (47904) *(G-10702)*

Stylish Unique Salon LLC 317 938-1273
935 N Pennsylvania St Indianapolis (46204) *(G-9519)*

Styrene Solutions LLC 270 317-2427
317 Capital Ave Mishawaka (46544) *(G-12009)*

Styrene Solutions LLC 574 876-4610
115 E Windsor Ave Elkhart (46514) *(G-3703)*

Sub Blanks Society LLC 877 405-6406
429 E Dupont Rd Ste 1078 Fort Wayne (46825) *(G-5449)*

Subaru Indiana Automotive Inc (HQ) 765 449-1111
5500 State Road 38 E Lafayette (47905) *(G-10703)*

Submicron LLC 800 609-1390
1434 Hedge Ct Greenfield (46140) *(G-6560)*

Substrate Treatments & Lubr 574 258-0904
1309 S Byrkit Ave Mishawaka (46544) *(G-12010)*

Subterranean Mbf, Fort Wayne *Also Called: Nsignia Screen Printing (G-5278)*

Success Express 317 750-1747
1501 S Catlin Rd Rockville (47872) *(G-14357)*

Success Holding Group Corp USA 260 490-9990
6461 N 100 E Ossian (46777) *(G-13435)*

Success Holding Group Intl Inc 260 450-1982
215 N Jefferson St Ossian (46777) *(G-13436)*

Sue & Kims Pies LLC 219 779-2140
5409 Dexter Dr Merrillville (46410) *(G-11562)*

Sue S Sheep Quarters 765 998-2067
11320 S Wheeling Pike Fairmount (46928) *(G-4413)*

Sugar Abd Bruno, Indianapolis *Also Called: Progressive Design Apparel Inc (G-9225)*

Sugar and Bruno Inc 317 991-4422
7260 Georgetown Rd Indianapolis (46268) *(G-9520)*

Sugar Coded Software LLC 858 652-0797
604 E 7th St Burlington (46915) *(G-1446)*

Sugar Creek Fabricators Inc 765 361-0891
503 W 300 N Crawfordsville (47933) *(G-2620)*

Sugar Creek Hops LLC 317 319-1164
1128 Laurelwood Carmel (46032) *(G-1772)*

Sugar Creek Vinyrd Winery Inc 317 844-3785
1324 Helford Ln Carmel (46032) *(G-1773)*

Sugar Daddys Sweet Shop 812 824-2253
5340 S Old State Road 37 Bloomington (47401) *(G-982)*

Sugar Tree Incorporated 260 417-3362
9185 Lima Rd Fort Wayne (46818) *(G-5450)*

Sugarcube Systems Inc 765 543-6709
2746 Margesson Xing Lafayette (47909) *(G-10704)*

Sugarpaste 574 276-8703
2211 S Michigan St South Bend (46613) *(G-15272)*

Suggs Custom Design Solutions 574 549-2174
336 W Garfield Ave Elkhart (46516) *(G-3704)*

Suitable Stylez 765 409-9375
2660 Hastings Ct Apt C Lafayette (47905) *(G-10705)*

Sullair Corporation 219 861-5005
1000 Kieffer Rd Michigan City (46360) *(G-11674)*

Sullair Training Center, Michigan City *Also Called: Hitachi Global Air Pwr US LLC (G-11625)*

Sullivan Daily Times, Sullivan *Also Called: Pierce Oil Co Inc (G-15416)*

Sullivan Engineered Services 812 294-1724
316 Mount Zion Rd Henryville (47126) *(G-7116)*

Sullivan Group, Nappanee *Also Called: Farwall Tsg LLC (G-12596)*

Sullivan IMI 812 268-3306
939 S Section St Sullivan (47882) *(G-15423)*

Sullivan-Palatek Inc 219 874-2497
1201 W Us Highway 20 Michigan City (46360) *(G-11675)*

Sumco LLC 317 241-7600
1351 S Girls School Rd Indianapolis (46231) *(G-9521)*

Sumco Group LLC 317 241-7600
1351 S Girls School Rd Indianapolis (46231) *(G-9522)*

Summer Cottage Inc 317 873-4176
7750 Zionsville Rd Ste 850 Indianapolis (46268) *(G-9523)*

Summerlot Engineered Pdts Inc 812 466-7266
11655 N U S 41 Rosedale Rosedale (47874) *(G-14383)*

Summers Metals & More 812 689-7088
315 Wilson St Osgood (47037) *(G-13417)*

Summerville Miniature Work Sp 317 326-8355
2145 Melody Ln Greenfield (46140) *(G-6561)*

Summerville Miniature Workshop, Greenfield *Also Called: Summerville Miniature Work Sp (G-6561)*

Summit, Logansport *Also Called: Summit/Ems Corporation (G-11108)*

Summit LLC 574 287-7468
660 County Road 15 Elkhart (46516) *(G-3705)*

Summit Brands, Fort Wayne *Also Called: Iron Out Inc (G-5118)*

Summit Brands, Fort Wayne *Also Called: Iron Out Inc (G-5119)*

Summit Business Products Inc 260 244-1820
4506 S State Road 9 57 Churubusco (46723) *(G-1987)*

ALPHABETIC SECTION

Summit Cy Precision Machining.. 260 258-0855
  815 Lawrence Dr Fort Wayne (46804) *(G-5451)*
Summit Foundry Systems Inc... 260 749-7740
  2100 Wayne Haven St Fort Wayne (46803) *(G-5452)*
Summit Industrial Tech Inc... 260 494-3461
  501 W Van Buren St Ste C Columbia City (46725) *(G-2204)*
Summit Manufacturing Corp... 260 428-2600
  2320 Meyer Rd Fort Wayne (46803) *(G-5453)*
Summit Manufacturing Corp... 317 823-2848
  10586 E 59th St Indianapolis (46236) *(G-9524)*
Summit Mfg & Machining Inc... 574 546-4571
  723 High Rd Bremen (46506) *(G-1225)*
Summit Pedorthics LLC.. 260 348-7268
  6207 Monarch Dr Fort Wayne (46815) *(G-5454)*
Summit Seating Inc... 574 264-9636
  2601 Northland Dr Elkhart (46514) *(G-3706)*
Summit/Ems Corporation.. 574 722-1317
  1509 Woodlawn Ave Logansport (46947) *(G-11108)*
Summt Outdoors.. 260 483-2519
  6714 Pointe Inverness Way Ste 200 Fort Wayne (46804) *(G-5455)*
Sun Chemical, Terre Haute *Also Called: Sun Chemical Corporation (G-15717)*
Sun Chemical Corporation.. 972 270-6735
  2642 W State Road 28 Frankfort (46041) *(G-5695)*
Sun Chemical Corporation.. 765 659-6000
  2642 W State Road 28 Frankfort (46041) *(G-5696)*
Sun Chemical Corporation.. 812 235-8031
  1350 N Fruitridge Ave Terre Haute (47804) *(G-15717)*
Sun Control Center LLC.. 260 490-9902
  6032 Highview Dr Ste E Fort Wayne (46818) *(G-5456)*
Sun Cosmetics LLC... 219 531-5359
  4901 Evans Ave Valparaiso (46383) *(G-16060)*
Sun Energy Services LLC... 765 251-1526
  213 E 33rd St Marion (46953) *(G-11339)*
Sun Engineering Inc... 219 962-1191
  950 Marquette Rd Lake Station (46405) *(G-10778)*
Sun King Brewing Company LLC... 317 602-3702
  135 N College Ave Indianapolis (46202) *(G-9525)*
Sun Polymers.. 219 426-1220
  2415 Pennsylvania St Fort Wayne (46803) *(G-5457)*
Sun Polymers International Inc (HQ).. 317 834-6410
  100 Sun Polymers Dr Mooresville (46158) *(G-12246)*
Sun Power Technologies LLC.. 317 399-8113
  17406 Tiller Ct Ste 900 Westfield (46074) *(G-16730)*
Sun Rise Metal Shop... 260 463-4026
  3070 W 350 S Topeka (46571) *(G-15820)*
Sunbeam Packaging Services LLC... 812 867-3551
  12518 Oak Gate Rd Evansville (47725) *(G-4337)*
Sunburst Stained Glass Co Inc.. 812 853-0460
  20 W Jennings St Newburgh (47630) *(G-13024)*
Suncoast Coffee Inc (PA)... 317 251-3198
  1114 E 52nd St Indianapolis (46205) *(G-9526)*
Suncoke Energy Inc... 219 397-0243
  3210 Watling St East Chicago (46312) *(G-3042)*
Suncoke Lake Terminal LLC.. 630 824-1963
  3210 Watling St East Chicago (46312) *(G-3043)*
Sundae's, Indianapolis *Also Called: Buckner Inc (G-7699)*
Sundance Signs.. 765 420-7446
  1116b S 4th St Lafayette (47905) *(G-10706)*
Sunequinox, Harlan *Also Called: Our Country Home Entps Inc (G-7058)*
Sunman Engineering Inc.. 812 623-4072
  131 W Washington St Sunman (47041) *(G-15446)*
Sunnybrook Rv, Middlebury *Also Called: Winnebago of Indiana LLC (G-11759)*
Sunocs LLC... 219 286-7081
  5907 Murvihill Rd Valparaiso (46383) *(G-16061)*
Sunpress South, Morgantown *Also Called: All 4u Printing LLC (G-12251)*
Sunpress South, Morgantown *Also Called: Kmls LLC (G-12259)*
Sunright America Inc... 812 342-3430
  6205 S International Dr Columbus (47201) *(G-2398)*
Sunright Solar Inc... 317 503-9253
  5342 W Vermont St Indianapolis (46224) *(G-9527)*
Sunrise Coal LLC.. 812 745-2002
  6331 E Freelandville Rd Oaktown (47561) *(G-13329)*
Sunrise Coal LLC (HQ).. 812 299-2800
  1183 E Canvasback Dr Terre Haute (47802) *(G-15718)*
Sunrise Energy LLC.. 812 886-9990
  1290 N State Road 67 Vincennes (47591) *(G-16156)*
Sunrise Pigment USA LLC... 773 449-8265
  13173 N Brick Chapel Dr Camby (46113) *(G-1515)*
Sunrise Wood Products LLC... 260 463-4822
  3565 S 300 W Lagrange (46761) *(G-10765)*
Sunrooms of Indiana Inc... 317 891-3232
  115 Shadowlawn Dr Fishers (46038) *(G-4608)*
Suns Out Inc... 765 205-5645
  1000 N Park Ave Marion (46952) *(G-11340)*
Super Blend Inc.. 260 463-7486
  105 S 500 E Lagrange (46761) *(G-10766)*
Super Spa Xclusives LLC.. 219 448-1486
  7616 Jarnecke Ave Hammond (46324) *(G-7016)*
Super-Pufft Snacks Usa Inc.. 850 295-9891
  705 W Dustman Rd Bluffton (46714) *(G-1059)*
Superb Horticulture LLC... 800 567-8264
  2811 Us Highway 31 Plymouth (46563) *(G-13815)*
Superb Tooling Inc... 812 367-2102
  250 Scenic Industrial Dr Ferdinand (47532) *(G-4449)*
Superioir Essex, Franklin *Also Called: Essex Frkawa Mgnt Wire USA LLC (G-5729)*
Superior, Elkhart *Also Called: Superior Tool & Die Co Inc (G-3710)*
Superior AG Resources Coop Inc... 812 724-4455
  504 S 2nd St Owensville (47665) *(G-13473)*
Superior Aluminum, New Haven *Also Called: Superior Aluminum Alloys LLC (G-12921)*
Superior Aluminum Alloys LLC... 260 749-7599
  14214 Edgerton Rd New Haven (46774) *(G-12921)*
Superior Axle LLC... 574 295-1905
  3001 Tuscany Dr Elkhart (46514) *(G-3707)*
Superior Canopy Corporation.. 260 488-4065
  2435 E Bellefontaine Rd Hamilton (46742) *(G-6862)*
Superior Coatings Inc... 574 546-0591
  1730 W Dewey St Bremen (46506) *(G-1226)*
Superior Concepts Indus LLC... 765 628-2956
  11763 E 300 S Greentown (46936) *(G-6649)*
Superior Distribution.. 317 308-5525
  2570 N Shadeland Ave Indianapolis (46219) *(G-9528)*
Superior Equipment & Mfg... 260 925-0152
  717 Lakeshore Dr Auburn (46706) *(G-427)*
Superior Essex, Fort Wayne *Also Called: Essex Frkawa Mgnt Wire USA LLC (G-4964)*
Superior Essex Inc... 260 420-1565
  3405 Meyer Rd Ste 170 Fort Wayne (46803) *(G-5458)*
SUPERIOR ESSEX INTERNATIONAL LP, Fort Wayne *Also Called: Superior Essex Intl LP (G-5459)*
Superior Essex Intl LP.. 260 461-4000
  1700 Swinney Ave Fort Wayne (46802) *(G-5459)*
Superior Fiberglass & Resins, Elkhart *Also Called: Superior Indus Solutions Inc (G-3708)*
Superior Forest Products LLC... 765 245-2895
  6429 W 100 N Montezuma (47862) *(G-12083)*
Superior Hardwoods, Montezuma *Also Called: Superior Forest Products LLC (G-12083)*
Superior Hardwoods, Montezuma *Also Called: Timberland Resources Inc (G-12084)*
Superior Indus Solutions Inc... 574 264-0161
  1030 All Pro Dr Elkhart (46514) *(G-3708)*
Superior Indus Solutions Inc (PA)... 317 781-4400
  1411 Roosevelt Ave Ste 250 Indianapolis (46201) *(G-9529)*
Superior Kreations Inc... 765 635-3729
  1926 E 53rd St Anderson (46013) *(G-202)*
Superior Laminating Inc... 574 361-7266
  60894 County Road 19 Goshen (46528) *(G-6261)*
Superior Layout.. 812 371-1709
  1417 Chestnut St Columbus (47201) *(G-2399)*
Superior Machine & Tool Co... 260 493-4517
  6911 Trafalgar Dr Fort Wayne (46803) *(G-5460)*
Superior Machine Incorporated... 574 654-8243
  33721 Early Rd New Carlisle (46552) *(G-12846)*
Superior Metal Tech LLC.. 317 897-9850
  9850 E 30th St Indianapolis (46229) *(G-9530)*
Superior Mfg Inc... 812 983-9900
  11333 Elberfeld Rd Elberfeld (47613) *(G-3121)*

Superior Piece Parts Inc 574 277-4236
54015 Fir Rd Mishawaka (46545) *(G-12011)*

Superior Plastics LLC 317 698-6422
9502 E 100 S Zionsville (46077) *(G-17055)*

Superior Print Inc 812 246-6311
840 S Indiana Ave Sellersburg (47172) *(G-14617)*

Superior Radiant Products Inc 800 527-4328
315 N Madison St Fortville (46040) *(G-5606)*

Superior Sample Co Inc 260 894-3136
520 Gerber St Ligonier (46767) *(G-11025)*

Superior Seating Inc 574 389-9011
21468 C St Elkhart (46516) *(G-3709)*

Superior Solvents and Chem, Indianapolis *Also Called: Superior Indus Solutions Inc (G-9529)*

Superior Source Woodworks LLC 574 773-4841
2881 E County Line Rd Nappanee (46550) *(G-12647)*

Superior Tool & Die Co Inc (PA) 574 293-2591
2325 S Nappanee St Elkhart (46517) *(G-3710)*

Superior Truss & Panel Inc 708 339-1200
7592 Melton Rd Gary (46403) *(G-6016)*

Superior Veneer & Plywood LLC 812 941-8850
1819 Dewey St New Albany (47150) *(G-12819)*

Superior Wood Products, Warsaw *Also Called: Rbk Development Inc (G-16417)*

Superior Woodcrafts LLC 260 357-3743
1111 S Franklin St Garrett (46738) *(G-5877)*

Supernova International Inc 317 969-8246
4444 Decatur Blvd Ste 1200 Indianapolis (46241) *(G-9531)*

Supersweet Farm Service, Nappanee *Also Called: AG Processing A Cooperative (G-12577)*

Supplieriq, South Bend *Also Called: Supplieriq LLC (G-15273)*

Supplieriq LLC 574 323-0707
1007 Chapin St South Bend (46601) *(G-15273)*

Suppress TEC LLC 812 453-5813
7599 Saint Johns Rd Elberfeld (47613) *(G-3122)*

Supreme, Goshen *Also Called: Supreme Industries Inc (G-6265)*

Supreme Corporation 574 642-4888
2581 Kercher Rd Goshen (46528) *(G-6262)*

Supreme Corporation (DH) 574 642-4888
2581 Kercher Rd Goshen (46528) *(G-6263)*

Supreme Corporation 260 894-9191
1491 Gerber St Ligonier (46767) *(G-11026)*

Supreme Corporation Georgia 574 228-4130
2581 Kercher Rd Goshen (46528) *(G-6264)*

Supreme Industries Inc (HQ) 574 642-3070
2581 Kercher Rd Goshen (46528) *(G-6265)*

Supreme Signs Inc 219 384-0198
265 Springhill Dr Valparaiso (46385) *(G-16062)*

Supremex Midwest Inc 317 253-4321
5331 N Tacoma Ave Indianapolis (46220) *(G-9532)*

Supremex Midwest LLC (HQ) 317 253-4321
5331 N Tacoma Ave Indianapolis (46220) *(G-9533)*

Supremex Midwest LLC 317 898-2000
7915 E 30th St Indianapolis (46219) *(G-9534)*

Supremex USA Inc (HQ) 317 253-4321
5331 N Tacoma Ave Indianapolis (46220) *(G-9535)*

Sur-Loc Inc 260 495-4065
501 E Swager St Fremont (46737) *(G-5836)*

Surclean Inc 248 791-2226
463 Southpoint Cir Ste 300 Brownsburg (46112) *(G-1405)*

Sure Tool & Engineering Inc 260 693-2193
302 W Pleasant St Churubusco (46723) *(G-1988)*

Sure-Flo Seamless Gutters Inc 260 622-4372
9192 N 750 E Ossian (46777) *(G-13437)*

Surestep LLC 574 233-3352
17530 Dugdale Dr South Bend (46635) *(G-15274)*

Surface Elements Inc 574 546-5455
506 E North St Bremen (46506) *(G-1227)*

Surface Enhancements Inc 574 269-1366
125 W 250 N Warsaw (46582) *(G-16432)*

Surface Generation Tech LLC 765 425-2741
56 Beauvoir Cir Anderson (46011) *(G-203)*

Surfis Inc 260 357-3475
Auburn (46706) *(G-428)*

Surplus Store and Exchange 765 447-0200
1650 Main St Lafayette (47904) *(G-10707)*

SUS Cast Products Inc 574 753-4111
1825 W Market St Logansport (46947) *(G-11109)*

Sushiya-US 260 444-4263
14328 Brafferton Pkwy Fort Wayne (46814) *(G-5461)*

Sustainable Sourcing LLC 765 505-2338
10500 S State Road 63 Clinton (47842) *(G-2078)*

Sustainables LLC 502 741-4834
6106 Evanston Ave Indianapolis (46220) *(G-9536)*

Sutton Custom Molds Inc 260 463-2772
4770 E 100 N Lagrange (46761) *(G-10767)*

SUv Parts & Accessories Inc 765 457-1345
2109 N Wabash Ave Kokomo (46901) *(G-10344)*

Suzuki Garphyttan Corp 574 232-8800
4404 Nimtz Pkwy South Bend (46628) *(G-15275)*

SW Watkins Limited 260 484-4844
918 W Cook Rd Fort Wayne (46825) *(G-5462)*

Swag's Screen Prtg Sportswear, Terre Haute *Also Called: Swagerle Screen Printing (G-15719)*

Swager Communications Inc 260 495-2515
501 E Swager St Fremont (46737) *(G-5837)*

Swagerle Screen Printing 812 232-6947
2950 S 7th St Terre Haute (47802) *(G-15719)*

Swags Welding Services LLC 260 417-7510
6650 E Mcguire Rd Churubusco (46723) *(G-1989)*

Swan Real Estate Mgmt Inc 765 664-1478
815 N Western Ave Marion (46952) *(G-11341)*

Swanel Beverage, Hammond *Also Called: Swanel Inc (G-7017)*

Swanel Inc (PA) 219 932-7676
6044 Erie Ave Hammond (46320) *(G-7017)*

Swanson Woodworking 765 585-0328
2949 E 950 N Attica (47918) *(G-354)*

Swansons Service Center 574 858-9406
U S 30 & County Road 650 W Atwood (46502) *(G-358)*

Swarovski North America Ltd 317 841-0037
6020 E 82nd St Ste 430 Indianapolis (46250) *(G-9537)*

Swartzentruber Sawmill LLC 812 486-3350
5912 N 900 E Montgomery (47558) *(G-12125)*

Swartzndrber Hrdwood Creat LLC 574 534-2502
17229 County Road 18 Goshen (46528) *(G-6266)*

Sweet Keepsakes 219 872-8467
319 Black Oak Dr Trail Creek (46360) *(G-15840)*

Sweet Moon Macaron LLC 219 484-9851
109 N Broad St Griffith (46319) *(G-6817)*

Sweet Obsssons Bake Shoppe LLC 260 273-2145
111 E Market St Bluffton (46714) *(G-1060)*

Sweet Properties LLC 812 283-8367
347 Spring St Jeffersonville (47130) *(G-10062)*

Sweet Scents LLC 219 902-6853
800 Sycamore St Evansville (47708) *(G-4338)*

Sweet Things Candy & Gifts, Carmel *Also Called: Sweet Things Inc (G-1774)*

Sweet Things Inc (PA) 317 872-8720
1481 Sunray Dr Apt 105 Carmel (46280) *(G-1774)*

Sweet Tooth LLC 317 986-3764
4543 E 38th St Indianapolis (46218) *(G-9538)*

Sweetener Supply Corporation 708 588-8400
11048 Mac Park Dr Wolcott (47995) *(G-16935)*

Sweetjoy Company LLC 502 821-0511
1809 Depauw Ave New Albany (47150) *(G-12820)*

Sweetwater Productions, Fort Wayne *Also Called: Sweetwater Sound LLC (G-5463)*

Sweetwater Sound LLC (PA) 260 432-8176
5501 Us Highway 30 W Fort Wayne (46818) *(G-5463)*

Swi 812 342-2409
3475 W International Ct Columbus (47201) *(G-2400)*

Swift Fuels LLC 765 464-8336
1435 Win Hentschel Blvd Ste 205 West Lafayette (47906) *(G-16632)*

Swiss Alps Printing & Off Sups, Vevay *Also Called: Swiss Alps Printing Inc (G-16113)*

Swiss Alps Printing Inc 812 427-3844
108 W Pike St Vevay (47043) *(G-16113)*

Swiss Caps, Patriot *Also Called: Switzerland Hills Inc (G-13511)*

ALPHABETIC SECTION — T-Flyerz Printing and Prom LLC

Swiss Labs Machine & Engrg Inc 317 346-6190
2854 N Graham Rd Franklin (46131) *(G-5780)*

Swiss Metal Spinning Co 260 692-1401
2301 W 200 S Monroe (46772) *(G-12064)*

Swiss Perfection LLC 574 457-4457
100 S Huntington St Syracuse (46567) *(G-15481)*

Swiss Woodworking LLC 260 849-9669
371 W 500 S Berne (46711) *(G-729)*

Switzer Buildings, Bremen *Also Called: Bremen Composites LLC (G-1177)*

Switzerland Hills Inc 812 594-2810
19091 State Road 250 Patriot (47038) *(G-13511)*

Swva Kentucky LLC 260 969-3500
7575 W Jefferson Blvd Fort Wayne (46804) *(G-5464)*

Sx4 .... 812 967-2502
3363 E Wetzel Rd Palmyra (47164) *(G-13486)*

Sycamore Coal Inc 812 491-4000
1183 E Canvasback Dr Terre Haute (47802) *(G-15720)*

Sycamore Enterprises Inc 812 477-2266
2214 Saint Joseph Ind Park Dr Evansville (47720) *(G-4339)*

Sycamore Winery LLC 812 243-0565
1320 Durkees Ferry Rd West Terre Haute (47885) *(G-16655)*

Syltech Experimental 765 489-1777
13931 Clyde Oler Rd Hagerstown (47346) *(G-6843)*

Sylvan Marine Inc (PA) 574 831-2950
68143 Clunette St New Paris (46553) *(G-12970)*

Sylvia Kay Hartley (PA) 317 984-3424
103 E Main St Arcadia (46030) *(G-318)*

Symantec, Indianapolis *Also Called: Gen Digital Inc (G-8268)*

Symmetry Medical Inc (DH) 574 267-8700
3724 N State Road 15 Warsaw (46582) *(G-16433)*

Symmetry Medical Inc 574 267-8700
486 W 350 N Warsaw (46582) *(G-16434)*

Symmetry Medical Mfg Inc 574 371-2284
3724 N State Road 15 Warsaw (46582) *(G-16435)*

Symmetry Medical USA Inc 574 267-8700
3724 N State Road 15 Warsaw (46582) *(G-16436)*

Syndicate Sales Inc (PA) 765 457-7277
2025 N Wabash Ave Kokomo (46901) *(G-10345)*

Synergy Composites LLC 217 454-9711
9034 Caminito Ct Indianapolis (46234) *(G-9539)*

Synergy Feeds LLC 260 723-5141
401 N Main St South Whitley (46787) *(G-15330)*

Synergy Industries Inc 574 320-2754
59264 Wilray Dr Elkhart (46517) *(G-3711)*

Synermed International Inc 317 896-1565
17408 Tiller Ct Ste 1900 Westfield (46074) *(G-16731)*

Syntag Rfld 317 685-5292
602 N Park Ave Indianapolis (46204) *(G-9540)*

Synthes USA, Warsaw *Also Called: Depuy Synthes Inc (G-16349)*

Synthypnion Press LLC 317 885-8394
8144 S Pennsylvania St Indianapolis (46227) *(G-9541)*

Syracuse Glass Inc 574 457-5516
1107 S Huntington St Ste D Syracuse (46567) *(G-15482)*

Syscon International Inc 574 232-3900
1108 High St South Bend (46601) *(G-15276)*

Syscon-Plantstar, South Bend *Also Called: Syscon International Inc (G-15276)*

Sysgenomics LLC 574 302-5396
51210 Lexingham Dr Granger (46530) *(G-6384)*

Systec Conveyors, Indianapolis *Also Called: Systec Corporation (G-9542)*

Systec Corporation 317 890-9230
3245 N Mitthoefer Rd Indianapolis (46235) *(G-9542)*

System Science Institute 260 436-6096
4710 Arden Dr Fl 1 Fort Wayne (46804) *(G-5465)*

System Solutions Inc 317 877-7572
4 Forest Bay Ln Cicero (46034) *(G-2001)*

Systems & Services of Michiana (PA) 574 273-1111
3505 W Mcgill St South Bend (46628) *(G-15277)*

Systems & Services of Michiana 574 277-3355
325 N Dixie Way Ste 300 South Bend (46637) *(G-15278)*

Systems and Services, South Bend *Also Called: Systems & Services of Michiana (G-15278)*

Systems Contracting Corp 765 361-2991
4537 S Nucor Rd Crawfordsville (47933) *(G-2621)*

Systems Engineering and Sls Co 260 422-1671
3805 E Pontiac St Fort Wayne (46803) *(G-5466)*

T & D Printing, Fishers *Also Called: T N D Printing (G-4609)*

T & E Welding Inc 812 324-0140
10 W Locust St Petersburg (47567) *(G-13627)*

T & G Games Inc 574 297-5455
4900 N Boxman Pl Monticello (47960) *(G-12171)*

T & I Tool LLC 765 489-6293
99 N Sycamore St Hagerstown (47346) *(G-6844)*

T & L Sharpening Inc 574 583-3868
2663 S Freeman Rd Monticello (47960) *(G-12172)*

T & L Tool & Die II Inc 574 722-6246
911 Calla St Logansport (46947) *(G-11110)*

T & M, Merrillville *Also Called: T & M Equipment Company Inc (G-11563)*

T & M Equipment Company Inc 317 293-9255
6501 Guion Rd Indianapolis (46268) *(G-9543)*

T & M Equipment Company Inc (PA) 219 942-2299
2880 E 83rd Pl Merrillville (46410) *(G-11563)*

T & M Precision Inc (PA) 812 689-5769
1861 S Us Highway 421 Versailles (47042) *(G-16104)*

T & M Precision Inc 513 253-2274
1861 S Us Highway 421 Versailles (47042) *(G-16105)*

T & M Rubber Inc 574 533-3173
1102 S 10th St Goshen (46526) *(G-6267)*

T & S Equipment Company 260 665-9521
2999 N Wayne St Angola (46703) *(G-297)*

T & T Hydraulics Inc 765 548-2355
7443 S 625 W Rosedale (47874) *(G-14384)*

T A T Apparel and Promotions, Indianapolis *Also Called: Thoughts Are Things Inc (G-9599)*

T and J Printing Supply 317 986-4765
5739 W 85th St Indianapolis (46278) *(G-9544)*

T B K Tarp Sales & Service, Gary *Also Called: T K Sales & Service (G-6017)*

T F & T Inc 765 874-1628
603 W Linden St Lynn (47355) *(G-11188)*

T G R Finishings, Kokomo *Also Called: Tgr Inc (G-10348)*

T I B Inc 574 892-5151
775 N Michigan St Argos (46501) *(G-327)*

T J B Inc 219 293-8030
2926 Paul Dr Elkhart (46514) *(G-3712)*

T K Fabricating 765 866-0755
6331 W 200 S Crawfordsville (47933) *(G-2622)*

T K M Triple K Machining 765 629-2805
6972 S 200 W Rushville (46173) *(G-14414)*

T K Sales & Service 219 962-8982
669 S Grand Blvd Gary (46403) *(G-6017)*

T K T Inc 574 825-5233
420 N Main St Middlebury (46540) *(G-11753)*

T L Tate Manufacturing Inc 765 452-8283
1500 N Webster St Kokomo (46901) *(G-10346)*

T Logistics, Greenwood *Also Called: T Organization Inc (G-6771)*

T N D Printing 260 493-4949
12634 Walrond Rd Fishers (46037) *(G-4609)*

T Organization Inc 463 204-5118
624 Nicole Dr Apt D Greenwood (46143) *(G-6771)*

T Productions Inc 574 257-8610
504 S Byrkit St Mishawaka (46544) *(G-12012)*

T R Bulger Inc 219 879-8525
3123 E Michigan Blvd Trail Creek (46360) *(G-15841)*

T S Manufacturing 574 831-6647
68563 County Road 17 New Paris (46553) *(G-12971)*

T Shirt 1 Inc 812 232-5046
2319 N 25th St Terre Haute (47804) *(G-15721)*

T Shorter Manufacturing Inc 574 264-4131
2931 Dexter Dr Elkhart (46514) *(G-3713)*

T W Brackett & Assoc LLC 765 769-3000
103 N Perry St Attica (47918) *(G-355)*

T W Machine & Grinding 260 799-4236
7150 N 350 W Columbia City (46725) *(G-2205)*

T-A Wind Down Inc 708 839-1400
9200 Calumet Ave Ste N1 Munster (46321) *(G-12566)*

T-Flyerz Printing and Prom LLC 260 729-7392
6073 N Us Highway 27 Bryant (47326) *(G-1437)*

T-H Licensing Inc

T-H Licensing Inc..765 772-4128
2400 Sagamore Pkwy S Lafayette (47905) *(G-10708)*

T-Mack Machinery LLC..765 728-8655
418 W Oil St Montpelier (47359) *(G-12183)*

T-N-T Performance Mch Sp LLC......................................574 457-5056
210 E Maple Grove St Syracuse (46567) *(G-15483)*

T. E. Scott, Rockville Also Called: Scott Pet Products Inc *(G-14354)*

T.K.O. Graphix, Plainfield Also Called: Tko Enterprises Inc *(G-13736)*

T&S Group LLC..219 310-0364
1141 Paradise Way N Unit B Greenwood (46143) *(G-6772)*

T&S Midwest Beverage LLC..317 690-1705
3428 N Brandywine Rd Shelbyville (46176) *(G-14802)*

T&T Elite Construction LLC...317 657-8898
4652 Falcon Run Way Indianapolis (46254) *(G-9545)*

T1design, Indianapolis Also Called: Travis Britton *(G-9632)*

Tab Software Corp..260 490-7132
8118 Victoria Woods Pl Fort Wayne (46825) *(G-5467)*

Tabco Business Forms Inc...812 882-2836
638 Broadway St Vincennes (47591) *(G-16157)*

Taberts Machine Shop..765 464-9181
5833 E Old Us Highway 52 Templeton (47986) *(G-15522)*

Table Thyme Designs LLC..317 634-0281
217 W 10th St Ste 125 Indianapolis (46202) *(G-9546)*

Tacair Publications LLC..260 429-7975
15922 Wappes Rd Churubusco (46723) *(G-1990)*

Tackle Service Center, Mooresville Also Called: Robert J Matt *(G-12239)*

Tactical Wldg Fabrication LLC...317 457-5340
3620 Developers Rd Indianapolis (46227) *(G-9547)*

Tactile Engineering Inc...765 233-6620
3601 Sagamore Pkwy N Ste C Lafayette (47904) *(G-10709)*

Tactive, Indianapolis Also Called: Print Resources Inc *(G-9202)*

Tads Construction Clean Up, Marion Also Called: Trevares D Smith *(G-11343)*

Taggarts Custom Sndblst LLC..765 825-4584
1740 Georgia Ave Connersville (47331) *(G-2471)*

Taghleef Industries Inc..302 326-5500
3600 E Head Ave Rosedale (47874) *(G-14385)*

Taghleef Industries Inc..812 460-5657
425 N Brown Ave Terre Haute (47803) *(G-15722)*

Takeda..812 972-0957
1205 Todd Ln Nw Corydon (47112) *(G-2517)*

Takeda Pharmaceuticals USA Inc..................................812 738-0452
1860 Andrew Ct Nw Corydon (47112) *(G-2518)*

Talbert Manufacturing, Rensselaer Also Called: Liberty Trailers LLC *(G-14058)*

Talbert Manufacturing Inc (PA)......................................800 348-5232
1628 W State Road 114 Rensselaer (47978) *(G-14071)*

Talent Cabinet LLC..317 733-2149
10903 Yorktown Xing Carmel (46032) *(G-1775)*

Tall Cotton Marketing LLC..312 320-5862
3522 S State Road 104 La Porte (46350) *(G-10486)*

Tall Oaks Woodworking..708 275-5723
12608 Tall Oaks Dr Cedar Lake (46303) *(G-1839)*

Talon Products LLC..574 218-0100
1690 Commerce Dr Bristol (46507) *(G-1294)*

Talon Systems Inc..765 393-1711
6548 N 100 W Alexandria (46001) *(G-63)*

Talon Terra LLC...219 393-1400
399 E Hupp Rd La Porte (46350) *(G-10487)*

Tamco Manufacturing Co..574 294-1909
2717 Oakland Ave Elkhart (46517) *(G-3714)*

Tamwall Demountable Partitions, Indianapolis Also Called: Tamwall Inc *(G-9548)*

Tamwall Inc...317 546-5055
4362 Sellers St Indianapolis (46226) *(G-9548)*

Tangent Rail Products Inc...412 325-0202
2901 Ohio Blvd Ste 252 Terre Haute (47803) *(G-15723)*

Tangent Rail Products Inc...812 789-5331
3818 S County Road 50 E Winslow (47598) *(G-16925)*

Tanglewood LLC..607 621-1189
4742 W County Road 1060 N Boonville (47601) *(G-1099)*

Tanglewood Press, Indianapolis Also Called: Tanglewood Publishing Inc *(G-9549)*

Tanglewood Publishing Inc..812 877-9488
1060 N Capitol Ave Ste E395 Indianapolis (46204) *(G-9549)*

ALPHABETIC SECTION

Tangoe, Indianapolis Also Called: Tangoe Us Inc *(G-9550)*

Tangoe Us Inc...203 859-9300
8888 Keystone Xing Ste 1300 Indianapolis (46240) *(G-9550)*

Tangoe Us Inc (DH)..973 257-0300
8888 Keystone Xing Ste 1300 Indianapolis (46240) *(G-9551)*

Tanguero Inc...415 236-2642
3315 S Daniel Ct Bloomington (47401) *(G-983)*

Tanimura & Antle, Plymouth Also Called: Ready Pac Foods Inc *(G-13810)*

Tank Construction & Service Co...................................317 509-6294
6145 S Indianapolis Rd Whitestown (46075) *(G-16823)*

Tao Tao USA, Indianapolis Also Called: Taotao Usa Inc *(G-9552)*

Taotao Usa Inc..317 856-8628
8207 Zionsville Rd Indianapolis (46268) *(G-9552)*

Tap-A-Lite Inc..219 932-8067
820 165th St Hammond (46324) *(G-7018)*

Tap, The, Bloomington Also Called: Myfin Inc *(G-928)*

Targamite LLC..260 489-0046
6917 Innovation Blvd Fort Wayne (46818) *(G-5468)*

Target Metal Blanking Inc..812 346-1700
1 Steel Way North Vernon (47265) *(G-13298)*

Target Printing Inc...260 744-6038
3233 Lafayette St Fort Wayne (46806) *(G-5469)*

Tarpenning-Lafollette Co Inc...317 780-1500
4212 W 71st St Ste B Indianapolis (46268) *(G-9553)*

Tartan Properties LLC..317 714-7337
3419 Roosevelt Ave Indianapolis (46218) *(G-9554)*

Tarver Wolff LLC..765 265-7416
1149 Brookhaven Rd Brookville (47012) *(G-1336)*

TAs Welding and Grn Svcs LLC.....................................765 210-4274
5459 W Old 24 Wabash (46992) *(G-16216)*

Tasco Industries Inc..219 922-6100
10018 Express Dr Highland (46322) *(G-7157)*

Tascon Corp..317 547-6127
2213 Duke St Indianapolis (46205) *(G-9555)*

Task Force Tips Inc..219 462-6161
3701 Innovation Way Valparaiso (46383) *(G-16063)*

Task Force Tips LLC (PA)...219 462-6161
3701 Innovation Way Valparaiso (46383) *(G-16064)*

Taste of Joy LLC...219 501-0157
2031 Arrowhead Dr Apt 1a Merrillville (46410) *(G-11564)*

Tasty Treats Bakery LLC..317 622-8829
8251 Dogwood Circle East Dr Indianapolis (46268) *(G-9556)*

Tasus Corporation (HQ)...812 333-6500
300 N Daniels Way Bloomington (47404) *(G-984)*

Tate Soaps & Surfactants Inc..765 868-4488
1500 N Webster St Kokomo (46901) *(G-10347)*

Tatianas Embroidery...574 875-1654
59018 Jasmine Ct Elkhart (46517) *(G-3715)*

Tatman Inc..765 825-2164
815 N Central Ave Connersville (47331) *(G-2472)*

Taulman3d LLC..401 996-8868
1600 A St Ne Ste 18 Linton (47441) *(G-11047)*

Taunyas Creative Cuts...812 574-7722
220 Clifty Dr Madison (47250) *(G-11253)*

Taurus Tech & Engrg LLC..765 282-2090
4401 S Delaware Dr Muncie (47302) *(G-12498)*

Taurus Tool & Engineering Inc......................................765 282-2090
4401 S Delaware Dr Muncie (47302) *(G-12499)*

Tavistock Restaurants LLC..317 488-1230
49 W Maryland St Ste 104 Indianapolis (46204) *(G-9557)*

Tayco Brace Inc..574 850-7910
205 W Western Ave # 101 South Bend (46601) *(G-15279)*

Taylor & Francis..765 364-1300
5500 W 74th St Indianapolis (46268) *(G-9558)*

Taylor Chain, East Chicago Also Called: Grc Enterprises Inc *(G-3012)*

Taylor Communications Inc...317 392-3235
1750 Miller Ave Shelbyville (46176) *(G-14803)*

Taylor Gary..812 895-0715
3561 E Crystal Valley Dr Vincennes (47591) *(G-16158)*

Taylor Made Awards, Greencastle Also Called: Taylor Made Enterprises Inc *(G-6433)*

Taylor Made Candles..812 663-6634
7864 W County Road 80 N Greensburg (47240) *(G-6634)*

ALPHABETIC SECTION — Techseal Division

Taylor Made Enterprises Inc.. 765 653-8481
1292 N Jackson St Greencastle (46135) *(G-6433)*

Taylor Made Fabrics, Elkhart *Also Called: Taylor Made Group LLC (G-3716)*

Taylor Made Group LLC... 574 535-1125
3501 County Road 6 E Elkhart (46514) *(G-3716)*

Taylor Tire Treading Co Inc.. 317 634-9476
2101 Massachusetts Ave Indianapolis (46218) *(G-9559)*

Taylor Welding... 765 659-2955
3342 Washington Ave Frankfort (46041) *(G-5697)*

Tb Plastic Extrusions Inc... 574 266-7409
54432 Adams St Elkhart (46514) *(G-3717)*

Tbi, Wheatfield *Also Called: Tefft Bridge and Iron LLC (G-16773)*

Tbin LLC... 812 491-9100
1698 S 100 W Princeton (47670) *(G-14013)*

Tbk America Inc... 765 962-0147
3700 W Industries Rd Richmond (47374) *(G-14210)*

Tc Graphics, Evansville *Also Called: Schaffsteins Truck Clean LLC (G-4298)*

Tc Heartland LLC (PA)... 317 566-9750
14390 Clay Terrace Blvd Ste 205 Carmel (46032) *(G-1776)*

Tc Heartland LLC... 317 876-7121
4635 W 84th St Ste 300 Indianapolis (46268) *(G-9560)*

Tc Pallets & Peddler Sweet LLC... 812 283-1090
1414 E 10th St Jeffersonville (47130) *(G-10063)*

Tc4 LLC... 317 709-5429
9217 Muir Ln Fishers (46037) *(G-4610)*

Tcb Enterprises LLC... 574 522-3971
51165 Greenfield Pkwy Middlebury (46540) *(G-11754)*

Tcb Industries Inc... 574 522-3971
4519 Wyland Dr Elkhart (46516) *(G-3718)*

Tcb International LLC... 502 619-3191
12378 Bridgewater Rd Indianapolis (46256) *(G-9561)*

Tclogic LLC... 317 464-5152
519 E Mccarty St Indianapolis (46203) *(G-9562)*

TCS Cabinets... 765 208-5350
557 E 1450 N Summitville (46070) *(G-15433)*

Tct Technologies, Indianapolis *Also Called: Tct Technologies LLC (G-9563)*

Tct Technologies LLC... 317 833-6730
8435 Keystone Xing Ste 230 Indianapolis (46240) *(G-9563)*

Tdc Logging LLC.. 574 289-4243
24890 Edison Rd South Bend (46628) *(G-15280)*

Tdk Graphics, Crown Point *Also Called: Tdk Graphics Inc (G-2762)*

Tdk Graphics Inc... 219 663-7799
1180 N Main St Crown Point (46307) *(G-2762)*

TDS, Brookston *Also Called: Terra Drive Systems Inc (G-1313)*

Tdy Industries LLC.. 260 726-8121
250 E Lafayette St Portland (47371) *(G-13968)*

TE Custom Woodwork LLC.. 317 910-6906
10480 Lookout Ln Indianapolis (46234) *(G-9564)*

Teach ME Stuff.. 317 550-6319
355 Andscott Dr Brownsburg (46112) *(G-1406)*

Teaco Inc... 219 874-6234
2117 Ohio St Michigan City (46360) *(G-11676)*

Teague Concrete Backhoe... 765 674-4692
105 W 3rd St Jonesboro (46938) *(G-10081)*

Teal Lake Iron Mining Company.. 574 273-7000
4100 Edison Lakes Pkwy Mishawaka (46545) *(G-12013)*

Team Gear Printing LLC.. 765 935-4748
3451 Dorothy Ln Richmond (47374) *(G-14211)*

Team Gear Printing LLC (PA).. 765 977-2995
4714 National Rd E Richmond (47374) *(G-14212)*

Team Green Inc.. 317 872-2700
7615 Zionsville Rd Indianapolis (46268) *(G-9565)*

Team Handy, Evansville *Also Called: Team Handy LLC (G-4340)*

Team Handy LLC.. 812 962-3630
14215 N Green River Rd Evansville (47725) *(G-4340)*

Team Hillman LLC.. 260 426-2626
414 E Wayne St Fort Wayne (46802) *(G-5470)*

Team Image.. 317 477-0027
18 W South St Greenfield (46140) *(G-6562)*

Team Image LLC (PA)... 317 468-0802
121 S Pennsylvania St Greenfield (46140) *(G-6563)*

Team Image LLC... 317 477-7468
212 E Main St Greenfield (46140) *(G-6564)*

Team Mantra Wear LLC... 260 273-0421
979 N Main St Bluffton (46714) *(G-1061)*

Team Mantra Wear LLC... 260 827-0061
4126 N 100 E Bluffton (46714) *(G-1062)*

Team Oneway.. 574 387-5417
12911 Industrial Park Dr Unit 9 Granger (46530) *(G-6385)*

Team Pride Athletic AP Corp.. 574 224-8326
2196 Sweetgum Rd Rochester (46975) *(G-14327)*

Team Rocket Aircraft, Cutler *Also Called: Frazier Aviation LLC (G-2784)*

Team Spirit.. 219 924-6272
10429 Columbia Ave Munster (46321) *(G-12567)*

Teamair Mro Ltd... 812 584-3733
12978 Josephs Field Ln Moores Hill (47032) *(G-12188)*

TEC Air Inc.. 219 301-7084
9200 Calumet Ave Ste Nw1 Munster (46321) *(G-12568)*

TEC Hoist LLC.. 708 598-2300
1349 E Main St Griffith (46319) *(G-6818)*

TEC Photography... 812 332-9847
1011 W Gourley Pike Bloomington (47404) *(G-985)*

TEC-Air LLC.. 219 301-7084
9200 Calumet Ave Ste Nw01 Munster (46321) *(G-12569)*

Tech Castings LLC.. 765 535-4100
1102 South St Shirley (47384) *(G-14902)*

Tech Innovation LLC... 317 506-8343
8517 Oakmont Ln Indianapolis (46260) *(G-9566)*

Tech Solutions and Sales Inc.. 317 536-5846
6898 Hawthorn Park Dr Indianapolis (46220) *(G-9567)*

Tech Tronic LLC.. 260 750-7992
2100 Saint Marys Ave Apt 308 Fort Wayne (46808) *(G-5471)*

Tech Weigh Manufacturing, Griffith *Also Called: Technical Weighing Svcs Inc (G-6819)*

Techbrokers/Techchic, Scottsburg *Also Called: Donna Dalton (G-14553)*

Techcom Inc.. 812 372-0960
4630 Progress Dr Columbus (47201) *(G-2401)*

Techknowledgey Inc.. 574 202-0362
1711 W Clinton St Goshen (46526) *(G-6268)*

Techknowledgey Inc (PA)... 574 971-4267
1840 W Lincoln Ave Goshen (46526) *(G-6269)*

Techna Fit of Indiana... 317 350-2153
493 Southpoint Cir # B Brownsburg (46112) *(G-1407)*

Techna-Fit Inc... 317 350-2153
493 Southpoint Cir # B Brownsburg (46112) *(G-1408)*

Technalysis Inc... 317 291-1985
7172 Waldemar Dr Indianapolis (46268) *(G-9568)*

Techncal Cntrols/Solutions Inc....................................... 260 416-0329
2640 N 825 E Churubusco (46723) *(G-1991)*

Technical Equipment Sales LLC..................................... 260 445-1008
4501 Earhart Dr Ste A Fort Wayne (46809) *(G-5472)*

Technical Water Treatment Inc....................................... 574 277-1949
51431 Autumn Ridge Dr Granger (46530) *(G-6386)*

Technical Weighing Svcs Inc (PA).................................. 219 924-3366
1004 Reder Rd Griffith (46319) *(G-6819)*

Technicoat LLC... 574 339-1745
4421 N 1150 E Grovertown (46531) *(G-6824)*

Technicote Inc.. 812 466-9844
3200 N 25th St Terre Haute (47804) *(G-15724)*

Technidyne Corporation (PA)... 812 948-2884
100 Quality Ave New Albany (47150) *(G-12821)*

Technifab, Brazil *Also Called: Technifab Products Inc (G-1166)*

Technifab Products Inc (PA)... 812 442-0520
10339 N Industrial Park Dr Brazil (47834) *(G-1166)*

Techniplas, Mishawaka *Also Called: TP Remainco In Inc (G-12015)*

Technology, Indianapolis *Also Called: Innovative Media Sciences Inc (G-8556)*

Technology Cons Group LLC.. 219 525-4064
1500 E 89th Ave Bldg B Merrillville (46410) *(G-11565)*

Technology Dynamics.. 317 524-6338
9105 E 56th St Ste 2150 Indianapolis (46216) *(G-9569)*

Techryan Inc... 317 721-4835
2680 E Main St Ste 100 Plainfield (46168) *(G-13734)*

Techseal Division, Goshen *Also Called: Parker-Hannifin Corporation (G-6236)*

Techshot | **ALPHABETIC SECTION**

Techshot, Greenville *Also Called: Redwire Space Technologies Inc (G-6653)*
Techshot Lighting LLC 812 923-9591
5605 Featheringill Rd Ste 102 Floyds Knobs (47119) *(G-4695)*
Teck Machine LLC 574 773-7004
70793 County Road 11 Nappanee (46550) *(G-12648)*
Teck USA Inc 888 995-1972
715 W Southern Ave Indianapolis (46225) *(G-9570)*
Tecnoplast Usa LLC 317 769-4929
3619 W 73rd St Ste 1 Anderson (46011) *(G-204)*
Tecumseh Peerless Gear Mch Div, Salem *Also Called: Tecumseh Products Company LLC (G-14502)*
Tecumseh Products Company LLC 812 883-3575
1555 S Jackson St Salem (47167) *(G-14502)*
Ted Bostick 765 458-6555
2230 W Snake Hill Rd Liberty (47353) *(G-10999)*
Tedco Inc 765 489-5807
303 W Main St Hagerstown (47346) *(G-6845)*
Tedco Inc (PA) 765 489-4527
498 S Washington St Hagerstown (47346) *(G-6846)*
Tedco Inc 401 461-1118
5167 E 65th St Indianapolis (46220) *(G-9571)*
Tedco Toys, Hagerstown *Also Called: Tedco Inc (G-6846)*
Tedrows Wood Products Inc 812 247-2260
7910 Coal Hollow Rd Shoals (47581) *(G-14912)*
Tee Trudys Rainbow Palac 765 273-7571
701 E 8th St Muncie (47302) *(G-12500)*
Teejays Sweet Tooth LLC 219 208-5229
8660 Purdue Rd Ste 8660-600 Indianapolis (46268) *(G-9572)*
Teeki Hut Custom Tees Inc 317 205-3589
807 Broad Ripple Ave Indianapolis (46220) *(G-9573)*
Tees and Blues LLC 765 808-4081
3715 N Bennington Ct Apt F Muncie (47303) *(G-12501)*
Tefft Bridge and Iron LLC 219 828-4011
12632 N 400 E Wheatfield (46392) *(G-16773)*
Teg Holdings Inc 574 264-7514
1210 County Road 6 W Elkhart (46514) *(G-3719)*
Tegeler Welding Services LLC 765 409-6446
6143 Druley Rd Richmond (47374) *(G-14213)*
Teijin Automotive Tech Inc 260 627-0890
13811 Roth Rd Grabill (46741) *(G-6325)*
Teijin Automotive Tech Inc 260 355-4011
1890 Riverfork Dr Huntington (46750) *(G-7373)*
Tejas Tubular Products Inc 574 249-0623
31140 Edison Rd New Carlisle (46552) *(G-12847)*
Tek Coat and Spray LLC 260 748-0314
3900 Transportation Dr Fort Wayne (46818) *(G-5473)*
Tek Print LLC 812 336-2525
812 14th St Bedford (47421) *(G-677)*
Teklad Diets, Indianapolis *Also Called: Envigo Rms Inc (G-8125)*
Tekmodo LLC 574 970-5800
1701 Conant St Elkhart (46516) *(G-3720)*
Tekmodo Oz Holdings LLC 574 970-5800
1701 Conant St Elkhart (46516) *(G-3721)*
Tekmodo Structures LLC 574 970-5800
1701 Conant St Elkhart (46516) *(G-3722)*
Telamon Corporation (PA) 317 818-6888
1000 E 116th St Carmel (46032) *(G-1777)*
Telamon Corporation 317 818-6888
4656 Anson Blvd Whitestown (46075) *(G-16824)*
Telamon Entp Ventures LLC 317 818-6888
1000 E 116th St Carmel (46032) *(G-1778)*
Telamon International, Carmel *Also Called: Telamon Technologies Corp (G-1781)*
Telamon International Corp (HQ) 317 818-6888
1000 E 116th St Carmel (46032) *(G-1779)*
Telamon Spv LLC 800 788-6680
1000 E 116th St Carmel (46032) *(G-1780)*
Telamon Technologies Corp 317 818-6888
1000 E 116th St Carmel (46032) *(G-1781)*
Telecommunications, Indianapolis *Also Called: Vertical Steel Maintenance LLC (G-9711)*
Telecommunications Pdts Div, Fort Wayne *Also Called: Essex Frkawa Mgnt Wire USA LLC (G-4962)*

Telectro-Mek Inc 260 747-0586
2700 Nuttman Ave Fort Wayne (46802) *(G-5474)*
Teledyne Flir LLC 412 423-2100
3495 Kent Ave Ste Q100 West Lafayette (47906) *(G-16633)*
Teledyne Flir Defense Inc 765 775-1701
3495 Kent Ave Ste V100 West Lafayette (47906) *(G-16634)*
Teledyne Flir Detection Inc 765 775-1701
3495 Kent Ave Ste V100 West Lafayette (47906) *(G-16635)*
Teleios Inc 317 509-1596
191 Aspen Way Carmel (46032) *(G-1782)*
Telix Pharmaceuticals US Inc (HQ) 317 588-9700
11700 Exit 5 Pkwy Ste 200 Fishers (46037) *(G-4611)*
Tell City Concrete Supply, Tell City *Also Called: Mulzer Crushed Stone Inc (G-15513)*
Temperature Control Svcs LLC 765 325-2439
4240 W 50 S Lebanon (46052) *(G-10945)*
Tempest Technical Sales Inc (PA) 317 844-9236
13295 Illinois St Ste 329 Carmel (46032) *(G-1783)*
Tempest Tool & Machine Inc 812 346-6464
7235 W Us Highway 50 North Vernon (47265) *(G-13299)*
Tempesta Media LLC 312 371-0555
315 Washington Park Blvd Michigan City (46360) *(G-11677)*
Temple, Elkhart *Also Called: Postle Operating LLC (G-3613)*
Temple Inland 765 362-1074
801 N Englewood Dr Crawfordsville (47933) *(G-2623)*
Temple-Inland Inc 765 675-6732
815 Industrial Dr Tipton (46072) *(G-15793)*
Temple-Island 901 419-9000
2135 Stout Field East Dr Indianapolis (46241) *(G-9574)*
Templeton Coal Company Inc (PA) 812 232-7037
701 Wabash Ave Ste 501 Terre Haute (47807) *(G-15725)*
Templeton Coal Company Inc 812 232-7037
711 Hulman St Terre Haute (47802) *(G-15726)*
Templeton Myers Inc 317 898-6688
351 S Post Rd Indianapolis (46219) *(G-9575)*
Temptek Inc 317 887-6352
525 E Stop 18 Rd Greenwood (46143) *(G-6773)*
Tempur Production Usa LLC 859 455-1000
3200 Comfort Dr Crawfordsville (47933) *(G-2624)*
Tempus Nova LLC (HQ) 877 379-7376
111 Monument Cir Ste 202 Indianapolis (46204) *(G-9576)*
Ten Cate Enbi Inc (indiana) 317 398-3267
1703 Mccall Dr Shelbyville (46176) *(G-14804)*
Ten Point Trim Corp 317 875-5424
4750 Nw Plaza West Dr Zionsville (46077) *(G-17056)*
Tendre Press LLC 812 606-9563
134 N Overhill Dr Bloomington (47408) *(G-986)*
Tenneco, Angola *Also Called: Pullman Company (G-290)*
Tenneco, Elkhart *Also Called: Tenneco Automotive Oper Co Inc (G-3723)*
Tenneco, Indianapolis *Also Called: Tenneco Inc (G-9577)*
Tenneco, South Bend *Also Called: Federal-Mogul Powertrain LLC (G-15032)*
Tenneco Automotive Oper Co Inc 574 296-9400
4825 Hoffman St Elkhart (46516) *(G-3723)*
Tenneco Automotive Oper Co Inc 260 894-9214
1490 Gerber St Ligonier (46767) *(G-11027)*
Tenneco Inc 317 842-5550
7002 Graham Rd Ste 128 Indianapolis (46220) *(G-9577)*
Tennplasco, Edinburgh *Also Called: Manar Inc (G-3092)*
Teragraphics Ink LLC 765 430-2863
204 E Pine Ave West Lafayette (47906) *(G-16636)*
Teras Sporty Ink 219 369-6276
515 Lincolnway La Porte (46350) *(G-10488)*
Teresa L Powell CPA 765 962-1862
321 Sw 1st St Richmond (47374) *(G-14214)*
Terex, Bourbon *Also Called: Terex Corporation (G-1129)*
Terex Advance Mixer Inc 260 497-0728
7727 Freedom Way Fort Wayne (46818) *(G-5475)*
Terex Corporation 574 342-0086
4470 Lincoln Hwy Bourbon (46504) *(G-1129)*
Terex Corporation 260 497-0728
7727 Freedom Way Fort Wayne (46818) *(G-5476)*
Terhune Welding Shop 260 565-3446
3390 N State Road 1 Bluffton (46714) *(G-1063)*

ALPHABETIC SECTION

Terick Sales 574 626-3173
3519 E County Road 800 S Walton (46994) *(G-16283)*

Terick Sales & Service, Walton Also Called: Terick Sales *(G-16283)*

Ternet Metal Finishing Inc 260 897-3903
150 Green Dr Avilla (46710) *(G-496)*

Terra Drive Systems Inc 219 279-2801
9098 W 800 S Brookston (47923) *(G-1313)*

Terra Health North America LLC 317 675-9990
725 W 21st St Connersville (47331) *(G-2473)*

Terrance A Smith Distributing 765 644-3396
2215 N Madison Ave Anderson (46011) *(G-205)*

Terrapin Mfg 717 339-6007
4109 Evard Rd Fort Wayne (46835) *(G-5477)*

Terre Hute Wlbert Brial Vlt In 812 235-0339
509 E Preston St Terre Haute (47802) *(G-15727)*

Terrecorp Inc 317 951-8325
2121 Hillside Ave Indianapolis (46218) *(G-9578)*

Terrel Automotive Machine Inc 812 883-3859
707 S Main St Salem (47167) *(G-14503)*

Terremax Farms LLC (PA) 812 242-0276
3260 Red Barn Rd Terre Haute (47805) *(G-15728)*

Terri Logan Studios 765 966-7876
2101 Reeveston Rd Richmond (47374) *(G-14215)*

Terronics Development Corp Inc 765 552-0808
7565 W 900 N Elwood (46036) *(G-3838)*

Terry Haute Propane Plant 812 877-3406
6625 E Margaret Dr Terre Haute (47803) *(G-15729)*

Terry L Ray 765 342-3180
340 S Sycamore St Martinsville (46151) *(G-11430)*

Terry Liquidation III Inc (PA) 219 362-9908
210 Philadelphia St La Porte (46350) *(G-10489)*

Terry Liquidation III Inc 219 362-3557
28 Industrial Pkwy La Porte (46350) *(G-10490)*

Terrys Sewer Service 219 756-5238
8235 Lincoln St Merrillville (46410) *(G-11566)*

Terrys Welding Inc 765 564-3331
9176 W 132 N Delphi (46923) *(G-2909)*

Tesco, Syracuse Also Called: Thomas Strickler *(G-15485)*

Tesla Inc 317 558-8431
8280 Castleton Corner Dr Indianapolis (46250) *(G-9579)*

Tessellated Inc 304 277-8896
1400 E Angela Blvd South Bend (46617) *(G-15281)*

Test Gauge & Backflow Supply, Indianapolis Also Called: Prosperus LLC *(G-9233)*

Test Publications, Noblesville Also Called: Metheny Enterprises Inc *(G-13135)*

Test Rite Systems & Mfg Co LLC 317 736-9192
1650 N 800 E Franklin (46131) *(G-5781)*

Testimony Publications LLC 812 602-3031
901 Jobes Ln Evansville (47712) *(G-4341)*

Tetrafab Corporation 812 258-0000
3429 Knobs Valley Dr Floyds Knobs (47119) *(G-4696)*

Tetrasolv Inc 765 643-3941
444 E 29th St Anderson (46016) *(G-206)*

Tetrasolv Filtration, Anderson Also Called: Tetrasolv Inc *(G-206)*

Texacon Cut Stone LLC 812 824-3211
4790 Fluck Mill Rd Bloomington (47403) *(G-987)*

Texas Industrial Services, Whitestown Also Called: Indiana Industrial Svcs LLC *(G-16810)*

Texas Instruments, Carmel Also Called: Texas Instruments Incorporated *(G-1784)*

Texas Instruments Incorporated 317 574-2611
12900 N Meridian St Ste 175 Carmel (46032) *(G-1784)*

Texas Monthly, Indianapolis Also Called: Emmis Publishing LP *(G-8108)*

Texmo Blank, Warsaw Also Called: Texmo Blank USA Inc *(G-16437)*

Texmo Blank USA Inc 574 696-9990
596 E 200 N Warsaw (46582) *(G-16437)*

Textile Conservation Services, Indianapolis Also Called: Harold Mailand *(G-8364)*

Textron Aviation Inc 317 241-2893
6911 Pierson Dr Indianapolis (46241) *(G-9580)*

Textron Aviation Inc 317 227-3621
6911 Pierson Dr Indianapolis (46241) *(G-9581)*

Textron Outdoor Power Eqp Inc (HQ) 704 504-6600
6302 E County Road 100 N Coatesville (46121) *(G-2110)*

Texys America LLC 317 469-4828
7301 Georgetown Rd Ste 125 Indianapolis (46268) *(G-9582)*

Texys Sensors LLC 317 469-4828
8425 Woodfield Crossing Blvd Ste 100 Indianapolis (46240) *(G-9583)*

Tf Fulfillment, Whitestown Also Called: Tfi Inc *(G-16825)*

Tfco Incorporated (PA) 219 324-4166
2606 N State Road 39 La Porte (46350) *(G-10491)*

Tfco Incorporated 219 324-4166
207 N State Road 39 La Porte (46350) *(G-10492)*

Tfi Inc 317 290-1333
4257 S 500 E Whitestown (46075) *(G-16825)*

Tfp Inc 219 513-9572
1950 N Griffith Blvd Ste A Griffith (46319) *(G-6820)*

Tfp Unlimited LLC 317 414-8819
9433 E Washington St Indianapolis (46229) *(G-9584)*

Tfs Inc 260 422-5896
1808 W Main St Fort Wayne (46808) *(G-5478)*

Tfx Plating Company Llc 765 289-2436
2401 N Executive Park Dr Yorktown (47396) *(G-16983)*

Tgc Auto Care Products Inc 765 962-7725
421 S 33rd St Richmond (47374) *(G-14216)*

Tge Puzzle Pieces In Life 219 345-2193
2026 E 1130 N Demotte (46310) *(G-2930)*

Tgf Enterprises LLC 440 840-9704
11075 Woods Bay Ln Indianapolis (46236) *(G-9585)*

Tgm Manufacturing Inc 260 758-3055
5980 N 400 W Uniondale (46791) *(G-15873)*

Tgr Inc 765 452-8225
1257 E Morgan St Kokomo (46901) *(G-10348)*

Tgs, Fort Wayne Also Called: Trellis Growing Systems LLC *(G-5504)*

Tgx Medical Systems LLC 317 575-0300
1016 Pine Hill Way Carmel (46032) *(G-1785)*

Th Custom Printing 765 251-3986
871 E 1550 N Summitville (46070) *(G-15434)*

Thach LLC 317 373-3734
14939 Maggie Ct Westfield (46074) *(G-16732)*

Thadco, Bloomington Also Called: Winters Assoc Prmtnal Pdts Inc *(G-1015)*

Thaddeus Luxury Hbags & HM ACC 907 301-1373
101 E Main St Syracuse (46567) *(G-15484)*

Thanatos Manufacturing LLC 260 251-8498
4263 W 200 S Portland (47371) *(G-13969)*

Thank You Lord LLC 317 319-1271
9538 Oakley Dr Indianapolis (46260) *(G-9586)*

That Beverage Company LLC 260 413-9660
810 Donnell Ave Ste 102 Fort Wayne (46808) *(G-5479)*

That Print Lady LLC 317 339-7411
4517 Jamestown Ct Apt D Indianapolis (46226) *(G-9587)*

Thatcher Engineering Corp 219 949-2084
7100 Industrial Hwy Gary (46406) *(G-6018)*

The Akron Equipment Company 260 622-4150
6935 N State Road 1 Ossian (46777) *(G-13438)*

The Baldus Company Inc 260 424-2366
440 E Brackenridge St Fort Wayne (46802) *(G-5480)*

The Commodore Corporation (PA) 574 533-7100
58096 County Road 7 Elkhart (46517) *(G-3724)*

THE CRITERION NEWSPAPER, Indianapolis Also Called: Criterion Press Inc *(G-7904)*

The Dalton Corporation (HQ) 574 267-8111
1900 E Jefferson St Warsaw (46580) *(G-16438)*

The Deaton Family Company 815 726-6234
318 E 7th St Auburn (46706) *(G-429)*

The Education Connection, Clay City Also Called: Waite Adel (marlane) *(G-2048)*

The Eminence Hair Collectn LLC 317 300-6051
8404 Penbrooke Pl Indianapolis (46237) *(G-9588)*

THE FALCON MINT, Portland Also Called: Collegiate Pride Inc *(G-13932)*

The Findlay Publishing Co 812 222-8000
133 S Main St Batesville (47006) *(G-606)*

The Ford Meter Box Company Inc (PA) 260 563-3171
775 Manchester Ave Wabash (46992) *(G-16217)*

The Goshen News, Goshen Also Called: Triple Crown Media LLC *(G-6273)*

The Harrison Steel Castings Co (PA) 765 762-2481
900 S Mound St Attica (47918) *(G-356)*

ALPHABETIC SECTION

The Killion Corporation..317 271-4536
1755 Midwest Blvd Indianapolis (46214) *(G-9589)*

The Office Shop Inc (PA)...812 934-5611
131 Batesville Shopping Vlg Batesville (47006) *(G-607)*

The Paper, Wabash *Also Called: Paper of Wabash County Inc (G-16208)*

The Papers Inc (PA)...574 658-4111
206 S Main St Milford (46542) *(G-11807)*

The Pro Shear Corporation Corp..................................260 408-1010
3405 Meyer Rd Ste 100 Fort Wayne (46803) *(G-5481)*

Thedailygrind LLC..317 531-1276
607 S Main St Whitestown (46075) *(G-16826)*

Thegoosecompany LLC..708 280-7512
8547 Monroe Ave Munster (46321) *(G-12570)*

Therametric Technologies Inc (PA)..............................317 565-8065
9880 Douglas Floyd Pkwy Noblesville (46060) *(G-13181)*

Therma-Tru Corp..260 562-1009
8055 N State Road 9 Howe (46746) *(G-7243)*

Thermal Ceramics Inc...574 296-3500
2730 Industrial Pkwy Elkhart (46516) *(G-3725)*

Thermal Product Solutions...708 758-6530
1470 Mackinaw Pl Schererville (46375) *(G-14546)*

Thermal Structures Inc..317 876-7213
5705 W 80th St Indianapolis (46278) *(G-9590)*

Thermal Structures Inc..951 736-9911
2800 Airwest Blvd Ste 100 Plainfield (46168) *(G-13735)*

Thermal Tech & Temp Inc..219 213-2093
880 N Madison St Crown Point (46307) *(G-2763)*

Thermax Inc..978 844-2528
1725 N Graham Rd Franklin (46131) *(G-5782)*

Thermco Instrument Corporation...............................219 362-6258
1201 W Us Highway 20 La Porte (46350) *(G-10493)*

Thermo - Transfer Inc..317 398-3503
1601 Miller Ave Shelbyville (46176) *(G-14805)*

Thermo Bond Buildings LLC.......................................574 295-1214
58120 County Road 3 Elkhart (46517) *(G-3726)*

Thermo Cube Incorporated..574 936-5096
2255 Walter Glaub Dr Plymouth (46563) *(G-13816)*

Thermo Fisher Scientific Inc......................................812 477-2760
958 S Kenmore Dr Ste C Evansville (47714) *(G-4342)*

Thermo-Cycler Industries Inc (PA).............................219 767-2990
111 E Hamilton St Union Mills (46382) *(G-15868)*

Thermodyne Food Svc Pdts Inc..................................260 428-2535
4418 New Haven Ave Fort Wayne (46803) *(G-5482)*

Thermoplastic Division, Goshen *Also Called: Triangle Rubber Co LLC (G-6272)*

Thermoset Plastics Division, Indianapolis *Also Called: Lord Corporation (G-8782)*

Thermphyscal Prpts RES Lab Inc................................765 463-1581
3080 Kent Ave West Lafayette (47906) *(G-16637)*

Thermtron Mfg Inc..260 622-6000
1625 Baker Dr Ossian (46777) *(G-13439)*

Thermwood Corporation..812 937-4476
904 Buffaloville Rd Dale (47523) *(G-2794)*

Think North America Inc...313 565-6781
3221 Magnum Dr Elkhart (46516) *(G-3727)*

Thinkshortcut Publishing LLC....................................765 935-1127
2695 Inke Rd Richmond (47374) *(G-14217)*

This & That Products...812 299-2688
3784 Hotel St Terre Haute (47802) *(G-15730)*

This Old Farm, Colfax *Also Called: This Old Farm Inc (G-2113)*

This Old Farm Inc...765 324-2161
9572 W County Road 650 S Colfax (46035) *(G-2113)*

This That EMB Screen Prtg LLC..................................317 541-8548
3724 N Dequincy St Indianapolis (46218) *(G-9591)*

Thomas & Skinner Inc (PA)..317 923-2501
1120 E 23rd St Indianapolis (46205) *(G-9592)*

Thomas & Skinner Inc...812 689-4811
525 Western Ave Osgood (47037) *(G-13418)*

Thomas Cubit Inc..219 933-0566
110 Brunswick St Hammond (46327) *(G-7019)*

Thomas Custom Lighting..765 378-5472
207 South St Chesterfield (46017) *(G-1899)*

Thomas E Slade Inc..812 437-5233
6220 Vogel Rd Evansville (47715) *(G-4343)*

Thomas Green LLC..317 337-0000
7517 Winton Dr Indianapolis (46268) *(G-9593)*

Thomas Himebaugh..812 246-0197
3502 Fairview Knob Rd Sellersburg (47172) *(G-14618)*

Thomas L Wehr...317 835-7824
8192 W 700 N Fairland (46126) *(G-4403)*

Thomas Madison...312 625-9152
450 St John Rd Ste 201-5 Michigan City (46360) *(G-11678)*

Thomas Medical, Indianapolis *Also Called: Catheter Research Inc (G-7760)*

Thomas Monuments Inc..317 244-6525
7009 W Washington St Indianapolis (46241) *(G-9594)*

Thomas Products & Services Inc................................217 463-3999
109 W Harrison St Clinton (47842) *(G-2079)*

Thomas R Clark...219 508-7412
1812 Beech St Valparaiso (46383) *(G-16065)*

Thomas Strickler...574 457-2473
6749 E Cornelius Rd Syracuse (46567) *(G-15485)*

Thomas Taylor..317 557-3287
3220 Halifax Dr Indianapolis (46222) *(G-9595)*

Thomas/Euclid Industries Inc....................................317 783-7171
2575 Bethel Ave Indianapolis (46203) *(G-9596)*

Thomasville Furniture Inds Inc..................................336 476-2175
442 165th St Hammond (46324) *(G-7020)*

Thomco Inc...317 359-3539
1414 Sadlier Circle West Dr Indianapolis (46239) *(G-9597)*

Thompson...219 942-8133
421 Driftwood Dr Hobart (46342) *(G-7211)*

Thompson Machining Svcs Inc...................................765 647-3451
11040 State Road 101 Brookville (47012) *(G-1337)*

Thompson Printing Service Inc..................................317 783-7448
447 E Elbert St Indianapolis (46227) *(G-9598)*

Thomson Industries Inc..574 529-2496
1209 Shore Ln Syracuse (46567) *(G-15486)*

Thomson Reuters Corporation...................................317 570-9387
8670 Harrison Pkwy Fishers (46038) *(G-4612)*

Thor, Elkhart *Also Called: Thor Industries Inc (G-3730)*

Thor Industries Inc...574 264-2900
52570 Paul Dr Elkhart (46514) *(G-3728)*

Thor Industries Inc...574 266-1111
4221 Pine Creek Rd Elkhart (46516) *(G-3729)*

Thor Industries Inc (PA)..574 970-7460
601 E Beardsley Ave Elkhart (46514) *(G-3730)*

Thor Industries Inc...574 262-2624
28719 Jami St Elkhart (46514) *(G-3731)*

Thor Industries Inc...574 584-2151
505 Ward St Wakarusa (46573) *(G-16253)*

Thor Industries Inc...800 860-5658
606 Nelsons Pkwy Wakarusa (46573) *(G-16254)*

Thor Industries Data Center......................................574 970-7460
3080 Windsor Ct Elkhart (46514) *(G-3732)*

THOR INDUSTRIES, INC., Wakarusa *Also Called: Thor Industries Inc (G-16253)*

Thor Motor Coach, Elkhart *Also Called: Thor Industries Inc (G-3728)*

Thor Motor Coach, Elkhart *Also Called: Thor Industries Inc (G-3731)*

Thor Motor Coach Inc (HQ).......................................574 266-1111
701 County Road 15 Ste 100 Elkhart (46516) *(G-3733)*

Thor Motor Coach Inc...800 860-5658
510 Ward St Wakarusa (46573) *(G-16255)*

Thorgren Tool & Molding Co......................................219 462-1801
912 Roosevelt Rd Valparaiso (46383) *(G-16066)*

Thorgren Tool & Molding Co......................................219 462-1801
1100 Evans Ave Valparaiso (46383) *(G-16067)*

Thormax Enterprises LLC..812 530-7744
101 W Laurel St Seymour (47274) *(G-14699)*

Thornbury Software..765 546-8640
205 W Franklin St Winchester (47394) *(G-16900)*

Thornes Homes Inc...812 275-4656
3211 State Road 37 S Bedford (47421) *(G-678)*

Thoughts Are Things Inc...317 585-8053
8035 Clearwater Dr Indianapolis (46256) *(G-9599)*

Thousand One Inc..765 962-3636
1001 Se St Richmond (47374) *(G-14218)*

ALPHABETIC SECTION — Tippy Creek Winery LLC

Thrasher Welding and Mch Sp 260 475-5550
2085 S 600 W Angola (46703) *(G-298)*

Thread Bear Publishing, South Whitley Also Called: Wish Factory Inc *(G-15332)*

Three Cups LLC 317 633-8082
310 W Michigan St Ste A Indianapolis (46202) *(G-9600)*

Three Daughters Corp 260 925-2128
5005 County Road 29 Auburn (46706) *(G-430)*

Three Floyds Distilling Co LLC 219 922-3565
9750 Indiana Pkwy Munster (46321) *(G-12571)*

Three K Racing Enterprises 765 482-4273
2685 S 25 W Lebanon (46052) *(G-10946)*

Three Little Monkeys 765 778-9370
129 S Pendleton Ave Stop 3 Pendleton (46064) *(G-13557)*

Three Moons Fiberworks LLC 219 841-5387
402 Broadway Chesterton (46304) *(G-1960)*

Three Rivers Distilling Co LLC 260 745-9355
220 E Wallace St Fort Wayne (46803) *(G-5483)*

Thrift Products Heating Spc, Peru Also Called: Ebert Machine Company Inc *(G-13581)*

Thrifty Nickel Want ADS, Greenwood Also Called: American Classifieds *(G-6667)*

Throttle Jockey, Kokomo Also Called: Graphics Lab Uv Printing Inc *(G-10272)*

Thrush Co Inc 765 472-3351
340 W 8th St Peru (46970) *(G-13604)*

Thrust Industries, Evansville Also Called: Bmg Inc *(G-3936)*

Thrust Industries Inc 812 437-3643
10334 Hedden Rd Evansville (47725) *(G-4344)*

Thugs Inc Choppers 317 454-3762
735 N Lynhurst Dr Indianapolis (46224) *(G-9601)*

Thunder Pro 317 498-0241
1439 W Us Highway 40 Greenfield (46140) *(G-6565)*

Thunder Rolls Express 812 667-5111
13449 State Road 129 Canaan (47224) *(G-1528)*

Thunderbird Aviation LLC 847 303-3100
8623 E Washington St Indianapolis (46219) *(G-9602)*

Thunderbird Products, Decatur Also Called: Porter Inc *(G-2876)*

Thundrbird Traditional Archery 812 699-1099
306 N Ohio St Culver (46511) *(G-2782)*

Thursday Pools LLC 317 973-0200
840 Commerce Pkwy Ste 2 Fortville (46040) *(G-5607)*

Thyme In Kitchen LLC 812 624-0344
2308 W Franklin St Ste A Evansville (47712) *(G-4345)*

Thyme In The Kitchen, Evansville Also Called: Thyme In Kitchen LLC *(G-4345)*

TI Automotive 260 622-7372
6879 N State Road 1 Ossian (46777) *(G-13440)*

TI Automotive Inc 260 587-6100
507 H L Thompson Jr Dr Ashley (46705) *(G-337)*

TI Automotive Ligonier Corp 260 894-3163
925 N Main St Ligonier (46767) *(G-11028)*

TI Group Auto Systems LLC 260 587-6100
507 H L Thompson Jr Dr Ashley (46705) *(G-338)*

TI Group Auto Systems LLC 260 622-7900
1200 Baker Dr Ossian (46777) *(G-13441)*

Tibbs Enterprises LLC 574 360-9552
508 Cloudmont Dr Osceola (46561) *(G-13403)*

Tic Toc Trophy Shop inc 574 893-4234
930 E Rochester St Akron (46910) *(G-10)*

Ticzkus Electronic and Mfg 574 542-2325
8100 W Olson Rd Rochester (46975) *(G-14328)*

Tidy Janitorial Services LLC 502 807-8647
1450 Blackiston View Dr Clarksville (47129) *(G-2039)*

Tiedemann-Bevs Industries LLC 765 962-4914
4225 W Industries Rd Richmond (47374) *(G-14219)*

Tiedmann and Sons, Richmond Also Called: Tiedemann-Bevs Industries LLC *(G-14219)*

Tilted Compass Winery LLC 812 691-1766
1461 W State Road 246 Clay City (47841) *(G-2047)*

Tim Weberding Woodworking LLC 865 430-8811
117 N Main St Batesville (47006) *(G-608)*

Timber & Logging, Mauckport Also Called: Michael Skaggs *(G-11438)*

Timber Arts LLC 765 522-4121
3057 E County Road 800 N Bainbridge (46105) *(G-564)*

Timber Creek Design Co Inc 317 297-5336
7230 Guion Rd Indianapolis (46268) *(G-9603)*

Timber Hawk Bows Inc 812 837-9340
7895 S State Road 446 Bloomington (47401) *(G-988)*

Timber Line Crating LP 260 238-3075
17501 Campbell Rd Spencerville (46788) *(G-15375)*

Timberland Resources Inc 765 245-2634
6429 W 100 N Montezuma (47862) *(G-12084)*

Timberlight Manufacturing Co 317 694-1317
8146 Grassy Meadow Ct Indianapolis (46259) *(G-9604)*

Timberline Industries, Brazil Also Called: Timberline Industries LLC *(G-1167)*

Timberline Industries LLC 812 442-0949
1892 E Us Highway 40 Brazil (47834) *(G-1167)*

Timbers Custom Signs 812 866-6655
3660 W State Road 56 Hanover (47243) *(G-7046)*

Time Out Trailers Inc 574 294-7671
4636 Chester Dr Elkhart (46516) *(G-3734)*

Timecpsual Antiq GL Cllctables 317 902-6201
6142 Crystal View Dr Indianapolis (46237) *(G-9605)*

Timelessmusicgroup LLC 317 721-6671
9758 Innisbrook Blvd Carmel (46032) *(G-1786)*

Times 765 659-4622
62 N Main St Ste 104 Frankfort (46041) *(G-5698)*

Times 10 Associates LLC 800 773-6432
1101 Cumberland Xing Ste 252 Valparaiso (46383) *(G-16068)*

Times Leader Publications LLC 317 300-8782
5252 E Main St Avon (46123) *(G-552)*

Times, The, Martinsville Also Called: Mooresville Times *(G-11415)*

Times, The, Munster Also Called: Lee Enterprises Inc Times *(G-12547)*

Timken Company 574 287-1566
3010 Mishawaka Ave South Bend (46615) *(G-15282)*

Timken Furnaces Agency, South Bend Also Called: Timken Company *(G-15282)*

Timothy D Goin 317 771-0404
8240 E 75th St Indianapolis (46256) *(G-9606)*

Timothy Hoover Industries LLC 812 987-6342
1701 Village Green Blvd Jeffersonville (47130) *(G-10064)*

Timothy Reed Carry ME Mus Pubg 812 322-7187
610 S Washington St Apt D Bloomington (47401) *(G-989)*

Timothy White 765 689-8270
191 S Elm St Bunker Hill (46914) *(G-1444)*

Tims Tees 317 503-5736
10310 Majestic Perch Ct Indianapolis (46234) *(G-9607)*

Tin Man Shtmtl & Roofg LLC 513 276-1716
26170 Sawdon Ridge Rd Guilford (47022) *(G-6830)*

Tinas Ceramics & Things 812 917-4190
1001 N 3rd St Terre Haute (47807) *(G-15731)*

Tinchers Creative Woodworks 765 344-0062
11206 E Ferndale Rd Rockville (47872) *(G-14358)*

Tint Masters 260 704-2676
5015 Speedway Dr Fort Wayne (46825) *(G-5484)*

Tints & Prints By Tierney LLC 317 769-5895
4211 Honeysuckle Ln Zionsville (46077) *(G-17057)*

Tiny Timbers, Deputy Also Called: Homestead Properties Inc *(G-2941)*

Tip To Tail Aerospace LLC 765 437-6556
1697 W Hoosier Blvd Peru (46970) *(G-13605)*

Tippecanoe Laboratories, Lafayette Also Called: Evonik Corporation *(G-10575)*

Tippecanoe Press Inc 317 392-1207
230 N Knightstown Rd Shelbyville (46176) *(G-14806)*

Tippecanoe Tire Service Inc 765 884-0920
219 E 5th St Fowler (47944) *(G-5634)*

Tippmann, Fort Wayne Also Called: Tippmann Sports LLC *(G-5488)*

Tippmann Arms Company LLC 260 245-0602
2955 S Maplecrest Rd Fort Wayne (46803) *(G-5485)*

Tippmann Brothers LLC 260 403-1911
8834 Mayhew Rd Fort Wayne (46835) *(G-5486)*

Tippmann Ordnance, Fort Wayne Also Called: Allied Mfg Partners Inc *(G-4745)*

Tippmann Products LLC 260 438-7946
3905 Goeglein Rd Fort Wayne (46815) *(G-5487)*

Tippmann Sports LLC (DH) 800 533-4831
4230 Lake Ave Fort Wayne (46815) *(G-5488)*

Tippmann US Holdco Inc (HQ) 260 749-6022
4230 Lake Ave Fort Wayne (46815) *(G-5489)*

Tippy Creek Winery LLC 574 253-1862
5998 N 200 E Leesburg (46538) *(G-10962)*

Tipsy Glass LLC 260 251-0021
1756 W State Road 67 Portland (47371) *(G-13970)*

Tipton Electric Motor Services 765 963-3380
113 S Washington St Sharpsville (46068) *(G-14713)*

Tipton Engrg Elc Mtr Svcs Inc 765 963-3380
159 W Vine St Sharpsville (46068) *(G-14714)*

Tipton Mills, Columbus Also Called: Tipton Mills Foods LLC *(G-2402)*

Tipton Mills Foods LLC 812 372-0900
835 S Mapleton St Columbus (47201) *(G-2402)*

Tipton Tribune 765 675-2115
116 S Main St Ste A Tipton (46072) *(G-15794)*

Tire Center, Portland Also Called: Tire Center of Portland Inc *(G-13971)*

Tire Center of Portland Inc 260 726-8947
421 N Meridian St Portland (47371) *(G-13971)*

Tire Central and Service Avon 317 966-0662
214 S Raceway Rd Indianapolis (46231) *(G-9608)*

Tire Rack Inc (HQ) 888 541-1777
7101 Vorden Pkwy South Bend (46628) *(G-15283)*

Tire Rack, The, South Bend Also Called: Tire Rack Inc *(G-15283)*

Tires Enterprises Corp 866 807-4930
3716 W Ridge Rd Gary (46408) *(G-6019)*

Tis Holding Inc 317 946-6354
1132 Southeastern Ave Indianapolis (46202) *(G-9609)*

Tisa, Princeton Also Called: Toyota Boshoku Indiana LLC *(G-14014)*

Tishler Industries Inc 317 581-8811
500 E 96th St Ste 475 Indianapolis (46240) *(G-9610)*

Tishler Industries Inc (PA) 765 286-5454
1810 S Macedonia Ave Muncie (47302) *(G-12502)*

Tissue Source LLC 765 746-6679
7163 Whitestown Pkwy Box 221 Zionsville (46077) *(G-17058)*

Titan Bats LLC 317 670-8380
14045 Pecos Ct Carmel (46033) *(G-1787)*

Titan Graphics LLC 317 496-2188
10036 Olio Rd Mccordsville (46055) *(G-11457)*

Titan Metal Spinning Inc 260 665-1067
1000 Crestview Dr Angola (46703) *(G-299)*

Titan Metal Worx LLC 260 422-4433
5225 New Haven Ave Fort Wayne (46803) *(G-5490)*

Titanium LLC 765 236-6906
847 N 300 E Kokomo (46901) *(G-10349)*

Titanium Rails Nutrition LLC 219 940-3704
1709 E 37th Ave Hobart (46342) *(G-7212)*

Title Ten Manufacturing LLC 765 388-2482
401 W Willard St Muncie (47302) *(G-12503)*

Titus Inc 574 936-3345
9887 6b Rd Plymouth (46563) *(G-13817)*

Titus Mfg LLC 574 286-1928
7991 Lilac Rd Plymouth (46563) *(G-13818)*

Titus Plus, Columbia City Also Called: Titus Tool Company Inc *(G-2207)*

Titus Precision Company 260 244-6114
900 W Connexion Way Columbia City (46725) *(G-2206)*

Titus Tool Company Inc 206 447-1489
900 W Connexion Way Columbia City (46725) *(G-2207)*

Tj Constructions LLC 470 406-2804
2020 Winter Ave Indianapolis (46218) *(G-9611)*

Tj Haase Winery Ltd Lblty Co 765 505-1382
8249 Hannah Ave Terre Haute (47805) *(G-15732)*

Tj Maintenance LLC 219 776-8427
8591 N 300 W Lake Village (46349) *(G-10784)*

Tj Mobile Service, Madison Also Called: Triumphant Jrney MBL Ntary Svc *(G-11254)*

Tj Performance LLC 765 580-0481
4331 N Jobe Rd Brownsville (47325) *(G-1432)*

Tjr Fabrication LLC 765 384-4455
2749 W 2nd St Marion (46952) *(G-11342)*

Tk Elevator Corporation 317 595-1125
8665 Bash St Indianapolis (46256) *(G-9612)*

Tk Finishing LLC 574 233-1617
3702 W Sample St Ste 4045 South Bend (46619) *(G-15284)*

Tk Metal Forming Inc 574 293-2907
57433 Nagy Dr Elkhart (46517) *(G-3735)*

Tk Software Inc (PA) 317 569-8887
11495 Pennsylvania St Ste 220 Carmel (46032) *(G-1788)*

Tko Enterprises Inc (PA) 317 271-1398
2751 Stafford Rd Plainfield (46168) *(G-13736)*

Tl Industries Inc 419 666-8144
21746 Buckingham Rd Elkhart (46516) *(G-3736)*

Tl Mold Inc 574 596-7875
24242 State Line Rd Elkhart (46514) *(G-3737)*

Tla Signs Inc 260 833-2402
2175 W 175 N Angola (46703) *(G-300)*

TLC Candle Co LLC 317 313-3029
11650 Olio Rd Ste 1000 Fishers (46037) *(G-4613)*

TLC Metals Inc 317 894-8684
2155 Fields Blvd Greenfield (46140) *(G-6566)*

Tlk Precision Inc 317 427-0123
9609 N Pumpkinvine Rd Fairland (46126) *(G-4404)*

Tls By Design LLC 765 683-1971
10737 Sand Key Cir Indianapolis (46256) *(G-9613)*

TM Shadow Publishing LLC 502 794-8435
5534 Saint Joe Rd Fort Wayne (46835) *(G-5491)*

Tma Enterprises Inc 317 272-0694
7900 E Us Highway 36 Ste C Avon (46123) *(G-553)*

Tmak Inc 219 874-7661
200 Winski Dr Michigan City (46360) *(G-11679)*

Tmf Center Inc 765 762-3800
105 Slauter Ln Williamsport (47993) *(G-16854)*

Tmf Center Inc (PA) 765 762-1000
300 W Washington St Williamsport (47993) *(G-16855)*

Tmgg LLC 812 687-7444
714 5th St Plainville (47568) *(G-13746)*

TMI 574 533-4741
14578 State Road 4 Goshen (46528) *(G-6270)*

TMI Contractors, Mount Vernon Also Called: Tron Mechanical Incorporated *(G-12324)*

Tmk Manufacturing LLC 765 763-6754
307 E Fletcher St Morristown (46161) *(G-12281)*

Tmmi, Princeton Also Called: Toyota Motor Mfg Ind Inc *(G-14015)*

Tmmi, Princeton Also Called: Toyota Motor Mfg Ind Inc *(G-14016)*

Tmr Group, Whitestown Also Called: Tank Construction & Service Co *(G-16823)*

Tms International LLC 219 787-5220
251 E Us Rt 12 Burns Harbor (46304) *(G-1456)*

Tms International LLC 219 881-0155
3001 Dickey Rd East Chicago (46312) *(G-3044)*

Tms International LLC 219 881-0155
Truck Stop 749 Gary (46402) *(G-6020)*

Tms International LLC 219 881-0266
1 N Broadway Gary (46402) *(G-6021)*

Tms International LLC 219 762-2176
2901 Carlson Dr # 100 Hammond (46323) *(G-7021)*

Tmx Healthcare Tech LLC (DH) 877 874-6339
5451 Lakeview Parkway South Dr Indianapolis (46268) *(G-9614)*

Tnemec Company Inc 317 884-1806
458 Park 800 Dr Greenwood (46143) *(G-6774)*

TNT Construction 260 726-2643
114 Jack Imel Ave Portland (47371) *(G-13972)*

TNT Fabricating LLC 574 540-2465
9841 Sunnyside Dr Plymouth (46563) *(G-13819)*

TNT Top Notch Tees 219 775-3812
1552 Happy Valley Rd Crown Point (46307) *(G-2764)*

TNT Truck Accessories LLC 812 305-0714
152 W 1275 S Haubstadt (47639) *(G-7090)*

To A Tee Inc 317 757-8842
7125 Girls School Ave Indianapolis (46241) *(G-9615)*

TOA (usa) LLC 317 834-0522
2000 Pleiades Dr Mooresville (46158) *(G-12247)*

TOA Winchester LLC 765 584-7639
200 Inks Dr Winchester (47394) *(G-16901)*

Toco Inc 317 627-8854
4307 Blackwood Ct Greenwood (46143) *(G-6775)*

Todays Signs and Graphics 765 288-4771
1804 N Wheeling Ave Ste 1 Muncie (47303) *(G-12504)*

Todd Enterprise Inc 317 209-6610
6220 Edenshall Ln Noblesville (46062) *(G-13182)*

Todd K Hockemeyer Inc 260 639-3591
12108 S Us Highway 27 Fort Wayne (46816) *(G-5492)*

ALPHABETIC SECTION

Todd L Wise..260 799-4828
5440 W 450 S Albion (46701) *(G-46)*

Todd's Wldg & Stl Fabricator, Bloomington *Also Called: Todds Wldg & Stl Fabrication (G-990)*

Toddler Timer LLC..216 282-7247
920 E 62nd St Apt U4 Indianapolis (46220) *(G-9616)*

Todds Hydrlcs RPR & Stl Fbrct..812 466-3457
3904 4th Pkwy Terre Haute (47804) *(G-15733)*

Todds Wldg & Stl Fabrication...812 824-2407
4810 S Old State Road 37 Bloomington (47401) *(G-990)*

Togs Powder Coating...574 266-2850
1200 Oak St Elkhart (46514) *(G-3738)*

Tokumei LLC..765 772-0073
4955 State Road 43 N West Lafayette (47906) *(G-16638)*

Tom Cooks, Evansville *Also Called: Industrial Sewing Machine Co (G-4124)*

Tom Doherty Company Inc..317 352-8200
2402 N Shadeland Ave Ste A Indianapolis (46219) *(G-9617)*

Tom West Farms..812 986-2162
8235 E State Road 42 Poland (47868) *(G-13838)*

Tom West Repair, Poland *Also Called: Tom West Farms (G-13838)*

Tomahawk Log & County Homes..................................260 833-6429
280 Lane 100 Pine Canyon Lk Angola (46703) *(G-301)*

Tomken Plastic Tech Inc..765 284-2472
4601 N Superior Dr Muncie (47303) *(G-12505)*

Tomlinson Manufacturing Co..765 719-3700
1421 Amy Ln Franklin (46131) *(G-5783)*

Toms Printing Service..260 438-3721
Ossian (46777) *(G-13442)*

Toner Tek, Crawfordsville *Also Called: BOM Corporation (G-2549)*

Tonis Touch LLC..317 992-1280
2448 Meadowlark Way Apt C Plainfield (46168) *(G-13737)*

Tonne Winery Incorporated..765 896-9821
101 W Royerton Rd Muncie (47303) *(G-12506)*

Tony London Co Inc..812 373-0748
4630 Progress Dr # A Columbus (47201) *(G-2403)*

Tony Stewart Racing Entps LLC..................................317 858-8620
438 Southpoint Cir Brownsburg (46112) *(G-1409)*

Tonya Gerhardt...260 434-1370
6134 Constitution Dr Fort Wayne (46804) *(G-5493)*

Too Tuft LLC...317 719-2182
8465 Keystone Xing Indianapolis (46240) *(G-9618)*

Tool Dynamics LLC..812 379-4243
835 S Marr Rd Columbus (47201) *(G-2404)*

Tool Room Service...765 287-0062
1403 S Liberty St Muncie (47302) *(G-12507)*

Tool Source Inc..765 778-0777
9279 S State Road 13 Pendleton (46064) *(G-13558)*

Toolcraft LLC...260 749-0454
2620 S Maplecrest Rd Fort Wayne (46803) *(G-5494)*

Toolmasters Inc...574 256-1881
1203 E 6th St Mishawaka (46544) *(G-12014)*

Toomuchfun Rubberstamps Inc..................................260 557-4808
11738 Winchester Rd Fort Wayne (46819) *(G-5495)*

Tooties Zenergy Candles LLC....................................317 437-9936
5941 Winston Dr Indianapolis (46226) *(G-9619)*

Top Cat Printing Inc..812 683-2773
6636 S 585w Huntingburg (47542) *(G-7293)*

Top Design Cnc Inc..219 662-2915
41 N 400 E Valparaiso (46383) *(G-16069)*

Top Fuel Crossfit Inc..219 281-7001
1674 E North St Crown Point (46307) *(G-2765)*

Top In Sound Inc..765 649-8111
3273 N State Road 9 Anderson (46012) *(G-207)*

Top Lock Corporation...317 831-2000
319 Harlan Dr Mooresville (46158) *(G-12248)*

Top Notch Embroidery, Valparaiso *Also Called: Nancy Ferber (G-16007)*

Top Notch Tool and Engrg Inc...................................812 663-2184
930 E Main St Greensburg (47240) *(G-6635)*

Top of Hill Performance LLC....................................812 637-3693
28730 Chappelow Hill Rd West Harrison (47060) *(G-16552)*

Top Shelf Acoustics LLC..317 512-4569
8175 Ehlerbrook Rd Indianapolis (46237) *(G-9620)*

Topics Newspapers Inc...888 357-7827
13095 Publishers Dr Fishers (46038) *(G-4614)*

Topnotch Locs LLC..260 557-9628
728 E 22nd St Indianapolis (46202) *(G-9621)*

Topp Industries Incorporated....................................574 223-3681
420 N State Road 25 Rochester (46975) *(G-14329)*

Toppan Photomasks Inc...765 854-7500
1901 E Morgan St Kokomo (46901) *(G-10350)*

Topps Safety Apparel, Inc., Rochester *Also Called: Btq Manufacturing Inc (G-14281)*

Topstitch Inc
921 Summa Dr Elkhart (46516) *(G-3739)*

Toralgen Inc..812 820-3374
1220 Waterway Blvd Ste H123 Indianapolis (46202) *(G-9622)*

Toray Resin Company (DH).....................................317 398-7833
821 W Mausoleum Rd Shelbyville (46176) *(G-14807)*

Torch Newspapers Inc..765 569-2033
125 W High St Rockville (47872) *(G-14359)*

Tordilleria Del Valle..765 654-9590
905 Walnut Ave Frankfort (46041) *(G-5699)*

Tornier Inc..574 268-0861
100 Capital Dr Ste 201 Warsaw (46582) *(G-16439)*

Torque Engineering Corporation.............................574 264-2628
2932 Thorne Dr Elkhart (46514) *(G-3740)*

Torrid, Merrillville *Also Called: Torrid LLC (G-11567)*

Torrid LLC..219 769-1192
2109 Southlake Mall Spc 324 Merrillville (46410) *(G-11567)*

Tortillas Nuevo Leon, Hammond *Also Called: O-M Distributors Inc (G-6988)*

Total Cleaning Solutions LLC.................................260 471-7761
4620 Lima Rd Fort Wayne (46808) *(G-5496)*

Total Concepts Design Inc.....................................812 752-6534
1054 S Taylor Mill Rd Scottsburg (47170) *(G-14582)*

Total Control Systems, Fort Wayne *Also Called: Murray Equipment Inc (G-5252)*

Total Home Control LLC..317 430-3679
7369 Yorkshire Blvd N Indianapolis (46229) *(G-9623)*

Total Quality Pallets Inc...317 822-9888
1401 Newman St Indianapolis (46201) *(G-9624)*

Total Tote Inc..260 982-8318
11606 N State Road 15 North Manchester (46962) *(G-13252)*

Touch 4 Life, Indianapolis *Also Called: Beverly Harris (G-7619)*

Touch of Class Interiors..765 452-5879
802 E Sycamore St Kokomo (46901) *(G-10351)*

Touch Plate Led, Fort Wayne *Also Called: Touchplate Technologies Inc (G-5497)*

Touchdown Machining Inc....................................812 378-0300
432 S Mapleton Dr Columbus (47201) *(G-2405)*

Touchplate Technologies Inc.................................260 426-1565
4822 Projects Dr Fort Wayne (46825) *(G-5497)*

Touchtronics Inc...574 294-2570
57315 Nagy Dr Ste A Elkhart (46517) *(G-3741)*

Tower Advertising Products Inc (PA)....................260 593-2103
1015 W Lake St Topeka (46571) *(G-15821)*

Tower Atmtive Oprtons USA II L...........................260 920-1500
801 W 15th St Auburn (46706) *(G-431)*

Tower Automotive, Auburn *Also Called: Tower Atmtive Oprtons USA II L (G-431)*

Tower Ribbons, Topeka *Also Called: Tower Advertising Products Inc (G-15821)*

Tower Structural Laminating, Ligonier *Also Called: Supreme Corporation (G-11026)*

Town & Country Industries Inc.............................219 712-0893
10187 Florida Ln Crown Point (46307) *(G-2766)*

Town & Country Press Inc...................................574 936-9505
1920 Jim Neu Dr Plymouth (46563) *(G-13820)*

Town & Country Printing, Crown Point *Also Called: Town & Country Industries Inc (G-2766)*

Town of Saratoga...765 584-1576
107 N Barber St Saratoga (47382) *(G-14509)*

Town Planner..317 888-6750
410 N Us Highway 31 Ste 3 Whiteland (46184) *(G-16798)*

Town Planner, Columbus *Also Called: Brent Devers (G-2229)*

Town Welder...219 945-1311
9306 Grand Blvd Crown Point (46307) *(G-2767)*

Towne Air Freight, South Bend *Also Called: Clp Towne Inc (G-14977)*

Towne Post Network Inc.....................................317 288-7101
11216 Fall Creek Rd Ste 125 Indianapolis (46256) *(G-9625)*

Townsends Disposal.. 765 985-2126	**Trane, Bloomington** *Also Called: Trane US Inc (G-992)*
2444 W Main St Mexico (46958) *(G-11573)*	**Trane, Evansville** *Also Called: Trane US Inc (G-4346)*
Toyo Seiko North America Inc..................................... 574 288-2000	**Trane, Fishers** *Also Called: Trane US Inc (G-4615)*
3585 Moreau Ct South Bend (46628) *(G-15285)*	**Trane, Fort Wayne** *Also Called: Trane US Inc (G-5498)*
Toyoshima Special Steel USA, Indianapolis *Also Called: Ichinen USA Corporation (G-8450)*	**Trane, Rushville** *Also Called: Trane US Inc (G-14415)*
Toyota, Columbus *Also Called: Toyota Material Handling Inc (G-2406)*	**Trane, South Bend** *Also Called: Trane US Inc (G-15286)*
Toyota Boshoku Indiana, Princeton *Also Called: Tbin LLC (G-14013)*	**Trane US Inc**... 800 285-2487
Toyota Boshoku Indiana LLC.. 812 491-9100	1458 S Liberty Dr Bloomington (47403) *(G-992)*
1698 S 100 W Princeton (47670) *(G-14014)*	**Trane US Inc**... 812 421-8725
Toyota Material Handling Inc (DH).............................. 800 381-5879	1024 E Sycamore St Evansville (47714) *(G-4346)*
5559 Inwood Dr Columbus (47201) *(G-2406)*	**Trane US Inc**... 317 255-8777
Toyota Motor Mfg Ind Inc (HQ)..................................... 812 387-2266	8100 E 106th St Fishers (46038) *(G-4615)*
4000 S Tulip Tree Dr Princeton (47670) *(G-14015)*	**Trane US Inc**... 260 489-0884
Toyota Motor Mfg Ind Inc... 812 385-5153	6602 Innovation Blvd Fort Wayne (46818) *(G-5498)*
528 W Poplar Ave Princeton (47670) *(G-14016)*	**Trane US Inc**... 765 932-7200
Toyota Tsusho America Inc... 765 449-3500	1300 N Benjamin St Rushville (46173) *(G-14415)*
5440 Haggerty Ln Colburn (47905) *(G-2111)*	**Trane US Inc**... 574 282-4880
TP Orthodontics Inc (PA)... 219 785-2591	3725 Cleveland Rd Ste 300 South Bend (46628) *(G-15286)*
100 Center Plz La Porte (46350) *(G-10494)*	**Trans Atlantic Products LLC**... 574 262-0165
TP Remainco In Inc (HQ)... 574 256-1521	2778 Faith Ave Elkhart (46514) *(G-3743)*
616 W Mckinley Ave Mishawaka (46545) *(G-12015)*	**Trans-Flo, Fort Wayne** *Also Called: Im Indiana Holdings Inc (G-5093)*
Tp/Elm Acquisition Sbusid Inc (HQ)............................ 260 728-2161	**Transcend Orthtics Prsthtics L**..................................... 574 233-3352
2110 Patterson St Decatur (46733) *(G-2886)*	417 Fernhill Ave Fort Wayne (46805) *(G-5499)*
TPC Software Inc.. 317 844-1480	**Transcend Orthtics Prsthtics L**..................................... 317 300-9016
490 Tulip Poplar Crst Carmel (46033) *(G-1789)*	595 S Emerson Ave Ste 300 Greenwood (46143) *(G-6776)*
Tpg Mt Vernon Marine LLC... 317 631-0234	**Transcend Orthtics Prsthtics L**..................................... 317 334-1114
1341 N Capitol Ave Indianapolis (46202) *(G-9626)*	3445 W 96th St Indianapolis (46268) *(G-9629)*
Tprl, West Lafayette *Also Called: Thermphyscal Prpts RES Lab Inc (G-16637)*	**Transcend Orthtics Prsthtics L**..................................... 219 736-9960
Tr Manufacturing LLC.. 260 357-4679	112 E 90th Dr Merrillville (46410) *(G-11569)*
1106 S Cowen St Garrett (46738) *(G-5878)*	**Transcend Orthtics Prsthtics L (HQ)**............................ 574 233-3352
Tracaron Designs Inc... 317 839-9006	17530 Dugdale Dr South Bend (46635) *(G-15287)*
6498 Crystal Springs Dr Avon (46123) *(G-554)*	**Transcendia Inc**.. 765 935-1520
Trace Engineering Inc.. 765 354-4351	300 Industrial Pkwy Richmond (47374) *(G-14220)*
400 Locust St Middletown (47356) *(G-11777)*	**Transco Railway Products Inc**...................................... 574 753-6227
Trachsels Embroidery.. 260 982-2376	1331 S 18th St Logansport (46947) *(G-11111)*
905 N Market St North Manchester (46962) *(G-13253)*	**Transfoam LLC**.. 631 747-0255
Tracy K Hullett... 765 472-3349	1210 Waterway Blvd Indianapolis (46202) *(G-9630)*
268 W 3rd St Peru (46970) *(G-13606)*	**Transformation Industries LLC**..................................... 574 457-9320
Trade & Industrial Supply Inc....................................... 812 537-1300	615 Cushing St South Bend (46616) *(G-15288)*
1101 N Pocket Rd Batesville (47006) *(G-609)*	**Transformations, Fort Wayne** *Also Called: Transformations By Wieland Inc (G-5500)*
Tradebe, East Chicago *Also Called: Tradebe Industrial Svcs LLC (G-3046)*	**Transformations By Wieland Inc**.................................. 800 440-9337
Tradebe Environmental Svcs LLC (DH)...................... 800 388-7242	310 Racquet Dr Fort Wayne (46825) *(G-5500)*
1433 E 83rd Ave Ste 200 Merrillville (46410) *(G-11568)*	**Transhield Inc (HQ)**.. 574 266-4118
Tradebe GP.. 800 388-7242	2932 Thorne Dr Elkhart (46514) *(G-3744)*
4343 Kennedy Ave East Chicago (46312) *(G-3045)*	**Transilwrap, Richmond** *Also Called: Transcendia Inc (G-14220)*
Tradebe Industrial Svcs LLC.. 800 388-7242	**Transmed Associates Inc (PA)**...................................... 317 293-9993
1433 E 83rd Ave Ste 200 East Chicago (46312) *(G-3046)*	8131 Kingston St Ste 700 Avon (46123) *(G-555)*
Tradeline Fabricating Inc.. 812 637-1444	**Transportation Tech Inds (DH)**..................................... 812 962-5000
22422 Stateline Rd Lawrenceburg (47025) *(G-10862)*	7140 Office Cir Evansville (47715) *(G-4347)*
Trademark, Indianapolis *Also Called: Indiana Chemical LLC (G-8476)*	**Transtex LLC**... 877 960-2644
Trading Post.. 574 935-5460	8219 Northwest Blvd Ste 100 Indianapolis (46278) *(G-9631)*
523 E Jefferson St Plymouth (46563) *(G-13821)*	**Transwheel Corporation (HQ)**...................................... 260 358-8660
Traffic Sign Co Inc... 317 845-9305	3000 Yeoman Way Huntington (46750) *(G-7374)*
9402 Uptown Dr Ste 1500 Indianapolis (46256) *(G-9627)*	**Transworks Inc**... 619 441-0133
Traffic Signal Company, Carmel *Also Called: Doron Distribution Inc (G-1610)*	9910 Dupont Circle Dr E Ste 200 Fort Wayne (46825) *(G-5501)*
Traffic Technical Support Inc....................................... 260 665-1575	**Tranter Graphics Inc**.. 574 834-2626
840 S 650 W Angola (46703) *(G-302)*	8094 N State Road 13 Syracuse (46567) *(G-15487)*
Trafford Holdings Ltd.. 888 232-4444	**Travel Lite Inc**... 574 831-3000
1663 S Liberty Dr Bloomington (47403) *(G-991)*	107 E Innovation Blvd Syracuse (46567) *(G-15488)*
Trafford Publishing, Bloomington *Also Called: Trafford Holdings Ltd (G-991)*	**Travel Star Products, Goshen** *Also Called: Exton Inc (G-6132)*
Trail Creek Leather.. 219 874-6702	**Travelhost Mag Indianapolis**.. 317 416-7780
315 Johnson Rd Trail Creek (46360) *(G-15842)*	10254 Tammer Dr Carmel (46032) *(G-1790)*
Trail Software Inc.. 888 854-0933	**Travis Britton**.. 317 762-6018
5724 Birtz Rd Ste 1 Indianapolis (46216) *(G-9628)*	315 N Franklin Rd Indianapolis (46219) *(G-9632)*
Trail's End Popcorn Company, Indianapolis *Also Called: Popcorn Weaver Mfg LLC (G-9162)*	**Travis C and Jan B Page**.. 812 398-5507
Train Co, La Porte *Also Called: Kenco Plastics Inc (G-10433)*	9606 S County Road 18 Sw Carlisle (47838) *(G-1544)*
Trained Thoughts Pubg LLC... 773 661-7237	**Travis Industries Inc**.. 260 479-7807
4028 Hohman Ave Hammond (46327) *(G-7022)*	2000 Summit St New Haven (46774) *(G-12922)*
Trams Design LLC... 574 206-3232	**Traylor Industrial LLC (HQ)**... 812 428-3708
22834 Pine Arbor Dr Apt 1b Elkhart (46516) *(G-3742)*	835 N Congress Ave Evansville (47715) *(G-4348)*

ALPHABETIC SECTION

Trazcor, Goshen *Also Called: Lippert Components Inc (G-6204)*
TRC Mfg Inc 574 262-9299
  17460 Fleetwood Ln South Bend (46635) *(G-15289)*
Tre Paper Company 765 649-2536
  5395 S 50 W Anderson (46013) *(G-208)*
Treat America Roche Diagnostic 317 521-1490
  10300 Kincaid Dr Fishers (46037) *(G-4616)*
Tredegar Corporation 574 262-4685
  2551 County Road 10 W Elkhart (46514) *(G-3745)*
Tredegar Corporation 812 466-0266
  3400 Fort Harrison Rd Terre Haute (47804) *(G-15734)*
Tree City Saw Mill 812 663-6363
  2663 E County Road 500 S Greensburg (47240) *(G-6636)*
Tree City Sawmill, Greensburg *Also Called: Tree City Saw Mill (G-6636)*
Tree City Tool & Engrg Co Inc 812 663-4196
  1954 N Montgomery Rd Greensburg (47240) *(G-6637)*
Tree Pro, West Lafayette *Also Called: Lafayette Marketing Inc (G-16600)*
Treehugger Maple Syrup LLC 765 698-3728
  15203 Ott Rd Laurel (47024) *(G-10826)*
Trek Pools LLC 317 896-0493
  5142 W State Road 38 New Castle (47362) *(G-12883)*
Trellborg Sling Sltions US Inc 260 748-5895
  2531 Bremer Rd Fort Wayne (46803) *(G-5502)*
Trellborg Sling Sltions US Inc (DH) 260 749-9631
  2531 Bremer Rd Fort Wayne (46803) *(G-5503)*
Trelleborg Sealing Solutions, Fort Wayne *Also Called: Trellborg Sling Sltions US Inc (G-5502)*
Trellis Growing Systems LLC 260 241-3128
  2427 S Hadley Rd Fort Wayne (46804) *(G-5504)*
Tremain Ceramic Tile & Flr Cvg 317 542-1491
  8105 E 47th St Indianapolis (46226) *(G-9633)*
Tremike Enterprises 317 547-6308
  5869 Meadowlark Dr Indianapolis (46226) *(G-9634)*
Trendsettin Tees LLC 219 201-1410
  1127 Ridgepointe Dr Indianapolis (46234) *(G-9635)*
Trenwa Inc 812 427-2217
  13268 Innovation Dr Florence (47020) *(G-4667)*
Trevares D Smith 765 603-0468
  1426 W 2nd St Marion (46952) *(G-11343)*
Trey Exploration Inc 812 858-3146
  2699 State Route 261 Newburgh (47630) *(G-13025)*
Trg Wind 507 829-6695
  210 Amhurst Cir Noblesville (46062) *(G-13183)*
Trh Software Inc 812 264-2428
  1503 7th Ave Terre Haute (47807) *(G-15735)*
Tri Aerospace LLC 812 872-2400
  1055 S Hunt St Terre Haute (47803) *(G-15736)*
Tri Star Embroidery, Fort Branch *Also Called: Barrett Manufacturing Inc (G-4702)*
Tri State Flasher Co, Evansville *Also Called: TSF Co Inc (G-4354)*
Tri State Mold 859 240-7643
  7255 State Route 56 W Rising Sun (47040) *(G-14246)*
Tri State Monument Company 812 386-7303
  425 N Main St Princeton (47670) *(G-14017)*
Tri State Optical Inc 765 289-4475
  1608 W Mcgalliard Rd Muncie (47304) *(G-12508)*
Tri State Printing & Embroider 812 316-0094
  24 N 1st St Vincennes (47591) *(G-16159)*
Tri State Timber LLC 812 327-8161
  3490 E Saddlebrook Ct Bloomington (47401) *(G-993)*
Tri-Esco Inc 765 446-7937
  101 N 36th St Colburn (47905) *(G-2112)*
Tri-Gen Inc 317 849-5612
  16565 River Rd Noblesville (46062) *(G-13184)*
Tri-K Machining, Danville *Also Called: Tri-K Machining Inc (G-2829)*
Tri-K Machining Inc 317 244-7724
  120 Commerce Dr Danville (46122) *(G-2829)*
Tri-Lakes Container Corp 574 594-2217
  533 S First St Pierceton (46562) *(G-13641)*
Tri-Pac Inc 574 855-2197
  3333 N Kenmore St South Bend (46628) *(G-15290)*
Tri-Pac Inc 574 855-2197
  3333 N Kenmore St South Bend (46628) *(G-15291)*

Tri-Plastics, Saint Anthony *Also Called: Bch Image USA Inc (G-14426)*
Tri-Sky LLC 812 746-1678
  13031 Balboa Dr Evansville (47725) *(G-4349)*
Tri-Star Filtration Inc 317 337-0940
  5319 W 86th St Indianapolis (46268) *(G-9636)*
Tri-Star Glove, Plainville *Also Called: Tmgg LLC (G-13746)*
Tri-State Cylinder Head, Evansville *Also Called: Sequoia National LLC (G-4306)*
Tri-State Forest Products Inc 317 328-1850
  6740 Guion Rd Indianapolis (46268) *(G-9637)*
Tri-State Guttertopper Inc 812 455-1460
  6901 Briar Ct Evansville (47711) *(G-4350)*
Tri-State Industries Inc 219 933-1710
  4923 Columbia Ave Hammond (46327) *(G-7023)*
Tri-State Machining Inc 260 422-2508
  2515 Mcdonald St Fort Wayne (46803) *(G-5505)*
Tri-State Mechanical Inc 260 471-0345
  4530 Secretary Dr Fort Wayne (46808) *(G-5506)*
Tri-State Metal Inc 219 397-0470
  220 W Chicago Ave East Chicago (46312) *(G-3047)*
Tri-State Powder Coating LLC 812 425-7010
  800 Bayse St Evansville (47713) *(G-4351)*
Tri-State Power Supply LLC 812 537-2500
  48 Doughty Rd Lawrenceburg (47025) *(G-10863)*
Tri-State Shtmtl & Mfg LLC 260 402-8831
  1738 Traders Xing Fort Wayne (46845) *(G-5507)*
Tri-State Trophies, Evansville *Also Called: Jef Enterprises Inc (G-4140)*
Tri-State Valve LLC (PA) 901 388-1550
  9355 Delegates Row Indianapolis (46240) *(G-9638)*
Tri-State Veterinary Sup Inc 812 477-4793
  3300 Interstate Dr Evansville (47715) *(G-4352)*
Triad Mining Inc 812 328-2117
  1216 E County Road 900 S Oakland City (47660) *(G-13324)*
Triangle Asphalt Paving Corp 765 482-5701
  501 Sam Ralston Rd Lebanon (46052) *(G-10947)*
Triangle Engineering Corp 317 243-8549
  2206 Production Dr Indianapolis (46241) *(G-9639)*
Triangle Machine Inc 574 246-0165
  3702 W Sample St Ste 1125 South Bend (46619) *(G-15292)*
Triangle Publishing 765 677-2544
  4201 S Washington St Marion (46953) *(G-11344)*
Triangle Rubber Co LLC 574 533-3118
  5333 E Beck Dr Elkhart (46516) *(G-3746)*
Triangle Rubber Co LLC 574 533-3118
  1801 Eisenhower Dr N Goshen (46526) *(G-6271)*
Triangle Rubber Co LLC (PA) 574 533-3118
  1924 Elkhart Rd Goshen (46526) *(G-6272)*
Tribejewels LLC 574 298-7162
  424 S Michigan St South Bend (46624) *(G-15293)*
Tribine Industries LLC 316 282-8011
  6991 E 750 N Logansport (46947) *(G-11112)*
Tribune Star, Terre Haute *Also Called: Newspaper Holding Inc (G-15651)*
Tribune, The, Seymour *Also Called: Seymour Trbune A Cal Ltd Prtnr (G-14691)*
Tribute Precast Systems LLC 260 587-9555
  110 Canopy Dr Ashley (46705) *(G-339)*
Tricias Embroidery 574 583-4371
  4789 Shenandoah Ct Monticello (47960) *(G-12173)*
Trident Engraving Inc 812 282-2098
  3114 New Chapel Rd Jeffersonville (47130) *(G-10065)*
Tridien Medical, Batesville *Also Called: Anodyne Medical Device Inc (G-578)*
Trifab & Construction Inc (PA) 219 845-1300
  2433 167th St Hammond (46323) *(G-7024)*
Trignetra Inc 765 637-8447
  1032 Onyx St West Lafayette (47906) *(G-16639)*
Trijent LLC 502 544-4250
  1774 W 1000 N Macy (46951) *(G-11196)*
Trilithic 317 536-1071
  9027 Pinecreek Way Indianapolis (46256) *(G-9640)*
Trilithic Inc 317 895-3600
  5808 Churchman Byp Indianapolis (46203) *(G-9641)*
Trill Machine LLC 219 730-0744
  104 W Washington St Kentland (47951) *(G-10164)*

ALPHABETIC SECTION

Trillium Cabinet Company Inc.. 317 471-8870
  4357 W 96th St Indianapolis (46268) *(G-9642)*
Trilogy Gallery, Nashville *Also Called: Pgs LLC (G-12678)*
Trilogy Technologies LLC... 317 769-0215
  5583 Wafer Ash Dr Whitestown (46075) *(G-16827)*
Trim-A-Door Corporation... 317 769-8746
  238 N 29th St Elwood (46036) *(G-3839)*
Trim-A-Door Corporation (PA)... 574 254-0300
  1824 N Home St Mishawaka (46545) *(G-12016)*
Trim-A-Seal of Indiana Inc (PA)... 219 883-2180
  1500 Polk St Gary (46407) *(G-6022)*
Trim-Lok Inc... 574 227-1143
  1642 Gateway Ct Elkhart (46514) *(G-3747)*
Trimas Corporation... 260 925-3700
  500 W 7th St Auburn (46706) *(G-432)*
Trimax Machine LLC... 812 887-9281
  5852 N Rod And Gun Clb Bruceville (47516) *(G-1433)*
Trimble Combustion Systems Inc.. 812 623-4545
  215 Nieman St Ste 2 Sunman (47041) *(G-15447)*
Trimedx, Indianapolis *Also Called: Tmx Healthcare Tech LLC (G-9614)*
Trinette Clark Agency Corp... 317 671-6097
  10733 Chenille Ct Indianapolis (46235) *(G-9643)*
Trinity Cmmnications Group Inc.. 260 484-1029
  2524 Merivale St Fort Wayne (46805) *(G-5508)*
Trinity Cstm Built Pallets LLC... 260 466-4625
  12802 Irving Rd New Haven (46774) *(G-12923)*
Trinity Displays, Chesterton *Also Called: Trinity Displays LLC (G-1961)*
Trinity Displays LLC... 219 201-8733
  1579 S Calumet Rd Chesterton (46304) *(G-1961)*
Trinity Metals LLC (PA).. 317 358-8265
  6400 English Ave Indianapolis (46219) *(G-9644)*
Trinity Metals LLC Inc... 317 358-8265
  2440 N Shadeland Ave Indianapolis (46219) *(G-9645)*
Trinity Products LLC.. 636 639-5244
  425 W 151st St East Chicago (46312) *(G-3048)*
Trinity Woodworking... 513 535-1964
  23036 Stateline Rd Lawrenceburg (47025) *(G-10864)*
Trion Coatings LLC.. 312 342-2004
  1400 E Angela Blvd # 331 South Bend (46617) *(G-15294)*
Triple A Sporting Goods, Laotto *Also Called: Zrp LLC (G-10813)*
Triple Crown Media LLC.. 574 533-2151
  114 S Main St Goshen (46526) *(G-6273)*
Triple H Tool Co... 812 567-4600
  7677 Folsomville Rd Tennyson (47637) *(G-15525)*
Triple J Ironworks Inc.. 765 544-9152
  211 S Main St Carthage (46115) *(G-1819)*
Triple J Machining and Mfg Inc... 574 586-7500
  324 Liberty St Walkerton (46574) *(G-16277)*
Triple Js Express Transport... 317 667-2368
  4029 Congaree Dr Indianapolis (46235) *(G-9646)*
Triple Js Transport LLC... 708 513-8389
  5534 Saint Joe Rd Saint John (46373) *(G-14459)*
Triple M Leather LLC... 260 238-5850
  6454 County Road 71 Saint Joe (46785) *(G-14444)*
Triple S Logging, Decatur *Also Called: Joseph M Schmidt (G-2865)*
Triple Xxx Root Beer Corp... 765 743-5373
  20 N Salisbury St West Lafayette (47906) *(G-16640)*
Triplex Industries Inc... 574 256-9253
  55901 Currant Rd Mishawaka (46545) *(G-12017)*
Triplex Plating Inc.. 219 874-3209
  1555 E Us Highway 12 Michigan City (46360) *(G-11680)*
Tristate Bolt Company... 260 357-5541
  1110 Fuller Dr Garrett (46738) *(G-5879)*
Triton Energy LLC
  205 Industrial Pkwy Waterloo (46793) *(G-16532)*
Triton Metal Products Inc.. 260 488-1800
  7790 S Homestead Dr Hamilton (46742) *(G-6863)*
Triton Plant, Angola *Also Called: BSC Vntres Acquisition Sub LLC (G-237)*
Triumph Controls LLC... 317 421-8760
  1960 N Michigan Rd Shelbyville (46176) *(G-14808)*
Triumph Thermal Systems LLC... 419 273-1192
  1960 N Michigan Rd Shelbyville (46176) *(G-14809)*

Triumphant Jrney MBL Ntary Svc... 608 208-5604
  923 W Main St Madison (47250) *(G-11254)*
Triunity LLC.. 317 703-1147
  15209 Herriman Blvd Noblesville (46060) *(G-13185)*
Trivalence Technologies LLC.. 800 209-2517
  3001 Maxx Rd Evansville (47711) *(G-4353)*
Trivector Manufacturing Inc... 260 637-0141
  4404 Engle Ridge Dr Fort Wayne (46804) *(G-5509)*
Trivett Contracting Inc... 317 539-5150
  5981 Liberty Pkwy Clayton (46118) *(G-2062)*
Trojan Battery... 317 561-5650
  923 Whitaker Rd Plainfield (46168) *(G-13738)*
Tron Mechanical Incorporated... 812 838-4715
  331 W 2nd St Mount Vernon (47620) *(G-12324)*
Troop Enterprises, Clarksville *Also Called: Judkins Sr Renaldo G (G-2022)*
Trophy Case LLC... 812 853-5087
  5388 Epworth Rd Newburgh (47630) *(G-13026)*
Trophy Homes Inc... 574 264-4911
  2730 Almac Ct Elkhart (46514) *(G-3748)*
Tropical Delights LLC.. 317 261-1001
  3703 Commercial Dr Indianapolis (46222) *(G-9647)*
Trot, Morocco *Also Called: Road Alert Systems LLC (G-12269)*
Trouw Nutrition Usa LLC.. 618 654-2070
  2601 Fortune Cir E Ste 200c Indianapolis (46241) *(G-9648)*
Troy Meggitt Inc (HQ).. 812 547-7071
  3 Industrial Dr Troy (47588) *(G-15843)*
Troy Stuart... 812 887-0403
  1 Fountain View Est Bldg 2 Washington (47501) *(G-16510)*
Troyc-Industries LLC... 317 531-1660
  10947 Echo Grove Cir Indianapolis (46236) *(G-9649)*
Troyer Brothers.. 260 589-2244
  6691 W State Road 124 Decatur (46733) *(G-2887)*
Troyer Brothers Inc... 260 565-2244
  6691 W State Rd 124 Bluffton (46714) *(G-1064)*
Troyer Products, Elkhart *Also Called: Samaron Corp (G-3661)*
Trs, Fortville *Also Called: Registration System LLC (G-5605)*
Tru Bore Company.. 317 442-6766
  213 E Main St Brownsburg (46112) *(G-1410)*
Tru-Cut Inc.. 765 683-9920
  3111 S Madison Ave Anderson (46016) *(G-209)*
Tru-Cut Machine & Tool Inc... 260 569-1802
  556 E Baumbauer Rd Lot 41 Wabash (46992) *(G-16218)*
Tru-Flex LLC.. 812 526-5600
  955 S Walnut St Edinburgh (46124) *(G-3106)*
Tru-Flex LLC (HQ)... 765 893-4403
  2391 S State Road 263 West Lebanon (47991) *(G-16649)*
Tru-Flex Real Estate Holdings LLC.. 765 893-4403
  2391 S State Rd Ste 263 West Lebanon (47991) *(G-16650)*
Tru-Form, Elkhart *Also Called: Tru-Form Metal Products Inc (G-3749)*
Tru-Form Metal Products Inc.. 574 266-8020
  27200 D I Dr Elkhart (46514) *(G-3749)*
Tru-Form Steel & Wire Inc (PA).. 765 348-5001
  1204 Gilkey Ave Hartford City (47348) *(G-7078)*
Tru-Form Steel & Wire Inc... 765 348-5001
  1822 Joe Bonham Dr Hartford City (47348) *(G-7079)*
Truck Lettering... 317 787-7875
  5102 Sandhurst Dr Indianapolis (46217) *(G-9650)*
Truck Stylin & Collision, Rochester *Also Called: Truck Stylin Unlimited (G-14330)*
Truck Stylin Unlimited.. 574 223-8800
  2123 Southway 31 Rochester (46975) *(G-14330)*
Truck Trailer Repair Indy LLC... 317 755-2177
  11357 N Pheasant Run Fairland (46126) *(G-4405)*
Truckin4ya LLC... 812 225-2640
  4001 Williams Crossing Way Jeffersonville (47130) *(G-10066)*
Trucking, Fishers *Also Called: C&C Transportation Service LLC (G-4479)*
Trucking, Jeffersonville *Also Called: Truckin4ya LLC (G-10066)*
Truckpro LLC... 765 482-6525
  450 N Enterprise Blvd Lebanon (46052) *(G-10948)*
Trucustom Cabinets LLC... 812 486-2861
  5161 N 900 E Montgomery (47558) *(G-12126)*
True Anlytics Mfg Slutions LLC... 317 995-3220
  2230 Stafford Rd Ste 115 Plainfield (46168) *(G-13739)*

ALPHABETIC SECTION — Tuskin Equipment Corporation

True Blue Company LLC 219 324-8482
229 Factory St La Porte (46350) *(G-10495)*

True Chem Inc 317 769-2701
283 Innisbrooke Ave Greenwood (46142) *(G-6777)*

True Colors Pubg & Design, Berne *Also Called: Annies Publishing LLC (G-704)*

True Essence Foods Inc 317 430-3156
1125 Brookside Ave Ste D2 Indianapolis (46202) *(G-9651)*

True North Group LLC 574 247-1866
1409 E Day Rd Mishawaka (46545) *(G-12018)*

True Precision Tech Inc 765 432-2177
1602 E Havens St Kokomo (46901) *(G-10352)*

True Royalty Boutique LLC 260 706-5121
513 E Jefferson Blvd Fort Wayne (46802) *(G-5510)*

True Stories Publishing Co LLC 765 425-8224
48 N Whitcomb Ave Indianapolis (46224) *(G-9652)*

True You Naturally Inc 317 518-2268
107 Northwood Dr Fishers (46038) *(G-4617)*

Trufab Stainless Inc 812 287-8278
2126 W Industrial Park Dr Bloomington (47404) *(G-994)*

Truss Systems Inc 812 897-3064
3555 Hwy 62 W Boonville (47601) *(G-1100)*

Trusslink 219 362-3968
512 Washington St La Porte (46350) *(G-10496)*

Trusted Solutions Group Inc 260 622-6000
1625 Baker Dr Ossian (46777) *(G-13443)*

Trustees Indiana University 812 855-7995
211 S Indiana Ave Rm 9 Bloomington (47405) *(G-995)*

Trustees Indiana University 812 855-0763
120 Ernie Pyle Hall Ind University Bloomington (47405) *(G-996)*

Trustees Indiana University 812 855-3439
465 Ballantine Hall 1020 E Kirkwood Ave Bloomington (47405) *(G-997)*

Trustees Indiana University 812 856-4186
2611 E 10th St Rm 160 Bloomington (47408) *(G-998)*

Trustees Indiana University 812 855-4848
900 E 7th St Bloomington (47405) *(G-999)*

Trusty Sons Tire Inc/Goodyear, Corydon *Also Called: Trusty Tires Inc (G-2519)*

Trusty Tires Inc 812 738-4212
1074 Old Forest Rd Nw Corydon (47112) *(G-2519)*

Trutex Equestrian LLC 812 350-6368
7448 W Old State Road 252 Edinburgh (46124) *(G-3107)*

Trutex Footing, Edinburgh *Also Called: Trutex Equestrian LLC (G-3107)*

Truth Publishing Company Inc (PA) 574 294-1661
421 S 2nd St Ste 100 Elkhart (46516) *(G-3750)*

Truth Publishing Company Inc 765 653-5151
100 N Jackson St Greencastle (46135) *(G-6434)*

Trutle Run Winery, Corydon *Also Called: Pfeiffer Winery & Vineyard Inc (G-2511)*

Truu Confidence LLC 317 795-0042
456 N Meridian St Ste 44741 Indianapolis (46204) *(G-9653)*

TRW Atmtive Coml String System, Lafayette *Also Called: ZF Active Safety & Elec US LLC (G-10724)*

TRW Commercial Steering 765 423-5377
800 Heath St Lafayette (47904) *(G-10710)*

TS Tech, New Castle *Also Called: TS Tech Indiana LLC (G-12884)*

TS Tech Indiana LLC 765 465-4294
3800 Brooks Dr New Castle (47362) *(G-12884)*

Tsb LLC 812 314-8331
12550 N Presidential Way Edinburgh (46124) *(G-3108)*

TSF Co Inc 812 985-2630
2930 Saint Philip Rd S Evansville (47712) *(G-4354)*

Tspdesign LLC 317 785-8663
1029 Redrock Dr Anderson (46013) *(G-210)*

Tssi, Shelburn *Also Called: Signaling Solution Inc (G-14721)*

Tsuda USA Corporation 317 468-9177
2934 Jannetides Blvd Greenfield (46140) *(G-6567)*

Tsune America LLC 812 378-9875
12550 N Presidential Way Edinburgh (46124) *(G-3109)*

Tsys Isolutions, Jeffersonville *Also Called: Procard Inc (G-10042)*

TT Machining & Fabricating LLC 219 878-0399
228 Indiana Highway 212 Michigan City (46360) *(G-11681)*

Tt2 LLC 260 438-4575
14516 Lima Rd Fort Wayne (46818) *(G-5511)*

Tu Jinghua 812 327-3819
3405 E Longview Ave # 10 Bloomington (47408) *(G-1000)*

Tube Fabrication Inds Inc 574 753-6377
130 E Industrial Blvd Logansport (46947) *(G-11113)*

Tube Form Solutions LLC (PA) 574 295-5041
435 Roske Dr Elkhart (46516) *(G-3751)*

Tube Form Solutions LLC 574 266-5230
4221 Pine Creek Rd Elkhart (46516) *(G-3752)*

Tube Processing Corp 317 787-1321
604 E Legrande Ave Indianapolis (46203) *(G-9654)*

Tube Processing Corp 317 787-5747
604 E Legrande Ave Indianapolis (46203) *(G-9655)*

Tube Processing Corp 317 782-9486
2840 Fortune Cir W Ste A Indianapolis (46241) *(G-9656)*

Tube Processing Corp 317 264-7760
2840 Fortune Cir W Ste A Indianapolis (46241) *(G-9657)*

Tube Processing Corp (PA) 317 787-1321
604 E Legrande Ave Indianapolis (46203) *(G-9658)*

Tubesock, Inc., Shelbyville *Also Called: Rob Nolley Inc (G-14792)*

Tucker Publishing Group Inc 812 426-2115
25 Nw Riverside Dr Ste 200 Evansville (47708) *(G-4355)*

Tuff Shed Inc 317 481-8388
4250 W Morris St Indianapolis (46241) *(G-9659)*

Tuff Shed Inc 317 774-2981
15274 Herriman Blvd Noblesville (46060) *(G-13186)*

Tuff Stuff Sales and Svc Inc 765 354-4151
8520 W State Road 236 Middletown (47356) *(G-11778)*

Tuff Tool Inc 262 612-8300
6003 Highgate Pl Fort Wayne (46815) *(G-5512)*

Tuggle Publishing 678 702-2139
5904 Meadows Dr Fort Wayne (46804) *(G-5513)*

Tulip Tree Creamery LLC 317 331-5469
6330 Corporate Dr Ste D Indianapolis (46278) *(G-9660)*

Tulox Plastics Corporation 765 664-5155
1007 W Overlook Rd Marion (46952) *(G-11345)*

Tumacs LLC 574 264-5000
3505 Cooper Dr Elkhart (46514) *(G-3753)*

Tumacs Covers, Elkhart *Also Called: Tumacs LLC (G-3753)*

Turbines Inc 812 877-2587
7303 Maynard Wheeler Ln Terre Haute (47803) *(G-15737)*

Turbonetics, Crown Point *Also Called: Turbonetics Holdings Inc (G-2768)*

Turbonetics Holdings Inc (HQ) 805 581-0333
9401 Georgia St Ste 2 Crown Point (46307) *(G-2768)*

Turkey Run Distillery LLC 765 505-2044
992 E State Road 47 Bloomingdale (47832) *(G-762)*

Turn & Burn Welding, Otwell *Also Called: Turn & Burn Welding Inc (G-13458)*

Turn & Burn Welding Inc 812 766-0641
3668 N State Road 257 Otwell (47564) *(G-13458)*

Turnbow Prosthetics LLC 260 396-2234
522 W 1000 S Columbia City (46725) *(G-2208)*

Turner Machine Co 317 751-5105
1951 Bloyd Ave Indianapolis (46218) *(G-9661)*

Turner Mining Group LLC 812 277-9077
304 W Kirkwood Ave Apt 100 Bloomington (47404) *(G-1001)*

Turner Paving Company 765 962-4408
1458 Nw 5th St Richmond (47374) *(G-14221)*

Turners Machining Specialties Inc 812 372-9472
820 Repp Dr Columbus (47201) *(G-2407)*

Turning Over A New Leaf LLC 765 573-3366
313 W Main St Gas City (46933) *(G-6040)*

Turnomat, Wakarusa *Also Called: Provident Tool & Die Inc (G-16245)*

Turonis Forget-Me-Not Inc 812 477-7500
4 N Weinbach Ave Evansville (47711) *(G-4356)*

Turtle Top, Goshen *Also Called: Independent Protection Co (G-6172)*

Turtle Top, New Paris *Also Called: Independent Protection Co (G-12960)*

Turtlefish Clothing Co LLC 812 896-2805
3010 S Middle Fork Ln Salem (47167) *(G-14504)*

Tusca 2 .... 812 876-2857
3815 N Collins Dr Bloomington (47404) *(G-1002)*

Tuskin Equipment Corporation 630 466-5590
616 S 4th St Elkhart (46516) *(G-3754)*

(PA)=Parent Co (HQ)=Headquarters (DH)=Div Headquarters

2024 Harris Indiana Industrial Directory

Tuthill Corporation 260 747-7529
  8825 Aviation Dr Fort Wayne (46809) *(G-5514)*
Tuthill Corporation 260 747-7529
  8825 Aviation Dr Fort Wayne (46809) *(G-5515)*
Tuthill Transfer Systems, Fort Wayne Also Called: Tuthill Corporation *(G-5514)*
Tuttle Aluminum & Bronze Inc 317 842-2420
  120 Shadowlawn Dr Fishers (46038) *(G-4618)*
Tuttle Railing Systems, Fishers Also Called: Tuttle Aluminum & Bronze Inc *(G-4618)*
TV Excel Inc 323 797-8538
  3215 Stellhorn Rd Fort Wayne (46815) *(G-5516)*
TW Enterprises LLC 513 520-8453
  9021 Meyer Rd Brookville (47012) *(G-1338)*
Tway Company Incorporated 317 636-2591
  1609 Oliver Ave Indianapolis (46221) *(G-9662)*
Tway Lifting Products, Indianapolis Also Called: Tway Company Incorporated *(G-9662)*
Twb of Indiana 812 342-6000
  3030 Barker Dr Columbus (47201) *(G-2408)*
Twe Nonwovens Us Inc 260 747-0990
  9403 Avionics Dr Fort Wayne (46809) *(G-5517)*
Twe Wholesale Inc 317 450-5409
  9777 Colonial Dr Carmel (46032) *(G-1791)*
Twice Daily LLC 812 484-5417
  640 S Bennighof Ave Evansville (47714) *(G-4357)*
Twigg, Martinsville Also Called: Twigg Corporation *(G-11431)*
Twigg Corporation (PA) 765 342-7126
  659 E York St Martinsville (46151) *(G-11431)*
Twin City Journal Reporter 765 674-0070
  407 E Main St Gas City (46933) *(G-6041)*
Twin Coatings & Finishes LLC 317 557-0633
  10216 E 25th St Indianapolis (46229) *(G-9663)*
Twin Hill, Jeffersonville Also Called: Twin Hill Acquisition Co Inc *(G-10067)*
Twin Hill Acquisition Co Inc 888 206-0699
  401 Salem Rd Jeffersonville (47130) *(G-10067)*
Twin Lakes Canvas Inc 574 583-2000
  1103 N 6th St Monticello (47960) *(G-12174)*
Twin Prints Inc 765 742-8656
  701 Main St Lafayette (47901) *(G-10711)*
Twin W Enterprise, Veedersburg Also Called: Robert Warrick *(G-16090)*
Twin Willows LLC 812 497-0254
  7603 W County Road 925 N Freetown (47235) *(G-5805)*
Twin-Air Products Inc 574 295-1129
  4602 Chester Dr Elkhart (46516) *(G-3755)*
Twinrocker Hand Made Paper Inc 765 563-3119
  100 E 3rd St Brookston (47923) *(G-1314)*
Twisod Wick Candle Company 317 490-4789
  1115 Twin Br Martinsville (46151) *(G-11432)*
Twisted Jute LLC 317 885-4276
  41 National Ave Indianapolis (46227) *(G-9664)*
Twisted Kilts Tees & Such Inc 317 413-8900
  4627 Eagles Watch Ln Indianapolis (46254) *(G-9665)*
Twisted Mtal Fbrction Svcs Inc 219 923-8045
  1331 Azalea Dr Munster (46321) *(G-12572)*
Twisted Stitcher 765 330-1083
  7681 E 100 S Hartford City (47348) *(G-7080)*
Twisted Stixx LLC 317 435-5034
  8018 Witherington Rd Indianapolis (46268) *(G-9666)*
Twisted Wick Candle Co 317 490-4789
  102 S Van Buren St Nashville (47448) *(G-12681)*
Two B Enterprises Inc 260 245-0119
  6926 Quemetco Ct Fort Wayne (46803) *(G-5518)*
Two Ees Winery 260 672-2000
  6808 N Us Highway 24 E Huntington (46750) *(G-7435)*
Two Guys Mechanical Contrs Inc 574 946-7671
  461 E Rosser Rd Winamac (46996) *(G-16878)*
Two Sticks Inc 219 926-7910
  147 E Us Highway 20 Chesterton (46304) *(G-1962)*
Tww Fabricaton & Machine LLC 985 637-8234
  55 Mardale Dr Brownsburg (46112) *(G-1411)*
Ty Bowells Farrier Service 812 537-3990
  170 Us Highway 50 E Greendale (47025) *(G-6456)*
Ty Specialized LLC 317 734-7900
  11423 Narrowleaf Dr Indianapolis (46235) *(G-9667)*

Tyco Welding 812 988-8770
  6473 State Road 46 E Nashville (47448) *(G-12682)*
Tycoon Logistics LLC 317 749-1381
  3620 Donald Ave Indianapolis (46224) *(G-9668)*
Tydenbrooks, Angola Also Called: EJ Brooks Company *(G-247)*
Tylayculture, Highland Also Called: Tylayculture LLC *(G-7158)*
Tylayculture LLC 219 678-8359
  9445 Indianapolis Blvd Highland (46322) *(G-7158)*
Tyler Truss LLC 765 221-5050
  1810 Fairfield Ln Pendleton (46064) *(G-13559)*
Tyler Truss Systems Inc 765 221-5050
  1810 Fairfield Ln Pendleton (46064) *(G-13560)*
Type Galley, The, Warren Also Called: Debra Lindhorst *(G-16296)*
Tysoft LLC 765 405-0098
  2211 S Walnut St Yorktown (47396) *(G-16984)*
Tyson, Indianapolis Also Called: Tyson Foods *(G-9669)*
Tyson, Logansport Also Called: Tyson Fresh Meats Inc *(G-11114)*
Tyson, Ramsey Also Called: Tyson Chicken Inc *(G-14027)*
Tyson Chicken Inc 812 347-2452
  495 Highway 64 Nw Ramsey (47166) *(G-14027)*
Tyson Foods 317 791-8430
  1301 S Keystone Ave Indianapolis (46203) *(G-9669)*
Tyson Foods Inc 812 738-3219
  545 Valley Rd Corydon (47112) *(G-2520)*
Tyson Foods Inc 260 726-3118
  1355 W Tyson Rd Portland (47371) *(G-13973)*
Tyson Fresh Meats Inc 765 339-4512
  38 E 900 N Linden (47955) *(G-11033)*
Tyson Fresh Meats Inc 574 753-6121
  2125 S County Road 125 W Logansport (46947) *(G-11114)*
Tyson Fresh Meats Inc 574 753-6134
  Hwy 35 S Logansport (46947) *(G-11115)*
Tyson Fresh Meats Inc 765 379-3102
  6870 S Us Highway 421 Rossville (46065) *(G-14388)*
Tyson Fresh Meats Inc 812 486-2800
  Rr 3 Washington (47501) *(G-16511)*
Tyson Mexican Original Inc 260 726-3118
  1355 W Tyson Rd Portland (47371) *(G-13974)*
Tyson Sales and Dist Inc 479 290-7776
  1301 S Keystone Ave Indianapolis (46203) *(G-9670)*
U B Klem Furniture Co Inc 812 326-2236
  3861 E Schnellville Rd Saint Anthony (47575) *(G-14432)*
U B Machine Inc 260 493-3381
  1615 Lincoln Hwy E New Haven (46774) *(G-12924)*
U F P, Granger Also Called: Ufp Granger LLC *(G-6387)*
U S Accu-Met Inc 765 533-4219
  6949 N County Road 400 W Middletown (47356) *(G-11779)*
U S Aggregates Inc 765 564-2282
  Us 421n Delphi (46923) *(G-2910)*
U S Aggregates Inc 765 436-7665
  6990 N 875 W Thorntown (46071) *(G-15757)*
U S Filter 317 280-4251
  6125 Guion Rd Indianapolis (46254) *(G-9671)*
U S Filter Distribution 317 271-1463
  1680 Expo Ln Indianapolis (46214) *(G-9672)*
U S Granules Corporation (PA) 574 936-2146
  1433 Western Ave Plymouth (46563) *(G-13822)*
U S Ink Division, Frankfort Also Called: Sun Chemical Corporation *(G-5695)*
U S S Inc 260 693-1172
  9745 E State Road 205-57 Churubusco (46723) *(G-1992)*
U Want Icecream LLC 317 577-4057
  8320 Shoe Overlook Dr Fishers (46038) *(G-4619)*
U-Bolts Engineering, Summitville Also Called: R & R Engineering Co Inc *(G-15429)*
U-Haul, Chesterton Also Called: Stout Plastic Weld *(G-1959)*
U-Haul, Zionsville Also Called: Imel John *(G-17017)*
U-Nitt LLC 812 251-9980
  13640 Akers Dr Carmel (46074) *(G-1792)*
U. S. Signcrafters, Osceola Also Called: US Signcrafters Inc *(G-13404)*
U. S. Steel, Gary Also Called: United States Steel Corp *(G-6023)*
U.S.I. Custom Blinds, Clarksville Also Called: United Services Inc *(G-2040)*

U.S.I. Custom Blinds, Jeffersonville Also Called: United Services Inc *(G-10068)*
Uaw/Rolls-Royce Training Ctr, Indianapolis Also Called: Rolls-Royce Corporation *(G-9325)*
Ubackoff.. 317 557-3951
7121 E 46th St Indianapolis (46226) *(G-9673)*
Ubelhor Construction Inc.. 812 357-2220
26018 State Road 145 Bristow (47515) *(G-1301)*
Ubelhor Woodworking, Bristow Also Called: Ubelhor Construction Inc *(G-1301)*
UC Ink LLC.. 765 220-5502
6549 S Kirker Rd West College Corner (47003) *(G-16544)*
Ucom Inc.. 260 829-1294
9725 W Maple St Orland (46776) *(G-13373)*
Uebelhors Golf.. 317 881-4109
7611 S Meridian St Indianapolis (46217) *(G-9674)*
Ufp Granger LLC.. 574 277-7670
50415 Herbert St Granger (46530) *(G-6387)*
Ufp LLC.. 219 697-2900
3126 E 500 S Brook (47922) *(G-1307)*
Ufp Nappanee LLC.. 574 773-2505
493 Shawnee St Nappanee (46550) *(G-12649)*
Ufp Structural Packaging LLC... 574 773-2505
493 Shawnee St Nappanee (46550) *(G-12650)*
UFS Corporation.. 219 464-2027
330 N 400 E Valparaiso (46383) *(G-16070)*
Ugo Bars LLC.. 812 322-3499
1019 W Howe St Bloomington (47403) *(G-1003)*
UHS USA Inc... 833 459-9403
10715 Andrade Dr Zionsville (46077) *(G-17059)*
Uinspire LLC.. 574 575-6949
1201 County Road 15 Elkhart (46516) *(G-3756)*
Uiw Supply, Columbus Also Called: United Industrial & Wldg LLC *(G-2410)*
Ulerys Fireworks Inc... 574 722-9119
1030 N 3rd St Logansport (46947) *(G-11116)*
Ullom Woodworks.. 765 610-3188
4740 E 200 N Anderson (46012) *(G-211)*
Ullom Woodworks.. 217 369-5769
18891 Stockton Dr Noblesville (46062) *(G-13187)*
Ulrich Chemical Inc.. 317 898-8632
3111 N Post Rd Indianapolis (46226) *(G-9675)*
Ultima Plastics LLC.. 812 459-1430
5401 Highway 41 N Ste B Evansville (47711) *(G-4358)*
Ultimate Bowling Products, Greenwood Also Called: Rbc Holding Inc *(G-6759)*
Ultimate Exhibits... 317 353-7374
3499 Firethorn Dr Whitestown (46075) *(G-16828)*
Ultimate Mfg... 765 517-1160
4794 S Lincoln Blvd Marion (46953) *(G-11346)*
Ultimate Sports Inc... 765 423-2984
820 Hillcrest Rd West Lafayette (47906) *(G-16641)*
Ultimate Wldg Fabrication LLC.. 317 379-2676
17625 River Rd Noblesville (46062) *(G-13188)*
Ultra Athlete LLC... 317 520-9898
2800 N Meridian St Ste 125 Carmel (46032) *(G-1793)*
Ultra Electronics, Columbia City Also Called: Undersea Sensor Systems Inc *(G-2209)*
Ultra Infiltrant, Zionsville Also Called: LLC 2 Holdings Limited LLC *(G-17030)*
Ultra Manufacturing, Walkerton Also Called: Austin & Austin Inc *(G-16264)*
Ultra Manufacturing Inc.. 574 586-2320
648 Stephens St Walkerton (46574) *(G-16278)*
Ultra Mfg LLC... 574 354-2564
68120 County Road 17 New Paris (46553) *(G-12972)*
Ultra-Fab Acquisitions Inc.. 574 294-7571
57985 State Road 19 Elkhart (46517) *(G-3757)*
Ultra/Glas of Lakeville Inc.. 574 784-8958
520 Industrial Dr Lakeville (46536) *(G-10793)*
Ultramontane Associates Inc.. 574 289-9786
206 Marquette Ave South Bend (46617) *(G-15295)*
Un Seen Press Co... 317 867-5594
17272 Futch Way Westfield (46074) *(G-16733)*
Un Seen Tesh, Westfield Also Called: Un Seen Press Co *(G-16733)*
Uncle Alberts Amplifier Inc.. 317 845-3037
7709 Hague Rd Indianapolis (46256) *(G-9676)*
Uncle Als Breading, Converse Also Called: JW Packaging LLC *(G-2477)*

Underdog Diner LLP... 812 598-2970
2800 Lake Dr Evansville (47711) *(G-4359)*
Underground Printing, Bloomington Also Called: A-1 Screenprinting LLC *(G-769)*
Underground Printing, West Lafayette Also Called: A-1 Screenprinting LLC *(G-16554)*
Undersea Sensor Systems Inc (DH)................................... 260 248-3500
4868 E Park 30 Dr Columbia City (46725) *(G-2209)*
Uniflex Relay Systems LLC... 765 232-4675
526 W Division St Union City (47390) *(G-15861)*
Uniform Hood Lace Inc... 317 896-9555
18881 Immi Way Ste B Westfield (46074) *(G-16734)*
Unifrax I LLC... 574 654-7100
54401 Smilax Rd New Carlisle (46552) *(G-12848)*
Unilever Hpc USA, Hammond Also Called: Unilever United States Inc *(G-7025)*
Unilever United States Inc.. 219 659-3200
1200 Calumet Ave Hammond (46320) *(G-7025)*
Union City Coatings LLC... 765 717-3919
301 S Jackson Pike Ste C Union City (47390) *(G-15862)*
Union Electric Steel Corp.. 219 464-1031
3702 Montdale Dr Valparaiso (46383) *(G-16071)*
Union Optical Eyecare Ctr Inc... 812 279-3466
3343 Michael Ave Bedford (47421) *(G-679)*
Union Tank Car Co... 219 880-5248
2815 Indianapolis Blvd Whiting (46394) *(G-16839)*
Union Tool Corp.. 574 267-3211
1144 N Detroit St Warsaw (46580) *(G-16440)*
Unique Global Solutions LLC.. 765 779-5030
5729 S 200 E Anderson (46017) *(G-212)*
Unique Graphic Designs Inc.. 574 583-7119
1279 N State Road 39 Monticello (47960) *(G-12175)*
Unique Jewelry and More LLC.. 317 244-3732
9209 Mccarty St Indianapolis (46231) *(G-9677)*
Unique Outdoor Products LLC... 260 486-4955
4211 Chetham Dr Fort Wayne (46835) *(G-5519)*
Unique Products... 812 376-8887
3129 25th St Columbus (47203) *(G-2409)*
Unique Signs.. 812 384-4967
1650 N Warren Rd Bloomfield (47424) *(G-758)*
Unique Specialty Services LLC.. 219 395-8898
307 S 18th St Chesterton (46304) *(G-1963)*
Unique Tooling Inc... 574 656-3585
101 S Maple Ave North Liberty (46554) *(G-13226)*
Uniquely Divine Yonis LLC... 317 918-9112
4050 Candy Apple Blvd Indianapolis (46235) *(G-9678)*
Uniseal, Evansville Also Called: Uniseal Inc *(G-4361)*
Uniseal Inc... 812 425-1361
1000 Grove St Evansville (47710) *(G-4360)*
Uniseal Inc (HQ).. 812 425-1361
1014 Uhlhorn St Evansville (47710) *(G-4361)*
Unison Engine Components, Terre Haute Also Called: Unison Engine Components Inc *(G-15738)*
Unison Engine Components Inc....................................... 904 739-4000
333 S 3rd St Terre Haute (47807) *(G-15738)*
Unit Step, Indianapolis Also Called: S S M Inc *(G-9356)*
United Animal Health, Sheridan Also Called: United Animal Health Inc *(G-14830)*
United Animal Health Inc (PA)... 317 758-4495
322 S Main St Sheridan (46069) *(G-14830)*
United Cabinet Corporation Nit.. 812 482-2561
1 Masterbrand Cabinets Dr Jasper (47546) *(G-9915)*
United Ccp Inc... 812 442-7468
301 N Murphy Ave Brazil (47834) *(G-1168)*
United Coatings, Indianapolis Also Called: United Coatings Mfg Co *(G-9679)*
United Coatings Mfg Co... 317 845-8830
5839 Barnstable Ct Indianapolis (46250) *(G-9679)*
United Coatings Tech Inc... 574 287-4774
1011 S Main St South Bend (46601) *(G-15296)*
United Drugs, Bloomington Also Called: Williams Bros Hlth Care Phrm I *(G-1012)*
United Feeds... 317 627-5637
1513 Brook Mill Ct Carmel (46032) *(G-1794)*
United Hero Apparel Printing... 812 306-1998
928 Beverly Ave Evansville (47710) *(G-4362)*
United Home Supply Inc.. 765 288-2737
3600 N Everbrook Ln Ste C Muncie (47304) *(G-12509)*

United Industrial & Wldg LLC	812 526-4050
8720 N Us Highway 31 Columbus (47201) *(G-2410)*	
United Leak Detection Inc	317 848-4447
Carmel (46082) *(G-1795)*	
United Machine & Tool LLC	260 749-8880
5431 New Haven Ave Fort Wayne (46803) *(G-5520)*	
United Machine Corporation	219 548-8050
753 Axe Ave Valparaiso (46383) *(G-16072)*	
United Minerals and Prpts Inc	812 838-5236
2700 Bluff Rd Mount Vernon (47620) *(G-12325)*	
United Minerals Inc	812 683-5024
409 N Van Buren St Huntingburg (47542) *(G-7294)*	
United Oil Corp	260 489-3511
Hwy 33 And Washington Center Rd Fort Wayne (46808) *(G-5521)*	
United Parcel Service Inc	317 776-9494
14350 Mundy Dr Ste 800 Noblesville (46060) *(G-13189)*	
United Pet Foods Inc	574 674-5981
30809 Corwin Rd Elkhart (46514) *(G-3758)*	
United Pie, Elkhart *Also Called: United Pies of Elkhart Inc (G-3759)*	
United Pies of Elkhart Inc	574 294-3419
1016 Middlebury St Elkhart (46516) *(G-3759)*	
United Precision Gear Co, Indianapolis *Also Called: United Precision Gear Co Inc (G-9680)*	
United Precision Gear Co Inc	317 784-4665
4937 Camden St Indianapolis (46227) *(G-9680)*	
United Ribtype Company, Fort Wayne *Also Called: Indiana Stamp Co Inc (G-5104)*	
United Roll Forming Corp	574 294-2800
58288 County Road 3 Elkhart (46517) *(G-3760)*	
United Seams Apparel Cnstr LLC	773 397-3831
7231 Northcote Ave Hammond (46324) *(G-7026)*	
United Services Inc (PA)	812 989-3320
118 W Lewis And Clark Pkwy Clarksville (47129) *(G-2040)*	
United Services Inc	812 989-3320
2626 America Place Jeffersonville (47130) *(G-10068)*	
United Shade LLC	574 262-0954
2780 County Road 6 W Elkhart (46514) *(G-3761)*	
United Sign Advertising, Indianapolis *Also Called: Stackman Signs/Graphics Inc (G-9489)*	
United States Cold Storage Inc	765 482-2653
415 S Mount Zion Rd Lebanon (46052) *(G-10949)*	
United States Dept of Navy	812 854-1762
300 Highway 36 Crane (47522) *(G-2541)*	
United States Gypsum Company	219 392-4600
301 Riley Rd East Chicago (46312) *(G-3049)*	
United States Gypsum Company	812 388-6866
8754 E State Road 450 Shoals (47581) *(G-14913)*	
United States Gypsum Company	812 247-2101
12802 Deep Cut Lake Rd Shoals (47581) *(G-14914)*	
United States Steel Corp	219 391-2045
101 E 129th St East Chicago (46312) *(G-3050)*	
United States Steel Corp	219 888-2000
1 N Broadway Gary (46402) *(G-6023)*	
United States Steel Corp	219 762-3131
6300 Us Highway 12 Portage (46368) *(G-13917)*	
United Technology Corp	317 481-5784
7304 W Morris St Indianapolis (46231) *(G-9681)*	
United Tool & Engineering Inc	574 259-1953
337 Campbell St Mishawaka (46544) *(G-12019)*	
United Tool Company Inc	260 563-3143
838 Lafontaine Ave Wabash (46992) *(G-16219)*	
United Turf Alliance LLC	770 335-3015
12840 Ford Dr Fishers (46038) *(G-4620)*	
United-Ah II LLC	317 758-4495
322 S Main St Sheridan (46069) *(G-14831)*	
Universal Air Products LLC (PA)	502 451-1825
7235 Novas Lndg Sellersburg (47172) *(G-14619)*	
Universal Bearing, Bremen *Also Called: Hanwha Machinery America Corp (G-1195)*	
Universal Blower Pac Inc	317 773-7256
440 Park 32 W Dr Noblesville (46062) *(G-13190)*	
Universal Coatings LLC	574 520-3403
1204 Pierina Dr Elkhart (46514) *(G-3762)*	
Universal Door Carrier Inc	317 241-3447
1609 S Sigsbee St Indianapolis (46241) *(G-9682)*	
Universal Export Partnr LLC	219 939-9529
5528 Melton Rd Gary (46403) *(G-6024)*	
Universal Frest Pdts Ind Ltd P	574 273-6326
51070 Bittersweet Rd Granger (46530) *(G-6388)*	
Universal Metalcraft Inc	260 547-4457
4215 W 750 N Decatur (46733) *(G-2888)*	
Universal Operating Inc	812 477-1584
1521 S Green River Rd Evansville (47715) *(G-4363)*	
Universal Package LLC	812 937-3605
435 Virginia St Ferdinand (47532) *(G-4450)*	
Universal Package Systems, Ferdinand *Also Called: Universal Package LLC (G-4450)*	
Universal Packg Systems Inc	260 829-6721
9880 W Naples St Orland (46776) *(G-13374)*	
Universal Precision Instrs Inc	574 264-3997
2921 Lavanture Pl Elkhart (46514) *(G-3763)*	
Universal Services Inc	219 397-4373
475 E 151st St East Chicago (46312) *(G-3051)*	
Universal Tool & Engrg Co	317 842-8999
105 Rush Ct Fishers (46038) *(G-4621)*	
Universal Transparent Bag Inc	317 634-6425
230 W Mccarty St Indianapolis (46225) *(G-9683)*	
University Loft Company, Greenfield *Also Called: J Squared Inc (G-6521)*	
University Notre Dame Du Lac	574 631-7471
024 S Dinnina Hall Notre Dame (46556) *(G-13317)*	
University Notre Dame Du Lac	574 631-6346
310 Flanner Hall Fl 3 Notre Dame (46556) *(G-13318)*	
University Publishing Corp	812 339-9033
310 S Washington St Bloomington (47401) *(G-1004)*	
Univertical Holdings Inc (HQ)	260 665-1500
203 Weatherhead St Angola (46703) *(G-303)*	
Univertical LLC	260 665-1500
203 Weatherhead St Angola (46703) *(G-304)*	
Unjust LLC	317 443-2584
10854 Nature Trail Dr Apt 101 Fishers (46038) *(G-4622)*	
Unlimited Manufacturing LLC	260 515-3332
702 N Main St Avilla (46710) *(G-497)*	
Unlimited Vending LLC	765 288-5952
3504 W Moore Rd Muncie (47304) *(G-12510)*	
Unplug Soy Candles	217 520-2658
16250 Remington Dr Fishers (46037) *(G-4623)*	
Unplug Soy Candles LLC	317 650-5776
1360 E Broadway St Ste C Fortville (46040) *(G-5608)*	
Unrivaled Interiors LLC (PA)	317 509-0496
24000 Twilight Hills Dr Cicero (46034) *(G-2002)*	
Unrivaled Interiors LLC	317 509-0496
24000 Twilight Hills Dr Cicero (46034) *(G-2003)*	
Upanaway LLC	866 218-7143
7284 W 200 N Greenfield (46140) *(G-6568)*	
Upcycle Industrial Inc	574 825-4990
221 W Us Highway 20 Ste B Middlebury (46540) *(G-11755)*	
Upg Enterprises LLC	708 594-9200
700 Chase St Gary (46404) *(G-6025)*	
Upland Brewing Co., Bloomington *Also Called: Upland Brewing Company Inc (G-1005)*	
Upland Brewing Company Inc (PA)	812 330-7421
350 W 11th St Bloomington (47404) *(G-1005)*	
Upland Print and Stitch	765 506-7011
230 N Main St Upland (46989) *(G-15882)*	
Upland Print Stitch	765 506-7011
40 E Berry Ave Upland (46989) *(G-15883)*	
Upland Tire & Service Ctr Inc	765 998-0871
148 S Main St Upland (46989) *(G-15884)*	
Upper Level Networks Inc	317 863-0955
16545 Southpark Dr Westfield (46074) *(G-16735)*	
Upper Level Sports LLC	317 681-3754
2303 E Riverside Dr Indianapolis (46208) *(G-9684)*	
Upright Iron Works Inc	219 922-1994
1941 N Woodlawn Ave Griffith (46319) *(G-6821)*	
Uprizing LLC	317 500-9359
5706 Vicksburg Dr Indianapolis (46254) *(G-9685)*	
UPS, Noblesville *Also Called: United Parcel Service Inc (G-13189)*	
UPS Store 5219	219 750-9597
417 W 81st Ave Merrillville (46410) *(G-11570)*	

ALPHABETIC SECTION — Vahala Foam Inc

UPS Store 6991, Zionsville *Also Called: P413 Corporation (G-17039)*
Upshaw Freight LLC.. 317 200-8655
  9702 E Washington St Ste 400 # 142 Indianapolis (46229) *(G-9686)*
Uptgraft Welding... 260 824-4624
  3295 E 450 S Bluffton (46714) *(G-1065)*
Urban Logging Company LLC.................................. 317 710-4070
  404 W 44th St Indianapolis (46208) *(G-9687)*
Urban Rustic Farmhouse LLC................................... 317 238-0945
  3114 S 500 W New Palestine (46163) *(G-12944)*
Urban Times, Indianapolis *Also Called: Brooks Publications Inc (G-7688)*
Urban Vines LLC... 317 763-0678
  120 E 161st St Westfield (46074) *(G-16736)*
Urschel Laboratories Inc (PA).................................. 219 464-4811
  1200 Cutting Edge Dr Chesterton (46304) *(G-1964)*
Urschelair Leasing LLC... 219 464-4811
  1200 Cutting Edge Dr Chesterton (46304) *(G-1965)*
US Automation LLC... 260 338-1100
  7143 State Road 3 Huntertown (46748) *(G-7267)*
US Biopsy, Indianapolis *Also Called: Promex Technologies LLC (G-9230)*
US Enzyme LLC... 317 268-4975
  137 Production Dr Ste A Avon (46123) *(G-556)*
US Lbm Operating Co 3009 LLC............................... 812 464-2428
  1700 N Kentucky Ave Evansville (47711) *(G-4364)*
US Leisure, Anderson *Also Called: Keter Us Inc (G-142)*
US Metals Inc... 219 398-1350
  425 W 151st St Ste 2 East Chicago (46312) *(G-3052)*
US Metals Inc... 219 802-8465
  940 150th St Hammond (46327) *(G-7027)*
US Molders Inc.. 219 984-5058
  59 W 100 N Reynolds (47980) *(G-14077)*
US Nano LLC.. 941 360-2161
  1400 E Angela Blvd Unit 125 South Bend (46617) *(G-15297)*
US Oilfield Company LLC... 888 584-7565
  8925 N Meridian Ste Ste 120 Carmel (46032) *(G-1796)*
Us Premier Business LLC... 540 822-0329
  8188 Durbin Ter Apt D Crown Point (46307) *(G-2769)*
US Rod Manufacturing LLC...................................... 574 227-1288
  502 S Oakland Ave Nappanee (46550) *(G-12651)*
US Signcrafters Inc.. 574 674-5055
  216 Lincolnway E Osceola (46561) *(G-13404)*
US Silicones LLC.. 260 497-0819
  623 Airport North Office Park Fort Wayne (46825) *(G-5522)*
US Silicones LLC (PA).. 260 480-0171
  3508 Independence Dr Fort Wayne (46808) *(G-5523)*
US Solids Control, Carmel *Also Called: US Oilfield Company LLC (G-1796)*
US Truck Trailer Service.. 574 232-2014
  1311 S Olive St South Bend (46619) *(G-15298)*
US Valves Inc.. 812 476-6662
  640 S Hebron Ave Evansville (47714) *(G-4365)*
US Water Systems Inc.. 317 209-0889
  1209 Country Club Rd Indianapolis (46234) *(G-9688)*
USA, Fishers *Also Called: True You Naturally Inc (G-4617)*
USA Bassin LLC.. 812 276-8043
  Bedford (47421) *(G-680)*
USA Flap, Aurora *Also Called: Specialty Adhesive Film Co (G-455)*
USA Medical Suppliers Ltd....................................... 608 782-1855
  9658 Oakhaven Ct Indianapolis (46256) *(G-9689)*
USA Today.. 212 715-2188
  13095 Publishers Dr Fishers (46038) *(G-4624)*
USA Travel Magazine.. 317 834-3683
  7213 Bethany Park Martinsville (46151) *(G-11433)*
USA Vision Systems Inc... 949 583-1519
  12550 Promise Creek Ln Ste 116 Fishers (46038) *(G-4625)*
Usalco Michigan City Plant LLC................................ 219 873-0914
  1750 E Us Highway 12 Michigan City (46360) *(G-11682)*
Use What Youve Got Ministry................................... 317 924-4124
  3549 Boulevard Pl Indianapolis (46208) *(G-9690)*
Useful Home Products LLC....................................... 765 459-0095
  186 Champagne Ct Kokomo (46901) *(G-10353)*
Useful Products LLC.. 877 304-9036
  429 W Jasper St Goodland (47948) *(G-6083)*

Uselman Packing Co... 765 832-2112
  75 E 4th St Clinton (47842) *(G-2080)*
USI, West Lafayette *Also Called: Ultimate Sports Inc (G-16641)*
Uskert Welding... 219 759-2794
  211 N 750 W Valparaiso (46385) *(G-16073)*
Usmpc Buyer Inc.. 260 356-2040
  701 N Broadway St Huntington (46750) *(G-7376)*
Usv Optical Inc.. 260 482-5033
  4201 Coldwater Rd Ste 4 Fort Wayne (46805) *(G-5524)*
Usw Lu 6103-07... 219 762-4433
  1919 Willowcreek Rd Portage (46368) *(G-13918)*
UT Electronic Controls, Huntington *Also Called: Utec Inc (G-7377)*
Utec Inc... 260 359-3514
  3650 W 200 N Huntington (46750) *(G-7377)*
Utilimaster Holdings Inc... 800 237-7806
  603 Earthway Blvd Bristol (46507) *(G-1295)*
Utilimaster Services LLC... 800 582-3454
  603 Earthway Blvd Bristol (46507) *(G-1296)*
Utilities AVI Specialists Inc..................................... 219 662-8175
  401 W Summit St Crown Point (46307) *(G-2770)*
Utility Access Solutions Inc..................................... 765 744-6528
  205 S Walnut St Ridgeville (47380) *(G-14238)*
Utility Body Werks, Elkhart *Also Called: Luxe Trucks LLC (G-3504)*
Utility Pipe Sales Indiana Inc................................... 317 224-2300
  2821 N Catherwood Ave Indianapolis (46219) *(G-9691)*
Utility Systems Inc (PA).. 317 842-9000
  8431 Castlewood Dr Indianapolis (46250) *(G-9692)*
Utility Systems Specialists, Churubusco *Also Called: U S S Inc (G-1992)*
Utility Test Equipment Company, Lafayette *Also Called: Radian Research Inc (G-10675)*
Utopian Coffee Company LLC.................................. 888 558-8674
  2001 S Calhoun St Fort Wayne (46802) *(G-5525)*
Utter's, Martinsville *Also Called: Sharon K Utter (G-11427)*
Utz Quality Foods LLC... 717 443-7230
  1955 Lancaster St Ste 1 Bluffton (46714) *(G-1066)*
Utz Quality Foods LLC... 812 430-5751
  9595 State Road 64 Georgetown (47122) *(G-6076)*
Utz Quality Foods LLC... 717 443-7230
  2801 Fortune Cir E Ste N-Q Indianapolis (46241) *(G-9693)*
Utz Quality Foods LLC... 717 982-3066
  4600 N Superior Dr Muncie (47303) *(G-12511)*
Uva Software LLC.. 877 927-1115
  11650 Olio Rd Ste 1000 Fishers (46037) *(G-4626)*
Uway Extrusion LLC... 765 592-6089
  48 N Parke Ave Marshall (47859) *(G-11375)*
V & H Fiberglass Repair... 574 772-4920
  680 N Us Highway 35 Knox (46534) *(G-10227)*
V & P Printing... 260 495-3741
  3655 N 300 E Fremont (46737) *(G-5838)*
V Art Grafix LLC.. 317 513-5522
  5102 Sandhurst Dr Indianapolis (46217) *(G-9694)*
V Global Holdings LLC (HQ).................................... 317 247-8141
  201 N Illinois St Ste 1800 Indianapolis (46204) *(G-9695)*
V I P Tooling Inc... 317 398-0753
  739 E Franklin St Shelbyville (46176) *(G-14810)*
V J Shimp Optical, Indianapolis *Also Called: Shimp Optical Corp (G-9420)*
V Luxuries LLC.. 877 308-5988
  16751 Clover Rd Noblesville (46060) *(G-13191)*
V M Integrated... 877 296-0621
  8501 Bash St Ste 1000 Indianapolis (46250) *(G-9696)*
V N C Inc... 219 696-5031
  585 N Nichols St Lowell (46356) *(G-11179)*
V-T Industries Inc.. 712 368-4381
  1406 Meridian St Shelbyville (46176) *(G-14811)*
V-Tech Engineering Inc.. 260 824-4322
  118 E Wabash St Bluffton (46714) *(G-1067)*
VA Optical Laboratory, Indianapolis *Also Called: Sitewise Inc (G-9444)*
Vacuum Technique LLC (HQ)................................... 800 848-4511
  935 S Woodland Ave Michigan City (46360) *(G-11683)*
Vadens Firearms & Ammun LLC................................ 317 840-5799
  4485 E 10th St Indianapolis (46201) *(G-9697)*
Vahala Foam Inc.. 574 293-1287
  930 Herman St Elkhart (46516) *(G-3764)*

ALPHABETIC SECTION

Val Rollers Incorporated.. 317 542-1968
2345 N Butler Ave Indianapolis (46218) *(G-9698)*

Valad McHning Cntrless Grnding..................................... 574 291-5541
2825 S Main St South Bend (46614) *(G-15299)*

Valentine Woodworking LLC.. 574 206-0697
25810 Miner Rd Elkhart (46514) *(G-3765)*

Valeo, Seymour *Also Called: Valeo North America Inc (G-14702)*

Valeo Eng Coolant Aftermarket, Greensburg *Also Called: Valeo North America Inc (G-6639)*

Valeo Engine Cooling, Greensburg *Also Called: Valeo North America Inc (G-6640)*

Valeo Engine Cooling Inc.. 812 663-8541
1100 E Barachel Ln Greensburg (47240) *(G-6638)*

Valeo Lighting Systems N Amer, Seymour *Also Called: Valeo North America Inc (G-14701)*

Valeo Ltg Systems N Amer LLC.. 812 523-5200
1231 A Ave N Seymour (47274) *(G-14700)*

Valeo North America Inc... 800 677-6004
1580 E Commerce Dr Greensburg (47240) *(G-6639)*

Valeo North America Inc... 812 663-8541
1100 E Barachel Ln Greensburg (47240) *(G-6640)*

Valeo North America Inc... 812 524-5198
2010 2nd Ave Seymour (47274) *(G-14701)*

Valeo North America Inc... 248 619-8300
1231 A Ave N Seymour (47274) *(G-14702)*

Valeo Thrmal Coml Vhcles N Ame, Elkhart *Also Called: Spheros North America Inc (G-3693)*

Valero Bluffton Ethanol Plant, Bluffton *Also Called: Valero Renewable Fuels Co LLC (G-1068)*

Valero Renewable Fuels Co LLC..................................... 260 846-0011
1441 S Adams St Bluffton (46714) *(G-1068)*

Valero Renewable Fuels Co LLC..................................... 812 833-3900
7201 Port Rd Mount Vernon (47620) *(G-12326)*

Valesco Manufacturing Inc.. 812 636-6001
7857 N 1100 E Loogootee (47553) *(G-11152)*

Valesco Manufacturing Inc (PA)..................................... 765 522-2740
9875 N County Road 600 E Roachdale (46172) *(G-14249)*

Valgotech LLC.. 850 339-8877
11079 Village Square Ln Fishers (46038) *(G-4627)*

Validated Custom Solutions LLC (PA)............................. 317 259-7604
905 N Capitol Ave # 200 Indianapolis (46204) *(G-9699)*

Valley Asphalt Corporation... 812 926-1471
110 Forest Ave Aurora (47001) *(G-458)*

Valley Distributing Inc.. 574 266-4455
2820 Lillian Ave Elkhart (46514) *(G-3766)*

Valley Line Wood Products LLC..................................... 260 768-7807
2935 N 500 W Shipshewana (46565) *(G-14895)*

Valley Manufacturing, Elkhart *Also Called: Valley Distributing Inc (G-3766)*

Valley Scale Company LLC.. 812 282-5269
751 W Kenwood Ave Clarksville (47129) *(G-2041)*

Valley Screen Process Co Inc.. 574 256-0901
58740 Executive Dr Mishawaka (46544) *(G-12020)*

Valley Sharpening Inc.. 574 674-9077
102 Osceola Ave Osceola (46561) *(G-13405)*

Valley Tile Corporation... 812 268-3328
2437 N Section St Sullivan (47882) *(G-15424)*

Valley Tool & Die Stampings.. 574 722-4566
6408 W Us Highway 24 Logansport (46947) *(G-11117)*

Valmont Industries Inc... 574 295-6942
3403 Charlotte Ave Elkhart (46517) *(G-3767)*

Valmont Site Pro 1, Plymouth *Also Called: Valmont Telecommunications Inc (G-13824)*

Valmont Structures, Plymouth *Also Called: Valmont Telecommunications Inc (G-13823)*

Valmont Telecommunications Inc (HQ)........................... 574 936-7221
1545 Pidco Dr Plymouth (46563) *(G-13823)*

Valmont Telecommunications Inc................................... 877 467-4763
2400 Walter Glaub Dr Plymouth (46563) *(G-13824)*

Valor Defense Solutions Inc... 812 617-0362
15484 N 1350 E Odon (47562) *(G-13354)*

Valparaiso Fire Fighters, Valparaiso *Also Called: City of Valparaiso (G-15928)*

Valparaiso II LLC.. 219 464-0431
2710 Laporte Ave Valparaiso (46383) *(G-16074)*

Valpariso Area Apprntcship Adv..................................... 219 613-6226
739 S Arbogast St Griffith (46319) *(G-6822)*

Valpo Velvet Shoppe, Valparaiso *Also Called: Browns Dairy Inc (G-15921)*

Value Production Inc.. 574 246-1913
2629 Foundation Dr South Bend (46628) *(G-15300)*

Value Tool & Engineering Inc (PA).................................. 574 246-1913
2629 Foundation Dr South Bend (46628) *(G-15301)*

Valve Serve LLC.. 260 421-1927
2020 E Washington Blvd Ste 550 Fort Wayne (46803) *(G-5526)*

Van Co... 574 271-8432
1030 N Merrifield Ave Mishawaka (46545) *(G-12021)*

Van Der Weele Jon D... 574 892-5005
200 W Walnut St Argos (46501) *(G-328)*

Van Duyne Block and Gravel... 574 223-6656
2602 S 500 E Rochester (46975) *(G-14331)*

Van Explorer Company Inc (PA)..................................... 574 267-7666
2749 N Fox Farm Rd Warsaw (46580) *(G-16441)*

Van Gard Vault Co Inc... 219 980-6233
4401 W Ridge Rd Gary (46408) *(G-6026)*

Van Gard Vault Company Inc... 219 949-7723
5100 Industrial Hwy Gary (46406) *(G-6027)*

Van Guard Vault, Gary *Also Called: Van Gard Vault Company Inc (G-6027)*

Van Schouwen Farms LLC.. 219 696-0877
19306 Clay St Hebron (46341) *(G-7107)*

Van Westrum Corporation... 317 926-3200
1750 E 37th St Indianapolis (46218) *(G-9700)*

Van Zandt Enterprises Inc.. 812 423-3511
1701 N Kentucky Ave Evansville (47711) *(G-4366)*

Van's Home Center, Auburn *Also Called: Vans TV & Appliance Inc (G-433)*

Vanair, Michigan City *Also Called: Vanair Manufacturing Inc (G-11684)*

Vanair Manufacturing Inc (PA)....................................... 219 879-5100
10896 W 300 N Michigan City (46360) *(G-11684)*

Vance Products Incorporated.. 812 829-4891
1100 W Morgan St Spencer (47460) *(G-15364)*

Vandelay Industries Ind Inc.. 574 202-2367
802 W Vistula St Bristol (46507) *(G-1297)*

Vandelay Properties LLC... 574 529-4795
101 E Main St Ste A101 Syracuse (46567) *(G-15489)*

Vandeleigh Industries LLC... 574 326-3254
318 S Elkhart Ave Apt 409 Elkhart (46516) *(G-3768)*

Vander Parts Co, Evansville *Also Called: Vandergriff & Associates Inc (G-4367)*

Vanderbilt Luxury Pontoons LLC.................................... 260 478-7227
4422 Airport Expy Ste 220 Fort Wayne (46809) *(G-5527)*

Vandergriff & Associates Inc.. 812 422-6033
1930 Allens Ln Evansville (47720) *(G-4367)*

Vandor Corporation (PA)... 765 966-7676
4251 W Industries Rd Richmond (47374) *(G-14222)*

Vandor Corporation... 765 683-9760
4251 W Industries Rd Richmond (47374) *(G-14223)*

Vanessa Collins LLC... 219 985-5705
2015 Leanders Rd Floyds Knobs (47119) *(G-4697)*

Vanex Color, Brazil *Also Called: Vanex Inc (G-1169)*

Vanex Inc.. 618 244-1413
1825 E National Ave Brazil (47834) *(G-1169)*

Vanguard Machine Inc... 260 508-6044
965 W Ryan Rd Columbia City (46725) *(G-2210)*

Vanguard National Trailer Corp (DH).............................. 219 253-2000
289 Water Tower Dr Monon (47959) *(G-12058)*

Vanilla Bean LLC.. 260 415-4652
7513 Leswood Ct Fort Wayne (46816) *(G-5528)*

Vanity Fair Brands LP.. 219 861-0205
1500 Lighthouse Pl Michigan City (46360) *(G-11685)*

Vanmeter and Son Lures LLC....................................... 812 653-0497
5341 E County Road 875 S Marengo (47140) *(G-11266)*

Vans Cabinet Shop Inc.. 574 658-9625
1704 E Mock Rd Milford (46542) *(G-11808)*

Vans Industrial Inc.. 219 931-4881
231 Condit St Hammond (46320) *(G-7028)*

Vans TV & Appliance Inc... 260 927-8267
106 Peckhart Ct Auburn (46706) *(G-433)*

Varied Products Indiana Inc... 219 763-2526
2180 N State Road 149 Chesterton (46304) *(G-1966)*

Variotech Corp.. 404 566-2935
8804 Bash St Ste C Indianapolis (46256) *(G-9701)*

Varsity Sports Inc.. 219 987-7200
603 N Halleck St Demotte (46310) *(G-2931)*

ALPHABETIC SECTION

Vase Candle, Campbellsburg *Also Called: Greene Woodworking & Glass LLC (G-1523)*

Vasmo Inc 317 549-3722
4101 E 30th St Ste 2 Indianapolis (46218) *(G-9702)*

Vauterbuilt Inc 219 712-2384
16448 Clay St Hebron (46341) *(G-7108)*

Vb Air Suspension North Amer, Elkhart *Also Called: Liftco Inc (G-3488)*

Vco Inc 812 235-3540
1210 Wabash Ave Terre Haute (47807) *(G-15739)*

Vdb Creative Publishing LLC 317 441-9204
1240 W 75th Court Ter Apt G Indianapolis (46260) *(G-9703)*

Vdk Printing LLC 260 602-8212
3822 Live Oak Blvd Fort Wayne (46804) *(G-5529)*

Veada Industries Inc 574 831-4775
19240 Tarman Rd New Paris (46553) *(G-12973)*

Vector Graphics Inc 317 255-9800
7409 Steinmeier Dr Indianapolis (46250) *(G-9704)*

Vectren, Evansville *Also Called: Vectren LLC (G-4368)*

Vectren LLC (HQ) 812 491-4000
1 Vectren Sq Evansville (47708) *(G-4368)*

Vectren LLC 812 424-6411
20 Nw 4th St Evansville (47708) *(G-4369)*

Vectren Fuels, Inc., Terre Haute *Also Called: Sycamore Coal Inc (G-15720)*

Vectren Power Supply 812 491-4310
Evansville (47708) *(G-4370)*

Vee Engineering Inc (PA) 765 778-7895
3620 W 73rd St Anderson (46011) *(G-213)*

Vee Engineering Inc 260 424-6635
3805 Reynolds St Fort Wayne (46803) *(G-5530)*

Vehicle Service Group LLC 800 445-9262
996 Industrial Dr Madison (47250) *(G-11255)*

Vehicle Service Group LLC (HQ) 800 640-5438
2700 Lanier Dr Madison (47250) *(G-11256)*

Vehicle Service Group LLC 812 273-1622
2700 Lanier Dr Madison (47250) *(G-11257)*

Velazquez Wldg Solutions LLC 812 391-9892
1515 Ekin Ave New Albany (47150) *(G-12822)*

Velko Hinge Inc 219 924-6363
9325 Kennedy Ct Munster (46321) *(G-12573)*

Vemme Kart Usa LLC 317 407-7172
6163 E Neitzel Rd Mooresville (46158) *(G-12249)*

Veneer Curry Sales LLC 812 945-6623
1014 E 6th St New Albany (47150) *(G-12823)*

Veneer Services LLC 317 346-0711
5851 S Harding St Indianapolis (46217) *(G-9705)*

Venture & Alliance Group, Carmel *Also Called: Telamon International Corp (G-1779)*

Veolia Wts Usa Inc 219 397-0554
3210 Watling St East Chicago (46312) *(G-3053)*

Veolia Wts Usa Inc 219 746-4060
109 Fairview Ave Valparaiso (46383) *(G-16075)*

Vera Bradley Inc (PA) 877 708-8372
12420 Stonebridge Rd Roanoke (46783) *(G-14272)*

Vera Bradley International LLC (HQ) 260 482-4673
12420 Stonebridge Rd Roanoke (46783) *(G-14273)*

Verallia Henrico Co, Muncie *Also Called: Ardagh Glass Inc (G-12344)*

Verallia North America, Indianapolis *Also Called: Ardagh Glass Inc (G-7542)*

Verbott Trucking & Transportat 317 363-9698
5883 Jamestown Square Ln Indianapolis (46234) *(G-9706)*

Verdure Sciences Inc 317 776-3600
17150 Metro Park Ct Noblesville (46060) *(G-13192)*

Vergence LLC 317 547-4417
9365 Counselors Row Indianapolis (46240) *(G-9707)*

Verista Inc 317 849-0330
9100 Fall View Dr Fishers (46037) *(G-4628)*

Verizon Business, Noblesville *Also Called: MCI Screwdriver Systems Inc (G-13132)*

Vermont Foundry Company, Kendallville *Also Called: Mahoney Foundries Inc (G-10134)*

Vernatherm By Vernet, Columbus *Also Called: Vernatherm LLC (G-2411)*

Vernatherm LLC 860 582-6776
910 S Gladstone Ave Columbus (47201) *(G-2411)*

Verne Lambright 260 593-0250
1390 S 700 W Topeka (46571) *(G-15822)*

Vernet Group, Columbus *Also Called: Vernet US Corporation (G-2413)*

Vernet US Corporation 812 372-0281
835 S Marr Rd Columbus (47201) *(G-2412)*

Vernet US Corporation (DH) 812 372-0281
910 S Gladstone Ave Columbus (47201) *(G-2413)*

Vernon A Stevens 812 626-0010
3901 Bergdolt Rd Evansville (47711) *(G-4371)*

Vernon Greyber 812 636-7880
9808 E 1100 N Odon (47562) *(G-13355)*

Vernon L Goedecke Company Inc 812 421-9633
1011 E Columbia St Evansville (47711) *(G-4372)*

Vernon Sharp 317 398-0631
2202 W Mckay Rd Shelbyville (46176) *(G-14812)*

Verns Woodworking 574 773-7930
491 4th Rd Bremen (46506) *(G-1228)*

Verona LLC 317 248-9888
2346 S Lynhurst Dr Ste C101 Indianapolis (46241) *(G-9708)*

Versatile Cab Solid Surfc Inc 574 753-2359
108 E Ottawa St Logansport (46947) *(G-11118)*

Versatile Fabrication LLC 574 293-8504
4431 Pine Creek Rd Elkhart (46516) *(G-3769)*

Versatile Metal Works LLC 765 754-7470
1403 S Liberty St Muncie (47302) *(G-12512)*

Versteel, Jasper *Also Called: Ditto Sales Inc (G-9832)*

Vertellus, Indianapolis *Also Called: V Global Holdings LLC (G-9695)*

Vertellus Agrculture Ntrtn Spc, Indianapolis *Also Called: Aurorium Holdings LLC (G-7564)*

Vertellus Agriculture & Ntrtn, Indianapolis *Also Called: VSI Liquidating Inc (G-9731)*

Vertellus Health & Specialty Products LLC 317 247-8141
201 N Illinois St Ste 1800 Indianapolis (46204) *(G-9709)*

Vertellus Intgrted Pyrdnes LLC, Indianapolis *Also Called: 1500 South Tibbs LLC (G-7384)*

Vertex Mdrnztion Sstinment LLC 601 607-6866
6125 E 21st St Indianapolis (46219) *(G-9710)*

Vertical Power Co 574 276-8094
10254 Jefferson Rd Osceola (46561) *(G-13406)*

Vertical Sale 260 438-4299
3838 Sherman Blvd Fort Wayne (46808) *(G-5531)*

Vertical Steel Maintenance LLC 912 710-0626
8465 Keystone Xing Ste 115 Indianapolis (46240) *(G-9711)*

Vertical Vegetation MGT LLC 765 366-4447
6655 E N 700 Darlington (47940) *(G-2835)*

Very Vocal Viking 317 919-8903
948 E Chambers Pike Bloomington (47408) *(G-1006)*

Vesco, Richmond *Also Called: Martin Ekwlor Phrmcuticals Inc (G-14159)*

Vesta, Indianapolis *Also Called: Vesta Pharmaceuticals Inc (G-9713)*

Vesta Ingredients Inc 317 895-9000
5767 Thunderbird Rd Indianapolis (46236) *(G-9712)*

Vesta Pharmaceuticals Inc 317 895-9000
5767 Thunderbird Rd Indianapolis (46236) *(G-9713)*

Vestil Manufacturing Corp 260 665-7586
749 Growth Pkwy Angola (46703) *(G-305)*

Vestil Manufacturing Corp (PA) 260 665-7586
2999 N Wayne St Angola (46703) *(G-306)*

Vestil Manufacturing Corp 800 348-0860
705 W Maumee St Angola (46703) *(G-307)*

Veterans Fabrication LLC 317 604-7704
12655 Federal Pl Fishers (46037) *(G-4629)*

Veterans Industries and Arts 317 730-1815
5380 N College Ave Indianapolis (46220) *(G-9714)*

Veterans Promise Cnstr LLC 317 501-4570
10904 Tallow Wood Ln Indianapolis (46236) *(G-9715)*

Vevay Newspapers Inc 812 427-2311
111 W Market St Vevay (47043) *(G-16114)*

Vgmc, Fort Wayne *Also Called: Geneva Manufacturing Inc (G-5021)*

Vhc Ltd (HQ) 765 584-2101
300 W Martin St Winchester (47394) *(G-16902)*

Vhgi Holdings Inc
103 N Court St Sullivan (47882) *(G-15425)*

Via Development Corp 888 225-5842
867 E 38th St Marion (46953) *(G-11347)*

Viant 317 788-7225
3735 N Arlington Ave Indianapolis (46218) *(G-9716)*

Viant Medical LLC ... 317 454-8824
  3735 N Arlington Ave Indianapolis (46218) *(G-9717)*

Viariloc Distributors Inc ... 317 273-0089
  1717 Expo Ln Indianapolis (46214) *(G-9718)*

Viavi Solutions Inc ... 317 788-9351
  5808 Churchman Byp Indianapolis (46203) *(G-9719)*

Vibcon Corporation ... 317 984-3543
  6660 E 266th St Ste 200 Arcadia (46030) *(G-319)*

Vibromatic Company Inc (PA) ... 317 773-3885
  1301 S 6th St Noblesville (46060) *(G-13193)*

Vibronics Inc ... 812 853-2300
  10744 State Route 662 W Newburgh (47630) *(G-13027)*

Vice Bros Pattern Sp & Fndry ... 260 782-2585
  1010 W State Road 524 Lagro (46941) *(G-10770)*

Vickers Graphics Inc ... 765 868-4646
  329 S 00 Ew Kokomo (46902) *(G-10354)*

Vickery Tape & Label Co Inc ... 765 472-1974
  3107 Barrett Rd Rochester (46975) *(G-14332)*

Vicki Wright and Company ... 317 372-7136
  247 Andrews Boulevard East Dr Plainfield (46168) *(G-13740)*

Vickie Hildreth ... 812 350-3575
  2331 N Marr Rd Columbus (47203) *(G-2414)*

Vicksmetal Armco Associates (PA) ... 765 659-5555
  150 S County Road 300 W Frankfort (46041) *(G-5700)*

Victor Oolitic Stone Company ... 812 275-3341
  301 Main St Oolitic (47451) *(G-13360)*

Victor R Gallagher ... 812 425-8256
  Evansville (47706) *(G-4373)*

Victor Reinz Valve Seals LLC ... 260 897-2827
  301 Progress Way Avilla (46710) *(G-498)*

Victorian House Scones LLC ... 765 586-6295
  1305 Richards St Lafayette (47904) *(G-10712)*

Victory Crunch Granola Snacks ... 219 613-3594
  7003 Broadway Merrillville (46410) *(G-11571)*

Victoza, Indianapolis *Also Called: Wisemed Inc* *(G-9778)*

Vidicom Corporation ... 219 923-7475
  124 Sibley St Hammond (46320) *(G-7029)*

Vidimos Inc ... 219 397-2728
  3858 Indiana Harbor Dr East Chicago (46312) *(G-3054)*

Vierks Fine Jewelry, Lafayette *Also Called: Surplus Store and Exchange* *(G-10707)*

Viewrail ... 574 742-1030
  1722 Eisenhower Dr N Goshen (46526) *(G-6274)*

Viewrail, Goshen *Also Called: Iron Baluster LLC* *(G-6177)*

Vigo Coal Company, Evansville *Also Called: Vigo Coal Operating Co Inc* *(G-4374)*

Vigo Coal Operating Co Inc (HQ) ... 812 759-8446
  250 N Cross Pointe Blvd Evansville (47715) *(G-4374)*

Vigo Machine Shop Inc ... 812 235-8393
  3920 Locust St Terre Haute (47803) *(G-15740)*

Vigred Sports, Auburn *Also Called: Baron Embroidery Corp* *(G-368)*

Viking Business Ventures Inc ... 260 489-7787
  7530 Disalle Blvd Fort Wayne (46825) *(G-5532)*

Viking Formed Products, Elkhart *Also Called: All American Group Inc* *(G-3160)*

Viking Group Inc ... 812 256-8500
  105 Quality Ct Charlestown (47111) *(G-1895)*

Viking Inc ... 260 244-6141
  2740 E Business 30 Columbia City (46725) *(G-2211)*

Viking Paper, Plymouth *Also Called: Viking Paper Company* *(G-13825)*

Viking Paper Company ... 574 936-6300
  1001 Pidco Dr Plymouth (46563) *(G-13825)*

Viking Plastics, Scottsburg *Also Called: Genesis Plastics and Engineering LLC* *(G-14556)*

Viking Plastics Indiana, Scottsburg *Also Called: VPI Acquisition LLC* *(G-14583)*

Village Custom Embroidery Inc ... 317 733-3110
  80 N First St Zionsville (46077) *(G-17060)*

Village Workshop Inc ... 812 933-1527
  3047 Washington St Oldenburg (47036) *(G-13359)*

Vin Elite Imports Inc ... 317 264-9250
  55 S State Ave Ste 358 Indianapolis (46201) *(G-9720)*

Vince Rogers Signs Inc ... 574 264-0542
  400 W Crawford St Elkhart (46514) *(G-3770)*

Vincennes Sun-Commercial, Vincennes *Also Called: Indiana Newspapers LLC* *(G-16131)*

Vincennes Welding Co Inc ... 812 882-9682
  923 N 13th St Vincennes (47591) *(G-16160)*

Vincent Aliano Elc & Hvac Inc ... 812 332-3332
  5128 W Vernal Pike Bloomington (47404) *(G-1007)*

Vineyard Fishery Products LLC ... 317 902-0753
  3032 Ruckle St Indianapolis (46205) *(G-9721)*

Vino of Indiana LLC ... 260 710-7464
  305 S Main St Wolcottville (46795) *(G-16943)*

Vintage AVI Publications LLC (PA) ... 260 440-3144
  1355 Waco Dr Huntington (46750) *(G-7378)*

Vintage AVI Publications LLC ... 260 440-3144
  442 N Jefferson St Huntington (46750) *(G-7379)*

Vintage Baked Modern LLC ... 219 252-9820
  601 Lincolnway Ste 1e Valparaiso (46383) *(G-16076)*

Vintage Chemical Inc ... 260 745-7272
  2007 Bremer Rd Fort Wayne (46803) *(G-5533)*

Vintage Publishing LLC ... 812 719-7200
  7643 Miranda Dr Evansville (47711) *(G-4375)*

Vintage Road Candles ... 765 621-3561
  413 W 11th St Apt A8 Alexandria (46001) *(G-64)*

Vinyl Creator ... 260 475-2012
  4698 S East Riley Sq Pleasant Lake (46779) *(G-13748)*

Vinyl Creator ... 260 318-5133
  11889 N Angling Rd 57 - 57 Wolcottville (46795) *(G-16944)*

Vinyl Therm of Indiana, Rushville *Also Called: Keith Ison* *(G-14403)*

Vinzant Software Inc ... 219 942-9544
  904 W Old Ridge Rd Ste 1 Hobart (46342) *(G-7213)*

Violet Sky LLC ... 574 850-5070
  1211 Mishawaka Ave South Bend (46615) *(G-15302)*

Viper USA Inc ... 765 742-4200
  345 Burnetts Rd West Lafayette (47906) *(G-16642)*

Virago Logistix Llc ... 800 767-2090
  5233 Hohman Ave Ste 202 Hammond (46320) *(G-7030)*

Vires Backhoe and Dumptruc ... 812 595-1630
  2571 E Doty Mill Rd Deputy (47230) *(G-2942)*

Virtu Fine Art Services Inc ... 317 822-1800
  212 W 10th St Ste B100 Indianapolis (46202) *(G-9722)*

Visable Vinyl ... 765 717-9678
  4635 E 250 N Hartford City (47348) *(G-7081)*

Vishay Americas Inc ... 765 778-4878
  555 S Pendleton Ave Pendleton (46064) *(G-13561)*

Vision Aid Systems Inc ... 317 888-0323
  916 E Main St Ste 114 Greenwood (46143) *(G-6778)*

Vision IV Inc ... 812 423-0119
  14110 Castle Brook Rd Evansville (47725) *(G-4376)*

Vision Machine Works Inc ... 574 259-6500
  56641 Twin Branch Dr Mishawaka (46545) *(G-12022)*

Vision Quest, Gary *Also Called: Jackson Vision Quest* *(G-5967)*

Vision Training Products Inc ... 574 259-2070
  4016 N Home St Mishawaka (46545) *(G-12023)*

Vispalexo Inc ... 330 323-4138
  450 E Vermont St Indianapolis (46202) *(G-9723)*

Vista Manufacturing Inc (PA) ... 574 264-0711
  53345 Columbia Dr Elkhart (46514) *(G-3771)*

Vista Plastic, Bristol *Also Called: Avr Products Inc* *(G-1247)*

Vista Worldwide LLC ... 574 264-0711
  53345 Columbia Dr Elkhart (46514) *(G-3772)*

Visual Communication Mfg, Crown Point *Also Called: Signs AP & Awards On Time LLC* *(G-2752)*

Visual Components, Carmel *Also Called: Visual Components N Amer Corp* *(G-1797)*

Visual Components N Amer Corp ... 855 823-3746
  550 Congressional Blvd Ste 350 Carmel (46032) *(G-1797)*

Visual Impact ... 812 432-3524
  8595 Huesseman Rd Dillsboro (47018) *(G-2953)*

Visual Values, New Castle *Also Called: R&S Sign Design* *(G-12881)*

Vita Plus Corp ... 574 595-0901
  3836 N 215 E Winamac (46996) *(G-16879)*

Vital Indus Solutions Corp ... 219 916-7648
  225 W Dunes Hwy Burns Harbor (46304) *(G-1457)*

Vital Signs LLC ... 219 548-1605
  4411 Evans Ave Ste D Valparaiso (46383) *(G-16077)*

ALPHABETIC SECTION — W.M. Kelley Co. Inc.

Vitalswap Technologies LLC 725 234-0077
  6401 Gateway Dr Indianapolis (46253) *(G-9724)*
Vitamins Inc 219 879-7356
  1700 E Us Highway 12 Michigan City (46360) *(G-11686)*
Vitracoat America Inc (PA) 574 262-2188
  2807 Marina Dr Elkhart (46514) *(G-3773)*
Vitruvian Composition LLC 317 447-8383
  6330 Hythe Rd Indianapolis (46220) *(G-9725)*
Viva Tia Maria, Zionsville Also Called: Viva Tia Maria LLC *(G-17061)*
Viva Tia Maria LLC 317 509-2650
  4738 Northwestern Dr Zionsville (46077) *(G-17061)*
Vivid Dragonfly Press LLC 609 954-1010
  5534 Saint Joe Rd Fort Wayne (46835) *(G-5534)*
Vivid Internet Publishing 317 858-3882
  4105 N County Road 900 E Brownsburg (46112) *(G-1412)*
Vivid Social Group LLC 317 447-7319
  6817 Ridge Vale Pl Apt 1f Indianapolis (46237) *(G-9726)*
Vivint Inc 317 983-0112
  3902 Hanna Cir Ste A Indianapolis (46241) *(G-9727)*
Vivolac Cultures Corporation 317 866-9528
  6108 W Stoner Dr Greenfield (46140) *(G-6569)*
Vixen, Elkhart Also Called: Vixen Composites LLC *(G-3774)*
Vixen Composites LLC 574 970-1224
  2965 Lavanture Pl Elkhart (46514) *(G-3774)*
Vk Press LLC 317 400-6883
  930 Prospect St Apt 206 Indianapolis (46203) *(G-9728)*
Vk Studios 317 224-6867
  10251 Landis Blvd Fishers (46040) *(G-4653)*
Vkf Renzel Usa Corp 219 661-6300
  1311 Merrillville Rd Crown Point (46307) *(G-2771)*
Vlb Group North America LLC 317 642-3425
  435 Roske Dr Elkhart (46516) *(G-3775)*
Vlc Services LLC 260 459-9501
  4807 Willow Brook Dr Fort Wayne (46835) *(G-5535)*
VMS Products Inc 888 321-4698
  6055 S White Oaks Dr Anderson (46013) *(G-214)*
Vmw Tooling Group LLC 574 293-5090
  56641 Twin Branch Dr Mishawaka (46545) *(G-12024)*
Vocel Inc 858 774-2063
  10240 Summerlin Way Fishers (46037) *(G-4630)*
Voege Precision Machine Pdts, Westfield Also Called: Voege Precision Mch Pdts LLC *(G-16737)*
Voege Precision Mch Pdts LLC 317 867-4699
  17808 Commerce Dr Westfield (46074) *(G-16737)*
Voegele Auto Supply LLC 765 647-3541
  12 Murphy St Brookville (47012) *(G-1339)*
Vogel Brothers Corporation 812 376-2775
  860 Repp Dr Columbus (47201) *(G-2415)*
Voges Machine 812 299-1546
  4876 W Kennett Dr Terre Haute (47802) *(G-15741)*
Voges Machine Shop, Terre Haute Also Called: Voges Machine *(G-15741)*
Voges Restoration and Wdwkg 812 299-1546
  5696 W Cantrell Dr Terre Haute (47802) *(G-15742)*
Vogler Copperworks LLC 812 630-9010
  308 S Vine St Haubstadt (47639) *(G-7091)*
Vogler Metalwork & Design Inc 812 615-0042
  1944 E 1200 S Haubstadt (47639) *(G-7092)*
Voice of God Recordings Inc 812 246-2137
  5911 Charlestown Pike Jeffersonville (47130) *(G-10069)*
Voluforms, Jeffersonville Also Called: Stewart Graphics Inc *(G-10060)*
Volunteer Fabricators, Inc., Indianapolis Also Called: Hackney Home Furnishings Inc *(G-8352)*
Von Duprin LLC 317 429-2866
  2720 Tobey Dr Indianapolis (46219) *(G-9729)*
Vorzeigen Machining Inc 765 827-1500
  5650 Industrial Ave S Connersville (47331) *(G-2474)*
Voss Automotive Inc (DH) 260 373-2277
  4640 Hillegas Rd Fort Wayne (46818) *(G-5536)*
Voss Industries, Jeffersonville Also Called: Pgp Corp *(G-10036)*
Voter Registration 219 755-3795
  2293 N Main St Crown Point (46307) *(G-2772)*

Voyant Beauty, Elkhart Also Called: Accra-Pac Inc *(G-3151)*
VPI Acquisition LLC 812 283-4435
  2200 Centennial Blvd Jeffersonville (47130) *(G-10070)*
VPI Acquisition LLC 812 752-6742
  640 N Wilson Rd Scottsburg (47170) *(G-14583)*
VSC, Clarksville Also Called: Valley Scale Company LLC *(G-2041)*
VSI Acquisition Corp 317 247-8141
  201 N Illinois St Indianapolis (46204) *(G-9730)*
VSI Liquidating Inc 317 247-8141
  201 N Illinois St Ste 1800 Indianapolis (46204) *(G-9731)*
Vti Packaging Specialties 574 277-4119
  12912 Industrial Park Dr Granger (46530) *(G-6389)*
Vulcraft Division, Saint Joe Also Called: Nucor Corporation *(G-14440)*
Vuteq Usa Inc 502 863-6322
  400 W 550 S Princeton (47670) *(G-14018)*
Vuteq Usa Inc 812 385-2584
  819 E 350 S Princeton (47670) *(G-14019)*
Vw Co 812 397-0102
  6521 N Us Highway 41 Shelburn (47879) *(G-14723)*
Vxa Apparel 219 259-6279
  8465 Keystone Xing Indianapolis (46240) *(G-9732)*
Vytec Inc 574 277-4295
  12912 Industrial Park Dr Granger (46530) *(G-6390)*
W & J Sawmill Llc 812 486-2719
  9533 E 600 N Montgomery (47558) *(G-12127)*
W & M Enterprises Inc 812 537-4656
  370 Industrial Dr Lawrenceburg (47025) *(G-10865)*
W & M Manufacturing, Bluffton Also Called: Carrera Manufacturing Inc *(G-1033)*
W & M Woodworking 260 854-3126
  3180 E 450 S Lagrange (46761) *(G-10768)*
W & S Woodworking LLC 812 486-3673
  6460 N 1100 E Loogootee (47553) *(G-11153)*
W & W Fabricating Inc 765 362-2182
  2597 S Us Highway 231 Crawfordsville (47933) *(G-2625)*
W & W Locker 260 344-3400
  8896 W 600 N Andrews (46702) *(G-222)*
W & W Pallet Co LLC 812 486-3548
  7799 E 300 N Montgomery (47558) *(G-12128)*
W A P LLC 317 421-3180
  705 W Mausoleum Rd Shelbyville (46176) *(G-14813)*
W A P Company, Martinsville Also Called: Wallace Construction Inc *(G-11434)*
W Ay-FM Media Group Inc 812 945-1043
  3211 Grant Line Rd Ste 1 New Albany (47150) *(G-12824)*
W B I, Liberty Also Called: Winslow-Browning Inc *(G-11000)*
W F Meyers Company Inc 812 275-4485
  1008 13th St Bedford (47421) *(G-681)*
W H I, Westfield Also Called: Wholesale Hrdwood Intriors Inc *(G-16740)*
W J Hagerty & Sons Ltd Inc 574 288-4991
  3801 Linden Ave South Bend (46619) *(G-15303)*
W Kendall & Sons Inc (PA) 219 733-2412
  10270 W Us Highway 30 Wanatah (46390) *(G-16292)*
W M G, Indianapolis Also Called: World Media Group Inc *(G-9790)*
W M Kelley Co Inc (PA) 812 945-3529
  620 Durgee Rd New Albany (47150) *(G-12825)*
W Michael Ssan Wlls Fndtion I 317 844-6006
  4929 Deer Ridge Dr S Carmel (46033) *(G-1798)*
W N T, Fort Wayne Also Called: Wnt *(G-5573)*
W R Grace & Co-Conn 219 398-2040
  5215 Kennedy Ave East Chicago (46312) *(G-3055)*
W R Grace Davison Chemical Div, East Chicago Also Called: W R Grace & Co-Conn *(G-3055)*
W T Boone Enterprises Inc 317 738-0275
  159 Cincinnati St Franklin (46131) *(G-5784)*
W W G Inc 317 783-6413
  5602 Elmwood Ave Ste 222 Indianapolis (46203) *(G-9733)*
W W Williams Company LLC 260 827-0553
  5415 State Road 930 Fort Wayne (46803) *(G-5537)*
W-M Lumber and Wood Pdts Inc 812 944-6711
  1801 E Main St New Albany (47150) *(G-12826)*
W.A. Zimmer Company, Huntington Also Called: Huntington Exteriors Inc *(G-7322)*
W.M. Kelley Co. Inc., New Albany Also Called: Lauyans Holdings Inc *(G-12763)*

W/S Packaging Group Inc ALPHABETIC SECTION

W/S Packaging Group Inc 317 578-4454
  6231 Avalon Lane East Dr Indianapolis (46220) *(G-9734)*

Wabash, Lafayette *Also Called: Wabash National Corporation (G-10716)*

Wabash Castings LLC 260 563-8371
  3837 Mill St Wabash (46992) *(G-16220)*

Wabash Club Raybestos Pdts Co 765 359-2862
  1204 Darlington Ave Crawfordsville (47933) *(G-2626)*

Wabash Heritage Mfg LLC 812 886-0147
  2525 N 6th St Vincennes (47591) *(G-16161)*

Wabash National LP (HQ) 765 771-5300
  1000 Sagamore Pkwy S Lafayette (47905) *(G-10713)*

Wabash National Corporation 800 937-4784
  3550 Veterans Memorial Pkwy S Lafayette (47909) *(G-10714)*

Wabash National Corporation 765 771-5300
  3000 Main St Lafayette (47904) *(G-10715)*

Wabash National Corporation (PA) 765 771-5310
  3900 Mccarty Ln Ste 202 Lafayette (47905) *(G-10716)*

Wabash National Mfg LP 765 771-5310
  1000 Sagamore Pkwy S Lafayette (47905) *(G-10717)*

Wabash Plain Dealer Co LLC 260 563-2131
  123 W Canal St Wabash (46992) *(G-16221)*

Wabash Plastics Inc (PA) 812 428-9300
  600 N Cross Pointe Blvd Evansville (47715) *(G-4377)*

Wabash Plastics Inc 812 867-2447
  1300 Burch Dr Evansville (47725) *(G-4378)*

Wabash River Energy LLC 812 535-6067
  444 W Sandford Ave West Terre Haute (47885) *(G-16656)*

Wabash Snacks, Bluffton *Also Called: Poore Brothers - Bluffton LLC (G-1048)*

Wabash Steel LLC 317 818-1622
  2007 Oliphant Dr Vincennes (47591) *(G-16162)*

Wabash Valley Cabinet Company 765 337-2859
  3218 N 775 W West Lafayette (47906) *(G-16643)*

Wabash Valley Motor & Mch Inc 812 466-7400
  3909 N Fruitridge Ave Terre Haute (47805) *(G-15743)*

Wabash Valley Packaging Corp 812 299-7181
  1303 E Industrial Dr Terre Haute (47802) *(G-15744)*

Wabash Valley Publishing LLC 812 494-2152
  611 N 7th St Vincennes (47591) *(G-16163)*

Wabash Valley Resources LLC 929 400-5230
  444 W Sandford Ave West Terre Haute (47885) *(G-16657)*

Wabash Valley Tool & Engrg 260 563-7690
  1253 S State Road 115 Wabash (46992) *(G-16222)*

Wabash Vly Woodworkers CLB Inc 317 538-2956
  2738 Westminster Ct West Lafayette (47906) *(G-16644)*

Wabash Welding Services Inc (PA) 260 563-2363
  150 Smith St Wabash (46992) *(G-16223)*

Wabtec Corporation 317 556-4116
  1110 Smith Rd Plainfield (46168) *(G-13741)*

Wabtec Plainfield Dcm, Plainfield *Also Called: Wabtec Corporation (G-13741)*

Waddell Printing Co, Lagrange *Also Called: La Grange Publishing Co Inc (G-10747)*

Waelz Sustainable Products LLC 317 334-7067
  3440 W Co Rd 300 S Logansport (46947) *(G-11119)*

Wag-Way Tool Incorporated 812 886-0598
  483 N Mount Zion Rd Vincennes (47591) *(G-16164)*

Waggway Tool, Vincennes *Also Called: Birdeye Inc (G-16115)*

Wagler Carriages & Wagons, Odon *Also Called: Norman Wagler (G-13346)*

Wagler Competition Pdts LLC 812 486-9360
  9612 N 675 E Odon (47562) *(G-13356)*

Wagler Custom Cabinets LLC 812 486-2878
  8152 E 200 N Montgomery (47558) *(G-12129)*

Wagler Machining LLC 812 866-2904
  11778 W State Road 256 Lexington (47138) *(G-10982)*

Wagler Mini Barn Products LLC 812 687-7372
  8972 N 550 E Plainville (47568) *(G-13747)*

Wagler Woodworking 812 486-6357
  19866 Us Highway 231 Loogootee (47553) *(G-11154)*

Waglers Custom WD Turnings LLC 812 687-7758
  8593 N 775 E Odon (47562) *(G-13357)*

Wagner Electric Fort Wayne Inc 260 484-5532
  3610 N Clinton St Fort Wayne (46805) *(G-5538)*

Wagner Signs Inc 317 788-0202
  2802 E Troy Ave Indianapolis (46203) *(G-9735)*

Wagner Tool Grinding Inc 260 426-5145
  419 High St Fort Wayne (46808) *(G-5539)*

Wagner Truss Manufacturing Inc 812 852-2206
  9410 N Us 421 Napoleon (47034) *(G-12576)*

Wagner Zip-Change Inc 708 681-4100
  913 Arbordale Pl Fort Wayne (46825) *(G-5540)*

Wagners Plasti Craft Co 260 627-3147
  5705 Union Chapel Rd Fort Wayne (46845) *(G-5541)*

Wagners Tree Service 219 608-1525
  1511 E State Road 2 La Porte (46350) *(G-10497)*

Wagners Tree Svc & Clean Up, La Porte *Also Called: Wagners Tree Service (G-10497)*

Wahs Candle Studio 734 846-5654
  111 Wood Dr Sharpsville (46068) *(G-14715)*

Wait Industries LLC 574 347-4320
  2500 Ada Dr Elkhart (46514) *(G-3776)*

Waite Adel (marlane) 812 939-2252
  4810 S Whippoorwill Lk Dr Clay City (47841) *(G-2048)*

Waka Manufacturing Inc 574 258-0019
  945 E 5th St Mishawaka (46544) *(G-12025)*

Wakarusa Ag LLC 574 862-1163
  905 Nelsons Pkwy Wakarusa (46573) *(G-16256)*

Wakelam John 812 752-5243
  160 E State Road 356 Scottsburg (47170) *(G-14584)*

Wakelam Lumber Company, Scottsburg *Also Called: Wakelam John (G-14584)*

Walburn Kitchens, Muncie *Also Called: Walburn Services Inc (G-12513)*

Walburn Services Inc 765 289-3383
  109 S Claypool Rd Muncie (47303) *(G-12513)*

Walerko Tool and Engrg Com 574 295-2233
  1935 W Lusher Ave Elkhart (46517) *(G-3777)*

Walker Family Enterprises LLC 812 385-2945
  1607 W Broadway St Princeton (47670) *(G-14020)*

Walkerton Plant, Walkerton *Also Called: American Roller Company LLC (G-16263)*

Walkerton Tool & Die Inc 574 586-3162
  106 Industrial Park Dr Walkerton (46574) *(G-16279)*

Wall Control Services Inc 260 450-6411
  2826 Longwood Ct Fort Wayne (46845) *(G-5542)*

Wall's Enterprises, Whiteland *Also Called: Walls Lawn & Garden Inc (G-16799)*

Wallace Construction Inc 317 422-5356
  9790 Old State Road 37 N Martinsville (46151) *(G-11434)*

Wallace Grain Company Inc 317 758-4434
  604 S Main St Sheridan (46069) *(G-14832)*

Wallace Legacy 1 Inc 812 944-9368
  4345 Security Pkwy New Albany (47150) *(G-12827)*

Wallace Legacy 2 LLC 812 944-9368
  4345 Security Pkwy New Albany (47150) *(G-12828)*

Wallace Processing LLC 765 397-3363
  3737 S State Road 341 Hillsboro (47949) *(G-7162)*

Wallar Additions Inc (PA) 574 262-1989
  30012 County Road 10 Elkhart (46514) *(G-3778)*

Walls Lawn & Garden Inc 317 535-9059
  201 N Us Highway 31 Whiteland (46184) *(G-16799)*

Wallys Construction 812 254-4154
  1279 South 3t Washington (47501) *(G-16512)*

Wallys Lockshop 765 748-2282
  606 W 11th St Muncie (47302) *(G-12514)*

Walnut Acres Sawmill LLC 765 344-0027
  757 E 200 S Rockville (47872) *(G-14360)*

Walnut Creek Fabrication Inc 765 749-1226
  4891 S 475 E Portland (47371) *(G-13975)*

Walnut Lane Woodworking 574 633-2114
  12530 Shively Rd Bremen (46506) *(G-1229)*

Walter Ostermeyer 260 705-1960
  6210 Beaver Creek Ct Fort Wayne (46814) *(G-5543)*

Walter Piano Company Inc 574 266-0615
  1705 County Road 6 E Ste 200 Elkhart (46514) *(G-3779)*

Walters Cabinet Shop 765 452-9634
  471 E 1300 S Kokomo (46901) *(G-10355)*

Walters Development Co LLC 260 747-7531
  6600 Ardmore Ave Fort Wayne (46809) *(G-5544)*

Walters', Kokomo *Also Called: Walters Cabinet Shop (G-10355)*

Walton Industrial Park Inc 574 626-2929
  7585 S Us Hwy 35 Walton (46994) *(G-16284)*

ALPHABETIC SECTION — Waupaca Foundry Inc

Walton Logging 812 365-9635
991 S State Road 66 Marengo (47140) *(G-11267)*

Wampum Hardware, Pennville *Also Called: Dyno Nobel Inc (G-13563)*

Wanafeed Corporation 317 862-4032
4410 Northeastern Ave Indianapolis (46239) *(G-9736)*

Wanamaker Feed & Seed Company, Indianapolis *Also Called: Wanafeed Corporation (G-9736)*

Wanda Harrington 765 642-1628
5215 S 100 W Anderson (46013) *(G-215)*

Waninger & Sons Timber Co, Fulda *Also Called: Waninger Knneth Sons Log Tmber (G-5850)*

Waninger Knneth Sons Log Tmber 812 357-5200
Hwy 545 Fulda (47536) *(G-5850)*

Wannemuehler Distribution Inc 812 422-3251
516 N 7th Ave Evansville (47710) *(G-4379)*

Wap Inc 877 421-3187
705 W Mausoleum Rd Shelbyville (46176) *(G-14814)*

WAr - LLC- Westville Prtg 219 785-2821
361 W Main St Westville (46391) *(G-16765)*

Warburton Wood Works LLC 317 318-9113
1347 Pauls Dr Greenfield (46140) *(G-6570)*

Ward, Fort Wayne *Also Called: Ward Pattern & Engineering Inc (G-5547)*

Ward Corporation (PA) 260 426-8700
642 Growth Ave Fort Wayne (46808) *(G-5545)*

Ward Corporation 260 489-2281
7603 Opportunity Dr Fort Wayne (46825) *(G-5546)*

Ward Electric LLC 219 462-8780
1858 Hayes Leonard Rd Valparaiso (46385) *(G-16078)*

Ward Forging Company Inc 812 923-7463
3311 E Luther Rd Floyds Knobs (47119) *(G-4698)*

Ward Heat Treating, Fort Wayne *Also Called: Ward Corporation (G-5546)*

Ward Industries Inc 574 825-2548
58582 State Road 13 Middlebury (46540) *(G-11756)*

Ward Pattern & Engineering Inc 260 426-8700
642 Growth Ave Fort Wayne (46808) *(G-5547)*

Ward Production Machine, Fort Wayne *Also Called: Ward Corporation (G-5545)*

Ware Industries Inc 219 378-7100
4245 Railroad Ave East Chicago (46312) *(G-3056)*

WARE INDUSTRIES INC., East Chicago *Also Called: Ware Industries Inc (G-3056)*

Warm Glow Candle Company 765 855-5483
519 W Water St Centerville (47330) *(G-1855)*

Warm Glow Candle Outlet 765 855-2000
2131 N Centerville Rd Centerville (47330) *(G-1856)*

Warm Socks Inc 309 868-3398
3545 Hollow Run Cir Apt 226 Indianapolis (46214) *(G-9737)*

Warner Bodies, Elwood *Also Called: Manasek Acquisition Co LLC (G-3830)*

Warner Bodies, Noblesville *Also Called: Boice Manufacturing Inc (G-13044)*

Warner Press Inc 800 741-7721
2902 Enterprise Dr Anderson (46013) *(G-216)*

Warnock Welding & Fabg LLC 812 498-5408
4484 E State Road 258 Seymour (47274) *(G-14703)*

Warren Homes Inc 812 882-1059
2807 Adams Meyer Ln Vincennes (47591) *(G-16165)*

Warren Power Attachments 317 892-4737
4614 E County Road 1000 N Pittsboro (46167) *(G-13655)*

Warren Printing Services LLC 812 738-6508
217 E Chestnut St Corydon (47112) *(G-2521)*

Warrick Newco LLC 812 853-6111
4400 W State Route 66 Newburgh (47630) *(G-13028)*

Warrior Rack, Muncie *Also Called: Title Ten Manufacturing LLC (G-12503)*

Warsaw Black Oxide Inc 574 491-2975
310 S Walnut St Burket (46508) *(G-1445)*

Warsaw Chemical Company Inc 574 267-3251
390 Argonne Rd Warsaw (46580) *(G-16442)*

Warsaw Coil Co Inc 574 267-6041
1809 W Winona Ave Warsaw (46580) *(G-16443)*

Warsaw Custom Cabinet (PA) 574 267-5794
1697 W 350 S Warsaw (46580) *(G-16444)*

Warsaw Custom Cabinet 574 267-5794
904 Chestnut Ave Winona Lake (46590) *(G-16916)*

Warsaw Cut Glass Company Inc 574 267-6581
505 S Detroit St Warsaw (46580) *(G-16445)*

Warsaw Electropolishing, Warsaw *Also Called: Surface Enhancements Inc (G-16432)*

Warsaw Foundry Company Inc 574 267-8772
1212 N Detroit St Warsaw (46580) *(G-16446)*

Warsaw Manufacturing Facility, Warsaw *Also Called: Dalton Corp Warsaw Mfg Fcilty (G-16344)*

Warsaw Metal Products Inc 574 269-6211
3589 E 100 S Pierceton (46562) *(G-13642)*

Warsaw Mfg Div, Warsaw *Also Called: R R Donnelley & Sons Company (G-16414)*

Warsaw Orthopedic Inc 901 396-3133
2500 Silveus Xing Warsaw (46582) *(G-16447)*

Waseve LLC 443 204-7976
12750 Horseferry Rd Ste 100 Carmel (46032) *(G-1799)*

Wash Systems LLC (PA) 317 201-2625
11088 Plum Hollow Cir Fishers (46037) *(G-4631)*

Wash.systems, Fishers *Also Called: Wash Systems LLC (G-4631)*

Washburn Heating & AC 574 825-7697
54761 County Road 8 Middlebury (46540) *(G-11757)*

Washington and Scoville 317 798-2911
450 E 96th St Indianapolis (46240) *(G-9738)*

Washington Prcoessing Plant, Washington *Also Called: Perdue Farms Inc (G-16503)*

Washington Times Herald, Washington *Also Called: Newspaper Holding Inc (G-16496)*

Washmuth Cabinet Company 765 932-2701
507 N Morgan St Rushville (46173) *(G-14416)*

Wasser Brewing Company LLC 765 653-3240
102 E Franklin St Greencastle (46135) *(G-6435)*

Waste 1 .... 765 477-9138
3304 Concord Rd Lafayette (47909) *(G-10718)*

Wastequip Manufacturing Co LLC 574 946-6631
480 E 150 S Winamac (46996) *(G-16880)*

Wasu Inc 765 448-4450
4418 Lake Villa Dr West Lafayette (47906) *(G-16645)*

Watchdog Manufacturing LLC 574 218-6604
21601 Durham Way Bristol (46507) *(G-1298)*

Watchdog Manufacturing LLC 574 536-2445
57039 Rutledge Ct Elkhart (46516) *(G-3780)*

Watcon Inc (PA) 574 287-3397
2215 S Main St South Bend (46613) *(G-15304)*

Water Energizers, Jeffersonville *Also Called: Water Energizers Inc (G-10071)*

Water Energizers Inc 812 288-6900
3008 Middle Rd Ste A Jeffersonville (47130) *(G-10071)*

Water Front Rabbitry, Odon *Also Called: Graber (G-13336)*

Water Pump Specialists 317 270-9360
5108 W Vermont St Indianapolis (46224) *(G-9739)*

Water Sciences Inc 260 485-4655
3208 Caprice Ct Fort Wayne (46808) *(G-5548)*

Water Treatment Systems, Indianapolis *Also Called: Earthsmarte Water Indiana Inc (G-8035)*

Waterax, Valparaiso *Also Called: Waterax Corporation (G-16079)*

Waterax Corporation 360 574-1818
3701 Innovation Way Valparaiso (46383) *(G-16079)*

Waterfield Automotive, Muncie *Also Called: Waterfield Automotive Mch Sp (G-12515)*

Waterfield Automotive Mch Sp 765 288-6262
3600 S Meeker Ave Muncie (47302) *(G-12515)*

Waterfurnace International Inc 260 478-5667
9000 Conservation Way Fort Wayne (46809) *(G-5549)*

Waterfurnace Renewable Energy, Fort Wayne *Also Called: Waterfurnace International Inc (G-5549)*

Waterjet Cutting Indiana Inc 317 328-8444
10760 E Us Highway 136 Indianapolis (46234) *(G-9740)*

Waterjet Fabricating LLC 765 288-4575
1725 W Kilgore Ave Muncie (47304) *(G-12516)*

Watermelon World Publishing 574 267-2505
307 Administration Blvd Winona Lake (46590) *(G-16917)*

Watershipblue LLC 317 910-8585
4021 Ruckle St Indianapolis (46205) *(G-9741)*

Waterways Equipment Exch Inc (PA) 812 925-8104
1699 S Stevenson Station Rd Chandler (47610) *(G-1868)*

Wattre Inc 260 657-3701
9301 Roberts Rd Woodburn (46797) *(G-16956)*

Waupaca Foundry Inc 812 547-0700
9856 W State Road 66 Tell City (47586) *(G-15518)*

ALPHABETIC SECTION

Wauseon MCHne&mfg-Kndlvlle Div 260 347-5095
708 S Orchard St Kendallville (46755) *(G-10154)*

Wave Express 574 642-0630
67952 Us Highway 33 Goshen (46526) *(G-6275)*

Wawasee Aluminum Works Inc 574 457-2082
206 S Front St Syracuse (46567) *(G-15490)*

Wax Connections Inc 219 778-2325
3628 E Us Highway 20 Rolling Prairie (46371) *(G-14372)*

Way Interglobal, Elkhart *Also Called: Next Gen Power Holdings LLC (G-3568)*

Wayne Black Oxide Inc 260 484-0280
4505 Executive Blvd Fort Wayne (46808) *(G-5550)*

Wayne Burial Vault Company Inc 317 357-4656
602 S Emerson Ave Indianapolis (46203) *(G-9742)*

Wayne Chemical Inc 260 432-1120
7114 Homestead Rd Fort Wayne (46814) *(G-5551)*

Wayne Combustion Systems, Fort Wayne *Also Called: Wayne/Scott Fetzer Company (G-5555)*

Wayne Concept Mfg Inc 260 482-8615
5005 Speedway Dr Fort Wayne (46825) *(G-5552)*

Wayne David Incorporated 317 417-7165
2441 S 25 W Franklin (46131) *(G-5785)*

Wayne Machine Mfrs Inc 765 962-0459
1747 S 5th St Richmond (47374) *(G-14224)*

Wayne Manufacturing LLC 260 637-5586
6505 State Road 205 Laotto (46763) *(G-10811)*

Wayne Meats, Milan *Also Called: Milan Food Bank (G-11781)*

Wayne Metals LLC (PA) 260 758-3121
400 E Logan St Markle (46770) *(G-11364)*

Wayne Newspapers, Cambridge City *Also Called: Janis Buhl (G-1497)*

Wayne Press Incorporated 260 744-3022
1716 S Harrison St Fort Wayne (46802) *(G-5553)*

Wayne Steel Supply Inc 260 489-6249
7707 Freedom Way Fort Wayne (46818) *(G-5554)*

Wayne Tool Design, Laotto *Also Called: Wayne Manufacturing LLC (G-10811)*

Wayne/Scott Fetzer Company 260 425-9200
801 Glasgow Ave Fort Wayne (46803) *(G-5555)*

Waynedale News Inc 260 747-4535
2505 Lower Huntington Rd Ste A Fort Wayne (46809) *(G-5556)*

Wayseeker LLC 574 529-0199
9521 N Koher Rd E Syracuse (46567) *(G-15491)*

Wb Automotive Holdings Inc 734 604-8962
3405 Meyer Rd Fort Wayne (46803) *(G-5557)*

Wb Frozen Us LLC 317 858-9000
1760 Industrial Dr Greenwood (46143) *(G-6779)*

Wb Refractory Service Inc 317 450-7386
826 E Sumner Ave Indianapolis (46227) *(G-9743)*

WC Redmon Co Inc 765 473-6683
200 Harrison Ave Peru (46970) *(G-13607)*

Wcm Tool & Machine Inc 812 422-2315
810 E Division St Evansville (47711) *(G-4380)*

Wdb Enterprises Inc 219 844-4224
7917 New Jersey Ave Hammond (46323) *(G-7031)*

Wdmi Inc 574 936-2136
2341 W Jefferson St Plymouth (46563) *(G-13826)*

We Do Everything, Bloomington *Also Called: Mobile Power Washing LLC (G-922)*

We Greater Courier Svcs LLC 317 966-1043
9165 Otis Ave Ste 263 Indianapolis (46216) *(G-9744)*

Wear Haus Designs, Lagrange *Also Called: Picture It Inc (G-10758)*

Wearly Monuments, Muncie *Also Called: Wearly Monuments Inc (G-12517)*

Wearly Monuments Inc (PA) 765 284-9796
4000 W Kilgore Ave Muncie (47304) *(G-12517)*

Weas Engineering Inc 317 867-4477
17297 Oak Ridge Rd Westfield (46074) *(G-16738)*

Weatherall Company, Charlestown *Also Called: Weatherall Indiana Inc (G-1896)*

Weatherall Indiana Inc 812 256-3378
106 Industrial Way Charlestown (47111) *(G-1896)*

Weatherford Engineered 812 858-3147
Newburgh (47629) *(G-13029)*

Weaver Air Products LLC 317 848-4420
1033 3rd Ave Sw Ste 212 Carmel (46032) *(G-1800)*

Weaver Fine Furn Cabinets Inc 812 342-4833
14400 W Georgetown Rd Columbus (47201) *(G-2416)*

Weaver Logging Incorporated 260 589-9985
2896 West St Berne (46711) *(G-730)*

Weaver Popcorn Bulk LLC (PA) 765 357-8413
303 Congressional Blvd Pmb 200 Carmel (46032) *(G-1801)*

Weaver Woodworking 260 565-3647
7795 E 300 S Bluffton (46714) *(G-1069)*

Weavers Dtch Cntry Ssnings LLC 260 768-7550
7450 W 050 N Lagrange (46761) *(G-10769)*

Weavers Welding 812 438-3425
4572 Salem Rdg Aurora (47001) *(G-459)*

Web Converting, Fort Wayne *Also Called: Web Industries Dallas Inc (G-5558)*

Web Converting of Fort Wayne, Fort Wayne *Also Called: Web Industries Fort Wayne Inc (G-5559)*

Web Design and Developer, Merrillville *Also Called: Cambridge Enterprise Inc (G-11496)*

Web Industries Dallas Inc 260 432-0027
3925 Ardmore Ave Fort Wayne (46802) *(G-5558)*

Web Industries Fort Wayne Inc 260 432-0027
3925 Ardmore Ave Fort Wayne (46802) *(G-5559)*

Web Printing Connection Inc 260 637-4037
11706 Trails End Ct Fort Wayne (46845) *(G-5560)*

Web Products 816 777-3735
229 Factory St La Porte (46350) *(G-10498)*

Web Software LLC 765 452-3936
2115 W Alto Rd Ste A Kokomo (46902) *(G-10356)*

Webb Wheel Products Inc 812 548-0477
50 Scenic Industrial Dr Ferdinand (47532) *(G-4451)*

Webb Wheel Products Inc 812 548-0477
9840 W State Road 66 Tell City (47586) *(G-15519)*

Webb, Danny Plumbing & Heating, Plymouth *Also Called: Danny Webb Plumbing (G-13769)*

Webber Manufacturing Company 317 357-8681
8498 Brookville Rd Indianapolis (46239) *(G-9745)*

Weber Vintage Sound Tech Inc 765 452-1249
329 E Firmin St Kokomo (46902) *(G-10357)*

Weber Woodworking 765 967-3665
148 S 21st St Richmond (47374) *(G-14225)*

Weberdings Carving Shop Inc 812 934-3710
1230 State Road 46 E Batesville (47006) *(G-610)*

Webster Custom Canvas, North Webster *Also Called: Webster Custom Canvas Inc (G-13314)*

Webster Custom Canvas Inc 574 834-4497
221 N Main St North Webster (46555) *(G-13314)*

Webster West Inc 812 346-5666
1050 Rodgers Park Dr North Vernon (47265) *(G-13300)*

Webster West Packaging, North Vernon *Also Called: Webster West Inc (G-13300)*

Webster's Billing Services, Chesterton *Also Called: Websters Protective Cases Inc (G-1967)*

Websters Protective Cases Inc 219 263-3039
709 Plaza Dr Ste 2-224 Chesterton (46304) *(G-1967)*

Websters Tom Custom WD Turning, Indianapolis *Also Called: Prized Possession (G-9214)*

Wedge Guys LLC 708 362-0731
11121 Hickory Grove Rd Cedar Lake (46303) *(G-1840)*

Wedj-FM, Indianapolis *Also Called: Continntal Broadcast Group LLC (G-7858)*

Wee Engineer Inc 765 449-4280
282 Delaware St Dayton (47941) *(G-2838)*

Weekly Herald, The, Madison *Also Called: Madison Courier (G-11237)*

Weg Commercial Motors, Bluffton *Also Called: Weg Electric Corp (G-1070)*

Weg Electric Corp 260 827-2200
410 E Spring St Bluffton (46714) *(G-1070)*

Wegener Steel and Fabricating 219 462-3911
906 Evans Ave Valparaiso (46383) *(G-16080)*

Wehr Engineering, Fairland *Also Called: Thomas L Wehr (G-4403)*

Wehr Welding & Repair Shop, Jasper *Also Called: Robert L Wehr (G-9905)*

Weights & Measures 812 349-2566
119 W 7th St Bloomington (47404) *(G-1008)*

Weissair 260 466-7693
905 Bluffview Dr Angola (46703) *(G-308)*

Welbilt Fdsrvice Companies LLC 260 459-8200
1111 N Hadley Rd Fort Wayne (46804) *(G-5561)*

Welbilt Fdsrvice Companies LLC 812 406-4527
600 Patrol Rd Ste 500 Jeffersonville (47130) *(G-10072)*

Welch Packaging, Marion *Also Called: Welch Packaging Marion LLC (G-11348)*

Welch Packaging Kentucky LLC (HQ) 574 295-2460
1020 Herman St Elkhart (46516) *(G-3781)*

ALPHABETIC SECTION

Welch Packaging Marion LLC.. 765 651-2600
2409 W 2nd St Marion (46952) *(G-11348)*

Welch Winery LLC.. 707 327-8038
8600 E Windsor Rd Selma (47383) *(G-14623)*

Welcome Friends, Terre Haute Also Called: Mikro Furniture *(G-15646)*

Weld & Fabrication Shop, Batesville Also Called: Red Forge Inc *(G-602)*

Welder On Way LLC... 260 920-4705
351 County Road 35 Ashley (46705) *(G-340)*

Welders Choice... 219 880-5470
5713 Pointe Dr Hammond (46320) *(G-7032)*

Welding Center... 219 921-1509
1951 Jacob Ln Chesterton (46304) *(G-1968)*

Welding Insptn Cnslting Trning, Solsberry Also Called: Flynn Welding & Inspection LLC *(G-14925)*

Welding Plus LLC... 317 902-0883
7239 Shelbyville Rd Indianapolis (46259) *(G-9746)*

Welding Services/Training, Hammond Also Called: Strike & Walk Da Cup Wldg LLC *(G-7015)*

Welding Shop... 260 593-2544
5157 W 1100 N Ligonier (46767) *(G-11029)*

Welding Unlimited LLC.. 812 582-0777
2278 E County Road 650 N Petersburg (47567) *(G-13628)*

Weldors Inc.. 765 289-9074
2702 S Monroe St Muncie (47302) *(G-12518)*

Weldy Enterprises, Wakarusa Also Called: Hahn Enterprises Inc *(G-16234)*

Welformed, Elkhart Also Called: Genesis Products LLC *(G-3374)*

Well Done Industries LLC.. 219 838-5201
1679 Jonquil Dr Lowell (46356) *(G-11180)*

Well Groomed Mens Care LLC.. 317 908-4451
1705 N Shadeland Ave Indianapolis (46219) *(G-9747)*

Well Ink.. 765 743-3413
360 Brown St West Lafayette (47906) *(G-16646)*

Well Spring Automation LLC (PA)....................................... 317 324-1119
366 Ridgepoint Dr Carmel (46032) *(G-1802)*

Wellco Holdings Inc (DH)... 574 264-9661
1503 Mcnaughton Ave Elkhart (46514) *(G-3782)*

Wellington Global LLC.. 317 590-1755
2136 N Catherwood Ave Apt 2b Indianapolis (46219) *(G-9748)*

Wellman Furnaces, Shelbyville Also Called: Precious Technology Group LLC *(G-14787)*

Wellness Pet LLC.. 574 259-7834
1025 W 11th St Mishawaka (46544) *(G-12026)*

Wells Robe Sales & Rental... 317 542-9062
5702 E 40th St Indianapolis (46226) *(G-9749)*

Wells Trckg A Div Wlls Assoc I... 317 250-2616
2901 N Euclid Ave Indianapolis (46218) *(G-9750)*

Wells Unlimited Robes Service, Indianapolis Also Called: Wells Robe Sales & Rental *(G-9749)*

Wellsource Nutraceuticals LLC... 219 213-6173
9800 Connecticut Dr Crown Point (46307) *(G-2773)*

Wellspring Components LLC.. 260 768-7336
1085 N 850 W Shipshewana (46565) *(G-14896)*

Wellspring Water Services LLC.. 337 962-5767
366 Ridgepoint Dr Carmel (46032) *(G-1803)*

Welshco, Union Mills Also Called: Welshco LLC *(G-15869)*

Welshco LLC.. 219 767-2786
3637 W 900 S Union Mills (46382) *(G-15869)*

Wendell Conger... 812 282-2564
3018 Grand Pointe Jeffersonville (47130) *(G-10073)*

Wendell Denton... 317 736-8397
4257 S 200 E Franklin (46131) *(G-5786)*

Wentworth Software... 812 218-0052
3410 Lakewood Blvd Jeffersonville (47130) *(G-10074)*

Wenzel Acquisition Inc... 260 495-9898
5610 N West St Fremont (46737) *(G-5839)*

Wenzel Metal Spinning, Fremont Also Called: Wenzel Metal Spinning Inc *(G-5840)*

Wenzel Metal Spinning, Fremont Also Called: Wenzel Metal Spinning Inc Ind *(G-5841)*

Wenzel Metal Spinning Inc (PA)... 260 495-9898
701 W Water St Fremont (46737) *(G-5840)*

Wenzel Metal Spinning Inc Ind.. 260 495-9898
701 W Water St Fremont (46737) *(G-5841)*

Werner Custom Woodworking.. 812 852-0029
3589 W Napoleon Main St Batesville (47006) *(G-611)*

Werner Sawmill Inc... 812 482-7565
3545 N 550w Jasper (47546) *(G-9916)*

Werrco Inc.. 812 497-3500
5994 W State Road 58 Brownstown (47220) *(G-1428)*

Werrco Tools & Machines, Brownstown Also Called: Werrco Inc *(G-1428)*

Werzalit, Syracuse Also Called: Werzalit of America Inc *(G-15492)*

Werzalit of America Inc... 814 362-3881
501 W Railroad Ave Syracuse (46567) *(G-15492)*

Wes Group Inc... 219 932-5200
1225 Martin Luther King Dr Gary (46402) *(G-6028)*

Wesley Publishing House, The, Fishers Also Called: Wesleyan Church Corporation *(G-4632)*

Wesleyan Church Corporation (PA)................................... 317 774-7900
13300 Olio Rd Ste X Fishers (46037) *(G-4632)*

Wesleys Pallets & Heat Treat... 812 526-0377
6181 S 550 E Franklin (46131) *(G-5787)*

Wessels Company... 317 888-9800
101 Tank St Greenwood (46143) *(G-6780)*

West Allis Ductile Iron, Auburn Also Called: Milwaukee Ductile Iron Inc *(G-410)*

West Allis Gray Iron.. 260 925-4717
1401 S Grandstaff Dr Auburn (46706) *(G-434)*

West Executive Offices, Mishawaka Also Called: Patrick Industries Inc *(G-11970)*

West Fork Whiskey Co.. 812 583-9797
1660 Bellefontaine St Indianapolis (46202) *(G-9751)*

West Lakes Boat Mart, Rome City Also Called: West Lakes Marine Inc *(G-14378)*

West Lakes Marine Inc (PA)... 260 854-2525
85 E Holiday Pt Rome City (46784) *(G-14378)*

West Phrm Svcs AZ Inc.. 765 650-2300
2810 W State Road 28 Frankfort (46041) *(G-5701)*

West Plains Distribution LLC... 260 563-9500
1600 S Olive St Wabash (46992) *(G-16224)*

West Plains Mining LLC... 260 563-9500
6601 W Old 24 Wabash (46992) *(G-16225)*

West Point Woodworking LLC.. 260 768-4750
6565 W 200 N Shipshewana (46565) *(G-14897)*

West Side Community News, Indianapolis Also Called: Community Papers Inc *(G-7841)*

West Vigo Machine Shop Inc.. 812 533-1961
339 N 4th St West Terre Haute (47885) *(G-16658)*

Westbow Press.. 866 928-1240
1663 S Liberty Dr Bloomington (47403) *(G-1009)*

Westech Building Products Inc.. 812 985-3628
7451 Highway 62 E Mount Vernon (47620) *(G-12327)*

Westerley Inc
1300 E 86th St Ste 14 # 340 Indianapolis (46240) *(G-9752)*

Western Consolidated Tech Inc (DH)................................ 260 495-9866
700 W Swager St Fremont (46737) *(G-5842)*

Western Excelsior Corporation (PA)................................. 970 533-7412
4609 E Boonville New Harmony Rd Evansville (47725) *(G-4381)*

Western Green, Evansville Also Called: Western Excelsior Corporation *(G-4381)*

Western Kentucky Drilling... 812 457-5639
600 S Cullen Ave Apt 810 Evansville (47715) *(G-4382)*

Western Products Indiana Inc... 765 529-6230
387 W State Road 38 New Castle (47362) *(G-12885)*

Western Wayne News.. 765 478-5448
26 W Church St Cambridge City (47327) *(G-1504)*

Western Wyne Rgonal Sewage Dst................................... 765 478-3788
200 S Plum St Cambridge City (47327) *(G-1505)*

Western-Cullen-Hayes Inc... 765 962-0526
120 N 3rd St Richmond (47374) *(G-14226)*

Westfield Donuts.. 317 896-5856
212 E Main St Westfield (46074) *(G-16739)*

Westfield Outdoor Inc.. 317 334-0364
8675 Purdue Rd Indianapolis (46268) *(G-9753)*

Westfield Steel Inc... 812 466-3500
3345 Fort Harrison Rd Terre Haute (47804) *(G-15745)*

Westlund Concepts... 317 819-0611
806 N Woodward St Lapel (46051) *(G-10818)*

Weston Foods US Holdings LLC (HQ)................................ 317 858-9000
50 Maplehurst Dr Brownsburg (46112) *(G-1413)*

Westrock Company... 219 229-0981
1000 Pidco Dr Plymouth (46563) *(G-13827)*

Westrock Cp LLC... 812 372-8873
3101 State St Columbus (47201) *(G-2417)*

Westrock Cp LLC   ALPHABETIC SECTION

Westrock Cp LLC 574 772-5545
   6595 E State Road 10 Knox (46534) *(G-10228)*

Westrock Cp LLC 574 256-0318
   1925 Stone Ct Mishawaka (46545) *(G-12027)*

Westrock Cp LLC 574 936-2118
   1100 Pidco Dr Plymouth (46563) *(G-13828)*

Westrock Cp LLC 219 762-4855
   5900 Carlson Ave Portage (46368) *(G-13919)*

Westrock Mwv LLC 317 787-3361
   6302 Churchman Byp Indianapolis (46203) *(G-9754)*

Westrock Rkt LLC 812 372-8873
   3101 State St Columbus (47201) *(G-2418)*

Westrock Rkt LLC 574 936-2118
   1810 Pidco Dr Plymouth (46563) *(G-13829)*

Westside Automation Inc 812 768-6878
   78 W 1100 S Haubstadt (47639) *(G-7093)*

Westwood Paper Company 317 843-1212
   4489 Camborne Dr Carmel (46033) *(G-1804)*

Wethington 317 594-6000
   4162 N Ems Blvd Greenfield (46140) *(G-6571)*

Wetwillies Bubbles LLC 260 633-0064
   15486 Bears Breech Ct Huntertown (46748) *(G-7268)*

Wg Machine & Tool 317 994-5556
   317 W Main St Lizton (46149) *(G-11051)*

Wgs Global Services LC 812 548-4446
   840 5th St Tell City (47586) *(G-15520)*

Wgs Global Services LC 810 239-4947
   9856 W State Road 66 Tell City (47586) *(G-15521)*

Wh International Casting LLC 562 521-0727
   181 Burkart Blvd Seymour (47274) *(G-14704)*

WH International Casting, LLC, Seymour *Also Called: Wh International Casting LLC (G-14704)*

Whallon Machinery Inc 574 643-9561
   205 N. Chicago Street (Us Hwy 35) Royal Center (46978) *(G-14394)*

Whatever It Tkes HM Imprvs LLC 317 494-9568
   10625 Tilford Dr Apt 2e Camby (46113) *(G-1516)*

Whatzthat Vending LLC 317 362-9088
   5168 Alpine Violet Way Indianapolis (46254) *(G-9755)*

Whatzup LLC 260 407-3198
   5501 Us Highway 30 W Fort Wayne (46818) *(G-5562)*

Wheel Group Holdings LLC 317 780-1661
   5720 Kopetsky Dr Ste I Indianapolis (46217) *(G-9756)*

Wheel Horse Sales & Service 574 272-4242
   51465 Indiana State Route 933 South Bend (46637) *(G-15305)*

Wheel One, Indianapolis *Also Called: Wheel Group Holdings LLC (G-9756)*

Wheelchair Help LLC 574 295-2220
   28423 Old Us 33 Elkhart (46516) *(G-3783)*

Wheelchair of Indiana 317 627-6560
   4717 Boulevard Pl Indianapolis (46208) *(G-9757)*

Wheeler Corporation (PA) 317 398-7500
   841 Elston Dr Shelbyville (46176) *(G-14815)*

Wheelock Manufacturing Inc 219 285-8540
   2505 Dekko Dr Garrett (46738) *(G-5880)*

Wheels 4 Tots Inc 219 987-6812
   10700 W 1300 N Demotte (46310) *(G-2932)*

Wheels In Sky 812 249-8233
   1026 Monterey Ave Terre Haute (47803) *(G-15746)*

Whimet Inc 574 267-8062
   2100 N Detroit St Warsaw (46580) *(G-16448)*

Whimsical Gardens 317 257-4704
   5464 N Capitol Ave Indianapolis (46208) *(G-9758)*

Whimsicals Inc 317 773-6130
   1606 Chestnut Ct Noblesville (46062) *(G-13194)*

Whipp In Holdings LLC (PA) 260 478-2363
   3405 Engle Rd Fort Wayne (46809) *(G-5563)*

Whirlpool, Plainfield *Also Called: Whirlpool Corporation (G-13742)*

Whirlpool Corporation 812 426-4000
   5401 Us Hwy 41n Evansville (47711) *(G-4383)*

Whirlpool Corporation 317 837-5700
   2801 Airwest Blvd Plainfield (46168) *(G-13742)*

Whisler Custom Leather Co 765 212-8932
   1108 E Royerton Rd Muncie (47303) *(G-12519)*

Whistle Stop 219 253-4100
   10012 N Us Highway 421 Monon (47959) *(G-12059)*

Whitaker Glass & Mirror LLC 765 482-1500
   104 E Superior St Lebanon (46052) *(G-10950)*

Whitaker Skid and Crate, Corydon *Also Called: Whitakerr Dalemon (G-2522)*

Whitakerr Dalemon 812 738-2396
   1240 Old North Bridge Rd Ne Corydon (47112) *(G-2522)*

Whitcomb Yard, Valparaiso *Also Called: Legacy Vulcan LLC (G-15996)*

Whitcraft Enterprises Inc 260 422-6518
   4323 Merchant Rd Fort Wayne (46818) *(G-5564)*

Whitcraft Welding 574 867-6021
   7915 E 300 N Grovertown (46531) *(G-6825)*

White ARC Welding, Hammond *Also Called: Clinton Parker (G-6903)*

White Cap 153, Fort Wayne *Also Called: White Cap LP (G-5565)*

White Cap LLC 812 425-6221
   2201 W Maryland St Evansville (47712) *(G-4384)*

White Cap LP 260 471-7619
   3333 Independence Dr Fort Wayne (46808) *(G-5565)*

White Eagle Indus Group LLC 270 577-2415
   205 W Poplar St Corydon (47112) *(G-2523)*

White House Ventures LLC 260 693-3032
   4960 S 600 E-57 Churubusco (46723) *(G-1993)*

White Machine Inc 574 267-5895
   1903 White Industrial Dr Warsaw (46580) *(G-16449)*

White Oak Land & Timber LLC 812 482-5102
   560 E 25th St Jasper (47546) *(G-9917)*

White River Outfitters LLC 812 787-0921
   314 Main St Shoals (47581) *(G-14915)*

White River Press Inc 317 507-4684
   914 Park Ave Anderson (46012) *(G-217)*

White Rver Fndry/Creative Arts, Spencer *Also Called: Mark Parmenter (G-15355)*

White Sand & Gravel Inc 317 882-7791
   7229 Lake Rd Indianapolis (46217) *(G-9759)*

White Surgical Inc 260 755-5800
   14520 Egrets Ct Fort Wayne (46814) *(G-5566)*

White Water Truss Llc 765 489-6261
   79 Paul R Foulke Pkwy Hagerstown (47346) *(G-6847)*

Whiteco Industries Inc (PA) 219 769-6601
   701 E 83rd Ave Ste 17 Merrillville (46410) *(G-11572)*

Whitehead Signs Inc 317 632-1800
   1801 Deloss St Indianapolis (46201) *(G-9760)*

Whiteman Embroidery 574 342-3697
   8091 Elm Rd Bourbon (46504) *(G-1130)*

Whites Welding & Machining LLC 765 987-7984
   1591 E County Road 600 S Straughn (47387) *(G-15400)*

Whites Woodworks 765 341-6678
   1835 Pumpkinvine Hill Rd Martinsville (46151) *(G-11435)*

Whitesell Prcsion Cmpnents Inc 812 282-4014
   100 Technology Way Jeffersonville (47130) *(G-10075)*

Whitestown - Precast, Whitestown *Also Called: Hydro Conduit of Texas LP (G-16809)*

Whitetail Heartbeat 260 336-1052
   61755 State Road 13 Middlebury (46540) *(G-11758)*

Whitewater Print Solutions LLC 513 405-3452
   10108 State Road 101 Brookville (47012) *(G-1340)*

Whitewater Publications Inc 765 647-4221
   531 Main St Brookville (47012) *(G-1341)*

Whiting Clean Energy Inc 219 473-0653
   2155 Standard Ave Whiting (46394) *(G-16840)*

Whiting Metals LLC 219 659-6955
   2230 Indianapolis Blvd Whiting (46394) *(G-16841)*

Whitley Evergreen Inc (HQ) 260 723-5131
   201 W First St South Whitley (46787) *(G-15331)*

Whitley Feeds Div, South Whitley *Also Called: Nutritional Research Assoc (G-15322)*

Whitlocks Pressure Wash 765 825-5868
   5649 Industrial Ave S Connersville (47331) *(G-2475)*

Whitman Publications Inc 574 268-2062
   401 Kings Hwy Winona Lake (46590) *(G-16918)*

Whitman Publishing 574 267-3941
   302 E Winona Ave Warsaw (46580) *(G-16450)*

Whitney Tool Company Inc 812 275-4491
   906 R St Bedford (47421) *(G-682)*

ALPHABETIC SECTION

Whitt Photo Service, Indianapolis *Also Called: Rick Whitt (G-9305)*

Wholeaf Aloe Distributors.. 219 322-7217
46 Oak Ct Schererville (46375) *(G-14547)*

Wholebody Wholesoul, Merrillville *Also Called: Blessed Humbled Beginnings LLC (G-11490)*

Wholesale, Crown Point *Also Called: Us Premier Business LLC (G-2769)*

Wholesale Drainage Supply Inc... 812 397-5100
8300 N Us Highway 41 Shelburn (47879) *(G-14724)*

Wholesale Hrdwood Intriors Inc... 317 867-3660
17715 Commerce Dr Ste 300 Westfield (46074) *(G-16740)*

Wholistic Gardens.. 260 573-1088
4840 County Road 4 Waterloo (46793) *(G-16533)*

Whyte Haus... 260 484-5666
1629 Channel Pl Fort Wayne (46825) *(G-5567)*

Whyte Horse Winery LLC... 574 583-2345
1510 S Airport Rd Monticello (47960) *(G-12176)*

Wible Lumber Inc.. 260 351-2441
7155 S State Rte 3 South Milford (46786) *(G-15314)*

Wible U-Pick Hardwoods, South Milford *Also Called: Wible Lumber Inc (G-15314)*

Wiburn Jones Construction, Brazil *Also Called: Pool Shop (G-1162)*

Wichman Woodworking Inc... 812 522-8450
8305 N County Road 300 E Seymour (47274) *(G-14705)*

Wick - Fab Inc... 260 897-3303
307 E Fourth St Avilla (46710) *(G-499)*

Wickey Canvas Outdoor Cooking.. 260 223-8890
747 E 350 S Berne (46711) *(G-731)*

Wickfab Steel Fabrication, Avilla *Also Called: Wick - Fab Inc (G-499)*

Wicone.. 219 218-5199
7604 Mccook Ave Hammond (46323) *(G-7033)*

Wieland Designs, Indianapolis *Also Called: Logic Furniture LLC (G-8777)*

Wieland Designs Inc.. 574 533-2168
901 E Madison St Goshen (46528) *(G-6276)*

Wiers Fleet Partners Inc (PA)..574 936-4076
2111 Jim Neu Dr Plymouth (46563) *(G-13830)*

Wiese, Indianapolis *Also Called: Wiese Holding Company (G-9761)*

Wiese Holding Company... 317 241-8600
4549 W Bradbury Ave Indianapolis (46241) *(G-9761)*

Wilbert Burial Vault Co, Indianapolis *Also Called: Wilbert Burial Vault Co Inc (G-9762)*

Wilbert Burial Vault Co Inc.. 317 547-1387
2165 N Sherman Dr Indianapolis (46218) *(G-9762)*

Wilbert Sexton Corporation... 812 334-0883
2332 W 3rd St Bloomington (47404) *(G-1010)*

Wilbert Sexton Corporation (PA)..812 336-6469
1908 W Allen St Bloomington (47403) *(G-1011)*

Wilbert Sexton Corporation... 812 372-3210
3100 S Us Highway 31 Columbus (47201) *(G-2419)*

Wilbert Sexton Corporation... 812 882-3555
426 S 15th St Vincennes (47591) *(G-16166)*

Wilco Corporation... 317 228-9320
5352 W 79th St Indianapolis (46268) *(G-9763)*

Wilcoxen Machine & Tool Inc... 317 784-4665
4937 Camden St Indianapolis (46227) *(G-9764)*

Wild Birds Unlimited, Granger *Also Called: Birds Nest Inc (G-6337)*

Wild Boar Mine... 812 922-1015
2277 Tecumseh Rd Lynnville (47619) *(G-11193)*

Wild Child Organics LLC... 574 213-5204
1143 E Ireland Rd South Bend (46614) *(G-15306)*

Wild Flavors Inc.. 859 991-5229
6326 Calais Dr Indianapolis (46220) *(G-9765)*

Wild Grain Woodworks LLC.. 317 626-3939
17159 Linda Way Noblesville (46062) *(G-13195)*

Wild Hair Canvas Shop... 812 290-1086
605 Green Blvd Aurora (47001) *(G-460)*

Wild Hunnits Group Inc... 312 609-9433
6945 Patricia Ln Hammond (46323) *(G-7034)*

Wild Spirit Coffee Company, Owensburg *Also Called: Michael Filley (G-13463)*

Wildcat Creek Winery, Lafayette *Also Called: Rick Black Associates LLC (G-10680)*

Wildcat Java LLC (PA)...765 438-3682
716 Michigan Rd Burlington (46915) *(G-1447)*

Wildebeest LLC... 812 391-5631
4128 S Calhoun St Fort Wayne (46807) *(G-5568)*

Wildman Business Group LLC (PA)..................................... 866 369-1552
800 S Buffalo St Warsaw (46580) *(G-16451)*

Wildman Corporate Apparel, Warsaw *Also Called: Wildman Business Group LLC (G-16451)*

Wildwood Millwork LLC.. 574 535-9104
2408 Lincolnway E Goshen (46526) *(G-6277)*

Wiley.. 317 794-6765
12162 Talon Trce Fishers (46037) *(G-4633)*

Wiley Young & Associates.. 574 269-7006
121 W Market St Ste B Warsaw (46580) *(G-16452)*

Wiley Industries Incorporated... 317 574-1477
1311 Woodgate Dr Carmel (46033) *(G-1805)*

Wiley Metal Fabricating Inc.. 765 674-9707
816 W 34th St Marion (46953) *(G-11349)*

Wiley Metal Fabricating Inc (PA)... 765 671-7865
4589 N Wabash Rd Marion (46952) *(G-11350)*

Wiley Publishing, Indianapolis *Also Called: John Wiley & Sons Inc (G-8631)*

Wilhelm AG Lime, Peru *Also Called: Jolene D Pavey (G-13588)*

Wilhelm Gravel, Waterloo *Also Called: Country Stone (G-16518)*

Wilhelm Gravel Co Inc.. 260 837-6511
2280 County Road 27 Waterloo (46793) *(G-16534)*

Wilhite Industries Inc.. 812 853-8771
5833 S Yankeetown Rd Boonville (47601) *(G-1101)*

Wilhoite Monuments Inc... 765 286-7423
4710 S Madison St Muncie (47302) *(G-12520)*

Wilkerson Logging Inc.. 812 988-4960
4263 Hoover Rd Nashville (47448) *(G-12683)*

Wilkerson Sawmill.. 812 988-7436
5400 Hoover Rd Nashville (47448) *(G-12684)*

Willemin Macodel... 317 219-6113
15250 Endeavor Dr Noblesville (46060) *(G-13196)*

William Browning... 765 647-6397
7015 Jefferson St Brookville (47012) *(G-1342)*

William D Darr.. 574 518-0453
5416 E 950 N Syracuse (46567) *(G-15493)*

William Donson.. 765 628-3236
7636 E 300 N Kokomo (46901) *(G-10358)*

William E Steiner.. 317 575-9018
5254 Faye Ct Carmel (46033) *(G-1806)*

William F Bane Co, Indianapolis *Also Called: Bane-Clene Corp (G-7595)*

William F Shirley.. 812 426-2599
2721 W Mill Rd Evansville (47720) *(G-4385)*

William H Sadlier Inc.. 219 465-0453
4405 Blair Ln Valparaiso (46383) *(G-16081)*

William L Theby.. 812 477-6673
650 Salem Ct Evansville (47715) *(G-4386)*

William Leman Co (PA)...574 546-2371
114 N Center St Bremen (46506) *(G-1230)*

William R Arvin... 812 486-5255
699 S County Road 700 E Winslow (47598) *(G-16926)*

William Wsley Prof Oral Prstht.. 317 635-1000
5605 W 73rd St Indianapolis (46278) *(G-9766)*

Williams Bros Hlth Care Phrm I... 812 335-0000
574 S Landmark Ave Bloomington (47403) *(G-1012)*

Williams Bros Hlth Care Phrm I (PA)...................................812 254-2497
10 Williams Brothers Dr Washington (47501) *(G-16513)*

Williams Bros Logging LLC... 270 547-0266
2880 Overlook Dr Sw Mauckport (47142) *(G-11442)*

Williams Distribution LLC.. 317 749-0006
1642 Mccollough Ct Indianapolis (46260) *(G-9767)*

Williams Jewelers Inc... 812 475-1705
3101 Covert Ave Evansville (47714) *(G-4387)*

Williams Printing Inc.. 765 468-6033
201 E Henry St Farmland (47340) *(G-4427)*

Williams Prprty Prsrvation LLC... 219 336-3047
548 Circle Dr La Porte (46350) *(G-10499)*

Williams Quality Pallets Inc.. 770 265-1030
15414 Delphinium Pl Huntertown (46748) *(G-7269)*

Williams Scotsman Inc... 260 749-6611
5314 Maumee Rd Fort Wayne (46803) *(G-5569)*

Williams Scotsman Inc... 317 782-2463
2301 S Holt Rd Indianapolis (46241) *(G-9768)*

Williams Signs, Dayton *Also Called: Wee Engineer Inc (G-2838)*

Williams Tool & Machine Corp.. 765 676-5859
54 W Main St Jamestown (46147) *(G-9821)*

Williams Weld Service LLC.. 812 865-3298
3824 E County Road 625 N Orleans (47452) *(G-13383)*

Williams West & Witts Pdts Co.. 219 879-8236
3501 W Dunes Hwy Michigan City (46360) *(G-11687)*

Williams Woods Pubg Svcs LLC.. 317 270-0976
3921 English Ave Indianapolis (46201) *(G-9769)*

Williams Woodshop.. 574 686-2324
2171 E 300 N Camden (46917) *(G-1522)*

Williamsburg Furniture Inc (HQ)... 800 582-8183
2096 Cheyenne St Nappanee (46550) *(G-12652)*

Williamsburg Furniture Inc.. 574 387-5691
3300 W Sample St South Bend (46619) *(G-15307)*

Williamsburg Marine LLC.. 574 658-3409
2096 Cheyenne St Nappanee (46550) *(G-12653)*

Willie Lehman... 574 935-2809
24793 County Road 52 Nappanee (46550) *(G-12654)*

Willis Machining Inc.. 812 744-1100
18395 Hogan Hill Rd Aurora (47001) *(G-461)*

Willoughby Industries Inc... 317 875-0830
5105 W 78th St Indianapolis (46268) *(G-9770)*

Willow Creek Crossing Inc.. 219 809-8952
3574 W Us Highway 20 La Porte (46350) *(G-10500)*

Willow Way LLC... 765 886-4642
520 W Main St Hagerstown (47346) *(G-6848)*

Willow Way LLC... 765 886-4640
12873 We Oler Rd Hagerstown (47346) *(G-6849)*

Willowgreen Inc.. 260 490-2222
2209 Saint Joe Center Rd Apt 166 Fort Wayne (46825) *(G-5570)*

Willows and More.. 812 560-1088
8094 W County Road 1270 S Westport (47283) *(G-16753)*

Wilson Autotech, Crawfordsville *Also Called: Wilson Enterprises Inc (G-2627)*

Wilson Burial Vault Inc... 260 356-5722
446 W Markle Rd Huntington (46750) *(G-7380)*

Wilson Enterprises Inc... 765 362-1089
2008 Indianapolis Rd Crawfordsville (47933) *(G-2627)*

Wilson Fertilizer & Grain Inc (PA)...574 223-3175
1827 E Lucas St Rochester (46975) *(G-14333)*

Wilson Industries.. 313 330-0643
1602 Crestview Dr New Albany (47150) *(G-12829)*

Wilson Iron Works, Crown Point *Also Called: Deg Corp (G-2675)*

Wilson Machine Shop Inc... 812 392-2774
7780 W County Road 800 N Elizabethtown (47232) *(G-3134)*

Wilson Media Group Inc... 765 452-0055
515 W Sycamore St Kokomo (46901) *(G-10359)*

Wilson Printing... 317 745-5868
527 N County Road 50 E Danville (46122) *(G-2830)*

Wilson Welding & Piping LLC.. 317 397-4865
4774 Olive Branch Rd Greenwood (46143) *(G-6781)*

Wilsons Hearing Aid Center LLC.. 765 747-4131
3716 N Wheeling Ave Muncie (47304) *(G-12521)*

Wilsons Locker & Proc Plant.. 812 358-2632
2018 Blue Spring Caverns Rd Bedford (47421) *(G-683)*

Wilsons Slaughtering & Proc, Bedford *Also Called: Wilsons Locker & Proc Plant (G-683)*

Wimmer Lime Service Inc... 765 948-4001
7497 S 150 E Fairmount (46928) *(G-4414)*

Wimmer Mfg Inc.. 765 465-9846
201 County Rd 100 S New Castle (47362) *(G-12886)*

Winamac Coil Spring Inc.. 574 653-2186
512 N Smith St Kewanna (46939) *(G-10168)*

Winamac Cold Draw, Winamac *Also Called: Plymouth Tube Company (G-16871)*

Winandy Greenhouse Company.. 765 935-2111
2211 Peacock Rd Richmond (47374) *(G-14227)*

Winbush Refreshments LLC... 317 762-8236
433 N Capitol Ave Indianapolis (46204) *(G-9771)*

Winchester Steel.. 812 591-2071
10622 S County Road 100 W Westport (47283) *(G-16754)*

Winco Printing & Gift Shop, Roanoke *Also Called: James David Inc (G-14271)*

Wind Deco, Zionsville *Also Called: Fanimation Inc (G-17007)*

Window Makeover, Indianapolis *Also Called: Harrell Family LLC (G-8366)*

Windsor Steel Inc.. 574 294-1060
2210 Middlebury St Elkhart (46516) *(G-3784)*

Windsor Wartcare... 574 266-6555
3100 Windsor Ct Elkhart (46514) *(G-3785)*

Windstream Technologies Inc (PA).. 812 953-1481
819 Buckeye St North Vernon (47265) *(G-13301)*

Windy City Coml Tire & Svc LLC.. 773 530-1246
444 E Chicago Ave East Chicago (46312) *(G-3057)*

Wine & Canvas South Bend LLC.. 574 807-1562
51213 County Road 11 Elkhart (46514) *(G-3786)*

Wine and Canvas.. 574 514-9942
51197 Channel Ct Elkhart (46514) *(G-3787)*

Wine and Canvas, Indianapolis *Also Called: Wine and Canvas Dev LLC (G-9773)*

Wine and Canvas Dev LLC.. 812 345-1019
135 N Gates Dr Ste 3 Bloomington (47404) *(G-1013)*

Wine and Canvas Dev LLC.. 317 914-2806
1005 Hawthorne Dr Columbus (47203) *(G-2420)*

Wine and Canvas Dev LLC.. 765 278-0432
6411 Kentucky Ave Indianapolis (46221) *(G-9772)*

Wine and Canvas Dev LLC (PA)... 317 345-1567
1760 Cholla Ter Indianapolis (46240) *(G-9773)*

Wine N Vine... 765 282-3300
1524 E Mcgalliard Rd Muncie (47303) *(G-12522)*

Winfield American, The, Crown Point *Also Called: Region Communications Inc (G-2743)*

Winfield Solutions LLC... 317 838-3733
923 Whitaker Rd Ste G Plainfield (46168) *(G-13743)*

Wingards SA... 260 768-4656
3670 N State Road 5 Shipshewana (46565) *(G-14898)*

Wingards Sales LLC.. 260 768-7961
3715 N State Road 5 Shipshewana (46565) *(G-14899)*

Wingate Enterprise LLC... 513 293-9833
278 Ivy Hill Dr Lawrenceburg (47025) *(G-10866)*

Winingers Manufacturing LLC... 812 887-6129
1117 Ritterskamp Ave Vincennes (47591) *(G-16167)*

Wink Anti Tip LLC... 812 305-3165
4936 Countrylane Dr Evansville (47715) *(G-4388)*

Winn Machine Inc... 219 324-2978
1712 Genesis Dr La Porte (46350) *(G-10501)*

Winndeavor LLC.. 219 324-2978
1712 Genesis Dr La Porte (46350) *(G-10502)*

Winnebago of Indiana LLC... 574 825-5250
201 14th Ave Middlebury (46540) *(G-11759)*

Winner's Circle, Spencer *Also Called: Crescendo Inc (G-15344)*

Winning Edge, Rochester *Also Called: Winning Edge of Rochester Inc (G-14334)*

Winning Edge of Rochester Inc... 574 223-6090
221 Rouch Place Dr Rochester (46975) *(G-14334)*

Winona Building Products LLC... 574 822-0100
506 North St Plymouth (46563) *(G-13831)*

Winona Powder Coating Inc (PA).. 574 267-8311
9876 W Old Road 30 Etna Green (46524) *(G-3851)*

Winona Pvd Coatings LLC.. 574 269-3255
1180 Polk Dr Warsaw (46582) *(G-16453)*

Winski Brothers Inc.. 765 654-5323
751 W Washington St Frankfort (46041) *(G-5702)*

Winslow Scale Company.. 812 466-5265
1355 Aberdeen St Terre Haute (47804) *(G-15747)*

Winslow-Browning Inc... 765 458-5157
215 Brownsville Ave Liberty (47353) *(G-11000)*

Winspear Publishing LLC... 812 204-7973
209 E Grimes Ln Bloomington (47401) *(G-1014)*

Winters Assoc Prmtnal Pdts Inc (PA)..................................... 812 330-7000
1048 W 17th St Bloomington (47404) *(G-1015)*

Winters Publishing... 812 663-4948
330 E Central Ave Greensburg (47240) *(G-6641)*

Winzerwald Winery LLC... 812 357-7000
26300 N Indian Lake Rd Bristow (47515) *(G-1302)*

Wipbeatz LLC... 866 676-1465
5625 N German Church Rd Indianapolis (46235) *(G-9774)*

Wirco Inc (PA).. 260 897-3768
105 Progress Way Avilla (46710) *(G-500)*

ALPHABETIC SECTION — Woodland Ridge Woodworking LLC

Wire Design, Elkhart *Also Called: Patrick Industries Inc (G-3599)*

Wire-Tek Inc 812 623-8300
234 Industrial Dr Sunman (47041) *(G-15448)*

Wireamerica Inc 260 969-1700
1613 E Wallace St Fort Wayne (46803) *(G-5571)*

Wirecut Technologies Inc 317 885-9915
5328 Commerce Square Dr Indianapolis (46237) *(G-9775)*

Wise Business Forms Inc 260 489-1561
4301 Merchant Rd Fort Wayne (46818) *(G-5572)*

Wise Energy LLC 317 475-0305
5999 Medora Dr Indianapolis (46228) *(G-9776)*

Wise Printing Inc (PA) 317 351-9477
1429 Sadlier Circle West Dr Indianapolis (46239) *(G-9777)*

Wiseguys Seating & Accessry Co 574 294-6030
2701 Industrial Pkwy Elkhart (46516) *(G-3788)*

Wiseman Custom Cabinets Inc 812 678-3601
4501 E State Road 56 Dubois (47527) *(G-2955)*

Wisemed Inc 317 644-1169
1192 Chelsey Village Ct Unit D Indianapolis (46260) *(G-9778)*

Wish Factory Inc 260 745-2550
509 S Main St South Whitley (46787) *(G-15332)*

Wishbone Medical Inc (PA) 574 306-4006
100 Capital Dr Warsaw (46582) *(G-16454)*

Wishful Thinking, Nashville *Also Called: Crystal Source (G-12669)*

With Love Bath Bombs 317 523-9197
7903 Wildcat Run Ln Indianapolis (46239) *(G-9779)*

Witham Anthony J Sign Prod 317 984-3765
26266 Devaney Rd Arcadia (46030) *(G-320)*

Witham Machine LLC 317 835-2076
8429 W 525 N Boggstown (46110) *(G-1077)*

Witherspoon Farms Inc 812 882-5272
2263 E Shawnee Dr Vincennes (47591) *(G-16168)*

Witt Galvanizing 574 935-4500
2631 Jim Neu Dr Plymouth (46563) *(G-13832)*

Witt Industries Inc 765 289-3427
2415 S Walnut St Muncie (47302) *(G-12523)*

Witt Industries Inc 574 935-4500
2631 Jim Neu Dr Plymouth (46563) *(G-13833)*

Wittmer Woodworking LLC 812 486-3115
4637 E 200 N Montgomery (47558) *(G-12130)*

Wiw Inc 219 663-7900
424 Wessex Rd Crown Point (46307) *(G-2774)*

Wjh Investments Inc
102 Enterprise Dr Warsaw (46580) *(G-16455)*

Wk-Rpe Inc 317 739-3543
1424 Commerce Pkwy Franklin (46131) *(G-5788)*

Wm Express LLP 773 647-5305
1111 Merrill St Hammond (46320) *(G-7035)*

Wnc of Dayton LLC 937 999-8868
3969 E 82nd St Indianapolis (46240) *(G-9780)*

Wnt 260 440-0485
3009 Parnell Ave Fort Wayne (46805) *(G-5573)*

Woehr Tool & Die 408 313-1708
110 Pennsylvania St Elizabethtown (47232) *(G-3135)*

Wolf Corporation 260 749-9393
3434 Maplecrest Rd Fort Wayne (46803) *(G-5574)*

Wolf Technical Engineering LLC 800 783-9653
9855 Crosspoint Blvd Ste 126 Indianapolis (46256) *(G-9781)*

Wolfe and Swickard Mch Co Inc 317 241-2589
1344 S Tibbs Ave Indianapolis (46241) *(G-9782)*

Wolfe Diversified Inds LLC (PA) 765 683-9374
9408 W Constellation Dr Pendleton (46064) *(G-13562)*

Wolfe Engineered Plastics LLC 812 623-8403
215 Nieman St Sunman (47041) *(G-15449)*

Wolfgang Software 317 443-5147
10401 Cotton Blossom Dr Fishers (46038) *(G-4634)*

Wolfpack Chassis LLC 260 349-1887
800 Weston Ave Kendallville (46755) *(G-10155)*

Wonning Cabinets 812 522-1608
5875 E County Road 875 N Seymour (47274) *(G-14706)*

Wood & More LLC 260 350-1537
20386 County Road 38 Goshen (46526) *(G-6278)*

Wood Block Press Inc 405 742-7308
330 S 28th St Richmond (47374) *(G-14228)*

Wood Creat By Delagrange Inc 260 657-5525
15818 Darling Rd New Haven (46774) *(G-12925)*

Wood Creations Inc 574 522-7765
800 Industrial Pkwy Elkhart (46516) *(G-3789)*

Wood Kovers, Valparaiso *Also Called: Heat Wagons Inc (G-15961)*

Wood Lighter Cases LLC 812 969-3908
7705 Pine Hill Dr Se Elizabeth (47117) *(G-3131)*

Wood Parts Inc 574 326-3631
4340 Pine Creek Rd Elkhart (46516) *(G-3790)*

Wood Pile Pallet Company LLC 317 750-9272
637 S Lincoln Blvd Marion (46953) *(G-11351)*

Wood Shapes Unlimited Inc 317 861-1775
20 S Westside Dr Ste D New Palestine (46163) *(G-12945)*

Wood Shop, Indianapolis *Also Called: Greypaint LLC (G-8327)*

Wood Shoppe 260 758-3453
2107 S 600 E Huntington (46750) *(G-7381)*

Wood Sign Products 574 234-1218
56956 Oak Rd South Bend (46619) *(G-15308)*

Wood Spc By Fehrenbacher Inc 812 963-9414
8920 Big Cynthiana Rd Evansville (47720) *(G-4389)*

Wood Technologies LLC 260 627-8858
13804 Antwerp Rd Grabill (46741) *(G-6326)*

Wood Truss Systems Inc 765 751-9990
784 Eden Woods Pl Carmel (46033) *(G-1807)*

Wood Wiz Inc 317 834-9079
6 W Main St Mooresville (46158) *(G-12250)*

Wood-Mizer, Indianapolis *Also Called: Wood-Mizer LLC (G-9783)*

Wood-Mizer LLC 317 271-1542
8180 W 10th St Indianapolis (46214) *(G-9783)*

Wood-Mizer Holdings Inc 812 663-5257
8829 E State Road 46 Greensburg (47240) *(G-6642)*

Wood-Mizer Holdings Inc (PA) 317 271-1542
8180 W 10th St Indianapolis (46214) *(G-9784)*

Wood-Mizer Holdings Inc 317 892-4444
7865 N County Road 100 E Lizton (46149) *(G-11052)*

Woodberry Family Freight LLC 317 665-6917
5919 Parkwood Ct Apt 8 Indianapolis (46254) *(G-9785)*

Woodbox & Bin, Pendleton *Also Called: Larry Conover (G-13540)*

Woodburn Diamond Die Inc (PA) 260 632-4217
23012 Tile Mill Rd Woodburn (46797) *(G-16957)*

Woodburn Graphics Inc 812 232-0323
25 S 6th St Terre Haute (47807) *(G-15748)*

Woodcraft Manufacturing Co 812 882-2354
810 S 17th St Vincennes (47591) *(G-16169)*

Woodcrafters LLC 765 469-5103
8472 N 100 E Denver (46926) *(G-2936)*

Woodcrafters Home Products LLC 812 482-2527
1 Masterbrand Cabinets Dr Jasper (47546) *(G-9918)*

Woodcrest Manufacturing Inc 765 472-4471
150 E Washington Ave Peru (46970) *(G-13608)*

Wooden Signs 317 506-6991
2013 Beach Ave Indianapolis (46240) *(G-9786)*

Woodenware Usa Inc 574 372-8400
9151 W 750 N Etna Green (46524) *(G-3852)*

Woodfield Printing Inc 317 848-2000
9700 Lake Shore Dr E Ste E Carmel (46280) *(G-1808)*

Woodgrain Construction Inc 317 873-5608
3380 S 875 E Zionsville (46077) *(G-17062)*

Woodhollow LLC 219 384-2802
9603 Spring St Rear Highland (46322) *(G-7159)*

Woodie's Coverup, Middlebury *Also Called: T K T Inc (G-11753)*

Woodland Lbor Rltons Cnslting 219 879-6095
15 Bristol Dr Michigan City (46360) *(G-11688)*

Woodland Manufacturing & Sup 317 271-2266
10896 E Us Highway 36 Avon (46123) *(G-557)*

Woodland Park Inc 574 825-2104
111 Crystal Heights Blvd Middlebury (46540) *(G-11760)*

Woodland Ridge Woodworking LLC 812 821-8032
5182 W Woodland Rd Ellettsville (47429) *(G-3812)*

Woodland Standard Inc..812 945-4122
  901 Park Pl New Albany (47150) *(G-12830)*

Woodmizer Products, Greensburg *Also Called: Wood-Mizer Holdings Inc (G-6642)*

Woodpart International, Elkhart *Also Called: Woodparts International Corp (G-3791)*

Woodparts International Corp....................................... 574 293-0566
  729 Mason St Elkhart (46516) *(G-3791)*

Woodruff Automotive LLC.. 812 636-4908
  10298 N 700 E Odon (47562) *(G-13358)*

Woods Cabinets.. 812 279-6494
  2615 Broadview Dr Bedford (47421) *(G-684)*

Woods Enterprises... 574 232-7449
  26795 State Road 2 South Bend (46619) *(G-15309)*

Woods of Amber... 765 763-6926
  632 S Washington St Morristown (46161) *(G-12282)*

Woods Printing Company Inc.. 812 536-2261
  601 W Main St Holland (47541) *(G-7215)*

Woods Unlimited Inc... 574 656-3382
  67850 Sycamore Rd North Liberty (46554) *(G-13227)*

Woodside Woodworks LLC... 260 499-3220
  4795 S 200 W Wolcottville (46795) *(G-16945)*

Woodward Tire Sales & Svc Inc.................................... 260 432-0694
  3111 Covington Rd Fort Wayne (46802) *(G-5575)*

Woodward Tire Service, Fort Wayne *Also Called: Woodward Tire Sales & Svc Inc (G-5575)*

Woodworking... 574 825-5858
  900 S 1075 W Middlebury (46540) *(G-11761)*

Woodworking By Design, Hoagland *Also Called: Knapke & Sons Inc (G-7169)*

Woodwright Door & Trim Inc... 574 522-1667
  808 9th St Elkhart (46516) *(G-3792)*

Woody Enterprises LLC.. 765 498-7300
  7880 N Roaring Creek Rd Bloomingdale (47832) *(G-763)*

Woodys Hot Rodz LLC.. 812 637-1933
  23950 Salt Fork Rd Lawrenceburg (47025) *(G-10867)*

Woodys Paint Spot Ltd... 574 255-0348
  3860 W Shore Dr Bremen (46506) *(G-1231)*

Woof and Purr Naturals, Mishawaka *Also Called: Bella Food Sales LLC (G-11849)*

Word 4 Word LLC.. 317 601-3995
  218 W Morris St Indianapolis (46225) *(G-9787)*

Wordpro Communication Services................................ 847 296-3964
  6525 Emerald Hill Ct Indianapolis (46237) *(G-9788)*

Work Field Collaborative Inc.. 360 581-9476
  2834 E Washington St Indianapolis (46201) *(G-9789)*

Work Room.. 765 268-2634
  1415 E 400 S Bringhurst (46913) *(G-1238)*

Workflow Solutions LLC.. 502 627-0257
  3211 Grant Line Rd Ste 2 New Albany (47150) *(G-12831)*

Working Pitbull Kennell... 708 762-9725
  4319 Indianapolis Blvd East Chicago (46312) *(G-3058)*

Workrite Machine & Tool Inc... 260 489-4778
  6319 Discount Dr Fort Wayne (46818) *(G-5576)*

Workroom Inc.. 574 269-6624
  204 13th St Winona Lake (46590) *(G-16919)*

World Arts Inc... 812 829-2255
  156 E Franklin St Spencer (47460) *(G-15365)*

World Class Fiberglass... 317 512-3343
  5694 N Private Road 660 W Fairland (46126) *(G-4406)*

World Graffix LLC.. 574 936-1927
  14717 Lincoln Hwy Plymouth (46563) *(G-13834)*

World Media Group Inc.. 317 549-8484
  2301 Whispering Dr Indianapolis (46239) *(G-9790)*

World Missionary Press Inc.. 574 831-2111
  19168 County Road 146 New Paris (46553) *(G-12974)*

World Rdo Mssnary Fllwship Inc.................................. 574 970-4252
  2830 17th St Elkhart (46517) *(G-3793)*

Worldcell Extrusions, Elkhart *Also Called: Worldwide Foam Ltd (G-3796)*

Worldcell Extrusions LLC... 574 333-2249
  318 S Elkhart Ave Elkhart (46516) *(G-3794)*

Worlds Best Pallets, The, Carmel *Also Called: Artistic Composite Pallets LLC (G-1565)*

Worldwide Battery Company LLC................................. 248 830-8537
  2804 Jeanwood Dr Ste 5a Elkhart (46514) *(G-3795)*

Worldwide Battery Company LLC................................. 812 475-1326
  6050 Wedeking Ave Ste 5 Evansville (47715) *(G-4390)*

Worldwide Door Cmpnnts Ind Inc................................. 219 992-9225
  8218 N 279 W Lake Village (46349) *(G-10785)*

Worldwide Foam Ltd (DH)... 574 968-8268
  1806 Conant St Elkhart (46516) *(G-3796)*

Worley Lumber Company Inc....................................... 812 967-3521
  5803 E Hurst Rd Pekin (47165) *(G-13523)*

Worth Publications LLC.. 219 808-4001
  13398 Hayes Ct Crown Point (46307) *(G-2775)*

Worth Tax and Financial Svc....................................... 574 267-4687
  3201 E Center Street Ext Warsaw (46582) *(G-16456)*

Worthington Industries Inc.. 219 465-6107
  1445 N Michigan Ave Greensburg (47240) *(G-6643)*

Worthington Steel Company.. 219 929-4000
  100 Worthington Dr Porter (46304) *(G-13925)*

Worwag Coatings... 765 746-6037
  2330 S 30th St Lafayette (47909) *(G-10719)*

Woundvision LLC... 317 775-6054
  10585 N Meridian St Ste 110 Carmel (46290) *(G-1809)*

Wp Beverages LLC.. 574 722-6207
  1031 N 3rd St Logansport (46947) *(G-11120)*

Wpr Services LLC.. 317 513-5269
  9059 Technology Ln Fishers (46038) *(G-4635)*

Wpta Television Inc... 217 221-3353
  3401 Butler Rd Fort Wayne (46808) *(G-5577)*

Wraco Enterprises Inc... 812 339-3987
  125 S Westplex Ave Bloomington (47404) *(G-1016)*

Wraith Arms Resolutions LLC..................................... 812 380-1208
  9602 E 475s Velpen (47590) *(G-16095)*

Wreath Inc.. 812 939-3439
  500 E 10th St Clay City (47841) *(G-2049)*

Wrg Publishing.. 317 839-6520
  912 Walton Dr Plainfield (46168) *(G-13744)*

Wri, Peru *Also Called: Borgwarner (pds) Peru Inc (G-13568)*

Wrib Manufacturing Inc... 765 294-2841
  110 E Jackson St Veedersburg (47987) *(G-16092)*

Wright Coatings Corporation...................................... 317 937-6768
  8620 W 82nd St Indianapolis (46278) *(G-9791)*

Wright Horizon Enterprises LLC................................. 317 779-8182
  9 English Grn Westfield (46074) *(G-16741)*

Wright Implement I LLC.. 812 522-1922
  1250 W 2nd St Seymour (47274) *(G-14707)*

Wright Repairs Inc.. 765 674-3300
  5900 Eastside Parkway Dr Gas City (46933) *(G-6042)*

Wright Woodworks, Westfield *Also Called: Wright Horizon Enterprises LLC (G-16741)*

Wrights Timber Products.. 812 383-7138
  201 S Hymera Church St Shelburn (47879) *(G-14725)*

Wrights Woodworking.. 765 723-1546
  8862 E 500 S New Ross (47968) *(G-12981)*

Writ Labs Inc... 650 560-5008
  433 N Capitol Ave Ste 100 Indianapolis (46204) *(G-9792)*

Write Word... 219 987-5254
  6834 Mercedes Ln Demotte (46310) *(G-2933)*

Writeguard Business Systems.................................... 317 849-7292
  5102 E 65th St Indianapolis (46220) *(G-9793)*

Writers of Vision.. 812 239-6347
  4118 W County Road 975 N Farmersburg (47850) *(G-4421)*

Wrought Iron Werks LLC.. 219 779-7476
  6873 W 700 N Lake Village (46349) *(G-10786)*

Wrr Inc... 317 577-1149
  8908 Gary Pl Indianapolis (46256) *(G-9794)*

Wsg Manufacturing LLC... 765 934-2101
  4485 Perry Worth Rd Whitestown (46075) *(G-16829)*

Wunder Company Inc... 219 962-8573
  3200 E 37th Ave Lake Station (46405) *(G-10779)*

Wurth Additive Group Inc... 551 269-7695
  598 Chaney Ave Greenwood (46143) *(G-6782)*

Wws Fabricating Inc... 765 506-7341
  506 S Lenfesty Ave Marion (46953) *(G-11352)*

Www Writing Co.. 317 498-4041
  10700 N Carthage Pike Carthage (46115) *(G-1820)*

Www.crssrdsfreightsolutionscom, Fishers *Also Called: Crossroads Frt Solutions LLC (G-4497)*

ALPHABETIC SECTION

Www.psychmxgrafix.com, Greenfield *Also Called: Moan Racing Products LLC (G-6530)*
Wyatt Farm Center Inc 574 354-2998
  26545 County Road 52 Nappanee (46550) *(G-12655)*
Wyatt Survival Supply LLC 765 318-2872
  1750 S Conservation Club Rd Morgantown (46160) *(G-12266)*
Wynn Jones Mining Tools L L C 812 858-5394
  7022 Jenner Rd Newburgh (47630) *(G-13030)*
Wynn Wire Die Services Inc 260 471-1395
  1919 Lakeview Dr Fort Wayne (46808) *(G-5578)*
Wyrco LLC 317 691-2832
  13603 E 131st St Fishers (46037) *(G-4636)*
X-L Box Inc 219 763-3736
  1035 N State Road 149 Valparaiso (46385) *(G-16082)*
X-Press Printing, Portage *Also Called: Express Printing & Copying (G-13862)*
X-Treme Lazer Tag 812 238-8412
  844 W Johnson Dr Terre Haute (47802) *(G-15749)*
X-Y Tool and Die Inc 260 357-3365
  6492 State Road 205 Laotto (46763) *(G-10812)*
Xantrex LLC (HQ) 800 670-0707
  541 Roske Dr Ste A Elkhart (46516) *(G-3797)*
Xantrex LLC 800 670-0707
  541 Roske Dr Ste A Elkhart (46516) *(G-3798)*
XCEL Clean of Indiana, Indianapolis *Also Called: Nighthawk Enterprises LLC (G-9011)*
Xcelerix Corp 317 208-2320
  9000 Keystone Xing Ste 900 Indianapolis (46201) *(G-9795)*
Xennovate Medical LLC (PA) 765 939-2037
  1080 University Blvd Richmond (47374) *(G-14229)*
Xerox Corp 765 494-6511
  698 Ahlers Dr Lafayette (47907) *(G-10720)*
Xetex Bottling Group, Valparaiso *Also Called: Ira William Scott (G-15977)*
Xfmrs Inc 317 834-1066
  7570 E Landersdale Rd Camby (46113) *(G-1517)*
Xfmrs Holdings Inc (PA) 317 834-1066
  7570 E Landersdale Rd Camby (46113) *(G-1518)*
Xl Graphics Inc 317 738-3434
  170 Commerce Dr Franklin (46131) *(G-5789)*
Xlibris Corporation 812 671-9162
  1663 S Liberty Dr Ste 200 Bloomington (47403) *(G-1017)*
Xoxo Invites 773 744-2504
  1958 Springvale Dr Crown Point (46307) *(G-2776)*
Xpedited Bulk Carriers LLC 708 490-7539
  2043 Martha St Highland (46322) *(G-7160)*
Xpedited Trucking Inc 463 223-7366
  880 Monon Green Blvd Carmel (46032) *(G-1810)*
Xpressvending LLC 331 264-3541
  2228 Harbor Dr Indianapolis (46229) *(G-9796)*
Xtrac Inc 317 472-2451
  6183 W 80th St Indianapolis (46278) *(G-9797)*
Xtreme ADS Limited 765 644-7323
  1735 W 53rd St Anderson (46013) *(G-218)*
Xtreme Alternative Def Systems, Anderson *Also Called: Xtreme ADS Limited (G-218)*
Xtreme Graphics 812 989-6948
  3301 Justinian Jeffersonville (47130) *(G-10076)*
Xtreme Graphics, Indianapolis *Also Called: Xtreme Signs & Graphics LLC (G-9798)*
Xtreme Signs & Graphics LLC 317 299-5622
  3350 N High School Rd Ste J Indianapolis (46224) *(G-9798)*
Xwind LLC 317 350-2080
  1185 E Northfield Dr Ste C Brownsburg (46112) *(G-1414)*
Xylem Vue Inc 574 360-1093
  12441 Beckley St Ste 6 Granger (46530) *(G-6391)*
Xylem Vue Inc (HQ) 574 855-1012
  3725 Foundation Ct Ste E South Bend (46628) *(G-15310)*
XYZ Machining Inc 574 269-5541
  5141 W 100 S Warsaw (46580) *(G-16457)*
XYZ Model Works 260 413-1873
  10334 N 500 W Decatur (46733) *(G-2889)*
Yager & Associates LLC 260 413-9571
  2601 E Gump Rd Fort Wayne (46845) *(G-5579)*
Yalel Unbland LLC 404 232-9139
  1075 Broad Ripple Ave 120 Indianapolis (46220) *(G-9799)*
Yamaguchi Mfg Usa Inc 765 973-9130
  1771 Sheridan St Richmond (47374) *(G-14230)*

Yamaha Mar Precision Propeller, Indianapolis *Also Called: Yamaha Motor Corporation USA (G-9800)*
Yamaha Motor Corporation USA 317 545-9080
  2427 N Ritter Ave Indianapolis (46218) *(G-9800)*
Yandt Boat Works LLC 219 851-8311
  308 Grayson Rd La Porte (46350) *(G-10503)*
Yaney Mktg Graphic Design LLC 317 776-0676
  136 S 9th St Ste 18 Noblesville (46060) *(G-13197)*
Yanfeng US Auto Intr Systems I 260 347-0500
  300 S Progress Dr E Kendallville (46755) *(G-10156)*
YANFENG US AUTOMOTIVE INTERIOR SYSTEMS I LLC, Kendallville *Also Called: Yanfeng US Auto Intr Systems I (G-10156)*
Yankee Candle Company Inc 812 526-5195
  11740 Ne Executive Dr Edinburgh (46124) *(G-3110)*
Yankee Made Woodworks LLC 513 607-3152
  13141 Springfield Rd Bath (47010) *(G-612)*
Yard Signs 317 736-7446
  6840 S 300 W Trafalgar (46181) *(G-15834)*
Yard Signs Inc 317 535-7000
  1444 Demaree Rd Greenwood (46143) *(G-6783)*
Year, Indianapolis *Also Called: Thomas Taylor (G-9595)*
Yellow Cat LLC 913 213-4570
  1419 S Winfield Rd Bloomington (47401) *(G-1018)*
Yellow Creek Gravel Service, Goshen *Also Called: Harrison Hauling Inc (G-6162)*
Yellow Cup LLC 260 403-3489
  228 E Collins Rd Ste C Fort Wayne (46825) *(G-5580)*
Yellow Dog Anodizing 574 343-2247
  2730 Almac Ct Elkhart (46514) *(G-3799)*
Yellow Fellow Safety Signs LLC 813 557-6428
  1415 E 8th St Jeffersonville (47130) *(G-10077)*
Yellowstone Rv, Nappanee *Also Called: Gulf Stream Coach Inc (G-12603)*
Yer Brands Inc 239 307-2925
  1350 N Commerce Dr Ste B Rushville (46173) *(G-14417)*
Yes Feed & Supply LLC 765 361-9821
  2065 S Nucor Rd Crawfordsville (47933) *(G-2628)*
Yes Yes Trucking LLC 800 971-3633
  10475 Crosspoint Blvd Ste 250 Indianapolis (46256) *(G-9801)*
Yesco LLC 812 469-2292
  1300 N Royal Ave Evansville (47715) *(G-4391)*
Yesco Sign & Lighting Service 317 559-3374
  8621 Bash St Ste A Indianapolis (46256) *(G-9802)*
Yesco Sing Lighting Service 812 577-0904
  1090 W Eads Pkwy Lawrenceburg (47025) *(G-10868)*
Yinroot LLC 317 379-9529
  12174 E 141st St Noblesville (46060) *(G-13198)*
Ynwa Industries Inc 574 295-6641
  555 County Road 15 Elkhart (46516) *(G-3800)*
Yoder Fiberglass LLC 260 593-0234
  9755 W 600 S Topeka (46571) *(G-15823)*
Yoder Kitchen Corp (PA) 574 773-3197
  501 S Main St Nappanee (46550) *(G-12656)*
Yoder Software Inc 574 302-6232
  1121 N Notre Dame Ave South Bend (46617) *(G-15311)*
Yoder Woodworking 574 825-0402
  60157 County Road 35 Middlebury (46540) *(G-11762)*
Yoder Woodworking Inc 574 546-5100
  2534 State Road 331 Bremen (46506) *(G-1232)*
Yoder's Lockworks, New Paris *Also Called: Yoders Custom Service (G-12975)*
Yoder's Meat Shop, Shipshewana *Also Called: Yoders Meats Inc (G-14900)*
Yoders & Sons Repair Shop 260 593-2727
  6035 W 800 S Topeka (46571) *(G-15824)*
Yoders Cabinets 812 486-3826
  5207 N 775 E Montgomery (47558) *(G-12131)*
Yoders Custom Service 574 831-4717
  18638 County Road 46 New Paris (46553) *(G-12975)*
Yoders Meats Inc 260 768-4715
  435 S Van Buren St Shipshewana (46565) *(G-14900)*
Yoders Quality Barns LLC 260 565-4122
  7207 E State Road 124 Bluffton (46714) *(G-1071)*
Yoders Wood Shop LLC 260 768-3246
  1675 N 675 W Shipshewana (46565) *(G-14901)*

(PA)=Parent Co (HQ)=Headquarters (DH)=Div Headquarters

Yoders Woodworking LLC 574 773-0699
13941 N 700 W Nappanee (46550) *(G-12657)*

Yogurtz 317 853-6600
12561 N Meridian St Carmel (46032) *(G-1811)*

Yolanda Denise LLC 317 457-6831
6137 Crawfordsville Rd Ste F179 Indianapolis (46224) *(G-9803)*

Yongli America LLC 219 763-7920
6625 Daniel Burnham Dr Ste A Portage (46368) *(G-13920)*

Yongs Audio Connection LLC 317 298-8333
3851 Kevin Way Indianapolis (46254) *(G-9804)*

York & Sons Welding LLC 812 577-6352
1437 N County Line Rd Moores Hill (47032) *(G-12189)*

York Group Inc 765 966-0077
1620 Rich Rd Richmond (47374) *(G-14231)*

York Group Inc 765 966-1576
620 S J St Richmond (47374) *(G-14232)*

York Tank and Mfg LLC 765 401-0667
4438 S Roberts St Kingman (47952) *(G-10175)*

York Technology, Richmond *Also Called: York Group Inc (G-14231)*

Yosira LLC 260 241-1203
14017 Pendleton Mills Ct Fort Wayne (46814) *(G-5581)*

You Can Do It Printer, Columbus *Also Called: Prestige Printing Inc (G-2381)*

Young & Kenady Incorporated 317 852-6300
463 Southpoint Cir Ste 600 Brownsburg (46112) *(G-1415)*

Young Cimtech LLC 812 948-1472
325 Park East Blvd New Albany (47150) *(G-12832)*

Young Machine Company Inc 812 944-5807
904 Industrial Blvd New Albany (47150) *(G-12833)*

Youngs Freight & Logistics LLC 765 639-7888
4511 Columbus Ave Apt B-12 Anderson (46013) *(G-219)*

Your Face Our Place Print Shop 812 567-4510
3877 State Road 161 N Tennyson (47637) *(G-15526)*

Your Mane Nails, Indianapolis *Also Called: Burton Debiceious (G-7702)*

Yourbodygetsit LLC 317 908-7445
3354 Graceland Ave Indianapolis (46208) *(G-9805)*

Yourspace LLC 260 702-9595
6320 Highview Dr Fort Wayne (46818) *(G-5582)*

Youth JAM LLC 765 644-6375
2017 Heather Rd Anderson (46012) *(G-220)*

Yudu, Fort Wayne *Also Called: Tt2 LLC (G-5511)*

Yuma, Shelbyville *Also Called: Yushiro Manufacturing Amer Inc (G-14816)*

Yurts of America, Indianapolis *Also Called: J&K Yurts Inc (G-8610)*

Yushiro Manufacturing Amer Inc 317 398-9862
783 W Mausoleum Rd Shelbyville (46176) *(G-14816)*

Z Grills Inc 909 295-5264
6161 Decatur Blvd Ste A Indianapolis (46241) *(G-9806)*

Z Rodz & Customs LLC 574 806-5774
4015 E 200 N Knox (46534) *(G-10229)*

Z-Athletic, Westfield *Also Called: Global USA Inc (G-16692)*

Zachary T Laffin 317 480-2248
2181 N West Bay Dr Apt A Greenfield (46140) *(G-6572)*

Zaffer Industries LLC 317 910-4958
854 Sunbow Cir Indianapolis (46231) *(G-9807)*

Zana Peabody Publishing LLC 463 210-5111
550 Congressional Blvd Ste 115 Carmel (46032) *(G-1812)*

Zebra Express LLC 317 828-9277
605 Summer Wood Ln Apt 4 Indianapolis (46229) *(G-9808)*

Zehrhaus Inc 260 486-3198
8516 Samantha Dr Fort Wayne (46835) *(G-5583)*

Zeising Winery 812 518-0607
8715 S 500w Huntingburg (47542) *(G-7295)*

Zeller LLC 317 343-2930
8888 Keystone Xing Ste 650 Indianapolis (46240) *(G-9809)*

Zeller Elevator Co 812 985-5888
8875 Meinschein Rd Mount Vernon (47620) *(G-12328)*

Zeller Polymer Solutions, LLC, Indianapolis *Also Called: Zeller LLC (G-9809)*

Zels 219 864-1011
7889 W Lincoln Hwy Schererville (46375) *(G-14548)*

Zendigo Boutique LLC 574 314-8328
1143 E Ireland Rd South Bend (46614) *(G-15312)*

Zeno Companies Inc 219 728-5126
505 Grant Ave Chesterton (46304) *(G-1969)*

Zeno Signs LLC 219 250-2896
119 Broadway Chesterton (46304) *(G-1970)*

Zentis, Plymouth *Also Called: Zentis North America Holdg LLC (G-13836)*

Zentis North America LLC 574 941-1100
2050 N Oak Dr Plymouth (46563) *(G-13835)*

Zentis North America Holdg LLC 574 941-1100
2050 N Oak Dr Plymouth (46563) *(G-13836)*

Zepps Predator Calls LLC 574 971-8371
11935 W 710 N Middlebury (46540) *(G-11763)*

Zepps Predator Calls LLC (PA) 574 971-8371
10334 State Road 120 Middlebury (46540) *(G-11764)*

Zepto Systems Incorporated 812 323-0642
3110 S Mulberry Ln Bloomington (47401) *(G-1019)*

Zergnet 317 201-0889
17279 Bluestone Dr Noblesville (46062) *(G-13199)*

Zerocarb LLC 812 214-1084
318 Main St Ste 101 Evansville (47708) *(G-4392)*

ZF Active Safety & Elec US LLC 260 357-6327
817 N Taylor Rd Garrett (46738) *(G-5881)*

ZF Active Safety & Elec US LLC 765 429-1984
4820 Dale Dr Lafayette (47905) *(G-10721)*

ZF Active Safety & Elec US LLC 765 429-1678
9th & Greenbush Lafayette (47904) *(G-10722)*

ZF Active Safety & Elec US LLC 765 429-1936
1450 N 9th St Lafayette (47904) *(G-10723)*

ZF Active Safety & Elec US LLC 765 423-5377
800 Heath St Lafayette (47904) *(G-10724)*

ZF Automotive 260 357-1148
817 N Taylor Rd Garrett (46738) *(G-5882)*

ZF North America Inc 765 429-1622
1450 N 9th St Lafayette (47904) *(G-10725)*

Ziehl-Abegg Inc 317 219-3014
802 Mulberry St Ste Gb-07 Noblesville (46060) *(G-13200)*

Zieman Manufacturing Company Inc (HQ) 574 535-1125
2703 College Ave Goshen (46528) *(G-6279)*

Zig-Zag Crnr Qilts Baskets LLC 317 326-3115
7872 N Troy Rd Greenfield (46140) *(G-6573)*

Ziggity Systems Inc 574 825-5849
101 Industrial Pkwy E Middlebury (46540) *(G-11765)*

Zim Corp 260 438-2110
5715 Garman Rd Auburn (46706) *(G-435)*

Zimco Materials Inc 219 883-0870
2555 E 15th Ave Gary (46402) *(G-6029)*

Zimmer Inc 574 267-2038
56 E Bell Dr Warsaw (46582) *(G-16458)*

Zimmer Inc 800 348-9500
2094 N Boeing Rd Warsaw (46582) *(G-16459)*

Zimmer Inc 574 267-6131
1800 W Center St Warsaw (46580) *(G-16460)*

Zimmer Inc 574 267-6131
1777 W Center St Warsaw (46580) *(G-16461)*

Zimmer Inc 574 527-7297
1535 W Center St Bldg 19 Warsaw (46580) *(G-16462)*

Zimmer Inc 574 371-1557
1113 W Lake St Warsaw (46580) *(G-16463)*

Zimmer Inc (HQ) 800 348-9500
1800 W Center St Warsaw (46580) *(G-16464)*

Zimmer Biomet 574 453-1326
6016 Highview Dr Fort Wayne (46818) *(G-5584)*

Zimmer Biomet, Warsaw *Also Called: Biomet Inc (G-16323)*

Zimmer Biomet, Warsaw *Also Called: Zimmer Inc (G-16459)*

Zimmer Biomet, Warsaw *Also Called: Zimmer Inc (G-16460)*

Zimmer Biomet, Warsaw *Also Called: Zimmer Inc (G-16462)*

Zimmer Biomet, Warsaw *Also Called: Zimmer Inc (G-16464)*

Zimmer Biomet, Warsaw *Also Called: Zimmer Biomet Holdings Inc (G-16466)*

Zimmer Biomet, Warsaw *Also Called: Zimmer Production Inc (G-16468)*

Zimmer Biomet, Warsaw *Also Called: Zimmer Us Inc (G-16471)*

Zimmer Biomet Hibbard 574 267-0670
3550 E Us Highway 30 Warsaw (46580) *(G-16465)*

Zimmer Biomet Hibbard LLC 800 352-2982
3209 Cascade Dr Ste H Valparaiso (46383) *(G-16083)*

Zimmer Biomet Holdings Inc 317 872-8484
  6825 Hillsdale Ct Indianapolis (46250) *(G-9810)*

Zimmer Biomet Holdings Inc (PA) 574 267-6131
  345 E Main St Warsaw (46580) *(G-16466)*

Zimmer Biomet Indiana, Indianapolis *Also Called: Zimmer Biomet Holdings Inc (G-9810)*

Zimmer Bmet Connected Hlth LLC 800 613-6131
  345 E Main St Warsaw (46580) *(G-16467)*

Zimmer Custom Made Packaging, Ossian *Also Called: Zimmer Holdings LLC (G-13444)*

Zimmer Custom-Made Packaging, Indianapolis *Also Called: Zimmer Paper Products Del LLC (G-9811)*
  2687 E 500 N Ossian (46777) *(G-13444)*

Zimmer Medwest, Warsaw *Also Called: Wiley Young & Associates (G-16452)*

Zimmer Metal Sales LLC 574 862-1800
  64470 State Road 19 Goshen (46526) *(G-6280)*

Zimmer Paper Products Del LLC (PA) 317 263-3420
  1450 E 20th St Indianapolis (46218) *(G-9811)*

Zimmer Production Inc 574 267-6131
  56 E Bell Dr Bldg A Warsaw (46582) *(G-16468)*

Zimmer Production Inc (HQ) 574 267-6131
  345 E Main St Warsaw (46580) *(G-16469)*

Zimmer Spine Inc 800 655-2614
  1800 W Center St Bldg 5 Warsaw (46580) *(G-16470)*

Zimmer Us Inc 574 267-6131
  1800 W Center St Warsaw (46580) *(G-16471)*

Zimmer Welding LLC 317 632-5212
  16 N Harding St Indianapolis (46222) *(G-9812)*

Zimmerman Art Glass LLC 812 738-2206
  300 E Chestnut St Corydon (47112) *(G-2524)*

Zing Polymer Formations LLC 317 598-0480
  8907 Tynan Way Fishers (46038) *(G-4637)*

Zinn Cabinets Plus, Bringhurst *Also Called: Zinn Kitchens Inc (G-1239)*

Zinn Kitchens Inc 574 967-4179
  1211 S Center St Bringhurst (46913) *(G-1239)*

Zionsville Custom Cabinets LLC 317 339-0380
  10830 Bennett Pkwy Ste E Zionsville (46077) *(G-17063)*

Zionsville Times Sentinel, Lebanon *Also Called: Community Holdings Indiana Inc (G-10886)*

Zionsville Towing Inc 317 873-4550
  4901 W 106th St Zionsville (46077) *(G-17064)*

Zip Zone Gone LLC 812 604-0041
  815 John St Ste 110 # 1017 Evansville (47713) *(G-4393)*

Zipp Print, Mishawaka *Also Called: Zipp Printing LLC (G-12028)*

Zipp Printing LLC 574 256-0059
  235 E Mckinley Ave Ste 2 Mishawaka (46545) *(G-12028)*

Zipp Speed Weaponry, Indianapolis *Also Called: Compositech Inc (G-7846)*

Zoetis 574 232-9927
  6879 Enterprise Dr Ste 500 South Bend (46628) *(G-15313)*

Zogman Enterprises Inc 317 873-6809
  170 W Hawthorne St Zionsville (46077) *(G-17065)*

Zojila Ltd Liability Company 765 404-3767
  2004 N 9th St Lafayette (47904) *(G-10726)*

Zollman, Indianapolis *Also Called: Zollman Plastic Surgery PC (G-9813)*

Zollman Plastic Surgery PC 317 328-1100
  6848 Fox Lake Dr N Indianapolis (46278) *(G-9813)*

Zoo Zone, Evansville *Also Called: Ad Vision Graphics Inc (G-3873)*

Zoofari Gardens, Indianapolis *Also Called: Industrial Sales & Supply Inc (G-8519)*

Zotic Scents LLC 317 766-6501
  832 Park Central Ct Indianapolis (46260) *(G-9814)*

Zps America LLC 317 452-4030
  4950 W 79th St Indianapolis (46268) *(G-9815)*

Zr Tactical Solutions LLC 317 721-9787
  15223 Herriman Blvd Ste 4 Noblesville (46060) *(G-13201)*

Zrp LLC 888 824-5587
  11750 E State Road 205 Laotto (46763) *(G-10813)*

Zrts, Noblesville *Also Called: Zr Tactical Solutions LLC (G-13201)*

Zs Systems LLC 765 588-4528
  675 N 36th St Lafayette (47905) *(G-10727)*

Zvibleman, Barry, Indianapolis *Also Called: Onion Enterprises Inc (G-9056)*

PRODUCT INDEX

• Product categories are listed in alphabetical order.

A

ABRASIVES
ABRASIVES: sandpaper
ACCELERATION INDICATORS & SYSTEM COMPONENTS: Aerospace
ACCELERATORS, RUBBER PROCESSING: Cyclic or Acyclic
ACIDS: Boric
ACRYLONITRILE BUTADIENE STYRENE RESINS
ACTUATORS: Indl, NEC
ADAPTERS: Well
ADHESIVES
ADHESIVES & SEALANTS
ADHESIVES & SEALANTS WHOLESALERS
ADHESIVES: Epoxy
ADVERTISING AGENCIES
ADVERTISING AGENCIES: Consultants
ADVERTISING DISPLAY PRDTS
ADVERTISING MATERIAL DISTRIBUTION
ADVERTISING REPRESENTATIVES: Newspaper
ADVERTISING SPECIALTIES, WHOLESALE
ADVERTISING SVCS: Direct Mail
ADVERTISING SVCS: Outdoor
ADVERTISING SVCS: Transit
AERIAL WORK PLATFORMS
AEROSOLS
AGENTS, BROKERS & BUREAUS: Personal Service
AGRICULTURAL DISINFECTANTS
AGRICULTURAL EQPT: BARN, SILO, POULTRY, DAIRY/LIVESTOCK MACH
AGRICULTURAL EQPT: Elevators, Farm
AGRICULTURAL EQPT: Fertilizng, Sprayng, Dustng/Irrigatn Mach
AGRICULTURAL EQPT: Grounds Mowing Eqpt
AGRICULTURAL EQPT: Trailers & Wagons, Farm
AGRICULTURAL EQPT: Turf & Grounds Eqpt
AGRICULTURAL MACHINERY & EQPT: Wholesalers
AIR CLEANING SYSTEMS
AIR CONDITIONERS: Motor Vehicle
AIR CONDITIONING & VENTILATION EQPT & SPLYS: Wholesales
AIR CONDITIONING EQPT
AIR CONDITIONING EQPT, WHOLE HOUSE: Wholesalers
AIR CONDITIONING UNITS: Complete, Domestic Or Indl
AIR COOLERS: Metal Plate
AIR DUCT CLEANING SVCS
AIR MATTRESSES: Plastic
AIR POLLUTION MEASURING SVCS
AIR PURIFICATION EQPT
AIRCRAFT & AEROSPACE FLIGHT INSTRUMENTS & GUIDANCE SYSTEMS
AIRCRAFT & HEAVY EQPT REPAIR SVCS
AIRCRAFT ASSEMBLY PLANTS
AIRCRAFT ENGINES & ENGINE PARTS: Air Scoops
AIRCRAFT ENGINES & ENGINE PARTS: Exhaust Systems
AIRCRAFT ENGINES & ENGINE PARTS: Research & Development, Mfr
AIRCRAFT ENGINES & PARTS
AIRCRAFT FLIGHT INSTRUMENT REPAIR SVCS
AIRCRAFT PARTS & AUXILIARY EQPT: Assys, Subassemblies/Parts
AIRCRAFT PARTS & AUXILIARY EQPT: Body & Wing Assys & Parts
AIRCRAFT PARTS & AUXILIARY EQPT: Body Assemblies & Parts
AIRCRAFT PARTS & AUXILIARY EQPT: Deicing Eqpt
AIRCRAFT PARTS & AUXILIARY EQPT: Gears, Power Transmission
AIRCRAFT PARTS & AUXILIARY EQPT: Military Eqpt & Armament
AIRCRAFT PARTS & AUXILIARY EQPT: Nacelles
AIRCRAFT PARTS & AUXILIARY EQPT: Research & Development, Mfr
AIRCRAFT PARTS & EQPT, NEC
AIRCRAFT SEATS
AIRCRAFT SERVICING & REPAIRING
AIRCRAFT TURBINES
AIRCRAFT UPHOLSTERY REPAIR SVCS
AIRCRAFT: Airplanes, Fixed Or Rotary Wing
AIRCRAFT: Motorized
ALARMS: Burglar
ALARMS: Fire
ALCOHOL, GRAIN: For Beverage Purposes
ALCOHOL, INDL: Grain
ALCOHOL: Ethyl & Ethanol
ALKALIES & CHLORINE
ALTERNATORS & GENERATORS: Battery Charging
ALTERNATORS: Automotive
ALUMINUM
ALUMINUM PRDTS
ALUMINUM: Coil & Sheet
ALUMINUM: Rolling & Drawing
AMMUNITION
Ammunition Loading & Assembling Plant
AMMUNITION: Components
AMMUNITION: Small Arms
AMPLIFIERS
AMUSEMENT & RECREATION SVCS: Exposition Operation
AMUSEMENT MACHINES: Coin Operated
AMUSEMENT PARK DEVICES & RIDES
ANALGESICS
ANALYZERS: Network
ANALYZERS: Respiratory
ANESTHESIA EQPT
ANIMAL BASED MEDICINAL CHEMICAL PRDTS
ANIMAL FEED & SUPPLEMENTS: Livestock & Poultry
ANIMAL FEED: Wholesalers
ANIMAL FOOD & SUPPLEMENTS: Bird Food, Prepared
ANIMAL FOOD & SUPPLEMENTS: Bone Meal
ANIMAL FOOD & SUPPLEMENTS: Cat
ANIMAL FOOD & SUPPLEMENTS: Chicken Feeds, Prepared
ANIMAL FOOD & SUPPLEMENTS: Dog
ANIMAL FOOD & SUPPLEMENTS: Dog & Cat
ANIMAL FOOD & SUPPLEMENTS: Feed Premixes
ANIMAL FOOD & SUPPLEMENTS: Feed Supplements
ANIMAL FOOD & SUPPLEMENTS: Livestock
ANIMAL FOOD & SUPPLEMENTS: Pet, Exc Dog & Cat, Canned
ANIMAL FOOD & SUPPLEMENTS: Poultry
ANIMAL FOOD/SUPPLEMENTS: Feeds Fm Meat/Meat/Veg Combnd Meals
ANNEALING: Metal
ANODIZING SVC
ANTENNAS: Receiving
ANTIFREEZE
APPLIANCE PARTS: Porcelain Enameled
APPLIANCES, HOUSEHOLD OR COIN OPERATED: Laundry Dryers
APPLIANCES, HOUSEHOLD: Kitchen, Major, Exc Refrigs & Stoves
APPLIANCES, HOUSEHOLD: Sewing Machines & Attchmnts, Domestic
APPLIANCES: Household, Refrigerators & Freezers
APPLIANCES: Major, Cooking
APPLIANCES: Small, Electric
APPLICATIONS SOFTWARE PROGRAMMING
AQUARIUM ACCESS, METAL
AQUARIUMS & ACCESS: Glass
ARCHITECTURAL SVCS
ARCHITECTURAL SVCS: Engineering
ARMATURE REPAIRING & REWINDING SVC
ARMOR PLATES
ART DEALERS & GALLERIES
ART GOODS & SPLYS WHOLESALERS
ART GOODS, WHOLESALE
ART SPLY STORES
ARTIST'S MATERIALS & SPLYS
ARTWORK: Framed
ASBESTOS REMOVAL EQPT
ASPHALT & ASPHALT PRDTS
ASPHALT COATINGS & SEALERS
ASPHALT MINING & BITUMINOUS STONE QUARRYING SVCS
ASPHALT PLANTS INCLUDING GRAVEL MIX TYPE
ASSEMBLING & PACKAGING SVCS: Cosmetic Kits
ASSEMBLING SVC: Plumbing Fixture Fittings, Plastic
ASSOCIATION FOR THE HANDICAPPED
ASSOCIATIONS: Business
ASSOCIATIONS: Manufacturers'
ASSOCIATIONS: Real Estate Management
ASSOCIATIONS: Trade
ATOMIZERS
AUDIO & VIDEO EQPT, EXC COMMERCIAL
AUDIO COMPONENTS
AUDIO ELECTRONIC SYSTEMS
AUDIO-VISUAL PROGRAM PRODUCTION SVCS
AUTO & HOME SUPPLY STORES: Auto & Truck Eqpt & Parts
AUTO & HOME SUPPLY STORES: Automotive Access
AUTO & HOME SUPPLY STORES: Automotive parts
AUTO & HOME SUPPLY STORES: Batteries, Automotive & Truck
AUTO & HOME SUPPLY STORES: Speed Shops, Incl Race Car Splys
AUTO & HOME SUPPLY STORES: Trailer Hitches, Automotive
AUTO & HOME SUPPLY STORES: Truck Eqpt & Parts
AUTOCLAVES: Laboratory
AUTOMATED TELLER MACHINE NETWORK
AUTOMATIC REGULATING CONTROL: Building Svcs Monitoring, Auto
AUTOMATIC REGULATING CONTROLS: AC & Refrigeration
AUTOMATIC REGULATING CONTROLS: Appliance, Exc AirCond/Refr
AUTOMATIC REGULATING CONTROLS: Hardware, Environmental Reg
AUTOMATIC REGULATING CONTROLS: Pneumatic Relays, Air-Cond
AUTOMATIC TELLER MACHINES
AUTOMOBILES & OTHER MOTOR VEHICLES WHOLESALERS
AUTOMOBILES: Wholesalers
AUTOMOTIVE & TRUCK GENERAL REPAIR SVC
AUTOMOTIVE BODY SHOP
AUTOMOTIVE BODY, PAINT & INTERIOR REPAIR & MAINTENANCE SVC
AUTOMOTIVE CUSTOMIZING SVCS, NONFACTORY BASIS
AUTOMOTIVE GLASS REPLACEMENT SHOPS
AUTOMOTIVE PARTS, ACCESS & SPLYS
AUTOMOTIVE PARTS: Plastic
AUTOMOTIVE PRDTS: Rubber
AUTOMOTIVE REPAIR SHOPS: Diesel Engine Repair
AUTOMOTIVE REPAIR SHOPS: Electrical Svcs
AUTOMOTIVE REPAIR SHOPS: Engine Rebuilding
AUTOMOTIVE REPAIR SHOPS: Engine Repair
AUTOMOTIVE REPAIR SHOPS: Machine Shop
AUTOMOTIVE REPAIR SHOPS: Muffler Shop, Sale/Rpr/Installation
AUTOMOTIVE REPAIR SHOPS: Rebuilding & Retreading Tires
AUTOMOTIVE REPAIR SHOPS: Springs, Rebuilding & Repair
AUTOMOTIVE REPAIR SHOPS: Tire Recapping
AUTOMOTIVE REPAIR SHOPS: Tire Repair Shop
AUTOMOTIVE REPAIR SHOPS: Trailer Repair
AUTOMOTIVE REPAIR SHOPS: Wheel Alignment
AUTOMOTIVE REPAIR SVC
AUTOMOTIVE SPLYS & PARTS, NEW, WHOL: Auto Servicing Eqpt
AUTOMOTIVE SPLYS & PARTS, NEW, WHOLESALE: Engines/Eng Parts
AUTOMOTIVE SPLYS & PARTS, NEW, WHOLESALE: Filters, Air & Oil
AUTOMOTIVE SPLYS & PARTS, NEW, WHOLESALE: Hardware
AUTOMOTIVE SPLYS & PARTS, NEW, WHOLESALE: Trailer Parts
AUTOMOTIVE SPLYS & PARTS, NEW, WHOLESALE: Wheels
AUTOMOTIVE SPLYS & PARTS, WHOLESALE, NEC
AUTOMOTIVE SVCS, EXC REPAIR & CARWASHES: Insp & Diagnostic
AUTOMOTIVE SVCS, EXC REPAIR & CARWASHES: Lubrication

PRODUCT INDEX

AUTOMOTIVE SVCS, EXC RPR/CARWASHES: High Perf Auto Rpr/Svc
AUTOMOTIVE TOWING SVCS
AUTOMOTIVE TRANSMISSION REPAIR SVC
AUTOMOTIVE WELDING SVCS
AUTOMOTIVE: Bodies
AUTOMOTIVE: Seating
AWNINGS & CANOPIES
AWNINGS & CANOPIES: Awnings, Fabric, From Purchased Matls
AWNINGS & CANOPIES: Canopies, Fabric, From Purchased Matls
AWNINGS: Fiberglass
AWNINGS: Metal
AXLES
AXLES: Rolled Or Forged, Made In Steel Mills

B

BACKHOES
BAGS: Canvas
BAGS: Paper
BAGS: Paper, Made From Purchased Materials
BAGS: Plastic
BAGS: Plastic & Pliofilm
BAGS: Plastic, Made From Purchased Materials
BAGS: Rubber Or Rubberized Fabric
BAGS: Trash, Plastic Film, Made From Purchased Materials
BAKERIES, COMMERCIAL: On Premises Baking Only
BAKERIES: On Premises Baking & Consumption
BAKERY MACHINERY
BAKERY PRDTS, FROZEN: Wholesalers
BAKERY PRDTS: Bagels, Fresh Or Frozen
BAKERY PRDTS: Bakery Prdts, Partially Cooked, Exc frozen
BAKERY PRDTS: Biscuits, Baked, Baking Powder & Raised
BAKERY PRDTS: Bread, All Types, Fresh Or Frozen
BAKERY PRDTS: Buns, Bread Type, Fresh Or Frozen
BAKERY PRDTS: Cakes, Bakery, Exc Frozen
BAKERY PRDTS: Cones, Ice Cream
BAKERY PRDTS: Cookies
BAKERY PRDTS: Cookies & crackers
BAKERY PRDTS: Doughnuts, Exc Frozen
BAKERY PRDTS: Dry
BAKERY PRDTS: Frozen
BAKERY PRDTS: Pies, Bakery, Frozen
BAKERY PRDTS: Pies, Exc Frozen
BAKERY PRDTS: Pretzels
BAKERY PRDTS: Wholesalers
BAKERY: Wholesale Or Wholesale & Retail Combined
BANNERS: Fabric
BANQUET HALL FACILITIES
BAR JOISTS & CONCRETE REINFORCING BARS: Fabricated
BARBECUE EQPT
BARGES BUILDING & REPAIR
BARRICADES: Metal
BARS, COLD FINISHED: Steel, From Purchased Hot-Rolled
BARS, PLATES & SHEETS: Zinc & Zinc Alloy Bars, Plates, Etc
BARS: Concrete Reinforcing, Fabricated Steel
BASES, BEVERAGE
BATH SALTS
BATHROOM FIXTURES: Plastic
BATTERIES, EXC AUTOMOTIVE: Wholesalers
BATTERIES: Alkaline, Cell Storage
BATTERIES: Lead Acid, Storage
BATTERIES: Rechargeable
BATTERIES: Storage
BATTERIES: Wet
BATTERY CASES: Plastic Or Plastics Combination
BATTERY CHARGERS
BATTERY CHARGERS: Storage, Motor & Engine Generator Type
BAUXITE MINING
BEARINGS & PARTS Ball
BEARINGS: Ball & Roller
BEARINGS: Roller & Parts
BEAUTY & BARBER SHOP EQPT
BEAUTY & BARBER SHOP EQPT & SPLYS WHOLESALERS
BEAUTY SALONS
BEDDING & BEDSPRINGS STORES
BEDDING, BEDSPREADS, BLANKETS & SHEETS
BEDS: Institutional

BEDSPREADS & BED SETS, FROM PURCHASED MATERIALS
BEER & ALE WHOLESALERS
BEER & ALE, WHOLESALE: Beer & Other Fermented Malt Liquors
BEER, WINE & LIQUOR STORES
BEER, WINE & LIQUOR STORES: Beer, Packaged
BELTING: Rubber
BELTS: Conveyor, Made From Purchased Wire
BELTS: Seat, Automotive & Aircraft
BERYLLIUM
BEVERAGE BASES & SYRUPS
BEVERAGE STORES
BEVERAGES, ALCOHOLIC: Ale
BEVERAGES, ALCOHOLIC: Beer
BEVERAGES, ALCOHOLIC: Beer & Ale
BEVERAGES, ALCOHOLIC: Bourbon Whiskey
BEVERAGES, ALCOHOLIC: Brandy & Brandy Spirits
BEVERAGES, ALCOHOLIC: Distilled Liquors
BEVERAGES, ALCOHOLIC: Wines
BEVERAGES, MALT
BEVERAGES, NONALCOHOLIC: Bottled & canned soft drinks
BEVERAGES, NONALCOHOLIC: Carbonated
BEVERAGES, NONALCOHOLIC: Carbonated, Canned & Bottled, Etc
BEVERAGES, NONALCOHOLIC: Cider
BEVERAGES, NONALCOHOLIC: Flavoring extracts & syrups, nec
BEVERAGES, NONALCOHOLIC: Fruit Drnks, Under 100% Juice, Can
BEVERAGES, NONALCOHOLIC: Soft Drinks, Canned & Bottled, Etc
BEVERAGES, WINE & DISTILLED ALCOHOLIC, WHOLESALE: Liquor
BEVERAGES, WINE & DISTILLED ALCOHOLIC, WHOLESALE: Wine
BICYCLE ASSEMBLY SVCS
BICYCLES WHOLESALERS
BICYCLES, PARTS & ACCESS
BILLIARD TABLE REPAIR SVCS
BILLING & BOOKKEEPING SVCS
BINDING SVC: Books & Manuals
BINDING SVC: Trade
BINS: Prefabricated, Metal Plate
BIOLOGICAL PRDTS: Blood Derivatives
BIOLOGICAL PRDTS: Exc Diagnostic
BIOLOGICAL PRDTS: Vaccines
BIOLOGICAL PRDTS: Vaccines & Immunizing
BIOLOGICAL PRDTS: Veterinary
BLADES: Knife
BLADES: Saw, Hand Or Power
BLANKBOOKS & LOOSELEAF BINDERS
BLANKBOOKS: Albums
BLANKBOOKS: Albums, Record
BLANKETS & BLANKETING, COTTON
BLANKETS, INSULATING: Aircraft, Asbestos
BLAST FURNACE & RELATED PRDTS
BLASTING SVC: Sand, Metal Parts
BLINDS & SHADES: Vertical
BLINDS : Window
BLOCKS & BRICKS: Concrete
BLOCKS: Landscape Or Retaining Wall, Concrete
BLOCKS: Paving, Concrete
BLOCKS: Standard, Concrete Or Cinder
BLOWERS & FANS
BLOWERS & FANS
BLUEPRINTING SVCS
BOAT & BARGE COMPONENTS: Metal, Prefabricated
BOAT BUILDING & REPAIR
BOAT BUILDING & REPAIRING: Fiberglass
BOAT BUILDING & REPAIRING: Motorboats, Inboard Or Outboard
BOAT BUILDING & REPAIRING: Motorized
BOAT BUILDING & REPAIRING: Non-Motorized
BOAT BUILDING & REPAIRING: Pontoons, Exc Aircraft & Inflat
BOAT BUILDING & REPAIRING: Yachts
BOAT DEALERS
BOAT DEALERS: Marine Splys & Eqpt
BOAT DEALERS: Motor
BOAT LIFTS
BOATS & OTHER MARINE EQPT: Plastic
BODIES: Truck & Bus

BODY PARTS: Automobile, Stamped Metal
BOILER & HEATING REPAIR SVCS
BOILER REPAIR SHOP
BOILERS: Low-Pressure Heating, Steam Or Hot Water
BOLTS: Metal
BOOK STORES
BOOKS, WHOLESALE
BORING MILL
BOTTLED GAS DEALERS: Liquefied Petro, Dlvrd To Customers
BOTTLED GAS DEALERS: Propane
BOTTLES: Plastic
BOXES & CRATES: Rectangular, Wood
BOXES & SHOOK: Nailed Wood
BOXES: Ammunition, Metal
BOXES: Corrugated
BOXES: Paperboard, Folding
BOXES: Paperboard, Set-Up
BOXES: Plastic
BOXES: Solid Fiber
BOXES: Wirebound, Wood
BOXES: Wooden
BRAKES & BRAKE PARTS
BRAKES: Electromagnetic
BRAKES: Metal Forming
BRAKES: Press
BRASS & BRONZE PRDTS: Die-casted
BRASS FOUNDRY, NEC
BRAZING SVCS
BRAZING: Metal
BRICK, STONE & RELATED PRDTS WHOLESALERS
BRICKS & BLOCKS: Structural
BRICKS : Ceramic Glazed, Clay
BRICKS : Flooring, Clay
BRIDGE COMPONENTS: Bridge sections, prefabricated, highway
BROADCASTING & COMMS EQPT: Antennas, Transmitting/Comms
BROADCASTING & COMMUNICATION EQPT: Transmit-Receiver, Radio
BROADCASTING & COMMUNICATIONS EQPT: Studio Eqpt, Radio & TV
BROADCASTING & COMMUNICATIONS EQPT: Transmitting, Radio/TV
BROKERS: Loan
BROKERS: Printing
BRONZE FOUNDRY, NEC
BROOMS & BRUSHES
BROOMS & BRUSHES: Household Or Indl
BROOMS & BRUSHES: Street Sweeping, Hand Or Machine
BRUSHES
BUILDING & OFFICE CLEANING SVCS
BUILDING & STRUCTURAL WOOD MEMBERS
BUILDING BOARD: Gypsum
BUILDING CLEANING & MAINTENANCE SVCS
BUILDING COMPONENTS: Structural Steel
BUILDING MAINTENANCE SVCS, EXC REPAIRS
BUILDING PRDTS & MATERIALS DEALERS
BUILDING PRDTS: Concrete
BUILDING PRDTS: Stone
BUILDINGS & COMPONENTS: Prefabricated Metal
BUILDINGS: Mobile, For Commercial Use
BUILDINGS: Portable
BUILDINGS: Prefabricated, Metal
BUILDINGS: Prefabricated, Wood
BUMPERS: Motor Vehicle
BURIAL VAULTS: Concrete Or Precast Terrazzo
BURNERS: Gas, Indl
BURNERS: Gas-Oil, Combination
BURNERS: Oil, Domestic Or Indl
BUSHINGS & BEARINGS
BUSINESS ACTIVITIES: Non-Commercial Site
BUSINESS FORMS WHOLESALERS
BUSINESS FORMS: Printed, Continuous
BUSINESS FORMS: Printed, Manifold
BUSINESS MACHINE REPAIR, ELECTRIC
BUSINESS TRAINING SVCS
BUTTER WHOLESALERS

C

CABINETS & CASES: Show, Display & Storage, Exc Wood
CABINETS: Bathroom Vanities, Wood

PRODUCT INDEX

CABINETS: Entertainment
CABINETS: Entertainment Units, Household, Wood
CABINETS: Factory
CABINETS: Kitchen, Metal
CABINETS: Kitchen, Wood
CABINETS: Office, Wood
CABINETS: Show, Display, Etc, Wood, Exc Refrigerated
CABINETS: Stereo, Wood
CABLE & OTHER PAY TELEVISION DISTRIBUTION
CABLE & PAY TELEVISION SVCS: Direct Broadcast Satellite
CABLE TELEVISION
CABLE WIRING SETS: Battery, Internal Combustion Engines
CABLE: Aluminum, Made In Rolling Mills
CABLE: Fiber Optic
CABLE: Noninsulated
CABLE: Steel, Insulated Or Armored
CACAO BEAN PROCESSING
CAFES
CALCULATING & ACCOUNTING EQPT
CALIBRATING SVCS, NEC
CAMPERS: Truck Mounted
CAMSHAFTS
CAN LIDS & ENDS
CANDLE SHOPS
CANDLES
CANDLES: Wholesalers
CANDY & CONFECTIONS: Candy Bars, Including Chocolate Covered
CANDY & CONFECTIONS: Chocolate Candy, Exc Solid Chocolate
CANDY & CONFECTIONS: Popcorn Balls/Other Trtd Popcorn Prdts
CANDY, NUT & CONFECTIONERY STORES: Candy
CANDY: Soft
CANNED SPECIALTIES
CANS: Metal
CANVAS PRDTS
CANVAS PRDTS: Convertible Tops, Car/Boat, Fm Purchased Mtrl
CAPACITORS: NEC
CAPS: Plastic
CAR WASH EQPT
CAR WASH EQPT & SPLYS WHOLESALERS
CARBIDES
CARBON & GRAPHITE PRDTS, NEC
CARBON BLACK
CARBURETORS
CARDIOVASCULAR SYSTEM DRUGS, EXC DIAGNOSTIC
CARDS: Color
CARDS: Greeting
CARDS: Identification
CARDS: Playing
CARPET & UPHOLSTERY CLEANING SVCS
CARPETS, RUGS & FLOOR COVERING
CARPETS: Textile Fiber
CARRIERS: Infant, Textile
CARS: Electric
CASEMENTS: Aluminum
CASES: Carrying
CASES: Carrying, Clothing & Apparel
CASES: Jewelry
CASES: Plastic
CASES: Shipping, Nailed Or Lock Corner, Wood
CASINGS: Sheet Metal
CASINGS: Storage, Missile & Missile Components
CASKETS & ACCESS
CAST STONE: Concrete
CASTINGS GRINDING: For The Trade
CASTINGS: Aerospace, Aluminum
CASTINGS: Aerospace, Nonferrous, Exc Aluminum
CASTINGS: Aluminum
CASTINGS: Brass, NEC, Exc Die
CASTINGS: Commercial Investment, Ferrous
CASTINGS: Die, Aluminum
CASTINGS: Die, Nonferrous
CASTINGS: Ductile
CASTINGS: Gray Iron
CASTINGS: Machinery, Aluminum
CASTINGS: Steel
CASTINGS: Titanium
CATALOG & MAIL-ORDER HOUSES
CATALOG SALES
CATALOG SHOWROOMS

CATALYSTS: Chemical
CATAPULTS
CATERERS
CATTLE WHOLESALERS
CAULKING COMPOUNDS
CEMENT & CONCRETE RELATED PRDTS & EQPT: Bituminous
CEMENT ROCK: Crushed & Broken
CEMENT: Hydraulic
CEMENT: Natural
CEMENT: Portland
CERAMIC FIBER
CHAIN: Tire, Made From Purchased Wire
CHAIN: Welded, Made From Purchased Wire
CHANGE MAKING MACHINES
CHASSIS: Motor Vehicle
CHASSIS: Travel Trailer
CHEMICAL CLEANING SVCS
CHEMICAL ELEMENTS
CHEMICAL PROCESSING MACHINERY & EQPT
CHEMICALS & ALLIED PRDTS WHOLESALERS, NEC
CHEMICALS & ALLIED PRDTS, WHOLESALE: Adhesives
CHEMICALS & ALLIED PRDTS, WHOLESALE: Chemical Additives
CHEMICALS & ALLIED PRDTS, WHOLESALE: Chemicals, Indl
CHEMICALS & ALLIED PRDTS, WHOLESALE: Chemicals, Indl & Heavy
CHEMICALS & ALLIED PRDTS, WHOLESALE: Detergent/ Soap
CHEMICALS & ALLIED PRDTS, WHOLESALE: Indl Gases
CHEMICALS & ALLIED PRDTS, WHOLESALE: Oil Additives
CHEMICALS & ALLIED PRDTS, WHOLESALE: Oxygen
CHEMICALS & ALLIED PRDTS, WHOLESALE: Plastics Film
CHEMICALS & ALLIED PRDTS, WHOLESALE: Plastics Materials, NEC
CHEMICALS & ALLIED PRDTS, WHOLESALE: Plastics Prdts, NEC
CHEMICALS & ALLIED PRDTS, WHOLESALE: Plastics Sheets & Rods
CHEMICALS & ALLIED PRDTS, WHOLESALE: Polyurethane Prdts
CHEMICALS & ALLIED PRDTS, WHOLESALE: Resins
CHEMICALS & ALLIED PRDTS, WHOLESALE: Resins, Plastics
CHEMICALS & ALLIED PRDTS, WHOLESALE: Spec Clean/ Sanitation
CHEMICALS & ALLIED PRDTS, WHOLESALE: Syn Resin, Rub/Plastic
CHEMICALS & ALLIED PRDTS, WHOLESALE: Waxes, Exc Petroleum
CHEMICALS & OTHER PRDTS DERIVED FROM COKING
CHEMICALS, AGRICULTURE: Wholesalers
CHEMICALS: Agricultural
CHEMICALS: Aluminum Compounds
CHEMICALS: Ammonium Salts & Compounds
CHEMICALS: Bromine, Elemental
CHEMICALS: Fire Retardant
CHEMICALS: High Purity, Refined From Technical Grade
CHEMICALS: Inorganic, NEC
CHEMICALS: Magnesium Compounds Or Salts, Inorganic
CHEMICALS: Medicinal
CHEMICALS: Medicinal, Organic, Uncompounded, Bulk
CHEMICALS: NEC
CHEMICALS: Organic, NEC
CHEMICALS: Phenol
CHEMICALS: Reagent Grade, Refined From Technical Grade
CHEMICALS: Soda Ash
CHEMICALS: Water Treatment
CHICKEN SLAUGHTERING & PROCESSING
CHILDREN'S & INFANTS' CLOTHING STORES
CHOCOLATE, EXC CANDY FROM BEANS: Chips, Powder, Block, Syrup
CHOCOLATE, EXC CANDY FROM PURCH CHOC: Chips, Powder, Block
CHROMATOGRAPHY EQPT
CHUCKS
CHURCHES
CIGARETTE & CIGAR PRDTS & ACCESS
CIRCUIT BOARD REPAIR SVCS
CIRCUIT BOARDS: Wiring
CIRCUITS: Electronic
CLAMPS & COUPLINGS: Hose

CLAMPS: Metal
CLAY: Ground Or Treated
CLEANING EQPT: Commercial
CLEANING EQPT: Floor Washing & Polishing, Commercial
CLEANING EQPT: High Pressure
CLEANING OR POLISHING PREPARATIONS, NEC
CLEANING PRDTS: Automobile Polish
CLEANING PRDTS: Degreasing Solvent
CLEANING PRDTS: Disinfectants, Household Or Indl Plant
CLEANING PRDTS: Drain Pipe Solvents Or Cleaners
CLEANING PRDTS: Laundry Preparations
CLEANING PRDTS: Sanitation Preparations
CLEANING PRDTS: Sanitation Preps, Disinfectants/ Deodorants
CLEANING PRDTS: Specialty
CLEANING PRDTS: Stain Removers
CLEANING SVCS: Industrial Or Commercial
CLIPPERS: Fingernail & Toenail
CLOSURES: Closures, Stamped Metal
CLOSURES: Plastic
CLOTHING & ACCESS, WOMEN, CHILDREN & INFANT, WHOL: Handbags
CLOTHING & ACCESS, WOMEN, CHILDREN & INFANT, WHOL: Uniforms
CLOTHING & ACCESS, WOMEN, CHILDREN/INFANT, WHOL: Baby Goods
CLOTHING & ACCESS: Costumes, Theatrical
CLOTHING & ACCESS: Handicapped
CLOTHING & ACCESS: Men's Miscellaneous Access
CLOTHING & APPAREL STORES: Custom
CLOTHING & FURNISHINGS, MEN'S & BOYS', WHOLESALE: Uniforms
CLOTHING & FURNISHINGS, MENS & BOYS, WHOL: Sportswear/Work
CLOTHING STORES: Designer Apparel
CLOTHING STORES: T-Shirts, Printed, Custom
CLOTHING STORES: Uniforms & Work
CLOTHING STORES: Unisex
CLOTHING: Access, Women's & Misses'
CLOTHING: Aprons, Exc Rubber/Plastic, Women, Misses, Junior
CLOTHING: Athletic & Sportswear, Men's & Boys'
CLOTHING: Athletic & Sportswear, Women's & Girls'
CLOTHING: Baker, Barber, Lab/Svc Ind Apparel, Washable, Men
CLOTHING: Band Uniforms
CLOTHING: Blouses, Women's & Girls'
CLOTHING: Children's, Girls'
CLOTHING: Coats & Suits, Men's & Boys'
CLOTHING: Costumes
CLOTHING: Dresses
CLOTHING: Hats & Headwear, Knit
CLOTHING: Hospital, Men's
CLOTHING: Leather
CLOTHING: Maternity
CLOTHING: Neckwear
CLOTHING: Outerwear, Women's & Misses' NEC
CLOTHING: Robes & Dressing Gowns
CLOTHING: Shirts
CLOTHING: Shirts & T-Shirts, Knit
CLOTHING: Shirts, Dress, Men's & Boys'
CLOTHING: Socks
CLOTHING: Suits & Skirts, Women's & Misses'
CLOTHING: T-Shirts & Tops, Knit
CLOTHING: Tailored Suits & Formal Jackets
CLOTHING: Trousers & Slacks, Men's & Boys'
CLOTHING: Uniforms & Vestments
CLOTHING: Uniforms, Ex Athletic, Women's, Misses' & Juniors'
CLOTHING: Uniforms, Men's & Boys'
CLOTHING: Uniforms, Military, Men/Youth, Purchased Materials
CLOTHING: Uniforms, Team Athletic
CLOTHING: Uniforms, Work
CLOTHING: Waterproof Outerwear
CLOTHING: Work Apparel, Exc Uniforms
COAL & OTHER MINERALS & ORES WHOLESALERS
COAL GASIFICATION
COAL MINING SERVICES
COAL MINING: Bituminous & Lignite Surface
COAL MINING: Bituminous Coal & Lignite-Surface Mining
COAL MINING: Bituminous, Surface, NEC
COAL PREPARATION PLANT: Bituminous or Lignite

PRODUCT INDEX

COAL, MINERALS & ORES, WHOLESALE: Coal
COATING COMPOUNDS: Tar
COATING OR WRAPPING SVC: Steel Pipe
COATING SVC: Metals, With Plastic Or Resins
COATINGS: Polyurethane
COFFEE SVCS
COIL WINDING SVC
COILS & ROD: Extruded, Aluminum
COILS & TRANSFORMERS
COILS: Electric Motors Or Generators
COILS: Pipe
COLOR PIGMENTS
COLORS: Pigments, Inorganic
COMBINED ELEMENTARY & SECONDARY SCHOOLS, PRIVATE
COMFORTERS & QUILTS, FROM MANMADE FIBER OR SILK
COMMERCIAL & OFFICE BUILDINGS RENOVATION & REPAIR
COMMERCIAL ART & GRAPHIC DESIGN SVCS
COMMERCIAL ART & ILLUSTRATION SVCS
COMMERCIAL CONTAINERS WHOLESALERS
COMMERCIAL EQPT WHOLESALERS, NEC
COMMERCIAL EQPT, WHOLESALE: Restaurant, NEC
COMMERCIAL EQPT, WHOLESALE: Scales, Exc Laboratory
COMMERCIAL EQPT, WHOLESALE: Store Fixtures & Display Eqpt
COMMERCIAL EQPT, WHOLESALE: Vending Machines, Coin-Operated
COMMERCIAL PRINTING & NEWSPAPER PUBLISHING
COMMON SAND MINING
COMMUNICATIONS EQPT WHOLESALERS
COMMUNICATIONS EQPT: Microwave
COMMUNICATIONS SVCS
COMMUNICATIONS SVCS: Data
COMMUNICATIONS SVCS: Internet Connectivity Svcs
COMMUNICATIONS SVCS: Internet Host Svcs
COMMUNICATIONS SVCS: Online Svc Providers
COMMUNICATIONS SVCS: Proprietary Online Svcs Networks
COMMUNICATIONS SVCS: Signal Enhancement Network Svcs
COMMUNICATIONS SVCS: Telephone, Voice
COMPACT LASER DISCS: Prerecorded
COMPOSITION STONE: Plastic
COMPOST
COMPRESSORS: Air & Gas
COMPRESSORS: Air & Gas, Including Vacuum Pumps
COMPRESSORS: Refrigeration & Air Conditioning Eqpt
COMPUTER & COMPUTER SOFTWARE STORES
COMPUTER & COMPUTER SOFTWARE STORES: Software & Access
COMPUTER & COMPUTER SOFTWARE STORES: Software, Bus/Non-Game
COMPUTER & COMPUTER SOFTWARE STORES: Software, Computer Game
COMPUTER & DATA PROCESSING EQPT REPAIR & MAINTENANCE
COMPUTER & OFFICE MACHINE MAINTENANCE & REPAIR
COMPUTER CODE AUTHORS
COMPUTER FACILITIES MANAGEMENT SVCS
COMPUTER FORMS
COMPUTER GRAPHICS SVCS
COMPUTER PERIPHERAL EQPT REPAIR & MAINTENANCE
COMPUTER PERIPHERAL EQPT, NEC
COMPUTER PERIPHERAL EQPT, WHOLESALE
COMPUTER PERIPHERAL EQPT: Input Or Output
COMPUTER PROGRAMMING SVCS: Custom
COMPUTER RELATED MAINTENANCE SVCS
COMPUTER SOFTWARE DEVELOPMENT
COMPUTER SOFTWARE DEVELOPMENT & APPLICATIONS
COMPUTER SOFTWARE SYSTEMS ANALYSIS & DESIGN: Custom
COMPUTER STORAGE DEVICES, NEC
COMPUTER SYSTEMS ANALYSIS & DESIGN
COMPUTER TERMINALS
COMPUTERS, NEC
COMPUTERS, NEC, WHOLESALE
COMPUTERS, PERIPHERALS & SOFTWARE, WHOLESALE: Mainframe
COMPUTERS, PERIPHERALS & SOFTWARE, WHOLESALE: Software
COMPUTERS: Personal
CONCRETE BUILDING PRDTS WHOLESALERS
CONCRETE PLANTS
CONCRETE PRDTS
CONCRETE PRDTS, PRECAST, NEC
CONCRETE: Asphaltic, Not From Refineries
CONCRETE: Ready-Mixed
CONDUITS & FITTINGS: Electric
CONFINEMENT SURVEILLANCE SYS MAINTENANCE & MONITORING SVCS
CONNECTORS: Cord, Electric
CONNECTORS: Electronic
CONSTRUCTION & MINING MACHINERY WHOLESALERS
CONSTRUCTION & ROAD MAINTENANCE EQPT: Drags, Road
CONSTRUCTION EQPT REPAIR SVCS
CONSTRUCTION EQPT: Attachments, Snow Plow
CONSTRUCTION EQPT: Finishers & Spreaders
CONSTRUCTION EQPT: Graders, Road
CONSTRUCTION EQPT: Tractors
CONSTRUCTION MATERIALS, WHOLESALE: Aggregate
CONSTRUCTION MATERIALS, WHOLESALE: Air Ducts, Sheet Metal
CONSTRUCTION MATERIALS, WHOLESALE: Architectural Metalwork
CONSTRUCTION MATERIALS, WHOLESALE: Asphalt Felts & coating
CONSTRUCTION MATERIALS, WHOLESALE: Awnings
CONSTRUCTION MATERIALS, WHOLESALE: Building Stone
CONSTRUCTION MATERIALS, WHOLESALE: Building, Exterior
CONSTRUCTION MATERIALS, WHOLESALE: Building, Interior
CONSTRUCTION MATERIALS, WHOLESALE: Concrete Mixtures
CONSTRUCTION MATERIALS, WHOLESALE: Door Frames
CONSTRUCTION MATERIALS, WHOLESALE: Fiberglass Building Mat
CONSTRUCTION MATERIALS, WHOLESALE: Glass
CONSTRUCTION MATERIALS, WHOLESALE: Gravel
CONSTRUCTION MATERIALS, WHOLESALE: Limestone
CONSTRUCTION MATERIALS, WHOLESALE: Molding, All Materials
CONSTRUCTION MATERIALS, WHOLESALE: Pallets, Wood
CONSTRUCTION MATERIALS, WHOLESALE: Particleboard
CONSTRUCTION MATERIALS, WHOLESALE: Paving Materials
CONSTRUCTION MATERIALS, WHOLESALE: Plywood
CONSTRUCTION MATERIALS, WHOLESALE: Prefabricated Structures
CONSTRUCTION MATERIALS, WHOLESALE: Roofing & Siding Material
CONSTRUCTION MATERIALS, WHOLESALE: Sand
CONSTRUCTION MATERIALS, WHOLESALE: Septic Tanks
CONSTRUCTION MATERIALS, WHOLESALE: Sewer Pipe, Clay
CONSTRUCTION MATERIALS, WHOLESALE: Siding, Exc Wood
CONSTRUCTION MATERIALS, WHOLESALE: Stone, Crushed Or Broken
CONSTRUCTION MATERIALS, WHOLESALE: Tile & Clay Prdts
CONSTRUCTION MATERIALS, WHOLESALE: Veneer
CONSTRUCTION MATERIALS, WHOLESALE: Windows
CONSTRUCTION MATLS, WHOL: Composite Board Prdts, Woodboard
CONSTRUCTION MATLS, WHOL: Doors, Combination, Screen-Storm
CONSTRUCTION SAND MINING
CONSTRUCTION: Agricultural Building
CONSTRUCTION: Athletic & Recreation Facilities
CONSTRUCTION: Bridge
CONSTRUCTION: Commercial & Office Building, New
CONSTRUCTION: Commercial & Office Buildings, Prefabricated
CONSTRUCTION: Dams, Waterways, Docks & Other Marine
CONSTRUCTION: Drainage System
CONSTRUCTION: Farm Building
CONSTRUCTION: Food Prdts Manufacturing or Packing Plant
CONSTRUCTION: Foundation & Retaining Wall
CONSTRUCTION: Heavy Highway & Street
CONSTRUCTION: Indl Buildings, New, NEC
CONSTRUCTION: Indl Plant
CONSTRUCTION: Pipeline, NEC
CONSTRUCTION: Power & Communication Transmission Tower
CONSTRUCTION: Residential, Nec
CONSTRUCTION: Scaffolding
CONSTRUCTION: Sewer Line
CONSTRUCTION: Single-Family Housing
CONSTRUCTION: Single-family Housing, New
CONSTRUCTION: Swimming Pools
CONSTRUCTION: Transmitting Tower, Telecommunication
CONSTRUCTION: Warehouse
CONSTRUCTION: Waste Water & Sewage Treatment Plant
CONSTRUCTION: Water & Sewer Line
CONSULTING SVC: Business, NEC
CONSULTING SVC: Educational
CONSULTING SVC: Financial Management
CONSULTING SVC: Management
CONSULTING SVCS, BUSINESS: Communications
CONSULTING SVCS, BUSINESS: Energy Conservation
CONSULTING SVCS, BUSINESS: Environmental
CONSULTING SVCS, BUSINESS: Safety Training Svcs
CONSULTING SVCS, BUSINESS: Sys Engnrg, Exc Computer/ Prof
CONSULTING SVCS, BUSINESS: Systems Analysis & Engineering
CONSULTING SVCS, BUSINESS: Systems Analysis Or Design
CONSULTING SVCS: Scientific
CONTACTS: Electrical
CONTAINERS: Cargo, Wood & Metal Combination
CONTAINERS: Food & Beverage
CONTAINERS: Food, Folding, Made From Purchased Materials
CONTAINERS: Food, Liquid Tight, Including Milk
CONTAINERS: Frozen Food & Ice Cream
CONTAINERS: Glass
CONTAINERS: Ice Cream, Made From Purchased Materials
CONTAINERS: Laminated Phenolic & Vulcanized Fiber
CONTAINERS: Metal
CONTAINERS: Plastic
CONTAINERS: Sanitary, Food
CONTAINERS: Shipping, Bombs, Metal Plate
CONTAINERS: Wood
CONTRACT FOOD SVCS
CONTRACTOR: Dredging
CONTRACTOR: Rigging & Scaffolding
CONTRACTORS: Building Site Preparation
CONTRACTORS: Cable Laying
CONTRACTORS: Carpentry Work
CONTRACTORS: Carpentry, Cabinet & Finish Work
CONTRACTORS: Closet Organizers, Installation & Design
CONTRACTORS: Coating, Caulking & Weather, Water & Fire
CONTRACTORS: Commercial & Office Building
CONTRACTORS: Communications Svcs
CONTRACTORS: Computerized Controls Installation
CONTRACTORS: Directional Oil & Gas Well Drilling Svc
CONTRACTORS: Drywall
CONTRACTORS: Electronic Controls Installation
CONTRACTORS: Energy Management Control
CONTRACTORS: Excavating Slush Pits & Cellars Svcs
CONTRACTORS: Fence Construction
CONTRACTORS: Fiber Optic Cable Installation
CONTRACTORS: Fire Detection & Burglar Alarm Systems
CONTRACTORS: Floor Laying & Other Floor Work
CONTRACTORS: Food Svcs Eqpt Installation
CONTRACTORS: Foundation & Footing
CONTRACTORS: Gas Field Svcs, NEC
CONTRACTORS: General Electric
CONTRACTORS: Glass Tinting, Architectural & Automotive
CONTRACTORS: Grave Excavation
CONTRACTORS: Heating & Air Conditioning
CONTRACTORS: Heating Systems Repair & Maintenance Svc
CONTRACTORS: Highway & Street Construction, General
CONTRACTORS: Highway & Street Paving
CONTRACTORS: Kitchen Cabinet Installation
CONTRACTORS: Machine Rigging & Moving
CONTRACTORS: Machinery Installation
CONTRACTORS: Masonry & Stonework
CONTRACTORS: Oil & Gas Aerial Geophysical Exploration Svcs

PRODUCT INDEX

CONTRACTORS: Oil & Gas Building, Repairing & Dismantling Svc
CONTRACTORS: Oil & Gas Field Geological Exploration Svcs
CONTRACTORS: Oil & Gas Wells Pumping Svcs
CONTRACTORS: Oil & Gas Wells Svcs
CONTRACTORS: Oil Field Haulage Svcs
CONTRACTORS: Oil Field Mud Drilling Svcs
CONTRACTORS: Painting, Commercial
CONTRACTORS: Painting, Indl
CONTRACTORS: Petroleum Storage Tanks, Pumping & Draining
CONTRACTORS: Pile Driving
CONTRACTORS: Plumbing
CONTRACTORS: Power Generating Eqpt Installation
CONTRACTORS: Prefabricated Window & Door Installation
CONTRACTORS: Process Piping
CONTRACTORS: Refractory or Acid Brick Masonry
CONTRACTORS: Renovation, Aircraft Interiors
CONTRACTORS: Seismograph Survey Svcs
CONTRACTORS: Septic System
CONTRACTORS: Sheet Metal Work, NEC
CONTRACTORS: Ship Boiler & Tank Cleaning & Repair
CONTRACTORS: Siding
CONTRACTORS: Structural Iron Work, Structural
CONTRACTORS: Structural Steel Erection
CONTRACTORS: Terrazzo Work
CONTRACTORS: Tile Installation, Ceramic
CONTRACTORS: Underground Utilities
CONTRACTORS: Ventilation & Duct Work
CONTRACTORS: Vinyl Flooring Installation, Tile & Sheet
CONTRACTORS: Warm Air Heating & Air Conditioning
CONTRACTORS: Water Well Drilling
CONTRACTORS: Wood Floor Installation & Refinishing
CONTRACTORS: Wrecking & Demolition
CONTROL EQPT: Electric
CONTROL EQPT: Electric Buses & Locomotives
CONTROL EQPT: Noise
CONTROLS & ACCESS: Indl, Electric
CONTROLS & ACCESS: Motor
CONTROLS: Automatic Temperature
CONTROLS: Electric Motor
CONTROLS: Environmental
CONTROLS: Marine & Navy, Auxiliary
CONVENIENCE STORES
CONVERTERS: Torque, Exc Auto
CONVEYOR SYSTEMS
CONVEYOR SYSTEMS: Belt, General Indl Use
CONVEYOR SYSTEMS: Bulk Handling
CONVEYOR SYSTEMS: Pneumatic Tube
CONVEYOR SYSTEMS: Robotic
CONVEYORS & CONVEYING EQPT
COOKING & FOODWARMING EQPT: Commercial
COOKWARE, STONEWARE: Coarse Earthenware & Pottery
COOLING TOWERS: Metal
COOLING TOWERS: Wood
COPPER: Rolling & Drawing
COPYRIGHT BUYING & LICENSING
CORRUGATING MACHINES
COSMETIC PREPARATIONS
COSMETICS & TOILETRIES
COSMETICS WHOLESALERS
COSMETOLOGY & PERSONAL HYGIENE SALONS
COUNTER & SINK TOPS
COUNTERS OR COUNTER DISPLAY CASES, EXC WOOD
COUNTERS OR COUNTER DISPLAY CASES, WOOD
COUNTERS: Mechanical
COUNTING DEVICES: Controls, Revolution & Timing
COUNTING DEVICES: Tachometer, Centrifugal
COUNTRY CLUBS
COUPLINGS: Hose & Tube, Hydraulic Or Pneumatic
COUPLINGS: Shaft
COVERS: Automobile Seat
COVERS: Automotive, Exc Seat & Tire
CRANE & AERIAL LIFT SVCS
CRANES: Indl Plant
CRANES: Overhead
CREDIT CARD SVCS
CROWNS & CLOSURES
CRUDE PETROLEUM & NATURAL GAS PRODUCTION
CRUDE PETROLEUM PRODUCTION
CRYOGENIC COOLING DEVICES: Infrared Detectors, Masers
CULTURE MEDIA

CULVERTS: Sheet Metal
CUPOLAS: Metal Plate
CUPS & PLATES: Foamed Plastics
CURBING: Granite Or Stone
CURTAIN & DRAPERY FIXTURES: Poles, Rods & Rollers
CURTAIN WALLS: Building, Steel
CURTAINS: Window, From Purchased Materials
CUSHIONS & PILLOWS
CUSTOM COMPOUNDING OF RUBBER MATERIALS
CUT STONE & STONE PRODUCTS
CUTLERY
CYCLIC CRUDES & INTERMEDIATES
CYLINDER & ACTUATORS: Fluid Power
CYLINDERS: Pump

D

DAIRY PRDTS STORE: Butter
DAIRY PRDTS STORE: Cheese
DAIRY PRDTS STORE: Ice Cream, Packaged
DAIRY PRDTS STORES
DAIRY PRDTS: Butter
DAIRY PRDTS: Cheese
DAIRY PRDTS: Dairy Based Desserts, Frozen
DAIRY PRDTS: Dietary Supplements, Dairy & Non-Dairy Based
DAIRY PRDTS: Dried & Powdered Milk & Milk Prdts
DAIRY PRDTS: Fermented & Cultured Milk Prdts
DAIRY PRDTS: Ice Cream, Bulk
DAIRY PRDTS: Ice Cream, Packaged, Molded, On Sticks, Etc.
DAIRY PRDTS: Milk, Condensed & Evaporated
DAIRY PRDTS: Natural Cheese
DAIRY PRDTS: Processed Cheese
DAIRY PRDTS: Whipped Topping, Exc Frozen Or Dry Mix
DANCE INSTRUCTOR & SCHOOL
DATA PROCESSING & PREPARATION SVCS
DATA PROCESSING SVCS
DECORATIVE WOOD & WOODWORK
DEFENSE SYSTEMS & EQPT
DEGREASING MACHINES
DEICING OR DEFROSTING FLUID
DENTAL EQPT
DENTAL EQPT & SPLYS
DENTAL EQPT & SPLYS WHOLESALERS
DENTAL EQPT & SPLYS: Dental Hand Instruments, NEC
DENTAL EQPT & SPLYS: Dental Materials
DENTAL EQPT & SPLYS: Enamels
DENTAL EQPT & SPLYS: Orthodontic Appliances
DENTAL INSTRUMENT REPAIR SVCS
DENTISTS' OFFICES & CLINICS
DEODORANTS: Personal
DERMATOLOGICALS
DESIGN SVCS, NEC
DESIGN SVCS: Commercial & Indl
DESIGN SVCS: Computer Integrated Systems
DIAGNOSTIC SUBSTANCES
DIAGNOSTIC SUBSTANCES OR AGENTS: Blood Derivative
DIAGNOSTIC SUBSTANCES OR AGENTS: Enzyme & Isoenzyme
DIAGNOSTIC SUBSTANCES OR AGENTS: In Vitro
DIAGNOSTIC SUBSTANCES OR AGENTS: Microbiology & Virology
DIAGNOSTIC SUBSTANCES OR AGENTS: Radioactive
DIAGNOSTIC SUBSTANCES OR AGENTS: Veterinary
DIAMONDS, GEMS, WHOLESALE
DIE CUTTING SVC: Paper
DIE SETS: Presses, Metal Stamping
DIES & TOOLS: Special
DIES: Cutting, Exc Metal
DIES: Diamond, Metalworking
DIES: Extrusion
DIES: Paper Cutting
DIES: Plastic Forming
DIES: Steel Rule
DIODES & RECTIFIERS
DIODES: Light Emitting
DIRECT SELLING ESTABLISHMENTS, NEC
DIRECT SELLING ESTABLISHMENTS: Food Svcs
DISCS & TAPE: Optical, Blank
DISPLAY ITEMS: Corrugated, Made From Purchased Materials
DISTRIBUTORS: Motor Vehicle Engine
DOCK EQPT & SPLYS, INDL

DOCKS: Floating, Wood
DOOR FRAMES: Wood
DOORS & WINDOWS: Storm, Metal
DOORS: Fire, Metal
DOORS: Folding, Plastic Or Plastic Coated Fabric
DOORS: Garage, Overhead, Metal
DOORS: Garage, Overhead, Wood
DOORS: Glass
DOORS: Screen, Metal
DRAPERIES & CURTAINS
DRAPERIES: Plastic & Textile, From Purchased Materials
DRAPERY & UPHOLSTERY STORES: Draperies
DRILL BITS
DRILLING MACHINERY & EQPT: Oil & Gas
DRINKING PLACES: Bars & Lounges
DRIVE SHAFTS
DRIVES: High Speed Indl, Exc Hydrostatic
DRIVES: Hydrostatic
DRUG STORES
DRUGS & DRUG PROPRIETARIES, WHOLESALE: Animal Medicines
DRUGS & DRUG PROPRIETARIES, WHOLESALE: Pharmaceuticals
DRUGS & DRUG PROPRIETARIES, WHOLESALE: Vitamins & Minerals
DRUGS: Parasitic & Infective Disease Affecting
DUCTING: Plastic
DUCTS: Sheet Metal
DUMPSTERS: Garbage
DUST OR FUME COLLECTING EQPT: Indl
DYES & PIGMENTS: Organic

E

EATING PLACES
EDITING SVCS
EDUCATIONAL SVCS
ELECTRIC MOTOR & GENERATOR AUXILIARY PARTS
ELECTRIC MOTOR REPAIR SVCS
ELECTRIC SERVICES
ELECTRIC SVCS, NEC: Power Generation
ELECTRICAL APPARATUS & EQPT WHOLESALERS
ELECTRICAL DISCHARGE MACHINING, EDM
ELECTRICAL EQPT REPAIR SVCS
ELECTRICAL EQPT REPAIR SVCS: High Voltage
ELECTRICAL EQPT: Automotive, NEC
ELECTRICAL GOODS, WHOLESALE: Electrical Appliances, Major
ELECTRICAL GOODS, WHOLESALE: Fittings & Construction Mat
ELECTRICAL GOODS, WHOLESALE: Generators
ELECTRICAL GOODS, WHOLESALE: Light Bulbs & Related Splys
ELECTRICAL GOODS, WHOLESALE: Security Control Eqpt & Systems
ELECTRICAL GOODS, WHOLESALE: Signaling, Eqpt
ELECTRICAL GOODS, WHOLESALE: Switchgear
ELECTRICAL GOODS, WHOLESALE: Wire & Cable
ELECTRICAL MEASURING INSTRUMENT REPAIR & CALIBRATION SVCS
ELECTRICAL SPLYS
ELECTRICAL SUPPLIES: Porcelain
ELECTROMEDICAL EQPT
ELECTRON TUBES
ELECTRONIC DEVICES: Solid State, NEC
ELECTRONIC EQPT REPAIR SVCS
ELECTRONIC LOADS & POWER SPLYS
ELECTRONIC PARTS & EQPT WHOLESALERS
ELECTRONIC SHOPPING
ELECTRONIC TRAINING DEVICES
ELEMENTARY & SECONDARY SCHOOLS, PUBLIC
ELEVATORS & EQPT
ELEVATORS WHOLESALERS
ELEVATORS: Installation & Conversion
EMBLEMS: Embroidered
EMBROIDERY ADVERTISING SVCS
EMBROIDERY KITS
EMERGENCY ALARMS
EMPLOYMENT SVCS: Labor Contractors
ENAMELS
ENCLOSURES: Electronic
ENGINE REBUILDING: Diesel
ENGINEERING SVCS
ENGINEERING SVCS: Acoustical

PRODUCT INDEX

ENGINEERING SVCS: Building Construction
ENGINEERING SVCS: Electrical Or Electronic
ENGINEERING SVCS: Machine Tool Design
ENGINEERING SVCS: Mechanical
ENGINEERING SVCS: Petroleum
ENGINEERING SVCS: Structural
ENGINES: Diesel & Semi-Diesel Or Duel Fuel
ENGINES: Gasoline, NEC
ENGINES: Internal Combustion, NEC
ENGINES: Marine
ENGRAVING SVC, NEC
ENGRAVING SVCS
ENVELOPES
ENVELOPES WHOLESALERS
ENZYMES
EPOXY RESINS
EQUIPMENT: Pedestrian Traffic Control
EQUIPMENT: Rental & Leasing, NEC
ETCHING & ENGRAVING SVC
ETHYLENE-PROPYLENE RUBBERS: EPDM Polymers
EXHAUST SYSTEMS: Eqpt & Parts
EXPLORATION, METAL MINING
EXPLOSIVES
EXTRACTS, FLAVORING

F

FABRIC STORES
FABRICS & CLOTH: Quilted
FABRICS: Apparel & Outerwear, Broadwoven
FABRICS: Apparel & Outerwear, Cotton
FABRICS: Bags & Bagging, Cotton
FABRICS: Basket Weave, Cotton
FABRICS: Bonded-Fiber, Exc Felt
FABRICS: Denims
FABRICS: Fiberglass, Broadwoven
FABRICS: Nonwoven
FABRICS: Resin Or Plastic Coated
FABRICS: Scrub Cloths
FABRICS: Underwear, Cotton
FABRICS: Upholstery, Cotton
FABRICS: Upholstery, Wool
FACILITIES SUPPORT SVCS
FAMILY CLOTHING STORES
FANS, BLOWING: Indl Or Commercial
FANS, VENTILATING: Indl Or Commercial
FANS: Ceiling
FARM & GARDEN MACHINERY WHOLESALERS
FARM MACHINERY REPAIR SVCS
FARM PRDTS, RAW MATERIALS, WHOLESALE: Feathers
FARM SPLYS WHOLESALERS
FARM SPLYS, WHOLESALE: Feed
FARM SPLYS, WHOLESALE: Fertilizers & Agricultural Chemicals
FARM SPLYS, WHOLESALE: Garden Splys
FASTENERS WHOLESALERS
FASTENERS: Metal
FASTENERS: Metal
FAUCETS & SPIGOTS: Metal & Plastic
FEATHERS & FEATHER PRODUCTS
FENCES OR POSTS: Ornamental Iron Or Steel
FENCING MATERIALS: Docks & Other Outdoor Prdts, Wood
FENCING MATERIALS: Wood
FENCING: Chain Link
FENDERS: Automobile, Stamped Or Pressed Metal
FERTILIZER, AGRICULTURAL: Wholesalers
FERTILIZERS: Nitrogenous
FERTILIZERS: Phosphatic
FIBER & FIBER PRDTS: Protein
FIBER & FIBER PRDTS: Vinyl
FIBERS: Carbon & Graphite
FILTER ELEMENTS: Fluid & Hydraulic Line
FILTERS
FILTERS & SOFTENERS: Water, Household
FILTERS: Air
FILTERS: Air Intake, Internal Combustion Engine, Exc Auto
FILTERS: General Line, Indl
FILTRATION DEVICES: Electronic
FINANCIAL SVCS
FINISHING AGENTS
FINISHING SVCS
FIRE ALARM MAINTENANCE & MONITORING SVCS
FIRE ARMS, SMALL: Guns Or Gun Parts, 30 mm & Below
FIRE ARMS, SMALL: Rifles Or Rifle Parts, 30 mm & below

FIRE CONTROL OR BOMBING EQPT: Electronic
FIRE EXTINGUISHERS, WHOLESALE
FIRE EXTINGUISHERS: Portable
FIRE OR BURGLARY RESISTIVE PRDTS
FIREARMS & AMMUNITION, EXC SPORTING, WHOLESALE
FIREFIGHTING APPARATUS
FIREPLACE EQPT & ACCESS
FIREWORKS
FIRST AID SPLYS, WHOLESALE
FISH FOOD
FISHING EQPT: Lures
FITTINGS & ASSEMBLIES: Hose & Tube, Hydraulic Or Pneumatic
FITTINGS & SPECIALTIES: Steam
FITTINGS: Pipe
FITTINGS: Pipe, Fabricated
FIXTURES & EQPT: Kitchen, Metal, Exc Cast Aluminum
FLAGPOLES
FLAGS: Fabric
FLAGSTONES
FLAT GLASS: Construction
FLAT GLASS: Sheet
FLAT GLASS: Window, Clear & Colored
FLOOR COVERING STORES
FLOOR COVERING STORES: Carpets
FLOOR COVERINGS WHOLESALERS
FLOOR COVERINGS: Rubber
FLOOR COVERINGS: Textile Fiber
FLOOR COVERINGS: Twisted Paper, Grass, Reed, Coir, Etc
FLOORING & SIDING: Metal
FLOORING: Hardwood
FLOORING: Rubber
FLORIST: Flowers, Fresh
FLOWERS, ARTIFICIAL, WHOLESALE
FLUES & PIPES: Stove Or Furnace
FLUID METERS & COUNTING DEVICES
FLUID POWER PUMPS & MOTORS
FLUID POWER VALVES & HOSE FITTINGS
FOAM RUBBER
FOAMS & RUBBER, WHOLESALE
FOIL & LEAF: Metal
FOIL: Aluminum
FOIL: Laminated To Paper Or Other Materials
FOOD COLORINGS
FOOD PRDTS, CANNED: Barbecue Sauce
FOOD PRDTS, CANNED: Beans & Bean Sprouts
FOOD PRDTS, CANNED: Fruits
FOOD PRDTS, CANNED: Fruits & Fruit Prdts
FOOD PRDTS, CANNED: Jams, Including Imitation
FOOD PRDTS, CANNED: Jams, Jellies & Preserves
FOOD PRDTS, CANNED: Mexican, NEC
FOOD PRDTS, CANNED: Soups, Exc Seafood
FOOD PRDTS, CANNED: Spaghetti & Other Pasta Sauce
FOOD PRDTS, CONFECTIONERY, WHOLESALE: Snack Foods
FOOD PRDTS, FISH & SEAFOOD: Prepared Cakes & Sticks
FOOD PRDTS, FROZEN: Fruits, Juices & Vegetables
FOOD PRDTS, WHOLESALE: Beverages, Exc Coffee & Tea
FOOD PRDTS, WHOLESALE: Coffee & Tea
FOOD PRDTS, WHOLESALE: Coffee, Green Or Roasted
FOOD PRDTS, WHOLESALE: Dried or Canned Foods
FOOD PRDTS, WHOLESALE: Grain Elevators
FOOD PRDTS, WHOLESALE: Grains
FOOD PRDTS, WHOLESALE: Organic & Diet
FOOD PRDTS, WHOLESALE: Salt, Edible
FOOD PRDTS, WHOLESALE: Sauces
FOOD PRDTS, WHOLESALE: Specialty
FOOD PRDTS, WHOLESALE: Spices & Seasonings
FOOD PRDTS, WHOLESALE: Water, Distilled
FOOD PRDTS: Almond Pastes
FOOD PRDTS: Animal & marine fats & oils
FOOD PRDTS: Baking Powder
FOOD PRDTS: Box Lunches, For Sale Off Premises
FOOD PRDTS: Butter, Renovated & Processed
FOOD PRDTS: Cheese Curls & Puffs
FOOD PRDTS: Chicken, Processed, Fresh
FOOD PRDTS: Chili Pepper Or Powder
FOOD PRDTS: Coffee
FOOD PRDTS: Corn & other vegetable starches
FOOD PRDTS: Corn Chips & Other Corn-Based Snacks
FOOD PRDTS: Corn Meal
FOOD PRDTS: Corn Oil, Refined
FOOD PRDTS: Dessert Mixes & Fillings

FOOD PRDTS: Dips, Exc Cheese & Sour Cream Based
FOOD PRDTS: Doughs, Frozen Or Refrig From Purchased Flour
FOOD PRDTS: Dressings, Salad, Raw & Cooked Exc Dry Mixes
FOOD PRDTS: Dried & Dehydrated Fruits, Vegetables & Soup Mix
FOOD PRDTS: Duck Slaughtering & Processing
FOOD PRDTS: Edible fats & oils
FOOD PRDTS: Edible Oil Prdts, Exc Corn Oil
FOOD PRDTS: Fish Oil
FOOD PRDTS: Flour & Other Grain Mill Products
FOOD PRDTS: Flour Mixes & Doughs
FOOD PRDTS: Fruit Juices
FOOD PRDTS: Fruits & Vegetables, Pickled
FOOD PRDTS: Ice, Cubes
FOOD PRDTS: Malt
FOOD PRDTS: Mixes, Pancake From Purchased Flour
FOOD PRDTS: Mixes, Pizza
FOOD PRDTS: Mixes, Sauces, Dry
FOOD PRDTS: Mixes, Seasonings, Dry
FOOD PRDTS: Oil, Hydrogenated, Edible
FOOD PRDTS: Olive Oil
FOOD PRDTS: Pasta, Uncooked, Packaged With Other Ingredients
FOOD PRDTS: Peanut Butter
FOOD PRDTS: Pickles, Vinegar
FOOD PRDTS: Potato Chips & Other Potato-Based Snacks
FOOD PRDTS: Sandwiches
FOOD PRDTS: Seasonings & Spices
FOOD PRDTS: Starch, Corn
FOOD PRDTS: Sugar
FOOD PRDTS: Syrup, Maple
FOOD PRDTS: Syrups
FOOD PRDTS: Tea
FOOD PRDTS: Vegetable Oil Mills, NEC
FOOD PRDTS: Wheat Flour
FOOD PRODUCTS MACHINERY
FOOD STORES: Grocery, Chain
FOOD STORES: Grocery, Independent
FOOD STORES: Supermarkets, Chain
FOOD STORES: Supermarkets, Independent
FOOD WARMING EQPT: Commercial
FOOTWEAR, WHOLESALE: Boots
FOOTWEAR: Cut Stock
FORGINGS: Aluminum
FORGINGS: Automotive & Internal Combustion Engine
FORGINGS: Bearing & Bearing Race, Nonferrous
FORGINGS: Construction Or Mining Eqpt, Ferrous
FORGINGS: Engine Or Turbine, Nonferrous
FORGINGS: Gear & Chain
FORGINGS: Iron & Steel
FORGINGS: Machinery, Nonferrous
FORGINGS: Metal , Ornamental, Ferrous
FORGINGS: Nonferrous
FORGINGS: Nuclear Power Plant, Ferrous
FORGINGS: Pump & Compressor, Ferrous
FORMS: Concrete, Sheet Metal
FOUNDRIES: Aluminum
FOUNDRIES: Gray & Ductile Iron
FOUNDRIES: Iron
FOUNDRIES: Nonferrous
FOUNDRIES: Steel
FOUNDRIES: Steel Investment
FOUNDRY MACHINERY & EQPT
FRACTIONATION PRDTS OF CRUDE PETROLEUM, HYDROCARBONS, NEC
FRAMES & FRAMING WHOLESALE
FRAMES: Chair, Metal
FRICTION MATERIAL, MADE FROM POWDERED METAL
FUEL ADDITIVES
FUEL BRIQUETTES & WAXES
FUEL CELLS: Solid State
FUEL DEALERS: Coal
FUEL OIL DEALERS
FUELS: Diesel
FUELS: Nuclear
FUNGICIDES OR HERBICIDES
FURNACE CASINGS: Sheet Metal
FURNACES & OVENS: Indl
FURNACES: Indl, Electric
FURNITURE COMPONENTS: Porcelain Enameled
FURNITURE PARTS: Metal

PRODUCT INDEX

FURNITURE REPAIR & MAINTENANCE SVCS
FURNITURE STOCK & PARTS: Hardwood
FURNITURE STOCK & PARTS: Turnings, Wood
FURNITURE STORES
FURNITURE WHOLESALERS
FURNITURE, HOUSEHOLD: Wholesalers
FURNITURE, OFFICE: Wholesalers
FURNITURE, OUTDOOR & LAWN: Wholesalers
FURNITURE, WHOLESALE: Lockers
FURNITURE: Bedroom, Wood
FURNITURE: Box Springs, Assembled
FURNITURE: Cabinets & Filing Drawers, Office, Exc Wood
FURNITURE: Cabinets & Vanities, Medicine, Metal
FURNITURE: Chair & Couch Springs, Assembled
FURNITURE: Chairs, Household Upholstered
FURNITURE: Chairs, Household Wood
FURNITURE: Chairs, Office Wood
FURNITURE: Console Tables, Wood
FURNITURE: Dining Room, Wood
FURNITURE: Fiberglass & Plastic
FURNITURE: Foundations & Platforms
FURNITURE: Garden, Exc Wood, Metal, Stone Or Concrete
FURNITURE: Hotel
FURNITURE: Household, Metal
FURNITURE: Household, Upholstered, Exc Wood Or Metal
FURNITURE: Juvenile, Wood
FURNITURE: Laboratory
FURNITURE: Living Room, Upholstered On Wood Frames
FURNITURE: Mattresses & Foundations
FURNITURE: Mattresses, Box & Bedsprings
FURNITURE: Mattresses, Innerspring Or Box Spring
FURNITURE: Novelty, Wood
FURNITURE: Office, Exc Wood
FURNITURE: Office, Wood
FURNITURE: Picnic Tables Or Benches, Park
FURNITURE: Recliners, Upholstered On Wood Frames
FURNITURE: School
FURNITURE: Sofa Beds Or Convertible Sofas)
FURNITURE: Storage Chests, Household, Wood
FURNITURE: Table Tops, Marble
FURNITURE: Tables, Household, Metal
FURNITURE: Tables, Office, Wood
FURNITURE: Upholstered
FURNITURE: Vehicle
FURNITURE: Waterbed Frames, Wood
FUSES & FUSE EQPT

G

GAMES & TOYS: Baby Carriages & Restraint Seats
GAMES & TOYS: Board Games, Children's & Adults'
GAMES & TOYS: Child Restraint Seats, Automotive
GAMES & TOYS: Craft & Hobby Kits & Sets
GAMES & TOYS: Electronic
GARBAGE CONTAINERS: Plastic
GAS & OIL FIELD EXPLORATION SVCS
GAS & OIL FIELD SVCS, NEC
GAS FIELD MACHINERY & EQPT
GAS PRODUCTION & DISTRIBUTION: Coke Oven
GAS: Refinery
GASES & LIQUIFIED PETROLEUM GASES
GASES: Carbon Dioxide
GASES: Indl
GASES: Nitrogen
GASES: Oxygen
GASKET MATERIALS
GASKETS
GASKETS & SEALING DEVICES
GASOLINE FILLING STATIONS
GEARS
GEARS & GEAR UNITS: Reduction, Exc Auto
GEARS: Power Transmission, Exc Auto
GENERATING APPARATUS & PARTS: Electrical
GENERATION EQPT: Electronic
GENERATORS SETS: Steam
GENERATORS: Gas
GENERATORS: Vehicles, Gas-Electric Or Oil-Electric
GIFT SHOP
GIFT WRAP: Paper, Made From Purchased Materials
GIFT, NOVELTY & SOUVENIR STORES: Gifts & Novelties
GIFTS & NOVELTIES: Wholesalers
GLASS PRDTS, FROM PURCHASED GLASS: Glassware
GLASS PRDTS, FROM PURCHASED GLASS: Mirrored

GLASS PRDTS, FROM PURCHASED GLASS: Mirrors, Framed
GLASS PRDTS, FROM PURCHASED GLASS: Windshields
GLASS PRDTS, FROM PURCHD GLASS: Strengthened Or Reinforced
GLASS PRDTS, PRESSED OR BLOWN: Furnishings & Access
GLASS PRDTS, PRESSED OR BLOWN: Glass Fibers, Textile
GLASS PRDTS, PRESSED OR BLOWN: Glassware, Art Or Decorative
GLASS: Fiber
GLASS: Flat
GLASS: Leaded
GLASS: Pressed & Blown, NEC
GOLF CARTS: Wholesalers
GOLF COURSES: Public
GOLF EQPT
GOLF GOODS & EQPT
GOURMET FOOD STORES
GRADING SVCS
GRANITE: Cut & Shaped
GRAPHIC ARTS & RELATED DESIGN SVCS
GRATINGS: Tread, Fabricated Metal
GRAVEL MINING
GREASES: Lubricating
GREENHOUSES: Prefabricated Metal
GRINDING SVC: Precision, Commercial Or Indl
GRINDING SVCS: Ophthalmic Lens, Exc Prescription
GROCERIES, GENERAL LINE WHOLESALERS
GUARD PROTECTIVE SVCS
GUIDED MISSILES & SPACE VEHICLES
GUIDED MISSILES & SPACE VEHICLES: Research & Development
GUM & WOOD CHEMICALS
GUTTERS: Sheet Metal
GYPSUM BOARD
GYPSUM PRDTS

H

HAIR & HAIR BASED PRDTS
HAIR CARE PRDTS
HAIR DRESSING, FOR THE TRADE
HAND TOOLS, NEC: Wholesalers
HANDBAGS
HANDBAGS: Women's
HANDYMAN SVCS
HARDWARE
HARDWARE & BUILDING PRDTS: Plastic
HARDWARE & EQPT: Stage, Exc Lighting
HARDWARE STORES
HARDWARE STORES: Builders'
HARDWARE STORES: Pumps & Pumping Eqpt
HARDWARE STORES: Tools
HARDWARE WHOLESALERS
HARDWARE, WHOLESALE: Builders', NEC
HARDWARE, WHOLESALE: Chains
HARDWARE, WHOLESALE: Security Devices, Locks
HARDWARE: Aircraft
HARDWARE: Builders'
HARDWARE: Casket
HARDWARE: Door Opening & Closing Devices, Exc Electrical
HARDWARE: Furniture
HARDWARE: Furniture, Builders' & Other Household
HARNESS ASSEMBLIES: Cable & Wire
HARNESS WIRING SETS: Internal Combustion Engines
HEALTH AIDS: Exercise Eqpt
HEARING AIDS
HEAT EXCHANGERS: After Or Inter Coolers Or Condensers, Etc
HEAT TREATING: Metal
HEATERS: Space, Exc Electric
HEATING & AIR CONDITIONING UNITS, COMBINATION
HEATING EQPT: Complete
HEATING EQPT: Induction
HEATING PADS: Nonelectric
HEATING UNITS & DEVICES: Indl, Electric
HELICOPTERS
HELMETS: Athletic
HELMETS: Steel
HITCHES: Trailer
HOBBY, TOY & GAME STORES: Arts & Crafts & Splys
HOISTING SLINGS
HOISTS

HOLDING COMPANIES: Investment, Exc Banks
HOLDING COMPANIES: Personal, Exc Banks
HOME ENTERTAINMENT EQPT: Electronic, NEC
HOME HEALTH CARE SVCS
HOMEFURNISHING STORES: Pottery
HOMEFURNISHING STORES: Venetian Blinds
HOMEFURNISHINGS, WHOLESALE: Blinds, Vertical
HOMEFURNISHINGS, WHOLESALE: Carpets
HOMEFURNISHINGS, WHOLESALE: Decorating Splys
HOMEFURNISHINGS, WHOLESALE: Draperies
HOMEFURNISHINGS, WHOLESALE: Wood Flooring
HOMES: Log Cabins
HONING & LAPPING MACHINES
HORSESHOES
HOSE: Flexible Metal
HOSE: Plastic
HOSE: Pneumatic, Rubber Or Rubberized Fabric, NEC
HOSE: Rubber
HOT TUBS
HOT TUBS: Plastic & Fiberglass
HOTELS & MOTELS
HOUSEHOLD APPLIANCE STORES: Appliance Parts
HOUSEHOLD ARTICLES, EXC KITCHEN: Pottery
HOUSEHOLD ARTICLES: Metal
HOUSEHOLD FURNISHINGS, NEC
HOUSEHOLD SEWING MACHINES WHOLESALERS: Electric
HOUSEWARES, ELECTRIC: Cooking Appliances
HOUSEWARES, ELECTRIC: Fans, Exhaust & Ventilating
HOUSEWARES, ELECTRIC: Heating Units, Electric Appliances
HOUSEWARES: Dishes, Plastic
HOUSINGS: Business Machine, Sheet Metal
HYDRAULIC EQPT REPAIR SVC

I

ICE
IGNITER GRAINS: Boron Potassium Nitrate
IGNITION SYSTEMS: High Frequency
INDL & PERSONAL SVC PAPER WHOLESALERS
INDL & PERSONAL SVC PAPER, WHOLESALE: Boxes & Containers
INDL & PERSONAL SVC PAPER, WHOLESALE: Shipping Splys
INDL EQPT SVCS
INDL GASES WHOLESALERS
INDL MACHINERY & EQPT WHOLESALERS
INDL PATTERNS: Foundry Cores
INDL PATTERNS: Foundry Patternmaking
INDL PROCESS INSTRUMENTS: Analyzers
INDL PROCESS INSTRUMENTS: Control
INDL PROCESS INSTRUMENTS: Moisture Meters
INDL PROCESS INSTRUMENTS: On-Stream Gas Or Liquid Analysis
INDL SPLYS WHOLESALERS
INDL SPLYS, WHOLESALE: Abrasives
INDL SPLYS, WHOLESALE: Adhesives, Tape & Plasters
INDL SPLYS, WHOLESALE: Bearings
INDL SPLYS, WHOLESALE: Bins & Containers, Storage
INDL SPLYS, WHOLESALE: Fasteners & Fastening Eqpt
INDL SPLYS, WHOLESALE: Gaskets
INDL SPLYS, WHOLESALE: Gaskets & Seals
INDL SPLYS, WHOLESALE: Gears
INDL SPLYS, WHOLESALE: Power Transmission, Eqpt & Apparatus
INDL SPLYS, WHOLESALE: Rubber Goods, Mechanical
INDL SPLYS, WHOLESALE: Seals
INDL SPLYS, WHOLESALE: Tools
INDL SPLYS, WHOLESALE: Tools, NEC
INDL SPLYS, WHOLESALE: Valves & Fittings
INDL TRUCK REPAIR SVCS
INDUSTRIAL & COMMERCIAL EQPT INSPECTION SVCS
INFORMATION RETRIEVAL SERVICES
INFORMATION SVCS: Consumer
INGOT, EXTRUSION: Extrusion ingot, aluminum: rolling mills
INK: Printing
INSECTICIDES & PESTICIDES
INSPECTION & TESTING SVCS
INSTRUMENTS, LABORATORY: Differential Thermal Analysis
INSTRUMENTS, LABORATORY: Spectrometers
INSTRUMENTS, MEASURING & CNTRL: Radiation & Testing, Nuclear

PRODUCT INDEX

INSTRUMENTS, MEASURING & CNTRLG: Aircraft & Motor Vehicle
INSTRUMENTS, MEASURING & CONTROLLING: Gas Detectors
INSTRUMENTS, MEASURING & CONTROLLING: Ion Chambers
INSTRUMENTS, SURGICAL & MED: Fixation Appliances, Internal
INSTRUMENTS, SURGICAL & MED: Needles & Syringes, Hypodermic
INSTRUMENTS, SURGICAL & MEDICAL: Blood & Bone Work
INSTRUMENTS, SURGICAL & MEDICAL: Blood Transfusion
INSTRUMENTS, SURGICAL & MEDICAL: Catheters
INSTRUMENTS, SURGICAL & MEDICAL: Inhalation Therapy
INSTRUMENTS, SURGICAL & MEDICAL: IV Transfusion
INSTRUMENTS, SURGICAL & MEDICAL: Muscle Exercise, Ophthalmic
INSTRUMENTS, SURGICAL & MEDICAL: Ophthalmic
INSTRUMENTS, SURGICAL & MEDICAL: Plates & Screws, Bone
INSTRUMENTS: Analytical
INSTRUMENTS: Flow, Indl Process
INSTRUMENTS: Indl Process Control
INSTRUMENTS: Laser, Scientific & Engineering
INSTRUMENTS: Measurement, Indl Process
INSTRUMENTS: Measuring, Electrical Energy
INSTRUMENTS: Medical & Surgical
INSTRUMENTS: Nautical
INSTRUMENTS: Power Measuring, Electrical
INSTRUMENTS: Pressure Measurement, Indl
INSTRUMENTS: Temperature Measurement, Indl
INSTRUMENTS: Test, Electrical, Engine
INSTRUMENTS: Test, Electronic & Electric Measurement
INSTRUMENTS: Test, Electronic & Electrical Circuits
INSULATION & ROOFING MATERIALS: Wood, Reconstituted
INSULATION MATERIALS WHOLESALERS
INSULATION: Fiberglass
INSULATORS & INSULATION MATERIALS: Electrical
INSURANCE AGENTS, NEC
INTEGRATED CIRCUITS, SEMICONDUCTOR NETWORKS, ETC
INTERIOR DECORATING SVCS
INTERIOR DESIGN SVCS, NEC
INTRAVENOUS SOLUTIONS
INVERTERS: Nonrotating Electrical
INVESTORS, NEC
INVESTORS: Real Estate, Exc Property Operators
IRON & STEEL PRDTS: Hot-Rolled
IRON ORE MINING
IRON ORES
IRRADIATION EQPT

J

JACKS: Hydraulic
JEWELRY REPAIR SVCS
JEWELRY STORES
JEWELRY STORES: Precious Stones & Precious Metals
JEWELRY STORES: Silverware
JEWELRY STORES: Watches
JEWELRY, PRECIOUS METAL: Rings, Finger
JEWELRY, PRECIOUS METAL: Settings & Mountings
JEWELRY, WHOLESALE
JEWELRY: Precious Metal
JIGS & FIXTURES
JOB PRINTING & NEWSPAPER PUBLISHING COMBINED
JOB TRAINING SVCS
JOISTS: Long-Span Series, Open Web Steel

K

KILNS & FURNACES: Ceramic
KITCHEN CABINETS WHOLESALERS
KITCHEN UTENSILS: Food Handling & Processing Prdts, Wood
KITCHENWARE STORES
KITCHENWARE: Plastic
KNIVES: Agricultural Or indl

L

LABELS: Cotton, Printed
LABELS: Paper, Made From Purchased Materials
LABORATORIES, TESTING: Food
LABORATORIES, TESTING: Pollution
LABORATORIES, TESTING: Product Testing
LABORATORIES, TESTING: Product Testing, Safety/Performance
LABORATORIES, TESTING: Radiation
LABORATORIES: Biological
LABORATORIES: Biotechnology
LABORATORIES: Commercial Nonphysical Research
LABORATORIES: Dental, Crown & Bridge Production
LABORATORIES: Electronic Research
LABORATORIES: Noncommercial Research
LABORATORIES: Physical Research, Commercial
LABORATORIES: Testing
LABORATORIES: Testing
LABORATORY APPARATUS & FURNITURE
LABORATORY APPARATUS, EXC HEATING & MEASURING
LABORATORY APPARATUS: Pipettes, Hemocytometer
LABORATORY CHEMICALS: Organic
LABORATORY EQPT, EXC MEDICAL: Wholesalers
LABORATORY EQPT: Chemical
LABORATORY EQPT: Clinical Instruments Exc Medical
LABORATORY EQPT: Incubators
LABORATORY EQPT: Sterilizers
LADDERS: Metal
LADDERS: Permanent Installation, Metal
LAMINATED PLASTICS: Plate, Sheet, Rod & Tubes
LAMINATING MATERIALS
LAMINATING SVCS
LAMP & LIGHT BULBS & TUBES
LAMP BULBS & TUBES, ELECTRIC: For Specialized Applications
LAMP BULBS & TUBES, ELECTRIC: Light, Complete
LAMP BULBS & TUBES/PARTS, ELECTRIC: Generalized Applications
LAMP SHADES: Glass
LAND SUBDIVIDERS & DEVELOPERS: Commercial
LASER SYSTEMS & EQPT
LASERS: Welding, Drilling & Cutting Eqpt
LAUNDRY EQPT: Commercial
LAUNDRY EQPT: Household
LAWN & GARDEN EQPT
LAWN & GARDEN EQPT: Blowers & Vacuums
LAWN & GARDEN EQPT: Grass Catchers, Lawn Mower
LAWN & GARDEN EQPT: Lawnmowers, Residential, Hand Or Power
LAWN & GARDEN EQPT: Tractors & Eqpt
LEAD
LEAD PENCILS & ART GOODS
LEASING & RENTAL: Construction & Mining Eqpt
LEASING & RENTAL: Medical Machinery & Eqpt
LEASING & RENTAL: Trucks, Without Drivers
LEASING: Passenger Car
LEATHER GOODS: Garments
LEATHER GOODS: Holsters
LEATHER GOODS: Personal
LEATHER GOODS: Safety Belts
LEATHER GOODS: Straps
LEATHER TANNING & FINISHING
LEATHER: Accessory Prdts
LEGAL & TAX SVCS
LEGAL OFFICES & SVCS
LICENSE TAGS: Automobile, Stamped Metal
LIFE SAVING & SURVIVAL EQPT REPAIR SVCS, NONMEDICAL
LIFESAVING & SURVIVAL EQPT, EXC MEDICAL, WHOLESALE
LIGHTING EQPT: Flashlights
LIGHTING EQPT: Motor Vehicle, Headlights
LIGHTING EQPT: Motor Vehicle, NEC
LIGHTING FIXTURES WHOLESALERS
LIGHTING FIXTURES, NEC
LIGHTING FIXTURES: Decorative Area
LIGHTING FIXTURES: Fluorescent, Commercial
LIGHTING FIXTURES: Indl & Commercial
LIGHTING FIXTURES: Motor Vehicle
LIGHTING FIXTURES: Public
LIGHTING MAINTENANCE SVC
LIME
LIMESTONE: Crushed & Broken
LIMESTONE: Cut & Shaped
LIMESTONE: Dimension
LIMESTONE: Ground
LINERS & COVERS: Fabric
LININGS: Fabric, Apparel & Other, Exc Millinery
LIP BALMS
LIQUEFIED PETROLEUM GAS DEALERS
LITHOGRAPHIC PLATES
LIVESTOCK WHOLESALERS, NEC
LOCKERS
LOCKS
LOCKS & LOCK SETS, WHOLESALE
LOCKS: Coin-Operated
LOCKSMITHS
LOCOMOTIVES & PARTS
LOGGING
LOGGING CAMPS & CONTRACTORS
LOGGING: Timber, Cut At Logging Camp
LOGGING: Wooden Logs
LOTIONS OR CREAMS: Face
LOTIONS: SHAVING
LOUDSPEAKERS
LUBRICANTS: Corrosion Preventive
LUBRICATING EQPT: Indl
LUBRICATING OIL & GREASE WHOLESALERS
LUBRICATION SYSTEMS & EQPT
LUGGAGE & BRIEFCASES
LUGGAGE: Traveling Bags
LUMBER & BLDG MATLS DEALER, RET: Electric Constructn Matls
LUMBER & BLDG MATLS DEALER, RET: Garage Doors, Sell/Install
LUMBER & BLDG MATRLS DEALERS, RET: Bath Fixtures, Eqpt/Sply
LUMBER & BLDG MTRLS DEALERS, RET: Planing Mill Prdts/Lumber
LUMBER & BUILDING MATERIAL DEALERS, RETAIL: Roofing Material
LUMBER & BUILDING MATERIALS DEALER, RET: Door & Window Prdts
LUMBER & BUILDING MATERIALS DEALER, RET: Masonry Matls/Splys
LUMBER & BUILDING MATERIALS DEALERS, RET: Solar Heating Eqpt
LUMBER & BUILDING MATERIALS DEALERS, RETAIL: Brick
LUMBER & BUILDING MATERIALS DEALERS, RETAIL: Cement
LUMBER & BUILDING MATERIALS DEALERS, RETAIL: Modular Homes
LUMBER & BUILDING MATERIALS DEALERS, RETAIL: Sand & Gravel
LUMBER & BUILDING MATERIALS DEALERS, RETAIL: Siding
LUMBER & BUILDING MATERIALS RET DEALERS: Millwork & Lumber
LUMBER & BUILDING MATLS DEALERS, RET: Concrete/Cinder Block
LUMBER: Dimension, Hardwood
LUMBER: Fiberboard
LUMBER: Hardwood Dimension
LUMBER: Hardwood Dimension & Flooring Mills
LUMBER: Kiln Dried
LUMBER: Panels, Plywood, Softwood
LUMBER: Plywood, Hardwood
LUMBER: Plywood, Hardwood or Hardwood Faced
LUMBER: Plywood, Prefinished, Hardwood
LUMBER: Plywood, Softwood
LUMBER: Rails, Fence, Round Or Split
LUMBER: Resawn, Small Dimension
LUMBER: Treated
LUMBER: Veneer, Softwood

M

MACHINE PARTS: Stamped Or Pressed Metal
MACHINE TOOL ACCESS: Cams
MACHINE TOOL ACCESS: Drills
MACHINE TOOL ACCESS: Files
MACHINE TOOL ACCESS: Tools & Access
MACHINE TOOL ATTACHMENTS & ACCESS
MACHINE TOOLS & ACCESS
MACHINE TOOLS, METAL CUTTING: Exotic, Including Explosive
MACHINE TOOLS, METAL CUTTING: Home Workshop
MACHINE TOOLS, METAL CUTTING: Lathes
MACHINE TOOLS, METAL CUTTING: Numerically Controlled
MACHINE TOOLS, METAL CUTTING: Plasma Process
MACHINE TOOLS, METAL CUTTING: Saws, Power

PRODUCT INDEX

MACHINE TOOLS, METAL CUTTING: Tool Replacement & Rpr Parts
MACHINE TOOLS, METAL CUTTING: Vertical Turning & Boring
MACHINE TOOLS, METAL FORMING: Headers
MACHINE TOOLS, METAL FORMING: Magnetic Forming
MACHINE TOOLS, METAL FORMING: Marking
MACHINE TOOLS, METAL FORMING: Mechanical, Pneumatic Or Hyd
MACHINE TOOLS, METAL FORMING: Pressing
MACHINE TOOLS, METAL FORMING: Punching & Shearing
MACHINE TOOLS, METAL FORMING: Rebuilt
MACHINE TOOLS: Metal Cutting
MACHINE TOOLS: Metal Forming
MACHINERY & EQPT, AGRICULTURAL, WHOLESALE: Landscaping Eqpt
MACHINERY & EQPT, AGRICULTURAL, WHOLESALE: Lawn
MACHINERY & EQPT, AGRICULTURAL, WHOLESALE: Lawn & Garden
MACHINERY & EQPT, INDL, WHOLESALE: Chemical Process
MACHINERY & EQPT, INDL, WHOLESALE: Conveyor Systems
MACHINERY & EQPT, INDL, WHOLESALE: Engines & Parts, Diesel
MACHINERY & EQPT, INDL, WHOLESALE: Engs/ Transportation Eqpt
MACHINERY & EQPT, INDL, WHOLESALE: Heat Exchange
MACHINERY & EQPT, INDL, WHOLESALE: Hydraulic Systems
MACHINERY & EQPT, INDL, WHOLESALE: Indl Machine Parts
MACHINERY & EQPT, INDL, WHOLESALE: Instruments & Cntrl Eqpt
MACHINERY & EQPT, INDL, WHOLESALE: Lift Trucks & Parts
MACHINERY & EQPT, INDL, WHOLESALE: Machine Tools & Access
MACHINERY & EQPT, INDL, WHOLESALE: Machine Tools & Metalwork
MACHINERY & EQPT, INDL, WHOLESALE: Measure/Test, Electric
MACHINERY & EQPT, INDL, WHOLESALE: Petroleum Industry
MACHINERY & EQPT, INDL, WHOLESALE: Processing & Packaging
MACHINERY & EQPT, INDL, WHOLESALE: Safety Eqpt
MACHINERY & EQPT, INDL, WHOLESALE: Sawmill
MACHINERY & EQPT, INDL, WHOLESALE: Sewing
MACHINERY & EQPT, INDL, WHOLESALE: Trailers, Indl
MACHINERY & EQPT, INDL, WHOLESALE: Water Pumps
MACHINERY & EQPT, WHOLESALE: Construction, General
MACHINERY & EQPT: Farm
MACHINERY & EQPT: Liquid Automation
MACHINERY, EQPT & SUPPLIES: Parking Facility
MACHINERY, FOOD PRDTS: Cutting, Chopping, Grinding, Mixing
MACHINERY, FOOD PRDTS: Dairy & Milk
MACHINERY, FOOD PRDTS: Ovens, Bakery
MACHINERY, MAILING: Postage Meters
MACHINERY, METALWORKING: Coilers, Metalworking
MACHINERY, PAPER INDUSTRY: Converting, Die Cutting & Stampng
MACHINERY, PRINTING TRADES: Plates
MACHINERY, WOODWORKING: Sanding, Exc Portable Floor Sanders
MACHINERY: Ammunition & Explosives Loading
MACHINERY: Automotive Related
MACHINERY: Bridge Or Gate, Hydraulic
MACHINERY: Construction
MACHINERY: Cryogenic, Industrial
MACHINERY: Custom
MACHINERY: Desalination Eqpt
MACHINERY: Electronic Component Making
MACHINERY: Gas Separators
MACHINERY: Ice Cream
MACHINERY: Ice Making
MACHINERY: Metalworking
MACHINERY: Mining
MACHINERY: Packaging
MACHINERY: Paint Making
MACHINERY: Plastic Working
MACHINERY: Pottery Making
MACHINERY: Printing Presses
MACHINERY: Recycling
MACHINERY: Road Construction & Maintenance
MACHINERY: Rubber Working
MACHINERY: Semiconductor Manufacturing
MACHINERY: Textile
MACHINERY: Wire Drawing
MACHINERY: Woodworking
MACHINISTS' TOOLS & MACHINES: Measuring, Metalworking Type
MACHINISTS' TOOLS: Precision
MAGAZINES, WHOLESALE
MAGNESIUM
MAGNETIC SHIELDS, METAL
MAGNETIC TAPE, AUDIO: Prerecorded
MAGNETS: Permanent
MAIL-ORDER HOUSE, NEC
MAIL-ORDER HOUSES: Educational Splys & Eqpt
MAIL-ORDER HOUSES: Fitness & Sporting Goods
MAILBOX RENTAL & RELATED SVCS
MAILING SVCS, NEC
MANAGEMENT CONSULTING SVCS: Administrative
MANAGEMENT CONSULTING SVCS: Automation & Robotics
MANAGEMENT CONSULTING SVCS: Business
MANAGEMENT CONSULTING SVCS: Construction Project
MANAGEMENT CONSULTING SVCS: Distribution Channels
MANAGEMENT CONSULTING SVCS: General
MANAGEMENT CONSULTING SVCS: Hospital & Health
MANAGEMENT CONSULTING SVCS: Industrial
MANAGEMENT CONSULTING SVCS: Industrial & Labor
MANAGEMENT CONSULTING SVCS: Industry Specialist
MANAGEMENT CONSULTING SVCS: Information Systems
MANAGEMENT CONSULTING SVCS: Manufacturing
MANAGEMENT CONSULTING SVCS: Quality Assurance
MANAGEMENT CONSULTING SVCS: Real Estate
MANAGEMENT CONSULTING SVCS: Training & Development
MANAGEMENT CONSULTING SVCS: Transportation
MANAGEMENT SERVICES
MANAGEMENT SVCS: Business
MANAGEMENT SVCS: Construction
MANPOWER TRAINING
MANUFACTURING INDUSTRIES, NEC
MARBLE, BUILDING: Cut & Shaped
MARINAS
MARINE CARGO HANDLING SVCS
MARINE CARGO HANDLING SVCS: Marine Terminal
MARINE HARDWARE
MARINE RELATED EQPT
MARINE SPLYS WHOLESALERS
MARKETS: Meat & fish
MARKING DEVICES
MARKING DEVICES: Canceling Stamps, Hand, Rubber Or Metal
MARKING DEVICES: Embossing Seals & Hand Stamps
MATS OR MATTING, NEC: Rubber
MATS, MATTING & PADS: Nonwoven
MEAT MARKETS
MEAT PRDTS: Boxed Beef, From Slaughtered Meat
MEAT PRDTS: Dried Beef, From Purchased Meat
MEAT PRDTS: Frozen
MEAT PRDTS: Prepared Beef Prdts From Purchased Beef
MEAT PRDTS: Roast Beef, From Purchased Meat
MEAT PRDTS: Sausages & Related Prdts, From Purchased Meat
MEAT PRDTS: Snack Sticks, Incl Jerky, From Purchased Meat
MECHANISMS: Coin-Operated Machines
MEDIA: Magnetic & Optical Recording
MEDICAL & HOSPITAL EQPT WHOLESALERS
MEDICAL & SURGICAL SPLYS: Bandages & Dressings
MEDICAL & SURGICAL SPLYS: Braces, Orthopedic
MEDICAL & SURGICAL SPLYS: Clothing, Fire Resistant & Protect
MEDICAL & SURGICAL SPLYS: Ear Plugs
MEDICAL & SURGICAL SPLYS: Limbs, Artificial
MEDICAL & SURGICAL SPLYS: Orthopedic Appliances
MEDICAL & SURGICAL SPLYS: Personal Safety Eqpt
MEDICAL & SURGICAL SPLYS: Prosthetic Appliances
MEDICAL CENTERS
MEDICAL EQPT REPAIR SVCS, NON-ELECTRIC
MEDICAL EQPT: Diagnostic
MEDICAL EQPT: Electromedical Apparatus
MEDICAL EQPT: Electrotherapeutic Apparatus
MEDICAL EQPT: Sterilizers
MEDICAL EQPT: Ultrasonic Scanning Devices
MEDICAL EQPT: Ultrasonic, Exc Cleaning
MEDICAL SUNDRIES: Rubber
MEMBERSHIP ORGANIZATIONS, NEC: Personal Interest
MEMBERSHIP ORGANIZATIONS, PROFESSIONAL: Health Association
MEMBERSHIP ORGANIZATIONS, RELIGIOUS: Baptist Church
MEMBERSHIP ORGANIZATIONS, RELIGIOUS: Catholic Church
MEMBERSHIP ORGANIZATIONS, RELIGIOUS: Methodist Church
MEMBERSHIP ORGS, RELIGIOUS: Non-Denominational Church
MEN'S & BOYS' CLOTHING ACCESS STORES
MEN'S & BOYS' CLOTHING WHOLESALERS, NEC
MEN'S & BOYS' SPORTSWEAR CLOTHING STORES
METAL & STEEL PRDTS: Abrasive
METAL COMPONENTS: Prefabricated
METAL DETECTORS
METAL FABRICATORS: Plate
METAL FINISHING SVCS
METAL MINING SVCS
METAL SERVICE CENTERS & OFFICES
METAL STAMPING, FOR THE TRADE
METAL STAMPINGS: Perforated
METAL TREATING COMPOUNDS
METALS SVC CENTERS & WHOLESALERS: Cable, Wire
METALS SVC CENTERS & WHOLESALERS: Ferrous Metals
METALS SVC CENTERS & WHOLESALERS: Flat Prdts, Iron Or Steel
METALS SVC CENTERS & WHOLESALERS: Foundry Prdts
METALS SVC CENTERS & WHOLESALERS: Pipe & Tubing, Steel
METALS SVC CENTERS & WHOLESALERS: Sheets, Metal
METALS SVC CENTERS & WHOLESALERS: Steel
METALS SVC CENTERS & WHOLESALERS: Tubing, Metal
METALS: Antifriction Bearing, Lead-Base
METALS: Precious NEC
METALS: Primary Nonferrous, NEC
METALWORK: Miscellaneous
METALWORK: Ornamental
METALWORKING MACHINERY WHOLESALERS
METERING DEVICES: Gasoline Dispensing
METERING DEVICES: Water Quality Monitoring & Control Systems
MICROCIRCUITS, INTEGRATED: Semiconductor
MICROWAVE COMPONENTS
MILITARY GOODS & REGALIA STORES
MILITARY INSIGNIA, TEXTILE
MILL PRDTS: Structural & Rail
MILLWORK
MINE & QUARRY SVCS: Nonmetallic Minerals
MINE DEVELOPMENT, METAL
MINE PREPARATION SVCS
MINERAL WOOL
MINERALS: Ground Or Otherwise Treated
MINERALS: Ground or Treated
MINIATURES
MINING EXPLORATION & DEVELOPMENT SVCS
MINING MACHINERY & EQPT WHOLESALERS
MISSILE GUIDANCE SYSTEMS & EQPT
MIXTURES & BLOCKS: Asphalt Paving
MOBILE COMMUNICATIONS EQPT
MOBILE HOME FRAMES
MOBILE HOMES
MOBILE HOMES: Personal Or Private Use
MODELS: General, Exc Toy
MODULES: Computer Logic
MOLDED RUBBER PRDTS
MOLDING COMPOUNDS
MOLDINGS & TRIM: Wood
MOLDINGS OR TRIM: Automobile, Stamped Metal
MOLDS: Indl
MONUMENTS & GRAVE MARKERS, WHOLESALE
MOPS: Floor & Dust
MOTION PICTURE & VIDEO DISTRIBUTION
MOTION PICTURE & VIDEO PRODUCTION SVCS
MOTION PICTURE & VIDEO PRODUCTION SVCS: Educational
MOTOR & GENERATOR PARTS: Electric

PRODUCT INDEX

MOTOR HOMES
MOTOR VEHICLE ASSEMBLY, COMPLETE: Ambulances
MOTOR VEHICLE ASSEMBLY, COMPLETE: Buses, All Types
MOTOR VEHICLE ASSEMBLY, COMPLETE: Fire Department Vehicles
MOTOR VEHICLE ASSEMBLY, COMPLETE: Military Motor Vehicle
MOTOR VEHICLE ASSEMBLY, COMPLETE: Universal Carriers, Mil
MOTOR VEHICLE ASSEMBLY, COMPLETE: Wreckers, Tow Truck
MOTOR VEHICLE DEALERS: Automobiles, New & Used
MOTOR VEHICLE PARTS & ACCESS: Air Conditioner Parts
MOTOR VEHICLE PARTS & ACCESS: Anti-Sway Devices
MOTOR VEHICLE PARTS & ACCESS: Bearings
MOTOR VEHICLE PARTS & ACCESS: Body Components & Frames
MOTOR VEHICLE PARTS & ACCESS: Brakes, Air
MOTOR VEHICLE PARTS & ACCESS: Clutches
MOTOR VEHICLE PARTS & ACCESS: Connecting Rods
MOTOR VEHICLE PARTS & ACCESS: Cylinder Heads
MOTOR VEHICLE PARTS & ACCESS: Electrical Eqpt
MOTOR VEHICLE PARTS & ACCESS: Engines & Parts
MOTOR VEHICLE PARTS & ACCESS: Engs & Trans,Factory, Rebuilt
MOTOR VEHICLE PARTS & ACCESS: Fuel Pumps
MOTOR VEHICLE PARTS & ACCESS: Fuel Systems & Parts
MOTOR VEHICLE PARTS & ACCESS: Gas Tanks
MOTOR VEHICLE PARTS & ACCESS: Gears
MOTOR VEHICLE PARTS & ACCESS: Instrument Board Assemblies
MOTOR VEHICLE PARTS & ACCESS: Lifting Mechanisms, Dump Truck
MOTOR VEHICLE PARTS & ACCESS: Mufflers, Exhaust
MOTOR VEHICLE PARTS & ACCESS: Oil Pumps
MOTOR VEHICLE PARTS & ACCESS: Propane Conversion Eqpt
MOTOR VEHICLE PARTS & ACCESS: Rear Axel Housings
MOTOR VEHICLE PARTS & ACCESS: Thermostats
MOTOR VEHICLE PARTS & ACCESS: Trailer Hitches
MOTOR VEHICLE PARTS & ACCESS: Transmission Housings Or Parts
MOTOR VEHICLE PARTS & ACCESS: Transmissions
MOTOR VEHICLE PARTS & ACCESS: Wipers, Windshield
MOTOR VEHICLE PARTS & ACCESS: Wiring Harness Sets
MOTOR VEHICLE RACING & DRIVER SVCS
MOTOR VEHICLE SPLYS & PARTS WHOLESALERS: New
MOTOR VEHICLE SPLYS & PARTS WHOLESALERS: Used
MOTOR VEHICLE: Hardware
MOTOR VEHICLE: Radiators
MOTOR VEHICLE: Shock Absorbers
MOTOR VEHICLE: Steering Mechanisms
MOTOR VEHICLE: Wheels
MOTOR VEHICLES & CAR BODIES
MOTOR VEHICLES, WHOLESALE: Fire Trucks
MOTOR VEHICLES, WHOLESALE: Truck tractors
MOTOR VEHICLES, WHOLESALE: Trucks, commercial
MOTORCYCLE ACCESS
MOTORCYCLE DEALERS
MOTORCYCLES & RELATED PARTS
MOTORS: Electric
MOTORS: Generators
MOUNTING SVC: Swatches & Samples
MULTIPLEXERS: Telephone & Telegraph
MUSIC DISTRIBUTION APPARATUS
MUSIC LICENSING TO RADIO STATIONS
MUSICAL INSTRUMENTS & ACCESS: Carrying Cases
MUSICAL INSTRUMENTS & ACCESS: NEC
MUSICAL INSTRUMENTS & ACCESS: Pianos
MUSICAL INSTRUMENTS & PARTS: Percussion
MUSICAL INSTRUMENTS & SPLYS STORES: Pianos
MUSICAL INSTRUMENTS WHOLESALERS
MUSICAL INSTRUMENTS: Bassoons
MUSICAL INSTRUMENTS: Guitars & Parts, Electric & Acoustic

N

NAILS WHOLESALERS
NAILS: Steel, Wire Or Cut
NAME PLATES: Engraved Or Etched
NATURAL GAS DISTRIBUTION TO CONSUMERS
NATURAL GAS LIQUIDS PRODUCTION
NATURAL GAS PRODUCTION
NATURAL LIQUEFIED PETROLEUM GAS PRODUCTION
NATURAL PROPANE PRODUCTION
NEW & USED CAR DEALERS
NICKEL
NONCURRENT CARRYING WIRING DEVICES
NONFERROUS: Rolling & Drawing, NEC
NOTEBOOKS, MADE FROM PURCHASED MATERIALS
NOVELTIES
NOVELTIES & SPECIALTIES: Metal
NOVELTIES: Plastic
NOZZLES: Fire Fighting
NURSERIES & LAWN & GARDEN SPLY STORES, RETAIL: Fertilizer
NYLON FIBERS
NYLON RESINS

O

OFFICE EQPT WHOLESALERS
OFFICE EQPT, WHOLESALE: Photocopy Machines
OFFICE SPLY & STATIONERY STORES: Office Forms & Splys
OFFICE SPLYS, NEC, WHOLESALE
OFFICES & CLINICS OF DOCTORS OF MEDICINE: Radiologist
OIL & GAS FIELD EQPT: Drill Rigs
OIL & GAS FIELD MACHINERY
OIL FIELD MACHINERY & EQPT
OIL FIELD SVCS, NEC
OIL TREATING COMPOUNDS
OILS & ESSENTIAL OILS
OILS: Cutting
OINTMENTS
OPHTHALMIC GOODS
OPHTHALMIC GOODS WHOLESALERS
OPHTHALMIC GOODS: Frames & Parts, Eyeglass & Spectacle
OPHTHALMIC GOODS: Lenses, Ophthalmic
OPTICAL GOODS STORES
OPTICAL GOODS STORES: Contact Lenses, Prescription
OPTICAL GOODS STORES: Eyeglasses, Prescription
OPTICAL GOODS STORES: Opticians
OPTICAL INSTRUMENTS & APPARATUS
OPTICAL INSTRUMENTS & LENSES
OPTICAL ISOLATORS
ORGANIZATIONS: Medical Research
ORGANIZATIONS: Religious
ORGANIZATIONS: Research Institute

P

PACKAGE DESIGN SVCS
PACKAGING & LABELING SVCS
PACKAGING MATERIALS, WHOLESALE
PACKAGING MATERIALS: Paper
PACKAGING MATERIALS: Paper, Coated Or Laminated
PACKAGING MATERIALS: Plastic Film, Coated Or Laminated
PACKING & CRATING SVC
PACKING MATERIALS: Mechanical
PACKING: Rubber
PADDING: Foamed Plastics
PAINTS & ADDITIVES
PAINTS & ALLIED PRODUCTS
PAINTS & VARNISHES: Plastics Based
PAINTS, VARNISHES & SPLYS WHOLESALERS
PAINTS, VARNISHES & SPLYS, WHOLESALE: Paints
PAINTS: Oil Or Alkyd Vehicle Or Water Thinned
PAINTS: Waterproof
PALLET REPAIR SVCS
PALLETS & SKIDS: Wood
PALLETS: Plastic
PALLETS: Wood & Metal Combination
PANEL & DISTRIBUTION BOARDS & OTHER RELATED APPARATUS
PANEL & DISTRIBUTION BOARDS: Electric
PANELS & SECTIONS: Prefabricated, Concrete
PANELS: Building, Metal
PANELS: Building, Plastic, NEC
PAPER & BOARD: Die-cut
PAPER PRDTS: Infant & Baby Prdts
PAPER PRDTS: Molded Pulp Prdts
PAPER PRDTS: Napkins, Sanitary, Made From Purchased Material
PAPER PRDTS: Sanitary Tissue Paper
PAPER, WHOLESALE: Printing
PAPER: Adding Machine Rolls, Made From Purchased Materials
PAPER: Adhesive
PAPER: Business Form
PAPER: Cardboard
PAPER: Coated & Laminated, NEC
PAPER: Coated, Exc Photographic, Carbon Or Abrasive
PAPER: Corrugated
PAPER: Newsprint
PAPER: Specialty Or Chemically Treated
PAPER: Wallpaper
PAPER: Waxed, Made From Purchased Materials
PAPER: Wrapping & Packaging
PAPERBOARD PRDTS: Folding Boxboard
PAPERBOARD PRDTS: Packaging Board
PARTITIONS & FIXTURES: Except Wood
PARTITIONS: Wood & Fixtures
PARTS: Metal
PATENT OWNERS & LESSORS
PATTERNS: Indl
PAVERS
PAVING MIXTURES
PENCILS & PENS WHOLESALERS
PERFUME: Perfumes, Natural Or Synthetic
PERFUMES
PERSONAL CREDIT INSTITUTIONS: Consumer Finance Companies
PERSONAL SVCS
PEST CONTROL IN STRUCTURES SVCS
PET FOOD WHOLESALERS
PET SPLYS
PETROLEUM & PETROLEUM PRDTS, WHOLESALE: Bulk Stations
PETROLEUM BULK STATIONS & TERMINALS
PHARMACEUTICAL PREPARATIONS: Druggists' Preparations
PHARMACEUTICAL PREPARATIONS: Pills
PHARMACEUTICAL PREPARATIONS: Proprietary Drug
PHARMACEUTICAL PREPARATIONS: Solutions
PHARMACEUTICAL PREPARATIONS: Tablets
PHARMACEUTICALS
PHOTOCOPYING & DUPLICATING SVCS
PHOTOGRAPHIC & OPTICAL GOODS EQPT REPAIR SVCS
PHOTOGRAPHIC EQPT & SPLYS
PHOTOGRAPHIC EQPT & SPLYS WHOLESALERS
PHOTOGRAPHIC EQPT & SPLYS: Printing Eqpt
PHOTOGRAPHY SVCS: Commercial
PHYSICAL EXAMINATION & TESTING SVCS
PHYSICIANS' OFFICES & CLINICS: Medical doctors
PICTURE FRAMES: Metal
PICTURE FRAMES: Wood
PICTURE FRAMING SVCS, CUSTOM
PIECE GOODS & NOTIONS WHOLESALERS
PIECE GOODS, NOTIONS & DRY GOODS, WHOL: Textiles, Woven
PIECE GOODS, NOTIONS & OTHER DRY GOODS, WHOLESALE: Fabrics
PILOT SVCS: Aviation
PINS
PIPE & TUBES: Copper & Copper Alloy
PIPE & TUBES: Seamless
PIPE CLEANERS
PIPE FITTINGS: Plastic
PIPE, SEWER: Concrete
PIPE: Concrete
PIPE: Copper
PIPE: Plastic
PIPE: Sheet Metal
PIPE: Water, Cast Iron
PIPELINES: Natural Gas
PIPES & TUBES
PIPES & TUBES: Steel
PIPES & TUBES: Welded
PIPES: Steel & Iron
PISTONS & PISTON RINGS
PLAQUES: Picture, Laminated
PLASMAS
PLASTICIZERS, ORGANIC: Cyclic & Acyclic
PLASTICS FILM & SHEET
PLASTICS FILM & SHEET: Polyethylene
PLASTICS FILM & SHEET: Polypropylene
PLASTICS FILM & SHEET: Polyvinyl
PLASTICS FILM & SHEET: Vinyl

PRODUCT INDEX

PLASTICS FINISHED PRDTS: Laminated
PLASTICS MATERIAL & RESINS
PLASTICS MATERIALS, BASIC FORMS & SHAPES WHOLESALERS
PLASTICS PROCESSING
PLASTICS: Blow Molded
PLASTICS: Extruded
PLASTICS: Finished Injection Molded
PLASTICS: Molded
PLASTICS: Polystyrene Foam
PLASTICS: Thermoformed
PLATES: Aluminum
PLATES: Steel
PLATES: Truss, Metal
PLATING & POLISHING SVC
PLATING COMPOUNDS
PLATING SVC: Chromium, Metals Or Formed Prdts
PLAYGROUND EQPT
PLEATING & STITCHING FOR THE TRADE: Decorative & Novelty
PLEATING & STITCHING SVC
PLUGS: Electric
PLUMBING FIXTURES
PLUMBING FIXTURES: Plastic
PLUMBING FIXTURES: Vitreous
POINT OF SALE DEVICES
POLISHING SVC: Metals Or Formed Prdts
POLYETHYLENE RESINS
POLYSTYRENE RESINS
POLYURETHANE RESINS
POLYVINYL CHLORIDE RESINS
POSTERS
POULTRY & POULTRY PRDTS WHOLESALERS
POULTRY & SMALL GAME SLAUGHTERING & PROCESSING
POULTRY SLAUGHTERING & PROCESSING
POWDER: Aluminum Atomized
POWDER: Iron
POWDER: Metal
POWER GENERATORS
POWER TRANSMISSION EQPT: Aircraft
PRECAST TERRAZZO OR CONCRETE PRDTS
PRECIOUS METALS
PRERECORDED TAPE, CD/RECORD STORES: Audio Tapes, Prerecorded
PRESSED FIBER & MOLDED PULP PRDTS, EXC FOOD
PRESTRESSED CONCRETE PRDTS
PRIMARY FINISHED OR SEMIFINISHED SHAPES
PRINT CARTRIDGES: Laser & Other Computer Printers
PRINTED CIRCUIT BOARDS
PRINTERS' SVCS: Folding, Collating, Etc
PRINTERS: Computer
PRINTERS: Magnetic Ink, Bar Code
PRINTING & BINDING: Book Music
PRINTING & BINDING: Books
PRINTING & ENGRAVING: Card, Exc Greeting
PRINTING & ENGRAVING: Financial Notes & Certificates
PRINTING & STAMPING: Fabric Articles
PRINTING & WRITING PAPER WHOLESALERS
PRINTING MACHINERY
PRINTING, COMMERCIAL: Business Forms, NEC
PRINTING, COMMERCIAL: Decals, NEC
PRINTING, COMMERCIAL: Envelopes, NEC
PRINTING, COMMERCIAL: Imprinting
PRINTING, COMMERCIAL: Labels & Seals, NEC
PRINTING, COMMERCIAL: Letterpress & Screen
PRINTING, COMMERCIAL: Literature, Advertising, NEC
PRINTING, COMMERCIAL: Magazines, NEC
PRINTING, COMMERCIAL: Periodicals, NEC
PRINTING, COMMERCIAL: Promotional
PRINTING, COMMERCIAL: Screen
PRINTING, COMMERCIAL: Stationery, NEC
PRINTING, LITHOGRAPHIC: Advertising Posters
PRINTING, LITHOGRAPHIC: Calendars
PRINTING, LITHOGRAPHIC: Forms, Business
PRINTING, LITHOGRAPHIC: Offset & photolithographic printing
PRINTING, LITHOGRAPHIC: Promotional
PRINTING, LITHOGRAPHIC: Tickets
PRINTING: Books
PRINTING: Books
PRINTING: Broadwoven Fabrics. Cotton
PRINTING: Checkbooks

PRINTING: Commercial, NEC
PRINTING: Flexographic
PRINTING: Gravure, Cards, Exc Greeting
PRINTING: Gravure, Forms, Business
PRINTING: Gravure, Labels
PRINTING: Gravure, Rotogravure
PRINTING: Laser
PRINTING: Letterpress
PRINTING: Lithographic
PRINTING: Manmade Fiber & Silk, Broadwoven Fabric
PRINTING: Offset
PRINTING: Screen, Broadwoven Fabrics, Cotton
PRINTING: Screen, Fabric
PRINTING: Screen, Manmade Fiber & Silk, Broadwoven Fabric
PRINTING: Thermography
PROFESSIONAL EQPT & SPLYS, WHOLESALE: Analytical Instruments
PROFESSIONAL EQPT & SPLYS, WHOLESALE: Engineers', NEC
PROFESSIONAL EQPT & SPLYS, WHOLESALE: Optical Goods
PROFESSIONAL INSTRUMENT REPAIR SVCS
PROFILE SHAPES: Unsupported Plastics
PROMOTION SVCS
PROPELLERS: Boat & Ship, Machined
PROTECTION EQPT: Lightning
PUBLIC RELATIONS & PUBLICITY SVCS
PUBLIC RELATIONS SVCS
PUBLISHERS: Art Copy & Poster
PUBLISHERS: Music Book & Sheet Music
PUBLISHERS: Music, Sheet
PUBLISHERS: Patterns, Paper
PUBLISHERS: Sheet Music
PUBLISHERS: Telephone & Other Directory
PUBLISHING & BROADCASTING: Internet Only
PUBLISHING & PRINTING: Art Copy
PUBLISHING & PRINTING: Book Music
PUBLISHING & PRINTING: Books
PUBLISHING & PRINTING: Magazines: publishing & printing
PUBLISHING & PRINTING: Music, Book
PUBLISHING & PRINTING: Newsletters, Business Svc
PUBLISHING & PRINTING: Newspapers
PUBLISHING & PRINTING: Pamphlets
PUBLISHING & PRINTING: Periodical Statistical Reports
PUBLISHING & PRINTING: Shopping News
PUBLISHING & PRINTING: Textbooks
PUBLISHING & PRINTING: Trade Journals
PUBLISHING & PRINTING: Yearbooks
PULP MILLS
PULP MILLS: Mechanical & Recycling Processing
PUMPS & PARTS: Indl
PUMPS & PUMPING EQPT REPAIR SVCS
PUMPS & PUMPING EQPT WHOLESALERS
PUMPS, HEAT: Electric
PUMPS: Domestic, Water Or Sump
PUMPS: Measuring & Dispensing
PUMPS: Oil Well & Field
PUMPS: Oil, Measuring Or Dispensing
PUMPS: Vacuum, Exc Laboratory
PURCHASING SVCS
PURIFICATION & DUST COLLECTION EQPT

Q

QUICKLIME
QUILTING: Individuals

R

RACE CAR OWNERS
RACEWAYS
RADAR SYSTEMS & EQPT
RADIO BROADCASTING & COMMUNICATIONS EQPT
RADIO BROADCASTING STATIONS
RADIO COMMUNICATIONS: Airborne Eqpt
RADIO COMMUNICATIONS: Carrier Eqpt
RAILINGS: Prefabricated, Metal
RAILROAD EQPT
RAILROAD EQPT & SPLYS WHOLESALERS
RAILROAD EQPT: Cars & Eqpt, Train, Freight Or Passenger
RAILROAD EQPT: Locomotives & Parts, Indl
RAILROAD MAINTENANCE & REPAIR SVCS
RAMPS: Prefabricated Metal
REAL ESTATE AGENCIES & BROKERS

REAL ESTATE AGENCIES: Rental
REAL ESTATE AGENTS & MANAGERS
RECORDING HEADS: Speech & Musical Eqpt
RECORDS & TAPES: Prerecorded
RECOVERY SVC: Iron Ore, From Open Hearth Slag
RECREATIONAL VEHICLE DEALERS
RECREATIONAL VEHICLE PARTS & ACCESS STORES
REELS: Cable, Metal
REFINING: Petroleum
REFRACTORIES: Clay
REFRACTORIES: Foundry, Clay
REFRACTORIES: Nonclay
REFRACTORIES: Tile & Brick, Exc Plastic
REFRACTORY MATERIALS WHOLESALERS
REFRIGERATION & HEATING EQUIPMENT
REFRIGERATION EQPT & SPLYS WHOLESALERS
REFRIGERATION EQPT: Complete
REFRIGERATION SVC & REPAIR
REFRIGERATOR REPAIR SVCS
REFUSE SYSTEMS
REGISTERS: Air, Metal
REGULATORS: Transmission & Distribution Voltage
REHABILITATION CTR, RESIDENTIAL WITH HEALTH CARE INCIDENTAL
REHABILITATION SVCS
RELAYS & SWITCHES: Indl, Electric
RELIGIOUS SPLYS WHOLESALERS
RELOCATION SVCS
REMOVERS & CLEANERS
REMOVERS: Paint
RENTAL SVCS: Audio-Visual Eqpt & Sply
RENTAL SVCS: Business Machine & Electronic Eqpt
RENTAL SVCS: Costume
RENTAL SVCS: Oil Eqpt
RENTAL SVCS: Recreational Vehicle
RENTAL SVCS: Tent & Tarpaulin
RENTAL SVCS: Work Zone Traffic Eqpt, Flags, Cones, Etc
RENTAL: Portable Toilet
RENTAL: Video Tape & Disc
RESEARCH, DEVELOPMENT & TESTING SVCS, COMM: Agricultural
RESEARCH, DEVELOPMENT & TESTING SVCS, COMMERCIAL: Energy
RESEARCH, DEVELOPMENT & TESTING SVCS, COMMERCIAL: Medical
RESEARCH, DEVELOPMENT & TESTING SVCS, COMMERCIAL: Physical
RESINS: Custom Compound Purchased
RESPIRATORS
RESTAURANT EQPT: Sheet Metal
RESTAURANTS: Fast Food
RESTAURANTS:Full Svc, American
RETAIL BAKERY: Bread
RETAIL BAKERY: Cakes
RETAIL BAKERY: Cookies
RETAIL BAKERY: Doughnuts
RETAIL BAKERY: Pretzels
RETAIL STORES: Artificial Limbs
RETAIL STORES: Audio-Visual Eqpt & Splys
RETAIL STORES: Batteries, Non-Automotive
RETAIL STORES: Business Machines & Eqpt
RETAIL STORES: Cake Decorating Splys
RETAIL STORES: Christmas Lights & Decorations
RETAIL STORES: Cleaning Eqpt & Splys
RETAIL STORES: Concrete Prdts, Precast
RETAIL STORES: Cosmetics
RETAIL STORES: Decals
RETAIL STORES: Educational Aids & Electronic Training Mat
RETAIL STORES: Electronic Parts & Eqpt
RETAIL STORES: Flags
RETAIL STORES: Hearing Aids
RETAIL STORES: Ice
RETAIL STORES: Infant Furnishings & Eqpt
RETAIL STORES: Medical Apparatus & Splys
RETAIL STORES: Orthopedic & Prosthesis Applications
RETAIL STORES: Perfumes & Colognes
RETAIL STORES: Pet Food
RETAIL STORES: Pet Splys
RETAIL STORES: Safety Splys & Eqpt
RETAIL STORES: Spas & Hot Tubs
RETAIL STORES: Telephone & Communication Eqpt
RETAIL STORES: Tents
RETAIL STORES: Water Purification Eqpt

PRODUCT INDEX

RETAIL STORES: Welding Splys
REUPHOLSTERY & FURNITURE REPAIR
RIBBONS, NEC
ROAD CONSTRUCTION EQUIPMENT WHOLESALERS
ROBOTS: Assembly Line
RODS: Extruded, Aluminum
RODS: Steel & Iron, Made In Steel Mills
ROLL FORMED SHAPES: Custom
ROLLING MILL EQPT: Finishing
ROLLING MILL MACHINERY
ROLLING MILL ROLLS: Cast Steel
ROLLS & BLANKETS, PRINTERS': Rubber Or Rubberized Fabric
ROOFING GRANULES
RUBBER PRDTS: Appliance, Mechanical
RUBBER PRDTS: Automotive, Mechanical
RUBBER PRDTS: Silicone
RUBBER PRDTS: Sponge
RUBBER STRUCTURES: Air-Supported
RUGS : Hand & Machine Made

S

SAFE DEPOSIT BOXES
SAFES & VAULTS: Metal
SAFETY EQPT & SPLYS WHOLESALERS
SALES PROMOTION SVCS
SALT
SAMPLE BOOKS
SAND & GRAVEL
SAND LIME PRDTS
SAND MINING
SANDBLASTING EQPT
SANITARY SVCS: Hazardous Waste, Collection & Disposal
SANITARY SVCS: Medical Waste Disposal
SANITARY SVCS: Refuse Collection & Disposal Svcs
SANITARY SVCS: Rubbish Collection & Disposal
SANITARY SVCS: Waste Materials, Recycling
SATELLITES: Communications
SAWDUST & SHAVINGS
SAWMILL MACHINES
SAWS & SAWING EQPT
SCAFFOLDS: Mobile Or Stationary, Metal
SCALE REPAIR SVCS
SCALES & BALANCES, EXC LABORATORY
SCALES: Indl
SCHOOLS: Vocational, NEC
SCIENTIFIC INSTRUMENTS WHOLESALERS
SCISSORS: Hand
SCRAP & WASTE MATERIALS, WHOLESALE: Ferrous Metal
SCRAP & WASTE MATERIALS, WHOLESALE: Metal
SCRAP & WASTE MATERIALS, WHOLESALE: Nonferrous Metals Scrap
SCRAP & WASTE MATERIALS, WHOLESALE: Paper
SCRAP STEEL CUTTING
SCREENS: Projection
SCREW MACHINE PRDTS
SCREWS: Metal
SEALANTS
SEALING COMPOUNDS: Sealing, synthetic rubber or plastic
SEALS: Oil, Rubber
SEARCH & NAVIGATION SYSTEMS
SEAT BELTS: Automobile & Aircraft
SEATING: Stadium
SECURITY CONTROL EQPT & SYSTEMS
SECURITY DEVICES
SECURITY GUARD SVCS
SECURITY SYSTEMS SERVICES
SEEDS & BULBS WHOLESALERS
SEMICONDUCTORS & RELATED DEVICES
SENSORS: Infrared, Solid State
SENSORS: Radiation
SENSORS: Temperature, Exc Indl Process
SEPTIC TANK CLEANING SVCS
SEPTIC TANKS: Concrete
SEWAGE & WATER TREATMENT EQPT
SEWER CLEANING EQPT: Power
SEWING MACHINE REPAIR SHOP
SEWING MACHINES & PARTS: Indl
SHADES: Window
SHALE: Expanded
SHAPES & PILINGS, STRUCTURAL: Steel
SHAPES: Extruded, Aluminum, NEC
SHAVING PREPARATIONS

SHEET METAL SPECIALTIES, EXC STAMPED
SHELVING, MADE FROM PURCHASED WIRE
SHELVING: Office & Store, Exc Wood
SHIELDS OR ENCLOSURES: Radiator, Sheet Metal
SHIMS: Metal
SHIP BUILDING & REPAIRING: Cargo, Commercial
SHIP BUILDING & REPAIRING: Dredges
SHIP BUILDING & REPAIRING: Ferryboats
SHOE STORES
SHOE STORES: Athletic
SHOE STORES: Boots, Men's
SHOES: Athletic, Exc Rubber Or Plastic
SHOES: Men's
SHOES: Men's, Dress
SHOES: Plastic Or Rubber
SHOES: Women's
SHOT PEENING SVC
SHOWCASES & DISPLAY FIXTURES: Office & Store
SHOWER STALLS: Plastic & Fiberglass
SHREDDERS: Indl & Commercial
SHUTTERS, DOOR & WINDOW: Metal
SHUTTERS, DOOR & WINDOW: Plastic
SIDING: Sheet Metal
SIGN PAINTING & LETTERING SHOP
SIGNALING APPARATUS: Electric
SIGNALS: Traffic Control, Electric
SIGNS & ADVERTISING SPECIALTIES
SIGNS & ADVERTISING SPECIALTIES: Artwork, Advertising
SIGNS & ADVERTISING SPECIALTIES: Letters For Signs, Metal
SIGNS & ADVERTISING SPECIALTIES: Novelties
SIGNS & ADVERTISING SPECIALTIES: Scoreboards, Electric
SIGNS, ELECTRICAL: Wholesalers
SIGNS, EXC ELECTRIC, WHOLESALE
SIGNS: Electrical
SIGNS: Neon
SILICONES
SILK SCREEN DESIGN SVCS
SILVERWARE & PLATED WARE
SIMULATORS: Flight
SIZES
SKILL TRAINING CENTER
SKIN CARE PRDTS: Suntan Lotions & Oils
SLABS: Steel
SLAG: Crushed Or Ground
SMOKE DETECTORS
SOFT DRINKS WHOLESALERS
SOFTWARE PUBLISHERS: Home Entertainment
SOFTWARE PUBLISHERS: Operating Systems
SOFTWARE TRAINING, COMPUTER
SOIL TESTING KITS
SOLAR CELLS
SOLAR HEATING EQPT
SOLVENTS
SOLVENTS: Organic
SONAR SYSTEMS & EQPT
SOUND EFFECTS & MUSIC PRODUCTION: Motion Picture
SOUND EQPT: Electric
SOUND REPRODUCING EQPT
SPACE PROPULSION UNITS & PARTS
SPAS
SPEAKER SYSTEMS
SPECIALIZED LIBRARIES
SPECIALTY FOOD STORES: Coffee
SPECIALTY FOOD STORES: Health & Dietetic Food
SPECIALTY FOOD STORES: Vitamin
SPECIALTY SAWMILL PRDTS
SPORTING & ATHLETIC GOODS: Arrows, Archery
SPORTING & ATHLETIC GOODS: Basketball Eqpt & Splys, NEC
SPORTING & ATHLETIC GOODS: Batons
SPORTING & ATHLETIC GOODS: Bowling Balls
SPORTING & ATHLETIC GOODS: Camping Eqpt & Splys
SPORTING & ATHLETIC GOODS: Fishing Tackle, General
SPORTING & ATHLETIC GOODS: Football Eqpt & Splys, NEC
SPORTING & ATHLETIC GOODS: Gymnasium Eqpt
SPORTING & ATHLETIC GOODS: Hunting Eqpt
SPORTING & ATHLETIC GOODS: Shafts, Golf Club
SPORTING & ATHLETIC GOODS: Shooting Eqpt & Splys, General

SPORTING & ATHLETIC GOODS: Targets, Archery & Rifle Shooting
SPORTING & ATHLETIC GOODS: Team Sports Eqpt
SPORTING & ATHLETIC GOODS: Trap Racks, Clay Targets
SPORTING & ATHLETIC GOODS: Water Sports Eqpt
SPORTING & REC GOODS, WHOLESALE: Camping Eqpt & Splys
SPORTING & RECREATIONAL GOODS, WHOLESALE: Athletic Goods
SPORTING CAMPS
SPORTING FIREARMS WHOLESALERS
SPORTING GOODS STORES, NEC
SPORTING GOODS STORES: Camping & Backpacking Eqpt
SPORTING GOODS STORES: Firearms
SPORTING GOODS STORES: Playground Eqpt
SPORTING GOODS STORES: Specialty Sport Splys, NEC
SPORTS APPAREL STORES
SPORTS CLUBS, MANAGERS & PROMOTERS
SPORTS PROMOTION SVCS
SPRINGS: Coiled Flat
SPRINGS: Mechanical, Precision
SPRINGS: Precision
SPRINGS: Steel
SPRINGS: Torsion Bar
SPRINGS: Wire
STACKING MACHINES: Automatic
STAINLESS STEEL
STAIRCASES & STAIRS, WOOD
STAMPINGS: Automotive
STAMPINGS: Metal
STATIONERY & OFFICE SPLYS WHOLESALERS
STATIONERY: Made From Purchased Materials
STATORS REWINDING SVCS
STATUARY & OTHER DECORATIVE PRDTS: Nonmetallic
STEEL & ALLOYS: Tool & Die
STEEL WOOL
STEEL, COLD-ROLLED: Sheet Or Strip, From Own HotRolled
STEEL, COLD-ROLLED: Strip NEC, From Purchased HotRolled
STEEL, COLD-ROLLED: Strip Or Wire
STEEL, HOT-ROLLED: Sheet Or Strip
STONE: Dimension, NEC
STONE: Quarrying & Processing, Own Stone Prdts
STONEWARE PRDTS: Pottery
STORE FIXTURES: Exc Wood
STORE FIXTURES: Wood
STORES: Auto & Home Supply
STOVES: Wood & Coal Burning
STRAWS: Drinking, Made From Purchased Materials
STRUCTURAL SUPPORT & BUILDING MATERIAL: Concrete
STUDS & JOISTS: Sheet Metal
STYRENE
SUNDRIES & RELATED PRDTS: Medical & Laboratory, Rubber
SURFACE ACTIVE AGENTS
SURGICAL APPLIANCES & SPLYS
SURGICAL APPLIANCES & SPLYS
SURGICAL IMPLANTS
SUSPENSION SYSTEMS: Acoustical, Metal
SVC ESTABLISHMENT EQPT, WHOLESALE: Firefighting Eqpt
SWEEPING COMPOUNDS
SWIMMING POOL EQPT: Filters & Water Conditioning Systems
SWIMMING POOLS, EQPT & SPLYS: Wholesalers
SWITCHES: Electric Power
SWITCHES: Electric Power, Exc Snap, Push Button, Etc
SWITCHES: Electronic
SWITCHES: Electronic Applications
SWITCHGEAR & SWITCHBOARD APPARATUS
SWITCHGEAR & SWITCHGEAR ACCESS, NEC
SYNTHETIC RESIN FINISHED PRDTS, NEC
SYSTEMS ENGINEERING: Computer Related
SYSTEMS INTEGRATION SVCS
SYSTEMS INTEGRATION SVCS: Local Area Network
SYSTEMS SOFTWARE DEVELOPMENT SVCS

T

TABLE OR COUNTERTOPS, PLASTIC LAMINATED
TABLES: Lift, Hydraulic
TAGS & LABELS: Paper
TANK REPAIR SVCS
TANKS & OTHER TRACKED VEHICLE CMPNTS

PRODUCT INDEX

TANKS: Cryogenic, Metal
TANKS: Fuel, Including Oil & Gas, Metal Plate
TANKS: Lined, Metal
TANKS: Plastic & Fiberglass
TANKS: Standard Or Custom Fabricated, Metal Plate
TANKS: Storage, Farm, Metal Plate
TANKS: Water, Metal Plate
TAPE STORAGE UNITS: Computer
TAPES, ADHESIVE: Cellophane, Made From Purchased Materials
TAPES: Pressure Sensitive, Rubber
TARGET DRONES
TARPAULINS
TARPAULINS, WHOLESALE
TELECOMMUNICATION EQPT REPAIR SVCS, EXC TELEPHONES
TELEPHONE EQPT: Modems
TELEPHONE EQPT: NEC
TELEPHONE SVCS
TELEVISION BROADCASTING & COMMUNICATIONS EQPT
TELEVISION BROADCASTING STATIONS
TELEVISION SETS
TELEVISION: Closed Circuit Eqpt
TEMPERING: Metal
TEMPORARY HELP SVCS
TESTERS: Battery
TESTERS: Physical Property
TEXTILE & APPAREL SVCS
TEXTILES: Bagging, Jute
THEATRICAL PRODUCTION SVCS
THERMOCOUPLES
THERMOPLASTIC MATERIALS
THERMOSETTING MATERIALS
THERMOSTAT REPAIR SVCS
TILE: Brick & Structural, Clay
TILE: Rubber
TIN
TIRE & INNER TUBE MATERIALS & RELATED PRDTS
TIRE INFLATORS: Hand Or Compressor Operated
TIRES & INNER TUBES
TIRES & TUBES WHOLESALERS
TIRES & TUBES, WHOLESALE: Automotive
TOBACCO: Chewing
TOBACCO: Cigarettes
TOBACCO: Smoking
TOILETRIES, WHOLESALE: Toilet Soap
TOILETRIES, WHOLESALE: Toiletries
TOILETS: Portable Chemical, Plastics
TOOL & DIE STEEL
TOOLS: Hand, Mechanics
TOWERS, SECTIONS: Transmission, Radio & Television
TOWING & TUGBOAT SVC
TOYS & HOBBY GOODS & SPLYS, WHOL: Toy Novelties & Amusements
TOYS & HOBBY GOODS & SPLYS, WHOLESALE: Playing Cards
TOYS & HOBBY GOODS & SPLYS, WHOLESALE: Toys & Games
TOYS & HOBBY GOODS & SPLYS, WHOLESALE: Video Games
TOYS: Dolls, Stuffed Animals & Parts
TOYS: Electronic
TRADING STAMP PROMOTION & REDEMPTION
TRAILER COACHES: Automobile
TRAILERS & CHASSIS: Camping
TRAILERS & PARTS: Boat
TRAILERS & PARTS: Horse
TRAILERS & TRAILER EQPT
TRAILERS: Camping, Tent-Type
TRAILERS: Demountable Cargo Containers
TRAILERS: House, Exc Permanent Dwellings
TRAILERS: Semitrailers, Truck Tractors
TRAILERS: Truck, Chassis
TRANSDUCERS: Electrical Properties
TRANSFORMERS: Distribution
TRANSFORMERS: Specialty
TRANSFORMERS: Voltage Regulating
TRANSMISSIONS: Motor Vehicle
TRANSPORTATION EQPT & SPLYS WHOLESALERS, NEC
TRANSPORTATION SVCS, WATER: Canal Barge Operations
TRAP ROCK: Crushed & Broken
TRAVEL AGENCIES
TRAVEL TRAILERS & CAMPERS

TRAYS: Plastic
TROPHIES, NEC
TROPHIES, WHOLESALE
TROPHIES: Metal, Exc Silver
TRUCK & BUS BODIES: Garbage Or Refuse Truck
TRUCK & BUS BODIES: Motor Vehicle, Specialty
TRUCK & BUS BODIES: Truck Beds
TRUCK BODIES: Body Parts
TRUCK GENERAL REPAIR SVC
TRUCK PARTS & ACCESSORIES: Wholesalers
TRUCKING & HAULING SVCS: Building Materials
TRUCKING & HAULING SVCS: Contract Basis
TRUCKING & HAULING SVCS: Heavy Machinery, Local
TRUCKING & HAULING SVCS: Heavy, NEC
TRUCKING & HAULING SVCS: Lumber & Log, Local
TRUCKING: Except Local
TRUCKING: Local, With Storage
TRUCKING: Local, Without Storage
TRUCKS & TRACTORS: Industrial
TRUCKS: Forklift
TRUCKS: Indl
TRUSSES & FRAMING: Prefabricated Metal
TRUSSES: Wood, Floor
TUBES: Extruded Or Drawn, Aluminum
TUBES: Light Sensing & Emitting
TUBES: Paper
TUBES: Steel & Iron
TUBES: Television
TUBES: Wrought, Welded Or Lock Joint
TUBING: Flexible, Metallic
TUBING: Rubber
TURBINES & TURBINE GENERATOR SET UNITS, COMPLETE
TURBINES & TURBINE GENERATOR SET UNITS: Gas, Complete
TURBINES & TURBINE GENERATOR SETS
TURBINES & TURBINE GENERATOR SETS & PARTS
TYPESETTING SVC
TYPESETTING SVC: Computer

U

UNIFORM SPLY SVCS: Indl
UNIFORM STORES
UNISEX HAIR SALONS
UNIVERSITY
UNSUPPORTED PLASTICS: Floor Or Wall Covering
UPHOLSTERY WORK SVCS
URNS: Cut Stone
USED CAR DEALERS
USED MERCHANDISE STORES
UTENSILS: Household, Cooking & Kitchen, Metal
UTILITY TRAILER DEALERS

V

VACUUM CLEANERS: Indl Type
VACUUM SYSTEMS: Air Extraction, Indl
VALUE-ADDED RESELLERS: Computer Systems
VALVE REPAIR SVCS, INDL
VALVES
VALVES & PARTS: Gas, Indl
VALVES & PIPE FITTINGS
VALVES & REGULATORS: Pressure, Indl
VALVES: Aerosol, Metal
VALVES: Aircraft, Control, Hydraulic & Pneumatic
VALVES: Control, Automatic
VALVES: Fluid Power, Control, Hydraulic & pneumatic
VALVES: Indl
VALVES: Plumbing & Heating
VALVES: Regulating & Control, Automatic
VALVES: Water Works
VAN CONVERSIONS
VAN CONVERSIONS
VARIETY STORES
VAULTS & SAFES WHOLESALERS
VEHICLES: All Terrain
VEHICLES: Recreational
VENDING MACHINE REPAIR SVCS
VENDING MACHINES & PARTS
VETERINARY PHARMACEUTICAL PREPARATIONS
VETERINARY PRDTS: Instruments & Apparatus
VIALS: Glass
VIDEO & AUDIO EQPT, WHOLESALE
VIDEO EQPT

VIDEO PRODUCTION SVCS
VIDEO TAPE PRODUCTION SVCS
VIDEO TRIGGERS: Remote Control TV Devices
VINYL RESINS, NEC
VISUAL COMMUNICATIONS SYSTEMS
VITAMINS: Natural Or Synthetic, Uncompounded, Bulk
VOCATIONAL REHABILITATION AGENCY

W

WALL COVERINGS WHOLESALERS
WALLBOARD: Decorated, Made From Purchased Materials
WALLBOARD: Gypsum
WALLPAPER STORE
WALLS: Curtain, Metal
WAREHOUSING & STORAGE FACILITIES, NEC
WAREHOUSING & STORAGE, REFRIGERATED: Cold Storage Or Refrig
WAREHOUSING & STORAGE: Bulk St & Termnls, Hire, Petro/Chem
WAREHOUSING & STORAGE: Farm Prdts
WAREHOUSING & STORAGE: General
WAREHOUSING & STORAGE: Miniwarehouse
WAREHOUSING & STORAGE: Self Storage
WARM AIR HEAT & AC EQPT & SPLYS, WHOLESALE Fan, Heat & Vent
WARM AIR HEATING/AC EQPT/SPLYS, WHOL Warm Air Htg Eqpt/Splys
WASHERS
WASHERS: Plastic
WATCH REPAIR SVCS
WATER HEATERS
WATER PURIFICATION EQPT: Household
WATER TREATMENT EQPT: Indl
WATER: Distilled
WATER: Mineral, Carbonated, Canned & Bottled, Etc
WATER: Pasteurized, Canned & Bottled, Etc
WATERPROOFING COMPOUNDS
WAXES: Petroleum, Not Produced In Petroleum Refineries
WEATHER STRIP: Sponge Rubber
WEIGHING MACHINERY & APPARATUS
WELDING & CUTTING APPARATUS & ACCESS, NEC
WELDING EQPT
WELDING EQPT & SPLYS WHOLESALERS
WELDING EQPT & SPLYS: Gas
WELDING EQPT REPAIR SVCS
WELDING EQPT: Electric
WELDING EQPT: Electrical
WELDING MACHINES & EQPT: Ultrasonic
WELDING REPAIR SVC
WELDING SPLYS, EXC GASES: Wholesalers
WELDMENTS
WELL LOGGING EQPT
WET CORN MILLING
WHEEL BALANCING EQPT: Automotive
WHEELCHAIR LIFTS
WHEELCHAIRS
WHEELS & PARTS
WHEELS: Abrasive
WHEELS: Disc, Wheelbarrow, Stroller, Etc, Stamped Metal
WHIRLPOOL BATHS: Hydrotherapy
WINCHES
WINDINGS: Coil, Electronic
WINDOW & DOOR FRAMES
WINDOW FRAMES & SASHES: Plastic
WINDOW FRAMES, MOLDING & TRIM: Vinyl
WINDOWS, LOUVER: Metal
WINDOWS: Frames, Wood
WINDOWS: Wood
WINDSHIELD WIPER SYSTEMS
WIRE
WIRE & CABLE: Nonferrous, Aircraft
WIRE & CABLE: Nonferrous, Automotive, Exc Ignition Sets
WIRE & CABLE: Nonferrous, Building
WIRE & WIRE PRDTS
WIRE FABRIC: Welded Steel
WIRE MATERIALS: Copper
WIRE MATERIALS: Steel
WIRE PRDTS: Ferrous Or Iron, Made In Wiredrawing Plants
WIRE PRDTS: Steel & Iron
WIRE: Communication
WIRE: Magnet
WIRE: Mesh
WIRE: Nonferrous

PRODUCT INDEX

WIRE: Nonferrous, Appliance Fixture
WIRE: Steel, Insulated Or Armored
WIRE: Wire, Ferrous Or Iron
WOMEN'S & CHILDREN'S CLOTHING WHOLESALERS, NEC
WOMEN'S & GIRLS' SPORTSWEAR WHOLESALERS
WOMEN'S CLOTHING STORES
WOMEN'S CLOTHING STORES: Ready-To-Wear
WOMEN'S SPECIALTY CLOTHING STORES
WOOD & WOOD BY-PRDTS, WHOLESALE
WOOD PRDTS: Applicators
WOOD PRDTS: Mantels
WOOD PRDTS: Moldings, Unfinished & Prefinished
WOOD PRDTS: Mulch Or Sawdust
WOOD PRDTS: Mulch, Wood & Bark
WOOD PRDTS: Outdoor, Structural
WOOD PRDTS: Panel Work
WOOD PRDTS: Signboards
WOOD PRDTS: Trophy Bases
WOOD PRODUCTS: Reconstituted
WOOD TREATING: Creosoting
WOOD TREATING: Railroad Cross Bridges & Switch Ties
WOOD TREATING: Railroad Cross-Ties
WOOD TREATING: Structural Lumber & Timber
WOOD TREATING: Wood Prdts, Creosoted
WOODWORK & TRIM: Interior & Ornamental
WOODWORK: Interior & Ornamental, NEC
WORD PROCESSING EQPT
WOVEN WIRE PRDTS, NEC

X

X-RAY EQPT & TUBES
X-RAY EQPT REPAIR SVCS

Y

YARN & YARN SPINNING
YARN MILLS: Texturizing, Throwing & Twisting

PRODUCT SECTION

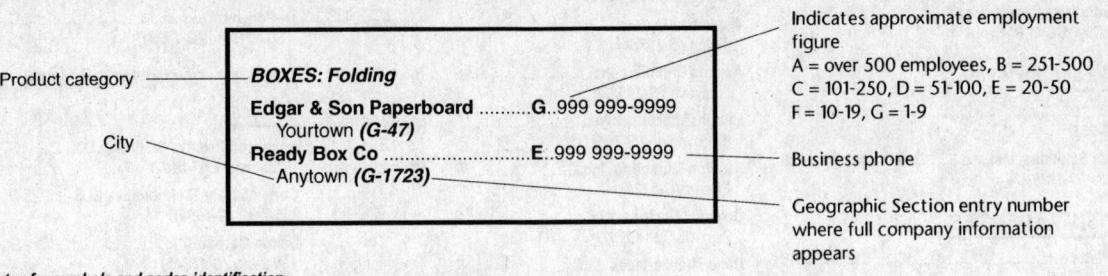

See footnotes for symbols and codes identification.
• Refer to the Industrial Product Index preceding this section to locate product headings.

ABRASIVES

10x Engineered Materials LLC............... F 260 209-1207
  Wabash *(G-16170)*
3M Company... E 765 348-3200
  Hartford City *(G-7060)*
3M Company... B 317 692-6666
  Indianapolis *(G-7388)*
Advanced Cutting Systems Inc................ E 260 423-3394
  Fort Wayne *(G-4725)*
Andersons Agriculture Group LP.............. F 765 564-6135
  Delphi *(G-2890)*
Chance Abrasives.................................... G 219 871-0977
  Michigan City *(G-11587)*
Enviri Corporation.................................... F 219 944-6250
  Gary *(G-5928)*
Plymouth Pdts Acquisition Inc................. G 574 936-4757
  Plymouth *(G-13804)*
Royer Enterprises Inc.............................. G 260 359-0689
  Huntington *(G-7362)*
Saint-Gobain Abrasives Inc..................... D 317 837-0700
  Plainfield *(G-13726)*
Schaffner Manufacturing Co.................... F 601 366-9902
  Richmond *(G-14202)*
Surface Generation Tech LLC................. G 765 425-2741
  Anderson *(G-203)*
Woodburn Diamond Die Inc.................... E 260 632-4217
  Woodburn *(G-16957)*

ABRASIVES: sandpaper

Sandpaper Studio LLC............................. G 317 435-7479
  Whiteland *(G-16795)*

ACCELERATION INDICATORS & SYSTEM COMPONENTS: Aerospace

Federal-Mogul Powertrain LLC................ G 574 272-5900
  South Bend *(G-15032)*
First Gear Inc... E 260 490-3238
  Fort Wayne *(G-4984)*
Rolls-Royce Defense Svcs Inc................. D 317 230-5006
  Indianapolis *(G-9330)*

ACCELERATORS, RUBBER PROCESSING: Cyclic or Acyclic

Coeus Technology Inc.............................. G 765 203-2304
  Anderson *(G-96)*

ACIDS: Boric

Eco Services Operations Corp................. E 219 932-7651
  Hammond *(G-6919)*

ACRYLONITRILE BUTADIENE STYRENE RESINS

Envalior Engineering Materials Inc........... C 800 333-4237
  Evansville *(G-4039)*
Envalior Engineering Mtls Inc................... G 812 435-7500
  Evansville *(G-4041)*

ACTUATORS: Indl, NEC

Flosource Inc... E 800 752-5959
  Mooresville *(G-12208)*
Micro-Precision Operations..................... F 260 589-2136
  Berne *(G-719)*
SMC Corporation of America................... B 317 899-4440
  Noblesville *(G-13176)*

ADAPTERS: Well

Paulus Plastic Co Inc.............................. G 574 834-7663
  North Webster *(G-13312)*

ADHESIVES

Adhesive Solutions Company LLC........... G 260 691-0304
  Columbia City *(G-2117)*
Big Dog Adhesives LLC........................... F 574 350-2237
  Elkhart *(G-3224)*
Bondline Adhesives Inc........................... F 812 423-4651
  Evansville *(G-3939)*
Capital Adhesives & Packg Corp............. F 317 834-5415
  Mooresville *(G-12197)*
Chem Tech Inc.. F 574 848-1001
  Bristol *(G-1253)*
Covalnce Spcalty Adhesives LLC............ B 812 424-2904
  Evansville *(G-3987)*
Evans Adhesive Corporation................... G 812 859-4245
  Spencer *(G-15345)*
Heartland Adhesives Inc.......................... G 219 310-8645
  Crown Point *(G-2692)*
Industrial Adhesives Indiana.................... G 317 271-2100
  Indianapolis *(G-8516)*
Lomont Holdings Co Inc.......................... E 800 545-9023
  Angola *(G-273)*
Lord Corporation..................................... D 317 259-4161
  Indianapolis *(G-8782)*
Parr Corp... F 574 264-9614
  Elkhart *(G-3584)*
Parr Technologies LLC............................ G 574 264-9614
  Elkhart *(G-3586)*
Parson Adhesives Inc.............................. G 812 401-7277
  Evansville *(G-4234)*
Patrick Industries Inc............................... F 574 295-5206
  Elkhart *(G-3588)*
Patrick Industries Inc............................... D 574 294-8828
  Elkhart *(G-3592)*
Patrick Industries Inc............................... B 574 294-7511
  Elkhart *(G-3593)*
Royal Holdings Inc................................... C 574 246-5000
  South Bend *(G-15227)*

Saimax Products Inc................................ G 248 299-5585
  Evansville *(G-4296)*
SealCorpUSA Inc..................................... D 866 868-0791
  Evansville *(G-4303)*
Technicote Inc... E 812 466-9844
  Terre Haute *(G-15724)*
Xennovate Medical LLC........................... G 765 939-2037
  Richmond *(G-14229)*

ADHESIVES & SEALANTS

3M Company... B 317 692-6666
  Indianapolis *(G-7388)*
Abtrex Industries Inc............................... F 734 728-0550
  South Bend *(G-14934)*
American Sealants Inc............................. E 800 325-7040
  Fort Wayne *(G-4757)*
Cast Products LP.................................... E 574 294-2684
  Elkhart *(G-3249)*
Coleman Cable LLC................................ D 765 449-7227
  Lafayette *(G-10553)*
Custom Building Products LLC................ C 765 656-0234
  Frankfort *(G-5659)*
Davies-Imperial Coatings Inc................... E 219 933-0877
  Hammond *(G-6911)*
Federal Process Corp.............................. G 574 288-0607
  South Bend *(G-15030)*
Gdc Inc.. C 574 533-3128
  Goshen *(G-6143)*
Hco Holding I Corporation....................... G 317 248-1344
  Indianapolis *(G-8373)*
Howmet Corporation................................ G 219 325-4143
  La Porte *(G-10424)*
Iron Out Inc... E 800 654-0791
  Fort Wayne *(G-5119)*
Laticrete International Inc........................ G 317 298-8510
  Indianapolis *(G-8726)*
Morgan Adhesives Company LLC........... B 812 342-2004
  Columbus *(G-2357)*
Parr Holdings LLC................................... E 423 468-1855
  Elkhart *(G-3585)*
Precoat Metals.. F 219 763-1504
  Portage *(G-13906)*
PSC Industries Inc................................... G 317 547-5439
  Indianapolis *(G-9237)*
Royal Adhesives & Sealants LLC............ D 574 246-5000
  South Bend *(G-15226)*
Saran LP.. C
  Indianapolis *(G-9373)*
Seal Corp... G 812 868-0790
  Evansville *(G-4302)*
Transcendia Inc....................................... C 765 935-1520
  Richmond *(G-14220)*
Warsaw Chemical Company Inc............. D 574 267-3251
  Warsaw *(G-16442)*

Employee Codes: A=Over 500 employees, B=251-500
C=101-250, D=51-100, E=20-50, F=10-19, G=1-9

2024 Harris Indiana Industrial Directory

1239

ADHESIVES & SEALANTS WHOLESALERS — PRODUCT SECTION

ADHESIVES & SEALANTS WHOLESALERS

Adhesive Solutions Company LLC.......... G 260 691-0304
  Columbia City *(G-2117)*

ADHESIVES: Epoxy

Freda Inc.. F 260 665-8431
  Angola *(G-253)*
Mito Material Solutions Inc....................... G 855 344-6486
  Indianapolis *(G-8936)*

ADVERTISING AGENCIES

Charles E Watts... G 812 547-8516
  Tell City *(G-15498)*
Clondalkin Pharma & Healthcare Inc...... A 336 292-4555
  Indianapolis *(G-7824)*
Degler Mktg & Mailing Svcs...................... G 317 873-5550
  Zionsville *(G-17002)*
Dow Theory Forecasts Inc......................... E 219 931-6480
  Hammond *(G-6915)*
Em Global LLC .... G 812 258-9993
  Jeffersonville *(G-9976)*
Goldleaf Promotional Pdts Inc.................. G 317 202-2754
  Indianapolis *(G-8302)*
Ovation Communications Inc.................... G 812 401-9100
  Evansville *(G-4230)*
Printing Creations Inc................................ G 765 759-9679
  Yorktown *(G-16982)*
Rick Singleton... F 574 259-5555
  Mishawaka *(G-11986)*
Rowland Printing Co Inc............................. F 317 773-1829
  Noblesville *(G-13168)*
Shilling Sales Inc.. E 260 426-2626
  Fort Wayne *(G-5413)*

ADVERTISING AGENCIES: Consultants

Baxter Design & Advertising..................... G 219 464-9237
  Valparaiso *(G-15912)*
Digital Design Genius.................................. G 317 515-3680
  Camby *(G-1509)*
Sexton Advertising LLC............................... G 812 522-4059
  Seymour *(G-14688)*
Tremike Enterprises .... G 317 547-6308
  Indianapolis *(G-9634)*
Yaney Mktg Graphic Design LLC.............. G 317 776-0676
  Noblesville *(G-13197)*

ADVERTISING DISPLAY PRDTS

Hoosier Family Living LLC......................... G 812 396-7880
  Vincennes *(G-16129)*
Trinity Displays LLC..................................... G 219 201-8733
  Chesterton *(G-1961)*

ADVERTISING MATERIAL DISTRIBUTION

C & W Inkd... F 317 352-1000
  Indianapolis *(G-7706)*
Professional Gifting Inc.............................. F 800 350-1796
  Indianapolis *(G-9221)*
Sampco Inc.. G 413 442-4043
  South Bend *(G-15230)*

ADVERTISING REPRESENTATIVES: Newspaper

Aim Media Indiana Oper LLC..................... E 317 736-7101
  Franklin *(G-5704)*
Newspaper Holding Inc............................... G 270 678-5171
  Jeffersonville *(G-10024)*

ADVERTISING SPECIALTIES, WHOLESALE

Abracadabra Graphics................................. G 812 336-1971
  Bloomington *(G-771)*

Apparel Plus Inc.. G 812 951-2111
  Georgetown *(G-6054)*
Apple Group Inc.. E 765 675-4777
  Tipton *(G-15764)*
Awards Unlimited Inc.................................. G 765 447-9413
  Lafayette *(G-10532)*
Baugh Enterprises Inc................................. F 812 334-8189
  Bloomington *(G-796)*
Burston Marketing Inc................................. F 574 262-4005
  Elkhart *(G-3238)*
Celestial Designs LLC.................................. G 317 733-3110
  Zionsville *(G-16997)*
Dimo Multiservices LLC.............................. F 463 256-0561
  Avon *(G-513)*
Discount Labels LLC.................................... A 812 945-2617
  New Albany *(G-12720)*
Favor It Promotions Inc.............................. F 317 733-1112
  Carmel *(G-1634)*
Flag & Banner Company Inc..................... F 317 299-4880
  Indianapolis *(G-8199)*
Garco Graphics.. G 219 980-1113
  Gary *(G-5935)*
Integrity Sign Solutions Inc....................... G 502 233-8755
  New Albany *(G-12749)*
Jer-Maur Corporation................................... G 812 384-8290
  Bloomfield *(G-750)*
Omnisource Marketing Group Inc........... E 317 575-3300
  Indianapolis *(G-9050)*
Paust Inc.. F 765 962-1507
  Richmond *(G-14180)*
Premiere Advertising.................................... G 317 722-2400
  Indianapolis *(G-9193)*
Printing Solutions Inc................................. G 812 923-0756
  Floyds Knobs *(G-4689)*
Professional Gifting Inc.............................. F 800 350-1796
  Indianapolis *(G-9221)*
Shilling Sales Inc.. E 260 426-2626
  Fort Wayne *(G-5413)*
Smiling Cross Inc.. G 812 323-9290
  Bloomington *(G-976)*
Star Quality Awards Inc............................. G 812 273-1740
  Madison *(G-11252)*
Winters Assoc Prmtnal Pdts Inc.............. F 812 330-7000
  Bloomington *(G-1015)*

ADVERTISING SVCS: Direct Mail

American Ex Trvl Rlted Svcs In................ G 812 523-0106
  Seymour *(G-14629)*
Crossrads Rhbilitation Ctr Inc.................. C 317 897-7320
  Indianapolis *(G-7910)*
Degler Mktg & Mailing Svcs...................... G 317 873-5550
  Zionsville *(G-17002)*
Harmony Press Inc...................................... E 800 525-3742
  Bourbon *(G-1122)*
Ovation Communications Inc.................... G 812 401-9100
  Evansville *(G-4230)*
Presstime Graphics Inc.............................. F 812 234-3815
  Terre Haute *(G-15669)*
Printwerk Graphics & Design.................... G 219 322-7722
  Dyer *(G-2981)*

ADVERTISING SVCS: Outdoor

Sig Media LLC... F 317 858-7624
  Indianapolis *(G-9426)*

ADVERTISING SVCS: Transit

Sig Media LLC... F 317 858-7624
  Indianapolis *(G-9426)*

AERIAL WORK PLATFORMS

Altec Industries Inc..................................... C 317 872-3460
  Indianapolis *(G-7493)*

AEROSOLS

Tri-Pac Inc... C 574 855-2197
  South Bend *(G-15291)*

AGENTS, BROKERS & BUREAUS: Personal Service

Advanced Prtctive Slutions LLC................ G 765 720-9574
  Coatesville *(G-2102)*
Cortex Safety Technologies LLC.............. G 317 414-5607
  Carmel *(G-1598)*
Dalton Corporation....................................... F 574 267-8111
  Warsaw *(G-16345)*
Distance Learning Systems Ind............... E 888 955-3276
  Greenwood *(G-6686)*

AGRICULTURAL DISINFECTANTS

Koch Industries Inc...................................... G 260 356-7191
  Huntington *(G-7335)*
Sepro Corporation.. E 317 580-8282
  Carmel *(G-1758)*

AGRICULTURAL EQPT: BARN, SILO, POULTRY, DAIRY/LIVESTOCK MACH

Applegate Livestock Eqp Inc..................... D 765 964-3715
  Union City *(G-15848)*
Cardinal Services Inc Indiana.................... D 574 267-3823
  Warsaw *(G-16333)*
Dpc Inc... E 765 564-3752
  Delphi *(G-2895)*
Rhinehart Development Corp.................... E 260 238-4442
  Spencerville *(G-15373)*
Swiss Perfection LLC................................... F 574 457-4457
  Syracuse *(G-15481)*

AGRICULTURAL EQPT: Elevators, Farm

Haines Engineering Inc.............................. G 260 589-3388
  Berne *(G-713)*

AGRICULTURAL EQPT: Fertilizng, Sprayng, Dustng/Irrigatn Mach

Gvm Inc.. G 765 689-5010
  Bunker Hill *(G-1441)*

AGRICULTURAL EQPT: Grounds Mowing Eqpt

Barry Stuckwisch... G 812 525-1052
  Seymour *(G-14631)*

AGRICULTURAL EQPT: Trailers & Wagons, Farm

Cornelius Manufacturing Inc..................... D 812 636-4319
  Washington *(G-16474)*
K & B Trailer Sales & Mfg Inc.................. G 574 946-4382
  Monterey *(G-12080)*
Norman Wagler.. G 812 636-8015
  Odon *(G-13346)*
Par-Kan Company LLC................................ D 260 352-2141
  Silver Lake *(G-14920)*

AGRICULTURAL EQPT: Turf & Grounds Eqpt

SA Heinen LLC.. G 317 416-7818
  Indianapolis *(G-9358)*

AGRICULTURAL MACHINERY & EQPT: Wholesalers

Bonnell Grain Handling Inc....................... E 574 595-7827
  Star City *(G-15396)*
Chester Inc.. F 574 896-5600
  North Judson *(G-13209)*

PRODUCT SECTION

AIRCRAFT ENGINES & PARTS

Deer Country Equipment LLC............... E 812 522-1922
Seymour *(G-14646)*

Delphi Products Co Inc......................... F 800 382-7903
Delphi *(G-2894)*

Dennis Polk & Associates Inc................ G 574 831-3555
New Paris *(G-12950)*

Miles Farm Supply LLC......................... D 812 359-4463
Boonville *(G-1090)*

National Equipment Inc......................... G 219 462-1205
Valparaiso *(G-16009)*

Schlatters Inc.. G 219 567-9158
Francesville *(G-5645)*

Seaflo Marine & Rv N Amer LLC........... E 844 473-2356
South Bend *(G-15236)*

T W Brackett & Assoc LLC................... G 765 769-3000
Attica *(G-355)*

Wright Implement I LLC........................ G 812 522-1922
Seymour *(G-14707)*

AIR CLEANING SYSTEMS

3-T Corp.. F 812 424-7878
Evansville *(G-3856)*

Clarcor Air Filtration Products Inc........ A 502 969-2304
Jeffersonville *(G-9952)*

Protect Plus Industries.......................... G 219 324-8482
La Porte *(G-10467)*

AIR CONDITIONERS: Motor Vehicle

Auto Temp Ctrl Specialists Inc.............. G 812 333-2963
Bloomington *(G-787)*

Deans Place.. G 765 282-5712
Muncie *(G-12375)*

Hitachi Astemo Indiana Inc.................. C 765 213-4915
Muncie *(G-12417)*

Proair LLC... D 574 264-5494
Elkhart *(G-3622)*

Schnell Service Center.......................... G 812 683-2461
Huntingburg *(G-7290)*

Twin-Air Products Inc........................... G 574 295-1129
Elkhart *(G-3755)*

AIR CONDITIONING & VENTILATION EQPT & SPLYS: Wholesales

Aero-Flo Industries Inc......................... G 219 393-3555
La Porte *(G-10378)*

Spheros North America Inc.................. G 734 218-7350
Elkhart *(G-3693)*

AIR CONDITIONING EQPT

Reearth Technologies............................ G 812 219-6517
Bloomington *(G-953)*

AIR CONDITIONING EQPT, WHOLE HOUSE: Wholesalers

Koch Enterprises Inc............................ G 812 465-9800
Evansville *(G-4159)*

AIR CONDITIONING UNITS: Complete, Domestic Or Indl

Crown Products & Services Inc............ G 317 564-4799
Carmel *(G-1601)*

Dometic Corporation............................ B 260 463-7657
Elkhart *(G-3301)*

AIR COOLERS: Metal Plate

Caliente LLC... E 260 426-3800
Fort Wayne *(G-4830)*

AIR DUCT CLEANING SVCS

Poynter Sheet Metal Inc....................... B 317 893-1193
Greenwood *(G-6753)*

AIR MATTRESSES: Plastic

Allen Apr Plastics Repair Inc................ E 260 482-8523
Fort Wayne *(G-4741)*

Brianza USA Corp................................. G 574 855-9520
Elkhart *(G-3235)*

Vixen Composites LLC.......................... G 574 970-1224
Elkhart *(G-3774)*

AIR POLLUTION MEASURING SVCS

Chapman Environmental Controls........ G 574 674-8706
Osceola *(G-13386)*

AIR PURIFICATION EQPT

Air-Tech Industrial Design.................... G 317 797-1804
Monrovia *(G-12076)*

Airbotx Inc.. G 317 981-1811
Westfield *(G-16663)*

Iaire LLC.. G 317 806-2750
Indianapolis *(G-8447)*

Midwest Purification LLC..................... G 317 536-7445
Greenwood *(G-6740)*

Natures Way.. G 317 839-4566
Plainfield *(G-13707)*

Pond Doctors Inc.................................. G 812 744-5258
Aurora *(G-453)*

Submicron LLC..................................... G 800 609-1390
Greenfield *(G-6560)*

AIRCRAFT & AEROSPACE FLIGHT INSTRUMENTS & GUIDANCE SYSTEMS

7th Leadership Organization................ G 219 938-6906
Gary *(G-5883)*

Corvette Aerospace LLC....................... G 317 512-4616
Shelbyville *(G-14747)*

Cyclone Adg LLC.................................. G 520 403-2927
New Albany *(G-12718)*

Hoosier Industrial Supply..................... G 574 535-0712
Goshen *(G-6167)*

Silicis Technologies Inc........................ E 317 896-5044
Westfield *(G-16728)*

United Technology Corp....................... F 317 481-5784
Indianapolis *(G-9681)*

AIRCRAFT & HEAVY EQPT REPAIR SVCS

Newlins Wldg & Tank Maint LLC.......... G 765 245-2741
Montezuma *(G-12082)*

Orton-Mccullough Crane Company...... G 260 356-7900
Huntington *(G-7347)*

AIRCRAFT ASSEMBLY PLANTS

Airbuoyant LLC..................................... G 765 623-9815
Anderson *(G-74)*

Airplane Annuals................................... G 817 528-6545
Bainbridge *(G-558)*

Bae Systems Controls Inc.................... A 260 434-5195
Fort Wayne *(G-4787)*

Boeing Company................................... G 219 977-4354
Gary *(G-5905)*

Charlie N83 Inc..................................... G 260 625-4211
Fort Wayne *(G-4843)*

Dean Baldwin Pntg Ltd Partnr.............. D 765 681-1800
Peru *(G-13578)*

Hoosier Industrial Supply..................... G 574 535-0712
Goshen *(G-6167)*

Mw Aircraft Inc..................................... G 317 873-4627
Zionsville *(G-17034)*

Quo Vadis Aerospace LLC.................... G 575 621-2372
Indianapolis *(G-9253)*

Rollison Airplane Company Inc............ G 812 384-4972
Bloomfield *(G-756)*

Textron Aviation Inc............................. E 317 241-2893
Indianapolis *(G-9580)*

Textron Aviation Inc............................. E 317 227-3621
Indianapolis *(G-9581)*

Thunderbird Aviation LLC.................... G 847 303-3100
Indianapolis *(G-9602)*

Tip To Tail Aerospace LLC................... G 765 437-6556
Peru *(G-13605)*

AIRCRAFT ENGINES & ENGINE PARTS: Air Scoops

Tri Aerospace LLC................................. E 812 872-2400
Terre Haute *(G-15736)*

AIRCRAFT ENGINES & ENGINE PARTS: Exhaust Systems

Integrated Energy Technologies Inc...... E 812 421-7810
Evansville *(G-4128)*

AIRCRAFT ENGINES & ENGINE PARTS: Research & Development, Mfr

Rolls-Royce Corporation....................... E 317 230-4118
Indianapolis *(G-9327)*

Rolls-Royce Corporation....................... C 317 230-4118
Indianapolis *(G-9328)*

Rolls-Royce Corporation....................... A 317 230-2000
Indianapolis *(G-9329)*

AIRCRAFT ENGINES & PARTS

Aerodyn Engineering LLC..................... E 317 334-1523
Indianapolis *(G-7451)*

Allens Therapuetic Services................. G 317 820-3600
Indianapolis *(G-7481)*

Bel-Mar Products Corporation.............. G 317 769-3262
Whitestown *(G-16801)*

Cuda II Inc... F 317 839-1515
Indianapolis *(G-7921)*

Enjet Aero Terre Haute LLC................. D 913 717-7390
Terre Haute *(G-15586)*

GE Aviation Systems LLC..................... G 765 432-5917
Lafayette *(G-10588)*

Goodrich Corporation........................... D 812 704-5200
Jeffersonville *(G-9993)*

Honeywell International Inc................. E 812 854-4450
Crane *(G-2538)*

Honeywell International Inc................. F 317 580-6165
Indianapolis *(G-8408)*

Honeywell International Inc................. E 765 284-3300
Muncie *(G-12419)*

Honeywell International Inc................. G 219 836-3803
Munster *(G-12540)*

Honeywell International Inc................. G 574 935-0200
Plymouth *(G-13782)*

Honeywell International Inc................. G 574 231-3322
South Bend *(G-15066)*

Honeywell International Inc................. A 574 231-3000
South Bend *(G-15067)*

IBC Materials & Tech LLC.................... E 765 481-2900
Lebanon *(G-10899)*

Jds International Inc............................ F 317 753-4427
Noblesville *(G-13112)*

N Rolls-Royce Amercn Tech Inc........... D 317 230-4347
Indianapolis *(G-8978)*

Ngh Retail LLC...................................... G 219 476-0772
Valparaiso *(G-16012)*

Nori Metals... G 574 213-4344
South Bend *(G-15168)*

Employee Codes: A=Over 500 employees, B=251-500
C=101-250, D=51-100, E=20-50, F=10-19, G=1-9

AIRCRAFT ENGINES & PARTS

PRODUCT SECTION

Polycraft Products Inc.............................. E 812 577-3401
  Greendale *(G-6452)*
Precoat Metals.. F 219 763-1504
  Portage *(G-13906)*
Robert Perez... G 317 291-7311
  Indianapolis *(G-9314)*
Rolls-Royce Corporation......................... E 812 421-7810
  Evansville *(G-4292)*
Rolls-Royce Corporation......................... D 317 230-2000
  Indianapolis *(G-9326)*
Rolls-Royce Corporation......................... E 317 657-0267
  Plainfield *(G-13723)*
Rolls-Royce Corporation......................... E 317 230-2736
  Zionsville *(G-17048)*
Rtx Corporation....................................... B 260 589-7207
  Berne *(G-723)*
Rtx Corporation....................................... G 260 358-0888
  Huntington *(G-7364)*
Simpson Alloy Services Inc..................... G 812 969-2766
  Elizabeth *(G-3129)*
Smiths Arospc Components Haute......... G 812 235-5210
  Terre Haute *(G-15698)*
Teamair Mro Ltd..................................... G 812 584-3733
  Moores Hill *(G-12188)*
Thermal Structures Inc........................... F 951 736-9911
  Plainfield *(G-13735)*
Turbines Inc.. E 812 877-2587
  Terre Haute *(G-15737)*
Twigg Corporation................................... G 765 342-7126
  Martinsville *(G-11431)*
Unison Engine Components Inc.............. C 904 739-4000
  Terre Haute *(G-15738)*
Walerko Tool and Engrg Corp.................. E 574 295-2233
  Elkhart *(G-3777)*
Westerley Inc.. E
  Indianapolis *(G-9752)*

AIRCRAFT FLIGHT INSTRUMENT REPAIR SVCS

Troy Meggitt Inc...................................... D 812 547-7071
  Troy *(G-15843)*

AIRCRAFT PARTS & AUXILIARY EQPT: Assys, Subassemblies/Parts

Iasa Group LLC....................................... G 260 484-1322
  Fort Wayne *(G-5090)*
Mears Machine Corp............................... D 317 271-6041
  Avon *(G-537)*

AIRCRAFT PARTS & AUXILIARY EQPT: Body & Wing Assys & Parts

Tri Aerospace LLC................................... E 812 872-2400
  Terre Haute *(G-15736)*

AIRCRAFT PARTS & AUXILIARY EQPT: Body Assemblies & Parts

Dean Baldwin Pntg Ltd Partnr.................. D 765 681-1800
  Peru *(G-13578)*

AIRCRAFT PARTS & AUXILIARY EQPT: Deicing Eqpt

Smart Manufacturing Inc......................... G 765 482-7481
  Lebanon *(G-10943)*

AIRCRAFT PARTS & AUXILIARY EQPT: Gears, Power Transmission

First Gear Inc.. E 260 490-3238
  Fort Wayne *(G-4984)*
Master Power Transmission Inc.............. E 812 378-2270
  Columbus *(G-2350)*

AIRCRAFT PARTS & AUXILIARY EQPT: Military Eqpt & Armament

Mvo Usa Inc.. F 317 585-5785
  Indianapolis *(G-8974)*

AIRCRAFT PARTS & AUXILIARY EQPT: Nacelles

Safran Nclles Svcs Amricas LLC............. G 317 827-0859
  Plainfield *(G-13725)*

AIRCRAFT PARTS & AUXILIARY EQPT: Research & Development, Mfr

U S S Inc... G 260 693-1172
  Churubusco *(G-1992)*
Vertex Mdrnztion Sstinment LLC............ A 601 607-6866
  Indianapolis *(G-9710)*
Wolf Technical Engineering LLC.............. G 800 783-9653
  Indianapolis *(G-9781)*

AIRCRAFT PARTS & EQPT, NEC

Aar LLC... G 260 591-0100
  Peru *(G-13565)*
AAR Corp.. G 317 227-5000
  Indianapolis *(G-7409)*
AAR Supply Chain Inc............................. F 317 227-5000
  Indianapolis *(G-7410)*
Aero Innovations LLC.............................. G 812 233-0384
  Terre Haute *(G-15534)*
Air Kit LLC.. G 317 745-0656
  Danville *(G-2806)*
Airtomic LLC... E 317 738-0148
  Franklin *(G-5706)*
Airtomic Repair Station........................... G 317 738-0148
  Franklin *(G-5707)*
Avt Composites....................................... G 317 286-7575
  Brownsburg *(G-1349)*
Avt Composites....................................... G 219 742-0865
  Lebanon *(G-10878)*
B-D Industries Inc................................... F 574 295-1420
  Elkhart *(G-3214)*
C F Roark Wldg Engrg Co Inc.................. C 317 852-3163
  Brownsburg *(G-1356)*
Cnc Industries Inc.................................. E 260 490-5700
  Fort Wayne *(G-4863)*
Composites Unlimited............................. G 812 475-8621
  Evansville *(G-3977)*
Cook Aircraft Leasing Inc........................ G 812 339-2044
  Bloomington *(G-836)*
Cuda II Inc.. F 317 839-1515
  Indianapolis *(G-7921)*
Eyc Drones LLC...................................... G 812 890-9068
  Vincennes *(G-16124)*
Frazier Aviation LLC................................ G 888 835-9269
  Cutler *(G-2784)*
GMI LLC.. G 260 209-6676
  Fort Wayne *(G-5028)*
Golden-Helvey Holdings Inc.................... D 574 266-4500
  Elkhart *(G-3384)*
Goodrich Corporation.............................. D 812 704-5200
  Jeffersonville *(G-9993)*
Honeywell International Inc..................... G 574 231-2000
  South Bend *(G-15068)*
Hupp & Associates Inc........................... E 260 748-8282
  New Haven *(G-12906)*
Indiana Aircraft Hardware Co.................. G 317 485-6500
  Fortville *(G-5600)*

Integrated De Icing Servi........................ G 317 517-1643
  Indianapolis *(G-8567)*
Jds International Inc............................... F 317 753-4427
  Noblesville *(G-13112)*
Kem Krest Defense LLC.......................... F 574 389-2650
  Elkhart *(G-3450)*
L&E Engineering LLC.............................. A 937 746-6696
  Greenwood *(G-6727)*
Lift Works Inc... G 812 797-0479
  Franklin *(G-5753)*
Mack Tool & Engineering Inc.................. E 574 233-8424
  South Bend *(G-15133)*
Midwest Aerospace Ltd.......................... F 219 365-7250
  Lowell *(G-11173)*
MSP Aviation Inc.................................... E 812 333-6100
  Bloomington *(G-926)*
Odyssian Technology LLC...................... G 574 257-7555
  South Bend *(G-15176)*
Precision Piece Parts Inc........................ D 574 255-3185
  Mishawaka *(G-11978)*
Pynco Inc... E 812 275-0900
  Bedford *(G-661)*
Q Air Inc... G 219 476-7048
  Valparaiso *(G-16032)*
Radius Aerospace Inc............................. G 317 392-5000
  Shelbyville *(G-14790)*
Rayco Mch & Engrg Group Inc................ E 317 291-7848
  Indianapolis *(G-9268)*
Regent Aerospace Corporation............... C 317 837-4000
  Plainfield *(G-13721)*
Rjv Investments Inc................................ E 574 234-1063
  South Bend *(G-15223)*
Rolls-Royce Corporation......................... E 812 421-7810
  Evansville *(G-4292)*
Saab Aeronautics Indiana LLC................ E 315 445-5009
  West Lafayette *(G-16627)*
Triumph Controls LLC............................. F 317 421-8760
  Shelbyville *(G-14808)*
Triumph Thermal Systems LLC............... G 419 273-1192
  Shelbyville *(G-14809)*
Tube Processing Corp............................. G 317 264-7760
  Indianapolis *(G-9657)*
Tube Processing Corp............................. B 317 787-1321
  Indianapolis *(G-9658)*
Value Production Inc............................... E 574 246-1913
  South Bend *(G-15300)*

AIRCRAFT SEATS

Mj Aircraft Inc.. F 765 378-7700
  Anderson *(G-156)*
Wolf Technical Engineering LLC.............. G 800 783-9653
  Indianapolis *(G-9781)*

AIRCRAFT SERVICING & REPAIRING

Mj Aircraft Inc.. F 765 378-7700
  Anderson *(G-156)*

AIRCRAFT TURBINES

Allison Transmission Inc........................ A 317 242-5000
  Indianapolis *(G-7491)*
Ares Division LLC................................... G 260 349-9803
  Waterloo *(G-16514)*

AIRCRAFT UPHOLSTERY REPAIR SVCS

Indy Aerospace Inc................................. G 817 521-6508
  Indianapolis *(G-8522)*

AIRCRAFT: Airplanes, Fixed Or Rotary Wing

Boeing Company..................................... G 317 484-1363
  Indianapolis *(G-7656)*
Golden Age Aeroplane Works LLC........... G 812 358-5778
  Brownstown *(G-1423)*

PRODUCT SECTION
AMMUNITION: Small Arms

Hull Aircraft Support LLC........................ G 219 324-6247
  La Porte *(G-10426)*

AIRCRAFT: Motorized

Drone Works LLC.................................... G 812 917-4691
  Terre Haute *(G-15579)*

Infinity Drones LLC................................. G 812 457-7140
  Poseyville *(G-13978)*

ALARMS: Burglar

L3harris Technologies Inc..................... G 260 451-5597
  Fort Wayne *(G-5169)*

Logical Concepts.................................... F 317 885-6330
  Greenwood *(G-6730)*

Sentinel Alarm Inc................................ G 219 874-6051
  Trail Creek *(G-15839)*

ALARMS: Fire

American Fire Company......................... G 219 840-0630
  Valparaiso *(G-15899)*

ALCOHOL, GRAIN: For Beverage Purposes

Grain Processing Corporation................ E 812 257-0480
  Washington *(G-16481)*

ALCOHOL, INDL: Grain

Grain Processing Corporation................ E 812 257-0480
  Washington *(G-16481)*

ALCOHOL: Ethyl & Ethanol

Andersons Clymers Ethanol LLC............ G 574 722-2627
  Logansport *(G-11057)*

Cardinal Ethanol LLC............................ D 765 964-3137
  Union City *(G-15850)*

Green Plains Grain Company LLC.......... E 812 985-7480
  Mount Vernon *(G-12298)*

Green Plains Inc................................... E 812 985-7480
  Mount Vernon *(G-12299)*

Hoosier Ethanol Energy LLC.................. G 260 407-6161
  Fort Wayne *(G-5077)*

New Energy Corp................................... C 574 233-3116
  South Bend *(G-15165)*

Poet Borefining - Portland LLC............... G 260 726-2681
  Portland *(G-13961)*

Poet Brfining - Alexandria LLC............... G 765 724-4384
  Alexandria *(G-57)*

Poet Brfining - Cloverdale LLC............... D 765 795-3235
  Cloverdale *(G-2093)*

Poet Brfining - N Mnchester LLC............ G 260 774-3532
  North Manchester *(G-13247)*

Poet Brfining - Shelbyville LLC............... G 317 699-4199
  Shelbyville *(G-14786)*

Valero Renewable Fuels Co LLC............. D 260 846-0011
  Bluffton *(G-1068)*

Valero Renewable Fuels Co LLC............. G 812 833-3900
  Mount Vernon *(G-12326)*

Williams Distribution LLC..................... G 317 749-0006
  Indianapolis *(G-9767)*

ALKALIES & CHLORINE

Warsaw Chemical Company Inc............. D 574 267-3251
  Warsaw *(G-16442)*

ALTERNATORS & GENERATORS: Battery Charging

Borgwarner Pds (indiana) Inc................ C 765 778-6696
  Noblesville *(G-13045)*

Borgwarner Reman Holdings LLC.......... A 800 372-5131
  Pendleton *(G-13527)*

Old Remco Holdings LLC...................... C 765 778-6499
  Pendleton *(G-13548)*

ALTERNATORS: Automotive

B & M Electrical Company Inc................ F 765 448-4532
  Lafayette *(G-10533)*

D & E Auto Electric Inc......................... F 219 763-3892
  Portage *(G-13858)*

Hitachi Astemo Americas Inc................ D 859 734-9451
  Ligonier *(G-11017)*

ALUMINUM

Alcoa Corporation................................. E 812 853-6111
  Newburgh *(G-12992)*

Alcoa Corporation................................. E 812 842-3350
  Newburgh *(G-12993)*

Alcoa Power Generating Inc................. G 812 842-3350
  Newburgh *(G-12994)*

Closure Systems Intl Hldngs In.............. G 765 364-6300
  Crawfordsville *(G-2553)*

Closure Systems Intl Inc....................... B 765 364-6300
  Crawfordsville *(G-2554)*

Closure Systems Intl Inc....................... C 317 390-5000
  Indianapolis *(G-7825)*

G & L Machine LLP............................... G 260 488-2100
  Hamilton *(G-6854)*

Howmet Aerospace Inc......................... B 812 853-6111
  Newburgh *(G-13004)*

Howmet Aerospace Inc......................... B 412 553-4545
  Newburgh *(G-13005)*

Industrial Sales & Supply Inc................ E 317 240-0560
  Indianapolis *(G-8519)*

K-TEC Corp.. G 317 398-6684
  Shelbyville *(G-14766)*

Kingsford Products Inc......................... F 740 862-4450
  Decatur *(G-2866)*

Nanshan Amer Advnced Alum Tech...... C 765 838-8645
  Lafayette *(G-10657)*

Scepter Inc... F 812 735-2600
  Bicknell *(G-737)*

ALUMINUM PRDTS

Alexandria Extrsion Mdmrica LL............ G 317 545-1221
  Indianapolis *(G-7470)*

Alliance Aluminum Products Inc........... D 574 848-4300
  Bristol *(G-1242)*

Altec LLC... D 812 282-8256
  Jeffersonville *(G-9928)*

Alumina Products Incorporated............ G 727 934-9781
  Terre Haute *(G-15539)*

Aluminum Dynamics LLC...................... G 260 969-3500
  Fort Wayne *(G-4746)*

Aluminum Extrusions........................... G 574 206-0100
  Elkhart *(G-3168)*

Aluminum Insights LLC....................... E 574 534-5547
  Syracuse *(G-15454)*

Bonnell Aluminum Inc......................... A 815 351-6802
  Kentland *(G-10157)*

Brazeway LLC...................................... A 317 392-2533
  Shelbyville *(G-14740)*

Gusa Holdings Inc................................ D 317 545-1221
  Indianapolis *(G-8343)*

Hautau Tube Cutoff Systems LLC........... F 765 647-1600
  Brookville *(G-1323)*

Hydro Extrusion Usa LLC...................... C 765 825-1141
  Connersville *(G-2442)*

Hydro Extrusion Usa LLC...................... C 574 262-2667
  Elkhart *(G-3415)*

Indalex Inc.. G 765 457-1117
  Kokomo *(G-10286)*

Indiana Gratings Inc............................ F 765 342-7191
  Martinsville *(G-11404)*

Indilex Aluminum Solutions.................. G 765 825-1141
  Connersville *(G-2445)*

Lakemaster Inc.................................... F 765 288-3718
  Muncie *(G-12437)*

Matalco Bluffton LLC............................ D 260 353-3100
  Bluffton *(G-1040)*

Napier & Napier................................... G 765 580-9116
  Liberty *(G-10992)*

Parco Incorporated.............................. F 260 451-0810
  Fort Wayne *(G-5296)*

Patrick Industries Inc........................... C 574 534-5300
  Goshen *(G-6237)*

Patrick Industries Inc........................... G 574 255-9692
  Mishawaka *(G-11971)*

Plymouth Tube Company...................... D 574 946-6191
  Winamac *(G-16871)*

Specialty Blanks Inc............................. E 812 232-8775
  Terre Haute *(G-15708)*

Stalcop LLC... E 765 436-7926
  Thorntown *(G-15756)*

Tredegar Corporation........................... D 812 466-0266
  Terre Haute *(G-15734)*

ALUMINUM: Coil & Sheet

New Process Steel LP........................... E 260 868-1445
  Butler *(G-1474)*

ALUMINUM: Rolling & Drawing

Alcoa Corporation................................. G 765 983-9200
  Richmond *(G-14085)*

Alconex Specialty Products................... E 260 744-3446
  Fort Wayne *(G-4737)*

Arconic US LLC..................................... A 412 553-2500
  Lafayette *(G-10526)*

Elektrsola Dr Gerd Schldbach G............. B 765 477-8000
  Lafayette *(G-10574)*

Kaiser Aluminum Warrick LLC............... A 412 315-2900
  Newburgh *(G-13011)*

Rockport Roll Shop LLC........................ E 812 362-6419
  Rockport *(G-14348)*

Southwire Company LLC....................... D 574 546-5115
  Bremen *(G-1222)*

Spectra Metal Sales Inc........................ G 317 822-8291
  Indianapolis *(G-9476)*

AMMUNITION

Bobcat Armament and Mfg LLC............. G 317 699-6127
  Shelbyville *(G-14738)*

Pine Valley Munitions Inc..................... G 260 818-6113
  Columbia City *(G-2181)*

Popguns Inc.. G 317 897-8660
  Indianapolis *(G-9163)*

Standard Issue Armory LLC.................. F 812 364-1466
  Greenville *(G-6657)*

Ammunition Loading & Assembling Plant

Bobcat Armament and Mfg LLC............. G 317 699-6127
  Shelbyville *(G-14738)*

AMMUNITION: Components

Lomatt Dynamics LLC........................... G 574 500-2517
  Leesburg *(G-10957)*

Pine Valley Munitions Inc..................... G 260 818-6113
  Columbia City *(G-2181)*

AMMUNITION: Small Arms

Adam L Hoskins.................................... G 765 580-0345
  Liberty *(G-10983)*

Armorite Ammo LLC.............................. G 765 825-7527
  Connersville *(G-2425)*

Cgf Enterprises LLC.............................. G 574 889-2074
  Logansport *(G-11067)*

Dalren Enterprises LLC......................... G 502 396-0346
  Pekin *(G-13515)*

AMMUNITION: Small Arms

Hoosier Bullets LLC................................ G 317 694-1257
Trafalgar *(G-15828)*

Lomatt Dynamics LLC............................ G 574 500-2517
Leesburg *(G-10957)*

Northern Indiana Ordnance Co.............. G 574 289-5938
South Bend *(G-15173)*

Paraklese Technologies LLC.................. F 502 357-0735
Georgetown *(G-6073)*

Sons of Thunder..................................... G 812 897-4908
Boonville *(G-1098)*

AMPLIFIERS

American Mobile Sound Ind LLC........... G 765 288-1500
Muncie *(G-12341)*

ASA Electronics LLC............................... C 574 264-3135
Elkhart *(G-3192)*

Crown Audio Inc..................................... B 800 342-6939
Elkhart *(G-3273)*

Harman Professional Inc........................ B 574 294-8000
Elkhart *(G-3398)*

Uncle Alberts Amplifier Inc..................... G 317 845-3037
Indianapolis *(G-9676)*

Vergence LLC... F 317 547-4417
Indianapolis *(G-9707)*

AMUSEMENT & RECREATION SVCS: Exposition Operation

Hamilton County Business Mag.............. G 317 774-7747
Noblesville *(G-13092)*

AMUSEMENT MACHINES: Coin Operated

Action Amusement.................................. G 812 422-9029
Evansville *(G-3872)*

Advance Green Mfg Co Inc.................... G 574 457-2695
Goshen *(G-6088)*

C & P Distributing LLC........................... F 574 256-1138
Mishawaka *(G-11857)*

Grand Products Inc................................ C 317 870-3122
Indianapolis *(G-8312)*

AMUSEMENT PARK DEVICES & RIDES

Adkins Amusements................................ G 765 939-0285
Richmond *(G-14083)*

County Line Companies LLC.................. G 866 959-7866
Kokomo *(G-10250)*

Ham Enterprise LLC............................... G 317 831-2902
Martinsville *(G-11398)*

Russell L Rooksberry.............................. G 812 659-1683
Carlisle *(G-1543)*

Tri Aerospace LLC.................................. E 812 872-2400
Terre Haute *(G-15736)*

ANALGESICS

Pipe Dream Innovations LLC.................. G 503 910-8815
Marion *(G-11328)*

ANALYZERS: Network

Avid Operations Inc................................ G 260 220-2001
Fort Wayne *(G-4784)*

Donald Pape... G 260 484-6088
Fort Wayne *(G-4924)*

ANALYZERS: Respiratory

Breath of Life Home Medical.................. F 317 896-3048
Westfield *(G-16671)*

Faztech LLC.. G 812 327-0926
Bloomington *(G-864)*

ANESTHESIA EQPT

Flw Plastics Inc....................................... F 812 546-0050
Hope *(G-7224)*

King Systems Corporation...................... B 317 776-6823
Noblesville *(G-13120)*

ANIMAL BASED MEDICINAL CHEMICAL PRDTS

Animalsinkcom LLC................................ G 317 496-8467
Brownsburg *(G-1347)*

Wisemed Inc... G 317 644-1169
Indianapolis *(G-9778)*

ANIMAL FEED & SUPPLEMENTS: Livestock & Poultry

B S R Inc... G 812 235-4444
Terre Haute *(G-15547)*

B S R Inc... G 812 235-4444
Terre Haute *(G-15548)*

B S R Inc... E 812 235-4444
Terre Haute *(G-15549)*

Belstra Milling Co Inc.............................. G 219 766-2284
Kouts *(G-10361)*

Belstra Milling Co Inc.............................. E 219 987-4343
Demotte *(G-2911)*

Blue River Farm Supply Inc.................... G 812 364-6675
Palmyra *(G-13478)*

Bristow Milling Co LLC........................... G 812 843-5176
Bristow *(G-1299)*

Bundy Bros and Sons Inc....................... F 812 966-2551
Medora *(G-11462)*

C D C P Inc... E 219 766-2284
Kouts *(G-10362)*

Cargill Incorporated................................ G 765 665-3326
Dana *(G-2803)*

Cargill Incorporated................................ B 402 533-4227
Hammond *(G-6895)*

Cargill Incorporated................................ G 574 353-7623
Mentone *(G-11470)*

Cargill Incorporated................................ G 574 353-7621
Mentone *(G-11471)*

Commodity Blenders LLC...................... G 260 375-3202
Warren *(G-16294)*

Egg Innovations LLC.............................. D 574 267-7545
Warsaw *(G-16355)*

Elanco US Inc... G 812 242-5999
Terre Haute *(G-15584)*

Envigo Rms Inc...................................... G 317 806-6080
Greenfield *(G-6500)*

Envigo Rms Inc...................................... G 317 806-6060
Greenfield *(G-6501)*

Envigo Rms Inc...................................... C 317 806-6080
Indianapolis *(G-8125)*

Frick Services Inc................................... E 260 761-3311
Wawaka *(G-16539)*

Griffin Industries LLC.............................. D 812 379-9528
Columbus *(G-2315)*

Griffin Industries LLC.............................. D 812 659-3399
Newberry *(G-12989)*

HMS Zoo Diets Inc................................. G 260 824-5157
Bluffton *(G-1037)*

Hog Slat Incorporated............................ D 574 967-4145
Camden *(G-1520)*

Innovative Concepts Group Inc.............. G 317 408-0292
Indianapolis *(G-8554)*

Jbs United Inc... F 317 758-2609
Sheridan *(G-14824)*

Keystone Cooperative Inc...................... G 765 489-4141
Hagerstown *(G-6838)*

Lambrights Inc.. G 260 463-2178
Lagrange *(G-10750)*

Land OLakes Inc.................................... F 574 967-3064
Flora *(G-4660)*

Land OLakes Inc.................................... E 765 962-9561
Richmond *(G-14155)*

Laughery Valley AG Co-Op Inc.............. G 812 689-4401
Osgood *(G-13412)*

Mainstreet Marketing Entps LLC............ G 765 482-6815
Lebanon *(G-10912)*

Mark Hackman....................................... G 812 522-8257
Brownstown *(G-1425)*

Midwestern Pet Foods Inc...................... F 812 867-7466
Evansville *(G-4205)*

Nutritional Research Assoc.................... F 260 723-4931
South Whitley *(G-15322)*

Pine Manor Inc....................................... G 574 533-4186
Goshen *(G-6238)*

Purina Animal Nutrition LLC................... G 812 424-5501
Evansville *(G-4265)*

Purina Animal Nutrition LLC................... G 765 659-4791
Frankfort *(G-5692)*

Purina Animal Nutrition LLC................... G 574 658-4137
Milford *(G-11804)*

Purina Animal Nutrition LLC................... G 765 373-9377
Richmond *(G-14191)*

Purina Animal Nutrition LLC................... G 765 962-9561
Richmond *(G-14192)*

Purina Animal Nutrition LLC................... F 765 962-9561
Richmond *(G-14193)*

Reconserve of Indiana Inc..................... G 812 299-2191
Mooresville *(G-12238)*

Regal Mills Odon.................................... G 812 295-2299
Loogootee *(G-11149)*

Scotts Miracle-Gro Company.................. G 219 984-6110
Reynolds *(G-14076)*

Trouw Nutrition Usa LLC........................ D 618 654-2070
Indianapolis *(G-9648)*

United Feeds.. G 317 627-5637
Carmel *(G-1794)*

United Pet Foods Inc.............................. F 574 674-5981
Elkhart *(G-3758)*

Vita Plus Corp... G 574 595-0901
Winamac *(G-16879)*

Wallace Grain Company Inc................... F 317 758-4434
Sheridan *(G-14832)*

Wilson Fertilizer & Grain Inc................... G 574 223-3175
Rochester *(G-14333)*

ANIMAL FEED: Wholesalers

AG Processing A Cooperative................ G 574 773-4138
Nappanee *(G-12577)*

B S R Inc... G 812 235-4444
Terre Haute *(G-15548)*

B S R Inc... E 812 235-4444
Terre Haute *(G-15549)*

Elanco Animal Health Inc....................... A 877 352-6261
Greenfield *(G-6493)*

Elanco International Inc......................... D 877 352-6261
Greenfield *(G-6494)*

Flinn Frms Bdford Feed Seed In............ G 812 279-4136
Bedford *(G-636)*

Lambrights Inc.. G 260 463-2178
Lagrange *(G-10750)*

Nutritional Research Assoc.................... F 260 723-4931
South Whitley *(G-15322)*

Synergy Feeds LLC................................ E 260 723-5141
South Whitley *(G-15330)*

Wilson Fertilizer & Grain Inc................... G 574 223-3175
Rochester *(G-14333)*

ANIMAL FOOD & SUPPLEMENTS: Bird Food, Prepared

Audubon Workshop................................ G 812 537-3583
Greendale *(G-6438)*

PRODUCT SECTION

Birds Nest Inc.. G 574 247-0201
  Granger *(G-6337)*
Global Harvest Foods LLC..................... E 219 984-6110
  Reynolds *(G-14073)*
Mitchell Marketing Group Inc................. G 317 816-7010
  Carmel *(G-1700)*
Sappers Market and Greenhouses......... G 219 942-4995
  Hobart *(G-7206)*

ANIMAL FOOD & SUPPLEMENTS: Bone Meal

Synergy Feeds LLC................................. E 260 723-5141
  South Whitley *(G-15330)*

ANIMAL FOOD & SUPPLEMENTS: Cat

Saturn Petcare Inc.................................. G 812 872-5646
  Terre Haute *(G-15689)*

ANIMAL FOOD & SUPPLEMENTS: Chicken Feeds, Prepared

Egg Innvtons Organic Feeds LLC........... G 800 337-1951
  Gary *(G-5927)*

ANIMAL FOOD & SUPPLEMENTS: Dog

Albrecht Incorporated............................. G 260 422-9440
  Fort Wayne *(G-4736)*
Canines Choice Inc................................ G 765 662-2633
  Marion *(G-11276)*
Eagle Pet Products Inc........................... D 574 259-7834
  Mishawaka *(G-11888)*
Good Poppi LLC..................................... G 812 319-1660
  Evansville *(G-4093)*
Midwestern Pet Foods Inc...................... F 812 867-7466
  Evansville *(G-4205)*
Scott Pet Products Inc........................... D 765 569-4702
  Hillsdale *(G-7164)*
Scott Pet Products Inc........................... G 765 569-4636
  Rockville *(G-14355)*
Underdog Diner LLP............................... G 812 598-2970
  Evansville *(G-4359)*

ANIMAL FOOD & SUPPLEMENTS: Dog & Cat

Bhj Usa LLC.. G 574 722-3933
  Logansport *(G-11062)*
Blue Buffalo Company Ltd..................... B 203 665-3500
  Richmond *(G-14099)*
Heartland Pet Food Mfg Ind LLC............ F 765 209-4140
  Richmond *(G-14132)*
Hills Pet Nutrition Inc............................. E 765 935-7071
  Richmond *(G-14133)*
Macor.. G 574 255-2658
  Mishawaka *(G-11935)*
Nick-Em Builders LLC............................ F 574 992-8313
  Logansport *(G-11099)*
Nick-Em Builders LLC............................ E 574 516-1060
  Logansport *(G-11100)*
Nutritional Research Assoc.................... F 260 723-4931
  South Whitley *(G-15322)*
Phillips Feed Service Inc........................ E 610 250-2099
  Indianapolis *(G-9137)*
Purina Mills LLC..................................... D 812 424-5501
  Evansville *(G-4266)*
Purina Mills LLC..................................... E 574 658-4137
  Milford *(G-11805)*
Saturn Petcare Inc.................................. G 812 263-5646
  Terre Haute *(G-15687)*
Saturn Petcare Inc.................................. C 812 872-5646
  Terre Haute *(G-15688)*
Schell & Kampeter Inc............................ F 765 570-4262
  Rushville *(G-14411)*
Wellness Pet LLC.................................... E 574 259-7834
  Mishawaka *(G-12026)*

ANIMAL FOOD & SUPPLEMENTS: Feed Premixes

Gem Elevator Inc..................................... G 317 894-7722
  Greenfield *(G-6505)*
Gro-Tec Inc.. F 765 853-1246
  Modoc *(G-12051)*

ANIMAL FOOD & SUPPLEMENTS: Feed Supplements

Micronutrients USA LLC......................... D 317 486-5880
  Indianapolis *(G-8903)*
Shaklee Authorized Distributor............... G 260 471-8232
  Fort Wayne *(G-5410)*
Super Blend Inc...................................... G 260 463-7486
  Lagrange *(G-10766)*

ANIMAL FOOD & SUPPLEMENTS: Livestock

Alliance Feed LLC.................................. G 260 244-6100
  Columbia City *(G-2119)*
Cargill Dry Corn Ingrdents Inc................ E 317 632-1481
  Indianapolis *(G-7744)*
Flinn Frms Bdford Feed Seed In............. G 812 279-4136
  Bedford *(G-636)*
Kent Nutrition Group Inc........................ F 574 722-5368
  Logansport *(G-11087)*
Ridley USA Inc.. F 260 768-4103
  Shipshewana *(G-14883)*
Strauss Veal Feeds Inc........................... E 260 982-8611
  North Manchester *(G-13251)*
United Animal Health Inc....................... D 317 758-4495
  Sheridan *(G-14830)*
Wanafeed Corporation............................ G 317 862-4032
  Indianapolis *(G-9736)*

ANIMAL FOOD & SUPPLEMENTS: Pet, Exc Dog & Cat, Canned

Hoosier Processing LLC......................... F 260 422-9440
  Fort Wayne *(G-5080)*

ANIMAL FOOD & SUPPLEMENTS: Poultry

Pine Manor Inc.. B 800 532-4186
  Orland *(G-13370)*

ANIMAL FOOD/SUPPLEMENTS: Feeds Fm Meat/Meat/Veg Combnd Meals

Tyson Foods Inc..................................... G 260 726-3118
  Portland *(G-13973)*

ANNEALING: Metal

Atmosphere Annealing LLC................... E 812 346-1275
  North Vernon *(G-13256)*
H & H Commercial Heat Treating........... G 765 288-3618
  Muncie *(G-12407)*

ANODIZING SVC

B-D Industries Inc................................... F 574 295-1420
  Elkhart *(G-3214)*
Bearcat Anodizing LLC.......................... G 574 533-0448
  Goshen *(G-6097)*
Brunswick Corporation............................ D 260 459-8200
  Fort Wayne *(G-4821)*
Quick Turn Anodizing LLC..................... F 877 716-1150
  Edinburgh *(G-3099)*
Southern Alum Finshg Co Inc................ G 800 357-9016
  Indianapolis *(G-9464)*
Superior Metal Tech LLC....................... D 317 897-9850
  Indianapolis *(G-9530)*
Yellow Dog Anodizing............................. G 574 343-2247
  Elkhart *(G-3799)*

ANTENNAS: Receiving

Toyota Tsusho America Inc.................... D 765 449-3500
  Colburn *(G-2111)*

ANTIFREEZE

Universal Services Inc............................ G 219 397-4373
  East Chicago *(G-3051)*

APPLIANCE PARTS: Porcelain Enameled

Long Item Development Corp................ G 317 780-1077
  Indianapolis *(G-8780)*

APPLIANCES, HOUSEHOLD OR COIN OPERATED: Laundry Dryers

Bonzell Combs.. G 872 248-4123
  Highland *(G-7125)*
Laundry On US LLC................................ G 812 567-3653
  Terre Haute *(G-15630)*
Megans Wash and Fold LLC.................. G 317 903-5253
  Pendleton *(G-13543)*
Whirlpool Corporation............................. E 317 837-5300
  Plainfield *(G-13742)*

APPLIANCES, HOUSEHOLD: Kitchen, Major, Exc Refrigs & Stoves

Keith Miller... G 260 982-6858
  North Manchester *(G-13237)*
Solfire Contract Mfg Inc......................... F 260 755-2115
  Fort Wayne *(G-5424)*

APPLIANCES, HOUSEHOLD: Sewing Machines & Attchmnts, Domestic

Sailrite Enterprises Inc.......................... F 260 244-4647
  Columbia City *(G-2195)*

APPLIANCES: Household, Refrigerators & Freezers

Freezing Systems and Svc Inc............... F 219 879-6236
  Michigan City *(G-11615)*
JC Refrigeration LLC.............................. G 260 768-4067
  Shipshewana *(G-14855)*

APPLIANCES: Major, Cooking

Sterling Manufacturing LLC................... G 260 451-9760
  Fort Wayne *(G-5442)*
Thermodyne Food Svc Pdts Inc............. E 260 428-2535
  Fort Wayne *(G-5482)*
Z Grills Inc.. G 909 295-5264
  Indianapolis *(G-9806)*

APPLIANCES: Small, Electric

Battle Creek Equipment Co.................... E 260 495-3472
  Fremont *(G-5810)*
Electric Plus Inc..................................... D 317 718-0100
  Avon *(G-516)*
Exhale Fans LLC..................................... G 812 366-3351
  Georgetown *(G-6059)*
Royal Spa Corporation............................ D 317 781-0828
  Indianapolis *(G-9341)*
Ward Electric LLC................................... G 219 462-8780
  Valparaiso *(G-16078)*

APPLICATIONS SOFTWARE PROGRAMMING

Authenticx Inc.. D 317 296-6238
  Indianapolis *(G-7570)*
Binarie LLC... G 317 496-8836
  Greenwood *(G-6676)*
Center For Ethcal Rbtics A Nnt.............. G 219 741-9374
  Hammond *(G-6897)*

Employee Codes: A=Over 500 employees, B=251-500
C=101-250, D=51-100, E=20-50, F=10-19, G=1-9

APPLICATIONS SOFTWARE PROGRAMMING

Ksn Technologies Inc .... E 219 877-4770
Chesterton *(G-1942)*

Lifedata LLC .... G 925 800-3381
Marion *(G-11309)*

Prevounce Health Inc .... F 800 618-7738
Indianapolis *(G-9195)*

Robocfi LLC .... G 317 612-7889
Fort Wayne *(G-5388)*

Wall Control Services Inc .... G 260 450-6411
Fort Wayne *(G-5542)*

AQUARIUM ACCESS, METAL

Spectrum Brands Inc .... E 317 773-6627
Noblesville *(G-13179)*

AQUARIUMS & ACCESS: Glass

Spectrum Brands Inc .... E 317 773-6627
Noblesville *(G-13179)*

ARCHITECTURAL SVCS

Meyer Custom Woodworking Inc ..... G 812 695-2021
Dubois *(G-2954)*

Werzalit of America Inc .... D 814 362-3881
Syracuse *(G-15492)*

ARCHITECTURAL SVCS: Engineering

Architura Corporation .... G 317 348-1000
Indianapolis *(G-7541)*

ARMATURE REPAIRING & REWINDING SVC

Flanders Electric Mtr Svc LLC .... D 812 421-4300
Evansville *(G-4078)*

Gorrepati Service Systems .... G 317 299-7590
Indianapolis *(G-8308)*

Ies Subsidiary Holdings Inc .... G 330 830-3500
South Bend *(G-15074)*

Machine Rebuilders & Service .... F 260 482-8168
Fort Wayne *(G-5197)*

ARMOR PLATES

By The Sword Inc .... F 877 433-9368
Huntingburg *(G-7271)*

ART DEALERS & GALLERIES

Gibbs Susie Framing & Art .... G 765 428-2434
Lafayette *(G-10589)*

H J J Inc .... G 219 362-4421
La Porte *(G-10414)*

Noel Studio Inc .... F 317 297-1117
Indianapolis *(G-9019)*

Pfortune Art & Design Inc .... G 317 872-4123
Indianapolis *(G-9133)*

Randall Corp .... G 812 425-7122
Evansville *(G-4272)*

ART GOODS & SPLYS WHOLESALERS

Bottom Line Management Inc .... F 812 944-7388
Clarksville *(G-2010)*

ART GOODS, WHOLESALE

Noel Studio Inc .... F 317 297-1117
Indianapolis *(G-9019)*

ART SPLY STORES

Colophon Book Arts Supply LLC ..... G 812 671-0577
Bloomington *(G-834)*

Stitch N Frame .... G 260 478-1301
Fort Wayne *(G-5443)*

Twinrocker Hand Made Paper Inc ... G 765 563-3119
Brookston *(G-1314)*

ARTIST'S MATERIALS & SPLYS

Double E Distributing Co Inc .... G 812 334-2220
Bloomington *(G-858)*

ARTWORK: Framed

Horizon Anim LLC .... G 317 742-4917
Indianapolis *(G-8413)*

ASBESTOS REMOVAL EQPT

Wall Control Services Inc .... G 260 450-6411
Fort Wayne *(G-5542)*

ASPHALT & ASPHALT PRDTS

Asphalt Materials Inc .... G 317 875-4670
Indianapolis *(G-7553)*

Asphalt Materials Inc .... B 317 872-6010
Indianapolis *(G-7552)*

Calcar Quarries Incorporated .... F 812 723-2109
Paoli *(G-13491)*

E & B Paving Inc .... E 765 643-5358
Anderson *(G-112)*

Hotmix Inc .... G 812 663-2020
Greensburg *(G-6605)*

Hotmix Inc .... G 812 926-1471
Aurora *(G-445)*

Milestone Contractors N Inc .... G 219 924-5900
South Bend *(G-15151)*

Niblock Excavating Inc .... D 574 848-4437
Bristol *(G-1281)*

Paul H Rohe Company Inc .... E 812 926-1471
Aurora *(G-451)*

Rogers Group Inc .... E 812 882-3640
Vincennes *(G-16150)*

Triangle Asphalt Paving Corp .... E 765 482-5701
Lebanon *(G-10947)*

ASPHALT COATINGS & SEALERS

Alphajak LLC .... G 574 800-4810
Mishawaka *(G-11839)*

Central States Mfg Inc .... C 219 879-4770
Michigan City *(G-11586)*

Dave OMara Paving Inc .... G 812 346-1214
North Vernon *(G-13264)*

Dupouy Enterprises LLC .... G 765 453-1466
Kokomo *(G-10260)*

K Tech Specialty Coatings Inc .... F 260 587-3888
Ashley *(G-333)*

Prophalt Sealcoating LLC .... G 502 356-3238
Henryville *(G-7114)*

R & J Excvtg & Sealcoating LLC ..... G 812 799-1849
Columbus *(G-2385)*

Sampco Inc .... G 413 442-4043
South Bend *(G-15230)*

Schmidt Contracting Inc .... E 812 482-3923
Jasper *(G-9908)*

Standard Industries Inc .... G 219 872-1111
Michigan City *(G-11672)*

Triangle Asphalt Paving Corp .... E 765 482-5701
Lebanon *(G-10947)*

ASPHALT MINING & BITUMINOUS STONE QUARRYING SVCS

Hanson Agrigoods Midwest Inc .... G 317 635-9048
Cloverdale *(G-2085)*

ASPHALT PLANTS INCLUDING GRAVEL MIX TYPE

Harding Group LLC .... G 317 846-7401
Indianapolis *(G-8356)*

PRODUCT SECTION

Harding Materials Inc .... G 317 849-9666
Indianapolis *(G-8358)*

ASSEMBLING & PACKAGING SVCS: Cosmetic Kits

Elite Packaging LLC .... G 502 232-2596
Jeffersonville *(G-9975)*

ASSEMBLING SVC: Plumbing Fixture Fittings, Plastic

Buckaroos Inc .... G 317 899-9100
Indianapolis *(G-7696)*

LGS Plumbing Inc .... E 219 663-2177
Crown Point *(G-2718)*

ASSOCIATION FOR THE HANDICAPPED

Knox Cnty Assn For Rmrkble Ctz .... D 812 886-4312
Vincennes *(G-16136)*

ASSOCIATIONS: Business

News-Banner Publications Inc .... E 260 824-0224
Bluffton *(G-1046)*

Super Blend Inc .... G 260 463-7486
Lagrange *(G-10766)*

ASSOCIATIONS: Manufacturers'

Abda Incorporated .... G 317 273-8343
Indianapolis *(G-7416)*

ASSOCIATIONS: Real Estate Management

Heritage Financial Group Inc .... E 574 522-8000
Elkhart *(G-3404)*

Millwork Specialties Co Inc .... G 219 362-2960
La Porte *(G-10453)*

Project Field Solutions Inc .... G 317 590-7678
Fishers *(G-4584)*

ASSOCIATIONS: Trade

American Maint & Training Inc .... F 812 738-4230
Corydon *(G-2485)*

Automobile Dealers Assn of Ind ..... G 317 635-1441
Indianapolis *(G-7576)*

ATOMIZERS

All Rvs Manufacturing Inc .... G 574 538-1559
Shipshewana *(G-14833)*

All-State Industries Inc .... G 574 522-4245
Elkhart *(G-3165)*

ARC of Greater Boone Cnty Inc ...... F 765 482-0051
Lebanon *(G-10875)*

Aspire Industries .... F 812 542-1561
New Albany *(G-12693)*

BF Goodrich Tire Manufacturing ..... G 260 493-8100
Woodburn *(G-16946)*

Crr Industries LLC .... G 219 947-2052
Hobart *(G-7184)*

Derby Industries LLC .... G 765 778-6104
Anderson *(G-102)*

Incipio Devices LLC .... D 260 200-1970
Huntington *(G-7325)*

International Game Technology ...... G 317 731-3791
Indianapolis *(G-8577)*

LCI Industries .... G 574 535-1125
Elkhart *(G-3475)*

Madden Engineered Products LLC .. G 574 295-4292
Elkhart *(G-3509)*

Nemcomed Instrs & Implants .... F 800 255-4576
Fort Wayne *(G-5265)*

Nf Industries Inc .... G 317 738-2558
Franklin *(G-5759)*

PRODUCT SECTION
AUTOMOBILES & OTHER MOTOR VEHICLES WHOLESALERS

Nfi Industries Inc .... G 765 483-9741
　Lebanon *(G-10926)*
Patterson Products LLC .... G 812 309-3614
　Otwell *(G-13457)*
Squareframe Industries LLC .... G 765 430-3301
　Lafayette *(G-10696)*
True Precision Tech Inc .... G 765 432-2177
　Kokomo *(G-10352)*

AUDIO & VIDEO EQPT, EXC COMMERCIAL

Adaptive Tech Solutions LLC .... G 317 762-4363
　Carmel *(G-1549)*
Damping Technologies Inc .... F 574 258-7916
　Mishawaka *(G-11880)*
Ebey Sales & Service .... G 260 636-3286
　Albion *(G-25)*
Electronics Research Inc .... C 812 925-6000
　Chandler *(G-1861)*
Image Vault LLC .... G 812 948-8400
　New Albany *(G-12743)*
Loys Sales Inc .... G 765 552-7250
　Elwood *(G-3829)*
RB Annis Instruments Inc .... G 765 848-1621
　Greencastle *(G-6428)*
Record / Play Tek Inc .... G 574 848-5233
　Bristol *(G-1284)*
Sony Dadc US Inc .... A 812 462-8100
　Terre Haute *(G-15706)*
Sports Select Usa Inc .... G 317 631-4011
　Indianapolis *(G-9482)*
Technology Cons Group LLC .... G 219 525-4064
　Merrillville *(G-11565)*
Total Home Control LLC .... G 317 430-3679
　Indianapolis *(G-9623)*

AUDIO COMPONENTS

A E Techron Inc .... F 574 295-9495
　Elkhart *(G-3139)*

AUDIO ELECTRONIC SYSTEMS

Audience Response Systems Inc .... F 812 479-7507
　Evansville *(G-3902)*
Boyer Enterprises Inc .... G 812 773-3295
　Evansville *(G-3943)*
Csd Group LLC .... G 260 918-3500
　New Haven *(G-12901)*
Dream Systems LLC .... F 715 241-8332
　New Palestine *(G-12936)*
Harman Embedded Audio LLC .... F 317 849-8175
　Indianapolis *(G-8363)*
Lea LLC .... F 574 216-1622
　South Bend *(G-15120)*
Lexicon Incorporated .... C 203 328-3500
　Elkhart *(G-3486)*
St Joe Group Inc .... E 260 918-3500
　New Haven *(G-12920)*
Tech Solutions and Sales Inc .... G 317 536-5846
　Indianapolis *(G-9567)*
Yongs Audio Connection LLC .... G 317 298-8333
　Indianapolis *(G-9804)*

AUDIO-VISUAL PROGRAM PRODUCTION SVCS

Sizzlin Sound Productions LLC .... G 765 376-0129
　Crawfordsville *(G-2615)*
Technology Cons Group LLC .... G 219 525-4064
　Merrillville *(G-11565)*
Top In Sound Inc .... G 765 649-8111
　Anderson *(G-207)*

AUTO & HOME SUPPLY STORES: Auto & Truck Eqpt & Parts

Advance Stores Company Inc .... G 317 253-5034
　Indianapolis *(G-7436)*
Engler Machine & Tool Inc .... F 812 386-6254
　Princeton *(G-13992)*

AUTO & HOME SUPPLY STORES: Automotive Access

Broadway Auto Glass LLC .... F 219 884-5277
　Merrillville *(G-11493)*

AUTO & HOME SUPPLY STORES: Automotive parts

Component Machine Inc .... G 317 635-8929
　Indianapolis *(G-7845)*
Ferguson Equipment Inc .... G 574 234-4303
　South Bend *(G-15033)*
Fortville Automotive Sup Inc .... G 317 485-5114
　Fortville *(G-5594)*
Greys Automotive Inc .... G 317 632-3562
　Indianapolis *(G-8328)*
KOI Enterprises Inc .... D 812 537-2335
　Lawrenceburg *(G-10843)*
Lingenfelter Prfmce Engrg Inc .... E 260 724-2552
　Decatur *(G-2869)*
Mastersbilt Chassis Inc .... G 812 793-3666
　Crothersville *(G-2642)*
Promotor Engines & Components .... G 574 533-9898
　Goshen *(G-6243)*

AUTO & HOME SUPPLY STORES: Batteries, Automotive & Truck

Batteries Plus .... G 317 219-0007
　Noblesville *(G-13040)*
Tri-State Power Supply LLC .... G 812 537-2500
　Lawrenceburg *(G-10863)*

AUTO & HOME SUPPLY STORES: Speed Shops, Incl Race Car Splys

Motorsport Price Engineering .... G 812 546-4220
　Hope *(G-7229)*
Olson Race Cars .... G 765 529-6933
　New Castle *(G-12878)*

AUTO & HOME SUPPLY STORES: Trailer Hitches, Automotive

Pyramid Equipment Inc .... F 219 778-2591
　Rolling Prairie *(G-14371)*

AUTO & HOME SUPPLY STORES: Truck Eqpt & Parts

Advance Prtective Coatings Inc .... G 317 228-0123
　Indianapolis *(G-7435)*
Dubois County Liners LLP .... G 812 634-1294
　Jasper *(G-9835)*
Hellmans Auto Supply Co Inc .... G 219 885-7655
　Gary *(G-5949)*
Line-X .... G 812 491-9475
　Evansville *(G-4170)*
Line-X of Schererville Inc .... F 219 865-1000
　Schererville *(G-14530)*
Mid-State Truck Equipment Inc .... E 317 849-4903
　Fishers *(G-4566)*
Nicks Automotive Inc .... F 765 964-6843
　Union City *(G-15856)*
RPM Machinery LLC .... G 574 271-0800
　South Bend *(G-15228)*
Truck Stylin Unlimited .... F 574 223-8800
　Rochester *(G-14330)*

AUTOCLAVES: Laboratory

Helmer Scientific LLC .... C 317 773-9073
　Noblesville *(G-13094)*

AUTOMATED TELLER MACHINE NETWORK

Retro Atm LLC .... G 317 752-6915
　Indianapolis *(G-9294)*

AUTOMATIC REGULATING CONTROL: Building Svcs Monitoring, Auto

Johnson Controls Inc .... F 812 868-1374
　Evansville *(G-4144)*
Johnson Controls Inc .... G 317 917-5043
　Pittsboro *(G-13649)*
Vivint Inc .... B 317 983-0112
　Indianapolis *(G-9727)*
Wise Energy LLC .... G 317 475-0305
　Indianapolis *(G-9776)*

AUTOMATIC REGULATING CONTROLS: AC & Refrigeration

Elliott-Williams Company Inc .... E 317 453-2295
　Indianapolis *(G-8097)*
Gillespie Mrrell Gen Contg LLC .... G 765 618-4084
　Marion *(G-11288)*
Siemens Industry Inc .... E 317 381-0734
　Indianapolis *(G-9425)*

AUTOMATIC REGULATING CONTROLS: Appliance, Exc AirCond/Refr

Johnson Sales Corp .... G 219 322-9558
　Schererville *(G-14525)*

AUTOMATIC REGULATING CONTROLS: Hardware, Environmental Reg

Dwyer Instruments LLC .... C 219 879-8868
　Michigan City *(G-11604)*

AUTOMATIC REGULATING CONTROLS: Pneumatic Relays, Air-Cond

SMC Corporation of America .... B 317 899-4440
　Noblesville *(G-13176)*

AUTOMATIC TELLER MACHINES

Chase Beford .... G 812 277-7028
　Bedford *(G-626)*
Chase N Corydon .... F 812 738-3032
　Corydon *(G-2490)*
Chase Southport Emerson .... G 317 266-7470
　Indianapolis *(G-7787)*
Elmos .... G 574 371-2050
　Warsaw *(G-16358)*
Fairfield Gas Way .... G 260 744-2186
　Fort Wayne *(G-4973)*
Retro Atm LLC .... G 317 752-6915
　Indianapolis *(G-9294)*

AUTOMOBILES & OTHER MOTOR VEHICLES WHOLESALERS

Coachmen Recrtl Vhcl Co LLC .... G 574 825-5821
　Middlebury *(G-11704)*
Fenwick Motor Sports .... G 765 522-1354
　Bainbridge *(G-562)*

AUTOMOBILES & OTHER MOTOR VEHICLES WHOLESALERS

Wabash National Corporation.............. E 765 771-5300
  Lafayette *(G-10715)*

Wabash National Corporation.............. A 765 771-5310
  Lafayette *(G-10716)*

AUTOMOBILES: Wholesalers

Grouper Wild LLC................................. C 574 534-1499
  Goshen *(G-6156)*

AUTOMOTIVE & TRUCK GENERAL REPAIR SVC

Auto Express Vale............................... E 317 897-6618
  Indianapolis *(G-7572)*

Auto Specialty Lafayette Inc................ G 765 446-2311
  Lafayette *(G-10531)*

Awol Metal Contorsion LLC.................. G 260 909-0411
  Kendallville *(G-10093)*

Barry Seat Cover & Auto GL Co............ F 574 288-4603
  South Bend *(G-14956)*

Bills Gar & Auto Refinishing................. G 765 296-4978
  Lafayette *(G-10537)*

Bridgestone Ret Operations LLC.......... G 317 773-2761
  Noblesville *(G-13048)*

Hendershot Service Center Inc............. F 765 653-2600
  Greencastle *(G-6412)*

Hobbs Auto Diagnostics & Repr........... G 765 606-1490
  Anderson *(G-127)*

Jasper Engine Exchange Inc................ A 812 482-1041
  Jasper *(G-9853)*

Kerns Speed Shop................................ G 812 275-4289
  Bedford *(G-652)*

Leonards Auto Service.......................... G 812 879-4802
  Gosport *(G-6286)*

Macallister Machinery Co Inc................ C 260 483-6469
  Fort Wayne *(G-5195)*

Marmon Highway Tech LLC................... E 317 787-0718
  Indianapolis *(G-8839)*

Midwest Auto Repair Inc....................... F 219 322-0364
  Schererville *(G-14534)*

Mikesmobimech LLC............................. G 317 753-0492
  Indianapolis *(G-8918)*

Mitchell Smith Racing........................... G 765 640-0237
  Anderson *(G-155)*

Mooresville Tire & Service Ctr............... G 317 831-1215
  Mooresville *(G-12224)*

OHM Automotive LLC............................ G 812 879-5455
  Bloomington *(G-934)*

Pfm Automotive Management Inc......... G 317 733-3977
  Zionsville *(G-17040)*

Pfm Car & Truck Castleton Inc.............. E 317 577-7777
  Indianapolis *(G-9131)*

Schnell Service Center......................... G 812 683-2461
  Huntingburg *(G-7290)*

Selking International LLC..................... E 260 482-3000
  Fort Wayne *(G-5408)*

Selking International Inc....................... G 574 522-2001
  Elkhart *(G-3668)*

Upland Tire & Service Ctr Inc................ G 765 998-0871
  Upland *(G-15884)*

Woodward Tire Sales & Svc Inc............ G 260 432-0694
  Fort Wayne *(G-5575)*

AUTOMOTIVE BODY SHOP

Nicks Automotive Inc........................... F 765 964-6843
  Union City *(G-15856)*

AUTOMOTIVE BODY, PAINT & INTERIOR REPAIR & MAINTENANCE SVC

Indiana Custom Trucks LLC.................. E 260 463-3244
  Shipshewana *(G-14852)*

Marmon Highway Tech LLC................... E 317 787-0718
  Indianapolis *(G-8839)*

Northern Ind Indus Catings LLC........... G 574 893-4621
  Akron *(G-6)*

AUTOMOTIVE CUSTOMIZING SVCS, NONFACTORY BASIS

K & D Custom Coach Inc...................... E 574 537-1716
  Goshen *(G-6182)*

AUTOMOTIVE GLASS REPLACEMENT SHOPS

Barry Seat Cover & Auto GL Co............ F 574 288-4603
  South Bend *(G-14956)*

Broadway Auto Glass LLC..................... F 219 884-5277
  Merrillville *(G-11493)*

AUTOMOTIVE PARTS, ACCESS & SPLYS

1 Composites LLC............................... G 260 665-6112
  Bourbon *(G-1119)*

4 Piston Racing.................................... G 317 902-0200
  Danville *(G-2805)*

A-Fab LLC... F 812 897-0900
  Boonville *(G-1078)*

Acadia... G 260 894-7125
  Ligonier *(G-11001)*

Accuride Emi LLC................................ E 940 565-8505
  Evansville *(G-3868)*

Action Machine Inc............................. F 574 287-9650
  South Bend *(G-14935)*

Adell Group LLC.................................. G 317 507-6158
  Carmel *(G-1550)*

Aero Industries Inc.............................. D 317 244-2433
  Indianapolis *(G-7448)*

Aeromotive Tech Inc........................... G 260 723-5646
  South Whitley *(G-15315)*

Airfx USA LLC...................................... F 812 917-5573
  Terre Haute *(G-15536)*

Airfx USA LLC...................................... G 812 878-8135
  Brazil *(G-1132)*

Airtek LLC... C 219 947-1664
  Hobart *(G-7172)*

All American Group Inc........................ E 574 262-0123
  Elkhart *(G-3160)*

Allied Tube & Conduit Corp.................. F 812 265-9255
  Madison *(G-11201)*

Allison Transmission Inc...................... C 317 242-5000
  Indianapolis *(G-7487)*

Allison Transmission Inc...................... G 317 821-5104
  Indianapolis *(G-7488)*

Allison Transmission Inc...................... C 317 280-6206
  Indianapolis *(G-7489)*

AM General Holdings LLC..................... A 574 237-6222
  South Bend *(G-14940)*

AM General LLC................................... G 574 258-6699
  South Bend *(G-14941)*

AM General LLC................................... D 574 237-6222
  South Bend *(G-14942)*

American Axle & Mfg Inc...................... E 260 824-6800
  Bluffton *(G-1024)*

Amsafe Partners Inc............................ D 574 266-8330
  Elkhart *(G-3180)*

Aptiv Services Us LLC......................... C 765 451-0732
  Carmel *(G-1562)*

Aptiv Services Us LLC......................... A 765 451-5011
  Kokomo *(G-10233)*

Ares Division LLC................................ G 260 349-9803
  Waterloo *(G-16514)*

Aristo LLC... E
  Hobart *(G-7173)*

Attc Manufacturing Inc........................ B 812 547-5060
  Tell City *(G-15497)*

Atwood Mobile Products Inc................ A 574 264-2131
  Elkhart *(G-3202)*

Atwood Mobile Products LLC................ D 574 266-4848
  Elkhart *(G-3203)*

Atwood Mobile Products LLC................ D 574 264-2131
  Elkhart *(G-3204)*

Atwood Mobile Products LLC................ D 574 264-2131
  Elkhart *(G-3205)*

Atwood Mobile Products LLC................ D 574 264-2131
  Elkhart *(G-3206)*

Auburn Manufacturing Inc................... E 260 925-8651
  Auburn *(G-364)*

Auto Bumper Exchange Inc.................. G 260 493-4408
  Fort Wayne *(G-4780)*

Autoform Tool & Mfg LLC..................... C 260 624-2014
  Angola *(G-232)*

Autoliv Asp Inc.................................... B 801 620-8018
  Columbia City *(G-2121)*

Autoneum North America Inc............... G 248 848-0100
  Jeffersonville *(G-9937)*

Avg North America Inc........................ F 765 748-3162
  Gas City *(G-6033)*

Avionic Structures Indiana Inc............. F 765 671-7865
  Marion *(G-11273)*

Axle Inc.. G 574 264-9434
  Elkhart *(G-3209)*

B & B Manufacturing Inc..................... D 219 324-0247
  La Porte *(G-10387)*

Barry Seat Cover & Auto GL Co............ F 574 288-4603
  South Bend *(G-14956)*

Bender Products Inc........................... E 574 255-5350
  Mishawaka *(G-11852)*

Bendix Coml Vhcl Systems LLC............ E 260 356-9720
  Huntington *(G-7301)*

Bentz Transport Products Inc.............. F 260 622-9100
  Zionsville *(G-16996)*

Borgwarner Noblesville LLC.................. G 765 451-0400
  Kokomo *(G-10240)*

Borgwarner Propulsion II LLC............... G 765 236-0025
  Kokomo *(G-10241)*

BRC Rubber & Plastics Inc................... F 260 203-5300
  Churubusco *(G-1974)*

BRC Rubber & Plastics Inc................... E 260 894-4121
  Ligonier *(G-11007)*

BRC Rubber & Plastics Inc................... C 260 693-2171
  Fort Wayne *(G-4815)*

Brindle Products Inc........................... F 260 627-2156
  Grabill *(G-6290)*

Cardinal Services Inc Indiana............... D 574 267-3823
  Warsaw *(G-16333)*

Carter Fuel Systems LLC..................... G 574 735-0235
  Logansport *(G-11065)*

CCT Enterprises LLC........................... E 260 925-1420
  Auburn *(G-375)*

Cedar Creek Studios Inc...................... G 260 627-7320
  Leo *(G-10966)*

Chemtrusion Inc.................................. E 812 280-2910
  Jeffersonville *(G-9951)*

Chiyoda USA Corporation..................... C 765 653-9098
  Greencastle *(G-6396)*

Colbin Tool Company Inc..................... E 574 457-3183
  Syracuse *(G-15459)*

Component Machine Inc...................... G 317 635-8929
  Indianapolis *(G-7845)*

Compositech Inc................................. E 800 231-6755
  Indianapolis *(G-7846)*

Concept Design & Fabrication.............. G 812 481-1142
  Jasper *(G-9829)*

Continental Manufacturing LLC............ E 765 778-9999
  Anderson *(G-98)*

PRODUCT SECTION — AUTOMOTIVE PARTS, ACCESS & SPLYS

Conversion Components Inc............... G 574 264-4181
Elkhart *(G-3266)*

Cooper-Standard Automotive Inc......... E 260 637-5824
Auburn *(G-380)*

Cooper-Standard Automotive Inc......... E 260 247-7703
Fort Wayne *(G-4872)*

Covidien LP... C 317 837-8199
Plainfield *(G-13674)*

Csr Suspension LLC............................ G 812 346-8620
North Vernon *(G-13261)*

Cummins Cdc Holding Inc.................... A 812 312-3162
Columbus *(G-2251)*

Cummins Engine Company Inc............ E 812 522-9366
Seymour *(G-14643)*

Cummins Engine Holding Company..... B 812 377-5000
Columbus *(G-2255)*

Cummins Franchise Holdco LLC......... D 812 377-5000
Columbus *(G-2257)*

Cummins Holding Group LLC.............. G 765 962-6332
Richmond *(G-14112)*

Cummins Inc... D 812 377-5298
Columbus *(G-2258)*

Cummins Inc... G 812 377-2932
Columbus *(G-2259)*

Cummins Inc... G 812 377-9914
Columbus *(G-2260)*

Cummins Inc... G 812 377-0150
Columbus *(G-2261)*

Cummins Inc... G 765 430-0093
Columbus *(G-2262)*

Cummins Inc... F 812 376-0742
Columbus *(G-2263)*

Cummins Inc... G 812 377-8601
Columbus *(G-2272)*

Cummins Inc... F 812 378-2874
Columbus *(G-2273)*

Cummins Inc... G 260 482-3691
Fort Wayne *(G-4895)*

Cummins Inc... F 317 610-2493
Indianapolis *(G-7927)*

Cummins Inc... G 317 244-7251
Indianapolis *(G-7928)*

Cummins Inc... G 812 524-6381
Seymour *(G-14644)*

Cummins Inc... G 260 657-1436
Woodburn *(G-16947)*

Cummins Power Systems LLC............ A 410 590-8700
Columbus *(G-2274)*

Cummins Sales Svc............................. G 260 482-3691
Fort Wayne *(G-4896)*

Cummins Sales Svc............................. G 574 252-2154
Mishawaka *(G-11870)*

Cummins-Scania Xpi Mfg LLC............. G 812 377-5000
Columbus *(G-2275)*

Curtis-Maruyasu America Inc.............. B 812 544-2021
Santa Claus *(G-14507)*

Cushman Performance Parts LLC...... G 765 653-3054
Greencastle *(G-6400)*

Custom Wood Products Inc................. D 574 522-3300
Elkhart *(G-3283)*

Dacco/Detroit Indiana Inc..................... G 317 545-5334
Indianapolis *(G-7945)*

Daechang Seat Co Ltd USA................ E 317 755-3663
Indianapolis *(G-7946)*

Dallara LLC.. F 317 388-5400
Speedway *(G-15334)*

Dana Driveshaft Products LLC............ G 260 432-2903
Marion *(G-11280)*

Dana Incorporated................................ G 260 897-2827
Avilla *(G-474)*

Dana Incorporated................................ C 260 481-3597
Fort Wayne *(G-4903)*

Dana Incorporated................................ G 765 772-4000
Lafayette *(G-10568)*

Dana Light Axle Products LLC............ F 260 483-7174
Fort Wayne *(G-4904)*

Danta Inc.. G 219 369-9190
La Porte *(G-10398)*

Delco Electronics................................. G 765 455-9713
Kokomo *(G-10255)*

Delphi Electronics Safety..................... G 765 883-7795
Kokomo *(G-10256)*

Delphi Technologies............................. F 765 451-0670
Kokomo *(G-10257)*

Delphi Technologies............................. E 765 480-1993
Kokomo *(G-10258)*

Diamet.. G 812 379-4606
Columbus *(G-2283)*

Diesel Punk Core................................. G 812 631-0606
Bloomington *(G-855)*

Dometic.. C 574 266-4848
Elkhart *(G-3300)*

Dometic Corporation............................ B 260 463-7657
Elkhart *(G-3301)*

Double T Manufacturing Corp............. F 574 262-1340
Elkhart *(G-3302)*

Dynamic Axle LLC............................... G 574 226-0242
Elkhart *(G-3308)*

Dynomax.. G 317 835-3813
Fishers *(G-4506)*

E-Motion LLC....................................... G 317 379-5761
Carmel *(G-1617)*

Eaton Corporation................................ G 317 704-2520
Indianapolis *(G-8043)*

Eco Vehicle Systems LLC................... E 765 964-6009
Union City *(G-15852)*

Engineered Machined Pdts Inc............ G 317 462-8894
Greenfield *(G-6498)*

Enovapremier LLC............................... E 812 385-0576
Princeton *(G-13993)*

Faurecia Emssons Ctrl Tech USA....... A 812 348-4305
Columbus *(G-2303)*

FCA North America Holdings LLC...... B 765 454-0018
Kokomo *(G-10264)*

FCA US LLC... C 765 454-1005
Kokomo *(G-10267)*

Federal-Mogul Motorparts LLC........... G 317 875-7259
Indianapolis *(G-8171)*

Federal-Mogul Powertrain LLC........... G 765 659-7207
Frankfort *(G-5662)*

Fenwick Motor Sports.......................... G 765 522-1354
Bainbridge *(G-562)*

Fiber Forged Composites LLC............ G 574 772-0107
Knox *(G-10207)*

Fisher & Company Incorporated.......... D 586 746-2000
Evansville *(G-4070)*

Flex-N-Gate LLC.................................. G 260 665-8288
Angola *(G-251)*

Flex-N-Gate LLC.................................. G 765 793-5732
Covington *(G-2530)*

Ford Motor Company........................... F 901 368-8821
Plainfield *(G-13680)*

Four Woods Laminating Inc................ E 260 593-2246
Topeka *(G-15806)*

Frank Wiss Racg Components Inc..... G 317 243-9585
Indianapolis *(G-8222)*

Freudenberg-Nok General Partnr....... G 765 763-7246
Morristown *(G-12277)*

Freudenberg-Nok General Partnr....... C 317 421-3400
Shelbyville *(G-14756)*

Freudenberg-Nok General Partnr....... C 734 354-5504
Shelbyville *(G-14757)*

G N U Inc... C 219 464-7813
Valparaiso *(G-15952)*

Gac Enterprises Usa LLC.................... F 317 839-9525
Plainfield *(G-13682)*

Gearbox Lm Holdings Inc.................... G 765 362-3500
Crawfordsville *(G-2569)*

General Motors LLC............................. F 260 673-2048
Roanoke *(G-14267)*

GKN Sinter Metals LLC....................... C 812 883-3381
Salem *(G-14479)*

Global Forming LLC............................. E 317 290-1000
Indianapolis *(G-8289)*

GM Components Holdings LLC........... G 765 451-8440
Kokomo *(G-10270)*

Grede LLC.. C 765 521-8000
New Castle *(G-12865)*

Greg Moser Engineering Inc................ E 260 726-6689
Portland *(G-13949)*

Grouper Wild LLC................................ C 574 534-1499
Goshen *(G-6156)*

Gulf Stream Coach Inc........................ C 574 773-7761
Nappanee *(G-12603)*

Hart Plastics Inc................................... E 574 264-7060
Elkhart *(G-3400)*

Heartland Automotive........................... G 765 446-2311
Lafayette *(G-10595)*

Heartland Automotive Inc.................... A 765 653-4263
Greencastle *(G-6409)*

Heartland Automotive LLC................... E 765 653-4263
Greencastle *(G-6410)*

Hendrickson Engineering LLC............. G 765 404-9132
West Lafayette *(G-16592)*

Hendrickson International.................... E 260 349-6400
Kendallville *(G-10115)*

Hendrickson International Corp........... G 260 868-2131
Butler *(G-1466)*

Hendrickson International Corp........... E 260 349-6400
Kendallville *(G-10116)*

Hendrickson International Corp........... E 260 349-6400
Kendallville *(G-10117)*

Hendrickson International Corp........... C 765 483-5350
Lebanon *(G-10896)*

Hendrickson International Corp........... G 765 483-7217
Lebanon *(G-10897)*

Hisada America Inc.............................. C 812 526-0756
Edinburgh *(G-3086)*

Hitachi Astemo Americas Inc.............. D 859 734-9451
Ligonier *(G-11017)*

Hoehn Engineered Products LLC........ G 260 223-9158
Decatur *(G-2863)*

Honda Dev & Mfg Amer LLC............... A 812 222-6000
Greensburg *(G-6604)*

Hoosier Industrial Supply Inc.............. F 574 533-8565
Goshen *(G-6168)*

Horner Industrial Services Inc............. F 317 634-7165
Indianapolis *(G-8418)*

Icon Metal Forming LLC...................... B 812 738-5900
Corydon *(G-2499)*

Ifok Inc... F 219 477-5107
Valparaiso *(G-15968)*

IGP North America LLC....................... G 812 670-3483
Jeffersonville *(G-10001)*

Indiana Automotive Fas Inc................. B 317 467-0100
Greenfield *(G-6511)*

Indiana Custom Trucks LLC................ E 260 463-3244
Shipshewana *(G-14852)*

Indiana Marujun LLC........................... D 765 584-7639
Winchester *(G-16891)*

Indiana Mills & Manufacturing.............. B 317 896-9531
Westfield *(G-16699)*

Indiana Precision Technology............. G 317 462-3015
Greenfield *(G-6514)*

Indiana Transmission........................... G 765 854-4201
Kokomo *(G-10287)*

Employee Codes: A=Over 500 employees, B=251-500
C=101-250, D=51-100, E=20-50, F=10-19, G=1-9

AUTOMOTIVE PARTS, ACCESS & SPLYS — PRODUCT SECTION

Inter-Cntnntal Gear Brake USA............... D 317 268-0040
  Plainfield *(G-13693)*

Interstate Power Systems Inc................. G 952 854-2044
  Gary *(G-5964)*

Jason Incorporated................................. G 248 455-7919
  Richmond *(G-14148)*

Jasper Holdings Inc................................. F 812 482-1041
  Jasper *(G-9854)*

Jasper Willow Springs Mo LLC............. G 800 827-7455
  Jasper *(G-9860)*

Jlm Lubricants Usa LLC......................... G 317 500-1012
  Brownsburg *(G-1377)*

Jrz Industries Inc.................................... G 574 834-4543
  North Webster *(G-13308)*

Kinedyne... G 260 403-5149
  Auburn *(G-399)*

Kinetech LLC... G 317 441-1924
  Westfield *(G-16704)*

Kirby Risk Corporation........................... D 765 447-1402
  Lafayette *(G-10621)*

Kp Holdings LLC..................................... B 317 867-0234
  Westfield *(G-16706)*

Kph Engineered Systems Inc................. B 317 867-0234
  Westfield *(G-16707)*

Kumar Brothers Inc................................ G 317 410-2450
  Avon *(G-535)*

KYB Americas Corporation..................... B 317 881-7772
  Greenwood *(G-6726)*

Lakepark Industries Ind Inc.................... D
  Shipshewana *(G-14861)*

Laminat LLC.. G 574 233-1534
  South Bend *(G-15114)*

Lau Holdings LLC................................... D 574 223-3181
  Rochester *(G-14300)*

LCI Industries... G 574 264-3521
  Elkhart *(G-3477)*

LCI Industries... G 574 312-6116
  Elkhart *(G-3478)*

LCI Industries... A 574 535-1125
  Elkhart *(G-3476)*

Lear Corporation..................................... D 260 244-1700
  Columbia City *(G-2167)*

Lear Corporation..................................... G 765 653-2511
  Greencastle *(G-6417)*

Lear Corporation..................................... B 219 852-0014
  Hammond *(G-6969)*

Lear Corporation..................................... D 574 935-3818
  Plymouth *(G-13792)*

Linamar Strctures USA Mich Inc............ G 248 372-9018
  Albion *(G-32)*

Lingenfelter Prfmce Engrg Inc................ E 260 724-2552
  Decatur *(G-2869)*

Lippert Components............................... G 574 226-4088
  Elkhart *(G-3490)*

Lippert Components Inc......................... G 574 535-1125
  Elkhart *(G-3492)*

Lippert Components Inc......................... D 574 535-1125
  Goshen *(G-6202)*

Lippert Components Inc......................... G 574 849-0869
  Goshen *(G-6206)*

Lippert Components Inc......................... F 574 971-4320
  Goshen *(G-6207)*

Lippert Components Inc......................... E 574 312-7445
  Middlebury *(G-11734)*

Lippert Components Inc......................... E 800 551-9149
  Mishawaka *(G-11930)*

Lippert Components Inc......................... D 574 537-8900
  Mishawaka *(G-11931)*

Lippert Components Inc......................... F 260 234-4303
  Yoder *(G-16966)*

Lippert Components Inc......................... B 574 535-1125
  Elkhart *(G-3493)*

Liquivinyl LLC... G 765 283-6265
  Yorktown *(G-16975)*

Lund International Holding Co................ G 888 477-3729
  Jasper *(G-9884)*

Magna Powertrain America Inc.............. E 765 587-1300
  Muncie *(G-12443)*

Magna Powertrain America Inc.............. C 765 587-1300
  Muncie *(G-12444)*

Make It Mobile LLC................................ G 260 562-1045
  Howe *(G-7239)*

Makuta Inc.. F 317 642-0001
  Shelbyville *(G-14773)*

Mancor Indiana Inc................................ E 765 779-4800
  Anderson *(G-151)*

Martinrea Industries Inc......................... C 812 346-5750
  North Vernon *(G-13285)*

Mastersbilt Chassis Inc.......................... G 812 793-3666
  Crothersville *(G-2642)*

Meritor Inc.. G 317 279-2180
  Plainfield *(G-13706)*

Metaldyne Snterforged Pdts LLC........... G 812 346-1566
  North Vernon *(G-13287)*

Metzler Enterprise.................................. G 574 293-9267
  Elkhart *(G-3529)*

Miata Hubs LLC...................................... G 240 298-7368
  Brownsburg *(G-1388)*

Midwest Auto Repair Inc........................ F 219 322-0364
  Schererville *(G-14534)*

Min Ko Kyaw LLC................................... F 574 296-3500
  Elkhart *(G-3545)*

Mobile Dynamometer LLC...................... G 765 271-5080
  Kokomo *(G-10311)*

Mobility Ventures LLC............................ G 734 367-3714
  South Bend *(G-15153)*

Morryde International Inc....................... F 574 293-1581
  Elkhart *(G-3553)*

Morryde International Inc....................... F 574 293-1581
  Elkhart *(G-3554)*

Mosey Manufacturing Co Inc................. C 765 983-8889
  Richmond *(G-14170)*

Motorama Auto Ctr Inc.......................... G 317 831-0036
  Mooresville *(G-12226)*

Motorsport Price Engineering................. G 812 546-4220
  Hope *(G-7229)*

Muncie Power Products Inc................... G 785 284-7721
  Muncie *(G-12465)*

Muncie Power Products Inc................... E 765 284-7721
  Muncie *(G-12464)*

Mvp Usa Inc... F 317 585-5785
  Indianapolis *(G-8974)*

Nalon Power Development LLC............. G 317 450-7564
  Pittsboro *(G-13652)*

Nelson Global Products Inc.................... C 317 782-9486
  Indianapolis *(G-8999)*

Next Gnrtion Dlrshp Warsaw LLC......... G 463 234-9400
  Indianapolis *(G-9008)*

Norco Industries Inc............................... C 574 262-3400
  Elkhart *(G-3573)*

North American Mfg Inc......................... G 765 948-3337
  Fairmount *(G-4411)*

NSK Corporation.................................... D 765 458-5000
  Liberty *(G-10993)*

NSK Precision America Inc.................... D 317 738-5000
  Franklin *(G-5762)*

NSK Services Inc.................................... G 812 695-2004
  Jasper *(G-9899)*

NTN Driveshaft Inc................................ A 812 342-7000
  Columbus *(G-2362)*

Nyx LLC... A 734 838-3570
  New Albany *(G-12786)*

Pailton Inc.. G 219 476-0085
  Valparaiso *(G-16021)*

Pana-Pacific.. G 260 482-6607
  Fort Wayne *(G-5293)*

Perfection Wheel LLC............................. G 260 358-9239
  Huntington *(G-7355)*

Performance Brake Parts Inc................. G 260 410-1404
  Grabill *(G-6320)*

Peterson Sanko Corp.............................. G 765 966-9656
  Richmond *(G-14182)*

Phillips Company Inc............................. F 812 526-8250
  Edinburgh *(G-3098)*

Phillips Company Inc............................. E 812 378-3797
  Columbus *(G-2377)*

Phinia Delphi USA LLC........................... G 317 203-4602
  Plainfield *(G-13714)*

Phinia USA LLC...................................... B 765 778-6879
  Anderson *(G-177)*

Power Plant Service Inc......................... E 260 432-6716
  Fort Wayne *(G-5328)*

Power Train Corp Fort Wayne................ F 317 241-9393
  Indianapolis *(G-9167)*

Pridgeon & Clay Inc............................... G 317 738-4885
  Franklin *(G-5770)*

Quality Converters Inc........................... E 260 829-6541
  Orland *(G-13371)*

Race Engineering................................... G 219 661-8904
  Crown Point *(G-2740)*

Ramco Engineering Inc.......................... E 574 266-1455
  Elkhart *(G-3638)*

Raybestos Aftermarket Pdts Co............. G 765 359-1943
  Crawfordsville *(G-2608)*

Raybestos Powertrain............................ D 765 362-3500
  Crawfordsville *(G-2609)*

Raybestos Powertrain LLC..................... G 812 268-0322
  Sullivan *(G-15418)*

Raybestos Powertrain LLC..................... G 812 268-0322
  Sullivan *(G-15419)*

Rayco Mch & Engrg Group Inc............... E 317 291-7848
  Indianapolis *(G-9268)*

Raytech Corp.. G 765 359-2882
  Crawfordsville *(G-2610)*

Reflexallen USA Inc................................ E 317 870-3610
  Indianapolis *(G-9280)*

Resonac Powdered Metals Americ......... E 812 663-5058
  Greensburg *(G-6628)*

Rexnord Industries LLC......................... G 414 643-2559
  Plainfield *(G-13722)*

Rgr Engines.. G 630 488-7966
  Monticello *(G-12169)*

Rich Bures.. G 317 270-9360
  Indianapolis *(G-9300)*

Riverside Mfg Inc.................................... C 260 637-4470
  Fort Wayne *(G-5387)*

Robert Bosch LLC................................... G 574 654-4000
  New Carlisle *(G-12844)*

Robert Bosch LLC................................... G 574 654-4000
  New Carlisle *(G-12845)*

Rochester Manufacturing LLC................ G 574 224-2044
  Rochester *(G-14318)*

Rt Acquisition Corp................................ D 812 482-2932
  Jasper *(G-9907)*

Sacoma Properties LLC.......................... F 812 526-5600
  Edinburgh *(G-3102)*

Safe Fleet Mirrors................................... E 574 266-3700
  Elkhart *(G-3659)*

Shield Restraint Systems Inc................. C 574 266-8330
  Elkhart *(G-3673)*

SMI Seller Inc... A 765 825-3121
  Connersville *(G-2466)*

SMR Management Inc............................ G 765 252-0257
  Lafayette *(G-10692)*

SPD Performance Plus LLC.................... G 260 433-6192
  Bluffton *(G-1055)*

PRODUCT SECTION

AUTOMOTIVE REPAIR SHOPS: Engine Repair

Spears Holdings Inc............................ G..... 765 378-4908
  Anderson *(G-196)*

Specialty Rim Supply Inc..................... G..... 812 234-3002
  Terre Haute *(G-15710)*

Spitzer Racing Enterprises................... F..... 317 894-9533
  Greenfield *(G-6559)*

Splendor Boats LLC............................ F..... 260 352-2835
  Silver Lake *(G-14923)*

Standard Industrial Supply Inc.............. E..... 574 946-6661
  Winamac *(G-16876)*

Standard Intgrted Slutions Inc.............. F..... 574 946-6661
  Winamac *(G-16877)*

Standard Motor Products Inc................ D..... 574 259-6253
  Mishawaka *(G-12007)*

Stant Corporation................................ D..... 765 825-3122
  Connersville *(G-2467)*

Stant USA Corp.................................. B..... 765 825-3121
  Connersville *(G-2469)*

Stant USA Corp.................................. C..... 765 825-3121
  Connersville *(G-2470)*

Starcraft Corporation........................... G..... 574 534-7705
  Goshen *(G-6259)*

Starcraft Corporation........................... G..... 574 534-7827
  Goshen *(G-6260)*

Steel Tank & Fabricating Corp............... E..... 260 248-8971
  Columbia City *(G-2203)*

Surface Generation Tech LLC................ G..... 765 425-2741
  Anderson *(G-203)*

T K T Inc... G..... 574 825-5233
  Middlebury *(G-11753)*

Taylor Made Group LLC....................... D..... 574 535-1125
  Elkhart *(G-3716)*

Team Oneway..................................... G..... 574 387-5417
  Granger *(G-6385)*

Tenneco Inc....................................... G..... 317 842-5550
  Indianapolis *(G-9577)*

The Pro Shear Corporation Corp........... G..... 260 408-1010
  Fort Wayne *(G-5481)*

Thermal Ceramics Inc.......................... E..... 574 296-3500
  Elkhart *(G-3725)*

TI Automotive...................................... G..... 260 622-7372
  Ossian *(G-13440)*

TI Automotive Inc................................ G..... 260 587-6100
  Ashley *(G-337)*

TI Automotive Ligonier Corp.................. A..... 260 894-3163
  Ligonier *(G-11028)*

TI Group Auto Systems LLC.................. D..... 260 587-6100
  Ashley *(G-338)*

TI Group Auto Systems LLC.................. B..... 260 622-7900
  Ossian *(G-13441)*

TNT Truck Accessories LLC.................. G..... 812 305-0714
  Haubstadt *(G-7090)*

Trans Atlantic Products LLC.................. F..... 574 262-0165
  Elkhart *(G-3743)*

Tru-Flex LLC...................................... G..... 812 526-5600
  Edinburgh *(G-3106)*

Tru-Flex LLC...................................... C..... 765 893-4403
  West Lebanon *(G-16649)*

Tru-Flex Real Estate Holdings LLC......... D..... 765 893-4403
  West Lebanon *(G-16650)*

Truckpro LLC..................................... F..... 765 482-6525
  Lebanon *(G-10948)*

TRW Commercial Steering.................... E..... 765 423-5377
  Lafayette *(G-10710)*

Twb of Indiana.................................... G..... 812 342-6000
  Columbus *(G-2408)*

U B Machine Inc.................................. F..... 260 493-3381
  New Haven *(G-12924)*

Ultimate Sports Inc............................. G..... 765 423-2984
  West Lafayette *(G-16641)*

Valeo Engine Cooling Inc..................... A..... 812 663-8541
  Greensburg *(G-6638)*

Valeo Ltg Systems N Amer LLC............. A..... 812 523-5200
  Seymour *(G-14700)*

Valeo North America Inc...................... C..... 800 677-6004
  Greensburg *(G-6639)*

Valeo North America Inc...................... B..... 248 619-8300
  Seymour *(G-14702)*

Vee Engineering Inc............................ D..... 260 424-6635
  Fort Wayne *(G-5530)*

Vehicle Service Group LLC................... E..... 800 445-9262
  Madison *(G-11255)*

Viariloc Distributors Inc........................ G..... 317 273-0089
  Indianapolis *(G-9718)*

Voegele Auto Supply LLC..................... G..... 765 647-3541
  Brookville *(G-1339)*

Wabash Club Raybestos Pdts Co.......... G..... 765 359-2862
  Crawfordsville *(G-2626)*

Wabash National Corporation............... E..... 765 771-5300
  Lafayette *(G-10715)*

Wabash National Corporation............... A..... 765 771-5310
  Lafayette *(G-10716)*

Wagler Competition Pdts LLC............... F..... 812 486-9360
  Odon *(G-13356)*

Water Pump Specialists....................... G..... 317 270-9360
  Indianapolis *(G-9739)*

Wayne David Incorporated................... G..... 317 417-7165
  Franklin *(G-5785)*

Webb Wheel Products Inc.................... C..... 812 548-0477
  Tell City *(G-15519)*

Wellspring Components LLC................. G..... 260 768-7336
  Shipshewana *(G-14896)*

Xtrac Inc... F..... 317 472-2451
  Indianapolis *(G-9797)*

ZF Active Safety & Elec US LLC............ D..... 260 357-6327
  Garrett *(G-5881)*

ZF Active Safety & Elec US LLC............ E..... 765 429-1678
  Lafayette *(G-10722)*

ZF Active Safety & Elec US LLC............ D..... 765 429-1936
  Lafayette *(G-10723)*

ZF Active Safety & Elec US LLC............ A..... 765 423-5377
  Lafayette *(G-10724)*

ZF Automotive.................................... F..... 260 357-1148
  Garrett *(G-5882)*

ZF North America Inc.......................... E..... 765 429-1622
  Lafayette *(G-10725)*

AUTOMOTIVE PARTS: Plastic

Ace Mobility Inc.................................. F..... 317 241-2444
  Indianapolis *(G-7421)*

Bremen Composites LLC..................... D..... 574 546-3791
  Bremen *(G-1177)*

Diversity - Vuteq LLC.......................... C..... 812 761-0210
  Princeton *(G-13989)*

Enovapremier LLC............................... E..... 812 385-0576
  Princeton *(G-13993)*

Futaba Indiana America Corp............... B..... 812 895-4700
  Vincennes *(G-16127)*

Gmv LLC.. G..... 765 635-4842
  Carmel *(G-1642)*

Hinseys Pro Paint Inc.......................... G..... 260 407-2000
  Fort Wayne *(G-5068)*

Indy Parts Inc.................................... G..... 317 243-7171
  Indianapolis *(G-8532)*

J L Wickey Corp.................................. G..... 260 627-3109
  Grabill *(G-6303)*

JMS Engineered Plastics Inc................. G..... 574 277-3228
  South Bend *(G-15093)*

JMS Engineered Plastics Inc................. G..... 574 277-3228
  South Bend *(G-15094)*

M&M Performance Inc......................... G..... 574 536-6103
  Goshen *(G-6208)*

Midwest Willys LLC............................. G..... 765 362-2247
  Crawfordsville *(G-2590)*

Nyx Fort Wayne LLC........................... D..... 260 484-0595
  Mishawaka *(G-11968)*

Odyssey Machine Inc.......................... G..... 812 951-1160
  Georgetown *(G-6072)*

Sasaki Coating North Amer Inc............. F..... 317 956-2232
  Indianapolis *(G-9374)*

Voss Automotive Inc........................... D..... 260 373-2277
  Fort Wayne *(G-5536)*

AUTOMOTIVE PRDTS: Rubber

American Rubber Corp......................... G..... 317 548-8455
  Anderson *(G-77)*

Central Rubber & Plastics Inc............... E..... 574 534-6411
  Goshen *(G-6110)*

Exactseal Inc..................................... G..... 317 559-2220
  Indianapolis *(G-8148)*

Goodtime Technology Dev Ltd.............. G..... 317 876-3661
  Indianapolis *(G-8306)*

Klh Holding Corporation....................... E..... 317 634-3976
  Indianapolis *(G-8693)*

No-Sail Splash Guard Co Inc................ G..... 765 522-2100
  Roachdale *(G-14248)*

Servaas Inc....................................... G..... 317 633-2020
  Indianapolis *(G-9405)*

AUTOMOTIVE REPAIR SHOPS: Diesel Engine Repair

Cummins Crosspoint LLC..................... E..... 317 243-7979
  Indianapolis *(G-7925)*

Cummins Cumberland Inc.................... B..... 317 243-7979
  Indianapolis *(G-7926)*

Indiana Mobile Marine LLC................... G..... 317 961-1881
  Indianapolis *(G-8483)*

Jolliff Diesel Service LLC...................... G..... 812 692-5725
  Elnora *(G-3815)*

AUTOMOTIVE REPAIR SHOPS: Electrical Svcs

Deans Place....................................... G..... 765 282-5712
  Muncie *(G-12375)*

AUTOMOTIVE REPAIR SHOPS: Engine Rebuilding

C & P Machine Service Inc................... F..... 260 484-7723
  Fort Wayne *(G-4827)*

Chappos Inc....................................... G..... 219 942-8101
  Hobart *(G-7181)*

Dons Automotive and Mch Inc.............. G..... 812 547-6292
  Tell City *(G-15500)*

Performance Technology Inc................. G..... 574 862-2116
  Wakarusa *(G-16242)*

Sauers Racing Auto Machines............... G..... 812 265-2803
  Madison *(G-11251)*

Three K Racing Enterprises.................. G..... 765 482-4273
  Lebanon *(G-10946)*

Woodruff Automotive LLC..................... G..... 812 636-4908
  Odon *(G-13358)*

AUTOMOTIVE REPAIR SHOPS: Engine Repair

Auto Center Inc.................................. G..... 317 545-3360
  Indianapolis *(G-7571)*

Indian Creek Outdoor Power LLC........... G..... 812 597-3055
  Morgantown *(G-12258)*

Morgan Automotive.............................. G..... 765 378-0593
  Chesterfield *(G-1897)*

Pfm Onsite Services Inc....................... G..... 317 784-7777
  Indianapolis *(G-9132)*

Pyramid Equipment Inc........................ F..... 219 778-2591
  Rolling Prairie *(G-14371)*

AUTOMOTIVE REPAIR SHOPS: Engine Repair

Reed Auto - Indy Mich LLC................F.....317 872-1132
  Indianapolis (G-9279)

AUTOMOTIVE REPAIR SHOPS: Machine Shop

BCI Solutions Inc................C.....574 546-2411
  Bremen (G-1174)
Brent Morris................G.....812 282-6945
  Jeffersonville (G-9946)
CCT Enterprises LLC................E.....260 925-1420
  Auburn (G-375)
Champion Racing Engines LLC................G.....317 335-2491
  Mccordsville (G-11446)
Frank Wiss Racg Components Inc................G.....317 243-9585
  Indianapolis (G-8222)
Greg Moser Engineering Inc................E.....260 726-6689
  Portland (G-13949)
H & E Machined Specialties................F.....260 424-2527
  Fort Wayne (G-5045)
Numerical Productions Inc................D.....317 783-1362
  Indianapolis (G-9034)
Three Daughters Corp................E.....260 925-2128
  Auburn (G-430)
Waterfield Automotive Mch Sp................G.....765 288-6262
  Muncie (G-12515)

AUTOMOTIVE REPAIR SHOPS: Muffler Shop, Sale/Rpr/Installation

Auto Specialty Lafayette Inc................G.....765 446-2311
  Lafayette (G-10531)
Mighty Muffler LLC................G.....765 966-6833
  Richmond (G-14166)
Reed Auto - Indy Mich LLC................F.....317 872-1132
  Indianapolis (G-9279)

AUTOMOTIVE REPAIR SHOPS: Rebuilding & Retreading Tires

Best-One Kentuckiana Inc................G.....812 282-4799
  Jeffersonville (G-9942)
Bridgestone Ret Operations LLC................F.....812 332-2119
  Bloomington (G-815)
Bridgestone Ret Operations LLC................G.....260 447-2596
  Columbia City (G-2127)
Bridgestone Ret Operations LLC................G.....812 477-8818
  Evansville (G-3951)
Bridgestone Ret Operations LLC................G.....317 846-6516
  Indianapolis (G-7681)
Bridgestone Ret Operations LLC................G.....765 447-5041
  Lafayette (G-10542)
Bridgestone Ret Operations LLC................G.....812 232-9478
  Terre Haute (G-15554)
K Tech Supply................G.....812 793-3352
  Crothersville (G-2641)
Loves Travel Stops................F.....574 935-4103
  Plymouth (G-13793)
Premier Bandage 3 Inc................F.....574 257-0248
  South Bend (G-15202)
Taylor Tire Treading Co Inc................G.....317 634-9476
  Indianapolis (G-9559)

AUTOMOTIVE REPAIR SHOPS: Springs, Rebuilding & Repair

Mikesmobimech LLC................G.....317 753-0492
  Indianapolis (G-8918)

AUTOMOTIVE REPAIR SHOPS: Tire Recapping

E & M Tire Salvage Inc................G.....260 745-3016
  Fort Wayne (G-4936)

Hughes Tire Service Inc................F.....812 883-4981
  Salem (G-14481)

AUTOMOTIVE REPAIR SHOPS: Tire Repair Shop

Atr Tire and Repair LLC................G.....574 349-4462
  New Paris (G-12946)
Auto Express Vale................E.....317 897-6618
  Indianapolis (G-7572)
Ben Tire Distributors Ltd................E.....317 798-2013
  Indianapolis (G-7612)
Bernard Burns................G.....574 382-5019
  Macy (G-11194)
Best-One Kentuckiana Inc................E.....812 285-5400
  Jeffersonville (G-9941)
Best-One Lt LLC................G.....812 471-8473
  Evansville (G-3928)
Best-One Tire & Auto Care of A................G.....260 665-7330
  Angola (G-234)
Best-One Tire & Svc Auburn Inc................G.....260 925-2782
  Auburn (G-369)
Bridgestone Ret Operations LLC................F.....812 423-4451
  Evansville (G-3952)
Bridgestone Ret Operations LLC................G.....317 849-9120
  Indianapolis (G-7682)
Clark Tire Fishers Inc................G.....317 842-0544
  Fishers (G-4490)
Cunningham Tire Services Inc................G.....765 473-9200
  Peru (G-13576)
D & D Tire Shop LLC................G.....219 354-0402
  East Chicago (G-3002)
Dales Goodyear Tire & Service................G.....574 272-3779
  South Bend (G-14995)
Daviess County Tire Inc................G.....812 254-1035
  Washington (G-16476)
Double D................G.....765 569-6822
  Rockville (G-14351)
Gentis Tire & Service Inc................E.....765 348-2400
  Hartford City (G-7066)
Goodyear Tire Center................G.....260 726-9321
  Portland (G-13946)
Indiana Discount Tire Company................G.....574 875-8547
  Elkhart (G-3421)
McCord Tire Service Inc................F.....812 235-8016
  Terre Haute (G-15639)
Midwest Tire & Service LLC................G.....502 377-3722
  Salem (G-14492)
Mooresville Tire & Service Ctr................G.....317 831-1215
  Mooresville (G-12224)
Parish Tire & Battery Shop................G.....765 793-3191
  Covington (G-2532)
Paul Nunez Road Service................G.....765 584-1628
  Winchester (G-16898)
Penner Tire & Service LLC................G.....812 653-0029
  Hardinsburg (G-7048)
Portland Tire & Service Inc................G.....260 726-9321
  Portland (G-13962)
Reed Auto - Indy Mich LLC................F.....317 872-1132
  Indianapolis (G-9279)
Reis Tire Sales Inc................E.....812 425-2229
  Evansville (G-4283)
Smith Tire Inc................F.....574 267-8261
  Warsaw (G-16427)
Tippecanoe Tire Service Inc................G.....765 884-0920
  Fowler (G-5634)
Tire Center of Portland Inc................G.....260 726-8947
  Portland (G-13971)
Tire Central and Service Avon................G.....317 966-0662
  Indianapolis (G-9608)
Tires Enterprises Corp................F.....866 807-4930
  Gary (G-6019)

Trusty Tires Inc................G.....812 738-4212
  Corydon (G-2519)
Upland Tire & Service Ctr Inc................G.....765 998-0871
  Upland (G-15884)
Woodward Tire Sales & Svc Inc................G.....260 432-0694
  Fort Wayne (G-5575)

AUTOMOTIVE REPAIR SHOPS: Trailer Repair

Forks Rv Inc................D.....574 825-7467
  Shipshewana (G-14846)
Rugged Steel Works LLC................F.....260 444-4241
  Fort Wayne (G-5390)

AUTOMOTIVE REPAIR SHOPS: Wheel Alignment

Parish Tire & Battery Shop................G.....765 793-3191
  Covington (G-2532)

AUTOMOTIVE REPAIR SVC

Anthony Smith................G.....765 478-5325
  Cambridge City (G-1490)
B & M Electrical Company Inc................F.....765 448-4532
  Lafayette (G-10533)
Best Weld Inc................G.....765 641-7720
  Anderson (G-83)
Lances Drvshaft Components Inc................G.....219 762-2531
  Portage (G-13881)
Mc Ginley Fire Apparatus................G.....765 482-3152
  Lebanon (G-10915)
Midwest Auto Repair Inc................F.....219 322-0364
  Schererville (G-14534)
Morgan Automotive................G.....765 378-0593
  Chesterfield (G-1897)
Next Gnrtion Dlrshp Warsaw LLC................G.....463 234-9400
  Indianapolis (G-9008)

AUTOMOTIVE SPLYS & PARTS, NEW, WHOL: Auto Servicing Eqpt

C & P Machine Service Inc................F.....260 484-7723
  Fort Wayne (G-4827)
Voss Automotive Inc................D.....260 373-2277
  Fort Wayne (G-5536)

AUTOMOTIVE SPLYS & PARTS, NEW, WHOLESALE: Engines/Eng Parts

Mirrus Corporation Inc................F.....812 689-1411
  Versailles (G-16102)

AUTOMOTIVE SPLYS & PARTS, NEW, WHOLESALE: Filters, Air & Oil

Indianapolis In................E.....855 628-3458
  Indianapolis (G-8502)

AUTOMOTIVE SPLYS & PARTS, NEW, WHOLESALE: Hardware

Conversion Components Inc................G.....574 264-4181
  Elkhart (G-3266)
Wb Automotive Holdings Inc................G.....734 604-8962
  Fort Wayne (G-5557)

AUTOMOTIVE SPLYS & PARTS, NEW, WHOLESALE: Trailer Parts

Axis Products Inc................C.....574 266-8282
  Elkhart (G-3207)
Chubbs Steel Sales Inc................E.....574 295-3166
  Elkhart (G-3252)
Jayco Inc................A.....574 825-5861
  Middlebury (G-11727)

PRODUCT SECTION

AUTOMOTIVE SPLYS & PARTS, NEW, WHOLESALE: Wheels

Best Tires & Wheels .... F 317 306-3379
Franklin (G-5715)

Richards Liquidation Corp .... F 574 807-8588
Mishawaka (G-11985)

Wheels In Sky .... G 812 249-8233
Terre Haute (G-15746)

AUTOMOTIVE SPLYS & PARTS, WHOLESALE, NEC

Action Machine Inc .... F 574 287-9650
South Bend (G-14935)

Afco Performance Group LLC .... F 812 897-0900
Boonville (G-1079)

Allied Enterprises LLC .... E 765 288-8849
Muncie (G-12339)

Ben Tire Distributors Ltd .... E 317 798-2013
Indianapolis (G-7612)

Boyer Machine & Tool Co Inc .... E 812 379-9581
Columbus (G-2228)

Chiyoda USA Corporation .... C 765 653-9098
Greencastle (G-6396)

KOI Enterprises Inc .... D 812 537-2335
Lawrenceburg (G-10843)

Meritor Inc .... G 317 279-2180
Plainfield (G-13706)

Midwest Mat Company .... G 765 286-0831
Muncie (G-12455)

Motsinger Auto Supply Inc .... G 317 782-8484
Indianapolis (G-8960)

Promotor Engines & Components .... G 574 533-9898
Goshen (G-6243)

Stant USA Corp .... C 765 825-3121
Connersville (G-2470)

Staples Pipe & Muffler .... G 812 522-3569
Butlerville (G-1488)

AUTOMOTIVE SVCS, EXC REPAIR & CARWASHES: Insp & Diagnostic

Auto Specialty Lafayette Inc .... G 765 446-2311
Lafayette (G-10531)

Deans Place .... G 765 282-5712
Muncie (G-12375)

Qualitex Inc .... F 260 244-7839
Columbia City (G-2186)

AUTOMOTIVE SVCS, EXC REPAIR & CARWASHES: Lubrication

Gorrepati Service Systems .... G 317 299-7590
Indianapolis (G-8308)

Illinois Lubricants LLC .... G 260 436-2444
Fort Wayne (G-5092)

AUTOMOTIVE SVCS, EXC RPR/ CARWASHES: High Perf Auto Rpr/Svc

Lingenfelter Prfmce Engrg Inc .... E 260 724-2552
Decatur (G-2869)

Mitchell Smith Racing .... G 765 640-0237
Anderson (G-155)

Rhyne Engines Inc .... G 219 845-1218
Gary (G-6004)

AUTOMOTIVE TOWING SVCS

Chads LLC .... G 812 323-7377
Ellettsville (G-3802)

Grahams Wrecker Service Inc .... G 317 736-4355
Whiteland (G-16787)

Parish Tire & Battery Shop .... G 765 793-3191
Covington (G-2532)

Sparkling Clean Inc .... G 812 422-4871
Evansville (G-4326)

Zionsville Towing Inc .... G 317 873-4550
Zionsville (G-17064)

AUTOMOTIVE TRANSMISSION REPAIR SVC

Hobbs Auto Diagnostics & Repr .... G 765 606-1490
Anderson (G-127)

Metaldyne M&A Bluffton LLC .... D 260 824-6800
Bluffton (G-1042)

Mikesmobimech LLC .... G 317 753-0492
Indianapolis (G-8918)

Northern Trans & Differential .... G 219 764-4009
Portage (G-13900)

Tecumseh Products Company LLC .... G 812 883-3575
Salem (G-14502)

Truckpro LLC .... F 765 482-6525
Lebanon (G-10948)

AUTOMOTIVE WELDING SVCS

Chappos Inc .... G 219 942-8101
Hobart (G-7181)

Ernies Welding Shop LLC .... G 812 326-2600
Saint Anthony (G-14427)

Mikesmobimech LLC .... G 317 753-0492
Indianapolis (G-8918)

Mooresville Welding Inc .... G 317 831-2265
Mooresville (G-12225)

Shank Welding Inc .... G 260 897-2068
Avilla (G-495)

T K Sales & Service .... G 219 962-8982
Gary (G-6017)

AUTOMOTIVE: Bodies

KFC Composite Engineering Co .... G 219 369-9093
La Porte (G-10436)

Revenge Designs Inc .... G 260 724-4000
Decatur (G-2881)

AUTOMOTIVE: Seating

Bald Spot Racing LLC .... G 317 402-7188
Zionsville (G-16995)

Clarios LLC .... E 260 485-9999
Fort Wayne (G-4851)

Clarios LLC .... C 260 479-4400
Fort Wayne (G-4852)

Clarios LLC .... B 317 638-7611
Indianapolis (G-7816)

Johnson Controls Inc .... F 219 736-7105
Crown Point (G-2704)

Johnson Controls Inc .... G 812 868-1374
Evansville (G-4144)

Johnson Controls Inc .... F 317 917-5043
Pittsboro (G-13649)

Johnson Controls Inc .... F 812 362-6901
Rockport (G-14343)

Nhk Seating of America Inc .... G 765 605-2443
Frankfort (G-5683)

Nhk Seating of America Inc .... E 765 659-4781
Frankfort (G-5684)

Pauls Seating Inc .... G 574 522-0630
Elkhart (G-3601)

Superior Seating Inc .... F 574 389-9011
Elkhart (G-3709)

Toyota Boshoku Indiana LLC .... A 812 491-9100
Princeton (G-14014)

TS Tech Indiana LLC .... G 765 465-4294
New Castle (G-12884)

AWNINGS & CANOPIES

A Shade Faster Products LLC .... G 574 584-5744
Elkhart (G-3142)

All American Tent & Awning Inc .... E 812 232-4206
Terre Haute (G-15537)

Awningtec Usa Incorporated .... E 812 734-0423
Corydon (G-2486)

AWNINGS & CANOPIES: Awnings, Fabric, From Purchased Matls

Blessing Enterprises Inc .... F 219 736-9800
Merrillville (G-11491)

Canvas Shop LLC .... G 260 768-7755
Shipshewana (G-14840)

Cool Planet LLC .... G 317 927-9000
Indianapolis (G-7868)

Lafayette Tents & Events LLC .... E 765 742-4277
Lafayette (G-10630)

Larrys Canvas Cleaning .... G 260 463-2220
Lagrange (G-10751)

Laudeman Place Inc .... F 574 546-4404
Bremen (G-1203)

Lomont Holdings Co Inc .... E 800 545-9023
Angola (G-273)

Marion Tent & Awning Co .... G 765 664-7722
Marion (G-11317)

Twin Lakes Canvas Inc .... G 574 583-2000
Monticello (G-12174)

Webster Custom Canvas Inc .... G 574 834-4497
North Webster (G-13314)

AWNINGS & CANOPIES: Canopies, Fabric, From Purchased Matls

Marine Mooring Inc .... E 574 594-5787
Warsaw (G-16390)

AWNINGS: Fiberglass

American Window and Glass Inc .... C 812 464-9400
Evansville (G-3886)

AWNINGS: Metal

H & H Home Improvement Inc .... G 812 288-8700
Clarksville (G-2017)

Key Sheet Metal Inc .... G 317 546-7151
Indianapolis (G-8677)

Marion Tent & Awning Co .... G 765 664-7722
Marion (G-11317)

AXLES

Axis Products Inc .... C 574 266-8282
Elkhart (G-3207)

Dexter Axle Company LLC .... C 260 636-2195
Albion (G-23)

Dexter Axle Company LLC .... D 574 294-6651
Elkhart (G-3291)

Dexter Axle Company LLC .... D 574 295-7888
Elkhart (G-3292)

Graber Manufacturing .... G 812 636-7725
Odon (G-13337)

Industrial Axle Company LLC .... E 574 294-6651
Elkhart (G-3423)

Industrial Axle Company LLC .... D 574 295-6077
Elkhart (G-3424)

Mullets Fencing and Supplies .... G 574 646-3300
Nappanee (G-12628)

Peerless Gear LLC .... G 812 883-7900
Salem (G-14497)

AXLES: Rolled Or Forged, Made In Steel Mills

Employee Codes: A=Over 500 employees, B=251-500
C=101-250, D=51-100, E=20-50, F=10-19, G=1-9

2024 Harris Indiana Industrial Directory

1253

Ntk Precision Axle Corporation............ B 765 656-1000
Frankfort (G-5687)

BACKHOES

Ramar Industries Inc...................... G 765 288-7319
Muncie (G-12483)

Tracy K Hullett................................. G 765 472-3349
Peru (G-13606)

Vires Backhoe and Dumptruc............ G 812 595-1630
Deputy (G-2942)

BAGS: Canvas

B&C Distributor Inc.......................... G 609 293-3257
Indianapolis (G-7585)

Websters Protective Cases Inc......... G 219 263-3039
Chesterton (G-1967)

BAGS: Paper

Viking Paper Company..................... E 574 936-6300
Plymouth (G-13825)

BAGS: Paper, Made From Purchased Materials

Hilex Poly Co LLC............................ C 812 346-1066
North Vernon (G-13277)

BAGS: Plastic

Gen Enterprises............................... G 574 498-6777
Tippecanoe (G-15759)

Inteplast Group Corporation............. G 219 220-2528
Remington (G-14035)

Midwest Sandbags LLC.................... G 847 366-6555
Elkhart (G-3541)

Printpack Inc.................................... C 812 663-5091
Greensburg (G-6625)

Witham Machine LLC....................... G 317 835-2076
Boggstown (G-1077)

BAGS: Plastic & Pliofilm

Grrk Holdings Inc............................. E 317 872-0172
Indianapolis (G-8336)

Npx One LLC................................... D 201 791-7600
Indianapolis (G-9031)

BAGS: Plastic, Made From Purchased Materials

Bagbarn Co...................................... F 847 850-2592
Madison (G-11204)

Cougar Bag Eb LLC......................... E 317 831-9720
Mooresville (G-12200)

Cpg - Ohio LLC................................ F 260 829-6721
Orland (G-13363)

D & M Enterprises LLC................... F 260 483-4008
Fort Wayne (G-4901)

Eagle Industries Inc......................... F 812 282-1393
Jeffersonville (G-9973)

Hilex Poly Co LLC............................ C 812 346-1066
North Vernon (G-13277)

Putnam Plastics Inc......................... E 765 795-6102
Cloverdale (G-2094)

Universal Transparent Bag Inc......... G 317 634-6425
Indianapolis (G-9683)

BAGS: Rubber Or Rubberized Fabric

LTI Holdings Inc............................... G 574 389-1878
Elkhart (G-3502)

Rubber Products Distrs Inc.............. F 317 883-6700
Greenwood (G-6762)

BAGS: Trash, Plastic Film, Made From Purchased Materials

Berry Global Group Inc.................... A 812 424-2904
Evansville (G-3921)

BAKERIES, COMMERCIAL: On Premises Baking Only

Almiras Bakery................................. F 219 844-4334
Hammond (G-6872)

B&B Goodiez.................................... G 765 338-6833
Connersville (G-2427)

Babbs Supermarket Inc.................... E 812 829-2231
Spencer (G-15339)

Colonial Baking Co Inc..................... G 812 232-4466
Terre Haute (G-15565)

Concannons Pastry Shop................. F 765 288-8551
Muncie (G-12369)

Enjoy Life Natural Brands LLC........ G 844 624-7162
Jeffersonville (G-9978)

Fingerhut Bakery Inc........................ F 574 896-5937
North Judson (G-13212)

Ganal Corporation............................ G 260 749-2161
New Haven (G-12903)

Gutierrez Mexican Bky Mkt Inc......... G 574 534-9979
Goshen (G-6158)

Harlan Bakeries LLC....................... C 317 272-3600
Indianapolis (G-8361)

Harlan Bakeries LLC....................... G 317 272-3600
Avon (G-523)

Harlan Bakeries-Avon LLC.............. B 317 272-3600
Avon (G-524)

Hearthside Food Solutions LLC...... B 219 878-1522
Michigan City (G-11622)

Heyerly Brothers Inc........................ F 260 622-4196
Ossian (G-13426)

Holsum of Fort Wayne Inc................ A 219 362-4561
La Porte (G-10421)

Houchens Industries Inc.................. F 812 467-7255
Evansville (G-4111)

Klosterman Baking Co...................... F 317 359-5545
Indianapolis (G-8696)

Kroger Co... G 574 294-6092
Elkhart (G-3460)

Kroger Co... G 574 291-0740
South Bend (G-15107)

Lakeshore Foods Corp..................... D 219 362-8513
La Porte (G-10444)

Lewis Brothers Bakeries Inc............ C 812 886-6533
Vincennes (G-16137)

Miller Distributions Inc..................... F 574 533-1940
Goshen (G-6224)

Neeta Sweet Cupcakes n Minis........ G 574 286-7032
Granger (G-6366)

Ohana Donuts and Ice Cream LLC... G 317 288-0922
Fishers (G-4570)

Organic Bread of Heaven LLC......... F 219 883-5126
Gary (G-5991)

Peace Love Cupcakes...................... G 812 239-1591
Terre Haute (G-15659)

Perfection Bakeries Inc.................... G 219 789-4816
Valparaiso (G-16023)

Schnuck Markets Inc........................ C 812 853-9505
Newburgh (G-13019)

Shipshewana Bread Box Corp......... G 260 768-4629
Shipshewana (G-14887)

Tyson Mexican Original Inc............. D 260 726-3118
Portland (G-13974)

Vanilla Bean LLC.............................. G 260 415-4652
Fort Wayne (G-5528)

BAKERIES: On Premises Baking & Consumption

A Pinch of Sweetness LLC................ G 765 838-2358
Lafayette (G-10513)

Black Rose Pastries LLC.................. G 773 708-3650
Gary (G-5901)

Craftmark Bakery LLC..................... C 317 548-3929
Indianapolis (G-7898)

Donut Bank Inc................................ E 812 426-0011
Evansville (G-4019)

Eat Da Cake LLC.............................. G 765 479-4985
Merrillville (G-11510)

Grabers Kountry Korner LLC........... F 812 636-4399
Odon (G-13339)

Heyerly Brothers Inc........................ F 260 622-4196
Ossian (G-13426)

Organic Bread of Heaven LLC......... F 219 883-5126
Gary (G-5991)

Richards Bakery............................... F 260 424-4012
Fort Wayne (G-5383)

BAKERY MACHINERY

A M Manufacturing Co Inc............... E 219 472-7272
Munster (G-12526)

Reading Bakery Systems Inc........... F 317 337-0000
Indianapolis (G-9277)

BAKERY PRDTS, FROZEN: Wholesalers

Cookie Please................................... G 317 879-6589
Indianapolis (G-7867)

BAKERY PRDTS: Bagels, Fresh Or Frozen

Ernestine Foods Inc......................... G 219 274-0188
Crown Point (G-2681)

BAKERY PRDTS: Bakery Prdts, Partially Cooked, Exc frozen

Baked With Billie LLC....................... G 317 517-1575
Indianapolis (G-7591)

BAKERY PRDTS: Biscuits, Baked, Baking Powder & Raised

Always Fresh Baked Goods Inc........ E 317 319-4747
Martinsville (G-11380)

Cookie Please................................... G 317 879-6589
Indianapolis (G-7867)

BAKERY PRDTS: Bread, All Types, Fresh Or Frozen

Flowers Baking Co Ohio LLC.......... G 502 350-4700
Hobart (G-7188)

Flowers Baking Co Ohio LLC.......... G 502 350-4700
Marion (G-11286)

Flowers Baking Co Ohio LLC.......... G 502 350-4700
South Bend (G-15037)

Flowers Bkg Co Bardstown LLC...... G 502 350-4700
Seymour (G-14654)

Hartford Bakery Inc.......................... D 812 425-4642
Evansville (G-4104)

Holsum of Fort Wayne Inc................ C 260 456-2130
Fort Wayne (G-5071)

Lewis Brothers Bakeries Inc............ C 812 425-4642
Evansville (G-4166)

Perfection Bakeries Inc.................... C 260 424-8245
Fort Wayne (G-5306)

Weston Foods US Holdings LLC...... A 317 858-9000
Brownsburg (G-1413)

PRODUCT SECTION   BAR JOISTS & CONCRETE REINFORCING BARS: Fabricated

BAKERY PRDTS: Buns, Bread Type, Fresh Or Frozen

Kbi Inc .... D 765 763-6114
  Morristown *(G-12278)*

BAKERY PRDTS: Cakes, Bakery, Exc Frozen

A Pinch of Sweetness LLC .... G 765 838-2358
  Lafayette *(G-10513)*

Cassie Cakes LLC .... G 219 308-3320
  Hammond *(G-6896)*

Dlicous Dsserts By Deedee LLC .... G 317 515-1858
  South Bend *(G-15002)*

Jay C Food 84 .... G 812 886-9311
  Vincennes *(G-16133)*

Nanas Cakes and Sweets LLC .... G 317 694-4271
  Indianapolis *(G-8982)*

Pasteleria Gresil LLC .... G 317 299-8801
  Indianapolis *(G-9096)*

Rhondas Tasty Treats LLC .... G 574 315-4011
  South Bend *(G-15218)*

Royal Couture Treats Btq Ltd .... G 812 914-9057
  New Albany *(G-12809)*

Sweet Tooth LLC .... G 317 986-3764
  Indianapolis *(G-9538)*

Tasty Treats Bakery LLC .... G 317 622-8829
  Indianapolis *(G-9556)*

BAKERY PRDTS: Cones, Ice Cream

Hartzells Homemade Ice Cream .... G 812 332-3502
  Bloomington *(G-875)*

BAKERY PRDTS: Cookies

Blondies Cookies Inc .... F 765 628-3978
  Greentown *(G-6645)*

Darlington Cookie Company .... G 800 754-2202
  Indianapolis *(G-7952)*

Debra M Lewis .... G 219 937-4240
  Hammond *(G-6912)*

Ellison Bakery LLC .... C 800 711-8091
  Fort Wayne *(G-4946)*

Hearthside Food Solutions LLC .... B 219 878-1522
  Michigan City *(G-11622)*

Hometown Products .... G 317 625-2447
  Pittsboro *(G-13648)*

Lance Snyder .... G 717 632-4477
  Indianapolis *(G-8720)*

Richmond Baking Co .... C 765 962-8535
  Richmond *(G-14197)*

Snyders-Lance Inc .... G 317 270-7599
  Fishers *(G-4605)*

Snyders-Lance Inc .... G 812 285-0939
  Jeffersonville *(G-10055)*

BAKERY PRDTS: Cookies & crackers

Almiras Bakery .... F 219 844-4334
  Hammond *(G-6872)*

Bloomington Cookies LLC .... D 812 668-7779
  Bloomington *(G-811)*

Clif Bar & Company .... D 510 596-6451
  Indianapolis *(G-7822)*

Fingerhut Bakery Inc .... F 574 896-5937
  North Judson *(G-13212)*

Grace Island Spcalty Foods Inc .... G 260 357-3336
  Garrett *(G-5863)*

Heaven Sent Gurmet Cookies Inc .... G 219 980-1066
  Gary *(G-5948)*

Heyerly Brothers Inc .... F 260 622-4196
  Ossian *(G-13426)*

Houchens Industries Inc .... F 812 467-7455
  Evansville *(G-4111)*

Richmond Baking Georgia Inc .... G 765 962-8535
  Richmond *(G-14198)*

Schnuck Markets Inc .... C 812 853-9505
  Newburgh *(G-13019)*

Shipshewana Bread Box Corp .... G 260 768-4629
  Shipshewana *(G-14887)*

Weston Foods US Holdings LLC .... A 317 858-9000
  Brownsburg *(G-1413)*

BAKERY PRDTS: Doughnuts, Exc Frozen

Donut Bank Inc .... E 812 426-0011
  Evansville *(G-4019)*

Square Donuts Inc .... G 812 232-6463
  Terre Haute *(G-15714)*

Westfield Donuts .... G 317 896-5856
  Westfield *(G-16739)*

BAKERY PRDTS: Dry

Somethin Sweet Llc .... G 317 804-4894
  Indianapolis *(G-9460)*

Sugar Daddys Sweet Shop .... G 812 824-2253
  Bloomington *(G-982)*

Victorian House Scones LLC .... G 765 586-6295
  Lafayette *(G-10712)*

BAKERY PRDTS: Frozen

Alpha Baking Co Inc .... C 219 324-7440
  La Porte *(G-10381)*

Lewis Brothers Bakeries Inc .... C 812 886-6533
  Vincennes *(G-16137)*

Moms Pound Cakes LLC .... G 773 220-3822
  Merrillville *(G-11544)*

Phoenix Press Inc .... D 765 644-3959
  Anderson *(G-178)*

Sue & Kims Pies LLC .... G 317 779-2140
  Merrillville *(G-11562)*

BAKERY PRDTS: Pies, Bakery, Frozen

Moores Pie Shop Inc .... G 765 457-2428
  Kokomo *(G-10314)*

United Pies of Elkhart Inc .... G 574 294-3419
  Elkhart *(G-3759)*

BAKERY PRDTS: Pies, Exc Frozen

Bea MA Bkes Spclty Dsserts LLC .... G 219 302-6716
  Merrillville *(G-11487)*

Moores Pie Shop Inc .... G 765 457-2428
  Kokomo *(G-10314)*

On-Time LLC .... G 708 890-0230
  Hammond *(G-6989)*

United Pies of Elkhart Inc .... G 574 294-3419
  Elkhart *(G-3759)*

BAKERY PRDTS: Pretzels

Brilliant Blondes LLC .... F 765 288-8077
  Muncie *(G-12357)*

Chestnut Land Company .... G 574 271-8740
  Mishawaka *(G-11860)*

Mike-Sells West Virginia Inc .... G 317 241-7422
  Indianapolis *(G-8917)*

Perfect Twist Pretzels LLC .... G 574 248-1715
  Nappanee *(G-12636)*

Pretzels LLC .... C 800 456-4838
  Bluffton *(G-1049)*

Snyders-Lance Inc .... G 317 858-2209
  Indianapolis *(G-9456)*

BAKERY PRDTS: Wholesalers

Harlan Bakeries LLC .... C 317 272-3600
  Indianapolis *(G-8361)*

Harlan Bakeries LLC .... G 317 272-3600
  Avon *(G-523)*

Harlan Bakeries-Avon LLC .... B 317 272-3600
  Avon *(G-524)*

Lewis Brothers Bakeries Inc .... C 812 886-6533
  Vincennes *(G-16137)*

BAKERY: Wholesale Or Wholesale & Retail Combined

Alexson LLC .... G 219 210-3642
  Michigan City *(G-11576)*

Alpha Baking Co Inc .... G 574 234-0188
  South Bend *(G-14938)*

Bavettes Meat Company LLC .... G 312 590-7141
  Noblesville *(G-13041)*

Bimbo Bakeries Usa Inc .... G 317 570-1741
  Indianapolis *(G-7627)*

Black Rose Pastries LLC .... G 773 708-3650
  Gary *(G-5901)*

Blue Dolphin Ffy LLC .... G 773 255-3591
  Hammond *(G-6887)*

C Johnson Group LLC .... G 219 512-0619
  Indianapolis *(G-7708)*

Cornerstone Bread Co .... G 317 897-9671
  Indianapolis *(G-7877)*

Dutch Waffle Company LLC .... F 574 312-4578
  Plymouth *(G-13773)*

Eat Da Cake LLC .... G 765 479-4985
  Merrillville *(G-11510)*

Fountain Acres Foods .... G 765 847-1897
  Fountain City *(G-5611)*

Froet Group LLC .... F 317 414-2538
  Whitestown *(G-16807)*

Indiana Baking Co .... F 260 483-5997
  Fort Wayne *(G-5098)*

Indiana Grocery Group LLC .... E 219 462-5147
  Valparaiso *(G-15971)*

Kt Cakes .... G 812 442-6047
  Rosedale *(G-14381)*

Loves Enterprise LLC .... G 219 307-9191
  Gary *(G-5978)*

Maurices Sgnture Chsecakes LLC .... G 708 879-0031
  Valparaiso *(G-16000)*

May Suu Mon LLC .... G 786 556-8295
  Fort Wayne *(G-5209)*

Mel-Rhon Inc .... G 574 546-4559
  Bremen *(G-1205)*

Michael Greene .... G 317 753-7226
  Ladoga *(G-10508)*

Namsou Lims LLC .... G 347 641-5886
  Indianapolis *(G-8981)*

New Horizons Baking Co LLC .... C 260 495-7055
  Fremont *(G-5828)*

Richards Bakery .... F 260 424-4012
  Fort Wayne *(G-5383)*

Sea Salt & Cinnamon LLC .... F 727 481-4024
  Muncie *(G-12491)*

Sib Inc .... F 812 331-6029
  Bloomington *(G-969)*

Sweet Obsssons Bake Shoppe LLC .... G 260 273-2145
  Bluffton *(G-1060)*

Wb Frozen Us LLC .... A 317 858-9000
  Greenwood *(G-6779)*

BANNERS: Fabric

Eastern Banner Supply Corp .... G 812 448-2222
  Brazil *(G-1140)*

BANQUET HALL FACILITIES

Grafton Peek Incorporated .... F 317 557-8377
  Greenwood *(G-6709)*

Reset Family Solutions LLC .... G 317 699-2990
  Carthage *(G-1817)*

Employee Codes: A=Over 500 employees, B=251-500
C=101-250, D=51-100, E=20-50, F=10-19, G=1-9

BAR JOISTS & CONCRETE REINFORCING BARS: Fabricated

BAR JOISTS & CONCRETE REINFORCING BARS: Fabricated

6 Twenty-Six Inc... F..... 260 471-2002
  Fort Wayne *(G-4713)*

Rebar Corp of Indiana.................................... G..... 260 471-2002
  Fort Wayne *(G-5371)*

BARBECUE EQPT

Betos Bar Inc... G..... 219 397-8247
  East Chicago *(G-2993)*

Onward Manufacturing Company............... E..... 260 358-4111
  Huntington *(G-7346)*

Steven Ray Hughes...................................... G..... 574 491-2128
  Claypool *(G-2058)*

BARGES BUILDING & REPAIR

Acbl Holding Corporation............................ A..... 310 712-1850
  Jeffersonville *(G-9921)*

Acl Sales Corporation.................................. G..... 812 288-0100
  Jeffersonville *(G-9923)*

American Barge Line Company.................. G..... 812 288-0100
  Jeffersonville *(G-9930)*

American Coml Barge Line LLC................ C..... 812 288-0100
  Jeffersonville *(G-9931)*

American Commercial Lines Inc................ C..... 812 288-0100
  Jeffersonville *(G-9932)*

Commercial Barge Line Company............. E..... 812 288-0100
  Jeffersonville *(G-9956)*

Corn Island Shipyard Inc............................. G..... 812 362-8808
  Grandview *(G-6327)*

Estill Smith Marine Svcs Inc....................... G..... 812 282-7944
  Jeffersonville *(G-9983)*

BARRICADES: Metal

Rose Black... G..... 317 636-7459
  Indianapolis *(G-9332)*

BARS, COLD FINISHED: Steel, From Purchased Hot-Rolled

Ward Forging Company Inc........................ G..... 812 923-7463
  Floyds Knobs *(G-4698)*

BARS, PLATES & SHEETS: Zinc & Zinc Alloy Bars, Plates, Etc

Metal Source LLC.. E..... 260 563-8833
  Wabash *(G-16200)*

BARS: Concrete Reinforcing, Fabricated Steel

Anderson Fab Llc... G..... 317 534-7306
  Martinsville *(G-11381)*

CMa Steel & Fabrication Inc...................... F..... 260 207-9000
  Fort Wayne *(G-4861)*

Elliott Mfg & Fabrication............................. G..... 812 865-0516
  Paoli *(G-13493)*

Fabtration LLC... F..... 812 989-6730
  Georgetown *(G-6060)*

Ironhorse Detailing Inc................................ G..... 812 939-3300
  Clay City *(G-2044)*

J & F Steel Corporation............................... G..... 219 764-3500
  Burns Harbor *(G-1453)*

Morryde International Inc........................... C..... 574 293-1581
  Elkhart *(G-3555)*

Right Angle Stl & Fabrication.................... E..... 574 773-7148
  Nappanee *(G-12641)*

Rkdjrt Inc.. E..... 812 354-8899
  Petersburg *(G-13624)*

Sherman Enterprises Inc............................. G..... 260 636-6225
  Albion *(G-45)*

Stolz Structural Inc..................................... G..... 812 983-4720
  Elberfeld *(G-3118)*

Stoutco Inc... D..... 574 848-4411
  Bristol *(G-1293)*

Trivett Contracting Inc................................ E..... 317 539-5150
  Clayton *(G-2062)*

US Metals Inc... G..... 219 398-1350
  East Chicago *(G-3052)*

Z Rodz & Customs LLC.............................. G..... 574 806-5774
  Knox *(G-10229)*

BASES, BEVERAGE

Mbv-Midwest LLC.. G..... 800 400-3090
  Indianapolis *(G-8859)*

BATH SALTS

Blush Bath Bombs By Amor....................... G..... 219 313-3993
  Crown Point *(G-2657)*

With Love Bath Bombs................................ G..... 317 523-9197
  Indianapolis *(G-9779)*

BATHROOM FIXTURES: Plastic

Hotel Vanities Intl LLC............................... G..... 317 787-2330
  Indianapolis *(G-8423)*

Hotel Vanities Intl LLC............................... F..... 317 787-2330
  Indianapolis *(G-8424)*

Royal Spa Corporation................................ D..... 317 781-0828
  Indianapolis *(G-9341)*

BATTERIES, EXC AUTOMOTIVE: Wholesalers

Batteries Plus... G..... 317 219-0007
  Noblesville *(G-13040)*

Ocella Inc.. G..... 845 842-8185
  Newberry *(G-12990)*

Worldwide Battery Company LLC............. G..... 248 830-8537
  Elkhart *(G-3795)*

Worldwide Battery Company LLC............. G..... 812 475-1326
  Evansville *(G-4390)*

BATTERIES: Alkaline, Cell Storage

Dd Dannar LLC.. F..... 765 216-7191
  Muncie *(G-12374)*

BATTERIES: Lead Acid, Storage

Exide Technologies LLC............................. G..... 317 876-7475
  Indianapolis *(G-8155)*

Johnson Controls Inc.................................. F..... 317 917-5043
  Pittsboro *(G-13649)*

BATTERIES: Rechargeable

Enpower Inc.. E..... 463 213-3200
  Indianapolis *(G-8123)*

Ocella Inc.. G..... 845 842-8185
  Newberry *(G-12990)*

BATTERIES: Storage

B T Bttery Charger Systems Inc................ G..... 574 533-6030
  Goshen *(G-6093)*

Batteries Plus... G..... 317 219-0007
  Noblesville *(G-13040)*

Bulldog Battery Corporation...................... D..... 260 563-0551
  Wabash *(G-16176)*

Bw Energy & Innovation LLC..................... G..... 214 223-2459
  Greenfield *(G-6474)*

C&D Technologies Inc................................ C..... 765 762-2461
  Attica *(G-345)*

Crown Battery Manufacturing Co.............. G..... 260 423-3358
  Fort Wayne *(G-4888)*

Greatbatch Ltd... G..... 260 755-7484
  Warsaw *(G-16371)*

Integer Holdings Corporation..................... G..... 260 373-1664
  Fort Wayne *(G-5114)*

Knk Battery LLC... G..... 765 426-2016
  Otterbein *(G-13454)*

Tri-State Power Supply LLC....................... G..... 812 537-2500
  Lawrenceburg *(G-10863)*

Trojan Battery.. F..... 317 561-5650
  Plainfield *(G-13738)*

Worldwide Battery Company LLC............. G..... 248 830-8537
  Elkhart *(G-3795)*

Worldwide Battery Company LLC............. G..... 812 475-1326
  Evansville *(G-4390)*

BATTERIES: Wet

C&D Technologies Inc................................ C..... 765 762-2461
  Attica *(G-345)*

Greatbatch Ltd... G..... 260 755-7484
  Warsaw *(G-16371)*

Integer Holdings Corporation..................... G..... 260 373-1664
  Fort Wayne *(G-5114)*

Ocella Inc.. G..... 845 842-8185
  Newberry *(G-12990)*

BATTERY CASES: Plastic Or Plastics Combination

Captive Holdings LLC................................ D..... 812 424-2904
  Evansville *(G-3962)*

BATTERY CHARGERS

Energy Access Incorporated...................... F..... 317 329-1676
  Indianapolis *(G-8115)*

Exide Technologies LLC............................. G..... 317 876-7475
  Indianapolis *(G-8155)*

Flat Electronics LLC................................... G..... 765 414-6635
  Fishers *(G-4524)*

Go Electric Inc... G..... 765 400-1347
  Anderson *(G-122)*

BATTERY CHARGERS: Storage, Motor & Engine Generator Type

Rpg Energy Group Inc................................ F..... 317 614-0054
  Indianapolis *(G-9342)*

BAUXITE MINING

Howmet Aerospace Inc............................... B..... 412 553-4545
  Newburgh *(G-13005)*

BEARINGS & PARTS Ball

NSK Corporation.. D..... 765 458-5000
  Liberty *(G-10993)*

BEARINGS: Ball & Roller

Emerson Industrial Automation.................. G..... 574 583-9171
  Monticello *(G-12148)*

McGill Manufacturing Co Inc..................... A..... 219 465-2200
  Monticello *(G-12157)*

Menon Bearings Limited............................. G..... 866 556-3666
  Fishers *(G-4564)*

Nachi Technology Inc.................................. G..... 317 535-5000
  Greenwood *(G-6744)*

NSK Precision America Inc........................ D..... 317 738-5000
  Franklin *(G-5762)*

Rbc Bearings Incorporated......................... G..... 574 935-3027
  Plymouth *(G-13808)*

Rbc Prcsion Pdts - Plymouth Inc............... D..... 574 935-3027
  Plymouth *(G-13809)*

Regal Beloit America Inc............................ E..... 219 465-2200
  Monticello *(G-12167)*

Regal Beloit America Inc............................ E..... 219 465-2200
  Valparaiso *(G-16035)*

PRODUCT SECTION

BEVERAGES, ALCOHOLIC: Beer

Timken Company.................................. G 574 287-1566
South Bend *(G-15282)*

BEARINGS: Roller & Parts

Hsm Eagle Ltd..................................... G 812 491-9667
Evansville *(G-4112)*

Standard Locknut LLC......................... C 317 399-2230
Westfield *(G-16729)*

BEAUTY & BARBER SHOP EQPT

Accutemp Products Inc........................ G 260 493-6831
New Haven *(G-12890)*

Advanced Manufacturing In................. G 260 273-9669
Geneva *(G-6047)*

Afm Industries LLC............................... E 574 910-0982
Walkerton *(G-16262)*

AM Manufacturing Company Ind......... F 800 342-6744
Munster *(G-12528)*

Anchor Industries Inc........................... C 812 867-2421
Evansville *(G-3892)*

Containmed Inc.................................... G 317 487-8800
Indianapolis *(G-7854)*

Coolstream Rv Ducting Inc.................. F 574 361-4271
Elkhart *(G-3267)*

Dynatect Manufacturing Inc................. E 219 462-0822
Valparaiso *(G-15936)*

Dynatect Manufacturing Inc................. F 219 465-1898
Valparaiso *(G-15937)*

East Industries LLC.............................. G 812 273-4358
Madison *(G-11216)*

Foamiture... G 574 831-4775
New Paris *(G-12953)*

H A Industries....................................... G 219 931-6304
Hammond *(G-6937)*

Ilpea Industries Inc............................... C 812 752-2526
Evansville *(G-4116)*

Indiana Manufacturing Inst.................. G 765 494-4935
West Lafayette *(G-16595)*

Indiana Materials Proc LLC.................. F 260 244-6026
Columbia City *(G-2155)*

Mark Peiser Manufacturing Inc............ G 317 698-5376
Brownsburg *(G-1385)*

Nuwave Manufacturing......................... G 317 987-8229
Indianapolis *(G-9036)*

Park 100 Foods Inc.............................. E 765 763-6064
Morristown *(G-12280)*

Raven Industries Inc............................. G 877 923-5832
Wakarusa *(G-16246)*

Raw Barbers and Company LLC......... G 925 383-6212
Hammond *(G-6995)*

Reachpoint Industries Corp.................. G 219 707-3514
Highland *(G-7152)*

State Beauty Supply............................. G 260 755-6361
Fort Wayne *(G-5436)*

Steel Green Manufacturing LLC........... E 765 481-2890
Lebanon *(G-10944)*

Stylish Unique Salon LLC..................... G 317 938-1273
Indianapolis *(G-9519)*

Taunyas Creative Cuts......................... G 812 574-7722
Madison *(G-11253)*

Tbin LLC... G 812 491-9100
Princeton *(G-14013)*

Troyc-Industries LLC............................ G 317 531-1660
Indianapolis *(G-9649)*

Tspdesign LLC..................................... G 317 785-8663
Anderson *(G-210)*

Yankee Candle Company Inc.............. G 812 526-5195
Edinburgh *(G-3110)*

Yellow Cup LLC.................................... G 260 403-3489
Fort Wayne *(G-5580)*

BEAUTY & BARBER SHOP EQPT & SPLYS WHOLESALERS

Bedlam Beard Company LLC.............. G 317 800-9631
Lizton *(G-11048)*

Black Lavish Essentials LLC................ G 800 214-8664
Indianapolis *(G-7639)*

Divine Essentials LLC.......................... G 765 400-8609
Muncie *(G-12385)*

Kill Her Set LLC.................................... F 317 992-2220
Indianapolis *(G-8682)*

BEAUTY SALONS

Anderson Shykia................................. G 773 304-6852
Gary *(G-5894)*

Beautybyneyadior LLC......................... G 800 988-2592
Gary *(G-5898)*

Bettys Daughter Inc............................. G 317 500-1490
Plainfield *(G-13661)*

Cheri-Theree Inc.................................. G 812 529-8132
Lamar *(G-10795)*

Divine Essentials LLC.......................... G 765 400-8609
Muncie *(G-12385)*

Kenra Professional LLC....................... F 800 428-8073
Indianapolis *(G-8673)*

Kjs Beauty Lounge LLC....................... G 317 426-0621
Indianapolis *(G-8692)*

Majesty Hair Care System LLC............ G 317 900-6789
Indianapolis *(G-8818)*

Tonis Touch LLC.................................. G 317 992-1280
Plainfield *(G-13737)*

BEDDING & BEDSPRINGS STORES

Futon Factory Inc.................................. F 317 549-8639
Indianapolis *(G-8245)*

BEDDING, BEDSPREADS, BLANKETS & SHEETS

Capeable Sensory Products LLC......... G 260 387-5939
Fort Wayne *(G-4832)*

BEDS: Institutional

Anodyne Medical Device Inc............... D 954 340-0500
Batesville *(G-578)*

Hill-Rom Inc.. A 812 934-7777
Batesville *(G-589)*

BEDSPREADS & BED SETS, FROM PURCHASED MATERIALS

Artisan Interiors Inc.............................. D 574 825-9494
Middlebury *(G-11699)*

Ascot Enterprises Inc........................... E 877 773-7751
Nappanee *(G-12582)*

Katherine Mackey................................ G 765 825-0634
Connersville *(G-2448)*

BEER & ALE WHOLESALERS

Barley Island Brewing Co..................... G 317 770-5280
Noblesville *(G-13039)*

Calumet Breweries Inc......................... E 219 845-2242
Hammond *(G-6891)*

Indiana City Brewing LLC..................... F 317 643-1103
Carmel *(G-1666)*

Mishawaka Brewing Company............ G 574 256-9993
Granger *(G-6362)*

Tavistock Restaurants LLC.................. G 317 488-1230
Indianapolis *(G-9557)*

BEER & ALE, WHOLESALE: Beer & Other Fermented Malt Liquors

Sun King Brewing Company LLC........ D 317 602-3702
Indianapolis *(G-9525)*

Terrance A Smith Distributing.............. E 765 644-3396
Anderson *(G-205)*

BEER, WINE & LIQUOR STORES

Big Red Liquors Inc.............................. G 812 339-9552
Bloomington *(G-806)*

Crankshaft Brewing Co........................ G 317 939-0138
Brownsburg *(G-1361)*

Rihm Inc... G 765 478-3426
Cambridge City *(G-1502)*

BEER, WINE & LIQUOR STORES: Beer, Packaged

Lost Hollow Beer Co LLC..................... G 317 796-9516
Greencastle *(G-6420)*

BELTING: Rubber

Dunham Rubber Belting Corp.............. G 317 604-5313
Shelbyville *(G-14753)*

BELTS: Conveyor, Made From Purchased Wire

Engineering and Industrial................... E 574 722-3714
Logansport *(G-11073)*

Pro Tech Automation Inc..................... G 317 201-3875
Monrovia *(G-12079)*

Yongli America LLC............................. G 219 763-7920
Portage *(G-13920)*

BELTS: Seat, Automotive & Aircraft

Gerardot Performance Pdts Inc........... G 260 623-3048
Monroeville *(G-12069)*

Wolf Technical Engineering LLC.......... G 800 783-9653
Indianapolis *(G-9781)*

BERYLLIUM

Goldman Machine Services................. G 812 359-5440
Richland *(G-14078)*

BEVERAGE BASES & SYRUPS

Ambrotos LLC...................................... G 413 887-1058
Otwell *(G-13456)*

DWG Global Services LLC.................. G 469 605-0567
Avon *(G-514)*

Tc Heartland LLC................................. A 317 566-9750
Carmel *(G-1776)*

BEVERAGE STORES

Max of All Trades LLC.......................... G 317 703-4242
Kokomo *(G-10305)*

BEVERAGES, ALCOHOLIC: Ale

Ash & Elm Cider Company LLC........... G 317 600-3164
Indianapolis *(G-7550)*

Pepito Miller Bev Imports LLC............. G 317 416-3215
Plainfield *(G-13713)*

BEVERAGES, ALCOHOLIC: Beer

Barley Island Brewing Co..................... G 317 770-5280
Noblesville *(G-13039)*

Beach House Beverages LLC............. G 260 969-1064
Fort Wayne *(G-4789)*

Best Beers LLC.................................... E 812 332-1234
Bloomington *(G-803)*

BEVERAGES, ALCOHOLIC: Beer

Black Acre Brewing Company LLC......... E 317 207-6266
  Indianapolis *(G-7637)*
Calumet Breweries Inc........................ E 219 845-2242
  Hammond *(G-6891)*
Centerpoint Brewing Co LLC................. F 317 602-8386
  Indianapolis *(G-7768)*
Daredevil Brewing Company LLC........... G 765 602-1067
  Speedway *(G-15336)*
Eder Bros LLC................................. G 219 718-3335
  Schererville *(G-14520)*
Ekos Manufacturing LLC..................... G 847 630-9717
  Indianapolis *(G-8068)*
Indiana City Brewing LLC..................... F 317 643-1103
  Carmel *(G-1666)*
Lennies Inc.................................... E 812 323-2112
  Bloomington *(G-910)*
Lost Hollow Beer Co LLC..................... G 317 796-9516
  Greencastle *(G-6420)*
Melanie Brewery Company Inc.............. G 219 762-9652
  Portage *(G-13886)*
Mishawaka Brewing Company............... G 574 256-9993
  Granger *(G-6362)*
Monarch Distributing LLC .... A 800 382-9851
  Indianapolis *(G-8947)*
Myfin Inc...................................... F 812 287-8579
  Bloomington *(G-928)*
Rapid View LLC............................... G 574 224-3373
  Rochester *(G-14315)*
Round Town Brewery LLC................... G 317 657-6397
  Indianapolis *(G-9337)*
South Bend Brew Werks LLC................ G 801 209-2987
  South Bend *(G-15250)*
Sun King Brewing Company LLC........... D 317 602-3702
  Indianapolis *(G-9525)*
Tavistock Restaurants LLC.................. G 317 488-1230
  Indianapolis *(G-9557)*
Upland Brewing Company Inc.............. F 812 330-7421
  Bloomington *(G-1005)*
Wasser Brewing Company LLC............. F 765 653-3240
  Greencastle *(G-6435)*

BEVERAGES, ALCOHOLIC: Beer & Ale

Chapmans Cider Company LLC............. G 260 444-1194
  Angola *(G-239)*
Charles Wnngs DBA Dassault AVI......... G 928 276-4983
  Indianapolis *(G-7786)*
City Wineworks................................ G 765 460-5563
  Peru *(G-13572)*
Crankshaft Brewing Co....................... G 317 939-0138
  Brownsburg *(G-1361)*
Dockside....................................... G 574 400-0848
  South Bend *(G-15003)*
Drinkgp LLC.................................... G 317 410-4748
  Indianapolis *(G-8009)*
Floyd County Brewing Co LLC............... F 502 724-3202
  New Albany *(G-12731)*
Jaszy Drinks LLC.............................. G 219 742-5013
  Gary *(G-5969)*
Laotto Brewing LLC........................... G 260 897-3152
  Avilla *(G-486)*
Michigan City Brewing Co Inc............... G 219 879-4677
  Michigan City *(G-11637)*
Oaken Barrel Brewing Co Inc................ E 317 887-2287
  Greenwood *(G-6748)*
Sugar Creek Hops LLC....................... G 317 319-1164
  Carmel *(G-1772)*
Terrance A Smith Distributing............... E 765 644-3396
  Anderson *(G-205)*
Turonis Forget-Me-Not Inc................... F 812 477-7500
  Evansville *(G-4356)*

BEVERAGES, ALCOHOLIC: Bourbon Whiskey

West Fork Whiskey Co........................ G 812 583-9797
  Indianapolis *(G-9751)*

BEVERAGES, ALCOHOLIC: Brandy & Brandy Spirits

Hotel Tango Whiskey Inc..................... E 317 653-1806
  Indianapolis *(G-8422)*

BEVERAGES, ALCOHOLIC: Distilled Liquors

12-05 Distillery LLC........................... G 317 402-4818
  Indianapolis *(G-7383)*
1205 Distillery................................. G 317 804-5675
  Westfield *(G-16659)*
18th Street Distillery LLC..................... F 219 803-0820
  Hammond *(G-6865)*
8th Day Distillery LLC......................... G 317 690-2202
  Indianapolis *(G-7394)*
Bear Wallow Distillery........................ G 812 657-4923
  Nashville *(G-12662)*
Bemis Distillers LLC.......................... G 317 619-0711
  Greenwood *(G-6675)*
Cardinal Spirits LLC........................... E 812 202-6789
  Bloomington *(G-820)*
Distillery 64 LLC............................... G 502 536-7485
  New Albany *(G-12721)*
Easley Enterprises Inc........................ G 317 636-4516
  Indianapolis *(G-8036)*
Edwin Coe LLC................................ G 260 438-7678
  Churubusco *(G-1984)*
Hard Truth Distilling Co LLC................. D 812 720-4840
  Nashville *(G-12670)*
Hotel Tango Whiskey Inc..................... E 317 653-1806
  Indianapolis *(G-8422)*
Hunt Club Distillery........................... G 317 441-7194
  Sheridan *(G-14823)*
Indiana Natural Infusions LLC............... G 847 754-9277
  Lowell *(G-11163)*
Indiana Whiskey Co........................... G 574 339-1737
  South Bend *(G-15079)*
McCracken Curve Distillery LLC............ G 812 486-3651
  Montgomery *(G-12113)*
Mgpi Processing Inc.......................... F 812 532-4100
  Greendale *(G-6448)*
Oakley Brothers Distillery.................... G 765 274-5590
  Anderson *(G-171)*
Old Fort Distillery Inc......................... G 260 705-5128
  Grabill *(G-6317)*
Repeal 1205 LLC.............................. G 317 402-4818
  Indianapolis *(G-9292)*
Royal Inc....................................... F 812 424-4925
  Evansville *(G-4295)*
Southern In Distillery......................... G 812 454-0135
  Mount Vernon *(G-12322)*
Streven Distilling Company LLC............. G 574 527-4061
  Warsaw *(G-16431)*
Three Floyds Distilling Co LLC.............. F 219 922-3565
  Munster *(G-12571)*
Three Rivers Distilling Co LLC.............. E 260 745-9355
  Fort Wayne *(G-5483)*
Turkey Run Distillery LLC.................... G 765 505-2044
  Bloomingdale *(G-762)*

BEVERAGES, ALCOHOLIC: Wines

Aftermath Cidery and Winery................ G 219 299-8463
  Valparaiso *(G-15894)*
Ambrosia Orchard Inc........................ G 260 639-4101
  Hoagland *(G-7165)*
Ancient Cellars................................ G 503 437-4827
  Indianapolis *(G-7515)*
At The Barn Winery........................... G 513 310-8810
  Lawrenceburg *(G-10829)*
B and C Enterprises.......................... G 260 691-2171
  Albion *(G-18)*
Bacchus Winery Golf Vinyrd LLC........... G 574 732-4663
  Logansport *(G-11059)*
Bacchus Winery LLC......................... G 574 722-1416
  Logansport *(G-11060)*
Belgian Horse Winery LLC................... G 765 779-3002
  Middletown *(G-11767)*
Best Vineyards LLC........................... G 812 969-9463
  Elizabeth *(G-3124)*
Blue Heron Vineyards LLC................... G 812 619-6045
  Cannelton *(G-1533)*
Bonaccorsi Wine Company LLC............ G 310 777-3704
  Carmel *(G-1570)*
Brandywine Creek............................. G 317 868-0563
  Indianapolis *(G-7672)*
Brandywine Creek Vnyrds Wnery........... G 317 403-5669
  New Palestine *(G-12934)*
Briali Vineyards LLC.......................... G 260 316-5156
  Fremont *(G-5812)*
Brown County Wine Company Inc......... G 812 988-6144
  Nashville *(G-12666)*
Butler Vineyards............................... G 219 929-1400
  Chesterton *(G-1907)*
Butler Vineyards............................... G 812 332-6660
  Bloomington *(G-819)*
Carousel Winery............................... G 812 849-1005
  Mitchell *(G-12035)*
Cedar Creek Winery.......................... G 765 342-9000
  Martinsville *(G-11385)*
Cedar Creek Winery.......................... G 812 988-1111
  Nashville *(G-12667)*
Chateau De Pique Inc........................ G 812 522-9296
  Seymour *(G-14638)*
Chateau Thomas Winery Inc................ F 317 837-9463
  Plainfield *(G-13668)*
Cherry Hill Vineyard LLC.................... G 317 846-5170
  Carmel *(G-1586)*
Copia Vineyards and Winery LLC.......... G 805 835-6094
  Indianapolis *(G-7870)*
Country Hritg Wnery Vinyrd Inc............. F 260 637-2980
  Laotto *(G-10803)*
Country Moon Winery LLC.................. G 317 773-7942
  Noblesville *(G-13064)*
Cupkas Bee Good Meadery LLC........... G 260 927-3837
  Auburn *(G-381)*
Cupkas Bee Good Meadery LLC........... G 260 927-3837
  Auburn *(G-382)*
Daniels Vineyard LLC......................... F 317 894-6860
  Greenfield *(G-6487)*
Dulcius Vineyards LLC....................... G 260 602-9259
  Columbia City *(G-2140)*
Dune Ridge Winery LLC...................... G 219 548-4605
  Chesterton *(G-1921)*
Ertel Cellars Winery Inc...................... G 812 933-1500
  Batesville *(G-588)*
Evangeline Orchard & Winery............... G 574 278-6301
  Monticello *(G-12149)*
Family Vineyard LLC.......................... G 812 322-1720
  Indianapolis *(G-8165)*
Finley Creek Vineyards LLC................. G 317 769-5483
  Zionsville *(G-17008)*
First Miracle LLC.............................. G 812 472-3527
  Fredericksburg *(G-5793)*
Four Corners Winery LLC.................... G 219 730-5311
  Valparaiso *(G-15950)*
Frogs Leap..................................... G 812 235-5759
  Terre Haute *(G-15592)*

PRODUCT SECTION

BEVERAGES, NONALCOHOLIC: Carbonated

Fruit Hills Winery Orchrd LLC......................... G 574 848-9463
   Bristol *(G-1262)*

Graybull Organic Wines Inc........................... G 317 797-2186
   Indianapolis *(G-8316)*

Harmony Winery... G 317 585-9463
   Knightstown *(G-10196)*

Heagy Vineyards LLC...................................... G 317 752-4484
   Carmel *(G-1652)*

Home - Little Creek Winery.............................. G 812 319-3951
   Evansville *(G-4107)*

Hooker Corner Winery LLC............................. G 765 585-1225
   Pine Village *(G-13643)*

Hopwood Cellars Winery LLC......................... G 317 873-4099
   Zionsville *(G-17016)*

Huckleberry Winery... G 317 850-4445
   Bargersville *(G-568)*

Hunters Ridge Winery LLC.............................. G 812 967-9463
   Salem *(G-14482)*

Indian Trail Wines LLC..................................... G 574 889-2509
   Royal Center *(G-14391)*

Indiana Artisan Inc... G 317 607-8715
   Carmel *(G-1665)*

Indiana Whl Wine & Lq Co Inc........................ G 317 667-0231
   Indianapolis *(G-8501)*

J & J Winery... G 765 969-1188
   Richmond *(G-14143)*

James Lake Vineyard Inc................................ G 260 495-9463
   Fremont *(G-5824)*

Laker Winery LLC... G 812 934-4633
   Sunman *(G-15440)*

Lane Byler Inc... G 260 920-4377
   Auburn *(G-402)*

Lane Legacy Vineyard...................................... G 937 902-7738
   Brookville *(G-1328)*

Lanthier Winery LLC... G 502 663-2399
   Madison *(G-11234)*

Lanthier Winery & Restaurant......................... G 812 273-2409
   Madison *(G-11235)*

Lasalles Landing Vineyard LLC...................... G 574 277-2711
   South Bend *(G-15117)*

Manic Meadery.. G 219 614-1846
   Crown Point *(G-2722)*

Meier Winery & Vinyard LLC........................... G 812 382-4220
   Sullivan *(G-15414)*

Monkey Hollow.. G 812 998-2112
   Saint Meinrad *(G-14463)*

Mystique Winery and Vinyrd LLC................... G 812 922-5612
   Lynnville *(G-11190)*

Nashville Tasting Room.................................... G 812 720-7080
   Nashville *(G-12677)*

New Day Meadery LLC..................................... G 317 602-7030
   Indianapolis *(G-9004)*

Oak Hill Winery LLC.. G 765 395-3632
   Converse *(G-2479)*

Oliver Wine Company Inc................................. D 812 876-5800
   Bloomington *(G-935)*

Owen Valley Winery LLC.................................. G 812 828-0883
   Spencer *(G-15356)*

Pacheco Winery Ltd Lblty Co.......................... F 812 799-0683
   Columbus *(G-2369)*

Peace Water Winery LLC................................ G 317 810-1330
   Noblesville *(G-13154)*

Peppers Ridge LLC.. G 812 499-3743
   Rockport *(G-14347)*

Pfeiffer Winery & Vineyard Inc....................... G 812 952-2650
   Corydon *(G-2511)*

Plainfield Winery Tstng Rm............................ G 317 837-9463
   Plainfield *(G-13716)*

Prairie Sun Vineyard LLC................................ G 219 741-5918
   Rolling Prairie *(G-14368)*

Preston Leaderbrand.. F 812 828-0883
   Spencer *(G-15357)*

Prp Wine International..................................... F 317 288-0005
   Indianapolis *(G-9234)*

Red Gate Farms Inc... G 812 277-9750
   Bedford *(G-667)*

Rick Black Associates LLC............................. G 765 838-3498
   Lafayette *(G-10680)*

Ridge Winery Inc.. G 812 427-3380
   Vevay *(G-16111)*

Running Vines Winery..................................... G 219 617-2429
   Valparaiso *(G-16041)*

S L Thomas Family Winery Inc...................... G 812 273-3755
   Madison *(G-11250)*

Schmitt Bennett... G 812 459-8523
   Haubstadt *(G-7089)*

Scout Mountain Farm - Hideaway.................. G 812 738-7196
   Corydon *(G-2515)*

Shady Creek Vineyard LLC............................. G 219 874-9463
   Michigan City *(G-11666)*

Simmons Winery & Farm Mkt Inc.................. G 812 546-0091
   Columbus *(G-2393)*

Stoney Creek Winery LLC............................... G 574 642-4454
   Millersburg *(G-11819)*

Sugar Creek Vinyrd Winery Inc..................... G 317 844-3785
   Carmel *(G-1773)*

Sycamore Winery LLC..................................... G 812 243-0565
   West Terre Haute *(G-16655)*

Tilted Compass Winery LLC........................... G 812 691-1766
   Clay City *(G-2047)*

Tippy Creek Winery LLC................................. G 574 253-1862
   Leesburg *(G-10962)*

Tipsy Glass LLC... G 260 251-0021
   Portland *(G-13970)*

Tj Haase Winery Ltd Lblty Co......................... G 765 505-1382
   Terre Haute *(G-15732)*

Tonne Winery Incorporated............................ G 765 896-9821
   Muncie *(G-12506)*

Twe Wholesale Inc... G 317 450-5409
   Carmel *(G-1791)*

Twin Willows LLC.. G 812 497-0254
   Freetown *(G-5805)*

Two Ees Winery.. F 260 672-2000
   Huntington *(G-7375)*

Urban Vines LLC... G 317 763-0678
   Westfield *(G-16736)*

Vineyard Fishery Products LLC..................... G 317 902-0753
   Indianapolis *(G-9721)*

Welch Winery LLC.. G 707 327-8038
   Selma *(G-14623)*

Whyte Horse Winery LLC................................ G 574 583-2345
   Monticello *(G-12176)*

Winzerwald Winery LLC................................... G 812 357-7000
   Bristow *(G-1302)*

Zeising Winery... G 812 518-0607
   Huntingburg *(G-7295)*

BEVERAGES, MALT

Proximo Distillers LLC..................................... D 201 204-1718
   Lawrenceburg *(G-10855)*

Triple Xxx Root Beer Corp.............................. G 765 743-5373
   West Lafayette *(G-16640)*

BEVERAGES, NONALCOHOLIC: Bottled & canned soft drinks

American Bottling Company........................... D 574 291-9000
   South Bend *(G-14943)*

Blended LLC.. G 317 268-8005
   Danville *(G-2808)*

Central Coca-Cola Btlg Co Inc....................... D 765 642-9951
   Anderson *(G-91)*

Central Coca-Cola Btlg Co Inc....................... E 800 241-2653
   Bloomington *(G-828)*

Central Coca-Cola Btlg Co Inc....................... D 260 478-2978
   Fort Wayne *(G-4840)*

Central Coca-Cola Btlg Co Inc....................... D 317 398-0129
   Indianapolis *(G-7771)*

Central Coca-Cola Btlg Co Inc....................... E 317 243-3771
   Indianapolis *(G-7772)*

Central Coca-Cola Btlg Co Inc....................... E 812 482-7475
   Jasper *(G-9827)*

Central Coca-Cola Btlg Co Inc....................... E 260 726-7126
   Portland *(G-13930)*

Central Coca-Cola Btlg Co Inc....................... G 800 241-2653
   Shelbyville *(G-14744)*

Central Coca-Cola Btlg Co Inc....................... E 574 291-1511
   South Bend *(G-14969)*

Clark Foods Inc.. E 812 949-3075
   New Albany *(G-12714)*

Coca Cola Bottling Company I........................ G 812 376-3381
   Columbus *(G-2240)*

Coca Cola Btlg Co Kokomo Ind...................... E 574 936-3220
   Plymouth *(G-13764)*

Coca Cola Btlg Co Kokomo Ind...................... D 765 457-4421
   Kokomo *(G-10248)*

Coca-Cola Bottling Co..................................... E 812 332-4434
   Bloomington *(G-831)*

Coca-Cola Bottling Co..................................... G 800 688-2053
   Richmond *(G-14108)*

Coca-Cola Bottling Co Portland..................... E 260 729-6124
   Portland *(G-13931)*

Coca-Cola Consolidated Inc........................... C 812 228-3200
   Evansville *(G-3974)*

Coca-Cola Enterprises..................................... G 574 291-1511
   South Bend *(G-14978)*

Indianapolis Gatorade..................................... G 317 821-6400
   Indianapolis *(G-8505)*

Ira William Scott.. G 219 241-5674
   Valparaiso *(G-15977)*

Northeast Bottling Co...................................... G 260 343-0208
   Kendallville *(G-10139)*

Party Cask... G 812 234-3008
   Terre Haute *(G-15657)*

PD Kangaroo Inc... G 317 417-7143
   Indianapolis *(G-9109)*

Quaker Oats Company..................................... C 317 821-6442
   Indianapolis *(G-9245)*

Snapple Beverage Corp................................... G 812 424-7978
   Evansville *(G-4323)*

Success Holding Group Intl Inc..................... G 260 450-1982
   Ossian *(G-13436)*

BEVERAGES, NONALCOHOLIC: Carbonated

Capitol Source Network................................... G 260 248-9747
   Columbia City *(G-2129)*

Dads Root Beer Company LLC...................... G 812 482-5352
   Jasper *(G-9830)*

P-Americas LLC.. G 812 794-4455
   Austin *(G-468)*

P-Americas LLC.. G 812 332-1200
   Bloomington *(G-940)*

P-Americas LLC.. G 765 647-3576
   Brookville *(G-1332)*

P-Americas LLC.. G 765 289-0270
   Indianapolis *(G-9081)*

P-Americas LLC.. C 219 836-1800
   Munster *(G-12556)*

P-Americas LLC.. G 812 522-3421
   Seymour *(G-14670)*

Pepsi 3449... F 317 760-7335
   Indianapolis *(G-9117)*

Pepsi Beverages Company............................. E 260 428-9156
   Fort Wayne *(G-5301)*

Pepsi Beverages Company............................. E 219 836-1800
   Munster *(G-12557)*

Employee Codes: A=Over 500 employees, B=251-500
C=101-250, D=51-100, E=20-50, F=10-19, G=1-9

BEVERAGES, NONALCOHOLIC: Carbonated

Pepsi Bottling Ventures LLC	E	765 659-7313	
Frankfort (G-5690)			
Pepsi-Cola	G	812 634-1844	
Jasper (G-9902)			
Pepsi-Cola Metro Btlg Co Inc	F	812 332-1200	
Bloomington (G-945)			
Pepsico	G	260 750-9106	
Fort Wayne (G-5302)			
Pepsico	C	317 821-6400	
Indianapolis (G-9118)			
Pepsico	E	317 334-0153	
Whitestown (G-16813)			
Pepsico Inc	E	260 579-3461	
Fort Wayne (G-5303)			
Pepsico Inc	G	317 830-4011	
Indianapolis (G-9119)			
Pepsico Inc	G	765 345-7668	
Knightstown (G-10201)			
Pepsico Beverage Sales LLC	C	574 314-6001	
South Bend (G-15190)			
Refreshment Services Inc	D	812 466-0602	
Terre Haute (G-15677)			
Wp Beverages LLC	F	574 722-6207	
Logansport (G-11120)			

BEVERAGES, NONALCOHOLIC: Carbonated, Canned & Bottled, Etc

Circle City Sonorans LLC	G	317 395-3693	
Indianapolis (G-7807)			
Gamer Energy LLC	G	317 660-9262	
Carmel (G-1639)			
Liquid Ninja Energy LLC	F	812 746-2830	
Evansville (G-4171)			
Vin Elite Imports Inc	G	317 264-9250	
Indianapolis (G-9720)			

BEVERAGES, NONALCOHOLIC: Cider

Adrian Orchards Inc	G	317 784-0550	
Indianapolis (G-7434)			
Millers Mill	G	574 825-2010	
Middlebury (G-11738)			

BEVERAGES, NONALCOHOLIC: Flavoring extracts & syrups, nec

Central Coca-Cola Btlg Co Inc	E	317 243-3771	
Indianapolis (G-7772)			
Common Collabs LLC	G	574 249-9182	
North Judson (G-13210)			
First Creative Ingredients Inc	G	219 764-0202	
Portage (G-13865)			
International Bakers Service	E	574 287-7111	
South Bend (G-15083)			
Moseley Laboratories Inc	F	317 866-8460	
Greenfield (G-6533)			
Partlow Farms LLC	G	317 919-8064	
Noblesville (G-13151)			
Pepsico Inc	G	317 830-4011	
Indianapolis (G-9119)			
Savor Flavor LLC	G	812 667-1030	
Dillsboro (G-2952)			
Vitamins Inc	E	219 879-7356	
Michigan City (G-11686)			
Wild Flavors Inc	G	859 991-5229	
Indianapolis (G-9765)			

BEVERAGES, NONALCOHOLIC: Fruit Drnks, Under 100% Juice, Can

Better Blacc Wall Streetz LLC	F	812 927-0712	
Seymour (G-14632)			

BEVERAGES, NONALCOHOLIC: Soft Drinks, Canned & Bottled, Etc

American Bottling Company	D	260 484-4177	
Fort Wayne (G-4752)			
American Bottling Company	C	317 875-4900	
Indianapolis (G-7500)			
American Bottling Company	D	765 987-7800	
Spiceland (G-15376)			
Bollygood Inc	G	317 215-5616	
Indianapolis (G-7658)			
Central Coca-Cola Btlg Co Inc	E	800 241-2653	
Indianapolis (G-7770)			
Dr Pepper Bottling Co	G	765 647-3576	
Brookville (G-1319)			
Dr Pepper Snapple Group	G	574 291-9000	
South Bend (G-15005)			
Dr Pepper Snapple Group I	G	260 484-4177	
Fort Wayne (G-4927)			
Interactions Incorporated	D	574 722-6207	
Logansport (G-11083)			
Keurig Dr Pepper Inc	G	812 522-3823	
Seymour (G-14661)			
Qtg Pepsi Co Larry Davi	G	317 830-4020	
Indianapolis (G-9244)			
RC Transportation LLC	D	812 424-7978	
Evansville (G-4274)			
Refresco Beverages US Inc	F	812 537-7300	
Greendale (G-6455)			
Royal Crown Bottling Corp	C	812 424-7978	
Evansville (G-4294)			
Swanel Inc	E	219 932-7676	
Hammond (G-7017)			

BEVERAGES, WINE & DISTILLED ALCOHOLIC, WHOLESALE: Liquor

Clancys of Portage	E	219 764-4995	
Portage (G-13856)			

BEVERAGES, WINE & DISTILLED ALCOHOLIC, WHOLESALE: Wine

Durm Vineyard Inc	G	317 862-9463	
Indianapolis (G-8021)			
Indiana Whl Wine & Lq Co Inc	G	317 667-0231	
Indianapolis (G-8501)			
Prp Wine International	F	317 288-0005	
Indianapolis (G-9234)			
Vin Elite Imports Inc	G	317 264-9250	
Indianapolis (G-9720)			

BICYCLE ASSEMBLY SVCS

Walton Industrial Park Inc	F	574 626-2929	
Walton (G-16284)			

BICYCLES WHOLESALERS

America Wild LLC	G	888 485-2589	
Fort Wayne (G-4751)			

BICYCLES, PARTS & ACCESS

America Wild LLC	G	888 485-2589	
Fort Wayne (G-4751)			
Best Bicycle Inc	G	812 336-2724	
Bloomington (G-804)			
David Tortora	G	317 506-6902	
Carmel (G-1605)			

BILLIARD TABLE REPAIR SVCS

Jay Orner Sons Billiard Co Inc	G	317 243-0046	
Indianapolis (G-8618)			

BILLING & BOOKKEEPING SVCS

Groupone Health Source Inc	D	800 769-5288	
Indianapolis (G-8334)			
Lil Red Studios LLC	G	317 443-4932	
Indianapolis (G-8753)			

BINDING SVC: Books & Manuals

A-1 Awards Inc	F	317 546-9000	
Indianapolis (G-7406)			
Acclaim Graphics Inc	G	812 424-5035	
Evansville (G-3866)			
Art Bookbinders of America	F	312 226-4100	
Hammond (G-6880)			
Baxter Printing Incorporated	G	219 923-1999	
Griffith (G-6793)			
Brand Prtg & Photo-Litho Co	G	317 921-4095	
New Palestine (G-12933)			
C J P Corporation	G	219 924-1685	
Highland (G-7127)			
Cecils Printing & Off Sups Inc	G	812 683-4416	
Huntingburg (G-7273)			
Ckmt Associates Inc	F	219 924-2820	
Hammond (G-6902)			
Classic Graphics Inc	F	260 482-3487	
Fort Wayne (G-4853)			
Colophon Book Arts Supply LLC	G	812 671-0577	
Bloomington (G-834)			
Consolidated Printing Svcs Inc	G	765 468-6033	
Farmland (G-4424)			
Courier Printing Co Allen Cnty	G	260 627-2728	
Grabill (G-6293)			
Creative Concept Ventures Inc	G	812 282-9442	
Jeffersonville (G-9964)			
Crossrads Rhbilitation Ctr Inc	C	317 897-7320	
Indianapolis (G-7910)			
Digital Printing Incorporated	G	812 265-2205	
Madison (G-11214)			
Doerr Printing Co	G	317 568-0135	
Indianapolis (G-7994)			
Dynamark Graphics Group Inc	E	317 328-2555	
Indianapolis (G-8023)			
Ed Sons Inc	F	317 897-8821	
Indianapolis (G-8051)			
Epi Printers Inc	D	317 579-4870	
Indianapolis (G-8129)			
Evansville Bindery Inc	G	812 423-2222	
Evansville (G-4048)			
Ewing Printing Company Inc	F	812 882-2415	
Vincennes (G-16120)			
Express Press Indiana Inc	E	574 277-3355	
South Bend (G-15023)			
Faulkenberg Printing Co Inc	F	317 638-1359	
Franklin (G-5730)			
Fedex Office & Print Svcs Inc	G	317 849-9683	
Indianapolis (G-8174)			
Fedex Office & Print Svcs Inc	G	317 885-6480	
Indianapolis (G-8175)			
Fedex Office & Print Svcs Inc	G	317 295-1063	
Indianapolis (G-8176)			
Fedex Office & Print Svcs Inc	G	317 337-2679	
Indianapolis (G-8177)			
Fedex Office & Print Svcs Inc	G	317 631-6862	
Indianapolis (G-8178)			
Fedex Office & Print Svcs Inc	G	317 251-2406	
Indianapolis (G-8179)			
Fedex Office & Print Svcs Inc	F	765 449-4950	
Lafayette (G-10579)			
Goetz Printing	G	812 243-2086	
Terre Haute (G-15600)			
Granger Gazette Inc	G	574 277-2679	
Granger (G-6350)			

PRODUCT SECTION

BLANKBOOKS & LOOSELEAF BINDERS

Green Banner Publications Inc............... E 812 967-3176
  Borden *(G-1109)*
Greencastle Offset Inc............................ G 765 653-4026
  Greencastle *(G-6406)*
Greensburg Printing Co Inc..................... G 812 663-8265
  Greensburg *(G-6598)*
Hardesty Printing Co Inc......................... F 574 267-7591
  Warsaw *(G-16374)*
Hardesty Printing Co Inc......................... F 574 223-4553
  Rochester *(G-14293)*
Hetty Incorporated................................. ..... 219 933-0833
  Hammond *(G-6945)*
Hetty Incorporated................................. G 219 836-2517
  Munster *(G-12539)*
Hf Group LLC.. B 260 982-2107
  North Manchester *(G-13234)*
Hiatt Enterprises Inc.............................. G 765 289-2700
  Muncie *(G-12416)*
Hiatt Enterprises Inc.............................. F 765 289-7756
  Muncie *(G-12415)*
Hinen Printing Co.................................. G 260 248-8984
  Columbia City *(G-2150)*
Home Mountain Publishing Co Inc........... E 219 462-6601
  Valparaiso *(G-15962)*
Howard Print Shop LLC.......................... G 765 453-6161
  Kokomo *(G-10283)*
Infobind Systems Inc............................. G 260 248-4989
  Fort Wayne *(G-5106)*
Journal & Chronicle Inc.......................... G 812 752-5060
  Scottsburg *(G-14566)*
Kendallville Custom Printing.................... F 260 347-9233
  Kendallville *(G-10125)*
Kistner Enterprises Inc........................... G 317 773-7733
  Noblesville *(G-13123)*
L & L Press Inc..................................... F 765 664-3162
  Marion *(G-11305)*
La Grange Publishing Co Inc................... F 260 463-3243
  Lagrange *(G-10747)*
Lamco Finishers Inc.............................. E 317 471-1010
  Indianapolis *(G-8717)*
Largus Speedy Print Corp....................... E 219 922-8414
  Munster *(G-12546)*
Lincoln Printing Corporation.................... A 260 424-5200
  Fort Wayne *(G-5186)*
Ludwick Graphics Inc............................. G 574 233-2165
  South Bend *(G-15131)*
Masco Corporation of Indiana.................. E 317 848-1812
  Indianapolis *(G-8847)*
Maureen Sharp..................................... G 765 379-3644
  Rossville *(G-14387)*
Maury Boyd & Associates Inc.................. F 317 849-6110
  Indianapolis *(G-8853)*
Mignone Communications Incorporated C 260 358-0266
  Huntington *(G-7344)*
Millcraft Paper Company......................... G 317 240-3500
  Indianapolis *(G-8920)*
Montgomery & Associates Inc.................. F 219 879-0088
  Michigan City *(G-11641)*
Offset House Inc................................... F 317 849-5155
  Indianapolis *(G-9042)*
Offset One Inc...................................... F 260 456-8828
  Fort Wayne *(G-5282)*
Overgaards Artcraft Printers.................... G 574 234-8464
  South Bend *(G-15183)*
Parrot Press Inc.................................... E 260 422-6402
  Fort Wayne *(G-5298)*
Phoenix Press Inc................................. D 765 644-3959
  Anderson *(G-178)*
PIP Marketing Signs Print....................... G 317 843-5755
  Carmel *(G-1719)*
Presstime Graphics Inc.......................... F 812 234-3815
  Terre Haute *(G-15669)*

Printing Place Inc.................................. F 260 665-8444
  Angola *(G-289)*
Progressive Printing Co Inc..................... G 765 653-3814
  Greencastle *(G-6427)*
Quality Printing of NW Ind...................... G 219 322-6677
  Schererville *(G-14540)*
R R Donnelley & Sons Company.............. C 765 362-1300
  Crawfordsville *(G-2607)*
Reprocomm Inc..................................... G 765 423-2578
  Lafayette *(G-10679)*
Reprocomm Inc..................................... G 765 472-5700
  Peru *(G-13598)*
Rhr Corporation.................................... G 317 788-1504
  Indianapolis *(G-9298)*
Riden Inc.. G 219 362-5511
  La Porte *(G-10473)*
Rink Printing Company........................... E 574 232-7935
  South Bend *(G-15220)*
Rise Inc... D 260 665-9408
  Angola *(G-292)*
Rowland Printing Co Inc......................... F 317 773-1829
  Noblesville *(G-13168)*
Schutte Lithography Inc.......................... F 812 469-3500
  Evansville *(G-4300)*
Service Graphics Inc.............................. D 317 471-8246
  Indianapolis *(G-9408)*
Service Printers Inc............................... E 574 266-6710
  Elkhart *(G-3669)*
Specialized Printed Products................... G 260 483-7075
  Fort Wayne *(G-5428)*
Spi-Binding Company Inc........................ F 765 794-4992
  Darlington *(G-2834)*
Stines Printing Inc................................. G 260 356-5994
  Huntington *(G-7371)*
Tabco Business Forms Inc...................... F 812 882-2836
  Vincennes *(G-16157)*
Tatman Inc... E 765 825-2164
  Connersville *(G-2472)*
Thomas E Slade Inc............................... F 812 437-5233
  Evansville *(G-4343)*
Tippecanoe Press Inc............................. G 317 392-1207
  Shelbyville *(G-14806)*
University Publishing Corp....................... E 812 339-9033
  Bloomington *(G-1004)*
Voice of God Recordings Inc................... D 812 246-2137
  Jeffersonville *(G-10069)*
WAr - LLC- Westville Prtg...................... G 219 785-2821
  Westville *(G-16765)*
Whitewater Publications Inc..................... F 765 647-4221
  Brookville *(G-1341)*
Woodburn Graphics Inc.......................... F 812 232-0323
  Terre Haute *(G-15748)*

BINDING SVC: Trade

Blasted Works....................................... G 574 583-3211
  Monticello *(G-12138)*
Gateway Builders & Properties................ G 574 295-9944
  Elkhart *(G-3367)*

BINS: Prefabricated, Metal Plate

Ctb Inc.. G 574 658-4191
  Milford *(G-11789)*
Ctb Inc.. A 574 658-4191
  Milford *(G-11790)*

BIOLOGICAL PRDTS: Blood Derivatives

Immunotek Bio Centers LLC................... G 337 500-1294
  Indianapolis *(G-8467)*
Immunotek Bio Centers LLC................... G 337 500-1294
  Jeffersonville *(G-10002)*

BIOLOGICAL PRDTS: Exc Diagnostic

Acro Biomedical Co Ltd......................... G 317 286-6788
  Fishers *(G-4460)*
Apotex Corp... F 317 334-1314
  Indianapolis *(G-7526)*
Apotex Corp... E 317 839-6550
  Plainfield *(G-13658)*
Arkley Biotek LLC.................................. G 317 331-7580
  Indianapolis *(G-7545)*
Biosafe Engineering LLC........................ E 317 858-8099
  Indianapolis *(G-7629)*
Bioscience Vaccines Inc......................... G 765 464-5890
  West Lafayette *(G-16566)*
Corebiologic LLC................................... G 260 437-0353
  Fort Wayne *(G-4878)*
Geniphys Inc.. G 317 973-0523
  Zionsville *(G-17013)*
Harlan Development Company................ G 317 352-1583
  Indianapolis *(G-8362)*
Pucl Bindley Bioscience Ctr.................... G 765 496-3975
  West Lafayette *(G-16621)*
Tissue Source LLC................................ G 765 746-6679
  Zionsville *(G-17058)*
Vasmo Inc.. F 317 549-3722
  Indianapolis *(G-9702)*

BIOLOGICAL PRDTS: Vaccines

Mwi Veterinary Supply Co....................... G 317 769-7771
  Lebanon *(G-10924)*

BIOLOGICAL PRDTS: Vaccines & Immunizing

Rimedion Inc.. G 415 513-5535
  Indianapolis *(G-9308)*

BIOLOGICAL PRDTS: Veterinary

Aratana Therapeutics Inc........................ D 913 353-1000
  Greenfield *(G-6466)*
Envigo Rms Inc..................................... ..... 317 806-6080
  Greenfield *(G-6500)*
Envigo Rms Inc..................................... C 317 806-6080
  Indianapolis *(G-8125)*
Indy Medical Supplies LLC...................... G 866 744-9013
  Zionsville *(G-17019)*
Stem Point Inc..................................... G 352 870-0122
  Franklin *(G-5778)*

BLADES: Knife

Bose Knife Works.................................. G 812 397-5114
  Shelburn *(G-14717)*
Part Solutions LLC................................ G 219 477-5101
  South Bend *(G-15186)*
Pettigrew... G 260 868-2032
  Butler *(G-1475)*

BLADES: Saw, Hand Or Power

Milwaukee Electric Tool Corp................... E 800 729-3878
  Greenwood *(G-6742)*

BLANKBOOKS & LOOSELEAF BINDERS

Clarke Harland Corp.............................. G 812 283-9598
  Jeffersonville *(G-9953)*
Delux Illumination................................. G 219 331-9525
  Chesterton *(G-1917)*
Deluxe Detail LLC.................................. G 574 292-8968
  South Bend *(G-14996)*
Eckhart & Company Inc.......................... E 317 347-2665
  Indianapolis *(G-8046)*
Futurex Industries Inc............................ E 765 498-8900
  Bloomingdale *(G-759)*

Employee Codes: A=Over 500 employees, B=251-500
C=101-250, D=51-100, E=20-50, F=10-19, G=1-9

2024 Harris Indiana
Industrial Directory

BLANKBOOKS & LOOSELEAF BINDERS

PRODUCT SECTION

Harcourt Industries Inc .... E 765 629-2625
Milroy *(G-11824)*

Lamco Finishers Inc .... E 317 471-1010
Indianapolis *(G-8717)*

Leed Selling Tools Corp .... C 812 482-7888
Ireland *(G-9816)*

Nussmeier Engraving Company .... E 812 425-1339
Evansville *(G-4224)*

Raine Inc .... F 765 622-7687
Anderson *(G-182)*

Spi-Binding Company Inc .... F 765 794-4992
Darlington *(G-2834)*

BLANKBOOKS: Albums

Neu Scrapbooking Store LLC .... G 317 781-7970
Indianapolis *(G-9000)*

BLANKBOOKS: Albums, Record

Hard Hustla Muzik LLC .... G 812 214-1995
Evansville *(G-4103)*

Lovett Entertainment LLC .... G 773 208-9608
Schererville *(G-14532)*

Timelessmusicgroup LLC .... G 317 721-6671
Carmel *(G-1786)*

BLANKETS & BLANKETING, COTTON

East Cast Erosion Holdings LLC .... G 812 867-4873
Evansville *(G-4026)*

BLANKETS, INSULATING: Aircraft, Asbestos

Thermal Structures Inc .... F 317 876-7213
Indianapolis *(G-9590)*

BLAST FURNACE & RELATED PRDTS

Worthington Steel Company .... G 219 929-4000
Porter *(G-13925)*

BLASTING SVC: Sand, Metal Parts

Abrasive Processing & Tech LLC .... G 317 485-5157
Fortville *(G-5587)*

Chief Metal Works Inc .... G 765 932-2134
Rushville *(G-14396)*

Complete Finish Inc .... F 260 587-3588
Ashley *(G-331)*

Klinge Enameling Company Inc .... E 317 359-8291
Indianapolis *(G-8694)*

Midwest Surface Prep LLC .... G 317 726-1336
Indianapolis *(G-8915)*

Performance Powder Coating .... G 765 438-5224
Kokomo *(G-10320)*

Schaffsteins Truck Clean LLC .... F 812 464-2424
Evansville *(G-4298)*

Steve Reiff Inc .... E 260 723-4360
South Whitley *(G-15328)*

W Kendall & Sons Inc .... G 219 733-2412
Wanatah *(G-16292)*

BLINDS & SHADES: Vertical

Mitchell Fabrics Inc .... E 309 674-8631
Lafayette *(G-10651)*

Oxford House Incorporated .... D 765 884-3265
Fowler *(G-5629)*

Vertical Sale .... G 260 438-4299
Fort Wayne *(G-5531)*

Vertical Vegetation MGT LLC .... F 765 366-4447
Darlington *(G-2835)*

BLINDS : Window

Best Blinds .... G 260 490-4422
Fort Wayne *(G-4796)*

Blinds At Home LLC .... G 317 489-8133
Indianapolis *(G-7641)*

Custom Blind and Shade Company .... G 812 867-9280
Evansville *(G-4001)*

Essex .... G 317 201-7099
Indianapolis *(G-8136)*

Irvine Shade & Door Inc .... D 574 522-1446
Elkhart *(G-3430)*

J P Whitt Inc .... G 765 759-0521
Muncie *(G-12430)*

Lafayette Venetian Blind Inc .... A 765 464-2500
West Lafayette *(G-16601)*

Merin Interiors Indianapolis .... G 317 251-6603
Indianapolis *(G-8877)*

Midwest Blind & Shade Co .... G 574 271-0770
Mishawaka *(G-11947)*

Nacjam Interior Blinds Inc .... G 765 449-8035
Lafayette *(G-10656)*

Sharon S Cheesecakes .... G 219 477-5773
Valparaiso *(G-16047)*

United Services Inc .... G 812 989-3320
Jeffersonville *(G-10068)*

United Services Inc .... G 812 989-3320
Clarksville *(G-2040)*

BLOCKS & BRICKS: Concrete

Camilles Studio .... G 219 365-5902
Cedar Lake *(G-1828)*

Crown Brick & Supply Inc .... E 219 663-7880
Crown Point *(G-2668)*

Devening Block Inc .... E 812 372-4458
Columbus *(G-2282)*

Dubois Cnty Block & Brick Inc .... F 812 482-6293
Jasper *(G-9834)*

Hanson Aggregates Wrp Inc .... E 502 244-7550
Sellersburg *(G-14596)*

Hydro Conduit .... G 561 651-7177
Greenfield *(G-6510)*

Irving Materials Inc .... D 317 326-3101
Greenfield *(G-6518)*

Majestic Block & Supply Inc .... G 317 842-6602
Fishers *(G-4560)*

Slon Inc .... E 765 884-1792
Fowler *(G-5633)*

Southfield Corporation .... E 812 824-1355
Bloomington *(G-978)*

BLOCKS: Landscape Or Retaining Wall, Concrete

Engineered Products Inc .... G 219 662-2080
Crown Point *(G-2680)*

Glen-Gery Corporation .... F 317 784-2505
Indianapolis *(G-8285)*

Menard Inc .... C 812 466-1234
Terre Haute *(G-15641)*

Rose HI Lawn Care Ldscpg Snow .... G 812 230-0024
Terre Haute *(G-15684)*

BLOCKS: Paving, Concrete

Hessit Works Inc .... G 812 829-6246
Freedom *(G-5801)*

Stotlar Hill LLC .... F 260 497-0808
Fort Wayne *(G-5446)*

BLOCKS: Standard, Concrete Or Cinder

Carters Concrete Block Inc .... G 574 583-7811
Monticello *(G-12142)*

Cash Concrete Products Inc .... F 765 653-4007
Greencastle *(G-6395)*

Holcim (us) Inc .... G 219 378-1193
East Chicago *(G-3017)*

Jones and Sons Inc .... E 812 254-4731
Washington *(G-16489)*

Shelby Gravel Inc .... F 317 738-3445
Franklin *(G-5776)*

Slater Concrete Products Inc .... G 260 347-0164
Kendallville *(G-10152)*

St Henry Tile Co Inc .... E 260 589-2880
Berne *(G-728)*

St Henry Tile Co Inc .... G 765 966-7771
Richmond *(G-14207)*

Van Duyne Block and Gravel .... G 574 223-6656
Rochester *(G-14331)*

Wheeler Corporation .... F 317 398-7500
Shelbyville *(G-14815)*

BLOWERS & FANS

Air Side Systems LLC .... G 765 778-7895
Anderson *(G-73)*

Blocksom & Co .... G 219 878-4458
Trail Creek *(G-15835)*

CJ Magers Enterprises LLC .... G 219 778-4884
La Porte *(G-10394)*

Cor-A-Vent Inc .... F 574 258-6161
Mishawaka *(G-11865)*

CTB MN Investment Co Inc .... E 574 658-4191
Milford *(G-11794)*

Cummins Filtration Ip Inc .... G 615 514-7339
Columbus *(G-2256)*

Donaldson Company Inc .... A 765 659-4766
Frankfort *(G-5660)*

Donaldson Company Inc .... G 952 887-3131
Monticello *(G-12146)*

Dustex .... G 812 725-0808
Jeffersonville *(G-9972)*

Eta Fabrication Inc .... F 260 897-3711
Avilla *(G-476)*

Fan-Tastic Vent .... G 800 521-0298
Elkhart *(G-3342)*

Kabert Industries Inc .... D 765 874-2335
Lynn *(G-11184)*

Kch Services Inc .... G 260 463-3100
Lagrange *(G-10745)*

Spectrum Brands Inc .... E 317 773-6627
Noblesville *(G-13179)*

Terronics Development Corp Inc .... G 765 552-0808
Elwood *(G-3838)*

Aero-Flo Industries Inc .... G 219 393-3555
La Porte *(G-10378)*

Dack Blower Manufacturing Inc .... G 574 867-2025
Grovertown *(G-6823)*

Horton Fan Systems Inc .... C 317 249-9100
Carmel *(G-1659)*

Mechanovent Corporation .... G 219 326-1767
La Porte *(G-10449)*

Roots Blowers LLC .... D 765 827-9200
Connersville *(G-2465)*

BLUEPRINTING SVCS

Blue Print Specialties Inc .... G 765 742-6976
Lafayette *(G-10539)*

Copy Solutions Inc .... G 260 436-2679
Fort Wayne *(G-4874)*

Eastern Engineering Supply Inc .... F 260 426-3119
Fort Wayne *(G-4938)*

J & L Dimensional Services Inc .... E 219 325-3588
La Porte *(G-10430)*

Maco Reprograhics LLC .... G 812 464-8108
Evansville *(G-4183)*

BOAT & BARGE COMPONENTS: Metal, Prefabricated

J & J Boat Works Inc .... G 812 667-5902
Madison *(G-11231)*

PRODUCT SECTION

Marion Metal Products Inc...............F 765 662-8333
Marion *(G-11313)*

BOAT BUILDING & REPAIR

Angola Canvas Co...............F 260 665-9913
Angola *(G-227)*

Boat Works...............G 574 457-4034
Syracuse *(G-15457)*

Brunswick Corporation...............G 866 278-6942
Brownsburg *(G-1353)*

Chief Powerboats Inc...............G 219 775-7024
Crown Point *(G-2665)*

Culvers Port Side Marina...............G 574 223-5090
Rochester *(G-14285)*

Evansville Marine Service Inc...............E 812 424-9278
Evansville *(G-4053)*

Fiberglass Pdts & Boat Repr...............G 260 627-3209
Grabill *(G-6295)*

Gonzales Enterprises Inc...............G 219 841-1756
Portage *(G-13870)*

Handypro of Northwest Indiana...............G 219 707-8240
Portage *(G-13875)*

Harris Flotebote...............G 260 432-4555
Fort Wayne *(G-5050)*

Heatherwood Enterprises Inc...............G 812 294-7270
Memphis *(G-11464)*

Highwater Marine LLC...............E 574 457-2082
Syracuse *(G-15463)*

Hoosier Marine...............G 812 879-5549
Quincy *(G-14021)*

Indiana Mobile Marine LLC...............G 317 961-1881
Indianapolis *(G-8483)*

J & J Boat Works Inc...............G 812 667-5902
Madison *(G-11231)*

Marine Group LLC...............C 574 622-0490
Bristol *(G-1272)*

Neoteric Incorporated...............F 812 234-1120
Terre Haute *(G-15650)*

Pontoon Boat LLC...............D 574 264-6336
Elkhart *(G-3608)*

Pro Wake Watersports Indianap...............G 801 691-2153
Noblesville *(G-13159)*

Pro Wake Watersports Syracuse...............G 801 691-2153
Syracuse *(G-15475)*

Propaganda Motorcycles Inc...............G 765 997-8787
Richmond *(G-14188)*

Robert Engle...............G 317 522-7761
Westfield *(G-16723)*

Sparrow Group Incorporated...............G 574 968-7335
Warsaw *(G-16428)*

Sylvan Marine Inc...............B 574 831-2950
New Paris *(G-12970)*

Thunder Pro...............G 317 498-0241
Greenfield *(G-6565)*

Veada Industries Inc...............A 574 831-4775
New Paris *(G-12973)*

West Lakes Marine Inc...............F 260 854-2525
Rome City *(G-14378)*

Yandt Boat Works LLC...............G 219 851-8311
La Porte *(G-10503)*

BOAT BUILDING & REPAIRING: Fiberglass

Highwater Marine LLC...............D 574 522-8381
Elkhart *(G-3406)*

Splendor Boats LLC...............F 260 352-2835
Silver Lake *(G-14923)*

World Class Fiberglass...............G 317 512-3343
Fairland *(G-4406)*

Yoder Fiberglass LLC...............G 260 593-0234
Topeka *(G-15823)*

BOAT BUILDING & REPAIRING: Motorboats, Inboard Or Outboard

Porter Inc...............A 800 736-7685
Decatur *(G-2876)*

BOAT BUILDING & REPAIRING: Motorized

Smoker Craft Inc...............B 574 831-2103
New Paris *(G-12968)*

Vanderbilt Luxury Pontoons LLC...............F 260 478-7227
Fort Wayne *(G-5527)*

Wawasee Aluminum Works Inc...............E 574 457-2082
Syracuse *(G-15490)*

BOAT BUILDING & REPAIRING: Non-Motorized

Sherms Marine Inc...............F 260 563-8051
Wabash *(G-16215)*

BOAT BUILDING & REPAIRING: Pontoons, Exc Aircraft & Inflat

Brunswick Corporation...............D 260 459-8200
Fort Wayne *(G-4821)*

J C Mfg Inc...............E 574 834-2881
North Webster *(G-13307)*

BOAT BUILDING & REPAIRING: Yachts

Atlatl Group LLC...............E 602 233-2628
Washington *(G-16472)*

Kentuckiana Yacht Services LLC...............G 812 282-7579
Jeffersonville *(G-10007)*

Rolls-Royce Corporation...............E 317 230-2000
Indianapolis *(G-9325)*

Rolls-Royce Corporation...............E 317 230-8515
West Lafayette *(G-16626)*

BOAT DEALERS

Smoker Craft Inc...............B 574 831-2103
New Paris *(G-12968)*

Splendor Boats LLC...............F 260 352-2835
Silver Lake *(G-14923)*

Webster Custom Canvas Inc...............G 574 834-4497
North Webster *(G-13314)*

BOAT DEALERS: Marine Splys & Eqpt

Lake Lite Inc...............G 260 918-2758
Avilla *(G-485)*

BOAT DEALERS: Motor

Culvers Port Side Marina...............G 574 223-5090
Rochester *(G-14285)*

Sherms Marine Inc...............F 260 563-8051
Wabash *(G-16215)*

West Lakes Marine Inc...............F 260 854-2525
Rome City *(G-14378)*

BOAT LIFTS

Boat Lift Guys Inc...............G 260 667-3057
Angola *(G-235)*

D & S Boat Lifts...............G 574 583-8972
Monticello *(G-12144)*

Deatons Waterfront Svcs LLC...............F 317 336-7180
Fortville *(G-5591)*

Lakeland Pier and Lift LLC...............F 574 377-3481
Warsaw *(G-16385)*

BOATS & OTHER MARINE EQPT: Plastic

Poppy Co...............G 317 442-2491
Brownsburg *(G-1395)*

Rookstools Pier Shop Inc...............E 574 453-4771
Leesburg *(G-10960)*

BODIES: Truck & Bus

Accubuilt Plant I...............G 574 389-9000
Elkhart *(G-3152)*

Accuride Emi LLC...............E 940 565-8505
Evansville *(G-3868)*

Arboc Specialty Vehicles LLC...............D 574 825-1720
Middlebury *(G-11697)*

Braun Motor Works LLC...............G 574 205-0102
Winamac *(G-16858)*

Dana Driveshaft Products LLC...............G 260 432-2903
Marion *(G-11280)*

Eaton Corporation...............C 260 925-3800
Auburn *(G-387)*

Eaton Corporation...............C 317 704-2520
Indianapolis *(G-8043)*

Federal-Mogul Motorparts LLC...............G 219 872-5150
Michigan City *(G-11611)*

Ford Motor Company...............F 901 368-8821
Plainfield *(G-13680)*

General Motors LLC...............B 260 672-1224
Roanoke *(G-14268)*

Gravel Conveyors Inc...............F 317 873-8686
Zionsville *(G-17014)*

Hendrickson International Corp...............C 260 349-6400
Kendallville *(G-10117)*

Hendrickson International Corp...............C 765 483-5350
Lebanon *(G-10896)*

Independent Protection Co...............C 574 831-5680
New Paris *(G-12960)*

International Brake Inds Inc...............D 419 905-7468
South Bend *(G-15084)*

Lund International Holding Co...............E 765 742-7200
Lafayette *(G-10641)*

Luxe Trucks LLC...............F 574 522-8422
Elkhart *(G-3504)*

Marmon Highway Tech LLC...............E 317 787-0718
Indianapolis *(G-8839)*

Original Tractor Cab Co Inc...............F 765 663-2214
Arlington *(G-329)*

Quality Tank Trucks & Eqp Inc...............G 317 635-0000
Indianapolis *(G-9247)*

Ramco Engineering Inc...............E 574 266-1455
Elkhart *(G-3638)*

Shyft Group Usa Inc...............G 574 848-2000
Bristol *(G-1291)*

Starcraft Corporation...............G 574 534-7827
Goshen *(G-6260)*

Supreme Industries Inc...............C 574 642-3070
Goshen *(G-6265)*

Utilimaster Holdings Inc...............A 800 237-7806
Bristol *(G-1295)*

Vanair Manufacturing Inc...............C 219 879-5100
Michigan City *(G-11684)*

BODY PARTS: Automobile, Stamped Metal

Afco Performance Group LLC...............F 812 897-0900
Boonville *(G-1079)*

Auto Extras Inc...............G 574 855-2370
South Bend *(G-14952)*

Fukai Toyotetsu Indiana Corp...............D 765 676-4800
Jamestown *(G-9817)*

Futaba Indiana America Corp...............B 812 895-4700
Vincennes *(G-16127)*

Heritage Products Inc...............C 765 364-9002
Crawfordsville *(G-2577)*

Jason Holdings Inc...............C 414 277-9300
Richmond *(G-14147)*

Kousei Usa Inc...............G 812 373-7315
Columbus *(G-2336)*

BODY PARTS: Automobile, Stamped Metal

Metal Fab Engineering Inc .... E 574 278-7150
  Winamac *(G-16867)*
Multimatic Indiana Inc .... E 260 868-1000
  Butler *(G-1472)*
Omr North America Inc .... D 317 510-9700
  Speedway *(G-15337)*
Oreca North America Inc .... G 317 517-2948
  Indianapolis *(G-9069)*
Pk USA Inc .... B 317 395-5500
  Shelbyville *(G-14784)*
Sanoh America Inc .... G 419 425-2600
  Lafayette *(G-10683)*
Spheros North America Inc .... G 734 218-7350
  Elkhart *(G-3693)*
Techna Fit of Indiana .... G 317 350-2153
  Brownsburg *(G-1407)*

BOILER & HEATING REPAIR SVCS

Complete Controls Inc .... G 260 489-0852
  Fort Wayne *(G-4868)*
Griffin Clark LLC .... G 765 491-9059
  Bloomington *(G-871)*

BOILER REPAIR SHOP

Power Plant Service Inc .... E 260 432-6716
  Fort Wayne *(G-5328)*

BOILERS: Low-Pressure Heating, Steam Or Hot Water

Canvas Mw LLC .... D 630 560-3703
  Michigan City *(G-11585)*

BOLTS: Metal

Agrati - Park Forest LLC .... D 219 531-2202
  Valparaiso *(G-15895)*
B K & M Inc .... G 219 924-0184
  Griffith *(G-6792)*
Cold Heading Co .... E 260 495-7003
  Fremont *(G-5816)*
Cold Heading Co .... E 260 495-4222
  Fremont *(G-5817)*
Cold Heading Co .... E 260 587-3231
  Hudson *(G-7244)*
Elgin Fastener Group LLC .... G 812 689-8917
  Versailles *(G-16099)*
Fontana Fasteners Inc .... C 765 654-0477
  Frankfort *(G-5664)*
Mc Coy Bolt Works Inc .... D 260 482-4476
  Fort Wayne *(G-5210)*
R & R Engineering Co Inc .... E 765 536-2331
  Summitville *(G-15429)*
Rohder Machine & Tool Inc .... E 219 663-3697
  Crown Point *(G-2747)*
Steve Mitchell .... G 574 831-4848
  New Paris *(G-12969)*
Tristate Bolt Company .... F 260 357-5541
  Garrett *(G-5879)*

BOOK STORES

Embroidme .... G 219 465-1400
  Valparaiso *(G-15943)*
Prairie Creek Prtg & Bk Str .... G 812 636-7243
  Montgomery *(G-12119)*

BOOKS, WHOLESALE

Tom Doherty Company Inc .... G 317 352-8200
  Indianapolis *(G-9617)*

BORING MILL

Hy-Tech Machining Systems LLC ...... E 765 649-6852
  Anderson *(G-131)*

BOTTLED GAS DEALERS: Liquefied Petro, Dlvrd To Customers

Ferrellgas LP .... G 574 936-2725
  Crawfordsville *(G-2566)*

BOTTLED GAS DEALERS: Propane

Crestwood Equity Partners LP .... G 812 265-3313
  Madison *(G-11212)*
Oeding Corporation .... G 812 367-1271
  Ferdinand *(G-4446)*

BOTTLES: Plastic

Ahf Industries Inc .... C 812 936-9988
  French Lick *(G-5843)*
Amcor Rigid Packaging Usa LLC .... G 317 736-4313
  Greenwood *(G-6666)*
Berry Global Group Inc .... A 812 424-2904
  Evansville *(G-3921)*
Crown Packaging International Inc ..... D 219 738-1000
  Merrillville *(G-11499)*
North America Packaging Corp .... G 317 291-2396
  Indianapolis *(G-9021)*
Plastic Recycl Export Ltd LLC .... G 301 758-6885
  Fort Wayne *(G-5318)*
Polycon Industries Inc .... C 219 738-1000
  Merrillville *(G-11551)*
Setco LLC .... B 812 424-2904
  Evansville *(G-4307)*
Silgan Plastics LLC .... F 812 522-0900
  Seymour *(G-14693)*
Specialty Mfg Ind Inc .... E 812 256-4633
  Charlestown *(G-1894)*

BOXES & CRATES: Rectangular, Wood

Bryan Ward .... G 812 696-5126
  Farmersburg *(G-4417)*
Knights Woodworking LLC .... G 812 988-2106
  Nashville *(G-12673)*

BOXES & SHOOK: Nailed Wood

A S M Inc .... G 260 724-8220
  Decatur *(G-2839)*
American Fibertech Corporation .... D 219 261-3586
  Lafayette *(G-10521)*
C & C Mailbox Products .... G 765 358-4880
  Gaston *(G-6044)*
C E Kersting & Sons .... G 574 896-2766
  North Judson *(G-13207)*
Findley Foster Corp .... G 812 524-7279
  Seymour *(G-14653)*
Hoosier Box and Skid Inc .... G 574 256-2111
  Mishawaka *(G-11908)*
Indiana Wood Products Inc .... D 574 825-2129
  Middlebury *(G-11724)*
Industrial Woodkraft Inc .... E 812 897-4893
  Boonville *(G-1087)*
Leclere Manufacturing Inc .... G 812 683-5627
  Jasper *(G-9882)*

BOXES: Ammunition, Metal

Bway Corporation .... G 219 462-8915
  Valparaiso *(G-15923)*

BOXES: Corrugated

American Containers Inc .... D 574 936-4068
  Plymouth *(G-13755)*
American Corrugated .... G 812 425-4056
  Evansville *(G-3885)*
Arrow Container LLC .... D 317 882-6444
  Indianapolis *(G-7548)*
B&H Capital Inc .... B 812 376-9301
  Columbus *(G-2225)*
Buckeye Corrugated Inc .... D 317 856-3701
  Indianapolis *(G-7697)*
Capitol City Container Corp .... E 317 875-0290
  Indianapolis *(G-7735)*
Cardinal Container Corp .... E 317 898-2715
  Indianapolis *(G-7739)*
Color-Box LLC .... A 765 966-7588
  Richmond *(G-14109)*
Container Service Corp .... D 574 232-7474
  South Bend *(G-14982)*
Corrugated Concepts LLC .... G 317 290-1140
  Indianapolis *(G-7880)*
Cps Inc .... F 317 804-2300
  Indianapolis *(G-7895)*
CRA-Wal Inc .... D 317 856-3701
  Indianapolis *(G-7896)*
Csc-Indiana LLC .... E 708 625-3255
  New Haven *(G-12900)*
Custom Packaging Inc .... F 317 876-9559
  Indianapolis *(G-7933)*
Five Star Sheets LLC .... D 574 654-8058
  New Carlisle *(G-12840)*
Galaxy Container LLC .... G 574 936-6300
  Plymouth *(G-13778)*
Hackett & Hackett LLC .... G 574 370-7191
  South Bend *(G-15057)*
Hoosier Container Inc .... E 765 966-2541
  Richmond *(G-14136)*
Indiana Box Company .... E 317 462-7743
  Greenfield *(G-6512)*
Indiana Box Company .... E 260 356-9660
  Huntington *(G-7326)*
Indiana Carton Company Inc .... D 574 546-3848
  Bremen *(G-1197)*
Inland Container .... G 317 876-0768
  Indianapolis *(G-8549)*
Innovative Packaging Inc .... E 260 356-6577
  Huntington *(G-7329)*
Innovative Packaging Assoc Inc .... E 260 356-6577
  Huntington *(G-7330)*
International Paper Company .... G 765 492-3341
  Cayuga *(G-1822)*
International Paper Company .... D 765 364-5342
  Crawfordsville *(G-2580)*
International Paper Company .... D 317 390-3300
  Indianapolis *(G-8582)*
International Paper Company .... G 812 326-2125
  Saint Anthony *(G-14429)*
International Paper Company .... D 800 643-7244
  Terre Haute *(G-15619)*
Jamil Packaging Corporation .... E 574 256-2600
  Mishawaka *(G-11917)*
Jcmz Enterprises Inc .... E 812 372-0288
  Columbus *(G-2329)*
Kelly Box and Packaging Corp .... G 317 804-7044
  Indianapolis *(G-8668)*
Kelly Box and Packaging Corp .... D 260 432-4570
  Fort Wayne *(G-5145)*
Lacap Container Corp .... G 317 835-4282
  Shelbyville *(G-14771)*
Marion Paper Box Company .... F 765 664-6435
  Marion *(G-11314)*
Menasha Packaging Company LLC ...... G 877 818-2016
  Richmond *(G-14163)*
Met-Pak Specialties Corp .... E 260 420-2217
  Fort Wayne *(G-5215)*
Michigan City Paper Box Co .... D 219 872-8383
  Michigan City *(G-11638)*
Northern Box Company Inc .... E 574 264-2161
  Elkhart *(G-3574)*

PRODUCT SECTION   BRICKS : Flooring, Clay

Northern Indiana Packg Co Inc............... E 260 356-9660
  Huntington *(G-7345)*
Nova Packaging Group Inc....................... E 765 651-2600
  Marion *(G-11321)*
Orora Packaging Solutions...................... F 317 879-4628
  Indianapolis *(G-9071)*
Packaging Corporation America............. B 812 376-9301
  Columbus *(G-2370)*
Packaging Corporation America............. G 812 526-5919
  Edinburgh *(G-3095)*
Packaging Corporation America............. D 765 674-9781
  Gas City *(G-6039)*
Packaging Corporation America............. G 317 247-0193
  Indianapolis *(G-9084)*
Packaging Corporation America............. G 812 482-4598
  Jasper *(G-9901)*
Packaging Corporation America............. G 812 522-3100
  Seymour *(G-14671)*
Packaging Corporation America............. G 812 522-3100
  Seymour *(G-14672)*
Packaging Corporation America............. C 812 882-7631
  Vincennes *(G-16142)*
Packaging Lgstics Slutions LLC............... G 502 807-8346
  Jeffersonville *(G-10033)*
Paperworks Industries Inc....................... C 260 563-3102
  Wabash *(G-16210)*
PCA Suthern Ind Corrugated LLC............ E 812 376-9301
  Columbus *(G-2373)*
Pli LLC... E 219 326-1350
  La Porte *(G-10463)*
Pratt (jet Corr) Inc.................................... B 219 548-9191
  Valparaiso *(G-16030)*
Royal Box Group LLC................................ C 317 462-7743
  Greenfield *(G-6545)*
Royal Box Group LLC................................ C 765 728-2416
  Huntington *(G-7361)*
Schwarz Partners Packaging LLC............ G 812 523-6600
  Seymour *(G-14685)*
Servants Inc.. D 812 634-2201
  Jasper *(G-9910)*
Sisco Corporation...................................... D 812 422-2090
  Evansville *(G-4316)*
Southland Container Corp......................... C 812 385-0774
  Princeton *(G-14012)*
Temple-Island... G 901 419-9000
  Indianapolis *(G-9574)*
Wabash Valley Packaging Corp................ F 812 299-7181
  Terre Haute *(G-15744)*
Webster West Inc..................................... E 812 346-5666
  North Vernon *(G-13300)*
Welch Packaging Marion LLC.................. G 765 651-2600
  Marion *(G-11348)*
Westrock Company.................................. G 219 229-0981
  Plymouth *(G-13827)*
Westrock Cp LLC...................................... G 812 372-8873
  Columbus *(G-2417)*
Westrock Cp LLC...................................... E 574 772-5545
  Knox *(G-10228)*
Westrock Cp LLC...................................... G 574 256-0318
  Mishawaka *(G-12027)*
Westrock Cp LLC...................................... G 219 762-4855
  Portage *(G-13919)*
Westrock Mwv LLC.................................. G 317 787-3361
  Indianapolis *(G-9754)*
Westrock Rkt LLC.................................... G 574 936-2118
  Plymouth *(G-13829)*

BOXES: Paperboard, Folding

Americraft Carton Inc.............................. A 812 537-1784
  Lawrenceburg *(G-10828)*
Colbert Packaging Corporation................ D 574 295-6605
  Elkhart *(G-3256)*

Combined Technologies Inc..................... G 847 968-4855
  Bristol *(G-1254)*
Custom Carton Inc.................................... F 260 563-7411
  Wabash *(G-16179)*
Tre Paper Company.................................. G 765 649-2536
  Anderson *(G-208)*
Westrock Cp LLC...................................... G 574 936-2118
  Plymouth *(G-13828)*

BOXES: Paperboard, Set-Up

American Containers Inc......................... D 574 936-4068
  Plymouth *(G-13755)*
Artistic Carton... F 260 925-6060
  Kendallville *(G-10091)*
Colbert Packaging Corporation................ D 574 295-6605
  Elkhart *(G-3256)*
Jessup Paper Box LLC.............................. F 765 588-9137
  Lafayette *(G-10615)*
Pathfinder Services Inc........................... E 260 356-0500
  Huntington *(G-7354)*

BOXES: Plastic

Resin Partners Inc.................................... C 765 298-6800
  Anderson *(G-185)*

BOXES: Solid Fiber

Carton Craft Corporation.......................... D 812 949-4393
  New Albany *(G-12709)*
Smith Consulting Inc................................ E 765 728-5980
  Montpelier *(G-12181)*

BOXES: Wirebound, Wood

JR Graber & Sons LLC.............................. G 260 657-1071
  Grabill *(G-6306)*
Zehrhaus Inc... G 260 486-3198
  Fort Wayne *(G-5583)*

BOXES: Wooden

Ash-Lin Inc... F 317 861-1540
  Fountaintown *(G-5613)*
JR Grber Sons Fmly Ltd Prtnr.................. G 260 657-1071
  Grabill *(G-6307)*
Millers Wood Specialties Inc................... E 765 478-3248
  Cambridge City *(G-1499)*
Whitakerr Dalemon................................... G 812 738-2396
  Corydon *(G-2522)*

BRAKES & BRAKE PARTS

Bludot Inc... G 574 277-2306
  South Bend *(G-14959)*
BWI INDIANA INC...................................... E 937 260-2460
  Greenfield *(G-6475)*
Carlisle Indus Brake Frction I.................. B 812 336-3811
  Bloomington *(G-822)*
D & D Brake Sales Inc............................. E 317 485-5177
  Fortville *(G-5590)*
Indiana Precision Forge LLC................... E 317 421-0102
  Shelbyville *(G-14760)*
International Brake Inds Inc.................... D 419 905-7468
  South Bend *(G-15084)*
NERP LLC... G 574 303-6377
  South Bend *(G-15163)*
Techna-Fit Inc... G 317 350-2153
  Brownsburg *(G-1408)*
Webb Wheel Products Inc....................... G 812 548-0477
  Ferdinand *(G-4451)*

BRAKES: Electromagnetic

Altra Industrial Motion Corp..................... E 219 874-5248
  Michigan City *(G-11577)*

BRAKES: Metal Forming

Altra Industrial Motion Corp..................... E 219 874-5248
  Michigan City *(G-11577)*

BRAKES: Press

Press Brake Safety LLC............................ G 317 413-7593
  Zionsville *(G-17044)*

BRASS & BRONZE PRDTS: Die-casted

Aero Metals Inc... B 219 326-1976
  La Porte *(G-10377)*

BRASS FOUNDRY, NEC

Sterling Sales and Engrg Inc................... G 765 376-0454
  Veedersburg *(G-16091)*

BRAZING SVCS

Applied Metals & Mch Works Inc............ E 260 424-4834
  Fort Wayne *(G-4766)*
Brazing Preforms LLC.............................. G 317 705-6455
  Noblesville *(G-13047)*
Tube Processing Corp.............................. G 317 264-7760
  Indianapolis *(G-9657)*
Tube Processing Corp.............................. B 317 787-1321
  Indianapolis *(G-9658)*

BRAZING: Metal

D & D Industries Inc................................. E 219 844-5600
  Hammond *(G-6910)*
Electro Seal Corporation.......................... G 219 926-8606
  Chesterton *(G-1922)*
Exotic Metal Treating Inc........................ F 317 784-8565
  Indianapolis *(G-8156)*
Quality Steel Treating Co Inc.................. E 317 357-8691
  Tipton *(G-15788)*

BRICK, STONE & RELATED PRDTS WHOLESALERS

Brampton Brick Inc................................... E 812 397-2190
  Farmersburg *(G-4416)*
Camilles Studio... G 219 365-5902
  Cedar Lake *(G-1828)*
Crown Brick & Supply Inc........................ E 219 663-7880
  Crown Point *(G-2668)*
Devening Block Inc................................... E 812 372-4458
  Columbus *(G-2282)*
Dubois Cnty Block & Brick Inc................ F 812 482-6293
  Jasper *(G-9834)*
Hanson Aggregates Wrp Inc.................... E 502 244-7550
  Sellersburg *(G-14596)*
Hydro Conduit... G 561 651-7177
  Greenfield *(G-6510)*
Mulzer Crushed Stone Inc....................... E 812 256-3346
  Charlestown *(G-1886)*
Ozinga Indiana Rdymx Con Inc................ F 219 949-9800
  Gary *(G-5993)*
Parke County Aggregates LLC................. G 765 245-2344
  Rockville *(G-14353)*

BRICKS & BLOCKS: Structural

Ceramica Inc... F 317 546-0087
  Indianapolis *(G-7777)*
Heb Development LLC............................. E 616 363-3825
  Centerpoint *(G-1845)*

BRICKS : Ceramic Glazed, Clay

Whimsical Gardens................................... G 317 257-4704
  Indianapolis *(G-9758)*

BRICKS : Flooring, Clay

Employee Codes: A=Over 500 employees, B=251-500
C=101-250, D=51-100, E=20-50, F=10-19, G=1-9

2024 Harris Indiana
Industrial Directory

1265

BRIDGE COMPONENTS: Bridge sections, prefabricated, highway

Santarossa Mosaic Tile Co Inc..................C..... 317 632-9494
  Indianapolis *(G-9371)*

BRIDGE COMPONENTS: Bridge sections, prefabricated, highway

Bedford Crane Service LLC...................F..... 812 275-4411
  Bedford *(G-622)*
Indiana Steel & Engrg Inc......................E..... 812 275-3363
  Bedford *(G-647)*
Wabash Steel LLC...................................G..... 317 818-1622
  Vincennes *(G-16162)*

BROADCASTING & COMMS EQPT: Antennas, Transmitting/Comms

Electronics Research Inc........................C..... 812 925-6000
  Chandler *(G-1861)*
Telamon Corporation..............................G..... 317 818-6888
  Whitestown *(G-16824)*

BROADCASTING & COMMUNICATION EQPT: Transmit-Receiver, Radio

World Rdo Mssnary Fllwship Inc...........G..... 574 970-4252
  Elkhart *(G-3793)*

BROADCASTING & COMMUNICATIONS EQPT: Studio Eqpt, Radio & TV

Anderson Shykia.....................................G..... 773 304-6852
  Gary *(G-5894)*
Grand Master Llc....................................G..... 574 288-8273
  South Bend *(G-15048)*

BROADCASTING & COMMUNICATIONS EQPT: Transmitting, Radio/TV

Crown Audio Inc......................................B..... 800 342-6939
  Elkhart *(G-3273)*
Harman Professional Inc.......................B..... 574 294-8000
  Elkhart *(G-3398)*
International Rdo & Elec Corp...............G..... 866 262-8910
  Elkhart *(G-3429)*

BROKERS: Loan

Wallar Additions Inc................................G..... 574 262-1989
  Elkhart *(G-3778)*

BROKERS: Printing

C E M Printing & Specialities................G..... 269 684-6898
  South Bend *(G-14964)*
Dynamark Graphics Group Inc.............E..... 317 328-2555
  Indianapolis *(G-8023)*
Hiatt Enterprises Inc..............................F..... 765 289-7756
  Muncie *(G-12415)*
Maury Boyd & Associates Inc...............F..... 317 849-6110
  Indianapolis *(G-8853)*
Specialized Printed Products................G..... 260 483-7075
  Fort Wayne *(G-5428)*

BRONZE FOUNDRY, NEC

Mark Parmenter......................................G..... 812 829-6583
  Spencer *(G-15355)*
Wilhoite Monuments Inc........................G..... 765 286-7423
  Muncie *(G-12520)*

BROOMS

Brian Newton..G..... 812 200-3149
  Nashville *(G-12663)*

BROOMS & BRUSHES

Midwest Finishing Systems Inc............E..... 574 257-0099
  Mishawaka *(G-11949)*

Reit-Price Mfg Co Incorporated.............G..... 765 964-3252
  Union City *(G-15860)*

BROOMS & BRUSHES: Household Or Indl

Jason Incorporated.................................D..... 765 965-5333
  Richmond *(G-14149)*

BROOMS & BRUSHES: Street Sweeping, Hand Or Machine

City of Fort Wayne..................................E..... 260 427-1235
  Fort Wayne *(G-4849)*

BRUSHES

American Way Marketing Llc................F..... 574 295-6633
  Elkhart *(G-3178)*
Royal Brush Manufacturing Inc............F..... 219 660-4170
  Munster *(G-12562)*

BUILDING & OFFICE CLEANING SVCS

Lady Q LLC-S..G..... 219 304-8404
  Indianapolis *(G-8712)*

BUILDING & STRUCTURAL WOOD MEMBERS

Continntal Crpntry Cmpnnts LLC..........E..... 219 733-0367
  Wanatah *(G-16289)*
Glue-Lam Erectors Inc..........................F..... 317 878-9717
  Trafalgar *(G-15827)*
James G Henager...................................G..... 812 795-2230
  Elberfeld *(G-3115)*
Northern Indiana Truss LLC..................E..... 574 858-0505
  Warsaw *(G-16402)*
Osterholt Construction Inc....................G..... 260 672-3493
  Huntington *(G-7348)*
Trusslink..G..... 219 362-3968
  La Porte *(G-10496)*
Tyler Truss Systems Inc........................F..... 765 221-5050
  Pendleton *(G-13560)*
Ufp Granger LLC....................................E..... 574 277-7670
  Granger *(G-6387)*
US Lbm Operating Co 3009 LLC..........G..... 812 464-2428
  Evansville *(G-4364)*

BUILDING BOARD: Gypsum

Proform Finishing Products LLC..........E..... 219 866-7570
  Rensselaer *(G-14063)*

BUILDING CLEANING & MAINTENANCE SVCS

A & H Enterprises LLC..........................G..... 317 398-3070
  Shelbyville *(G-14729)*
American Maint & Training Inc............F..... 812 738-4230
  Corydon *(G-2485)*
Chem-Dry of Allen County....................G..... 260 490-2705
  Fort Wayne *(G-4844)*
Complete Property Care LLC...............G..... 765 288-0890
  Muncie *(G-12368)*
Mold Removers LLC..............................G..... 317 846-0977
  Indianapolis *(G-8946)*
Onsite Construction Services...............E..... 312 723-8060
  Chesterton *(G-1951)*
Professional Grade Svcs LLC..............G..... 317 688-8898
  Indianapolis *(G-9222)*
Wise Energy LLC....................................G..... 317 475-0305
  Indianapolis *(G-9776)*

BUILDING COMPONENTS: Structural Steel

Aggreate Systems..................................G..... 260 854-4711
  Rome City *(G-14374)*

Almet Inc..D..... 260 493-1556
  New Haven *(G-12891)*
Alum-Elec Structures Inc......................G..... 260 347-9362
  Kendallville *(G-10088)*
Benchmark Inc..F..... 812 238-0659
  Terre Haute *(G-15551)*
C & C Iron Inc...E..... 219 769-2511
  Merrillville *(G-11495)*
Cives Corporation...................................C..... 219 279-4000
  Wolcott *(G-16927)*
Evans Metal Products Co Inc...............F..... 574 264-2166
  Elkhart *(G-3335)*
Four Star Fabricators Inc......................D..... 812 354-9995
  Petersburg *(G-13612)*
Gary Bridge and Iron Co Inc.................G..... 219 884-3792
  Gary *(G-5936)*
Geiger & Peters Inc...............................D..... 317 322-7740
  Indianapolis *(G-8266)*
Harpring Steel Inc..................................G..... 812 256-6326
  Charlestown *(G-1878)*
Helgeson Steel Inc.................................F..... 574 293-5576
  Elkhart *(G-3403)*
M & S Steel Corp....................................E..... 260 357-5184
  Garrett *(G-5869)*
Marion Steel Fabrication Inc................E..... 765 664-1478
  Marion *(G-11315)*
Mr2 Performance LLC...........................G..... 765 483-9371
  Lebanon *(G-10921)*
Munster Steel Co Inc.............................E..... 219 924-5198
  Hammond *(G-6984)*
P H Drew Incorporated..........................E..... 317 297-5152
  Indianapolis *(G-9080)*
Preferred Tank & Tower Inc.................G..... 270 826-7950
  Evansville *(G-4256)*
Productivity Fabricators Inc.................F..... 765 966-2896
  Richmond *(G-14187)*
Rex Alton & Companies Inc.................F..... 812 882-8519
  Vincennes *(G-16149)*
Sigma Steel Inc.......................................E..... 812 275-4489
  Bedford *(G-672)*
Sisson Steel Inc......................................F..... 812 354-8701
  Winslow *(G-16922)*
Stahl Equipment Inc..............................F..... 812 925-3341
  Gentryville *(G-6053)*
Worthington Industries Inc...................E..... 219 465-6107
  Greensburg *(G-6643)*

BUILDING MAINTENANCE SVCS, EXC REPAIRS

D J Investments Inc...............................G..... 260 726-7346
  Portland *(G-13936)*
Padgett Inc..C..... 812 945-2391
  New Albany *(G-12790)*

BUILDING PRDTS & MATERIALS DEALERS

Gutter One Supply..................................F..... 317 872-1257
  Indianapolis *(G-8344)*
Hydro Conduit...G..... 561 651-7177
  Greenfield *(G-6510)*
Kuntry Lumber and Farm Sup Ltd.......F..... 260 463-3242
  Lagrange *(G-10746)*
Maher Supply Inc...................................G..... 812 234-7699
  Terre Haute *(G-15635)*
Omega Cabinets Ltd.............................A..... 319 235-5700
  Jasper *(G-9900)*
Richardson Molding LLC......................G..... 317 787-9463
  Indianapolis *(G-9303)*
Steinkamp Warehouses Inc.................E..... 812 683-3860
  Huntingburg *(G-7292)*
Tremain Ceramic Tile & Flr Cvg..........E..... 317 542-1491
  Indianapolis *(G-9633)*

PRODUCT SECTION

BURIAL VAULTS: Concrete Or Precast Terrazzo

Tri-State Guttertopper Inc .... G 812 455-1460
  Evansville *(G-4350)*

Tyler Truss LLC .... D 765 221-5050
  Pendleton *(G-13559)*

Woodland Manufacturing & Sup .... F 317 271-2266
  Avon *(G-557)*

BUILDING PRDTS: Concrete

Flyover Enterprises Inc .... G 317 417-1747
  Pendleton *(G-13532)*

Homeowners Equity & Rlty Corp .... G 219 981-1700
  Gary *(G-5952)*

Quikrete Companies LLC .... E 317 251-2281
  Indianapolis *(G-9252)*

Southern Indiana Supply Inc .... F 812 482-2267
  Jasper *(G-9914)*

BUILDING PRDTS: Stone

Superior Canopy Corporation .... E 260 488-4065
  Hamilton *(G-6862)*

BUILDINGS & COMPONENTS: Prefabricated Metal

123carportz .... G 574 376-0470
  Mishawaka *(G-11833)*

Agricon LLC .... F 219 261-2157
  Remington *(G-14032)*

All American Group Inc .... G 260 724-7391
  Decatur *(G-2842)*

American Steel Carports Inc .... G 419 737-1331
  Mount Summit *(G-12284)*

Asphalt Equipment Company Inc .... E 260 672-3004
  Fort Wayne *(G-4775)*

Biologics Modular LLC .... G 317 626-4093
  Brownsburg *(G-1350)*

Burns Construction Inc .... E 574 382-2315
  Macy *(G-11195)*

Classic Buildings Inc .... E 812 944-5821
  Clarksville *(G-2013)*

CTB MN Investment Co Inc .... E 574 658-4191
  Milford *(G-11794)*

Daily Co .... G 574 546-5126
  Bremen *(G-1185)*

Dytec-Nci LLC .... G 317 919-0000
  Fishers *(G-4507)*

Heartland Industries Inc .... G 317 569-1718
  Carmel *(G-1653)*

Jobsite Trailer Corporation .... E 574 224-4000
  Rochester *(G-14298)*

Koontz-Wagner Custom Contro .... D 574 387-5802
  South Bend *(G-15104)*

Kw Custom Controls LLC .... E 312 343-3920
  South Bend *(G-15112)*

Lacopa International Inc .... G 317 410-1483
  Pittsboro *(G-13650)*

Laidig Inc .... E 574 256-0204
  Mishawaka *(G-11925)*

Lakemaster Inc .... F 765 288-3718
  Muncie *(G-12437)*

Martins Mini Barns LLC .... G 574 238-0045
  Goshen *(G-6214)*

Maurer Constructors Inc .... G 812 236-5950
  Brazil *(G-1152)*

Mbci Inc .... C 317 835-2201
  Shelbyville *(G-14775)*

Midwestern Structures LLC .... G 574 835-9733
  Muncie *(G-12456)*

Miller Brothers Builders Inc .... E 574 533-8602
  Goshen *(G-6222)*

Millers Mini-Barns LLC .... G 812 883-8072
  Salem *(G-14493)*

Morton Buildings Inc .... F 765 653-9781
  Cloverdale *(G-2090)*

Morton Buildings Inc .... F 800 447-7436
  Jasper *(G-9893)*

Morton Buildings Inc .... F 260 563-2118
  Wabash *(G-16204)*

Northedge Steel LLC .... G 765 444-6021
  Yorktown *(G-16979)*

Sigma Steel Inc .... E 812 275-4489
  Bedford *(G-672)*

Slabaugh Storage Barns Inc .... G 260 768-7989
  Shipshewana *(G-14890)*

Wagler Mini Barn Products LLC .... G 812 687-7372
  Plainville *(G-13747)*

Williams Scotsman Inc .... E 260 749-6611
  Fort Wayne *(G-5569)*

Woodland Manufacturing & Sup .... F 317 271-2266
  Avon *(G-557)*

Yoders Quality Barns LLC .... G 260 565-4122
  Bluffton *(G-1071)*

BUILDINGS: Mobile, For Commercial Use

Commercial Structures Corp .... G 574 773-7931
  Goshen *(G-6115)*

Commercial Structures Corp .... E 574 773-7931
  Nappanee *(G-12590)*

Jobsite Trailer Corporation .... E 574 224-4000
  Rochester *(G-14298)*

Mark-Line Industries LLC .... C 574 825-5851
  Bristol *(G-1273)*

Thermo Bond Buildings LLC .... D 574 295-1214
  Elkhart *(G-3726)*

Whitley Evergreen Inc .... F 260 723-5131
  South Whitley *(G-15331)*

BUILDINGS: Portable

(ebs Cmpstes Engnred Bnded Str .... F 574 266-3471
  Elkhart *(G-3136)*

All Steel Carports Inc .... G 765 284-0694
  Muncie *(G-12337)*

Century Industries LLC .... E 812 246-3371
  Sellersburg *(G-14590)*

Chief Industries Inc .... C 219 866-4121
  Rensselaer *(G-14047)*

Five Starr Inc .... G 812 367-1554
  Ferdinand *(G-4433)*

Rollin Mini Barns LLC .... G 812 687-7581
  Odon *(G-13348)*

Williams Scotsman Inc .... F 317 782-2463
  Indianapolis *(G-9768)*

BUILDINGS: Prefabricated, Metal

All Star Manufacturing Inc .... G 574 293-8141
  Culver *(G-2779)*

BUILDINGS: Prefabricated, Wood

(ebs Cmpstes Engnred Bnded Str .... F 574 266-3471
  Elkhart *(G-3136)*

Affordable Luxury Homes Inc .... D 260 758-2141
  Markle *(G-11353)*

Burns Construction Inc .... E 574 382-2315
  Macy *(G-11195)*

Classic Buildings Inc .... E 812 944-5821
  Clarksville *(G-2013)*

Continntal Crpntry Cmpnnts LLC .... E 219 733-0367
  Wanatah *(G-16289)*

Custom Sheds Plus LLC .... G 260 215-3988
  Syracuse *(G-15460)*

Lakeside Manor .... E 219 362-3956
  La Porte *(G-10445)*

Landmark Home & Land Company .... G 219 874-4065
  Michigan City *(G-11630)*

Lawrenceburg Mini Barns .... G 513 290-5794
  Lawrenceburg *(G-10844)*

Light House Center Inc .... F 765 448-4502
  Lafayette *(G-10636)*

Mbsi Holdings LLC .... G 574 295-1214
  Elkhart *(G-3520)*

Midwest Fast Structures LLC .... G 812 886-3060
  Vincennes *(G-16139)*

Miller Brothers Builders Inc .... E 574 533-8602
  Goshen *(G-6222)*

Mobile/Modular Express II LLC .... G 574 295-1214
  Elkhart *(G-3548)*

Modular Builders Inc .... G 574 223-4934
  Rochester *(G-14309)*

Morton Buildings Inc .... F 260 563-2118
  Wabash *(G-16204)*

Mosier Pallet & Lumber Co .... G 812 366-4817
  Corydon *(G-2506)*

Permabase Building Pdts LLC .... G 765 828-0898
  Clinton *(G-2075)*

RPI Components Inc .... G 574 536-2283
  Elkhart *(G-3653)*

Skyline Champion Corporation .... G 574 294-6521
  Elkhart *(G-3681)*

TNT Construction .... G 260 726-2643
  Portland *(G-13972)*

Tuff Shed Inc .... G 317 481-8388
  Indianapolis *(G-9659)*

Tuff Shed Inc .... F 317 774-2981
  Noblesville *(G-13186)*

BUMPERS: Motor Vehicle

Lod LLC .... G 765 385-0631
  Fowler *(G-5626)*

Ynwa Industries Inc .... D 574 295-6641
  Elkhart *(G-3800)*

BURIAL VAULTS: Concrete Or Precast Terrazzo

Akron Concrete Products Inc .... G 574 893-4841
  Akron *(G-1)*

Anderson Memorial Park Inc .... F 765 643-3211
  Anderson *(G-78)*

Arrow Vault Co Inc .... G 765 742-1704
  Lafayette *(G-10527)*

Calumet Wilbert Vault Co Inc .... F 219 980-1173
  Gary *(G-5910)*

Century Grave & Vault Service .... G 812 967-2110
  Pekin *(G-13513)*

Columbus Vault Co .... G 812 372-3210
  Columbus *(G-2247)*

Forsyth Brothers Con Pdts Inc .... G 812 466-4080
  Terre Haute *(G-15590)*

Forsyth Puttmann LLC .... G 812 466-2925
  Terre Haute *(G-15591)*

Grable Burial Vault Svc Inc .... G 574 753-4514
  Logansport *(G-11075)*

Harris Burial Service Inc .... G 812 939-3605
  Clay City *(G-2043)*

Harris Precast Inc .... G 219 362-2457
  La Porte *(G-10416)*

Harris Precast Inc .... G 219 362-9671
  La Porte *(G-10417)*

Indiana Green Burial LLC .... G 812 961-1960
  Worthington *(G-16961)*

Johnsons Burial Designs .... G 317 549-2148
  Indianapolis *(G-8636)*

Lebanon Berg Vault Co Inc .... G 765 482-0302
  Lebanon *(G-10909)*

Mark Concrete Products Inc .... G 317 398-8616
  Shelbyville *(G-14774)*

BURIAL VAULTS: Concrete Or Precast Terrazzo

Minnick Services Corp............................. E 260 432-5031
  Fort Wayne *(G-5231)*

Monticello Vault Burial Co....................... G 574 583-3206
  Monticello *(G-12159)*

Quality Vault Company............................ G 812 336-8127
  Bloomington *(G-949)*

Rosskovenski Concrete & Rdymx............ G 765 832-6103
  Clinton *(G-2077)*

Terre Hute Wlbert Brial Vlt In.................. F 812 235-0339
  Terre Haute *(G-15727)*

Van Gard Vault Co Inc............................ G 219 980-6233
  Gary *(G-6026)*

Van Gard Vault Company Inc.................. F 219 949-7723
  Gary *(G-6027)*

Wayne Burial Vault Company Inc............ G 317 357-4656
  Indianapolis *(G-9742)*

Wilbert Burial Vault Co Inc..................... E 317 547-1387
  Indianapolis *(G-9762)*

Wilbert Sexton Corporation..................... G 812 372-3210
  Columbus *(G-2419)*

Wilbert Sexton Corporation..................... G 812 882-3555
  Vincennes *(G-16166)*

Wilbert Sexton Corporation..................... G 812 336-6469
  Bloomington *(G-1011)*

Wilson Burial Vault Inc........................... G 260 356-5722
  Huntington *(G-7380)*

BURNERS: Gas, Indl

Maxon Corporation.................................. C 765 284-3304
  Muncie *(G-12449)*

Trimble Combustion Systems Inc........... G 812 623-4545
  Sunman *(G-15447)*

BURNERS: Gas-Oil, Combination

Eclipse Inc... D
  Muncie *(G-12389)*

BURNERS: Oil, Domestic Or Indl

Wayne/Scott Fetzer Company................ D 260 425-9200
  Fort Wayne *(G-5555)*

BUSHINGS & BEARINGS

Complete Drives Inc............................... F 260 489-6033
  Fort Wayne *(G-4869)*

BUSINESS ACTIVITIES: Non-Commercial Site

103 Collection LLC................................. G 800 896-2945
  Schererville *(G-14510)*

1globalds LLC... F 765 413-2211
  Westfield *(G-16660)*

1st Choice Contractors LLC.................... G 317 628-4721
  Indianapolis *(G-7385)*

3jm Hauling LLC..................................... G 317 518-0750
  Avon *(G-501)*

3oe Scientific LLC.................................. F 317 869-7602
  Carmel *(G-1545)*

3sevens LLC... G 502 594-2312
  Henryville *(G-7112)*

4ever Chosen LLC.................................. G 765 431-7548
  Kokomo *(G-10230)*

651 Emergency Lighting......................... G 765 748-6664
  Yorktown *(G-16967)*

A Snack Above Rest LLC....................... G 219 455-3335
  Gary *(G-5884)*

A-1vet LLC.. G 317 498-1804
  Indianapolis *(G-7407)*

A&J Development Group LLC................ G 317 767-1182
  Indianapolis *(G-7404)*

A1 Deliveries LLC................................... G 317 828-3951
  Indianapolis *(G-7408)*

Abacus Printingngraphics Inc................. E 915 223-5166
  Indianapolis *(G-7412)*

Acdc Control LLC................................... G 219 801-3900
  East Chicago *(G-2988)*

Aesthtcally Pleasing Skin Soak.............. G 317 551-0156
  Indianapolis *(G-7454)*

Afr Equipment LLC................................. G 888 519-9899
  Laurel *(G-10824)*

All Things Jchari LLC............................. G 260 414-4065
  Fort Wayne *(G-4740)*

All Things Kingdom LLC........................ G 312 200-4569
  Highland *(G-7120)*

Allons-Y For Inv & Tech LLC................. G 260 206-4445
  Bloomington *(G-777)*

Alpha Matrix LLC.................................... G 812 686-1640
  Lamar *(G-10794)*

Amish Country Dairy LLC...................... G 574 323-1701
  Shipshewana *(G-14835)*

Avari Reef Labs LLC.............................. G 317 201-9615
  Anderson *(G-80)*

B & N Rentals LLC................................. G 219 850-3304
  Chesterton *(G-1906)*

B&C Distributor Inc................................ G 609 293-3257
  Indianapolis *(G-7585)*

Bass Farms LLC..................................... G 317 401-4700
  Shelbyville *(G-14734)*

Bawaenterprises LLC............................ G 269 228-1258
  Granger *(G-6336)*

Bell Transportation LLC......................... G 317 833-0745
  Indianapolis *(G-7610)*

Beyond Distributions LLC...................... G 631 960-1745
  Indianapolis *(G-7621)*

Big Brick House Bakery LLP................. G 260 563-1071
  Fort Wayne *(G-4799)*

Big Bruhs Seasoning LLP...................... G 502 751-5516
  Clarksville *(G-2009)*

Bizness As Usual Pubg LLC.................. G 463 701-6433
  Indianapolis *(G-7634)*

Blackmon Metal Fabrication LLC........... G 346 254-9500
  Gary *(G-5902)*

Blueprint Restoration LLC...................... G 301 730-4727
  Indianapolis *(G-7650)*

Borrv Concepts LLC.............................. G 317 405-9121
  Indianapolis *(G-7661)*

Boudoir Lash Parlor LLC....................... G 330 259-5696
  Indianapolis *(G-7664)*

Brayden Shedron.................................... G 765 480-7675
  Walton *(G-16281)*

Browmi By Misha LLC............................ G 317 801-3911
  Indianapolis *(G-7689)*

BTS Dispatching LLC............................. G 317 300-4594
  Indianapolis *(G-7695)*

Bulent Gumusel...................................... G 812 803-5912
  Bloomington *(G-818)*

Byler Sawmill.. G 812 577-5761
  Bennington *(G-702)*

C Johnson Group LLC........................... G 219 512-0619
  Indianapolis *(G-7708)*

Captivated LLC....................................... G 317 554-7400
  Carmel *(G-1579)*

Cater To You Catering LLC................... G 219 301-1091
  Hobart *(G-7179)*

Cbrk LLC... G 317 601-8546
  Indianapolis *(G-7764)*

Certified Choice Truckers LLC............... G 260 615-3437
  Fort Wayne *(G-4841)*

Cfn 260 LLC... G 260 241-5678
  Fort Wayne *(G-4842)*

Chef Hymie Inc....................................... G 201 218-4378
  New Albany *(G-12711)*

CHG Developments LLC....................... G 720 480-0957
  Indianapolis *(G-7797)*

Clearspring Manufacturing LLC............. F 260 593-2086
  Topeka *(G-15796)*

Clif Allred.. G 765 244-8082
  Peru *(G-13573)*

Cooper Transit LLC............................... G 260 797-3003
  Fort Wayne *(G-4871)*

Corlens Inc... G 843 822-6174
  Terre Haute *(G-15568)*

Corner Sto LLC...................................... G 219 798-2822
  Indianapolis *(G-7876)*

Covington and Martin LLC..................... G 812 946-3846
  Jeffersonville *(G-9963)*

Crume Industries LLC............................ G 574 747-7683
  Elkhart *(G-3275)*

D I Hair Extensions LLC........................ G 219 742-3611
  Merrillville *(G-11503)*

Dajac Inc.. G 317 608-0500
  Sheridan *(G-14821)*

Dark Source Records LLC..................... G 616 378-6060
  Indianapolis *(G-7950)*

Dash CAM Fusion LLC.......................... G 708 365-8553
  Indianapolis *(G-7953)*

David M Pszonka................................... G 219 988-2235
  Hebron *(G-7098)*

Death Enn LLC....................................... G 219 402-4436
  Merrillville *(G-11504)*

Deep Three Inc...................................... G 260 705-2283
  Spencerville *(G-15369)*

Dem Guys LLC....................................... G 708 552-3056
  Greenwood *(G-6684)*

Digistitch... G 574 538-3960
  Goshen *(G-6121)*

Diverse Machine Services LLC............. G 317 670-1381
  Indianapolis *(G-7980)*

Diverse Sales Solutions LLC................. G 317 514-2403
  Indianapolis *(G-7981)*

Divine Grace Homecare......................... G 219 290-5911
  Gary *(G-5923)*

Divine Machine LLC............................... G 812 709-5246
  Shoals *(G-14906)*

Dlb Transporters LLC............................ G 317 667-3368
  Indianapolis *(G-7992)*

Dodson Logistics LLC............................ G 937 657-7490
  Richmond *(G-14115)*

Drava Underwater LLC.......................... G 812 622-0432
  Owensville *(G-13466)*

Drinkgp LLC... G 317 410-4748
  Indianapolis *(G-8009)*

Driverz For Life(d 4 L) LLC.................... G 317 619-4513
  Indianapolis *(G-8010)*

Ds Mgmt Group LLC.............................. G 317 946-8646
  Indianapolis *(G-8014)*

Efurnituremax LLC................................. G 317 697-9504
  Indianapolis *(G-8058)*

Elegant Eyes LLC.................................. G 317 640-1995
  Greenwood *(G-6692)*

Elite Construction Northwest................. F 888 811-0212
  Merrillville *(G-11512)*

Elizabeth A Taylor.................................. G 815 353-4798
  Freedom *(G-5799)*

Ellerbrock Welding LLC......................... G 559 978-2651
  New Castle *(G-12860)*

Emmanuel Michael................................. G 806 559-5673
  Greenwood *(G-6694)*

Empirical Themes LLC.......................... G 260 431-1437
  Fort Wayne *(G-4950)*

Environ Corporation............................... G 317 774-0541
  Carmel *(G-1625)*

Evans Herron... G 317 492-1384
  Indianapolis *(G-8140)*

Everything Else LLC.............................. G 574 350-7383
  Elkhart *(G-3336)*

PRODUCT SECTION

BUSINESS ACTIVITIES: Non-Commercial Site

Exclusive Stylez LLC .... G 470 406-2804
Indianapolis *(G-8151)*

Extensive Design LLC .... G 260 267-6752
Fort Wayne *(G-4969)*

F D McCrary Operator Inc .... G 812 354-6520
Petersburg *(G-13611)*

Father Son Sanders Trnspt LLC .... G 773 899-8078
Hammond *(G-6926)*

Fex LLC .... G 317 308-8820
Indianapolis *(G-8182)*

Finalmile-Logistics LLC .... G 773 259-0727
Portage *(G-13864)*

Fischer Fleet Wash LLC .... G 812 661-9947
Rockport *(G-14340)*

Foxxie Planner L L C .... G 260 247-6303
Fort Wayne *(G-5004)*

Galbe Magazine LLC .... G 248 742-5231
Carmel *(G-1638)*

Gems Quality Extensions LLC .... G 219 501-6320
East Chicago *(G-3010)*

Genes Transport LLC .... G 404 227-5178
Indianapolis *(G-8274)*

Gerald S Zins .... G 812 623-4980
Osgood *(G-13409)*

Get Right Home Solutions LLC .... G 574 374-2001
Goshen *(G-6148)*

Givestr Inc .... G 202 997-5862
Indianapolis *(G-8283)*

Glens Pact LLC .... G 317 540-5869
Indianapolis *(G-8286)*

Graber .... G 812 636-7699
Odon *(G-13336)*

Graber Lumber LP .... E 260 238-4124
Spencerville *(G-15370)*

Greene County Pallets Inc .... F 812 384-8362
Bloomfield *(G-746)*

Grnwman LLC .... G 219 359-9237
Chesterton *(G-1933)*

Grumble Games LLC .... G 317 941-6433
Carmel *(G-1645)*

Hdh Manufacturing Inc .... G 317 918-4088
Indianapolis *(G-8376)*

Hearts Rmned Lifestyle Cir LLC .... G 800 807-0485
Gary *(G-5947)*

Help Help LLC .... G 317 910-6631
Avon *(G-525)*

Herextensions LLC .... G 219 466-4273
East Chicago *(G-3016)*

HM Lowry Enterprises LLC .... G 765 524-8435
Cambridge City *(G-1495)*

Hobbs Transport Services LLC .... G 317 607-5590
Indianapolis *(G-8401)*

Hoehn Engineered Products LLC .... G 260 223-9158
Decatur *(G-2863)*

Horizon Anim LLC .... G 317 742-4917
Indianapolis *(G-8413)*

Hush Clothing 317 LLC .... G 317 935-2184
Indianapolis *(G-8438)*

Hydration Turbine Inc .... G 317 491-0656
Indianapolis *(G-8440)*

Idonix Solutions Inc .... G 317 544-8171
Fishers *(G-4542)*

Imma Jerk LLC .... G 219 885-8613
Gary *(G-5958)*

Indiana Chemical LLC .... G 317 912-3800
Indianapolis *(G-8476)*

Innovations By .... G 260 413-1869
Fort Wayne *(G-5109)*

Intimusic LLC .... G 574 210-4562
South Bend *(G-15086)*

Jacksons 33 Transporting LLC .... G 901 628-7803
Indianapolis *(G-8616)*

James Harper .... G 812 267-4251
Depauw *(G-2939)*

Jaszy Drinks LLC .... G 219 742-5013
Gary *(G-5969)*

Jeshsoft LLC .... G 812 431-8603
Evansville *(G-4142)*

Jet Fast Carriers LLC .... G 219 218-3021
Indianapolis *(G-8623)*

Jle Fabricating LLC .... G 574 341-4034
Argos *(G-324)*

John F Semrau .... G 765 337-8831
Medaryville *(G-11459)*

Jtex Cnstr & Consulting LLC .... G 812 486-9123
Velpen *(G-16093)*

Just Perfection LLC .... G 347 559-5878
Indianapolis *(G-8650)*

Kala Mindfulness LLC .... G 720 351-9664
Indianapolis *(G-8657)*

Keenville & Company LLC .... G 219 916-6737
Valparaiso *(G-15984)*

Kelwood Designs LLC .... G 574 862-2472
Goshen *(G-6184)*

Ladybugz Bookstore LLC .... G 469 459-1780
Noblesville *(G-13125)*

Lakeland Pier and Lift LLC .... F 574 377-3481
Warsaw *(G-16385)*

Lane Wright LLC .... G 317 473-4783
Indianapolis *(G-8722)*

Lewis & Lee Presents LLC .... G 219 484-5298
Hammond *(G-6971)*

Lgndz Customs LLC .... G 765 293-9303
Marion *(G-11308)*

Little Super Findings .... G 812 430-3353
Evansville *(G-4173)*

Lj Motive LLC .... F 219 588-5480
Hobart *(G-7200)*

Lord Fms Games LLC .... G 317 710-2253
Indianapolis *(G-8783)*

Loves Enterprise LLC .... G 219 307-9191
Gary *(G-5978)*

Lovett Entertainment LLC .... G 773 208-9608
Schererville *(G-14532)*

Lux Beauty Den LLC .... G 708 793-0871
Merrillville *(G-11534)*

Luxetrend LLC .... G 502 208-9344
Evansville *(G-4178)*

Magaws of Boston .... G 765 935-6170
Richmond *(G-14158)*

Magical Moments LLC .... G 463 209-5766
Greenwood *(G-6731)*

Makingmoves Transports LLC .... G 260 579-5584
Fort Wayne *(G-5200)*

Mantra Enterprise LLC .... G 201 428-8709
Fishers *(G-4561)*

Marie Collective LLC .... G 317 683-0408
Indianapolis *(G-8832)*

Martin Uniforms LLC .... G 317 408-9186
Indianapolis *(G-8843)*

Mast Services Lafayette LLC .... G 765 464-6940
Lafayette *(G-10643)*

Masters Apps LLC .... G 574 312-5233
Goshen *(G-6217)*

Maurices Sgnture Chsecakes LLC .... G 708 879-0031
Valparaiso *(G-16000)*

McGuires Magic Cleaning LLC .... G 317 504-7739
Indianapolis *(G-8866)*

Meadowlark Wdwkg Cabinetry LLC .... G 765 541-3660
Connersville *(G-2456)*

Melvin McCullough .... G 765 577-0083
Jamestown *(G-9819)*

Michael Cary Ross .... G 765 631-2565
Martinsville *(G-11413)*

Michael Filley .... G 956 443-6364
Owensburg *(G-13463)*

Michael Hazeltine .... F 317 750-5091
Greenwood *(G-6739)*

Michael Holland .... G 317 538-1776
Indianapolis *(G-8897)*

Micro Businessware Inc .... G 502 424-6613
Sellersburg *(G-14607)*

Midwest Tire & Service LLC .... G 502 377-3722
Salem *(G-14492)*

Midwestern Structures LLC .... G 574 835-9733
Muncie *(G-12456)*

Modular Green Systems LLC .... G 260 547-4121
Craigville *(G-2535)*

Moodys Logistics Services LLC .... G 812 512-2772
Linton *(G-11040)*

Morganblair Logistics LLC .... G 219 249-2689
Munster *(G-12550)*

Muzfeed Inc .... G 815 252-7676
Fort Wayne *(G-5253)*

Mvctc .... G 765 969-8921
Richmond *(G-14173)*

My Goodies Snack Vending LLC .... G 317 653-7395
Anderson *(G-164)*

Myfoodmixer LLC .... G 219 229-7036
Michigan City *(G-11644)*

Naporamic LLC .... G 463 249-8265
Indianapolis *(G-8984)*

Naya Trans LLC .... G 317 720-8602
Indianapolis *(G-8995)*

Next Level Candles LLC .... G 574 347-1030
South Bend *(G-15167)*

Next Reformation Publishing Co .... G 317 650-1364
Plainfield *(G-13708)*

Nicholas Mendel .... G 574 870-8856
Delphi *(G-2904)*

No More Bugs .... G 317 658-6096
Indianapolis *(G-9014)*

Nobleman Logistics LLC .... G 317 340-7406
Indianapolis *(G-9017)*

North Coast Organics LLC .... G 260 246-0289
Fort Wayne *(G-5274)*

Nut House Woodworks LLC .... G 317 345-7177
Summitville *(G-15426)*

Oakleaf Industries Inc .... G 317 414-2040
Fishers *(G-4645)*

Octobers Firm Label LLC .... G 317 778-1447
Noblesville *(G-13147)*

Olympus Management LLC .... G 317 412-7977
Westfield *(G-16715)*

Omega One Connect Inc .... G 317 626-3445
Indianapolis *(G-9048)*

On Point Precision LLC .... G 317 590-2510
Indianapolis *(G-9052)*

Only Get Better Logistics LLC .... G 317 835-5606
Indianapolis *(G-9057)*

Operation 1 Veteran Inc .... G 574 536-5536
Goshen *(G-6231)*

Out The Box Transit Inc .... G 317 523-0061
Carmel *(G-1713)*

Owen County Pallet LLC .... G 812 384-6568
Worthington *(G-16962)*

Owens Property Solutions LLC .... G 708 374-2626
Gary *(G-5992)*

P&C Prime LLC .... F 231 420-3650
Fredericksburg *(G-5795)*

Pappas Construction LLC .... G 219 314-7068
Hobart *(G-7203)*

Paris Black Fashion LLC .... G 317 529-7119
Greencastle *(G-6423)*

Passions Fruitopia LLC .... G 800 515-1891
Highland *(G-7151)*

Employee Codes: A=Over 500 employees, B=251-500
C=101-250, D=51-100, E=20-50, F=10-19, G=1-9

2024 Harris Indiana Industrial Directory

BUSINESS ACTIVITIES: Non-Commercial Site — PRODUCT SECTION

Peterson Mfg LLC .... G 574 876-1427
   Wheatfield *(G-16771)*
Polley Tech LLC .... G 812 524-0688
   Seymour *(G-14675)*
Potorti Enterprises Inc .... G 812 989-8528
   Floyds Knobs *(G-4688)*
Premium Corporation .... E 219 258-0141
   South Bend *(G-15203)*
Presidential Bath & Fix LLC .... G 812 259-9817
   Evansville *(G-4257)*
Print It Inc .... G 317 774-6848
   Indianapolis *(G-9200)*
Proapse Software .... G 260 615-9839
   Fort Wayne *(G-5352)*
Purspec Technologies Inc .... G 765 532-2208
   West Lafayette *(G-16623)*
Qualtronics LLC .... E 812 375-8880
   Columbus *(G-2384)*
Quickspace Transportation LLC .... G 812 585-2317
   Indianapolis *(G-9250)*
R&H Metalworks LLC .... G 317 513-8733
   Fairland *(G-4402)*
Rai LLC .... G 765 227-0111
   Indianapolis *(G-9263)*
Rakk LLC .... G 812 271-4300
   Austin *(G-470)*
Rapar Inc .... G 812 254-9886
   Washington *(G-16506)*
Rayes Rpid Rslts - MBL DRG ALC .... G 317 721-1065
   Indianapolis *(G-9270)*
RC Enterprise LLC .... G 317 935-5628
   Carmel *(G-1735)*
Reloaded Activewear LLC .... G 317 652-7394
   Indianapolis *(G-9289)*
Renegade Dispatching LLC .... G 260 797-5423
   Fort Wayne *(G-5380)*
Respect Da Flava LLC .... G 765 243-1629
   Indianapolis *(G-9293)*
Ricktom Promotions LLC .... G 812 430-0282
   Evansville *(G-4289)*
Rlay Express Inc .... G 754 265-8555
   Avon *(G-548)*
Rob Nolley Inc .... F 317 825-5211
   Shelbyville *(G-14792)*
Ronald Lee Allen .... G 812 644-7649
   Loogootee *(G-11150)*
Rose Sharon All Naturals LLC .... G 317 500-4725
   Indianapolis *(G-9334)*
Rowe Tech .... G 317 453-0015
   Indianapolis *(G-9339)*
Royal Barbie Blinks LLC .... G 765 400-6205
   Lafayette *(G-10681)*
RTC .... G 260 503-9770
   Columbia City *(G-2193)*
Rustic Fisher Creations LLC .... G 574 279-5754
   North Liberty *(G-13222)*
Sams Tech Tire LLC .... G 219 942-7317
   Hobart *(G-7205)*
Samuel Powell .... G 812 887-6813
   French Lick *(G-5849)*
Selektd Worx LLC .... G 317 227-9337
   Indianapolis *(G-9401)*
Sengo LLC .... G 574 383-9833
   South Bend *(G-15238)*
Shelovexempress LLC .... G 317 490-2097
   Evansville *(G-4309)*
Silverthorn Handyman Svcs LLC .... G 812 896-4201
   Salem *(G-14498)*
Sky Cryptoassets LLC .... G 949 903-6896
   Carmel *(G-1763)*
SL Beauty LLC .... G 317 969-0341
   Indianapolis *(G-9446)*

Spagheady Inc .... G 317 499-6184
   Indianapolis *(G-9467)*
Speak Abilities LLP .... G 303 827-8269
   West Lafayette *(G-16630)*
Steele Roofing Co LLC .... G 219 243-1563
   Valparaiso *(G-16058)*
Stem Point LLC .... G 352 870-0122
   Franklin *(G-5778)*
Still Safety Products LLC .... G 855 249-0009
   Evanston *(G-3855)*
Study Studsters LLC .... G 574 635-1018
   Elkhart *(G-3702)*
Sugarcube Systems Inc .... G 765 543-6709
   Lafayette *(G-10704)*
Suitable Stylez .... G 765 409-9375
   Lafayette *(G-10705)*
T&S Group LLC .... G 219 310-0364
   Greenwood *(G-6772)*
Tc4 LLC .... G 317 709-5429
   Fishers *(G-4610)*
Timelessmusicgroup LLC .... G 317 721-6671
   Carmel *(G-1786)*
Timothy D Goin .... G 317 771-0404
   Indianapolis *(G-9606)*
Todd Enterprise Inc .... F 317 209-6610
   Noblesville *(G-13182)*
Trevares D Smith .... G 765 603-0468
   Marion *(G-11343)*
Trill Machine LLC .... G 219 730-0744
   Kentland *(G-10164)*
Trinity Displays LLC .... G 219 201-8733
   Chesterton *(G-1961)*
Tspdesign LLC .... G 317 785-8663
   Anderson *(G-210)*
Tt2 LLC .... G 260 438-4575
   Fort Wayne *(G-5511)*
TW Enterprises LLC .... G 513 520-8453
   Brookville *(G-1338)*
Underdog Diner LLP .... G 812 598-2970
   Evansville *(G-4359)*
Urban Rustic Farmhouse LLC .... G 317 238-0945
   New Palestine *(G-12944)*
Virago Logistix Llc .... G 800 767-2090
   Hammond *(G-7030)*
Warnock Welding & Fabg LLC .... G 812 498-5408
   Seymour *(G-14703)*
Wildebeest LLC .... G 812 391-5631
   Fort Wayne *(G-5568)*
Williams Woodshop .... G 574 686-2324
   Camden *(G-1522)*
Wm Express LLP .... G 773 647-5305
   Hammond *(G-7035)*
Woodberry Family Freight LLC .... G 317 665-6917
   Indianapolis *(G-9785)*
Youngs Freight & Logistics LLC .... G 765 639-7888
   Anderson *(G-219)*
Zachary T Laffin .... G 317 480-2248
   Greenfield *(G-6572)*

BUSINESS FORMS WHOLESALERS

Allison Pymnt Systems LLC DBA .... C 317 808-2400
   Indianapolis *(G-7485)*
Altstadt Business Forms Inc .... F 812 425-3393
   Evansville *(G-3882)*
Brand Prtg & Photo-Litho Co .... G 317 921-4095
   New Palestine *(G-12933)*
Custom Forms Inc .... F 765 463-6162
   Lafayette *(G-10565)*
Diversified Bus Systems Inc .... G 317 254-8668
   Indianapolis *(G-7984)*
Excel Business Printing Inc .... G 317 259-1075
   Indianapolis *(G-8149)*

Finest Grade Products .... G 812 421-1976
   Evansville *(G-4069)*
Perdue Printed Products Inc .... G 260 456-7575
   Fort Wayne *(G-5304)*
Stewart Graphics Inc .... E 812 283-0455
   Jeffersonville *(G-10060)*

BUSINESS FORMS: Printed, Continuous

Highland Computer Forms Inc .... F 260 665-6268
   Angola *(G-259)*
Writeguard Business Systems .... G 317 849-7292
   Indianapolis *(G-9793)*

BUSINESS FORMS: Printed, Manifold

Altstadt Business Forms Inc .... F 812 425-3393
   Evansville *(G-3882)*
Anchor Enterprises .... G 812 282-7220
   Jeffersonville *(G-9933)*
Falls Cities Printing Inc .... F 812 949-9051
   New Albany *(G-12728)*
International Label Mfg LLC .... F 812 235-5071
   Terre Haute *(G-15618)*
Kendallville Custom Printing .... F 260 347-9233
   Kendallville *(G-10125)*
Label Tech Inc .... E 765 747-1234
   Muncie *(G-12436)*
Lincoln Printing Corporation .... A 260 424-5200
   Fort Wayne *(G-5186)*
NP Converters Inc .... D 812 448-2555
   Brazil *(G-1158)*
Pengad/West Inc .... E 765 286-3000
   Muncie *(G-12473)*
R R Donnelley & Sons Company .... B 260 624-2350
   Angola *(G-291)*
Stewart Graphics Inc .... E 812 283-0455
   Jeffersonville *(G-10060)*
Taylor Communications Inc .... E 317 392-3235
   Shelbyville *(G-14803)*
Tippecanoe Press Inc .... G 317 392-1207
   Shelbyville *(G-14806)*
Wise Business Forms Inc .... D 260 489-1561
   Fort Wayne *(G-5572)*
Woodburn Graphics Inc .... F 812 232-0323
   Terre Haute *(G-15748)*

BUSINESS MACHINE REPAIR, ELECTRIC

Cummins - Allison Corp .... G 317 872-6244
   Indianapolis *(G-7922)*
Lasertone Inc .... F 812 473-5945
   Evansville *(G-4162)*
Mid-America Environmental LLC .... F 812 475-1644
   Evansville *(G-4204)*
Shearer Printing Service Inc .... E 765 457-3274
   Kokomo *(G-10334)*
The Office Shop Inc .... E 812 934-5611
   Batesville *(G-607)*

BUSINESS TRAINING SVCS

Nechanna One Productions Corp .... G 317 400-8908
   Indianapolis *(G-8997)*

BUTTER WHOLESALERS

Revival LLC .... G 812 345-4317
   Indianapolis *(G-9296)*

CABINETS & CASES: Show, Display & Storage, Exc Wood

Barns Unlimited LLC .... G 765 489-6282
   New Castle *(G-12851)*
Cabinets & Counters Inc .... E 812 858-3300
   Newburgh *(G-12995)*

PRODUCT SECTION

CABINETS: Kitchen, Wood

Metal Dynamics Ltd .... E 812 949-7998
  New Albany *(G-12775)*

CABINETS: Bathroom Vanities, Wood

Academy Inc .... G 574 293-7113
  Elkhart *(G-3147)*
Bremtown Fine Cstm Cbnetry Inc .... D 574 546-2781
  Bremen *(G-1179)*
Double T Manufacturing Corp .... F 574 262-1340
  Elkhart *(G-3302)*
H-C Liquidating Corp .... A 574 535-9300
  Goshen *(G-6159)*
Haas Cabinet Co Inc .... C 812 246-4431
  Sellersburg *(G-14594)*
J Miller Cabinet Company Inc .... G 260 691-2032
  Columbia City *(G-2158)*
Jds Pughs Cabinets Inc .... G 317 835-2910
  Trafalgar *(G-15830)*
Kitchen Kompact Inc .... C 812 282-6681
  Jeffersonville *(G-10011)*
Masterbrand Cabinets LLC .... E 812 367-1104
  Ferdinand *(G-4443)*
Norcraft Companies Inc .... D 800 297-0661
  Jasper *(G-9896)*
Norcraft Companies LP .... B 812 482-2527
  Jasper *(G-9897)*
Omega Cabinets Ltd .... A 319 235-5700
  Jasper *(G-9900)*
Radel Wood Products Inc .... F 765 472-2940
  Peru *(G-13597)*
Saco Industries Inc .... B 219 690-9900
  Lowell *(G-11178)*
Shamrock Cabinets Inc .... E 812 482-7969
  Jasper *(G-9911)*
Warsaw Custom Cabinet .... G 574 267-5794
  Warsaw *(G-16444)*
Yoder Kitchen Corp .... E 574 773-3197
  Nappanee *(G-12656)*

CABINETS: Entertainment

Eds Wood Craft .... G 812 768-6617
  Haubstadt *(G-7084)*
Fehrenbacher Cabinets Inc .... E 812 963-3377
  Evansville *(G-4066)*
Heather Sound Amplification .... G 574 255-6100
  Mishawaka *(G-11906)*
Innovative Corp .... E 317 804-5977
  Westfield *(G-16701)*
Lewis & Lee Presents LLC .... G 219 484-5298
  Hammond *(G-6971)*
M Bryant Denisa .... G 317 350-3878
  Indianapolis *(G-8805)*
Madison Cabinets Inc .... G 260 639-3915
  Hoagland *(G-7170)*
Shamrock Cabinets Inc .... E 812 482-7969
  Jasper *(G-9911)*
Walters Cabinet Shop .... G 765 452-9634
  Kokomo *(G-10355)*

CABINETS: Entertainment Units, Household, Wood

Graber Cabinetry LLC .... E 260 627-2243
  Grabill *(G-6297)*
J & J Woodcrafters .... G 765 436-2466
  Thorntown *(G-15752)*
Larry Graber Cabinets .... G 812 486-2713
  Montgomery *(G-12109)*
Rbk Development Inc .... E 574 267-5879
  Warsaw *(G-16417)*

CABINETS: Factory

Country Corner Woodworks LLC .... G 574 825-6782
  Middlebury *(G-11706)*
Country Mill Cabinet Co Inc .... F 260 693-9289
  Laotto *(G-10804)*
Creative Woodworks LLC .... G 260 450-1742
  Fort Wayne *(G-4887)*
Deerwood Group .... G 219 866-5521
  Monon *(G-12055)*
HB International .... G 574 773-8200
  Nappanee *(G-12606)*
Rabb and Howe Cabinet Top Co .... F 317 926-6442
  Indianapolis *(G-9258)*
Signet Millwork LLC .... E 812 248-0612
  Sellersburg *(G-14615)*
Top Design Cnc Inc .... G 219 662-2915
  Valparaiso *(G-16069)*
United Cabinet Corporation Nit .... G 812 482-2561
  Jasper *(G-9915)*
United Home Supply Inc .... G 765 288-2737
  Muncie *(G-12509)*

CABINETS: Kitchen, Metal

Warren Homes Inc .... G 812 882-1059
  Vincennes *(G-16165)*

CABINETS: Kitchen, Wood

Acme Cabinet Corporation .... G 219 924-1800
  Griffith *(G-6785)*
Acpi Wood Products LLC .... D 574 842-2066
  Culver *(G-2777)*
Advanced Cabinet Systems Inc .... D 765 677-8000
  Marion *(G-11268)*
All About Organizing .... G 513 238-8157
  Lawrenceburg *(G-10827)*
American Cabinet Refacing Inc .... G 317 875-7453
  Zionsville *(G-16990)*
American Woodmark Corporation .... B 765 677-1690
  Gas City *(G-6031)*
Americas Cabinet Co Ind Inc .... F 317 788-9533
  Greenfield *(G-6461)*
Anderson Amish Cabinets LLC .... G 317 575-9277
  Carmel *(G-1560)*
Aristocrat Inc .... G 812 634-0460
  Jasper *(G-9824)*
Aristoline Cabinets Inc .... E 260 482-9719
  Fort Wayne *(G-4771)*
B & L Custom Cabinets Inc .... G 765 379-2471
  Rossville *(G-14386)*
Barker Kitchen & Bath Cabinets .... G 812 493-4693
  Hanover *(G-7039)*
Beattys Custom Woods .... G 574 722-2752
  Logansport *(G-11061)*
Beebe Cabinet Co Inc .... F 574 293-3580
  Elkhart *(G-3222)*
Best Custom Cabinet Refacing .... G 260 459-1448
  Columbia City *(G-2123)*
Bkb Custom Cabinetry LLC .... G 317 439-9427
  Mooresville *(G-12195)*
Boger Cabinetry & Design Inc .... G 317 588-6954
  Fishers *(G-4476)*
Brandenberger Door Mfg .... G 260 657-1494
  Grabill *(G-6289)*
Brookwood Cabinet Company Inc .... F 260 749-5012
  Fort Wayne *(G-4819)*
Burns Cabinets and Disp Inc .... G 260 897-2219
  Avilla *(G-473)*
C & J Cabinets .... G 574 255-5812
  Mishawaka *(G-11856)*
C & R Woodworks .... G 317 422-9603
  Martinsville *(G-11382)*
Cabinet and Stone Expo .... G 317 879-1688
  Indianapolis *(G-7712)*

Cabinet and Stone Expo LLC .... G 317 879-1688
  Indianapolis *(G-7713)*
Cabinet Barn 2com .... G 317 421-1750
  Shelbyville *(G-14743)*
Cabinet Barn Inc .... G 812 246-5237
  Sellersburg *(G-14589)*
Cabinet Crafters Corp .... G 765 724-7074
  Alexandria *(G-47)*
Cabinet Expressions .... G 317 366-7669
  Noblesville *(G-13053)*
Cabinet Fctories Outl Richmond .... G 765 966-3875
  Richmond *(G-14102)*
Cabinetmaker Inc .... G 812 723-3461
  Paoli *(G-13490)*
Cabinetry Green LLC .... G 317 842-1550
  Fishers *(G-4480)*
Cabinetry Ideas Inc .... G 317 722-1300
  Indianapolis *(G-7714)*
Cabinetry Solutions LLC .... G 574 326-3699
  Elkhart *(G-3245)*
Cabinets By Rick Inc .... G 812 945-2220
  New Albany *(G-12708)*
Cabinets Inc .... G 219 322-3900
  Schererville *(G-14518)*
Cabinets Plus By Ptrick Geer I .... F 765 642-0329
  Anderson *(G-87)*
Cabinets To Go LLC .... G 317 486-0888
  Indianapolis *(G-7715)*
Cabinets Unlimited Corporation .... G 219 558-2210
  Saint John *(G-14446)*
Cabinets Unlimited Inc .... G 260 925-5555
  Saint Joe *(G-14437)*
Carriage House Woodworking Inc .... G 317 406-3042
  Coatesville *(G-2104)*
Carter Cabinet Company Inc .... G 317 985-5782
  New Palestine *(G-12935)*
Cedar Woodworking .... G 812 486-2765
  Montgomery *(G-12088)*
Claires Cabinet Refinishing .... G 317 495-5406
  Indianapolis *(G-7815)*
Classic Cabinets LLC .... G 317 507-3775
  Carmel *(G-1589)*
Coblentz Cabinet LLC .... G 812 687-7525
  Montgomery *(G-12089)*
Cochran Custom Woodworking LLC .... G 765 523-3220
  Stockwell *(G-15399)*
Columbus Cabinetry LLC .... G 812 447-1005
  Columbus *(G-2241)*
Columbus Cstm Cbinets Furn LLC .... G 812 379-9411
  Columbus *(G-2242)*
Commercial Electric Co Inc .... E 260 726-9357
  Portland *(G-13933)*
Concept Cabinet Shop .... G 765 653-1080
  Greencastle *(G-6398)*
Concepts Cabinet Shop Inc .... G 317 272-7430
  Avon *(G-511)*
Corbetts Custom Cabinetry LLC .... G 812 670-6211
  Jeffersonville *(G-9961)*
Corner Cabinet .... G 317 859-6336
  Greenwood *(G-6682)*
Cornerstone Cabinets .... G 317 718-0050
  Plainfield *(G-13671)*
Corsi Cabinet Company Inc .... D 317 786-1434
  Indianapolis *(G-7881)*
Counter Design Co Inc .... E 812 477-1243
  Evansville *(G-3985)*
Counterfitters Inc .... G 219 531-0848
  Valparaiso *(G-15929)*
Countertop Connections Inc .... G 317 822-9858
  Franklin *(G-5723)*
Countertop Manufacturing Inc .... E 765 966-4969
  Richmond *(G-14111)*

CABINETS: Kitchen, Wood

Company	Section	Phone
Countertop Shoppe Inc	G	574 936-1423
Plymouth *(G-13766)*		
Country Cabinets LLC	G	260 694-6777
Poneto *(G-13840)*		
Country Craft Cabinets LLC	G	574 596-8624
Bristol *(G-1255)*		
Country View Cabinets LLC	G	574 825-3150
Goshen *(G-6116)*		
Countryside Cabinetry LLC	G	765 597-2391
Marshall *(G-11371)*		
County Line Cabinetry LLC	G	574 642-1202
Middlebury *(G-11707)*		
Creative Cabinets	G	574 264-9041
Elkhart *(G-3270)*		
Creative Concepts Cabinetry	G	812 522-0204
Seymour *(G-14642)*		
Cregg Custom Cabinets	G	812 342-3605
Columbus *(G-2249)*		
Crickys Country Cabinets LLC	G	812 486-3705
Loogootee *(G-11129)*		
Crossrads Cntrtops Cbnetry LLC	G	317 908-9254
Indianapolis *(G-7909)*		
Custom Cabinets & Furn LLC	F	812 486-2503
Montgomery *(G-12092)*		
Custom Design Laminates Inc	F	574 674-9174
Osceola *(G-13388)*		
Custom Tables & Cabinets	G	812 486-3831
Montgomery *(G-12093)*		
D & B Cabinet Sales Inc	G	317 392-2870
Shelbyville *(G-14750)*		
D & E Cabinets	G	812 486-2961
Montgomery *(G-12094)*		
D L Miller Woodworking	G	260 562-9329
Shipshewana *(G-14842)*		
Daugherty Cabinets	G	574 272-9205
Granger *(G-6343)*		
Davis Cabinet and Flooring LLC	G	765 530-8170
Hagerstown *(G-6836)*		
Dennys Woodcraft Inc	G	812 883-0770
Salem *(G-14477)*		
Distinctive Kitchen & Bath Inc	G	317 882-7100
Greenwood *(G-6687)*		
Doors & Drawers Inc	F	574 533-3509
Goshen *(G-6125)*		
Douglas Dye and Associates Inc	G	317 844-1709
Carmel *(G-1611)*		
DS Woods Custom Cabinets	G	260 692-6565
Decatur *(G-2853)*		
Dutch Made Inc	G	260 657-3331
Harlan *(G-7054)*		
Dutch Made Inc	C	260 657-3311
Grabill *(G-6294)*		
E & S Wood Creations LLC	F	260 768-3033
Lagrange *(G-10736)*		
Eds Wood Craft	G	812 768-6617
Haubstadt *(G-7084)*		
Elko Inc	F	812 473-8400
Evansville *(G-4030)*		
Evia Custom Cabinets LLC	G	317 987-5504
Carmel *(G-1630)*		
Faes Cabinet LLC	G	567 259-8571
Fort Wayne *(G-4972)*		
Fehrenbacher Cabinets Inc	E	812 963-3377
Evansville *(G-4066)*		
Fergys Cabinets	G	765 529-0116
New Castle *(G-12861)*		
Finish Alternatives	G	317 440-2899
Indianapolis *(G-8189)*		
Genrich Custom Cabinetry Mllwk	F	317 351-0991
Indianapolis *(G-8277)*		
Gentrys Cabinet Inc	G	765 643-6461
Anderson *(G-120)*		
Goings Properties LLC	G	765 294-2380
Veedersburg *(G-16087)*		
Graber Cabinetry LLC	E	260 627-2243
Grabill *(G-6297)*		
Graber Furniture	G	812 295-4939
Loogootee *(G-11136)*		
Graber Woodworks Inc	G	812 486-2861
Montgomery *(G-12100)*		
Granitech	G	574 674-6988
Elkhart *(G-3386)*		
Hardwood Door Mfg LLC	G	812 486-3313
Montgomery *(G-12102)*		
Harlan Cabinets Inc	F	260 657-5154
Harlan *(G-7056)*		
Healey Custom Cabinetry LLC	G	574 946-4000
Winamac *(G-16863)*		
Herb Rahman & Sons Inc	G	812 367-2513
Ferdinand *(G-4435)*		
High Caliber Cabinetry LLC	G	812 246-5550
Sellersburg *(G-14600)*		
Homemark Cabinetry LLC	E	678 234-4519
Connersville *(G-2440)*		
Hoosier House Furnishings LLC	G	574 975-0357
Goshen *(G-6166)*		
Houck Industries Inc	F	812 663-5675
Greensburg *(G-6606)*		
Hurst Custom Cabinets Inc	G	812 683-3378
Huntingburg *(G-7283)*		
Independent Cabinets	G	502 594-6026
Memphis *(G-11465)*		
Innovative Corp	E	317 804-5977
Westfield *(G-16701)*		
Interior Fixs & Mllwk Co Inc	G	812 446-0933
Knightsville *(G-10202)*		
J & J Woodcrafters	G	765 436-2466
Thorntown *(G-15752)*		
J and G Enterprises	G	219 778-4319
Rolling Prairie *(G-14365)*		
J G Cabinet & Counter Inc	G	260 723-4275
Larwill *(G-10820)*		
James G Henager	G	812 795-2230
Elberfeld *(G-3115)*		
Janice Cabinetry LLC	G	219 741-8120
Valparaiso *(G-15980)*		
Jerry Hillenburg Co	G	317 422-8884
Martinsville *(G-11409)*		
Johnny Graber Woodworking	G	260 466-4957
Grabill *(G-6305)*		
JP Custom Cabinetry Inc	G	219 956-3587
Wheatfield *(G-16769)*		
Jrs Custom Cabinets Co	E	219 696-7205
Lowell *(G-11164)*		
K & K Cabinets & Supply	G	317 852-4808
Brownsburg *(G-1379)*		
Ka Crown Point Inc	F	219 595-5276
Crown Point *(G-2707)*		
Kelwood Designs LLC	G	574 862-2472
Goshen *(G-6184)*		
Key Millwork Inc	G	260 426-6501
Fort Wayne *(G-5147)*		
Kitchens By Gregory Ltd	G	219 769-1551
Merrillville *(G-11527)*		
Kline Cabinet Makers LLC	F	317 326-3049
Maxwell *(G-11444)*		
Klomp Construction Company	G	219 308-8372
Saint John *(G-14454)*		
Kountry Wood Products LLC	C	574 773-5673
Nappanee *(G-12618)*		
Kramer Furn & Cab Makers Inc	E	812 526-2711
Edinburgh *(G-3089)*		
Lakeside Woodworking	G	812 687-7901
Freedom *(G-5802)*		
Lambright Woodworking LLC	F	260 593-2721
Topeka *(G-15811)*		
Lami-Crafts Inc	G	812 232-3012
Terre Haute *(G-15628)*		
Laminique Inc	F	765 482-4222
Zionsville *(G-17029)*		
Leroy E Doty Cabinet Shop	G	219 663-1139
Crown Point *(G-2717)*		
Level Set Cabinet Works LLC	G	812 787-0830
Washington *(G-16491)*		
Lockerbie Square Cab Co Inc	G	317 635-1134
Indianapolis *(G-8775)*		
Lue Manufacturing Corporation	F	574 862-4249
Wakarusa *(G-16238)*		
Madison Cabinets Inc	G	260 639-3915
Hoagland *(G-7170)*		
Madison County Cabinets Inc	F	765 778-4646
Pendleton *(G-13541)*		
Marcotte Cabinets	G	574 520-1342
Granger *(G-6359)*		
Martinson Cabinet Shop	G	219 926-1566
Chesterton *(G-1947)*		
Masterbrand Inc	B	812 482-2527
Jasper *(G-9887)*		
Masterbrand Cabinets LLC	F	812 482-2527
Celestine *(G-1842)*		
Masterbrand Cabinets LLC	G	812 367-1104
Ferdinand *(G-4442)*		
Masterbrand Cabinets LLC	G	574 535-9300
Goshen *(G-6216)*		
Masterbrand Cabinets LLC	D	812 482-2527
Huntingburg *(G-7287)*		
Masterbrand Cabinets LLC	D	812 482-2513
Jasper *(G-9888)*		
Masterbrand Cabinets LLC	F	765 966-3940
Richmond *(G-14160)*		
Masterbrand US Holdings Corp	C	812 482-2527
Jasper *(G-9889)*		
Mc Custom Cabinets Inc	G	502 641-1528
Underwood *(G-15845)*		
Medallion Cabinetry	F	574 842-2066
Culver *(G-2781)*		
Meyer Custom Woodworking Inc	G	812 695-2021
Dubois *(G-2954)*		
Micka Cabinets	G	219 838-5450
Highland *(G-7144)*		
Mid Continent Cabinetry		866 527-0141
Jasper *(G-9891)*		
Midwest Country Cabinets	G	812 486-8580
Loogootee *(G-11146)*		
Milestone Cabinetry	F	219 947-0600
Merrillville *(G-11539)*		
Miller Cabinetry & Furn LLC	G	260 657-5052
Grabill *(G-6315)*		
Miller Maid Cabinets Inc	G	317 780-8280
Indianapolis *(G-8922)*		
Millers Custom Cabinets	G	260 768-7830
Shipshewana *(G-14869)*		
Mouron & Company Inc	F	317 243-7955
Indianapolis *(G-8962)*		
Muncie Cabinet Discounters	G	765 216-7367
Muncie *(G-12460)*		
Myers Cabinet Company	G	765 342-7781
Martinsville *(G-11418)*		
New Image Cabinet Coating	G	812 228-4666
Floyds Knobs *(G-4686)*		
Nka Cabinet Designs LLC	G	765 490-4661
Lafayette *(G-10659)*		
Nut House Woodworks LLC	G	317 345-7177
Summitville *(G-15426)*		
Oehlers Woods	G	317 848-2698
Carmel *(G-1710)*		

2024 Harris Indiana Industrial Directory

(G-0000) Company's Geographic Section entry number

PRODUCT SECTION

CABLE: Noninsulated

Orchard Lane Cabinets............................. G 574 825-7568
  Goshen *(G-6232)*
Orr Cabinet Co .... G 260 636-7757
  Albion *(G-39)*
Oxford Cabinet Company LLC................. G 765 223-2101
  Liberty *(G-10995)*
Patrick Industries Inc............................... G 574 293-1521
  Elkhart *(G-3589)*
Paynes Fine Cabrinetry .... G 765 589-9176
  Lafayette *(G-10665)*
Peace Valley Cabinets Inc....................... G 812 486-3831
  Montgomery *(G-12118)*
Philip Konrad & Sons Inc......................... F 574 772-3966
  Knox *(G-10219)*
Phoenix Custom Kitchens Inc.................. G 812 523-1890
  Seymour *(G-14674)*
Ponderosa Cabinet Company LLC........... G 260 349-2509
  Kendallville *(G-10143)*
Pumpkin Patch Market Inc....................... G 574 825-3312
  Middlebury *(G-11747)*
R & R Custom Woodworking Inc.............. G 574 773-5436
  Nappanee *(G-12640)*
Rabb and Howe Cabinet Top Co.............. F 317 926-6442
  Indianapolis *(G-9258)*
Rbk Development Inc............................... E 574 267-5879
  Warsaw *(G-16417)*
Rentown Cabinets LLC............................. G 574 546-2569
  Bremen *(G-1218)*
Richeson Contracting Inc......................... E 317 889-5995
  Indianapolis *(G-9304)*
Rmg Cabinetry Inc .... G 219 712-6129
  Hammond *(G-6999)*
Robert C Kueber...................................... G 812 838-5813
  Mount Vernon *(G-12317)*
Rogers Cabinetry .... G 574 664-9931
  Logansport *(G-11105)*
ROH Custom Cabinetry LLC.................... G 260 802-1158
  Silver Lake *(G-14921)*
Ronald Chileen Furniture......................... G 574 542-4505
  Rochester *(G-14321)*
Roomworks LLC....................................... G 317 846-2090
  Carmel *(G-1745)*
Royal Design Custom Kitchens &............. G 260 593-0508
  Topeka *(G-15816)*
Rush County Wood Products................... G 765 629-0603
  Milroy *(G-11831)*
S & H Cabinets... G 574 773-7465
  Nappanee *(G-12643)*
Schertz Craftsmen Inc.............................. C 877 472-2782
  Grabill *(G-6324)*
Schmidt Cabinetry & Furn LLC................. G 574 862-2200
  Wakarusa *(G-16249)*
Schrock... G 812 636-7842
  Odon *(G-13349)*
Scott Bernth .... G 219 926-4836
  Otis *(G-13445)*
Shelby Custom Cabinets Inc.................... G 317 398-0344
  Shelbyville *(G-14796)*
Signet Cabinetry Inc .... G 812 248-0612
  Sellersburg *(G-14614)*
Sims Cabinet Co Inc................................ E 317 634-1747
  Danville *(G-2828)*
Smith Custom Cabinets............................ G 812 342-4797
  Columbus *(G-2394)*
Southern Indiana Wdwkg LLC.................. G 812 636-0127
  Odon *(G-13352)*
Spiceland Wood Products Inc.................. F 765 987-8156
  Spiceland *(G-15379)*
Strohbeck Cabinet Install......................... G 812 923-5013
  Floyds Knobs *(G-4694)*
Superior Laminating Inc........................... G 574 361-7266
  Goshen *(G-6261)*
Talent Cabinet LLC .... G 317 733-2149
  Carmel *(G-1775)*
TCS Cabinets... G 765 208-5350
  Summitville *(G-15433)*
Tracaron Designs Inc............................... G 317 839-9006
  Avon *(G-554)*
Trillium Cabinet Company Inc.................. G 317 471-8870
  Indianapolis *(G-9642)*
Trucustom Cabinets LLC.......................... G 812 486-2861
  Montgomery *(G-12126)*
V-T Industries Inc..................................... G 712 368-4381
  Shelbyville *(G-14811)*
Vans Cabinet Shop Inc............................. G 574 658-9625
  Milford *(G-11808)*
Versatile Cab Solid Surfc Inc .... G 574 753-2359
  Logansport *(G-11118)*
Village Workshop Inc................................ G 812 933-1527
  Oldenburg *(G-13359)*
Wabash Valley Cabinet Company............ G 765 337-2859
  West Lafayette *(G-16643)*
Wagler Custom Cabinets LLC.................. G 812 486-2878
  Montgomery *(G-12129)*
Walburn Services Inc............................... G 765 289-3383
  Muncie *(G-12513)*
Walters Cabinet Shop............................... G 765 452-9634
  Kokomo *(G-10355)*
Warsaw Custom Cabinet.......................... G 574 267-5794
  Winona Lake *(G-16916)*
Washmuth Cabinet Company................... G 765 932-2701
  Rushville *(G-14416)*
William R Arvin... G 812 486-5255
  Winslow *(G-16926)*
Wiseman Custom Cabinets Inc................ G 812 678-3601
  Dubois *(G-2955)*
Wonning Cabinets.................................... G 812 522-1608
  Seymour *(G-14706)*
Wood Creat By Delagrange Inc .... G 260 657-5525
  New Haven *(G-12925)*
Wood Shapes Unlimited Inc..................... G 317 861-1775
  New Palestine *(G-12945)*
Wood Shoppe... G 260 758-3453
  Huntington *(G-7381)*
Woods Cabinets....................................... G 812 279-6494
  Bedford *(G-684)*
Yoders Cabinets....................................... G 812 486-3826
  Montgomery *(G-12131)*
Zinn Kitchens Inc .... E 574 967-4179
  Bringhurst *(G-1239)*
Zionsville Custom Cabinets LLC .... G 317 339-0380
  Zionsville *(G-17063)*

CABINETS: Office, Wood

ALE Enterprises Inc................................. G 317 856-2981
  Indianapolis *(G-7467)*
Delbert Kemp... F 812 486-3325
  Montgomery *(G-12095)*
Eds Wood Craft.. G 812 768-6617
  Haubstadt *(G-7084)*
Gehl Industries Inc................................... F 574 773-7663
  Nappanee *(G-12598)*
George Gardner....................................... G 317 270-8036
  Plainfield *(G-13683)*
Hensley Custom Cabinetry....................... G 219 843-5331
  Rensselaer *(G-14053)*
Leroy E Doty Cabinet Shop...................... G 219 663-1139
  Crown Point *(G-2717)*
Rabb and Howe Cabinet Top Co.............. F 317 926-6442
  Indianapolis *(G-9258)*
Steffy Wood Products Inc......................... F 260 665-8016
  Angola *(G-294)*

CABINETS: Show, Display, Etc, Wood, Exc Refrigerated

Beebe Cabinet Co Inc.............................. F 574 293-3580
  Elkhart *(G-3222)*
Carl Fox Cabinets Inc............................... G 812 342-3020
  Jonesville *(G-10084)*
Countertop Manufacturing Inc.................. E 765 966-4969
  Richmond *(G-14111)*
Deem & Loureiro Inc................................ G 770 652-9871
  Indianapolis *(G-7961)*
Freedom Valley Cabinets......................... G 717 606-2811
  Freedom *(G-5800)*
Graber Cabinetry LLC.............................. E 260 627-2243
  Grabill *(G-6297)*
Jensen Cabinet Inc.................................. E 260 456-2131
  Fort Wayne *(G-5134)*
Mhp Holdings Inc..................................... C 574 825-9524
  Middlebury *(G-11736)*
Wagners Plasti Craft Co........................... G 260 627-3147
  Fort Wayne *(G-5541)*
Woods Unlimited Inc................................ G 574 656-3382
  North Liberty *(G-13227)*
Zehrhaus Inc.. G 260 486-3198
  Fort Wayne *(G-5583)*

CABINETS: Stereo, Wood

Kimball International Inc.......................... C 812 482-1600
  Jasper *(G-9878)*

CABLE & OTHER PAY TELEVISION DISTRIBUTION

Vectren LLC... G 812 424-6411
  Evansville *(G-4369)*
Vision Aid Systems Inc............................. G 317 888-0323
  Greenwood *(G-6778)*

CABLE & PAY TELEVISION SVCS: Direct Broadcast Satellite

Woody Enterprises LLC............................ G 765 498-7300
  Bloomingdale *(G-763)*

CABLE TELEVISION

Essex Frkawa Mgnt Wire USA LLC.......... G 260 424-1708
  Columbia City *(G-2144)*
Times.. E 765 659-4622
  Frankfort *(G-5698)*

CABLE WIRING SETS: Battery, Internal Combustion Engines

East Penn Manufacturing Co.................... G 317 236-6288
  Indianapolis *(G-8038)*

CABLE: Aluminum, Made In Rolling Mills

L-Source Ltd LLC..................................... G 260 459-1971
  Fort Wayne *(G-5168)*

CABLE: Fiber Optic

Belden Inc.. G 978 537-9961
  Richmond *(G-14091)*
Dx Hammond Opco LLC........................... G 219 501-0905
  Whiting *(G-16834)*
Precision Utilities Group Inc..................... D 260 485-8300
  Fort Wayne *(G-5342)*

CABLE: Noninsulated

Alliance Group Tech Inc........................... D 260 375-2810
  Warren *(G-16293)*
Khorporate Holdings Inc.......................... C 260 357-3365
  Laotto *(G-10807)*

CABLE: Steel, Insulated Or Armored

Sanlo Inc.. D 219 879-0241
  Michigan City *(G-11664)*
Tway Company Incorporated................. E 317 636-2591
  Indianapolis *(G-9662)*

CACAO BEAN PROCESSING

Violet Sky LLC... G 574 850-5070
  South Bend *(G-15302)*

CAFES

Anns Boba Tea LLC................................ G 317 681-3143
  Indianapolis *(G-7520)*
Harvest Cafe Coffee & Tea LLC............ G 317 585-9162
  Indianapolis *(G-8369)*
South Bend Chocolate Co Inc............... F 574 233-2577
  South Bend *(G-15251)*

CALCULATING & ACCOUNTING EQPT

Cinq LLC... G 405 361-0097
  New Albany *(G-12713)*

CALIBRATING SVCS, NEC

Qig LLC... E 260 244-3591
  Columbia City *(G-2185)*

CAMPERS: Truck Mounted

Indiana Interstate Entps LLC................. G 260 463-8100
  Lagrange *(G-10743)*

CAMSHAFTS

Hapco Rebuilders Inc.............................. G 812 232-2550
  Terre Haute *(G-15604)*

CAN LIDS & ENDS

Ball Metal Beverage Cont Corp.............. C 574 583-9418
  Monticello *(G-12137)*

CANDLE SHOPS

Aesthtcally Pleasing Skin Soak............. G 317 551-0156
  Indianapolis *(G-7454)*
Emma Pearls Creations LLC.................. G 219 200-2277
  Highland *(G-7135)*
Paula Rosenbaum.................................. G 319 484-2941
  Valparaiso *(G-16022)*
Taylor Made Candles.............................. G 812 663-6634
  Greensburg *(G-6634)*
Yankee Candle Company Inc................ G 812 526-5195
  Edinburgh *(G-3110)*

CANDLES

Abboo Candle Co LLC............................ G 317 395-4404
  Fortville *(G-5586)*
Antique Candle Works Inc..................... E 765 250-8481
  Lafayette *(G-10523)*
Antique Candle Works LLC................... G 765 586-6013
  Porter *(G-13921)*
Astral Auras LLC..................................... G 219 628-5258
  Crown Point *(G-2652)*
B Honey & Candles................................. G 574 642-1145
  Shipshewana *(G-14838)*
Baerden Primitives LLC.......................... G 502 909-7045
  Clarksville *(G-2007)*
Bask Aroma Co LLC................................ G 765 404-7582
  Lafayette *(G-10535)*
Beckys Orgnl Pppts Gs Cls.................... G 219 934-0895
  Highland *(G-7124)*
Bee Kind Candles................................... G 765 618-5819
  Fort Wayne *(G-4793)*
Birch and Stitch LLC............................... G 317 353-7786
  Indianapolis *(G-7630)*

Birch Candle Company LLC.................. G 765 296-9425
  Dayton *(G-2837)*
Brighttany Pollitt..................................... G 217 597-1624
  Greenfield *(G-6472)*
Candle Chef LLC..................................... G 317 406-3391
  Plainfield *(G-13664)*
Celestial Candle..................................... G 812 886-4819
  Vincennes *(G-16117)*
Christian Candle Company................... G 317 427-8070
  Indianapolis *(G-7800)*
Coral Dog Candles................................. G 812 797-4050
  Bedford *(G-627)*
Country Valley Candles......................... G 574 702-1302
  Royal Center *(G-14390)*
Damor & Co LLC..................................... G 317 790-8360
  Indianapolis *(G-7947)*
Emma Pearls Creations LLC.................. G 219 200-2277
  Highland *(G-7135)*
Fancy Candle Soy LLC........................... G 765 769-4042
  Anderson *(G-117)*
Flickers Candle Shop............................. G 317 403-5045
  Indianapolis *(G-8203)*
Fresh Bakery Candles LLC.................... G 317 899-2377
  Indianapolis *(G-8232)*
Gem Industries Inc................................. G 574 773-4513
  Nappanee *(G-12599)*
Gold Canyon Candles............................ G 812 267-4477
  Elizabeth *(G-3125)*
Green Way Candle Company LLC........ G 574 536-3802
  Goshen *(G-6155)*
Hey Heys Candles LLC........................... G 812 484-9956
  Evansville *(G-4106)*
Hungry Candle LLC................................ G 773 656-1774
  Indianapolis *(G-8434)*
Indigo Candles....................................... G 317 457-9814
  Indianapolis *(G-8514)*
J&K Generations..................................... G 812 508-1094
  Bedford *(G-650)*
Jewelry In Candles................................. G 765 401-6228
  Waynetown *(G-16541)*
Jps Candles LLC..................................... G 219 728-8210
  Chesterton *(G-1940)*
Jwcandle Co LLC.................................... G 317 661-1066
  Beech Grove *(G-695)*
KS Kreations.. G 574 514-7366
  Georgetown *(G-6066)*
Laymon Industries LLC.......................... G 574 277-4536
  South Bend *(G-15119)*
Light of Life Gel Candles....................... G 574 310-3777
  Mishawaka *(G-11929)*
Linneas Lights LLC................................. G 317 324-4002
  Carmel *(G-1684)*
Lit By Neek... G 317 775-5574
  Indianapolis *(G-8767)*
Magic Candle Inc.................................... G 317 357-1101
  Indianapolis *(G-8809)*
Mallang Spa Essentials.......................... G 219 902-9788
  Hammond *(G-6976)*
ME Time Candle Co LLC........................ G 317 378-5533
  Indianapolis *(G-8867)*
Merrywood Group LLC........................... G 765 729-5927
  Muncie *(G-12451)*
Moco Fragrances LLC............................ G 317 642-9014
  Flat Rock *(G-4656)*
Moody Candles LLC............................... G 317 535-2969
  Bargersville *(G-570)*
Murphys Townhouse Candles LLC....... G 260 318-0504
  Kendallville *(G-10137)*
Next Level Candles LLC......................... G 574 347-1030
  South Bend *(G-15167)*
Night Lights Company LLC................... G 574 606-4288
  Indianapolis *(G-9010)*

Oreo Effect LLC....................................... G 574 404-4800
  South Bend *(G-15180)*
Otter Creek Candle LLC......................... G 812 750-4129
  Holton *(G-7219)*
Paula Rosenbaum.................................. G 319 484-2941
  Valparaiso *(G-16022)*
Penn & Beech Candle Co...................... G 317 645-8732
  Indianapolis *(G-9114)*
Prominent Promotional Pdts LLC......... G 317 376-5772
  Quincy *(G-14022)*
Purple Vertigo Candles LLC.................. G 502 807-6619
  New Salisbury *(G-12986)*
Raven Lake Originals Candles.............. G 765 419-1473
  Greentown *(G-6648)*
Redmaster Fusion LLC........................... G 260 273-5819
  Fort Wayne *(G-5374)*
Rosmarino Candles LLC........................ G 970 218-2835
  Bloomington *(G-963)*
Rustic Glow Candle Co LLC.................. G 317 696-4264
  Indianapolis *(G-9349)*
Schwartz Manufacturing Inc................. G 260 589-3865
  Berne *(G-725)*
Simple Glow Candle Co......................... G 260 435-0062
  Fort Wayne *(G-5418)*
Soy Magnifiscents.................................. G 765 746-6358
  Lafayette *(G-10694)*
Soyful Fragrant Candles LLC............... G 219 588-2685
  Gary *(G-6014)*
Stoney Ridgs Candles............................ G 574 453-6807
  Etna Green *(G-3850)*
Sweetjoy Company LLC......................... G 502 821-0511
  New Albany *(G-12820)*
Taylor Made Candles.............................. G 812 663-6634
  Greensburg *(G-6634)*
Timberlight Manufacturing Co.............. G 317 694-1317
  Indianapolis *(G-9604)*
TLC Candle Co LLC................................ G 317 313-3029
  Fishers *(G-4613)*
Tooties Zenergy Candles LLC............... G 317 437-9936
  Indianapolis *(G-9619)*
Twisod Wick Candle Company............. G 317 490-4789
  Martinsville *(G-11432)*
Twisted Wick Candle Co........................ G 317 490-4789
  Nashville *(G-12681)*
Unplug Soy Candles............................... G 217 520-2658
  Fishers *(G-4623)*
Unplug Soy Candles LLC....................... G 317 650-5776
  Fortville *(G-5608)*
Vintage Road Candles........................... G 765 621-3561
  Alexandria *(G-64)*
Wahs Candle Studio............................... G 734 846-5654
  Sharpsville *(G-14715)*
Warm Glow Candle Company............... E 765 855-5483
  Centerville *(G-1855)*
Warm Glow Candle Outlet..................... G 765 855-2000
  Centerville *(G-1856)*
Wicone... G 219 218-5199
  Hammond *(G-7033)*

CANDLES: Wholesalers

Antique Candle Works Inc..................... E 765 250-8481
  Lafayette *(G-10523)*
Yankee Candle Company Inc................ G 812 526-5195
  Edinburgh *(G-3110)*

CANDY & CONFECTIONS: Candy Bars, Including Chocolate Covered

Donaldsons Chocolates Inc................... G 765 482-3334
  Lebanon *(G-10891)*

PRODUCT SECTION

CARPETS, RUGS & FLOOR COVERING

CANDY & CONFECTIONS: Chocolate Candy, Exc Solid Chocolate

Debrand Inc..D..... 260 969-8333
Fort Wayne *(G-4909)*

CANDY & CONFECTIONS: Popcorn Balls/ Other Trtd Popcorn Prdts

Gary Poppins LLC.................................E..... 866 354-1300
Knox *(G-10209)*

Poptique Popcorn LLC.........................G..... 260 244-3745
Columbia City *(G-2182)*

Wsg Manufacturing LLC......................G..... 765 934-2101
Whitestown *(G-16829)*

CANDY, NUT & CONFECTIONERY STORES: Candy

Abbotts Candy and Gifts Inc................E..... 765 489-4442
Hagerstown *(G-6832)*

Lowerys Home Made Candies Inc......G..... 765 288-7300
Muncie *(G-12441)*

Olympia Candy Kitchen LLC...............G..... 574 533-5040
Goshen *(G-6230)*

Schimpffs Confectionery LLC.............F..... 812 283-8367
Jeffersonville *(G-10052)*

South Bend Chocolate Co Inc.............F..... 574 233-2577
South Bend *(G-15251)*

Stephen Libs Candy Company Inc.....F..... 812 473-0048
Evansville *(G-4331)*

Sweet Things Inc..................................F..... 317 872-8720
Carmel *(G-1774)*

CANDY: Soft

Catalent Wellness Indiana LLC..........F..... 812 537-5203
Greendale *(G-6443)*

CANNED SPECIALTIES

Frito-Lay North America Inc................B..... 765 659-1831
Frankfort *(G-5669)*

Mead Johnson & Company LLC.........C..... 812 429-5000
Evansville *(G-4193)*

Vitamins Inc..E..... 219 879-7356
Michigan City *(G-11686)*

CANS: Metal

Ardagh Glass Inc.................................G..... 610 341-7885
Muncie *(G-12344)*

Armor Products Inc.............................C..... 502 228-1458
Madison *(G-11202)*

Ball Corporation...................................F..... 574 583-9418
Monticello *(G-12136)*

Ball Inc..A..... 317 736-8236
Franklin *(G-5712)*

Bway Corporation................................G..... 219 462-8915
Valparaiso *(G-15923)*

Canpack US LLC..................................A..... 272 226-7225
Muncie *(G-12364)*

Crown Cork & Seal Usa Inc................C..... 765 362-3200
Crawfordsville *(G-2560)*

Indianapolis Container Company.......G..... 317 580-5000
Indianapolis *(G-8503)*

Industrial Container Svcs LLC............F..... 812 283-7659
Alton *(G-65)*

Norton Packaging Inc..........................E..... 574 867-6002
Hamlet *(G-6864)*

Powell Systems Inc..............................G..... 765 884-0613
Fowler *(G-5631)*

R & M Welding & Fabricating Sp........G..... 812 295-9130
Loogootee *(G-11148)*

Sangsin Indiana Inc.............................G..... 765 432-4143
Kokomo *(G-10329)*

Silgan Containers Mfg Corp................E..... 219 845-1500
Hammond *(G-7006)*

Silgan Containers Mfg Corp................E..... 219 362-7002
La Porte *(G-10483)*

Silgan White Cap LLC.........................C..... 812 425-6222
Evansville *(G-4314)*

Silgan White Cap LLC.........................B..... 765 983-9200
Richmond *(G-14205)*

CANVAS PRDTS

Anchor Industries Inc..........................D..... 812 867-2421
Evansville *(G-3891)*

Canvas Vinyl Creations Inc................G..... 317 371-4227
Noblesville *(G-13054)*

Coverite-Custom Covers.....................G..... 574 278-7152
Monticello *(G-12143)*

Dometic Corporation............................B..... 260 463-7657
Elkhart *(G-3301)*

Donna McCormick.................................G..... 574 278-3152
Monticello *(G-12147)*

Lc Covers LLC......................................G..... 260 463-2220
Lagrange *(G-10752)*

Meese Inc..F..... 800 829-4535
Madison *(G-11241)*

Nose and Mustache LLC....................G..... 260 758-8800
Markle *(G-11360)*

Wickey Canvas Outdoor Cooking.......G..... 260 223-8890
Berne *(G-731)*

Wild Hair Canvas Shop........................G..... 812 290-1086
Aurora *(G-460)*

CANVAS PRDTS: Convertible Tops, Car/ Boat, Fm Purchased Mtrl

Angola Canvas Co................................F..... 260 665-9913
Angola *(G-227)*

Tumacs LLC..E..... 574 264-5000
Elkhart *(G-3753)*

CAPACITORS: NEC

A C Mallory Capacitors LLC................G..... 317 612-1000
Indianapolis *(G-7397)*

Greatbatch Ltd.....................................G..... 260 755-7484
Warsaw *(G-16371)*

Integer Holdings Corporation..............G..... 260 373-1664
Fort Wayne *(G-5114)*

Kirby Risk Corporation.........................D..... 317 398-9713
Shelbyville *(G-14768)*

Tempest Technical Sales Inc..............G..... 317 844-9236
Carmel *(G-1783)*

Zepto Systems Incorporated...............G..... 812 323-0642
Bloomington *(G-1019)*

CAPS: Plastic

Drug Plastics Closures Inc.................E..... 812 526-0555
Edinburgh *(G-3080)*

Rfbp Inc...B
Evansville *(G-4288)*

CAR WASH EQPT

A&E Klassic Detailing LLC..................G..... 219 363-6671
Michigan City *(G-11574)*

Elite Hand Car Wash & More LLC......G..... 317 500-8308
Avon *(G-517)*

James Morris..G..... 574 387-2615
South Bend *(G-15090)*

Laserwash..G..... 765 359-0582
Crawfordsville *(G-2584)*

Michiana Carwash Systems LLC.......G..... 574 320-2331
Goshen *(G-6219)*

Region Auto Detailing LLC..................G..... 219 427-6318
East Chicago *(G-3039)*

CAR WASH EQPT & SPLYS WHOLESALERS

Whitlocks Pressure Wash....................F..... 765 825-5868
Connersville *(G-2475)*

CARBIDES

Gill Carbide Saw & Tl Svc LLC...........G..... 317 698-6787
Martinsville *(G-11397)*

CARBON & GRAPHITE PRDTS, NEC

Aerodine Composites LLC..................E..... 317 271-1207
Indianapolis *(G-7450)*

Friction Products Company LLC.........A..... 765 362-3500
Crawfordsville *(G-2568)*

Graphite Customs LLC........................G..... 260 402-8690
Fort Wayne *(G-5036)*

Hickman Williams & Company............G..... 219 379-5199
La Porte *(G-10419)*

Hickman Williams & Company............G..... 812 522-6293
Seymour *(G-14656)*

CARBON BLACK

Dean Co Inc..G..... 317 891-2518
Greenfield *(G-6488)*

CARBURETORS

Tecumseh Products Company LLC....F..... 812 883-3575
Salem *(G-14502)*

CARDIOVASCULAR SYSTEM DRUGS, EXC DIAGNOSTIC

Midwest Pediatric Crdiolgy PC............D..... 219 836-1355
Munster *(G-12549)*

CARDS: Color

Colwell Inc..C..... 260 347-1981
Kendallville *(G-10100)*

Colwell Inc..C..... 260 347-1981
Kendallville *(G-10099)*

CARDS: Greeting

Behning Inc...G..... 260 672-2663
Roanoke *(G-14260)*

Kellmark Corporation...........................F..... 574 264-9695
Elkhart *(G-3449)*

Mejjm Inc...G..... 317 893-6929
Indianapolis *(G-8873)*

Nussmeier Engraving Company.........E..... 812 425-1339
Evansville *(G-4224)*

CARDS: Identification

CPI Card Group - Indiana Inc..............C..... 260 424-4920
Fort Wayne *(G-4881)*

Gieseck+dvrent Epymnts Amer In......G..... 866 484-0611
Fort Wayne *(G-5024)*

Roi Marketing Company Inc................G..... 317 644-0797
Indianapolis *(G-9321)*

Stoffel Seals Corporation....................E..... 845 353-3800
Angola *(G-296)*

CARDS: Playing

Thach LLC...G..... 317 373-3734
Westfield *(G-16732)*

CARPET & UPHOLSTERY CLEANING SVCS

Bane-Clene Corp..................................G..... 317 546-5448
Indianapolis *(G-7594)*

Kings-Qlity Rstrtion Svcs LLC............F..... 812 944-4347
New Albany *(G-12760)*

Employee Codes: A=Over 500 employees, B=251-500
C=101-250, D=51-100, E=20-50, F=10-19, G=1-9

CARPETS, RUGS & FLOOR COVERING

CARPETS, RUGS & FLOOR COVERING

Advanced Services LLC .... F 317 780-6909
  Indianapolis *(G-7441)*

All Day Carpet Binding LLC .... G 219 851-8071
  Lafayette *(G-10518)*

Bock Engineering Company Inc .... G 574 522-3191
  Elkhart *(G-3229)*

Envirotech Extrusion Inc .... E 765 966-8068
  Richmond *(G-14120)*

Indiana Rug Company .... G 574 252-4653
  Mishawaka *(G-11911)*

Jpc LLC .... F 574 293-8030
  Elkhart *(G-3437)*

Manta Rugs .... G 765 869-5940
  Boswell *(G-1118)*

Mohawk Group LLC .... G 765 250-5458
  West Lafayette *(G-16611)*

Taylor Gary .... G 812 895-0715
  Vincennes *(G-16158)*

Todd K Hockemeyer Inc .... G 260 639-3591
  Fort Wayne *(G-5492)*

CARPETS: Textile Fiber

Tekmodo Oz Holdings LLC .... G 574 970-5800
  Elkhart *(G-3721)*

CARRIERS: Infant, Textile

Upanaway LLC .... G 866 218-7143
  Greenfield *(G-6568)*

CARS: Electric

M-TEC Corporation .... D 574 294-1060
  Elkhart *(G-3507)*

CASEMENTS: Aluminum

Meridian Metalform Inc .... G 812 422-1524
  Evansville *(G-4196)*

CASES: Carrying

CH Ellis Co Inc .... E 317 636-3351
  Indianapolis *(G-7782)*

Derby Inc .... D 574 233-4500
  South Bend *(G-14997)*

Frances Monforte .... G 317 875-0880
  Indianapolis *(G-8221)*

MTS Products Corp .... E 574 295-3142
  Elkhart *(G-3559)*

Smor Cases Inc .... E 574 291-0346
  South Bend *(G-15248)*

CASES: Carrying, Clothing & Apparel

4ever Chosen LLC .... G 765 431-7548
  Kokomo *(G-10230)*

B Word LLC .... G 317 654-6873
  Indianapolis *(G-7583)*

Bag Corporation .... G 317 699-5523
  Indianapolis *(G-7590)*

Bbliss & Jus Be Zany .... G 215 251-9235
  Indianapolis *(G-7599)*

Death Enn LLC .... G 219 402-4436
  Merrillville *(G-11504)*

East Coast Treasure Finds LLC .... G 845 879-8744
  Carmel *(G-1618)*

Hotricity LLC .... G 765 212-0411
  Muncie *(G-12422)*

Howse Ov Drmrs LLC .... G 574 366-2406
  South Bend *(G-15073)*

Imagine Like God LLC .... G 574 575-5023
  Elkhart *(G-3418)*

Intellectual Quality LLC .... G 708 979-3127
  Lafayette *(G-10609)*

Melaninwisdomgarment .... G 574 315-3081
  South Bend *(G-15147)*

Oxford Industries Inc .... G 317 569-0866
  Indianapolis *(G-9077)*

Porter Case Inc .... G 219 289-2616
  South Bend *(G-15200)*

Ramo & Co LLC .... G 219 381-1843
  Gary *(G-5999)*

Sarah Johnson Nettles .... G 317 778-0023
  Indianapolis *(G-9372)*

Tetrafab Corporation .... F 812 258-0000
  Floyds Knobs *(G-4696)*

Word 4 Word LLC .... G 317 601-3995
  Indianapolis *(G-9787)*

Zotic Scents LLC .... G 317 766-6501
  Indianapolis *(G-9814)*

CASES: Jewelry

Luxetrend LLC .... G 502 208-9344
  Evansville *(G-4178)*

CASES: Plastic

Shadowhouse Jiu-Jitsu Inc .... G 219 873-4556
  La Porte *(G-10481)*

CASES: Shipping, Nailed Or Lock Corner, Wood

Monrovlle Box Pllet WD Pdts LL .... E 260 623-3128
  Monroeville *(G-12071)*

CASINGS: Sheet Metal

Auto Truck Group LLC .... G 260 493-1800
  Roanoke *(G-14259)*

CASINGS: Storage, Missile & Missile Components

C F Roark Wldg Engrg Co Inc .... C 317 852-3163
  Brownsburg *(G-1356)*

CASKETS & ACCESS

Astral Carrier Inc .... E 765 874-1406
  Lynn *(G-11181)*

Astral Industries Inc .... C 765 874-2525
  Lynn *(G-11182)*

Aurora Casket Company LLC .... G 812 926-1110
  Aurora *(G-438)*

Aurora Casket Company LLC .... B 800 457-1111
  Aurora *(G-439)*

Batesville Casket Company LLC .... A 800 622-8373
  Batesville *(G-580)*

Batesville Casket Company Inc .... F 812 934-7010
  Batesville *(G-581)*

Batesville Interactive LLC .... G 812 932-0164
  Batesville *(G-582)*

Batesville Services LLC .... C 800 622-8373
  Batesville *(G-583)*

Hillenbrand Luxembourg Inc .... E 812 934-7500
  Batesville *(G-591)*

JM Hutton & Co Inc .... E 765 962-3506
  Richmond *(G-14151)*

JM Hutton & Co Inc .... D 765 962-3591
  Richmond *(G-14152)*

Matthews International Corp .... D 765 966-1576
  Richmond *(G-14161)*

Milso Industries Inc .... F 765 966-8012
  Richmond *(G-14167)*

Paragon Casket Inc .... D 888 855-3601
  Richmond *(G-14179)*

Pontone Industries LLC .... C 765 966-8012
  Richmond *(G-14183)*

Romark Industries Inc .... G 765 966-6211
  Richmond *(G-14200)*

Vandor Corporation .... E 765 683-9760
  Richmond *(G-14223)*

Werzalit of America Inc .... D 814 362-3881
  Syracuse *(G-15492)*

York Group Inc .... C 765 966-1576
  Richmond *(G-14232)*

CAST STONE: Concrete

Custom Cast Stone Inc .... D 317 896-1700
  Westfield *(G-16682)*

Monumental Stone Works Inc .... F 765 866-0658
  New Market *(G-12927)*

CASTINGS GRINDING: For The Trade

Med Grind Inc .... G 574 965-4040
  Delphi *(G-2903)*

Stump & Grind .... G 812 453-2121
  Elberfeld *(G-3120)*

T W Machine & Grinding .... G 260 799-4236
  Columbia City *(G-2205)*

CASTINGS: Aerospace, Aluminum

Cuda II Inc .... G 317 514-0885
  Indianapolis *(G-7920)*

Engel Manufacturing Co Inc .... E 574 232-3800
  South Bend *(G-15015)*

Kessington LLC .... D 574 266-4500
  Elkhart *(G-3452)*

Midwest Aerospace Casting LLC .... G 708 597-1300
  Crown Point *(G-2725)*

CASTINGS: Aerospace, Nonferrous, Exc Aluminum

Engel Manufacturing Co Inc .... E 574 232-3800
  South Bend *(G-15015)*

Lite Magnesium Products Inc .... G 765 299-3644
  Indianapolis *(G-8768)*

CASTINGS: Aluminum

Ball Brass and Aluminum Foundry Inc .. E 260 925-3515
  Auburn *(G-367)*

Bud LLC .... E 574 534-5300
  Goshen *(G-6103)*

Dillon Pattern Works Inc .... F 765 642-3549
  Anderson *(G-103)*

Ewing Light Metals Co Inc .... E 317 926-4591
  Indianapolis *(G-8146)*

Foley Pattern Company Inc .... E 260 925-4113
  Auburn *(G-391)*

General Aluminum Mfg Company ...... C 260 356-3900
  Huntington *(G-7314)*

Mahoney Foundries Inc .... E 260 347-1768
  Kendallville *(G-10134)*

Minneapolis Die Casting LLC .... C 763 536-5500
  Auburn *(G-411)*

Muncie Casting Corp .... E 765 288-2611
  Muncie *(G-12461)*

Phillips Pattern & Casting Inc .... F 765 288-2319
  Muncie *(G-12475)*

Valmont Telecommunications Inc ...... F 877 467-4763
  Plymouth *(G-13824)*

Valmont Telecommunications Inc ...... F 574 936-7221
  Plymouth *(G-13823)*

Vice Bros Pattern Sp & Fndry .... G 260 782-2585
  Lagro *(G-10770)*

Wingards Sales LLC .... G 260 768-7961
  Shipshewana *(G-14899)*

CASTINGS: Brass, NEC, Exc Die

PRODUCT SECTION — CEMENT: Portland

Ball Brass and Aluminum Foundry Inc.. E 260 925-3515
Auburn *(G-367)*

Ewing Light Metals Co Inc................ E 317 926-4591
Indianapolis *(G-8146)*

Mahoney Foundries Inc...................... E 260 347-1768
Kendallville *(G-10134)*

Phillips Pattern & Casting Inc............ F 765 288-2319
Muncie *(G-12475)*

CASTINGS: Commercial Investment, Ferrous

Aero Metals Inc................................... B 219 326-1976
La Porte *(G-10377)*

J & T Marine Specialists Inc............. G 317 890-9444
Indianapolis *(G-8600)*

Texmo Blank USA Inc........................ D 574 696-9990
Warsaw *(G-16437)*

CASTINGS: Die, Aluminum

Batesville Products Inc..................... D 513 381-2057
Lawrenceburg *(G-10831)*

Enkei America Moldings Inc............. G 812 373-7000
Columbus *(G-2299)*

FCA US LLC....................................... C 765 454-1005
Kokomo *(G-10267)*

General Aluminum Mfg Company..... C 260 495-2600
Fremont *(G-5822)*

General Motors LLC............................ B 812 279-7321
Bedford *(G-638)*

Grandview Aluminum Products......... F 812 649-2569
Grandview *(G-6328)*

Heartland Castings Inc...................... E 260 837-8311
Waterloo *(G-16521)*

Indiana Cast Stone Company............ F 317 847-5429
Spencer *(G-15350)*

Kitchen-Quip Inc................................ E 260 837-8311
Kendallville *(G-10129)*

Koch Enterprises Inc......................... G 812 465-9800
Evansville *(G-4159)*

Madison Precision Products Inc....... B 812 273-4702
Madison *(G-11238)*

Noblitt International Corp.................. E 812 372-9969
Columbus *(G-2361)*

Old Rev LLC....................................... G 317 580-2420
Westfield *(G-16714)*

Ryobi Die Casting (usa) Inc.............. A 317 398-3398
Shelbyville *(G-14794)*

SUS Cast Products Inc...................... D 574 753-4111
Logansport *(G-11109)*

CASTINGS: Die, Nonferrous

Accurate Castings Inc....................... D 219 362-8531
La Porte *(G-10373)*

Indiana Gratings Inc.......................... F 765 342-7191
Martinsville *(G-11404)*

S P X Corp.. G 574 594-9681
Pierceton *(G-13640)*

CASTINGS: Ductile

Accurate Castings Inc....................... E 219 393-3122
La Porte *(G-10374)*

BCI Solutions Inc............................... C 574 546-2411
Bremen *(G-1174)*

In Ductile LLC.................................... F 317 776-8000
Noblesville *(G-13101)*

Intat Precision Inc............................. B 765 932-5323
Rushville *(G-14401)*

Milwaukee Ductile Iron Inc............... G 260 925-4717
Auburn *(G-410)*

Transportation Tech Inds.................. F 812 962-5000
Evansville *(G-4347)*

CASTINGS: Gray Iron

Accucast Inc...................................... G 317 849-5521
Fishers *(G-4459)*

Atlas Foundry Company Inc............. C 765 662-2525
Marion *(G-11272)*

Bahr Bros Mfg Inc............................. E 765 664-6235
Marion *(G-11274)*

Dalton Corp Kndllvlle Mfg Fclt......... C 260 637-6047
Kendallville *(G-10108)*

Gartland Foundry Company Inc....... C 812 232-0226
Terre Haute *(G-15594)*

Kitley Company................................. E 317 546-2427
Indianapolis *(G-8691)*

Metal Technologies Inc Alabama..... D 260 925-4717
Auburn *(G-408)*

Minneapolis Die Casting LLC........... C 763 536-5500
Auburn *(G-411)*

Navistar Cmponent Holdings LLC... A 317 352-4500
Indianapolis *(G-8994)*

New Dalton Foundry LLC................. F 574 267-8111
Warsaw *(G-16400)*

Plymouth Foundry Inc...................... E 574 936-2106
Plymouth *(G-13801)*

Richmond Casting Company........... E 765 935-4090
Richmond *(G-14199)*

Rochester Metal Products Corp...... B 574 223-3164
Rochester *(G-14319)*

The Dalton Corporation.................... D 574 267-8111
Warsaw *(G-16438)*

Warsaw Foundry Company Inc....... D 574 267-8772
Warsaw *(G-16446)*

Waupaca Foundry Inc...................... A 812 547-0700
Tell City *(G-15518)*

CASTINGS: Machinery, Aluminum

Linamar Strctures USA Mich Inc..... G 260 636-7030
Avilla *(G-487)*

Mpi Products LLC.............................. E 248 237-3007
Knox *(G-10218)*

CASTINGS: Steel

Shenango LLC................................... F 812 235-2058
Terre Haute *(G-15691)*

The Harrison Steel Castings Co...... A 765 762-2481
Attica *(G-356)*

CASTINGS: Titanium

GKN Aerospace Muncie Inc............. E 765 747-7147
Muncie *(G-12402)*

Titanium LLC...................................... G 765 236-6906
Kokomo *(G-10349)*

Titanium Rails Nutrition LLC............ G 219 940-3704
Hobart *(G-7212)*

CATALOG & MAIL-ORDER HOUSES

Johnny Lemas................................... G 260 833-8850
Angola *(G-264)*

Rose Sharon All Naturals LLC......... G 317 500-4725
Indianapolis *(G-9334)*

Sacred Selections............................. G 260 347-3758
Kendallville *(G-10151)*

Sailrite Enterprises Inc.................... F 260 244-4647
Columbia City *(G-2195)*

CATALOG SALES

American Legion National He........... D 317 630-1200
Indianapolis *(G-7505)*

Annies Publishing LLC..................... C 260 589-4000
Berne *(G-704)*

Dauenhauer Glass Company Inc.... G 260 433-5876
Fort Wayne *(G-4906)*

Joseph Matthew Biaso..................... G 812 277-6871
Mitchell *(G-12041)*

Rva LLC.. G 317 800-9800
Fishers *(G-4602)*

CATALOG SHOWROOMS

Dutch Made Inc.................................. G 260 657-3331
Harlan *(G-7054)*

CATALYSTS: Chemical

Shell Catalysts & Tech LP................ C 219 874-6211
Michigan City *(G-11667)*

CATAPULTS

Egenolf Contg & Rigging II Inc........ F 317 787-5301
Indianapolis *(G-8059)*

CATERERS

Grafton Peek Incorporated............... F 317 557-8377
Greenwood *(G-6709)*

Heaven Sent Gurmet Cookies Inc... G 219 980-1066
Gary *(G-5948)*

Milan Food Bank................................ G 812 654-3682
Milan *(G-11781)*

Parretts Meat Proc & Catrg Inc....... F 574 967-3711
Flora *(G-4663)*

Roller-Wilson Industries LLC........... G 317 377-4900
Indianapolis *(G-9324)*

CATTLE WHOLESALERS

P & R Farms Llc................................ G 812 326-2010
Saint Anthony *(G-14430)*

CAULKING COMPOUNDS

Cast Products LP.............................. G 574 255-9619
Mishawaka *(G-11859)*

Colorimetric Inc................................. F 574 255-9619
Mishawaka *(G-11862)*

Dehco Inc... D 574 294-2684
Elkhart *(G-3288)*

Weatherall Indiana Inc..................... F 812 256-3378
Charlestown *(G-1896)*

CEMENT & CONCRETE RELATED PRDTS & EQPT: Bituminous

Nobbe Concrete Products Inc......... G 765 647-4017
Brookville *(G-1329)*

CEMENT ROCK: Crushed & Broken

Rock Creek Stone LLC..................... D 260 694-6880
Bluffton *(G-1052)*

CEMENT: Hydraulic

Busters Cement Products Inc......... G 765 529-0287
New Castle *(G-12854)*

D and D Custom Concrete Inc......... G 574 274-6013
Mishawaka *(G-11875)*

Heidelberg Mtls US Cem LLC........... B 812 849-2191
Mitchell *(G-12040)*

Irving Materials Inc.......................... F 765 922-7285
Kokomo *(G-10291)*

Light House Center Inc.................... F 765 448-4502
Lafayette *(G-10636)*

CEMENT: Natural

Southfield Corporation...................... E 317 846-6060
Carmel *(G-1767)*

CEMENT: Portland

Buzzi Unicem USA Inc...................... E 317 706-3352
Carmel *(G-1577)*

Employee Codes: A=Over 500 employees, B=251-500
C=101-250, D=51-100, E=20-50, F=10-19, G=1-9

CEMENT: Portland

Buzzi Unicem USA Inc .... G 574 674-8873
  Elkhart *(G-3239)*
Buzzi Unicem USA Inc .... C 765 653-9766
  Greencastle *(G-6393)*
Buzzi Unicem USA Inc .... E 317 780-9860
  Indianapolis *(G-7705)*
Heidelberg Mtls US Cem LLC .... C 574 753-5121
  Logansport *(G-11076)*
Holcim (us) Inc .... G 219 378-1193
  East Chicago *(G-3017)*
Lone Star Industries Inc .... G 574 674-8873
  Elkhart *(G-3499)*
Lone Star Industries Inc .... G 260 482-4559
  Fort Wayne *(G-5190)*
Lone Star Industries Inc .... G 765 653-9766
  Greencastle *(G-6419)*
Lone Star Industries Inc .... G 317 780-9860
  Indianapolis *(G-8778)*
Lone Star Industries Inc .... D 317 706-3314
  Carmel *(G-1685)*
River Cement Sales Company .... G 812 285-1003
  Jeffersonville *(G-10048)*

CERAMIC FIBER

Ceramic Fiber Enterprises Inc .... G 765 362-2179
  Crawfordsville *(G-2551)*
Thermal Ceramics Inc .... E 574 296-3500
  Elkhart *(G-3725)*
Unifrax I LLC .... C 574 654-7100
  New Carlisle *(G-12848)*

CHAIN: Tire, Made From Purchased Wire

Onspot of North America Inc .... G 203 377-0777
  North Vernon *(G-13290)*

CHAIN: Welded, Made From Purchased Wire

Grc Enterprises Inc .... E 219 932-2220
  East Chicago *(G-3012)*

CHANGE MAKING MACHINES

James R McNutt .... G 317 899-6955
  Indianapolis *(G-8617)*
Standard Change-Makers Inc .... F 317 899-6955
  Indianapolis *(G-9492)*
Standard Change-Makers Inc .... C 317 899-6955
  Indianapolis *(G-9491)*

CHASSIS: Motor Vehicle

Aje Suspension Inc .... F 812 346-7356
  North Vernon *(G-13255)*
Checkered Racing & Chrome LLC .... F 812 275-2875
  Spencer *(G-15341)*
LCI Industries .... A 574 535-1125
  Elkhart *(G-3476)*
Lcm Realty LLC .... G 574 535-1125
  Elkhart *(G-3479)*
Lippert Cmponents Intl Sls Inc .... G 574 312-7480
  Elkhart *(G-3489)*
Lippert Components Inc .... G 574 295-1483
  Elkhart *(G-3491)*
Lippert Components Inc .... G 574 535-1125
  Elkhart *(G-3492)*
Lippert Components Inc .... D 574 535-1125
  Goshen *(G-6202)*
Lippert Components Inc .... C 574 537-8900
  Goshen *(G-6205)*
Lippert Components Inc .... G 574 849-0869
  Goshen *(G-6206)*
Lippert Components Inc .... F 574 971-4320
  Goshen *(G-6207)*
Lippert Components Inc .... E 574 312-7445
  Middlebury *(G-11734)*
Lippert Components Inc .... E 800 551-9149
  Mishawaka *(G-11930)*
Lippert Components Inc .... F 574 312-6654
  South Bend *(G-15125)*
Lippert Components Inc .... F 260 234-4303
  Yoder *(G-16966)*
Lippert Components Inc .... B 574 535-1125
  Elkhart *(G-3493)*
Lippert Components Mfg Inc .... D 574 535-1125
  Elkhart *(G-3495)*
U B Machine Inc .... F 260 493-3381
  New Haven *(G-12924)*
Vehicle Service Group LLC .... C 812 273-1622
  Madison *(G-11257)*
Vehicle Service Group LLC .... C 800 640-5438
  Madison *(G-11256)*
Wb Automotive Holdings Inc .... G 734 604-8962
  Fort Wayne *(G-5557)*

CHASSIS: Travel Trailer

Dmi Holding Corp .... C 574 534-1224
  Goshen *(G-6123)*
Hy-Line Enterprises Intl Inc .... E 574 294-1112
  Elkhart *(G-3413)*
Keystone Rv Company .... C 574 535-2100
  Wakarusa *(G-16237)*
Keystone Rv Company .... D 574 534-9430
  Goshen *(G-6191)*

CHEMICAL CLEANING SVCS

Paradigm Industries Inc .... G 317 574-8590
  Carmel *(G-1714)*

CHEMICAL ELEMENTS

Ashleys Elements LLC .... G 765 480-2168
  Tipton *(G-15765)*
Element Armament .... G 317 530-9013
  Whiteland *(G-16784)*
Element Clumbus .... G 812 526-2329
  Columbus *(G-2296)*
Machine Elements Inc .... G 219 508-3968
  Valparaiso *(G-15999)*
Sengo LLC .... G 574 383-9833
  South Bend *(G-15238)*
Surface Elements Inc .... F 574 546-5455
  Bremen *(G-1227)*

CHEMICAL PROCESSING MACHINERY & EQPT

Shar Systems Inc .... E 260 432-5312
  Fort Wayne *(G-5412)*
Wayne Chemical Inc .... E 260 432-1120
  Fort Wayne *(G-5551)*

CHEMICALS & ALLIED PRDTS WHOLESALERS, NEC

Accra-Pac Inc .... G 574 295-0000
  Elkhart *(G-3149)*
Adhesive Products Inc .... G 317 899-0565
  Indianapolis *(G-7432)*
Airgas Usa LLC .... G 812 474-0440
  Evansville *(G-3878)*
Apg Inc .... D 574 295-0000
  Elkhart *(G-3185)*
B S R Inc .... G 812 235-4444
  Terre Haute *(G-15548)*
B S R Inc .... E 812 235-4444
  Terre Haute *(G-15549)*
Bane-Clene Corp .... G 317 546-5448
  Indianapolis *(G-7594)*
Bane-Clene Corp .... F 317 546-5448
  Indianapolis *(G-7595)*
Bangs Laboratories Inc .... F 317 570-7020
  Fishers *(G-4470)*
Cast Products LP .... E 574 294-2684
  Elkhart *(G-3249)*
Craft Laboratories Inc .... E 260 432-9467
  Fort Wayne *(G-4882)*
Hydrite Chemical Co .... D 812 232-5411
  Terre Haute *(G-15611)*
Koehler Welding Supply Inc .... F 812 574-4103
  Madison *(G-11233)*
Linde Gas & Equipment Inc .... G 812 376-3314
  Columbus *(G-2343)*
Pendry Coatings LLC .... G 574 268-2956
  Warsaw *(G-16410)*
Superior Indus Solutions Inc .... E 317 781-4400
  Indianapolis *(G-9529)*

CHEMICALS & ALLIED PRDTS, WHOLESALE: Adhesives

Cerline Ceramic Corp .... G 765 649-7222
  Anderson *(G-92)*

CHEMICALS & ALLIED PRDTS, WHOLESALE: Chemical Additives

Paradigm Industries Inc .... G 317 574-8590
  Carmel *(G-1714)*

CHEMICALS & ALLIED PRDTS, WHOLESALE: Chemicals, Indl

1500 South Tibbs LLC .... C 317 247-8141
  Indianapolis *(G-7384)*
Ink - LLC .... G 317 502-6473
  Franklin *(G-5746)*
J 2 Systems and Supply LLC .... G 317 602-3940
  Indianapolis *(G-8601)*
Kml Inc .... G 260 897-3723
  Laotto *(G-10808)*
Nochar Inc .... G 317 613-3046
  Indianapolis *(G-9018)*
Sdf Engineering LLC .... G 317 674-2643
  Carmel *(G-1755)*
Substrate Treatments & Lubr .... F 574 258-0904
  Mishawaka *(G-12010)*
Warsaw Chemical Company Inc .... D 574 267-3251
  Warsaw *(G-16442)*

CHEMICALS & ALLIED PRDTS, WHOLESALE: Chemicals, Indl & Heavy

J & K Supply Inc .... G 765 448-1188
  Lafayette *(G-10611)*
Magnum International Inc .... E 708 889-9999
  Crown Point *(G-2721)*
Ulrich Chemical Inc .... E 317 898-8632
  Indianapolis *(G-9675)*

CHEMICALS & ALLIED PRDTS, WHOLESALE: Detergent/Soap

J&K Generations .... G 812 508-1094
  Bedford *(G-650)*

CHEMICALS & ALLIED PRDTS, WHOLESALE: Indl Gases

Messer LLC .... G 574 234-4887
  South Bend *(G-15148)*

CHEMICALS: Inorganic, NEC

CHEMICALS & ALLIED PRDTS, WHOLESALE: Oil Additives

Lucas Oil Products Inc .... C 951 270-0154
Indianapolis *(G-8793)*

CHEMICALS & ALLIED PRDTS, WHOLESALE: Oxygen

Air Products and Chemicals Inc .... G 812 466-6492
Terre Haute *(G-15535)*

Williams Bros Hlth Care Phrm I .... E 812 335-0000
Bloomington *(G-1012)*

Williams Bros Hlth Care Phrm I .... E 812 254-2497
Washington *(G-16513)*

CHEMICALS & ALLIED PRDTS, WHOLESALE: Plastics Film

American Renolit Corporation .... C 219 324-6886
La Porte *(G-10384)*

Plastics Family Holdings Inc .... G 317 890-1808
Indianapolis *(G-9153)*

CHEMICALS & ALLIED PRDTS, WHOLESALE: Plastics Materials, NEC

Celestial Designs LLC .... G 317 733-3110
Zionsville *(G-16997)*

Magnum International Inc .... E 708 889-9999
Crown Point *(G-2721)*

Superior Indus Solutions Inc .... E 317 781-4400
Indianapolis *(G-9529)*

CHEMICALS & ALLIED PRDTS, WHOLESALE: Plastics Prdts, NEC

A S V Plastics Inc .... F 574 264-9694
Elkhart *(G-3141)*

Ameri-Kart Corp .... C 574 848-7462
Bristol *(G-1244)*

Nibco Inc .... C 574 296-1240
Goshen *(G-6227)*

CHEMICALS & ALLIED PRDTS, WHOLESALE: Plastics Sheets & Rods

Parkland Plastics Inc .... E 574 825-4336
Middlebury *(G-11745)*

CHEMICALS & ALLIED PRDTS, WHOLESALE: Polyurethane Prdts

Pinder Polyurethane & Plas Inc .... G 219 397-8248
East Chicago *(G-3034)*

CHEMICALS & ALLIED PRDTS, WHOLESALE: Resins

Innovations Amplified LLC .... G 317 339-4685
Indianapolis *(G-8552)*

CHEMICALS & ALLIED PRDTS, WHOLESALE: Resins, Plastics

General Rbr Plas of Evansville .... E 812 464-5153
Evansville *(G-4087)*

CHEMICALS & ALLIED PRDTS, WHOLESALE: Spec Clean/Sanitation

Online Packaging Incorporated .... E 219 872-0925
Michigan City *(G-11648)*

Sorbtech Inc .... G 812 944-9108
Clarksville *(G-2037)*

Tgc Auto Care Products Inc .... G 765 962-7725
Richmond *(G-14216)*

CHEMICALS & ALLIED PRDTS, WHOLESALE: Syn Resin, Rub/Plastic

Ampacet Corporation .... D 812 466-5231
Terre Haute *(G-15544)*

Independent Plastic Inc .... G 765 521-2251
New Castle *(G-12869)*

CHEMICALS & ALLIED PRDTS, WHOLESALE: Waxes, Exc Petroleum

Jzj Services LLC .... E 812 424-8268
Evansville *(G-4147)*

CHEMICALS & OTHER PRDTS DERIVED FROM COKING

Citizens Energy Group .... F 317 261-8794
Indianapolis *(G-7812)*

Hawkins Inc .... G 765 288-8930
Muncie *(G-12409)*

CHEMICALS, AGRICULTURE: Wholesalers

1500 South Tibbs LLC .... C 317 247-8141
Indianapolis *(G-7384)*

Biodyne-Midwest LLC .... F 888 970-0955
Fort Wayne *(G-4801)*

Helena Agri-Enterprises LLC .... G 765 869-5518
Ambia *(G-66)*

Helena Agri-Enterprises LLC .... G 812 654-3177
Dillsboro *(G-2946)*

Helena Agri-Enterprises LLC .... G 574 268-4762
Huntington *(G-7317)*

Helena Agri-Enterprises LLC .... G 765 583-4458
Otterbein *(G-13452)*

Miles Farm Supply LLC .... D 812 359-4463
Boonville *(G-1090)*

Winfield Solutions LLC .... G 317 838-3733
Plainfield *(G-13743)*

CHEMICALS: Agricultural

Bayer Great Lakes Prod Co LLC .... E 317 945-7121
Windfall *(G-16903)*

Dintec Agrichemicals .... G 317 337-7870
Indianapolis *(G-7976)*

Dow Agroscience .... G 765 743-0015
West Lafayette *(G-16577)*

Dow Agrosciences .... G 765 775-2918
West Lafayette *(G-16578)*

Dow Agrosciences LLC .... G 317 846-7873
Carmel *(G-1612)*

Dow Agrosciences LLC .... E 317 252-5602
Indianapolis *(G-8000)*

Dow Elanco Sciences .... G 317 337-3691
Indianapolis *(G-8002)*

Dupont and Tonkel Partners LLC .... G 260 444-2264
Fort Wayne *(G-4932)*

Dupont Circle III .... G 260 489-9508
Fort Wayne *(G-4933)*

Dupont Commons LLC .... G 260 637-3215
Fort Wayne *(G-4934)*

Eidp Inc .... A 833 267-8382
Indianapolis *(G-8064)*

Eli Lilly International Corp .... F 317 276-2000
Indianapolis *(G-8091)*

Helena Agri-Enterprises LLC .... G 574 268-4762
Huntington *(G-7317)*

Kep Chem Inc .... G 574 739-0501
Logansport *(G-11088)*

Keystone Cooperative Inc .... G 765 489-4141
Hagerstown *(G-6838)*

Landec Ag Inc .... F 765 385-1000
Oxford *(G-13475)*

Monsanto Company .... G 229 759-0034
Evansville *(G-4209)*

Monsanto Company .... G 323 265-1025
Lafayette *(G-10653)*

Monsanto Company .... G 574 870-0397
Reynolds *(G-14074)*

Monsanto Company .... G 219 733-2938
Union Mills *(G-15866)*

Monsanto Whitestown Seed .... G 317 692-9485
Whitestown *(G-16812)*

Mycogen Corporation .... F 317 337-3000
Indianapolis *(G-8977)*

Roy Umbarger and Sons Inc .... F 317 422-5195
Franklin *(G-5775)*

Southern Indiana Chemical Inc .... G 812 687-7118
Washington *(G-16509)*

Superior AG Resources Coop Inc .... G 812 724-4455
Owensville *(G-13473)*

Wellington Global LLC .... G 317 590-1755
Indianapolis *(G-9748)*

CHEMICALS: Aluminum Compounds

Chemtrade Solutions LLC .... G 317 917-0319
Indianapolis *(G-7794)*

Mobex Global US Inc .... G 319 269-3848
Albion *(G-35)*

CHEMICALS: Ammonium Salts & Compounds

V Global Holdings LLC .... E 317 247-8141
Indianapolis *(G-9695)*

CHEMICALS: Bromine, Elemental

Glcc Laurel LLC .... G 765 497-6100
West Lafayette *(G-16584)*

CHEMICALS: Fire Retardant

Prt Inc .... G 765 938-3333
Rushville *(G-14407)*

CHEMICALS: High Purity, Refined From Technical Grade

Helena Agri-Enterprises LLC .... G 765 583-4458
Otterbein *(G-13452)*

Kml Inc .... G 260 897-3723
Laotto *(G-10808)*

Lightcrafters Nanotech LLC .... G 610 844-8341
Crown Point *(G-2719)*

Soulbrain Mi Inc .... F 248 869-3079
Kokomo *(G-10336)*

CHEMICALS: Inorganic, NEC

Addenda LLC .... F 317 290-5007
Indianapolis *(G-7430)*

Airgas Usa Inc .... G 812 362-7593
Rockport *(G-14335)*

Akzo Nobel Coatings Inc .... E 574 372-2000
Warsaw *(G-16310)*

Arch Wood Protection Inc .... G 219 464-3949
Valparaiso *(G-15904)*

Astec Corp .... G 317 872-7550
Indianapolis *(G-7557)*

Basic Elements LLC .... G 219 838-1325
Munster *(G-12532)*

Benchmark Chemical Corp .... G 317 875-0051
Indianapolis *(G-7613)*

CHEMICALS: Inorganic, NEC

Celanese Corporation.................................. G 812 421-8900
  Evansville *(G-3967)*
Central Indiana Ethanol LLC.................. G 765 384-4001
  Carmel *(G-1584)*
Craft Laboratories Inc............................. E 260 432-9467
  Fort Wayne *(G-4882)*
Davies-Imperial Coatings Inc.................. E 219 933-0877
  Hammond *(G-6911)*
Dover Chemical Corporation.................. G 219 852-0042
  Hammond *(G-6914)*
Eidp Inc... G 812 299-6700
  Terre Haute *(G-15583)*
Eidp Inc... G 219 462-4587
  Valparaiso *(G-15938)*
EJ Bognar Incorporated.......................... G 412 344-9900
  Schneider *(G-14549)*
Element Armament LLC.......................... G 317 442-7924
  Bargersville *(G-565)*
Elemental S A Protection......................... G 765 717-7325
  Muncie *(G-12391)*
Elements Elearning LLC.......................... G 317 986-2113
  Indianapolis *(G-8070)*
G&S Research Inc................................... G 317 815-1443
  Carmel *(G-1637)*
Giles Manufacturing Company............... G 812 537-4852
  Greendale *(G-6446)*
Helena Agri-Enterprises LLC.................. G 765 869-5518
  Ambia *(G-66)*
Helena Agri-Enterprises LLC.................. G 812 654-3177
  Dillsboro *(G-2946)*
Hydrite Chemical Co................................ D 812 232-5411
  Terre Haute *(G-15611)*
Industrial Water MGT Inc......................... G 317 889-0836
  Indianapolis *(G-8521)*
J 2 Systems and Supply LLC.................. G 317 602-3940
  Indianapolis *(G-8601)*
Jci Jones Chemicals Inc......................... E 317 787-8382
  Beech Grove *(G-694)*
Kemira Water Solutions Inc.................... D 219 397-2646
  East Chicago *(G-3024)*
Metalworking Lubricants Co.................... C 317 269-2444
  Indianapolis *(G-8891)*
New Elements LLC................................... G 219 465-1389
  Valparaiso *(G-16011)*
Nochar Inc... G 317 613-3046
  Indianapolis *(G-9018)*
PQ LLC... D 812 288-7186
  Clarksville *(G-2027)*
Pure Elements LLC................................... G 317 503-0411
  Indianapolis *(G-9241)*
Reagent Chemical & RES Inc................. D 574 772-7424
  Knox *(G-10220)*
Servaas Manufacturing Corp.................. G 317 253-0454
  Indianapolis *(G-9407)*
Shoremet LLC... F 219 390-3336
  Valparaiso *(G-16049)*
Silberline Mfg Co Inc................................ E 260 728-2111
  Decatur *(G-2883)*
Substrate Treatments & Lubr.................. F 574 258-0904
  Mishawaka *(G-12010)*
Thomas R Clark.. G 219 508-7412
  Valparaiso *(G-16065)*
Usalco Michigan City Plant LLC............ G 219 873-0914
  Michigan City *(G-11682)*
W R Grace & Co-Conn............................. E 219 398-2040
  East Chicago *(G-3055)*
Wayne Chemical Inc................................. E 260 432-1120
  Fort Wayne *(G-5551)*

CHEMICALS: Magnesium Compounds Or Salts, Inorganic

Dallas Group of America Inc................... B 812 283-6675
  Jeffersonville *(G-9968)*
Giles Chemical Corporation.................... G 812 537-4852
  Greendale *(G-6445)*

CHEMICALS: Medicinal

1500 South Tibbs LLC.............................. C 317 247-8141
  Indianapolis *(G-7384)*
Cgenetech Inc... G 317 295-1925
  Indianapolis *(G-7781)*
Efil Pharmaceuticals Corp....................... G 765 491-7247
  West Lafayette *(G-16579)*

CHEMICALS: Medicinal, Organic, Uncompounded, Bulk

VSI Acquisition Corp................................. C 317 247-8141
  Indianapolis *(G-9730)*

CHEMICALS: NEC

Amalgamated Incorporated..................... G 260 489-2549
  Fort Wayne *(G-4747)*
Arch Chemicals Inc................................... G 219 464-3949
  Valparaiso *(G-15903)*
Arch Wood Protection Inc........................ G 219 464-3949
  Valparaiso *(G-15904)*
Atmosphere Dynamics Corp................... G 317 392-6262
  Shelbyville *(G-14731)*
Bangs Laboratories Inc........................... F 317 570-7020
  Fishers *(G-4470)*
Boomers... G 765 741-4031
  Muncie *(G-12355)*
Chemicals Inc USA................................... G 317 334-1000
  Indianapolis *(G-7792)*
Chemque Inc.. G 800 268-6111
  Indianapolis *(G-7793)*
Chemtec LLC... F 812 499-8408
  Newburgh *(G-12997)*
Custom Building Products LLC............... C 765 656-0234
  Frankfort *(G-5659)*
Dow Chemical Company.......................... C 317 337-3819
  Indianapolis *(G-8001)*
Eco Services Operations Corp................ E 219 932-7651
  Hammond *(G-6919)*
Enviri Corporation..................................... F 219 397-0200
  East Chicago *(G-3007)*
H&G Legacy Co... G 317 241-9233
  Indianapolis *(G-8348)*
Heidelberg Mtls US Cem LLC................. C 574 753-5121
  Logansport *(G-11076)*
Honey & Salt LLC..................................... G 317 625-1135
  Indianapolis *(G-8407)*
Hydrite Chemical Co................................ D 812 232-5411
  Terre Haute *(G-15611)*
Ifs Coatings... G 317 471-5122
  Indianapolis *(G-8455)*
Innovative Chem Resources Inc............. G 317 695-6001
  Indianapolis *(G-8553)*
Insultech LLC.. F 317 389-5134
  Indianapolis *(G-8565)*
Interrachem LLC....................................... E 812 858-3147
  Newburgh *(G-13009)*
Kaze Energy LLC...................................... G 502 664-5519
  Georgetown *(G-6064)*
Kemco International Inc........................... F 260 829-1263
  Orland *(G-13367)*
Kenra Professional LLC........................... F 800 428-8073
  Indianapolis *(G-8673)*
Klinge Enameling Company Inc.............. E 317 359-8291
  Indianapolis *(G-8694)*
Le Kem of Indiana Inc.............................. G 812 932-5536
  Batesville *(G-595)*
Metals and Additives LLC........................ G 812 446-2525
  Brazil *(G-1153)*
Metals and Additives LLC........................ F 317 290-5007
  Indianapolis *(G-8890)*
Metalworking Lubricants Co.................... C 317 269-2444
  Indianapolis *(G-8891)*
Midwest Custom Chemicals Inc............. G 812 858-3147
  Newburgh *(G-13013)*
Miller Chemical Tech & MGT Inc............ G 317 560-5437
  Franklin *(G-5757)*
Nochar Inc... G 317 613-3046
  Indianapolis *(G-9018)*
Polyfusion LLC.. G 260 624-7659
  Angola *(G-285)*
Quaker Chemical Corp............................. G 765 668-2441
  Marion *(G-11332)*
Ricca Chemical Company LLC............... E 812 932-1161
  Batesville *(G-603)*
Sanco Industries Inc................................ G 260 467-1791
  Fort Wayne *(G-5397)*
Sanco Industries Inc................................ G 260 426-6281
  Fort Wayne *(G-5398)*
Sunocs LLC... G 219 286-7081
  Valparaiso *(G-16061)*
Superior Indus Solutions Inc.................. E 317 781-4400
  Indianapolis *(G-9529)*
Total Cleaning Solutions LLC................. G 260 471-7761
  Fort Wayne *(G-5496)*
Tri-Pac Inc... C 574 855-2197
  South Bend *(G-15291)*
Univertical LLC.. F 260 665-1500
  Angola *(G-304)*
William L Theby... G 812 477-6673
  Evansville *(G-4386)*
Yushiro Manufacturing Amer Inc............ E 317 398-9862
  Shelbyville *(G-14816)*
Zeller LLC.. G 317 343-2930
  Indianapolis *(G-9809)*

CHEMICALS: Organic, NEC

Green Tek LLC.. F 317 294-1614
  Carmel *(G-1644)*

CHEMICALS: Phenol

Eco Services Operations Corp................ E 219 932-7651
  Hammond *(G-6919)*

CHEMICALS: Reagent Grade, Refined From Technical Grade

Omicron Biochemicals Inc....................... E 574 287-6910
  South Bend *(G-15177)*

CHEMICALS: Soda Ash

Eco Services Operations Corp................ E 219 932-7651
  Hammond *(G-6919)*

CHEMICALS: Water Treatment

Astbury Water Technology Inc................ G 260 668-8900
  Angola *(G-231)*
Craig Hydraulic Enterprises.................... G 812 432-5108
  Dillsboro *(G-2944)*
Driessen Water Inc................................... G 765 529-4905
  Muncie *(G-12386)*
GCI LLC... G 317 574-4970
  Carmel *(G-1640)*
Iron Out Inc... G 260 483-2519
  Fort Wayne *(G-5118)*
Iron Out Inc... E 800 654-0791
  Fort Wayne *(G-5119)*
Sheung T Cheng....................................... G 646 220-2195
  Portage *(G-13913)*

PRODUCT SECTION **CLEANING OR POLISHING PREPARATIONS, NEC**

Watcon Inc .... G 574 287-3397
 South Bend *(G-15304)*

Water Sciences Inc .... G 260 485-4655
 Fort Wayne *(G-5548)*

Weas Engineering Inc .... F 317 867-4477
 Westfield *(G-16738)*

CHICKEN SLAUGHTERING & PROCESSING

Perdue Farms Inc .... C 765 436-7990
 Thorntown *(G-15754)*

Tyson Foods Inc .... E 812 738-3219
 Corydon *(G-2520)*

Tyson Foods Inc .... G 260 726-3118
 Portland *(G-13973)*

Tyson Sales and Dist Inc .... C 479 290-7776
 Indianapolis *(G-9670)*

CHILDREN'S & INFANTS' CLOTHING STORES

Shop Lulu Bean LLC .... G 219 525-5336
 Merrillville *(G-11559)*

CHOCOLATE, EXC CANDY FROM BEANS: Chips, Powder, Block, Syrup

Abbotts Candy and Gifts Inc .... E 765 489-4442
 Hagerstown *(G-6832)*

Debrand Inc .... D 260 969-8333
 Fort Wayne *(G-4909)*

Donaldsons Chocolates Inc .... G 765 482-3334
 Lebanon *(G-10891)*

El Popular Inc .... F 219 397-3728
 East Chicago *(G-3005)*

LLC Tipton Mills .... G
 Columbus *(G-2345)*

Lowerys Home Made Candies Inc .... G 765 288-7300
 Muncie *(G-12441)*

Olympia Candy Kitchen LLC .... G 574 533-5040
 Goshen *(G-6230)*

Stephen Libs Candy Company Inc .... F 812 473-0048
 Evansville *(G-4331)*

Sweet Things Inc .... F 317 872-8720
 Carmel *(G-1774)*

True Essence Foods Inc .... F 317 430-3156
 Indianapolis *(G-9651)*

CHOCOLATE, EXC CANDY FROM PURCH CHOC: Chips, Powder, Block

Claeys Candy Inc .... F 574 287-1818
 South Bend *(G-14974)*

Deco Chem Inc .... F 574 255-2366
 Mishawaka *(G-11883)*

South Bend Chocolate Co Inc .... F 574 233-2577
 South Bend *(G-15251)*

CHROMATOGRAPHY EQPT

Inchromatics LLC .... G 317 872-7401
 Indianapolis *(G-8470)*

CHUCKS

Chuck Stace-Allen Inc .... E 317 632-2401
 Indianapolis *(G-7803)*

CHURCHES

Fresh Start Inc .... F 812 254-3398
 Washington *(G-16479)*

CIGARETTE & CIGAR PRDTS & ACCESS

Churchill Cigars .... G 812 273-2249
 Madison *(G-11209)*

Smoke Smoke Smoke .... G 219 942-3331
 Hobart *(G-7209)*

CIRCUIT BOARD REPAIR SVCS

Cinq LLC .... G 405 361-0097
 New Albany *(G-12713)*

CIRCUIT BOARDS: Wiring

Pinder Instruments Company Inc .... G 219 924-7070
 Munster *(G-12558)*

CIRCUITS: Electronic

Acterna LLC .... E 317 788-9351
 Indianapolis *(G-7425)*

Autosem Inc .... E 574 288-8866
 South Bend *(G-14953)*

B Q Products Inc .... F 317 786-5500
 Indianapolis *(G-7582)*

Carson Manufacturing Co Inc .... F 317 257-3191
 Indianapolis *(G-7750)*

Circuits Repair LLC .... G 317 512-1026
 Shelbyville *(G-14745)*

Compal Electronics Na Inc .... E 574 992-8793
 Logansport *(G-11069)*

Competition Electronic Systems .... G 317 291-2823
 Indianapolis *(G-7844)*

CTS Elctrnic Cmponents Cal Inc .... G 574 523-3800
 Elkhart *(G-3278)*

Electronic Services LLC .... E 765 457-3894
 Kokomo *(G-10262)*

Heather Sound Amplification .... G 574 255-6100
 Mishawaka *(G-11906)*

Indiana Integrated Circuits In .... G 574 217-4612
 South Bend *(G-15077)*

Investwell Electronics Inc .... G 765 457-1911
 Kokomo *(G-10289)*

K I B Enterprises Corp .... C 574 262-0518
 Elkhart *(G-3443)*

Kendrion (mishawaka) LLC .... E 574 257-2422
 Mishawaka *(G-11922)*

Kimball Electronics Tampa Inc .... G 812 634-4000
 Jasper *(G-9870)*

KK Hall Inc .... G 317 839-8329
 Clayton *(G-2061)*

Leoni LLC .... G 574 315-0503
 Mishawaka *(G-11928)*

Mallory Sonalert Products Inc .... E 317 612-1000
 Indianapolis *(G-8822)*

Microform Inc .... G 574 522-9851
 Elkhart *(G-3536)*

Mier Products Inc .... E 765 457-0223
 Kokomo *(G-10307)*

Orion Global Sourcing Inc .... G 812 332-3338
 Bloomington *(G-939)*

R C Systems Inc .... G 812 282-4898
 Jeffersonville *(G-10044)*

Redwire Space Technologies Inc .... E 812 923-9591
 Greenville *(G-6653)*

Samtec Inc .... A 812 944-6733
 New Albany *(G-12812)*

Schumaker Technical Assembly .... G 765 742-7176
 Lafayette *(G-10687)*

Smg Global Inc .... G 765 250-0081
 Lafayette *(G-10691)*

Toppan Photomasks Inc .... C 765 854-7500
 Kokomo *(G-10350)*

Trignetra Inc .... G 765 637-8447
 West Lafayette *(G-16639)*

Wilco Corporation .... F 317 228-9320
 Indianapolis *(G-9763)*

CLAMPS & COUPLINGS: Hose

Guardian Ind Inc .... E 219 874-5248
 Michigan City *(G-11618)*

CLAMPS: Metal

Grrreat Creations .... E 574 773-5331
 Nappanee *(G-12601)*

Indiana Custom Trucks LLC .... E 260 463-3244
 Shipshewana *(G-14852)*

CLAY: Ground Or Treated

American Art Clay Co Inc .... C 317 244-6871
 Indianapolis *(G-7499)*

Enviro Group Inc .... G 317 882-9360
 Greenwood *(G-6702)*

CLEANING EQPT: Commercial

A&M Commercial Cleaning LLC .... G 765 720-3737
 Greencastle *(G-6392)*

McGuires Magic Cleaning LLC .... G 317 504-7739
 Indianapolis *(G-8866)*

Nighthawk Enterprises LLC .... E 317 576-9235
 Indianapolis *(G-9011)*

CLEANING EQPT: Floor Washing & Polishing, Commercial

Hawk Enterprises Elkhart Inc .... G 574 294-1910
 Elkhart *(G-3402)*

CLEANING EQPT: High Pressure

Aqua Blast Corp .... F 260 728-4433
 Decatur *(G-2844)*

Cox Cleaning Services .... G 260 804-9001
 Fort Wayne *(G-4880)*

Michrochem LLC .... G 812 838-1832
 Mount Vernon *(G-12309)*

CLEANING OR POLISHING PREPARATIONS, NEC

Arden Companies LLC .... D 260 747-1657
 Fort Wayne *(G-4770)*

Astec Corp .... G 317 872-7550
 Indianapolis *(G-7557)*

Blue Ribbon Products Inc .... G 317 972-7970
 Indianapolis *(G-7648)*

Brulin & Company Inc .... D 317 923-3211
 Indianapolis *(G-7691)*

Brulin Holding Company Inc .... E 317 923-3211
 Indianapolis *(G-7692)*

Danny Webb Plumbing .... G 574 936-2746
 Plymouth *(G-13769)*

F B C Inc .... E 574 848-5288
 Bristol *(G-1260)*

Gillis Company .... G 574 273-9086
 Granger *(G-6349)*

Holloway House Inc .... E 317 485-4272
 Fortville *(G-5599)*

Kleen-Rite Supply Inc .... F 812 422-7483
 Evansville *(G-4156)*

Osborn LLC .... D 414 277-9300
 Richmond *(G-14178)*

Parts Cleaning Tech LLC .... G 317 243-4205
 Indianapolis *(G-9095)*

Professionally Polished LLC .... G 219 779-7664
 Crown Point *(G-2738)*

Servaas Laboratories Inc .... E 317 636-7760
 Indianapolis *(G-9406)*

Tate Soaps & Surfactants Inc .... G 765 868-4488
 Kokomo *(G-10347)*

CLEANING OR POLISHING PREPARATIONS, NEC

W J Hagerty & Sons Ltd Inc................ E 574 288-4991
South Bend *(G-15303)*

Warsaw Chemical Company Inc........... D 574 267-3251
Warsaw *(G-16442)*

CLEANING PRDTS: Automobile Polish

A 2 Z Universal Solutions....................... G 317 496-7435
Union City *(G-15846)*

Michael Montgomery............................. G 317 478-6080
Indianapolis *(G-8898)*

CLEANING PRDTS: Degreasing Solvent

Tgc Auto Care Products Inc.................... G 765 962-7725
Richmond *(G-14216)*

CLEANING PRDTS: Disinfectants, Household Or Indl Plant

Aqua Utility Services LLC...................... G 812 284-9243
New Albany *(G-12690)*

Disaster Masters Inc............................. G 317 385-2216
Fishers *(G-4504)*

Ecolab Inc.. E 260 359-3280
Huntington *(G-7308)*

CLEANING PRDTS: Drain Pipe Solvents Or Cleaners

L&S Sanitation Service.......................... G 765 932-5410
Rushville *(G-14404)*

CLEANING PRDTS: Laundry Preparations

Aon(all or Nothing) LLC......................... G 219 405-0163
Indianapolis *(G-7524)*

First Image... G 219 791-9900
Merrillville *(G-11517)*

Sand Dcl LLC....................................... G 260 459-9565
Fort Wayne *(G-5399)*

CLEANING PRDTS: Sanitation Preparations

Smart Systems..................................... G 800 348-0823
Mishawaka *(G-11997)*

CLEANING PRDTS: Sanitation Preps, Disinfectants/Deodorants

Global Ozone Innovations LLC.............. G 574 294-5797
Elkhart *(G-3383)*

Monofoilusa LLC.................................. G 317 340-9951
Elwood *(G-3832)*

Relevo Labs LLC.................................. G 317 900-6949
Carmel *(G-1739)*

Steritech-Usa Inc.................................. G 260 745-7272
Fort Wayne *(G-5441)*

CLEANING PRDTS: Specialty

Blueprint Restoration LLC..................... G 301 730-4727
Indianapolis *(G-7650)*

Custom Bottling & Packg Inc................. E 877 401-7195
Ashley *(G-332)*

Geberts Cleaning Service...................... G 812 254-4658
Washington *(G-16480)*

Golden Ventures Inc............................. E 317 872-2705
Indianapolis *(G-8300)*

K2 Industrial Services Inc..................... F 219 933-1100
Highland *(G-7141)*

Kings-Qlity Rstrtion Svcs LLC................ F 812 944-4347
New Albany *(G-12760)*

Opportunities Inc.................................. G 574 518-0606
North Webster *(G-13311)*

Powerclean Inc..................................... E 260 483-1375
Fort Wayne *(G-5329)*

Rexford Rand Corp............................... E 219 872-5561
Michigan City *(G-11657)*

CLEANING PRDTS: Stain Removers

Mold Removers LLC............................. G 317 846-0977
Indianapolis *(G-8946)*

CLEANING SVCS: Industrial Or Commercial

Clean By Design Inc............................. G 260 414-4444
Fort Wayne *(G-4857)*

CLIPPERS: Fingernail & Toenail

Kjs Beauty Lounge LLC......................... G 317 426-0621
Indianapolis *(G-8692)*

CLOSURES: Closures, Stamped Metal

Charmaran Company LLC..................... F 260 347-3347
Kendallville *(G-10098)*

Rieke LLC.. B 260 925-3700
Auburn *(G-419)*

CLOSURES: Plastic

Kerr Group LLC.................................... C 812 424-2904
Evansville *(G-4149)*

Poly-Seal LLC...................................... D 812 306-2573
Evansville *(G-4247)*

CLOTHING & ACCESS, WOMEN, CHILDREN & INFANT, WHOL: Handbags

Cinda B USA LLC................................. G 260 469-0803
Fort Wayne *(G-4848)*

CLOTHING & ACCESS, WOMEN, CHILDREN & INFANT, WHOL: Uniforms

National Fdrtion State High SC.............. E 317 972-6900
Indianapolis *(G-8988)*

CLOTHING & ACCESS, WOMEN, CHILDREN/ INFANT, WHOL: Baby Goods

Diaper Stone Opco LLC........................ G 866 221-2145
Greenfield *(G-6489)*

CLOTHING & ACCESS: Costumes, Theatrical

Rittenhouse Square.............................. G 260 824-4200
Bluffton *(G-1051)*

CLOTHING & ACCESS: Handicapped

Nebo Ridge Enterprises LLC................. G 317 471-1089
Carmel *(G-1703)*

Unjust LLC.. G 317 443-2584
Fishers *(G-4622)*

CLOTHING & ACCESS: Men's Miscellaneous Access

Haus Love Inc...................................... G 317 601-6521
Indianapolis *(G-8370)*

Him Gentlemans Boutique..................... G 812 924-7441
New Albany *(G-12741)*

Kinney Dancewear................................ G 317 581-1800
Noblesville *(G-13121)*

Marie Collective LLC............................ G 317 683-0408
Indianapolis *(G-8832)*

Regal Inc... G 765 284-5722
Muncie *(G-12487)*

CLOTHING & APPAREL STORES: Custom

Celestial Designs LLC.......................... G 317 733-3110
Zionsville *(G-16997)*

Eliba Collections LLC........................... G 646 675-6196
Whiteland *(G-16785)*

Graphic Fx Inc..................................... E 812 234-0000
Terre Haute *(G-15601)*

Hoogies Sports House Inc.................... G 574 533-9875
Goshen *(G-6165)*

Kennyleeholmescom............................. G 574 612-2526
Elkhart *(G-3451)*

Professional Gifting Inc........................ G 800 350-1796
Indianapolis *(G-9221)*

Ram Graphics Inc................................. F 765 724-7783
Alexandria *(G-58)*

Select Embroidery/Top It Off.................. F 812 337-8049
Bloomington *(G-968)*

CLOTHING & FURNISHINGS, MEN'S & BOYS', WHOLESALE: Uniforms

National Fdrtion State High SC.............. E 317 972-6900
Indianapolis *(G-8988)*

CLOTHING & FURNISHINGS, MENS & BOYS, WHOL: Sportswear/Work

Smiling Cross Inc................................. G 812 323-9290
Bloomington *(G-976)*

CLOTHING STORES: Designer Apparel

Better Blacc Wall Streetz LLC................ F 812 927-0712
Seymour *(G-14632)*

Legacy Enterprises Inc......................... G 219 484-9483
Merrillville *(G-11531)*

CLOTHING STORES: T-Shirts, Printed, Custom

4ink Fullfillment Services...................... G 812 738-4465
Corydon *(G-2483)*

All Things Custom LLC......................... G 765 618-5332
Sweetser *(G-15453)*

Country Stitches Embroidery................. G 219 324-7625
La Porte *(G-10396)*

Paul Miller... G 765 449-4893
Lafayette *(G-10664)*

Pretty Chique LLC................................ G 317 922-5899
Indianapolis *(G-9194)*

Sportsmania Sales Inc.......................... G 317 873-5501
Zionsville *(G-17052)*

CLOTHING STORES: Uniforms & Work

Geckos.. G 765 762-0822
Attica *(G-349)*

Masbez LLC... G 855 962-7239
Frankfort *(G-5681)*

CLOTHING STORES: Unisex

Torrid LLC... F 219 769-1192
Merrillville *(G-11567)*

CLOTHING: Access, Women's & Misses'

CM Reed LLC....................................... G 517 546-4100
Greendale *(G-6444)*

Grnwman LLC....................................... G 219 359-9237
Chesterton *(G-1933)*

Hidinghilda LLC................................... G 260 760-7093
Kendallville *(G-10118)*

Rustic Fisher Creations LLC.................. G 574 279-5754
North Liberty *(G-13222)*

Zendigo Boutique LLC.......................... G 574 314-8328
South Bend *(G-15312)*

CLOTHING: Aprons, Exc Rubber/Plastic, Women, Misses, Junior

Still Safety Products LLC...................... G 855 249-0009
Evanston *(G-3855)*

PRODUCT SECTION

CLOTHING: Uniforms, Military, Men/Youth, Purchased Materials

CLOTHING: Athletic & Sportswear, Men's & Boys'

Fanatics Lids College LLC...................... E 888 814-4287
  Indianapolis *(G-8166)*
Hush Clothing 317 LLC.......................... G 317 935-2184
  Indianapolis *(G-8438)*
Sports Licensed Division....................... A 317 895-7000
  Indianapolis *(G-9481)*

CLOTHING: Athletic & Sportswear, Women's & Girls'

Best Friends Inc...................................... G 765 985-3872
  Denver *(G-2934)*
Fanatics Lids College LLC...................... E 888 814-4287
  Indianapolis *(G-8166)*
Legends Maingate LLC........................... F 317 243-2000
  Indianapolis *(G-8735)*
Maingate LLC... D
  Indianapolis *(G-8814)*
Scrubs2therescue LLC............................ G 317 748-7677
  Indianapolis *(G-9397)*
Sports Licensed Division....................... A 317 895-7000
  Indianapolis *(G-9481)*
True Royalty Boutique LLC..................... F 260 706-5121
  Fort Wayne *(G-5510)*
Truu Confidence LLC.............................. G 317 795-0042
  Indianapolis *(G-9653)*

CLOTHING: Baker, Barber, Lab/Svc Ind Apparel, Washable, Men

Browmi By Misha LLC............................ G 317 801-3911
  Indianapolis *(G-7689)*

CLOTHING: Band Uniforms

Pearison Inc... D 812 963-8890
  Cynthiana *(G-2788)*

CLOTHING: Blouses, Women's & Girls'

Anita Lorrain LLC.................................... G 574 621-0531
  South Bend *(G-14946)*
August Gill Apparel LLC......................... G 317 342-2800
  Fort Wayne *(G-4779)*
Luxe Fashion Palace LLC....................... G 317 379-1372
  Indianapolis *(G-8799)*
Working Pitbull Kennell.......................... G 708 762-9725
  East Chicago *(G-3058)*

CLOTHING: Children's, Girls'

Indiana Knitwear Corporation................. E 317 462-4413
  Greenfield *(G-6513)*
Lubber Dubbers...................................... G 812 475-1725
  Evansville *(G-4176)*

CLOTHING: Coats & Suits, Men's & Boys'

Legacy Enterprises Inc........................... G 219 484-9483
  Merrillville *(G-11531)*

CLOTHING: Costumes

Costumes By Design.............................. G 812 334-2029
  Bloomington *(G-849)*
Ghost Forge L T D.................................. G 765 362-8654
  Crawfordsville *(G-2570)*
Higgins Dyan.. G 812 876-0754
  Ellettsville *(G-3809)*
Patchwork Costumes LLC...................... G 317 750-6162
  Indianapolis *(G-9097)*
Rivars Inc... E 765 789-6119
  Indianapolis *(G-9309)*

CLOTHING: Dresses

Elysian Company LLC............................ G 574 267-2259
  Warsaw *(G-16359)*
House of Delrenee LLC.......................... G 219 670-1153
  Indianapolis *(G-8427)*
Kitwana Kouture LLC............................. G 812 589-7135
  Evansville *(G-4155)*
Kurvy Kurves Kouture LLC..................... F 812 340-6090
  Bloomington *(G-904)*
Lj Motive LLC.. F 219 588-5480
  Hobart *(G-7200)*

CLOTHING: Hats & Headwear, Knit

Mammoth Hats Inc.................................. F 812 849-2772
  Mitchell *(G-12044)*

CLOTHING: Hospital, Men's

Clinical Scrubs LLC................................ G 317 607-3991
  Indianapolis *(G-7823)*
Creative Mnds Work Pblctons LL.......... G 317 759-1002
  Indianapolis *(G-7901)*
Nitas Scrubs Zone LLC........................... G 317 204-6576
  Indianapolis *(G-9012)*

CLOTHING: Leather

Hilltop Leather.. G 317 508-3404
  Martinsville *(G-11401)*
Martin Uniforms LLC.............................. G 317 408-9186
  Indianapolis *(G-8843)*

CLOTHING: Maternity

Three Little Monkeys.............................. G 765 778-9370
  Pendleton *(G-13557)*

CLOTHING: Neckwear

Farwall Tsg LLC...................................... F 574 773-2108
  Nappanee *(G-12596)*
Impulse of Jasper Inc............................. G 812 481-2880
  Jasper *(G-9844)*
Provisa International Inc........................ G 812 207-9137
  Charlestown *(G-1892)*
Sugar and Bruno Inc............................... F 317 991-4422
  Indianapolis *(G-9520)*

CLOTHING: Outerwear, Women's & Misses' NEC

Berne Apparel Company........................ E 260 622-1500
  Ossian *(G-13419)*
Dance Sophisticates Inc........................ E 317 634-7728
  Indianapolis *(G-7948)*
Eliba Collections LLC............................ G 646 675-6196
  Whiteland *(G-16785)*
Farwall Tsg LLC...................................... F 574 773-2108
  Nappanee *(G-12596)*
Hoogies Sports House Inc..................... G 574 533-9875
  Goshen *(G-6165)*

CLOTHING: Robes & Dressing Gowns

Wells Robe Sales & Rental..................... G 317 542-9062
  Indianapolis *(G-9749)*

CLOTHING: Shirts

Abbott Industrial Sewing LLC................ G 574 383-1588
  South Bend *(G-14932)*
Eliba Collections LLC............................ G 646 675-6196
  Whiteland *(G-16785)*
Hoogies Sports House Inc..................... G 574 533-9875
  Goshen *(G-6165)*

CLOTHING: Shirts & T-Shirts, Knit

Dontstoptillyougetenough LLC.............. G 812 250-8262
  Evansville *(G-4018)*

CLOTHING: Shirts, Dress, Men's & Boys'

European Concepts LLC........................ G 888 797-9005
  Fort Wayne *(G-4966)*
Him Gentlemans Boutique..................... G 812 924-7441
  New Albany *(G-12741)*

CLOTHING: Socks

Aeromind LLC... G 800 905-2157
  Indianapolis *(G-7453)*
For Bare Feet LLC.................................. G 812 322-9317
  Martinsville *(G-11393)*
Just Standout LLC.................................. G 317 531-6956
  Indianapolis *(G-8651)*
Standout Socks...................................... G 317 531-6950
  Indianapolis *(G-9494)*
Warm Socks Inc...................................... G 309 868-3398
  Indianapolis *(G-9737)*

CLOTHING: Suits & Skirts, Women's & Misses'

Legacy Enterprises Inc........................... G 219 484-9483
  Merrillville *(G-11531)*

CLOTHING: T-Shirts & Tops, Knit

All Things Kingdom LLC........................ G 312 200-4569
  Highland *(G-7120)*
Dyer Signwerks Inc................................ G 219 322-7722
  Dyer *(G-2971)*
Professional Gifting Inc......................... F 800 350-1796
  Indianapolis *(G-9221)*

CLOTHING: Tailored Suits & Formal Jackets

Hearts Rmned Lifestyle Ctr LLC............ G 800 807-0485
  Gary *(G-5947)*
Impact Racing Inc................................... D 317 852-3067
  Indianapolis *(G-8468)*
Kevin Koch.. G 574 971-8094
  Goshen *(G-6187)*
Sugar Tree Incorporated........................ G 260 417-3362
  Fort Wayne *(G-5450)*

CLOTHING: Trousers & Slacks, Men's & Boys'

Berne Apparel Company........................ E 260 622-1500
  Ossian *(G-13419)*

CLOTHING: Uniforms & Vestments

Dance Sophisticates Inc........................ E 317 634-7728
  Indianapolis *(G-7948)*
Designs 4 U Inc...................................... G 765 793-3026
  Covington *(G-2528)*
Fall Creek Corporation........................... G 765 482-1861
  Lebanon *(G-10893)*

CLOTHING: Uniforms, Ex Athletic, Women's, Misses' & Juniors'

Classy Stitches...................................... G 317 856-3261
  Indianapolis *(G-7821)*

CLOTHING: Uniforms, Men's & Boys'

Ashley Worldwide Inc............................ G 574 259-2481
  Granger *(G-6332)*
United Seams Apparel Cnstr LLC.......... G 773 397-3831
  Hammond *(G-7026)*

CLOTHING: Uniforms, Military, Men/Youth, Purchased Materials

Raine Inc... F 765 622-7687
  Anderson *(G-182)*

CLOTHING: Uniforms, Team Athletic

Designs 4 U Inc .... G 765 793-3026
  Covington (G-2528)
Official Sports Intl Inc .... F 574 269-1404
  Warsaw (G-16403)

CLOTHING: Uniforms, Work

Twin Hill Acquisition Co Inc .... E 888 206-0699
  Jeffersonville (G-10067)

CLOTHING: Waterproof Outerwear

Mad Dasher Inc .... E 260 747-0545
  Fort Wayne (G-5198)
Nasco Industries Inc .... C 812 254-7393
  Washington (G-16494)

CLOTHING: Work Apparel, Exc Uniforms

Berne Apparel Company .... E 260 622-1500
  Ossian (G-13419)
Gohn Bros Manufacturing Co .... G 574 825-2400
  Middlebury (G-11718)

COAL & OTHER MINERALS & ORES WHOLESALERS

Covey Rise Minerals LLC .... G 812 897-2356
  Boonville (G-1086)

COAL GASIFICATION

Sg Solutions LLC .... E 812 535-6000
  West Terre Haute (G-16654)
Wabash River Energy LLC .... D 812 535-6067
  West Terre Haute (G-16656)
Wabash Valley Resources LLC .... G 929 400-5230
  West Terre Haute (G-16657)

COAL MINING SERVICES

Al Perry Enterprises Inc .... G 812 867-7727
  Evansville (G-3879)
B B Mining Inc .... G 812 845-2717
  Cynthiana (G-2785)
Black Panther Mining LLC .... G 812 745-2920
  Oaktown (G-13325)
Eagle River Coal LLC .... G 618 252-0490
  Evansville (G-4024)
English Resources Inc .... G 812 423-6716
  Evansville (G-4038)
Fretina Corporation .... F 812 547-6471
  Tell City (G-15504)
Gibson County Coal LLC .... B 812 385-1816
  Owensville (G-13467)
Hallador Energy Company .... E 812 299-2800
  Terre Haute (G-15603)
K Q Servicing LLC .... G 812 486-9244
  Loogootee (G-11140)
Lily Group Inc .... G 812 268-5459
  Sullivan (G-15412)
Mt Vernon Transfer Trml LLC .... G 812 838-5531
  Mount Vernon (G-12311)
Peabody Energy Corporation .... G 314 342-3400
  Lynnville (G-11191)
Peabody Midwest Mining LLC .... E 812 297-7661
  Lynnville (G-11192)
Rogers Group Inc .... C 812 333-6324
  Bloomington (G-959)
Stone Coal Services LLC .... G 812 455-8215
  Elberfeld (G-3119)
Sycamore Coal Inc .... G 812 491-2000
  Terre Haute (G-15720)
Triad Mining Inc .... G 812 328-2117
  Oakland City (G-13324)

Vectren LLC .... G 812 424-6411
  Evansville (G-4369)
Vectren LLC .... A 812 491-4000
  Evansville (G-4368)

COAL MINING: Bituminous & Lignite Surface

Gibson County Coal LLC .... B 812 385-1816
  Owensville (G-13467)
Peabody Midwest Mining LLC .... B 812 782-3209
  Francisco (G-5646)
Peabody Midwest Mining LLC .... G 812 254-7714
  Washington (G-16500)
Peabody Midwest Mining LLC .... E 812 297-7661
  Lynnville (G-11192)
Phoenix Natural Resources Inc .... G 636 537-0283
  Jasper (G-9903)

COAL MINING: Bituminous Coal & Lignite-Surface Mining

ANR Pipeline Company .... G 260 463-3342
  Lagrange (G-10728)
Mt Vernon Coal Transfer Co .... E 812 838-5531
  Mount Vernon (G-12310)
Peabody Bear Run Mining LLC .... C 314 342-7676
  Carlisle (G-1542)
Rogers Group Inc .... D 812 332-6341
  Bloomington (G-960)
Sandy Little Coal Company Inc .... G 812 529-8216
  Evanston (G-3854)
Sunrise Coal LLC .... G 812 299-2800
  Terre Haute (G-15718)

COAL MINING: Bituminous, Surface, NEC

Vigo Coal Operating Co Inc .... C 812 759-8446
  Evansville (G-4374)

COAL PREPARATION PLANT: Bituminous or Lignite

American Resources Corporation .... C 317 855-9926
  Fishers (G-4463)
Hickman Williams & Company .... G 219 379-5199
  La Porte (G-10419)
Mt Vernon Transfer Trml LLC .... G 812 838-5531
  Mount Vernon (G-12311)

COAL, MINERALS & ORES, WHOLESALE: Coal

Al Perry Enterprises Inc .... G 812 867-7727
  Evansville (G-3879)

COATING COMPOUNDS: Tar

Asphalt Cutbacks Inc .... F 219 398-4230
  East Chicago (G-2991)
United Coatings Mfg Co .... G 317 845-8830
  Indianapolis (G-9679)

COATING OR WRAPPING SVC: Steel Pipe

Bi-State Asphalt .... G 765 832-5000
  Clinton (G-2064)
Chemcoaters LLC .... E 219 977-1929
  Gary (G-5916)

COATING SVC: Metals, With Plastic Or Resins

Evansville Metal Products Inc .... D 812 423-5632
  Evansville (G-4054)
Henkel US Operations Corp .... C 765 284-5050
  Muncie (G-12413)
Job Shop Coatings Inc .... F 317 462-9714
  Greenfield (G-6522)

Magna-Tech Manufacturing Corporation C 765 284-5050
  Muncie (G-12445)
Saran LP C
  Indianapolis (G-9373)

COATINGS: Polyurethane

Masson Inc .... F 317 632-8021
  Indianapolis (G-8848)
Pinder Polyurethane & Plas Inc .... G 219 397-8248
  East Chicago (G-3034)

COFFEE SVCS

Suncoast Coffee Inc .... E 317 251-3198
  Indianapolis (G-9526)

COIL WINDING SVC

Q P Inc .... F 574 295-6884
  Elkhart (G-3626)

COILS & ROD: Extruded, Aluminum

Jupiter Aluminum Corporation .... C 219 932-3322
  Hammond (G-6962)

COILS & TRANSFORMERS

Andover Coils LLC .... D 765 447-1157
  Fishers (G-4464)
Coil-Tran LLC .... D 219 942-8511
  Hobart (G-7182)
Custom Magnetics Inc .... E 260 982-8508
  North Manchester (G-13231)
Hermetic Coil Co Inc .... E 812 735-2400
  Bicknell (G-734)
Kane Usa Inc .... E 800 547-5740
  Indianapolis (G-8660)
Kendrion (mishawaka) LLC .... E 574 257-2422
  Mishawaka (G-11922)
Lesea Inc .... G 574 344-8215
  South Bend (G-15124)
Midwest Coil LLC .... G 765 807-5429
  Lafayette (G-10648)
Performance Mstr Coil Proc Inc .... E 765 364-1300
  Crawfordsville (G-2603)
RB Annis Instruments Inc .... G 765 848-1621
  Greencastle (G-6428)
Southern Electric Coil LLC .... E 219 931-5500
  Hammond (G-7011)
Tempest Technical Sales Inc .... G 317 844-9236
  Carmel (G-1783)
Warsaw Coil Co Inc .... D 574 267-6041
  Warsaw (G-16443)

COILS: Electric Motors Or Generators

Southern Electric Coil LLC .... E 219 931-5500
  Hammond (G-7011)

COILS: Pipe

Alliance Steel LLC .... C 219 427-5400
  Gary (G-5889)

COLOR PIGMENTS

Kibbechem Inc .... E 574 266-1234
  Elkhart (G-3454)

COLORS: Pigments, Inorganic

Altair Nanotechnologies Inc .... A 317 333-7617
  Anderson (G-75)
Icl Specialty Products Inc .... G 219 933-1560
  Hammond (G-6951)
Lyondllbsell Advnced Plymers I .... E 574 935-5131
  Plymouth (G-13794)
Sunrise Pigment USA LLC .... G 773 449-8265
  Camby (G-1515)

PRODUCT SECTION

COMMERCIAL PRINTING & NEWSPAPER PUBLISHING

United Minerals and Prpts Inc............... G 812 838-5236
Mount Vernon *(G-12325)*

COMBINED ELEMENTARY & SECONDARY SCHOOLS, PRIVATE

Boeke Road Baptist Church Inc............ G 812 479-5342
Evansville *(G-3938)*

COMFORTERS & QUILTS, FROM MANMADE FIBER OR SILK

Joseph Fisher................................... G 765 435-7231
Waveland *(G-16535)*

COMMERCIAL & OFFICE BUILDINGS RENOVATION & REPAIR

Bc Countertops Inc........................... E 317 637-4427
Indianapolis *(G-7600)*
DC Construction Services Inc............ E 317 577-0276
Indianapolis *(G-7958)*
Reed Contracting Company................ E 765 452-2638
Kokomo *(G-10326)*

COMMERCIAL ART & GRAPHIC DESIGN SVCS

Chromasource Inc............................. C 260 420-3000
Columbia City *(G-2130)*
Classic Graphics Inc.......................... F 260 482-3487
Fort Wayne *(G-4853)*
Cs Kern Inc...................................... E 765 289-8600
Muncie *(G-12370)*
Debra Richard................................... G 812 379-4927
Columbus *(G-2281)*
Digital Design Genius......................... G 317 515-3680
Camby *(G-1509)*
Freckles Grphics Lafayette Inc............ F 765 448-4692
Lafayette *(G-10581)*
Gibson Innovations LLC..................... G 317 561-0932
Terre Haute *(G-15597)*
Grayson Graphics.............................. G 574 264-6466
Elkhart *(G-3388)*
Karemar Productions......................... G 765 766-5117
Mooreland *(G-12185)*
Kennyleeholmescom......................... G 574 612-2526
Elkhart *(G-3451)*
Marketing Services Group Inc............ B 317 381-2268
Indianapolis *(G-8838)*
Optiviz Media LLC............................. G 812 681-1711
Vincennes *(G-16141)*
Schaffsteins Truck Clean LLC............. F 812 464-2424
Evansville *(G-4298)*
Sexton Advertising LLC..................... G 812 522-4059
Seymour *(G-14688)*
Thomas E Slade Inc.......................... F 812 437-5233
Evansville *(G-4343)*
Titan Graphics LLC........................... G 317 496-2188
Mccordsville *(G-11457)*
Young & Kenady Incorporated........... G 317 852-6300
Brownsburg *(G-1415)*

COMMERCIAL ART & ILLUSTRATION SVCS

Indianapolis Signworks Inc................. E 317 872-8722
Indianapolis *(G-8508)*
Shadow Graphix Inc.......................... G 317 481-9710
Indianapolis *(G-9411)*

COMMERCIAL CONTAINERS WHOLESALERS

Crown Packaging International Inc...... D 219 738-1000
Merrillville *(G-11499)*

COMMERCIAL EQPT WHOLESALERS, NEC

North Central Equipment C................. G 574 825-2006
Middlebury *(G-11741)*
Playfair Shuffleboard Company........... F 260 747-7288
Fort Wayne *(G-5319)*
Storageworks Inc.............................. G 317 577-3511
Fishers *(G-4607)*
Thermodyne Food Svc Pdts Inc.......... E 260 428-2535
Fort Wayne *(G-5482)*
Willow Way LLC............................... G 765 886-4642
Hagerstown *(G-6848)*

COMMERCIAL EQPT, WHOLESALE: Restaurant, NEC

Indy Hoods LLC................................ F 317 731-7170
Indianapolis *(G-8529)*
MD Holdings LLC.............................. G 317 831-7030
Mooresville *(G-12220)*
US Water Systems Inc...................... E 317 209-0889
Indianapolis *(G-9688)*

COMMERCIAL EQPT, WHOLESALE: Scales, Exc Laboratory

Indiana Scale Company Inc................ F 812 232-0893
Terre Haute *(G-15617)*
Technical Weighing Svcs Inc.............. E 219 924-3366
Griffith *(G-6819)*

COMMERCIAL EQPT, WHOLESALE: Store Fixtures & Display Eqpt

Markley Enterprise Inc....................... D 574 295-4195
Elkhart *(G-3513)*
Wood Technologies LLC..................... E 260 627-8858
Grabill *(G-6326)*

COMMERCIAL EQPT, WHOLESALE: Vending Machines, Coin-Operated

Small World Enterprises LLC.............. G 312 550-1717
Lake Station *(G-10776)*
Unlimited Vending LLC...................... G 765 288-5952
Muncie *(G-12510)*
Whatzthat Vending LLC..................... G 317 362-9088
Indianapolis *(G-9755)*

COMMERCIAL PRINTING & NEWSPAPER PUBLISHING

411 Newspaper................................. G 219 922-8846
Munster *(G-12524)*
Aim Media Indiana Oper LLC............. G 812 358-2111
Brownstown *(G-1416)*
Aim Media Indiana Oper LLC............. D 812 372-7811
Columbus *(G-2215)*
Aim Media Indiana Oper LLC............. G 812 736-7101
Franklin *(G-5705)*
Aim Media Indiana Oper LLC............. G 317 462-5528
Greenfield *(G-6459)*
Aim Media Indiana Oper LLC............. E 317 462-5528
Greenfield *(G-6460)*
Aim Media Indiana Oper LLC............. G 812 988-2221
Nashville *(G-12659)*
Aim Media Indiana Oper LLC............. G 765 778-2324
Pendleton *(G-13524)*
Aim Media Indiana Oper LLC............. F 812 522-4871
Seymour *(G-14626)*
Aim Media Indiana Oper LLC............. D 812 372-7811
Columbus *(G-2216)*
All Printing and Publications............... G 260 636-2727
Albion *(G-17)*

Citiview Publications LLC................... G 502 296-1623
Floyds Knobs *(G-4672)*
Ckmt Associates Inc.......................... F 219 924-2820
Hammond *(G-6902)*
Cnhi LLC.. G 574 936-3101
Plymouth *(G-13763)*
Colormax Digital Imaging Inc............. F 812 477-3805
Evansville *(G-3975)*
Delphos Herald of Indiana Inc............ E 812 537-0063
Lawrenceburg *(G-10833)*
Elwood Publishing Company Inc......... E 765 552-3355
Elwood *(G-3823)*
George P Stewart Printing Co............ E 317 924-5143
Indianapolis *(G-8278)*
Graphic Printing Co Inc..................... E 260 726-8141
Portland *(G-13947)*
Herald Argus.................................... G 219 362-2161
Michigan City *(G-11623)*
Indiana Newspapers LLC................... D 317 444-3800
Indianapolis *(G-8486)*
Indiana Newspapers LLC................... A 317 444-4000
Indianapolis *(G-8487)*
Kankakee Valley Publishing Co.......... G 219 866-5111
Rensselaer *(G-14056)*
Kpc Media Group Inc......................... C 260 347-0400
Kendallville *(G-10130)*
La Grange Publishing Co Inc.............. F 260 463-3243
Lagrange *(G-10747)*
Life Path Numerology Center............. G 317 638-9752
Indianapolis *(G-8747)*
Manchester North News Journal........ G 260 982-6383
North Manchester *(G-13238)*
Paper of Montgomery County............. G 765 361-8888
Crawfordsville *(G-2600)*
Paper of Wabash County Inc.............. F 260 563-8326
Wabash *(G-16208)*
Paxton Media Group LLC................... G 765 664-5111
Marion *(G-11324)*
Pierce Oil Co Inc............................... F 812 268-6356
Sullivan *(G-15416)*
Princeton Publishing Inc..................... G 812 385-2525
Princeton *(G-14010)*
Purdue Student Pubg Foundation........ D 765 743-1111
West Lafayette *(G-16622)*
R R Donnelley Inc............................. F 317 614-2508
Indianapolis *(G-9256)*
RE Wilson LLC................................. G 317 730-4846
Zionsville *(G-17045)*
Republic Inc...................................... E 812 342-8028
Columbus *(G-2386)*
Russ Publishing................................. F 812 847-4487
Linton *(G-11045)*
Schurz Communications Inc............... E 574 235-6496
South Bend *(G-15235)*
Shelbyville Newspapers Inc................ E 317 398-6631
Shelbyville *(G-14798)*
South Bend Tribune Corp................... B 574 235-6161
South Bend *(G-15257)*
Southsider.. G 317 781-0023
Indianapolis *(G-9465)*
Spencer Evening World...................... D 812 829-2255
Spencer *(G-15362)*
Teragraphics Ink LLC......................... G 765 430-2863
West Lafayette *(G-16636)*
That Print Lady LLC........................... G 317 339-7411
Indianapolis *(G-9587)*
Tipton Tribune.................................. G 765 675-2115
Tipton *(G-15794)*
Triple Crown Media LLC..................... G 574 533-2151
Goshen *(G-6273)*
Wabash Plain Dealer Co LLC.............. E 260 563-2131
Wabash *(G-16221)*

Employee Codes: A=Over 500 employees, B=251-500
C=101-250, D=51-100, E=20-50, F=10-19, G=1-9

COMMON SAND MINING

Country Stone................................F 260 837-7134
Waterloo *(G-16518)*

Harrison Sand and Gravel Co................G 812 663-2021
Greensburg *(G-6600)*

Shelby Gravel Inc................................E 317 398-4485
Shelbyville *(G-14797)*

Southfield Corporation........................E 317 846-6060
Carmel *(G-1767)*

COMMUNICATIONS EQPT WHOLESALERS

Emergency Radio Service LLC..............G 800 377-2929
Ligonier *(G-11011)*

Emergency Radio Service LLC..............E 206 894-4145
Ligonier *(G-11012)*

Lionfish Cyber Hldngs LLC-S Ln...........G 877 732-6772
Indianapolis *(G-8766)*

Sneaky Micro Video Divisio.................G 317 925-1496
Indianapolis *(G-9454)*

COMMUNICATIONS EQPT: Microwave

Commtineo LLC....................................F 219 476-3667
Wanatah *(G-16288)*

COMMUNICATIONS SVCS

Trilithic Inc...C 317 895-3600
Indianapolis *(G-9641)*

COMMUNICATIONS SVCS: Data

American Eagle Security Inc.................G 219 980-1177
Merrillville *(G-11482)*

Loud Clear Communications LLC..........G 260 433-9479
Auburn *(G-403)*

COMMUNICATIONS SVCS: Internet Connectivity Svcs

Indy Web Inc.......................................G 317 536-1201
Indianapolis *(G-8537)*

COMMUNICATIONS SVCS: Internet Host Svcs

Sky Cryptoassets LLC..........................G 949 903-6896
Carmel *(G-1763)*

COMMUNICATIONS SVCS: Online Svc Providers

Flight1 Aviation Tech Inc......................G 404 504-7010
Wabash *(G-16186)*

Hoosier Times Inc................................C 812 331-4270
Bloomington *(G-882)*

Scanpower LLC....................................G 765 277-2308
Richmond *(G-14201)*

Slingshot Media LLC............................G 765 778-6848
Pendleton *(G-13555)*

COMMUNICATIONS SVCS: Proprietary Online Svcs Networks

Telamon Corporation...........................C 317 818-6888
Carmel *(G-1777)*

Telamon Spv LLC.................................G 800 788-6680
Carmel *(G-1780)*

COMMUNICATIONS SVCS: Signal Enhancement Network Svcs

Slingshot Media LLC............................G 765 778-6848
Pendleton *(G-13555)*

COMMUNICATIONS SVCS: Telephone, Voice

Plum Group Inc....................................F 617 712-3000
Indianapolis *(G-9155)*

COMPACT LASER DISCS: Prerecorded

Sony Dadc US Inc.................................A 812 462-8100
Terre Haute *(G-15706)*

COMPOSITION STONE: Plastic

Tekmodo LLC.......................................F 574 970-5800
Elkhart *(G-3720)*

Tekmodo Structures LLC......................G 574 970-5800
Elkhart *(G-3722)*

COMPOST

Creative Ldscp & Compost Co..............G 317 776-2909
Noblesville *(G-13065)*

Earth Mama Compost..........................G 317 759-4589
Indianapolis *(G-8033)*

Elvin L Nuest Sales and Servic.............G 219 863-5216
Francesville *(G-5639)*

Farmer Automatic America Inc............G 574 857-3116
Rochester *(G-14289)*

Greencycle Inc.....................................G 317 773-3350
Noblesville *(G-13089)*

COMPRESSORS: Air & Gas

ABB Flexible Automation Inc................G 317 876-9090
Indianapolis *(G-7414)*

Abro Industries Inc..............................E 574 232-8289
South Bend *(G-14933)*

Atlas Copco Compressors....................G 574 264-1033
Elkhart *(G-3199)*

Bkb Manufacturing Inc........................G 260 982-8524
North Manchester *(G-13229)*

Boss Industries LLC............................E 219 324-7776
La Porte *(G-10390)*

Brama Inc..F 317 786-7770
Indianapolis *(G-7671)*

Cohesant Technologies Inc...................G 317 871-7611
Indianapolis *(G-7833)*

Cook Compression LLC........................G 502 515-6900
Jeffersonville *(G-9960)*

Custom Compressor Svcs Corp.............G 219 879-4966
Michigan City *(G-11592)*

Midwest Finishing Systems Inc............E 574 257-0099
Mishawaka *(G-11949)*

Precisionair LLC..................................G 219 380-9267
La Porte *(G-10464)*

Roots Blowers LLC..............................D 765 827-9200
Connersville *(G-2465)*

Sullair Corporation..............................G 219 861-5005
Michigan City *(G-11674)*

Systems Engineering and Sls Co..........G 260 422-1671
Fort Wayne *(G-5466)*

COMPRESSORS: Air & Gas, Including Vacuum Pumps

Air Fixtures Inc....................................F 260 982-2169
North Manchester *(G-13228)*

Hitachi Global Air Pwr US LLC.............G 219 861-5207
Michigan City *(G-11625)*

Hitachi Global Air Pwr US LLC.............C 219 879-5451
Michigan City *(G-11626)*

K Grimmer Industries Inc.....................C 317 736-3800
Leo *(G-10968)*

Kobelco Cmpsr Mfg Ind Inc..................D 574 295-3145
Elkhart *(G-3459)*

Sullivan-Palatek Inc............................C 219 874-2497
Michigan City *(G-11675)*

Vanair Manufacturing Inc.....................C 219 879-5100
Michigan City *(G-11684)*

COMPRESSORS: Refrigeration & Air Conditioning Eqpt

Griffen Plmbng-Heating-Cooling...........E 574 295-2440
Elkhart *(G-3392)*

COMPUTER & COMPUTER SOFTWARE STORES

3btech Inc...E 574 233-0508
South Bend *(G-14927)*

Blue Byte Tech Solutions LLC...............G 574 903-5637
Elkhart *(G-3227)*

Country Club Computer.......................G 317 271-4000
Indianapolis *(G-7889)*

Coy & Associates.................................G 317 787-5089
Indianapolis *(G-7893)*

The Office Shop Inc.............................E 812 934-5611
Batesville *(G-607)*

COMPUTER & COMPUTER SOFTWARE STORES: Software & Access

Riddell Technologies LLC.....................G 219 213-9602
Crown Point *(G-2745)*

COMPUTER & COMPUTER SOFTWARE STORES: Software, Bus/Non-Game

Cbf Forensics LLC...............................G 708 383-8320
Hobart *(G-7180)*

Intelligent Software Inc.......................G 219 923-6166
Munster *(G-12543)*

Money Tree Software Ltd....................E 541 754-3701
Muncie *(G-12458)*

COMPUTER & COMPUTER SOFTWARE STORES: Software, Computer Game

Tokumei LLC.......................................G 765 772-0073
West Lafayette *(G-16638)*

COMPUTER & DATA PROCESSING EQPT REPAIR & MAINTENANCE

C & P Distributing LLC........................F 574 256-1138
Mishawaka *(G-11857)*

COMPUTER & OFFICE MACHINE MAINTENANCE & REPAIR

Compumark Industries Inc...................G 219 365-0508
Saint John *(G-14448)*

Lasertech Inc......................................G 812 277-1321
Bedford *(G-656)*

Riddell Technologies LLC.....................G 219 213-9602
Crown Point *(G-2745)*

Rob Nolley Inc.....................................F 317 825-5211
Shelbyville *(G-14792)*

Simplex Computer Services..................G 260 570-7062
Auburn *(G-423)*

COMPUTER CODE AUTHORS

Wildebeest LLC...................................G 812 391-5631
Fort Wayne *(G-5568)*

COMPUTER FACILITIES MANAGEMENT SVCS

Computer Solutions Systems Inc..........F 812 235-9008
Terre Haute *(G-15566)*

Rob Nolley Inc.....................................F 317 825-5211
Shelbyville *(G-14792)*

COMPUTER FORMS

Iu East Business Office .... E 765 973-8218
  Richmond *(G-14141)*

COMPUTER GRAPHICS SVCS

Big Picture Data Imaging LLC .... G 812 235-0202
  Terre Haute *(G-15553)*
Blasted Works .... G 574 583-3211
  Monticello *(G-12138)*
Blue Byte Tech Solutions LLC .... G 574 903-5637
  Elkhart *(G-3227)*
Cooperative Ventures Ind Corp .... G 317 564-4695
  Carmel *(G-1596)*
Long Tail Corporation .... G 260 918-0489
  Fort Wayne *(G-5191)*

COMPUTER PERIPHERAL EQPT REPAIR & MAINTENANCE

Diverse Tech Services Inc .... E 317 432-6444
  Indianapolis *(G-7982)*

COMPUTER PERIPHERAL EQPT, NEC

Axon Network Services LLC .... G 317 818-9000
  Indianapolis *(G-7580)*
Carson Manufacturing Co Inc .... F 317 257-3191
  Indianapolis *(G-7750)*
Clovis LLC .... G 812 944-4791
  Floyds Knobs *(G-4674)*
Dbisp LLC .... G 317 222-1671
  Indianapolis *(G-7957)*
Environmental Technology Inc .... E 574 233-1202
  South Bend *(G-15016)*
Federal Provider LLC .... G 317 710-3997
  Indianapolis *(G-8170)*
Impact Cnc LLC .... D 260 244-5511
  Columbia City *(G-2154)*
Paradise Ink Inc .... G 812 402-4465
  Evansville *(G-4233)*
Scott Billman .... G 317 293-9921
  Indianapolis *(G-9394)*
Sony Dadc US Inc .... A 812 462-8100
  Terre Haute *(G-15706)*
Whyte Haus .... G 260 484-5666
  Fort Wayne *(G-5567)*
Xerox Corp .... F 765 494-6511
  Lafayette *(G-10720)*

COMPUTER PERIPHERAL EQPT, WHOLESALE

Osc Holdings LLC .... G 765 751-7000
  Muncie *(G-12470)*

COMPUTER PERIPHERAL EQPT: Input Or Output

Accups LLC .... G 765 586-5021
  West Lafayette *(G-16555)*

COMPUTER PROGRAMMING SVCS: Custom

Cyberia Ltd .... G 317 721-2582
  Indianapolis *(G-7938)*
Edutronics .... G 765 529-6751
  New Castle *(G-12859)*
Tempus Nova LLC .... F 877 379-7376
  Indianapolis *(G-9576)*

COMPUTER RELATED MAINTENANCE SVCS

Sim2k Inc .... E 317 251-7920
  Indianapolis *(G-9440)*

COMPUTER SOFTWARE DEVELOPMENT

39 Degrees North LLC .... F 855 447-3939
  Bloomington *(G-765)*
Advanced Designs Corp .... F 812 333-1922
  Bloomington *(G-773)*
App Press LLC .... G 317 661-4759
  Indianapolis *(G-7528)*
Benjamin Carrier .... G 337 366-2603
  Jeffersonville *(G-9940)*
Concrete Monkey Studios LLC .... G 812 630-2339
  Evansville *(G-3978)*
Custom Software Solutions Inc .... G 260 637-8393
  Fort Wayne *(G-4900)*
Eric Isaacson .... G 812 339-1811
  Bloomington *(G-862)*
Ilab LLC .... D 317 218-3258
  Indianapolis *(G-8459)*
Ler Techforce LLC .... C 812 373-0870
  Columbus *(G-2340)*
Lord Fms Games LLC .... G 317 710-2253
  Indianapolis *(G-8783)*
Mirage Computers Inc .... G 260 665-5072
  Angola *(G-276)*
Policystat LLC .... D 317 644-1296
  Carmel *(G-1720)*
Regional Data Services Inc .... F 219 661-3200
  Crown Point *(G-2744)*
Riddell Technologies LLC .... G 219 213-9602
  Crown Point *(G-2745)*
Sahasra Technologies Corp .... E 317 845-5326
  Carmel *(G-1751)*
SGS Cybermetrix Inc .... G 800 713-1203
  Columbus *(G-2391)*
Sharpen Technologies Inc .... E 855 249-3357
  Indianapolis *(G-9413)*
Sk Marktng Strtgies LLC DBA A .... G 812 962-0900
  Evansville *(G-4317)*
Technalysis Inc .... G 317 291-1985
  Indianapolis *(G-9568)*
Tysoft LLC .... G 765 405-0098
  Yorktown *(G-16984)*

COMPUTER SOFTWARE DEVELOPMENT & APPLICATIONS

Conversightai .... F 201 294-1896
  Indianapolis *(G-7865)*
Dry Heat Coffee LLC .... G 760 422-9865
  Indianapolis *(G-8013)*
Flat Electronics LLC .... G 765 414-6635
  Fishers *(G-4524)*
Leaning Palms LLC .... G 630 886-8924
  Crown Point *(G-2715)*
Life Less Ordinary LLC .... G 317 727-4277
  Indianapolis *(G-8746)*
Money Tree Software Ltd .... E 541 754-3701
  Muncie *(G-12458)*
On Call McGraw LLC .... G 317 938-8777
  Indianapolis *(G-9051)*
Paragon Medical Inc .... C 574 594-2140
  Pierceton *(G-13638)*
Peter Stone Company .... G 260 768-9150
  Shipshewana *(G-14879)*
Pillar Innovations LLC .... G 812 474-9080
  Evansville *(G-4244)*
Previnex LLC .... G 877 212-0310
  Carmel *(G-1729)*
Procard Inc .... D 303 279-2255
  Jeffersonville *(G-10042)*

COMPUTER SOFTWARE SYSTEMS ANALYSIS & DESIGN: Custom

Agora Brands Group Inc .... E 615 802-0086
  Borden *(G-1104)*
Aunalytics Inc .... D 574 307-9230
  South Bend *(G-14951)*
Baugh Enterprises Inc .... F 812 334-8189
  Bloomington *(G-796)*
Center For The Study Knwldge D .... G 812 361-4424
  Bloomington *(G-827)*
Diverse Tech Services Inc .... E 317 432-6444
  Indianapolis *(G-7982)*
Flynn Media LLC .... G 317 536-2972
  Indianapolis *(G-8210)*
Goldenmarc LLC .... G 317 855-1651
  Indianapolis *(G-8301)*
Image Vault LLC .... G 812 948-8400
  New Albany *(G-12743)*
Infinite Ai Inc .... G 317 965-4850
  Carmel *(G-1669)*
Perspicacity LLC .... G 812 650-2080
  Bloomington *(G-946)*
Simplex Computer Services .... G 260 570-7062
  Auburn *(G-423)*
Tipton Engrg Elc Mtr Svcs Inc .... G 765 963-3380
  Sharpsville *(G-14714)*
W T Boone Enterprises Inc .... G 317 738-0275
  Franklin *(G-5784)*
Web Software LLC .... F 765 452-3936
  Kokomo *(G-10356)*

COMPUTER STORAGE DEVICES, NEC

Emc2 .... G 317 435-8021
  Indianapolis *(G-8102)*
Integrity Qntum Innvations LLC .... G 765 537-9037
  Martinsville *(G-11407)*
Quantum 7 Group LLC .... G 812 824-9378
  Bloomington *(G-950)*
Quantumtech LLC .... G 786 512-0827
  Indianapolis *(G-9248)*
RB Annis Instruments Inc .... G 765 848-1621
  Greencastle *(G-6428)*
Scale Computing Inc .... E 317 856-9959
  Indianapolis *(G-9385)*
Sony Dadc US Inc .... A 812 462-8100
  Terre Haute *(G-15706)*
Techknowledgey Inc .... G 574 202-0362
  Goshen *(G-6268)*
Techknowledgey Inc .... G 574 971-4267
  Goshen *(G-6269)*

COMPUTER SYSTEMS ANALYSIS & DESIGN

Compumark Industries Inc .... G 219 365-0508
  Saint John *(G-14448)*
Diverse Tech Services Inc .... E 317 432-6444
  Indianapolis *(G-7982)*
Edutronics .... G 765 529-6751
  New Castle *(G-12859)*
Mirage Computers Inc .... G 260 665-5072
  Angola *(G-276)*

COMPUTER TERMINALS

CIS Holdings Inc .... G 703 996-0500
  Indianapolis *(G-7810)*
Kristopher Cox .... G 502 930-9162
  Scottsburg *(G-14569)*

COMPUTERS, NEC

3btech Inc .... E 574 233-0508
  South Bend *(G-14927)*

COMPUTERS, NEC

Acdc Control LLC	G	219 801-3900
East Chicago *(G-2988)*		
Apple III LLC	G	317 691-2869
Carmel *(G-1561)*		
Apple Terrace LLC	G	260 347-9400
Kendallville *(G-10089)*		
Apple-Ly Ever After Inc	G	219 838-9397
Highland *(G-7122)*		
Bromire Technology	G	317 294-9083
Greenfield *(G-6473)*		
Computer Solutions Systems Inc	F	812 235-9008
Terre Haute *(G-15566)*		
Country Club Computer	G	317 271-4000
Indianapolis *(G-7889)*		
David Askew	G	574 273-0184
Granger *(G-6344)*		
Dcs Car Audio	G	812 437-8488
Evansville *(G-4009)*		
Dec Co Ecumenical Agape Center	G	812 222-0392
Greensburg *(G-6590)*		
Emmanuel Michael	G	806 559-5673
Greenwood *(G-6694)*		
Futuretek	G	317 631-0098
Indianapolis *(G-8246)*		
General Dynmics Mssion Systems	F	260 434-9500
Fort Wayne *(G-5020)*		
Green Apple Active LLC	G	910 585-1151
Westfield *(G-16693)*		
Jacyl Technology Inc	G	260 471-6067
Fort Wayne *(G-5128)*		
Keys Computers Inc	F	317 750-5071
Indianapolis *(G-8678)*		
Kimball Electronics Inc	A	812 634-4200
Jasper *(G-9865)*		
L5 Solutions LLC	G	317 436-1044
Indianapolis *(G-8706)*		
Milani Custom Homes LLC	G	219 455-5804
Merrillville *(G-11538)*		
Mvctc	G	765 969-8921
Richmond *(G-14173)*		
Omnicell Co	G	812 376-0747
Columbus *(G-2365)*		
P F Apple LLC	G	317 773-8683
Noblesville *(G-13149)*		
Premium Corporation	E	219 258-0141
South Bend *(G-15203)*		
Q-Edge Corporation	E	317 203-6800
Plainfield *(G-13718)*		

COMPUTERS, NEC, WHOLESALE

C & P Distributing LLC	F	574 256-1138
Mishawaka *(G-11857)*		
Mirage Computers Inc	G	260 665-5072
Angola *(G-276)*		

COMPUTERS, PERIPHERALS & SOFTWARE, WHOLESALE: Mainframe

Maddenco Inc	F	812 474-6245
Evansville *(G-4184)*		

COMPUTERS, PERIPHERALS & SOFTWARE, WHOLESALE: Software

Ilab LLC	D	317 218-3258
Indianapolis *(G-8459)*		
Money Tree Software Ltd	E	541 754-3701
Muncie *(G-12458)*		
Tclogic LLC	G	317 464-5152
Indianapolis *(G-9562)*		

COMPUTERS: Personal

Apple--day Cstm Hndcrfted Pdts	G	219 841-6602
Valparaiso *(G-15901)*		
Cybernaut Industria LLC	G	317 664-5316
Indianapolis *(G-7939)*		
HP Inc	G	317 566-6200
Carmel *(G-1662)*		
HP Inc	F	317 334-3400
Plainfield *(G-13687)*		
Indy Web Inc	G	317 536-1201
Indianapolis *(G-8537)*		

CONCRETE BUILDING PRDTS WHOLESALERS

CMa Supply Co Fort Wayne Inc	E	260 471-9000
Fort Wayne *(G-4862)*		
Irving Materials Inc	G	812 254-0820
Washington *(G-16486)*		
Kuert Concrete Inc	F	574 293-0430
Goshen *(G-6193)*		
Kuert Concrete Inc	E	574 232-9911
South Bend *(G-15109)*		
Minnick Services Corp	E	260 432-5031
Fort Wayne *(G-5231)*		
Monumental Stone Works Inc	F	765 866-6658
New Market *(G-12927)*		

CONCRETE PLANTS

Korte Bros Inc	F	260 497-0500
Fort Wayne *(G-5157)*		

CONCRETE PRDTS

AK Industries Inc	D	574 936-6022
Plymouth *(G-13752)*		
Beaver Gravel Corporation	D	317 773-0679
Noblesville *(G-13042)*		
Beazer East Inc	G	260 490-9006
Fort Wayne *(G-4791)*		
Carters LLC	F	260 432-3568
Fort Wayne *(G-4835)*		
Cash Concrete Products Inc	F	765 653-4007
Greencastle *(G-6395)*		
Cast Stone	G	317 617-1088
Indianapolis *(G-7756)*		
Cheetah Building Products	G	812 466-1234
Terre Haute *(G-15562)*		
Combi Institiute Inc	G	602 269-2288
Carmel *(G-1592)*		
Concrete Supply LLC	E	812 474-6715
Evansville *(G-3979)*		
Erie-Haven Inc	D	260 478-1674
Fort Wayne *(G-4959)*		
Forterra Concrete Inds Inc	E	859 254-4242
Whitestown *(G-16806)*		
Hi-Tech Concrete Inc	G	765 477-5550
Lafayette *(G-10597)*		
Hog Slat Incorporated	D	765 828-0828
Universal *(G-15875)*		
Holcim (us) Inc	G	219 378-1193
East Chicago *(G-3017)*		
Hydro Conduit of Texas LP	G	317 769-2261
Whitestown *(G-16809)*		
Jones & Sons Inc	E	812 882-2957
Vincennes *(G-16135)*		
Legacy Vulcan LLC	G	219 987-3040
Demotte *(G-2922)*		
Legacy Vulcan LLC	G	219 462-5832
Valparaiso *(G-15995)*		
Midwest Tile and Concrete Pdts	G	260 749-5173
Woodburn *(G-16952)*		
Mjs Concrete	G	260 341-5640
Woodburn *(G-16954)*		
Northfield Block Company	G	800 424-0190
Indianapolis *(G-9023)*		
Plaster Shak	G	317 881-6518
Greenwood *(G-6752)*		
Precast Specialties Inc	F	260 623-6131
Monroeville *(G-12072)*		
Quikrete Companies LLC	E	317 241-8237
Indianapolis *(G-9251)*		
Rogers Group Inc	G	765 342-6898
Martinsville *(G-11424)*		
Sion Inc	E	765 884-1792
Fowler *(G-5633)*		
Spider Tie	G	574 596-3073
Syracuse *(G-15479)*		
St Regis Culvert Inc	F	317 353-8065
Indianapolis *(G-9487)*		
Vernon L Goedecke Company Inc	G	812 421-9633
Evansville *(G-4372)*		
White Cap LP	E	260 471-7619
Fort Wayne *(G-5565)*		

CONCRETE PRDTS, PRECAST, NEC

Beaver Products Inc	F	317 773-0679
Noblesville *(G-13043)*		
Brickworks Supply Center LLC	E	317 786-9208
Carmel *(G-1573)*		
Concrete Lady Inc	E	812 256-2765
Otisco *(G-13447)*		
Coreslab Strctres Indnplis Inc	D	317 353-2118
Indianapolis *(G-7875)*		
Dyer Vault Company Inc	E	219 865-2521
Dyer *(G-2972)*		
Eavk Legacy Inc	E	812 246-4461
New Albany *(G-12723)*		
Hessit Works Inc	G	812 829-6246
Freedom *(G-5801)*		
Horn Pre-Cast Inc	F	812 372-4458
Columbus *(G-2320)*		
Howard & Sons Cement Pdts Inc	G	574 293-1906
Elkhart *(G-3412)*		
Jjs Concrete Construction LLC	E	812 636-0173
Montgomery *(G-12103)*		
Jones & Sons Inc	E	812 299-2287
Terre Haute *(G-15622)*		
Lowell Concrete Products Inc	E	219 696-3339
Lowell *(G-11169)*		
McCreary Concrete Products Inc	E	765 932-3058
Tipton *(G-15784)*		
Pavers Inc	G	317 271-0823
Indianapolis *(G-9104)*		
Reams Concrete	G	812 752-3746
Scottsburg *(G-14575)*		
S & M Precast Inc	D	812 246-6258
Henryville *(G-7115)*		
S & S Precast Inc	E	574 946-4123
Winamac *(G-16874)*		
S S M Inc	G	317 357-4552
Indianapolis *(G-9356)*		
Trenwa Inc	F	812 427-2217
Florence *(G-4667)*		

CONCRETE: Asphaltic, Not From Refineries

Concrete & Asphalt Recycl Inc	G	574 237-1928
Mishawaka *(G-11864)*		

CONCRETE: Ready-Mixed

A & T Concrete Supply Inc	E	812 753-4252
Fort Branch *(G-4701)*		
All-Rite Ready Mix Inc	F	812 926-0920
Aurora *(G-437)*		
Armstrongs	G	219 977-8368
Gary *(G-5896)*		

PRODUCT SECTION

CONCRETE: Ready-Mixed

Atkins Quarry... G 972 653-5550
   Jeffersonville *(G-9936)*

Attica Ready Mixed Concrete................... F 765 762-2424
   Attica *(G-343)*

Beaver Gravel Corporation....................... D 317 773-0679
   Noblesville *(G-13042)*

Brim Concrete Inc...................................... G 765 564-4975
   Delphi *(G-2891)*

Builders Concrete & Supply Co Inc........ C 317 570-6201
   Fishers *(G-4478)*

Busters Cement Products Inc................... G 765 529-0287
   New Castle *(G-12854)*

Cash Concrete Products Inc..................... G 765 653-4887
   Greencastle *(G-6394)*

Cash Concrete Products Inc..................... F 765 653-4007
   Greencastle *(G-6395)*

Cemex... F 317 351-9912
   Indianapolis *(G-7766)*

Cemex Materials LLC................................ C 317 891-7500
   Greenfield *(G-6477)*

Cemex Materials LLC................................ C 317 891-3015
   Indianapolis *(G-7767)*

Cemex Materials LLC................................ D 317 769-5801
   Whitestown *(G-16803)*

Center Concrete Inc.................................. G 800 453-4224
   Butler *(G-1460)*

Central Concrete Supply LLC.................. F 812 481-2331
   Jasper *(G-9828)*

Century Concrete Inc................................ G 765 739-6210
   Bainbridge *(G-560)*

Concrete Supply LLC................................ E 812 474-6715
   Evansville *(G-3979)*

County Materials Corp.............................. G 317 769-5503
   Whitestown *(G-16804)*

Crawford County Concrete...................... G 812 739-2707
   Leavenworth *(G-10869)*

Elkhart County Gravel Inc....................... G 574 825-7913
   Middlebury *(G-11714)*

Environ Corporation................................. G 317 774-0541
   Carmel *(G-1625)*

Erie Haven Inc... G 260 665-2052
   Angola *(G-249)*

Erie-Haven Inc... G 260 478-1674
   Auburn *(G-389)*

Erie-Haven Inc... F 260 353-1133
   Bluffton *(G-1036)*

Erie-Haven Inc... G 260 483-3865
   Fort Wayne *(G-4958)*

Erie-Haven Inc... D 260 478-1674
   Fort Wayne *(G-4959)*

Ernst Enterprises Inc................................ G 260 726-8282
   Portland *(G-13938)*

Ernst Enterprises Inc................................ G 812 284-5205
   Sellersburg *(G-14592)*

Ernst Enterprises Inc................................ G 765 584-5700
   Winchester *(G-16886)*

Gra-Rock Redi Mix Precast LLC............ F 765 395-7275
   Amboy *(G-67)*

Hanson Aggregates Wrp Inc................... E 502 244-7550
   Sellersburg *(G-14596)*

Harrison Concrete..................................... G 812 275-6682
   Bedford *(G-640)*

Heidelberg Mtls Mdwest Agg Inc........... G 260 747-3105
   Fort Wayne *(G-5061)*

Heidelberg Mtls Mdwest Agg Inc........... F 765 653-1956
   Greencastle *(G-6411)*

Heidelberg Mtls Mdwest Agg Inc........... G 812 689-5017
   Versailles *(G-16100)*

Heidelberg Mtls Sthwest Agg LL............. G 260 665-2626
   Angola *(G-257)*

Heidelberg Mtls Sthwest Agg LL............. G 260 747-5011
   Fort Wayne *(G-5062)*

Heidelberg Mtls Sthwest Agg LL............. G 812 246-4481
   Sellersburg *(G-14598)*

Heidelberg Mtls US Cem LLC................. B 812 849-2191
   Mitchell *(G-12040)*

Heidelberg Mtls US Cem LLC................. E 812 246-5472
   Sellersburg *(G-14599)*

Hilltop Basic Resources Inc.................... G 812 594-2293
   Patriot *(G-13510)*

Holcim - Mwr Inc....................................... G 260 665-2052
   Angola *(G-260)*

Holcim (us) Inc... G 219 378-1193
   East Chicago *(G-3017)*

Hollingshead Mixer Company LLC........ D 260 897-4397
   Avilla *(G-477)*

Holzer Ready Mix LLC............................. F 317 306-9327
   Indianapolis *(G-8403)*

Hoosier Ready Mix LLC........................... F 812 254-7625
   Washington *(G-16484)*

Hopkins Gravel Sand & Concrete........... G 317 831-2704
   Mooresville *(G-12211)*

I MI Erie Stone.. G 765 728-5335
   Montpelier *(G-12178)*

Im Indiana Holdings Inc.......................... G 260 478-1674
   Fort Wayne *(G-5093)*

IMI Bloomfield... G 812 384-0045
   Bloomfield *(G-749)*

IMI Riving Materials Inc......................... G 812 753-4201
   Fort Branch *(G-4704)*

IMI South LLC.. G 812 284-9732
   Clarksville *(G-2019)*

IMI South LLC.. G 812 738-4173
   Corydon *(G-2500)*

IMI South LLC.. G 812 273-1428
   Madison *(G-11229)*

IMI South LLC.. E 812 945-6605
   New Albany *(G-12744)*

IMI Southwest Inc.................................... E 812 424-3554
   Evansville *(G-4118)*

Indiana Im Holdings Inc......................... E 260 637-3101
   Fort Wayne *(G-5101)*

Interstate Block Corporation.................. G 812 273-1742
   Madison *(G-11230)*

Irving Materials Inc................................. G 765 644-8819
   Anderson *(G-135)*

Irving Materials Inc................................. F 765 778-4760
   Anderson *(G-136)*

Irving Materials Inc................................. G 812 275-7450
   Bedford *(G-649)*

Irving Materials Inc................................. F 812 333-8530
   Bloomington *(G-892)*

Irving Materials Inc................................. F 260 824-3428
   Bluffton *(G-1039)*

Irving Materials Inc................................. G 812 443-4661
   Brazil *(G-1148)*

Irving Materials Inc................................. G 765 647-6533
   Brookville *(G-1327)*

Irving Materials Inc................................. G 765 478-4914
   Cambridge City *(G-1496)*

Irving Materials Inc................................. G 765 825-2581
   Connersville *(G-2446)*

Irving Materials Inc................................. G 765 362-6904
   Crawfordsville *(G-2581)*

Irving Materials Inc................................. G 765 552-5041
   Elwood *(G-3826)*

Irving Materials Inc................................. G 812 424-3551
   Evansville *(G-4132)*

Irving Materials Inc................................. F 317 326-3101
   Fort Wayne *(G-5120)*

Irving Materials Inc................................. F 765 654-5333
   Frankfort *(G-5675)*

Irving Materials Inc................................. G 317 888-0157
   Greenwood *(G-6717)*

Irving Materials Inc................................. G 812 683-4444
   Huntingburg *(G-7284)*

Irving Materials Inc................................. F 260 356-7214
   Huntington *(G-7331)*

Irving Materials Inc................................. G 317 843-2944
   Indianapolis *(G-8589)*

Irving Materials Inc................................. G 317 872-0152
   Indianapolis *(G-8590)*

Irving Materials Inc................................. G 317 783-3381
   Indianapolis *(G-8591)*

Irving Materials Inc................................. G 317 243-7391
   Indianapolis *(G-8592)*

Irving Materials Inc................................. G 317 899-2187
   Indianapolis *(G-8593)*

Irving Materials Inc................................. G 765 452-4044
   Kokomo *(G-10290)*

Irving Materials Inc................................. F 765 922-7285
   Kokomo *(G-10291)*

Irving Materials Inc................................. G 765 423-2533
   Lafayette *(G-10610)*

Irving Materials Inc................................. G 765 482-5620
   Lebanon *(G-10903)*

Irving Materials Inc................................. G 574 722-3420
   Logansport *(G-11084)*

Irving Materials Inc................................. G 765 674-2271
   Marion *(G-11296)*

Irving Materials Inc................................. G 765 342-3369
   Martinsville *(G-11408)*

Irving Materials Inc................................. G 765 728-5335
   Montpelier *(G-12179)*

Irving Materials Inc................................. F 317 831-0224
   Mooresville *(G-12216)*

Irving Materials Inc................................. G 765 836-4007
   Muncie *(G-12426)*

Irving Materials Inc................................. G 765 288-5566
   Muncie *(G-12427)*

Irving Materials Inc................................. G 765 288-0288
   Muncie *(G-12428)*

Irving Materials Inc................................. F 317 770-1745
   Noblesville *(G-13108)*

Irving Materials Inc................................. G 317 773-3640
   Noblesville *(G-13109)*

Irving Materials Inc................................. G 574 936-2975
   Plymouth *(G-13788)*

Irving Materials Inc................................. G 219 261-2441
   Remington *(G-14037)*

Irving Materials Inc................................. G 812 883-4242
   Scottsburg *(G-14565)*

Irving Materials Inc................................. G 812 829-9445
   Spencer *(G-15353)*

Irving Materials Inc................................. G 765 755-3447
   Springport *(G-15380)*

Irving Materials Inc................................. G 765 922-7931
   Swayzee *(G-15451)*

Irving Materials Inc................................. F 765 922-7991
   Swayzee *(G-15452)*

Irving Materials Inc................................. G 765 675-6327
   Tipton *(G-15777)*

Irving Materials Inc................................. G 812 254-0820
   Washington *(G-16486)*

Irving Materials Inc................................. G 765 743-3806
   West Lafayette *(G-16596)*

Irving Materials Inc................................. G 317 535-7566
   Whiteland *(G-16790)*

Irving Materials Inc................................. F 574 946-3754
   Winamac *(G-16864)*

Irving Materials Inc................................. D 317 326-3101
   Greenfield *(G-6518)*

Irving Materials Inc................................. E 260 356-7214
   Huntington *(G-7332)*

J & K Supply Inc....................................... G 765 448-1188
   Lafayette *(G-10611)*

CONCRETE: Ready-Mixed

Jack Mix .... G 812 923-8679
  Floyds Knobs *(G-4682)*

Jjs Concrete Construction LLC .... E 812 636-0173
  Montgomery *(G-12103)*

Johnson & Johnson Incorporated .... F 317 539-8420
  Mooresville *(G-12218)*

Jones & Sons Inc .... E 812 299-2287
  Terre Haute *(G-15622)*

Jones & Sons Inc .... E 812 882-2957
  Vincennes *(G-16135)*

Jones and Sons Inc .... E 812 254-4731
  Washington *(G-16489)*

Kentucky Concrete Indiana LLC .... E 812 282-6671
  Jeffersonville *(G-10008)*

Keystone Concrete Inc .... E 260 693-6437
  Churubusco *(G-1986)*

Kuert Concrete Inc .... F 574 293-0430
  Goshen *(G-6193)*

Kuert Concrete Inc .... G 574 223-2414
  Rochester *(G-14299)*

Kuert Concrete Inc .... G 574 453-3993
  Warsaw *(G-16384)*

Kuert Concrete Inc .... E 574 232-9911
  South Bend *(G-15109)*

Lees Ready-Mix & Trucking .... E
  Shelbyville *(G-14772)*

Lees Ready-Mix & Trucking Inc .... F 812 372-1800
  Columbus *(G-2339)*

Legacy Vulcan LLC .... G 574 293-1536
  Elkhart *(G-3483)*

Legacy Vulcan LLC .... G 219 567-9155
  Francesville *(G-5643)*

Legacy Vulcan LLC .... G 219 696-5467
  Lowell *(G-11167)*

Legacy Vulcan LLC .... G 219 253-6686
  Monon *(G-12056)*

Legacy Vulcan LLC .... G 219 465-3066
  Valparaiso *(G-15996)*

Lewis Jerry Cnstr & Excvtg .... G 765 653-2800
  Greencastle *(G-6418)*

Lone Star Industries Inc .... D 317 706-3314
  Carmel *(G-1685)*

Ma-Ri-Al Corp .... E 317 773-0679
  Noblesville *(G-13129)*

Martin Marietta Materials Inc .... F 765 883-8172
  Russiaville *(G-14424)*

McClure Concrete .... G 765 525-6098
  Flat Rock *(G-4655)*

McIntire Concrete .... F 765 759-7111
  Muncie *(G-12450)*

Mendozas Incorporated .... G 219 791-9034
  Merrillville *(G-11537)*

Mes Legacy Pc Inc .... E 317 769-5503
  Indianapolis *(G-8880)*

Meuth Construction Supply Inc .... G 812 424-8554
  Evansville *(G-4199)*

Meuth Construction Supply Inc .... G 270 826-8554
  Princeton *(G-14004)*

Mix On Site .... G 765 607-2140
  West Lafayette *(G-16608)*

Mulzer Crushed Stone Inc .... E 812 547-3467
  Tell City *(G-15512)*

Mulzer Crushed Stone Inc .... E 812 547-7921
  Tell City *(G-15513)*

N E W Interstate Concrete Inc .... F 812 234-5983
  Terre Haute *(G-15649)*

Ohio Valley Ready Mix Inc .... E 812 282-6671
  Jeffersonville *(G-10028)*

Ozinga - Concrete .... G 574 291-7100
  South Bend *(G-15184)*

Ozinga Bros Inc .... E 574 546-2550
  Bremen *(G-1211)*

Ozinga Bros Inc .... E 219 662-0925
  Crown Point *(G-2728)*

Ozinga Bros Inc .... E 574 971-8239
  Goshen *(G-6233)*

Ozinga Bros Inc .... E 574 642-4455
  Goshen *(G-6234)*

Ozinga Bros Inc .... C 219 949-9800
  Portage *(G-13901)*

Ozinga Bros Inc .... E 219 956-3418
  Wheatfield *(G-16770)*

Ozinga Inc .... G 219 324-2286
  La Porte *(G-10461)*

Ozinga Indiana Rdymx Con Inc .... F 219 949-9800
  Gary *(G-5993)*

Pepcon Concrete Inc .... G 765 964-6572
  Union City *(G-15858)*

Prairie Group .... G 812 877-9886
  Terre Haute *(G-15666)*

Prairie Group Inc .... G 812 824-1355
  Bloomington *(G-948)*

Precast Solutions Inc .... F 317 545-6557
  Whitestown *(G-16816)*

Primed & Ready LLC .... G 317 694-2028
  Indianapolis *(G-9197)*

Prmi 1 Inc .... G 219 474-5022
  Kentland *(G-10162)*

Purdy Concrete Inc .... G 765 477-7687
  Lafayette *(G-10672)*

Purdy Materials Inc .... E 765 474-8993
  Lafayette *(G-10673)*

Quikrete Companies LLC .... E 317 251-2281
  Indianapolis *(G-9252)*

Raver Ready Mix Concrete LLC .... G 812 662-7900
  Batesville *(G-601)*

Ready Set Go Inc .... G 765 564-2847
  Delphi *(G-2907)*

Rosskovenski Concrete & Rdymx .... G 765 832-6103
  Clinton *(G-2077)*

Sagamore Ready-Mix LLC .... G 765 759-8999
  Daleville *(G-2802)*

Sagamore Ready-Mix LLC .... G 317 570-6201
  Fishers *(G-4603)*

Schmaltz Ready Mix Concrete .... G 812 689-5140
  Osgood *(G-13415)*

Shelby Gravel Inc .... F 317 738-3445
  Franklin *(G-5776)*

Shelby Gravel Inc .... F 317 784-6678
  Indianapolis *(G-9417)*

Shelby Gravel Inc .... F 317 216-7556
  Indianapolis *(G-9418)*

Shelby Gravel Inc .... G 765 932-3292
  Rushville *(G-14412)*

Shelby Gravel Inc .... F 317 804-8100
  Westfield *(G-16726)*

Shelby Gravel Inc .... E 317 398-4485
  Shelbyville *(G-14797)*

Shoreline East Inc .... G 219 878-9991
  Michigan City *(G-11668)*

Smith Ready Mix Inc .... F 219 462-3191
  Valparaiso *(G-16054)*

Southfield Corporation .... E 812 824-1355
  Bloomington *(G-978)*

Southfield Corporation .... E 317 846-6060
  Carmel *(G-1767)*

Southfield Corporation .... E 317 773-5340
  Noblesville *(G-13177)*

Speedway Redi Mix Inc .... G 260 665-5999
  Angola *(G-293)*

Speedway Redi Mix Inc .... G 260 244-7205
  Columbia City *(G-2201)*

Speedway Redi-Mix Inc .... G 260 356-5600
  Huntington *(G-7370)*

Speedway Redi-Mix Inc .... F 260 496-8877
  Fort Wayne *(G-5430)*

Spurlino Mtls Indianapolis LLC .... G 765 339-4055
  Linden *(G-11032)*

St Henry Tile Co Inc .... E 260 589-2880
  Berne *(G-728)*

Sullivan IMI .... G 812 268-3306
  Sullivan *(G-15423)*

Wdmi Inc .... D 574 936-2136
  Plymouth *(G-13826)*

Zimco Materials Inc .... G 219 883-0870
  Gary *(G-6029)*

CONDUITS & FITTINGS: Electric

Linear Solutions Inc .... F 219 237-2399
  Griffith *(G-6812)*

Regal Rexnord Corporation .... E 574 583-9171
  Monticello *(G-12168)*

CONFINEMENT SURVEILLANCE SYS MAINTENANCE & MONITORING SVCS

Applied Technology Group Inc .... F 260 482-2844
  Fort Wayne *(G-4767)*

CONNECTORS: Cord, Electric

E M F Corp .... E 260 665-9541
  Angola *(G-246)*

CONNECTORS: Electronic

Telamon International Corp .... D 317 818-6888
  Carmel *(G-1779)*

CONSTRUCTION & MINING MACHINERY WHOLESALERS

Caterpillar Inc .... E 630 743-4094
  Greenfield *(G-6476)*

Cbizze LLC .... G 623 204-9782
  South Bend *(G-14968)*

Macallister Machinery Co Inc .... F 765 966-0759
  Richmond *(G-14157)*

Paulus Plastic Co Inc .... G 574 834-7663
  North Webster *(G-13312)*

Square 1 Dsign Manufacture Inc .... F 866 647-7771
  Shelbyville *(G-14800)*

CONSTRUCTION & ROAD MAINTENANCE EQPT: Drags, Road

Linkel Company .... G 812 934-5190
  Batesville *(G-596)*

CONSTRUCTION EQPT REPAIR SVCS

Cindon Inc .... F 812 853-5450
  Newburgh *(G-12998)*

Halyard Corporation .... E 219 515-2820
  Portage *(G-13873)*

CONSTRUCTION EQPT: Attachments, Snow Plow

Express Steel Inc .... F 317 657-5017
  Martinsville *(G-11390)*

CONSTRUCTION EQPT: Finishers & Spreaders

American Industrial Co LLC .... E 317 859-9900
  Greenwood *(G-6668)*

Road Widener LLC .... G 844 494-3363
  Floyds Knobs *(G-4691)*

CONSTRUCTION EQPT: Graders, Road

AF Ohab Company Inc.................................. E 317 225-4740
Indianapolis (G-7455)

CONSTRUCTION EQPT: Tractors

Wakarusa Ag LLC.. F 574 862-1163
Wakarusa (G-16256)

CONSTRUCTION MATERIALS, WHOLESALE: Aggregate

Garrity Stone Inc.. G 317 546-0893
Indianapolis (G-8263)
Hanson Agrigoods Midwest Inc................... G 317 635-9048
Cloverdale (G-2085)
Irving Materials Inc..................................... G 765 288-0288
Muncie (G-12428)
Korte Bros Inc... F 260 497-0500
Fort Wayne (G-5157)
Wyatt Farm Center Inc................................ G 574 354-2998
Nappanee (G-12655)

CONSTRUCTION MATERIALS, WHOLESALE: Air Ducts, Sheet Metal

Cbizze LLC... G 623 204-9782
South Bend (G-14968)
River Valley Sheet Metal Inc........................ F 574 259-2538
Mishawaka (G-11988)

CONSTRUCTION MATERIALS, WHOLESALE: Architectural Metalwork

Johns Archtctral Met Solutions..................... F 219 440-2116
Crown Point (G-2703)
Tuttle Aluminum & Bronze Inc..................... D 317 842-2420
Fishers (G-4618)

CONSTRUCTION MATERIALS, WHOLESALE: Asphalt Felts & coating

Monument Chemical LLC............................ D 317 223-2630
Indianapolis (G-8952)

CONSTRUCTION MATERIALS, WHOLESALE: Awnings

Classic Sign & Awning................................ G 260 665-6663
Angola (G-241)
Mofab Inc.. G 765 649-5577
Anderson (G-157)
Ruby Enterprises Inc.................................. G 765 649-2060
Anderson (G-186)

CONSTRUCTION MATERIALS, WHOLESALE: Building Stone

Heritage Ldscp Sup Group Inc..................... E 317 849-9100
Indianapolis (G-8389)

CONSTRUCTION MATERIALS, WHOLESALE: Building, Exterior

Amgi LLC.. G 317 447-1524
New Palestine (G-12928)
Hunter Nutrition Inc.................................... F 765 563-1003
Brookston (G-1311)
Patrick Industries Inc.................................. D 574 294-8828
Elkhart (G-3592)
Patrick Industries Inc.................................. B 574 294-7511
Elkhart (G-3593)
Spohn Associates Inc................................. G 317 921-2445
Indianapolis (G-9480)

CONSTRUCTION MATERIALS, WHOLESALE: Building, Interior

Borkholder Corporation............................... E 574 773-4083
Nappanee (G-12585)
Faulkens Floorcover.................................... F 574 300-4260
South Bend (G-15027)

CONSTRUCTION MATERIALS, WHOLESALE: Concrete Mixtures

Shelby Gravel Inc.. F 812 526-2731
Edinburgh (G-3104)

CONSTRUCTION MATERIALS, WHOLESALE: Door Frames

Trim-A-Door Corporation............................. G 317 769-8746
Elwood (G-3839)

CONSTRUCTION MATERIALS, WHOLESALE: Fiberglass Building Mat

Craft Metal Products Inc.............................. G 317 545-3252
Indianapolis (G-7897)
Trivector Manufacturing Inc......................... E 260 637-0141
Fort Wayne (G-5509)

CONSTRUCTION MATERIALS, WHOLESALE: Glass

Glass City Inc.. G 219 887-2100
Gary (G-5943)
Hartford TEC Glass Co Inc.......................... E 765 348-1282
Hartford City (G-7068)
Indy Glass Center Inc................................. E 317 591-5000
Indianapolis (G-8527)
Keusch Glass Inc.. E 812 482-2566
Jasper (G-9864)

CONSTRUCTION MATERIALS, WHOLESALE: Gravel

Rogers Group Inc.. E 765 893-4463
Williamsport (G-16853)

CONSTRUCTION MATERIALS, WHOLESALE: Limestone

Heidelberg Mtls Mdwest Agg Inc.................. G 260 632-1410
Woodburn (G-16948)
Ionic Cut Stone Incorporated...................... G 812 829-3416
Spencer (G-15352)
U S Aggregates Inc..................................... E 765 564-2282
Delphi (G-2910)

CONSTRUCTION MATERIALS, WHOLESALE: Molding, All Materials

Lasalle Bristol Corporation........................... F 574 293-5526
Elkhart (G-3470)
Phoenix Closures Inc.................................. F 765 658-1800
Greencastle (G-6424)
Reeds Plastic Tops Inc................................ G 765 282-1471
Muncie (G-12486)

CONSTRUCTION MATERIALS, WHOLESALE: Pallets, Wood

Buckingham Pallets Inc............................... G 317 846-8601
Carmel (G-1574)
Commercial Pallet Recycl Inc...................... G 260 668-6208
Hudson (G-7245)
Commercial Pallet Recycl Inc...................... F 260 829-1021
Orland (G-13362)

K & S Pallet Inc... E 260 422-1264
Fort Wayne (G-5141)
Rick Hollingshead....................................... G 765 833-2846
Roann (G-14253)

CONSTRUCTION MATERIALS, WHOLESALE: Particleboard

Kay Company Inc.. E 765 659-3388
Frankfort (G-5677)

CONSTRUCTION MATERIALS, WHOLESALE: Paving Materials

Scotts Grant County Asp Inc........................ G 765 664-2754
Marion (G-11337)

CONSTRUCTION MATERIALS, WHOLESALE: Plywood

National Products Inc.................................. E 574 457-4565
Syracuse (G-15469)
Robert Weed Plywood Corp........................ B 574 848-7631
Bristol (G-1288)

CONSTRUCTION MATERIALS, WHOLESALE: Prefabricated Structures

Biologics Modular LLC................................ G 317 626-4093
Brownsburg (G-1350)
Morton Buildings Inc................................... F 260 563-2118
Wabash (G-16204)

CONSTRUCTION MATERIALS, WHOLESALE: Roofing & Siding Material

Patrick Industries Inc.................................. D 574 294-8828
Elkhart (G-3592)
Patrick Industries Inc.................................. B 574 294-7511
Elkhart (G-3593)

CONSTRUCTION MATERIALS, WHOLESALE: Sand

Irving Materials Inc..................................... D 317 326-3101
Greenfield (G-6518)
Old Dutch Sand Co Inc............................... G 219 938-7020
Gary (G-5988)

CONSTRUCTION MATERIALS, WHOLESALE: Septic Tanks

Creed & Dyer Precast Inc........................... G 574 784-3361
Lakeville (G-10789)
Mnt Delivery Company................................ G 574 518-6250
Osceola (G-13399)

CONSTRUCTION MATERIALS, WHOLESALE: Sewer Pipe, Clay

Amgi LLC.. G 317 447-1524
New Palestine (G-12928)
Midwest Tile and Concrete Pdts.................. G 260 749-5173
Woodburn (G-16953)

CONSTRUCTION MATERIALS, WHOLESALE: Siding, Exc Wood

Arran Isle Inc.. E 574 295-4400
Elkhart (G-3191)
C & K United Shtmtl & Mech...................... E 812 423-5090
Evansville (G-3958)
Lasalle Bristol Corporation........................... C 574 295-8400
Elkhart (G-3469)

CONSTRUCTION MATERIALS, WHOLESALE: Stone, Crushed Or Broken

Aggrock Quarries Inc	G	812 246-2582
Charlestown *(G-1870)*		
Barrett Paving Materials Inc	G	765 935-3060
Richmond *(G-14090)*		
Crawford County Concrete	G	812 739-2707
Leavenworth *(G-10869)*		
Heidelberg Mtls Mdwest Agg Inc	G	765 653-7205
Cloverdale *(G-2086)*		
Heidelberg Mtls Mdwest Agg Inc	F	765 653-1956
Greencastle *(G-6411)*		
Irving Materials Inc	F	765 778-4760
Anderson *(G-136)*		
Jones & Sons Inc	E	812 882-2957
Vincennes *(G-16135)*		
Mulzer Crushed Stone Inc	E	812 547-3467
Tell City *(G-15512)*		
Rogers Group Inc	C	812 333-6324
Bloomington *(G-959)*		
Rogers Group Inc	D	812 332-6341
Bloomington *(G-960)*		
Rogers Group Inc	D	812 333-8560
Bloomington *(G-961)*		
Rogers Group Inc	D	219 474-5125
Kentland *(G-10163)*		
Rogers Group Inc	D	812 849-3530
Mitchell *(G-12047)*		

CONSTRUCTION MATERIALS, WHOLESALE: Tile & Clay Prdts

Evansville Block Co Inc	E	812 422-2864
Evansville *(G-4049)*		

CONSTRUCTION MATERIALS, WHOLESALE: Veneer

Dimension Plywood Inc	G	812 944-6491
New Albany *(G-12719)*		
Heitink Veneers Incorporated	E	812 336-6436
Bloomington *(G-876)*		

CONSTRUCTION MATERIALS, WHOLESALE: Windows

Therma-Tru Corp	F	260 562-1009
Howe *(G-7243)*		

CONSTRUCTION MATLS, WHOL: Composite Board Prdts, Woodboard

Gutter One Supply	F	317 872-1257
Indianapolis *(G-8344)*		
Wolfe Engineered Plastics LLC	G	812 623-8403
Sunman *(G-15449)*		

CONSTRUCTION MATLS, WHOL: Doors, Combination, Screen-Storm

All-Weather Products Inc	G	812 867-6403
Evansville *(G-3880)*		
Benthall Bros Inc	E	800 488-5995
Evansville *(G-3915)*		

CONSTRUCTION SAND MINING

Krafft Gravel Inc	G	260 238-4653
Spencerville *(G-15372)*		
Old Dutch Sand Co Inc	G	219 938-7020
Gary *(G-5988)*		
Utility Access Solutions Inc	G	765 744-6528
Ridgeville *(G-14238)*		
White Sand & Gravel Inc	G	317 882-7791
Indianapolis *(G-9759)*		

CONSTRUCTION: Agricultural Building

Cozy Cat Inc	G	765 463-1254
Lafayette *(G-10559)*		
Indiana Mobile Welding LLC	G	317 771-8900
Noblesville *(G-13102)*		

CONSTRUCTION: Athletic & Recreation Facilities

Bleacherpro LLC	G	813 394-5316
Fort Wayne *(G-4806)*		
Maddox Industrial Contg LLC	E	812 544-2156
Santa Claus *(G-14508)*		
Radon Environmental Inc	G	317 843-0804
Elkhart *(G-3637)*		
Wallar Additions Inc	G	574 262-1989
Elkhart *(G-3778)*		

CONSTRUCTION: Bridge

Beer and Slabaugh Inc	E	574 773-3413
Nappanee *(G-12584)*		
C & R Cnstr & Consulting LLC	G	812 738-4493
Corydon *(G-2489)*		
Milestone Contractors LP	D	812 579-5248
Columbus *(G-2356)*		

CONSTRUCTION: Commercial & Office Building, New

ALE Enterprises Inc	G	317 856-2981
Indianapolis *(G-7467)*		
Burns Construction Inc	E	574 382-2315
Macy *(G-11195)*		
J G Bowers Inc	E	765 677-1000
Marion *(G-11297)*		
North Webster Construction Inc	E	574 834-4448
North Webster *(G-13310)*		
Tri-Esco Inc	F	765 446-7937
Colburn *(G-2112)*		

CONSTRUCTION: Commercial & Office Buildings, Prefabricated

Classic Buildings Inc	E	812 944-5821
Clarksville *(G-2013)*		

CONSTRUCTION: Dams, Waterways, Docks & Other Marine

Hampton Equipment LLC	G	260 740-8704
Fort Wayne *(G-5049)*		
Lakemaster Inc	F	765 288-3718
Muncie *(G-12437)*		

CONSTRUCTION: Drainage System

Parke County Aggregates LLC	G	765 245-2344
Rockville *(G-14353)*		
Randall K Dike	G	812 664-4942
Owensville *(G-13471)*		

CONSTRUCTION: Farm Building

Lowes Pellets and Grain Inc	E	812 663-7863
Greensburg *(G-6615)*		

CONSTRUCTION: Food Prdts Manufacturing or Packing Plant

Better Blacc Wall Streetz LLC	F	812 927-0712
Seymour *(G-14632)*		
Dmp LLC	G	812 699-0086
Worthington *(G-16959)*		

CONSTRUCTION: Foundation & Retaining Wall

Thatcher Engineering Corp	D	219 949-2084
Gary *(G-6018)*		

CONSTRUCTION: Heavy Highway & Street

Niblock Excavating Inc	G	260 248-2100
Columbia City *(G-2174)*		

CONSTRUCTION: Indl Buildings, New, NEC

Empire Contractors Inc	D	812 424-3865
Evansville *(G-4035)*		
Sterling Industrial LLC	C	812 423-7832
Evansville *(G-4333)*		

CONSTRUCTION: Indl Plant

Honeywell International Inc	G	219 836-3803
Munster *(G-12540)*		

CONSTRUCTION: Pipeline, NEC

GI Properties Inc	G	219 763-1177
Portage *(G-13868)*		

CONSTRUCTION: Power & Communication Transmission Tower

Benson Tower LLC	G	270 577-7598
Evansville *(G-3914)*		

CONSTRUCTION: Residential, Nec

Alexander Thompson	G	218 577-7627
Hammond *(G-6870)*		
Kings-Qlity Rstrtion Svcs LLC	F	812 944-4347
New Albany *(G-12760)*		

CONSTRUCTION: Scaffolding

Top Lock Corporation	G	317 831-2000
Mooresville *(G-12248)*		

CONSTRUCTION: Sewer Line

Beer and Slabaugh Inc	E	574 773-3413
Nappanee *(G-12584)*		

CONSTRUCTION: Single-Family Housing

All American Group Inc	E	574 262-0123
Elkhart *(G-3160)*		
Bigg Dawg Construction LLC	G	317 506-1436
Indianapolis *(G-7624)*		
Expedition Log Homes	G	219 663-5555
Crown Point *(G-2683)*		
H & H Home Improvement Inc	G	812 288-8700
Clarksville *(G-2017)*		
Landmark Home & Land Company	G	219 874-4065
Michigan City *(G-11630)*		

CONSTRUCTION: Single-family Housing, New

American Adventures Inc	G	574 875-6850
Elkhart *(G-3170)*		
Benakovich Builders	G	219 204-2777
Thorntown *(G-15750)*		
E & L Construction Inc	G	765 525-7081
Manilla *(G-11260)*		
Ettensohn & Company LLC	G	812 547-5491
Tell City *(G-15501)*		
Klomp Construction Company	G	219 308-8372
Saint John *(G-14454)*		
Miller Brothers Builders Inc	E	574 533-8602
Goshen *(G-6222)*		

PRODUCT SECTION

CONSTRUCTION: Swimming Pools

Chester Pool Systems Inc .... E 812 949-7333
New Albany *(G-12712)*

Pool Shop .... G 812 446-0026
Brazil *(G-1162)*

Sparkle Pools Inc .... F 812 232-1292
Terre Haute *(G-15707)*

Thursday Pools LLC .... G 317 973-0200
Fortville *(G-5607)*

CONSTRUCTION: Transmitting Tower, Telecommunication

Commtineo LLC .... F 219 476-3667
Wanatah *(G-16288)*

Swager Communications Inc .... E 260 495-2515
Fremont *(G-5837)*

CONSTRUCTION: Warehouse

Csa Racking LLC .... G 414 241-3585
Hammond *(G-6908)*

CONSTRUCTION: Waste Water & Sewage Treatment Plant

Astbury Water Technology Inc .... D 317 328-7153
Indianapolis *(G-7556)*

CONSTRUCTION: Water & Sewer Line

Watershipblue LLC .... G 317 910-8585
Indianapolis *(G-9741)*

CONSULTING SVC: Business, NEC

Abundant Life Publications LLC .... G 219 730-7621
Gary *(G-5887)*

Agi International Inc .... F 317 536-2415
Indianapolis *(G-7458)*

Aunalytics Inc .... D 574 307-9230
South Bend *(G-14951)*

Automobile Dealers Assn of Ind .... G 317 635-1441
Indianapolis *(G-7576)*

Carelogiq Corp .... G 219 682-6327
Munster *(G-12534)*

Cr Publications .... G 219 931-6700
Hammond *(G-6906)*

Crown Training and Dev Inc .... F 219 947-0845
Merrillville *(G-11500)*

Detroit Holdings LLC .... G 202 309-9681
North Liberty *(G-13216)*

Dieng Group LLC .... G 317 699-1909
Indianapolis *(G-7973)*

Drake Enterprises LLC .... G 317 460-5991
Pittsboro *(G-13644)*

Enterprise MGT Solutions LLC .... G 219 545-8544
Merrillville *(G-11513)*

Goldenmarc LLC .... G 317 855-1651
Indianapolis *(G-8301)*

Indiana Auto Dealers Assn Svcs .... G 317 635-1441
Indianapolis *(G-8473)*

Jdh Logistics LLC .... G 573 529-2005
Fort Branch *(G-4705)*

John R Bowen & Associates .... G 812 544-2267
Newburgh *(G-13010)*

Ksn Technologies Inc .... E 219 877-4770
Chesterton *(G-1942)*

Nebo Ridge Enterprises LLC .... G 317 471-1089
Carmel *(G-1703)*

Peerless Gear LLC .... G 812 883-7900
Salem *(G-14497)*

Pyrotek Incorporated .... D 260 248-4141
Columbia City *(G-2184)*

RAD Cube LLC .... F 317 456-7560
Indianapolis *(G-9260)*

Rebound Project LLP .... G 765 621-5604
Anderson *(G-183)*

Registration System LLC .... G 317 966-6919
Fortville *(G-5605)*

Sailor Group LLC .... G 574 226-0362
Elkhart *(G-3660)*

Samaron Corp .... E 574 970-7070
Elkhart *(G-3661)*

Sentinel Services Inc .... E 574 360-5279
Granger *(G-6376)*

Turning Over A New Leaf LLC .... G 765 573-3366
Gas City *(G-6040)*

Vigo Coal Operating Co Inc .... C 812 759-8446
Evansville *(G-4374)*

CONSULTING SVC: Educational

DMC Distribution LLC .... G 219 926-6401
Porter *(G-13924)*

Standard For Success LLC .... F 844 737-3825
Cloverdale *(G-2099)*

CONSULTING SVC: Financial Management

Triumphant Jrney MBL Ntary Svc .... G 608 208-5604
Madison *(G-11254)*

CONSULTING SVC: Management

Advanced Prtctive Slutions LLC .... G 765 720-9574
Coatesville *(G-2102)*

American Eagle Health LLC .... G 812 921-9224
Floyds Knobs *(G-4668)*

American Veteran Group LLC .... G 317 600-4749
Westfield *(G-16664)*

Arroyo Industries LLC .... G 317 605-4163
Greenwood *(G-6671)*

Deberry MGT & Consulting LLC .... G 317 767-4703
Indianapolis *(G-7959)*

Destiny Solutions Inc .... G 502 384-0031
Georgetown *(G-6057)*

Enpak LLC .... G 574 268-7273
Warsaw *(G-16360)*

Enterprise MGT Solutions LLC .... G 219 545-8544
Merrillville *(G-11513)*

Froet Group LLC .... F 317 414-2538
Whitestown *(G-16807)*

Innovations Amplified LLC .... G 317 339-4685
Indianapolis *(G-8552)*

Jtex Cnstr & Consulting LLC .... G 812 486-9123
Velpen *(G-16093)*

Printing Inc Louisville KY .... F 800 237-5894
Jeffersonville *(G-10041)*

Project Field Solutions Inc .... G 317 590-7678
Fishers *(G-4584)*

Sk Markting Strtgies LLC DBA A .... G 812 962-0900
Evansville *(G-4317)*

Spring Ventures Infovation LLC .... G 317 847-1117
Greenwood *(G-6770)*

Tippmann US Holdco Inc .... E 260 749-6022
Fort Wayne *(G-5489)*

CONSULTING SVCS, BUSINESS: Communications

Sk Markting Strtgies LLC DBA A .... G 812 962-0900
Evansville *(G-4317)*

CONSULTING SVCS, BUSINESS: Energy Conservation

Al Perry Enterprises Inc .... G 812 867-7727
Evansville *(G-3879)*

CONSULTING SVCS, BUSINESS: Environmental

Anaerobic Innovations LLC .... G 765 491-1174
West Lafayette *(G-16561)*

Assurance Waste Management LLC .... G 765 341-4431
Cloverdale *(G-2082)*

F D Deskins Company Inc .... F 317 284-4014
Fishers *(G-4520)*

Sorbtech Inc .... G 812 944-9108
Clarksville *(G-2037)*

CONSULTING SVCS, BUSINESS: Safety Training Svcs

Asphalt Materials Inc .... G 317 875-4670
Indianapolis *(G-7553)*

CONSULTING SVCS, BUSINESS: Sys Engnrg, Exc Computer/ Prof

Corvano LLC .... G 317 403-0471
Fishers *(G-4495)*

Cybernaut Industria LLC .... G 317 664-5316
Indianapolis *(G-7939)*

Indy Web Inc .... G 317 536-1201
Indianapolis *(G-8537)*

CONSULTING SVCS, BUSINESS: Systems Analysis & Engineering

Agora Brands Group Inc .... E 615 802-0086
Borden *(G-1104)*

American Eagle Health LLC .... G 812 921-9224
Floyds Knobs *(G-4668)*

Binarie LLC .... G 317 496-8836
Greenwood *(G-6676)*

Indigo Industries LLC .... G 480 747-4560
Greenwood *(G-6715)*

Ipheion Development Corp .... G 240 281-1619
Indianapolis *(G-8587)*

Spring Ventures Infovation LLC .... G 317 847-1117
Greenwood *(G-6770)*

CONSULTING SVCS, BUSINESS: Systems Analysis Or Design

Radian Research Inc .... D 765 449-5500
Lafayette *(G-10675)*

CONSULTING SVCS: Scientific

Ipheion Development Corp .... G 240 281-1619
Indianapolis *(G-8587)*

Telamon Entp Ventures LLC .... F 317 818-6888
Carmel *(G-1778)*

CONTACTS: Electrical

Contact Fabricators Ind Inc .... G 317 366-7274
Middletown *(G-11768)*

CONTAINERS: Cargo, Wood & Metal Combination

H & A Products Inc .... G 574 226-0079
Elkhart *(G-3394)*

H & M Bay Inc .... F 410 463-5430
Fort Wayne *(G-5046)*

Satco Inc .... D 317 856-0301
Indianapolis *(G-9377)*

CONTAINERS: Food & Beverage

J&K Generations .... G 812 508-1094
Bedford *(G-650)*

CONTAINERS: Food, Folding, Made From Purchased Materials

Red Gold LP .... E 765 754-8750
Alexandria (G-59)

CONTAINERS: Food, Folding, Made From Purchased Materials

Glenmark Industries Inc .... C 574 936-5788
Plymouth (G-13780)

CONTAINERS: Food, Liquid Tight, Including Milk

International Paper Company .... D 800 643-7244
Terre Haute (G-15619)

CONTAINERS: Frozen Food & Ice Cream

Viva Tia Maria LLC .... E 317 509-2650
Zionsville (G-17061)

CONTAINERS: Glass

Anchor Glass Container Corp .... D 812 537-1655
Greendale (G-6437)
Ardagh Glass Inc .... G 765 768-7891
Dunkirk (G-2960)
Ardagh Glass Packaging Inc .... G 317 558-1002
Indianapolis (G-7543)
Indianapolis Container Company ...... G 317 580-5000
Indianapolis (G-8503)

CONTAINERS: Ice Cream, Made From Purchased Materials

Wethington .... G 317 594-6000
Greenfield (G-6571)

CONTAINERS: Laminated Phenolic & Vulcanized Fiber

Great Lakes Lamination Inc .... G 574 389-9663
Elkhart (G-3390)
Great Lakes Lamination Inc .... G 574 389-9663
Bristol (G-1265)

CONTAINERS: Metal

Diversified Qulty Svcs Ind LLC .... G 765 644-7712
Anderson (G-105)
W & M Enterprises Inc .... F 812 537-4656
Lawrenceburg (G-10865)

CONTAINERS: Plastic

Amcor Rigid Packaging Usa LLC ...... G 317 736-4313
Franklin (G-5708)
Assmann Corporation America .... E 260 357-3181
Garrett (G-5854)
Berry Film Products Co Inc .... C 812 306-2690
Evansville (G-3917)
Berry Global Inc .... G 260 495-2000
Fremont (G-5811)
Berry Global Inc .... E 812 558-3510
Odon (G-13331)
Berry Global Inc .... A 812 424-2904
Evansville (G-3918)
Berry Global Escrow Corp .... G 812 424-2904
Evansville (G-3920)
Berry Global Group Inc .... F 812 868-7429
Princeton (G-13984)
Berry Global Group Inc .... A 812 424-2904
Evansville (G-3921)
Berry Plastics Group Inc .... E 812 424-2904
Evansville (G-3924)
Bprex Healthcare Packaging Inc .... F 812 424-2904
Evansville (G-3948)
Captive Plastics LLC .... C 812 424-2904
Evansville (G-3963)

CPI Holding Corporation .... F 812 424-2904
Evansville (G-3990)
D&W Fine Pack LLC .... D 260 432-3027
Fort Wayne (G-4902)
Drug Plastics and Glass Co Inc .... E 765 385-0035
Oxford (G-13474)
Fibertech Plastics LLC .... D 812 983-2642
Elberfeld (G-3113)
Fti Inc .... D 812 983-2642
Elberfeld (G-3114)
Full Tank Freedom Inc .... E 317 485-7887
Fortville (G-5596)
Genpak LLC .... F 812 256-7040
Jeffersonville (G-9991)
Genpak LLC .... G 812 752-3111
Scottsburg (G-14557)
Grafco Industries Ltd Partnr .... C 812 424-2904
Evansville (G-4095)
Indianapolis Container Company ...... G 317 580-5000
Indianapolis (G-8503)
Letica Corporation .... A 812 421-3136
Evansville (G-4165)
Mad Dasher Inc .... E 260 747-0545
Fort Wayne (G-5198)
Mauser Packaging Solutions .... G 317 297-4638
Indianapolis (G-8854)
Meese Inc .... F 800 829-4535
Madison (G-11241)
Mytex Polymers US Corp .... E 812 280-2900
Jeffersonville (G-10021)
Norton Packaging Inc .... E 574 867-6002
Hamlet (G-6864)
Paragon Medical Inc .... C 574 594-2140
Pierceton (G-13637)
Paragon Medical Inc .... C 574 594-2140
Pierceton (G-13638)
Placon Corporation .... F 608 278-4920
Elkhart (G-3606)
Polycon Industries Inc .... C 219 738-1000
Merrillville (G-11551)
PRC - Desoto International Inc .... E 317 290-1600
Indianapolis (G-9177)
Remco Products Corporation .... D 317 876-9856
Zionsville (G-17046)
Revolution Materials (in) LLC .... D 812 234-2724
Terre Haute (G-15680)
Ser North America LLC .... F 765 639-0300
Anderson (G-190)
Silgan Plastics LLC .... D 260 894-7814
Ligonier (G-11023)
Silgan Plastics LLC .... G 812 522-0900
Seymour (G-14692)
Silgan Plastics LLC .... F 812 522-0900
Seymour (G-14693)
Variotech Corp .... G 404 566-2935
Indianapolis (G-9701)

CONTAINERS: Sanitary, Food

Affinis Group LLC .... G 317 831-3830
Mooresville (G-12191)
Divine Grace Homecare .... G 219 290-5911
Gary (G-5923)
Genpak LLC .... G 812 752-3111
Scottsburg (G-14557)
Letica Corporation .... A 812 421-3136
Evansville (G-4165)

CONTAINERS: Shipping, Bombs, Metal Plate

Armor Products Inc .... C 502 228-1458
Madison (G-11202)
Meese Inc .... F 800 829-4535
Madison (G-11241)

Sabre Manufacturing LLC .... C 574 772-5380
Knox (G-10222)

CONTAINERS: Wood

A S M Inc .... G 260 724-8220
Decatur (G-2839)
A-1 Pallet Co of Clarksville .... G 812 288-6339
Clarksville (G-2006)
American Fibertech Corporation .... D 219 261-3586
Lafayette (G-10521)
Anthony Wyne Rhblttion Ctr For .... D 260 744-6145
Fort Wayne (G-4762)
Conner Sawmill Inc .... F 574 626-3227
Walton (G-16282)
Gordon Lumber Company .... G 219 924-0500
Griffith (G-6804)
Industrial Woodkraft Inc .... E 812 897-4893
Boonville (G-1087)
Southern Indiana Hardwoods Inc ..... E 812 326-2053
Huntingburg (G-7291)
Star Case Manufacturing Co LLC ..... E 219 922-4440
Munster (G-12565)
W & M Enterprises Inc .... F 812 537-4656
Lawrenceburg (G-10865)

CONTRACT FOOD SVCS

Deonta Walker .... G 317 970-3586
Indianapolis (G-7965)
Passions Fruitopia LLC .... G 800 515-1891
Highland (G-7151)

CONTRACTOR: Dredging

Paf Construction LLC .... E 812 496-4669
Columbus (G-2371)

CONTRACTOR: Rigging & Scaffolding

Bishop Lifting Products Inc .... G 260 478-4700
Fort Wayne (G-4805)

CONTRACTORS: Building Site Preparation

Landmark Home & Land Company ... G 219 874-4065
Michigan City (G-11630)

CONTRACTORS: Cable Laying

Avid Operations Inc .... G 260 220-2001
Fort Wayne (G-4784)

CONTRACTORS: Carpentry Work

Benakovich Builders .... G 219 204-2777
Thorntown (G-15750)
Continntal Crpntry Cmpnnts LLC ...... E 219 733-0367
Wanatah (G-16289)
Dutch Country Woodworking Inc ..... G 260 499-4847
Lagrange (G-10734)
Empire Contractors Inc .... D 812 424-3865
Evansville (G-4035)
Gary E Ellsworth .... G 260 639-3078
Hoagland (G-7168)
Marquise Enterprises Ltd .... G 317 578-3400
Indianapolis (G-8840)
Rodeswood LLC .... G 574 457-4496
Syracuse (G-15476)

CONTRACTORS: Carpentry, Cabinet & Finish Work

Academy Inc .... G 574 293-7113
Elkhart (G-3147)
Claridges Wood Shop .... G 812 536-2569
Stendal (G-15398)
Douglas Dye and Associates Inc ..... G 317 844-1709
Carmel (G-1611)

PRODUCT SECTION — CONTRACTORS: Highway & Street Construction, General

Ettensohn & Company LLC .... G 812 547-5491
Tell City *(G-15501)*

Freedom Valley Cabinets .... G 717 606-2811
Freedom *(G-5800)*

Innovative Corp .... E 317 804-5977
Westfield *(G-16701)*

Klomp Construction Company .... G 219 308-8372
Saint John *(G-14454)*

Kostyo Woodworking Inc .... G 812 466-7350
Terre Haute *(G-15625)*

M & H Woodworking LLC .... G 812 486-2570
Montgomery *(G-12111)*

Mhp Holdings Inc .... C 574 825-9524
Middlebury *(G-11736)*

CONTRACTORS: Closet Organizers, Installation & Design

All About Organizing .... G 513 238-8157
Lawrenceburg *(G-10827)*

CONTRACTORS: Coating, Caulking & Weather, Water & Fire

K2 Industrial Services Inc .... F 219 933-1100
Highland *(G-7141)*

Midwest Pipecoating Inc .... D 219 322-4564
Schererville *(G-14535)*

CONTRACTORS: Commercial & Office Building

K Q Servicing LLC .... G 812 486-9244
Loogootee *(G-11140)*

Marshall Companies Indiana .... G 317 769-2666
Lebanon *(G-10913)*

Max of All Trades LLC .... G 317 703-4242
Kokomo *(G-10305)*

Miller Brothers Builders Inc .... E 574 533-8602
Goshen *(G-6222)*

Over Top Roofing and Rmdlg LLC .... G 513 704-5422
Lawrenceburg *(G-10851)*

T Organization Inc .... E 463 204-5118
Greenwood *(G-6771)*

CONTRACTORS: Communications Svcs

Trilithic Inc .... C 317 895-3600
Indianapolis *(G-9641)*

CONTRACTORS: Computerized Controls Installation

Custom Controls & Engrg Inc .... G 812 663-0755
Greensburg *(G-6587)*

CONTRACTORS: Directional Oil & Gas Well Drilling Svc

G & B Directional Boring LLC .... F 574 538-8132
Shipshewana *(G-14847)*

Tru Bore Company .... G 317 442-6766
Brownsburg *(G-1410)*

US Oilfield Company LLC .... F 888 584-7465
Carmel *(G-1796)*

CONTRACTORS: Drywall

All-Phase Construction Co LLC .... G 317 345-7057
Fishers *(G-4461)*

Clean Lines Painting LLC .... G 708 200-2210
Michigan City *(G-11588)*

Dr Restorations Inc .... G 317 646-7150
Clermont *(G-2063)*

CONTRACTORS: Electronic Controls Installation

Complete Controls Inc .... G 260 489-0852
Fort Wayne *(G-4868)*

Liberty Automation LLC .... G 574 524-0436
Albion *(G-31)*

Quantum Technologies LLC .... G 765 426-0156
Elizabethtown *(G-3132)*

Rex Byers Htg & Coolg Systems .... F 765 459-8858
Kokomo *(G-10328)*

CONTRACTORS: Energy Management Control

Watershipblue LLC .... G 317 910-8585
Indianapolis *(G-9741)*

CONTRACTORS: Excavating Slush Pits & Cellars Svcs

E Z Choice .... G 219 852-4281
Hammond *(G-6917)*

Filson Earthwork Company .... F 317 774-3180
Noblesville *(G-13078)*

CONTRACTORS: Fence Construction

Fencescapes LLC .... F 317 210-3912
Avon *(G-519)*

K & K Fence Inc .... E 317 359-5425
Indianapolis *(G-8652)*

Mofab Inc .... G 765 649-5577
Anderson *(G-157)*

Mullets Fencing and Supplies .... G 574 646-3300
Nappanee *(G-12628)*

Quality Fence Ltd .... G 260 768-4986
Shipshewana *(G-14880)*

Safeguard Solutions LLC .... G 317 519-0255
Greenfield *(G-6548)*

CONTRACTORS: Fiber Optic Cable Installation

Belden Inc .... G 978 537-9961
Richmond *(G-14091)*

Loud Clear Communications LLC .... G 260 433-9479
Auburn *(G-403)*

CONTRACTORS: Fire Detection & Burglar Alarm Systems

American Fire Company .... G 219 840-0630
Valparaiso *(G-15899)*

Johnson Cntrls Fire Prtction L .... G 317 826-2130
Indianapolis *(G-8633)*

Phil & Son Inc .... G 219 663-5757
Crown Point *(G-2730)*

Sentinel Alarm Inc .... G 219 874-6051
Trail Creek *(G-15839)*

CONTRACTORS: Floor Laying & Other Floor Work

Doris Drapery Boutique .... G 765 472-5850
Peru *(G-13580)*

Santarossa Mosaic Tile Co Inc .... C 317 632-9494
Indianapolis *(G-9371)*

CONTRACTORS: Food Svcs Eqpt Installation

Carmel Engineering Inc .... F 765 279-8955
Kirklin *(G-10187)*

Conover Custom Fabrication Inc .... F 317 784-1904
Indianapolis *(G-7853)*

CONTRACTORS: Foundation & Footing

Niblock Excavating Inc .... D 574 848-4437
Bristol *(G-1281)*

CONTRACTORS: Gas Field Svcs, NEC

Pinnacle Oil Trading LLC .... E 317 875-9465
Indianapolis *(G-9147)*

CONTRACTORS: General Electric

B & D Electric Inc .... F 812 254-2122
Shoals *(G-14903)*

Boone County Electric Inc .... G 765 482-1430
Lebanon *(G-10880)*

Current Electric Inc .... F 219 872-7736
Michigan City *(G-11591)*

Electric Plus Inc .... D 317 718-0100
Avon *(G-516)*

Electronic Services LLC .... E 765 457-3894
Kokomo *(G-10262)*

Gottman Electric Company Inc .... G 812 838-0037
Mount Vernon *(G-12297)*

Hoosier Industrial Electric .... F 812 346-2232
North Vernon *(G-13278)*

Hubbard Inc .... G 317 535-1926
Whiteland *(G-16788)*

J V Crane & Engineering Inc .... E 219 942-8566
Portage *(G-13879)*

Link Electrical Service .... G 812 288-8184
Jeffersonville *(G-10013)*

Nrk Inc .... E 812 232-1800
Terre Haute *(G-15653)*

CONTRACTORS: Glass Tinting, Architectural & Automotive

Broadway Auto Glass LLC .... F 219 884-5277
Merrillville *(G-11493)*

CONTRACTORS: Grave Excavation

Wilson Burial Vault Inc .... G 260 356-5722
Huntington *(G-7380)*

CONTRACTORS: Heating & Air Conditioning

A & A Prcsion Htg Colg Rfrgn L .... G 812 401-1711
Evansville *(G-3859)*

Fletcher Heating & Cooling .... G 812 865-2984
Paoli *(G-13494)*

Geo-Flo Corporation .... F 812 275-8513
Bedford *(G-639)*

Hayward & Sams LLP .... G 260 351-4166
Stroh *(G-15401)*

Paniccia Heating & Cooling Inc .... G 219 872-2198
Michigan City *(G-11650)*

T R Bulger Inc .... G 219 879-8525
Trail Creek *(G-15841)*

Washburn Heating & AC .... G 574 825-7697
Middlebury *(G-11757)*

CONTRACTORS: Heating Systems Repair & Maintenance Svc

All Pro Property Services LLC .... G 317 721-1227
Indianapolis *(G-7474)*

Economy Electric Htg & Coolg .... G 219 923-4441
Highland *(G-7134)*

Vincent Aliano Elc & Hvac Inc .... G 812 332-3332
Bloomington *(G-1007)*

CONTRACTORS: Highway & Street Construction, General

CONTRACTORS: Highway & Street Construction, General

Rogers Group Inc .... F 812 333-8550
Bloomington *(G-962)*

Sssi Inc .... F 219 880-0818
Gary *(G-6015)*

Utility Access Solutions Inc .... G 765 744-6528
Ridgeville *(G-14238)*

Vans Industrial Inc .... E 219 931-4881
Hammond *(G-7028)*

CONTRACTORS: Highway & Street Paving

E & B Paving Inc .... E 765 674-5848
Marion *(G-11284)*

E & B Paving Inc .... E 765 643-5358
Anderson *(G-112)*

Milestone Contractors LP .... D 812 579-5248
Columbus *(G-2356)*

Milestone Contractors LP .... D 765 772-7500
Lafayette *(G-10650)*

Niblock Excavating Inc .... D 574 848-4437
Bristol *(G-1281)*

Phend and Brown Inc .... E 574 658-4166
Milford *(G-11802)*

Wallace Construction Inc .... F 317 422-5356
Martinsville *(G-11434)*

CONTRACTORS: Kitchen Cabinet Installation

Johnny Graber Woodworking .... G 260 466-4957
Grabill *(G-6305)*

CONTRACTORS: Machine Rigging & Moving

Egenolf Contg & Rigging II Inc .... F 317 787-5301
Indianapolis *(G-8059)*

Egenolf Machine Inc .... F 317 787-5301
Indianapolis *(G-8061)*

Padgett Inc .... C 812 945-2391
New Albany *(G-12790)*

Precision Surveillance Corp .... E 219 397-4295
East Chicago *(G-3035)*

Trivett Contracting Inc .... E 317 539-5150
Clayton *(G-2062)*

CONTRACTORS: Machinery Installation

Daifuku Intrlgistics Amer Corp .... D 219 777-2220
Hobart *(G-7186)*

Engineered Conveyors Inc .... F 765 459-4545
Kokomo *(G-10263)*

Indiana Industrial Svcs LLC .... D 317 769-6099
Whitestown *(G-16810)*

Mid-State Automation Inc .... G 765 795-5500
Cloverdale *(G-2089)*

V-Tech Engineering Inc .... F 260 824-4322
Bluffton *(G-1067)*

CONTRACTORS: Masonry & Stonework

Charles Coons .... G 765 362-6509
Crawfordsville *(G-2552)*

Empire Contractors Inc .... D 812 424-3865
Evansville *(G-4035)*

Tremain Ceramic Tile & Flr Cvg .... E 317 542-1491
Indianapolis *(G-9633)*

CONTRACTORS: Oil & Gas Aerial Geophysical Exploration Svcs

Countrymark Ref Logistics LLC .... B 812 838-4341
Mount Vernon *(G-12295)*

CONTRACTORS: Oil & Gas Building, Repairing & Dismantling Svc

Helvie and Sons Inc .... G 765 674-1372
Marion *(G-11292)*

Nupointe Energy LLC .... F 765 981-2664
Warren *(G-16302)*

Sunrise Energy LLC .... G 812 886-9990
Vincennes *(G-16156)*

CONTRACTORS: Oil & Gas Field Geological Exploration Svcs

Domco LLC .... G 317 902-4404
Carmel *(G-1609)*

CONTRACTORS: Oil & Gas Wells Pumping Svcs

Cheri-Theree Inc .... G 812 529-8132
Lamar *(G-10795)*

JTI Inc .... G 317 797-9698
Indianapolis *(G-8647)*

K S Oil Corp .... G 812 453-3026
Mount Vernon *(G-12305)*

CONTRACTORS: Oil & Gas Wells Svcs

Imperial Petroleum Inc .... E 812 867-1433
Darmstadt *(G-2836)*

CONTRACTORS: Oil Field Haulage Svcs

Imel John .... G 317 873-8764
Zionsville *(G-17017)*

CONTRACTORS: Oil Field Mud Drilling Svcs

A A A Mudjackers Inc .... G 317 574-1990
Sharpsville *(G-14708)*

CONTRACTORS: Painting, Commercial

Csi Manufacturing Inc .... F 574 825-7891
Middlebury *(G-11708)*

Helming Bros Inc .... G 812 634-9797
Jasper *(G-9842)*

Quality Pnt Prstned Fnshes Inc .... G 574 294-6944
Elkhart *(G-3633)*

Van Zandt Enterprises Inc .... F 812 423-3511
Evansville *(G-4366)*

CONTRACTORS: Painting, Indl

Creative Liquid Coatings Inc .... B 260 349-1862
Kendallville *(G-10105)*

Northern Ind Indus Catings LLC .... G 574 893-4621
Akron *(G-6)*

Rex Alton & Companies Inc .... F 812 882-8519
Vincennes *(G-16149)*

Saran LP C
Indianapolis *(G-9373)*

CONTRACTORS: Petroleum Storage Tanks, Pumping & Draining

Tank Construction & Service Co .... F 317 509-6294
Whitestown *(G-16823)*

CONTRACTORS: Pile Driving

Thatcher Engineering Corp .... D 219 949-2084
Gary *(G-6018)*

CONTRACTORS: Plumbing

Danny Webb Plumbing .... G 574 936-2746
Plymouth *(G-13769)*

Griffen Plmbng-Heating-Cooling .... E 574 295-2440
Elkhart *(G-3392)*

Huntingburg Machine Works Inc .... F 812 683-3531
Huntingburg *(G-7282)*

Rcate Plbg Mech Ltd Lblty Co .... G 812 613-0895
Sellersburg *(G-14611)*

US Metals Inc .... G 219 802-8465
Hammond *(G-7027)*

CONTRACTORS: Power Generating Eqpt Installation

Discount Power Equipment .... G 765 642-0040
Anderson *(G-104)*

CONTRACTORS: Prefabricated Window & Door Installation

Concord Realstate Corp .... F 765 423-5555
Lafayette *(G-10554)*

H & H Home Improvement Inc .... G 812 288-8700
Clarksville *(G-2017)*

Huntington Exteriors Inc .... F 260 356-1621
Huntington *(G-7322)*

CONTRACTORS: Process Piping

Tron Mechanical Incorporated .... C 812 838-4715
Mount Vernon *(G-12324)*

CONTRACTORS: Refractory or Acid Brick Masonry

Pyro Industrial Services Inc .... E 219 787-5700
Portage *(G-13907)*

CONTRACTORS: Renovation, Aircraft Interiors

Indy Aerospace Inc .... G 817 521-6508
Indianapolis *(G-8522)*

Regent Aerospace Corporation .... C 317 837-4000
Plainfield *(G-13721)*

CONTRACTORS: Seismograph Survey Svcs

Seismic Vision LLC .... G 219 548-8704
Valparaiso *(G-16043)*

CONTRACTORS: Septic System

Eaton Septic Tank Company .... G 765 396-3275
Eaton *(G-3060)*

Jones & Sons Inc .... E 812 299-2287
Terre Haute *(G-15622)*

Mnt Delivery Company .... G 574 518-6250
Osceola *(G-13399)*

Russells Excvtg Sptc Tnks Inc .... F 812 838-2471
Mount Vernon *(G-12318)*

CONTRACTORS: Sheet Metal Work, NEC

Arrow Metals Inc .... E 765 825-4443
Connersville *(G-2426)*

Bright Sheet Metal Company Inc .... D 317 783-3181
Indianapolis *(G-7683)*

Bright Sheet Metal Company Inc .... D 317 291-7600
Indianapolis *(G-7684)*

C & K United Shtmtl & Mech .... E 812 423-5090
Evansville *(G-3958)*

Clover Sheet Metal Company .... F 574 293-5912
Elkhart *(G-3255)*

Helming Bros Inc .... G 812 634-9797
Jasper *(G-9842)*

Icon Metal Forming LLC .... B 812 738-5900
Corydon *(G-2499)*

J Coffey Metal Masters Inc .... D 317 780-1864
Indianapolis *(G-8604)*

Pb Metal Works .... G 765 489-1311
Hagerstown *(G-6841)*

Seib Machine & Tool Co Inc .... G 812 453-6174
Evansville *(G-4304)*

SW Watkins Limited .... D 260 484-4844
Fort Wayne *(G-5462)*

PRODUCT SECTION

CONTROLS: Electric Motor

Vidimos Inc .... D 219 397-2728
  East Chicago *(G-3054)*

CONTRACTORS: Ship Boiler & Tank Cleaning & Repair

Tradebe Environmental Svcs LLC .... E 800 388-7242
  Merrillville *(G-11568)*
Tradebe GP .... A 800 388-7242
  East Chicago *(G-3045)*
Tradebe Industrial Svcs LLC .... D 800 388-7242
  East Chicago *(G-3046)*

CONTRACTORS: Siding

H & H Home Improvement Inc .... G 812 288-8700
  Clarksville *(G-2017)*
Huntington Exteriors Inc .... F 260 356-1621
  Huntington *(G-7322)*

CONTRACTORS: Structural Iron Work, Structural

Buhrt Engineering & Cnstr .... E 574 267-3720
  Warsaw *(G-16331)*
Precision Surveillance Corp .... E 219 397-4295
  East Chicago *(G-3035)*
Reese Forge Orna Ironwork .... G 219 775-1039
  Lake Village *(G-10782)*

CONTRACTORS: Structural Steel Erection

Arrow Metals Inc .... E 765 825-4443
  Connersville *(G-2426)*
D & M Systems Inc .... G 812 327-2384
  Owensburg *(G-13461)*
Ellerbrock Welding LLC .... G 559 978-2651
  New Castle *(G-12860)*
Harpring Steel Inc .... G 812 256-6326
  Charlestown *(G-1878)*
Hgmc Supply Inc .... F 317 351-9500
  Indianapolis *(G-8394)*
Padgett Inc .... C 812 945-2391
  New Albany *(G-12790)*
Triple J Ironworks Inc .... G 765 544-9152
  Carthage *(G-1819)*

CONTRACTORS: Terrazzo Work

Santarossa Mosaic Tile Co Inc .... C 317 632-9494
  Indianapolis *(G-9371)*

CONTRACTORS: Tile Installation, Ceramic

Concepts In Stone & Tile Inc .... G 574 267-4712
  Warsaw *(G-16337)*
Max of All Trades LLC .... G 317 703-4242
  Kokomo *(G-10305)*
Tremain Ceramic Tile & Flr Cvg .... E 317 542-1491
  Indianapolis *(G-9633)*

CONTRACTORS: Underground Utilities

LGS Plumbing Inc .... E 219 663-2177
  Crown Point *(G-2718)*

CONTRACTORS: Ventilation & Duct Work

ABC Industries Inc .... D 800 426-0921
  Winona Lake *(G-16907)*
Cor-A-Vent Inc .... F 574 255-1910
  Mishawaka *(G-11866)*
Evansville Sheet Metal Works Inc .... D 812 423-7871
  Evansville *(G-4057)*
JO Mory Inc .... G 260 347-3753
  Kendallville *(G-10121)*
Millenium Sheet Metal Inc .... F 574 935-9101
  Plymouth *(G-13797)*

Superior Distribution .... G 317 308-5525
  Indianapolis *(G-9528)*

CONTRACTORS: Vinyl Flooring Installation, Tile & Sheet

Coronado Stone Inc .... E 812 284-2845
  Jeffersonville *(G-9962)*

CONTRACTORS: Warm Air Heating & Air Conditioning

Horner Industrial Services Inc .... F 317 634-7165
  Indianapolis *(G-8418)*

CONTRACTORS: Water Well Drilling

Bonar Inc .... G 260 636-7430
  Albion *(G-19)*
Gentry Well & Pump Service LLC .... G 260 563-1907
  Wabash *(G-16189)*
Hoover Well Drilling Inc .... G 574 831-4901
  New Paris *(G-12959)*
McGrews Well Drilling Inc .... G 574 857-3875
  Rochester *(G-14306)*
Remmler Well Drilling LLC .... G 812 663-8178
  Greensburg *(G-6627)*
Rose-Wall Mfg Inc .... G 317 894-4497
  Greenfield *(G-6544)*

CONTRACTORS: Wood Floor Installation & Refinishing

Jeff Hury Hrdwood Flors Pntg S .... G 812 204-8650
  Evansville *(G-4141)*
Milani Custom Homes LLC .... G 219 455-5804
  Merrillville *(G-11538)*

CONTRACTORS: Wrecking & Demolition

A & T Cnstr & Excvtg Inc .... G 219 314-2439
  Cedar Lake *(G-1826)*
C & R Cnstr & Consulting LLC .... G 812 738-4493
  Corydon *(G-2489)*

CONTROL EQPT: Electric

Advantage Electronics Inc .... F 317 888-1946
  Greenwood *(G-6659)*
Automation & Control Svcs Inc .... F 219 558-2060
  Schererville *(G-14514)*
Control Consultants of America .... G 219 989-3311
  Hammond *(G-6905)*
Doron Distribution Inc .... G 317 594-9259
  Carmel *(G-1610)*
Electronics Incorporated .... E 574 256-5001
  Mishawaka *(G-11891)*
Enginring Cncpts Unlimited Inc .... G 317 849-8470
  Fishers *(G-4514)*
ITT LLC .... G 260 451-6000
  Fort Wayne *(G-5122)*
Kreuter Manufacturing Co Inc .... G 574 831-4626
  New Paris *(G-12964)*
L3harris Technologies Inc .... G 260 451-6000
  Fort Wayne *(G-5171)*
Liberty Automation LLC .... G 574 524-0436
  Albion *(G-31)*
Rockwell Automation Inc .... D 219 924-3002
  Munster *(G-12561)*
Touchplate Technologies Inc .... E 260 426-1565
  Fort Wayne *(G-5497)*

CONTROL EQPT: Electric Buses & Locomotives

Illinois Tool Works Inc .... G 317 298-5000
  Indianapolis *(G-8461)*

Protron LLC .... G 765 313-1595
  Anderson *(G-181)*

CONTROL EQPT: Noise

Damping Technologies Inc .... F 574 258-7916
  Mishawaka *(G-11880)*
Damping Technologies Inc .... E 574 258-7916
  Mishawaka *(G-11879)*
Jason Holdings Inc .... C 414 277-9300
  Richmond *(G-14147)*

CONTROLS & ACCESS: Indl, Electric

Direct Control Systems Inc .... G 765 282-7474
  Muncie *(G-12384)*
Duesenburg Inc .... G 260 496-9650
  Fort Wayne *(G-4931)*
Dwyer Instruments LLC .... C 219 879-8868
  Michigan City *(G-11604)*
E C T Franklin Control Systems .... G 765 939-2531
  Richmond *(G-14117)*
Elkhart Electronics .... G 574 679-4627
  Osceola *(G-13390)*
Freelance Services LLC .... G 317 727-2669
  Pittsboro *(G-13647)*
Horner Apg LLC .... F 317 916-4274
  Indianapolis *(G-8414)*
Horner Industrial Services Inc .... G 260 434-1189
  Fort Wayne *(G-5083)*
Horner Industrial Services Inc .... G 812 466-5281
  Terre Haute *(G-15607)*
Horner Industrial Services Inc .... G 317 639-4261
  Indianapolis *(G-8416)*
JMS Electronics Corporation .... E 574 522-0246
  Elkhart *(G-3434)*
Master Filter Corporation .... G 317 545-3335
  Indianapolis *(G-8849)*
Top of Hill Performance LLC .... G 812 637-3693
  West Harrison *(G-16552)*

CONTROLS & ACCESS: Motor

Danfoss Power Solutions II LLC .... G 260 248-5800
  Columbia City *(G-2136)*
Eaton Corporation .... E 574 283-5004
  South Bend *(G-15009)*
Kcma & Services LLC .... G 260 645-0885
  Waterloo *(G-16522)*

CONTROLS: Automatic Temperature

Abbott Controls Inc .... G 317 697-7102
  Indianapolis *(G-7415)*
Advantage Engineering Inc .... D 317 887-0729
  Greenwood *(G-6660)*
Automated Logic Corporation .... F 765 286-1993
  Muncie *(G-12347)*
Building Temp Solutions LLC .... F 260 449-9201
  Fort Wayne *(G-4823)*
Jackson Systems LLC .... C 888 359-0365
  Indianapolis *(G-8615)*
Open Control Systems LLC .... G 317 429-0627
  Indianapolis *(G-9062)*
Pinder Instruments Company Inc .... G 219 924-7070
  Munster *(G-12558)*
Schneider Elc Systems USA Inc .... G 317 372-2839
  Indianapolis *(G-9390)*
Temperature Control Svcs LLC .... G 765 325-2439
  Lebanon *(G-10945)*
Temptek Inc .... G 317 887-6352
  Greenwood *(G-6773)*

CONTROLS: Electric Motor

Nidec Motor Corporation .... D 812 385-2564
  Princeton *(G-14007)*

CONTROLS: Electric Motor

SGS Cybermetrix Inc.. G 800 713-1203
  Columbus *(G-2391)*

CONTROLS: Environmental

OMI Industries Inc.. G 812 438-9218
  Rising Sun *(G-14244)*
Pyromation LLC.. C 260 484-2580
  Fort Wayne *(G-5358)*
Rees Inc.. F 260 495-9811
  Fremont *(G-5832)*
Ruskin... F 574 223-3181
  Rochester *(G-14322)*
Seminole Energy Services.................................. G 219 923-2131
  Highland *(G-7153)*
Spyder Controls Inc... G 866 919-9092
  South Bend *(G-15262)*
Thatcher Engineering Corp.................................. D 219 949-2084
  Gary *(G-6018)*
Utec Inc... A 260 359-3514
  Huntington *(G-7377)*
Vernet US Corporation... D 812 372-0281
  Columbus *(G-2412)*
Vernet US Corporation... C 812 372-0281
  Columbus *(G-2413)*

CONTROLS: Marine & Navy, Auxiliary

Electromechanical RES Labs................................ E 812 948-8484
  New Albany *(G-12724)*

CONVENIENCE STORES

Premier AG Co-Op Inc... E 812 522-4911
  Seymour *(G-14677)*

CONVERTERS: Torque, Exc Auto

Aisin Drivetrain Inc.. C 812 793-2427
  Crothersville *(G-2636)*
Champ Torque Converters Inc............................. G 812 424-2602
  Evansville *(G-3969)*

CONVEYOR SYSTEMS

Frontier Engineering.. G 317 823-6885
  Indianapolis *(G-8235)*
General Material Handling Co.............................. G 317 888-5735
  Indianapolis *(G-8272)*
Iron Bull Manufacturing LLC................................ G 765 597-2480
  Marshall *(G-11374)*
Martin Grgory Cnvyor Engrg LLC........................ G 812 923-9814
  Georgetown *(G-6068)*
S TEC Group Inc... F 219 844-7030
  Hammond *(G-7002)*
Systec Corporation.. D 317 890-9230
  Indianapolis *(G-9542)*

CONVEYOR SYSTEMS: Belt, General Indl Use

Bastian Solutions LLC... F 317 575-9992
  Westfield *(G-16668)*

CONVEYOR SYSTEMS: Bulk Handling

Summerlot Engineered Pdts Inc.......................... F 812 466-7266
  Rosedale *(G-14383)*

CONVEYOR SYSTEMS: Pneumatic Tube

Berendsen Inc... G 812 423-6468
  Evansville *(G-3916)*
Ctb Inc... E 765 654-8517
  Frankfort *(G-5657)*
CTB MN Investment Co Inc................................. A 765 654-8517
  Frankfort *(G-5658)*
Indiana Im Holdings Inc....................................... E 260 637-3101
  Fort Wayne *(G-5101)*

CONVEYOR SYSTEMS: Robotic

Butterworth Industries Inc................................... E 765 677-6725
  Gas City *(G-6034)*
Pia Automation US Inc.. E 812 485-5500
  Evansville *(G-4242)*

CONVEYORS & CONVEYING EQPT

1st Source Products Inc...................................... F 812 288-7466
  Jeffersonville *(G-9919)*
Advance Fabricators Inc...................................... E 812 944-6941
  New Albany *(G-12686)*
Aggregate Systems... F 260 854-4711
  Rome City *(G-14373)*
Applicon Company Incorporated......................... F 317 635-7843
  Indianapolis *(G-7532)*
Banks Machine & Engrg LLC.............................. D 317 642-4980
  Shelbyville *(G-14732)*
Belt Tech Industrial Inc.. E 812 258-5959
  Washington *(G-16473)*
C & P Engineering and Mfg Inc........................... F 765 825-4293
  Connersville *(G-2430)*
C&M Conveyor Inc.. C 812 849-5647
  Mitchell *(G-12034)*
Carman Industries Inc... E 812 288-4710
  Jeffersonville *(G-9950)*
Conveyors Inc... G 317 539-5472
  Danville *(G-2809)*
CPM Conveyor LLC... E 317 875-1919
  Indianapolis *(G-7894)*
Custom Conveyor Inc.. F 812 663-2023
  Greensburg *(G-6588)*
Daifuku Intrlgistics Amer Corp............................. D 219 777-2220
  Hobart *(G-7186)*
Direct Conveyors LLC.. E 317 346-7777
  Franklin *(G-5725)*
Fabricated Steel Corporation............................... G 317 899-0012
  Indianapolis *(G-8162)*
George Koch Sons LLC....................................... D 812 465-9600
  Evansville *(G-4089)*
Gravel Conveyors Inc.. F 317 873-8686
  Zionsville *(G-17014)*
H & H Design & Tool Inc..................................... G 765 886-6199
  Economy *(G-3066)*
Halo LLC... D 317 575-9992
  Carmel *(G-1647)*
Hirata Corporation of America............................. E 317 856-8600
  Indianapolis *(G-8399)*
Hoosier Conveyor Company LLC........................ G 765 445-3337
  Knightstown *(G-10197)*
Hovair Automotive LLC....................................... E 317 738-0485
  Franklin *(G-5742)*
Industrial Transmission Eqp................................ E 574 936-3028
  Plymouth *(G-13785)*
Interntnal Mtl Hdlg Systems In............................ F 812 222-4488
  Greensburg *(G-6609)*
Keener Corporation... E 765 825-2100
  Connersville *(G-2449)*
Kelco Steel Fabrication Inc.................................. G 317 248-9229
  Indianapolis *(G-8667)*
Koehler Welding Supply Inc................................ F 812 574-4103
  Madison *(G-11233)*
Lauyans Holdings Inc.. E
  New Albany *(G-12763)*
M Pro LLC... G 765 459-4750
  Kokomo *(G-10302)*
Mainline Conveyor Systems Inc.......................... F 317 831-2795
  Mooresville *(G-12219)*
Manchester Inc.. G 260 982-2202
  Roann *(G-14252)*
McClamroch Ag LLC.. G 765 362-4495
  Crawfordsville *(G-2588)*
McGinty Conveyors Inc....................................... G 317 240-4315
  Indianapolis *(G-8865)*
Prime Conveyor Inc... E 219 736-1994
  Merrillville *(G-11552)*
Rowe Conveyor LLC.. E 317 602-1024
  Indianapolis *(G-9338)*
Rowe Conveyor LLC.. E 317 602-1024
  Greenwood *(G-6761)*
Sager Metal Strip Company LLC......................... E 219 874-3609
  Michigan City *(G-11659)*
Screw Conveyor Corporation............................... E 219 931-1450
  Hammond *(G-7003)*
Screw Conveyor Pacific Corp.............................. E 219 931-1450
  Hammond *(G-7004)*
Shuttleworth LLC... D 260 356-8500
  Huntington *(G-7368)*
Smock Materials Handling Co............................. F 317 890-3200
  Indianapolis *(G-9452)*
Sparks Belting Company Inc............................... G 800 451-4537
  Hammond *(G-7012)*
Stahl Equipment Inc.. F 812 925-3341
  Gentryville *(G-6053)*
Vestil Manufacturing Corp................................... C 260 665-7586
  Angola *(G-306)*
Vibcon Corporation.. F 317 984-3543
  Arcadia *(G-319)*
W M Kelley Co Inc... D 812 945-3529
  New Albany *(G-12825)*
Webber Manufacturing Company......................... E 317 357-8681
  Indianapolis *(G-9745)*

COOKING & FOODWARMING EQPT: Commercial

Accutemp Products Inc....................................... D 260 493-0415
  New Haven *(G-12889)*
Bottom Line Management Inc.............................. F 812 944-7388
  Clarksville *(G-2010)*
MD Holdings LLC.. G 317 831-7030
  Mooresville *(G-12220)*

COOKWARE, STONEWARE: Coarse Earthenware & Pottery

Carol Burt... G 765 282-5383
  Muncie *(G-12365)*
Molded Acstcal Pdts Easton Inc......................... E 574 968-3124
  Granger *(G-6363)*

COOLING TOWERS: Metal

Advantage Engineering Inc.................................. D 317 887-0729
  Greenwood *(G-6660)*
SPX Corporation.. D 219 879-6561
  Michigan City *(G-11671)*
SPX Corporation.. G 812 849-5647
  Mitchell *(G-12048)*

COOLING TOWERS: Wood

Action Cooling Towers Inc................................... G 219 285-2660
  Morocco *(G-12267)*
Cleveland-Cliffs Kote LP..................................... B 574 654-1000
  New Carlisle *(G-12837)*

COPPER: Rolling & Drawing

Alconex Specialty Products................................ E 260 744-3446
  Fort Wayne *(G-4738)*
Brand Sheet Metal Works Inc.............................. G 765 284-5594
  Muncie *(G-12356)*
Southwire Company LLC..................................... D 574 546-5115
  Bremen *(G-1222)*
Southwire Company LLC..................................... E 765 449-7227
  Lafayette *(G-10693)*

PRODUCT SECTION

DIES & TOOLS: Special

Knitting Mill Inc.................................G.....219 942-8031
   Hobart *(G-7198)*

DENTAL EQPT & SPLYS: Enamels

Kathy Zuccarelli..............................G.....219 865-4095
   Schererville *(G-14526)*

Michael J Meyer D M D P C...............G.....812 275-7112
   Bedford *(G-658)*

Ronald L Miller................................G.....765 662-3881
   Marion *(G-11336)*

DENTAL EQPT & SPLYS: Orthodontic Appliances

Growing Smiles Inc..........................G.....317 787-6404
   Indianapolis *(G-8335)*

Orthodontic Design & Prod Inc...........E.....317 346-6655
   Franklin *(G-5763)*

Protero Corporation.........................E.....219 393-5591
   Kingsford Heights *(G-10186)*

Rmo Inc...C.....303 592-8200
   Franklin *(G-5774)*

TP Orthodontics Inc.........................B.....219 785-2591
   La Porte *(G-10494)*

DENTAL INSTRUMENT REPAIR SVCS

Fidelity Dental Handpiece Svc............G.....317 254-0277
   Indianapolis *(G-8185)*

DENTISTS' OFFICES & CLINICS

National Dentex LLC........................C.....317 849-5143
   Indianapolis *(G-8987)*

Somer Inc......................................E.....317 873-1111
   Zionsville *(G-17051)*

DEODORANTS: Personal

Relevo Labs LLC.............................G.....317 900-6949
   Carmel *(G-1739)*

DERMATOLOGICALS

Noah Worcester Derm Society............G.....317 257-5907
   Indianapolis *(G-9015)*

DESIGN SVCS, NEC

Clean By Design Inc........................G.....260 414-4444
   Fort Wayne *(G-4857)*

Concept Prints Inc...........................F.....317 290-1222
   Indianapolis *(G-7851)*

Costumes By Design.......................G.....812 334-2029
   Bloomington *(G-849)*

Digital Design Genius......................G.....317 515-3680
   Camby *(G-1509)*

Menard Inc.....................................C.....812 466-1234
   Terre Haute *(G-15641)*

Midwest Design Hydraulic.................G.....765 714-3016
   West Lafayette *(G-16605)*

Nka Cabinet Designs LLC.................G.....765 490-4661
   Lafayette *(G-10659)*

Olson Custom Designs LLC...............E.....317 892-6400
   Indianapolis *(G-9046)*

Squeegeepie Merch Co LLC..............G.....765 376-6358
   Crawfordsville *(G-2618)*

Travis Britton.................................G.....317 762-6018
   Indianapolis *(G-9632)*

Westlund Concepts.........................F.....317 819-0611
   Lapel *(G-10818)*

Whimsicals Inc...............................G.....317 773-6130
   Noblesville *(G-13194)*

Zojila Ltd Liability Company..............G.....765 404-3767
   Lafayette *(G-10726)*

DESIGN SVCS: Commercial & Indl

K C Creations.................................G.....937 418-1859
   Indianapolis *(G-8653)*

King Investments Inc.......................G.....812 752-6000
   Scottsburg *(G-14568)*

Sampco Inc....................................G.....413 442-4043
   South Bend *(G-15230)*

DESIGN SVCS: Computer Integrated Systems

Blue Byte Tech Solutions LLC............G.....574 903-5637
   Elkhart *(G-3227)*

Crown Training and Dev Inc...............F.....219 947-0845
   Merrillville *(G-11500)*

Fiserv Mrtg Servicing Systems...........C.....574 282-3300
   South Bend *(G-15034)*

Flynn Media LLC............................G.....317 536-2972
   Indianapolis *(G-8210)*

Gta Enterprises Inc..........................E.....260 478-7800
   Fort Wayne *(G-5044)*

Long Tail Corporation......................G.....260 918-0489
   Fort Wayne *(G-5191)*

Orion Global Sourcing Inc.................G.....812 332-3338
   Bloomington *(G-939)*

Rob Nolley Inc................................F.....317 825-5211
   Shelbyville *(G-14792)*

DIAGNOSTIC SUBSTANCES

Cardinal Health 414 LLC...................F.....317 981-4100
   Indianapolis *(G-7740)*

Intervention Diagnostics Inc...............G.....317 432-6091
   Indianapolis *(G-8584)*

R 2 Diagnostics Inc.........................G.....574 288-4377
   South Bend *(G-15212)*

Roche Diagnostics Corporation..........A.....800 428-5076
   Indianapolis *(G-9319)*

Siemens Hlthcare Dgnostics Inc.........G.....574 262-6139
   Elkhart *(G-3675)*

Strand Diagnostics LLC....................G.....317 455-2100
   Indianapolis *(G-9517)*

DIAGNOSTIC SUBSTANCES OR AGENTS: Blood Derivative

Chematics Inc.................................F.....574 834-2406
   North Webster *(G-13303)*

DIAGNOSTIC SUBSTANCES OR AGENTS: Enzyme & Isoenzyme

Stanbio Laboratory LP.....................G.....830 249-0772
   Elkhart *(G-3695)*

DIAGNOSTIC SUBSTANCES OR AGENTS: In Vitro

Synermed International Inc................G.....317 896-1565
   Westfield *(G-16731)*

Sysgenomics LLC...........................G.....574 302-5396
   Granger *(G-6384)*

DIAGNOSTIC SUBSTANCES OR AGENTS: Microbiology & Virology

Core Biologic LLC...........................G.....888 390-8838
   Fort Wayne *(G-4875)*

Microworks Inc...............................G.....219 661-8620
   Crown Point *(G-2724)*

Poly Group LLC..............................G.....812 590-4750
   New Albany *(G-12796)*

DIAGNOSTIC SUBSTANCES OR AGENTS: Radioactive

Petnet Indiana LLC..........................E.....865 218-2000
   Indianapolis *(G-9129)*

DIAGNOSTIC SUBSTANCES OR AGENTS: Veterinary

Mwi Veterinary Supply Co.................G.....317 769-7771
   Lebanon *(G-10924)*

DIAMONDS, GEMS, WHOLESALE

Downey Creations LLC....................F.....317 248-9888
   Indianapolis *(G-8003)*

Nina Gail Diamonds LLC..................G.....765 591-0477
   Muncie *(G-12469)*

DIE CUTTING SVC: Paper

Bruce Payne..................................G.....260 492-2259
   Fort Wayne *(G-4820)*

DIE SETS: Presses, Metal Stamping

Budco Tool & Die Inc.......................E.....574 522-4004
   Elkhart *(G-3237)*

Little Engineering LLC.....................G.....317 517-3323
   Whiteland *(G-16791)*

Standard Die Supply of Indiana Inc.....D.....317 236-6200
   Indianapolis *(G-9493)*

DIES & TOOLS: Special

A & A Custom Automation Inc............D.....812 464-3650
   Evansville *(G-3858)*

AAA Tool and Die Company Inc..........F.....574 246-1222
   South Bend *(G-14931)*

Accutech Mold & Machine Inc............C.....260 471-6102
   Fort Wayne *(G-4722)*

Ahaus Tool & Engineering Inc............D.....765 962-3573
   Richmond *(G-14084)*

Ajax Tool Inc..................................G.....260 747-7482
   Fort Wayne *(G-4735)*

Allegiance Tool and Die Inc...............G.....574 277-1819
   Granger *(G-6331)*

Ameri-Tek Manufacturing Inc............F.....574 753-8058
   Logansport *(G-11055)*

Apex Tool and Manufacturing............E.....812 425-8121
   Evansville *(G-3894)*

Ark Model and Stampings Inc............F.....317 549-3394
   New Palestine *(G-12931)*

Artisan Tool & Die Inc......................E.....765 288-6653
   Muncie *(G-12346)*

Atkisson Enterprises Inc...................F.....765 675-7593
   Tipton *(G-15766)*

Aul In The Family Tool and Die..........G.....765 759-5161
   Yorktown *(G-16969)*

B & B Engineering Inc.....................G.....765 566-3460
   Bringhurst *(G-1235)*

B & D Manufacturing Inc..................G.....765 452-2761
   Kokomo *(G-10234)*

B & J Specialty Inc..........................D.....260 761-5011
   Wawaka *(G-16536)*

B B & H Tool of Columbus Inc............F.....812 372-3707
   Columbus *(G-2224)*

B/C Precision Tool Inc.....................G.....812 577-0642
   Greendale *(G-6439)*

B&J Rocket America Inc...................E.....574 825-5802
   Middlebury *(G-11700)*

Batesville Tool & Die Inc...................B.....812 934-5616
   Batesville *(G-584)*

Beckys Die Cutting Inc....................G.....260 467-1714
   Fort Wayne *(G-4792)*

Berkey Machine Corporation.............G.....260 761-4002
   Wawaka *(G-16538)*

Blessing Tool & Die Inc....................G.....574 875-1982
   Elkhart *(G-3226)*

DIES & TOOLS: Special

Bmg Inc .... G 812 437-3643
   Evansville *(G-3936)*

Britt Tool Inc .... D 812 446-0503
   Brazil *(G-1136)*

Bst Enterprises Inc .... G 260 493-4313
   New Haven *(G-12895)*

Btd Manufacturing Inc .... G 812 934-5616
   Batesville *(G-585)*

Butler Tool & Design Inc .... F 219 297-4531
   Goodland *(G-6080)*

C & G Tool Inc .... G 812 524-7061
   Jonesville *(G-10083)*

Center Line Mold & Tool Inc .... F 812 526-0970
   Edinburgh *(G-3070)*

Century Tool & Engr Inc .... G 317 685-0942
   Indianapolis *(G-7776)*

Chiyoda Montrow Die Mfg Inc .... G 812 767-1885
   North Vernon *(G-13257)*

Claymore Tools Inc .... G 574 255-6483
   South Bend *(G-14975)*

Clifty Engineering and Tool Co .... C 812 273-3272
   Madison *(G-11210)*

Collins Tl & Die Ltd Lblty Co .... G 812 273-4765
   Madison *(G-11211)*

Competition Tl & Engrg II Inc .... G 812 524-1991
   Seymour *(G-14639)*

Continental Machining Pdts Inc .... G 219 474-5061
   Kentland *(G-10158)*

Corydon Machine & Tool Co Inc .... E 812 738-3107
   Corydon *(G-2495)*

Custom Engineering Inc .... F 812 424-3879
   Evansville *(G-4003)*

Cutting Edge Wire Edm Inc .... G 765 284-3820
   Muncie *(G-12371)*

D & E Machine Inc .... G 765 653-8919
   Greencastle *(G-6402)*

D & J Tool Co Inc .... G 260 636-2682
   Albion *(G-21)*

D & M Tool Corporation .... E 812 279-8882
   Springville *(G-15384)*

D A Hochstetler & Sons LLP .... F 574 642-1144
   Topeka *(G-15800)*

D1 Mold & Tool LLC .... F 765 378-0693
   Alexandria *(G-48)*

Dedrick Tool & Die Inc .... G 260 824-3334
   Bluffton *(G-1034)*

Defelice Engineering Inc .... G 317 834-2832
   Mooresville *(G-12201)*

Delta Tool Manufacturing Inc .... G 574 223-4863
   Rochester *(G-14286)*

Die-Rite Machine and Tool Corp .... G 574 522-2366
   Elkhart *(G-3297)*

Dieco of Indiana Inc .... F 765 825-4151
   Connersville *(G-2435)*

Dietech Corporation .... G 260 724-8946
   Decatur *(G-2852)*

Diversified Tools and Mchs Inc .... G 260 489-0272
   Fort Wayne *(G-4919)*

DOE Run Tooling Inc .... G 812 265-3057
   Madison *(G-11215)*

Double H Manufacturing Corp .... D 215 674-4100
   Marion *(G-11281)*

Drp Mold Inc .... G 765 349-3355
   Martinsville *(G-11389)*

Duel Tool & Gage Inc .... G 317 244-0129
   Indianapolis *(G-8018)*

dwg Design Services Corp .... G 812 372-0864
   Columbus *(G-2292)*

Dynamic Dies Inc .... E 419 861-5413
   Indianapolis *(G-8025)*

Dynamic Tool Machine .... G 765 730-0167
   Yorktown *(G-16973)*

E F M Corporation .... D 812 372-4421
   Columbus *(G-2293)*

Elkhart Laser Products LLC .... G 574 304-7242
   Elkhart *(G-3326)*

Elkhart Tool and Die Inc .... E 574 295-8500
   Elkhart *(G-3331)*

Evansville Tool & Die Inc .... F 812 422-7101
   Evansville *(G-4059)*

Evart Engineering Company Inc .... F 765 354-2232
   Middletown *(G-11769)*

Ex-Cut Technology LLC .... F 260 672-9602
   Roanoke *(G-14263)*

Fayette Tool and Engineering .... D 765 825-7518
   Connersville *(G-2438)*

Fisher Tool 2 Inc .... G 812 867-8350
   Evansville *(G-4071)*

Foil Die International Inc .... F 260 359-9011
   Huntington *(G-7310)*

Foil Form Inc .... G 260 359-9011
   Huntington *(G-7311)*

Fort Wayne Mold & Engrg Inc .... E 260 747-9168
   Fort Wayne *(G-4998)*

Franklin Stamping Inds Inc .... F 765 282-5138
   Muncie *(G-12397)*

Future Tool & Engrg Co Inc .... F 812 376-8699
   Columbus *(G-2311)*

Granite Engrg & Tl Co Inc .... F 812 375-9077
   Columbus *(G-2314)*

Grotrian Tool & Die .... G 260 894-3558
   Ligonier *(G-11016)*

Gta Enterprises Inc .... E 260 478-7800
   Fort Wayne *(G-5044)*

Gvs Technologies LLC .... F 574 293-0974
   Elkhart *(G-3393)*

H & H Design & Tool Inc .... G 765 886-6199
   Economy *(G-3066)*

H and M Tool & Die Inc .... F 812 663-8252
   Greensburg *(G-6599)*

Heritage Tool and Die Inc .... G 260 359-8121
   Huntington *(G-7318)*

Hermetic Coil Co Inc .... E 812 735-2400
   Bicknell *(G-734)*

Hipsher Tool & Die Inc .... F 260 563-4143
   Wabash *(G-16192)*

Hoosier Manufacturing LLC .... G 260 493-9990
   Fort Wayne *(G-5078)*

Hoosier Toolmaking & Engrg Inc .... G 260 493-9990
   Fort Wayne *(G-5081)*

Humphrey Tool Co Inc .... G 574 753-3853
   Logansport *(G-11079)*

Huntington Tool & Die Inc .... F 260 356-5940
   Van Buren *(G-16085)*

IAm Aw Tl Die Makers LL 229 .... G 574 333-5955
   Elkhart *(G-3416)*

Industrial Mlding Cnslting DSI .... G 574 653-2772
   Kewanna *(G-10165)*

Industrial Tool & Die Corp .... F 812 424-9971
   Evansville *(G-4125)*

Injection Plastics & Mfg Co .... E 574 784-2070
   Lapaz *(G-10816)*

Inson Tool & Machine Inc .... G 812 752-3754
   Scottsburg *(G-14564)*

J B Tool Die & Engineering Co .... C 260 483-9586
   Fort Wayne *(G-5123)*

J O Wolf Tool & Die Inc .... G 260 672-2605
   Huntington *(G-7333)*

J P Corporation .... G 317 783-1000
   Beech Grove *(G-693)*

J W Model & Engineering Inc .... G 317 788-7471
   Indianapolis *(G-8609)*

Jacobs Machine & Tool Co Inc .... F 317 831-2917
   Mooresville *(G-12217)*

Jj Machine .... G 765 723-1511
   New Ross *(G-12980)*

Jpg Machine & Tool LLC .... G 812 265-4512
   Madison *(G-11232)*

K & K Inc .... F 574 266-8040
   Elkhart *(G-3440)*

K & M Tool & Die Inc .... G 765 482-9464
   Lebanon *(G-10906)*

K-K Tool and Design Inc .... E 260 758-2940
   Markle *(G-11356)*

Kazmier Tooling Inc .... G 773 586-0300
   Hammond *(G-6965)*

Keller Tool .... G 812 873-7344
   Butlerville *(G-1486)*

Ken-Bar Tool & Engineering Inc .... E 765 284-4408
   Noblesville *(G-13119)*

Kent Machine Inc .... E 765 778-7777
   Pendleton *(G-13539)*

King Industrial Corporation .... F 812 522-3261
   Seymour *(G-14662)*

Kirby Machine Company LLC .... E 317 773-6700
   Noblesville *(G-13122)*

Krukemeier Machine & Tool Co .... E 317 784-7042
   Beech Grove *(G-697)*

Lafayette Tool & Die Inc .... G 765 429-6362
   Lafayette *(G-10631)*

Lake Tool & Die Inc .... G 574 457-8274
   Syracuse *(G-15467)*

Le-Hue Machine and Tool Co .... G 574 255-8404
   Mishawaka *(G-11927)*

Lehue Machine and Tool .... G 574 329-5456
   Osceola *(G-13397)*

Lex Tooling LLC .... G 765 675-6301
   Tipton *(G-15779)*

Lone Star Tool & Die Weld .... G 812 346-9681
   Vernon *(G-16097)*

Mac Machine & Metal Works Inc .... E 765 825-4121
   Connersville *(G-2453)*

Madison Tool and Die Inc .... D 812 273-2250
   Madison *(G-11239)*

Mark Tool & Die Inc .... F 765 533-4932
   Markleville *(G-11369)*

Matrix Manufacturing Inc .... G 260 854-4659
   Wolcottville *(G-16941)*

McGinn Tool & Engineering Co .... F 317 736-5512
   Franklin *(G-5755)*

Mdl Mold & Die Components Inc .... G 812 373-0021
   Columbus *(G-2351)*

Michiana Metal Fabrication Inc .... G 574 256-9010
   Elkhart *(G-3533)*

Michiana Plastics Inc .... E 574 259-6262
   Mishawaka *(G-11945)*

Midwest Tool & Die Corp .... E 260 414-1506
   Fort Wayne *(G-5226)*

Millennium Tool Inc .... E 812 701-5761
   Madison *(G-11244)*

Modern Drop Forge Company LLC .... B 708 489-4208
   Merrillville *(G-11541)*

Mold Service Inc .... G 260 868-2920
   Butler *(G-1471)*

Msk Mold Inc .... G 812 985-5457
   Wadesville *(G-16227)*

Norman Tool Inc .... G 812 867-3496
   Evansville *(G-4221)*

North-Side Machine & Tool Inc .... F 765 654-4538
   Frankfort *(G-5686)*

Northern Tool & Die LLC .... G 260 495-7314
   Fremont *(G-5830)*

O & R Precision Grinding Inc .... E 260 368-9394
   Berne *(G-721)*

Onxx Tool Inc .... G 260 897-3530
   Avilla *(G-491)*

PRODUCT SECTION — DOORS & WINDOWS: Storm, Metal

Overton & Sons Tl & Die Co Inc .... E 317 831-4542
Mooresville *(G-12232)*

Pace Tool & Engineering Inc .... G 812 373-9885
Hope *(G-7230)*

Perfection Mold & Tool Inc .... G 574 292-0824
South Bend *(G-15191)*

Perm Industries Inc .... E 219 365-5000
Saint John *(G-14456)*

Ploog Engineering Co Inc .... G 219 663-2854
Crown Point *(G-2731)*

Precision Tool & Die Inc .... G 765 664-4786
Marion *(G-11330)*

Precision Tubes Inc .... G 317 783-2339
Indianapolis *(G-9187)*

Premium Mold Tool .... G 812 967-3187
Pekin *(G-13521)*

Price Machine & Tool Inc .... G 260 338-1081
Huntertown *(G-7263)*

Proton Mold Tool Inc .... G 812 923-7263
Floyds Knobs *(G-4690)*

Quality Mold and Engrg Inc .... G 812 346-6577
Vernon *(G-16098)*

Quality Steel & Aluminium .... G 574 294-7221
Elkhart *(G-3635)*

Quality Tool & Die Inc .... G 219 324-2511
La Porte *(G-10469)*

R & M Tool Engineering Inc .... F 812 352-0240
North Vernon *(G-13294)*

Reich Tool & Design Inc .... F 574 849-6416
Elkhart *(G-3646)*

Richeys Mold and Tool Inc .... G 812 752-1059
Scottsburg *(G-14576)*

River Valley Plastics Inc .... E 574 262-5221
Elkhart *(G-3649)*

Robert Atkins .... G 765 536-4164
Summitville *(G-15430)*

Ross Engineering & Machine Inc .... E 574 586-7791
Walkerton *(G-16276)*

Specialty Engrg Tl & Die LLC .... G 260 356-2678
Huntington *(G-7369)*

Specialty Tool & Die Company .... F 765 452-9209
Kokomo *(G-10337)*

Specialty Tooling Inc .... F 812 464-8521
Evansville *(G-4328)*

Speedcraft Prototypes .... G 765 644-6449
Anderson *(G-198)*

Stamina Metal Products Inc .... G 574 534-7410
Goshen *(G-6258)*

Star Tool & Die Inc .... F 574 264-3815
Elkhart *(G-3698)*

Star Tool Inc .... E 812 372-6730
Columbus *(G-2395)*

Stolle Tool Incorporated .... F 765 935-5185
Richmond *(G-14209)*

Superior Tool & Die Co Inc .... E 574 293-2591
Elkhart *(G-3710)*

Sure Tool & Engineering Inc .... G 260 693-2193
Churubusco *(G-1988)*

T & I Tool LLC .... G 765 489-6293
Hagerstown *(G-6844)*

T & L Tool & Die II Inc .... G 574 722-6246
Logansport *(G-11110)*

Tempest Tool & Machine Inc .... E 812 346-6464
North Vernon *(G-13299)*

Thompson Machining Svcs Inc .... F 765 647-3451
Brookville *(G-1337)*

Tmak Inc .... E 219 874-7661
Michigan City *(G-11679)*

Toolcraft LLC .... E 260 749-0454
Fort Wayne *(G-5494)*

Toolmasters Inc .... G 574 256-1881
Mishawaka *(G-12014)*

Trace Engineering Inc .... G 765 354-4351
Middletown *(G-11777)*

United Tool & Engineering Inc .... E 574 259-1953
Mishawaka *(G-12019)*

W W G Inc .... G 317 783-6413
Indianapolis *(G-9733)*

Wabash Valley Tool & Engrg .... G 260 563-7690
Wabash *(G-16222)*

Walkerton Tool & Die Inc .... E 574 586-3162
Walkerton *(G-16279)*

DIES: Cutting, Exc Metal

Atlas Die LLC .... D 574 295-0050
Elkhart *(G-3200)*

Pro-Form Plastics Inc .... E 812 522-4433
Crothersville *(G-2644)*

DIES: Diamond, Metalworking

C & A Tool Engineering Inc .... C 260 693-2167
Auburn *(G-372)*

C & A Tool Engineering Inc .... G 260 693-2167
Churubusco *(G-1978)*

C & A Tool Engineering Inc .... G 260 693-2167
Churubusco *(G-1979)*

C & A Tool Engineering Inc .... G 260 693-2167
Churubusco *(G-1980)*

C & A Tool Engineering Inc .... G 260 693-2167
Churubusco *(G-1981)*

C & A Tool Engineering Inc .... B 260 693-2167
Churubusco *(G-1982)*

Fort Wayne Wire Die Inc .... C 260 747-1681
Fort Wayne *(G-5002)*

Heritage Wire Die Inc .... G 260 728-9300
Decatur *(G-2862)*

Woodburn Diamond Die Inc .... E 260 632-4217
Woodburn *(G-16957)*

DIES: Extrusion

Al-Ex Inc .... G 574 206-0100
Elkhart *(G-3157)*

Intertech Products Inc .... D 260 982-1544
North Manchester *(G-13235)*

DIES: Paper Cutting

Dynamic Dies Inc .... E 317 247-4706
Indianapolis *(G-8026)*

DIES: Plastic Forming

Delux Industries Inc .... E 812 867-0655
Evansville *(G-4011)*

Grimm Mold & Die Co Inc .... F 219 778-4211
Rolling Prairie *(G-14363)*

Herman Tool & Machine Inc .... F 574 594-5544
Pierceton *(G-13632)*

Smith Machine and Tool .... G 574 223-2318
Rochester *(G-14326)*

Wcm Tool & Machine Inc .... G 812 422-2315
Evansville *(G-4380)*

DIES: Steel Rule

Allied Steel Rule Dies Inc .... F 317 634-9835
Indianapolis *(G-7484)*

American Steel Rule Die Inc .... G 574 262-3437
Elkhart *(G-3175)*

Atlas Die LLC .... D 574 295-0050
Elkhart *(G-3200)*

Meck Die Inc .... G 574 262-5441
Elkhart *(G-3523)*

Midwest Stl Rule Cutng Die Inc .... E 317 780-4600
Indianapolis *(G-8914)*

DIODES & RECTIFIERS

Perfection Products Inc .... E 765 482-7786
Lebanon *(G-10932)*

DIODES: Light Emitting

Amerlight LLC .... F 812 602-3452
Evansville *(G-3889)*

Dti Services Ltd Liability Co .... G 765 745-0261
Indianapolis *(G-8015)*

Neoti LLC .... F 260 494-1499
Bluffton *(G-1045)*

DIRECT SELLING ESTABLISHMENTS, NEC

Big Red Liquors Inc .... G 812 339-9552
Bloomington *(G-806)*

DIRECT SELLING ESTABLISHMENTS: Food Svcs

Deonta Walker .... G 317 970-3586
Indianapolis *(G-7965)*

DISCS & TAPE: Optical, Blank

Sony Dadc US Inc .... F 812 462-8116
Terre Haute *(G-15704)*

Sony Dadc US Inc .... F 812 462-8784
Terre Haute *(G-15705)*

Sony Dadc US Inc .... A 812 462-8100
Terre Haute *(G-15706)*

DISPLAY ITEMS: Corrugated, Made From Purchased Materials

Cox John .... G 765 463-6396
West Lafayette *(G-16571)*

DISTRIBUTORS: Motor Vehicle Engine

Spectra Prmium Mblity Sltons L .... F 800 628-5442
Greenfield *(G-6557)*

DOCK EQPT & SPLYS, INDL

M & J Shelton Enterprises Inc .... G 260 745-1616
Fort Wayne *(G-5194)*

Red Earth LLC .... G 260 338-1439
Fort Wayne *(G-5373)*

T & S Equipment Company .... D 260 665-9521
Angola *(G-297)*

Tis Holding Inc .... G 317 946-6354
Indianapolis *(G-9609)*

Vestil Manufacturing Corp .... E 260 665-7586
Angola *(G-305)*

Vestil Manufacturing Corp .... C 260 665-7586
Angola *(G-306)*

DOCKS: Floating, Wood

Engineered Dock Systems Inc .... G 317 803-2443
Indianapolis *(G-8120)*

DOOR FRAMES: Wood

Fairmont Door Corp .... G 260 563-6307
Wabash *(G-16185)*

Licar America LLC .... E 812 256-6400
Jeffersonville *(G-10012)*

Mishawaka Door LLC .... G 574 259-2822
Mishawaka *(G-11954)*

DOORS & WINDOWS: Storm, Metal

All-Weather Products Inc .... G 812 867-6403
Evansville *(G-3880)*

Maher Supply Inc .... G 812 234-7699
Terre Haute *(G-15635)*

Employee Codes: A=Over 500 employees, B=251-500
C=101-250, D=51-100, E=20-50, F=10-19, G=1-9

DOORS & WINDOWS: Storm, Metal

Sun Control Center LLC.................................. F 260 490-9902
 Fort Wayne *(G-5456)*
Trim-A-Seal of Indiana Inc......................... F 219 883-2180
 Gary *(G-6022)*

DOORS: Fire, Metal

A & A Sheet Metal Products................... D 219 326-1288
 La Porte *(G-10371)*

DOORS: Folding, Plastic Or Plastic Coated Fabric

Irvine Shade & Door Inc........................... D 574 522-1446
 Elkhart *(G-3430)*

DOORS: Garage, Overhead, Metal

Ecpca Safe-Way LLC................................. D 574 267-4861
 Warsaw *(G-16354)*
Modern Door Corporation......................... D 574 586-3117
 Walkerton *(G-16271)*
Safe-Way Garage Doors LLC..................... E 574 267-4861
 Warsaw *(G-16420)*

DOORS: Garage, Overhead, Wood

Ecpca Safe-Way LLC................................. D 574 267-4861
 Warsaw *(G-16354)*
Pro Door Manufacturing LLC................... D 317 839-3050
 Plainfield *(G-13717)*

DOORS: Glass

Vernon Greyber... G 812 636-7880
 Odon *(G-13355)*

DOORS: Screen, Metal

Kinro Manufacturing Inc.......................... E 574 535-1125
 Elkhart *(G-3457)*

DRAPERIES & CURTAINS

Ascot Enterprises Inc............................... G 574 658-3000
 Milford *(G-11786)*
Ascot Enterprises Inc............................... D 260 593-3733
 Topeka *(G-15795)*
Designers Touch....................................... G 812 944-2267
 Floyds Knobs *(G-4676)*
Dixie Lee Drapery Co Inc........................ G 317 783-9869
 Indianapolis *(G-7989)*
Femyer Drapery Shop............................... G 765 282-3398
 Muncie *(G-12393)*
Industrial Sewing Machine Co................ G 812 425-2555
 Evansville *(G-4124)*
Jans Sewing Things................................. G 812 945-8113
 New Albany *(G-12752)*
K M Davis Inc... G 765 426-9227
 Lafayette *(G-10617)*
Katherine Mackey..................................... G 765 825-0634
 Connersville *(G-2448)*
M & D Draperies....................................... G 812 886-4608
 Vincennes *(G-16138)*
Majestic Draperies Inc............................. G 574 257-8465
 Elkhart *(G-3510)*
Majesty Enterprises Inc........................... G 812 752-6446
 Scottsburg *(G-14570)*
Merin Interiors Indianapolis................... G 317 251-6603
 Indianapolis *(G-8877)*
Ping Custom Drapery Workroom............. G 317 984-3251
 Cicero *(G-1999)*
Quality Drapery Corporation................... G 765 481-2370
 Lebanon *(G-10936)*
Work Room... G 765 268-2634
 Bringhurst *(G-1238)*

DRAPERIES: Plastic & Textile, From Purchased Materials

Artisan Interiors Inc................................ D 574 825-9494
 Middlebury *(G-11699)*
Ascot Enterprises Inc.............................. D 877 773-7751
 Elkhart *(G-3195)*
Custom Draperies of Indiana.................. G 219 924-2500
 Hammond *(G-6909)*
Doris Drapery Boutique........................... G 765 472-5850
 Peru *(G-13580)*
Lafayette Venetian Blind Inc.................. A 765 464-2500
 West Lafayette *(G-16601)*
Northwest Interiors Inc.......................... F 574 294-2326
 Elkhart *(G-3575)*
Schroer Drapery....................................... G 812 523-3633
 Brownstown *(G-1427)*
Silk Mountain Creations Inc.................. G 317 815-1660
 Carmel *(G-1761)*
Touch of Class Interiors......................... G 765 452-5879
 Kokomo *(G-10351)*

DRAPERY & UPHOLSTERY STORES: Draperies

Custom Sewing Service............................ G 812 428-7015
 Evansville *(G-4004)*
Dixie Lee Drapery Co Inc........................ G 317 783-9869
 Indianapolis *(G-7989)*
McL Window Coverings Inc..................... F 317 577-2670
 Fishers *(G-4563)*
Shelby Westside Upholstering................ G 317 631-8911
 Indianapolis *(G-9419)*

DRILL BITS

Drake Corporation.................................... F 636 464-5070
 Indianapolis *(G-8005)*

DRILLING MACHINERY & EQPT: Oil & Gas

Laibe Corporation.................................... D 317 231-2250
 Indianapolis *(G-8713)*
Mobile Drill Operating Co LLC................ E 317 260-8108
 Indianapolis *(G-8940)*

DRINKING PLACES: Bars & Lounges

Centerpoint Brewing Co LLC.................... F 317 602-8386
 Indianapolis *(G-7768)*
Daredevil Brewing Company LLC............. G 765 602-1067
 Speedway *(G-15336)*
Oaken Barrel Brewing Co Inc.................. E 317 887-2287
 Greenwood *(G-6748)*

DRIVE SHAFTS

D & E Auto Electric Inc.......................... F 219 763-3892
 Portage *(G-13858)*
Lances Drvshaft Components Inc........... G 219 762-2531
 Portage *(G-13881)*

DRIVES: High Speed Indl, Exc Hydrostatic

Moore Machine & Gear Inc...................... G 812 963-3074
 Evansville *(G-4212)*

DRIVES: Hydrostatic

Hydro-Gear Inc... G 317 821-0477
 Indianapolis *(G-8444)*
Terra Drive Systems Inc......................... C 219 279-2801
 Brookston *(G-1313)*

DRUG STORES

Kroger Co.. G 574 291-0740
 South Bend *(G-15107)*
Merrill Corporation.................................. E 574 255-2988
 Mishawaka *(G-11942)*
Williams Bros Hlth Care Phrm I............. E 812 335-0000
 Bloomington *(G-1012)*
Williams Bros Hlth Care Phrm I............. C 812 254-2497
 Washington *(G-16513)*

DRUGS & DRUG PROPRIETARIES, WHOLESALE: Animal Medicines

Elanco Animal Health Inc....................... A 877 352-6261
 Greenfield *(G-6493)*

DRUGS & DRUG PROPRIETARIES, WHOLESALE: Pharmaceuticals

Eli Lilly and Company............................. C 317 276-2000
 Indianapolis *(G-8089)*
Komodo Pharmaceuticals Inc.................. F 317 485-0023
 Fortville *(G-5602)*
Martin Ekwlor Phrmcuticals Inc.............. F 765 962-4410
 Richmond *(G-14159)*

DRUGS & DRUG PROPRIETARIES, WHOLESALE: Vitamins & Minerals

Wellsource Nutraceuticals LLC............... G 219 213-6173
 Crown Point *(G-2773)*

DRUGS: Parasitic & Infective Disease Affecting

Cretaceous Cures..................................... G 317 379-7744
 Westfield *(G-16680)*

DUCTING: Plastic

API Indiana Inc....................................... D 574 293-5574
 Elkhart *(G-3186)*
Arran Isle Inc... E 574 295-4400
 Elkhart *(G-3191)*
Lasalle Bristol Corporation..................... C 574 295-8400
 Elkhart *(G-3469)*

DUCTS: Sheet Metal

Ba Romines Sheetmetal Inc.................... E 260 657-5500
 Harlan *(G-7049)*
Chappelles Sheet Metal Shop.................. G 812 246-2121
 Borden *(G-1106)*
Koomler & Sons Inc.................................. F 260 482-7641
 Fort Wayne *(G-5155)*
Nash Sheet Metal Co................................ G 812 397-5306
 Shelburn *(G-14718)*
Rohrs Custom Metal................................. G 812 689-3764
 Holton *(G-7220)*
S & H Metal Products Inc...................... E 260 593-2565
 Topeka *(G-15817)*
Southwark Metal Mfg Co......................... C 317 823-5300
 Mccordsville *(G-11456)*

DUMPSTERS: Garbage

Assurance Waste Management LLC........ G 765 341-4431
 Cloverdale *(G-2082)*
Douglas Dumpster and Svcs LLC............ G 630 460-8727
 Portage *(G-13859)*
Dragon ESP Ltd....................................... E 574 893-1569
 Akron *(G-4)*
Estes Waste Solutions LLC..................... F 812 283-6400
 Jeffersonville *(G-9982)*
Galfab LLC.. F 574 946-7767
 Winamac *(G-16861)*
Hunts Maintenance Inc............................ G 219 785-2333
 Westville *(G-16762)*
Kumas Dumpster Rentals LLC................ G 662 422-1508
 Crown Point *(G-2713)*

PRODUCT SECTION

ELECTRICAL APPARATUS & EQPT WHOLESALERS

M A C Corporation .... D 317 545-3341
  Indianapolis *(G-8803)*
Mobile Disposal .... G 260 267-6348
  Fort Wayne *(G-5236)*
Mvp Dumpsters Inc .... G 317 502-3155
  Pendleton *(G-13545)*
Par-Kan Company LLC .... D 260 352-2141
  Silver Lake *(G-14920)*

DUST OR FUME COLLECTING EQPT: Indl

Honeyville Metal Inc .... D 800 593-8377
  Topeka *(G-15809)*
Precision Sheet Metal Inc .... F 269 663-8810
  Granger *(G-6371)*

DYES & PIGMENTS: Organic

Eidp Inc .... A 833 267-8382
  Indianapolis *(G-8064)*

EATING PLACES

Barley Island Brewing Co .... G 317 770-5280
  Noblesville *(G-13039)*
Frickers Inc .... G 765 965-6655
  Richmond *(G-14123)*
Kroger Co .... G 574 291-0740
  South Bend *(G-15107)*
Lanthier Winery & Restaurant .... G 812 273-2409
  Madison *(G-11235)*
Meats By Linz Inc .... E 708 862-0830
  Hammond *(G-6979)*
MI Tierra .... G 812 376-0668
  Columbus *(G-2353)*
Mishawaka Brewing Company .... G 574 256-9993
  Granger *(G-6362)*
Mishawaka Frozen Custard .... G 574 255-8000
  Mishawaka *(G-11956)*
Olympia Candy Kitchen LLC .... G 574 533-5040
  Goshen *(G-6230)*
Schnuck Markets Inc .... C 812 853-9505
  Newburgh *(G-13019)*
Tavistock Restaurants LLC .... G 317 488-1230
  Indianapolis *(G-9557)*
Upland Brewing Company Inc .... F 812 330-7421
  Bloomington *(G-1005)*
Wasser Brewing Company LLC .... F 765 653-3240
  Greencastle *(G-6435)*
Zels .... G 219 864-1011
  Schererville *(G-14548)*

EDITING SVCS

Precisely Write Inc .... G 317 585-7701
  Indianapolis *(G-9178)*

EDUCATIONAL SVCS

Friends of Third World Inc .... G 260 422-6821
  Fort Wayne *(G-5013)*
Kcma & Services LLC .... G 260 645-0885
  Waterloo *(G-16522)*
Worth Tax and Financial Svc .... G 574 267-4687
  Warsaw *(G-16456)*

ELECTRIC MOTOR & GENERATOR AUXILIARY PARTS

SUv Parts & Accessories Inc .... G 765 457-1345
  Kokomo *(G-10344)*

ELECTRIC MOTOR REPAIR SVCS

Altek Inc .... G 812 385-2561
  Princeton *(G-13981)*
B & D Electric Inc .... F 812 254-2122
  Shoals *(G-14903)*

Best Electric Motor Service .... G 765 583-2408
  Otterbein *(G-13450)*
Boone County Electric Inc .... G 765 482-1430
  Lebanon *(G-10880)*
C & L Electric Motor Repr Inc .... G 574 533-2643
  Elkhart *(G-3243)*
C&C Electric Motors LLC .... G 574 656-3898
  North Liberty *(G-13215)*
Columbus Industrial Electric .... F 812 372-8414
  Columbus *(G-2244)*
Electric Motor Services Inc .... E 219 931-2850
  Hammond *(G-6922)*
Electric Mtr Repr & Rewind Inc .... G 812 284-5059
  Jeffersonville *(G-9974)*
Electrical Motor Products Inc .... G 877 455-1599
  Fort Wayne *(G-4944)*
Electrik Connection Inc .... G 219 362-4581
  La Porte *(G-10404)*
Electro Corp .... F 219 393-5571
  Kingsbury *(G-10177)*
Enyart Electric Motor Repr Inc .... G 574 288-4731
  South Bend *(G-15017)*
Eps Enterprises Inc .... G 260 493-4913
  Fort Wayne *(G-4957)*
Evans Enterprises LLC .... G 317 986-2073
  Indianapolis *(G-8141)*
Flanders Inc .... F 812 867-7421
  Evansville *(G-4075)*
Flanders Electric Motor Service LLC .... C 812 867-7421
  Evansville *(G-4076)*
Flanders Electric Mtr Svc LLC .... E 812 867-4014
  Evansville *(G-4077)*
Gary Electric Motor Service Co .... F 219 884-6555
  Valparaiso *(G-15953)*
Gottman Electric Company Inc .... G 812 838-0037
  Mount Vernon *(G-12297)*
Harrison Electric Inc .... G 219 879-0444
  Michigan City *(G-11620)*
Hoosier Industrial Electric .... F 812 346-2232
  North Vernon *(G-13278)*
Horner Apg LLC .... F 317 916-4274
  Indianapolis *(G-8414)*
Horner Industrial Services Inc .... G 260 434-1189
  Fort Wayne *(G-5083)*
Horner Industrial Services Inc .... G 812 466-5281
  Terre Haute *(G-15607)*
Horner Industrial Services Inc .... C 317 639-4261
  Indianapolis *(G-8416)*
Illiana Electrical Svcs LLC .... G 219 276-1743
  Valparaiso *(G-15969)*
Illiana Indus Elc Mtr Svcs Inc .... F 219 286-3654
  Valparaiso *(G-15970)*
Industrial Motor & Tool LLC .... G 574 534-8282
  Goshen *(G-6174)*
Integrated Power Services LLC .... F 812 665-4400
  Poseyville *(G-13979)*
Jasper Electric Motor Inc .... F 812 482-1660
  Jasper *(G-9851)*
Jasper Electric Motor Inc .... F 812 482-1660
  Jasper *(G-9850)*
Kesters Electric Motor Svc LLC .... G 574 269-2889
  Warsaw *(G-16382)*
Kiemle-Hankins Company .... F 219 213-2643
  Crown Point *(G-2709)*
Kirby Risk Corporation .... D 765 423-4205
  Lafayette *(G-10622)*
Kirby Risk Corporation .... F 765 664-5185
  Marion *(G-11304)*
Kirby Risk Corporation .... D 765 448-4567
  Lafayette *(G-10623)*
Kochs Electric Inc .... E 317 639-5624
  Indianapolis *(G-8700)*

Kw Maintenance Services LLC .... E 574 232-2051
  South Bend *(G-15113)*
Magnetech Industrial Svcs Inc .... G 219 937-0100
  Hammond *(G-6975)*
Motor Electric Inc .... G 574 294-7123
  Elkhart *(G-3556)*
Northern Electric Company Inc .... E 574 289-7791
  South Bend *(G-15172)*
P H C Industries Inc .... G
  Fort Wayne *(G-5291)*
Peter Austin Co .... G 765 288-6397
  Muncie *(G-12474)*
Phase Three Electric Inc .... G 812 945-9922
  New Albany *(G-12793)*
Phazpak Inc .... G 260 692-6416
  Monroe *(G-12061)*
Precision Electric Inc .... E 574 256-1000
  Mishawaka *(G-11977)*
Pres-Del Electric Inc .... G 219 884-3146
  Gary *(G-5995)*
Quality Repair Services Inc .... F 317 881-0205
  Greenwood *(G-6756)*
Reliable Indus Sls & Svc LLC .... G 219 929-8295
  Valparaiso *(G-16037)*
Ritchie Electric Motor Co LLC .... G 219 866-5185
  Rensselaer *(G-14067)*
Robinson Industries Inc .... E 317 867-3214
  Westfield *(G-16724)*
Ronald Holloway .... G 574 223-6825
  Plymouth *(G-13812)*
Spina Enterprises Inc .... G 219 879-0444
  Michigan City *(G-11670)*
Tipton Electric Motor Services .... G 765 963-3380
  Sharpsville *(G-14713)*
Tipton Engrg Elc Mtr Svcs Inc .... G 765 963-3380
  Sharpsville *(G-14714)*
Wabash Valley Motor & Mch Inc .... G 812 466-7400
  Terre Haute *(G-15743)*
Wagner Electric Fort Wayne Inc .... G 260 484-5532
  Fort Wayne *(G-5538)*
Wright Repairs Inc .... F 765 674-3300
  Gas City *(G-6042)*

ELECTRIC SERVICES

P&C Prime LLC .... F 231 420-3650
  Fredericksburg *(G-5795)*
Vectren LLC .... G 812 424-6411
  Evansville *(G-4369)*
Vectren LLC .... A 812 491-4000
  Evansville *(G-4368)*

ELECTRIC SVCS, NEC: Power Generation

Futurewerks LLC .... G 305 926-3633
  Indianapolis *(G-8247)*

ELECTRICAL APPARATUS & EQPT WHOLESALERS

Academy Energy Group LLC .... G 312 931-7443
  Newburgh *(G-12991)*
Ademco Inc .... G 317 359-9505
  Indianapolis *(G-7431)*
Blackbird .... G 812 944-0799
  New Albany *(G-12702)*
Bryant Control Inc .... F 317 549-3355
  Fishers *(G-4477)*
Crume Industries LLC .... G 574 747-7683
  Elkhart *(G-3275)*
Cummins Inc .... G 260 482-3691
  Fort Wayne *(G-4895)*
Eaton Corporation .... G 317 704-2520
  Indianapolis *(G-8043)*

Employee Codes: A=Over 500 employees, B=251-500
C=101-250, D=51-100, E=20-50, F=10-19, G=1-9

2024 Harris Indiana Industrial Directory

ELECTRICAL APPARATUS & EQPT WHOLESALERS

Flanders Electric Mtr Svc LLC............... D 812 421-4300
Evansville *(G-4078)*

Gregory Thomas Inc............................... G 219 324-3801
La Porte *(G-10412)*

Hoosier Fire Equipment Inc.................... F 219 462-1707
Valparaiso *(G-15965)*

Horner Apg LLC..................................... F 317 916-4274
Indianapolis *(G-8414)*

Horner Electric Inc................................. E 317 639-4261
Indianapolis *(G-8415)*

Horner Industrial Services Inc............... G 260 434-1189
Fort Wayne *(G-5083)*

Horner Industrial Services Inc............... C 317 639-4261
Indianapolis *(G-8416)*

Logical Concepts.................................... F 317 885-6330
Greenwood *(G-6730)*

Robinson Industries Inc........................ E 317 867-3214
Westfield *(G-16724)*

ELECTRICAL DISCHARGE MACHINING, EDM

B&B Tool and Molding Co Inc................. E
Muncie *(G-12348)*

Clifty Engineering and Tool Co............... C 812 273-3272
Madison *(G-11210)*

Decatur Mold Tool and Engrg................ C 812 346-5188
North Vernon *(G-13266)*

Ex-Cut Technology LLC........................ F 260 672-9602
Roanoke *(G-14263)*

Photon Automation Inc........................... F 844 574-6866
Greenfield *(G-6538)*

Photon Automation Inc........................... C 844 574-6866
Greenfield *(G-6539)*

ELECTRICAL EQPT REPAIR SVCS

Agri-Tronix Corp..................................... F 317 738-4474
Franklin *(G-5703)*

Best Equipment Co Inc........................... E 317 823-3050
Indianapolis *(G-7617)*

I E M C... G 219 464-2890
Valparaiso *(G-15966)*

Sign Group Inc....................................... F 317 875-6969
Indianapolis *(G-9430)*

ELECTRICAL EQPT REPAIR SVCS: High Voltage

Horner Industrial Services Inc............... G 812 466-5281
Terre Haute *(G-15607)*

Horner Industrial Services Inc............... C 317 639-4261
Indianapolis *(G-8416)*

ELECTRICAL EQPT: Automotive, NEC

Cds LLC.. G 812 637-0900
West Harrison *(G-16545)*

Federal-Mogul Powertrain LLC............. G 574 272-5900
South Bend *(G-15032)*

GM Components Holdings LLC............ G 765 451-5011
Kokomo *(G-10269)*

Kimball Electronics Group LLC............. C 812 634-4000
Jasper *(G-9868)*

Noel-Smyser Engineering Corp............. E 317 293-2215
Indianapolis *(G-9020)*

R & R Regulators Inc............................. F 574 522-3500
Elkhart *(G-3636)*

ELECTRICAL GOODS, WHOLESALE: Electrical Appliances, Major

Long Item Development Corp................ G 317 780-1077
Indianapolis *(G-8780)*

ELECTRICAL GOODS, WHOLESALE: Fittings & Construction Mat

Kirby Risk Corporation........................... D 317 398-9713
Shelbyville *(G-14768)*

ELECTRICAL GOODS, WHOLESALE: Generators

Cummins Crosspoint LLC....................... D 812 867-4400
Evansville *(G-3999)*

Cummins Crosspoint LLC....................... E 317 243-7979
Indianapolis *(G-7925)*

Lancon Electric Inc................................. G 260 897-3285
Laotto *(G-10809)*

ELECTRICAL GOODS, WHOLESALE: Light Bulbs & Related Splys

Bonner & Associates.............................. G 317 571-1911
Carmel *(G-1571)*

Elkhart Supply Corp............................... E 574 264-4156
Elkhart *(G-3330)*

International Lighting LLC...................... F 219 989-0060
Hammond *(G-6958)*

National Handicapped Workshop........... F 765 287-8331
Muncie *(G-12468)*

ELECTRICAL GOODS, WHOLESALE: Security Control Eqpt & Systems

Allegion Public Ltd Company................. D 317 810-3700
Carmel *(G-1554)*

Brickhouse Electronics LLC................... F 212 643-7449
Indianapolis *(G-7678)*

ELECTRICAL GOODS, WHOLESALE: Signaling, Eqpt

Doron Distribution Inc............................ G 317 594-9259
Carmel *(G-1610)*

Dux Signal Kits LLC................................ G 260 623-3017
Monroeville *(G-12068)*

ELECTRICAL GOODS, WHOLESALE: Switchgear

Power Components of Midwest............. E 574 256-6990
Mishawaka *(G-11976)*

ELECTRICAL GOODS, WHOLESALE: Wire & Cable

Hessville Cable & Sling Co.................... E 773 768-8181
Gary *(G-5951)*

Kamdoer Inc.. E 574 293-2990
Elkhart *(G-3446)*

Patrick Industries Inc............................. D 574 293-2990
Elkhart *(G-3599)*

Rtw Enterprises Inc............................... E 574 294-3275
Elkhart *(G-3654)*

ELECTRICAL MEASURING INSTRUMENT REPAIR & CALIBRATION SVCS

Chance Ind Standards Lab Inc.............. F 317 787-6578
Indianapolis *(G-7783)*

ELECTRICAL SPLYS

Amgi LLC... G 317 447-1524
New Palestine *(G-12928)*

Babsco Supply Inc................................ G 574 267-8999
Warsaw *(G-16316)*

Controls Center Inc............................... G 317 634-2665
Indianapolis *(G-7863)*

Kirby Risk Corporation........................... G 765 643-3384
Anderson *(G-143)*

Kirby Risk Corporation........................... D 765 447-1402
Lafayette *(G-10621)*

Kirby Risk Corporation........................... D 765 423-4205
Lafayette *(G-10622)*

Kirby Risk Corporation........................... F 765 664-5185
Marion *(G-11304)*

Kirby Risk Corporation........................... F 765 254-5460
Muncie *(G-12435)*

Kirby Risk Corporation........................... G 765 448-4567
Lafayette *(G-10623)*

Mohler Technology Inc.......................... E 812 897-2900
Boonville *(G-1093)*

Schneider Electric Usa Inc.................... D 260 356-2060
Huntington *(G-7366)*

ELECTRICAL SUPPLIES: Porcelain

Insulation Specialties of Amer............... E 219 733-2502
Wanatah *(G-16290)*

Leco Corporation.................................... G 574 288-9017
South Bend *(G-15122)*

Thomas & Skinner Inc........................... C 812 689-4811
Osgood *(G-13418)*

ELECTROMEDICAL EQPT

B & J Specialty Inc................................. G 260 636-2067
Kendallville *(G-10095)*

Biomet Inc... A 574 267-6639
Warsaw *(G-16323)*

Cliniwave Inc.. G 812 923-9591
Floyds Knobs *(G-4673)*

Medishield... G 502 939-9903
New Albany *(G-12773)*

Mr-Link LLC... G 512 297-4582
Lafayette *(G-10654)*

Plastic Assembly Tech Inc..................... G 317 841-1202
Indianapolis *(G-9150)*

Purspec Technologies Inc..................... G 765 532-2208
West Lafayette *(G-16623)*

Telamon Entp Ventures LLC................. F 317 818-6888
Carmel *(G-1778)*

ELECTRON TUBES

Pantera Mfg Corporation....................... G 317 435-0422
Fishers *(G-4646)*

ELECTRONIC DEVICES: Solid State, NEC

Paul Nelson... G 765 352-0698
Martinsville *(G-11421)*

Payne-Sparkmanm Manufacturing........ F 812 944-4893
New Albany *(G-12792)*

ELECTRONIC EQPT REPAIR SVCS

Kouder Instrument Service Co.............. G 219 374-5935
Cedar Lake *(G-1833)*

R C Systems Inc..................................... G 812 282-4898
Jeffersonville *(G-10044)*

Richard J Bagan Inc.............................. E 260 244-5115
Columbia City *(G-2190)*

Teaco Inc.. G 219 874-6234
Michigan City *(G-11676)*

ELECTRONIC LOADS & POWER SPLYS

Adafill Global LLC................................... G 317 798-5378
Indianapolis *(G-7427)*

Green Cubes Technology LLC.............. E 502 416-1060
Kokomo *(G-10273)*

Wattre Inc... G 260 657-3701
Woodburn *(G-16956)*

PRODUCT SECTION
ENGINEERING SVCS

ELECTRONIC PARTS & EQPT WHOLESALERS

Acterna LLC .... E 317 788-9351
  Indianapolis (G-7425)
ASA Electronics LLC .... C 574 264-3135
  Elkhart (G-3192)
Coil-Tran LLC .... D 219 942-8511
  Hobart (G-7182)
Copper Mountain Tech LLC .... E 317 222-5400
  Indianapolis (G-7872)
Dti Services Ltd Liability Co .... G 765 745-0261
  Indianapolis (G-8015)
Elkhart Supply Corp .... E 574 264-4156
  Elkhart (G-3330)
Harman Embedded Audio LLC .... F 317 849-8175
  Indianapolis (G-8363)
Xfmrs Inc .... A 317 834-1066
  Camby (G-1517)

ELECTRONIC SHOPPING

Blessed Humbled Beginnings LLC ... G 219 255-3820
  Merrillville (G-11490)
Shop Lulu Bean LLC .... G 219 525-5336
  Merrillville (G-11559)
Spagheady Inc .... G 317 499-6184
  Indianapolis (G-9467)
Spobric LLC .... G 302 249-1045
  Indianapolis (G-9479)
Tonis Touch LLC .... G 317 992-1280
  Plainfield (G-13737)
VMS Products Inc .... G 888 321-4698
  Anderson (G-214)

ELECTRONIC TRAINING DEVICES

Allied Mfg Partners Inc .... G 260 428-2670
  Fort Wayne (G-4745)
Automation Consultants Inc .... G 502 552-4995
  Floyds Knobs (G-4669)
Curtis Life Research LLC .... G 317 873-4519
  Zionsville (G-16999)
Targamite LLC .... G 260 489-0046
  Fort Wayne (G-5468)
Terick Sales .... G 574 626-3173
  Walton (G-16283)

ELEMENTARY & SECONDARY SCHOOLS, PUBLIC

Lionfish Cyber Hldngs LLC-S Ln ..... G 877 732-6772
  Indianapolis (G-8766)

ELEVATORS & EQPT

Elevator One LLC .... G 317 634-8001
  Indianapolis (G-8071)

ELEVATORS WHOLESALERS

Tk Elevator Corporation .... D 317 595-1125
  Indianapolis (G-9612)

ELEVATORS: Installation & Conversion

Tk Elevator Corporation .... D 317 595-1125
  Indianapolis (G-9612)
Zeller Elevator Co .... G 812 985-5888
  Mount Vernon (G-12328)

EMBLEMS: Embroidered

Celestial Designs LLC .... G 317 733-3110
  Zionsville (G-16997)
Spectrum Marketing .... G 765 643-5566
  Anderson (G-197)

Sportsmania Sales Inc .... G 317 873-5501
  Zionsville (G-17052)

EMBROIDERY ADVERTISING SVCS

Athletic Edge Inc .... F 260 489-6613
  Fort Wayne (G-4778)
Em Global LLC .... G 812 258-9993
  Jeffersonville (G-9976)
G D Cox Inc .... G 317 398-0035
  Shelbyville (G-14758)
Kessler Concepts Inc .... F 317 630-9901
  Indianapolis (G-8675)
Profit Over Romance LLC .... G 219 900-3592
  Gary (G-5997)
Rookies Unlimited Inc .... G 765 536-2726
  Summitville (G-15431)
Smiling Cross Inc .... G 812 323-9290
  Bloomington (G-976)
Spark Marketing LLC .... G 219 301-0071
  Dyer (G-2983)
Spectrum Marketing .... G 765 643-5566
  Anderson (G-197)
Stien Designs & Graphics Inc .... G 260 347-9136
  Kendallville (G-10153)

EMBROIDERY KITS

Aus Embroidery Inc .... G 317 899-1225
  Indianapolis (G-7568)

EMERGENCY ALARMS

Ademco Inc .... G 317 359-9505
  Indianapolis (G-7431)
Advanced Protection Systems .... G 574 626-2939
  Walton (G-16280)
American Eagle Security Inc .... G 219 980-1177
  Merrillville (G-11482)
Esco Communications LLC .... D 317 298-2975
  Indianapolis (G-8130)
Molex LLC .... F 317 834-5600
  Mooresville (G-12223)

EMPLOYMENT SVCS: Labor Contractors

Vergence LLC .... F 317 547-4417
  Indianapolis (G-9707)

ENAMELS

IVc Industrial Coatings Inc .... C 812 442-5080
  Brazil (G-1149)

ENCLOSURES: Electronic

Koester Metals Inc .... E 260 495-1818
  Fremont (G-5825)
Mier Products Inc .... E 765 457-0223
  Kokomo (G-10307)
Star Case Manufacturing Co LLC .... E 219 922-4440
  Munster (G-12565)

ENGINE REBUILDING: Diesel

Hobbs Auto Diagnostics & Repr ...... G 765 606-1490
  Anderson (G-127)
Jolliff Diesel Service LLC .... G 812 692-5725
  Elnora (G-3815)
Stant USA Corp .... C 765 825-3121
  Connersville (G-2470)

ENGINEERING SVCS

Advanced Welding and Engrg .... G 317 820-3595
  Indianapolis (G-7443)
AM General Holdings LLC .... A 574 237-6222
  South Bend (G-14940)
AM General LLC .... D 574 237-6222
  South Bend (G-14942)

Apex AG Solutions LLC .... F 765 305-1930
  Winchester (G-16882)
Arroyo Industries LLC .... G 317 605-4163
  Greenwood (G-6671)
Binarie LLC .... G 317 496-8836
  Greenwood (G-6676)
Butler Tool & Design Inc .... F 219 297-4531
  Goodland (G-6080)
Crown Training and Dev Inc .... F 219 947-0845
  Merrillville (G-11500)
Crume Industries LLC .... G 574 747-7683
  Elkhart (G-3275)
Daifuku Intrlgistics Amer Corp .... D 219 777-2220
  Hobart (G-7186)
Damping Technologies Inc .... F 574 258-7916
  Mishawaka (G-11880)
Damping Technologies Inc .... E 574 258-7916
  Mishawaka (G-11879)
Daylight Engineering Inc .... G 812 983-2518
  Elberfeld (G-3111)
Design Engineering .... G 219 926-2170
  Chesterton (G-1919)
Divsys Aerospace & Engrg LLC ...... F 317 941-7777
  Indianapolis (G-7987)
Drake Enterprises LLC .... G 317 460-5991
  Pittsboro (G-13644)
Engineered Refr Shapes Svcs LLC . G 765 778-8040
  Pendleton (G-13531)
Enterprise MGT Solutions LLC .... G 219 545-8544
  Merrillville (G-11513)
Future Mold Inc .... F 812 941-8661
  New Albany (G-12735)
Gmp Holdings LLC .... G 317 353-6580
  Indianapolis (G-8294)
Halo LLC .... D 317 575-9992
  Carmel (G-1647)
Hgl Dynamics Inc .... G 317 782-3500
  Indianapolis (G-8393)
Hirata Corporation of America .... E 317 856-8600
  Indianapolis (G-8399)
Imagineering Enterprises Inc .... E 317 635-8565
  Indianapolis (G-8464)
Imagineering Enterprises Inc .... E 574 287-0642
  South Bend (G-15075)
Imagineering Enterprises Inc .... D 574 287-2941
  South Bend (G-15076)
Ipheion Development Corp .... G 240 281-1619
  Indianapolis (G-8587)
KYB Americas Corporation .... B 317 736-7774
  Franklin (G-5750)
Lingenfelter Prfmce Engrg Inc .... E 260 724-2552
  Decatur (G-2869)
Metal Fab Engineering Inc .... E 574 278-7150
  Winamac (G-16867)
Mobility Ventures LLC .... G 734 367-3714
  South Bend (G-15153)
Modern Forge Companies LLC .... A 708 388-1806
  Merrillville (G-11542)
Natare Corporation .... E 317 290-8828
  Indianapolis (G-8985)
Odyssian Technology LLC .... G 574 257-7555
  South Bend (G-15176)
Pia Automation US Inc .... E 812 485-5500
  Evansville (G-4242)
Quantum Technologies LLC .... G 765 426-0156
  Elizabethtown (G-3132)
Rd Rubber Products Inc .... G 260 357-3571
  Garrett (G-5875)
Ring-R Inc .... E 260 565-3347
  Decatur (G-2882)
Rob Passarelli .... G 317 340-8597
  Carmel (G-1743)

Employee Codes: A=Over 500 employees, B=251-500
C=101-250, D=51-100, E=20-50, F=10-19, G=1-9

2024 Harris Indiana Industrial Directory

ENGINEERING SVCS

Setco LLC... B 812 424-2904
  Evansville *(G-4307)*

Specialty Blanks Inc............................... G 812 232-8775
  Terre Haute *(G-15708)*

Stedman Machine Company Inc............ D 812 926-0038
  Aurora *(G-457)*

Superior Indus Solutions Inc................. E 317 781-4400
  Indianapolis *(G-9529)*

Telamon Corporation.............................. C 317 818-6888
  Carmel *(G-1777)*

World Rdo Mssnary Fllwship Inc........... G 574 970-4252
  Elkhart *(G-3793)*

Wpr Services LLC................................... G 317 513-5269
  Fishers *(G-4635)*

Xtreme ADS Limited............................... E 765 644-7323
  Anderson *(G-218)*

ENGINEERING SVCS: Acoustical

Metal Technologies Inc Alabama........... D 260 925-4717
  Auburn *(G-408)*

ENGINEERING SVCS: Building Construction

JMS Engineered Plastics Inc................. G 574 277-3228
  South Bend *(G-15093)*

JMS Engineered Plastics Inc................. D 574 277-3228
  South Bend *(G-15094)*

Royal Adhesives & Sealants LLC.......... D 574 246-5000
  South Bend *(G-15226)*

ENGINEERING SVCS: Electrical Or Electronic

Computer Age Engineering Inc.............. E 765 674-8551
  Marion *(G-11278)*

Crown Elec Svcs & Automtn Inc............ D 972 929-4700
  Portage *(G-13857)*

Direct Control Systems Inc.................... G 765 282-7474
  Muncie *(G-12384)*

Duesenburg Inc...................................... G 260 496-9650
  Fort Wayne *(G-4931)*

Llama Corporation.................................. G 888 701-7432
  Decatur *(G-2870)*

Mesh Systems LLC................................. E 317 661-4800
  Carmel *(G-1698)*

ENGINEERING SVCS: Machine Tool Design

Lyntech Engineering Inc........................ G 574 224-2300
  Rochester *(G-14303)*

ENGINEERING SVCS: Mechanical

7th Leadership Organization................. G 219 938-6906
  Gary *(G-5883)*

Biosafe Engineering LLC...................... E 317 858-8099
  Indianapolis *(G-7629)*

Ironworks Engineering LLC................... G 317 296-9359
  New Palestine *(G-12940)*

K&T Performance Engrg LLC................ G 765 437-0185
  Peru *(G-13589)*

Klinge Enameling Company Inc............ E 317 359-8291
  Indianapolis *(G-8694)*

Robert Perez... G 317 291-7311
  Indianapolis *(G-9314)*

Specialty Tooling Inc............................. F 812 464-8521
  Evansville *(G-4328)*

Wolf Technical Engineering LLC........... G 800 783-9653
  Indianapolis *(G-9781)*

ENGINEERING SVCS: Petroleum

Barger Engineering Inc......................... G 812 476-3077
  Evansville *(G-3909)*

Moore Engineering & Prod Co............... F 812 479-1051
  Evansville *(G-4211)*

Oilfield Research Inc............................. G 812 424-2907
  Evansville *(G-4226)*

Robinson Engineering & Oil Co............. F 812 477-1575
  Evansville *(G-4291)*

ENGINEERING SVCS: Structural

Precision Surveillance Corp.................. E 219 397-4295
  East Chicago *(G-3035)*

ENGINES: Diesel & Semi-Diesel Or Duel Fuel

Ccts Technology Group Inc................... G 305 209-5743
  Indianapolis *(G-7765)*

Mpc Global LLC...................................... G 816 399-4710
  Indianapolis *(G-8964)*

S & S Diesel Motorsport LLC................. G 812 216-3639
  Seymour *(G-14683)*

ENGINES: Gasoline, NEC

Brazil Auto & Electric............................. G 812 442-0060
  Brazil *(G-1135)*

Michael Dargie....................................... G 765 935-2241
  Richmond *(G-14165)*

ENGINES: Internal Combustion, NEC

Bes Racing Engines Inc........................ F 812 576-2371
  Guilford *(G-6827)*

Carlson Motorsports............................... G 765 339-4407
  Linden *(G-11030)*

Champion Racing Engines LLC............ G 317 335-2491
  Mccordsville *(G-11446)*

Cummins - Allison Corp......................... G 317 872-6244
  Indianapolis *(G-7922)*

Cummins Americas Inc.......................... G 812 377-5000
  Columbus *(G-2250)*

Cummins Crosspoint LLC...................... D 812 867-4400
  Evansville *(G-3999)*

Cummins Crosspoint LLC...................... E 260 482-3691
  Fort Wayne *(G-4894)*

Cummins Crosspoint LLC...................... E 317 484-2146
  Indianapolis *(G-7923)*

Cummins Crosspoint LLC...................... E 317 244-7251
  Indianapolis *(G-7924)*

Cummins Crosspoint LLC...................... E 574 252-2154
  Mishawaka *(G-11869)*

Cummins Crosspoint LLC...................... E 317 243-7979
  Indianapolis *(G-7925)*

Cummins Cumberland Inc...................... B 317 243-7979
  Indianapolis *(G-7926)*

Cummins Dist Holdco Inc....................... E 812 377-5000
  Columbus *(G-2252)*

Cummins Emission Solutions Inc.......... D 615 986-2596
  Columbus *(G-2253)*

Cummins Emssion Sltons Clmbus........ E 800 286-6467
  Columbus *(G-2254)*

Cummins Inc... ..... 812 524-6455
  Columbus *(G-2264)*

Cummins Inc... G 317 460-9843
  Columbus *(G-2265)*

Cummins Inc... G 812 377-7739
  Columbus *(G-2266)*

Cummins Inc... E 812 374-4774
  Columbus *(G-2267)*

Cummins Inc... G 812 377-6072
  Columbus *(G-2268)*

Cummins Inc... B 812 377-7000
  Columbus *(G-2269)*

Cummins Inc... G 812 312-3162
  Columbus *(G-2270)*

Cummins Inc... G 812 377-8601
  Columbus *(G-2272)*

Cummins Inc... F 812 378-2874
  Columbus *(G-2273)*

Cummins Inc... G 317 244-7251
  Indianapolis *(G-7928)*

Cummins Inc... G 317 751-4567
  Whiteland *(G-16782)*

Cummins Inc... A 812 377-5000
  Columbus *(G-2271)*

Cummins Power Generation Inc............ E 574 262-4611
  Elkhart *(G-3281)*

Cummins Repair Inc............................... G 260 632-4800
  Harlan *(G-7053)*

Cummins-Scania Xpi Mfg LLC............... G 812 377-5000
  Columbus *(G-2275)*

Engineered Machined Pdts Inc.............. G 317 462-8894
  Greenfield *(G-6498)*

FCA North America Holdings LLC........ B 765 454-0018
  Kokomo *(G-10264)*

Freedom Racing Engines....................... G 317 858-9937
  Pittsboro *(G-13646)*

Futurewerks LLC.................................... G 305 926-3633
  Indianapolis *(G-8247)*

Mitchell Smith Racing............................ G 765 640-0237
  Anderson *(G-155)*

Motorsport Price Engineering................ G 812 546-4220
  Hope *(G-7229)*

Powerhouse Engines LLC..................... G 765 576-1418
  Lynn *(G-11186)*

Spyder Controls Inc............................... G 866 919-9092
  South Bend *(G-15262)*

Stensland Engines Inc.......................... G 260 623-6859
  Monroeville *(G-12075)*

Unison Engine Components Inc............ C 904 739-4000
  Terre Haute *(G-15738)*

ENGINES: Marine

Torque Engineering Corporation........... F 574 264-2628
  Elkhart *(G-3740)*

ENGRAVING SVC, NEC

Bills Industries LLC............................... G 765 629-0227
  Milroy *(G-11821)*

Cedar Woodworking................................ G 812 486-2765
  Montgomery *(G-12088)*

Engraving and Stamp Center Inc........... G 812 336-0606
  Bloomington *(G-861)*

Gary Printing Inc.................................... G 219 886-1767
  Gary *(G-5938)*

Gogolaks Engraving................................ G 219 972-3995
  Hammond *(G-6935)*

Riverside Printing Co............................. G 812 275-1950
  Bedford *(G-669)*

Rock Garden Engraving.......................... G 765 647-3357
  Brookville *(G-1334)*

The Deaton Family Company................. D 815 726-6234
  Auburn *(G-429)*

ENGRAVING SVCS

Etched In Stone Engrv & EMB............... G 317 535-8160
  Whiteland *(G-16786)*

J P Corporation....................................... G 317 783-1000
  Beech Grove *(G-693)*

JP Industries Inc.................................... F 574 293-8763
  Elkhart *(G-3436)*

Laser Marking Technologies.................. G 812 852-7999
  Osgood *(G-13411)*

Maddox Engineering Inc........................ F 812 903-0048
  Greenville *(G-6652)*

Mains Enterprises Inc............................ G 765 425-0162
  Wilkinson *(G-16843)*

Ramifications LLC.................................. G 765 729-5484
  Muncie *(G-12484)*

Specialty Shoppe................................... G 574 772-7873
  Knox *(G-10225)*

Star Quality Awards Inc............................ G..... 812 273-1740
  Madison (G-11252)

ENVELOPES

Bowers Envelope Company Inc................ G..... 317 253-4321
  Indianapolis (G-7665)
BSC Vntres Acquisition Sub LLC.............. D..... 260 665-7521
  Angola (G-237)
Cenveo Worldwide Limited....................... D..... 800 995-9500
  New Albany (G-12710)
Double Envelope Corp............................. G..... 260 434-0500
  Fort Wayne (G-4926)
Envelope Service Inc................................ E..... 260 432-6277
  Fort Wayne (G-4952)
Gov 6 Corp.. G..... 317 847-4942
  Indianapolis (G-8310)
Our Sunday Visitor Apps LLC................. E..... 800 348-2440
  Huntington (G-7349)
Ray Envelope Company Inc...................... E..... 317 353-6251
  Indianapolis (G-9267)

ENVELOPES WHOLESALERS

Double Envelope Corp............................. G..... 260 434-0500
  Fort Wayne (G-4926)
Millcraft Paper Company.......................... G..... 317 240-3500
  Indianapolis (G-8920)

ENZYMES

Enzyme Solutions Inc............................... G..... 800 523-1323
  Fort Wayne (G-4955)
Midwest Bio-Products Inc......................... G..... 765 793-3426
  Covington (G-2531)
US Enzyme LLC....................................... G..... 317 268-4975
  Avon (G-556)

EPOXY RESINS

Leepoxy Plastics Inc................................ G..... 260 747-7411
  Fort Wayne (G-5180)
Star Technology Inc.................................. E..... 260 837-7833
  Waterloo (G-16531)
V Global Holdings LLC............................. E..... 317 247-8141
  Indianapolis (G-9695)

EQUIPMENT: Pedestrian Traffic Control

Highway Safety Services Inc.................... D..... 765 474-1000
  Lafayette (G-10599)

EQUIPMENT: Rental & Leasing, NEC

Airbotx LLC.. G..... 317 981-1811
  Westfield (G-16663)
Heat Wagons Inc...................................... F..... 219 464-8818
  Valparaiso (G-15961)
Macallister Machinery Co Inc.................... F..... 765 966-0759
  Richmond (G-14157)
McL Window Coverings Inc...................... F..... 317 577-2670
  Fishers (G-4563)
Motion Engineering Company Inc............. G..... 317 804-7990
  Westfield (G-16712)
Standard Change-Makers Inc................... C..... 317 899-6955
  Indianapolis (G-9491)
TSF Co Inc... E..... 812 985-2630
  Evansville (G-4354)

ETCHING & ENGRAVING SVC

Carmel Trophies Plus LLC....................... G..... 317 844-3770
  Carmel (G-1581)
Endless Creations.................................... G..... 812 623-0190
  Sunman (G-15437)
Fishers Laser Carvers LLC...................... G..... 317 845-0500
  Fishers (G-4523)
Northern Ind Indus Catings LLC............... G..... 574 893-4621
  Akron (G-6)

Star Quality Awards Inc............................ G..... 812 273-1740
  Madison (G-11252)
Trophy Case LLC..................................... G..... 812 853-5087
  Newburgh (G-13026)

ETHYLENE-PROPYLENE RUBBERS: EPDM Polymers

CT Polymers LLC..................................... F..... 574 598-6132
  Bourbon (G-1120)
Green Earth Polymers Inc......................... G..... 812 602-4070
  Evansville (G-4096)

EXHAUST SYSTEMS: Eqpt & Parts

Arvin Sango Inc.. A..... 812 265-2888
  Madison (G-11203)
Cummins Emission Solutions Inc............. D..... 615 986-2596
  Columbus (G-2253)
Elsa LLC.. B..... 765 552-5200
  Elwood (G-3821)
Elsa Corporation...................................... B..... 765 552-5200
  Elwood (G-3822)
Exhaust Productions Inc.......................... D..... 219 942-0069
  Merrillville (G-11516)
Faurecia Emssons Ctrl Tech USA............ B..... 812 565-5214
  Columbus (G-2304)
Faurecia Emssons Ctrl Tech USA............ B..... 812 341-2000
  Columbus (G-2305)
Faurecia Emssons Ctrl Tech USA............ D..... 248 758-8160
  Fort Wayne (G-4978)
Faurecia Exhaust Systems LLC............... C..... 812 341-2079
  Columbus (G-2306)
Heavy Duty Manufacturing Inc................. F..... 260 432-2480
  Fort Wayne (G-5056)
Integrated Energy Technologies Inc......... E..... 812 421-7810
  Evansville (G-4128)
Viking Inc... E..... 260 244-6141
  Columbia City (G-2211)

EXPLORATION, METAL MINING

P M I LLC... G..... 812 374-3856
  Edinburgh (G-3094)
Vhgi Holdings Inc..................................... G
  Sullivan (G-15425)

EXPLOSIVES

Dyno Nobel Inc... G..... 260 731-4431
  Pennville (G-13563)
Ireco Metals Inc.. G..... 574 936-2146
  Plymouth (G-13787)
Nelson Brothers....................................... G..... 812 250-7520
  Evansville (G-4220)

EXTRACTS, FLAVORING

Callisons Inc.. G..... 574 896-5074
  North Judson (G-13208)
Dairychem Laboratories Inc..................... E..... 317 849-8400
  Fishers (G-4501)
William Leman Co.................................... E..... 574 546-2371
  Bremen (G-1230)

FABRIC STORES

Gohn Bros Manufacturing Co................... G..... 574 825-2400
  Middlebury (G-11718)

FABRICS & CLOTH: Quilted

Lavender Patch Fabr Quilts LLC.............. G..... 574 848-0011
  Bristol (G-1270)

FABRICS: Apparel & Outerwear, Broadwoven

Bw Wholesale LLC................................... G..... 775 856-3522
  Greenwood (G-6678)

RB Concepts.. G..... 317 735-2172
  Bloomington (G-952)
Spobric LLC... G..... 302 249-1045
  Indianapolis (G-9479)

FABRICS: Apparel & Outerwear, Cotton

Lee Reed Holdings LLC........................... G..... 219 255-0555
  Hammond (G-6970)
Moore Shirts LLC..................................... G..... 317 350-4342
  Fort Wayne (G-5241)
Savage Yet Civilized LLC........................ G..... 855 560-9223
  Merrillville (G-11556)
Spobric LLC... G..... 302 249-1045
  Indianapolis (G-9479)
Unjust LLC.. G..... 317 443-2584
  Fishers (G-4622)
Word 4 Word LLC.................................... G..... 317 601-3995
  Indianapolis (G-9787)

FABRICS: Bags & Bagging, Cotton

Midwest Sandbags LLC........................... G..... 847 366-6555
  Elkhart (G-3541)

FABRICS: Basket Weave, Cotton

Zig-Zag Crnr Qilts Baskets LLC............... G..... 317 326-3115
  Greenfield (G-6573)

FABRICS: Bonded-Fiber, Exc Felt

Fiber Bond Operating LLC....................... C..... 219 879-4541
  Trail Creek (G-15837)

FABRICS: Denims

Denim and Honey..................................... G..... 812 222-2009
  Greensburg (G-6591)
Perfect World Denim LLC......................... G..... 260 449-9099
  Fort Wayne (G-5305)

FABRICS: Fiberglass, Broadwoven

Altec Engineering Inc............................... E..... 574 293-1965
  Elkhart (G-3167)
Goldshield Fiber Glass Inc....................... C..... 260 728-2476
  Decatur (G-2859)
Kabert Industries Inc............................... D..... 765 874-2335
  Lynn (G-11184)
Sampson Fiberglass Inc........................... E..... 574 255-4356
  Mishawaka (G-11990)
Structural Composites Ind Inc.................. D..... 260 894-4083
  Ligonier (G-11024)

FABRICS: Nonwoven

Carver Non-Woven Indiana LLC.............. G..... 260 627-0033
  Fremont (G-5814)
Carver Non-Woven Tech LLC................... C..... 260 627-0033
  Fremont (G-5815)
Gaius Julius Crassus Inc......................... G..... 219 879-4541
  Trail Creek (G-15838)
Jason Holdings Inc.................................. C..... 414 277-9300
  Richmond (G-14147)
Midwest Nonwovens Indiana LLC............ E..... 317 241-8956
  Indianapolis (G-8912)
Twe Nonwovens Us Inc........................... E..... 260 747-0990
  Fort Wayne (G-5517)

FABRICS: Resin Or Plastic Coated

CP Polymer Solutions LLC....................... G..... 812 426-1350
  Evansville (G-3989)
Elite Crete Systems Inc........................... F..... 219 465-7671
  Valparaiso (G-15942)
Sirmax North America Inc........................ D..... 765 639-0300
  Anderson (G-194)

FABRICS: Scrub Cloths

Creative Mnds Work Pblctns LL........... G 317 759-1002
  Indianapolis *(G-7901)*
Ninas Scrub Boutique LLC.................... G 833 445-1955
  Anderson *(G-169)*
Sassy Scrubz LLC.................................. G 463 224-5693
  Indianapolis *(G-9376)*
Uinspire LLC... G 574 575-6949
  Elkhart *(G-3756)*

FABRICS: Underwear, Cotton

Enduring Endeavors LLC....................... G 260 410-1025
  Fort Wayne *(G-4951)*

FABRICS: Upholstery, Cotton

Lazzerini Corporation............................. F 574 206-4769
  Elkhart *(G-3474)*

FABRICS: Upholstery, Wool

Kds Industries LLC................................. G 574 333-2720
  Elkhart *(G-3448)*

FACILITIES SUPPORT SVCS

Fiserv Mrtg Servicing Systems............. C 574 282-3300
  South Bend *(G-15034)*
Johnson Controls Inc............................. F 812 868-1374
  Evansville *(G-4144)*
Johnson Controls Inc............................. F 317 917-5043
  Pittsboro *(G-13649)*

FAMILY CLOTHING STORES

Cool Cayenne LLC.................................. G 765 282-0977
  Albany *(G-12)*
Operation 1 Veteran Inc......................... G 574 536-5536
  Goshen *(G-6231)*
Yalel Unbland LLC.................................. G 404 232-9139
  Indianapolis *(G-9799)*

FANS, BLOWING: Indl Or Commercial

Eclipse Inc.. D
  Muncie *(G-12389)*
Horner Industrial Services Inc................ F 317 634-7165
  Indianapolis *(G-8418)*
Universal Blower Pac Inc....................... E 317 773-7256
  Noblesville *(G-13190)*

FANS, VENTILATING: Indl Or Commercial

Airjet Inc... D 574 264-0123
  Elkhart *(G-3155)*
Lau Holdings LLC................................... D 574 223-3181
  Rochester *(G-14300)*
New York Blower Company.................... C 217 347-3233
  La Porte *(G-10457)*
Thermo-Cycler Industries Inc................ G 219 767-2990
  Union Mills *(G-15868)*

FANS: Ceiling

Fanimation Inc.. E 317 733-4113
  Zionsville *(G-17007)*

FARM & GARDEN MACHINERY WHOLESALERS

Bane-Welker Equipment LLC................ F 812 234-2627
  Terre Haute *(G-15550)*
Hahn Enterprises Inc............................. G 574 862-4491
  Wakarusa *(G-16234)*

FARM MACHINERY REPAIR SVCS

Bickels Garage & Welding..................... G 765 853-5457
  Modoc *(G-12050)*

Buffington Electric Motors...................... G 574 935-5453
  Plymouth *(G-13762)*
Fayette Welding Service Inc.................. G 317 852-2929
  Brownsburg *(G-1366)*
Pwi Corp... E 574 646-2015
  Nappanee *(G-12638)*
Whitcraft Welding................................... G 574 867-6021
  Grovertown *(G-6825)*

FARM PRDTS, RAW MATERIALS, WHOLESALE: Feathers

Maple Leaf Inc.. B 574 453-4455
  Leesburg *(G-10958)*

FARM SPLYS WHOLESALERS

Archer-Daniels-Midland Company........ E 260 824-0079
  Bluffton *(G-1025)*
Belstra Milling Co Inc............................. E 219 987-4343
  Demotte *(G-2911)*
Blue River Farm Supply Inc................... G 812 364-6675
  Palmyra *(G-13478)*
Bristow Milling Co LLC........................... G 812 843-5176
  Bristow *(G-1299)*
International A I Inc............................... F 812 824-2473
  Bloomington *(G-891)*
Keystone Cooperative Inc...................... G 765 659-2596
  Frankfort *(G-5678)*
Kuntry Lumber and Farm Sup Ltd........ F 260 463-3242
  Lagrange *(G-10746)*
Northwest Farm Fertilizers.................... G 219 785-2331
  Westville *(G-16764)*
Pine Manor Inc....................................... G 574 533-4186
  Goshen *(G-6238)*
Premier AG Co-Op Inc........................... E 812 522-4911
  Seymour *(G-14677)*
Russell E Martin.................................... G 574 354-2563
  Akron *(G-8)*
Sun Rise Metal Shop............................. G 260 463-4026
  Topeka *(G-15820)*

FARM SPLYS, WHOLESALE: Feed

Bundy Bros and Sons Inc...................... F 812 966-2551
  Medora *(G-11462)*
Hunter Nutrition Inc............................... F 765 563-1003
  Brookston *(G-1311)*
Keystone Cooperative Inc...................... G 765 249-2233
  Michigantown *(G-11691)*
Keystone Cooperative Inc...................... G 800 525-0272
  Indianapolis *(G-8680)*
Laughery Valley AG Co-Op Inc.............. G 812 689-4401
  Osgood *(G-13412)*
Salamonie Mills Inc............................... F 260 375-2200
  Warren *(G-16304)*
Wallace Grain Company Inc.................. F 317 758-4434
  Sheridan *(G-14832)*

FARM SPLYS, WHOLESALE: Fertilizers & Agricultural Chemicals

Keystone Cooperative Inc...................... G 765 489-4141
  Hagerstown *(G-6838)*

FARM SPLYS, WHOLESALE: Garden Splys

Earth First Kentuckiana Inc................... F 812 923-1227
  Charlestown *(G-1875)*
U-Nitt LLC... G 812 251-9980
  Carmel *(G-1792)*

FASTENERS WHOLESALERS

Archimedes Inc...................................... F 260 347-3903
  Kendallville *(G-10090)*

B & H Industries Corporation................ G 765 794-4428
  Darlington *(G-2832)*
Bollhoff Inc... D 260 347-3903
  Kendallville *(G-10097)*
General Fasteners Co............................ G 574 343-2413
  Elkhart *(G-3372)*
K&M Fasteners LLC.............................. G 260 525-8989
  Berne *(G-717)*
Rightway Fasteners Inc......................... C 812 342-2700
  Columbus *(G-2387)*
Scotts Fasteners & Supply LLC............. G 317 372-8743
  Danville *(G-2827)*
Smart Machine Inc................................ G 219 922-0706
  Hammond *(G-7009)*

FASTENERS: Metal

Elgin Fastener Group LLC..................... G 812 689-8917
  Versailles *(G-16099)*
Indiana Whitesell Corporation............... B 317 279-3278
  Indianapolis *(G-8500)*
Rdd Properties Inc................................ E 317 870-1940
  Waterloo *(G-16529)*

FAUCETS & SPIGOTS: Metal & Plastic

Lasalle Bristol Corporation.................... F 574 936-9894
  Plymouth *(G-13791)*
Rcate Plbg Mech Ltd Lblty Co.............. G 812 613-0386
  Sellersburg *(G-14611)*

FEATHERS & FEATHER PRODUCTS

LSI Wallcovering Inc............................. D 502 458-1502
  New Albany *(G-12767)*
Speedhook Specialists Inc.................... G 219 378-6369
  Beverly Shores *(G-732)*

FENCES OR POSTS: Ornamental Iron Or Steel

Ironcraft Co Inc...................................... G 574 272-0866
  South Bend *(G-15088)*
K & K Fence Inc..................................... E 317 359-5425
  Indianapolis *(G-8652)*

FENCING MATERIALS: Docks & Other Outdoor Prdts, Wood

Holman Lumber LLC.............................. G 260 337-0338
  Saint Joe *(G-14438)*
Rookstools Pier Shop Inc...................... E 574 453-4771
  Leesburg *(G-10960)*

FENCING MATERIALS: Wood

Menard Inc... C 812 466-1234
  Terre Haute *(G-15641)*
Quality Fence Ltd.................................. G 260 768-4986
  Shipshewana *(G-14880)*

FENCING: Chain Link

Ifc Fence LLC... G 219 977-4000
  Gary *(G-5956)*

FENDERS: Automobile, Stamped Or Pressed Metal

Body Panels Co...................................... F 812 962-6262
  Evansville *(G-3937)*
Fenders Inc.. G 574 293-3717
  Elkhart *(G-3344)*
Tru-Form Metal Products Inc................ F 574 266-8020
  Elkhart *(G-3749)*

FERTILIZER, AGRICULTURAL: Wholesalers

PRODUCT SECTION

FIRE ARMS, SMALL: Rifles Or Rifle Parts, 30 mm & below

AG Plus Inc .... G 260 623-6121
  Monroeville *(G-12066)*
AG Plus Inc .... E 260 723-5141
  South Whitley *(G-15316)*
Andersons Agriculture Group LP .... F 765 564-6135
  Delphi *(G-2890)*
Andersons Agriculture Group LP .... G 574 626-2522
  Galveston *(G-5851)*
Andersons Fertilizer Service .... G 765 538-3285
  Romney *(G-14379)*
Clunette Elevator Co Inc .... F 574 858-2281
  Leesburg *(G-10952)*
Don Hartman Oil Co Inc .... G 765 643-5026
  Anderson *(G-106)*
Frick Services Inc .... E 260 761-3311
  Wawaka *(G-16539)*
Kova Fertilizer Inc .... E 812 663-5081
  Greensburg *(G-6613)*
Roy Umbarger and Sons Inc .... F 317 422-5195
  Franklin *(G-5775)*
Superior AG Resources Coop Inc .... G 812 724-4455
  Owensville *(G-13473)*

FERTILIZERS: Nitrogenous

Andersons Agriculture Group LP .... G 574 753-4974
  Logansport *(G-11056)*
Keystone Cooperative Inc .... G 765 659-2596
  Frankfort *(G-5678)*
Knox Fertilizer Company Inc .... C 574 772-6275
  Knox *(G-10213)*

FERTILIZERS: Phosphatic

Andersons Agriculture Group LP .... G 574 753-4974
  Logansport *(G-11056)*
Wilson Fertilizer & Grain Inc .... G 574 223-3175
  Rochester *(G-14333)*

FIBER & FIBER PRDTS: Protein

Butterfield Foods LLC .... C 317 776-4775
  Noblesville *(G-13051)*

FIBER & FIBER PRDTS: Vinyl

Fdc Graphics Films Inc .... E 800 634-7523
  South Bend *(G-15029)*

FIBERS: Carbon & Graphite

Applied Composites Engrg Inc .... E 317 243-4225
  Indianapolis *(G-7533)*
Composite Specialties .... G 317 852-1408
  Brownsburg *(G-1360)*
Indy Prfmce Composites Inc .... G 317 858-7793
  Brownsburg *(G-1373)*

FILTER ELEMENTS: Fluid & Hydraulic Line

Hook Industrial Sales Inc .... D 260 432-9441
  Fort Wayne *(G-5075)*
Hy-Pro Corporation .... D 317 849-3535
  Anderson *(G-130)*

FILTERS

Advance Filter LLC .... G 317 565-7009
  Anderson *(G-72)*
Asl Technologies LLC .... G 219 733-2777
  Wanatah *(G-16286)*
Burgess Enterprises LLC .... G 260 615-5194
  Albion *(G-20)*
Butlers General Repair .... G 812 268-5631
  Sullivan *(G-15403)*
Clear Decision Filtration Inc .... G 219 567-2008
  Francesville *(G-5637)*
Cpp Filter Corporation .... G 765 446-8416
  Lafayette *(G-10560)*
Don Detzer LLC .... G 812 362-7599
  Tennyson *(G-15523)*
F D Deskins Company Inc .... F 317 284-4014
  Fishers *(G-4520)*
GLS Machining & Design LLC .... G 765 754-8248
  Alexandria *(G-52)*
Gvs Filter Technology Inc .... G 317 442-3925
  Zionsville *(G-17015)*
Heartland Filled Machine LLC .... G 574 223-6931
  Rochester *(G-14295)*
Indianapolis In .... E 855 628-3458
  Indianapolis *(G-8502)*
McCullagh Corporation .... F 877 645-7676
  Long Beach *(G-11124)*
Spencer Machine and TI Co Inc .... E 812 282-6300
  Jeffersonville *(G-10057)*
SRK Filters LLC .... G 765 647-9962
  Cedar Grove *(G-1825)*
T & T Hydraulics Inc .... G 765 548-2355
  Rosedale *(G-14384)*
U S Filter .... G 317 280-4251
  Indianapolis *(G-9671)*
U S Filter Distribution .... G 317 271-1463
  Indianapolis *(G-9672)*
Web Products .... G 816 777-3735
  La Porte *(G-10498)*

FILTERS & SOFTENERS: Water, Household

American Melt Blown Filtration .... E 219 866-3500
  Rensselaer *(G-14041)*
Astbury Water Technology Inc .... D 317 328-7153
  Indianapolis *(G-7556)*
Leach & Sons WaterCare .... G 317 248-8954
  Danville *(G-2818)*
New Aqua LLC .... D 317 272-3000
  Avon *(G-540)*
On The Go Portable Water Softe .... F 260 482-9614
  Bloomington *(G-936)*
Puritan Water Conditioning .... F 765 362-6340
  Crawfordsville *(G-2606)*

FILTERS: Air

American Melt Blown Filtration .... E 219 866-3500
  Rensselaer *(G-14041)*
Anthony Group LLC .... F 317 536-7445
  Greenwood *(G-6669)*
Indianapolis In .... E 855 628-3458
  Indianapolis *(G-8502)*

FILTERS: Air Intake, Internal Combustion Engine, Exc Auto

Donaldson Company Inc .... G 765 635-2285
  Anderson *(G-107)*
JW Machining LLC .... G 812 344-6753
  Columbus *(G-2332)*
Rayco Mch & Engrg Group Inc .... E 317 291-7848
  Indianapolis *(G-9268)*
True Blue Company LLC .... E 219 324-8482
  La Porte *(G-10495)*

FILTERS: General Line, Indl

Action Filtration Inc .... G 812 546-6262
  Hope *(G-7222)*
Bofrebo Industries Inc .... E 219 322-1550
  Schererville *(G-14516)*
Enviro Filtration Inc .... G 815 469-2871
  Gary *(G-5929)*
Filter Fabrics Inc .... F
  Goshen *(G-6136)*
Filtration Plus Inc .... F 219 879-0663
  Michigan City *(G-11612)*
Gvs Filter Technology Inc .... E 317 471-3700
  Indianapolis *(G-8345)*
Hitachi Global Air Pwr US LLC .... C 219 879-5451
  Michigan City *(G-11626)*
Lesac Corporation .... E 219 879-3215
  Michigan City *(G-11632)*
Pittsfield Products Inc .... D 260 488-2124
  Hamilton *(G-6859)*

FILTRATION DEVICES: Electronic

Andon Specialties Inc .... G 317 983-1700
  Indianapolis *(G-7516)*
Chemtrex LLC .... G 317 508-4223
  Noblesville *(G-13058)*
Separation Technologies Inc .... G 219 548-5814
  Valparaiso *(G-16046)*
Sonicu LLC .... G 317 468-2345
  Greenfield *(G-6556)*
Tetrasolv Inc .... F 765 643-3941
  Anderson *(G-206)*
Tri-Star Filtration Inc .... G 317 337-0940
  Indianapolis *(G-9636)*

FINANCIAL SVCS

Oxinas Partners LLC .... G 812 725-8649
  Jeffersonville *(G-10032)*
Sentinel Services Inc .... E 574 360-5279
  Granger *(G-6376)*

FINISHING AGENTS

J & B Sales & Induction Srvcs .... G 765 965-2500
  Richmond *(G-14142)*

FINISHING SVCS

Crossrads Rhbilitation Ctr Inc .... C 317 897-7320
  Indianapolis *(G-7910)*

FIRE ALARM MAINTENANCE & MONITORING SVCS

American Eagle Security Inc .... G 219 980-1177
  Merrillville *(G-11482)*
American Fire Company .... G 219 840-0630
  Valparaiso *(G-15899)*

FIRE ARMS, SMALL: Guns Or Gun Parts, 30 mm & Below

Acme Sports Inc .... G 812 522-4008
  Seymour *(G-14625)*
Blythes Sport Shop Inc .... F 219 924-4403
  Griffith *(G-6795)*
Calumet Arsenal LLC .... G 219 256-9885
  Whiting *(G-16833)*
CF Gunworks LLC .... G 317 538-1122
  Frankfort *(G-5653)*
Dave Brown Customs LLC .... G 812 727-5560
  Palmyra *(G-13479)*
Michael Hazeltine .... F 317 750-5091
  Greenwood *(G-6739)*
Namacle LLC .... G 574 320-1436
  South Bend *(G-15158)*
Red Bull Armory LLC .... G 757 287-7738
  Mitchell *(G-12046)*
Suppress TEC LLC .... G 812 453-5813
  Elberfeld *(G-3122)*
Vadens Firearms & Ammun LLC .... G 317 840-5799
  Indianapolis *(G-9697)*
Wraith Arms Resolutions LLC .... G 812 380-1208
  Velpen *(G-16095)*

FIRE ARMS, SMALL: Rifles Or Rifle Parts, 30 mm & below

Zrp LLC.. G..... 888 824-5587
Laotto *(G-10813)*

FIRE CONTROL OR BOMBING EQPT: Electronic

T Shorter Manufacturing Inc................. G..... 574 264-4131
Elkhart *(G-3713)*

FIRE EXTINGUISHERS, WHOLESALE

Abro Industries Inc............................... E..... 574 232-8289
South Bend *(G-14933)*

FIRE EXTINGUISHERS: Portable

Carl Abbott.. G..... 317 590-4143
Indianapolis *(G-7745)*

FIRE OR BURGLARY RESISTIVE PRDTS

Davis Hezakih Corp............................... F..... 260 768-7300
Shipshewana *(G-14843)*

E & H Bridge and Grating Inc................. G..... 812 277-8343
Bedford *(G-632)*

Rko Enterprises LLC............................. G..... 812 273-8813
Madison *(G-11248)*

S C Pryor Inc... F..... 317 352-1281
Indianapolis *(G-9354)*

Sacoma Properties LLC......................... F..... 812 526-5600
Edinburgh *(G-3102)*

Schafer Industries Inc........................... D..... 574 234-4116
South Bend *(G-15234)*

Tru-Flex LLC... C..... 765 893-4403
West Lebanon *(G-16649)*

FIREARMS & AMMUNITION, EXC SPORTING, WHOLESALE

Blythes Sport Shop Inc.......................... F..... 219 924-4403
Griffith *(G-6795)*

Pine Valley Munitions Inc...................... G..... 260 818-6113
Columbia City *(G-2181)*

Vadens Firearms & Ammun LLC............ G..... 317 840-5799
Indianapolis *(G-9697)*

FIREFIGHTING APPARATUS

Elkhart Brass Manufacturing.................. C..... 574 295-8330
Elkhart *(G-3322)*

Safe Fleet Holdings LLC........................ G..... 574 849-4619
Elkhart *(G-3658)*

FIREPLACE EQPT & ACCESS

American Flame LLC............................. D..... 260 459-1703
Fort Wayne *(G-4754)*

Bottom Line Management Inc................ F..... 812 944-7388
Clarksville *(G-2010)*

Gibson Brothers Welding Inc................. F..... 765 948-5775
Fairmount *(G-4410)*

Seymour Manufacturing Co Inc.............. C..... 812 522-2900
Seymour *(G-14689)*

FIREWORKS

Bada Boom Fireworks LLC.................... G..... 219 472-6700
Gary *(G-5897)*

Jackson Hewitt Tax Service.................... F..... 574 255-2200
Mishawaka *(G-11915)*

Johnny Lemas....................................... G..... 260 833-8850
Angola *(G-264)*

Millennial Fireworks.............................. G..... 812 732-5126
Mauckport *(G-11439)*

Ulerys Fireworks Inc............................. G..... 574 722-9119
Logansport *(G-11116)*

Vw Co... G..... 812 397-0102
Shelburn *(G-14723)*

FIRST AID SPLYS, WHOLESALE

Wildman Business Group LLC................ G..... 866 369-1552
Warsaw *(G-16451)*

Workflow Solutions LLC......................... G..... 502 627-0257
New Albany *(G-12831)*

FISH FOOD

Avari Reef Labs LLC.............................. G..... 317 201-9615
Anderson *(G-80)*

FISHING EQPT: Lures

Harpoon Lure Co DBA Forming T............ G..... 812 371-3550
North Vernon *(G-13275)*

Lure Ventures Inc.................................. G..... 219 313-5325
Mishawaka *(G-11934)*

Meredith Hughes................................... G..... 317 354-6073
Plainfield *(G-13705)*

PH Custom Lures LLC........................... G..... 765 541-0726
Connersville *(G-2461)*

Vanmeter and Son Lures LLC................ G..... 812 653-0497
Marengo *(G-11266)*

FITTINGS & ASSEMBLIES: Hose & Tube, Hydraulic Or Pneumatic

Cindon Inc.. F..... 812 853-5450
Newburgh *(G-12998)*

Dependable Rubber Industrial............... G..... 765 447-5654
Lafayette *(G-10569)*

Kilgore Manufacturing Co Inc................ D..... 260 248-2002
Columbia City *(G-2162)*

Kobaltec LLC... G..... 219 462-1483
Valparaiso *(G-15988)*

Macallister Machinery Co Inc................. C..... 260 483-6469
Fort Wayne *(G-5195)*

Mary Jonas... F..... 317 500-0600
Indianapolis *(G-8845)*

Metal Powder Products Co LLP.............. F..... 317 805-3764
Noblesville *(G-13133)*

P H C Industries Inc.............................. G
Fort Wayne *(G-5291)*

Parker-Hannifin Corporation.................. A..... 260 748-6000
Fort Wayne *(G-5297)*

River Bend Hose Specialty Inc............... E..... 574 233-1133
South Bend *(G-15222)*

Techna-Fit Inc....................................... G..... 317 350-2153
Brownsburg *(G-1408)*

Terry Liquidation III Inc......................... D..... 219 362-9908
La Porte *(G-10489)*

FITTINGS & SPECIALTIES: Steam

Modbar LLC... F..... 206 450-4743
Fort Wayne *(G-5239)*

FITTINGS: Pipe

JM Fittings LLC..................................... E..... 260 747-9200
Fort Wayne *(G-5137)*

Nibco Inc.. B..... 574 295-3000
Elkhart *(G-3570)*

R2b2 Industries LLC............................. G..... 812 436-4840
Evansville *(G-4270)*

FITTINGS: Pipe, Fabricated

Barry Company Inc................................ G..... 317 578-2486
Fishers *(G-4471)*

FIXTURES & EQPT: Kitchen, Metal, Exc Cast Aluminum

Kitchen & Bath Fixtures......................... G..... 574 296-7617
Elkhart *(G-3458)*

Premier Concepts Inc............................ G..... 574 269-7570
Warsaw *(G-16413)*

Zojila Ltd Liability Company.................. G..... 765 404-3767
Lafayette *(G-10726)*

FLAGPOLES

Original Tractor Cab Co Inc................... F..... 765 663-2214
Arlington *(G-329)*

FLAGS: Fabric

Classy Stitches..................................... G..... 317 856-3261
Indianapolis *(G-7821)*

FLAGSTONES

Flagstone Village LLC............................ G..... 219 989-3265
Hammond *(G-6930)*

FLAT GLASS: Construction

Pilkington North America Inc................ G..... 317 346-0621
Franklin *(G-5766)*

Spohn Associates Inc............................ G..... 317 921-2445
Indianapolis *(G-9480)*

FLAT GLASS: Sheet

Calumite Company LLC......................... G..... 219 787-8667
Portage *(G-13852)*

FLAT GLASS: Window, Clear & Colored

Cloudmaker Studio Inc.......................... G..... 219 879-1724
Michigan City *(G-11589)*

Midwest Fade Control............................ G..... 219 926-5043
Lafayette *(G-10649)*

Mr Tintz.. G..... 219 844-5500
Hammond *(G-6983)*

Tint Masters... G..... 260 704-2676
Fort Wayne *(G-5484)*

FLOOR COVERING STORES

Faulkens Floorcover.............................. F..... 574 300-4260
South Bend *(G-15027)*

Indiana Rug Company........................... G..... 574 252-4653
Mishawaka *(G-11911)*

Jack Laurie Coml Floors Inc................... G..... 317 569-2095
Indianapolis *(G-8613)*

K M Davis Inc....................................... G..... 765 426-9227
Lafayette *(G-10617)*

Neighborhood Floors & More LLC.......... G..... 219 510-5737
Portage *(G-13895)*

Todd K Hockemeyer Inc......................... G..... 260 639-3591
Fort Wayne *(G-5492)*

FLOOR COVERING STORES: Carpets

Fashion Flooring and Ltg Inc................. G
Valparaiso *(G-15947)*

Indiana Lumber Inc............................... G..... 812 837-9493
Bloomington *(G-889)*

Shelby Westside Upholstering................ G..... 317 631-8911
Indianapolis *(G-9419)*

Touch of Class Interiors......................... G..... 765 452-5879
Kokomo *(G-10351)*

FLOOR COVERINGS WHOLESALERS

Arran Isle Inc.. E..... 574 295-4400
Elkhart *(G-3191)*

Bock Engineering Company Inc............. G..... 574 522-3191
Elkhart *(G-3229)*

PRODUCT SECTION

FOOD PRDTS, CANNED: Soups, Exc Seafood

Faulkens Floorcover.................................. F 574 300-4260
  South Bend *(G-15027)*

Lasalle Bristol Corporation...................... F 574 295-4400
  Bristol *(G-1269)*

Lasalle Bristol Corporation...................... F 574 936-9894
  Plymouth *(G-13791)*

Lasalle Bristol Corporation...................... C 574 295-8400
  Elkhart *(G-3469)*

Todd K Hockemeyer Inc......................... G 260 639-3591
  Fort Wayne *(G-5492)*

FLOOR COVERINGS: Rubber

Excell Usa Inc.. D 812 895-1687
  Vincennes *(G-16121)*

FLOOR COVERINGS: Textile Fiber

Faulkens Floorcover.................................. F 574 300-4260
  South Bend *(G-15027)*

Georgia Direct Carpet Inc........................ F 765 966-2548
  Richmond *(G-14125)*

FLOOR COVERINGS: Twisted Paper, Grass, Reed, Coir, Etc

Recreation Insites LLC........................... G 317 578-0588
  Fishers *(G-4592)*

FLOORING & SIDING: Metal

Michael D Metz....................................... G 812 526-9606
  Columbus *(G-2354)*

FLOORING: Hardwood

Cross Country Hardwood LLC.................. F 812 571-4226
  Vevay *(G-16108)*

Hillcrest Enterprises LLC........................ G 812 875-2500
  Worthington *(G-16960)*

James A Andrew Inc............................... G 765 269-9807
  Lafayette *(G-10614)*

Jeff Hury Hrdwood Flors Pntg S.............. G 812 204-8650
  Evansville *(G-4141)*

Knies Sawmill Inc.................................... G 812 683-3402
  Huntingburg *(G-7285)*

Santarossa Mosaic Tile Co Inc................ C 317 632-9494
  Indianapolis *(G-9371)*

FLOORING: Rubber

Recreation Insites LLC........................... G 317 578-0588
  Fishers *(G-4592)*

FLORIST: Flowers, Fresh

Larry Flowers Wholesale......................... G 765 747-5156
  Muncie *(G-12438)*

FLOWERS, ARTIFICIAL, WHOLESALE

Jadco Ltd... F 219 661-2065
  Crown Point *(G-2699)*

FLUES & PIPES: Stove Or Furnace

Kitchen Queen LLC.................................. G 812 662-8399
  Saint Paul *(G-14465)*

FLUID METERS & COUNTING DEVICES

Dwyer Instruments LLC........................... C 219 879-8868
  Michigan City *(G-11604)*

FLUID POWER PUMPS & MOTORS

Crown Elec Svcs & Automtn Inc.............. D 972 929-4700
  Portage *(G-13857)*

D A Hochstetler & Sons LLP................... F 574 642-1144
  Topeka *(G-15800)*

Dresser LLC.. D 765 827-9200
  Connersville *(G-2436)*

Elevator Equipment Corporation.............. D 765 966-7761
  Richmond *(G-14119)*

Freudenberg-Nok General Partnr............. C 260 894-7183
  Ligonier *(G-11015)*

Gravel Conveyors Inc.............................. F 317 873-8686
  Zionsville *(G-17014)*

Jomar Machining & Fabg Inc................... E 574 825-9837
  Middlebury *(G-11728)*

Met-Pro Technologies LLC...................... G 317 293-2930
  Indianapolis *(G-8882)*

Murray Equipment Inc............................. C 260 484-0382
  Fort Wayne *(G-5252)*

Nidec Motor Corporation......................... D 812 385-2564
  Princeton *(G-14007)*

Parker-Hannifin Corporation.................... E 866 247-4827
  Jeffersonville *(G-10034)*

Parker-Hannifin Corporation.................... F 219 736-0400
  Merrillville *(G-11549)*

Parker-Hannifin Corporation.................... G 317 776-7600
  Noblesville *(G-13150)*

Parker-Hannifin Corporation.................... C 574 528-9400
  Syracuse *(G-15470)*

Steel Parts Corporation........................... A 765 675-2191
  Tipton *(G-15791)*

Terry Liquidation III Inc.......................... F 219 362-3557
  La Porte *(G-10490)*

FLUID POWER VALVES & HOSE FITTINGS

Bilfinger Airvac Water Technologies Inc D 574 223-3980
  Rochester *(G-14279)*

JM Fittings LLC....................................... E 260 747-9200
  Fort Wayne *(G-5137)*

Midwest Design Hydraulic....................... G 765 714-3016
  West Lafayette *(G-16605)*

Neff Group Distributors Inc..................... F 260 489-6007
  Fort Wayne *(G-5259)*

Nrp Jones LLC....................................... G 219 362-9908
  La Porte *(G-10459)*

Proportion-Air Inc.................................... D 317 335-2602
  Mccordsville *(G-11454)*

Seals & Components Inc........................ G 708 895-5222
  La Porte *(G-10478)*

Slb Corporation...................................... F 574 255-9774
  Mishawaka *(G-11996)*

FOAM RUBBER

Exemplary Foam Inc............................... F 574 295-8888
  Elkhart *(G-3338)*

Foamcraft Inc.. E 574 534-4343
  Goshen *(G-6139)*

Hi-Tech Foam Products LLC................... E 317 737-2298
  Indianapolis *(G-8396)*

Pactiv LLC.. E 574 936-7065
  Plymouth *(G-13800)*

FOAMS & RUBBER, WHOLESALE

Foam Rubber LLC................................... C 765 521-2000
  New Castle *(G-12862)*

Foamcraft Inc.. E 574 293-8569
  Elkhart *(G-3352)*

Foamcraft Inc.. E 574 534-4343
  Goshen *(G-6139)*

Vahala Foam Inc..................................... D 574 293-1287
  Elkhart *(G-3764)*

FOIL & LEAF: Metal

Avery Dennison Corporation.................... D 219 696-7777
  Lowell *(G-11155)*

Old Rev LLC... G 317 580-2420
  Westfield *(G-16714)*

FOIL: Aluminum

Gusa Holdings Inc................................... D 317 545-1221
  Indianapolis *(G-8343)*

FOIL: Laminated To Paper Or Other Materials

Foil Laminating Inc.................................. E
  Plymouth *(G-13777)*

FOOD COLORINGS

Sugarpaste.. G 574 276-8703
  South Bend *(G-15272)*

FOOD PRDTS, CANNED: Barbecue Sauce

Douglas K Gresham................................. G 812 445-3174
  Seymour *(G-14649)*

Kens Foods Inc....................................... D 765 505-7900
  Lebanon *(G-10908)*

Smoked Q LLC.. G 260 494-5029
  Fort Wayne *(G-5423)*

FOOD PRDTS, CANNED: Beans & Bean Sprouts

Eden Foods Inc....................................... E 765 396-3344
  Eaton *(G-3061)*

FOOD PRDTS, CANNED: Fruits

Bay Valley Foods LLC............................. C 574 935-3097
  Plymouth *(G-13757)*

Eden Foods Inc....................................... E 765 396-3344
  Eaton *(G-3061)*

Kraft Heinz Foods Company.................... D 260 347-1300
  Kendallville *(G-10131)*

Lakeside Foods....................................... G 219 924-4860
  Highland *(G-7142)*

Millers Mill... G 574 825-2010
  Middlebury *(G-11738)*

Red Gold Inc... G 765 557-5500
  Elwood *(G-3834)*

Red Gold Inc... C 260 368-9017
  Geneva *(G-6050)*

Youth JAM LLC....................................... G 765 644-6375
  Anderson *(G-220)*

Zentis North America LLC....................... B 574 941-1100
  Plymouth *(G-13835)*

Zentis North America Holdg LLC............. C 574 941-1100
  Plymouth *(G-13836)*

FOOD PRDTS, CANNED: Fruits & Fruit Prdts

Rays Juice Company............................... G 219 809-7400
  Michigan City *(G-11656)*

FOOD PRDTS, CANNED: Jams, Including Imitation

Dutch Kettle LLC..................................... F 574 546-4033
  Bremen *(G-1188)*

FOOD PRDTS, CANNED: Jams, Jellies & Preserves

Schergers Kttle Jams Jellies -................. G 800 447-6475
  Shipshewana *(G-14885)*

FOOD PRDTS, CANNED: Mexican, NEC

Tyson Mexican Original Inc..................... D 260 726-3118
  Portland *(G-13974)*

FOOD PRDTS, CANNED: Soups, Exc Seafood

Morgan Foods Inc.................................... A 812 794-1170
  Austin *(G-467)*

Employee Codes: A=Over 500 employees, B=251-500, C=101-250, D=51-100, E=20-50, F=10-19, G=1-9

FOOD PRDTS, CANNED: Soups, Exc Seafood

Park 100 Foods Inc................................. E 317 549-4545
   Indianapolis *(G-9093)*
Park 100 Foods Inc................................. D 765 675-3480
   Tipton *(G-15786)*

FOOD PRDTS, CANNED: Spaghetti & Other Pasta Sauce

Sprigati LLC.. G 219 484-9455
   Munster *(G-12564)*

FOOD PRDTS, CONFECTIONERY, WHOLESALE: Snack Foods

Dieng Group LLC................................... G 317 699-1909
   Indianapolis *(G-7973)*
Snax In Pax Inc..................................... E 260 593-3066
   Topeka *(G-15819)*

FOOD PRDTS, FISH & SEAFOOD: Prepared Cakes & Sticks

H & H Partnership Inc.......................... G 765 513-4739
   Kokomo *(G-10274)*

FOOD PRDTS, FROZEN: Fruits, Juices & Vegetables

Frozen Garden LLC............................... F 219 286-3578
   Valparaiso *(G-15951)*
Hawaiian Smoothie LLC......................... G 317 881-7290
   Fishers *(G-4537)*
Pepsico Inc.. G 317 830-4011
   Indianapolis *(G-9119)*
Zentis North America Holdg LLC.......... C 574 941-1100
   Plymouth *(G-13836)*

FOOD PRDTS, WHOLESALE: Beverages, Exc Coffee & Tea

Pepsi-Cola Metro Btlg Co Inc................ F 812 332-1200
   Bloomington *(G-945)*

FOOD PRDTS, WHOLESALE: Coffee & Tea

Allen Street Roasters LLC..................... G 815 955-7872
   La Porte *(G-10380)*
Buckner Inc.. E 317 570-0533
   Indianapolis *(G-7699)*
Harvest Cafe Coffee & Tea LLC............. G 317 585-9162
   Indianapolis *(G-8369)*

FOOD PRDTS, WHOLESALE: Coffee, Green Or Roasted

Suncoast Coffee Inc.............................. E 317 251-3198
   Indianapolis *(G-9526)*

FOOD PRDTS, WHOLESALE: Dried or Canned Foods

Dieng Group LLC................................... G 317 699-1909
   Indianapolis *(G-7973)*

FOOD PRDTS, WHOLESALE: Grain Elevators

AG Plus Inc.. G 260 623-6121
   Monroeville *(G-12066)*
AG Plus Inc.. E 260 723-5141
   South Whitley *(G-15316)*
Archer-Daniels-Midland Company......... G 765 299-1672
   Fowler *(G-5618)*
B S R Inc... E 812 235-4444
   Terre Haute *(G-15549)*
Bundy Bros and Sons Inc...................... F 812 966-2551
   Medora *(G-11462)*
Clunette Elevator Co Inc....................... F 574 858-2281
   Leesburg *(G-10952)*
Gem Elevator Inc................................... G 317 894-7722
   Greenfield *(G-6505)*
Northwest Farm Fertilizers.................... G 219 785-2331
   Westville *(G-16764)*
Premier AG Co-Op Inc.......................... E 812 522-4911
   Seymour *(G-14677)*
Roy Umbarger and Sons Inc.................. F 317 422-5195
   Franklin *(G-5775)*
Salamonie Mills Inc............................... F 260 375-2200
   Warren *(G-16304)*

FOOD PRDTS, WHOLESALE: Grains

Archer-Daniels-Midland Company......... E 765 654-4411
   Frankfort *(G-5649)*
Frick Services Inc.................................. E 260 761-3311
   Wawaka *(G-16539)*
Keystone Cooperative Inc...................... G 765 249-2233
   Michigantown *(G-11691)*
Keystone Cooperative Inc...................... C 800 525-0272
   Indianapolis *(G-8680)*
Langeland Farms Inc............................. G 812 663-9546
   Greensburg *(G-6614)*
Laughery Valley AG Co-Op Inc.............. G 812 689-4401
   Osgood *(G-13412)*
Lowes Pellets and Grain Inc.................. E 812 663-7863
   Greensburg *(G-6615)*
United Animal Health Inc....................... D 317 758-4495
   Sheridan *(G-14830)*
Wallace Grain Company Inc.................. F 317 758-4434
   Sheridan *(G-14832)*
Wilson Fertilizer & Grain Inc................. G 574 223-3175
   Rochester *(G-14333)*

FOOD PRDTS, WHOLESALE: Organic & Diet

Lebermuth Company Inc........................ D 574 259-7000
   South Bend *(G-15121)*

FOOD PRDTS, WHOLESALE: Salt, Edible

B S R Inc... E 812 235-4444
   Terre Haute *(G-15549)*

FOOD PRDTS, WHOLESALE: Sauces

Joey Chestnut Foods LLC..................... G 317 602-4830
   Indianapolis *(G-8629)*

FOOD PRDTS, WHOLESALE: Specialty

Passions Fruitopia LLC.......................... G 800 515-1891
   Highland *(G-7151)*

FOOD PRDTS, WHOLESALE: Spices & Seasonings

Reidco Inc.. E 812 358-3000
   Brownstown *(G-1426)*

FOOD PRDTS, WHOLESALE: Water, Distilled

Beverly Harris.. G 317 910-0542
   Indianapolis *(G-7619)*
Dribot LLC... G 317 885-6330
   Indianapolis *(G-8007)*
Majestic Water Company....................... G 317 790-2448
   Indianapolis *(G-8817)*

FOOD PRDTS: Almond Pastes

Pgp International Inc............................. E 812 449-0650
   Evansville *(G-4238)*

FOOD PRDTS: Animal & marine fats & oils

Bunge North America East LLC............. D 260 724-2101
   Decatur *(G-2849)*
Darling Ingredients Inc.......................... G 317 708-3070
   Columbus *(G-2279)*
Darling Ingredients Inc.......................... E 317 784-4486
   Indianapolis *(G-7951)*
Darling Ingredients Inc.......................... G 812 659-3399
   Newberry *(G-12988)*
Darling Ingredients Inc.......................... E 913 321-9328
   Plymouth *(G-13770)*
Geo Pfaus Sons Company Inc............... E 800 732-8645
   Jeffersonville *(G-9992)*
Griffin Industries LLC............................ D 812 659-3399
   Newberry *(G-12989)*
Hrr Enterprises Inc................................ E 219 362-9050
   La Porte *(G-10425)*
L & R Marine LLC.................................. G 260 768-8094
   Shipshewana *(G-14859)*
Nutritional Research Assoc................... F 260 723-4931
   South Whitley *(G-15322)*
Sustainable Sourcing LLC..................... E 765 505-2338
   Clinton *(G-2078)*

FOOD PRDTS: Baking Powder

Clabber Girl Corporation....................... D 812 232-9446
   Terre Haute *(G-15563)*
Hulman & Company................................ G 812 232-9446
   Terre Haute *(G-15608)*
Hulman & Company................................ C 812 232-9446
   Terre Haute *(G-15609)*

FOOD PRDTS: Box Lunches, For Sale Off Premises

Gleaners Food Bank of Ind Inc.............. D 317 925-0191
   Indianapolis *(G-8284)*

FOOD PRDTS: Butter, Renovated & Processed

Revival LLC... G 812 345-4317
   Indianapolis *(G-9296)*

FOOD PRDTS: Cheese Curls & Puffs

Super-Pufft Snacks Usa Inc................... G 850 295-9891
   Bluffton *(G-1059)*

FOOD PRDTS: Chicken, Processed, Fresh

Perdue Farms Inc................................. G 765 325-2997
   Lebanon *(G-10931)*

FOOD PRDTS: Chili Pepper Or Powder

G and G Peppers LLC............................ E 765 358-4519
   Gaston *(G-6045)*
Global Packaging LLC........................... E 317 896-2089
   Westfield *(G-16691)*

FOOD PRDTS: Coffee

Copper Moon Coffee LLC...................... D 317 541-9000
   Lafayette *(G-10555)*
Dry Heat Coffee LLC............................. G 760 422-9865
   Indianapolis *(G-8013)*
Grinds Manufacturing LLC..................... F 510 763-1088
   Westfield *(G-16694)*
Harvest Cafe Coffee & Tea LLC............. G 317 585-9162
   Indianapolis *(G-8369)*
Hoosier Roaster Llc.............................. G 574 257-1415
   Mishawaka *(G-11909)*
Michael Filley....................................... G 956 443-6364
   Owensburg *(G-13463)*
Rich Halstead....................................... G 219 462-8888
   Valparaiso *(G-16039)*
Roast Haus Coffee LLC......................... G 224 544-9550
   Crown Point *(G-2746)*

PRODUCT SECTION

FOOD PRDTS: Potato Chips & Other Potato-Based Snacks

Thedailygrind LLC.. G 317 531-1276
Whitestown *(G-16826)*

FOOD PRDTS: Corn & other vegetable starches

Ingredion Incorporated.. F 800 713-0208
Whiteland *(G-16789)*

FOOD PRDTS: Corn Chips & Other Corn-Based Snacks

Mike-Sells West Virginia Inc................................ G 317 241-7422
Indianapolis *(G-8917)*

Specialty Food Group LLC.................................. D 219 531-2142
Valparaiso *(G-16055)*

FOOD PRDTS: Corn Meal

Cargill Dry Corn Ingrdents Inc............................. E 317 632-1481
Indianapolis *(G-7744)*

Nutramaize LLC.. G 765 273-8274
West Lafayette *(G-16615)*

FOOD PRDTS: Corn Oil, Refined

Cargill Incorporated.. B 402 533-4227
Hammond *(G-6895)*

FOOD PRDTS: Dessert Mixes & Fillings

Conagra Brands Inc.. C 402 240-5000
Indianapolis *(G-7848)*

FOOD PRDTS: Dips, Exc Cheese & Sour Cream Based

Chicken and Salsa Inc.. G 812 480-6580
Evansville *(G-3971)*

Studio Digital Salsa LLC...................................... G 317 439-8994
Plainfield *(G-13733)*

FOOD PRDTS: Doughs, Frozen Or Refrig From Purchased Flour

Loaded Dough Cookie Co LLC........................... G 765 969-6513
Centerville *(G-1851)*

FOOD PRDTS: Dressings, Salad, Raw & Cooked Exc Dry Mixes

Grafton Peek Incorporated................................... F 317 557-8377
Greenwood *(G-6709)*

Richards Restaurant Inc...................................... F 260 997-6823
Bryant *(G-1436)*

FOOD PRDTS: Dried & Dehydrated Fruits, Vegetables & Soup Mix

Arneys Freeze-Dried Treats LLC......................... G 812 801-1386
Fort Wayne *(G-4772)*

Bella Food Sales LLC.. G 574 229-8803
Mishawaka *(G-11849)*

Eggpress LLC... G 574 267-2847
Warsaw *(G-16356)*

N K Hurst Co Inc.. E 317 634-6425
Zionsville *(G-17035)*

FOOD PRDTS: Duck Slaughtering & Processing

Culver Duck Farms Inc.. C 574 825-9537
Middlebury *(G-11709)*

Maple Leaf Farms Inc.. C 574 658-4121
Milford *(G-11799)*

Maple Leaf Farms Inc.. A 574 453-4500
Milford *(G-11798)*

FOOD PRDTS: Edible fats & oils

Blackpoint Distribution Co LLC............................ E 260 414-9096
Leo *(G-10964)*

Bunge North America East LLC.......................... D 260 724-2101
Decatur *(G-2849)*

FOOD PRDTS: Edible Oil Prdts, Exc Corn Oil

Northern Indiana Oil LLC..................................... F 317 966-0288
Indianapolis *(G-9022)*

FOOD PRDTS: Fish Oil

USA Bassin LLC... F 812 276-8043
Bedford *(G-680)*

FOOD PRDTS: Flour & Other Grain Mill Products

AG Plus Inc... G 260 623-6121
Monroeville *(G-12066)*

AG Plus Inc... E 260 723-5141
South Whitley *(G-15316)*

Archer-Daniels-Midland Company....................... G 317 783-3321
Beech Grove *(G-686)*

Archer-Daniels-Midland Company....................... E 260 824-0079
Bluffton *(G-1025)*

Archer-Daniels-Midland Company....................... G 765 362-2965
Crawfordsville *(G-2545)*

Archer-Daniels-Midland Company....................... G 574 773-4138
Nappanee *(G-12580)*

Archer-Daniels-Midland Company....................... G 219 866-2810
Rensselaer *(G-14043)*

Archer-Daniels-Midland Company....................... G 219 866-3939
Rensselaer *(G-14044)*

Azteca Milling LP... G 812 867-3190
Evansville *(G-3905)*

Cargill Incorporated.. G 574 353-7621
Mentone *(G-11471)*

Clunette Elevator Co Inc...................................... F 574 858-2281
Leesburg *(G-10952)*

Dillman Farm Incorporated.................................. G 812 825-5525
Bloomington *(G-857)*

Laughery Valley AG Co-Op Inc........................... G 812 689-4401
Osgood *(G-13412)*

Martinsville Milling Co Inc.................................... G 317 253-2581
Indianapolis *(G-8844)*

New Carbon Company LLC................................. G 574 247-2270
South Bend *(G-15164)*

Roy Umbarger and Sons Inc............................... F 317 422-5195
Franklin *(G-5775)*

Salamonie Mills Inc.. F 260 375-2200
Warren *(G-16304)*

Wallace Grain Company Inc................................ F 317 758-4434
Sheridan *(G-14832)*

FOOD PRDTS: Flour Mixes & Doughs

Clabber Girl Corporation...................................... D 812 232-9446
Terre Haute *(G-15563)*

Harlan Bakeries LLC.. C 317 272-3600
Indianapolis *(G-8361)*

Harlan Bakeries LLC.. G 317 272-3600
Avon *(G-523)*

Harlan Bakeries-Avon LLC.................................. B 317 272-3600
Avon *(G-524)*

JW Packaging LLC... G 317 414-9038
Converse *(G-2477)*

M&C Wndrink Rverside Farms Inc...................... G 928 897-0061
Lowell *(G-11170)*

Vintage Baked Modern LLC................................ G 219 252-9820
Valparaiso *(G-16076)*

FOOD PRDTS: Fruit Juices

Caj Food Products Inc... G 888 524-6882
Fishers *(G-4481)*

FOOD PRDTS: Fruits & Vegetables, Pickled

Christina Ann Clark.. G 317 778-7832
Indianapolis *(G-7802)*

Pickle Bites LLC... G 773 780-7559
Hammond *(G-6992)*

Pickled Pedaler... G 317 877-0624
Noblesville *(G-13155)*

FOOD PRDTS: Ice, Cubes

Bryant Ice Co Inc.. G 765 459-4543
Kokomo *(G-10242)*

FOOD PRDTS: Malt

Archer-Daniels-Midland Company....................... G 765 299-1672
Fowler *(G-5618)*

FOOD PRDTS: Mixes, Pancake From Purchased Flour

New Carbon Company LLC................................. G 574 247-2270
Indianapolis *(G-9002)*

FOOD PRDTS: Mixes, Pizza

Crust N More Inc.. F 317 890-7878
Indianapolis *(G-7915)*

FOOD PRDTS: Mixes, Sauces, Dry

Chef Hymie Inc... G 201 218-4378
New Albany *(G-12711)*

FOOD PRDTS: Mixes, Seasonings, Dry

Big Bruhs Seasoning LLP.................................... G 502 751-5516
Clarksville *(G-2009)*

FOOD PRDTS: Oil, Hydrogenated, Edible

Heartland Harvest Proc LLC................................ G 260 228-0736
Hartford City *(G-7069)*

Heartland Harvest Proc LLC................................ G 260 228-0736
Gas City *(G-6038)*

FOOD PRDTS: Olive Oil

A Wild Hare LLC... F 812 988-9453
Nashville *(G-12658)*

Debbies Handmade Soap.................................... G 765 747-5090
Muncie *(G-12376)*

FOOD PRDTS: Pasta, Uncooked, Packaged With Other Ingredients

C & G Salsa Company LLC................................. G 317 569-9099
Noblesville *(G-13052)*

FOOD PRDTS: Peanut Butter

B Happy Peanut Butter LLC................................ G 317 733-3831
Zionsville *(G-16994)*

Pacific Beach Peanut BTR LLC.......................... G 858 522-9297
Indianapolis *(G-9082)*

Peanut Butter Ministries Inc................................. G 260 627-0777
Leo *(G-10970)*

FOOD PRDTS: Pickles, Vinegar

Rickles Pickles LLC... G 260 495-9024
Fremont *(G-5834)*

Sechlers Pickles Inc... E 260 337-5461
Saint Joe *(G-14443)*

FOOD PRDTS: Potato Chips & Other Potato-Based Snacks

FOOD PRDTS: Potato Chips & Other Potato-Based Snacks

Broad Ripple Chip Co LLC .... G 317 590-7687
Indianapolis *(G-7687)*

Magic Company .... E 260 747-1502
Fort Wayne *(G-5199)*

Utz Quality Foods LLC .... G 812 430-5751
Georgetown *(G-6076)*

Utz Quality Foods LLC .... G 717 443-7230
Indianapolis *(G-9693)*

FOOD PRDTS: Sandwiches

Butterfield Foods LLC .... C 317 776-4775
Noblesville *(G-13051)*

Pb & J Factory LLC .... G 317 504-4714
Indianapolis *(G-9107)*

FOOD PRDTS: Seasonings & Spices

El Popular Inc .... F 219 397-3728
East Chicago *(G-3005)*

Kalustyan Corporation .... F 908 688-6111
Hobart *(G-7195)*

Reidco Inc .... E 812 358-3000
Brownstown *(G-1426)*

Sdgs Rubs & Spices LLC .... G 773 531-5497
Hammond *(G-7005)*

FOOD PRDTS: Starch, Corn

Clabber Girl Corporation .... D 812 232-9446
Terre Haute *(G-15563)*

Grain Processing Corporation .... E 812 257-0480
Washington *(G-16481)*

Ingredion Incorporated .... D 317 635-4455
Indianapolis *(G-8545)*

Ingredion Incorporated .... B 317 295-4122
Indianapolis *(G-8546)*

FOOD PRDTS: Sugar

California Sugars LLC .... F 219 886-9151
Gary *(G-5909)*

Combined Technologies Inc .... G 847 968-4855
Bristol *(G-1254)*

FOOD PRDTS: Syrup, Maple

Front Porch Sugarhouse .... F 574 831-5753
New Paris *(G-12954)*

Kcma & Services LLC .... G 260 645-0885
Waterloo *(G-16522)*

Lm Sugarbush LLC .... G 812 967-4491
Borden *(G-1115)*

Michael Ramer .... G 574 538-8010
New Paris *(G-12965)*

Treehugger Maple Syrup LLC .... G 765 698-3728
Laurel *(G-10826)*

FOOD PRDTS: Syrups

Dragonwood LLC .... G 765 947-0097
Kempton *(G-10086)*

FOOD PRDTS: Tea

Anns Boba Tea LLC .... G 317 681-3143
Indianapolis *(G-7520)*

That Beverage Company LLC .... G 260 413-9660
Fort Wayne *(G-5479)*

FOOD PRDTS: Vegetable Oil Mills, NEC

Matthew Schlachter .... G 812 686-5486
Bristow *(G-1300)*

Solae LLC .... D 800 325-7108
Remington *(G-14038)*

FOOD PRDTS: Wheat Flour

Archer-Daniels-Midland Company ..... G 765 299-1672
Fowler *(G-5618)*

Big Brick House Bakery LLP .... G 260 563-1071
Fort Wayne *(G-4799)*

PHM Brands LLC .... E 219 879-7356
Michigan City *(G-11651)*

FOOD PRODUCTS MACHINERY

American Equipment Corp .... G 888 321-0117
Fort Wayne *(G-4753)*

Carmel Engineering Inc .... F 765 279-8955
Kirklin *(G-10187)*

CTB MN Investment Co Inc .... E 574 658-4191
Milford *(G-11794)*

Hillenbrand Inc .... A 812 931-5000
Batesville *(G-590)*

Kitchen-Quip Inc .... E 260 837-8311
Kendallville *(G-10129)*

Linco Group LLC .... G 765 418-5567
Williamsport *(G-16851)*

Mssh Inc .... G 812 663-2180
Greensburg *(G-6620)*

Nemco Food Equipment Ltd .... G 260 399-6692
Fort Wayne *(G-5262)*

Norris Thermal Tech Inc .... G 574 353-7855
Tippecanoe *(G-15762)*

Pacmoore Process Tech LLC .... G 317 831-2666
Mooresville *(G-12233)*

Palmer Caning .... G 773 394-4913
Lafayette *(G-10662)*

Skipper Rota Corporation .... F 708 331-0660
Crown Point *(G-2758)*

Thomas Green LLC .... G 317 337-0000
Indianapolis *(G-9593)*

Urschelair Leasing LLC .... G 219 464-4811
Chesterton *(G-1965)*

FOOD STORES: Grocery, Chain

Lakeshore Foods Corp .... D 219 362-8513
La Porte *(G-10444)*

FOOD STORES: Grocery, Independent

Babbs Supermarket Inc .... E 812 829-2231
Spencer *(G-15339)*

Rihm Inc .... G 765 478-3426
Cambridge City *(G-1502)*

FOOD STORES: Supermarkets, Chain

Kroger Co .... G 574 294-6092
Elkhart *(G-3460)*

Kroger Co .... G 574 291-0740
South Bend *(G-15107)*

Schnuck Markets Inc .... C 812 853-9505
Newburgh *(G-13019)*

FOOD STORES: Supermarkets, Independent

Houchens Industries Inc .... F 812 467-7255
Evansville *(G-4111)*

FOOD WARMING EQPT: Commercial

Edelweiss Edge LLC .... G 260 399-6692
Fort Wayne *(G-4942)*

FOOTWEAR, WHOLESALE: Boots

Bootmakers LLC .... G 765 412-7243
West Lafayette *(G-16568)*

Cowpokes Inc .... E 765 642-3911
Anderson *(G-99)*

FOOTWEAR: Cut Stock

Bootmakers LLC .... G 765 412-7243
West Lafayette *(G-16568)*

Four Quarters RE LLC .... G 765 474-2295
Lafayette *(G-10580)*

Upper Level Networks Inc .... G 317 863-0955
Westfield *(G-16735)*

Upper Level Sports LLC .... G 317 681-3754
Indianapolis *(G-9684)*

FORGINGS: Aluminum

Harvey Industries LLC .... B 260 563-8371
Wabash *(G-16190)*

FORGINGS: Automotive & Internal Combustion Engine

Federal-Mogul Powertrain LLC .... G 574 272-5900
South Bend *(G-15032)*

Spectra Prmium Mblity Sltons U .... G 800 628-5442
Greenfield *(G-6558)*

FORGINGS: Bearing & Bearing Race, Nonferrous

Terrecorp Inc .... F 317 951-8325
Indianapolis *(G-9578)*

FORGINGS: Construction Or Mining Eqpt, Ferrous

Deister Concentrator Na LLC .... F 260 747-2700
Fort Wayne *(G-4911)*

Harrell Family LLC .... F 317 770-4550
Indianapolis *(G-8366)*

FORGINGS: Engine Or Turbine, Nonferrous

CMI Pgi Holdings LLC .... F 812 377-5000
Columbus *(G-2238)*

FORGINGS: Gear & Chain

Emco Gears Inc .... G 317 243-3836
Indianapolis *(G-8103)*

Fairfield Manufacturing Co Inc .... A 765 772-4000
Lafayette *(G-10576)*

Indiana Tool & Mfg Co Inc .... C 574 936-2112
Plymouth *(G-13784)*

T-H Licensing Inc .... E 765 772-4128
Lafayette *(G-10708)*

FORGINGS: Iron & Steel

Modern Forge Companies LLC .... A 708 388-1806
Merrillville *(G-11542)*

Premier Forge Group LLC .... D 800 727-8121
Portland *(G-13963)*

FORGINGS: Machinery, Nonferrous

Fountaintown Forge Inc .... E 317 861-5403
Fountaintown *(G-5614)*

FORGINGS: Metal, Ornamental, Ferrous

Horneco Fabrication Inc .... G 260 672-2064
Fort Wayne *(G-5082)*

McCallister Industries Inc .... G 317 417-7365
Indianapolis *(G-8861)*

FORGINGS: Nonferrous

Impact Forge Group Inc .... G 812 342-4437
Columbus *(G-2322)*

JM Fittings LLC .... E 260 747-9200
Fort Wayne *(G-5137)*

Parker-Hannifin Corporation .... D 260 636-2104
Albion *(G-40)*

R P Imel .... G 260 543-2465
Uniondale *(G-15872)*

Symmetry Medical Mfg Inc .... C 574 371-2284
Warsaw *(G-16435)*

PRODUCT SECTION

FRICTION MATERIAL, MADE FROM POWDERED METAL

Tdy Industries LLC............................B......260 726-8121
  Portland *(G-13968)*

FORGINGS: Nuclear Power Plant, Ferrous

Bwxt Nclear Oprtions Group Inc..............C......812 838-1200
  Mount Vernon *(G-12294)*
Rolls-Royce Corporation......................E......317 230-2000
  Indianapolis *(G-9325)*
Rolls-Royce Corporation......................E......317 230-8515
  West Lafayette *(G-16626)*

FORGINGS: Pump & Compressor, Ferrous

H & H Manufacturing Inc.....................G......812 664-3582
  Patoka *(G-13508)*

FORMS: Concrete, Sheet Metal

Carroll Distrg & Cnstr Sup Inc..............G......317 984-2400
  Noblesville *(G-13055)*
CMa Supply Co Fort Wayne Inc...............E......260 471-9000
  Fort Wayne *(G-4862)*
Larry Atwood..................................G......765 525-6851
  Waldron *(G-16260)*

FOUNDRIES: Aluminum

12154 Holding Corp...........................C......260 563-8371
  Wabash *(G-16171)*
Batesville Products Inc......................F......812 926-4230
  Aurora *(G-440)*
Ce Systems Inc................................E......812 372-8234
  Columbus *(G-2235)*
Dualtech Inc...................................E......317 738-9043
  Franklin *(G-5727)*
Duplicast Metalworks Inc....................G......317 926-0745
  Indianapolis *(G-8020)*
Enkei America Inc.............................A......812 373-7000
  Columbus *(G-2298)*
FCA North America Holdings LLC............B......765 454-0018
  Kokomo *(G-10264)*
FCA US LLC....................................C......765 454-1005
  Kokomo *(G-10267)*
General Aluminum Mfg Company............C......260 495-2600
  Fremont *(G-5822)*
Global...G......317 494-6174
  Franklin *(G-5732)*
Grandview Aluminum Products...............F......812 649-2569
  Grandview *(G-6328)*
Harvey Industries LLC........................B......260 563-8371
  Wabash *(G-16190)*
Heartland Aluminum Inc.....................E......260 375-4652
  Huntington *(G-7316)*
Innovative Casting Tech Inc..................F......317 738-5966
  Franklin *(G-5748)*
Madison Precision Products Inc............B......812 273-4702
  Madison *(G-11238)*
New Point Products Inc......................G......812 663-6311
  New Point *(G-12976)*
Ryobi Die Casting (usa) Inc.................A......317 398-3398
  Shelbyville *(G-14794)*
SUS Cast Products Inc.......................D......574 753-4111
  Logansport *(G-11109)*
Wabash Castings LLC.........................F......260 563-8371
  Wabash *(G-16220)*
Ward Corporation.............................C......260 426-8700
  Fort Wayne *(G-5545)*
Ward Pattern & Engineering Inc...........C......260 426-8700
  Fort Wayne *(G-5547)*

FOUNDRIES: Gray & Ductile Iron

Ce Systems Inc................................E......812 372-8234
  Columbus *(G-2235)*
Dalton Corp Warsaw Mfg Fcilty..............G......574 267-8111
  Warsaw *(G-16344)*

Dalton Corporation............................F......574 267-8111
  Warsaw *(G-16345)*
Grede LLC......................................C......765 521-8000
  New Castle *(G-12865)*
J A Smit Inc....................................G......812 424-8141
  Evansville *(G-4133)*
La Porte Technologies LLC..................F......219 362-1000
  La Porte *(G-10442)*
Leons Fabrication Inc........................F......219 365-5272
  Schererville *(G-14528)*
Metal Technologies Indiana LLC...........C......260 925-4717
  Auburn *(G-409)*
North Vernon Industry........................B......812 346-8772
  North Vernon *(G-13289)*
West Allis Gray Iron..........................E......260 925-4717
  Auburn *(G-434)*
Wh International Casting LLC..............G......562 521-0727
  Seymour *(G-14704)*

FOUNDRIES: Iron

Accurate Castings Inc........................E......219 393-3122
  La Porte *(G-10374)*
Ce Systems Inc................................E......812 372-8234
  Columbus *(G-2235)*
Dalton Corporation............................F......574 267-8111
  Warsaw *(G-16345)*
Ewing Light Metals Co Inc...................E......317 926-4591
  Indianapolis *(G-8146)*
Grede LLC......................................C......765 521-8000
  New Castle *(G-12865)*
Mosey Manufacturing Co Inc................C......765 983-8889
  Richmond *(G-14170)*
Muncie Casting Corp.........................E......765 288-2611
  Muncie *(G-12461)*
Plymouth Foundry Inc.......................E......574 936-2106
  Plymouth *(G-13801)*
Wirco Inc.......................................C......260 897-3768
  Avilla *(G-500)*

FOUNDRIES: Nonferrous

Accurate Castings Inc........................E......219 393-3122
  La Porte *(G-10374)*
Batesville Products Inc......................F......812 926-4230
  Aurora *(G-440)*
Batesville Products Inc......................D......513 381-2057
  Lawrenceburg *(G-10831)*
Cole Energy Incorporated...................G......317 839-9688
  Plainfield *(G-13670)*
Crosbie Foundry Company Inc.............F......574 262-1502
  Elkhart *(G-3272)*
Ewing Light Metals Co Inc...................E......317 926-4591
  Indianapolis *(G-8146)*
Excel Manufacturing Inc.....................D......812 523-6764
  Seymour *(G-14650)*
General Products Delaware C..............B......260 668-1440
  Angola *(G-255)*
Howmet Aerospace Inc......................A......219 326-7400
  La Porte *(G-10423)*
Kitchen-Quip Inc..............................E......260 837-8311
  Kendallville *(G-10129)*
New Point Products Inc......................G......812 663-6311
  New Point *(G-12976)*
Nonferrous Products Inc....................E......317 738-2558
  Franklin *(G-5761)*
Orthodontic Design & Prod Inc............E......317 346-6655
  Franklin *(G-5763)*
Ward Corporation.............................C......260 426-8700
  Fort Wayne *(G-5545)*

FOUNDRIES: Steel

Bahr Bros Mfg Inc.............................E......765 664-6235
  Marion *(G-11274)*

Ball Brass and Aluminum Foundry Inc....E......260 925-3515
  Auburn *(G-367)*
CM Tech...G......765 584-6501
  Winchester *(G-16885)*
FCA North America Holdings LLC............B......765 454-0018
  Kokomo *(G-10264)*
Hoosier Engineering Co Inc.................G......260 694-6887
  Poneto *(G-13841)*
IBC US Holdings Inc.........................G......317 738-2558
  Franklin *(G-5743)*
Jec Steel Company............................G......574 326-3829
  Goshen *(G-6179)*
Jec Steel Company............................G......574 326-3829
  Bristol *(G-1268)*
Southland Metals Inc.........................G......574 252-4441
  Mishawaka *(G-12004)*
Trusted Solutions Group Inc................D......260 622-6000
  Ossian *(G-13443)*
United States Steel Corp.....................F......219 391-2045
  East Chicago *(G-3050)*
United States Steel Corp.....................G......219 888-2000
  Gary *(G-6023)*
West Allis Gray Iron..........................E......260 925-4717
  Auburn *(G-434)*
Wrib Manufacturing Inc......................G......765 294-2841
  Veedersburg *(G-16092)*

FOUNDRIES: Steel Investment

Howmet Aerospace Inc......................A......219 326-7400
  La Porte *(G-10423)*
Wegener Steel and Fabricating.............G......219 462-3911
  Valparaiso *(G-16080)*
Winchester Steel..............................G......812 591-2071
  Westport *(G-16754)*

FOUNDRY MACHINERY & EQPT

Chuck Bivens Services Inc..................F......260 747-6195
  Fort Wayne *(G-4846)*
Summit Foundry Systems Inc..............F......260 749-7740
  Fort Wayne *(G-5452)*
Wrib Manufacturing Inc......................G......765 294-2841
  Veedersburg *(G-16092)*

FRACTIONATION PRDTS OF CRUDE PETROLEUM, HYDROCARBONS, NEC

HK Petroleum Ltd.............................G......229 366-1313
  Madison *(G-11226)*

FRAMES & FRAMING WHOLESALE

Editions Ltd Gllery Fine Art I................G......317 466-9940
  Indianapolis *(G-8055)*

FRAMES: Chair, Metal

Moyers Inc......................................F......574 264-3119
  Elkhart *(G-3557)*

FRICTION MATERIAL, MADE FROM POWDERED METAL

Aisin Chemical Indiana LLC.................E......812 793-2888
  Crothersville *(G-2635)*
Arrayed Additive Inc..........................G......317 981-5982
  Indianapolis *(G-7547)*
B6 Manufacturing LLC......................G......317 549-4290
  Indianapolis *(G-7587)*
Cmbf LLC.......................................G......812 336-3811
  Bloomington *(G-830)*
GKN Sinter Metals LLC......................C......812 883-3381
  Salem *(G-14479)*
Hibbing International Friction..............F......765 529-7001
  New Castle *(G-12867)*

Employee Codes: A=Over 500 employees, B=251-500
C=101-250, D=51-100, E=20-50, F=10-19, G=1-9

FRICTION MATERIAL, MADE FROM POWDERED METAL

Innovative 3d Mfg LLC............................ G 317 560-5080
  Franklin *(G-5747)*

Nst Campbellsburg LLC............................ G 812 755-4501
  Noblesville *(G-13145)*

FUEL ADDITIVES

Keil Chemical Corporation...................... E 219 931-2630
  Hammond *(G-6966)*

Petroleum Solutions Inc.......................... G 574 546-2133
  Bremen *(G-1214)*

FUEL BRIQUETTES & WAXES

Calumet Shreveport Fuels Llc................. D 317 328-5660
  Indianapolis *(G-7726)*

Calumet Superior LLC............................. C 317 328-5660
  Indianapolis *(G-7729)*

FUEL CELLS: Solid State

Toyota Tsusho America Inc..................... D 765 449-3500
  Colburn *(G-2111)*

FUEL DEALERS: Coal

Carter Fuel Systems LLC........................ B 800 342-6125
  Logansport *(G-11064)*

FUEL OIL DEALERS

Calumet Shreveport Fuels Llc................. D 317 328-5660
  Indianapolis *(G-7726)*

Calumet Superior LLC............................. C 317 328-5660
  Indianapolis *(G-7729)*

Jolliff Diesel Service LLC........................ G 812 692-5725
  Elnora *(G-3815)*

Spence/Banks Holdings Inc.................... F 812 235-8123
  Terre Haute *(G-15713)*

FUELS: Diesel

Emerald Cast Rnewable Fuel LLC........... G 765 942-5019
  Ladoga *(G-10507)*

Imperial Petroleum Inc............................ E 812 867-1433
  Darmstadt *(G-2836)*

Triton Energy LLC.................................... G
  Waterloo *(G-16532)*

FUELS: Nuclear

Central Indiana Ethanol LLC.................... E 765 384-4001
  Marion *(G-11277)*

FUNGICIDES OR HERBICIDES

Corteva Inc... G 765 586-4077
  Indianapolis *(G-7882)*

Corteva Inc... A 833 267-8382
  Indianapolis *(G-7883)*

United Turf Alliance LLC......................... G 770 335-3015
  Fishers *(G-4620)*

FURNACE CASINGS: Sheet Metal

D Martin Enterprises Inc......................... F 219 872-8211
  Michigan City *(G-11596)*

T R Bulger Inc.. G 219 879-8525
  Trail Creek *(G-15841)*

FURNACES & OVENS: Indl

Austin-Westran LLC................................ E 815 234-2811
  Indianapolis *(G-7569)*

Brouillette Htg Coolg Plbg LLC............... G 765 884-0176
  Fowler *(G-5622)*

George Koch Sons LLC.......................... D 812 465-9600
  Evansville *(G-4089)*

Green Fast Cure LLC.............................. G 812 486-2510
  Montgomery *(G-12101)*

Heat Wagons Inc.................................... F 219 464-8818
  Valparaiso *(G-15961)*

Industrial Combustn Engineers............... E 219 949-5066
  Gary *(G-5960)*

Light Beam Technology Inc.................... G 260 635-2195
  Kimmell *(G-10170)*

Midwest Finishing Systems Inc.............. E 574 257-0099
  Mishawaka *(G-11949)*

Precious Technology Group LLC............ F 317 398-4411
  Shelbyville *(G-14787)*

Rogers Engineering and Mfg Co............ E 765 478-5444
  Cambridge City *(G-1503)*

Thermal Product Solutions..................... G 708 758-6530
  Schererville *(G-14546)*

Universal Door Carrier Inc...................... G 317 241-3447
  Indianapolis *(G-9682)*

Wax Connections Inc............................. G 219 778-2325
  Rolling Prairie *(G-14372)*

FURNACES: Indl, Electric

Gillespie Mrrell Gen Contg LLC.............. G 765 618-4084
  Marion *(G-11288)*

FURNITURE COMPONENTS: Porcelain Enameled

Ffesar Inc... G 812 378-4220
  Mccordsville *(G-11448)*

FURNITURE PARTS: Metal

Ditto Sales Inc....................................... E 812 482-3043
  Jasper *(G-9832)*

DStyle Inc... F 619 662-0560
  Jasper *(G-9833)*

Shrock Manufacturing Inc....................... E 574 264-4126
  Elkhart *(G-3674)*

FURNITURE REPAIR & MAINTENANCE SVCS

Claridges Wood Shop............................. G 812 536-2569
  Stendal *(G-15398)*

Douglas Dye and Associates Inc............ G 317 844-1709
  Carmel *(G-1611)*

FURNITURE STOCK & PARTS: Hardwood

Graber Furniture..................................... G 812 295-4939
  Loogootee *(G-11136)*

R & R Custom Woodworking Inc........... G 574 773-5436
  Nappanee *(G-12640)*

Swartzndrber Hrdwood Creat LLC......... G 574 534-2502
  Goshen *(G-6266)*

Werzalit of America Inc.......................... D 814 362-3881
  Syracuse *(G-15492)*

FURNITURE STOCK & PARTS: Turnings, Wood

Brown Ridge Studio................................ G 812 335-0643
  Bloomington *(G-816)*

Prized Possession.................................. G 317 842-1498
  Indianapolis *(G-9214)*

FURNITURE STORES

American Natural Resources LLC.......... F 219 922-6444
  Griffith *(G-6790)*

Best Chairs Incorporated....................... D 812 367-1761
  Paoli *(G-13489)*

Bollock Interprises Inc........................... F 765 448-6000
  Lafayette *(G-10541)*

Chris Schwartz...................................... G 260 615-9574
  Grabill *(G-6292)*

Classic Kitchen and Gran LLC................ G 317 575-8883
  Westfield *(G-16676)*

Coffeys Custom Upholstery.................... G 812 948-8611
  New Albany *(G-12715)*

Crossroads Furniture Co LLC................. F 765 307-2095
  Crawfordsville *(G-2558)*

Graber Furniture..................................... G 812 295-4939
  Loogootee *(G-11136)*

Indiana Furniture Industries Inc.............. D 812 482-5727
  Jasper *(G-9845)*

K M Davis Inc... G 765 426-9227
  Lafayette *(G-10617)*

Lambright Woodworking LLC.................. F 260 593-2721
  Topeka *(G-15811)*

Oeding Corporation................................ G 812 367-1271
  Ferdinand *(G-4446)*

REM Industries Inc................................. F 574 862-2127
  Wakarusa *(G-16247)*

Roudebush Co Inc.................................. G 574 595-7115
  Star City *(G-15397)*

Sylvia Kay Hartley.................................. G 317 984-3424
  Arcadia *(G-318)*

FURNITURE WHOLESALERS

American Natural Resources LLC.......... F 219 922-6444
  Griffith *(G-6790)*

DStyle Inc... F 619 662-0560
  Jasper *(G-9833)*

Family Leisurecom Inc........................... F 317 823-4448
  Indianapolis *(G-8164)*

Ffesar Inc... G 812 378-4220
  Mccordsville *(G-11448)*

J Squared Inc.. D 317 866-5638
  Greenfield *(G-6521)*

Martins Wood Works.............................. G 574 862-4080
  Goshen *(G-6215)*

Spectrum Finishing LLC......................... G 260 463-7300
  Lagrange *(G-10762)*

FURNITURE, HOUSEHOLD: Wholesalers

Arran Isle Inc... G 574 295-4400
  Elkhart *(G-3191)*

Candles By Dar Inc................................ F 260 482-2099
  Fort Wayne *(G-4831)*

Lasalle Bristol Corporation..................... C 574 295-8400
  Elkhart *(G-3469)*

Oakleaf Industries Inc............................ G 317 414-2040
  Fishers *(G-4645)*

FURNITURE, OFFICE: Wholesalers

Altstadt Business Forms Inc.................. F 812 425-3393
  Evansville *(G-3882)*

Furniture Distributors Inc....................... F 317 357-8508
  Indianapolis *(G-8243)*

Jofco Inc.. G 812 482-5154
  Jasper *(G-9861)*

Smith & Butterfield Co Inc..................... F 812 422-3261
  Evansville *(G-4320)*

FURNITURE, OUTDOOR & LAWN: Wholesalers

C & C Mailbox Products......................... G 765 358-4880
  Gaston *(G-6044)*

Durogreen Outdoor LLC......................... F 574 327-6943
  Elkhart *(G-3307)*

Jordan Manufacturing Co Inc................ C 800 328-6522
  Monticello *(G-12155)*

FURNITURE, WHOLESALE: Lockers

Pinnacle Mailing Products...................... F 765 405-1194
  Yorktown *(G-16980)*

FURNITURE: Bedroom, Wood

Borkholder Corporation.......................... E 574 773-4083
  Nappanee *(G-12585)*

PRODUCT SECTION

FURNITURE: Foundations & Platforms

E & S Wood Creations LLC .... F 260 768-3033
  Lagrange (G-10736)
Furniture Distributors Inc .... F 317 357-8508
  Indianapolis (G-8243)
Mobel Inc .... C 812 367-1214
  Ferdinand (G-4445)
Sampler Inc .... F 765 663-2233
  Homer (G-7221)
Streamside Woodshop LLC .... G 260 768-7887
  Shipshewana (G-14894)

FURNITURE: Box Springs, Assembled

Leggett & Platt Incorporated .... C 219 866-7181
  Rensselaer (G-14057)

FURNITURE: Cabinets & Filing Drawers, Office, Exc Wood

P-Kelco Inc .... E 260 356-6326
  Huntington (G-7353)

FURNITURE: Cabinets & Vanities, Medicine, Metal

J Borinstein Inc .... G 317 252-0875
  Shelbyville (G-14764)

FURNITURE: Chair & Couch Springs, Assembled

Loewenstein Furniture Inc .... F 800 521-5381
  Huntingburg (G-7286)

FURNITURE: Chairs, Household Upholstered

Best Chairs Incorporated .... C 812 367-1761
  Cannelton (G-1532)
Best Chairs Incorporated .... D 812 367-1761
  Paoli (G-13489)
Best Chairs Incorporated .... A 812 367-1761
  Ferdinand (G-4429)
Custom Wood Products Inc .... D 574 522-3300
  Elkhart (G-3283)
Indiana Furniture Industries Inc .... D 812 482-5727
  Jasper (G-9845)

FURNITURE: Chairs, Household Wood

ALE Enterprises Inc .... G 317 856-2981
  Indianapolis (G-7467)
Als Woodcraft Inc .... F 812 967-4458
  Borden (G-1105)
Antreasian Design Inc .... F 317 546-3234
  Indianapolis (G-7523)
Barry A Wilcox .... G 260 495-3677
  Fremont (G-5809)
Beebe Cabinet Co Inc .... F 574 293-3580
  Elkhart (G-3222)
Best Chairs Incorporated .... C 812 367-1761
  Cannelton (G-1532)
Bills Furniture .... G 317 695-8347
  Bloomington (G-807)
C & P Woodworking Inc .... G 260 637-3088
  Auburn (G-373)
Cabinetmaker Inc .... G 812 723-3461
  Paoli (G-13490)
Cherished Woodcraft .... G 317 502-4451
  Greenfield (G-6480)
Chuppville Carving .... G 574 354-7642
  Nappanee (G-12589)
Commercial Electric Co Inc .... E 260 726-9357
  Portland (G-13933)
Country Cabinets LLC .... G 260 694-6777
  Poneto (G-13840)

Country View Furn Mfg & Uphl .... G 812 636-5024
  Odon (G-13333)
Douglas Dye and Associates Inc .... G 317 844-1709
  Carmel (G-1611)
Ecojacks LLC .... G 574 306-0414
  South Whitley (G-15317)
Ed Lloyd Co .... G 812 342-2505
  Columbus (G-2294)
Efurnituremax LLC .... G 317 697-9504
  Indianapolis (G-8058)
Fehrenbacher Cabinets Inc .... E 812 963-3377
  Evansville (G-4066)
From Trees To These Inc .... G 260 592-7397
  Decatur (G-2856)
Gloria J Burnworth .... G 765 366-3950
  Attica (G-350)
Graber Woodworks Inc .... G 812 486-2861
  Montgomery (G-12100)
Haas Cabinet Co Inc .... C 812 246-4431
  Sellersburg (G-14594)
Hickory Furniture Designs Inc .... G 765 642-0700
  Shelbyville (G-14759)
Hoosier Wood Creations Inc .... F 574 831-6330
  New Paris (G-12958)
Indiana Architectural Plywood .... E 317 878-4822
  Trafalgar (G-15829)
J Miller Cabinet Company Inc .... G 260 691-2032
  Columbia City (G-2158)
J Squared Inc .... D 317 866-5638
  Greenfield (G-6521)
Jasper Chair Company .... D 812 482-5239
  Jasper (G-9848)
Kasnak Restorations Inc .... G 317 852-9770
  Brownsburg (G-1381)
Kelco Steel Fabrication Inc .... G 317 248-9229
  Indianapolis (G-8667)
Kimball International Inc .... C 812 482-1600
  Jasper (G-9878)
Kountry Kraft Wood Pdts LLC .... G 574 831-6736
  New Paris (G-12963)
Kramer Furn & Cab Makers Inc .... E 812 526-2711
  Edinburgh (G-3089)
L R Nisley & Sons .... G 574 642-1245
  Goshen (G-6195)
Lambright Woodworking LLC .... F 260 593-2721
  Topeka (G-15811)
Leibering Dimension Inc .... G 812 367-2971
  Ferdinand (G-4440)
Lockerbie Square Cab Co Inc .... G 317 635-1134
  Indianapolis (G-8775)
Logic Furniture LLC .... B 574 975-0007
  Indianapolis (G-8777)
Madison Cabinets Inc .... G 260 639-3915
  Hoagland (G-7170)
Martins Wood Works .... G 574 862-4080
  Goshen (G-6215)
Moores Country Wood Crafting .... F 317 984-3326
  Arcadia (G-315)
Oeding Corporation .... G 812 367-1271
  Ferdinand (G-4446)
Oehlers Woods .... G 317 848-2698
  Carmel (G-1710)
Ofs Brands Holdings Inc .... D 800 521-5381
  Huntingburg (G-7289)
Old Guy Woodcrafters LLC .... G 574 527-9044
  Winona Lake (G-16913)
Old Hickory Furniture Company Inc .... D 317 398-3151
  Shelbyville (G-14781)
Patrick Industries Inc .... G 574 293-1521
  Elkhart (G-3589)
Pinetree Woodcraft LLC .... G 765 886-1177
  Greens Fork (G-6576)

Rbk Development Inc .... E 574 267-5879
  Warsaw (G-16417)
REM Industries Inc .... F 574 862-2127
  Wakarusa (G-16247)
Richcraft Wood Products LLC .... G 812 320-7884
  Bloomington (G-957)
Rock Creek 2019 Inc .... E 812 933-0388
  Batesville (G-604)
Rodeswood LLC .... G 574 457-4496
  Syracuse (G-15476)
Roudebush Co Inc .... G 574 595-7115
  Star City (G-15397)
Schertz Craftsmen Inc .... C 877 472-2782
  Grabill (G-6324)
Stump Home Specialties Mfg Inc .... G 574 291-0050
  South Bend (G-15271)
Superior Woodcrafts LLC .... G 260 357-3743
  Garrett (G-5877)
Swartzndrber Hrdwood Creat LLC .... G 574 534-2502
  Goshen (G-6266)
Thomasville Furniture Inds Inc .... G 336 476-2175
  Hammond (G-7020)
Timber Creek Design Co Inc .... G 317 297-5336
  Indianapolis (G-9603)
U B Klem Furniture Co Inc .... D 812 326-2236
  Saint Anthony (G-14432)
Walters Cabinet Shop .... G 765 452-9634
  Kokomo (G-10355)
Weberdings Carving Shop Inc .... F 812 934-3710
  Batesville (G-610)
Werzalit of America Inc .... G 814 362-3881
  Syracuse (G-15492)
Woodcrafters LLC .... G 765 469-5103
  Denver (G-2936)
Yoders Wood Shop LLC .... G 260 768-3246
  Shipshewana (G-14901)

FURNITURE: Chairs, Office Wood

Jasper Chair Company .... D 812 482-5239
  Jasper (G-9848)
Jasper Seating Company Inc .... C 812 936-9977
  French Lick (G-5847)
Jasper Seating Company Inc .... C 812 482-3204
  Jasper (G-9858)
Jofco Inc .... C 812 482-5154
  Jasper (G-9861)

FURNITURE: Console Tables, Wood

Dorel Home Furnishings Inc .... D 812 372-0141
  Columbus (G-2285)

FURNITURE: Dining Room, Wood

Custom Wood Products Inc .... D 574 522-3300
  Elkhart (G-3283)

FURNITURE: Fiberglass & Plastic

Fibertech Plastics LLC .... D 812 983-2642
  Elberfeld (G-3113)
Keter Us Inc .... C 317 575-4700
  Anderson (G-142)
Laminique Inc .... F 765 482-4222
  Zionsville (G-17029)
Resin Partners Inc .... D 765 724-7761
  Alexandria (G-61)

FURNITURE: Foundations & Platforms

Firesmoke Org .... G 317 690-2542
  Indianapolis (G-8190)
Helping Hrts Helping Hands Inc .... G 248 980-5090
  Middlebury (G-11720)
Kimalco Inc .... G 812 463-3105
  Evansville (G-4153)

Employee Codes: A=Over 500 employees, B=251-500
C=101-250, D=51-100, E=20-50, F=10-19, G=1-9

FURNITURE: Garden, Exc Wood, Metal, Stone Or Concrete

FURNITURE: Garden, Exc Wood, Metal, Stone Or Concrete

Beachfront Furniture Inc......................... G 574 875-0817
Elkhart (G-3219)

FURNITURE: Hotel

Csr Associates LLC .... G 317 255-2247
Indianapolis (G-7918)

Troy Stuart .... G 812 887-0403
Washington (G-16510)

FURNITURE: Household, Metal

Benz Custom Metal LLC........................ G 812 365-2613
Marengo (G-11261)

Best Chairs Incorporated........................ C 812 367-1761
Cannelton (G-1532)

Bo-Mar Industries Inc............................. E 317 899-1240
Indianapolis (G-7651)

Flambeau Inc .... G 812 372-4899
Columbus (G-2310)

Lakemaster Inc....................................... F 765 288-3718
Muncie (G-12437)

Mastercraft Inc.. C 260 463-8702
Lagrange (G-10755)

Mouron & Company Inc......................... F 317 243-7955
Indianapolis (G-8962)

Poly-Wood LLC...................................... G 877 457-3284
Syracuse (G-15473)

Poly-Wood LLC...................................... D 574 457-3284
Syracuse (G-15474)

Sills Custom Works & Fab LLC............. G 219 200-9813
Knox (G-10224)

FURNITURE: Household, Upholstered, Exc Wood Or Metal

Columbus Cstm Cbinets Furn LLC......... G 812 379-9411
Columbus (G-2242)

Ditto Sales Inc.. G 812 424-4098
Evansville (G-4015)

Philipps Wood Processing...................... G 812 357-2824
Ferdinand (G-4447)

Weaver Fine Furn Cabinets Inc.............. G 812 342-4833
Columbus (G-2416)

FURNITURE: Juvenile, Wood

Woodcrest Manufacturing Inc................ C 765 472-4471
Peru (G-13608)

FURNITURE: Laboratory

Modular Dvcs Acquisition LLC............... D 317 818-4480
Indianapolis (G-8943)

FURNITURE: Living Room, Upholstered On Wood Frames

Furniture Distributors Inc........................ F 317 357-8508
Indianapolis (G-8243)

Shelby Westside Upholstering................ G 317 631-8911
Indianapolis (G-9419)

FURNITURE: Mattresses & Foundations

Crossroads Furniture Co LLC................. F 765 307-2095
Crawfordsville (G-2558)

Holder Bedding Inc................................. G 765 447-7907
Lafayette (G-10600)

Idgas Inc... G 317 839-1133
Plainfield (G-13688)

May and Co Inc...................................... E 317 236-6500
Greenwood (G-6735)

Vans TV & Appliance Inc....................... F 260 927-8267
Auburn (G-433)

Williamsburg Furniture Inc..................... E 574 387-5691
South Bend (G-15307)

Williamsburg Furniture Inc..................... D 800 582-8183
Nappanee (G-12652)

FURNITURE: Mattresses, Box & Bedsprings

Futon Factory Inc................................... F 317 549-8639
Indianapolis (G-8245)

KMC Corporation.................................... E 574 267-7033
Warsaw (G-16383)

Leggett & Platt Incorporated.................. D 260 347-2600
Kendallville (G-10133)

Leggett & Platt Incorporated.................. E 219 766-2261
Kouts (G-10363)

Sleepmadecom LLC............................... E 662 350-0999
Evansville (G-4318)

Tempur Production Usa LLC................. D 859 455-1000
Crawfordsville (G-2624)

FURNITURE: Mattresses, Innerspring Or Box Spring

Blue Bell Mattress Company LLC........... C 260 749-9393
Fort Wayne (G-4808)

Bowles Mattress Company Inc............... G 812 288-8614
Jeffersonville (G-9945)

Derby Inc... D 574 233-4500
South Bend (G-14997)

Elkhart Bedding Co Inc.......................... F 574 293-6200
Elkhart (G-3318)

Mastercraft Inc.. C 260 463-8702
Lagrange (G-10755)

Wolf Corporation..................................... E 260 749-9393
Fort Wayne (G-5574)

FURNITURE: Novelty, Wood

Dubois Wood Products Inc.................... C 812 683-3613
Huntingburg (G-7277)

FURNITURE: Office, Exc Wood

David Edward Furniture Inc................... C 812 482-1600
Jasper (G-9831)

Deer Creek Village................................. G 574 699-6327
Peru (G-13579)

Edsal Manufacturing Co LLC................. C 773 254-0600
Gary (G-5926)

Evansville Corp Design Inc.................... G 812 426-0911
Evansville (G-4050)

Global... G 317 494-6174
Franklin (G-5732)

Jasper Chair Company........................... D 812 482-5239
Jasper (G-9848)

Jasper Seating Company Inc................. C 812 723-1323
Paoli (G-13498)

Kimball Furniture Group LLC................. E 812 482-8517
Jasper (G-9873)

Kimball Furniture Group LLC................. C 812 634-3526
Jasper (G-9874)

Kimball Furniture Group LLC................. B 812 482-1600
Jasper (G-9872)

Kimball Hospitality Inc............................ B 812 482-8090
Jasper (G-9876)

Kimball Inc.. A 812 482-1600
Jasper (G-9877)

Kimball International Inc........................ E 812 937-3284
Jasper (G-9879)

Kimball International Inc........................ C 812 482-1600
Jasper (G-9878)

Kimball International Transit.................. C 812 634-3346
Jasper (G-9880)

Lui Plus.. G 812 309-9350
Indianapolis (G-8795)

Ofs Brands Holdings Inc........................ D 800 521-5381
Huntingburg (G-7289)

Rivers Resources LLC........................... G 317 572-5029
Indianapolis (G-9310)

Unique Global Solutions LLC................. G 765 779-5030
Anderson (G-212)

FURNITURE: Office, Wood

Antreasian Design Inc........................... F 317 546-3234
Indianapolis (G-7523)

Aynes Upholstery LLC............................ G 812 829-1321
Freedom (G-5798)

Beebe Cabinet Co Inc............................ F 574 293-3580
Elkhart (G-3222)

Ckh Two Inc... E 317 841-7800
Fishers (G-4489)

Custom Wood Products Inc................... D 574 522-3300
Elkhart (G-3283)

David Edward Furniture Inc................... C 812 482-1600
Jasper (G-9831)

Double T Manufacturing Corp................ F 574 262-1340
Elkhart (G-3302)

Ecojacks LLC... G 574 306-0414
South Whitley (G-15317)

Environmental Products Inc................... F 219 393-3446
Kingsbury (G-10178)

Graber Cabinetry LLC............................ E 260 627-2243
Grabill (G-6297)

Inwood Office Furniture Inc................... D 812 482-6121
Jasper (G-9847)

J Squared Inc... D 317 866-5638
Greenfield (G-6521)

Jasper Seating Company Inc................. C 812 771-4500
Jasper (G-9857)

Jasper Seating Company Inc................. C 812 723-1323
Paoli (G-13498)

Johnco Corp... G 317 576-4417
Indianapolis (G-8632)

Kimball Furniture Group LLC................. B 812 482-1600
Jasper (G-9872)

Kimball Hospitality Inc............................ E 812 482-8090
Jasper (G-9875)

Kimball International Inc........................ C 812 482-1600
Jasper (G-9878)

Klomp Construction Company................ G 219 308-8372
Saint John (G-14454)

Millmade Incorporated............................ G 812 424-7778
Evansville (G-4206)

Ofs Brands Holdings Inc........................ D 800 521-5381
Huntingburg (G-7289)

Old Hickory Furniture Company Inc...... D 317 398-3151
Shelbyville (G-14781)

Robert M Kolarich.................................. G 317 596-9753
Fishers (G-4597)

Shamrock Cabinets Inc.......................... E 812 482-7969
Jasper (G-9911)

Swartzndrber Hrdwood Creat LLC......... G 574 534-2502
Goshen (G-6266)

FURNITURE: Picnic Tables Or Benches, Park

County of Steuben.................................. G 260 833-2401
Angola (G-243)

Nvb Playgrounds Inc.............................. G 317 826-2777
Indianapolis (G-9037)

Recreation Insites LLC.......................... G 317 578-0588
Fishers (G-4592)

FURNITURE: Recliners, Upholstered On Wood Frames

Seating Technology Inc.......................... D 574 971-4100
Goshen (G-6253)

FURNITURE: School

Indiana Furniture Industries Inc............... D 812 482-5727
  Jasper *(G-9845)*
Inwood Office Furniture Inc.................... D 812 482-6121
  Jasper *(G-9847)*
Jasper Chair Company........................... D 812 482-5239
  Jasper *(G-9848)*
Jasper Seating Company Inc.................... C 812 482-3204
  Jasper *(G-9858)*

FURNITURE: Sofa Beds Or Convertible Sofas)

Seating Technology Inc......................... D 574 971-4100
  Goshen *(G-6253)*

FURNITURE: Storage Chests, Household, Wood

Graber Manufacturing LLC...................... G 260 657-3400
  Grabill *(G-6298)*
Mission Woodworking Inc....................... E 574 848-5697
  Bristol *(G-1274)*

FURNITURE: Table Tops, Marble

Marstone Products Ltd.......................... E 800 466-7465
  Fairland *(G-4400)*
One Source Fabrication LLC.................... G 574 259-6011
  South Bend *(G-15178)*

FURNITURE: Tables, Household, Metal

Austin-Westran LLC.............................. E 815 234-2811
  Indianapolis *(G-7569)*

FURNITURE: Tables, Office, Wood

Mouron & Company Inc.......................... F 317 243-7955
  Indianapolis *(G-8962)*

FURNITURE: Upholstered

Aaron Company Inc.............................. F 219 838-0852
  Gary *(G-5886)*
Coffeys Custom Upholstery..................... G 812 948-8611
  New Albany *(G-12715)*
Country View Furn Mfg & Uphl................. G 812 636-5024
  Odon *(G-13333)*
David Edward Furniture Inc.................... C 812 482-1600
  Jasper *(G-9831)*
Furniture Sales & Marketing................... G 317 849-1508
  Indianapolis *(G-8244)*
Home Reserve LLC............................... F 260 969-6939
  Fort Wayne *(G-5072)*
Jasper Chair Company........................... D 812 482-5239
  Jasper *(G-9848)*
Kimball International Inc...................... C 812 482-1600
  Jasper *(G-9878)*
KMC Corporation................................ E 574 267-7033
  Warsaw *(G-16383)*
La-Z-Boy Inc.................................... G 812 367-0190
  Ferdinand *(G-4439)*
Love Upholstery LLC............................ G 812 639-3789
  Jasper *(G-9883)*
Mastercraft Inc................................. C 260 463-8702
  Lagrange *(G-10755)*
Red Chair Designs.............................. G 317 852-9880
  Brownsburg *(G-1397)*
Smith Brothers Berne Inc...................... A 260 589-2131
  Berne *(G-726)*
Sylvia Kay Hartley............................. G 317 984-3424
  Arcadia *(G-318)*
Tls By Design LLC.............................. E 765 683-1971
  Indianapolis *(G-9613)*

Transformations By Wieland Inc................ D 800 440-9337
  Fort Wayne *(G-5500)*
Vans TV & Appliance Inc....................... F 260 927-8267
  Auburn *(G-433)*
Williamsburg Furniture Inc.................... E 574 387-5691
  South Bend *(G-15307)*
Williamsburg Furniture Inc.................... D 800 582-8183
  Nappanee *(G-12652)*

FURNITURE: Vehicle

Fbsa LLC.. G 800 443-4540
  Rochester *(G-14290)*
Flair Interiors Inc............................. D 574 534-2163
  Goshen *(G-6137)*
Lexington LLC.................................. E 574 295-8166
  Elkhart *(G-3487)*
Lippert Components Inc........................ E 574 295-8166
  Elkhart *(G-3494)*
Lippert Components Inc........................ D 574 534-8177
  Goshen *(G-6201)*
Transportation Tech Inds...................... F 812 962-5000
  Evansville *(G-4347)*
Veada Industries Inc........................... A 574 831-4775
  New Paris *(G-12973)*

FURNITURE: Waterbed Frames, Wood

Merrill Manufacturing Inc..................... F 812 752-6688
  Scottsburg *(G-14571)*

FUSES & FUSE EQPT

Hoffmaster Electric Inc........................ G 219 616-1313
  Schererville *(G-14523)*

GAMES & TOYS: Baby Carriages & Restraint Seats

Dorel Juvenile Group Inc...................... F 812 314-6629
  Columbus *(G-2288)*
Dorel Juvenile Group Inc...................... C 800 457-5276
  Columbus *(G-2289)*
Peg Perego USA Inc............................. D 800 671-1701
  Fort Wayne *(G-5300)*

GAMES & TOYS: Board Games, Children's & Adults'

Cloak Gaming LLC............................... G 502 563-8790
  Corydon *(G-2492)*
Fundex Games Ltd............................... E 317 248-1080
  Indianapolis *(G-8241)*
Ludo Fact USA LLC.............................. E 765 588-9137
  Lafayette *(G-10640)*

GAMES & TOYS: Child Restraint Seats, Automotive

EVS Ltd... F 574 233-5707
  South Bend *(G-15019)*
Merritt Manufacturing Inc..................... G 317 409-0148
  Indianapolis *(G-8878)*

GAMES & TOYS: Craft & Hobby Kits & Sets

Country Cabin LLC.............................. G 812 232-4635
  Terre Haute *(G-15569)*
Country Woodcrafts Inc........................ G 260 244-7578
  Columbia City *(G-2135)*
Haan Crafts LLC................................ F 765 583-4496
  Otterbein *(G-13451)*
Indy Products Company......................... G 317 831-1114
  Mooresville *(G-12214)*
K&D Crafts..................................... G 812 667-2575
  Dillsboro *(G-2948)*

KBK Magik LLC.................................. G 219 512-4040
  Indianapolis *(G-8663)*
Libra Elite LLC................................ G 706 831-5753
  Indianapolis *(G-8745)*
Lil Red Studios LLC............................ G 317 443-4932
  Indianapolis *(G-8753)*
Melissa Townsend............................... G 317 797-7992
  Indianapolis *(G-8875)*
No Limits Just Pssbilities LLC................ G 930 465-1218
  Princeton *(G-14008)*
Shepherds Loft................................. G 812 486-2304
  Montgomery *(G-12122)*
Sub Blanks Society LLC......................... G 877 405-6406
  Fort Wayne *(G-5449)*

GAMES & TOYS: Electronic

Fex LLC... G 317 308-8820
  Indianapolis *(G-8182)*
Lightuptoyscom LLC............................. E 812 246-1916
  Sellersburg *(G-14604)*
Tokumei LLC.................................... G 765 772-0073
  West Lafayette *(G-16638)*

GARBAGE CONTAINERS: Plastic

Ameri-Kart Corp................................ C 574 848-7462
  Bristol *(G-1244)*
Waste 1.. F 765 477-9138
  Lafayette *(G-10718)*

GAS & OIL FIELD EXPLORATION SVCS

Barger Engineering Inc......................... G 812 476-3077
  Evansville *(G-3909)*
Black and Gold Energy LLC..................... G 812 618-6744
  Evansville *(G-3933)*
Black Gold Ventures Ind LLC................... G 260 820-0771
  Bluffton *(G-1029)*
Carlisle Mine.................................. G 812 398-2200
  Carlisle *(G-1540)*
Core Minerals Operating Co Inc................ G 812 759-6950
  Evansville *(G-3983)*
Covey Rise Minerals LLC....................... G 812 897-2356
  Boonville *(G-1086)*
Enviropeel USA................................. G 317 631-9100
  Indianapolis *(G-8126)*
Freeport Minerals Corporation................. G 260 421-5400
  Fort Wayne *(G-5010)*
Gemini Oil LLC................................. G 260 571-8388
  Warren *(G-16298)*
Hallador Energy Company....................... E 812 299-2800
  Terre Haute *(G-15603)*
Hjr Oil Inc.................................... G 317 849-4503
  Fishers *(G-4539)*
Imperial Petroleum Inc......................... E 812 867-1433
  Darmstadt *(G-2836)*
J R and D Exploration Inc..................... G 812 677-2895
  Princeton *(G-14002)*
Legacy Resources Co LP........................ G 317 328-5660
  Indianapolis *(G-8734)*
Magnum Exploration Inc........................ G 812 673-4914
  New Harmony *(G-12887)*
Mannon Oil LLC................................. F 812 867-5946
  Evansville *(G-4188)*
Michael R Harris............................... G 812 425-9411
  Evansville *(G-4201)*
Pioneer Oil Company Inc....................... F 812 494-2800
  Vincennes *(G-16144)*
Plymouth Oil and Gas Inc...................... G 574 875-4808
  Goshen *(G-6241)*
Richard M Judd................................. G 916 704-3364
  Bloomington *(G-955)*
Riverside Petroleum Ind LLC................... G 812 639-0859
  Washington *(G-16507)*

GAS & OIL FIELD EXPLORATION SVCS

Sun Energy Services LLC .... G 765 251-1526
  Marion *(G-11339)*

Trey Exploration Inc .... G 812 858-3146
  Newburgh *(G-13025)*

United Minerals Inc .... G 812 683-5024
  Huntingburg *(G-7294)*

Wellspring Water Services LLC .... G 337 962-5767
  Carmel *(G-1803)*

GAS & OIL FIELD SVCS, NEC

M2i LLC .... G 765 618-2162
  Marion *(G-11311)*

Quest Energy Inc .... F 317 318-5737
  Fishers *(G-4589)*

Rs Used Oil Services Inc .... F 866 778-7336
  Carmel *(G-1748)*

GAS FIELD MACHINERY & EQPT

Daylight Engineering Inc .... G 812 983-2518
  Elberfeld *(G-3111)*

Gesco Group LLC .... G 260 747-5088
  Fort Wayne *(G-5023)*

Llama Corporation .... G 888 701-7432
  Decatur *(G-2870)*

GAS PRODUCTION & DISTRIBUTION: Coke Oven

Sssi Inc .... F 219 880-0818
  Gary *(G-6015)*

GAS: Refinery

Shell Pipe Line Corporation .... G 765 962-1329
  Richmond *(G-14204)*

GASES & LIQUIFIED PETROLEUM GASES

Hometown Energy LLC .... G 812 663-3391
  Greensburg *(G-6603)*

GASES: Carbon Dioxide

Jt Composites LLC .... G 317 297-9520
  Indianapolis *(G-8645)*

Linde Gas & Equipment Inc .... G 260 423-4468
  Fort Wayne *(G-5187)*

Linde Gas & Equipment Inc .... G 317 481-4550
  Indianapolis *(G-8761)*

GASES: Indl

A G A Gas Inc .... G 317 783-2331
  Indianapolis *(G-7399)*

Airgas Usa LLC .... G 812 474-0440
  Evansville *(G-3878)*

Airgas Usa LLC .... F 260 749-9576
  Fort Wayne *(G-4733)*

Airgas Usa LLC .... G 317 248-8072
  Indianapolis *(G-7464)*

Airgas Usa LLC .... G 812 362-7593
  Rockport *(G-14335)*

Ferrellgas LP .... G 574 936-2725
  Crawfordsville *(G-2566)*

Indiana Oxygen Company Inc .... D 317 290-0003
  Indianapolis *(G-8488)*

Linde Gas & Equipment Inc .... G 574 537-1366
  Goshen *(G-6198)*

Linde Inc .... G 317 984-7002
  Cicero *(G-1998)*

Linde Inc .... E 219 391-5100
  East Chicago *(G-3027)*

Linde Inc .... G 317 881-6825
  Indianapolis *(G-8762)*

Linde Inc .... G 765 456-1128
  Kokomo *(G-10297)*

Linde Inc .... G 812 524-0173
  Seymour *(G-14664)*

Messer LLC .... G 574 234-4887
  South Bend *(G-15148)*

Petrogas International Corp .... G 260 484-0859
  Auburn *(G-416)*

Weaver Air Products LLC .... G 317 848-4420
  Carmel *(G-1800)*

GASES: Nitrogen

Air Products and Chemicals Inc .... G 812 466-6492
  Terre Haute *(G-15535)*

Linde Gas & Equipment Inc .... G 317 782-4661
  Indianapolis *(G-8760)*

Matheson Tri-Gas Inc .... G 812 838-5518
  Mount Vernon *(G-12307)*

Matheson Tri-Gas Inc .... G 317 892-5221
  Pittsboro *(G-13651)*

Messer LLC .... E 908 464-8100
  Indianapolis *(G-8881)*

Messer LLC .... D 219 324-0498
  La Porte *(G-10450)*

GASES: Oxygen

Alig LLC .... G 812 362-7593
  Rockport *(G-14336)*

Linde Inc .... F 219 326-7808
  La Porte *(G-10446)*

GASKET MATERIALS

American Rubber Corp .... G 317 548-8455
  Anderson *(G-77)*

Tfco Incorporated .... G 219 324-4166
  La Porte *(G-10492)*

Tfco Incorporated .... G 219 324-4166
  La Porte *(G-10491)*

GASKETS

Bonar Inc .... G 260 636-7430
  Albion *(G-19)*

Breiner Company Inc .... F 317 272-2521
  Avon *(G-509)*

Cannon Fabrication Company .... F 765 629-2277
  Milroy *(G-11822)*

Freudenberg-Nok General Partnr .... C 765 763-7246
  Morristown *(G-12277)*

Gaska Tape Inc .... D 574 294-5431
  Elkhart *(G-3366)*

Gindor Inc .... G 574 642-4004
  Goshen *(G-6149)*

Hoosier Gasket Corporation .... D 317 545-2000
  Indianapolis *(G-8409)*

Ilpea Industries Inc .... D 812 752-2526
  Scottsburg *(G-14561)*

Ilpea Industries Inc .... D 812 752-2526
  Scottsburg *(G-14562)*

Jeans Extrusions Inc .... C 812 883-2581
  Salem *(G-14486)*

Metallic Seals Inc .... G 317 780-0773
  Indianapolis *(G-8889)*

Midwest Gasket Corporation .... E 765 629-2221
  Milroy *(G-11826)*

Parker-Hannifin Corporation .... D 574 533-1111
  Goshen *(G-6236)*

Seals & Components Inc .... G 708 895-5222
  La Porte *(G-10478)*

GASKETS & SEALING DEVICES

American Elkhart LLC .... F 574 293-0333
  Elkhart *(G-3172)*

EJ Brooks Company .... D 800 348-4777
  Angola *(G-247)*

Federal-Mogul Powertrain LLC .... B 574 271-5954
  South Bend *(G-15031)*

Hi-Tech Foam Products LLC .... E 317 737-2298
  Indianapolis *(G-8396)*

Triangle Rubber Co LLC .... C 574 533-3118
  Goshen *(G-6272)*

Trifab & Construction Inc .... G 219 845-1300
  Hammond *(G-7024)*

GASOLINE FILLING STATIONS

Smith Tire Inc .... F 574 267-8261
  Warsaw *(G-16427)*

GEARS

Kanoff Enterprises .... G 574 575-6787
  Mishawaka *(G-11921)*

Mtr Machining Concept Inc .... G 260 587-3381
  Ashley *(G-334)*

Schafer Industries Inc .... D 574 234-4116
  South Bend *(G-15234)*

GEARS & GEAR UNITS: Reduction, Exc Auto

Dana Sac Usa Inc .... F 765 759-2300
  Yorktown *(G-16972)*

GEARS: Power Transmission, Exc Auto

United Precision Gear Co Inc .... G 317 784-4665
  Indianapolis *(G-9680)*

GENERATING APPARATUS & PARTS: Electrical

Hendershot Service Center Inc .... F 765 653-2600
  Greencastle *(G-6412)*

Liberty Green Renewables LLP .... G 812 951-3143
  Georgetown *(G-6067)*

Summit/Ems Corporation .... E 574 722-1317
  Logansport *(G-11108)*

GENERATION EQPT: Electronic

Amerawhip Inc .... G 317 639-5248
  Indianapolis *(G-7497)*

Empro Manufacturing Co Inc .... E 317 823-3000
  Indianapolis *(G-8110)*

Enerfuel Inc .... E
  Greenfield *(G-6497)*

Motion & Control Entps LLC .... F 219 844-4224
  Munster *(G-12551)*

RB Annis Instruments Inc .... G 765 848-1621
  Greencastle *(G-6428)*

Wdb Enterprises Inc .... F 219 844-4224
  Hammond *(G-7031)*

GENERATORS SETS: Steam

Helmuth Quality Power System .... G 574 457-2002
  Syracuse *(G-15462)*

GENERATORS: Gas

Current Electric Inc .... F 219 872-7736
  Michigan City *(G-11591)*

GENERATORS: Vehicles, Gas-Electric Or Oil-Electric

Go Electric Inc .... G 765 400-1347
  Anderson *(G-122)*

GIFT SHOP

Abbotts Candy and Gifts Inc .... E 765 489-4442
  Hagerstown *(G-6832)*

Alan W Long .... G 812 265-6717
  Madison *(G-11198)*

PRODUCT SECTION

GRAPHIC ARTS & RELATED DESIGN SVCS

Concrete Lady Inc .... E 812 256-2765
  Otisco (G-13447)
Cowpokes Inc .... E 765 642-3911
  Anderson (G-99)
Friends of Third World Inc .... G 260 422-6821
  Fort Wayne (G-5013)
Mercantile Store .... G 812 988-6939
  Nashville (G-12675)
Mishawaka Art & Frame Gallery .... G 574 259-9320
  Mishawaka (G-11953)
Pgs LLC .... F 812 988-4030
  Nashville (G-12678)

GIFT WRAP: Paper, Made From Purchased Materials

Asc Inc .... C 765 473-4438
  Peru (G-13567)
Hoosier Miracle Inc .... G 765 473-4438
  Peru (G-13586)

GIFT, NOVELTY & SOUVENIR STORES: Gifts & Novelties

Bbs Celebration Center .... G 765 730-6575
  Yorktown (G-16971)
Crystal Source .... G 812 988-7009
  Nashville (G-12669)
Entertainment Express .... G 219 763-3610
  Portage (G-13861)
Kenneth Raber .... G 812 486-3102
  Montgomery (G-12105)
Lil Red Studios LLC .... G 317 443-4932
  Indianapolis (G-8753)

GIFTS & NOVELTIES: Wholesalers

Bbs Celebration Center .... G 765 730-6575
  Yorktown (G-16971)
Howe House Ltd Editions Inc .... G 765 742-6831
  Lafayette (G-10602)

GLASS PRDTS, FROM PURCHASED GLASS: Glassware

Warsaw Cut Glass Company Inc .... G 574 267-6581
  Warsaw (G-16445)

GLASS PRDTS, FROM PURCHASED GLASS: Mirrored

D & W Inc .... D 574 264-9674
  Elkhart (G-3284)
Omega National Products LLC .... C 574 295-5353
  Elkhart (G-3579)

GLASS PRDTS, FROM PURCHASED GLASS: Mirrors, Framed

Sherwood Industries Inc .... E 574 262-2639
  Elkhart (G-3672)

GLASS PRDTS, FROM PURCHASED GLASS: Windshields

Carlex Glass America LLC .... B 260 925-5656
  Auburn (G-374)
Glass Surgeons Inc .... G 219 374-2500
  Cedar Lake (G-1831)
Vuteq Usa Inc .... B 502 863-6322
  Princeton (G-14018)

GLASS PRDTS, FROM PURCHD GLASS: Strengthened Or Reinforced

Cleer Vision Windows Inc .... E 574 262-0449
  Elkhart (G-3254)
Creative Industries Inc .... E 317 248-1102
  Plainfield (G-13676)
State Wide Aluminum Inc .... C 574 262-2594
  Elkhart (G-3699)

GLASS PRDTS, PRESSED OR BLOWN: Furnishings & Access

HH Rellim Inc .... G 812 662-9944
  Greensburg (G-6602)

GLASS PRDTS, PRESSED OR BLOWN: Glass Fibers, Textile

Global Composites Inc .... C 574 522-9956
  Elkhart (G-3380)

GLASS PRDTS, PRESSED OR BLOWN: Glassware, Art Or Decorative

Ink Dawgz LLC .... G 219 781-6972
  Valparaiso (G-15974)
Inspired Fire GL Stdio Gllery .... G 765 474-1981
  Lafayette (G-10608)
Zimmerman Art Glass LLC .... G 812 738-2206
  Corydon (G-2524)

GLASS: Fiber

B Thystrup US Corporation .... G 574 834-2554
  North Webster (G-13302)
Palmetto Planters LLC .... G 765 396-4446
  Eaton (G-3065)
Pyrotek Incorporated .... D 260 248-4141
  Columbia City (G-2184)
Stability America Inc .... G 574 642-3029
  Goshen (G-6257)
Talon Products LLC .... F 574 218-0100
  Bristol (G-1294)
V & H Fiberglass Repair .... G 574 772-4920
  Knox (G-10227)

GLASS: Flat

Carlex Glass America LLC .... B 260 925-5656
  Auburn (G-374)
Chicago Bifold .... G 708 532-4365
  Highland (G-7129)
Indiana Bevel Inc .... G 317 596-0001
  Fishers (G-4544)
Pilkington North America Inc .... D 317 392-7000
  Shelbyville (G-14783)
Pilkington North America Inc .... G 574 273-5457
  South Bend (G-15195)
Wallar Additions Inc .... G 574 262-1989
  Elkhart (G-3778)

GLASS: Leaded

Larry Robertson Associates .... F 812 537-4090
  Indianapolis (G-8723)

GLASS: Pressed & Blown, NEC

Anchor Glass Container Corp .... D 765 584-6101
  Winchester (G-16881)
Apollo Design Technology Inc .... D 260 497-9191
  Fort Wayne (G-4763)
Creations In Glass .... G 219 326-7941
  La Porte (G-10397)
Diversified Ophthalmics Inc .... E 317 780-1677
  Indianapolis (G-7985)
Jerry Oppered .... G 574 269-5363
  Warsaw (G-16381)

Maul Technology Co .... F 765 584-2101
  Winchester (G-16894)
Naptown Etching Inc .... G 317 733-8776
  Zionsville (G-17036)
Northern Indiana Manufacturing .... E 574 342-2105
  Bourbon (G-1125)
S & S Optical Co Inc .... F 260 749-9614
  New Haven (G-12915)
Spectrum Brands Inc .... E 317 773-6627
  Noblesville (G-13179)
Toppan Photomasks Inc .... C 765 854-7500
  Kokomo (G-10350)

GOLF CARTS: Wholesalers

Indian Creek Outdoor Power LLC .... G 812 597-3055
  Morgantown (G-12258)
Mid America Powered Vehicles .... G 812 925-7745
  Chandler (G-1864)

GOLF COURSES: Public

Stone Quary .... E 765 473-5578
  Peru (G-13603)

GOLF EQPT

Triunity LLC .... G 317 703-1147
  Noblesville (G-13185)
Uebelhors Golf .... G 317 881-4109
  Indianapolis (G-9674)
Yourbodygetsit LLC .... G 317 908-7445
  Indianapolis (G-9805)

GOLF GOODS & EQPT

Fairway Custom Golf .... G 317 842-0017
  Fishers (G-4521)
Golf Plus Inc .... G 812 477-7529
  Evansville (G-4092)
Uebelhors Golf .... G 317 881-4109
  Indianapolis (G-9674)

GOURMET FOOD STORES

Ernestine Foods Inc .... G 219 274-0188
  Crown Point (G-2681)

GRADING SVCS

Globe Asphalt Paving Co Inc .... E 317 568-4344
  Indianapolis (G-8293)

GRANITE: Cut & Shaped

Classic Kitchen and Gran LLC .... G 317 575-8883
  Westfield (G-16676)
Michael and Sons Incorporated .... F 812 876-4736
  Bloomfield (G-752)

GRAPHIC ARTS & RELATED DESIGN SVCS

Annual Reports Inc .... G 317 736-8838
  Franklin (G-5709)
Aon(all or Nothing) LLC .... G 219 405-0163
  Indianapolis (G-7524)
Burston Marketing Inc .... F 574 262-4005
  Elkhart (G-3238)
Business Art & Designs Inc .... G 317 782-9108
  Beech Grove (G-688)
Cyclone Custom Prouducts LLC .... G 765 246-6523
  Greencastle (G-6401)
Drs Graphix Group Inc .... G 317 569-1855
  Indianapolis (G-8011)
Epic Graphics and Printing .... G 219 545-1240
  Gary (G-5930)
Founders West Inc .... G 812 936-7446
  Mccordsville (G-11449)
Grace Henderson .... G 765 661-9063
  Marion (G-11289)

Employee Codes: A=Over 500 employees, B=251-500
C=101-250, D=51-100, E=20-50, F=10-19, G=1-9

GRAPHIC ARTS & RELATED DESIGN SVCS

Graphic Visions.................................. G..... 812 331-7446
  Bloomington *(G-869)*
Hetty Incorporated............................. G..... 219 933-0833
  Hammond *(G-6945)*
Hetty Incorporated............................. G..... 219 836-2517
  Munster *(G-12539)*
Indiana Dimensional Pdts LLC......... E..... 574 834-7681
  North Webster *(G-13306)*
Mid West Digital Express Inc............ F..... 317 733-1214
  Zionsville *(G-17033)*
Moose Lake Products Co Inc.............. F..... 260 432-2768
  Fort Wayne *(G-5242)*
Pam C Jones Enterprises Inc............. G..... 812 294-1862
  Borden *(G-1117)*
Raging Rocket Web Design LLC......... G..... 219 381-5027
  Crown Point *(G-2741)*
Reinforcements Design...................... G..... 219 866-8626
  Rensselaer *(G-14064)*
Rlr Associates Inc............................... G..... 317 632-1300
  Indianapolis *(G-9312)*
Sig Media LLC................................... F..... 317 858-7624
  Indianapolis *(G-9426)*
Techcom Inc...................................... F..... 812 372-0960
  Columbus *(G-2401)*
Whimsicals Inc.................................. G..... 317 773-6130
  Noblesville *(G-13194)*
World Graffix LLC............................ G..... 574 936-1927
  Plymouth *(G-13834)*

GRATINGS: Tread, Fabricated Metal

Barnett-Bates Corporation................. F..... 815 726-5223
  Anderson *(G-82)*
E & H Bridge and Grating Inc............ G..... 812 277-8343
  Bedford *(G-632)*
Hilltop Metal Fabricating LLC........... G..... 574 773-4975
  Nappanee *(G-12610)*

GRAVEL MINING

Beaver Gravel Corporation................ D..... 317 773-0679
  Noblesville *(G-13042)*
Cgs Services Inc................................ G..... 765 763-6258
  Morristown *(G-12273)*
D Robertson Gravel Co Inc................. F..... 765 832-2768
  Clinton *(G-2065)*
Greensboro Sand & Gravel LLC......... G..... 765 624-9342
  Knightstown *(G-10195)*
Hopkins Gravel Sand & Concrete........ G..... 317 831-2704
  Mooresville *(G-12211)*
Lafontaine Gravel Inc....................... G..... 765 981-4849
  La Fontaine *(G-10369)*
LPI Paving & Excavating.................... G..... 260 726-9564
  Portland *(G-13955)*
Paddack Brothers Inc........................ G..... 765 659-4777
  Frankfort *(G-5689)*
Rogers Group Inc.............................. F..... 812 275-7860
  Springville *(G-15392)*
Roskovenski Sand & Gravel Inc......... G..... 765 832-6748
  Clinton *(G-2076)*
Schrock Aggregate Company Inc........ G..... 574 862-4167
  Wakarusa *(G-16250)*
Schrock Excavating Inc..................... E..... 574 862-4167
  Wakarusa *(G-16251)*
Shelby Gravel Inc............................. F..... 812 526-2731
  Edinburgh *(G-3104)*
Spray Sand & Gravel Inc.................... G..... 812 523-8081
  Seymour *(G-14697)*
U S Aggregates Inc............................ E..... 765 564-2282
  Delphi *(G-2910)*
Van Duyne Block and Gravel............. G..... 574 223-6656
  Rochester *(G-14331)*
West Plains Distribution LLC............. F..... 260 563-9500
  Wabash *(G-16224)*

Wilhelm Gravel Co Inc....................... E..... 260 837-6511
  Waterloo *(G-16534)*

GREASES: Lubricating

Steelco Industrial Lubricants............ G..... 219 462-0333
  Valparaiso *(G-16057)*
Times 10 Associates LLC.................... G..... 800 773-6432
  Valparaiso *(G-16068)*
Universal Services Inc....................... G..... 219 397-4373
  East Chicago *(G-3051)*

GREENHOUSES: Prefabricated Metal

Winandy Greenhouse Company.......... E..... 765 935-2111
  Richmond *(G-14227)*

GRINDING SVC: Precision, Commercial Or Indl

A & A Machine Service Inc................. G..... 317 745-7367
  Avon *(G-502)*
Beverly Industrial Service Inc............ E..... 812 667-5047
  Dillsboro *(G-2943)*
Fort Wayne Diamond Pdts Inc............ G..... 260 747-1681
  Fort Wayne *(G-4991)*
Huth Tool... G..... 260 749-9411
  Fort Wayne *(G-5085)*
Huth Tool & Machine Corp................. G..... 260 749-9411
  Fort Wayne *(G-5086)*
Illiana Grinding Machining Inc......... G..... 219 306-0253
  East Chicago *(G-3019)*
Midwest Accurate Grinding Svc......... F..... 219 696-4060
  Lowell *(G-11172)*
P & J Tool Co Inc............................... G..... 317 546-4858
  Indianapolis *(G-9078)*
Riverside Tool Corp........................... E..... 574 522-6798
  Elkhart *(G-3650)*
Schuler Precision Tool LLC................ G..... 260 982-2704
  North Manchester *(G-13249)*

GRINDING SVCS: Ophthalmic Lens, Exc Prescription

City Optical Co Inc............................ G..... 317 788-4243
  Indianapolis *(G-7814)*
Shimp Optical Corp............................ G..... 317 636-4448
  Indianapolis *(G-9420)*

GROCERIES, GENERAL LINE WHOLESALERS

Albanese Conf Group Inc.................. E..... 219 947-3070
  Merrillville *(G-11479)*
Albanese Conf Group Inc.................. G..... 219 947-3070
  Merrillville *(G-11480)*
MI Tierra.. G..... 812 376-0668
  Columbus *(G-2353)*

GUARD PROTECTIVE SVCS

Advanced Prtctve Slutions LLC.......... G..... 765 720-9574
  Coatesville *(G-2102)*

GUIDED MISSILES & SPACE VEHICLES

Cypress Springs Entps Inc................. G..... 812 743-8888
  Wheatland *(G-16774)*

GUIDED MISSILES & SPACE VEHICLES: Research & Development

Raytheon Company............................ G..... 310 647-9438
  Fort Wayne *(G-5369)*
Raytheon Company............................ G..... 317 306-4633
  Indianapolis *(G-9275)*

GUM & WOOD CHEMICALS

Arch Wood Protection Inc.................. G..... 219 464-3949
  Valparaiso *(G-15904)*
Jefferson Homebuilders Inc.............. G..... 317 398-3125
  Shelbyville *(G-14765)*
Pag Holdings Inc............................... G..... 814 446-2525
  Brazil *(G-1161)*
Pag Holdings LLC.............................. G..... 317 290-5006
  Indianapolis *(G-9087)*

GUTTERS: Sheet Metal

HB Gutters LLC.................................. G..... 765 414-5698
  Winamac *(G-16862)*
Over Top Roofing and Rmdlg LLC..... G..... 513 704-5422
  Lawrenceburg *(G-10851)*
Sure-Flo Seamless Gutters Inc........... G..... 260 622-4372
  Ossian *(G-13437)*

GYPSUM BOARD

Esco Industries Inc........................... F..... 574 522-4500
  Elkhart *(G-3334)*

GYPSUM PRDTS

Georgia-Pacific LLC.......................... D..... 219 956-3100
  Wheatfield *(G-16767)*
Ng Operations LLC............................ E..... 765 828-0898
  Clinton *(G-2073)*
Ng Operations LLC............................ D..... 765 828-0371
  Clinton *(G-2074)*
Patrick Industries Inc....................... G..... 574 294-1975
  Elkhart *(G-3590)*
Patrick Industries Inc....................... F..... 574 295-9660
  Elkhart *(G-3591)*
Patrick Industries Inc....................... G..... 574 294-8828
  Elkhart *(G-3592)*
Patrick Industries Inc....................... B..... 574 294-7511
  Elkhart *(G-3593)*
Precast Solutions Inc........................ F..... 317 545-6557
  Whitestown *(G-16816)*
Structural Composites LLC................ E..... 574 294-7511
  Elkhart *(G-3701)*
United States Gypsum Company........ D..... 219 392-4600
  East Chicago *(G-3049)*
United States Gypsum Company........ E..... 812 388-6866
  Shoals *(G-14913)*
United States Gypsum Company........ C..... 812 247-2101
  Shoals *(G-14914)*
Westech Building Products Inc.......... E..... 812 985-3628
  Mount Vernon *(G-12327)*

HAIR & HAIR BASED PRDTS

Beautybyneyadior LLC...................... G..... 800 988-2592
  Gary *(G-5898)*
Becoming Her LLC............................. G..... 317 200-0165
  Indianapolis *(G-7608)*
Bold Solutions LLC............................ G..... 708 740-8577
  Merrillville *(G-11492)*
Candice Jefferson............................. G..... 219 315-8629
  Hammond *(G-6892)*
Carla Clark....................................... G..... 812 598-4687
  Evansville *(G-3964)*
D I Hair Extensions LLC.................... G..... 219 742-3611
  Merrillville *(G-11503)*
Diamond Lush Extensions LLC.......... G..... 773 984-1003
  Merrillville *(G-11506)*
Divine Confidence LLC...................... G..... 574 218-1279
  Goshen *(G-6122)*
Dropship My Bundles LLC................. G..... 219 381-8061
  Gary *(G-5924)*
Exclusive Stylez LLC......................... G..... 470 406-2804
  Indianapolis *(G-8151)*

PRODUCT SECTION

HARDWARE & EQPT: Stage, Exc Lighting

Expressions Braids By Gwen LLC......... G..... 260 312-6037
  Fort Wayne (G-4968)
Flawless Units LLC............................... G..... 317 833-5975
  Indianapolis (G-8201)
Gale Industries Insltn Matl.................... G..... 765 447-1191
  Lafayette (G-10583)
Hair Necessities.................................... G..... 812 288-5887
  Clarksville (G-2018)
Her Majesty Crown LLC........................ G..... 260 218-2255
  Fort Wayne (G-5064)
Herextensions LLC............................... G..... 219 466-4273
  East Chicago (G-3016)
Janelle Davis.. G..... 765 635-6233
  Anderson (G-139)
London Hair Bundles LLC..................... G..... 317 953-3888
  Fishers (G-4557)
Luxurylinks LLC.................................... G..... 260 258-2814
  Fort Wayne (G-5193)
Minks & Beyond LLC............................ G..... 219 402-7011
  Valparaiso (G-16003)
Naturalee Twisted LLC......................... G..... 317 523-1012
  Beech Grove (G-700)
Naturally LLC.. G..... 317 667-5690
  Indianapolis (G-8991)
Pretty Xquisite Hair LLC....................... G..... 765 760-6948
  Muncie (G-12478)
Pure Beautee Bundlez Inc.................... G..... 574 204-3979
  Indianapolis (G-9240)
The Eminence Hair Collectn LLC.......... G..... 317 300-6051
  Indianapolis (G-9588)
Topnotch Locs LLC.............................. G..... 260 557-9628
  Indianapolis (G-9621)

HAIR CARE PRDTS

Adjust Your Crown Hair Care Pd........... G..... 317 970-1144
  Indianapolis (G-7433)
Amorlai Organics LLC........................... G..... 219 595-9102
  Highland (G-7121)
Chanel J Luxury Collection LLC............ G..... 470 210-4706
  Indianapolis (G-7784)
Divine Essentials LLC........................... G..... 765 400-8609
  Muncie (G-12385)
Gems Quality Extensions LLC.............. G..... 219 501-6320
  East Chicago (G-3010)
Icon Beauty Supply Inc......................... G..... 317 209-6550
  Noblesville (G-13099)
Kenra Professional LLC........................ F..... 800 428-8073
  Indianapolis (G-8673)
Majesty Hair Care System LLC............. G..... 317 900-6789
  Indianapolis (G-8818)
Malibu Wellness Inc.............................. E..... 317 624-7560
  Indianapolis (G-8821)
Maverick Packaging Inc........................ E..... 574 264-2891
  Elkhart (G-3519)
Signature Formulations LLC................. G..... 317 878-4086
  Trafalgar (G-15833)
Tonis Touch LLC................................... G..... 317 992-1280
  Plainfield (G-13737)
Wild Child Organics LLC....................... G..... 574 213-5204
  South Bend (G-15306)

HAIR DRESSING, FOR THE TRADE

Brittany Bushong.................................. G..... 574 457-4970
  Syracuse (G-15458)
Jewels Hair & Accessories LLC............ G..... 260 310-9915
  Fort Wayne (G-5135)
Krowned By Qwan LLC........................ G..... 317 813-9914
  Indianapolis (G-8704)
Tonis Touch LLC................................... G..... 317 992-1280
  Plainfield (G-13737)
Vickie Hildreth...................................... G..... 812 350-3575
  Columbus (G-2414)

HAND TOOLS, NEC: Wholesalers

Buckaroos Inc...................................... G..... 317 899-9100
  Indianapolis (G-7696)
Tartan Properties LLC........................... G..... 317 714-7337
  Indianapolis (G-9554)

HANDBAGS

Amanda Elizabeth LLC.......................... G..... 602 317-9633
  Fort Wayne (G-4748)
Arm Kandy LLC..................................... G..... 317 975-1576
  Indianapolis (G-7546)
CM Reed LLC....................................... G..... 517 546-4100
  Greendale (G-6444)
Vera Bradley Inc................................... B..... 877 708-8372
  Roanoke (G-14272)
Vera Bradley International LLC............. G..... 260 482-4673
  Roanoke (G-14273)

HANDBAGS: Women's

Aubry Lane LLC.................................... G..... 317 644-6372
  Indianapolis (G-7561)

HANDYMAN SVCS

Cruz Electric & Handy Svc LLC............. G..... 219 308-7117
  Hobart (G-7185)
Mast Services Lafayette LLC................. G..... 765 464-6940
  Lafayette (G-10643)
Northern Indiana Ordnance Co............. G..... 574 289-5938
  South Bend (G-15173)
Rackcollections LLC............................. G..... 317 779-4302
  Indianapolis (G-9259)

HARDWARE

Araymond Mfg Ctr N Amer Inc............. C..... 574 722-5168
  Logansport (G-11058)
Batesville Products Inc......................... D..... 513 381-2057
  Lawrenceburg (G-10831)
Crossroads Door & Hardware Inc......... G..... 812 234-9751
  Terre Haute (G-15570)
Dorma... G..... 317 468-6742
  Greenfield (G-6491)
Engineered Dock Systems Inc.............. G..... 317 803-2443
  Indianapolis (G-8120)
Fiedeke Vinyl Coverings Inc.................. F..... 574 534-3408
  Goshen (G-6135)
Grace Manufacturing Inc....................... F..... 574 267-8000
  Warsaw (G-16369)
Hart Plastics Inc................................... E..... 574 264-7060
  Elkhart (G-3400)
Holland Metal Fab Inc.......................... F..... 574 522-1434
  Elkhart (G-3409)
Indiana Architectural Plywood.............. E..... 317 878-4822
  Trafalgar (G-15829)
JM Fittings LLC..................................... E..... 260 747-9200
  Fort Wayne (G-5137)
L & W Engineering Inc.......................... C..... 574 825-5351
  Middlebury (G-11730)
Maurer Specialty Pools and Con.......... G..... 574 320-2429
  Mishawaka (G-11940)
Modern Forge Companies LLC............. A..... 708 388-1806
  Merrillville (G-11542)
Osr Inc.. F..... 812 342-7642
  Columbus (G-2368)
Parker-Hannifin Corporation................. A..... 260 748-6000
  Fort Wayne (G-5297)
Pridgeon & Clay Inc.............................. G..... 317 738-4885
  Franklin (G-5770)
Quality Converters Inc.......................... E..... 260 829-6541
  Orland (G-13371)
R & R Regulators Inc............................ F..... 574 522-3500
  Elkhart (G-3636)

Reelcraft Industries Inc......................... C..... 855 634-9109
  Columbia City (G-2188)
S C Pryor Inc.. F..... 317 352-1281
  Indianapolis (G-9354)
Samaron Corp....................................... E..... 574 970-7070
  Elkhart (G-3661)
Slb Corporation.................................... F..... 574 255-9774
  Mishawaka (G-11996)
Sparks Belting Company Inc................ G..... 800 451-4537
  Hammond (G-7012)
Standard Fusee Corporation................ D..... 765 472-4375
  Peru (G-13602)
Steel Parts Corporation........................ A..... 765 675-2191
  Tipton (G-15791)
Summer Cottage Inc............................. G..... 317 873-4176
  Indianapolis (G-9523)
Sur-Loc Inc... F..... 260 495-4065
  Fremont (G-5836)
Terry Liquidation III Inc......................... F..... 219 362-3557
  La Porte (G-10490)
Titus Tool Company Inc....................... F..... 206 447-1489
  Columbia City (G-2207)
Tru-Flex Real Estate Holdings LLC....... D..... 765 893-4403
  West Lebanon (G-16650)
Velko Hinge Inc..................................... E..... 219 924-6363
  Munster (G-12573)
Viking Inc.. E..... 260 244-6141
  Columbia City (G-2211)
Ward Industries Inc.............................. F..... 574 825-2548
  Middlebury (G-11756)
Western Products Indiana Inc.............. F..... 765 529-6230
  New Castle (G-12885)
Wood & More LLC................................. G..... 260 350-1537
  Goshen (G-6278)

HARDWARE & BUILDING PRDTS: Plastic

Avr Products Inc................................... G..... 574 294-6101
  Bristol (G-1247)
Buc Construction Supply Inc............... G..... 574 532-9345
  Lafayette (G-10547)
Cor-A-Vent Inc...................................... F..... 574 258-6161
  Mishawaka (G-11865)
Deflecto LLC... B..... 317 849-9555
  Indianapolis (G-7962)
Digger Specialties Inc........................... G..... 574 546-2811
  Bremen (G-1186)
Digger Specialties Inc........................... D..... 574 546-5999
  Bremen (G-1187)
First Place Trophy Inc........................... G..... 574 293-6147
  Elkhart (G-3347)
General Fabricators Inc......................... G..... 317 787-9354
  Indianapolis (G-8271)
Hancor Inc.. E..... 812 443-2080
  Brazil (G-1144)
J Plus Products Inc............................... G..... 317 660-1003
  Carmel (G-1675)
Konrady Plastics Inc............................. E..... 219 763-7001
  Portage (G-13880)
Life Management Inc............................ G..... 260 747-7408
  Fort Wayne (G-5185)
Nibco Inc.. B..... 574 295-3000
  Elkhart (G-3570)
Outsource Technologies Inc................. F..... 574 233-1303
  South Bend (G-15182)
Permalatt Products Inc......................... G..... 574 546-6311
  Bremen (G-1213)

HARDWARE & EQPT: Stage, Exc Lighting

Energy Saver Lights Inc....................... F..... 202 544-7868
  Indianapolis (G-8118)
Ler Techforce LLC................................ C..... 812 373-0870
  Columbus (G-2340)

HARDWARE & EQPT: Stage, Exc Lighting

Sizzlin Sound Productions LLC............... G..... 765 376-0129
 Crawfordsville *(G-2615)*
Tyler Truss LLC................................. D..... 765 221-5050
 Pendleton *(G-13559)*

HARDWARE STORES

Attica Ready Mixed Concrete................. F..... 765 762-2424
 Attica *(G-343)*
Barry Company Inc........................... G..... 812 333-1850
 Bloomington *(G-795)*
Boger Cabinetry & Design Inc............... G..... 317 588-6954
 Fishers *(G-4476)*
CRS-Drs Corporation......................... G..... 260 478-7555
 Fort Wayne *(G-4891)*
Johnco Corp................................... G..... 317 576-4417
 Indianapolis *(G-8632)*
Leeps Supply Co Inc.......................... E..... 219 756-5337
 Merrillville *(G-11530)*
Neumayr Lumber Co Inc...................... F..... 765 764-4148
 Attica *(G-353)*
Robinson Industries Inc...................... E..... 317 867-3214
 Westfield *(G-16724)*
T K Sales & Service.......................... G..... 219 962-8982
 Gary *(G-6017)*

HARDWARE STORES: Builders'

Tartan Properties LLC........................ G..... 317 714-7337
 Indianapolis *(G-9554)*

HARDWARE STORES: Pumps & Pumping Eqpt

McGrews Well Drilling Inc................... G..... 574 857-3875
 Rochester *(G-14306)*
Progress Group Inc........................... D..... 219 322-3700
 Schererville *(G-14539)*

HARDWARE STORES: Tools

All-Rite Ready Mix Inc....................... F..... 812 926-0920
 Aurora *(G-437)*
Dkl Tool & Manufacturing LLC.............. G..... 574 289-2291
 South Bend *(G-15001)*
Earth First Kentuckiana Inc.................. F..... 812 923-1227
 Charlestown *(G-1875)*
Grotrian Tool & Die........................... G..... 260 894-3558
 Ligonier *(G-11016)*
Stanley Black & Decker Inc.................. D..... 860 225-5111
 Indianapolis *(G-9495)*

HARDWARE WHOLESALERS

Dbisp LLC..................................... G..... 317 222-1671
 Indianapolis *(G-7957)*
Ditto Sales Inc................................ E..... 812 482-3043
 Jasper *(G-9832)*

HARDWARE, WHOLESALE: Builders', NEC

Tamco Manufacturing Co..................... G..... 574 294-1909
 Elkhart *(G-3714)*

HARDWARE, WHOLESALE: Chains

Kentuckiana Wire Rope & Supply........... F..... 812 282-3667
 Jeffersonville *(G-10005)*
Onspot of North America Inc................ G..... 203 377-0777
 North Vernon *(G-13290)*

HARDWARE, WHOLESALE: Security Devices, Locks

Standard Change-Makers Inc................ F..... 317 899-6955
 Indianapolis *(G-9492)*

HARDWARE: Aircraft

Govparts LLC.................................. G..... 260 449-9741
 Fort Wayne *(G-5031)*
Indy Aerospace Inc............................ G..... 817 521-6508
 Indianapolis *(G-8522)*

HARDWARE: Builders'

Hingecraft Corporation....................... E..... 574 293-6543
 Elkhart *(G-3407)*
L & S Lumber................................. F..... 765 886-1452
 Greens Fork *(G-6575)*
Von Duprin LLC............................... A..... 317 429-2866
 Indianapolis *(G-9729)*

HARDWARE: Casket

Geneva Manufacturing Inc................... E..... 260 368-7555
 Fort Wayne *(G-5021)*
Timberline Industries LLC.................... G..... 812 442-0949
 Brazil *(G-1167)*

HARDWARE: Door Opening & Closing Devices, Exc Electrical

Bloomfield Mfg Co Inc........................ E..... 812 384-4441
 Bloomfield *(G-740)*
L E Johnson Products Inc..................... G..... 574 293-5664
 Elkhart *(G-3461)*
L E Johnson Products Inc..................... C..... 574 293-5664
 Elkhart *(G-3462)*
Oak Security Group LLC..................... F..... 317 585-9830
 Indianapolis *(G-9040)*

HARDWARE: Furniture

Olon Industries Inc (us)...................... G..... 812 254-0427
 Washington *(G-16497)*
REM Industries Inc............................ F..... 574 862-2127
 Wakarusa *(G-16247)*

HARDWARE: Furniture, Builders' & Other Household

Benakovich Builders........................... G..... 219 204-2777
 Thorntown *(G-15750)*
Elkhart Hinge Co Inc.......................... F..... 574 293-2841
 Elkhart *(G-3325)*
J Game Ventures LLC........................ G..... 812 241-7096
 Danville *(G-2814)*
Pk USA Inc.................................... B..... 317 395-5500
 Shelbyville *(G-14784)*

HARNESS ASSEMBLIES: Cable & Wire

A-1vet LLC.................................... G..... 317 498-1804
 Indianapolis *(G-7407)*
Advanced Harn & Assembly LLC............ F..... 574 722-4040
 Logansport *(G-11054)*
Alliance Group Tech Inc...................... D..... 260 375-2810
 Warren *(G-16293)*
Almega/Tru-Flex Inc.......................... E..... 574 546-2113
 Bremen *(G-1172)*
Alpine Electronics Manufact................. A..... 956 217-3200
 Greenwood *(G-6665)*
Assembly Masters Inc........................ G..... 574 293-9026
 Elkhart *(G-3198)*
C & G Wiring Inc.............................. F..... 574 333-3433
 Elkhart *(G-3241)*
Caddo Connections Inc....................... E..... 219 874-8119
 La Porte *(G-10393)*
Electric-Tec LLC.............................. E..... 260 665-1252
 Angola *(G-248)*
Freedom Acres Inc........................... F..... 260 856-3059
 Cromwell *(G-2630)*
Fruition Industries LLC....................... F..... 260 854-2325
 Rome City *(G-14375)*

Gartech Enterprises Inc....................... F..... 812 794-4796
 Austin *(G-465)*
Group Dekko Inc.............................. E..... 260 854-4783
 Rome City *(G-14376)*
HB Connect Inc................................ G..... 855 503-9159
 Fort Wayne *(G-5051)*
HB Connect Inc................................ D..... 260 422-1212
 Fort Wayne *(G-5052)*
Hermac Incorporated......................... E..... 260 925-0312
 Auburn *(G-396)*
Hi-Pro Inc..................................... F..... 260 665-5038
 Angola *(G-258)*
Jag Wire LLC................................. F..... 260 463-8537
 Lagrange *(G-10744)*
Kamdoer Inc................................... E..... 574 293-2990
 Elkhart *(G-3446)*
Kauffman Engineering LLC.................. D..... 574 732-2154
 Bremen *(G-1201)*
Kauffman Engineering LLC.................. D..... 765 482-5640
 Lebanon *(G-10907)*
Kauffman Engineering Inc................... D..... 574 722-3800
 Logansport *(G-11086)*
Kirby Risk Corporation....................... D..... 765 448-4567
 Lafayette *(G-10623)*
Kra International LLC........................ D..... 574 259-3550
 Mishawaka *(G-11923)*
Laketronics Inc................................ E..... 260 856-4588
 Cromwell *(G-2631)*
Mssl Wiring System Inc....................... D..... 330 856-3366
 Portland *(G-13958)*
Mursix Corporation........................... C..... 765 282-2221
 Yorktown *(G-16977)*
Northwind Electronics LLC................... F..... 317 288-0787
 Indianapolis *(G-9024)*
Parkway Investor Group Inc................. E..... 260 665-1252
 Angola *(G-281)*
Patrick Industries Inc......................... D..... 574 293-2990
 Elkhart *(G-3599)*
Pent Assemblies............................... E..... 260 347-5828
 Kendallville *(G-10141)*
Pinder Instruments Company Inc........... G..... 219 924-7070
 Munster *(G-12558)*
Precision Wire Assemblies Inc............... D..... 765 489-6302
 Hagerstown *(G-6842)*
Precision Wire Supply LLC................... E..... 574 834-7545
 North Webster *(G-13313)*
Protron LLC................................... G..... 765 313-1595
 Anderson *(G-181)*
Quality Plas Engrg Acqstion Co............. E..... 574 262-2621
 Elkhart *(G-3632)*
Rayconn LLC.................................. G..... 317 809-5788
 Indianapolis *(G-9269)*
Rtw Enterprises Inc........................... E..... 574 294-3275
 Elkhart *(G-3654)*
Tap-A-Lite Inc................................. E..... 219 932-8067
 Hammond *(G-7018)*
Walton Industrial Park Inc.................... F..... 574 626-2929
 Walton *(G-16284)*
Wheelock Manufacturing Inc................ E..... 219 285-8540
 Garrett *(G-5880)*

HARNESS WIRING SETS: Internal Combustion Engines

Cpx Inc.. B..... 219 474-5280
 Kentland *(G-10159)*
Patrick Industries Inc......................... D..... 260 665-6112
 Angola *(G-282)*
Qualtronics LLC............................... E..... 812 375-8880
 Columbus *(G-2384)*

HEALTH AIDS: Exercise Eqpt

CL Holding LLC.. G 317 736-4414
  Franklin (G-5720)

HEARING AIDS

Accurate Hearing Aid Svcs LLC................... G 219 464-1937
  Valparaiso (G-15891)
Audio Diagnostics Inc.................................... G 765 477-7016
  Lafayette (G-10529)
Belltone Hearing Care Center....................... G 317 462-9999
  Greenfield (G-6470)
D J Investments Inc...................................... G 765 348-3558
  Hartford City (G-7064)
D J Investments Inc...................................... G 260 726-7346
  Portland (G-13936)
D J Investments Inc...................................... G 765 348-4381
  Hartford City (G-7063)
Integrity Hearing... G 317 882-9151
  Noblesville (G-13107)
Leahy Adology Hearing Aids LLC................. G 765 601-4003
  Frankfort (G-5679)
McMillin Hearing Aid Inc............................... G 812 847-2470
  Linton (G-11039)
Starkey Laboratories Inc............................... F 952 828-6934
  Plainfield (G-13731)
Wilsons Hearing Aid Center LLC.................. G 765 747-4131
  Muncie (G-12521)

HEAT EXCHANGERS: After Or Inter Coolers Or Condensers, Etc

Hale Industries Inc.. F 317 577-0337
  Fortville (G-5598)
Heat Exchanger Design Inc........................... E 317 686-9000
  Indianapolis (G-8379)

HEAT TREATING: Metal

Al-Fe Heat Treating LLC............................... F 260 563-8321
  Wabash (G-16173)
Albany Metal Treating Inc............................. F 765 789-6470
  Albany (G-11)
Applied Thermal Tech Inc.............................. E 574 269-7116
  Warsaw (G-16173)
Araymond Mfg Ctr N Amer Inc..................... C 574 722-5168
  Logansport (G-11058)
ATI Flat Rlled Pdts Hldngs LLC..................... F 765 529-9570
  New Castle (G-12850)
B&J Rocket America Inc............................... E 574 825-5802
  Middlebury (G-11700)
Bodycote Testing Group Inc......................... G 219 882-4283
  Gary (G-5904)
Bodycote Thermal Proc Inc.......................... E 574 295-2491
  Elkhart (G-3231)
Bodycote Thermal Proc Inc.......................... E 260 423-1691
  Fort Wayne (G-4811)
Bodycote Thermal Proc Inc.......................... E 812 662-0500
  Greensburg (G-6582)
Bodycote Thermal Proc Inc.......................... E 317 924-4321
  Indianapolis (G-7654)
Boyd Machine and Repair Co....................... E 260 635-2195
  Kimmell (G-10169)
Bwt LLC... F 574 232-3338
  South Bend (G-14963)
Circle City Heat Treating Inc........................ G 317 440-9102
  Indianapolis (G-7805)
Dependable Metal Treating Inc..................... F 260 347-5744
  Kendallville (G-10110)
Fremont Coatings Div................................... G 260 495-4445
  Fremont (G-5821)
Gerdau Macsteel Inc..................................... E 260 356-9520
  Huntington (G-7315)
Harbor Metals LLC.. E 574 232-3338
  South Bend (G-15058)

Hartford Heat Treatment............................... G 812 725-8272
  New Albany (G-12740)
HTI... F 574 722-2814
  Logansport (G-11078)
Indianna... G 219 947-9533
  Hobart (G-7192)
Learman Elctrnic Tl Assctesinc.................... G 574 293-4641
  Elkhart (G-3480)
Learman Electronic Tool Assoc.................... G 574 226-0420
  Elkhart (G-3481)
Leed Thermal Processing Inc...................... G 317 637-5102
  Indianapolis (G-8733)
Legacy Heat Treatment LLC........................ D 219 237-4500
  Griffith (G-6811)
McLaughlin Services LLC............................. G 260 897-4328
  Avilla (G-489)
Melting Point Metalworks LLC...................... G 317 984-0037
  Brownsburg (G-1387)
Nitrex Inc... E 317 346-7700
  Franklin (G-5760)
Northern Indiana Manufacturing................... E 574 342-2105
  Bourbon (G-1125)
Ooley Products Inc....................................... E 317 787-9351
  Indianapolis (G-9059)
Precision Heat Treating Corp....................... E 260 749-5125
  Fort Wayne (G-5338)
Rogers Engineering and Mfg Co................... E 765 478-5444
  Cambridge City (G-1503)
Sinden Racing Service Inc........................... F 317 243-7171
  Indianapolis (G-9443)
South Bend Heat Treat Inc........................... G 574 288-4794
  South Bend (G-15254)
Specilty Blnks Inc An Ind Corp..................... C 812 234-3002
  Terre Haute (G-15711)
Steel Technologies LLC................................ C 502 245-2110
  Portage (G-13916)
Sturm Heat Treating Inc............................... F 317 357-2368
  Indianapolis (G-9518)
Tool Dynamics LLC...................................... E 812 379-4243
  Columbus (G-2404)
Tri-State Metal Inc....................................... E 219 397-0470
  East Chicago (G-3047)
Ward Corporation... F 260 489-2281
  Fort Wayne (G-5546)
Wesleys Pallets & Heat Treat....................... G 812 526-0377
  Franklin (G-5787)

HEATERS: Space, Exc Electric

Heat Wagons Inc.. F 219 464-8818
  Valparaiso (G-15961)

HEATING & AIR CONDITIONING UNITS, COMBINATION

Crosspoint Solutions LLC............................. E 877 826-9399
  Indianapolis (G-7908)
Fletcher Heating & Cooling.......................... G 812 865-2984
  Paoli (G-13494)
Grayson Thermal Systems Corp................... C 317 739-3290
  Franklin (G-5736)
M Jones Consulting LLC............................... G 317 353-3823
  Monrovia (G-12078)
Master Filter Corporation.............................. G 317 545-3335
  Indianapolis (G-8849)
MD Moxie LLC.. F 260 347-1203
  Kendallville (G-10136)
Mr Heat Inc.. G 219 345-5629
  Demotte (G-2925)
Validated Custom Solutions LLC.................. G 317 259-7604
  Indianapolis (G-9699)
Washburn Heating & AC............................... G 574 825-7697
  Middlebury (G-11757)

HEATING EQPT: Complete

All Pro Property Services LLC..................... G 317 721-1227
  Indianapolis (G-7474)
Caliente LLC.. E 260 426-3800
  Fort Wayne (G-4830)
Hrezo Industrial Eqp & Engrg....................... F 812 537-4700
  Greendale (G-6447)
Jackson Systems LLC.................................. C 888 359-0365
  Indianapolis (G-8615)
Superior Distribution.................................... G 317 308-5525
  Indianapolis (G-9528)
Templeton Coal Company Inc...................... C 812 232-7037
  Terre Haute (G-15726)

HEATING EQPT: Induction

Thermal Tech & Temp Inc............................ F 219 213-2093
  Crown Point (G-2763)

HEATING PADS: Nonelectric

Fit Tight Covers Company Inc..................... E 812 492-3370
  Evansville (G-4072)
Gribbins Specialty Group Inc....................... G 812 422-3340
  Evansville (G-4099)

HEATING UNITS & DEVICES: Indl, Electric

Contour Hardening Inc................................. E 888 867-2184
  Indianapolis (G-7861)
Sherwood-Templeton Inc.............................. G 812 232-7037
  Terre Haute (G-15692)
Templeton Coal Company Inc...................... G 812 232-7037
  Terre Haute (G-15725)

HELICOPTERS

Hoosier Helicopter Svcs Inc........................ G 812 935-5296
  Bloomington (G-880)
Utilities AVI Specialists Inc.......................... G 219 662-8175
  Crown Point (G-2770)

HELMETS: Athletic

Cheercussion LLC.. F 317 762-4009
  Carmel (G-1585)

HELMETS: Steel

Mahan Technical Design LLC....................... G 765 341-0533
  Martinsville (G-11410)

HITCHES: Trailer

Southern Ind Lnngs Catings Inc................... G 812 206-7250
  Charlestown (G-1893)
Trimas Corporation....................................... F 260 925-3700
  Auburn (G-432)

HOBBY, TOY & GAME STORES: Arts & Crafts & Splys

Mishawaka Art & Frame Gallery................... G 574 259-9320
  Mishawaka (G-11953)
Stitch N Frame... G 260 478-1301
  Fort Wayne (G-5443)

HOISTING SLINGS

TEC Hoist LLC... E 708 598-2300
  Griffith (G-6818)

HOISTS

Cranewerks Inc.. D 765 663-2909
  Morristown (G-12274)
Mooresville Welding Inc............................... G 317 831-2265
  Mooresville (G-12225)

HOLDING COMPANIES: Investment, Exc Banks

Better Blacc Wall Streetz LLC............... F 812 927-0712
  Seymour *(G-14632)*
Navistar Cmponent Holdings LLC.......... A 317 352-4500
  Indianapolis *(G-8994)*
Rbc Holding Inc............................... F 317 340-3845
  Greenwood *(G-6759)*
V Global Holdings LLC....................... E 317 247-8141
  Indianapolis *(G-9695)*

HOLDING COMPANIES: Personal, Exc Banks

Specialty Steel Holdco Inc................... A 877 289-2277
  Hammond *(G-7013)*
Wright Horizon Enterprises LLC............ G 317 779-8182
  Westfield *(G-16741)*

HOME ENTERTAINMENT EQPT: Electronic, NEC

Jerome Pagell................................. G 219 226-0591
  Crown Point *(G-2702)*
JP Technology Inc........................... G 219 947-2525
  Crown Point *(G-2706)*
Kas Satellite & Cable Inc.................... G 260 833-3941
  Angola *(G-267)*
Smarter Home Technology Inc............. G 815 677-6885
  Chandler *(G-1866)*

HOME HEALTH CARE SVCS

Borrv Concepts LLC.......................... G 317 405-9121
  Indianapolis *(G-7661)*

HOMEFURNISHING STORES: Pottery

Schmidt Marken Designs..................... G 219 785-4238
  La Porte *(G-10477)*
Strawtown Pottery & Antq Inc.............. G 317 984-5080
  Noblesville *(G-13180)*

HOMEFURNISHING STORES: Venetian Blinds

Abda Incorporated........................... G 317 273-8343
  Indianapolis *(G-7416)*
Doris Drapery Boutique...................... G 765 472-5850
  Peru *(G-13580)*
Otter Creek Christian Church................ G 812 446-5300
  Brazil *(G-1159)*
Pool Shop..................................... G 812 446-0026
  Brazil *(G-1162)*

HOMEFURNISHINGS, WHOLESALE: Blinds, Vertical

Midwest Blind & Shade Co................... G 574 271-0770
  Mishawaka *(G-11947)*

HOMEFURNISHINGS, WHOLESALE: Carpets

Craft Metal Products Inc..................... G 317 545-3252
  Indianapolis *(G-7897)*
Georgia Direct Carpet Inc.................... F 765 966-2548
  Richmond *(G-14125)*
Santarossa Mosaic Tile Co Inc............... C 317 632-9494
  Indianapolis *(G-9371)*

HOMEFURNISHINGS, WHOLESALE: Decorating Splys

Country Cabin LLC............................ G 812 232-4635
  Terre Haute *(G-15569)*
Willows and More............................ G 812 560-1088
  Westport *(G-16753)*

Zing Polymer Formations LLC............... G 317 598-0480
  Fishers *(G-4637)*

HOMEFURNISHINGS, WHOLESALE: Draperies

Quality Drapery Corporation................. G 765 481-2370
  Lebanon *(G-10936)*

HOMEFURNISHINGS, WHOLESALE: Wood Flooring

Brenco LLC.................................... G 219 844-9570
  Schererville *(G-14517)*

HOMES: Log Cabins

Appalachian Log Structures.................. G 812 744-5711
  Moores Hill *(G-12186)*
Colluci Construction-Log Homes............ G 812 843-5607
  English *(G-3840)*
Country Charm................................ G 765 572-2588
  Attica *(G-347)*
Countrymark Log Homes Inc................ G 866 468-3301
  Vevay *(G-16107)*
E & L Construction Inc....................... G 765 525-7081
  Manilla *(G-11260)*
Expedition Log Homes........................ G 219 663-5555
  Crown Point *(G-2683)*
Heritage Log Homes.......................... G 812 427-2591
  Vevay *(G-16110)*
Lauer Log Homes Inc........................ G 260 486-7010
  Fort Wayne *(G-5176)*
Napoleon Lumber Co.......................... G 812 852-4545
  Napoleon *(G-12575)*
Schroeder Log Home Supply Inc............ G 574 825-1054
  Middlebury *(G-11749)*
Sidney & Janice Bond......................... G 812 366-8160
  Floyds Knobs *(G-4693)*
Tomahawk Log & County Homes........... G 260 833-6429
  Angola *(G-301)*
Wagler Mini Barn Products LLC............. G 812 687-7372
  Plainville *(G-13747)*

HONING & LAPPING MACHINES

Rx Honing Machine Corp..................... G 574 259-1606
  Mishawaka *(G-11989)*

HORSESHOES

Bowmans Hoof Trimming..................... G 574 522-2838
  Elkhart *(G-3233)*
Ty Bowells Farrier Service................... G 812 537-3990
  Greendale *(G-6456)*

HOSE: Flexible Metal

Engineered Industrial Products.............. G 317 684-4280
  Indianapolis *(G-8121)*
Esco Enterprises Indiana Inc................. F 317 241-0318
  Indianapolis *(G-8131)*
Hose Technology Inc......................... E 765 762-5501
  Williamsport *(G-16848)*
Tru-Flex Real Estate Holdings LLC......... D 765 893-4403
  West Lebanon *(G-16650)*

HOSE: Plastic

Mitsubishi Chemical Advncd Mtr............ C 260 479-4100
  Fort Wayne *(G-5233)*
Mitsubshi Chem Advnced Mtls In.......... D 260 479-4700
  Fort Wayne *(G-5234)*

HOSE: Pneumatic, Rubber Or Rubberized Fabric, NEC

Clean-Seal Inc................................. E 574 299-1888
  South Bend *(G-14976)*

HOSE: Rubber

American Rubber Corp........................ G 317 548-8455
  Anderson *(G-77)*
Flexible Technologies Inc.................... G 574 936-2432
  Plymouth *(G-13776)*
Omega Products Inc.......................... E 574 546-5606
  Bremen *(G-1210)*
Radiator Specialty Company................. D 574 546-5606
  Bremen *(G-1216)*
S & R Welding Inc............................ G 317 710-0360
  Indianapolis *(G-9353)*
Slb Corporation................................ F 574 255-9774
  Mishawaka *(G-11996)*

HOT TUBS

Masterspas LLC................................ C 260 436-9100
  Fort Wayne *(G-5207)*
Masterspas LLC................................ D 260 436-9100
  Fort Wayne *(G-5206)*

HOT TUBS: Plastic & Fiberglass

Thursday Pools LLC........................... G 317 973-0200
  Fortville *(G-5607)*

HOTELS & MOTELS

Colluci Construction-Log Homes............ G 812 843-5607
  English *(G-3840)*
Whiteco Industries Inc....................... A 219 769-6601
  Merrillville *(G-11572)*

HOUSEHOLD APPLIANCE STORES: Appliance Parts

3sevens LLC................................... G 502 594-2312
  Henryville *(G-7112)*

HOUSEHOLD ARTICLES, EXC KITCHEN: Pottery

Schmidt Marken Designs..................... G 219 785-4238
  La Porte *(G-10477)*

HOUSEHOLD ARTICLES: Metal

Aircom Manufacturing Inc.................... B 317 545-5383
  Indianapolis *(G-7462)*
B Stevens Service LLC....................... G 812 622-2039
  Cynthiana *(G-2786)*
Grace Manufacturing Inc..................... F 574 267-8000
  Warsaw *(G-16369)*
Kimball Electronics Inc....................... D 317 545-5383
  Indianapolis *(G-8686)*
Outsource Technologies Inc................. F 574 233-1303
  South Bend *(G-15182)*
R&H Metalworks LLC......................... G 317 513-8733
  Fairland *(G-4402)*
Samuel Powell................................. G 812 887-6813
  French Lick *(G-5849)*

HOUSEHOLD FURNISHINGS, NEC

Anderson Creations Inc...................... G 574 223-8932
  Rochester *(G-14276)*
Baird Home Corporation...................... G 812 883-1141
  Salem *(G-14473)*
Coronado Casuals LLC........................ G 615 470-5718
  Plainfield *(G-13672)*
Inhabit Inc..................................... G 317 636-1699
  Indianapolis *(G-8548)*
K M Davis Inc................................. G 765 426-9227
  Lafayette *(G-10617)*

PRODUCT SECTION

INDL MACHINERY & EQPT WHOLESALERS

Keter North America Inc .... D 765 298-6800
  Anderson (G-141)
Nice-Pak Products Inc .... A 845 365-1700
  Mooresville (G-12228)
Pgs LLC .... F 812 988-4030
  Nashville (G-12678)
Reit Price Co .... G 765 964-3252
  Union City (G-15859)
Veada Industries Inc .... A 574 831-4775
  New Paris (G-12973)
Vera Bradley Inc .... B 877 708-8372
  Roanoke (G-14272)

HOUSEHOLD SEWING MACHINES WHOLESALERS: Electric

Rebuilding Cnslting Pckg Slton .... G 574 389-1966
  Elkhart (G-3641)

HOUSEWARES, ELECTRIC: Cooking Appliances

Hyndman Industrial Pdts Inc .... E 260 483-6042
  Fort Wayne (G-5089)
Mwss Inc .... G 574 287-3365
  Elkhart (G-3560)

HOUSEWARES, ELECTRIC: Fans, Exhaust & Ventilating

Enerlinc Inc .... G 317 574-1009
  Fortville (G-5593)

HOUSEWARES, ELECTRIC: Heating Units, Electric Appliances

Southeast Specialties Inc .... G 706 667-0422
  Indianapolis (G-9463)

HOUSEWARES: Dishes, Plastic

Galleyware Company Inc .... G 302 996-9480
  Zionsville (G-17009)

HOUSINGS: Business Machine, Sheet Metal

T Organization Inc .... E 463 204-5118
  Greenwood (G-6771)

HYDRAULIC EQPT REPAIR SVC

B & C Machining Inc .... E 219 866-7091
  Rensselaer (G-14045)
Dependable Rubber Industrial .... G 765 447-5654
  Lafayette (G-10569)
Five Star Hydraulics Inc .... E 219 762-1619
  Portage (G-13866)
Fourman Enterprises Inc .... F 812 546-5734
  Hope (G-7225)
Industrial Hydraulics Inc .... E 317 247-4421
  Indianapolis (G-8518)
K M Specialty Pumps Inc .... F 812 925-3000
  Chandler (G-1863)
Macallister Machinery Co Inc .... C 260 483-6469
  Fort Wayne (G-5195)
Motion & Control Entps LLC .... F 219 844-4224
  Munster (G-12551)
Ottosons Industries Inc .... G 219 365-8330
  Cedar Lake (G-1835)
T & T Hydraulics Inc .... G 765 548-2355
  Rosedale (G-14384)
Wdb Enterprises Inc .... F 219 844-4224
  Hammond (G-7031)

ICE

Airgas Inc .... G 317 632-7106
  Indianapolis (G-7463)
Arctic Glacier USA Inc .... F 800 562-1990
  Bedford (G-620)
Arctic Ice Express Inc .... F 812 333-0423
  Bloomington (G-783)
Celebration Ice LLC .... F 812 634-9801
  Jasper (G-9826)
Home City Ice Company .... F 765 762-6096
  Attica (G-352)
Home City Ice Company .... G 317 926-2451
  Indianapolis (G-8404)
Industrial and Coml Contg Inc .... F 219 405-8599
  Valparaiso (G-15973)
Quikset Bollard Company .... G 502 648-6734
  New Albany (G-12801)

IGNITER GRAINS: Boron Potassium Nitrate

Scp Holdings Inc .... G 260 925-2588
  Auburn (G-421)

IGNITION SYSTEMS: High Frequency

Group Dekko Inc .... E 574 834-2818
  North Webster (G-13305)

INDL & PERSONAL SVC PAPER WHOLESALERS

Farm Boy Meats of Evansville .... D 812 425-5231
  Evansville (G-4064)
Millcraft Paper Company .... F 317 240-3500
  Indianapolis (G-8920)
Servants Inc .... D 812 634-2201
  Jasper (G-9910)

INDL & PERSONAL SVC PAPER, WHOLESALE: Boxes & Containers

Gta Containers LLC .... E 574 288-3459
  South Bend (G-15054)
Indianapolis Container Company ... G 317 580-5000
  Indianapolis (G-8503)

INDL & PERSONAL SVC PAPER, WHOLESALE: Shipping Splys

PSC Industries Inc .... F 812 425-9071
  Evansville (G-4263)

INDL EQPT SVCS

3-T Corp .... F 812 424-7878
  Evansville (G-3856)
Automation Consultants Inc .... G 502 552-4995
  Floyds Knobs (G-4669)
B & H Electric and Supply Inc .... E 812 522-5607
  Seymour (G-14630)
Bastian Automation Engrg LLC ...... D 317 467-2583
  Greenfield (G-6468)
Buhrt Engineering & Cnstr .... E 574 267-3720
  Warsaw (G-16331)
Evansville Assn For The Blind .... C 812 422-1181
  Evansville (G-4047)
Line-X .... G 812 491-9475
  Evansville (G-4170)
Mtr Machining Concept Inc .... G 260 587-3381
  Ashley (G-334)
Refractory Service Corporation ...... E 219 397-7108
  East Chicago (G-3038)
Southlake Machine Corp .... G 219 285-6150
  Morocco (G-12270)
Stanley Black & Decker Inc .... D 860 225-5111
  Indianapolis (G-9495)
Storageworks Inc .... G 317 577-3511
  Fishers (G-4607)

T & M Equipment Company Inc ...... F 317 293-9255
  Indianapolis (G-9543)
Tarpenning-Lafollette Co Inc .... E 317 780-1500
  Indianapolis (G-9553)

INDL GASES WHOLESALERS

Airgas Usa LLC .... G 812 362-7593
  Rockport (G-14335)
Indiana Oxygen Company Inc .... G 765 662-8700
  Marion (G-11295)
Indiana Oxygen Company Inc .... D 317 290-0003
  Indianapolis (G-8488)

INDL MACHINERY & EQPT WHOLESALERS

Aam-Equipco Inc .... G 574 272-8886
  Granger (G-6329)
American Veteran Group LLC .... G 317 600-4749
  Westfield (G-16664)
Asphalt Equipment Company Inc ... E 260 672-3004
  Fort Wayne (G-4775)
Autoform Tool & Mfg LLC .... C 260 624-2014
  Angola (G-232)
Banks Machine & Engrg LLC .... D 317 642-4980
  Shelbyville (G-14732)
Brake Supply Company Inc .... C 812 467-1000
  Evansville (G-3950)
Buskirk Engineering Inc .... F 260 622-5550
  Ossian (G-13420)
Capital Adhesives & Packg Corp .... F 317 834-5415
  Mooresville (G-12197)
Clarke Industrial Systems Inc .... E 260 489-4575
  Fishers (G-4491)
Craft Laboratories Inc .... E 260 432-9467
  Fort Wayne (G-4882)
Gearbox Group Inc .... G 812 268-0322
  Sullivan (G-15406)
Hawkins Darryal .... G 765 282-6021
  Muncie (G-12410)
Hoffman Sls & Specialty Co Inc ...... G 317 846-6428
  Carmel (G-1656)
Hoosier Fire Equipment Inc .... F 219 462-1707
  Valparaiso (G-15965)
Hoosier Metal Polish Inc .... F 219 474-6011
  Kentland (G-10160)
Horner Industrial Services Inc .... F 317 634-7165
  Indianapolis (G-8418)
Indco Inc .... G 812 945-4383
  New Albany (G-12746)
Interstate Power Systems Inc .... E 952 854-2044
  Gary (G-5964)
Koch Enterprises Inc .... G 812 465-9800
  Evansville (G-4159)
Landis Equipment & Tool Rental .... G 812 847-2582
  Linton (G-11037)
Logansport Machine Co Inc .... E 574 735-0225
  Logansport (G-11090)
Machine Tool Service Inc .... F 812 232-1912
  Terre Haute (G-15634)
Mainline Conveyor Systems Inc ..... F 317 831-2795
  Mooresville (G-12219)
Ogden Welding Systems Inc .... E 219 322-5252
  Schererville (G-14537)
Pathfinder Cutting Tech LLC .... F 424 342-9723
  Indianapolis (G-9099)
Pyramid Equipment Inc .... F 219 778-2591
  Rolling Prairie (G-14371)
Robinson Industries Inc .... E 317 867-3214
  Westfield (G-16724)
Rochester Cement Products Inc .... G 574 223-3917
  Rochester (G-14316)
Specialty Tool LLC .... F 260 493-6351
  Indianapolis (G-9471)

Employee Codes: A=Over 500 employees, B=251-500
C=101-250, D=51-100, E=20-50, F=10-19, G=1-9

INDL MACHINERY & EQPT WHOLESALERS

Storageworks Inc .... G 317 577-3511
Fishers (G-4607)

Systems Engineering and Sls Co .... G 260 422-1671
Fort Wayne (G-5466)

T & M Equipment Company Inc .... F 317 293-9255
Indianapolis (G-9543)

Technical Water Treatment Inc .... G 574 277-1949
Granger (G-6386)

Tsune America LLC .... F 812 378-9875
Edinburgh (G-3109)

W M Kelley Co Inc .... D 812 945-3529
New Albany (G-12825)

INDL PATTERNS: Foundry Cores

American Bronze Craft Inc .... F 501 729-3018
Indianapolis (G-7501)

Shells Inc .... D 574 342-2673
Bourbon (G-1127)

INDL PATTERNS: Foundry Patternmaking

Baseline Tool Company .... F 260 761-4932
Wawaka (G-16537)

Charles Bane .... G 765 855-5100
Centerville (G-1848)

Diversified Pattern Engrg Inc .... E 260 897-3771
Avilla (G-475)

Maxwell Engineering Inc .... G 260 745-4991
Fort Wayne (G-5208)

Nvsd LLC .... G 502 561-0007
New Albany (G-12785)

Ward Pattern & Engineering Inc .... C 260 426-8700
Fort Wayne (G-5547)

INDL PROCESS INSTRUMENTS: Analyzers

Analyticalab Inc .... G 219 473-9777
Whiting (G-16831)

Crown Audio Inc .... B 800 342-6939
Elkhart (G-3273)

Harman Professional Inc .... B 574 294-8000
Elkhart (G-3398)

Syscon International Inc .... C 574 232-3900
South Bend (G-15276)

INDL PROCESS INSTRUMENTS: Control

Axis Controls Incorporated .... G 260 414-4028
Fort Wayne (G-4785)

Industrial Controls Corp .... G 219 884-1141
Gary (G-5961)

INDL PROCESS INSTRUMENTS: Moisture Meters

T W Brackett & Assoc LLC .... G 765 769-3000
Attica (G-355)

INDL PROCESS INSTRUMENTS: On-Stream Gas Or Liquid Analysis

Thermco Instrument Corporation .... F 219 362-6258
La Porte (G-10493)

INDL SPLYS WHOLESALERS

Airgas Usa LLC .... G 812 474-0440
Evansville (G-3878)

Hoosier Industrial Supply Inc .... F 574 533-8565
Goshen (G-6168)

Indiana Whitesell Corporation .... B 317 279-3278
Indianapolis (G-8500)

Jac Jmr Inc .... G 219 663-6700
Crown Point (G-2698)

Kaiser Tool Company Inc .... E 260 484-3620
Fort Wayne (G-5142)

Midwest Design Hydraulic .... G 765 714-3016
West Lafayette (G-16605)

Mulzer Crushed Stone Inc .... E 812 547-7921
Tell City (G-15513)

Puck Supply & Machine LLC .... F 574 293-3333
Elkhart (G-3625)

River Bend Hose Specialty Inc .... E 574 233-1133
South Bend (G-15222)

Standard Die Supply of Indiana Inc .... D 317 236-6200
Indianapolis (G-9493)

Steelco Industrial Lubricants .... G 219 462-0333
Valparaiso (G-16057)

Terry Liquidation III Inc .... D 219 362-9908
La Porte (G-10489)

Tri-State Power Supply LLC .... G 812 537-2500
Lawrenceburg (G-10863)

VMS Products Inc .... G 888 321-4698
Anderson (G-214)

INDL SPLYS, WHOLESALE: Abrasives

Daylight Engineering Inc .... G 812 983-2518
Elberfeld (G-3111)

INDL SPLYS, WHOLESALE: Adhesives, Tape & Plasters

Abro Industries Inc .... E 574 232-8289
South Bend (G-14933)

Adhesive Solutions Company LLC .... G 260 691-0304
Columbia City (G-2117)

Capital Adhesives & Packg Corp .... F 317 834-5415
Mooresville (G-12197)

Custom Building Products LLC .... C 765 656-0234
Frankfort (G-5659)

INDL SPLYS, WHOLESALE: Bearings

Bearing Service Company PA .... G 773 734-5132
Griffith (G-6794)

Hanwha Machinery America Corp .... D 574 546-2261
Bremen (G-1195)

Headco Industries Inc .... G 219 924-7758
Highland (G-7140)

Headco Industries Inc .... G 574 288-4471
South Bend (G-15062)

Hoosier Industrial Supply .... G 574 535-0712
Goshen (G-6167)

NSK Corporation .... D 765 458-5000
Liberty (G-10993)

INDL SPLYS, WHOLESALE: Bins & Containers, Storage

Universal Package LLC .... F 812 937-3605
Ferdinand (G-4450)

INDL SPLYS, WHOLESALE: Fasteners & Fastening Eqpt

McFeelys Inc .... F 800 443-7937
Aurora (G-449)

Titus Tool Company Inc .... F 206 447-1489
Columbia City (G-2207)

INDL SPLYS, WHOLESALE: Gaskets

Avr Products Inc .... G 574 294-6101
Bristol (G-1247)

Freudenberg-Nok General Partnr .... C 317 421-3400
Shelbyville (G-14756)

INDL SPLYS, WHOLESALE: Gaskets & Seals

American Rubber Corp .... G 317 548-8455
Anderson (G-77)

Clean-Seal Inc .... E 574 299-1888
South Bend (G-14976)

Nitto Inc .... G 317 879-2840
Zionsville (G-17037)

Polymod Technologies Inc .... F 260 436-1322
Fort Wayne (G-5325)

Press-Seal Corporation .... C 260 436-0521
Fort Wayne (G-5350)

Rits Ltd Brokers Inc .... G 260 348-0786
Fort Wayne (G-5385)

INDL SPLYS, WHOLESALE: Gears

Fairfield Manufacturing Co Inc .... A 765 772-4000
Lafayette (G-10576)

Somaschini North America LLC .... E 574 968-0273
South Bend (G-15249)

INDL SPLYS, WHOLESALE: Power Transmission, Eqpt & Apparatus

Altra Industrial Motion Corp .... E 219 874-5248
Michigan City (G-11577)

P H C Industries Inc .... G
Fort Wayne (G-5291)

INDL SPLYS, WHOLESALE: Rubber Goods, Mechanical

Ace Extrusion LLC .... F 812 868-8640
Evansville (G-3869)

Bluffton Rubber .... G 260 824-4501
Bluffton (G-1031)

BRC Rubber & Plastics Inc .... E 260 894-4121
Ligonier (G-11007)

BRC Rubber & Plastics Inc .... F 765 728-8510
Montpelier (G-12177)

BRC Rubber Plastics Inc .... G 260 894-7263
Ligonier (G-11008)

Coleman Cable LLC .... D 765 449-7227
Lafayette (G-10553)

Contitech Usa Inc .... B 260 925-0700
Auburn (G-378)

Contitech Usa Inc .... B 260 925-0700
Auburn (G-379)

Envirotech Extrusion Inc .... E 765 966-8068
Richmond (G-14120)

Freudenberg-Nok General Partnr .... C 765 763-7246
Morristown (G-12277)

Freudenberg-Nok General Partnr .... C 734 354-5504
Shelbyville (G-14757)

Iris Rubber Co Inc .... F 317 984-3561
Cicero (G-1997)

Jasper Rubber Products Inc .... D 812 482-3242
Jasper (G-9855)

Jasper Rubber Products Inc .... B 812 482-3242
Jasper (G-9856)

Mid-States Rubber Products Inc .... B 812 385-3473
Princeton (G-14005)

Parker-Hannifin Corporation .... D 574 533-1111
Goshen (G-6236)

Parker-Hannifin Corporation .... C 574 528-9400
Syracuse (G-15470)

Polycraft Products Inc .... E 812 577-3401
Greendale (G-6452)

Rd Rubber Products Inc .... G 260 357-3571
Garrett (G-5875)

Rubber Shop Inc .... G 574 291-6440
South Bend (G-15229)

T & M Rubber Inc .... E 574 533-3173
Goshen (G-6267)

Triangle Rubber Co LLC .... C 574 533-3118
Goshen (G-6272)

INSTRUMENTS, SURGICAL & MEDICAL: Inhalation Therapy

Viking Inc... E 260 244-6141
  Columbia City *(G-2211)*
Worldcell Extrusions LLC................................. G 574 333-2249
  Elkhart *(G-3794)*

INDL SPLYS, WHOLESALE: Seals

Hook Industrial Sales Inc................................ D 260 432-9441
  Fort Wayne *(G-5075)*

INDL SPLYS, WHOLESALE: Tools

Rusach International Inc................................ F 317 638-0298
  Hope *(G-7232)*
Stanley Black & Decker Inc........................... D 860 225-5111
  Indianapolis *(G-9495)*

INDL SPLYS, WHOLESALE: Tools, NEC

Earth First Kentuckiana Inc........................... F 812 923-1227
  Charlestown *(G-1875)*
Peter Austin Co.. G 765 288-6397
  Muncie *(G-12474)*

INDL SPLYS, WHOLESALE: Valves & Fittings

Barnett-Bates Corporation............................. F 815 726-5223
  Anderson *(G-82)*

INDL TRUCK REPAIR SVCS

Black Equipment Company S Inc.................. C 812 477-6481
  Evansville *(G-3934)*
Fire Apparatus Service Inc............................ G 219 985-0788
  Gary *(G-5933)*

INDUSTRIAL & COMMERCIAL EQPT INSPECTION SVCS

Dearborn Crane and Engrg Co...................... E 574 259-2444
  Mishawaka *(G-11882)*
Hmt LLC.. G 219 736-9901
  Merrillville *(G-11522)*

INFORMATION RETRIEVAL SERVICES

First Databank Inc... G 317 571-7200
  Carmel *(G-1636)*
Gannett Co Inc... G 765 423-5511
  Lafayette *(G-10584)*
Xlibris Corporation... B 812 671-9162
  Bloomington *(G-1017)*

INFORMATION SVCS: Consumer

Plum Group Inc.. F 617 712-3000
  Indianapolis *(G-9155)*

INGOT, EXTRUSION: Extrusion ingot, aluminum: rolling mills

A/C Fabricating Corp..................................... E 574 534-1415
  Goshen *(G-6086)*
Alconex Specialty Products........................... E 260 744-3446
  Fort Wayne *(G-4738)*
Postle Operating LLC.................................... D 574 266-7720
  Elkhart *(G-3612)*
Postle Operating LLC.................................... D 574 389-0800
  Elkhart *(G-3613)*

INK: Printing

Actega North America Inc............................. G 800 426-4657
  Schererville *(G-14512)*
Braden Sutphin Ink Co.................................. G 317 352-8781
  Indianapolis *(G-7669)*
Budget Inks LLC.. G 877 636-4657
  Angola *(G-238)*
Enviro Ink... G 260 748-0636
  Fort Wayne *(G-4953)*
Flint CPS Inks North Amer LLC..................... E 317 870-4422
  Indianapolis *(G-8204)*
Flint Group US LLC....................................... F 574 269-4603
  Warsaw *(G-16363)*
Industrial Organic Inks Inc............................ G 219 878-0613
  Chesterton *(G-1938)*
INX International Ink Co................................ G 765 939-6625
  Richmond *(G-14140)*
INX LLC.. G 219 779-0508
  Gary *(G-5965)*
Nor-Cote International Inc............................ G 800 488-9180
  Crawfordsville *(G-2596)*
North American Ink.. G 765 659-6000
  Frankfort *(G-5685)*
Peafield Products Inc.................................... F 317 839-8473
  Plainfield *(G-13711)*
Stamp N Scrap Ink Corp............................... G 219 440-7239
  Dyer *(G-2984)*
Sun Chemical Corporation............................ E 972 270-6735
  Frankfort *(G-5695)*
Sun Chemical Corporation............................ E 765 659-6000
  Frankfort *(G-5696)*
Sun Chemical Corporation............................ G 812 235-8031
  Terre Haute *(G-15717)*
Sun Cosmetics LLC....................................... D 219 531-5359
  Valparaiso *(G-16060)*

INSECTICIDES & PESTICIDES

Agriselect Evansville LLC............................. G 812 453-2235
  Evansville *(G-3877)*
Corteva Agriscience LLC.............................. A 317 337-3000
  Indianapolis *(G-7884)*
Monofoilusa LLC... G 317 340-9951
  Elwood *(G-3832)*
Prime Source LLC... G 812 867-8921
  Evansville *(G-4258)*
V Global Holdings LLC.................................. E 317 247-8141
  Indianapolis *(G-9695)*

INSPECTION & TESTING SVCS

Red Bull Armory LLC..................................... G 757 287-7738
  Mitchell *(G-12046)*
Solid Rock LLC.. G 260 755-2687
  Fort Wayne *(G-5425)*
Teaco Inc... G 219 874-6234
  Michigan City *(G-11676)*
Watcon Inc... G 574 287-3397
  South Bend *(G-15304)*

INSTRUMENTS, LABORATORY: Differential Thermal Analysis

Peli Biothermal LLC...................................... G 763 412-4800
  Plainfield *(G-13712)*

INSTRUMENTS, LABORATORY: Spectrometers

Anasazi Instruments Inc............................... F 317 861-7657
  New Palestine *(G-12930)*

INSTRUMENTS, MEASURING & CNTRL: Radiation & Testing, Nuclear

Nuclear Measurements Corp......................... G 317 546-2415
  Indianapolis *(G-9032)*

INSTRUMENTS, MEASURING & CNTRLG: Aircraft & Motor Vehicle

Cvg Sprague Devices LLC............................ C 614 289-5360
  Michigan City *(G-11593)*

INSTRUMENTS, MEASURING & CONTROLLING: Gas Detectors

J and N Enterprises Inc................................ G 219 465-2700
  Valparaiso *(G-15978)*

INSTRUMENTS, MEASURING & CONTROLLING: Ion Chambers

Containment Tech Group Inc........................ G 317 862-5945
  Indianapolis *(G-7855)*

INSTRUMENTS, SURGICAL & MED: Fixation Appliances, Internal

Nexxt Spine LLC.. F 317 436-7801
  Noblesville *(G-13141)*

INSTRUMENTS, SURGICAL & MED: Needles & Syringes, Hypodermic

Becton Dickinson and Company.................... D 317 561-2900
  Plainfield *(G-13660)*

INSTRUMENTS, SURGICAL & MEDICAL: Blood & Bone Work

Advanced Mbility Solutions LLC................... F 812 438-2338
  Rising Sun *(G-14240)*
Arcamed LLC... E 317 375-7733
  Indianapolis *(G-7538)*
Bd Medical Development Inc........................ G 219 310-8551
  Crown Point *(G-2653)*
Biomet Europe Ltd.. E 574 267-2038
  Warsaw *(G-16325)*
Catalent Pharma Solutions Inc..................... D 812 355-4498
  Bloomington *(G-825)*
Cook Incorporated... A 812 339-2235
  Bloomington *(G-841)*
Depuy Synthes Inc.. C 574 267-8143
  Warsaw *(G-16349)*
Freudenberg Medical Mis Inc....................... C 812 280-2400
  Jeffersonville *(G-9987)*
Lvb Acquisition Holding LLC......................... A 574 267-6639
  Warsaw *(G-16389)*
Yager & Associates LLC............................... G 260 413-9571
  Fort Wayne *(G-5579)*
Yosira LLC... G 260 241-1203
  Fort Wayne *(G-5581)*

INSTRUMENTS, SURGICAL & MEDICAL: Blood Transfusion

Helmer Scientific LLC................................... C 317 773-9073
  Noblesville *(G-13094)*

INSTRUMENTS, SURGICAL & MEDICAL: Catheters

Cook Incorporated... G 812 339-2235
  Ellettsville *(G-3806)*
Cook Incorporated... A 812 339-2235
  Bloomington *(G-840)*
Cook Medical LLC... A 812 323-4500
  Bloomington *(G-846)*
Cook Medical LLC... B 812 339-2235
  Bloomington *(G-845)*
Vance Products Incorporated....................... C 812 829-4891
  Spencer *(G-15364)*

INSTRUMENTS, SURGICAL & MEDICAL: Inhalation Therapy

Rgr Medical Solutions Inc............................. C 317 285-9703
  Fishers *(G-4596)*

INSTRUMENTS, SURGICAL & MEDICAL: Inhalation Therapy

Rusher Medical LLC .... G 260 341-6514
 Fort Wayne *(G-5391)*

INSTRUMENTS, SURGICAL & MEDICAL: IV Transfusion

Mira Vista Diagnostics LLC .... E 317 856-2681
 Indianapolis *(G-8932)*

INSTRUMENTS, SURGICAL & MEDICAL: Muscle Exercise, Ophthalmic

Jemarkel Health-Tech LLC .... G 219 548-5881
 Valparaiso *(G-15981)*
Vertical Power Co .... G 574 276-8094
 Osceola *(G-13406)*

INSTRUMENTS, SURGICAL & MEDICAL: Ophthalmic

Tri-Pac Inc .... C 574 855-2197
 South Bend *(G-15291)*
Vision Training Products Inc .... F 574 259-2070
 Mishawaka *(G-12023)*

INSTRUMENTS, SURGICAL & MEDICAL: Plates & Screws, Bone

Tayco Brace Inc .... E 574 850-7910
 South Bend *(G-15279)*

INSTRUMENTS: Analytical

Animated Dynamics Inc .... G 765 418-5359
 West Lafayette *(G-16563)*
Arch Med Sltions - Elkhart LLC .... F 574 264-3997
 Elkhart *(G-3188)*
Beckman Coulter Inc .... F 317 808-4200
 Indianapolis *(G-7604)*
Beckman Coulter Inc .... D 317 808-4200
 Indianapolis *(G-7605)*
Beckman Coulter Inc .... D 317 471-8029
 Indianapolis *(G-7606)*
Beckman Coulter Life Sciences .... D 408 747-2000
 Indianapolis *(G-7607)*
Capital Envmtl Entps Inc .... E 317 240-8085
 Indianapolis *(G-7733)*
Cubed Laboratories LLC .... G 866 935-6165
 South Bend *(G-14987)*
Flir Security Inc .... G 443 936-9108
 Indianapolis *(G-8205)*
Griffin Analytical Technologies LLC .... E 765 775-1701
 West Lafayette *(G-16588)*
Infrared Lab Systems LLC .... G 317 896-1565
 Westfield *(G-16700)*
Ipheion Development Corp .... G 240 281-1619
 Indianapolis *(G-8587)*
Kprime Technologies LLC .... G 260 399-1337
 Fort Wayne *(G-5159)*
Leco Corporation .... G 574 288-9017
 South Bend *(G-15122)*
Lloyd Jr Frank P and Assoc .... G 317 388-9225
 Indianapolis *(G-8773)*
Perkinelmer Hlth Sciences Inc .... G 800 385-1555
 South Bend *(G-15193)*
Purspec Technologies Inc .... G 765 532-2208
 West Lafayette *(G-16623)*
Teledyne Flir Defense Inc .... E 765 775-1701
 West Lafayette *(G-16634)*
Teledyne Flir Detection Inc .... E 765 775-1701
 West Lafayette *(G-16635)*
Templeton Coal Company Inc .... C 812 232-7037
 Terre Haute *(G-15726)*
Thermo Fisher Scientific Inc .... F 812 477-2760
 Evansville *(G-4342)*

Trilithic Inc .... C 317 895-3600
 Indianapolis *(G-9641)*

INSTRUMENTS: Flow, Indl Process

AMG LLC .... F 317 329-4004
 Indianapolis *(G-7513)*
Endress + Hser Flwtec AG Div U .... C 317 535-7138
 Greenwood *(G-6698)*

INSTRUMENTS: Indl Process Control

Hillenbrand Inc .... A 812 931-5000
 Batesville *(G-590)*

INSTRUMENTS: Laser, Scientific & Engineering

Axis Industries Usa LLC .... F 317 739-3390
 Franklin *(G-5711)*

INSTRUMENTS: Measurement, Indl Process

Industrial Physics Inc .... F 812 981-3133
 New Albany *(G-12747)*

INSTRUMENTS: Measuring, Electrical Energy

Technical Weighing Svcs Inc .... E 219 924-3366
 Griffith *(G-6819)*

INSTRUMENTS: Medical & Surgical

34 Lives Pbc .... G 303 550-9989
 West Lafayette *(G-16553)*
Accu-Mold LLC .... E 269 323-0388
 Mishawaka *(G-11834)*
Advanced Vscular Therapies Inc .... G 765 423-1720
 Lafayette *(G-10516)*
Advantis Medical Inc .... C 317 859-2300
 Greenwood *(G-6661)*
After Action Med Dntl Sup LLC .... G 800 892-5352
 Indianapolis *(G-7457)*
Airgas Usa LLC .... G 317 248-8072
 Indianapolis *(G-7464)*
Allen Medical Systems Inc .... G 978 266-4286
 Batesville *(G-576)*
Allen Medical Systems Inc .... G 812 931-2512
 Batesville *(G-577)*
American Veteran Group LLC .... G 317 600-4749
 Westfield *(G-16664)*
Ameriflo2 Inc .... F 317 844-2019
 Indianapolis *(G-7511)*
Ash Access Technology Inc .... G 765 742-4813
 Lafayette *(G-10528)*
Ats Manufacturing Inc .... G
 Elkhart *(G-3201)*
Avalign Technologies Inc .... G 260 484-1500
 Fort Wayne *(G-4782)*
Avalign Technologies Inc .... G 888 625-4497
 Greenwood *(G-6673)*
B & J Medical LLC .... E 260 349-1275
 Kendallville *(G-10094)*
Bamboo US Bidco LLC .... A 812 333-0887
 Bloomington *(G-794)*
Baxter Healthcare Corporation .... G 219 942-8136
 Hobart *(G-7174)*
Baxter Healthcare Corporation .... G 317 291-0620
 Indianapolis *(G-7598)*
Baxter Phrm Solutions LLC .... A 812 355-7167
 Bloomington *(G-799)*
Biomedix-Inc .... F 812 355-7000
 Bloomington *(G-808)*
Biomet Inc .... A 574 267-6639
 Warsaw *(G-16323)*
Boston Scientific Corp .... G 951 914-2400
 Indianapolis *(G-7663)*

Boston Scientific Corporation .... A 812 829-4877
 Spencer *(G-15340)*
Breg Inc .... G 760 505-0521
 Indianapolis *(G-7675)*
Breg Inc .... E 317 559-0479
 Indianapolis *(G-7676)*
Catheter Research Inc .... C 317 872-0074
 Indianapolis *(G-7760)*
Center For Dagnstc Imaging CDI .... G 812 331-7727
 Bloomington *(G-826)*
Century Pharmaceuticals Inc .... E 317 849-4210
 Indianapolis *(G-7775)*
Circle M Spring Inc .... E 574 267-2883
 Warsaw *(G-16335)*
Circle Medical Products Inc .... G 317 271-2626
 Indianapolis *(G-7809)*
CNA Tool Engineering Inc .... G 260 927-2298
 Auburn *(G-377)*
Compassionate Procedures LLC .... G 317 259-4656
 Indianapolis *(G-7843)*
Cook Biodevice LLC .... G 800 265-0945
 Bloomington *(G-837)*
Cook Capital Equipment LLC .... F 800 457-4500
 Spencer *(G-15342)*
Cook General Biotechnology LLC .... F 317 917-3450
 Indianapolis *(G-7866)*
Cook Group Incorporated .... F 812 331-1025
 Ellettsville *(G-3805)*
Cook Incorporated .... G 812 339-2235
 Bloomington *(G-839)*
Cook Incorporated .... G 812 829-4891
 Spencer *(G-15343)*
Cook Medical Inc .... D 812 822-1402
 Bloomington *(G-843)*
Cook Medical LLC .... A 812 339-2235
 Bloomington *(G-844)*
Cook Medical Technologies LLC .... F 812 339-2235
 Bloomington *(G-847)*
Cook Regentec LLC .... D 800 265-0945
 Bloomington *(G-848)*
Covidien LP .... C 317 837-8199
 Plainfield *(G-13674)*
Cspine Inc .... G 574 936-7893
 South Bend *(G-14986)*
Depuy Synthes Products Inc .... F 574 267-8143
 Warsaw *(G-16350)*
Eli Lilly International Corp .... F 317 276-2000
 Indianapolis *(G-8091)*
Engineered Medical Systems .... D 317 246-5500
 Indianapolis *(G-8122)*
Esaote North America Inc .... D 317 813-6000
 Fishers *(G-4517)*
Ferrellok Lifesciences LLC .... G 765 716-0056
 Muncie *(G-12394)*
First Gear Inc .... E 260 490-3238
 Fort Wayne *(G-4984)*
GMI LLC .... G 260 209-6676
 Fort Wayne *(G-5028)*
Greatbatch Ltd .... G 260 755-7300
 Fort Wayne *(G-5040)*
Group Dekko Inc .... G 260 599-3405
 Kendallville *(G-10114)*
Hansa Medical Products Inc .... G 317 815-0708
 Carmel *(G-1649)*
Hemocleanse Inc .... F 765 742-4813
 Lafayette *(G-10596)*
Holgin Technologies LLC .... F 317 774-5181
 Noblesville *(G-13095)*
I V S .... G 765 914-5268
 Connersville *(G-2443)*
Innotek Custom Solutions LLC .... G 260 341-8691
 Fort Wayne *(G-5108)*

PRODUCT SECTION

INSURANCE AGENTS, NEC

Innovtive Nurological Dvcs LLC............ G 317 674-2999
Carmel *(G-1670)*

Innovtive Surgical Designs Inc............. F 812 369-4252
Spencer *(G-15351)*

Inotiv Inc... G 812 985-5900
Mount Vernon *(G-12302)*

Inscope Medical Solutions Inc.............. G 502 882-0183
New Albany *(G-12748)*

Integer Holdings Corporation................ F 317 454-8800
Indianapolis *(G-8566)*

Inventory Solutions Inc........................ G 212 749-5027
Indianapolis *(G-8585)*

Kilgore Manufacturing Co Inc............... D 260 248-2002
Columbia City *(G-2162)*

Mach Medical LLC............................. E 260 229-1514
Columbia City *(G-2169)*

Mattox and Moore Inc......................... G 317 632-7534
Indianapolis *(G-8852)*

McClinton Life Sciences Inc................. G 317 903-4230
Indianapolis *(G-8862)*

Med Devices LLC.............................. G 317 508-1699
Indianapolis *(G-8869)*

Med-Cut Inc..................................... D 574 269-1982
Warsaw *(G-16394)*

Med2950 LLC................................... E 317 545-5383
Indianapolis *(G-8870)*

Medical Systems Corp Indiana.............. E 317 856-1340
Indianapolis *(G-8872)*

Medline Industries LP......................... G 800 633-5463
Charlestown *(G-1882)*

Medtrnic Sofamor Danek USA Inc......... G 317 837-8142
Plainfield *(G-13702)*

Medtrnic Sofamor Danek USA Inc......... G 574 267-6826
Warsaw *(G-16396)*

Medtronic.. G 317 837-8664
Plainfield *(G-13703)*

Micropulse Inc.................................. C 260 625-3304
Columbia City *(G-2171)*

Nanovis LLC.................................... G 260 625-1502
Columbia City *(G-2173)*

Nemco Medical Ltd........................... E 260 484-1500
Fort Wayne *(G-5263)*

Newcomed Inc.................................. G 260 484-1500
Fort Wayne *(G-5269)*

Nginstruments LLC............................ D 574 268-2112
Warsaw *(G-16401)*

Omnitech Systems Inc........................ E 219 531-5532
Valparaiso *(G-16018)*

Paragon Medical Inc.......................... C 574 594-2140
Pierceton *(G-13637)*

Paragon Medical Inc.......................... C 574 594-2140
Pierceton *(G-13638)*

Performance Cnc LLC........................ G 574 780-4864
Bourbon *(G-1126)*

Philips Ultrasound Inc......................... F 317 591-5242
Indianapolis *(G-9135)*

Point Medical Corporation.................... A 219 663-1775
Crown Point *(G-2732)*

Precision Edge Srgcal Pdts LLC........... D 260 624-3123
Angola *(G-287)*

Promex Technologies LLC................... E 317 736-0128
Indianapolis *(G-9230)*

Prp Technologies LLC........................ G 260 433-3769
Fort Wayne *(G-5355)*

Rmi Holdings LLC............................. F 317 214-7076
Warsaw *(G-16419)*

Rx Help Centers LLC......................... G 866 478-9593
Indianapolis *(G-9350)*

Scott G Kirk.................................... G 317 843-1703
Carmel *(G-1754)*

Single Source Medical LLC................. E 574 656-3400
North Liberty *(G-13224)*

Smed - Ta/Td LLC............................ G 260 625-3347
Columbia City *(G-2198)*

Smith & Nephew Inc.......................... G 800 357-6155
Indianapolis *(G-9449)*

Smiths Medical Asd Inc...................... E 219 554-2196
Gary *(G-6011)*

Sophysa USA Inc.............................. G 219 663-7711
Crown Point *(G-2761)*

Ste Acquisition LLC........................... E 260 925-1382
Auburn *(G-426)*

Stryker Corporation........................... G 832 509-9988
Mooresville *(G-12244)*

Symmetry Medical Inc........................ G 574 267-8700
Warsaw *(G-16433)*

Symmetry Medical USA Inc................. G 574 267-8700
Warsaw *(G-16436)*

Tri-Pac Inc..................................... G 574 855-2197
South Bend *(G-15290)*

Universal Precision Instrs Inc............... G 574 264-3997
Elkhart *(G-3763)*

Vasmo Inc...................................... F 317 549-3722
Indianapolis *(G-9702)*

Verista Inc..................................... A 317 849-0330
Fishers *(G-4628)*

Viant... F 317 788-7225
Indianapolis *(G-9716)*

Viant Medical LLC............................ E 317 454-8824
Indianapolis *(G-9717)*

White Surgical Inc............................. G 260 755-5800
Fort Wayne *(G-5566)*

INSTRUMENTS: Nautical

Undersea Sensor Systems Inc............. E 260 248-3500
Columbia City *(G-2209)*

INSTRUMENTS: Power Measuring, Electrical

Radian Research Inc.......................... D 765 449-5500
Lafayette *(G-10675)*

INSTRUMENTS: Pressure Measurement, Indl

Dwyer Instruments Inc........................ G 219 279-2031
Wolcott *(G-16928)*

INSTRUMENTS: Temperature Measurement, Indl

Capital Tech Solutions LLC.................. F 812 303-4357
Evansville *(G-3961)*

Complete Controls Inc........................ G 260 489-0852
Fort Wayne *(G-4868)*

Environmental Technology Inc.............. E 574 233-1202
South Bend *(G-15016)*

Heraeus Electro-Nite Co LLC............... C 765 473-8275
Peru *(G-13584)*

INSTRUMENTS: Test, Electrical, Engine

Indiana Research Institute................... G 812 378-5363
Columbus *(G-2325)*

Indiana Research Institute................... G 812 378-4221
Columbus *(G-2326)*

P&C Prime LLC................................ F 231 420-3650
Fredericksburg *(G-5795)*

Precision Systems............................. G 812 283-4904
Clarksville *(G-2029)*

Renk Systems Corporation.................. E 317 455-1367
Camby *(G-1513)*

Ticzkus Electronic and Mfg.................. G 574 542-2325
Rochester *(G-14328)*

INSTRUMENTS: Test, Electronic & Electric Measurement

Advantage Electronics Inc................... F 317 888-1946
Greenwood *(G-6659)*

Chance Ind Standards Lab Inc............. F 317 787-6578
Indianapolis *(G-7783)*

Contact Products Inc......................... G 219 838-1911
Munster *(G-12536)*

Hilevel Technology Inc....................... G 765 349-1650
Martinsville *(G-11400)*

Noel-Smyser Engineering Corp............. E 317 293-2215
Indianapolis *(G-9020)*

Solid Rock LLC................................ G 260 755-2687
Fort Wayne *(G-5425)*

Utility Systems Inc............................ E 317 842-9000
Indianapolis *(G-9692)*

INSTRUMENTS: Test, Electronic & Electrical Circuits

Createch/Rehder Development Co......... G 765 252-0257
West Lafayette *(G-16572)*

INSULATION & ROOFING MATERIALS: Wood, Reconstituted

Proline Spray Foam Inc....................... G 317 981-2158
Indianapolis *(G-9229)*

Standard Industries Inc....................... G 219 872-1111
Michigan City *(G-11672)*

Standard Industries Inc....................... G 812 838-4861
Mount Vernon *(G-12323)*

INSULATION MATERIALS WHOLESALERS

Innovative Energy Inc......................... E 219 696-3639
Crown Point *(G-2697)*

INSULATION: Fiberglass

API Indiana Inc................................. D 574 293-5574
Elkhart *(G-3186)*

Hy-TEC Fiberglass Inc....................... G 260 489-6601
Fort Wayne *(G-5087)*

Insul-Coustic Corporation.................... E 260 420-1480
Fort Wayne *(G-5113)*

Insulation Fabricators Inc.................... D 219 845-2008
Hammond *(G-6956)*

Johns Manville Corporation.................. D 765 973-5200
Richmond *(G-14153)*

Knauf Insulation Inc........................... C 317 398-4434
Shelbyville *(G-14770)*

Molded Acstcal Pdts Easton Inc........... E 610 253-7135
Elkhart *(G-3550)*

Owens Corning Sales LLC.................. G 260 665-7318
Angola *(G-279)*

Owens Corning Sales LLC.................. C 765 647-4131
Brookville *(G-1331)*

Owens Corning Sales LLC.................. G 219 465-4324
Valparaiso *(G-16020)*

Owens Corning Sales LLC.................. G 260 563-2111
Wabash *(G-16207)*

INSULATORS & INSULATION MATERIALS: Electrical

Bo-Witt Products Inc.......................... E 812 526-5561
Edinburgh *(G-3069)*

Gund Company Inc............................ E 219 374-9944
Cedar Lake *(G-1832)*

Napier & Napier................................ G 765 580-9116
Liberty *(G-10992)*

Surfis Inc....................................... G 260 357-3475
Auburn *(G-428)*

Winona Building Products LLC............. F 574 822-0100
Plymouth *(G-13831)*

INSURANCE AGENTS, NEC

Cook Group Incorporated.................... F 812 339-2235
Bloomington *(G-838)*

INTEGRATED CIRCUITS, SEMICONDUCTOR NETWORKS, ETC

Alliance Group Tech Inc.................... D 260 375-2810
Warren *(G-16293)*

Jones International Inc..................... G 219 746-1478
Gary *(G-5971)*

Linear Technology LLC..................... G 317 443-1169
Arcadia *(G-314)*

Magellan Integration Inc................... E 812 492-4400
Evansville *(G-4185)*

INTERIOR DECORATING SVCS

Custom Interior Dynamics LLC............ F 317 632-0477
Indianapolis *(G-7930)*

Touch of Class Interiors..................... G 765 452-5879
Kokomo *(G-10351)*

INTERIOR DESIGN SVCS, NEC

Botti Stdio Archtctral Arts In.............. E 847 869-5933
La Porte *(G-10391)*

Deem & Loureiro Inc....................... G 770 652-9871
Indianapolis *(G-7961)*

Rlr Associates Inc.......................... G 317 632-1300
Indianapolis *(G-9312)*

Unrivaled Interiors LLC.................... G 317 509-0496
Cicero *(G-2003)*

INTRAVENOUS SOLUTIONS

Caicos Solutions LLC....................... G 317 314-3776
Indianapolis *(G-7716)*

INVERTERS: Nonrotating Electrical

Xantrex LLC................................ C 800 670-0707
Elkhart *(G-3798)*

Xantrex LLC................................ E 800 670-0707
Elkhart *(G-3797)*

INVESTORS, NEC

Integrity Marketing Team Inc.............. G 317 517-0012
Plainfield *(G-13691)*

Rios Investment Services LLC............. G 574 514-3999
South Bend *(G-15221)*

Sater Enterprises........................... G 812 477-1529
Evansville *(G-4297)*

INVESTORS: Real Estate, Exc Property Operators

Deedgrabbercom Inc........................ G 219 712-9722
Munster *(G-12538)*

Tylayculture LLC........................... G 219 678-8359
Highland *(G-7158)*

IRON & STEEL PRDTS: Hot-Rolled

Elkhart Steel Service Inc................... E 574 262-2552
Elkhart *(G-3329)*

Gerdau Ameristeel US Inc.................. E 765 286-5454
Muncie *(G-12400)*

Nlmk Indiana LLC........................... B 219 787-8200
Portage *(G-13899)*

IRON ORE MINING

National Steel Pellet Company............ G 574 273-7000
Mishawaka *(G-11963)*

IRON ORES

Arcelormittal Holdings LLC................. D 219 399-1200
East Chicago *(G-2990)*

IRRADIATION EQPT

Jason Holdings Inc......................... C 414 277-9300
Richmond *(G-14147)*

JACKS: Hydraulic

Norco Industries Inc....................... G 574 262-3400
Elkhart *(G-3571)*

Norco Industries Inc....................... G 800 347-2232
Elkhart *(G-3572)*

JEWELRY REPAIR SVCS

Ginas Creative Jewelry Inc................ G 317 272-0032
Avon *(G-521)*

GNB Studio Inc............................ G 317 356-4834
Indianapolis *(G-8295)*

Golden Lion Inc............................ G 765 446-9557
Lafayette *(G-10592)*

Goldstone Jewelry Inc..................... G 765 742-1975
West Lafayette *(G-16585)*

Interntnal Damnd Gold Exch Ltd........... G 317 872-6666
Indianapolis *(G-8583)*

Khamis Fine Jewelers Inc.................. G 317 841-8440
Indianapolis *(G-8681)*

Mark Edward Hails.......................... G 812 437-1030
Evansville *(G-4189)*

Rogers Enterprises Inc..................... G 317 851-5500
Greenwood *(G-6760)*

Sisson & Son Mfg Jewelers................. G 574 967-4331
Flora *(G-4665)*

Williams Jewelers Inc...................... G 812 475-1705
Evansville *(G-4387)*

JEWELRY STORES

Collegiate Pride Inc........................ G 260 726-7818
Portland *(G-13932)*

Golden Lion Inc............................ G 765 446-9557
Lafayette *(G-10592)*

Jewelers Boutique Inc..................... G 317 788-7679
Indianapolis *(G-8624)*

Ralph Privoznik Jewelry Art................ G 765 742-4904
Lafayette *(G-10676)*

JEWELRY STORES: Precious Stones & Precious Metals

Alan W Long................................ G 812 265-6717
Madison *(G-11198)*

Argentum Jewelry Inc....................... G 812 336-3100
Bloomington *(G-784)*

Ashleys Jewelry By Design Ltd............ G 219 926-9039
Chesterton *(G-1904)*

Brinker Mfg Jewelers Inc................... F 812 476-0651
Evansville *(G-3954)*

Crystal Source.............................. G 812 988-7009
Nashville *(G-12669)*

David Gonzales............................. G 765 284-6960
Muncie *(G-12373)*

Design Msa Inc............................ G 317 817-9000
Carmel *(G-1606)*

Edward E Petri Company.................... G 317 636-5007
Indianapolis *(G-8057)*

G Thrapp Jewelers Inc...................... G 317 255-5555
Indianapolis *(G-8254)*

Ginas Creative Jewelry Inc................. G 317 272-0032
Avon *(G-521)*

Goldstone Jewelry Inc...................... G 765 742-1975
West Lafayette *(G-16585)*

Interntnal Damnd Gold Exch Ltd........... G 317 872-6666
Indianapolis *(G-8583)*

J C Sipe Inc................................ G 317 848-0215
Indianapolis *(G-8603)*

Khamis Fine Jewelers Inc.................. G 317 841-8440
Indianapolis *(G-8681)*

Legacy Enterprises Inc..................... G 219 484-9483
Merrillville *(G-11531)*

Peter Franklin Jewelers Inc................ G 260 749-4315
New Haven *(G-12913)*

Rogers Enterprises Inc..................... G 317 851-5500
Greenwood *(G-6760)*

Ronaldo Designer Jewelry Inc............. F 812 972-7220
New Albany *(G-12808)*

Sisson & Son Mfg Jewelers................. G 574 967-4331
Flora *(G-4665)*

Surplus Store and Exchange................ F 765 447-0200
Lafayette *(G-10707)*

Williams Jewelers Inc...................... G 812 475-1705
Evansville *(G-4387)*

JEWELRY STORES: Silverware

Simply Silver............................... G 260 824-4667
Bluffton *(G-1053)*

JEWELRY STORES: Watches

Stall & Kessler Inc......................... G 765 742-1259
Lafayette *(G-10698)*

JEWELRY, PRECIOUS METAL: Rings, Finger

Herff Jones LLC............................ C 317 297-3741
Indianapolis *(G-8383)*

JEWELRY, PRECIOUS METAL: Settings & Mountings

Downey Creations LLC...................... F 317 248-9888
Indianapolis *(G-8003)*

J C Sipe Inc................................ G 317 848-0215
Indianapolis *(G-8603)*

Surplus Store and Exchange................ F 765 447-0200
Lafayette *(G-10707)*

JEWELRY, WHOLESALE

Ronaldo Designer Jewelry Inc............. F 812 972-7220
New Albany *(G-12808)*

Surplus Store and Exchange................ F 765 447-0200
Lafayette *(G-10707)*

JEWELRY: Precious Metal

Argentum Jewelry Inc....................... G 812 336-3100
Bloomington *(G-784)*

Ashleys Jewelry By Design Ltd............ G 219 926-9039
Chesterton *(G-1904)*

Clarity Industry Co LLC..................... G 678 389-5006
Indianapolis *(G-7817)*

Collegiate Pride Inc........................ G 260 726-7818
Portland *(G-13932)*

Crystal Source.............................. G 812 988-7009
Nashville *(G-12669)*

David Gonzales............................. G 765 284-6960
Muncie *(G-12373)*

Ed Stump Assembly Inc.................... G 574 291-0058
South Bend *(G-15011)*

Edward E Petri Company.................... G 317 636-5007
Indianapolis *(G-8057)*

G Thrapp Jewelers Inc...................... G 317 255-5555
Indianapolis *(G-8254)*

Ginas Creative Jewelry Inc................. G 317 272-0032
Avon *(G-521)*

Gold N Gems............................... G 317 895-6002
Indianapolis *(G-8296)*

Golden Lion Inc............................ G 765 446-9557
Lafayette *(G-10592)*

PRODUCT SECTION
LABORATORIES: Noncommercial Research

Goldstone Jewelry Inc................................ G 765 742-1975
West Lafayette *(G-16585)*

Herff Jones Co Indiana - Inc.................... E 317 297-3740
Indianapolis *(G-8385)*

Intelliquote.. G 530 669-6840
Roanoke *(G-14270)*

Interntnal Damnd Gold Exch Ltd............. G 317 872-6666
Indianapolis *(G-8583)*

Jack Forney.. G 812 334-1259
Bloomington *(G-895)*

Janette Walker.. G 219 937-9160
Hammond *(G-6961)*

Jewelers Boutique Inc............................... G 317 788-7679
Indianapolis *(G-8624)*

Kensington Watch Services...................... G 219 306-5499
Crown Point *(G-2708)*

Little Super Findings................................. G 812 430-3353
Evansville *(G-4173)*

Mark Edward Hails..................................... G 812 437-1030
Evansville *(G-4189)*

O C Tanner Company................................ G 317 575-8553
Indianapolis *(G-9038)*

P&E Enterprises... G 219 226-9524
Crown Point *(G-2729)*

Peter Franklin Jewelers Inc...................... G 260 749-4315
New Haven *(G-12913)*

Ralph Privoznik Jewelry Art..................... G 765 742-4904
Lafayette *(G-10676)*

Ronaldo Designer Jewelry Inc................. F 812 972-7220
New Albany *(G-12808)*

Stall & Kessler Inc..................................... G 765 742-1259
Lafayette *(G-10698)*

Terri Logan Studios................................... G 765 966-7876
Richmond *(G-14215)*

Williams Jewelers Inc............................... G 812 475-1705
Evansville *(G-4387)*

JIGS & FIXTURES

City Pattern and Foundry Company Inc. D 574 273-3000
Granger *(G-6339)*

CL Tech Inc... G 812 526-0995
Edinburgh *(G-3072)*

H & P Tool Co Inc....................................... E 765 962-4504
Richmond *(G-14129)*

Jus Rite Engineering Inc........................... E 574 522-9600
Elkhart *(G-3438)*

K C Machine Inc... G 574 293-1822
Elkhart *(G-3442)*

Kain Tool Inc... G 260 829-6569
Orland *(G-13366)*

Merit Tool & Manufacturing Inc................ F 765 396-9566
Eaton *(G-3063)*

Nixon Tool Company Inc............................ E 765 966-6608
Richmond *(G-14175)*

Reber Machine & Tool Co Inc................... E 765 288-0297
Muncie *(G-12485)*

Taurus Tech & Engrg LLC......................... E 765 282-2090
Muncie *(G-12498)*

JOB PRINTING & NEWSPAPER PUBLISHING COMBINED

Courier Printing Co Allen Cnty................. G 260 627-2728
Grabill *(G-6293)*

Dubois-Spncer Cunties Pubg Inc............. F 812 367-2041
Ferdinand *(G-4430)*

Exchange Publishing Corp....................... F 574 831-2138
New Paris *(G-12952)*

Indiana News Media LLC........................... G 812 703-2025
Columbus *(G-2323)*

Indiana News Media LLC........................... G 812 546-4940
Hope *(G-7228)*

Midcountry Media Inc................................ D 765 345-5133
Knightstown *(G-10200)*

News-Gazette.. F 765 584-4501
Winchester *(G-16895)*

OBannon Publishing Company................ E 812 738-4552
Corydon *(G-2508)*

Posey County News................................... G 812 682-3950
New Harmony *(G-12888)*

Whitewater Publications Inc..................... F 765 647-4221
Brookville *(G-1341)*

JOB TRAINING SVCS

Cardinal Services Inc Indiana.................. D 574 267-3823
Warsaw *(G-16333)*

Rauch Inc... E 812 945-4063
New Albany *(G-12803)*

JOISTS: Long-Span Series, Open Web Steel

New Millennium Bldg Systems LLC......... C 260 868-6000
Butler *(G-1473)*

New Millennium Bldg Systems LLC......... G 260 969-3500
Fort Wayne *(G-5267)*

KILNS & FURNACES: Ceramic

Hoosier Metal Polish Inc........................... F 219 474-6011
Kentland *(G-10160)*

KITCHEN CABINETS WHOLESALERS

Countertop Manufacturing Inc.................. E 765 966-4969
Richmond *(G-14111)*

Country Woodshop LLC............................ E 574 642-3681
Goshen *(G-6117)*

Elko Inc.. F 812 473-8400
Evansville *(G-4030)*

Kountry Wood Products LLC.................... C 574 773-5673
Nappanee *(G-12618)*

Sims-Lohman Inc.. G 317 467-0710
Greenfield *(G-6553)*

Superior Laminating Inc............................ G 574 361-7266
Goshen *(G-6261)*

KITCHEN UTENSILS: Food Handling & Processing Prdts, Wood

Anndys Paradise LLC................................. G 317 258-7531
Indianapolis *(G-7519)*

Deonta Walker... G 317 970-3586
Indianapolis *(G-7965)*

Rpf Inc.. G 317 727-6386
Boggstown *(G-1076)*

KITCHENWARE STORES

Woodland Manufacturing & Sup.............. F 317 271-2266
Avon *(G-557)*

KITCHENWARE: Plastic

Styles Kitchen LLC..................................... G 765 405-6875
Lafayette *(G-10701)*

KNIVES: Agricultural Or indl

Illiana Grinding Machining Inc................. G 219 306-0253
East Chicago *(G-3019)*

LABELS: Cotton, Printed

Graphic22 Inc.. G 219 921-5409
Chesterton *(G-1930)*

Tt2 LLC... G 260 438-4575
Fort Wayne *(G-5511)*

LABELS: Paper, Made From Purchased Materials

Associated Label Inc.................................. G 812 877-3682
Terre Haute *(G-15546)*

Discount Labels LLC.................................. A 812 945-2617
New Albany *(G-12720)*

Hi-Tech Label Inc....................................... F 765 659-1800
Frankfort *(G-5673)*

Label Tech Inc... E 765 747-1234
Muncie *(G-12436)*

Patriot Label Inc... G 812 877-1611
Terre Haute *(G-15658)*

LABORATORIES, TESTING: Food

Rapid View LLC... G 574 224-3373
Rochester *(G-14315)*

LABORATORIES, TESTING: Pollution

Mold Removers LLC................................... G 317 846-0977
Indianapolis *(G-8946)*

LABORATORIES, TESTING: Product Testing

Moseley Laboratories Inc.......................... F 317 866-8460
Greenfield *(G-6533)*

LABORATORIES, TESTING: Product Testing, Safety/Performance

Cortex Safety Technologies LLC............. G 317 414-5607
Carmel *(G-1598)*

Thermphyscal Prpts RES Lab Inc............ G 765 463-1581
West Lafayette *(G-16637)*

LABORATORIES, TESTING: Radiation

Radon Environmental Inc.......................... G 317 843-0804
Elkhart *(G-3637)*

LABORATORIES: Biological

Toralgen Inc... G 812 820-3374
Indianapolis *(G-9622)*

LABORATORIES: Biotechnology

Catalent Indiana LLC................................. B 812 355-6746
Bloomington *(G-824)*

MBX Biosciences Inc................................. E 317 659-0200
Carmel *(G-1695)*

LABORATORIES: Commercial Nonphysical Research

Enviri Corporation...................................... G 317 983-5353
Pittsboro *(G-13645)*

SealCorpUSA Inc.. D 866 868-0791
Evansville *(G-4303)*

LABORATORIES: Dental, Crown & Bridge Production

Dental Professional Laboratory............... E 219 769-6225
Merrillville *(G-11505)*

National Dentex LLC.................................. C 317 849-5143
Indianapolis *(G-8987)*

Somer Inc... E 317 873-1111
Zionsville *(G-17051)*

LABORATORIES: Electronic Research

Pynco Inc... E 812 275-0900
Bedford *(G-661)*

Silicis Technologies Inc............................. E 317 896-5044
Westfield *(G-16728)*

LABORATORIES: Noncommercial Research

Center For The Study Knwldge D............ G 812 361-4424
Bloomington *(G-827)*

Employee Codes: A=Over 500 employees, B=251-500
C=101-250, D=51-100, E=20-50, F=10-19, G=1-9

LABORATORIES: Physical Research, Commercial

Cyberia Ltd .... G 317 721-2582
  Indianapolis *(G-7938)*

LABORATORIES: Physical Research, Commercial

Ampacet Corporation .... E 812 466-9828
  Terre Haute *(G-15543)*
Bangs Laboratories Inc .... F 317 570-7020
  Fishers *(G-4470)*
Eli Lilly International Corp .... F 317 276-2000
  Indianapolis *(G-8091)*
Faztech LLC .... G 812 327-0926
  Bloomington *(G-864)*
IBC Materials & Tech LLC .... E 765 481-2900
  Lebanon *(G-10899)*
Kp Pharmaceutical Tech Inc .... E 812 330-8121
  Bloomington *(G-903)*
Pfizer Inc .... D 212 733-2323
  Terre Haute *(G-15660)*
Polymod Technologies Inc .... F 260 436-1322
  Fort Wayne *(G-5325)*

LABORATORIES: Testing

Acterna LLC .... E 317 788-9351
  Indianapolis *(G-7425)*
Bundoo Laboratories LLC .... G 317 978-5574
  Beech Grove *(G-687)*
Divsys Intl - Icape LLC .... E 317 405-9427
  Indianapolis *(G-7988)*
Eminence Hlth Care Stffing AGC .... G 866 350-6400
  South Bend *(G-15013)*
Flynn Welding & Inspection LLC .... G 812 327-7437
  Solsberry *(G-14925)*
Indiana Research Institute .... G 812 378-4221
  Columbus *(G-2326)*
Integrated Instrument Svcs Inc .... F 317 248-1958
  Indianapolis *(G-8568)*
Northern Indiana Ordnance Co .... G 574 289-5938
  South Bend *(G-15173)*
Odyssian Technology LLC .... G 574 257-7555
  South Bend *(G-15176)*
Mira Vista Diagnostics LLC .... E 317 856-2681
  Indianapolis *(G-8932)*
Sober Scientific LLC .... G 765 465-9803
  Sheridan *(G-14829)*

LABORATORY APPARATUS & FURNITURE

Current Technologies Inc .... F 765 364-0490
  Crawfordsville *(G-2561)*
Envigo Rms Inc .... G 317 806-6080
  Greenfield *(G-6500)*
Envigo Rms Inc .... G 317 806-6060
  Greenfield *(G-6501)*
Envigo Rms Inc .... C 317 806-6080
  Indianapolis *(G-8125)*
Fast Track Technologies LLC .... F 317 229-6080
  Noblesville *(G-13075)*
Harry J Kloeppel & Associates .... G 317 578-1300
  Indianapolis *(G-8368)*
I2r .... G 812 235-6167
  Terre Haute *(G-15612)*
Poly-Wood LLC .... G 877 457-3284
  Syracuse *(G-15473)*
Poly-Wood LLC .... D 574 457-3284
  Syracuse *(G-15474)*
Templeton Coal Company Inc .... C 812 232-7037
  Terre Haute *(G-15726)*

LABORATORY APPARATUS, EXC HEATING & MEASURING

Cbf Forensics LLC .... G 708 383-8320
  Hobart *(G-7180)*
Leco Corporation .... G 574 288-9017
  South Bend *(G-15122)*

LABORATORY APPARATUS: Pipettes, Hemocytometer

Cook Group Incorporated .... F 812 339-2235
  Bloomington *(G-838)*

LABORATORY CHEMICALS: Organic

Beckman Coulter Inc .... D 317 471-8029
  Indianapolis *(G-7606)*

LABORATORY EQPT, EXC MEDICAL: Wholesalers

Williams Distribution LLC .... G 317 749-0006
  Indianapolis *(G-9767)*

LABORATORY EQPT: Chemical

Beckman Coulter Inc .... D 317 471-8029
  Indianapolis *(G-7606)*

LABORATORY EQPT: Clinical Instruments Exc Medical

Care Test Lab LLC .... G 574 326-1082
  Indianapolis *(G-7742)*

LABORATORY EQPT: Incubators

Ameribrace Orthopedic LLC .... G 260 704-6027
  Fort Wayne *(G-4750)*

LABORATORY EQPT: Sterilizers

Merss Corporation .... G 317 632-7299
  Indianapolis *(G-8879)*

LADDERS: Metal

Briter Products Inc .... G 574 386-8167
  South Bend *(G-14962)*
L & W Engineering Inc .... C 574 825-5351
  Middlebury *(G-11730)*
Miller Mfg Corp .... E 574 773-4136
  Nappanee *(G-12626)*

LADDERS: Permanent Installation, Metal

Evans Metal Products Co Inc .... F 574 264-2166
  Elkhart *(G-3335)*

LAMINATED PLASTICS: Plate, Sheet, Rod & Tubes

Ameri-Kart Corp .... D 225 642-7874
  Bristol *(G-1243)*
Applied Composites Engrg Inc .... E 317 243-4225
  Indianapolis *(G-7533)*
Berry Global Group Inc .... A 812 424-2904
  Evansville *(G-3921)*
Elko Inc .... F 812 473-8400
  Evansville *(G-4030)*
Envalior Engineering Materials Inc .... C 800 333-4237
  Evansville *(G-4039)*
Envalior Engineering Mtls Inc .... G 812 435-7500
  Evansville *(G-4041)*
Experimental Nylon Products .... E 574 674-8747
  Osceola *(G-13391)*
F Robert Gardner Co Inc .... G 317 634-2333
  Indianapolis *(G-8161)*
General Fabricators Inc .... G 317 787-9354
  Indianapolis *(G-8271)*
Hancor Inc .... E 812 443-2080
  Brazil *(G-1144)*

Hartson-Kennedy Cabinet Top Co .... B 765 668-8144
  Marion *(G-11291)*
Heywood Williams Inc .... G 574 295-8400
  Elkhart *(G-3405)*
Jaeger-Ntek Sling Slutions Inc .... D 219 324-1111
  La Porte *(G-10431)*
Lockerbie Square Cab Co Inc .... G 317 635-1134
  Indianapolis *(G-8775)*
Miller Waste Mills Inc .... G 507 454-6900
  Indianapolis *(G-8924)*
Omni Plastics LLC .... D 812 422-0888
  Evansville *(G-4227)*
Positron Corporation .... E 574 295-8777
  Elkhart *(G-3610)*
Sabic Innovative Plas US LLC .... D 812 372-0197
  Columbus *(G-2388)*
Sabin Corporation .... C 812 323-4500
  Bloomington *(G-965)*
Skips Bumper Repair .... G 773 289-2255
  Gary *(G-6010)*
Sonoco Products Company .... D 812 526-5511
  Edinburgh *(G-3105)*
Thrust Industries Inc .... F 812 437-3643
  Evansville *(G-4344)*
Triangle Rubber Co LLC .... C 574 533-3118
  Goshen *(G-6272)*

LAMINATING MATERIALS

Specialty Adhesive Film Co .... E 812 926-0156
  Aurora *(G-455)*

LAMINATING SVCS

Genesis Products LLC .... C 574 266-8293
  Elkhart *(G-3373)*
Genesis Products LLC .... C 877 266-8292
  Goshen *(G-6146)*
Jknk Ventures Inc .... E 812 246-0900
  Sellersburg *(G-14603)*
Lamco Finishers Inc .... E 317 471-1010
  Indianapolis *(G-8717)*
Patrick Industries Inc .... G 574 293-1521
  Elkhart *(G-3589)*

LAMP & LIGHT BULBS & TUBES

Acuity Brands Lighting Inc .... B 765 362-1837
  Crawfordsville *(G-2543)*
Lomont Holdings Co Inc .... E 800 545-9023
  Angola *(G-273)*
Pent Plastics Inc .... C 260 897-3775
  Kendallville *(G-10142)*
Tap-A-Lite Inc .... E 219 932-8067
  Hammond *(G-7018)*
Valeo Ltg Systems N Amer LLC .... A 812 523-5200
  Seymour *(G-14700)*

LAMP BULBS & TUBES, ELECTRIC: For Specialized Applications

Lampliter .... G 317 827-0250
  Indianapolis *(G-8719)*

LAMP BULBS & TUBES, ELECTRIC: Light, Complete

6605 E State LLC .... G 260 433-7007
  Fort Wayne *(G-4714)*
Energy Saver Lights Inc .... F 202 544-7868
  Indianapolis *(G-8118)*

LAMP BULBS & TUBES/PARTS, ELECTRIC: Generalized Applications

PRODUCT SECTION

LEGAL OFFICES & SVCS

International Lighting LLC............F.....219 989-0060
 Hammond *(G-6958)*

LAMP SHADES: Glass

Glass City Inc............G.....219 887-2100
 Gary *(G-5943)*
Moss L Glass Co Inc............F.....765 642-4946
 Indianapolis *(G-8957)*
Oldcastle Buildingenvelope Inc............D.....317 876-1155
 Indianapolis *(G-9044)*
Otter Creek Christian Church............G.....812 446-5300
 Brazil *(G-1159)*
Pool Shop............G.....812 446-0026
 Brazil *(G-1162)*

LAND SUBDIVIDERS & DEVELOPERS: Commercial

R E Casebeer & Sons Inc............G.....812 829-3284
 Spencer *(G-15359)*
Whiteco Industries Inc............A.....219 769-6601
 Merrillville *(G-11572)*

LASER SYSTEMS & EQPT

Accuracy Laser Fabrication LLC............G.....812 322-6431
 Bedford *(G-616)*
Automated Laser Corporation............G.....260 637-4140
 Fort Wayne *(G-4781)*
Directed Photonics Inc............G.....317 877-3142
 Noblesville *(G-13072)*
Fairway Laser Systems Inc............G.....219 462-6892
 Valparaiso *(G-15946)*
Supernova International Inc............G.....317 969-8246
 Indianapolis *(G-9531)*
X-Treme Lazer Tag............G.....812 238-8412
 Terre Haute *(G-15749)*

LASERS: Welding, Drilling & Cutting Eqpt

Advanced Metal Etching Inc............E.....260 894-4189
 Ligonier *(G-11003)*
Troyer Brothers Inc............E.....260 565-2244
 Bluffton *(G-1064)*

LAUNDRY EQPT: Commercial

Hansford Prevent LLC............G.....317 985-2346
 Indianapolis *(G-8354)*
Randolph Carpet-Tile Cleaning............G.....317 401-2300
 Cicero *(G-2000)*
Security Integrated Corp............G.....219 942-9666
 Munster *(G-12563)*

LAUNDRY EQPT: Household

Accra-Pac Inc............D.....574 295-0000
 Elkhart *(G-3151)*
Accra-Pac Inc............D.....574 295-0000
 Elkhart *(G-3150)*

LAWN & GARDEN EQPT

Alm Services Inc............G.....765 288-6624
 Muncie *(G-12340)*
Deer Country Equipment LLC............E.....812 522-1922
 Seymour *(G-14646)*
Discount Power Equipment............G.....765 642-0040
 Anderson *(G-104)*
Everything Else LLC............G.....574 350-7383
 Elkhart *(G-3336)*
Forest Commodities Inc............G.....765 349-3291
 Martinsville *(G-11394)*
Great States Corp............G.....765 288-6624
 Muncie *(G-12406)*
Husqvrna Cnsmr Otdr Prod NA............C.....812 883-3575
 Salem *(G-14483)*

Mide Products............G.....574 326-3060
 Elkhart *(G-3538)*
Midwest Equipment Mfg Inc............F.....765 436-2496
 Thorntown *(G-15753)*
Mtd Products Inc............F.....317 986-2042
 Indianapolis *(G-8970)*
Novae Corp............F.....260 982-7075
 North Manchester *(G-13245)*
Rich Manufacturing Inc............G.....765 436-2744
 Lebanon *(G-10937)*
Talon Terra LLC............G.....219 393-1400
 La Porte *(G-10487)*
Textron Outdoor Power Eqp Inc............G.....704 504-6600
 Coatesville *(G-2110)*
Wheel Horse Sales & Service............G.....574 272-4242
 South Bend *(G-15305)*
Wright Implement I LLC............G.....812 522-1922
 Seymour *(G-14707)*

LAWN & GARDEN EQPT: Blowers & Vacuums

Palmor Products Inc............E.....800 872-2822
 Lebanon *(G-10928)*

LAWN & GARDEN EQPT: Grass Catchers, Lawn Mower

Bane-Welker Equipment LLC............F.....812 234-2627
 Terre Haute *(G-15550)*

LAWN & GARDEN EQPT: Lawnmowers, Residential, Hand Or Power

Rochester Metal Products Corp............E.....765 288-6624
 Muncie *(G-12490)*

LAWN & GARDEN EQPT: Tractors & Eqpt

Egenolf Enterprise Inc............F.....317 501-5069
 Indianapolis *(G-8060)*
Lafayette Marketing Inc............F.....765 474-5374
 West Lafayette *(G-16600)*
Peters Enterprises............G.....260 493-6435
 New Haven *(G-12914)*

LEAD

Eco-Bat America LLC............C.....317 247-1303
 Indianapolis *(G-8048)*

LEAD PENCILS & ART GOODS

The Killion Corporation............D.....317 271-4536
 Indianapolis *(G-9589)*

LEASING & RENTAL: Construction & Mining Eqpt

GI Properties Inc............G.....219 763-1177
 Portage *(G-13868)*
Hampton Equipment LLC............G.....260 740-8704
 Fort Wayne *(G-5049)*
Macallister Machinery Co Inc............C.....260 483-6469
 Fort Wayne *(G-5195)*
Macallister Machinery Co Inc............F.....765 966-0759
 Richmond *(G-14157)*
Pittman Mine Service LLC............G.....812 847-2340
 Linton *(G-11042)*
Poseidon LLC............C.....260 422-8767
 Berne *(G-722)*
Wyatt Farm Center Inc............G.....574 354-2998
 Nappanee *(G-12655)*

LEASING & RENTAL: Medical Machinery & Eqpt

Hill-Rom Inc............A.....812 934-7777
 Batesville *(G-589)*
Williams Bros Hlth Care Phrm I............E.....812 335-0000
 Bloomington *(G-1012)*
Williams Bros Hlth Care Phrm I............C.....812 254-2497
 Washington *(G-16513)*

LEASING & RENTAL: Trucks, Without Drivers

Carmel Welding and Sup Co Inc............E.....317 846-3493
 Carmel *(G-1582)*
Imel John............G.....317 873-8764
 Zionsville *(G-17017)*
Landis Equipment & Tool Rental............G.....812 847-2582
 Linton *(G-11037)*
Mid-State Truck Equipment Inc............E.....317 849-4903
 Fishers *(G-4566)*
Stout Plastic Weld............F.....219 926-7622
 Chesterton *(G-1959)*
Upland Tire & Service Ctr Inc............G.....765 998-0871
 Upland *(G-15884)*

LEASING: Passenger Car

Ford Motor Company............F.....901 368-8821
 Plainfield *(G-13680)*

LEATHER GOODS: Garments

Hilltop Leather............G.....317 508-3404
 Martinsville *(G-11401)*

LEATHER GOODS: Holsters

Bear Arms Holsters............G.....260 310-2376
 Fort Wayne *(G-4790)*
Daltech Enterprises Inc............G.....260 527-4590
 Fremont *(G-5818)*
Fast Holster LLC............G.....317 727-5243
 Carmel *(G-1633)*

LEATHER GOODS: Personal

Long Leather Works LLC............G.....812 336-5309
 Bloomington *(G-913)*
Moses Leathers............G.....260 203-8799
 Fort Wayne *(G-5245)*

LEATHER GOODS: Safety Belts

Superior Concepts Indus LLC............F.....765 628-2956
 Greentown *(G-6649)*

LEATHER GOODS: Straps

David W Imhoff............G.....574 862-4375
 Goshen *(G-6119)*
L M Products Inc............E.....765 643-3802
 Anderson *(G-145)*

LEATHER TANNING & FINISHING

Color Glo............G.....812 926-2639
 Aurora *(G-441)*
Trail Creek Leather............G.....219 874-6702
 Trail Creek *(G-15842)*

LEATHER: Accessory Prdts

Midwest Leather LLC............G.....435 257-7880
 Grabill *(G-6314)*
Vera Bradley Inc............B.....877 708-8372
 Roanoke *(G-14272)*

LEGAL & TAX SVCS

Mellon Tax Service............G.....219 947-1660
 Hobart *(G-7201)*

LEGAL OFFICES & SVCS

Eaton Corporation............G.....317 704-2520
 Indianapolis *(G-8043)*

LEGAL OFFICES & SVCS

Enterprise MGT Solutions LLC............ G..... 219 545-8544
 Merrillville (G-11513)

LICENSE TAGS: Automobile, Stamped Metal

Irwin Hodson Group Indiana LLC........ G..... 260 482-8052
 Fort Wayne (G-5121)

LIFE SAVING & SURVIVAL EQPT REPAIR SVCS, NONMEDICAL

Recovery Force LLC........................... G..... 866 604-6458
 Fishers (G-4591)

LIFESAVING & SURVIVAL EQPT, EXC MEDICAL, WHOLESALE

Speedhook Specialists Inc................. G..... 219 378-6369
 Beverly Shores (G-732)
Wyatt Survival Supply LLC................. G..... 765 318-2872
 Morgantown (G-12266)

LIGHTING EQPT: Flashlights

Cloud Defensive LLC........................ G..... 813 492-5683
 Chandler (G-1859)
Cloud Defensive LLC........................ E..... 812 646-1762
 Evansville (G-3973)
Orka Technologies LLC..................... G..... 812 378-9842
 Columbus (G-2367)

LIGHTING EQPT: Motor Vehicle, Headlights

Dajac Inc.. G..... 317 608-0500
 Sheridan (G-14821)
Lund International Holding Co............ E..... 765 742-7200
 Lafayette (G-10641)

LIGHTING EQPT: Motor Vehicle, NEC

J J Lites... G..... 765 966-3252
 Richmond (G-14144)

LIGHTING FIXTURES WHOLESALERS

A Homestead Shoppe Inc................. E..... 574 784-2307
 Lapaz (G-10814)
Amerlight LLC.................................. F..... 812 602-3452
 Evansville (G-3889)
Vista Manufacturing Inc.................... E..... 574 264-0711
 Elkhart (G-3771)

LIGHTING FIXTURES, NEC

B&D Lighting LLC............................. G..... 317 414-8056
 Indianapolis (G-7586)
Badger Daylighting Corp................... G..... 219 762-9177
 Portage (G-13848)
Blackbird.. G..... 812 944-0799
 New Albany (G-12702)
Brighter Design Inc.......................... G..... 765 447-9494
 Lafayette (G-10544)
Circle City Lighting Inc..................... G..... 317 439-0824
 Noblesville (G-13060)
Festive Lights LLC............................ G..... 317 998-0627
 Indianapolis (G-8181)
Gmp Holdings LLC........................... G..... 317 353-6580
 Indianapolis (G-8294)
Ikio Led Lighting LLC........................ A..... 765 414-0835
 Indianapolis (G-8458)
Indiana Emergency Lighting LLC........ G..... 260 463-1277
 Marion (G-11294)
Ledgedge Lighting Inc..................... G..... 805 383-8493
 Angola (G-272)
Lumen Cache Inc............................. F..... 317 222-1314
 Indianapolis (G-8796)
Lunarglo LLC................................... G..... 574 294-2624
 Elkhart (G-3503)

Mid-America Sound Corporation........ F..... 317 947-9880
 Greenfield (G-6528)
Nu Led Lighting............................... G..... 317 989-7352
 Greenwood (G-6747)
Spectrum Brands Inc....................... E..... 317 773-6627
 Noblesville (G-13179)
Spotlight On Drama LLC................... G..... 765 643-7170
 Anderson (G-199)
Touchplate Technologies Inc............. E..... 260 426-1565
 Fort Wayne (G-5497)
Vista Worldwide LLC........................ G..... 574 264-0711
 Elkhart (G-3772)

LIGHTING FIXTURES: Decorative Area

Around Campus LLC......................... G..... 574 360-6571
 South Bend (G-14949)
Lawncreations LLC........................... G..... 574 536-1546
 Millersburg (G-11815)

LIGHTING FIXTURES: Fluorescent, Commercial

Lomont Holdings Co Inc................... E..... 800 545-9023
 Angola (G-273)
Professional Grade Svcs LLC............. G..... 317 688-8898
 Indianapolis (G-9222)

LIGHTING FIXTURES: Indl & Commercial

55 West LLC................................... F
 Indianapolis (G-7392)
Acuity Brands Inc............................ G..... 765 362-1837
 Crawfordsville (G-2542)
Acuity Brands Lighting Inc................ B..... 765 362-1837
 Crawfordsville (G-2543)
Advance Leds LLC........................... G..... 844 815-8898
 Evansville (G-3874)
Amerlight LLC................................. F..... 812 602-3452
 Evansville (G-3889)
Craft Metal Products Inc................... G..... 317 545-3252
 Indianapolis (G-7897)
Dream Lighting Inc.......................... F..... 574 206-4888
 Elkhart (G-3303)
Eco Parking Technologies LLC........... F..... 866 897-1234
 Indianapolis (G-8047)
Energy Harness Corporation.............. G..... 239 246-1958
 Carmel (G-1622)
Energy Harness Corporation.............. G..... 317 999-5561
 Indianapolis (G-8116)
Green Illuminating Systems Inc......... G..... 317 869-7430
 Noblesville (G-13088)
Martin Professional Inc..................... G..... 574 294-8000
 Elkhart (G-3516)
Metalite Corporation........................ E..... 812 944-6600
 New Albany (G-12776)
Rpg Energy Group Inc...................... F..... 317 614-0054
 Indianapolis (G-9342)
Semcor Inc..................................... E..... 219 362-0222
 La Porte (G-10479)
Source Products Inc......................... G..... 260 424-0864
 Columbia City (G-2200)
Specified Ltg Systems Ind Inc........... F..... 317 577-8100
 Indianapolis (G-9472)
Thomas Custom Lighting.................. G..... 765 378-5472
 Chesterfield (G-1899)
Ward Industries Inc......................... F..... 574 825-2548
 Middlebury (G-11756)

LIGHTING FIXTURES: Motor Vehicle

David Murray.................................. G..... 765 766-5229
 Mooreland (G-12184)
Grote Industries Inc......................... A..... 812 273-2121
 Madison (G-11222)

Grote Industries LLC........................ A..... 812 265-8273
 Madison (G-11223)
North American Lighting Inc.............. B..... 812 983-2663
 Elberfeld (G-3116)
Roadworks Maufacturing................... G..... 765 742-7200
 West Lafayette (G-16625)
Tcb Enterprises LLC......................... F..... 574 522-3971
 Middlebury (G-11754)
Techshot Lighting LLC...................... G..... 812 923-9591
 Floyds Knobs (G-4695)
Yellow Cat LLC................................. G..... 913 213-4570
 Bloomington (G-1018)

LIGHTING FIXTURES: Public

Kc Innovations LLC.......................... F..... 888 290-8920
 Loogootee (G-11141)

LIGHTING MAINTENANCE SVC

Ikio Led Lighting LLC........................ A..... 765 414-0835
 Indianapolis (G-8458)
Loves Travel Stops........................... F..... 574 935-4103
 Plymouth (G-13793)

LIME

Calcar Quarries Incorporated............. F..... 812 723-2109
 Paoli (G-13491)
Dotted Lime Resale LLC.................... G..... 317 908-3905
 Westfield (G-16686)
Harris Stone Service Inc.................... F..... 765 522-6241
 Bainbridge (G-563)
Heidelberg Mtls Mdwest Agg Inc........ G..... 812 889-2120
 Lexington (G-10977)
Jolene D Pavey............................... G..... 765 473-6171
 Peru (G-13588)
Mulzer Crushed Stone Inc................. E..... 812 365-2145
 English (G-3844)
Rogers Group Inc............................ D..... 219 474-5125
 Kentland (G-10163)
Rogers Group Inc............................ G..... 765 342-6898
 Martinsville (G-11424)
Rogers Group Inc............................ D..... 812 849-3530
 Mitchell (G-12047)
Rogers Group Inc............................ E..... 812 882-3640
 Vincennes (G-16150)
Rush County Stone Co Inc................ G..... 765 629-2211
 Milroy (G-11830)

LIMESTONE: Crushed & Broken

Aggrock Quarries Inc....................... G..... 812 246-2582
 Charlestown (G-1870)
Barrett Paving Materials Inc.............. G..... 765 935-3060
 Richmond (G-14090)
Bedford Limestone Suppliers............. F..... 812 279-9120
 Bedford (G-623)
Bens Quarry LLC............................. G..... 812 824-3730
 Springville (G-15382)
Brummett Enterprises LLC................ G..... 812 325-6993
 Bloomington (G-817)
Carmeuse Lime Inc.......................... D..... 219 949-1450
 Gary (G-5912)
Cave Quarries Inc............................ F..... 812 936-7743
 Paoli (G-13492)
Francesville Vulcan Materials............. G..... 219 567-9155
 Francesville (G-5640)
Global Stone Portage LLC................. F..... 219 787-9190
 Portage (G-13869)
Handson.. F..... 812 246-4481
 Sellersburg (G-14595)
Hanson Aggregates Wrp Inc.............. E..... 502 244-7550
 Sellersburg (G-14596)
Harris Stone Service Inc.................... F..... 765 522-6241
 Bainbridge (G-563)

PRODUCT SECTION

Heidelberg Mtls Mdwest Agg Inc............ F 765 653-1956
  Greencastle *(G-6411)*

Heidelberg Mtls Mdwest Agg Inc............ G 812 246-1942
  Sellersburg *(G-14597)*

Iowa Limestone Company...................... F 317 981-7919
  Cloverdale *(G-2087)*

Kellers Limestone Service Inc................. G 219 326-1688
  La Porte *(G-10432)*

LLC Ward Stone..................................... E 812 587-0272
  Flat Rock *(G-4654)*

Marietta Martin Materials Inc.................. G 317 789-4020
  Indianapolis *(G-8834)*

Marietta Martin Materials Inc.................. F 765 459-3194
  Kokomo *(G-10304)*

Marietta Martin Materials Inc.................. G 317 831-7391
  Martinsville *(G-11411)*

Marietta Martin Materials Inc.................. F 317 776-4460
  Noblesville *(G-13130)*

Martin Marietta Materials Inc.................. G 317 846-8540
  Carmel *(G-1692)*

Martin Marietta Materials Inc.................. F 317 573-4460
  Carmel *(G-1693)*

Martin Marietta Materials Inc.................. F 317 846-5942
  Carmel *(G-1694)*

Martin Marietta Materials Inc.................. G 317 244-4460
  Indianapolis *(G-8841)*

Meshberger Brothers Stone C................. D 260 334-5311
  Bluffton *(G-1041)*

Mulzer Crushed Stone Inc....................... E 812 256-3346
  Charlestown *(G-1886)*

Mulzer Crushed Stone Inc....................... G 812 937-2442
  Dale *(G-2791)*

Mulzer Crushed Stone Inc....................... E 812 739-4777
  Leavenworth *(G-10871)*

Mulzer Crushed Stone Inc....................... E 812 732-1002
  Mauckport *(G-11440)*

Mulzer Crushed Stone Inc....................... G 812 838-3472
  Mount Vernon *(G-12312)*

Mulzer Crushed Stone Inc....................... G 812 354-9650
  Petersburg *(G-13619)*

Mulzer Crushed Stone Inc....................... E 812 547-7921
  Tell City *(G-15513)*

Nalc LLC.. G 502 548-9590
  Cloverdale *(G-2091)*

New Point Stone Co Inc......................... G 812 852-4225
  Batesville *(G-598)*

New Point Stone Co Inc......................... G 765 698-2227
  Laurel *(G-10825)*

New Point Stone Co Inc......................... F 812 663-2021
  Greensburg *(G-6622)*

Paul H Rohe Company Inc..................... E 812 926-1471
  Aurora *(G-451)*

Robertson Crushed Stone Inc................. E 812 633-4881
  Milltown *(G-11820)*

Rogers Group Inc.................................. D 812 333-8560
  Bloomington *(G-961)*

Stone Quary.. E 765 473-5578
  Peru *(G-13603)*

U S Aggregates Inc................................ E 765 564-2282
  Delphi *(G-2910)*

U S Aggregates Inc................................ G 765 436-7665
  Thorntown *(G-15757)*

LIMESTONE: Cut & Shaped

3d Stone Purchaser Inc.......................... F 812 824-5805
  Bloomington *(G-767)*

Accent Limestone & Carving Inc............. G 812 876-7040
  Bloomington *(G-772)*

Bedford Stonecrafters Inc...................... G 812 275-2646
  Bedford *(G-625)*

Bybee Stone Company Inc..................... D 812 876-2215
  Ellettsville *(G-3801)*

Indiana Cut Stone Inc............................ F 812 275-0264
  Bedford *(G-643)*

Indiana Lmstone Acqisition LLC............. D 812 275-5556
  Bedford *(G-645)*

Ionic Cut Stone Incorporated................. G 812 829-3416
  Spencer *(G-15352)*

Justin Blackwell.................................... F 812 834-6350
  Norman *(G-13203)*

LIMESTONE: Dimension

B G Hoadley Quarries Inc....................... E 812 332-1447
  Bloomington *(G-790)*

Independent Limestone Co LLC.............. E 812 824-4951
  Bloomington *(G-887)*

Indiana Lmstone Acqisition LLC............. D 812 275-5556
  Bedford *(G-645)*

Indiana Lmstone Acqisition LLC............. E 812 275-3341
  Bloomington *(G-888)*

Indiana Stone Works............................. G 812 279-0448
  Bedford *(G-648)*

Reed Quarries Inc.................................. F 812 332-2771
  Bloomington *(G-954)*

Rush County Stone Co Inc..................... G 765 629-2211
  Milroy *(G-11830)*

Victor Oolitic Stone Company................ C 812 275-3341
  Oolitic *(G-13360)*

LIMESTONE: Ground

3d Stone Inc... E 812 824-5805
  Bloomington *(G-766)*

Big Creek LLC....................................... F 812 876-0835
  Gosport *(G-6283)*

Calcar Quarries Incorporated................. F 812 723-2109
  Paoli *(G-13491)*

Heidelberg Mtls Mdwest Agg Inc............ G 765 653-7205
  Cloverdale *(G-2086)*

Heidelberg Mtls Mdwest Agg Inc............ G 812 889-2120
  Lexington *(G-10977)*

Heidelberg Mtls Mdwest Agg Inc............ G 812 346-6100
  North Vernon *(G-13276)*

Heidelberg Mtls Mdwest Agg Inc............ G 260 632-1410
  Woodburn *(G-16948)*

Heidelberg Mtls Sthast Agg LLC............. E 317 788-4086
  Indianapolis *(G-8380)*

Heritage Aggregates LLC....................... G 317 434-4600
  Indianapolis *(G-8386)*

Heritage Aggregates LLC....................... G 765 436-7665
  Thorntown *(G-15751)*

Heritage Aggregates LLC....................... G 317 872-6010
  Indianapolis *(G-8387)*

Mulzer Crushed Stone Inc....................... E 812 365-2145
  English *(G-3844)*

Mulzer Crushed Stone Inc....................... G 844 480-6803
  Evansville *(G-4216)*

Rogers Group Inc.................................. D 219 474-5125
  Kentland *(G-10163)*

Seminole Stone Inc............................... F 812 634-7115
  Jasper *(G-9909)*

Stone-Street Quarries Inc...................... F 260 639-6511
  Hoagland *(G-7171)*

West Plains Mining LLC......................... E 260 563-9500
  Wabash *(G-16225)*

LINERS & COVERS: Fabric

Transhield Inc....................................... E 574 266-4118
  Elkhart *(G-3744)*

LININGS: Fabric, Apparel & Other, Exc Millinery

H3r Garage LLC.................................... G 317 519-1368
  Indianapolis *(G-8349)*

LIP BALMS

Damor & Co LLC................................... G 317 790-8360
  Indianapolis *(G-7947)*

LIQUEFIED PETROLEUM GAS DEALERS

Industrial Sewing Machine Co................ G 812 425-2255
  Evansville *(G-4124)*

LITHOGRAPHIC PLATES

Graphik Mechanix Inc............................ G 260 426-7001
  Fort Wayne *(G-5035)*

LIVESTOCK WHOLESALERS, NEC

D Rinker Transport LLC......................... G 765 749-4120
  Dunkirk *(G-2961)*

LOCKERS

A & A Sheet Metal Products................... D 219 326-1288
  La Porte *(G-10371)*

LOCKS

Allegion S&S Holding Co Inc.................. B 317 810-3700
  Carmel *(G-1555)*

Allegion US Holding Co Inc.................... E 317 810-3700
  Carmel *(G-1556)*

Armored Locks Inc................................ G 219 798-6502
  Michigan City *(G-11579)*

Avis Industrial Corporation.................... E 765 998-8100
  Upland *(G-15876)*

Fki Security Group LLC.......................... B 812 948-8400
  New Albany *(G-12730)*

Schlage Lock Company LLC................... B 317 810-3700
  Carmel *(G-1752)*

Top Lock Corporation............................ G 317 831-2000
  Mooresville *(G-12248)*

Wallys Lockshop................................... G 765 748-2282
  Muncie *(G-12514)*

LOCKS & LOCK SETS, WHOLESALE

S C Pryor Inc.. F 317 352-1281
  Indianapolis *(G-9354)*

LOCKS: Coin-Operated

Standard Change-Makers Inc................. C 317 899-6955
  Indianapolis *(G-9491)*

LOCKSMITHS

Control Key Plus................................... G 317 567-2194
  Indianapolis *(G-7862)*

G E C O M Corp.................................... A 812 663-2270
  Greensburg *(G-6595)*

Key Made Now...................................... G 317 664-8582
  Indianapolis *(G-8676)*

Keys R US.. G 317 616-0267
  Indianapolis *(G-8679)*

LOCOMOTIVES & PARTS

Hadady Corporation.............................. E 219 322-7417
  Dyer *(G-2976)*

Powerrail Holdings Inc.......................... G 765 827-4660
  Connersville *(G-2463)*

Professnl Locomotive Svcs Inc............... E 219 398-9123
  East Chicago *(G-3036)*

LOGGING

A & S Logging Inc................................. G 574 896-3136
  North Judson *(G-13205)*

Arboramerica Inc.................................. F 765 572-1212
  Westpoint *(G-16743)*

Baldwin Logging Inc............................. G 812 834-1040
  Norman *(G-13202)*

LOGGING

Brocks Incorporated .... G 765 721-3068
  Bainbridge *(G-559)*

Burton Lumber Co Inc .... F 812 866-4438
  Lexington *(G-10975)*

Calhoun Logging Corporation .... G 260 839-0268
  Claypool *(G-2051)*

Christman Logging .... G 502 525-2649
  Madison *(G-11208)*

CJ Logging LLC .... G 812 360-0163
  Morgantown *(G-12256)*

Cory Williamson .... G 812 242-0400
  Clay City *(G-2042)*

Crone Logging LLC .... G 765 346-0025
  Martinsville *(G-11386)*

Ferree Logging LLC .... G 812 786-1676
  Corydon *(G-2496)*

Gabhart Logging LLC .... G 812 365-2425
  Marengo *(G-11263)*

Howard Logging .... G 260 327-3862
  Pierceton *(G-13633)*

J Robert Switzer .... G 765 474-1307
  Lafayette *(G-10612)*

Jim Graber Logging LLC .... G 812 636-7000
  Odon *(G-13341)*

Jim McCarter Logging .... G 812 321-5661
  Wheatland *(G-16775)*

Jim Rhodes Logging .... G 812 739-4221
  English *(G-3841)*

Keller Logging LLC .... G 219 309-0379
  Valparaiso *(G-15985)*

Kelsie Pierce .... G 812 279-1335
  Bedford *(G-651)*

Loggers Incorporated .... E 812 939-2797
  Clay City *(G-2045)*

Logging .... G 812 216-3544
  Seymour *(G-14666)*

Louanna Stilwell .... G 812 631-0647
  Velpen *(G-16094)*

Mark A Morin Logging Inc .... G 812 327-4917
  West Baden Springs *(G-16542)*

Michael L Baker .... G 812 967-2160
  Salem *(G-14491)*

Michael Skaggs .... G 812 732-8809
  Mauckport *(G-11438)*

Mike Gross .... G 574 529-2201
  New Paris *(G-12966)*

Mitchell L Kline .... G 812 449-6518
  Evanston *(G-3853)*

Odon Sawmill Inc .... E 812 636-7314
  Odon *(G-13347)*

PFC Farm Services Inc .... G 260 235-0817
  Fremont *(G-5831)*

Pingleton Logging Inc .... G 765 653-2878
  Greencastle *(G-6425)*

Pingleton Sawmill Inc .... E 765 653-2878
  Greencastle *(G-6426)*

R E Casebeer & Sons Inc .... G 812 829-3284
  Spencer *(G-15359)*

Ralph Ransom Veneers .... G 812 858-9956
  Newburgh *(G-13018)*

Rays Logging LLC .... G 812 935-5307
  Spencer *(G-15360)*

Robert Cody Jacobs .... G 812 606-5195
  Nashville *(G-12679)*

Robert L Young .... G 812 863-4475
  Springville *(G-15391)*

Ronald Lee Allen .... G 812 644-7649
  Loogootee *(G-11150)*

Ronald Wright Logging LLC .... G 812 338-2665
  English *(G-3847)*

Russell Beeman Logging Inc .... G 765 387-0464
  Anderson *(G-188)*

Tri-State Forest Products Inc .... F 317 328-1850
  Indianapolis *(G-9637)*

Universal Frest Pdts Ind Ltd P .... E 574 273-6326
  Granger *(G-6388)*

Walton Logging .... G 812 365-9635
  Marengo *(G-11267)*

Waninger Knneth Sons Log Tmber .... G 812 357-5200
  Fulda *(G-5850)*

LOGGING CAMPS & CONTRACTORS

Andis Logging Inc .... F 812 723-2357
  Paoli *(G-13487)*

Anthony D Etienne Logging .... G 812 843-5872
  Magnet *(G-11258)*

Artys Logging Inc .... G 812 969-3124
  Elizabeth *(G-3123)*

AS Logging LLC .... G 812 613-0577
  Taswell *(G-15494)*

Bear Hollow Wood Carvers LLC .... G 812 843-5549
  Saint Croix *(G-14433)*

Billy R Ransom .... G 812 897-5921
  Boonville *(G-1082)*

Boondocks Logging LLC .... G 812 247-3363
  Shoals *(G-14904)*

Bray Logging .... G 812 863-7947
  Owensburg *(G-13459)*

Campbell Logging LLC .... G 812 972-6280
  Birdseye *(G-738)*

Carr Logging .... G 812 863-7585
  Owensburg *(G-13460)*

Cash Logging LLC .... G 812 843-5335
  Mount Pleasant *(G-12283)*

Charles Kolb Logging .... G 765 458-7766
  Liberty *(G-10985)*

Charles Kolb Sons Logging .... G 765 647-4309
  Brookville *(G-1317)*

Coffman Dallas Log & Excvtg .... G 812 738-1528
  Corydon *(G-2493)*

Coffman Logging .... G 812 732-4857
  Corydon *(G-2494)*

Coleman Logging .... G 765 458-7219
  Liberty *(G-10986)*

Daniel Steffy .... G 812 726-4769
  Vincennes *(G-16118)*

Delmar Knepp Logging .... G 812 486-2565
  Loogootee *(G-11131)*

Dennis Etiennes Logging Inc .... G 812 843-4518
  Cannelton *(G-1535)*

Dennis K Marvell .... G 812 779-5107
  Patoka *(G-13507)*

Dwight Smith Logging .... G 812 834-5546
  Heltonville *(G-7110)*

George Voyles Sawmill Inc .... G 812 472-3968
  Salem *(G-14478)*

Goodrick Timber .... G 765 778-7442
  Pendleton *(G-13535)*

Gordon D Browning .... G 765 458-7792
  Liberty *(G-10988)*

Graber Lumber LP .... E 260 238-4124
  Spencerville *(G-15370)*

Graber Ronald D Yoder & .... G 574 268-9512
  Warsaw *(G-16368)*

Greg Abplanalp Logging LLC .... G 812 873-8463
  Butlerville *(G-1483)*

Hartman Logging .... G 765 653-3889
  Greencastle *(G-6408)*

John Collier Logging Inc .... G 317 539-9663
  Fillmore *(G-4454)*

Joseph M Schmidt .... G 260 223-3498
  Decatur *(G-2865)*

Keith Bixler .... G 812 866-1637
  Lexington *(G-10978)*

Kelly Bixler Logging .... G 812 752-6636
  Scottsburg *(G-14567)*

Kinser Timber Products Inc .... G 812 876-4775
  Gosport *(G-6285)*

Knepps Logging Bandmilling .... G 812 486-7721
  Montgomery *(G-12106)*

Marvell Logging Company LLC .... G 812 779-5107
  Patoka *(G-13509)*

Michael Deom Professional .... G 812 836-2206
  Tell City *(G-15511)*

Michael L Reynolds .... G 812 528-7844
  Medora *(G-11463)*

Midwest Logging & Veneer .... G 765 342-2774
  Martinsville *(G-11414)*

Mike Fisher Logging .... G 812 357-2169
  Ferdinand *(G-4444)*

NJ Logging LLC .... G 812 597-0782
  Morgantown *(G-12261)*

Ohio River Veneer LLC .... F 812 824-7928
  Bloomington *(G-933)*

Peacock Logging Inc .... G 812 794-3579
  Austin *(G-469)*

Rodney Sloan Logging Inc .... G 812 934-5321
  Batesville *(G-605)*

Shady Oaks Logging LLC .... G 317 902-9741
  Morgantown *(G-12263)*

Slabach Logging LLC .... G 260 768-4644
  Shipshewana *(G-14889)*

Spencer Logging .... G 812 595-0987
  Scottsburg *(G-14581)*

Tdc Logging .... G 574 289-4243
  South Bend *(G-15280)*

Weaver Logging Incorporated .... G 260 589-9985
  Berne *(G-730)*

Wilkerson Logging Inc .... G 812 988-4960
  Nashville *(G-12683)*

William Browning .... G 765 647-6397
  Brookville *(G-1342)*

Williams Bros Logging LLC .... G 270 547-0266
  Mauckport *(G-11442)*

LOGGING: Timber, Cut At Logging Camp

Blue River Timber LLC .... G 812 291-0411
  Evansville *(G-3935)*

Cannon Timber LLC .... G 219 754-1088
  La Crosse *(G-10364)*

D Timber Inc .... G 219 374-8085
  Crown Point *(G-2672)*

Knepp Logging LLC .... G 812 486-3741
  Loogootee *(G-11142)*

White Oak Land & Timber LLC .... G 812 482-5102
  Jasper *(G-9917)*

LOGGING: Wooden Logs

Orla Bontrater .... G 260 768-7553
  Shipshewana *(G-14873)*

LOTIONS OR CREAMS: Face

Be Body Butters LLC .... G 317 362-9248
  Indianapolis *(G-7602)*

Damor & Co LLC .... G 317 790-8360
  Indianapolis *(G-7947)*

Simply Saidahs LLC .... G 317 650-4256
  Carmel *(G-1762)*

Wholeaf Aloe Distributors .... G 219 322-7217
  Schererville *(G-14547)*

LOTIONS: SHAVING

Redmaster Fusion LLC .... G 260 273-5819
  Fort Wayne *(G-5374)*

Serendipity Sanctuary .... G 765 541-2364
  Richmond *(G-14203)*

PRODUCT SECTION

LUMBER: Hardwood Dimension & Flooring Mills

LOUDSPEAKERS
Klipsch Group Inc .... C 317 860-8100
Indianapolis (G-8695)

LUBRICANTS: Corrosion Preventive
Gabriel Products Inc .... G 502 291-5388
Jeffersonville (G-9989)

LUBRICATING EQPT: Indl
Leasenet Incorporated .... G 317 575-4098
Indianapolis (G-8731)

LUBRICATING OIL & GREASE WHOLESALERS
D-A Lubricant Company Inc .... E 317 923-5321
Lebanon (G-10890)
Jolliff Diesel Service LLC .... G 812 692-5725
Elnora (G-3815)
Miller Industrial Fluids LLC .... E 317 634-7300
Indianapolis (G-8921)
Petrochoice Holdings Inc .... E 317 634-7300
Indianapolis (G-9130)
Petroleum Solutions Inc .... G 574 546-2133
Bremen (G-1214)
Pinnacle Oil Holdings LLC .... C 317 875-9465
Indianapolis (G-9144)
Pinnacle Oil Holdings LLC .... E 317 875-9465
Indianapolis (G-9145)

LUBRICATION SYSTEMS & EQPT
Lubrication Devices .... G 574 234-4674
South Bend (G-15130)
Perma Lubrication .... G 317 241-0797
Indianapolis (G-9126)
Perma Lubrication .... G 219 531-9155
Valparaiso (G-16024)
Summit Manufacturing Corp .... G 317 823-2848
Indianapolis (G-9524)
Systems Engineering and Sls Co .... G 260 422-1671
Fort Wayne (G-5466)

LUGGAGE & BRIEFCASES
C H Ellis LLC .... G 317 636-3351
Indianapolis (G-7707)
Leed Selling Tools Corp .... C 812 482-7888
Ireland (G-9816)
Raine Inc .... F 765 622-7687
Anderson (G-182)

LUGGAGE: Traveling Bags
Cinda B USA LLC .... G 260 469-0803
Fort Wayne (G-4848)
One-Stop Travel Shop Inc .... G 812 339-9496
Bloomington (G-937)
Rva LLC .... G 317 800-9800
Fishers (G-4602)

LUMBER & BLDG MATLS DEALER, RET: Electric Constructn Matls
Rees Inc .... F 260 495-9811
Fremont (G-5832)

LUMBER & BLDG MATLS DEALER, RET: Garage Doors, Sell/Install
Ecpca Safe-Way LLC .... D 574 267-4861
Warsaw (G-16354)
Safe-Way Garage Doors LLC .... E 574 267-4861
Warsaw (G-16420)

LUMBER & BLDG MATRLS DEALERS, RET: Bath Fixtures, Eqpt/Sply
United Home Supply Inc .... G 765 288-2737
Muncie (G-12509)

LUMBER & BLDG MTRLS DEALERS, RET: Planing Mill Prdts/Lumber
Pike Lumber Company Inc .... E 574 893-4511
Carbon (G-1538)

LUMBER & BUILDING MATERIAL DEALERS, RETAIL: Roofing Material
Gillespie Mrrell Gen Contg LLC .... G 765 618-4084
Marion (G-11288)

LUMBER & BUILDING MATERIALS DEALER, RET: Door & Window Prdts
A-1 Door Specialties Inc .... G 260 749-1635
South Bend (G-14930)
Concord Realstate Corp .... F 765 423-5555
Lafayette (G-10554)
Hoosier Interior Doors Inc .... G 574 534-3072
Goshen (G-6169)
Woodwright Door & Trim Inc .... G 574 522-1667
Elkhart (G-3792)

LUMBER & BUILDING MATERIALS DEALER, RET: Masonry Matls/Splys
Heritage Ldscp Sup Group Inc .... E 317 849-9100
Indianapolis (G-8389)
Jjs Concrete Construction LLC .... E 812 636-0173
Montgomery (G-12103)

LUMBER & BUILDING MATERIALS DEALERS, RET: Solar Heating Eqpt
Inovateus Solar LLC .... E 574 485-1400
South Bend (G-15081)

LUMBER & BUILDING MATERIALS DEALERS, RETAIL: Brick
Brickworks Supply Center LLC .... E 317 786-9208
Carmel (G-1573)
Carters Concrete Block Inc .... E 574 722-2644
Fort Wayne (G-4836)
Eavk Legacy Inc .... E 812 246-4461
New Albany (G-12723)
Prairie Group .... F 812 877-9886
Terre Haute (G-15666)

LUMBER & BUILDING MATERIALS DEALERS, RETAIL: Cement
Shelby Gravel Inc .... F 317 216-7556
Indianapolis (G-9418)
Shelby Gravel Inc .... F 317 804-8100
Westfield (G-16726)
St Henry Tile Co Inc .... E 260 589-2880
Berne (G-728)
Zimco Materials Inc .... G 219 883-0870
Gary (G-6029)

LUMBER & BUILDING MATERIALS DEALERS, RETAIL: Modular Homes
Light House Center Inc .... F 765 448-4502
Lafayette (G-10636)

LUMBER & BUILDING MATERIALS DEALERS, RETAIL: Sand & Gravel
D Robertson Gravel Co Inc .... F 765 832-2768
Clinton (G-2065)
Martins Lime Service Inc .... G 574 784-2270
Plymouth (G-13796)
Merritt Sand and Gravel Inc .... F 260 665-2513
Waterloo (G-16524)

LUMBER & BUILDING MATERIALS DEALERS, RETAIL: Siding
Zimmer Metal Sales LLC .... G 574 862-1800
Goshen (G-6280)

LUMBER & BUILDING MATERIALS RET DEALERS: Millwork & Lumber
John Gebhart Woodworkings .... G 765 492-3898
Cayuga (G-1823)

LUMBER & BUILDING MATLS DEALERS, RET: Concrete/Cinder Block
McIntire Concrete .... F 765 759-7111
Muncie (G-12450)
Slater Concrete Products Inc .... G 260 347-0164
Kendallville (G-10152)

LUMBER: Dimension, Hardwood
Als Woodcraft Inc .... F 812 967-4458
Borden (G-1105)
Mould-Rite Inc .... G 812 967-3200
Pekin (G-13520)

LUMBER: Fiberboard
Kay Company Inc .... E 765 659-3388
Frankfort (G-5677)

LUMBER: Hardwood Dimension
Ecojacks LLC .... G 574 306-0414
South Whitley (G-15317)
Indiana Wood Products Inc .... D 574 825-2129
Middlebury (G-11724)
Palletone of Indiana Inc .... D 260 768-4021
Shipshewana (G-14877)
Salt Creek Harvest LLC .... G 708 927-5569
Valparaiso (G-16042)

LUMBER: Hardwood Dimension & Flooring Mills
A New Covenant Woodwork LLC .... G 812 737-2929
Laconia (G-10504)
Cabinetmaker Inc .... G 812 723-3461
Paoli (G-13490)
Champion Wood Products Inc .... G 812 282-9460
Sellersburg (G-14591)
Chisholm Lumber & Supply Co .... E 317 547-3535
Indianapolis (G-7799)
Coopers Wood Heat Supply LLC .... G 765 918-1039
Crawfordsville (G-2555)
Dehart Pallet & Lumber Co .... F 812 794-2974
Austin (G-464)
Dutch Made Inc .... G 260 657-3331
Harlan (G-7054)
Ford Sawmills Inc .... F 812 324-2134
Vincennes (G-16125)
Forest Products Group Inc .... F 765 659-1807
Frankfort (G-5665)
Frank Miller Lumber Co Inc .... C 800 345-2643
Union City (G-15853)

LUMBER: Hardwood Dimension & Flooring Mills

George Voyles Sawmill Inc................................G..... 812 472-3968
  Salem (G-14478)
Helmsburg Sawmill Inc.....................................E..... 812 988-6161
  Nashville (G-12671)
Herberts Sawmill Inc...F..... 812 663-9347
  Greensburg (G-6601)
Heritage Hardwoods KY Inc..........................D..... 812 288-5855
  Jeffersonville (G-9994)
Homestead Properties Inc.............................F..... 812 866-4415
  Deputy (G-2941)
Jackson Brothers Lumber Co........................F..... 812 847-7812
  Linton (G-11036)
Mikro Furniture..G..... 812 877-9550
  Terre Haute (G-15646)
Norstam Veneers Inc......................................D..... 812 732-4391
  Mauckport (G-11441)
Odon Sawmill Inc..E..... 812 636-7314
  Odon (G-13347)
Olon Industries Inc (us)..................................G..... 812 254-0427
  Washington (G-16497)
Phil Etiennes Timber Harvest.......................E..... 812 843-5132
  Saint Croix (G-14435)
Pike Lumber Company Inc............................E..... 574 893-4511
  Carbon (G-1538)
Pingleton Sawmill Inc.....................................E..... 765 653-2878
  Greencastle (G-6426)
Quality Hardwood Products Inc...................F..... 260 982-2043
  Claypool (G-2056)
R E Casebeer & Sons Inc..............................E..... 812 829-3284
  Spencer (G-15359)
Randall Lowe Sons Sawmill LLC.................F..... 812 936-2254
  French Lick (G-5848)
Rogers Group Inc..C..... 812 333-6324
  Bloomington (G-959)
Stateline Woodturnings LLC.........................G..... 260 768-4507
  Shipshewana (G-14892)
Stemwood Corp...E..... 812 945-6646
  New Albany (G-12818)
Superior Forest Products LLC.......................F..... 765 245-2895
  Montezuma (G-12083)
Universal Frest Pdts Ind Ltd P......................E..... 574 273-6326
  Granger (G-6388)
US Lbm Operating Co 3009 LLC..................G..... 812 464-2428
  Evansville (G-4364)
Werner Sawmill Inc...E..... 812 482-7565
  Jasper (G-9916)

LUMBER: Kiln Dried

C C Cook and Son Lbr Co Inc......................E..... 765 672-4235
  Reelsville (G-14030)
Pike Lumber Company Inc............................C..... 574 893-4511
  Akron (G-7)

LUMBER: Panels, Plywood, Softwood

FM Holdings LLC...G..... 574 773-2814
  Nappanee (G-12597)

LUMBER: Plywood, Hardwood

Besse Veneers Inc..E..... 906 428-3113
  Trafalgar (G-15826)
Chisholm Lumber & Supply Co....................E..... 317 547-3535
  Indianapolis (G-7799)
Danzer Services Inc..G..... 812 526-2601
  Edinburgh (G-3074)
Danzer Veneer Americas Inc........................F..... 812 526-6789
  Edinburgh (G-3075)
Flexible Materials Inc.....................................D..... 812 280-7000
  Jeffersonville (G-9984)
Kimball Furniture Group LLC.......................B..... 812 482-8401
  Jasper (G-9871)
Land of Indiana Inc..F..... 812 788-1560
  Bedford (G-654)

Miller Veneers Inc...C..... 317 638-2326
  Indianapolis (G-8923)
Patrick Industries Inc.....................................D..... 574 522-7710
  Elkhart (G-3598)
Sexton Plywood & Veneer Co......................G..... 812 454-0488
  Evansville (G-4308)
Sims-Lohman Inc...G..... 317 467-0710
  Greenfield (G-6553)
Superior Veneer & Plywood LLC..................G..... 812 941-8850
  New Albany (G-12819)
Universal Frest Pdts Ind Ltd P......................E..... 574 273-6326
  Granger (G-6388)
Veneer Curry Sales LLC.................................F..... 812 945-6623
  New Albany (G-12823)
Wible Lumber Inc...E..... 260 351-2441
  South Milford (G-15314)

LUMBER: Plywood, Hardwood or Hardwood Faced

D & M Sales LLC..G..... 574 825-9024
  Middlebury (G-11710)
Dimension Plywood Inc..................................G..... 812 944-6491
  New Albany (G-12719)
Grizzly Ridge Hardwoods LLC....................G..... 574 546-3600
  Bremen (G-1194)
Hoehn Hardwoods..G..... 812 968-3242
  Corydon (G-2498)
Indiana Architectural Plywood....................E..... 317 878-4822
  Trafalgar (G-15829)
Patrick Industries Inc.....................................D..... 574 294-8828
  Elkhart (G-3592)
Patrick Industries Inc.....................................B..... 574 294-7511
  Elkhart (G-3593)
Wholesale Hrdwood Intriors Inc...................F..... 317 867-3660
  Westfield (G-16740)

LUMBER: Plywood, Prefinished, Hardwood

Custom Plywood Inc..E..... 812 944-7300
  New Albany (G-12717)
Heritage Unlimited LLC..................................G..... 574 538-8021
  Goshen (G-6164)

LUMBER: Plywood, Softwood

JDC Veneers Inc...D..... 812 284-9775
  Jeffersonville (G-10003)

LUMBER: Rails, Fence, Round Or Split

IMI Southwest Inc..F..... 260 432-3973
  Fort Wayne (G-5095)

LUMBER: Resawn, Small Dimension

Great Lakes Forest Pdts Inc.........................C..... 574 389-9663
  Elkhart (G-3389)

LUMBER: Treated

Kustom Kilms LLC..G..... 317 512-5813
  Columbus (G-2337)
Preserving Past..G..... 574 835-0833
  Elkhart (G-3618)
Rookstools Pier Shop Inc..............................E..... 574 453-4771
  Leesburg (G-10960)
Southeast Wood Treating Inc.......................C..... 765 962-4077
  Richmond (G-14206)
Tangent Rail Products Inc............................E..... 412 325-0202
  Terre Haute (G-15723)
Universal Frest Pdts Ind Ltd P......................E..... 574 273-6326
  Granger (G-6388)

LUMBER: Veneer, Softwood

Douglas Dye and Associates Inc................G..... 317 844-1709
  Carmel (G-1611)

Pleasant Hill Veneer Corp.............................G..... 812 725-8924
  Jeffersonville (G-10039)

MACHINE PARTS: Stamped Or Pressed Metal

Charmaran Company LLC.............................F..... 260 347-3347
  Kendallville (G-10098)
Cnc Industries Inc...E..... 260 490-5700
  Fort Wayne (G-4863)
Computer Technology.....................................G..... 812 283-5094
  Jeffersonville (G-9959)
Countryside Tool...G..... 260 357-3839
  Garrett (G-5857)
Haven Manufacturing Ind LLC.....................F..... 260 622-4150
  Ossian (G-13425)
J & K Associates Inc.......................................G..... 317 255-3588
  Indianapolis (G-8599)
Kable Tool & Engineering..............................G..... 260 726-9670
  Portland (G-13954)
KMC Enterprises Inc.......................................G..... 765 584-1533
  Winchester (G-16893)
Mpi Engineered Tech LLC..............................B..... 574 772-3850
  Knox (G-10215)
P & A Machine Company Inc.......................G..... 317 634-3673
  Bargersville (G-571)
Perfecto Tool & Engineering Co..................E..... 765 644-2821
  Anderson (G-176)
The Akron Equipment Company..................E..... 260 622-4150
  Ossian (G-13438)
Tube Processing Corp....................................G..... 317 264-7760
  Indianapolis (G-9657)
Tube Processing Corp....................................B..... 317 787-1321
  Indianapolis (G-9658)
Ultra Manufacturing Inc.................................E..... 574 586-2320
  Walkerton (G-16278)

MACHINE TOOL ACCESS: Cams

Precision Cams Inc...G..... 317 634-3521
  Indianapolis (G-9180)

MACHINE TOOL ACCESS: Drills

Nachi Tool America Inc..................................E..... 317 535-0320
  Greenwood (G-6745)

MACHINE TOOL ACCESS: Files

T & L Sharpening Inc......................................F..... 574 583-3868
  Monticello (G-12172)

MACHINE TOOL ACCESS: Tools & Access

Bel-Mar Products Corporation.....................G..... 317 769-3262
  Whitestown (G-16801)
Budco Tool & Die Inc......................................E..... 574 522-4004
  Elkhart (G-3237)
Butler Tool & Design Inc................................F..... 219 297-4531
  Goodland (G-6080)
Eagle Precision LLC..F..... 260 637-4649
  Huntertown (G-7254)
General Crafts Corp..G..... 574 533-1936
  Goshen (G-6144)
H & P Tool Co Inc...E..... 765 962-4504
  Richmond (G-14129)
Nap Asset Holdings Ltd.................................D..... 812 482-2000
  Jasper (G-9894)
Riverside Tool Corp...E..... 574 522-6798
  Elkhart (G-3650)
Stanley Black & Decker Inc..........................D..... 860 225-5111
  Indianapolis (G-9495)
Teague Concrete Backhoe............................G..... 765 674-4692
  Jonesboro (G-10081)

MACHINE TOOL ATTACHMENTS & ACCESS

Aeromet Industries Inc..................................D..... 219 924-7442
  Griffith (G-6787)

PRODUCT SECTION

MACHINE TOOLS, METAL FORMING: Punching & Shearing

Fastener Equipment Corporation.............. G 708 957-5100
  Valparaiso *(G-15948)*
Hoosier Spline Broach Corp..................... E 765 452-8273
  Kokomo *(G-10281)*
Indiana Tool & Mfg Co Inc........................ C 574 936-2112
  Plymouth *(G-13784)*
Kaiser Tool Company Inc.......................... E 260 484-3620
  Fort Wayne *(G-5142)*
Logansport Machine Co Inc...................... E 574 735-0225
  Logansport *(G-11090)*
Rusach International Inc......................... F 317 638-0298
  Hope *(G-7232)*
Scg Acquisition Company LLC................... E 574 294-1506
  Elkhart *(G-3664)*
Tri-State Industries Inc........................... D 219 933-1710
  Hammond *(G-7023)*
Willemin Macodel..................................... G 317 219-6113
  Noblesville *(G-13196)*

MACHINE TOOLS & ACCESS

Berkey Machine Corporation................... G 260 761-4002
  Wawaka *(G-16538)*
Bristol Tool and Die Inc.......................... F 574 848-5354
  Bristol *(G-1252)*
C & A Tool Engineering Inc..................... C 260 693-2167
  Auburn *(G-372)*
C & A Tool Engineering Inc..................... B 260 693-2167
  Churubusco *(G-1982)*
C-Way Tool and Die Inc........................... G 812 256-6341
  Charlestown *(G-1872)*
Capital Machine Company Inc.................. F 317 638-6661
  Indianapolis *(G-7734)*
Century Tool & Engr Inc........................... G 317 685-0942
  Indianapolis *(G-7776)*
Claymore Tools Inc................................. G 574 255-6483
  South Bend *(G-14975)*
Earthchain Magnetic Pro......................... G 317 803-8034
  Indianapolis *(G-8034)*
Fairfield Manufacturing Co Inc............... G 815 508-7353
  Lafayette *(G-10577)*
Feddema Industries Inc.......................... E 260 665-6463
  Angola *(G-250)*
G & S Super Abrasives Inc....................... E 260 665-5562
  Angola *(G-254)*
General Aluminum Mfg Company............. C 260 495-2600
  Fremont *(G-5822)*
Grimm Mold & Die Co Inc......................... F 219 778-4211
  Rolling Prairie *(G-14363)*
Herman Tool & Machine Inc..................... F 574 594-5544
  Pierceton *(G-13632)*
Hoosier Tool & Die Co Inc........................ D 812 376-8286
  Edinburgh *(G-3087)*
Industrial Sales & Supply Inc.................. E 317 240-0560
  Indianapolis *(G-8519)*
Jones Machine & Tool Inc........................ E 812 364-4588
  Fredericksburg *(G-5794)*
K-K Tool and Design Inc.......................... E 260 758-2940
  Markle *(G-11356)*
Kennametal Inc....................................... G 317 696-8798
  Indianapolis *(G-8670)*
Liberty Tool and Engrg Inc...................... G 765 354-9550
  Middletown *(G-11772)*
M4 Sciences LLC...................................... G 765 479-6215
  West Lafayette *(G-16603)*
M4 Sciences Corporation......................... G 765 479-6215
  West Lafayette *(G-16604)*
Micro-Precision Operations.................... F 260 589-2136
  Berne *(G-719)*
Morris Mold and Machine Co................... G 317 923-6653
  Indianapolis *(G-8955)*
Nachi America Inc.................................... E 877 622-4487
  Greenwood *(G-6743)*

Nst Technologies Mim LLC...................... C 812 755-4501
  Campbellsburg *(G-1526)*
Overton & Sons Tl & Die Co Inc................ E 317 831-4542
  Mooresville *(G-12232)*
Pannell & Son Welding Inc...................... G 765 948-3606
  Summitville *(G-15427)*
Pontiac Engraving................................... G 630 834-4424
  Plymouth *(G-13805)*
Precision Surfacing Solutions................. G 317 841-2400
  Noblesville *(G-13157)*
Precision Tubes Inc................................ G 317 783-2339
  Indianapolis *(G-9187)*
Qualtech Tool & Engrg Inc....................... F 260 726-6572
  Portland *(G-13965)*
R B Tool & Machinery Co......................... G 574 679-0082
  Osceola *(G-13401)*
Rimsmith Tool LLC................................... G 219 926-8665
  Chesterton *(G-1957)*
Specialty Tool LLC................................... F 260 493-6351
  Indianapolis *(G-9471)*
Spectrum Services Inc............................ G 574 272-7605
  Granger *(G-6380)*
Superior Tool & Die Co Inc....................... E 574 293-2591
  Elkhart *(G-3710)*
Surclean Inc.. F 248 791-2226
  Brownsburg *(G-1405)*
Sure Tool & Engineering Inc.................... G 260 693-2193
  Churubusco *(G-1988)*
Thomas L Wehr... G 317 835-7824
  Fairland *(G-4403)*
Toolcraft LLC... E 260 749-0454
  Fort Wayne *(G-5494)*
Tsune America LLC.................................. F 812 378-9875
  Edinburgh *(G-3109)*

MACHINE TOOLS, METAL CUTTING: Exotic, Including Explosive

Claymore Tools Inc................................. G 574 255-6483
  South Bend *(G-14975)*
Extreme Tool Supply............................... G 219 362-5129
  La Porte *(G-10407)*

MACHINE TOOLS, METAL CUTTING: Home Workshop

Cyberia Ltd... G 317 721-2582
  Indianapolis *(G-7938)*
Solomon M Eicher.................................... G 812 289-1252
  Marysville *(G-11436)*

MACHINE TOOLS, METAL CUTTING: Lathes

Lionshead Precision Metals LLC.............. D 317 787-6358
  Greenwood *(G-6729)*

MACHINE TOOLS, METAL CUTTING: Numerically Controlled

Killer Machining Solutions LLC................ G 813 786-2309
  Brownsburg *(G-1383)*
Masbez LLC.. G 855 962-7239
  Frankfort *(G-5681)*
Milltronics Mfg Co Inc............................. C 952 442-1410
  Indianapolis *(G-8926)*

MACHINE TOOLS, METAL CUTTING: Plasma Process

ARC Angle Welding/Fabrication............... F 812 619-1731
  Tell City *(G-15496)*
Tri-State Industries Inc........................... D 219 933-1710
  Hammond *(G-7023)*

MACHINE TOOLS, METAL CUTTING: Saws, Power

Continental Diamond Tool Corp............... F 260 493-1294
  New Haven *(G-12899)*
Nap Asset Holdings Ltd........................... D 812 482-2000
  Jasper *(G-9894)*

MACHINE TOOLS, METAL CUTTING: Tool Replacement & Rpr Parts

American Tool Service Inc....................... F 260 493-6351
  Fort Wayne *(G-4758)*
Cnm Machine Tool Repair........................ G 765 552-3255
  Elwood *(G-3819)*
Creative Tool Inc.................................... G 260 338-1222
  Huntertown *(G-7251)*
Eagle Precision Machining Inc................ G 260 637-4649
  Huntertown *(G-7255)*
Indiana Handpiece Repair Inc................. G 260 436-0765
  Fort Wayne *(G-5100)*
Pathfinder Cutting Tech LLC.................... F 424 342-9723
  Indianapolis *(G-9099)*
S&S Machinery Repair LLC...................... G 812 521-2368
  Norman *(G-13204)*
Tom West Farms...................................... G 812 986-2162
  Poland *(G-13838)*

MACHINE TOOLS, METAL CUTTING: Vertical Turning & Boring

Danubius Machine Inc............................. G 219 662-7787
  Crown Point *(G-2673)*
Lmr Industries LLC.................................. G 219 765-4157
  Hammond *(G-6973)*
Zps America LLC...................................... E 317 452-4030
  Indianapolis *(G-9815)*

MACHINE TOOLS, METAL FORMING: Headers

A & M Systems Inc................................... F 574 522-5000
  Elkhart *(G-3138)*
A/C Fabricating Corp............................... E 574 534-1415
  Goshen *(G-6086)*

MACHINE TOOLS, METAL FORMING: Magnetic Forming

Mishawaka LLC.. F 574 259-1981
  Mishawaka *(G-11952)*

MACHINE TOOLS, METAL FORMING: Marking

Masson Inc.. F 317 632-8021
  Indianapolis *(G-8848)*

MACHINE TOOLS, METAL FORMING: Mechanical, Pneumatic Or Hyd

Independent Rail Corporation................. E 317 780-8480
  Indianapolis *(G-8472)*
Roadhog Inc.. E 317 858-7050
  Brownsburg *(G-1398)*
Southern Mechatronics Co Inc................ G
  Brownsburg *(G-1404)*

MACHINE TOOLS, METAL FORMING: Pressing

Precision Industries Corp........................ F 574 522-2626
  Elkhart *(G-3615)*

MACHINE TOOLS, METAL FORMING: Punching & Shearing

Beatty International Inc .... E 219 931-3000
  Hammond *(G-6882)*
Beatty Machine & Mfg Co .... E 219 931-3000
  Hammond *(G-6883)*
Masbez LLC .... G 855 962-7239
  Frankfort *(G-5681)*

MACHINE TOOLS, METAL FORMING: Rebuilt

Applied Metals & Mch Works Inc .... E 260 424-4834
  Fort Wayne *(G-4766)*
Quality Die Set Corp .... E 574 967-4411
  Logansport *(G-11104)*

MACHINE TOOLS: Metal Cutting

Baker Prototype Engrg Inc .... G 574 266-7223
  Elkhart *(G-3215)*
Butler Tool & Design Inc .... F 219 297-4531
  Goodland *(G-6080)*
Capital Machine Company Inc .... F 317 638-6661
  Indianapolis *(G-7734)*
Charleston Metal Products Inc .... F 260 837-8211
  Waterloo *(G-16516)*
Cut-Pro Indexable Tooling LLC .... G 260 668-2400
  Angola *(G-245)*
Dmg Mori Usa Inc .... G 317 913-0978
  Indianapolis *(G-7993)*
Dunes Investment Inc .... F 219 764-4270
  Portage *(G-13860)*
Edge Technologies Inc .... G 317 408-0116
  Indianapolis *(G-8053)*
EDM Specialties Inc .... G 317 856-4700
  Indianapolis *(G-8056)*
Epco Products Inc .... E 260 747-8888
  Fort Wayne *(G-4956)*
Express Machine .... G 812 719-5979
  Cannelton *(G-1536)*
GMI LLC .... G 260 209-6676
  Fort Wayne *(G-5028)*
Grinding and Polsg McHy Corp ...... F 317 898-0750
  Indianapolis *(G-8331)*
Hoosier Spline Broach Corp .... E 765 452-8273
  Kokomo *(G-10281)*
Indiana Oxygen Company Inc .... G 765 662-8700
  Marion *(G-11295)*
Kaiser Tool Company Inc .... E 260 484-3620
  Fort Wayne *(G-5142)*
Macallister Machinery Co Inc .... F 765 966-0759
  Richmond *(G-14157)*
Micro Tool & Machine Co Inc .... G 574 272-9141
  Granger *(G-6360)*
Micro-Precision Operations .... F 260 589-2136
  Berne *(G-719)*
Mosey Manufacturing Co Inc .... G 765 983-8870
  Richmond *(G-14168)*
Mosey Manufacturing Co Inc .... C 765 983-8870
  Richmond *(G-14169)*
Mosey Manufacturing Co Inc .... C 765 983-8889
  Richmond *(G-14170)*
Mosey Manufacturing Co Inc .... C 765 983-8870
  Richmond *(G-14171)*
Mrg Robotics .... G 814 341-4334
  Indianapolis *(G-8967)*
Palmary America LLC .... G 317 494-1415
  Franklin *(G-5764)*
Peerless Machinery Inc .... G 574 210-5990
  South Bend *(G-15188)*
Qig LLC .... E 260 244-3591
  Columbia City *(G-2185)*
R P Imel .... G 260 543-2465
  Uniondale *(G-15872)*
Reeder & Kline Machine Co Inc ...... F 317 846-6591
  Carmel *(G-1737)*
Roeder Industries .... G 812 654-3322
  Milan *(G-11783)*
Specialty Tool LLC .... F 260 493-6351
  Indianapolis *(G-9471)*
Standard Locknut LLC .... C 317 399-2230
  Westfield *(G-16729)*
Stanley Engnered Fastening LLC ... C 765 728-2433
  Montpelier *(G-12182)*
Stedman Machine Company Inc .... D 812 926-0038
  Aurora *(G-457)*
Surclean Inc .... F 248 791-2226
  Brownsburg *(G-1405)*
Tascon Corp .... F 317 547-6127
  Indianapolis *(G-9555)*
Titus Inc .... F 574 936-3345
  Plymouth *(G-13817)*
Versatile Metal Works LLC .... F 765 754-7470
  Muncie *(G-12512)*
Whitesell Prcsion Cmpnents Inc .... C 812 282-4014
  Jeffersonville *(G-10075)*
Winndeavor LLC .... G 219 324-2978
  La Porte *(G-10502)*
Wyrco LLC .... G 317 691-2832
  Fishers *(G-4636)*

MACHINE TOOLS: Metal Forming

Ahern Electric Inc .... G 219 874-3508
  Westville *(G-16755)*
Allfab LLC .... G 317 359-3539
  Indianapolis *(G-7482)*
Ayco Panel .... G 765 635-8106
  Jasonville *(G-9822)*
Bemcor Inc .... F 219 937-1600
  Hammond *(G-6885)*
Beulah Inc .... G 219 309-5635
  Valparaiso *(G-15913)*
Davis Machine and Tool Inc .... F 812 526-2674
  Edinburgh *(G-3076)*
Die-Mensional Metal Stampg Inc .. F 812 265-3946
  Madison *(G-11213)*
Egenolf Machine Inc .... F 317 787-5301
  Indianapolis *(G-8061)*
Ferguson Equipment Inc .... G 574 234-4303
  South Bend *(G-15033)*
Fortville Automotive Sup Inc .... G 317 485-5114
  Fortville *(G-5594)*
Frech U S A Inc .... F 219 874-2812
  Michigan City *(G-11614)*
Nachi America Inc .... E 877 622-4487
  Greenwood *(G-6743)*
Olympus Manufacturing Systems .. G 219 465-1520
  Valparaiso *(G-16017)*
Smgf LLC .... E 812 354-8899
  Petersburg *(G-13625)*
Sullivan Engineered Services .... G 812 294-1724
  Henryville *(G-7116)*
Tk Metal Forming Inc .... F 574 293-2907
  Elkhart *(G-3735)*
Toolmasters Inc .... G 574 256-1881
  Mishawaka *(G-12014)*
Tru-Cut Machine & Tool Inc .... G 260 569-1802
  Wabash *(G-16218)*
United Machine Corporation .... E 219 548-8050
  Valparaiso *(G-16072)*
Versatile Metal Works LLC .... F 765 754-7470
  Muncie *(G-12512)*
Vlb Group North America LLC .... E 317 642-3425
  Elkhart *(G-3775)*

MACHINERY & EQPT, AGRICULTURAL, WHOLESALE: Landscaping Eqpt

Jones & Sons Inc .... E 812 299-2287
  Terre Haute *(G-15622)*

MACHINERY & EQPT, AGRICULTURAL, WHOLESALE: Lawn

A1 Campers and Trlrs Mfg LLC .... G 574 227-2200
  Elkhart *(G-3143)*

MACHINERY & EQPT, AGRICULTURAL, WHOLESALE: Lawn & Garden

Al-Ko Kober LLC .... C 574 294-6651
  Elkhart *(G-3158)*
Dexter Axle Company LLC .... C 574 294-6651
  Elkhart *(G-3293)*
Siteone Landscape Supply LLC ...... G 219 769-2351
  Merrillville *(G-11560)*

MACHINERY & EQPT, INDL, WHOLESALE: Chemical Process

Industrial Water MGT Inc .... G 317 889-0836
  Indianapolis *(G-8521)*
Mixer Direct LLC .... D 812 202-4047
  Jeffersonville *(G-10020)*
Separation Technologies Inc .... G 219 548-5814
  Valparaiso *(G-16046)*

MACHINERY & EQPT, INDL, WHOLESALE: Conveyor Systems

C&M Conveyor Inc .... C 812 849-5647
  Mitchell *(G-12034)*

MACHINERY & EQPT, INDL, WHOLESALE: Engines & Parts, Diesel

Ccts Technology Group Inc .... G 305 209-5743
  Indianapolis *(G-7765)*
Cummins Americas Inc .... G 812 377-5000
  Columbus *(G-2250)*
Cummins Crosspoint LLC .... D 812 867-4400
  Evansville *(G-3999)*
Cummins Crosspoint LLC .... E 260 482-3691
  Fort Wayne *(G-4894)*
Cummins Crosspoint LLC .... E 317 484-2146
  Indianapolis *(G-7923)*
Cummins Crosspoint LLC .... E 317 244-7251
  Indianapolis *(G-7924)*
Cummins Crosspoint LLC .... E 574 252-2154
  Mishawaka *(G-11869)*
Cummins Crosspoint LLC .... E 317 243-7979
  Indianapolis *(G-7925)*
Cummins Cumberland Inc .... B 317 243-7979
  Indianapolis *(G-7926)*
Macallister Machinery Co Inc .... C 260 483-6469
  Fort Wayne *(G-5195)*
S & S Diesel Motorsport LLC .... G 812 216-3639
  Seymour *(G-14683)*

MACHINERY & EQPT, INDL, WHOLESALE: Engs/Transportation Eqpt

Allied Enterprises LLC .... E 765 288-8849
  Muncie *(G-12339)*
Global Parts Network LLC .... G 574 855-5000
  South Bend *(G-15044)*

MACHINERY & EQPT, INDL, WHOLESALE: Heat Exchange

MACHINERY & EQPT: Farm

Hale Industries Inc .... F 317 577-0337
Fortville (G-5598)

Waterfurnace International Inc .... B 260 478-5667
Fort Wayne (G-5549)

MACHINERY & EQPT, INDL, WHOLESALE: Hydraulic Systems

Berendsen Inc .... G 812 423-6468
Evansville (G-3916)

Carver Inc .... G 260 563-7577
Wabash (G-16177)

Headco Industries Inc .... G 219 924-7758
Highland (G-7140)

Headco Industries Inc .... G 574 288-4471
South Bend (G-15062)

Motion & Control Entps LLC .... F 219 844-4224
Munster (G-12551)

National Consolidated Corp .... F 574 289-7885
South Bend (G-15159)

Terra Drive Systems Inc .... C 219 279-2801
Brookston (G-1313)

Terry Liquidation III Inc .... F 219 362-3557
La Porte (G-10490)

Troyer Brothers Inc .... E 260 565-2244
Bluffton (G-1064)

Wdb Enterprises Inc .... G 219 844-4224
Hammond (G-7031)

MACHINERY & EQPT, INDL, WHOLESALE: Indl Machine Parts

Aqua Blast Corp .... F 260 728-4433
Decatur (G-2844)

Mantra Enterprise LLC .... G 201 428-8709
Fishers (G-4561)

R B Tool & Machinery Co .... G 574 679-0082
Osceola (G-13401)

MACHINERY & EQPT, INDL, WHOLESALE: Instruments & Cntrl Eqpt

Cast Products LP .... E 574 294-2684
Elkhart (G-3249)

Dehco Inc .... D 574 294-2684
Elkhart (G-3288)

Richard J Bagan Inc .... E 260 244-5115
Columbia City (G-2190)

MACHINERY & EQPT, INDL, WHOLESALE: Lift Trucks & Parts

Black Equipment Company S Inc .... C 812 477-6481
Evansville (G-3934)

MACHINERY & EQPT, INDL, WHOLESALE: Machine Tools & Access

Ayco Panel .... G 765 635-8106
Jasonville (G-9822)

Fastener Equipment Corporation .... G 708 957-5100
Valparaiso (G-15948)

Macallister Machinery Co Inc .... F 765 966-0759
Richmond (G-14157)

Roeder Industries .... G 812 654-3322
Milan (G-11783)

SSd Control Technology Inc .... E 574 289-5942
South Bend (G-15264)

MACHINERY & EQPT, INDL, WHOLESALE: Machine Tools & Metalwork

Surclean Inc .... F 248 791-2226
Brownsburg (G-1405)

MACHINERY & EQPT, INDL, WHOLESALE: Measure/Test, Electric

Kane Usa Inc .... E 800 547-5740
Indianapolis (G-8660)

MACHINERY & EQPT, INDL, WHOLESALE: Petroleum Industry

Steel Tank & Fabricating Corp .... E 260 248-8971
Columbia City (G-2203)

MACHINERY & EQPT, INDL, WHOLESALE: Processing & Packaging

Magnum Venus Products Inc .... G 727 573-2955
Goshen (G-6210)

MACHINERY & EQPT, INDL, WHOLESALE: Safety Eqpt

Western-Cullen-Hayes Inc .... F 765 962-0526
Richmond (G-14226)

MACHINERY & EQPT, INDL, WHOLESALE: Sawmill

Square 1 Dsign Manufacture Inc .... F 866 647-7771
Shelbyville (G-14800)

MACHINERY & EQPT, INDL, WHOLESALE: Sewing

Hope Hardwoods Inc .... F 812 546-4427
Hope (G-7226)

Industrial Sewing Machine Co .... G 812 425-2255
Evansville (G-4124)

MACHINERY & EQPT, INDL, WHOLESALE: Trailers, Indl

Novae LLC .... E 260 758-9838
Markle (G-11361)

MACHINERY & EQPT, INDL, WHOLESALE: Water Pumps

3w Enterprises LLC .... G 847 366-6555
Elkhart (G-3137)

MACHINERY & EQPT, WHOLESALE: Construction, General

AF Ohab Company Inc .... E 317 225-4740
Indianapolis (G-7455)

Delphi Body Works .... F 765 564-2212
Delphi (G-2893)

ITR America LLC .... D 219 947-8230
Hobart (G-7193)

Masbez LLC .... G 855 962-7239
Frankfort (G-5681)

Schlatters Inc .... G 219 567-9158
Francesville (G-5645)

MACHINERY & EQPT: Farm

Agri-Power Inc .... F 812 874-3316
Poseyville (G-13976)

Andersons Agriculture Group LP .... F 765 564-6135
Delphi (G-2890)

AT Ferrell Company Inc .... E 260 824-3400
Bluffton (G-1026)

Azland Inc .... G 765 429-6200
West Lafayette (G-16564)

Bonnell Grain Handling Inc .... E 574 595-7827
Star City (G-15396)

Bruning Enterprises Inc .... G 317 835-7591
Shelbyville (G-14742)

Case Lineage Management .... G 317 721-1764
Indianapolis (G-7754)

Case New Holland LLC .... E 765 482-5446
Lebanon (G-10881)

Case Weinkauff .... G 219 733-9484
Valparaiso (G-15925)

Cases Marine Service Inc .... G 317 379-0020
Arcadia (G-310)

Chief Metal Works Inc .... G 765 932-2134
Rushville (G-14396)

Churchill Equipment .... G 812 347-2592
Depauw (G-2937)

City Welding & Fabrication .... G 765 569-5403
Rockville (G-14350)

Cnh Industrial America LLC .... C 765 482-5409
Lebanon (G-10884)

Cowco Inc .... G 812 346-8993
North Vernon (G-13260)

Ctb Inc .... E 574 658-4191
Milford (G-11791)

CTB MN Investment Co Inc .... E 574 658-4191
Milford (G-11794)

D A Hochstetler & Sons LLP .... F 574 642-1144
Topeka (G-15800)

Danko Farm Supply & Feed Inc .... G 812 870-7413
Sullivan (G-15404)

Davaus LLC .... G 260 245-5006
Hoagland (G-7166)

Davern Machine Shop .... G 765 505-1051
Dana (G-2804)

Delphi Products Co Inc .... F 800 382-7903
Delphi (G-2894)

Earthway Products LLC .... D 574 848-7491
Bristol (G-1258)

Et AG Center LLC .... F 317 834-4500
Mooresville (G-12205)

Farm Innovators Inc .... E 574 936-5096
Plymouth (G-13774)

Franklin Olin .... G 765 342-9040
Martinsville (G-11396)

Garver Manufacturing Inc .... G 765 964-5828
Union City (G-15854)

Gator Cases Inc .... F 260 627-8070
Columbia City (G-2148)

Goliath Ag LLC .... F 765 305-1141
Winchester (G-16888)

Greensbroom .... G 317 416-7818
Indianapolis (G-8322)

Hahn Enterprises Inc .... G 574 862-4491
Wakarusa (G-16234)

Hampton Equipment LLC .... G 260 740-8704
Fort Wayne (G-5049)

Headsight Inc .... G 574 546-5022
Bremen (G-1196)

Hog Slat Incorporated .... E 574 967-3776
Flora (G-4659)

Honeyville Metal Inc .... D 800 593-8377
Topeka (G-15809)

Hunter Industries .... G 630 200-7581
Noblesville (G-13097)

Hurricane Ditcher Company Inc .... F 812 886-9663
Vincennes (G-16130)

Jacobs Mfg LLC .... G 574 583-3883
Monticello (G-12154)

Jeffs Farm Svc .... G 812 254-1980
Washington (G-16487)

JI Manfcturing Fabrication Inc .... G 260 589-3723
Berne (G-716)

Koenig Equipment Inc .... G 765 962-7330
Richmond (G-14154)

MACHINERY & EQPT: Farm

Land Enterprises .... G 317 774-9475
　Noblesville *(G-13126)*
Living Prairie Equipment LLC .... G 765 479-0759
　Wolcott *(G-16933)*
Madison Manufacturing Inc .... E 574 633-4433
　Bremen *(G-1204)*
McKillip Machinery Inc .... G 260 330-2842
　Wabash *(G-16199)*
McM Manufacturing .... G 574 339-6994
　South Bend *(G-15146)*
Modern AG Solutions LLC .... G 765 221-1011
　Pendleton *(G-13544)*
Mooresville Welding Inc .... G 317 831-2265
　Mooresville *(G-12225)*
National Equipment Inc .... G 219 462-1205
　Valparaiso *(G-16009)*
New Holland Richmond Inc .... F 765 962-7724
　Richmond *(G-14174)*
Onyett Welding & Machine Inc .... G 812 582-2999
　Petersburg *(G-13620)*
Oxbo International Corporation .... G 260 768-3217
　Shipshewana *(G-14874)*
Perma-Green Supreme Inc .... E 219 548-3801
　Valparaiso *(G-16025)*
Peterson Mfg LLC .... G 574 876-1427
　Wheatfield *(G-16771)*
Shobe Cases LLC .... G 317 363-9006
　Indianapolis *(G-9421)*
Spankys Paintball .... G 812 752-7375
　Scottsburg *(G-14580)*
Superb Horticulture LLC .... F 800 567-8264
　Plymouth *(G-13815)*
Whitcraft Welding .... G 574 867-6021
　Grovertown *(G-6825)*
Wood Lighter Cases LLC .... G 812 969-3908
　Elizabeth *(G-3131)*
Writers of Vision .... G 812 239-6347
　Farmersburg *(G-4421)*

MACHINERY & EQPT: Liquid Automation

Automated Proc Eqp Svcs LLC .... G 219 206-2517
　Union Mills *(G-15863)*
Duesenberg Inc .... G 260 496-9650
　Fort Wayne *(G-4931)*
Faztech LLC .... G 812 327-0926
　Bloomington *(G-864)*
Mixer Direct LLC .... D 812 202-4047
　Jeffersonville *(G-10020)*
Ryoei USA Inc .... F 317 912-4498
　Indianapolis *(G-9352)*

MACHINERY, EQPT & SUPPLIES: Parking Facility

Bright Line Striping LLC .... G 765 404-1402
　Lafayette *(G-10543)*
City of Anderson .... G 765 648-6715
　Anderson *(G-93)*
Rexing-Goedde Electric Service .... G 812 963-5725
　Wadesville *(G-16229)*

MACHINERY, FOOD PRDTS: Cutting, Chopping, Grinding, Mixing

Urschel Laboratories Inc .... B 219 464-4811
　Chesterton *(G-1964)*
Willow Way LLC .... G 765 886-4640
　Hagerstown *(G-6849)*

MACHINERY, FOOD PRDTS: Dairy & Milk

Kaeb Sales Inc .... G 574 862-2477
　Wakarusa *(G-16236)*

Metzger Dairy Inc .... F 260 564-5445
　Kimmell *(G-10171)*

MACHINERY, FOOD PRDTS: Ovens, Bakery

Roost .... G 317 842-3735
　Fishers *(G-4599)*

MACHINERY, MAILING: Postage Meters

Pitney Bowes Inc .... G 260 436-7395
　Indianapolis *(G-9148)*
Vernon A Stevens .... G 812 626-0010
　Evansville *(G-4371)*

MACHINERY, METALWORKING: Coilers, Metalworking

Rci Hv Inc .... D 724 538-3180
　Chesterton *(G-1956)*

MACHINERY, PAPER INDUSTRY: Converting, Die Cutting & Stampng

C & W Inkd .... F 317 352-1000
　Indianapolis *(G-7706)*

MACHINERY, PRINTING TRADES: Plates

Precision Rubber Plate Co Inc .... D 317 783-3226
　Indianapolis *(G-9186)*

MACHINERY, WOODWORKING: Sanding, Exc Portable Floor Sanders

Sandman Products LLC .... G 574 264-7700
　Elkhart *(G-3662)*

MACHINERY: Ammunition & Explosives Loading

Bobcat Armament and Mfg LLC .... G 317 699-6127
　Shelbyville *(G-14738)*

MACHINERY: Automotive Related

3g Concepts LLC .... G 574 267-6100
　Warsaw *(G-16306)*
AMI Industries Inc .... G 989 786-3755
　Angola *(G-226)*
Automatic Fastner Tools .... G 317 784-4111
　Indianapolis *(G-7575)*
Computer Age Engineering Inc .... E 765 674-8551
　Marion *(G-11278)*
D W Stewart .... G 260 463-2607
　Lagrange *(G-10733)*
Eagle Consulting Inc .... G 317 590-0485
　Indianapolis *(G-8031)*
First Gear Inc .... E 260 490-3238
　Fort Wayne *(G-4984)*
Lyntech Engineering Inc .... G 574 224-2300
　Rochester *(G-14303)*
Metal Technologies Inc .... D 812 384-9800
　Auburn *(G-406)*
Mvo Usa Inc .... F 317 585-5785
　Indianapolis *(G-8974)*
Sinden Racing Service Inc .... F 317 243-7171
　Indianapolis *(G-9443)*
SMC Corporation of America .... B 317 899-4440
　Noblesville *(G-13176)*
Trimax Machine LLC .... G 812 887-9281
　Bruceville *(G-1433)*
Vauterbuilt Inc .... G 219 712-2384
　Hebron *(G-7108)*

MACHINERY: Bridge Or Gate, Hydraulic

Beatty International Inc .... E 219 931-3000
　Hammond *(G-6882)*

Bemcor Inc .... F 219 937-1600
　Hammond *(G-6885)*

MACHINERY: Construction

1109 169th LLC .... G 219 671-5052
　Crown Point *(G-2647)*
AMA Usa Inc .... G 317 329-6590
　Indianapolis *(G-7494)*
Avis Industrial Corporation .... E 765 998-8100
　Upland *(G-15876)*
Birdeye Inc .... F 812 886-0598
　Vincennes *(G-16115)*
Boarder Magic By J & A .... G 317 545-4401
　Indianapolis *(G-7652)*
Border Mgic By Wlden Entps Inc .... G 317 628-2314
　Indianapolis *(G-7660)*
Caterpillar Inc .... E 630 743-4094
　Greenfield *(G-6476)*
Caterpillar Inc .... C 765 448-5000
　Lafayette *(G-10549)*
Caterpillar Inc .... G 765 447-6816
　Lafayette *(G-10550)*
Colby L Stanger .... G 574 536-5835
　Goshen *(G-6114)*
Galfab LLC .... F 574 946-7767
　Winamac *(G-16861)*
Highland Park Services Inc .... G 317 954-0456
　Indianapolis *(G-8398)*
Howard Materials LLC .... G 317 849-9666
　Indianapolis *(G-8430)*
Indco Inc .... G 812 945-4383
　New Albany *(G-12746)*
ITR America LLC .... D 219 947-8230
　Hobart *(G-7193)*
Kentuckiana Machine and Tl Inc .... G 502 301-9005
　Lanesville *(G-10800)*
Keystone Engrg & Mfg Corp .... F 317 271-6192
　Avon *(G-532)*
Maddox Industrial Contg LLC .... E 812 544-2156
　Santa Claus *(G-14508)*
Mittler Supply Inc .... G 765 289-6341
　Muncie *(G-12457)*
Road Alert Systems LLC .... G 219 669-1206
　Morocco *(G-12269)*
Schaefer Yard Care Ldscpg LLC .... G 812 215-6424
　Oakland City *(G-13322)*
Smith Excavating .... G 812 636-0054
　Odon *(G-13351)*
Speedway Construction Pdts LLC .... G 260 203-9806
　Fort Wayne *(G-5429)*
Square 1 Dsign Manufacture Inc .... F 866 647-7771
　Shelbyville *(G-14800)*
Stedman Machine Company Inc .... D 812 926-0038
　Aurora *(G-457)*
Summerlot Engineered Pdts Inc .... F 812 466-7266
　Rosedale *(G-14383)*
Templeton Coal Company Inc .... C 812 232-7037
　Terre Haute *(G-15726)*
Terex Advance Mixer Inc .... D 260 497-0728
　Fort Wayne *(G-5475)*
Terex Corporation .... G 574 342-0086
　Bourbon *(G-1129)*
Terex Corporation .... C 260 497-0728
　Fort Wayne *(G-5476)*
Unrivaled Interiors LLC .... G 317 509-0496
　Cicero *(G-2002)*

MACHINERY: Cryogenic, Industrial

Technifab Products Inc .... E 812 442-0520
　Brazil *(G-1166)*

MACHINERY: Custom

Ahaus Tool & Engineering Inc.............. D 765 962-3573
Richmond *(G-14084)*

American Industrial McHy Inc................. F 219 755-4090
Merrillville *(G-11483)*

Bcd and Associates LLC...................... G 317 873-5394
Indianapolis *(G-7601)*

Carl A Nix Welding Service Inc.............. F 812 386-6281
Princeton *(G-13987)*

Carmel Engineering Inc......................... F 765 279-8955
Kirklin *(G-10187)*

CL Tech Inc.. G 812 526-0995
Edinburgh *(G-3072)*

Custom Mch Motioneering Inc................ E 574 251-0292
South Bend *(G-14993)*

Davis Tool & Machine LLC.................... F 317 896-9278
Westfield *(G-16684)*

Evart Engineering Company Inc............. F 765 354-2232
Middletown *(G-11769)*

Fortville Feeders Inc............................ D 317 485-5195
Fortville *(G-5595)*

Fourman Enterprises Inc....................... F 812 546-5734
Hope *(G-7225)*

Grindco Inc.. E 219 763-6130
Chesterton *(G-1932)*

Industrial Hydraulics Inc....................... E 317 247-4421
Indianapolis *(G-8518)*

Injection Plastics & Mfg Co.................... E 574 784-2070
Lapaz *(G-10816)*

Jennerjahn Machine Inc....................... D 765 998-2733
Marion *(G-11300)*

JMS Machine Inc................................. G 260 244-0077
Columbia City *(G-2161)*

K C Cmponents Wldg Fabrication........... G 317 539-6067
Greencastle *(G-6416)*

Keller Machine & Welding Inc............... E 219 464-4915
Valparaiso *(G-15986)*

King Investments Inc........................... G 812 752-6000
Scottsburg *(G-14568)*

Kokomo Metal Fabricators Inc............... G 765 459-8173
Kokomo *(G-10292)*

Lynn Tool Company Inc........................ G 765 874-2471
Lynn *(G-11185)*

Mechancal Engrg Cntrls Atmtn C........... E 574 294-7580
Elkhart *(G-3522)*

Metaltec Inc.. G 219 362-9811
La Porte *(G-10452)*

Micromatic LLC.................................... D 260 589-2136
Berne *(G-720)*

Millers Wldg & Mech Svcs Inc............... G 812 923-3359
Pekin *(G-13519)*

Mitchum-Schaefer Inc.......................... E 317 546-4081
Indianapolis *(G-8935)*

Novamatiq Inc..................................... E 260 483-1153
Fort Wayne *(G-5277)*

Oakley Industries LLC.......................... G 812 246-2600
Sellersburg *(G-14608)*

Perfecto Tool & Engineering Co............. G 765 644-2821
Anderson *(G-176)*

Pinson Manufacturing Co LLC................ G 217 273-8819
Albany *(G-14)*

Piper Flyers II Inc................................ E 317 858-9538
Zionsville *(G-17042)*

Prodigy Mold & Tool Inc....................... G 812 753-3029
Haubstadt *(G-7088)*

Qig LLC... E 260 244-3591
Columbia City *(G-2185)*

Reynolds & Co Inc............................... E 812 232-5313
Terre Haute *(G-15681)*

Selco Engineering Inc........................... F
Shelbyville *(G-14795)*

Square 1 Dsign Manufacture Inc............ F 866 647-7711
Shelbyville *(G-14800)*

SSd Control Technology Inc.................. E 574 289-5942
South Bend *(G-15264)*

T & M Precision Inc.............................. G 812 689-5769
Versailles *(G-16104)*

T K Fabricating.................................... G 765 866-0755
Crawfordsville *(G-2622)*

Titus Inc... F 574 936-3345
Plymouth *(G-13817)*

Tmak Inc... E 219 874-7661
Michigan City *(G-11679)*

Total Tote Inc...................................... G 260 982-8318
North Manchester *(G-13252)*

Tree City Tool & Engrg Co Inc............... E 812 663-4196
Greensburg *(G-6637)*

Union Tool Corp................................... E 574 267-3211
Warsaw *(G-16440)*

US Valves Inc...................................... G 812 476-6662
Evansville *(G-4365)*

Uway Extrusion LLC............................. G 765 592-6089
Marshall *(G-11375)*

MACHINERY: Desalination Eqpt

Watershipblue LLC.............................. G 317 910-8585
Indianapolis *(G-9741)*

MACHINERY: Electronic Component Making

Moorfeed Corporation........................... E 317 545-7171
Greenfield *(G-6532)*

MACHINERY: Gas Separators

Separation By Design Inc..................... E 812 424-1239
Evansville *(G-4305)*

MACHINERY: Ice Cream

Flavor Burst LLC.................................. E 317 745-2952
Danville *(G-2812)*

MD Holdings LLC.................................. G 317 831-7030
Mooresville *(G-12220)*

MACHINERY: Ice Making

Manitowoc Beverage Eqp Inc................ C 812 246-7000
New Albany *(G-12770)*

MACHINERY: Metalworking

Aam-Equipco Inc.................................. G 574 272-8886
Granger *(G-6329)*

Aaron McWhirter................................... G 307 256-0070
Camby *(G-1506)*

Abell Tool Co Inc.................................. G 317 887-0021
Greenwood *(G-6658)*

Concept Machinery Inc......................... G 317 845-5588
Indianapolis *(G-7850)*

Finite Filtation Company....................... G 219 789-8084
Crown Point *(G-2684)*

George Koch Sons LLC.......................... D 812 465-9600
Evansville *(G-4089)*

Glaze Tool and Engineering Inc............. E 260 493-4557
New Haven *(G-12905)*

Grinding and Polsg McHy Corp.............. F 317 898-0750
Indianapolis *(G-8331)*

Gsw Press Automation Inc.................... G 419 733-5230
North Vernon *(G-13273)*

Innovative Mold & Machine Inc.............. G 317 634-1177
Indianapolis *(G-8557)*

McBroom Electric Co Inc....................... D 317 926-3451
Indianapolis *(G-8860)*

Meriwether Tool & Engrg Inc................. E 260 744-6955
Fort Wayne *(G-5214)*

Pia Automation US Inc......................... E 812 485-5500
Evansville *(G-4242)*

Precision Automation Company............. E 812 283-7963
Clarksville *(G-2028)*

Quality Industrial Supplies................... G 219 324-2654
La Porte *(G-10468)*

Star Tool Inc....................................... E 812 372-6730
Columbus *(G-2395)*

Walkerton Tool & Die Inc...................... E 574 586-3162
Walkerton *(G-16279)*

Wastequip Manufacturing Co LLC.......... D 574 946-6631
Winamac *(G-16880)*

X-Y Tool and Die Inc............................. D 260 357-3365
Laotto *(G-10812)*

MACHINERY: Mining

Brake Supply Company Inc................... C 812 467-1000
Evansville *(G-3950)*

Claymore Tools Inc............................... G 574 255-6483
South Bend *(G-14975)*

Jenmar Enterprises LLC........................ G 219 306-3149
Noblesville *(G-13113)*

Jones Trucking Inc............................... G 765 537-2279
Paragon *(G-13502)*

K-Tron America Inc.............................. D 812 934-7000
Batesville *(G-594)*

Keystone Engrg & Mfg Corp................. F 317 271-6192
Avon *(G-532)*

Mine System Solutions LLC.................. G 270 952-5422
Boonville *(G-1091)*

Pillar Innovations LLC.......................... G 812 474-9080
Evansville *(G-4244)*

S & S Machine Shop Inc....................... E 812 897-5343
Boonville *(G-1096)*

Wyatt Farm Center Inc......................... G 574 354-2998
Nappanee *(G-12655)*

MACHINERY: Packaging

All Packaging Equipment Corp.............. G 574 294-3371
Elkhart *(G-3163)*

Apex Filling Systems Inc...................... G 219 575-7493
Michigan City *(G-11578)*

Chicago Automated Labeling Inc............ G 219 531-0646
Valparaiso *(G-15926)*

Christ Packing Systems Corp................ G 574 243-9110
South Bend *(G-14972)*

Grrk Holdings Inc................................. E 317 872-0172
Indianapolis *(G-8336)*

Kwik Lok Corporation........................... E 260 493-1220
New Haven *(G-12909)*

Lindal North America Inc...................... D 812 657-7142
Columbus *(G-2342)*

Monosol LLC.. G 219 763-7589
Portage *(G-13891)*

Morgan Adhesives Company LLC........... B 812 342-2004
Columbus *(G-2357)*

Nyx LLC.. A 734 838-3570
New Albany *(G-12786)*

Packaging Systems Indiana Inc............. G 765 449-1011
Lafayette *(G-10661)*

Parkway Industrial Entps LLC................ F 260 622-7200
Ossian *(G-13430)*

Powell Systems Inc.............................. E 765 884-0980
Fowler *(G-5630)*

Precision Automation Company............. E 812 283-7963
Clarksville *(G-2028)*

Precision Products Group Inc................ F 317 663-4590
Indianapolis *(G-9184)*

Webber Manufacturing Company........... E 317 357-8681
Indianapolis *(G-9745)*

MACHINERY: Paint Making

Indco Inc... G 812 945-4383
New Albany *(G-12746)*

MACHINERY: Paint Making

UFS Corporation... F 219 464-2027
Valparaiso *(G-16070)*

MACHINERY: Plastic Working

Cutting Edge Machine & Tl Inc.................... D 866 514-1620
New Paris *(G-12949)*

Hermetic Coil Co Inc..................................... E 812 735-2400
Bicknell *(G-734)*

Honey Creek Machine Inc........................... E 812 299-5255
Terre Haute *(G-15605)*

Kenco Plastics Inc.. F 219 324-6621
La Porte *(G-10433)*

Peerless Machine & Tool Corp.................... D 765 662-2586
Marion *(G-11326)*

Summit Industrial Tech Inc.......................... G 260 494-3461
Columbia City *(G-2204)*

Tamco Manufacturing Co............................. G 574 294-1909
Elkhart *(G-3714)*

Tuskin Equipment Corporation.................... G 630 466-5590
Elkhart *(G-3754)*

MACHINERY: Pottery Making

American Art Clay Co Inc............................. C 317 244-6871
Indianapolis *(G-7499)*

MACHINERY: Printing Presses

Abacus Printingngraphics Inc...................... E 915 223-5166
Indianapolis *(G-7412)*

Indiana Imprint LLC...................................... G 812 704-2773
French Lick *(G-5846)*

Kbc Machine... G 317 446-6163
Greenfield *(G-6523)*

Print Queens LLC... G 317 285-8934
Indianapolis *(G-9201)*

Scalable Press Inc....................................... G 877 752-9060
Indianapolis *(G-9384)*

MACHINERY: Recycling

Hillenbrand Inc.. A 812 931-5000
Batesville *(G-590)*

Sortera Technologies Inc............................. E 260 330-7100
Markle *(G-11362)*

MACHINERY: Road Construction & Maintenance

County of Lagrange...................................... F 260 499-6353
Lagrange *(G-10732)*

MACHINERY: Rubber Working

Engineering and Industrial .... E 574 722-3714
Logansport *(G-11073)*

MACHINERY: Semiconductor Manufacturing

Anatolia Group Ltd Partnership.................... G 203 343-7808
Indianapolis *(G-7514)*

Applied Electronic Mtls LLC......................... G 260 438-8632
Fort Wayne *(G-4765)*

Hirata Corporation of America..................... E 317 856-8600
Indianapolis *(G-8399)*

Siddhi Integrated Mfg Svcs Inc.................... G 502 298-8640
Clarksville *(G-2036)*

Sugarcube Systems Inc............................... G 765 543-6709
Lafayette *(G-10704)*

MACHINERY: Textile

Machining Solutions..................................... G 574 292-3227
South Bend *(G-15132)*

Precision Additive Solutions........................ G 419 320-6978
Carmel *(G-1727)*

Southern Mechatronics Co Inc..................... G
Brownsburg *(G-1404)*

MACHINERY: Wire Drawing

Bell Machine Company Inc.......................... E 765 654-5225
Frankfort *(G-5652)*

Dwd Industries LLC..................................... G 260 639-3254
Hoagland *(G-7167)*

Dwd Industries LLC..................................... E 260 728-9272
Decatur *(G-2854)*

Esteves-Dwd LLC.. D 260 728-9272
Decatur *(G-2855)*

Precision Die Technologies LLC.................. F 260 482-5001
Fort Wayne *(G-5336)*

Premier Consulting Inc................................ F 260 496-9300
Fort Wayne *(G-5343)*

Royer Enterprises Inc.................................. G 260 359-0689
Huntington *(G-7362)*

Wynn Wire Die Services Inc........................ G 260 471-1395
Fort Wayne *(G-5578)*

MACHINERY: Woodworking

Core Wood Components LLC...................... G 574 370-4457
Elkhart *(G-3268)*

Grinding and Polsg McHy Corp................... F 317 898-0750
Indianapolis *(G-8331)*

Lozier Machinery Incorporated.................... G 812 945-2558
New Albany *(G-12766)*

McFeelys Inc.. F 800 443-7937
Aurora *(G-449)*

Nobbe Concrete Products Inc..................... G 765 647-4017
Brookville *(G-1329)*

Northtech Machine LLC............................... F 812 967-7400
Borden *(G-1116)*

PDQ Workholding LLC................................ E 260 244-2919
Columbia City *(G-2179)*

Squirrel Daddy Inc....................................... G 260 723-4946
South Whitley *(G-15326)*

MACHINISTS' TOOLS & MACHINES: Measuring, Metalworking Type

Clarks Cnc LLC.. G 812 508-1773
Springville *(G-15383)*

Picketts Place Inc.. G 317 763-1168
Westfield *(G-16717)*

MACHINISTS' TOOLS: Precision

Advent Precision Inc.................................... G 317 908-6937
Indianapolis *(G-7445)*

Beverly Industrial Service Inc...................... E 812 667-5047
Dillsboro *(G-2943)*

CPR Machining LLC.................................... E 574 299-0222
South Bend *(G-14984)*

Scheidler Machine Incorporated.................. G 812 662-6555
Greensburg *(G-6630)*

Stapert Tool & Machine Co Inc.................... G 317 787-2387
Indianapolis *(G-9497)*

Yamaguchi Mfg Usa Inc............................... G 765 973-9130
Richmond *(G-14230)*

MAGAZINES, WHOLESALE

Great Deals Magazine.................................. F 765 649-3302
Anderson *(G-123)*

Magazine Fulfillment Corp........................... F 219 874-4245
Michigan City *(G-11636)*

MAGNESIUM

Liteauto Inc... G 317 813-5045
Indianapolis *(G-8769)*

MAGNETIC SHIELDS, METAL

Ad-Vance Magnetics Inc.............................. E 574 223-3158
Rochester *(G-14274)*

MAGNETIC TAPE, AUDIO: Prerecorded

Boeke Road Baptist Church Inc.................. G 812 479-5342
Evansville *(G-3938)*

MAGNETS: Permanent

Magnequench Inc... E 765 778-7809
Pendleton *(G-13542)*

Magnets R US Inc.. G 574 633-0061
South Bend *(G-15135)*

Thomas & Skinner Inc................................. C 317 923-2501
Indianapolis *(G-9592)*

MAIL-ORDER HOUSE, NEC

Indiana Botanic Gardens Inc....................... C 219 947-4040
Hobart *(G-7191)*

Summerville Miniature Work Sp................... G 317 326-8355
Greenfield *(G-6561)*

MAIL-ORDER HOUSES: Educational Splys & Eqpt

DMC Distribution LLC.................................. G 219 926-6401
Porter *(G-13924)*

MAIL-ORDER HOUSES: Fitness & Sporting Goods

Official Sports Intl Inc.................................. F 574 269-1404
Warsaw *(G-16403)*

MAILBOX RENTAL & RELATED SVCS

Noblesville Pack & Ship............................... G 317 776-6306
Noblesville *(G-13144)*

P413 Corporation... G 317 769-0679
Zionsville *(G-17039)*

PostNet Postal & Business Svcs................ G 317 462-7118
Greenfield *(G-6541)*

MAILING SVCS, NEC

Anthony Wayne Rhblttion Ctr For............... C 317 972-1000
Indianapolis *(G-7522)*

Anthony Wayne Rhblttion Ctr For............... D 260 744-6145
Fort Wayne *(G-4762)*

Baugh Enterprises Inc................................. F 812 334-8189
Bloomington *(G-796)*

Cozy Cat Inc... G 765 463-1254
Lafayette *(G-10559)*

Data Mail Incorporated................................ E 812 424-7835
Evansville *(G-4007)*

Delp Printing & Mailing Inc......................... G 317 872-9744
Indianapolis *(G-7963)*

Faris Mailing Inc.. F 317 246-3315
Indianapolis *(G-8167)*

Fineline Graphics Incorporated................... D 317 872-4490
Indianapolis *(G-8188)*

Lori Hicks... G 574 291-6341
South Bend *(G-15129)*

Printing Partners Inc................................... D 317 635-2282
Indianapolis *(G-9206)*

Service Graphics Inc................................... D 317 471-8246
Indianapolis *(G-9408)*

MANAGEMENT CONSULTING SVCS: Administrative

Gibson Nehemiah Group Inc....................... F 317 643-3838
Muncie *(G-12401)*

MANAGEMENT CONSULTING SVCS: Automation & Robotics

General Automation Company..................... F 317 849-7483
Noblesville *(G-13085)*

PRODUCT SECTION
MANUFACTURING INDUSTRIES, NEC

Liberty Automation LLC.......................... G 574 524-0436
　Albion (G-31)
Plum Group Inc...................................... F 617 712-3000
　Indianapolis (G-9155)
Quantum Technologies LLC.................... G 765 426-0156
　Elizabethtown (G-3132)

MANAGEMENT CONSULTING SVCS: Business

Eli Lilly International Corp....................... F 317 276-2000
　Indianapolis (G-8091)
Mpp Holdings Inc................................... G 317 805-3764
　Noblesville (G-13140)
Tgf Enterprises LLC............................... G 440 840-9704
　Indianapolis (G-9585)
Winfield Solutions LLC........................... G 317 838-3733
　Plainfield (G-13743)

MANAGEMENT CONSULTING SVCS: Construction Project

Assured General Contg LLC................... G 260 740-4744
　Fort Wayne (G-4776)
Maddox Industrial Contg LLC................. E 812 544-2156
　Santa Claus (G-14508)

MANAGEMENT CONSULTING SVCS: Distribution Channels

Blackpoint Distribution Co LLC............... E 260 414-9096
　Leo (G-10964)
Georg Utz Inc.. E 812 526-2240
　Edinburgh (G-3085)

MANAGEMENT CONSULTING SVCS: General

Digital Carvings LLC.............................. G 812 269-6123
　Ellettsville (G-3807)
Life Path Numerology Center.................. G 317 638-9752
　Indianapolis (G-8747)

MANAGEMENT CONSULTING SVCS: Hospital & Health

Carelogiq Corp...................................... G 219 682-6327
　Munster (G-12534)
Clinical Architecture LLC....................... E 317 580-8400
　Carmel (G-1590)
Tmx Healthcare Tech LLC...................... F 877 874-6339
　Indianapolis (G-9614)

MANAGEMENT CONSULTING SVCS: Industrial

McNeil Coatings Cons Inc....................... G 317 885-1557
　Greenwood (G-6736)

MANAGEMENT CONSULTING SVCS: Industrial & Labor

Machining & Repr Resource Inc.............. G 219 588-7395
　Highland (G-7143)

MANAGEMENT CONSULTING SVCS: Industry Specialist

Northern Indiana Ordnance Co................ G 574 289-5938
　South Bend (G-15173)

MANAGEMENT CONSULTING SVCS: Information Systems

Waseve LLC.. G 443 204-7976
　Carmel (G-1799)

MANAGEMENT CONSULTING SVCS: Manufacturing

Ditech Inc.. E 812 526-0850
　Edinburgh (G-3077)

MANAGEMENT CONSULTING SVCS: Quality Assurance

Smith Consulting Inc.............................. E 765 728-5980
　Montpelier (G-12181)

MANAGEMENT CONSULTING SVCS: Real Estate

Adafill Global LLC.................................. G 317 798-5378
　Indianapolis (G-7427)

MANAGEMENT CONSULTING SVCS: Training & Development

Christian Sound & Song Inc.................... G 574 294-2893
　Elkhart (G-3251)

MANAGEMENT CONSULTING SVCS: Transportation

Dock Bumpers Inc.................................. G 312 597-9282
　Highland (G-7132)
Rios Investment Services LLC................. G 574 514-3999
　South Bend (G-15221)
Sorbtech Inc.. G 812 944-9108
　Clarksville (G-2037)

MANAGEMENT SERVICES

Agi International Inc............................... F 317 536-2415
　Indianapolis (G-7458)
Automated Laser Corporation................. G 260 637-4140
　Fort Wayne (G-4781)
Central Coca-Cola Btlg Co Inc................ E 800 241-2653
　Bloomington (G-828)
Central Coca-Cola Btlg Co Inc................ E 800 241-2653
　Indianapolis (G-7770)
Central Coca-Cola Btlg Co Inc................ E 812 482-7475
　Jasper (G-9827)
Central Coca-Cola Btlg Co Inc................ E 260 726-7126
　Portland (G-13930)
Central Coca-Cola Btlg Co Inc................ E 800 241-2653
　Shelbyville (G-14744)
Crown Training and Dev Inc.................... G 219 947-0845
　Merrillville (G-11500)
Fretina Corporation................................ F 812 547-6471
　Tell City (G-15504)
Indiana Scale Company Inc.................... F 812 232-0893
　Terre Haute (G-15617)
LH Industries Corp................................. E 260 432-5563
　Fort Wayne (G-5181)
Patrick Industries Inc............................. G 574 293-1521
　Elkhart (G-3597)

MANAGEMENT SVCS: Business

Agora Brands Group Inc......................... E 615 802-0086
　Borden (G-1104)
Commtineo LLC..................................... F 219 476-3667
　Wanatah (G-16288)
Paragon Force Inc.................................. D 812 384-3040
　Bloomfield (G-755)

MANAGEMENT SVCS: Construction

Assured General Contg LLC................... G 260 740-4744
　Fort Wayne (G-4776)
Hgmc Supply Inc.................................... F 317 351-9500
　Indianapolis (G-8394)

Pittman Mine Service LLC...................... G 812 847-2340
　Linton (G-11042)

MANPOWER TRAINING

Cooperative Ventures Ind Corp............... G 317 564-4695
　Carmel (G-1596)

MANUFACTURING INDUSTRIES, NEC

4 Lens Partnerships LLC........................ G 317 490-1389
　Indianapolis (G-7390)
Abbott L Abbott Nutrition....................... G 765 935-8650
　Richmond (G-14082)
ABS Mfg Rep Inc.................................... G 317 407-0406
　Carmel (G-1548)
Accra Pac Holding Co LLC..................... G 765 326-0005
　Fort Wayne (G-4719)
Achates LLC.. F 317 852-6978
　Brownsburg (G-1343)
Acme Firearms Mfg LLC......................... G 812 522-4008
　Seymour (G-14624)
Adept LLC... G 812 275-8899
　Bedford (G-618)
Advanced Mfg Solutions LLC.................. G 812 691-2030
　Shelburn (G-14716)
Advantage Manufacturing LLC................ G 317 831-2902
　Martinsville (G-11377)
Agile Mfg Inc... G 417 845-6065
　Milford (G-11785)
Alliance Studios LLC............................. G 317 525-8487
　Indianapolis (G-7483)
Alpha Matrix LLC................................... G 812 686-1640
　Lamar (G-10794)
America Corn Cutter............................... G 219 733-0885
　Wanatah (G-16285)
American Axle Manufacturi.................... F 812 418-7726
　Columbus (G-2217)
Anchor Industries.................................. G 812 664-0772
　Owensville (G-13465)
Anglers Manufacturing........................... G 812 988-8040
　Nashville (G-12660)
Apex Industries LLC.............................. G 260 624-5003
　Angola (G-230)
ARC Industries...................................... G 812 471-1633
　Evansville (G-3897)
ARC Industries LLC............................... G 317 753-1607
　Carmel (G-1563)
Archer Industries LLC............................ G 317 418-1260
　Indianapolis (G-7539)
Armor Contract Mfg Inc.......................... F 574 327-2962
　Elkhart (G-3189)
Artistic Stone Mfg LLC........................... G 574 546-3771
　Bremen (G-1173)
Aunt Netts Country Candles LLC............ G 765 557-2770
　Elwood (G-3818)
Austins Metal Mafia Inc.......................... G 812 619-6115
　Cannelton (G-1531)
B Industries Inc..................................... G 574 264-3290
　Elkhart (G-3211)
B&R Manufacturing Inc........................... G 574 293-5669
　Elkhart (G-3213)
B2 Manufacturing LLC........................... G 765 993-4519
　Fountain City (G-5609)
Bantam Industries Inc............................ G 714 561-6122
　Indianapolis (G-7596)
Barnwood Masters LLC......................... G 260 414-9790
　Mentone (G-11469)
Basin Material Handling LLC.................. G 812 849-0124
　Mitchell (G-12032)
Bbs Celebration Center.......................... G 765 730-6575
　Yorktown (G-16971)
Bells and Whistles LLC.......................... G 317 315-3129
　Bloomington (G-801)

MANUFACTURING INDUSTRIES, NEC

Brothers Industries LLC.................................. G 812 560-6224
Greensburg (G-6583)

Browell Bellhousing Inc................................... G 765 447-2292
Lafayette (G-10545)

Buck Hollow Cnc LLC..................................... G 717 269-9322
Brownsville (G-1430)

Buehrer Industries LLC.................................. G 260 563-2181
Wabash (G-16175)

Bunny Flaming Industries............................... G 317 554-7143
Indianapolis (G-7700)

C & B Industries LLC..................................... G 260 490-3000
Fort Wayne (G-4824)

C & C Industries.. G 260 804-6518
Fort Wayne (G-4825)

C & F Industries LLC..................................... G 765 580-0378
Liberty (G-10984)

C & J K Industries Inc.................................... G 219 746-5760
Munster (G-12533)

Carousel Industries.. G 317 674-8111
Fishers (G-4483)

Carter Enterprises Inc.................................... G 317 984-1497
Arcadia (G-309)

Carters Manufacturing & Weld....................... G 630 464-1520
Knox (G-10203)

Casting Company Inc..................................... G 317 509-4311
Indianapolis (G-7757)

CCM Industries Inc.. G 765 545-0597
Winchester (G-16884)

Centerline Manufacturing Inc.......................... G 260 348-7400
Fort Wayne (G-4839)

Circle S Industries LLC.................................. G 317 727-6752
Morgantown (G-12255)

Cobo Industries... G 812 341-4318
Indianapolis (G-7830)

Commercial Technical Svcs Inc....................... G 260 436-9898
Fort Wayne (G-4867)

Corporatestars Industries LLC........................ G 317 783-0614
Indianapolis (G-7879)

Cosology LLC.. G 812 630-3084
Lamar (G-10796)

Cross Match Technologies Inc......................... G 317 596-3260
Indianapolis (G-7905)

Crossroads Mfg LLC...................................... G 765 592-6456
Marshall (G-11372)

CSM Industries LLC....................................... G 219 465-2009
Valparaiso (G-15931)

Csn Industries Inc.. G 317 697-6549
Morgantown (G-12257)

Custom Fitz LLC.. G 219 405-0896
Porter (G-13922)

Custom Mfg & Fabrication LLC....................... G 260 908-1088
Auburn (G-383)

Czech Industries LLC..................................... G 317 946-1380
Indianapolis (G-7940)

Damage Industries II LLC............................... G 574 256-7006
Mishawaka (G-11877)

Damage Industries LLC.................................. G 574 256-7006
Mishawaka (G-11878)

Dargo Industries.. G 765 716-9272
Muncie (G-12372)

Daugherty Box Factory................................... G 260 375-2810
Warren (G-16295)

Davis Industries Inc....................................... G 317 871-0103
Indianapolis (G-7955)

Diamondback Metalcrafts Inc.......................... G 317 363-7760
Mooresville (G-12202)

Dkd Mfg Inc.. G 574 298-9592
Lakeville (G-10790)

Dmp Industries LLC....................................... G 260 413-6701
Warsaw (G-16353)

Domain Industries LLC.................................. G 800 227-5437
Fort Wayne (G-4922)

Down To Fabricate LLC.................................. G 812 249-1825
Guilford (G-6828)

Dragon Industries Inc.................................... G 574 772-2243
Knox (G-10205)

Dragon Industries Incorporated..................... G 574 772-3508
Knox (G-10206)

Drk Global Manufacturing LLC....................... G 574 387-6264
Mishawaka (G-11886)

Dubois Manufacturing Inc.............................. G 574 674-6988
Elkhart (G-3304)

Due North Industries Corp............................. G 812 306-4043
Evansville (G-4021)

Dw Inc.. G 812 696-2149
Farmersburg (G-4418)

Ebp and Associates Inc.................................. G 812 386-7062
Princeton (G-13990)

Edsal Inc... F 219 427-1294
Gary (G-5925)

Eften Inc... G 260 982-1544
North Manchester (G-13233)

Eis Packaging Machinery Inc.......................... G 574 870-0087
Logansport (G-11072)

Elite Industries LLC....................................... F 317 407-6869
Indianapolis (G-8092)

Elkhart Brass.. E 574 266-3700
Elkhart (G-3320)

Ellinger Mfg Tech LLC................................... G 574 303-2086
Mishawaka (G-11893)

Empire Industries Inc.................................... F 260 908-0996
Butler (G-1463)

Enhanced Mfg Solutions Inc........................... G 812 932-1101
Batesville (G-587)

Estes Aws LLC.. G 317 995-9742
Indianapolis (G-8137)

Fabcore Industries LLC.................................. G 260 438-3431
Fort Wayne (G-4971)

Fast Manufacturing LLC................................. G 219 778-8238
Rolling Prairie (G-14361)

Fcs Industries Incorporated........................... G 574 288-5150
South Bend (G-15028)

Fenris Forge LLC... G 260 422-9044
Fort Wayne (G-4980)

Fillmanns Industries LLC............................... G 765 744-4772
Daleville (G-2799)

Fink Industries LLC....................................... G 219 923-2015
Highland (G-7136)

Fire Star Industries LLC................................. G 317 432-3212
Greenwood (G-6704)

First Source Manufacturing............................ G 574 527-7192
Pierceton (G-13631)

Fix-Ur-6 LLC... G 812 989-4310
Floyds Knobs (G-4677)

Fortune Diversified Industries........................ G 317 532-3644
Indianapolis (G-8216)

Fox Manufacturing LLC.................................. G 317 430-1493
Pendleton (G-13533)

Foy Industries... G 317 727-3905
Indianapolis (G-8218)

Fuel Fabrication LLC..................................... G 219 390-7022
Crown Point (G-2688)

Future Manufacturing Inc............................... G 260 454-0222
Huntington (G-7312)

Fuzion Industries... G 812 430-4037
Evansville (G-4082)

FWD Technologies LLC.................................. G 360 907-9755
Huntington (G-7313)

Gdp Industries LLC....................................... G 260 414-4003
Fort Wayne (G-5017)

Gdt Terre Haute Mfg...................................... G 812 460-7706
Terre Haute (G-15595)

Gen Y Hitch.. G 574 218-6363
Bremen (G-1192)

Gifford Mfg Advisors LLC............................... G 918 809-4116
Floyds Knobs (G-4680)

Ginger White LLC.. G 773 818-8740
Gary (G-5942)

Gladieux Trading Mfg Co................................ G 260 417-6774
Fort Wayne (G-5026)

Gold Standard Truss LLC.............................. G 219 987-7781
Demotte (G-2918)

Goodlife Industries Inc.................................. G 317 339-6341
Indianapolis (G-8304)

Goodloe Industry Svc.................................... G 317 258-5534
Indianapolis (G-8305)

Goshen Mfg Co Inc.. G 574 533-1357
Goshen (G-6152)

Graysville Mfg Inc... G 812 382-4616
Sullivan (G-15407)

Great Lakes Waterjet Inc............................... G 574 651-2158
Granger (G-6351)

Green Mountain Industries LLC..................... G 812 585-1531
Centerpoint (G-1844)

Grit Into Grace Inc.. G 317 331-8334
Indianapolis (G-8333)

Hager Industries Inc...................................... G 317 219-6622
Noblesville (G-13091)

Hammertechracecars LLC............................. G 765 412-8824
Avon (G-522)

Hart Industries Inc.. G 574 575-4657
Elkhart (G-3399)

Hdh Manfacturing... G 317 918-4088
Indianapolis (G-8374)

Hefter Industries... G 219 728-1159
Chesterton (G-1935)

Hensley Composites LLC............................... G 574 202-3840
Mishawaka (G-11907)

Hestad Industries Inc.................................... G 574 271-7609
Granger (G-6352)

Hi-Def Coatings... G 812 801-4895
Hanover (G-7043)

Hidden Electrical LLC................................... G 317 628-4233
Westfield (G-16697)

HK Manufacturing Inc.................................... G 260 925-1680
Auburn (G-397)

Hlb1 LLC... F 219 575-7534
La Porte (G-10420)

Hmh Manufacturing LLC................................ G 765 553-5447
Kokomo (G-10280)

Hollowheart Industries LLC........................... G 812 737-4002
Spencer (G-15349)

Howa USA Inc... G 765 962-7855
Richmond (G-14137)

Huber Industries... G 812 537-2275
Lawrenceburg (G-10841)

Hurst Enterprise... G 812 853-0901
Newburgh (G-13006)

Infinite Lifts LLC... G 260 388-2868
Huntington (G-7328)

Infinity Uv Inc... G 269 625-3423
Elkhart (G-3425)

Innovative Slots LLC..................................... G 317 520-7374
Indianapolis (G-8558)

Insulpedia LLC.. G 317 459-4030
Fishers (G-4548)

Iron Men Industries Inc................................. G 574 596-2251
Russiaville (G-14423)

Jacobs Mfg LLC.. G 765 490-6111
Lafayette (G-10613)

Jani Industries Inc.. G 317 985-3916
Avon (G-528)

Jaz Industrial LLC... F 812 305-5692
Evansville (G-4138)

Jcj Fabrication LLC....................................... G 765 621-9556
Anderson (G-140)

PRODUCT SECTION — MANUFACTURING INDUSTRIES, NEC

Jcs Technologies Inc .... G 317 201-5064
 Fishers *(G-4549)*

Jdb Manufacturing LLC .... G 317 752-8756
 Indianapolis *(G-8620)*

Jedeu Industries LLC .... G 317 660-5526
 Mishawaka *(G-11920)*

Joe May Industries LLC .... G 260 494-8735
 Huntertown *(G-7258)*

Jrds Industries .... G 260 729-5037
 Portland *(G-13953)*

K & P Industries LLC .... G 317 881-9245
 Greenwood *(G-6720)*

Karma Industries Inc .... G 765 742-9200
 Lafayette *(G-10619)*

Keenville & Company LLC .... G 219 916-6737
 Valparaiso *(G-15984)*

Kemco Manufacturing LLC .... G 574 546-2025
 Bremen *(G-1202)*

Kermit Usa Inc .... G 765 288-3334
 Indianapolis *(G-8674)*

Kerria Industries Inc .... G 317 852-4542
 Brownsburg *(G-1382)*

Keystone Engineering & Mfg LLC .... G 317 319-7639
 Avon *(G-531)*

Kidstar Safety .... G 800 785-6015
 Osceola *(G-13396)*

Kien Industries LLP .... G 260 471-1098
 Fort Wayne *(G-5149)*

Kimmel Fabrication Studio LLC .... G 260 403-5691
 Fort Wayne *(G-5150)*

Kipin Industries .... G 317 510-1181
 Indianapolis *(G-8688)*

Kore Industries LLC .... G 773 343-5966
 Gary *(G-5975)*

Kreider Manufacturing .... G 260 894-7120
 Ligonier *(G-11018)*

Kt Industries LLC .... G 260 432-0027
 Fort Wayne *(G-5162)*

Kyann Manufacturing Group LLC .... G 260 724-9721
 Decatur *(G-2867)*

Lamarvis Industries LLC .... G 317 797-0483
 Terre Haute *(G-15627)*

Lamon Brewster Industries LLC .... G 818 668-4298
 Indianapolis *(G-8718)*

Lang Capital LLC .... G 812 325-2177
 Floyds Knobs *(G-4684)*

Larck Industries LLC .... G 574 993-5502
 Mishawaka *(G-11926)*

Larry Zoeller .... G 502 439-0812
 Lanesville *(G-10802)*

Leland Manufacturing .... G 812 367-2068
 Ferdinand *(G-4441)*

Lennon Industries .... G 219 996-6024
 Hebron *(G-7102)*

LH Industries Corp .... G 260 432-5563
 Fort Wayne *(G-5182)*

Licensed Eliquid Mfg LLC .... F 260 245-6442
 Fort Wayne *(G-5184)*

Life43 LLC .... F 708 335-7329
 Merrillville *(G-11533)*

Lippert Extrusions .... F 574 312-6467
 Elkhart *(G-3496)*

Lite Magnesium Products Inc .... G 765 299-3644
 Indianapolis *(G-8768)*

Little Mfg LLC .... G 812 453-8137
 Boonville *(G-1089)*

Locc Industries LLC .... G 219 575-2727
 Portage *(G-13882)*

Luckmann Industries .... G 317 464-0323
 Indianapolis *(G-8794)*

M & S Curtis LLC .... G 317 946-8440
 Indianapolis *(G-8802)*

M G Industries .... G 812 362-7593
 Rockport *(G-14344)*

M2 Industries LLC .... G 812 246-0651
 Jeffersonville *(G-10014)*

Mane Reserved LLC .... G 219 516-5800
 Indianapolis *(G-8825)*

Manu Sangha Inc .... G 219 262-5400
 Elkhart *(G-3511)*

Manufacturing Solution Intl .... G 219 841-9434
 Chesterton *(G-1946)*

Mari Manu Corp .... G 219 804-3294
 Hammond *(G-6977)*

Maron Products Inc .... G 574 254-0840
 Mishawaka *(G-11937)*

Martin Industries .... G 502 553-6599
 New Albany *(G-12772)*

Martin Industries LLC .... G 502 553-6599
 Sellersburg *(G-14605)*

McPheeters and Associates Inc .... G 812 988-2840
 Freetown *(G-5804)*

ME Fabrication LLP .... G 574 594-2801
 Pierceton *(G-13634)*

Medical Structures Mfg Corp .... G 574 612-0353
 Elkhart *(G-3524)*

Metalworking Machinery LLC .... G 317 752-0981
 Indianapolis *(G-8892)*

Mfd Express Inc .... G 765 717-3539
 Springport *(G-15381)*

Milstrata Manufacturing LLC .... G 260 209-4415
 Fort Wayne *(G-5229)*

Mje Industries Inc .... G 219 299-3535
 Valparaiso *(G-16004)*

Mk Mfg LLC .... G 260 768-4678
 Shipshewana *(G-14870)*

Moosein Industries LLC .... G 219 406-7306
 Portage *(G-13892)*

Nakoma Products LLC .... G 317 357-5715
 Indianapolis *(G-8980)*

Nalin Manufacturing LLC .... G 812 401-9187
 Evansville *(G-4218)*

Natural Pharmaceutical Mfg LLC .... F 812 689-3309
 Osgood *(G-13413)*

Naturespire LLC .... G 463 266-0395
 Indianapolis *(G-8992)*

Netshape Technologies LLC .... E 317 805-3764
 Campbellsburg *(G-1525)*

Norine S Herbs .... G 574 642-4272
 Goshen *(G-6229)*

Notetech Industries LLC .... G 574 326-3188
 Elkhart *(G-3577)*

Nova Manufacturing .... G 512 750-5165
 Avon *(G-542)*

NPS Xofigo Mfg Plant 5889 .... G 317 981-4129
 Indianapolis *(G-9030)*

Nu Wave Manufacturing LLC .... G 317 989-4703
 Danville *(G-2821)*

Omega Co .... G 317 831-4471
 Mooresville *(G-12231)*

Osterfeld Industries .... G 219 926-4646
 Chesterton *(G-1952)*

Outdoor Industries .... G 574 551-5936
 Warsaw *(G-16407)*

P & M Fabrication .... G 812 232-7640
 Terre Haute *(G-15656)*

P & T Manufacturing Corp .... G 260 442-9304
 Kendallville *(G-10140)*

P P G Industries Inc .... F 812 442-5080
 Brazil *(G-1160)*

P2 Precision Mfg LLC .... G 260 609-6295
 Pierceton *(G-13636)*

Packrat Industries LLC .... G 317 295-0208
 Indianapolis *(G-9085)*

Pangaea Industries LLC .... G 574 850-5841
 South Bend *(G-15185)*

Peerless Manufacturing LLC .... G 260 760-0880
 Avilla *(G-492)*

Phantom Industries LLC .... G 812 276-5956
 Jeffersonville *(G-10037)*

Phtal Aoy Industries LLC .... G 260 267-0025
 Warsaw *(G-16411)*

Plastic Recycl Export Ltd LLC .... G 301 758-6885
 Fort Wayne *(G-5318)*

Platinum Industries LLC .... G 765 744-8323
 Fishers *(G-4577)*

Polar Information Tech LLC .... G 303 725-8015
 Fishers *(G-4578)*

Politan Steel Fabrication Inc .... G 317 714-6800
 Fishers *(G-4647)*

Potorti Enterprises Inc .... G 812 989-8528
 Floyds Knobs *(G-4688)*

Predator Percussion LLC .... G 317 919-7659
 New Whiteland *(G-12987)*

Premium Manufacturing LLC .... G 219 258-0141
 La Porte *(G-10466)*

Premium Vinyl Mfg .... G 219 922-6501
 Griffith *(G-6815)*

Prestige Tooling LLC .... G 269 470-4525
 Elkhart *(G-3619)*

Prevounce Health Inc .... F 800 618-7738
 Indianapolis *(G-9195)*

Prime Time Manufacturing .... G 574 862-3001
 Wakarusa *(G-16243)*

Pro Series Products LLC .... G 812 793-3506
 Crothersville *(G-2643)*

Procoat Products LLC .... G 812 352-6083
 North Vernon *(G-13293)*

Prowler Industries LLC .... F 877 477-6953
 Greensburg *(G-6626)*

Pwi .... D 574 646-2015
 Nappanee *(G-12637)*

Quiet Storm Productions LLC .... G 219 448-1998
 Michigan City *(G-11654)*

R M Mfg Housing Svc .... G 574 288-5207
 South Bend *(G-15214)*

R N A Industries Corp .... G 765 288-4413
 Redkey *(G-14029)*

Rappid Mfg Inc .... G 317 440-8084
 Indianapolis *(G-9266)*

RE Industries Inc .... G 219 987-1764
 Demotte *(G-2928)*

Redab Industries Inc .... G 219 484-8382
 Crown Point *(G-2742)*

Resourcemfg .... G 812 574-5500
 Madison *(G-11247)*

Resourcemfg .... G 812 523-2100
 Seymour *(G-14681)*

Resourcemfg .... G 812 231-8500
 Terre Haute *(G-15679)*

Revere Industries .... G 317 638-1521
 Indianapolis *(G-9295)*

RFI Mfg Co .... G 812 207-6939
 New Albany *(G-12805)*

Ribbe Welding & Mfg Inc .... G 765 390-4044
 Kingman *(G-10173)*

Ric Corporation D/B/A .... G 260 432-0799
 Fort Wayne *(G-5382)*

Richey M A Mfg Co Sprtng Gds .... G 765 659-5389
 Frankfort *(G-5693)*

Ridge Iron LLC .... G 646 450-0092
 Plymouth *(G-13811)*

Ring Industries Inc .... G 219 204-1577
 Lake Village *(G-10783)*

Robinson Auto Parts Mfg .... G 317 921-0076
 Indianapolis *(G-9315)*

Employee Codes: A=Over 500 employees, B=251-500
C=101-250, D=51-100, E=20-50, F=10-19, G=1-9

MANUFACTURING INDUSTRIES, NEC

PRODUCT SECTION

Rocca Industries LLC .... G 812 576-1011
  Brookville *(G-1333)*
Roller-Wilson Industries LLC .... G 317 377-4900
  Indianapolis *(G-9324)*
Ronlewhorn Industries LLC .... G 765 661-9343
  Indianapolis *(G-9331)*
Rowan Industries LLC .... G 574 302-1203
  South Bend *(G-15225)*
RPM .... G 309 798-1856
  Hammond *(G-7001)*
S L Manufacturing LLC .... G 260 657-3392
  Grabill *(G-6323)*
Safeguard Nursery Products LLC .... G 502 648-7922
  New Albany *(G-12810)*
Sanco Industries .... G 219 426-3922
  Fort Wayne *(G-5396)*
Sanlo Manufacturing .... G 219 879-0241
  Michigan City *(G-11665)*
Satellite Industries .... G 800 328-3332
  Elkhart *(G-3663)*
Saul Goode Industries LLC .... F 317 929-1111
  Indianapolis *(G-9380)*
Scaggs Moto Designs .... G 765 426-2526
  Lafayette *(G-10684)*
Schmigbob LLC .... G 219 781-7991
  Crown Point *(G-2748)*
Seibertspace Industries LLC .... G 317 566-0014
  Carmel *(G-1757)*
Shark-Co Mfg LLC .... G 317 670-6397
  Lebanon *(G-10941)*
Shields Mech & Fabrication LLC .... G 219 863-3972
  Demotte *(G-2929)*
Shophouse Fabrication LLC .... G 260 367-2156
  Howe *(G-7242)*
SM Industries LLC .... G 219 613-5295
  Saint John *(G-14458)*
Smart Pergola .... G 317 987-7750
  Carmel *(G-1764)*
Snake Sandbags LLC .... G 317 721-1006
  Carmel *(G-1765)*
Snowbird Industries LLC .... G 716 481-1142
  Indianapolis *(G-9455)*
So Industries LLC .... G 765 606-7596
  Pendleton *(G-13556)*
Solae LLC .... F 219 986-6119
  Remington *(G-14039)*
Solar Freeze LLC .... E 260 499-4973
  Lagrange *(G-10761)*
Spear Industries Inc .... G 317 717-1957
  Greenwood *(G-6769)*
Specialty Manufacturing .... G 317 587-4999
  Carmel *(G-1769)*
Star Manufacturing LLC .... G 574 329-6042
  Elkhart *(G-3697)*
Steel Box Co LLC .... G 812 620-7043
  Salem *(G-14500)*
Strobel Mfg Inc .... G 812 282-4388
  Jeffersonville *(G-10061)*
Strykeril Industries LLC .... G 219 321-0400
  Fort Wayne *(G-5447)*
Super Spa Xclusives LLC .... G 219 448-1486
  Hammond *(G-7016)*
Synergy Industries Inc .... G 574 320-2754
  Elkhart *(G-3711)*
T S Manufacturing .... G 574 831-6647
  New Paris *(G-12971)*
Teach ME Stuff .... G 317 550-6319
  Brownsburg *(G-1406)*
Tech Tronic LLC .... G 260 750-7992
  Fort Wayne *(G-5471)*
Terrapin Mfg .... G 717 339-6007
  Fort Wayne *(G-5477)*

Thanatos Manufacturing LLC .... G 260 251-8498
  Portland *(G-13969)*
Thermtron Mfg Inc .... G 260 622-6000
  Ossian *(G-13439)*
Thomas Products & Services Inc .... G 217 463-3999
  Clinton *(G-2079)*
Thomas Strickler .... G 574 457-2473
  Syracuse *(G-15485)*
Thomson Industries Inc .... G 574 529-2496
  Syracuse *(G-15486)*
Timothy Hoover Industries LLC .... G 812 987-6342
  Jeffersonville *(G-10064)*
Titus Mfg LLC .... G 574 286-1928
  Plymouth *(G-13818)*
Tmk Manufacturing LLC .... G 765 763-6754
  Morristown *(G-12281)*
Transformation Industries LLC .... G 574 457-9320
  South Bend *(G-15288)*
Travis Industries Inc .... G 260 479-7807
  New Haven *(G-12922)*
Trellis Growing Systems LLC .... G 260 241-3128
  Fort Wayne *(G-5504)*
Tri-State Shtmtl & Mfg LLC .... G 260 402-8831
  Fort Wayne *(G-5507)*
Ubackoff .... G 317 557-3951
  Indianapolis *(G-9673)*
Ultimate Mfg .... G 765 517-1160
  Marion *(G-11346)*
Ultra Mfg LLC .... G 574 354-2564
  New Paris *(G-12972)*
Union City Coatings LLC .... G 765 717-3919
  Union City *(G-15862)*
Unlimited Manufacturing LLC .... G 260 515-3332
  Avilla *(G-497)*
Upcycle Industrial Inc .... G 574 825-4990
  Middlebury *(G-11755)*
Urban Rustic Farmhouse LLC .... G 317 238-0945
  New Palestine *(G-12944)*
Vandelay Industries Ind Inc .... G 574 202-2367
  Bristol *(G-1297)*
Vandelay Properties LLC .... G 574 529-4795
  Syracuse *(G-15489)*
Vandeleigh Industries LLC .... G 574 326-3254
  Elkhart *(G-3768)*
Vemme Kart Usa LLC .... G 317 407-7172
  Mooresville *(G-12249)*
Vestil Manufacturing Corp .... G 800 348-0860
  Angola *(G-307)*
Veterans Industries and Arts .... G 317 730-1815
  Indianapolis *(G-9714)*
Wagners Tree Service .... G 219 608-1525
  La Porte *(G-10497)*
Walnut Creek Fabrication Inc .... G 765 749-1226
  Portland *(G-13975)*
Watchdog Manufacturing LLC .... G 574 218-6604
  Bristol *(G-1298)*
Watchdog Manufacturing LLC .... G 574 536-2445
  Elkhart *(G-3780)*
Well Done Industries LLC .... G 219 838-5201
  Lowell *(G-11180)*
White Cap LLC .... G 812 425-6221
  Evansville *(G-4384)*
Wiley Industries Incorporated .... G 317 574-1477
  Carmel *(G-1805)*
Wilson Industries .... G 313 330-0643
  New Albany *(G-12829)*
Wimmer Mfg Inc .... G 765 465-9846
  New Castle *(G-12886)*
Wink Anti Tip LLC .... G 812 305-3165
  Evansville *(G-4388)*
Yes Feed & Supply LLC .... G 765 361-9821
  Crawfordsville *(G-2628)*

York Tank and Mfg LLC .... F 765 401-0667
  Kingman *(G-10175)*
Zaffer Industries LLC .... G 317 910-4958
  Indianapolis *(G-9807)*

MARBLE, BUILDING: Cut & Shaped

Botti Stdio Archtctral Arts In .... E 847 869-5933
  La Porte *(G-10391)*
Granitech .... G 574 674-6988
  Elkhart *(G-3386)*

MARINAS

Culvers Port Side Marina .... G 574 223-5090
  Rochester *(G-14285)*
West Lakes Marine Inc .... F 260 854-2525
  Rome City *(G-14378)*

MARINE CARGO HANDLING SVCS

Acl Professional Services Inc .... C 812 288-0100
  Jeffersonville *(G-9922)*
VMS Products Inc .... G 888 321-4698
  Anderson *(G-214)*

MARINE CARGO HANDLING SVCS: Marine Terminal

Acbl Holding Corporation .... A 310 712-1850
  Jeffersonville *(G-9921)*
Acl Sales Corporation .... G 812 288-0100
  Jeffersonville *(G-9923)*
American Barge Line Company .... G 812 288-0100
  Jeffersonville *(G-9930)*
American Coml Barge Line LLC .... C 812 288-0100
  Jeffersonville *(G-9931)*
American Commercial Lines Inc .... C 812 288-0100
  Jeffersonville *(G-9932)*
Commercial Barge Line Company .... E 812 288-0100
  Jeffersonville *(G-9956)*

MARINE HARDWARE

Epco Products Inc .... E 260 747-8888
  Fort Wayne *(G-4956)*
Rookstools Pier Shop Inc .... E 574 453-4771
  Leesburg *(G-10960)*

MARINE RELATED EQPT

Old JB LLC .... C 812 288-0200
  Jeffersonville *(G-10029)*

MARINE SPLYS WHOLESALERS

Hoosier Industrial Supply Inc .... F 574 533-8565
  Goshen *(G-6168)*
Porter Inc .... A 800 736-7685
  Decatur *(G-2876)*

MARKETS: Meat & fish

Kroger Co .... G 574 291-0740
  South Bend *(G-15107)*
Lengerich Meats Inc .... F 260 638-4123
  Zanesville *(G-16986)*
Moody Meats .... G 317 272-4533
  Avon *(G-538)*
Royal Center Locker Plant Inc .... G 574 643-3275
  Royal Center *(G-14392)*

MARKING DEVICES

Arben Corporation .... E 812 477-7763
  Evansville *(G-3896)*
Clear Stamp Inc .... G 219 324-3800
  La Porte *(G-10395)*
Koehler .... G 219 462-4128
  Valparaiso *(G-15989)*

PRODUCT SECTION
MEDICAL & SURGICAL SPLYS: Orthopedic Appliances

Riverside Printing Co............................. G 812 275-1950
  Bedford *(G-669)*

S & T Fulfillment LLC......................... E 812 466-4900
  Terre Haute *(G-15686)*

Sign A Rama.. G 812 477-7763
  Evansville *(G-4310)*

Wagner Zip-Change Inc .... E 708 681-4100
  Fort Wayne *(G-5540)*

MARKING DEVICES: Canceling Stamps, Hand, Rubber Or Metal

Toomuchfun Rubberstamps Inc........ G 260 557-4808
  Fort Wayne *(G-5495)*

MARKING DEVICES: Embossing Seals & Hand Stamps

A & M Rubber Stamps Inc.................. G 219 836-0892
  Munster *(G-12525)*

Indiana Stamp Co Inc .... E 260 424-8973
  Fort Wayne *(G-5104)*

Stamp Works .... G 765 962-5201
  Richmond *(G-14208)*

MATS OR MATTING, NEC: Rubber

Jpc LLC .... F 574 293-8030
  Elkhart *(G-3437)*

Midwest Mat Company .... G 765 286-0831
  Muncie *(G-12455)*

Pierceton Rubber Products Inc.......... F 574 594-3002
  Pierceton *(G-13639)*

MATS, MATTING & PADS: Nonwoven

Mat Matrs of Indiana Inc................... G 260 624-2882
  Angola *(G-274)*

Mountville Mats.................................. G 574 753-8858
  Logansport *(G-11094)*

Rtw Enterprises Inc........................... E 574 294-3275
  Elkhart *(G-3654)*

MEAT MARKETS

Brook Locker Plant............................. G 219 275-2611
  Brook *(G-1303)*

Dewig Bros Packing Co Inc................ E 812 768-6208
  Haubstadt *(G-7083)*

Fisher Packing Company .... E 260 726-7355
  Portland *(G-13941)*

Johns Butcher Shop Inc .... F 574 773-4632
  Nappanee *(G-12615)*

Manley Meats Inc................................ F 260 592-7313
  Decatur *(G-2871)*

Merkley & Sons Inc............................. E 812 482-7020
  Jasper *(G-9890)*

Parretts Meat Proc & Catrg Inc.......... F 574 967-3711
  Flora *(G-4663)*

Rices Quality Farm Meats Inc............ G 812 829-4562
  Spencer *(G-15361)*

Yoders Meats Inc................................ G 260 768-4715
  Shipshewana *(G-14900)*

MEAT PRDTS: Boxed Beef, From Slaughtered Meat

Tyson Fresh Meats Inc....................... C 574 753-6121
  Logansport *(G-11114)*

MEAT PRDTS: Dried Beef, From Purchased Meat

Farm Boy Meats of Evansville............ D 812 425-5231
  Evansville *(G-4064)*

MEAT PRDTS: Frozen

Farm Boy Meats of Evansville............ D 812 425-5231
  Evansville *(G-4064)*

Myers Frz Foods Provisioners .... G 765 525-6304
  Saint Paul *(G-14467)*

MEAT PRDTS: Prepared Beef Prdts From Purchased Beef

This Old Farm Inc............................... E 765 324-2161
  Colfax *(G-2113)*

MEAT PRDTS: Roast Beef, From Purchased Meat

Zels.. G 219 864-1011
  Schererville *(G-14548)*

MEAT PRDTS: Sausages & Related Prdts, From Purchased Meat

Saint Adrian Meats Sausage LLC........ G 317 403-3305
  Lebanon *(G-10938)*

MEAT PRDTS: Snack Sticks, Incl Jerky, From Purchased Meat

Cosmos Superior Foods LLC............. E 317 975-2747
  Indianapolis *(G-7886)*

Grandpas Beef Jerky LLC................. G 317 258-3209
  Fishers *(G-4534)*

Nates Beef Jerky .... G 765 348-6569
  Upland *(G-15879)*

Red Beard Beef Jerky .... G 574 596-7054
  Elkhart *(G-3645)*

MECHANISMS: Coin-Operated Machines

C & P Distributing LLC....................... F 574 256-1138
  Mishawaka *(G-11857)*

MEDIA: Magnetic & Optical Recording

Cinram Inc... A 416 298-8190
  Richmond *(G-14104)*

RB Annis Instruments Inc.................. G 765 848-1621
  Greencastle *(G-6428)*

Sony Corporation of America............. F 812 462-8726
  Terre Haute *(G-15703)*

MEDICAL & HOSPITAL EQPT WHOLESALERS

All About Organizing.......................... G 513 238-8157
  Lawrenceburg *(G-10827)*

American Eagle Health LLC............... G 812 921-9224
  Floyds Knobs *(G-4668)*

Breath of Life Home Medical.............. F 317 896-3048
  Westfield *(G-16671)*

Kilgore Manufacturing Co Inc .... D 260 248-2002
  Columbia City *(G-2162)*

Merrill Corporation............................. E 574 255-2988
  Mishawaka *(G-11942)*

Sober Scientific LLC.......................... G 765 465-9803
  Sheridan *(G-14829)*

Standard Fusee Corporation.............. D 765 472-4375
  Peru *(G-13602)*

MEDICAL & SURGICAL SPLYS: Bandages & Dressings

3M Company .... B 317 692-6666
  Indianapolis *(G-7388)*

Current Technologies Inc................... F 765 364-0490
  Crawfordsville *(G-2561)*

Romaine Incorporated........................ F 574 294-7101
  Elkhart *(G-3651)*

MEDICAL & SURGICAL SPLYS: Braces, Orthopedic

Advanced Orthopro Inc...................... E 317 924-4444
  Indianapolis *(G-7439)*

Calumet Orthpd Prosthetics Co......... G 219 942-2148
  Hobart *(G-7177)*

Central Brace & Limb Co Inc............. G 812 232-2145
  Terre Haute *(G-15558)*

Circle City Medical Inc....................... G 317 228-1144
  Carmel *(G-1587)*

Ultra Athlete LLC............................... G 317 520-9898
  Carmel *(G-1793)*

Vispalexo Inc...................................... G 330 323-4138
  Indianapolis *(G-9723)*

MEDICAL & SURGICAL SPLYS: Clothing, Fire Resistant & Protect

1st Choice Safety LLC........................ G 260 797-5338
  Fort Wayne *(G-4711)*

Brayden Shedron................................ G 765 480-7675
  Walton *(G-16281)*

MEDICAL & SURGICAL SPLYS: Ear Plugs

Aearo Technologies LLC.................... A 612 284-1232
  Indianapolis *(G-7446)*

Custom Outfitted Protection.............. G 317 373-2092
  Indianapolis *(G-7932)*

MEDICAL & SURGICAL SPLYS: Limbs, Artificial

Advanced Orthopro Inc...................... G 812 478-3656
  Terre Haute *(G-15531)*

Advanced Wund Limb Care Ctr In...... G 812 232-0957
  Terre Haute *(G-15532)*

American Limb & Orthopedic Co........ G 574 522-3643
  Elkhart *(G-3173)*

Central Brace & Limb Co Inc............. G 765 457-4868
  Kokomo *(G-10243)*

Hanger Prsthetcs & Ortho Inc........... F 219 844-2021
  Hammond *(G-6944)*

Hanger Prsthtics Orthotics Inc.......... G 765 966-5069
  Richmond *(G-14131)*

Mobile Limb & Brace Inc.................... G 765 463-4100
  West Lafayette *(G-16610)*

Orthotic & Prosthetic Lab................... F 812 479-6298
  Evansville *(G-4229)*

Orthotic Prosthetic Specialist............ G 219 836-8668
  Munster *(G-12555)*

Rehabltttion Inst Indnpolis Inc........... G 888 456-7440
  Terre Haute *(G-15678)*

Stride Prosthetics LLC....................... G 317 520-2652
  Plainfield *(G-13732)*

Summit Pedorthics LLC...................... G 260 348-7268
  Fort Wayne *(G-5454)*

Transmed Associates Inc................... G 317 293-9993
  Avon *(G-555)*

MEDICAL & SURGICAL SPLYS: Orthopedic Appliances

Biomet... F 574 551-8959
  Warsaw *(G-16321)*

Biomet Inc... F 574 371-3760
  Warsaw *(G-16322)*

Biomet Inc... A 574 267-6639
  Warsaw *(G-16323)*

Biomet Biologics LLC......................... E 574 267-2038
  Warsaw *(G-16324)*

MEDICAL & SURGICAL SPLYS: Orthopedic Appliances

Biomet Leasing Inc .... E 574 267-6639
  Warsaw *(G-16326)*
Biomet Orthopedics LLC .... E 574 267-6639
  Warsaw *(G-16327)*
Biomet Sports Medicine LLC .... D 574 267-6639
  Warsaw *(G-16328)*
Biomet Trauma LLC .... F 574 267-6639
  Warsaw *(G-16329)*
Biomet US Reconstruction LLC .... F 800 348-9500
  Warsaw *(G-16330)*
Biopoly LLC .... F 260 999-6135
  Fort Wayne *(G-4802)*
Central Brace & Limb Co Inc .... F 317 925-4296
  Indianapolis *(G-7769)*
Crossroads Orthotics & Cnsltn .... G 765 359-0041
  Crawfordsville *(G-2559)*
Del Palma Orthopedics Llc .... G 260 625-3169
  Columbia City *(G-2137)*
Johnsons Orthtics Prsthtics LL .... G 812 372-2800
  Columbus *(G-2331)*
Northern Brace Company Inc .... G 574 233-4221
  South Bend *(G-15171)*
Rayco Steel Process Inc .... F 574 267-7676
  Warsaw *(G-16415)*
Rmi Holdings LLC .... F 317 214-7076
  Warsaw *(G-16419)*
Symmetry Medical Inc .... G 574 267-8700
  Warsaw *(G-16433)*
Transcend Orthtics Prsthtics L .... G 219 736-9960
  Merrillville *(G-11569)*
Wiley Young & Associates .... G 574 269-7006
  Warsaw *(G-16452)*
Zimmer Inc .... G 574 267-2038
  Warsaw *(G-16458)*
Zimmer Inc .... G 800 348-9500
  Warsaw *(G-16459)*
Zimmer Inc .... G 574 267-6131
  Warsaw *(G-16460)*
Zimmer Inc .... G 574 267-6131
  Warsaw *(G-16461)*
Zimmer Inc .... G 574 527-7297
  Warsaw *(G-16462)*
Zimmer Inc .... F 574 371-1557
  Warsaw *(G-16463)*
Zimmer Inc .... B 800 348-9500
  Warsaw *(G-16464)*
Zimmer Biomet .... F 574 453-1326
  Fort Wayne *(G-5584)*
Zimmer Biomet Hibbard .... F 574 267-0670
  Warsaw *(G-16465)*
Zimmer Biomet Hibbard LLC .... G 800 352-2982
  Valparaiso *(G-16083)*
Zimmer Biomet Holdings Inc .... G 317 872-8484
  Indianapolis *(G-9810)*
Zimmer Biomet Holdings Inc .... A 574 267-6131
  Warsaw *(G-16466)*
Zimmer Bmet Connected Hlth LLC .... E 800 613-6131
  Warsaw *(G-16467)*
Zimmer Production Inc .... G 574 267-6131
  Warsaw *(G-16468)*
Zimmer Production Inc .... G 574 267-6131
  Warsaw *(G-16469)*
Zimmer Spine Inc .... E 800 655-2614
  Warsaw *(G-16470)*
Zimmer Us Inc .... C 574 267-6131
  Warsaw *(G-16471)*

MEDICAL & SURGICAL SPLYS: Personal Safety Eqpt

Accra-Pac Inc .... D 574 295-0000
  Elkhart *(G-3151)*

Cortex Safety Technologies LLC .... G 317 414-5607
  Carmel *(G-1598)*
Great Lake Sales & Marketing .... G 219 325-0637
  La Porte *(G-10411)*
Infinity Products Inc .... G 317 272-3435
  Plainfield *(G-13690)*
Peyton Technical Services LLC .... F 812 738-2016
  Corydon *(G-2510)*
Steel Grip Inc .... G 765 793-3652
  Covington *(G-2534)*
Steel Grip Inc .... G 765 397-3344
  Kingman *(G-10174)*
TW Enterprises LLC .... G 513 520-8453
  Brookville *(G-1338)*

MEDICAL & SURGICAL SPLYS: Prosthetic Appliances

Bionic Prosthetics and Ortho .... G 219 221-6119
  Michigan City *(G-11582)*
Bionic Prsthtics Orthtics Grou .... G 219 791-9200
  Merrillville *(G-11488)*
Magnolia .... G 317 831-3220
  Jasper *(G-9886)*
Northern Prosthetics Inc .... G 574 233-2459
  South Bend *(G-15174)*
Prevail Prsthtics Orthtics Inc .... G 765 668-0890
  Fort Wayne *(G-5351)*
Turnbow Prosthetics LLC .... G 260 396-2234
  Columbia City *(G-2208)*

MEDICAL CENTERS

Advanced Mbility Solutions LLC .... F 812 438-2338
  Rising Sun *(G-14240)*

MEDICAL EQPT REPAIR SVCS, NON-ELECTRIC

Merss Corporation .... G 317 632-7299
  Indianapolis *(G-8879)*
Protron LLC .... G 765 313-1595
  Anderson *(G-181)*

MEDICAL EQPT: Diagnostic

Center For Diagnostic Imaging .... F 812 234-0555
  Terre Haute *(G-15557)*
Tmx Healthcare Tech LLC .... F 877 874-6339
  Indianapolis *(G-9614)*

MEDICAL EQPT: Electromedical Apparatus

Biomet Europe Ltd .... E 574 267-2038
  Warsaw *(G-16325)*
Covidien LP .... C 317 837-8199
  Plainfield *(G-13674)*
Lvb Acquisition Holding LLC .... A 574 267-6639
  Warsaw *(G-16389)*

MEDICAL EQPT: Electrotherapeutic Apparatus

Bionode LLC .... G 317 292-7686
  Indianapolis *(G-7628)*

MEDICAL EQPT: Sterilizers

Steris Corporation .... D 440 354-2600
  Indianapolis *(G-9503)*

MEDICAL EQPT: Ultrasonic Scanning Devices

Nanosonics Inc .... E 844 876-7466
  Indianapolis *(G-8983)*
Orthoconcepts Inc .... G 317 727-0100
  Indianapolis *(G-9072)*

Radiation Physics Cnslting Inc .... G 317 251-0193
  Indianapolis *(G-9262)*

MEDICAL EQPT: Ultrasonic, Exc Cleaning

Esaote North America Inc .... D 317 813-6000
  Fishers *(G-4517)*

MEDICAL SUNDRIES: Rubber

Terra Health North America LLC .... G 317 675-9990
  Connersville *(G-2473)*

MEMBERSHIP ORGANIZATIONS, NEC: Personal Interest

Academy of Mdel Aronautics Inc .... D 765 287-1256
  Muncie *(G-12334)*

MEMBERSHIP ORGANIZATIONS, PROFESSIONAL: Health Association

34 Lives Pbc .... G 303 550-9989
  West Lafayette *(G-16553)*
American School Health Assn .... G 703 506-7675
  Bloomington *(G-779)*

MEMBERSHIP ORGANIZATIONS, RELIGIOUS: Baptist Church

Boeke Road Baptist Church Inc .... G 812 479-5342
  Evansville *(G-3938)*

MEMBERSHIP ORGANIZATIONS, RELIGIOUS: Catholic Church

Otter Creek Christian Church .... G 812 446-5300
  Brazil *(G-1159)*

MEMBERSHIP ORGANIZATIONS, RELIGIOUS: Methodist Church

Wesleyan Church Corporation .... E 317 774-7900
  Fishers *(G-4632)*

MEMBERSHIP ORGS, RELIGIOUS: Non-Denominational Church

Advancing Chrsts Kngdom Globl ...... G 219 765-3586
  Merrillville *(G-11478)*
World Rdo Mssnary Fllwship Inc ...... G 574 970-4252
  Elkhart *(G-3793)*

MEN'S & BOYS' CLOTHING ACCESS STORES

Gohn Bros Manufacturing Co .... G 574 825-2400
  Middlebury *(G-11718)*

MEN'S & BOYS' CLOTHING WHOLESALERS, NEC

Ram Graphics Inc .... F 765 724-7783
  Alexandria *(G-58)*

MEN'S & BOYS' SPORTSWEAR CLOTHING STORES

Golf Plus Inc .... G 812 477-7529
  Evansville *(G-4092)*
Goods On Target Sporting Inc .... G 812 623-2300
  Sunman *(G-15438)*
Profit Over Romance LLC .... G 219 900-3592
  Gary *(G-5997)*
Truu Confidence LLC .... G 317 795-0042
  Indianapolis *(G-9653)*
Unjust LLC .... G 317 443-2584
  Fishers *(G-4622)*

PRODUCT SECTION

METAL STAMPING, FOR THE TRADE

METAL & STEEL PRDTS: Abrasive

EMJ Metals .... G 317 838-8899
Plainfield *(G-13679)*

Grace Steel LLC .... F 574 387-4612
South Bend *(G-15046)*

Grace Steel Corporation .... G 574 218-6600
Bristol *(G-1264)*

Keener Metal Fabricating LLC .... E 765 825-2100
Connersville *(G-2450)*

Mid-West Metal Products Co Inc .... E 888 741-1044
Muncie *(G-12454)*

Nicorr LLC .... G 574 342-0700
Bourbon *(G-1124)*

Nucor Harris Rebar Midwest LLC .... F 317 831-2456
Mooresville *(G-12229)*

Phoenix Corporation .... F 513 727-4763
Hammond *(G-6991)*

METAL COMPONENTS: Prefabricated

Beh IL Corp .... G 219 886-2710
Gary *(G-5899)*

McElroy Metal Mill Inc .... G 317 823-6895
Indianapolis *(G-8864)*

Mpi Products Holdings LLC .... G 248 237-3007
Knox *(G-10217)*

Mpp Holdings Inc .... G 317 805-3764
Noblesville *(G-13140)*

RPI Components Inc .... G 574 536-2283
Elkhart *(G-3653)*

METAL DETECTORS

Mikes Metal Dectors .... G 812 366-3558
Georgetown *(G-6070)*

New Concept Metal Detector .... G 765 447-2681
Lafayette *(G-10658)*

METAL FABRICATORS: Plate

Gldn Rule Truss & Metal Sales .... G 812 866-1800
Lexington *(G-10976)*

METAL FINISHING SVCS

Andritz Herr-Voss Stamco Inc .... G 219 764-8586
Chesterton *(G-1902)*

Anodizing Technologies Inc .... G 317 253-5725
Indianapolis *(G-7521)*

Koch Enterprises Inc .... G 812 465-9800
Evansville *(G-4159)*

Plating Products Inc .... G 775 241-0416
Kokomo *(G-10322)*

Union Tool Corp .... E 574 267-3211
Warsaw *(G-16440)*

METAL MINING SVCS

Diamond Mining Lead .... G 317 340-7760
Indianapolis *(G-7970)*

Postle Aluminum Company LLC .... E 574 389-0800
Elkhart *(G-3611)*

Richard M Judd .... G 916 704-3364
Bloomington *(G-955)*

Turner Mining Group LLC .... C 812 277-9077
Bloomington *(G-1001)*

METAL SERVICE CENTERS & OFFICES

Angola Wire Products Inc .... G 260 665-3061
Angola *(G-228)*

Bar Processing Corporation .... F 219 931-0702
Hammond *(G-6881)*

Calpipe Industries LLC .... E 219 844-6800
Hobart *(G-7176)*

Chicago Steel Ltd Partnership .... E 219 949-1111
Gary *(G-5918)*

Edcoat Limited Partnership .... E 574 654-9105
New Carlisle *(G-12839)*

High Performance Alloys Inc .... E 765 945-8230
Windfall *(G-16905)*

Indiana Cast Metals Assn Inc .... G 317 974-1830
Indianapolis *(G-8475)*

Keywest Metal .... G 219 654-4063
Hobart *(G-7197)*

National Material LP .... G 219 397-5088
East Chicago *(G-3031)*

New Process Steel LP .... E 260 868-1445
Butler *(G-1474)*

Newco Metals Inc .... G 765 644-6649
Anderson *(G-168)*

Newco Metals Inc .... E 317 485-7721
Pendleton *(G-13546)*

Robinson Steel Co Inc .... C 219 398-4600
East Chicago *(G-3040)*

S&S Steel Services Inc .... C 765 622-4545
Anderson *(G-189)*

US Metals Inc .... G 219 398-1350
East Chicago *(G-3052)*

Veterans Fabrication LLC .... G 317 604-7704
Fishers *(G-4629)*

METAL STAMPING, FOR THE TRADE

Advanced Metal Fabricators Inc .... F 574 259-1263
Mishawaka *(G-11835)*

Ameri-Tek Manufacturing Inc .... F 574 753-8058
Logansport *(G-11055)*

Ark Model and Stampings Inc .... F 317 549-3394
New Palestine *(G-12931)*

Aul Brothers Tool & Die Inc .... F 765 759-5124
Yorktown *(G-16968)*

Austin Tri-Hawk Automotive Inc .... C 812 794-0062
Austin *(G-463)*

B Walter & Company Inc .... E 260 563-2181
Wabash *(G-16174)*

B&J Rocket America Inc .... E 574 825-5802
Middlebury *(G-11700)*

Batesville Tool & Die Inc .... B 812 934-5616
Batesville *(G-584)*

Btd Manufacturing Inc .... E 812 934-5616
Batesville *(G-585)*

C E R Metal Marking Corp .... G 219 924-9710
Highland *(G-7126)*

Capco LLC .... D 812 375-1700
Columbus *(G-2233)*

Curtis Tom Tool and Dye .... G 574 293-3832
Elkhart *(G-3282)*

Da-Mar Industries Inc .... F 260 347-1662
Kendallville *(G-10107)*

Die-Mensional Metal Stampg Inc .... F 812 265-3946
Madison *(G-11213)*

Domar Machine & Tool Inc .... G 574 295-8791
Elkhart *(G-3299)*

Evansville Metal Products Inc .... D 812 423-5632
Evansville *(G-4054)*

First Metals & Plastics Tec .... E 812 379-4400
Columbus *(G-2308)*

Franklin Stamping Inds Inc .... F 765 282-5138
Muncie *(G-12397)*

Gammons Metal & Mfg Co Inc .... E 317 546-7091
Indianapolis *(G-8258)*

Gbo Corporation .... F 574 825-7670
Middlebury *(G-11717)*

Gt Stamping Inc .... D 574 533-4108
Goshen *(G-6157)*

Harold Precision Products Inc .... E 765 348-2710
Hartford City *(G-7067)*

Hasser Enterprises Inc .... G 765 583-1444
West Lafayette *(G-16590)*

Hoosier Stamping LLC .... G 812 426-2778
Chandler *(G-1862)*

Hoosier Stamping & Mfg Corp .... E 812 426-2778
Evansville *(G-4110)*

Hoosier Washer .... G 317 460-8354
Waldron *(G-16259)*

Humphrey Tool Co Inc .... G 574 753-3853
Logansport *(G-11079)*

Imh Fabrication LLC .... G 317 508-7462
Indianapolis *(G-8466)*

Imperial Stamping Corporation .... D 574 294-3780
Elkhart *(G-3419)*

Indiana Fine Blanking .... G 574 772-3850
Knox *(G-10211)*

Indiana Metal Stamping Co .... E 574 936-2964
Plymouth *(G-13783)*

Indianapolis Metal Spinning Co .... F 317 273-7440
Indianapolis *(G-8507)*

J M Hutton .... G 765 935-4817
Richmond *(G-14145)*

L H Stamping Corporation .... E 260 432-5563
Fort Wayne *(G-5167)*

LH Industries Corp .... E 260 432-5563
Fort Wayne *(G-5181)*

Lippert Components Inc .... G 574 535-1125
Elkhart *(G-3492)*

Lippert Components Inc .... D 574 535-1125
Goshen *(G-6202)*

Lippert Components Inc .... G 574 849-0869
Goshen *(G-6206)*

Lippert Components Inc .... F 574 971-4320
Goshen *(G-6207)*

Lippert Components Inc .... F 574 312-7445
Middlebury *(G-11734)*

Lippert Components Inc .... E 800 551-9149
Mishawaka *(G-11930)*

Lippert Components Inc .... F 260 234-4303
Yoder *(G-16966)*

Lippert Components Inc .... B 574 535-1125
Elkhart *(G-3493)*

Logan Stampings Inc .... G 574 722-3101
Peru *(G-13590)*

Logan Stampings Inc .... E 574 722-3101
Logansport *(G-11089)*

MA Metal Co Inc .... E 812 526-2666
Edinburgh *(G-3091)*

Maron Products Incorporated .... D 574 259-1971
Mishawaka *(G-11938)*

Master Manufacturing Company .... E 812 425-1561
Evansville *(G-4191)*

Mc Metalcraft Inc .... G 574 259-8101
Mishawaka *(G-11941)*

Metal Fab Engineering Inc .... E 574 278-7150
Winamac *(G-16867)*

Mid-West Spring Mfg Co .... D 574 353-1409
Mentone *(G-11474)*

Mpi Engineered Tech Win LLC .... G 574 772-3850
Knox *(G-10216)*

Mursix Corporation .... C 765 282-2221
Yorktown *(G-16977)*

Phoenix Stamping Group LLC .... E 404 699-2882
Fort Wayne *(G-5314)*

Precision Stamping Inc .... F 574 522-8987
Elkhart *(G-3616)*

Precision Stmping Slutions LLC .... G 317 501-4436
Fishers *(G-4583)*

Quality Die Set Corp .... E 574 967-4411
Logansport *(G-11104)*

Rbm Manufacturing Inc .... G 765 364-6933
Crawfordsville *(G-2613)*

Reber Enterprises LLC .... G 260 356-6826
Huntington *(G-7360)*

Employee Codes: A=Over 500 employees, B=251-500
C=101-250, D=51-100, E=20-50, F=10-19, G=1-9

METAL STAMPING, FOR THE TRADE

Rhinehart Development Corp............... E 260 238-4442
  Spencerville (G-15373)
Samco Inc.. E 812 279-8131
  Bedford (G-671)
Sha-Do Corp... G 574 848-9296
  Bristol (G-1290)
Shakour Industries Inc.......................... G 574 289-0100
  South Bend (G-15239)
Stamina Metal Products Inc................. G 574 534-7410
  Goshen (G-6258)
Stampede Enterprises Inc.................... D 574 232-5997
  South Bend (G-15266)
Stone City Products Inc........................ D 812 275-3373
  Bedford (G-676)
Titan Metal Spinning Inc....................... G 260 665-1067
  Angola (G-299)
Valley Tool & Die Stampings................ E 574 722-4566
  Logansport (G-11117)
Wayne Manufacturing LLC................... D 260 637-5586
  Laotto (G-10811)
Wenzel Metal Spinning Inc................... D 260 495-9898
  Fremont (G-5840)
York Group Inc..................................... C 765 966-1576
  Richmond (G-14232)

METAL STAMPINGS: Perforated

Diamond Manufacturing Company........ D 219 874-2374
  Michigan City (G-11600)

METAL TREATING COMPOUNDS

Blue Grass Chemical Spc LLC.............. F 812 948-1115
  New Albany (G-12703)
Opta (usa) Inc....................................... E 716 446-8888
  Kingsbury (G-10184)

METALS SVC CENTERS & WHOLESALERS: Cable, Wire

Rankin Pump and Supply Co Inc........... G 812 238-2535
  Terre Haute (G-15675)
Tway Company Incorporated................ E 317 636-2591
  Indianapolis (G-9662)

METALS SVC CENTERS & WHOLESALERS: Ferrous Metals

Dixie Metal Spinning Corp..................... G 317 541-1330
  Indianapolis (G-7990)
Univertical Holdings Inc........................ G 260 665-1500
  Angola (G-303)

METALS SVC CENTERS & WHOLESALERS: Flat Prdts, Iron Or Steel

Feralloy Corporation............................. D 219 787-9698
  Portage (G-13863)

METALS SVC CENTERS & WHOLESALERS: Foundry Prdts

Sterling Sales and Engrg Inc................. G 765 376-0454
  Veedersburg (G-16091)

METALS SVC CENTERS & WHOLESALERS: Pipe & Tubing, Steel

Hancor Inc.. E 812 443-2080
  Brazil (G-1144)

METALS SVC CENTERS & WHOLESALERS: Sheets, Metal

Flexco Products Inc.............................. C 574 294-2502
  Elkhart (G-3348)

Preferred Metal Service Inc.................. G 219 988-2386
  Crown Point (G-2735)

METALS SVC CENTERS & WHOLESALERS: Steel

A2 Sales LLC.. E 708 924-1200
  Gary (G-5885)
Alro Steel Corporation.......................... E 260 749-9661
  Yoder (G-16964)
Ambassador Steel Corporation............. F 317 834-3434
  Mooresville (G-12193)
Barks Wldg Sups & Farming Inc........... G 812 732-4366
  Corydon (G-2487)
Bobcat Steel LLC................................. G 317 699-6127
  Shelbyville (G-14739)
Central Illinois Steel Company.............. G 219 882-1026
  Gary (G-5915)
Central Steel and Wire Co LLC............. G 219 787-5000
  Portage (G-13854)
Dz Investments LLC............................. E 317 895-4141
  Indianapolis (G-8027)
Elkhart Steel Service Inc...................... E 574 262-2552
  Elkhart (G-3329)
Evansville Sheet Metal Works Inc........ D 812 423-7871
  Evansville (G-4057)
Friedman Industries Inc........................ E 219 392-3400
  East Chicago (G-3008)
Grant County Steel Inc......................... F 765 668-7547
  Marion (G-11290)
Heidtman Steel Products Inc............... E 219 256-7426
  East Chicago (G-3015)
Kammerer Inc....................................... D 260 349-9098
  Kendallville (G-10124)
Lenex Steel Company.......................... E 317 818-1622
  Terre Haute (G-15632)
Mill Steel Co... F 765 622-4545
  Anderson (G-154)
Mofab Inc.. F 765 649-1288
  Anderson (G-158)
Mofab Inc.. E 765 649-5577
  Anderson (G-159)
New Castle Stainless Plate LLC........... D 765 529-0120
  New Castle (G-12876)
Pgp Corp... D 812 285-7700
  Jeffersonville (G-10036)
Quality Steel & Alum Pdts Inc............... E 574 295-8715
  Elkhart (G-3634)
Ryerson Tull Inc.................................... D 219 764-3500
  Burns Harbor (G-1455)
Special Metals Corporation................... B 574 262-3451
  Elkhart (G-3690)
Steel Storage Inc.................................. E 574 282-2618
  South Bend (G-15268)
Summerlot Engineered Pdts Inc........... F 812 466-7266
  Rosedale (G-14383)
Upg Enterprises LLC............................ D 708 594-9200
  Gary (G-6025)
W & W Fabricating Inc.......................... G 765 362-2182
  Crawfordsville (G-2625)
Wegener Steel and Fabricating............. G 219 462-3911
  Valparaiso (G-16080)
Westfield Steel Inc................................ G 812 466-3500
  Terre Haute (G-15745)
Winski Brothers Inc.............................. G 765 654-5323
  Frankfort (G-5702)

METALS SVC CENTERS & WHOLESALERS: Tubing, Metal

Aluminum Wldg & Mch Works Inc........ G 219 787-8066
  Chesterton (G-1901)

PRODUCT SECTION

Fluid Handling Technology Inc............. G 317 216-9629
  Indianapolis (G-8207)
G and P Enterprises Ind Inc................. G 812 723-3837
  Paoli (G-13495)

METALS: Antifriction Bearing, Lead-Base

ABM Advanced Bearing Mtls LLC........ G 812 663-3401
  Greensburg (G-6578)

METALS: Precious NEC

Get Down Get Arund Prcous Mtls........ G 219 243-2105
  Westville (G-16759)
Precious Gems Metals.......................... G 260 563-4780
  Wabash (G-16213)

METALS: Primary Nonferrous, NEC

Dallas Group of America Inc................ B 812 283-6675
  Jeffersonville (G-9968)
Univertical Holdings Inc....................... G 260 665-1500
  Angola (G-303)
Whiting Metals LLC.............................. G 219 659-6955
  Whiting (G-16841)

METALWORK: Miscellaneous

Alexander Screw Products Inc............. E 317 898-5313
  Indianapolis (G-7469)
Aluminum Wldg & Mch Works Inc........ G 219 787-8066
  Chesterton (G-1901)
Ambassador Steel Corporation............ F 317 834-3434
  Mooresville (G-12193)
Coffee Lomont & Moyer Inc................ F 260 422-7825
  Fort Wayne (G-4865)
Complex Structures Group LLC.......... E 219 947-3939
  Merrillville (G-11498)
Delta Tool Manufacturing Inc............... G 574 223-4863
  Rochester (G-14286)
Divine Machine..................................... G 812 388-6323
  Shoals (G-14905)
Double E Enterprise Inc....................... G 812 689-0671
  Osgood (G-13407)
General Crafts Corp.............................. G 574 533-1936
  Goshen (G-6144)
Induction Iron Incorporated.................. F 813 969-3300
  Evansville (G-4122)
Interntnal Mtl Hdlg Systems In.............. F 812 222-4488
  Greensburg (G-6609)
K & S Farm Machine Shop Inc............ F 812 663-8567
  Greensburg (G-6610)
Made-Rite Manufacturing Inc............... G 812 967-2652
  Salem (G-14488)
McD Machine Incorporated.................. G 812 339-1240
  Bloomington (G-916)
Metal Spinners Inc............................... F 260 665-2158
  Angola (G-275)
Midland Metal Products Co.................. D 773 927-5700
  Hammond (G-6981)
Midwest Roll Forming & Mfg Inc.......... C 574 594-2100
  Pierceton (G-13635)
Performance Tool Inc........................... F 260 726-6572
  Portland (G-13959)
Polley Tech LLC................................... G 812 524-0688
  Seymour (G-14675)
Qfs Holdings LLC................................. G 317 634-2543
  Indianapolis (G-9243)
Scheffler Hartmut Romanus.................. G 765 855-2917
  Centerville (G-1853)
Structral Cmpnnts Fbrction Inc............ F 765 342-9188
  Martinsville (G-11429)
Ten Point Trim Corp............................. E 317 875-5424
  Zionsville (G-17056)
Voges Restoration and Wdwkg............. G 812 299-1546
  Terre Haute (G-15742)

MILLWORK

Willie Lehman .... G 574 935-2809
  Nappanee (G-12654)

METALWORK: Ornamental

Centrum Force Fabrication .... G 574 295-5367
  Goshen (G-6111)
Hamilton Iron Works Inc .... G 574 533-3784
  Goshen (G-6160)
Herman Tool & Machine Inc .... F 574 594-5544
  Pierceton (G-13632)
Mofab Inc .... E 765 649-5577
  Anderson (G-159)
Muncie Metal Spinning Inc .... F 765 288-1937
  Muncie (G-12462)
Schouten Metal Craft Inc .... G 317 546-2639
  Indianapolis (G-9391)
Signature Metals Inc .... G 317 335-2207
  Mccordsville (G-11455)
Sugar Creek Fabricators Inc .... G 765 361-0891
  Crawfordsville (G-2620)
Upright Iron Works Inc .... G 219 922-1994
  Griffith (G-6821)
Wrought Iron Werks LLC .... G 219 779-7476
  Lake Village (G-10786)

METALWORKING MACHINERY WHOLESALERS

Beatty International Inc .... E 219 931-3000
  Hammond (G-6882)
Bemcor Inc .... F 219 937-1600
  Hammond (G-6885)
Contour Hardening Inc .... E 888 867-2184
  Indianapolis (G-7861)

METERING DEVICES: Gasoline Dispensing

Phoenix America LLC .... E 260 432-9664
  Fort Wayne (G-5311)

METERING DEVICES: Water Quality Monitoring & Control Systems

Monitoring Solutions Inc .... E 317 856-9400
  Indianapolis (G-8948)
Ray Kammer .... G 219 938-1708
  Gary (G-6000)

MICROCIRCUITS, INTEGRATED: Semiconductor

Maxim Integrated Products Inc .... G 252 227-7202
  Westfield (G-16710)

MICROWAVE COMPONENTS

Mann Made Microwave LLC .... G 317 407-1223
  Franklin (G-5754)
Microwave Devices Inc .... G 317 868-8833
  Franklin (G-5756)
Tempest Technical Sales Inc .... G 317 844-9236
  Carmel (G-1783)

MILITARY GOODS & REGALIA STORES

Operation 1 Veteran Inc .... G 574 536-5536
  Goshen (G-6231)

MILITARY INSIGNIA, TEXTILE

Team Spirit .... G 219 924-6272
  Munster (G-12567)

MILL PRDTS: Structural & Rail

Progress Rail Mfg Corp .... C 765 281-2685
  Muncie (G-12480)

Progress Rail Services Corp .... C 219 397-5326
  East Chicago (G-3037)

MILLWORK

A & M Woodworking .... G 574 642-4555
  Millersburg (G-11810)
A AMP R Woodworking .... G 574 849-1477
  Goshen (G-6084)
A J Schnell Wood Works LLC .... G 317 370-8890
  Zionsville (G-16988)
A&J Woodworking LLC .... G 574 642-4551
  Goshen (G-6085)
Aaron Dickinson .... G 317 503-0922
  Greenfield (G-6457)
Acorn Woodworks .... G 317 867-4377
  Westfield (G-16662)
American Millwork LLC .... G 574 295-4158
  Elkhart (G-3174)
Amish Woodworking LLC .... G 574 941-4439
  Plymouth (G-13756)
An Squared LLC .... G 317 517-7139
  New Palestine (G-12929)
Antreasian Design Inc .... F 317 546-3234
  Indianapolis (G-7523)
Arnold Family Woodworks .... G 765 246-6593
  Fillmore (G-4452)
Auto Wood Restoration .... G 219 797-3775
  Hanna (G-7036)
B Nickell Woodworking LLC .... G 574 333-2863
  Elkhart (G-3212)
B&M Wood Inc .... G 574 535-0024
  Goshen (G-6095)
Bawling Acres Woodworking LLC .... G 260 768-3214
  Middlebury (G-11702)
Bc Countertops Inc .... E 317 637-4427
  Indianapolis (G-7600)
Bear Hollow Wood Carvers .... G 812 936-3030
  French Lick (G-5844)
Beeline Woodworking .... G 260 894-3806
  Ligonier (G-11005)
Bentz Woodworking .... G 765 525-4946
  Waldron (G-16257)
Bittersweet LLC .... G 317 254-0677
  Indianapolis (G-7632)
Bloomers Woodworking Inc .... G 317 502-9360
  Indianapolis (G-7643)
Bowtie Woodworks LLC .... G 765 667-1934
  Indianapolis (G-7666)
Bratco Inc .... G 812 536-4071
  Holland (G-7214)
Brewers Contg & Wdwrk LLC .... G 812 620-8961
  Pekin (G-13502)
Browns Woodworking Limited .... G 260 693-2868
  Churubusco (G-1975)
Bryan Snyder Inc .... G 574 238-4481
  Goshen (G-6102)
Byler Family Wood Working .... G 574 825-3339
  Goshen (G-6107)
C&M Woodworking LLC .... G 260 403-4555
  Leo (G-10965)
Carriage House Woodworking .... G 765 352-8514
  Martinsville (G-11383)
Cash & Carry Lumber Co Inc .... E 765 378-7575
  Daleville (G-2797)
Catholic Woodworker .... G 317 413-4276
  Carmel (G-1583)
Cedar Creek Woodworking LLC .... G 812 687-7556
  Odon (G-13332)
Centerline Woodworking .... G 260 768-4116
  Lagrange (G-10731)
Central Indiana Woodworkers .... G 317 407-9228
  Indianapolis (G-7773)

Chase Manufacturing LLC .... C 574 546-4776
  Nappanee (G-12588)
Chisholm Lumber & Supply Co .... E 317 547-3535
  Indianapolis (G-7799)
Circle City Woodworking .... G 765 637-6687
  Indianapolis (G-7808)
Ckh Two Inc .... E 317 841-7800
  Fishers (G-4489)
Clinton Custom Wood Turning .... G 574 535-0543
  Goshen (G-6112)
Cns Custom Woodworks Inc .... G 812 350-2431
  Columbus (G-2239)
Cois Coillte Woodworking LLC .... G 812 340-3718
  Bloomington (G-832)
Cornerstone Mill Work .... G 260 357-0754
  Garrett (G-5856)
Couden Woodworks Inc .... G 317 370-0835
  Noblesville (G-13063)
Country Craftsman Wdwkg LLC .... G 574 773-4911
  Nappanee (G-12591)
Country Woodworking LLC .... G 812 636-6004
  Odon (G-13334)
Cox Interior Inc .... G 317 896-2227
  Indianapolis (G-7892)
Crestview Woodworking LLC .... G 260 768-4707
  Shipshewana (G-14841)
Cumberland Millwork & Supply .... G 260 471-6936
  Fort Wayne (G-4892)
Custom Draperies of Indiana .... G 219 924-2500
  Hammond (G-6909)
Custom Millwork & Display Inc .... F 574 289-4000
  South Bend (G-14994)
Custom Wood Creations LLC .... G 765 860-1983
  Kokomo (G-10254)
Custom Woodworking .... G 812 339-6601
  Bloomington (G-851)
Custom Woodworking .... G 812 422-6786
  Evansville (G-4005)
Dan Barnett Woodworking LLC .... G 765 724-7828
  Alexandria (G-49)
Dickinson Woodworking LLC .... G 317 519-5254
  Greenfield (G-6490)
Diverse Woodworking LLC .... G 812 366-3000
  Georgetown (G-6058)
Divine Heritage Barns LLC .... G 812 709-0066
  Rushville (G-14399)
Dnh Woodworking .... G 260 593-0439
  Topeka (G-15802)
Dobbins Interior Woodworks .... G 812 221-0058
  Dillsboro (G-2945)
Double E Woodworking LLC .... G 260 593-0522
  Topeka (G-15803)
Double J Woodworking .... G 812 290-8877
  Lawrenceburg (G-10834)
Double L Woodworking LLC .... F 260 768-3155
  Goshen (G-6126)
Drew It Yourself Wood Working .... G 317 250-6548
  Noblesville (G-13074)
Dutch Craft Woodwork LLC .... G 812 486-3675
  Montgomery (G-12096)
Dutch Made Inc .... G 260 657-3331
  Harlan (G-7054)
Dutchcraft Corporation .... G 260 463-8366
  Lagrange (G-10735)
Dutchmaid Woodworking LLC .... G 260 768-7442
  Shipshewana (G-14844)
E M Woodworking .... G 812 486-2696
  Montgomery (G-12097)
Englehardt Custom Wdwkg LLC .... G 812 425-9282
  Evansville (G-4037)
Ettensohn & Company LLC .... G 812 547-5491
  Tell City (G-15501)

Employee Codes: A=Over 500 employees, B=251-500
C=101-250, D=51-100, E=20-50, F=10-19, G=1-9

2024 Harris Indiana Industrial Directory

MILLWORK — PRODUCT SECTION

Expert Woodworks .... G 219 345-2705
  Lake Village *(G-10780)*
Fairview Woodworking .... G 260 768-3255
  Shipshewana *(G-14845)*
Ferry Street Woodworks .... G 812 427-9663
  Vevay *(G-16109)*
Fine Woodworks .... G 765 346-2630
  Martinsville *(G-11392)*
First Age Woodworking LLC .... G 765 667-1847
  Indianapolis *(G-8191)*
Fitzpatrick Sons Woodworks LLC .... G 219 987-2223
  Demotte *(G-2916)*
Flp Woodworks .... G 260 424-3904
  Fort Wayne *(G-4987)*
Flying Pig Woodworks LLC .... G 219 242-5557
  Union Mills *(G-15864)*
Forest Products Group Inc .... F 765 659-1807
  Frankfort *(G-5665)*
Four Daughters LLC .... G 805 868-7456
  New Albany *(G-12733)*
Four Woods Laminating Inc .... E 260 593-2246
  Topeka *(G-15806)*
Frontier Woodworks .... G 260 463-2049
  Lagrange *(G-10739)*
G & R Woodworking LLC .... G 812 687-7701
  Montgomery *(G-12098)*
G & S Rural Woodworking .... G 765 348-7781
  Hartford City *(G-7065)*
Gary E Ellsworth .... G 260 639-3078
  Hoagland *(G-7168)*
Gauger Woodworking Plus .... G 812 421-8223
  Evansville *(G-4085)*
Genesis Products LLC .... B 574 533-5089
  Goshen *(G-6145)*
Georgia-Pacific LLC .... D 219 956-3100
  Wheatfield *(G-16767)*
Gilpin Custom Woodworking LLC .... G 260 413-6618
  Roanoke *(G-14269)*
Gold Seale Woodworking .... G 765 744-4159
  Muncie *(G-12404)*
Goosecreek Woodworking LLC .... G 317 557-9189
  Carthage *(G-1814)*
Graef Custom Homes LLC .... G 574 807-5859
  South Bend *(G-15047)*
Grampas Cedar Works LLC .... G 317 372-0816
  Monrovia *(G-12077)*
Grundy Woodworks .... G 765 337-4596
  Crawfordsville *(G-2572)*
Gutter One Supply .... F 317 872-1257
  Indianapolis *(G-8344)*
Hd Woodworking .... G 260 310-9327
  Fort Wayne *(G-5053)*
Heidenreich Woodworking Inc .... G 317 861-9331
  New Palestine *(G-12937)*
Helmuths Woodworking LLC .... G 574 825-0073
  Shipshewana *(G-14849)*
Hickory Valley Woodworking LLC .... G 812 486-2857
  Loogootee *(G-11138)*
Hochstetler Woodworking LLC .... G 260 593-3255
  Topeka *(G-15808)*
Hoosier Custom Woodworking .... G 574 642-3764
  Millersburg *(G-11814)*
Hoosier Reclaimed Timber .... G 812 322-3912
  Bloomington *(G-881)*
Hoosier Wood Works .... G 812 325-9823
  Bloomington *(G-884)*
Hudec Construction Company .... E 219 922-9811
  Griffith *(G-6807)*
Indiana Southern Millwork Inc .... E 812 346-6129
  North Vernon *(G-13280)*
Indianapolis Woodworking .... G 317 345-4180
  Fishers *(G-4546)*

Integrity Woodcrafting .... G 260 562-2067
  Shipshewana *(G-14853)*
Interior Fixs & Mllwk Co Inc .... G 812 446-0933
  Knightsville *(G-10202)*
International Wood Inc .... F 260 248-1491
  Albion *(G-29)*
Iron Timbers LLC .... G 812 614-0467
  Versailles *(G-16101)*
Irvine Shade & Door Inc .... D 574 522-1446
  Elkhart *(G-3430)*
J T Woodworking LLC .... G 513 543-1130
  Lawrenceburg *(G-10842)*
Jackson Brothers Lumber Co .... F 812 847-7812
  Linton *(G-11036)*
Jacksons Woodworks LLC .... G 765 623-0638
  Elwood *(G-3827)*
James G Henager .... G 812 795-2230
  Elberfeld *(G-3115)*
Jays Woodworking Direct LLC .... G 219 345-3335
  Lake Village *(G-10781)*
Jbj Custom Woodworking Inc .... G 260 450-7295
  Monroeville *(G-12070)*
JI Woodworking LLC .... G 317 910-2976
  Carmel *(G-1678)*
JM Woodworking Enterprise LLC .... G 574 773-0444
  Milford *(G-11795)*
JM Woodworking LLC .... G 574 354-7093
  Syracuse *(G-15464)*
John G Wagler .... G 812 709-1681
  Odon *(G-13342)*
Jri Woodworks .... G 812 401-1234
  Evansville *(G-4145)*
Kaizen Woodworks .... G 714 350-6281
  Granger *(G-6356)*
Kentucky Wood Floors LLC .... G 812 256-2164
  Borden *(G-1111)*
Knothole Woodworks LLC .... G 317 600-8151
  Kirklin *(G-10191)*
Kostyo Woodworking Inc .... G 812 466-7350
  Terre Haute *(G-15625)*
Kraigs Custom Woodworking .... G 574 904-7501
  Mishawaka *(G-11924)*
Kuntry Lumber and Farm Sup Ltd .... F 260 463-3242
  Lagrange *(G-10746)*
L & N Woodworking LLC .... G 260 768-7008
  Shipshewana *(G-14858)*
L & W Woodworking LLC .... G 260 463-8938
  Wolcottville *(G-16940)*
LA Woodworking LLC .... G 574 825-5580
  Middlebury *(G-11731)*
Lakeview Woodworking .... G 574 642-1335
  Goshen *(G-6196)*
LAMB Woodworking LLC .... G 260 768-7992
  Shipshewana *(G-14862)*
Lambert Wood Works LLC .... G 812 952-4204
  Lanesville *(G-10801)*
Learning Cedar Woodworking .... G 574 862-1864
  Elkhart *(G-3482)*
Legacy Wood Creations LLC .... G 574 773-4405
  Nappanee *(G-12620)*
Light House Woodworking DBA .... G 260 704-0589
  Saint Joe *(G-14439)*
Ligonier Woodworking .... G 260 894-9969
  Ligonier *(G-11019)*
Limitless Woodworking LLC .... G 317 702-1763
  Noblesville *(G-13128)*
Limon Woodworking LLC .... G 317 362-9179
  Indianapolis *(G-8757)*
Lions Pride Customs LLC .... G 765 490-8296
  Lafayette *(G-10637)*
Lockerbie Square Cab Co Inc .... G 317 635-1134
  Indianapolis *(G-8775)*

Loggers Incorporated .... E 812 939-2797
  Clay City *(G-2045)*
Lucky Man Wdwkg Hndyman Svcs L .... G 810 247-3099
  Fishers *(G-4559)*
M & D Woodworking .... G 260 450-0484
  Grabill *(G-6312)*
M & M Tabletops LLC .... G 502 396-9236
  New Albany *(G-12769)*
Madison Millwork Inc .... G 765 649-7883
  Anderson *(G-150)*
Makers Hand Woodworking .... G 317 797-8776
  Albany *(G-13)*
Marc Woodworking Inc .... D 317 635-9663
  Indianapolis *(G-8827)*
Marquise Enterprises Ltd .... G 317 578-3400
  Indianapolis *(G-8840)*
Martell & Co .... G 317 752-2847
  Greenwood *(G-6733)*
Marvelous Woodworking LLC .... G 317 679-5890
  Lebanon *(G-10914)*
Maschino Woodworks LLC .... G 812 230-7428
  Terre Haute *(G-15637)*
Mast Woodworking .... G 812 636-7938
  Odon *(G-13343)*
Mata Custom Woodworking .... G 812 987-2676
  Jeffersonville *(G-10018)*
Meadowlark Wdwkg Cabinetry LLC .... G 765 541-3660
  Connersville *(G-2456)*
Medlin Custom Woodworking Inc .... F 765 939-0923
  Richmond *(G-14162)*
Miami Gardens Millwork .... G 812 208-4541
  Terre Haute *(G-15644)*
Mikes Creative Woodworks LLC .... G 502 649-3665
  Charlestown *(G-1884)*
Mill Creek Lumber Co .... G 765 347-8546
  Hartford City *(G-7072)*
Miller Cabins and Barns LLC .... G 574 773-7661
  Nappanee *(G-12623)*
Millrose Custom Woodworking .... G 812 699-5101
  Bloomfield *(G-754)*
Mo-Wood Products Inc .... G 812 482-5625
  Jasper *(G-9892)*
Molargik Woodworking Inc .... G 260 357-6625
  Garrett *(G-5871)*
Mountjoy Wooding .... G 317 897-6792
  Indianapolis *(G-8961)*
Mustard Seed Woodworking LLC .... G 765 336-4423
  Lebanon *(G-10922)*
N & R Woodworking Llc .... G 812 787-0644
  Odon *(G-13345)*
Newtons Legacy Wdwkg Engrv LLC .... G 812 322-3360
  Bloomington *(G-930)*
Noble Woodworks .... G 765 525-4226
  Saint Paul *(G-14468)*
Northeast Woodworking .... G 260 665-1986
  Angola *(G-278)*
Nov Oak Woodworking .... G 812 422-1973
  Evansville *(G-4222)*
Nuevopoly LLC .... G 317 260-0026
  Indianapolis *(G-9033)*
Oconnorwoodworking .... G 812 364-1022
  Palmyra *(G-13483)*
Odon Sawmill Inc .... E 812 636-7314
  Odon *(G-13347)*
Olon Industries Inc (us) .... G 812 254-0427
  Washington *(G-16497)*
Omega National Products LLC .... C 574 295-5353
  Elkhart *(G-3579)*
Owen Woodworking .... G 317 331-6936
  Danville *(G-2822)*
Pax Custom Woodworking LLC .... G 805 300-3720
  Indianapolis *(G-9106)*

PRODUCT SECTION

MINERALS: Ground or Treated

Philip Konrad & Sons Inc .... F 574 772-3966
  Knox (G-10219)
Phoenix Woodworking Co LLC .... G 317 340-0726
  Carmel (G-1717)
Pickslays Woodworking .... G 530 388-8697
  Winona Lake (G-16914)
Powell Woodworking LLC .... G 812 279-5029
  Bedford (G-660)
Power Plant Service Inc .... E 260 432-6716
  Fort Wayne (G-5328)
Prospect Distribution Inc .... E 317 359-9551
  Indianapolis (G-9231)
PTG Inc .... G 317 892-4625
  Brownsburg (G-1396)
Raad Custom Woodworking LLC .... G 765 432-1385
  Kokomo (G-10325)
Randys Tooling & Wdwkg LLC .... G 812 326-2204
  Saint Anthony (G-14431)
Redlin Custom Woodworking LLC .... G 317 578-1852
  Fishers (G-4593)
Regenbogen Woodworks LLC .... G 317 902-8221
  Indianapolis (G-9282)
RH Yoder Enterprises LLC .... G 574 825-6183
  Shipshewana (G-14882)
Riddle Ridge Woodworks .... G 812 596-4503
  English (G-3846)
RI Strahm Woodworking Inc .... G 260 623-3228
  Monroeville (G-12073)
Ro-Vic Wood Products Inc .... F 812 283-9199
  Jeffersonville (G-10049)
Rockwell Diversified Woodworks .... G 317 758-4797
  Sheridan (G-14827)
Rogers Group Inc .... C 812 333-6324
  Bloomington (G-959)
Rst Custom Woodworking LL .... G 317 602-2490
  Indianapolis (G-9344)
Rustic Creations LLC .... G 574 349-8156
  Nappanee (G-12642)
Sandwabi Woodworking LLC .... G 765 891-0774
  Lebanon (G-10939)
Sawdust Farms Woodworking LLC .... G 574 946-3399
  Winamac (G-16875)
SAWs Woodworking LLC .... G 574 773-4216
  Nappanee (G-12644)
Schindler Woodwork .... G 513 314-5943
  Cedar Grove (G-1824)
Schmucker Woodworking LLC .... G 260 413-9784
  New Haven (G-12918)
Schwan Products LLC .... G 260 350-4764
  Topeka (G-15818)
Schwartz Woodworking .... G 260 593-3193
  Millersburg (G-11817)
Schwartz Woodworking LLC .... G 260 854-9457
  Wolcottville (G-16942)
Scp Building Products LLC .... G 574 772-2955
  Knox (G-10223)
Sego Woodworking .... G 317 431-9087
  Indianapolis (G-9399)
Shiloh Custom Woodworks .... G 812 636-0100
  Odon (G-13350)
Shipshewana Woodworks LLC .... G 260 768-7034
  Shipshewana (G-14888)
Sorg Millwork .... G 260 639-3223
  Fort Wayne (G-5427)
South Bend Woodworks LLC .... F 574 232-8875
  South Bend (G-15258)
Spectrum Finishing LLC .... G 260 463-7300
  Lagrange (G-10762)
State Line Woodworking .... G 260 768-4577
  Shipshewana (G-14891)
Steven Block .... G 765 749-5394
  Muncie (G-12497)

Steves Woodworking LLC .... G 317 507-4194
  Martinsville (G-11428)
Stolls Woodworking LLC .... G 812 486-5117
  Odon (G-13353)
Stoney Acres Woodworking LLC .... F 260 768-4367
  Shipshewana (G-14893)
Studabker Spclty Woodworks LLC .... G 260 273-1326
  Bluffton (G-1058)
Superior Source Woodworks LLC .... G 574 773-4841
  Nappanee (G-12647)
Swanson Woodworking .... G 765 585-0328
  Attica (G-354)
Swiss Woodworking LLC .... G 260 849-9669
  Berne (G-729)
Tall Oaks Woodworking .... G 708 275-5723
  Cedar Lake (G-1839)
TE Custom Woodwork LLC .... G 317 910-6906
  Indianapolis (G-9564)
Tim Weberding Woodworking LLC .... G 865 430-8811
  Batesville (G-608)
Timber Arts LLC .... G 765 522-4121
  Bainbridge (G-564)
Trim-A-Door Corporation .... E 574 254-0300
  Mishawaka (G-12016)
Trinity Woodworking .... G 513 535-1964
  Lawrenceburg (G-10864)
Tru-Cut Inc .... E 765 683-9920
  Anderson (G-209)
Ullom Woodworks .... G 765 610-3188
  Anderson (G-211)
Ullom Woodworks .... G 217 369-5769
  Noblesville (G-13187)
Universal Door Carrier Inc .... G 317 241-3447
  Indianapolis (G-9682)
Universal Frest Pdts Ind Ltd P .... E 574 273-6326
  Granger (G-6388)
US Lbm Operating Co 3009 LLC .... G 812 464-2428
  Evansville (G-4364)
Verns Woodworking .... G 574 773-7930
  Bremen (G-1228)
Vk Studios .... G 317 224-6867
  Fishers (G-4653)
W & M Woodworking .... G 260 854-3126
  Lagrange (G-10768)
Wabash Vly Woodworkers CLB Inc .... G 317 538-2956
  West Lafayette (G-16644)
Wagler Woodworking .... G 812 486-6357
  Loogootee (G-11154)
Walnut Lane Woodworking .... G 574 633-2114
  Bremen (G-1229)
Warburton Wood Works LLC .... G 317 318-9113
  Greenfield (G-6570)
Weaver Woodworking .... G 260 565-3647
  Bluffton (G-1069)
Weber Woodworking .... G 765 967-3665
  Richmond (G-14225)
Weberdings Carving Shop Inc .... F 812 934-3710
  Batesville (G-610)
Werner Custom Woodworking .... G 812 852-0029
  Batesville (G-611)
West Point Woodworking LLC .... G 260 768-4750
  Shipshewana (G-14897)
Whites Woodworks .... G 765 341-6678
  Martinsville (G-11435)
Wible Lumber Inc .... E 260 351-2441
  South Milford (G-15314)
Wichman Woodworking Inc .... G 812 522-8450
  Seymour (G-14705)
Wild Grain Woodworks LLC .... G 317 626-3939
  Noblesville (G-13195)
Wildwood Millwork LLC .... G 574 535-9104
  Goshen (G-6277)

Wood Creations Inc .... G 574 522-7765
  Elkhart (G-3789)
Wood Wiz Inc .... G 317 834-9079
  Mooresville (G-12250)
Woodgrain Construction Inc .... G 317 873-5608
  Zionsville (G-17062)
Woodland Ridge Woodworking LLC .... G 812 821-8032
  Ellettsville (G-3812)
Woodside Woodworks LLC .... G 260 499-3220
  Wolcottville (G-16945)
Woodworking .... G 574 825-5858
  Middlebury (G-11761)
Wrights Woodworking .... G 765 723-1546
  New Ross (G-12981)
Yankee Made Woodworks LLC .... G 513 607-3152
  Bath (G-612)
Yoder Woodworking .... G 574 825-0402
  Middlebury (G-11762)
Yoders Woodworking LLC .... G 574 773-0699
  Nappanee (G-12657)

MINE & QUARRY SVCS: Nonmetallic Minerals

243 Quarry .... G 765 653-4100
  Cloverdale (G-2081)

MINE DEVELOPMENT, METAL

James F Reilly 3 Ent .... G 574 277-8267
  Mishawaka (G-11916)

MINE PREPARATION SVCS

Shaal John .... G 812 882-2396
  Vincennes (G-16153)

MINERAL WOOL

Aearo Technologies LLC .... C 317 692-6666
  Indianapolis (G-7447)
Global Composites Inc .... G 574 294-7681
  Elkhart (G-3381)
Insulation Specialties of Amer .... E 219 733-2502
  Wanatah (G-16290)
Owens Corning Sales LLC .... G 765 647-2857
  Brookville (G-1330)
PSC Industries Inc .... G 317 547-5439
  Indianapolis (G-9237)
Unifrax I LLC .... C 574 654-7100
  New Carlisle (G-12848)
Usmpc Buyer Inc .... E 260 356-2040
  Huntington (G-7376)

MINERALS: Ground Or Otherwise Treated

Calcean LLC .... G 812 672-4995
  Seymour (G-14636)
Performance Minerals Corp .... G 219 365-8356
  Saint John (G-14455)

MINERALS: Ground or Treated

Arcosa Lw Hpb LLC .... E 317 831-0710
  Mooresville (G-12194)
Beemsterboer Slag Corp .... E 773 785-6000
  Hammond (G-6884)
Covia Holdings Corporation .... G 812 683-2179
  Huntingburg (G-7275)
Grefco Minerals Inc .... F 765 362-6000
  Crawfordsville (G-2571)
Hydraulic Press Brick Company .... C 317 290-1140
  Mooresville (G-12212)
Irving Materials Inc .... F 765 922-7285
  Kokomo (G-10291)
Reed Minerals .... G 219 944-6250
  Gary (G-6001)

MINERALS: Ground or Treated

Rogers Group Inc..................................... D 812 849-3530
  Mitchell *(G-12047)*
United Minerals and Prpts Inc.................. G 812 838-5236
  Mount Vernon *(G-12325)*
Veolia Wts Usa Inc................................... G 219 397-0554
  East Chicago *(G-3053)*

MINIATURES

Mid America Prototyping Inc.................... G 765 643-3200
  Anderson *(G-153)*
Summerville Miniature Work Sp............... G 317 326-8355
  Greenfield *(G-6561)*

MINING EXPLORATION & DEVELOPMENT SVCS

A-Rose Consultants LLC......................... F 765 650-8700
  Frankfort *(G-5648)*
GES Services LLC................................... G 812 270-3090
  Evansville *(G-4090)*
Hydro Vac Services LLC........................ E 317 345-2120
  Indianapolis *(G-8443)*

MINING MACHINERY & EQPT WHOLESALERS

Brake Supply Company Inc..................... C 812 467-1000
  Evansville *(G-3950)*
Mining Machine Parts Inc........................ G 812 897-1256
  Boonville *(G-1092)*
Mpc Global LLC...................................... G 816 399-4710
  Indianapolis *(G-8964)*
Vandergriff & Associates Inc................... G 812 422-6033
  Evansville *(G-4367)*

MISSILE GUIDANCE SYSTEMS & EQPT

Rjv Investments Inc................................ E 574 234-1063
  South Bend *(G-15223)*

MIXTURES & BLOCKS: Asphalt Paving

Allterrain Paving & Cnstr LLC.................. E 502 265-4731
  New Albany *(G-12687)*
Armor Coat LLC....................................... G 260 210-1307
  Huntington *(G-7298)*
Asphalt Cutbacks Inc............................... F 219 398-4230
  East Chicago *(G-2991)*
Asphalt Materials Inc............................... G 317 243-8304
  Indianapolis *(G-7551)*
Bituminous Materials & Sup LP............... G 317 228-8203
  Indianapolis *(G-7633)*
Blaney Sealcoating................................ G 219 241-3622
  La Porte *(G-10389)*
C & R Cnstr & Consulting LLC................ G 812 738-4493
  Corydon *(G-2489)*
Dave OMara Paving Inc........................... G 812 346-1214
  North Vernon *(G-13264)*
DC Construction Services Inc................. E 317 577-0276
  Indianapolis *(G-7958)*
E & B Paving Inc..................................... E 765 674-5848
  Marion *(G-11284)*
Harding Group LLC................................. D 317 536-8364
  Indianapolis *(G-8357)*
Hco Holding I Corporation....................... G 317 248-1344
  Indianapolis *(G-8373)*
Heidelberg Mtls Mdwest Agg Inc............. G 260 632-4252
  Woodburn *(G-16949)*
Heritage Asphalt Llc............................... G 317 872-6010
  Indianapolis *(G-8388)*
Holcim (us) Inc....................................... G 219 378-1193
  East Chicago *(G-3017)*
Jenstar Asphalt LLC................................ G 219 963-4260
  Gary *(G-5970)*

Laketon Refining Corporation.................. F 260 982-0703
  Laketon *(G-10787)*
Lewis Sealing & Cleaning....................... G 317 783-1424
  Indianapolis *(G-8742)*
Milestone Contractors LP........................ D 812 579-5248
  Columbus *(G-2356)*
Milestone Contractors LP........................ D 765 772-7500
  Lafayette *(G-10650)*
Monument Chemical LLC........................ G 317 223-2630
  Indianapolis *(G-8952)*
Niblock Excavating Inc............................ G 260 248-2100
  Columbia City *(G-2174)*
Parsleys Seal Coating Inc....................... G 812 876-5450
  Ellettsville *(G-3811)*
Paving Plus Company............................. G 317 784-1857
  Indianapolis *(G-9105)*
Powco Inc... F 765 334-4210
  Cambridge City *(G-1500)*
Rieth-Riley Cnstr Co Inc......................... E 574 875-5183
  Gary *(G-6005)*
Rieth-Riley Cnstr Co Inc......................... F 574 288-8321
  South Bend *(G-15219)*
Rogers Group Inc.................................... F 812 333-8550
  Bloomington *(G-962)*
Rogers Group Inc.................................... G 765 342-6898
  Martinsville *(G-11424)*
Scotts Grant County Asp Inc................... G 765 664-2754
  Marion *(G-11337)*
Semmaterials LP.................................... G 574 267-5076
  Warsaw *(G-16421)*
Valley Asphalt Corporation..................... G 812 926-1471
  Aurora *(G-458)*
Walters Development Co LLC................ G 260 747-7531
  Fort Wayne *(G-5544)*

MOBILE COMMUNICATIONS EQPT

Haven Technologies Inc......................... E 317 740-0419
  Carmel *(G-1651)*
Star Tracks Command............................ G 574 596-5331
  Valparaiso *(G-16056)*

MOBILE HOME FRAMES

Beck Industries LP................................ D 574 294-5621
  Elkhart *(G-3221)*

MOBILE HOMES

Accent Complex Inc............................... G 574 522-2368
  Elkhart *(G-3148)*
Autumn Makers Mobile HM Subdv......... G 765 759-7878
  Yorktown *(G-16970)*
Bayview Estates.................................... G 574 457-4136
  Syracuse *(G-15456)*
Bilbees Service and Supply Inc.............. G 317 895-8288
  Indianapolis *(G-7625)*
Dutchtown Homes Inc............................ G 812 354-2197
  Petersburg *(G-13610)*
Fr Chinook LLC...................................... G 317 356-1666
  Indianapolis *(G-8219)*
Gulf Stream Coach Inc........................... C 574 773-7761
  Nappanee *(G-12603)*
Heritage Financial Group Inc................. E 574 522-8000
  Elkhart *(G-3404)*
Home Phone Inc.................................... G 812 941-8551
  Jeffersonville *(G-9997)*
Kropf Industries Inc................................ E 574 533-2171
  Goshen *(G-6192)*
Lcf Enterprises LLC................................ G 260 483-3248
  Fort Wayne *(G-5179)*
Rev Recreation Group Inc...................... D 260 724-4217
  Decatur *(G-2879)*
Schult Homes Corp................................ F 574 825-5880
  Middlebury *(G-11750)*

Skyline Corporation................................ C 574 294-2463
  Elkhart *(G-3682)*
Skyline Homes Inc................................. E 574 294-6521
  Elkhart *(G-3683)*
Softexpert Usa LLC................................ G 260 925-7674
  Auburn *(G-424)*
Thornes Homes Inc................................ G 812 275-4656
  Bedford *(G-678)*
Trophy Homes Inc.................................. E 574 264-4911
  Elkhart *(G-3748)*
Zieman Manufacturing Company Inc...... C 574 535-1125
  Goshen *(G-6279)*

MOBILE HOMES: Personal Or Private Use

Rochester Homes Inc............................. C 574 223-4321
  Rochester *(G-14317)*
Willow Creek Crossing Inc..................... G 219 809-8952
  La Porte *(G-10500)*
Woodland Park Inc................................. E 574 825-2104
  Middlebury *(G-11760)*

MODELS: General, Exc Toy

Maxwell Engineering Inc........................ G 260 745-4991
  Fort Wayne *(G-5208)*
Realize Inc... F 317 915-0295
  Noblesville *(G-13165)*
Techcom Inc.. F 812 372-0960
  Columbus *(G-2401)*

MODULES: Computer Logic

Federal-Mogul Powertrain LLC............... G 574 272-5900
  South Bend *(G-15032)*

MOLDED RUBBER PRDTS

Acme Masking Company Inc.................. E 317 272-6202
  Avon *(G-503)*
BRC Rubber & Plastics Inc..................... E 260 827-0871
  Bluffton *(G-1032)*
Field Rubber Products Inc...................... F 317 773-3787
  Noblesville *(G-13077)*
Gorilla Plastic Rbr Group LLC................ F 317 635-9616
  Indianapolis *(G-8307)*
Griffith Rbr Mills of Garrett..................... C 260 357-0876
  Garrett *(G-5865)*
H A King Co Inc..................................... G 260 482-6376
  Fort Wayne *(G-5047)*
Hawkins Darryal..................................... G 765 282-6021
  Muncie *(G-12410)*
Iris Rubber Co Inc.................................. F 317 984-3561
  Cicero *(G-1997)*
McCammon Engineering Corp................ G 812 356-4455
  Sullivan *(G-15413)*
Phoenix Closures Inc............................. F 765 658-1800
  Greencastle *(G-6424)*
Protective Coatings Inc......................... E 260 424-2900
  Fort Wayne *(G-5354)*
Schacht-Pfister Inc................................ G 260 356-9775
  Huntington *(G-7365)*
Specialty Products & Polymers.............. G 269 684-5931
  South Bend *(G-15260)*
Ten Cate Enbi Inc (indiana).................... C 317 398-3267
  Shelbyville *(G-14804)*
Vestil Manufacturing Corp..................... C 260 665-7586
  Angola *(G-306)*

MOLDING COMPOUNDS

Alterra Plastics LLC................................ F 812 271-1890
  Seymour *(G-14628)*
Bd Medical Development Inc.................. G 219 310-8551
  Crown Point *(G-2653)*
Industrial Dielectrics Inc........................ B 317 773-1766
  Noblesville *(G-13103)*

PRODUCT SECTION — MOTOR HOMES

Lyondllbsell Advnced Plymers I............ E 812 202-1968
  Evansville *(G-4179)*
Matrix Tool Inc.. F 574 259-3093
  Mishawaka *(G-11939)*
Replas of Texas Inc................................... G 812 421-3600
  Evansville *(G-4284)*
Sabic Innovative Plas US LLC................. D 812 372-0197
  Columbus *(G-2388)*
Stenidy Industries Inc............................... G 317 873-5343
  Zionsville *(G-17054)*

MOLDINGS & TRIM: Wood

AMC Acquisition Corporation................. D 215 572-0738
  Elkhart *(G-3169)*
Clark Millworks.. G 260 665-1270
  Angola *(G-240)*
Eckhart Woodworking Inc....................... E 260 692-6218
  Monroe *(G-12060)*
Louisiana-Pacific Corporation................. D 574 825-5845
  Middlebury *(G-11735)*
Quality Hardwood Sales LLC................... D 574 773-2505
  Nappanee *(G-12639)*
Robert Weed Plywood Corp..................... B 574 848-7631
  Bristol *(G-1288)*
Rodeswood LLC... G 574 457-4496
  Syracuse *(G-15476)*
Ufp Nappanee LLC....................................... D 574 773-2505
  Nappanee *(G-12649)*

MOLDINGS OR TRIM: Automobile, Stamped Metal

Hitchcock Tool LLC.................................... G 513 276-7345
  Richmond *(G-14134)*

MOLDS: Indl

Acme Masking Company Inc.................... E 317 272-6202
  Avon *(G-503)*
Advanced Mold & Engineering................ F 812 342-9000
  Columbus *(G-2214)*
Applied Composites Engrg Inc................ E 317 243-4225
  Indianapolis *(G-7533)*
Ar-Tee Enterprises Inc............................... G 574 848-5543
  Bristol *(G-1246)*
Axis Mold Inc.. G 574 292-8904
  New Carlisle *(G-12834)*
Boe Knows Mold... G 260 760-7136
  New Haven *(G-12894)*
Broken Mold Customs Inc........................ G 219 863-1008
  Demotte *(G-2913)*
Classic City Tool & Engineering Inc....... F 260 925-1420
  Auburn *(G-376)*
Constellation Mold Inc............................. F 812 424-5338
  Evansville *(G-3982)*
Davis Machine and Tool Inc..................... F 812 526-2674
  Edinburgh *(G-3076)*
Dme Manufacturing Pa Inc...................... F 219 872-8211
  Michigan City *(G-11601)*
Eagle Mold & Tool...................................... G 574 862-1966
  Wakarusa *(G-16232)*
Epw LLC... F 574 293-5090
  Elkhart *(G-3333)*
Glaze Tool and Engineering Inc.............. E 260 493-4557
  New Haven *(G-12905)*
Global Mold Solutions Inc........................ F 574 259-6262
  Mishawaka *(G-11901)*
Guardian Mold Prevent Corp.................. G 708 878-5788
  Dyer *(G-2975)*
Huth Tool & Machine Corp...................... G 260 749-9411
  Fort Wayne *(G-5086)*
Injection Mold Inc...................................... G 812 346-7002
  North Vernon *(G-13282)*

Jones Machine & Tool Inc........................ E 812 364-4588
  Fredericksburg *(G-5794)*
Journeyman Tool & Mold Inc.................. G 574 237-1880
  South Bend *(G-15097)*
Kendon Corporation.................................. E 765 282-1515
  Muncie *(G-12433)*
Kitterman Machine Co Inc....................... G 317 773-2283
  Noblesville *(G-13124)*
Lb Mold Inc... E 812 526-2030
  Edinburgh *(G-3090)*
Lorentson Manufacturing Co.................. E 765 452-4425
  Kokomo *(G-10300)*
Matchless Machine & Tool Co................. E 765 342-4550
  Martinsville *(G-11412)*
Maxwell Engineering Inc.......................... G 260 745-4991
  Fort Wayne *(G-5208)*
Michiana Global Mold Inc........................ F 574 259-6262
  Mishawaka *(G-11944)*
Micro Tool & Machine Co Inc.................. G 574 272-9141
  Granger *(G-6360)*
Midwest Mold Remediation Inc............. G 502 386-6559
  Jeffersonville *(G-10019)*
MO Money Mold Co Inc............................ G 812 256-2681
  Otisco *(G-13449)*
Mold Stoppers of Indiana........................ G 812 325-1609
  Bloomington *(G-923)*
Moonlight Mold & Machine Inc.............. G 765 868-9860
  Kokomo *(G-10313)*
Morris Mold and Machine Co.................. G 317 923-6653
  Indianapolis *(G-8955)*
Omega Enterprises Inc.............................. E 765 584-1990
  Winchester *(G-16896)*
Precision Plastics Indiana Inc.................. C 260 244-6114
  Columbia City *(G-2183)*
R & D Mold and Engineering Inc............ G 574 257-1070
  Mishawaka *(G-11983)*
Shakour Industries Inc.............................. G 574 289-0100
  South Bend *(G-15239)*
Sutton Custom Molds Inc........................ G 260 463-2772
  Lagrange *(G-10767)*
TI Mold Inc... G 574 596-7875
  Elkhart *(G-3737)*
Tri State Mold.. G 859 240-7643
  Rising Sun *(G-14246)*
Triple H Tool Co.. G 812 567-4600
  Tennyson *(G-15525)*
Triplex Industries Inc................................. G 574 256-9253
  Mishawaka *(G-12017)*
Wirco Inc... C 260 897-3768
  Avilla *(G-500)*

MONUMENTS & GRAVE MARKERS, WHOLESALE

American Urn Inc....................................... G 812 379-5555
  Columbus *(G-2218)*

MOPS: Floor & Dust

Evansville Assn For The Blind................. C 812 422-1181
  Evansville *(G-4047)*
Reit-Price Mfg Co Incorporated............. G 765 964-3252
  Union City *(G-15860)*

MOTION PICTURE & VIDEO DISTRIBUTION

Sweetwater Sound LLC............................ G 260 432-8176
  Fort Wayne *(G-5463)*

MOTION PICTURE & VIDEO PRODUCTION SVCS

Motion Engineering Company Inc......... G 317 804-7990
  Westfield *(G-16712)*

MOTION PICTURE & VIDEO PRODUCTION SVCS: Educational

DMC Distribution LLC............................... G 219 926-6401
  Porter *(G-13924)*

MOTOR & GENERATOR PARTS: Electric

Electrocraft Inc... D 812 385-3013
  Princeton *(G-13991)*
Flanders Inc.. F 812 867-7421
  Evansville *(G-4075)*
Flanders Electric Motor Service LLC...... C 812 867-7421
  Evansville *(G-4076)*
MO Trailer Corporation............................ F 574 533-0824
  Goshen *(G-6226)*
Regal Beloit Logistics LLC....................... F 317 837-1150
  Plainfield *(G-13719)*
Ritchie Electric Motor Co LLC................. G 219 866-5185
  Rensselaer *(G-14067)*

MOTOR HOMES

Aip/Fw Funding Inc................................... G 212 627-2360
  Decatur *(G-2840)*
All American Group Inc............................ G 574 262-9889
  Elkhart *(G-3159)*
All American Group Inc............................ G 574 825-1720
  Middlebury *(G-11693)*
All American Group Inc............................ G 574 825-5821
  Middlebury *(G-11694)*
All American Group Inc............................ G 574 262-0123
  Elkhart *(G-3160)*
Bison Horse Trailers LLC.......................... G 574 658-4161
  Milford *(G-11788)*
Coachmen Recrtl Vhcl Co LLC................. G 574 825-5821
  Middlebury *(G-11704)*
Damon Corporation................................... A 574 262-2624
  Elkhart *(G-3285)*
Ds Corp... D 260 593-3850
  Topeka *(G-15804)*
Fiber-Tron Corp... F 574 294-8545
  Elkhart *(G-3345)*
Forest River Inc... A 574 296-7700
  Elkhart *(G-3353)*
Forest River Inc... A 574 262-3474
  Elkhart *(G-3355)*
Forest River Inc... C 574 642-2640
  Millersburg *(G-11812)*
Gulf Stream Coach Inc.............................. A 574 773-7761
  Nappanee *(G-12602)*
Jayco Inc.. A 574 825-5861
  Middlebury *(G-11727)*
Milford Property LLC................................. F 574 970-7460
  Elkhart *(G-3543)*
Newmar Corporation................................ G 574 773-7791
  Nappanee *(G-12631)*
Pen Products Miami Cor Fcility.............. G 765 689-8920
  Bunker Hill *(G-1443)*
Phoenix Usa Inc.. E 574 266-2020
  Elkhart *(G-3603)*
Quality Concepts.. G 574 215-6391
  Goshen *(G-6244)*
Rev Recreation Group Inc....................... D 260 724-4217
  Decatur *(G-2879)*
Starcraft Corporation................................ G 574 534-7827
  Goshen *(G-6260)*
Thor Industries Inc.................................... E 574 264-2900
  Elkhart *(G-3728)*
Thor Industries Inc.................................... G 574 266-1111
  Elkhart *(G-3729)*
Thor Industries Inc.................................... F 574 262-2624
  Elkhart *(G-3731)*

Employee Codes: A=Over 500 employees, B=251-500
C=101-250, D=51-100, E=20-50, F=10-19, G=1-9

2024 Harris Indiana Industrial Directory

MOTOR HOMES

Thor Industries Inc..................................... G 800 860-5658
Wakarusa *(G-16254)*

Thor Industries Inc..................................... B 574 970-7460
Elkhart *(G-3730)*

MOTOR VEHICLE ASSEMBLY, COMPLETE: Ambulances

Autofarm Mobility LLC............................... G 317 410-0070
Daleville *(G-2795)*

City of Valparaiso...................................... G 219 462-5291
Valparaiso *(G-15928)*

Medix Specialty Vehicles LLC.................. C 574 266-0911
Elkhart *(G-3525)*

Rev Renegade LLC................................... E 574 966-0166
Bristol *(G-1286)*

MOTOR VEHICLE ASSEMBLY, COMPLETE: Buses, All Types

Besi Manufacturing Inc............................ G 812 427-4114
Vevay *(G-16106)*

Capital City Transit LLC........................... G 317 813-5800
Mooresville *(G-12198)*

Eldorado National Kansas Inc................. C 785 827-1033
Goshen *(G-6130)*

Forest River Inc....................................... D 574 262-5466
Elkhart *(G-3354)*

Independent Protection Co...................... E 574 533-4116
Goshen *(G-6172)*

Thor Industries Inc................................... E 574 264-2900
Elkhart *(G-3728)*

Thor Industries Inc................................... B 574 970-7460
Elkhart *(G-3730)*

MOTOR VEHICLE ASSEMBLY, COMPLETE: Fire Department Vehicles

1st Attack Engineering Inc....................... G 260 837-2435
Auburn *(G-359)*

Fishers Fire Station 92............................ G 317 595-3292
Fishers *(G-4522)*

Lake Ridge Vlntr Fire Dept Inc................. E 219 980-8620
Gary *(G-5976)*

Mc Ginley Fire Apparatus........................ G 765 482-3152
Lebanon *(G-10915)*

Renewed Performance Company............ F 765 675-7586
Tipton *(G-15789)*

MOTOR VEHICLE ASSEMBLY, COMPLETE: Military Motor Vehicle

AM General Holdings LLC........................ A 574 237-6222
South Bend *(G-14940)*

AM General LLC....................................... A 574 258-7523
Mishawaka *(G-11840)*

AM General LLC....................................... G 574 258-6699
South Bend *(G-14941)*

AM General LLC....................................... D 574 237-6222
South Bend *(G-14942)*

MOTOR VEHICLE ASSEMBLY, COMPLETE: Universal Carriers, Mil

7th Leadership Organization................... G 219 938-6906
Gary *(G-5883)*

MOTOR VEHICLE ASSEMBLY, COMPLETE: Wreckers, Tow Truck

B & B Industries Inc................................ E 574 262-8551
Elkhart *(G-3210)*

Sparkling Clean Inc................................. G 812 422-4871
Evansville *(G-4326)*

MOTOR VEHICLE DEALERS: Automobiles, New & Used

Autofarm Mobility LLC............................... G 317 410-0070
Daleville *(G-2795)*

Ford Motor Company................................ F 901 368-8821
Plainfield *(G-13680)*

General Motors LLC................................. B 765 668-2000
Marion *(G-11287)*

General Motors LLC................................. B 260 672-1224
Roanoke *(G-14268)*

Sternberg Inc... E 812 867-0077
Evansville *(G-4335)*

Subaru Indiana Automotive Inc............... A 765 449-1111
Lafayette *(G-10703)*

MOTOR VEHICLE PARTS & ACCESS: Air Conditioner Parts

Faurecia Emssons Ctrl Tech USA........... B 812 341-2000
Columbus *(G-2302)*

Keihin Aircon North America.................. C 765 213-4915
Muncie *(G-12432)*

MOTOR VEHICLE PARTS & ACCESS: Anti-Sway Devices

Raytech Powertrain LLC......................... C 812 268-0322
Crawfordsville *(G-2611)*

MOTOR VEHICLE PARTS & ACCESS: Bearings

Hanwha Machinery America Corp........... D 574 546-2261
Bremen *(G-1195)*

MOTOR VEHICLE PARTS & ACCESS: Body Components & Frames

Camaco LLC... G 248 657-0246
Portage *(G-13853)*

Creative Liquid Coatings Inc.................. B 260 349-1862
Kendallville *(G-10105)*

Decker Sales Inc.................................... G 812 330-1580
Bloomington *(G-853)*

Dwyer Enterprises.................................. G 317 573-9628
Carmel *(G-1614)*

Flora Racing... G 574 233-0642
South Bend *(G-15036)*

G E C O M Corp..................................... A 812 663-2270
Greensburg *(G-6595)*

Global Glass Inc..................................... F 574 294-7681
Elkhart *(G-3382)*

J & L Future Fiberglass Co..................... G 574 784-2900
Lapaz *(G-10817)*

Kampco Steel Products Inc.................... E 574 294-5466
Elkhart *(G-3447)*

L & W Engineering Inc........................... C 574 825-5351
Middlebury *(G-11730)*

Madison Manufacturing Inc.................... E 574 633-4433
Bremen *(G-1204)*

Rance Aluminum Fabrication.................. E 574 266-9028
Elkhart *(G-3639)*

S & H Metal Products Inc...................... E 260 593-2565
Topeka *(G-15817)*

State Wide Aluminum Inc....................... C 574 262-2594
Elkhart *(G-3699)*

Valley Distributing Inc............................ E 574 266-4455
Elkhart *(G-3766)*

MOTOR VEHICLE PARTS & ACCESS: Brakes, Air

Advics Manufacturing Ind LLC................ B 812 298-1617
Terre Haute *(G-15533)*

TOA (usa) LLC....................................... B 317 834-0522
Mooresville *(G-12247)*

MOTOR VEHICLE PARTS & ACCESS: Clutches

Eaton Corporation................................... C 260 925-3800
Auburn *(G-387)*

FCC (adams) LLC................................... B 260 589-8555
Berne *(G-711)*

FCC (indiana) LLC.................................. A 260 726-8023
Portland *(G-13939)*

South Bend Clutch Inc............................ E 574 256-5064
Mishawaka *(G-12002)*

MOTOR VEHICLE PARTS & ACCESS: Connecting Rods

Performance Rod & Custom Inc.............. G 812 897-5805
Boonville *(G-1095)*

MOTOR VEHICLE PARTS & ACCESS: Cylinder Heads

Indy Cylinder Head Inc........................... E 317 862-3724
Indianapolis *(G-8526)*

MOTOR VEHICLE PARTS & ACCESS: Electrical Eqpt

Lear Corporation..................................... E 317 481-0530
Indianapolis *(G-8730)*

MOTOR VEHICLE PARTS & ACCESS: Engines & Parts

Aisin USA Mfg Inc................................... A 812 523-1969
Seymour *(G-14627)*

Beachy Machine Inc................................ G 765 452-9051
Kokomo *(G-10235)*

Borgwarner Pds (indiana) Inc................ C 765 778-6696
Noblesville *(G-13045)*

Borgwarner Reman Holdings LLC.......... A 800 372-5131
Pendleton *(G-13527)*

Champion Racing Engines LLC............. G 317 335-2491
Mccordsville *(G-11446)*

Freudenberg-Nok General Partnr.......... C 260 894-7183
Ligonier *(G-11015)*

Heads First... G 219 785-4100
Westville *(G-16761)*

Keller Performance Center.................... G 765 827-5225
Connersville *(G-2451)*

Metaldyne M&A Bluffton LLC................. D 260 824-6800
Bluffton *(G-1042)*

Mpt Muncie LLC..................................... E 765 587-1300
Muncie *(G-12459)*

Old Remco Holdings LLC....................... G 765 778-6499
Pendleton *(G-13548)*

Performance Technology Inc................. G 574 862-2116
Wakarusa *(G-16242)*

Pk USA Inc... B 317 395-5500
Shelbyville *(G-14784)*

PMG Indiana LLC................................... C 812 379-4606
Columbus *(G-2379)*

Raybestos Powertrain LLC.................... F 812 268-1211
Sullivan *(G-15420)*

Rayburn Automotive Inc........................ G 317 535-8232
Greenwood *(G-6758)*

Roadwin Parts Inc................................. G 630 742-4098
Hammond *(G-7000)*

Robert Bosch LLC................................. G 260 636-1005
Albion *(G-44)*

PRODUCT SECTION

MOTOR VEHICLE: Steering Mechanisms

Tenneco Automotive Oper Co Inc............ C 574 296-9400
  Elkhart (G-3723)
Tri Aerospace LLC.. E 812 872-2400
  Terre Haute (G-15736)

MOTOR VEHICLE PARTS & ACCESS: Engs & Trans, Factory, Rebuilt

Borgwarner (pds) Peru Inc......................... D 765 472-2002
  Peru (G-13568)
Caterpillar Remn Powrtrn Indna............. B 317 738-2117
  Franklin (G-5718)
Indiana Research Institute........................ G 812 378-5363
  Columbus (G-2325)
Jasper Engine Exchange Inc..................... G 812 482-1041
  Leavenworth (G-10870)
Jasper Engine Exchange Inc..................... A 812 482-1041
  Jasper (G-9853)
Transworks Inc... G 619 441-0133
  Fort Wayne (G-5501)

MOTOR VEHICLE PARTS & ACCESS: Fuel Pumps

Avis Industrial Corporation..................... E 765 998-8100
  Upland (G-15876)
Carter Fuel Systems LLC........................... B 800 342-6125
  Logansport (G-11064)

MOTOR VEHICLE PARTS & ACCESS: Fuel Systems & Parts

Hitachi Astemo Indiana Inc..................... A 317 462-3015
  Greenfield (G-6509)
Smart Technologies LLC............................ G 317 738-4338
  Franklin (G-5777)

MOTOR VEHICLE PARTS & ACCESS: Gas Tanks

Kautex Inc... G 260 897-3250
  Avilla (G-481)

MOTOR VEHICLE PARTS & ACCESS: Gears

Al-Ko Kober LLC... C 574 294-6651
  Elkhart (G-3158)
Dexter Axle Company LLC........................ C 574 294-6651
  Elkhart (G-3293)
Fairfield Manufacturing Co Inc................ A 765 772-4000
  Lafayette (G-10576)
Somaschini North America LLC............. E 574 968-0273
  South Bend (G-15249)

MOTOR VEHICLE PARTS & ACCESS: Instrument Board Assemblies

Aptiv Services Us LLC................................ A 765 867-4435
  Westfield (G-16665)
Killer Camaros Custom Camaro.............. G 260 255-2425
  New Haven (G-12908)
Proto-Fab Acquisition Inc........................ E 574 522-4245
  Elkhart (G-3624)

MOTOR VEHICLE PARTS & ACCESS: Lifting Mechanisms, Dump Truck

Gbj Holdings LLC... G 317 483-1896
  Highland (G-7137)

MOTOR VEHICLE PARTS & ACCESS: Mufflers, Exhaust

Staples Pipe & Muffler............................... G 812 346-2474
  North Vernon (G-13296)

Tenneco Automotive Oper Co Inc............ C 260 894-9214
  Ligonier (G-11027)

MOTOR VEHICLE PARTS & ACCESS: Oil Pumps

Engineered Machined Pdts Inc................ D 317 462-8894
  Greenfield (G-6499)

MOTOR VEHICLE PARTS & ACCESS: Propane Conversion Eqpt

Joe Wade Customs....................................... G 765 548-0333
  Rosedale (G-14380)
Woodys Hot Rodz LLC................................ G 812 637-1933
  Lawrenceburg (G-10867)

MOTOR VEHICLE PARTS & ACCESS: Rear Axel Housings

American Axle & Mfg Inc........................... E 260 495-4315
  Fremont (G-5808)

MOTOR VEHICLE PARTS & ACCESS: Thermostats

Vernet US Corporation............................... D 812 372-0281
  Columbus (G-2412)
Vernet US Corporation............................... C 812 372-0281
  Columbus (G-2413)

MOTOR VEHICLE PARTS & ACCESS: Trailer Hitches

Cardinal Services Inc Indiana................. D 574 267-3823
  Warsaw (G-16332)
Pulliam Enterprises Inc............................. E 574 259-1520
  Mishawaka (G-11982)

MOTOR VEHICLE PARTS & ACCESS: Transmission Housings Or Parts

Henman Engineering and Machine Inc.. D 765 288-8098
  Muncie (G-12414)
Parker-Hannifin Corporation................... E 260 894-7125
  Syracuse (G-15471)
Ryobi Die Casting (usa) Inc...................... G 317 398-3398
  Shelbyville (G-14793)
Ryobi Die Casting (usa) Inc...................... A 317 398-3398
  Shelbyville (G-14794)

MOTOR VEHICLE PARTS & ACCESS: Transmissions

Aisin Drivetrain Inc................................... C 812 793-2427
  Crothersville (G-2636)
Allison Transmission Inc......................... D 317 242-2080
  Indianapolis (G-7490)
Allison Transmission Inc......................... A 317 242-5000
  Indianapolis (G-7491)
FCA North America Holdings LLC......... G 765 854-4234
  Kokomo (G-10266)
FCC (north America) Inc........................... E 260 726-8023
  Portland (G-13940)
Steel Parts Manufacturing Inc................ C 765 675-2191
  Tipton (G-15792)
Stephen G Morrow Inc............................... G 812 876-7837
  Spencer (G-15363)
Tsuda USA Corporation............................. F 317 468-9177
  Greenfield (G-6567)

MOTOR VEHICLE PARTS & ACCESS: Wipers, Windshield

Federal-Mogul Motorparts LLC............... G 219 872-5150
  Michigan City (G-11611)

MOTOR VEHICLE PARTS & ACCESS: Wiring Harness Sets

Gartech Enterprises Inc............................ F 812 794-4796
  Austin (G-465)
Motherson Sumi Systems Limited......... A 260 726-6501
  Portland (G-13957)
Northwind Electronics LLC...................... F 317 288-0787
  Indianapolis (G-9024)

MOTOR VEHICLE RACING & DRIVER SVCS

Team Green Inc.. F 317 872-2700
  Indianapolis (G-9565)

MOTOR VEHICLE SPLYS & PARTS WHOLESALERS: New

Abro Industries Inc.................................... E 574 232-8289
  South Bend (G-14933)
Asc Inc.. C 765 473-4438
  Peru (G-13567)
Cummins Inc... G 812 524-6455
  Columbus (G-2264)
Frank Wiss Racg Components Inc........ G 317 243-9585
  Indianapolis (G-8222)
Hoosier Fire Equipment Inc.................... F 219 462-1707
  Valparaiso (G-15965)
Muncie Power Products Inc.................... E 765 284-7721
  Muncie (G-12464)
Pfm Automotive Management Inc........ G 317 733-3977
  Zionsville (G-17040)
Pfm Car & Truck Castleton Inc.............. E 317 577-7777
  Indianapolis (G-9131)
Pfm Onsite Services Inc.......................... G 317 784-7777
  Indianapolis (G-9132)
Phoenix Assembly LLC.............................. D 317 884-3600
  Greenwood (G-6751)
T & M Equipment Company Inc............. F 317 293-9255
  Indianapolis (G-9543)

MOTOR VEHICLE SPLYS & PARTS WHOLESALERS: Used

A-Fab LLC.. F 812 897-0900
  Boonville (G-1078)
KOI Enterprises Inc.................................... D 812 537-2335
  Lawrenceburg (G-10843)
Power Train Corp Fort Wayne................. F 317 241-9393
  Indianapolis (G-9167)

MOTOR VEHICLE: Hardware

Allegion Public Ltd Company.................. D 317 810-3700
  Carmel (G-1554)
Qmp Inc.. E 574 262-1575
  Elkhart (G-3627)
Ultra-Fab Acquisitions Inc...................... F 574 294-7571
  Elkhart (G-3757)

MOTOR VEHICLE: Radiators

Anthony Smith.. G 765 478-5325
  Cambridge City (G-1490)
Indiana Heat Transfer Corporation........ C 574 936-3171
  Salem (G-14484)
Saldana Racing Tanks Inc....................... F 317 852-4193
  Indianapolis (G-9365)
Valeo North America Inc.......................... B 812 663-8541
  Greensburg (G-6640)

MOTOR VEHICLE: Shock Absorbers

Advanced Racg Suspensions Inc........... F 317 896-3306
  Indianapolis (G-7440)
KYB Americas Corporation...................... B 317 736-7774
  Franklin (G-5750)

MOTOR VEHICLE: Steering Mechanisms

Industrial Steering Pdts Inc.................. F 260 488-1880
  Hamilton *(G-6856)*

MOTOR VEHICLE: Wheels

Accuride Corporation..................... C 812 962-5000
  Evansville *(G-3867)*
Enkei America Inc........................ A 812 373-7000
  Columbus *(G-2298)*
Reliable Tool & Machine Co............. E 260 343-7150
  Kendallville *(G-10150)*
Transwheel Corporation................. C 260 358-8660
  Huntington *(G-7374)*

MOTOR VEHICLES & CAR BODIES

ABC Truck & Equipment LLC............ G 260 565-3307
  Bluffton *(G-1021)*
American Reliance Inds Co.............. E 260 768-4704
  Shipshewana *(G-14834)*
Damon Motor Coach..................... E 574 536-3781
  Elkhart *(G-3286)*
Franke Motorsports Inc.................. G 317 357-6995
  Indianapolis *(G-8223)*
Gearbox Group Inc........................ G 812 268-0322
  Sullivan *(G-15406)*
General Motors LLC..................... B 765 668-2000
  Marion *(G-11287)*
Independent Protection Co............. C 574 831-5680
  New Paris *(G-12960)*
K C Cmponents Wldg Fabrication...... G 317 539-6067
  Greencastle *(G-6416)*
Navistar Inc.............................. G 317 787-3113
  Indianapolis *(G-8993)*
NRC Modifications Inc................... F 574 825-3646
  Middlebury *(G-11742)*
Rebel Devil Customs LLP................ G 303 921-7131
  Sharpsville *(G-14712)*
Rev Recreation Group Inc.............. E 260 724-2418
  Decatur *(G-2880)*
Speedsters................................ G 574 546-4656
  Bremen *(G-1223)*
Taotao Usa Inc........................... G 317 856-8628
  Indianapolis *(G-9552)*
Tesla Inc.................................. G 317 558-8431
  Indianapolis *(G-9579)*
Think North America Inc................ E 313 565-6781
  Elkhart *(G-3727)*
Utilimaster Holdings Inc................ A 800 237-7806
  Bristol *(G-1295)*
Wave Express............................. G 574 642-0630
  Goshen *(G-6275)*

MOTOR VEHICLES, WHOLESALE: Fire Trucks

Fire Apparatus Service Inc............. G 219 985-0788
  Gary *(G-5933)*

MOTOR VEHICLES, WHOLESALE: Truck tractors

Wakarusa Ag LLC......................... F 574 862-1163
  Wakarusa *(G-16256)*

MOTOR VEHICLES, WHOLESALE: Trucks, commercial

Bulk Truck & Transport Service........ E 812 866-2155
  Hanover *(G-7040)*
Selking International LLC.............. E 260 482-3000
  Fort Wayne *(G-5408)*

Selking International Inc.............. G 574 522-2001
  Elkhart *(G-3668)*
Wee Engineer Inc........................ F 765 449-4280
  Dayton *(G-2838)*

MOTORCYCLE ACCESS

Custom Cycle of Indiana................ G 812 256-9089
  Otisco *(G-13448)*
Orr Motor Sports......................... G 260 244-2681
  Columbia City *(G-2178)*
SJ Sales Inc.............................. G 260 433-5947
  Fort Wayne *(G-5419)*
Time Out Trailers Inc................... G 574 294-7671
  Elkhart *(G-3734)*

MOTORCYCLE DEALERS

Graphics Lab Uv Printing Inc........... F 765 457-5784
  Kokomo *(G-10272)*

MOTORCYCLES & RELATED PARTS

Faith Forgotten Firearms LLC.......... G 614 940-9145
  New Albany *(G-12727)*
Iron Hawg................................. G 317 462-0991
  Greenfield *(G-6517)*
Jrotten Chopper Inc..................... G 765 517-1779
  Jonesboro *(G-10080)*
Kdz Kustoms LLC......................... G 260 927-0533
  Auburn *(G-398)*
Outdoor Performance................... F 765 732-3335
  Liberty *(G-10994)*
Reality Motor Sports Inc............... G 765 662-3000
  Marion *(G-11335)*
Red Hawk Choppers Inc................. G 765 307-2269
  Crawfordsville *(G-2614)*
Ss Custom Choppers LLC................ G 260 415-3793
  Fort Wayne *(G-5433)*
Thugs Inc Choppers...................... G 317 454-3762
  Indianapolis *(G-9601)*

MOTORS: Electric

B & H Electric and Supply Inc.......... E 812 522-5607
  Seymour *(G-14630)*
Bluffton Motor Works LLC............... G 260 827-2200
  Bluffton *(G-1030)*
Burt Products Inc........................ G 812 386-6890
  Princeton *(G-13986)*
Electric Motors and Spc................. C 260 357-4141
  Garrett *(G-5860)*
Franklin Electric Co Inc................. B 260 824-2900
  Fort Wayne *(G-5006)*
Hansen Corporation...................... B 812 385-3000
  Princeton *(G-13997)*
Mohler Technology Inc................... E 812 897-2900
  Boonville *(G-1093)*
OH Hunt Lines Inc........................ G 260 856-2125
  Cromwell *(G-2632)*
Pete D Limkemann....................... G 260 403-4297
  Fort Wayne *(G-5307)*
Regal Rexnord Corporation............. E 574 583-9171
  Monticello *(G-12168)*
Scottorsville Sales and Svc............. G 765 250-5245
  Lafayette *(G-10688)*
Sterling Electric Inc..................... E 317 872-0471
  Indianapolis *(G-9505)*

MOTORS: Generators

An-Mar Wiring Systems Inc.............. F 574 255-5923
  Mishawaka *(G-11842)*
Clipper Country.......................... G 765 935-2344
  Richmond *(G-14106)*
Coil-Tran LLC............................ D 219 942-8511
  Hobart *(G-7182)*

Contour Hardening Inc................... E 888 867-2184
  Indianapolis *(G-7861)*
Controls Center Inc..................... G 317 634-2665
  Indianapolis *(G-7863)*
Cummins Inc.............................. D 812 522-9366
  Seymour *(G-14645)*
Custom Magnetics Inc................... E 260 982-8508
  North Manchester *(G-13231)*
Dayton-Phoenix Group Inc.............. D 765 742-4410
  West Lafayette *(G-16575)*
Electro Corp.............................. F 219 393-5571
  Kingsbury *(G-10177)*
Elevator Equipment Corporation....... D 765 966-7761
  Richmond *(G-14119)*
Franklin Electric Intl.................... F 260 824-2900
  Fort Wayne *(G-5007)*
Futurewerks LLC......................... G 305 926-3633
  Indianapolis *(G-8247)*
Ies Subsidiary Holdings Inc............ G 330 830-3500
  South Bend *(G-15074)*
JMS Electronics Corporation........... E 574 522-0246
  Elkhart *(G-3434)*
Jones Engineering Inc................... G 812 254-6456
  Washington *(G-16490)*
Kane Usa Inc............................. E 800 547-5740
  Indianapolis *(G-8660)*
Kendrion (mishawaka) LLC.............. E 574 257-2422
  Mishawaka *(G-11922)*
Leeson Electric Corporation........... E 317 821-3700
  Plainfield *(G-13697)*
Light Engineering....................... F 317 471-1800
  Indianapolis *(G-8749)*
Marathon Electric........................ G 317 837-2523
  Plainfield *(G-13699)*
Mighty-Quip Industries.................. G 260 615-1899
  Fort Wayne *(G-5228)*
Q P Inc................................... F 574 295-6884
  Elkhart *(G-3626)*
Regal Beloit America Inc................ F 260 416-5400
  Fort Wayne *(G-5377)*
Regal Rexnord Corporation............. E 608 364-8800
  Fort Wayne *(G-5378)*
Regal Rexnord Corporation............. F 317 837-2667
  Plainfield *(G-13720)*
Regal-Beloit Electric Motors Inc....... A 260 416-5400
  Fort Wayne *(G-5379)*
Siemens Industry Inc.................... D 219 763-7927
  Portage *(G-13914)*
Vanair Manufacturing Inc............... C 219 879-5100
  Michigan City *(G-11684)*

MOUNTING SVC: Swatches & Samples

Leed Selling Tools Corp................. E 812 867-4340
  Evansville *(G-4164)*
Superior Sample Co Inc.................. E 260 894-3136
  Ligonier *(G-11025)*

MULTIPLEXERS: Telephone & Telegraph

C&D Technologies Inc................... C 765 762-2461
  Attica *(G-345)*
International Resources Inc............ G 317 813-5300
  Greenwood *(G-6716)*
Nexvoo Inc............................... G 866 910-8366
  Indianapolis *(G-9009)*
Omnion Power Inc........................ G 317 259-9264
  Indianapolis *(G-9049)*

MUSIC DISTRIBUTION APPARATUS

Associated World Music LLC............ G 219 512-4511
  Crown Point *(G-2651)*
Haven Technologies Inc................. E 317 740-0419
  Carmel *(G-1651)*

PRODUCT SECTION NOZZLES: Fire Fighting

Hole N Wall Entertainment LLC............... G 317 586-1037
Indianapolis (G-8402)
Octobers Firm Label LLC..................... G 317 778-1447
Noblesville (G-13147)
Wipbeatz LLC............................ G 866 676-1465
Indianapolis (G-9774)

MUSIC LICENSING TO RADIO STATIONS

Rebound Project LLP....................... G 765 621-5604
Anderson (G-183)

MUSICAL INSTRUMENTS & ACCESS: Carrying Cases

Elkcases Inc.............................. G 574 295-7700
Elkhart (G-3317)
Humes & Berg Mfg Co Inc................. G 219 391-5880
East Chicago (G-3018)
L M Products Inc........................... E 765 643-3802
Anderson (G-145)

MUSICAL INSTRUMENTS & ACCESS: NEC

CJS Muzic Company-The Spot LLC........ G 219 487-9873
Hammond (G-6901)
Conn-Selmer Inc........................... D 574 522-1675
Elkhart (G-3261)
Grem USA Corporation.................... G 260 456-2354
Fort Wayne (G-5041)
Kimmel Music............................. G 260 302-3082
Kendallville (G-10128)
Main Music............................... G 812 295-2020
Loogootee (G-11145)
Sorley Horns LLC......................... G 317 258-2718
Bargersville (G-574)
Sweetwater Sound LLC................... G 260 432-8176
Fort Wayne (G-5463)
T Shorter Manufacturing Inc.............. G 574 264-4131
Elkhart (G-3713)
Uniflex Relay Systems LLC................ G 765 232-4675
Union City (G-15861)

MUSICAL INSTRUMENTS & ACCESS: Pianos

Conn-Selmer Inc........................... D 574 522-1675
Elkhart (G-3262)
Steinway Piano Company Inc............. D 574 522-1675
Elkhart (G-3700)
Walter Piano Company Inc................ F 574 266-0615
Elkhart (G-3779)

MUSICAL INSTRUMENTS & PARTS: Percussion

Stone Custom Drum LLC................. G 260 403-7519
Fort Wayne (G-5445)

MUSICAL INSTRUMENTS & SPLYS STORES: Pianos

Conn-Selmer Inc........................... D 574 522-1675
Elkhart (G-3262)
Walter Piano Company Inc................ F 574 266-0615
Elkhart (G-3779)

MUSICAL INSTRUMENTS WHOLESALERS

Conn-Selmer Inc........................... E 574 295-6730
Elkhart (G-3263)
Rees Harps Inc............................ F 812 438-3032
Rising Sun (G-14245)

MUSICAL INSTRUMENTS: Bassoons

Fox Products Corporation................. C 260 723-4888
South Whitley (G-15318)

MUSICAL INSTRUMENTS: Guitars & Parts, Electric & Acoustic

Ataraxis Music LLC....................... G 626 945-6441
Fishers (G-4466)
Conn-Selmer Inc........................... E 574 295-6730
Elkhart (G-3263)
Eddie S Guitars........................... G 219 689-7007
Dyer (G-2973)
Lucas Custom Instruments LLC.......... G 812 342-3093
Columbus (G-2347)
Stradella String Instrs Inc................ G 219 464-3390
Valparaiso (G-16059)

NAILS WHOLESALERS

Burton Debiceious........................ G 317 495-0123
Indianapolis (G-7702)

NAILS: Steel, Wire Or Cut

Fuzion Products LLC...................... G 317 536-0745
Indianapolis (G-8248)

NAME PLATES: Engraved Or Etched

Crichlow Industries Inc................... G 317 925-5178
Indianapolis (G-7903)

NATURAL GAS DISTRIBUTION TO CONSUMERS

K Grimmer Industries Inc.................. C 317 736-3800
Leo (G-10968)
Vectren LLC.............................. G 812 424-6411
Evansville (G-4369)
Vectren LLC.............................. A 812 491-4000
Evansville (G-4368)

NATURAL GAS LIQUIDS PRODUCTION

Citizens By-Products Coal Co.............. F 317 927-4738
Indianapolis (G-7811)
Nicholas Bryant.......................... G 765 366-0108
Hillsboro (G-7161)

NATURAL GAS PRODUCTION

Ah Medora Lfg LLC....................... G 346 440-1416
Medora (G-11460)
Green Cow Power LLC.................... G 219 984-5915
Goshen (G-6154)
Indy High Btu LLC......................... G 317 749-0732
Indianapolis (G-8528)
Pulse Energy Systems LLC................ G 618 392-5502
Evansville (G-4264)
Responsble Enrgy Oprations LLC........ G 812 354-8776
Petersburg (G-13623)
South Bend Ethanol LLC.................. D 574 703-3360
South Bend (G-15252)

NATURAL LIQUEFIED PETROLEUM GAS PRODUCTION

Jackson-Jennings LLC.................... G 812 522-4911
Seymour (G-14659)

NATURAL PROPANE PRODUCTION

Trade & Industrial Supply Inc............. G 812 537-1300
Batesville (G-609)

NEW & USED CAR DEALERS

American Steel Carports Inc.............. G 419 737-1331
Mount Summit (G-12284)
Rolls-Royce Corporation.................. E 317 230-2000
Indianapolis (G-9325)

Rolls-Royce Corporation.................. E 317 230-8515
West Lafayette (G-16626)

NICKEL

Ed Nickels................................ G 219 887-6128
Merrillville (G-11511)
Haynes International Inc.................. F 219 326-8530
La Porte (G-10418)
Haynes International Inc.................. A 765 456-6000
Kokomo (G-10278)
Patricia J Nickels Inc..................... G 502 489-4358
Charlestown (G-1890)

NONCURRENT CARRYING WIRING DEVICES

Appleton Grp LLC......................... G 219 326-5936
La Porte (G-10386)
Ronard Industries Inc..................... F 219 874-4801
Michigan City (G-11658)

NONFERROUS: Rolling & Drawing, NEC

Eco-Bat America LLC...................... C 317 247-1303
Indianapolis (G-8048)
Exeon Processors LLC..................... F 765 674-2266
Jonesboro (G-10078)
Hammond Group Inc...................... G 219 931-9360
Hammond (G-6939)
Hammond Group Inc...................... E 219 845-0031
Hammond (G-6940)
Metals and Additives LLC................. G 812 446-2525
Brazil (G-1153)
Rdd Properties Inc........................ E 317 870-1940
Waterloo (G-16529)
TI Group Auto Systems LLC.............. D 260 587-6100
Ashley (G-338)
Wagner Zip-Change Inc................... E 708 681-4100
Fort Wayne (G-5540)

NOTEBOOKS, MADE FROM PURCHASED MATERIALS

Rose & Petal LLC......................... G 260 704-5731
Fort Wayne (G-5389)

NOVELTIES

Buztronics Inc............................ E 317 876-3413
Brownsburg (G-1355)
Candles By Dar Inc....................... F 260 482-2099
Fort Wayne (G-4831)
Eastons Lettering Service................. G 219 942-5101
Hobart (G-7187)
Graphic Barn LLC......................... G 812 952-3826
Lanesville (G-10798)
XYZ Model Works......................... G 260 413-1873
Decatur (G-2889)

NOVELTIES & SPECIALTIES: Metal

4board LLC............................... G 317 997-3354
Indianapolis (G-7391)
Metal Fab Engineering Inc................ E 574 278-7150
Winamac (G-16867)

NOVELTIES: Plastic

Hot Stamping & Printing.................. G 219 767-2429
Union Mills (G-15865)
Royer Corporation........................ D 800 457-8997
Madison (G-11249)
Ultima Plastics LLC....................... G 812 459-1430
Evansville (G-4358)

NOZZLES: Fire Fighting

Elkhart Brass Manufacturing.............. C 574 295-8330
Elkhart (G-3322)

NOZZLES: Fire Fighting

Task Force Tips Inc.................................. F 219 462-6161
Valparaiso *(G-16063)*

Task Force Tips LLC................................. C 219 462-6161
Valparaiso *(G-16064)*

NURSERIES & LAWN & GARDEN SPLY STORES, RETAIL: Fertilizer

Agbest Cooperative Inc........................... G 765 358-3388
Gaston *(G-6043)*

Andersons Agriculture Group LP............. G 574 626-2522
Galveston *(G-5851)*

Bristow Milling Co LLC............................. G 812 843-5176
Bristow *(G-1299)*

Frick Services Inc.................................... E 260 761-3311
Wawaka *(G-16539)*

Keystone Cooperative Inc....................... G 317 861-5080
Fountaintown *(G-5615)*

Nachurs Alpine Solutions LLC................. G 812 738-1333
Corydon *(G-2507)*

Wanafeed Corporation............................. G 317 862-4032
Indianapolis *(G-9736)*

NYLON FIBERS

Eidp Inc... A 833 267-8382
Indianapolis *(G-8064)*

Mitsubishi Chemical Advncd Mtr.............. C 260 479-4100
Fort Wayne *(G-5233)*

Mitsubshi Chem Advnced Mtls In............ D 260 479-4700
Fort Wayne *(G-5234)*

NYLON RESINS

Mitsubishi Chemical Advncd Mtr.............. C 260 479-4100
Fort Wayne *(G-5233)*

Mitsubshi Chem Advnced Mtls In............ D 260 479-4700
Fort Wayne *(G-5234)*

OFFICE EQPT WHOLESALERS

Business Systems Mgt Corp.................... G 219 938-0166
Gary *(G-5908)*

Cummins - Allison Corp........................... G 317 872-6244
Indianapolis *(G-7922)*

Marketing and Retail Sales...................... G 812 883-1813
Salem *(G-14489)*

Office Sup of Southern Ind Inc................. G 812 283-5523
Jeffersonville *(G-10027)*

Pinnacle Mailing Products....................... F 765 405-1194
Yorktown *(G-16980)*

OFFICE EQPT, WHOLESALE: Photocopy Machines

Classic Products Corp............................. E 260 484-2695
Fort Wayne *(G-4855)*

OFFICE SPLY & STATIONERY STORES: Office Forms & Splys

A & H Enterprises LLC............................. G 317 398-3070
Shelbyville *(G-14729)*

Automobile Dealers Assn of Ind............... G 317 635-1441
Indianapolis *(G-7576)*

Bryant Printing LLC.................................. G 765 521-3379
New Castle *(G-12853)*

Cecils Printing & Off Sups Inc.................. G 812 683-4416
Huntingburg *(G-7273)*

Coy & Associates.................................... G 317 787-5089
Indianapolis *(G-7893)*

Indiana Auto Dealers Assn Svcs.............. G 317 635-1441
Indianapolis *(G-8473)*

Journal & Chronicle Inc........................... G 812 752-5060
Scottsburg *(G-14566)*

Marketing and Retail Sales...................... G 812 883-1813
Salem *(G-14489)*

Premier Print & Svcs Group Inc............... F 574 273-2525
Granger *(G-6372)*

Qgraphics Inc.. G 765 564-2314
Delphi *(G-2906)*

Scott Culbertson..................................... G 260 357-6430
Garrett *(G-5876)*

Shearer Printing Service Inc.................... E 765 457-3274
Kokomo *(G-10334)*

Smith & Butterfield Co Inc....................... F 812 422-3261
Evansville *(G-4320)*

The Office Shop Inc................................. E 812 934-5611
Batesville *(G-607)*

Tippecanoe Press Inc.............................. G 317 392-1207
Shelbyville *(G-14806)*

OFFICE SPLYS, NEC, WHOLESALE

Dbisp LLC.. G 317 222-1671
Indianapolis *(G-7957)*

I4 Identity LLC... G 317 662-0448
Fishers *(G-4541)*

Office Sup of Southern Ind Inc................. G 812 283-5523
Jeffersonville *(G-10027)*

Peerless Printing Corporation.................. G 765 664-8341
Marion *(G-11327)*

Systems & Services of Michiana.............. G 574 277-3355
South Bend *(G-15278)*

Systems & Services of Michiana.............. G 574 273-1111
South Bend *(G-15277)*

OFFICES & CLINICS OF DOCTORS OF MEDICINE: Radiologist

Fort Wyne Rdlgy Assn Fundation............ F 260 266-8120
Fort Wayne *(G-5003)*

OIL & GAS FIELD EQPT: Drill Rigs

Diedrich Drill Inc..................................... E 219 326-7788
La Porte *(G-10401)*

OIL & GAS FIELD MACHINERY

F D McCrary Operator Inc....................... G 812 354-6520
Petersburg *(G-13611)*

Fiberx Incorporated................................. G 317 501-5619
Hammond *(G-6928)*

M&C Tech Indiana Corporation............... E 812 674-2122
Washington *(G-16493)*

Nov Inc.. G 317 897-3099
Indianapolis *(G-9027)*

Systems Engineering and Sls Co............ G 260 422-1671
Fort Wayne *(G-5466)*

OIL FIELD MACHINERY & EQPT

Ares Division LLC.................................... G 260 349-9803
Waterloo *(G-16514)*

Emquip Corporation................................ G 317 849-3977
Indianapolis *(G-8111)*

Nrp Jones LLC.. D 800 348-8868
La Porte *(G-10460)*

OIL FIELD SVCS, NEC

Baker Petrolite LLC................................. G 219 473-5329
Whiting *(G-16832)*

Bst Corp.. G 812 925-7911
Boonville *(G-1083)*

Core Laboratories LP.............................. G 260 312-0455
Fort Wayne *(G-4876)*

Diane Vander Vliet.................................. G 574 389-9360
Elkhart *(G-3296)*

Franklin Well Service LLC....................... F 877 943-4680
Vincennes *(G-16126)*

Jay Costas Companies Inc..................... G 219 663-4364
Crown Point *(G-2700)*

JE Mnnix Well Srvcing Mini E.................. G 765 855-5464
Centerville *(G-1850)*

Minnix J E Well Servicing........................ G 765 855-5464
Centerville *(G-1852)*

Morgan Excavating................................. G 812 385-6036
Oakland City *(G-13321)*

Newpark Resources Inc.......................... G 765 546-9473
Ridgeville *(G-14236)*

Oilfield Research Inc............................... G 812 424-2907
Evansville *(G-4226)*

Pioneer Oilfield Services LLC.................. F 812 882-0999
Vincennes *(G-16145)*

Saybolt.. G 812 944-5001
Clarksville *(G-2033)*

Saybolt LP... G 812 282-7242
Clarksville *(G-2034)*

Stealth Energy Group LLC...................... G 316 260-0064
Zionsville *(G-17053)*

Strategic Tanks Incorporated.................. F 574 807-2403
Notre Dame *(G-13316)*

United Oil Corp....................................... G 260 489-3511
Fort Wayne *(G-5521)*

US Oilfield Company LLC....................... F 888 584-7565
Carmel *(G-1796)*

Weatherford Engineered......................... G 812 858-3147
Newburgh *(G-13029)*

OIL TREATING COMPOUNDS

Consolidated Recycling Co Inc................ D 812 547-7951
Evansville *(G-3981)*

OILS & ESSENTIAL OILS

Bedlam Beard Company LLC.................. G 317 800-9631
Lizton *(G-11048)*

Sassy Organics Collection LLC............... G 231 942-0751
Indianapolis *(G-9375)*

Sol Melanin Beauty LLC.......................... G 317 354-3977
Indianapolis *(G-9459)*

OILS: Cutting

Metalworking Lubricants Co.................... C 317 269-2444
Indianapolis *(G-8891)*

OINTMENTS

Bloom Pharmaceutical............................ G 260 615-2633
Fort Wayne *(G-4807)*

Merrill Corporation.................................. E 574 255-2988
Mishawaka *(G-11942)*

OPHTHALMIC GOODS

City Optical Co Inc.................................. D 317 924-1300
Indianapolis *(G-7813)*

Diversified Ophthalmics Inc.................... E 317 780-1677
Indianapolis *(G-7985)*

Luxottica of America Inc......................... G 317 293-9999
Indianapolis *(G-8800)*

Luxottica of America Inc......................... G 219 736-0141
Merrillville *(G-11535)*

Plainfield Eye Care................................. F 317 839-2368
Plainfield *(G-13715)*

Singer Optical Company Inc................... F 812 423-1179
Evansville *(G-4315)*

Tri State Optical Inc................................ D 765 289-4475
Muncie *(G-12508)*

OPHTHALMIC GOODS WHOLESALERS

City Optical Co Inc.................................. D 317 924-1300
Indianapolis *(G-7813)*

Diversified Ophthalmics Inc.................... E 317 780-1677
Indianapolis *(G-7985)*

PRODUCT SECTION — PACKAGING MATERIALS: Plastic Film, Coated Or Laminated

Kokomo Optical Company Inc .... G 765 459-5137
Kokomo *(G-10293)*

Singer Optical Company Inc .... F 812 423-1179
Evansville *(G-4315)*

Vision Training Products Inc .... F 574 259-2070
Mishawaka *(G-12023)*

OPHTHALMIC GOODS: Frames & Parts, Eyeglass & Spectacle

Usv Optical Inc .... G 260 482-5033
Fort Wayne *(G-5524)*

OPHTHALMIC GOODS: Lenses, Ophthalmic

Harmon Hrmon Uysugi Optmtrists .... F 812 723-4752
Paoli *(G-13496)*

OPTICAL GOODS STORES

City Optical Co Inc .... D 317 924-1300
Indianapolis *(G-7813)*

Jackson Vision Quest .... G 219 882-9397
Gary *(G-5967)*

OPTICAL GOODS STORES: Contact Lenses, Prescription

Better Visions PC .... F 260 244-7542
Columbia City *(G-2124)*

Better Visions PC .... F 260 627-2669
Leo *(G-10963)*

OPTICAL GOODS STORES: Eyeglasses, Prescription

Columbus Optical Service Inc .... G 812 372-4117
Columbus *(G-2245)*

Kokomo Optical Company Inc .... G 765 459-5137
Kokomo *(G-10293)*

Luxottica of America Inc .... G 317 293-9999
Indianapolis *(G-8800)*

Luxottica of America Inc .... G 219 736-0141
Merrillville *(G-11535)*

Shimp Optical Corp .... G 317 636-4448
Indianapolis *(G-9420)*

Usv Optical Inc .... G 260 482-5033
Fort Wayne *(G-5524)*

OPTICAL GOODS STORES: Opticians

Tri State Optical Inc .... D 765 289-4475
Muncie *(G-12508)*

OPTICAL INSTRUMENTS & APPARATUS

Dave Jones Machinists LLC .... G 574 256-5500
Mishawaka *(G-11881)*

Vision Aid Systems Inc .... G 317 888-0323
Greenwood *(G-6778)*

OPTICAL INSTRUMENTS & LENSES

Corlens Inc .... G 843 822-6174
Terre Haute *(G-15568)*

General Optics LLC .... G 765 637-5578
Zionsville *(G-17012)*

Optical Solutions LLC LLC .... G 317 525-8308
Fishers *(G-4571)*

S & S Optical Co Inc .... F 260 749-9614
New Haven *(G-12915)*

OPTICAL ISOLATORS

Jdsu Acterna Holdings LLC .... G 317 788-9351
Indianapolis *(G-8621)*

Viavi Solutions Inc .... E 317 788-9351
Indianapolis *(G-9719)*

ORGANIZATIONS: Medical Research

Ash Access Technology Inc .... G 765 742-4813
Lafayette *(G-10528)*

ORGANIZATIONS: Religious

Christian Sound & Song Inc .... G 574 294-2893
Elkhart *(G-3251)*

Gospel Echoes Team Association .... G 574 533-0221
Goshen *(G-6153)*

ORGANIZATIONS: Research Institute

Ampacet Corporation .... E 812 466-9828
Terre Haute *(G-15543)*

PACKAGE DESIGN SVCS

Catalent Wellness Indiana LLC .... F 812 537-5203
Greendale *(G-6443)*

PACKAGING & LABELING SVCS

Accra-Pac Inc .... G 574 295-0000
Elkhart *(G-3149)*

Ahf Industries Inc .... C 812 936-9988
French Lick *(G-5843)*

Apg Inc .... D 574 295-0000
Elkhart *(G-3185)*

Asempac Inc .... E 812 945-6303
New Albany *(G-12692)*

Black Lavish Essentials LLC .... G 800 214-8664
Indianapolis *(G-7639)*

Century Pharmaceuticals Inc .... E 317 849-4210
Indianapolis *(G-7775)*

Custom Bottling & Packg Inc .... E 877 401-7195
Ashley *(G-332)*

Custom Carton Inc .... F 260 563-7411
Wabash *(G-16179)*

Data Mail Incorporated .... E 812 424-7835
Evansville *(G-4007)*

Ditech Inc .... E 812 526-0850
Edinburgh *(G-3077)*

Fedex Office & Print Svcs Inc .... G 317 974-0378
Indianapolis *(G-8172)*

Fedex Office & Print Svcs Inc .... G 317 917-1529
Indianapolis *(G-8173)*

Insertec Inc .... D 800 556-1911
Indianapolis *(G-8560)*

L M Corporation .... E 574 535-0581
Goshen *(G-6194)*

National Products LLC .... G 219 393-5536
Kingsbury *(G-10182)*

Pathfinder Services Inc .... E 260 356-0500
Huntington *(G-7354)*

Precision Products Group Inc .... F 317 663-4590
Indianapolis *(G-9184)*

Rauch Inc .... E 812 945-4063
New Albany *(G-12803)*

Royal Adhesives & Sealants LLC .... D 574 246-5000
South Bend *(G-15226)*

Service Graphics Inc .... D 317 471-8246
Indianapolis *(G-9408)*

Universal Packg Systems Inc .... C 260 829-6721
Orland *(G-13374)*

PACKAGING MATERIALS, WHOLESALE

ABC Industries Inc .... D 800 426-0921
Winona Lake *(G-16907)*

Bethlehem Packg Die Cutng Inc .... E 812 282-8740
New Albany *(G-12700)*

Cluster Packaging LLC .... G 612 803-1056
Crown Point *(G-2666)*

Huhtamaki Inc .... D 765 677-0395
Marion *(G-11293)*

ISI of Indiana Inc .... G 317 241-2999
Indianapolis *(G-8595)*

Jamil Packaging Corporation .... E 574 256-2600
Mishawaka *(G-11917)*

Kelly Box and Packaging Corp .... D 260 432-4570
Fort Wayne *(G-5145)*

Pregis LLC .... G 574 936-7065
Plymouth *(G-13806)*

PACKAGING MATERIALS: Paper

3M Company .... E 765 348-3200
Hartford City *(G-7060)*

Accu-Label Inc .... E 260 482-5223
Fort Wayne *(G-4720)*

American Containers Inc .... D 574 936-4068
Plymouth *(G-13755)*

Bprex Closures LLC .... D 812 386-1525
Princeton *(G-13985)*

Crichlow Industries Inc .... G 317 925-5178
Indianapolis *(G-7903)*

Custom Packaging Inc .... F 317 876-9559
Indianapolis *(G-7933)*

Dynamic Packg Solutions Inc .... C 574 848-1410
Bristol *(G-1257)*

Eagle Packaging Inc .... G 260 281-2333
Goshen *(G-6128)*

Elite Packaging LLC .... G 502 232-2596
Jeffersonville *(G-9975)*

Filmtech Inc .... G 888 399-7442
Greensburg *(G-6592)*

G & T Industries Inc .... E 812 634-2252
Jasper *(G-9839)*

Huhtamaki Inc .... C 219 972-4264
Hammond *(G-6950)*

Innovative Energy Inc .... E 219 696-3639
Crown Point *(G-2697)*

Label Tech Inc .... E 765 747-1234
Muncie *(G-12436)*

MSI Express Inc .... E 219 871-9882
Portage *(G-13894)*

NP Converters Inc .... D 812 448-2555
Brazil *(G-1158)*

Nyx LLC .... A 734 838-3570
New Albany *(G-12786)*

Pactiv LLC .... E 574 936-7065
Plymouth *(G-13800)*

Pennplastics LLC .... G 574 286-0705
Mishawaka *(G-11973)*

PSC Industries Inc .... F 812 425-9071
Evansville *(G-4263)*

Sonoco Products Company .... D 812 526-5511
Edinburgh *(G-3105)*

Stoffel Seals Corporation .... E 845 353-3800
Angola *(G-296)*

Taghleef Industries Inc .... A 302 326-5500
Rosedale *(G-14385)*

Vti Packaging Specialties .... G 574 277-4119
Granger *(G-6389)*

Westrock Cp Inc .... G 574 936-2118
Plymouth *(G-13828)*

PACKAGING MATERIALS: Paper, Coated Or Laminated

Supremex Midwest LLC .... G 317 898-2000
Indianapolis *(G-9534)*

PACKAGING MATERIALS: Plastic Film, Coated Or Laminated

Bowers Envelope Company Inc .... G 317 253-4321
Indianapolis *(G-7665)*

PACKAGING MATERIALS: Plastic Film, Coated Or Laminated

Cpg - Ohio LLC	F	260 829-6721
Orland *(G-13363)*		
Interactive Surface Tech LLC	G	812 246-0900
Sellersburg *(G-14602)*		
Max Katz Bag Company Inc	D	317 635-9561
Indianapolis *(G-8855)*		
Monosol LLC	G	219 324-9459
La Porte *(G-10454)*		
Monosol LLC	G	219 763-7589
Portage *(G-13891)*		
Sabert Corporation	G	260 747-3149
Fort Wayne *(G-5395)*		
Spartech LLC	D	765 281-5100
Muncie *(G-12495)*		
Universal Package LLC	F	812 937-3605
Ferdinand *(G-4450)*		
Universal Packg Systems Inc	C	260 829-6721
Orland *(G-13374)*		

PACKING & CRATING SVC

Packaging Group Corp	F	219 879-2500
Michigan City *(G-11649)*		
VMS Products Inc	G	888 321-4698
Anderson *(G-214)*		

PACKING MATERIALS: Mechanical

Uniform Hood Lace Inc	G	317 896-9555
Westfield *(G-16734)*		

PACKING: Rubber

Griffith Rbr Mills of Garrett	C	260 357-0876
Garrett *(G-5865)*		

PADDING: Foamed Plastics

Aqua Lily Products LLC	G	951 246-9610
Elkhart *(G-3187)*		
Foamcraft Inc	E	574 293-8569
Elkhart *(G-3352)*		
Residue West Inc	F	731 587-9596
Evansville *(G-4285)*		

PAINTS & ADDITIVES

Advanced Protective Tech LLC	G	888 531-4527
Valparaiso *(G-15892)*		
D & L Industrial Finishes Inc	G	765 458-5157
Liberty *(G-10987)*		
Davies-Imperial Coatings Inc	E	219 933-0877
Hammond *(G-6911)*		
Nanochem Technologies LLC	E	574 970-2436
Elkhart *(G-3563)*		
Red Spot Paint & Varnish Co	G	812 428-9100
Evansville *(G-4279)*		
United Coatings Tech Inc	F	574 287-4774
South Bend *(G-15296)*		
Wurth Additive Group Inc	F	551 269-7695
Greenwood *(G-6782)*		

PAINTS & ALLIED PRODUCTS

3b Photonics LLC	G	574 702-2620
Logansport *(G-11053)*		
Abtrex Industries Inc	F	734 728-0550
South Bend *(G-14934)*		
Ampacet Corporation	E	812 466-9828
Terre Haute *(G-15543)*		
Ampacet Corporation	D	812 466-5231
Terre Haute *(G-15544)*		
Aoc LLC	D	219 465-4384
Valparaiso *(G-15900)*		
Belden Inc	C	724 222-7060
Richmond *(G-14092)*		
Bloomington Con Surfaces Corp	G	812 345-0011
Bloomington *(G-810)*		
Bondline Adhesives Inc	F	812 423-4651
Evansville *(G-3939)*		
Connersville Paint Mfgco	G	765 825-4111
Connersville *(G-2433)*		
Contego International Inc	G	317 580-0665
Carmel *(G-1594)*		
Contego International Inc	G	574 223-5989
Rochester *(G-14283)*		
Cp Inc	E	765 825-4111
Connersville *(G-2434)*		
Dse Inc	E	812 376-0310
Columbus *(G-2291)*		
Icl Specialty Products Inc	G	219 933-1560
Hammond *(G-6951)*		
Katalyst Corporation	G	317 783-6500
Beech Grove *(G-696)*		
Margco International LLC	G	317 568-4274
Indianapolis *(G-8828)*		
Mautz Paint Factory	G	574 289-2497
South Bend *(G-15141)*		
Midwest Pipecoating Inc	D	219 322-4564
Schererville *(G-14535)*		
Ncp Coatings Inc	G	574 255-9678
Mishawaka *(G-11964)*		
Polytek Development Corp	G	317 494-6420
Franklin *(G-5767)*		
PPG Architectural Finishes Inc	G	317 745-0427
Avon *(G-545)*		
PPG Architectural Finishes Inc	G	317 575-8011
Carmel *(G-1722)*		
PPG Architectural Finishes Inc	G	317 575-8011
Carmel *(G-1723)*		
PPG Architectural Finishes Inc	G	317 471-8250
Carmel *(G-1724)*		
PPG Architectural Finishes Inc	G	812 473-0339
Evansville *(G-4251)*		
PPG Architectural Finishes Inc	G	260 436-1854
Fort Wayne *(G-5330)*		
PPG Architectural Finishes Inc	G	260 436-1854
Fort Wayne *(G-5331)*		
PPG Architectural Finishes Inc	G	260 373-2373
Fort Wayne *(G-5332)*		
PPG Architectural Finishes Inc	G	317 634-2547
Indianapolis *(G-9168)*		
PPG Architectural Finishes Inc	G	317 787-9393
Indianapolis *(G-9169)*		
PPG Architectural Finishes Inc	G	765 447-9334
Lafayette *(G-10669)*		
PPG Architectural Finishes Inc	G	812 232-0672
Terre Haute *(G-15664)*		
PPG Architectural Finishes Inc	G	812 882-0440
Vincennes *(G-16146)*		
PPG Holdings Inc	G	317 663-4590
Indianapolis *(G-9170)*		
PPG Industries Inc	G	317 745-0427
Avon *(G-546)*		
PPG Industries Inc	G	317 870-0345
Carmel *(G-1725)*		
PPG Industries Inc	G	812 948-9253
Clarksville *(G-2026)*		
PPG Industries Inc	G	812 867-6601
Evansville *(G-4252)*		
PPG Industries Inc	G	812 424-4774
Evansville *(G-4253)*		
PPG Industries Inc	G	812 473-0339
Evansville *(G-4254)*		
PPG Industries Inc	G	317 598-9448
Fishers *(G-4581)*		
PPG Industries Inc	G	317 577-2344
Fishers *(G-4582)*		
PPG Industries Inc	G	260 373-2373
Fort Wayne *(G-5333)*		
PPG Industries Inc	E	260 432-6900
Fort Wayne *(G-5334)*		
PPG Industries Inc	G	317 251-9494
Indianapolis *(G-9171)*		
PPG Industries Inc	G	317 267-0511
Indianapolis *(G-9172)*		
PPG Industries Inc	G	317 897-3836
Indianapolis *(G-9173)*		
PPG Industries Inc	G	317 787-9393
Indianapolis *(G-9174)*		
PPG Industries Inc	G	317 546-5714
Indianapolis *(G-9175)*		
PPG Industries Inc	G	765 282-0316
Muncie *(G-12476)*		
PPG Industries Inc	G	812 944-4164
New Albany *(G-12797)*		
PPG Industries Inc	G	812 232-0672
Terre Haute *(G-15665)*		
PPG Industries Inc	G	812 882-0440
Vincennes *(G-16147)*		
PPG Industries Inc	G	317 867-5934
Westfield *(G-16719)*		
Precoat Metals	F	219 763-1504
Portage *(G-13906)*		
Protech Powder Coatings Inc	G	814 456-1243
Liberty *(G-10997)*		
Rbc Holding Inc	F	317 340-3845
Greenwood *(G-6759)*		
Red Spot Paint & Varnish Co	G	812 428-9100
Evansville *(G-4278)*		
Redspot Paint and Varnish Co	E	812 428-9100
Evansville *(G-4282)*		
Rollie Williams Paint Spot	G	812 827-2488
Jasper *(G-9906)*		
Sonoco Products Company	D	812 526-5511
Edinburgh *(G-3105)*		
Technicote Inc	E	812 466-9844
Terre Haute *(G-15724)*		
Transcendia Inc	C	765 935-1520
Richmond *(G-14220)*		
United Coatings Mfg Co	G	317 845-8830
Indianapolis *(G-9679)*		
United Minerals and Prpts Inc	G	812 838-5236
Mount Vernon *(G-12325)*		
Van Zandt Enterprises Inc	F	812 423-3511
Evansville *(G-4366)*		
Woodys Paint Spot Ltd	G	574 255-0348
Bremen *(G-1231)*		
Worwag Coatings	G	765 746-6037
Lafayette *(G-10719)*		

PAINTS & VARNISHES: Plastics Based

Red Spot Paint & Varnish Co	G	812 428-9100
Evansville *(G-4280)*		
Red Spot Paint & Varnish Co	B	812 428-9100
Evansville *(G-4281)*		

PAINTS, VARNISHES & SPLYS WHOLESALERS

Jack Laurie Coml Floors Inc	G	317 569-2095
Indianapolis *(G-8613)*		

PAINTS, VARNISHES & SPLYS, WHOLESALE: Paints

Mautz Paint Factory	G	574 289-2497
South Bend *(G-15141)*		

PAINTS: Oil Or Alkyd Vehicle Or Water Thinned

Freeband Custom Paint LLC.................G..... 219 216-2553
Indianapolis (G-8226)

Quality Coatings Inc..................F..... 812 925-3314
Chandler (G-1865)

Vanex Inc..................E..... 618 244-1413
Brazil (G-1169)

PAINTS: Waterproof

Dist Council 91..................G..... 812 962-9191
Evansville (G-4014)

PALLET REPAIR SVCS

American Pallet & Recycl Inc..................G..... 219 322-4391
Dyer (G-2966)

Clm Pallet Recycling Inc..................G..... 317 485-4080
Fortville (G-5589)

Green Stream Company..................C..... 574 293-1949
Elkhart (G-3391)

J & J Pallet Corp..................E..... 812 944-8670
New Albany (G-12750)

Millers Wood Specialties Inc..................E..... 765 478-3248
Cambridge City (G-1499)

X-L Box Inc..................F..... 219 763-3736
Valparaiso (G-16082)

PALLETS & SKIDS: Wood

A S M Inc..................G..... 260 724-8220
Decatur (G-2839)

A-1 Pallet Co of Clarksville..................G..... 812 288-6339
Clarksville (G-2006)

Anthony Wyne Rhblttion Ctr For..................D..... 260 744-6145
Fort Wayne (G-4762)

Danwood Industries..................G..... 219 369-1484
La Porte (G-10399)

H H Pallet..................G..... 765 505-1682
Crawfordsville (G-2575)

Powell Systems Inc..................E..... 765 884-0980
Fowler (G-5630)

Servants Inc..................D..... 812 634-2201
Jasper (G-9910)

Ufp Granger LLC..................E..... 574 277-7670
Granger (G-6387)

Wabash Heritage Mfg LLC..................G..... 812 886-0147
Vincennes (G-16161)

PALLETS: Plastic

Flambeau Inc..................G..... 812 372-4899
Columbus (G-2310)

Greystone Logistics Inc..................G..... 812 459-9978
Evansville (G-4098)

Paxxal Inc..................G..... 317 296-7724
Noblesville (G-13153)

Perfect Manufacturing LLC..................G..... 317 924-5284
Indianapolis (G-9122)

Polymer Logistics Inc..................D..... 219 706-5985
Portage (G-13904)

PALLETS: Wood & Metal Combination

Henry Street LLC..................D..... 317 788-7225
Franklin (G-5738)

Matco Pallets..................G..... 260 223-0585
Decatur (G-2872)

Rhino Shipping Solutions LLC..................G..... 317 721-9476
Fishers (G-4649)

PANEL & DISTRIBUTION BOARDS & OTHER RELATED APPARATUS

American Technology Compone..................C..... 800 238-2687
Elkhart (G-3177)

J & J Industrial Service Inc..................G..... 219 362-4973
La Porte (G-10429)

Mechancal Engrg Cntrls Atmtn C..................E..... 574 294-7580
Elkhart (G-3522)

Pinder Instruments Company Inc..................G..... 219 924-7070
Munster (G-12558)

Richard J Bagan Inc..................E..... 260 244-5115
Columbia City (G-2190)

Semcor Inc..................E..... 219 362-0222
La Porte (G-10479)

PANEL & DISTRIBUTION BOARDS: Electric

Leman Engrg & Consulting Inc..................G..... 574 870-7732
Brookston (G-1312)

PANELS & SECTIONS: Prefabricated, Concrete

Ram North America Inc..................F..... 317 984-1971
Arcadia (G-316)

PANELS: Building, Metal

Central States Mfg Inc..................C..... 219 879-4770
Michigan City (G-11586)

PANELS: Building, Plastic, NEC

Crane Composites Inc..................G..... 574 295-9391
Elkhart (G-3269)

Crane Composites Inc..................G..... 815 467-8600
Goshen (G-6118)

Panolam Industries Inc..................D..... 574 264-0702
Elkhart (G-3582)

Ram North America Inc..................F..... 317 984-1971
Arcadia (G-316)

PAPER & BOARD: Die-cut

A-1 Graphics Inc..................G..... 765 289-1851
Muncie (G-12332)

AK Tool and Die Inc..................G..... 574 286-9010
Mishawaka (G-11836)

American Steel Rule Die Inc..................G..... 574 262-3437
Elkhart (G-3175)

C & W Inkd..................F..... 317 352-1000
Indianapolis (G-7706)

Graphix Unlimited Inc..................G..... 574 546-3770
Bremen (G-1193)

Harcourt Industries Inc..................E..... 765 629-2625
Milroy (G-11824)

Millcraft Paper Company..................G..... 317 240-3500
Indianapolis (G-8920)

Rink Printing Company..................E..... 574 232-7935
South Bend (G-15220)

Ross-Gage Inc..................E..... 317 283-2323
Indianapolis (G-9335)

Tre Paper Company..................G..... 765 649-2536
Anderson (G-208)

Westrock Rkt LLC..................E..... 812 372-8873
Columbus (G-2418)

PAPER PRDTS: Infant & Baby Prdts

Bobby Little Creations..................G..... 219 313-5102
Crown Point (G-2658)

Diaper Stone Opco LLC..................G..... 866 221-2145
Greenfield (G-6489)

PAPER PRDTS: Molded Pulp Prdts

Huhtamaki Inc..................C..... 219 972-4264
Hammond (G-6950)

PAPER PRDTS: Napkins, Sanitary, Made From Purchased Material

Med Pad Incorporated..................G..... 812 422-6154
Evansville (G-4195)

PAPER PRDTS: Sanitary Tissue Paper

Nice-Pak Products Inc..................E..... 317 839-0373
Plainfield (G-13710)

PAPER, WHOLESALE: Printing

Millcraft Paper Company..................G..... 317 240-3500
Indianapolis (G-8920)

PAPER: Adding Machine Rolls, Made From Purchased Materials

Gov 6 Corp..................G..... 317 847-4942
Indianapolis (G-8310)

PAPER: Adhesive

Avery Dennison Corporation..................C..... 260 481-4500
Fort Wayne (G-4783)

Avery Dennison Corporation..................D..... 219 696-7777
Lowell (G-11155)

Eckart America Corporation..................G..... 219 864-4861
Schererville (G-14519)

Quality Engineered Pdts Inc..................F..... 574 294-6943
Elkhart (G-3630)

PAPER: Business Form

Roi Marketing Company Inc..................G..... 317 644-0797
Indianapolis (G-9321)

PAPER: Cardboard

Cardboard Apothecary..................G..... 574 309-3007
South Bend (G-14966)

Guy Cardboard..................G..... 812 989-4809
Elizabeth (G-3127)

PAPER: Coated & Laminated, NEC

3M Company..................E..... 765 348-3200
Hartford City (G-7060)

Abro Industries Inc..................E..... 574 232-8289
South Bend (G-14933)

Accu-Label Inc..................E..... 260 482-5223
Fort Wayne (G-4720)

Daubert Vci Inc..................E..... 574 772-9310
Knox (G-10204)

F Robert Gardner Co Inc..................G..... 317 634-2333
Indianapolis (G-8161)

Fedex Office & Print Svcs Inc..................G..... 317 337-2679
Indianapolis (G-8177)

Gindor Inc..................G..... 574 642-4004
Goshen (G-6149)

Hi-Tech Label Inc..................F..... 765 659-1800
Frankfort (G-5673)

International Paper Company..................D..... 800 643-7244
Terre Haute (G-15619)

Jknk Ventures Inc..................E..... 812 246-0900
Sellersburg (G-14603)

L & L Press Inc..................F..... 765 664-3162
Marion (G-11305)

Label Tech Inc..................E..... 765 747-1234
Muncie (G-12436)

Lambel Corporation..................G..... 317 849-6828
Indianapolis (G-8716)

Lamco Finishers Inc..................E..... 317 471-1010
Indianapolis (G-8717)

Mito-Craft Inc..................G..... 574 287-4555
South Bend (G-15152)

Morgan Adhesives Company LLC..................B..... 812 342-2004
Columbus (G-2357)

NP Converters Inc..................D..... 812 448-2555
Brazil (G-1158)

R R Donnelley & Sons Company..................B..... 260 624-2350
Angola (G-291)

PAPER: Coated & Laminated, NEC

Tippecanoe Press Inc .... G 317 392-1207
  Shelbyville *(G-14806)*

Westrock Cp LLC .... G 574 936-2118
  Plymouth *(G-13828)*

Zimmer Paper Products Del LLC .... D 317 263-3420
  Indianapolis *(G-9811)*

PAPER: Coated, Exc Photographic, Carbon Or Abrasive

Covalnce Spcialty Coatings LLC .... E 812 424-2904
  Evansville *(G-3988)*

PAPER: Corrugated

Flutes Inc .... D 844 317-2021
  Indianapolis *(G-8209)*

Flutes Inc .... D 317 870-6010
  Indianapolis *(G-8208)*

Georgia-Pacific Corrugated III LLC .... G
  Indianapolis *(G-8279)*

Georgia-Pacific LLC .... G 219 776-0069
  Wheatfield *(G-16766)*

Sheets LLC .... G 317 290-1140
  Carmel *(G-1759)*

Sinflex Paper Co Inc .... E 765 789-6688
  Muncie *(G-12493)*

Welch Packaging Kentucky LLC .... E 574 295-2460
  Elkhart *(G-3781)*

PAPER: Newsprint

Freddie Powell .... G 574 658-3345
  Lafayette *(G-10582)*

PAPER: Specialty Or Chemically Treated

Noblesville Pack & Ship .... G 317 776-6306
  Noblesville *(G-13144)*

PAPER: Wallpaper

Girls .... G 812 299-1382
  Terre Haute *(G-15598)*

Panel Solutions Inc .... G 574 389-8494
  Elkhart *(G-3580)*

Staltari Enterprises Inc .... G 574 522-1988
  Elkhart *(G-3694)*

PAPER: Waxed, Made From Purchased Materials

Bomarko Inc .... C 574 936-9901
  Plymouth *(G-13758)*

Zimmer Holdings LLC .... G
  Ossian *(G-13444)*

Zimmer Paper Products Del LLC .... D 317 263-3420
  Indianapolis *(G-9811)*

PAPER: Wrapping & Packaging

Bmk Investments Inc .... G 574 282-2538
  South Bend *(G-14960)*

Cascades Holding US Inc .... B 219 697-2900
  Brook *(G-1304)*

Inland Paper Board & Packaging .... G 317 879-9710
  Indianapolis *(G-8550)*

Jodo Investments Inc .... E 765 651-0200
  Marion *(G-11301)*

New-Indy Hartford City LLC .... D 765 348-5440
  Hartford City *(G-7073)*

PAPERBOARD PRDTS: Folding Boxboard

Clondalkin Pharma & Healthcare Inc ...... A 336 292-4555
  Indianapolis *(G-7824)*

PAPERBOARD PRDTS: Packaging Board

Custom Kraft Pack LLC .... F 502 595-8146
  Jeffersonville *(G-9966)*

PARTITIONS & FIXTURES: Except Wood

Burns Cabinets and Disp Inc .... G 260 897-2219
  Avilla *(G-473)*

Creative Industries Inc .... E 317 248-1102
  Plainfield *(G-13676)*

Elkhart Brass Manufacturing Co .... E 800 346-0250
  Elkhart *(G-3321)*

Flambeau Inc .... G 812 372-4899
  Columbus *(G-2310)*

Michiana Laminated Products .... E 260 562-2871
  Howe *(G-7240)*

Organized Living Inc .... C 812 334-8839
  Bloomington *(G-938)*

Out of Box Solutions Inc .... G 317 605-8719
  Indianapolis *(G-9076)*

Patrick Industries Inc .... G 574 293-1521
  Elkhart *(G-3589)*

Shamrock Cabinets Inc .... E 812 482-7969
  Jasper *(G-9911)*

Shed Craft Creations LLC .... G 765 993-1161
  Winchester *(G-16899)*

Tru-Form Steel & Wire Inc .... E 765 348-5001
  Hartford City *(G-7078)*

Ynwa Industries Inc .... D 574 295-6641
  Elkhart *(G-3800)*

PARTITIONS: Wood & Fixtures

Eds Wood Craft .... G 812 768-6617
  Haubstadt *(G-7084)*

Elko Inc .... F 812 473-8400
  Evansville *(G-4030)*

Fehrenbacher Cabinets Inc .... E 812 963-3377
  Evansville *(G-4066)*

Garyrae Inc .... F 574 255-7141
  Mishawaka *(G-11898)*

Indiana Southern Millwork Inc .... E 812 346-6129
  North Vernon *(G-13280)*

Kline Cabinet Makers LLC .... F 317 326-3049
  Maxwell *(G-11444)*

Lambright Woodworking LLC .... F 260 593-2721
  Topeka *(G-15811)*

Laminated Tops Central Ind Inc .... E 812 824-6299
  Bloomington *(G-906)*

Laminique Inc .... F 765 482-4222
  Zionsville *(G-17029)*

Lawrence Shirks .... G 574 223-5118
  Rochester *(G-14301)*

Oehlers Woods .... G 317 848-2698
  Carmel *(G-1710)*

Our Country Home Entps Inc .... D 260 657-5605
  Grabill *(G-6318)*

Our Country Home Entps Inc .... E 260 657-5605
  Harlan *(G-7058)*

Patrick Industries Inc .... G 574 293-1521
  Elkhart *(G-3589)*

Patrick Industries Inc .... G 574 294-5758
  Elkhart *(G-3596)*

Rabb and Howe Cabinet Top Co .... F 317 926-6442
  Indianapolis *(G-9258)*

Rbk Development Inc .... E 574 267-5879
  Warsaw *(G-16417)*

Sims Cabinet Co Inc .... E 317 634-1747
  Danville *(G-2828)*

SJS Components LLC .... G 260 578-0192
  Warsaw *(G-16426)*

Solid Surface Craftsmen Inc .... G 317 535-2333
  Whiteland *(G-16797)*

Tremain Ceramic Tile & Flr Cvg .... E 317 542-1491
  Indianapolis *(G-9633)*

Walters Cabinet Shop .... G 765 452-9634
  Kokomo *(G-10355)*

Yourspace LLC .... G 260 702-9595
  Fort Wayne *(G-5582)*

PARTS: Metal

D & T Tool Special Machine .... G 260 597-7216
  Ossian *(G-13422)*

Metal Technologies Indiana LLC .... C 260 925-4717
  Auburn *(G-409)*

Production Partners Inc .... F 574 229-5960
  Mishawaka *(G-11980)*

Small Parts Inc .... B 574 753-6323
  Logansport *(G-11107)*

Steel Storage Inc .... F 574 282-2618
  South Bend *(G-15268)*

Summit Manufacturing Corp .... E 260 428-2600
  Fort Wayne *(G-5453)*

Versatile Metal Works LLC .... F 765 754-7470
  Muncie *(G-12512)*

Warsaw Metal Products Inc .... F 574 269-6211
  Pierceton *(G-13642)*

Wayne Metals LLC .... D 260 758-3121
  Markle *(G-11364)*

PATENT OWNERS & LESSORS

Odyssian Technology LLC .... G 574 257-7555
  South Bend *(G-15176)*

PATTERNS: Indl

Armour Pattern Inc .... G 219 374-9325
  Cedar Lake *(G-1827)*

Charles E Obryan .... G 812 536-2399
  Huntingburg *(G-7274)*

Cindys Crossstitch & Patterns .... G 317 410-0764
  Indianapolis *(G-7804)*

Core-Tech Inc .... D 260 748-4477
  Fort Wayne *(G-4877)*

Cunningham Pattern & Engrg Inc .... F 812 379-9571
  Columbus *(G-2276)*

Dillon Pattern Works Inc .... F 765 642-3549
  Anderson *(G-103)*

Foley Pattern Company Inc .... E 260 925-4113
  Auburn *(G-391)*

K & K Inc .... F 574 266-8040
  Elkhart *(G-3440)*

Muncie Casting Corp .... E 765 288-2611
  Muncie *(G-12461)*

New Point Products Inc .... G 812 663-6311
  New Point *(G-12976)*

Northbend Pattern Works Inc .... E 812 637-3000
  West Harrison *(G-16550)*

Northside Pattern Works Inc .... G 317 290-0501
  Brownsburg *(G-1391)*

Ooten Pattern Works .... G 317 244-7348
  Indianapolis *(G-9061)*

Owings Patterns Inc .... F 812 944-5577
  Sellersburg *(G-14609)*

Peerless Pattern & Machine Co .... G 765 477-7719
  Lafayette *(G-10666)*

Standard Pattern Company Inc .... G 260 456-4870
  Fort Wayne *(G-5435)*

Weberdings Carving Shop Inc .... F 812 934-3710
  Batesville *(G-610)*

PAVERS

Paver Rescue Inc .... G 317 259-4880
  Indianapolis *(G-9103)*

Turner Paving Company .... G 765 962-4408
  Richmond *(G-14221)*

PRODUCT SECTION

PHARMACEUTICALS

PAVING MIXTURES

Meshberger Brothers Stone C............... D 260 334-5311
Bluffton (G-1041)

Schrock Aggregate Company Inc........... G 574 862-4167
Wakarusa (G-16250)

Schrock Excavating Inc........................... E 574 862-4167
Wakarusa (G-16251)

Wallace Construction Inc........................ F 317 422-5356
Martinsville (G-11434)

PENCILS & PENS WHOLESALERS

Harcourt Industries Inc........................... E 765 629-2625
Milroy (G-11824)

PERFUME: Perfumes, Natural Or Synthetic

Annie Oakley Enterprises Inc.................. F 260 894-7100
Ligonier (G-11004)

PERFUMES

Legacy Enterprises Inc........................... G 219 484-9483
Merrillville (G-11531)

Oil Palace Limited................................... G 317 679-9187
Indianapolis (G-9043)

PERSONAL CREDIT INSTITUTIONS: Consumer Finance Companies

Heritage Financial Group Inc.................. E 574 522-8000
Elkhart (G-3404)

PERSONAL SVCS

Hot Shot Multimedia Entps LLC.............. G 317 537-7527
South Bend (G-15072)

PEST CONTROL IN STRUCTURES SVCS

Corteva Inc... G 765 586-4077
Indianapolis (G-7882)

Corteva Inc... A 833 267-8382
Indianapolis (G-7883)

PET FOOD WHOLESALERS

Bhj Usa LLC... G 574 722-3933
Logansport (G-11062)

Blue Buffalo Company Ltd..................... B 203 665-3500
Richmond (G-14099)

Hoosier Processing LLC......................... F 260 422-9440
Fort Wayne (G-5080)

PET SPLYS

All Pet Supplies Inc................................ G 219 885-9670
Gary (G-5888)

Always Full LLC..................................... G 317 727-9639
Carmel (G-1559)

Becks Bird Feeders................................ G 765 874-1496
Markleville (G-11367)

Midwest Dachshund Rescue Inc............ G 815 260-6734
Highland (G-7145)

Planet Pets... G 812 539-7316
Lawrenceburg (G-10853)

Sittin Pretty LLC..................................... G 219 947-4121
Crown Point (G-2757)

Tri-State Veterinary Sup Inc................... G 812 477-4793
Evansville (G-4352)

PETROLEUM & PETROLEUM PRDTS, WHOLESALE: Bulk Stations

AMP Americas LLC................................ G 312 300-6700
Fair Oaks (G-4394)

Hoosier Penn Oil Co Inc......................... G 812 284-9433
Jeffersonville (G-9998)

PETROLEUM BULK STATIONS & TERMINALS

Keystone Cooperative Inc...................... G 765 249-2233
Michigantown (G-11691)

Keystone Cooperative Inc...................... C 800 525-0272
Indianapolis (G-8680)

PHARMACEUTICAL PREPARATIONS: Druggists' Preparations

Bruce A Hodson..................................... G 765 212-7757
Attica (G-344)

Vesta Ingredients Inc............................. G 317 895-9000
Indianapolis (G-9712)

PHARMACEUTICAL PREPARATIONS: Pills

American Family Pharmacy LLC............ G 317 334-1933
Indianapolis (G-7503)

PHARMACEUTICAL PREPARATIONS: Proprietary Drug

Naturegenic Inc..................................... G 765 807-5525
West Lafayette (G-16612)

Tri-Pac Inc... C 574 855-2197
South Bend (G-15290)

Tri-Pac Inc... C 574 855-2197
South Bend (G-15291)

PHARMACEUTICAL PREPARATIONS: Solutions

Ips-Integrated Prj Svcs LLC................... G 317 247-1200
Indianapolis (G-8588)

Lodos Theranostics LLC........................ G 765 427-2492
West Lafayette (G-16602)

PHARMACEUTICAL PREPARATIONS: Tablets

Biokorf LLC.. G 765 727-0782
West Lafayette (G-16565)

Kremers Urban Phrmcuticals Inc........... D
Seymour (G-14663)

PHARMACEUTICALS

Abbott Inc... D 765 647-2523
Brookville (G-1315)

Accra-Pac Inc.. D 574 295-0000
Elkhart (G-3151)

Accra-Pac Inc.. D 574 295-0000
Elkhart (G-3150)

Acura Pharmaceutical Tech................... G 574 842-3305
Culver (G-2778)

Akina Inc... F 765 464-0501
West Lafayette (G-16559)

Allergan Sales LLC................................ F 888 786-6471
Charlestown (G-1871)

Amatsigroup Inc..................................... G 617 576-2005
Terre Haute (G-15541)

Applied Laboratories Inc........................ E 812 372-2607
Columbus (G-2221)

Aquestive Therapeutics Inc................... E 219 762-4143
Portage (G-13844)

Aquestive Therapeutics Inc................... E 219 762-3165
Portage (G-13845)

Aratana Therapeutics Inc...................... D 913 353-1000
Greenfield (G-6466)

Ardena Company................................... G 219 926-1018
Chesterton (G-1903)

Areva Pharmaceuticals Inc.................... F 855 853-4760
Georgetown (G-6055)

Astellas Pharma Us Inc......................... G 574 595-7569
Star City (G-15395)

Astrazeneca Pharmaceuticals LP........... G 240 252-0125
Mount Vernon (G-12287)

Astrazeneca Pharmaceuticals LP........... E 812 429-5000
Mount Vernon (G-12288)

Bamboo US Bidco LLC.......................... G 812 355-5289
Bloomington (G-793)

Baxter Intl.. G 812 355-4283
Bloomington (G-797)

Baxter Phrm Solutions LLC................... C 812 333-0887
Bloomington (G-798)

Bayer Healthcare LLC........................... E 574 262-6136
Elkhart (G-3218)

Bayer Healthcare LLC........................... E 574 252-4735
Mishawaka (G-11846)

Bayer Healthcare LLC........................... E 574 252-4734
Mishawaka (G-11847)

Biota Biosciences Inc........................... G 765 702-3744
Cambridge City (G-1491)

Bristol Myers... F 812 428-1927
Evansville (G-3955)

Bristol-Myers Squibb Company.............. F 812 429-5505
Evansville (G-3956)

Bristol-Myers Squibb Company.............. G 260 432-2764
Fort Wayne (G-4818)

Bristol-Myers Squibb Company.............. C 812 307-2000
Mount Vernon (G-12293)

Brogan Pharmaceuticals LLC................ F 219 644-3693
Crown Point (G-2662)

Bulent Gumusel..................................... G 812 803-5912
Bloomington (G-818)

Cardinal Health 414 LLC....................... F 317 981-4100
Indianapolis (G-7740)

Catalent Indiana LLC............................ G 812 355-6746
Bloomington (G-823)

Catalent Indiana LLC............................ B 812 355-6746
Bloomington (G-824)

Catalent Pharma Solutions Inc.............. D 812 355-4498
Bloomington (G-825)

Catalent Wellness Holdings LLC........... D 800 344-6225
Greendale (G-6442)

Colorcon Inc.. G 317 545-6211
Indianapolis (G-7836)

Colorcon Inc.. D 317 545-6211
Indianapolis (G-7837)

Confluence Pharmaceuticals LLC.......... G 317 379-7498
Arcadia (G-311)

Corange International............................ G
Indianapolis (G-7874)

Crossroads Biologicals LLC.................. G 765 239-9113
Lafayette (G-10562)

Crosswind Pharmacy............................. G 812 381-4815
Indianapolis (G-7912)

Curia Indiana LLC................................. D 765 463-0112
West Lafayette (G-16574)

Dickey Consumer Products Inc............. F 317 773-8330
Noblesville (G-13071)

DSM Enterprises LLC............................ G 317 698-3317
Lebanon (G-10892)

Eidp Inc... A 833 267-8382
Indianapolis (G-8064)

Elan Corp PLC....................................... G 317 442-1502
Fishers (G-4509)

Elanco US Inc....................................... G 765 832-4400
Clinton (G-2066)

Elanco US Inc....................................... C 877 352-6261
Greenfield (G-6495)

Eli Lilly and Company........................... G 317 748-1622
Fishers (G-4511)

Eli Lilly and Company........................... G 317 276-2000
Indianapolis (G-8072)

Eli Lilly and Company........................... G 317 276-7907
Indianapolis (G-8073)

PHARMACEUTICALS

Eli Lilly and Company .... G 317 276-2118
  Indianapolis *(G-8074)*

Eli Lilly and Company .... G 317 276-2000
  Indianapolis *(G-8075)*

Eli Lilly and Company .... G 317 276-2000
  Indianapolis *(G-8076)*

Eli Lilly and Company .... G 317 276-5925
  Indianapolis *(G-8077)*

Eli Lilly and Company .... F 317 276-2000
  Indianapolis *(G-8078)*

Eli Lilly and Company .... F 317 651-7790
  Indianapolis *(G-8079)*

Eli Lilly and Company .... F 317 277-0147
  Indianapolis *(G-8080)*

Eli Lilly and Company .... F 317 276-2000
  Indianapolis *(G-8081)*

Eli Lilly and Company .... F 317 276-2000
  Indianapolis *(G-8082)*

Eli Lilly and Company .... F 317 276-2000
  Indianapolis *(G-8083)*

Eli Lilly and Company .... F 317 276-7907
  Indianapolis *(G-8084)*

Eli Lilly and Company .... E 317 276-2000
  Indianapolis *(G-8085)*

Eli Lilly and Company .... D 317 277-1307
  Indianapolis *(G-8086)*

Eli Lilly and Company .... C 317 276-2000
  Indianapolis *(G-8087)*

Eli Lilly and Company .... C 317 276-2000
  Indianapolis *(G-8089)*

Eli Lilly and Company .... E 317 433-3624
  Plainfield *(G-13678)*

Eli Lilly and Company .... G 812 242-5900
  Terre Haute *(G-15585)*

Eli Lilly and Company .... A 317 276-2000
  Indianapolis *(G-8088)*

Eli Lilly Interamerica Inc .... F 317 276-2000
  Indianapolis *(G-8090)*

Eli Lilly International Corp .... F 317 276-2000
  Indianapolis *(G-8091)*

Energy Delivery Solutions LLC .... G 502 271-8753
  Jeffersonville *(G-9977)*

Evecxia Therapeutics Inc .... G 919 597-8762
  Westfield *(G-16689)*

Exelead Inc .... D 317 612-2900
  Indianapolis *(G-8154)*

Exelead Inc .... E 317 347-2800
  Indianapolis *(G-8153)*

F Hoffmann-La Roche Ltd .... F 317 370-8578
  Indianapolis *(G-8160)*

F Hoffmann-La Roche Ltd .... G 317 370-8578
  Indianapolis *(G-8159)*

Fenwick Pharma LLC .... G 765 412-1889
  West Lafayette *(G-16580)*

Fisher Clinical Services Inc .... E 317 277-0337
  Indianapolis *(G-8197)*

Genoa Healthcare LLC .... G 219 427-1837
  Gary *(G-5940)*

Giles Manufacturing Company .... G 812 537-4852
  Greendale *(G-6446)*

Horizon Biotechnologies LLC .... G 317 534-2540
  Greenwood *(G-6712)*

Incog Biopharma Services Inc .... F 812 320-4236
  Fishers *(G-4543)*

Indiana Univ Schl Medicine .... F 317 278-6518
  Indianapolis *(G-8498)*

Ingenus LLC .... F 317 430-1855
  Indianapolis *(G-8543)*

Inspire LLC .... G 317 339-7718
  Indianapolis *(G-8562)*

International Infusion LP .... G 708 710-9200
  Munster *(G-12544)*

Jbs United Inc .... G 765 296-4539
  Frankfort *(G-5676)*

Jnj Blue Enterprise LLC .... G 502 593-8464
  New Albany *(G-12754)*

Komodo Pharmaceuticals Inc .... F 317 485-0023
  Fortville *(G-5602)*

Kp Pharmaceutical Tech Inc .... E 812 330-8121
  Bloomington *(G-903)*

Lexington Pharmaceuticals .... G 317 870-0370
  Indianapolis *(G-8743)*

Lexington Phrmcticals Labs LLC .... G 317 566-9750
  Carmel *(G-1683)*

Lgenia Inc .... F 317 861-8850
  Fortville *(G-5603)*

Lilly Research Laboratories .... G 317 276-0127
  Indianapolis *(G-8754)*

Lilly Usa LLC .... C 317 276-2000
  Indianapolis *(G-8755)*

Lilly Ventures .... G 317 651-3050
  Indianapolis *(G-8756)*

Martin Ekwlor Phrmcuticals Inc .... F 765 962-4410
  Richmond *(G-14159)*

MBX Biosciences Inc .... E 317 659-0200
  Carmel *(G-1695)*

Mead Johnson & Company LLC .... G 812 429-5000
  Mount Vernon *(G-12308)*

Mead Johnson & Company LLC .... C 812 429-5000
  Evansville *(G-4193)*

Med-Pharm Pharmacy .... G 812 232-2086
  Terre Haute *(G-15640)*

Merck Sharp & Dohme LLC .... G 908 740-4000
  Plainfield *(G-13704)*

Millipore Sigma .... F 317 453-5490
  Indianapolis *(G-8925)*

Msd Group LLC .... G 260 444-4658
  Fort Wayne *(G-5249)*

Mvk Pharmaceuticals LLC .... G 317 374-2178
  Indianapolis *(G-8973)*

Northwind Pharmaceuticals LLC .... G 317 436-8522
  Indianapolis *(G-9025)*

Northwind Pharmaceuticals LLC .... G 800 722-0772
  Indianapolis *(G-9026)*

Novartis Corporation .... G 317 852-3839
  Brownsburg *(G-1392)*

Novo Nrdisk RES Ctr Indnplis I .... G 541 520-8030
  Indianapolis *(G-9029)*

Npm Holdings Inc .... G 812 689-3309
  Osgood *(G-13414)*

Nukemed Inc .... G 765 437-1631
  Bunker Hill *(G-1442)*

Nukemed Inc .... E 574 271-2800
  South Bend *(G-15175)*

Nutritional Research Assoc .... F 260 723-4931
  South Whitley *(G-15322)*

Optum Pharmacy 702 LLC .... D 812 256-8600
  Jeffersonville *(G-10031)*

Orano Med LLC .... G 469 638-0632
  Brownsburg *(G-1393)*

Osram Inc .... G 317 847-6268
  Westfield *(G-16716)*

Parsolex Gmp Center Inc .... F 765 464-8414
  West Lafayette *(G-16617)*

Pd Sub LLC .... E 812 524-0534
  Seymour *(G-14673)*

Peli Biothermal LLC .... G 763 412-4800
  Plainfield *(G-13712)*

Pfizer Inc .... G 574 232-9927
  South Bend *(G-15194)*

Pfizer Inc .... D 212 733-2323
  Terre Haute *(G-15660)*

Pharma Form Finders LLC .... G 317 362-1191
  Fishers *(G-4574)*

PRODUCT SECTION

Phytoption LLC .... G 765 490-7738
  West Lafayette *(G-16620)*

Point Biopharma Global Inc .... F 317 543-9957
  Indianapolis *(G-9158)*

Point Biopharma Inc .... E 833 544-2637
  Indianapolis *(G-9159)*

Point Biopharma USA Inc .... G 317 543-9957
  Indianapolis *(G-9160)*

R J Smithey LLC .... G 317 435-8473
  Greenwood *(G-6757)*

R2 Pharma LLC .... G 317 810-6205
  Carmel *(G-1733)*

Relevo Inc .... G 317 644-0099
  Carmel *(G-1738)*

Robert J Stankovich .... G 317 844-0886
  Carmel *(G-1744)*

Roche Diabetes Care Inc .... D 317 521-2000
  Indianapolis *(G-9316)*

Roche Diagnostics Corp .... E 317 521-2000
  Indianapolis *(G-9317)*

Roche Diagnostics Corporation .... C 317 521-2000
  Indianapolis *(G-9318)*

Roche Operations Ltd .... D 787 285-0170
  Indianapolis *(G-9320)*

Rph On Call LLC .... G 317 622-4800
  Greenfield *(G-6546)*

Safetynet LLC .... G 502 609-3339
  New Albany *(G-12811)*

Sanofi US Services Inc .... D 317 228-5750
  Indianapolis *(G-9370)*

Schwarz Pharma .... F 812 523-3457
  Seymour *(G-14686)*

Sepracor Inc .... G 317 513-6257
  Fishers *(G-4651)*

Somersaults LLC .... G 317 747-7496
  Fishers *(G-4652)*

Spirrow Therapeutics LLC .... G 317 750-8879
  West Lafayette *(G-16631)*

Sysgenomics LLC .... G 574 302-5396
  Granger *(G-6384)*

Takeda .... F 812 972-0957
  Corydon *(G-2517)*

Takeda Pharmaceuticals USA Inc .... G 812 738-0452
  Corydon *(G-2518)*

Telix Pharmaceuticals US Inc .... D 317 588-9700
  Fishers *(G-4611)*

Treat America Roche Diagnostic .... G 317 521-1490
  Fishers *(G-4616)*

United-Ah II LLC .... F 317 758-4495
  Sheridan *(G-14831)*

Verista Inc .... A 317 849-0330
  Fishers *(G-4628)*

Vesta Pharmaceuticals Inc .... E 317 895-9000
  Indianapolis *(G-9713)*

Vitamins Inc .... E 219 879-7356
  Michigan City *(G-11686)*

Yinroot LLC .... G 317 379-9529
  Noblesville *(G-13198)*

Zoetis .... G 574 232-9927
  South Bend *(G-15313)*

PHOTOCOPYING & DUPLICATING SVCS

Art Bookbinders of America .... F 312 226-4100
  Hammond *(G-6880)*

Blue River Printing Inc .... G 317 392-3676
  Shelbyville *(G-14736)*

Commercial Print Shop Inc .... G 260 724-3722
  Decatur *(G-2850)*

Copy-Print Shop Inc .... E 765 447-6868
  Lafayette *(G-10556)*

Copymat Services Inc .... G 765 743-5995
  Lafayette *(G-10557)*

PRODUCT SECTION   PIPE: Plastic

Creative Concept Ventures Inc........................ G..... 812 282-9442
 Jeffersonville (G-9964)
David Camp.. G..... 812 346-6255
 North Vernon (G-13265)
Dynamark Graphics Group Inc........................ E..... 317 328-2555
 Indianapolis (G-8023)
Ed Sons Inc... F..... 317 897-8821
 Indianapolis (G-8051)
Express Press Inc.. G..... 812 882-3278
 Vincennes (G-16122)
Fedex Office & Print Svcs Inc......................... G..... 317 974-0378
 Indianapolis (G-8172)
Fedex Office & Print Svcs Inc......................... G..... 317 917-1529
 Indianapolis (G-8173)
Fedex Office & Print Svcs Inc......................... G..... 317 849-9683
 Indianapolis (G-8174)
Fedex Office & Print Svcs Inc......................... G..... 317 885-6480
 Indianapolis (G-8175)
Fedex Office & Print Svcs Inc......................... G..... 317 295-1063
 Indianapolis (G-8176)
Fedex Office & Print Svcs Inc......................... G..... 317 337-2679
 Indianapolis (G-8177)
Fedex Office & Print Svcs Inc......................... G..... 317 631-6862
 Indianapolis (G-8178)
Fedex Office & Print Svcs Inc......................... G..... 317 251-2406
 Indianapolis (G-8179)
Fedex Office & Print Svcs Inc......................... F..... 765 449-4950
 Lafayette (G-10579)
Hiatt Enterprises Inc....................................... G..... 765 289-2700
 Muncie (G-12416)
Hiatt Enterprises Inc....................................... F..... 765 289-7756
 Muncie (G-12415)
MPS Printing Incorporated............................. G..... 812 273-4446
 Madison (G-11245)
Mr Copy Inc.. G..... 812 334-2679
 Bloomington (G-925)
Novaprints LLC.. F..... 317 577-6682
 Indianapolis (G-9028)
Ovation Communications Inc.......................... G..... 812 401-9100
 Evansville (G-4230)
Paper Chase.. G..... 812 385-4757
 Princeton (G-14009)
Perfect Impressions Printing.......................... G..... 317 923-1756
 Indianapolis (G-9121)
Printing Partners East Inc.............................. G..... 317 356-2522
 Indianapolis (G-9207)
Priority Press Inc... G..... 317 240-0103
 Indianapolis (G-9212)
Randall Corp.. G..... 812 425-7122
 Evansville (G-4272)
Rebecca L Hamann & Associates.................... G..... 219 763-1233
 Portage (G-13910)
Rhr Corporation.. G..... 317 788-1504
 Indianapolis (G-9298)
Rrc Corporation.. F..... 317 687-8325
 Indianapolis (G-9343)
Sharp Printing Services Inc............................ G..... 317 842-5159
 Fishers (G-4604)
Tdk Graphics Inc... G..... 219 663-7799
 Crown Point (G-2762)

PHOTOGRAPHIC & OPTICAL GOODS EQPT REPAIR SVCS

Blasted Works.. G..... 574 583-3211
 Monticello (G-12138)

PHOTOGRAPHIC EQPT & SPLYS

BOM Corporation.. E..... 765 361-0382
 Crawfordsville (G-2549)
Insight Lpr LLC... F..... 855 862-5468
 Carmel (G-1671)

Ionpcs LLC.. G..... 219 510-2073
 Portage (G-13878)
Jackson Technologies LLC............................. G..... 812 258-9939
 New Albany (G-12751)
Techryan Inc... G..... 317 721-4835
 Plainfield (G-13734)

PHOTOGRAPHIC EQPT & SPLYS WHOLESALERS

Insight Lpr LLC... F..... 855 862-5468
 Carmel (G-1671)

PHOTOGRAPHIC EQPT & SPLYS: Printing Eqpt

Business Systems Mgt Corp........................... G..... 219 938-0166
 Gary (G-5908)
Image Inks Company...................................... G..... 317 432-5041
 Indianapolis (G-8462)

PHOTOGRAPHY SVCS: Commercial

Scher Maihem Publishing Ltd......................... G..... 260 897-2697
 Avilla (G-494)

PHYSICAL EXAMINATION & TESTING SVCS

Workflow Solutions LLC.................................. G..... 502 627-0257
 New Albany (G-12831)

PHYSICIANS' OFFICES & CLINICS: Medical doctors

Advanced Orthopro Inc.................................. E..... 317 924-4444
 Indianapolis (G-7439)
Groupone Health Source Inc......................... D..... 800 769-5288
 Indianapolis (G-8334)

PICTURE FRAMES: Metal

Mishawaka Art & Frame Gallery..................... G..... 574 259-9320
 Mishawaka (G-11953)

PICTURE FRAMES: Wood

Grace Henderson.. G..... 765 661-9063
 Marion (G-11289)
H J J Inc... G..... 219 362-4421
 La Porte (G-10414)
Herff Jones LLC... C..... 317 297-3741
 Indianapolis (G-8383)
Stitch N Frame.. G..... 260 478-1301
 Fort Wayne (G-5443)

PICTURE FRAMING SVCS, CUSTOM

Randall Corp.. G..... 812 425-7122
 Evansville (G-4272)

PIECE GOODS & NOTIONS WHOLESALERS

Custom Sewing Service.................................. G..... 812 428-7015
 Evansville (G-4004)
J Ennis Fabrics Inc (usa)................................ G..... 877 953-6647
 Plainfield (G-13695)
Samaron Corp.. E..... 574 970-7070
 Elkhart (G-3661)

PIECE GOODS, NOTIONS & DRY GOODS, WHOL: Textiles, Woven

Georg Utz Inc.. E..... 812 526-2240
 Edinburgh (G-3085)

PIECE GOODS, NOTIONS & OTHER DRY GOODS, WHOLESALE: Fabrics

Tiedemann-Bevs Industries LLC..................... E..... 765 962-4914
 Richmond (G-14219)

PILOT SVCS: Aviation

Indigo Industries LLC..................................... G..... 480 747-4560
 Greenwood (G-6715)

PINS

Blush and Bobby Pins LLC.............................. G..... 317 789-5166
 Carmel (G-1568)
Hadady Corporation.. E..... 219 322-7417
 Dyer (G-2976)
Herff Jones Co Indiana - Inc......................... E..... 317 297-3740
 Indianapolis (G-8385)
Mr Pin Shi Peter Lee....................................... G..... 574 264-9754
 Elkhart (G-3558)
Philip Pins.. G..... 219 769-1059
 Merrillville (G-11550)
Pin Oak Group LLC.. G..... 260 637-7778
 Fort Wayne (G-5315)
Pin Point Av LLC... G..... 317 750-3120
 Indianapolis (G-9142)
Pin-Up Curls LLC... G..... 260 241-5871
 Fort Wayne (G-5316)

PIPE & TUBES: Copper & Copper Alloy

Essex Frkawa Mgnt Wire USA LLC................. E..... 260 461-4000
 Fort Wayne (G-4962)

PIPE & TUBES: Seamless

37 Pipe & Supply LLC.................................... G..... 812 275-5676
 Bedford (G-615)
Moyers Inc... F..... 574 264-3119
 Elkhart (G-3557)

PIPE CLEANERS

Forterra Concrete Inds Inc............................. E..... 812 426-5353
 Evansville (G-4080)

PIPE FITTINGS: Plastic

Fairview Fittings & Mfg.................................. G..... 574 206-8884
 Elkhart (G-3341)
Filtration Parts Incorporated......................... F..... 704 661-8135
 Rensselaer (G-14052)
Green Leaf Inc.. C..... 812 877-1546
 Fontanet (G-4699)
Nibco Inc... F..... 812 256-8500
 Charlestown (G-1888)
Nibco Inc... C..... 574 296-1240
 Goshen (G-6227)
Rieke LLC.. B..... 260 925-3700
 Auburn (G-419)
Viking Group Inc... B..... 812 256-8500
 Charlestown (G-1895)

PIPE, SEWER: Concrete

Terrys Sewer Service...................................... G..... 219 756-5238
 Merrillville (G-11566)

PIPE: Concrete

Ace Extrusion LLC... E..... 812 436-4840
 Evansville (G-3870)
County Materials Corp.................................... E..... 317 323-6000
 Maxwell (G-11443)
ICP Liquidating Company............................... D..... 419 841-3361
 Indianapolis (G-8451)
Independent Concrete Pipe Company........... E..... 317 262-4920
 Indianapolis (G-8471)

PIPE: Copper

F J Rettig & Sons Inc..................................... G..... 260 563-6603
 Wabash (G-16184)

PIPE: Plastic

Ace Extrusion LLC	E	812 463-5230	
Evansville *(G-3871)*			
Advanced Drainage Systems Inc	G	812 443-2080	
Brazil *(G-1131)*			
Advanced Drainage Systems Inc	G	317 917-7960	
Indianapolis *(G-7438)*			
Blair Industries LLC	G	765 215-2735	
Muncie *(G-12354)*			
Corrosion Technologies Inc	G	317 894-0627	
Greenfield *(G-6484)*			
Cresline Plastic Pipe Co Inc	E	812 428-9300	
Evansville *(G-3994)*			
Cresline-Northwest LLC	F	812 428-9300	
Evansville *(G-3995)*			
Cresline-West Inc	G	812 428-9300	
Evansville *(G-3996)*			
Diamond Plastics Corporation	D	765 287-9234	
Muncie *(G-12382)*			
Fratco Inc	D	800 854-7120	
Monticello *(G-12150)*			
Hancor Inc	E	812 443-2080	
Brazil *(G-1144)*			
Kuri TEC Manufacturing Inc	E	765 764-6000	
Williamsport *(G-16850)*			
Liner Products LLC	F	812 723-0244	
Paoli *(G-13499)*			
Plastic Pipe Technologies LLC	G	317 674-5944	
New Palestine *(G-12942)*			
Uniseal Inc	E	812 425-1361	
Evansville *(G-4360)*			
Viking Group Inc	B	812 256-8500	
Charlestown *(G-1895)*			

PIPE: Sheet Metal

- 37 Pipe & Supply LLC .... G 812 275-5676
  Bedford *(G-615)*
- J T D Spiral Inc .... G 260 497-1300
  Fort Wayne *(G-5125)*
- Kalenborn Abresist Corporation ... E 800 348-0717
  Urbana *(G-15886)*

PIPE: Water, Cast Iron

- 37 Pipe & Supply LLC .... G 812 275-5676
  Bedford *(G-615)*

PIPELINES: Natural Gas

- ANR Pipeline Company .... G 260 463-3342
  Lagrange *(G-10728)*

PIPES & TUBES

- Interntional Pipe Cons Sls LLC ... F 765 388-2222
  New Castle *(G-12870)*
- Kanoff Enterprises .... G 574 575-6787
  Mishawaka *(G-11921)*
- Norres North America Inc .... E 855 667-7370
  South Bend *(G-15169)*

PIPES & TUBES: Steel

- Cal Pipe Manufacturing Inc .... G 219 844-6800
  Hobart *(G-7175)*
- Century Tube LLC .... C 812 265-9255
  Madison *(G-11206)*
- Clevelnd-Clffs Tblar Cmpnnts L ... C 812 341-3200
  Columbus *(G-2237)*
- Down Range Industries LLC ... G 219 895-0834
  Cedar Lake *(G-1830)*
- Hd Mechanical Inc .... F 219 924-6050
  Griffith *(G-6806)*
- Illinois Ni Cast LLC .... F 260 897-3768
  Avilla *(G-478)*
- Indiana Tube Corporation .... B 812 467-7155
  Evansville *(G-4121)*
- Ist Liquidating Inc .... E 812 358-3894
  Brownstown *(G-1424)*
- Kalenborn Abresist Corporation ... E 800 348-0717
  Urbana *(G-15886)*
- Martinrea Industries Inc .... C 812 346-5750
  North Vernon *(G-13285)*
- Napier & Napier .... G 765 580-9116
  Liberty *(G-10992)*
- Nelson Global Products Inc .... C 317 782-9486
  Indianapolis *(G-8999)*
- Nucor Tubular Products .... E 812 265-7548
  Madison *(G-11246)*
- Paragon Tube Corporation ..... E 260 424-1266
  Fort Wayne *(G-5295)*
- Plymouth Tube Company .... D 574 946-6191
  Winamac *(G-16871)*
- Ptc Alliance Corporation .... F 765 259-3334
  Richmond *(G-14189)*
- Ptc Tubular Products LLC .... D 765 259-3334
  Richmond *(G-14190)*
- Rookstools Pier Shop Inc .... E 574 453-4771
  Leesburg *(G-10960)*
- Tejas Tubular Products Inc .... C 574 249-0623
  New Carlisle *(G-12847)*
- Thormax Enterprises LLC .... G 812 530-7744
  Seymour *(G-14699)*
- Tube Processing Corp .... C 317 782-9486
  Indianapolis *(G-9656)*
- Utility Pipe Sales Indiana Inc ... G 317 224-2300
  Indianapolis *(G-9691)*

PIPES & TUBES: Welded

- Allied Tube & Conduit Corp .... F 812 265-9255
  Madison *(G-11201)*
- Applegate Livestock Eqp Inc ... D 765 964-3715
  Union City *(G-15848)*
- Lock Joint Tube LLC .... C 574 299-5326
  South Bend *(G-15127)*
- Steuben County Welding & Fabg ... G 260 665-3001
  Angola *(G-295)*

PIPES: Steel & Iron

- Protherm Supply Inc .... G 812 492-3386
  Evansville *(G-4262)*

PISTONS & PISTON RINGS

- Federal-Mogul Powertrain LLC ... B 574 271-5954
  South Bend *(G-15031)*
- Precision Rings Incorporated ... E 317 247-4786
  Indianapolis *(G-9185)*

PLAQUES: Picture, Laminated

- Awards America Inc .... F 219 462-7903
  Valparaiso *(G-15906)*
- Lamco Finishers Inc .... E 317 471-1010
  Indianapolis *(G-8717)*
- Lloyds of Indiana Inc .... G 317 251-5430
  Indianapolis *(G-8774)*
- Plaquemaker Plus Inc .... G 317 594-5556
  Fishers *(G-4576)*

PLASMAS

- Gcam Inc .... G 714 738-6462
  Indianapolis *(G-8265)*

PLASTICIZERS, ORGANIC: Cyclic & Acyclic

- ACS Technical Products Inc .... E 219 924-4370
  Griffith *(G-6786)*

PLASTICS FILM & SHEET

- American Renolit Corporation ... C 219 324-6886
  La Porte *(G-10384)*
- Berry Global Group Inc .... A 812 424-2904
  Evansville *(G-3921)*
- Foil Laminating Inc .... E
  Plymouth *(G-13777)*
- Futurex Industries Inc .... E 765 597-2221
  Marshall *(G-11373)*
- Futurex Industries Inc .... E 812 299-5708
  Terre Haute *(G-15593)*
- Futurex Industries Inc .... C 765 498-3900
  Bloomingdale *(G-760)*
- Primex Plastics Corporation ... B 765 966-7774
  Richmond *(G-14186)*
- Printpack Inc .... C 812 663-5091
  Greensburg *(G-6625)*
- Tredegar Corporation .... G 574 262-4685
  Elkhart *(G-3745)*

PLASTICS FILM & SHEET: Polyethylene

- Amcor Flexibles North Amer Inc ... B 812 466-2213
  Terre Haute *(G-15542)*
- Tessellated Inc .... G 304 277-8896
  South Bend *(G-15281)*
- Tredegar Corporation .... D 812 466-0266
  Terre Haute *(G-15734)*

PLASTICS FILM & SHEET: Polypropylene

- Mirwec Film Incorporated ..... F 812 331-7194
  Bloomington *(G-920)*
- Taghleef Industries Inc .... A 302 326-5500
  Rosedale *(G-14385)*

PLASTICS FILM & SHEET: Polyvinyl

- Transcendia Inc .... C 765 935-1520
  Richmond *(G-14220)*

PLASTICS FILM & SHEET: Vinyl

- American Renolit Corp La ...... G 856 241-4901
  La Porte *(G-10383)*

PLASTICS FINISHED PRDTS: Laminated

- American Art Clay Co Inc .... C 317 244-6871
  Indianapolis *(G-7499)*
- Brownsburg Custom Cabinets Inc ... G 317 271-1887
  Indianapolis *(G-7690)*
- Parkland Plastics Inc .... E 574 825-4336
  Middlebury *(G-11745)*
- Patrick Industries Inc .... E 574 825-4336
  Middlebury *(G-11746)*
- Plasticraft-Complete Acrylics ... G 765 610-9502
  Anderson *(G-180)*
- Sims Cabinet Co Inc .... E 317 634-1747
  Danville *(G-2828)*

PLASTICS MATERIAL & RESINS

- Addivant USA LLC .... G 765 497-6020
  West Lafayette *(G-16556)*
- Advance Prtective Coatings Inc ... G 317 228-0123
  Indianapolis *(G-7435)*
- Aearo Technologies LLC .... C 317 692-6666
  Indianapolis *(G-7447)*
- Akzo Nobel Coatings Inc .... E 574 372-2000
  Warsaw *(G-16310)*
- Ameri-Kart Corp .... D 225 642-7874
  Bristol *(G-1243)*
- Ameri-Kart Corp .... C 574 848-7462
  Bristol *(G-1244)*
- Ampacet Corporation .... D 812 466-5231
  Terre Haute *(G-15544)*

PRODUCT SECTION

PLASTICS PROCESSING

Aoc LLC .... D 219 465-4384
Valparaiso *(G-15900)*

Apr Plastics Inc .... F 812 258-8888
Evansville *(G-3895)*

Atc Plastics LLC .... G 317 469-7552
Indianapolis *(G-7558)*

Avient Corporation .... E 574 267-1100
Warsaw *(G-16315)*

B&F Plastics Inc .... D 765 962-6125
Richmond *(G-14089)*

Bdc Enterprise LLC .... G 317 395-6740
Shelbyville *(G-14735)*

Better Way Products .... G 574 546-2868
Bremen *(G-1175)*

Blehm Plastics .... G 317 736-4090
Franklin *(G-5717)*

Bpc Manufacturing Operation .... G 574 936-9894
Plymouth *(G-13761)*

C4 Polymers Inc .... G 440 543-3866
Muncie *(G-12359)*

Cabinets & Counters Inc .... E 812 858-3300
Newburgh *(G-12995)*

Cereplast Inc .... F 310 615-1900
Seymour *(G-14637)*

Chase Plastic Services Inc .... G 574 239-4090
South Bend *(G-14971)*

Complete Packaging Group Inc .... G 765 547-1300
Brookville *(G-1318)*

Covestro LLC .... G 765 659-4721
Frankfort *(G-5656)*

Createc Corporation .... B 317 566-0022
Indianapolis *(G-7899)*

Crossroads Sourcing Group Ltd .... G 847 940-4123
Carmel *(G-1600)*

Custom Fiber Composites LLC .... G 765 376-1360
Lebanon *(G-10889)*

Double H Plastics Inc .... F 765 664-9090
Marion *(G-11282)*

Dubois County Liners LLP .... G 812 634-1294
Jasper *(G-9835)*

Echo Engrg & Prod Sups Inc .... E 317 876-8848
Indianapolis *(G-8045)*

Efficient Plas Solutions Inc .... G 574 965-4690
Delphi *(G-2896)*

Envalior Engineering Mtls Inc .... G 812 435-7500
Evansville *(G-4040)*

Erj Composites LLC .... G 574 360-3517
Mishawaka *(G-11895)*

Evoqua Water Technologies LLC .... E 317 280-4251
Indianapolis *(G-8144)*

Fiber Technologies LLC .... G 812 569-4641
Bloomington *(G-866)*

Foamcraft Inc .... E 574 534-4343
Goshen *(G-6139)*

Freudenberg-Nok General Partnr .... C 734 354-5504
Shelbyville *(G-14757)*

G & T Industries Inc .... G 812 634-2252
Jasper *(G-9839)*

Glass City Inc .... G 219 887-2100
Gary *(G-5943)*

Graber Cabinetry LLC .... E 260 627-2243
Grabill *(G-6297)*

Green Tree Plastics LLC .... G 812 402-4127
Evansville *(G-4097)*

Henry Holsters LLC .... F 812 369-2266
Spencer *(G-15348)*

Hoehn Plastics Inc .... D 812 874-3646
Poseyville *(G-13977)*

Huntsman Intl Trdg Corp .... D 812 334-7090
Bloomington *(G-885)*

Indiana Polymers Inc .... G 219 762-9550
Valparaiso *(G-15972)*

Industrial Dlctrics Hldngs Inc .... G 317 773-1766
Noblesville *(G-13104)*

Industrial Plastics Group LLC .... E 812 831-4053
Evansville *(G-4123)*

Innovative Composites Ltd .... F 574 857-2224
Rochester *(G-14297)*

Integral Technologies Inc .... G 812 550-1770
Evansville *(G-4127)*

Ip Corporation .... F 574 259-1505
Mishawaka *(G-11913)*

Ip Corporation .... E 574 234-1105
South Bend *(G-15087)*

Ip Moulding Inc .... D 574 825-5845
Middlebury *(G-11726)*

Jp Incorporated - Indiana .... B 574 457-2062
Syracuse *(G-15465)*

Kvk US Technologies Inc .... G 765 529-1100
New Castle *(G-12871)*

Line-X of Schererville Inc .... F 219 865-1000
Schererville *(G-14530)*

Lucent Polymers Inc .... D 812 421-2216
Evansville *(G-4177)*

Makuta Inc .... F 317 642-0001
Shelbyville *(G-14773)*

Martin Holding Company LLC .... E 812 401-9988
Evansville *(G-4190)*

Meyer Plastics Inc .... F 260 482-4595
Fort Wayne *(G-5219)*

Monosol LLC .... G 765 485-5400
Lebanon *(G-10918)*

Monosol LLC .... G 219 762-3165
Portage *(G-13890)*

Monosol LLC .... F 219 762-3165
Merrillville *(G-11546)*

Naturespire LLC .... G 463 266-0395
Indianapolis *(G-8992)*

Omni Plastics LLC .... D 812 422-0888
Evansville *(G-4227)*

Omni Technologies Inc .... F 812 539-4144
Greendale *(G-6451)*

OTech Corporation .... C 219 778-8001
Rolling Prairie *(G-14367)*

Pactiv LLC .... E 574 936-7065
Plymouth *(G-13800)*

Plastic Recycl Export Ltd LLC .... G 301 758-6885
Fort Wayne *(G-5318)*

Plastic Recycling Inc .... E 317 780-6100
Indianapolis *(G-9151)*

Polyfusion LLC .... G 260 624-7659
Angola *(G-284)*

Polymod Technologies Inc .... F 260 436-1322
Fort Wayne *(G-5325)*

Polytek Development Corp .... G 317 494-6420
Franklin *(G-5767)*

Precision Colors LLC .... F 260 969-6402
Fort Wayne *(G-5335)*

Primex Clor Cmpnding Addtves C .... E 800 222-5116
Richmond *(G-14184)*

Process Systems & Services .... G 812 427-2331
Florence *(G-4666)*

Rainmaker Polymers LLC .... G 574 268-0010
Winona Lake *(G-16915)*

Rbc Holding Inc .... F 317 340-3845
Greenwood *(G-6759)*

Rtp Enterprise Inc .... G 317 258-3213
Noblesville *(G-13169)*

Sabic Innovative Plas US LLC .... B 812 831-4054
Mount Vernon *(G-12319)*

Sabic Innvtive Plas Mt Vrnon L .... A 812 838-4385
Mount Vernon *(G-12320)*

Shaw Polymers Holdings LLC .... G 219 779-9450
Crown Point *(G-2750)*

Silcotec Inc .... F 219 324-4411
La Porte *(G-10482)*

Solid Surface Craftsmen Inc .... G 317 535-2333
Whiteland *(G-16797)*

Spartech LLC .... D 765 281-5100
Muncie *(G-12495)*

Sun Polymers .... G 219 426-1220
Fort Wayne *(G-5457)*

Toray Resin Company .... D 317 398-7833
Shelbyville *(G-14807)*

Triangle Rubber Co LLC .... E 574 533-3118
Elkhart *(G-3746)*

Triangle Rubber Co LLC .... G 574 533-3118
Goshen *(G-6271)*

Vahala Foam Inc .... D 574 293-1287
Elkhart *(G-3764)*

PLASTICS MATERIALS, BASIC FORMS & SHAPES WHOLESALERS

Arrowhead Plastic Engrg Inc .... F 765 396-9113
Eaton *(G-3059)*

Brunk LLC .... D 800 227-4156
Goshen *(G-6101)*

CRS-Drs Corporation .... G 260 478-7555
Fort Wayne *(G-4891)*

Meyer Plastics Inc .... D 317 259-4131
Indianapolis *(G-8895)*

Plastic Recycl Export Ltd LLC .... D 301 758-6885
Fort Wayne *(G-5318)*

Polymer Logistics Inc .... D 219 706-5985
Portage *(G-13904)*

Shaw Polymers Holdings LLC .... G 219 779-9450
Crown Point *(G-2750)*

PLASTICS PROCESSING

A S V Plastics Inc .... F 574 264-9694
Elkhart *(G-3141)*

Accelerated Curing Inc .... F 260 726-3202
Portland *(G-13926)*

Butler-Macdonald Inc .... D 317 872-5115
Indianapolis *(G-7704)*

Diamond Manufacturing Company .... D 219 874-2374
Michigan City *(G-11600)*

Earthwise Plastics Inc .... E 765 673-0308
Gas City *(G-6036)*

Eis Fibercoating Inc .... E 574 722-5192
Logansport *(G-11071)*

Elkcases Inc .... G 574 295-7700
Elkhart *(G-3317)*

Fibergrate Composite .... G 317 752-2500
Indianapolis *(G-8184)*

First Metals & Plastics Inc .... E 812 379-4400
Columbus *(G-2307)*

Independent Plastic Inc .... G 765 521-2251
New Castle *(G-12869)*

Inside Systems .... G 317 831-3772
Mooresville *(G-12215)*

Kendrion (mishawaka) LLC .... E 574 257-2422
Mishawaka *(G-11922)*

Lawson Design Inc .... G 812 967-2810
Henryville *(G-7113)*

Mar-Kan Marketing Inc .... G 317 228-9335
Indianapolis *(G-8826)*

Patrick Industries Inc .... G 574 294-8828
Elkhart *(G-3594)*

Penz Inc .... E 574 255-4736
Mishawaka *(G-11974)*

Production Partners Inc .... F 574 229-5960
Mishawaka *(G-11980)*

Reschcor Inc .... G 574 295-2413
Elkhart *(G-3647)*

Employee Codes: A=Over 500 employees, B=251-500
C=101-250, D=51-100, E=20-50, F=10-19, G=1-9

2024 Harris Indiana Industrial Directory

PLASTICS PROCESSING — PRODUCT SECTION

Splendor Boats LLC .... F 260 352-2835
 Silver Lake *(G-14923)*
Taghleef Industries Inc .... A 302 326-5500
 Rosedale *(G-14385)*
The Killion Corporation .... D 317 271-4536
 Indianapolis *(G-9589)*
Tredegar Corporation .... D 812 466-0266
 Terre Haute *(G-15734)*
Trellborg Sling Sltions US Inc .... E 260 749-9631
 Fort Wayne *(G-5503)*
Tru-Form Steel & Wire Inc .... F 765 348-5001
 Hartford City *(G-7079)*
Tru-Form Steel & Wire Inc .... E 765 348-5001
 Hartford City *(G-7078)*
Western Consolidated Tech Inc .... D 260 495-9866
 Fremont *(G-5842)*
ZF Active Safety & Elec US LLC .... D 765 429-1984
 Lafayette *(G-10721)*

PLASTICS: Blow Molded

Cluster Packaging LLC .... G 612 803-1056
 Crown Point *(G-2666)*
Fort Wayne Plastics Inc .... C 260 432-2520
 Fort Wayne *(G-5000)*
Kn Platech America Corporation .... D 317 392-7707
 Shelbyville *(G-14769)*

PLASTICS: Extruded

Cor-A-Vent Inc .... F 574 255-1910
 Mishawaka *(G-11866)*
Flexseals Mfg LLC .... G 574 293-0333
 Elkhart *(G-3351)*
JD Engineered Products LLC .... G 260 316-2907
 Hamilton *(G-6857)*
Kibbechem Inc .... E 574 266-1234
 Elkhart *(G-3454)*
Newell Industrial LLC .... E 260 636-3336
 Albion *(G-36)*
North American Extrusn & Assem .... G 260 636-3336
 Albion *(G-37)*
Plastic Extrusions Company .... G 812 479-3232
 Evansville *(G-4245)*
Reschcor Inc .... D 574 295-2413
 Bristol *(G-1285)*
Seals & Components Inc .... G 708 895-5222
 La Porte *(G-10478)*
Vytec Inc .... E 574 277-4295
 Granger *(G-6390)*

PLASTICS: Finished Injection Molded

Aircom Manufacturing Inc .... B 317 545-5383
 Indianapolis *(G-7462)*
Akka Plastics Inc .... E 812 849-9256
 Mitchell *(G-12030)*
Ar-Tee Enterprises Inc .... G 574 848-5543
 Bristol *(G-1246)*
Artek Inc .... E 260 484-4222
 Fort Wayne *(G-4773)*
Burco Molding Inc .... D 317 773-5699
 Noblesville *(G-13050)*
Cedar Plastics Inc .... F 765 483-3260
 Lebanon *(G-10882)*
Concept Assembly Solutions LLC .... F 574 855-2534
 Mishawaka *(G-11863)*
Custom Urethanes Inc .... G 219 924-1644
 Highland *(G-7131)*
Decatur Mold Tool and Engrg .... C 812 346-5188
 North Vernon *(G-13266)*
Exton Inc .... F 574 533-0447
 Goshen *(G-6132)*
Genesis Molding Inc .... D 574 256-9271
 Mishawaka *(G-11899)*

Hartland Products Inc .... F 219 778-9034
 Rolling Prairie *(G-14364)*
Infinity Molding & Assembly Inc .... D 812 838-0370
 Mount Vernon *(G-12300)*
Interactive Engineering Inc .... G 574 272-5851
 Granger *(G-6354)*
Jones Machine & Tool Inc .... G 812 364-4588
 Fredericksburg *(G-5794)*
Kemper Tool Inc .... G 812 744-8633
 Moores Hill *(G-12187)*
Kenco Plastics Inc .... F 219 324-6621
 La Porte *(G-10433)*
Kimball Electronics Inc .... E 317 357-3175
 Indianapolis *(G-8685)*
Kimball Electronics Inc .... D 317 545-5383
 Indianapolis *(G-8686)*
Mary Jonas .... F 317 500-0600
 Indianapolis *(G-8845)*
Meer Enterprises Inc .... D 574 522-7527
 Elkhart *(G-3526)*
Moriroku Technology N Amer Inc .... G 765 221-7576
 Anderson *(G-161)*
New Market Plastics Inc .... F 317 758-5494
 Crawfordsville *(G-2593)*
Nexgen Mold & Tool Inc .... E 812 945-3375
 New Albany *(G-12784)*
Plastics Research and Dev Inc .... E 812 279-8885
 Springville *(G-15390)*
Precision Plastics Indiana Inc .... C 260 244-6114
 Columbia City *(G-2183)*
Srg Global Trim Inc .... A 812 473-6200
 Evansville *(G-4329)*
Standard Plastic Corporation .... F 260 824-0214
 Bluffton *(G-1056)*
T-A Wind Down Inc .... C 708 839-1400
 Munster *(G-12566)*
TEC-Air LLC .... D 219 301-7084
 Munster *(G-12569)*
Templeton Coal Company Inc .... G 812 232-7037
 Terre Haute *(G-15725)*
Vee Engineering Inc .... D 260 424-6635
 Fort Wayne *(G-5530)*
Vee Engineering Inc .... G 765 778-7895
 Anderson *(G-213)*
Wabash Plastics Inc .... G 812 428-9300
 Evansville *(G-4377)*
York Group Inc .... D 765 966-0077
 Richmond *(G-14231)*

PLASTICS: Molded

Adkev Inc .... F 574 583-4420
 Monticello *(G-12132)*
Adkev Inc .... D 219 297-4484
 Goodland *(G-6078)*
Alex Virok DBA Intec .... G 317 770-7559
 Noblesville *(G-13034)*
Altec Engineering Inc .... E 574 293-1965
 Elkhart *(G-3167)*
Ashley Industrial Molding Inc .... D 260 587-9155
 Ashley *(G-330)*
Auburn Hardwood Molding .... G 260 925-5959
 Auburn *(G-363)*
B Plus Enterprises Inc .... G 219 733-9404
 Wanatah *(G-16287)*
Cambridge Molding Inc .... G 574 546-4311
 Nappanee *(G-12587)*
Cpx Inc .... B 219 474-5280
 Kentland *(G-10159)*
Eagle Mold & Tool .... G 574 862-1966
 Wakarusa *(G-16232)*
Futurex Industries Inc .... E 765 498-8900
 Bloomingdale *(G-759)*

Glass Molders Pottery Pla .... G 812 398-6222
 Carlisle *(G-1541)*
Group Dekko Inc .... D 260 357-3621
 Fort Wayne *(G-5042)*
Hewitt Tool & Die Inc .... D 765 453-3889
 Oakford *(G-13319)*
Manar Inc .... D 812 526-2891
 Edinburgh *(G-3092)*
Neptune Flotation LLC .... F 317 588-3600
 Carmel *(G-1704)*
Pent Plastics Inc .... C 260 897-3775
 Kendallville *(G-10142)*
Red Star Contract Mfg Inc .... E 260 327-3145
 Larwill *(G-10822)*
Richardson Molding LLC .... G 317 787-9463
 Indianapolis *(G-9303)*
Sabin Corporation .... C 812 323-4500
 Bloomington *(G-965)*
Smiths Enterprises Inc .... G 765 378-6267
 Chesterfield *(G-1898)*
Trim-Lok Inc .... F 574 227-1143
 Elkhart *(G-3747)*
US Molders Inc .... E 219 984-5058
 Reynolds *(G-14077)*

PLASTICS: Polystyrene Foam

Abbp LLC .... G 812 402-2000
 Evansville *(G-3864)*
Aearo Technologies LLC .... C 317 692-6666
 Indianapolis *(G-7447)*
American Whitetail Inc .... F 812 937-7185
 Ferdinand *(G-4428)*
Cellofoam North America Inc .... D 317 535-9008
 Whiteland *(G-16778)*
Efp LLC .... E 812 602-0019
 Evansville *(G-4029)*
Foam Fabricators Inc .... G 812 948-1696
 New Albany *(G-12732)*
Foamcraft Inc .... E 574 534-4343
 Goshen *(G-6139)*
Foamcraft Inc .... E 812 849-3350
 Mitchell *(G-12039)*
Foamcraft Inc .... F 317 545-3626
 Indianapolis *(G-8212)*
Foamex LP .... E 800 417-4257
 Fort Wayne *(G-4990)*
Forefront Foam LLC .... F 574 343-1146
 Mishawaka *(G-11897)*
Fxi Inc .... G 260 925-1073
 Auburn *(G-392)*
Fxi Auburn .... G 260 925-1073
 Auburn *(G-393)*
Gdc Inc .... C 574 533-3128
 Goshen *(G-6143)*
Innocor Foam Tech - Acp Inc .... G 574 294-7694
 Elkhart *(G-3427)*
Johns Manville Corporation .... G 574 546-4666
 Bremen *(G-1200)*
Kibbechem Inc .... E 574 266-1234
 Elkhart *(G-3454)*
Knox Enterprises Inc .... G 317 714-3073
 Indianapolis *(G-8699)*
Lifoam Industries LLC .... D 410 889-1023
 Fishers *(G-4556)*
Molded Foam LLC .... E 574 848-1500
 Bristol *(G-1275)*
Mossberg Industries Inc .... D 260 357-5141
 Garrett *(G-5873)*
Opflex Solutions Inc .... F 800 568-7036
 Indianapolis *(G-9064)*
Opflex Technologies LLC .... F 518 568-7036
 Indianapolis *(G-9065)*

PRODUCT SECTION

PLUMBING FIXTURES

PSC Industries Inc.. F 812 425-9071
Evansville *(G-4263)*

Security Paks Intl LLC..................................... F 317 536-2662
Carmel *(G-1756)*

Sonoco Prtective Solutions Inc................... E 260 726-9333
Portland *(G-13967)*

PLASTICS: Thermoformed

Arrowhead Plastic Engrg Inc........................ F 765 396-9113
Eaton *(G-3059)*

Artistic Composite Pallets LLC.................... E 317 960-5813
Carmel *(G-1565)*

Crescent Plastics Inc..................................... C 812 428-9305
Evansville *(G-3992)*

Hart Plastics Inc... E 574 264-7060
Elkhart *(G-3400)*

Hightec Solar Inc.. F 219 814-4279
Michigan City *(G-11624)*

Hoosier Fiberglass Industries...................... F 812 232-5027
Terre Haute *(G-15606)*

Imp Holdings LLC... D 260 665-6112
Angola *(G-263)*

Meyer Plastics Inc.. D 317 259-4131
Indianapolis *(G-8895)*

Osborn Manufacturing Corp......................... F 574 267-6156
Warsaw *(G-16406)*

Patrick Industries Inc.................................... D 260 665-6112
Angola *(G-282)*

Pro-Form Plastics Inc.................................... E 812 522-4433
Crothersville *(G-2644)*

Spectron MRC LLC... G 574 271-2800
South Bend *(G-15261)*

Spencer Industries Inc.................................. C 812 937-4561
Dale *(G-2792)*

PLATES: Aluminum

Taylor Made Enterprises Inc....................... G 765 653-8481
Greencastle *(G-6433)*

PLATES: Steel

McCombs and Son Company....................... G 765 825-4581
Connersville *(G-2454)*

PLATES: Truss, Metal

Gldn Rule Truss & Metal Sales................... G 812 866-1800
Lexington *(G-10976)*

Grabill Truss Incorporated........................... G 260 627-0933
Grabill *(G-6301)*

PLATING & POLISHING SVC

Albany Metal Treating Inc............................ F 765 789-6470
Albany *(G-11)*

Alliance Steel Corporation............................ E 708 924-1200
Gary *(G-5890)*

Altec LLC.. D 812 282-8256
Jeffersonville *(G-9928)*

Araymond Mfg Ctr N Amer Inc................... C 574 722-5168
Logansport *(G-11058)*

ATI Flat Rlled Pdts Hldngs LLC................... F 765 529-9570
New Castle *(G-12850)*

Bare Metal Inc.. F 812 948-1313
New Albany *(G-12696)*

Batesville Products Inc................................. D 513 381-2057
Lawrenceburg *(G-10831)*

Bonnell Aluminum Inc................................... A 815 351-6802
Kentland *(G-10157)*

C & J Plating & Grinding LLC..................... G 765 288-8728
Muncie *(G-12358)*

Ceramica Inc... F 317 546-0087
Indianapolis *(G-7777)*

Circle City Heat Treating Inc....................... F 317 440-9102
Indianapolis *(G-7805)*

Commercial Finishing Corp.......................... F 317 267-0377
Indianapolis *(G-7840)*

Heidtman Steel Products Inc....................... D 419 691-4646
Butler *(G-1465)*

Hydro Extrusion Usa LLC............................. B 888 935-5757
North Liberty *(G-13217)*

J & J Welding Inc... E 812 838-4391
Mount Vernon *(G-12303)*

Just Perfection LLC....................................... G 347 559-5878
Indianapolis *(G-8650)*

Linden Machine Shop LLC........................... G 765 339-7244
Linden *(G-11031)*

Napier & Napier... G 765 580-9116
Liberty *(G-10992)*

National Material LP...................................... C 219 397-5088
East Chicago *(G-3031)*

Neo Industries LLC.. G 219 762-6075
Portage *(G-13896)*

Poiry Partners LLC.. G 260 436-7070
Fort Wayne *(G-5321)*

Rci Hv Inc.. D 724 538-3180
Chesterton *(G-1956)*

Saran LP.. C
Indianapolis *(G-9373)*

Sterling Industrial LLC.................................. C 812 423-7832
Evansville *(G-4333)*

United States Steel Corp............................. G 219 762-3131
Portage *(G-13917)*

Whitlocks Pressure Wash............................ F 765 825-5868
Connersville *(G-2475)*

Worthington Steel Company....................... G 219 929-4000
Porter *(G-13925)*

PLATING COMPOUNDS

Warsaw Black Oxide Inc............................... E 574 491-2975
Burket *(G-1445)*

PLATING SVC: Chromium, Metals Or Formed Prdts

Chrome Deposit Corporation....................... E 219 763-1571
Portage *(G-13855)*

G and P Enterprises Ind Inc....................... G 812 723-3837
Paoli *(G-13495)*

P & J Industries Inc...................................... E 260 894-7143
Ligonier *(G-11021)*

Wrr Inc... E 317 577-1149
Indianapolis *(G-9794)*

PLAYGROUND EQPT

Kidstuff Playsystems Inc.............................. D 219 938-3331
Gary *(G-5974)*

Recreation Insites LLC................................. G 317 578-0588
Fishers *(G-4592)*

S & W Swing Sets.. G 260 414-6200
New Haven *(G-12916)*

Sb Finishing.. G 317 598-0965
Indianapolis *(G-9382)*

PLEATING & STITCHING FOR THE TRADE: Decorative & Novelty

Fanim Industries Inc..................................... F 888 567-2055
Zionsville *(G-17006)*

PLEATING & STITCHING SVC

A-1 Awards Inc... F 317 546-9000
Indianapolis *(G-7406)*

Arizona Sport Shirts Inc............................... E 317 481-2160
Indianapolis *(G-7544)*

Champions Image.. G 317 501-3617
Noblesville *(G-13057)*

Charles Coons.. G 765 362-6509
Crawfordsville *(G-2552)*

Coachs Connection Inc................................. G 260 356-0400
Huntington *(G-7306)*

Connies Satin Stitch Inc............................... G 219 942-1887
Hobart *(G-7183)*

Crescendo Inc... G 812 829-4759
Spencer *(G-15344)*

Dave Turner.. G 765 674-3360
Gas City *(G-6035)*

Drike Inc.. F 574 259-8822
Mishawaka *(G-11885)*

Embroidery By Jackie.................................... G 765 438-6240
Forest *(G-4700)*

Imperial Trophy & Awards Co..................... G 260 432-8161
Fort Wayne *(G-5096)*

Kerham Inc.. E 260 483-5444
Fort Wayne *(G-5146)*

Ram Graphics Inc... F 765 724-7783
Alexandria *(G-58)*

Safety Vehicle Emblem Inc.......................... F 317 885-7565
Indianapolis *(G-9364)*

Sharon K Utter... G 765 349-8991
Martinsville *(G-11427)*

Shilling Sales Inc.. E 260 426-2626
Fort Wayne *(G-5413)*

Stoffel Seals Corporation.............................. E 845 353-3800
Angola *(G-296)*

Winters Assoc Prmtnal Pdts Inc................. F 812 330-7000
Bloomington *(G-1015)*

PLUGS: Electric

Aearo Technologies LLC............................... A 612 284-1232
Indianapolis *(G-7446)*

Tap-A-Lite Inc... E 219 932-8067
Hammond *(G-7018)*

PLUMBING FIXTURES

Ashley F Ward Inc... G 574 294-1502
Elkhart *(G-3196)*

Ashley F Ward Inc... G 219 879-4177
Michigan City *(G-11580)*

Barry Company Inc.. G 812 333-1850
Bloomington *(G-795)*

Bath Gallery Showroom................................ G 219 531-2150
Valparaiso *(G-15911)*

Bootz Manufacturing Co LLC....................... C 812 425-4646
Evansville *(G-3942)*

City Supply Inc... G 574 259-6028
Mishawaka *(G-11861)*

Ferguson Enterprises LLC............................ G 219 440-5254
Schererville *(G-14521)*

Josam Company... D 219 872-5531
Michigan City *(G-11628)*

Kipps Plumbing Inc....................................... G 219 661-9320
Crown Point *(G-2710)*

Lee Supply Corp... F 812 333-4343
Bloomington *(G-909)*

Mark Miller.. G 317 626-9441
Indianapolis *(G-8836)*

Nibco Inc... F 574 296-1240
Goshen *(G-6227)*

Parker-Hannifin Corporation........................ D 260 636-2104
Albion *(G-40)*

Rex Byers Htg & Coolg Systems................ F 765 459-8858
Kokomo *(G-10328)*

Schmidt Contracting Inc.............................. E 812 482-3923
Jasper *(G-9908)*

St Regis Culvert Inc...................................... F 317 353-8065
Indianapolis *(G-9487)*

Stanley Oliver Products LLC........................ G 260 499-3506
Lagrange *(G-10764)*

PLUMBING FIXTURES

US Metals Inc .... G 219 802-8465
  Hammond (G-7027)
Willoughby Industries Inc .... C 317 875-0830
  Indianapolis (G-9770)

PLUMBING FIXTURES: Plastic

Abtrex Industries Inc .... F 734 728-0550
  South Bend (G-14934)
Altec Engineering Inc .... E 574 293-1965
  Elkhart (G-3167)
Frontline Mfg Inc .... E 574 269-6751
  Warsaw (G-16365)
Nibco Inc .... C 574 296-1240
  Goshen (G-6227)
Shidler Associates .... G 574 232-7357
  South Bend (G-15241)

PLUMBING FIXTURES: Vitreous

Bootz Manufacturing Co LLC .... C 812 425-4646
  Evansville (G-3942)
Coast OEM LLC .... G 765 553-5904
  Kokomo (G-10247)
Josam Company .... D 219 872-5531
  Michigan City (G-11628)
Leeps Supply Co Inc .... E 219 756-5337
  Merrillville (G-11530)
Patriot Porcelain LLC .... G 574 583-5128
  Monticello (G-12164)

POINT OF SALE DEVICES

Front End Digital Inc .... G 317 652-6134
  Fishers (G-4528)

POLISHING SVC: Metals Or Formed Prdts

502 Mold Polishing LLC .... G 502 436-0239
  Greenville (G-6650)
Allfab LLC .... G 317 359-3539
  Indianapolis (G-7482)
Custom Polish & Chrome .... G 260 665-7448
  Angola (G-244)
Db Polishing .... G 574 518-2443
  Nappanee (G-12593)
Doug Wilcox .... G 812 476-1957
  Lynnville (G-11189)
Evans Herron .... G 317 492-1384
  Indianapolis (G-8140)

POLYETHYLENE RESINS

Sun Polymers International Inc .... F 317 834-6410
  Mooresville (G-12246)

POLYSTYRENE RESINS

Apexx Enterprises LLC .... F 812 486-2443
  Montgomery (G-12085)
Cellofoam North America Inc .... D 317 535-9008
  Whiteland (G-16778)
Foam Fabricators Inc .... G 812 948-1696
  New Albany (G-12732)

POLYURETHANE RESINS

Future Foam Inc .... E 574 294-7694
  Elkhart (G-3363)
Molded Foam Products Inc .... F 574 848-1500
  Bristol (G-1276)

POLYVINYL CHLORIDE RESINS

AM Stabilizers Corporation .... G 219 844-3980
  Valparaiso (G-15896)
Aqseptence Group Inc .... G 574 208-5866
  Rochester (G-14277)

POSTERS

Phantom Neon LLC .... G 765 362-2221
  Crawfordsville (G-2604)

POULTRY & POULTRY PRDTS WHOLESALERS

Jfs Milling Inc .... G 812 683-4200
  Vincennes (G-16134)

POULTRY & SMALL GAME SLAUGHTERING & PROCESSING

Cargill Incorporated .... B 402 533-4227
  Hammond (G-6895)
Crystal Valley Farms LLC .... D 260 829-6550
  Orland (G-13364)
Farbest Farms Inc .... F 812 481-1034
  Huntingburg (G-7279)
Hy-Line North America LLC .... D 260 375-3041
  Warren (G-16300)
Jfs Milling Inc .... G 812 683-4200
  Vincennes (G-16134)
Koch Foods .... G 574 457-4384
  Syracuse (G-15466)
Lambrights Inc .... G 260 463-2178
  Lagrange (G-10750)
Maple Leaf Inc .... G 260 982-8655
  North Manchester (G-13241)
Perdue Farms Inc .... D 812 886-0593
  Vincennes (G-16143)
Perdue Farms Inc .... E 757 787-5210
  Washington (G-16501)
Tyson Chicken Inc .... A 812 347-2452
  Ramsey (G-14027)

POULTRY SLAUGHTERING & PROCESSING

Perdue Farms Inc .... A 812 254-8500
  Washington (G-16502)
Pine Manor Inc .... B 800 532-4186
  Orland (G-13370)

POWDER: Aluminum Atomized

Algalco LLC .... G 317 361-2787
  Indianapolis (G-7471)
Metal Powder Products LLC .... F 317 805-3764
  Noblesville (G-13134)
National Material Company LLC .... E 219 397-5088
  East Chicago (G-3030)
Old Rev LLC .... G 317 580-2420
  Westfield (G-16714)

POWDER: Iron

Powdertech Corp .... D 219 462-4141
  Valparaiso (G-16028)

POWDER: Metal

Creative Powder Coatings LLC .... D 260 489-3580
  Fort Wayne (G-4884)
Hawk Precision Components Inc .... G 812 755-4501
  Campbellsburg (G-1524)
ITW Gema .... F 317 298-5000
  Indianapolis (G-8598)
Jbs Powder Coating LLC .... G 812 952-1204
  Lanesville (G-10799)
LLC 2 Holdings Limited LLC .... G 317 319-9825
  Zionsville (G-17030)
Metal Powder Products LLC .... G 317 214-8120
  Indianapolis (G-8887)
Nst Technologies Mim LLC .... C 812 755-4501
  Campbellsburg (G-1526)

Powder Processing & Tech LLC .... E 219 462-4141
  Valparaiso (G-16027)

POWER GENERATORS

Ipower Technologies Inc .... G 317 574-0103
  Anderson (G-134)

POWER TRANSMISSION EQPT: Aircraft

Allison Transmission Inc .... C 317 280-6206
  Indianapolis (G-7489)

PRECAST TERRAZZO OR CONCRETE PRDTS

Hanson Pipe Precast .... G 219 873-9509
  Michigan City (G-11619)
Indiana Precast Inc .... E 812 372-7771
  Columbus (G-2324)
Tribute Precast Systems LLC .... G 260 587-9555
  Ashley (G-339)

PRECIOUS METALS

Dnm Converters & Cores .... G 502 599-5225
  Clarksville (G-2015)

PRERECORDED TAPE, CD/RECORD STORES: Audio Tapes, Prerecorded

Audio Flow LLC .... G 219 230-6330
  Portage (G-13846)

PRESSED FIBER & MOLDED PULP PRDTS, EXC FOOD

Avery Dennison Corporation .... D 219 696-7777
  Lowell (G-11155)
Ufp LLC .... G 219 697-2900
  Brook (G-1307)

PRESTRESSED CONCRETE PRDTS

Prestress Services Inc .... C 260 724-7117
  Decatur (G-2877)
Strescore Inc .... E 574 233-1117
  South Bend (G-15270)

PRIMARY FINISHED OR SEMIFINISHED SHAPES

Iron Dynamics Inc .... C 260 868-8800
  Butler (G-1469)

PRINT CARTRIDGES: Laser & Other Computer Printers

BOM Corporation .... E 765 361-0382
  Crawfordsville (G-2549)
Gallagher Environmental Inc .... G 773 791-4670
  Saint John (G-14450)
Lasertech Inc .... G 812 277-1321
  Bedford (G-656)

PRINTED CIRCUIT BOARDS

Carrier Corporation .... F 260 358-0888
  Huntington (G-7304)
Cil Electronics LLC .... E 765 457-3894
  Kokomo (G-10244)
David Kechel .... G 260 627-2749
  Leo (G-10967)
Divsys Aerospace & Engrg LLC .... F 317 941-7777
  Indianapolis (G-7987)
Divsys Intl - Icape LLC .... E 317 405-9427
  Indianapolis (G-7988)
Dpict Imaging Inc .... G 317 436-8411
  Indianapolis (G-8004)

PRINTING, COMMERCIAL: Periodicals, NEC

Icape-Usa LLC .... G 765 431-1271
Indianapolis *(G-8449)*

Jtd Enterprises Inc .... F 574 533-9438
Goshen *(G-6180)*

Key Electronics Inc .... C 812 206-2500
Jeffersonville *(G-10009)*

Kimball Elec Indianapolis Inc .... D 812 634-4000
Indianapolis *(G-8684)*

Kimball Electronics Inc .... A 812 634-4200
Jasper *(G-9865)*

Kimball Electronics Inc .... B 812 634-4000
Jasper *(G-9866)*

Kimball Electronics Group LLC .... G 812 634-4200
Jasper *(G-9867)*

Kimball Electronics Mfg Inc .... A 812 482-1600
Jasper *(G-9869)*

Kimball Electronics Tampa Inc .... G 812 634-4000
Jasper *(G-9870)*

Proto Engineering Llc .... G 800 522-6752
Mooresville *(G-12237)*

Semiconductor Test Supply LLC .... G 317 513-7393
Martinsville *(G-11426)*

Teaco Inc .... G 219 874-6234
Michigan City *(G-11676)*

Vector Graphics Inc .... G 317 255-9800
Indianapolis *(G-9704)*

PRINTERS' SVCS: Folding, Collating, Etc

Ao Inc .... G 317 280-3000
Avon *(G-504)*

Edwin Rahn .... G 260 622-7178
Ossian *(G-13423)*

Tdk Graphics Inc .... F 219 663-7799
Crown Point *(G-2762)*

PRINTERS: Computer

Laser Plus Inc .... G 574 269-1246
Warsaw *(G-16386)*

Midwest Office Solutions LLC .... G 262 658-2679
Mooresville *(G-12222)*

PRINTERS: Magnetic Ink, Bar Code

Marteck Inc .... E 800 569-9849
Zionsville *(G-17031)*

Syntag Rfid .... G 317 685-5292
Indianapolis *(G-9540)*

PRINTING & BINDING: Book Music

C-Point Inc .... C 260 478-9551
Fort Wayne *(G-4828)*

PRINTING & BINDING: Books

Biblical Enterprises LLC .... G 812 391-0071
Bloomington *(G-805)*

Codybro LLC .... G 765 827-5441
Connersville *(G-2432)*

Solema USA Inc .... G 765 361-0806
Crawfordsville *(G-2616)*

PRINTING & ENGRAVING: Card, Exc Greeting

Hiatt Enterprises Inc .... F 765 289-7756
Muncie *(G-12415)*

PRINTING & ENGRAVING: Financial Notes & Certificates

Triumphant Jrney MBL Ntary Svc ...... G 608 208-5604
Madison *(G-11254)*

PRINTING & STAMPING: Fabric Articles

Apple Group Inc .... E 765 675-4777
Tipton *(G-15764)*

Diverse Sales Solutions LLC .... G 317 514-2403
Indianapolis *(G-7981)*

EDS Teez LLC .... G 224 518-3388
Hammond *(G-6921)*

F Robert Gardner Co Inc .... G 317 634-2333
Indianapolis *(G-8161)*

Homelife Forever Inc .... G 765 307-0416
Roachdale *(G-14247)*

Lomont Holdings Co Inc .... E 800 545-9023
Angola *(G-273)*

Specialty Shoppe .... G 574 772-7873
Knox *(G-10225)*

Titan Graphics LLC .... G 317 496-2188
Mccordsville *(G-11457)*

PRINTING & WRITING PAPER WHOLESALERS

Mecom Ltd Inc .... D 317 218-2600
Indianapolis *(G-8868)*

Reprocomm Inc .... G 765 472-5700
Peru *(G-13598)*

PRINTING MACHINERY

Acutech LLC .... F 574 262-8228
Elkhart *(G-3153)*

Blue Grass Chemical Spc LLC .... F 812 948-1115
New Albany *(G-12703)*

Crunchtech Holdings LLC .... G 818 583-0004
Kendallville *(G-10106)*

Egenolf Machine Inc .... F 317 787-5301
Indianapolis *(G-8061)*

Finzer Roller Inc .... G 219 325-8808
La Porte *(G-10408)*

Numerical Concepts Inc .... E 812 466-5261
Terre Haute *(G-15654)*

Perfecta USA .... F 317 862-7371
Indianapolis *(G-9124)*

PRINTING, COMMERCIAL: Business Forms, NEC

Evansville Bindery Inc .... G 812 423-2222
Evansville *(G-4048)*

In Business For Life Inc .... G 317 691-6169
Carmel *(G-1664)*

Premier Print & Svcs Group Inc .... F 574 273-2525
Granger *(G-6372)*

Taylor Communications Inc .... E 317 392-3235
Shelbyville *(G-14803)*

Toms Printing Service .... G 260 438-3721
Ossian *(G-13442)*

PRINTING, COMMERCIAL: Decals, NEC

Graphix Unlimited Inc .... E 574 546-3770
Bremen *(G-1193)*

Maple-Hunter Decals .... G 812 894-9759
Riley *(G-14239)*

PRINTING, COMMERCIAL: Envelopes, NEC

Stines Printing Inc .... G 260 356-5994
Huntington *(G-7371)*

PRINTING, COMMERCIAL: Imprinting

1z2z Imprints .... G 303 918-8979
Bloomington *(G-764)*

PRINTING, COMMERCIAL: Labels & Seals, NEC

American Label Products Inc .... G 317 873-9850
Zionsville *(G-16991)*

Cenveo Worldwide Limited .... D 800 995-9500
New Albany *(G-12710)*

Data Label Inc .... C 800 457-0676
Terre Haute *(G-15577)*

Headlands Ltd .... G 260 426-9884
Wolcottville *(G-16937)*

Indilabel LLC .... F 317 839-8814
Plainfield *(G-13689)*

International Label Mfg LLC .... F 812 235-5071
Terre Haute *(G-15618)*

Label Logic Inc .... E 574 266-6007
Elkhart *(G-3464)*

Label Tech Inc .... G 765 747-1234
Muncie *(G-12436)*

Lambel Corporation .... G 317 849-6828
Indianapolis *(G-8716)*

Liberty Book & Bb Manufactures .... E 317 633-1450
Indianapolis *(G-8744)*

Matrix Label Systems Inc .... E 317 839-1973
Plainfield *(G-13700)*

Multi-Color Corporation .... C 513 396-5600
Scottsburg *(G-14572)*

Multi-Color Corporation .... E 812 752-0586
Scottsburg *(G-14573)*

Robert Copeland .... G 951 245-0041
Zionsville *(G-17047)*

Standard Label Co Inc .... F 574 522-3548
Elkhart *(G-3696)*

Stranco Inc .... F 219 874-5221
Michigan City *(G-11673)*

Vickery Tape & Label Co Inc .... F 765 472-1974
Rochester *(G-14332)*

W/S Packaging Group Inc .... G 317 578-4454
Indianapolis *(G-9734)*

PRINTING, COMMERCIAL: Letterpress & Screen

Graphic22 Inc .... G 219 921-5409
Chesterton *(G-1930)*

Krafty Bravo LLC .... G 317 366-3485
South Bend *(G-15105)*

Nicholas Mendel .... G 574 870-8856
Delphi *(G-2904)*

Outfitters Inc .... G 765 778-9097
Pendleton *(G-13549)*

Perfect Apparel LLC .... G 317 389-5553
Indianapolis *(G-9120)*

Sign Art Quality Advertising .... G 219 763-6122
Hobart *(G-7207)*

Siman Promotions Inc .... G 260 637-5621
Fort Wayne *(G-5417)*

Spark Marketing LLC .... G 219 301-0071
Dyer *(G-2983)*

PRINTING, COMMERCIAL: Literature, Advertising, NEC

MPS Indianapolis Inc .... C 317 241-2020
Indianapolis *(G-8966)*

Optiviz Media LLC .... G 812 681-1711
Vincennes *(G-16141)*

Printwerk Graphics & Design .... G 219 322-7722
Dyer *(G-2981)*

PRINTING, COMMERCIAL: Magazines, NEC

Rubenstein LLC .... G 317 946-2752
Indianapolis *(G-9346)*

Singing Pines Projects Inc .... G 812 988-8807
Nashville *(G-12680)*

PRINTING, COMMERCIAL: Periodicals, NEC

12 Stone Ventures Inc .... G 765 573-4605
 Converse *(G-2476)*
Baxter Design & Advertising .... G 219 464-9237
 Valparaiso *(G-15912)*
Boilers Inc .... G 765 742-5855
 West Lafayette *(G-16567)*
Diamond Hoosier .... G 317 773-1411
 Noblesville *(G-13070)*
Endowment Development Services .... F 317 542-9829
 Indianapolis *(G-8114)*
Greencastle Offset Inc .... G 765 653-4026
 Greencastle *(G-6406)*
Horizon Publishing Company LLC .... F 219 852-3200
 Hammond *(G-6949)*
Indiana State Medical Assn .... E 317 261-2060
 Indianapolis *(G-8494)*
International English Inc .... G 260 868-2670
 Butler *(G-1467)*
Magazine Fulfillment Corp .... F 219 874-4245
 Michigan City *(G-11636)*
Our Sunday Visitor Inc .... B 260 359-2564
 Huntington *(G-7350)*
Pearson Education Inc .... G 765 483-6738
 Lebanon *(G-10929)*
Relx Inc .... G 317 849-9806
 Fishers *(G-4595)*
Sophistcted Lving Indianapolis .... F 317 565-4555
 Carmel *(G-1766)*
Travelhost Mag Indianapolis .... G 317 416-7780
 Carmel *(G-1790)*
University Notre Dame Du Lac .... E 574 631-6346
 Notre Dame *(G-13318)*

PRINTING, COMMERCIAL: Promotional

Adlink Promotions .... G 574 271-7003
 Granger *(G-6330)*
B-Hive Printing .... G 812 897-3905
 Boonville *(G-1081)*
Brenmeer LLC .... G 260 267-0249
 Fort Wayne *(G-4816)*
Dimensional Imprinting Inc .... G 260 417-0202
 Milton *(G-11832)*
Distinct Images Inc .... F 317 613-4413
 Indianapolis *(G-7977)*
Everything Under Sun LLC .... G 812 438-3397
 Rising Sun *(G-14242)*
Graphic Fx Inc .... E 812 234-0000
 Terre Haute *(G-15601)*
Masco Corporation of Indiana .... E 317 848-1812
 Indianapolis *(G-8847)*
Moose Lake Products Co Inc .... F 260 432-2768
 Fort Wayne *(G-5242)*
Nielsen Enterprises Inc .... G 574 277-3748
 Granger *(G-6367)*
Printing Inc Louisville KY .... F 800 237-5894
 Jeffersonville *(G-10041)*
Thoughts Are Things Inc .... G 317 585-8053
 Indianapolis *(G-9599)*
Xl Graphics Inc .... F 317 738-3434
 Franklin *(G-5789)*

PRINTING, COMMERCIAL: Screen

18 Threads LLC .... F 260 409-2923
 Fort Wayne *(G-4710)*
47tee LLC .... G 317 373-8070
 Fishers *(G-4457)*
4ink Fullfillment Services .... G 812 738-4465
 Corydon *(G-2483)*
A & M Innovations LLC .... G 317 306-6118
 Whiteland *(G-16776)*
A-1 Screenprinting LLC .... G 812 558-0286
 Bloomington *(G-769)*
A-1 Screenprinting LLC .... G 765 588-3851
 West Lafayette *(G-16554)*
A&A Screen Printing .... G 765 473-8783
 Peru *(G-13564)*
A+ Images Inc .... G 317 405-8955
 Indianapolis *(G-7405)*
Aardvark Graphics .... G 574 267-4799
 Warsaw *(G-16307)*
Abr Images Inc .... F 866 342-4764
 Bloomington *(G-770)*
Abracadabra Graphics .... G 812 336-1971
 Bloomington *(G-771)*
Advantex Inc .... G 812 339-6479
 Bloomington *(G-774)*
After Hours Embroidery .... G 812 926-9355
 Aurora *(G-436)*
All Gussied Up Embroidery .... G 317 517-1557
 Indianapolis *(G-7473)*
Allsports .... G 812 883-3561
 Salem *(G-14470)*
Almost Famous Printing .... G 219 793-6388
 Whiting *(G-16830)*
Andresen Graphic Processors .... F 317 291-7071
 Brownsburg *(G-1346)*
Apparel Design Group .... G 812 339-3355
 Bloomington *(G-781)*
As You Wish Custom .... G 502 216-3144
 Jeffersonville *(G-9935)*
Asahi TEC America Corporation .... G 765 962-8399
 Richmond *(G-14087)*
Ascl Printwear LLC .... G 317 507-0548
 Avon *(G-505)*
Axe Head Threads LLC .... G 317 607-6330
 New Palestine *(G-12932)*
Bartons Screen Printing .... G 812 422-4303
 Evansville *(G-3910)*
Baxter Printing Incorporated .... G 219 923-1999
 Griffith *(G-6793)*
Bex Screen Printing Inc .... G 317 791-0375
 Indianapolis *(G-7620)*
Big Picture Data Imaging LLC .... G 812 235-0202
 Terre Haute *(G-15553)*
Black Dog Printing LLC .... G 812 955-0577
 Richmond *(G-14098)*
Blue Octopus Printing Company .... F 317 247-1997
 Indianapolis *(G-7646)*
Blue River Services Inc .... E 812 738-2437
 Corydon *(G-2488)*
Brandwise LLC .... G 317 574-0066
 Noblesville *(G-13046)*
Broken Tee LLC .... G 812 559-0741
 Jasper *(G-9825)*
BT Management Inc .... G 219 794-9546
 Merrillville *(G-11494)*
California Colors Inc .... G 317 435-1351
 Fishers *(G-4482)*
Cause Printing Company .... G 765 573-3330
 Huntington *(G-7305)*
CD Grafix LLC .... G 812 945-4443
 Clarksville *(G-2011)*
Cdb Screen Printing Inc .... G 765 472-4404
 Peru *(G-13570)*
Celestial Designs LLC .... G 317 733-3110
 Zionsville *(G-16997)*
Coffey Connection LLC .... G 317 300-9639
 Greenwood *(G-6681)*
Colorrush Inc .... G 317 374-3494
 Indianapolis *(G-7838)*
Cool Cayenne .... G 260 376-0927
 Portland *(G-13934)*
Cool Cayenne LLC .... G 765 282-0977
 Albany *(G-12)*
Countryside Printing LLC .... G 812 486-2454
 Montgomery *(G-12090)*
County West Sports .... G 317 839-4076
 Plainfield *(G-13673)*
Craigs Printing Co .... G 812 358-5010
 Brownstown *(G-1421)*
Custom Ink Writers .... G 260 202-9350
 Portland *(G-13935)*
Custom Prints and Tees LLC .... G 317 891-4550
 Indianapolis *(G-7935)*
D S Custom Tees .... G 219 802-3127
 Gary *(G-5921)*
Daisy Tees LLC .... G 574 259-1933
 Mishawaka *(G-11876)*
Dec-O-Art Inc .... E 574 294-6451
 Elkhart *(G-3287)*
Denneycreative .... G 260 494-0862
 Wabash *(G-16180)*
Dirty Squeegee Screen Prtg LLC .... G 574 358-0003
 Middlebury *(G-11712)*
Dna Designs LLC .... G 812 329-1310
 Bedford *(G-631)*
Drike Inc .... F 574 259-8822
 Mishawaka *(G-11885)*
Dse Inc .... E 812 376-0310
 Columbus *(G-2291)*
El Shaddai Inc .... G 260 359-9080
 Huntington *(G-7309)*
Elegan Graphics .... G 219 462-9921
 Valparaiso *(G-15940)*
Elengas Customwear .... G 317 577-1677
 Fishers *(G-4510)*
Em Global LLC .... G 812 258-9993
 Jeffersonville *(G-9976)*
Embroidme .... G 219 465-1400
 Valparaiso *(G-15943)*
Evansvlle Print Specialist Inc .... G 812 423-5831
 Evansville *(G-4060)*
Excell Color Graphics Inc .... E 260 482-2720
 Fort Wayne *(G-4967)*
Expressions Custom Tees .... G 317 205-6229
 Indianapolis *(G-8158)*
Extensive Design LLC .... G 260 267-6752
 Fort Wayne *(G-4969)*
Faith Walkers .... G 219 873-1900
 Michigan City *(G-11610)*
Fired Up Tees LLC .... G 317 412-4113
 Bargersville *(G-566)*
Freckles Grphics Lafayette Inc .... F 765 448-4692
 Lafayette *(G-10581)*
Fresh Printz Incorporated .... F 812 352-6400
 North Vernon *(G-13271)*
G D Cox Inc .... G 317 398-0035
 Shelbyville *(G-14758)*
Gettelfinger Holdings LLC .... G 812 923-9065
 Floyds Knobs *(G-4679)*
Giraffe-X Graphics Inc .... G 317 546-4944
 Indianapolis *(G-8282)*
Glittered Pig LLC .... G 812 779-6154
 Princeton *(G-13995)*
Goldden Corporation .... F 765 423-4366
 Lafayette *(G-10591)*
Goose Graphics L L C .... G 260 563-4516
 Fort Wayne *(G-5029)*
Grafac Industries Inc .... G 812 474-0930
 Evansville *(G-4094)*
Graphic Visions .... G 812 331-7446
 Bloomington *(G-869)*
Graphics Lab Uv Printing Inc .... F 765 457-5784
 Kokomo *(G-10272)*

PRODUCT SECTION — PRINTING, COMMERCIAL: Screen

Company	Emp	Phone
Graphics Unlmted McRpublishing — Angola *(G-256)*	G	260 665-3443
H M C Screen Printing Inc — Noblesville *(G-13090)*	E	317 773-8532
Happy Tees LLC — Indianapolis *(G-8355)*	G	317 465-0122
Hat Plug US — Elkhart *(G-3401)*	G	574 575-2520
Hinen Printing Co — Columbia City *(G-2150)*	G	260 248-8984
Hoosier Daddy Custom Tees — Portage *(G-13876)*	G	218 308-3544
Hot Cake — Indianapolis *(G-8419)*	E	317 889-2253
Ics Inks LLP — Indianapolis *(G-8452)*	G	317 690-9254
IM Impressed — Munster *(G-12542)*	G	219 838-7959
Image Plus Original LLC — Indianapolis *(G-8463)*	G	800 226-7316
Imagination Graphics — Evansville *(G-4117)*	G	812 423-6503
Imprint It All — Terre Haute *(G-15614)*	G	812 234-0024
Ink Dawgz LLC — Valparaiso *(G-15974)*	G	219 781-6972
Inkworks Studio LLC — Evansville *(G-4126)*	G	812 401-6203
Insana Tees — Portage *(G-13877)*	G	219 801-5104
J Tees — Seymour *(G-14658)*	G	812 524-9292
J&J Sprts Screen Prtg Sprit Wr — Evansville *(G-4135)*	G	812 909-2686
J&P Custom Designs Inc — Indianapolis *(G-8611)*	G	317 253-2198
Jer-Maur Corporation — Bloomfield *(G-750)*	G	812 384-8290
Jeremy Parker — Muncie *(G-12431)*	G	765 284-5414
Keen Screen — New Albany *(G-12757)*	G	812 989-8885
Keen Screen — New Albany *(G-12758)*	G	812 945-5336
Kennyleeholmescom — Elkhart *(G-3451)*	G	574 612-2526
Kessler Concepts Inc — Indianapolis *(G-8675)*	F	317 630-9901
Kewanna Screen Printing Inc — Kewanna *(G-10167)*	G	574 653-2683
Kirchoff Custom Sports Inc — Evansville *(G-4154)*	G	812 434-0355
Knoy Apparel — Lafayette *(G-10624)*	G	765 448-1031
Leap Frogz Ink LLC — Greenwood *(G-6728)*	G	317 786-2441
Lee Reed Holdings LLC — Hammond *(G-6970)*	G	219 255-0555
Legacy Enterprises Inc — Merrillville *(G-11531)*	G	219 484-9483
Legacy Screen Printing Promoti — Chesterton *(G-1944)*	G	219 262-4000
Liberty Screen Printing — Madison *(G-11236)*	G	812 273-4358
Lightning Printing — Crawfordsville *(G-2585)*	G	765 362-5999
Lila J Athletic Wear — Floyds Knobs *(G-4685)*	G	502 619-2898
Logo USA Corporation — Westfield *(G-16708)*	F	317 867-8518
Logo Zone Inc — Logansport *(G-11091)*	G	574 753-7569
Logos Express Inc — Lebanon *(G-10911)*	G	317 272-1200
Logowear LLC — Greenfield *(G-6525)*	G	317 462-3376
M M Printing Plus — Milford *(G-11797)*	G	574 658-9345
Macdesign Inc — Carmel *(G-1689)*	G	317 580-9390
Mama Fox Tee Company — Fort Wayne *(G-5201)*	G	260 438-4054
Mandala Screen Printing Inc — Winamac *(G-16866)*	G	574 946-6290
Mexabilly Brothers LLC — Anderson *(G-152)*	G	765 621-6334
Mg Impressions LLC — Noblesville *(G-13138)*	G	317 219-5118
Midnite Grafix — Princeton *(G-14006)*	G	812 386-9430
Minds Eye Graphics Inc — Decatur *(G-2874)*	F	260 724-2050
Mito-Craft Inc — South Bend *(G-15152)*	G	574 287-4555
New End Zone Sporting Goods — Washington *(G-16495)*	G	812 254-1895
New Haven Trophies & Shirts — New Haven *(G-12911)*	G	260 749-0269
New Process Graphics LLC — Fort Wayne *(G-5268)*	E	260 489-1700
Next Level Logo Store Inc — La Porte *(G-10458)*	G	219 344-5141
Next Phase Graphics — Huntertown *(G-7259)*	G	260 627-6259
Nickprint Inc — Carmel *(G-1705)*	G	317 489-3033
Nite Owl Promotions Inc — Ellettsville *(G-3810)*	G	812 876-3888
Nsignia Screen Printing — Fort Wayne *(G-5278)*	G	260 420-0500
Ohio Vly Screen Prtrs EMB Engr — Lawrenceburg *(G-10850)*	G	812 539-3307
Old Fort Tee Company LLC — Fort Wayne *(G-5283)*	G	248 506-3762
Ooshirts Inc — Indianapolis *(G-9060)*	G	317 246-9083
Outfitter — Muncie *(G-12471)*	G	765 289-6456
Parlor City Trophy & AP Inc — Bluffton *(G-1047)*	G	260 824-0216
Pearl Screen Printing — Evansville *(G-4235)*	G	812 429-1686
Perdue Printed Products Inc — Fort Wayne *(G-5304)*	G	260 456-7575
Personal Impressions Inc — Fortville *(G-5604)*	G	317 485-4409
Phil Irwin Advertising Inc — Indianapolis *(G-9134)*	F	317 547-5117
Photo Screen Service Inc — Indianapolis *(G-9140)*	G	317 636-7712
Photo Specialties — New Albany *(G-12794)*	G	812 944-5111
Plastimatic Arts Corp — Mishawaka *(G-11975)*	E	574 254-9000
Play 2 Win Screenprinting LLC — Oxford *(G-13476)*	G	765 426-0679
Portage Custom Wear LLC — Portage *(G-13905)*	G	219 841-9070
Ppi Acquisition LLC — Marion *(G-11329)*	E	765 674-8627
Prentice Products Holdings LLC — Fort Wayne *(G-5346)*	E	260 747-3195
Reckon With It Tees Stuff LLC — Covington *(G-2533)*	G	765 585-3610
Rivera Screenprinting — Burney *(G-1448)*	G	812 663-0816
Romanart Incorporated — Merrillville *(G-11555)*	G	219 736-9150
Rookies Unlimited Inc — Summitville *(G-15431)*	G	765 536-2726
Rtees LLC — Plainfield *(G-13724)*	G	317 345-7445
Running Around Screen Prtg LLC — Columbia City *(G-2194)*	G	260 248-1216
Sampan Group LLC — Jeffersonville *(G-10050)*	G	812 280-6094
Sampan Screen Print New Image — Jeffersonville *(G-10051)*	G	812 282-8499
Screen Printing Super Store — Westfield *(G-16725)*	G	317 804-9904
Screenprint Special Tees LLC — Indianapolis *(G-9396)*	G	317 396-0349
Screens — Fredericksburg *(G-5796)*	G	812 472-3274
Shadow Screen Printing — Terre Haute *(G-15690)*	G	812 234-3104
Shodas Tees & Gifts — South Whitley *(G-15323)*	G	260 418-8448
Signs AP & Awards On Time LLC — Crown Point *(G-2752)*	G	219 661-4488
Single Inc — Terre Haute *(G-15697)*	G	812 877-2220
Sir Graphics Inc — Granger *(G-6379)*	G	574 272-9330
Six Six Sublimation LLC — Brownsburg *(G-1403)*	G	317 858-5211
Sledgehammer Printing Corp — Newburgh *(G-13022)*	G	812 629-2160
South Bend Screen Process Inc — Mishawaka *(G-12003)*	G	574 254-9000
Southwest Grafix and AP Inc — Evansville *(G-4325)*	F	812 425-5104
Sports Screen Impact — Aurora *(G-456)*	G	812 926-9355
Sports Unlimited Printed AP — Knox *(G-10226)*	G	574 772-4239
Squeegeepie Merch Co LLC — Crawfordsville *(G-2618)*	G	765 376-6358
Standout Creations LLC — Anderson *(G-200)*	G	765 203-9110
Sterling Impressions Inc — Indianapolis *(G-9507)*	G	317 329-9773
Steve Weaver Art — Bremen *(G-1224)*	G	574 546-3530
Swagerle Screen Printing — Terre Haute *(G-15719)*	G	812 232-6947
T Productions Inc — Mishawaka *(G-12012)*	G	574 257-8610
T Shirt 1 Inc — Terre Haute *(G-15721)*	G	812 232-5046
Table Thyme Designs LLC — Indianapolis *(G-9546)*	G	317 634-0281
Team Image LLC — Greenfield *(G-6564)*	E	317 477-7468
Team Image LLC — Greenfield *(G-6563)*	G	317 468-0802
Team Mantra Wear LLC — Bluffton *(G-1061)*	G	260 273-0421
Team Mantra Wear LLC — Bluffton *(G-1062)*	G	260 827-0061
Team Pride Athletic AP Corp — Rochester *(G-14327)*	G	574 224-8326
Tee Trudys Rainbow Palac — Muncie *(G-12500)*	G	765 273-7571
Teeki Hut Custom Tees Inc — Indianapolis *(G-9573)*	G	317 205-3589

Employee Codes: A=Over 500 employees, B=251-500, C=101-250, D=51-100, E=20-50, F=10-19, G=1-9

PRINTING, COMMERCIAL: Screen

Tees and Blues LLC .... G 765 808-4081
  Muncie (G-12501)
Teras Sporty Ink .... G 219 369-6276
  La Porte (G-10488)
Tims Tees .... G 317 503-5736
  Indianapolis (G-9607)
Tma Enterprises Inc .... G 317 272-0694
  Avon (G-553)
TNT Top Notch Tees .... G 219 775-3812
  Crown Point (G-2764)
To A Tee Inc .... F 317 757-8842
  Indianapolis (G-9615)
Top Cat Printing Inc .... G 812 683-2773
  Huntingburg (G-7293)
Topstitch Inc .... F
  Elkhart (G-3739)
Travis Britton .... G 317 762-6018
  Indianapolis (G-9632)
Trendsettin Tees LLC .... G 219 201-1410
  Indianapolis (G-9635)
Tri State Printing & Embroider .... G 812 316-0094
  Vincennes (G-16159)
Triple Js Transport LLC .... G 708 513-8389
  Saint John (G-14459)
Turtlefish Clothing Co LLC .... G 812 896-2805
  Salem (G-14504)
Unique Graphic Designs Inc .... G 574 583-7119
  Monticello (G-12175)
Upland Print and Stitch .... G 765 506-7011
  Upland (G-15882)
Upland Print Stitch .... G 765 506-7011
  Upland (G-15883)
Varsity Sports Inc .... G 219 987-7200
  Demotte (G-2931)
Vickers Graphics Inc .... G 765 868-4646
  Kokomo (G-10354)
Vivid Social Group LLC .... G 317 447-7319
  Indianapolis (G-9726)
WAr- LLC- Westville Prtg .... G 219 785-2821
  Westville (G-16765)
Warren Printing Services LLC .... F 812 738-6508
  Corydon (G-2521)
Wildman Business Group LLC .... G 866 369-1552
  Warsaw (G-16451)
Wilson Enterprises Inc .... G 765 362-1089
  Crawfordsville (G-2627)
Xtreme Graphics .... G 812 989-6948
  Jeffersonville (G-10076)

PRINTING, COMMERCIAL: Stationery, NEC

Altstadt Business Forms Inc .... F 812 425-3393
  Evansville (G-3882)
Asc Inc .... E 765 472-5331
  Peru (G-13566)
Avery Dennison Corporation .... D 219 696-7777
  Lowell (G-11155)
Gov 6 Corp .... G 317 847-4942
  Indianapolis (G-8310)
Judkins Sr Renaldo G .... G 812 944-4251
  Clarksville (G-2022)

PRINTING, LITHOGRAPHIC: Advertising Posters

C-Point Inc .... C 260 478-9551
  Fort Wayne (G-4828)
Franklin Barry Gallery .... G 317 822-8455
  Indianapolis (G-8224)
Whitewater Print Solutions LLC .... G 513 405-3452
  Brookville (G-1340)

PRINTING, LITHOGRAPHIC: Calendars

Kellmark Corporation .... F 574 264-9695
  Elkhart (G-3449)

PRINTING, LITHOGRAPHIC: Forms, Business

Altstadt Business Forms Inc .... F 812 425-3393
  Evansville (G-3882)

PRINTING, LITHOGRAPHIC: Offset & photolithographic printing

AR Shot It LLC .... G 317 654-0187
  Indianapolis (G-7537)
B-Hive Printing .... G 812 897-3905
  Boonville (G-1081)

PRINTING, LITHOGRAPHIC: Promotional

Drike Inc .... F 574 259-8822
  Mishawaka (G-11885)
Giles Agency Incorporated .... G 317 842-5546
  Indianapolis (G-8281)
Smiling Cross Inc .... G 812 323-9290
  Bloomington (G-976)
Town & Country Industries Inc .... E 219 712-0893
  Crown Point (G-2766)

PRINTING, LITHOGRAPHIC: Tickets

Trinity Cmmnications Group Inc .... G 260 484-1029
  Fort Wayne (G-5508)

PRINTING: Books

Annies Publishing LLC .... C 260 589-4000
  Berne (G-704)
Direct Point LLC .... G 260 705-2279
  Fort Wayne (G-4917)
Diversified Bus Systems Inc .... G 317 254-8668
  Indianapolis (G-7984)
Herff Jones Inc .... E 317 612-3400
  Indianapolis (G-8384)
Kendallville Custom Printing .... F 260 347-9233
  Kendallville (G-10125)
Lsc Communications Inc .... C 765 364-2247
  Crawfordsville (G-2586)
Lsc Communications Inc .... G 812 234-1585
  Terre Haute (G-15633)
Lsc Communications Us LLC .... G 765 362-1300
  Crawfordsville (G-2587)
Michael L Jerrell .... G 812 354-9297
  Petersburg (G-13617)
Mitchell-Fleming Printing Inc .... F 317 462-5467
  Greenfield (G-6529)
University Publishing Corp .... E 812 339-9033
  Bloomington (G-1004)
Augustin Prtg & Design Svcs .... G 765 966-7130
  Richmond (G-14088)
R R Donnelley & Sons Company .... C 765 362-1300
  Crawfordsville (G-2607)
Wayseeker LLC .... G 574 529-0199
  Syracuse (G-15491)

PRINTING: Broadwoven Fabrics. Cotton

Bens Creative Ventures LLC .... G 574 279-1057
  Fort Wayne (G-4795)
Graphic22 Inc .... G 219 921-5409
  Chesterton (G-1930)
Pretty Chique LLC .... G 317 922-5899
  Indianapolis (G-9194)

PRINTING: Checkbooks

Clarke Harland Corp .... G 812 283-9598
  Jeffersonville (G-9954)

Deluxe Wheel Company .... G 219 395-8003
  Chesterton (G-1918)
Segundo Deluxe LLC .... G 260 414-7820
  Indianapolis (G-9400)
Writeguard Business Systems .... G 317 849-7292
  Indianapolis (G-9793)

PRINTING: Commercial, NEC

Acclaim Graphics Inc .... G 812 424-5035
  Evansville (G-3866)
Adams Smith .... G 219 661-2812
  Crown Point (G-2648)
Advanced Digital Imaging .... G 765 491-9434
  West Lafayette (G-16558)
Altstadt Business Forms Inc .... F 812 425-3393
  Evansville (G-3882)
American Printing Indiana LLC .... G 765 825-7600
  Anderson (G-76)
American Veteran Group LLC .... G 317 600-4749
  Westfield (G-16664)
Bartel Printing Company Inc .... G 574 267-7421
  Warsaw (G-16317)
Bartons Teez .... G 812 422-4303
  Evansville (G-3911)
Bell Graphics and Design LLC .... G 765 827-5441
  Connersville (G-2428)
Bennett Printing .... G 812 966-2917
  Medora (G-11461)
Bev Can Printers LLC .... G 219 617-6181
  La Porte (G-10388)
Black Hustle Holdings Corp .... G 800 988-7067
  Indianapolis (G-7638)
Blue River Printing Inc .... G 317 392-3676
  Shelbyville (G-14736)
Bm Creations Inc .... E 219 922-8935
  Griffith (G-6796)
Brand Prtg & Photo-Litho Co .... G 317 921-4095
  New Palestine (G-12933)
Bredensteiner & Associates .... G 317 921-2226
  Indianapolis (G-7673)
C E M Printing & Specialities .... G 269 684-6898
  South Bend (G-14964)
Campbell Printing Company .... G 219 866-5913
  Rensselaer (G-14046)
Ccmp Inc .... E 219 922-8935
  Griffith (G-6799)
Classic Graphics Inc .... F 260 482-3487
  Fort Wayne (G-4853)
Clover Printing LLC .... G 260 657-3003
  Harlan (G-7052)
Coachs Connection Inc .... G 260 356-0400
  Huntington (G-7306)
Consolidated Printing Svcs Inc .... G 765 468-6033
  Farmland (G-4424)
Courier Printing Co Allen Cnty .... G 260 627-2728
  Grabill (G-6293)
Courier-Times Inc .... D 765 529-1111
  New Castle (G-12856)
Criterion Press Inc .... E 317 236-1570
  Indianapolis (G-7904)
Cs Kern Inc .... E 765 289-8600
  Muncie (G-12370)
Custom Packaging Inc .... F 317 876-9559
  Indianapolis (G-7933)
Dale Flora .... G 260 982-7233
  North Manchester (G-13232)
Dance World Bazaar Corporation .... G 812 663-7679
  Greensburg (G-6589)
David Camp .... G 812 346-6255
  North Vernon (G-13265)
Defining Trndstting Cstm Print .... G 260 755-1038
  Fort Wayne (G-4910)

PRINTING: Commercial, NEC

Direct Printing Co .... G 317 831-1047
Mooresville (G-12203)

Doerr Printing Co .... G 317 568-0135
Indianapolis (G-7994)

Douglas P Terrell .... G 812 254-1976
Washington (G-16478)

Eastern Engineering Supply Inc .... F 260 426-3119
Fort Wayne (G-4938)

Ed Sons Inc .... F 317 897-8821
Indianapolis (G-8051)

Epic Graphics and Printing .... G 219 545-1240
Gary (G-5930)

Esther Reid .... G 314 504-6659
South Bend (G-15018)

Ewing Printing Company Inc .... F 812 882-2415
Vincennes (G-16120)

F Robert Gardner Co Inc .... G 317 634-2333
Indianapolis (G-8161)

Faulkenberg Printing Co Inc .... F 317 638-1359
Franklin (G-5730)

Fedex Office & Print Svcs Inc .... G 317 251-2406
Indianapolis (G-8179)

First Class Printing .... G 317 808-2222
Indianapolis (G-8192)

Fort Wayne Newspapers Inc .... B 260 461-8444
Fort Wayne (G-4999)

Goldleaf Promotional Pdts Inc .... G 317 202-2754
Indianapolis (G-8302)

Graphic 2000 Forms Labels .... G 260 387-5943
Fort Wayne (G-5033)

Graphic Menus Inc .... F 765 396-3003
Eaton (G-3062)

Greensburg Printing Co Inc .... G 812 663-8265
Greensburg (G-6598)

Harcourt Industries Inc .... E 765 629-2625
Milroy (G-11824)

Hi-Tech Label Inc .... F 765 659-1800
Frankfort (G-5673)

Hiatt Enterprises Inc .... G 765 289-2700
Muncie (G-12416)

Hot Off Press .... G 317 253-5987
Indianapolis (G-8420)

Jac Jmr Inc .... G 219 663-6700
Crown Point (G-2698)

JB Graphics Inc .... G 317 819-0008
Westfield (G-16702)

John R Bowen & Associates .... G 812 544-2267
Newburgh (G-13010)

Jomark Inc .... F 248 478-2600
Angola (G-265)

Jones & Webb Associates Inc .... G 317 236-9755
Indianapolis (G-8637)

Journal & Chronicle Inc .... G 812 752-5060
Scottsburg (G-14566)

Jt Printing LLC .... G 317 271-7700
Avon (G-529)

Kendallville Custom Printing .... F 260 347-9233
Kendallville (G-10125)

Kingery Group Inc .... G 317 823-9585
Indianapolis (G-8687)

Kmls LLC .... G 317 845-2955
Morgantown (G-12259)

L & L Press Inc .... F 765 664-3162
Marion (G-11305)

L R Green Co Inc .... D 317 781-4200
Indianapolis (G-8705)

La Grange Publishing Co Inc .... F 260 463-3243
Lagrange (G-10747)

Laconia Laser Engraving .... G 812 786-3641
Laconia (G-10506)

Largus Speedy Print Corp .... E 219 922-8414
Munster (G-12546)

Leader Publishing Co of Salem .... E 812 883-3281
Salem (G-14487)

Lincoln Printing Corporation .... A 260 424-5200
Fort Wayne (G-5186)

Louies Companies Inc .... G 765 448-4300
Lafayette (G-10639)

Lsc Communications Us LLC .... G 812 256-3396
Charlestown (G-1880)

Marketing Services Group Inc .... B 317 381-2268
Indianapolis (G-8838)

Minuteman Press .... F 317 209-1677
Indianapolis (G-8931)

Mossberg & Company Inc .... F 260 755-6283
Fort Wayne (G-5246)

MPS Printing Incorporated .... G 812 273-4446
Madison (G-11245)

Multi Packaging Solutions Inc .... G 317 241-2020
Indianapolis (G-8971)

Npp Packaging Graphics .... G 317 522-2010
Zionsville (G-17038)

Nussmeier Engraving Company .... E 812 425-1339
Evansville (G-4224)

Occasions Group Inc .... G 812 623-2225
Sunman (G-15442)

Offset One Inc .... F 260 456-8828
Fort Wayne (G-5282)

Omnisource Marketing Group Inc .... E 317 575-3300
Indianapolis (G-9050)

P413 Corporation .... G 317 769-0679
Zionsville (G-17039)

Paper Chase .... G 812 385-4757
Princeton (G-14009)

Pengad/West Inc .... E 765 286-3000
Muncie (G-12473)

Pentzer Printing Inc .... F 812 372-2896
Columbus (G-2375)

Perfect Plastic Printing Corp .... G 317 888-9447
Greenwood (G-6750)

Pharmaprinter Inc .... G 765 543-1520
West Lafayette (G-16619)

Phillip Westrick .... G 219 232-8337
Kentland (G-10161)

Pierce Oil Co Inc .... F 812 268-6356
Sullivan (G-15416)

Planks Printing Service Inc .... G 574 533-1739
Goshen (G-6240)

Pontiac Engraving .... G 630 834-4424
Plymouth (G-13805)

Pratt Visual Solutions Company .... E 800 428-7728
Indianapolis (G-9176)

Precision Label Incorporated .... F 812 877-3811
Terre Haute (G-15668)

Premiere Advertising .... G 317 722-2400
Indianapolis (G-9193)

Prentice Products Inc .... E 260 747-3195
Fort Wayne (G-5347)

Presstime Graphics Inc .... F 812 234-3815
Terre Haute (G-15669)

Prince Manufacturing Corp .... D 260 357-4484
Garrett (G-5874)

Printing Place Inc .... F 260 665-8444
Angola (G-289)

Printing Services Inc .... G 317 300-0363
Indianapolis (G-9208)

Printpack Inc .... C 812 663-5091
Greensburg (G-6625)

Priority Press Inc .... G 317 848-9695
Carmel (G-1730)

Priority Press Inc .... G 317 240-0103
Indianapolis (G-9212)

Priority Press Inc .... E 317 241-4234
Indianapolis (G-9211)

Pro Link .... G 765 225-1051
Crawfordsville (G-2605)

Progressive Printing Co Inc .... G 765 653-3814
Greencastle (G-6427)

Quality Imagination Corp .... G 317 753-0042
Indianapolis (G-9246)

Quality Printing of NW Ind .... G 219 322-6677
Schererville (G-14540)

R R Donnelley & Sons Company .... F 812 523-1800
Seymour (G-14679)

R R Donnelley & Sons Company .... D 574 267-7101
Warsaw (G-16414)

Rayco Marketing .... G 574 293-8416
Elkhart (G-3640)

Raymond Little Print Shop .... G 317 246-9083
Indianapolis (G-9271)

Reprocomm Inc .... G 765 472-5700
Peru (G-13598)

Rogers Marketing & Prtg Inc .... G 317 838-7203
Avon (G-549)

Rowland Printing Co Inc .... F 317 773-1829
Noblesville (G-13168)

Schutte Lithography Inc .... G 812 469-3500
Evansville (G-4300)

Seedline International Inc .... G 765 795-2500
Greencastle (G-6430)

Selby Publishing & Printing .... G 765 453-5417
Kokomo (G-10332)

Service Graphics Inc .... D 317 471-8246
Indianapolis (G-9408)

Sonoco Products Company .... D 812 526-5511
Edinburgh (G-3105)

Spectrum MGT Holdg Co LLC .... G 812 941-6899
New Albany (G-12817)

Stage Door Graphics .... G 317 398-9011
Shelbyville (G-14801)

Stoffel Seals Corporation .... E 845 353-3800
Angola (G-296)

Studio Printers .... G 574 772-0900
North Judson (G-13214)

Tabco Business Forms Inc .... G 812 882-2836
Vincennes (G-16157)

Taulman3d LLC .... G 401 996-8868
Linton (G-11047)

Thomas E Slade Inc .... F 812 437-5233
Evansville (G-4343)

Tko Enterprises Inc .... D 317 271-1398
Plainfield (G-13736)

Trident Engraving Inc .... G 812 282-2098
Jeffersonville (G-10065)

Triple Crown Media LLC .... G 574 533-2151
Goshen (G-6273)

V & P Printing .... G 260 495-3741
Fremont (G-5838)

Vinyl Creator .... G 260 318-5133
Wolcottville (G-16944)

Werzalit of America Inc .... D 814 362-3881
Syracuse (G-15492)

White River Press Inc .... G 317 507-4684
Anderson (G-217)

Whitewater Publications Inc .... F 765 647-4221
Brookville (G-1341)

Wise Business Forms Inc .... D 260 489-1561
Fort Wayne (G-5572)

Woodburn Graphics Inc .... F 812 232-0323
Terre Haute (G-15748)

Woodfield Printing Inc .... G 317 848-2000
Carmel (G-1808)

Writeguard Business Systems .... G 317 849-7292
Indianapolis (G-9793)

Zimmer Paper Products Del LLC .... D 317 263-3420
Indianapolis (G-9811)

Employee Codes: A=Over 500 employees, B=251-500
C=101-250, D=51-100, E=20-50, F=10-19, G=1-9

2024 Harris Indiana
Industrial Directory

PRINTING: Flexographic

Accu-Label Inc.. E 260 482-5223
  Fort Wayne (G-4720)
Tranter Graphics Inc.. D 574 834-2626
  Syracuse (G-15487)
Useful Products LLC....................................... E 877 304-9036
  Goodland (G-6083)

PRINTING: Gravure, Cards, Exc Greeting

I4 Identity LLC... G 317 662-0448
  Fishers (G-4541)

PRINTING: Gravure, Forms, Business

Viking Business Ventures Inc........................ G 260 489-7787
  Fort Wayne (G-5532)

PRINTING: Gravure, Labels

Gary Printing Inc.. G 219 886-1767
  Gary (G-5938)

PRINTING: Gravure, Rotogravure

Multi-Color Corporation................................. E 812 752-0586
  Scottsburg (G-14573)
Proedge Inc... E 219 552-9550
  Shelby (G-14727)
Stien Designs & Graphics Inc....................... G 260 347-9136
  Kendallville (G-10153)

PRINTING: Laser

Anthony Wyne Rhbltttion Ctr For................. C 317 972-1000
  Indianapolis (G-7522)
Lamco Finishers Inc....................................... E 317 471-1010
  Indianapolis (G-8717)
Laser Marking Technologies......................... G 812 852-7999
  Osgood (G-13411)
Shakour Industries Inc.................................. G 574 289-0100
  South Bend (G-15239)
Simplified Imaging LLC................................. G 219 663-5122
  Crown Point (G-2756)

PRINTING: Letterpress

Anchor Enterprises.. G 812 282-7220
  Jeffersonville (G-9933)
Apollo Prtg & Graphics Ctr Inc..................... E 574 287-3707
  South Bend (G-14948)
Bloomington Letter Shop.............................. G 812 824-6363
  Bloomington (G-812)
Burkert-Walton Inc... G 812 425-7157
  Evansville (G-3957)
Cecils Printing & Off Sups Inc...................... G 812 683-4416
  Huntingburg (G-7273)
Commercial Print Shop Inc........................... G 260 724-3722
  Decatur (G-2850)
Fehring F N & Son Printers........................... G 219 933-0439
  Valparaiso (G-15949)
Garco Graphics... G 219 980-1113
  Gary (G-5935)
Harmony Press Inc... E 800 525-3742
  Bourbon (G-1122)
Hartley J Company Inc.................................. G 812 376-9708
  Hartsville (G-7082)
Haywood Printing Co..................................... G 812 384-8639
  Bloomfield (G-747)
Haywood Printing Co Inc.............................. E 765 742-4085
  Indianapolis (G-8372)
Highway Press Inc.. G 812 283-6462
  Jeffersonville (G-9996)
Hoosier Jiffy Print.. G 260 563-8715
  Wabash (G-16193)
Kozs Quality Printing Inc.............................. G 219 696-6711
  Lowell (G-11166)

Maco Press Inc... G 317 846-5754
  Carmel (G-1690)
Mooney Copy Service Inc............................. G 812 423-6626
  Evansville (G-4210)
Mossberg & Company Inc............................ D 574 289-9253
  South Bend (G-15155)
Overgaards Artcraft Printers........................ G 574 234-8464
  South Bend (G-15183)
Parrot Press Inc.. E 260 422-6402
  Fort Wayne (G-5298)
Printcrafters Inc.. G 812 838-4106
  Mount Vernon (G-12315)
Printing Partners Inc..................................... D 317 635-2282
  Indianapolis (G-9206)
Rink Printing Company................................. E 574 232-7935
  South Bend (G-15220)
Tatman Inc... E 765 825-2164
  Connersville (G-2472)
TEC Photography... G 812 332-9847
  Bloomington (G-985)
Tippecanoe Press Inc.................................... G 317 392-1207
  Shelbyville (G-14806)
Town & Country Press Inc............................ F 574 936-9505
  Plymouth (G-13820)
Wayne Press Incorporated............................ G 260 744-3022
  Fort Wayne (G-5553)

PRINTING: Lithographic

3stax Printing & EMB LLC............................. G 317 612-7122
  Indianapolis (G-7389)
Accent Complex Inc...................................... G 574 522-2368
  Elkhart (G-3148)
Acclaim Graphics Inc.................................... G 812 424-5035
  Evansville (G-3866)
Accu-Label Inc.. E 260 482-5223
  Fort Wayne (G-4720)
Advantage Print Solutions........................... F 812 473-5945
  Evansville (G-3876)
Affordable Screen Printing EMB.................. G 574 278-7885
  Monticello (G-12133)
Aim Media Indiana Oper LLC....................... E 317 736-7101
  Franklin (G-5704)
Aim Media Indiana Oper LLC....................... E 317 462-5528
  Greenfield (G-6458)
Aj Screen Printing LLC.................................. G 574 274-4333
  Bremen (G-1171)
All Printing and Publications....................... G 260 636-2727
  Albion (G-17)
American Elite Printing LLC......................... G 765 513-0889
  Fishers (G-4639)
American Ex Trvl Rlted Svcs In.................... G 812 523-0106
  Seymour (G-14629)
Angies Printing LLC....................................... G 765 966-6237
  Richmond (G-14086)
Apparel Design Group................................... G 812 339-3355
  Bloomington (G-781)
Beast Custom Athletic Printing................... G 765 610-6802
  Fairmount (G-4408)
Belcher Printing Services............................. G 812 305-1093
  Evansville (G-3913)
Blue Print Specialties Inc............................. G 765 742-6976
  Lafayette (G-10539)
Blue Print University Inc.............................. G 317 446-8715
  Speedway (G-15333)
Bright Corp.. F 765 642-3114
  Griffith (G-6797)
Browns Simply Printings............................... G 317 490-7493
  Mooresville (G-12196)
Bryan Janky.. G 708 921-7676
  Valparaiso (G-15922)
Business Connection LLC............................ G 219 762-5660
  Portage (G-13850)

Cave Company Printing Inc......................... G 812 863-4333
  Bloomfield (G-743)
Cenveo Worldwide Limited.......................... D 800 995-9500
  New Albany (G-12710)
Chameleon Lifestyles LLC............................ G 317 468-3246
  Greenfield (G-6479)
City South Bend Building Corp................... G 574 235-9977
  South Bend (G-14973)
Ckmt Associates Inc...................................... F 219 924-2820
  Hammond (G-6902)
Classic LLC... G 260 241-4353
  Fort Wayne (G-4854)
Cnhi LLC.. G 812 944-6481
  Jeffersonville (G-9955)
Coachs Connection Inc................................ G 260 356-0400
  Huntington (G-7306)
Colormax Digital Imaging Inc..................... F 812 477-3805
  Evansville (G-3975)
Community Holdings Indiana Inc............... G 812 663-3111
  Greensburg (G-6585)
Community Holdings Indiana Inc............... G 765 482-4650
  Lebanon (G-10885)
Community Holdings Indiana Inc............... G 574 722-5000
  Logansport (G-11068)
Copy Solutions Inc.. G 260 436-2679
  Fort Wayne (G-4874)
Courier Printing Co Allen Cnty................... G 260 627-2728
  Grabill (G-6293)
Crescendo Inc... G 812 829-4759
  Spencer (G-15344)
Crossroads Imprints Inc............................... G 765 482-2931
  Lebanon (G-10887)
Data Mail Incorporated................................. E 812 424-7835
  Evansville (G-4007)
Delp Printing & Mailing Inc......................... G 317 872-9744
  Indianapolis (G-7963)
Delphos Herald of Indiana Inc.................... E 812 537-0063
  Lawrenceburg (G-10833)
Digital Image Editions.................................. G 812 876-4770
  Bloomington (G-856)
Discover Putnam County.............................. G 765 653-4026
  Greencastle (G-6403)
Dla Document Services................................ G 812 854-1465
  Crane (G-2537)
Eight Ten Twelve LLC.................................... G 317 773-8532
  Indianapolis (G-8065)
Em Printing & Embroidery LLC................... G 812 373-0082
  Columbus (G-2297)
Evansvlle Print Specialist Inc...................... G 812 423-5831
  Evansville (G-4060)
Excell Color Graphics Inc............................. E 260 482-2720
  Fort Wayne (G-4967)
Faris Mailing Inc... F 317 246-3315
  Indianapolis (G-8167)
Fedex Office & Print Svcs Inc...................... G 317 974-0378
  Indianapolis (G-8172)
Fedex Office & Print Svcs Inc...................... G 317 917-1529
  Indianapolis (G-8173)
Fedex Office & Print Svcs Inc...................... G 317 631-6862
  Indianapolis (G-8178)
Fedex Office & Print Svcs Inc...................... F 765 449-4950
  Lafayette (G-10579)
Firehouse Printing LLC................................. G 812 547-3109
  Tell City (G-15503)
Four Star Screen Printing LLC..................... G 765 533-3006
  New Castle (G-12863)
Friends of Third World Inc.......................... G 260 422-6821
  Fort Wayne (G-5013)
Gannett Media Corp...................................... C 765 423-5512
  Lafayette (G-10585)
Giant Paw Prints Inc..................................... G 219 241-9299
  Valparaiso (G-15955)

PRODUCT SECTION
PRINTING: Lithographic

Giant Paw Prints Rescue.................. G 219 241-9299
  Westville (G-16760)
Goatee Shirt Printing LLC............... G 219 916-2443
  Valparaiso (G-15958)
Grace Amazing Graphics................. G 812 737-2841
  Laconia (G-10505)
Gracies Paw Prints........................... G 317 910-9969
  Fishers (G-4532)
Granger Gazette Inc......................... G 574 277-2679
  Granger (G-6350)
Graphic Expressions........................ G 219 663-2085
  Merrillville (G-11520)
Gryphon Print Studio LLC................ G 574 514-1644
  South Bend (G-15049)
Hatch Prints.. G 312 952-1908
  South Bend (G-15059)
Haywood Printing Co........................ G 812 384-8639
  Bloomfield (G-747)
Hennessey Montage Prints............. G 317 841-7562
  Carmel (G-1654)
Herff Jones LLC.................................. E 317 612-3400
  Indianapolis (G-8384)
Hiatt Enterprises Inc......................... G 765 289-2700
  Muncie (G-12416)
Hiatt Enterprises Inc......................... F 765 289-7756
  Muncie (G-12415)
Hinen Printing Co............................... G 260 248-8984
  Columbia City (G-2150)
Hoffman Quality Graphics............... G 574 223-5738
  Rochester (G-14296)
Hoosier Times Inc............................... C 812 275-3372
  Bedford (G-641)
Hoosier Times Inc............................... C 812 331-4270
  Bloomington (G-882)
Impressions LLC................................. G 765 490-2575
  Lafayette (G-10604)
Indiana Business People LLC............ G 317 455-4040
  Indianapolis (G-8474)
Indiana Newspapers LLC.................... D 812 886-9955
  Vincennes (G-16131)
Indiana Newspapers LLC.................... A 317 444-4000
  Indianapolis (G-8487)
Indy Color Printing LLC..................... G 317 371-8829
  Indianapolis (G-8524)
Inline Shirt Printing LLC................... G 765 647-6356
  Brookville (G-1326)
Innerprint Inc..................................... G 317 509-6511
  Fishers (G-4643)
Instant Warehouse........................... G 765 342-3430
  Martinsville (G-11406)
Insty-Prints.. G 317 788-1504
  Indianapolis (G-8564)
J A Davis... G 812 354-9129
  Petersburg (G-13616)
J4 Printing LLC.................................. G 260 417-5382
  Fort Wayne (G-5127)
Jackson Group Inc............................ C 317 791-9000
  Indianapolis (G-8614)
Jacob Adams..................................... G 765 564-2314
  Delphi (G-2900)
Jacobs Company LLC....................... F 317 818-8500
  Carmel (G-1676)
JC Printing.. G 574 721-9000
  Logansport (G-11085)
Joans Tshirt Printing LLC................ G 812 934-2616
  Batesville (G-593)
Journal & Chronicle Inc.................... G 812 752-5060
  Scottsburg (G-14566)
Just Install LLC................................. G 317 607-3911
  Noblesville (G-13115)
K Irpcheadstart Program................. G 219 345-2011
  Demotte (G-2919)

Kankakee Valley Publishing Co........ G 219 866-5111
  Rensselaer (G-14056)
Kasting Printing Service.................. G 317 881-9411
  Indianapolis (G-8662)
Kendallville Custom Printing........... F 260 347-9233
  Kendallville (G-10125)
Kile Enterprises Inc.......................... F 317 844-6629
  Carmel (G-1681)
Kim Print LLC..................................... G 812 223-5333
  Indianapolis (G-8683)
Kinkos Inc... G 765 449-4950
  Lafayette (G-10620)
Knots & Spots Inc............................. G 574 946-6000
  Winamac (G-16865)
Kpc Media Group Inc........................ F 260 426-2640
  Fort Wayne (G-5158)
Kpc Media Group Inc........................ C 260 347-0400
  Kendallville (G-10130)
L and P Brothers............................... G 219 313-6946
  Hammond (G-6967)
La Grange Publishing Co Inc........... F 260 463-3243
  Lagrange (G-10747)
Langley Fine Art Prints.................... G 219 872-0087
  Long Beach (G-11123)
Lc Screen Printing LLC.................... G 812 687-7476
  Montgomery (G-12110)
Legacy Screen Prtg Prmtons LLC... F 219 262-4000
  Michigan City (G-11631)
Lithocraft Inc.................................... E 812 948-1608
  New Albany (G-12764)
Longhorn Marketing Group............ G 765 650-4430
  Frankfort (G-5680)
Lsc Communications Us LLC.......... G 574 267-7101
  Warsaw (G-16388)
Madison Courier................................ E 812 265-3641
  Madison (G-11237)
Marketing and Retail Sales............. G 812 883-1813
  Salem (G-14489)
Marketing Kreativo.......................... G 574 370-5410
  Goshen (G-6213)
Masco Corporation of Indiana........ E 317 848-1812
  Indianapolis (G-8847)
Maury Boyd & Associates Inc......... F 317 849-6110
  Indianapolis (G-8853)
Maximum Business Solutions Inc... G 219 933-1809
  Hammond (G-6978)
Mecom Ltd Inc................................... D 317 218-2600
  Indianapolis (G-8868)
Messenger LLC.................................. C 260 925-1700
  Auburn (G-405)
Metro Printed Products Inc............. G 317 885-0077
  Greenwood (G-6738)
Mid America Print Council Inc........ G 765 463-3971
  Lafayette (G-10647)
Mignone Communications Incorporated C 260 358-0266
  Huntington (G-7344)
Mik Mocha Prints LLC....................... G 812 376-8891
  Columbus (G-2355)
Minuteman Press............................. F 317 209-1677
  Indianapolis (G-8931)
Mito-Craft Inc................................... G 574 287-4555
  South Bend (G-15152)
Movie Poster Print........................... G 812 679-7301
  Columbus (G-2358)
Multi Packaging Solutions Inc........ G 317 241-2020
  Indianapolis (G-8971)
Muncie Novelty Company Inc......... D 765 288-8301
  Muncie (G-12463)
Nelmar Printing Co........................... G 317 504-7840
  Avon (G-539)
News-Banner Publications Inc........ E 260 824-0224
  Bluffton (G-1046)

Nielsen Company............................. G 812 889-3493
  Lexington (G-10979)
Nussmeier Engraving Company..... E 812 425-1339
  Evansville (G-4224)
Ordonez Construccion Svcs LLC... G 317 771-1213
  Indianapolis (G-9068)
Pack Printing LLC............................ G 317 437-9779
  Indianapolis (G-9083)
Panda Prints..................................... G 574 322-1050
  Bristol (G-1282)
Pandora Printing.............................. G 574 551-9624
  Warsaw (G-16408)
Parrot Press Inc............................... E 260 422-6402
  Fort Wayne (G-5298)
PC Imprints LLC................................ G 812 622-0855
  Poseyville (G-13980)
Pengad/West Inc.............................. E 765 286-3000
  Muncie (G-12473)
Phan Gear Prints LLC...................... G 260 450-2539
  Fort Wayne (G-5308)
Piccolo Printing................................ G 888 901-8648
  Evansville (G-4243)
Pinpoint Printer............................... G 812 577-0630
  Aurora (G-452)
Plastic Cardz LLC............................. G 260 431-6380
  Fort Wayne (G-5317)
Posters 2 Prints LLC....................... E 317 414-8972
  Indianapolis (G-9166)
Posters 2 Prints LLC....................... G 800 598-5837
  Indianapolis (G-9165)
Posters 2 Prints LLC....................... G 317 769-3784
  Zionsville (G-17043)
Precision Print LLC.......................... G 765 789-8799
  Albany (G-15)
Prentice Products Inc..................... E 260 747-3195
  Fort Wayne (G-5347)
Primal Prints LLC............................. G 260 494-8435
  Huntertown (G-7264)
Princeton Publishing Inc................. G 812 385-2525
  Princeton (G-14010)
Print 2 Finish LLC............................ G 812 256-5515
  Charlestown (G-1891)
Print It Inc... G 317 774-6848
  Indianapolis (G-9200)
Print It Wear It Inc.......................... G 317 946-1456
  Shelbyville (G-14788)
Print My Merch LLC......................... G 765 269-6772
  Mishawaka (G-11979)
Print Sharp Enterprises Inc........... G 317 899-2754
  Indianapolis (G-9203)
Print2promo Group Inc.................. G 219 778-4649
  Rolling Prairie (G-14369)
Printed By Erik Inc.......................... G 574 295-1203
  Elkhart (G-3621)
Printing Partners East Inc............. G 317 356-2522
  Indianapolis (G-9207)
Printing Technologies Inc.............. E 800 428-3786
  Indianapolis (G-9209)
Printsource...................................... G 317 507-6526
  Indianapolis (G-9210)
Pro Prints... G 812 932-3800
  Batesville (G-600)
Professional Design LLC................ G 765 529-1590
  New Castle (G-12879)
Proforma Print Promo Group........ G 574 931-2941
  South Bend (G-15207)
Publishers Consulting Corp........... F 219 874-4245
  Michigan City (G-11652)
Quality Printing of NW Ind............ G 219 322-6677
  Schererville (G-14540)
Rasure Prints LLC............................ G 812 454-6222
  Evansville (G-4273)

Employee Codes: A=Over 500 employees, B=251-500
C=101-250, D=51-100, E=20-50, F=10-19, G=1-9

2024 Harris Indiana
Industrial Directory

PRINTING: Lithographic

Redrum Incorporated .... G 859 489-1516
  New Albany (G-12804)
Rightcolors LLC .... G 812 675-8775
  Bedford (G-668)
Rock Hard Stnes Cstm Prtg Rhns .... G 219 613-0112
  Merrillville (G-11554)
Ronnie Elmore Jr. .... G 765 719-1681
  Cloverdale (G-2095)
Roteck Enterprises Inc .... G 219 322-4132
  Dyer (G-2982)
Scott Printing LLC .... G 812 306-7477
  Evansville (G-4301)
Screenbroidery LLC .... E 317 546-1900
  Noblesville (G-13173)
Shadow Screen Printing .... G 812 234-3104
  Terre Haute (G-15690)
Sharon K Utter .... G 765 349-8991
  Martinsville (G-11427)
Shirt Print Ave .... G 812 882-9610
  Vincennes (G-16154)
Small Town Printers LLC .... G 812 596-1536
  Elizabeth (G-3130)
Smith & Butterfield Co Inc .... F 812 422-3261
  Evansville (G-4320)
Smith & Butterfield Co Inc .... G 812 422-3261
  Evansville (G-4321)
Solutions For Print LLC .... G 812 584-2701
  Fountaintown (G-5616)
Speedy-Screen LLC .... G 317 910-0724
  Indianapolis (G-9478)
Starlight Printing .... G 812 486-3905
  Montgomery (G-12124)
State Cleaning Solutions .... G 812 336-4817
  Indianapolis (G-9500)
Stines Printing Inc .... G 260 356-5994
  Huntington (G-7371)
Stump Printing Co .... F 260 723-5171
  South Whitley (G-15329)
Success Express .... G 317 750-1747
  Rockville (G-14357)
Summit LLC .... G 574 287-7468
  Elkhart (G-3705)
Swagerle Screen Printing .... G 812 232-6947
  Terre Haute (G-15719)
T and J Printing Supply .... G 317 986-4765
  Indianapolis (G-9544)
T-Flyerz Printing and Prom LLC .... G 260 729-7392
  Bryant (G-1437)
Team Gear Printing LLC .... G 765 935-4748
  Richmond (G-14211)
Team Gear Printing LLC .... G 765 977-2995
  Richmond (G-14212)
Templeton Myers Inc .... E 317 898-6688
  Indianapolis (G-9575)
Th Custom Printing .... G 765 251-3986
  Summitville (G-15434)
The Deaton Family Company .... D 815 726-6234
  Auburn (G-429)
The Office Shop Inc .... E 812 934-5611
  Batesville (G-607)
This That EMB Screen Prtg LLC .... G 317 541-8548
  Indianapolis (G-9591)
Thomas E Slade Inc .... F 812 437-5233
  Evansville (G-4343)
Thomas Madison .... G 312 625-9152
  Michigan City (G-11678)
Times .... E 765 659-4622
  Frankfort (G-5698)
Tints & Prints By Tierney LLC .... G 317 769-5895
  Zionsville (G-17057)
Tko Enterprises Inc .... D 317 271-1398
  Plainfield (G-13736)

Tonya Gerhardt .... G 260 434-1370
  Fort Wayne (G-5493)
Triple Crown Media LLC .... G 574 533-2151
  Goshen (G-6273)
Truth Publishing Company Inc .... G 765 653-5151
  Greencastle (G-6434)
United Hero Apparel Printing .... G 812 306-1998
  Evansville (G-4362)
United Parcel Service Inc .... G 317 776-9494
  Noblesville (G-13189)
University Publishing Corp .... E 812 339-9033
  Bloomington (G-1004)
V & P Printing .... G 260 495-3741
  Fremont (G-5838)
Valley Screen Process Co Inc .... D 574 256-0901
  Mishawaka (G-12020)
Voice of God Recordings Inc .... D 812 246-2137
  Jeffersonville (G-10069)
Wabash Plain Dealer Co LLC .... E 260 563-2131
  Wabash (G-16221)
WAr - LLC- Westville Prtg .... G 219 785-2821
  Westville (G-16765)
Whitewater Publications Inc .... F 765 647-4221
  Brookville (G-1341)
William E Steiner .... G 317 575-9018
  Carmel (G-1806)
Wise Business Forms Inc .... D 260 489-1561
  Fort Wayne (G-5572)
Work Field Collaborative Inc .... G 360 581-9476
  Indianapolis (G-9789)
Writeguard Business Systems .... G 317 849-7292
  Indianapolis (G-9793)

PRINTING: Manmade Fiber & Silk, Broadwoven Fabric

Graphic22 Inc .... G 219 921-5409
  Chesterton (G-1930)

PRINTING: Offset

323ink LLC .... G 812 282-3620
  Jeffersonville (G-9920)
A-1 Graphics Inc .... G 765 289-1851
  Muncie (G-12332)
A-R-T Printing .... G 812 235-8600
  Terre Haute (G-15529)
AC Printing Inc .... G 708 418-9100
  Highland (G-7118)
Accuprint of Kentuckiana Inc .... G 812 944-8603
  New Albany (G-12685)
Ace Printing .... G 812 275-3412
  Bedford (G-617)
AG Apparel and Screen Prtg LLC .... G 260 483-3817
  Fort Wayne (G-4732)
AG Printing Specialists LLC .... G 866 445-6824
  Lafayette (G-10517)
All 4u Printing LLC .... G 317 845-2955
  Morgantown (G-12251)
Allegra Marketing Print Mail .... G 317 643-6248
  Indianapolis (G-7479)
Allen C Terhune & Associates .... G 765 948-4164
  Fairmount (G-4407)
Allison Pymnt Systems LLC DBA .... C 317 808-2400
  Indianapolis (G-7485)
AMA Design Print .... G 219 462-8683
  Valparaiso (G-15897)
American Business Forms I .... G 317 852-8956
  Brownsburg (G-1345)
American Printing .... G 219 836-5600
  Munster (G-12530)
American Printing & Advg Inc .... F 219 937-1844
  Hammond (G-6874)

American Printing Company .... G 574 533-5399
  Goshen (G-6092)
Anchor Enterprises .... G 812 282-7220
  Jeffersonville (G-9933)
Apple Press Inc .... G 317 253-7752
  Indianapolis (G-7530)
Augustin Prtg & Design Svcs .... G 765 966-7130
  Richmond (G-14088)
Ave Maria Press Inc .... D 574 287-2831
  Notre Dame (G-13315)
Aztec Printing Inc .... G 812 422-1462
  Wadesville (G-16226)
Bartel Printing Company Inc .... G 574 267-7421
  Warsaw (G-16317)
Baugh Enterprises Inc .... F 812 334-8189
  Bloomington (G-796)
Baxter Printing Incorporated .... G 219 923-1999
  Griffith (G-6793)
Bhar Printing Incorporated .... G 317 899-1020
  Indianapolis (G-7622)
Biela Printing .... G 219 874-8094
  Michigan City (G-11581)
Bills Printing .... G 765 962-7674
  Richmond (G-14097)
Bizcard .... G 317 436-8649
  Greenfield (G-6471)
Blasted Works .... G 574 583-3211
  Monticello (G-12138)
Bloomington Letter Shop .... G 812 824-6363
  Bloomington (G-812)
Bobilyn Printing .... G 219 926-7087
  Westville (G-16756)
Bowen Printing Inc .... G 574 936-3924
  Plymouth (G-13759)
Boy-Conn Printers Incorporated .... G 219 462-2665
  Valparaiso (G-15920)
Brainstorm Print LLC .... G 317 466-1600
  Indianapolis (G-7670)
Bredensteiner Imaging Inc .... G 317 921-1900
  Indianapolis (G-7674)
Brinkman Press Inc .... G 317 722-0305
  Indianapolis (G-7686)
Broadway Press LLC .... G 765 644-8813
  Anderson (G-85)
Bryant Printing LLC .... G 765 521-3379
  New Castle (G-12853)
Budget Printing Centers Inc .... G 812 282-8832
  Jeffersonville (G-9948)
Buis Enterprises Inc .... G 317 839-7394
  Plainfield (G-13663)
Burkert-Walton Inc .... G 812 425-7157
  Evansville (G-3957)
C J P Corporation .... G 219 924-1685
  Highland (G-7127)
C R Graphics .... G 317 881-6192
  Greenwood (G-6679)
Campbell Printing Company .... G 219 866-5913
  Rensselaer (G-14046)
Cardcarecom .... G 574 315-5294
  Mishawaka (G-11858)
Carlton Ventures Inc .... G 317 637-2590
  Indianapolis (G-7746)
Cecils Printing & Off Sups Inc .... G 812 683-4416
  Huntingburg (G-7273)
Chesterton Printing Co .... G 219 250-2896
  Chesterton (G-1910)
Chromasource Inc .... C 260 420-3000
  Columbia City (G-2130)
Circle Printing LLC .... G 812 663-7367
  Greensburg (G-6584)
CJ Printing .... G 219 924-1685
  Hammond (G-6900)

PRODUCT SECTION

PRINTING: Offset

Classic Graphics Inc .... F 260 482-3487
  Fort Wayne *(G-4853)*
Clondalkin Pharma & Healthcare Inc ...... A 336 292-4555
  Indianapolis *(G-7824)*
Commercial Print Shop Inc .... G 260 724-3722
  Decatur *(G-2850)*
Complete Prtg Solutions Inc .... G 812 285-9200
  Jeffersonville *(G-9958)*
Consolidated Printing Svcs Inc .... G 765 468-6033
  Farmland *(G-4424)*
Copies Plus LLC .... G 317 545-5083
  Indianapolis *(G-7871)*
Copy-Print Shop Inc .... E 765 447-6868
  Lafayette *(G-10556)*
Copymat Services Inc .... G 765 743-5995
  Lafayette *(G-10557)*
Cornerstone Business Prtg LLC .... G 574 642-4060
  Middlebury *(G-11705)*
CPC .... G 812 358-5010
  Brownstown *(G-1420)*
Craigs Printing Co .... G 812 358-5010
  Brownstown *(G-1421)*
Creative Concept Ventures Inc .... G 812 282-9442
  Jeffersonville *(G-9964)*
Crown Point Printing LLC .... G 219 226-0900
  Crown Point *(G-2670)*
Crystal Graphics Inc .... G 317 535-9202
  Whiteland *(G-16780)*
Custom Forms Inc .... F 765 463-6162
  Lafayette *(G-10565)*
D & E Printing Company Inc .... G 317 852-9048
  Brownsburg *(G-1362)*
D & M Printing Inc .... G 812 847-4837
  Linton *(G-11034)*
D-J Printing Specialists Inc .... G 219 465-1164
  Valparaiso *(G-15935)*
Damalak Printing Inc .... G 317 896-5337
  Westfield *(G-16683)*
Data Print Initiatives LLC .... G 260 489-2665
  Fort Wayne *(G-4905)*
Digital Printing Incorporated .... G 812 265-2205
  Madison *(G-11214)*
Discount Copy Services Inc .... G 317 773-8783
  Noblesville *(G-13073)*
Diverse Sales Solutions LLC .... G 317 514-2403
  Indianapolis *(G-7981)*
Diversfied Cmmnctons Group Inc .... F 317 755-3191
  Indianapolis *(G-7983)*
Diversified Bus Systems Inc .... G 317 254-8668
  Indianapolis *(G-7984)*
Diversity Press LLC .... G 317 241-4234
  Indianapolis *(G-7986)*
Docu-Tech Services Inc .... G 219 769-7115
  Merrillville *(G-11508)*
Doerr Printing Co .... G 317 568-0135
  Indianapolis *(G-7994)*
Dove Printing Services Inc .... G 317 469-7546
  Indianapolis *(G-7999)*
Dps Printing LLC .... G 260 503-9681
  Columbia City *(G-2139)*
Dragon Printing LLC .... G 317 919-9619
  Greenwood *(G-6690)*
Drs Graphix Group Inc .... G 317 569-1855
  Indianapolis *(G-8011)*
Duley Press Inc .... E 574 259-5203
  Mishawaka *(G-11887)*
Dynamark Graphics Group Inc .... G 317 569-1855
  Indianapolis *(G-8024)*
Dynamark Graphics Group Inc .... E 317 328-2555
  Indianapolis *(G-8023)*
E D H Inc .... G 219 712-5145
  Lake Station *(G-10772)*

Economy Offset Printers Inc .... G 574 534-6270
  Goshen *(G-6129)*
Ed Sons Inc .... F 317 897-8821
  Indianapolis *(G-8051)*
Elite Printing Inc .... G 317 781-9701
  Indianapolis *(G-8093)*
Elite Printing Inc .... G 317 257-2744
  Indianapolis *(G-8094)*
Envision Graphics Inc .... G 260 925-2266
  Auburn *(G-388)*
EP Graphics Inc .... C 877 589-2145
  Berne *(G-710)*
Epi Printers Inc .... D 317 579-4870
  Indianapolis *(G-8129)*
Evansville Bindery Inc .... G 812 423-2222
  Evansville *(G-4048)*
Evansville Lithograph Co Inc .... G 812 477-0506
  Evansville *(G-4052)*
Ewing Printing Company Inc .... F 812 882-2415
  Vincennes *(G-16120)*
Excel Business Printing Inc .... G 317 259-1075
  Indianapolis *(G-8149)*
Express Press Inc .... G 812 882-3278
  Vincennes *(G-16122)*
Express Press Indiana Inc .... G 219 874-2223
  South Bend *(G-15022)*
Express Press Indiana Inc .... E 574 277-3355
  South Bend *(G-15023)*
Express Printing & Copying .... G 219 762-3508
  Portage *(G-13862)*
F Robert Gardner Co Inc .... G 317 634-2333
  Indianapolis *(G-8161)*
Falls Cities Printing Inc .... F 812 949-9051
  New Albany *(G-12728)*
Fast Print Incorporated .... G 260 484-5487
  Fort Wayne *(G-4976)*
Faulkenberg Printing Co Inc .... F 317 638-1359
  Franklin *(G-5730)*
Fehring F N & Son Printers .... G 219 933-0439
  Valparaiso *(G-15949)*
Figtree Print LLC .... G 978 503-1779
  Evansville *(G-4068)*
Fineline Digital Group Inc .... E 317 872-4490
  Indianapolis *(G-8187)*
Fineline Graphics Incorporated .... D 317 872-4490
  Indianapolis *(G-8188)*
First Quality Printing Inc .... G 317 506-8633
  Indianapolis *(G-8195)*
First Quality Printing Center .... G 317 546-5531
  Indianapolis *(G-8196)*
Four Part Inc .... G 219 926-7777
  Chesterton *(G-1928)*
Four Star Printing .... G 765 620-9728
  Frankton *(G-5791)*
Garco Graphics .... G 219 980-1113
  Gary *(G-5935)*
Garrett Prtg & Graphics Inc .... G 812 422-6005
  Evansville *(G-4084)*
Gary Printing Inc .... G 219 886-1767
  Gary *(G-5938)*
Gen-Twelve Corporation .... G 260 483-7075
  Fort Wayne *(G-5018)*
Get Printing Inc .... G 574 533-6827
  Goshen *(G-6147)*
Gkb Holdings Inc .... E 260 471-7744
  Fort Wayne *(G-5025)*
Go Print LLC .... G 765 778-1111
  Pendleton *(G-13534)*
Goetz Printing .... G 812 243-2086
  Terre Haute *(G-15600)*
Gold Star Printing LLC .... G 260 768-7920
  Shipshewana *(G-14848)*

Gospel Echoes Team Association .... G 574 533-0221
  Goshen *(G-6153)*
Grafcor Inc .... F 765 966-7030
  Richmond *(G-14127)*
Graphic Expressions Inc .... G 317 577-9622
  Fishers *(G-4535)*
Graphics Unlimited .... G 765 288-6816
  Muncie *(G-12405)*
Green Banner Publications Inc .... E 812 967-3176
  Borden *(G-1109)*
Greencastle Offset Inc .... G 765 653-4026
  Greencastle *(G-6406)*
Greenline Screen Printing .... G 317 572-1155
  Indianapolis *(G-8321)*
Greensburg Printing Co Inc .... G 812 663-8265
  Greensburg *(G-6598)*
Hardesty Printing Co Inc .... F 574 267-7591
  Warsaw *(G-16374)*
Hardesty Printing Co Inc .... F 574 223-4553
  Rochester *(G-14293)*
Hardingpoorman Inc .... C 317 876-3355
  Indianapolis *(G-8359)*
Hardingpoorman Group Inc .... G 317 876-3355
  Indianapolis *(G-8360)*
Harmony Press Inc .... E 800 525-3742
  Bourbon *(G-1122)*
Hartford City News Times .... F 765 348-0110
  Winchester *(G-16889)*
Haywood Printing Co Inc .... E 765 742-4085
  Indianapolis *(G-8372)*
Heckley Printing Inc .... G 260 434-1370
  Fort Wayne *(G-5058)*
Hetty Incorporated .... G 219 933-0833
  Hammond *(G-6945)*
Hetty Incorporated .... G 219 836-2517
  Munster *(G-12539)*
Highway Press Inc .... G 812 283-6462
  Jeffersonville *(G-9996)*
Home Mountain Publishing Co Inc .... E 219 462-6601
  Valparaiso *(G-15962)*
Home News Enterprises LLC .... B 800 876-7811
  Columbus *(G-2318)*
Hoosier Jiffy Print .... G 260 563-8715
  Wabash *(G-16193)*
Hoosier Press Inc .... G 765 649-3716
  Anderson *(G-129)*
Horoho Printing Company Inc .... G 765 452-8862
  Kokomo *(G-10282)*
Howard Print Shop LLC .... G 765 453-6161
  Kokomo *(G-10283)*
Huelseman Printing Co .... G 765 647-3947
  Brookton *(G-1324)*
Hugh K Eagan .... G 574 269-5411
  Warsaw *(G-16375)*
Iiiimpressions That Count Inc .... G 317 423-0581
  Indianapolis *(G-8457)*
Impression Printing .... G 765 342-6977
  Martinsville *(G-11403)*
Impressions Printing Inc .... G 812 634-2574
  Jasper *(G-9843)*
Impressive Printing .... G 812 913-1101
  New Albany *(G-12745)*
In-Print .... G 219 956-3001
  Wheatfield *(G-16768)*
Infinitprint Solutions Inc .... E 765 962-1507
  Richmond *(G-14139)*
Ink Spot .... G 260 482-4492
  Fort Wayne *(G-5107)*
Ink Spot Tattoo .... G 260 244-0025
  Columbia City *(G-2156)*
Innovative Printing Svcs Inc .... G 812 443-1007
  Brazil *(G-1147)*

Employee Codes: A=Over 500 employees, B=251-500
C=101-250, D=51-100, E=20-50, F=10-19, G=1-9

2024 Harris Indiana
Industrial Directory

1389

PRINTING: Offset — PRODUCT SECTION

Inter Print At Ions .... G 765 404-0887
  Brownsburg (G-1376)
International Label Mfg LLC .... F 812 235-5071
  Terre Haute (G-15618)
J & J Printing Co .... G 765 642-6642
  Anderson (G-137)
Jam Printing Inc .... F 765 649-9292
  Anderson (G-138)
James David Inc .... G 260 744-0579
  Roanoke (G-14271)
Jem Printing Inc .... G 812 376-9264
  Columbus (G-2330)
Jewett Printing LLC .... G 812 232-0087
  Farmersburg (G-4419)
Jkp Printing Inc .... G 574 246-1650
  South Bend (G-15092)
Jomark Inc .... F 248 478-2600
  Angola (G-265)
Josh Rowland .... G 574 596-6754
  Noblesville (G-13114)
JP Ownership Group Inc .... D 317 791-1122
  Indianapolis (G-8643)
Kalems Enterprises Inc .... G 317 399-1645
  Indianapolis (G-8658)
Kc Designs .... G 812 876-4020
  Bloomington (G-899)
Keefer Printing Company Inc .... E 260 424-4543
  Fort Wayne (G-5144)
Kevin M Walters .... G 317 565-9564
  Fishers (G-4554)
Kill-N-Em Inc .... G 574 233-6655
  South Bend (G-15100)
Kistner Enterprises Inc .... G 317 773-7733
  Noblesville (G-13123)
Kozs Quality Printing Inc .... G 219 696-6711
  Lowell (G-11166)
L & L Press Inc .... F 765 664-3162
  Marion (G-11305)
Lagnaippe LLC .... G 812 288-9291
  New Albany (G-12762)
Lagwana Printing Inc .... G 260 463-4901
  Shipshewana (G-14860)
Lagwana Printing Inc .... G 260 463-4901
  Lagrange (G-10748)
Largus Speedy Print Corp .... E 219 922-8414
  Munster (G-12546)
Lbw Printing & Dtp .... G 260 347-9053
  Kendallville (G-10132)
Leader Publishing Co of Salem .... E 812 883-3281
  Salem (G-14487)
Leed Samples-Fulfillment .... F 812 867-4340
  Evansville (G-4163)
Lesha and Wade Printing Svcs .... G 317 738-4992
  Franklin (G-5752)
Light & Ink Corporation .... G 812 421-1400
  Evansville (G-4168)
Light Printing Co .... G 815 429-3724
  Brook (G-1305)
Lincoln Printing Corporation .... A 260 424-5200
  Fort Wayne (G-5186)
Link Printing Services LLC .... G 317 902-6374
  Indianapolis (G-8765)
Link Printing Services LLC .... G 317 826-9852
  Indianapolis (G-8764)
Litho Press Inc .... E 317 634-6468
  Indianapolis (G-8771)
Lithogrphic Communications LLC .... E 219 924-9779
  Munster (G-12548)
Lithotone Inc .... E 574 294-5521
  Elkhart (G-3497)
Livings Graphics Inc .... G 574 264-4114
  Elkhart (G-3498)

Ludwick Graphics Inc .... G 574 233-2165
  South Bend (G-15131)
Maco Press Inc .... G 317 846-5754
  Carmel (G-1690)
Maco Reprograhics LLC .... G 812 464-8108
  Evansville (G-4183)
Maple Leaf Graphics Inc .... G 317 410-0321
  Carmel (G-1691)
Maple Leaf Printing Co Inc .... G 574 534-7790
  Goshen (G-6212)
McCormack Prtg Impressions Inc .... G 765 675-9556
  Tipton (G-15783)
McCrory Publishing .... G 260 485-1812
  Fort Wayne (G-5211)
MD Laird Inc .... G 317 842-6338
  Greenwood (G-6737)
Metropolitan Printing Svcs LLC .... C 812 332-7279
  Bloomington (G-917)
Mid West Digital Express Inc .... F 317 733-1214
  Zionsville (G-17033)
Midwest Color Printing LLC .... G 812 822-2947
  Bloomington (G-919)
Midwest Empire LLC .... G 317 786-7446
  Indianapolis (G-8908)
Midwest Graphics Inc .... E 317 780-4600
  Indianapolis (G-8910)
Midwest Printing .... G 812 238-1641
  Terre Haute (G-15645)
Mike Mugler .... G 812 945-4266
  Clarksville (G-2023)
Miles Printing Corporation .... F 317 243-8571
  Indianapolis (G-8919)
Milliner Printing Company Inc .... G 260 563-5717
  Wabash (G-16203)
Minute Print It Inc .... G 765 482-9019
  Lebanon (G-10916)
Mitchell-Fleming Printing Inc .... F 317 462-5467
  Greenfield (G-6529)
Mla Printing Inc .... G 219 398-8888
  Merrillville (G-11540)
Moeller Printing Co Inc .... E 317 353-2224
  Indianapolis (G-8944)
Montgomery & Associates Inc .... F 219 879-0088
  Michigan City (G-11641)
Mooney Copy Service Inc .... G 812 423-6626
  Evansville (G-4210)
Moore Services Incorporated .... G 317 571-9800
  Carmel (G-1702)
Moore-Langen Printing Company Inc .... D 812 234-1585
  Terre Haute (G-15648)
Morris Printing Company Inc .... G 317 639-5553
  Indianapolis (G-8956)
Mossberg & Company Inc .... F 574 236-1094
  South Bend (G-15154)
Mossberg & Company Inc .... D 574 289-9253
  South Bend (G-15155)
Mossberg Co .... F 574 850-6285
  South Bend (G-15156)
MPS Printing Incorporated .... G 812 273-4446
  Madison (G-11245)
Mr Copy Inc .... G 812 334-2679
  Bloomington (G-925)
Mr Copyrite .... G 219 462-1108
  Valparaiso (G-16005)
Nai Print Solutions .... G 317 392-1207
  Shelbyville (G-14779)
Nea LLC .... G 574 295-0024
  Elkhart (G-3565)
New Image Prtg & Design Inc .... F 260 969-0410
  Fort Wayne (G-5266)
Newsletter Express Ltd .... G 317 876-8916
  Indianapolis (G-9006)

Next Offset Solutions Inc .... G 773 844-1784
  West Lafayette (G-16613)
Nicholson and Sons Prtg Inc .... E 812 283-1200
  Jeffersonville (G-10026)
Novaprints LLC .... F 317 577-6682
  Indianapolis (G-9028)
Nwi Print & Mail LLC .... G 219 916-1358
  Dyer (G-2979)
Oce Corporate Printing Div .... G 260 436-7395
  Fort Wayne (G-5280)
Office Sup of Southern Ind Inc .... G 812 283-5523
  Jeffersonville (G-10027)
Offset House Inc .... F 317 849-5155
  Indianapolis (G-9042)
Offset One Inc .... F 260 456-8828
  Fort Wayne (G-5282)
Old Capital Printing LLC .... G 812 946-9444
  New Albany (G-12789)
Outfield Prsnized Spt Blls Inc .... G 219 661-8942
  Crown Point (G-2727)
Ovation Communications Inc .... G 812 401-9100
  Evansville (G-4230)
Overgaards Artcraft Printers .... G 574 234-8464
  South Bend (G-15183)
P A Rogers Printing Service .... G 317 823-7627
  Indianapolis (G-9079)
Pagels-Kelley Enterprises LLC .... F 219 872-8552
  Long Beach (G-11126)
Pam C Jones Enterprises Inc .... G 812 294-1862
  Borden (G-1117)
Panther Graphics LLC .... G 317 223-3845
  Indianapolis (G-9089)
Par Digital Imaging Inc .... G 317 787-3330
  Greenwood (G-6749)
Paragon Printing Center Inc .... G 574 533-5835
  Osceola (G-13400)
Paust Inc .... F 765 962-1507
  Richmond (G-14180)
Pearson Printing Company .... G 765 664-8769
  Marion (G-11325)
Peerless Printing Corporation .... G 765 664-8341
  Marion (G-11327)
Pentzer Printing Inc .... F 812 372-2896
  Columbus (G-2375)
Perdue Printed Products Inc .... G 260 456-7575
  Fort Wayne (G-5304)
Perfect Impressions Printing .... G 317 923-1756
  Indianapolis (G-9121)
Pettit Printing Inc .... G 260 563-2346
  Wabash (G-16212)
Phoenix Color Corp .... F 812 238-1551
  Terre Haute (G-15661)
Phoenix Color Corp .... D 812 234-1585
  Terre Haute (G-15662)
Phoenix Press Inc .... D 765 644-3959
  Anderson (G-178)
Picture Perfect Printing .... G 765 482-4241
  Lebanon (G-10933)
PIP Marketing Signs Print .... G 317 843-5755
  Carmel (G-1719)
Prairie Creek Prtg & Bk Str .... G 812 636-7243
  Montgomery (G-12119)
Prairieton Printing .... G 812 299-9611
  Terre Haute (G-15667)
Preferred Print .... G 317 371-8829
  Indianapolis (G-9189)
Premier Label Company Inc .... F 765 289-5000
  Muncie (G-12477)
Premier Printing .... G 765 459-8339
  Kokomo (G-10323)
Premier Prints LLC .... G 812 987-1129
  Jeffersonville (G-10040)

PRINTING: Screen, Broadwoven Fabrics, Cotton

Presstime Graphics Inc .... F 812 234-3815
  Terre Haute (G-15669)
Prestige Printing Inc .... E 812 372-2500
  Columbus (G-2381)
Print Center Inc .... G 219 874-9683
  Long Beach (G-11128)
Print Ideas .... G 317 299-8766
  Indianapolis (G-9199)
Print It Plus Inc .... G 812 466-7446
  Terre Haute (G-15670)
Print Management Solutions Inc .... G 574 234-7269
  South Bend (G-15205)
Print Resources Inc .... D 317 833-7000
  Indianapolis (G-9202)
Print Shop Inc .... G 574 264-0023
  Elkhart (G-3620)
Print Solutions of Indiana .... G 219 988-4186
  Crown Point (G-2736)
Print Source Corporation .... G 260 824-3911
  Bluffton (G-1050)
Printcraft Press Inc .... G 765 457-2141
  Kokomo (G-10324)
Printcrafters Inc .... G 812 838-4106
  Mount Vernon (G-12315)
Printing All Stars .... G 812 288-9291
  New Albany (G-12798)
Printing Center Inc .... G 317 545-8518
  Indianapolis (G-9204)
Printing Company LLC .... G 812 367-2668
  Ferdinand (G-4448)
Printing Concepts Inc .... G 317 899-2754
  Indianapolis (G-9205)
Printing Creations Inc .... G 765 759-9679
  Yorktown (G-16982)
Printing Impression .... G 812 537-4077
  Lawrenceburg (G-10854)
Printing In Time Inc .... G 502 807-3545
  Elizabeth (G-3128)
Printing Partners Inc .... D 317 635-2282
  Indianapolis (G-9206)
Printing Place Inc .... F 260 665-8444
  Angola (G-289)
Printing Solutions Inc .... G 812 923-0756
  Floyds Knobs (G-4689)
Printworks Inc .... G 317 535-1250
  Whiteland (G-16793)
Priority Press Inc .... G 317 240-0103
  Indianapolis (G-9212)
Priority Printing LLC .... G 317 241-4234
  Indianapolis (G-9213)
Proforma Premier Printing .... G 317 842-9181
  Indianapolis (G-9224)
Progressive Printing Co Inc .... G 765 653-3814
  Greencastle (G-6427)
Proprint Forms LLC .... G 317 861-8701
  New Palestine (G-12943)
Pulaski County Press Inc .... G 574 946-6628
  Winamac (G-16872)
Qgraphics Inc .... G 765 564-2314
  Delphi (G-2906)
Quad/Graphics Inc .... G 260 748-5300
  Fort Wayne (G-5361)
Quality Graphics Corp .... G 219 845-7084
  Hammond (G-6994)
R & B Fine Printing Inc .... G 219 365-9490
  Saint John (G-14457)
Rainbow Printing LLC .... F 812 275-3372
  Bedford (G-663)
Randall Corp .... G 812 425-7122
  Evansville (G-4272)
Red Line Graphics Incorporated .... E 317 784-7455
  Indianapolis (G-9278)

Rensselaer Print Co .... G 219 866-5000
  Rensselaer (G-14066)
Reprocomm Inc .... G 765 423-2578
  Lafayette (G-10679)
Reprocomm Inc .... G 765 472-5700
  Peru (G-13598)
Rhr Corporation .... G 317 788-1504
  Indianapolis (G-9298)
Richards Printery .... G 812 406-0295
  Greenville (G-6654)
Riden Inc .... G 219 362-5511
  La Porte (G-10473)
Rink Printing Company .... E 574 232-7935
  South Bend (G-15220)
Riverside Printing Co .... G 812 275-1950
  Bedford (G-669)
Rj Partners of Indiana Inc C
  Indianapolis (G-9311)
Row Printing Inc .... G 317 796-3289
  Brownsburg (G-1399)
Row Printing Inc .... G 317 441-4301
  Brownsburg (G-1400)
Rowland Printing Co Inc .... F 317 773-1829
  Noblesville (G-13168)
Rrc Corporation .... F 317 687-8325
  Indianapolis (G-9343)
Russ Print Shp/Hbron Advrtser .... F 219 996-3142
  Hebron (G-7106)
Samuel Wahli .... G 260 749-2288
  New Haven (G-12917)
Service Printers Inc .... E 574 266-6710
  Elkhart (G-3669)
Shackelford Graphics .... G 317 783-3582
  Indianapolis (G-9409)
Sharp Printing Services Inc .... G 317 842-5159
  Fishers (G-4604)
Shearer Printing Service Inc .... E 765 457-3274
  Kokomo (G-10334)
Shelbyville Newspapers Inc .... E 317 398-6631
  Shelbyville (G-14798)
Smith Business Supply Inc .... G 765 654-4442
  Frankfort (G-5694)
Smitson Cmmnications Group LLC .... G 317 876-8916
  Indianapolis (G-9451)
Sound & Graphics .... G 219 963-7293
  Lake Station (G-10777)
Specialized Printed Products .... G 260 483-7075
  Fort Wayne (G-5428)
Spectrum Print and Mktg LLC .... G 317 908-7471
  Avon (G-551)
Spencer Evening World .... D 812 829-2255
  Spencer (G-15362)
Spencer Printing Inc .... G 765 288-6111
  Muncie (G-12496)
St Clair Press .... G 317 612-9100
  Indianapolis (G-9484)
Stage Door Graphics .... G 317 398-9011
  Shelbyville (G-14801)
Steve Weaver Art .... G 574 546-3530
  Bremen (G-1224)
Summit Business Products Inc .... G 260 244-1820
  Churubusco (G-1987)
Superior Print Inc .... E 812 246-6311
  Sellersburg (G-14617)
Swiss Alps Printing Inc .... G 812 427-3844
  Vevay (G-16113)
Systems & Services of Michiana .... G 574 277-3355
  South Bend (G-15278)
Systems & Services of Michiana .... G 574 273-1911
  South Bend (G-15277)
T N D Printing .... G 260 493-4949
  Fishers (G-4609)

Tabco Business Forms Inc .... G 812 882-2836
  Vincennes (G-16157)
Target Printing Inc .... G 260 744-6038
  Fort Wayne (G-5469)
Tatman Inc .... E 765 825-2164
  Connersville (G-2472)
Tdk Graphics Inc .... F 219 663-7799
  Crown Point (G-2762)
Tek Print LLC .... G 812 336-2525
  Bedford (G-677)
Thompson Printing Service Inc .... G 317 783-7448
  Indianapolis (G-9598)
Tippecanoe Press Inc .... G 317 392-1207
  Shelbyville (G-14806)
Town & Country Press Inc .... F 574 936-9505
  Plymouth (G-13820)
Twin Prints Inc .... G 765 742-8656
  Lafayette (G-10711)
Two B Enterprises Inc .... F 260 245-0119
  Fort Wayne (G-5518)
Vdk Printing LLC .... G 260 602-8212
  Fort Wayne (G-5529)
Virtu Fine Art Services Inc .... G 317 822-1800
  Indianapolis (G-9722)
Wayne Press Incorporated .... G 260 744-3022
  Fort Wayne (G-5553)
Web Printing Connection Inc .... G 260 637-4037
  Fort Wayne (G-5560)
Well Ink .... G 765 743-3413
  West Lafayette (G-16646)
Williams Printing Inc .... G 765 468-6033
  Farmland (G-4427)
Wilson Printing .... G 317 745-5868
  Danville (G-2830)
Wise Printing Inc .... G 317 351-9477
  Indianapolis (G-9777)
Woodburn Graphics Inc .... F 812 232-0323
  Terre Haute (G-15748)
Woodfield Printing Inc .... G 317 848-2000
  Carmel (G-1808)
Woods Printing Company Inc .... F 812 536-2261
  Holland (G-7215)
World Arts Inc .... D 812 829-2255
  Spencer (G-15365)
Wraco Enterprises Inc .... G 812 339-3987
  Bloomington (G-1016)
Xl Graphics Inc .... F 317 738-3434
  Franklin (G-5789)
Your Face Our Place Print Shop .... G 812 567-4510
  Tennyson (G-15526)
Zogman Enterprises Inc .... G 317 873-6809
  Zionsville (G-17065)

PRINTING: Screen, Broadwoven Fabrics, Cotton

323ink LLC .... G 812 282-3620
  Jeffersonville (G-9920)
A D I Screen Printing .... G 765 457-8580
  Kokomo (G-10231)
Action Embroidery Inc .... G 850 626-1796
  Charlestown (G-1869)
All Things Custom LLC .... G 765 618-5332
  Sweetser (G-15453)
Concept Prints Inc .... F 317 290-1222
  Indianapolis (G-7851)
ID Graphics Incorporated .... G 765 649-9988
  Anderson (G-133)
Ink Dawgz LLC .... G 219 781-6972
  Valparaiso (G-15974)
OHaras Sports Inc .... G 219 836-5554
  Munster (G-12554)

Employee Codes: A=Over 500 employees, B=251-500
C=101-250, D=51-100, E=20-50, F=10-19, G=1-9

PRINTING: Screen, Broadwoven Fabrics, Cotton | PRODUCT SECTION

Printwise LLC .... G 765 244-1983
  Peru *(G-13595)*

Tony London Co Inc .... G 812 373-0748
  Columbus *(G-2403)*

UC Ink LLC .... G 765 220-5502
  West College Corner *(G-16544)*

PRINTING: Screen, Fabric

American Keeper Corporation .... E 765 521-2080
  New Castle *(G-12849)*

Athletic Edge Inc .... F 260 489-6613
  Fort Wayne *(G-4778)*

Burston Marketing Inc .... F 574 262-4005
  Elkhart *(G-3238)*

Codybro LLC .... G 765 827-5441
  Connersville *(G-2432)*

Cross Printwear Inc .... G 317 293-1776
  Indianapolis *(G-7906)*

Custom Imprint Corporation .... F 800 378-3397
  Merrillville *(G-11502)*

Dance World Bazaar Corporation .... G 812 663-7679
  Greensburg *(G-6589)*

Elegan Sportswear Inc .... E 219 464-8416
  Valparaiso *(G-15941)*

Flag & Banner Company Inc .... F 317 299-4880
  Indianapolis *(G-8199)*

Game Plan Graphics LLC .... G 812 663-3238
  Greensburg *(G-6596)*

Hometown Shirts & Graphix LLC .... G 765 564-3066
  Delphi *(G-2898)*

In Case of Emergency Press .... G 812 650-3352
  Bloomington *(G-886)*

Ink Dawgz LLC .... G 219 781-6972
  Valparaiso *(G-15974)*

Jasper EMB & Screen Prtg .... G 812 482-4787
  Jasper *(G-9852)*

Jer-Maur Corporation .... G 812 384-8290
  Bloomfield *(G-750)*

Kennyleeholmescom .... G 574 612-2526
  Elkhart *(G-3451)*

Lady Q LLC-S .... G 219 304-8404
  Indianapolis *(G-8712)*

Legends Maingate LLC .... F 317 243-2000
  Indianapolis *(G-8735)*

Locoli Inc .... E 219 515-6900
  Schererville *(G-14531)*

Maingate LLC .... D
  Indianapolis *(G-8814)*

Progressive Design Apparel Inc ...... E 317 293-5888
  Indianapolis *(G-9225)*

Ram Graphics Inc .... F 765 724-7783
  Alexandria *(G-58)*

Rbs Tees Co .... G 812 522-8675
  Seymour *(G-14680)*

Robert Burkhart .... G 219 448-0365
  Alexandria *(G-62)*

Spectrum Marketing .... G 765 643-5566
  Anderson *(G-197)*

Sport Form Inc .... G 260 589-2200
  Berne *(G-727)*

Sportscenter Inc .... G 260 436-6198
  Fort Wayne *(G-5432)*

Star Quality Awards Inc .... G 812 273-1740
  Madison *(G-11252)*

Sycamore Enterprises Inc .... G 812 477-2266
  Evansville *(G-4339)*

Travis Britton .... G 317 762-6018
  Indianapolis *(G-9632)*

Winning Edge of Rochester Inc ...... F 574 223-6090
  Rochester *(G-14334)*

Woods Enterprises .... G 574 232-7449
  South Bend *(G-15309)*

PRINTING: Screen, Manmade Fiber & Silk, Broadwoven Fabric

Classic Products Corp .... E 260 484-2695
  Fort Wayne *(G-4855)*

Ink Dawgz LLC .... G 219 781-6972
  Valparaiso *(G-15974)*

Main Event Mdsg Group LLC .... F 317 570-8900
  Indianapolis *(G-8812)*

PRINTING: Thermography

Kwik Kopy Printing .... G 219 663-7799
  Crown Point *(G-2714)*

PROFESSIONAL EQPT & SPLYS, WHOLESALE: Analytical Instruments

Lazar Scientific Incorporated .... G 574 271-7020
  Granger *(G-6358)*

PROFESSIONAL EQPT & SPLYS, WHOLESALE: Engineers', NEC

Blue Print Specialties Inc .... G 765 742-6976
  Lafayette *(G-10539)*

Maco Reprograhics LLC .... G 812 464-8108
  Evansville *(G-4183)*

Priority Press Inc .... G 317 848-9695
  Carmel *(G-1730)*

Priority Press Inc .... E 317 241-4234
  Indianapolis *(G-9211)*

PROFESSIONAL EQPT & SPLYS, WHOLESALE: Optical Goods

City Optical Co Inc .... G 317 788-4243
  Indianapolis *(G-7814)*

City Optical Co Inc .... D 317 924-1300
  Indianapolis *(G-7813)*

Vision Training Products Inc .... F 574 259-2070
  Mishawaka *(G-12023)*

PROFESSIONAL INSTRUMENT REPAIR SVCS

Gary M Brown .... G 765 831-2536
  New Castle *(G-12864)*

Heads First .... G 219 785-4100
  Westville *(G-16761)*

Indiana Handpiece Repair Inc .... G 260 436-0765
  Fort Wayne *(G-5100)*

T & L Sharpening Inc .... F 574 583-3868
  Monticello *(G-12172)*

Uncle Alberts Amplifier Inc .... G 317 845-3037
  Indianapolis *(G-9676)*

PROFILE SHAPES: Unsupported Plastics

3d Parts Mfg LLC .... G 317 860-6941
  Anderson *(G-68)*

Mitsubishi Chemical Advncd Mtr .... C 260 479-4100
  Fort Wayne *(G-5233)*

Mitsubshi Chem Advnced Mtls In .. D 260 479-4700
  Fort Wayne *(G-5234)*

Polygon Company .... D 574 586-3145
  Walkerton *(G-16274)*

Polygon Company .... C 574 586-3145
  Walkerton *(G-16275)*

Prolon Inc .... E 574 522-8900
  Elkhart *(G-3623)*

Specialty Mfg Ind Inc .... E 812 256-4633
  Charlestown *(G-1894)*

PROMOTION SVCS

Digital Design Genius .... G 317 515-3680
  Camby *(G-1509)*

Kessler Concepts Inc .... F 317 630-9901
  Indianapolis *(G-8675)*

PROPELLERS: Boat & Ship, Machined

Hoverstream LLC .... G 317 489-0075
  Indianapolis *(G-8428)*

PROTECTION EQPT: Lightning

Emp Solutions Inc .... G 937 608-0283
  Fishers *(G-4512)*

Independent Protection Co .... C 574 831-5680
  New Paris *(G-12960)*

Independent Protection Co .... E 574 533-4116
  Goshen *(G-6172)*

Llama Corporation .... G 888 701-7432
  Decatur *(G-2870)*

PUBLIC RELATIONS & PUBLICITY SVCS

Kamrex Inc .... E 317 204-3779
  Avon *(G-530)*

PUBLIC RELATIONS SVCS

Annual Reports Inc .... G 317 736-8838
  Franklin *(G-5709)*

Printing Creations Inc .... G 765 759-9679
  Yorktown *(G-16982)*

PUBLISHERS: Art Copy & Poster

Folk Art To Go .... G 317 753-8553
  Indianapolis *(G-8213)*

PUBLISHERS: Music Book & Sheet Music

Cola Voce Music Inc .... G 317 466-0624
  Indianapolis *(G-7834)*

Intimusic LLC .... G 574 210-4562
  South Bend *(G-15086)*

PCA Publishing Inc .... G 317 658-2055
  Indianapolis *(G-9108)*

Performers Edition LLC .... G 317 429-1300
  Indianapolis *(G-9125)*

Trinette Clark Agency Corp .... G 317 671-6097
  Indianapolis *(G-9643)*

PUBLISHERS: Music, Sheet

Tylayculture LLC .... G 219 678-8359
  Highland *(G-7158)*

PUBLISHERS: Patterns, Paper

Temple Inland .... G 765 362-1074
  Crawfordsville *(G-2623)*

PUBLISHERS: Sheet Music

Dark Source Records LLC .... G 616 378-6060
  Indianapolis *(G-7950)*

PUBLISHERS: Telephone & Other Directory

Agate Workshop .... G 812 333-0900
  Bloomington *(G-775)*

Nationwide Publishing Company .... G 260 312-3924
  Fort Wayne *(G-5258)*

PUBLISHING & BROADCASTING: Internet Only

Breadmansrt Llc .... G 219 238-9169
  Gary *(G-5906)*

Brill Stuff LLC .... G 502 889-9705
  New Albany *(G-12705)*

Crawl Before You Walk LLC .... G 219 413-6623
  Plainfield *(G-13675)*

PRODUCT SECTION

PUBLISHING & PRINTING: Newspapers

Domaindress LLC...................................G.....812 430-4856
  Evansville *(G-4017)*
Dungan Aerial Service Inc...................G.....765 827-1355
  Connersville *(G-2437)*
Gibson Nehemiah Group Inc................F.....317 643-3838
  Muncie *(G-12401)*
Indiana Interactive LLC.......................E.....317 233-2010
  Indianapolis *(G-8480)*
Indianapolis Social SEC Off..................G.....800 772-1213
  Indianapolis *(G-8509)*
Lemonwire LLC...................................G.....317 243-1758
  Indianapolis *(G-8737)*
Mavrick Entrmt Netwrk Inc...................G.....317 779-1237
  Brownsburg *(G-1386)*
Porchlight Group Inc............................G.....317 804-1166
  Fishers *(G-4579)*
Raging Rocket Web Design LLC..........G.....219 381-5027
  Crown Point *(G-2741)*
Scanpower LLC...................................G.....765 277-2308
  Richmond *(G-14201)*
SL Terrastar Group LLC.......................G.....317 702-7240
  Indianapolis *(G-9447)*
Street Dreams Production Inc.............G.....574 440-9136
  South Bend *(G-15269)*
Teck USA Inc......................................G.....888 995-1972
  Indianapolis *(G-9570)*
Tempesta Media LLC..........................G.....312 371-0555
  Michigan City *(G-11677)*
TV Excel Inc...D.....323 797-8538
  Fort Wayne *(G-5516)*
Zachary T Laffin..................................G.....317 480-2248
  Greenfield *(G-6572)*

PUBLISHING & PRINTING: Art Copy

Lori Hicks..G.....574 291-6341
  South Bend *(G-15129)*
Rough Notes Company Inc.................E.....317 582-1600
  Carmel *(G-1746)*

PUBLISHING & PRINTING: Book Music

Performers Edition LLC.......................G.....317 429-1300
  Indianapolis *(G-9125)*

PUBLISHING & PRINTING: Books

AM Publishing Inc..............................G.....317 806-0001
  Fishers *(G-4462)*
Apologia Eductl Ministries Inc............E.....765 608-3280
  Anderson *(G-79)*
Ave Maria Press Inc...........................D.....574 287-2831
  Notre Dame *(G-13315)*
Beacon House....................................G.....219 756-2131
  Schererville *(G-14515)*
Book of US LLC..................................G.....331 256-5953
  Crown Point *(G-2660)*
Brendacurtis Recipe Books LLC.........E.....574 216-2261
  Indianapolis *(G-7677)*
Helping Hands...................................G.....219 696-4564
  Lowell *(G-11162)*
Mbpc Progressive Consultants...........G.....765 301-1864
  Greencastle *(G-6421)*
No-Load Fund Investor Inc.................G.....317 571-1471
  Carmel *(G-1707)*
Our Sunday Visitor Apps LLC............E.....800 348-2440
  Huntington *(G-7349)*
Pearson Education Inc.......................F.....317 428-3049
  Indianapolis *(G-9110)*
Wesleyan Church Corporation............E.....317 774-7900
  Fishers *(G-4632)*
World Missionary Press Inc................E.....574 831-2111
  New Paris *(G-12974)*

PUBLISHING & PRINTING: Magazines: publishing & printing

1632 Inc..G.....219 398-4155
  East Chicago *(G-2987)*
American Legion National He.............D.....317 630-1200
  Indianapolis *(G-7505)*
Athletes Management & Services.......G.....317 925-8200
  Indianapolis *(G-7559)*
Christian Sound & Song Inc..............G.....574 294-2893
  Elkhart *(G-3251)*
Dynamic Resource Group Inc............E.....260 589-4000
  Berne *(G-709)*
Emp of Evansville...............................F.....812 962-1309
  Evansville *(G-4034)*
Fort Wayne Newspapers Inc..............B.....260 461-8444
  Fort Wayne *(G-4999)*
Galbe Magazine LLC..........................G.....248 742-5231
  Carmel *(G-1638)*
Literature Sales..................................G.....219 873-3093
  Michigan City *(G-11635)*
Lsc Communications Inc....................C.....765 364-2247
  Crawfordsville *(G-2586)*
Lsc Communications Us LLC............G.....765 362-1300
  Crawfordsville *(G-2587)*
Market Place Publications..................G.....219 769-7733
  Merrillville *(G-11536)*
Omega One Connect Inc....................G.....317 626-3445
  Indianapolis *(G-9048)*
Pages Editorial Services Inc...............F.....765 674-4212
  Marion *(G-11323)*

PUBLISHING & PRINTING: Music, Book

Tom Doherty Company Inc................G.....317 352-8200
  Indianapolis *(G-9617)*

PUBLISHING & PRINTING: Newsletters, Business Svc

Abundant Life Publications LLC.........G.....219 730-7621
  Gary *(G-5887)*
Automobile Dealers Assn of Ind.........G.....317 635-1441
  Indianapolis *(G-7576)*
Clutch Graphics..................................G.....812 244-9673
  Carbon *(G-1537)*
Cupprint LLC......................................F.....574 323-5250
  South Bend *(G-14988)*
Dow Theory Forecasts Inc..................E.....219 931-6480
  Hammond *(G-6915)*
Edwin Rahn..G.....260 622-7178
  Ossian *(G-13423)*
Goldenmarc LLC................................G.....317 855-1651
  Indianapolis *(G-8301)*
Hammer Marketing..............................G.....317 841-1567
  Fishers *(G-4536)*
Horizon Management Svcs Inc..........G.....219 852-3200
  Hammond *(G-6948)*
Indiana Auto Dealers Assn Svcs........G.....317 635-1441
  Indianapolis *(G-8473)*
Photoprose Productions Inc..............G.....316 371-4634
  Jeffersonville *(G-10038)*

PUBLISHING & PRINTING: Newspapers

Aim Media Indiana Oper LLC............E.....317 736-7101
  Franklin *(G-5704)*
Aim Media Indiana Oper LLC............E.....317 462-5528
  Greenfield *(G-6458)*
Alan Daily..G.....574 595-6253
  Star City *(G-15394)*
American Senior Homecare...............G.....317 849-4968
  Indianapolis *(G-7507)*
Benton Review Newspaper................G.....765 884-1902
  Fowler *(G-5619)*
Bingo Bugle.......................................G.....765 348-2859
  Hartford City *(G-7062)*
BJ Corporation of Indiana LLC...........G.....317 507-6672
  Indianapolis *(G-7635)*
Cnhi LLC..G.....765 640-4893
  Anderson *(G-95)*
Cnhi LLC..G.....812 944-6481
  Jeffersonville *(G-9955)*
Community Holdings Indiana Inc.......F.....765 622-1212
  Anderson *(G-97)*
Community Holdings Indiana Inc.......G.....812 663-3111
  Greensburg *(G-6585)*
Community Holdings Indiana Inc.......G.....317 873-6397
  Lebanon *(G-10886)*
Community Holdings Indiana Inc.......G.....574 722-5000
  Logansport *(G-11068)*
Cornerstone Fllwship Kndllvlle...........G.....260 347-0615
  Kendallville *(G-10102)*
Courier-Times Inc...............................D.....765 529-1111
  New Castle *(G-12856)*
Crothersville Times.............................G.....812 793-2188
  Crothersville *(G-2639)*
Daily II Larry.......................................G.....765 884-9355
  Fowler *(G-5623)*
Daily Money Managers Ind LLC.........G.....317 797-0012
  Carmel *(G-1604)*
Daily Peru Tribune Pubg Co...............F.....765 473-6641
  Peru *(G-13577)*
Daily Rental..G.....773 881-7762
  Munster *(G-12537)*
Decatur Publishing Co Inc..................E.....260 724-2121
  Decatur *(G-2851)*
Delphos Herald of Indiana Inc............C.....812 438-2011
  Rising Sun *(G-14241)*
Don Taylor...G.....219 662-0597
  Crown Point *(G-2678)*
Eastside Vice Cmnty News Mdia........G.....317 356-2222
  Indianapolis *(G-8041)*
Ebony & Co Inc..................................G.....260 246-4691
  Fort Wayne *(G-4940)*
Elwood Publishing Company Inc........G.....765 724-4469
  Alexandria *(G-50)*
Elwood Publishing Company Inc........G.....765 675-2115
  Tipton *(G-15772)*
Evansville Courier Co........................B.....812 464-7500
  Evansville *(G-4051)*
Evansville Thunderbolts......................F.....812 435-0872
  Evansville *(G-4058)*
Fairmount News..................................G.....765 948-4164
  Fairmount *(G-4409)*
Fort Wayne Newspapers Inc..............B.....260 461-8444
  Fort Wayne *(G-4999)*
Fountain County Neighbor..................G.....765 762-2411
  Attica *(G-348)*
Frankfort Newspaper..........................G.....859 254-2385
  Frankfort *(G-5666)*
Franklin Township Civic League.........G.....317 862-1774
  Indianapolis *(G-8225)*
Fresh News LLC.................................G.....219 929-5558
  Chesterton *(G-1929)*
Ft Wayne Reader................................G.....260 420-8580
  Fort Wayne *(G-5014)*
Gannett Co Inc...................................G.....765 423-5511
  Lafayette *(G-10584)*
Gannett Media Corp............................G.....765 962-1575
  Richmond *(G-14124)*
Granger Gazette Inc...........................G.....574 277-2679
  Granger *(G-6350)*
Green Banner Publications Inc..........E.....812 967-3176
  Borden *(G-1109)*

Employee Codes: A=Over 500 employees, B=251-500
C=101-250, D=51-100, E=20-50, F=10-19, G=1-9

2024 Harris Indiana Industrial Directory

PUBLISHING & PRINTING: Newspapers

Growing Child Inc... G 765 463-1696
West Lafayette *(G-16589)*

Harrison Press... G 513 367-4582
Lawrenceburg *(G-10839)*

Hartford City News Times....................... F 765 348-0110
Winchester *(G-16889)*

Home News Enterprises LLC.................. B 800 876-7811
Columbus *(G-2318)*

Hoosier Times Inc... F 812 332-4401
Beech Grove *(G-691)*

Hoosier Times Inc... C 765 342-3311
Martinsville *(G-11402)*

Horizon Publications Inc............................ G 260 244-5153
Columbia City *(G-2152)*

Huntington County Tab Inc...................... G 260 356-1107
Huntington *(G-7321)*

Illinois Agri-News.. G 317 726-5391
Indianapolis *(G-8460)*

Indiana Newspapers LLC............................ D 765 213-5700
Muncie *(G-12425)*

Indiana Newspapers LLC............................ D 812 886-9955
Vincennes *(G-16131)*

Indianapolis Power... G 317 834-3871
Martinsville *(G-11405)*

Indianplis Legislative Insight................... G 317 955-9997
Indianapolis *(G-8510)*

Info Publishing Impact LLC...................... G 317 912-3642
Fishers *(G-4547)*

Innovative Media Sciences Inc............. G 317 366-4371
Indianapolis *(G-8556)*

Iu International Svc Ctr................................ F 812 855-9086
Bloomington *(G-893)*

James Smith.. G 260 414-1237
Fort Wayne *(G-5132)*

Journal of Teaching Writing..................... G 317 274-0092
Indianapolis *(G-8640)*

Kankakee Valley Post News..................... G 219 987-5111
Demotte *(G-2920)*

Kpc Media Group Inc.................................... F 678 645-0000
Angola *(G-270)*

Kpc Media Group Inc.................................... G 260 868-5501
Auburn *(G-401)*

Kpc Media Group Inc.................................... F 260 426-2640
Fort Wayne *(G-5158)*

La Ola Latino Americana............................ F 317 822-0345
Indianapolis *(G-8707)*

La Voz De Indiana Inc.................................. G 317 636-7970
Indianapolis *(G-8708)*

La Voz De Indiana Inc.................................. G 317 423-0957
Indianapolis *(G-8709)*

Laff Worx LLC.. G 812 267-0430
New Salisbury *(G-12985)*

Leader Publishing Co of Salem.............. E 812 883-3281
Salem *(G-14487)*

Lee Enterprises Inc Times......................... E 219 933-3200
Munster *(G-12547)*

Lee Publications Inc....................................... G 219 462-5151
Valparaiso *(G-15994)*

Liberty Herald... G 765 458-5114
Liberty *(G-10991)*

Macednian Ptrtic Orgnztion of............... G 260 422-5900
Fort Wayne *(G-5196)*

Mayhill Publications Inc.............................. E 765 345-5133
Knightstown *(G-10199)*

Mittera Group Inc.. G 812 256-3396
Charlestown *(G-1885)*

Montgomery & Associates Inc............... F 219 879-0088
Michigan City *(G-11641)*

Mooresville Times.. E 317 831-0280
Martinsville *(G-11415)*

My Daily Wedding Deals LLC.................. G 812 603-6149
Indianapolis *(G-8975)*

Myers Enterprises Inc................................... G 812 636-7350
Odon *(G-13344)*

New Time Inc.. G 219 655-5041
Whiting *(G-16836)*

News and Tribune.. F 812 206-2168
Jeffersonville *(G-10023)*

News Dispatch... C 219 874-7211
Michigan City *(G-11645)*

News Examiner Circulation Dept.......... G 765 825-2914
Connersville *(G-2458)*

News Publishing Company LLC............. G 502 633-4334
Tell City *(G-15515)*

News Publishing Company Inc............... G 260 461-8444
Fort Wayne *(G-5270)*

News Reminder.. G 574 583-5121
Monticello *(G-12161)*

News-Herald Inc.. G 765 425-8903
Marion *(G-11320)*

Newsnow Dubois County............................ G 812 827-6131
Jasper *(G-9895)*

Newspaper Holding Inc................................ G 270 678-5171
Jeffersonville *(G-10024)*

Newspaper Holding Inc................................ G 812 231-4200
Terre Haute *(G-15651)*

Newspaper Holding Inc................................ G 812 254-0480
Washington *(G-16496)*

Northwest Indiana Newsppr Inc........... G 574 722-5000
Logansport *(G-11101)*

Northwest News & Printing..................... G 260 637-9003
Fort Wayne *(G-5276)*

Nwhoodtales Corp... G 708 858-0598
Highland *(G-7148)*

Nwitimescom.. E 219 933-3200
Munster *(G-12553)*

Odb Inc.. G 260 673-0062
Fort Wayne *(G-5281)*

Patriot Inc.. G 317 462-5172
Greenfield *(G-6535)*

Pendleton Times.. G 765 778-2324
Pendleton *(G-13552)*

Planet Goshen LLC... G 574 830-5797
Goshen *(G-6239)*

Poultry Press... G 765 827-0932
Connersville *(G-2462)*

Progress Examiner... G 812 865-3242
Orleans *(G-13381)*

Pudders LLC.. G 317 402-3507
Shelbyville *(G-14789)*

Rebecca L Hamann & Associates........... G 219 763-1233
Portage *(G-13910)*

Reno LLC.. G 708 846-7821
Schererville *(G-14542)*

Republican.. G 317 745-2777
Danville *(G-2825)*

Richard K Williams... G 616 745-9319
Albion *(G-43)*

Schurz Communications Inc.................... F 574 247-7237
Mishawaka *(G-11992)*

Seymour Trbune A Cal Ltd Prtnr........... F 812 522-4871
Seymour *(G-14691)*

Shopping Guide News Inc.......................... F 574 223-5417
Rochester *(G-14324)*

South Bend Tribune Corp........................... F 574 971-5651
Goshen *(G-6256)*

South Gibson Star-Times Inc................... F 812 753-3553
Fort Branch *(G-4707)*

South Whtley Trbune Prcton New........ G 260 723-4771
South Whitley *(G-15325)*

Southern Indiana Bus Source.................. G 812 206-6397
Jeffersonville *(G-10056)*

Static Media Inc.. G 212 366-4500
Fishers *(G-4606)*

The Papers Inc... C 574 658-4111
Milford *(G-11807)*

Times... E 765 659-4622
Frankfort *(G-5698)*

Times Leader Publications LLC............. F 317 300-8782
Avon *(G-552)*

Topics Newspapers Inc................................ F 888 357-7827
Fishers *(G-4614)*

Torch Newspapers Inc.................................. G 765 569-2033
Rockville *(G-14359)*

Town of Saratoga... G 765 584-1576
Saratoga *(G-14509)*

Trustees Indiana University..................... G 812 855-7995
Bloomington *(G-995)*

Truth Publishing Company Inc............... C 574 294-1661
Elkhart *(G-3750)*

Twice Daily LLC.. G 812 484-5417
Evansville *(G-4357)*

University Notre Dame Du Lac.............. F 574 631-7471
Notre Dame *(G-13317)*

USA Today.. G 212 715-2188
Fishers *(G-4624)*

Vevay Newspapers Inc................................. G 812 427-2311
Vevay *(G-16114)*

Waynedale News Inc..................................... G 260 747-4535
Fort Wayne *(G-5556)*

Western Wayne News.................................. G 765 478-5448
Cambridge City *(G-1504)*

Whatzup LLC... G 260 407-3198
Fort Wayne *(G-5562)*

Wilson Media Group Inc............................. F 765 452-0055
Kokomo *(G-10359)*

Wpta Television Inc...................................... D 217 221-3353
Fort Wayne *(G-5577)*

Zergnet.. G 317 201-0889
Noblesville *(G-13199)*

PUBLISHING & PRINTING: Pamphlets

Main1media LLC.. G 317 841-7000
Indianapolis *(G-8813)*

Old Paths Tract Society Inc....................... G 812 247-2560
Shoals *(G-14909)*

PUBLISHING & PRINTING: Periodical Statistical Reports

Americas Coml Trnsp RES Co LLC........ F 812 379-2085
Columbus *(G-2219)*

PUBLISHING & PRINTING: Shopping News

Crown Point Shopping News.................... G 219 663-4212
Crown Point *(G-2671)*

PUBLISHING & PRINTING: Textbooks

Sdi Innovations Inc.. C 765 471-8883
Lafayette *(G-10689)*

PUBLISHING & PRINTING: Trade Journals

Michiana Executive Journal..................... G 574 256-6666
Mishawaka *(G-11943)*

Rough Notes Company Inc........................ E 317 582-1600
Carmel *(G-1746)*

Trustees Indiana University..................... G 812 856-4186
Bloomington *(G-998)*

PUBLISHING & PRINTING: Yearbooks

Herff Jones LLC.. E 317 612-3400
Indianapolis *(G-8384)*

Herff Jones LLC.. C 317 297-3741
Indianapolis *(G-8383)*

PULP MILLS

International Paper Company.................. D 800 643-7244
Terre Haute *(G-15619)*

Recycling Center Inc............................. D 765 966-8295
Richmond *(G-14195)*

Recycling Works LLC........................... F 574 293-3751
Elkhart *(G-3644)*

PULP MILLS: Mechanical & Recycling Processing

Chesapeake Recycling Inc..................... E 574 946-6602
Winamac *(G-16859)*

Integrity Fiber Supply LLC...................... E 317 290-1140
Carmel *(G-1672)*

Jeda Equipment Services Inc................. G 317 842-9377
Fishers *(G-4550)*

Premier Scrap Processing LLC............. F 317 242-9502
Indianapolis *(G-9191)*

Welder On Way LLC.............................. G 260 920-4705
Ashley *(G-340)*

PUMPS & PARTS: Indl

Aeromind LLC.. G 800 905-2157
Indianapolis *(G-7453)*

Autoform Tool & Mfg LLC....................... C 260 624-2014
Angola *(G-232)*

Flint & Walling Inc................................. E 800 345-9422
Kendallville *(G-10111)*

Gardner Denver Inc............................... E 219 558-0354
Saint John *(G-14451)*

Grundfos Pumps Mfg Corp..................... G 317 925-9661
Indianapolis *(G-8337)*

Hy-Flex Corporation............................... E 765 571-5125
Knightstown *(G-10198)*

Mantra Enterprise LLC........................... G 201 428-8709
Fishers *(G-4561)*

Picketts Place Inc.................................. G 317 763-1168
Westfield *(G-16717)*

Tuskin Equipment Corporation................ G 630 466-5590
Elkhart *(G-3754)*

Wee Engineer Inc.................................. F 765 449-4280
Dayton *(G-2838)*

PUMPS & PUMPING EQPT REPAIR SVCS

Altek Inc.. G 812 385-2561
Princeton *(G-13981)*

Hamilton Bros Inc.................................. F 317 241-2571
Indianapolis *(G-8353)*

Horner Industrial Services Inc................. G 260 434-1189
Fort Wayne *(G-5083)*

Horner Industrial Services Inc................. G 812 466-5281
Terre Haute *(G-15607)*

Horner Industrial Services Inc................. C 317 639-4261
Indianapolis *(G-8416)*

Kochs Electric Inc.................................. E 317 639-5624
Indianapolis *(G-8700)*

Progress Group Inc............................... D 219 322-3700
Schererville *(G-14539)*

Rankin Pump and Supply Co Inc............. G 812 238-2535
Terre Haute *(G-15675)*

PUMPS & PUMPING EQPT WHOLESALERS

All-Pro Pump & Repair Inc..................... G 317 738-4203
Morgantown *(G-12252)*

Allegion S&S Holding Co Inc.................. E 317 429-2299
Indianapolis *(G-7478)*

Automatic Pool Covers Inc..................... E 317 579-2000
Westfield *(G-16666)*

Banjo Corporation.................................. C 765 362-7367
Crawfordsville *(G-2546)*

Dresser LLC.. D 765 827-9200
Connersville *(G-2436)*

Dura Products Inc.................................. F 855 502-3872
Arcadia *(G-313)*

Fill-Rite Company................................... E 260 747-7529
Fort Wayne *(G-4982)*

FL Smidth... G 812 402-9210
Evansville *(G-4073)*

Flowserve Corporation........................... G 219 763-1000
Portage *(G-13867)*

Franklin Electric Co Inc.......................... B 260 824-2900
Fort Wayne *(G-5006)*

Hoosier Fire Equipment Inc.................... F 219 462-1707
Valparaiso *(G-15965)*

Met-Pro Technologies LLC..................... G 317 293-2930
Indianapolis *(G-8882)*

Nst Technologies Mim LLC.................... C 812 755-4501
Campbellsburg *(G-1526)*

Ohio Transmission Corporation.............. G 812 466-2734
Terre Haute *(G-15655)*

Parker-Hannifin Corporation................... D 260 636-2104
Albion *(G-40)*

R B Tool & Machinery Co....................... G 574 679-0082
Osceola *(G-13401)*

Rankin Pump and Supply Co Inc............. G 812 238-2535
Terre Haute *(G-15675)*

Shoemaker Welding Company................ G 574 656-4412
North Liberty *(G-13223)*

Specialty Mfg Ind Inc.............................. E 812 256-4633
Charlestown *(G-1894)*

Sterling Fluid Systems USA LLC............ C 317 925-9661
Indianapolis *(G-9506)*

Tbk America Inc.................................... E 765 962-0147
Richmond *(G-14210)*

Thrush Co Inc....................................... E 765 472-3351
Peru *(G-13604)*

Tuthill Corporation................................. G 260 747-7529
Fort Wayne *(G-5514)*

Tuthill Corporation................................. C 260 747-7529
Fort Wayne *(G-5515)*

Waterax Corporation.............................. G 360 574-1818
Valparaiso *(G-16079)*

Xylem Vue Inc....................................... D 574 855-1012
South Bend *(G-15310)*

PUMPS, HEAT: Electric

Waterfurnace International Inc................ B 260 478-5667
Fort Wayne *(G-5549)*

PUMPS: Domestic, Water Or Sump

3w Enterprises LLC............................... G 847 366-6555
Elkhart *(G-3137)*

Hayward & Sams LLP............................ G 260 351-4166
Stroh *(G-15401)*

PUMPS: Measuring & Dispensing

Chemical Control Systems Inc................ G 219 465-5103
Griffith *(G-6800)*

Cortex Safety Technologies LLC............. G 317 414-5607
Carmel *(G-1598)*

Gfi Innovations LLC............................... G 847 263-9000
Plymouth *(G-13779)*

Indco Inc... G 812 945-4383
New Albany *(G-12746)*

Separation By Design Inc...................... E 812 424-1239
Evansville *(G-4305)*

PUMPS: Oil Well & Field

Jj Energy Inc... G 630 401-7026
Lebanon *(G-10905)*

Oasis Pumps Mfg Co............................. G 812 783-2146
Mount Vernon *(G-12313)*

PUMPS: Oil, Measuring Or Dispensing

Rj Fuel Services Inc.............................. G 812 350-2897
Edinburgh *(G-3101)*

PUMPS: Vacuum, Exc Laboratory

Vacuum Technique LLC......................... E 800 848-4511
Michigan City *(G-11683)*

PURCHASING SVCS

Finvantage LLC...................................... F 317 500-4949
Carmel *(G-1635)*

PURIFICATION & DUST COLLECTION EQPT

Gbi Air Systems Inc............................... G 574 272-0600
Granger *(G-6348)*

Universal Air Products LLC.................... G 502 451-1825
Sellersburg *(G-14619)*

QUICKLIME

Mississippi Lime Company..................... G 800 437-5463
Portage *(G-13889)*

QUILTING: Individuals

Zig-Zag Crnr Qilts Baskets LLC.............. G 317 326-3115
Greenfield *(G-6573)*

RACE CAR OWNERS

Chip Ganassi Racing Teams Inc............. D 317 802-0000
Indianapolis *(G-7798)*

RACEWAYS

E Squared Motorsports LLC................... G 317 626-2937
Avon *(G-515)*

Miller Raceway...................................... G 219 939-9688
Gary *(G-5982)*

Raceway Hand Car Wash LLC................ G 260 242-9866
Kendallville *(G-10147)*

RADAR SYSTEMS & EQPT

Radar Associates Corporation................ G 219 838-8030
Munster *(G-12560)*

RADIO BROADCASTING & COMMUNICATIONS EQPT

Telectro-Mek Inc.................................... G 260 747-0586
Fort Wayne *(G-5474)*

RADIO BROADCASTING STATIONS

Continntal Broadcast Group LLC............ E 317 924-1071
Indianapolis *(G-7858)*

Emmis Corporation................................ D 317 266-0100
Indianapolis *(G-8106)*

Emmis Operating Company.................... E 317 266-0100
Indianapolis *(G-8107)*

The Findlay Publishing Co..................... G 812 222-8000
Batesville *(G-606)*

World Rdo Mssnary Fllwship Inc............. G 574 970-4252
Elkhart *(G-3793)*

RADIO COMMUNICATIONS: Airborne Eqpt

Gwin Enterprises.................................... G 317 881-6401
Indianapolis *(G-8346)*

Nello Capital Inc.................................... G 574 288-3632
South Bend *(G-15160)*

RADIO COMMUNICATIONS: Carrier Eqpt

Cohda Wireless America LLC................. G 248 513-2105
Indianapolis *(G-7832)*

RAILINGS: Prefabricated, Metal

RAILROAD EQPT

Colbin Tool Company Inc.......................... E 574 457-3183
Syracuse *(G-15459)*

RAILROAD EQPT

Amsted Graphite Materials LLC................. D 219 931-1900
Hammond *(G-6877)*

Arbor Preservative Systems LLC................ F 812 232-2316
Terre Haute *(G-15545)*

General Signals Inc.................................... E 812 474-4256
Evansville *(G-4088)*

Illiana Railcar Services LLC........................ G 812 264-4687
Terre Haute *(G-15613)*

JP Industries Inc....................................... F 574 293-8763
Elkhart *(G-3436)*

Kasgro Rail Car Management..................... G 812 347-3888
Corydon *(G-2503)*

Progress Rail Locomotive Inc..................... F 765 281-2685
Muncie *(G-12479)*

Progress Rail Services Corp....................... D 765 472-2002
Peru *(G-13596)*

Tangent Rail Products Inc.......................... E 412 325-0202
Terre Haute *(G-15723)*

Transco Railway Products Inc.................... E 574 753-6227
Logansport *(G-11111)*

Union Tank Car Co.................................... G 219 880-5248
Whiting *(G-16839)*

Veterans Fabrication LLC........................... G 317 604-7704
Fishers *(G-4629)*

Wabtec Corporation................................... G 317 556-4116
Plainfield *(G-13741)*

Western-Cullen-Hayes Inc.......................... F 765 962-0526
Richmond *(G-14226)*

RAILROAD EQPT & SPLYS WHOLESALERS

General Signals Inc.................................... E 812 474-4256
Evansville *(G-4088)*

RAILROAD EQPT: Cars & Eqpt, Train, Freight Or Passenger

Adams & Westlake Ltd................................ E 574 264-1141
Elkhart *(G-3154)*

RAILROAD EQPT: Locomotives & Parts, Indl

American Maint & Training Inc.................... F 812 738-4230
Corydon *(G-2485)*

RAILROAD MAINTENANCE & REPAIR SVCS

Professnl Locomotive Svcs Inc................... E 219 398-9123
East Chicago *(G-3036)*

Progress Rail Mfg Corp.............................. C 765 281-2685
Muncie *(G-12480)*

Progress Rail Services Corp....................... C 219 397-5326
East Chicago *(G-3037)*

RAMPS: Prefabricated Metal

Full Metal Solutions LLC............................. F 812 725-9660
Jeffersonville *(G-9988)*

T & S Equipment Company........................ D 260 665-9521
Angola *(G-297)*

REAL ESTATE AGENCIES & BROKERS

Complete Property Care LLC...................... G 765 288-0890
Muncie *(G-12368)*

Land of Indiana Inc.................................... F 812 788-1560
Bedford *(G-654)*

REAL ESTATE AGENCIES: Rental

Daily Rental... G 773 881-7762
Munster *(G-12537)*

REAL ESTATE AGENTS & MANAGERS

Brockwood Farm.. G 812 837-9607
Nashville *(G-12664)*

RECORDING HEADS: Speech & Musical Eqpt

Music Store.. G 812 949-3004
Clarksville *(G-2024)*

RECORDS & TAPES: Prerecorded

Chatterup LLC.. G 317 213-6283
Westfield *(G-16675)*

Cinram Inc... A 416 298-8190
Richmond *(G-14104)*

Cliff A Ostermeyer..................................... G 615 361-7902
Fort Wayne *(G-4860)*

Counterpart.. D 317 587-1621
Fishers *(G-4496)*

Lifedata LLC.. G 925 800-3381
Marion *(G-11309)*

M&M Interactive Inc................................... G 317 708-1250
Carmel *(G-1688)*

Optical Disc Solutions Inc.......................... E 765 935-7574
Richmond *(G-14177)*

Peerview Data Inc..................................... G 317 238-3234
Indianapolis *(G-9112)*

Photonic LLC... G 502 930-9544
Sellersburg *(G-14610)*

Rpdm Solutions Inc.................................... G 317 608-2938
Huntington *(G-7363)*

Voice of God Recordings Inc...................... D 812 246-2137
Jeffersonville *(G-10069)*

Wish Factory Inc.. F 260 745-2550
South Whitley *(G-15332)*

World Media Group Inc.............................. D 317 549-8484
Indianapolis *(G-9790)*

RECOVERY SVC: Iron Ore, From Open Hearth Slag

Golden Beam Metals LLC.......................... G 317 806-2750
Indianapolis *(G-8297)*

Phoenix Services LLC................................ E 219 787-0019
Portage *(G-13903)*

Tjr Fabrication LLC..................................... F 765 384-4455
Marion *(G-11342)*

RECREATIONAL VEHICLE DEALERS

Forest River Inc... C 574 533-5934
Goshen *(G-6141)*

Forest River Inc... E 574 389-4600
Elkhart *(G-3356)*

Patrick Industries Inc................................. E 574 825-4336
Middlebury *(G-11746)*

RECREATIONAL VEHICLE PARTS & ACCESS STORES

Bilbees Service and Supply Inc.................. G 317 895-8288
Indianapolis *(G-7625)*

Dg Manufacturing Inc................................. D 574 294-7550
Elkhart *(G-3295)*

Eash LLC... F 574 295-4450
Elkhart *(G-3311)*

Jpc LLC... F 574 293-8030
Elkhart *(G-3437)*

Kentuckiana Yacht Services LLC................ G 812 282-7579
Jeffersonville *(G-10007)*

REELS: Cable, Metal

Hosetract Industries Ltd............................. F 260 489-8828
Fort Wayne *(G-5084)*

Murpac of Fort Wayne LLC........................ G 260 424-2299
Fort Wayne *(G-5251)*

Reelcraft Industries Inc............................... C 855 634-9109
Columbia City *(G-2188)*

REFINING: Petroleum

Airgas Inc... G 317 632-7106
Indianapolis *(G-7463)*

Apollo America... G 812 284-3300
Jeffersonville *(G-9934)*

Calumet Inc.. E 317 328-5660
Indianapolis *(G-7717)*

Calumet Finance Corp............................... E 317 328-5660
Indianapolis *(G-7718)*

Calumet Gp LLC.. E 317 328-5660
Indianapolis *(G-7719)*

Calumet International Inc........................... G 317 328-5660
Indianapolis *(G-7720)*

Calumet Karns City Ref LLC...................... E 317 328-5660
Indianapolis *(G-7721)*

Calumet Operating LLC............................. E 317 328-5660
Indianapolis *(G-7723)*

Calumet Refining LLC................................ G 765 587-4618
Muncie *(G-12362)*

Calumet Refining LLC................................ E 317 328-5660
Indianapolis *(G-7724)*

Calumet Shreveport Llc.............................. G 317 328-5660
Indianapolis *(G-7725)*

Calumet Shreveport Ref LLC..................... F 317 328-5660
Indianapolis *(G-7727)*

Cjs Stop N Go... G 317 877-0681
Noblesville *(G-13061)*

Countrymark Ref Logistics LLC.................. B 812 838-4341
Mount Vernon *(G-12295)*

Don Hartman Oil Co Inc............................. G 765 643-5026
Anderson *(G-106)*

Exxon Mobil Corporation............................. G 574 217-7630
South Bend *(G-15024)*

Heritage-Crystal Clean Inc......................... G 317 390-3642
Indianapolis *(G-8390)*

Leesburg Stop-N-Go LLC.......................... G 574 453-3004
Leesburg *(G-10956)*

Oxbow Carbon & Minerals......................... G 219 473-0359
Whiting *(G-16837)*

Superior Indus Solutions Inc...................... F 574 264-0161
Elkhart *(G-3708)*

REFRACTORIES: Clay

Can-Clay Corp... E
Cannelton *(G-1534)*

Champion Target....................................... F 765 966-7745
Richmond *(G-14103)*

Harbisonwalker Intl Inc............................... G 219 881-4440
Gary *(G-5945)*

Quikrete Companies LLC........................... E 317 251-2281
Indianapolis *(G-9252)*

R T W Refractory Inc................................. F 812 468-4299
Evansville *(G-4269)*

Refractory Engineers Inc............................ E 317 273-2000
Indianapolis *(G-9281)*

Resco Products Inc.................................... F 219 844-7830
Hammond *(G-6997)*

REFRACTORIES: Foundry, Clay

Wb Refractory Service Inc......................... G 317 450-7386
Indianapolis *(G-9743)*

REFRACTORIES: Nonclay

Allied Mineral Products Inc........................ F 219 923-5875
Griffith *(G-6789)*

EJ Bognar Incorporated............................. G 412 344-9900
Schneider *(G-14549)*

Indiana Refractories Inc............................. E 260 426-3286
Fort Wayne *(G-5102)*

PRODUCT SECTION — RENTAL: Portable Toilet

Insulation Specialties of Amer................ E 219 733-2502
  Wanatah (G-16290)
Magneco/Metrel Inc........................... D 219 885-4190
  Gary (G-5979)
Minteq International Inc..................... G 219 886-9555
  Gary (G-5984)
Minteq Shapes and Services Inc.......... D 219 762-4863
  Portage (G-13888)
One Eight Seven Incorporated............. G 219 886-2060
  Gary (G-5989)
Pyro Industrial Services Inc................ E 219 787-5700
  Portage (G-13907)
Refractory Service Corporation............ E 219 853-0885
  Hammond (G-6996)
Simko & Sons Inc............................. F 219 933-9100
  Hammond (G-7007)

REFRACTORIES: Tile & Brick, Exc Plastic

Ht Enterprises Inc............................. G 765 794-4174
  Crawfordsville (G-2578)

REFRACTORY MATERIALS WHOLESALERS

D Martin Enterprises Inc..................... F 219 872-8211
  Michigan City (G-11596)
Magneco/Metrel Inc........................... D 219 885-4190
  Gary (G-5979)
Pyro Industrial Services Inc................ E 219 787-5700
  Portage (G-13907)
Refractory Service Corporation............ E 219 853-0885
  Hammond (G-6996)

REFRIGERATION & HEATING EQUIPMENT

A & A Prcsion Htg Colg Rfrgn L........... G 812 401-1711
  Evansville (G-3859)
Air Systems Compents LP................... G 765 483-5841
  Lebanon (G-10873)
B & K Beverage Service Inc................ G 317 209-9842
  Lebanon (G-10879)
Carrier Corporation........................... D 317 243-0851
  Indianapolis (G-7749)
Crosspoint Power and Rfrgn LLC......... F 317 240-1967
  Indianapolis (G-7907)
Delivery Concepts Inc........................ E 574 522-3981
  Elkhart (G-3289)
Evansville Metal Products Inc............. G 812 421-6589
  Evansville (G-4055)
Evansville Metal Products Inc............. D 812 423-5632
  Evansville (G-4054)
Flow Center Products Inc.................... G 765 364-9460
  Crawfordsville (G-2567)
Geo-Flo Corporation.......................... F 812 275-8513
  Bedford (G-639)
Ilpea Industries Inc........................... D 812 752-2526
  Scottsburg (G-14561)
Industrial Combustn Engineers............ E 219 949-5066
  Gary (G-5960)
Jlb Industrial LLC............................. G 765 561-1751
  Rushville (G-14402)
Lennox International Inc..................... E 219 756-3709
  Merrillville (G-11532)
Lennox Nat Account Svcs LLC............. G 800 333-4001
  Indianapolis (G-8739)
Lennoxs Legacy Rescue Inc................ G 260 223-3115
  Decatur (G-2868)
Parker-Hannifin Corporation............... A 260 748-6000
  Fort Wayne (G-5297)
Ram Services Rfrgn & Mech................ G 317 679-8541
  Indianapolis (G-9264)
Redi/Controls Inc.............................. G 317 494-6600
  Franklin (G-5773)
Refrigeration Design Ind LLC............... G 317 498-3435
  Rushville (G-14409)

Rheem Sales Company Inc.................. G 479 648-4900
  Indianapolis (G-9297)
Supreme Corporation......................... G 260 894-9191
  Ligonier (G-11026)
Supreme Corporation......................... C 574 642-4888
  Goshen (G-6263)
Trane US Inc.................................... G 800 285-2487
  Bloomington (G-992)
Trane US Inc.................................... F 812 421-8725
  Evansville (G-4346)
Trane US Inc.................................... D 317 255-8777
  Fishers (G-4615)
Trane US Inc.................................... F 260 489-0884
  Fort Wayne (G-5498)
Trane US Inc.................................... D 765 932-7200
  Rushville (G-14415)
Trane US Inc.................................... G 574 282-4880
  South Bend (G-15286)
Webber Manufacturing Company......... E 317 357-8681
  Indianapolis (G-9745)
Welbilt Fdsrvice Companies LLC......... B 260 459-8200
  Fort Wayne (G-5561)
Welbilt Fdsrvice Companies LLC......... B 812 406-4527
  Jeffersonville (G-10072)

REFRIGERATION EQPT & SPLYS WHOLESALERS

Elliott-Williams Company Inc............... E 317 453-2295
  Indianapolis (G-8097)
Stanton and Associates Inc................. G 574 247-5522
  Granger (G-6383)

REFRIGERATION EQPT: Complete

Advantage Engineering Inc.................. D 317 887-0729
  Greenwood (G-6660)
Duncan Supply Co Inc........................ G 765 446-0105
  Lafayette (G-10572)
Elliott-Williams Company Inc............... E 317 453-2295
  Indianapolis (G-8097)
Stanton and Associates Inc................. G 574 247-5522
  Granger (G-6383)
Whirlpool Corporation........................ D 812 426-4000
  Evansville (G-4383)

REFRIGERATION SVC & REPAIR

Expert Electrical Services LLC............. G 765 664-6642
  Marion (G-11285)

REFRIGERATOR REPAIR SVCS

JC Refrigeration LLC......................... G 260 768-4067
  Shipshewana (G-14855)

REFUSE SYSTEMS

Ecobat Resources Cal Inc.................... B 317 247-1303
  Indianapolis (G-8049)
Enviri Corporation............................. F 219 397-0200
  East Chicago (G-3007)
K & S Pallet Inc................................ E 260 422-1264
  Fort Wayne (G-5141)
Recycling Works LLC......................... F 574 293-3751
  Elkhart (G-3644)

REGISTERS: Air, Metal

Continental Industries Inc................... D 574 262-4511
  Elkhart (G-3265)

REGULATORS: Transmission & Distribution Voltage

General Transmission Pdts LLC............ G 574 284-2917
  South Bend (G-15043)

REHABILITATION CTR, RESIDENTIAL WITH HEALTH CARE INCIDENTAL

Cardinal Services Inc Indiana.............. D 574 267-3823
  Warsaw (G-16333)

REHABILITATION SVCS

ARC of Greater Boone Cnty Inc............ F 765 482-0051
  Lebanon (G-10875)

RELAYS & SWITCHES: Indl, Electric

Riverside Mfg LLC............................. B 260 637-4470
  Fort Wayne (G-5386)

RELIGIOUS SPLYS WHOLESALERS

Dicksons Inc.................................... C 812 522-1308
  Seymour (G-14647)
Templeton Coal Company Inc.............. G 812 232-7037
  Terre Haute (G-15725)

RELOCATION SVCS

Owens Machinery Inc......................... G 812 968-3285
  Corydon (G-2509)

REMOVERS & CLEANERS

Chad Simons.................................... G 219 405-1620
  Chesterton (G-1909)
Snow Management Group.................... G 574 252-5253
  Mishawaka (G-12000)

REMOVERS: Paint

Sansher Corporation.......................... G 260 484-2000
  Fort Wayne (G-5400)

RENTAL SVCS: Audio-Visual Eqpt & Sply

Sizzlin Sound Productions LLC............. G 765 376-0129
  Crawfordsville (G-2615)

RENTAL SVCS: Business Machine & Electronic Eqpt

Pitney Bowes Inc............................... G 260 436-7395
  Indianapolis (G-9148)

RENTAL SVCS: Costume

Higgins Dyan................................... G 812 876-0754
  Ellettsville (G-3809)

RENTAL SVCS: Oil Eqpt

Gesco Group LLC.............................. G 260 747-5088
  Fort Wayne (G-5023)

RENTAL SVCS: Recreational Vehicle

Grand Design Rv LLC......................... C 574 825-8000
  Middlebury (G-11719)

RENTAL SVCS: Tent & Tarpaulin

All American Tent & Awning Inc........... E 812 232-4206
  Terre Haute (G-15537)
Phil Irwin Advertising Inc................... F 317 547-5117
  Indianapolis (G-9134)

RENTAL SVCS: Work Zone Traffic Eqpt, Flags, Cones, Etc

Highway Safety Services Inc................ D 765 474-1000
  Lafayette (G-10599)
Road Alert Systems LLC..................... G 219 669-1206
  Morocco (G-12269)

RENTAL: Portable Toilet

RENTAL: Video Tape & Disc

Nix Sanitary Service.................................. G 812 785-1158
  Boonville *(G-1094)*

RENTAL: Video Tape & Disc

Royal Inc... F 812 424-4925
  Evansville *(G-4295)*

RESEARCH, DEVELOPMENT & TESTING SVCS, COMM: Agricultural

Corteva Agriscience LLC....................... A 317 337-3000
  Indianapolis *(G-7884)*
Mycogen Corporation............................ F 317 337-3000
  Indianapolis *(G-8977)*
Naturegenic Inc..................................... G 765 807-5525
  West Lafayette *(G-16612)*

RESEARCH, DEVELOPMENT & TESTING SVCS, COMMERCIAL: Energy

Durhat Transportation LLC..................... G 463 204-9119
  Greenwood *(G-6691)*

RESEARCH, DEVELOPMENT & TESTING SVCS, COMMERCIAL: Medical

Biokorf LLC.. G 765 727-0782
  West Lafayette *(G-16565)*
Biopoly LLC... F 260 999-6135
  Fort Wayne *(G-4802)*
Cook Medical Holdings LLC.................. G 812 339-2235
  Bloomington *(G-842)*
Inotiv Inc... G 812 985-5900
  Mount Vernon *(G-12302)*

RESEARCH, DEVELOPMENT & TESTING SVCS, COMMERCIAL: Physical

Contour Hardening Inc........................... E 888 867-2184
  Indianapolis *(G-7861)*

RESINS: Custom Compound Purchased

Color Master Inc.................................. D 260 868-2320
  Butler *(G-1461)*
Crosspoint Polymer Tech LLC............... E 812 426-1350
  Evansville *(G-3997)*
Envalior Engineering Materials Inc......... C 800 333-4237
  Evansville *(G-4039)*
Envalior Engineering Mtls Inc................ G 812 435-7500
  Evansville *(G-4041)*
Enviroplas LLC..................................... D 812 868-0808
  Evansville *(G-4043)*
Enviroplas LLC..................................... D 812 868-0808
  Evansville *(G-4044)*
Geon Performance Solutions LLC.......... G 812 466-5116
  Terre Haute *(G-15596)*
Innovations Amplified LLC..................... G 317 339-4685
  Indianapolis *(G-8552)*
Lush & Luxe Creations LLC.................. G 317 561-0574
  Indianapolis *(G-8798)*
Matrixx-Qtr Inc...................................... D 812 429-0901
  Evansville *(G-4192)*
McCammon Engineering Corp............... G 812 356-4455
  Sullivan *(G-15413)*
Miller Waste Mills Inc............................ G 507 454-6900
  Indianapolis *(G-8924)*
Mwf LLC... G 812 936-5303
  Bloomington *(G-927)*
Polyram Compounds LLC...................... F 812 401-5830
  Evansville *(G-4248)*
Polytek Development Corp.................... G 317 494-6420
  Franklin *(G-5767)*
Rbc Holding Inc.................................... F 317 340-3845
  Greenwood *(G-6759)*

Sabic Innovative Plas US LLC................ B 812 831-4054
  Mount Vernon *(G-12319)*
Sabic Innvtive Plas Mt Vrnon L............... A 812 838-4385
  Mount Vernon *(G-12320)*

RESPIRATORS

Airgas Usa LLC.................................... G 317 248-8072
  Indianapolis *(G-7464)*

RESTAURANT EQPT: Sheet Metal

Indy Hoods LLC.................................... F 317 731-7170
  Indianapolis *(G-8529)*

RESTAURANTS: Fast Food

Dugdale Beef Company Inc................... E 317 291-9660
  Indianapolis *(G-8019)*

RESTAURANTS: Full Svc, American

Clancys of Portage................................. E 219 764-4995
  Portage *(G-13856)*

RETAIL BAKERY: Bread

Always Fresh Baked Goods Inc.............. E 317 319-4747
  Martinsville *(G-11380)*
Cornerstone Bread Co............................ G 317 897-9671
  Indianapolis *(G-7877)*
Ganal Corporation.................................. G 260 749-2161
  New Haven *(G-12903)*
Shipshewana Bread Box Corp................ G 260 768-4629
  Shipshewana *(G-14887)*

RETAIL BAKERY: Cakes

Almiras Bakery..................................... F 219 844-4334
  Hammond *(G-6872)*
Concannons Pastry Shop....................... F 765 288-8551
  Muncie *(G-12369)*
Fingerhut Bakery Inc............................. F 574 896-5937
  North Judson *(G-13212)*
Moms Pound Cakes LLC....................... G 773 220-3822
  Merrillville *(G-11544)*

RETAIL BAKERY: Cookies

Blondies Cookies Inc............................ F 765 628-3978
  Greentown *(G-6645)*
Loaded Dough Cookie Co LLC.............. G 765 969-6513
  Centerville *(G-1851)*

RETAIL BAKERY: Doughnuts

Square Donuts Inc................................. G 812 232-6463
  Terre Haute *(G-15714)*
Westfield Donuts................................... G 317 896-5856
  Westfield *(G-16739)*

RETAIL BAKERY: Pretzels

Brilliant Blondes LLC............................ F 765 288-8077
  Muncie *(G-12357)*
Chestnut Land Company........................ G 574 271-8740
  Mishawaka *(G-11860)*
Pretzels Inc... E 574 941-2201
  Plymouth *(G-13807)*

RETAIL STORES: Artificial Limbs

Advanced Orthopro Inc......................... G 812 478-3656
  Terre Haute *(G-15531)*
Northern Prosthetics Inc....................... G 574 233-2459
  South Bend *(G-15174)*

RETAIL STORES: Audio-Visual Eqpt & Splys

Technology Cons Group LLC................ G 219 525-4064
  Merrillville *(G-11565)*

RETAIL STORES: Batteries, Non-Automotive

Ocella Inc... G 845 842-8185
  Newberry *(G-12990)*

RETAIL STORES: Business Machines & Eqpt

Gesco Group LLC................................ G 260 747-5088
  Fort Wayne *(G-5023)*
Rose-Wall Mfg Inc................................ G 317 894-4497
  Greenfield *(G-6544)*
The Office Shop Inc............................. E 812 934-5611
  Batesville *(G-607)*

RETAIL STORES: Cake Decorating Splys

Black Rose Pastries LLC....................... G 773 708-3650
  Gary *(G-5901)*

RETAIL STORES: Christmas Lights & Decorations

Candles By Dar Inc............................... F 260 482-2099
  Fort Wayne *(G-4831)*
Herman Tool & Machine Inc................. F 574 594-5544
  Pierceton *(G-13632)*
Pgs LLC.. F 812 988-4030
  Nashville *(G-12678)*

RETAIL STORES: Cleaning Eqpt & Splys

Modrak Products Company Inc............. F 219 838-0308
  Gary *(G-5985)*

RETAIL STORES: Concrete Prdts, Precast

P3 Polymers LLC................................. G 812 674-2051
  Washington *(G-16499)*
Reams Concrete.................................... G 812 752-3746
  Scottsburg *(G-14575)*

RETAIL STORES: Cosmetics

Love-Toi LLC....................................... G 317 537-7635
  Anderson *(G-149)*
Majesty Hair Care System LLC............. G 317 900-6789
  Indianapolis *(G-8818)*

RETAIL STORES: Decals

Pyramid Sign & Design Inc................... G 765 447-4174
  Lafayette *(G-10674)*

RETAIL STORES: Educational Aids & Electronic Training Mat

Abundant Life Publications LLC............ G 219 730-7621
  Gary *(G-5887)*

RETAIL STORES: Electronic Parts & Eqpt

Cybernaut Industria LLC....................... G 317 664-5316
  Indianapolis *(G-7939)*
Northwind Electronics LLC.................... F 317 288-0787
  Indianapolis *(G-9024)*

RETAIL STORES: Flags

Flag & Banner Company Inc................. F 317 299-4880
  Indianapolis *(G-8199)*
Flags International Inc........................... G 574 674-5125
  Osceola *(G-13392)*

RETAIL STORES: Hearing Aids

Belltone Hearing Care Center................ G 317 462-9999
  Greenfield *(G-6470)*
D J Investments Inc.............................. G 765 348-3558
  Hartford City *(G-7064)*
D J Investments Inc.............................. G 765 348-4381
  Hartford City *(G-7063)*

PRODUCT SECTION

RUBBER PRDTS: Silicone

Integrity Hearing................................. G 317 882-9151
Noblesville *(G-13107)*

Starkey Laboratories Inc...................... F 952 828-6943
Plainfield *(G-13731)*

Wilsons Hearing Aid Center LLC............ G 765 747-4131
Muncie *(G-12521)*

RETAIL STORES: Ice

Home City Ice Company........................ G 317 926-2451
Indianapolis *(G-8404)*

RETAIL STORES: Infant Furnishings & Eqpt

Wasu Inc... G 765 448-4450
West Lafayette *(G-16645)*

RETAIL STORES: Medical Apparatus & Splys

Gvs Filter Technology Inc...................... E 317 471-3700
Indianapolis *(G-8345)*

Mold Removers LLC............................... G 317 846-0977
Indianapolis *(G-8946)*

Vintage Chemical Inc............................. G 260 745-7272
Fort Wayne *(G-5533)*

RETAIL STORES: Orthopedic & Prosthesis Applications

American Limb & Orthopedic Co............. G 574 522-3643
Elkhart *(G-3173)*

Central Brace & Limb Co Inc................. G 812 232-2145
Terre Haute *(G-15558)*

Central Brace & Limb Co Inc................. F 317 925-4296
Indianapolis *(G-7769)*

Hanger Prsthetcs & Ortho Inc................ F 219 844-2021
Hammond *(G-6944)*

Hanger Prsthtics Orthotics Inc............... G 765 966-5069
Richmond *(G-14131)*

Northern Brace Company Inc................. G 574 233-4221
South Bend *(G-15171)*

Tornier Inc.. G 574 268-0861
Warsaw *(G-16439)*

RETAIL STORES: Perfumes & Colognes

Bath & Body Works LLC......................... F 317 209-1517
Avon *(G-506)*

Bath & Body Works LLC......................... F 317 468-0834
Greenfield *(G-6469)*

Bath & Body Works LLC......................... F 219 531-2146
Valparaiso *(G-15910)*

RETAIL STORES: Pet Food

Hoosier Processing LLC......................... F 260 422-9440
Fort Wayne *(G-5080)*

RETAIL STORES: Pet Splys

Scott Pet Products Inc.......................... C 765 569-4636
Rockville *(G-14354)*

RETAIL STORES: Safety Splys & Eqpt

Advanced Lf Spport Innvtons LL............. G 574 538-1688
Goshen *(G-6090)*

Roberson Fire & Safety Inc................... G 317 879-3119
Indianapolis *(G-9313)*

RETAIL STORES: Spas & Hot Tubs

Masterspas LLC..................................... C 260 436-9100
Fort Wayne *(G-5207)*

Masterspas LLC..................................... D 260 436-9100
Fort Wayne *(G-5206)*

Pool Shop... G 812 446-0026
Brazil *(G-1162)*

RETAIL STORES: Telephone & Communication Eqpt

Williams Bros Hlth Care Phrm I............. E 812 335-0000
Bloomington *(G-1012)*

Williams Bros Hlth Care Phrm I............. C 812 254-2497
Washington *(G-16513)*

RETAIL STORES: Tents

Lafayette Tents & Events LLC............... E 765 742-4277
Lafayette *(G-10630)*

Montgomery Tent & Awning Co.............. F 317 357-9759
Indianapolis *(G-8951)*

RETAIL STORES: Water Purification Eqpt

Driessen Water Inc............................... G 765 529-4905
Muncie *(G-12386)*

Markle Water Treatment Plant............... G 260 758-3482
Markle *(G-11358)*

New Aqua LLC...................................... D 317 272-3000
Avon *(G-540)*

Puritan Water Conditioning.................... F 765 362-6340
Crawfordsville *(G-2606)*

Rayne Water Conditioning..................... G 765 742-8967
Lafayette *(G-10677)*

US Water Systems Inc.......................... E 317 209-0889
Indianapolis *(G-9688)*

RETAIL STORES: Welding Splys

Linde Gas & Equipment Inc................... G 260 423-4468
Fort Wayne *(G-5187)*

Linde Gas & Equipment Inc................... G 317 481-4550
Indianapolis *(G-8761)*

REUPHOLSTERY & FURNITURE REPAIR

Spectrum Marketing.............................. G 765 643-5566
Anderson *(G-197)*

RIBBONS, NEC

Indiana Ribbon Inc................................ E 219 279-2112
Wolcott *(G-16931)*

Tower Advertising Products Inc............. D 260 593-2103
Topeka *(G-15821)*

ROAD CONSTRUCTION EQUIPMENT WHOLESALERS

Simmons Equipment Sales Inc............... F 260 625-3308
Columbia City *(G-2197)*

ROBOTS: Assembly Line

ABB Flexible Automation Inc................. G 317 876-9090
Indianapolis *(G-7414)*

Amatrol Inc.. G 800 264-8285
Jeffersonville *(G-9929)*

Arbuckle Industries Inc......................... G 317 835-7489
Fairland *(G-4396)*

Banks Machine & Engrg LLC.................. D 317 642-4980
Shelbyville *(G-14732)*

Crume Industries LLC............................ G 574 747-7683
Elkhart *(G-3275)*

Enpak LLC.. G 574 268-7273
Warsaw *(G-16360)*

Flow International Corporation.............. F 253 850-3500
Jeffersonville *(G-9985)*

Nachi America Inc................................. E 877 622-4487
Greenwood *(G-6743)*

Probotech Inc....................................... G 317 849-6197
Indianapolis *(G-9217)*

Via Development Corp........................... D 888 225-5842
Marion *(G-11347)*

Wall Control Services Inc...................... G 260 450-6411
Fort Wayne *(G-5542)*

RODS: Extruded, Aluminum

Hydro Extrusion Usa LLC....................... B 888 935-5757
North Liberty *(G-13217)*

RODS: Steel & Iron, Made In Steel Mills

EVille Iron Street Rods Ltd................... G 812 428-3764
Evansville *(G-4062)*

ROLL FORMED SHAPES: Custom

Hoosier Trim Products LLC.................... E 317 271-4007
Indianapolis *(G-8412)*

Rfc LLC.. D 812 284-0650
Jeffersonville *(G-10046)*

United Roll Forming Corp...................... E 574 294-2800
Elkhart *(G-3760)*

ROLLING MILL EQPT: Finishing

Enbi Global Inc..................................... F 317 395-7324
Shelbyville *(G-14754)*

ROLLING MILL MACHINERY

Gsw Press Automation Inc..................... G 419 733-5230
North Vernon *(G-13273)*

Hoosier Roll Shop Services LLC............. F 219 844-8077
Hammond *(G-6947)*

ROLLING MILL ROLLS: Cast Steel

Cleveland-Cliffs Steel LLC..................... D 219 787-2120
Chesterton *(G-1914)*

Union Electric Steel Corp...................... G 219 464-1031
Valparaiso *(G-16071)*

ROLLS & BLANKETS, PRINTERS': Rubber Or Rubberized Fabric

ENBI INDIANA INC................................. C 317 398-3267
Shelbyville *(G-14755)*

ROOFING GRANULES

Enviri Corporation................................. F 219 944-6250
Gary *(G-5928)*

RUBBER PRDTS: Appliance, Mechanical

Griffith Rbr Mills of Garrett................... E 260 357-3125
Garrett *(G-5864)*

RUBBER PRDTS: Automotive, Mechanical

Ati Inc... G 812 520-5409
Mount Vernon *(G-12290)*

Ati Inc... G 812 431-5409
Mount Vernon *(G-12289)*

Bawaenterprises LLC............................. G 269 228-1258
Granger *(G-6336)*

BRC Rubber & Plastics Inc.................... E 260 827-0871
Bluffton *(G-1032)*

BRC Rubber & Plastics Inc.................... F 260 203-5300
Churubusco *(G-1974)*

BRC Rubber & Plastics Inc.................... C 260 693-2171
Fort Wayne *(G-4815)*

Fellwocks Automotive............................ G 812 867-3658
Evansville *(G-4067)*

Western Consolidated Tech Inc............. D 260 495-9866
Fremont *(G-5842)*

RUBBER PRDTS: Silicone

Exactseal Inc....................................... G 317 559-2220
Indianapolis *(G-8148)*

Gumena LLC... G 574 339-6510
Mishawaka *(G-11903)*

RUBBER PRDTS: Silicone

PTG Silicones Inc.................................. F 812 948-8719
New Albany *(G-12800)*

Sealwrap Systems LLC........................ G 317 462-3310
Greenfield *(G-6549)*

RUBBER PRDTS: Sponge

Obelisk Re-Play Opco LLC................... G 866 228-1485
Greenfield *(G-6534)*

RUBBER STRUCTURES: Air-Supported

Indianapolis Industrial Pdts.................. G 317 359-3078
Indianapolis *(G-8506)*

RUGS : Hand & Machine Made

Too Tuft LLC... G 317 719-2182
Indianapolis *(G-9618)*

SAFE DEPOSIT BOXES

PSI LLC.. G 765 483-0954
Lebanon *(G-10935)*

Risco Products Inc.............................. G 317 392-6150
Shelbyville *(G-14791)*

SAFES & VAULTS: Metal

Customer 1st LLC................................ G 812 733-4638
Borden *(G-1107)*

Customer 1st LLC................................ G 877 768-9970
Pekin *(G-13514)*

Fire King International LLC................... E 812 822-5574
New Albany *(G-12729)*

Fki Security Group LLC........................ B 812 948-8400
New Albany *(G-12730)*

Johnson Safe Company LLC................ G 317 876-7233
Zionsville *(G-17025)*

Meilink Safe Company......................... D 812 941-0024
New Albany *(G-12774)*

Tuff Stuff Sales and Svc Inc.................. F 765 354-4151
Middletown *(G-11778)*

SAFETY EQPT & SPLYS WHOLESALERS

Asphalt Materials Inc........................... G 317 875-4670
Indianapolis *(G-7553)*

Region Signs Inc................................. F 219 473-1616
Whiting *(G-16838)*

SALES PROMOTION SVCS

Gs Sales Inc.. G 317 595-6750
Westfield *(G-16695)*

Minute Print It Inc................................. G 765 482-9019
Lebanon *(G-10916)*

Plaquemaker Plus Inc.......................... G 317 594-5556
Fishers *(G-4576)*

SALT

Alebro LLC... F 317 876-9212
Indianapolis *(G-7468)*

Es Deicing... G 260 422-2020
Fort Wayne *(G-4960)*

Giles Chemical Corporation................. G 812 537-4852
Greendale *(G-6445)*

Morton Salt Inc.................................... D 219 477-0461
New Haven *(G-12910)*

SAMPLE BOOKS

Leed Selling Tools Corp....................... E 812 867-4340
Evansville *(G-4164)*

SAND & GRAVEL

Beer and Slabaugh Inc........................ E 574 773-3413
Nappanee *(G-12584)*

Chuck Shane Gravel LLC..................... G 574 893-4110
Silver Lake *(G-14918)*

Cimentos N Votorantim Amer Inc.......... E 812 384-9463
Bloomfield *(G-744)*

D H Gravel Company............................ G 765 893-4914
Williamsport *(G-16847)*

Engineering Aggregates Corp.............. G 765 249-3073
Michigantown *(G-11690)*

Flynn & Sons Sand & Gravel LLC......... G 812 636-4400
Odon *(G-13335)*

GCI Slingers LLC.................................. F 317 873-8686
Zionsville *(G-17011)*

Gibson County Sand & Grav Inc............ G 812 851-5800
Haubstadt *(G-7085)*

Gravel Doctor Indianapolis LLC............ G 317 399-4585
Indianapolis *(G-8313)*

Greenfield Gravel Inc........................... G 317 326-4003
Greenfield *(G-6506)*

Handson.. F 812 246-4481
Sellersburg *(G-14595)*

Happy Valley Sand and Grav Inc........... G 317 839-6800
Plainfield *(G-13684)*

Harrison Hauling Inc............................ G 574 862-3196
Goshen *(G-6162)*

Harrison Sand and Gravel Co............... G 812 656-8149
West Harrison *(G-16547)*

Hassenplug & Son Sand & Gravel........ G 574 223-5230
Rochester *(G-14294)*

Henschen Sand and Gravel.................. G 260 367-2636
Howe *(G-7236)*

Holcim (us) Inc.................................... G 219 378-1193
East Chicago *(G-3017)*

Hydraulic Press Brick Company........... C 317 290-1140
Mooresville *(G-12212)*

Indiana Gravel LLC.............................. G 574 538-7152
Goshen *(G-6173)*

Ingram Road Quarry LLC..................... G 812 824-3730
Springville *(G-15386)*

Irving Materials Inc.............................. F 765 778-4760
Anderson *(G-136)*

Irving Materials Inc.............................. F 765 922-7285
Kokomo *(G-10291)*

Lake County Sand & Gravel LLC.......... G 219 988-4540
Merrillville *(G-11528)*

Lees Ready-Mix & Trucking Inc............ F 812 372-1800
Columbus *(G-2339)*

Longhorn Sand and Gravel LLC........... G 574 532-2788
North Liberty *(G-13218)*

Marietta Martin Materials Inc............... G 317 831-7391
Martinsville *(G-11411)*

Marietta Martin Materials Inc............... F 317 776-4460
Noblesville *(G-13130)*

Michele L Gravel................................. G 317 889-0521
Indianapolis *(G-8899)*

Mulzer Crushed Stone Inc................... E 844 480-6803
Evansville *(G-4216)*

Muncie Sand & Gravel Inc................... G 765 282-6422
Muncie *(G-12466)*

Paul H Rohe Company Inc................... E 812 926-1471
Aurora *(G-451)*

Quikrete Companies LLC..................... E 317 251-2281
Indianapolis *(G-9252)*

Rex Alton & Companies Inc................. F 812 882-8519
Vincennes *(G-16149)*

Rogers Group Inc................................ C 812 333-6324
Bloomington *(G-959)*

Rogers Group Inc................................ G 765 342-6898
Martinsville *(G-11424)*

Rogers Group Inc................................ D 812 849-3530
Mitchell *(G-12047)*

Rogers Group Inc................................ E 812 882-3640
Vincennes *(G-16150)*

Rogers Group Inc................................ E 765 893-4863
Williamsport *(G-16853)*

S & G Excavating Inc........................... F 812 234-4848
Terre Haute *(G-15685)*

Shelby Gravel Inc................................ F 317 738-3445
Franklin *(G-5776)*

Southfield Corporation......................... E 812 824-1355
Bloomington *(G-978)*

Speedway Sand & Gravel Inc............... G 574 893-7355
Silver Lake *(G-14922)*

Spray Inc... F 812 346-3197
Seymour *(G-14695)*

Spray Sand & Gravel Inc...................... G 812 522-5417
Seymour *(G-14696)*

Steele Roofing Co LLC........................ G 219 243-1563
Valparaiso *(G-16058)*

Stone Quary.. G 574 936-2975
Plymouth *(G-13814)*

Todd L Wise.. G 260 799-4828
Albion *(G-46)*

Wallace Construction Inc..................... F 317 422-5356
Martinsville *(G-11434)*

Wells Trckg A Div Wlls Assoc I............. G 317 250-2616
Indianapolis *(G-9750)*

SAND LIME PRDTS

Martins Lime Service Inc..................... G 574 784-2270
Plymouth *(G-13796)*

SAND MINING

Asphalt Materials Inc........................... G 317 875-4670
Indianapolis *(G-7553)*

Asphalt Materials Inc........................... B 317 872-6010
Indianapolis *(G-7552)*

Brookfield Sand & Gravel Inc............... E 317 835-2235
Fairland *(G-4398)*

Crisman Sand Company Inc................ G 219 462-3114
Valparaiso *(G-15930)*

Elkhart County Gravel Inc.................... G 574 831-2815
Warsaw *(G-16357)*

Elkhart County Gravel Inc.................... G 574 831-2815
New Paris *(G-12951)*

Heidelberg Mtls Sthast Agg LLC........... E 317 788-4086
Indianapolis *(G-8380)*

Illiana Remedial Action Inc.................. G 219 844-4862
Hammond *(G-6954)*

Merritt Sand and Gravel Inc................. F 260 665-2513
Waterloo *(G-16524)*

North America Frac Sand Inc............... G 260 490-9990
Ossian *(G-13429)*

Schmaltz Ready Mix Concrete.............. G 812 689-5140
Osgood *(G-13415)*

Stone Quary.. E 765 473-5578
Peru *(G-13603)*

SANDBLASTING EQPT

Forecast Sales Inc............................... F 317 829-0147
Indianapolis *(G-8214)*

Taggarts Custom Sndblst LLC.............. G 765 825-4584
Connersville *(G-2471)*

SANITARY SVCS: Hazardous Waste, Collection & Disposal

Tradebe Environmental Svcs LLC......... E 800 388-7242
Merrillville *(G-11568)*

Tradebe GP... A 800 388-7242
East Chicago *(G-3045)*

Winski Brothers Inc.............................. G 765 654-5323
Frankfort *(G-5702)*

SANITARY SVCS: Medical Waste Disposal

Circle Medical Products Inc................. G 317 271-2626
Indianapolis *(G-7809)*

PRODUCT SECTION
SCREW MACHINE PRDTS

SANITARY SVCS: Refuse Collection & Disposal Svcs

Recycling Center Inc.................................. D 765 966-8295
Richmond *(G-14195)*

SANITARY SVCS: Rubbish Collection & Disposal

Hunts Maintenance Inc............................. G 219 785-2333
Westville *(G-16762)*

SANITARY SVCS: Waste Materials, Recycling

Blackwood Solutions LLC........................ D 812 676-8770
Bloomington *(G-809)*
Concrete & Asphalt Recycl Inc................. G 574 237-1928
Mishawaka *(G-11864)*
Green Stream Company............................ C 574 293-1949
Elkhart *(G-3391)*
Mervis Industries Inc.............................. G 812 232-1251
Terre Haute *(G-15643)*
Plastic Recycling Inc............................... E 317 780-6100
Indianapolis *(G-9151)*

SATELLITES: Communications

Midwest Comm Solutions LLP................. G 800 880-5847
Fort Wayne *(G-5224)*
Woody Enterprises LLC........................... G 765 498-7300
Bloomingdale *(G-763)*

SAWDUST & SHAVINGS

North Central Ind Shavings LLC............... G 765 395-3875
Converse *(G-2478)*

SAWMILL MACHINES

Wood-Mizer Holdings Inc........................ D 812 663-5257
Greensburg *(G-6642)*
Wood-Mizer Holdings Inc........................ C 317 271-1542
Indianapolis *(G-9784)*

SAWS & SAWING EQPT

Beckler Power Equipment........................ G 260 356-1188
Huntington *(G-7300)*
Drake Corporation................................... F 636 464-5070
Indianapolis *(G-8005)*
Otter Creek Christian Church................... G 812 446-5300
Brazil *(G-1159)*
Pool Shop... G 812 446-0026
Brazil *(G-1162)*

SCAFFOLDS: Mobile Or Stationary, Metal

Sonny Scaffolds Inc................................. F 317 831-3900
Mooresville *(G-12243)*

SCALE REPAIR SVCS

Technical Weighing Svcs Inc.................... E 219 924-3366
Griffith *(G-6819)*
Valley Scale Company LLC...................... F 812 282-5269
Clarksville *(G-2041)*

SCALES & BALANCES, EXC LABORATORY

Powell Systems Inc................................. E 765 884-0980
Fowler *(G-5630)*
Raco Industries LLC................................ G 812 232-3676
Terre Haute *(G-15674)*
Sinden Racing Service Inc....................... F 317 243-7171
Indianapolis *(G-9443)*
Weights & Measures............................... G 812 349-2566
Bloomington *(G-1008)*

SCALES: Indl

A H Emery Company............................... G 812 466-5265
Terre Haute *(G-15527)*
Indiana Scale Company Inc..................... F 812 232-0893
Terre Haute *(G-15617)*
Richards Scale Company Inc................... G 812 246-3354
Sellersburg *(G-14612)*
Winslow Scale Company.......................... E 812 466-5265
Terre Haute *(G-15747)*

SCHOOLS: Vocational, NEC

Crown Training and Dev Inc.................... F 219 947-0845
Merrillville *(G-11500)*

SCIENTIFIC INSTRUMENTS WHOLESALERS

Lk Technologies Inc................................. G 812 332-4449
Bloomington *(G-912)*

SCISSORS: Hand

Allen-Davis Enterprises Inc..................... G 574 303-2173
Mishawaka *(G-11837)*

SCRAP & WASTE MATERIALS, WHOLESALE: Ferrous Metal

J Trockman & Sons Inc........................... E 812 425-5271
Evansville *(G-4134)*
Joe W Morgan Inc................................... D 812 423-5914
Evansville *(G-4143)*
Mervis Industries Inc.............................. G 765 454-5800
Kokomo *(G-10306)*
Omnisource LLC..................................... G 574 654-7561
New Carlisle *(G-12843)*
Omnisource LLC..................................... C 260 422-5541
Fort Wayne *(G-5286)*
P & H Iron & Supply Inc.......................... F 219 853-0240
Hammond *(G-6990)*
Porter County Ir & Met Recycle................ F 219 996-7630
Hebron *(G-7104)*
Recycling Center Inc............................... D 765 966-8295
Richmond *(G-14195)*
Winski Brothers Inc................................. G 765 654-5323
Frankfort *(G-5702)*

SCRAP & WASTE MATERIALS, WHOLESALE: Metal

American Scrap Processing Inc................ C 219 398-1444
East Chicago *(G-2989)*
D Martin Enterprises Inc......................... F 219 872-8211
Michigan City *(G-11596)*
Kendallville Iron & Metal Inc................... F 260 347-1958
Kendallville *(G-10126)*
Mervis Industries Inc.............................. G 812 232-1251
Terre Haute *(G-15643)*
Remedium Services Group LLC................ F 317 660-6868
Carmel *(G-1741)*

SCRAP & WASTE MATERIALS, WHOLESALE: Nonferrous Metals Scrap

Newco Metals Inc.................................... G 765 644-6649
Anderson *(G-168)*
Newco Metals Inc.................................... E 317 485-7721
Pendleton *(G-13546)*

SCRAP & WASTE MATERIALS, WHOLESALE: Paper

Recycling Works LLC............................... F 574 293-3751
Elkhart *(G-3644)*

SCRAP STEEL CUTTING

Steel Dynamics Inc.................................. B 260 969-3500
Fort Wayne *(G-5438)*

SCREENS: Projection

Da-Lite Screen Company LLC................... B 574 267-8101
Warsaw *(G-16342)*
Legrand AV Inc....................................... B 574 267-8101
Warsaw *(G-16387)*

SCREW MACHINE PRDTS

Accurate Mnfctred Pdts Group I............... E 317 472-9000
Indianapolis *(G-7420)*
Aegis Sales and Engineering................... F 260 483-4160
Fort Wayne *(G-4731)*
Alexander Screw Products Inc................. E 317 898-5313
Indianapolis *(G-7469)*
Ashley F Ward Inc................................... G 574 294-1502
Elkhart *(G-3196)*
Ashley F Ward Inc................................... G 219 879-4177
Michigan City *(G-11580)*
Auburn Manufacturing Inc....................... E 260 925-8651
Auburn *(G-364)*
Bar-Wal Products.................................... G 574 457-5311
Syracuse *(G-15455)*
Beckett Bronze Company Inc................... E 765 282-2261
Muncie *(G-12350)*
Biddle Precision Components Inc............ C 317 758-4451
Sheridan *(G-14817)*
Charleston Metal Products Inc................. E 260 837-8211
Waterloo *(G-16516)*
Charleston Metal Products Inc................. D 260 837-8211
Waterloo *(G-16517)*
D & S Machine Products Inc.................... E 812 926-6250
Aurora *(G-442)*
Ds Products Inc....................................... E 260 563-9030
Wabash *(G-16182)*
Dual Machine Corporation....................... F 317 921-9850
Indianapolis *(G-8017)*
Ebert Machine Company Inc.................... E 765 473-3728
Peru *(G-13581)*
EMC Precision Machining II LLC.............. D 317 758-4451
Sheridan *(G-14822)*
Epco Products Inc................................... E 260 747-8888
Fort Wayne *(G-4956)*
Exactifab.. G 812 420-2723
Brazil *(G-1142)*
F & F Screw Machine Products................ E 574 293-0362
Elkhart *(G-3340)*
Fitech Inc... E 513 398-1414
Michigan City *(G-11613)*
Gapco Inc... G 317 787-6440
Indianapolis *(G-8259)*
H & E Machined Specialties..................... F 260 424-2527
Fort Wayne *(G-5045)*
Ham Enterprises Machine Co................... G 765 342-7966
Martinsville *(G-11399)*
Jerden Industries Inc.............................. E 812 332-1762
Bloomington *(G-896)*
Jessen Manufacturing Co Inc................... D 574 295-3836
Elkhart *(G-3432)*
Jrp Machine Co....................................... G 317 955-1905
Indianapolis *(G-8644)*
Kent Brenneke.. G 260 446-5383
Harlan *(G-7057)*
Madison Tool and Die Inc........................ D 812 273-2250
Madison *(G-11239)*
Mid America Screw Products................... F 574 294-6905
Elkhart *(G-3537)*
Mitchel & Scott Machine Co..................... F 317 639-5331
Indianapolis *(G-8933)*
Mitchel Group Incorporated..................... C 317 639-5331
Indianapolis *(G-8934)*
National Consolidated Corp..................... F 574 289-7885
South Bend *(G-15159)*

SCREW MACHINE PRDTS

Northern Indiana Manufacturing............ E 574 342-2105
  Bourbon *(G-1125)*
Performance Cnc LLC........................... G 574 780-4864
  Bourbon *(G-1126)*
Point Machine Products Inc................... G 574 289-2429
  South Bend *(G-15199)*
Precision Piece Parts Inc....................... D 574 255-3185
  Mishawaka *(G-11978)*
Prodigy Mold & Tool Inc....................... E 812 753-3029
  Haubstadt *(G-7088)*
RCO-Reed Corporation.......................... E 317 736-8014
  Franklin *(G-5771)*
RD Smith Manufacturing Inc.................. G 260 829-6709
  Orland *(G-13372)*
RTC... G 260 503-9770
  Columbia City *(G-2193)*
S H Leggitt Company............................. G 574 264-0230
  Elkhart *(G-3656)*
Sierra Machine...................................... G 574 232-5694
  South Bend *(G-15242)*
Standard Locknut LLC........................... C 317 399-2230
  Westfield *(G-16729)*
Terry Liquidation III Inc........................ F 219 362-3557
  La Porte *(G-10490)*
Tri Aerospace LLC................................. E 812 872-2400
  Terre Haute *(G-15736)*
Winn Machine Inc.................................. G 219 324-2978
  La Porte *(G-10501)*

SCREWS: Metal

Indiana Automotive Fas Inc................... B 317 467-0100
  Greenfield *(G-6511)*

SEALANTS

Ace Extrusion LLC................................. E 812 463-5230
  Evansville *(G-3871)*
Aeromind LLC....................................... G 800 905-2157
  Indianapolis *(G-7453)*
Geocel Holdings Corporation................. D 574 264-0645
  Elkhart *(G-3376)*
Koch Enterprises Inc............................. G 812 465-9800
  Evansville *(G-4159)*
Multiseal Inc... C 812 428-3422
  Evansville *(G-4215)*
Uniseal Inc.. E 812 425-1361
  Evansville *(G-4360)*
Uniseal Inc.. C 812 425-1361
  Evansville *(G-4361)*

SEALING COMPOUNDS: Sealing, synthetic rubber or plastic

Franco Corporation............................... G 765 675-6691
  Tipton *(G-15774)*
PRC - Desoto International Inc.............. E 317 290-1600
  Indianapolis *(G-9177)*
Trelleborg Sling Sltions US Inc.............. C 260 748-5895
  Fort Wayne *(G-5502)*

SEALS: Oil, Rubber

Freudenberg-Nok General Partnr........... C 317 421-3400
  Shelbyville *(G-14756)*
Press-Seal Corporation......................... G 260 436-0521
  Fort Wayne *(G-5349)*
Press-Seal Corporation......................... C 260 436-0521
  Fort Wayne *(G-5350)*
T & M Rubber Inc.................................. E 574 533-3173
  Goshen *(G-6267)*

SEARCH & NAVIGATION SYSTEMS

Aerogage Inc.. G 978 422-8224
  Martinsville *(G-11378)*

Bae Systems Controls Inc...................... A 260 434-5195
  Fort Wayne *(G-4787)*
L3harris Technologies Inc..................... G 812 202-5171
  Crane *(G-2540)*
L3harris Technologies Inc..................... G 260 451-5597
  Fort Wayne *(G-5169)*
Lockheed Martin Corporation................ G 317 821-4000
  Indianapolis *(G-8776)*
Outdoor Technologies LLC..................... G 812 654-4399
  Milan *(G-11782)*
Pyromation LLC..................................... C 260 484-2580
  Fort Wayne *(G-5358)*
Raytheon Company............................... A 310 647-9438
  Fort Wayne *(G-5366)*
Raytheon Company............................... C 317 306-8471
  Indianapolis *(G-9273)*

SEAT BELTS: Automobile & Aircraft

Gerardot Performance Pdts Inc.............. G 260 623-3048
  Monroeville *(G-12069)*
Wolf Technical Engineering LLC............ G 800 783-9653
  Indianapolis *(G-9781)*

SEATING: Stadium

Preferred Seating Company LLC............ G 317 782-3323
  Indianapolis *(G-9190)*

SECURITY CONTROL EQPT & SYSTEMS

AV Solutions Indy LLC............................ G 317 509-5930
  Indianapolis *(G-7578)*
Center For Ethcal Rbtics A Nnt.............. G 219 741-9374
  Hammond *(G-6897)*
Johnson Cntrls SEC Sltions LLC............. G 800 238-2455
  Indianapolis *(G-8634)*
Magnasphere Corporation..................... G 574 533-1310
  Goshen *(G-6209)*
Nrk Inc.. E 812 232-1800
  Terre Haute *(G-15653)*
Phil & Son Inc....................................... G 219 663-5757
  Crown Point *(G-2730)*
Sitewise Inc.. G 317 988-1630
  Indianapolis *(G-9444)*
USA Vision Systems Inc........................ G 949 583-1519
  Fishers *(G-4625)*

SECURITY DEVICES

Allegion LLC.. E 317 810-3700
  Carmel *(G-1553)*
Applied Technology Group Inc.............. F 260 482-2844
  Fort Wayne *(G-4767)*
Conzer Security Inc.............................. G 317 580-9460
  Carmel *(G-1595)*
Loud Clear Communications LLC........... G 260 433-9479
  Auburn *(G-403)*
Poolguard/Pbm Industries Inc............... F 812 346-2648
  North Vernon *(G-13292)*
Quick Panic Release LLC...................... G 812 841-5733
  Terre Haute *(G-15673)*
Qumulex Inc... E 317 207-0520
  Fishers *(G-4590)*
Reese Forge Orna Ironwork................... G 219 775-1039
  Lake Village *(G-10782)*

SECURITY GUARD SVCS

AM General LLC.................................... A 574 258-7523
  Mishawaka *(G-11840)*

SECURITY SYSTEMS SERVICES

Lionfish Cyber Hldngs LLC-S Ln............ G 877 732-6772
  Indianapolis *(G-8766)*
Loud Clear Communications LLC........... G 260 433-9479
  Auburn *(G-403)*

Phil & Son Inc....................................... G 219 663-5757
  Crown Point *(G-2730)*
Pro It Solutions LLC.............................. F 574 862-0021
  Wakarusa *(G-16244)*
Roi Marketing Company Inc................... G 317 644-0797
  Indianapolis *(G-9321)*

SEEDS & BULBS WHOLESALERS

Corteva Agriscience LLC....................... A 317 337-3000
  Indianapolis *(G-7884)*

SEMICONDUCTORS & RELATED DEVICES

3 Micron Laser Technology LLC............. G 317 677-8958
  Indianapolis *(G-7387)*
Advanced Control Tech Inc.................... G 317 806-2750
  Indianapolis *(G-7437)*
Allegro Microsystems LLC..................... G 765 854-2263
  Carmel *(G-1557)*
Autosem Inc.. E 574 288-8866
  South Bend *(G-14953)*
Bandgap Semiconductor LLC................. G 317 652-3250
  Noblesville *(G-13038)*
Bowmar LLC.. E 260 747-3121
  Fort Wayne *(G-4813)*
Ca Inc... E 317 844-7221
  Indianapolis *(G-7711)*
Convergent Consulting LLC................... G 202 441-6453
  Indianapolis *(G-7864)*
Environmental Technology Inc............... E 574 233-1202
  South Bend *(G-15016)*
Express Controls................................... G 574 831-3497
  Goshen *(G-6131)*
Fireflies Ltd... G 219 728-6245
  Chesterton *(G-1926)*
Gen Digital Inc..................................... G 317 575-4010
  Indianapolis *(G-8268)*
Heraeus Electro-Nite Co LLC................ C 765 473-8275
  Peru *(G-13584)*
Hoosier Cab Company LLC.................... G 812 822-2508
  Bloomington *(G-879)*
Indiana Intgrated Circuits LLC.............. G 574 217-4612
  South Bend *(G-15078)*
Infineon Tech Americas Corp................ G 866 951-9519
  Kokomo *(G-10288)*
Microchip Technology Inc..................... G 317 842-1676
  Indianapolis *(G-8901)*
Microchip Technology Inc..................... G 317 773-8323
  Noblesville *(G-13139)*
Microscreen LLC.................................... E 574 232-4358
  South Bend *(G-15150)*
Netegrity Inc.. F 219 763-6400
  Portage *(G-13898)*
Nxp Usa Inc.. G 765 459-5355
  Kokomo *(G-10318)*
Power Components of Midwest.............. E 574 256-6990
  Mishawaka *(G-11976)*
Pyromation LLC..................................... C 260 484-2580
  Fort Wayne *(G-5358)*
Sanders Pulsed Power LLC.................... G 630 313-2378
  South Bend *(G-15232)*
Semicndctor Cmponents Inds LLC......... G 765 868-5015
  Kokomo *(G-10333)*
Texas Instruments Incorporated............ G 317 574-2611
  Carmel *(G-1784)*
Toppan Photomasks Inc........................ C 765 854-7500
  Kokomo *(G-10350)*
US Nano LLC... G 941 360-2161
  South Bend *(G-15297)*
Vishay Americas Inc.............................. G 765 778-4878
  Pendleton *(G-13561)*

PRODUCT SECTION　　　　　　　　　　　　　　　　　　　　　　　　　SHOE STORES: Boots, Men's

SENSORS: Infrared, Solid State

Hartsock Industrial Sales Inc................. G 317 858-8250
　Westfield *(G-16696)*

SENSORS: Radiation

Mark Lamaster... G 765 534-4185
　Noblesville *(G-13131)*

SENSORS: Temperature, Exc Indl Process

Honeywell International Inc................... G 812 473-4163
　Evansville *(G-4108)*
Pyromation LLC....................................... C 260 484-2580
　Fort Wayne *(G-5358)*

SEPTIC TANK CLEANING SVCS

Mnt Delivery Company............................ G 574 518-6250
　Osceola *(G-13399)*

SEPTIC TANKS: Concrete

Bowsman Tank Co.................................. G 260 244-7129
　Columbia City *(G-2125)*
Carter Septic Tank Inc............................ G 574 583-5796
　Monticello *(G-12141)*
Creed & Dyer Precast Inc....................... G 574 784-3361
　Lakeville *(G-10789)*
Eaton Septic Tank Company................. G 765 396-3275
　Eaton *(G-3060)*
Farmer Legacy Inc................................. G 574 264-4625
　Elkhart *(G-3343)*
Holman Sptic Tank Sls Rdymix I........... F 812 689-1913
　Holton *(G-7217)*
Midwest Tile and Concrete Pdts............ G 260 749-5173
　Woodburn *(G-16953)*
Quality Tank Trucks & Eqp Inc.............. G 317 635-0000
　Indianapolis *(G-9247)*
Rochester Cement Products Inc............ G 574 223-3917
　Rochester *(G-14316)*
Russells Excvtg Sptic Tnks Inc............. F 812 838-2471
　Mount Vernon *(G-12318)*

SEWAGE & WATER TREATMENT EQPT

American Hydro Systems Inc................ F 866 357-5063
　Fort Wayne *(G-4755)*
Aqseptence Group Inc.......................... D 574 223-3980
　Rochester *(G-14278)*
Canature Watergroup USA Inc.............. G 877 771-6789
　Whitestown *(G-16802)*
Clute Enterprises Inc............................. G 260 413-0810
　Huntertown *(G-7250)*
Crawford Water Care.............................. G 317 758-6017
　Sheridan *(G-14820)*
Davis Water Services Inc...................... G 219 394-2270
　Rensselaer *(G-14050)*
Evoqua Water Technologies LLC.......... E 317 280-4255
　Indianapolis *(G-8145)*
Fluid-Tech International Corp................ G 260 420-5000
　Fort Wayne *(G-4988)*
Leistner Aquatic Services Inc............... G 317 535-6099
　Morgantown *(G-12160)*
Monroe County Regional Sewer........... G 812 824-9005
　Bloomington *(G-924)*
Technical Water Treatment Inc.............. G 574 277-1949
　Granger *(G-6186)*

SEWER CLEANING EQPT: Power

Brockwood Farm..................................... G 812 837-9607
　Nashville *(G-12664)*
SDP Manufacturing Inc.......................... E 765 768-5000
　Dunkirk *(G-2963)*
Sewer Optical Services Inc................... G 765 242-3768
　Lebanon *(G-10940)*

SEWING MACHINE REPAIR SHOP

Spectrum Services Inc........................... G 574 272-7605
　Granger *(G-6380)*

SEWING MACHINES & PARTS: Indl

Kirby Risk Corporation........................... F 765 664-5185
　Marion *(G-11304)*

SHADES: Window

Ascot Enterprises Inc............................. E 574 773-7751
　Nappanee *(G-12581)*
Ascot Enterprises Inc............................. E 877 773-7751
　Nappanee *(G-12582)*
United Shade LLC.................................. D 574 262-0954
　Elkhart *(G-3761)*

SHALE: Expanded

Hydraulic Press Brick Company............ E 317 290-1140
　Indianapolis *(G-8441)*

SHAPES & PILINGS, STRUCTURAL: Steel

Indiana Steel Fabricating Inc................. F 765 742-1031
　Lafayette *(G-10606)*
Viper USA Inc... D 765 742-4200
　West Lafayette *(G-16642)*

SHAPES: Extruded, Aluminum, NEC

80/20 LLC... B 260 248-8030
　Columbia City *(G-2114)*
Hoosier Trim Products LLC................... E 317 271-4007
　Indianapolis *(G-8412)*

SHAVING PREPARATIONS

103 Collection LLC................................ G 800 896-2945
　Schererville *(G-14510)*

SHEET METAL SPECIALTIES, EXC STAMPED

Bearcat Corp... E 574 533-0448
　Goshen *(G-6098)*
Bo-Mar Industries Inc............................. E 317 899-1240
　Indianapolis *(G-7651)*
Brand Sheet Metal Works Inc................ G 765 284-5594
　Muncie *(G-12356)*
Cartesian Corp....................................... E 765 742-0293
　Lafayette *(G-10548)*
Cyclone Manufacturing Co Inc.............. F 260 774-3311
　Urbana *(G-15885)*
D & V Precision Sheetmetal.................. E 317 462-2601
　Greenfield *(G-6485)*
Dud(e)s N Roses LLC............................ G 260 739-9053
　Fort Wayne *(G-4930)*
EH Baare Corporation............................ G 765 778-7895
　Anderson *(G-113)*
Enconco Inc.. E 317 251-1251
　Indianapolis *(G-8112)*
Estes Design and Mfg Inc..................... D 317 899-2203
　Indianapolis *(G-8138)*
Flexco Products Inc............................... C 574 294-2502
　Elkhart *(G-3348)*
Floor Works Mfg & Fab.......................... G 812 394-2311
　Fairbanks *(G-4395)*
Gary Metal Mfg LLC............................... E 219 885-3232
　Gary *(G-5937)*
Girtz Industries Inc................................. C 844 464-4789
　Monticello *(G-12151)*
Huntington Sheet Metal Inc................... D 260 356-9011
　Huntington *(G-7323)*
Imh Fabrication LLC............................... E 317 252-5566
　Indianapolis *(G-8465)*
Imh Fabrication LLC............................... F 317 508-7462
　Indianapolis *(G-8466)*

Lauck Manufacturing Co Inc.................. F 317 787-6269
　Indianapolis *(G-8727)*
Loyal Mfg Corp....................................... F 317 359-3185
　Indianapolis *(G-8788)*
Matrix Manufacturing Inc....................... G 260 854-4659
　Wolcottville *(G-16941)*
Noble Industries Inc............................... E 317 773-1926
　Noblesville *(G-13142)*
Pro-Fab Sheet Metal Ind Inc................. G
　Crown Point *(G-2737)*
Sam Mouron Equipment Co Inc............ F 317 776-1799
　Noblesville *(G-13171)*
Schuster Sheet Metal Inc...................... G 574 293-4802
　Elkhart *(G-3665)*
Sheet Metal Models Inc......................... F 317 783-1303
　Indianapolis *(G-9415)*
Tarpenning-Lafollette Co Inc................. E 317 780-1500
　Indianapolis *(G-9553)*
Tomlinson Manufacturing Co................. G 765 719-3700
　Franklin *(G-5783)*

SHELVING, MADE FROM PURCHASED WIRE

Angola Wire Products Inc...................... C 260 665-9447
　Angola *(G-229)*
Lafayette Wire Products Inc.................. D 765 474-7896
　Lafayette *(G-10632)*

SHELVING: Office & Store, Exc Wood

Cottom Automated Bus Soluti............... G 317 853-6531
　Carmel *(G-1599)*
Edsal Manufacturing Co LLC................ C 773 254-0600
　Gary *(G-5926)*

SHIELDS OR ENCLOSURES: Radiator, Sheet Metal

Mary Jonas.. F 317 500-0600
　Indianapolis *(G-8845)*

SHIMS: Metal

Agi International Inc............................... F 317 536-2415
　Indianapolis *(G-7458)*

SHIP BUILDING & REPAIRING: Cargo, Commercial

Branch Express Trucking LLC............... G 574 807-2212
　South Bend *(G-14961)*
Cargo Skiff Corporation......................... G 812 873-6349
　Butlerville *(G-1482)*

SHIP BUILDING & REPAIRING: Dredges

Paf Construction LLC............................ E 812 496-4669
　Columbus *(G-2371)*

SHIP BUILDING & REPAIRING: Ferryboats

Smoker Craft Inc.................................... B 574 831-2103
　New Paris *(G-12968)*

SHOE STORES

Amos D Graber & Sons.......................... F 260 749-0526
　New Haven *(G-12892)*
Cbrk LLC.. G 317 601-8546
　Indianapolis *(G-7764)*
Kinney Dancewear.................................. G 317 581-1800
　Noblesville *(G-13121)*

SHOE STORES: Athletic

Buddy Covers Inc................................... G 317 846-5766
　Carmel *(G-1575)*
Game Plan Graphics LLC...................... G 812 663-3238
　Greensburg *(G-6596)*

SHOE STORES: Boots, Men's

Discount Boots & Tack.................... G 812 522-9770
Seymour *(G-14648)*

SHOES: Athletic, Exc Rubber Or Plastic

Drillmaster Corp.............................. G 732 919-3088
Cynthiana *(G-2787)*

Onfield Apparel Group LLC.............. G 317 895-7249
Indianapolis *(G-9055)*

SHOES: Men's

Orb LLC... G 833 946-4672
Indianapolis *(G-9067)*

SHOES: Men's, Dress

Him Gentlemans Boutique................ G 812 924-7441
New Albany *(G-12741)*

SHOES: Plastic Or Rubber

Nike Inc.. G 219 879-1320
Michigan City *(G-11646)*

Orb LLC... G 833 946-4672
Indianapolis *(G-9067)*

Piro Shoes LLC............................... F 888 849-0916
Fishers *(G-4575)*

SHOES: Women's

Orb LLC... G 833 946-4672
Indianapolis *(G-9067)*

SHOT PEENING SVC

Metal Improvement Company LLC..... G 317 875-6030
Indianapolis *(G-8886)*

Toyo Seiko North America Inc.......... G 574 288-2000
South Bend *(G-15285)*

SHOWCASES & DISPLAY FIXTURES: Office & Store

Deflecto LLC.................................... B 317 849-9555
Indianapolis *(G-7962)*

SHOWER STALLS: Plastic & Fiberglass

Composite Tech Assemblies LLC...... E 574 948-0004
Plymouth *(G-13765)*

Frontline Mfg Inc............................. D 574 453-2902
Warsaw *(G-16366)*

Oasis Lifestyle LLC......................... F 574 948-0004
Plymouth *(G-13799)*

Ultra/Glas of Lakeville Inc................ F 574 784-8958
Lakeville *(G-10793)*

SHREDDERS: Indl & Commercial

Olympia Business Systems Inc........ F 800 225-5644
Wabash *(G-16206)*

SSP Technologies Inc..................... G 888 548-4668
Chesterton *(G-1958)*

SHUTTERS, DOOR & WINDOW: Metal

A Shutter In Time LLC..................... G 317 512-6753
Manilla *(G-11259)*

HB International LLC....................... G 574 773-8200
Nappanee *(G-12604)*

HB International LLC....................... D 574 773-0470
Nappanee *(G-12605)*

Heartland Shutter Company LLC...... G 317 710-3350
Indianapolis *(G-8378)*

Kinro Manufacturing Inc.................. E 574 535-1125
Elkhart *(G-3456)*

SHUTTERS, DOOR & WINDOW: Plastic

V N C Inc... F 219 696-5031
Lowell *(G-11179)*

SIDING: Sheet Metal

Johns Archtctral Met Solutions......... F 219 440-2116
Crown Point *(G-2703)*

Zimmer Metal Sales LLC................. G 574 862-1800
Goshen *(G-6280)*

SIGN PAINTING & LETTERING SHOP

Adams Signs Inc............................. G 219 972-0700
Highland *(G-7119)*

Alveys Sign Co Inc.......................... E 812 867-2567
Evansville *(G-3883)*

Christys Design & Sign Inc.............. G 317 882-5444
Greenwood *(G-6680)*

Marshall G Smith Sign Painting........ G 260 744-9492
Fort Wayne *(G-5203)*

Reed Sign Service Inc..................... G 765 459-4033
Kokomo *(G-10327)*

Signs AP & Awards On Time LLC..... G 219 661-4488
Crown Point *(G-2752)*

Wagner Signs Inc............................ E 317 788-0202
Indianapolis *(G-9735)*

Whitehead Signs Inc........................ F 317 632-1800
Indianapolis *(G-9760)*

SIGNALING APPARATUS: Electric

Dux Signal Kits LLC........................ G 260 623-3017
Monroeville *(G-12068)*

Pumpalarmcom LLC........................ G 888 454-5051
Indianapolis *(G-9239)*

SIGNALS: Traffic Control, Electric

Master Filter Corporation................. G 317 545-3335
Indianapolis *(G-8849)*

SC Supply Company LLC................. G 574 287-0252
Mishawaka *(G-11991)*

Traffic Technical Support Inc........... G 260 665-1575
Angola *(G-302)*

SIGNS & ADVERTISING SPECIALTIES

1 Stop Signs................................... G 765 748-2902
Muncie *(G-12331)*

1globalds LLC................................. F 765 413-2211
Westfield *(G-16660)*

20 Minute Signs Plus Inc................. G 765 413-1046
Lafayette *(G-10512)*

8105 Georgia LLC........................... G 219 757-3532
Merrillville *(G-11475)*

A Harris Verl Inc.............................. G 317 736-4680
Indianapolis *(G-7400)*

A One Signs & Graphics.................. G 574 293-7104
Elkhart *(G-3140)*

A Plus Sign Area Ltg Spcalists......... G 765 966-4857
Richmond *(G-14080)*

A S P Parrott Signs......................... G 812 325-9102
Bloomington *(G-768)*

A Sign Above................................... G 317 392-2144
Laurel *(G-10823)*

A Sign Odyssey LLC........................ G 219 962-1247
Lake Station *(G-10771)*

A Sign of Tymes.............................. G 317 251-0792
Indianapolis *(G-7402)*

A To Z Sign Shop............................ G 219 462-7489
Valparaiso *(G-15889)*

A Yard Art....................................... G 317 862-1486
Carmel *(G-1546)*

AAA Black Signs LLC...................... G 765 315-9569
Martinsville *(G-11376)*

Aardvark Vinyl Signs....................... G 260 833-0800
Angola *(G-224)*

Aarvee Associates LLC.................... G 312 222-5665
Indianapolis *(G-7411)*

Absograph Sign Co......................... G 630 940-4093
Valparaiso *(G-15890)*

Ace Sign Company Inc.................... G 812 232-4206
Terre Haute *(G-15530)*

ACS Sign Solution........................... E 317 201-4838
Indianapolis *(G-7423)*

Action Printing Sign Co................... G 219 362-9729
La Porte *(G-10375)*

Ad Vision Graphics Inc.................... G 812 476-4932
Evansville *(G-3873)*

Adams Signs Inc............................. G 219 972-0700
Highland *(G-7119)*

Adlink Promotions........................... G 574 271-7003
Granger *(G-6330)*

ADM Custom Creations LLC............ G 765 499-0584
Hartford City *(G-7061)*

Advanced Digital Signs LLC............. G 260 704-0319
Fort Wayne *(G-4726)*

Advanced Sign & Ltg Svc Inc........... G 812 430-2817
Evansville *(G-3875)*

Affordable Sign & Neon Inc.............. G 219 853-1855
Hammond *(G-6869)*

Affordable Signs Incorporated.......... G 260 349-1710
Kendallville *(G-10087)*

Alan Sutton Graphic Design............. G 219 567-2764
Francesville *(G-5636)*

American Sign Design..................... G 574 287-4387
South Bend *(G-14944)*

AMS Embroidery & Signs LLC......... G 513 313-1613
Brookville *(G-1316)*

Apex Electric & Sign Inc.................. G 317 326-1325
Greenfield *(G-6462)*

Apex Electric & Sign Inc.................. G 317 326-1325
Morristown *(G-12271)*

Arizona Sport Shirts Inc.................. E 317 481-2160
Indianapolis *(G-7544)*

Asa Above Rest............................... G 317 392-2144
Shelbyville *(G-14730)*

Asd Signs & Graphics LLC.............. G 317 437-6921
Indianapolis *(G-7549)*

Asempac Inc................................... E 812 945-6303
New Albany *(G-12692)*

Atrium Web Services LLC................ G 812 322-6904
Bloomington *(G-785)*

Auto & Sign Specialties Inc.............. G 260 824-1987
Bluffton *(G-1027)*

Auto Art & Signs............................. G 765 448-6800
Lafayette *(G-10530)*

Awards Unlimited Inc...................... G 765 447-9413
Lafayette *(G-10532)*

B & B Signs.................................... G 812 282-5366
Floyds Knobs *(G-4670)*

B & L Lighting and Sign Inc............. G 317 984-4206
Noblesville *(G-13037)*

B2c2 LLC.. G 808 533-4128
Bloomington *(G-791)*

Baller Signs Inc.............................. G 260 824-1987
Bluffton *(G-1028)*

Banners Unlimited........................... G 574 825-8070
Middlebury *(G-11701)*

Bassett Signs LLC.......................... G 812 946-0017
Jeffersonville *(G-9939)*

Baugh Enterprises Inc..................... F 812 334-8189
Bloomington *(G-796)*

Baumbauer Signs............................ G 260 368-7537
Geneva *(G-6048)*

Beacon Sign Company LLC.............. G 317 272-2388
Avon *(G-507)*

Bill Banner Signs............................ G 765 209-2642
Falmouth *(G-4415)*

PRODUCT SECTION — SIGNS & ADVERTISING SPECIALTIES

Company	Code	Phone
Biltz Signs — Warsaw (G-16320)	G	574 594-2703
Bml Graphics LLC — Tipton (G-15767)	F	317 984-5500
Bo-Mar Industries Inc — Indianapolis (G-7651)	E	317 899-1240
Bob Prescott — Valparaiso (G-15918)	G	219 736-7804
Boezeman Enterprises Inc — Demotte (G-2912)	G	219 345-2732
Booth Signs Inc — Columbus (G-2227)	G	812 376-7446
Bottom Sign LLC — New Albany (G-12704)	G	812 949-7446
Boyd Sign Company — Angola (G-236)	G	260 833-2257
Brett Tishner — Tipton (G-15769)	G	765 675-2180
Brick Street Embroidery — Leesburg (G-10951)	G	574 453-3729
Bright Signs and More — Fort Wayne (G-4817)	G	260 203-2444
Broadway Auto Glass LLC — Merrillville (G-11493)	F	219 884-5277
Broken Vessel Sign Co LLC — Decatur (G-2847)	G	260 273-2780
Bully Graphics and Signs — Monticello (G-12140)	G	574 870-0783
Business Art & Designs Inc — Beech Grove (G-688)	G	317 782-9108
Buttons Galore Inc — Brownsburg (G-1354)	F	800 626-8168
Buy Bulk Displays — Mishawaka (G-11855)	G	574 855-3522
Buy Bulk Displays LLC — Osceola (G-13384)	G	574 222-4378
C & H Sign Inc Corporation — Anderson (G-86)	G	765 642-7777
C4 Custom Creation LLC — Pierceton (G-13630)	G	574 551-3904
Capital Custom Signs — Peru (G-13569)	G	765 689-7170
Cardinal Sign Service — Newburgh (G-12996)	G	812 499-0311
Cardwell Signs LLC — Sheridan (G-14819)	G	414 698-3992
Castleton Village Center Inc — Indianapolis (G-7758)	G	317 577-1995
Classic Sign & Awning — Angola (G-241)	G	260 665-6663
Clifford Signs Inc — Kokomo (G-10245)	G	765 453-0745
Coats Wright De Sign — Carmel (G-1591)	G	317 569-5980
Connectons Sign Lngage Intrprt — Evansville (G-3980)	G	812 449-7140
Courtney Signs — Indianapolis (G-7890)	F	317 653-5146
Creative Inc — Lafayette (G-10561)	G	765 447-3500
Creative Sign Resources LLC — Fort Wayne (G-4885)	E	260 425-9618
Creative Signs — Fort Wayne (G-4886)	G	260 438-6352
Cumulus Intrmdate Holdings Inc — Kokomo (G-10252)	G	765 452-5704
Custom Creations MGT LLC — Fort Wayne (G-4897)	G	765 491-8434
Custom Inspirational Signs — Bicknell (G-733)	G	315 715-1893
Custombannerlab — Carmel (G-1603)	G	317 956-3898
D D Signs Inc — Terre Haute (G-15572)	G	812 243-0084
Dailey Signs LLC — Fishers (G-4500)	G	317 436-7550
DBC Imaging — Indianapolis (G-7956)	G	317 757-5298
Debra Richard — Columbus (G-2281)	G	812 379-4927
Designs 4 U Inc — Covington (G-2528)	G	765 793-3026
Directions Promotions — Evansville (G-4013)	G	812 746-2505
DK Earlen Signs LLC — Newburgh (G-13000)	G	812 490-8423
Don Anderson — Monticello (G-12145)	G	574 278-7243
Doty Graphics — Morristown (G-12275)	G	765 763-7178
Dupre Capital LLC — Jeffersonville (G-9971)	F	812 291-1141
Dxd Signs — Highland (G-7133)	G	219 588-4403
Economy Signs Incorporated — Hammond (G-6920)	G	219 932-1233
Edinburgh Signs & Grapics — Edinburgh (G-3083)	G	812 526-6626
Elliott Smith Interiors LLC — Zionsville (G-17005)	G	317 966-5101
Embosstek — Fort Wayne (G-4948)	G	260 484-7700
Enyart Signs — Rochester (G-14288)	G	574 223-8254
Essential Archtctral Signs Inc — Indianapolis (G-8135)	F	317 253-6000
Everywhere Signs LLC — Bloomington (G-863)	G	812 323-1471
F & S Signage Solutions Inc — Danville (G-2811)	G	317 539-2086
Fast Grafix — Newburgh (G-13001)	G	812 305-3464
Fast Signs — South Bend (G-15026)	G	574 254-0545
Fastsigns — Fort Wayne (G-4977)	G	260 373-0911
Fastsigns — Indianapolis (G-8169)	G	317 280-3041
Fellers Inc — Indianapolis (G-8180)	G	317 876-3008
Fine Guys Inc — Tell City (G-15502)	G	812 547-8630
First Place Trophies — Princeton (G-13994)	G	812 385-3279
Flag & Banner Company Inc — Indianapolis (G-8199)	F	317 299-4880
Founders West Inc — Mccordsville (G-11449)	G	812 936-7446
Frank Balensiefer — Earl Park (G-2986)	G	219 474-6419
Freelance Lettering Inc — Indianapolis (G-8229)	F	317 244-9272
Freeman Signs — Danville (G-2813)	G	317 386-3453
French Lick Auto Signs — French Lick (G-5845)	G	812 936-7777
G C Solutions Inc — Indianapolis (G-8252)	G	317 334-1149
Gardner Graphics & Signs — Greencastle (G-6404)	G	765 630-8475
Gast Sign Co — Valparaiso (G-15954)	G	219 759-4336
Geckos — Attica (G-349)	G	765 762-0822
Get Noticed Portable Signs — Anderson (G-121)	G	765 649-6645
Gindor Inc — Goshen (G-6149)	G	574 642-4004
Glgraphix — Lafayette (G-10590)	G	765 446-8600
Golden Signworks Lighting — Indianapolis (G-8299)	G	317 358-4791
Good Signs — Franklin (G-5735)	G	317 738-4663
Grace Fths Clbratory Signs LLC — Indianapolis (G-8311)	G	463 701-7673
Grandview Aluminum Products — Grandview (G-6328)	F	812 649-2569
Granite Tee Signs LLC — Fort Branch (G-4703)	G	317 670-4967
Graphex International — Lowell (G-11161)	G	219 696-4849
Graphic Shack Signs — Greencastle (G-6405)	G	765 721-4317
Graphic Visions — Bloomington (G-869)	G	812 331-7446
Graphically Speaking — Chesterton (G-1931)	G	219 921-1572
Graphics Emporium — Bringhurst (G-1236)	G	574 967-4627
Graphics Factory — Elkhart (G-3387)	G	574 264-0542
Graphics Systems Inc — Fort Wayne (G-5034)	G	260 485-9667
Graycraft Signs Plus Inc — Warsaw (G-16370)	G	574 269-3780
Grayson Graphics — Elkhart (G-3388)	G	574 264-6466
Greenwood Light & Sign Service — Boggstown (G-1073)	G	317 840-5729
Guaranteed Lighting & Signs — Crawfordsville (G-2573)	G	765 866-1229
H L Signworks — Ellettsville (G-3808)	G	812 325-5750
Hanks Sign Shop LLC — Ferdinand (G-4434)	G	812 367-2851
Hayes Design Company LLC — South Bend (G-15060)	E	574 236-5615
Helix Signworx LLC — Anderson (G-125)	G	765 203-1381
Hi-Rise Sign & Lighting LLC — Bloomington (G-877)	G	812 825-4448
Holloway Vinyl Signs Grap — Yorktown (G-16974)	G	765 717-1581
Hot Rod Car Care LLC — Indianapolis (G-8421)	G	317 660-2077
Hubbard Services Inc — Greenwood (G-6713)	G	317 881-2828
Huston Signs LLC — Westfield (G-16698)	E	317 804-9009
Hydrojet Signs — Winchester (G-16890)	G	765 584-2125
I F S Corp — Indianapolis (G-8445)	G	317 898-6118
Icon International Inc — Fort Wayne (G-5091)	D	260 482-8700
Ideal Sign Corp — Valparaiso (G-15967)	G	219 406-2092
Illiana Signs — Saint John (G-14453)	G	708 862-9164
Imperial Trophy & Awards Co — Fort Wayne (G-5096)	G	260 432-8161
In Tex Signs and Graphics — Princeton (G-14001)	G	812 385-2471
Indiana Logo Sign Group — Indianapolis (G-8481)	G	800 950-1093

Employee Codes: A=Over 500 employees, B=251-500, C=101-250, D=51-100, E=20-50, F=10-19, G=1-9

2024 Harris Indiana Industrial Directory

SIGNS & ADVERTISING SPECIALTIES — PRODUCT SECTION

Indiana Sign & Barricade Inc .... E 317 377-8000
Indianapolis *(G-8492)*

Indiana Stamp Co Inc .... G 260 407-4165
Fort Wayne *(G-5103)*

Indiana Stamp Co Inc .... E 260 424-8973
Fort Wayne *(G-5104)*

Indiana Wrap Company LLC .... G 219 902-4997
Merrillville *(G-11525)*

Indianapolis Signworks Inc .... E 317 872-8722
Indianapolis *(G-8508)*

Indy Imaging Inc .... E 317 917-7938
Indianapolis *(G-8530)*

Indy Wide Format .... G 317 912-1385
Indianapolis *(G-8538)*

Indys Pro Graphix Inc .... E 317 769-3205
Zionsville *(G-17020)*

Indys Sign Source Inc .... G 317 372-2260
Indianapolis *(G-8540)*

Ink Trax Promotional Solutions .... G 317 336-6921
Mccordsville *(G-11452)*

Innovative Signs Llc .... G 317 747-4454
Pendleton *(G-13537)*

Insign Inc .... G 317 251-0131
Indianapolis *(G-8561)*

Integrity Sign Solutions Inc .... G 502 233-8755
New Albany *(G-12749)*

J R Sign Company and Services .... G 260 414-0510
Fort Wayne *(G-5124)*

J W P Vinyl Designs .... G 812 873-8744
Dupont *(G-2964)*

Jabra Signs & Graphics .... G 765 584-7100
Winchester *(G-16892)*

Jake Eddies Signs .... G 765 962-1892
Richmond *(G-14146)*

James Wafford .... G 317 773-7200
Noblesville *(G-13111)*

Jason Babbs .... G 812 595-9073
Austin *(G-466)*

Jbl Signals and Lighting LLC .... G 574 855-2251
South Bend *(G-15091)*

Jef Enterprises Inc .... F 812 425-0628
Evansville *(G-4140)*

Johnny White .... G 260 441-0077
Fort Wayne *(G-5138)*

Johnson Engraving & Trophies .... G 260 982-7868
North Manchester *(G-13236)*

Joyful Sign Company LLC .... G 317 529-1020
Indianapolis *(G-8642)*

Joyfully Said Signs LLC .... G 574 596-9949
Middlebury *(G-11729)*

Karbach Holdings Corporation .... F 219 924-2454
Hobart *(G-7196)*

Kellmark Corporation .... F 574 264-9695
Elkhart *(G-3449)*

Kerham Inc .... E 260 483-5444
Fort Wayne *(G-5146)*

King Signs .... G 317 882-0785
Greenwood *(G-6723)*

Klem Signs & Restyling LLC .... G 812 357-2222
Saint Meinrad *(G-14461)*

Klems Graphic Designs .... G 812 357-2222
Saint Meinrad *(G-14462)*

Kokomo Thrift & Gift LLC .... G 765 553-5973
Kokomo *(G-10295)*

Konrady Graphics Inc .... G 219 662-0436
Crown Point *(G-2712)*

Lafayette Sign Guy LLC .... G 765 771-9900
Lafayette *(G-10629)*

Legacy Sign Group LLC .... E 219 728-5102
Westville *(G-16763)*

Linda Harmon De Sign Studi .... G 765 573-6138
Marion *(G-11310)*

Link Electrical Service .... G 812 288-8184
Jeffersonville *(G-10013)*

Literature Display Systems .... G 317 841-4398
Indianapolis *(G-8770)*

Lloyd Werking Sign Painting .... G 765 354-2881
Middletown *(G-11773)*

Lotus Designs LLC .... G 812 206-7281
Charlestown *(G-1879)*

M F Y Designs Inc .... G 260 563-6662
Wabash *(G-16196)*

Markle Music .... G 812 847-2103
Linton *(G-11038)*

Marshall G Smith Sign Painting .... G 260 744-9492
Fort Wayne *(G-5203)*

Masco Corporation of Indiana .... E 317 848-1812
Indianapolis *(G-8847)*

McCaffery Sign Designs .... G 574 232-9991
South Bend *(G-15142)*

McCord Signs LLC .... E 812 537-5516
Lawrenceburg *(G-10846)*

Michiana Signs and Lighting .... G 574 520-1254
Mishawaka *(G-11946)*

Midwest Graphix LLC .... G 812 649-2522
Rockport *(G-14345)*

Midwest Sign Company Inc .... G 317 931-9535
Seymour *(G-14668)*

Mindys Brownsburg Signs Inc .... G 317 939-0921
Brownsburg *(G-1389)*

Mjs Businesses LLC .... G 317 845-1932
Indianapolis *(G-8938)*

MO Signs LLC .... G 574 780-4075
Plymouth *(G-13798)*

Monticello Signs & Scrn .... G 815 848-4111
Monticello *(G-12158)*

Morgan Commercial Lettering .... G 260 482-6430
Fort Wayne *(G-5243)*

Mullin Sign Studio .... G 219 926-8937
Chesterton *(G-1949)*

New Hope Services Inc .... D 812 752-4892
Scottsburg *(G-14574)*

New Hope Services Inc .... E 812 288-8248
Jeffersonville *(G-10022)*

Next Day Signs .... G 574 259-7446
Mishawaka *(G-11965)*

Next Products LLC .... G 317 392-4701
Shelbyville *(G-14780)*

Nitro Alley Graphix LLC .... G 317 286-3294
Brownsburg *(G-1390)*

No Limit Outdoor Sign Co LLC .... G 765 457-1877
Kokomo *(G-10317)*

No-Sail Splash Guard Co Inc .... G 765 522-2100
Roachdale *(G-14248)*

Northwest Indus Specialist Inc .... F 219 397-7446
East Chicago *(G-3033)*

Nwi Signs .... G 219 796-0948
Cedar Lake *(G-1834)*

Ovation Communications Inc .... G 812 401-9100
Evansville *(G-4230)*

Over Hill & Dale Sign Studio .... G 812 867-1664
Evansville *(G-4231)*

P3 Graphix LLC .... G 812 641-1294
Salem *(G-14495)*

Paint Town Graphics Inc .... E 260 422-9152
Fort Wayne *(G-5292)*

Pathfinder Communications Corp .... G 574 266-5115
South Bend *(G-15187)*

Pathfinder Communications Corp .... E 574 295-2500
Elkhart *(G-3587)*

Peytons Barricade Sign Co LLC .... G 812 283-6461
Jeffersonville *(G-10035)*

Phillips Signs & Graphics .... G 812 499-3607
Evansville *(G-4241)*

Pink Signs LLC .... G 317 509-8805
Mooresville *(G-12235)*

Pitcher Enterprises LLC .... G 574 242-1113
Winamac *(G-16870)*

Pjw Inc .... G 574 295-1203
Elkhart *(G-3605)*

Porter Signs .... G 812 222-0283
Greensburg *(G-6624)*

Premier Signs LLC .... G 888 518-2498
Uniondale *(G-15870)*

Premiere Signs LLC .... G 260 543-2612
Uniondale *(G-15871)*

Prentice Products Inc .... E 260 747-3195
Fort Wayne *(G-5347)*

Print Plus Express Inc .... G 812 466-6150
Terre Haute *(G-15671)*

Printing Inc Louisville KY .... F 800 237-5894
Jeffersonville *(G-10041)*

Pro Signs & Graphics .... G 765 675-7446
Tipton *(G-15787)*

Professional Permits .... G 574 257-2954
Mishawaka *(G-11981)*

Progressive Design Apparel Inc .... E 317 293-5888
Indianapolis *(G-9225)*

Pyramid Sign & Design Inc .... G 765 447-4174
Lafayette *(G-10674)*

R W Moran Express Inc .... G 317 445-5861
Indianapolis *(G-9257)*

R&S Sign Design .... G 765 520-5594
New Castle *(G-12881)*

Ray Marketing LLC .... G 317 782-0940
Beech Grove *(G-701)*

Recognition Plus .... G 812 232-2372
Terre Haute *(G-15676)*

Red Hen Signs .... G 812 430-0956
Evansville *(G-4277)*

Reddington Design Inc .... G 574 272-0790
South Bend *(G-15217)*

Reed Sign Service Inc .... G 765 459-4033
Kokomo *(G-10327)*

Reinforcements Design .... G 219 866-8626
Rensselaer *(G-14064)*

Richard Butterfield .... G 765 754-3129
Orestes *(G-13361)*

Richardson Entps Blmington LLC .... G 812 287-8179
Bloomington *(G-956)*

Riley Signs & Sheet Metal LLC .... G 317 359-7446
Indianapolis *(G-9307)*

Rlr Associates Inc .... G 317 632-1300
Indianapolis *(G-9312)*

Roesler Fine Art Services .... G 219 797-4955
Union Mills *(G-15867)*

Roger Harper Signs .... G 812 945-1581
New Albany *(G-12807)*

Ron Glasscock .... G 812 986-2342
Poland *(G-13837)*

Ron Nawrocki .... G 260 437-5323
Avilla *(G-493)*

Rookies Unlimited Inc .... G 765 536-2726
Summitville *(G-15431)*

Ryan Osborne Inc .... G 317 535-4881
Greenwood *(G-6764)*

Sampco Inc .... G 413 442-4043
South Bend *(G-15230)*

Schaefer Sign Works .... G 317 292-9373
Indianapolis *(G-9387)*

Scott Signs LLC .... G 574 533-7524
Goshen *(G-6252)*

Seaton Springs Inc .... G 812 282-2440
Clarksville *(G-2035)*

Selectric Signs .... G 812 378-6129
Columbus *(G-2389)*

PRODUCT SECTION

SIGNS & ADVERTISING SPECIALTIES

Sexton Advertising LLC .... G 812 522-4059
  Seymour *(G-14688)*

Shadow Signs .... G 317 481-9710
  Indianapolis *(G-9412)*

Shads Signs .... G 812 512-6066
  Linton *(G-11046)*

Shirts and Stuffs Happens .... G 812 217-8390
  Boonville *(G-1097)*

Sign A Rama .... G 812 477-7763
  Evansville *(G-4310)*

Sign A Rama .... G 812 537-5516
  Lawrenceburg *(G-10860)*

Sign Arama .... G 812 657-7449
  Columbus *(G-2392)*

Sign Art LLC .... G 317 247-0333
  Indianapolis *(G-9427)*

Sign Art Quality Advertising .... G 219 763-6122
  Hobart *(G-7207)*

Sign Creations .... G 574 204-2179
  Mishawaka *(G-11993)*

Sign Creations LLC .... G 574 855-1246
  South Bend *(G-15243)*

Sign Deals Delivered .... G 574 276-7404
  Bremen *(G-1221)*

Sign Deals Delivered Inc .... G 574 276-7404
  South Bend *(G-15244)*

Sign Exchange .... G 812 662-9469
  Greensburg *(G-6631)*

Sign Exchange .... G 812 621-2527
  Milan *(G-11784)*

Sign Factory .... G 574 255-7446
  Mishawaka *(G-11994)*

Sign For It LLC .... G 317 834-4636
  Mooresville *(G-12242)*

Sign Guy .... G 812 345-2515
  Bloomington *(G-970)*

Sign Guys Inc .... G 317 875-7446
  Greenwood *(G-6767)*

Sign Gypsies Louisville LLC .... G 281 743-2137
  New Albany *(G-12813)*

Sign Here Ltd .... G 317 487-8001
  Indianapolis *(G-9431)*

Sign Lighting .... G 502 664-6655
  New Albany *(G-12814)*

Sign Pros .... G 765 289-2177
  Muncie *(G-12492)*

Sign Pros Inc .... G 765 642-1175
  Anderson *(G-192)*

Sign Pros of Marion .... G 765 677-1234
  Marion *(G-11338)*

Sign Services .... G 317 546-1111
  Indianapolis *(G-9432)*

Sign Solutions Inc .... F 317 535-5757
  Whiteland *(G-16796)*

Sign Stop LLC .... G 812 460-0119
  Terre Haute *(G-15693)*

Sign Store Inc .... G 812 537-0102
  Lawrenceburg *(G-10861)*

Sign Together .... G 812 219-2338
  Bloomington *(G-971)*

Sign Up 4 Fun .... G 317 800-3535
  Indianapolis *(G-9433)*

Sign-A-Rama .... G 317 477-2400
  Greenfield *(G-6551)*

Signart & Vinyl LLC .... G 765 644-5290
  Anderson *(G-193)*

Signified Signs Inc .... G 219 712-7385
  Crown Point *(G-2751)*

Signified Signs Inc .... G 219 712-7385
  Portage *(G-13915)*

Signplex LLC .... G 765 795-7446
  Cloverdale *(G-2098)*

Signrite .... G 812 320-5245
  Bloomington *(G-972)*

Signs & Designs By Lewis .... G 574 223-9403
  Rochester *(G-14325)*

Signs & Stripes By Carr .... G 317 432-9215
  Jamestown *(G-9820)*

Signs By Don .... G 219 374-6754
  Cedar Lake *(G-1837)*

Signs By Sulane Inc .... G 765 565-6773
  Carthage *(G-1818)*

Signs By Susie .... G 812 385-2739
  Princeton *(G-14011)*

Signs By TM LLC .... G 317 872-3220
  Indianapolis *(G-9436)*

Signs Etc .... G 574 674-9671
  Osceola *(G-13402)*

Signs In Time By Greg Inc .... G 260 749-7446
  Fort Wayne *(G-5416)*

Signs Inc International .... G 317 925-2835
  Indianapolis *(G-9437)*

Signs Magic LLC .... G 812 473-5155
  Evansville *(G-4313)*

Signs Now .... G 812 323-2776
  Bloomington *(G-973)*

Signs Now Jeffersonville .... G 812 282-2440
  Jeffersonville *(G-10054)*

Signs of Progress LLC .... G 317 340-7225
  Carmel *(G-1760)*

Signs of Seasons .... G 219 866-4507
  Rensselaer *(G-14068)*

Signs of Times LLC .... G 812 981-3000
  New Albany *(G-12815)*

Signs Overnite Inc .... G 219 365-4088
  Crown Point *(G-2754)*

Signs Success .... G 765 427-1437
  Otterbein *(G-13455)*

Signs To Go .... G 502 533-0090
  Sellersburg *(G-14616)*

Signs Unlimited .... G 574 255-0500
  Mishawaka *(G-11995)*

Signtech Sign Services Inc .... G 574 537-8080
  Goshen *(G-6255)*

Signworks LLC .... F 317 872-8722
  Indianapolis *(G-9438)*

Simko Signs LLC .... G 219 308-6000
  Crown Point *(G-2755)*

Simple Sign Solutions Inc .... G 317 272-5224
  Noblesville *(G-13175)*

Simply Swank HM Dcor Signs LLC .... G 574 204-2339
  Granger *(G-6377)*

Sister Pines Signs) .... G 219 242-1824
  Valparaiso *(G-16053)*

Sky High Graphix LLC .... G 260 267-0724
  Fort Wayne *(G-5420)*

Sky High Sign Service .... G 765 436-7012
  Thorntown *(G-15755)*

Skyline Signs Inc .... G 765 564-4422
  Delphi *(G-2908)*

Slingshot Media LLC .... G 765 778-6848
  Pendleton *(G-13555)*

Smart Displays LLC .... G 812 322-3912
  Bloomington *(G-975)*

Sna LLC .... G 317 931-1022
  Indianapolis *(G-9453)*

Snep Sign Co .... G 260 982-6016
  North Manchester *(G-13250)*

Snykin Inc .... G 317 845-5051
  Indianapolis *(G-9457)*

Spark Marketing LLC .... G 219 301-0071
  Dyer *(G-2983)*

Speckin Sign Service Inc .... G 317 539-5133
  Greencastle *(G-6431)*

Speedpro Imaging .... G 765 446-8600
  Lafayette *(G-10695)*

Steve Stamper .... G 765 653-8786
  Greencastle *(G-6432)*

Stingel Enterprises Inc .... F 812 883-0054
  Salem *(G-14501)*

Stoffel Seals Corporation .... E 845 353-3800
  Angola *(G-296)*

Strategic Solutions Inc .... G 812 853-8525
  Newburgh *(G-13023)*

Sundance Signs .... G 765 420-7446
  Lafayette *(G-10706)*

Superior Kreations Inc .... G 765 635-3729
  Anderson *(G-202)*

Supreme Signs Inc .... G 219 384-0198
  Valparaiso *(G-16062)*

Synergy Composites LLC .... G 217 454-9711
  Indianapolis *(G-9539)*

Tc4 LLC .... G 317 709-5429
  Fishers *(G-4610)*

Team Hillman LLC .... G 260 426-2626
  Fort Wayne *(G-5470)*

Tfp Unlimited LLC .... G 317 414-8819
  Indianapolis *(G-9584)*

Tgr Inc .... F 765 452-8225
  Kokomo *(G-10348)*

The Killion Corporation .... D 317 271-4536
  Indianapolis *(G-9589)*

Thousand One Inc .... G 765 962-3636
  Richmond *(G-14218)*

Tko Enterprises Inc .... D 317 271-1398
  Plainfield *(G-13736)*

Tla Signs Inc .... G 260 833-2402
  Angola *(G-300)*

Todays Signs and Graphics .... G 765 288-4771
  Muncie *(G-12504)*

Tower Advertising Products Inc .... D 260 593-2103
  Topeka *(G-15821)*

Town & Country Industries Inc .... E 219 712-0893
  Crown Point *(G-2766)*

Traffic Sign Co Inc .... G 317 845-9305
  Indianapolis *(G-9627)*

Truck Lettering .... G 317 787-7875
  Indianapolis *(G-9650)*

Ultimate Exhibits .... G 317 353-7374
  Whitestown *(G-16828)*

Unique Signs .... G 812 384-4967
  Bloomfield *(G-758)*

V Art Grafix LLC .... G 317 513-5522
  Indianapolis *(G-9694)*

Van Der Weele Jon D .... G 574 892-5005
  Argos *(G-328)*

Vince Rogers Signs Inc .... G 574 264-0542
  Elkhart *(G-3770)*

Vinyl Creator .... G 260 475-2012
  Pleasant Lake *(G-13748)*

Visable Vinyl .... G 765 717-9678
  Hartford City *(G-7081)*

Visual Impact .... G 812 432-3524
  Dillsboro *(G-2953)*

Vkf Renzel Usa Corp .... F 219 661-6300
  Crown Point *(G-2771)*

Wagner Signs Inc .... E 317 788-0202
  Indianapolis *(G-9735)*

Ward Industries Inc .... F 574 825-2548
  Middlebury *(G-11756)*

Westlund Concepts .... F 317 819-0611
  Lapel *(G-10818)*

Whiteco Industries Inc .... A 219 769-6601
  Merrillville *(G-11572)*

Winters Assoc Prmtnal Pdts Inc .... F 812 330-7000
  Bloomington *(G-1015)*

Employee Codes: A=Over 500 employees, B=251-500
C=101-250, D=51-100, E=20-50, F=10-19, G=1-9

SIGNS & ADVERTISING SPECIALTIES

PRODUCT SECTION

Witham Anthony J Sign Prod..............G..... 317 984-3765
 Arcadia *(G-320)*
Wooden Signs..............................G..... 317 506-6991
 Indianapolis *(G-9786)*
World Graffix LLC........................G..... 574 936-1927
 Plymouth *(G-13834)*
XI Graphics Inc............................F..... 317 738-3434
 Franklin *(G-5789)*
Xtreme Signs & Graphics LLC........G..... 317 299-5622
 Indianapolis *(G-9798)*
Yard Signs....................................G..... 317 736-7446
 Trafalgar *(G-15834)*
Yard Signs Inc...............................G..... 317 535-7000
 Greenwood *(G-6783)*
Yellow Fellow Safety Signs LLC......G..... 813 557-6428
 Jeffersonville *(G-10077)*
Yesco LLC.....................................G..... 812 469-2292
 Evansville *(G-4391)*
Yesco Sign & Lighting Service.........G..... 317 559-3374
 Indianapolis *(G-9802)*
Yesco Sing Lighting Service.............G..... 812 577-0904
 Lawrenceburg *(G-10868)*
Young & Kenady Incorporated........G..... 317 852-6300
 Brownsburg *(G-1415)*
Zeno Companies Inc......................G..... 219 728-5126
 Chesterton *(G-1969)*
Zeno Signs LLC.............................G..... 219 250-2896
 Chesterton *(G-1970)*

SIGNS & ADVERTISING SPECIALTIES: Artwork, Advertising

Clients Choice Ltd........................G..... 812 853-2911
 Boonville *(G-1085)*
Dezigns By Cindy Ziese..................G..... 219 819-8786
 Rensselaer *(G-14051)*
Image One LLC............................D..... 317 576-2700
 Mccordsville *(G-11451)*
Sweet Keepsakes...........................G..... 219 872-8467
 Trail Creek *(G-15840)*

SIGNS & ADVERTISING SPECIALTIES: Letters For Signs, Metal

Titan Graphics LLC........................G..... 317 496-2188
 Mccordsville *(G-11457)*
Wagner Zip-Change Inc..................E..... 708 681-4100
 Fort Wayne *(G-5540)*

SIGNS & ADVERTISING SPECIALTIES: Novelties

American Spcialty Bus Intl LLC.......G..... 317 271-5000
 Zionsville *(G-16992)*
Athletic Edge Inc...........................F..... 260 489-6613
 Fort Wayne *(G-4778)*
Business & Industrial Pdts Co..........G..... 812 376-6149
 Columbus *(G-2231)*
Indiana Dimensional Pdts LLC........E..... 574 834-7681
 North Webster *(G-13306)*
Indiana Metal Craft Inc..................D..... 812 336-2362
 Bloomington *(G-890)*
Ricktom Promotions LLC...............G..... 812 430-0282
 Evansville *(G-4289)*
Sig Media LLC...............................F..... 317 858-7624
 Indianapolis *(G-9426)*
Tremike Enterprises........................G..... 317 547-6308
 Indianapolis *(G-9634)*

SIGNS & ADVERTISING SPECIALTIES: Scoreboards, Electric

Sign Group Inc..............................G..... 317 228-8049
 Indianapolis *(G-9429)*

SIGNS, ELECTRICAL: Wholesalers

Sign Craft Industries Inc.................E..... 317 842-8664
 Indianapolis *(G-9428)*
Signdoc Identity LLC.....................G..... 317 247-9670
 Indianapolis *(G-9435)*
Signrite..G..... 812 320-5245
 Bloomington *(G-972)*

SIGNS, EXC ELECTRIC, WHOLESALE

Economy Signs Incorporated..........G..... 219 932-1233
 Hammond *(G-6920)*
Fedex Office & Print Svcs Inc..........G..... 317 974-0378
 Indianapolis *(G-8172)*
Fedex Office & Print Svcs Inc..........G..... 317 917-1529
 Indianapolis *(G-8173)*
Graphic22 Inc................................G..... 219 921-5409
 Chesterton *(G-1930)*
Link Electrical Service....................G..... 812 288-8184
 Jeffersonville *(G-10013)*
Northwest Indus Specialist Inc.........F..... 219 397-7446
 East Chicago *(G-3033)*
Over Hill & Dale Sign Studio...........G..... 812 867-1664
 Evansville *(G-4231)*
Traffic Sign Co Inc.........................G..... 317 845-9305
 Indianapolis *(G-9627)*
Wagner Zip-Change Inc..................E..... 708 681-4100
 Fort Wayne *(G-5540)*

SIGNS: Electrical

A Sign-By-Design Inc....................F..... 317 876-7900
 Lebanon *(G-10872)*
ACS Sign Solution.........................G..... 317 925-2835
 Indianapolis *(G-7424)*
All American Tent & Awning Inc.....E..... 812 232-4206
 Terre Haute *(G-15537)*
Alveys Sign Co Inc.........................E..... 812 867-2567
 Evansville *(G-3883)*
Awning Partners Mfg Group LLC....E..... 317 644-3793
 Indianapolis *(G-7579)*
Begley Sign Painting Inc.................G..... 317 835-2027
 Fairland *(G-4397)*
Chads Signs Installations Inc...........G..... 317 867-2737
 Noblesville *(G-13056)*
Chuck Cable..................................G..... 765 981-2800
 La Fontaine *(G-10367)*
Clover Signs Co.............................F..... 812 442-7446
 Brazil *(G-1139)*
Custom Sign & Engineeri................E..... 812 401-1550
 Newburgh *(G-12999)*
Custom Signs Unlimited Co............G..... 260 483-4444
 Fort Wayne *(G-4899)*
Cyclone Custom Prouducts LLC.....G..... 765 246-6523
 Greencastle *(G-6401)*
Digital Dynamics LLC....................G..... 317 407-9658
 Martinsville *(G-11388)*
Earl Park Sign Shop LLC................G..... 219 474-6419
 Earl Park *(G-2985)*
Green Sign Co Inc.........................F..... 812 663-2550
 Greensburg *(G-6597)*
Greenfield Signs Inc.......................G..... 317 469-3095
 Greenfield *(G-6507)*
Hutchison Signs & Elec Co Inc........E..... 317 894-8877
 Indianapolis *(G-8439)*
Isf Inc...E..... 317 251-1219
 Indianapolis *(G-8594)*
Johnson Bros S Whitley Sign Co.....F..... 260 723-5161
 South Whitley *(G-15319)*
Jrowe Signs...................................G..... 260 668-7100
 Angola *(G-266)*
Landmark Signs Inc.......................D..... 219 762-9577
 Chesterton *(G-1943)*

Martin Signs & Crane Services........G..... 317 908-9708
 Indianapolis *(G-8842)*
Mg Electric and Sign LLC...............G..... 317 538-0455
 Greenfield *(G-6527)*
Neoti LLC.....................................F..... 260 494-1499
 Bluffton *(G-1045)*
North American Signs Inc...............D..... 574 234-5252
 South Bend *(G-15170)*
Phoenix Sign Works Inc.................G..... 317 432-4027
 Indianapolis *(G-9139)*
Premier Sign Group Inc..................G..... 317 613-4411
 Indianapolis *(G-9192)*
Premiere Signs Co Inc....................G..... 574 533-8585
 Goshen *(G-6242)*
Sign Craft Industries Inc.................E..... 317 842-8664
 Indianapolis *(G-9428)*
Sign Group Inc..............................F..... 317 875-6969
 Indianapolis *(G-9430)*
Sign Solutions Inc..........................F..... 317 881-1818
 Greenwood *(G-6768)*
Sign Source One Group Inc............G..... 219 736-5865
 Hobart *(G-7208)*
Sign Write Signs LLC.....................G..... 219 477-3840
 Valparaiso *(G-16050)*
Signcenter Inc................................G..... 812 232-4994
 Terre Haute *(G-15694)*
Signcrafters Inc..............................G..... 317 579-4800
 Indianapolis *(G-9434)*
Signcrafters Inc..............................E..... 812 424-9011
 Evansville *(G-4312)*
Signdoc Identity LLC.....................G..... 317 247-9670
 Indianapolis *(G-9435)*
Sojane Technologies Inc.................G..... 317 915-1059
 Indianapolis *(G-9458)*
Square 1 Designs & Signs...............G..... 219 552-0079
 Shelby *(G-14728)*
Stackman Signs/Graphics Inc..........F..... 317 784-6120
 Indianapolis *(G-9489)*
Steindler Signs & Graphix LLC.......G..... 219 733-2551
 Wanatah *(G-16291)*
The Baldus Company Inc................G..... 260 424-2366
 Fort Wayne *(G-5480)*
US Signcrafters Inc........................F..... 574 674-5055
 Osceola *(G-13404)*
Wendell Conger.............................G..... 812 282-2564
 Jeffersonville *(G-10073)*

SIGNS: Neon

Advanced Sign & Graphics Inc........F..... 765 284-8360
 Muncie *(G-12336)*
Affordable Neon Services................G..... 317 299-6061
 Indianapolis *(G-7456)*
Billy R Phillips..............................F..... 317 828-5058
 Indianapolis *(G-7626)*
Columbus Signs.............................G..... 812 376-7877
 Nashville *(G-12668)*
Delaplane & Son Neon & Sign........G..... 574 859-3431
 Camden *(G-1519)*
Express Sign & Neon Llc................G..... 812 882-0104
 Vincennes *(G-16123)*
Lamar Advertising Company...........F..... 260 482-9566
 Fort Wayne *(G-5173)*
Military Neon Signs.......................G..... 574 258-9804
 Mishawaka *(G-11951)*
Neon Attractions Incorporated........G..... 812 843-5881
 Tell City *(G-15514)*
Phantom Neon LLC.......................G..... 765 362-2221
 Crawfordsville *(G-2604)*
Sign-Age Inc..................................G..... 765 778-5254
 Pendleton *(G-13553)*
Whitehead Signs Inc......................F..... 317 632-1800
 Indianapolis *(G-9760)*

SILICONES

Momentive Performance Mtls Inc............ B 260 357-2000
Garrett *(G-5872)*

Precision Medical Inds Inc..................... G 260 234-3112
Albion *(G-41)*

US Silicones LLC................................. G 260 497-0819
Fort Wayne *(G-5522)*

US Silicones LLC................................. F 260 480-0171
Fort Wayne *(G-5523)*

SILK SCREEN DESIGN SVCS

Asempac Inc.. E 812 945-6303
New Albany *(G-12692)*

Custom TS & Trophies......................... G 219 926-4174
Porter *(G-13923)*

Dave Turner.. G 765 674-3360
Gas City *(G-6035)*

East 40 Sports Apparel Inc................... G 812 877-3695
Terre Haute *(G-15580)*

Logo Boys Inc..................................... G 574 256-6844
Mishawaka *(G-11932)*

Main Event Mdsg Group LLC................. F 317 570-8900
Indianapolis *(G-8812)*

Smiling Cross Inc................................ G 812 323-9290
Bloomington *(G-976)*

Squeegeepie Merch Co LLC.................. G 765 376-6358
Crawfordsville *(G-2618)*

Stien Designs & Graphics Inc................ G 260 347-9136
Kendallville *(G-10153)*

Tranter Graphics Inc............................ D 574 834-2626
Syracuse *(G-15487)*

Wagner Signs Inc................................ E 317 788-0202
Indianapolis *(G-9735)*

SILVERWARE & PLATED WARE

Sincerely Naiya LLC........................... G 602 518-3870
Hartford City *(G-7076)*

Stephen L Capper & Associates............ G 317 546-9000
Indianapolis *(G-9502)*

SIMULATORS: Flight

Xwind LLC... G 317 350-2080
Brownsburg *(G-1414)*

SIZES

Veolia Wts Usa Inc.............................. G 219 746-4060
Valparaiso *(G-16075)*

SKILL TRAINING CENTER

Cabinetmaker Inc................................ G 812 723-3461
Paoli *(G-13490)*

SKIN CARE PRDTS: Suntan Lotions & Oils

Seductive Lifestyle LLC...................... G 708 990-0720
Gary *(G-6008)*

SLABS: Steel

Steel Avenue Inc................................. G
Mishawaka *(G-12008)*

SLAG: Crushed Or Ground

Beemsterboer Slag Corp...................... C 219 392-1930
East Chicago *(G-2992)*

Edw C Levy Co.................................... G 765 364-9251
Crawfordsville *(G-2565)*

Levy Environmental Services Co........... E 260 868-5123
Butler *(G-1470)*

Levy Environmental Services Co........... E 260 625-4930
Columbia City *(G-2168)*

South Shore Slag LLC......................... E 219 881-6544
Hammond *(G-7010)*

SMOKE DETECTORS

St Louis Group LLC............................. G 317 975-3121
Indianapolis *(G-9485)*

SOFT DRINKS WHOLESALERS

American Bottling Company.................. D 574 291-9000
South Bend *(G-14943)*

Central Coca-Cola Btlg Co Inc............... E 800 241-2653
Indianapolis *(G-7770)*

Clark Foods Inc.................................. E 812 949-3075
New Albany *(G-12714)*

P-Americas LLC.................................. G 765 289-0270
Indianapolis *(G-9081)*

SOFTWARE PUBLISHERS: Home Entertainment

Freehold Games LLC.......................... G 574 656-9031
Walkerton *(G-16266)*

Lord Fms Games LLC.......................... G 317 710-2253
Indianapolis *(G-8783)*

Roajer LLC... G 317 348-4640
Carmel *(G-1742)*

SOFTWARE PUBLISHERS: Operating Systems

Kristine Willoughby............................. G 574 850-5145
South Bend *(G-15106)*

SOFTWARE TRAINING, COMPUTER

Cad/CAM Technologies Inc................... G 765 778-2020
Pendleton *(G-13528)*

Gary M Brown..................................... G 765 831-2536
New Castle *(G-12864)*

SOIL TESTING KITS

Ploog Engineering Co Inc..................... G 219 663-2854
Crown Point *(G-2731)*

SOLAR CELLS

Reearth Technologies.......................... G 812 219-6517
Bloomington *(G-953)*

Sunright Solar Inc............................... G 317 503-9253
Indianapolis *(G-9527)*

SOLAR HEATING EQPT

Crossroads Solar Entps LLC................. F 607 759-1058
South Bend *(G-14985)*

Gmp Holdings LLC............................... G 317 353-6580
Indianapolis *(G-8294)*

Inovateus Solar LLC............................ E 574 485-1400
South Bend *(G-15081)*

Our Country Home Entps Inc................. E 260 657-5605
Harlan *(G-7058)*

SOLVENTS

Calumet Missouri LLC.......................... E 318 795-3800
Indianapolis *(G-7722)*

Calumet Spclty Pdts Prtners LP............. C 317 328-5660
Indianapolis *(G-7728)*

Hoosier Penn Oil Co Inc....................... E 317 390-5406
Indianapolis *(G-8411)*

SOLVENTS: Organic

Hoosier Penn Oil Co Inc....................... G 812 284-9433
Jeffersonville *(G-9998)*

SONAR SYSTEMS & EQPT

Raytheon Company.............................. G 260 429-6000
Fort Wayne *(G-5367)*

Raytheon Company.............................. A 260 429-6000
Fort Wayne *(G-5368)*

Raytheon Company.............................. G 317 306-7492
Indianapolis *(G-9274)*

SOUND EFFECTS & MUSIC PRODUCTION: Motion Picture

Hard Hustla Muzik LLC......................... G 812 214-1995
Evansville *(G-4103)*

SOUND EQPT: Electric

Top In Sound Inc................................. G 765 649-8111
Anderson *(G-207)*

SOUND REPRODUCING EQPT

Esco Communications LLC................... D 317 298-2975
Indianapolis *(G-8130)*

SPACE PROPULSION UNITS & PARTS

Adranos Energetics LLC....................... G 208 539-2439
West Lafayette *(G-16557)*

In Space LLC...................................... G 765 775-2107
Lafayette *(G-10605)*

SPAS

Tylayculture LLC................................. G 219 678-8359
Highland *(G-7158)*

SPEAKER SYSTEMS

Alpine Electronics Manufact.................. A 956 217-3200
Greenwood *(G-6665)*

Kelley Global Brands LLC..................... G 833 554-8326
Noblesville *(G-13118)*

MTS Products Corp.............................. E 574 295-3142
Elkhart *(G-3559)*

Weber Vintage Sound Tech Inc.............. G 765 452-1249
Kokomo *(G-10357)*

SPECIALIZED LIBRARIES

Center For The Study Knwldge D........... G 812 361-4424
Bloomington *(G-827)*

SPECIALTY FOOD STORES: Coffee

Allen Street Roasters LLC.................... G 815 955-7872
La Porte *(G-10380)*

Ambrotos LLC..................................... G 413 887-1058
Otwell *(G-13456)*

Copper Moon Coffee LLC..................... D 317 541-9000
Lafayette *(G-10555)*

Utopian Coffee Company LLC................ G 888 558-8674
Fort Wayne *(G-5525)*

SPECIALTY FOOD STORES: Health & Dietetic Food

Serendipity Sanctuary......................... G 765 541-2364
Richmond *(G-14203)*

SPECIALTY FOOD STORES: Vitamin

Wellsource Nutraceuticals LLC.............. G 219 213-6173
Crown Point *(G-2773)*

SPECIALTY SAWMILL PRDTS

Woodparts International Corp................ F 574 293-0566
Elkhart *(G-3791)*

SPORTING & ATHLETIC GOODS: Arrows, Archery

Pieniadze Inc...................................... G 888 226-6241
Zionsville *(G-17041)*

SPORTING & ATHLETIC GOODS: Basketball Eqpt & Splys, NEC

Dick Baumgartners Basket................ E 765 220-1767
  Richmond *(G-14114)*

SPORTING & ATHLETIC GOODS: Batons

Comfort Suites Baton Rouge............... G 317 247-5500
  Indianapolis *(G-7839)*
Sharps Baton Mfg Corp...................... G 574 214-9389
  Elkhart *(G-3671)*

SPORTING & ATHLETIC GOODS: Bowling Balls

Rbg Inc... G 812 866-3983
  Lexington *(G-10980)*

SPORTING & ATHLETIC GOODS: Camping Eqpt & Splys

Pathfinder School LLC........................ G 317 791-8777
  Indianapolis *(G-9100)*
Westfield Outdoor Inc......................... C 317 334-0364
  Indianapolis *(G-9753)*

SPORTING & ATHLETIC GOODS: Fishing Tackle, General

Fisherman S Lurecraft Shop Inc........... F 260 829-1274
  Orland *(G-13365)*

SPORTING & ATHLETIC GOODS: Football Eqpt & Splys, NEC

Schutt Sports LLC.............................. C 217 324-2712
  Plainfield *(G-13727)*

SPORTING & ATHLETIC GOODS: Gymnasium Eqpt

Midwest Gym Supply Inc..................... F 812 265-4099
  Madison *(G-11242)*

SPORTING & ATHLETIC GOODS: Hunting Eqpt

Centurion Arms LLC............................ F 619 994-5756
  Morgantown *(G-12254)*
Kes LLC... G 812 728-8101
  Floyds Knobs *(G-4683)*

SPORTING & ATHLETIC GOODS: Shafts, Golf Club

Brickyard Crossing............................. G 317 492-6573
  Indianapolis *(G-7679)*
Dauenhauer Glass Company Inc........... G 260 433-5876
  Fort Wayne *(G-4906)*
Delilah Club Covers LLC..................... G 812 401-0012
  Evansville *(G-4010)*
Fairway Custom Golf........................... G 317 842-0017
  Fishers *(G-4521)*
Indiana Sction of The Prof Glf.............. F 317 738-9696
  Franklin *(G-5744)*

SPORTING & ATHLETIC GOODS: Shooting Eqpt & Splys, General

Cloud Defensive LLC........................... G 813 492-5683
  Chandler *(G-1859)*
Dave Brown Customs LLC................... G 812 727-5560
  Palmyra *(G-13479)*
L&N Supply LLC................................ G 219 397-9500
  East Chicago *(G-3026)*

SPORTING & ATHLETIC GOODS: Targets, Archery & Rifle Shooting

Axecalibur LLC................................... G 812 822-1157
  Bloomington *(G-788)*
Deer Track Archery Inc...................... G 765 643-6847
  Anderson *(G-101)*
Paraklese Technolcgies LLC................. F 502 357-0735
  Georgetown *(G-6073)*
Reagent Chemical & RES Inc............... G 574 772-7424
  Knox *(G-10221)*
Shull Tactical Concepts Inc.................. G 260 316-9224
  Butler *(G-1478)*

SPORTING & ATHLETIC GOODS: Team Sports Eqpt

Certor Sports LLC.............................. D 800 426-9784
  Plainfield *(G-13667)*
Dmp LLC.. G 812 699-0086
  Worthington *(G-16959)*
Fanatics Lids College LLC................... E 888 814-4287
  Indianapolis *(G-8166)*
Graphic Fx Inc................................... E 812 234-0000
  Terre Haute *(G-15601)*
Tarver Wolff LLC................................ G 765 265-7416
  Brookville *(G-1336)*

SPORTING & ATHLETIC GOODS: Trap Racks, Clay Targets

Federal Cartridge Company.................. C 765 966-7745
  Richmond *(G-14121)*

SPORTING & ATHLETIC GOODS: Water Sports Eqpt

Destro Machines LLC.......................... G 412 999-1619
  Carmel *(G-1607)*
Dunn-Rite Products Inc....................... F 765 552-9433
  Elwood *(G-3820)*
Hudson Aquatic Systems LLC............... F 260 665-1635
  Angola *(G-262)*
Leisure Pool & Spa LLC...................... G 812 537-0071
  Lawrenceburg *(G-10845)*
Natare Corporation............................. E 317 290-8828
  Indianapolis *(G-8985)*

SPORTING & REC GOODS, WHOLESALE: Camping Eqpt & Splys

Wyatt Survival Supply LLC.................. G 765 318-2872
  Morgantown *(G-12266)*

SPORTING & RECREATIONAL GOODS, WHOLESALE: Athletic Goods

Buddy Covers Inc............................... G 317 846-5766
  Carmel *(G-1575)*
Midwest Gym Supply Inc..................... F 812 265-4099
  Madison *(G-11242)*
Ppi Acquisition LLC............................ E 765 674-8627
  Marion *(G-11329)*

SPORTING CAMPS

Dick Baumgartners Basket................... E 765 220-1767
  Richmond *(G-14114)*

SPORTING FIREARMS WHOLESALERS

Lomatt Dynamics LLC......................... G 574 500-2517
  Leesburg *(G-10957)*
Sisk Rifles Manufacturing LLC............. G 812 686-8067
  Tell City *(G-15517)*

SPORTING GOODS STORES, NEC

Global Ozone Innovations LLC.............. G 574 294-5797
  Elkhart *(G-3383)*

SPORTING GOODS STORES: Camping & Backpacking Eqpt

Montgomery Tent & Awning Co............. F 317 357-9759
  Indianapolis *(G-8951)*

SPORTING GOODS STORES: Firearms

Blythes Sport Shop Inc....................... E 219 476-0026
  Valparaiso *(G-15916)*
Centurion Arms LLC............................ F 619 994-5756
  Morgantown *(G-12254)*
Vadens Firearms & Ammun LLC............ G 317 840-5799
  Indianapolis *(G-9697)*

SPORTING GOODS STORES: Playground Eqpt

Kidstuff Playsystems Inc..................... D 219 938-3331
  Gary *(G-5974)*
Nvb Playgrounds Inc........................... G 317 826-2777
  Indianapolis *(G-9037)*

SPORTING GOODS STORES: Specialty Sport Splys, NEC

Rookies Unlimited Inc......................... G 765 536-2726
  Summitville *(G-15431)*

SPORTS APPAREL STORES

Dear Athletes Inc................................ G 615 682-3332
  Noblesville *(G-13069)*
Dugout.. G 765 642-8528
  Anderson *(G-111)*
Goldden Corporation........................... F 765 423-4366
  Lafayette *(G-10591)*
Hoosier Racing Tire Corp..................... G 574 784-3152
  Lakeville *(G-10792)*
Locoli Inc... E 219 515-6900
  Schererville *(G-14531)*
Marketing and Retail Sales................... G 812 883-1813
  Salem *(G-14489)*
Mercantile Store................................. G 812 988-6939
  Nashville *(G-12675)*
Next Level Logo Store Inc.................... G 219 344-5141
  La Porte *(G-10458)*
Spobric LLC....................................... G 302 249-1045
  Indianapolis *(G-9479)*
Xtreme Graphics................................. G 812 989-6948
  Jeffersonville *(G-10076)*

SPORTS CLUBS, MANAGERS & PROMOTERS

Athletes Management & Services.......... G 317 925-8200
  Indianapolis *(G-7559)*

SPORTS PROMOTION SVCS

Diamond Hoosier................................. G 317 773-1411
  Noblesville *(G-13070)*

SPRINGS: Coiled Flat

Kokomo Spring Company Inc................ F 765 459-5156
  Kokomo *(G-10294)*

SPRINGS: Mechanical, Precision

Drc Machining LLC.............................. G 812 825-5783
  Bloomington *(G-859)*
Leggett & Platt Incorporated................. D 260 347-2600
  Kendallville *(G-10133)*

PRODUCT SECTIONSTEEL, COLD-ROLLED: Sheet Or Strip, From Own HotRolled

Myers Spring Co IncE574 753-5105
　Logansport *(G-11096)*
Winamac Coil Spring IncC574 653-2186
　Kewanna *(G-10168)*

SPRINGS: Precision

Forward Lift / A Dover CompanyG812 273-7325
　Madison *(G-11221)*
Hoosier Spring Co IncC574 291-7550
　South Bend *(G-15070)*
Pepka Spring Company IncF765 459-3114
　Kokomo *(G-10319)*
Suzuki Garphyttan CorpD574 232-8800
　South Bend *(G-15275)*
Titus Precision CompanyG260 244-6114
　Columbia City *(G-2206)*
Walton Industrial Park IncF574 626-2929
　Walton *(G-16284)*

SPRINGS: Steel

Ferguson Equipment IncG574 234-4303
　South Bend *(G-15033)*
Matthew Warren IncD574 722-8200
　Logansport *(G-11093)*
Muehlhausen Spring CompanyG574 859-2481
　Flora *(G-4662)*
Myers Spring Co IncE574 753-5105
　Logansport *(G-11096)*
Pepka Spring Company IncF765 459-3114
　Kokomo *(G-10319)*
Preferred Metal Service IncG219 988-2386
　Crown Point *(G-2735)*
Specialty Wire TechnologiesF260 750-1418
　Elkhart *(G-3692)*
Valley Tool & Die StampingsE574 722-4566
　Logansport *(G-11117)*
Wellspring Components LLCG260 768-7336
　Shipshewana *(G-14896)*
Winamac Coil Spring IncC574 653-2186
　Kewanna *(G-10168)*

SPRINGS: Torsion Bar

Cargo Systems IncG574 264-1600
　Elkhart *(G-3247)*
M-3 and Associates IncE574 294-3988
　Elkhart *(G-3506)*
McGowan Wire Specialties IncG574 232-7110
　South Bend *(G-15145)*
Mid-West Spring Mfg CoG800 424-0244
　Mentone *(G-11473)*

SPRINGS: Wire

A J Coil IncG574 353-7174
　Tippecanoe *(G-15758)*
A J Kay CoF224 475-0370
　South Bend *(G-14928)*
Araymond Mfg Ctr N Amer IncC574 722-5168
　Logansport *(G-11058)*
Circle M Spring IncE574 267-2883
　Warsaw *(G-16335)*
Mid-West Spring Mfg CoD574 353-1409
　Mentone *(G-11474)*
Mid-West Spring Mfg CoG800 424-0244
　Mentone *(G-11473)*
Pimmler Holdings IncG574 583-8090
　Monticello *(G-12165)*
Spring Monticello CorporationD574 583-8090
　Monticello *(G-12170)*
Valley Tool & Die StampingsE574 722-4566
　Logansport *(G-11117)*

STACKING MACHINES: Automatic

Rowe Conveyor LLCG317 602-1024
　Greenwood *(G-6761)*

STAINLESS STEEL

3d Parts Mfg LLCG317 860-6941
　Anderson *(G-68)*
ATIF317 238-3073
　Indianapolis *(G-7560)*
ATI Flat Rlled Pdts Hldngs LLCF765 529-9570
　New Castle *(G-12850)*
Bahr Bros Mfg IncE765 664-6235
　Marion *(G-11274)*
Calbrite IndustriesG219 844-6800
　Hammond *(G-6890)*
Cleveland-Cliffs Steel CorpC812 362-6000
　Rockport *(G-14338)*
Hebron Ventures North AmericaG260 437-7733
　Fort Wayne *(G-5057)*
Ima Inox Market America LLCE765 896-4411
　Muncie *(G-12423)*
Nachi America IncE877 622-4487
　Greenwood *(G-6743)*
New Castle Stainless Plate LLCD765 529-0120
　New Castle *(G-12876)*
Pope SteelG317 498-0504
　Greenfield *(G-6540)*
Ratner Steel Supply CoG219 787-6700
　Portage *(G-13909)*
SwiG812 342-2409
　Columbus *(G-2400)*
Thomas HimebaughG812 246-0197
　Sellersburg *(G-14618)*

STAIRCASES & STAIRS, WOOD

JW Woodworking IncG574 831-3033
　New Paris *(G-12962)*
Shinabargar Custom StairsG219 462-1735
　Valparaiso *(G-16048)*

STAMPINGS: Automotive

Almco Steel Products CorpC260 824-1118
　Bluffton *(G-1023)*
Aludyne North America LLCB260 925-4711
　Auburn *(G-361)*
Aludyne North America LLCC574 594-9681
　Pierceton *(G-13629)*
Blue River Stamping IncD317 395-5600
　Shelbyville *(G-14737)*
Fayette Tool and EngineeringD765 825-7518
　Connersville *(G-2438)*
Flex-N-Gate LLCG260 665-8288
　Angola *(G-251)*
Fogwell Technologies IncG260 410-1898
　Roanoke *(G-14266)*
Francine Bond Insur Agcy IncG317 262-2250
　Brownsburg *(G-1369)*
Grouper Wild LLCC574 534-1499
　Goshen *(G-6156)*
Gt Industries IncE734 241-7242
　North Vernon *(G-13274)*
Hudson Industries IncC260 587-3288
　Hudson *(G-7246)*
Lakepark Industries Ind IncD
　Shipshewana *(G-14861)*
Lcm Realty IV LLCG574 312-6182
　Goshen *(G-6197)*
Mpi Engineered Tech Win LLCG574 772-3850
　Knox *(G-10216)*
Multimatic Indiana IncC260 749-3700
　Fort Wayne *(G-5250)*

Nasg Indiana LLCE765 381-4310
　Muncie *(G-12467)*
Pridgeon & Clay IncG317 738-4885
　Franklin *(G-5770)*
Pro-Tech Tool & Stamping IncG765 258-3613
　Frankfort *(G-5691)*
Robert AtkinsG765 536-4164
　Summitville *(G-15430)*
Shiloh Susiebell LLCG574 936-8412
　Plymouth *(G-13813)*
Specialty Blanks IncG812 232-8775
　Terre Haute *(G-15708)*
Specialty Rim Supply IncG812 234-3002
　Terre Haute *(G-15709)*
Steel Parts CorporationA765 675-2191
　Tipton *(G-15791)*
TOA Winchester LLCB765 584-7639
　Winchester *(G-16901)*
Tower Atmtve Oprtons USA II LC260 920-1500
　Auburn *(G-431)*

STAMPINGS: Metal

Pro-Tech Tool & Stamping IncG765 258-3613
　Frankfort *(G-5691)*

STATIONERY & OFFICE SPLYS WHOLESALERS

Johnco CorpG317 576-4417
　Indianapolis *(G-8632)*
Label Tech IncE765 747-1234
　Muncie *(G-12436)*
Rivers Resources LLCG317 572-5029
　Indianapolis *(G-9310)*
Smith & Butterfield Co IncF812 422-3261
　Evansville *(G-4320)*
Smith & Butterfield Co IncF812 422-3261
　Evansville *(G-4321)*

STATIONERY: Made From Purchased Materials

Bowers Envelope Company IncG317 253-4321
　Indianapolis *(G-7665)*
Foxxie Planner L L CG260 247-6303
　Fort Wayne *(G-5004)*

STATORS REWINDING SVCS

Buffington Electric MotorsG574 935-5453
　Plymouth *(G-13762)*
Kirby Risk CorporationG765 643-3384
　Anderson *(G-143)*

STATUARY & OTHER DECORATIVE PRDTS: Nonmetallic

Zing Polymer Formations LLCG317 598-0480
　Fishers *(G-4637)*

STEEL & ALLOYS: Tool & Die

Indiana Tool IncF765 825-7117
　Connersville *(G-2444)*
Qualtech Tool & Engrg IncF260 726-6572
　Portland *(G-13965)*

STEEL WOOL

Hilltop Specialties LLCG574 773-4975
　Nappanee *(G-12611)*

STEEL, COLD-ROLLED: Sheet Or Strip, From Own HotRolled

Insight Equity Holdings LLCB219 378-1930
　East Chicago *(G-3023)*

STEEL, COLD-ROLLED: Strip NEC, From Purchased HotRolled

Heidtman Steel Products Inc................... E 219 256-7426
East Chicago *(G-3015)*

STEEL, COLD-ROLLED: Strip Or Wire

Mill Steel Co... F 765 622-4545
Anderson *(G-154)*

S&S Steel Services Inc............................. C 765 622-4545
Anderson *(G-189)*

STEEL DYNAMICS HEARTLAND LLC.... C 812 299-8866
Terre Haute *(G-15716)*

Steel Technologies LLC............................ C 765 362-3110
Crawfordsville *(G-2619)*

STEEL, HOT-ROLLED: Sheet Or Strip

Great Lakes Steel Corporation................. G 574 273-7000
Mishawaka *(G-11902)*

Ingleside Holdings L P............................. G 574 273-7000
Mishawaka *(G-11912)*

Lana Hudelson.. G 812 865-3951
Orleans *(G-13377)*

National Caster Acquisition...................... G 574 273-7000
Mishawaka *(G-11958)*

National Casting Corporation................... G 574 273-7000
Mishawaka *(G-11959)*

National Coating Line Corp...................... F 574 273-7000
Mishawaka *(G-11960)*

National Mtls Procurement Corp.............. G 574 273-7000
Mishawaka *(G-11961)*

National Steel Funding Corp.................... G 574 273-7000
Mishawaka *(G-11962)*

NS Holdings Corporation......................... G 574 273-7000
Mishawaka *(G-11966)*

NS Land Company.................................. G 574 273-7000
Mishawaka *(G-11967)*

Robinson Steel Co Inc............................. C 219 398-4600
East Chicago *(G-3040)*

Steel Technologies LLC........................... C 765 362-3110
Crawfordsville *(G-2619)*

Teal Lake Iron Mining Company.............. G 574 273-7000
Mishawaka *(G-12013)*

United States Steel Corp........................ G 219 762-3131
Portage *(G-13917)*

STONE: Dimension, NEC

Demotte Decorative Stone Inc................. G 219 987-5461
Demotte *(G-2915)*

Garrity Stone Inc.................................... G 317 546-0893
Indianapolis *(G-8263)*

Heritage Ldscp Sup Group Inc................ E 317 849-9100
Indianapolis *(G-8389)*

Indiana Quarriers & Carvers.................... F 812 935-8383
Bedford *(G-646)*

Marietta Martin Materials Inc................... F 317 776-4460
Noblesville *(G-13130)*

Tremain Ceramic Tile & Flr Cvg.............. E 317 542-1491
Indianapolis *(G-9233)*

STONE: Quarrying & Processing, Own Stone Prdts

New Point Stone Co Inc.......................... G 765 698-2227
Laurel *(G-10825)*

Slon Inc.. E 765 884-1792
Fowler *(G-5633)*

STONEWARE PRDTS: Pottery

Davis Vachon Artworks........................... G 260 489-9160
Fort Wayne *(G-4907)*

Scottsburg Stoneware LLC...................... G 812 752-6353
Scottsburg *(G-14578)*

Shafer Stoneware.................................. G 765 855-2409
Centerville *(G-1854)*

STORE FIXTURES: Exc Wood

Precision Millwork & Plas Inc.................. E 574 243-8720
South Bend *(G-15201)*

STORE FIXTURES: Wood

JC Moag Corporation.............................. D 812 284-8400
Georgetown *(G-6063)*

Platinum Display Group.......................... G 317 731-5026
Indianapolis *(G-9154)*

Precision Millwork & Plas Inc.................. E 574 243-8720
South Bend *(G-15201)*

STORES: Auto & Home Supply

C & P Machine Service Inc..................... F 260 484-7723
Fort Wayne *(G-4827)*

Daviess County Tire & Sup Inc............... G 812 254-1035
Washington *(G-16475)*

J & P Custom Plating Inc....................... G 260 726-9696
Portland *(G-13951)*

U B Machine Inc.................................... F 260 493-3381
New Haven *(G-12924)*

STOVES: Wood & Coal Burning

Hitzer Inc.. F 260 589-8536
Berne *(G-714)*

Oesterling Chimney Sweep Inc............... G 812 372-3512
Columbus *(G-2364)*

STRAWS: Drinking, Made From Purchased Materials

Hoffmaster Group Inc............................. D 855 230-5281
Fort Wayne *(G-5070)*

Sustainables LLC................................... G 502 741-4834
Indianapolis *(G-9536)*

STRUCTURAL SUPPORT & BUILDING MATERIAL: Concrete

Carters Concrete Block Inc..................... E 574 722-2644
Fort Wayne *(G-4836)*

Specification Products Inc...................... G 888 881-1726
Noblesville *(G-13178)*

STUDS & JOISTS: Sheet Metal

Rite-Way Steel Inc................................. F 574 262-3465
Elkhart *(G-3648)*

STYRENE

Futurex Industries Inc............................. E 812 299-5708
Terre Haute *(G-15593)*

Futurex Industries Inc............................. C 765 498-3900
Bloomingdale *(G-760)*

Styrene Solutions LLC............................ G 270 317-2427
Mishawaka *(G-12009)*

Styrene Solutions LLC............................ G 574 876-4610
Elkhart *(G-3703)*

SUNDRIES & RELATED PRDTS: Medical & Laboratory, Rubber

Gdc Inc.. C 574 533-3128
Goshen *(G-6143)*

Midwest Rubber Sales Inc...................... G 765 468-7105
Farmland *(G-4426)*

North American Latex Corp.................... D 812 268-6608
Sullivan *(G-15415)*

SURFACE ACTIVE AGENTS

Classic Chemical Corp............................ G 812 934-3289
Indianapolis *(G-7819)*

Dse Inc.. E 812 376-0310
Columbus *(G-2291)*

SURGICAL APPLIANCES & SPLYS

Bryton Corporation................................. F 317 334-8700
Indianapolis *(G-7694)*

3oe Scientific LLC.................................. F 317 869-7602
Carmel *(G-1545)*

Accra-Pac Inc... D 574 295-0000
Elkhart *(G-3150)*

American Eagle Health LLC..................... G 812 921-9224
Floyds Knobs *(G-4668)*

American Veteran Group LLC................. G 317 600-4749
Westfield *(G-16664)*

Battle Creek Equipment Co..................... E 260 495-3472
Fremont *(G-5810)*

Bionic Prosthetics and Ortho.................. G 219 791-9200
Elkhart *(G-3225)*

Bionic Prosthetics and Ortho.................. G 765 838-8222
Lafayette *(G-10538)*

Bionic Prosthetics and Ortho.................. G 219 791-9200
Valparaiso *(G-15914)*

Bionic Prsthtics Orthtics Grou................. G 219 940-3104
Merrillville *(G-11489)*

Bleys Prosthetics & Orthotics................. G 812 704-3894
Seymour *(G-14634)*

Borrv Concepts LLC............................... G 317 405-9121
Indianapolis *(G-7661)*

Braun Corporation.................................. D 574 946-7413
Winamac *(G-16856)*

Center For Orthtic Prsthtic Ex................ G 219 365-0248
Highland *(G-7128)*

Cook Medical Holdings LLC..................... G 812 339-2235
Bloomington *(G-842)*

Cook Medical LLC.................................. A 812 339-2235
Bloomington *(G-844)*

Cook Medical LLC.................................. A 812 323-4500
Bloomington *(G-846)*

Cook Medical LLC.................................. B 812 339-2235
Bloomington *(G-845)*

Coventure I LLC..................................... G 800 570-0072
Mishawaka *(G-11867)*

Depuy Inc... G 574 372-7010
Winona Lake *(G-16910)*

Depuy Orthopaedics Inc......................... E 574 267-8143
Warsaw *(G-16347)*

Depuy Products Inc................................ C 574 267-8143
Warsaw *(G-16348)*

Depuy Synthes Sales Inc....................... G 574 267-8143
Warsaw *(G-16351)*

Dienen Inc.. C 574 233-3352
South Bend *(G-14999)*

Ehob LLC... C 317 972-4600
Indianapolis *(G-8062)*

Fort Wayne Metals RES Pdts LLC.......... G 260 747-4154
Fort Wayne *(G-4997)*

Hill-Rom Inc... A 812 934-7777
Batesville *(G-589)*

Howmedica Osteonics Corp.................... G 317 587-2008
Carmel *(G-1661)*

Invacare Corporation............................. F 317 838-5500
Plainfield *(G-13694)*

Kenney Orthopedics Carmel LLC............ G 317 993-3664
Carmel *(G-1680)*

Kenney Orthopedics Seymour LLC......... G 812 271-1627
Seymour *(G-14660)*

Kenney Orthpdics Blmington LLC........... G 812 727-3651
Bloomington *(G-900)*

Kenney Orthpdics Indnpolis LLC............. G 859 241-1015
Indianapolis *(G-8672)*

PRODUCT SECTION

TABLE OR COUNTERTOPS, PLASTIC LAMINATED

Kenney Orthpdics Indnpolis LLC............ G..... 317 300-0814
 Greenwood *(G-6722)*
Kenney Orthpedics Columbus LLC......... F..... 812 214-4623
 Columbus *(G-2334)*
Medical Device Bus Svcs Inc................... G..... 317 596-3320
 Indianapolis *(G-8871)*
Medical Device Bus Svcs Inc................... A..... 574 267-8143
 Warsaw *(G-16395)*
Mtek Armor Group LLC............................ G..... 765 341-0933
 Martinsville *(G-11416)*
National Dentex LLC................................ C..... 317 849-5143
 Indianapolis *(G-8987)*
Nemcomed Instrs & Implants................... F..... 800 255-4576
 Fort Wayne *(G-5265)*
Orthopediatrics Corp.................................. G..... 574 268-6379
 Warsaw *(G-16404)*
Orthopediatrics US Dist............................. E..... 574 268-6379
 Warsaw *(G-16405)*
OSI Specialties Inc................................... F..... 317 293-4858
 Indianapolis *(G-9074)*
Paragon Medical Inc................................. C..... 317 570-5830
 Indianapolis *(G-9092)*
Point Medical Corporation........................ A..... 219 663-1775
 Crown Point *(G-2732)*
Precision Piece Parts Inc......................... D..... 574 255-3185
 Mishawaka *(G-11978)*
Recovery Force LLC................................. G..... 866 604-6458
 Fishers *(G-4591)*
Somer Inc... E..... 317 873-1111
 Zionsville *(G-17051)*
Standard Fusee Corporation..................... D..... 765 472-4375
 Peru *(G-13602)*
Surestep LLC.. C..... 574 233-3352
 South Bend *(G-15274)*
Transcend Orthtics Prsthtics L.................. G..... 574 233-3352
 Fort Wayne *(G-5499)*
Transcend Orthtics Prsthtics L.................. G..... 317 300-9016
 Greenwood *(G-6776)*
Transcend Orthtics Prsthtics L.................. G..... 317 334-1114
 Indianapolis *(G-9629)*
Transcend Orthtics Prsthtics L.................. F..... 574 233-3352
 South Bend *(G-15287)*
USA Medical Suppliers Ltd....................... G..... 608 782-1855
 Indianapolis *(G-9689)*
Wishbone Medical Inc.............................. G..... 574 306-4006
 Warsaw *(G-16454)*

SURGICAL IMPLANTS

Biomet Europe Ltd.................................... E..... 574 267-2038
 Warsaw *(G-16325)*
Golden-Helvey Holdings Inc..................... D..... 574 266-4500
 Elkhart *(G-3384)*
Lvb Acquisition Holding LLC..................... A..... 574 267-6639
 Warsaw *(G-16389)*
Maitland Engineering Inc.......................... E..... 574 287-0155
 South Bend *(G-15137)*
Nemcomed Fw LLC.................................. E..... 260 480-5226
 Fort Wayne *(G-5264)*
Tornier Inc.. G..... 574 268-0861
 Warsaw *(G-16439)*
Warsaw Orthopedic Inc............................ D..... 901 396-3133
 Warsaw *(G-16447)*
Zollman Plastic Surgery PC...................... F..... 317 328-1100
 Indianapolis *(G-9813)*

SUSPENSION SYSTEMS: Acoustical, Metal

Liquidspring LLC....................................... G..... 765 474-7816
 Lafayette *(G-10638)*

SVC ESTABLISHMENT EQPT, WHOLESALE: Firefighting Eqpt

Elkhart Brass Manufacturing Co............... E..... 800 346-0250
 Elkhart *(G-3321)*
Hoosier Fire Equipment Inc...................... F..... 219 462-1707
 Valparaiso *(G-15965)*
Roberson Fire & Safety Inc...................... G..... 317 879-3119
 Indianapolis *(G-9313)*

SWEEPING COMPOUNDS

Sorbtech Inc... G..... 812 944-9108
 Clarksville *(G-2037)*

SWIMMING POOL EQPT: Filters & Water Conditioning Systems

Canature USA Inc.................................... G..... 877 771-6789
 Carmel *(G-1578)*

SWIMMING POOLS, EQPT & SPLYS: Wholesalers

Automatic Pool Covers Inc....................... E..... 317 579-2000
 Westfield *(G-16666)*
Dunn-Rite Products Inc............................ F..... 765 552-9433
 Elwood *(G-3820)*
Fort Wayne Pools..................................... C..... 260 459-4100
 Fort Wayne *(G-5001)*
Leisure Pool & Spa LLC.......................... G..... 812 537-0071
 Lawrenceburg *(G-10845)*
Natare Corporation................................... E..... 317 290-8828
 Indianapolis *(G-8985)*
Sparkle Pools Inc..................................... F..... 812 232-1292
 Terre Haute *(G-15707)*

SWITCHES: Electric Power

Power Components of Midwest................ E..... 574 256-6990
 Mishawaka *(G-11976)*
Sigma Switches Plus Inc......................... F..... 574 294-5776
 Elkhart *(G-3676)*

SWITCHES: Electric Power, Exc Snap, Push Button, Etc

Burt Products Inc..................................... G..... 812 386-6890
 Princeton *(G-13986)*
Ms Sedco Inc... E..... 317 842-2545
 Indianapolis *(G-8968)*

SWITCHES: Electronic

American Technology Compone............... C..... 800 238-2687
 Elkhart *(G-3177)*
Dwyer Instruments Inc............................. G..... 219 393-5250
 La Porte *(G-10402)*
Infinias LLC.. G..... 317 348-1249
 Indianapolis *(G-8541)*
Intelliray Inc.. G..... 260 547-4399
 Decatur *(G-2864)*
Stuart Manufacturing Inc.......................... E..... 260 403-2003
 Fort Wayne *(G-5448)*
V-Tech Engineering Inc............................ F..... 260 824-4322
 Bluffton *(G-1067)*
ZF Active Safety & Elec US LLC.............. D..... 765 429-1984
 Lafayette *(G-10721)*

SWITCHES: Electronic Applications

AEL/Span LLC... E..... 317 203-4602
 Plainfield *(G-13656)*
Tempest Technical Sales Inc.................... G..... 317 844-9236
 Carmel *(G-1783)*
Touchtronics Inc....................................... F..... 574 294-2570
 Elkhart *(G-3741)*

SWITCHGEAR & SWITCHBOARD APPARATUS

CTS Corporation....................................... G..... 574 293-7511
 Berne *(G-707)*
Direct Control Systems Inc....................... G..... 765 282-7474
 Muncie *(G-12384)*
Extrasurplus LLC...................................... G..... 252 619-8604
 Gary *(G-5931)*
Sigma Switches Plus Inc......................... F..... 574 294-5776
 Elkhart *(G-3676)*
Standard Fusee Corporation..................... D..... 765 472-4375
 Peru *(G-13602)*
Teaco Inc.. G..... 219 874-6234
 Michigan City *(G-11676)*
Touchplate Technologies Inc.................... E..... 260 426-1565
 Fort Wayne *(G-5497)*
Western Consolidated Tech Inc................ D..... 260 495-9866
 Fremont *(G-5842)*

SWITCHGEAR & SWITCHGEAR ACCESS, NEC

Integrity Marketing Team Inc.................... G..... 317 517-0012
 Plainfield *(G-13691)*
Siemens Industry Inc............................... D..... 219 763-7927
 Portage *(G-13914)*

SYNTHETIC RESIN FINISHED PRDTS, NEC

Calico Precision Molding LLC.................. E..... 260 484-4500
 Fort Wayne *(G-4829)*

SYSTEMS ENGINEERING: Computer Related

Binarie LLC.. G..... 317 496-8836
 Greenwood *(G-6676)*
Vergence LLC... F..... 317 547-4417
 Indianapolis *(G-9707)*

SYSTEMS INTEGRATION SVCS

Adaptive Tech Solutions LLC................... G..... 317 762-4363
 Carmel *(G-1549)*
Drs Graphix Group Inc............................. G..... 317 569-1855
 Indianapolis *(G-8011)*
Ers Automation Inc................................... G..... 260 341-8114
 Columbia City *(G-2143)*
Frakes Engineering Inc............................ E..... 317 577-3000
 Indianapolis *(G-8220)*

SYSTEMS INTEGRATION SVCS: Local Area Network

Business Systems Mgt Corp..................... G..... 219 938-0166
 Gary *(G-5908)*

SYSTEMS SOFTWARE DEVELOPMENT SVCS

Agora Brands Group Inc.......................... E..... 615 802-0086
 Borden *(G-1104)*

TABLE OR COUNTERTOPS, PLASTIC LAMINATED

Boardworks Inc... G..... 219 464-8111
 Valparaiso *(G-15917)*
Cabinets & Counters Inc.......................... E..... 812 858-3300
 Newburgh *(G-12995)*
Countertop Connections Inc..................... G..... 317 822-9858
 Franklin *(G-5723)*
Custom Design Laminates Inc................. F..... 574 674-9174
 Osceola *(G-13388)*
Eash LLC.. F..... 574 295-4450
 Elkhart *(G-3311)*

TABLE OR COUNTERTOPS, PLASTIC LAMINATED

H & S Custom Countertops Inc............... G 812 422-6314
  Evansville *(G-4100)*
Hackney Home Furnishings Inc............. C 317 895-4300
  Indianapolis *(G-8352)*
Mission Woodworking Inc....................... E 574 848-5697
  Bristol *(G-1274)*
Molargik Woodworking Inc..................... G 260 357-6625
  Garrett *(G-5871)*
Newlett Inc... D 574 294-8899
  Elkhart *(G-3567)*
Patrick Industries Inc............................. G 574 266-8400
  Elkhart *(G-3595)*
Plastic Top Fabricators Inc..................... G 317 786-4367
  Indianapolis *(G-9152)*

TABLES: Lift, Hydraulic

Ameri-Kart Corp...................................... C 574 848-7462
  Bristol *(G-1244)*

TAGS & LABELS: Paper

Shelf Tag Supply Corporation................. G 317 580-4030
  Westfield *(G-16727)*

TANK REPAIR SVCS

Bulk Truck & Transport Service.............. E 812 866-2155
  Hanover *(G-7040)*
Hmt LLC... G 219 736-9901
  Merrillville *(G-11522)*
Tank Construction & Service Co............ F 317 509-6294
  Whitestown *(G-16823)*
Trifab & Construction Inc........................ G 219 845-1300
  Hammond *(G-7024)*

TANKS & OTHER TRACKED VEHICLE CMPNTS

AM General LLC..................................... A 574 258-7523
  Mishawaka *(G-11840)*
Jds International Inc............................... F 317 753-4427
  Noblesville *(G-13112)*
Nix Sanitary Service................................ G 812 785-1158
  Boonville *(G-1094)*
Sleegers Engineered Pdts Inc................ G 317 786-7770
  Indianapolis *(G-9448)*
Surface Generation Tech LLC................ G 765 425-2741
  Anderson *(G-203)*

TANKS: Cryogenic, Metal

Alloy Custom Products LLC................... D 765 564-4684
  Lafayette *(G-10520)*
Precision Cryogenic Systems................. F 317 273-2800
  Indianapolis *(G-9182)*

TANKS: Fuel, Including Oil & Gas, Metal Plate

Hmt LLC... G 219 736-9901
  Merrillville *(G-11522)*

TANKS: Lined, Metal

Axis Unlimited LLC................................. G 574 370-8923
  Elkhart *(G-3208)*
Lagrange Products Inc........................... C 260 495-3025
  Fremont *(G-5826)*

TANKS: Plastic & Fiberglass

AK Industries Inc.................................... D 574 936-6022
  Plymouth *(G-13752)*
Apexx Enterprises LLC........................... F 812 486-2443
  Montgomery *(G-12085)*
Composites Syndicate LLC.................... F 260 484-3139
  Fort Wayne *(G-4870)*

Tj Maintenance LLC................................ G 219 776-8427
  Lake Village *(G-10784)*

TANKS: Standard Or Custom Fabricated, Metal Plate

Abtrex Industries Inc............................... F 734 728-0550
  South Bend *(G-14934)*
Bulk Truck & Transport Service.............. E 812 866-2155
  Hanover *(G-7040)*
Hensley Fabricating & Eqp Co................ E 574 498-6514
  Tippecanoe *(G-15760)*
Hoosier Tank and Mfg LLC..................... D 574 232-8368
  South Bend *(G-15071)*
Kennedy Tank & Mfg Co......................... C 317 787-1311
  Indianapolis *(G-8671)*
Norman Stein & Associates................... G 260 749-5468
  New Haven *(G-12912)*
Ottenweller Co Inc.................................. C 260 484-3166
  Fort Wayne *(G-5289)*
Penway Inc.. E 812 526-2645
  Edinburgh *(G-3097)*
Quick Tanks Inc...................................... D 260 347-3850
  Kendallville *(G-10146)*
Wessels Company.................................. D 317 888-9800
  Greenwood *(G-6780)*

TANKS: Storage, Farm, Metal Plate

CTB MN Investment Co Inc.................... E 574 658-4191
  Milford *(G-11794)*

TANKS: Water, Metal Plate

Phoenix Fbrcators Erectors LLC............ C 317 271-7002
  Avon *(G-544)*

TAPE STORAGE UNITS: Computer

Leroy R Sollars....................................... G 765 284-9417
  Selma *(G-14622)*

TAPES, ADHESIVE: Cellophane, Made From Purchased Materials

Bruno Cb Inc... G 317 619-7467
  Indianapolis *(G-7693)*

TAPES: Pressure Sensitive, Rubber

3M Company... B 317 692-6666
  Indianapolis *(G-7388)*

TARGET DRONES

Indigo Industries LLC............................. G 480 747-4560
  Greenwood *(G-6715)*

TARPAULINS

Gosport Manufacturing Co Inc................ E 800 457-4406
  Gosport *(G-6284)*
Gta Containers LLC................................ E 574 288-3459
  South Bend *(G-15054)*
Mosiers Tarps LLC.................................. G 260 563-3332
  Wabash *(G-16205)*
T K Sales & Service................................ G 219 962-8982
  Gary *(G-6017)*

TARPAULINS, WHOLESALE

T K Sales & Service................................ G 219 962-8982
  Gary *(G-6017)*

TELECOMMUNICATION EQPT REPAIR SVCS, EXC TELEPHONES

Vertical Steel Maintenance LLC............. G 912 710-0626
  Indianapolis *(G-9711)*

TELEPHONE EQPT: Modems

Great Deals Magazine............................. F 765 649-3302
  Anderson *(G-123)*

TELEPHONE EQPT: NEC

Esco Communications LLC.................... D 317 298-2975
  Indianapolis *(G-8130)*
Stg Networks LLC................................... G 317 667-0865
  Indianapolis *(G-9509)*
Telamon Technologies Corp................... A 317 818-6888
  Carmel *(G-1781)*

TELEPHONE SVCS

Accent Complex Inc................................ G 574 522-2368
  Elkhart *(G-3148)*

TELEVISION BROADCASTING & COMMUNICATIONS EQPT

Channel 40 Network LLC........................ G 317 794-6150
  Indianapolis *(G-7785)*

TELEVISION BROADCASTING STATIONS

Emmis Operating Company.................... E 317 266-0100
  Indianapolis *(G-8107)*
Schurz Communications Inc.................. F 574 247-7237
  Mishawaka *(G-11992)*

TELEVISION SETS

Vidicom Corporation............................... G 219 923-7475
  Hammond *(G-7029)*

TELEVISION: Closed Circuit Eqpt

Sneaky Micro Video Divisio.................... G 317 925-1496
  Indianapolis *(G-9454)*

TEMPERING: Metal

Gerdau McSteel Atmsphere Annli.......... E 812 346-1275
  North Vernon *(G-13272)*
Simpson Alloy Services Inc.................... G 812 969-2766
  Elizabeth *(G-3129)*

TEMPORARY HELP SVCS

Goldenmarc LLC..................................... G 317 855-1651
  Indianapolis *(G-8301)*

TESTERS: Battery

Advance Stores Company Inc................. G 317 253-5034
  Indianapolis *(G-7436)*

TESTERS: Physical Property

Deprisco Ventures Inc............................ E 260 637-8660
  Fort Wayne *(G-4916)*
Magwerks Corporation........................... F 317 241-8011
  Danville *(G-2819)*
Moyer Process & Controls Co................ G 260 495-2405
  Fremont *(G-5827)*
Sonam Technologies LLC....................... G 844 887-6626
  Crown Point *(G-2760)*

TEXTILE & APPAREL SVCS

Paige Marschall...................................... G 574 277-1631
  Granger *(G-6368)*

TEXTILES: Bagging, Jute

Midwest Sandbags LLC.......................... G 847 366-6555
  Elkhart *(G-3541)*

THEATRICAL PRODUCTION SVCS

Whiteco Industries Inc........................... A 219 769-6601
  Merrillville *(G-11572)*

TOILETS: Portable Chemical, Plastics

THERMOCOUPLES

Intech Automation Systems Corp............ G..... 209 836-8610
Peru *(G-13587)*

THERMOPLASTIC MATERIALS

Chemtrusion Inc................................. E..... 812 280-2910
Jeffersonville *(G-9951)*

Eidp Inc... A..... 833 267-8382
Indianapolis *(G-8064)*

Encom Polymers LLC........................ E..... 812 421-7700
Evansville *(G-4036)*

Gaska Tape Inc................................. D..... 574 294-5431
Elkhart *(G-3366)*

Geon Performance Solutions LLC........ G..... 812 466-5116
Terre Haute *(G-15596)*

Jamplast Inc.................................... F..... 812 838-8562
Mount Vernon *(G-12304)*

Monument Chemical LLC................... D..... 317 223-2630
Indianapolis *(G-8952)*

Nova Polymers Incorporated.............. E..... 812 476-0339
Evansville *(G-4223)*

Primex Plastics Corporation............... B..... 765 966-7774
Richmond *(G-14186)*

THERMOSETTING MATERIALS

Transfoam LLC................................. G..... 631 747-0255
Indianapolis *(G-9630)*

THERMOSTAT REPAIR SVCS

Grayson Thermal Systems Corp......... C..... 317 739-3290
Franklin *(G-5736)*

TILE: Brick & Structural, Clay

Meridian Brick LLC............................ E..... 812 894-2454
Terre Haute *(G-15642)*

TILE: Rubber

Valley Tile Corporation...................... G..... 812 268-3328
Sullivan *(G-15424)*

TIN

Cleveland-Cliffs Steel LLC................. D..... 219 787-2120
Chesterton *(G-1914)*

Murrays Tin Cup................................ G..... 260 349-1002
Kendallville *(G-10138)*

TIRE & INNER TUBE MATERIALS & RELATED PRDTS

E & D Tire & Repair LLC.................... G..... 812 486-6493
Loogootee *(G-11134)*

Sams Tech Tire LLC.......................... G..... 219 942-7317
Hobart *(G-7205)*

Simon and Sons................................ G..... 812 852-3636
Osgood *(G-13416)*

TIRE INFLATORS: Hand Or Compressor Operated

Wee Engineer Inc.............................. F..... 765 449-4280
Dayton *(G-2838)*

TIRES & INNER TUBES

Hoosier Racing Tire Corp................... G..... 574 784-3152
Lakeville *(G-10792)*

Lionshead Specialty Tire & Whe......... F..... 574 533-6169
Goshen *(G-6200)*

Michelin North America Inc................ A..... 260 493-8100
Woodburn *(G-16951)*

Rubber Shop Inc............................... G..... 574 291-6440
South Bend *(G-15229)*

T K T Inc.. G..... 574 825-5233
Middlebury *(G-11753)*

TIRES & TUBES WHOLESALERS

Cast Products LP.............................. E..... 574 294-2684
Elkhart *(G-3249)*

Dehco Inc... D..... 574 294-2684
Elkhart *(G-3288)*

Midwest Auto Repair Inc.................... F..... 219 322-0364
Schererville *(G-14534)*

Pomps Tire Service Inc..................... E..... 260 489-5252
Fort Wayne *(G-5326)*

Portland Tire & Service Inc................ G..... 260 726-9321
Portland *(G-13962)*

TIRES & TUBES, WHOLESALE: Automotive

Ben Tire Distributors Ltd................... E..... 317 798-2013
Indianapolis *(G-7612)*

Bernard Burns.................................. G..... 574 382-5019
Macy *(G-11194)*

Best One Tire & Svc S Bend Inc......... G..... 574 246-4021
South Bend *(G-14958)*

Best-One Lt LLC............................... G..... 812 471-8473
Evansville *(G-3928)*

Best-One Tire & Auto Care of A......... G..... 260 665-7330
Angola *(G-234)*

Best-One Tire & Svc Auburn Inc........ G..... 260 925-2782
Auburn *(G-369)*

BF Goodrich Tire Manufacturing........ G..... 260 493-8100
Woodburn *(G-16946)*

Bridgestone Ret Operations LLC........ F..... 812 332-2119
Bloomington *(G-815)*

Bridgestone Ret Operations LLC........ G..... 260 447-2596
Columbia City *(G-2127)*

Bridgestone Ret Operations LLC........ G..... 812 477-8818
Evansville *(G-3951)*

Bridgestone Ret Operations LLC........ F..... 812 423-4451
Evansville *(G-3952)*

Bridgestone Ret Operations LLC........ G..... 317 846-6516
Indianapolis *(G-7681)*

Bridgestone Ret Operations LLC........ G..... 317 849-9120
Indianapolis *(G-7682)*

Bridgestone Ret Operations LLC........ G..... 765 447-5041
Lafayette *(G-10542)*

Bridgestone Ret Operations LLC........ G..... 317 773-2761
Noblesville *(G-13048)*

Bridgestone Ret Operations LLC........ G..... 812 232-9478
Terre Haute *(G-15554)*

Clark Tire Fishers Inc....................... G..... 317 842-0544
Fishers *(G-4490)*

D & D Tire Shop LLC........................ G..... 219 354-0402
East Chicago *(G-3002)*

Dales Goodyear Tire & Service.......... G..... 574 272-3779
South Bend *(G-14995)*

Daviess County Tire Inc.................... G..... 812 254-1035
Washington *(G-16476)*

Double D.. G..... 765 569-6822
Rockville *(G-14351)*

E & M Tire Salvage Inc..................... G..... 260 745-3016
Fort Wayne *(G-4936)*

Ferentino Tire USA Inc...................... G..... 574 316-6116
Plymouth *(G-13775)*

Gentis Tire & Service Inc................... E..... 765 348-2400
Hartford City *(G-7066)*

Goodyear Tire & Rubber Company..... G..... 219 762-0651
Portage *(G-13871)*

Goodyear Tire Center........................ G..... 260 726-9321
Portland *(G-13946)*

Hoosier Racing Tire Corp................... G..... 574 784-3152
Lakeville *(G-10792)*

Hoosier Tire & Retreading Inc............ F..... 812 876-8286
Bloomington *(G-883)*

Hughes Tire Service Inc.................... F..... 812 883-4981
Salem *(G-14481)*

Indiana Discount Tire Company.......... G..... 574 875-8547
Elkhart *(G-3421)*

Lionshead Specialty Tire & Whe......... F..... 574 533-6169
Goshen *(G-6200)*

McCord Tire Service Inc.................... F..... 812 235-8016
Terre Haute *(G-15639)*

Midwest Auto Repair Inc.................... F..... 219 322-0364
Schererville *(G-14534)*

Mooresville Tire & Service Ctr............ G..... 317 831-1215
Mooresville *(G-12224)*

Parish Tire & Battery Shop................. G..... 765 793-3191
Covington *(G-2532)*

Penner Tire & Service LLC................. G..... 812 653-0029
Hardinsburg *(G-7048)*

Pomps Tire Service Inc..................... E..... 260 489-5252
Fort Wayne *(G-5326)*

Portland Tire & Service Inc................ G..... 260 726-9321
Portland *(G-13962)*

Raben Tire Co LLC........................... F..... 812 465-5555
Evansville *(G-4271)*

Reed Auto - Indy Mich LLC................ G..... 317 872-1132
Indianapolis *(G-9279)*

Reis Tire Sales Inc............................ E..... 812 425-2229
Evansville *(G-4283)*

Smith Tire Inc................................... F..... 574 267-8261
Warsaw *(G-16427)*

Snider Tire Inc.................................. D..... 260 824-4520
Bluffton *(G-1054)*

Tippecanoe Tire Service Inc............... G..... 765 884-0920
Fowler *(G-5634)*

Tire Center of Portland Inc................. G..... 260 726-8947
Portland *(G-13971)*

Trusty Tires Inc................................ G..... 812 738-4212
Corydon *(G-2519)*

Upland Tire & Service Ctr Inc............. G..... 765 998-0871
Upland *(G-15884)*

Windy City Coml Tire & Svc LLC........ G..... 773 530-1246
East Chicago *(G-3057)*

Woodward Tire Sales & Svc Inc......... G..... 260 432-0694
Fort Wayne *(G-5575)*

TOBACCO: Chewing

Black Swan Vapors LLC.................... G..... 317 645-5210
Pendleton *(G-13526)*

TOBACCO: Cigarettes

Big Red Liquors Inc........................... G..... 812 339-9552
Bloomington *(G-806)*

Liggett Group LLC............................. G..... 812 479-7635
Evansville *(G-4167)*

Smoker Friendly................................ G..... 812 556-0244
Jasper *(G-9912)*

South Bend Smoke Time Inc.............. F..... 574 318-4837
South Bend *(G-15256)*

TOBACCO: Smoking

La Porte Smokes and Beverages........ G..... 219 575-7754
La Porte *(G-10441)*

TOILETRIES, WHOLESALE: Toilet Soap

Tall Cotton Marketing LLC.................. G..... 312 320-5862
La Porte *(G-10486)*

TOILETRIES, WHOLESALE: Toiletries

North Coast Organics LLC.................. G..... 260 246-0289
Fort Wayne *(G-5274)*

Rugged Company............................. G..... 317 441-0927
Anderson *(G-187)*

TOILETS: Portable Chemical, Plastics

Olympic Fiberglass Industries................. F 574 223-3101
Rochester *(G-14310)*

TOOL & DIE STEEL

101 Tool & Die LLC................................. G 260 203-2981
Fort Wayne *(G-4708)*

Advanced Engineering Inc...................... F 260 356-8077
Huntington *(G-7296)*

Classic Industries Inc............................. G 812 421-4006
Evansville *(G-3972)*

Kretler Tool & Engineering Inc................ G 260 897-2662
Avilla *(G-484)*

Meriwether Tool & Engrg Inc................... E 260 744-6955
Fort Wayne *(G-5214)*

True Precision Tech Inc.......................... G 765 432-2177
Kokomo *(G-10352)*

United Ccp Inc.. E 812 442-7468
Brazil *(G-1168)*

TOOLS: Hand, Mechanics

Indy Side Piece LLC................................ G 317 426-3927
Indianapolis *(G-8534)*

TOWERS, SECTIONS: Transmission, Radio & Television

Emergency Radio Service LLC................ G 800 377-2929
Ligonier *(G-11011)*

Emergency Radio Service LLC................ E 206 894-4145
Ligonier *(G-11012)*

Ers Holding Company Inc....................... G 260 894-4145
Ligonier *(G-11013)*

Ers Tower LLC....................................... E 260 894-4145
Ligonier *(G-11014)*

Sabre Integrated Services...................... G 317 844-9100
Indianapolis *(G-9361)*

Swager Communications Inc.................. E 260 495-2515
Fremont *(G-5837)*

Valmont Telecommunications Inc............ F 877 467-4763
Plymouth *(G-13824)*

Valmont Telecommunications Inc............ F 574 936-7221
Plymouth *(G-13823)*

Vertical Steel Maintenance LLC.............. G 912 710-0626
Indianapolis *(G-9711)*

TOWING & TUGBOAT SVC

Evansville Marine Service Inc.................. E 812 424-9278
Evansville *(G-4053)*

TOYS & HOBBY GOODS & SPLYS, WHOL: Toy Novelties & Amusements

Summerville Miniature Work Sp.............. G 317 326-8355
Greenfield *(G-6561)*

TOYS & HOBBY GOODS & SPLYS, WHOLESALE: Playing Cards

Thach LLC... G 317 373-3734
Westfield *(G-16732)*

TOYS & HOBBY GOODS & SPLYS, WHOLESALE: Toys & Games

Gener8 LLC... G 317 253-8737
Indianapolis *(G-8269)*

Litko Aerosystems Inc............................ G 219 462-9295
Valparaiso *(G-15998)*

Suns Out Inc.. E 765 205-5645
Marion *(G-11340)*

TOYS & HOBBY GOODS & SPLYS, WHOLESALE: Video Games

Tokumei LLC... G 765 772-0073
West Lafayette *(G-16638)*

TOYS: Dolls, Stuffed Animals & Parts

Red Wagon.. G 260 768-3090
Shipshewana *(G-14881)*

TOYS: Electronic

RC Fun Parks LLC................................. G 574 217-7715
Granger *(G-6374)*

TRADING STAMP PROMOTION & REDEMPTION

Tasus Corporation.................................. C 812 333-6500
Bloomington *(G-984)*

TRAILER COACHES: Automobile

Girard Products LLC.............................. G 574 534-3328
Elkhart *(G-3378)*

Kzrv LP.. B 260 768-4016
Shipshewana *(G-14856)*

Winnebago of Indiana LLC...................... C 574 825-5250
Middlebury *(G-11759)*

TRAILERS & CHASSIS: Camping

Highland Ridge Rv Inc............................ B 260 768-7771
Shipshewana *(G-14850)*

Wolfpack Chassis LLC............................ E 260 349-1887
Kendallville *(G-10155)*

TRAILERS & PARTS: Boat

Spreuer & Son Inc.................................. F 260 463-3513
Lagrange *(G-10763)*

T I B Inc.. E 574 892-5151
Argos *(G-327)*

TRAILERS & PARTS: Horse

Miller Carriage Company LLC.................. G 260 768-4553
Shipshewana *(G-14867)*

Sierra Motor Corp.................................. D 574 848-1300
Bristol *(G-1292)*

TRAILERS & TRAILER EQPT

Aluminum Trailer Company..................... C 574 773-2440
Nappanee *(G-12579)*

Beck Industries LP................................. D 574 294-5621
Elkhart *(G-3221)*

Chubbs Steel Sales Inc.......................... E 574 295-3166
Elkhart *(G-3252)*

Collins Trailers Inc................................. G 574 294-2561
Elkhart *(G-3257)*

Dexter Chassis Group Inc....................... D 574 266-7356
Elkhart *(G-3294)*

Flj Transport LLC................................... G 574 642-0200
Goshen *(G-6138)*

Garry Mertz... G 260 837-6451
Waterloo *(G-16520)*

Global Parts Network LLC...................... G 574 855-5000
South Bend *(G-15044)*

Hadley Products LLC............................. G 574 266-3700
Elkhart *(G-3396)*

Hobbs Transport Services LLC............... G 317 607-5590
Indianapolis *(G-8401)*

Iea Equipment Management LLC............ B 765 832-2800
Clinton *(G-2069)*

Iea Management Services Inc................. G 765 832-8526
Clinton *(G-2070)*

Intech Trailers Inc................................... D 574 221-8231
Nappanee *(G-12614)*

JC Creations LLC.................................. G 574 248-0126
Bremen *(G-1199)*

Legacy Trailer Rentals LLC..................... G 812 873-5218
North Vernon *(G-13284)*

Liberty Inds Investments LLC.................. D 765 246-4031
Fillmore *(G-4455)*

Logistick Inc.. G 800 758-5840
South Bend *(G-15128)*

Metalcrafters Inc.................................... F 574 294-2502
Elkhart *(G-3528)*

MO Trailer Corporation........................... F 574 533-0824
Goshen *(G-6226)*

Olympic Fiberglass Industries................. F 574 223-3101
Rochester *(G-14310)*

P R F.. G 219 477-8660
Portage *(G-13902)*

Rios Investment Services LLC................ G 574 514-3999
South Bend *(G-15221)*

Supreme Industries Inc........................... C 574 642-3070
Goshen *(G-6265)*

Zieman Manufacturing Company Inc........ C 574 535-1125
Goshen *(G-6279)*

TRAILERS: Camping, Tent-Type

Forest River Inc...................................... B 574 848-1335
Bristol *(G-1261)*

Forest River Inc...................................... C 574 642-2640
Millersburg *(G-11812)*

J&K Yurts Inc... G 317 377-9878
Indianapolis *(G-8610)*

TRAILERS: Demountable Cargo Containers

Band Brothers Transport LLC.................. G 317 709-4415
Indianapolis *(G-7592)*

Forest River Inc...................................... B 574 848-1335
Bristol *(G-1261)*

Pace American Enterprises Inc............... D 800 247-5767
Middlebury *(G-11744)*

Wellco Holdings Inc............................... C 574 264-9661
Elkhart *(G-3782)*

TRAILERS: House, Exc Permanent Dwellings

Jayco Inc.. A 574 825-5861
Middlebury *(G-11727)*

Kropf Industries Inc................................ E 574 533-2171
Goshen *(G-6192)*

Trophy Homes Inc.................................. E 574 264-4911
Elkhart *(G-3748)*

TRAILERS: Semitrailers, Truck Tractors

Dock Bumpers Inc................................. G 312 597-9282
Highland *(G-7132)*

Rail Protection Plus LLC........................ G 812 399-1084
New Albany *(G-12802)*

Virago Logistix Llc................................. G 800 767-2090
Hammond *(G-7030)*

TRAILERS: Truck, Chassis

Zieman Manufacturing Company Inc........ C 574 535-1125
Goshen *(G-6279)*

TRANSDUCERS: Electrical Properties

Hartsock Industrial Sales Inc................... G 317 858-8250
Westfield *(G-16696)*

TRANSFORMERS: Distribution

Hoffmaster Electric Inc........................... G 219 616-1313
Schererville *(G-14523)*

Weg Electric Corp.................................. D 260 827-2200
Bluffton *(G-1070)*

PRODUCT SECTION

TRANSFORMERS: Specialty

Custom Magnetics Inc.................................. E 260 982-8508
North Manchester (G-13231)

TRANSFORMERS: Voltage Regulating

Protron LLC... G 765 313-1595
Anderson (G-181)

TRANSMISSIONS: Motor Vehicle

Allied Enterprises LLC............................... E 765 288-8849
Muncie (G-12339)

Allison Transm Holdings Inc..................... A 317 242-5000
Indianapolis (G-7486)

Allomatic Products Company.................... G 800 686-4729
Sullivan (G-15402)

FCA North America Holdings LLC........... D 765 454-1705
Kokomo (G-10265)

Mor/Ryde Inc... C 574 293-1581
Elkhart (G-3551)

Morris Holding Company LLC................... C 812 446-6141
Brazil (G-1154)

Morris Mfg & Sls Corp.............................. C 812 446-6141
Brazil (G-1155)

Morryde International Inc.......................... C 574 293-1581
Elkhart (G-3555)

Mosey Manufacturing Co Inc.................... C 765 983-8870
Richmond (G-14171)

Nagakura Engrg Works Co Inc................. C 812 375-1382
Columbus (G-2359)

Pullman Company...................................... B 260 667-2200
Angola (G-290)

TRANSPORTATION EQPT & SPLYS WHOLESALERS, NEC

Gbj Holdings LLC...................................... G 317 483-1896
Highland (G-7137)

Turbines Inc... E 812 877-2587
Terre Haute (G-15737)

TRANSPORTATION SVCS, WATER: Canal Barge Operations

Acbl Holding Corporation.......................... A 310 712-1850
Jeffersonville (G-9921)

Acl Sales Corporation................................ G 812 288-0100
Jeffersonville (G-9923)

American Barge Line Company................. G 812 288-0100
Jeffersonville (G-9930)

American Coml Barge Line LLC............... C 812 288-0100
Jeffersonville (G-9931)

American Commercial Lines Inc............... C 812 288-0100
Jeffersonville (G-9932)

Commercial Barge Line Company............ E 812 288-0100
Jeffersonville (G-9956)

TRAP ROCK: Crushed & Broken

S & G Excavating Inc................................ F 812 234-4848
Terre Haute (G-15685)

TRAVEL AGENCIES

American Ex Trvl Rlted Svcs In................ G 812 523-0106
Seymour (G-14629)

R Drew & Co Inc....................................... G 765 420-7237
West Lafayette (G-16624)

Safe Travels Solutions LLC...................... G 317 640-4576
Indianapolis (G-9363)

TRAVEL TRAILERS & CAMPERS

All American Group Inc............................. G 574 825-5821
Middlebury (G-11694)

All American Group Inc............................. G 574 825-8555
Middlebury (G-11695)

All American Group Inc............................. E 574 262-0123
Elkhart (G-3160)

Bison Coach LLC...................................... E 574 658-4161
Milford (G-11787)

Coachmen Recrtl Vhcl Co LLC................. G 574 825-5821
Middlebury (G-11704)

Damon Corporation.................................. A 574 262-2624
Elkhart (G-3285)

Dna Enterprises Inc................................... E 574 534-0034
Elkhart (G-3298)

Donald Lloyd... G 937 304-5683
Indianapolis (G-7996)

Ds Corp... D 260 593-3850
Topeka (G-15804)

Forest River Inc... A 574 296-7700
Elkhart (G-3353)

Forest River Inc... A 574 262-3474
Elkhart (G-3355)

Forest River Inc... A 574 642-3112
Goshen (G-6140)

Forest River Inc... C 574 533-5934
Goshen (G-6141)

Forest River Cherokee Inc........................ G 260 593-2566
Topeka (G-15805)

Forest River Custom Extrusions............... G 574 975-0206
Goshen (G-6142)

Forks Rv Inc.. D 574 825-7467
Shipshewana (G-14846)

Gulf Stream Coach Inc.............................. C 574 773-7761
Nappanee (G-12603)

Gulf Stream Parts & Service..................... G 574 858-2850
Etna Green (G-3849)

Heart Breaker Sales LLC.......................... G 765 489-4048
Hagerstown (G-6837)

Homette Corporation................................. G 574 294-6521
Elkhart (G-3410)

Independent Protection Co....................... C 574 831-5680
New Paris (G-12960)

Keystone Rv Company.............................. D 574 537-0600
Goshen (G-6188)

Keystone Rv Company.............................. B 574 535-2100
Goshen (G-6189)

Keystone Rv Company.............................. B 574 535-2100
Goshen (G-6190)

Layton Homes Corporation....................... C 574 294-6521
Elkhart (G-3473)

Layton Homes Corporation....................... G 574 294-6521
Elkhart (G-3472)

Lippert Components Inc........................... F 574 971-4320
Goshen (G-6207)

Livin Lite Corp... E 574 862-2228
Shipshewana (G-14865)

Lsr Conversions LLC................................ F 574 206-9610
Elkhart (G-3501)

Marathon Homes Corporation................... E 574 294-6441
Elkhart (G-3512)

Newmar Corporation................................. G 574 773-7791
Nappanee (G-12631)

Next Gen Power Holdings LLC................. G 574 971-4490
Elkhart (G-3568)

Recreation By Design LLC....................... D 574 294-2117
Elkhart (G-3642)

Skyline Corporation.................................. C 574 294-2463
Elkhart (G-3682)

Skyline Homes Inc.................................... E 574 294-6521
Elkhart (G-3683)

Starcraft Corporation................................ G 574 534-7827
Goshen (G-6260)

Supreme Corporation................................ G 260 894-9191
Ligonier (G-11026)

Supreme Corporation................................ C 574 642-4888
Goshen (G-6263)

Thor Industries Inc.................................... G 574 584-2151
Wakarusa (G-16253)

Thor Industries Inc.................................... G 800 860-5658
Wakarusa (G-16254)

Thor Motor Coach Inc............................... E 800 860-5658
Wakarusa (G-16255)

Thor Motor Coach Inc............................... C 574 266-1111
Elkhart (G-3733)

TI Industries Inc.. E 419 666-8144
Elkhart (G-3736)

Wabash National LP................................. E 765 771-5300
Lafayette (G-10713)

TRAYS: Plastic

MCP Usa Inc.. G 219 734-6598
Portage (G-13885)

Sabert Corporation................................... E 260 222-0758
Fort Wayne (G-5394)

TROPHIES, NEC

Bruce Fox Inc.. C 812 945-3511
New Albany (G-12706)

TROPHIES, WHOLESALE

Bruce Fox Inc.. C 812 945-3511
New Albany (G-12706)

First Place Trophy Inc............................... G 574 293-6147
Elkhart (G-3347)

Imperial Trophy & Awards Co................... G 260 432-8161
Fort Wayne (G-5096)

Ram Graphics Inc...................................... F 765 724-7783
Alexandria (G-58)

Tower Advertising Products Inc................ D 260 593-2103
Topeka (G-15821)

TROPHIES: Metal, Exc Silver

Awardmakersnet Inc.................................. G 260 925-4672
Auburn (G-366)

Professional Bowling Ball Svc.................. G 317 786-4329
Indianapolis (G-9220)

Tic Toc Trophy Shop Inc........................... G 574 893-4234
Akron (G-10)

TRUCK & BUS BODIES: Garbage Or Refuse Truck

Autocar LLC... E 765 489-5499
Hagerstown (G-6833)

Townsends Disposal................................. G 765 985-2126
Mexico (G-11573)

TRUCK & BUS BODIES: Motor Vehicle, Specialty

Delivery Concepts Inc............................... E 574 522-3981
Elkhart (G-3289)

Mavron Inc... F 574 267-3044
Warsaw (G-16392)

Mobility Ventures LLC............................... G 734 367-3714
South Bend (G-15153)

Sharp Wraps LLC...................................... G 317 989-8447
Zionsville (G-17049)

TLC Metals Inc.. D 317 894-8684
Greenfield (G-6566)

TRUCK & BUS BODIES: Truck Beds

Mooresville Welding Inc............................ G 317 831-2265
Mooresville (G-12225)

TRUCK BODIES: Body Parts

Armor Parent Corp.................................... F 812 962-5000
Evansville (G-3900)

Employee Codes: A=Over 500 employees, B=251-500
C=101-250, D=51-100, E=20-50, F=10-19, G=1-9

TRUCK BODIES: Body Parts

Bentz Transport Products Inc............... F 260 622-9100
  Zionsville *(G-16996)*

Braun Companies LLC.................... E 765 332-2084
  New Castle *(G-12852)*

Kneppers Inc.................................. G 260 636-2180
  Albion *(G-30)*

Kneppers Inc.................................. G 260 636-2180
  Avilla *(G-483)*

Mantra Enterprise LLC.................... G 201 428-8709
  Fishers *(G-4561)*

Vanguard National Trailer Corp........... E 219 253-2000
  Monon *(G-12058)*

TRUCK GENERAL REPAIR SVC

CD & Ws Bordner Entps Inc.............. G 765 268-2120
  Cutler *(G-2783)*

Tire Central and Service Avon............ G 317 966-0662
  Indianapolis *(G-9608)*

TRUCK PARTS & ACCESSORIES: Wholesalers

Brake Supply Company Inc............... C 812 467-1000
  Evansville *(G-3950)*

Mid-State Truck Equipment Inc............ E 317 849-4903
  Fishers *(G-4566)*

Switzerland Hills Inc........................... E 812 594-2810
  Patriot *(G-13511)*

TRUCKING & HAULING SVCS: Building Materials

Cresline Plastic Pipe Co Inc............... E 812 428-9300
  Evansville *(G-3994)*

TRUCKING & HAULING SVCS: Contract Basis

Haas Cabinet Co Inc........................ C 812 246-4431
  Sellersburg *(G-14594)*

TRUCKING & HAULING SVCS: Heavy Machinery, Local

Industrial Mint Wldg Machining............ E 219 393-5531
  Kingsbury *(G-10179)*

TRUCKING & HAULING SVCS: Heavy, NEC

Full Throttle Enterprise Inc................. G 317 779-3887
  Indianapolis *(G-8240)*

TRUCKING & HAULING SVCS: Lumber & Log, Local

Blackwood Solutions LLC.................. D 812 676-8770
  Bloomington *(G-809)*

TRUCKING: Except Local

Accra-Pac Inc................................. G 574 295-0000
  Elkhart *(G-3149)*

CDP Logistics Inc............................ G 773 968-1455
  Avon *(G-510)*

Frick Services Inc............................ E 260 761-3311
  Wawaka *(G-16539)*

Jdh Logistics LLC............................ G 573 529-2005
  Fort Branch *(G-4705)*

Jennings County Pallets Inc............... E 812 458-6288
  Butlerville *(G-1484)*

Popcorn Weaver Mfg LLC................. C 765 934-2101
  Indianapolis *(G-9162)*

Southlake Lift Truck......................... G 219 962-4695
  Gary *(G-6013)*

T Organization Inc........................... E 463 204-5118
  Greenwood *(G-6771)*

Zip Zone Gone LLC.......................... G 812 604-0041
  Evansville *(G-4393)*

TRUCKING: Local, With Storage

Blackwood Solutions LLC.................. D 812 676-8770
  Bloomington *(G-809)*

Kic LLC... E 360 823-4440
  Evansville *(G-4152)*

Simmons Equipment Sales Inc............ F 260 625-3308
  Columbia City *(G-2197)*

TRUCKING: Local, Without Storage

All American Ex Solutions LLC............ E 317 789-3070
  Indianapolis *(G-7472)*

Band Brothers Transport LLC............. G 317 709-4415
  Indianapolis *(G-7592)*

C & C Pallets and Lumber LLC........... G 765 524-3214
  New Castle *(G-12855)*

Carmichael Welding Inc.................... G 812 825-5156
  Bloomfield *(G-742)*

Kendallville Iron & Metal Inc............... F 260 347-1958
  Kendallville *(G-10126)*

Krafft Gravel Inc.............................. G 260 238-4653
  Spencerville *(G-15372)*

Lees Ready-Mix & Trucking............... E
  Shelbyville *(G-14772)*

Paddack Brothers Inc....................... G 765 659-4777
  Frankfort *(G-5689)*

R & R Trucking & Freight LLC............ G 888 477-8782
  Indianapolis *(G-9254)*

Raymone Sanders Fmly Trckg LLC...... G 317 400-3545
  Indianapolis *(G-9272)*

Rex Alton & Companies Inc.............. F 812 882-8519
  Vincennes *(G-16149)*

TRUCKS & TRACTORS: Industrial

Alta Equipment Holdings Inc.............. G 269 578-3182
  South Bend *(G-14939)*

Aluminum Trailer Company............... C 574 773-2440
  Nappanee *(G-12579)*

AM General LLC............................. A 574 258-7523
  Mishawaka *(G-11840)*

Bemcor Inc.................................... F 219 937-1600
  Hammond *(G-6885)*

Buhrt Engineering & Cnstr................. E 574 267-3720
  Warsaw *(G-16331)*

Century Industries LLC..................... E 812 246-3371
  Sellersburg *(G-14590)*

Eaton Corporation........................... C 260 925-3800
  Auburn *(G-387)*

Elpers Truck Equipment LLC.............. F 812 423-5787
  Evansville *(G-4031)*

Galfab LLC..................................... F 574 946-7767
  Winamac *(G-16861)*

Great Dane LLC.............................. A 812 443-4711
  Brazil *(G-1143)*

Hirata Corporation of America............ E 317 856-8600
  Indianapolis *(G-8399)*

Hy-TEC Fiberglass Inc..................... G 260 489-6601
  Fort Wayne *(G-5087)*

Industrial Transmission Eqp............... E 574 936-3028
  Plymouth *(G-13785)*

JD Materials.................................. G 219 662-1418
  Crown Point *(G-2701)*

Joyce/Dayton Corp.......................... E 260 726-9361
  Portland *(G-13952)*

Kenneth E Ziegler........................... G 765 675-2222
  Tipton *(G-15778)*

Lafayette Wire Products Inc............... D 765 474-7896
  Lafayette *(G-10632)*

Laidig Inc...................................... E 574 256-0204
  Mishawaka *(G-11925)*

Major Tool and Machine Inc............... C 317 636-6433
  Indianapolis *(G-8820)*

Mooresville Welding Inc.................... G 317 831-2265
  Mooresville *(G-12225)*

Nelson J Hochstetler........................ G 260 499-0315
  Lagrange *(G-10756)*

Ogden Welding Systems Inc.............. E 219 322-5252
  Schererville *(G-14537)*

Pierce Tracy.................................. G 765 748-2361
  Anderson *(G-179)*

Rance Aluminum Fabrication.............. E 574 266-9028
  Elkhart *(G-3639)*

S and SM Achine USA LLC............... G 708 758-8300
  Gary *(G-6006)*

Selking International LLC................... E 260 482-3000
  Fort Wayne *(G-5408)*

Selking International Inc.................... G 574 522-2001
  Elkhart *(G-3668)*

Showtime Conversions Inc................ E 574 825-1130
  Middlebury *(G-11752)*

Stahl Equipment Inc......................... F 812 925-3341
  Gentryville *(G-6053)*

Storageworks Inc............................ G 317 577-3511
  Fishers *(G-4607)*

Supreme Industries Inc..................... C 574 642-3070
  Goshen *(G-6265)*

Utilimaster Services LLC................... B 800 582-3454
  Bristol *(G-1296)*

Wiese Holding Company................... D 317 241-8600
  Indianapolis *(G-9761)*

TRUCKS: Forklift

Michiana Forklift Inc......................... F 574 326-3702
  Elkhart *(G-3532)*

North Central Equipment C................ G 574 825-2006
  Middlebury *(G-11741)*

Southlake Lift Truck......................... G 219 962-4695
  Gary *(G-6013)*

Toyota Material Handling Inc.............. D 800 381-5879
  Columbus *(G-2406)*

TRUCKS: Indl

141 Trucking LLC............................ G 312 581-5121
  Schererville *(G-14511)*

5 Star Logistics LLC......................... G 708 926-4251
  Highland *(G-7117)*

7r Express LLC............................... G 833 611-3497
  Evansville *(G-3857)*

A Divine Image Enterprise LLC........... G 317 397-8132
  Indianapolis *(G-7398)*

A&J Logistic LLC............................. G 708 314-6817
  Dyer *(G-2965)*

Abs Freight Lines LLC...................... G 317 691-6846
  Indianapolis *(G-7417)*

All Shppers Are Prrity Trckg L............ G 317 525-6954
  Indianapolis *(G-7476)*

Anderson & Anderson Trckg Inc......... G 219 661-7547
  Crown Point *(G-2650)*

Bell Transportation LLC.................... G 317 833-0745
  Indianapolis *(G-7610)*

Beyond Distributions LLC.................. G 631 960-1745
  Indianapolis *(G-7621)*

Cedric Morris................................. G 678 718-0012
  Fishers *(G-4485)*

Citrine Dispatch LLC........................ G 219 689-8293
  Hammond *(G-6899)*

Clp Towne Inc................................ G 574 233-3183
  South Bend *(G-14977)*

Cmoss Transport LLC...................... G 317 656-1846
  Indianapolis *(G-7828)*

Cooper Transit LLC......................... G 260 797-3003
  Fort Wayne *(G-4871)*

PRODUCT SECTION

D Rinker Transport LLC......................... G 765 749-4120
Dunkirk *(G-2961)*

Diamonds & Pearls Trnsp LLC.............. G 504 295-2701
Indianapolis *(G-7972)*

Dodson Logistics LLC............................ G 937 657-7490
Richmond *(G-14115)*

Dohrn Transfer Company......................... E 574 941-4484
Plymouth *(G-13771)*

Extreme Trailer Service LLC .... E 812 406-1984
Charlestown *(G-1876)*

Forever Young Trckg Svcs LLC .... G 616 350-4053
Indianapolis *(G-8215)*

Ftn Logistics LLC..................................... G 317 488-7446
Indianapolis *(G-8237)*

Fuentes Distributing Inc......................... G 219 808-2147
Hammond *(G-6933)*

Generation Logistics LLC .... G 877 238-7380
Indianapolis *(G-8273)*

Genertonal Outreach Gaming LLC........ G 872 777-6882
Gary *(G-5939)*

Gypsum Express Ltd............................... G 812 247-2648
Shoals *(G-14908)*

Its Family Trucking LLC .... G 219 277-7162
Hammond *(G-6960)*

Jacksons 33 Transporting LLC............... G 901 628-7803
Indianapolis *(G-8616)*

John S Cotter.. G 765 584-2521
Ridgeville *(G-14234)*

Jpc Trucking LLC................................... G 219 207-2300
Valparaiso *(G-15982)*

Kath Enterprise LLC .... G 877 641-6990
Gary *(G-5972)*

Ksm Logistics LLC................................. G 574 318-2040
South Bend *(G-15108)*

Leggits LLC... G 269 447-3500
South Bend *(G-15123)*

Lifted Loads LLC .... G 317 432-1542
Indianapolis *(G-8748)*

M-Famouz Logistics LLC .... G 219 501-1921
Hammond *(G-6974)*

MHp Distribution LLC.............................. F 312 731-8380
Gary *(G-5981)*

Midwest Transit Authority LLC................ G 765 414-5097
West Lafayette *(G-16606)*

Moodys Logistics Services LLC .... G 812 512-2772
Linton *(G-11040)*

O&T Alliance Group LLC .... G 302 287-0953
Indianapolis *(G-9039)*

On The Go Logistics LLC........................ G 765 810-7454
Anderson *(G-173)*

One Little Truck LLC .... G 872 276-0014
Highland *(G-7149)*

Prosperer Trucking LLC......................... G 317 551-5691
Indianapolis *(G-9232)*

Qme LLC... G 773 263-9830
Gary *(G-5998)*

R & R Trucking & Freight LLC................. G 888 477-8782
Indianapolis *(G-9254)*

Renegade Dispatching LLC................... G 260 797-5423
Fort Wayne *(G-5380)*

Right Direction Trckg Ex LLC................. G 502 912-2504
Jeffersonville *(G-10047)*

S & Y Trucking LLC................................ G 317 642-6222
Noblesville *(G-13170)*

Shalom Trans LLC .... E 317 712-6765
Avon *(G-550)*

Ssm Logistics LLC................................. G 812 354-4509
Winslow *(G-16923)*

Tidy Janitorial Services LLC................... G 502 807-9847
Clarksville *(G-2039)*

Transtex LLC.. G 877 960-2644
Indianapolis *(G-9631)*

Truckin4ya LLC...................................... G 812 225-2640
Jeffersonville *(G-10066)*

Two Sticks Inc.. G 219 926-7910
Chesterton *(G-1962)*

Verbott Trucking & Transportat.............. G 317 363-9698
Indianapolis *(G-9706)*

Wild Hunnits Group Inc.......................... G 312 609-9433
Hammond *(G-7034)*

Yes Yes Trucking LLC............................. G 800 971-3633
Indianapolis *(G-9801)*

Youngs Freight & Logistics LLC .... G 765 639-7888
Anderson *(G-219)*

TRUSSES & FRAMING: Prefabricated Metal

B & A Cnstr & Design Inc........................ F 812 683-4600
Huntingburg *(G-7270)*

Carter-Lee Building Components .... E 317 639-5431
Indianapolis *(G-7752)*

TRUSSES: Wood, Floor

Beachwood Lumber Co Inc..................... G 574 858-9325
Warsaw *(G-16319)*

Georgetown Truss Company Inc............ E 812 951-2647
Georgetown *(G-6061)*

Kerkhoff Associates Inc.......................... E 765 583-4491
Otterbein *(G-13453)*

TUBES: Extruded Or Drawn, Aluminum

Alconex Specialty Products..................... E 260 744-3446
Fort Wayne *(G-4738)*

Arconic US LLC...................................... A 765 771-3600
Lafayette *(G-10525)*

TUBES: Light Sensing & Emitting

HB Connect Inc....................................... G 855 503-9159
Fort Wayne *(G-5051)*

HB Connect Inc....................................... D 260 422-1212
Fort Wayne *(G-5052)*

TUBES: Paper

Precision Products Group Inc................. F 317 663-4590
Indianapolis *(G-9184)*

TUBES: Steel & Iron

Allied Tube & Conduit Corp..................... F 765 459-8811
Kokomo *(G-10232)*

Avis Industrial Corporation..................... E 765 998-8100
Upland *(G-15876)*

Midwest Tube Mills Inc........................... D 812 265-1553
Madison *(G-11243)*

Nelson Acquisition LLC.......................... E 574 753-6377
Logansport *(G-11097)*

Nippon Steel Pipe America Inc............... B 812 523-0842
Seymour *(G-14669)*

TUBES: Television

J & L Uebelhor Enterprises LLC.............. G 812 367-1591
Ferdinand *(G-4436)*

TUBES: Wrought, Welded Or Lock Joint

Bock Industries Inc................................. E 574 295-8070
Elkhart *(G-3230)*

Ljt Texas LLC... D 800 257-6859
South Bend *(G-15126)*

TUBING: Flexible, Metallic

OHM Enterprise LLC............................... G 812 879-5455
Gosport *(G-6288)*

Parker-Hannifin Corporation................... E 260 587-9102
Ashley *(G-335)*

TUBING: Rubber

Fluid Handling Technology Inc................ G 317 216-9629
Indianapolis *(G-8207)*

TURBINES & TURBINE GENERATOR SET UNITS, COMPLETE

Iet Global Inc.. E 812 421-7810
Evansville *(G-4114)*

Tri Aerospace LLC................................. E 812 872-2400
Terre Haute *(G-15736)*

Windstream Technologies Inc................ F 812 953-1481
North Vernon *(G-13301)*

TURBINES & TURBINE GENERATOR SET UNITS: Gas, Complete

Caterpillar Inc... G 765 447-6816
Lafayette *(G-10550)*

Siemens Energy Inc................................ C 317 677-1340
Indianapolis *(G-9424)*

TURBINES & TURBINE GENERATOR SETS

Allison Transmission Inc......................... C 317 821-5104
Indianapolis *(G-7488)*

Allison Transmission Inc......................... A 317 242-5000
Indianapolis *(G-7491)*

B&W Environmental................................ G 260 766-4135
Portland *(G-13929)*

Babcock.. G 219 462-8851
Valparaiso *(G-15907)*

Clayhill Wind & Solar LLC .... G 765 437-2395
Sharpsville *(G-14709)*

Cummins Inc... D 812 522-9366
Seymour *(G-14645)*

Design Engineering................................. G 219 926-2170
Chesterton *(G-1919)*

Drive Process Services Inc..................... G 765 741-9717
Muncie *(G-12387)*

Falcon Manufacturing LLC .... F 317 884-3600
Columbus *(G-2301)*

Mantech Manifold.................................... G 260 479-2383
Fort Wayne *(G-5202)*

Petal Solutions LLC................................ G 765 404-7747
West Lafayette *(G-16618)*

Power Wall Systems LLC....................... G 317 348-1260
Fishers *(G-4580)*

Prime Tech Inc.. F 317 715-1162
Indianapolis *(G-9196)*

TURBINES & TURBINE GENERATOR SETS & PARTS

Integrated Energy Technologies Inc........ E 812 421-7810
Evansville *(G-4128)*

TYPESETTING SVC

Acclaim Graphics Inc.............................. G 812 424-5035
Evansville *(G-3866)*

Advantage Productions........................... G 219 879-6892
La Porte *(G-10376)*

Aim Media Indiana Oper LLC.................. E 317 462-5528
Greenfield *(G-6458)*

Brand Prtg & Photo-Litho Co.................. G 317 921-4095
New Palestine *(G-12933)*

BSC Vntres Acquisition Sub LLC........... D 260 665-7521
Angola *(G-237)*

C J P Corporation................................... G 219 924-1685
Highland *(G-7127)*

Cecils Printing & Off Sups Inc................ G 812 683-4416
Huntingburg *(G-7273)*

Employee Codes: A=Over 500 employees, B=251-500
C=101-250, D=51-100, E=20-50, F=10-19, G=1-9

2024 Harris Indiana
Industrial Directory

TYPESETTING SVC

PRODUCT SECTION

Ckmt Associates Inc .... F 219 924-2820
 Hammond *(G-6902)*

Classic Graphics Inc .... F 260 482-3487
 Fort Wayne *(G-4853)*

Cnhi LLC .... G 812 944-6481
 Jeffersonville *(G-9955)*

Community Holdings Indiana Inc .... G 812 663-3111
 Greensburg *(G-6585)*

Community Holdings Indiana Inc .... G 765 482-4650
 Lebanon *(G-10885)*

Community Papers Inc .... G 317 241-7363
 Indianapolis *(G-7841)*

Composition LLC .... G 317 979-7214
 Fishers *(G-4493)*

Consolidated Printing Svcs Inc .... G 765 468-6033
 Farmland *(G-4424)*

Copyfire Typesetting Inc .... G 317 894-0408
 Indianapolis *(G-7873)*

Copymat Services Inc .... G 765 743-5995
 Lafayette *(G-10557)*

Courier Printing Co Allen Cnty .... G 260 627-2728
 Grabill *(G-6293)*

Courier-Times Inc .... D 765 529-1111
 New Castle *(G-12856)*

Coy & Associates .... G 317 787-5089
 Indianapolis *(G-7893)*

Creative Concept Ventures Inc .... G 812 282-9442
 Jeffersonville *(G-9964)*

Crescendo Inc .... G 812 829-4759
 Spencer *(G-15344)*

D & M Printing Inc .... G 812 847-4837
 Linton *(G-11034)*

Debra Lindhorst .... G 260 375-3285
 Warren *(G-16296)*

Digital Printing Incorporated .... G 812 265-2205
 Madison *(G-11214)*

Doerr Printing Co .... G 317 568-0135
 Indianapolis *(G-7994)*

Dynamark Graphics Group Inc .... E 317 328-2555
 Indianapolis *(G-8023)*

Ed Sons Inc .... F 317 897-8821
 Indianapolis *(G-8051)*

Evansville Bindery Inc .... G 812 423-2222
 Evansville *(G-4048)*

Evansville Courier Co .... B 812 464-7500
 Evansville *(G-4051)*

Ewing Printing Company Inc .... F 812 882-2415
 Vincennes *(G-16120)*

Excell Color Graphics Inc .... E 260 482-2720
 Fort Wayne *(G-4967)*

Express Press Indiana Inc .... E 574 277-3355
 South Bend *(G-15023)*

Fedex Office & Print Svcs Inc .... G 317 849-9683
 Indianapolis *(G-8174)*

Fedex Office & Print Svcs Inc .... G 317 885-6480
 Indianapolis *(G-8175)*

Fedex Office & Print Svcs Inc .... G 317 295-1063
 Indianapolis *(G-8176)*

Fedex Office & Print Svcs Inc .... G 317 337-2679
 Indianapolis *(G-8177)*

Fedex Office & Print Svcs Inc .... G 317 631-6862
 Indianapolis *(G-8178)*

Fedex Office & Print Svcs Inc .... G 317 251-2406
 Indianapolis *(G-8179)*

Fedex Office & Print Svcs Inc .... F 765 449-4950
 Lafayette *(G-10579)*

Fineline Graphics Incorporated .... G 317 872-4490
 Indianapolis *(G-8188)*

First Quality Printing Inc .... G 317 506-8633
 Indianapolis *(G-8195)*

Gary Printing Inc .... G 219 886-1767
 Gary *(G-5938)*

Gkb Holdings Inc .... E 260 471-7744
 Fort Wayne *(G-5025)*

Goetz Printing .... G 812 243-2086
 Terre Haute *(G-15600)*

Granger Gazette Inc .... G 574 277-2679
 Granger *(G-6350)*

Green Banner Publications Inc .... E 812 967-3176
 Borden *(G-1109)*

Greensburg Printing Co Inc .... G 812 663-8265
 Greensburg *(G-6598)*

Hardesty Printing Co Inc .... F 574 267-7591
 Warsaw *(G-16374)*

Hardesty Printing Co Inc .... F 574 223-4553
 Rochester *(G-14293)*

Hetty Incorporated .... G 219 933-0833
 Hammond *(G-6945)*

Hetty Incorporated .... G 219 836-2517
 Munster *(G-12539)*

Hiatt Enterprises Inc .... G 765 289-2700
 Muncie *(G-12416)*

Hiatt Enterprises Inc .... F 765 289-7756
 Muncie *(G-12415)*

Hinen Printing Co .... G 260 248-8984
 Columbia City *(G-2150)*

Home Mountain Publishing Co Inc .... E 219 462-6601
 Valparaiso *(G-15962)*

Hoosier Times Inc .... C 812 331-4270
 Bloomington *(G-882)*

Howard Print Shop LLC .... G 765 453-6161
 Kokomo *(G-10283)*

Indiana Newspapers LLC .... D 812 886-9955
 Vincennes *(G-16131)*

J Jarrett Engineering Inc .... G 812 268-3338
 Sullivan *(G-15408)*

Jomark Inc .... F 248 478-2600
 Angola *(G-265)*

Journal & Chronicle Inc .... G 812 752-5060
 Scottsburg *(G-14566)*

Kendallville Custom Printing .... F 260 347-9233
 Kendallville *(G-10125)*

Kistner Enterprises Inc .... G 317 773-7733
 Noblesville *(G-13123)*

Kpc Media Group Inc .... F 260 426-2640
 Fort Wayne *(G-5158)*

Kpc Media Group Inc .... C 260 347-0400
 Kendallville *(G-10130)*

L & L Press Inc .... F 765 664-3162
 Marion *(G-11305)*

La Grange Publishing Co Inc .... F 260 463-3243
 Lagrange *(G-10747)*

Largus Speedy Print Corp .... E 219 922-8414
 Munster *(G-12546)*

Leader Publishing Co of Salem .... E 812 883-3281
 Salem *(G-14487)*

Light Printing Co .... G 815 429-3724
 Brook *(G-1305)*

Lincoln Printing Corporation .... A 260 424-5200
 Fort Wayne *(G-5186)*

Ludwick Graphics Inc .... G 574 233-2165
 South Bend *(G-15131)*

Maury Boyd & Associates Inc .... F 317 849-6110
 Indianapolis *(G-8853)*

Minute Print It Inc .... G 765 482-9019
 Lebanon *(G-10916)*

Muncie Novelty Company Inc .... D 765 288-8301
 Muncie *(G-12463)*

News Publishing Company LLC .... G 812 649-4440
 Rockport *(G-14346)*

Nussmeier Engraving Company .... E 812 425-1339
 Evansville *(G-4224)*

Offset House Inc .... F 317 849-5155
 Indianapolis *(G-9042)*

Offset One Inc .... F 260 456-8828
 Fort Wayne *(G-5282)*

Overgaards Artcraft Printers .... G 574 234-8464
 South Bend *(G-15183)*

Pierce Oil Co Inc .... F 812 268-6356
 Sullivan *(G-15416)*

PIP Marketing Signs Print .... G 317 843-5755
 Carmel *(G-1719)*

Presstime Graphics Inc .... F 812 234-3815
 Terre Haute *(G-15669)*

Printing Place Inc .... F 260 665-8444
 Angola *(G-289)*

Progressive Printing Co Inc .... G 765 653-3814
 Greencastle *(G-6427)*

Publishers Consulting Corp .... F 219 874-4245
 Michigan City *(G-11652)*

Qgraphics Inc .... G 574 967-3733
 Flora *(G-4664)*

Quality Printing of NW Ind .... G 219 322-6677
 Schererville *(G-14540)*

Reprocomm Inc .... G 765 472-5700
 Peru *(G-13598)*

Rhr Corporation .... G 317 788-1504
 Indianapolis *(G-9298)*

Rick Whitt .... G 317 873-5507
 Indianapolis *(G-9305)*

Riden Inc .... G 219 362-5511
 La Porte *(G-10473)*

Rink Printing Company .... E 574 232-7935
 South Bend *(G-15220)*

Rrc Corporation .... F 317 687-8325
 Indianapolis *(G-9343)*

Russ Print Shp/Hbron Advrtser .... F 219 996-3142
 Hebron *(G-7106)*

Service Printers Inc .... E 574 266-6710
 Elkhart *(G-3669)*

Specialized Printed Products .... G 260 483-7075
 Fort Wayne *(G-5428)*

Spencer Evening World .... D 812 829-2255
 Spencer *(G-15362)*

Stines Printing Inc .... G 260 356-5994
 Huntington *(G-7371)*

Tabco Business Forms Inc .... G 812 882-2836
 Vincennes *(G-16157)*

Tatman Inc .... E 765 825-2164
 Connersville *(G-2472)*

The Deaton Family Company .... D 815 726-6234
 Auburn *(G-429)*

Thomas E Slade Inc .... F 812 437-5233
 Evansville *(G-4343)*

Times .... E 765 659-4622
 Frankfort *(G-5698)*

Town & Country Press Inc .... F 574 936-9505
 Plymouth *(G-13820)*

Triple Crown Media LLC .... G 574 533-2151
 Goshen *(G-6273)*

Truth Publishing Company Inc .... G 765 653-5151
 Greencastle *(G-6434)*

University Publishing Corp .... E 812 339-9033
 Bloomington *(G-1004)*

Vitruvian Composition LLC .... G 317 447-8383
 Indianapolis *(G-9725)*

Voice of God Recordings Inc .... D 812 246-2137
 Jeffersonville *(G-10069)*

WAr - LLC- Westville Prtg .... G 219 785-2821
 Westville *(G-16765)*

Woodburn Graphics Inc .... F 812 232-0323
 Terre Haute *(G-15748)*

Writeguard Business Systems .... G 317 849-7292
 Indianapolis *(G-9793)*

Zipp Printing LLC .... G 574 256-0059
 Mishawaka *(G-12028)*

2024 Harris Indiana Industrial Directory

(G-0000) Company's Geographic Section entry number

PRODUCT SECTION

TYPESETTING SVC: Computer

Annual Reports Inc.................................. G 317 736-8838
Franklin *(G-5709)*

Rowland Printing Co Inc.......................... F 317 773-1829
Noblesville *(G-13168)*

UNIFORM SPLY SVCS: Indl

Wildman Business Group LLC.............. G 866 369-1552
Warsaw *(G-16451)*

UNIFORM STORES

J B Hinchman Inc.................................... G 317 359-1808
Indianapolis *(G-8602)*

OHaras Sports Inc................................... G 219 836-5554
Munster *(G-12554)*

Winning Edge of Rochester Inc.............. F 574 223-6090
Rochester *(G-14334)*

UNISEX HAIR SALONS

Best Electric Motor Service..................... G 765 583-2408
Otterbein *(G-13450)*

Classique Hair Style................................ G 317 738-2104
Franklin *(G-5721)*

UNIVERSITY

Ball State University................................ G 765 285-8218
Muncie *(G-12349)*

Trustees Indiana University..................... G 812 855-7995
Bloomington *(G-995)*

Trustees Indiana University..................... G 812 855-3439
Bloomington *(G-997)*

Trustees Indiana University..................... G 812 856-4186
Bloomington *(G-998)*

Trustees Indiana University..................... F 812 855-4848
Bloomington *(G-999)*

University Notre Dame Du Lac................ F 574 631-7471
Notre Dame *(G-13317)*

University Notre Dame Du Lac................ E 574 631-6346
Notre Dame *(G-13318)*

UNSUPPORTED PLASTICS: Floor Or Wall Covering

Custom Covers Inc.................................. G 765 481-7800
Lebanon *(G-10888)*

Jack Laurie Coml Floors Inc.................... G 317 569-2095
Indianapolis *(G-8613)*

UPHOLSTERY WORK SVCS

Industrial Sewing Machine Co................. G 812 425-2255
Evansville *(G-4124)*

Love Upholstery LLC............................... G 812 639-3789
Jasper *(G-9883)*

URNS: Cut Stone

American Urn Inc..................................... G 812 379-5555
Columbus *(G-2218)*

Aurora Casket Company LLC................ B 800 457-1111
Aurora *(G-439)*

USED CAR DEALERS

Futurex Industries Inc............................. E 765 597-2221
Marshall *(G-11373)*

Heritage Financial Group Inc.................. E 574 522-8000
Elkhart *(G-3404)*

Oxford House Incorporated..................... D 765 884-3265
Fowler *(G-5629)*

Transwheel Corporation........................... C 260 358-8660
Huntington *(G-7374)*

USED MERCHANDISE STORES

Fall Creek Corporation............................. G 765 482-1861
Lebanon *(G-10893)*

UTENSILS: Household, Cooking & Kitchen, Metal

Gentec LLC... G 260 436-7333
Fort Wayne *(G-5022)*

UTILITY TRAILER DEALERS

Aluminum Trailer Company..................... C 574 773-2440
Nappanee *(G-12579)*

Chief Metal Works Inc............................. G 765 932-2134
Rushville *(G-14396)*

Collins Trailers Inc................................... G 574 294-2561
Elkhart *(G-3257)*

Holiday House LLC.................................. F 574 206-0016
Elkhart *(G-3408)*

Intech Trailers Inc.................................... D 574 221-8231
Nappanee *(G-12614)*

LGS Industries LLC................................. E 574 848-5665
Middlebury *(G-11733)*

Nexgen Group Inc.................................... G 574 218-6363
Nappanee *(G-12632)*

Schwartzs Trailer Sales Inc..................... G 317 773-2608
Noblesville *(G-13172)*

Talbert Manufacturing Inc........................ C 800 348-5232
Rensselaer *(G-14071)*

VACUUM CLEANERS: Indl Type

Clover Industrial Services LLC................ G 317 879-5001
Indianapolis *(G-7826)*

VACUUM SYSTEMS: Air Extraction, Indl

Dekker Vacuum Technologies Inc........... D 219 861-0661
Michigan City *(G-11598)*

VALUE-ADDED RESELLERS: Computer Systems

Cybernaut Industria LLC......................... G 317 664-5316
Indianapolis *(G-7939)*

Gary M Brown... G 765 831-2536
New Castle *(G-12864)*

Knowledge Diffusion Games LLC........... G 812 361-4424
Bloomington *(G-902)*

VALVE REPAIR SVCS, INDL

Tri-State Valve LLC.................................. F 901 388-1550
Indianapolis *(G-9638)*

VALVES

Valve Serve LLC....................................... G 260 421-1927
Fort Wayne *(G-5526)*

VALVES & PARTS: Gas, Indl

S H Leggitt Company............................... G 574 264-0230
Elkhart *(G-3656)*

Specilzed Cmpnent Prts Ltd LLC........... C 260 925-2588
Auburn *(G-425)*

VALVES & PIPE FITTINGS

Air Fixtures Inc... F 260 982-2169
North Manchester *(G-13228)*

Ameriflo Inc.. F 317 844-2019
Indianapolis *(G-7510)*

Ashley F Ward Inc................................... G 574 294-1502
Elkhart *(G-3196)*

Ashley F Ward Inc................................... G 219 879-4177
Michigan City *(G-11580)*

Banjo Corporation..................................... C 765 362-7367
Crawfordsville *(G-2546)*

Dresser LLC... D 765 827-9200
Connersville *(G-2436)*

Eclipse Inc... D
Muncie *(G-12389)*

Epco Products Inc.................................... E 260 747-8888
Fort Wayne *(G-4956)*

Eti LLC... F 260 368-7246
Geneva *(G-6049)*

Flotec Inc.. E 317 273-6960
Indianapolis *(G-8206)*

Hancor Inc.. E 812 443-2080
Brazil *(G-1144)*

Honeywell International Inc..................... G 574 231-2000
South Bend *(G-15068)*

Midwest Design Hydraulic....................... G 765 714-3016
West Lafayette *(G-16605)*

Parker-Hannifin Corporation.................... A 260 748-6000
Fort Wayne *(G-5297)*

PHD Inc... F 260 356-0120
Huntington *(G-7356)*

Strahman Holdings Inc............................ G 317 818-5030
Carmel *(G-1771)*

The Ford Meter Box Company Inc.......... C 260 563-3171
Wabash *(G-16217)*

VALVES & REGULATORS: Pressure, Indl

SMC Corporation of America................... B 317 899-4440
Noblesville *(G-13176)*

VALVES: Aerosol, Metal

Csi Manufacturing Inc.............................. F 574 825-7891
Middlebury *(G-11708)*

H & H Sales Company Inc....................... F 260 637-3177
Huntertown *(G-7257)*

Indy Aerospace Inc.................................. G 817 521-6508
Indianapolis *(G-8522)*

VALVES: Aircraft, Control, Hydraulic & Pneumatic

Nrp Jones LLC... D 800 348-8868
La Porte *(G-10460)*

VALVES: Control, Automatic

Shoemaker Inc.. F 260 625-4321
Fort Wayne *(G-5414)*

US Valves Inc... G 812 476-6662
Evansville *(G-4365)*

VALVES: Fluid Power, Control, Hydraulic & pneumatic

Hydro Systems Mfg Inc............................ G 260 436-4476
Fort Wayne *(G-5088)*

Noble Composites Inc............................. G 574 533-1462
Goshen *(G-6228)*

SMC Corporation of America................... B 317 899-4440
Noblesville *(G-13176)*

VALVES: Indl

Aalberts Hydrnic Flow Ctrl Inc................ E 317 257-6050
Fishers *(G-4458)*

AMG LLC... F 317 329-4004
Indianapolis *(G-7513)*

Dresser LLC... D 765 827-9200
Connersville *(G-2436)*

Electronics Incorporated.......................... E 574 256-5001
Mishawaka *(G-11891)*

Fitch Inc.. F 260 637-0835
Huntertown *(G-7256)*

Flosource Inc.. E 800 752-5959
Mooresville *(G-12208)*

Employee Codes: A=Over 500 employees, B=251-500
C=101-250, D=51-100, E=20-50, F=10-19, G=1-9

2024 Harris Indiana
Industrial Directory

VALVES: Indl

Frew Process Group LLC .... G 317 565-5000
  Noblesville *(G-13081)*
Hoerbiger Service .... F 574 855-4112
  South Bend *(G-15065)*
Kaman Corporation .... D 714 696-3750
  Fort Wayne *(G-5143)*
MH Vale PC .... G 219 661-0867
  Crown Point *(G-2723)*
Nibco Inc .... B 574 295-3000
  Elkhart *(G-3570)*
Parker-Hannifin Corporation .... D 260 636-2104
  Albion *(G-40)*
Pentair .... G 574 278-7161
  Winamac *(G-16869)*
Picketts Place Inc .... G 317 763-1168
  Westfield *(G-16717)*
Proportion-Air Inc .... D 317 335-2602
  Mccordsville *(G-11454)*
Stingray Systems LLC .... G 317 238-6508
  Indianapolis *(G-9511)*
Tri-State Valve LLC .... F 901 388-1550
  Indianapolis *(G-9638)*
Vernatherm LLC .... E 860 582-6776
  Columbus *(G-2411)*

VALVES: Plumbing & Heating

Maxon Corporation .... C 765 284-3304
  Muncie *(G-12449)*

VALVES: Regulating & Control, Automatic

Dwyer Instruments LLC .... C 219 879-8868
  Michigan City *(G-11604)*
Stant Manufacturing Inc .... A 870 247-5480
  Connersville *(G-2468)*

VALVES: Water Works

Emond Eldon .... G 219 279-2442
  Wolcott *(G-16930)*
Randall K Dike .... G 812 664-4942
  Owensville *(G-13471)*

VAN CONVERSIONS

Coach Line Motors .... G 765 825-7893
  Connersville *(G-2431)*
Gulf Stream Coach Inc .... C 574 773-7761
  Nappanee *(G-12603)*
Independent Protection Co .... C 574 831-5680
  New Paris *(G-12960)*
Southside Mini Storage .... G 574 293-3270
  Elkhart *(G-3688)*
Thor Motor Coach Inc .... E 800 860-5658
  Wakarusa *(G-16255)*
Thor Motor Coach Inc .... C 574 266-1111
  Elkhart *(G-3733)*
Van Explorer Company Inc .... E 574 267-7666
  Warsaw *(G-16441)*
C M I Enterprises Inc .... D 305 685-9651
  Elkhart *(G-3244)*
Fiedeke Vinyl Coverings Inc .... F 574 534-3408
  Goshen *(G-6135)*
Independent Protection Co .... C 574 831-5680
  New Paris *(G-12960)*
Independent Protection Co .... E 574 533-4116
  Goshen *(G-6172)*
Twin-Air Products Inc .... G 574 295-1129
  Elkhart *(G-3755)*

VARIETY STORES

Circle Printing LLC .... G 812 663-7367
  Greensburg *(G-6584)*
Gohn Bros Manufacturing Co .... G 574 825-2400
  Middlebury *(G-11718)*

VAULTS & SAFES WHOLESALERS

Fire King International LLC .... E 812 822-5574
  New Albany *(G-12729)*
Fki Security Group LLC .... B 812 948-8400
  New Albany *(G-12730)*
Meilink Safe Company .... D 812 941-0024
  New Albany *(G-12774)*
S C Pryor Inc .... F 317 352-1281
  Indianapolis *(G-9354)*

VEHICLES: All Terrain

Atv Parts Barn LLC .... G 812 251-6113
  Brazil *(G-1133)*

VEHICLES: Recreational

Alliance Rv LLC .... E 574 312-5215
  Elkhart *(G-3166)*
Asw LLC .... C 260 432-1596
  Columbia City *(G-2120)*
Beco Inc .... G 765 778-3426
  Pendleton *(G-13525)*
Bridgeview Manufacturing LLC .... F 574 970-0116
  Elkhart *(G-3236)*
Creative Manufacturing Rv LLC .... F 574 333-3302
  Elkhart *(G-3271)*
D Rv Luxury Suites LLC .... F 260 562-1075
  Howe *(G-7233)*
East-T-West North-To-South Inc .... D 574 264-6664
  Elkhart *(G-3312)*
Ember Recrtl Vehicles Inc .... D 844 732-4204
  Bristol *(G-1259)*
Encore Rv LLC .... E 574 327-6540
  Elkhart *(G-3332)*
Fiber-Tron Corp .... F 574 294-8545
  Elkhart *(G-3345)*
Forest River Inc .... E 574 389-4600
  Elkhart *(G-3356)*
Gardiner Rentals Bill .... G 765 447-5111
  Lafayette *(G-10586)*
Grand Design Rv LLC .... C 574 825-8000
  Middlebury *(G-11719)*
H L Enterprise Inc .... G 574 294-1112
  Elkhart *(G-3395)*
Highland Ridge Rv Inc .... B 260 768-7771
  Shipshewana *(G-14850)*
Holiday House LLC .... F 574 206-0016
  Elkhart *(G-3408)*
Hymer Group Usa LLC .... G 574 970-7460
  Bristol *(G-1267)*
IKON Group .... G 574 326-3661
  Elkhart *(G-3417)*
Keyline Sales Inc .... G 574 294-5611
  Elkhart *(G-3453)*
Landjet International .... G 574 970-7805
  Elkhart *(G-3468)*
Mudd-Ox Inc .... F 260 768-7221
  Shipshewana *(G-14871)*
Open Range Rv Company .... E 260 768-7771
  Shipshewana *(G-14872)*
Parallax Group Inc .... G 800 443-4859
  Anderson *(G-175)*
Quality Concepts .... G 574 215-6391
  Goshen *(G-6244)*
Recreation Vhcl Technical Inst .... G 574 549-9068
  Elkhart *(G-3643)*
Recreational Customs Inc .... G 574 642-0632
  Goshen *(G-6246)*
Seaflo Marine & Rv N Amer LLC .... E 844 473-2356
  South Bend *(G-1199)*
Showhaulers Trucks Inc .... E 574 825-6764
  Middlebury *(G-11751)*

Slicers .... G 812 255-0655
  Vincennes *(G-16155)*
Structural Composites Ind Inc .... D 260 894-4083
  Ligonier *(G-11024)*
Thor Industries Inc .... B 574 970-7460
  Elkhart *(G-3730)*
TRC Mfg Inc .... G 574 262-9299
  South Bend *(G-15289)*
Use What Youve Got Ministry .... G 317 924-4124
  Indianapolis *(G-9690)*

VENDING MACHINE REPAIR SVCS

C & P Distributing LLC .... F 574 256-1138
  Mishawaka *(G-11857)*
Standard Change-Makers Inc .... F 317 899-6955
  Indianapolis *(G-9492)*

VENDING MACHINES & PARTS

A Snack Above Rest LLC .... G 219 455-3335
  Gary *(G-5884)*
Ds Mgmt Group LLC .... G 317 946-8646
  Indianapolis *(G-8014)*
Evelyns Enterprise .... G 219 980-8799
  Merrillville *(G-11515)*
Key Enhancement LLC .... G 502 403-5661
  Jeffersonville *(G-10010)*
My Goodies Snack Vending LLC .... G 317 653-7395
  Anderson *(G-164)*
Styles Versatility LLC .... G 765 270-2217
  Lafayette *(G-10702)*
Taste of Joy LLC .... G 219 501-0157
  Merrillville *(G-11564)*
Unlimited Vending LLC .... G 765 288-5952
  Muncie *(G-12510)*
Whatzthat Vending LLC .... G 317 362-9088
  Indianapolis *(G-9755)*
White House Ventures LLC .... G 260 693-3032
  Churubusco *(G-1993)*
Winbush Refreshments LLC .... G 317 762-8236
  Indianapolis *(G-9771)*
Xpressvending LLC .... G 331 264-3541
  Indianapolis *(G-9796)*

VETERINARY PHARMACEUTICAL PREPARATIONS

Elanco Animal Health Inc .... A 877 352-6261
  Greenfield *(G-6493)*
Elanco International Inc .... D 877 352-6261
  Greenfield *(G-6494)*
Hawthorne Products Inc .... G 765 768-6585
  Dunkirk *(G-2962)*
Kindred Biosciences Inc .... D 650 701-7901
  Greenfield *(G-6524)*
Mattox and Moore Inc .... G 317 632-7534
  Indianapolis *(G-8852)*
Mwi Veterinary Supply Co .... G 317 769-7771
  Lebanon *(G-10923)*
Mwi Veterinary Supply Co .... G 317 769-7771
  Lebanon *(G-10924)*

VETERINARY PRDTS: Instruments & Apparatus

Thompson .... G 219 942-8133
  Hobart *(G-7211)*

VIALS: Glass

Amcor Phrm Packg USA LLC .... D 812 591-2332
  Westport *(G-16748)*
Nipro Phrmpckging Amricas Corp .... D 812 591-2332
  Westport *(G-16749)*

PRODUCT SECTION

VIDEO & AUDIO EQPT, WHOLESALE
St Joe Group Inc.............................. E 260 918-3500
New Haven (G-12920)

VIDEO EQPT
Motion Engineering Company Inc.......... G 317 804-7990
Westfield (G-16712)

VIDEO PRODUCTION SVCS
Heart Breaker Sales LLC...................... G 765 489-4048
Hagerstown (G-6837)

VIDEO TAPE PRODUCTION SVCS
Bird Publishing Company..................... G 219 462-6330
Valparaiso (G-15915)
National Fdrtion State High SC............... E 317 972-6900
Indianapolis (G-8988)

VIDEO TRIGGERS: Remote Control TV Devices
Skytech II LLC.................................. E 260 459-1703
Fort Wayne (G-5421)
Skytech-Systems Inc........................... F 260 459-1703
Fort Wayne (G-5422)

VINYL RESINS, NEC
Innovations Amplified LLC.................... G 317 339-4685
Indianapolis (G-8552)

VISUAL COMMUNICATIONS SYSTEMS
Tct Technologies LLC.......................... F 317 833-6730
Indianapolis (G-9563)

VITAMINS: Natural Or Synthetic, Uncompounded, Bulk
Herbs G&W Inc................................. G 574 646-2134
Nappanee (G-12609)
Vitamins Inc..................................... E 219 879-7356
Michigan City (G-11686)

VOCATIONAL REHABILITATION AGENCY
Anthony Wyne Rhbltition Ctr For............. D 260 744-6145
Fort Wayne (G-4762)
Pathfinder Services Inc........................ E 260 356-0500
Huntington (G-7354)

WALL COVERINGS WHOLESALERS
Blumling Design & Graphics Inc.............. G 765 477-7446
Lafayette (G-10540)

WALLBOARD: Decorated, Made From Purchased Materials
Hoosier Wallbeds Incorporated............... G 812 747-7154
Lawrenceburg (G-10840)
S R Wood Inc.................................... E 812 288-9201
Clarksville (G-2032)

WALLBOARD: Gypsum
Proform Finishing Products LLC.............. D 812 247-2424
Shoals (G-14910)

WALLPAPER STORE
Doris Drapery Boutique........................ G 765 472-5850
Peru (G-13580)
K M Davis Inc.................................... G 765 426-9277
Lafayette (G-10617)

WALLS: Curtain, Metal

Ertl Fabricating Inc............................ F 765 393-1376
Anderson (G-116)

WAREHOUSING & STORAGE FACILITIES, NEC
Coca-Cola Bottling Co......................... E 812 332-4434
Bloomington (G-831)
P-Americas LLC................................. G 812 522-3421
Seymour (G-14670)
Wireamerica Inc................................. G 260 969-1700
Fort Wayne (G-5571)

WAREHOUSING & STORAGE, REFRIGERATED: Cold Storage Or Refrig
United States Cold Storage Inc............... E 765 482-2653
Lebanon (G-10949)

WAREHOUSING & STORAGE: Bulk St & Termnls, Hire, Petro/Chem
Quaker Chemical Corp......................... G 765 668-2441
Marion (G-11332)

WAREHOUSING & STORAGE: Farm Prdts
Frick Services Inc............................... E 260 761-3311
Wawaka (G-16539)

WAREHOUSING & STORAGE: General
AEL/Span LLC................................... E 317 203-4602
Plainfield (G-13656)
Agi International Inc........................... F 317 536-2415
Indianapolis (G-7458)
Alpha Baking Co Inc........................... G 574 234-0188
South Bend (G-14938)
Bendix Coml Vhcl Systems LLC.............. E 260 356-9720
Huntington (G-7301)
Bootz Manufacturing Co LLC................. C 812 425-4646
Evansville (G-3942)
Indiana Research Institute.................... G 812 378-5363
Columbus (G-2325)
KYB Americas Corporation.................... B 317 881-7772
Greenwood (G-6726)
Pridgeon & Clay Inc............................ G 317 738-4885
Franklin (G-5770)
Proedge Inc..................................... E 219 552-9550
Shelby (G-14727)
Revolution Materials (in) LLC................ D 812 234-2724
Terre Haute (G-15680)
Westrock Cp LLC............................... G 574 936-2118
Plymouth (G-13828)

WAREHOUSING & STORAGE: Miniwarehouse
Thormax Enterprises LLC...................... G 812 530-7744
Seymour (G-14699)

WAREHOUSING & STORAGE: Self Storage
Georg Utz Inc................................... E 812 526-2240
Edinburgh (G-3085)
Mark Concrete Products Inc.................. G 317 398-8616
Shelbyville (G-14774)
Toyota Tsusho America Inc................... G 765 449-3500
Colburn (G-2111)

WARM AIR HEAT & AC EQPT & SPLYS, WHOLESALE Fan, Heat & Vent
Poynter Sheet Metal Inc....................... B 317 893-1193
Greenwood (G-6753)

WARM AIR HEATING/AC EQPT/SPLYS, WHOL Warm Air Htg Eqpt/Splys
Air Energy Systems Inc........................ G 317 290-8500
Indianapolis (G-7460)
D & W Inc....................................... D 574 264-9674
Elkhart (G-3284)
Lasalle Bristol Corporation.................... F 574 293-5526
Elkhart (G-3470)
Superior Distribution........................... G 317 308-5525
Indianapolis (G-9528)
Thermo-Cycler Industries Inc................. G 219 767-2990
Union Mills (G-15868)

WASHERS
Hoosier Gasket Corporation................... D 317 545-2000
Indianapolis (G-8409)
Schafer Power Washing........................ G 812 866-1956
Lexington (G-10981)

WASHERS: Plastic
Fred Schock Company Inc..................... F 765 647-4648
Brookville (G-1320)

WATCH REPAIR SVCS
Kensington Watch Services.................... G 219 306-5499
Crown Point (G-2708)

WATER HEATERS
Ebert Machine Company Inc................... E 765 473-3728
Peru (G-13581)

WATER PURIFICATION EQPT: Household
Kendle Custom Inc.............................. G 812 985-5917
Evansville (G-4148)
Lonn Manufacturing Inc........................ G 317 897-1440
Indianapolis (G-8781)
Onesource Water................................ G 866 917-7873
Indianapolis (G-9054)
Samco Inc....................................... G 812 926-4282
Sunman (G-15444)
True Chem Inc.................................. G 317 769-2701
Greenwood (G-6777)
US Water Systems Inc.......................... E 317 209-0889
Indianapolis (G-9688)

WATER TREATMENT EQPT: Indl
Amgi LLC.. G 317 447-1524
New Palestine (G-12928)
Anaerobic Innovations LLC.................... G 765 491-1174
West Lafayette (G-16561)
Assured Water Care Company................. G 317 997-5790
Indianapolis (G-7555)
Bio-Response Solutions Inc................... F 317 386-3500
Danville (G-2807)
Chem-Aqua...................................... G 317 899-3660
Indianapolis (G-7791)
Chemical Control Systems Inc................ G 219 465-5103
Griffith (G-6800)
CHS Legacy Company........................... G 260 456-3596
Columbia City (G-2131)
City of Anderson................................ D 765 648-6560
Anderson (G-94)
City of Columbia City.......................... G 260 248-5118
Columbia City (G-2132)
Crestwood Equity Partners LP................ G 812 265-3313
Madison (G-11212)
Earthsmarte Water Indiana Inc............... G 317 800-8442
Indianapolis (G-8035)
Eco Water of Southern Indiana............... G 812 734-1407
New Salisbury (G-12984)

WATER TREATMENT EQPT: Indl

Environmental MGT & Dev Inc .... G 765 874-1539
Lynn *(G-11183)*

Envmtl Franke Systems LLC .... G 260 710-6491
Fort Wayne *(G-4954)*

Filter Sciences LLC .... G 260 387-7709
Fort Wayne *(G-4983)*

Flora Wastewater Treatment .... G 574 967-3005
Flora *(G-4658)*

Freije Treatment Systems Inc .... E 888 766-7258
Fishers *(G-4527)*

Freije Treatment Systems Inc .... G 317 508-3848
Indianapolis *(G-8230)*

Global Water Technologies Inc .... G 317 452-4488
Indianapolis *(G-8292)*

Kirklin Waste Water Treatment .... G 765 279-5251
Kirklin *(G-10190)*

M J Markiewicz & Associates .... G 765 452-6562
Kokomo *(G-10301)*

Markle Water Treatment Plant .... G 260 758-3482
Markle *(G-11358)*

Mid State Water Treatment .... G 765 884-1220
Fowler *(G-5627)*

Mohawk Laboratories .... G 317 899-3660
Indianapolis *(G-8945)*

Molden Associates Inc .... G 219 879-8425
Long Beach *(G-11125)*

Onion Enterprises Inc .... G 317 762-6007
Indianapolis *(G-9056)*

Over Globe LLC .... G 305 607-6472
Brownsburg *(G-1394)*

Phoenix Pure Holdings LLC .... G 219 448-0142
Long Beach *(G-11127)*

Watcon Inc .... G 574 287-3397
South Bend *(G-15304)*

Water Energizers Inc .... F 812 288-6900
Jeffersonville *(G-10071)*

Western Wyne Rgonal Sewage Dst .... G 765 478-3788
Cambridge City *(G-1505)*

WATER: Distilled

New Aqua LLC .... D 317 272-3000
Avon *(G-540)*

WATER: Mineral, Carbonated, Canned & Bottled, Etc

Rolling Hills Springs LLC .... G 844 454-6866
Linton *(G-11044)*

WATER: Pasteurized, Canned & Bottled, Etc

Niagara Bottling LLC .... G 909 230-5000
Jeffersonville *(G-10025)*

Niagara Bottling LLC .... G 909 758-5313
Plainfield *(G-13709)*

WATERPROOFING COMPOUNDS

Merediths Inc .... E 765 966-5084
Richmond *(G-14164)*

WAXES: Petroleum, Not Produced In Petroleum Refineries

Calumet Paralogics LLC .... F 765 587-4618
Muncie *(G-12361)*

Paralogics LLC .... E 765 587-4618
Muncie *(G-12472)*

WEATHER STRIP: Sponge Rubber

Ilpea Industries Inc .... D 812 752-2526
Scottsburg *(G-14561)*

Nishikawa Cooper LLC .... C 260 593-2156
Fort Wayne *(G-5271)*

Nishikawa Cooper LLC .... C 248 978-6953
Fort Wayne *(G-5272)*

Nishikawa Cooper LLC .... B 260 593-2156
Topeka *(G-15813)*

Nishikawa of America Inc .... G 260 593-2156
Topeka *(G-15814)*

WEIGHING MACHINERY & APPARATUS

Cullman Casting Corporation .... G 256 735-0900
North Vernon *(G-13262)*

Technical Weighing Svcs Inc .... E 219 924-3366
Griffith *(G-6819)*

WELDING & CUTTING APPARATUS & ACCESS, NEC

Souder Deryl Co .... G 765 565-6719
Anderson *(G-195)*

WELDING EQPT

Best Equipment & Welding Co .... E 317 271-8652
Indianapolis *(G-7616)*

Blackmon Metal Fabrication LLC .... G 346 254-9500
Gary *(G-5902)*

Bryant Machining & Welding LLC .... G 260 997-6059
Bryant *(G-1434)*

Coleman Cable LLC .... D 765 449-7227
Lafayette *(G-10553)*

GC Fuller Mfg Co Inc .... F 812 539-2831
Lawrenceburg *(G-10838)*

Ken Anliker .... G 219 984-5676
Chalmers *(G-1858)*

Kennametal Inc .... E 574 534-2585
Goshen *(G-6185)*

Laser Welder Company .... G 816 807-6971
South Bend *(G-15118)*

Linde Gas & Equipment Inc .... G 812 376-3314
Columbus *(G-2343)*

Manufacturing Technology Inc .... C 574 230-0258
South Bend *(G-15138)*

Ogden Welding Systems Inc .... E 219 322-5252
Schererville *(G-14537)*

Precision Wldg Solutions LLC .... G 317 698-7522
Martinsville *(G-11422)*

WELDING EQPT & SPLYS WHOLESALERS

Airgas Usa LLC .... G 812 362-7593
Rockport *(G-14335)*

Aluminum Wldg & Mch Works Inc .... G 219 787-8066
Chesterton *(G-1901)*

Indiana Oxygen Company Inc .... G 765 662-8700
Marion *(G-11295)*

Indiana Oxygen Company Inc .... D 317 290-0003
Indianapolis *(G-8488)*

Linde Gas & Equipment Inc .... G 812 376-3314
Columbus *(G-2343)*

Linde Gas & Equipment Inc .... G 260 423-4468
Fort Wayne *(G-5187)*

Linde Gas & Equipment Inc .... G 317 481-4550
Indianapolis *(G-8761)*

Matheson Tri-Gas Inc .... G 812 838-5518
Mount Vernon *(G-12307)*

Matheson Tri-Gas Inc .... G 317 892-5221
Pittsboro *(G-13651)*

WELDING EQPT & SPLYS: Gas

Tri-State Industries Inc .... D 219 933-1710
Hammond *(G-7023)*

WELDING EQPT REPAIR SVCS

Dx 4 LLC .... F 260 749-0632
Fort Wayne *(G-4935)*

Flanders Electric Mtr Svc LLC .... D 812 421-4300
Evansville *(G-4078)*

WELDING EQPT: Electric

Linde Advanced Material Techno .... C 317 240-2500
Indianapolis *(G-8758)*

Microtech Holding Corp .... G 260 490-4005
Fort Wayne *(G-5221)*

S T Praxair Technology Inc .... E 317 240-2500
Indianapolis *(G-9357)*

Warnock Welding & Fabg LLC .... G 812 498-5408
Seymour *(G-14703)*

WELDING EQPT: Electrical

Marian Suzhou LLC .... G 317 638-6525
Indianapolis *(G-8830)*

Masbez LLC .... G 855 962-7239
Frankfort *(G-5681)*

Ogden Welding Systems Inc .... E 219 322-5252
Schererville *(G-14537)*

WELDING MACHINES & EQPT: Ultrasonic

B Y M Electronics Inc .... G 574 674-5096
Granger *(G-6335)*

Best Equipment Co Inc .... E 317 823-3050
Indianapolis *(G-7617)*

WELDING REPAIR SVC

104 Welding .... G 219 393-0801
La Porte *(G-10370)*

A & A Industries Inc .... G 812 663-5584
Greensburg *(G-6577)*

AAA Welding Inc .... G 574 293-5294
Elkhart *(G-3144)*

Aarons Welding LLC .... G 574 529-3885
Warsaw *(G-16308)*

ABC Fix-N-Fab Welding LLC .... G 765 230-6492
Covington *(G-2526)*

ABF Welding & Pipe LLC .... G 765 977-7349
Cambridge City *(G-1489)*

Absolute Fabrication Inc .... G 574 848-0300
Elkhart *(G-3146)*

Absolute Welding Inc .... F 812 923-8001
Borden *(G-1103)*

AC Welding Mscellaneous Ir Inc .... G 317 491-2898
Indianapolis *(G-7419)*

Accu-Built Tooling and Weld .... G 574 825-7878
Goshen *(G-6087)*

Ace Welding and Machine Inc .... G 812 379-9625
Columbus *(G-2213)*

Acro Engineering Inc .... E 812 663-6236
Greensburg *(G-6579)*

Action Welding & Machine Svcs .... G 219 766-0406
Kouts *(G-10360)*

Acwelding & Misc Iron Inc .... G 317 491-2898
Indianapolis *(G-7426)*

Advanced Welding and Engrg .... G 317 820-3595
Indianapolis *(G-7443)*

Allfab LLC .... G 317 359-3539
Indianapolis *(G-7482)*

American Machine & Fabg Co Inc .... G 812 944-4136
New Albany *(G-12688)*

Amos D Graber & Sons .... F 260 749-0526
New Haven *(G-12892)*

Amos Welding LLC .... G 765 561-2359
Rushville *(G-14395)*

Angel ARC Welding .... G 812 322-9027
Columbus *(G-2220)*

Annette Balfour .... G 765 286-1910
Muncie *(G-12342)*

APL Welding & Fabrication LLC .... G 765 572-1088
Westpoint *(G-16742)*

PRODUCT SECTION — WELDING REPAIR SVC

ARC Angle Welding/Fabrication............ F 812 619-1731
  Tell City *(G-15496)*

Arcpro Welding & Prop Repair................ G 812 867-6383
  Evansville *(G-3898)*

Area Welding Inc LLC............................. G 219 669-0981
  Dyer *(G-2967)*

Area Welding Innovations LLC............. G 219 789-2209
  Gary *(G-5895)*

Ash Welding.. G 219 808-7139
  Hebron *(G-7096)*

Atp Welding Inc...................................... G 765 483-9273
  Lebanon *(G-10877)*

Auto Truck Group LLC.......................... G 260 356-1610
  Huntington *(G-7299)*

Auto Truck Group LLC.......................... G 260 493-1800
  Roanoke *(G-14259)*

Automated Welding Services Inc........... G 812 464-8784
  Evansville *(G-3903)*

B C Welding Inc..................................... G 574 272-9008
  Granger *(G-6334)*

B&M Millwright Inc................................. G 765 883-8177
  Russiaville *(G-14420)*

Bair Welding LLC................................... G 260 485-1452
  Fort Wayne *(G-4788)*

Bare Bones Custom Welding................. G 502 773-2338
  New Albany *(G-12695)*

Bargers Welding Shop........................... G 812 889-2095
  Lexington *(G-10974)*

Barks Wldg Sups & Farming Inc............ G 812 732-4366
  Corydon *(G-2487)*

Bates Machine Inc................................. G 574 264-3997
  Elkhart *(G-3216)*

Beards Welding & Fabrication................ G 317 374-4779
  Franklin *(G-5713)*

Beasley Fabricating & McHnng.............. G 219 297-4000
  Goodland *(G-6079)*

Beasley Welding.................................... G 812 883-2573
  Salem *(G-14474)*

Bel-Mar Products Corporation............... G 317 769-3262
  Whitestown *(G-16801)*

Bergren & Associates............................ G 219 852-1500
  Hammond *(G-6886)*

Best Equipment & Welding Co............... E 317 271-8652
  Indianapolis *(G-7616)*

Bever Wldg & Fabrication LLC.............. G 765 524-4597
  Knightstown *(G-10194)*

Beyond Welding Inspection Inc............. G 812 849-4410
  Mitchell *(G-12033)*

Boat Worx of Monticello......................... G 574 297-7961
  Monticello *(G-12139)*

Bobs Welding & Repair LLC.................. G 765 744-4192
  Farmland *(G-4422)*

Bontrager Welding................................. G 260 463-8950
  Lagrange *(G-10730)*

Bordners Aut Serv................................. G 260 483-4084
  Fort Wayne *(G-4812)*

Brand Sheet Metal Works Inc................ G 765 284-5594
  Muncie *(G-12356)*

Bryant Welding & Fabrication................ G 765 935-4281
  Richmond *(G-14101)*

Buchanan Iron Works Inc...................... G 219 785-4480
  Westville *(G-16757)*

Butlers General Repair.......................... G 812 268-5631
  Sullivan *(G-15403)*

C & C Welding & Fabg Inc.................... G 812 384-8089
  Bloomfield *(G-741)*

C-Mar Welding....................................... G 260 410-8104
  New Haven *(G-12896)*

C-Way Tool and Die Inc........................ G 812 256-6341
  Charlestown *(G-1872)*

C&W Fabrication LLC............................ D 812 282-0488
  Jeffersonville *(G-9949)*

Calumet Welding Center Inc.................. G 219 923-9353
  Griffith *(G-6798)*

Camm Machine and Welding LLC......... G 812 347-2040
  Ramsey *(G-14024)*

Campbells Welding & Machine.............. G 574 643-6705
  Royal Center *(G-14389)*

Carmel Welding and Sup Co Inc........... E 317 846-3493
  Carmel *(G-1582)*

Carmichael Welding Inc....................... G 812 825-5156
  Bloomfield *(G-742)*

Century Tool & Engr Inc........................ G 317 685-0942
  Indianapolis *(G-7776)*

Certified Welding Company Inc............. G 765 522-3238
  Bainbridge *(G-561)*

Cesars Welding LLC............................. G 317 938-8830
  Indianapolis *(G-7780)*

Chesterfield Tool & Engrg Inc............... E 765 378-5101
  Daleville *(G-2798)*

Chief Metal Works Inc.......................... G 765 932-2134
  Rushville *(G-14396)*

City Welding & Fabrication.................... G 765 569-5403
  Rockville *(G-14350)*

Clearspring Welding.............................. G 260 463-8754
  Wolcottville *(G-16936)*

Cline Brothers Welding Inc.................... G 812 738-3537
  Corydon *(G-2491)*

Clinton Parker.. G 219 877-5096
  Hammond *(G-6903)*

CM Welding Inc.................................... G 765 258-4024
  Frankfort *(G-5654)*

Collins Tl & Die Ltd Lblty Co.................. G 812 273-4765
  Madison *(G-11211)*

Conley Welding Specialties Inc............. G 260 343-9051
  Kendallville *(G-10101)*

Constant Voltage Welding Inc............... G 765 339-7914
  New Richmond *(G-12977)*

Continental Welding Sup Corp.............. G 812 232-2488
  Terre Haute *(G-15567)*

Country Welding.................................... G 812 358-4402
  Seymour *(G-14640)*

Country Welding LLC............................ G 260 352-2938
  Silver Lake *(G-14919)*

Craig Welding and Mfg Inc.................... E 574 353-7912
  Mentone *(G-11472)*

Crow Welding and Fabrication............... G 317 619-3190
  Indianapolis *(G-7913)*

Custom Fab & Weld Inc....................... G 574 277-8877
  Granger *(G-6341)*

Custom Machining Services Inc............ G 219 462-6128
  Valparaiso *(G-15932)*

Custom Machining Services Inc............ E 219 462-6128
  Valparaiso *(G-15933)*

D & J Fabrication and Welding.............. G 260 414-0300
  Auburn *(G-384)*

D & S Metal Fab & Welding LLC........... G 317 862-2503
  Indianapolis *(G-7942)*

D&M Repair and Welding LLC.............. G 765 533-4565
  Markleville *(G-11368)*

Da-Mar Industries Inc........................... F 260 347-1662
  Kendallville *(G-10107)*

Dalam Welding LLC............................... G 260 593-0167
  Topeka *(G-15801)*

Darlage Metalworx LLC......................... G 812 341-5530
  Columbus *(G-2278)*

Davids Inc... F 812 376-6870
  Columbus *(G-2280)*

Davis Custom Welding.......................... G 765 847-2407
  Richmond *(G-14113)*

Davis Tool & Machine LLC.................... F 317 896-9278
  Westfield *(G-16684)*

Davron Fabricating................................ G 765 339-7303
  New Richmond *(G-12978)*

DB&h Welding and Fabrication............. G 765 617-8474
  Wilkinson *(G-16842)*

Diamond Welding................................... G 765 741-2760
  Muncie *(G-12383)*

Dianne Forrest Welding Company......... G 219 381-1667
  Gary *(G-5922)*

Ditech Inc... E 812 379-9756
  Edinburgh *(G-3078)*

DLM Fabrication.................................... G 219 393-8820
  Chesterton *(G-1920)*

Dons Specialty Welding LLC................. G 260 557-3492
  Fort Wayne *(G-4925)*

Douglas Drudge..................................... G 574 566-2210
  Claypool *(G-2052)*

Downeys Welding Repair...................... G 765 778-4727
  Pendleton *(G-13530)*

Drake Enterprises LLC......................... G 317 460-5991
  Pittsboro *(G-13644)*

Dransfield & Associates Wldg................ G 317 736-6281
  Franklin *(G-5726)*

Du-Mar Welding LLC............................. G 574 223-9889
  Rochester *(G-14287)*

Dunes Investment Inc........................... F 219 764-4270
  Portage *(G-13860)*

E & H Industrial Services LLC.............. F 317 569-8819
  Carmel *(G-1616)*

E & H Industrial Services Inc................ E 317 670-4456
  Indianapolis *(G-8028)*

E Z Welding... G 574 892-6417
  Argos *(G-321)*

East Side Welding Inc.......................... G 317 823-4065
  Indianapolis *(G-8039)*

Ebwa Industries Inc.............................. F 317 637-5860
  Indianapolis *(G-8044)*

Eckstein Welding & Fabrication............. G 812 934-2059
  Batesville *(G-586)*

Edco Welding and Hydraulic Inc........... F 317 783-2323
  Indianapolis *(G-8052)*

Eds Crane Service................................. G 317 535-7385
  Whiteland *(G-16783)*

Egenolf Machine Inc.............................. F 317 787-5301
  Indianapolis *(G-8061)*

Ellerbrock Welding LLC......................... G 559 978-2651
  New Castle *(G-12860)*

Epic Welding LLC................................. G 502 554-6326
  Jeffersonville *(G-9979)*

Ernstberger Enterprises Inc.................. D 812 282-0488
  Jeffersonville *(G-9981)*

Evers Welding Company Inc................. G 812 576-2232
  Guilford *(G-6829)*

Fabcreation.. G 812 246-6222
  Sellersburg *(G-14593)*

Fancil Welding LLC............................... G 574 267-8627
  Warsaw *(G-16361)*

Farmway Welding.................................. G 574 498-6147
  Argos *(G-322)*

Fayette Welding Service Inc................. G 317 852-2929
  Brownsburg *(G-1366)*

Flare Precision LLC............................... E 260 490-1101
  Fort Wayne *(G-4985)*

Flynn Welding & Inspection LLC........... G 812 327-7437
  Solsberry *(G-14925)*

Four Star Welding................................. G 574 825-3856
  Middlebury *(G-11716)*

Freedom Industrial Welding LLC........... G 812 686-9802
  Rockport *(G-14341)*

Friths Custom Weld............................... G 812 937-2618
  Dale *(G-2790)*

Frye Welding LLC.................................. G 260 908-4766
  Kendallville *(G-10112)*

Fullenkamp Machine & Mfg Inc............. F 260 726-8345
  Portland *(G-13944)*

Employee Codes: A=Over 500 employees, B=251-500
C=101-250, D=51-100, E=20-50, F=10-19, G=1-9

WELDING REPAIR SVC

Company	Section	Phone
Galbreath Industrial Svcs LLC	G	574 737-8159
Logansport *(G-11074)*		
Galloweld LLC	G	219 215-2006
Hammond *(G-6934)*		
Gary Simons	G	812 852-4316
Osgood *(G-13408)*		
Garys Welding & Machining LLC	G	812 279-6780
Bedford *(G-637)*		
General Sheet Metal Works Inc	E	574 288-0611
South Bend *(G-15042)*		
Georges Welding & Mech Svc	G	219 989-0781
Gary *(G-5941)*		
Gibson Brothers Welding Inc	F	765 948-5775
Fairmount *(G-4410)*		
Gilleys Repair and Welding	G	812 374-6009
Columbus *(G-2313)*		
Gilleys Wldg & Fabrication LLC	G	765 720-0554
Fillmore *(G-4453)*		
Gillum Machine & Tool Inc	F	765 893-4426
West Lebanon *(G-16648)*		
GL Custom Welding LLC	G	260 593-0253
Topeka *(G-15807)*		
Glens Mobile Welding	G	219 663-2668
Crown Point *(G-2689)*		
Glicks Miracles Inc	G	260 436-6671
Fort Wayne *(G-5027)*		
Gravelton Machine Shop Inc	G	574 773-3413
Nappanee *(G-12600)*		
Greenwood Models Inc	G	317 859-2988
Greenwood *(G-6710)*		
H & H Design & Tool Inc	G	765 886-6199
Economy *(G-3066)*		
H & S Fabrication LLC	G	260 724-3656
Decatur *(G-2860)*		
Hammond Machine Works Inc	E	219 933-0479
Hammond *(G-6942)*		
Hartware Technologies	G	317 439-5816
Carmel *(G-1650)*		
Hasty Welding	G	765 482-8925
Lebanon *(G-10895)*		
Heise Welding Service	G	574 652-4631
Burrows *(G-1458)*		
Hepton Welding LLC	G	800 570-4238
Nappanee *(G-12608)*		
Herman Tool & Machine Inc	F	574 594-5544
Pierceton *(G-13632)*		
Hershberger Welding	G	574 642-3994
Millersburg *(G-11813)*		
Hetsco	G	317 530-5331
Greenwood *(G-6711)*		
Hickory Corner Custom Wldg LLC	G	812 890-2926
Vincennes *(G-16128)*		
Highball Fabricators LLC	G	574 831-6647
New Paris *(G-12957)*		
Highland Machine Tool Inc	E	812 923-8884
Floyds Knobs *(G-4681)*		
Hill Top Welding LLC	G	765 585-2549
Attica *(G-351)*		
Hite Welding & Chassis	G	765 741-0046
Muncie *(G-12418)*		
Hively Welding Company Inc	G	219 843-5111
Medaryville *(G-11458)*		
Hochstetler Welding	G	260 463-2793
Lagrange *(G-10741)*		
Hochstetler Welding LLC	G	574 773-0600
Nappanee *(G-12612)*		
Hoke Weld	G	812 569-0587
Paoli *(G-13497)*		
Hollers Welding Llc	G	812 825-9834
Bloomington *(G-878)*		
Hoosier Machine & Welding Inc	F	317 638-6286
Indianapolis *(G-8410)*		
Hoosier Spline Broach Corp	E	765 452-8273
Kokomo *(G-10281)*		
Hoosier Welding	G	765 521-4539
New Castle *(G-12868)*		
Hubbard Welding	G	317 539-2758
Clayton *(G-2059)*		
Huehls Salcoating Lawncare LLC	G	317 782-4069
Indianapolis *(G-8433)*		
Huffman Metalworks LLC	G	574 835-0783
Brookville *(G-1325)*		
Hughes Welding and Fabrication	G	812 385-2770
Princeton *(G-13999)*		
Huntington Sheet Metal Inc	D	260 356-9011
Huntington *(G-4553)*		
I M S I Rental Svcs & Repair	G	765 522-1223
North Salem *(G-13254)*		
Impact Racing Inc	D	317 852-3067
Indianapolis *(G-8468)*		
Imperial Stamping Corporation	D	574 294-3780
Elkhart *(G-3419)*		
Indiana Industrial Svcs LLC	G	317 769-6099
Whitestown *(G-16810)*		
Indiana Mobile Welding LLC	G	317 771-8900
Noblesville *(G-13102)*		
Indianplis Wldg Fbrication LLC	G	317 999-7856
Indianapolis *(G-8512)*		
Industrial Mint Wldg Machining	E	219 393-5531
Kingsbury *(G-10179)*		
Innovative Metalworks LLC	G	260 839-0295
Sidney *(G-14916)*		
Innovative Welding LLC	G	574 642-4537
Goshen *(G-6175)*		
Instate Welding Service Inc	G	260 437-2894
Fort Wayne *(G-5112)*		
IWP LLC	G	812 756-0303
Holton *(G-7218)*		
J & J Repair	G	574 831-3075
Goshen *(G-6178)*		
J & J Welding	G	219 872-7282
Michigan City *(G-11627)*		
J & J Welding Inc	E	812 838-4391
Mount Vernon *(G-12303)*		
J & R Welding	G	574 862-1590
Wakarusa *(G-16235)*		
J A Smit Inc	G	812 424-8141
Evansville *(G-4133)*		
James Conner Welding LLC	G	765 230-0455
Darlington *(G-2833)*		
Jarrod Zachary Weld	G	765 230-6424
Crawfordsville *(G-2582)*		
Jbs Welding	G	317 946-8676
Greenwood *(G-6718)*		
Jerry Lambert	G	765 378-7599
Daleville *(G-2800)*		
Jims Welding & Repair LLC	G	765 564-1797
Bringhurst *(G-1237)*		
Jlr Mechanical Inc	G	502 551-6879
Clarksville *(G-2021)*		
Joe Woodrow	G	765 866-0436
New Market *(G-12926)*		
Johns Portable Siiop Weld	G	574 936-1702
Plymouth *(G-13789)*		
Johns Welding and Fabrication	G	574 936-1702
Plymouth *(G-13790)*		
Johnsons Welding Inc	G	317 835-2438
Boggstown *(G-1074)*		
Jomar Machining & Fabg Inc	E	574 825-9837
Middlebury *(G-11728)*		
JRS Custom Fabrication	G	317 852-4964
Brownsburg *(G-1378)*		
K & B Trailer Sales & Mfg Inc	G	574 946-4382
Monterey *(G-12080)*		
K & M Weld Fab	G	219 362-3736
Rolling Prairie *(G-14366)*		
K C Cmponents Wldg Fabrication	G	317 539-6067
Greencastle *(G-6416)*		
K-K Tool and Design Inc	E	260 758-2940
Markle *(G-11356)*		
Kammerer Inc	D	260 349-9098
Kendallville *(G-10124)*		
Kammerer Inc	F	260 347-0389
Kendallville *(G-10123)*		
Kark Welding	G	574 400-3989
Granger *(G-6357)*		
Kc Mig Welding LLC	G	317 739-1051
Fishers *(G-4553)*		
Kevin Chumbley Enterprises	G	502 548-2544
Palmyra *(G-13481)*		
Kleihege Welding Machine	G	812 849-5056
Mitchell *(G-12042)*		
Klingerman Welding	G	574 342-7375
Bourbon *(G-1123)*		
Knepps Custom Welding	G	765 525-5130
Saint Paul *(G-14466)*		
Knip Welding	G	219 987-5123
Demotte *(G-2921)*		
Kocsis Brothers Machine Co	G	219 397-8400
East Chicago *(G-3025)*		
Kortzendorf Machine & Tool	F	317 783-5449
Greenwood *(G-6725)*		
Kyle Fabrication & Welding LLC	G	317 627-8537
Franklin *(G-5751)*		
Kz Welding	G	260 350-7397
Hudson *(G-7247)*		
L & C Welding LLC	G	260 593-3410
Shipshewana *(G-14857)*		
L & L Engineering Co Inc	G	317 786-6886
Beech Grove *(G-698)*		
L & R Machine Co Inc	G	317 787-7251
Beech Grove *(G-699)*		
L L Welding	G	812 499-2961
Tell City *(G-15506)*		
L&N Welding LLC	G	317 372-9554
Danville *(G-2817)*		
Lane Shady Welding LLC	G	574 825-5553
Middlebury *(G-11732)*		
Larry Shorts Welding	G	812 664-4910
Owensville *(G-13470)*		
Lauck Manufacturing Co Inc	F	317 787-6269
Indianapolis *(G-8727)*		
Lawson Welding Shop	G	812 448-8984
Harmony *(G-7059)*		
Lee Crawford Welding	G	317 490-8009
Indianapolis *(G-8732)*		
Lengachers Welding LLC	G	260 438-9033
Grabill *(G-6310)*		
Leons Fabrication Inc	F	219 365-5272
Schererville *(G-14528)*		
Linden Machine Shop LLC	G	765 339-7244
Linden *(G-11031)*		
Little Creations LLC	G	765 868-9656
Kokomo *(G-10299)*		
Loading Dock Maintenance LLC	G	260 424-3635
Fort Wayne *(G-5188)*		
Lockwood Welding Incorporated	G	260 925-2086
Waterloo *(G-16523)*		
Lozano Wldg & Fabrication LLC	G	812 550-1706
Evansville *(G-4175)*		
Lozano Wldg & Fabrication LLC	G	812 629-2000
Newburgh *(G-13012)*		
M & M Service Co Wldg & Repr	G	812 328-6195
Freelandville *(G-5803)*		
Major Tool and Machine Inc	C	317 636-6433
Indianapolis *(G-8820)*		

2024 Harris Indiana Industrial Directory

(G-0000) Company's Geographic Section entry number

PRODUCT SECTION WELDING REPAIR SVC

Company	Code	Phone
Manier Wldg & Fabrication LLC Tipton (G-15782)	G	765 675-6078
Manufacturing Technology Inc South Bend (G-15138)	C	574 230-0258
Mapco Cloverdale (G-2088)	G	765 795-3179
Martin Welding Shop Wakarusa (G-16240)	G	574 862-2578
Martinez Custom Welding Warsaw (G-16391)	G	574 377-2251
Mattox Machine & Welding Inc Salem (G-14490)	G	812 883-6460
Matts Repair Inc Lowell (G-11171)	F	219 696-6765
McGinn Tool & Engineering Co Franklin (G-5755)	F	317 736-5512
Melching Machine Inc Ossian (G-13428)	E	260 622-4315
Mengel Welding Company Demotte (G-2923)	G	219 987-4079
Mervin M Burkholder Wakarusa (G-16241)	G	574 862-4144
Metal Head Welding Winslow (G-16920)	G	812 582-4234
Metcalf Engineering Inc Indianapolis (G-8893)	G	765 342-6792
Mg Iron Welding Inc Hammond (G-6980)	G	708 916-1344
Microtech Welding Corp Warsaw (G-16398)	G	574 268-5314
Microtech Welding Corp Fort Wayne (G-5222)	F	260 490-4005
Midwest Machining & Fabg Griffith (G-6814)	F	219 924-0206
Midwest Welding Fabrication Elkhart (G-3542)	G	574 226-8306
Midwest Welding Fabrication Warren (G-16301)	G	260 355-9354
Miller Custom Metals LLC Wolcott (G-16934)	G	219 279-2671
Miller Machine and Welding LLC Vincennes (G-16140)	G	812 882-7566
Miller Welding Kokomo (G-10309)	G	765 628-2463
Miller Welding LLC Bloomfield (G-753)	G	812 381-0800
Millers Wldg & Mech Svcs Inc Pekin (G-13519)	G	812 923-3359
Misner Welding & Cnstr Inc Dugger (G-2958)	G	812 648-2980
Mitchum-Schaefer Inc Indianapolis (G-8935)	E	317 546-4081
Modern Wldg & Boiler Works Inc Terre Haute (G-15647)	G	812 232-5039
Monogram Metal Shop LLC Grabill (G-6316)	G	260 797-3307
Montgomery Welding Inc Montgomery (G-12116)	G	812 486-3710
Moores Welding Service Inc Leo (G-10969)	G	260 627-2177
Morgan Nye Corydon (G-2505)	G	812 738-4587
Morris Machine & Tool Rensselaer (G-14060)	G	219 866-3018
Motsinger Auto Supply Inc Indianapolis (G-8960)	G	317 782-8484
Mrrx Mobile Railcar Repair LLC Clinton (G-2072)	G	812 251-0055
Mtm Machining Inc Michigan City (G-11642)	F	219 872-6477
Mullets Welding LLC Nappanee (G-12629)	G	574 773-0189
Ncs Welding Inc Winamac (G-16868)	G	574 946-7485
Nector Machine & Fabricating Schererville (G-14536)	G	219 322-6878
Neil Silke Fort Wayne (G-5260)	G	574 999-4866
Newlins Wldg & Tank Maint LLC Montezuma (G-12082)	G	765 245-2741
Newton Wldg & Fabrication LLC Crawfordsville (G-2594)	G	765 365-5129
Nichols Mfg Co Inc Lowell (G-11174)	F	219 696-8577
Nix & Company LLC Munster (G-12552)	G	219 595-5541
Nk Welding Products Inc Fort Wayne (G-5273)	G	260 424-1901
Noble County Welding Inc Avilla (G-490)	F	260 897-4082
Northeast Enterprises Inc Fort Wayne (G-5275)	G	260 485-8011
Northside Machining Inc Huntingburg (G-7288)	G	812 683-3500
Northside Wldg Fabrication LLC Carmel (G-1708)	G	317 844-2240
O & R Precision Grinding Inc Berne (G-721)	E	260 368-9394
Oakes Marion (G-11322)	G	765 384-5317
OBrien Jack & Pat Enterprises Greencastle (G-6422)	G	765 653-5070
OHM Automotive LLC Bloomington (G-934)	G	812 879-5455
On Site Welding & Maintenance Campbellsburg (G-1527)	G	812 755-4184
On The Spot Welding LLC Indianapolis (G-9053)	G	317 746-6699
On-Site Wldg Mllright Svcs LLC Carmel (G-1711)	G	317 843-9773
Onyett Welding & Machine Inc Petersburg (G-13620)	G	812 582-2999
Overton & Sons Tl & Die Co Inc Mooresville (G-12232)	E	317 831-4542
Owens Welding & Machine Monticello (G-12163)	G	574 583-9566
Pannell & Son Welding Inc Summitville (G-15427)	G	765 948-3606
Parsons Welding Service Morgantown (G-12262)	G	812 597-4914
Patrick Welding LLC New Albany (G-12791)	G	812 557-7299
Peerless Pattern & Machine Co Lafayette (G-10666)	G	765 477-7719
Penn Central Welding LLC Lagrange (G-10757)	G	260 463-2490
Pfeiffer Welding & Fabrication Sharpsville (G-14711)	G	765 434-1983
Phipps Sons Welding Gary (G-5994)	G	219 776-3810
Portable Welding Solutions Indianapolis (G-9164)	G	714 381-1690
Powerweld Inc Valparaiso (G-16029)	G	219 462-8700
Prairie Welding & Repair Leesburg (G-10959)	G	574 858-0509
Precision Pulse LLC Peru (G-13593)	G	765 472-6002
Precision Tubes Inc Indianapolis (G-9187)	G	317 783-2339
Precision Welding Corp Huntertown (G-7261)	G	260 637-5814
Professional Sndblst & Wldg Logansport (G-11103)	G	574 355-9825
Pyramid Equipment Rolling Prairie (G-14370)	G	219 778-4253
Pyramid Equipment Inc Rolling Prairie (G-14371)	F	219 778-2591
Pyro Micro Welding LLC Evansville (G-4267)	G	812 431-3330
Quality Die Set Corp Logansport (G-11104)	E	574 967-4411
R & M Welding & Fabricating Sp Loogootee (G-11148)	G	812 295-9130
R & R Welding Fort Wayne (G-5364)	G	260 424-3635
Raber Buggy Shop LLC Montgomery (G-12120)	G	812 486-3789
Red Forge Inc Batesville (G-602)	G	812 934-9641
Ribbe Welding & Mfg Inc Kingman (G-10173)	G	765 390-4044
Richard Myers Mllwrght Russiaville (G-14425)	G	765 883-8177
Robert L Wehr Jasper (G-9905)	G	812 482-2673
Robert Warrick Veedersburg (G-16090)	G	765 294-4335
Roberts C Wldg Trck Hvy Equip Sunman (G-15443)	G	812 623-1525
Rods Welding Shop Coal City (G-2101)	G	812 859-4250
Roembke Mfg & Design Inc Ossian (G-13433)	F	260 622-4030
Roger Baber Portable Wldg LLC Galveston (G-5853)	G	574 859-4520
Rogers Engineering and Mfg Co Cambridge City (G-1503)	E	765 478-5444
Ron Mendenhall Ladoga (G-10509)	G	765 866-8283
Rons General Repair West College Corner (G-16543)	G	765 732-3805
Royers General Wldg & Repr LLC Goshen (G-6250)	G	574 862-2707
Russs Custom Welding Corp Cloverdale (G-2096)	G	765 795-5795
Rusty Shelden Duwane Washington (G-16508)	G	812 890-5780
S-Tech Inc Crothersville (G-2645)	G	812 793-3506
Saliwnchik Sons Wldg Fbrction La Porte (G-10476)	G	219 362-9009
Schenk and Sons Tree Svc Inc Mount Vernon (G-12321)	G	812 985-3954
Schuler Precision Tool LLC North Manchester (G-13249)	G	260 982-2704
Seib Machine & Tool Co Inc Evansville (G-4304)	G	812 453-6174
Seiler Excavating Inc Auburn (G-422)	G	260 925-0507
Shipshe Welding Shipshewana (G-14886)	G	260 768-7267
Shoemaker Welding Company North Liberty (G-13223)	G	574 656-4412
Shucks Wldg & Fabrication LLC Atlanta (G-342)	G	317 409-8526
Sifford Custom Welding Lynn (G-11187)	G	765 969-3473
Six Mile Welding LLC Lagrange (G-10759)	G	260 768-3126
Skipper Rota Corporation Crown Point (G-2758)	F	708 331-0660
Slabaugh Welding LLC Milford (G-11806)	G	574 773-5410
Smith Welding Tipton (G-15790)	G	765 438-4173

Employee Codes: A=Over 500 employees, B=251-500
C=101-250, D=51-100, E=20-50, F=10-19, G=1-9

2024 Harris Indiana Industrial Directory

WELDING REPAIR SVC

Snyders Prtble Wldg Fbrication................ G 574 258-4015
  Mishawaka *(G-12001)*
Southwest Welding LLC....................... G 574 862-4453
  Wakarusa *(G-16252)*
Sovern Machining & Welding................. G 812 392-2532
  Scipio *(G-14551)*
Speedcraft Prototypes........................... G 765 644-6449
  Anderson *(G-198)*
Star Engineering & Mch Co Inc.............. E 260 824-4825
  Bluffton *(G-1057)*
Starkey Welding Inc............................... G 765 932-2005
  Rushville *(G-14413)*
Stephens Welding LLC......................... G 812 925-6033
  Chandler *(G-1867)*
Stolle Tool Incorporated........................ F 765 935-5185
  Richmond *(G-14209)*
Stoltzfus Custom Welding LLC.............. G 765 569-2362
  Rockville *(G-14356)*
Stonebraker Welding Servi.................... G 574 453-7630
  Leesburg *(G-10961)*
Stout Plastic Weld.................................. F 219 926-7622
  Chesterton *(G-1959)*
Stowers Wldg Indus Piping LLC............ G 765 279-5002
  Kirklin *(G-10192)*
Stricker Welding LLC............................. G 812 207-3800
  Memphis *(G-11467)*
Strike & Walk Da Cup Wldg LLC........... G 219 455-4683
  Hammond *(G-7015)*
Summerlot Engineered Pdts Inc............ F 812 466-7266
  Rosedale *(G-14383)*
Summers Metals & More........................ G 812 689-7088
  Osgood *(G-13417)*
Sun Engineering Inc.............................. E 219 962-1191
  Lake Station *(G-10778)*
SW Watkins Limited.............................. D 260 484-4844
  Fort Wayne *(G-5462)*
Swags Welding Services LLC................ G 260 417-7510
  Churubusco *(G-1989)*
T & E Welding Inc.................................. F 812 324-0140
  Petersburg *(G-13627)*
Tactical Wldg Fabrication LLC............... G 317 457-5340
  Indianapolis *(G-9547)*
TAs Welding and Grn Svcs LLC............ G 765 210-4274
  Wabash *(G-16216)*
Taylor Welding....................................... G 765 659-2955
  Frankfort *(G-5697)*
Teck Machine LLC................................. G 574 773-7004
  Nappanee *(G-12648)*
Ted Bostick... G 765 458-6555
  Liberty *(G-10999)*
Tegeler Welding Services LLC.............. G 765 409-6446
  Richmond *(G-14213)*
Terhune Welding Shop.......................... G 260 565-3446
  Bluffton *(G-1063)*
Terrys Welding Inc................................ G 765 564-3331
  Delphi *(G-2909)*
Tfp Inc... G 219 513-9572
  Griffith *(G-6820)*
Thomas Cubit Inc.................................. G 219 933-0566
  Hammond *(G-7019)*
Thrasher Welding and Mch Sp............... G 260 475-5550
  Angola *(G-298)*
Titus Inc.. F 574 936-3345
  Plymouth *(G-13817)*
TNT Fabricating LLC............................. G 574 540-2465
  Plymouth *(G-13819)*
Todds Wldg & Stl Fabrication................ G 812 824-2407
  Bloomington *(G-990)*
Toolcraft LLC.. E 260 749-0454
  Fort Wayne *(G-5494)*
Total Concepts Design Inc.................... D 812 752-6534
  Scottsburg *(G-14582)*

Town Welder.. G 219 945-1311
  Crown Point *(G-2767)*
Tradeline Fabricating Inc...................... E 812 637-1444
  Lawrenceburg *(G-10862)*
Tri-Esco Inc.. F 765 446-7937
  Colburn *(G-2112)*
Turn & Burn Welding Inc...................... G 812 766-0641
  Otwell *(G-13458)*
Turners Machining Specialties Inc........ E 812 372-9472
  Columbus *(G-2407)*
Tuttle Aluminum & Bronze Inc.............. D 317 842-2420
  Fishers *(G-4618)*
Two Guys Mechanical Contrs Inc.......... E 574 946-7671
  Winamac *(G-16878)*
Tyco Welding... G 812 988-8770
  Nashville *(G-12682)*
Ultimate Wldg Fabrication LLC............. G 317 379-2676
  Noblesville *(G-13188)*
United Industrial & Wldg LLC................ G 812 526-4050
  Columbus *(G-2410)*
United Tool Company Inc...................... F 260 563-3143
  Wabash *(G-16219)*
Uptgraft Welding................................... G 260 824-4624
  Bluffton *(G-1065)*
Uskert Welding...................................... G 219 759-2794
  Valparaiso *(G-16073)*
Velazquez Wldg Solutions LLC............. G 812 391-9892
  New Albany *(G-12822)*
Vincennes Welding Co Inc.................... F 812 882-9682
  Vincennes *(G-16160)*
Vision Machine Works Inc..................... G 574 259-6500
  Mishawaka *(G-12022)*
Weavers Welding................................... G 812 438-3425
  Aurora *(G-459)*
Welders Choice..................................... G 219 880-5470
  Hammond *(G-7032)*
Welding Center..................................... G 219 921-1509
  Chesterton *(G-1968)*
Welding Plus LLC................................. G 317 902-0883
  Indianapolis *(G-9746)*
Welding Shop.. G 260 593-2544
  Ligonier *(G-11029)*
Welding Unlimited LLC......................... G 812 582-0777
  Petersburg *(G-13628)*
Weldors Inc... G 765 289-9074
  Muncie *(G-12518)*
Welshco LLC.. G 219 767-2786
  Union Mills *(G-15869)*
West Vigo Machine Shop Inc................ F 812 533-1961
  West Terre Haute *(G-16658)*
Whites Welding & Machining LLC........ G 765 987-7984
  Straughn *(G-15400)*
William F Shirley................................... G 812 426-2599
  Evansville *(G-4385)*
Williams Weld Service LLC................... G 812 865-3298
  Orleans *(G-13383)*
Wilson Machine Shop Inc...................... G 812 392-2774
  Elizabethtown *(G-3134)*
Wilson Welding & Piping LLC............... G 317 397-4865
  Greenwood *(G-6781)*
Wrib Manufacturing Inc........................ G 765 294-2841
  Veedersburg *(G-16092)*
Wws Fabricating Inc............................. G 765 506-7341
  Marion *(G-11352)*
X-Y Tool and Die Inc............................. D 260 357-3365
  Laotto *(G-10812)*
Yoders & Sons Repair Shop................. G 260 593-2727
  Topeka *(G-15824)*
York & Sons Welding LLC..................... G 812 577-6352
  Moores Hill *(G-12189)*
Zimmer Welding LLC............................ G 317 632-5212
  Indianapolis *(G-9812)*

Zionsville Towing Inc............................. G 317 873-4550
  Zionsville *(G-17064)*

WELDING SPLYS, EXC GASES: Wholesalers

Airgas Usa LLC.................................... F 260 749-9576
  Fort Wayne *(G-4733)*
Airgas Usa LLC.................................... F 812 362-7593
  Rockport *(G-14335)*
Koehler Welding Supply Inc................. F 812 574-4103
  Madison *(G-11233)*

WELDMENTS

Dx 4 LLC.. F 260 749-0632
  Fort Wayne *(G-4935)*
Lynn Tool Company Inc........................ G 765 874-2471
  Lynn *(G-11185)*

WELL LOGGING EQPT

Lucas Oil Racing Inc............................. F 812 738-1147
  Corydon *(G-2504)*

WET CORN MILLING

Archer-Daniels-Midland Company......... G 765 299-1672
  Fowler *(G-5618)*
Archer-Daniels-Midland Company......... G 260 749-0022
  New Haven *(G-12893)*
Colorcon Inc... D 317 545-6211
  Indianapolis *(G-7837)*
Primary Pdts Ingrdnts Amrcas L........... D 765 448-7123
  Lafayette *(G-10670)*
Primary Pdts Ingrdnts Amrcas L........... B 765 474-5474
  Lafayette *(G-10671)*

WHEEL BALANCING EQPT: Automotive

Integrated Technology LLC................... F 574 300-9412
  Elkhart *(G-3428)*

WHEELCHAIR LIFTS

Adaptive Mobility Inc............................ F 317 347-6400
  Indianapolis *(G-7429)*
Braun Corporation................................ B 574 946-6153
  Winamac *(G-16857)*
Covidien LP.. C 317 837-8199
  Plainfield *(G-13674)*
Life Essentials Inc................................ F 765 423-4192
  Wolcott *(G-16932)*
Mobility Svm LLC................................. E 260 434-4777
  Fort Wayne *(G-5237)*
Tk Elevator Corporation....................... D 317 595-1125
  Indianapolis *(G-9612)*
Todds Hydrlcs RPR & Stl Fbrct............ G 812 466-3457
  Terre Haute *(G-15733)*
Williams Bros Hlth Care Phrm I............ E 812 335-0000
  Bloomington *(G-1012)*
Williams Bros Hlth Care Phrm I............ C 812 254-2497
  Washington *(G-16513)*

WHEELCHAIRS

Equippe Advanced Mobility.................. G 317 807-6789
  Greenwood *(G-6703)*
Ms Wheelchair Indiana Inc................... G 317 408-0947
  Indianapolis *(G-8969)*
Operation 1 Veteran Inc....................... G 574 536-5536
  Goshen *(G-6231)*
Ring-Co Mobile LLC............................. G 317 641-7050
  Trafalgar *(G-15832)*
Wheelchair Help LLC........................... G 574 295-2220
  Elkhart *(G-3783)*
Wheelchair of Indiana.......................... G 317 627-6560
  Indianapolis *(G-9757)*

WHEELS & PARTS

FTC Products Corp..................... G 219 567-2441
Francesville (G-5642)

Miller Mfg Corp........................... E 574 773-4136
Nappanee (G-12626)

Tire Rack Inc.............................. B 888 541-1777
South Bend (G-15283)

Transportation Tech Inds........... F 812 962-5000
Evansville (G-4347)

Wheels 4 Tots Inc...................... G 219 987-6812
Demotte (G-2932)

WHEELS: Abrasive

Sandusky Abrasive Wheel Co..... E 219 879-6601
Michigan City (G-11663)

WHEELS: Disc, Wheelbarrow, Stroller, Etc, Stamped Metal

Gleason Corporation................... C 574 533-1141
Goshen (G-6150)

WHIRLPOOL BATHS: Hydrotherapy

Kaldewei Usa Inc....................... G 866 822-2527
Fishers (G-4552)

Masco Bath Corporation............. A 317 254-5959
Indianapolis (G-8846)

Oasis Lifestyle LLC.................... F 574 948-0004
Plymouth (G-13799)

WINCHES

Chads LLC................................. G 812 323-7377
Ellettsville (G-3802)

WINDINGS: Coil, Electronic

Q P Inc...................................... F 574 295-6884
Elkhart (G-3626)

WINDOW & DOOR FRAMES

Advantage Manufacturing Inc..... F 773 626-2200
South Bend (G-14936)

Davis Exteriors Inc.................... G 260 786-1600
Andrews (G-221)

Door Service Supply.................. G 317 496-0391
Greenwood (G-6689)

Global Building Products LLC.... E 574 296-6868
Elkhart (G-3379)

Graber Thermoloc Windows LLC ..... G 812 486-3273
Montgomery (G-12099)

Imperial Products LLC................ E 765 966-0322
Richmond (G-14138)

Invign LLC................................. G 574 971-5498
Goshen (G-6176)

LCI Industries............................ A 574 535-1125
Elkhart (G-3476)

Mx5 & Associates Inc................ F 574 226-0733
Elkhart (G-3561)

Quanex Homeshield LLC........... E 765 966-4400
Richmond (G-14194)

WINDOW FRAMES & SASHES: Plastic

Graber Manufacturing LLC......... G 260 657-3400
Grabill (G-6298)

Ilpea Industries Inc.................... D 812 752-2526
Scottsburg (G-14562)

WINDOW FRAMES, MOLDING & TRIM: Vinyl

Bee Window Incorporated.......... C 317 283-8522
Fishers (G-4473)

Home Guard Industries Inc........ D 260 627-6060
Grabill (G-6302)

Keusch Glass Inc...................... E 812 482-2566
Jasper (G-9864)

Plastics Family Holdings Inc...... G 317 890-1808
Indianapolis (G-9153)

WINDOWS, LOUVER: Metal

Classee Vinyl Windows LLC....... G 574 825-7863
Middlebury (G-11703)

WINDOWS: Frames, Wood

Clear View Cstm Wndows Dors In......... G 812 877-1000
Terre Haute (G-15564)

Dr Restorations Inc.................... G 317 646-7150
Clermont (G-2063)

WINDOWS: Wood

Andersen Corporation................ G 260 694-6861
Poneto (G-13839)

WINDSHIELD WIPER SYSTEMS

Cvg Sprague Devices LLC......... C 614 289-5360
Michigan City (G-11593)

WIRE

Group Dekko Inc........................ D 260 357-3621
Fort Wayne (G-5042)

McGowan Wire Specialties Inc... G 574 232-7110
South Bend (G-15145)

Tru-Form Steel & Wire Inc......... E 765 348-5001
Hartford City (G-7078)

WIRE & CABLE: Nonferrous, Aircraft

Sandin Mfg LLC......................... D 219 872-2253
Michigan City (G-11662)

WIRE & CABLE: Nonferrous, Automotive, Exc Ignition Sets

Sigma Wire International LLC..... G 574 295-9660
Elkhart (G-3677)

WIRE & CABLE: Nonferrous, Building

Belden Inc.................................. A 765 962-7561
Richmond (G-14094)

Essex Frkawa Mgnt Wire USA LLC..... F 260 248-5500
Columbia City (G-2146)

Essex Frkawa Mgnt Wire USA LLC..... E 260 461-4000
Fort Wayne (G-4962)

WIRE & WIRE PRDTS

A J Kay Co................................. F 224 475-0370
South Bend (G-14928)

Accel International..................... F 260 897-9990
Avilla (G-471)

Accent Wire Products................ G 765 628-3587
Greentown (G-6644)

Advantage Wire & Machine Inc.... G 765 698-4643
Connersville (G-2424)

American Rigging Rental........... G 317 721-9553
Indianapolis (G-7506)

American Wire Rope Sling of In.. G 260 478-4700
Fort Wayne (G-4759)

American Wire Rope Sling of In.. G 574 257-9424
Mishawaka (G-11841)

American Wire Rope Sling of In.. F 877 634-2545
Indianapolis (G-7508)

Angola Wire Products Inc.......... G 260 665-3061
Angola (G-228)

Automation Enclosures LLC...... G 812 453-8480
Evansville (G-3904)

B & G Entity Inc........................ F 260 724-8874
Decatur (G-2845)

Belden Inc.................................. A 765 962-7561
Richmond (G-14094)

Bender Products Inc................... E 574 255-5350
Mishawaka (G-11852)

Benthall Bros Inc....................... E 800 488-5995
Evansville (G-3915)

Bettner Wire Coating Dies Inc.... F 812 372-2732
Columbus (G-2226)

Bishop Lifting Products Inc........ G 317 634-2545
Indianapolis (G-7631)

Braid Den Inc............................. E 260 244-2995
Columbia City (G-2126)

Cmj & Associates Corporation... G 765 962-1947
Richmond (G-14107)

Ecp American Steel LLC............ G 574 257-9424
Mishawaka (G-11890)

Ecp American Steel LLC............ E 260 478-9101
Fort Wayne (G-4941)

Elektrisola Incorporated............. G 317 375-8192
Indianapolis (G-8069)

Elevator Equipment Corporation.. D 765 966-7761
Richmond (G-14119)

Essex Frkawa Mgnt Wire USA LLC..... F 260 248-5500
Columbia City (G-2146)

Fab Solutions LLC..................... G 765 744-2671
Redkey (G-14028)

Group Dekko Holdings Inc......... G 800 829-3101
Fort Wayne (G-5043)

Hessville Cable & Sling Co........ E 773 768-8181
Gary (G-5951)

Hewitt Manufacturing Company..... F 765 525-9829
Waldron (G-16258)

Kingsford Products Inc.............. F 740 862-4450
Decatur (G-2866)

Lake Cable of Indiana LLC........ C 847 238-3000
Valparaiso (G-15990)

Lauck Manufacturing Co Inc...... F 317 787-6269
Indianapolis (G-8727)

Macpactor Inc............................ G 502 643-7845
Jeffersonville (G-10015)

Madsen Wire LLC...................... F 260 829-6561
Orland (G-13368)

Merchants Metals LLC............... F 317 783-7678
Indianapolis (G-8876)

Mid-West Spring Mfg Co........... D 574 353-1409
Mentone (G-11474)

Myers Spring Co Inc.................. E 574 753-5105
Logansport (G-11096)

Noble Wire Products Inc............ G 317 773-1926
Orland (G-13369)

Outtadaway LLC........................ G 219 866-8885
Rensselaer (G-14062)

Pwt Group LLC......................... E 260 490-6477
Fort Wayne (G-5357)

R & R Engineering Co Inc......... E 765 536-2331
Summitville (G-15429)

Reelcraft Industries Inc.............. C 855 634-9109
Columbia City (G-2188)

S & J Manufacturing LLC........... F 812 662-6640
Greensburg (G-6629)

Sandin Mfg LLC......................... D 219 872-2253
Michigan City (G-11662)

Sanlo Inc.................................... D 219 879-0241
Michigan City (G-11664)

Valley Tool & Die Stampings...... E 574 722-4566
Logansport (G-11117)

Winamac Coil Spring Inc........... C 574 653-2186
Kewanna (G-10168)

Wire-Tek Inc............................... G 812 623-8300
Sunman (G-15448)

WIRE FABRIC: Welded Steel

WIRE FABRIC: Welded Steel
Four Star Field Services Inc.................... G 812 354-9995
  Petersburg *(G-13613)*
Warren Power Attachments.................... G 317 892-4737
  Pittsboro *(G-13655)*

WIRE MATERIALS: Copper
Cerro Wire LLC.. D 812 793-2929
  Crothersville *(G-2638)*
E M F Corp... E 260 488-2479
  Hamilton *(G-6852)*
Elektrsola Dr Gerd Schldbach G............ B 765 477-8000
  Lafayette *(G-10574)*
International Wire Group Inc.................. E 574 546-4680
  Bremen *(G-1198)*
Lake Copper Conductors LLC................ F 847 238-3000
  Elkhart *(G-3466)*

WIRE MATERIALS: Steel
Accel International..................................... F 260 897-9990
  Avilla *(G-471)*
Belden Inc.. C 724 222-7060
  Richmond *(G-14092)*
Belden Inc.. A 765 962-7561
  Richmond *(G-14094)*
Best Weld Inc.. G 765 641-7720
  Anderson *(G-83)*
Cablecraft Motion Controls LLC............. C 260 749-5105
  New Haven *(G-12897)*
D Martin Enterprises Inc........................... F 219 872-8211
  Michigan City *(G-11596)*
Elektrsola Dr Gerd Schldbach G............ B 765 477-8000
  Lafayette *(G-10574)*
Essex Frkawa Mgnt Wire USA LLC....... G 260 424-1708
  Columbia City *(G-2144)*
Essex Frkawa Mgnt Wire USA LLC....... F 260 248-5500
  Columbia City *(G-2146)*
Fort Wayne Metals RES Pdts.................. G 260 747-4154
  Fort Wayne *(G-4994)*
Hammond Steel Components LLC......... F 630 816-1343
  Hammond *(G-6943)*
Kingsford Products Inc.............................. F 740 862-4450
  Decatur *(G-2866)*
Metal Technologies Auburn LLC............ B 260 527-1410
  Auburn *(G-407)*
Nsci.. G 317 820-6526
  Carmel *(G-1709)*
Pwt Group LLC... E 260 490-6477
  Fort Wayne *(G-5357)*
Suggs Custom Design Solutions............ G 574 549-2174
  Elkhart *(G-3704)*
Truckpro LLC... F 765 482-6525
  Lebanon *(G-10948)*
Wolfpack Chassis LLC.............................. E 260 349-1887
  Kendallville *(G-10155)*

WIRE PRDTS: Ferrous Or Iron, Made In Wiredrawing Plants
EH Baare Corporation............................... G 765 778-7895
  Anderson *(G-113)*

WIRE PRDTS: Steel & Iron
Extrasurplus LLC.. G 252 619-8604
  Gary *(G-5931)*

WIRE: Communication
Belden Inc.. G 765 983-5200
  Richmond *(G-14093)*
Prysmian Cbles Systems USA LLC........ D 317 271-8447
  Indianapolis *(G-9236)*
Prysmian Cbles Systems USA LLC........ C 765 664-2321
  Marion *(G-11331)*
Telamon Corporation................................. C 317 818-6888
  Carmel *(G-1777)*
Telamon Spv LLC....................................... G 800 788-6680
  Carmel *(G-1780)*
Wireamerica Inc.. G 260 969-1700
  Fort Wayne *(G-5571)*

WIRE: Magnet
Alconex Specialty Products..................... E 260 744-3446
  Fort Wayne *(G-4738)*
Essex Frkawa Mgnt Wire USA LLC....... G 260 461-4000
  Fort Wayne *(G-4963)*
Essex Frkawa Mgnt Wire USA LLC....... G 260 461-4183
  Fort Wayne *(G-4964)*
Essex Frkawa Mgnt Wire USA LLC....... E 317 738-4365
  Franklin *(G-5729)*
REA Magnet Wire Company Inc............. D 800 732-9473
  Fort Wayne *(G-5370)*

WIRE: Mesh
Spaceguard Inc... D 812 523-3044
  Seymour *(G-14694)*

WIRE: Nonferrous
Accel International..................................... F 260 897-9990
  Avilla *(G-471)*
Almega/Tru-Flex Inc.................................. E 574 546-2113
  Bremen *(G-1172)*
Belden Inc.. C 317 818-6300
  Carmel *(G-1566)*
Belden Inc.. C 724 222-7060
  Richmond *(G-14092)*
Belden Wire & Cable Company LLC...... E 765 983-5200
  Richmond *(G-14095)*
Cerro Wire LLC.. D 812 793-2929
  Crothersville *(G-2638)*
Elektrsola Dr Gerd Schldbach G............ B 260 421-5400
  Fort Wayne *(G-4945)*
Elektrsola Dr Gerd Schldbach G............ B 765 477-8000
  Lafayette *(G-10574)*
Essex Brownell LLC................................... B 260 424-1708
  Fort Wayne *(G-4961)*
Essex Frkawa Mgnt Wire USA LLC....... E 260 248-5500
  Columbia City *(G-2145)*
Essex Services Inc.................................... B 260 461-4000
  Fort Wayne *(G-4965)*
Flex Appeals Family and Frien............... G 219 863-3830
  Demotte *(G-2917)*
Installed Building Pdts LLC..................... G 317 398-3216
  Shelbyville *(G-14762)*
International Wire Group Inc.................. E 574 546-4680
  Bremen *(G-1198)*
Latch Gard Co Inc..................................... G 574 862-2373
  Elkhart *(G-3471)*
Prysmian Cbles Systems USA LLC........ D 317 271-8447
  Indianapolis *(G-9235)*
Prysmian Cbles Systems USA LLC........ D 765 483-1760
  Lebanon *(G-10934)*
Sanlo Inc.. D 219 879-0241
  Michigan City *(G-11664)*
Southwire Company LLC......................... D 574 546-5915
  Bremen *(G-1222)*
Southwire Company LLC......................... E 317 445-2722
  Plainfield *(G-13730)*
Superior Essex Inc.................................... C 260 420-1565
  Fort Wayne *(G-5458)*
Superior Essex Intl LP.............................. C 260 461-4000
  Fort Wayne *(G-5459)*
W Michael Ssan Wlls Fndtion I............... G 317 844-6006
  Carmel *(G-1798)*

WIRE: Nonferrous, Appliance Fixture
Indy Wiring Services LLC........................ G 317 371-7044
  Brownsburg *(G-1374)*

WIRE: Steel, Insulated Or Armored
Fort Wayne Metals RES Pdts LLC......... G 260 747-4154
  Columbia City *(G-2147)*
Fort Wayne Metals RES Pdts LLC......... G 260 747-4154
  Fort Wayne *(G-4995)*
Fort Wayne Metals RES Pdts LLC......... G 260 747-4154
  Fort Wayne *(G-4997)*
Fort Wayne Metals RES Pdts LLC......... A 260 747-4154
  Fort Wayne *(G-4996)*
Kokoku Wire Industries Corp.................. E 574 287-5610
  South Bend *(G-15103)*
Mid-West Metal Products Co Inc........... E 765 741-3140
  Muncie *(G-12453)*
Midwest Bale Ties Inc.............................. F 765 364-0113
  Crawfordsville *(G-2589)*

WIRE: Wire, Ferrous Or Iron
National Material Company LLC............ E 219 397-5088
  East Chicago *(G-3030)*

WOMEN'S & CHILDREN'S CLOTHING WHOLESALERS, NEC
Hoogies Sports House Inc....................... G 574 533-9875
  Goshen *(G-6165)*
Ontime Toys Inc... G 317 598-9333
  Indianapolis *(G-9058)*
Ram Graphics Inc...................................... F 765 724-7783
  Alexandria *(G-58)*

WOMEN'S & GIRLS' SPORTSWEAR WHOLESALERS
Arizona Sport Shirts Inc........................... E 317 481-2160
  Indianapolis *(G-7544)*
Locoli Inc... E 219 515-6900
  Schererville *(G-14531)*
Sport Form Inc... G 260 589-2200
  Berne *(G-727)*

WOMEN'S CLOTHING STORES
Anita Lorrain LLC....................................... G 574 621-0531
  South Bend *(G-14946)*
Janelle Davis... G 765 635-6233
  Anderson *(G-139)*

WOMEN'S CLOTHING STORES: Ready-To-Wear
Marie Collective LLC................................. G 317 683-0408
  Indianapolis *(G-8832)*
Savage Yet Civilized LLC......................... G 855 560-9223
  Merrillville *(G-11556)*
Signs AP & Awards On Time LLC.......... G 219 661-4488
  Crown Point *(G-2752)*

WOMEN'S SPECIALTY CLOTHING STORES
CM Reed LLC... G 517 546-4100
  Greendale *(G-6444)*

WOOD & WOOD BY-PRDTS, WHOLESALE
Acpi Wood Products LLC........................ D 574 842-2066
  Culver *(G-2777)*
Core Wood Components LLC................. G 574 370-4457
  Elkhart *(G-3268)*

WOOD PRDTS: Applicators
Hilltop Wood Working............................... G 270 604-1962
  Madison *(G-11225)*

PRODUCT SECTION

WOVEN WIRE PRDTS, NEC

Rab Wood Products..................................G..... 574 206-5001
  South Bend *(G-15215)*

Voges Restoration and Wdwkg..............G..... 812 299-1546
  Terre Haute *(G-15742)*

Wood Sign Products................................G..... 574 234-1218
  South Bend *(G-15308)*

WOOD PRDTS: Mantels

R P Wakefield Company Inc...................E..... 260 837-8841
  Waterloo *(G-16528)*

Shamrock Cabinets Inc............................E..... 812 482-7969
  Jasper *(G-9911)*

WOOD PRDTS: Moldings, Unfinished & Prefinished

Alexandria Mw LLC..................................G..... 219 324-9541
  La Porte *(G-10379)*

Barkman Custom Woodworking..............F..... 574 773-9212
  Nappanee *(G-12583)*

Borkholder Wood Products Inc................G..... 574 546-2613
  Bremen *(G-1176)*

Branik Inc..G..... 260 467-1808
  Fort Wayne *(G-4814)*

By-Pass Paint Shop Inc............................F..... 574 264-5334
  Elkhart *(G-3240)*

Champion Wood Products Inc.................G..... 812 282-9460
  Sellersburg *(G-14591)*

Cornerstone Moulding Inc.......................E..... 574 546-4249
  Bremen *(G-1182)*

Faske Wood Moulding Inc.......................F..... 812 923-5601
  Borden *(G-1108)*

House of Fara Incorporated....................D..... 219 362-8544
  La Porte *(G-10422)*

Indiana Lumber Inc..................................G..... 812 837-9493
  Bloomington *(G-889)*

Jeff Goodnight...G..... 765 779-4867
  Middletown *(G-11771)*

Knapke & Sons Inc..................................E..... 260 639-0112
  Hoagland *(G-7169)*

Mervin Knepps Molding...........................G..... 812 486-2971
  Montgomery *(G-12114)*

Mullet Custom Interior LLC.....................F..... 574 773-9442
  Nappanee *(G-12627)*

New Style of Crossroads LLC................F..... 260 593-3800
  Topeka *(G-15812)*

Specialized Wood Products Inc..............E..... 574 522-6376
  Elkhart *(G-3691)*

Sunrise Wood Products LLC...................G..... 260 463-4822
  Lagrange *(G-10765)*

Ubelhor Construction Inc........................F..... 812 357-2220
  Bristow *(G-1301)*

Warsaw Foundry Company Inc...............D..... 574 267-8772
  Warsaw *(G-16446)*

Woodwright Door & Trim Inc..................G..... 574 522-1667
  Elkhart *(G-3792)*

WOOD PRDTS: Mulch Or Sawdust

Earth First Kentuckiana Inc.....................F..... 812 923-1227
  Charlestown *(G-1875)*

Greencycle of Indiana Inc.......................G..... 317 780-8175
  Indianapolis *(G-8318)*

Greencycle of Indiana Inc.......................G..... 317 769-5668
  Whitestown *(G-16808)*

WOOD PRDTS: Mulch, Wood & Bark

Clm Pallet Recycling Inc........................G..... 317 485-4080
  Fortville *(G-5589)*

Ostler Enterprises Inc.............................G..... 765 656-1275
  Frankfort *(G-5688)*

Pgc Mulch LLC..G..... 812 455-0700
  Evansville *(G-4236)*

WOOD PRDTS: Outdoor, Structural

Better Built Barns Inc..............................G..... 812 477-2001
  Evansville *(G-3929)*

Classic Manufacturing Co LLC................E..... 765 344-1619
  Brazil *(G-1138)*

Modular Green Systems LLC..................G..... 260 547-4121
  Craigville *(G-2535)*

Tangent Rail Products Inc......................E..... 812 789-5331
  Winslow *(G-16925)*

WOOD PRDTS: Panel Work

Cac Wallpanels LLC................................G..... 260 437-4003
  Harlan *(G-7051)*

Indiana Dimension Inc............................D..... 574 739-2319
  Logansport *(G-11082)*

Kerkhoff Associates Inc..........................E..... 765 583-4491
  Otterbein *(G-13453)*

Schertz Craftsmen Inc............................C..... 877 472-2782
  Grabill *(G-6324)*

WOOD PRDTS: Signboards

Joseph Northern.....................................G..... 574 309-5508
  South Bend *(G-15096)*

WOOD PRDTS: Trophy Bases

Deer Ridgewood Craft LLC.....................G..... 812 535-3744
  West Terre Haute *(G-16651)*

Dynamic Designs Scottys.......................G..... 219 809-7268
  Michigan City *(G-11605)*

NP Awards LLC.......................................G..... 317 861-0825
  New Palestine *(G-12941)*

Schug Awards LLC..................................G..... 765 447-0002
  Lafayette *(G-10686)*

WOOD PRODUCTS: Reconstituted

GAF...G..... 219 872-1111
  Michigan City *(G-11616)*

Good Earth Compost LLC........................G..... 812 824-7928
  Bloomington *(G-868)*

Michiana Column & Truss LLC................G..... 574 862-2828
  Goshen *(G-6220)*

Patrick Industries Inc..............................D..... 574 294-8828
  Elkhart *(G-3592)*

Patrick Industries Inc..............................G..... 574 294-5758
  Elkhart *(G-3596)*

Patrick Industries Inc..............................B..... 574 294-7511
  Elkhart *(G-3593)*

Structural Composites LLC.....................E..... 574 294-7511
  Elkhart *(G-3701)*

WOOD TREATING: Creosoting

Steinkamp Warehouses Inc.....................E..... 812 683-3860
  Huntingburg *(G-7292)*

WOOD TREATING: Railroad Cross Bridges & Switch Ties

Stella-Jones Corporation........................E..... 812 789-5331
  Winslow *(G-16924)*

WOOD TREATING: Railroad Cross-Ties

Primix Corporation..................................G..... 574 858-0069
  Atwood *(G-357)*

WOOD TREATING: Structural Lumber & Timber

Birch Wood..G..... 260 432-0011
  Fort Wayne *(G-4803)*

Jefferson Homebuilders Inc....................G..... 317 398-3125
  Shelbyville *(G-14765)*

WOOD TREATING: Wood Prdts, Creosoted

FTC Liquidation Inc.................................F..... 574 295-6700
  Elkhart *(G-3359)*

Hampels Woodland Products..................G..... 574 293-2124
  Elkhart *(G-3397)*

Pumpkin Patch Market Inc......................G..... 574 825-3312
  Middlebury *(G-11747)*

WOODWORK & TRIM: Interior & Ornamental

Creative Wood Designs Inc....................E..... 260 894-4533
  Ligonier *(G-11010)*

Custom Interior Dynamics LLC...............F..... 317 632-0477
  Indianapolis *(G-7930)*

Dairyland Woodworks LLC......................G..... 715 271-2110
  Warsaw *(G-16343)*

Ed Lloyd Co..G..... 812 342-2505
  Columbus *(G-2294)*

L & L Woodworking LLC..........................G..... 574 535-4613
  Nappanee *(G-12619)*

Real Wood Works....................................G..... 812 277-1462
  Bedford *(G-665)*

Woods Enterprises..................................G..... 574 232-7449
  South Bend *(G-15309)*

Wright Horizon Enterprises LLC.............G..... 317 779-8182
  Westfield *(G-16741)*

WOODWORK: Interior & Ornamental, NEC

Borkholder Lavon....................................G..... 574 773-3714
  Nappanee *(G-12586)*

Burks Door & Sash Inc............................E..... 317 844-2484
  Carmel *(G-1576)*

Chris Schwartz..G..... 260 615-9574
  Grabill *(G-6292)*

Comptons Woodworking LLC..................G..... 765 712-0568
  Cloverdale *(G-2084)*

Fischer Woodcraft Incorporated..............G..... 317 627-6035
  Beech Grove *(G-689)*

Franklin Garage Ltd.................................G..... 260 442-2439
  Fort Wayne *(G-5008)*

From Woods...G..... 765 468-7387
  Farmland *(G-4425)*

Guys Wood N Things...............................G..... 812 689-0433
  Holton *(G-7216)*

Jeff Hurst Custom Wdwkg Inc................G..... 812 367-1430
  Ferdinand *(G-4437)*

John Gebhart Woodworkings..................G..... 765 492-3898
  Cayuga *(G-1823)*

Kleeman Cabinetry..................................G..... 812 926-0428
  Aurora *(G-447)*

M & M Woodworking................................G..... 812 486-2418
  Washington *(G-16492)*

Mark Foster..G..... 574 965-4558
  Delphi *(G-2902)*

Mdl Woodworking LLC.............................G..... 260 242-1824
  Fort Wayne *(G-5213)*

Schuhler Woodworking LLC....................G..... 317 626-0452
  Danville *(G-2826)*

Tinchers Creative Woodworks................G..... 765 344-0062
  Rockville *(G-14358)*

Uniquely Divine Yonis LLC......................G..... 317 918-9112
  Indianapolis *(G-9678)*

Wittmer Woodworking LLC......................G..... 812 486-3115
  Montgomery *(G-12130)*

WORD PROCESSING EQPT

Automated Bus Solutions Inc..................F..... 317 257-9062
  Fishers *(G-4468)*

WOVEN WIRE PRDTS, NEC

Bridon-American Corporation..................D..... 812 749-3115
  Oakland City *(G-13320)*

Employee Codes: A=Over 500 employees, B=251-500
C=101-250, D=51-100, E=20-50, F=10-19, G=1-9

2024 Harris Indiana Industrial Directory

WOVEN WIRE PRDTS, NEC

Mathews Wire Inc................................. F 765 659-3542
Frankfort *(G-5682)*
Sommer Metalcraft LLC....................... D 765 362-6200
Crawfordsville *(G-2617)*
Wirco Inc... C 260 897-3768
Avilla *(G-500)*

X-RAY EQPT & TUBES

American Eagle Health LLC................. G 812 921-9224
Floyds Knobs *(G-4668)*
CXR Company Inc................................ F 574 269-6020
Warsaw *(G-16341)*
Golden Engineering Inc....................... E 765 855-3493
Centerville *(G-1849)*

X-RAY EQPT REPAIR SVCS

CXR Company Inc................................ F 574 269-6020
Warsaw *(G-16341)*

YARN & YARN SPINNING

Regal Manufacturing Company............ G 765 334-8118
Cambridge City *(G-1501)*

YARN MILLS: Texturizing, Throwing & Twisting

BP Wind Energy North Amer Inc........... G 765 884-1000
Fowler *(G-5621)*
Elmotec-Statolmat................................ G 260 758-8300
Markle *(G-11355)*